OVERSIZE

PETERSON'S GRADUATE PROGRAMS IN ENGINEERING & APPLIED SCIENCES

2012

PETERSON'S

Publishing

PETERSON'S
Publishing

About Peterson's Publishing
To succeed on your lifelong educational journey, you will need accurate, dependable, and practical tools and resources. That is why Peterson's is everywhere education happens. Because whenever and however you need education content delivered, you can rely on Peterson's to provide the information, know-how, and guidance to help you reach your goals. Tools to match the right students with the right school. It's here. Personalized resources and expert guidance. It's here. Comprehensive and dependable education content—delivered whenever and however you need it. It's all here.

For more information, contact Peterson's, 2000 Lenox Drive, Lawrenceville, NJ 08648; 800-338-3282 Ext. 54229; or find us online at www.petersonspublishing.com.

Bernadette Webster, Director of Publishing; Jill C. Schwartz, Editor; Ken Britschge, Research Project Manager; Nicole Gallo, Amy L. Weber, Research Associates; Phyllis Johnson, Software Engineer; Ray Golaszewski, Publishing Operations Manager; Linda M. Williams, Composition Manager; Karen Mount, Fulfillment Coordinator; Danielle Vreeland, Shannon White, Client Relations Representatives

ISSN 1097-1068
ISBN-13: 978-0-7689-3284-3
ISBN-10: 0-7689-3284-X

Printed in the United States of America

10 9 8 7 6 5 4 3 2 1   14 13 12

Forty-sixth Edition

Sustainability—Its Importance to Peterson's Publishing

What does sustainability mean to Peterson's Publishing? As a leading publisher, we are aware that our business has a direct impact on vital resources—most especially the trees that are used to make our books. Peterson's Publishing is proud that its products are certified by the Sustainable Forestry Initiative (SFI) and that all of its books are printed on paper that is 40 percent post-consumer waste using vegetable-based ink.

Being a part of the Sustainable Forestry Initiative (SFI) means that all of our vendors—from paper suppliers to printers—have undergone rigorous audits to demonstrate that they are maintaining a sustainable environment.

Peterson's Publishing continuously strives to find new ways to incorporate sustainability throughout all aspects of its business.

CONTENTS

SPECIAL ADVERTISING SECTION

Thomas Jefferson University School of Population Health

University of Medicine and Dentistry of New Jersey

Saint Louis University

St. Mary's University

The Winston Preparatory Schools

A Note from the Peterson's Editors

The six volumes of Peterson's *Graduate and Professional Programs*, the only annually updated reference work of its kind, provide wide-ranging information on the graduate and professional programs offered by accredited colleges and universities in the United States, U.S. territories, and Canada and by those institutions outside the United States that are accredited by U.S. accrediting bodies. More than 44,000 individual academic and professional programs at more than 2,200 institutions are listed. Peterson's *Graduate and Professional Programs* have been used for more than forty years by prospective graduate and professional students, placement counselors, faculty advisers, and all others interested in postbaccalaureate education.

Graduate & Professional Programs: An Overview contains information on institutions as a whole, while the other books in the series are devoted to specific academic and professional fields:

Graduate Programs in the Humanities, Arts & Social Sciences
Graduate Programs in the Biological Sciences
Graduate Programs in the Physical Sciences, Mathematics, Agricultural Sciences, the Environment & Natural Resources
Graduate Programs in Engineering & Applied Sciences
Graduate Programs in Business, Education, Health, Information Studies, Law & Social Work

The books may be used individually or as a set. For example, if you have chosen a field of study but do not know what institution you want to attend or if you have a college or university in mind but have not chosen an academic field of study, it is best to begin with the Overview guide.

Graduate & Professional Programs: An Overview presents several directories to help you identify programs of study that might interest you; you can then research those programs further in the other books in the series by using the Directory of Graduate and Professional Programs by Field, which lists 500 fields and gives the names of those institutions that offer graduate degree programs in each.

For geographical or financial reasons, you may be interested in attending a particular institution and will want to know what it has to offer. You should turn to the Directory of Institutions and Their Offerings, which lists the degree programs available at each institution. As in the Directory of Graduate and Professional Programs by Field, the level of degrees offered is also indicated.

All books in the series include advice on graduate education, including topics such as admissions tests, financial aid, and accreditation. **The Graduate Adviser** includes two essays and information about accreditation. The first essay, "The Admissions Process," discusses general admission requirements, admission tests, factors to consider when selecting a graduate school or program, when and how to apply, and how admission decisions are made. Special information for international students and tips for minority students are also included. The second essay, "Financial Support," is an overview of the broad range of support available at the graduate level. Fellowships, scholarships, and grants; assistantships and internships; federal and private loan programs, as well as Federal Work-Study; and the GI bill are detailed. This essay concludes with advice on applying for need-based financial aid. "Accreditation and Accrediting Agencies" gives information on accreditation and its purpose and lists institutional accrediting agencies first and then specialized accrediting agencies relevant to each volume's specific fields of study.

With information on more than 44,000 graduate programs in 500 disciplines, Peterson's *Graduate and Professional Programs* give you all the information you need about the programs that are of interest to you in three formats: **Profiles** (capsule summaries of basic information), **Displays** (information that an institution or program wants to emphasize), and **Close-Ups** (written by administrators, with more expansive information than the **Profiles**, emphasizing different aspects of the programs). By using these various formats of program information, coupled with **Appendixes** and **Indexes** covering directories and subject areas for all six books, you will find that these guides provide the most comprehensive, accurate, and up-to-date graduate study information available.

At the end of the book, you'll find a special section of ads placed by Peterson's preferred clients. Their financial support makes it possible for Peterson's Publishing to continue to provide you with the highest-quality educational exploration, test-prep, financial aid, and career-preparation resources you need to succeed on your educational journey.

Find Us on Facebook®

Join the grad school conversation on Facebook® at www.facebook.com/petersonspublishing. Peterson's expert resources are available to help you as you search for the right graduate program for you.

Peterson's publishes a full line of resources with information you need to guide you through the graduate admissions process. Peterson's publications can be found at college libraries and career centers and your local bookstore or library—or visit us on the Web at www.petersonspublishing.com. Peterson's books are now also available as eBooks.

Colleges and universities will be pleased to know that Peterson's helped you in your selection. Admissions staff members are more than happy to answer questions, address specific problems, and help in any way they can. The editors at Peterson's wish you great success in your graduate program search!

THE GRADUATE ADVISER

The Admissions Process

Generalizations about graduate admissions practices are not always helpful because each institution has its own set of guidelines and procedures. Nevertheless, some broad statements can be made about the admissions process that may help you plan your strategy.

Factors Involved in Selecting a Graduate School or Program

Selecting a graduate school and a specific program of study is a complex matter. Quality of the faculty; program and course offerings; the nature, size, and location of the institution; admission requirements; cost; and the availability of financial assistance are among the many factors that affect one's choice of institution. Other considerations are job placement and achievements of the program's graduates and the institution's resources, such as libraries, laboratories, and computer facilities. If you are to make the best possible choice, you need to learn as much as you can about the schools and programs you are considering before you apply.

The following steps may help you narrow your choices.

- Talk to alumni of the programs or institutions you are considering to get their impressions of how well they were prepared for work in their fields of study.
- Remember that graduate school requirements change, so be sure to get the most up-to-date information possible.
- Talk to department faculty members and the graduate adviser at your undergraduate institution. They often have information about programs of study at other institutions.
- Visit the Web sites of the graduate schools in which you are interested to request a graduate catalog. Contact the department chair in your chosen field of study for additional information about the department and the field.
- Visit as many campuses as possible. Call ahead for an appointment with the graduate adviser in your field of interest and be sure to check out the facilities and talk to students.

General Requirements

Graduate schools and departments have requirements that applicants for admission must meet. Typically, these requirements include undergraduate transcripts (which provide information about undergraduate grade point average and course work applied toward a major), admission test scores, and letters of recommendation. Most graduate programs also ask for an essay or personal statement that describes your personal reasons for seeking graduate study. In some fields, such as art and music, portfolios or auditions may be required in addition to other evidence of talent. Some institutions require that the applicant have an undergraduate degree in the same subject as the intended graduate major.

Most institutions evaluate each applicant on the basis of the applicant's total record, and the weight accorded any given factor varies widely from institution to institution and from program to program.

The Application Process

You should begin the application process at least one year before you expect to begin your graduate study. Find out the application deadline for each institution (many are provided in the **Profile** section of this guide). Go to the institution's Web site and find out if you can apply online. If not, request a paper application form. Fill out this form thoroughly and neatly. Assume that the school needs all the information it is requesting and that the admissions officer will be sensitive to the neatness and overall quality of what you submit. Do not supply more information than the school requires.

The institution may ask at least one question that will require a three- or four-paragraph answer. Compose your response on the assumption that the admissions officer is interested in both what you think and how you express yourself. Keep your statement brief and to the point, but, at the same time, include all pertinent information about your past experiences and your educational goals. Individual statements vary greatly in style and content, which helps admissions officers differentiate among applicants. Many graduate departments give considerable weight to the statement in making their admissions decisions, so be sure to take the time to prepare a thoughtful and concise statement.

If recommendations are a part of the admissions requirements, carefully choose the individuals you ask to write them. It is generally best to ask current or former professors to write the recommendations, provided they are able to attest to your intellectual ability and motivation for doing the work required of a graduate student. It is advisable to provide stamped, preaddressed envelopes to people being asked to submit recommendations on your behalf.

Completed applications, including references, transcripts, and admission test scores, should be received at the institution by the specified date.

Be advised that institutions do not usually make admissions decisions until all materials have been received. Enclose a self-addressed postcard with your application, requesting confirmation of receipt. Allow at least ten days for the return of the postcard before making further inquiries.

If you plan to apply for financial support, it is imperative that you file your application early.

ADMISSION TESTS

The major testing program used in graduate admissions is the Graduate Record Examinations (GRE) testing program, sponsored by the GRE Board and administered by Educational Testing Service, Princeton, New Jersey.

The Graduate Record Examinations testing program consists of a General Test and eight Subject Tests. The General Test measures critical thinking, verbal reasoning, quantitative reasoning, and analytical writing skills. It is offered as an Internet-based test (iBT) in the United States, Canada, and many other countries.

The typical computer-based General Test consists of one 30-minute verbal reasoning section, one 45-minute quantitative reasoning sections, one 45-minute issue analysis (writing) section, and one 30-minute argument analysis (writing) section. In addition, an unidentified verbal or quantitative section that doesn't count toward a score may be included and an identified research section that is not scored may also be included.

The Subject Tests measure achievement and assume undergraduate majors or extensive background in the following eight disciplines:

- Biochemistry, Cell and Molecular Biology
- Biology
- Chemistry
- Computer Science
- Literature in English
- Mathematics
- Physics
- Psychology

The Subject Tests are available three times per year as paper-based administrations around the world. Testing time is approximately 2 hours and 50 minutes. You can obtain more information about the GRE by visiting the ETS Web site at www.ets.org or consulting the *GRE Information and Registration Bulletin*. The *Bulletin* can be obtained at many undergraduate colleges. You can also download it from the ETS Web site or obtain it by contacting Graduate Record Examinations, Educational Testing Service, P.O. Box 6000, Princeton, NJ 08541-6000; phone: 609-771-7670.

If you expect to apply for admission to a program that requires any of the GRE tests, you should select a test date well in advance of the application deadline. Scores on the computer-based General Test are reported within ten to fifteen days; scores on the paper-based Subject Tests are reported within six weeks.

Another testing program, the Miller Analogies Test (MAT), is administered at more than 500 Controlled Testing Centers, licensed by Harcourt Assessment, Inc., in the United States, Canada, and other countries. The MAT computer-based test is now available. Testing time is 60 minutes. The test consists of 120 partial analogies. You can obtain the *Candidate Information Booklet,* which contains a list of test centers and instructions for taking the test, from http://www.milleranalogies.com or by calling 800-622-3231 (toll-free).

Check the specific requirements of the programs to which you are applying.

How Admission Decisions Are Made

The program you apply to is directly involved in the admissions process. Although the final decision is usually made by the graduate dean (or an associate) or the faculty admissions committee, recommendations from faculty members in your intended field are important. At some institutions, an interview is incorporated into the decision process.

A Special Note for International Students

In addition to the steps already described, there are some special considerations for international students who intend to apply for graduate study in the United States. All graduate schools require an indication of competence in English. The purpose of the Test of English as a Foreign Language (TOEFL) is to evaluate the English proficiency of people who are nonnative speakers of English and want to study at colleges and universities where English is the language of instruction. The TOEFL is administered by Educational Testing Service (ETS) under the general direction of a policy board established by the College Board and the Graduate Record Examinations Board.

The TOEFL iBT assesses the four basic language skills: listening, reading, writing, and speaking. It was administered for the first time in September 2005, and ETS continues to introduce the TOEFL iBT in selected cities. The Internet-based test is administered at secure, official test centers. The testing time is approximately 4 hours. Because the TOEFL iBT includes a speaking section, the Test of Spoken English (TSE) is no longer needed.

The TOEFL is also offered in the paper-based format in areas of the world where Internet-based testing is not available. The paper-based TOEFL consists of three sections—listening comprehension, structure and written expression, and reading comprehension. The testing time is approximately 3 hours. The Test of Written English (TWE) is also given. The TWE is a 30-minute essay that measures the examinee's ability to compose in English. Examinees receive a TWE score separate from their TOEFL score. The *Information Bulletin* contains information on local fees and registration procedures.

Additional information and registration materials are available from TOEFL Services, Educational Testing Service, P.O. Box 6151, Princeton, New Jersey 08541-6151. Phone: 609-771-7100. Web site: www.toefl.org.

International students should apply especially early because of the number of steps required to complete the admissions process. Furthermore, many United States graduate schools have a limited number of spaces for international students, and many more students apply than the schools can accommodate.

International students may find financial assistance from institutions very limited. The U.S. government requires international applicants to submit a certification of support, which is a statement attesting to the applicant's financial resources. In addition, international students *must* have health insurance coverage.

Tips for Minority Students

Indicators of a university's values in terms of diversity are found both in its recruitment programs and its resources directed to student success. Important questions: Does the institution vigorously recruit minorities for its graduate programs? Is there funding available to help with the costs associated with visiting the school? Are minorities represented in the institution's brochures or Web site or on their faculty rolls? What campus-based resources or services (including assistance in locating housing or career counseling and placement) are available? Is funding available to members of underrepresented groups?

At the program level, it is particularly important for minority students to investigate the "climate" of a program under consideration. How many minority students are enrolled and how many have graduated? What opportunities are there to work with diverse faculty and mentors whose research interests match yours? How are conflicts resolved or concerns addressed? How interested are faculty in building strong and supportive relations with students? "Climate" concerns should be addressed by posing questions to various individuals, including faculty members, current students, and alumni.

Information is also available through various organizations, such as the Hispanic Association of Colleges & Universities (HACU), and publications such as *Diverse Issues in Higher Education* and *Hispanic Outlook* magazine. There are also books devoted to this topic, such as *The Multicultural Student's Guide to Colleges* by Robert Mitchell.

Financial Support

The range of financial support at the graduate level is very broad. The following descriptions will give you a general idea of what you might expect and what will be expected of you as a financial support recipient.

Fellowships, Scholarships, and Grants

These are usually outright awards of a few hundred to many thousands of dollars with no service to the institution required in return. Fellowships and scholarships are usually awarded on the basis of merit and are highly competitive. Grants are made on the basis of financial need or special talent in a field of study. Many fellowships, scholarships, and grants not only cover tuition, fees, and supplies but also include stipends for living expenses with allowances for dependents. However, the terms of each should be examined because some do not permit recipients to supplement their income with outside work. Fellowships, scholarships, and grants may vary in the number of years for which they are awarded.

In addition to the availability of these funds at the university or program level, many excellent fellowship programs are available at the national level and may be applied for before and during enrollment in a graduate program. A listing of many of these programs can be found at the Council of Graduate Schools' Web site: http://www.cgsnet.org. There is a wealth of information in the "Programs" and "Awards" sections.

Assistantships and Internships

Many graduate students receive financial support through assistantships, particularly involving teaching or research duties. It is important to recognize that such appointments should not be viewed simply as employment relationships but rather should constitute an integral and important part of a student's graduate education. As such, the appointments should be accompanied by strong faculty mentoring and increasingly responsible apprenticeship experiences. The specific nature of these appointments in a given program should be considered in selecting that graduate program.

TEACHING ASSISTANTSHIPS

These usually provide a salary and full or partial tuition remission and may also provide health benefits. Unlike fellowships, scholarships, and grants, which require no service to the institution, teaching assistantships require recipients to provide the institution with a specific amount of undergraduate teaching, ideally related to the student's field of study. Some teaching assistants are limited to grading papers, compiling bibliographies, taking notes, or monitoring laboratories. At some graduate schools, teaching assistants must carry lighter course loads than regular full-time students.

RESEARCH ASSISTANTSHIPS

These are very similar to teaching assistantships in the manner in which financial assistance is provided. The difference is that recipients are given basic research assignments in their disciplines rather than teaching responsibilities. The work required is normally related to the student's field of study; in most instances, the assistantship supports the student's thesis or dissertation research.

ADMINISTRATIVE INTERNSHIPS

These are similar to assistantships in application of financial assistance funds, but the student is given an assignment on a part-time basis, usually as a special assistant with one of the university's administrative offices. The assignment may not necessarily be directly related to the recipient's discipline.

RESIDENCE HALL AND COUNSELING ASSISTANTSHIPS

These assistantships are frequently assigned to graduate students in psychology, counseling, and social work, but they may be offered to students in other disciplines, especially if the student has worked in this capacity during his or her undergraduate years. Duties can vary from being available in a dean's office for a specific number of hours for consultation with undergraduates to living in campus residences and being responsible for both counseling and administrative tasks or advising student activity groups. Residence hall assistantships often include a room and board allowance and, in some cases, tuition assistance and stipends. Contact the Housing and Student Life Office for more information.

Health Insurance

The availability and affordability of health insurance is an important issue and one that should be considered in an applicant's choice of institution and program. While often included with assistantships and fellowships, this is not always the case and, even if provided, the benefits may be limited. It is important to note that the U.S. government requires international students to have health insurance.

The GI Bill

This provides financial assistance for students who are veterans of the United States armed forces. If you are a veteran, contact your local Veterans Administration office to determine your eligibility and to get full details about benefits. There are a number of programs that offer educational benefits to current military enlistees. Some states have tuition assistance programs for members of the National Guard. Contact the VA office at the college for more information.

Federal Work-Study Program (FWS)

Employment is another way some students finance their graduate studies. The federally funded Federal Work-Study Program provides eligible students with employment opportunities, usually in public and private nonprofit organizations. Federal funds pay up to 75 percent of the wages, with the remainder paid by the employing agency. FWS is available to graduate students who demonstrate financial need. Not all schools have these funds, and some only award them to undergraduates. Each school sets its application deadline and work-study earnings limits. Wages vary and are related to the type of work done. You must file the Free Application for Federal Student Aid (FAFSA) to be eligible for this program.

Loans

Many graduate students borrow to finance their graduate programs when other sources of assistance (which do not have to be repaid) prove insufficient. You should always read and understand the terms of any loan program before submitting your application.

FEDERAL DIRECT LOANS

Federal Direct Stafford Loans. The Federal Direct Stafford Loan Program offers low-interest loans to students with the Department of Education acting as the lender.

There are two components of the Federal Stafford Loan program. Under the *subsidized* component of the program, the federal government pays the interest on the loan while you are enrolled in graduate school on at least a half-time basis, during the six-month grace period after you drop below half-time enrollment, as well as during any period of deferment. Under the *unsubsidized* component of the program, you pay the interest on the loan from the day proceeds are issued. Eligibility for the federal subsidy is based on demonstrated financial need as determined by the financial aid office from the information you provide on the FAFSA. A cosigner is not required, since the loan is not based on creditworthiness.

Although *unsubsidized* Federal Direct Stafford Loans may not be as desirable as *subsidized* Federal Direct Stafford Loans from the student's perspective, they are a useful source of support for those who may not qualify for the subsidized loans or who need additional financial assistance.

Graduate students may borrow up to $20,500 per year through the Direct Stafford Loan Program, up to a cumulative maximum of $138,500, including undergraduate borrowing. This may include up to $8,500 in *subsidized* Direct Stafford Loans annually, depending on eligibility, up to a cumulative maximum of $65,500, including undergraduate borrowing. The amount of the loan borrowed through the *unsubsidized* Direct Stafford Loan Program equals the total amount of the loan (as much as $20,500) minus your eligibility for a *subsidized* Direct Loan (as much as $8,500). You may borrow up to the cost of attendance at the school in which you are enrolled or will attend, minus estimated financial assistance from other federal, state, and private sources, up to a maximum of $20,500.

Direct Stafford Loans made on or after July 1, 2006, carry a fixed interest rate of 6.8% both for in-school and in-repayment borrowers.

A fee is deducted from the loan proceeds upon disbursement. Loans with a first disbursement on or after July 1, 2010, have a borrower origination fee of 1 percent. The Department of Education offers a 0.5 percent origination fee rebate incentive. Borrowers must make their first twelve payments on time in order to retain the rebate.

Under the *subsidized* Federal Direct Stafford Loan Program, repayment begins six months after your last date of enrollment on at least a half-time basis. Under the *unsubsidized* program, repayment of interest begins within thirty days from disbursement of the loan proceeds, and repayment of the principal begins six months after your last enrollment on at least a half-time basis. Some borrowers may choose to defer interest payments while they are in school. The accrued interest is added to the loan balance when the borrower begins repayment. There are several repayment options.

Federal Perkins Loans. The Federal Perkins Loan is available to students demonstrating financial need and is administered directly by the school. Not all schools have these funds, and some may award them to undergraduates only. Eligibility is determined from the information you provide on the FAFSA. The school will notify you of your eligibility.

Eligible graduate students may borrow up to $6,000 per year, up to a maximum of $40,000, including undergraduate borrowing (even if your previous Perkins Loans have been repaid). The interest rate for Federal Perkins Loans is 5 percent, and no interest accrues while you remain in school at least half-time. There are no guarantee, loan, or disbursement fees. Repayment begins nine months after your last date of enrollment on at least a half-time basis and may extend over a maximum of ten years with no prepayment penalty.

Federal Direct Graduate PLUS Loans. Effective July 1, 2006, graduate and professional students are eligible for Graduate PLUS loans. This program allows students to borrow up to the cost of attendance, less any other aid received. These loans have a fixed interest rate of 7.9 percent, and interest begins to accrue at the time of disbursement. The PLUS loans do involve a credit check; a PLUS borrower may obtain a loan with a cosigner if his or her credit is not good enough. Grad PLUS loans may be deferred while a student in school and for the six months following a drop below half-time enrollment. For more information, contact your college financial aid office.

Deferring Your Federal Loan Repayments. If you borrowed under the Federal Direct Stafford Loan Program, Federal Direct PLUS Loan Program, or the Federal Perkins Loan Program for previous undergraduate or graduate study, your payments may be deferred when you return to graduate school, depending on when you borrowed and under which program.

There are other deferment options available if you are temporarily unable to repay your loan. Information about these deferments is provided at your entrance and exit interviews. If you believe you are eligible for a deferment of your loan payments, you must contact your lender or loan servicer to request a deferment. The deferment must be filed prior to the time your payment is due, and it must be refiled when it expires if you remain eligible for deferment at that time.

SUPPLEMENTAL (PRIVATE) LOANS

Many lending institutions offer supplemental loan programs and other financing plans, such as the ones described here, to students seeking additional assistance in meeting their education expenses. Some loan programs target all types of graduate students; others are designed specifically for business, law, or medical students. In addition, you can use private loans not specifically designed for education to help finance your graduate degree.

If you are considering borrowing through a supplemental or private loan program, you should carefully consider the terms and be sure to "read the fine print." Check with the program sponsor for the most current terms that will be applicable to the amounts you intend to borrow for graduate study. Most supplemental loan programs for graduate study offer unsubsidized, credit-based loans. In general, a credit-ready borrower is one who has a satisfactory credit history or no credit history at all. A creditworthy borrower generally must pass a credit test to be eligible to borrow or act as a cosigner for the loan funds.

Many supplemental loan programs have minimum and maximum annual loan limits. Some offer amounts equal to the cost of attendance minus any other aid you will receive for graduate study. If you are planning to borrow for several years of graduate study, consider whether there is a cumulative or aggregate limit on the amount you may borrow. Often this cumulative or aggregate limit will include any amounts you borrowed and have not repaid for undergraduate or previous graduate study.

The combination of the annual interest rate, loan fees, and the repayment terms you choose will determine how much you will repay over time. Compare these features in combination before you decide which loan program to use. Some loans offer interest rates that are adjusted monthly, some quarterly, some annually. Some offer interest rates that are lower during the in-school, grace, and deferment periods and then increase when you begin repayment. Some programs include a loan "origination" fee, which is usually deducted from the principal amount you receive when the loan is disbursed and must be repaid along with the interest and other principal when you graduate, withdraw from school, or drop below half-time study. Sometimes the loan fees are reduced if you borrow with a qualified cosigner. Some programs allow you to defer interest and/or principal payments while you are enrolled in graduate school. Many programs allow you to capitalize your interest payments; the interest due on your loan is added to the outstanding balance of your loan, so you don't have to repay immediately, but this increases the amount you owe. Other programs allow you to pay the interest as you go, which reduces the amount you later have to repay. The private loan market is very competitive, and your financial aid office can help you evaluate these programs.

Applying for Need-Based Financial Aid

Schools that award federal and institutional financial assistance based on need will require you to complete the FAFSA and, in some cases, an institutional financial aid application.

If you are applying for federal student assistance, you **must** complete the FAFSA. A service of the U.S. Department of Education, the FAFSA is free to all applicants. Most applicants apply online at www.fafsa.ed.gov. Paper applications are available at the financial aid office of your local college.

After your FAFSA information has been processed, you will receive a Student Aid Report (SAR). If you provided an e-mail address on the FAFSA, this will be sent to you electronically; otherwise, it will be mailed to your home address.

Follow the instructions on the SAR if you need to correct information reported on your original application. If your situation changes after you file your FAFSA, contact your financial aid officer to discuss amending your information. You can also appeal your financial aid award if you have extenuating circumstances.

If you would like more information on federal student financial aid, visit the FAFSA Web site or download the most recent version of *Funding Education Beyond High School: The Guide to Federal Student Aid* at http://studentaid.ed.gov/students/publications/student_guide/index.html. This guide is also available in Spanish.

The U.S. Department of Education also has a toll-free number for questions concerning federal student aid programs. The number is 1-800-4-FED AID (1-800-433-3243). If you are hearing impaired, call toll-free, 1-800-730-8913.

Summary

Remember that these are generalized statements about financial assistance at the graduate level. Because each institution allots its aid differently, you should communicate directly with the school and the specific department of interest to you. It is not unusual, for example, to find that an endowment vested within a specific department supports one or more fellowships. You may fit its requirements and specifications precisely.

Accreditation and Accrediting Agencies

Colleges and universities in the United States, and their individual academic and professional programs, are accredited by nongovernmental agencies concerned with monitoring the quality of education in this country. Agencies with both regional and national jurisdictions grant accreditation to institutions as a whole, while specialized bodies acting on a nationwide basis—often national professional associations—grant accreditation to departments and programs in specific fields.

Institutional and specialized accrediting agencies share the same basic concerns: the purpose an academic unit—whether university or program—has set for itself and how well it fulfills that purpose, the adequacy of its financial and other resources, the quality of its academic offerings, and the level of services it provides. Agencies that grant institutional accreditation take a broader view, of course, and examine university-wide or college-wide services with which a specialized agency may not concern itself.

Both types of agencies follow the same general procedures when considering an application for accreditation. The academic unit prepares a self-evaluation, focusing on the concerns mentioned above and usually including an assessment of both its strengths and weaknesses; a team of representatives of the accrediting body reviews this evaluation, visits the campus, and makes its own report; and finally, the accrediting body makes a decision on the application. Often, even when accreditation is granted, the agency makes a recommendation regarding how the institution or program can improve. All institutions and programs are also reviewed every few years to determine whether they continue to meet established standards; if they do not, they may lose their accreditation.

Accrediting agencies themselves are reviewed and evaluated periodically by the U.S. Department of Education and the Council for Higher Education Accreditation (CHEA). Recognized agencies adhere to certain standards and practices, and their authority in matters of accreditation is widely accepted in the educational community.

This does not mean, however, that accreditation is a simple matter, either for schools wishing to become accredited or for students deciding where to apply. Indeed, in certain fields the very meaning and methods of accreditation are the subject of a good deal of debate. For their part, those applying to graduate school should be aware of the safeguards provided by regional accreditation, especially in terms of degree acceptance and institutional longevity. Beyond this, applicants should understand the role that specialized accreditation plays in their field, as this varies considerably from one discipline to another. In certain professional fields, it is necessary to have graduated from a program that is accredited in order to be eligible for a license to practice, and in some fields the federal government also makes this a hiring requirement. In other disciplines, however, accreditation is not as essential, and there can be excellent programs that are not accredited. In fact, some programs choose not to seek accreditation, although most do.

Institutions and programs that present themselves for accreditation are sometimes granted the status of candidate for accreditation, or what is known as "preaccreditation." This may happen, for example, when an academic unit is too new to have met all the requirements for accreditation. Such status signifies initial recognition and indicates that the school or program in question is working to fulfill all requirements; it does not, however, guarantee that accreditation will be granted.

Institutional Accrediting Agencies—Regional

MIDDLE STATES ASSOCIATION OF COLLEGES AND SCHOOLS
Accredits institutions in Delaware, District of Columbia, Maryland, New Jersey, New York, Pennsylvania, Puerto Rico, and the Virgin Islands.
Dr. Elizabeth Sibolski, President
Middle States Commission on Higher Education
3624 Market Street, Second Floor West
Philadelphia, Pennsylvania 19104
Phone: 267-284-5000
Fax: 215-662-5501
E-mail: info@msche.org
Web: www.msche.org

NEW ENGLAND ASSOCIATION OF SCHOOLS AND COLLEGES
Accredits institutions in Connecticut, Maine, Massachusetts, New Hampshire, Rhode Island, and Vermont.
Barbara E. Brittingham, Director
Commission on Institutions of Higher Education
209 Burlington Road, Suite 201
Bedford, Massachusetts 01730-1433
Phone: 781-271-0022
Fax: 781-271-0950
E-mail: kwillis@neasc.org
Web: www.neasc.org

NORTH CENTRAL ASSOCIATION OF COLLEGES AND SCHOOLS
Accredits institutions in Arizona, Arkansas, Colorado, Illinois, Indiana, Iowa, Kansas, Michigan, Minnesota, Missouri, Nebraska, New Mexico, North Dakota, Ohio, Oklahoma, South Dakota, West Virginia, Wisconsin, and Wyoming.
Dr. Sylvia Manning, President
The Higher Learning Commission
230 South LaSalle Street, Suite 7-500
Chicago, Illinois 60604-1413
Phone: 312-263-0456
Fax: 312-263-7462
E-mail: smanning@hlcommission.org
Web: www.ncahlc.org

NORTHWEST COMMISSION ON COLLEGES AND UNIVERSITIES
Accredits institutions in Alaska, Idaho, Montana, Nevada, Oregon, Utah, and Washington.
Dr. Sandra E. Elman, President
8060 165th Avenue, NE, Suite 100
Redmond, Washington 98052
Phone: 425-558-4224
Fax: 425-376-0596
E-mail: selman@nwccu.org
Web: www.nwccu.org

SOUTHERN ASSOCIATION OF COLLEGES AND SCHOOLS
Accredits institutions in Alabama, Florida, Georgia, Kentucky, Louisiana, Mississippi, North Carolina, South Carolina, Tennessee, Texas, and Virginia.
Belle S. Wheelan, President
Commission on Colleges
1866 Southern Lane
Decatur, Georgia 30033-4097
Phone: 404-679-4500
Fax: 404-679-4558
E-mail: questions@sacscoc.org
Web: www.sacscoc.org

WESTERN ASSOCIATION OF SCHOOLS AND COLLEGES
Accredits institutions in California, Guam, and Hawaii.
Ralph A. Wolff, President and Executive Director
Accrediting Commission for Senior Colleges and Universities
985 Atlantic Avenue, Suite 100
Alameda, California 94501
Phone: 510-748-9001
Fax: 510-748-9797
E-mail: www.wascsenior.org/contact
Web: www.wascweb.org/contact

Institutional Accrediting Agencies—Other

ACCREDITING COUNCIL FOR INDEPENDENT COLLEGES AND SCHOOLS
Albert C. Gray, Ph.D., Executive Director and CEO
750 First Street, NE, Suite 980
Washington, DC 20002-4241
Phone: 202-336-6780
Fax: 202-842-2593
E-mail: info@acics.org
Web: www.acics.org

DISTANCE EDUCATION AND TRAINING COUNCIL (DETC)
Accrediting Commission
Michael P. Lambert, Executive Director
1601 18th Street, NW, Suite 2
Washington, DC 20009
Phone: 202-234-5100
Fax: 202-332-1386
E-mail: Brianna@detc.org
Web: www.detc.org

Specialized Accrediting Agencies

[Only *Graduate & Professional Programs: An Overview* of *Peterson's Graduate and Professional Programs* Series includes the complete list of specialized accrediting groups recognized by the U.S. Department of Education and the Council on Higher Education Accreditation (CHEA). The list in this book is abridged.]

ENGINEERING
Michael Milligan, Ph.D., PE, Executive Director
Accreditation Board for Engineering and Technology, Inc. (ABET)
111 Market Place, Suite 1050
Baltimore, Maryland 21202
Phone: 410-347-7700
Fax: 410-625-2238
E-mail: accreditation@abet.org
Web: www.abet.org

TECHNOLOGY
Michale S. McComis, Ed.D., Executive Director
Accrediting Commission of Career Schools and Colleges
2101 Wilson Boulevard, Suite 302
Arlington, Virginia 22201
Phone: 703-247-4212
Fax: 703-247-4533
E-mail: mccomis@accsc.org
Web: www.accsc.org

How to Use These Guides

As you identify the particular programs and institutions that interest you, you can use both the *Graduate & Professional Programs: An Overview* volume and the specialized volumes in the series to obtain detailed information.

- *Graduate Programs in the Physical Sciences, Mathematics, Agricultural Sciences, the Environment & Natural Resources*
- *Graduate Programs in Engineering & Applied Sciences*
- *Graduate Programs the Humanities, Arts & Social Sciences*
- *Graduate Programs in the Biological Sciences*
- *Graduate Programs in Business, Education, Health, Information Studies, Law & Social Work*

Each of the specialized volumes in the series is divided into sections that contain one or more directories devoted to programs in a particular field. If you do not find a directory devoted to your field of interest in a specific volume, consult "Directories and Subject Areas" (located at the end of each volume). After you have identified the correct volume, consult the "Directories and Subject Areas in This Book" index, which shows (as does the more general directory) what directories cover subjects not specifically named in a directory or section title.

Each of the specialized volumes in the series has a number of general directories. These directories have entries for the largest unit at an institution granting graduate degrees in that field. For example, the general Engineering and Applied Sciences directory in the *Graduate Programs in Engineering & Applied Sciences* volume consists of **Profiles** for colleges, schools, and departments of engineering and applied sciences.

General directories are followed by other directories, or sections, that give more detailed information about programs in particular areas of the general field that has been covered. The general Engineering and Applied Sciences directory, in the previous example, is followed by nineteen sections with directories in specific areas of engineering, such as Chemical Engineering, Industrial/Management Engineering, and Mechanical Engineering.

Because of the broad nature of many fields, any system of organization is bound to involve a certain amount of overlap. Environmental studies, for example, is a field whose various aspects are studied in several types of departments and schools. Readers interested in such studies will find information on relevant programs in the *Graduate Programs in the Biological Sciences* volume under Ecology and Environmental Biology; in the *Graduate Programs in the Physical Sciences, Mathematics, Agricultural Sciences, the Environment & Natural Resources* volume under Environmental Management and Policy and Natural Resources; in the *Graduate Programs in Engineering & Applied Sciences* volume under Energy Management and Policy and Environmental Engineering; and in the *Graduate Programs in Business, Education, Health, Information Studies, Law & Social Work* volume under Environmental and Occupational Health. To help you find all of the programs of interest to you, the introduction to each section within the specialized volumes includes, if applicable, a paragraph suggesting other sections and directories with information on related areas of study.

Directory of Institutions with Programs in Engineering and Applied Sciences

This directory lists institutions in alphabetical order and includes beneath each name the academic fields in which each institution offers graduate programs. The degree level in each field is also indicated, provided that the institution has supplied that information in response to Peterson's Annual Survey of Graduate and Professional Institutions. An M indicates that a master's degree program is offered; a D indicates that a doctoral degree program is offered; a P indicates that the first professional degree is offered; an O signifies that other advanced degrees (e.g., certificates or specialist degrees) are offered; and an * (asterisk) indicates that a **Close-Up** and/or **Display** is located in this volume. See the index, "Close-Ups and Displays," for the specific page number.

Profiles of Academic and Professional Programs in the Specialized Volumes

Each section of **Profiles** has a table of contents that lists the Program Directories, **Displays**, and **Close-Ups.** Program Directories consist of the **Profiles** of programs in the relevant fields, with **Displays** following if programs have chosen to include them. **Close-Ups,** which are more individualized statements, again if programs have chosen to submit them, are also listed.

The **Profiles** found in the 500 directories in the specialized volumes provide basic data about the graduate units in capsule form for quick reference. To make these directories as useful as possible, **Profiles** are generally listed for an institution's smallest academic unit within a subject area. In other words, if an institution has a College of Liberal Arts that administers many related programs, the **Profile** for the individual program (e.g., Program in History), not the entire College, appears in the directory.

There are some programs that do not fit into any current directory and are not given individual **Profiles**. The directory structure is reviewed annually in order to keep this number to a minimum and to accommodate major trends in graduate education.

The following outline describes the **Profile** information found in the guides and explains how best to use that information. Any item that does not apply to or was not provided by a graduate unit is omitted from its listing. The format of the **Profiles** is constant, making it easy to compare one institution with another and one program with another.

Identifying Information. The institution's name, in boldface type, is followed by a complete listing of the administrative structure for that field of study. (For example, University of Akron, Buchtel College of Arts and Sciences, Department of Theoretical and Applied Mathematics, Program in Mathematics.) The last unit listed is the one to which all information in the **Profile** pertains. The institution's city, state, and zip code follow.

Offerings. Each field of study offered by the unit is listed with all postbaccalaureate degrees awarded. Degrees that are not preceded by a specific concentration are awarded in the general field listed in the unit name. Frequently, fields of study are broken down into subspecializations, and those appear following the degrees awarded; for example, "Offerings in secondary education (M.Ed.), including English education, mathematics education, science education." Students enrolled in the M.Ed. program would be able to specialize in any of the three fields mentioned.

Professional Accreditation. Some **Profiles** indicate whether a program is professionally accredited. Because it is possible for a program to receive or lose professional accreditation at any time, students entering fields in which accreditation is important to a career should verify the status of programs by contacting either the chairperson or the appropriate accrediting association.

Jointly Offered Degrees. Explanatory statements concerning programs that are offered in cooperation with other institutions are included in the list of degrees offered. This occurs most commonly on a regional basis (for example, two state universities offering a cooperative Ph.D. in special education) or where the specialized nature of the institutions encourages joint efforts (a J.D./M.B.A. offered by a law school at an institution with no formal business programs and an institution with a business school but lacking a law school). Only programs that are truly cooperative are listed; those involving only limited course work at another institution are not. Interested students should contact the heads of such units for further information.

Part-Time and Evening/Weekend Programs. When information regarding the availability of part-time or evening/weekend study appears in the **Profile**, it means that students are able to earn a degree exclusively through such study.

Postbaccalaureate Distance Learning Degrees. A postbaccalaureate distance learning degree program signifies that course requirements can be fulfilled with minimal or no on-campus study.

Faculty. Figures on the number of faculty members actively involved with graduate students through teaching or research are separated into full-and part-time as well as men and women whenever the information has been supplied.

Students. Figures for the number of students enrolled in graduate and professional programs pertain to the semester of highest enrollment from the 2010–11 academic year. These figures are broken down into full-and part-time and men and women whenever the data have been supplied. Information on the number of matriculated students enrolled in the unit who are members of a minority group or are international students appears here. The average age of the matriculated students is followed by the number of applicants, the percentage accepted, and the number enrolled for fall 2010.

Degrees Awarded. The number of degrees awarded in the calendar year is listed. Many doctoral programs offer a terminal master's degree if students leave the program after completing only part of the requirements for a doctoral degree; that is indicated here. All degrees are classified into one of four types: master's, doctoral, first professional, and other advanced degrees. A unit may award one or several degrees at a given level; however, the data are only collected by type and may therefore represent several different degree programs.

Degree Requirements. The information in this section is also broken down by type of degree, and all information for a degree level pertains to all degrees of that type unless otherwise specified. Degree requirements are collected in a simplified form to provide some very basic information on the nature of the program and on foreign language, thesis or dissertation, comprehensive exam, and registration requirements. Many units also provide a short list of additional requirements, such as fieldwork or an internship. For complete information on graduation requirements, contact the graduate school or program directly.

Entrance Requirements. Entrance requirements are broken down into the four degree levels of master's, doctoral, first professional, and other advanced degrees. Within each level, information may be provided in two basic categories: entrance exams and other requirements. The entrance exams are identified by the standard acronyms used by the testing agencies, unless they are not well known. Other entrance requirements are quite varied, but they often contain an undergraduate or graduate grade point average (GPA). Unless otherwise stated, the GPA is calculated on a 4.0 scale and is listed as a minimum required for admission. Additional exam requirements/recommendations for international students may be listed here. Application deadlines for domestic and international students, the application fee, and whether electronic applications are accepted may be listed here. Note that the deadline should be used for reference only; these dates are subject to change, and students interested in applying should always contact the graduate unit directly about application procedures and deadlines.

Expenses. The typical cost of study for the 2010–11 academic year is given in two basic categories: tuition and fees. Cost of study may be quite complex at a graduate institution. There are often sliding scales for part-time study, a different cost for first-year students, and other variables that make it impossible to completely cover the cost of study for each graduate program. To provide the most usable information, figures are given for full-time study for a full year where available and for part-time study in terms of a per-unit rate (per credit, per semester hour, etc.). Occasionally, variances may be noted in tuition and fees for reasons such as the type of program, whether courses are taken during the day or evening, whether courses are at the master's or doctoral level, or other institution-specific reasons. Expenses are usually subject to change; for exact costs at any given time, contact your chosen schools and programs directly. Keep in mind that the tuition of Canadian institutions is usually given in Canadian dollars.

Financial Support. This section contains data on the number of awards administered by the institution and given to graduate students during the 2010–11 academic year. The first figure given represents the total number of students receiving financial support enrolled in that unit. If the unit has provided information on graduate appoint- ments, these are broken down into three major categories: fellowships give money to graduate students to cover the cost of study and living expenses and are not based on a work obligation or research commitment, research assistantships provide stipends to graduate students for assistance in a formal research project with a faculty member, and teaching assistantships provide stipends to graduate students for teaching or for assisting faculty members in teaching undergraduate classes. Within each category, figures are given for the total number of awards, the average yearly amount per award, and whether full or partial tuition reimbursements are awarded. In addition to graduate appointments, the availability of several other financial aid sources is covered in this section. Tuition waivers are routinely part of a graduate appointment, but units sometimes waive part or all of a student's tuition even if a graduate appointment is not available. Federal Work-Study is made available to students who demonstrate need and meet the federal guidelines; this form of aid normally includes 10 or more hours of work per week in an office of the institution. Institutionally sponsored loans are low-interest loans available to graduate students to cover both educational and living expenses. Career-related internships or fieldwork offer money to students who are participating in a formal off-campus research project or practicum. Grants, scholarships, traineeships, unspecified assistantships, and other awards may also be noted. The availability of financial support to part-time students is also indicated here.

Some programs list the financial aid application deadline and the forms that need to be completed for students to be eligible for financial awards. There are two forms: FAFSA, the Free Application for Federal Student Aid, which is required for federal aid, and the CSS PROFILE®.

Faculty Research. Each unit has the opportunity to list several keyword phrases describing the current research involving faculty members and graduate students. Space limitations prevent the unit from listing complete information on all research programs. The total expenditure for funded research from the previous academic year may also be included.

Unit Head and Application Contact. The head of the graduate program for each unit is listed with academic title and telephone and fax numbers and e-mail address if available. In addition to the unit head, many graduate programs list a separate contact for application and admission information, which follows the listing for the unit head. If no unit head or application contact is given, you should contact the overall institution for information on graduate admissions.

Displays and Close-Ups

The **Displays** and **Close-Ups** are supplementary insertions submitted by deans, chairs, and other administrators who wish to offer an additional, more individualized statement to readers. A number of graduate school and program administrators have attached a **Display** ad near the **Profile** listing. Here you will find information that an institution or program wants to emphasize. The **Close-Ups** are by their very nature more expansive and flexible than the **Profiles**, and the administrators who have written them may emphasize different aspects of their programs. All of the **Close-Ups** are organized in the same way (with the exception of a few that describe research and training opportunities instead of degree programs), and in each one you will find information on the same basic topics, such as programs of study, research facilities, tuition and fees, financial aid, and application procedures. If an institution or program has submitted a **Close-Up**, a boldface cross-reference appears below its **Profile**. As with the **Displays**, all of the **Close-Ups** in the guides have been submitted by choice; the absence of a **Display** or **Close-Up** does not reflect any type of editorial judgment on the part of Peterson's, and their presence in the guides should not be taken as an indication of status, quality, or approval. Statements regarding a university's objectives and accomplishments are a reflection of its own beliefs and are not the opinions of the Peterson's editors.

Appendixes

This section contains two appendixes. The first, "Institutional Changes Since the 2011 Edition," lists institutions that have closed, merged, or changed their name or status since the last edition of the guides. The second, "Abbreviations Used in the Guides," gives abbreviations of degree names, along with what those abbreviations stand for. These appendixes are identical in all six volumes of *Peterson's Graduate and Professional Programs*.

Indexes

There are three indexes presented here. The first index, "Close-Ups and Displays," gives page references for all programs that have chosen to place **Close-Ups** and **Displays** in this volume. It is arranged alphabetically by institution; within institutions, the arrangement is alphabetical by subject area. It is not an index to all programs in the book's directories of **Profiles**; readers must refer to the directories themselves for **Profile** information on programs that have not submitted the additional, more individualized statements. The second index, "Directories and Subject Areas in Other Books in This Series", gives book references for the directories in the specialized volumes and also includes cross-references for subject area names not used in the directory structure, for example, "Computing Technology (see Computer Science)." The third index, "Directories and Subject Areas in This Book," gives page references for the directories in this volume and cross-references for subject area names not used in this volume's directory structure.

Data Collection Procedures

The information published in the directories and **Profiles** of all the books is collected through Peterson's Annual Survey of Graduate and Professional Institutions. The survey is sent each spring to nearly 2,400 institutions offering postbaccalaureate degree programs, including accredited institutions in the United States, U.S. territories, and Canada and those institutions outside the United States that are accredited by U.S. accrediting bodies. Deans and other administrators complete these surveys, providing information on programs in the 500 academic and professional fields covered in the guides as well as overall institutional information. While every effort has been made to ensure the accuracy and completeness of the data, information is sometimes unavailable or changes occur after publication deadlines. All usable information received in time for publication has been included. The omission of any particular item from a directory or **Profile** signifies either that the item is not applicable to the institution or program or that information was not available. **Profiles** of programs scheduled to begin during the 2011–12 academic year cannot, obviously, include statistics on enrollment or, in many cases, the number of faculty members. If no usable data were submitted by an institution, its name, address, and program name appear in order to indicate the availability of graduate work.

Criteria for Inclusion in This Guide

To be included in this guide, an institution must have full accreditation or be a candidate for accreditation (preaccreditation) status by an institutional or specialized accrediting body recognized by the U.S. Department of Education or the Council for Higher Education Accreditation (CHEA). Institutional accrediting bodies, which review each institution as a whole, include the six regional associations of schools and colleges (Middle States, New England, North Central, Northwest, Southern, and Western), each of which is responsible for a specified portion of the United States and its territories. Other institutional accrediting bodies are national in scope and accredit specific kinds of institutions (e.g., Bible colleges, independent colleges, and rabbinical and Talmudic schools). Program registration by the New York State Board of Regents is considered to be the equivalent of institutional accreditation, since the board requires that all programs offered by an institution meet its standards before recognition is granted. A Canadian institution must be chartered and authorized to grant degrees by the provincial government, affiliated with a chartered institution, or accredited by a recognized U.S. accrediting body. This guide also includes institutions outside the United States that are accredited by these U.S. accrediting bodies. There are recognized specialized or professional accrediting bodies in more than fifty different fields, each of which is authorized to accredit institutions or specific programs in its particular field. For specialized institutions that offer programs in one field only, we designate this to be the equivalent of institutional accreditation. A full explanation of the accrediting process and complete information on recognized institutional (regional and national) and specialized accrediting bodies can be found online at www.chea.org or at www.ed.gov/admins/finaid/accred/index.html.

DIRECTORY OF INSTITUTIONS WITH PROGRAMS IN ENGINEERING & APPLIED SCIENCES

ACADEMY OF ART UNIVERSITY

Game Design and Development	M
Modeling and Simulation	M

ACADIA UNIVERSITY

Computer Science	M

AIR FORCE INSTITUTE OF TECHNOLOGY

Aerospace/Aeronautical Engineering	M,D
Computer Engineering	M,D
Computer Science	M,D
Electrical Engineering	M,D
Engineering and Applied Sciences—General	M,D
Engineering Management	M
Engineering Physics	M,D
Environmental Engineering	M
Management of Technology	M,D
Materials Sciences	M,D
Nuclear Engineering	M,D
Operations Research	M,D
Systems Engineering	M,D

ALABAMA AGRICULTURAL AND MECHANICAL UNIVERSITY

Computer Science	M
Engineering and Applied Sciences—General	M
Materials Sciences	M,D

ALASKA PACIFIC UNIVERSITY

Telecommunications Management	M

ALBANY COLLEGE OF PHARMACY AND HEALTH SCIENCES

Biotechnology	P,M

ALCORN STATE UNIVERSITY

Computer Science	M
Information Science	M

ALFRED UNIVERSITY

Bioengineering	M,D
Ceramic Sciences and Engineering	M,D
Electrical Engineering	M,D
Engineering and Applied Sciences—General	M,D
Materials Sciences	M,D
Mechanical Engineering	M,D

ALLIANT INTERNATIONAL UNIVERSITY–SAN DIEGO

Management of Technology	M,D

AMERICAN INTERCONTINENTAL UNIVERSITY ATLANTA

Information Science	M

AMERICAN INTERCONTINENTAL UNIVERSITY ONLINE

Computer and Information Systems Security	M
Information Science	M

AMERICAN INTERCONTINENTAL UNIVERSITY SOUTH FLORIDA

Computer and Information Systems Security	M
Information Science	M

AMERICAN SENTINEL UNIVERSITY

Computer Science	M
Health Informatics	M

AMERICAN UNIVERSITY

Applied Science and Technology	M
Computer Science	M,O

THE AMERICAN UNIVERSITY IN CAIRO

Computer Science	M
Construction Engineering	M
Electrical Engineering	M
Engineering and Applied Sciences—General	M,D,O
Management of Technology	M
Mechanical Engineering	M

THE AMERICAN UNIVERSITY IN DUBAI

Construction Management	M

THE AMERICAN UNIVERSITY OF ATHENS

Computer Science	M
Engineering and Applied Sciences—General	M
Systems Engineering	M
Telecommunications	M

AMERICAN UNIVERSITY OF BEIRUT

Civil Engineering	M,D
Computer Engineering	M,D
Computer Science	M
Electrical Engineering	M,D
Engineering and Applied Sciences—General	M,D
Engineering Management	M,D
Mechanical Engineering	M,D
Water Resources Engineering	M,D

AMERICAN UNIVERSITY OF SHARJAH

Chemical Engineering	M
Civil Engineering	M
Computer Engineering	M
Electrical Engineering	M
Mechanical Engineering	M

ANDREWS UNIVERSITY

Engineering and Applied Sciences—General	M
Software Engineering	M

ANNA MARIA COLLEGE

Fire Protection Engineering	M

APPALACHIAN STATE UNIVERSITY

Computer Science	M
Engineering Physics	M

ARIZONA STATE UNIVERSITY

Aerospace/Aeronautical Engineering	M,D
Bioinformatics	M,D
Biomedical Engineering	M,D
Biotechnology	P,M
Chemical Engineering	M,D
Civil Engineering	M,D
Computer Science	M,D
Construction Engineering	M,D
Construction Management	M,D
Electrical Engineering	M,D,O
Engineering and Applied Sciences—General	M,D,O
Environmental Engineering	M,D
Ergonomics and Human Factors	M
Geological Engineering	M,D
Industrial/Management Engineering	M,D
Information Science	M
Management of Technology	M
Manufacturing Engineering	M
Materials Engineering	M,D
Materials Sciences	M,D
Mechanical Engineering	M,D
Medical Informatics	M,D
Modeling and Simulation	M,D
Nanotechnology	M,D
Nuclear Engineering	M,D,O
Reliability Engineering	M
Software Engineering	M
Systems Engineering	M
Systems Science	M
Technology and Public Policy	M
Transportation and Highway Engineering	M,D,O

ARKANSAS STATE UNIVERSITY

Biotechnology	D,O
Computer Science	M
Engineering and Applied Sciences—General	M

ARKANSAS TECH UNIVERSITY

Engineering and Applied Sciences—General	M
Health Informatics	M
Information Science	M

ARMSTRONG ATLANTIC STATE UNIVERSITY

Computer Science	M

ASPEN UNIVERSITY

Information Science	M,O

ATHABASCA UNIVERSITY

Information Science	M
Management of Technology	M,O

AUBURN UNIVERSITY

Aerospace/Aeronautical Engineering	M,D
Chemical Engineering	M,D
Civil Engineering	M,D
Computer Engineering	M,D
Computer Science	M,D
Construction Engineering	M,D
Construction Management	M
Electrical Engineering	M,D
Engineering and Applied Sciences—General	M,D

Environmental Engineering — M,D

Geotechnical Engineering	M,D
Hydraulics	M,D
Industrial/Management Engineering	M,D
Materials Engineering	M,D
Mechanical Engineering	M,D
Software Engineering	M,D
Structural Engineering	M,D
Systems Engineering	M,D
Textile Sciences and Engineering	D
Transportation and Highway Engineering	M,D

BALL STATE UNIVERSITY

Computer Science	M
Information Science	M
Telecommunications	M

BARRY UNIVERSITY

Health Informatics	O
Information Science	M

BAYLOR COLLEGE OF MEDICINE

Bioengineering	D
Biomedical Engineering	D

BAYLOR UNIVERSITY

Biomedical Engineering	M,D
Computer Engineering	M,D
Computer Science	M
Electrical Engineering	M,D
Engineering and Applied Sciences—General	M,D
Mechanical Engineering	M,D

BELLEVUE UNIVERSITY

Information Science	M

BENEDICTINE UNIVERSITY

Computer and Information Systems Security	M
Health Informatics	M

BENTLEY UNIVERSITY

Ergonomics and Human Factors	M
Information Science	M

BOISE STATE UNIVERSITY

Civil Engineering	M
Computer Engineering	M,D
Computer Science	M
Electrical Engineering	M,D
Engineering and Applied Sciences—General	M,D
Materials Engineering	M
Mechanical Engineering	M

BOSTON UNIVERSITY

Bioinformatics	M,D
Biomedical Engineering	M,D
Computer and Information Systems Security	M
Computer Engineering	M,D
Computer Science	M,D
Database Systems	M
Electrical Engineering	M,D
Engineering and Applied Sciences—General	M,D
Health Informatics	M
Management of Technology	M
Manufacturing Engineering	M,D

Materials Engineering	M,D
Materials Sciences	M,D
Mechanical Engineering	M,D
Systems Engineering	M,D
Telecommunications Management	M
Telecommunications	M

BOWIE STATE UNIVERSITY

Computer Science	M,D

BOWLING GREEN STATE UNIVERSITY

Computer Science	M
Construction Management	M
Manufacturing Engineering	M
Operations Research	M
Software Engineering	M

BRADLEY UNIVERSITY

Civil Engineering	M
Computer Science	M
Construction Engineering	M
Electrical Engineering	M
Engineering and Applied Sciences—General	M
Industrial/Management Engineering	M
Information Science	M
Manufacturing Engineering	M
Mechanical Engineering	M

BRANDEIS UNIVERSITY

Bioinformatics	M,O
Biotechnology	M
Computer and Information Systems Security	M,O
Computer Science	M,D,O
Health Informatics	M,O
Software Engineering	M,O

BRIDGEWATER STATE UNIVERSITY

Computer Science	M

BRIGHAM YOUNG UNIVERSITY

Biotechnology	M,D
Chemical Engineering	M,D
Civil Engineering	M,D
Computer Engineering	M,D
Computer Science	M,D
Construction Management	M
Electrical Engineering	M,D
Engineering and Applied Sciences—General	M,D
Information Science	M
Mechanical Engineering	M,D

BROCK UNIVERSITY

Biotechnology	M,D
Computer Science	M

BROOKLYN COLLEGE OF THE CITY UNIVERSITY OF NEW YORK

Computer Science	M,D,O
Information Science	M,D,O

BROWN UNIVERSITY

Biomedical Engineering	M,D
Biotechnology	M,D
Chemical Engineering	M,D
Computer Engineering	M,D
Computer Science	M,D
Electrical Engineering	M,D
Engineering and Applied Sciences—General	M,D
Materials Sciences	M,D

Mechanical Engineering	M,D
Mechanics	M,D

BUCKNELL UNIVERSITY

Chemical Engineering	M
Civil Engineering	M
Electrical Engineering	M
Engineering and Applied Sciences—General	M
Mechanical Engineering	M

BUFFALO STATE COLLEGE, STATE UNIVERSITY OF NEW YORK

Industrial/Management Engineering	M

CALIFORNIA INSTITUTE OF TECHNOLOGY

Aerospace/Aeronautical Engineering	M,D,O
Bioengineering	M,D
Chemical Engineering	M,D
Civil Engineering	M,D,O
Computer Science	M,D
Electrical Engineering	M,D,O
Engineering and Applied Sciences—General	M,D,O
Environmental Engineering	M,D
Materials Sciences	M,D
Mechanical Engineering	M,D,O
Mechanics	M,D
Systems Engineering	M,D

CALIFORNIA LUTHERAN UNIVERSITY

Management of Technology	M,O

CALIFORNIA MIRAMAR UNIVERSITY

Telecommunications Management	M
Telecommunications	M

CALIFORNIA NATIONAL UNIVERSITY FOR ADVANCED STUDIES

Engineering and Applied Sciences—General	M
Engineering Management	M

CALIFORNIA POLYTECHNIC STATE UNIVERSITY, SAN LUIS OBISPO

Aerospace/Aeronautical Engineering	M
Civil Engineering	M
Computer Science	M
Electrical Engineering	M
Engineering and Applied Sciences—General	M
Environmental Engineering	M
Industrial/Management Engineering	M
Mechanical Engineering	M
Polymer Science and Engineering	M

CALIFORNIA STATE POLYTECHNIC UNIVERSITY, POMONA

Aerospace/Aeronautical Engineering	M
Biotechnology	M
Civil Engineering	M
Computer Science	M

Electrical Engineering	M
Engineering Management	M
Mechanical Engineering	M

CALIFORNIA STATE UNIVERSITY CHANNEL ISLANDS

Bioinformatics	M
Biotechnology	M
Computer Science	M

CALIFORNIA STATE UNIVERSITY, CHICO

Computer Engineering	M
Computer Science	M
Electrical Engineering	M
Engineering and Applied Sciences—General	M
Modeling and Simulation	M

CALIFORNIA STATE UNIVERSITY, DOMINGUEZ HILLS

Bioinformatics	M
Computer Science	M

CALIFORNIA STATE UNIVERSITY, EAST BAY

Computer Science	M
Construction Management	M
Engineering and Applied Sciences—General	M
Engineering Management	M
Operations Research	M

CALIFORNIA STATE UNIVERSITY, FRESNO

Civil Engineering	M
Computer Science	M
Electrical Engineering	M
Engineering and Applied Sciences—General	M
Industrial/Management Engineering	M
Mechanical Engineering	M

CALIFORNIA STATE UNIVERSITY, FULLERTON

Civil Engineering	M
Computer Science	M
Electrical Engineering	M
Engineering and Applied Sciences—General	M
Information Science	M
Mechanical Engineering	M
Mechanics	M
Software Engineering	M
Systems Engineering	M

CALIFORNIA STATE UNIVERSITY, LONG BEACH

Aerospace/Aeronautical Engineering	M
Chemical Engineering	M
Civil Engineering	M
Computer Engineering	M
Computer Science	M
Electrical Engineering	M
Engineering Management	M,D
Ergonomics and Human Factors	M
Mechanical Engineering	M,D

CALIFORNIA STATE UNIVERSITY, LOS ANGELES

Civil Engineering	M
Computer Science	M
Electrical Engineering	M
Engineering and Applied Sciences—General	M*

Management of Technology	M
Mechanical Engineering	M

CALIFORNIA STATE UNIVERSITY, NORTHRIDGE

Artificial Intelligence/Robotics	M
Civil Engineering	M
Computer Science	M
Electrical Engineering	M
Engineering and Applied Sciences—General	M
Engineering Management	M
Ergonomics and Human Factors	M
Industrial/Management Engineering	M
Manufacturing Engineering	M
Materials Engineering	M
Mechanical Engineering	M
Software Engineering	M
Structural Engineering	M
Systems Engineering	M

CALIFORNIA STATE UNIVERSITY, SACRAMENTO

Civil Engineering	M
Computer Science	M
Electrical Engineering	M
Engineering and Applied Sciences—General	M
Mechanical Engineering	M
Software Engineering	M

CALIFORNIA STATE UNIVERSITY, SAN BERNARDINO

Computer Science	M

CALIFORNIA STATE UNIVERSITY, SAN MARCOS

Computer Science	M

CAMBRIDGE COLLEGE

Management of Technology	M
Medical Informatics	M

CAPELLA UNIVERSITY

Computer and Information Systems Security	M,D,O
Management of Technology	M,D,O

CAPITOL COLLEGE

Computer and Information Systems Security	M
Computer Science	M
Electrical Engineering	M
Information Science	M
Telecommunications Management	M

CARLETON UNIVERSITY

Aerospace/Aeronautical Engineering	M,D
Biomedical Engineering	M,D
Civil Engineering	M,D
Computer Science	M,D
Electrical Engineering	M,D
Engineering and Applied Sciences—General	M,D
Environmental Engineering	M,D
Information Science	M,D
Management of Technology	M
Materials Engineering	M,D

Mechanical Engineering	M,D
Systems Engineering	M,D
Systems Science	M,D

CARNEGIE MELLON UNIVERSITY

Architectural Engineering	M,D
Artificial Intelligence/ Robotics	M,D
Bioengineering	M,D
Biomedical Engineering	M,D
Biotechnology	M,D
Chemical Engineering	M,D
Civil Engineering	M,D
Computer and Information Systems Security	M
Computer Engineering	M,D*
Computer Science	M,D
Construction Management	M,D
Electrical Engineering	M,D
Environmental Engineering	M,D
Human-Computer Interaction	M,D
Information Science	M,D
Management of Technology	M,D
Materials Engineering	M,D
Materials Sciences	M,D
Mechanical Engineering	M,D
Mechanics	M,D
Operations Research	D
Polymer Science and Engineering	M,D
Software Engineering	M,D
Systems Engineering	M
Technology and Public Policy	M,D*
Telecommunications Management	M

CARROLL UNIVERSITY

Software Engineering	M

CASE WESTERN RESERVE UNIVERSITY

Aerospace/Aeronautical Engineering	M,D
Biomedical Engineering	M,D*
Chemical Engineering	M,D
Civil Engineering	M,D
Computer Engineering	M,D
Computer Science	M,D
Electrical Engineering	M,D
Engineering and Applied Sciences—General	M,D
Engineering Management	M
Information Science	M,D
Materials Engineering	M,D
Materials Sciences	M,D
Mechanical Engineering	M,D
Operations Research	M
Polymer Science and Engineering	M,D
Systems Engineering	M,D

THE CATHOLIC UNIVERSITY OF AMERICA

Biomedical Engineering	M,D
Civil Engineering	M,D
Computer Science	M,D
Electrical Engineering	M,D
Engineering and Applied Sciences—General	M,D,O
Engineering Management	M,O
Environmental Engineering	M,D
Ergonomics and Human Factors	M,D
Materials Engineering	M

Materials Sciences	M
Mechanical Engineering	M,D

CENTRAL CONNECTICUT STATE UNIVERSITY

Computer Science	M,O
Construction Management	M,O
Engineering and Applied Sciences—General	M,O
Management of Technology	M,O

CENTRAL MICHIGAN UNIVERSITY

Automotive Engineering	M,O
Computer Science	M
Engineering and Applied Sciences—General	M
Materials Sciences	D

CENTRAL WASHINGTON UNIVERSITY

Engineering and Applied Sciences—General	M
Industrial/Management Engineering	M

CHAMPLAIN COLLEGE

Management of Technology	M

CHICAGO STATE UNIVERSITY

Computer Science	M

CHRISTIAN BROTHERS UNIVERSITY

Engineering and Applied Sciences—General	M

CHRISTOPHER NEWPORT UNIVERSITY

Computer Science	M

THE CITADEL, THE MILITARY COLLEGE OF SOUTH CAROLINA

Computer Science	M
Information Science	M

CITY COLLEGE OF THE CITY UNIVERSITY OF NEW YORK

Biomedical Engineering	M,D
Chemical Engineering	M,D
Civil Engineering	M,D
Computer Science	M,D
Electrical Engineering	M,D
Engineering and Applied Sciences—General	M,D
Mechanical Engineering	M,D

CITY UNIVERSITY OF SEATTLE

Computer and Information Systems Security	M,O
Computer Science	M,O
Management of Technology	M,O

CLAFLIN UNIVERSITY

Biotechnology	M

CLAREMONT GRADUATE UNIVERSITY

Financial Engineering	M
Health Informatics	M,D,O
Information Science	M,D,O

Operations Research	M,D
Systems Science	M,D,O
Telecommunications	M,D,O

CLARK ATLANTA UNIVERSITY

Computer Science	M
Information Science	M

CLARKSON UNIVERSITY

Chemical Engineering	M,D
Civil Engineering	M
Computer Engineering	M,D
Computer Science	M
Electrical Engineering	M,D
Engineering and Applied Sciences—General	M,D*
Engineering Management	M
Environmental Engineering	M,D
Information Science	M*
Mechanical Engineering	M,D

CLARK UNIVERSITY

Information Science	M

CLEMSON UNIVERSITY

Automotive Engineering	M,D
Bioengineering	M,D
Biosystems Engineering	M,D
Chemical Engineering	M,D
Civil Engineering	M,D
Computer Engineering	M,D
Computer Science	M,D
Construction Management	M
Electrical Engineering	M,D
Engineering and Applied Sciences—General	M,D
Environmental Engineering	M,D
Ergonomics and Human Factors	D
Industrial/Management Engineering	M,D
Manufacturing Engineering	M
Materials Engineering	M,D
Materials Sciences	M,D
Mechanical Engineering	M,D
Operations Research	M,D

CLEVELAND STATE UNIVERSITY

Biomedical Engineering	D
Chemical Engineering	M,D
Civil Engineering	M,D
Computer Science	M,D
Electrical Engineering	M,D
Engineering and Applied Sciences—General	M,D
Environmental Engineering	M,D
Industrial/Management Engineering	M,D
Information Science	M,D
Mechanical Engineering	M,D
Software Engineering	M,D

COLEMAN UNIVERSITY

Information Science	M
Management of Technology	M

COLLEGE OF CHARLESTON

Computer Science	M

THE COLLEGE OF SAINT ROSE

Computer Science	M
Information Science	M

THE COLLEGE OF ST. SCHOLASTICA

Health Informatics	M,O

COLLEGE OF STATEN ISLAND OF THE CITY UNIVERSITY OF NEW YORK

Computer Science	M

THE COLLEGE OF WILLIAM AND MARY

Applied Science and Technology	M,D
Computer Science	M,D
Operations Research	M

COLORADO CHRISTIAN UNIVERSITY

Computer and Information Systems Security	M

COLORADO SCHOOL OF MINES

Chemical Engineering	M,D
Computer Science	M,D
Electronic Materials	M,D
Engineering and Applied Sciences—General	M,D,O
Engineering Management	M,D
Environmental Engineering	M,D
Geological Engineering	M,D
Management of Technology	M,D
Materials Engineering	M,D
Materials Sciences	M,D
Metallurgical Engineering and Metallurgy	M,D
Mineral/Mining Engineering	M,D
Nuclear Engineering	M,D
Petroleum Engineering	M,D
Systems Engineering	M,D

COLORADO STATE UNIVERSITY

Biomedical Engineering	M,D
Chemical Engineering	M,D
Civil Engineering	M,D
Computer Science	M,D
Construction Management	M
Electrical Engineering	M,D
Engineering and Applied Sciences—General	M,D
Mechanical Engineering	M,D

COLORADO STATE UNIVERSITY–PUEBLO

Applied Science and Technology	M
Engineering and Applied Sciences—General	M
Industrial/Management Engineering	M
Systems Engineering	M

COLORADO TECHNICAL UNIVERSITY COLORADO SPRINGS

Computer and Information Systems Security	M,D
Computer Engineering	M
Computer Science	M,D
Database Systems	M,D
Electrical Engineering	M
Management of Technology	M,D
Software Engineering	M,D
Systems Engineering	M

COLORADO TECHNICAL UNIVERSITY DENVER

Computer and Information Systems Security	M
Computer Engineering	M
Computer Science	M
Database Systems	M
Electrical Engineering	M
Management of Technology	M
Software Engineering	M
Systems Engineering	M

COLORADO TECHNICAL UNIVERSITY SIOUX FALLS

Computer and Information Systems Security	M
Computer Science	M
Management of Technology	M
Software Engineering	M

COLUMBIA UNIVERSITY

Biomedical Engineering	M,D
Chemical Engineering	M,D
Civil Engineering	M,D,O
Computer Engineering	M,D,O
Computer Science	M,D,O*
Construction Engineering	M,D,O
Construction Management	M,D,O
Electrical Engineering	M,D,O*
Engineering and Applied Sciences—General	M,D,O
Environmental Engineering	M,D,O
Financial Engineering	M,D,O
Industrial/Management Engineering	M,D,O
Management of Technology	M
Materials Engineering	M,D,O
Materials Sciences	M,D,O
Mechanical Engineering	M,D,O
Mechanics	M,D,O
Medical Informatics	M,D,O
Metallurgical Engineering and Metallurgy	M,D,O
Mineral/Mining Engineering	M,D,O
Operations Research	M,D,O

COLUMBUS STATE UNIVERSITY

Computer Science	M,O
Modeling and Simulation	M,O

CONCORDIA UNIVERSITY (CANADA)

Aerospace/Aeronautical Engineering	M
Biotechnology	M,D,O
Civil Engineering	M,D,O
Computer and Information Systems Security	M,O
Computer Engineering	M,D
Computer Science	M,D,O
Construction Engineering	M,D,O
Electrical Engineering	M,D
Engineering and Applied Sciences—General	M,D,O
Environmental Engineering	M,D,O
Game Design and Development	M,O
Industrial/Management Engineering	M,D,O
Mechanical Engineering	M,D,O
Software Engineering	M,D,O
Systems Engineering	M,O
Telecommunications Management	M,O

CONCORDIA UNIVERSITY COLLEGE OF ALBERTA

Computer and Information Systems Security	M

COOPER UNION FOR THE ADVANCEMENT OF SCIENCE AND ART

Chemical Engineering	M
Civil Engineering	M
Electrical Engineering	M
Engineering and Applied Sciences—General	M
Mechanical Engineering	M

CORNELL UNIVERSITY

Aerospace/Aeronautical Engineering	M,D
Agricultural Engineering	M,D
Artificial Intelligence/ Robotics	M,D
Biochemical Engineering	M,D
Bioengineering	M,D
Biomedical Engineering	M,D
Chemical Engineering	M,D
Civil Engineering	M,D
Computer Engineering	M,D
Computer Science	M,D
Electrical Engineering	M,D
Engineering and Applied Sciences—General	M,D
Engineering Management	M,D
Engineering Physics	M,D
Environmental Engineering	M,D
Ergonomics and Human Factors	M
Geotechnical Engineering	M,D
Human-Computer Interaction	D
Industrial/Management Engineering	M,D
Information Science	D
Manufacturing Engineering	M,D
Materials Engineering	M,D
Materials Sciences	M,D
Mechanical Engineering	M,D
Mechanics	M,D
Operations Research	M,D
Polymer Science and Engineering	M,D
Structural Engineering	M,D
Systems Engineering	M
Textile Sciences and Engineering	M,D
Transportation and Highway Engineering	M,D
Water Resources Engineering	M,D

DAKOTA STATE UNIVERSITY

Information Science	M,D*

DALHOUSIE UNIVERSITY

Agricultural Engineering	M,D
Bioengineering	M,D
Bioinformatics	M,D
Biomedical Engineering	M,D
Chemical Engineering	M,D
Civil Engineering	M,D
Computer Engineering	M,D
Computer Science	M,D
Electrical Engineering	M,D
Engineering and Applied Sciences—General	M,D
Environmental Engineering	M,D
Human-Computer Interaction	M
Industrial/Management Engineering	M,D

Materials Engineering	M,D
Mechanical Engineering	M,D
Medical Informatics	M,D
Mineral/Mining Engineering	M,D

DALLAS BAPTIST UNIVERSITY

Engineering Management	M
Management of Technology	M

DARTMOUTH COLLEGE

Biochemical Engineering	M,D
Biomedical Engineering	M,D
Biotechnology	M,D
Computer Engineering	M,D
Computer Science	M,D
Electrical Engineering	M,D
Engineering and Applied Sciences—General	M,D
Engineering Management	M
Engineering Physics	M,D
Environmental Engineering	M,D
Manufacturing Engineering	M,D
Materials Engineering	M,D
Materials Sciences	M,D
Mechanical Engineering	M,D

DAVENPORT UNIVERSITY

Computer and Information Systems Security	M

DAVENPORT UNIVERSITY

Computer and Information Systems Security	M

DAVENPORT UNIVERSITY

Computer and Information Systems Security	M

DEPAUL UNIVERSITY

Computer and Information Systems Security	M,D
Computer Science	M,D
Game Design and Development	M,D
Human-Computer Interaction	M,D
Information Science	M,D
Management of Technology	M,D
Polymer Science and Engineering	M
Software Engineering	M,D

DESALES UNIVERSITY

Information Science	M

DIGIPEN INSTITUTE OF TECHNOLOGY

Computer Science	M

DREXEL UNIVERSITY

Architectural Engineering	M,D
Biochemical Engineering	M
Biomedical Engineering	M,D
Chemical Engineering	M,D
Civil Engineering	M,D
Computer Engineering	M
Computer Science	M,D
Construction Management	M
Electrical Engineering	M
Engineering and Applied Sciences—General	M,D,O
Engineering Management	M,O

Environmental Engineering	M,D
Geotechnical Engineering	M,D
Hydraulics	M,D
Information Science	M,D
Materials Engineering	M,D
Mechanical Engineering	M,D
Mechanics	M,D
Medical Informatics	M,D,O
Software Engineering	M,D,O
Structural Engineering	M,D
Telecommunications	M

DUKE UNIVERSITY

Bioinformatics	D,O
Biomedical Engineering	M,D
Civil Engineering	M,D
Computer Engineering	M,D
Computer Science	M,D
Electrical Engineering	M,D*
Engineering and Applied Sciences—General	M
Engineering Management	M
Environmental Engineering	M,D
Materials Engineering	M
Materials Sciences	M,D
Mechanical Engineering	M,D

DUQUESNE UNIVERSITY

Biotechnology	M

EAST CAROLINA UNIVERSITY

Biotechnology	M
Computer Science	M,D,O
Industrial/Management Engineering	M,D,O
Information Science	M
Management of Technology	M,D,O
Manufacturing Engineering	M,D,O

EASTERN ILLINOIS UNIVERSITY

Computer and Information Systems Security	M,O
Computer Science	M,O
Engineering and Applied Sciences—General	M,O
Systems Science	M,O

EASTERN KENTUCKY UNIVERSITY

Industrial/Management Engineering	M
Manufacturing Engineering	M

EASTERN MICHIGAN UNIVERSITY

Artificial Intelligence/ Robotics	M,O
Computer and Information Systems Security	M,O
Computer Science	M,O
Construction Management	M
Engineering and Applied Sciences—General	M
Engineering Management	M
Management of Technology	D
Polymer Science and Engineering	M
Technology and Public Policy	M

EASTERN WASHINGTON UNIVERSITY

Computer Science	M

EAST STROUDSBURG UNIVERSITY OF PENNSYLVANIA
Computer Science — M

EAST TENNESSEE STATE UNIVERSITY
Computer Science — M
Information Science — M
Manufacturing Engineering — M,O

ÉCOLE POLYTECHNIQUE DE MONTRÉAL
Aerospace/Aeronautical Engineering — M,D,O
Biomedical Engineering — M,D,O
Chemical Engineering — M,D,O
Civil Engineering — M,D,O
Computer Engineering — M,D,O
Computer Science — M,D,O
Electrical Engineering — M,D,O
Engineering and Applied Sciences—General — M,D,O
Engineering Physics — M,D,O
Environmental Engineering — M,D,O
Geotechnical Engineering — M,D,O
Hydraulics — M,D,O
Industrial/Management Engineering — M,D,O
Management of Technology — M,D,O
Mechanical Engineering — M,D,O
Mechanics — M,D,O
Nuclear Engineering — M,D,O
Operations Research — M,D,O
Structural Engineering — M,D,O
Transportation and Highway Engineering — M,D,O

ELMHURST COLLEGE
Computer Science — M

EMBRY-RIDDLE AERONAUTICAL UNIVERSITY–DAYTONA
Aerospace/Aeronautical Engineering — M
Computer Engineering — M
Electrical Engineering — M
Engineering Physics — D
Ergonomics and Human Factors — M
Mechanical Engineering — M
Software Engineering — M
Systems Engineering — M

EMBRY-RIDDLE AERONAUTICAL UNIVERSITY–PRESCOTT
Safety Engineering — M

EMBRY-RIDDLE AERONAUTICAL UNIVERSITY–WORLDWIDE
Aerospace/Aeronautical Engineering — M
Aviation — D
Management of Technology — M

EMORY UNIVERSITY
Computer Science — M,D
Health Informatics — M,D

EVERGLADES UNIVERSITY
Aviation — M
Information Science — M

EXCELSIOR COLLEGE
Medical Informatics — O

FAIRFIELD UNIVERSITY
Computer Engineering — M
Electrical Engineering — M
Engineering and Applied Sciences—General — M
Management of Technology — M
Mechanical Engineering — M
Software Engineering — M

FAIRLEIGH DICKINSON UNIVERSITY, COLLEGE AT FLORHAM
Chemical Engineering — M,O
Computer Science — M
Management of Technology — M,O

FAIRLEIGH DICKINSON UNIVERSITY, METROPOLITAN CAMPUS
Computer Engineering — M
Computer Science — M
Electrical Engineering — M
Engineering and Applied Sciences—General — M
Systems Science — M

FERRIS STATE UNIVERSITY
Computer Science — M
Database Systems — M

FITCHBURG STATE UNIVERSITY
Computer Science — M

FLORIDA AGRICULTURAL AND MECHANICAL UNIVERSITY
Biomedical Engineering — M,D
Chemical Engineering — M,D
Civil Engineering — M,D
Electrical Engineering — M,D
Engineering and Applied Sciences—General — M,D
Environmental Engineering — M,D
Industrial/Management Engineering — M,D
Mechanical Engineering — M,D
Software Engineering — M

FLORIDA ATLANTIC UNIVERSITY
Civil Engineering — M
Computer Engineering — M,D
Computer Science — M,D
Electrical Engineering — M,D
Engineering and Applied Sciences—General — M,D
Mechanical Engineering — M,D
Ocean Engineering — M,D

FLORIDA GULF COAST UNIVERSITY
Computer Science — M
Information Science — M

FLORIDA INSTITUTE OF TECHNOLOGY
Aerospace/Aeronautical Engineering — M,D
Biotechnology — M,D
Chemical Engineering — M,D
Civil Engineering — M,D

(continued)
Computer Engineering — M,D
Computer Science — M,D
Electrical Engineering — M,D
Engineering and Applied Sciences—General — M,D
Engineering Management — M,D
Ergonomics and Human Factors — M
Management of Technology — M
Mechanical Engineering — M,D
Ocean Engineering — M,D
Operations Research — M,D
Software Engineering — M,D
Systems Engineering — M,D

FLORIDA INTERNATIONAL UNIVERSITY
Biomedical Engineering — M,D
Civil Engineering — M,D
Computer Engineering — M
Computer Science — M,D
Construction Management — M
Electrical Engineering — M,D
Engineering and Applied Sciences—General — M,D*
Environmental Engineering — M
Information Science — M,D
Materials Engineering — M,D
Materials Sciences — M,D
Mechanical Engineering — M,D
Telecommunications — M,D

FLORIDA STATE UNIVERSITY
Biomedical Engineering — M,D
Chemical Engineering — M,D
Civil Engineering — M,D
Computer and Information Systems Security — M,D
Computer Science — M,D
Electrical Engineering — M,D
Energy and Power Engineering — M,D
Engineering and Applied Sciences—General — M,D
Environmental Engineering — M,D
Industrial/Management Engineering — M,D
Manufacturing Engineering — M,D
Materials Sciences — M,D
Mechanical Engineering — M,D
Polymer Science and Engineering — M

FORDHAM UNIVERSITY
Computer Science — M

FRANKLIN PIERCE UNIVERSITY
Telecommunications — M,D,O

FRANKLIN UNIVERSITY
Computer Science — M

FROSTBURG STATE UNIVERSITY
Computer Science — M

FULL SAIL UNIVERSITY
Game Design and Development — M

GANNON UNIVERSITY
Computer Science — M
Electrical Engineering — M
Engineering Management — M

(continued)
Environmental Engineering — M
Information Science — M
Mechanical Engineering — M
Software Engineering — M

GEORGE MASON UNIVERSITY
Bioinformatics — M,D,O
Civil Engineering — M,D,O
Computer and Information Systems Security — M,D,O
Computer Engineering — M,D,O
Computer Science — M,D,O
Database Systems — M,D,O
Electrical Engineering — M,D,O
Engineering and Applied Sciences—General — M,D,O
Engineering Physics — M,D
Game Design and Development — M,D,O
Health Informatics — M,O
Information Science — M,D,O
Management of Technology — M,D
Modeling and Simulation — M,D,O
Operations Research — M,D,O
Software Engineering — M,D,O
Systems Engineering — M,D,O
Telecommunications Management — M,D,O
Telecommunications — M,D,O
Water Resources Engineering — M,D,O

GEORGETOWN UNIVERSITY
Bioinformatics — M
Computer Science — M
Materials Sciences — D

THE GEORGE WASHINGTON UNIVERSITY
Aerospace/Aeronautical Engineering — M,D,O
Bioinformatics — M
Biotechnology — M
Civil Engineering — M,D,O
Computer Engineering — M,D
Computer Science — M,D
Electrical Engineering — M,D
Engineering and Applied Sciences—General — M,D,O
Engineering Management — M,D,O
Environmental Engineering — M,D,O
Management of Technology — M,D
Materials Sciences — M,D
Mechanical Engineering — M,D,O
Systems Engineering — M,D,O
Technology and Public Policy — M
Telecommunications — M,D

GEORGIA HEALTH SCIENCES UNIVERSITY
Health Informatics — M

GEORGIA INSTITUTE OF TECHNOLOGY
Aerospace/Aeronautical Engineering — M,D
Bioengineering — M,D
Bioinformatics — M,D
Biomedical Engineering — D
Chemical Engineering — M,D
Civil Engineering — M,D
Computer and Information Systems Security — M,D
Computer Engineering — M,D

---

*M—master's degree; P—first professional degree; D—doctorate; O—other advanced degree; *—Close-Up and/or Display*

Computer Science M,D
Electrical Engineering M,D
Engineering and Applied Sciences—General M,D
Environmental Engineering M,D
Ergonomics and Human Factors M,D
Human-Computer Interaction M
Industrial/Management Engineering M,D
Management of Technology M,O
Materials Engineering M,D
Mechanical Engineering M,D
Mechanics M,D
Nuclear Engineering M,D
Operations Research M,D
Polymer Science and Engineering M,D
Systems Engineering M,D
Textile Sciences and Engineering M,D

GEORGIA SOUTHERN UNIVERSITY
Computer Science M
Electrical Engineering M,O
Mechanical Engineering M,O

GEORGIA SOUTHWESTERN STATE UNIVERSITY
Computer Science M
Information Science M

GEORGIA STATE UNIVERSITY
Computer Science M,D
Information Science M
Operations Research M,D

GOLDEN GATE UNIVERSITY
Health Informatics M,D,O
Management of Technology M,D,O

GOVERNORS STATE UNIVERSITY
Computer Science M

GRADUATE SCHOOL AND UNIVERSITY CENTER OF THE CITY UNIVERSITY OF NEW YORK
Biomedical Engineering D
Chemical Engineering D
Civil Engineering D
Computer Science D
Electrical Engineering D
Engineering and Applied Sciences—General D
Mechanical Engineering D

GRAND CANYON UNIVERSITY
Health Informatics M

GRAND VALLEY STATE UNIVERSITY
Bioinformatics M
Computer Engineering M
Computer Science M
Electrical Engineering M
Engineering and Applied Sciences—General M
Information Science M
Manufacturing Engineering M
Mechanical Engineering M
Medical Informatics M
Software Engineering M

HAMPTON UNIVERSITY
Computer Science M

HARDING UNIVERSITY
Management of Technology M

HARRISBURG UNIVERSITY OF SCIENCE AND TECHNOLOGY
Construction Management M
Management of Technology M
Systems Engineering M

HARVARD UNIVERSITY
Applied Science and Technology M,O
Biomedical Engineering M,D
Biotechnology M,O
Computer Science M,D
Engineering and Applied Sciences—General M,D
Information Science M,D,O
Management of Technology D
Medical Informatics M

HAWAI'I PACIFIC UNIVERSITY
Software Engineering M
Telecommunications Management M

HEC MONTREAL
Financial Engineering M
Operations Research M

HENLEY-PUTNAM UNIVERSITY
Computer and Information Systems Security M

HERZING UNIVERSITY ONLINE
Management of Technology M

HODGES UNIVERSITY
Management of Technology M

HOFSTRA UNIVERSITY
Computer Science M

HOLY NAMES UNIVERSITY
Energy Management and Policy M

HOOD COLLEGE
Biotechnology M,O
Computer and Information Systems Security M,O
Computer Science M,O
Information Science M,O
Systems Science M

HOWARD UNIVERSITY
Biotechnology M,D
Chemical Engineering M
Civil Engineering M
Computer Science M
Electrical Engineering M,D
Engineering and Applied Sciences—General M,D
Mechanical Engineering M,D

HUMBOLDT STATE UNIVERSITY
Hazardous Materials Management M

IDAHO STATE UNIVERSITY
Civil Engineering M
Engineering and Applied Sciences—General M,D,O
Environmental Engineering M
Hazardous Materials Management M
Management of Technology M
Mechanical Engineering M
Nuclear Engineering M,D,O
Operations Research M

ILLINOIS INSTITUTE OF TECHNOLOGY
Aerospace/Aeronautical Engineering M,D
Agricultural Engineering M,D
Architectural Engineering M,D
Bioengineering M,D
Biomedical Engineering D
Biotechnology M,D
Chemical Engineering M,D
Civil Engineering M,D
Computer Engineering M,D
Computer Science M,D
Construction Engineering M,D
Construction Management M,D
Electrical Engineering M,D
Engineering and Applied Sciences—General M,D
Environmental Engineering M,D
Geotechnical Engineering M,D
Manufacturing Engineering M,D
Materials Engineering M,D
Materials Sciences M,D
Mechanical Engineering M,D
Software Engineering M,D
Structural Engineering M,D
Telecommunications M,D
Transportation and Highway Engineering M,D

ILLINOIS STATE UNIVERSITY
Biotechnology M
Industrial/Management Engineering M
Management of Technology M

INDIANA STATE UNIVERSITY
Computer Engineering M
Computer Science M
Engineering and Applied Sciences—General M
Industrial/Management Engineering M
Management of Technology D

INDIANA UNIVERSITY BLOOMINGTON
Bioinformatics M,D
Biotechnology M,D
Computer Science M,D
Energy Management and Policy M,D,O
Ergonomics and Human Factors M,D
Health Informatics M,D
Human-Computer Interaction M,D
Information Science M,D,O
Materials Sciences M,D

Safety Engineering M,D
Telecommunications M
Water Resources Engineering M,D

INDIANA UNIVERSITY–PURDUE UNIVERSITY FORT WAYNE
Computer Engineering M
Computer Science M
Construction Management M
Electrical Engineering M
Engineering and Applied Sciences—General M,O
Industrial/Management Engineering M
Information Science M
Mechanical Engineering M
Operations Research M,O
Systems Engineering M

INDIANA UNIVERSITY–PURDUE UNIVERSITY INDIANAPOLIS
Artificial Intelligence/Robotics M,D
Biomedical Engineering M,D,O
Computer Engineering M,D
Computer Science M,D
Electrical Engineering M,D
Information Science M,D
Mechanical Engineering M,D,O

INDIANA UNIVERSITY SOUTH BEND
Computer Science M

INSTITUTO CENTROAMERICANO DE ADMINISTRACIÓN DE EMPRESAS
Management of Technology M

INSTITUTO TECNOLOGICO DE SANTO DOMINGO
Construction Management M,O
Energy and Power Engineering M,D,O
Energy Management and Policy M,D,O
Engineering and Applied Sciences—General M,O
Environmental Engineering M,O
Industrial/Management Engineering M,O
Information Science M,O
Software Engineering M,O
Structural Engineering M,O
Telecommunications M,O

INSTITUTO TECNOLÓGICO Y DE ESTUDIOS SUPERIORES DE MONTERREY, CAMPUS CENTRAL DE VERACRUZ
Computer Science M
Management of Technology M

INSTITUTO TECNOLÓGICO Y DE ESTUDIOS SUPERIORES DE MONTERREY, CAMPUS CHIHUAHUA
Computer Engineering M,O
Electrical Engineering M,O
Engineering Management M,O
Industrial/Management Engineering M,O
Mechanical Engineering M,O
Systems Engineering M,O

INSTITUTO TECNOLÓGICO Y DE ESTUDIOS SUPERIORES DE MONTERREY, CAMPUS CIUDAD DE MÉXICO

Computer Science	M,D
Environmental Engineering	M,D
Industrial/Management Engineering	M,D
Telecommunications Management	M

INSTITUTO TECNOLÓGICO Y DE ESTUDIOS SUPERIORES DE MONTERREY, CAMPUS CIUDAD OBREGÓN

Engineering and Applied Sciences—General	M
Telecommunications Management	M

INSTITUTO TECNOLÓGICO Y DE ESTUDIOS SUPERIORES DE MONTERREY, CAMPUS CUERNAVACA

Computer Science	M,D
Information Science	M,D
Management of Technology	M,D

INSTITUTO TECNOLÓGICO Y DE ESTUDIOS SUPERIORES DE MONTERREY, CAMPUS ESTADO DE MÉXICO

Computer Science	M,D
Information Science	M,D
Materials Engineering	M,D
Materials Sciences	M,D
Telecommunications Management	M,D

INSTITUTO TECNOLÓGICO Y DE ESTUDIOS SUPERIORES DE MONTERREY, CAMPUS IRAPUATO

Computer Science	M,D
Information Science	M,D
Management of Technology	M,D
Telecommunications Management	M,D

INSTITUTO TECNOLÓGICO Y DE ESTUDIOS SUPERIORES DE MONTERREY, CAMPUS LAGUNA

Industrial/Management Engineering	M

INSTITUTO TECNOLÓGICO Y DE ESTUDIOS SUPERIORES DE MONTERREY, CAMPUS MONTERREY

Agricultural Engineering	M,D
Artificial Intelligence/Robotics	M,D
Biotechnology	M,D
Chemical Engineering	M,D
Civil Engineering	M,D
Computer Science	M,D
Electrical Engineering	M,D
Engineering and Applied Sciences—General	M,D
Environmental Engineering	M,D
Industrial/Management Engineering	M,D
Information Science	M,D
Manufacturing Engineering	M,D
Mechanical Engineering	M,D

Systems Engineering	M,D

INSTITUTO TECNOLÓGICO Y DE ESTUDIOS SUPERIORES DE MONTERREY, CAMPUS SONORA NORTE

Information Science	M

INTER AMERICAN UNIVERSITY OF PUERTO RICO, BAYAMÓN CAMPUS

Biotechnology	M

INTER AMERICAN UNIVERSITY OF PUERTO RICO, GUAYAMA CAMPUS

Computer and Information Systems Security	M
Computer Science	M

INTER AMERICAN UNIVERSITY OF PUERTO RICO, METROPOLITAN CAMPUS

Computer Science	M

INTERNATIONAL TECHNOLOGICAL UNIVERSITY

Computer Engineering	M
Computer Science	M
Electrical Engineering	M,D
Engineering Management	M
Software Engineering	M,D

THE INTERNATIONAL UNIVERSITY OF MONACO

Financial Engineering	M

IONA COLLEGE

Computer Science	M
Management of Technology	M,O
Telecommunications	M

IOWA STATE UNIVERSITY OF SCIENCE AND TECHNOLOGY

Aerospace/Aeronautical Engineering	M,D
Agricultural Engineering	M,D
Bioengineering	M,D
Bioinformatics	M,D
Biosystems Engineering	M,D
Chemical Engineering	M,D
Civil Engineering	M,D
Computer Engineering	M,D
Computer Science	M,D
Construction Engineering	M,D
Electrical Engineering	M,D
Engineering and Applied Sciences—General	M,D
Environmental Engineering	M,D
Geotechnical Engineering	M,D
Human-Computer Interaction	M,D
Industrial/Management Engineering	M,D
Information Science	M
Materials Engineering	M,D
Materials Sciences	M,D
Mechanical Engineering	M,D
Mechanics	M,D
Operations Research	M,D
Structural Engineering	M,D
Systems Engineering	M
Transportation and Highway Engineering	M,D

JACKSON STATE UNIVERSITY

Computer Science	M
Materials Sciences	M

JACKSONVILLE STATE UNIVERSITY

Computer Science	M
Software Engineering	M

JAMES MADISON UNIVERSITY

Applied Science and Technology	M
Computer Science	M

THE JOHNS HOPKINS UNIVERSITY

Bioengineering	M,D
Bioinformatics	M,D,O
Biomedical Engineering	M,D,O
Biotechnology	M
Chemical Engineering	M,D
Civil Engineering	M,D
Computer and Information Systems Security	M,O
Computer Engineering	M,D,O
Computer Science	M,D,O
Electrical Engineering	M,D,O
Engineering and Applied Sciences—General	M,D,O
Engineering Management	M
Environmental Engineering	M,D,O
Health Informatics	M
Information Science	M
Management of Technology	M,O
Materials Engineering	M,D
Materials Sciences	M,D
Mechanical Engineering	M,D
Mechanics	M
Nanotechnology	M
Operations Research	M,D
Systems Engineering	M,O
Telecommunications	M,O

JONES INTERNATIONAL UNIVERSITY

Computer and Information Systems Security	M
Management of Technology	M

KANSAS STATE UNIVERSITY

Agricultural Engineering	M,D
Architectural Engineering	M
Bioengineering	M,D
Chemical Engineering	M,D
Civil Engineering	M,D
Computer Science	M,D
Electrical Engineering	M,D
Engineering and Applied Sciences—General	M,D*
Engineering Management	M,D
Industrial/Management Engineering	M,D
Information Science	M,D
Manufacturing Engineering	M,D
Mechanical Engineering	M,D
Nuclear Engineering	M,D
Operations Research	M,D
Software Engineering	M,D

KAPLAN UNIVERSITY, DAVENPORT CAMPUS

Computer and Information Systems Security	M

KEAN UNIVERSITY

Biotechnology	M

KENNESAW STATE UNIVERSITY

Computer Science	M
Information Science	M

KENT STATE UNIVERSITY

Computer Science	M,D
Engineering and Applied Sciences—General	M
Financial Engineering	M
Information Science	M

KENTUCKY STATE UNIVERSITY

Computer and Information Systems Security	M
Computer Science	M
Information Science	M

KETTERING UNIVERSITY

Electrical Engineering	M
Engineering Management	M
Manufacturing Engineering	M
Mechanical Engineering	M

KNOWLEDGE SYSTEMS INSTITUTE

Computer Science	M
Information Science	M

KUTZTOWN UNIVERSITY OF PENNSYLVANIA

Computer Science	M

LAKEHEAD UNIVERSITY

Computer Engineering	M
Computer Science	M
Electrical Engineering	M
Engineering and Applied Sciences—General	M
Environmental Engineering	M

LAMAR UNIVERSITY

Chemical Engineering	M,D
Civil Engineering	M,D
Computer Science	M
Electrical Engineering	M,D
Engineering and Applied Sciences—General	M,D
Engineering Management	M,D
Environmental Engineering	M,D
Industrial/Management Engineering	M,D
Information Science	M
Mechanical Engineering	M,D

LA SALLE UNIVERSITY

Computer Science	M
Management of Technology	M

LAURENTIAN UNIVERSITY

Engineering and Applied Sciences—General	M,D
Mineral/Mining Engineering	M,D

LAWRENCE TECHNOLOGICAL UNIVERSITY

Architectural Engineering	M,D
Automotive Engineering	M,D

*M—master's degree; P—first professional degree; D—doctorate; O—other advanced degree; *—Close-Up and/or Display*

Civil Engineering	M,D
Computer Engineering	M,D
Computer Science	M
Electrical Engineering	M,D
Engineering and Applied Sciences—General	M,D
Engineering Management	M,D
Industrial/Management Engineering	M,D
Management of Technology	M,D
Manufacturing Engineering	M,D
Mechanical Engineering	M,D

LEBANESE AMERICAN UNIVERSITY

Computer Science	M

LEHIGH UNIVERSITY

Bioengineering	M,D
Chemical Engineering	M,D
Civil Engineering	M,D
Computer Engineering	M,D
Computer Science	M,D
Electrical Engineering	M,D
Energy and Power Engineering	M
Engineering and Applied Sciences—General	M,D
Engineering Management	M,D
Environmental Engineering	M,D
Industrial/Management Engineering	M,D
Information Science	M
Manufacturing Engineering	M
Materials Engineering	M,D
Materials Sciences	M,D
Mechanical Engineering	M,D
Mechanics	M,D
Polymer Science and Engineering	M,D
Structural Engineering	M,D
Systems Engineering	M,D

LEHMAN COLLEGE OF THE CITY UNIVERSITY OF NEW YORK

Computer Science	M

LETOURNEAU UNIVERSITY

Engineering and Applied Sciences—General	M

LEWIS UNIVERSITY

Aviation	M
Computer and Information Systems Security	M
Management of Technology	M

LONG ISLAND UNIVERSITY, BROOKLYN CAMPUS

Computer Science	M

LONG ISLAND UNIVERSITY, C.W. POST CAMPUS

Computer Science	M
Engineering Management	M
Information Science	M

LOUISIANA STATE UNIVERSITY AND AGRICULTURAL AND MECHANICAL COLLEGE

Agricultural Engineering	M,D
Applied Science and Technology	M
Bioengineering	M,D
Chemical Engineering	M,D

Civil Engineering	M,D
Computer Engineering	M,D
Computer Science	M,D
Electrical Engineering	M,D
Engineering and Applied Sciences—General	M,D
Environmental Engineering	M,D
Geotechnical Engineering	M,D
Industrial/Management Engineering	M,D
Mechanical Engineering	M,D
Mechanics	M,D
Petroleum Engineering	M,D
Structural Engineering	M,D
Systems Science	M,D
Transportation and Highway Engineering	M,D
Water Resources Engineering	M,D

LOUISIANA STATE UNIVERSITY IN SHREVEPORT

Computer Science	M
Systems Science	M

LOUISIANA TECH UNIVERSITY

Biomedical Engineering	M,D
Chemical Engineering	M,D
Civil Engineering	M,D
Computer Science	M
Electrical Engineering	M,D
Engineering and Applied Sciences—General	M,D
Industrial/Management Engineering	M
Mechanical Engineering	M,D
Modeling and Simulation	M,D

LOYOLA MARYMOUNT UNIVERSITY

Civil Engineering	M
Computer Science	M
Electrical Engineering	M
Engineering Management	M
Mechanical Engineering	M
Systems Engineering	M

LOYOLA UNIVERSITY CHICAGO

Computer Science	M
Information Science	M
Software Engineering	M

LOYOLA UNIVERSITY MARYLAND

Computer Science	M
Software Engineering	M

MAHARISHI UNIVERSITY OF MANAGEMENT

Computer Science	M

MANHATTAN COLLEGE

Chemical Engineering	M
Civil Engineering	M
Computer Engineering	M
Electrical Engineering	M
Engineering and Applied Sciences—General	M
Environmental Engineering	M
Mechanical Engineering	M

MARIST COLLEGE

Computer Science	M,O
Management of Technology	M,O
Software Engineering	M,O

MARLBORO COLLEGE

Information Science	M,O

MARQUETTE UNIVERSITY

Bioinformatics	M,D
Biomedical Engineering	M,D
Civil Engineering	M,D,O
Computer Engineering	M,D,O
Computer Science	M,D
Construction Engineering	M,D,O
Construction Management	M,D,O
Electrical Engineering	M,D,O
Engineering and Applied Sciences—General	M,D,O
Engineering Management	M,D,O
Environmental Engineering	M,D,O
Geotechnical Engineering	M,D,O
Hazardous Materials Management	M,D,O
Management of Technology	M,D
Mechanical Engineering	M,D,O
Structural Engineering	M,D,O
Transportation and Highway Engineering	M,D,O
Water Resources Engineering	M,D,O

MARSHALL UNIVERSITY

Engineering and Applied Sciences—General	M
Engineering Management	M
Environmental Engineering	M
Information Science	M
Management of Technology	M

MARYLHURST UNIVERSITY

Energy and Power Engineering	M

MARYMOUNT UNIVERSITY

Computer and Information Systems Security	M,O
Medical Informatics	M,O

MARYWOOD UNIVERSITY

Biotechnology	M
Information Science	M,O

MASSACHUSETTS INSTITUTE OF TECHNOLOGY

Aerospace/Aeronautical Engineering	M,D,O
Bioengineering	M,D
Biomedical Engineering	M,D
Chemical Engineering	M,D
Civil Engineering	M,D,O
Computer Engineering	M,D,O
Computer Science	M,D,O
Construction Engineering	M,D,O
Electrical Engineering	M,D,O
Electronic Materials	M,D,O
Engineering and Applied Sciences—General	M,D,O
Engineering Management	M,D
Environmental Engineering	M,D,O
Geotechnical Engineering	M,D,O
Information Science	M,D,O
Manufacturing Engineering	M,D,O
Materials Engineering	M,D,O
Materials Sciences	M,D,O
Mechanical Engineering	M,D,O
Medical Informatics	M
Metallurgical Engineering and Metallurgy	M,D,O

Nuclear Engineering	M,D,O
Ocean Engineering	M,D,O
Operations Research	M,D
Polymer Science and Engineering	M,D,O
Structural Engineering	M,D,O
Systems Engineering	M,D
Technology and Public Policy	M,D
Transportation and Highway Engineering	M,D,O

MAYO GRADUATE SCHOOL

Biomedical Engineering	D

MCGILL UNIVERSITY

Aerospace/Aeronautical Engineering	M,D
Agricultural Engineering	M,D
Bioengineering	M,D
Bioinformatics	M,D
Biomedical Engineering	M,D
Biotechnology	M,D,O
Chemical Engineering	M,D
Civil Engineering	M,D
Computer Engineering	M,D
Computer Science	M,D
Electrical Engineering	M,D
Engineering and Applied Sciences—General	M,D,O
Environmental Engineering	M,D
Geotechnical Engineering	M,D
Hydraulics	M,D
Materials Engineering	M,D,O
Mechanical Engineering	M,D
Mechanics	M,D
Mineral/Mining Engineering	M,D,O
Structural Engineering	M,D
Water Resources Engineering	M,D

MCMASTER UNIVERSITY

Chemical Engineering	M,D
Civil Engineering	M,D
Computer Science	M,D
Electrical Engineering	M,D
Engineering and Applied Sciences—General	M,D
Engineering Physics	M,D
Materials Engineering	M,D
Materials Sciences	M,D
Mechanical Engineering	M,D
Nuclear Engineering	M,D
Software Engineering	M,D

MCNEESE STATE UNIVERSITY

Chemical Engineering	M
Civil Engineering	M
Computer Science	M
Electrical Engineering	M
Engineering and Applied Sciences—General	M
Engineering Management	M
Mechanical Engineering	M

MEDICAL COLLEGE OF WISCONSIN

Bioinformatics	M
Medical Informatics	M

MEMORIAL UNIVERSITY OF NEWFOUNDLAND

Civil Engineering	M,D
Computer Engineering	M,D
Computer Science	M,D
Electrical Engineering	M,D

Engineering and Applied Sciences—General	M,D
Environmental Engineering	M
Mechanical Engineering	M,D
Ocean Engineering	M,D

MERCER UNIVERSITY

Biomedical Engineering	M
Computer Engineering	M
Electrical Engineering	M
Engineering and Applied Sciences—General	M
Engineering Management	M
Environmental Engineering	M
Management of Technology	M
Mechanical Engineering	M
Software Engineering	M

MERCY COLLEGE

Computer and Information Systems Security	M

METROPOLITAN STATE UNIVERSITY

Computer and Information Systems Security	M,D,O
Computer Science	M

MIAMI UNIVERSITY

Engineering and Applied Sciences—General	M,O
Paper and Pulp Engineering	M
Software Engineering	M,O
Systems Science	M

MICHIGAN STATE UNIVERSITY

Biosystems Engineering	M,D
Chemical Engineering	M,D
Civil Engineering	M,D
Computer Science	M,D
Construction Management	M,D
Electrical Engineering	M,D
Engineering and Applied Sciences—General	M,D
Environmental Engineering	M,D
Game Design and Development	M
Manufacturing Engineering	M,D
Materials Engineering	M,D
Materials Sciences	M,D
Mechanical Engineering	M,D
Mechanics	M,D
Telecommunications	M

MICHIGAN TECHNOLOGICAL UNIVERSITY

Biomedical Engineering	D
Chemical Engineering	M,D
Civil Engineering	M,D
Computer Engineering	D
Computer Science	M,D
Electrical Engineering	M,D
Engineering and Applied Sciences—General	M,D
Engineering Physics	D
Environmental Engineering	M,D
Geological Engineering	M,D
Materials Engineering	M,D
Mechanical Engineering	M,D
Mechanics	M
Metallurgical Engineering and Metallurgy	M,D

Mineral/Mining Engineering	M,D

MIDDLE TENNESSEE STATE UNIVERSITY

Aerospace/Aeronautical Engineering	M
Computer Science	M
Medical Informatics	M

MIDWESTERN STATE UNIVERSITY

Computer Science	M

MILLS COLLEGE

Computer Science	M,O

MILWAUKEE SCHOOL OF ENGINEERING

Civil Engineering	M
Engineering and Applied Sciences—General	M
Engineering Management	M
Environmental Engineering	M
Medical Informatics	M
Structural Engineering	M

MINNESOTA STATE UNIVERSITY MANKATO

Automotive Engineering	M
Database Systems	M,O
Electrical Engineering	M
Manufacturing Engineering	M

MISSISSIPPI COLLEGE

Computer Science	M

MISSISSIPPI STATE UNIVERSITY

Aerospace/Aeronautical Engineering	M,D
Bioengineering	M,D
Biomedical Engineering	M,D
Chemical Engineering	M,D
Civil Engineering	M,D
Computer Engineering	M,D
Computer Science	M,D
Electrical Engineering	M,D
Engineering and Applied Sciences—General	M,D
Industrial/Management Engineering	M,D
Mechanical Engineering	M,D
Systems Engineering	M,D

MISSISSIPPI VALLEY STATE UNIVERSITY

Bioinformatics	M

MISSOURI STATE UNIVERSITY

Applied Science and Technology	M
Computer Science	M
Construction Management	M
Materials Sciences	M

MISSOURI UNIVERSITY OF SCIENCE AND TECHNOLOGY

Aerospace/Aeronautical Engineering	M,D
Ceramic Sciences and Engineering	M,D
Chemical Engineering	M,D
Civil Engineering	M,D
Computer Engineering	M,D
Computer Science	M,D

Construction Engineering	M,D
Electrical Engineering	M,D
Engineering and Applied Sciences—General	M,D
Engineering Management	M,D
Environmental Engineering	M,D
Geological Engineering	M,D
Geotechnical Engineering	M,D
Hydraulics	M,D
Information Science	M
Manufacturing Engineering	M,D
Mechanical Engineering	M,D
Mechanics	M,D
Metallurgical Engineering and Metallurgy	M,D
Mineral/Mining Engineering	M,D
Nuclear Engineering	M,D
Petroleum Engineering	M,D
Systems Engineering	M,D

MISSOURI WESTERN STATE UNIVERSITY

Engineering and Applied Sciences—General	M
Ergonomics and Human Factors	M

MONMOUTH UNIVERSITY

Computer Science	M,O
Software Engineering	M,O

MONTANA STATE UNIVERSITY

Chemical Engineering	M,D
Civil Engineering	M,D
Computer Engineering	M,D
Computer Science	M,D
Construction Engineering	M,D
Electrical Engineering	M,D
Engineering and Applied Sciences—General	M,D
Environmental Engineering	M,D
Industrial/Management Engineering	M,D
Mechanical Engineering	M,D
Mechanics	M,D

MONTANA TECH OF THE UNIVERSITY OF MONTANA

Electrical Engineering	M
Engineering and Applied Sciences—General	M
Environmental Engineering	M
Geological Engineering	M
Industrial/Management Engineering	M
Metallurgical Engineering and Metallurgy	M
Mineral/Mining Engineering	M
Petroleum Engineering	M

MONTCLAIR STATE UNIVERSITY

Computer Science	M,O
Information Science	M,O

MOREHEAD STATE UNIVERSITY

Industrial/Management Engineering	M

MORGAN STATE UNIVERSITY

Bioinformatics	M
Civil Engineering	M,D
Electrical Engineering	M,D

Engineering and Applied Sciences—General	M,D
Industrial/Management Engineering	M,D
Telecommunications Management	M
Transportation and Highway Engineering	M

MURRAY STATE UNIVERSITY

Management of Technology	M
Safety Engineering	M
Telecommunications Management	M

NATIONAL UNIVERSITY

Computer Science	M
Database Systems	M
Engineering and Applied Sciences—General	M
Engineering Management	M
Environmental Engineering	M
Game Design and Development	M
Health Informatics	M
Information Science	M
Management of Technology	M
Safety Engineering	M
Software Engineering	M
Systems Engineering	M
Telecommunications	M

NAVAL POSTGRADUATE SCHOOL

Aerospace/Aeronautical Engineering	M
Applied Science and Technology	M
Computer Engineering	M,D,O
Computer Science	M,D
Electrical Engineering	M,D,O
Information Science	M,O
Mechanical Engineering	M,D,O
Modeling and Simulation	M,D
Operations Research	M,D
Software Engineering	M,D
Systems Engineering	M,D,O

NEW JERSEY INSTITUTE OF TECHNOLOGY

Bioinformatics	M,D
Biomedical Engineering	M,D
Chemical Engineering	M,D
Civil Engineering	M,D
Computer Engineering	M,D
Computer Science	M,D
Electrical Engineering	M,D
Energy and Power Engineering	M
Engineering and Applied Sciences—General	M,D,O
Engineering Management	M
Environmental Engineering	M,D
Industrial/Management Engineering	M,D
Information Science	M,D
Internet Engineering	M
Management of Technology	M
Manufacturing Engineering	M
Materials Engineering	M,D
Materials Sciences	M,D
Mechanical Engineering	M,D,O
Pharmaceutical Engineering	M
Safety Engineering	M

Software Engineering	M,D
Transportation and Highway Engineering	M,D

NEW MEXICO HIGHLANDS UNIVERSITY

Computer Science	M

NEW MEXICO INSTITUTE OF MINING AND TECHNOLOGY

Computer Science	M,D
Electrical Engineering	M
Engineering Management	M
Environmental Engineering	M
Hazardous Materials Management	M
Materials Engineering	M,D
Mechanics	M
Mineral/Mining Engineering	M
Operations Research	M,D
Petroleum Engineering	M,D
Water Resources Engineering	M

NEW MEXICO STATE UNIVERSITY

Bioinformatics	M,D
Biotechnology	M,D
Chemical Engineering	M,D
Civil Engineering	M,D
Computer Engineering	M,D
Computer Science	M,D
Electrical Engineering	M,D
Engineering and Applied Sciences—General	M,D
Environmental Engineering	M,D
Industrial/Management Engineering	M,D
Mechanical Engineering	M,D

NEW YORK INSTITUTE OF TECHNOLOGY

Computer and Information Systems Security	M
Computer Engineering	M
Computer Science	M
Electrical Engineering	M
Energy and Power Engineering	M,O
Energy Management and Policy	M,O
Engineering and Applied Sciences—General	M,O
Environmental Engineering	M

NEW YORK UNIVERSITY

Agricultural Engineering	M,D
Computer Science	M,D
Construction Management	M,O
Database Systems	M,O
Ergonomics and Human Factors	M,D

NICHOLLS STATE UNIVERSITY

Computer Science	M

NORFOLK STATE UNIVERSITY

Computer Engineering	M
Computer Science	M
Electrical Engineering	M
Materials Sciences	M

NORTH CAROLINA AGRICULTURAL AND TECHNICAL STATE UNIVERSITY

Chemical Engineering	M,D
Civil Engineering	M
Computer Engineering	M,D
Computer Science	M
Construction Management	M
Electrical Engineering	M,D
Energy and Power Engineering	M,D
Engineering and Applied Sciences—General	M,D
Industrial/Management Engineering	M,D
Management of Technology	M,D
Mechanical Engineering	M,D
Systems Engineering	M,D

NORTH CAROLINA STATE UNIVERSITY

Aerospace/Aeronautical Engineering	M,D
Agricultural Engineering	M,D,O
Bioengineering	M,D,O
Bioinformatics	M,D
Biomedical Engineering	M,D
Biotechnology	M
Chemical Engineering	M,D
Civil Engineering	M,D
Computer Engineering	M,D
Computer Science	M,D
Electrical Engineering	M,D
Engineering and Applied Sciences—General	M,D*
Ergonomics and Human Factors	D
Financial Engineering	M
Industrial/Management Engineering	M,D
Management of Technology	D
Manufacturing Engineering	M
Materials Engineering	M,D
Materials Sciences	M,D
Mechanical Engineering	M,D*
Nuclear Engineering	M,D
Operations Research	M,D
Paper and Pulp Engineering	M,D
Polymer Science and Engineering	D
Textile Sciences and Engineering	M,D

NORTH CENTRAL COLLEGE

Computer Science	M

NORTH DAKOTA STATE UNIVERSITY

Agricultural Engineering	M,D
Bioinformatics	M,D
Biosystems Engineering	M,D
Civil Engineering	M,D
Computer Engineering	M,D
Computer Science	M,D,O
Construction Management	M
Electrical Engineering	M,D
Engineering and Applied Sciences—General	M,D
Environmental Engineering	M,D
Industrial/Management Engineering	M,D
Manufacturing Engineering	M,D
Materials Sciences	D
Mechanical Engineering	M,D
Mechanics	M,D
Nanotechnology	D

Operations Research	M,D,O
Polymer Science and Engineering	M,D
Software Engineering	M,D,O

NORTHEASTERN ILLINOIS UNIVERSITY

Computer Science	M

NORTHEASTERN UNIVERSITY

Bioinformatics	M
Biotechnology	M
Chemical Engineering	M,D
Civil Engineering	M,D
Computer Engineering	M,D
Computer Science	M,D
Electrical Engineering	M,D
Energy and Power Engineering	M
Engineering and Applied Sciences—General	M,D,O
Engineering Management	M,D
Environmental Engineering	M,D
Health Informatics	M,D
Industrial/Management Engineering	M,D
Information Science	M,D,O
Manufacturing Engineering	M,D
Mechanical Engineering	M,D
Operations Research	M,D
Telecommunications Management	M

NORTHERN ARIZONA UNIVERSITY

Civil Engineering	M
Computer Science	M
Electrical Engineering	M
Engineering and Applied Sciences—General	M,D,O
Environmental Engineering	M
Mechanical Engineering	M

NORTHERN ILLINOIS UNIVERSITY

Computer Science	M
Electrical Engineering	M
Engineering and Applied Sciences—General	M
Industrial/Management Engineering	M
Mechanical Engineering	M

NORTHERN KENTUCKY UNIVERSITY

Computer and Information Systems Security	M,O
Computer Science	M,O
Health Informatics	M,O
Information Science	M,O
Management of Technology	M
Software Engineering	M,O

NORTHWESTERN POLYTECHNIC UNIVERSITY

Computer Engineering	M
Computer Science	M
Electrical Engineering	M
Engineering and Applied Sciences—General	M

NORTHWESTERN UNIVERSITY

Biomedical Engineering	M,D
Biotechnology	D
Chemical Engineering	M,D
Civil Engineering	M,D

Computer and Information Systems Security	M
Computer Engineering	M,D,O
Computer Science	M,D,O
Database Systems	M
Electrical Engineering	M,D,O
Electronic Materials	M,D,O
Engineering and Applied Sciences—General	M,D,O
Engineering Design	M
Engineering Management	M
Environmental Engineering	M,D
Geotechnical Engineering	M,D
Industrial/Management Engineering	M,D
Information Science	M
Materials Engineering	M,D,O
Materials Sciences	M,D,O
Mechanical Engineering	M,D
Mechanics	M,D
Medical Informatics	M
Software Engineering	M
Structural Engineering	M,D
Transportation and Highway Engineering	M,D

NORTHWEST MISSOURI STATE UNIVERSITY

Computer Science	M,O

NORWICH UNIVERSITY

Civil Engineering	M
Computer and Information Systems Security	M
Construction Management	M
Environmental Engineering	M
Geotechnical Engineering	M
Structural Engineering	M
Water Resources Engineering	M

NOVA SOUTHEASTERN UNIVERSITY

Bioinformatics	M,O
Computer and Information Systems Security	M,D
Computer Science	M,D
Health Informatics	M,O
Information Science	M,D
Medical Informatics	M,O

OAKLAND UNIVERSITY

Computer Engineering	M
Computer Science	M
Electrical Engineering	M
Engineering and Applied Sciences—General	M,D
Engineering Management	M
Mechanical Engineering	M,D
Software Engineering	M
Systems Engineering	M,D
Systems Science	M

OGI SCHOOL OF SCIENCE & ENGINEERING AT OREGON HEALTH & SCIENCE UNIVERSITY

Biomedical Engineering	M,D
Computer Engineering	M,D
Computer Science	M,D
Electrical Engineering	M,D
Environmental Engineering	M,D
Management of Technology	M,O
Ocean Engineering	M,D

THE OHIO STATE UNIVERSITY

Agricultural Engineering	M,D
Bioengineering	M,D
Biomedical Engineering	M,D
Chemical Engineering	M,D
Civil Engineering	M,D
Computer Engineering	M,D
Computer Science	M,D
Electrical Engineering	M,D
Engineering and Applied Sciences—General	M,D
Industrial/Management Engineering	M,D
Information Science	M,D
Materials Engineering	M,D
Materials Sciences	M,D
Mechanical Engineering	M,D
Metallurgical Engineering and Metallurgy	M,D
Nuclear Engineering	M,D
Operations Research	M
Surveying Science and Engineering	M,D
Systems Engineering	M,D

OHIO UNIVERSITY

Biomedical Engineering	M,D
Chemical Engineering	M,D
Civil Engineering	M,D
Computer Science	M,D
Construction Engineering	M,D
Electrical Engineering	M,D
Engineering and Applied Sciences—General	M,D
Environmental Engineering	M,D
Geotechnical Engineering	M,D
Industrial/Management Engineering	M,D
Mechanical Engineering	M,D
Mechanics	M,D
Structural Engineering	M,D
Systems Engineering	M
Telecommunications	M
Transportation and Highway Engineering	M,D
Water Resources Engineering	M,D

OKLAHOMA CITY UNIVERSITY

Computer Science	M

OKLAHOMA STATE UNIVERSITY

Agricultural Engineering	M,D
Applied Science and Technology	M,D,O
Bioengineering	M,D
Chemical Engineering	M,D
Civil Engineering	M,D
Computer Engineering	M,D
Computer Science	M,D
Electrical Engineering	M,D
Engineering and Applied Sciences—General	M,D*
Environmental Engineering	M,D
Fire Protection Engineering	M,D
Industrial/Management Engineering	M,D
Information Science	M,D
Mechanical Engineering	M,D
Telecommunications Management	M,D

OLD DOMINION UNIVERSITY

Aerospace/Aeronautical Engineering	M,D

Civil Engineering	M,D
Computer Engineering	M,D
Computer Science	M,D
Electrical Engineering	M,D
Engineering and Applied Sciences—General	M,D
Engineering Management	M,D
Environmental Engineering	M,D
Ergonomics and Human Factors	D
Human-Computer Interaction	M,D
Information Science	D
Management of Technology	M
Manufacturing Engineering	M,D
Mechanical Engineering	M,D
Modeling and Simulation	M,D
Systems Engineering	M,D

OREGON HEALTH & SCIENCE UNIVERSITY

Biomedical Engineering	M,D
Computer Engineering	M,D
Computer Science	M,D
Electrical Engineering	M,D
Environmental Engineering	M,D
Health Informatics	M,D,O
Management of Technology	M
Medical Informatics	M,D,O

OREGON STATE UNIVERSITY

Bioengineering	M,D
Chemical Engineering	M,D
Civil Engineering	M,D
Computer Engineering	M,D
Computer Science	M,D
Construction Engineering	M,D
Electrical Engineering	M,D
Engineering and Applied Sciences—General	M,D
Environmental Engineering	M,D
Geotechnical Engineering	M,D
Industrial/Management Engineering	M,D
Manufacturing Engineering	M,D
Materials Sciences	M,D
Mechanical Engineering	M,D
Nanotechnology	M,D
Nuclear Engineering	M,D
Ocean Engineering	M,D
Operations Research	M,D
Paper and Pulp Engineering	M,D
Structural Engineering	M,D
Systems Engineering	M,D
Transportation and Highway Engineering	M,D
Water Resources Engineering	M,D

OUR LADY OF THE LAKE UNIVERSITY OF SAN ANTONIO

Computer and Information Systems Security	M

PACE UNIVERSITY

Computer and Information Systems Security	M,D,O
Computer Science	M,D,O
Information Science	M,D,O
Software Engineering	M,D,O
Telecommunications	M,D,O

PACIFIC LUTHERAN UNIVERSITY

Management of Technology	M

PACIFIC STATES UNIVERSITY

Computer Science	M
Management of Technology	M,D

PENN STATE ERIE, THE BEHREND COLLEGE

Engineering and Applied Sciences—General	M

PENN STATE GREAT VALLEY

Engineering and Applied Sciences—General	M

PENN STATE HARRISBURG

Engineering and Applied Sciences—General	M

PENN STATE HERSHEY MEDICAL CENTER

Bioengineering	M,D

PENN STATE UNIVERSITY PARK

Aerospace/Aeronautical Engineering	M,D
Agricultural Engineering	M,D
Architectural Engineering	M,D
Bioengineering	M,D
Chemical Engineering	M,D
Civil Engineering	M,D
Computer Engineering	M,D
Computer Science	M,D
Electrical Engineering	M,D
Engineering and Applied Sciences—General	M,D
Environmental Engineering	M,D
Geotechnical Engineering	M,D
Industrial/Management Engineering	M,D
Information Science	M,D
Manufacturing Engineering	M,D
Materials Engineering	M,D
Materials Sciences	M,D
Mechanical Engineering	M,D
Mechanics	M,D
Mineral/Mining Engineering	M,D
Nuclear Engineering	M,D

PHILADELPHIA UNIVERSITY

Construction Management	M
Textile Sciences and Engineering	M,D

PITTSBURG STATE UNIVERSITY

Construction Engineering	M
Engineering and Applied Sciences—General	M

POINT PARK UNIVERSITY

Engineering Management	M

POLYTECHNIC INSTITUTE OF NYU

Bioinformatics	M
Biomedical Engineering	M,D
Biotechnology	M
Chemical Engineering	M,D
Civil Engineering	M,D

Computer and Information Systems Security	O
Computer Engineering	M,O
Computer Science	M,D
Construction Management	M,D,O
Electrical Engineering	M,D
Engineering Physics	M
Environmental Engineering	M
Financial Engineering	M,O
Industrial/Management Engineering	M
Management of Technology	M,D,O
Manufacturing Engineering	M
Mechanical Engineering	M,D
Polymer Science and Engineering	M
Software Engineering	O
Systems Engineering	M
Telecommunications Management	M
Telecommunications	M
Transportation and Highway Engineering	M,D

POLYTECHNIC INSTITUTE OF NYU, LONG ISLAND GRADUATE CENTER

Aerospace/Aeronautical Engineering	M
Bioinformatics	M
Chemical Engineering	M
Civil Engineering	M
Computer Engineering	M
Computer Science	M
Construction Management	M
Electrical Engineering	M
Engineering Design	M
Engineering Physics	M
Environmental Engineering	M
Financial Engineering	M,O
Industrial/Management Engineering	M
Management of Technology	M
Manufacturing Engineering	M
Mechanical Engineering	M
Systems Engineering	M
Telecommunications	M
Transportation and Highway Engineering	M

POLYTECHNIC INSTITUTE OF NYU, WESTCHESTER GRADUATE CENTER

Bioinformatics	M
Computer Engineering	M
Computer Science	M
Electrical Engineering	M
Financial Engineering	M,O
Industrial/Management Engineering	M
Information Science	M
Management of Technology	M
Manufacturing Engineering	M
Telecommunications	M

POLYTECHNIC UNIVERSITY OF PUERTO RICO

Civil Engineering	M
Computer Engineering	M
Computer Science	M
Electrical Engineering	M
Engineering Management	M
Management of Technology	M
Manufacturing Engineering	M
Mechanical Engineering	M

POLYTECHNIC UNIVERSITY OF PUERTO RICO, MIAMI CAMPUS

Construction Management	M
Environmental Engineering	M

POLYTECHNIC UNIVERSITY OF PUERTO RICO, ORLANDO CAMPUS

Construction Management	M
Engineering Management	M
Environmental Engineering	M
Management of Technology	M

PONTIFICIA UNIVERSIDAD CATOLICA MADRE Y MAESTRA

Engineering and Applied Sciences—General	M
Structural Engineering	M

PORTLAND STATE UNIVERSITY

Artificial Intelligence/ Robotics	M,D,O
Civil Engineering	M,D,O
Computer Engineering	M,D
Computer Science	M,D
Electrical Engineering	M,D
Engineering and Applied Sciences—General	M,D,O
Engineering Management	M,D,O
Environmental Engineering	M,D
Management of Technology	M,D
Manufacturing Engineering	M,D
Mechanical Engineering	M,D,O
Modeling and Simulation	M,D,O
Software Engineering	M,D
Systems Engineering	M,O
Systems Science	M,D,O

PRAIRIE VIEW A&M UNIVERSITY

Computer Science	M,D
Electrical Engineering	M,D
Engineering and Applied Sciences—General	M,D

PRINCETON UNIVERSITY

Aerospace/Aeronautical Engineering	M,D
Chemical Engineering	M,D
Civil Engineering	M,D
Computer Science	M,D
Electrical Engineering	M,D
Electronic Materials	D
Engineering and Applied Sciences—General	M,D
Financial Engineering	M,D
Materials Sciences	D
Mechanical Engineering	M,D
Ocean Engineering	D
Operations Research	M,D

PURDUE UNIVERSITY

Aerospace/Aeronautical Engineering	M,D
Agricultural Engineering	M,D
Biomedical Engineering	M,D
Chemical Engineering	M,D
Civil Engineering	M,D
Computer and Information Systems Security	M
Computer Engineering	M,D
Computer Science	M,D
Electrical Engineering	M,D
Engineering and Applied Sciences—General	M,D,O
Industrial/Management Engineering	M,D
Materials Engineering	M,D
Mechanical Engineering	M,D,O
Nuclear Engineering	M,D

PURDUE UNIVERSITY CALUMET

Biotechnology	M
Computer Engineering	M
Computer Science	M
Electrical Engineering	M
Engineering and Applied Sciences—General	M
Mechanical Engineering	M

QUEENS COLLEGE OF THE CITY UNIVERSITY OF NEW YORK

Computer Science	M

QUEEN'S UNIVERSITY AT KINGSTON

Chemical Engineering	M,D
Civil Engineering	M,D
Computer Engineering	M,D
Computer Science	M,D
Electrical Engineering	M,D
Engineering and Applied Sciences—General	M,D
Mechanical Engineering	M,D
Mineral/Mining Engineering	M,D

REGIS COLLEGE (MA)

Biotechnology	M

REGIS UNIVERSITY

Computer and Information Systems Security	M,O
Computer Science	M,O
Database Systems	M,O
Information Science	M,O
Management of Technology	M,O
Software Engineering	M,O
Systems Engineering	M,O

RENSSELAER AT HARTFORD

Computer Engineering	M
Computer Science	M
Electrical Engineering	M
Engineering and Applied Sciences—General	M
Information Science	M
Mechanical Engineering	M
Systems Science	M

RENSSELAER POLYTECHNIC INSTITUTE

Aerospace/Aeronautical Engineering	M,D
Bioengineering	M,D
Biomedical Engineering	M,D
Ceramic Sciences and Engineering	M,D
Chemical Engineering	M,D
Civil Engineering	M,D
Computer Engineering	M,D
Computer Science	M,D
Electrical Engineering	M,D
Engineering and Applied Sciences—General	M,D
Engineering Management	M,D
Engineering Physics	M,D
Environmental Engineering	M,D
Financial Engineering	M,D
Geotechnical Engineering	M,D
Human-Computer Interaction	M

Industrial/Management Engineering	M,D
Materials Engineering	M,D
Mechanical Engineering	M,D,O
Nuclear Engineering	M,D

PURDUE UNIVERSITY (continued in column 3)

Industrial/Management Engineering	M,D
Information Science	M
Materials Engineering	M,D
Materials Sciences	M,D
Mechanical Engineering	M,D
Metallurgical Engineering and Metallurgy	M,D
Nuclear Engineering	M,D
Polymer Science and Engineering	M,D
Structural Engineering	M,D
Systems Engineering	M,D
Technology and Public Policy	M,D
Transportation and Highway Engineering	M,D

RICE UNIVERSITY

Bioengineering	M,D
Bioinformatics	M,D
Biomedical Engineering	M,D
Chemical Engineering	M,D
Civil Engineering	M,D
Computer Engineering	M,D
Computer Science	M,D
Electrical Engineering	M,D
Engineering and Applied Sciences—General	M,D
Environmental Engineering	M,D
Materials Sciences	M,D
Mechanical Engineering	M,D

RIVIER COLLEGE

Computer Science	M

ROBERT MORRIS UNIVERSITY

Computer and Information Systems Security	M,D
Engineering and Applied Sciences—General	M
Engineering Management	M
Information Science	M,D

ROCHESTER INSTITUTE OF TECHNOLOGY

Bioinformatics	M
Computer and Information Systems Security	M,O
Computer Engineering	M
Computer Science	M,D,O
Database Systems	M,O
Electrical Engineering	M
Engineering and Applied Sciences—General	M,D,O
Engineering Design	M
Engineering Management	M
Game Design and Development	M
Human-Computer Interaction	M
Industrial/Management Engineering	M
Information Science	M,D
Manufacturing Engineering	M
Materials Engineering	M
Materials Sciences	M
Mechanical Engineering	M
Medical Informatics	M
Software Engineering	M
Systems Engineering	M,D
Technology and Public Policy	M
Telecommunications	M

ROGER WILLIAMS UNIVERSITY

Construction Management	M

ROLLINS COLLEGE

Management of Technology	M

ROOSEVELT UNIVERSITY

Biotechnology	M
Computer Science	M
Telecommunications	M

ROSE-HULMAN INSTITUTE OF TECHNOLOGY

Biomedical Engineering	M
Chemical Engineering	M
Civil Engineering	M
Computer Engineering	M
Electrical Engineering	M
Engineering and Applied Sciences—General	M
Engineering Management	M
Environmental Engineering	M
Mechanical Engineering	M
Software Engineering	M

ROWAN UNIVERSITY

Chemical Engineering	M
Civil Engineering	M
Construction Management	M
Electrical Engineering	M
Engineering and Applied Sciences—General	M
Engineering Management	M
Mechanical Engineering	M

ROYAL MILITARY COLLEGE OF CANADA

Chemical Engineering	M,D
Civil Engineering	M,D
Computer Engineering	M,D
Computer Science	M
Electrical Engineering	M,D
Engineering and Applied Sciences—General	M,D
Environmental Engineering	M,D
Materials Sciences	M,D
Mechanical Engineering	M,D
Nuclear Engineering	M,D
Software Engineering	M,D

RUTGERS, THE STATE UNIVERSITY OF NEW JERSEY, CAMDEN

Computer Science	M

RUTGERS, THE STATE UNIVERSITY OF NEW JERSEY, NEWARK

Management of Technology	D

RUTGERS, THE STATE UNIVERSITY OF NEW JERSEY, NEW BRUNSWICK

Aerospace/Aeronautical Engineering	M,D
Biochemical Engineering	M,D
Biomedical Engineering	M,D
Chemical Engineering	M,D
Civil Engineering	M,D
Computer Engineering	M,D
Computer Science	M,D
Electrical Engineering	M,D
Environmental Engineering	M,D
Hazardous Materials Management	M,D

Industrial/Management Engineering	M,D
Materials Engineering	M,D
Materials Sciences	M,D
Mechanical Engineering	M,D
Mechanics	M,D
Operations Research	D
Systems Engineering	M,D

SACRED HEART UNIVERSITY

Computer and Information Systems Security	M,O
Computer Science	M,O
Database Systems	M,O
Information Science	M,O

ST. AMBROSE UNIVERSITY

Management of Technology	M

ST. CLOUD STATE UNIVERSITY

Biomedical Engineering	M
Computer and Information Systems Security	M
Computer Science	M
Electrical Engineering	M
Engineering and Applied Sciences—General	M
Engineering Management	M
Mechanical Engineering	M
Technology and Public Policy	M

ST. FRANCIS XAVIER UNIVERSITY

Computer Science	M

ST. JOHN'S UNIVERSITY (NY)

Biotechnology	M
Computer Science	M

SAINT JOSEPH'S UNIVERSITY

Computer Science	M,O
Health Informatics	M,O

SAINT LEO UNIVERSITY

Computer and Information Systems Security	M

SAINT LOUIS UNIVERSITY

Biomedical Engineering	M,D

SAINT MARTIN'S UNIVERSITY

Civil Engineering	M
Engineering Management	M

SAINT MARY'S UNIVERSITY (CANADA)

Applied Science and Technology	M

ST. MARY'S UNIVERSITY (UNITED STATES)

Computer Engineering	M
Computer Science	M
Electrical Engineering	M
Engineering and Applied Sciences—General	M
Engineering Management	M
Industrial/Management Engineering	M
Information Science	M
Operations Research	M
Software Engineering	M

SAINT MARY'S UNIVERSITY OF MINNESOTA

Telecommunications	M

SAINT XAVIER UNIVERSITY

Computer Science	M
Information Science	M

SALEM INTERNATIONAL UNIVERSITY

Computer and Information Systems Security	M

SAM HOUSTON STATE UNIVERSITY

Computer Science	M
Industrial/Management Engineering	M
Information Science	M

SAN DIEGO STATE UNIVERSITY

Aerospace/Aeronautical Engineering	M,D
Civil Engineering	M
Computer Science	M
Electrical Engineering	M
Engineering and Applied Sciences—General	M,D
Engineering Design	M,D
Mechanical Engineering	M,D
Mechanics	M,D
Telecommunications Management	M

SAN FRANCISCO STATE UNIVERSITY

Biotechnology	M
Computer Science	M
Engineering and Applied Sciences—General	M
Software Engineering	M

SAN JOSE STATE UNIVERSITY

Aerospace/Aeronautical Engineering	M
Chemical Engineering	M
Civil Engineering	M
Computer Engineering	M
Computer Science	M
Electrical Engineering	M
Engineering and Applied Sciences—General	M
Industrial/Management Engineering	M
Materials Engineering	M
Mechanical Engineering	M
Software Engineering	M
Systems Engineering	M

SANTA CLARA UNIVERSITY

Civil Engineering	M
Computer Engineering	M,D,O
Computer Science	M,D,O
Electrical Engineering	M,D,O
Energy and Power Engineering	M,D,O
Energy Management and Policy	M,D,O
Engineering and Applied Sciences—General	M,D,O
Engineering Design	M,D,O
Engineering Management	M
Management of Technology	M
Materials Engineering	M,D,O
Mechanical Engineering	M,D,O
Software Engineering	M,D,O

SAVANNAH COLLEGE OF ART AND DESIGN

Game Design and Development	M,O

SCHOOL OF THE ART INSTITUTE OF CHICAGO

Materials Sciences	M

SEATTLE UNIVERSITY

Engineering and Applied Sciences—General	M
Software Engineering	M

SETON HALL UNIVERSITY

Management of Technology	M

SHIPPENSBURG UNIVERSITY OF PENNSYLVANIA

Computer Science	M

SILICON VALLEY UNIVERSITY

Computer Engineering	M
Computer Science	M

SIMON FRASER UNIVERSITY

Biotechnology	M,D
Computer Science	M,D
Engineering and Applied Sciences—General	M,D
Information Science	M,D
Management of Technology	M,D

SOUTH CAROLINA STATE UNIVERSITY

Civil Engineering	M
Mechanical Engineering	M
Transportation and Highway Engineering	M

SOUTH DAKOTA SCHOOL OF MINES AND TECHNOLOGY

Artificial Intelligence/ Robotics	M
Bioengineering	D
Biomedical Engineering	M,D
Chemical Engineering	M,D
Civil Engineering	M
Construction Management	M
Electrical Engineering	M
Engineering and Applied Sciences—General	M,D
Engineering Management	M
Geological Engineering	M,D
Management of Technology	M
Materials Engineering	M,D
Materials Sciences	M,D
Mechanical Engineering	M,D
Nanotechnology	D

SOUTH DAKOTA STATE UNIVERSITY

Agricultural Engineering	M,D
Biosystems Engineering	M,D
Civil Engineering	M
Electrical Engineering	M,D
Engineering and Applied Sciences—General	M,D
Industrial/Management Engineering	M
Mechanical Engineering	M

SOUTHEASTERN LOUISIANA UNIVERSITY

Applied Science and Technology	M
Computer Science	M

SOUTHEASTERN OKLAHOMA STATE UNIVERSITY

Aviation	M
Biotechnology	M

SOUTHEAST MISSOURI STATE UNIVERSITY

Management of Technology	M

SOUTHERN ARKANSAS UNIVERSITY–MAGNOLIA

Computer Science	M

SOUTHERN CONNECTICUT STATE UNIVERSITY

Computer Science	M

SOUTHERN ILLINOIS UNIVERSITY CARBONDALE

Biomedical Engineering	M
Civil Engineering	M
Computer Engineering	M,D
Computer Science	M,D
Electrical Engineering	M,D
Energy and Power Engineering	D
Engineering and Applied Sciences—General	M,D
Manufacturing Engineering	M
Mechanical Engineering	M
Mechanics	M,D
Mineral/Mining Engineering	M

SOUTHERN ILLINOIS UNIVERSITY EDWARDSVILLE

Biotechnology	M
Civil Engineering	M
Computer Science	M
Electrical Engineering	M
Engineering and Applied Sciences—General	M
Industrial/Management Engineering	M
Mechanical Engineering	M

SOUTHERN METHODIST UNIVERSITY

Applied Science and Technology	M,D
Civil Engineering	M,D
Computer Engineering	M,D
Computer Science	M,D
Electrical Engineering	M,D
Engineering and Applied Sciences—General	M,D
Engineering Management	M,D
Environmental Engineering	M,D
Information Science	M,D
Manufacturing Engineering	M,D
Mechanical Engineering	M,D
Operations Research	M,D
Software Engineering	M,D
Systems Engineering	M,D
Systems Science	M,D
Telecommunications	M,D

*M—master's degree; P—first professional degree; D—doctorate; O—other advanced degree; *—Close-Up and/or Display*

SOUTHERN OREGON UNIVERSITY

Computer Science	M

SOUTHERN POLYTECHNIC STATE UNIVERSITY

Computer and Information Systems Security	M,O
Computer Engineering	M
Computer Science	M,O
Construction Management	M
Electrical Engineering	M
Engineering and Applied Sciences—General	M,O
Industrial/Management Engineering	M,O
Information Science	M,O
Software Engineering	M,O
Systems Engineering	M,O

SOUTHERN UNIVERSITY AND AGRICULTURAL AND MECHANICAL COLLEGE

Computer Science	M
Engineering and Applied Sciences—General	M

STANFORD UNIVERSITY

Aerospace/Aeronautical Engineering	M,D,O
Bioengineering	M,D
Biomedical Engineering	M
Chemical Engineering	M,D,O
Civil Engineering	M,D,O
Computer Science	M,D
Electrical Engineering	M,D,O
Engineering and Applied Sciences—General	M,D,O
Engineering Design	M
Engineering Management	M,D
Environmental Engineering	M,D,O
Industrial/Management Engineering	M,D
Materials Engineering	M,D,O
Materials Sciences	M,D,O
Mechanical Engineering	M,D,O
Medical Informatics	M,D
Petroleum Engineering	M,D,O

STATE UNIVERSITY OF NEW YORK AT BINGHAMTON

Biomedical Engineering	M,D
Computer Science	M,D
Electrical Engineering	M,D
Engineering and Applied Sciences—General	M,D
Industrial/Management Engineering	M,D
Materials Engineering	M,D
Materials Sciences	M,D
Mechanical Engineering	M,D
Systems Science	M,D

STATE UNIVERSITY OF NEW YORK AT NEW PALTZ

Computer Science	M
Electrical Engineering	M

STATE UNIVERSITY OF NEW YORK AT OSWEGO

Human-Computer Interaction	M

STATE UNIVERSITY OF NEW YORK COLLEGE OF ENVIRONMENTAL SCIENCE AND FORESTRY

Construction Management	M,D

Environmental Engineering	M,D
Paper and Pulp Engineering	M,D
Water Resources Engineering	M,D

STATE UNIVERSITY OF NEW YORK DOWNSTATE MEDICAL CENTER

Biomedical Engineering	M,D

STATE UNIVERSITY OF NEW YORK INSTITUTE OF TECHNOLOGY

Computer Science	M
Engineering and Applied Sciences—General	M
Information Science	M
Management of Technology	M
Telecommunications	M

STEPHEN F. AUSTIN STATE UNIVERSITY

Biotechnology	M
Computer Science	M

STEPHENS COLLEGE

Health Informatics	M,O

STEVENS INSTITUTE OF TECHNOLOGY

Aerospace/Aeronautical Engineering	M,O
Bioinformatics	M,D,O
Biomedical Engineering	M,O
Chemical Engineering	M,D,O
Civil Engineering	M,D,O
Computer and Information Systems Security	M,D,O
Computer Engineering	M,D,O
Computer Science	M,D,O
Construction Engineering	M,O
Construction Management	M,O
Database Systems	M,D,O
Electrical Engineering	M,D,O
Engineering and Applied Sciences—General	M,D,O
Engineering Design	M
Engineering Management	M,D
Engineering Physics	M,D,O
Environmental Engineering	M,D,O
Financial Engineering	M
Health Informatics	M,D,O
Information Science	M,O
Management of Technology	M,D,O
Manufacturing Engineering	M
Materials Engineering	M,D
Mechanical Engineering	M,D,O
Modeling and Simulation	M,D,O
Ocean Engineering	M,D
Polymer Science and Engineering	M,D,O
Software Engineering	M,D,O
Structural Engineering	M,D,O
Systems Engineering	M,D,O
Systems Science	M,D
Telecommunications Management	M,D,O
Telecommunications	M,D,O
Water Resources Engineering	M,D,O

STEVENSON UNIVERSITY

Management of Technology	M

STONY BROOK UNIVERSITY, STATE UNIVERSITY OF NEW YORK

Biomedical Engineering	M,D,O
Computer Engineering	M,D,O
Computer Science	M,D,O
Electrical Engineering	M,D
Engineering and Applied Sciences—General	M,D,O
Hazardous Materials Management	M,O
Management of Technology	M
Materials Engineering	M,D
Materials Sciences	M,D
Mechanical Engineering	M,D
Software Engineering	M,D,O
Systems Engineering	M
Technology and Public Policy	D

STRATFORD UNIVERSITY

Computer and Information Systems Security	M
Software Engineering	M
Telecommunications	M

STRAYER UNIVERSITY

Computer and Information Systems Security	M
Information Science	M
Software Engineering	M
Systems Science	M
Telecommunications Management	M

SUFFOLK UNIVERSITY

Computer Science	M

SULLIVAN UNIVERSITY

Management of Technology	P,M,D

SYRACUSE UNIVERSITY

Aerospace/Aeronautical Engineering	M,D
Bioengineering	M,D
Chemical Engineering	M,D
Civil Engineering	M,D
Computer and Information Systems Security	O
Computer Engineering	M,D,O
Computer Science	M
Electrical Engineering	M,D,O
Engineering and Applied Sciences—General	M,D,O
Engineering Management	M
Environmental Engineering	M
Information Science	D,O
Mechanical Engineering	M,D
Telecommunications Management	M,O
Telecommunications	M

TEACHERS COLLEGE, COLUMBIA UNIVERSITY

Management of Technology	M

TÉLÉ-UNIVERSITÉ

Computer Science	M,D

TEMPLE UNIVERSITY

Civil Engineering	M
Computer Engineering	M
Computer Science	M,D
Electrical Engineering	M

Engineering and Applied Sciences—General	M,D
Financial Engineering	M
Health Informatics	M
Information Science	M,D
Mechanical Engineering	M

TENNESSEE STATE UNIVERSITY

Engineering and Applied Sciences—General	M,D

TENNESSEE TECHNOLOGICAL UNIVERSITY

Chemical Engineering	M,D
Civil Engineering	M,D
Computer Science	M
Electrical Engineering	M,D
Engineering and Applied Sciences—General	M,D
Mechanical Engineering	M,D

TEXAS A&M HEALTH SCIENCE CENTER

Materials Sciences	M

TEXAS A&M UNIVERSITY

Aerospace/Aeronautical Engineering	M,D
Agricultural Engineering	M,D
Bioengineering	M,D
Biomedical Engineering	M,D
Chemical Engineering	M,D
Civil Engineering	M,D
Computer Engineering	M,D
Computer Science	M,D
Construction Engineering	M,D
Construction Management	M,D
Electrical Engineering	M,D
Engineering and Applied Sciences—General	M,D
Environmental Engineering	M,D
Geotechnical Engineering	M,D
Industrial/Management Engineering	M,D
Manufacturing Engineering	M
Materials Engineering	M,D
Mechanical Engineering	M,D
Nuclear Engineering	M,D
Ocean Engineering	M,D
Petroleum Engineering	M,D
Structural Engineering	M,D
Transportation and Highway Engineering	M,D
Water Resources Engineering	M,D

TEXAS A&M UNIVERSITY–COMMERCE

Computer Science	M
Industrial/Management Engineering	M
Management of Technology	M

TEXAS A&M UNIVERSITY–CORPUS CHRISTI

Computer Science	M

TEXAS A&M UNIVERSITY–KINGSVILLE

Chemical Engineering	M
Civil Engineering	M
Computer Science	M
Electrical Engineering	M
Engineering and Applied Sciences—General	M,D
Environmental Engineering	M,D

Industrial/Management	
Engineering	M
Mechanical Engineering	M
Petroleum Engineering	M

TEXAS A&M UNIVERSITY–SAN ANTONIO

Computer and Information	
Systems Security	M

TEXAS SOUTHERN UNIVERSITY

Computer Science	M
Industrial/Management	
Engineering	M
Transportation and	
Highway Engineering	M

TEXAS STATE UNIVERSITY–SAN MARCOS

Computer Science	M
Industrial/Management	
Engineering	M
Management of	
Technology	M
Materials Sciences	D
Software Engineering	M

TEXAS TECH UNIVERSITY

Biotechnology	M
Chemical Engineering	M,D
Civil Engineering	M,D
Computer Science	M,D
Electrical Engineering	M,D
Engineering and Applied	
Sciences—General	M,D
Engineering Management	M,D
Environmental	
Engineering	M,D
Industrial/Management	
Engineering	M,D
Manufacturing Engineering	M,D
Mechanical Engineering	M,D
Petroleum Engineering	M,D
Software Engineering	M,D
Systems Engineering	M,D

TEXAS TECH UNIVERSITY HEALTH SCIENCES CENTER

Biotechnology	M

THOMAS EDISON STATE COLLEGE

Applied Science and	
Technology	O

THOMAS JEFFERSON UNIVERSITY

Biomedical Engineering	D
Biotechnology	D

TOWSON UNIVERSITY

Computer and Information	
Systems Security	M,D,O
Computer Science	M
Database Systems	M,D,O
Information Science	M,D,O
Software Engineering	M,D,O

TOYOTA TECHNOLOGICAL INSTITUTE OF CHICAGO

Computer Science	D

TRENT UNIVERSITY

Computer Science	M
Materials Sciences	M
Modeling and Simulation	M,D

TREVECCA NAZARENE UNIVERSITY

Information Science	M
Management of	
Technology	M

TRINE UNIVERSITY

Civil Engineering	M
Engineering and Applied	
Sciences—General	M
Mechanical Engineering	M

TROY UNIVERSITY

Computer Science	M

TUFTS UNIVERSITY

Bioengineering	M,D,O
Biomedical Engineering	M,D
Biotechnology	O
Chemical Engineering	M,D
Civil Engineering	M,D
Computer Science	M,D,O
Electrical Engineering	M,D,O
Engineering and Applied	
Sciences—General	M,D
Engineering Management	M
Environmental	
Engineering	M,D
Ergonomics and Human	
Factors	M,D
Geotechnical Engineering	M,D
Hazardous Materials	
Management	M,D
Human-Computer	
Interaction	O
Manufacturing Engineering	O
Mechanical Engineering	M,D
Structural Engineering	M,D
Water Resources	
Engineering	M,D

TUI UNIVERSITY

Computer and Information	
Systems Security	M,D
Health Informatics	M,D,O

TULANE UNIVERSITY

Biomedical Engineering	M,D
Chemical Engineering	D

TUSKEGEE UNIVERSITY

Electrical Engineering	M
Engineering and Applied	
Sciences—General	M,D
Materials Engineering	D
Mechanical Engineering	M

UNION GRADUATE COLLEGE

Computer Science	M
Electrical Engineering	M
Engineering and Applied	
Sciences—General	M
Engineering Management	M
Mechanical Engineering	M

UNIVERSIDAD AUTONOMA DE GUADALAJARA

Computer Science	M,D
Energy and Power	
Engineering	M,D
Manufacturing Engineering	M,D
Systems Science	M,D

UNIVERSIDAD CENTRAL DEL ESTE

Environmental	
Engineering	M

UNIVERSIDAD DE LAS AMÉRICAS–PUEBLA

Biotechnology	M
Chemical Engineering	M
Computer Science	M,D
Construction Management	M
Electrical Engineering	M
Engineering and Applied	
Sciences—General	M,D
Industrial/Management	
Engineering	M
Manufacturing Engineering	M

UNIVERSIDAD DEL ESTE

Computer and Information	
Systems Security	M

UNIVERSIDAD DEL TURABO

Telecommunications	M

UNIVERSIDAD NACIONAL PEDRO HENRIQUEZ URENA

Environmental	
Engineering	M

UNIVERSITÉ DE MONCTON

Civil Engineering	M
Computer Science	M,O
Electrical Engineering	M
Engineering and Applied	
Sciences—General	M
Industrial/Management	
Engineering	M
Mechanical Engineering	M

UNIVERSITÉ DE MONTRÉAL

Bioinformatics	M,D
Biomedical Engineering	M,D,O
Computer Science	M,D
Ergonomics and Human	
Factors	O

UNIVERSITÉ DE SHERBROOKE

Biotechnology	P,M,D,O
Chemical Engineering	M,D
Civil Engineering	M,D
Computer and Information	
Systems Security	M
Electrical Engineering	M,D
Engineering and Applied	
Sciences—General	M,D,O
Engineering Management	M,O
Environmental	
Engineering	M
Information Science	M,D
Mechanical Engineering	M,D

UNIVERSITÉ DU QUÉBEC À CHICOUTIMI

Engineering and Applied	
Sciences—General	M,D

UNIVERSITÉ DU QUÉBEC À MONTRÉAL

Ergonomics and Human	
Factors	O

UNIVERSITÉ DU QUÉBEC À RIMOUSKI

Engineering and Applied	
Sciences—General	M

UNIVERSITÉ DU QUÉBEC À TROIS-RIVIÈRES

Computer Science	M
Electrical Engineering	M,D
Industrial/Management	
Engineering	M,O

UNIVERSITÉ DU QUÉBEC, ÉCOLE DE TECHNOLOGIE SUPÉRIEURE

Engineering and Applied	
Sciences—General	M,D,O

UNIVERSITÉ DU QUÉBEC EN ABITIBI-TÉMISCAMINGUE

Engineering and Applied	
Sciences—General	M,O
Mineral/Mining	
Engineering	M,O

UNIVERSITÉ DU QUÉBEC EN OUTAOUAIS

Computer Science	M,D
Software Engineering	O

UNIVERSITÉ DU QUÉBEC, INSTITUT NATIONAL DE LA RECHERCHE SCIENTIFIQUE

Energy Management and	
Policy	M,D
Materials Sciences	M,D
Telecommunications	M,D

UNIVERSITÉ LAVAL

Aerospace/Aeronautical	
Engineering	M
Agricultural Engineering	M
Chemical Engineering	M,D
Civil Engineering	M,D,O
Computer Science	M,D
Electrical Engineering	M,D
Engineering and Applied	
Sciences—General	M,D,O
Environmental	
Engineering	M,D
Industrial/Management	
Engineering	O
Mechanical Engineering	M,D
Metallurgical Engineering	
and Metallurgy	M,D
Mineral/Mining	
Engineering	M,D
Modeling and Simulation	M,O
Software Engineering	O

UNIVERSITY AT ALBANY, STATE UNIVERSITY OF NEW YORK

Computer Science	M,D
Information Science	M,D,O
Management of	
Technology	M
Nanotechnology	M,D

UNIVERSITY AT BUFFALO, THE STATE UNIVERSITY OF NEW YORK

Aerospace/Aeronautical	
Engineering	M,D
Bioengineering	M,D
Biotechnology	M
Chemical Engineering	M,D
Civil Engineering	M,D
Computer Science	M,D

---

*M—master's degree; P—first professional degree; D—doctorate; O—other advanced degree; *—Close-Up and/or Display*

Electrical Engineering	M,D
Engineering and Applied	
Sciences—General	M,D*
Environmental	
Engineering	M,D
Financial Engineering	M,D,O
Industrial/Management	
Engineering	M,D
Materials Sciences	M
Mechanical Engineering	M,D
Modeling and Simulation	M,D,O
Structural Engineering	M,D

UNIVERSITY OF ADVANCING TECHNOLOGY

Computer and Information	
Systems Security	M
Computer Science	M
Game Design and	
Development	M
Management of	
Technology	M

THE UNIVERSITY OF AKRON

Biomedical Engineering	M,D
Chemical Engineering	M,D
Civil Engineering	M,D
Computer Engineering	M,D
Computer Science	M
Electrical Engineering	M,D
Engineering and Applied	
Sciences—General	M,D
Engineering Management	M
Management of	
Technology	M
Mechanical Engineering	M,D
Polymer Science and	
Engineering	M,D

THE UNIVERSITY OF ALABAMA

Aerospace/Aeronautical	
Engineering	M,D
Chemical Engineering	M,D
Civil Engineering	M,D
Computer Engineering	M,D
Computer Science	M,D
Construction Engineering	M,D
Electrical Engineering	M,D
Engineering and Applied	
Sciences—General	M,D
Environmental	
Engineering	M,D
Ergonomics and Human	
Factors	M
Materials Engineering	M,D
Materials Sciences	D
Mechanical Engineering	M,D
Mechanics	M,D
Metallurgical Engineering	
and Metallurgy	M,D

THE UNIVERSITY OF ALABAMA AT BIRMINGHAM

Biomedical Engineering	M,D
Civil Engineering	M,D
Computer and Information	
Systems Security	M
Computer Engineering	D
Computer Science	M,D
Construction Engineering	M
Electrical Engineering	M
Engineering and Applied	
Sciences—General	M,D
Health Informatics	M
Information Science	M,D
Materials Engineering	M,D
Materials Sciences	D
Mechanical Engineering	M
Safety Engineering	M

THE UNIVERSITY OF ALABAMA IN HUNTSVILLE

Aerospace/Aeronautical	
Engineering	M,D
Biotechnology	D
Chemical Engineering	M
Civil Engineering	M,D
Computer Engineering	M,D
Computer Science	M,D,O
Electrical Engineering	M,D
Engineering and Applied	
Sciences—General	M,D
Engineering Management	M,D
Environmental	
Engineering	M,D
Geotechnical Engineering	M,D
Industrial/Management	
Engineering	M,D
Materials Sciences	M,D
Mechanical Engineering	M,D
Modeling and Simulation	M,D,O
Operations Research	M
Software Engineering	M,D,O
Structural Engineering	M,D
Systems Engineering	M,D
Transportation and	
Highway Engineering	M,D
Water Resources	
Engineering	M,D

UNIVERSITY OF ALASKA ANCHORAGE

Civil Engineering	M,O
Engineering and Applied	
Sciences—General	M,O
Engineering Management	M
Environmental	
Engineering	M
Geological Engineering	M
Ocean Engineering	M,O

UNIVERSITY OF ALASKA FAIRBANKS

Civil Engineering	M,D
Computer Engineering	M,D
Computer Science	M
Electrical Engineering	M,D
Engineering and Applied	
Sciences—General	M,D
Engineering Management	M,D
Environmental	
Engineering	M,D
Geological Engineering	M,D
Mechanical Engineering	M,D
Mineral/Mining	
Engineering	M
Petroleum Engineering	M,D
Software Engineering	M

UNIVERSITY OF ALBERTA

Biomedical Engineering	M,D
Biotechnology	M,D
Chemical Engineering	M,D
Civil Engineering	M,D
Computer Engineering	M,D
Computer Science	M,D
Construction Engineering	M,D
Electrical Engineering	M,D
Energy and Power	
Engineering	M,D
Engineering Management	M,D
Environmental	
Engineering	M,D
Geotechnical Engineering	M,D
Materials Engineering	M,D
Mechanical Engineering	M,D
Mineral/Mining	
Engineering	M,D
Nanotechnology	M,D
Petroleum Engineering	M,D
Structural Engineering	M,D

Systems Engineering	M,D
Telecommunications	M,D
Water Resources	
Engineering	M,D

THE UNIVERSITY OF ARIZONA

Aerospace/Aeronautical	
Engineering	M,D
Agricultural Engineering	M,D
Biomedical Engineering	M,D
Biosystems Engineering	M,D
Chemical Engineering	M,D
Civil Engineering	M,D
Computer Engineering	M,D
Computer Science	M,D
Electrical Engineering	M,D
Engineering and Applied	
Sciences—General	M,D,O
Environmental	
Engineering	M,D
Geological Engineering	M,D,O
Industrial/Management	
Engineering	M,D
Materials Engineering	M,D
Materials Sciences	M,D
Mechanical Engineering	M,D
Mechanics	M,D
Medical Informatics	M,D,O
Mineral/Mining	
Engineering	M,O
Reliability Engineering	M
Systems Engineering	M,D

UNIVERSITY OF ARKANSAS

Agricultural Engineering	M,D
Bioengineering	M
Biomedical Engineering	M
Chemical Engineering	M,D
Civil Engineering	M,D
Computer Engineering	M,D
Computer Science	M,D
Electrical Engineering	M,D
Electronic Materials	M,D
Engineering and Applied	
Sciences—General	M,D
Environmental	
Engineering	M
Industrial/Management	
Engineering	M,D
Mechanical Engineering	M,D
Operations Research	M,D
Telecommunications	M,D
Transportation and	
Highway Engineering	M

UNIVERSITY OF ARKANSAS AT LITTLE ROCK

Applied Science and	
Technology	M,D
Bioinformatics	M,D
Computer Science	M
Construction Management	M,O
Information Science	M
Management of	
Technology	M,O
Systems Engineering	O

UNIVERSITY OF ATLANTA

Computer Science	P,M,D,O

UNIVERSITY OF BALTIMORE

Human-Computer	
Interaction	M,D
Information Science	M,D

UNIVERSITY OF BRIDGEPORT

Computer Engineering	M,D
Computer Science	M,D
Electrical Engineering	M

Engineering and Applied	
Sciences—General	M,D
Management of	
Technology	M
Mechanical Engineering	M

THE UNIVERSITY OF BRITISH COLUMBIA

Chemical Engineering	M,D
Civil Engineering	M,D
Computer Engineering	M,D
Computer Science	M,D
Electrical Engineering	M,D
Engineering and Applied	
Sciences—General	M,D
Engineering Physics	M
Geological Engineering	M,D
Materials Engineering	M,D
Materials Sciences	M,D
Mechanical Engineering	M,D
Metallurgical Engineering	
and Metallurgy	M,D
Mineral/Mining	
Engineering	M,D
Operations Research	M
Software Engineering	M

UNIVERSITY OF CALGARY

Biomedical Engineering	M,D
Biotechnology	M
Chemical Engineering	M,D
Civil Engineering	M,D
Computer Engineering	M,D
Computer Science	M,D
Electrical Engineering	M,D
Engineering and Applied	
Sciences—General	M,D
Geotechnical Engineering	M,D
Manufacturing Engineering	M,D
Mechanical Engineering	M,D
Petroleum Engineering	M,D
Software Engineering	M,D

UNIVERSITY OF CALIFORNIA, BERKELEY

Applied Science and	
Technology	D
Bioengineering	D
Chemical Engineering	M,D
Civil Engineering	M,D
Computer Science	M,D
Construction Management	O
Electrical Engineering	M,D
Energy Management and	
Policy	M,D
Engineering and Applied	
Sciences—General	M,D,O
Engineering Management	M,D
Environmental	
Engineering	M,D
Financial Engineering	M
Geotechnical Engineering	M,D
Industrial/Management	
Engineering	M,D
Materials Engineering	M,D
Materials Sciences	M,D
Mechanical Engineering	M,D
Mechanics	M,D
Nuclear Engineering	M,D
Operations Research	M,D
Structural Engineering	M,D
Transportation and	
Highway Engineering	M,D
Water Resources	
Engineering	M,D

UNIVERSITY OF CALIFORNIA, DAVIS

Aerospace/Aeronautical	
Engineering	M,D,O

Applied Science and Technology	M,D
Bioengineering	M,D
Biomedical Engineering	M,D
Chemical Engineering	M,D
Civil Engineering	M,D,O
Computer Engineering	M,D
Computer Science	M,D
Electrical Engineering	M,D
Engineering and Applied Sciences—General	M,D,O
Environmental Engineering	M,D,O
Materials Engineering	M,D
Materials Sciences	M,D
Mechanical Engineering	M,D,O
Medical Informatics	M
Transportation and Highway Engineering	M,D

UNIVERSITY OF CALIFORNIA, IRVINE

Aerospace/Aeronautical Engineering	M,D
Biochemical Engineering	M,D
Biomedical Engineering	M,D
Biotechnology	M
Chemical Engineering	M,D
Civil Engineering	M,D
Computer Science	M,D
Electrical Engineering	M,D
Engineering and Applied Sciences—General	M,D
Environmental Engineering	M,D
Information Science	M,D
Materials Engineering	M,D
Materials Sciences	M,D
Mechanical Engineering	M,D
Transportation and Highway Engineering	M,D

UNIVERSITY OF CALIFORNIA, LOS ANGELES

Aerospace/Aeronautical Engineering	M,D
Bioinformatics	M,D
Biomedical Engineering	M,D
Chemical Engineering	M,D
Civil Engineering	M,D
Computer Science	M,D
Electrical Engineering	M,D
Engineering and Applied Sciences—General	M,D
Environmental Engineering	M,D
Financial Engineering	M,D
Manufacturing Engineering	M
Materials Engineering	M,D
Materials Sciences	M,D
Mechanical Engineering	M,D

UNIVERSITY OF CALIFORNIA, MERCED

Bioengineering	M,D
Computer Science	M,D
Electrical Engineering	M,D
Engineering and Applied Sciences—General	M,D
Mechanical Engineering	M,D
Mechanics	M,D

UNIVERSITY OF CALIFORNIA, RIVERSIDE

Artificial Intelligence/ Robotics	M,D
Bioengineering	M,D
Bioinformatics	D
Chemical Engineering	M,D

Computer Engineering	M,D
Computer Science	M,D
Electrical Engineering	M,D
Environmental Engineering	M,D
Materials Engineering	M,D
Materials Sciences	M,D
Mechanical Engineering	M,D
Nanotechnology	M,D

UNIVERSITY OF CALIFORNIA, SAN DIEGO

Aerospace/Aeronautical Engineering	M,D
Artificial Intelligence/ Robotics	M,D
Bioengineering	M,D*
Bioinformatics	D
Chemical Engineering	M,D
Computer Engineering	M,D
Computer Science	M,D
Electrical Engineering	M,D
Engineering Physics	M,D
Materials Sciences	M,D
Mechanical Engineering	M,D
Mechanics	M,D
Modeling and Simulation	M,D
Ocean Engineering	M,D
Structural Engineering	M,D
Telecommunications	M,D

UNIVERSITY OF CALIFORNIA, SAN FRANCISCO

Bioengineering	D
Bioinformatics	D
Medical Informatics	D

UNIVERSITY OF CALIFORNIA, SANTA BARBARA

Bioengineering	D
Chemical Engineering	D
Computer Engineering	M,D
Computer Science	M,D
Electrical Engineering	M,D
Engineering and Applied Sciences—General	M,D
Materials Engineering	M,D
Materials Sciences	M,D
Mechanical Engineering	M,D

UNIVERSITY OF CALIFORNIA, SANTA CRUZ

Bioinformatics	M,D
Computer Engineering	M,D
Computer Science	M,D
Electrical Engineering	M,D
Engineering and Applied Sciences—General	M,D
Management of Technology	M,D
Telecommunications	M,D

UNIVERSITY OF CENTRAL ARKANSAS

Computer Science	M

UNIVERSITY OF CENTRAL FLORIDA

Aerospace/Aeronautical Engineering	M
Biotechnology	M
Civil Engineering	M,D,O
Computer Engineering	M,D
Computer Science	M,D
Construction Engineering	M,D,O
Electrical Engineering	M,D,O
Engineering and Applied Sciences—General	M,D,O

Engineering Design	M,D,O
Environmental Engineering	M,D
Ergonomics and Human Factors	M,D,O
Game Design and Development	M
Health Informatics	M,O
Industrial/Management Engineering	M,D,O
Materials Engineering	M,D
Materials Sciences	M,D
Mechanical Engineering	M,D,O
Modeling and Simulation	M,D,O
Operations Research	M,D,O
Structural Engineering	M,D,O
Systems Engineering	M,D,O
Transportation and Highway Engineering	M,D,O

UNIVERSITY OF CENTRAL MISSOURI

Aerospace/Aeronautical Engineering	M,D
Computer Science	M,D
Information Science	M,D,O
Management of Technology	M,D

UNIVERSITY OF CENTRAL OKLAHOMA

Computer Science	M
Engineering and Applied Sciences—General	M

UNIVERSITY OF CHICAGO

Computer Science	M

UNIVERSITY OF CINCINNATI

Aerospace/Aeronautical Engineering	M,D
Bioinformatics	D
Biomedical Engineering	D
Ceramic Sciences and Engineering	M,D
Chemical Engineering	M,D
Civil Engineering	M,D
Computer Engineering	M,D
Computer Science	M,D
Electrical Engineering	M,D
Engineering and Applied Sciences—General	M,D
Environmental Engineering	M,D
Ergonomics and Human Factors	M,D
Industrial/Management Engineering	M,D
Materials Engineering	M,D
Materials Sciences	M,D
Mechanical Engineering	M,D
Mechanics	M,D
Metallurgical Engineering and Metallurgy	M,D
Nuclear Engineering	M,D
Polymer Science and Engineering	M,D

UNIVERSITY OF COLORADO AT COLORADO SPRINGS

Aerospace/Aeronautical Engineering	M
Applied Science and Technology	M,D
Computer Science	M,D
Electrical Engineering	M,D
Engineering and Applied Sciences—General	M,D
Engineering Management	M

Information Science	M
Manufacturing Engineering	M
Mechanical Engineering	M
Software Engineering	M

UNIVERSITY OF COLORADO BOULDER

Aerospace/Aeronautical Engineering	M,D
Architectural Engineering	M,D
Chemical Engineering	M,D
Civil Engineering	M,D
Computer Engineering	M,D
Computer Science	M,D
Construction Engineering	M,D
Electrical Engineering	M,D
Engineering and Applied Sciences—General	M,D
Engineering Management	M
Environmental Engineering	M,D
Geotechnical Engineering	M,D
Mechanical Engineering	M,D
Operations Research	M
Structural Engineering	M,D
Telecommunications Management	M
Telecommunications	M
Water Resources Engineering	M,D

UNIVERSITY OF COLORADO DENVER

Applied Science and Technology	M
Bioengineering	M,D
Bioinformatics	D
Civil Engineering	M,D
Computer Science	M,D
Electrical Engineering	M
Energy Management and Policy	M
Engineering and Applied Sciences—General	M,D
Environmental Engineering	M,D
Geotechnical Engineering	M,D
Hazardous Materials Management	M
Hydraulics	M,D
Information Science	M,D
Management of Technology	M,D
Mechanical Engineering	M,D
Medical Informatics	M,D
Structural Engineering	M,D
Transportation and Highway Engineering	M,D

UNIVERSITY OF CONNECTICUT

Biomedical Engineering	M,D
Chemical Engineering	M,D
Civil Engineering	M,D
Computer Science	M,D
Electrical Engineering	M,D
Engineering and Applied Sciences—General	M,D
Environmental Engineering	M,D
Materials Engineering	M,D
Materials Sciences	M,D
Mechanical Engineering	M,D
Metallurgical Engineering and Metallurgy	M,D
Polymer Science and Engineering	M,D
Software Engineering	M,D

*M—master's degree; P—first professional degree; D—doctorate; O—other advanced degree; *—Close-Up and / or Display*

UNIVERSITY OF DALLAS

Management of Technology	M

UNIVERSITY OF DAYTON

Aerospace/Aeronautical Engineering	M,D
Agricultural Engineering	M
Bioengineering	M
Biosystems Engineering	M
Chemical Engineering	M
Civil Engineering	M
Computer and Information Systems Security	M
Computer Engineering	M,D
Computer Science	M
Electrical Engineering	M,D
Engineering and Applied Sciences—General	M,D
Engineering Management	M
Environmental Engineering	M
Materials Engineering	M,D
Mechanical Engineering	M,D
Mechanics	M
Structural Engineering	M
Transportation and Highway Engineering	M
Water Resources Engineering	M

UNIVERSITY OF DELAWARE

Biotechnology	M,D
Chemical Engineering	M,D
Civil Engineering	M,D
Computer Engineering	M,D
Computer Science	M,D
Electrical Engineering	M,D
Energy Management and Policy	M,D
Engineering and Applied Sciences—General	M,D
Environmental Engineering	M,D
Geotechnical Engineering	M,D
Information Science	M,D
Management of Technology	M
Materials Engineering	M,D
Materials Sciences	M,D
Mechanical Engineering	M,D
Ocean Engineering	M,D
Operations Research	M,D
Structural Engineering	M,D
Transportation and Highway Engineering	M,D
Water Resources Engineering	M,D

UNIVERSITY OF DENVER

Bioengineering	M,D
Computer and Information Systems Security	M,O
Computer Engineering	M,D
Computer Science	M,D
Construction Management	M
Database Systems	M,O
Electrical Engineering	M,D
Energy Management and Policy	M,O
Engineering and Applied Sciences—General	M,D
Internet Engineering	M,O
Management of Technology	M,O
Materials Engineering	M,D
Materials Sciences	M,D
Mechanical Engineering	M,D
Software Engineering	M,O
Systems Engineering	M,D
Telecommunications	M,O

UNIVERSITY OF DETROIT MERCY

Architectural Engineering	M
Civil Engineering	M,D
Computer Engineering	M,D
Computer Science	M
Electrical Engineering	M,D
Engineering and Applied Sciences—General	M,D
Engineering Management	M
Environmental Engineering	M,D
Information Science	M
Mechanical Engineering	M,D
Software Engineering	M

UNIVERSITY OF EVANSVILLE

Computer Science	M
Electrical Engineering	M
Engineering and Applied Sciences—General	M

UNIVERSITY OF FLORIDA

Aerospace/Aeronautical Engineering	M,D,O
Agricultural Engineering	M,D,O
Bioengineering	M,D,O
Biomedical Engineering	M,D,O
Chemical Engineering	M,D
Civil Engineering	M,D,O
Computer Engineering	M,D,O
Computer Science	M,D
Construction Engineering	M,D
Electrical Engineering	M,D,O
Engineering and Applied Sciences—General	M,D,O*
Environmental Engineering	M,D,O
Industrial/Management Engineering	M,D,O
Information Science	M,D
Materials Engineering	M,D,O
Materials Sciences	M,D,O
Mechanical Engineering	M,D,O
Nuclear Engineering	M,D,O
Ocean Engineering	M,D,O
Systems Engineering	M,D,O

UNIVERSITY OF GEORGIA

Agricultural Engineering	M,D
Artificial Intelligence/Robotics	M
Biochemical Engineering	M
Bioengineering	M,D
Bioinformatics	M,D,O
Computer Science	M,D
Environmental Engineering	M
Internet Engineering	M

UNIVERSITY OF GUELPH

Bioengineering	M,D
Biotechnology	M,D
Computer Science	M,D
Engineering and Applied Sciences—General	M,D
Environmental Engineering	M,D
Water Resources Engineering	M,D

UNIVERSITY OF HARTFORD

Engineering and Applied Sciences—General	M

UNIVERSITY OF HAWAII AT MANOA

Bioengineering	M
Civil Engineering	M,D
Computer Science	M,D,O

UNIVERSITY OF HOUSTON

Biomedical Engineering	D
Chemical Engineering	M,D
Civil Engineering	M,D
Computer and Information Systems Security	M
Computer Science	M,D
Construction Management	M
Electrical Engineering	M,D
Engineering and Applied Sciences—General	M,D
Industrial/Management Engineering	M,D
Information Science	M,D
Mechanical Engineering	M,D
Petroleum Engineering	M,D
Telecommunications	M

UNIVERSITY OF HOUSTON–CLEAR LAKE

Biotechnology	M
Computer Engineering	M
Computer Science	M
Information Science	M
Software Engineering	M
Systems Engineering	M

UNIVERSITY OF HOUSTON–VICTORIA

Computer Science	M

UNIVERSITY OF IDAHO

Agricultural Engineering	M,D
Bioengineering	M,D
Bioinformatics	M,D
Chemical Engineering	M,D
Civil Engineering	M,D
Computer Engineering	M
Computer Science	M,D
Electrical Engineering	M,D
Engineering and Applied Sciences—General	M,D
Engineering Management	M
Environmental Engineering	M
Geological Engineering	M
Materials Sciences	M,D
Metallurgical Engineering and Metallurgy	M,D
Mineral/Mining Engineering	M,D
Nuclear Engineering	M,D

UNIVERSITY OF ILLINOIS AT CHICAGO

Bioengineering	M,D
Biotechnology	D
Chemical Engineering	M,D
Civil Engineering	M,D
Computer Engineering	M,D
Computer Science	M,D
Electrical Engineering	M,D
Engineering and Applied Sciences—General	M,D
Health Informatics	M
Industrial/Management Engineering	M,D
Materials Engineering	M,D

Electrical Engineering	M,D
Engineering and Applied Sciences—General	M,D
Environmental Engineering	M,D
Financial Engineering	M
Geological Engineering	M,D
Information Science	M,D
Mechanical Engineering	M,D
Ocean Engineering	M,D
Telecommunications	O

UNIVERSITY OF ILLINOIS AT SPRINGFIELD

Computer Science	M

UNIVERSITY OF ILLINOIS AT URBANA–CHAMPAIGN

Aerospace/Aeronautical Engineering	M,D
Agricultural Engineering	M,D
Aviation	M
Bioengineering	M,D
Bioinformatics	M,D,O
Chemical Engineering	M,D
Civil Engineering	M,D
Computer Engineering	M,D
Computer Science	M,D
Electrical Engineering	M,D
Energy Management and Policy	M
Engineering and Applied Sciences—General	M,D
Environmental Engineering	M,D
Ergonomics and Human Factors	M
Financial Engineering	M
Health Informatics	M,D,O
Human-Computer Interaction	M,D,O
Industrial/Management Engineering	M,D
Information Science	M,D,O
Management of Technology	M,D
Materials Engineering	M,D
Materials Sciences	M,D
Mechanical Engineering	M,D
Mechanics	M,D
Medical Informatics	M,D,O
Nuclear Engineering	M,D
Systems Engineering	M,D

THE UNIVERSITY OF IOWA

Biochemical Engineering	M,D
Biomedical Engineering	M,D
Chemical Engineering	M,D
Civil Engineering	M,D
Computer Engineering	M,D
Computer Science	M,D
Electrical Engineering	M,D
Engineering and Applied Sciences—General	M,D*
Environmental Engineering	M,D
Ergonomics and Human Factors	M,D
Health Informatics	M,D,O
Industrial/Management Engineering	M,D
Information Science	M,D,O
Manufacturing Engineering	M,D
Mechanical Engineering	M,D
Operations Research	M,D

THE UNIVERSITY OF KANSAS

Aerospace/Aeronautical Engineering	M,D
Architectural Engineering	M
Bioengineering	M,D
Biotechnology	M
Chemical Engineering	M,D
Civil Engineering	M,D
Computer Engineering	M
Computer Science	M,D
Construction Management	M
Electrical Engineering	M,D
Engineering and Applied Sciences—General	M,D

Engineering Management M
Environmental
  Engineering M,D
Health Informatics M
Mechanical Engineering M,D
Medical Informatics M,D,O
Petroleum Engineering M,D

UNIVERSITY OF KENTUCKY

Agricultural Engineering M,D
Biomedical Engineering M,D
Chemical Engineering M,D
Civil Engineering M,D
Computer Science M,D
Electrical Engineering M,D
Engineering and Applied
  Sciences—General M,D
Manufacturing Engineering M
Materials Sciences M,D
Mechanical Engineering M,D
Mineral/Mining
  Engineering M,D

UNIVERSITY OF LA VERNE

Health Informatics M

UNIVERSITY OF LETHBRIDGE

Computer Science M,D

UNIVERSITY OF LOUISIANA AT LAFAYETTE

Architectural Engineering M
Chemical Engineering M
Civil Engineering M
Computer Engineering M,D
Computer Science M,D*
Engineering Management M
Mechanical Engineering M
Petroleum Engineering M
Telecommunications M

UNIVERSITY OF LOUISVILLE

Chemical Engineering M,D
Civil Engineering M,D
Computer and Information
  Systems Security M,D,O
Computer Engineering M,D,O
Computer Science M,D,O
Electrical Engineering M,D
Engineering and Applied
  Sciences—General M,D,O
Engineering Management M,D,O
Environmental
  Engineering M,D
Industrial/Management
  Engineering M,D,O
Mechanical Engineering M,D

UNIVERSITY OF MAINE

Bioengineering M
Biomedical Engineering D
Chemical Engineering M,D
Civil Engineering M,D
Computer Engineering M,D
Computer Science M,D
Electrical Engineering M,D
Engineering and Applied
  Sciences—General M,D
Engineering Physics M
Mechanical Engineering M,D
Ocean Engineering D
Water Resources
  Engineering M,D

UNIVERSITY OF MANAGEMENT AND TECHNOLOGY

Computer Science M,O

Information Science M,O
Software Engineering M,O

THE UNIVERSITY OF MANCHESTER

Aerospace/Aeronautical
  Engineering M,D
Biochemical Engineering M,D
Bioinformatics M,D
Biotechnology M,D
Chemical Engineering M,D
Civil Engineering M,D
Computer Science M,D
Electrical Engineering M,D
Engineering Management M,D
Environmental
  Engineering M,D
Hazardous Materials
  Management M,D
Materials Sciences M,D
Mechanical Engineering M,D
Metallurgical Engineering
  and Metallurgy M,D
Modeling and Simulation M,D
Nuclear Engineering M,D
Paper and Pulp
  Engineering M,D
Polymer Science and
  Engineering M,D
Structural Engineering M,D

UNIVERSITY OF MANITOBA

Biosystems Engineering M,D
Civil Engineering M,D
Computer Engineering M,D
Computer Science M,D
Electrical Engineering M,D
Engineering and Applied
  Sciences—General M,D
Industrial/Management
  Engineering M,D
Manufacturing Engineering M,D
Mechanical Engineering M,D

UNIVERSITY OF MARYLAND, BALTIMORE COUNTY

Biochemical Engineering M,D,O
Biotechnology O
Chemical Engineering M,D
Civil Engineering M,D
Computer Engineering M,D
Computer Science M,D
Electrical Engineering M,D
Engineering and Applied
  Sciences—General M,D,O
Engineering Management M,O
Information Science M,D
Mechanical Engineering M,D,O
Systems Engineering M,O

UNIVERSITY OF MARYLAND, COLLEGE PARK

Aerospace/Aeronautical
  Engineering M,D
Bioengineering M,D
Chemical Engineering M,D
Civil Engineering M,D
Computer Engineering M,D
Computer Science M,D
Electrical Engineering M,D
Engineering and Applied
  Sciences—General M
Environmental
  Engineering M,D
Fire Protection
  Engineering M
Manufacturing Engineering M,D
Materials Engineering M,D
Materials Sciences M,D

Mechanical Engineering M,D
Mechanics M,D
Nuclear Engineering M,D
Reliability Engineering M,D
Systems Engineering M
Telecommunications M

UNIVERSITY OF MARYLAND EASTERN SHORE

Computer Science M

UNIVERSITY OF MARYLAND UNIVERSITY COLLEGE

Biotechnology M,O
Computer and Information
  Systems Security M,O
Health Informatics M,O
Information Science M,O
Management of
  Technology M,O

UNIVERSITY OF MASSACHUSETTS AMHERST

Architectural Engineering M,D
Biotechnology M,D
Chemical Engineering M,D
Civil Engineering M,D
Computer Engineering M,D
Computer Science M,D
Electrical Engineering M,D
Engineering and Applied
  Sciences—General M,D
Engineering Management
Environmental
  Engineering M
Industrial/Management
  Engineering M,D
Mechanical Engineering M,D
Operations Research M,D
Polymer Science and
  Engineering M,D

UNIVERSITY OF MASSACHUSETTS BOSTON

Biotechnology M
Computer Science M,D

UNIVERSITY OF MASSACHUSETTS DARTMOUTH

Biomedical Engineering D
Biotechnology D
Civil Engineering M
Computer Engineering M,D,O
Computer Science M,O
Electrical Engineering M,D,O
Engineering and Applied
  Sciences—General M,D,O
Environmental
  Engineering M
Mechanical Engineering M
Software Engineering M,O
Telecommunications M,D,O
Textile Sciences and
  Engineering M

UNIVERSITY OF MASSACHUSETTS LOWELL

Biotechnology M,D
Chemical Engineering M,D
Civil Engineering M,D,O
Computer Engineering M
Computer Science M,D
Electrical Engineering M,D
Energy and Power
  Engineering M,D
Engineering and Applied
  Sciences—General M,D,O

Environmental
  Engineering M,D,O
Ergonomics and Human
  Factors M,D,O
Health Informatics M,O
Industrial/Management
  Engineering M,D,O
Materials Engineering M,D,O
Mechanical Engineering M,D
Mechanics M,D
Nuclear Engineering M,D
Polymer Science and
  Engineering M,D,O

UNIVERSITY OF MASSACHUSETTS WORCESTER

Bioinformatics M,D

UNIVERSITY OF MEDICINE AND DENTISTRY OF NEW JERSEY

Bioinformatics M,D
Biomedical Engineering M,D,O
Medical Informatics M,D,O

UNIVERSITY OF MEMPHIS

Biomedical Engineering M,D
Civil Engineering M,D
Computer Engineering M,D
Computer Science M,D
Electrical Engineering M,D
Energy and Power
  Engineering M,D
Engineering and Applied
  Sciences—General M,D
Environmental
  Engineering M,D
Industrial/Management
  Engineering M,D
Manufacturing Engineering M
Mechanical Engineering M,D
Structural Engineering M,D
Transportation and
  Highway Engineering M,D
Water Resources
  Engineering M,D

UNIVERSITY OF MIAMI

Aerospace/Aeronautical
  Engineering M,D
Architectural Engineering M,D
Biomedical Engineering M,D
Civil Engineering M,D
Computer Engineering M,D
Computer Science M,D
Electrical Engineering M,D
Engineering and Applied
  Sciences—General M,D
Ergonomics and Human
  Factors M
Industrial/Management
  Engineering M,D
Management of
  Technology M,D
Mechanical Engineering M,D

UNIVERSITY OF MICHIGAN

Aerospace/Aeronautical
  Engineering M,D
Bioinformatics M,D
Biomedical Engineering M,D
Chemical Engineering M,D,O
Civil Engineering M,D,O
Computer Engineering M,D
Computer Science M,D
Construction Engineering M,D,O
Electrical Engineering M,D
Engineering and Applied
  Sciences—General M,D,O

Environmental Engineering	M,D,O
Health Informatics	M,D
Human-Computer Interaction	M,D
Industrial/Management Engineering	M,D
Information Science	M,D
Materials Engineering	M,D
Materials Sciences	M,D*
Mechanical Engineering	M,D
Nuclear Engineering	M,D,O
Ocean Engineering	M,D,O
Operations Research	M,D
Structural Engineering	M,D,O

UNIVERSITY OF MICHIGAN–DEARBORN

Automotive Engineering	M,D
Computer Engineering	M
Computer Science	M
Electrical Engineering	M
Engineering and Applied Sciences—General	M,D
Engineering Management	M,D
Industrial/Management Engineering	M,D
Information Science	M,D
Manufacturing Engineering	M
Mechanical Engineering	M
Software Engineering	M
Systems Engineering	M,D
Systems Science	M,D

UNIVERSITY OF MICHIGAN–FLINT

Computer Science	M
Information Science	M

UNIVERSITY OF MINNESOTA, DULUTH

Computer Engineering	M
Computer Science	M
Electrical Engineering	M
Engineering Management	M
Safety Engineering	M

UNIVERSITY OF MINNESOTA, TWIN CITIES CAMPUS

Aerospace/Aeronautical Engineering	M,D
Biomedical Engineering	M,D
Biosystems Engineering	M,D
Biotechnology	M
Chemical Engineering	M,D
Civil Engineering	M,D
Computer and Information Systems Security	M
Computer Engineering	M,D
Computer Science	M,D
Electrical Engineering	M,D
Engineering and Applied Sciences—General	M,D
Geological Engineering	M,D
Health Informatics	M,D
Industrial/Management Engineering	M,D
Information Science	M,D
Management of Technology	M
Materials Engineering	M,D
Materials Sciences	M,D
Mechanical Engineering	M,D
Mechanics	M,D
Systems Engineering	M
Technology and Public Policy	M

UNIVERSITY OF MISSISSIPPI

Applied Science and Technology	M,D

Engineering and Applied Sciences—General	M,D

UNIVERSITY OF MISSOURI

Aerospace/Aeronautical Engineering	M,D
Agricultural Engineering	M,D
Bioengineering	M,D
Bioinformatics	D
Chemical Engineering	M,D
Civil Engineering	M,D
Computer Science	M,D*
Electrical Engineering	M,D
Engineering and Applied Sciences—General	M,D
Environmental Engineering	M,D
Geotechnical Engineering	M,D
Health Informatics	M
Industrial/Management Engineering	M,D
Manufacturing Engineering	M,D
Mechanical Engineering	M,D
Nuclear Engineering	M,D
Structural Engineering	M,D
Transportation and Highway Engineering	M,D
Water Resources Engineering	M,D

UNIVERSITY OF MISSOURI–KANSAS CITY

Bioinformatics	P,M,D
Civil Engineering	M,D
Computer Engineering	M,D
Computer Science	M,D
Electrical Engineering	M,D
Engineering and Applied Sciences—General	M,D
Mechanical Engineering	M,D
Polymer Science and Engineering	M,D
Software Engineering	M,D
Telecommunications	M,D

UNIVERSITY OF MISSOURI–ST. LOUIS

Biotechnology	M,D,O
Computer Science	M,D

THE UNIVERSITY OF MONTANA

Computer Science	M

UNIVERSITY OF NEBRASKA AT OMAHA

Computer Science	M
Information Science	M,D,O

UNIVERSITY OF NEBRASKA–LINCOLN

Agricultural Engineering	M,D
Architectural Engineering	M,D
Bioengineering	M,D
Bioinformatics	M,D
Chemical Engineering	M,D
Civil Engineering	M,D
Computer Engineering	M,D
Computer Science	M,D
Electrical Engineering	M,D
Engineering and Applied Sciences—General	M,D
Engineering Management	M,D
Environmental Engineering	M,D
Industrial/Management Engineering	M,D
Information Science	M,D
Manufacturing Engineering	M,D
Materials Engineering	M,D

Materials Sciences	M,D
Mechanical Engineering	M,D*
Mechanics	M,D
Metallurgical Engineering and Metallurgy	M,D

UNIVERSITY OF NEVADA, LAS VEGAS

Aerospace/Aeronautical Engineering	M,D
Biomedical Engineering	M,D
Civil Engineering	M,D
Computer Engineering	M,D
Computer Science	M,D
Construction Management	M
Electrical Engineering	M,D
Engineering and Applied Sciences—General	M,D
Environmental Engineering	M,D
Information Science	M,D
Materials Engineering	M,D
Mechanical Engineering	M,D
Nuclear Engineering	M,D
Transportation and Highway Engineering	M,D

UNIVERSITY OF NEVADA, RENO

Biomedical Engineering	M,D
Biotechnology	M
Chemical Engineering	M,D
Civil Engineering	M,D
Computer Engineering	M,D
Computer Science	M,D
Electrical Engineering	M,D
Engineering and Applied Sciences—General	M,D
Geological Engineering	M,D
Materials Engineering	M,D
Mechanical Engineering	M,D
Metallurgical Engineering and Metallurgy	M,D
Mineral/Mining Engineering	M

UNIVERSITY OF NEW BRUNSWICK FREDERICTON

Chemical Engineering	M,D
Civil Engineering	M,D
Computer Engineering	M,D
Computer Science	M,D
Construction Engineering	M,D
Electrical Engineering	M,D
Engineering and Applied Sciences—General	M,D,O
Engineering Management	M
Environmental Engineering	M,D
Geotechnical Engineering	M,D
Materials Sciences	M,D
Mechanical Engineering	M,D
Mechanics	M,D
Structural Engineering	M,D
Surveying Science and Engineering	M,D,O
Transportation and Highway Engineering	M,D

UNIVERSITY OF NEW HAMPSHIRE

Chemical Engineering	M,D
Civil Engineering	M,D
Computer Science	M,D,O
Electrical Engineering	M,D
Management of Technology	M,O
Materials Sciences	M,D
Mechanical Engineering	M,D
Ocean Engineering	M,D,O
Software Engineering	M,D,O

UNIVERSITY OF NEW HAVEN

Computer and Information Systems Security	M,O
Computer Engineering	M
Computer Science	M,D,O
Database Systems	M,O
Electrical Engineering	M
Engineering and Applied Sciences—General	M,O
Engineering Management	M
Environmental Engineering	M,O
Fire Protection Engineering	M,O
Hazardous Materials Management	M,O
Industrial/Management Engineering	M,O
Information Science	M,O
Mechanical Engineering	M
Software Engineering	M,O
Systems Engineering	M,O
Telecommunications Management	M,O
Water Resources Engineering	M,O

UNIVERSITY OF NEW MEXICO

Biomedical Engineering	D
Chemical Engineering	M,D
Civil Engineering	M,D
Computer and Information Systems Security	M
Computer Engineering	M,D,O
Computer Science	M,D
Construction Management	M
Electrical Engineering	M,D,O*
Engineering and Applied Sciences—General	M,D,O
Management of Technology	M
Manufacturing Engineering	M
Mechanical Engineering	M,D
Nanotechnology	M,D
Nuclear Engineering	M,D

UNIVERSITY OF NEW ORLEANS

Computer Science	M
Engineering and Applied Sciences—General	M,D,O
Engineering Management	M,O
Mechanical Engineering	M

THE UNIVERSITY OF NORTH CAROLINA AT CHAPEL HILL

Bioinformatics	D
Biomedical Engineering	M,D
Computer Science	M,D*
Environmental Engineering	M,D
Materials Sciences	M,D
Operations Research	M,D

THE UNIVERSITY OF NORTH CAROLINA AT CHARLOTTE

Bioinformatics	M,O
Civil Engineering	M,D
Computer and Information Systems Security	M,D,O
Computer Engineering	M,D
Computer Science	M,O
Database Systems	M,O
Electrical Engineering	M,D
Engineering and Applied Sciences—General	M,D
Engineering Management	M
Environmental Engineering	M,D
Game Design and Development	M,D,O
Health Informatics	M,D,O

Information Science M,D,O
Mechanical Engineering M,D
Systems Engineering M,D

THE UNIVERSITY OF NORTH CAROLINA AT GREENSBORO

Computer Science M

THE UNIVERSITY OF NORTH CAROLINA WILMINGTON

Computer Science M
Systems Science M

UNIVERSITY OF NORTH DAKOTA

Aviation M
Chemical Engineering M
Civil Engineering M
Computer Science M,D
Electrical Engineering M
Engineering and Applied
  Sciences—General D
Environmental
  Engineering M
Geological Engineering M
Management of
  Technology M
Mechanical Engineering M
Mineral/Mining
  Engineering M
Structural Engineering M

UNIVERSITY OF NORTHERN BRITISH COLUMBIA

Computer Science M,D,O

UNIVERSITY OF NORTHERN IOWA

Biotechnology M
Computer Science M
Modeling and Simulation M

UNIVERSITY OF NORTH FLORIDA

Civil Engineering M
Computer Science M
Construction Management M
Electrical Engineering M
Mechanical Engineering M
Software Engineering M

UNIVERSITY OF NORTH TEXAS

Computer Engineering M,D
Computer Science M,D
Electrical Engineering M
Engineering and Applied
  Sciences—General M
Materials Sciences M,D

UNIVERSITY OF NORTH TEXAS HEALTH SCIENCE CENTER AT FORT WORTH

Biotechnology M,D

UNIVERSITY OF NOTRE DAME

Aerospace/Aeronautical
  Engineering M,D
Bioengineering M,D
Chemical Engineering M,D
Civil Engineering M,D
Computer Engineering M,D
Computer Science M,D
Electrical Engineering M,D*
Engineering and Applied
  Sciences—General M,D
Environmental
  Engineering M,D
Mechanical Engineering M,D

UNIVERSITY OF OKLAHOMA

Aerospace/Aeronautical
  Engineering M,D
Bioengineering M,D
Bioinformatics M,D
Chemical Engineering M,D
Civil Engineering M,D
Computer Engineering M,D
Computer Science M,D
Construction Management M
Electrical Engineering M,D
Engineering and Applied
  Sciences—General M,D
Engineering Management M,D
Engineering Physics M,D
Environmental
  Engineering M,D
Geological Engineering M,D
Industrial/Management
  Engineering M,D
Mechanical Engineering M,D
Petroleum Engineering M,D
Telecommunications M

UNIVERSITY OF OREGON

Computer Science M,D
Information Science M,D

UNIVERSITY OF OTTAWA

Aerospace/Aeronautical
  Engineering M,D
Biomedical Engineering M
Chemical Engineering M,D
Civil Engineering M,D
Computer Engineering M,D
Computer Science M,D
Electrical Engineering M,D
Engineering and Applied
  Sciences—General M,D,O
Engineering Management M,O
Information Science M,O
Mechanical Engineering M,D
Systems Science M,D,O

UNIVERSITY OF PENNSYLVANIA

Bioengineering M,D
Biotechnology M
Chemical Engineering M,D
Computer Science M,D
Electrical Engineering M,D
Engineering and Applied
  Sciences—General M,D,O*
Information Science M,D
Management of
  Technology M
Materials Engineering M,D
Materials Sciences M,D
Mechanical Engineering M,D
Mechanics M,D
Systems Engineering M,D
Telecommunications
  Management M
Telecommunications M

UNIVERSITY OF PHOENIX

Energy Management and
  Policy M
Health Informatics M
Management of
  Technology M

UNIVERSITY OF PHOENIX–ATLANTA CAMPUS

Management of
  Technology M

UNIVERSITY OF PHOENIX–AUGUSTA CAMPUS

Management of
  Technology M

UNIVERSITY OF PHOENIX–AUSTIN CAMPUS

Management of
  Technology M

UNIVERSITY OF PHOENIX–BIRMINGHAM CAMPUS

Health Informatics M
Management of
  Technology M

UNIVERSITY OF PHOENIX–BOSTON CAMPUS

Management of
  Technology M

UNIVERSITY OF PHOENIX–CENTRAL FLORIDA CAMPUS

Management of
  Technology M

UNIVERSITY OF PHOENIX–CENTRAL MASSACHUSETTS CAMPUS

Management of
  Technology M

UNIVERSITY OF PHOENIX–CENTRAL VALLEY CAMPUS

Management of
  Technology M

UNIVERSITY OF PHOENIX–CHARLOTTE CAMPUS

Health Informatics M
Management of
  Technology M

UNIVERSITY OF PHOENIX–CHATTANOOGA CAMPUS

Management of
  Technology M

UNIVERSITY OF PHOENIX–CHEYENNE CAMPUS

Management of
  Technology M

UNIVERSITY OF PHOENIX–CHICAGO CAMPUS

Management of
  Technology M

UNIVERSITY OF PHOENIX–CINCINNATI CAMPUS

Information Science M
Management of
  Technology M

UNIVERSITY OF PHOENIX–CLEVELAND CAMPUS

Management of
  Technology M

UNIVERSITY OF PHOENIX–COLUMBIA CAMPUS

Management of
  Technology M

UNIVERSITY OF PHOENIX–COLUMBUS GEORGIA CAMPUS

Management of
  Technology M

UNIVERSITY OF PHOENIX–COLUMBUS OHIO CAMPUS

Management of
  Technology M

UNIVERSITY OF PHOENIX–DALLAS CAMPUS

Management of
  Technology M

UNIVERSITY OF PHOENIX–DENVER CAMPUS

Management of
  Technology M

UNIVERSITY OF PHOENIX–DES MOINES CAMPUS

Health Informatics M,D
Management of
  Technology M

UNIVERSITY OF PHOENIX–EASTERN WASHINGTON CAMPUS

Management of
  Technology M

UNIVERSITY OF PHOENIX–HARRISBURG CAMPUS

Management of
  Technology M

UNIVERSITY OF PHOENIX–HAWAII CAMPUS

Management of
  Technology M

UNIVERSITY OF PHOENIX–HOUSTON CAMPUS

Management of
  Technology M

UNIVERSITY OF PHOENIX–IDAHO CAMPUS

Management of
  Technology M

UNIVERSITY OF PHOENIX–INDIANAPOLIS CAMPUS

Management of
  Technology M

UNIVERSITY OF PHOENIX–JERSEY CITY CAMPUS

Management of
  Technology M

---

*M—master's degree; P—first professional degree; D—doctorate; O—other advanced degree; *—Close-Up and/or Display*

UNIVERSITY OF PHOENIX–KANSAS CITY CAMPUS

Management of Technology	M

UNIVERSITY OF PHOENIX–LAS VEGAS CAMPUS

Management of Technology	M

UNIVERSITY OF PHOENIX–LOUISIANA CAMPUS

Management of Technology	M

UNIVERSITY OF PHOENIX–LOUISVILLE CAMPUS

Health Informatics	M
Management of Technology	M

UNIVERSITY OF PHOENIX–MADISON CAMPUS

Management of Technology	M

UNIVERSITY OF PHOENIX–MARYLAND CAMPUS

Management of Technology	M

UNIVERSITY OF PHOENIX–MEMPHIS CAMPUS

Management of Technology	M

UNIVERSITY OF PHOENIX–MILWAUKEE CAMPUS

Health Informatics	M,D

UNIVERSITY OF PHOENIX–MINNEAPOLIS/ST. LOUIS PARK CAMPUS

Management of Technology	M

UNIVERSITY OF PHOENIX–NASHVILLE CAMPUS

Management of Technology	M

UNIVERSITY OF PHOENIX–NEW MEXICO CAMPUS

Management of Technology	M

UNIVERSITY OF PHOENIX–NORTHERN NEVADA CAMPUS

Management of Technology	M

UNIVERSITY OF PHOENIX–NORTHWEST ARKANSAS CAMPUS

Management of Technology	M

UNIVERSITY OF PHOENIX–OKLAHOMA CITY CAMPUS

Management of Technology	M

UNIVERSITY OF PHOENIX–OMAHA CAMPUS

Management of Technology	M

UNIVERSITY OF PHOENIX–OREGON CAMPUS

Management of Technology	M

UNIVERSITY OF PHOENIX–PHILADELPHIA CAMPUS

Management of Technology	M

UNIVERSITY OF PHOENIX–PITTSBURGH CAMPUS

Management of Technology	M

UNIVERSITY OF PHOENIX–PUERTO RICO CAMPUS

Energy Management and Policy	M
Management of Technology	M

UNIVERSITY OF PHOENIX–RALEIGH CAMPUS

Health Informatics	M,D
Management of Technology	M

UNIVERSITY OF PHOENIX–RICHMOND CAMPUS

Management of Technology	M

UNIVERSITY OF PHOENIX–SACRAMENTO VALLEY CAMPUS

Management of Technology	M

UNIVERSITY OF PHOENIX–SAN ANTONIO CAMPUS

Management of Technology	M

UNIVERSITY OF PHOENIX–SAN DIEGO CAMPUS

Management of Technology	M

UNIVERSITY OF PHOENIX–SAVANNAH CAMPUS

Management of Technology	M

UNIVERSITY OF PHOENIX–SOUTHERN ARIZONA CAMPUS

Management of Technology	M

UNIVERSITY OF PHOENIX–SOUTHERN COLORADO CAMPUS

Management of Technology	M

UNIVERSITY OF PHOENIX–SPRINGFIELD CAMPUS

Management of Technology	M

UNIVERSITY OF PHOENIX–TULSA CAMPUS

Management of Technology	M

UNIVERSITY OF PHOENIX–UTAH CAMPUS

Management of Technology	M

UNIVERSITY OF PHOENIX–VANCOUVER CAMPUS

Management of Technology	M

UNIVERSITY OF PHOENIX–WASHINGTON D.C. CAMPUS

Health Informatics	M,D

UNIVERSITY OF PHOENIX–WEST FLORIDA CAMPUS

Management of Technology	M

UNIVERSITY OF PITTSBURGH

Artificial Intelligence/ Robotics	M,D*
Bioengineering	M,D
Bioinformatics	M,D,O
Chemical Engineering	M,D
Civil Engineering	M,D
Computer Engineering	M,D
Computer Science	M,D
Electrical Engineering	M,D
Engineering and Applied Sciences—General	M,D
Environmental Engineering	M,D
Health Informatics	M
Industrial/Management Engineering	M,D
Information Science	M,D,O
Materials Sciences	M,D
Mechanical Engineering	M,D
Petroleum Engineering	M,D
Telecommunications	M,D,O

UNIVERSITY OF PORTLAND

Engineering and Applied Sciences—General	M
Management of Technology	M

UNIVERSITY OF PUERTO RICO, MAYAGÜEZ CAMPUS

Chemical Engineering	M,D
Civil Engineering	M,D
Computer Engineering	M,D
Computer Science	M,D
Electrical Engineering	M,D
Engineering and Applied Sciences—General	M,D
Industrial/Management Engineering	M
Information Science	M,D
Mechanical Engineering	M

UNIVERSITY OF PUERTO RICO, MEDICAL SCIENCES CAMPUS

Health Informatics	M

UNIVERSITY OF PUERTO RICO, RÍO PIEDRAS

Information Science	M,O

UNIVERSITY OF REGINA

Computer Engineering	M,D
Computer Science	M,D
Engineering and Applied Sciences—General	M,D
Environmental Engineering	M,D
Industrial/Management Engineering	M,D
Petroleum Engineering	M,D
Software Engineering	M,D
Systems Engineering	M,D

UNIVERSITY OF RHODE ISLAND

Biomedical Engineering	M,D,O
Biotechnology	M,D
Chemical Engineering	M,D
Civil Engineering	M,D
Computer Engineering	M,D,O
Computer Science	M,D,O
Electrical Engineering	M,D,O
Engineering and Applied Sciences—General	M,D,O
Environmental Engineering	M,D
Ocean Engineering	M,D

UNIVERSITY OF ROCHESTER

Biomedical Engineering	M,D
Chemical Engineering	M,D*
Computer Engineering	M,D
Computer Science	M,D
Electrical Engineering	
Energy and Power Engineering	
Engineering and Applied Sciences—General	M,D
Materials Sciences	M,D
Mechanical Engineering	M,D

UNIVERSITY OF ST. THOMAS (MN)

Computer and Information Systems Security	M,O
Engineering and Applied Sciences—General	M,O
Engineering Management	M,O
Management of Technology	M,O
Manufacturing Engineering	M,O
Mechanical Engineering	M,O
Software Engineering	M,O
Systems Engineering	M,O

UNIVERSITY OF SAN DIEGO

Health Informatics	M,D

UNIVERSITY OF SAN FRANCISCO

Computer Science	M
Internet Engineering	M
Telecommunications Management	M

UNIVERSITY OF SASKATCHEWAN

Agricultural Engineering	M,D
Biomedical Engineering	M,D
Biotechnology	M
Chemical Engineering	M,D
Civil Engineering	M,D
Computer Science	M,D
Electrical Engineering	M,D
Engineering and Applied Sciences—General	M,D,O
Engineering Physics	M,D
Environmental Engineering	M,D,O
Mechanical Engineering	M,D

THE UNIVERSITY OF SCRANTON

Software Engineering — M

UNIVERSITY OF SOUTH AFRICA

Chemical Engineering — M
Engineering and Applied Sciences—General — M
Information Science — M,D
Technology and Public Policy — M,D
Telecommunications Management — M,D

UNIVERSITY OF SOUTH ALABAMA

Chemical Engineering — M
Civil Engineering — M
Computer Science — M
Electrical Engineering — M
Engineering and Applied Sciences—General — M
Information Science — M
Mechanical Engineering — M

UNIVERSITY OF SOUTH CAROLINA

Chemical Engineering — M,D
Civil Engineering — M,D
Computer Engineering — M,D
Computer Science — M,D
Electrical Engineering — M,D
Engineering and Applied Sciences—General — M,D
Hazardous Materials Management — M,D
Mechanical Engineering — M,D
Nuclear Engineering — M,D
Software Engineering — M,D

THE UNIVERSITY OF SOUTH DAKOTA

Computer Science — M,D

UNIVERSITY OF SOUTHERN CALIFORNIA

Aerospace/Aeronautical Engineering — M,D,O
Artificial Intelligence/Robotics — M,D
Bioinformatics — D
Biomedical Engineering — M,D
Chemical Engineering — M,D,O
Civil Engineering — M,D,O
Computer and Information Systems Security — M,D
Computer Engineering — M,D,O
Computer Science — M,D
Construction Management — M,D,O
Electrical Engineering — M,D,O
Engineering and Applied Sciences—General — M,D,O
Engineering Management — M,D,O
Environmental Engineering — M,D,O
Game Design and Development — M,D
Hazardous Materials Management — M,D,O
Industrial/Management Engineering — M,D,O
Manufacturing Engineering — M,D,O
Materials Engineering — M,D,O
Materials Sciences — M,D,O
Mechanical Engineering — M,D,O
Mechanics — M,D,O
Modeling and Simulation — M,D
Operations Research — M,D,O
Petroleum Engineering — M,D,O
Safety Engineering — M,D,O

Software Engineering — M,D
Systems Engineering — M,D,O
Telecommunications — M,D,O
Transportation and Highway Engineering — M,D,O

UNIVERSITY OF SOUTHERN INDIANA

Engineering and Applied Sciences—General — M

UNIVERSITY OF SOUTHERN MAINE

Computer Science — M
Manufacturing Engineering — M

UNIVERSITY OF SOUTHERN MISSISSIPPI

Computer Science — M,D
Construction Engineering — M
Polymer Science and Engineering — M,D

UNIVERSITY OF SOUTH FLORIDA

Biomedical Engineering — M,D
Chemical Engineering — M,D
Civil Engineering — M,D
Computer Engineering — M,D
Computer Science — M,D
Electrical Engineering — M,D
Engineering and Applied Sciences—General — M,D
Engineering Management — M,D
Environmental Engineering — M,D
Industrial/Management Engineering — M,D
Mechanical Engineering — M,D
Polymer Science and Engineering — M,D

THE UNIVERSITY OF TENNESSEE

Aerospace/Aeronautical Engineering — M,D
Agricultural Engineering — M
Aviation — M
Biomedical Engineering — M,D
Biosystems Engineering — M,D
Chemical Engineering — M,D
Civil Engineering — M,D
Computer Engineering — M,D
Computer Science — M,D
Electrical Engineering — M,D
Engineering and Applied Sciences—General — M,D
Engineering Management — M,D
Environmental Engineering — M
Industrial/Management Engineering — M,D
Information Science — M,D
Materials Engineering — M,D
Materials Sciences — M,D
Mechanical Engineering — M,D
Nuclear Engineering — M,D
Polymer Science and Engineering — M,D
Reliability Engineering — M,D

THE UNIVERSITY OF TENNESSEE AT CHATTANOOGA

Chemical Engineering — M
Civil Engineering — M
Computer Science — M,O
Electrical Engineering — M
Energy and Power Engineering — M,O

Engineering and Applied Sciences—General — M,D,O
Engineering Management — M,O
Industrial/Management Engineering — M
Mechanical Engineering — M
Medical Informatics — M,D,O

THE UNIVERSITY OF TENNESSEE SPACE INSTITUTE

Aerospace/Aeronautical Engineering — M,D
Aviation — M
Computer Science — M,D
Electrical Engineering — M,D
Engineering and Applied Sciences—General — M,D
Engineering Management — M,D
Materials Engineering — M
Materials Sciences — M
Mechanical Engineering — M,D
Mechanics — M,D

THE UNIVERSITY OF TEXAS AT ARLINGTON

Aerospace/Aeronautical Engineering — M,D
Bioengineering — M,D
Civil Engineering — M,D
Computer Engineering — M,D
Computer Science — M,D
Electrical Engineering — M,D
Engineering and Applied Sciences—General — M,D
Engineering Management — M
Industrial/Management Engineering — M,D
Materials Engineering — M,D
Materials Sciences — M,D
Mechanical Engineering — M,D
Software Engineering — M,D
Systems Engineering — M

THE UNIVERSITY OF TEXAS AT AUSTIN

Aerospace/Aeronautical Engineering — M,D
Architectural Engineering — M
Biomedical Engineering — M,D
Chemical Engineering — M,D
Civil Engineering — M,D
Computer Engineering — M,D
Computer Science — M,D
Electrical Engineering — M,D
Engineering and Applied Sciences—General — M,D
Environmental Engineering — M,D
Geotechnical Engineering — M,D
Industrial/Management Engineering — M,D
Materials Engineering — M,D
Materials Sciences — M,D
Mechanical Engineering — M,D
Mechanics — M,D
Mineral/Mining Engineering — M
Operations Research — M,D
Petroleum Engineering — M,D
Technology and Public Policy — M
Textile Sciences and Engineering — M
Water Resources Engineering — M,D

THE UNIVERSITY OF TEXAS AT DALLAS

Biomedical Engineering — M,D

Biotechnology — M,D
Computer and Information Systems Security — M
Computer Engineering — M,D
Computer Science — M,D
Electrical Engineering — M,D
Engineering and Applied Sciences—General — M,D
Financial Engineering — M
Materials Engineering — M,D
Materials Sciences — M,D
Mechanical Engineering — M
Software Engineering — M,D
Systems Engineering — M
Telecommunications — M,D

THE UNIVERSITY OF TEXAS AT EL PASO

Bioinformatics — M,D
Civil Engineering — M,D,O
Computer Engineering — M,D
Computer Science — M,D
Construction Management — M,D,O
Electrical Engineering — M,D
Engineering and Applied Sciences—General — M,D,O
Environmental Engineering — M,D,O
Industrial/Management Engineering — M,O
Information Science — M,D
Manufacturing Engineering — M,O
Materials Engineering — M,D
Materials Sciences — M,D
Mechanical Engineering — M
Metallurgical Engineering and Metallurgy — M,D
Systems Engineering — M,O

THE UNIVERSITY OF TEXAS AT SAN ANTONIO

Biomedical Engineering — M,D*
Biotechnology — M,D
Civil Engineering — M,D*
Computer and Information Systems Security — M,D
Computer Engineering — M,D
Computer Science — M,D
Construction Management — M
Electrical Engineering — M,D*
Engineering and Applied Sciences—General — M,D
Environmental Engineering — M,D
Information Science — M
Management of Technology — M,D
Manufacturing Engineering — M*
Mechanical Engineering — M*
Software Engineering — M,D

THE UNIVERSITY OF TEXAS AT TYLER

Civil Engineering — M
Computer Science — M
Electrical Engineering — M
Environmental Engineering — M
Mechanical Engineering — M
Structural Engineering — M
Transportation and Highway Engineering — M
Water Resources Engineering — M

THE UNIVERSITY OF TEXAS HEALTH SCIENCE CENTER AT HOUSTON

Health Informatics — M,D,O

M—master's degree; P—first professional degree; D—doctorate; O—other advanced degree; *—Close-Up and/or Display

THE UNIVERSITY OF TEXAS MEDICAL BRANCH

Bioinformatics	D

THE UNIVERSITY OF TEXAS OF THE PERMIAN BASIN

Computer Science	M

THE UNIVERSITY OF TEXAS–PAN AMERICAN

Computer Science	M
Electrical Engineering	M
Manufacturing Engineering	M
Mechanical Engineering	M

THE UNIVERSITY OF TEXAS SOUTHWESTERN MEDICAL CENTER AT DALLAS

Biomedical Engineering	M,D

UNIVERSITY OF THE DISTRICT OF COLUMBIA

Computer Science	M
Electrical Engineering	M
Engineering and Applied Sciences—General	M

UNIVERSITY OF THE SACRED HEART

Information Science	O

UNIVERSITY OF THE SCIENCES IN PHILADELPHIA

Bioinformatics	M
Biotechnology	M,D

THE UNIVERSITY OF TOLEDO

Bioengineering	M,D
Bioinformatics	M,O
Biomedical Engineering	D
Chemical Engineering	M,D
Civil Engineering	M,D
Computer Science	M,D
Electrical Engineering	M,D
Engineering and Applied Sciences—General	M
Industrial/Management Engineering	M,D
Mechanical Engineering	M,D

UNIVERSITY OF TORONTO

Aerospace/Aeronautical Engineering	M,D
Biomedical Engineering	M,D
Biotechnology	M
Chemical Engineering	M,D
Civil Engineering	M,D
Computer Engineering	M,D
Computer Science	M,D
Electrical Engineering	M,D
Engineering and Applied Sciences—General	M,D
Health Informatics	M
Industrial/Management Engineering	M,D
Management of Technology	M
Manufacturing Engineering	M
Materials Engineering	M,D
Materials Sciences	M,D
Mechanical Engineering	M,D

UNIVERSITY OF TULSA

Chemical Engineering	M,D
Computer Science	M,D
Electrical Engineering	M

Energy Management and Policy	M
Engineering and Applied Sciences—General	M,D
Engineering Physics	M
Financial Engineering	M
Mechanical Engineering	M,D
Petroleum Engineering	M,D

UNIVERSITY OF UTAH

Bioengineering	M,D*
Bioinformatics	M,D,O
Biotechnology	M
Chemical Engineering	M,D
Civil Engineering	M,D*
Computer Science	M,D
Electrical Engineering	M,D
Engineering and Applied Sciences—General	M,D
Environmental Engineering	M,D
Geological Engineering	M,D
Materials Engineering	M,D
Materials Sciences	M,D
Mechanical Engineering	M,D
Metallurgical Engineering and Metallurgy	M,D
Mineral/Mining Engineering	M,D
Nuclear Engineering	M,D

UNIVERSITY OF VERMONT

Biomedical Engineering	M
Civil Engineering	M,D
Computer Science	M,D
Electrical Engineering	M,D
Engineering and Applied Sciences—General	M,D
Environmental Engineering	M,D
Materials Sciences	M,D
Mechanical Engineering	M,D

UNIVERSITY OF VICTORIA

Computer Engineering	M,D
Computer Science	M,D
Electrical Engineering	M,D
Engineering and Applied Sciences—General	M,D
Health Informatics	M
Mechanical Engineering	M,D

UNIVERSITY OF VIRGINIA

Aerospace/Aeronautical Engineering	M,D
Biomedical Engineering	M,D
Chemical Engineering	M,D
Civil Engineering	M,D
Computer Engineering	M,D
Computer Science	M,D
Electrical Engineering	M,D
Engineering and Applied Sciences—General	M,D
Engineering Physics	M,D
Health Informatics	M
Materials Sciences	M,D
Mechanical Engineering	M,D
Systems Engineering	M,D

UNIVERSITY OF WASHINGTON

Aerospace/Aeronautical Engineering	M,D
Bioengineering	M,D
Bioinformatics	M,D
Biomedical Engineering	M,D
Biotechnology	D
Ceramic Sciences and Engineering	M,D
Chemical Engineering	M,D
Civil Engineering	M,D

Computer Science	M,D
Construction Engineering	M,D
Construction Management	M
Electrical Engineering	M,D
Energy Management and Policy	M,D
Engineering and Applied Sciences—General	M,D
Environmental Engineering	M,D
Geotechnical Engineering	M,D
Health Informatics	M,D
Industrial/Management Engineering	M,D
Information Science	M,D
Management of Technology	M,D
Materials Engineering	M,D
Materials Sciences	M,D
Mechanical Engineering	M,D
Medical Informatics	M,D
Nanotechnology	M,D
Structural Engineering	M,D
Transportation and Highway Engineering	M,D
Water Resources Engineering	M,D

UNIVERSITY OF WASHINGTON, BOTHELL

Computer Engineering	M
Software Engineering	M

UNIVERSITY OF WASHINGTON, TACOMA

Computer Engineering	M
Software Engineering	M

UNIVERSITY OF WATERLOO

Chemical Engineering	M,D
Civil Engineering	M,D
Computer Engineering	M,D
Computer Science	M,D
Electrical Engineering	M,D
Engineering and Applied Sciences—General	M,D
Engineering Management	M,D
Environmental Engineering	M,D
Information Science	M,D
Management of Technology	M,D
Mechanical Engineering	M,D
Operations Research	M,D
Software Engineering	M,D
Systems Engineering	M,D

THE UNIVERSITY OF WESTERN ONTARIO

Biochemical Engineering	M,D
Chemical Engineering	M,D
Civil Engineering	M,D
Computer Engineering	M,D
Computer Science	M,D
Electrical Engineering	M,D
Engineering and Applied Sciences—General	M,D
Environmental Engineering	M,D
Materials Engineering	M,D
Mechanical Engineering	M,D

UNIVERSITY OF WEST FLORIDA

Biotechnology	M
Computer Science	M
Database Systems	M
Software Engineering	M

UNIVERSITY OF WEST GEORGIA

Computer Science	M,O
Software Engineering	M,O

UNIVERSITY OF WINDSOR

Civil Engineering	M,D
Computer Science	M,D
Electrical Engineering	M,D
Engineering and Applied Sciences—General	M,D
Environmental Engineering	M,D
Industrial/Management Engineering	M,D
Manufacturing Engineering	M,D
Materials Engineering	M,D
Mechanical Engineering	M,D

UNIVERSITY OF WISCONSIN–LA CROSSE

Software Engineering	M

UNIVERSITY OF WISCONSIN–MADISON

Agricultural Engineering	M,D
Bioengineering	M,D
Biomedical Engineering	M,D
Chemical Engineering	M,D
Civil Engineering	M,D
Computer and Information Systems Security	M
Computer Science	M,D
Electrical Engineering	M,D
Energy and Power Engineering	M,D
Engineering and Applied Sciences—General	M,D
Engineering Management	M
Engineering Physics	M,D
Environmental Engineering	M,D
Geological Engineering	M,D
Industrial/Management Engineering	M,D
Management of Technology	M
Manufacturing Engineering	M
Materials Engineering	M,D
Materials Sciences	M,D
Mechanical Engineering	M,D
Mechanics	M,D
Nuclear Engineering	M,D
Polymer Science and Engineering	M,D
Systems Engineering	M,D

UNIVERSITY OF WISCONSIN–MILWAUKEE

Civil Engineering	M,D,O
Computer Engineering	M,D,O
Computer Science	M,D
Electrical Engineering	M,D,O
Engineering and Applied Sciences—General	M,D,O
Engineering Management	M,D,O
Ergonomics and Human Factors	M,D,O
Health Informatics	M,O
Industrial/Management Engineering	M,D,O
Manufacturing Engineering	M,D,O
Materials Engineering	M,D,O
Mechanical Engineering	M,D,O
Mechanics	M,D,O
Medical Informatics	D

UNIVERSITY OF WISCONSIN–PARKSIDE

Computer Science	M
Information Science	M

UNIVERSITY OF WISCONSIN–PLATTEVILLE

Computer Science	M
Engineering and Applied Sciences—General	M

UNIVERSITY OF WISCONSIN–STOUT

Industrial/Management Engineering	M
Information Science	M
Management of Technology	M
Manufacturing Engineering	M
Telecommunications Management	M

UNIVERSITY OF WISCONSIN–WHITEWATER

Management of Technology	M

UNIVERSITY OF WYOMING

Biotechnology	D
Chemical Engineering	M,D
Civil Engineering	M,D
Computer Science	M,D
Electrical Engineering	M,D
Engineering and Applied Sciences—General	M,D
Environmental Engineering	M
Mechanical Engineering	M,D
Petroleum Engineering	M,D

UTAH STATE UNIVERSITY

Aerospace/Aeronautical Engineering	M,D
Agricultural Engineering	M,D
Civil Engineering	M,D,O
Computer Science	M,D
Electrical Engineering	M,D
Engineering and Applied Sciences—General	M,D,O
Environmental Engineering	M,D,O
Mechanical Engineering	M,D
Water Resources Engineering	M,D

UTICA COLLEGE

Computer and Information Systems Security	M

VALPARAISO UNIVERSITY

Engineering Management	M,O

VANDERBILT UNIVERSITY

Bioinformatics	M,D
Biomedical Engineering	M,D
Chemical Engineering	M,D
Civil Engineering	M,D
Computer Science	M,D
Electrical Engineering	M,D
Engineering and Applied Sciences—General	M,D
Environmental Engineering	M,D
Materials Sciences	M,D
Mechanical Engineering	M,D

VILLANOVA UNIVERSITY

Artificial Intelligence/Robotics	M,O
Biochemical Engineering	M,O
Chemical Engineering	M,O
Civil Engineering	M
Computer Engineering	M,O
Computer Science	M,O
Electrical Engineering	M,O
Engineering and Applied Sciences—General	M,D,O
Environmental Engineering	M,O
Manufacturing Engineering	M,O
Mechanical Engineering	M,O
Software Engineering	M
Water Resources Engineering	M,O

VIRGINIA COMMONWEALTH UNIVERSITY

Bioengineering	M,D
Bioinformatics	M,D
Biomedical Engineering	M,D
Chemical Engineering	M,D
Computer Science	M,D
Electrical Engineering	M,D
Engineering and Applied Sciences—General	M,D
Mechanical Engineering	M,D
Nanotechnology	M,D
Operations Research	M

VIRGINIA INTERNATIONAL UNIVERSITY

Computer Science	M

VIRGINIA POLYTECHNIC INSTITUTE AND STATE UNIVERSITY

Aerospace/Aeronautical Engineering	M,D,O
Agricultural Engineering	M,D
Bioengineering	M,D
Bioinformatics	D
Biotechnology	M
Chemical Engineering	M,D
Civil Engineering	M,D,O
Computer and Information Systems Security	M,D,O
Computer Engineering	M,D,O
Computer Science	M,O
Construction Engineering	M
Electrical Engineering	M,D,O
Engineering and Applied Sciences—General	M,D,O
Engineering Management	M,O
Environmental Engineering	M,D,O
Hazardous Materials Management	M,D,O
Human-Computer Interaction	M,D,O
Industrial/Management Engineering	M,D,O
Materials Engineering	M,D
Materials Sciences	M,D
Mechanical Engineering	M,D
Mechanics	M,D,O
Mineral/Mining Engineering	M,D
Ocean Engineering	M,O
Software Engineering	M,O
Systems Engineering	M,D,O
Transportation and Highway Engineering	M,D,O
Water Resources Engineering	M,D,O

VIRGINIA STATE UNIVERSITY

Computer Science	M

WAKE FOREST UNIVERSITY

Biomedical Engineering	M,D
Computer Science	M

WALDEN UNIVERSITY

Computer and Information Systems Security	M,D
Engineering Management	M,D
Health Informatics	M,D,O
Management of Technology	M,D
Software Engineering	M,D

WASHINGTON STATE UNIVERSITY

Agricultural Engineering	M,D
Bioengineering	M,D
Chemical Engineering	M,D
Civil Engineering	M,D
Computer Engineering	M,D
Computer Science	M,D
Electrical Engineering	M,D
Engineering and Applied Sciences—General	M,D
Environmental Engineering	M
Materials Engineering	M
Materials Sciences	M,D
Mechanical Engineering	M,D

WASHINGTON STATE UNIVERSITY SPOKANE

Engineering Management	M

WASHINGTON STATE UNIVERSITY TRI-CITIES

Computer Engineering	M,D
Computer Science	M,D
Electrical Engineering	M,D
Engineering and Applied Sciences—General	M,D
Mechanical Engineering	M,D

WASHINGTON STATE UNIVERSITY VANCOUVER

Computer Science	M
Engineering and Applied Sciences—General	M
Mechanical Engineering	M

WASHINGTON UNIVERSITY IN ST. LOUIS

Aerospace/Aeronautical Engineering	M,D
Biomedical Engineering	M,D
Chemical Engineering	M,D
Computer Engineering	M,D
Computer Science	M,D*
Electrical Engineering	M,D
Engineering and Applied Sciences—General	M,D
Environmental Engineering	M,D
Mechanical Engineering	M,D
Structural Engineering	M,D
Systems Science	M,D

WAYNE STATE UNIVERSITY

Automotive Engineering	M,O
Biomedical Engineering	M,D
Chemical Engineering	M,D
Civil Engineering	M,D
Computer Engineering	M,D
Computer Science	M,D,O
Electrical Engineering	M,D
Engineering and Applied Sciences—General	M,D,O
Engineering Management	M
Industrial/Management Engineering	M,D
Manufacturing Engineering	M
Materials Engineering	M,D,O
Materials Sciences	M,D,O

Mechanical Engineering	M,D
Metallurgical Engineering and Metallurgy	M,D,O
Polymer Science and Engineering	M,D,O

WEBSTER UNIVERSITY

Aerospace/Aeronautical Engineering	M,D,O
Computer Science	M,O
Engineering Management	M
Telecommunications Management	M,D,O

WENTWORTH INSTITUTE OF TECHNOLOGY

Construction Management	M*

WESLEYAN UNIVERSITY

Bioinformatics	D
Computer Science	M,D

WEST CHESTER UNIVERSITY OF PENNSYLVANIA

Computer and Information Systems Security	M,O
Computer Science	M,O

WESTERN CAROLINA UNIVERSITY

Computer Science	M
Construction Management	M
Industrial/Management Engineering	M

WESTERN GOVERNORS UNIVERSITY

Computer and Information Systems Security	M

WESTERN ILLINOIS UNIVERSITY

Computer Science	M
Manufacturing Engineering	M
Technology and Public Policy	M

WESTERN INTERNATIONAL UNIVERSITY

Systems Engineering	M

WESTERN KENTUCKY UNIVERSITY

Computer Science	M
Management of Technology	M

WESTERN MICHIGAN UNIVERSITY

Chemical Engineering	M,D
Civil Engineering	M
Computer Engineering	M,D
Computer Science	M,D
Construction Engineering	M
Construction Management	M
Electrical Engineering	M,D
Engineering and Applied Sciences—General	M,D
Engineering Management	M
Industrial/Management Engineering	M,D
Manufacturing Engineering	M
Mechanical Engineering	M,D
Paper and Pulp Engineering	M,D
Structural Engineering	M
Transportation and Highway Engineering	M

*M—master's degree; P—first professional degree; D—doctorate; O—other advanced degree; *—Close-Up and / or Display*

WESTERN NEW ENGLAND UNIVERSITY

Electrical Engineering	M
Engineering and Applied Sciences—General	M,D
Engineering Management	M,D
Industrial/Management Engineering	M
Manufacturing Engineering	M
Mechanical Engineering	M

WESTERN WASHINGTON UNIVERSITY

Computer Science	M

WESTMINSTER COLLEGE (UT)

Management of Technology	M,O

WEST TEXAS A&M UNIVERSITY

Engineering and Applied Sciences—General	M

WEST VIRGINIA STATE UNIVERSITY

Biotechnology	M

WEST VIRGINIA UNIVERSITY

Aerospace/Aeronautical Engineering	M,D
Chemical Engineering	M,D
Civil Engineering	M,D
Computer Engineering	D
Computer Science	M,D
Electrical Engineering	M,D
Engineering and Applied Sciences—General	M,D
Environmental Engineering	M,D
Industrial/Management Engineering	M,D
Mechanical Engineering	M,D
Mineral/Mining Engineering	M,D
Petroleum Engineering	M,D
Safety Engineering	M
Software Engineering	M

WEST VIRGINIA UNIVERSITY INSTITUTE OF TECHNOLOGY

Engineering and Applied Sciences—General	M
Systems Engineering	M

WICHITA STATE UNIVERSITY

Aerospace/Aeronautical Engineering	M,D
Computer Engineering	M,D
Computer Science	M,D
Electrical Engineering	M,D
Engineering and Applied Sciences—General	M,D
Industrial/Management Engineering	M,D
Manufacturing Engineering	M,D
Mechanical Engineering	M,D

WIDENER UNIVERSITY

Chemical Engineering	M
Civil Engineering	M
Computer Engineering	M
Engineering and Applied Sciences—General	M
Engineering Management	M
Mechanical Engineering	M
Software Engineering	M
Telecommunications	M

WILFRID LAURIER UNIVERSITY

Management of Technology	M,D

WILKES UNIVERSITY

Electrical Engineering	M
Engineering and Applied Sciences—General	M
Engineering Management	M
Mechanical Engineering	M

WILLIAM PATERSON UNIVERSITY OF NEW JERSEY

Biotechnology	M

WILMINGTON UNIVERSITY

Computer and Information Systems Security	M
Internet Engineering	M

WINSTON-SALEM STATE UNIVERSITY

Computer Science	M

WINTHROP UNIVERSITY

Software Engineering	M,O

WOODS HOLE OCEANOGRAPHIC INSTITUTION

Civil Engineering	M,D,O
Electrical Engineering	M,D,O
Mechanical Engineering	M,D,O
Ocean Engineering	M,D,O

WORCESTER POLYTECHNIC INSTITUTE

Artificial Intelligence/Robotics	M,D,O
Biomedical Engineering	M,D,O
Biotechnology	M,D
Chemical Engineering	M,D
Civil Engineering	M,D,O
Computer Engineering	M,D,O
Computer Science	M,D,O
Construction Management	M,D,O
Electrical Engineering	M,D,O
Energy and Power Engineering	M,D
Engineering and Applied Sciences—General	M,D,O
Engineering Design	M,O
Environmental Engineering	M,D,O
Fire Protection Engineering	M,D,O
Manufacturing Engineering	M,D
Materials Engineering	M,D
Materials Sciences	M,D
Mechanical Engineering	M,D,O
Modeling and Simulation	M,D
Systems Science	M,D,O

WORCESTER STATE UNIVERSITY

Biotechnology	M

WRIGHT STATE UNIVERSITY

Biomedical Engineering	M
Computer Engineering	M,D
Computer Science	M,D
Electrical Engineering	M
Engineering and Applied Sciences—General	M,D
Ergonomics and Human Factors	M,D
Materials Engineering	M
Materials Sciences	M
Mechanical Engineering	M

YALE UNIVERSITY

Bioinformatics	D
Biomedical Engineering	M,D
Chemical Engineering	M,D
Computer Science	M,D
Electrical Engineering	M,D
Engineering and Applied Sciences—General	M,D*
Engineering Physics	M,D
Environmental Engineering	M,D
Mechanical Engineering	M,D

YORK UNIVERSITY

Computer Science	M,D

YOUNGSTOWN STATE UNIVERSITY

Civil Engineering	M
Computer Engineering	M
Computer Science	M
Electrical Engineering	M
Engineering and Applied Sciences—General	M
Environmental Engineering	M
Industrial/Management Engineering	M
Information Science	M
Mechanical Engineering	M

ACADEMIC AND PROFESSIONAL PROGRAMS IN ENGINEERING & APPLIED SCIENCES

Section 1
Engineering and Applied Sciences

This section contains a directory of institutions offering graduate work in engineering and applied sciences, followed by in-depth entries submitted by institutions that chose to prepare detailed program descriptions. Additional information about programs listed in the directory but not augmented by an in-depth entry may be obtained by writing directly to the dean of a graduate school or chair of a department at the address given in the directory.

For programs in specific areas of engineering, see all other sections in this book. In the other guides in this series:

Graduate Programs in the Humanities, Arts & Social Sciences
See *Applied Arts and Design (Industrial Design)* and *Architecture (Environmental Design)*

Graduate Programs in the Biological Sciences
See *Ecology, Environmental Biology,* and *Evolutionary Biology*

Graduate Programs in the Physical Sciences, Mathematics, Agricultural Sciences, the Environment & Natural Resources
See *Agricultural and Food Sciences* and *Natural Resources*

CONTENTS

Engineering and Applied Sciences—General

Air Force Institute of Technology, Graduate School of Engineering and Management, Dayton, OH 45433-7765. Offers MS, PhD. *Accreditation:* ABET (one or more programs are accredited). Part-time programs available. *Degree requirements:* For master's, thesis; for doctorate, thesis/dissertation. *Entrance requirements:* For master's, GRE General Test, minimum GPA of 3.0; for doctorate, GRE General Test.

Alabama Agricultural and Mechanical University, School of Graduate Studies, School of Engineering and Technology, Huntsville, AL 35811. Offers M Ed, MS. Part-time and evening/weekend programs available. *Degree requirements:* For master's, comprehensive exam, thesis optional. *Entrance requirements:* For master's, GRE General Test. Additional exam requirements/recommendations for international students: Required—TOEFL (minimum score 500 paper-based; 173 computer-based; 61 iBT). Electronic applications accepted. *Faculty research:* Ionized gases, hypersonic flow phenomenology, robotics systems development.

Alfred University, Graduate School, New York State College of Ceramics, School of Engineering, Alfred, NY 14802-1205. Offers biomedical materials engineering science (MS); ceramic engineering (MS); ceramics (PhD); electrical engineering (MS); glass science (MS, PhD); materials science and engineering (MS, PhD); mechanical engineering (MS). *Degree requirements:* For master's, thesis; for doctorate, thesis/dissertation. *Entrance requirements:* Additional exam requirements/recommendations for international students: Required—TOEFL (minimum score 590 paper-based; 243 computer-based). Electronic applications accepted. *Expenses:* Contact institution. *Faculty research:* Fine-particle technology, x-ray diffraction, superconductivity, electronic materials.

The American University in Cairo, School of Sciences and Engineering, Cairo, Egypt. Offers M Comp, M Eng, MS, PhD, Diploma. Part-time programs available. *Faculty:* 27 full-time (5 women), 9 part-time/adjunct (0 women). *Students:* 91 full-time (42 women), 184 part-time (90 women). 375 applicants, 46% accepted, 102 enrolled. In 2010, 56 master's awarded. *Degree requirements:* For master's, thesis (for some programs); for doctorate, thesis/dissertation. *Entrance requirements:* Additional exam requirements/recommendations for international students: Required—TOEFL (minimum score 450 paper-based; 133 computer-based; 45 iBT). *Application deadline:* For fall admission, 2/1 priority date for domestic and international students; for spring admission, 11/1 priority date for domestic and international students. Applications are processed on a rolling basis. Application fee: $50. Electronic applications accepted. *Financial support:* Fellowships with partial tuition reimbursements, teaching assistantships, scholarships/grants and unspecified assistantships available. Financial award application deadline: 5/12. *Faculty research:* Construction management and technology, structural engineering, public works engineering. *Unit head:* Dr. Ezzat Fahmy, Dean, 202-2615 Ext. 2926, E-mail: ezzat@aucegypt.edu. *Application contact:* Wesley Clark, Director of North American Admissions &Financial Aid, 212-646-810-9433 Ext. 4547, E-mail: wclark@aucnyo.edu.

The American University of Athens, School of Graduate Studies, Athens, Greece. Offers biomedical sciences (MS); business (MBA); business communication (MA); computer sciences (MS); engineering and applied sciences (MS); politics and policy making (MA); systems engineering (MS); telecommunications (MS). *Entrance requirements:* For master's, resume, 2 recommendation letters. Additional exam requirements/recommendations for international students: Required—TOEFL (minimum score 550 paper-based; 213 computer-based). *Faculty research:* Nanotechnology, environmental sciences, rock mechanics, human skin studies, Monte Carlo algorithms and software.

American University of Beirut, Graduate Programs, Faculty of Engineering and Architecture, Beirut, Lebanon. Offers applied energy (MME); civil engineering (ME, PhD); electrical and computer engineering (ME, PhD); engineering management (MEM); environmental and water resources (ME); environmental and water resources engineering (PhD); environmental technology (MSES); mechanical engineering (ME, PhD); urban design (MUD); urban planning and policy (MUP). Part-time programs available. *Faculty:* 57 full-time (12 women), 3 part-time/adjunct (0 women). *Students:* 261 full-time (92 women), 58 part-time (20 women). Average age 25. 272 applicants, 79% accepted, 108 enrolled. In 2010, 70 master's, 1 doctorate awarded. *Degree requirements:* For master's, one foreign language, comprehensive exam, thesis (for some programs); for doctorate, one foreign language, comprehensive exam, thesis/dissertation, publications. *Entrance requirements:* For master's, GRE (for electrical and computer engineering), letters of recommendation; for doctorate, GRE, letters of recommendation, master's degree, transcripts, curriculum vitae, interview. Additional exam requirements/recommendations for international students: Required—TOEFL (minimum score 600 paper-based; 250 computer-based; 100 iBT), IELTS (minimum score 7.5). *Application deadline:* For fall admission, 2/5 priority date for domestic and international students; for spring admission, 11/1 priority date for domestic students, 11/1 for international students. Applications are processed on a rolling basis. Application fee: $50. Electronic applications accepted. *Expenses:* Tuition: Full-time $12,294; part-time $683 per credit. Required fees: $499; $499 per credit. Tuition and fees vary according to course load and program. *Financial support:* In 2010–11, 10 fellowships with full tuition reimbursements (averaging $24,800 per year), 33 research assistantships with full tuition reimbursements (averaging $24,800 per year), 70 teaching assistantships with full tuition reimbursements (averaging $9,800 per year) were awarded; career-related internships or fieldwork, institutionally sponsored loans, scholarships/grants, health care benefits, and unspecified assistantships also available. Total annual research expenditures: $586,131. *Unit head:* Fadl H. Moukalled, Acting Dean, 961-135-0000 Ext. 3400, Fax: 961-174-4462, E-mail: memouk@aub.edu.lb. *Application contact:* Dr. Salim Kanaan, Director, Admissions Office, 961-135-0000 Ext. 2594, Fax: 961-175-0775, E-mail: sk00@aub.edu.lb.

Andrews University, School of Graduate Studies, College of Technology, Berrien Springs, MI 49104. Offers MS. *Entrance requirements:* For master's, minimum GPA of 2.6. Additional exam requirements/recommendations for international students: Required—TOEFL (minimum score 550 paper-based).

Arizona State University, College of Technology and Innovation, Mesa, AZ 85212. Offers MCST, MS, PhD. Part-time and evening/weekend programs available. *Faculty:* 101 full-time (25 women), 9 part-time/adjunct (2 women). *Students:* 149 full-time (41 women), 288 part-time (126 women); includes 96 minority (21 Black or African American, non-Hispanic/Latino; 8 American Indian or Alaska Native, non-Hispanic/Latino; 29 Asian, non-Hispanic/Latino; 34 Hispanic/Latino; 4 Two or more races, non-Hispanic/Latino), 84 international. Average age 33. 433 applicants, 85% accepted, 109 enrolled. In 2010, 71 master's awarded. *Degree requirements:* For master's, thesis, interactive Program of Study (iPOS) submitted before completing 50 percent of required credit hours. *Entrance requirements:* For master's, GRE, minimum GPA of 3.0 or equivalent in last 2 years of work leading to bachelor's degree. Additional exam requirements/recommendations for international students: Required—TOEFL, IELTS, or Pearson Test of English. *Application deadline:* For fall admission, 7/1 for domestic and international students; for spring admission, 12/1 for domestic and international students. Applications are processed on a rolling basis. Application fee: $70 ($90 for international students). Electronic applications accepted. *Expenses:* Contact institution. *Financial support:* In 2010–11, 17 research assistantships with full and partial tuition reimbursements (averaging $13,230 per year), 2 teaching assistantships with full and partial tuition reimbursements (averaging $12,263 per year) were awarded; career-related internships or fieldwork, Federal Work-Study, scholarships/grants, health care benefits, tuition waivers (full and partial), and unspecified assistantships also available. Support available to part-time students. Financial award application deadline: 3/1; financial award applicants required to submit FAFSA. Total annual research expenditures: $5.8 million. *Unit head:* Dr. Mitzi Montoya, Vice Provost and Dean, 480-727-1955, Fax: 480-727-1089, E-mail: mitzi.montoya@asu.edu. *Application contact:* Graduate Admissions, 480-965-6113.

Arizona State University, Ira A. Fulton School of Engineering, Tempe, AZ 85287-9309. Offers M Eng, MA, MCS, MS, MSE, PhD, Graduate Certificate. Part-time and evening/weekend

programs available. Postbaccalaureate distance learning degree programs offered (minimal on-campus study). *Faculty:* 234 full-time (42 women), 34 part-time/adjunct (7 women). *Students:* 1,373 full-time (291 women), 824 part-time (141 women); includes 289 minority (41 Black or African American, non-Hispanic/Latino; 8 American Indian or Alaska Native, non-Hispanic/Latino; 125 Asian, non-Hispanic/Latino; 104 Hispanic/Latino; 1 Native Hawaiian or other Pacific Islander, non-Hispanic/Latino; 10 Two or more races, non-Hispanic/Latino), 1,141 international. Average age 28. 3,762 applicants, 59% accepted, 739 enrolled. In 2010, 521 master's, 115 doctorates awarded. Terminal master's awarded for partial completion of doctoral program. *Degree requirements:* For master's, comprehensive exam (for some programs), thesis (for some programs), interactive Program of Study (iPOS) submitted before completing 50 percent of required credit hours; for doctorate, comprehensive exam, thesis/dissertation, interactive Program of Study (iPOS) submitted before completing 50 percent of required credit hours. *Entrance requirements:* For master's and doctorate, GRE, minimum GPA of 3.0 or equivalent in last 2 years of work leading to bachelor's degree. Additional exam requirements/recommendations for international students: Required—TOEFL, IELTS, or Pearson Test of English. *Application deadline:* For fall admission, 1/31 for domestic and international students; for spring admission, 7/1 for domestic and international students. Applications are processed on a rolling basis. Application fee: $70 ($90 for international students). Electronic applications accepted. *Expenses:* Contact institution. *Financial support:* In 2010–11, 545 research assistantships with full and partial tuition reimbursements (averaging $14,785 per year), 122 teaching assistantships with full and partial tuition reimbursements (averaging $12,879 per year) were awarded; fellowships with full tuition reimbursements, career-related internships or fieldwork, Federal Work-Study, institutionally sponsored loans, scholarships/grants, and tuition waivers (full and partial) also available. Financial award application deadline: 3/1; financial award applicants required to submit FAFSA. Total annual research expenditures: $71.2 million. *Unit head:* Paul C. Johnson, Dean, 480-965-9235, E-mail: paul.c.johnson@asu.edu. *Application contact:* Graduate Admissions, 480-965-6113.

Arkansas State University, Graduate School, College of Engineering, Jonesboro, State University, AR 72467. Offers MEM. Part-time programs available. *Faculty:* 3 part-time/adjunct (0 women). *Students:* 8 full-time (0 women), 7 part-time (1 woman); includes 2 minority (1 Black or African American, non-Hispanic/Latino; 1 Asian, non-Hispanic/Latino), 12 international. Average age 26. 16 applicants, 88% accepted, 10 enrolled. In 2010, 11 master's awarded. *Degree requirements:* For master's, comprehensive exam. *Entrance requirements:* For master's, GRE, appropriate bachelor's degree, official transcript, letters of recommendation, resume, immunization records. Additional exam requirements/recommendations for international students: Required—TOEFL (minimum score 550 paper-based; 213 computer-based; 79 iBT), IELTS (minimum score 6), PTE: Pearson Test of English Academic (56). *Application deadline:* For fall admission, 6/1 for domestic and international students; for spring admission, 10/15 for domestic and international students. Applications are processed on a rolling basis. Application fee: $30 ($40 for international students). Electronic applications accepted. *Expenses:* Contact institution. *Financial support:* In 2010–11, 3 students received support. Career-related internships or fieldwork, scholarships/grants, and unspecified assistantships available. Financial award application deadline: 7/1; financial award applicants required to submit FAFSA. *Unit head:* Dr. David Beasley, Dean, 870-972-2088, Fax: 870-972-3539, E-mail: dbbeasley@astate.edu. *Application contact:* Dr. Andrew Sustich, Dean of the Graduate School, 870-972-3029, Fax: 870-972-3857, E-mail: sustich@astate.edu.

Arkansas Tech University, Graduate College, College of Applied Sciences, Russellville, AR 72801. Offers emergency management (MS); engineering (M Engr); information technology (MS). Part-time programs available. *Students:* 86 full-time (24 women), 53 part-time (21 women); includes 14 minority (5 Black or African American, non-Hispanic/Latino; 2 American Indian or Alaska Native, non-Hispanic/Latino; 1 Asian, non-Hispanic/Latino; 4 Hispanic/Latino; 2 Two or more races, non-Hispanic/Latino), 60 international. Average age 31. In 2010, 44 master's awarded. *Degree requirements:* For master's, comprehensive exam (for some programs), thesis (for some programs), internship. *Entrance requirements:* For master's, GRE General Test. Additional exam requirements/recommendations for international students: Required—TOEFL (minimum score 550 paper-based; 213 computer-based; 79 iBT), IELTS (minimum score 6). *Application deadline:* For fall admission, 3/1 priority date for domestic students, 5/1 priority date for international students; for spring admission, 10/1 priority date for domestic and international students. Applications are processed on a rolling basis. Application fee: $0 ($30 for international students). Electronic applications accepted. *Expenses:* Tuition, state resident: full-time $4680; part-time $195 per credit hour. Tuition, nonresident: full-time $9360; part-time $390 per credit hour. Required fees: $714; $14 per credit hour. One-time fee: $326 part-time. Tuition and fees vary according to course load. *Financial support:* In 2010–11, teaching assistantships with full tuition reimbursements (averaging $4,000 per year); research assistantships, career-related internships or fieldwork, Federal Work-Study, scholarships/grants, health care benefits, and unspecified assistantships also available. Support available to part-time students. Financial award application deadline: 4/15; financial award applicants required to submit FAFSA. *Unit head:* Dr. William Hoefler, Dean, 479-968-0353 Ext. 501, E-mail: whoeflerjr@atu.edu. *Application contact:* Dr. Mary B. Gunter, Dean of Graduate College, 479-968-0398, Fax: 479-964-0542, E-mail: graduate.school@atu.edu.

Auburn University, Graduate School, Ginn College of Engineering, Auburn University, AL 36849. Offers M Ch E, M Mtl E, MAE, MCE, MEE, MISE, MME, MS, MSWE, PhD. Part-time programs available. *Faculty:* 146 full-time (12 women), 17 part-time/adjunct (2 women). *Students:* 407 full-time (96 women), 347 part-time (70 women); includes 40 Black or African American, non-Hispanic/Latino; 2 American Indian or Alaska Native, non-Hispanic/Latino; 15 Asian, non-Hispanic/Latino; 8 Hispanic/Latino), 385 international. Average age 28. 1,512 applicants, 44% accepted, 162 enrolled. In 2010, 125 master's, 48 doctorates awarded. *Degree requirements:* For master's, thesis (for some programs); for doctorate, thesis/dissertation. *Entrance requirements:* For master's and doctorate, GRE General Test. *Application deadline:* For fall admission, 7/7 for domestic students; for spring admission, 11/24 for domestic students. Applications are processed on a rolling basis. Application fee: $50 ($60 for international students). Electronic applications accepted. *Expenses:* Tuition, state resident: full-time $7002. Tuition, nonresident: full-time $21,898. International tuition: $22,116 full-time. Required fees: $892. Tuition and fees vary according to course load and program. *Financial support:* Fellowships, research assistantships, teaching assistantships, Federal Work-Study available. Support available to part-time students. Financial award application deadline: 3/15; financial award applicants required to submit FAFSA. *Unit head:* Dr. Larry Benefield, Dean, 334-844-2308. *Application contact:* Dr. George Flowers, Dean of the Graduate School, 334-844-2125.

Baylor University, Graduate School, School of Engineering and Computer Science, Department of Engineering, Waco, TX 76798. Offers biomedical engineering (MSBE); electrical and computer engineering (MSECE, PhD); engineering (ME); mechanical engineering (MSME). *Faculty:* 14 full-time (1 woman). *Students:* 30 full-time (4 women), 6 part-time (0 women); includes 9 minority (3 Black or African American, non-Hispanic/Latino; 2 Asian, non-Hispanic/Latino; 1 Hispanic/Latino; 3 Two or more races, non-Hispanic/Latino), 7 international. In 2010, 7 master's awarded. *Unit head:* Dr. Mike Thompson, Graduate Director, 254-710-4188. *Application contact:* Linda Keer, Administrative Assistant, 254-710-4188, Fax: 254-710-3870, E-mail: linda_kerr@baylor.edu.

Boise State University, Graduate College, College of Engineering, Boise, ID 83725-0399. Offers M Engr, MS, PhD. Part-time programs available. Postbaccalaureate distance learning degree programs offered (no on-campus study). *Entrance requirements:* For master's, minimum GPA of 3.0. Electronic applications accepted.

Boston University, College of Engineering, Boston, MA 02215. Offers M Eng, MS, PhD, MD/PhD, MS/MBA. Part-time programs available. Postbaccalaureate distance learning degree programs offered (no on-campus study). *Faculty:* 112 full-time (12 women), 9 part-time/adjunct

(1 woman). *Students:* 551 full-time (112 women), 60 part-time (13 women); includes 75 minority (6 Black or African American, non-Hispanic/Latino; 1 American Indian or Alaska Native, non-Hispanic/Latino; 49 Asian, non-Hispanic/Latino; 17 Hispanic/Latino; 2 Two or more races, non-Hispanic/Latino), 271 international. Average age 26. 1,931 applicants, 25% accepted, 245 enrolled. In 2010, 124 master's, 41 doctorates awarded. Terminal master's awarded for partial completion of doctoral program. *Degree requirements:* For master's, thesis (for some programs); for doctorate, comprehensive exam, thesis/dissertation. *Entrance requirements:* For master's and doctorate, GRE General Test. Additional exam requirements/recommendations for international students: Required—TOEFL (minimum score 550 paper-based; 213 computer-based; 84 iBT) or IELTS (minimum score 6.0). *Application deadline:* For fall admission, 4/1 for domestic and international students; for spring admission, 10/1 for domestic and international students. Applications are processed on a rolling basis. Application fee: $70. Electronic applications accepted. *Expenses:* Tuition: Full-time $39,314; part-time $1228 per credit. Required fees: $40 per semester. *Financial support:* In 2010–11, 458 students received support, including 70 fellowships with full tuition reimbursements available (averaging $28,200 per year), 241 research assistantships with full tuition reimbursements available (averaging $18,800 per year), 62 teaching assistantships with full tuition reimbursements available (averaging $18,800 per year); career-related internships or fieldwork, Federal Work-Study, institutionally sponsored loans, scholarships/grants, traineeships, health care benefits, and tuition waivers (full and partial) also available. Financial award application deadline: 1/15; financial award applicants required to submit FAFSA. *Faculty research:* Photonics, bioengineering, computer and information systems, nanotechnology, materials science and engineering. *Unit head:* Dr. Kenneth R. Lutchen, Dean, 617-353-2800, Fax: 617-358-3468, E-mail: klutch@bu.edu. *Application contact:* Stephen Doherty, Director of Graduate Programs, 617-353-9760, Fax: 617-353-0259, E-mail: enggrad@bu.edu.

Bradley University, Graduate School, College of Engineering and Technology, Peoria, IL 61625-0002. Offers MSCE, MSEE, MSIE, MSME, MSMFE. Part-time and evening/weekend programs available. *Degree requirements:* For master's, comprehensive exam, thesis optional. *Entrance requirements:* For master's, minimum GPA of 3.0, 2 letters of recommendation. Additional exam requirements/recommendations for international students: Required—TOEFL (minimum score 550 paper-based; 213 computer-based; 79 iBT). *Expenses:* Contact institution.

Brigham Young University, Graduate Studies, Ira A. Fulton College of Engineering and Technology, Provo, UT 84602. Offers MS, PhD. *Faculty:* 104 full-time (1 woman), 14 part-time/adjunct (0 women). *Students:* 387 full-time (36 women), 41 part-time (5 women); includes 67 minority (4 Black or African American, non-Hispanic/Latino; 8 American Indian or Alaska Native, non-Hispanic/Latino; 34 Asian, non-Hispanic/Latino; 19 Hispanic/Latino; 2 Native Hawaiian or other Pacific Islander, non-Hispanic/Latino), 36 international. Average age 27. 227 applicants, 77% accepted, 133 enrolled. In 2010, 102 master's, 15 doctorates awarded. *Degree requirements:* For master's, comprehensive exam, thesis (for some programs); for doctorate, comprehensive exam, thesis/dissertation. *Entrance requirements:* For master's, GRE, at least 3 letters of recommendation; transcripts from each institution attended; ecclesiastical endorsement, complete department requirements; for doctorate, GRE, at least 3 letters of recommendation; ecclesiastical endorsement, complete department requirements. Additional exam requirements/recommendations for international students: Required—TOEFL (minimum score 580 paper-based; 237 computer-based; 85 iBT), IELTS (minimum score 7). *Application deadline:* For fall admission, 1/15 for domestic and international students; for winter admission, 6/15 for domestic and international students; for spring admission, 1/15 for domestic and international students. Application fee: $50. Electronic applications accepted. *Expenses:* Tuition: Full-time $5580; part-time $310 per credit hour. Tuition and fees vary according to program and student's religious affiliation. *Financial support:* In 2010–11, 197 students received support, including 22 fellowships with full and partial tuition reimbursements available (averaging $15,050 per year), 200 research assistantships with full and partial tuition reimbursements available (averaging $11,883 per year), 98 teaching assistantships with full and partial tuition reimbursements available (averaging $10,029 per year); career-related internships or fieldwork, institutionally sponsored loans, scholarships/grants, and unspecified assistantships also available. Support available to part-time students. Financial award application deadline: 6/30; financial award applicants required to submit FAFSA. *Faculty research:* Combustion, microwave remote sensing, structural optimization, biomedical engineering, networking. Total annual research expenditures: $8.9 million. *Unit head:* Dr. Alan R. Parkinson, Dean, 801-422-4327, Fax: 801-422-0218, E-mail: college@et.byu.edu. *Application contact:* Claire A. DeWitt, Adviser, 801-422-4541, Fax: 801-422-0270, E-mail: gradstudies@byu.edu.

Brown University, Graduate School, Division of Engineering, Providence, RI 02912. Offers biomedical engineering (Sc M, PhD); electrical sciences and computer engineering (Sc M, PhD); fluid, thermal and chemical processes (Sc M, PhD); materials science and engineering (Sc M, PhD); mechanics of solids (Sc M, PhD). *Degree requirements:* For doctorate, thesis/dissertation, preliminary exam.

Bucknell University, Graduate Studies, College of Engineering, Lewisburg, PA 17837. Offers MS, MS Ch E, MSCE, MSEE, MSEV, MSME. Part-time programs available. *Degree requirements:* For master's, thesis. *Entrance requirements:* For master's, GRE General Test, GRE Subject Test, minimum GPA of 2.8. Additional exam requirements/recommendations for international students: Required—TOEFL. *Expenses:* Tuition: Full-time $36,992; part-time $4624 per course.

California Institute of Technology, Division of Engineering and Applied Science, Pasadena, CA 91125. Offers aeronautics (MS, PhD, Engr); applied and computational mathematics (MS, PhD); applied mechanics (MS, PhD); applied physics (MS, PhD); bioengineering (MS, PhD); civil engineering (MS, PhD, Engr); computation and neural systems (MS, PhD); computer science (MS, PhD); control and dynamical systems (MS, PhD); electrical engineering (MS, PhD, Engr); environmental science and engineering (MS, PhD); materials science (MS, PhD); mechanical engineering (MS, PhD, Engr). *Faculty:* 85 full-time (11 women). *Students:* 556 full-time (128 women). 2,592 applicants, 8% accepted, 67 enrolled. In 2010, 71 master's, 84 doctorates awarded. Terminal master's awarded for partial completion of doctoral program. *Degree requirements:* For doctorate, thesis/dissertation. *Entrance requirements:* For master's and doctorate, GRE (strongly recommended), minimum GPA of 3.5. Additional exam requirements/recommendations for international students: Required—TOEFL; Recommended—TWE (minimum score 5). *Application deadline:* For fall admission, 1/1 for domestic students. Application fee: $50. Electronic applications accepted. *Financial support:* In 2010–11, 122 fellowships, 355 research assistantships, 110 teaching assistantships were awarded; Federal Work-Study and institutionally sponsored loans also available. Support available to part-time students. *Unit head:* Dr. Ares J. Rosakis, Chair, 626-395-4100, E-mail: arosakis@caltech.edu. *Application contact:* Natalie Gilmore, Assistant Dean of Graduate Studies, 626-395-3812, Fax: 626-577-9246, E-mail: ngilmore@caltech.edu.

California National University for Advanced Studies, College of Engineering, Northridge, CA 91325. Offers MS Eng. Part-time programs available. Postbaccalaureate distance learning degree programs offered (no on-campus study). *Degree requirements:* For master's, thesis or alternative, project. *Entrance requirements:* For master's, minimum GPA of 3.0. Electronic applications accepted.

California Polytechnic State University, San Luis Obispo, College of Engineering, Department of Biomedical and General Engineering, San Luis Obispo, CA 93407. Offers MS, MBA/MS, MCRP/MS. Part-time programs available. *Faculty:* 5 full-time (2 women). *Students:* 93 full-time (20 women), 36 part-time (8 women); includes 38 minority (2 Black or African American, non-Hispanic/Latino; 1 American Indian or Alaska Native, non-Hispanic/Latino; 20 Asian, non-Hispanic/Latino; 12 Hispanic/Latino; 3 Two or more races, non-Hispanic/Latino), 4 international. Average age 26. 108 applicants, 70% accepted, 54 enrolled. In 2010, 15 master's awarded. *Degree requirements:* For master's, comprehensive exam (for some programs), thesis (for some programs). *Entrance requirements:* For master's, minimum GPA of 2.5 in last 90 quarter units of course work. Additional exam requirements/recommendations for international students: Required—TOEFL (minimum score 550 paper-based; 213 computer-based), TWE (minimum score 4.5). *Application deadline:* For fall admission, 7/1 for domestic students, 11/30 for international students; for winter admission, 11/1 for domestic students, 6/30 for international students; for spring admission, 2/1 for domestic students. Applications are processed on a rolling basis. Application fee: $55. Electronic applications accepted. *Expenses:* Tuition, state resident: full-time $5386; part-time $3124 per year. Tuition, nonresident: full-time $11,160; part-time $248 per unit. Required fees: $2250; $614 per term. One-time fee: $2250 full-time; $1842 part-time. *Financial support:* Fellowships, research assistantships, teaching assistantships, Federal Work-Study and scholarships/grants available. Support available to part-time students. Financial award application deadline: 3/2; financial award applicants required to submit FAFSA. *Faculty research:* Biomedical engineering, materials engineering, water engineering. *Unit head:* Dr. David Clague, Graduate Coordinator, 805-756-5145, Fax: 805-756-6424, E-mail: dclague@calpoly.edu. *Application contact:* Dr. David Clague, Graduate Coordinator, 805-756-5145, Fax: 805-756-6424, E-mail: dclague@calpoly.edu.

California State University, Chico, Graduate School, College of Engineering, Computer Science, and Technology, Chico, CA 95929-0722. Offers MS. Part-time programs available. Postbaccalaureate distance learning degree programs offered. *Students:* 23 full-time (2 women), 18 part-time (1 woman); includes 1 Asian, non-Hispanic/Latino, 29 international. Average age 26. 123 applicants, 63% accepted, 13 enrolled. In 2010, 51 master's awarded. *Entrance requirements:* Additional exam requirements/recommendations for international students: Required—TOEFL (minimum score 550 paper-based; 213 computer-based; 80 iBT), IELTS (minimum score 6.5). *Application deadline:* For fall admission, 3/1 priority date for domestic students, 3/1 for international students; for spring admission, 9/15 priority date for domestic students, 9/15 for international students. Applications are processed on a rolling basis. Application fee: $55. Electronic applications accepted. *Financial support:* Fellowships, research assistantships, teaching assistantships, career-related internships or fieldwork and Federal Work-Study available. Support available to part-time students. *Unit head:* Dr. Kenneth Derucher, Dean, 530-898-5963. *Application contact:* School of Graduate, International, and Interdisciplinary Studies, 530-898-6880, Fax: 530-898-6889, E-mail: grin@csuchico.edu.

California State University, East Bay, Office of Academic Programs and Graduate Studies, College of Science, Engineering Department, Hayward, CA 94542-3000. Offers construction management (MS); engineering management (MS). *Faculty:* 4 full-time (2 women). *Students:* 30 full-time (12 women), 62 part-time (12 women); includes 24 minority (4 Black or African American, non-Hispanic/Latino; 9 Asian, non-Hispanic/Latino; 11 Hispanic/Latino), 30 international. Average age 32. 92 applicants, 78% accepted, 27 enrolled. In 2010, 23 master's awarded. *Entrance requirements:* For master's, GRE or GMAT, minimum GPA of 2.5. Additional exam requirements/recommendations for international students: Required—TOEFL (minimum score 550 paper-based; 213 computer-based). *Application deadline:* For fall admission, 6/30 for domestic and international students. Application fee: $55. Electronic applications accepted. *Financial support:* Federal Work-Study and institutionally sponsored loans available. Support available to part-time students. Financial award application deadline: 3/2; financial award applicants required to submit FAFSA. *Unit head:* Dr. Saeid Motavalli, Chair, 510-885-2654, Fax: 510-885-2678, E-mail: saeid.motavalli@csueastbay.edu. *Application contact:* Dr. Donna Wiley, Interim Associate Director, 510-885-2928, Fax: 510-885-4777, E-mail: donna.wiley@csueastbay.edu.

California State University, Fresno, Division of Graduate Studies, College of Engineering and Computer Science, Fresno, CA 93740-8027. Offers MS. Part-time and evening/weekend programs available. *Degree requirements:* For master's, thesis or alternative. *Entrance requirements:* For master's, GRE General Test, minimum GPA of 2.7. Additional exam requirements/recommendations for international students: Required—TOEFL. Electronic applications accepted. *Faculty research:* Exhaust emission, blended fuel testing, waste management.

California State University, Fullerton, Graduate Studies, College of Engineering and Computer Science, Fullerton, CA 92834-9480. Offers MS. Part-time programs available. *Students:* 210 full-time (38 women), 522 part-time (124 women); includes 17 Black or African American, non-Hispanic/Latino; 186 Asian, non-Hispanic/Latino; 47 Hispanic/Latino; 9 Two or more races, non-Hispanic/Latino, 268 international. Average age 29. 1,052 applicants, 67% accepted, 315 enrolled. In 2010, 207 master's awarded. *Degree requirements:* For master's, comprehensive exam, project or thesis. *Entrance requirements:* For master's, minimum undergraduate GPA of 2.5. Application fee: $55. *Financial support:* Career-related internships or fieldwork, Federal Work-Study, institutionally sponsored loans, and scholarships/grants available. Support available to part-time students. Financial award application deadline: 3/1; financial award applicants required to submit FAFSA. *Unit head:* Dr. Raman Unnikrishnan, Dean, 657-278-3362. *Application contact:* Admissions/Applications, 657-278-2371.

California State University, Los Angeles, Graduate Studies, College of Engineering, Computer Science, and Technology, Los Angeles, CA 90032-8530. Offers MA, MS. Part-time and evening/weekend programs available. *Faculty:* 16 full-time (5 women), 13 part-time/adjunct (2 women). *Students:* 172 full-time (51 women), 268 part-time (49 women); includes 160 minority (18 Black or African American, non-Hispanic/Latino; 82 Asian, non-Hispanic/Latino; 59 Hispanic/Latino; 1 Two or more races, non-Hispanic/Latino), 206 international. Average age 29. 308 applicants, 99% accepted, 123 enrolled. In 2010, 161 master's awarded. *Entrance requirements:* Additional exam requirements/recommendations for international students: Required—TOEFL (minimum score 550 paper-based). *Application deadline:* For fall admission, 5/1 for domestic and international students. Applications are processed on a rolling basis. Application fee: $55. Electronic applications accepted. *Financial support:* Federal Work-Study available. Support available to part-time students. Financial award application deadline: 3/1. *Unit head:* Dr. Keith Moo-Young, Dean, 323-343-4500, Fax: 323-343-4555, E-mail: kmooyou@exchange.calstatela.edu. *Application contact:* Dr. Alan Muchlinski, Dean of Graduate Studies, 323-343-3820, Fax: 323-343-5653, E-mail: amuchli@exchange.calstatela.edu.

See Display on next page and Close-Up on page 77.

California State University, Northridge, Graduate Studies, College of Engineering and Computer Science, Northridge, CA 91330. Offers MS. Part-time and evening/weekend programs available. *Entrance requirements:* For master's, GRE General Test, minimum GPA of 2.5. Additional exam requirements/recommendations for international students: Required—TOEFL.

California State University, Sacramento, Graduate Studies, College of Engineering and Computer Science, Sacramento, CA 95819. Offers MS. Part-time and evening/weekend programs available. *Degree requirements:* For master's, writing proficiency exam. *Entrance requirements:* Additional exam requirements/recommendations for international students: Required—TOEFL. Electronic applications accepted.

Carleton University, Faculty of Graduate Studies, Faculty of Engineering and Design, Ottawa, ON K1S 5B6, Canada. Offers M Arch, M Des, M Eng, M Sc, MA Sc, PhD. *Degree requirements:* For doctorate, thesis/dissertation. *Entrance requirements:* For master's, honors degree; for doctorate, MA Sc or M Eng. Additional exam requirements/recommendations for international students: Required—TOEFL.

Case Western Reserve University, School of Graduate Studies, Case School of Engineering, Cleveland, OH 44106. Offers ME, MEM, MS, PhD, MD/MS, MD/PhD. Part-time and evening/weekend programs available. Postbaccalaureate distance learning degree programs offered (minimal on-campus study). *Faculty:* 106 full-time (12 women). *Students:* 561 full-time (122 women), 84 part-time (21 women); includes 14 Black or African American, non-Hispanic/Latino; 3 American Indian or Alaska Native, non-Hispanic/Latino; 50 Asian, non-Hispanic/Latino; 9 Hispanic/Latino, 310 international. 1,480 applicants, 22% accepted, 105 enrolled. In 2010, 134 master's, 56 doctorates awarded. Terminal master's awarded for partial completion of doctoral program. *Degree requirements:* For master's, thesis (for some programs); for doctorate, thesis/dissertation, qualifying exam, teaching experience. *Entrance requirements:* For master's and doctorate, GRE General Test. Additional exam requirements/recommendations for international students: Required—TOEFL (minimum score 550 paper-based; 213 computer-

Engineering and Applied Sciences—General

based; 79 iBT), IELTS (minimum score 6.5). *Application deadline:* Applications are processed on a rolling basis. Application fee: $50. Electronic applications accepted. *Financial support:* Fellowships with full and partial tuition reimbursements, research assistantships with full and partial tuition reimbursements, teaching assistantships, career-related internships or fieldwork, Federal Work-Study, and institutionally sponsored loans available. Support available to part-time students. Financial award applicants required to submit FAFSA. *Faculty research:* Advanced materials, biomedical engineering and human health, electrical engineering and computer science, civil engineering, engineering management. Total annual research expenditures: $37.9 million. *Unit head:* Norman C. Tien, Dean and Nord Professor of Engineering, 216-368-4436, Fax: 216-368-6939, E-mail: norman.tien@case.edu. *Application contact:* Dr. Patrick Crago, Associate Dean and Professor of Biomedical Engineering, 216-368-4436, Fax: 216-368-6939, E-mail: cseinfo@case.edu.

The Catholic University of America, School of Engineering, Washington, DC 20064. Offers MBE, MCE, MEE, MME, MS, MSCS, MSE, D Engr, PhD, Certificate. Part-time programs available. *Faculty:* 28 full-time (4 women), 27 part-time/adjunct (1 woman). *Students:* 49 full-time (13 women), 116 part-time (27 women); includes 13 Black or African American, non-Hispanic/Latino; 7 Asian, non-Hispanic/Latino; 8 Hispanic/Latino, 47 international. Average age 32. 200 applicants, 53% accepted, 46 enrolled. In 2010, 67 master's, 3 doctorates awarded. *Degree requirements:* For master's, thesis optional; for doctorate, comprehensive exam, thesis/dissertation. *Entrance requirements:* For master's and doctorate, statement of purpose, official copies of academic transcripts, three letters of recommendation. Additional exam requirements/recommendations for international students: Required—TOEFL (minimum score 580 paper-based; 237 computer-based). *Application deadline:* For fall admission, 8/1 priority date for domestic students, 7/15 for international students; for spring admission, 12/1 priority date for domestic students, 10/15 for international students. Applications are processed on a rolling basis. Application fee: $55. Electronic applications accepted. *Expenses:* Contact institution. *Financial support:* Fellowships, research assistantships, teaching assistantships, Federal Work-Study, scholarships/grants, tuition waivers (full and partial), and unspecified assistantships available. Financial award application deadline: 2/1; financial award applicants required to submit FAFSA. *Faculty research:* Rehabilitation engineering, cardiopulmonary biomechanics, geotechnical engineering, signal and image processing, fluid mechanics. Total annual research expenditures: $2.9 million. *Unit head:* Dr. Charles C. Nguyen, Dean, 202-319-5160, Fax: 202-319-4499, E-mail: nguyen@cua.edu. *Application contact:* Andrew Woodall, Director of Graduate Admissions, 202-319-5057, Fax: 202-319-6533, E-mail: cua-admissions@cua.edu.

Central Connecticut State University, School of Graduate Studies, School of Technology, Department of Engineering, New Britain, CT 06050-4010. Offers MS. Part-time and evening/weekend programs available. *Faculty:* 13 full-time (1 woman), 9 part-time/adjunct (1 woman). *Students:* 4 full-time (1 woman), 16 part-time (2 women); includes 5 minority (4 Asian, non-Hispanic/Latino; 1 Hispanic/Latino), 1 international. Average age 35. 19 applicants, 74% accepted, 5 enrolled. In 2010, 10 master's awarded. *Degree requirements:* For master's, comprehensive exam, thesis or alternative. *Entrance requirements:* For master's, minimum undergraduate GPA of 2.7. Additional exam requirements/recommendations for international students: Required—TOEFL. *Application deadline:* For fall admission, 7/1 for domestic students; for spring admission, 12/1 for domestic students. Applications are processed on a rolling basis. Application fee: $50. Electronic applications accepted. *Expenses:* Tuition, area resident: Full-time $5012; part-time $470 per credit. Tuition, state resident: full-time $7518; part-time $482 per credit. Tuition, nonresident: full-time $13,962; part-time $482 per credit. Required fees: $3772. One-time fee: $62 part-time. *Financial support:* In 2010–11, 1 student received support. Career-related internships or fieldwork, Federal Work-Study, scholarships/grants, and unspecified assistantships available. Support available to part-time students. Financial award application deadline: 2/15; financial award applicants required to submit FAFSA. *Unit head:* Dr. Alfred Gates, Chair, 860-832-1815. *Application contact:* Dr. Alfred Gates, Chair, 860-832-1815.

Central Connecticut State University, School of Graduate Studies, School of Technology, Department of Technology Engineering Education, New Britain, CT 06050-4010. Offers MS, Certificate. Part-time and evening/weekend programs available. *Faculty:* 5 full-time (1 woman), 1 part-time/adjunct (0 women). *Students:* 3 full-time (0 women), 17 part-time (0 women); includes 2 minority (1 Black or African American, non-Hispanic/Latino; 1 Hispanic/Latino), 1 international. Average age 40. 10 applicants, 100% accepted, 4 enrolled. In 2010, 9 master's, 1 other advanced degree awarded. *Degree requirements:* For master's, comprehensive exam, thesis or alternative; for Certificate, qualifying exam. *Entrance requirements:* For master's, minimum undergraduate GPA of 2.7. Additional exam requirements/recommendations for international students: Required—TOEFL. *Application deadline:* For fall admission, 7/1 for domestic students; for spring admission, 12/1 for domestic students. Applications are processed on a rolling basis. Application fee: $50. Electronic applications accepted. *Expenses:* Tuition, area resident: Full-time $5012; part-time $470 per credit. Tuition, state resident: full-time $7518; part-time $482 per credit. Tuition, nonresident: full-time $13,962; part-time $482 per credit. Required fees: $3772. One-time fee: $62 part-time. *Financial support:* In 2010–11, 2 students received support. Career-related internships or fieldwork, Federal Work-Study, scholarships/grants, and unspecified assistantships available. Support available to part-time students. Financial award application deadline: 2/15; financial award applicants required to submit FAFSA. *Faculty research:* Instruction, curriculum development, administration, occupational training. *Unit head:* Dr. James DeLaura, Chair, 860-832-1850. *Application contact:* Dr. James DeLaura, Chair, 860-832-1850.

Central Michigan University, College of Graduate Studies, College of Science and Technology, Department of Engineering Technology, Mount Pleasant, MI 48859. Offers industrial management and technology (MA). Part-time programs available. *Faculty:* 5 full-time (0 women), 1 part-time/adjunct (0 women). *Students:* 5 full-time (1 woman), 7 part-time (1 woman); includes 1 Asian, non-Hispanic/Latino, 5 international. Average age 29. *Degree requirements:* For master's, thesis or alternative. *Application deadline:* For fall admission, 6/1 for international students; for spring admission, 10/1 for international students. Applications are processed on a rolling basis. Application fee: $35 ($45 for international students). Electronic applications accepted. *Expenses:* Tuition, state resident: full-time $8208; part-time $456 per credit hour. Tuition, nonresident: full-time $13,788; part-time $766 per credit hour. One-time fee: $25. *Financial support:* Fellowships with tuition reimbursements, research assistantships with tuition reimbursements, teaching assistantships with tuition reimbursements, career-related internships or fieldwork, Federal Work-Study, unspecified assistantships, and out-of-state merit awards, non-resident graduate awards available. *Faculty research:* Computer applications, manufacturing process control, mechanical engineering automation, industrial technology. *Unit head:* Dr. Terence Lerch, Chairperson, 989-774-3033, Fax: 989-774-4900, E-mail: lerch1t@cmich.edu. *Application contact:* Dr. David A. Lopez, Graduate Program Coordinator, 989-774-3210, Fax: 989-774-4900, E-mail: lopez1da@cmich.edu.

Central Washington University, Graduate Studies and Research, College of Education and Professional Studies, Department of Industrial and Engineering Technology, Ellensburg, WA 98926. Offers engineering technology (MS). Part-time programs available. *Degree requirements:* For master's, thesis or alternative. *Entrance requirements:* For master's, minimum GPA of 3.0. Additional exam requirements/recommendations for international students: Required—TOEFL (minimum score 550 paper-based; 213 computer-based; 79 iBT). Electronic applications accepted.

Christian Brothers University, School of Engineering, Memphis, TN 38104-5581. Offers MEM, MSEM. Part-time and evening/weekend programs available. Postbaccalaureate distance learning degree programs offered (no on-campus study). *Faculty:* 1 full-time (0 women), 2 part-time/adjunct (1 woman). *Students:* 4 full-time (1 woman), 70 part-time (20 women); includes 18 minority (14 Black or African American, non-Hispanic/Latino; 2 Asian, non-Hispanic/Latino; 1 Hispanic/Latino; 1 Two or more races, non-Hispanic/Latino), 31 international. Average age 33. In 2010, 9 master's awarded. *Degree requirements:* For master's, engineering management project. *Entrance requirements:* For master's, GRE. Additional exam requirements/

Engineering and Applied Sciences—General

recommendations for international students: Required—TOEFL. Application fee: $50. *Expenses:* Tuition: Full-time $11,520; part-time $640 per credit hour. Required fees: $140; $140 per course. $70 per semester. Tuition and fees vary according to program. *Financial support:* Institutionally sponsored loans available. *Unit head:* Dr. Eric B. Welch, Dean, 901-321-3425, Fax: 901-321-3402, E-mail: ewelch@cbu.edu. *Application contact:* Dr. Neal Jackson, Director, 901-321-3283, Fax: 901-321-3494, E-mail: njackson@cbu.edu.

City College of the City University of New York, Graduate School, Grove School of Engineering, New York, NY 10031-9198. Offers ME, MS, PhD. Part-time programs available. Terminal master's awarded for partial completion of doctoral program. *Degree requirements:* For master's, thesis optional; for doctorate, one foreign language, comprehensive exam, thesis/dissertation. *Entrance requirements:* For master's, GRE General Test, minimum B average in undergraduate coursework; for doctorate, GRE General Test, minimum GPA of 3.5. Additional exam requirements/recommendations for international students: Required—TOEFL (minimum score 500 paper-based; 173 computer-based; 61 iBT). *Faculty research:* Robotics, network systems, structures.

Clarkson University, Graduate School, Wallace H. Coulter School of Engineering, Potsdam, NY 13699. Offers ME, MS, PhD. Part-time programs available. *Faculty:* 77 full-time (18 women), 7 part-time/adjunct (4 women). *Students:* 170 full-time (34 women), 3 part-time (2 women); includes 9 minority (1 American Indian or Alaska Native, non-Hispanic/Latino; 3 Asian, non-Hispanic/Latino; 2 Hispanic/Latino; 3 Two or more races, non-Hispanic/Latino), 94 international. Average age 27. 387 applicants, 53% accepted, 37 enrolled. In 2010, 38 master's, 16 doctorates awarded. Terminal master's awarded for partial completion of doctoral program. *Degree requirements:* For master's, thesis (for some programs); for doctorate, comprehensive exam, thesis/dissertation, departmental qualifying exam. *Entrance requirements:* For master's and doctorate, GRE, transcripts of all college coursework, resume, personal statement, three letters of recommendation. Additional exam requirements/recommendations for international students: Required—TOEFL (minimum score 550 paper-based; 213 computer-based; 80 iBT), IELTS (minimum score 6.5). *Application deadline:* For fall admission, 1/30 priority date for domestic and international students; for spring admission, 9/1 priority date for domestic and international students. Applications are processed on a rolling basis. Application fee: $25 ($35 for international students). Electronic applications accepted. *Expenses:* Tuition: Part-time $1136 per credit hour. *Financial support:* In 2010–11, 144 students received support, including 13 fellowships with full tuition reimbursements available (averaging $21,580 per year), 84 research assistantships with full tuition reimbursements available (averaging $21,580 per year), 47 teaching assistantships with full tuition reimbursements available (averaging $21,580 per year); scholarships/grants, tuition waivers (partial), and unspecified assistantships also available. *Faculty research:* Advanced materials processing, renewable energy rehabilitation, environmental. Total annual research expenditures: $10.6 million. *Unit head:* Dr. Goodarz Ahmadi, Dean, 315-268-6446, Fax: 315-268-4494, E-mail: gahmadi@clarkson.edu. *Application contact:* Kelly Sharlow, Assistant to the Dean, 315-268-7929, Fax: 315-268-4494, E-mail: ksharlow@clarkson.edu.

See Display below and Close-Up on page 79.

Clemson University, Graduate School, College of Engineering and Science, Clemson, SC 29634. Offers M Eng, M Engr, MFA, MS, PhD. Part-time programs available. *Faculty:* 282 full-time (40 women), 41 part-time/adjunct (11 women). *Students:* 1,238 full-time (323 women), 214 part-time (62 women); includes 51 Black or African American, non-Hispanic/Latino; 5 American Indian or Alaska Native, non-Hispanic/Latino; 34 Asian, non-Hispanic/Latino; 11 Hispanic/Latino; 13 Two or more races, non-Hispanic/Latino, 699 international. Average age 28. 2,797 applicants, 51% accepted, 487 enrolled. In 2010, 281 master's, 86 doctorates awarded. *Degree requirements:* For doctorate, thesis/dissertation. *Entrance requirements:* For master's and doctorate, GRE General Test. Additional exam requirements/recommendations for international students: Required—TOEFL. Application fee: $70 ($80 for international students).

Electronic applications accepted. *Expenses:* Tuition, state resident: full-time $6492; part-time $400 per credit hour. Tuition, nonresident: full-time $13,634; part-time $800 per credit hour. Required fees: $262 per semester. Part-time tuition and fees vary according to course load and program. *Financial support:* In 2010–11, 1,014 students received support, including 83 fellowships with full and partial tuition reimbursements available, 498 research assistantships with partial tuition reimbursements available, 526 teaching assistantships with partial tuition reimbursements available; career-related internships or fieldwork, institutionally sponsored loans, scholarships/grants, health care benefits, and unspecified assistantships also available. Support available to part-time students. Financial award applicants required to submit FAFSA. Total annual research expenditures: $32.2 million. *Unit head:* Dr. Esin Gulari, Dean, 864-656-3202. *Application contact:* Dr. R. Larry Dooley, Associate Dean for Research and Graduate Studies, 864-656-3200, Fax: 864-656-4466, E-mail: dooley@eng.clemson.edu.

Cleveland State University, College of Graduate Studies, Fenn College of Engineering, Cleveland, OH 44115. Offers MS, D Eng. Part-time and evening/weekend programs available. *Faculty:* 54 full-time (5 women), 12 part-time/adjunct (0 women). *Students:* 129 full-time (31 women), 242 part-time (36 women); includes 9 Black or African American, non-Hispanic/Latino; 8 Asian, non-Hispanic/Latino; 2 Hispanic/Latino, 238 international. Average age 27. 686 applicants, 52% accepted, 80 enrolled. In 2010, 99 master's, 8 doctorates awarded. *Degree requirements:* For master's, thesis or alternative; for doctorate, thesis/dissertation, candidacy and qualifying exams. *Entrance requirements:* For master's, GRE General Test, BS in engineering, minimum GPA of 3.0 (2.75 for students from ABET/EAC-accredited programs from the U. S. and Canada); for doctorate, GRE General Test, MS in engineering, minimum GPA of 3.25. Additional exam requirements/recommendations for international students: Required—TOEFL (minimum score 525 paper-based; 197 computer-based). *Application deadline:* For fall admission, 7/15 for domestic students, 5/15 for international students; for spring admission, 12/5 for domestic students, 11/1 for international students. Applications are processed on a rolling basis. Application fee: $30. Electronic applications accepted. *Expenses:* Tuition, state resident: full-time $8447; part-time $469 per credit hour. Tuition, nonresident: full-time $16,020; part-time $890 per credit hour. Required fees: $50. *Financial support:* In 2010–11, 93 students received support, including 1 fellowship with full tuition reimbursement available, 120 research assistantships with full and partial tuition reimbursements available (averaging $8,694 per year), 20 teaching assistantships with full and partial tuition reimbursements available (averaging $8,082 per year); career-related internships or fieldwork, institutionally sponsored loans, scholarships/grants, tuition waivers (full and partial), and unspecified assistantships also available. Support available to part-time students. Financial award application deadline: 3/30. *Faculty research:* Structural analysis and design, dynamic system and controls, applied biomedical engineering, transportation, water resources, telecommunication, power electronics, computer engineering, industrial automation, engineering management, mechanical design, thermodynamics and fluid mechanics, material engineering, tribology. Total annual research expenditures: $7.2 million. *Unit head:* Dr. Paul P. Lin, Associate Dean, 216-687-2556, Fax: 216-687-9280, E-mail: p.lin@csuohio.edu. *Application contact:* Dr. Paul P. Lin, Associate Dean, 216-687-2556, Fax: 216-687-9280, E-mail: p.lin@csuohio.edu.

Colorado School of Mines, Graduate School, Golden, CO 80401. Offers ME, MIPER, MS, PMS, PhD, Graduate Certificate. Part-time programs available. *Faculty:* 323 full-time (74 women), 100 part-time/adjunct (26 women). *Students:* 1,052 full-time (289 women), 169 part-time (44 women); includes 98 minority (10 Black or African American, non-Hispanic/Latino; 10 American Indian or Alaska Native, non-Hispanic/Latino; 31 Asian, non-Hispanic/Latino; 44 Hispanic/Latino; 1 Native Hawaiian or other Pacific Islander, non-Hispanic/Latino; 2 Two or more races, non-Hispanic/Latino), 331 international. Average age 29. 1,751 applicants, 50% accepted, 416 enrolled. In 2010, 325 master's, 49 doctorates awarded. *Degree requirements:* For master's, thesis (for some programs); for doctorate, comprehensive exam, thesis/dissertation. *Entrance requirements:* For master's, doctorate, and Graduate Certificate, GRE General Test. Additional exam requirements/recommendations for international students: Required—TOEFL (minimum score 550 paper-based; 213 computer-based; 80 iBT). *Application*

Engineering and Applied Sciences—General

Colorado School of Mines (continued)
deadline: For fall admission, 1/15 priority date for domestic and international students; for spring admission, 10/15 priority date for domestic and international students. Application fee: $50 ($70 for international students). Electronic applications accepted. *Expenses:* Tuition, state resident: full-time $11,550; part-time $641 per credit. Tuition, nonresident: full-time $25,980; part-time $1444 per credit. Required fees: $1874; $937 per semester. *Financial support:* In 2010–11, 699 students received support, including 82 fellowships with full tuition reimbursements available (averaging $20,000 per year), 420 research assistantships with full tuition reimbursements available (averaging $20,000 per year), 197 teaching assistantships with full tuition reimbursements available (averaging $20,000 per year); career-related internships or fieldwork, Federal Work-Study, institutionally sponsored loans, scholarships/grants, health care benefits, and unspecified assistantships also available. Financial award application deadline: 1/15; financial award applicants required to submit FAFSA. *Faculty research:* Energy, environment, materials, minerals, engineering systems. Total annual research expenditures: $31.9 million. *Unit head:* Dr. Tom M. Boyd, Dean of Graduate Studies, 303-273-3020, Fax: 303-273-3244, E-mail: tboyd@mines.edu. *Application contact:* Kay Leaman, Graduate Admissions Coordinator, 303-273-3249, Fax: 303-273-3244, E-mail: grad-app@mines.edu.

Colorado State University, Graduate School, College of Engineering, Fort Colllins, CO 80523-1301. Offers ME, MEE, MS, PhD. *Accreditation:* ABET. Part-time programs available. *Faculty:* 94 full-time (11 women), 7 part-time/adjunct (0 women). *Students:* 310 full-time (81 women), 348 part-time (66 women); includes 52 minority (4 Black or African American, non-Hispanic/Latino; 1 American Indian or Alaska Native, non-Hispanic/Latino; 11 Asian, non-Hispanic/Latino; 22 Hispanic/Latino; 1 Native Hawaiian or other Pacific Islander, non-Hispanic/Latino; 13 Two or more races, non-Hispanic/Latino), 196 international. Average age 30. 764 applicants, 52% accepted, 192 enrolled. In 2010, 94 master's, 38 doctorates awarded. *Degree requirements:* For doctorate, thesis/dissertation. *Entrance requirements:* For master's, GRE General Test, minimum GPA of 3.0, 3 letters of recommendation; for doctorate, GRE General Test, minimum GPA of 3.0, transcripts, 3 letters of recommendation, statement of purpose with interests. Additional exam requirements/recommendations for international students: Required—TOEFL (minimum score 550 paper-based; 213 computer-based; 80 iBT), IELTS (minimum score 6.5). *Application deadline:* For fall admission, 2/1 priority date for domestic and international students; for spring admission, 9/1 priority date for domestic and international students. Applications are processed on a rolling basis. Application fee: $50. Electronic applications accepted. *Expenses:* Tuition, state resident: full-time $7434; part-time $413 per credit. Tuition, nonresident: full-time $19,022; part-time $1057 per credit. Required fees: $1729; $88 per credit. *Financial support:* In 2010–11, 297 students received support, including 28 fellowships with full tuition reimbursements available (averaging $29,656 per year), 223 research assistantships with full tuition reimbursements available (averaging $17,494 per year), 46 teaching assistantships with full tuition reimbursements available (averaging $9,102 per year); career-related internships or fieldwork, Federal Work-Study, institutionally sponsored loans, scholarships/grants, traineeships, health care benefits, and unspecified assistantships also available. Financial award application deadline: 1/15; financial award applicants required to submit FAFSA. *Faculty research:* Atmospheric science, biological engineering, civil and environmental engineering, electrical and computer engineering, mechanical and biomedical engineering. Total annual research expenditures: $57.9 million. *Unit head:* Dr. Sandra L. Woods, Dean, 970-491-3366, Fax: 970-491-5569, E-mail: sandra.woods@colostate.edu. *Application contact:* Dr. Tom Siller, Associate Dean, 970-491-6220, Fax: 970-491-3429, E-mail: thomas.siller@colostate.edu.

Colorado State University–Pueblo, College of Education, Engineering and Professional Studies, Pueblo, CO 81001-4901. Offers M Ed, MS. Part-time and evening/weekend programs available. *Degree requirements:* For master's, thesis optional. *Entrance requirements:* For master's, GRE General Test. Additional exam requirements/recommendations for international students: Required—TOEFL (minimum score 500 paper-based; 173 computer-based). Electronic applications accepted. *Expenses:* Contact institution. *Faculty research:* Nanotechnology, applied operations, research transportation, decision analysis.

Columbia University, Fu Foundation School of Engineering and Applied Science, New York, NY 10027. Offers MS, Eng Sc D, PhD, Engr, MS/MBA. Part-time programs available. Post-baccalaureate distance learning degree programs offered (no on-campus study). *Faculty:* 203 full-time (22 women), 148 part-time/adjunct (11 women). *Students:* 1,387 full-time (349 women), 452 part-time (118 women); includes 159 minority (12 Black or African American, non-Hispanic/Latino; 2 American Indian or Alaska Native, non-Hispanic/Latino; 108 Asian, non-Hispanic/Latino; 25 Hispanic/Latino; 12 Two or more races, non-Hispanic/Latino), 1,228 international. Average age 28. 5,142 applicants, 27% accepted, 727 enrolled. In 2010, 817 master's, 129 doctorates, 6 other advanced degrees awarded. Terminal master's awarded for partial completion of doctoral program. *Degree requirements:* For master's, comprehensive exam (for some programs), thesis (for some programs); for doctorate, comprehensive exam (for some programs), thesis/dissertation, qualifying exam; for Engr, thesis optional. *Entrance requirements:* For master's and Engr, GRE General Test; for doctorate, GRE General Test, GRE Subject Test (computer science and applied physics programs only). Additional exam requirements/recommendations for international students: Required—TOEFL, IELTS. *Application deadline:* For fall admission, 12/1 priority date for domestic and international students; for spring admission, 10/1 priority date for domestic and international students. Application fee: $95. Electronic applications accepted. *Financial support:* In 2010–11, 643 students received support, including 72 fellowships with full and partial tuition reimbursements available (averaging $25,954 per year), 424 research assistantships with full tuition reimbursements available (averaging $29,525 per year), 147 teaching assistantships with full and partial tuition reimbursements available (averaging $26,844 per year); career-related internships or fieldwork, traineeships, health care benefits, and unspecified assistantships also available. Financial award application deadline: 12/1; financial award applicants required to submit FAFSA. Total annual research expenditures: $117.2 million. *Unit head:* Dr. Feniosky Pena-Mora, Dean, 212-854-2993, Fax: 212-864-0104, E-mail: dean@seas.columbia.edu. *Application contact:* Jocelyn Morales, Assistant Director, 212-854-6901, Fax: 212-854-5900, E-mail: seasgradmit@columbia.edu.

Concordia University, School of Graduate Studies, Faculty of Engineering and Computer Science, Montréal, QC H3G 1M8, Canada. Offers M App Comp Sc, M Comp Sc, M Eng, MA Sc, PhD, Certificate, Diploma. *Degree requirements:* For doctorate, comprehensive exam, thesis/dissertation. *Expenses:* Contact institution.

Cooper Union for the Advancement of Science and Art, Albert Nerken School of Engineering, New York, NY 10003-7120. Offers chemical engineering (ME); civil engineering (ME); electrical engineering (ME); mechanical engineering (ME). Part-time programs available. *Faculty:* 27 full-time (1 woman), 15 part-time/adjunct (2 women). *Students:* 57 full-time (15 women), 25 part-time (1 woman); includes 2 Black or African American, non-Hispanic/Latino; 1 American Indian or Alaska Native, non-Hispanic/Latino; 22 Asian, non-Hispanic/Latino; 2 Hispanic/Latino, 16 international. Average age 24. 72 applicants, 39% accepted, 27 enrolled. In 2010, 25 master's awarded. *Degree requirements:* For master's, thesis. *Entrance requirements:* For master's, GRE, BE, minimum GPA of 3.5. Additional exam requirements/recommendations for international students: Required—TOEFL (minimum score 600 paper-based; 250 computer-based; 100 iBT). *Application deadline:* For fall admission, 2/15 for domestic and international students. Application fee: $65. *Expenses:* Tuition: Full-time $35,000; part-time $1100 per credit. Required fees: $825 per semester. *Financial support:* Fellowships with full tuition reimbursements, career-related internships or fieldwork, Federal Work-Study, tuition waivers (full), and all admitted students receive full-tuition scholarships available. Support available to part-time students. Financial award application deadline: 5/1; financial award applicants required to submit CSS PROFILE or FAFSA. *Faculty research:* Civil infrastructure, imaging and sensing technology, biomedical engineering, encryption technology, process engineering. *Unit head:* Dr. Simon Ben-Avi, Acting Dean, 212-353-4285, E-mail: benavi@cooper.edu. *Application contact:* Student Contact, 212-353-4120, E-mail: admissions@cooper.edu.

Cornell University, Graduate School, Graduate Fields of Engineering, Ithaca, NY 14853-0001. Offers M Eng, MPS, MS, PhD, M Eng/MBA. *Faculty:* 244 full-time (32 women). *Students:* 1,668 full-time (440 women); includes 24 Black or African American, non-Hispanic/Latino; 1 American Indian or Alaska Native, non-Hispanic/Latino; 195 Asian, non-Hispanic/Latino; 69 Hispanic/Latino, 785 international. Average age 25. 6,105 applicants, 34% accepted, 1006 enrolled. In 2010, 698 master's, 121 doctorates awarded. *Degree requirements:* For doctorate, comprehensive exam, thesis/dissertation. *Entrance requirements:* Additional exam requirements/recommendations for international students: Required—TOEFL. Application fee: $70. Electronic applications accepted. *Expenses:* Tuition: Full-time $29,500. Required fees: $76. Tuition and fees vary according to degree level and program. *Financial support:* In 2010–11, 740 students received support, including 240 fellowships with full tuition reimbursements available, 443 research assistantships with full tuition reimbursements available, 186 teaching assistantships with full tuition reimbursements available; career-related internships or fieldwork, institutionally sponsored loans, scholarships/grants, health care benefits, tuition waivers (full and partial), and unspecified assistantships also available. Financial award applicants required to submit FAFSA. *Application contact:* Graduate School Application Requests, Caldwell Hall, 607-255-5816.

Dalhousie University, Faculty of Engineering, Halifax, NS B3H 4R2, Canada. Offers M Eng, M Sc, MA Sc, PhD, M Eng/M Plan, MA Sc/M Plan, MBA/M Eng. *Entrance requirements:* Additional exam requirements/recommendations for international students: Required—TOEFL, IELTS, 1 of 5 approved tests: TOEFL, IELTS, CANTEST, CAEL, Michigan English Language Assessment Battery.

Dartmouth College, Thayer School of Engineering, Hanover, NH 03755. Offers MEM, MS, PhD, MBA/MEM. *Faculty:* 51 full-time (7 women), 36 part-time/adjunct (4 women). *Students:* 200 full-time (57 women); includes 3 Black or African American, non-Hispanic/Latino; 1 American Indian or Alaska Native, non-Hispanic/Latino; 10 Asian, non-Hispanic/Latino; 3 Hispanic/Latino; 1 Two or more races, non-Hispanic/Latino, 102 international. Average age 24. 583 applicants, 27% accepted, 70 enrolled. In 2010, 44 master's, 7 doctorates awarded. *Degree requirements:* For doctorate, thesis/dissertation, candidacy oral exam. *Entrance requirements:* For master's and doctorate, GRE General Test. Additional exam requirements/recommendations for international students: Required—TOEFL. *Application deadline:* For fall admission, 1/1 priority date for domestic and international students. Applications are processed on a rolling basis. Application fee: $45. Electronic applications accepted. *Financial support:* In 2010–11, 187 students received support, including 5 fellowships with full tuition reimbursements available (averaging $22,920 per year), 96 research assistantships with full tuition reimbursements available (averaging $22,920 per year), 40 teaching assistantships with partial tuition reimbursements available (averaging $7,200 per year); career-related internships or fieldwork, institutionally sponsored loans, scholarships/grants, and tuition waivers (full and partial) also available. Financial award application deadline: 2/15; financial award applicants required to submit CSS PROFILE. *Faculty research:* Biomedical engineering, biotechnology and biochemical engineering, electrical and computer engineering, engineering physics, environmental engineering, materials science and engineering, mechanical systems engineering. *Unit head:* Dr. Joseph J. Helbie, Dean, 603-646-2238, Fax: 603-646-2580, E-mail: joseph.j.helbie@dartmouth.edu. *Application contact:* Candace S. Potter, Graduate Admissions Administrator, 603-646-3844, Fax: 603-646-1620, E-mail: candace.potter@dartmouth.edu.

Drexel University, College of Engineering, Philadelphia, PA 19104-2875. Offers MS, MSEE, MSSE, PhD, Certificate. Part-time and evening/weekend programs available. *Degree requirements:* For doctorate, thesis/dissertation. *Entrance requirements:* Additional exam requirements/recommendations for international students: Required—TOEFL. Electronic applications accepted.

Drexel University, School of Technology and Professional Studies, Philadelphia, PA 19104-2875. Offers construction management (MS); engineering technology (MS); food science (MS); hospitality management (MS); professional studies: creativity studies (MS); professional studies: e-learning leadership (MS); professional studies: homeland security management (MS); project management (MS); property management (MS); sport management (MS). Post-baccalaureate distance learning degree programs offered.

Duke University, Graduate School, Pratt School of Engineering, Master of Engineering Program, Durham, NC 27708-0271. Offers biomedical engineering (M Eng); civil engineering (M Eng); electrical and computer engineering (M Eng); environmental engineering (M Eng); materials science and engineering (M Eng); mechanical engineering (M Eng); photonics and optical sciences (M Eng). Part-time programs available. *Faculty:* 123 full-time, 1 part-time/adjunct. *Students:* 9 full-time (4 women); includes 2 minority (both Asian, non-Hispanic/Latino), 3 international. Average age 24. *Entrance requirements:* For master's, GRE General Test, resume, 3 letters of recommendation, statement of purpose. Additional exam requirements/recommendations for international students: Required—TOEFL. *Application deadline:* For fall admission, 6/15 for domestic students, 2/15 for international students; for spring admission, 11/1 for domestic students, 9/1 for international students. Application fee: $75. *Financial support:* Merit scholarships/grants available. *Unit head:* Dr. Bradley A. Fox, Executive Director, 919-660-5455, Fax: 919-660-5456. *Application contact:* Erin Degerman, Admissions Coordinator, 919-668-6789, Fax: 919-660-5456, E-mail: erin.degerman@duke.edu.

Eastern Illinois University, Graduate School, Lumpkin College of Business and Applied Sciences, School of Technology, Charleston, IL 61920-3099. Offers computer technology (Certificate); quality systems (Certificate); technology (MS); technology security (Certificate); work performance improvement (Certificate). Part-time and evening/weekend programs available.

Eastern Michigan University, Graduate School, College of Technology, School of Engineering Technology, Programs in Computer Aided Engineering, Ypsilanti, MI 48197. Offers CAD/CAM (MS); computer aided technology (MS). Part-time and evening/weekend programs available. Postbaccalaureate distance learning degree programs offered (minimal on-campus study). *Students:* 3 full-time (1 woman), 19 part-time (3 women), 17 international. Average age 28. In 2010, 14 master's awarded. *Entrance requirements:* Additional exam requirements/recommendations for international students: Required—TOEFL. *Application deadline:* Applications are processed on a rolling basis. Application fee: $35. *Financial support:* Fellowships, research assistantships with full tuition reimbursements, teaching assistantships with full tuition reimbursements, tuition waivers (partial) available. Financial award applicants required to submit FAFSA. *Unit head:* Dr. Tony Fukuo Shay, Program Coordinator, 734-487-2040, Fax: 734-487-8755, E-mail: tony.shay@emich.edu. *Application contact:* Dr. Tony Fukuo Shay, Program Coordinator, 734-487-2040, Fax: 734-487-8755, E-mail: tony.shay@emich.edu.

École Polytechnique de Montréal, Graduate Programs, Montréal, QC H3C 3A7, Canada. Offers M Eng, M Sc A, PhD, DESS. Part-time and evening/weekend programs available. Terminal master's awarded for partial completion of doctoral program. *Degree requirements:* For master's, one foreign language, thesis; for doctorate, one foreign language, thesis/dissertation. *Entrance requirements:* For master's, minimum GPA of 2.75; for doctorate, minimum GPA of 3.0. Electronic applications accepted. *Faculty research:* Chemical engineering, environmental engineering, microelectronics and communications, biomedical engineering, engineering physics.

Fairfield University, School of Engineering, Fairfield, CT 06824-5195. Offers electrical and computer engineering (MS); management of technology (MS); mechanical engineering (MS); software engineering (MS). Part-time and evening/weekend programs available. *Faculty:* 8 full-time (1 woman), 11 part-time/adjunct (0 women). *Students:* 31 full-time (12 women), 98 part-time (20 women); includes 28 minority (5 Black or African American, non-Hispanic/Latino; 17 Asian, non-Hispanic/Latino; 4 Hispanic/Latino; 1 Native Hawaiian or other Pacific Islander, non-Hispanic/Latino; 1 Two or more races, non-Hispanic/Latino), 26 international. Average age 35. 120 applicants, 55% accepted, 15 enrolled. In 2010, 52 master's awarded. *Degree requirements:* For master's, thesis, capstone course. *Entrance requirements:* For master's, interview, minimum GPA of 2.8, resume, 2 recommendations. Additional exam requirements/recommendations for international students: Required—TOEFL (minimum score 550 paper-based; 213 computer-based; 80 iBT). *Application deadline:* For fall admission, 5/15 for international students; for spring admission, 10/15 for international students. Applications are processed on a rolling basis. Application fee: $60. Electronic applications accepted. *Expenses:* Contact institution. *Financial support:* In 2010–11, 25 students received support. Unspecified assistantships available. Financial award applicants required to submit FAFSA. *Faculty research:* Vehicle dynamics, image processing, multimedia in instruction, thermal packaging, character recognition, photovoltaics and nanotechnology, Web technology. *Unit head:* Dr. Jack Beal, Dean, 203-254-4000 Ext. 4147, Fax: 203-254-4013, E-mail: jwbeal@fairfield.edu. *Application contact:* Marianne Gumpper, Director of Graduate and Continuing Studies Admissions, 203-254-4184, Fax: 203-254-4073, E-mail: gradadmis@fairfield.edu.

Fairleigh Dickinson University, Metropolitan Campus, University College: Arts, Sciences, and Professional Studies, School of Computer Sciences and Engineering, Teaneck, NJ 07666-1914. Offers computer engineering (MS); computer science (MS); e-commerce (MS); electrical engineering (MSEE); management information systems (MS); mathematical foundation (MS). *Students:* 114 full-time (34 women), 51 part-time (26 women), 109 international. Average age 27. 441 applicants, 57% accepted, 55 enrolled. In 2010, 101 master's awarded. *Application deadline:* Applications are processed on a rolling basis. Application fee: $40. *Unit head:* Dr. Alfredo Tan, Director, 201-692-2000. *Application contact:* Susan Brooman, University Director of Graduate Admissions, 201-692-2554, Fax: 201-692-2560, E-mail: globaleducation@fdu.edu.

Florida Agricultural and Mechanical University, Division of Graduate Studies, Research, and Continuing Education, College of Engineering Science, Technology, and Agriculture, Division of Agricultural Sciences, Tallahassee, FL 32307-3200. Offers agribusiness (MS); animal science (MS); engineering technology (MS); entomology (MS); food science (MS); international programs (MS); plant science (MS). *Degree requirements:* For master's, thesis. *Entrance requirements:* For master's, GRE General Test, minimum GPA of 3.0. Additional exam requirements/recommendations for international students: Required—TOEFL (minimum score 500 paper-based).

Florida Agricultural and Mechanical University, Division of Graduate Studies, Research, and Continuing Education, FAMU-FSU College of Engineering, Tallahassee, FL 32307-3200. Offers MS, PhD. College administered jointly by Florida State University. *Entrance requirements:* For master's, GRE General Test, minimum GPA of 3.0. Additional exam requirements/recommendations for international students: Required—TOEFL (minimum score 550 paper-based; 213 computer-based).

Florida Atlantic University, College of Engineering and Computer Science, Boca Raton, FL 33431-0991. Offers MS, PhD. Part-time and evening/weekend programs available. Post-baccalaureate distance learning degree programs offered (minimal on-campus study). *Faculty:* 81 full-time (10 women), 10 part-time/adjunct (1 woman). *Students:* 158 full-time (33 women), 157 part-time (37 women); includes 96 minority (23 Black or African American, non-Hispanic/Latino; 1 American Indian or Alaska Native, non-Hispanic/Latino; 24 Asian, non-Hispanic/Latino; 46 Hispanic/Latino; 2 Two or more races, non-Hispanic/Latino), 88 international. Average age 30. 226 applicants, 50% accepted, 74 enrolled. In 2010, 88 master's, 14 doctorates awarded. Terminal master's awarded for partial completion of doctoral program. *Degree requirements:* For master's, thesis optional; for doctorate, thesis/dissertation, qualifying exam. *Entrance requirements:* For master's, GRE General Test, minimum GPA of 3.0; for doctorate, GRE General Test. Additional exam requirements/recommendations for international students: Required—TOEFL. *Application deadline:* For fall admission, 7/1 for domestic students, 2/15 for international students; for spring admission, 11/1 for domestic students, 7/15 for international students. Applications are processed on a rolling basis. Application fee: $30. *Expenses:* Tuition, area resident: Part-time $319.96 per credit. Tuition, state resident: part-time $319.96 per credit. Tuition, nonresident: part-time $926.42 per credit. *Financial support:* In 2010–11, research assistantships with partial tuition reimbursements (averaging $15,000 per year), teaching assistantships with partial tuition reimbursements (averaging $15,000 per year) were awarded; fellowships, career-related internships or fieldwork, Federal Work-Study, and unspecified assistantships also available. Support available to part-time students. Financial award applicants required to submit FAFSA. *Faculty research:* Automated underwater vehicles, communication systems, computer networks, materials, neural networks. *Unit head:* Dr. Karl K. Stevens, Dean, 561-297-3400, Fax: 561-297-2659, E-mail: stevens@fau.edu. *Application contact:* Dr. Karl K. Stevens, Dean, 561-297-3400, Fax: 561-297-2659, E-mail: stevens@fau.edu.

Florida Institute of Technology, Graduate Programs, College of Engineering, Melbourne, FL 32901-6975. Offers MS, PhD. Part-time and evening/weekend programs available. *Faculty:* 60 full-time (2 women), 6 part-time/adjunct (0 women). *Students:* 319 full-time (70 women), 183 part-time (37 women); includes 37 minority (13 Black or African American, non-Hispanic/Latino; 10 Asian, non-Hispanic/Latino; 11 Hispanic/Latino; 3 Two or more races, non-Hispanic/Latino), 261 international. Average age 29. 1,131 applicants, 53% accepted, 134 enrolled. In 2010, 185 master's, 12 doctorates awarded. Terminal master's awarded for partial completion of doctoral program. *Degree requirements:* For master's, comprehensive exam (for some programs), thesis (for some programs); for doctorate, comprehensive exam (for some programs), thesis/dissertation. *Entrance requirements:* For master's, GRE, minimum GPA of 3.0, 3 letters of recommendation, resume, statement of objectives; for doctorate, GRE, minimum GPA of 3.2, 3 letters of recommendation, resume, statement of objectives. Additional exam requirements/recommendations for international students: Required—TOEFL (minimum score 550 paper-based; 213 computer-based; 79 iBT). *Application deadline:* For fall admission, 4/1 for international students; for spring admission, 9/30 for international students. Applications are processed on a rolling basis. Application fee: $50. Electronic applications accepted. *Expenses:* Tuition: Part-time $1040 per credit hour. Tuition and fees vary according to campus/location. *Financial support:* In 2010–11, 5 fellowships with full and partial tuition reimbursements (averaging $7,240 per year), 23 research assistantships with full and partial tuition reimbursements (averaging $4,970 per year), 51 teaching assistantships with full and partial tuition reimbursements (averaging $6,698 per year) were awarded; career-related internships or fieldwork, institutionally sponsored loans, unspecified assistantships, and tuition remissions also available. Support available to part-time students. Financial award application deadline: 3/1; financial award applicants required to submit FAFSA. *Faculty research:* Electrical and computer science and engineering; aerospace, chemical, civil, mechanical, and ocean engineering; environmental science and oceanography. Total annual research expenditures: $4.6 million. *Unit head:* Dr. Fredric M. Ham, Interim Dean, 321-674-8138, Fax: 321-674-7270, E-mail: fmh@fit.edu. *Application contact:* Cheryl A. Brown, Associate Director of Graduate Admissions, 321-674-7581, Fax: 321-723-9468, E-mail: cbrown@fit.edu.

Florida International University, College of Engineering and Computing, Miami, FL 33175. Offers MS, PhD. Part-time and evening/weekend programs available. Postbaccalaureate distance learning degree programs offered. *Faculty:* 95 full-time (9 women), 31 part-time/adjunct (0 women). *Students:* 467 full-time (125 women), 360 part-time (87 women); includes 63 Black or African American, non-Hispanic/Latino; 1 American Indian or Alaska Native, non-Hispanic/Latino; 26 Asian, non-Hispanic/Latino; 242 Hispanic/Latino, 376 international. Average age 28. 1,840 applicants, 27% accepted, 394 enrolled. In 2010, 293 master's, 35 doctorates awarded. Terminal master's awarded for partial completion of doctoral program. *Degree requirements:* For master's, thesis (for some programs); for doctorate, comprehensive exam, thesis/dissertation. *Entrance requirements:* For master's, GRE (depending on program), minimum GPA of 3.0; for doctorate, GRE General Test, minimum GPA of 3.0. Additional exam requirements/recommendations for international students: Required—TOEFL (minimum score 550 paper-based; 80 iBT). *Application deadline:* For fall admission, 6/1 for domestic students, 4/1 for international students; for spring admission, 10/1 for domestic students, 9/1 for international students. Applications are processed on a rolling basis. Application fee: $30. Electronic applications accepted. *Financial support:* Career-related internships or fieldwork, Federal Work-Study, institutionally sponsored loans, scholarships/grants, and unspecified assistantships available. Financial award application deadline: 3/1; financial award applicants required to submit FAFSA. *Faculty research:* Databases, informatics, computing systems, software engineering, security, biosensors, imaging, tissue engineering, biomaterials and bionanotechnology, transportation, wind engineering, hydrology, environmental engineering, engineering management, sustainability and green construction, risk management and decision systems, infrastructure systems, digital signal processing, power systems, nanophotonics, embedded systems, image processing, nanotechnology. *Unit head:* Dr. Amir Mirmiran, Dean, 305-348-2522, Fax: 305-348-1401, E-mail: amir.mirmiran@fiu.edu. *Application contact:* Maria Parrilla, Assistant Director of Graduate Admissions, 305-348-1890, Fax: 305-348-6142, E-mail: grad_eng@fiu.edu.

See Display on next page and Close-Up on page 81.

Florida State University, The Graduate School, FAMU-FSU College of Engineering, Tallahassee, FL 32310-6046. Offers MS, PhD. Part-time programs available. *Faculty:* 76 full-time (9 women), 11 part-time/adjunct (2 women). *Students:* 251 full-time (54 women), 28 part-time (9 women); includes 41 Black or African American, non-Hispanic/Latino; 1 American Indian or Alaska Native, non-Hispanic/Latino; 5 Asian, non-Hispanic/Latino; 15 Hispanic/Latino, 124 international. Average age 29. 455 applicants, 43% accepted, 63 enrolled. In 2010, 53 master's, 23 doctorates awarded. *Degree requirements:* For master's, thesis (for some programs); for doctorate, comprehensive exam, thesis/dissertation, preliminary exam, qualifying exam. *Entrance requirements:* For master's and doctorate, GRE General Test. Additional exam requirements/recommendations for international students: Required—TOEFL (minimum score 550 paper-based; 213 computer-based). *Application deadline:* For fall admission, 7/1 for domestic and international students; for spring admission, 11/1 for domestic and international students. Applications are processed on a rolling basis. Application fee: $30. *Expenses:* Tuition, state resident: full-time $8238.24. *Financial support:* In 2010–11, 233 students received support, including 8 fellowships with full tuition reimbursements available (averaging $18,000 per year), 113 research assistantships with full tuition reimbursements available (averaging $15,000 per year), 73 teaching assistantships with full tuition reimbursements available (averaging $15,000 per year); career-related internships or fieldwork, institutionally sponsored loans, scholarships/grants, tuition waivers (full), and unspecified assistantships also available. Financial award application deadline: 6/15. *Faculty research:* Fluid mechanics, aerodynamics, electromagnetics, digital signal processing, polymer processing. Total annual research expenditures: $12.1 million. *Unit head:* Dr. John Collier, Interim Dean and Professor, 850-410-6161, Fax: 850-410-6546, E-mail: dean@eng.fsu.edu. *Application contact:* Dr. John Collier, Interim Dean and Professor, 850-410-6161, Fax: 850-410-6546, E-mail: dean@eng.fsu.edu.

George Mason University, Volgenau School of Engineering, Fairfax, VA 22030. Offers MS, PhD, Certificate, Engr. Part-time and evening/weekend programs available. *Faculty:* 147 full-time (29 women), 140 part-time/adjunct (23 women). *Students:* 328 full-time (87 women), 1,293 part-time (279 women); includes 75 Black or African American, non-Hispanic/Latino; 5 American Indian or Alaska Native, non-Hispanic/Latino; 192 Asian, non-Hispanic/Latino; 57 Hispanic/Latino; 7 Two or more races, non-Hispanic/Latino, 471 international. Average age 31. 1,791 applicants, 63% accepted, 441 enrolled. In 2010, 476 master's, 23 doctorates, 109 other advanced degrees awarded. *Degree requirements:* For master's, thesis optional; for doctorate, thesis/dissertation, comprehensive oral and written exams. *Entrance requirements:* For master's, minimum GPA of 3.0 in last 60 hours of course work; for doctorate, GRE General Test, minimum graduate GPA of 3.5. Additional exam requirements/recommendations for international students: Required—TOEFL (minimum score 570 paper-based; 230 computer-based; 88 iBT). Application fee: $100. Electronic applications accepted. *Expenses:* Tuition, state resident: full-time $8192; part-time $440 per credit hour. Tuition, nonresident: full-time $22,952; part-time $1055 per credit hour. Required fees: $2364; $99 per credit hour. *Financial support:* In 2010–11, 257 students received support, including 9 fellowships with full tuition reimbursements available (averaging $18,000 per year), 105 research assistantships with full and partial tuition reimbursements available (averaging $15,300 per year), 144 teaching assistantships with full and partial tuition reimbursements available (averaging $11,126 per year); career-related internships or fieldwork, Federal Work-Study, scholarships/grants, unspecified assistantships, and health care benefits (full-time research or teaching assistantship recipients) also available. Financial award application deadline: 3/1; financial award applicants required to submit FAFSA. *Faculty research:* Systems management, quality assurance, decision support systems, cognitive ergonomics. Total annual research expenditures: $18.2 million. *Unit head:* Lloyd Griffiths, Dean, 703-993-1500, Fax: 703-993-1734, E-mail: lgriff@gmu.edu. *Application contact:* Nicole Sealey, Graduate Admission & Enrollment Services Director, 703-993-3932, E-mail: nsealey@gmu.edu.

The George Washington University, School of Engineering and Applied Science, Washington, DC 20052. Offers MS, D Sc, App Sc, Engr, Graduate Certificate. Part-time and evening/weekend programs available. *Faculty:* 82 full-time (10 women), 66 part-time/adjunct (9 women). *Students:* 405 full-time (115 women), 1,516 part-time (355 women); includes 394 minority (162 Black or African American, non-Hispanic/Latino; 10 American Indian or Alaska Native, non-Hispanic/Latino; 148 Asian, non-Hispanic/Latino; 66 Hispanic/Latino; 6 Native Hawaiian or other Pacific Islander, non-Hispanic/Latino; 2 Two or more races, non-Hispanic/Latino), 417 international. Average age 33. 1,396 applicants, 81% accepted, 459 enrolled. In 2010, 520 master's, 47 doctorates, 169 other advanced degrees awarded. *Degree requirements:* For master's, thesis optional; for doctorate, thesis/dissertation, qualifying exam. *Entrance requirements:* For master's, appropriate bachelor's degree; for doctorate, appropriate bachelor's or master's degree, GRE if highest earned degree is BS; for other advanced degree, appropriate master's degree. Additional exam requirements/recommendations for international students: Required—TOEFL or The George Washington University English as a Foreign Language Test. *Application deadline:* For fall admission, 3/1 for domestic students; for spring admission, 10/1 for domestic students. Applications are processed on a rolling basis. Application fee: $75. *Financial support:* In 2010–11, 216 students received support; fellowships with full and partial tuition reimbursements available, research assistantships with full and partial tuition reimbursements available, teaching assistantships with full and partial tuition reimbursements available, career-related internships or fieldwork, Federal Work-Study, institutionally sponsored loans, and tuition waivers (full and partial) available. Financial award application deadline: 3/1; financial award applicants required to submit FAFSA. *Faculty research:* Fatigue fracture and structural reliability, computer-integrated manufacturing, materials engineering, artificial intelligence and expert systems, quality assurance. Total annual research expenditures: $6.3 million. *Unit head:* David S. Dolling, Dean, 202-994-6080, E-mail: dolling@gwu.edu. *Application contact:* Adina Lav, Marketing, Recruiting and Admissions, 202-994-5827, Fax: 202-994-0909, E-mail: engineering@gwu.edu.

Georgia Institute of Technology, Graduate Studies and Research, College of Engineering, Atlanta, GA 30332-0001. Offers MS, MS Bio E, MS Ch E, MS Env E, MS Poly, MS Stat, MSAE, MSCE, MSEE, MSESM, MSHS, MSIE, MSME, MSNE, MSOR, PhD, MD/PhD. *Accreditation:* ABET (one or more programs are accredited). Part-time programs available. Postbaccalaureate distance learning degree programs offered. Terminal master's awarded for partial completion of doctoral program. *Degree requirements:* For doctorate, thesis/dissertation. *Entrance requirements:* Additional exam requirements/recommendations for international students: Required—TOEFL. Electronic applications accepted.

Graduate School and University Center of the City University of New York, Graduate Studies, Program in Engineering, New York, NY 10016-4039. Offers biomedical engineering (PhD); chemical engineering (PhD); civil engineering (PhD); electrical engineering (PhD); mechanical engineering (PhD). *Degree requirements:* For doctorate, thesis/dissertation. *Entrance requirements:* For doctorate, GRE General Test. Additional exam requirements/recommendations for international students: Required—TOEFL. Electronic applications accepted.

Grand Valley State University, Padnos College of Engineering and Computing, School of Engineering, Allendale, MI 49401-9403. Offers electrical and computer engineering (MSE); manufacturing operations (MSE); mechanical engineering (MSE); product design and manufacturing engineering (MSE). Part-time and evening/weekend programs available. *Degree requirements:* For master's, project or thesis. *Entrance requirements:* For master's, engineering degree, minimum GPA of 3.0. Additional exam requirements/recommendations for inter-

Engineering and Applied Sciences—General

national students: Required—TOEFL. Electronic applications accepted. *Faculty research:* Digital signal processing, computer aided design, computer aided manufacturing, manufacturing simulation, biomechanics, product design.

Harvard University, Graduate School of Arts and Sciences, School of Engineering and Applied Sciences, Cambridge, MA 02138. Offers applied mathematics (ME, SM, PhD); applied physics (ME, SM, PhD); computer science (ME, SM, PhD); engineering science (ME); engineering sciences (SM, PhD). Part-time programs available. Terminal master's awarded for partial completion of doctoral program. *Degree requirements:* For master's, thesis optional; for doctorate, comprehensive exam, thesis/dissertation. *Entrance requirements:* For master's and doctorate, GRE General Test, GRE Subject Test (recommended), 3 letters of recommendation. Additional exam requirements/recommendations for international students: Required—TOEFL (minimum score 80 iBT). Electronic applications accepted. *Expenses:* Tuition: Full-time $34,976. Required fees: $1166. Full-time tuition and fees vary according to program. *Faculty research:* Applied mathematics, applied physics, computer science and electrical engineering, environmental engineering, mechanical and biomedical engineering.

Howard University, College of Engineering, Architecture, and Computer Sciences, School of Engineering and Computer Science, Washington, DC 20059-0002. Offers M Eng, MCS, MS, PhD. Part-time programs available. Terminal master's awarded for partial completion of doctoral program. *Degree requirements:* For doctorate, one foreign language, thesis/dissertation, preliminary exam. *Entrance requirements:* For master's and doctorate, GRE General Test, minimum GPA of 3.0. Additional exam requirements/recommendations for international students: Required—TOEFL. Electronic applications accepted. *Faculty research:* Environmental engineering, solid-state electronics, dynamics and control of large flexible space structures, power systems, reaction kinetics.

Idaho State University, Office of Graduate Studies, College of Engineering, Pocatello, ID 83209-8060. Offers MS, PhD, Postbaccalaureate Certificate. *Accreditation:* ABET. Part-time programs available. *Degree requirements:* For master's, comprehensive exam (for some programs), thesis, thesis project, 2 semesters of seminar; for doctorate, comprehensive exam, thesis/dissertation, oral presentation and defense of research, oral examination; for Postbaccalaureate Certificate, comprehensive exam (for some programs), thesis optional, oral exam or thesis defense. *Entrance requirements:* For master's, GRE General Test, minimum GPA of 3.0 in upper-division undergraduate classes; for doctorate, GRE General Test, master's degree in engineering or physics, 1-page statement of research interests, resume, 3 letters of reference, 1-page statement of career interests; for Postbaccalaureate Certificate, GRE (if GPA between 2.0 and 3.0), bachelor's degree, minimum GPA of 3.0 in upper-division courses. Additional exam requirements/recommendations for international students: Required—TOEFL (minimum score 550 paper-based; 213 computer-based; 80 iBT). Electronic applications accepted. *Faculty research:* Nuclear engineering, biomedical engineering, robotics, measurement and control, structural systems.

Illinois Institute of Technology, Graduate College, Armour College of Engineering, Chicago, IL 60616-3793. Offers M Arch E, M Ch E, M Env E, M Geoenv E, M Trans E, MBE, MBMI, MCEM, MECE, MEM, MFPE, MGE, MMAE, MME, MMME, MNE, MPE, MPW, MS, MSE, MTSE, MVM, PhD. Part-time and evening/weekend programs available. Postbaccalaureate distance learning degree programs offered (no on-campus study). *Faculty:* 93 full-time (8 women), 22 part-time/adjunct (3 women). *Students:* 931 full-time (231 women), 318 part-time (53 women); includes 78 minority (18 Black or African American, non-Hispanic/Latino; 1 American Indian or Alaska Native, non-Hispanic/Latino; 44 Asian, non-Hispanic/Latino; 12 Hispanic/Latino; 3 Two or more races, non-Hispanic/Latino), 884 international. Average age 26. 3,045 applicants, 58% accepted, 448 enrolled. In 2010, 380 master's, 37 doctorates awarded. Terminal master's awarded for partial completion of doctoral program. *Degree requirements:* For master's, comprehensive exam (for some programs), thesis (for some programs); for doctorate, comprehensive exam, thesis/dissertation. *Entrance requirements:* For master's and doctorate, GRE General Test, minimum undergraduate GPA of 3.0. Additional exam requirements/recommendations for international students: Required—TOEFL (minimum score 523 paper-based; 70 iBT); Recommended—IELTS (minimum score 5.5). *Application deadline:* For fall admission, 5/1 for domestic and international students; for spring admission, 10/15 for domestic and international students. Applications are processed on a rolling basis. Application fee: $50. Electronic applications accepted. *Expenses:* Tuition: Full-time $18,576; part-time $1032 per credit hour. Required fees: $583 per semester. One-time fee: $150. Tuition and fees vary according to program and student level. *Financial support:* In 2010–11, 8 fellowships with full and partial tuition reimbursements (averaging $6,850 per year), 160 research assistantships with full and partial tuition reimbursements (averaging $8,568 per year), 69 teaching assistantships with full and partial tuition reimbursements (averaging $6,471 per year) were awarded; career-related internships or fieldwork, Federal Work-Study, institutionally sponsored loans, scholarships/grants, health care benefits, tuition waivers (full and partial), and unspecified assistantships also available. Support available to part-time students. Financial award applicants required to submit FAFSA. Total annual research expenditures: $13 million. *Unit head:* Dr. Natacha DePaola, Dean, 312-567-3009, Fax: 312-567-7961, E-mail: engineering@iit.edu. *Application contact:* Deborah Gibson, Director, Graduate Admission, 866-472-3448, Fax: 312-567-3138, E-mail: inquiry.grad@iit.edu.

Indiana State University, College of Graduate and Professional Studies, College of Technology, Terre Haute, IN 47809. Offers MS, MA/MS. *Entrance requirements:* For master's, bachelor's degree in industrial technology or related field. Additional exam requirements/recommendations for international students: Required—TOEFL. Electronic applications accepted.

Indiana University–Purdue University Fort Wayne, College of Engineering, Technology, and Computer Science, Fort Wayne, IN 46805-1499. Offers MS, Certificate. Part-time programs available. *Faculty:* 45 full-time (12 women), 2 part-time/adjunct (0 women). *Students:* 21 full-time (8 women), 102 part-time (37 women); includes 14 minority (6 Black or African American, non-Hispanic/Latino; 5 Asian, non-Hispanic/Latino; 3 Hispanic/Latino), 12 international. Average age 31. 49 applicants, 92% accepted, 37 enrolled. In 2010, 20 master's awarded. *Entrance requirements:* For master's, GRE General Test, minimum GPA of 3.0. Additional exam requirements/recommendations for international students: Required—TOEFL (minimum score 550 paper-based; 213 computer-based; 77 iBT); Recommended—TWE. *Application deadline:* For fall admission, 7/15 for domestic students, 5/15 for international students; for spring admission, 12/1 for domestic students, 10/15 for international students. Applications are processed on a rolling basis. Application fee: $55 ($60 for international students). Electronic applications accepted. *Expenses:* Tuition, state resident: full-time $4824; part-time $268 per credit. Tuition, nonresident: full-time $11,625; part-time $646 per credit. Required fees: $555; $30.85 per credit. Tuition and fees vary according to course load. *Financial support:* In 2010–11, 6 research assistantships with partial tuition reimbursements (averaging $12,740 per year), 7 teaching assistantships with partial tuition reimbursements (averaging $12,740 per year) were awarded; career-related internships or fieldwork, scholarships/grants, and unspecified assistantships also available. Support available to part-time students. Financial award application deadline: 3/1; financial award applicants required to submit FAFSA. *Faculty research:* Secure virtual environment, risk assessment and highway bridges, Samba vs. Windows. Total annual research expenditures: $211,661. *Unit head:* Dr. Max Yen, Dean, 260-481-6839, Fax: 260-481-5734, E-mail: yens@ipfw.edu. *Application contact:* Dr. Max Yen, Dean, 260-481-6839, Fax: 260-481-5734, E-mail: yens@ipfw.edu.

Instituto Tecnologico de Santo Domingo, Graduate School, Area of Engineering, Santo Domingo, Dominican Republic. Offers construction administration (MS, Certificate); data telecommunications (M Eng, MS, Certificate); industrial engineering (M Eng, Certificate); industrial management (M Mgmt); information technology (Certificate); maintenance engineering (M Eng); occupational hazard prevention (M Mgmt); production management (Certificate); quantitative methods (Certificate); sanitary and environmental engineering (M Eng); structural engineering (M Eng); systems engineering and electronic data processing (Certificate); transportation (Certificate).

Instituto Tecnológico y de Estudios Superiores de Monterrey, Campus Ciudad Obregón, Program in Engineering, Ciudad Obregón, Mexico. Offers ME.

Instituto Tecnológico y de Estudios Superiores de Monterrey, Campus Monterrey, Graduate and Research Division, Programs in Engineering, Monterrey, Mexico. Offers applied statistics (M Eng); artificial intelligence (PhD); automation engineering (M Eng); chemical engineering (M Eng); civil engineering (M Eng); electrical engineering (M Eng); electronic engineering (M Eng); environmental engineering (M Eng); industrial engineering (M Eng, PhD); manufacturing engineering (M Eng); mechanical engineering (M Eng); systems and quality engineering (M Eng). M Eng program offered jointly with University of Waterloo; PhD in industrial engineering with Texas A&M University. Part-time and evening/weekend programs available. Terminal master's awarded for partial completion of doctoral program. *Degree requirements:* For master's, one foreign language, thesis; for doctorate, one foreign language, thesis/dissertation. *Entrance requirements:* For master's, EXADEP; for doctorate, GRE, master's degree in related field. Additional exam requirements/recommendations for international students: Required—TOEFL. *Faculty research:* Flexible manufacturing cells, materials, statistical methods, environmental prevention, control and evaluation.

Iowa State University of Science and Technology, Graduate College, College of Engineering, Ames, IA 50011. Offers M Eng, MS, PhD. Part-time programs available. *Faculty:* 264 full-time (29 women), 16 part-time/adjunct (3 women). *Students:* 787 full-time (179 women), 444 part-time (74 women); includes 31 Black or African American, non-Hispanic/Latino; 4 American Indian or Alaska Native, non-Hispanic/Latino; 33 Asian, non-Hispanic/Latino; 17 Hispanic/Latino, 611 international. 2,356 applicants, 16% accepted, 209 enrolled. In 2010, 199 master's, 73 doctorates awarded. *Degree requirements:* For doctorate, thesis/dissertation. *Entrance requirements:* Additional exam requirements/recommendations for international students: Required—TOEFL. Application fee: $40 ($90 for international students). Electronic applications accepted. *Financial support:* In 2010–11, 505 research assistantships with full and partial tuition reimbursements (averaging $10,849 per year), 105 teaching assistantships with full and partial tuition reimbursements (averaging $7,076 per year) were awarded; fellowships, Federal Work-Study, scholarships/grants, health care benefits, and unspecified assistantships also available. Support available to part-time students. *Unit head:* Dr. Jonathan Wickert, Dean, 515-294-9988. *Application contact:* Dr. Jonathan Wickert, Dean, 515-294-9988.

The Johns Hopkins University, Engineering for Professionals, Elkridge, MD 21075. Offers M Ch E, M Mat SE, MCE, MEE, MME, MS, MSE, Graduate Certificate, Post-Master's Certificate. Part-time and evening/weekend programs available. *Faculty:* 235 part-time/adjunct (30 women). *Students:* 68 full-time (22 women), 2,146 part-time (482 women); includes 690 minority (202 Black or African American, non-Hispanic/Latino; 6 American Indian or Alaska Native, non-Hispanic/Latino; 312 Asian, non-Hispanic/Latino; 127 Hispanic/Latino; 5 Native Hawaiian or other Pacific Islander, non-Hispanic/Latino; 38 Two or more races, non-Hispanic/Latino), 44 international. Average age 31. In 2010, 580 master's, 31 other advanced degrees awarded. *Application deadline:* Applications are processed on a rolling basis. Application fee: $75. Electronic applications accepted. *Unit head:* Dr. Allan Bjerkaas, Associate Dean, 410-516-2300, Fax: 410-579-8049, E-mail: bjerkaas@jhu.edu. *Application contact:* Priyanka Dwivedi, Admissions Manager, 410-516-2300, Fax: 410-579-8049, E-mail: pdwived1@jhu.edu.

The Johns Hopkins University, G. W. C. Whiting School of Engineering, Baltimore, MD 21218-2699. Offers M Ch E, M Mat SE, MA, MCE, MEE, MME, MS, MSE, MSEM, MSSI, PhD, Certificate, Post-Master's Certificate. *Faculty:* 190 full-time (37 women), 94 part-time/adjunct (16 women). *Students:* 777 full-time (209 women), 36 part-time (8 women); includes 111 minority (17 Black or African American, non-Hispanic/Latino; 1 American Indian or Alaska Native, non-Hispanic/Latino; 62 Asian, non-Hispanic/Latino; 21 Hispanic/Latino; 10 Two or more races, non-Hispanic/Latino), 445 international. Average age 26. 2,443 applicants, 37% accepted, 289 enrolled. In 2010, 218 master's, 53 doctorates awarded. Terminal master's awarded for partial completion of doctoral program. *Degree requirements:* For master's, comprehensive exam (for some programs), thesis (for some programs); for doctorate, comprehensive exam, thesis/dissertation, oral exam. *Entrance requirements:* For master's, GRE General Test, letters of recommendation, transcripts; for doctorate, GRE General Test, letters of recommendation. Additional exam requirements/recommendations for international students: Required—TOEFL (minimum score 600 paper-based; 250 computer-based; 100 iBT) or IELTS (minimum score 7). Application fee: $75. Electronic applications accepted. *Financial support:* In 2010–11, 107 fellowships with full tuition reimbursements (averaging $23,347 per year), 552 research assistantships with full tuition reimbursements (averaging $26,605 per year), 65 teaching assistantships with full tuition reimbursements (averaging $12,624 per year) were awarded; Federal Work-Study, institutionally sponsored loans, scholarships/grants, health care benefits, tuition waivers (full and partial), and unspecified assistantships also available. Support available to part-time students. Financial award applicants required to submit FAFSA. *Faculty research:* Biomedical engineering, environmental systems and engineering, materials science and engineering, signal and image processing, structural dynamics and geomechanics. Total annual research expenditures: $70.2 million. *Unit head:* Dr. Nicholas P. Jones, Interim Dean, 410-516-8350 Ext. 3, Fax: 410-516-8627. *Application contact:* Dennis McIver, Coordinator of Graduate Admissions, 410-516-8174, Fax: 410-516-0780, E-mail: graduateadmissions@jhu.edu.

Kansas State University, Graduate School, College of Engineering, Manhattan, KS 66506. Offers MEM, MS, MSE, PhD. Part-time programs available. Postbaccalaureate distance learning degree programs offered (minimal on-campus study). *Degree requirements:* For doctorate, thesis/dissertation. *Entrance requirements:* For master's and doctorate, GRE. Additional exam requirements/recommendations for international students: Required—TOEFL. Electronic applications accepted.

See Display on next page and Close-Up on page 83.

Kent State University, College of Technology, Kent, OH 44242-0001. Offers MT. Part-time programs available. Postbaccalaureate distance learning degree programs offered. *Degree requirements:* For master's, thesis optional. *Entrance requirements:* For master's, GRE, minimum GPA of 2.75. Electronic applications accepted. *Expenses:* Tuition, state resident: full-time $7866; part-time $437 per credit hour. Tuition, nonresident: full-time $14,022; part-time $779 per credit hour. *Faculty research:* Automation, robotics, CAD, CAM, CIM.

Lakehead University, Graduate Studies, Faculty of Engineering, Thunder Bay, ON P7B 5E1, Canada. Offers control engineering (M Sc Engr); electrical/computer engineering (M Sc Engr); environmental engineering (M Sc Engr). Part-time programs available. *Degree requirements:* For master's, thesis. *Entrance requirements:* For master's, bachelor's degree in chemical, electrical or mechanical engineering, minimum B average. Additional exam requirements/recommendations for international students: Required—TOEFL. *Faculty research:* Pulp and paper, adaptive/process control, robust/interactive learning control, vibration control.

Lamar University, College of Graduate Studies, College of Engineering, Beaumont, TX 77710. Offers ME, MEM, MES, MS, DE, PhD. Part-time and evening/weekend programs available. *Faculty:* 39 full-time (3 women). *Students:* 244 full-time (37 women), 160 part-time (31 women); includes 6 Black or African American, non-Hispanic/Latino; 21 Asian, non-Hispanic/Latino; 4 Hispanic/Latino, 284 international. Average age 26. 383 applicants, 54% accepted, 46 enrolled. In 2010, 206 master's, 3 doctorates awarded. Terminal master's awarded for partial completion of doctoral program. *Degree requirements:* For doctorate, thesis/dissertation. *Entrance requirements:* For master's and doctorate, GRE General Test. Additional exam requirements/recommendations for international students: Required—TOEFL. *Application deadline:* For fall admission, 5/15 priority date for domestic students; for spring admission, 10/1 priority date for domestic students. Applications are processed on a rolling basis. Application fee: $25 ($50 for international students). *Expenses:* Tuition, state resident: full-time $4160; part-time $208 per credit hour. Tuition, nonresident: full-time $10,360; part-time $518 per credit hour. *Financial support:* In 2010–11, fellowships with partial tuition reimbursements (averaging $6,000 per year), research assistantships with partial tuition reimbursements (averaging $7,500 per year), teaching assistantships with partial tuition reimbursements (averaging $7,500 per year) were awarded; career-related internships or fieldwork, Federal Work-Study, institutionally sponsored loans, scholarships/grants, tuition waivers (full and partial), and laboratory assistantships also available. Support available to part-time students. Financial award application deadline: 4/1. *Faculty research:* Energy alternatives; process analysis, design, and control; pollution prevention. *Unit head:* Dr. Jack Hopper, Chair, 409-880-8784, Fax: 409-880-2197, E-mail: che_dept@hal.lamar.edu. *Application contact:* Sandy Drane, Coordinator of Graduate Admissions, 409-880-8356, Fax: 409-880-8414, E-mail: gradmissions@hal.lamar.edu.

Laurentian University, School of Graduate Studies and Research, School of Engineering, Sudbury, ON P3E 2C6, Canada. Offers mineral resources engineering (M Eng, MA Sc); natural resources engineering (PhD). Part-time programs available. *Faculty research:* Mining engineering, rock mechanics (tunneling, rockbursts, rock support), metallurgy (mineral processing, hydro and pyrometallurgy), simulations and remote mining, simulations and scheduling.

Lawrence Technological University, College of Engineering, Southfield, MI 48075-1058. Offers architectural engineering (MS); automotive engineering (MS); civil engineering (MS); electrical and computer engineering (MS); engineering management (MEM); industrial engineering (MS); manufacturing systems (ME, DE); mechanical engineering (MS); mechatronic systems engineering (MS). Part-time and evening/weekend programs available. *Faculty:* 20 full-time (4 women), 12 part-time/adjunct (0 women). *Students:* 8 full-time (1 woman), 366 part-time (60 women); includes 29 Black or African American, non-Hispanic/Latino; 1 American Indian or Alaska Native, non-Hispanic/Latino; 36 Asian, non-Hispanic/Latino; 9 Hispanic/Latino; 4 Two or more races, non-Hispanic/Latino, 81 international. Average age 32. 398 applicants, 48% accepted, 87 enrolled. In 2010, 121 master's, 5 doctorates awarded. *Degree requirements:* For master's, thesis (for some programs). *Entrance requirements:* Additional exam requirements/recommendations for international students: Required—TOEFL (minimum score 550 paper-based; 213 computer-based; 79 iBT). *Application deadline:* For fall admission, 6/30 priority date for domestic students, 6/30 for international students; for spring admission, 11/15 priority date for domestic students, 11/15 for international students. Applications are processed on a rolling basis. Application fee: $50. Electronic applications accepted. *Financial support:* In 2010–11, 72 students received support. Federal Work-Study and institutionally sponsored loans available. Support available to part-time students. Financial award application deadline: 4/1; financial award applicants required to submit FAFSA. *Faculty research:* Advanced composite materials in bridges, strengthening existing bridges with carbon and glass fiber sheets, development of drive shafts using composite materials. *Unit head:* Dr. Nabil Grace, Interim Dean, 248-204-2500, Fax: 248-204-2509, E-mail: engrdean@ltu.edu. *Application contact:* Jane Rohrback, Director of Admissions, 248-204-3160, Fax: 248-204-2228, E-mail: admissions@ltu.edu.

Lehigh University, P.C. Rossin College of Engineering and Applied Science, Bethlehem, PA 18015. Offers M Eng, MS, PhD, MBA/E. Part-time programs available. Postbaccalaureate distance learning degree programs offered (no on-campus study). *Faculty:* 120 full-time (15 women), 5 part-time/adjunct (1 woman). *Students:* 497 full-time (114 women), 148 part-time (33 women); includes 40 minority (14 Black or African American, non-Hispanic/Latino; 16 Asian, non-Hispanic/Latino; 9 Hispanic/Latino; 1 Native Hawaiian or other Pacific Islander, non-Hispanic/Latino), 345 international. Average age 27. 2,623 applicants, 20% accepted, 262 enrolled. In 2010, 158 master's, 49 doctorates awarded. Terminal master's awarded for partial completion of doctoral program. *Degree requirements:* For master's, comprehensive exam (for some programs), thesis (for some programs); for doctorate, comprehensive exam (for some programs), thesis/dissertation. *Entrance requirements:* For master's and doctorate, GRE General Test, BS. Additional exam requirements/recommendations for international students: Required—TOEFL (minimum score 550 paper-based; 213 computer-based; 79 iBT). *Application deadline:* For fall admission, 7/15 for domestic and international students; for spring admission, 12/1 for domestic and international students. Applications are processed on a rolling basis. Application fee: $75. Electronic applications accepted. *Expenses:* Contact institution. *Financial support:* In 2010–11, 364 students received support, including 56 fellowships with full and partial tuition reimbursements available (averaging $17,460 per year), 211 research assistantships with full and partial tuition reimbursements available (averaging $21,600 per year), 58 teaching assistantships with full and partial tuition reimbursements available (averaging $18,360 per year); career-related internships or fieldwork, institutionally sponsored loans, scholarships/grants, tuition waivers (full and partial), and unspecified assistantships also available. Support available to part-time students. Financial award application deadline: 1/15. *Faculty research:* Advanced materials and nanotechnology, life sciences and bioengineering, environmental science and energy, information science and technology, large structural systems, optical technologies. *Unit head:* Dr. John P. Coulter, Associate Dean of Graduate Studies and Research, 610-758-6310, Fax: 610-758-5623, E-mail: john.coulter@lehigh.edu. *Application contact:* Brianne Lisk, Administrative Coordinator of Graduate Studies and Research, 610-758-6310, Fax: 610-758-5623, E-mail: brc3@lehigh.edu.

LeTourneau University, School of Graduate and Professional Studies, Longview, TX 75607-7001. Offers business administration (MBA); counseling (MA); curriculum and instruction (M Ed); educational administration (M Ed); engineering (M Sc); psychology (MA); strategic leadership (MSL); teaching and learning (M Ed). Part-time and evening/weekend programs available. Postbaccalaureate distance learning degree programs offered (no on-campus study). *Faculty:* 9 full-time (1 woman), 62 part-time/adjunct (26 women). *Students:* 329 full-time (233 women); includes 152 Black or African American, non-Hispanic/Latino; 1 American Indian or Alaska Native, non-Hispanic/Latino; 5 Asian, non-Hispanic/Latino; 23 Hispanic/Latino. Average age 36. 138 applicants, 90% accepted, 120 enrolled. In 2010, 129 master's awarded. *Entrance requirements:* For master's, GRE (for MA in counseling and M Sc in engineering), minimum GPA of 2.8. Additional exam requirements/recommendations for international students: Required—TOEFL. *Application deadline:* Applications are processed on a rolling basis. Application fee: $0. Electronic applications accepted. *Expenses:* Tuition: Full-time $13,020; part-time $620 per credit hour. *Financial support:* Applicants required to submit FAFSA. *Unit head:* Dr. Carol Green, Vice President, 903-233-4010, Fax: 903-233-3227, E-mail: carolgreen@letu.edu. *Application contact:* Chris Fontaine, Assistant Vice President for Enrollment Management and Marketing, 903-233-4071, Fax: 903-233-3227, E-mail: chrisfontaine@letu.edu.

Louisiana State University and Agricultural and Mechanical College, Graduate School, College of Agriculture, Department of Biological and Agricultural Engineering, Baton Rouge, LA 70803. Offers biological and agricultural engineering (MSBAE); engineering science (MS, PhD). Part-time programs available. *Faculty:* 12 full-time (2 women). *Students:* 13 full-time (3 women), 3 part-time (0 women); includes 1 Black or African American, non-Hispanic/Latino; 3 Asian, non-Hispanic/Latino; 1 Hispanic/Latino, 6 international. Average age 26. 12 applicants, 58% accepted, 2 enrolled. In 2010, 8 master's awarded. Terminal master's awarded for partial completion of doctoral program. *Degree requirements:* For master's, thesis; for doctorate, thesis/dissertation. *Entrance requirements:* For master's and doctorate, GRE General Test, minimum GPA of 3.0. Additional exam requirements/recommendations for international students: Required—TOEFL (minimum score 550 paper-based; 213 computer-based; 79 iBT) or IELTS (minimum score 6.5). *Application deadline:* For fall admission, 1/25 priority date for domestic students, 5/15 for international students; for spring admission, 10/15 for international students. Applications are processed on a rolling basis. Application fee: $50 ($70 for international students). Electronic applications accepted. *Financial support:* In 2010–11, 14 students received support, including 1 fellowship (averaging $24,803 per year), 12 research assistantships with partial tuition reimbursements available (averaging $16,391 per year); teaching assistantships with partial tuition reimbursements available, career-related internships or fieldwork, Federal Work-Study, institutionally sponsored loans, scholarships/grants, health care benefits, and unspecified assistantships also available. Financial award application deadline: 7/1; financial award applicants required to submit FAFSA. *Faculty research:* Bioenergy, bioprocess engineering, cellular and molecular engineering, drug delivery using nanotechnology, environmental engineering. Total annual research expenditures: $37,654. *Unit head:* Dr. Dan Thomas, Head, 225-578-3153, Fax: 225-578-3492, E-mail: dthomas@agcenter.lsu.edu. *Application*

Engineering and Applied Sciences—General

KANSAS STATE ENGINEERING

Kansas State College of Engineering graduate programs offer state-of-the-art facilities that support nationally and internationally recognized research endeavors. Faculty, staff and students share a keen focus on creating a supportive environment and optimal educational experience for all participants in its eight doctorate and 12 master's degree programs.

Graduate Degree Programs

http://www.engg.ksu.edu/graduate_programs2.php

- Architectural Engineering, M.S.
- Biological and Agricultural Engineering, M.S./Ph.D.
- Chemical Engineering, M.S/Ph.D.
- Civil Engineering, M.S./Ph.D.
- Computer Science, M.S./Ph.D.
- Electrical Engineering, M.S./Ph.D.
- Engineering Management, M.E.M.
- Industrial Engineering, M.S./Ph.D.
- Mechanical Engineering, M.S./Ph.D.
- Nuclear Engineering, M.S./Ph.D.
- Operations Research, M.S.
- Software Engineering, M.S.E.

KANSAS STATE UNIVERSITY

contact: Dr. Steven Hall, Graduate Coordinator, 225-578-1058, Fax: 225-578-3492, E-mail: sghall@agcenter.lsu.edu.

Louisiana State University and Agricultural and Mechanical College, Graduate School, College of Engineering, Department of Construction Management and Industrial Engineering, Baton Rouge, LA 70803. Offers engineering science (PhD); industrial engineering (MSIE). *Faculty:* 12 full-time (5 women), 1 part-time/adjunct (0 women). *Students:* 16 full-time (2 women), 2 part-time (0 women); includes 1 Black or African American, non-Hispanic/Latino, 15 international. Average age 24. 37 applicants, 65% accepted, 4 enrolled. In 2010, 7 master's awarded. Terminal master's awarded for partial completion of doctoral program. *Degree requirements:* For master's, thesis; for doctorate, thesis/dissertation. *Entrance requirements:* For master's and doctorate, GRE General Test, minimum GPA of 3.0. Additional exam requirements/recommendations for international students: Required—TOEFL (minimum score 550 paper-based; 213 computer-based; 79 iBT) or IELTS (minimum score 6.5). *Application deadline:* For fall admission, 1/25 priority date for domestic students, 5/15 for international students; for spring admission, 10/15 for international students. Applications are processed on a rolling basis. Application fee: $50 ($70 for international students). Electronic applications accepted. *Financial support:* In 2010–11, 10 students received support, including 8 research assistantships with partial tuition reimbursements available (averaging $11,760 per year), 3 teaching assistantships with partial tuition reimbursements available (averaging $10,962 per year); fellowships, Federal Work-Study, institutionally sponsored loans, health care benefits, and unspecified assistantships also available. Financial award application deadline: 5/1; financial award application applicants required to submit FAFSA. *Faculty research:* Ergonomics and occupational health, information technology, production systems, supply management, construction safety and methods. Total annual research expenditures: $249,966. *Unit head:* Dr. Craig Harvey, Chair, 225-578-5112, Fax: 225-578-5109, E-mail: harvey@lsu.edu. *Application contact:* Dr. Pius Egbelu, Graduate Adviser, 225-578-5112, Fax: 225-578-5109, E-mail: pegbelu@eng.lsu.edu.

Louisiana State University and Agricultural and Mechanical College, Graduate School, College of Engineering, Interdepartmental Programs in Engineering, Baton Rouge, LA 70803. Offers engineering science (MSES, PhD). Part-time and evening/weekend programs available. *Students:* 46 full-time (16 women), 12 part-time (3 women); includes 3 Black or African American, non-Hispanic/Latino; 2 Hispanic/Latino, 39 international. Average age 30. 33 applicants, 70% accepted, 8 enrolled. In 2010, 20 master's, 7 doctorates awarded. Terminal master's awarded for partial completion of doctoral program. *Degree requirements:* For master's, thesis optional; for doctorate, thesis/dissertation. *Entrance requirements:* For master's and doctorate, GRE General Test, minimum GPA of 3.0. Additional exam requirements/recommendations for international students: Required—TOEFL (minimum score 550 paper-based, 213 computer-based, 79 iBT) or IELTS (minimum score 6.5). *Application deadline:* For fall admission, 1/25 priority date for domestic students, 5/15 for international students; for spring admission, 10/15 for international students. Applications are processed on a rolling basis. Application fee: $50 ($70 for international students). *Financial support:* In 2010–11, 53 students received support, including 6 fellowships (averaging $13,725 per year), 19 research assistantships with full and partial tuition reimbursements available (averaging $15,667 per year), 15 teaching assistantships with full and partial tuition reimbursements available (averaging $17,280 per year); Federal Work-Study, scholarships/grants, health care benefits, tuition waivers (full and partial), and unspecified assistantships also available. Support available to part-time students. Financial award application deadline: 3/1; financial award applicants required to submit FAFSA. *Faculty research:* Environmental engineering, transportation engineering, enhanced oil recovery, microelectrical-mechanical systems, manufacturing. Total annual research expenditures: $150,965. *Unit head:* Dr. Warren Wagguespack, Associate Dean for Research and Graduate Studies, 225-578-5731, Fax: 225-578-9162, E-mail: mewagg@me.lsu.edu. *Application contact:* Dr. Warren Wagguespack, Associate Dean for Research and Graduate Studies, 225-578-5731, Fax: 225-578-9162, E-mail: mewagg@me.lsu.edu.

Louisiana Tech University, Graduate School, College of Engineering and Science, Ruston, LA 71272. Offers MS, PhD. Part-time programs available. Terminal master's awarded for partial completion of doctoral program. *Degree requirements:* For doctorate, thesis/dissertation. *Entrance requirements:* For master's, GRE General Test, minimum GPA of 3.0 in last 60 hours. Additional exam requirements/recommendations for international students: Required—TOEFL. *Faculty research:* Trenchless technology, micromanufacturing, radionuclide transport, microbial liquefaction, hazardous waste treatment.

Manhattan College, Graduate Division, School of Engineering, Riverdale, NY 10471. Offers chemical engineering (MS); civil engineering (MS); computer engineering (MS); electrical engineering (MS); environmental engineering (ME, MS); mechanical engineering (MS). Part-time and evening/weekend programs available. *Faculty:* 29 full-time (2 women), 14 part-time/adjunct (0 women). *Students:* 54 full-time (12 women), 104 part-time (31 women); includes 17 Black or African American, non-Hispanic/Latino; 2 Asian, non-Hispanic/Latino; 15 Hispanic/Latino; 3 Two or more races, non-Hispanic/Latino, 11 international. Average age 28. 126 applicants, 73% accepted, 70 enrolled. In 2010, 48 master's awarded. *Degree requirements:* For master's, thesis or alternative. *Entrance requirements:* For master's, GRE (recommended), minimum GPA of 3.0. Additional exam requirements/recommendations for international students: Required—TOEFL (minimum score 550 paper-based; 213 computer-based; 80 iBT), IELTS (minimum score 6). *Application deadline:* For fall admission, 8/10 priority date for domestic students, 8/10 for international students; for spring admission, 1/7 for domestic and international students. Applications are processed on a rolling basis. Application fee: $50. *Expenses:* Contact institution. *Financial support:* In 2010–11, 29 students received support; fellowships with partial tuition reimbursements available, research assistantships with partial tuition reimbursements available, teaching assistantships with partial tuition reimbursements available, career-related internships or fieldwork, Federal Work-Study, scholarships/grants, and laboratory assistantships available. Support available to part-time students. Financial award application deadline: 2/1. *Faculty research:* Environmental/water, nucleation, environmental/management, heat transfer. Total annual research expenditures: $400,000. *Unit head:* Dr. Tim J. Ward, Dean of Engineering, 718-862-7281, Fax: 718-862-8015, E-mail: deanengr@manhattan.edu. *Application contact:* Sheila M. Halpin, Information Contact, 718-862-7281, Fax: 718-862-8015, E-mail: deanengr@manhattan.edu.

Marquette University, Graduate School, College of Engineering, Milwaukee, WI 53201-1881. Offers ME, MS, MSEM, PhD, Certificate. Part-time and evening/weekend programs available. *Faculty:* 58 full-time (7 women), 15 part-time/adjunct (2 women). *Students:* 129 full-time (33 women), 106 part-time (17 women); includes 17 minority (4 Black or African American, non-Hispanic/Latino; 1 American Indian or Alaska Native, non-Hispanic/Latino; 8 Asian, non-Hispanic/Latino; 3 Hispanic/Latino; 1 Native Hawaiian or other Pacific Islander, non-Hispanic/Latino), 77 international. Average age 28. 327 applicants, 51% accepted, 50 enrolled. In 2010, 30 master's, 2 doctorates awarded. *Degree requirements:* For doctorate, thesis/dissertation. *Entrance requirements:* For master's, minimum GPA of 3.0; for doctorate, GRE General Test, minimum GPA of 3.0. Additional exam requirements/recommendations for international students: Required—TOEFL (minimum score 530 paper-based; 78 computer-based). *Application deadline:* Applications are processed on a rolling basis. Application fee: $40. Electronic applications accepted. *Expenses:* Tuition: Full-time $16,290; part-time $905 per credit hour. Tuition and fees vary according to program. *Financial support:* In 2010–11, 115 students received support, including 12 fellowships with tuition reimbursements available, 23 research assistantships with tuition reimbursements available, 43 teaching assistantships with tuition reimbursements available; Federal Work-Study, institutionally sponsored loans, scholarships/grants, and tuition waivers (full and partial) also available. Support available to part-time students. Financial award application deadline: 2/15. *Faculty research:* Urban watershed management, microsensors for environmental pollutants, orthopedic rehabilitation engineering, telemedicine, ergonomics. Total annual research expenditures: $3.8 million. *Unit head:* Dr. Robert Bishop, Dean, 414-288-6591, Fax: 414-288-7082, E-mail: robert.bishop@marquette.edu. *Application contact:* Erin Fox, Director of Graduate Admissions, 414-288-7182, Fax: 414-288-1902, E-mail: erin.fox@marquette.edu.

Marshall University, Academic Affairs Division, College of Information Technology and Engineering, Huntington, WV 25755. Offers MS, MSE. Part-time and evening/weekend programs available. *Faculty:* 16 full-time (2 women), 4 part-time/adjunct (0 women). *Students:* 78 full-time (12 women), 96 part-time (16 women); includes 6 Black or African American, non-Hispanic/Latino; 2 Asian, non-Hispanic/Latino; 3 Hispanic/Latino, 41 international. Average age 32. In 2010, 45 master's awarded. *Degree requirements:* For master's, final project, oral exam. Application fee: $40. *Expenses:* Contact institution. *Financial support:* Fellowships, tuition waivers (full) available. Support available to part-time students. Financial award application deadline: 8/1; financial award applicants required to submit FAFSA. *Unit head:* Dr. Betsy Dulin, Dean, 304-746-2087, E-mail: bdulin@marshall.edu. *Application contact:* Information Contact, 304-746-1900, Fax: 304-746-1902, E-mail: services@marshall.edu.

Marshall University, Academic Affairs Division, College of Information Technology and Engineering, Weisberg Division of Engineering and Computer Science, Program in Engineering, Huntington, WV 25755. Offers MSE. *Students:* 11 full-time (1 woman), 15 part-time (1 woman); includes 1 Black or African American, non-Hispanic/Latino; 2 Asian, non-Hispanic/Latino, 6 international. Average age 29. In 2010, 4 master's awarded. *Unit head:* Dr. Eldon R. Larsen, Professor, 304-746-2047, E-mail: larsen@marshall.edu. *Application contact:* Information Contact, 304-746-1900, Fax: 304-746-1902, E-mail: services@marshall.edu.

Massachusetts Institute of Technology, School of Engineering, Cambridge, MA 02139. Offers M Eng, SM, PhD, Sc D, CE, EAA, ECS, EE, Mat E, Mech E, Met E, NE, Naval E, SM/MBA. *Faculty:* 369 full-time (59 women), 1 part-time/adjunct (0 women). *Students:* 2,672 full-time (645 women), 5 part-time (1 woman); includes 456 minority (45 Black or African American, non-Hispanic/Latino; 5 American Indian or Alaska Native, non-Hispanic/Latino; 285 Asian, non-Hispanic/Latino; 97 Hispanic/Latino; 24 Two or more races, non-Hispanic/Latino), 1,145 international. Average age 27. 7,549 applicants, 18% accepted, 898 enrolled. In 2010, 771 master's, 297 doctorates, 17 other advanced degrees awarded. Terminal master's awarded for partial completion of doctoral program. *Degree requirements:* For master's, thesis (for some programs); for doctorate, comprehensive exam, thesis/dissertation; for other advanced degree, thesis. Application fee: $75. Electronic applications accepted. *Expenses:* Tuition: Full-time $38,940; part-time $605 per unit. Required fees: $272. *Financial support:* In 2010–11, 2,382 students received support, including 624 fellowships with tuition reimbursements available (averaging $28,558 per year), 1,531 research assistantships with tuition reimbursements available (averaging $28,814 per year), 236 teaching assistantships with tuition reimbursements available (averaging $30,032 per year); career-related internships or fieldwork, Federal Work-Study, institutionally sponsored loans, scholarships/grants, traineeships, health care benefits, and unspecified assistantships also available. Total annual research expenditures: $308.8 million. *Unit head:* Prof. Ian A. Waitz, Dean, 617-253-3291, Fax: 617-253-8549. *Application contact:* Graduate Admissions, 617-253-2917, Fax: 617-687-9174, E-mail: mitgrad@mit.edu.

McGill University, Faculty of Graduate and Postdoctoral Studies, Faculty of Engineering, Montréal, QC H3A 2T5, Canada. Offers M Arch I, M Arch II, M Eng, M Sc, MMM, MUP, PhD, Diploma.

McGill University, Faculty of Graduate and Postdoctoral Studies, Faculty of Science, Department of Mathematics and Statistics, Montréal, QC H3A 2T5, Canada. Offers computational science and engineering (M Sc); mathematics and statistics (M Sc, MA, PhD), including applied mathematics (M Sc, MA), pure mathematics (M Sc, MA), statistics (M Sc, MA).

McMaster University, School of Graduate Studies, Faculty of Engineering, Hamilton, ON L8S 4M2, Canada. Offers M Eng, M Sc, MA Sc, PhD. Part-time programs available. *Degree requirements:* For doctorate, comprehensive exam, thesis/dissertation. *Entrance requirements:* Additional exam requirements/recommendations for international students: Required—TOEFL (minimum score 550 paper-based; 213 computer-based). *Faculty research:* Computer process control, water resources engineering, elasticity, flow induced vibrations, microelectronics.

McNeese State University, Doré School of Graduate Studies, College of Engineering and Engineering Technology, Lake Charles, LA 70609. Offers chemical engineering (M Eng); civil engineering (M Eng); electrical engineering (M Eng); engineering management (M Eng); mechanical engineering (M Eng). Part-time and evening/weekend programs available. *Faculty:* 15 full-time (1 woman). *Students:* 37 full-time (10 women), 18 part-time (1 woman); includes 5 minority (3 Black or African American, non-Hispanic/Latino; 1 American Indian or Alaska Native, non-Hispanic/Latino; 1 Two or more races, non-Hispanic/Latino), 43 international. In 2010, 28 master's awarded. *Degree requirements:* For master's, thesis or alternative. *Entrance requirements:* For master's, GRE, minimum undergraduate GPA of 3.0. Additional exam requirements/recommendations for international students: Required—TOEFL (minimum score 560 paper-based; 220 computer-based; 83 iBT). *Application deadline:* For fall admission, 5/15 priority date for domestic and international students; for spring admission, 10/15 priority date for domestic and international students. Applications are processed on a rolling basis. Application fee: $20 ($30 for international students). Tuition and fees vary according to course load. *Financial support:* Federal Work-Study available. Support available to part-time students. Financial award application deadline: 5/1. *Unit head:* Dr. Nikos Kiritsis, Dean, 337-475-5875, Fax: 337-475-5237, E-mail: nikosk@mcneese.edu.

Memorial University of Newfoundland, School of Graduate Studies, Faculty of Engineering and Applied Science, St. John's, NL A1C 5S7, Canada. Offers civil engineering (M Eng, PhD); electrical and computer engineering (M Eng, PhD); mechanical engineering (M Eng, PhD); ocean and naval architecture engineering (M Eng, PhD). Part-time programs available. *Degree requirements:* For master's, thesis; for doctorate, comprehensive exam, thesis/dissertation, oral thesis defense. *Entrance requirements:* For master's, 2nd class degree; for doctorate, master's degree in engineering. Electronic applications accepted. *Faculty research:* Engineering analysis, environmental and hydrotechnical studies, manufacturing and robotics, mechanics, structures and materials.

Mercer University, Graduate Studies, Macon Campus, School of Engineering, Macon, GA 31207-0003. Offers biomedical engineering (MSE); computer engineering (MSE); electrical engineering (MSE); engineering management (MSE); environmental engineering (MSE); environmental systems (MS); mechanical engineering (MSE); software engineering (MSE); software systems (MS); technical communications management (MS); technical management (MS). Part-time and evening/weekend programs available. Postbaccalaureate distance learning degree programs offered (no on-campus study). *Faculty:* 18 full-time (4 women), 1 part-time/adjunct (0 women). *Students:* 11 full-time (2 women), 100 part-time (22 women); includes 26 minority (13 Black or African American, non-Hispanic/Latino; 12 Asian, non-Hispanic/Latino; 1 Hispanic/Latino), 3 international. Average age 32. In 2010, 46 master's awarded. *Degree requirements:* For master's, thesis or alternative. *Entrance requirements:* For master's, minimum undergraduate GPA of 3.0. Additional exam requirements/recommendations for international students: Required—TOEFL. *Application deadline:* For fall admission, 7/1 for domestic students; for spring admission, 11/15 for domestic students. Applications are processed on a rolling basis. Application fee: $35 ($50 for international students). Electronic applications accepted. *Expenses:* Contact institution. *Financial support:* Federal Work-Study available. *Unit head:* Dr. Wade H. Shaw, Dean, 478-301-2459, Fax: 478-301-5593, E-mail: shaw_wh@mercer.edu. *Application contact:* Greg Lofton, Graduate Program Coordinator, 478-301-5480, Fax: 478-301-5434, E-mail: lofton_g@mercer.edu.

Miami University, Graduate School, School of Engineering and Applied Science, Oxford, OH 45056. Offers chemical and paper engineering (MS); computational science and engineering (MS); computer science and software engineering (MCS), including computer science; software development (Certificate). *Students:* 40 full-time (11 women), 4 part-time (1 woman); includes 1 Black or African American, non-Hispanic/Latino; 1 Asian, non-Hispanic/Latino; 1 Hispanic/Latino, 23 international. Average age 25. In 2010, 14 master's awarded. *Entrance requirements:* For master's, GRE, minimum undergraduate GPA of 3.0 during previous 2 years or 2.75 overall. Additional exam requirements/recommendations for international students: Required—TOEFL. Application fee: $50. *Expenses:* Tuition, state resident: full-time $11,616; part-time $484 per credit hour. Tuition, nonresident: full-time $25,656; part-time $1069 per credit hour. Required fees: $528. *Financial support:* Fellowships with full tuition reimbursements, research assistantships, teaching assistantships, Federal Work-Study, health care benefits, tuition waivers (full), and unspecified assistantships available. Financial award application deadline: 3/1. *Unit head:* Dr. Marek Dollar, Dean, 513-529-0700, E-mail: seasfyi@muohio.edu. *Application contact:* Graduate Admission Coordinator, 513-529-3734, Fax: 513-529-3734, E-mail: gradschool@muohio.edu.

Michigan State University, The Graduate School, College of Engineering, East Lansing, MI 48824. Offers MS, PhD. Part-time programs available. Electronic applications accepted.

Michigan Technological University, Graduate School, College of Engineering, Houghton, MI 49931. Offers ME, MS, PhD. Part-time programs available. Postbaccalaureate distance learning degree programs offered (minimal on-campus study). Terminal master's awarded for partial completion of doctoral program. *Degree requirements:* For master's, comprehensive exam (for some programs), thesis (for some programs); for doctorate, comprehensive exam, thesis/dissertation. *Entrance requirements:* For master's, GRE. Additional exam requirements/recommendations for international students: Required—TOEFL (minimum score 550 paper-based; 213 computer-based). Electronic applications accepted.

Milwaukee School of Engineering, Department of Electrical Engineering and Computer Science, Program in Engineering, Milwaukee, WI 53202-3109. Offers MS. Part-time and evening/weekend programs available. *Faculty:* 3 full-time (0 women), 3 part-time/adjunct (1 woman). *Students:* 2 full-time (0 women), 39 part-time (3 women); includes 1 Black or African American, non-Hispanic/Latino; 2 Asian, non-Hispanic/Latino, 1 international. Average age 23. 11 applicants, 82% accepted, 7 enrolled. In 2010, 5 master's awarded. *Degree requirements:* For master's, design project. *Entrance requirements:* For master's, GRE General Test or GMAT, BS in engineering. Additional exam requirements/recommendations for international students: Required—TOEFL (minimum score 79 iBT). *Application deadline:* Applications are processed on a rolling basis. Application fee: $30. Electronic applications accepted. *Expenses:* Tuition: Full-time $17,550; part-time $650 per credit. One-time fee: $75. *Financial support:* In 2010–11, 14 students received support, including 4 research assistantships (averaging $15,000 per year); career-related internships or fieldwork also available. Support available to part-time students. Financial award applicants required to submit FAFSA. *Faculty research:* Microprocessors, materials, thermodynamics, artificial intelligence, fluid power/hydraulics. *Unit head:* Dr. Subha Kumpaty, Director, 414-277-7466, Fax: 414-277-2222, E-mail: kumpaty@msoe.edu. *Application contact:* David E. Tietyen, Graduate Admissions Director, 800-332-6763, Fax: 414-277-7475, E-mail: wp@msoe.edu.

Mississippi State University, Bagley College of Engineering, Mississippi State, MS 39762. Offers MS, PhD. Part-time programs available. Postbaccalaureate distance learning degree programs offered (no on-campus study). *Faculty:* 101 full-time (14 women), 10 part-time/adjunct (1 woman). *Students:* 387 full-time (78 women), 220 part-time (42 women); includes 71 minority (39 Black or African American, non-Hispanic/Latino; 17 Asian, non-Hispanic/Latino; 12 Hispanic/Latino; 1 Native Hawaiian or other Pacific Islander, non-Hispanic/Latino; 2 Two or more races, non-Hispanic/Latino), 230 international. Average age 29. 813 applicants, 32% accepted, 171 enrolled. In 2010, 101 master's, 41 doctorates awarded. *Degree requirements:* For master's, comprehensive exam (for some programs), thesis; for doctorate, comprehensive exam (for some programs), thesis/dissertation. *Entrance requirements:* For master's, GRE General Test, minimum GPA of 2.75; for doctorate, GRE General Test. Additional exam requirements/recommendations for international students: Required—TOEFL (minimum score 475 paper-based; 153 computer-based; 53 iBT); Recommended—IELTS (minimum score 4.5). *Application deadline:* For fall admission, 7/1 for domestic students, 5/1 for international students; for spring admission, 11/1 for domestic students, 9/1 for international students. Applications are processed on a rolling basis. Application fee: $40. Electronic applications accepted. *Expenses:* Tuition, state resident: full-time $2730.50; part-time $304 per credit hour. Tuition, nonresident: full-time $6901; part-time $767 per credit hour. *Financial support:* In 2010–11, 130 research assistantships with full tuition reimbursements (averaging $14,505 per year), 41 teaching assistantships with full tuition reimbursements (averaging $13,061 per year) were awarded; Federal Work-Study, institutionally sponsored loans, scholarships/grants, and unspecified assistantships also available. Financial award application deadline: 4/1; financial award applicants required to submit FAFSA. *Faculty research:* Fluid dynamics, combustion, composite materials, computer design, high-voltage phenomena. Total annual research expenditures: $61.8 million. *Unit head:* Dr. Sarah A. Rajala, Dean, 662-325-2270, Fax: 662-325-8573, E-mail: rajala@bagley.msstate.edu. *Application contact:* Rita Burrell, Manager, Graduate and Distance Education, 662-325-5923, Fax: 662-325-8573, E-mail: rburrell@bagley.msstate.edu.

Mississippi State University, College of Arts and Sciences, Department of Physics and Astronomy, Mississippi State, MS 39762. Offers engineering (PhD), including applied physics; physics (MS). PhD is interdisciplinary. Part-time programs available. *Faculty:* 11 full-time (0 women). *Students:* 38 full-time (8 women), 3 part-time (0 women); includes 3 minority (1 Black or African American, non-Hispanic/Latino; 2 Hispanic/Latino), 32 international. Average age 29. 38 applicants, 45% accepted, 10 enrolled. In 2010, 6 master's, 4 doctorates awarded. *Degree requirements:* For master's, thesis optional, comprehensive oral or written exam; for doctorate, thesis/dissertation, comprehensive oral or written exam. *Entrance requirements:* For master's, GRE, minimum GPA of 2.75 on last two years of undergraduate courses; for doctorate, GRE. Additional exam requirements/recommendations for international students: Required—TOEFL (minimum score 475 paper-based; 153 computer-based; 53 iBT); Recommended—IELTS (minimum score 4.5). *Application deadline:* For fall admission, 7/1 priority date for domestic students, 5/1 for international students; for spring admission, 11/1 priority date for domestic students, 9/1 for international students. Applications are processed on a rolling basis. Application fee: $40. Electronic applications accepted. *Expenses:* Tuition, state resident: full-time $2730.50; part-time $304 per credit hour. Tuition, nonresident: full-time $6901; part-time $767 per credit hour. *Financial support:* In 2010–11, 5 research assistantships with full tuition reimbursements (averaging $14,310 per year), 22 teaching assistantships with full tuition reimbursements (averaging $13,023 per year) were awarded; Federal Work-Study, institutionally sponsored loans, and unspecified assistantships also available. Financial award application deadline: 3/15; financial award applicants required to submit FAFSA. *Faculty research:* Atomic/molecular spectroscopy, theoretical optics, gamma-ray astronomy, experimental nuclear physics, computational physics. Total annual research expenditures: $2 million. *Unit head:* Dr. Mark A. Novotny, Department Head and Professor, 662-325-2806, Fax: 662-325-8898, E-mail: man40@ra.msstate.edu. *Application contact:* Dr. David Monts, Professor and Graduate Coordinator, 662-325-2931, Fax: 662-325-8898, E-mail: physics@msstate.edu.

Missouri University of Science and Technology, Graduate School, School of Engineering, Rolla, MO 65409. Offers M Eng, MS, DE, PhD. Part-time and evening/weekend programs available. Electronic applications accepted.

Missouri Western State University, Program in Applied Science, St. Joseph, MO 64507-2294. Offers chemistry (MAS); engineering technology management (MAS); human factors and usability testing (MAS); information technology management (MAS). *Expenses:* Tuition, state resident: full-time $5544; part-time $308 per credit hour. Tuition, nonresident: full-time $10,206; part-time $567 per credit hour. Required fees: $30 per semester. One-time fee: $45 full-time.

Montana State University, College of Graduate Studies, College of Engineering, Department of Chemical and Biological Engineering, Bozeman, MT 59717. Offers chemical engineering (MS); engineering (PhD), including chemical engineering option, environmental engineering option; environmental engineering (MS). Part-time programs available. *Faculty:* 9 full-time (2 women), 2 part-time/adjunct (0 women). *Students:* 6 full-time (2 women), 13 part-time (7 women); includes 3 minority (1 American Indian or Alaska Native, non-Hispanic/Latino; 1 Asian, non-Hispanic/Latino; 1 Two or more races, non-Hispanic/Latino), 4 international. Average

Engineering and Applied Sciences—General

Montana State University (continued)
age 27. 9 applicants, 33% accepted, 3 enrolled. In 2010, 2 master's, 6 doctorates awarded. *Degree requirements:* For master's, comprehensive exam, thesis (for some programs); for doctorate, comprehensive exam, thesis/dissertation. *Entrance requirements:* For master's and doctorate, GRE General Test. Additional exam requirements/recommendations for international students: Required—TOEFL (minimum score 550 paper-based; 213 computer-based). *Application deadline:* For fall admission, 7/15 priority date for domestic students, 5/15 priority date for international students; for spring admission, 12/1 priority date for domestic students, 10/1 priority date for international students. Applications are processed on a rolling basis. Application fee: $30. Electronic applications accepted. *Expenses:* Tuition, state resident: full-time $5553.90. Tuition, nonresident: full-time $14,646. Required fees: $1233. *Financial support:* In 2010–11, 1 fellowship with full tuition reimbursement (averaging $30,000 per year), 17 research assistantships with full tuition reimbursements (averaging $20,000 per year), 2 teaching assistantships with full tuition reimbursements (averaging $11,000 per year) were awarded; health care benefits also available. Financial award application deadline: 3/1; financial award applicants required to submit FAFSA. *Faculty research:* Biofuels, extremophilic bioprocessing, and situ biocatalyzed heavy metal transformations; metabolic network analysis and engineering; magnetic resonance microscopy; modeling of biological systems; the development of protective coatings on planar solid oxide fuel cell (SOFC) metallic interconnects; characterizing corrosion mechanisms of materials in precisely-controlled exposures; testing materials in poly-crystalline silicon production environments; environmental biotechnology and bioremediation. Total annual research expenditures: $1.3 million. *Unit head:* Dr. Ron W. Larson, Head, 406-994-2221, Fax: 406-994-5308, E-mail: ronl@coe.montana.edu. *Application contact:* Dr. Carl A. Fox, Vice Provost for Graduate Education, 406-994-4145, Fax: 406-994-7433, E-mail: gradstudy@montana.edu.

Montana State University, College of Graduate Studies, College of Engineering, Department of Civil Engineering, Bozeman, MT 59717. Offers civil engineering (MS); construction engineering management (MCEM); engineering (PhD), including applied mechanics option, civil engineering option. Part-time programs available. *Faculty:* 19 full-time (2 women), 5 part-time/adjunct (1 woman). *Students:* 26 full-time (6 women), 21 part-time (6 women); includes 2 minority (1 American Indian or Alaska Native, non-Hispanic/Latino; 1 Two or more races, non-Hispanic/Latino), 1 international. Average age 27. 43 applicants, 44% accepted, 17 enrolled. In 2010, 15 master's, 1 doctorate awarded. *Degree requirements:* For master's, comprehensive exam, thesis (for some programs); for doctorate, comprehensive exam, thesis/dissertation. *Entrance requirements:* For master's and doctorate, GRE General Test. Additional exam requirements/recommendations for international students: Required—TOEFL (minimum score 550 paper-based; 213 computer-based). *Application deadline:* For fall admission, 7/15 priority date for domestic students, 5/15 priority date for international students; for spring admission, 12/1 priority date for domestic students, 10/1 priority date for international students. Applications are processed on a rolling basis. Application fee: $30. Electronic applications accepted. *Expenses:* Tuition, state resident: full-time $5553.90. Tuition, nonresident: full-time $14,646. Required fees: $1233. *Financial support:* In 2010–11, 20 students received support, including 1 fellowship (averaging $15,000 per year), 5 research assistantships with partial tuition reimbursements available (averaging $12,000 per year), 6 teaching assistantships with partial tuition reimbursements available (averaging $8,000 per year); scholarships/grants and tuition waivers (partial) also available. Financial award application deadline: 3/1; financial award applicants required to submit FAFSA. *Faculty research:* Snow and ice mechanics, biofilm engineering, transportation, structural and geo materials, water resources. Total annual research expenditures: $54,392. *Unit head:* Dr. Brett Gunnick, Head, 406-994-2111, Fax: 406-994-6105, E-mail: bgunnick@ce.montana.edu. *Application contact:* Dr. Carl A. Fox, Vice Provost for Graduate Education, 406-994-4145, Fax: 406-994-7433, E-mail: gradstudy@montana.edu.

Montana State University, College of Graduate Studies, College of Engineering, Department of Mechanical and Industrial Engineering, Bozeman, MT 59717. Offers engineering (PhD), including industrial engineering option, mechanical engineering option; industrial and management engineering (MS); mechanical engineering (MS). Part-time programs available. *Faculty:* 16 full-time (2 women), 9 part-time/adjunct (2 women). *Students:* 18 full-time (0 women), 28 part-time (9 women); includes 3 minority (all Asian, non-Hispanic/Latino), 9 international. Average age 27. 51 applicants, 43% accepted, 12 enrolled. In 2010, 14 master's, 1 doctorate awarded. *Degree requirements:* For master's, comprehensive exam, thesis, oral exams; for doctorate, comprehensive exam, thesis/dissertation, qualifying exam. *Entrance requirements:* For master's, GRE, official transcript, minimum GPA of 3.0, demonstrated potential for success, statement of goals, three letters of recommendation, proof of funds affidavit; for doctorate, minimum undergraduate GPA of 3.0, 3.2 graduate; three letters of recommendation; statement of objectives. Additional exam requirements/recommendations for international students: Required—TOEFL or IELTS. *Application deadline:* For fall admission, 7/15 priority date for domestic students, 5/15 priority date for international students; for spring admission, 12/1 priority date for domestic students, 10/1 priority date for international students. Applications are processed on a rolling basis. Application fee: $30. Electronic applications accepted. *Expenses:* Tuition, state resident: full-time $5553.90. Tuition, nonresident: full-time $14,646. Required fees: $1233. *Financial support:* In 2010–11, 34 students received support, including 22 research assistantships with tuition reimbursements available (averaging $8,276 per year), 22 teaching assistantships with tuition reimbursements available (averaging $5,255 per year); health care benefits and unspecified assistantships also available. Support available to part-time students. Financial award application deadline: 3/1; financial award applicants required to submit FAFSA. *Faculty research:* Human factors engineering, energy, design and manufacture, systems modeling, materials and structures, measurement systems. Total annual research expenditures: $1 million. *Unit head:* Dr. Chris Jenkins, Head, 406-994-2203, Fax: 406-994-6292, E-mail: cjenkins@me.montana.edu. *Application contact:* Dr. Carl A. Fox, Vice Provost for Graduate Education, 406-994-4145, Fax: 406-994-7433, E-mail: gradstudy@montana.edu.

Montana Tech of The University of Montana, Graduate School, Department of General Engineering, Butte, MT 59701-8997. Offers MS. Part-time programs available. *Faculty:* 8 full-time (0 women), 5 part-time/adjunct (0 women). *Students:* 11 full-time (1 woman), 2 part-time (0 women); includes 1 Hispanic/Latino. 7 applicants, 100% accepted, 7 enrolled. *Degree requirements:* For master's, comprehensive exam (for some programs), thesis optional. *Entrance requirements:* For master's, minimum GPA of 3.0. Additional exam requirements/recommendations for international students: Required—TOEFL (minimum score 525 paper-based; 195 computer-based; 71 iBT). *Application deadline:* For fall admission, 4/1 priority date for domestic students, 3/1 priority date for international students; for spring admission, 10/1 priority date for domestic students, 7/1 priority date for international students. Applications are processed on a rolling basis. Application fee: $30. Electronic applications accepted. *Expenses:* Tuition, state resident: full-time $5084. Tuition, nonresident: full-time $15,104. *Financial support:* In 2010–11, 10 students received support, including 8 teaching assistantships with partial tuition reimbursements available (averaging $3,750 per year); research assistantships with partial tuition reimbursements available, career-related internships or fieldwork, tuition waivers (full and partial), and unspecified assistantships also available. Financial award application deadline: 4/1; financial award applicants required to submit FAFSA. *Faculty research:* Wind energy and power controls, robotics, concurrent engineering, remotely piloted aircraft, composite materials. *Unit head:* Dr. Richard Johnson, Head, 406-496-4109, Fax: 406-496-4650, E-mail: djohnson@mtech.edu. *Application contact:* Fred Sullivan, Administrator, Graduate School, 406-496-4304, Fax: 406-496-4710, E-mail: fsullivan@mtech.edu.

Morgan State University, School of Graduate Studies, Clarence M. Mitchell, Jr. School of Engineering, Baltimore, MD 21251. Offers civil engineering (M Eng, D Eng); electrical engineering (M Eng, D Eng); industrial engineering (M Eng, D Eng); transportation (MS). Part-time and evening/weekend programs available. *Degree requirements:* For master's, thesis, comprehensive exam or equivalent; for doctorate, thesis/dissertation, comprehensive exam or equivalent. *Entrance requirements:* For master's, GRE, minimum undergraduate GPA of 2.5; for doctorate, GRE, minimum GPA of 3.0. Additional exam requirements/recommendations for international students: Required—TOEFL (minimum score 550 paper-based; 213 computer-based).

National University, Academic Affairs, School of Engineering and Technology, Department of Applied Engineering, La Jolla, CA 92037-1011. Offers database administration (MS); engineering management (MS); environmental engineering (MS); homeland security and safety engineering (MS); system engineering (MS); wireless communications (MS). Part-time and evening/weekend programs available. Postbaccalaureate distance learning degree programs offered (no on-campus study). *Faculty:* 6 full-time (1 woman), 69 part-time/adjunct (12 women). *Students:* 82 full-time (16 women), 153 part-time (35 women); includes 87 minority (18 Black or African American, non-Hispanic/Latino; 1 American Indian or Alaska Native, non-Hispanic/Latino; 34 Asian, non-Hispanic/Latino; 28 Hispanic/Latino; 2 Native Hawaiian or other Pacific Islander, non-Hispanic/Latino; 4 Two or more races, non-Hispanic/Latino), 60 international. Average age 31. 166 applicants, 100% accepted, 106 enrolled. In 2010, 79 master's awarded. *Degree requirements:* For master's, thesis. *Entrance requirements:* For master's, interview, minimum GPA of 2.5. Additional exam requirements/recommendations for international students: Required—TOEFL (minimum score 550 paper-based; 213 computer-based; 79 iBT), IELTS (minimum score 6). *Application deadline:* Applications are processed on a rolling basis. Application fee: $60 ($65 for international students). Electronic applications accepted. *Expenses:* Tuition: Full-time $9450; part-time $350 per unit. Required fees: $350 per unit. One-time fee: $60. *Financial support:* Career-related internships or fieldwork, institutionally sponsored loans, scholarships/grants, and tuition waivers (partial) available. Support available to part-time students. Financial award application deadline: 6/30; financial award applicants required to submit FAFSA. *Unit head:* Dr. Shekar Viswanathan, Chair and Associate Professor, 858-309-8416, Fax: 858-309-3420, E-mail: sviswana@nu.edu. *Application contact:* Dominick Giovanniello, Associate Regional Dean—San Diego, 800-NAT-UNIV, Fax: 858-541-7792, E-mail: dgiovann@nu.edu.

New Jersey Institute of Technology, Office of Graduate Studies, Newark, NJ 07102. Offers M Arch, MA, MAT, MBA, MIP, MS, PhD, Engineer, M Arch/MIP, M Arch/MS. Part-time and evening/weekend programs available. *Faculty:* 408 full-time (75 women), 246 part-time/adjunct (50 women). *Students:* 1,619 full-time (510 women), 1,080 part-time (318 women); includes 222 Black or African American, non-Hispanic/Latino; 10 American Indian or Alaska Native, non-Hispanic/Latino; 376 Asian, non-Hispanic/Latino; 202 Hispanic/Latino, 1,120 international. Average age 29. 5,003 applicants, 85% accepted, 1078 enrolled. In 2010, 959 master's, 67 doctorates awarded. Terminal master's awarded for partial completion of doctoral program. *Degree requirements:* For master's, thesis optional; for doctorate, thesis/dissertation. *Entrance requirements:* For master's, GRE General Test, official transcripts and proof of degree completion from all colleges and universities attended; one letter of recommendation in sealed envelope; for doctorate, GRE General Test, official transcripts and proof of degree completion from all colleges and universities attended; three letters of recommendation in sealed envelopes; statement of purpose. Additional exam requirements/recommendations for international students: Required—TOEFL (minimum score 550 paper-based; 213 computer-based; 79 iBT). *Application deadline:* For fall admission, 6/5 priority date for domestic students, 4/1 for international students; for spring admission, 11/15 for domestic and international students. Applications are processed on a rolling basis. Application fee: $65. Electronic applications accepted. *Expenses:* Tuition, state resident: full-time $14,724; part-time $818 per credit. Tuition, nonresident: full-time $20,304; part-time $1128 per credit. Required fees: $2272; $209 per credit. $103 per semester. One-time fee: $312 full-time; $212 part-time. *Financial support:* Fellowships with full and partial tuition reimbursements, research assistantships with full and partial tuition reimbursements, teaching assistantships with full and partial tuition reimbursements, career-related internships or fieldwork, Federal Work-Study, institutionally sponsored loans, and unspecified assistantships available. Financial award application deadline: 3/15. *Faculty research:* Toxic and hazardous waste management, transportation, biomedical engineering, computer-integrated manufacturing, management of technology. Total annual research expenditures: $60.9 million. *Unit head:* Dr. Marino Xanthos, Associate Provost, 973-596-3462, E-mail: marinos.xanthos@njit.edu. *Application contact:* Kathryn Kelly, Director of Admissions, 973-596-3300, Fax: 973-596-3461, E-mail: admissions@njit.edu.

New Jersey Institute of Technology, Office of Graduate Studies, Newark College of Engineering, Interdisciplinary Program in Engineering Science, Newark, NJ 07102. Offers MS. Part-time and evening/weekend programs available. *Students:* 1 part-time (0 women); includes Black or African American, non-Hispanic/Latino. Average age 54. In 2010, 1 master's awarded. *Entrance requirements:* For master's, GRE General Test. Additional exam requirements/recommendations for international students: Required—TOEFL (minimum score 550 paper-based; 213 computer-based; 79 iBT). *Application deadline:* For fall admission, 6/5 priority date for domestic students, 4/1 for international students; for spring admission, 11/15 for domestic and international students. Applications are processed on a rolling basis. Application fee: $65. Electronic applications accepted. *Expenses:* Tuition, state resident: full-time $14,724; part-time $818 per credit. Tuition, nonresident: full-time $20,304; part-time $1128 per credit. Required fees: $2272; $209 per credit. $103 per semester. One-time fee: $312 full-time; $212 part-time. *Financial support:* Fellowships with full and partial tuition reimbursements, research assistantships with full and partial tuition reimbursements, teaching assistantships with full and partial tuition reimbursements, career-related internships or fieldwork, Federal Work-Study, institutionally sponsored loans, and unspecified assistantships available. Financial award application deadline: 3/15. *Unit head:* Dr. Sunil Saigal, Program Director, 973-596-5443, E-mail: sunil.saigal@njit.edu. *Application contact:* Kathryn Kelly, Director of Admissions, 973-596-3300, Fax: 973-596-3461, E-mail: admissions@njit.edu.

New Mexico State University, Graduate School, College of Engineering, Las Cruces, NM 88003-8001. Offers MS Ch E, MS Env E, MSCE, MSEE, MSIE, MSME, PhD. Part-time programs available. *Faculty:* 59 full-time (9 women), 3 part-time/adjunct (1 woman). *Students:* 280 full-time (58 women), 156 part-time (35 women); includes 105 minority (8 Black or African American, non-Hispanic/Latino; 4 American Indian or Alaska Native, non-Hispanic/Latino; 5 Asian, non-Hispanic/Latino; 86 Hispanic/Latino; 2 Two or more races, non-Hispanic/Latino), 210 international. Average age 29. 510 applicants, 79% accepted, 146 enrolled. In 2010, 128 master's, 13 doctorates awarded. *Degree requirements:* For doctorate, thesis/dissertation. *Application deadline:* For fall admission, 7/1 priority date for domestic students; for spring admission, 11/1 for domestic students. Applications are processed on a rolling basis. Application fee: $30 ($50 for international students). Electronic applications accepted. *Expenses:* Tuition, state resident: full-time $4536; part-time $242 per credit. Tuition, nonresident: full-time $15,816; part-time $712 per credit. Required fees: $636 per term. *Financial support:* In 2010–11, 98 research assistantships (averaging $9,276 per year), 103 teaching assistantships (averaging $7,551 per year) were awarded; fellowships, career-related internships or fieldwork, Federal Work-Study, and health care benefits also available. Support available to part-time students. Financial award application deadline: 3/1. *Faculty research:* Structures and nondestructive testing, environmental science and engineering, telecommunication theory and systems, manufacturing methods and systems, high performance computing and software engineering. *Unit head:* Dr. Ricardo Jacquez, Dean, 575-646-7234, Fax: 575-646-3549, E-mail: rjaquez@nmsu.edu. *Application contact:* Dr. Ricardo Jacquez, Dean, 575-646-7234, Fax: 575-646-3549, E-mail: rjaquez@nmsu.edu.

New York Institute of Technology, Graduate Division, School of Engineering and Computing Sciences, Old Westbury, NY 11568-8000. Offers MS, Advanced Certificate. Part-time and evening/weekend programs available. Postbaccalaureate distance learning degree programs offered. *Students:* 356 full-time (87 women), 284 part-time (54 women); includes 97 minority (40 Black or African American, non-Hispanic/Latino; 3 American Indian or Alaska Native, non-Hispanic/Latino; 32 Asian, non-Hispanic/Latino; 21 Hispanic/Latino; 1 Two or more races, non-Hispanic/Latino), 331 international. Average age 28. In 2010, 244 master's, 34 other advanced degrees awarded. *Entrance requirements:* Additional exam requirements/recommendations for international students: Required—TOEFL (minimum score 550 paper-based; 213 computer-based). *Application deadline:* For fall admission, 7/1 priority date for domestic students; for spring admission, 12/1 priority date for domestic students. Applications are processed on a rolling basis. Application fee: $50. Electronic applications accepted. *Expenses:* Tuition: Part-time $835 per credit. *Financial support:* Fellowships, research assistantships with partial tuition reimbursements, career-related internships or fieldwork, institutionally sponsored loans, tuition waivers (full and partial), and unspecified assistantships available. Support available to part-time students. Financial award applicants required to submit FAFSA. *Faculty research:* Hybrid vehicle development, system design of photovoltaic cells, prototype module of DTV application environment, adaptive target detection in nonhomogeneous environment. *Unit head:* Dr. Nada Anid, Dean, 516-686-7931, Fax: 516-625-7933, E-mail: nanid@nyit.edu. *Application contact:* Dr. Jacquelyn Nealon, Vice President for Enrollment Services, 516-686-7925, Fax: 516-686-7597, E-mail: jnealon@nyit.edu.

North Carolina Agricultural and Technical State University, Graduate School, College of Engineering, Greensboro, NC 27411. Offers MS Ch E, MSCE, MSCS, MSE, MSEE, MSIE, MSME, PhD. Part-time programs available.

North Carolina State University, Graduate School, College of Engineering, Raleigh, NC 27695. Offers M Ch E, M Eng, MC Sc, MCE, MIE, MIMS, MMSE, MNE, MOR, MS, PhD. Part-time programs available. Terminal master's awarded for partial completion of doctoral program. *Degree requirements:* For doctorate, thesis/dissertation. Electronic applications accepted.

See Display on next page and Close-Up on page 85.

North Dakota State University, College of Graduate and Interdisciplinary Studies, College of Engineering and Architecture, Fargo, ND 58108. Offers MS, PhD. Part-time programs available. *Faculty:* 72 full-time (9 women), 11 part-time/adjunct (0 women). *Students:* 197 full-time (44 women), 108 part-time (20 women). Average age 27. 297 applicants, 43% accepted. In 2010, 32 master's, 5 doctorates awarded. Terminal master's awarded for partial completion of doctoral program. *Degree requirements:* For master's, thesis; for doctorate, comprehensive exam, thesis/dissertation. *Entrance requirements:* For master's and doctorate, minimum GPA of 3.0. Additional exam requirements/recommendations for international students: Required—TOEFL. *Application deadline:* For fall admission, 4/1 priority date for domestic and international students; for spring admission, 10/1 priority date for domestic and international students. Applications are processed on a rolling basis. Application fee: $45 ($60 for international students). *Expenses:* Contact institution. *Financial support:* In 2010–11, 150 students received support, including fellowships with full tuition reimbursements available (averaging $15,000 per year), research assistantships with full tuition reimbursements available (averaging $9,000 per year), teaching assistantships with full tuition reimbursements available (averaging $8,000 per year); career-related internships or fieldwork, Federal Work-Study, institutionally sponsored loans, scholarships/grants, and tuition waivers (full) also available. Support available to part-time students. Financial award application deadline: 4/15. *Faculty research:* Theoretical mechanics, robotics, automation, environmental engineering, man-made materials. Total annual research expenditures: $2.6 million. *Unit head:* Dr. Gary R. Smith, Dean, 701-231-7494, Fax: 701-231-8957, E-mail: gary.smith@ndsu.edu. *Application contact:* Dr. David A. Wittrock, Dean, 701-231-7033, Fax: 701-231-6524.

Northeastern University, College of Engineering, Boston, MA 02115-5096. Offers MS, PhD, Certificate. Part-time programs available. *Faculty:* 120 full-time (23 women), 25 part-time/adjunct (1 woman). *Students:* 1,069 full-time (289 women), 298 part-time (51 women). 2,648 applicants, 62% accepted, 496 enrolled. In 2010, 360 master's, 27 doctorates awarded. *Entrance requirements:* For master's and doctorate, GRE General Test. Additional exam requirements/recommendations for international students: Required—TOEFL. *Application deadline:* For fall admission, 1/15 priority date for domestic and international students. Applications are processed on a rolling basis. Application fee: $50. Electronic applications accepted. *Expenses:* Contact institution. *Financial support:* In 2010–11, 268 students received support, including 4 fellowships with full tuition reimbursements available, 146 research assistantships with full tuition reimbursements available (averaging $18,320 per year), 117 teaching assistantships with full tuition reimbursements available (averaging $18,320 per year); career-related internships or fieldwork, Federal Work-Study, scholarships/grants, tuition waivers (full), and unspecified assistantships also available. Support available to part-time students. Financial award application deadline: 1/15; financial award applicants required to submit FAFSA. *Unit head:* Dr. Yaman Yener, Associate Dean of Engineering for Research and Graduate Studies, 617-373-2711, Fax: 617-373-2501. *Application contact:* Jeffery Hengel, Admissions Specialist, 617-373-2711, Fax: 617-373-2501, E-mail: grad-eng@coe.neu.edu.

Northern Arizona University, Graduate College, College of Engineering, Forestry and Natural Sciences, Flagstaff, AZ 86011. Offers M Ed, M Eng, MAST, MAT, MF, MS, MSE, MSF, PhD, Certificate. *Faculty:* 195 full-time (62 women). *Students:* 272 full-time (134 women), 91 part-time (45 women); includes 45 minority (3 Black or African American, non-Hispanic/Latino; 11 American Indian or Alaska Native, non-Hispanic/Latino; 5 Asian, non-Hispanic/Latino; 22 Hispanic/Latino; 4 Two or more races, non-Hispanic/Latino), 22 international. 291 applicants, 41% accepted, 88 enrolled. In 2010, 97 master's, 9 doctorates, 1 other advanced degree awarded. *Entrance requirements:* For master's, minimum GPA of 3.0 in final 60 hours of undergraduate course work. Application fee: $65. *Financial support:* In 2010–11, 32 students received support, including 23 fellowships, 62 research assistantships, 113 teaching assistantships. Financial award applicants required to submit FAFSA. *Unit head:* Paul W. Jagodzinski, Dean, 928-523-2701, Fax: 928-523-2300, E-mail: paul.jagodzinski@nau.edu. *Application contact:* Paul W. Jagodzinski, Dean, 928-523-2701, Fax: 928-523-2300, E-mail: paul.jagodzinski@nau.edu.

Northern Illinois University, Graduate School, College of Engineering and Engineering Technology, De Kalb, IL 60115-2854. Offers MS. Part-time and evening/weekend programs available. *Faculty:* 36 full-time (2 women), 2 part-time/adjunct (0 women). *Students:* 111 full-time (17 women), 146 part-time (35 women); includes 5 Black or African American, non-Hispanic/Latino; 8 Asian, non-Hispanic/Latino; 7 Hispanic/Latino; 5 Two or more races, non-Hispanic/Latino, 131 international. Average age 27. 551 applicants, 42% accepted, 76 enrolled. In 2010, 78 master's awarded. *Degree requirements:* For master's, comprehensive exam, thesis optional. *Entrance requirements:* For master's, GRE General Test, minimum GPA of 2.75. Additional exam requirements/recommendations for international students: Required—TOEFL (minimum score 550 paper-based; 213 computer-based). *Application deadline:* For fall admission, 6/1 for domestic students, 5/1 for international students; for spring admission, 11/1 for domestic students, 10/1 for international students. Applications are processed on a rolling basis. Application fee: $30. Electronic applications accepted. *Expenses:* Tuition, state resident: full-time $7200; part-time $300 per credit hour. Tuition, nonresident: full-time $14,400; part-time $600 per credit hour. Required fees: $79 per credit hour. *Financial support:* In 2010–11, 42 research assistantships with full tuition reimbursements, 10 teaching assistantships with full tuition reimbursements were awarded; fellowships with full tuition reimbursements, career-related internships or fieldwork, Federal Work-Study, scholarships/grants, tuition waivers (full), and unspecified assistantships also available. Support available to part-time students. Financial award applicants required to submit FAFSA. *Unit head:* Dr. Promod Vohra, Dean, 815-753-1281, Fax: 815-753-1310, E-mail: pvohra@niu.edu. *Application contact:* Graduate School Office, 815-753-0395, E-mail: gradsch@niu.edu.

Northwestern Polytechnic University, School of Engineering, Fremont, CA 94539-7482. Offers computer science (MS); computer systems engineering (MS); electrical engineering (MS). Part-time and evening/weekend programs available. *Degree requirements:* For master's, thesis optional. *Entrance requirements:* For master's, minimum GPA of 3.0. Additional exam requirements/recommendations for international students: Required—TOEFL (minimum score 550 paper-based; 213 computer-based; 79 iBT). *Faculty research:* Computer networking, database design, Internet technology, software engineering, digital signal processing.

Northwestern University, McCormick School of Engineering and Applied Science, Evanston, IL 60208. Offers MEM, MIT, MME, MMM, MPD, MS, PhD, Certificate. MS and PhD admissions and degrees offered through The Graduate School. Part-time and evening/weekend programs

available. *Faculty:* 173 full-time (20 women). *Students:* 1,179 full-time (342 women), 260 part-time (52 women); includes 240 minority (30 Black or African American, non-Hispanic/Latino; 3 American Indian or Alaska Native, non-Hispanic/Latino; 143 Asian, non-Hispanic/Latino; 52 Hispanic/Latino; 1 Native Hawaiian or other Pacific Islander, non-Hispanic/Latino; 11 Two or more races, non-Hispanic/Latino), 542 international. Average age 26. 3,516 applicants, 28% accepted, 476 enrolled. In 2010, 370 master's, 121 doctorates awarded. Terminal master's awarded for partial completion of doctoral program. *Degree requirements:* For master's, comprehensive exam (for some programs), thesis (for some programs); for doctorate, comprehensive exam, thesis/dissertation. *Entrance requirements:* For master's and doctorate, GRE General Test. Additional exam requirements/recommendations for international students: Required—TOEFL (minimum score 577 paper-based, 233 computer-based, 90 iBT) or IELTS (7). *Application deadline:* 12/31 for domestic and international students. Application fee: $75. Electronic applications accepted. *Financial support:* Fellowships with tuition reimbursements, research assistantships with tuition reimbursements, teaching assistantships with tuition reimbursements, career-related internships or fieldwork, Federal Work-Study, institutionally sponsored loans, traineeships, health care benefits, and unspecified assistantships available. Financial award application deadline: 1/15; financial award applicants required to submit FAFSA. Total annual research expenditures: $117 million. *Unit head:* Dr. Julio Ottino, Dean, 847-491-3558, Fax: 847-491-5220, E-mail: jm-ottino@northwestern.edu. *Application contact:* Dr. Bruce Alan Lindvall, Assistant Dean for Graduate Studies, 847-491-4547, Fax: 847-491-5341, E-mail: b-lindvall@northwestern.edu.

Oakland University, Graduate Study and Lifelong Learning, School of Engineering and Computer Science, Rochester, MI 48309-4401. Offers MS, PhD. Part-time and evening/weekend programs available. *Degree requirements:* For doctorate, thesis/dissertation. *Entrance requirements:* For master's and doctorate, minimum GPA of 3.0 for unconditional admission. Additional exam requirements/recommendations for international students: Required—TOEFL (minimum score 550 paper-based; 213 computer-based). Electronic applications accepted. *Expenses:* Contact institution. *Faculty research:* Acquisition of automotive antenna measurements instrumentation, high fidelity antenna model, development for LAAS Cat-1 siting criteria, cyber security, 3D imaging of neurochemical in rat brains.

The Ohio State University, Graduate School, College of Engineering, Columbus, OH 43210. Offers M Arch, M Land Arch, MCRP, MS, MWE, PhD. Part-time and evening/weekend programs available. *Faculty:* 475. *Students:* 1,309 full-time (297 women), 459 part-time (96 women); includes 24 Black or African American, non-Hispanic/Latino; 1 American Indian or Alaska Native, non-Hispanic/Latino; 56 Asian, non-Hispanic/Latino; 32 Hispanic/Latino; 5 Two or more races, non-Hispanic/Latino, 895 international. Average age 27. In 2010, 296 master's, 128 doctorates awarded. *Degree requirements:* For doctorate, thesis/dissertation. *Entrance requirements:* Additional exam requirements/recommendations for international students: Recommended—TOEFL (minimum score 600 paper-based; 250 computer-based). *Application deadline:* For fall admission, 8/15 priority date for domestic students, 7/1 priority date for international students; for winter admission, 12/1 priority date for domestic students, 11/1 priority date for international students; for spring admission, 3/1 priority date for domestic students, 2/1 priority date for international students. Applications are processed on a rolling basis. Application fee: $40 ($50 for international students). Electronic applications accepted. *Expenses:* Tuition, state resident: full-time $10,605. Tuition, nonresident: full-time $26,535. Tuition and fees vary according to course load and program. *Financial support:* Fellowships, research assistantships, teaching assistantships, career-related internships or fieldwork, Federal Work-Study, institutionally sponsored loans, and unspecified assistantships available. Support available to part-time students. *Unit head:* Dr. David B. Williams, Dean, 614-292-2836, Fax: 614-292-9379, E-mail: williams.4219@osu.edu. *Application contact:* 614-292-9444, Fax: 614-292-3895, E-mail: domestic.grad@osu.edu.

Ohio University, Graduate College, Russ College of Engineering and Technology, Athens, OH 45701-2979. Offers M Eng Mgt, MS, PhD. Part-time programs available. *Faculty:* 90 full-time (10 women), 13 part-time/adjunct (2 women). *Students:* 236 full-time (60 women), 77 part-time (9 women); includes 11 minority (2 Black or African American, non-Hispanic/Latino; 1 Asian, non-Hispanic/Latino; 5 Hispanic/Latino; 3 Two or more races, non-Hispanic/Latino), 185 international. 355 applicants, 54% accepted, 62 enrolled. In 2010, 51 master's, 12 doctorates awarded. *Degree requirements:* For master's, comprehensive exam (for some programs), thesis (for some programs); for doctorate, comprehensive exam, thesis/dissertation. *Entrance requirements:* For master's, GRE General Test, BS in engineering or related field; for doctorate, GRE General Test, MS in engineering or related field. Additional exam requirements/recommendations for international students: Required—TOEFL or IELTS. *Application deadline:* Applications are processed on a rolling basis. Application fee: $50 ($55 for international students). Electronic applications accepted. *Expenses:* Contact institution. *Financial support:* Fellowships with full tuition reimbursements, research assistantships with full tuition reimbursements, teaching assistantships with full tuition reimbursements, career-related internships or fieldwork, Federal Work-Study, institutionally sponsored loans, and unspecified assistantships available. Financial award application deadline: 3/15. *Faculty research:* Avionics engineering, coal research, transportation engineering, software systems integration, materials processing. Total annual research expenditures: $14.7 million. *Unit head:* Dr. Dennis Irwin, Dean, 740-593-1482, Fax: 740-593-0659, E-mail: irwind@ohio.edu. *Application contact:* Dr. Shawn Ostermann, Associate Dean, 740-593-1482, Fax: 740-593-0659, E-mail: ostermann@ohio.edu.

Oklahoma State University, College of Engineering, Architecture and Technology, Stillwater, OK 74078. Offers MS, PhD. Postbaccalaureate distance learning degree programs offered. *Faculty:* 112 full-time (12 women), 6 part-time/adjunct (1 woman). *Students:* 361 full-time (68 women), 448 part-time (69 women); includes 8 Black or African American, non-Hispanic/Latino; 15 American Indian or Alaska Native, non-Hispanic/Latino; 16 Asian, non-Hispanic/Latino; 10 Hispanic/Latino, 515 international. Average age 28. 1,174 applicants, 38% accepted, 193 enrolled. In 2010, 209 master's, 21 doctorates awarded. *Degree requirements:* For master's, thesis (for some programs); for doctorate, comprehensive exam, thesis/dissertation. *Entrance requirements:* For master's and doctorate, GRE or GMAT. Additional exam requirements/recommendations for international students: Required—TOEFL (minimum score 550 paper-based; 79 iBT). *Application deadline:* For fall admission, 3/1 priority date for international students; for spring admission, 8/1 priority date for international students. Applications are processed on a rolling basis. Application fee: $40 ($75 for international students). Electronic applications accepted. *Expenses:* Tuition, state resident: full-time $3716; part-time $154.85 per credit hour. Tuition, nonresident: full-time $14,892; part-time $621 per credit hour. Required fees: $2044; $85.20 per credit hour. One-time fee: $50. Tuition and fees vary according to course load and campus/location. *Financial support:* In 2010–11, 250 research assistantships (averaging $11,510 per year), 170 teaching assistantships (averaging $8,002 per year) were awarded; career-related internships or fieldwork, Federal Work-Study, scholarships/grants, health care benefits, tuition waivers (partial), and unspecified assistantships also available. Support available to part-time students. Financial award application deadline: 3/1; financial award applicants required to submit FAFSA. *Unit head:* Dr. Karl N. Reid, Dean, 405-744-5140. *Application contact:* Dr. Gordon Emslie, Dean, 405-744-6368, Fax: 405-744-0355, E-mail: grad-i@okstate.edu.

See Display on page 57 and Close-Up on page 87.

Old Dominion University, Frank Batten College of Engineering and Technology, Norfolk, VA 23529. Offers ME, MEM, MS, D Eng, PhD. Part-time and evening/weekend programs available. Postbaccalaureate distance learning degree programs offered. *Faculty:* 93 full-time (12 women), 32 part-time/adjunct (5 women). *Students:* 216 full-time (40 women), 530 part-time (92 women); includes 120 minority (57 Black or African American, non-Hispanic/Latino; 2 American Indian or Alaska Native, non-Hispanic/Latino; 23 Asian, non-Hispanic/Latino; 23 Hispanic/Latino; 2 Native Hawaiian or other Pacific Islander, non-Hispanic/Latino; 13 Two or more races, non-Hispanic/Latino), 205 international. Average age 32. 558 applicants, 63% accepted, 144 enrolled. In 2010, 220 master's, 31 doctorates awarded. *Degree requirements:* For master's, comprehensive exam, thesis (for some programs); for doctorate, thesis/dissertation, candidacy

exam. *Entrance requirements:* For master's, GRE, minimum GPA of 3.0; for doctorate, GRE, minimum GPA of 3.5. Additional exam requirements/recommendations for international students: Required—TOEFL (minimum score 550 paper-based). *Application deadline:* For fall admission, 6/1 for domestic students, 2/15 priority date for international students; for spring admission, 11/1 for domestic students, 10/1 for international students. Applications are processed on a rolling basis. Application fee: $40. Electronic applications accepted. *Expenses:* Tuition, state resident: full-time $8592; part-time $358 per credit. Tuition, nonresident: full-time $21,672; part-time $903 per credit. Required fees: $119 per semester. One-time fee: $50. *Financial support:* In 2010–11, 168 students received support, including 8 fellowships with full and partial tuition reimbursements available (averaging $15,000 per year), 92 research assistantships with full and partial tuition reimbursements available (averaging $15,000 per year), 68 teaching assistantships with full and partial tuition reimbursements available (averaging $15,000 per year); career-related internships or fieldwork, Federal Work-Study, institutionally sponsored loans, scholarships/grants, and unspecified assistantships also available. Support available to part-time students. Financial award applicants required to submit FAFSA. *Faculty research:* Physical electronics, computational applied mechanics, structural dynamics, computational fluid dynamics, coastal engineering of water resources. Total annual research expenditures: $32.4 million. *Unit head:* Dr. Oktay Baysal, Dean, 757-683-3789, Fax: 757-683-4898, E-mail: obaysal@odu.edu. *Application contact:* Dr. Linda Vahala, Associate Dean, 757-683-3789, Fax: 757-683-4898, E-mail: lvahala@odu.edu.

Oregon State University, Graduate School, College of Engineering, Corvallis, OR 97331. Offers M Eng, M Engr, M Oc E, MA, MAIS, MBE, MHP, MS, PhD. Part-time programs available. Terminal master's awarded for partial completion of doctoral program. *Degree requirements:* For doctorate, thesis/dissertation. *Entrance requirements:* For master's and doctorate, minimum GPA of 3.0 in last 90 hours. Additional exam requirements/recommendations for international students: Required—TOEFL (minimum score 550 paper-based; 213 computer-based). *Faculty research:* Molecular beam epitaxy, wave-structure interaction, pavement materials, toxic wastes, mechanical design methodology.

Penn State Erie, The Behrend College, Graduate School, Erie, PA 16563-0001. Offers business administration (MBA); engineering (M Eng). *Accreditation:* AACSB. Part-time programs available. *Students:* 48 full-time (9 women), 59 part-time (17 women). Average age 28. 70 applicants, 70% accepted, 35 enrolled. In 2010, 123 master's awarded. *Entrance requirements:* Additional exam requirements/recommendations for international students: Required—TOEFL (minimum score 550 paper-based; 213 computer-based; 80 iBT). *Application deadline:* Applications are processed on a rolling basis. Application fee: $65. Electronic applications accepted. *Financial support:* Federal Work-Study available. Financial award application deadline: 2/15; financial award applicants required to submit FAFSA. *Unit head:* Dr. John D. Burke, Chief Executive Officer/Dean, 814-898-6160, Fax: 814-898-6461, E-mail: jdb1@psu.edu. *Application contact:* Ann M. Burbules, Graduate Admissions Counselor, 814-898-7255, Fax: 814-898-6044, E-mail: amb29@psu.edu.

Penn State Great Valley, Graduate Studies, Engineering Division, Malvern, PA 19355-1488. Offers ME, MEM, MS, MSE. *Unit head:* Dr. James A. Nemes, Division Head, 610-648-3335 Ext. 610, Fax: 648-648-3377, E-mail: jan16@psu.edu. *Application contact:* Dr. James A. Nemes, Division Head, 610-648-3335 Ext. 610, Fax: 648-648-3377, E-mail: jan16@psu.edu.

Penn State Harrisburg, Graduate School, School of Science, Engineering and Technology, Middletown, PA 17057-4898. Offers M Eng, MEPC, MPS, MS, MEPC/JD. Evening/weekend programs available. *Unit head:* Dr. Omid Ansary, Director, 717-948-6353, E-mail: axa8@psu.edu. *Application contact:* Robert Coffman, Director of Admissions, 717-948-6250, Fax: 717-948-6325, E-mail: ric1@psu.edu.

Penn State University Park, Graduate School, College of Engineering, State College, University Park, PA 16802-1503. Offers M Eng, MAE, MS, PhD. *Students:* 1,169 full-time (235 women), 133 part-time (16 women). Average age 27. 3,916 applicants, 26% accepted, 369 enrolled. In 2010, 310 master's, 131 doctorates awarded. *Entrance requirements:* Additional exam requirements/recommendations for international students: Required—TOEFL (minimum score 550 paper-based; 213 computer-based; 80 iBT). *Application deadline:* Applications are processed on a rolling basis. Application fee: $65. Electronic applications accepted. *Financial support:* Fellowships, research assistantships, teaching assistantships available. Financial award applicants required to submit FAFSA. *Unit head:* Dr. David N. Wormley, Dean, 814-865-7537, Fax: 814-865-8767, E-mail: dnw2@engr.psu.edu. *Application contact:* Cynthia E. Nicosia, Director, Graduate Enrollment Services, 814-865-1834, E-mail: cey1@psu.edu.

Pittsburg State University, Graduate School, College of Technology, Department of Engineering Technology, Pittsburg, KS 66762. Offers MET. *Degree requirements:* For master's, thesis or alternative.

Pontificia Universidad Catolica Madre y Maestra, Graduate School, Faculty of Engineering Sciences, Santiago, Dominican Republic. Offers earthquake engineering (ME); logistics management (ME).

Portland State University, Graduate Studies, Maseeh College of Engineering and Computer Science, Portland, OR 97207-0751. Offers M Eng, ME, MS, MSE, PhD, Certificate, MS/MBA, MS/MS. Part-time and evening/weekend programs available. *Faculty:* 79 full-time (13 women), 18 part-time/adjunct (5 women). *Students:* 299 full-time (69 women), 349 part-time (80 women); includes 85 minority (9 Black or African American, non-Hispanic/Latino; 52 Asian, non-Hispanic/Latino; 20 Hispanic/Latino; 2 Native Hawaiian or other Pacific Islander, non-Hispanic/Latino; 2 Two or more races, non-Hispanic/Latino), 269 international. Average age 31. 458 applicants, 62% accepted, 139 enrolled. In 2010, 187 master's, 9 doctorates awarded. *Degree requirements:* For doctorate, one foreign language, thesis/dissertation, oral and written exams. *Entrance requirements:* For master's, minimum GPA of 3.0 in upper-division course work or 2.75 overall; for doctorate, GRE General Test, GRE Subject Test, minimum GPA of 3.0 in upper-division course work. Additional exam requirements/recommendations for international students: Required—TOEFL (minimum score 550 paper-based; 213 computer-based). *Application deadline:* For fall admission, 4/1 for domestic students, 3/1 for international students; for winter admission, 9/1 for domestic and international students; for spring admission, 2/1 for domestic and international students. Applications are processed on a rolling basis. Application fee: $50. *Expenses:* Tuition, state resident: full-time $8505; part-time $315 per credit. Tuition, nonresident: full-time $13,284; part-time $492 per credit. Required fees: $1482; $21 per credit. $99 per term. One-time fee: $120. Part-time tuition and fees vary according to course load and program. *Financial support:* In 2010–11, 32 research assistantships with full tuition reimbursements (averaging $14,238 per year), 4 teaching assistantships with full tuition reimbursements (averaging $11,440 per year) were awarded; career-related internships or fieldwork, Federal Work-Study, scholarships/grants, and unspecified assistantships also available. Support available to part-time students. Financial award application deadline: 3/1; financial award applicants required to submit FAFSA. Total annual research expenditures: $7.9 million. *Unit head:* Dr. Renjeng Su, Dean, 503-725-8393, Fax: 503-725-2825, E-mail: renjengs@pdx.edu. *Application contact:* Marcia Fischer, Assistant Dean for Enrollment, 503-725-4289, Fax: 503-725-4298, E-mail: fischerm@cecs.pdx.edu.

Prairie View A&M University, College of Engineering, Prairie View, TX 77446-0519. Offers computer information systems (MSCIS); computer science (MSCS); electrical engineering (MSEE, PhDEE); engineering (MS Engr). Part-time and evening/weekend programs available. *Faculty:* 19 full-time (0 women). *Students:* 89 full-time (26 women), 34 part-time (5 women); includes 45 Black or African American, non-Hispanic/Latino; 1 American Indian or Alaska Native, non-Hispanic/Latino; 13 Asian, non-Hispanic/Latino; 3 Hispanic/Latino, 53 international. Average age 32. 50 applicants, 84% accepted, 33 enrolled. In 2010, 8 master's, 2 doctorates awarded. *Degree requirements:* For master's, thesis (for some programs); for doctorate, comprehensive exam, thesis/dissertation. *Entrance requirements:* For master's, GRE General Test, bachelor's degree in engineering from an ABET accredited institution; for doctorate, GRE. Additional exam requirements/recommendations for international students: Required—

TOEFL (minimum score 550 paper-based). *Application deadline:* For fall admission, 7/1 priority date for domestic and international students; for spring admission, 11/1 priority date for domestic and international students. Application fee: $50. Electronic applications accepted. *Expenses:* Tuition, state resident: full-time $3586.14; part-time $119.06 per credit hour. Tuition, nonresident: part-time $511.23 per credit hour. *Financial support:* In 2010–11, 80 students received support, including 14 fellowships (averaging $1,050 per year), 16 research assistantships (averaging $16,150 per year), 13 teaching assistantships (averaging $14,000 per year); career-related internships or fieldwork, institutionally sponsored loans, scholarships/grants, health care benefits, tuition waivers (partial), and unspecified assistantships also available. Financial award application deadline: 3/1; financial award applicants required to submit FAFSA. *Faculty research:* Applied radiation research, thermal science, computational fluid dynamics, analog mixed signal, aerial space battlefield. Total annual research expenditures: $439,054. *Unit head:* Dr. Kendall T. Harris, Dean, 936-261-9956, Fax: 936-261-9869, E-mail: tharris@pvamu.edu. *Application contact:* Barbara A. Thompson, Administrative Assistant, 936-261-9896, Fax: 936-261-9869, E-mail: bathompson@pvamu.edu.

Princeton University, Graduate School, School of Engineering and Applied Science, Princeton, NJ 08544-1019. Offers M Eng, MSE, PhD. Terminal master's awarded for partial completion of doctoral program. *Degree requirements:* For master's, thesis (for some programs); for doctorate, thesis/dissertation, research, teaching, general exam. *Entrance requirements:* For master's and doctorate, GRE General Test, official transcript(s), 3 letters of recommendation, personal statement. Additional exam requirements/recommendations for international students: Required—TOEFL. Electronic applications accepted.

Purdue University, College of Engineering, West Lafayette, IN 47907-2045. Offers MS, MSAAE, MSABE, MSBME, MSCE, MSChE, MSE, MSECE, MSIE, MSME, MSMSE, MSNE, PhD, Certificate, MD/PhD. *Accreditation:* ABET. Part-time programs available. Postbaccalaureate distance learning degree programs offered (no on-campus study). Terminal master's awarded for partial completion of doctoral program. *Degree requirements:* For master's, thesis (for some programs); for doctorate, comprehensive exam, thesis/dissertation. *Entrance requirements:* Additional exam requirements/recommendations for international students: Required—TOEFL (minimum score 550 paper-based; 213 computer-based) or IELTS (minimum score 6.5); Recommended—TWE. Electronic applications accepted. *Expenses:* Contact institution. *Faculty research:* Nanotechnology, advanced materials manufacturing, tissue and cell engineering, intelligent infrastructures, global sustainable industrial systems.

Purdue University Calumet, Graduate Studies Office, School of Engineering, Mathematics, and Science, Department of Engineering, Hammond, IN 46323-2094. Offers computer engineering (MSE); electrical engineering (MSE); engineering (MS); mechanical engineering (MSE). Evening/weekend programs available. *Entrance requirements:* Additional exam requirements/recommendations for international students: Required—TOEFL. Application fee: $30. *Expenses:* Tuition, state resident: full-time $6867. Tuition, nonresident: full-time $14,157. *Financial support:* Career-related internships or fieldwork available. Financial award application deadline: 3/1. *Unit head:* Dr. Kaliappan Gopalan, Head, 219-989-2685, E-mail: gopalan@purduecal.edu. *Application contact:* Janice Novosel, Engineering Graduate Program Secretary, 219-989-3106, E-mail: janice.novosel@purduecal.edu.

Purdue University Calumet, Graduate Studies Office, School of Technology, Hammond, IN 46323-2094. Offers MS. *Expenses:* Tuition, state resident: full-time $6867. Tuition, nonresident: full-time $14,157. *Unit head:* Niaz Latif, Dean, 219-989-8320, E-mail: nlatif@purduecal.edu. *Application contact:* Margaret Greer, Coordinator of Admissions and Records, 219-989-2257, Fax: 219-989-4130, E-mail: margaret.greer@purduecal.edu.

Queen's University at Kingston, School of Graduate Studies and Research, Faculty of Applied Science, Kingston, ON K7L 3N6, Canada. Offers M Eng, M Sc, M Sc Eng, PhD. Part-time programs available. *Degree requirements:* For doctorate, comprehensive exam, thesis/dissertation. *Entrance requirements:* Additional exam requirements/recommendations for international students: Required—TOEFL. Electronic applications accepted.

Rensselaer at Hartford, Department of Engineering, Hartford, CT 06120-2991. Offers ME, MS. Part-time and evening/weekend programs available. *Entrance requirements:* For master's, GRE. Additional exam requirements/recommendations for international students: Required—TOEFL (minimum score 600 paper-based; 250 computer-based; 100 iBT). Electronic applications accepted.

Rensselaer Polytechnic Institute, Graduate School, School of Engineering, Troy, NY 12180-3590. Offers M Eng, MS, D Eng, PhD. Part-time and evening/weekend programs available. Postbaccalaureate distance learning degree programs offered (no on-campus study). *Faculty:* 131 full-time (15 women), 15 part-time/adjunct (0 women). *Students:* 473 full-time (99 women), 63 part-time (7 women); includes 33 minority (3 Black or African American, non-Hispanic/Latino; 18 Asian, non-Hispanic/Latino; 12 Hispanic/Latino), 271 international. Average age 26. 1,941 applicants, 21% accepted, 126 enrolled. In 2010, 114 master's, 71 doctorates awarded. Terminal master's awarded for partial completion of doctoral program. *Degree requirements:* For master's, comprehensive exam (for some programs), thesis (for some programs); for doctorate, comprehensive exam (for some programs), thesis/dissertation. *Entrance requirements:* For master's and doctorate, GRE. Additional exam requirements/recommendations for international students: Required—TOEFL (minimum score 570 paper-based; 230 computer-based; 89 iBT), IELTS (minimum score 6.5). *Application deadline:* For fall admission, 1/1 priority date for domestic and international students; for spring admission, 8/15 priority date for domestic and international students. Applications are processed on a rolling basis. Application fee: $75. Electronic applications accepted. *Expenses:* Tuition: Full-time $39,600; part-time $1650 per credit. Required fees: $1896. *Financial support:* In 2010–11, 38 fellowships with full tuition reimbursements (averaging $22,442 per year), 267 research assistantships with full and partial tuition reimbursements (averaging $19,068 per year), 135 teaching assistantships with full and partial tuition reimbursements (averaging $17,166 per year) were awarded; career-related internships or fieldwork, institutionally sponsored loans, scholarships/grants, tuition waivers (full and partial), and unspecified assistantships also available. Financial award application deadline: 2/1. *Faculty research:* Computer networking, materials, computational mechanics and modeling, microelectronic technology, data mining. Total annual research expenditures: $29.5 million. *Unit head:* Dr. Joe Chow, Acting Dean, 518-276-6374, Fax: 518-276-6261, E-mail: chowj@rpi.edu. *Application contact:* James G. Nondorf, Vice President for Enrollment, 518-276-6216, Fax: 518-276-4072, E-mail: admissions@rpi.edu.

Rice University, Graduate Programs, George R. Brown School of Engineering, Houston, TX 77251-1892. Offers M Ch E, M Stat, MA, MBE, MCAM, MCE, MCS, MEE, MEE, MES, MME, MMS, MS, PhD, MBA/M Stat, MBA/ME, MBA/MEE, MD/PhD. MD/PhD offered jointly with Baylor College of Medicine, The University of Texas Health Science Center at Houston. Part-time programs available. Terminal master's awarded for partial completion of doctoral program. *Degree requirements:* For master's, comprehensive exam (for some programs), thesis (for some programs); for doctorate, comprehensive exam (for some programs), thesis/dissertation. *Entrance requirements:* For master's and doctorate, GRE General Test. Additional exam requirements/recommendations for international students: Required—TOEFL (minimum score 600 paper-based; 250 computer-based). Electronic applications accepted. *Faculty research:* Digital signal processing, tissue engineering, groundwater remediation, computational engineering and high performance computing, nanoscale science and technology.

Robert Morris University, Graduate Studies, School of Engineering, Mathematics and Science, Moon Township, PA 15108-1189. Offers engineering management (MS). Part-time and evening/weekend programs available. *Entrance requirements:* For master's, letters of recommendation. Additional exam requirements/recommendations for international students: Required—TOEFL (minimum score 550 paper-based; 213 computer-based; 79 iBT). Electronic applications accepted. *Expenses:* Contact institution.

Engineering and Applied Sciences—General

Rochester Institute of Technology, Graduate Enrollment Services, College of Applied Science and Technology, Department of Electrical, Computer and Telecommunications Engineering Technology, Rochester, NY 14623-5603. Offers facility management (MS); manufacturing and mechanical systems integration (MS); telecommunications engineering technology (MS). Part-time and evening/weekend programs available. Postbaccalaureate distance learning degree programs offered (no on-campus study). *Students:* 67 full-time (14 women), 55 part-time (8 women); includes 3 Black or African American, non-Hispanic/Latino; 2 Asian, non-Hispanic/Latino; 5 Hispanic/Latino; 1 Two or more races, non-Hispanic/Latino, 60 international. Average age 30. 133 applicants, 57% accepted, 40 enrolled. In 2010, 30 master's awarded. *Degree requirements:* For master's, thesis. *Entrance requirements:* For master's, GRE, minimum GPA of 3.0. Additional exam requirements/recommendations for international students: Required—TOEFL (minimum score 550 paper-based; 213 computer-based; 79 iBT) or IELTS (minimum score 6.5). *Application deadline:* For fall admission, 2/15 priority date for domestic and international students; for winter admission, 11/1 for domestic and international students; for spring admission, 2/1 for domestic and international students. Applications are processed on a rolling basis. *Expenses:* Tuition: Full-time $33,234; part-time $924 per credit hour. Required fees: $219. *Financial support:* In 2010–11, 84 students received support; research assistantships with partial tuition reimbursements available, teaching assistantships with partial tuition reimbursements available, career-related internships or fieldwork and unspecified assistantships available. Support available to part-time students. Financial award application deadline: 2/15; financial award applicants required to submit FAFSA. *Faculty research:* Fiber optic networks, next generation networks, project management. *Unit head:* Michael Eastman, Department Chair, 585-475-7787, Fax: 585-475-2178, E-mail: mgeiee@rit.edu. *Application contact:* Diane Ellison, Assistant Vice President, Graduate Enrollment Services, 585-475-2229, Fax: 585-475-7164, E-mail: gradinfo@rit.edu.

Rochester Institute of Technology, Graduate Enrollment Services, Kate Gleason College of Engineering, Rochester, NY 14623-5603. Offers ME, MS, MSEE, PhD, AC. Part-time and evening/weekend programs available. Postbaccalaureate distance learning degree programs offered (no on-campus study). *Students:* 306 full-time (59 women), 264 part-time (37 women); includes 5 Black or African American, non-Hispanic/Latino; 1 American Indian or Alaska Native, non-Hispanic/Latino; 20 Asian, non-Hispanic/Latino; 12 Hispanic/Latino, 223 international. Average age 28. 887 applicants, 56% accepted, 181 enrolled. In 2010, 236 master's, 3 doctorates, 1 other advanced degree awarded. Terminal master's awarded for partial completion of doctoral program. *Entrance requirements:* For master's, minimum GPA of 3.0. Additional exam requirements/recommendations for international students: Required—TOEFL (minimum score 570 paper-based; 230 computer-based; 88 iBT) or IELTS (minimum score 6.5). *Application deadline:* For fall admission, 2/15 priority date for domestic and international students. Applications are processed on a rolling basis. Application fee: $50. Electronic applications accepted. *Expenses:* Tuition: Full-time $33,234; part-time $924 per credit hour. Required fees: $219. *Financial support:* In 2010–11, 346 students received support; fellowships with partial tuition reimbursements available, research assistantships with partial tuition reimbursements available, teaching assistantships with partial tuition reimbursements available, career-related internships or fieldwork, institutionally sponsored loans, scholarships/grants, tuition waivers (partial), and unspecified assistantships available. Support available to part-time students. Financial award applicants required to submit FAFSA. *Faculty research:* Microprocessors, energy, communication systems. *Unit head:* Dr. Harvey Palmer, Dean, 585-475-2145, Fax: 585-475-6879, E-mail: coe@rit.edu. *Application contact:* Diane Ellison, Assistant Vice President, Graduate Enrollment Services, 585-475-2229, Fax: 585-475-7164, E-mail: gradinfo@rit.edu.

Rose-Hulman Institute of Technology, Faculty of Engineering and Applied Sciences, Terre Haute, IN 47803-3999. Offers M Eng, MS, MD/MS. Part-time and evening/weekend programs available. Postbaccalaureate distance learning degree programs offered (minimal on-campus study). *Faculty:* 88 full-time (20 women), 5 part-time/adjunct (2 women). *Students:* 59 full-time (13 women), 46 part-time (8 women); includes 4 minority (all Asian, non-Hispanic/Latino), 27 international. Average age 25.77 applicants, 90% accepted, 42 enrolled. In 2010, 56 master's awarded. *Degree requirements:* For master's, thesis (for some programs). *Entrance requirements:* For master's, GRE, minimum GPA of 3.0. Additional exam requirements/recommendations for international students: Required—TOEFL (minimum score 580 paper-based; 237 computer-based; 92 iBT). *Application deadline:* For fall admission, 2/1 priority date for domestic students. Applications are processed on a rolling basis. Application fee: $0. *Expenses:* Tuition: Full-time $35,595; part-time $1038 per credit hour. *Financial support:* In 2010–11, 59 students received support; fellowships with full and partial tuition reimbursements available, research assistantships with full and partial tuition reimbursements available, institutionally sponsored loans, scholarships/grants, and tuition waivers (full and partial) available. *Faculty research:* Optical instrument design and prototypes, biomaterials, adsorption and adsorption-based separations, image and speech processing, groundwater, solid and hazardous waste. Total annual research expenditures: $1 million. *Unit head:* Dr. Daniel J. Moore, Associate Dean of the Faculty, 812-877-8110, Fax: 812-877-8061, E-mail: daniel.j.moore@rose-hulman.edu. *Application contact:* Dr. Daniel J. Moore, Associate Dean of the Faculty, 812-877-8110, Fax: 812-877-8061, E-mail: daniel.j.moore@rose-hulman.edu.

Rowan University, Graduate School, College of Engineering, Program in Engineering, Glassboro, NJ 08028-1701. Offers MS. Part-time and evening/weekend programs available. *Students:* 1 full-time (0 women), 4 part-time (0 women); includes 1 Asian, non-Hispanic/Latino. Average age 24. 1 applicant, 100% accepted, 1 enrolled. *Degree requirements:* For master's, thesis (for some programs). *Entrance requirements:* For master's, GRE General Test. Additional exam requirements/recommendations for international students: Required—TOEFL. *Application deadline:* Applications are processed on a rolling basis. Application fee: $65 ($200 for international students). Electronic applications accepted. *Expenses:* Tuition, area resident: Part-time $602 per semester hour. Tuition, nonresident: part-time $602 per semester hour. Required fees: $100 per semester hour. One-time fee: $10 part-time. *Financial support:* Career-related internships or fieldwork, scholarships/grants, health care benefits, and unspecified assistantships available. *Unit head:* Dr. Horacio Sosa, Dean, College of Graduate and Continuing Education, 856-256-4747, Fax: 856-256-5638, E-mail: sosa@rowan.edu. *Application contact:* Karen Haynes, Graduate Coordinator, 856-256-4052, E-mail: haynes@rowan.edu.

Royal Military College of Canada, Division of Graduate Studies and Research, Engineering Division, Kingston, ON K7K 7B4, Canada. Offers M Eng, M Sc, MA Sc, PhD. *Degree requirements:* For master's, thesis; for doctorate, comprehensive exam, thesis/dissertation. *Entrance requirements:* For master's, honours degree with second-class standing; for doctorate, master's degree. Electronic applications accepted.

St. Cloud State University, School of Graduate Studies, College of Science and Engineering, St. Cloud, MN 56301-4498. Offers MA, MEM, MS. *Degree requirements:* For master's, thesis or alternative. *Entrance requirements:* For master's, GRE General Test, minimum GPA of 2.75. Additional exam requirements/recommendations for international students: Required—TOEFL (minimum score 550 paper-based; 213 computer-based). Electronic applications accepted.

St. Mary's University, Graduate School, Department of Engineering, San Antonio, TX 78228-8507. Offers electrical engineering (MS), including electrical engineering, electrical/computer engineering; engineering administration (MS); engineering systems management (MS); industrial engineering (MS), including engineering computer applications, engineering management, industrial engineering, operations research; software engineering (MS); JD/MS. Part-time programs available. *Degree requirements:* For master's, comprehensive exam. *Entrance requirements:* For master's, GRE General Test. Additional exam requirements/recommendations for international students: Required—TOEFL (minimum score 550 paper-based; 213 computer-based). Electronic applications accepted. *Faculty research:* Image processing, control, communication, artificial intelligence, robotics.

San Diego State University, Graduate and Research Affairs, College of Engineering, San Diego, CA 92182. Offers MS, PhD. Part-time and evening/weekend programs available. Terminal master's awarded for partial completion of doctoral program. *Degree requirements:*

For master's, thesis optional; for doctorate, thesis/dissertation. *Entrance requirements:* For master's, GRE General Test; for doctorate, GRE, 3 letters of recommendation. Additional exam requirements/recommendations for international students: Required—TOEFL. Electronic applications accepted.

San Francisco State University, Division of Graduate Studies, College of Science and Engineering, School of Engineering, San Francisco, CA 94132-1722. Offers embedded electrical and computer systems (MS); structural/earthquake engineering (MS). Part-time programs available. *Application deadline:* Applications are processed on a rolling basis. Electronic applications accepted. *Unit head:* Dr. Wenshen Pong, Director, 415-338-7738, E-mail: engineer@sfsu.edu. *Application contact:* Dr. Hamid Shahnasser, Graduate Coordinator, 415-338-2124, E-mail: hamid@sfsu.edu.

San Jose State University, Graduate Studies and Research, Charles W. Davidson College of Engineering, Department of General Engineering, San Jose, CA 95192-0001. Offers MS. Electronic applications accepted.

Santa Clara University, School of Engineering, Santa Clara, CA 95053. Offers MS, PhD, Certificate, Engineer. Part-time and evening/weekend programs available. *Faculty:* 45 full-time (14 women), 59 part-time/adjunct (8 women). *Students:* 332 full-time (103 women), 475 part-time (108 women); includes 242 minority (14 Black or African American, non-Hispanic/Latino; 192 Asian, non-Hispanic/Latino; 24 Hispanic/Latino; 4 Native Hawaiian or other Pacific Islander, non-Hispanic/Latino; 8 Two or more races, non-Hispanic/Latino), 334 international. Average age 29. 737 applicants, 67% accepted, 269 enrolled. In 2010, 223 master's, 9 doctorates, 6 other advanced degrees awarded. *Degree requirements:* For master's, thesis (for some programs); for doctorate, thesis/dissertation; for other advanced degree, thesis. *Entrance requirements:* For master's, GRE (waiver may be available), transcript; for doctorate, GRE, master's degree or equivalent; for other advanced degree, master's degree, published paper. Additional exam requirements/recommendations for international students: Required—TOEFL (minimum score 550 paper-based; 213 computer-based; 79 iBT). *Application deadline:* For fall admission, 8/1 for domestic students, 7/15 for international students; for winter admission, 10/28 for domestic students, 9/23 for international students; for spring admission, 2/25 for domestic students, 1/21 for international students. Applications are processed on a rolling basis. Application fee: $60. Electronic applications accepted. *Expenses:* Contact institution. *Financial support:* Research assistantships, teaching assistantships available. Financial award application deadline: 3/2; financial award applicants required to submit FAFSA. *Faculty research:* Development of small satellite design, tests and operations technology, Thermal and Electrical Nanoscale Transport (TENT). Total annual research expenditures: $1.9 million. *Unit head:* Dr. Alex Zecevic, Associate Dean for Graduate Studies, 408-554-2394, E-mail: azecevic@scu.edu. *Application contact:* Stacey Tinker, Director of Enrollment Management, 408-554-4748, Fax: 408-554-4323, E-mail: stinker@scu.edu.

Seattle University, College of Science and Engineering, Seattle, WA 98122-1090. Offers MSE. Part-time and evening/weekend programs available. *Degree requirements:* For master's, thesis. *Entrance requirements:* For master's, GRE General Test, 2 years of related work experience. *Expenses:* Contact institution.

Simon Fraser University, Graduate Studies, Faculty of Applied Sciences, School of Engineering Science, Burnaby, BC V5A 1S6, Canada. Offers M Eng, MA Sc, PhD. *Degree requirements:* For master's, thesis (for some programs); for doctorate, thesis/dissertation, qualifying exam. *Entrance requirements:* For master's, GRE, minimum GPA of 3.0; for doctorate, GRE, minimum GPA of 3.5. Additional exam requirements/recommendations for international students: Required—TOEFL or IELTS. *Faculty research:* Signal processing, electronics, communications, systems and control.

South Dakota School of Mines and Technology, Graduate Division, College of Engineering, Rapid City, SD 57701-3995. Offers MS, PhD. Part-time programs available. *Degree requirements:* For doctorate, thesis/dissertation. *Entrance requirements:* For doctorate, minimum graduate GPA of 3.0. Additional exam requirements/recommendations for international students: Required—TOEFL, TWE. Electronic applications accepted.

South Dakota State University, Graduate School, College of Engineering, Brookings, SD 57007. Offers MS, PhD. Part-time programs available. *Degree requirements:* For master's, thesis, oral exam; for doctorate, thesis/dissertation, preliminary oral and written exams. *Entrance requirements:* Additional exam requirements/recommendations for international students: Required—TOEFL. *Faculty research:* Process control and management, ground source heat pumps, water quality, heat transfer, power systems.

Southern Illinois University Carbondale, Graduate School, College of Engineering, Carbondale, IL 62901-4701. Offers ME, MS, PhD. *Degree requirements:* For master's, comprehensive exam; for doctorate, thesis/dissertation. *Entrance requirements:* For master's, minimum GPA of 2.7; for doctorate, GRE General Test, minimum GPA of 3.5. Additional exam requirements/recommendations for international students: Required—TOEFL. *Faculty research:* Electrical systems, all facets of fossil energy, mechanics.

Southern Illinois University Edwardsville, Graduate School, School of Engineering, Edwardsville, IL 62026-0001. Offers MS. Part-time programs available. *Faculty:* 43 full-time (3 women). *Students:* 103 full-time (22 women), 127 part-time (25 women); includes 20 minority (9 Black or African American, non-Hispanic/Latino; 1 American Indian or Alaska Native, non-Hispanic/Latino; 7 Asian, non-Hispanic/Latino; 1 Hispanic/Latino; 2 Two or more races, non-Hispanic/Latino), 119 international. Average age 26. 375 applicants, 65% accepted. In 2010, 88 master's awarded. *Degree requirements:* For master's, thesis (for some programs), research paper, final exam. *Entrance requirements:* Additional exam requirements/recommendations for international students: Required—TOEFL (minimum score 550 paper-based; 213 computer-based; 79 iBT), IELTS (minimum score 6.5). *Application deadline:* For fall admission, 7/22 for domestic students, 6/1 for international students; for spring admission, 12/9 for domestic students, 10/1 for international students. Applications are processed on a rolling basis. Application fee: $30. Electronic applications accepted. *Expenses:* Tuition, state resident: full-time $6012; part-time $1503 per semester. Tuition, nonresident: full-time $15,030; part-time $3758 per semester. Required fees: $1711; $675 per semester. *Financial support:* In 2010–11, 4 fellowships with full tuition reimbursements (averaging $8,370 per year), 34 research assistantships with full tuition reimbursements (averaging $8,064 per year), 77 teaching assistantships with full tuition reimbursements (averaging $8,064 per year) were awarded; career-related internships or fieldwork, Federal Work-Study, institutionally sponsored loans, scholarships/grants, traineeships, and unspecified assistantships also available. Support available to part-time students. Financial award application deadline: 3/1; financial award applicants required to submit FAFSA. *Unit head:* Dr. Hasan Sevim, Dean, 618-650-2541, E-mail: hsevim@siue.edu. *Application contact:* Michelle Robinson, Coordinator of Graduate Recruitment, 618-650-2811, Fax: 618-650-3523, E-mail: michero@siue.edu.

Southern Methodist University, Bobby B. Lyle School of Engineering, Dallas, TX 75275. Offers MS, MS Cp E, MSEE, MSEM, MSIEM, MSME, DE, PhD. Part-time and evening/weekend programs available. Postbaccalaureate distance learning degree programs offered (no on-campus study). *Faculty:* 55 full-time (10 women), 61 part-time/adjunct (5 women). *Students:* 203 full-time (52 women), 669 part-time (144 women); includes 208 minority (57 Black or African American, non-Hispanic/Latino; 4 American Indian or Alaska Native, non-Hispanic/Latino; 76 Asian, non-Hispanic/Latino; 68 Hispanic/Latino; 2 Native Hawaiian or other Pacific Islander, non-Hispanic/Latino; 1 Two or more races, non-Hispanic/Latino), 216 international. Average age 32. 672 applicants, 54% accepted, 226 enrolled. In 2010, 315 master's, 16 doctorates awarded. Terminal master's awarded for partial completion of doctoral program. *Degree requirements:* For master's, thesis optional; for doctorate, thesis/dissertation, oral and written qualifying exams. *Entrance requirements:* For master's, GRE General Test, minimum GPA of 3.0 in last 2 years; bachelor's degree in engineering, mathematics, or sciences; for doctorate, bachelor's degree in related field. Additional exam requirements/

recommendations for international students: Required—TOEFL (minimum score 550 paper-based; 213 computer-based). *Application deadline:* For fall admission, 7/1 for domestic students, 5/15 for international students; for spring admission, 11/15 for domestic students, 9/1 for international students. Applications are processed on a rolling basis. Application fee: $75. *Expenses:* Contact institution. *Financial support:* In 2010–11, 72 students received support, including 35 research assistantships with full tuition reimbursements available (averaging $16,800 per year), 33 teaching assistantships with full tuition reimbursements available (averaging $12,600 per year); fellowships, career-related internships or fieldwork, Federal Work-Study, institutionally sponsored loans, scholarships/grants, and tuition waivers (full and partial) also available. Financial award applicants required to submit FAFSA. *Faculty research:* Mobile and fault-tolerant computing, manufacturing systems, telecommunications, solid state devices and materials, fluid and thermal sciences. Total annual research expenditures: $3 million. *Unit head:* Dr. Geoffrey Orsak, Dean, 214-768-3050, Fax: 214-768-3845. *Application contact:* Marc Valerin, Director of Graduate and Executive Admissions, 214-768-3042, E-mail: valerin@engr.smu.edu.

Southern Polytechnic State University, Division of Engineering, Marietta, GA 30060-2896. Offers systems engineering (MS, Advanced Certificate, Graduate Certificate). Part-time and evening/weekend programs available. *Faculty:* 3 full-time (1 woman), 4 part-time/adjunct (3 women). *Students:* 8 full-time (0 women), 42 part-time (9 women); includes 12 Black or African American, non-Hispanic/Latino; 2 Asian, non-Hispanic/Latino; 3 Hispanic/Latino, 2 international. Average age 39. 15 applicants, 93% accepted, 11 enrolled. In 2010, 12 master's awarded. *Entrance requirements:* Additional exam requirements/recommendations for international students: Required—TOEFL (minimum score 550 paper-based; 213 computer-based; 79 iBT), IELTS (minimum score 6.5). *Application deadline:* For fall admission, 7/1 priority date for domestic students, 5/1 priority date for international students; for spring admission, 11/1 priority date for domestic students, 9/1 priority date for international students. Applications are processed on a rolling basis. Application fee: $20. Electronic applications accepted. *Expenses:* Tuition, state resident: full-time $3690; part-time $205 per semester hour. Tuition, nonresident: full-time $13,428; part-time $746 per semester hour. Required fees: $598 per semester. *Unit head:* Dr. Tom Currin, Associate Dean, 678-915-7482, Fax: 678-915-5527, E-mail: tcurrin@spsu.edu. *Application contact:* Nikki Palamiotis, Director of Graduate Studies, 678-915-4276, Fax: 678-915-7292, E-mail: npalamio@spsu.edu.

Southern Polytechnic State University, School of Engineering Technology and Management, Marietta, GA 30060-2896. Offers MBA, MS, MSA, Graduate Certificate, Graduate Transition Certificate. Part-time and evening/weekend programs available. Postbaccalaureate distance learning degree programs offered. *Faculty:* 18 full-time (4 women), 12 part-time/adjunct (6 women). *Students:* 117 full-time (59 women), 188 part-time (84 women); includes 91 Black or African American, non-Hispanic/Latino; 26 Asian, non-Hispanic/Latino; 9 Hispanic/Latino; 2 Two or more races, non-Hispanic/Latino, 62 international. Average age 34. 173 applicants, 93% accepted, 119 enrolled. In 2010, 91 master's, 1 other advanced degree awarded. *Entrance requirements:* Additional exam requirements/recommendations for international students: Required—TOEFL (minimum score 550 paper-based; 213 computer-based; 79 iBT), IELTS (minimum score 6.5). *Application deadline:* For fall admission, 7/1 priority date for domestic students, 5/1 priority date for international students; for spring admission, 11/1 priority date for domestic students, 9/1 priority date for international students. Applications are processed on a rolling basis. Application fee: $20. Electronic applications accepted. *Expenses:* Tuition, state resident: full-time $3690; part-time $205 per semester hour. Tuition, nonresident: full-time $13,428; part-time $746 per semester hour. Required fees: $598 per semester. *Financial support:* Research assistantships with tuition reimbursements, teaching assistantships with tuition reimbursements, career-related internships or fieldwork, scholarships/grants, and unspecified assistantships available. Support available to part-time students. Financial award application deadline: 5/1; financial award applicants required to submit FAFSA. *Faculty research:* Ethics, virtual reality, sustainability, management of technology, quality management, capacity planning, human-computer interaction/interface, enterprise integration planning, economic impact of educational institutions, behavioral accounting, accounting ethics, taxation, information security, visualizational simulation, human-computer interaction, analog and digital communications, computer networking, analog and low power electronics design, control systems and digital signal processing. *Unit head:* Dr. Jeff Ray, Dean, 678-915-7205, Fax: 678-915-7134, E-mail: jray@spsu.edu. *Application contact:* Nikki Palamiotis, Director of Graduate Studies, 678-915-4276, Fax: 678-915-7292, E-mail: npalamio@spsu.edu.

Southern University and Agricultural and Mechanical College, Graduate School, College of Engineering, Baton Rouge, LA 70813. Offers ME. *Degree requirements:* For master's, thesis. *Entrance requirements:* For master's, GRE General Test. Additional exam requirements/recommendations for international students: Required—TOEFL (minimum score 525 paper-based; 193 computer-based).

Stanford University, School of Engineering, Stanford, CA 94305-9991. Offers MS, PhD, Eng. *Degree requirements:* For doctorate, thesis/dissertation; for Eng, thesis. *Entrance requirements:* For master's, doctorate, and Eng, GRE General Test. Additional exam requirements/recommendations for international students: Required—TOEFL. Electronic applications accepted. *Expenses:* Contact institution.

State University of New York at Binghamton, Graduate School, Thomas J. Watson School of Engineering and Applied Science, Binghamton, NY 13902-6000. Offers M Eng, MS, MSAT, PhD. Part-time and evening/weekend programs available. *Faculty:* 74 full-time (11 women), 13 part-time/adjunct (3 women). *Students:* 388 full-time (84 women), 392 part-time (60 women); includes 11 Black or African American, non-Hispanic/Latino; 2 American Indian or Alaska Native, non-Hispanic/Latino; 46 Asian, non-Hispanic/Latino; 9 Hispanic/Latino, 488 international. Average age 27. 883 applicants, 54% accepted, 210 enrolled. In 2010, 205 master's, 33 doctorates awarded. Terminal master's awarded for partial completion of doctoral program. *Degree requirements:* For doctorate, thesis/dissertation. *Entrance requirements:* For master's and doctorate, GRE General Test, GRE Subject Test. Additional exam requirements/recommendations for international students: Required—TOEFL (minimum score 550 paper-based; 213 computer-based; 80 iBT). *Application deadline:* Applications are processed on a rolling basis. Application fee: $60. Electronic applications accepted. *Financial support:* In 2010–11, 272 students received support, including 6 fellowships with full tuition reimbursements available (averaging $16,500 per year), 148 research assistantships with full tuition reimbursements available (averaging $16,500 per year), 84 teaching assistantships with full tuition reimbursements available (averaging $16,500 per year); career-related internships or fieldwork, Federal Work-Study, institutionally sponsored loans, scholarships/grants, health care benefits, tuition waivers (full and partial), and unspecified assistantships also available. Financial award application deadline: 2/15; financial award applicants required to submit FAFSA. *Unit head:* Dr. Hari Srihari, Dean, 607-777-2871, E-mail: hsrihari@binghamton.edu. *Application contact:* Catherine Smith, Recruiting and Admissions Coordinator, 607-777-2151, Fax: 607-777-2501, E-mail: cmsmith@binghamton.edu.

State University of New York Institute of Technology, School of Information Systems and Engineering Technology, Utica, NY 13504-3050. Offers advanced technology (MS); computer and information science (MS); telecommunications (MS). Part-time and evening/weekend programs available. *Entrance requirements:* For master's, GRE General Test, minimum GPA of 3.0. Additional exam requirements/recommendations for international students: Required—TOEFL (minimum score 550 paper-based; 213 computer-based). *Faculty research:* Systems security, operating systems, traffic management, nanotechnology, rehabilitation technology.

Stevens Institute of Technology, Graduate School, Charles V. Schaefer Jr. School of Engineering, Hoboken, NJ 07030. Offers M Eng, MS, PhD, Certificate, Engr. Part-time and evening/weekend programs available. Postbaccalaureate distance learning degree programs offered. *Students:* 940 full-time (237 women), 499 part-time (88 women); includes 24 Black or African American, non-Hispanic/Latino; 150 Asian, non-Hispanic/Latino; 54 Hispanic/Latino, 722 international. Average age 27. 664 applicants, 76% accepted.Terminal master's awarded for partial completion of doctoral program. *Degree requirements:* For doctorate, thesis/dissertation. *Entrance requirements:* Additional exam requirements/recommendations for international students: Required—TOEFL. *Application deadline:* Applications are processed on a rolling basis. Application fee: $50. Electronic applications accepted. *Financial support:* Fellowships, research assistantships, teaching assistantships, career-related internships or fieldwork, Federal Work-Study, institutionally sponsored loans, tuition waivers (partial), and unspecified assistantships available. *Unit head:* Dr. George Korfiatis, Dean, 201-216-5263. *Application contact:* Graduate Admissions, 800-496-4935, Fax: 201-216-8044, E-mail: gradadmissions@stevens.edu.

Stony Brook University, State University of New York, Graduate School, College of Engineering and Applied Sciences, Stony Brook, NY 11794. Offers MS, PhD, Advanced Certificate, Certificate. Part-time and evening/weekend programs available. *Faculty:* 135 full-time (21 women), 33 part-time/adjunct (5 women). *Students:* 982 full-time (269 women), 193 part-time (67 women); includes 19 Black or African American, non-Hispanic/Latino; 93 Asian, non-Hispanic/Latino; 22 Hispanic/Latino; 2 Two or more races, non-Hispanic/Latino, 844 international. 3,541 applicants, 40% accepted, 417 enrolled. In 2010, 332 master's, 57 doctorates awarded. *Degree requirements:* For doctorate, comprehensive exam, thesis/dissertation. *Entrance requirements:* For doctorate, GRE General Test. Additional exam requirements/recommendations for international students: Required—TOEFL. *Application deadline:* For fall admission, 1/15 for domestic students. Application fee: $100. *Expenses:* Tuition, state resident: full-time $8370; part-time $349 per credit. Tuition, nonresident: full-time $13,780; part-time $574 per credit. Required fees: $994. *Financial support:* In 2010–11, 263 research assistantships, 171 teaching assistantships were awarded; fellowships, career-related internships or fieldwork also available. Total annual research expenditures: $29.2 million. *Unit head:* Dr. Yacov Shamash, Dean, 631-632-8380. *Application contact:* Barbara Byrne, Assistant Dean for Finance and Budget; Admissions and Records, 631-632-4723, Fax: 631-632-7039, E-mail: barbara.byrne@stonybrook.edu.

Syracuse University, L. C. Smith College of Engineering and Computer Science, Syracuse, NY 13244. Offers MS, PhD, CAS, CE, EE. Part-time and evening/weekend programs available. *Faculty:* 72 full-time (7 women), 22 part-time/adjunct (1 woman). *Students:* 669 full-time (180 women), 153 part-time (24 women); includes 42 minority (8 Black or African American, non-Hispanic/Latino; 27 Asian, non-Hispanic/Latino; 7 Hispanic/Latino), 611 international. Average age 26. 1,815 applicants, 44% accepted, 270 enrolled. In 2010, 218 master's, 27 doctorates awarded. *Degree requirements:* For doctorate, thesis/dissertation. *Entrance requirements:* For master's and doctorate, GRE General Test. Additional exam requirements/recommendations for international students: Required—TOEFL (minimum score 100 iBT). *Application deadline:* For fall admission, 7/1 priority date for domestic students, 6/1 priority date for international students. Applications are processed on a rolling basis. Application fee: $75. Electronic applications accepted. *Expenses:* Tuition: Part-time $1162 per credit. *Financial support:* Fellowships with full tuition reimbursements, research assistantships with full and partial tuition reimbursements, teaching assistantships with full and partial tuition reimbursements, scholarships/grants and tuition waivers (partial) available. Financial award application deadline: 1/1; financial award applicants required to submit FAFSA. *Faculty research:* Environmental systems, information assurance, biomechanics, solid mechanics and materials, software engineering. *Unit head:* Dr. Laura J. Steinberg, Dean, 315-443-2545, E-mail: ljs@syr.edu. *Application contact:* Kathleen Joyce, Assistant Dean, 314-443-2219, E-mail: topgrads@syr.edu.

Temple University, College of Engineering, Philadelphia, PA 19122-6096. Offers MS, MSE, PhD. Part-time programs available. *Faculty:* 38 full-time (5 women). *Students:* 80 full-time (23 women), 36 part-time (7 women); includes 3 Black or African American, non-Hispanic/Latino; 2 American Indian or Alaska Native, non-Hispanic/Latino; 11 Asian, non-Hispanic/Latino; 1 Hispanic/Latino, 68 international. Average age 29. 176 applicants, 49% accepted, 30 enrolled. In 2010, 46 master's, 2 doctorates awarded. *Degree requirements:* For master's, thesis optional; for doctorate, comprehensive exam, thesis/dissertation, 2 published papers. *Entrance requirements:* For master's, GRE General Test, minimum undergraduate GPA of 3.0; for doctorate, GRE General Test, minimum graduate GPA of 3.5, MS. Additional exam requirements/recommendations for international students: Required—TOEFL (minimum score 550 paper-based; 213 computer-based; 79 iBT). *Application deadline:* For fall admission, 7/1 priority date for domestic students, 12/15 for international students; for spring admission, 11/1 priority date for domestic students, 8/1 for international students. Applications are processed on a rolling basis. Application fee: $50. Electronic applications accepted. *Financial support:* Fellowships with full tuition reimbursements, research assistantships with full tuition reimbursements, teaching assistantships with full tuition reimbursements, career-related internships or fieldwork, Federal Work-Study, and institutionally sponsored loans available. Financial award application deadline: 1/15. *Faculty research:* Computer engineering, digital systems, bioengineering, transportation, materials. *Unit head:* Dr. Keyanoush Sadeghipour, Dean, 215-204-5285, Fax: 215-204-6936, E-mail: keya@temple.edu. *Application contact:* Tara Schumacher, Coordinator of Outreach, 215-204-6575, Fax: 215-204-8781, E-mail: tara.schumacher@temple.edu.

Tennessee State University, The School of Graduate Studies and Research, College of Engineering, Technology, and Computer Science, Nashville, TN 37209-1561. Offers computer and information systems engineering (MS, PhD); engineering (ME). Part-time and evening/weekend programs available. *Degree requirements:* For master's, project; for doctorate, comprehensive exam, thesis/dissertation. *Entrance requirements:* For doctorate, minimum GPA of 3.3. *Faculty research:* Robotics, intelligent systems, human-computer interaction software systems, biomedical engineering, signal/image processing, probabilistic design, intelligent manufacturing, cooperative mobile robots, condition based maintenance, sensor fusion.

Tennessee Technological University, Graduate School, College of Engineering, Cookeville, TN 38505. Offers MS, PhD. Part-time programs available. *Faculty:* 76 full-time (2 women). *Students:* 87 full-time (9 women), 72 part-time (9 women); includes 19 Black or African American, non-Hispanic/Latino; 59 Asian, non-Hispanic/Latino; 3 Hispanic/Latino. Average age 28. 279 applicants, 52% accepted, 38 enrolled. In 2010, 38 master's, 13 doctorates awarded. *Degree requirements:* For master's, comprehensive exam, thesis; for doctorate, comprehensive exam, thesis/dissertation. *Entrance requirements:* For master's, GRE General Test; for doctorate, GRE, minimum GPA of 3.5. Additional exam requirements/recommendations for international students: Required—TOEFL (minimum score 550 paper-based; 79 iBT), IELTS (minimum score 5.5). *Application deadline:* For fall admission, 8/1 for domestic students, 5/1 for international students; for spring admission, 12/1 for domestic students, 10/1 for international students. Application fee: $25 ($30 for international students). Electronic applications accepted. *Expenses:* Tuition, state resident: full-time $7934; part-time $388 per credit hour. Tuition, nonresident: full-time $19,758; part-time $962 per credit hour. *Financial support:* In 2010–11, 3 fellowships (averaging $8,000 per year), 71 research assistantships (averaging $9,293 per year), 41 teaching assistantships (averaging $7,223 per year) were awarded; career-related internships or fieldwork also available. Support available to part-time students. Financial award application deadline: 4/1. *Unit head:* Dr. David Huddleston, Interim Dean. *Application contact:* Shelia K. Kendrick, Coordinator of Graduate Admissions, 931-372-3808, Fax: 931-372-3497, E-mail: skendrick@tntech.edu.

Texas A&M University, College of Engineering, College Station, TX 77843. Offers M En, M Eng, MCS, MID, MS, D Eng, PhD. Part-time programs available. Postbaccalaureate distance learning degree programs offered (minimal on-campus study). *Faculty:* 373. *Students:* 2,591 full-time (528 women), 310 part-time (50 women); includes 52 Black or African American, non-Hispanic/Latino; 5 American Indian or Alaska Native, non-Hispanic/Latino; 116 Asian, non-Hispanic/Latino; 133 Hispanic/Latino, 1,891 international. In 2010, 600 master's, 155 doctorates awarded. Terminal master's awarded for partial completion of doctoral program. *Entrance requirements:* For master's and doctorate, GRE General Test. Additional exam requirements/recommendations for international students: Required—TOEFL. Application fee: $50 ($75 for international students). Electronic applications accepted. *Financial support:* Fellowships, research assistantships, teaching assistantships, career-related internships or

Engineering and Applied Sciences—General

Texas A&M University (continued)
fieldwork, institutionally sponsored loans, scholarships/grants, and unspecified assistantships available. Financial award applicants required to submit FAFSA. *Unit head:* Dr. G. Kemble Bennett, Dean, 979-845-7203, Fax: 979-845-8986, E-mail: kem-bennett@tamu.edu. *Application contact:* Dr. G. Kemble Bennett, Dean, 979-845-7203, Fax: 979-845-8986, E-mail: kem-bennett@tamu.edu.

Texas A&M University–Kingsville, College of Graduate Studies, College of Engineering, Kingsville, TX 78363. Offers ME, MS, PhD. Part-time and evening/weekend programs available. *Degree requirements:* For master's, comprehensive exam. *Entrance requirements:* For master's, GRE General Test. Additional exam requirements/recommendations for international students: Required—TOEFL.

Texas Tech University, Graduate School, Edward E. Whitacre Jr. College of Engineering, Lubbock, TX 79409. Offers M Engr, MENVEGR, MS, MS Ch E, MSCE, MSEE, MSIE, MSME, MSMSE, MSPE, MSSEM, PhD. Part-time programs available. *Faculty:* 107 full-time (18 women), 6 part-time/adjunct (1 woman). *Students:* 585 full-time (111 women), 182 part-time (35 women); includes 8 Black or African American, non-Hispanic/Latino; 6 Asian, non-Hispanic/Latino; 25 Hispanic/Latino; 3 Two or more races, non-Hispanic/Latino, 510 international. Average age 26. 1,849 applicants, 35% accepted, 207 enrolled. In 2010, 213 master's, 51 doctorates awarded. *Degree requirements:* For master's, thesis (for some programs); for doctorate, thesis/dissertation. *Entrance requirements:* For master's and doctorate, GRE General Test, minimum GPA of 3.0. Additional exam requirements/recommendations for international students: Required—TOEFL (minimum score 550 paper-based; 213 computer-based; 79 iBT). *Application deadline:* For fall admission, 6/1 priority date for domestic students, 1/15 priority date for international students; for spring admission, 9/1 priority date for domestic students, 6/15 priority date for international students. Applications are processed on a rolling basis. Application fee: $50 ($75 for international students). Electronic applications accepted. *Expenses:* Contact institution. *Financial support:* In 2010–11, 414 students received support, including 170 research assistantships with partial tuition reimbursements available (averaging $4,118 per year), 34 teaching assistantships with partial tuition reimbursements available (averaging $3,836 per year); career-related internships or fieldwork, Federal Work-Study, institutionally sponsored loans, scholarships/grants, traineeships, health care benefits, and unspecified assistantships also available. Support available to part-time students. Financial award application deadline: 4/15; financial award applicants required to submit FAFSA. *Faculty research:* Pulsed power and power electronics; water resources; energy (wind, petroleum, etc.); nanophotonics and nanotechnology. Total annual research expenditures: $23.3 million. *Unit head:* Dr. Albert Sacco, Dean, 806-742-3451, Fax: 806-742-3493, E-mail: al.sacco-jr@ttu.edu. *Application contact:* Dr. John E. Kobza, Senior Associate Dean, 806-742-3451, Fax: 806-742-3493, E-mail: john.kobza@ttu.edu.

Trine University, Allen School of Engineering and Technology, Angola, IN 46703-1764. Offers civil engineering (ME); mechanical engineering (ME). Part-time and evening/weekend programs available. *Degree requirements:* For master's, comprehensive exam, thesis. *Faculty research:* CAD, computer aided MFG, computer numerical control, parametric modeling, megatronics.

Tufts University, School of Engineering, Medford, MA 02155. Offers ME, MS, MSEM, PhD. Part-time programs available. Terminal master's awarded for partial completion of doctoral program. *Degree requirements:* For master's, thesis (for some programs); for doctorate, thesis/dissertation. *Entrance requirements:* For master's and doctorate, GRE General Test. Additional exam requirements/recommendations for international students: Required—TOEFL (minimum score 550 paper-based; 213 computer-based; 80 iBT). Electronic applications accepted. *Expenses:* Tuition: Full-time $39,624; part-time $3962 per course. Required fees: $40 per year. Full-time tuition and fees vary according to degree level, program and student level. Part-time tuition and fees vary according to course load.

Tuskegee University, Graduate Programs, College of Engineering, Architecture and Physical Sciences, Tuskegee, AL 36088. Offers MSEE, MSME, PhD. *Faculty:* 19 full-time (0 women). *Students:* 60 full-time (19 women), 13 part-time (4 women); includes 37 Black or African American, non-Hispanic/Latino, 31 international. Average age 28. 104 applicants, 59% accepted. In 2010, 14 master's awarded. *Degree requirements:* For master's, thesis or alternative. *Entrance requirements:* For master's, GRE General Test, GRE Subject Test. Additional exam requirements/recommendations for international students: Required—TOEFL (minimum score 500 paper-based; 69 computer-based). *Application deadline:* For fall admission, 7/15 for domestic students. Applications are processed on a rolling basis. Application fee: $25 ($35 for international students). *Expenses:* Tuition: Full-time $16,100; part-time $665 per credit hour. Required fees: $650. *Financial support:* Fellowships, research assistantships, teaching assistantships, career-related internships or fieldwork, Federal Work-Study, and institutionally sponsored loans available. Support available to part-time students. Financial award application deadline: 4/15. *Unit head:* Dr. Legand L. Burge, Acting Dean, 334-727-8356. *Application contact:* Dr. Robert L. Laney, Vice President/Director of Admissions and Enrollment Management, 334-727-8580, Fax: 334-727-5750, E-mail: planey@tuskegee.edu.

Union Graduate College, School of Engineering and Computer Science, Schenectady, NY 12308-3107. Offers computer science (MS); electrical engineering (MS); engineering and management systems (MS); mechanical engineering (MS). Part-time and evening/weekend programs available. *Faculty:* 3 full-time (0 women), 9 part-time/adjunct (0 women). *Students:* 15 full-time (1 woman), 89 part-time (13 women); includes 1 Black or African American, non-Hispanic/Latino; 1 American Indian or Alaska Native, non-Hispanic/Latino; 7 Asian, non-Hispanic/Latino; 6 Hispanic/Latino, 2 international. Average age 27. 52 applicants, 79% accepted, 39 enrolled. In 2010, 24 master's awarded. *Degree requirements:* For master's, capstone course. *Entrance requirements:* For master's, minimum GPA of 3.0, letters of recommendation. Additional exam requirements/recommendations for international students: Required—TOEFL (minimum score 550 paper-based; 213 computer-based). *Application deadline:* Applications are processed on a rolling basis. Application fee: $60. Electronic applications accepted. *Expenses:* Contact institution. *Financial support:* Research assistantships, Federal Work-Study, scholarships/grants, health care benefits, and tuition waivers (full and partial) available. Support available to part-time students. Financial award applicants required to submit FAFSA. *Unit head:* Robert Kozik, Dean, 515-631-9881, Fax: 518-631-9902, E-mail: kozikr@union.edu. *Application contact:* Diane Trzaskos, Coordinator, Admissions, 518-631-9837, Fax: 518-631-9901, E-mail: trzaskod@uniongraduatecollege.edu.

Universidad de las Américas–Puebla, Division of Graduate Studies, School of Engineering, Puebla, Mexico. Offers M Adm, MS, PhD. Part-time and evening/weekend programs available. *Degree requirements:* For master's, one foreign language, thesis. *Faculty research:* Artificial intelligence, food technology, construction, telecommunications, computers in education, operations research.

Université de Moncton, Faculty of Engineering, Moncton, NB E1A 3E9, Canada. Offers civil engineering (M Sc A); electrical engineering (M Sc A); industrial engineering (M Sc A); mechanical engineering (M Sc A). *Degree requirements:* For master's, thesis, proficiency in French. *Faculty research:* Structures, energy, composite materials, quality control, geo-environment, telecommunications, instrumentation, analog and digital electronics.

Université de Sherbrooke, Faculty of Engineering, Sherbrooke, QC J1K 2R1, Canada. Offers M Eng, M Env, M Sc A, PhD, Diploma. Part-time programs available. *Degree requirements:* For master's, one foreign language, thesis; for doctorate, comprehensive exam, thesis/dissertation. *Entrance requirements:* For master's, bachelor's degree in engineering or equivalent. Electronic applications accepted.

Université du Québec à Chicoutimi, Graduate Programs, Program in Engineering, Chicoutimi, QC G7H 2B1, Canada. Offers M Sc A, PhD. Part-time programs available. *Degree requirements:* For master's, thesis; for doctorate, thesis/dissertation. *Entrance requirements:* For master's, appropriate bachelor's degree, proficiency in French.

Université du Québec à Rimouski, Graduate Programs, Program in Engineering, Rimouski, QC G5L 3A1, Canada. Offers M Sc A. Program offered jointly with Université du Québec à Chicoutimi.

Université du Québec, École de technologie supérieure, Graduate Programs, Montréal, QC H3C 1K3, Canada. Offers M Eng, PhD, Diploma. Postbaccalaureate distance learning degree programs offered (minimal on-campus study). *Entrance requirements:* For master's and Diploma, appropriate bachelor's degree, proficiency in French; for doctorate, appropriate master's degree, proficiency in French.

Université du Québec en Abitibi-Témiscamingue, Graduate Programs, Program in Engineering, Rouyn-Noranda, QC J9X 5E4, Canada. Offers engineering (ME); mineral engineering (ME); mining engineering (DESS).

Université Laval, Faculty of Sciences and Engineering, Québec, QC G1K 7P4, Canada. Offers M Sc, PhD, Diploma. Part-time programs available. *Degree requirements:* For doctorate, thesis/dissertation. Electronic applications accepted.

University at Buffalo, the State University of New York, Graduate School, School of Engineering and Applied Sciences, Buffalo, NY 14260. Offers ME, MS, PhD. Part-time and evening/weekend programs available. Postbaccalaureate distance learning degree programs offered (minimal on-campus study). *Faculty:* 147 full-time (18 women), 25 part-time/adjunct (2 women). *Students:* 1,132 full-time (224 women), 148 part-time (22 women); includes 13 Black or African American, non-Hispanic/Latino; 1 American Indian or Alaska Native, non-Hispanic/Latino; 30 Asian, non-Hispanic/Latino; 12 Hispanic/Latino, 936 international. Average age 26. 5,084 applicants, 29% accepted, 397 enrolled. In 2010, 298 master's, 42 doctorates awarded. Terminal master's awarded for partial completion of doctoral program. *Degree requirements:* For doctorate, thesis/dissertation. *Entrance requirements:* For master's and doctorate, GRE General Test. Additional exam requirements/recommendations for international students: Required—TOEFL (minimum score 550 paper-based; 217 computer-based; 79 iBT). *Application deadline:* Applications are processed on a rolling basis. Application fee: $50. Electronic applications accepted. *Financial support:* In 2010–11, 42 fellowships with full tuition reimbursements (averaging $28,908 per year), 210 research assistantships with full and partial tuition reimbursements (averaging $21,300 per year), 168 teaching assistantships with full tuition reimbursements (averaging $20,900 per year) were awarded; career-related internships or fieldwork, Federal Work-Study, institutionally sponsored loans, scholarships/grants, tuition waivers (full and partial), and unspecified assistantships also available. Support available to part-time students. Financial award applicants required to submit FAFSA. *Faculty research:* Bioengineering, infrastructure and environmental engineering, electronic and photonic materials, simulation and visualization, information technology and computing. Total annual research expenditures: $61.3 million. *Unit head:* Dr. Harvey G. Stenger, Dean, 716-645-2771, Fax: 716-645-2495, E-mail: dean@buffalo.edu. *Application contact:* Dr. Rajan Batta, Associate Dean for Graduate Education, 716-645-2772, Fax: 716-645-2495, E-mail: batta@buffalo.edu.

See Display on next page and Close-Up on page 89.

The University of Akron, Graduate School, College of Engineering, Akron, OH 44325. Offers MS, PhD, MD/PhD. Part-time and evening/weekend programs available. *Faculty:* 84 full-time (13 women), 16 part-time/adjunct (1 woman). *Students:* 270 full-time (62 women), 85 part-time (17 women); includes 16 minority (2 Black or African American, non-Hispanic/Latino; 11 Asian, non-Hispanic/Latino; 1 Hispanic/Latino; 1 Native Hawaiian or other Pacific Islander, non-Hispanic/Latino; 1 Two or more races, non-Hispanic/Latino), 207 international. Average age 27. 427 applicants, 58% accepted, 99 enrolled. In 2010, 56 master's, 18 doctorates awarded. Terminal master's awarded for partial completion of doctoral program. *Degree requirements:* For master's, thesis optional; for doctorate, one foreign language, thesis/dissertation, candidacy exam, qualifying exam. *Entrance requirements:* For master's, GRE, minimum GPA of 2.75, letters of recommendation, statement of purpose, resume; for doctorate, GRE, minimum GPA of 3.0 with bachelor's degree, 3.5 with master's degree; letters of recommendation; statement of purpose, resume. Additional exam requirements/recommendations for international students: Required—TOEFL (minimum score 550 paper-based; 213 computer-based; 79 iBT). *Application deadline:* Applications are processed on a rolling basis. Application fee: $30 ($40 for international students). Electronic applications accepted. *Expenses:* Tuition, state resident: full-time $6800; part-time $378 per credit hour. Tuition, nonresident: full-time $11,644; part-time $647 per credit hour. Required fees: $1265. One-time fee: $30 full-time. *Financial support:* In 2010–11, 4 fellowships with full tuition reimbursements, 74 research assistantships with full tuition reimbursements, 156 teaching assistantships with full tuition reimbursements were awarded; career-related internships or fieldwork and Federal Work-Study also available. *Faculty research:* Engineering materials, energy research, NEMS and MEMS, bio-engineering, computational methods. Total annual research expenditures: $6.9 million. *Unit head:* Dr. George Haritos, Dean, 330-972-6978, E-mail: haritos@uakron.edu. *Application contact:* Dr. Craig Menzemer, Associate Dean, 330-972-5536, E-mail: ccmenze@uakron.edu.

The University of Alabama, Graduate School, College of Engineering, Tuscaloosa, AL 35487. Offers MAE, MES, MS, MS Ch E, MS Met E, MSCE, PhD. Part-time programs available. Postbaccalaureate distance learning degree programs offered (no on-campus study). *Faculty:* 104 full-time (15 women), 1 part-time/adjunct (0 women). *Students:* 214 full-time (34 women), 105 part-time (18 women); includes 27 minority (17 Black or African American, non-Hispanic/Latino; 5 Asian, non-Hispanic/Latino; 3 Hispanic/Latino; 2 Two or more races, non-Hispanic/Latino), 139 international. Average age 28. 429 applicants, 49% accepted, 82 enrolled. In 2010, 79 master's, 28 doctorates awarded. Terminal master's awarded for partial completion of doctoral program. *Degree requirements:* For master's, comprehensive exam; for doctorate, thesis/dissertation. *Entrance requirements:* For master's and doctorate, minimum GPA of 3.0. Additional exam requirements/recommendations for international students: Required—TOEFL (minimum score 550 paper-based; 213 computer-based). *Application deadline:* For fall admission, 7/1 for domestic students, 4/15 for international students; for spring admission, 11/15 for domestic students, 9/1 for international students. Applications are processed on a rolling basis. Application fee: $50 ($60 for international students). Electronic applications accepted. *Expenses:* Tuition, state resident: full-time $7900. Tuition, nonresident: full-time $20,500. *Financial support:* In 2010–11, 188 students received support, including 23 fellowships with full tuition reimbursements available (averaging $16,022 per year), 85 research assistantships with full tuition reimbursements available (averaging $16,022 per year), 73 teaching assistantships with full tuition reimbursements available (averaging $16,022 per year); career-related internships or fieldwork, Federal Work-Study, and institutionally sponsored loans also available. Financial award application deadline: 2/15. *Faculty research:* Materials and biomaterials networks and sensors, transportation, energy. Total annual research expenditures: $16.8 million. *Unit head:* Dr. Charles Karr, Dean, 205-348-6405, Fax: 205-348-8573. *Application contact:* Dr. David A. Francko, Dean, 205-348-8280, Fax: 205-348-0400, E-mail: dfrancko@ua.edu.

The University of Alabama at Birmingham, School of Engineering, Birmingham, AL 35294. Offers M Eng, MS Mt E, MSBME, MSCE, MSEE, MSME, PhD. Evening/weekend programs available. *Students:* 117 full-time (33 women), 238 part-time (53 women); includes 103 minority (67 Black or African American, non-Hispanic/Latino; 1 American Indian or Alaska Native, non-Hispanic/Latino; 21 Asian, non-Hispanic/Latino; 12 Hispanic/Latino; 2 Two or more races, non-Hispanic/Latino), 66 international. Average age 32. 274 applicants, 69% accepted, 128 enrolled. In 2010, 134 master's, 6 doctorates awarded. *Degree requirements:* For doctorate, thesis/dissertation. *Entrance requirements:* For master's, GRE General Test. *Application deadline:* Applications are processed on a rolling basis. Electronic applications accepted. *Expenses:* Tuition, state resident: full-time $5482. Tuition, nonresident: full-time $12,430. Tuition and fees vary according to program. *Financial support:* Fellowships with full tuition reimbursements, research assistantships with full tuition reimbursements, career-related internships or fieldwork, Federal Work-Study, institutionally sponsored loans, and tuition waivers (full and partial) available. Support available to part-time students. *Unit head:* Dr. Melinda Lalor, Dean, 205-934-8410, Fax: 205-934-8437. *Application contact:* Julie Bryant, Director of Graduate Admissions, 205-934-8227, Fax: 205-934-8413, E-mail: jbryant@uab.edu.

Engineering and Applied Sciences—General

The University of Alabama in Huntsville, School of Graduate Studies, College of Engineering, Huntsville, AL 35899. Offers MS, MSE, MSOR, MSSE, PhD. Part-time and evening/weekend programs available. Postbaccalaureate distance learning degree programs offered (minimal on-campus study). *Faculty:* 63 full-time (7 women), 14 part-time/adjunct (2 women). *Students:* 138 full-time (32 women), 447 part-time (86 women); includes 66 minority (31 Black or African American, non-Hispanic/Latino; 5 American Indian or Alaska Native, non-Hispanic/Latino; 18 Asian, non-Hispanic/Latino; 9 Hispanic/Latino; 3 Two or more races, non-Hispanic/Latino), 69 international. Average age 32. 484 applicants, 62% accepted, 186 enrolled. In 2010, 124 master's, 15 doctorates awarded. *Degree requirements:* For master's, comprehensive exam, thesis or alternative, oral and written exams; for doctorate, comprehensive exam, thesis/dissertation, oral and written exams. *Entrance requirements:* For master's and doctorate, GRE General Test, minimum GPA of 3.0. Additional exam requirements/recommendations for international students: Required—TOEFL (minimum score 500 paper-based; 173 computer-based; 62 iBT). *Application deadline:* For fall admission, 7/15 for domestic students, 4/1 for international students; for spring admission, 11/30 for domestic students, 9/1 for international students. Applications are processed on a rolling basis. Application fee: $40 ($50 for international students). Electronic applications accepted. *Expenses:* Tuition, state resident: full-time $7250; part-time $407.75 per credit hour. Tuition, nonresident: full-time $17,358; part-time $970.05 per credit hour. Required fees: $246.80 per semester. Tuition and fees vary according to course load and program. *Financial support:* In 2010–11, 97 students received support, including 44 research assistantships with full and partial tuition reimbursements available (averaging $11,769 per year), 54 teaching assistantships with full and partial tuition reimbursements available (averaging $10,694 per year); career-related internships or fieldwork, Federal Work-Study, institutionally sponsored loans, scholarships/grants, health care benefits, tuition waivers, and unspecified assistantships also available. Support available to part-time students. Financial award application deadline: 4/1; financial award applicants required to submit FAFSA. *Faculty research:* Propulsion, missile systems, automation, robotics, plasma. Total annual research expenditures: $44.1 million. *Unit head:* Dr. Shankar Mahalingam, Dean, 256-824-6474, Fax: 256-824-6843, E-mail: shankar.mahalingam@uah.edu. *Application contact:* Kathy Biggs, Graduate Studies Admissions Manager, 256-824-6199, Fax: 256-824-6405, E-mail: deangrad@uah.edu.

University of Alaska Anchorage, School of Engineering, Anchorage, AK 99508. Offers M AEST, MCE, MS, Certificate. Part-time and evening/weekend programs available. *Degree requirements:* For master's, comprehensive exam (for some programs), thesis (for some programs). *Entrance requirements:* For master's, GRE General Test. Additional exam requirements/recommendations for international students: Required—TOEFL (minimum score 550 paper-based; 213 computer-based).

University of Alaska Fairbanks, College of Engineering and Mines, Department of Civil and Environmental Engineering, Program in Environmental Engineering, Fairbanks, AK 99775-5900. Offers engineering (PhD), including environmental engineering; environmental engineering (MS), including environmental contaminants, environmental science and management, water supply and waste treatment. Part-time programs available. *Students:* 3 full-time (all women), 3 part-time (2 women). Average age 28. 5 applicants, 60% accepted, 1 enrolled. In 2010, 3 master's, 1 doctorate awarded. *Degree requirements:* For master's, comprehensive exam, thesis or alternative; for doctorate, comprehensive exam, thesis/dissertation, oral exam, oral defense. *Entrance requirements:* For master's, basic computer techniques; for doctorate, GRE General Test. Additional exam requirements/recommendations for international students: Required—TOEFL (minimum score 575 paper-based; 213 computer-based). *Application deadline:* For fall admission, 6/1 for domestic students, 3/1 for international students; for spring admission, 10/15 for domestic students, 9/1 for international students. Applications are processed on a rolling basis. Application fee: $60. Electronic applications accepted. *Expenses:* Tuition, state resident: full-time $5688; part-time $316 per credit. Tuition, nonresident: full-time $11,628; part-time $646 per credit. Required fees: $289 per semester. Tuition and fees vary according to course load and reciprocity agreements. *Financial support:* In 2010–11, 4 research assistant-

ships (averaging $13,290 per year), 1 teaching assistantship (averaging $7,088 per year) were awarded; fellowships, career-related internships or fieldwork, Federal Work-Study, scholarships/grants, health care benefits, and unspecified assistantships also available. Support available to part-time students. Financial award application deadline: 7/1; financial award applicants required to submit FAFSA. *Unit head:* Dr. David Barnes, Department Chair, 907-474-7241, Fax: 907-474-6087, E-mail: fyeqe@uaf.edu. *Application contact:* Dr. David Barnes, Department Chair, 907-474-7241, Fax: 907-474-6087, E-mail: fyeqe@uaf.edu.

University of Alaska Fairbanks, College of Engineering and Mines, Department of Electrical and Computer Engineering, Fairbanks, AK 99775-5915. Offers electrical engineering (MEE, MS, PhD); engineering (PhD). Part-time programs available. *Faculty:* 8 full-time (1 woman). *Students:* 19 full-time (3 women), 1 part-time (0 women), 10 international. Average age 26. 20 applicants, 35% accepted, 6 enrolled. In 2010, 4 master's awarded. Terminal master's awarded for partial completion of doctoral program. *Degree requirements:* For master's, comprehensive exam, thesis or alternative; for doctorate, comprehensive exam, thesis/dissertation, oral exam, oral defense. *Entrance requirements:* For master's and doctorate, GRE General Test. Additional exam requirements/recommendations for international students: Required—TOEFL (minimum score 550 paper-based; 213 computer-based; 80 iBT). *Application deadline:* For fall admission, 6/1 for domestic students, 3/1 for international students; for spring admission, 10/15 for domestic students, 9/1 for international students. Applications are processed on a rolling basis. Application fee: $60. Electronic applications accepted. *Expenses:* Tuition, state resident: full-time $5688; part-time $316 per credit. Tuition, nonresident: full-time $11,628; part-time $646 per credit. Required fees: $289 per semester. Tuition and fees vary according to course load and reciprocity agreements. *Financial support:* In 2010–11, 13 research assistantships with tuition reimbursements (averaging $11,876 per year), 10 teaching assistantships with tuition reimbursements (averaging $6,644 per year) were awarded; fellowships with tuition reimbursements, career-related internships or fieldwork, Federal Work-Study, scholarships/grants, health care benefits, and unspecified assistantships also available. Support available to part-time students. Financial award application deadline: 7/1; financial award applicants required to submit FAFSA. *Faculty research:* Geomagnetically-induced currents in power lines, electromagnetic wave propagation, laser radar systems, bioinformatics, distributed sensor networks. *Unit head:* Dr. Charles Mayer, Chair, 907-474-7137, Fax: 907-474-5135, E-mail: fyee@uaf.edu. *Application contact:* Dr. Charles Mayer, Chair, 907-474-7137, Fax: 907-474-5135, E-mail: fyee@uaf.edu.

University of Alaska Fairbanks, College of Engineering and Mines, Department of Mechanical Engineering, Fairbanks, AK 99775-5905. Offers engineering (PhD); mechanical engineering (MS). Part-time programs available. *Faculty:* 9 full-time (3 women), 4 part-time (0 women); includes 3 minority (1 Black or African American, non-Hispanic/Latino; 1 Asian, non-Hispanic/Latino; 1 Two or more races, non-Hispanic/Latino). Average age 29. 24 applicants, 29% accepted, 5 enrolled. In 2010, 2 master's, 1 doctorate awarded. Terminal master's awarded for partial completion of doctoral program. *Degree requirements:* For master's, comprehensive exam, thesis or alternative; for doctorate, comprehensive exam, thesis/dissertation, oral exam, oral defense. *Entrance requirements:* For master's and doctorate, GRE General Test. Additional exam requirements/recommendations for international students: Required—TOEFL (minimum score 550 paper-based; 213 computer-based; 80 iBT). *Application deadline:* For fall admission, 6/1 for domestic students, 3/1 for international students; for spring admission, 10/15 for domestic students, 9/1 for international students. Applications are processed on a rolling basis. Application fee: $60. Electronic applications accepted. *Expenses:* Tuition, state resident: full-time $5688; part-time $316 per credit. Tuition, nonresident: full-time $11,628; part-time $646 per credit. Required fees: $289 per semester. Tuition and fees vary according to course load and reciprocity agreements. *Financial support:* In 2010–11, 3 research assistantships with tuition reimbursements (averaging $13,721 per year), 5 teaching assistantships with tuition reimbursements (averaging $7,302 per year) were awarded; fellowships with tuition reimbursements, career-related internships or fieldwork, Federal Work-Study, scholarships/grants, health care benefits, and unspecified assistantships

Engineering and Applied Sciences—General

University of Alaska Fairbanks (continued)
also available. Support available to part-time students. Financial award application deadline: 7/1; financial award applicants required to submit FAFSA. *Faculty research:* Cold regions engineering, fluid mechanics, heat transfer, energy systems, indoor air quality. *Unit head:* Dr. Jonah Lee, Department Chair, 907-474-7136, Fax: 907-474-6141, E-mail: fymech@uaf.edu. *Application contact:* Dr. Jonah Lee, Department Chair, 907-474-7136, Fax: 907-474-6141, E-mail: fymech@uaf.edu.

The University of Arizona, College of Engineering, Tucson, AZ 85721. Offers M Eng, ME, MS, PhD, Certificate. Part-time programs available. Postbaccalaureate distance learning degree programs offered (no on-campus study). *Faculty:* 99 full-time (11 women), 12 part-time/adjunct (2 women). *Students:* 408 full-time (93 women), 135 part-time (22 women); includes 14 Black or African American, non-Hispanic/Latino; 1 American Indian or Alaska Native, non-Hispanic/Latino; 14 Asian, non-Hispanic/Latino; 36 Hispanic/Latino; 27 Two or more races, non-Hispanic/Latino, 268 international. Average age 30. 1,110 applicants, 36% accepted, 109 enrolled. In 2010, 121 master's, 38 doctorates awarded. *Degree requirements:* For doctorate, thesis/dissertation. *Entrance requirements:* Additional exam requirements/recommendations for international students: Required—TOEFL (minimum score 550 paper-based; 213 computer-based; 79 iBT). Application fee: $75. *Expenses:* Tuition, state resident: full-time $7692. *Financial support:* In 2010–11, 236 research assistantships with full tuition reimbursements (averaging $23,836 per year), 57 teaching assistantships with full tuition reimbursements (averaging $23,586 per year) were awarded; institutionally sponsored loans, scholarships/grants, health care benefits, and unspecified assistantships also available. Total annual research expenditures: $18.4 million. *Unit head:* Dr. Thomas W. Peterson, Dean, 520-621-6594, Fax: 520-621-2232, E-mail: twp@engr.arizona.edu. *Application contact:* General Information, 520-621-3471, Fax: 520-621-7112, E-mail: gradadm@grad.arizona.edu.

University of Arkansas, Graduate School, College of Engineering, Fayetteville, AR 72701-1201. Offers MS, MS Cmp E, MS Ch E, MS En E, MS Tc E, MSBE, MSBME, MSCE, MSE, MSEE, MSIE, MSME, MSOR, MSTE, PhD. *Students:* 134 full-time (33 women), 630 part-time (144 women); includes 114 minority (70 Black or African American, non-Hispanic/Latino; 7 American Indian or Alaska Native, non-Hispanic/Latino; 24 Asian, non-Hispanic/Latino; 12 Hispanic/Latino; 1 Native Hawaiian or other Pacific Islander, non-Hispanic/Latino), 165 international. 421 applicants, 71% accepted. In 2010, 272 master's, 28 doctorates awarded. *Degree requirements:* For doctorate, one foreign language, thesis/dissertation. *Application deadline:* For fall admission, 4/1 for international students; for spring admission, 10/1 for international students. Applications are processed on a rolling basis. Application fee: $40 ($50 for international students). Electronic applications accepted. *Financial support:* In 2010–11, 39 fellowships with tuition reimbursements, 189 research assistantships, 23 teaching assistantships were awarded; career-related internships or fieldwork and Federal Work-Study also available. Support available to part-time students. Financial award application deadline: 4/1; financial award applicants required to submit FAFSA. *Unit head:* Dean Ashok Saxena, Dean, 479-575-4153, Fax: 479-575-4346, E-mail: asaxena@uark.edu. *Application contact:* Dr. Terry Martin, Associate Dean for Academic Affairs, 479-575-3052, E-mail: tmartin@uark.edu.

University of Bridgeport, School of Engineering, Bridgeport, CT 06604. Offers MS, PhD. Part-time and evening/weekend programs available. Postbaccalaureate distance learning degree programs offered (no on-campus study). *Degree requirements:* For master's, thesis optional; for doctorate, thesis/dissertation. *Entrance requirements:* Additional exam requirements/recommendations for international students: Recommended—TOEFL (minimum score 550 paper-based; 213 computer-based; 80 iBT), IELTS (minimum score 6.5). Electronic applications accepted. *Expenses:* Contact institution. *Faculty research:* Atmospheric chemistry, minicomputers, heat transfer.

The University of British Columbia, Faculty of Applied Science, Vancouver, BC V6T 1Z1, Canada. Offers M Arch, M Eng, M Sc, MA Sc, MASA, MASLA, MLA, MSN, MSS, PhD. Part-time programs available. *Degree requirements:* For master's, comprehensive exam (for some programs), thesis (for some programs); for doctorate, comprehensive exam, thesis/dissertation. *Entrance requirements:* Additional exam requirements/recommendations for international students: Required—TOEFL (minimum score 550 paper-based; 213 computer-based). Electronic applications accepted. Tuition charges are reported in Canadian dollars. *Expenses:* Tuition, area resident: Full-time $4179 Canadian dollars. International tuition: $7344 Canadian dollars full-time. *Faculty research:* Architecture, nursing, engineering, landscape architecture.

University of Calgary, Faculty of Graduate Studies, Schulich School of Engineering, Calgary, AB T2N 1N4, Canada. Offers M Eng, M Sc, MPM, PhD. Part-time and evening/weekend programs available. *Degree requirements:* For doctorate, comprehensive exam, thesis/dissertation, candidacy exam. *Entrance requirements:* For master's, minimum GPA of 3.0; for doctorate, minimum GPA of 3.5. Additional exam requirements/recommendations for international students: Required—TOEFL, IELTS. *Faculty research:* Chemical and petroleum engineering, civil engineering, electrical and computer engineering, geomatics engineering, mechanical engineering and computer-integrated manufacturing.

University of California, Berkeley, Graduate Division, College of Engineering, Berkeley, CA 94720-1500. Offers M Eng, MS, D Eng, PhD, M Arch/MS, MCP/MS, MPP/MS. *Degree requirements:* For doctorate, thesis/dissertation, exam. *Entrance requirements:* For master's and doctorate, GRE General Test, minimum GPA of 3.0, 3 letters of recommendation.

University of California, Berkeley, UC Berkeley Extension, Certificate Programs in Engineering, Construction and Facilities Management, Berkeley, CA 94720-1500. Offers construction management (Certificate); HVAC (Certificate); integrated circuit design and techniques (online) (Certificate). Postbaccalaureate distance learning degree programs offered.

University of California, Davis, College of Engineering, Davis, CA 95616. Offers M Engr, MS, D Engr, PhD, Certificate, M Engr/MBA. Part-time programs available. Terminal master's awarded for partial completion of doctoral program. *Degree requirements:* For master's, comprehensive exam (for some programs), thesis (for some programs); for doctorate, comprehensive exam, thesis/dissertation. *Entrance requirements:* For doctorate, GRE. Additional exam requirements/recommendations for international students: Required—TOEFL (minimum score 550 paper-based; 213 computer-based). Electronic applications accepted.

University of California, Irvine, School of Engineering, Irvine, CA 92697. Offers MS, PhD. Part-time programs available. *Students:* 647 full-time (138 women), 70 part-time (19 women); includes 175 minority (2 Black or African American, non-Hispanic/Latino; 2 American Indian or Alaska Native, non-Hispanic/Latino; 137 Asian, non-Hispanic/Latino; 26 Hispanic/Latino; 1 Native Hawaiian or other Pacific Islander, non-Hispanic/Latino; 7 Two or more races, non-Hispanic/Latino), 357 international. Average age 27. 2,410 applicants, 25% accepted, 215 enrolled. In 2010, 150 master's, 70 doctorates awarded. Terminal master's awarded for partial completion of doctoral program. *Degree requirements:* For doctorate, thesis/dissertation. *Entrance requirements:* For master's and doctorate, GRE General Test, minimum GPA of 3.0, 3 letters of recommendation. Additional exam requirements/recommendations for international students: Required—TOEFL (minimum score 550 paper-based; 213 computer-based). *Application deadline:* For fall admission, 1/15 priority date for domestic students, 1/15 for international students. Applications are processed on a rolling basis. Application fee: $80 ($100 for international students). Electronic applications accepted. *Financial support:* Fellowships with tuition reimbursements, research assistantships with full tuition reimbursements, teaching assistantships with tuition reimbursements, institutionally sponsored loans, traineeships, health care benefits, and unspecified assistantships available. Financial award application deadline: 3/1; financial award applicants required to submit FAFSA. *Faculty research:* Biomedical, chemical and biochemical, civil and environmental, electrical and computer, and mechanical and aerospace engineering. *Unit head:* Dr. Gregory Washington, Dean, 949-824-6002, Fax: 949-824-8200, E-mail: engineeringdean@uci.edu. *Application contact:* Prof. John C. LaRue, Associate Dean, 949-824-6737, Fax: 949-824-8585, E-mail: jclarue@uci.edu.

University of California, Los Angeles, Graduate Division, Henry Samueli School of Engineering and Applied Science, Los Angeles, CA 90095-1601. Offers MS, PhD, MBA/MS. Evening/weekend programs available. Postbaccalaureate distance learning degree programs offered (no on-campus study). *Faculty:* 155 full-time (19 women), 21 part-time/adjunct (0 women). *Students:* 1,783 full-time (360 women); includes 26 Black or African American, non-Hispanic/Latino; 1 American Indian or Alaska Native, non-Hispanic/Latino; 432 Asian, non-Hispanic/Latino; 59 Hispanic/Latino; 7 Native Hawaiian or other Pacific Islander, non-Hispanic/Latino, 737 international. 3,914 applicants, 38% accepted, 601 enrolled. In 2010, 438 master's, 164 doctorates awarded. Terminal master's awarded for partial completion of doctoral program. *Degree requirements:* For master's, comprehensive exam or thesis; for doctorate, thesis/dissertation, qualifying exams. *Entrance requirements:* For master's, GRE General Test, minimum GPA of 3.0; for doctorate, GRE General Test, minimum GPA of 3.25. Additional exam requirements/recommendations for international students: Required—TOEFL (minimum score 560 paper-based; 220 computer-based; 87 iBT). *Application deadline:* For fall admission, 12/15 for domestic and international students. Application fee: $70 ($90 for international students). Electronic applications accepted. *Financial support:* In 2010–11, 482 fellowships, 1,870 research assistantships, 448 teaching assistantships were awarded; career-related internships or fieldwork, Federal Work-Study, institutionally sponsored loans, and tuition waivers (full and partial) also available. Financial award application deadline: 3/2; financial award applicants required to submit FAFSA. Total annual research expenditures: $92.7 million. *Unit head:* Dr. Richard D. Wesel, Associate Dean, Academic and Student Affairs, 310-825-2942. *Application contact:* Jan LaBuda, Director, Office of Academic and Student Affairs, 310-825-2514, Fax: 310-825-2473, E-mail: jan@ea.ucla.edu.

University of California, Merced, Division of Graduate Studies, School of Engineering, Merced, CA 95343. Offers electrical engineering and computer science (MS, PhD).

University of California, Santa Barbara, Graduate Division, College of Engineering, Santa Barbara, CA 93106-5130. Offers MS, PhD, MS/PhD. *Faculty:* 145 full-time (16 women), 17 part-time/adjunct (3 women). *Students:* 663 full-time (133 women); includes 4 Black or African American, non-Hispanic/Latino; 2 American Indian or Alaska Native, non-Hispanic/Latino; 244 Asian, non-Hispanic/Latino; 23 Hispanic/Latino; 2 Native Hawaiian or other Pacific Islander, non-Hispanic/Latino. Average age 26. 2,463 applicants, 22% accepted, 176 enrolled. In 2010, 92 master's, 77 doctorates awarded. Terminal master's awarded for partial completion of doctoral program. *Degree requirements:* For doctorate, thesis/dissertation. *Entrance requirements:* For master's, GRE, 3 letters of recommendation, resume/curriculum vitae; for doctorate, GRE, 3 letters of recommendation, statement of purpose, personal achievements/contributions statement, resume/curriculum vitae, transcripts for post-secondary institutions attended. Additional exam requirements/recommendations for international students: Required—TOEFL, IELTS. Application fee: $70 ($90 for international students). Electronic applications accepted. *Financial support:* In 2010–11, 563 students received support, including 213 fellowships with full and partial tuition reimbursements available (averaging $9,216 per year), 455 research assistantships with full and partial tuition reimbursements available (averaging $14,350 per year), 204 teaching assistantships with partial tuition reimbursements available (averaging $8,128 per year); career-related internships or fieldwork, Federal Work-Study, institutionally sponsored loans, scholarships/grants, traineeships, health care benefits, tuition waivers (full and partial), and unspecified assistantships also available. Financial award applicants required to submit FAFSA. *Unit head:* Dr. Matthew Tirrell, Dean, 805-893-3141. *Application contact:* 805-893-3207, E-mail: engrdean@engineering.ucsb.edu.

University of California, Santa Cruz, Division of Graduate Studies, Jack Baskin School of Engineering, Santa Cruz, CA 95064. Offers MS, PhD. *Students:* 314 full-time (81 women), 51 part-time (3 women); includes 71 minority (3 Black or African American, non-Hispanic/Latino; 1 American Indian or Alaska Native, non-Hispanic/Latino; 42 Asian, non-Hispanic/Latino; 23 Hispanic/Latino; 2 Two or more races, non-Hispanic/Latino), 98 international. Average age 31. 718 applicants, 30% accepted, 67 enrolled. In 2010, 45 master's, 34 doctorates awarded. *Entrance requirements:* For master's and doctorate, GRE General Test. Additional exam requirements/recommendations for international students: Required—TOEFL (minimum score 570 paper-based; 230 computer-based; 89 iBT); Recommended—IELTS (minimum score 8). Application fee: $70 ($90 for international students). Electronic applications accepted. *Financial support:* Fellowships, research assistantships, teaching assistantships, institutionally sponsored loans and tuition waivers available. Financial award applicants required to submit FAFSA. *Unit head:* Dean Arthur Ramirez, Dean, 831-459-2158, Fax: 831-459-4046, E-mail: apr@soe.ucsc.edu. *Application contact:* Veronica Williams, Graduate Admissions Assistant, 831-459-5905, Fax: 831-459-4843, E-mail: gradadm@ucsc.edu.

University of Central Florida, College of Engineering and Computer Science, Orlando, FL 32816. Offers MS, MS Cp E, MS Env E, MSAE, MSCE, MSEE, MSIE, MSME, MSMSE, PhD, Certificate. Part-time and evening/weekend programs available. *Faculty:* 114 full-time (15 women), 40 part-time/adjunct (4 women). *Students:* 644 full-time (139 women), 654 part-time (145 women); includes 279 minority (69 Black or African American, non-Hispanic/Latino; 2 American Indian or Alaska Native, non-Hispanic/Latino; 73 Asian, non-Hispanic/Latino; 120 Hispanic/Latino; 2 Native Hawaiian or other Pacific Islander, non-Hispanic/Latino; 13 Two or more races, non-Hispanic/Latino), 377 international. Average age 30. 1,233 applicants, 71% accepted, 367 enrolled. In 2010, 250 master's, 67 doctorates, 35 other advanced degrees awarded. *Degree requirements:* For doctorate, thesis/dissertation, candidacy exam, departmental qualifying exam. *Entrance requirements:* For master's, GRE General Test, minimum GPA of 3.0 in last 60 hours; for doctorate, minimum GPA of 3.5 in last 60 hours, resume. Additional exam requirements/recommendations for international students: Required—TOEFL. *Application deadline:* For fall admission, 7/15 for domestic students; for spring admission, 12/1 for domestic students. Application fee: $30. Electronic applications accepted. *Expenses:* Tuition, state resident: part-time $256.56 per credit hour. Tuition, nonresident: part-time $1011.52 per credit hour. Part-time tuition and fees vary according to program. *Financial support:* In 2010–11, 320 students received support, including 64 fellowships with partial tuition reimbursements available (averaging $6,000 per year), 289 research assistantships with partial tuition reimbursements available (averaging $8,300 per year), 140 teaching assistantships with partial tuition reimbursements available (averaging $7,700 per year); career-related internships or fieldwork, Federal Work-Study, institutionally sponsored loans, tuition waivers (partial), and unspecified assistantships also available. Financial award application deadline: 3/1; financial award applicants required to submit FAFSA. *Faculty research:* Electro-optics, lasers, materials, simulation, microelectronics. *Unit head:* Dr. Marwan Simaan, IDean, 407-823-2156, E-mail: simaan@eecs.ucf.edu. *Application contact:* Dr. Marwan Simaan, IDean, 407-823-2156, E-mail: simaan@eecs.ucf.edu.

University of Central Oklahoma, College of Graduate Studies and Research, College of Mathematics and Science, Department of Physics and Engineering, Edmond, OK 73034-5209. Offers MS. Part-time programs available. *Degree requirements:* For master's, thesis optional. *Entrance requirements:* For master's, 24 hours of course work in physics. Additional exam requirements/recommendations for international students: Required—TOEFL (minimum score 550 paper-based; 213 computer-based). Electronic applications accepted. *Faculty research:* Acoustics, solid-state physics/optical properties, molecular dynamics, nuclear physics, crystallography.

University of Cincinnati, Graduate School, College of Engineering, Cincinnati, OH 45221. Offers MS, PhD, MBA/MS. *Accreditation:* ABET (one or more programs are accredited). Part-time and evening/weekend programs available. Terminal master's awarded for partial completion of doctoral program. *Degree requirements:* For master's, thesis or alternative; for doctorate, comprehensive exam, thesis/dissertation. *Entrance requirements:* For master's and doctorate, GRE General Test. Additional exam requirements/recommendations for international students: Required—TOEFL (minimum score 520 paper-based; 190 computer-based).

University of Colorado at Colorado Springs, College of Engineering and Applied Science, Colorado Springs, CO 80933-7150. Offers ME, MS, PhD. Part-time and evening/weekend programs available. *Faculty:* 30 full-time (5 women), 1 part-time/adjunct (0 women). *Students:* 166 full-time (27 women), 84 part-time (10 women); includes 5 Black or African American, non-Hispanic/Latino; 15 Asian, non-Hispanic/Latino; 11 Hispanic/Latino; 1 Two or more races, non-Hispanic/Latino, 25 international. Average age 33. 102 applicants, 79% accepted, 61 enrolled. In 2010, 59 master's, 3 doctorates awarded. *Degree requirements:* For doctorate, comprehensive exam, thesis/dissertation. *Entrance requirements:* For master's, GRE General Test, minimum GPA of 3.0; for doctorate, GRE General Test, minimum GPA of 3.3. Additional exam requirements/recommendations for international students: Required—TOEFL. *Application deadline:* For fall admission, 5/1 for domestic students; for spring admission, 10/1 for domestic students. Applications are processed on a rolling basis. Application fee: $60 ($75 for international students). *Expenses:* Contact institution. *Financial support:* Fellowships, research assistantships, teaching assistantships, career-related internships or fieldwork, Federal Work-Study, and scholarships/grants available. Support available to part-time students. Financial award application deadline: 3/1; financial award applicants required to submit FAFSA. *Faculty research:* Ferroelectronics, electronics communication, computer-aided design, electromagnetics. Total annual research expenditures: $2 million. *Unit head:* Dr. Ramaswami Dandapani, Dean, 719-255-3543, Fax: 719-255-3542, E-mail: rdan@cas.uccs.edu. *Application contact:* Tina Moore, Director, Office of Student Support, 719-255-3347, E-mail: tmoore@uccs.edu.

University of Colorado Boulder, Graduate School, College of Engineering and Applied Science, Boulder, CO 80309. Offers ME, MS, PhD, JD/MS, MBA/MS. Part-time programs available. Postbaccalaureate distance learning degree programs offered. *Faculty:* 179 full-time (32 women). *Students:* 1,245 full-time (259 women), 398 part-time (89 women); includes 15 Black or African American, non-Hispanic/Latino; 8 American Indian or Alaska Native, non-Hispanic/Latino; 82 Asian, non-Hispanic/Latino; 52 Hispanic/Latino; 6 Two or more races, non-Hispanic/Latino, 478 international. Average age 28. 2,497 applicants, 403 enrolled. In 2010, 445 master's, 109 doctorates awarded. *Degree requirements:* For doctorate, thesis/dissertation. Application fee: $50 ($60 for international students). Electronic applications accepted. *Expenses:* Contact institution. *Financial support:* In 2010–11, 247 fellowships with full tuition reimbursements (averaging $12,287 per year), 413 research assistantships with full tuition reimbursements (averaging $15,375 per year), 70 teaching assistantships with full tuition reimbursements (averaging $17,591 per year) were awarded; career-related internships or fieldwork, scholarships/grants, traineeships, and tuition waivers (full) also available. Total annual research expenditures: $54.4 million.

University of Colorado Denver, College of Engineering and Applied Science, Denver, CO 80217. Offers M Eng, MS, PhD. Part-time and evening/weekend programs available. *Faculty:* 44 full-time (5 women), 13 part-time/adjunct (3 women). *Students:* 268 full-time (70 women), 160 part-time (30 women); includes 18 Black or African American, non-Hispanic/Latino; 26 Asian, non-Hispanic/Latino; 19 Hispanic/Latino, 128 international. Average age 32. 335 applicants, 50% accepted, 105 enrolled. In 2010, 84 master's, 4 doctorates awarded. *Degree requirements:* For doctorate, comprehensive exam, thesis/dissertation. *Entrance requirements:* For master's, GRE, minimum undergraduate GPA of 2.75; for doctorate, GRE, minimum cumulative GPA of 3.0. Additional exam requirements/recommendations for international students: Required—TOEFL (minimum score 525 paper-based; 197 computer-based; 71 iBT). Application fee: $50 ($75 for international students). Electronic applications accepted. *Expenses:* Contact institution. *Financial support:* In 2010–11, 41 students received support; research assistantships, teaching assistantships, Federal Work-Study and scholarships/grants available. Financial award application deadline: 4/1; financial award applicants required to submit FAFSA. *Faculty research:* Civil engineering, bioengineering, mechanical engineering, electrical engineering, computer science. Total annual research expenditures: $2.2 million. *Unit head:* Dr. Paul Rakowski, Assistant Dean of Student Services, 303-556-6771, Fax: 303-556-2511, E-mail: paul.rakowski@ucdenver.edu. *Application contact:* Dr. Paul Rakowski, Assistant Dean of Student Services, 303-556-6771, Fax: 303-556-2511, E-mail: paul.rakowski@ucdenver.edu.

University of Connecticut, Graduate School, School of Engineering, Storrs, CT 06269. Offers M Eng, MS, PhD. Terminal master's awarded for partial completion of doctoral program. *Degree requirements:* For master's, comprehensive exam; for doctorate, thesis/dissertation. *Entrance requirements:* For master's and doctorate, GRE General Test. Additional exam requirements/recommendations for international students: Required—TOEFL (minimum score 550 paper-based; 213 computer-based). Electronic applications accepted.

University of Dayton, Graduate School, School of Engineering, Dayton, OH 45469-0228. Offers MS, MS Ch E, MS Mat E, MSAE, MSCE, MSE, MSEE, MSEM, MSEM, MSEO, MSME, MSMS, DE, PhD. Part-time and evening/weekend programs available. Postbaccalaureate distance learning degree programs offered (no on-campus study). *Faculty:* 50 full-time (4 women), 36 part-time/adjunct (3 women). *Students:* 394 full-time (94 women), 128 part-time (30 women); includes 59 minority (31 Black or African American, non-Hispanic/Latino; 17 Asian, non-Hispanic/Latino; 10 Hispanic/Latino; 1 Two or more races, non-Hispanic/Latino), 194 international. Average age 28. 597 applicants, 59% accepted, 163 enrolled. In 2010, 121 master's, 22 doctorates awarded. *Degree requirements:* For master's, thesis optional; for doctorate, thesis/dissertation, departmental qualifying exam. *Entrance requirements:* For doctorate, MS. Additional exam requirements/recommendations for international students: Required—TOEFL (minimum score 550 paper-based; 213 computer-based; 80 iBT). *Application deadline:* For fall admission, 8/1 priority date for domestic students, 3/1 priority date for international students; for winter admission, 7/1 priority date for international students; for spring admission, 1/1 priority date for international students. Applications are processed on a rolling basis. Application fee: $0 ($50 for international students). Electronic applications accepted. *Expenses:* Tuition: Full-time $7800; part-time $650 per credit hour. *Financial support:* In 2010–11, 105 students received support, including 7 fellowships with full tuition reimbursements available (averaging $28,000 per year), 84 research assistantships with full tuition reimbursements available (averaging $15,000 per year), 14 teaching assistantships with full tuition reimbursements available (averaging $9,000 per year); career-related internships or fieldwork, institutionally sponsored loans, health care benefits, tuition waivers (full and partial), and unspecified assistantships also available. Financial award applicants required to submit FAFSA. Total annual research expenditures: $6.1 million. *Unit head:* Dr. John Weber, Associate Dean, 937-229-2736, Fax: 937-229-2756, E-mail: john.weber@notes.udayton.edu. *Application contact:* Alexander Popovski, Associate Director of International and Graduate Admissions, 937-229-4411, Fax: 937-229-4729, E-mail: gradadmission@udayton.edu.

University of Delaware, College of Engineering, Newark, DE 19716. Offers M Ch E, MAS, MCE, MEM, MMSE, MS, MSECE, MSME, PhD. Part-time and evening/weekend programs available. Postbaccalaureate distance learning degree programs offered (minimal on-campus study). Terminal master's awarded for partial completion of doctoral program. *Degree requirements:* For master's, thesis (for some programs); for doctorate, thesis/dissertation. *Entrance requirements:* For master's and doctorate, GRE General Test. Additional exam requirements/recommendations for international students: Required—TOEFL (minimum score 550 paper-based; 213 computer-based). Electronic applications accepted. *Faculty research:* Biotechnology, photonics, transportation, composite materials, materials science.

University of Denver, School of Engineering and Computer Science, Denver, CO 80208. Offers MS, PhD. *Faculty:* 26 full-time (3 women), 7 part-time/adjunct (2 women). *Students:* 10 full-time (2 women), 231 part-time (39 women); includes 25 minority (3 Black or African American, non-Hispanic/Latino; 9 Asian, non-Hispanic/Latino; 12 Hispanic/Latino; 1 Two or more races, non-Hispanic/Latino), 55 international. Average age 32. 259 applicants, 71% accepted, 61 enrolled. In 2010, 53 master's, 6 doctorates awarded. *Entrance requirements:* For master's, GRE General Test. Additional exam requirements/recommendations for international students: Required—TOEFL (minimum score 550 paper-based; 80 iBT). *Application deadline:* Applications are processed on a rolling basis. Application fee: $60. Electronic applications accepted. *Expenses:* Tuition: Full-time $35,604; part-time $29,670 per year. Required fees: $687 per year. Tuition and fees vary according to program. *Financial support:* In 2010–11, 4 research assistantships with full and partial tuition reimbursements (averaging $10,772 per year), 2 teaching assistantships with full and partial tuition reimbursements (averaging $18,298 per year) were awarded; Federal Work-Study, scholarships/grants, and unspecified assistantships also available. Financial award applicants required to submit FAFSA. *Unit head:* Dr. Rahmat Shoureshi, Dean, 303-871-2621, E-mail: rshoures@du.edu. *Application contact:* Information Request, 303-871-2716, E-mail: secs@du.edu.

University of Detroit Mercy, College of Engineering and Science, Detroit, MI 48221. Offers M Eng Mgt, MATM, ME, MS, MSCS, DE. Part-time and evening/weekend programs available. *Degree requirements:* For doctorate, thesis/dissertation. *Expenses:* Contact institution.

University of Evansville, College of Engineering and Computer Science, Evansville, IN 47722. Offers MS. Part-time programs available. *Faculty:* 2 full-time (0 women). *Students:* 1 (woman) part-time. Average age 28. 1 applicant, 0% accepted, 0 enrolled. *Degree requirements:* For master's, thesis. *Entrance requirements:* For master's, GRE, minimum undergraduate GPA of 2.8, 2 letters of recommendation, BS in electrical engineering or computer science. Additional exam requirements/recommendations for international students: Required—TOEFL (minimum score 550 paper-based; 79 iBT), IELTS (minimum score 6.5). *Application deadline:* For fall admission, 5/1 priority date for domestic and international students. Applications are processed on a rolling basis. Application fee: $25 ($50 for international students). *Expenses:* Contact institution. *Financial support:* Scholarships/grants available. Financial award application deadline: 6/1; financial award applicants required to submit FAFSA. *Unit head:* Dr. Philip Gerhart, Dean, 812-488-2651, Fax: 812-488-2780, E-mail: pg3@evansville.edu. *Application contact:* Dr. Dick Blandford, Department Chair, 812-488-2570, Fax: 812-488-2662, E-mail: blandford@evansville.edu.

University of Florida, Graduate School, College of Engineering, Gainesville, FL 32611. Offers MCE, ME, MS, PhD, Certificate, Engr, JD/MS, MD/PhD. *Accreditation:* ABET (one or more programs are accredited). Part-time programs available. Postbaccalaureate distance learning degree programs offered (no on-campus study). *Faculty:* 235 full-time (25 women), 12 part-time/adjunct (3 women). *Students:* 2,461 full-time (525 women), 643 part-time (157 women); includes 68 Black or African American, non-Hispanic/Latino; 5 American Indian or Alaska Native, non-Hispanic/Latino; 125 Asian, non-Hispanic/Latino; 157 Hispanic/Latino, 1,773 international. Average age 27. 5,463 applicants, 43% accepted, 853 enrolled. In 2010, 893 master's, 224 doctorates awarded. *Entrance requirements:* For master's and doctorate, GRE General Test, minimum GPA of 3.0; for other advanced degree, GRE General Test. Additional exam requirements/recommendations for international students: Required—TOEFL (minimum score 550 paper-based; 213 computer-based; 80 iBT), IELTS (minimum score 6). *Application deadline:* Applications are processed on a rolling basis. Application fee: $30. Electronic applications accepted. *Expenses:* Tuition, state resident: full-time $10,915.92. Tuition, nonresident: full-time $28,309. *Financial support:* In 2010–11, 1,181 students received support, including 78 fellowships with full tuition reimbursements available, 976 research assistantships with full tuition reimbursements available (averaging $19,823 per year), 127 teaching assistantships with full tuition reimbursements available (averaging $17,179 per year); career-related internships or fieldwork, Federal Work-Study, institutionally sponsored loans, and unspecified assistantships also available. Support available to part-time students. Financial award applicants required to submit FAFSA. Total annual research expenditures: $104 million. *Unit head:* Cammy R. Abernathy, PhD, Dean, 352-392-6000, E-mail: caber@ufl.edu. *Application contact:* David Norton, PhD, Associate Dean for Research and Graduate Prorgrams, 352-392-0946, E-mail: dnort@eng.ufl.edu.

See Display on next page and Close-Up on page 91.

University of Guelph, Graduate Studies, College of Physical and Engineering Science, School of Engineering, Guelph, ON N1G 2W1, Canada. Offers biological engineering (M Eng, M Sc, MA Sc, PhD); engineering systems and computing (M Eng, M Sc, MA Sc, PhD); environmental engineering (M Eng, M Sc, MA Sc, PhD); water resources engineering (M Eng, M Sc, MA Sc, PhD). Part-time programs available. *Degree requirements:* For master's, thesis (for some programs); for doctorate, comprehensive exam, thesis/dissertation. *Entrance requirements:* For master's, minimum B- average during previous 2 years of course work; for doctorate, minimum B average. Additional exam requirements/recommendations for international students: Required—TOEFL (minimum score 550 paper-based; 213 computer-based; 89 iBT), IELTS (minimum score 6.5). Electronic applications accepted. *Faculty research:* Water and food safety, environmental contaminant fates and mechanisms, computer systems, robotics and mechatronics, waste treatment.

University of Hartford, College of Engineering, Technology and Architecture, Program in Engineering, West Hartford, CT 06117-1599. Offers M Eng. *Entrance requirements:* Additional exam requirements/recommendations for international students: Required—TOEFL.

University of Hawaii at Manoa, Graduate Division, College of Engineering, Honolulu, HI 96822. Offers MS, PhD. *Accreditation:* ABET (one or more programs are accredited). Part-time programs available. *Faculty:* 75 full-time (3 women). *Students:* 160 full-time (35 women), 45 part-time (11 women); includes 103 minority (1 Black or African American, non-Hispanic/Latino; 69 Asian, non-Hispanic/Latino; 3 Hispanic/Latino; 11 Native Hawaiian or other Pacific Islander, non-Hispanic/Latino; 19 Two or more races, non-Hispanic/Latino), 69 international. Average age 29. 208 applicants, 69% accepted, 84 enrolled. In 2010, 35 master's, 10 doctorates awarded. *Entrance requirements:* Additional exam requirements/recommendations for international students: Required—TOEFL or IELTS. *Application deadline:* Applications are processed on a rolling basis. *Financial support:* In 2010–11, 30 fellowships, 103 research assistantships, 21 teaching assistantships were awarded; career-related internships or fieldwork, Federal Work-Study, and tuition waivers (full and partial) also available. Financial award applicants required to submit FAFSA. Total annual research expenditures: $7.4 million. *Unit head:* Peter E. Crouch, Dean, 808-956-7727, Fax: 808-956-2291. *Application contact:* Peter E. Crouch, Dean, 808-956-7727, Fax: 808-956-2291.

University of Houston, Cullen College of Engineering, Houston, TX 77204. Offers M Pet E, MCE, MCHE, MEE, MIE, MME, MSEE, MSME, PhD. Part-time programs available. *Faculty:* 86 full-time (10 women), 24 part-time/adjunct (2 women). *Students:* 551 full-time (145 women), 242 part-time (57 women); includes 20 Black or African American, non-Hispanic/Latino; 66 Asian, non-Hispanic/Latino; 35 Hispanic/Latino; 2 Two or more races, non-Hispanic/Latino, 537 international. Average age 27. 1,215 applicants, 42% accepted, 182 enrolled. In 2010, 189 master's, 37 doctorates awarded. Terminal master's awarded for partial completion of doctoral program. *Degree requirements:* For master's, thesis (for some programs); for doctorate, thesis/dissertation, departmental qualifying exam. *Entrance requirements:* For master's and doctorate, GRE General Test. Application fee: $25 ($75 for international students). *Expenses:* Tuition, state resident: full-time $8592; part-time $358 per credit hour. Tuition, nonresident: full-time $16,032; part-time $668 per credit hour. Required fees: $2889. Tuition and fees vary according to course load and program. *Financial support:* In 2010–11, 24 fellowships with partial tuition reimbursements (averaging $3,933 per year), 144 research assistantships with partial tuition reimbursements (averaging $11,985 per year), 73 teaching assistantships with partial tuition reimbursements (averaging $9,909 per year) were awarded; career-related internships or fieldwork, Federal Work-Study, institutionally sponsored loans, scholarships/grants, health care benefits, and unspecified assistantships also available. Support available to part-time students. Financial award application deadline: 2/1. *Faculty research:* Superconducting materials, microantennas for space packs, direct numerical simulation of pairing vortices. *Unit head:* Dr. Joseph Tedesco, Dean, 713-743-4242, Fax: 713-743-4214, E-mail: jtedesco@uh.edu. *Application contact:* Dr. Joseph Tedesco, Dean, 713-743-4242, Fax: 713-743-4214, E-mail: jtedesco@uh.edu.

University of Idaho, College of Graduate Studies, College of Engineering, Moscow, ID 83844-2282. Offers M Engr, MS, PhD. *Faculty:* 74 full-time, 6 part-time/adjunct. *Students:* 188 full-time (24 women), 263 part-time (40 women). Average age 33. In 2010, 95 master's, 9 doctorates awarded. *Degree requirements:* For doctorate, thesis/dissertation. *Entrance requirements:* For doctorate, minimum undergraduate GPA of 2.8, graduate 3.0. *Application deadline:* For fall admission, 8/1 for domestic students; for spring admission, 12/15 for domestic

Engineering and Applied Sciences—General

University of Idaho *(continued)*
students. Applications are processed on a rolling basis. Application fee: $60. Electronic applications accepted. *Expenses:* Tuition, nonresident: part-time $580 per credit. Required fees: $306 per credit. *Financial support:* Fellowships, research assistantships, teaching assistantships, career-related internships or fieldwork and Federal Work-Study available. Support available to part-time students. Financial award applicants required to submit FAFSA. *Faculty research:* Robotics, micro-electronic packaging, water resources engineering and science, oscillating flows in macro- and micro-scale methods of mechanical separation, nuclear energy. *Unit head:* Dr. Donald Blackletter, Dean, 208-885-6470, E-mail: deanengr@uidaho.edu. *Application contact:* Dr. Donald Blackletter, Dean, 208-885-6470, E-mail: deanengr@uidaho.edu.

University of Illinois at Chicago, Graduate College, College of Engineering, Chicago, IL 60607-7128. Offers M Eng, MEE, MS, PhD. Part-time and evening/weekend programs available. Terminal master's awarded for partial completion of doctoral program. *Degree requirements:* For doctorate, thesis/dissertation. *Entrance requirements:* For doctorate, GRE. Additional exam requirements/recommendations for international students: Required—TOEFL. Electronic applications accepted. *Expenses:* Contact institution.

University of Illinois at Urbana–Champaign, Graduate College, College of Engineering, Champaign, IL 61820. Offers MCS, MS, PhD, M Arch/MS, MBA/MS, MCS/JD, MCS/M Arch, MCS/MBA, MS/MBA, PhD/MBA. *Faculty:* 365 full-time (39 women), 14 part-time/adjunct (0 women). *Students:* 2,097 full-time (365 women), 453 part-time (75 women); includes 17 Black or African American, non-Hispanic/Latino; 1 American Indian or Alaska Native, non-Hispanic/Latino; 180 Asian, non-Hispanic/Latino; 54 Hispanic/Latino; 19 Two or more races, non-Hispanic/Latino, 1,403 international. 6,259 applicants, 21% accepted, 586 enrolled. In 2010, 469 master's, 261 doctorates awarded. *Application deadline:* Applications are processed on a rolling basis. Application fee: $75 ($90 for international students). Electronic applications accepted. *Expenses:* Contact institution. *Financial support:* In 2010–11, 280 fellowships, 1,702 research assistantships, 690 teaching assistantships were awarded; tuition waivers (full and partial) also available. *Unit head:* Dr. Ilesanmi Adesida, Dean, 217-333-2150, Fax: 217-244-7705, E-mail: iadesida@illinois.edu. *Application contact:* Dr. Ilesanmi Adesida, Dean, 217-333-2150, Fax: 217-244-7705, E-mail: iadesida@illinois.edu.

The University of Iowa, Graduate College, College of Engineering, Iowa City, IA 52242-1527. Offers MS, PhD. *Faculty:* 83 full-time (10 women), 2 part-time/adjunct (1 woman). *Students:* 411 full-time (110 women); includes 28 minority (10 Black or African American, non-Hispanic/Latino; 13 Asian, non-Hispanic/Latino; 5 Hispanic/Latino), 196 international. Average age 26. 709 applicants, 30% accepted, 114 enrolled. In 2010, 65 master's, 42 doctorates awarded. *Degree requirements:* For master's, thesis optional, exam; for doctorate, comprehensive exam, thesis/dissertation. *Entrance requirements:* For master's and doctorate, GRE, official academic records/transcripts, 3 letters of recommendation, resume, statement of purpose. Additional exam requirements/recommendations for international students: Required—TOEFL (minimum score 550 paper-based; 213 computer-based; 81 iBT). *Application deadline:* For fall admission, 7/15 for domestic students, 4/15 for international students; for spring admission, 12/1 for domestic students, 10/1 for international students. Applications are processed on a rolling basis. Application fee: $60 ($100 for international students). Electronic applications accepted. *Financial support:* In 2010–11, 29 fellowships with partial tuition reimbursements (averaging $20,678 per year), 292 research assistantships with partial tuition reimbursements (averaging $20,739 per year), 84 teaching assistantships with partial tuition reimbursements (averaging $17,174 per year) were awarded; scholarships/grants, health care benefits, and unspecified assistantships also available. Financial award application deadline: 2/1; financial award applicants required to submit FAFSA. Total annual research expenditures: $49.1 million. *Unit head:* Dr. Alec Scranton, Interim Dean, 319-335-5766, Fax: 319-335-6086, E-mail: alec-scranton@uiowa.edu. *Application contact:* Michael Barron, Director of Admissions, 319-335-1525, Fax: 319-335-1535, E-mail: admissions@uiowa.edu.

See Display on next page and Close-Up on page 93.

The University of Kansas, Graduate Studies, School of Engineering, Lawrence, KS 66045. Offers MCE, MCM, ME, MS, DE, PhD. Part-time and evening/weekend programs available. Postbaccalaureate distance learning degree programs offered (no on-campus study). *Students:* 342 full-time (100 women), 298 part-time (53 women); includes 67 minority (13 Black or African American, non-Hispanic/Latino; 5 American Indian or Alaska Native, non-Hispanic/Latino; 27 Asian, non-Hispanic/Latino; 17 Hispanic/Latino; 1 Native Hawaiian or other Pacific Islander, non-Hispanic/Latino; 4 Two or more races, non-Hispanic/Latino), 215 international. Average age 29. 705 applicants, 39% accepted, 112 enrolled. In 2010, 134 master's, 22 doctorates awarded. Terminal master's awarded for partial completion of doctoral program. *Degree requirements:* For doctorate, comprehensive exam, thesis/dissertation. *Entrance requirements:* For master's, GRE, minimum GPA of 3.0; for doctorate, GRE, minimum GPA of 3.5. Additional exam requirements/recommendations for international students: Required—TOEFL. *Application deadline:* Applications are processed on a rolling basis. Application fee: $55 ($65 for international students). Electronic applications accepted. *Expenses:* Contact institution. *Financial support:* Fellowships, research assistantships with full and partial tuition reimbursements, teaching assistantships with full and partial tuition reimbursements, career-related internships or fieldwork, Federal Work-Study, scholarships/grants, and unspecified assistantships available. *Faculty research:* Telecommunications, oil recovery, airplane design, structured materials, robotics. *Unit head:* Dr. Stuart R. Bell, Dean, 785-864-3881, E-mail: kuengr@ku.edu. *Application contact:* Dr. Glen Marotz, Associate Dean, 785-864-2980, Fax: 785-864-5445, E-mail: gama@ku.edu.

University of Kentucky, Graduate School, College of Engineering, Lexington, KY 40506-0032. Offers M Eng, MCE, MME, MS, MS Ch E, MS Min, MSCE, MSEE, MSEM, MSMAE, MSME, MSMSE, PhD. Part-time programs available. *Degree requirements:* For master's, comprehensive exam; for doctorate, comprehensive exam, thesis/dissertation. *Entrance requirements:* For master's, GRE General Test, minimum undergraduate GPA of 2.75; for doctorate, GRE General Test, minimum undergraduate GPA of 3.0. Additional exam requirements/recommendations for international students: Required—TOEFL (minimum score 550 paper-based; 213 computer-based). Electronic applications accepted.

University of Louisville, J.B. Speed School of Engineering, Louisville, KY 40292-0001. Offers M Eng, MS, PhD, Certificate, M Eng/MBA. *Accreditation:* ABET (one or more programs are accredited). Part-time programs available. Postbaccalaureate distance learning degree programs offered (no on-campus study). *Faculty:* 74 full-time (9 women). *Students:* 375 full-time (74 women), 152 part-time (30 women); includes 413 Black or African American, non-Hispanic/Latino; 13 American Indian or Alaska Native, non-Hispanic/Latino; 194 Asian, non-Hispanic/Latino; 7 Hispanic/Latino; 61 Two or more races, non-Hispanic/Latino, 421 international. Average age 27. 241 applicants, 48% accepted, 60 enrolled. In 2010, 181 master's, 24 doctorates awarded. Terminal master's awarded for partial completion of doctoral program. *Degree requirements:* For master's, comprehensive exam (for some programs), thesis or alternative; for doctorate, comprehensive exam, thesis/dissertation, minimum GPA of 3.0. *Entrance requirements:* For master's, doctorate, and Certificate, GRE General Test. Additional exam requirements/recommendations for international students: Required—TOEFL (minimum score 550 paper-based; 213 computer-based; 80 iBT), IELTS (minimum score 6.5). *Application deadline:* For fall admission, 5/1 priority date for domestic and international students; for spring admission, 11/1 priority date for domestic and international students. Applications are processed on a rolling basis. Application fee: $50. Electronic applications accepted. *Expenses:* Tuition, state resident: full-time $9144; part-time $508 per credit hour. Tuition, nonresident: full-time $19,026; part-time $1057 per credit hour. Tuition and fees vary according to program and reciprocity agreements. *Financial support:* In 2010–11, 87 students received support, including 17 fellowships with full tuition reimbursements available (averaging $20,000 per year), 29 research assistantships with full tuition reimbursements available (averaging $20,000 per year), 41 teaching assistantships with full tuition reimbursements available (averaging $20,000 per year); scholarships/grants also available. Financial award application deadline: 1/25; financial award applicants required to submit FAFSA. *Faculty research:*

Bioengineering, civil infrastructure, computer engineering and computer science, logistics and distribution, materials management. Total annual research expenditures: $14.8 million. *Unit head:* Dr. Mickey R. Wilhelm, Dean, 502-852-6281, Fax: 502-852-7033, E-mail: wilhelm@ louisville.edu. *Application contact:* Dr. Michael Day, Associate Dean, 502-852-6195, Fax: 502-852-7294, E-mail: day@louisville.edu.

University of Maine, Graduate School, College of Engineering, Orono, ME 04469. Offers MS, PhD. Part-time programs available. *Faculty:* 65 full-time (6 women), 11 part-time/adjunct (5 women). *Students:* 97 full-time (18 women), 53 part-time (8 women); includes 8 minority (1 Black or African American, non-Hispanic/Latino; 2 American Indian or Alaska Native, non-Hispanic/Latino; 4 Asian, non-Hispanic/Latino; 1 Two or more races, non-Hispanic/Latino), 50 international. Average age 30. 136 applicants, 33% accepted, 34 enrolled. In 2010, 38 master's, 6 doctorates awarded. Terminal master's awarded for partial completion of doctoral program. *Degree requirements:* For doctorate, thesis/dissertation. *Entrance requirements:* For master's and doctorate, GRE General Test. Additional exam requirements/recommendations for international students: Required—TOEFL. *Application deadline:* For fall admission, 2/1 priority date for domestic students. Applications are processed on a rolling basis. Application fee: $65. Electronic applications accepted. *Expenses:* Tuition, state resident: full-time $400. Tuition, nonresident: full-time $1050. *Financial support:* In 2010–11, 1 research assistantship with tuition reimbursement (averaging $12,790 per year) was awarded; Federal Work-Study, institutionally sponsored loans, scholarships/grants, and tuition waivers (full and partial) also available. Financial award application deadline: 3/1. *Unit head:* Dr. Dana Humphrey, Interim Dean, 207-581-2216, Fax: 207-581-2220. *Application contact:* Scott G. Delcourt, Associate Dean of the Graduate School, 207-581-3291, Fax: 207-581-3232, E-mail: graduate@maine.edu.

University of Manitoba, Faculty of Graduate Studies, Faculty of Engineering, Winnipeg, MB R3T 2N2, Canada. Offers M Eng, M Sc, PhD.

University of Maryland, Baltimore County, Graduate School, College of Engineering and Information Technology, Baltimore, MD 21250. Offers MS, PhD, Postbaccalaureate Certificate. Part-time and evening/weekend programs available. Postbaccalaureate distance learning degree programs offered (no on-campus study). *Faculty:* 111 full-time (29 women), 39 part-time/adjunct (8 women). *Students:* 391 full-time (117 women), 515 part-time (149 women); includes 202 minority (96 Black or African American, non-Hispanic/Latino; 72 Asian, non-Hispanic/Latino; 28 Hispanic/Latino; 6 Two or more races, non-Hispanic/Latino), 263 international. Average age 30. 883 applicants, 58% accepted, 230 enrolled. In 2010, 172 master's, 30 doctorates, 25 other advanced degrees awarded. *Degree requirements:* For master's, comprehensive exam (for some programs), thesis (for some programs); for doctorate, comprehensive exam, thesis/dissertation. *Entrance requirements:* For master's and doctorate, GRE General Test, minimum GPA of 3.0. Additional exam requirements/recommendations for international students: Required—TOEFL (minimum score 550 paper-based; 213 computer-based; 80 iBT). *Application deadline:* For fall admission, 6/1 for domestic students, 1/1 for international students; for spring admission, 11/1 for domestic students, 6/1 for international students. Applications are processed on a rolling basis. Application fee: $50. Electronic applications accepted. *Financial support:* In 2010–11, 7 fellowships with full tuition reimbursements (averaging $25,000 per year), 113 research assistantships with full tuition reimbursements (averaging $22,000 per year), 82 teaching assistantships with full tuition reimbursements (averaging $17,000 per year) were awarded; career-related internships or fieldwork, Federal Work-Study, scholarships/grants, health care benefits, tuition waivers (partial), and unspecified assistantships also available. Support available to part-time students. Financial award application deadline: 6/30; financial award applicants required to submit FAFSA. *Faculty research:* Biomaterials engineering, water resources engineering, security and information assurance, human-centered computing, design and manufacturing. Total annual research expenditures: $12.6 million. *Unit head:* Dr. Warren R. DeVries, Dean, 410-455-3270, Fax: 410-455-3559, E-mail: wdevries@umbc.edu. *Application contact:* Graduate School, 410-455-2537, E-mail: umbcgrad@umbc.edu.

University of Maryland, College Park, Academic Affairs, A. James Clark School of Engineering and School of Public Policy, Program in Engineering and Public Policy, College Park, MD 20742. Offers MS. *Students:* 8 full-time (3 women), 10 part-time (1 woman); includes 3 minority (1 Asian, non-Hispanic/Latino; 2 Hispanic/Latino), 1 international. 39 applicants, 51% accepted, 9 enrolled. In 2010, 6 master's awarded. *Application deadline:* For fall admission, 4/1 for domestic students, 2/1 for international students; for spring admission, 10/15 for domestic students, 6/1 for international students. Application fee: $75. *Expenses:* Tuition, area resident: Part-time $471 per credit hour. Tuition, state resident: part-time $471 per credit hour. Tuition, nonresident: part-time $1016 per credit hour. Required fees: $337 per term. *Unit head:* Dr. Steven Gabriel, Co-Director, 301-405-3242, E-mail: sgabriel@umd.edu. *Application contact:* Dean of the Graduate School, 301-405-0358, Fax: 301-314-9305, E-mail: ccaramel@umd.edu.

University of Massachusetts Amherst, Graduate School, College of Engineering, Amherst, MA 01003. Offers MS, MSCE, MSChE, MSECE, MSME, PhD. *Accreditation:* ABET (one or more programs are accredited). Part-time programs available. *Faculty:* 119 full-time (12 women). *Students:* 410 full-time (108 women), 67 part-time (14 women); includes 30 minority (3 Black or African American, non-Hispanic/Latino; 8 Asian, non-Hispanic/Latino; 13 Hispanic/Latino; 1 Native Hawaiian or other Pacific Islander, non-Hispanic/Latino; 5 Two or more races, non-Hispanic/Latino), 286 international. Average age 26. 1,644 applicants, 31% accepted, 151 enrolled. In 2010, 72 master's, 30 doctorates awarded. Terminal master's awarded for partial completion of doctoral program. *Degree requirements:* For master's, thesis (for some programs); for doctorate, comprehensive exam, thesis/dissertation. *Entrance requirements:* For master's and doctorate, GRE General Test. Additional exam requirements/recommendations for international students: Required—TOEFL (minimum score 550 paper-based; 213 computer-based; 80 iBT), IELTS (minimum score 6.5). *Application deadline:* Applications are processed on a rolling basis. Application fee: $50 ($65 for international students). Electronic applications accepted. *Expenses:* Tuition, state resident: full-time $2640. Required fees: $8282. One-time fee: $357 full-time. *Financial support:* In 2010–11, 33 fellowships with full tuition reimbursements (averaging $12,641 per year), 350 research assistantships with full tuition reimbursements, 76 teaching assistantships with full tuition reimbursements (averaging $6,461 per year) were awarded; career-related internships or fieldwork, Federal Work-Study, scholarships/grants, traineeships, health care benefits, tuition waivers (full), and unspecified assistantships also available. Support available to part-time students. Financial award applicants required to submit FAFSA. *Unit head:* Dr. Michael Malone, Dean, 413-545-6388, Fax: 413-545-6388. *Application contact:* Jean M. Ames, Supervisor of Admissions, 413-545-0722, Fax: 413-577-0010, E-mail: gradadm@grad.umass.edu.

University of Massachusetts Dartmouth, Graduate School, College of Engineering, North Dartmouth, MA 02747-2300. Offers MS, PhD, Postbaccalaureate Certificate. Part-time programs available. *Faculty:* 60 full-time (9 women), 11 part-time/adjunct (4 women). *Students:* 100 full-time (23 women), 124 part-time (22 women); includes 2 Black or African American, non-Hispanic/Latino; 1 American Indian or Alaska Native, non-Hispanic/Latino; 4 Asian, non-Hispanic/Latino; 4 Hispanic/Latino, 120 international. Average age 26. 296 applicants, 81% accepted, 68 enrolled. In 2010, 28 master's, 1 doctorate, 1 other advanced degree awarded. *Degree requirements:* For master's, thesis or alternative; for doctorate, comprehensive exam, thesis/dissertation. *Entrance requirements:* For doctorate, GRE. Additional exam requirements/recommendations for international students: Required—TOEFL (minimum score 500 paper-based). *Application deadline:* Applications are processed on a rolling basis. Application fee: $40 ($60 for international students). Electronic applications accepted. *Expenses:* Tuition, state resident: full-time $2071; part-time $86 per credit. Tuition, nonresident: full-time $8099; part-time $337 per credit. Required fees: $9446; $394 per credit. One-time fee: $75. Part-time tuition and fees vary according to class time, course load, degree level and reciprocity agreements. *Financial support:* In 2010–11, 5 fellowships with full tuition reimbursements (averaging $12,707 per year), 52 research assistantships with full tuition reimbursements (averaging $9,501 per year), 37 teaching assistantships with full tuition reimbursements (averaging $10,140 per year) were awarded; Federal Work-Study and unspecified assistantships also available. Support

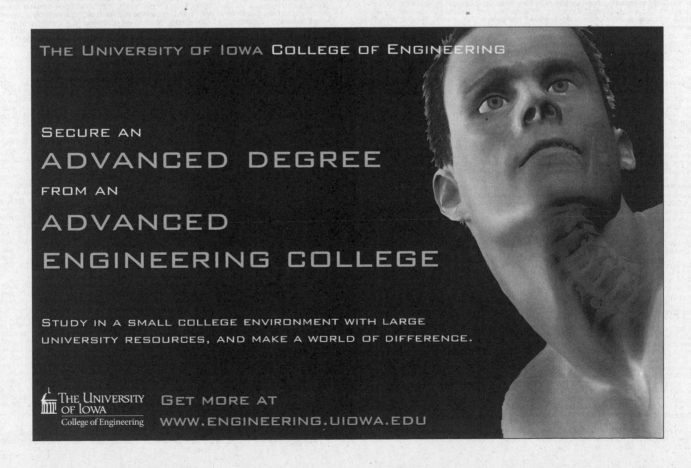

Engineering and Applied Sciences—General

University of Massachusetts Dartmouth (continued)
available to part-time students. Financial award application deadline: 3/1; financial award applicants required to submit FAFSA. *Faculty research:* Soil-geosynthetic systems, signals and systems, heat exchanger optimization, tracking of mesoscale features, blue light cures. Total annual research expenditures: $6 million. *Unit head:* Dr. Robert Peck, Dean, 508-999-8539, Fax: 508-999-9137, E-mail: rpeck@umassd.edu. *Application contact:* Elan Turcotte-Shamski, Graduate Admissions Officer, 508-999-8604, Fax: 508-999-8183, E-mail: graduate@umassd.edu.

University of Massachusetts Lowell, James B. Francis College of Engineering, Lowell, MA 01854-2881. Offers MS Eng, MSES, D Eng, PhD, Certificate, Graduate Certificate. Part-time and evening/weekend programs available. Terminal master's awarded for partial completion of doctoral program. *Degree requirements:* For doctorate, thesis/dissertation. *Entrance requirements:* For master's and doctorate, GRE General Test.

University of Memphis, Graduate School, Herff College of Engineering, Memphis, TN 38152. Offers MS, PhD. Part-time programs available. *Faculty:* 40 full-time (3 women), 4 part-time/adjunct (1 woman). *Students:* 117 full-time (35 women), 57 part-time (13 women); includes 13 Black or African American, non-Hispanic/Latino; 3 Asian, non-Hispanic/Latino; 1 Hispanic/Latino, 80 international. Average age 29. 77 applicants, 84% accepted, 62 enrolled. In 2010, 34 master's, 7 doctorates awarded. *Degree requirements:* For master's, comprehensive exam, thesis optional, 30-36 hours of course work, completion of course work within 6 years, continuous enrollment; for doctorate, comprehensive exam, thesis/dissertation, completion of degree within 12 years, residency, continuous enrollment. *Entrance requirements:* For master's, GRE, MAT, GMAT or PRAXIS; for doctorate, GRE, MAT, GMAT. Additional exam requirements/recommendations for international students: Required—TOEFL (minimum score 550 paper-based; 210 computer-based; 79 iBT). *Application deadline:* For fall admission, 7/1 for domestic students, 5/1 for international students; for spring admission, 12/1 for domestic students, 9/15 for international students. Application fee: $35 ($60 for international students). Electronic applications accepted. *Financial support:* In 2010–11, 30 students received support; fellowships with full tuition reimbursements available, research assistantships with full tuition reimbursements available, teaching assistantships with full tuition reimbursements available, career-related internships or fieldwork, Federal Work-Study, scholarships/grants, tuition waivers (full and partial), and unspecified assistantships available. Financial award application deadline: 2/15; financial award applicants required to submit FAFSA. *Faculty research:* Medical and biological applications of engineering; infrastructure, including transportation, ground water and GPS studies; computational intelligence and modeling; sensors. Total annual research expenditures: $4.5 million. *Unit head:* Dr. Richard C. Warder, Dean, 901-678-4306, Fax: 901-678-4180, E-mail: rcwarder@memphis.edu. *Application contact:* Dr. Deborah Hochstein, Associate Dean, 901-678-3298, Fax: 901-678-5030, E-mail: dhochstn@memphis.edu.

University of Miami, Graduate School, College of Engineering, Coral Gables, FL 33124. Offers MS, MSAE, MSBE, MSCE, MSECE, MSEVH, MSIE, MSME, MSOES, PhD, MBA/MSIE. Part-time and evening/weekend programs available. *Degree requirements:* For master's, thesis (for some programs); for doctorate, comprehensive exam, thesis/dissertation. *Entrance requirements:* For master's and doctorate, GRE General Test, minimum GPA of 3.0. Additional exam requirements/recommendations for international students: Required—TOEFL (minimum score 550 paper-based; 213 computer-based; 59 iBT). Electronic applications accepted.

University of Michigan, Horace H. Rackham School of Graduate Studies, College of Engineering, Ann Arbor, MI 48109. Offers M Eng, MS, MSE, D Eng, PhD, CE, Certificate, Ch E, Mar Eng, Nav Arch, Nuc E, M Arch/M Eng, M Arch/MSE, MBA/M Eng, MBA/MS, MBA/MSE. Part-time programs available. Postbaccalaureate distance learning degree programs offered (no on-campus study). *Faculty:* 353 full-time (56 women). *Students:* 2,618 full-time (567 women), 337 part-time (45 women). 6,449 applicants, 34% accepted, 901 enrolled. In 2010, 810 master's, 231 doctorates awarded. *Application deadline:* Applications are processed on a rolling basis. Application fee: $65 ($75 for international students). Electronic applications accepted. *Expenses:* Contact institution. *Financial support:* Fellowships, research assistantships, teaching assistantships, career-related internships or fieldwork, Federal Work-Study, institutionally sponsored loans, scholarships/grants, traineeships, health care benefits, tuition waivers (full and partial), and unspecified assistantships available. Support available to part-time students. Financial award applicants required to submit FAFSA. Total annual research expenditures: $180.6 million. *Unit head:* Prof. David C. Munson, Chair, 734-647-7010, Fax: 734-647-7009, E-mail: munson@umich.edu. *Application contact:* Mike Nazareth, Recruiting Contact, 734-647-7030, Fax: 734-647-7045, E-mail: mikenaz@umich.edu.

University of Michigan–Dearborn, College of Engineering and Computer Science, Dearborn, MI 48128-1491. Offers MS, MSE, PhD, MBA/MSE. Part-time and evening/weekend programs available. *Faculty:* 52 full-time (3 women), 12 part-time/adjunct (1 woman). *Students:* 63 full-time (9 women), 431 part-time (86 women); includes 23 Black or African American, non-Hispanic/Latino; 64 Asian, non-Hispanic/Latino; 19 Hispanic/Latino, 84 international. Average age 31. 230 applicants, 61% accepted, 105 enrolled. In 2010, 121 master's awarded. *Degree requirements:* For master's, thesis optional; for doctorate, thesis/dissertation. *Entrance requirements:* Additional exam requirements/recommendations for international students: Required—TOEFL (minimum score 560 paper-based; 220 computer-based; 84 iBT). *Application deadline:* For fall admission, 6/15 for domestic students, 4/1 for international students; for winter admission, 12/1 for domestic students, 10/15 for international students; for spring admission, 2/15 for domestic and international students. Applications are processed on a rolling basis. Application fee: $60 ($75 for international students). Electronic applications accepted. *Financial support:* In 2010–11, 12 students received support, including 7 fellowships (averaging $18,331 per year), 27 research assistantships with full tuition reimbursements available (averaging $56,894 per year), 12 teaching assistantships (averaging $3,400 per year); career-related internships or fieldwork and Federal Work-Study also available. Financial award application deadline: 4/1; financial award applicants required to submit FAFSA. *Faculty research:* CAD/CAM, expert systems, acoustics, vehicle electronics, engines and fuels. *Unit head:* Dr. Subrata Sengupta, Dean, 313-593-5290, Fax: 313-593-9967, E-mail: razal@engin.umd.umich.edu. *Application contact:* Dr. Keshav Varde, Associate Dean, 313-593-5117, Fax: 313-593-9967, E-mail: varde@engin.umd.umich.edu.

University of Minnesota, Twin Cities Campus, Institute of Technology, Minneapolis, MN 55455-0213. Offers M Aero E, M Ch E, M Comp E, M Geo E, M Mat SE, MA, MCE, MCIS, MCS, MEE, MS, MS Ch E, MS Mat SE, MSEE, MSIE, MSISE, MSME, MSMOT, MSST, PhD, MD/PhD. Part-time and evening/weekend programs available. Postbaccalaureate distance learning degree programs offered (minimal on-campus study). Electronic applications accepted.

University of Mississippi, Graduate School, School of Engineering, Oxford, University, MS 38677. Offers engineering science (MS, PhD). *Students:* 124 full-time (35 women), 37 part-time (9 women); includes 19 minority (11 Black or African American, non-Hispanic/Latino; 6 Asian, non-Hispanic/Latino; 2 Hispanic/Latino), 78 international. In 2010, 33 master's, 9 doctorates awarded. *Degree requirements:* For master's, thesis (for some programs); for doctorate, thesis/dissertation. *Entrance requirements:* For master's, GRE General Test, minimum GPA of 3.0; for doctorate, GRE General Test. Additional exam requirements/recommendations for international students: Required—TOEFL. *Application deadline:* For fall admission, 4/1 for domestic students; for spring admission, 10/1 for domestic students. Applications are processed on a rolling basis. Application fee: $25. Electronic applications accepted. *Financial support:* Scholarships/grants available. Financial award application deadline: 3/1; financial award applicants required to submit FAFSA. *Unit head:* Alexander Cheng, PhD, 662-915-7407, Fax: 662-915-1287, E-mail: engineer@olemiss.edu. *Application contact:* Dr. Christy M. Wyandt, Associate Dean, 662-915-7474, Fax: 662-915-7577, E-mail: cwyandt@olemiss.edu.

University of Missouri, Graduate School, College of Engineering, Columbia, MO 65211. Offers ME, MS, PhD. Part-time programs available. *Degree requirements:* For doctorate, thesis/dissertation. *Entrance requirements:* For master's and doctorate, GRE General Test. Additional exam requirements/recommendations for international students: Required—TOEFL.

University of Missouri–Kansas City, School of Computing and Engineering, Kansas City, MO 64110-2499. Offers civil engineering (MS); computer and electrical engineering (PhD); computer science (MS), including bioinformatics, software engineering, telecommunications networking; computer science and informatics (PhD); computing (PhD); electrical engineering (MS); engineering (PhD); mechanical engineering (MS); telecommunications (PhD). PhD (interdisciplinary) offered through the School of Graduate Studies. Part-time programs available. *Faculty:* 36 full-time (5 women), 21 part-time/adjunct (0 women). *Students:* 160 full-time (32 women), 194 part-time (41 women); includes 21 minority (5 Black or African American, non-Hispanic/Latino; 9 Asian, non-Hispanic/Latino; 6 Hispanic/Latino; 1 Two or more races, non-Hispanic/Latino), 273 international. Average age 25. 440 applicants, 55% accepted, 104 enrolled. In 2010, 135 master's awarded. *Degree requirements:* For doctorate, thesis/dissertation. *Entrance requirements:* For master's, GRE General Test, minimum GPA of 3.0, 3 letters of recommendation from professors; for doctorate, GRE General Test, minimum GPA of 3.5. Additional exam requirements/recommendations for international students: Required—TOEFL (minimum score 550 paper-based; 213 computer-based; 80 iBT). *Application deadline:* For fall admission, 1/15 priority date for domestic students, 1/15 for international students. Applications are processed on a rolling basis. Application fee: $45 ($50 for international students). *Expenses:* Tuition, state resident: full-time $5522.40; part-time $306.80 per credit hour. Tuition, nonresident: full-time $7128; part-time $792 per credit hour. Required fees: $261.15 per term. *Financial support:* In 2010–11, 35 research assistantships with partial tuition reimbursements (averaging $14,340 per year), 20 teaching assistantships with partial tuition reimbursements (averaging $13,351 per year) were awarded; career-related internships or fieldwork, Federal Work-Study, scholarships/grants, tuition waivers (partial), and unspecified assistantships also available. Support available to part-time students. Financial award application deadline: 3/1; financial award applicants required to submit FAFSA. *Faculty research:* Algorithms, bioinformatics and medical informatics, biomechanics/biomaterials, civil engineering materials, networking and telecommunications, thermal science. Total annual research expenditures: $1.1 million. *Unit head:* Dr. Kevin Z. Truman, Dean, 816-235-2399, Fax: 816-235-5159. *Application contact:* Dr. Kevin Z. Truman, Dean, 816-235-2399, Fax: 816-235-5159.

University of Nebraska–Lincoln, Graduate College, College of Engineering, Lincoln, NE 68588. Offers M Eng, MAE, MEE, MS, PhD. *Degree requirements:* For doctorate, comprehensive exam, thesis/dissertation. *Entrance requirements:* For master's and doctorate, GRE General Test. Additional exam requirements/recommendations for international students: Required—TOEFL. Electronic applications accepted.

University of Nevada, Las Vegas, Graduate College, Howard R. Hughes College of Engineering, Las Vegas, NV 89154-4005. Offers MS, MSE, PhD. Part-time programs available. *Faculty:* 67 full-time (9 women), 18 part-time/adjunct (0 women). *Students:* 149 full-time (29 women), 91 part-time (20 women); includes 67 minority (4 Black or African American, non-Hispanic/Latino; 2 American Indian or Alaska Native, non-Hispanic/Latino; 9 Asian, non-Hispanic/Latino; 12 Hispanic/Latino; 1 Native Hawaiian or other Pacific Islander, non-Hispanic/Latino; 39 Two or more races, non-Hispanic/Latino), 102 international. Average age 30. 148 applicants, 78% accepted, 67 enrolled. In 2010, 64 master's, 13 doctorates awarded. *Degree requirements:* For master's, comprehensive exam (for some programs), thesis (for some programs), final project; for doctorate, comprehensive exam, thesis/dissertation. *Entrance requirements:* Additional exam requirements/recommendations for international students: Required—TOEFL (minimum score 550 paper-based; 213 computer-based; 80 iBT), IELTS (minimum score 7). Application fee: $60 ($95 for international students). *Expenses:* Tuition, area resident: Part-time $239.50 per credit. Tuition, state resident: part-time $239.50 per credit. Tuition, nonresident: part-time $503 per credit. Required fees: $108 per semester. Tuition and fees vary according to course load, program and reciprocity agreements. *Financial support:* In 2010–11, 121 students received support, including 57 research assistantships with partial tuition reimbursements available (averaging $12,288 per year), 64 teaching assistantships with partial tuition reimbursements available (averaging $10,751 per year); institutionally sponsored loans, scholarships/grants, health care benefits, and unspecified assistantships also available. Financial award application deadline: 3/1. Total annual research expenditures: $7.4 million. *Unit head:* Dr. Rama Venkat, Interim Dean, 702-895-1094, Fax: 702-895-4059, E-mail: venkat@ee.unlv.edu. *Application contact:* Graduate College Admissions Evaluator, 702-895-3320, Fax: 702-895-4180, E-mail: gradcollege@unlv.edu.

University of Nevada, Reno, Graduate School, College of Engineering, Reno, NV 89557. Offers MS, PhD. Terminal master's awarded for partial completion of doctoral program. *Degree requirements:* For master's, thesis optional; for doctorate, thesis/dissertation. *Entrance requirements:* For master's, GRE General Test, minimum GPA of 2.75; for doctorate, GRE General Test, minimum GPA of 3.0. Additional exam requirements/recommendations for international students: Required—TOEFL (minimum score 500 paper-based; 173 computer-based; 61 iBT), IELTS (minimum score 6). Electronic applications accepted. *Expenses:* Tuition, state resident: full-time $2219; part-time $246 per credit. Tuition, nonresident: part-time $510 per credit. International tuition: $9009 full-time. Required fees: $59 per term. One-time fee: $101. Tuition and fees vary according to course load. *Faculty research:* Fabrication, development of new materials, structural and earthquake engineering, computer vision/virtual reality, acoustics, smart materials.

University of New Brunswick Fredericton, School of Graduate Studies, Faculty of Engineering, Fredericton, NB E3B 5A3, Canada. Offers M Eng, M Sc E, PhD, Certificate, Diploma. Part-time programs available. *Faculty:* 68 full-time (10 women), 17 part-time/adjunct (1 woman). *Students:* 234 full-time (47 women), 35 part-time (3 women). In 2010, 55 master's, 19 doctorates awarded. *Degree requirements:* For master's, thesis; for doctorate, comprehensive exam, thesis/dissertation, qualifying exam. *Entrance requirements:* For master's, minimum GPA of 3.0. Additional exam requirements/recommendations for international students: Required—TOEFL, TWE. *Application deadline:* For fall admission, 3/1 priority date for domestic students. Applications are processed on a rolling basis. Application fee: $50 Canadian dollars. *Expenses:* Tuition, area resident: Full-time $3708; part-time $927 per term. International tuition: $6300 full-time. Required fees: $50 per term. *Financial support:* In 2010–11, 284 research assistantships, 209 teaching assistantships were awarded; career-related internships or fieldwork also available. *Unit head:* Dr. David Coleman, Dean, 506-453-4570, Fax: 506-453-4569, E-mail: dcoleman@unb.ca. *Application contact:* Dr. David Coleman, Dean, 506-453-4570, Fax: 506-453-4569, E-mail: dcoleman@unb.ca.

University of New Haven, Graduate School, Tagliatela College of Engineering, West Haven, CT 06516-1916. Offers EMS, MS, MSIE, Certificate. Part-time and evening/weekend programs available. *Students:* 161 full-time (34 women), 91 part-time (10 women); includes 11 Black or African American, non-Hispanic/Latino; 9 Asian, non-Hispanic/Latino; 3 Hispanic/Latino, 153 international. Average age 29. 529 applicants, 99% accepted, 118 enrolled. In 2010, 78 master's, 9 other advanced degrees awarded. *Degree requirements:* For master's, thesis or alternative. *Entrance requirements:* Additional exam requirements/recommendations for international students: Required—TOEFL (minimum score 520 paper-based; 190 computer-based; 70 iBT); Recommended—IELTS (minimum score 5.5). *Application deadline:* For fall admission, 5/30 for international students; for winter admission, 10/15 for international students; for spring admission, 1/15 for international students. Applications are processed on a rolling basis. Application fee: $50. Electronic applications accepted. *Financial support:* Research assistantships with partial tuition reimbursements, teaching assistantships with partial tuition reimbursements, career-related internships or fieldwork, Federal Work-Study, scholarships/grants, tuition waivers, and unspecified assistantships available. Support available to part-time students. Financial award applicants required to submit FAFSA. *Unit head:* Dr. Barry Farbrother, Dean, 203-932-7167. *Application contact:* Eloise Gormley, Director of Graduate Admissions, 203-932-7449, Fax: 203-932-7137, E-mail: gradinfo@newhaven.edu.

University of New Mexico, Graduate School, School of Engineering, Albuquerque, NM 87131-2039. Offers MCM, MEME, MS, MSCE, PhD, Post-Doctoral Certificate, MBA/MEME.

Part-time and evening/weekend programs available. *Faculty:* 123 full-time (20 women), 30 part-time/adjunct (3 women). *Students:* 373 full-time (78 women), 191 part-time (31 women); includes 113 minority (6 Black or African American, non-Hispanic/Latino; 5 American Indian or Alaska Native, non-Hispanic/Latino; 17 Asian, non-Hispanic/Latino; 80 Hispanic/Latino; 1 Native Hawaiian or other Pacific Islander, non-Hispanic/Latino; 4 Two or more races, non-Hispanic/Latino), 182 international. Average age 31. 624 applicants, 32% accepted, 116 enrolled. In 2010, 117 master's, 36 doctorates awarded. *Application deadline:* Applications are processed on a rolling basis. Application fee: $50. Electronic applications accepted. *Expenses:* Tuition, state resident: full-time $5991; part-time $251 per credit hour. Tuition, nonresident: full-time $14,405; part-time $800.20 per credit hour. Tuition and fees vary according to course level, course load, program and reciprocity agreements. *Financial support:* In 2010–11, 357 students received support, including 16 fellowships (averaging $7,301 per year), 277 research assistantships (averaging $16,471 per year), 38 teaching assistantships (averaging $7,468 per year). Financial award application deadline: 3/1; financial award applicants required to submit FAFSA. Total annual research expenditures: $12.6 million. *Unit head:* Dr. Joseph L. Cecchi, Dean, 505-277-5522, Fax: 505-277-1422, E-mail: cecchi@unm.edu. *Application contact:* Dr. Joseph L. Cecchi, Dean, 505-277-5522, Fax: 505-277-1422, E-mail: cecchi@unm.edu.

University of New Orleans, Graduate School, College of Engineering, New Orleans, LA 70148. Offers MS, PhD, Certificate. Part-time programs available. Terminal master's awarded for partial completion of doctoral program. *Degree requirements:* For master's, comprehensive exam, thesis optional; for doctorate, comprehensive exam, thesis/dissertation. *Entrance requirements:* For master's, GRE General Test, minimum GPA of 3.0; for doctorate, GRE General Test. Additional exam requirements/recommendations for international students: Required—TOEFL (minimum score 550 paper-based; 213 computer-based; 79 iBT). Electronic applications accepted. *Faculty research:* Electrical, civil, environmental, mechanical, naval architecture, and marine engineering.

The University of North Carolina at Charlotte, Graduate School, The William States Lee College of Engineering, Charlotte, NC 28223-0001. Offers MS, MSCE, MSE, MSEE, MSME, PhD. Part-time and evening/weekend programs available. *Faculty:* 82 full-time (8 women), 1 (woman) part-time/adjunct. *Students:* 213 full-time (44 women), 173 part-time (37 women); includes 38 minority (18 Black or African American, non-Hispanic/Latino; 2 American Indian or Alaska Native, non-Hispanic/Latino; 8 Asian, non-Hispanic/Latino; 9 Hispanic/Latino; 1 Two or more races, non-Hispanic/Latino), 201 international. Average age 27. 431 applicants, 61% accepted, 64 enrolled. In 2010, 77 master's, 16 doctorates awarded. Terminal master's awarded for partial completion of doctoral program. *Degree requirements:* For master's, thesis or alternative; for doctorate, thesis/dissertation. *Entrance requirements:* For master's, GRE General Test. Additional exam requirements/recommendations for international students: Required—TOEFL (minimum score 557 paper-based; 220 computer-based; 83 iBT). *Application deadline:* For fall admission, 7/1 for domestic students, 5/1 for international students; for spring admission, 11/1 for domestic students, 10/1 for international students. Applications are processed on a rolling basis. Application fee: $55. Electronic applications accepted. *Expenses:* Tuition, state resident: full-time $3464. Tuition, nonresident: full-time $14,297. Required fees: $2094. Tuition and fees vary according to course load. *Financial support:* In 2010–11, 169 students received support, including 3 fellowships (averaging $31,815 per year), 65 research assistantships (averaging $7,814 per year), 101 teaching assistantships (averaging $8,748 per year); career-related internships or fieldwork, institutionally sponsored loans, scholarships/grants, and administrative assistantship also available. Support available to part-time students. Financial award application deadline: 4/1; financial award applicants required to submit FAFSA. *Faculty research:* Environmental engineering, structures and geotechnical engineering, precision engineering and precision metrology, optoelectronics and microelectronics, communications. Total annual research expenditures: $5.3 million. *Unit head:* Dr. Robert E. Johnson, Dean, 704-687-2301, Fax: 704-687-2352, E-mail: robejohn@.uncc.edu. *Application contact:* Kathy B. Giddings, Director of Graduate Admissions, 704-687-5503, Fax: 704-687-3279, E-mail: gradadm@uncc.edu.

University of North Dakota, Graduate School, School of Engineering and Mines, Program in Engineering, Grand Forks, ND 58202. Offers PhD. *Students:* 18 full-time (0 women), 7 part-time (1 woman), 19 international. Average age 31. 20 applicants, 40% accepted, 4 enrolled. In 2010, 2 doctorates awarded. *Degree requirements:* For doctorate, comprehensive exam, thesis/dissertation, final exam. *Entrance requirements:* For doctorate, minimum GPA of 3.0. Additional exam requirements/recommendations for international students: Required—TOEFL (minimum score 550 paper-based; 213 computer-based; 79 iBT), IELTS (minimum score 6.5). *Application deadline:* For fall admission, 8/1 priority date for domestic students, 5/1 priority date for international students; for spring admission, 12/1 priority date for domestic students, 9/1 priority date for international students. Applications are processed on a rolling basis. Application fee: $35. Electronic applications accepted. *Expenses:* Tuition, state resident: full-time $5857; part-time $306.74 per credit. Tuition, nonresident: full-time $15,666; part-time $729.77 per credit. Required fees: $53.42 per credit. Tuition and fees vary according to course load, program and reciprocity agreements. *Financial support:* In 2010–11, 21 students received support, including 15 research assistantships with full and partial tuition reimbursements available (averaging $8,274 per year), 6 teaching assistantships with full and partial tuition reimbursements available (averaging $5,206 per year); fellowships with full and partial tuition reimbursements available, career-related internships or fieldwork, Federal Work-Study, institutionally sponsored loans, scholarships/grants, and tuition waivers (full and partial) also available. Support available to part-time students. Financial award application deadline: 3/15; financial award applicants required to submit FAFSA. *Faculty research:* Combustion science, energy conversion, power transmission, environmental engineering. Total annual research expenditures: $90,175. *Unit head:* Dr. Hossein Salehfar, Graduate Director, 701-777-4331, Fax: 701-777-4838. *Application contact:* Staci Wells, Admissions Associate, 701-777-2945, Fax: 701-777-3619, E-mail: staci.wells@gradschool.und.edu.

University of North Texas, Toulouse Graduate School, College of Engineering, Department of Engineering Technology, Denton, TX 76203-5017. Offers MS. Part-time programs available. *Degree requirements:* For master's, comprehensive exam (for some programs), project or thesis. *Entrance requirements:* For master's, GRE General Test, BS in related field. Additional exam requirements/recommendations for international students: Recommended—TOEFL (minimum score 550 paper-based; 213 computer-based; 79 iBT), IELTS (minimum score 6.5). *Application deadline:* For fall admission, 2/1 for international students; for spring admission, 4/1 for international students. Applications are processed on a rolling basis. Electronic applications accepted. *Expenses:* Tuition, state resident: full-time $4298; part-time $239 per credit hour. Tuition, nonresident: full-time $10,782; part-time $549 per credit hour. Required fees: $1292; $270 per credit hour. *Financial support:* Fellowships, research assistantships with partial tuition reimbursements, teaching assistantships with partial tuition reimbursements available. Financial award application deadline: 4/15; financial award applicants required to submit FAFSA. *Faculty research:* Green design, steel structures, Piezoelectric system modeling, biophotonics, concrete pavement cracking. *Application contact:* Graduate Adviser, 940-565-2022, Fax: 940-565-2666, E-mail: kozak@unt.edu.

University of Notre Dame, Graduate School, College of Engineering, Notre Dame, IN 46556. Offers M Eng, MEME, MS, MS Aero E, MS Bio E, MS Ch E, MS Env E, MSCE, MSCSE, MSEE, MSME, PhD. Terminal master's awarded for partial completion of doctoral program. *Degree requirements:* For master's, comprehensive exam; for doctorate, thesis/dissertation. *Entrance requirements:* For master's and doctorate, GRE General Test. Additional exam requirements/recommendations for international students: Required—TOEFL. Electronic applications accepted.

University of Oklahoma, College of Engineering, Program in Engineering, Norman, OK 73019-0390. Offers MS, PhD. Part-time programs available. *Faculty:* 1 (woman) full-time. *Students:* 3 full-time (1 woman), 7 part-time (2 women); includes 2 minority (1 Black or African American, non-Hispanic/Latino; 1 American Indian or Alaska Native, non-Hispanic/Latino), 1 international. Average age 36. 2 applicants, 100% accepted, 2 enrolled. In 2010, 1 master's awarded. *Degree requirements:* For doctorate, comprehensive exam, thesis/dissertation, oral and qualifying exams. *Entrance requirements:* For doctorate, GRE. Additional exam requirements/recommendations for international students: Required—TOEFL (minimum score 550 paper-based; 213 computer-based; 79 iBT). *Application deadline:* For fall admission, 6/1 for domestic students, 4/1 for international students; for spring admission, 11/1 for domestic students, 9/1 for international students. Applications are processed on a rolling basis. Application fee: $40 ($90 for international students). Electronic applications accepted. *Expenses:* Tuition, state resident: full-time $3892.80; part-time $162.20 per credit hour. Tuition, nonresident: full-time $14,167; part-time $590.30 per credit hour. Required fees: $2523.40; $94.60 per credit hour. Tuition and fees vary according to course load and degree level. *Financial support:* Federal Work-Study, scholarships/grants, health care benefits, and unspecified assistantships available. Support available to part-time students. Financial award application deadline: 3/1; financial award applicants required to submit FAFSA. *Faculty research:* Bioengineering, energy, engineering education, infrastructure environment, nanotechnology and weather technology.

University of Ottawa, Faculty of Graduate and Postdoctoral Studies, Faculty of Engineering, Ottawa, ON K1N 6N5, Canada. Offers M Eng, MA Sc, MCS, PhD, Certificate. *Degree requirements:* For master's, thesis or alternative; for doctorate, thesis/dissertation. *Entrance requirements:* For master's, honors degree or equivalent, minimum B average. Electronic applications accepted.

University of Pennsylvania, School of Engineering and Applied Science, Philadelphia, PA 19104. Offers EMBA, MCIT, MS, MSE, PhD, AC, M Arch/MSE, MD/PhD, MSE/MBA, MSE/MCP, VMD/PhD. Part-time and evening/weekend programs available. *Faculty:* 105 full-time (14 women), 24 part-time/adjunct (1 woman). *Students:* 990 full-time (274 women), 315 part-time (67 women); includes 23 Black or African American, non-Hispanic/Latino; 1 American Indian or Alaska Native, non-Hispanic/Latino; 153 Asian, non-Hispanic/Latino; 24 Hispanic/Latino, 617 international. 3,875 applicants, 32% accepted, 621 enrolled. In 2010, 396 master's, 60 doctorates awarded. *Degree requirements:* For doctorate, thesis/dissertation. *Entrance requirements:* Additional exam requirements/recommendations for international students: Required—TOEFL. *Application deadline:* For fall admission, 6/1 priority date for domestic students, 5/1 priority date for international students; for spring admission, 11/1 priority date for domestic students, 10/1 priority date for international students. Applications are processed on a rolling basis. Application fee: $70. Electronic applications accepted. *Expenses:* Tuition: Full-time $25,660; part-time $4758 per course. Required fees: $2152; $270 per course. Tuition and fees vary according to course load, degree level and program. *Financial support:* In 2010–11, 393 students received support; fellowships, research assistantships, teaching assistantships, institutionally sponsored loans, scholarships/grants, traineeships, health care benefits, and unspecified assistantships available. Financial award application deadline: 12/15. *Unit head:* Eduardo D. Glandt, Dean, 215-898-7244, Fax: 215-573-2018, E-mail: seasdean@seas.upenn.edu. *Application contact:* Academic Programs Office, 215-898-4542, Fax: 215-573-5577, E-mail: engstats@seas.upenn.edu.

See Display on next page and Close-Up on page 95.

University of Pittsburgh, Katz Graduate School of Business, MBA/Master of Science in Engineering Dual-Degree Program, Pittsburgh, PA 15260. Offers MBA/MSE. *Accreditation:* AACSB. Part-time and evening/weekend programs available. *Faculty:* 60 full-time (18 women), 22 part-time/adjunct (5 women). *Students:* 12 full-time (2 women), 25 part-time (5 women); includes 1 Black or African American, non-Hispanic/Latino; 1 Hispanic/Latino. Average age 26. 33 applicants, 64% accepted, 11 enrolled. *Entrance requirements:* Additional exam requirements/recommendations for international students: Required—TOEFL (minimum 600 paper, 250 computer, 100 iBT) or IELTS. *Application deadline:* For fall admission, 4/1 for domestic students, 2/1 priority date for international students. Application fee: $50. Electronic applications accepted. *Expenses:* Tuition, state resident: full-time $17,304; part-time $701 per credit. Tuition, nonresident: full-time $29,554; part-time $1210 per credit. Required fees: $740; $214 per term. Tuition and fees vary according to program. *Financial support:* In 2010–11, 4 students received support. Career-related internships or fieldwork and scholarships/grants available. Financial award application deadline: 3/1; financial award applicants required to submit FAFSA. *Faculty research:* Diffusion of technology-driven innovation, customer-focused development of engineered and high-tech products and services, logistics and operations research, global supply chains, value innovation and sustainable innovation—green products for the planet's population. *Unit head:* William T. Valenta, Assistant Dean, Director of MBA Programs, 412-648-1610, Fax: 412-648-1659, E-mail: wtvalenta@katz.pitt.edu. *Application contact:* Cliff McCormick, Director MBA Admissions, 412-648-1700, Fax: 412-648-1659, E-mail: mba@katz.pitt.edu.

University of Pittsburgh, School of Engineering, Pittsburgh, PA 15260. Offers MS, MS Ch E, MSBENG, MSCEE, MSEE, MSIE, MSME, MSPE, PhD, MD/PhD, MS Ch E/MSPE. Part-time programs available. *Faculty:* 112 full-time (16 women), 192 part-time/adjunct (22 women). *Students:* 508 full-time (137 women), 307 part-time (51 women); includes 53 minority (17 Black or African American, non-Hispanic/Latino; 21 Asian, non-Hispanic/Latino; 15 Hispanic/Latino), 293 international. 2,154 applicants, 34% accepted, 237 enrolled. In 2010, 132 master's, 52 doctorates awarded. Terminal master's awarded for partial completion of doctoral program. *Degree requirements:* For doctorate, comprehensive exam, thesis/dissertation, final oral exams. *Entrance requirements:* Additional exam requirements/recommendations for international students: Required—TOEFL (minimum score 550 paper-based; 213 computer-based; 80 iBT). *Application deadline:* For fall admission, 3/1 priority date for domestic students; for spring admission, 7/1 priority date for domestic students. Applications are processed on a rolling basis. Application fee: $50. Electronic applications accepted. *Expenses:* Contact institution. *Financial support:* In 2010–11, 397 students received support, including 72 fellowships with full tuition reimbursements available (averaging $20,772 per year), 247 research assistantships with full tuition reimbursements available (averaging $22,000 per year), 78 teaching assistantships with full tuition reimbursements available (averaging $21,000 per year); scholarships/grants, traineeships, and tuition waivers (full and partial) also available. Financial award application deadline: 4/15. *Faculty research:* Artificial organs, biotechnology, signal processing, construction management, fluid dynamics. Total annual research expenditures: $74.8 million. *Unit head:* Dr. Gerald D. Holder, Dean, 412-624-9811, Fax: 412-624-0412, E-mail: holder@engrng.pitt.edu. *Application contact:* 412-624-9800, Fax: 412-624-9808, E-mail: admin@engrng.pitt.edu.

University of Portland, School of Engineering, Portland, OR 97203-5798. Offers ME. Part-time and evening/weekend programs available. *Faculty:* 2 full-time (0 women). *Students:* 1 full-time (0 women), all international. Average age 22. In 2010, 1 master's awarded. *Entrance requirements:* For master's, GRE General Test, minimum GPA of 3.0, 3 letters of recommendation, resume, statement of goals, official transcripts. Additional exam requirements/recommendations for international students: Required—TOEFL (minimum score 550 paper-based; 80 iBT), IELTS (minimum score 7). *Application deadline:* For fall admission, 7/15 priority date for domestic and international students; for spring admission, 12/15 priority date for domestic and international students. Applications are processed on a rolling basis. Application fee: $50. *Expenses:* Contact institution. *Financial support:* Teaching assistantships, career-related internships or fieldwork, Federal Work-Study, and scholarships/grants available. Support available to part-time students. Financial award application deadline: 3/1; financial award applicants required to submit FAFSA. *Unit head:* Dr. Zia Yamayee, Dean, 503-943-7314. *Application contact:* Dr. Khalid Khan, Director, 503-943-7276, E-mail: khan@up.edu.

University of Puerto Rico, Mayagüez Campus, Graduate Studies, College of Engineering, Mayagüez, PR 00681-9000. Offers ME, MS, PhD. Part-time programs available. *Students:* 365 full-time (129 women), 53 part-time (12 women); includes 293 Hispanic/Latino, 124 international. 112 applicants, 64% accepted, 32 enrolled. In 2010, 51 master's, 3 doctorates awarded. *Degree requirements:* For master's, comprehensive exam, thesis; for doctorate, one foreign language, thesis/dissertation. *Entrance requirements:* For doctorate, GRE. Additional exam requirements/recommendations for international students: Required—TOEFL or IELTS.

Engineering and Applied Sciences—General

Application deadline: For fall admission, 2/15 for domestic and international students; for spring admission, 9/15 for domestic and international students. Applications are processed on a rolling basis. Application fee: $25. *Expenses:* Tuition, state resident: full-time $1188. Tuition, nonresident: full-time $1188. International tuition: $6126 full-time. Tuition and fees vary according to course level and course load. *Financial support:* In 2010–11, 294 students received support, including 1 fellowship (averaging $12,000 per year), 185 research assistantships (averaging $15,000 per year), 108 teaching assistantships (averaging $8,500 per year); Federal Work-Study and institutionally sponsored loans also available. Total annual research expenditures: $10.7 million. *Unit head:* Dr. Jaime Seguel, Dean, 787-265-3823, Fax: 787-833-1190, E-mail: jaime.seguel@upr.edu. *Application contact:* Dr. Agustin Rullan, Graduate Affairs Officer, 787-265-3823, Fax: 787-833-6965, E-mail: agustin.rullan@upr.edu.

University of Regina, Faculty of Graduate Studies and Research, Faculty of Engineering and Applied Science, Regina, SK S4S 0A2, Canada. Offers M Eng, MA Sc, PhD. Part-time programs available. *Faculty:* 45 full-time (7 women), 2 part-time/adjunct (0 women). *Students:* 180 full-time (38 women), 27 part-time (6 women). 323 applicants, 46% accepted. In 2010, 35 master's, 11 doctorates awarded. *Degree requirements:* For master's, thesis (for some programs), project or thesis; for doctorate, comprehensive exam, thesis/dissertation. *Entrance requirements:* Additional exam requirements/recommendations for international students: Required—TOEFL (minimum score 550 paper-based; 80 iBT). *Application deadline:* For fall admission, 3/31 for domestic and international students; for winter admission, 7/31 for domestic and international students; for spring admission; 11/30 for domestic and international students. Application fee: $100. Electronic applications accepted. *Expenses:* Contact institution. *Financial support:* In 2010–11, 22 fellowships (averaging $18,955 per year), 12 research assistantships (averaging $17,125 per year), 32 teaching assistantships (averaging $6,893 per year) were awarded; career-related internships or fieldwork and scholarships/grants also available. Financial award application deadline: 6/15. *Unit head:* Dr. Paitoon Tontiwachwuthikul, Dean, 306-585-4160, Fax: 306-585-4855, E-mail: paitoon.tontiwachwuthikul@uregina.ca. *Application contact:* Melissa Dyck, Administrative Contact, 306-337-2603, Fax: 306-585-4855, E-mail: melissa.dyck@uregina.ca.

University of Rhode Island, Graduate School, College of Engineering, Kingston, RI 02881. Offers MS, PhD, Graduate Certificate. *Accreditation:* ABET (one or more programs are accredited). Part-time programs available. *Faculty:* 61 full-time (10 women), 8 part-time/adjunct (1 woman). *Students:* 127 full-time (24 women), 93 part-time (15 women); includes 25 minority (5 Black or African American, non-Hispanic/Latino; 1 American Indian or Alaska Native, non-Hispanic/Latino; 11 Asian, non-Hispanic/Latino; 6 Hispanic/Latino; 2 Two or more races, non-Hispanic/Latino), 54 international. In 2010, 53 master's, 8 doctorates awarded. *Entrance requirements:* Additional exam requirements/recommendations for international students: Required—TOEFL (minimum score 550 paper-based; 213 computer-based). Application fee: $65. Electronic applications accepted. *Expenses:* Tuition, state resident: full-time $9588; part-time $533 per credit hour. Tuition, nonresident: full-time $22,968; part-time $1276 per credit hour. Required fees: $1282; $68 per semester. Tuition and fees vary according to program. *Financial support:* In 2010–11, 37 research assistantships with full and partial tuition reimbursements (averaging $9,791 per year), 19 teaching assistantships with full and partial tuition reimbursements (averaging $9,033 per year) were awarded. Financial award applicants required to submit FAFSA. Total annual research expenditures: $7.1 million. *Unit head:* Dr. Raymond Wright, Dean, 401-874-2186, Fax: 401-782-1066, E-mail: dean@egr.uri.edu. *Application contact:* Dr. Raymond Wright, Dean, 401-874-2186, Fax: 401-782-1066, E-mail: dean@egr.uri.edu.

University of Rochester, Hajim School of Engineering and Applied Sciences, Rochester, NY 14627. Offers MS, PhD. Part-time programs available. Terminal master's awarded for partial completion of doctoral program. *Degree requirements:* For master's, comprehensive exam, thesis optional; for doctorate, thesis/dissertation, preliminary and oral exams. *Entrance requirements:* For master's and doctorate, GRE. Additional exam requirements/recommendations for international students: Required—TOEFL.

University of St. Thomas, Graduate Studies, School of Engineering, St. Paul, MN 55105-1096. Offers manufacturing engineering and operations (MS); mechanical engineering (MS); medical device development (Certificate); regulatory science (MS); software engineering (MS); software management (MS); software systems (MSS); systems engineering (MS); technology management (MS). *Accreditation:* ABET (one or more programs are accredited). *Entrance requirements:* For master's, resume, official transcripts. Additional exam requirements/recommendations for international students: Required—TOEFL (minimum score 550 paper-based). *Application deadline:* For fall admission, 8/1 priority date for domestic students; for spring admission, 1/1 priority date for domestic students. Applications are processed on a rolling basis. Application fee: $30. Electronic applications accepted. *Expenses:* Contact institution. *Financial support:* Fellowships, research assistantships, institutionally sponsored loans and scholarships/grants available. Support available to part-time students. Financial award application deadline: 4/1; financial award applicants required to submit FAFSA. *Unit head:* Don Weinkauf, Dean, 651-962-5760, Fax: 651-962-6419, E-mail: dhweinkauf@stthomas.edu. *Application contact:* Joyce A. Taylor, Graduate Programs Coordinator, 651-962-5756, Fax: 651-962-6419, E-mail: jataylor1@stthomas.edu.

University of Saskatchewan, College of Graduate Studies and Research, College of Engineering, Saskatoon, SK S7N 5A2, Canada. Offers M Eng, M Sc, PhD, Diploma. *Degree requirements:* For doctorate, thesis/dissertation. *Entrance requirements:* For master's and doctorate, GRE. Additional exam requirements/recommendations for international students: Required—TOEFL.

University of South Africa, College of Science, Engineering and Technology, Pretoria, South Africa. Offers chemical engineering (M Tech); information technology (M Tech).

University of South Alabama, Graduate School, College of Engineering, Mobile, AL 36688. Offers MS Ch E, MSCE, MSEE, MSME. Part-time programs available. *Faculty:* 28 full-time (2 women). *Students:* 114 full-time (16 women), 51 part-time (11 women); includes 9 minority (2 Black or African American, non-Hispanic/Latino; 4 Asian, non-Hispanic/Latino; 3 Hispanic/Latino), 121 international. 174 applicants, 50% accepted, 39 enrolled. In 2010, 63 master's awarded. *Degree requirements:* For master's, project or thesis. *Entrance requirements:* For master's, GRE General Test, BS in engineering, minimum GPA of 3.0. *Application deadline:* For fall admission, 7/15 priority date for domestic students, 6/15 for international students; for spring admission, 12/1 for domestic students, 11/1 for international students. Applications are processed on a rolling basis. Application fee: $35. *Expenses:* Tuition, state resident: part-time $300 per credit hour. Tuition, nonresident: part-time $600 per credit hour. Required fees: $150 per semester. *Financial support:* Research assistantships, career-related internships or fieldwork and institutionally sponsored loans available. Support available to part-time students. Financial award application deadline: 4/1. *Unit head:* Dr. Thomas G. Thomas, Director of Graduate Studies, 251-460-6140. *Application contact:* Dr. B. Keith Harrison, Director of Graduate Studies, 251-460-6160.

University of South Carolina, The Graduate School, College of Engineering and Computing, Columbia, SC 29208. Offers ME, MS, PhD. Part-time and evening/weekend programs available. Postbaccalaureate distance learning degree programs offered (minimal on-campus study). *Degree requirements:* For master's (for some programs); for doctorate, thesis/dissertation. *Entrance requirements:* For master's and doctorate, GRE General Test. Additional exam requirements/recommendations for international students: Required—TOEFL. Electronic applications accepted. *Faculty research:* Electrochemical engineering/fuel cell technology, fracture mechanics and nondestructive evaluation, virtual prototyping for electric power systems, wideband-gap electronics materials behavior/composites and smart materials.

University of Southern California, Graduate School, Viterbi School of Engineering, Los Angeles, CA 90089. Offers MCM, ME, MS, PhD, Engr, Graduate Certificate, MS/MBA. Part-time programs available. Postbaccalaureate distance learning degree programs offered (no on-campus study). *Students:* 2,688 full-time (585 women), 1,571 part-time (306 women); includes 648 minority (56 Black or African American, non-Hispanic/Latino; 422 Asian, non-Hispanic/Latino; 138 Hispanic/Latino; 32 Two or more races, non-Hispanic/Latino), 2,718 international. In 2010, 1,205 master's, 139 doctorates, 16 other advanced degrees awarded. Terminal master's awarded for partial completion of doctoral program. *Degree requirements:* For doctorate, comprehensive exam, thesis/dissertation. *Entrance requirements:* For master's and doctorate, GRE. *Application deadline:* Applications are processed on a rolling basis. Application fee: $85. Electronic applications accepted. *Expenses:* Contact institution. *Financial support:* Institutionally sponsored loans and scholarships/grants available. Financial award application deadline: 12/1. *Faculty research:* Mechanics and materials, aerodynamics of air/ground vehicles, gas dynamics, aerosols, astronautics and space science, geophysical and microgravity flows, planetary physics, power MEMs and MEMS vacuum pumps, heat transfer and combustion, health systems, transportation and logistics, manufacturing and automation, engineering systems design, risk and economic analysis, electromagnetic devices circuits and VLSI, MEMS and nanotechnology, electromagnetics and plasmas. *Unit head:* Dr. Yannis C. Yortsos, Dean, 213-740-0617, Fax: 213-740-8493, E-mail: engrdean@usc.edu. *Application contact:* Margery Berti, Associate Dean, 213-740-6241, Fax: 213-740-2367, E-mail: berti@usc.edu.

University of Southern Indiana, Graduate Studies, College of Science and Engineering, Evansville, IN 47712-3590. Offers MS. Part-time and evening/weekend programs available. *Faculty:* 5 full-time (2 women), 1 (woman) part-time/adjunct. *Students:* 12 part-time (4 women). Average age 33. 2 applicants, 100% accepted, 1 enrolled. In 2010, 1 master's awarded. *Degree requirements:* For master's, project. *Entrance requirements:* For master's, minimum GPA of 2.5, BS in engineering or engineering technology. Additional exam requirements/recommendations for international students: Required—TOEFL (minimum score 550 paper-based; 213 computer-based; 79 iBT), IELTS (minimum score 6). *Application deadline:* For fall admission, 8/15 priority date for domestic students, 3/1 priority date for international students. Applications are processed on a rolling basis. Application fee: $25. Electronic applications accepted. *Expenses:* Tuition, state resident: full-time $4823; part-time $267.95 per credit hour. Tuition, nonresident: full-time $9515; part-time $528.62 per credit hour. Required fees: $220; $22.75 per term. Tuition and fees vary according to course load and reciprocity agreements. *Financial support:* Federal Work-Study, scholarships/grants, tuition waivers (full and partial), and unspecified assistantships available. Financial award application deadline: 3/1; financial award applicants required to submit FAFSA. *Unit head:* Dr. Scott A. Gordon, Dean, 812-465-7137, E-mail: sgordon@usi.edu. *Application contact:* Dr. Peggy F. Harrel, Director, Graduate Studies, 812-465-7015, Fax: 812-464-1956, E-mail: pharrel@usi.edu.

University of South Florida, Graduate School, College of Engineering, Tampa, FL 33620-9951. Offers MCE, MCH, ME, MIE, MME, MSBE, MSBE, MSCE, MSCP, MSCS, MSEE, MSEM, MSES, MSIE, MSME, PhD. Part-time and evening/weekend programs available. *Faculty:* 84 full-time (11 women), 2 part-time/adjunct (0 women). *Students:* 527 full-time (148 women), 293 part-time (62 women); includes 184 minority (57 Black or African American, non-Hispanic/Latino; 46 Asian, non-Hispanic/Latino; 75 Hispanic/Latino; 2 Native Hawaiian or other Pacific Islander, non-Hispanic/Latino; 4 Two or more races, non-Hispanic/Latino), 314 international. Average age 30. 933 applicants, 53% accepted, 249 enrolled. In 2010, 181 master's, 51 doctorates awarded. Terminal master's awarded for partial completion of doctoral program. *Degree requirements:* For master's, comprehensive exam, thesis; for doctorate, comprehensive exam, thesis/dissertation. *Entrance requirements:* For master's, GRE General Test, minimum GPA of 3.0 in last 60 hours of coursework; for doctorate, GRE General Test, minimum GPA of 3.3 in last 60 hours of coursework. Additional exam requirements/recommendations for international students: Required—TOEFL (minimum score 550 paper-based; 213 computer-based). *Application deadline:* For fall admission, 2/15 for domestic students, 1/2 priority date for international students; for spring admission, 10/15 for domestic students, 6/1 priority date for international students. Applications are processed on a rolling basis. Application fee: $30. Electronic applications accepted. *Financial support:* Career-related internships or fieldwork, Federal Work-Study, scholarships/grants, health care benefits, and unspecified assistantships available. Financial award application deadline: 3/1; financial award applicants required to submit FAFSA. Total annual research expenditures: $71,627. *Unit head:* Dr. John Wieneck, Dean, 813-974-2530, Fax: 813-974-5094, E-mail: wieneck@eng.usf.edu. *Application contact:* Marsha L. Brett, Administrative Assistant, 813-974-3782, Fax: 813-974-5094, E-mail: brett@eng.usf.edu.

The University of Tennessee, Graduate School, College of Engineering, Knoxville, TN 37996. Offers MS, PhD, MS/MBA, MS/PhD. Part-time programs available. Postbaccalaureate distance learning degree programs offered (minimal on-campus study). *Faculty:* 148 full-time (15 women), 117 part-time/adjunct (5 women). *Students:* 599 full-time (113 women), 256 part-time (35 women); includes 28 Black or African American, non-Hispanic/Latino; 3 American Indian or Alaska Native, non-Hispanic/Latino; 23 Asian, non-Hispanic/Latino; 11 Hispanic/Latino, 314 international. Average age 26. 1,405 applicants, 29% accepted, 199 enrolled. In 2010, 154 master's, 63 doctorates awarded. *Degree requirements:* For master's, thesis or alternative; for doctorate, comprehensive exam, thesis/dissertation. *Entrance requirements:* For master's, GRE General Test, Minimum GPA of 2.7 (US degree holders); 3.0 (international degree holders); 3-References; Statement of purpose; for doctorate, GRE General Test, Minimum GPA of 3.0 (previous graduate course work); 3-References; Statement of purpose. Additional exam requirements/recommendations for international students: Required—TOEFL (minimum score 550 paper-based; 213 computer-based). *Application deadline:* For fall admission, 2/1 priority date for domestic and international students; for spring admission, 6/15 for domestic and international students. Applications are processed on a rolling basis. Application fee: $35. Electronic applications accepted. *Expenses:* Tuition, state resident: full-time $7440; part-time $414 per credit hour. Tuition, nonresident: full-time $22,478; part-time $1250 per credit hour. Required fees: $922; $43 per credit hour. Tuition and fees vary according to program. *Financial support:* In 2010–11, 484 students received support, including 53 fellowships with full tuition reimbursements available (averaging $17,140 per year), 390 research assistantships with full tuition reimbursements available (averaging $17,759 per year), 204 teaching assistantships with full tuition reimbursements available (averaging $13,560 per year); career-related internships or fieldwork, Federal Work-Study, institutionally sponsored loans, health care benefits, and unspecified assistantships also available. Financial award application deadline: 2/1; financial award applicants required to submit FAFSA. *Faculty research:* Chemical and biomolecular engineering; civil and environmental engineering; electrical engineering and computer science; nuclear engineering; materials science and engineering; mechanical, aerospace, and biomedical engineering; industrial and information engineering. Total annual research expenditures: $47.6 million. *Unit head:* Dr. Wayne T Davis, Dean, 865-974-5321, Fax: 865-974-8890, E-mail: way@utk.edu. *Application contact:* Dr. Masood Parang, Associate Dean of Student Affairs, 865-974-2454, Fax: 865-974-9871, E-mail: mparang@utk.edu.

The University of Tennessee at Chattanooga, Graduate School, College of Engineering and Computer Science, Chattanooga, TN 37403. Offers MS, MS Engr, PhD, Graduate Certificate. Part-time and evening/weekend programs available. Postbaccalaureate distance learning degree programs offered (no on-campus study). *Faculty:* 22 full-time (3 women), 2 part-time/adjunct (1 woman). *Students:* 61 full-time (11 women), 129 part-time (22 women); includes 24 minority (15 Black or African American, non-Hispanic/Latino; 4 Asian, non-Hispanic/Latino; 5 Hispanic/Latino), 32 international. Average age 30. 114 applicants, 75% accepted, 56 enrolled. In 2010, 46 master's, 1 doctorate, 22 other advanced degrees awarded. *Degree requirements:* For master's, comprehensive exam, thesis or alternative, capstone project; for doctorate, comprehensive exam, thesis/dissertation. *Entrance requirements:* For master's, GRE. Additional exam requirements/recommendations for international students: Required—TOEFL (minimum score 550 paper-based; 213 computer-based; 79 iBT), IELTS (minimum score 6). *Application deadline:* For fall admission, 8/1 priority date for domestic students, 6/1 for international students; for spring admission, 12/1 priority date for domestic students, 10/1 for international students. Applications are processed on a rolling basis. Application fee: $35. Electronic applications accepted. *Financial support:* In 2010–11, 39 research assistantships with full and partial tuition reimbursements (averaging $5,500 per year) were awarded; career-related internships or fieldwork, scholarships/grants, and unspecified assistantships also available. Support available to part-time students. *Faculty research:* Quality control and project management, aerodynamics, artificial intelligence, computational design, network security. Total annual research expenditures: $6.9 million. *Unit head:* Dr. William Sutton, Dean, 423-425-2256, Fax: 423-425-5229, E-mail: will-sutton@utc.edu. *Application contact:* Dr. Jerald Ainsworth, Dean of Graduate Studies, 423-425-4478, Fax: 423-425-5223, E-mail: jerald-ainsworth@utc.edu.

The University of Tennessee Space Institute, Graduate Programs, Tullahoma, TN 37388-9700. Offers MS, PhD. Part-time programs available. Postbaccalaureate distance learning degree programs offered. *Faculty:* 20 full-time (2 women), 25 part-time/adjunct (1 woman). *Students:* 54 full-time (8 women), 94 part-time (15 women); includes 12 minority (6 Black or African American, non-Hispanic/Latino; 5 Asian, non-Hispanic/Latino; 1 Native Hawaiian or other Pacific Islander, non-Hispanic/Latino), 23 international. 25 applicants, 88% accepted, 19 enrolled. In 2010, 59 master's, 3 doctorates awarded. Terminal master's awarded for partial completion of doctoral program. *Degree requirements:* For doctorate, one foreign language, thesis/dissertation. *Entrance requirements:* Additional exam requirements/recommendations for international students: Required—TOEFL (minimum score 550 paper-based; 213 computer-based; 80 iBT), IELTS (minimum score 6.5). *Application deadline:* For fall admission, 2/1 for international students; for spring admission, 6/15 for international students. Applications are processed on a rolling basis. Application fee: $35. Electronic applications accepted. *Financial support:* In 2010–11, 4 fellowships with full and partial tuition reimbursements (averaging $1,425 per year), 41 research assistantships with full tuition reimbursements (averaging $17,791 per year) were awarded; career-related internships or fieldwork, Federal Work-Study, institutionally sponsored loans, health care benefits, tuition waivers (full and partial), and unspecified assistantships also available. *Faculty research:* Materials processing, computational fluid dynamics, aerodynamics, laser applications. *Unit head:* Dr. Charles Johnson, Associate Executive Director, 931-393-7318, Fax: 931-393-7211, E-mail: cjohnson@utsi.edu. *Application contact:* Dee Merriman, Coordinator III, 931-393-7213, Fax: 931-393-7211, E-mail: dmerrima@utsi.edu.

The University of Texas at Arlington, Graduate School, College of Engineering, Arlington, TX 76019. Offers M Engr, MS, PhD. Part-time and evening/weekend programs available. Postbaccalaureate distance learning degree programs offered (minimal on-campus study). *Faculty:* 128 full-time (12 women), 8 part-time/adjunct (1 woman). *Students:* 995 full-time (235 women), 597 part-time (119 women); includes 165 minority (44 Black or African American, non-Hispanic/Latino; 77 Asian, non-Hispanic/Latino; 40 Hispanic/Latino; 1 Native Hawaiian or other Pacific Islander, non-Hispanic/Latino; 3 Two or more races, non-Hispanic/Latino), 1,127 international. Average age 27. 1,499 applicants, 72% accepted, 425 enrolled. In 2010, 481 master's, 56 doctorates awarded. Terminal master's awarded for partial completion of doctoral program. *Degree requirements:* For master's, thesis optional; for doctorate, thesis/dissertation. *Entrance requirements:* For master's, GRE General Test, minimum GPA of 3.0 in last 60 hours of coursework; for doctorate, GRE General Test. Additional exam requirements/recommendations for international students: Required—TOEFL (minimum score 550 paper-based; 213 computer-based). *Application deadline:* For fall admission, 6/6 for domestic students, 4/4 for international students; for spring admission, 10/15 for domestic students, 9/5 for international students. Applications are processed on a rolling basis. Application fee: $35 ($50 for international students). *Expenses:* Tuition, state resident: full-time $7500. Tuition, nonresident: full-time $13,080. International tuition: $13,250 full-time. *Financial support:* Fellowships, research assistantships, teaching assistantships, career-related internships or fieldwork, Federal Work-Study, institutionally sponsored loans, scholarships/grants, and tuition waivers (partial) available. Financial award application deadline: 6/1; financial award applicants required to submit FAFSA. *Faculty research:* Nanotechnology, mobile pervasive computing, bioinformatics intelligent systems. *Unit head:* Dr. Bill D. Carroll, Dean, 817-272-2571, Fax: 817-272-5110, E-mail: carroll@uta.edu. *Application contact:* Dr. Lynn L. Peterson, Associate Dean for Academic Affairs, 817-272-2571, Fax: 817-272-2548, E-mail: peterson@uta.edu.

The University of Texas at Austin, Graduate School, Cockrell School of Engineering, Austin, TX 78712-1111. Offers MA, MS, MSE, PhD, MBA/MSE, MD/PhD, MP Aff/MSE. *Accreditation:* ABET (one or more programs are accredited). Part-time and evening/weekend programs available. *Entrance requirements:* For master's and doctorate, GRE General Test. Additional exam requirements/recommendations for international students: Required—TOEFL (minimum score 550 paper-based; 213 computer-based). Electronic applications accepted.

The University of Texas at Dallas, Erik Jonsson School of Engineering and Computer Science, Richardson, TX 75080. Offers MS, MSEE, MSME, MSTE, PhD. Part-time and evening/weekend programs available. *Faculty:* 99 full-time (12 women), 3 part-time/adjunct (1 woman). *Students:* 865 full-time (195 women), 409 part-time (87 women); includes 135 minority (15 Black or African American, non-Hispanic/Latino; 1 American Indian or Alaska Native, non-Hispanic/Latino; 84 Asian, non-Hispanic/Latino; 32 Hispanic/Latino; 3 Two or more races, non-Hispanic/Latino), 908 international. Average age 27. 2,928 applicants, 49% accepted, 386 enrolled. In 2010, 377 master's, 56 doctorates awarded. *Degree requirements:* For master's, thesis optional; for doctorate, thesis/dissertation. *Entrance requirements:* For master's, GRE General Test, minimum GPA of 3.0 in related bachelor's course work; for doctorate, GRE General Test, minimum GPA of 3.5. Additional exam requirements/recommendations for international students: Required—TOEFL (minimum score 550 paper-based; 215 computer-based). *Application deadline:* For fall admission, 7/15 for domestic students, 5/1 priority date for international students; for spring admission, 11/15 for domestic students, 9/1 priority date for international students. Applications are processed on a rolling basis. Application fee: $50 ($100 for international students). Electronic applications accepted. *Expenses:* Tuition, state resident: full-time $10,248; part-time $569 per credit hour. Tuition, nonresident: full-time $18,544; part-time $1030 per credit hour. Tuition and fees vary according to course load. *Financial support:* In 2010–11, 428 students received support, including 6 fellowships with partial tuition reimbursements available (averaging $15,960 per year), 251 research assistantships with partial tuition reimbursements available (averaging $16,306 per year), 84 teaching assistantships with partial tuition reimbursements available (averaging $15,416 per year); career-related internships or fieldwork, Federal Work-Study, institutionally sponsored loans, scholarships/grants, and unspecified assistantships also available. Support available to part-time students. Financial award application deadline: 4/30; financial award applicants required to submit FAFSA. *Faculty research:* Semiconducting materials, nano-fabrication and bio-nanotechnology, biomedical devices and organic electronics, signal processing and language technology, cloud computing and IT security. Total annual research expenditures: $20.2 million. *Unit head:* Dr. Mark W. Spong, Dean, 972-883-2974, Fax: 972-883-2813, E-mail: ecsdean@utdallas.edu. *Application contact:* Dr. Cy Cantrell, Senior Associate Dean, 972-883-6234, Fax: 972-883-2813, E-mail: gradecs@utdallas.edu.

The University of Texas at El Paso, Graduate School, College of Engineering, El Paso, TX 79968-0001. Offers MEENE, MS, MSENE, MSIT, PhD, Certificate. Part-time and evening/weekend programs available. *Students:* 431 (97 women); includes 3 Black or African American, non-Hispanic/Latino; 8 Asian, non-Hispanic/Latino; 150 Hispanic/Latino, 250 international. Average age 28. 338 applicants, 49% accepted. In 2010, 116 master's, 8 doctorates awarded. *Degree requirements:* For master's, thesis optional; for doctorate, thesis/dissertation. *Entrance requirements:* For master's, GRE, minimum GPA of 3.0, letters of reference; for doctorate, GRE, statement of purpose, letters of reference. Additional exam requirements/recommendations for international students: Required—TOEFL; Recommended—IELTS. *Application deadline:* For fall admission, 8/1 priority date for domestic students, 3/1 for international students; for spring admission, 11/1 priority date for domestic students, 9/1 for international students. Applications are processed on a rolling basis. Application fee: $45 ($80 for international students). Electronic applications accepted. *Expenses:* Contact institution. *Financial support:* In 2010–11, research assistantships with partial tuition reimbursements (averaging $21,125 per year), teaching assistantships with partial tuition reimbursements (averaging $16,900 per year) were awarded; fellowships with partial tuition reimbursements, institutionally sponsored loans, scholarships/grants, health care benefits, tuition waivers (partial), and unspecified

Engineering and Applied Sciences—General

The University of Texas at El Paso *(continued)*
assistantships also available. Support available to part-time students. Financial award application deadline: 3/15; financial award applicants required to submit FAFSA. *Unit head:* Dr. Richard Schoephoerster, Dean, 915-747-6444, Fax: 915-747-5437, E-mail: schoephoerster@utep.edu. *Application contact:* Dr. Patricia D. Witherspoon, Dean of the Graduate School, 915-747-5491, Fax: 915-747-5788, E-mail: withersp@utep.edu.

The University of Texas at San Antonio, College of Engineering, San Antonio, TX 78249-0617. Offers MS, MSCE, PhD. Part-time and evening/weekend programs available. *Faculty:* 53 full-time (7 women), 7 part-time/adjunct (1 woman). *Students:* 206 full-time (53 women), 183 part-time (39 women); includes 88 minority (10 Black or African American, non-Hispanic/Latino; 16 Asian, non-Hispanic/Latino; 58 Hispanic/Latino; 4 Two or more races, non-Hispanic/Latino), 181 international. Average age 29. 325 applicants, 72% accepted, 115 enrolled. In 2010, 102 master's, 14 doctorates awarded. *Degree requirements:* For master's, comprehensive exam (for some programs), thesis (for some programs); for doctorate, comprehensive exam, thesis/dissertation. *Entrance requirements:* For master's, GRE General Test, minimum GPA of 3.0 in last 60 hours of bachelor's degree; for doctorate, GRE. Additional exam requirements/recommendations for international students: Required—TOEFL (minimum score 500 paper-based; 173 computer-based), IELTS (minimum score 5). *Application deadline:* For fall admission, 7/1 for domestic students, 4/1 for international students; for spring admission, 11/1 for domestic students, 9/1 for international students. Applications are processed on a rolling basis. Application fee: $45 ($80 for international students). Electronic applications accepted. *Expenses:* Tuition, state resident: full-time $4172; part-time $231.75 per credit hour. Tuition, nonresident: full-time $15,332; part-time $851.75 per credit hour. *Financial support:* In 2010–11, 144 students received support, including 22 fellowships (averaging $31,817 per year), 176 research assistantships (averaging $14,156 per year), 56 teaching assistantships (averaging $10,880 per year); career-related internships or fieldwork, institutionally sponsored loans, scholarships/grants, tuition waivers, and unspecified assistantships also available. Support available to part-time students. Financial award application deadline: 3/31. Total annual research expenditures: $2.5 million. *Unit head:* Dr. C. Mauli Agarwal, Dean, 210-458-4490, Fax: 210-458-5556, E-mail: mauli.agarwal@utsa.edu. *Application contact:* Veronica Ramirez, Assistant Dean, 210-458-4330, Fax: 210-458-4332, E-mail: graduatestudies@utsa.edu.

University of the District of Columbia, School of Engineering and Applied Science, Washington, DC 20008-1175. Offers MS. *Expenses:* Tuition, state resident: full-time $7580; part-time $421 per credit. Tuition, nonresident: full-time $14,580; part-time $810 per credit. Required fees: $620; $30 per credit. One-time fee: $100 part-time.

The University of Toledo, College of Graduate Studies, College of Engineering, Program in Engineering, Toledo, OH 43606-3390. Offers general engineering (MS). *Entrance requirements:* For master's, GRE General Test, minimum GPA of 2.7, industrial experience. *Expenses:* Tuition, state resident: full-time $11,426; part-time $476 per credit hour. Tuition, nonresident: full-time $21,660; part-time $903 per credit hour. One-time fee: $62.

University of Toronto, School of Graduate Studies, Physical Sciences Division, Faculty of Applied Science and Engineering, Toronto, ON M5S 1A1, Canada. Offers M Eng, MA Sc, MH Sc, PhD. Part-time programs available. *Degree requirements:* For doctorate, thesis/dissertation. *Expenses:* Contact institution.

University of Tulsa, Graduate School, College of Engineering and Natural Sciences, Tulsa, OK 74104-3189. Offers ME, MS, MSE, MTA, PhD, JD/MS, MBA/MS, MSF/MSAM. Part-time programs available. *Faculty:* 100 full-time (10 women), 2 part-time/adjunct (1 woman). *Students:* 232 full-time (61 women), 75 part-time (19 women); includes 17 minority (3 Black or African American, non-Hispanic/Latino; 9 American Indian or Alaska Native, non-Hispanic/Latino; 3 Asian, non-Hispanic/Latino; 2 Hispanic/Latino), 167 international. Average age 26. 542 applicants, 35% accepted, 76 enrolled. In 2010, 89 master's, 9 doctorates awarded. Terminal master's awarded for partial completion of doctoral program. *Degree requirements:* For master's, thesis (for some programs); for doctorate, comprehensive exam, thesis/dissertation. *Entrance requirements:* For master's and doctorate, GRE General Test. Additional exam requirements/recommendations for international students: Required—TOEFL (minimum score 550 paper-based; 213 computer-based), IELTS (minimum score 6). *Application deadline:* Applications are processed on a rolling basis. Application fee: $40. Electronic applications accepted. *Expenses:* Tuition: Full-time $16,902; part-time $939 per credit hour. Required fees: $1020; $4 per credit hour. Tuition and fees vary according to course load. *Financial support:* In 2010–11, 231 students received support, including 36 fellowships with full and partial tuition reimbursements available (averaging $4,439 per year), 151 research assistantships with full and partial tuition reimbursements available (averaging $10,677 per year), 99 teaching assistantships with full and partial tuition reimbursements available (averaging $10,018 per year); career-related internships or fieldwork, Federal Work-Study, scholarships/grants, health care benefits, tuition waivers (full and partial), and unspecified assistantships also available. Support available to part-time students. Financial award application deadline: 2/1; financial award applicants required to submit FAFSA. Total annual research expenditures: $18.2 million. *Unit head:* Dr. Steve J. Bellovich, Dean, 918-631-2288, E-mail: steven-bellovich@utulsa.edu. *Application contact:* Graduate School, 918-631-2336, Fax: 918-631-2156, E-mail: grad@utulsa.edu.

University of Utah, Graduate School, College of Engineering, Salt Lake City, UT 84112. Offers M Phil, ME, MS, PhD. *Accreditation:* ABET. *Faculty:* 153 full-time (19 women), 15 part-time/adjunct (0 women). *Students:* 688 full-time (90 women), 260 part-time (29 women); includes 47 minority (3 Black or African American, non-Hispanic/Latino; 1 American Indian or Alaska Native, non-Hispanic/Latino; 27 Asian, non-Hispanic/Latino; 15 Hispanic/Latino; 1 Two or more races, non-Hispanic/Latino), 360 international. Average age 28. 758 applicants, 55% accepted, 273 enrolled. In 2010, 210 master's, 60 doctorates awarded. *Application deadline:* Applications are processed on a rolling basis. Application fee: $55 ($65 for international students). *Expenses:* Contact institution. *Financial support:* Applicants required to submit FAFSA. *Faculty research:* Biomaterials, wastewater treatment, computer-aided graphics design, semiconductors, polymers. Total annual research expenditures: $37.8 million. *Unit head:* Dr. Richard B. Brown, Dean, 801-581-6912, E-mail: brown@coe.utah.edu. *Application contact:* Dianne Leonard, Coordinator, Administrative Program, 801-585-7769, Fax: 801-581-8692, E-mail: dleonard@coe.utah.edu.

University of Vermont, Graduate College, College of Engineering and Mathematics, Burlington, VT 05405. Offers MS, MST, PhD. Part-time programs available. *Students:* 168 (46 women); includes 1 Black or African American, non-Hispanic/Latino; 5 Asian, non-Hispanic/Latino; 1 Hispanic/Latino, 50 international. 297 applicants, 44% accepted, 36 enrolled. In 2010, 40 master's, 11 doctorates awarded. *Degree requirements:* For doctorate, thesis/dissertation. *Entrance requirements:* Additional exam requirements/recommendations for international students: Required—TOEFL (minimum score 550 paper-based; 213 computer-based; 80 iBT). *Application deadline:* For fall admission, 4/1 priority date for domestic students. Applications are processed on a rolling basis. Application fee: $40. Electronic applications accepted. *Expenses:* Tuition, state resident: part-time $537 per credit hour. Tuition, nonresident: part-time $1355 per credit hour. *Financial support:* Fellowships, research assistantships, teaching assistantships, Federal Work-Study available. Financial award application deadline: 3/1. *Unit head:* Prof. Jason Bates, Interim Director, 802-656-3333. *Application contact:* Prof. Jason Bates, Interim Director, 802-656-3333.

University of Victoria, Faculty of Graduate Studies, Faculty of Engineering, Victoria, BC V8W 2Y2, Canada. Offers M Eng, M Sc, MA Sc, PhD.

University of Virginia, School of Engineering and Applied Science, Charlottesville, VA 22903. Offers MCS, ME, MEP, MMSE, MS, PhD, ME/MBA. Part-time programs available. Postbaccalaureate distance learning degree programs offered (no on-campus study). *Faculty:* 142 full-time (16 women), 4 part-time/adjunct (0 women). *Students:* 600 full-time (144 women), 25 part-time (3 women); includes 72 minority (17 Black or African American, non-Hispanic/Latino;

40 Asian, non-Hispanic/Latino; 10 Hispanic/Latino; 5 Two or more races, non-Hispanic/Latino), 241 international. Average age 27. 1,570 applicants, 19% accepted, 114 enrolled. In 2010, 170 master's, 55 doctorates awarded. Terminal master's awarded for partial completion of doctoral program. *Degree requirements:* For doctorate, comprehensive exam, thesis/dissertation. *Entrance requirements:* For master's, GRE General Test, 3 letters of recommendation; for doctorate, GRE General Test, 3 letters of recommendation, essay. Additional exam requirements/recommendations for international students: Required—TOEFL (minimum score 600 paper-based; 250 computer-based; 90 iBT), IELTS (minimum score 7). *Application deadline:* For fall admission, 8/1 for domestic students, 4/1 for international students; for winter admission, 12/1 for domestic students, 8/1 for international students; for spring admission, 5/1 for domestic students, 1/1 for international students. Applications are processed on a rolling basis. Application fee: $60. Electronic applications accepted. *Financial support:* Fellowships with full tuition reimbursements, research assistantships with full tuition reimbursements, teaching assistantships with full tuition reimbursements, career-related internships or fieldwork available. Financial award application deadline: 1/15; financial award applicants required to submit FAFSA. *Unit head:* James H. Aylor, Dean, 434-924-3072, Fax: 434-243-2083. *Application contact:* Kathryn C. Thornton, Associate Dean for Graduate Programs, 434-924-3897, Fax: 434-982-3044, E-mail: seas-grad-admission@virginia.edu.

University of Washington, Graduate School, College of Engineering, Seattle, WA 98195-2180. Offers MAE, MME, MS, MSCE, MSE, MSME, PMS, PhD. Part-time programs available. Postbaccalaureate distance learning degree programs offered (no on-campus study). *Faculty:* 328 full-time (63 women), 80 part-time/adjunct (17 women). *Students:* 1,102 full-time (316 women), 697 part-time (146 women); includes 41 Black or African American, non-Hispanic/Latino; 4 American Indian or Alaska Native, non-Hispanic/Latino; 228 Asian, non-Hispanic/Latino; 58 Hispanic/Latino, 460 international. Average age 28. 4,490 applicants, 27% accepted, 517 enrolled. In 2010, 399 master's, 106 doctorates awarded. *Degree requirements:* For master's, comprehensive exam (for some programs), thesis optional, Teaching Assist. for 1 quarter, research project, final exam; for doctorate, comprehensive exam, thesis/dissertation, Qualifying, general & final exams; thesis defense, research/independent project, complete all work towards the degree within 10 years. *Entrance requirements:* For master's and doctorate, GRE General Test, Minimum GPA 3.0. Dept. requirements vary & include: letters of recommendation, statement of objectives/purpose, transcripts, resume or curriculum vitae. Additional exam requirements/recommendations for international students: Required—TOEFL (minimum score 580 paper-based; 237 computer-based; 92 iBT); Recommended—IELTS (minimum score 7). *Application deadline:* For fall admission, 12/15 for domestic students, 11/15 priority date for international students. Application fee: $75. Electronic applications accepted. *Financial support:* In 2010–11, 30 students received support, including 152 fellowships with full tuition reimbursements available (averaging $18,477 per year), 613 research assistantships with full tuition reimbursements available (averaging $17,217 per year), 153 teaching assistantships with full tuition reimbursements available (averaging $16,167 per year); career-related internships or fieldwork, Federal Work-Study, institutionally sponsored loans, scholarships/grants, traineeships, health care benefits, tuition waivers (full), unspecified assistantships, and stipend supplements also available. Financial award application deadline: 2/28; financial award applicants required to submit FAFSA. *Faculty research:* Biomaterials and tissue engineering, molecular energy processes, human-computer interaction, artificial intelligence, environmentally sensitive energy conversion. Total annual research expenditures: $110 million. *Unit head:* Dr. Matthew O'Donnell, Dean, 206-543-0340, Fax: 206-685-0666, E-mail: odonnel@uw.edu. *Application contact:* Dr. Eve Riskin, Associate Dean, Academic Affairs, 206-685-2313, Fax: 206-685-0666, E-mail: riskin@u.washington.edu.

University of Waterloo, Graduate Studies, Faculty of Engineering, Waterloo, ON N2L 3G1, Canada. Offers M Arch, M Eng, MA Sc, MBET, MMS, PhD. Part-time and evening/weekend programs available. Postbaccalaureate distance learning degree programs offered (no on-campus study). *Degree requirements:* For master's, research paper or thesis; for doctorate, comprehensive exam, thesis/dissertation. *Entrance requirements:* For master's, honors degree; for doctorate, master's degree, minimum A- average. Additional exam requirements/recommendations for international students: Required—TOEFL, TWE. Electronic applications accepted.

The University of Western Ontario, Faculty of Graduate Studies, Physical Sciences Division, Faculty of Engineering, London, ON N6A 5B8, Canada. Offers chemical and biochemical engineering (ME Sc, PhD); civil and environmental engineering (M Eng, ME Sc, PhD); electrical and computer engineering (M Eng, ME Sc, PhD); mechanical and materials engineering (M Eng, ME Sc, PhD). Part-time programs available. Terminal master's awarded for partial completion of doctoral program. *Degree requirements:* For master's, thesis; for doctorate, thesis/dissertation. *Entrance requirements:* For master's, minimum B average; for doctorate, minimum B+ average. *Faculty research:* Wind, geotechnical, chemical reactor engineering, applied electrostatics, biochemical engineering.

University of Windsor, Faculty of Graduate Studies, Faculty of Engineering, Windsor, ON N9B 3P4, Canada. Offers M Eng, MA Sc, PhD. Part-time programs available. *Degree requirements:* For doctorate, comprehensive exam, thesis/dissertation. *Entrance requirements:* For master's, minimum B average; for doctorate, master's degree. Additional exam requirements/recommendations for international students: Required—TOEFL. Electronic applications accepted.

University of Wisconsin–Madison, Graduate School, College of Engineering, Madison, WI 53706-1380. Offers ME, MS, PhD. Part-time programs available. Postbaccalaureate distance learning degree programs offered (minimal on-campus study). *Faculty:* 224 full-time (34 women), 93 part-time/adjunct (20 women). *Students:* 1,189 full-time (240 women), 83 part-time (15 women); includes 19 Black or African American, non-Hispanic/Latino; 3 American Indian or Alaska Native, non-Hispanic/Latino; 48 Asian, non-Hispanic/Latino; 34 Hispanic/Latino, 198 international. 3,671 applicants, 23% accepted, 282 enrolled. In 2010, 285 master's, 87 doctorates awarded. *Degree requirements:* For doctorate, thesis/dissertation. *Application deadline:* Applications are processed on a rolling basis. Application fee: $56. Electronic applications accepted. *Expenses:* Tuition, state resident: full-time $9887.36; part-time $617.96 per credit. Tuition, nonresident: full-time $24,054; part-time $1503.40 per credit. Required fees: $67.63 per credit. Tuition and fees vary according to reciprocity agreements. *Financial support:* Fellowships with full and partial tuition reimbursements, research assistantships with full tuition reimbursements, teaching assistantships with full tuition reimbursements, career-related internships or fieldwork, Federal Work-Study, institutionally sponsored loans, scholarships/grants, and unspecified assistantships available. Support available to part-time students. *Unit head:* Paul S. Peercy, Dean, 608-262-3482, Fax: 608-262-6400, E-mail: peercy@engr.wisc.edu.

University of Wisconsin–Madison, Graduate School, Department of Engineering Professional Development, Madison, WI 53706. Offers engine systems (ME); professional practice (ME). Part-time and evening/weekend programs available. Postbaccalaureate distance learning degree programs offered (minimal on-campus study). *Students:* 115 part-time (12 women). 75 applicants. In 2010, 44 master's awarded. *Entrance requirements:* For master's, ABET Accredited Engineering degree with GPA of 3.0 (out of 4.0) or higher; 4 years professional engineering experience. Additional exam requirements/recommendations for international students: Required—TOEFL (minimum score 580 paper-based; 243 computer-based). *Application deadline:* Applications are processed on a rolling basis. Application fee: $56. Electronic applications accepted. *Expenses:* Tuition, state resident: full-time $9887.36; part-time $617.96 per credit. Tuition, nonresident: full-time $24,054; part-time $1503.40 per credit. Required fees: $67.63 per credit. Tuition and fees vary according to reciprocity agreements. *Financial support:* Applicants required to submit FAFSA. *Unit head:* Wayne P. Pferdehirt, Director of Distance Degrees, 608-265-2361, E-mail: pferdehi@epd.engr.wisc.edu. *Application contact:* Gary R. Henderson, Director of Student Services, 608-262-0133, E-mail: henderson@epd.engr.wisc.edu.

University of Wisconsin–Milwaukee, Graduate School, College of Engineering and Applied Science, Milwaukee, WI 53201. Offers MS, PhD, Certificate, MUP/MS. Part-time programs available. *Faculty:* 80 full-time (9 women). *Students:* 186 full-time (37 women), 146 part-time (26 women); includes 15 Black or African American, non-Hispanic/Latino; 3 American Indian or Alaska Native, non-Hispanic/Latino; 8 Asian, non-Hispanic/Latino; 11 Hispanic/Latino, 33 international. Average age 31. 309 applicants, 65% accepted, 78 enrolled. In 2010, 55 master's, 19 doctorates awarded. *Degree requirements:* For master's, comprehensive exam (for some programs), thesis or alternative; for doctorate, thesis/dissertation, internship. *Entrance requirements:* For master's, GRE, minimum GPA of 2.75; for doctorate, GRE, minimum GPA of 3.5. Additional exam requirements/recommendations for international students: Required—TOEFL (minimum score 550 paper-based; 79 iBT), IELTS (minimum score 6.5). *Application deadline:* For fall admission, 1/1 priority date for domestic students; for spring admission, 9/1 for domestic students. Applications are processed on a rolling basis. Application fee: $56 ($96 for international students). *Financial support:* In 2010–11, 31 research assistantships, 82 teaching assistantships were awarded; fellowships, career-related internships or fieldwork, Federal Work-Study, and unspecified assistantships also available. Support available to part-time students. Financial award application deadline: 4/15. Total annual research expenditures: $17.6 million. *Unit head:* Dr. Tien-Chen Jen, Interim Dean, 414-229-4126, E-mail: jent@uwm.edu. *Application contact:* Betty Warras, General Information Contact, 414-229-6169, Fax: 414-229-6958, E-mail: ceas-graduate@uwm.edu.

University of Wisconsin–Platteville, School of Graduate Studies, Distance Learning Center, Online Master of Science in Engineering Program, Platteville, WI 53818-3099. Offers MS. Part-time and evening/weekend programs available. Postbaccalaureate distance learning degree programs offered (no on-campus study). *Students:* 3 full-time (0 women), 107 part-time (19 women); includes 9 minority (6 Black or African American, non-Hispanic/Latino; 1 American Indian or Alaska Native, non-Hispanic/Latino; 1 Asian, non-Hispanic/Latino; 1 Hispanic/Latino), 8 international. 42 applicants, 74% accepted, 23 enrolled. In 2010, 33 master's awarded. *Degree requirements:* For master's, thesis or alternative. *Entrance requirements:* Additional exam requirements/recommendations for international students: Required—TOEFL (minimum score 500 paper-based; 173 computer-based; 61 iBT). *Application deadline:* For fall admission, 7/1 priority date for domestic students; for spring admission, 11/1 priority date for domestic students. Applications are processed on a rolling basis. Application fee: $56. Electronic applications accepted. *Expenses:* Contact institution. *Financial support:* Scholarships/grants available. Support available to part-time students. *Unit head:* Dr. Lisa Riedle, Coordinator, 608-342-1686, Fax: 608-342-1566, E-mail: riedle@uwplatt.edu. *Application contact:* Information Contact, 608-342-1158, Fax: 608-342-1566, E-mail: engineering@uwplatt.edu.

University of Wyoming, College of Engineering and Applied Sciences, Laramie, WY 82070. Offers MS, PhD. Part-time programs available. *Entrance requirements:* For master's and doctorate, GRE General Test, minimum GPA of 3.0. Additional exam requirements/recommendations for international students: Required—TOEFL. Electronic applications accepted.

Utah State University, School of Graduate Studies, College of Engineering, Logan, UT 84322. Offers ME, MS, PhD, CE. Part-time and evening/weekend programs available. Terminal master's awarded for partial completion of doctoral program. *Degree requirements:* For master's, thesis (for some programs); for doctorate, thesis/dissertation. *Entrance requirements:* For master's and doctorate, GRE General Test, minimum GPA of 3.0. Additional exam requirements/recommendations for international students: Required—TOEFL. Electronic applications accepted. *Faculty research:* Crop-yield modeling, earthquake engineering, digital signal processing, technology and the public school, cryogenic cooling.

Vanderbilt University, School of Engineering, Nashville, TN 37235. Offers M Eng, MS, PhD, MD/PhD. MS and PhD offered through the Graduate School. Part-time programs available. *Faculty:* 121 full-time (22 women), 25 part-time/adjunct (2 women). *Students:* 352 full-time (99 women); includes 15 Black or African American, non-Hispanic/Latino; 2 American Indian or Alaska Native, non-Hispanic/Latino; 12 Asian, non-Hispanic/Latino; 9 Hispanic/Latino, 146 international. Average age 26. 1,314 applicants, 15% accepted, 106 enrolled. In 2010, 70 master's, 45 doctorates awarded. Terminal master's awarded for partial completion of doctoral program. *Degree requirements:* For master's, comprehensive exam (for some programs), thesis (for some programs); for doctorate, comprehensive exam (for some programs), thesis/dissertation. *Entrance requirements:* For master's and doctorate, GRE General Test. Additional exam requirements/recommendations for international students: Required—TOEFL. *Application deadline:* For fall admission, 1/15 for domestic and international students; for spring admission, 11/1 for domestic and international students. Application fee: $0. Electronic applications accepted. *Financial support:* Fellowships with full tuition reimbursements, research assistantships with full tuition reimbursements, teaching assistantships with full tuition reimbursements, career-related internships or fieldwork, Federal Work-Study, institutionally sponsored loans, scholarships/grants, traineeships, health care benefits, and tuition waivers (full and partial) available. Support available to part-time students. Financial award application deadline: 1/15; financial award applicants required to submit CSS PROFILE or FAFSA. *Faculty research:* Robotics, microelectronics, reliability in design, software engineering, medical imaging. Total annual research expenditures: $54.6 million. *Unit head:* Dean Kenneth F. Galloway, Dean, 615-322-0720, Fax: 615-343-8006, E-mail: kenneth.f.galloway@vanderbilt.edu. *Application contact:* Dolores A. Black, Coordinator, Graduate Student Recruiting, 615-343-3308, Fax: 615-343-8006, E-mail: dolores.black@vanderbilt.edu.

Villanova University, College of Engineering, Villanova, PA 19085-1699. Offers MSCPE, MSChE, MSEE, MSME, MSWREE, PhD, Certificate. Part-time and evening/weekend programs available. Postbaccalaureate distance learning degree programs offered (minimal on-campus study). *Faculty:* 72 full-time (11 women), 18 part-time/adjunct (2 women). *Students:* 75 full-time (13 women), 290 part-time (70 women); includes 13 Black or African American, non-Hispanic/Latino; 1 American Indian or Alaska Native, non-Hispanic/Latino; 18 Asian, non-Hispanic/Latino; 7 Hispanic/Latino, 49 international. Terminal master's awarded for partial completion of doctoral program. *Degree requirements:* For master's, thesis optional; for doctorate, thesis/dissertation. *Entrance requirements:* For master's, GRE General Test (for applicants with degrees from foreign universities), minimum GPA of 3.0; for doctorate, GRE General Test. Additional exam requirements/recommendations for international students: Required—TOEFL (minimum score 600 paper-based; 250 computer-based; 100 iBT). *Application deadline:* For fall admission, 8/1 priority date for domestic students, 4/1 priority date for international students; for spring admission, 12/1 for domestic students, 10/1 for international students. Applications are processed on a rolling basis. Application fee: $50. Electronic applications accepted. *Expenses:* Contact institution. *Financial support:* In 2010–11, research assistantships with full and partial tuition reimbursements (averaging $13,500 per year); Federal Work-Study, scholarships/grants, tuition waivers (full and partial), and unspecified assistantships also available. Support available to part-time students. Financial award application deadline: 1/15. *Faculty research:* Composite materials, economy and risk, heat transfer, signal detection. Total annual research expenditures: $3.9 million. *Unit head:* Dr. Gary A. Gabriele, Dean, 610-519-4960, Fax: 610-519-5859, E-mail: gary.gabriele@villanova.edu. *Application contact:* College of Engineering, Graduate Programs Office, 610-519-5840, Fax: 610-519-5859, E-mail: engineering.grad@villanova.edu.

Virginia Commonwealth University, Graduate School, School of Engineering, Richmond, VA 23284-9005. Offers MS, PhD, MD/PhD. *Faculty:* 50 full-time (8 women). *Students:* 157 full-time (50 women), 89 part-time (18 women); includes 50 minority (14 Black or African American, non-Hispanic/Latino; 24 Asian, non-Hispanic/Latino; 11 Hispanic/Latino; 1 Two or more races, non-Hispanic/Latino), 88 international. 245 applicants, 68% accepted, 108 enrolled. In 2010, 60 master's, 20 doctorates awarded. *Degree requirements:* For doctorate, thesis/dissertation, comprehensive oral and written exams. *Entrance requirements:* For master's and doctorate, GRE General Test. Additional exam requirements/recommendations for international students: Required—TOEFL (minimum score 600 paper-based; 250 computer-based; 100 iBT). *Application deadline:* For fall admission, 2/1 priority date for domestic students; for spring admission, 11/15 for domestic students. Application fee: $50. Electronic applications accepted. *Expenses:* Tuition, state resident: full-time $4308; part-time $479 per credit hour. Tuition, nonresident: full-time $8942; part-time $994 per credit hour. Required fees: $2000; $85 per credit hour. Tuition and fees vary according to course level, course load, degree level, campus/location and program. *Financial support:* Applicants required to submit FAFSA. *Faculty research:* Artificial hearts, orthopedic implants, medical imaging, medical instrumentation and sensors, cardiac monitoring. *Unit head:* Dr. Rosalyn S. Hobson, Associate Dean for Graduate Affairs, 804-828-3925, E-mail: rhobson@vcu.edu. *Application contact:* Mark D. Meadows, Director of Student Recruitment, 804-827-4005, E-mail: mdmeadows@vcu.edu.

Virginia Polytechnic Institute and State University, Graduate School, College of Engineering, Blacksburg, VA 24061. Offers M Eng, MEA, MS, PhD, Certificate. *Accreditation:* ABET (one or more programs are accredited). *Faculty:* 331 full-time (49 women), 1 part-time/adjunct (0 women). *Students:* 1,682 full-time (378 women), 402 part-time (79 women); includes 45 Black or African American, non-Hispanic/Latino; 92 Asian, non-Hispanic/Latino; 38 Hispanic/Latino, 955 international. Average age 28. 4,561 applicants, 20% accepted, 489 enrolled. In 2010, 452 master's, 154 doctorates awarded. *Degree requirements:* For master's, comprehensive exam (for some programs), thesis (for some programs); for doctorate, comprehensive exam (for some programs), thesis/dissertation (for some programs). *Entrance requirements:* For master's and doctorate, GRE. Additional exam requirements/recommendations for international students: Required—TOEFL (minimum score 550 paper-based; 213 computer-based). *Application deadline:* For fall admission, 7/1 for domestic and international students; for spring admission, 12/1 for domestic and international students. Applications are processed on a rolling basis. Application fee: $65. Electronic applications accepted. *Expenses:* Tuition, area resident: Full-time $9399; part-time $488 per credit hour. Tuition, state resident: full-time $9399; part-time $488 per credit hour. Tuition, nonresident: full-time $17,854; part-time $957.75 per credit hour. International tuition: $17,854 full-time. Required fees: $1534. Full-time tuition and fees vary according to program. *Financial support:* In 2010–11, 185 fellowships with full tuition reimbursements (averaging $6,315 per year), 841 research assistantships with full tuition reimbursements (averaging $20,820 per year), 197 teaching assistantships with full tuition reimbursements (averaging $16,737 per year) were awarded; career-related internships or fieldwork, Federal Work-Study, scholarships/grants, health care benefits, and unspecified assistantships also available. Financial award application deadline: 1/15. Total annual research expenditures: $87.3 million. *Unit head:* Dr. Richard C. Benson, Dean, 540-231-9752, Fax: 540-231-3362, E-mail: deaneng@vt.edu. *Application contact:* Linda Perkins, Contact, 540-231-9752, Fax: 540-231-3362, E-mail: lperkins@vt.edu.

Washington State University, Graduate School, College of Engineering and Architecture, Pullman, WA 99164. Offers M Arch, MS, PhD. *Faculty:* 106. *Students:* 386 full-time (107 women), 57 part-time (12 women); includes 25 minority (2 Black or African American, non-Hispanic/Latino; 1 American Indian or Alaska Native, non-Hispanic/Latino; 17 Asian, non-Hispanic/Latino; 4 Hispanic/Latino; 1 Two or more races, non-Hispanic/Latino), 235 international. Average age 27. 1,013 applicants, 17% accepted, 92 enrolled. In 2010, 132 master's, 25 doctorates awarded. Terminal master's awarded for partial completion of doctoral program. *Degree requirements:* For master's, comprehensive exam (for some programs), thesis (for some programs), oral exam; for doctorate, comprehensive exam, thesis/dissertation, oral exam. *Entrance requirements:* For master's, GRE, minimum GPA of 3.0, 3 letters of recommendation; for doctorate, GRE, minimum GPA of 3.4, 3 letters of recommendation. Additional exam requirements/recommendations for international students: Required—TOEFL (minimum score 520 paper-based; 190 computer-based). *Application deadline:* For fall admission, 3/1 priority date for domestic students, 3/1 for international students; for spring admission, 7/1 priority date for domestic students, 7/1 for international students. Applications are processed on a rolling basis. Application fee: $50. *Expenses:* Tuition, state resident: full-time $8552; part-time $443 per credit. Tuition, nonresident: full-time $21,650; part-time $1083 per credit. Required fees: $846. *Financial support:* In 2010–11, 141 research assistantships with full and partial tuition reimbursements (averaging $18,204 per year), 92 teaching assistantships with full and partial tuition reimbursements (averaging $18,204 per year) were awarded; career-related internships or fieldwork, Federal Work-Study, institutionally sponsored loans, tuition waivers (partial), and teaching associateships also available. Financial award application deadline: 4/1; financial award applicants required to submit FAFSA. Total annual research expenditures: $14.6 million. *Unit head:* Dr. Candis Claiborn, Dean, 509-335-5593, Fax: 509-335-7632, E-mail: claiborn@wsu.edu. *Application contact:* Graduate School Admissions, 800-GRADWSU, Fax: 509-335-1949, E-mail: gradsch@wsu.edu.

Washington State University Tri-Cities, Graduate Programs, College of Engineering and Computer Science, Richland, WA 99352. Offers computer science (MS, PhD); electrical and computer engineering (PhD); electrical engineering (MS); mechanical engineering (MS, PhD). Part-time programs available. *Faculty:* 28. *Students:* 4 full-time (0 women), 25 part-time (8 women); includes 2 Black or African American, non-Hispanic/Latino, 1 international. *Degree requirements:* For master's, comprehensive exam, thesis (for some programs); for doctorate, comprehensive exam, thesis/dissertation, oral exam. *Entrance requirements:* For master's and doctorate, GRE, minimum GPA of 3.0, 3 letters of recommendation. Additional exam requirements/recommendations for international students: Required—TOEFL (minimum score 550 paper-based; 213 computer-based). *Application deadline:* For fall admission, 1/10 priority date for domestic students, 1/10 for international students; for spring admission, 7/1 priority date for domestic students, 7/1 for international students. Application fee: $50. *Financial support:* Application deadline: 3/1. *Faculty research:* Positive ion track structure, biological systems computer simulations. *Unit head:* Dr. Ali Saberi, Chair, 509-372-7178, E-mail: sidra@eecs.wsu.edu. *Application contact:* Dr. Scott Hudson, Associate Director, 509-372-7254, Fax: 509-335-1949, E-mail: hudson@tricity.wsu.edu.

Washington State University Vancouver, Graduate Programs, School of Engineering and Computer Science, Vancouver, WA 98686. Offers computer science (MS); mechanical engineering (MS). Part-time programs available. *Faculty:* 9. *Students:* 14 full-time (1 woman), 5 part-time (1 woman); includes 1 Asian, non-Hispanic/Latino, 5 international. In 2010, 4 master's awarded. *Degree requirements:* For master's, comprehensive exam (for some programs), thesis, research project. *Entrance requirements:* For master's, minimum GPA of 3.0, 3 letters of recommendation with evaluation forms, resume. Additional exam requirements/recommendations for international students: Required—TOEFL (minimum score 550 paper-based). *Application deadline:* For fall admission, 1/10 priority date for domestic students, 1/10 for international students; for spring admission, 7/1 priority date for domestic students, 7/1 for international students. Applications are processed on a rolling basis. Application fee: $50. *Financial support:* In 2010–11, research assistantships with full tuition reimbursements (averaging $14,634 per year), teaching assistantships with full tuition reimbursements (averaging $13,383 per year) were awarded; health care benefits and unspecified assistantships also available. Financial award application deadline: 2/15. *Faculty research:* Software design, artificial intelligence, sensor networks, robotics, nanotechnology. Total annual research expenditures: $3.4 million. *Unit head:* Dr. Hakan Gurocak, Director, 360-546-9637, Fax: 360-546-9438, E-mail: hgurocak@vancouver.wsu.edu. *Application contact:* Peggy Moore, Academic Coordinator, 360-546-9638, Fax: 360-546-9438, E-mail: moorep@vancouver.wsu.edu.

Washington University in St. Louis, School of Engineering and Applied Science, Saint Louis, MO 63130-4899. Offers M Eng, MCE, MCM, MEM, MIM, MPM, MS, MSEE, MSEE, D Sc, PhD. Part-time and evening/weekend programs available. *Faculty:* 77 full-time, 74 part-time/adjunct. *Students:* 423 full-time (107 women), 297 part-time (61 women); includes 25 Black or African American, non-Hispanic/Latino; 2 American Indian or Alaska Native, non-Hispanic/Latino; 47 Asian, non-Hispanic/Latino; 18 Hispanic/Latino; 7 Two or more races, non-Hispanic/Latino, 209 international. 1,304 applicants, 34% accepted, 248 enrolled. In 2010, 187 master's, 50 doctorates awarded. Terminal master's awarded for partial completion of doctoral program. *Degree requirements:* For master's, comprehensive exam (for some programs), thesis (for some programs); for doctorate, comprehensive exam, thesis/dissertation. *Entrance requirements:* For master's and doctorate, GRE. Additional exam requirements/recommendations for international students: Required—TOEFL (minimum score 550 paper-based; 213 computer-based; 90 iBT), TWE. *Application deadline:* For fall admission, 1/15 for domestic and international students. Applications are processed on a rolling basis. Application fee: $60. Electronic applications accepted. *Financial support:* In 2010–11, 281 students received

Engineering and Applied Sciences—General

Washington University in St. Louis (continued)
support, including 31 fellowships with full tuition reimbursements available, 241 research assistantships with full tuition reimbursements available, 5 teaching assistantships with full tuition reimbursements available; career-related internships or fieldwork, Federal Work-Study, institutionally sponsored loans, scholarships/grants, health care benefits, tuition waivers (full and partial), and unspecified assistantships also available. Financial award applicants required to submit FAFSA. Total annual research expenditures: $24.7 million. *Unit head:* Ralph S. Quatrano, Dean, 314-935-6350, E-mail: rsq@wustl.edu. *Application contact:* Beth Schnettler, Director of Graduate Admissions, 314-935-7974, Fax: 314-719-4703, E-mail: bethschnettler@seas.wustl.edu.

Wayne State University, College of Engineering, Detroit, MI 48202. Offers MS, PhD, Certificate, Graduate Certificate. Part-time programs available. *Faculty:* 65 full-time (8 women), 17 part-time/adjunct (2 women). *Students:* 497 full-time (106 women), 309 part-time (84 women); includes 125 minority (46 Black or African American, non-Hispanic/Latino; 69 Asian, non-Hispanic/Latino; 7 Hispanic/Latino; 3 Two or more races, non-Hispanic/Latino), 336 international. Average age 30. 669 applicants, 56% accepted, 150 enrolled. In 2010, 190 master's, 29 doctorates, 2 other advanced degrees awarded. Terminal master's awarded for partial completion of doctoral program. *Degree requirements:* For master's, thesis optional; for doctorate, thesis/dissertation. *Entrance requirements:* Additional exam requirements/recommendations for international students: Required—TOEFL (minimum score 550 paper-based; 213 computer-based); Recommended—TWE (minimum score 6). *Application deadline:* For fall admission, 7/1 priority date for domestic students, 6/1 for international students; for winter admission, 10/1 for international students; for spring admission, 3/15 for domestic students, 2/1 for international students. Applications are processed on a rolling basis. Application fee: $30 ($50 for international students). *Expenses:* Tuition, state resident: full-time $7662; part-time $478.85 per credit hour. Tuition, nonresident: full-time $16,920; part-time $1057.55 per credit hour. Required fees: $571.20; $35.70 per credit hour. $188.05 per semester. Tuition and fees vary according to course load and program. *Financial support:* In 2010–11, 17 fellowships (averaging $16,990 per year), 80 research assistantships with tuition reimbursements (averaging $17,053 per year), 54 teaching assistantships with tuition reimbursements (averaging $17,067 per year) were awarded; career-related internships or fieldwork, Federal Work-Study, institutionally sponsored loans, scholarships/grants, and tuition waivers (full and partial) also available. Support available to part-time students. *Faculty research:* Smart sensors and integrated micro systems, biomedical engineering, civil infrastructures, nanotechnology, manufacturing and automotive engineering. *Unit head:* Dr. Ralph Kummler, Dean, 313-577-3861, Fax: 313-577-5300, E-mail: rkummler@eng.wayne.edu. *Application contact:* Dr. Gerald O. Thompkins, Associate Dean, 313-577-3780.

Western Michigan University, Graduate College, College of Engineering and Applied Sciences, Kalamazoo, MI 49008. Offers MS, MSE, PhD. Part-time programs available. *Degree requirements:* For doctorate, thesis/dissertation, oral exam. *Entrance requirements:* For master's, minimum GPA of 3.0; for doctorate, GRE General Test, minimum GPA of 3.0.

Western New England University, School of Engineering, Springfield, MA 01119. Offers MSE, MSEE, MSEM, PhD. Part-time and evening/weekend programs available. *Students:* 48 part-time (14 women); includes 1 Black or African American, non-Hispanic/Latino; 3 Asian, non-Hispanic/Latino; 2 Hispanic/Latino; 1 Two or more races, non-Hispanic/Latino, 2 international. In 2010, 15 master's awarded. *Degree requirements:* For master's, comprehensive exam, thesis optional. *Entrance requirements:* For master's, GRE, bachelor's degree in engineering or related field, letters of recommendation, resume. *Application deadline:* Applications are processed on a rolling basis. Application fee: $30. *Expenses:* Tuition: Full-time $35,582. *Financial support:* Available to part-time students. Applicants required to submit FAFSA. *Faculty research:* Fluid mechanics, control systems. *Unit head:* Dr. S. Hossein Cheraghi, Dean, 413-782-1272, E-mail: cheraghi@wnec.edu. *Application contact:* Matt Fox, Director of Recruiting and Marketing for Adult Learners, 413-782-1517, Fax: 413-782-1777, E-mail: study@wnec.edu.

West Texas A&M University, College of Agriculture, Nursing, and Natural Sciences, Department of Mathematics, Physical Sciences and Engineering Technology, Program in Engineering Technology, Canyon, TX 79016-0001. Offers MS. Part-time programs available. *Degree requirements:* For master's, comprehensive exam, thesis optional. *Entrance requirements:* For master's, GRE General Test. Additional exam requirements/recommendations for international students: Required—TOEFL (minimum score 550 paper-based). Electronic applications accepted. *Faculty research:* Composites, firearms technology, small arms research and development.

West Virginia University, College of Engineering and Mineral Resources, Morgantown, WV 26506. Offers MS, MS Ch E, MS Min E, MSAE, MSCE, MSCS, MSE, MSEE, MSIE, MSME, MSPNGE, MSSE, PhD. *Accreditation:* ABET (one or more programs are accredited). Part-time programs available. Terminal master's awarded for partial completion of doctoral program. *Degree requirements:* For master's, thesis optional; for doctorate, comprehensive exam, thesis/dissertation. *Entrance requirements:* Additional exam requirements/recommendations for international students: Required—TOEFL (minimum score 550 paper-based; 213 computer-based). *Expenses:* Contact institution. *Faculty research:* Composite materials, software engineering, information systems, aerodynamics, vehicle propulsion and emission.

West Virginia University Institute of Technology, College of Engineering, Montgomery, WV 25136. Offers MS. Part-time programs available. *Degree requirements:* For master's, thesis or alternative, fieldwork. *Entrance requirements:* For master's, GRE General Test, minimum GPA of 3.0. Additional exam requirements/recommendations for international students: Required—TOEFL.

Wichita State University, Graduate School, College of Engineering, Wichita, KS 67260. Offers MEM, MS, PhD. Part-time and evening/weekend programs available. *Unit head:* Dr. Zulma Toro-Ramos, Dean, 316-978-3400, Fax: 316-978-3853, E-mail: zulma.toro-ramos@

wichita.edu. *Application contact:* Dr. Zulma Toro-Ramos, Dean, 316-978-3400, Fax: 316-978-3853, E-mail: zulma.toro-ramos@wichita.edu.

Widener University, Graduate Programs in Engineering, Chester, PA 19013-5792. Offers chemical engineering (M Eng); civil engineering (M Eng); computer and software engineering (M Eng); engineering management (M Eng); management and technology (MSMT); mechanical engineering (M Eng); telecommunications engineering (M Eng); ME/MBA. Part-time and evening/weekend programs available. *Faculty:* 10 full-time (1 woman), 4 part-time/adjunct (0 women). *Students:* 10 full-time (0 women), 29 part-time (2 women); includes 7 Black or African American, non-Hispanic/Latino, 9 international. Average age 29. 439 applicants, 46% accepted, 23 enrolled. In 2010, 22 master's awarded. *Degree requirements:* For master's, thesis optional. *Entrance requirements:* Additional exam requirements/recommendations for international students: Required—TOEFL (minimum score 550 paper-based; 213 computer-based). *Application deadline:* For fall admission, 8/1 priority date for domestic students, 4/1 priority date for international students; for winter admission, 2/1 priority date for international students; for spring admission, 12/1 priority date for domestic students, 9/1 priority date for international students. Applications are processed on a rolling basis. Application fee: $25 ($300 for international students). *Expenses:* Contact institution. *Financial support:* In 2010–11, 5 teaching assistantships with partial tuition reimbursements (averaging $8,000 per year) were awarded; research assistantships, unspecified assistantships also available. Financial award application deadline: 3/15. *Faculty research:* Collagen, geosynthetics, mobile computing, image and signal processing. Total annual research expenditures: $490,773. *Unit head:* Nora J. Kogut, Assistant Dean, 610-499-4037, Fax: 610-499-4059, E-mail: njkogut@widener.edu. *Application contact:* Christine M. Weist, Assistant to Associate Provost for Graduate Studies, 610-499-4351, Fax: 610-499-4277, E-mail: christine.m.weist@widener.edu.

Wilkes University, College of Graduate and Professional Studies, College of Science and Engineering, Wilkes-Barre, PA 18766-0002. Offers MS, MS Ed, MSEE. Part-time programs available. *Students:* 14 full-time (1 woman), 18 part-time (2 women); includes 1 Asian, non-Hispanic/Latino; 1 Two or more races, non-Hispanic/Latino, 8 international. Average age 29. In 2010, 26 master's awarded. *Entrance requirements:* Additional exam requirements/recommendations for international students: Required—TOEFL (minimum score 550 paper-based; 213 computer-based; 79 iBT). *Application deadline:* Applications are processed on a rolling basis. Application fee: $45 ($65 for international students). Electronic applications accepted. Tuition and fees vary according to degree level and program. *Financial support:* Federal Work-Study and unspecified assistantships available. Financial award application deadline: 3/1; financial award applicants required to submit FAFSA. *Unit head:* Dr. Dale Bruns, Dean, 570-408-4600, Fax: 570-408-7860, E-mail: dale.bruns@wilkes.edu. *Application contact:* Kathleen Houlihan, Director of Graduate Studies, 570-408-3235, Fax: 570-408-7846, E-mail: kathleen.houlihan@wilkes.edu.

Worcester Polytechnic Institute, Graduate Studies and Research, Worcester, MA 01609-2280. Offers M Eng, MBA, ME, MME, MS, PhD, Advanced Certificate, Graduate Certificate. Part-time and evening/weekend programs available. Postbaccalaureate distance learning degree programs offered (no on-campus study). *Faculty:* 144 full-time (28 women), 33 part-time/adjunct (6 women). *Students:* 710 full-time (218 women), 644 part-time (134 women); includes 28 Black or African American, non-Hispanic/Latino; 1 American Indian or Alaska Native, non-Hispanic/Latino; 87 Asian, non-Hispanic/Latino; 31 Hispanic/Latino, 415 international. 2,612 applicants, 58% accepted, 566 enrolled. In 2010, 384 master's, 34 doctorates awarded. Terminal master's awarded for partial completion of doctoral program. *Degree requirements:* For master's, thesis (for some programs); for doctorate, thesis/dissertation. *Entrance requirements:* For master's and doctorate, 3 letters of recommendation. Additional exam requirements/recommendations for international students: Required—TOEFL (minimum score 550 paper-based; 213 computer-based; 79 iBT), IELTS (minimum score 6.5). *Application deadline:* For fall admission, 1/1 priority date for domestic and international students; for spring admission, 10/1 priority date for domestic and international students. Applications are processed on a rolling basis. Application fee: $70. Electronic applications accepted. *Expenses:* Tuition: Full-time $20,862; part-time $1159 per term. One-time fee: $15. *Financial support:* Institutionally sponsored loans, scholarships/grants, tuition waivers, and unspecified assistantships available. Financial award application deadline: 1/1; financial award applicants required to submit FAFSA. *Unit head:* Richard Sisson, Dean of Graduate Studies, 508-831-5633, Fax: 508-831-5178, E-mail: grad@wpi.edu. *Application contact:* Lynne Dougherty, Administrative Assistant, 508-831-5301, Fax: 508-831-5717, E-mail: grad@wpi.edu.

Wright State University, School of Graduate Studies, College of Engineering and Computer Science, Dayton, OH 45435. Offers MS, MSCE, MSE, PhD. Part-time and evening/weekend programs available. *Degree requirements:* For master's, thesis optional; for doctorate, thesis/dissertation, candidacy and general exams. *Entrance requirements:* For doctorate, GRE General Test, minimum GPA of 3.3. Additional exam requirements/recommendations for international students: Required—TOEFL. *Faculty research:* Robotics, heat transfer, fluid dynamics, microprocessors, mechanical vibrations.

Yale University, Graduate School of Arts and Sciences, School of Engineering and Applied Science, New Haven, CT 06520. Offers MS, PhD. Part-time programs available. Terminal master's awarded for partial completion of doctoral program. *Degree requirements:* For doctorate, thesis/dissertation, exam. *Entrance requirements:* For master's and doctorate, GRE General Test. Additional exam requirements/recommendations for international students: Required—TOEFL.

See Display on next page and Close-Up on page 97.

Youngstown State University, Graduate School, College of Science, Technology, Engineering and Mathematics, Youngstown, OH 44555-0001. Offers MCIS, MSE. Part-time and evening/weekend programs available. *Degree requirements:* For master's, thesis optional. *Entrance requirements:* For master's, minimum GPA of 2.75 in field. Additional exam requirements/recommendations for international students: Required—TOEFL. *Faculty research:* Structural mechanics, water quality, wetlands engineering, control systems, power systems, heat transfer, kinematics and dynamics.

Applied Science and Technology

American University, College of Arts and Sciences, Department of Biology, Washington, DC 20016-8007. Offers applied science (MS); biology (MA, MS); environmental science (MS), including environmental science, marine science. Part-time programs available. *Faculty:* 9 full-time (3 women), 3 part-time/adjunct (0 women). *Students:* 8 full-time (2 women), 8 part-time (6 women); includes 3 minority (1 Black or African American, non-Hispanic/Latino; 2 Asian, non-Hispanic/Latino), 2 international. Average age 25. 40 applicants, 53% accepted, 3 enrolled. In 2010, 10 master's awarded. *Degree requirements:* For master's, comprehensive exam, thesis (for some programs). *Entrance requirements:* For master's, GRE General Test, GRE Subject Test. Additional exam requirements/recommendations for international students: Required—TOEFL. *Application deadline:* For fall admission, 2/1 for domestic students; for spring admission, 10/1 for domestic students. Application fee: $80. *Financial support:* Fellowships, research assistantships with tuition reimbursements, teaching assistantships with tuition reimbursements, career-related internships or fieldwork, Federal Work-Study, and institutionally sponsored loans available. Financial award application deadline: 2/1. *Faculty research:* Neurobiology, cave biology, population genetics, vertebrate physiology. *Unit head:* Dr. David Carlini, Chair, 202-885-2194, Fax: 202-885-2182, E-mail: carlini@american.edu. *Application contact:* Kathleen Clowery, Director, Graduate Admissions, 202-885-3621, Fax: 202-885-1505.

The College of William and Mary, Faculty of Arts and Sciences, Department of Applied Science, Williamsburg, VA 23187-8795. Offers MS, PhD. *Faculty:* 10 full-time (2 women). *Students:* 33 full-time (12 women), 1 part-time (0 women); includes 2 minority (1 Black or African American, non-Hispanic/Latino; 1 Asian, non-Hispanic/Latino), 23 international. Average age 26. 41 applicants, 32% accepted, 9 enrolled. In 2010, 8 master's, 3 doctorates awarded. *Degree requirements:* For master's, comprehensive exam, thesis; for doctorate, comprehensive exam, thesis/dissertation, 4 core courses. *Entrance requirements:* For master's and doctorate, GRE General Test, GRE Subject Test. Additional exam requirements/recommendations for international students: Required—TOEFL, TWE. *Application deadline:* For fall admission, 2/3 priority date for domestic students, 2/3 for international students; for spring admission, 10/15 priority date for domestic students, 10/14 for international students. Applications are processed on a rolling basis. Application fee: $45. Electronic applications accepted. *Expenses:* Tuition, state resident: full-time $6400; part-time $345 per credit hour. Tuition, nonresident: full-time

Applied Science and Technology

$19,720; part-time $920 per credit hour. Required fees: $4368. *Financial support:* Fellowships, research assistantships, teaching assistantships, Federal Work-Study, health care benefits, tuition waivers (full), and unspecified assistantships available. Financial award application deadline: 4/15; financial award applicants required to submit FAFSA. *Faculty research:* Computational biology, non-destructive evaluation, neurophysiology, lasers 8 optics, solid state FTNMR. Total annual research expenditures: $1.6 million. *Unit head:* Dr. Mark Hinders, Chair, 757-221-1519, Fax: 757-221-2050, E-mail: hinders@as.wm.edu. *Application contact:* Rosario Fox, Education Support Specialist, 757-221-2563, Fax: 757-221-2050, E-mail: rxfoxx@wm.edu.

Colorado State University–Pueblo, College of Science and Mathematics, Pueblo, CO 81001-4901. Offers applied natural science (MS), including biochemistry, biology, chemistry. Part-time and evening/weekend programs available. *Degree requirements:* For master's, comprehensive exam (for some programs), thesis (for some programs), internship report (if non-thesis). *Entrance requirements:* For master's, GRE General Test (minimum score 1000), 2 letters of reference, minimum GPA of 3.0. Additional exam requirements/recommendations for international students: Required—TOEFL (minimum score 500 paper-based; 173 computer-based), IELTS (minimum score 5). *Faculty research:* Fungal cell walls, molecular biology, bioactive materials synthesis, atomic force microscopy-surface chemistry, nanoscience.

Harvard University, Extension School, Cambridge, MA 02138-3722. Offers applied sciences (CAS); biotechnology (ALM); educational technologies (ALM); educational technology (CET); English for graduate and professional studies (DGP); environmental management (ALM, CEM); information technology (ALM); journalism (ALM); liberal arts (ALM); management (ALM, CM); mathematics for teaching (ALM); museum studies (ALM); premedical studies (Diploma); publication and communication (CPC). Part-time and evening/weekend programs available. *Degree requirements:* For master's, thesis. *Entrance requirements:* For master's, 3 completed graduate courses with grade of B or higher. Additional exam requirements/recommendations for international students: Required—TOEFL (minimum score 600 paper-based; 250 computer-based), TWE (minimum score 5). *Expenses:* Contact institution.

James Madison University, The Graduate School, College of Integrated Science and Technology, Department of Integrated Science and Technology, Harrisonburg, VA 22807. Offers MS. *Faculty:* 15 full-time (2 women), 2 part-time/adjunct (both women). *Students:* 20 full-time (8 women), 34 part-time (13 women); includes 1 minority (Hispanic/Latino), 17 international. Average age 27. In 2010, 9 master's awarded. *Degree requirements:* For master's, thesis or alternative. *Entrance requirements:* For master's, GRE General Test. Additional exam requirements/recommendations for international students: Required—TOEFL. *Application deadline:* For fall admission, 5/1 priority date for domestic students; for spring admission, 9/1 priority date for domestic students. Applications are processed on a rolling basis. Application fee: $55. Electronic applications accepted. *Financial support:* In 2010–11, 7 students received support. Federal Work-Study and 7 graduate assistantships ($7382) available. Financial award application deadline: 3/1; financial award applicants required to submit FAFSA. *Unit head:* Dr. Eric H. Maslen, Interim Academic Unit Head, 540-568-2740, E-mail: masleneh@jmu.edu. *Application contact:* Lynette M. Bible, Director of Graduate Admissions, 540-568-6395, Fax: 540-568-7860, E-mail: biblelm@jmu.edu.

Louisiana State University and Agricultural and Mechanical College, Graduate School, College of Basic Sciences, Master of Natural Sciences Program, Baton Rouge, LA 70803. Offers MNS. Part-time programs available. *Students:* 16 full-time (12 women), 6 part-time (3 women); includes 6 Black or African American, non-Hispanic/Latino; 1 Asian, non-Hispanic/Latino. Average age 33. 2 applicants, 100% accepted, 0 enrolled. In 2010, 18 master's awarded. *Degree requirements:* For master's, comprehensive exam. *Entrance requirements:* For master's, GRE General Test, minimum GPA of 3.0. Additional exam requirements/recommendations for international students: Required—TOEFL (minimum score 550 paper-based; 213 computer-based; 79 iBT) or IELTS (minimum score 6.5). *Application deadline:* For fall admission, 5/15 priority date for domestic students, 5/15 for international students; for spring admission, 10/15 for international students. Applications are processed on a rolling basis. Application fee: $50 ($70 for international students). Electronic applications accepted. *Financial support:* In 2010–11, 21 students received support, including 14 research assistantships (averaging $33,786 per year); fellowships, teaching assistantships with partial tuition reimbursements available, Federal Work-Study, institutionally sponsored loans, and health care benefits also available. Financial award applicants required to submit FAFSA. Total annual research expenditures: $18,670. *Unit head:* Dr. Gary Byerly, Director, 225-578-4200, Fax: 225-578-8826, E-mail: glbyer@lsu.edu. *Application contact:* Dr. Gary Byerly, Director, 225-578-4200, Fax: 225-578-8826.

Missouri State University, Graduate College, College of Natural and Applied Sciences, Department of Agriculture, Springfield, MO 65897. Offers natural and applied science (MNAS), including agriculture (MNAS, MS Ed); plant science (MS); secondary education (MS Ed), including agriculture (MNAS, MS Ed). Part-time programs available. *Degree requirements:* For master's, comprehensive exam, thesis or alternative. *Entrance requirements:* For master's, GRE (MS plant science, MNAS), 9-12 teacher certification (MS Ed), minimum GPA of 3.0 (MS plant science, MNAS). Additional exam requirements/recommendations for international students: Required—TOEFL (minimum score 550 paper-based; 213 computer-based; 79 iBT). Electronic applications accepted. *Expenses:* Tuition, state resident: full-time $3348; part-time $186 per credit hour. Tuition, nonresident: full-time $6696; part-time $372 per credit hour. Required fees: $238 per semester. Tuition and fees vary according to course level, course load and program. *Faculty research:* Grapevine biotechnology, agricultural marketing, Asian elephant reproduction, poultry science, integrated pest management.

Missouri State University, Graduate College, College of Natural and Applied Sciences, Department of Biology, Springfield, MO 65897. Offers biology (MS); natural and applied science (MNAS), including biology (MNAS, MS Ed); secondary education (MS Ed), including biology (MNAS, MS Ed). *Degree requirements:* For master's, comprehensive exam, thesis or alternative. *Entrance requirements:* For master's, GRE (MS, MNAS), 24 hours of course work in biology (MS); minimum GPA of 3.0 (MS, MNAS), 9-12 teacher certification (MS Ed). Additional exam requirements/recommendations for international students: Required—TOEFL (minimum score 550 paper-based; 213 computer-based; 79 iBT). Electronic applications accepted. *Expenses:* Tuition, state resident: full-time $3348; part-time $186 per credit hour. Tuition, nonresident: full-time $6696; part-time $372 per credit hour. Required fees: $238 per semester. Tuition and fees vary according to course level, course load and program. *Faculty research:* Hibernation physiology of bats, behavioral ecology of salamanders, mussel conservation, plant evolution and systematics, cellular/molecular mechanisms involved in migraine pathology.

Missouri State University, Graduate College, College of Natural and Applied Sciences, Department of Chemistry, Springfield, MO 65897. Offers chemistry (MS); natural and applied science (MNAS), including chemistry (MNAS, MS Ed); secondary education (MS Ed), including chemistry (MNAS, MS Ed). Part-time programs available. *Degree requirements:* For master's, comprehensive exam, thesis. *Entrance requirements:* For master's, GRE General Test (MS, MNAS), minimum undergraduate GPA of 3.0 (MS and MNAS), 9-12 teacher certification (MS Ed). Additional exam requirements/recommendations for international students: Required—TOEFL (minimum score 550 paper-based; 213 computer-based; 79 iBT). Electronic applications accepted. *Expenses:* Tuition, state resident: full-time $3348; part-time $186 per credit hour. Tuition, nonresident: full-time $6696; part-time $372 per credit hour. Required fees: $238 per semester. Tuition and fees vary according to course level, course load and program. *Faculty research:* Polyethylene glycol derivatives, electrochemiluminescence of environmental systems, enzymology, environmental organic pollutants, DNA repair via NMR.

Missouri State University, Graduate College, College of Natural and Applied Sciences, Department of Geography, Geology, and Planning, Springfield, MO 65897. Offers geospatial

Applied Science and Technology

Missouri State University (continued)
sciences (MS); natural and applied science (MNAS), including geography, geology and planning; secondary education (MS Ed), including earth science, geography. Part-time and evening/weekend programs available. *Degree requirements:* For master's, comprehensive exam, thesis (for some programs). *Entrance requirements:* For master's, GRE General Test (MS, MNAS), minimum undergraduate GPA of 3.0 (MS, MNAS), 9-12 teacher certification (MS Ed). Additional exam requirements/recommendations for international students: Required—TOEFL (minimum score 550 paper-based; 213 computer-based; 79 iBT). Electronic applications accepted. *Expenses:* Tuition, state resident: full-time $3348; part-time $186 per credit hour. Tuition, nonresident: full-time $6696; part-time $372 per credit hour. Required fees: $238 per semester. Tuition and fees vary according to course level, course load and program. *Faculty research:* Stratigraphy and ancient meteorite impacts, environmental geochemistry of karst, hyper-spectral image processing, water quality, small town planning.

Missouri State University, Graduate College, College of Natural and Applied Sciences, Department of Mathematics, Springfield, MO 65897. Offers mathematics (MS); natural and applied science (MNAS), including mathematics (MNAS, MS Ed); secondary education (MS Ed), including mathematics (MNAS, MS Ed). Part-time programs available. *Degree requirements:* For master's, comprehensive exam, thesis or alternative. *Entrance requirements:* For master's, GRE (MS, MNAS), minimum undergraduate GPA of 3.0 (MS, MNAS), 9-12 teacher certification (MS Ed). Additional exam requirements/recommendations for international students: Required—TOEFL (minimum score 550 paper-based; 213 computer-based; 79 iBT). Electronic applications accepted. *Expenses:* Tuition, state resident: full-time $3348; part-time $186 per credit hour. Tuition, nonresident: full-time $6696; part-time $372 per credit hour. Required fees: $238 per semester. Tuition and fees vary according to course level, course load and program. *Faculty research:* Harmonic analysis, commutative algebra, number theory, K-theory, probability.

Naval Postgraduate School, Graduate Programs, Program in Undersea Warfare, Monterey, CA 93943. Offers applied science (MS); electrical engineering (MS); engineering acoustics (MS); operations research (MS); physical oceanography (MS). Program only open to commissioned officers of the United States and friendly nations and selected United States federal civilian employees. Part-time programs available. *Degree requirements:* For master's, thesis.

Oklahoma State University, Graduate College, Stillwater, OK 74078. Offers environmental science (MS); international studies (MS); natural and applied science (MS); photonics (PhD); plant science (PhD). Programs are interdisciplinary. *Faculty:* 2 full-time (1 woman). *Students:* 69 full-time (40 women), 131 part-time (68 women); includes 13 Black or African American, non-Hispanic/Latino; 15 American Indian or Alaska Native, non-Hispanic/Latino; 8 Asian, non-Hispanic/Latino; 8 Hispanic/Latino, 70 international. Average age 30. 690 applicants, 74% accepted, 75 enrolled. In 2010, 66 master's, 7 doctorates awarded. *Degree requirements:* For master's, thesis (for some programs); for doctorate, comprehensive exam, thesis/dissertation. *Entrance requirements:* For master's and doctorate, GRE or GMAT. Additional exam requirements/recommendations for international students: Required—TOEFL (minimum score 550 paper-based; 79 iBT). *Application deadline:* For fall admission, 3/1 priority date for international students; for spring admission, 8/1 priority date for international students. Applications are processed on a rolling basis. Application fee: $40 ($75 for international students). Electronic applications accepted. *Expenses:* Tuition, state resident: full-time $3716; part-time $154.85 per credit hour. Tuition, nonresident: full-time $14,892; part-time $621 per credit hour. Required fees: $2044; $85.20 per credit hour. One-time fee: $50. Tuition and fees vary according to course load and campus/location. *Financial support:* In 2010–11, 2 research assistantships (averaging $12,900 per year) were awarded; career-related internships or fieldwork, Federal Work-Study, scholarships/grants, health care benefits, tuition waivers (partial), and unspecified assistantships also available. Support available to part-time students. Financial award application deadline: 3/1; financial award applicants required to submit FAFSA. *Unit head:* Dr. Gordon Emslie, Dean, 405-744-6368, Fax: 405-744-0355, E-mail: grad-i@okstate.edu. *Application contact:* Dr. Susan Mathew, Coordinator of Admissions, 405-744-6368, Fax: 405-744-0355, E-mail: grad-i@okstate.edu.

Saint Mary's University, Faculty of Science, Interdisciplinary Program in Applied Science, Halifax, NS B3H 3C3, Canada. Offers M Sc.

Southeastern Louisiana University, College of Science and Technology, Program in Integrated Science and Technology, Hammond, LA 70402. Offers chemistry (MS); computer science (MS); information technology (MS); mathematics (MS); physics (MS). Part-time and evening/weekend programs available. *Faculty:* 11 full-time (3 women). *Students:* 13 full-time (5 women), 11 part-time (2 women); includes 1 minority (Asian, non-Hispanic/Latino), 8 international. Average age 32. 13 applicants, 46% accepted, 4 enrolled. In 2010, 5 master's awarded. *Degree requirements:* For master's, thesis (for some programs), 33-36 hours. *Entrance requirements:* For master's, GRE (minimum combined score 850), 2 letters of reference; minimum GPA of 2.75; 30 hours of course work including chemistry, physics, industrial technology, or mathematics. Additional exam requirements/recommendations for international students: Required—TOEFL (minimum score 500 paper-based; 173 computer-based; 61 iBT). *Application deadline:* For fall admission, 7/15 priority date for domestic students, 6/1 priority date for international students; for spring admission, 12/1 priority date for domestic students, 10/1 priority date for international students. Applications are processed on a rolling basis. Application fee: $20 ($30 for international students). Electronic applications accepted. *Expenses:* Tuition, state resident: full-time $3533. Tuition, nonresident: full-time $12,002. Required fees: $907. Tuition and fees vary according to degree level. *Financial support:* In 2010–11, 7 students received support, including 7 research assistantships (averaging $10,100 per year); career-related internships or fieldwork, Federal Work-Study, institutionally sponsored loans, and unspecified assistantships also available. Support available to part-time students. Financial award application deadline: 5/1; financial award applicants required to submit FAFSA. *Faculty research:* Computational statistics, medicinal chemistry, machine learning, optical interferometry,strength of materials and structure. *Unit head:* Dr. Ken Li, Coordinator, 985-549-3822, Fax: 985-549-2099, E-mail: kli@selu.edu. *Application contact:* Sandra Meyers, Graduate Admissions Analyst, 985-549-5620, Fax: 985-549-5632, E-mail: admissions@selu.edu.

Southern Methodist University, Bobby B. Lyle School of Engineering, Department of Engineering Management, Information, and Systems, Dallas, TX 75275. Offers applied science (MS); engineering management (MSEM, DE); information engineering and management (MSIEM); operations research (MS, PhD); systems engineering (MS, PhD). Part-time and evening/weekend programs available. Postbaccalaureate distance learning degree programs offered. *Faculty:* 8 full-time (1 woman), 22 part-time/adjunct (1 woman). *Students:* 47 full-time (12 women), 348 part-time (75 women); includes 114 minority (31 Black or African American, non-Hispanic/Latino; 2 American Indian or Alaska Native, non-Hispanic/Latino; 34 Asian, non-Hispanic/Latino; 44 Hispanic/Latino; 2 Native Hawaiian or other Pacific Islander, non-Hispanic/Latino; 1 Two or more races, non-Hispanic/Latino), 51 international. Average age 33. 208 applicants, 67% accepted, 92 enrolled. In 2010, 130 master's, 6 doctorates awarded. Terminal master's awarded for partial completion of doctoral program. *Degree requirements:* For master's, thesis optional; for doctorate, thesis/dissertation, oral and written qualifying exams. *Entrance requirements:* For master's, minimum GPA of 3.0 in last 2 years; bachelor's degree in engineering, mathematics, sciences, or technical area; for doctorate, GRE General Test (operations research, engineering management), bachelor's degree in related field. Additional exam requirements/recommendations for international students: Required—TOEFL. *Application deadline:* For fall admission, 7/1 for domestic students, 5/15 for international students; for spring admission, 11/15 for domestic students, 9/1 for international students. Applications are processed on a rolling basis. Application fee: $75. *Financial support:* In 2010–11, 6 students received support, including 4 research assistantships with full tuition reimbursements available (averaging $18,000 per year), 2 teaching assistantships with full tuition reimbursements available (averaging $18,000 per year); tuition waivers (full) also available. *Faculty research:* Telecommunications, decision systems, information engineering, operations research, software. Total annual research expenditures: $275,851. *Unit head:* Dr. Richard S. Barr, Chair, 214-768-1772, Fax: 214-768-1112, E-mail: emis@lyle.smu.edu. *Application contact:* Marc Valerin, Director of Graduate and Executive Admissions, 214-768-3042, E-mail: valerin@lyle.smu.edu.

Southern Methodist University, Bobby B. Lyle School of Engineering, Department of Environmental and Civil Engineering, Dallas, TX 75275-0340. Offers applied science (MS, PhD); civil and environmental engineering (PhD); civil engineering (MS); environmental engineering (MS); environmental science (MS), including environmental systems management. Part-time and evening/weekend programs available. Postbaccalaureate distance learning degree programs offered (no on-campus study). *Faculty:* 6 full-time (0 women), 11 part-time/adjunct (3 women). *Students:* 11 full-time (8 women), 47 part-time (21 women); includes 5 Black or African American, non-Hispanic/Latino; 2 Asian, non-Hispanic/Latino; 3 Hispanic/Latino, 6 international. Average age 37. 50 applicants, 86% accepted, 28 enrolled. In 2010, 26 master's awarded. Terminal master's awarded for partial completion of doctoral program. *Degree requirements:* For master's, thesis optional; for doctorate, thesis/dissertation, oral and written qualifying exams. *Entrance requirements:* For master's, GRE General Test, minimum GPA of 3.0 in last 2 years; bachelor's degree in engineering, mathematics, or sciences; for doctorate, GRE, BS and MS in related field, minimum GPA of 3.3. Additional exam requirements/recommendations for international students: Required—TOEFL. *Application deadline:* For fall admission, 7/1 for domestic students, 5/15 for international students; for spring admission, 11/15 for domestic students, 9/1 for international students. Applications are processed on a rolling basis. Application fee: $75. Electronic applications accepted. *Financial support:* In 2010–11, 9 students received support, including 2 research assistantships with full tuition reimbursements available (averaging $18,000 per year), 7 teaching assistantships with full tuition reimbursements available (averaging $18,000 per year); unspecified assistantships also available. *Faculty research:* Human and environmental health effects of endocrine disrupters, development of air pollution control systems for diesel engines, structural analysis and design, modeling and design of waste treatment systems. Total annual research expenditures: $100,000. *Unit head:* Prof. Khaled Abdelghany, Associate Chair, 214-768-3894, Fax: 214-768-2164, E-mail: khaled@lyle.smu.edu. *Application contact:* Marc Valerin, Director of Graduate and Executive Admissions, 214-768-3042, Fax: 214-768-3778, E-mail: valerin@lyle.smu.edu.

Thomas Edison State College, School of Applied Science and Technology, Trenton, NJ 08608-1176. Offers Graduate Certificate. Part-time programs available. Postbaccalaureate distance learning degree programs offered (no on-campus study). *Students:* 22 part-time (15 women); includes 3 Black or African American, non-Hispanic/Latino; 2 Asian, non-Hispanic/Latino; 3 Hispanic/Latino. Average age 42. In 2010, 3 Graduate Certificates awarded. *Entrance requirements:* Additional exam requirements/recommendations for international students: Required—TOEFL (minimum score 550 paper-based; 213 computer-based; 79 iBT). *Application deadline:* For fall admission, 8/15 priority date for domestic and international students; for winter admission, 11/15 priority date for domestic and international students; for spring admission, 2/15 priority date for domestic students, 1/15 priority date for international students. Applications are processed on a rolling basis. Application fee: $75. Electronic applications accepted. *Financial support:* Applicants required to submit FAFSA. *Unit head:* Dr. Marcus Tillery, Dean, School of Applied Science and Technology, 609-984-1130, Fax: 609-984-3898, E-mail: info@tesc.edu. *Application contact:* David Hoftiezer, Director of Admissions, 888-442-8372, Fax: 609-984-8447, E-mail: admissions@tesc.edu.

University of Arkansas at Little Rock, Graduate School, George W. Donughey College of Engineering and Information Technology, Department of Applied Science, Little Rock, AR 72204-1099. Offers MS, PhD. Part-time programs available. *Degree requirements:* For master's, comprehensive exam, thesis optional, oral exams; for doctorate, thesis/dissertation, 2 semesters of residency, candidacy exams. *Entrance requirements:* For master's, GRE General Test, interview, minimum GPA of 3.0; for doctorate, GRE General Test, interview, minimum graduate GPA of 3.5. Additional exam requirements/recommendations for international students: Required—TOEFL. *Faculty research:* Particle and powder science and technology, optical sensors, process control and automation, signal and image processing, biomedical measurement systems.

University of California, Berkeley, Graduate Division, College of Engineering, Group in Applied Science and Technology, Berkeley, CA 94720-1500. Offers PhD. *Degree requirements:* For doctorate, thesis/dissertation, preliminary exam, qualifying exam. *Entrance requirements:* For doctorate, GRE General Test, BA or BS in engineering, physics, mathematics, chemistry, or related field; minimum GPA of 3.0, 3 letters of recommendation.

University of California, Davis, College of Engineering, Program in Applied Science, Davis, CA 95616. Offers MS, PhD. Terminal master's awarded for partial completion of doctoral program. *Degree requirements:* For master's, comprehensive exam (for some programs), thesis (for some programs); for doctorate, thesis/dissertation. *Entrance requirements:* For master's and doctorate, GRE General Test, minimum GPA of 3.3. Additional exam requirements/recommendations for international students: Required—TOEFL (minimum score 550 paper-based; 213 computer-based). Electronic applications accepted. *Faculty research:* Plasma physics, scientific computing, fusion technology, laser physics and nonlinear optics.

University of Colorado at Colorado Springs, College of Letters, Arts and Sciences, Department of Mathematics, Colorado Springs, CO 80933-7150. Offers applied mathematics (MS); applied science (PhD); mathematics (M Sc). Part-time and evening/weekend programs available. *Faculty:* 11 full-time (1 woman), 1 (woman) part-time/adjunct. *Students:* 10 full-time (3 women), 10 part-time (6 women), 2 international. Average age 34. 9 applicants, 78% accepted, 6 enrolled. In 2010, 2 master's awarded. *Degree requirements:* For master's, thesis, qualifying exam. *Entrance requirements:* For master's, GRE General Test, minimum GPA of 3.0. Additional exam requirements/recommendations for international students: Required—TOEFL. *Application deadline:* For fall admission, 6/15 for domestic students. Applications are processed on a rolling basis. Application fee: $60 ($75 for international students). *Expenses:* Tuition, state resident: full-time $7916. Tuition, nonresident: full-time $16,610. Tuition and fees vary according to course load, degree level, program, reciprocity agreements and student level. *Financial support:* Teaching assistantships, Federal Work-Study and scholarships/grants available. Support available to part-time students. Financial award application deadline: 3/1; financial award applicants required to submit FAFSA. *Faculty research:* Abelian groups and noncommutative rings, hormone analysis and computer vision, probability and mathematical physics, stochastic dynamics, probability models. *Unit head:* Dr. Sarbarish Chakravarty, Chair, 719-255-3549, Fax: 719-255-3605, E-mail: schakrav@uccs.edu. *Application contact:* Elizabeth Buzo, Graduate Liaison, 719-255-3554, Fax: 719-255-3605, E-mail: ebuzo@uccs.edu.

University of Colorado Denver, College of Liberal Arts and Sciences, Program in Integrated Sciences, Denver, CO 80217-3364. Offers applied science (MIS); computer science (MIS); mathematics (MIS). Part-time and evening/weekend programs available. *Students:* 4 full-time (1 woman), 3 part-time (1 woman); includes 1 Hispanic/Latino. Average age 41. 4 applicants, 100% accepted, 2 enrolled. In 2010, 1 master's awarded. *Degree requirements:* For master's, thesis or alternative, 30 credit hours; thesis or project. *Entrance requirements:* For master's, GRE if undergraduate GPA is 2.75 or less, minimum of 40 semester hours in mathematics, computer science, physics, biology, chemistry and/or geology. *Application deadline:* For fall admission, 4/15 for domestic students; for spring admission, 10/15 for domestic students. Application fee: $50 ($75 for international students). Electronic applications accepted. *Expenses:* Tuition, state resident: full-time $7332; part-time $355 per credit hour. Tuition, nonresident: full-time $18,990; part-time $1055 per credit hour. Required fees: $998. Tuition and fees vary according to course level, course load, degree level, campus/location, program, reciprocity agreements and student level. *Financial support:* Application deadline: 4/1. *Faculty research:* Computer science, applied science, mathematics.

University of Mississippi, Graduate School, School of Applied Sciences, Oxford, University, MS 38677. Offers MA, MS, MSW, PhD. *Students:* 146 full-time (102 women), 75 part-time (53 women); includes 38 minority (32 Black or African American, non-Hispanic/Latino; 1 Hispanic/Latino; 1 Native Hawaiian or other Pacific Islander, non-Hispanic/Latino; 4 Two or more races, non-Hispanic/Latino), 10 international. In 2010, 34 master's, 1 doctorate awarded. *Entrance requirements:* For master's, GRE General Test, minimum GPA of 3.0. Additional exam requirements/recommendations for international students: Required—TOEFL. *Application deadline:* For fall admission, 4/1 for domestic students; for spring admission, 10/1 for domestic students. Applications are processed on a rolling basis. Application fee: $25. Electronic applications accepted. *Financial support:* Scholarships/grants available. Financial award application deadline: 3/1; financial award applicants required to submit FAFSA. *Unit head:* Dr. Linda Chitwood, Dean, 662-915-7916, Fax: 662-915-5717, E-mail: lchitwoo@olemiss.edu. *Application contact:* Dr. Christy M. Wyandt, Associate Dean, 662-915-7474, Fax: 662-915-7577, E-mail: cwyandt@olemiss.edu.

CALIFORNIA STATE UNIVERSITY, LOS ANGELES

College of Engineering, Computer Science, and Technology

Programs of Study

California State University, Los Angeles (CSULA) offers several Master of Science (M.S.) degree programs in civil, computer science, electrical, and mechanical engineering. The objective of these programs is to prepare students for employment in design, research, development, or teaching, and for further study toward doctoral degrees. Classes are offered year-round on the quarter system to accommodate the needs of working professionals.

The College of Engineering, Computer Science, and Technology offers some of the most exciting and progressive degree programs available today. It is committed to high standards, academic distinctiveness, and transforming dreams into reality. The College is renowned for research that culminates in new knowledge, academic rigor that makes a difference, and collaboration that transforms learning.

The M.S. in Civil Engineering program requires 45 units to complete, including at least 24 units of graduate (500 level) courses and a thesis or comprehensive examination. All students must satisfy the graduate writing assessment requirement (GWAR).

The M.S. in Electrical and Computer Engineering and the M.S. in Mechanical Engineering programs each require 45-quarter units to complete, including at least 24 units of graduate (500 level) courses. A minimum 3.0 grade point average is required. Completion of the programs requires passing the writing proficiency examination, if not passed as a requirement for the B.S. degree, and writing an acceptable thesis or completion of a comprehensive examination. Students should consult the CSULA general catalog for further information.

The M.S. in Computer Science program requires 45 to 52 units to complete. No more than 8 units of acceptable postbaccalaureate course work completed prior to entrance into classified standing may be included in the master's degree program.

The College offers ABET-accredited programs in civil, electrical, and mechanical engineering; and computer science. The information technology program is one of the only three in California. Faculty members are dedicated to teaching from the perspective of innovation, excellence, globalization, and integrity. Students are able to forge lifelong friendships that offer impeccable networking opportunities.

Research Facilities

The College of Engineering, Computer Science, and Technology at CSULA supports a diverse program of research at eight facilities that offer advanced technology and equipment and facilitate scientific collaboration and achievement. These laboratories include the Center for Energy and Sustainability (CE&S), Multidisciplinary Flight Dynamics and Control (MFDC) Laboratory, NASA University Research Center, National Center for Engineering and Technology (NCETE), Naval Seafloor Laboratory, Power, Energy, and Transportation (PET) Laboratory, Photonics Laboratory, and SPACE Laboratory.

Financial Aid

There are several financial aid opportunities available for graduate students. The Center for Student Financial Aid and the Office of Graduate Studies and Research offer the most current financial aid information. Additional information is available at http://www.calstatela.edu/univ/finaid/fedStateProgram.php.

Students are encouraged to apply for financial aid early and not wait until they are accepted into the degree program. The Free Application for Federal Student Aid (FAFSA) is used to determine financial aid eligibility. It must be filed yearly. In addition to the FAFSA, separate applications are required for scholarships and the Federal Direct Student Loan. Students must also submit CSULA's Certification of Graduate, Credential, or Postbaccalaureate Status form to the center.

Graduate students who are eligible for financial aid may be offered assistance from one or more of the following programs: State University Grant, Pell Grant Credential, Federal Perkins Loans, and Federal Direct Student Loans. Other options include the California State University, Los Angeles Graduate Equity Fellowship; the California State University, Los Angeles Excellence in Graduate Programs Initiative, the California Predoctoral Program, the California Forgivable Loan/Doctoral Incentive Program, and graduate assistantships. Aid listed here is subject to change without notice.

Cost of Study

In the 2011–12 academic year, tuition and fees for California students in the graduate and postbaccalaureate programs are $1510.70 (0–6 units) and $2454.70 (6.1 units or more). In addition, all nonresidents of California, including international students, must pay an additional $248 per unit nonresident tuition fee. All tuition and fees are subject to change without prior notice. For up-to-date fees information, visit www.calstatela.edu/univ/finaid.

Living and Housing Costs

On-campus student housing is available for more than 1,000 students. There are also opportunities for students to live in apartments and rooms in private homes or to share houses near the campus with other students. Students interested in living on campus or who need assistance in finding off-campus housing can call the Office of Residence Life and Housing Services at 323-343-4800.

Student Group

CSULA boasts more than 20,000 students and 185,000 alumni—with a wide variety of interests, ages, and backgrounds—who reflect the city's dynamic mix of populations. Students who are engaged in graduate and postbaccalaureate study constitute nearly one third of the total student body. Among enrolled students, 62 percent are women, 53 percent are Hispanic, almost 22 percent are Asian American/Pacific Islander, 8 percent are African American, and 16 percent are white, non-Hispanic.

The College of Engineering, Computer Science, and Technology strives to encourage and recognize the efforts of graduate students and has developed events, resources, and services specifically to support them. Graduate student organizations represent a wide array of social, cultural, and academic interests and include the American Society of Civil Engineers (ASCE), the Association for Computing Machinery (ACM), Chi Epsilon, the Institute of Electrical and Electronics Engineers (IEEE), the National Society of Black Engineers (NSBE), the Society of Automotive Engineers (SAE), the Society of Hispanic Engineering and Science Students (SHESS), the Society of Women Engineers (SWE), and Tau Beta Pi.

Student Outcomes

The College of ECST students incorporate their innovative learning experience and community service opportunities and leave CSULA humanizing engineering, computer science, and technology—well prepared to meet the challenges of a rapidly changing technological world and 21st-century workforce. Students are taught excellence, innovation, and distinctiveness from a global perspective, and graduates demonstrate internationally recognized leadership in applied research, advanced prototyping, and design.

Location

Near the edge of the city of Los Angeles, adjacent to the cities of Alhambra and Monterey Park, CSULA occupies 175 acres on a hilltop that offers views of Pasadena and the mountains to the north, the San Gabriel Valley to the east, metropolitan Los Angeles to the west, and the Palos Verdes Peninsula and Catalina Island to the south. Ample parking facilities are available, and public transportation to and from campus is excellent. The Cal State L.A. Transit Center makes the University accessible from more than thirty-five regional communities.

The campus was once one of California's thirty-six original adobes, built in 1776 by Franciscan missionaries and destroyed by fire in 1908. Around the 1850s, it was settled by the family of Juan Batista Batz, a Basque rancher from northern Spain as part of a Spanish land grant. Known as the Rancho Rosa Castilla, it was named, according to local historians, for the wild rose that grew near the home.

The University

The University offers over sixty graduate programs of study, and graduate study has been a major part of its academic commitment since its founding. CSULA continues to be a dynamic force in the education of students, setting a record of outstanding academic achievement for more than fifty years within the California State University system. Six colleges offer nationally recognized science, arts, business, criminal justice, engineering, nursing, education, and humanities programs, among others, led by an award-winning faculty.

CSULA is a regional leader in sustainable development and green initiatives with a $4.35-million hydrogen station. It has a Center of Excellence for Energy and Sustainability and hosts a NASA Space Center.

The University-Student Union, new in 2009, is home to offices of the Alumni Center and Associated Students, Inc. (ASI), as well as clubs and organizations. It has an expansive fitness center, theater, and meeting rooms that connect to the Golden Eagle through a third-floor bridge. The Golden Eagle includes a food court, a bookstore, and major conference facilities. Also in 2009, La Kretz Hall, the first building in the Wallis Annenberg Integrated Sciences Complex, was dedicated, with the second building currently under construction.

Applying

To apply, the student must have completed a four-year college course of study and hold an acceptable baccalaureate degree from an institution that is accredited by a regional accrediting association, or have completed equivalent academic preparation as determined by appropriate campus authorities. The student must have attained a grade point average of at least 2.5 (A=4.0) in the last 60 semester (90 quarter) units attempted.

Applicants should complete the online application for graduate students via CSU Mentor at http://www.csumentor.com/AdmissionApp/. An application fee of $55 in U.S. funds is required for each application filed.

Students should contact the program to which they are applying to learn about deadlines and requirements. Applicants must be admitted by a graduate program before they are admitted to the University.

Correspondence and Information

The College of Engineering, Computer Science, and Technology
California State University, Los Angeles
5151 State University Drive
Los Angeles, California 90032-8150

Phone: 323-343-4500
Fax: 323-343-4555
E-mail: engr@calstatela.edu
Web site: http://www.calstatela.edu
http://www.calstatela.edu/ecst

California State University, Los Angeles

THE FACULTY AND THEIR RESEARCH

The reputation California State University, Los Angeles, enjoys as an institution of higher learning is creditable largely to the high quality of its faculty members and their commitment to teaching and scholarship. These men and women have earned their highest degrees from leading universities throughout the world. Their achievements in their academic fields of specialization make them eminently qualified to teach students who possess a variety of academic interests. In addition, internationally acclaimed organizations serve on the College's advisory boards.

Mechanical Engineering

Tammy Chan. Environmental engineering.
Neda Fabris. Manufacturing, material science, mechanics, design.
Verica Gajic. Control systems, optimization, dynamics, design.
Darrell Guillaume. Fluid mechanics, thermodynamics, heat transfer, combustion.
Lin-Min Hsia. Kinematics of mechanisms, computer-aided design, robotics.
Samuel Landsberger. Design, kinematics, rehabilitation engineering.
Arturo Pacheco-Vega. Fluid mechanics, heat transfer, dynamical solutions, thermal control.
Trinh Pham. Fluid mechanics, thermodynamics, renewable energy, combustion.
Adel Sharif. Machine design, structural material.
Chivey Wu. Gas dynamics, fluid mechanics, aerodynamics.

Civil Engineering

Hassan Hashemian. Transportation and city planning.
Crist Khachikian. Environmental engineering.
Gustavo Menezes. Water quality and availability, modeling water and solute transport in groundwater in the vadose zone, measuring of unsaturated soil hydraulic properties, measuring of geohydrologic properties of using centrifugal forces, modeling environmental systems using geographic information system, environmental justice.
Rupa Purasinghe. Structural analysis.
Narendra Taly. Structural engineering, bridge design.
Mark Tufenkjian. Geotechnical engineering.

Electrical & Computer Engineering

Kodzo Abledu. Power systems, electrical machines, electronics.
Helen Boussallis. Communications, control systems.
Fred Daneshgaran. Communications, VLSI, optimization.
Jane Dong. Computer engineering.
Kamram Karimlou. Transportation, surveying.
Charles Liu. Computer systems architecture.

Lily Tabrizi. Communication systems, control systems.
Nancy Warter-Perez. Computer architecture, high performance processors and compilers.
Debra Won. Biomed engineering.

Technology

David Blekhman. Industrial technology, power, energy, and transportation.
Mauricio Castillo. Industrial technology, technology education.
Jai Hong. Industrial technology, manufacturing processes and automation.
Benjamin Lee. Graphic communications.
Ethan Lipton. Graphic communications, industrial technology, technology education.
Paul Liu. Industrial technology, manufacturing processes and automation.
Don Maurizio. Industrial technology, design, technology education.
Keith Mew. Aviation administration.
Stephanie Nelson. Industrial technology, technical communication, professional development.
Virgil Seaman. Industrial technology, computer-integrated design.
Ray Shackelford. Fire protection administration.
Le Tang. Industrial technology, internetworking, CISCO.

Computer Science

Russell Abbott. Artificial intelligence, Web, Java, complex systems.
Vladimir Akis. Computer graphics, topology, dynamical systems.
Valentino Crespi. Distributed computing, UAVs, tracking, hidden Markov models, machine learning, combinatorial optimization.
Huiping Guo. Computer networks, data security.
Jiang Guo. Software engineering, networks, operating systems.
Eun-Young (Elaine) Kang. Computer vision, computer graphics, image processing.
Raj Pamula. Fault tolerant computing, parallel processing.
Bedzad Parviz. General systems methodology, information theory, software engineering.
Chengyu Sun. Database performance optimization, communication, network applications.

College of Engineering, Computer Science, and Technology building.

Campus of California State University, Los Angeles.

CLARKSON UNIVERSITY

Coulter School of Engineering

Programs of Study	The Coulter School of Engineering, comprising departments of chemical and biomolecular, civil and environmental, electrical and computer, and mechanical and aeronautical engineering, offers programs of study leading to the Doctor of Philosophy (Ph.D.), Master of Science (M.S.), and Master of Engineering (M.E.) degrees. Interdisciplinary programs allow the student to specialize in such areas as materials processing, information technology, computer science, and environmental science and engineering. Descriptions of these programs can be found at http://www.clarkson.edu/engineering/graduate.

The Master of Science degree is awarded upon completion of 30 credit hours of graduate work, including a thesis. The Master of Engineering degree can be obtained in one calendar year; it includes the completion of a design-oriented project. In addition, Clarkson has initiated a two-year, two-degree program whereby students may obtain an M.E. degree in one year and continue on for an additional year to obtain an M.B.A.

The Ph.D. is awarded upon completion of a minimum of 90 credit hours of graduate work, corresponding to a minimum of three academic years of full-time study beyond the bachelor's degree. The candidacy procedure for the Ph.D. requires the presentation and defense of a proposal for the Ph.D. research. Candidates for the Ph.D. are required to prepare an original dissertation in an advanced research area and defend it in an oral examination.

The academic year consists of two semesters of fifteen weeks each. There is no formal summer session for graduate classes; graduate students and faculty members devote the summer entirely to research.

Research Facilities
The Department of Chemical and Biomolecular Engineering houses research labs for chemical-mechanical planarization (CMP); thin-film processing; bioengineering; nucleation; chemical metallurgy; chemical kinetics; process design; electrochemistry and electrochemical engineering; process intensification; experimental and computational fluid mechanics, including two research-grade wind tunnels; heat and mass transfer; and interfacial fluid mechanics, including a bubble column equipped with a motorized camera platform. The Department has a fuel-cell test laboratory and facilities for conducting research on alternate energy sources. In addition, excellent facilities are available for aerosol generation and ambient and indoor air pollution sampling and analysis, as well as tools for advanced data analysis.

The Department of Civil and Environmental Engineering has well-equipped environmental engineering laboratories with pilot plant facilities, walk-in constant-temperature rooms, and modern research instrumentation for organic and inorganic analyses; a hydraulics laboratory with a large automated tilting flume; temperature-controlled cold rooms and ice mechanics laboratories; a geomechanics laboratory with a wide array of laboratory and field testing equipment for geotechnical problems, including a number of specialized sensors, and a variety of loading systems, such as 200-kip closed-loop controlled stepping motor system and a 20-kip hydraulic closed-loop controlled servo-valve controlled axial-torsional system; structural and materials testing laboratories, including a unique strong floor and strong wall testing facility and an Instron 220-kip UTM; and soil mechanics and materials laboratories.

The Department of Electrical and Computer Engineering has laboratories for distributed computing networks, intelligent information processing, microelectronics, motion control, robotics, power electronics, electric machines and drives, liquid dielectric breakdown, biomedical signal and image processing, advanced visualization and networked multimedia and networked systems, and a 1-million-volt high-voltage measurement laboratory.

The Department of Mechanical and Aeronautical Engineering houses three wind tunnels, a clean room for microcontamination and nanotechnology research, and labs for fluid mechanics, heat transfer, aerosol and multiphase flow, CAD, image processing, energy conversion, vibrations, combustion, materials processing, manufacturing, and welding.

Much of the research work is conducted in conjunction with the University's interdisciplinary research centers: the New York State Center for Advanced Materials Processing (CAMP), Institute for the Sustainable Environment (ISE), Center for Sustainable Energy Systems (CRES), Center for Rehabilitation Engineering Science and Technology (CREST), and Center for Air Resources Engineering and Science (CARES). Computing facilities within the School of Engineering include an IBM series and a variety of Sun and IBM workstations, all interconnected to each office and laboratory by a high-speed wide-band network. Clarkson's Campus Information Services houses modern information storage and retrieval facilities, the computing center, and the library.

Financial Aid
Several forms of financial assistance are available, which permit a full-time program of study and provide a stipend plus tuition. Instructional assistantships involve an obligation of 12 hours per week of assistance in courses or laboratories. Research assistantships require research activity that is also used to satisfy thesis requirements. Partial-tuition scholarships are available for all degree programs.

Cost of Study
Tuition for graduate work is $1198 per credit hour in 2011–12. Fees are about $440 per year.

Living and Housing Costs
Graduate students can find rooms or apartments near the campus. The University maintains single and married student housing units. Off-campus apartments for 2 students rent for approximately $300 per month and up.

Student Group
There are approximately 200 students on campus pursuing graduate work in engineering. The total Graduate School enrollment is 400, and the undergraduate enrollment is 2,600.

Location
Potsdam, New York, is an attractive village located along the banks of the Raquette River on a rolling plain between the Adirondack Mountains and the St. Lawrence River. Three other colleges (one in Potsdam) provide a total college student body of 11,000 within a 12-mile radius. Potsdam is 100 miles from Montreal, 80 miles from Ottawa and Lake Placid, and 140 miles from Syracuse. The St. Lawrence Seaway, the Thousand Islands, and Adirondack resort areas are within a short drive. Opportunities for fishing, hiking, boating, golfing, camping, swimming, and skiing abound throughout the area.

The University
Clarkson University is a privately endowed school of science, engineering, and business. Master's degrees are offered in the engineering departments and in business administration, chemistry, computer science, mathematics, management systems, and physics; Ph.D. degrees are offered in chemical engineering, chemistry, civil and environmental engineering, electrical and computer engineering, engineering science, environmental science and engineering, materials science and engineering, mathematics, mechanical engineering, and physics.

Applying
It is recommended that applications be submitted by January 30 for the fall semester and September 15 for the spring semester to allow for full financial aid consideration. Study may begin in August, January, or June. Scores on the General Test of the GRE are required for all applications except those of Clarkson students. TOEFL scores of at least 550 (paper-based test), 213 (computer-based test), or 80 (Internet-based test) are required for all international applications.

Correspondence and Information
Wallace H. Coulter School of Engineering
Graduate Studies Office
Box 5700
Clarkson University
Potsdam, New York 13699-5700

Phone: 315-268-7929
Fax: 315-268-4494
E-mail: enggrad@clarkson.edu
Web site: http://www.clarkson.edu/engineering/graduate

Clarkson University

THE FACULTY AND THEIR RESEARCH

Department of Chemical and Biomolecular Engineering

S. V. Babu, Professor; Ph.D., SUNY at Stony Brook. Chemical-mechanical planarization of metal and dielectric films and thin films for photovoltaic applications.

Ruth E. Baltus, Professor; Ph.D., Carnegie Mellon. Transport in porous media, membrane separations, membrane characterization, room temperature ionic liquids and biosensors.

Sandra L. Harris, Associate Professor; Ph.D., California, Santa Barbara. Adaptive control, process control, and process identification; periodic processing; the control of systems having varying dead-times; the generation of input signals for efficient process identification.

Philip K. Hopke, Professor; Ph.D., Princeton. Multivariate statistical methods for data analysis; characterization of source/receptor relationships for ambient air pollutants; sampling, chemical, and physical characterization of airborne particles; experimental studies of homogeneous, heterogeneous, and ion-induced nucleation; indoor air quality; exposure and risk assessment.

R. J. J. Jachuck, Research Associate Professor; Ph.D., Newcastle Upon Tyne. Process intensification and miniaturization, intensified heat and mass transfer, polymerization.

Sitaraman Krishnan, Assistant Professor; Ph.D., Lehigh. Antifouling and biocompatible polymers, biomaterials, responsive materials, nanostructured material design using self-assembly, X-ray techniques for nanoscale materials characterization, multiphase polymerization kinetics.

Richard J. McCluskey, Associate Professor; Ph.D., Minnesota. Reaction kinetics and thermodynamics.

John B. McLaughlin, Professor; Ph.D., Harvard. Fluid mechanics, modeling of protective textiles, self-healing composite materials and the flow of air and suspended particles, electrostatic precipitator.

Don H. Rasmussen, Professor; Ph.D., Wisconsin–Madison. Nucleation and phase transformations, metal reduction, colloidal and interfacial phenomena.

R. Shankar Subramanian, Professor; Ph.D., Clarkson. Transport phenomena, colloidal and interfacial phenomena.

Ian Ivar Suni, Professor; Ph.D., Harvard. Electrochemical and electrochemical engineering with applications to biosensors, thin film growth and nanotechnology.

Ross Taylor, Professor; Ph.D., Manchester. Multicomponent mass transfer, separation process simulation, engineering applications of computer algebra.

Selma Mededovic Thagard, Assistant Professor; Ph.D., Florida State. Nonthermal plasma for air and wastewater treatment, plasma-assisted material synthesis, plasma chemistry, mathematical modeling of electrical discharges in gases and liquids.

William R. Wilcox, Professor and Co-Director, International Center for Gravity Materials Science and Applications; Ph.D., Berkeley. Materials processing, crystal growth.

Department of Civil and Environmental Engineering

Norbert L. Ackermann, Professor Emeritus; Ph.D., Carnegie Tech. Mechanics of granular flow, river hydraulics.

Christopher Bellona, Assistant Professor; Ph.D., Colorado School of Mines. Research and development of novel water treatment processes and systems.

James S. Bonner, Professor and Shipley Center for Innovation Fellow; Ph.D., Clarkson. Water quality and spill monitoring.

John P. Dempsey, Professor and Shipley Center for Innovation Fellow; Ph.D., Auckland (New Zealand). Fracture mechanics, tribology, ice-structure interaction.

Andrea Ferro, Associate Professor; Ph.D., Stanford. Air pollution, indoor air quality.

Stefan J. Grimberg, Associate Professor and Chair; Ph.D., North Carolina at Chapel Hill. Bioremediation, bioavailability of organic environmental pollutants.

Thomas M. Holsen, Professor; Ph.D., Berkeley. Fate and transport of chemicals in the environment.

Kerop Janoyan, Associate Professor and Executive Officer; Ph.D., UCLA. Geotechnical and structural engineering, soil-structural interactions, structural health monitoring.

Feng-Bor Lin, Professor; Ph.D., Carnegie Mellon. Modeling traffic operations, systems analysis.

Yongming Liu, Assistant Professor; Ph.D., Vanderbilt. Structural durability, multiscale damage modeling of materials.

Levon Minnetyan, Professor; Ph.D., Duke. Structural analysis and design.

Sulapha Peethamparan, Assistant Professor; Ph.D, Purdue. Characterization and control of cement and concrete materials.

Susan E. Powers, Professor and Associate Director for Sustainability; Ph.D., Michigan. Multiphase fluid flow; hazardous-waste management.

Shane Rogers, Assistant Professor; Ph.D., Iowa State. Fate and transport of etiological agents and anthropogenic compounds.

Hayley H. Shen, Professor; Ph.D., Clarkson; Ph.D., Iowa. Granular flow, sea ice processes.

Hung Tao Shen, Professor and Associate Dean for Research and Graduate Studies; Ph.D., Iowa. River hydraulics, river ice processes, mathematical modeling.

Lifeng Wang, Assistant Professor; Ph.D., Tsinghua (China). Mechanical properties of carbon nanotubes and related nanostructures.

Poojitha Yapa, Professor; Ph.D., Clarkson. Mathematical modeling of oil spills.

Department of Electrical and Computer Engineering

James J. Carroll, Associate Professor; Ph.D., Clemson. High-performance motion control, nonlinear control, control strategies.

Ming-Cheng Cheng, Associate Professor; Ph.D., Polytechnic. Device physics and modeling and simulation of electronic and thermal characteristics for advanced solid state devices.

Susan E. Conry, Associate Professor; Ph.D., Rice. Multiagent systems, distributed problem solving, design of coordination strategies.

Brian Dean, Assistant Professor; Ph.D., Wyoming. Biomimetics.

Daqing Hou, Assistant Professor; Ph.D., Alberta. Software design, program analysis, semantics of programming languages, software development environments and tools, software reuse, documentation, software evolution, formal methods.

William Jemison, Professor and Chair; Ph.D. Drexel. Microwave photonic systems and substations, microwave/mm-wave antenna design and measurement, radar systems, wireless and optical communications systems, lidar systems, biological applications of microwaves and photonics.

Abul N. Khondker, Associate Professor; Ph.D., Rice. Solid-state materials and device theory, modeling and characterization of semiconductor devices.

Jack Koplowitz, Associate Professor; Ph.D., Colorado. Image and signal processing, computer vision, pattern recognition.

Paul B. McGrath, Professor; Ph.D., London. Dielectric materials and high-voltage engineering, insulation problems.

Robert A. Meyer, Associate Professor; Ph.D., Rice. Artificial intelligence and distributed problem solving, verification of hardware designs, software engineering.

Thomas H. Ortmeyer, Professor; Ph.D., Iowa State. Power electronics, power quality, power system operation.

Vladimir Privman, Professor; D.Sci., Technion (Israel). Quantum devices: quantum computing, spintronics, nanoscale electronics; colloids and nanoparticles; synthesis and properties.

Liya L. Regel, Research Professor and Director, International Center for Gravity Materials Science and Applications; Ph.D., Irkutsk State (Russia); Doctorat, Ioffe Institute (Russia). Materials science and its influence on properties and device performance.

Jeremiah Remus, Assistant Professor; Ph.D., Duke. Statistical signal processing, model inversion and optimization, pattern recognition.

Charles J. Robinson, Founding Director, Center for Rehabilitation Engineering, Science, and Technology (CREST), and Herman L. Shulman Chair Professor; D.Sc., Washington (St. Louis). Combining the development of microdevices and nanodevices capable of measuring stroke sequences with fundamental research that characterizes the behavior of the nervous system, quantification of tremor through signal processing analysis of graphical drawings, and determining and describing the control systems employed in health and disease to permit upright standing in humans.

Edward Sazonov, Research Associate Professor; Ph.D., West Virginia. Computational intelligence, biomedical engineering, nondestructive testing.

Robert J. Schilling, Professor; Ph.D., Berkeley. Control, nonlinear systems, robotics, active control of acoustic noise, motion planning.

Stephanie Schuckers, Associate Professor; Ph.D., Michigan. Biomedical signal processing, medical devices, pattern recognition, large datasets.

James A. Svoboda, Associate Professor and Associate Chair; Ph.D., Wisconsin. Circuit theory, system theory, electronics, digital signal processing.

Lei Wu, Assistant Professor, Ph.D., IIT. Stochastic modeling and optimization of large-scale power systems, smart grid, high-penetration renewable energy applications, power systems reliability and economics, market power analysis and risk management.

Department of Mechanical and Aeronautical Engineering

Goodarz Ahmadi, Clarkson Distinguished Professor, Robert R. Hill '48 Professor, and Dean, Coulter School of Engineering; Ph.D., Purdue. Fluid mechanics, solid mechanics, multiphase flows, aerosols, microcontamination, surface cleaning.

Ajit Achuthan, Assistant Professor; Ph.D., Purdue. Solid mechanics, ferroelectrics, nanomechanics and smart structures and materials, fiber optic sensors.

Daryush Aidun, Professor and Chair; Ph.D., Rensselaer. Welding metallurgy and automation, corrosion, materials processing and solidification, reliability analysis of engineering components/systems.

Douglas Bohl, Assistant Professor; Ph.D., Michigan State. Experimental fluid mechanics and thermal science.

Frederick Carlson, Associate Professor; Ph.D., Connecticut. Heat transfer, crystal growth.

Cetin Cetinkaya, Professor; Ph.D., Illinois at Urbana-Champaign. Solid mechanics, stress wave propagation, surface cleaning and nanotechnology.

Suresh Dhaniyala, Associate Professor; Ph.D., Minnesota. Aerosols, nanoparticles, particle instrumentation, atmospheric aerosols, aircraft and ground-based sampling, fluid mechanics.

Kevin Fite, Assistant Professor; Ph.D., Vanderbilt. Dynamic systems and controls, robotics and mechatronics.

Brian Helenbrook, Associate Professor; Ph.D., Princeton. Computational fluid dynamics and combustion.

Kathleen Issen, Associate Professor; Ph.D., Northwestern. Solid mechanics, inelastic behavior and failure of geomaterials.

Ratneshwar Jha, Associate Professor; Ph.D., Arizona State. Solid mechanics, optimization, smart materials.

James Kane, Associate Professor; Ph.D., Connecticut. Solid mechanics, boundary-element methods.

Laurel Kuxhaus, Assistant Professor; Ph.D., Pittsburgh. Biomechanics; mechanics and control of the upper extremity, especially the elbow; elbow joint stiffness and its application to arthritis; prosthetic upper limb control and the diagnosis of Parkinson's disease; mathematical modeling of ligaments; mechanical properties of vertebral bone.

Ronald LaFleur, Associate Professor; Ph.D., Connecticut. Fluid mechanics, thermofluid design.

Sung P. Lin, Professor Emeritus; Ph.D., Michigan. Fluid mechanics, fluid dynamic stability.

Pier Marzocca, Associate Professor; Ph.D., Virginia Tech. Solid mechanics, nonlinear systems control.

John Moosbrugger, Professor and Associate Dean; Ph.D., Georgia Tech. Solid mechanics, plasticity.

David Morrison, Associate Professor; Ph.D., Michigan. Materials science, fracture mechanics.

Eric Thacher, Professor Emeritus and Senior Research Professor; Ph.D., New Mexico State. Thermal sciences, solar energy.

Daniel Valentine, Associate Professor and Executive Officer; Ph.D., Catholic University. Fluid mechanics, hydrodynamics.

Kenneth Visser, Associate Professor; Ph.D., Notre Dame. Experimental aerodynamics.

Kenneth Willmert, Professor; Ph.D., Case Western Reserve. Solid mechanics, optimal design.

Steven W. Yurgartis, Associate Professor; Ph.D., Rensselaer. Solid mechanics, composite materials.

Philip A. Yuya, Assistant Professor; Ph.D., Nebraska-Lincoln. Constitutive modeling and experimental mechanics of materials with special emphasis on biomaterials, nanofibers and polymers.

FLORIDA INTERNATIONAL UNIVERSITY

College of Engineering and Computing

Programs of Study

The College of Engineering and Computing is committed to educating professionals who can serve industry and the community at large in a wide variety of fields, as well as conduct innovative basic and applied research that meets the technical needs of industry and government, improves the quality of life, and contributes to the economic viability of Florida, the nation, and the world.

The College of Engineering and Computing consists of the School of Computing and Information Sciences and five academic departments: biomedical engineering, civil and environmental engineering, construction management, electrical and computer engineering, and mechanical and materials engineering. These academic departments offer programs leading to the Bachelor of Science (B.S.), the Master of Science (M.S.), and the Doctor of Philosophy (Ph.D.) degrees.

The College offers the Ph.D. in biomedical engineering, civil engineering electrical engineering, computer science, and mechanical engineering. The Master of Science is available in biomedical engineering, civil engineering, computer engineering, computer science, construction management, electrical engineering, engineering management, environmental engineering, information technology, materials science and engineering, mechanical engineering, and telecommunications and networking.

Research Facilities

The College of Engineering and Computing has numerous research institutes, centers, and laboratories that support its academic and research programs. The institutes include the Advanced Materials Research Institute (AMERI) and the Telecommunications and Information Technology Institute (IT2).

The research centers include the Applied Research Center (ARC), the Center for Advanced Distributed System Engineering (CADSE), the Center for Advanced Technology and Education (CATE), the Center for the Study of Matter at Extreme Conditions (CeSMEC), the Center for Energy and Technology of the Americas (CETA), the Center of Emerging Technologies for Advanced Information and High-Confidence Systems (CREST), the Engineering Information Center (EIC), the Engineering Manufacturing Center (EMC), the High Performance Database Research Center (HPDRC), the Lehman Center for Transportation Research (LCTR), and the IBM Latin American Supercomputing Consortium (LA GRID).

Research laboratories include the Autonomic Computing Research Laboratory (ACRL), the Construction and Structures Research and Testing Laboratory, the Distributed Multimedia Information System Laboratory (DMIS), the Digital Signal Processing Laboratory (DSP), the Enterprise Information Systems Research Laboratory, the Enterprise Systems Engineering Laboratory (ESE), the Graphic Simulation Laboratory (GSL), the Human Factors and Ergonomics Laboratory, the Information Systems Research Laboratory, the Laboratory for Wind Engineering Research (LWER), the Multidisciplinary Analysis, Inverse Design, Robust Optimal Control Laboratory (MAIDROC), the Optical Imaging and Tomography Laboratory, the Plasma Forming Laboratory (PFL), Bioinformatics Research Group (BioRG), and the Photonics Research Laboratory.

Affiliated Centers and Programs include the AMPATH International Exchange Point in Miami, CHEPREO: Center for High Energy Physics Research and Education Outreach, CIARA: Center for Internet Augmented Research and Assessment, CyberBridges, GEC: The Eugenio Pino and Family Global Entrepreneurship Center, IHRC: the International Hurricane Research Center, MOTOROLA Women in Engineering (MWIE), NASA All-Star Project, and Ware Foundation Neuro-Engineering and Brain Research Laboratory at Miami Children's Hospital.

Financial Aid

The College of Engineering and Computing offers a variety of merit-based fellowships, assistantships, and scholarships to qualified domestic and international students. These awards are highly competitive, and the amounts vary depending on the type of the award. Additional financial aid information is available from the Financial Aid Office at http://www.fiu.edu/orgs/finaid.

Cost of Study

For the 2011–12 academic year, tuition is $399.95 per credit for Florida residents and $904.03 per credit for out-of-state and international students. An additional $185 per semester is charged for student activity fees, a health fee, a photo ID, and parking. Books and supplies are estimated at $1400 per semester, and health insurance costs $1900 for two semesters.

Living and Housing Costs

Graduate student housing is available at University Park (305-348-4190) and the Biscayne Bay Campus (305-919-5587). On-campus housing ranges between $4900 and $6600 per semester, depending on the type of accommodation and meal plan selected. Additional information about on- and off-campus housing can be found through the Office of Housing and Residential Life Web site at http://www.fiu.edu/~housing.

Student Group

The College of Engineering and Computing has 892 graduate students, of whom 515 are full-time, 225 are women, and 431 are international students.

Location

Greater Miami is noted for its cultural diversity. Greater Miami has extensive cultural amenities, such as the New World Symphony, the Florida Grand Opera, and the Miami City Ballet, in addition to a tropical climate. The area has franchises in all major sports, and the University has inaugurated intercollegiate football to round out its extensive sports offerings. Miami is a major transportation hub with easy air and sea connections throughout the Americas and Europe.

The University and The College

Florida International University (FIU) is Miami's first public four-year university. With more than 39,000 students, almost 1100 full-time faculty members, and 124,000 alumni, FIU is the largest university in South Florida and one of the most dynamic institutions in the United States. The University's growth in enrollment and stature in the academic community are remarkable. In four decades, FIU has become nationally renowned as a doctoral-granting institution, with more than 200 degree programs. For the past five years, FIU was ranked among the top 100 public universities in *U.S. News & World Report*'s "America's Best Colleges," and it is also is ranked as a Research University in the High Research Activity category of the Carnegie Foundation's prestigious classification system. FIU recently graduated its first law class, and opened a medical school, attesting to the University's growth and recognition.

The College of Engineering and Computing is South Florida's leading engineering education resource. The College offers a full range of bachelor's, master's, and doctoral degree programs in engineering, construction, management, and computer sciences. Research is an integral part of the College's mission and its success, with more than $90 million in external research funding over the last five years from a variety of governmental and corporate sources.

Applying

In general, applicants must submit the completed application, the application fee, official transcripts, proof of degree, and GRE scores. In addition, some doctoral-program applicants must submit three letters of recommendation and a resume or curriculum vitae. International students must send in their TOEFL scores and have their transcripts evaluated. More information, including specific deadlines, is available from the College of Engineering and Computing.

Correspondence and Information

College of Engineering and Computing
Florida International University
10555 West Flagler Street, EC2430
Miami, Florida 33174-1630

Phone: 305-348-1890
Fax: 305-348-6142
E-mail: grad_eng@fiu.edu
Web site: http://cec.fiu.edu

Florida International University

THE FACULTY

School of Computing and Information Sciences

Walid Akache, Instructor; M.S., Miami (Florida).
David Barton, Professor; Ph.D., Cambridge.
Toby S. Berk, Professor Emeritus; Ph.D., Purdue.
Shu-Ching Chen, Associate Professor; Ph.D., Purdue.
Peter J. Clarke, Associate Professor; Ph.D., Clemson.
Tim Downey, Instructor; M.S., SUNY at Albany.
Xudong He, Professor; Ph.D., Virginia Tech.
Vagelis Hristidis, Assistant Professor; Ph.D., California, San Diego.
Kip Irvine, Instructor; M.S., Miami (Florida).
Sitharama Iyengar, Professor and Director; Ph.D., Mississippi State.
Sam Khalil, Visiting Instructor; Ph.D., Claude Bernard, Lyon (France).
Tao Li, Assistant Professor; Ph.D., Rochester.
Christine Lisetti, Associate Professor; Ph.D., Florida International.
Xiaowen Liu, Assistant Professor; Ph.D., Dartmouth.
Masoud Milani, Associate Professor; Ph.D., Central Florida.
Giri Narasimhan, Professor; Ph.D., Wisconsin–Madison.
Jainendra K. Navlakha, Professor; Ph.D., Case Western Reserve.
Deng Pan, Assistant Professor; Ph.D., SUNY at Stony Brook.
Ana Pasztor, Professor; Ph.D., Darmstadt (Germany).
Alex Pelin, Associate Professor; Ph.D., Pennsylvania.
Norman D. Pestaina, Instructor; M.S., Penn State.
Niki Pissinou, Professor; Ph.D., USC.
Nagarajan Prabakar, Associate Professor; Ph.D., Queensland (Australia).
Raju Rangaswami, Assistant Professor; Ph.D., California, Santa Barbara.
Naphtali Rishe, Professor; Ph.D., Tel Aviv.
S. Masoud Sadjadi, Assistant Professor; Ph.D., Michigan State.
Greg Shaw, Instructor; M.S., Barry.
Geoffrey Smith, Associate Professor; Ph.D., Cornell.
Joslyn Smith, Instructor; M.S., New Brunswick (Canada).
Jinpeng Wei, Assistant Professor; Ph.D., Georgia Tech.
Jill Weiss, Instructor; M.S., Barry.
Mark Allen Weiss, Professor and Associate Director; Ph.D., Princeton.
Ming Zhao, Assistant Professor; Ph.D., Florida.

Department of Biomedical Engineering

Michael Brown, Instructor; M.D./Ph.D., Miami (Florida).
James D. Byrne, Laboratory Instructor; Ph.D., Florida.
Michael Christie, Instructor and Undergraduate Adviser; Ph.D., Rutgers.
Anuradha Godavarty, Assistant Professor; Ph.D., Texas A&M.
Yen-Chi Huang, Assistant Professor; Ph.D. Michigan.
Ranu Jung, Chair; Ph.D., Case Western Reserve.
Chenzhong Li, Assistant Professor; Ph.D., Kumamoto (Japan).
Wei-Chiang Lin, Assistant Professor; Ph.D., Texas at Austin.
Anthony J. McGoron, Associate Professor; Ph.D., Louisiana Tech.
Sharan Ramaswamy, Assistant Professor; Ph.D., Iowa.
Nikolaos Tsoukias, Assistant Professor; Ph.D., California, Irvine.

Department of Civil and Environmental Engineering

Atorod Azizinamini, Chair; Ph.D., South Carolina.
Arindam Gan Chowdhury, Assistant Professor; Ph.D., Iowa State.
Hector R. Fuentes, Professor; Ph.D., Vanderbilt; PE, DEE.
Albert Gan, Associate Professor; Ph.D., Florida.
Mohammed Hadi, Assistant Professor; Ph.D., Florida; PE.
Sylvan C. Jolibois Jr., Associate Professor; Ph.D., Berkeley.
Shonali Laha, Associate Professor; Ph.D., Carnegie Mellon; PE.
Amir Mirmiran, Professor and Dean; Ph.D., Maryland; PE.
Caesar Abi Shdid, Undergraduate Advisor and Director, Center for Technology Transfer and Training (CT3); Ph.D., Florida.
L. David Shen, Professor, Associate Dean for Academic Programs, and Director, Lehman Center for Transportation Research; Ph.D., Clemson; PE, TE.
Nakin Suksawang, Assistant Professor; Ph.D., Rutgers.

Walter Z. Tang, Associate Professor; Ph.D., Delaware; PE.
Berrin Tansel, Associate Professor and Associate Director, Center for Diversity in Engineering; Ph.D., Wisconsin–Madison, 1985; PE.
Ton-Lo Wang, Professor and Undergraduate Program Director; Ph.D., IIT.

Department of Construction Management

Irtishad U. Ahmad, Associate Professor and Chairman; Ph.D., Cincinnati; PE.
Ronald A. Baier, Instructor and Undergraduate Advisor; M.E., Florida; PE.
Mehmet Emre Bayraktar, Assistant Professor; Ph.D., Purdue.
José A. Faria, Assistant Professor; Ph.D., Maryland.
Eugene D. Farmer, Associate Professor and Undergraduate Program Director; M.Arch., Illinois; RA, AIA.
Jose D. Mitrani, Associate Professor; M.E., Florida; PE, CPC, CGC.
Yimin Zhu, Assistant Professor; Ph.D., Florida; CCE.

Department of Electrical and Computer Engineering

Malek Adjouadi, Associate Professor and Director, CATE Center; Ph.D., Florida.
Jean Andrian, Associate Professor and Graduate Program Director; Ph.D., Florida.
Armando Barreto, Associate Professor and Director, Digital Signals Processing Lab; Ph.D., Florida.
Mirafzal Behrooz, Assistant Professor; Ph.D., Marquette.
Hai Deng, Assistant Professor; Ph.D., Texas at Austin.
Jeffrey Fan, Assistant Professor; Ph.D., California, Riverside.
Stravos V. Georgakopoulos, Assistant Professor; Ph.D., Arizona State.
W. Kinzy Jones, Professor; Ph.D., MIT.
Grover L. Larkins, Professor and Director; Ph.D., Case Western Reserve.
Chen Liu, Assistant Professor; Ph.D., California, Irvine.
Osama Mohammed, Professor; Ph.D., Virginia Tech.
Nezih Pala, Assistant Professor; Ph.D., Rensselaer.
Roberto R. Panepucci, Assistant Professor; Ph.D., Illinois at Urbana-Champaign.
Gang Quan, Associate Professor; Ph.D., Notre Dame.
Gustavo Roig, Professor; Ph.D., Florida.
Frank K. Urban, Associate Professor; Ph.D., Florida.
Kang K. Yen, Professor and Chair; Ph.D., Vanderbilt.

Department of Mechanical and Materials Engineering

Arvind Agarwal, Assistant Professor; Ph.D., Tennessee.
Yiding Cao, Associate Professor; Ph.D., Dayton.
Jiuhua Chen, Associate Professor and Graduate Program Director; Ph.D., Tennessee.
Won-Bong Choi, Associate Professor; Ph.D., North Carolina State.
George S. Dulikravich, Professor; Ph.D., Cornell.
Ali Ebadian, Professor; Ph.D., LSU.
Dennis Fan, Assistant Professor; Ph.D., SUNY at Stony Brook.
Gordon Hopkins, Professor; Ph.D., Alabama.
W. Kinzy Jones, Professor and Director, AMERI; Ph.D., MIT.
Cesar Levy, Professor and Chair; Ph.D., Stanford.
Norman D. H. Munroe, Associate Professor; Eng.Sc.D., Columbia.
Surendra K. Saxena, Professor; Ph.D., Uppsala (Sweden).
Carmen Schenck, Instructor/Counselor; M.S., Florida International.
Yong X. Tao, Professor and Undergraduate Program Director; Ph.D., Michigan.
Ibrahim Nur Tansel, Associate Professor; Ph.D., Wisconsin–Madison.
Sabri Tosunoglu, Associate Professor; Ph.D., Florida at Gainesville.
Igor Tsukanov, Assistant Professor, Ph.D., Northwestern.
Chunlei (Peggy) Wang, Assistant Professor; Ph.D., Jilin (China).
Kuang-Hsi Wu, Professor; Ph.D., Illinois at Urbana-Champaign.

KANSAS STATE UNIVERSITY

College of Engineering

Programs of Study

The College of Engineering's eight academic departments offer eight Ph.D. programs and eleven master's level programs. The M.S. and Ph.D. programs include: biological and agricultural engineering, chemical engineering, civil engineering, computing and information sciences, electrical engineering, industrial engineering, mechanical engineering, and nuclear engineering. Additional programs include the M.S. in architectural engineering, M.S. in operations research, Master of Software Engineering, and Master of Engineering Management.

Candidates for the M.S. degree are normally required to spend one academic year in residence; however, some M.S. degree programs are available partially or fully by distance. Subject to the approval of the major department, the candidate may choose one of the following options: (1) a minimum of 30 semester hours of graduate credit, including a master's thesis of 6 to 8 semester hours; (2) a minimum of 30 semester hours of graduate credit, including a written report of 2 semester hours, either of research or of problem work on a topic in the major field; or (3) a minimum of 30 semester hours of graduate credit in course work only, but including evidence of scholarly effort such as term papers and production of creative work, as determined by the student's supervisory committee.

Candidates for the Ph.D. degree normally devote at least three years of two semesters each to graduate study, or about 90 semester hours beyond the bachelor's degree. A dissertation is required. Ph.D. candidates must complete a year of full-time study in residence at Kansas State University. Furthermore, a minimum registration of 30 hours in research is required, not including work done toward a master's degree. Each candidate also must have completed at least 24 hours of course work at the University. The foreign language requirement is determined as a matter of policy by the graduate faculty in each department.

Research Facilities

Each of the eight departments in the College of Engineering has modern and fully equipped teaching and research laboratories. In addition, the College has several centers and institutes, including the Civil Infrastructure Systems Laboratory, the Advanced Manufacturing Institute, the Center for Sustainable Energy, the Center for Hazardous Substance Research, the Pollution Prevention Institute, the Institute for Environmental Research, and the National Gas Machinery Laboratory.

Financial Aid

The College of Engineering offers approximately 300 fellowships, traineeships, and assistantships each year. These awards are administered by individual departments.

Cost of Study

Fees for 2010–11 were $298 per credit hour for residents and $673 per credit hour for nonresidents. In addition, an $83 campus fee was charged for the first credit hour, with $25 charged for each additional credit hour, up to a maximum fee of $352 per semester. Students enrolled in the College of Engineering were assessed an engineering equipment fee of $19 per credit hour and a tuition surcharge of $20 per credit hour for engineering courses. Students with graduate assistantships may qualify for resident fees.

Living and Housing Costs

Residence hall rates for room and board for a double room with a fifteen-meal plan were $3432 per semester per student in 2010–11. A variety of apartments is also available at the Jardine complex, with monthly rent ranging from $378 for a one-bedroom unfurnished traditional apartment to $546 for a one-bedroom newly constructed apartment. In addition, there are scholarship housing units available that function as cooperatives in which students provide their own services. Complete information for Housing and Dining Services is available at http://housing.k-state.edu/. There are numerous privately owned apartments with a wide range of rental rates in the community.

Student Group

Kansas State University enrolls more than 23,000 students. The College of Engineering has approximately 3,000 undergraduate and 500 graduate students.

Location

The University's 664-acre campus is located in Manhattan, Kansas, a community of about 50,000 residents located in the scenic Flint Hills of northeast Kansas.

The University

Kansas State University was established in 1863 as the first land-grant institution under the Morrill Act. The University is composed of the Graduate School and the Colleges of Agriculture, Architecture and Design, Arts and Sciences, Business Administration, Education, Engineering, Human Ecology, Technology, and Veterinary Medicine. The College of Technology is located at Kansas State in Salina.

There are numerous cultural and entertainment activities associated with the University and the community. One of the most noteworthy is the Alfred M. Landon Lecture Series on Public Issues, which regularly brings outstanding speakers to the campus. The list of notables has included Tom Brokaw, George H. W. Bush, George W. Bush, Jimmy Carter, Bill Clinton, Bob Dole, Elizabeth Dole, Gerald Ford, Robert M. Gates, Mikhail Gorbachev, Billy Graham, Nancy Landon Kassebaum, Robert Kennedy, General Richard Myers, Richard Nixon, Sandra Day O'Connor, General David Petraeus, General Colin Powell, Dan Rather, Ronald Reagan, Sonia Sotomayor, Sheikh Yamani, and many others.

The University is a member of the Big Twelve Conference and provides numerous facilities for athletic activities.

Applying

The Graduate School has a nonrefundable application fee of $40 for domestic students and $55 for international students. Requirements vary according to department. Students interested in graduate study in the College of Engineering are invited to write to the Dean of Engineering, stating their area of interest.

Correspondence and Information

John R. English, Dean of Engineering
1046 Rathbone Hall
Kansas State University
Manhattan, Kansas 66506-5201

Phone: 785-532-5590
E-mail: ees@ksu.edu
Web site: http://www.ksu.edu

Kansas State University

FACULTY HEADS AND AREAS OF RESEARCH

Architectural Engineering. David R. Fritchen, Head; M.S., Washington (Seattle). (17 faculty members) Structural, mechanical, and electrical systems design for buildings: domestic water-supply and sanitation systems, fire protection, heating and air-conditioning systems, lighting and electrical systems, environmental control systems in buildings, communication and energy management systems for buildings. Building design and construction: integration of structural, mechanical, and electrical systems in buildings.

Biological and Agricultural Engineering. Joseph P. Harner, Head; Ph.D., Virginia Tech. (15 faculty members) Grain processing, handling, drying, and storage. Water and soil resources: irrigation systems, movement of pesticides and other chemicals in surface water and groundwater, improved water management techniques, erosion and sedimentation control, water quality and nonpoint pollution control, animal waste management. Off-highway vehicle systems: chemical application systems, site-specific and precision agriculture. Energy use in agriculture: efficient internal-combustion engine operation. Control systems: instrumentation and controls, sensor development, image processing, chemical spray metering and control. Animal environment: air quality, environmental modification, ventilation-fan performance. Process engineering: process design, cereal-based product development, properties of biological products, biobased fuels. Environmental engineering: constructed wetlands, vegetative filters, watershed modeling, bioremediation.

Chemical Engineering. James H. Edgar, Head; Ph.D., Florida. (10 faculty members) Bioconversion and bioprocessing: enzyme manipulation and reactor design, biomass conversion, biobased industrial products, separation and purification of biological systems, environmental engineering. Sensors and advanced materials: microelectronic materials, polymer science, adsorbents, catalysts, graphene technologies, bionanotechnology, and nanoelectronics. Alternative energy: catalysts and reactor design for hydrogen production, process synthesis, hydrogen and natural gas storage, artificial membranes for separation and purification.

Civil Engineering. Alok Bhandari, Head; Ph.D., Virginia Tech. (15 faculty members) Hydrology and hydraulic engineering: hydraulic and hydrologic modeling, overland flow hydraulics. Environmental engineering: physical, chemical, and biological processes for water, wastewater, and hazardous-waste treatment. Soil mechanics and foundation engineering: physical and mechanical properties of soil, soil stabilization, earth pressures and reactions, environmental geotechnology. Structural engineering: behavior and load-carrying capacity of steel and reinforced concrete members, fracture mechanics of concrete, finite-element methods, optimization applied to civil engineering structures, structural dynamics and earthquake engineering. Transportation engineering: urban transportation planning, transportation systems, analysis and simulation, geometric design of highways, highway safety, pavements and highway materials.

Computing and Information Sciences. Gurdip Singh, Head; Ph.D., SUNY at Stony Brook. (17 faculty members) Languages and software: high assurance software, software verification and certification, programming language and programming environment design. Cyber-security: language-based security, information assurance, enterprise systems security. Parallel and distributed computing systems: distributed mutual exclusion, real-time embedded systems, cluster computing, synchronization and concurrency, construction, distributed algorithms and protocols, operating systems, parallel programming languages and systems. Database systems: database design, object-oriented databases, artificial intelligence, data mining, bioinformatics. Software engineering: software life cycle, software environments and tools, software metrics, software specification, software testing, large software systems, computational science and engineering, agent-oriented software engineering.

Electrical and Computer Engineering. Don M. Gruenbacher, Head; Ph.D., Kansas State. (19 faculty members) Bioengineering: biomedicine, light-based bioinstrumentation, telemedicine. Communication systems: detection and estimation, analog/digital/RF circuits and systems, wireless telecommunications. Computer systems: computer vision, testing of digital systems, neural networks, computer architecture, noncontact sensing. Electromagnetics: device modeling and simulation, bioelectromagnetics. Instrumentation: computer-based instrumentation, sensors, intelligent instrumentation, microcontroller applications. Power systems: renewable energy, power system and stability, nonlinear dynamic systems, load management, distribution automation, power electronics, power devices, high-voltage circuits. Signal processing: adaptive signal processing, image processing. Solid-state electronics: sensors, device and process modeling, analog and digital integrated circuit design, infrared emitters and detectors, wide-bandgap semiconductors.

Industrial and Manufacturing Systems Engineering. Bradley A. Kramer, Head; Ph.D., Kansas State. (14 faculty members) Operations research: network optimization, graph theory, mathematical programming, health systems modeling and control, disaster recovery logistics, stochastic processes and queuing, fuzzy and uncertainty reasoning. Manufacturing systems engineering: advanced manufacturing processes, machining difficult materials, energy manufacturing, quality control. Ergonomics: highway safety, work environments. Engineering management: project management, management decision making.

Mechanical and Nuclear Engineering. Donald L. Fenton, Head; Ph.D., Illinois at Urbana-Champaign. (22 faculty members) Heat and mass transfer: fluid mechanics, room air diffusion. Machine design and materials science: acoustics, composite materials, dynamics, kinematics, rock mechanics, stress analysis, vibrations. Control systems: dynamic system modeling, stability, robust control, instrumentation and measurements, simulation and control, aircraft navigation and control. Heating, air conditioning, human comfort. Computer-assisted design and graphics. Nuclear reactor physics and engineering: radiation transport theory, neutron spectroscopy. Radiation detection and measurement: neutron activation analysis, X-ray and gamma-ray spectroscopy, nondestructive assay of fissile materials. Radiation protection: radiation shielding, environmental monitoring. Controlled thermonuclear power: radiation damage and materials problems.

Advanced Manufacturing Institute. Bradley A. Kramer, Director; Ph.D., Kansas State. The Advanced Manufacturing Institute (AMI) is dedicated to providing innovative and cost-effective engineering and business solutions. AMI offers a full spectrum of capabilities that integrate business and creative insight with design and engineering expertise. AMI works with entrepreneurs and businesses of all sizes—from startups to Fortune 500 companies—in every market imaginable, including manufacturing, transportation, aerospace, consumer products, agriculture, food, chemicals, plastics, bioprocessing, equipment, and machinery. AMI also manages a highly successful intern program that allows undergraduate and graduate students to gain real work experience in the company of experienced professionals. The program helps students increase their skills and knowledge and be more productive in the workplace upon graduation.

Center for Sustainable Energy. Mary Rezac, Co-director; Ph.D., Texas at Austin. The center is focused on efforts related to assessment, conversion, and/or utilization of sustainable energy resources such as biomass, wind, and solar. Faculty from the Colleges of Engineering, Agriculture, Arts and Sciences, and Business are involved in research and educational outreach efforts with biomass resource assessment, plant genetics for efficient biofuel production, and conversion and utilization of renewable resources to fuels for transportation and electricity.

Center for Hazardous Substance Research. Larry E. Erickson, Director; Ph.D., Kansas State. Handling and processing hazardous waste/materials; protection of water supplies: resource recovery, treatment, disposal, and storage of hazardous materials.

Health Care Operations Resource Center. David H. Ben Arieh, Director; Ph.D., Purdue. The Health Care Operations Resource Center conducts research and develops new technology and applied solutions to resolve operational issues that face the medical community. The center seeks to improve service quality, reduce costs, and improve patient care, and is engaged in improving health care operations at all levels of care from small rural clinics to large urban hospitals. The center engages both graduate and undergraduate students to work on these client projects and also involves students in research projects. The center emphasizes the use of operations research, analytical models, and information systems in its work.

Pollution Prevention Institute. Nancy Larson, Director; B.S., Montana State. Provides technical assistance and training in source reduction and environmental compliance to businesses, institutions, technical assistance groups, and private citizens throughout the Midwest. The institute also supports engineering interns, hosts an environmental management system (EMS) peer center, and serves as a meeting ground for KSU faculty members involved in pollution prevention and other related activities.

Institute for Environmental Research. Steven Eckels, Director; Ph.D., Iowa State. This internationally known lab studies the interaction between people and their thermal environment. With eight environmental chambers and special equipment such as sweating mannequins, IER focuses on factors affecting thermal comfort and thermal stress including environmental factors and HVAC systems; protective materials, clothing systems, and sleeping bags; and physical activity. Projects also deal with biothermal modeling, automobile environmental systems, and aircraft cabin environmental quality.

National Gas Machinery Laboratory. Byron W. Jones, Acting Director; Ph.D., Oklahoma State. This laboratory provides the natural gas industry with independent testing and research capabilities, knowledge databases, and educational programs. A premier turbocharger test and research facility has been developed through acquisition of gas turbine engines, instrumentation, and a laboratory building.

Civil Infrastructure Systems Laboratory. Alok Bhandari, Supervisor; Ph.D., Virginia Tech. The testing facility includes a pavement accelerated testing lab, a falling weight deflectometer state calibration station, and facilities for structural testing of bridge components and prestressed concrete girders. The facility is a center for cooperation between academia, industry, and state departments of transportation. The pavement research and testing activity is sponsored by a consortium called the Midwest States Accelerated Testing Pooled Funds Program that fulfills the needs of the surrounding states for full-scale testing and addresses research topics of national and international importance.

University Transportation Center. Robert W. Stokes, Director; Ph.D., Texas A&M. The University Transportation Center (UTC) coordinates interdisciplinary transportation education, research, training, and outreach efforts at K-State. The UTC's theme, "The sustainability and safety of rural transportation systems and infrastructure," emphasizes the unique needs of rural transportation systems. The UTC conducts research concerning local, state, regional, national, and international transportation problems through a coordinated effort between K-State, the Kansas Department of Transportation (KDOT), and the Research and Innovative Technology Administration (RITA) of the US Department of Transportation (USDOT). Dissemination of research information is achieved through the Center's Web site (http://transport.ksu.edu/), publication of reports, and through seminars for members of industry, government, and academia. Continuing education is also provided on transportation-related issues for licensed professional engineers. Training includes the development of short courses, handbooks, manuals, and other training materials developed under the Traffic Assistance Services for Kansas (TASK) Program and the American Concrete Institute (ACI) and Superpave certification training programs for personnel engaged in the construction of Kansas's highways. The Center also sponsors the annual Kansas Transportation Engineering Conference.

NORTH CAROLINA STATE UNIVERSITY

College of Engineering

Programs of Study

The College of Engineering comprises eleven degree-granting departments which are authorized to award the Master of Science, the Master of Engineering in a designated field, and the Doctor of Philosophy. Programs of graduate study leading to the M.S. and Ph.D. are aerospace engineering, biological and agricultural engineering, biomedical engineering (jointly with School of Medicine at the University of North Carolina at Chapel Hill), chemical engineering, civil engineering, computer science, electrical and computer engineering, industrial and systems engineering, materials science and engineering, mechanical engineering, and nuclear engineering; textile engineering offers the M.S. degree. Nonthesis master's degrees are also offered in most of the discipline areas and in the interdisciplinary program of integrated manufacturing systems engineering. Most nonthesis degrees require project or research work and a written technical report. The M.S. and Ph.D. degrees as well as the nonthesis master's degree are offered in the interdisciplinary program of operations research. Master's degrees are offered via distance learning through Engineering Online in aerospace engineering, chemical engineering, civil engineering, computer engineering, computer science, electrical engineering, industrial and systems engineering, integrated manufacturing systems engineering, materials science and engineering, mechanical engineering, and nuclear engineering. The Master of Engineering degree can be earned via distance education as well.

In most departments, the Master of Science degree is awarded for completing 30 credits of work, including a thesis. The Master of Engineering in a designated field is awarded for completing 30–36 course credits. A Ph.D. degree is awarded for completing a program of work, passing the oral preliminary examination, completing a research dissertation, and passing a final examination on the dissertation.

Research Facilities

Special research facilities and equipment include RAMAN and FIIR facilities; transmission electron microscopes; computerized SEM with full X-ray and image analysis capabilities; electron beam–induced current and cathodoluminescence microscopy equipment; a scanning laser microscope; laser MBE and pulsed laser depositions systems with full diagnostics; field emission electron beam lithography equipment; an imaging ion microscope for SIMS and 3-D ion imaging; a scanning Auger microprobe; an electron microprobe; complete X-ray analysis facilities including equipment for diffraction, topography, and radiography; a photoluminescence laboratory; MBE systems with in situ surface analysis; focused ion beam micromachinery; atomic resolution scanning tunneling microscopes; a precision engineering laboratory including diamond turning, ductile regime grinding, and surface metrology capabilities; a nuclear reactor with radiographic and neutron activation analysis; an applied energy laboratory; a plasma studies laboratory; a Freon simulator of a PWR fission reactor; a synthesis laboratory for III-V semiconductor materials; an organometallic chemical vapor deposition system; a semiconductor device fabrication laboratory; a deep UV mask aligner, and oxidation diffusion furnaces; a plasma and chemical etching and vapor deposition facility; computer systems for research in communications and signal processing and in microelectronics; a commercial computer design system for large integrated circuits; an EPA automated pollution and combustion gas facility; anechoic and reverberation chambers; a computer-controlled gas chromatograph–mass spectrometer; a robotics and automation laboratory; state-of-the-art multimedia, voice I/O, and software engineering labs; UNIX, Linux, and Windows workstations linked through Ethernet; a large structures-testing system; pavement wheel-track testing; superpave asphalt testing; a shake table; geotechnical test pits; plasmas for fusion; plasma propulsion; and laser-ablated plasmas for thin-film deposition. An engineering graduate research center features more than 120,000 square feet of dedicated laboratory facilities, including a class-10 clean room for processing.

Financial Aid

Approximately half of the engineering graduate students are provided assistantships with full support for studies, including tuition and health insurance.

Cost of Study

Tuition and fees for full-time study in 2011–12 are $3917.10 per semester for North Carolina residents and $9941.10 per semester for nonresidents. Students taking fewer than 9 credits pay reduced amounts. Most students appointed as teaching or research assistants qualify for tuition and health insurance support.

Living and Housing Costs

On-campus dormitory facilities are provided for unmarried graduate students. In 2010–11, the rent for double rooms started at $2600 per semester. Apartments for married students in King Village rented for $560 per month for a studio, $620 for a one-bedroom apartment, and $715 for a two-bedroom apartment.

Student Group

The College of Engineering had an enrollment of 6,365 undergraduate students and 2,586 graduate students in 2010–11. Most graduate students find full- or part-time support through fellowships, assistantships, and special duties with research organizations in the area. During the 2010–11 academic year, the College conferred 139 doctoral degrees, 615 master's degrees, and 1,086 Bachelor of Science degrees.

Location

Raleigh, the state capital of North Carolina, has a metropolitan population of over 500,000 and is ranked among the best places to live and work. Nearby is Research Triangle Park, one of the largest and fastest-growing research parks in the nation. The area offers numerous opportunities for recreation, sports, the arts, and other entertainment.

The University and The College

North Carolina State University is the principal technological institution of the University of North Carolina system. It is the home of the nationally acclaimed Centennial Campus, a model industry–government–university research park where students and professors work alongside industry leaders. The University's largest schools are the Colleges of Engineering, Agriculture and Life Sciences, Physical and Mathematical Sciences, and Humanities and Social Sciences. Total enrollment is more than 32,000. A cooperative relationship with Duke University and the University of North Carolina at Chapel Hill contributes to a rich academic and research atmosphere, as does the University's association with the Research Triangle Park and the Oak Ridge National Lab. The College has 300 faculty members with professorial rank.

Applying

Applications may be submitted at any time. Although the GRE General Test is not always required, it is helpful in making decisions concerning financial aid. An applicant desiring to visit the campus may request information concerning travel allowances by writing to the graduate administrator of the preferred program of study. Students may apply for fellowships or assistantships in their application for admission. Applications for all students are accepted online at http://www2.acs.ncsu.edu/grad/applygrad.htm.

Correspondence and Information

Dean of the Graduate School
North Carolina State University
P.O. Box 7102
Raleigh, North Carolina 27695-7102

Phone: 919-515-2872
Web site: https://www.ncsu.edu

North Carolina State University

THE FACULTY AND THEIR RESEARCH

BIOLOGICAL AND AGRICULTURAL ENGINEERING. R. Evans, Department Head. **Faculty:** D. Beasley, F. Birgand, M. Boyette, M. Burchell, L. Cartee, J. Cheng, G. Chescheir, M. Chinn, J. Classen, C. Daubert, B. Farkas, G. Grabow, S. Hale, R. Huffman, W. Hunt, G. Jennings, P. Kolar, T. Losordo, P. Mente, G. Roberson, S. Roe, K. Sandeep, S. Shah, R. Sharma, R. Skaggs, O. Simmons, J. Spooner, L. Stikeleather, K. Swartzel, M. Veal, L. Wang, P. Westerman, T. Whitaker, D. Willits, M. Youssef. **Research areas:** Bioinstrumentation, bioprocessing, materials handling, energy conservation and alternative fuels, environmental control, machine systems, microprocessor applications, water and waste management, hydrology, ecological and environmental engineering.

BIOMEDICAL ENGINEERING. N. Allbritton, Department Head. **Faculty:** A. Banes, T. Bateman, L. Cartee, P. Dayton, R. Dennis, O. Favorov, C. Finley, G. Forest, C. Gallippi, M. Gamcsik, M. Giddings, R. Goldberg, S. Gomez, E. Grant, D. Lalush, W. Lin, E. Loboa, J. Macdonald, T. Magnuson, G. McCarty, M. McCord, P. Mente, H. Troy Nagle, R. Narayan, H. Ozturk, H. Pillsbury, J. Ramsey, B. Steele, M. Tommerdahl, A. Veleva, G. Walker, P. Weinhold. **Affiliated Faculty:** A. Aleksandrov, N. Allen, D. Bitzer, M. Bourham, J. Brickley Jr., G. Buckner, B. Button, J. Cavanagh, E. Chaney, M. Chow, L. Clarke, S. Cooper, D. Cormier, S. Franzen, H. Fuchs, R. Gardner, R. Gorga, R. Grossfeld, M. Haider, A. Hale, O. Harrysson, A. Hickey, W. Holton, T. Johnson, J. Kimbell, C. Kleinstreuer, K. Kocis, H. Krim, A. Kuznetsov, G. Lazzi, S. Lubkin, N. Monteiro-Riviere, J. Muth, B. Oberhardt, T. O'Connell, A. Oldenburg, M. Olufsen, D. Padua, S. Pizer, B. Pourdeyhimi, J. Qi, A. Rabiei, M. Ramasubramanian, L. Reid, S. Roe, J. Rubin, M. Schoenfisch, S. Seelecke, D. Shen, C. Smith, W. Snyder, A. Spagnoli, L. Stikeleather, A. Stomp, M. Stoskopf, R. Superfine, J. Thompson, D. Thrall, A. Tonelli, A. Tropsha, B. Vaughn, M. Vouk, S. Washburn, D. Woodward, B. Yu. **Research areas:** Biomedical imaging, micro- and nano-systems engineering, rehabilitation engineering.

CHEMICAL AND BIOMOLECULAR ENGINEERING. P. Fedkiw, Department Head. **Faculty:** R. Carbonell, J. DeSimone, M. Dickey, J. Genzer, C. Grant, K. Gubbins, C. Hall, J. Haugh, W. Henderson, R. Kelly, S. Khan, H. Lamb, P. Lim, D. Ollis, G. Parsons, S. Peretti, B. Rao, G. Reeves, R. Spontak, O. Velev, P. Westmoreland. **Research areas:** Biomolecular engineering, biotechnology, biofuels and biomass conversion, electrochemical and reaction engineering, electronic materials, energy, green chemistry and engineering, innovative textiles, molecular simulations, nanotechnology and interfacial science, polymers and colloids, supercritical fluids.

CIVIL ENGINEERING. M. Barlaz, Department Head. V. Matzen, Director of Graduate Programs. **Faculty:** S. Arumugam, J. Baugh, C. Bobko, R. C. Borden, R. H. Borden, E. Downey Brill Jr., J. DeCarolis, F. de los Reyes, J. Ducoste, B. Edge, M. Evans, C. Frey, M. Gabr, M. Guddati, A. Gupta, T. Hassan, J. Hummer, D. Johnston, N. Khosla, Y. Kim, D. Knappe, M. Kowalsky, M. Leming, G. List, M. Liu, G. Mahinthakumar, J. Nau, M. Overton, S. Rahman, S. Ranjithan, W. Rasdorf, S. Rizkalla, N. Rouphail, R. Seracino, J. Stone, A. Tayebali, B. Williams, J. Yu. **Research areas:** Civil engineering systems, computer-aided engineering, construction engineering and management, construction materials, energy modeling, environmental engineering, geotechnical engineering, transportation systems and materials, solid mechanics, structural engineering, water resources and coastal engineering.

COMPUTER SCIENCE. M. Vouk, Department Head. **Faculty:** A. Anton, K. Anyanwu, D. Bahler, D. Bitzer, F. Brglez, R. Chirkova, J. Doyle, R. Dutta, R. Fornaro, V. Freeh, E. Gehringer, X. Gu, K. Harfoush, C. Healey, S. Heber, S. Heckman, T. Honeycutt, S. Iyer, X. Jiang, J. Lester, X. Ma, F. Mueller, E. Murphy-Hill, P. Ning, H. Perros, M. Rappa, D. Reeves, I. Rhee, D. Roberts, R. Rodman, G. Rouskas, N. Samatova, R. St. Amant, C. Savage, M. Singh, M. Stallmann, W. Stewart, A. Tharp, D. Thuente, B. Watson, L. Williams, T. Xie, R. Young, T. Yu. **Research areas:** Theory (algorithms, theory of computation), systems (computer architectures and operating systems, embedded and real-time systems, parallel and distributed systems, scientific and high performance computing), artificial intelligence (intelligent agents; data-mining, information and knowledge discovery, engineering and management; ecommerce technologies; information visualization, graphics and human-computer interaction), networks (networking and performance evaluation), security (software and network systems security, information assurance, privacy), software engineering (requirements, formal methods, reliability engineering, process and methods, programming languages), computer-based education.

ELECTRICAL AND COMPUTER ENGINEERING. D. Stancil, Department Head. **Faculty:** T. Alexander, W. Alexander, J. Baliga, M. Baran, D. Baron, S. Bedair, S. Bhattacharya, G. Bilbro, A. Bozkurt, J. Brickley, G. Byrd, A. Chakrabortty, M. Chow, H. Dai, R. Davis, A. Dean, M. Devetsikiotis, A. Duel-Hallen, M. Escuti, D. Eun, B. Floyd, P. Franzon, E. Gehringer, J. Grainger, E. Grant, B. Greene, A. Huang, B. Hughes, K. Kim, R. Kolbas, H. Krim, S. Lukic, L. Lunardi, N. Masnari, T. Miller, V. Misra, T. Mitchell, J. Muth, T. Nagle, A. Nilsson, H. Ozturk, M. Ozturk, E. Rotenberg, D. Schurig, M. Sichitiu, W. Snyder, Y. Solihin, M. Steer, C. Townsend, K. Townsend, R. Trew, J. Trussell, I. Viniotis, S. Walsh, W. Wang, C. Williams, G. Yu, H. Zhou. **Research areas:** Bioelectronics engineering; communications and digital signal processing; computer architecture and systems; control, robotics, and mechatronics; electronic circuits and systems; nanoelectronics and photonics; networking; power electronics and power systems.

INDUSTRIAL AND SYSTEMS ENGINEERING. P. Cohen, Department Head. **Faculty:** M. Ayoub, R. Bernhard, D. Cormier, T. Culbreth, B. Denton, J. Dong, S. Elmaghraby, S.-C. Fang, Y. Fathi, O. Harrysson, T. Hodgson, S. Hsiang, J. Ivy, D. Kaber, M. Kay, R. King, Y.-S. Lee, S. Roberts, E. Sanii, R. Uzsoy, J. Wilson, R. Young. **Research areas:** Medical device manufacturing; health systems; investment science; ergonomics; occupational safety; facilities design; production planning, scheduling, and control; logistics systems; supply chain design and management; material handling; concurrent engineering; manufacturing processes; rapid prototyping; optimization; soft computing; stochastic processes and simulation.

INTEGRATED MANUFACTURING SYSTEMS ENGINEERING. T. J. Hodgson, Director. S. D. Jackson, Associate Director. **Associate Faculty:** D. R. Bahler, P. Banks-Lee, R. L. Barker, K. Barletta, M. D. Boyette, C. Bozarth, G. D. Buckner, S. Chapman, Y. A. Chen, T. Clapp, T. Culbreth, B. Denton, M. Devetsikiotis, Y. Fathi, T. K. Ghosh, R. Handfield, O. L. A. Harrysson, G. L. Hodge, J. Ivy, M. G. Kay, R. E. King, J. P. Lavelle, J. W. Leach, Y.-S. Lee, R. L. Lemaster, K. Mitchell, M. Montoya-Weiss, M. K. Ramasubramanian, M. Rappa, W. J. Rasdorf, P. Ro, S. Roberts, R. Rodman, C. Rossetti, J. P. Rust, D. Saloni, E. T. Sanii, A. M. Seyam, L. M. Silverberg, E. Sumner, K. A. Thoney, J. R. Wilson, R. E. Young, C. F. Zorowski. **Adjunct Faculty:** J. A. Janet, J. Taheri. The Integrated Manufacturing Systems Engineering (IMSE) Institute was established in 1984. IMSE provides multidisciplinary graduate-level education and practical training opportunities in the theory and practice of integrated manufacturing systems engineering at the master's level. IMSE focuses on providing a manufacturing presence and a program environment in the College of Engineering where faculty, graduate students, and industry can engage cooperatively in multidisciplinary graduate education, basic and applied research, and technology transfer in areas of common interest related to modern manufacturing systems technology. The objective of the IMSE program is to offer students with traditional discipline backgrounds in engineering and the physical sciences an opportunity to broaden their understanding of the multidisciplinary area of manufacturing systems. Core areas of concentration are offered in manufacturing systems, logistics, mechatronics, and biomanufacturing. **Research areas:** Automation, CAD, CAM, CIM and advanced information technology, logistics, manufacturing system simulations, material handling, mechatronics, part fabrication, quality assurance and testing, process and facilities planning, product assembly, product design, robotics, scheduling and operations management, supply chain management.

MATERIALS SCIENCE AND ENGINEERING. J. Schwartz, Department Head. **Faculty:** C. M. Balik, D. Brenner, J. Cuomo, N. El-Masry, D. Irving, M. Johnson, J. Kasichainula, C. Koch, T. Luo, J. P. Maria, A. Melechko, K. L. Murty, J. Narayan, T. Rawanowicz, C. L. Reynolds, J. M. Rigsbee, G. Rozgonyi, R. Scattergood, Z. Sitar, R. Spontak, J. Tracy, Y. Yingling, Y. Zhu. **Emeritus Faculty:** K. Bachman, R. Benson Jr., C. Chiklis, H. Conrad, R. F. Davis, A. Fahmy, J. Hren, H. Palmour III, H. Stadelmaier. **Research areas:** Atomic resolution electronic microscopy and analytical techniques, advanced materials and processing methods, composite materials, computer simulation techniques, electronic materials, electrical and mechanical properties, metals, nanostructured materials, nonequilibrium processing, nuclear materials, polymers, biomaterials, structure-property relations, surface phenomena, thin-film processing and characterization.

MECHANICAL AND AEROSPACE ENGINEERING. R. Gould, Department Head. **Faculty:** G. Buckner, F. DeJarnette, T. Dow, T. Echekki, H. Eckerlin, J. Edwards Jr., J. Eischen, T. Fang, S. Ferguson, A. Gopalarathnam, C. Hall Jr., H. Hassan, H. Y. Huang, R. Keltie, E. Klang, C. Kleinstreuer, A. Kuznetsov, H. Luo, K. Lyons, A. Mazzoleni, R. Nagel, G. Ngaile, K. Peters, A. Rabiei, M. Ramasubramanian, P. Ro, W. Roberts, A. Saveliev, S. Seelecke, L. Silverberg, J. Strenkowski, R. Tolson, J. Tu, T. Ward, F. Wu, F. Yuan, Y. Zhu, M. Zikry. **Research areas:** Aerothermodynamics, autoadaptive systems, biofluid dynamics, biomechanics, combustion, composite structures, computational fluid dynamics, control systems, electromechanics, energy conversion, environmental engineering, flight dynamics and aircraft design, fluid/aero dynamics, fluid mechanics and two-phase flow, fracture mechanics, heat transfer, hypersonics, manufacturing, materials processing, mechanical and random vibrations, mechatronics, micro/nano mechanical and electrical systems, nano thermosystems, precision engineering, probabilistic mechanics, propulsion, risk and reliability, robotics, solid mechanics, space systems and dynamics, structural health monitoring, thermal management, theoretical and structural acoustics.

NUCLEAR ENGINEERING. Y. Y. Azmy, Department Head. **Faculty:** H. S. Abdel-Khalik, D. Anistratov, M. A. Bourham, D. G. Cacuci, J. M. Doster, J. Eapen, R. P. Gardner, J. G. Gilligan, A. I. Hawari, K. L. Murty, S. C. Shannon, P. J. Turinsky, M.-S. Yim. **Research areas:** Computational reactor physics; fuel management; plasma engineering; radiation effects in nuclear materials; nuclear power systems modeling; plasma-surface interactions; radiation transport; reactor dynamics, control, and safety; computational thermal hydraulics; nuclear waste management; radiological engineering; industrial radiation applications; medical radiation physics; plasmas for fusion; plasma propulsion; laser-ablated plasmas for thin-film deposition; nuclear environmental risk analysis; radiation measurements; neutron scattering and imaging; advanced nuclear fuel cycles; multiscale and multiphysics modeling.

OPERATIONS RESEARCH. T. J. Hodgson, Co-Director; N. Medhin, Co-Director. **Faculty:** J. Baugh, R. Bernhard, B. Bhattacharyya, J. Bishir, E. Brill Jr., R. Buche, S. Campbell, R. Chirkova, W. Chou, B. Denton, M. Devetsikiotis, J. Dunn, B. Edge, S. Elmaghraby, S. Fang, Y. Fathi, R. Funderlic, S. Ghosal, H. Gold, R. Handfield, R. Hartwig, P. Hersh, T. Hodgson, D. Holthausen, T. Honeycutt, S. Hsiang, I. Ipsen, K. Ito, J. Ivy, J. Joines, M. Kang, M. Kay, C. Kelley, R. King, J. Lavery, Z. Li, M. Liu, G. List, D. McAllister, C. Meyer Jr., A. Nilsson, H. Nuttle, T. Pang, H. Perros, K. Pollock, S. Ranjithan, M. Rappa, T. Reiland, S. Roberts, J. Roise, G. Rouskas, C. Savage, J. Scroggs, M. Singh, C. Smith, R. Smith, M. Stallmann, J. Stape, W. Stewart, J. Stone, M. Suh, W. Sun, J. Taheri, K. Thoney-Barletta, H. Tran, R. Uzsoy, I. Viniotis, M. Vouk, W. Wang, D. Warsing, J. Wilson, F. Wu, R. Young, T. Yu, Z. Zeng, D. Zenkov. **Research areas:** Mathematical programming, fuzzy optimization and decision making, networks, queuing, production planning, scheduling, project management, routing, simulation, stochastic processes and modeling, systems theory and optimal control, facilities layout and planning, logistics, inventory theory, supply chain management, financial engineering.

TEXTILE ENGINEERING. J. Rust, Department Head. H. Hamouda, Program Director. **Faculty:** R. Barker, K. Beck, T. Clapp, R. Gorga, B. Gupta, J. Hinestroza, W. Jasper, J. Joines, W. Krause, M. McCord, G. Mock, J. Rust. **Research areas:** Electromechanical design, real-time monitoring and control, studies in thermal and fluid sciences, polymer and fiber science, biomedical application of textiles, design and fabrication, process optimization, product/machine/system design, nanocomposites, nanolayer electrostatic self-assemblies, mathematical modeling of transport phenomena, rheology, polyelectrolytes, semi-crystalline polymers, carbon nanotube composite extrusion for enhanced mechanical/thermal/electrical properties, barrier fabrics, biopolymers, structure-property relationships.

OKLAHOMA STATE UNIVERSITY

College of Engineering, Architecture and Technology

Programs of Study

The College of Engineering, Architecture and Technology offers Master of Science and Doctor of Philosophy degree programs in biosystems, chemical, civil, computer, electrical, and mechanical engineering and industrial engineering and management. Master of Science degrees are also offered in engineering and technology management, and environmental engineering.

The master's degree may consist of 24 credit hours of course work plus 6 credit hours of thesis or 32 credit hours (35 credit hours for the Master of Science in mechanical engineering), including a creative component (independent study) of at least 2 hours.

The Doctor of Philosophy degree requires 90 credit hours beyond the B.S. or 60 beyond the master's, including 18 to 30 thesis credits. Preliminary, qualifying, and final examinations are required.

The master's degrees can be completed in twelve months but usually require more time. The Ph.D. requires from two to three years beyond the master's. The University offers two 16-week semesters plus an eight-week summer session each year.

Research Facilities

The College of Engineering's annual research budget is approximately $25 million. A wide variety of computer equipment and numerous minicomputers, microcomputers, and microprocessors, with interactive graphics capability, are available within the College. Extensive laboratory space and research equipment are available for use by students. The College's Office of Engineering Research provides administrative support services for more than 200 active research projects. These services include budget preparation, assistance with compliance issues, and production and fiscal reporting on contracts and grants. The University has a large central research library covering more than 6 acres of floor space, with a substantial amount devoted to engineering and physical science volumes. Research laboratories are located in the engineering schools in the Advanced Technology Research Center and in the Helmerich ATRC in Tulsa.

Financial Aid

Financial aid for graduate students includes fellowships, scholarships, and teaching and research assistantships. Stipends for half-time assistantships for the 2010–11 year ranged from $900 to $2400 per month for master's students and from $975 to $2800 per month for Ph.D. students. Nonresident tuition is waived for graduate assistants. Depending on the appointments, the resident tuition for up to 6 credits per semester may also be waived. The fellowship and scholarship application deadline is February 1 for the following academic year, but early application is encouraged.

Cost of Study

For 2010–11, tuition for graduate-level credit was $154.85 per credit hour for Oklahoma residents and $620.50 for nonresidents. Other miscellaneous per-credit-hour fees totaled approximately $1359.20 per semester. All engineering students pay a technology fee of $21.50 per credit hour to support high-end desktop computers available to students.

Living and Housing Costs

Residential hall single rooms were available for approximately $590 to $755 per month in 2010–11. Deluxe suites with private bedrooms and baths were available for approximately $715 per month. Apartments with private bedrooms and baths and shared kitchens and living rooms were available for approximately $735 per month. All rooms assume a twelve-month contract and include furnishings, basic utilities, cable television, and connection to the Internet. Family housing is also available. Meal plans were available for approximately $800 to $2000 per semester, depending on the number of meals requested. A single resident student should expect to spend approximately $8000 per semester for room, food, books, and miscellaneous expenses.

Student Group

The OSU enrollment is about 23,500 full-time on-campus students; approximately 5,000 of these are graduate students. Men constitute 52 percent and women, 48 percent of the student body. The College of Engineering, Architecture, and Technology has 3,769 students, including 809 graduate students in engineering.

Student Outcomes

While students receiving graduate degrees in engineering at Oklahoma State University are recruited in the national marketplace, increasing numbers of employment opportunities are available within the geographical area. Companies include Delphi in Wichita Falls, Texas; Koch Industries in Wichita, Kansas; Raytheon in the Dallas area; American Airlines, The Williams Companies, and the Corps of Engineers in Tulsa; and AT&T and Xerox in Oklahoma City.

Location

Stillwater, located 65 miles from both Tulsa and Oklahoma City, has a population of 45,000 and is essentially a university town. There are a number of lakes and recreational areas nearby that are usually not crowded. The climate is mild and pleasant, typical of the Sun Belt area.

The University

Founded in 1890, Oklahoma State University is a land-grant institution with eight colleges: Agricultural Sciences and Natural Resources; Arts and Sciences; Spears School of Business Administration; Education; Engineering, Architecture and Technology; Graduate Studies; Human Sciences; and Veterinary Medicine. The Stillwater campus has more than 100 buildings situated on 415 acres, plus the nearby Lake Carl Blackwell area of 19,364 acres. Cultural and recreational facilities are provided by the Seretean Center for the Performing Arts, the Valerie Colvin Physical Education Center, and the award-winning Student Union. The University participates in all major intercollegiate sports and ranks third nationally in the number of NCAA championships in varsity sports. OSU is a member of the Big Twelve Conference.

Applying

Application forms are available from the Graduate College or at https://app.it.okstate.edu/gradcollege/ and may be submitted online. Requests for financial aid should be made directly to the school of interest by February 1 for summer or fall admission and by October 1 for spring admission.

Correspondence and Information

Graduate Adviser
School of (specify)
Oklahoma State University
Stillwater, Oklahoma 74078
Web site: http://www.ceat.okstate.edu/

Dean of the Graduate College
202 Whitehurst Hall
Oklahoma State University
Stillwater, Oklahoma 74078

Oklahoma State University

FACULTY HEADS AND RESEARCH AREAS

Interim Dean, College of Engineering, Architecture and Technology: Khaled Gasem.
Associate Deans: David R. Thompson, Academics; D. Alan Tree, Research.

Biosystems Engineering. Professor Daniel Thomas, Head. Areas of emphasis include soil erosion, sediment control, nonpoint-source pollution, hydrology, stream processes, water quality, crop processing, bioconversion processes, renewable energy, animal-waste management, grain storage, food processing, physical properties of biological materials, sensors and control technology, mechatronics, machine vision, image processing, biosensors, energy conservation, equipment design, and precision agriculture. More information can be found at http://biosystems.okstate.edu.

Chemical Engineering. Professor R. Russell Rhinehart, Interim Head. The School of Chemical Engineering is involved in a variety of industrially relevant and fundamental research projects. Students have the opportunity to pursue traditional areas of chemical engineering, including vapor-liquid equilibrium thermodynamics, adsorption thermodynamics, and rheology. In addition, graduate research is available in areas such as computer-assisted process design, CPD methods for reactor design, ultrapure water processing, industrial ion exchange, artificial intelligence applied to process control and monitoring, biomedical applications, bioproduction of fuels, and development of design strategies for environmentally benign processes.

Civil and Environmental Engineering. Professor John Veenstra, Head. Research interests include structural analysis and design; expansive soils; dynamic compaction; biological and chemical treatment of industrial, domestic, and hazardous wastes; air and water pollution; groundwater pollution; aquifer restoration; geosynthetics; flexible and rigid pavements; "smart" bridges; construction material; offshore structures; computational mechanics; composites; lightweight concrete; construction scheduling and estimating; and alternate disputes resolution. The Oklahoma Transportation Center is a major research entity of the school.

Electrical and Computer Engineering. Professor Keith A. Teague, Head. The School of Electrical and Computer Engineering offers degrees and areas of study across the disciplines of electrical engineering and computer engineering. Graduate and research fields of specialization include control systems, system identification, optimization, neural networks, intelligent systems and fuzzy logic, telecommunication systems and networks, security and information assurance, communication theory, wireless communication systems and networking, error control coding, intelligent sensor networks, robotics, embedded systems, computer architecture, programmable and reconfigurable digital systems, high-speed computer arithmetic, compiler optimization for computer architecture, system-on-a-chip architectures, digital computer design, VLSI and mixed-signal VLSI, analog CMOS electronics, high-temperature VLSI, energy/power/renewable-energy systems, power economics, power electronics, statistical signal processing, image processing and machine vision, image coding, biomedical image processing and bioimaging, biosensors, speech coding and compression, digital signal processing, engineering reliability, estimation theory, electromagnetics/antennas/radar, numerical electromagnetics, electromagnetic compatibility, optical engineering, photonics and electrooptics, terahertz optoelectronics, MEMS, nanodevices and nanotechnology, thermoelectric devices, advanced electronic materials, microfabrication, ultrafast optics, fiber optics, and laser systems. Excellent research laboratories and facilities are available in photonics and terahertz optoelectronics, communications and signal processing, wireless communications and networks, image processing and machine vision, bioimaging and instrumentation, mixed-signal VLSI and high-temperature semiconductors, MEMS, nanodevices and nanofabrication, intelligent sensor networks, embedded systems and robotics, high-speed computer arithmetic, computer architecture, electromagnetic compatibility, numerical electromagnetics, intelligent control, and power and energy systems. Modern computer and laboratory facilities are readily available for use by graduate students and faculty members. More information can be found at http://www.ece.okstate.edu.

Engineering and Technology Management. Professor Camille DeYong, Ph.D., PE, Director. The Engineering and Technology Management program provides experienced engineers, scientists, and technical managers with career-enhancing management skills. This program is offered through distance learning and is not designed for full-time on-campus students. Objectives of the program are to improve the participants' ability to identify and act on strategic issues; strategically manage technologies; integrate company functions; implement management skills, knowledge, and tools; and manage an organization's intellectual capabilities and properties. Core topics include technology strategy development, forecasting, and integration; project management; change management; benchmarking and competitive analysis; technical employee leadership and motivation; organization systems; new product planning, development, and management; technology sourcing and transfer; team approaches; integrating product and process design; and global marketing and manufacturing. More information can be found on the program's Web site at http://etm.okstate.edu.

Industrial Engineering and Management. Professor William J. Kolarik, Head, and Professor Manjunath Kamath, Graduate Program Director. The Computer Integrated Manufacturing Center, the Center for Engineering Logistics and Distribution, the Oklahoma Industrial Assessment Center, and the Sensor Networks and Complex Manufacturing Systems Lab are among the school's research facilities. Focus areas of research and instruction include manufacturing systems, enterprise modeling and supply chains, quality and reliability, operations research, facilities and energy management, and management and organizational behavior. Sub-area specialization is available within each of the focus areas. Further details are available at the Web site: http://www.okstate.edu/ceat/iem. For further information, students may contact the program at IEM-GRAD@okstate.edu.

Mechanical and Aerospace Engineering. Professor Larry L. Hoberock, Head. The School of Mechanical and Aerospace Engineering is a major participant in the interdisciplinary Web Handling Research Center and houses research labs for manufacturing process materials, nanotechnology, solid mechanics, fluid mechanics, aerodynamics, composite materials controls, ultraprecision surfaces, robotics, indoor environmental research psychometrics, and biomedical engineering. Students without B.S.M.E. degrees may need prerequisite work at the undergraduate level. The research program covers a wide variety of topics. The research for manufacturing processes and materials includes ultraprecision machining and grinding, nontraditional machining, synthesis of diamond films and coatings, advanced ceramic finishing and processing, surface and subsurface characterization and metrology, and molecular dynamics modeling. For web handling, the research involves nip mechanics, roll defects, roll structure analysis and measurement, constituent properties of web stacks, winding mechanics, air entrainment, roll buckling and wrinkling, viscoelastic and hygroscopic material effects, online tension measurement and control, traction, web flutter, and lateral dynamics and control. The research for fluid mechanics, aerodynamics, and propulsion focuses on computational fluid dynamics, aeroservoelasticity, numerical modeling of airfoil performance, two-phase flow, filtration flows, slurry flows, micro-UAV propulsion, and unmanned aerospace vehicles and systems. The thrust areas for heat transfer, thermal, and environmental systems involve thermal system simulation and optimization, building simulation and load calculation, ground-source heat pumps, bridge de-icing, heat transfer in machining and grinding, refrigeration, psychometrics, numerical modeling of thermal reactors, and micro heat exchangers. The research topics for solid mechanics and materials are material characterization, nondestructive evaluation, viscoelastic material characterization, aerogel synthesis, high-speed slitting, nanoscale sensors, and composite materials. For dynamics and control, the thrust areas involve control of nonlinear uncertain systems, system identification and parameter estimation, robotic systems control, control of large interconnected systems, machine vision, target tracking, applied automation, web tension control, and lateral web guidance. For biomedical engineering, the thrust areas are artificial tissues, tissue scaffolding, blood-flow simulation, and endolithial blood-cell behavior.

UNIVERSITY AT BUFFALO, THE STATE UNIVERSITY OF NEW YORK

School of Engineering and Applied Sciences

Programs of Study

The University at Buffalo offers degrees in all major fields of engineering through the School of Engineering and Applied Sciences (SEAS). Students may pursue master's and doctoral degrees in the departments of chemical and biological engineering; civil, structural, and environmental engineering; computer science and engineering; electrical engineering; industrial and systems engineering; and mechanical and aerospace engineering. In the top 15 percent of the nation's 300 engineering schools, the School of Engineering and Applied Sciences offers a wide variety of excellent instruction, research opportunities, resources, and facilities to its students.

SEAS faculty members participate in many research activities, including extensive involvement in two major Integrative Graduate Education Research and Traineeship (IGERT) grants funded by the National Science Foundation.

Research Facilities

Research facilities are supported by the School of Engineering and Applied Sciences to give students the opportunity to conduct research specific to their area of study. The Center for Biomedical Engineering coordinates research in biomedical engineering through cooperation among engineering departments and other schools, especially medicine and pharmacy. Research at the Center of Excellence for Document Analysis and Recognition focuses on the theory and applications of pattern recognition, machine learning, and information retrieval. The Center for Excellence in Global Enterprise Management was established in 1998 to deliver leading-edge research driven by industrial need with results that have immediate practical impact. The Center for Unified Biometrics is focused on advancing the fundamental science of biometrics and providing key enabling technologies to build engineered systems. The goals of the Center for Excellence in Information Systems Assurance Research and Education are graduate education and coordinated research in computer security and information assurance by faculty members from several schools and departments at the University at Buffalo. Founded in 1987 as the New York State Center for Hazardous Waste Management, the Center for Integrated Waste Management was established by the New York State Legislation to initiate and coordinate research and technology development in the areas of toxic substances and hazardous wastes. The Center for Multisource Information Fusion serves as one focal point for the conduct of research and development in information fusion and as an incubation center for small businesses and professorial and individual entrepreneurial activities. The research focus of the Energy Systems Institute is the development of mechanisms to predict failure in electronic systems.

The mission of the Great Lakes Program is to develop, evaluate, and synthesize scientific and technical knowledge on the Great Lakes Ecosystem in support of public education and policy formation. The Multidisciplinary Center for Earthquake Engineering Research's overall goal is to enhance the seismic resiliency of communities through improved engineering and management tools for critical infrastructure systems (water supply, electric power, hospitals, and transportation systems). The New York State Center for Engineering Design and Industrial Innovation carries out research to develop state-of-the-art simulation techniques and tools for the design of products, complex systems, and scientific applications. The Center for Industrial Effectiveness forges a link between the University at Buffalo's technical resources and the business community.

Financial Aid

For highly qualified applicants, a variety of research appointments are available, as are University-supported assistantships and fellowships. Tuition scholarships are also available. Summer support is available for most research appointments. Work done as a research assistant is generally applicable to the student's thesis or dissertation.

Cost of Study

Tuition and fees for in-state residents total $9978 per academic year for full-time study. Out-of-state tuition and fees total $15,388 per academic year.

Living and Housing Costs

The University at Buffalo offers students residence hall accommodations as well as apartments at several complexes surrounding the campus. Housing costs vary, depending upon location.

Student Group

More than 1,200 graduate students are enrolled in degree programs through the School of Engineering and Applied Sciences. Approximately 420 students are enrolled in doctoral programs, while the remaining students are enrolled as master's degree candidates.

Location

The city of Buffalo, New York, is located on the banks of Lake Erie, within an hour's drive of Lake Ontario and just minutes from the majestic scenery of Niagara Falls. It is within easy driving distance of Toronto and lies directly in the middle of the Northeastern trade corridor that runs from Chicago to Boston. With more than 9 million residents, it is the third-largest trade market in North America and is home to several professional sports franchises, museums, art galleries, and numerous areas for outdoor recreation throughout the year.

The University and The School

The School of Engineering and Applied Sciences is part of the University at Buffalo, the largest comprehensive public university in the state of New York, and is located on the North Campus in Amherst, New York.

Applying

The fastest and easiest way to apply is through the University's interactive graduate application Web site at http://www.gradmit.buffalo.edu/grenglinks.htm. The deadline for application materials varies by each department. The academic year begins in August. Applicants must hold a bachelor's degree in a science or engineering-related field. All international applicants must be able to document their ability to meet all educational and living expenses for their entire length of study.

Applications for graduate study and other related information may be obtained via e-mail (seasgrad@buffalo.edu).

Correspondence and Information

University at Buffalo (SUNY)
School of Engineering and Applied Sciences
412 Bonner Hall
Buffalo, New York 14260-1900

Phone: 716-645-0956
E-mail: seasgrad@buffalo.edu
Web site: http://www.eng.buffalo.edu

University at Buffalo, the State University of New York

FACULTY HEADS AND AREAS OF RESEARCH

Chemical and Biological Engineering
Dr. Mark Swihart, Director of Graduate Study.

The Department of Chemical and Biological Engineering has attained international recognition for its excellence in research and teaching. Cutting-edge research projects span the areas of advanced materials and nanotechnology; molecular and multiscale modeling and simulation; and biochemical, biomolecular, and biomedical engineering. These projects are supported by federal agencies such as the National Science Foundation and the National Institutes of Health, and by industry. (Web site: http://www.cbe.buffalo.edu)

Civil, Structural, and Environmental Engineering
Dr. Gilberto Mosqueda, Director of Graduate Study.

Current research in the Department of Civil, Structural, and Environmental Engineering focuses on five key areas including computational mechanics; environmental and hydrosystems engineering (biological process analysis, bioremediation, drinking water, ecosystem restoration, groundwater, toxic substances fate, volatile organics, and wastewater treatment); geomechanics and geotechnical engineering (soil dynamics); structural and earthquake engineering (active and passive control of structures, blast-resistant design, bridge engineering, fiber-reinforced polymeric structures, nuclear structures, nonstructural systems, and steel and reinforced concrete structures); and transportation systems engineering (artificial intelligence applications, dynamic network modeling and control, freight modeling, integrated transportation and land-use modeling, intelligent transportation systems, traffic simulation, and traveler behavior modeling). The department is home to the Multidisciplinary Center for Earthquake Engineering Research (MCEER), the Great Lakes Program, and the Structural Engineering and Earthquake Simulation Laboratory, among others. (Web site: http://www.csee.buffalo.edu/)

Computer Science and Engineering
Dr. Jan Chomicki, Director of Graduate Study.

The Department of Computer Science and Engineering conducts research in algorithms and theory of computing, augmentative technology for the handicapped, bioinformatics and computational biology, biometrics, computational linguistics and cognitive science, computer networks and distributed systems, computer science education, computer security and information assurance, computer vision, cyberinfrastructure and computational science, databases, data fusion, data mining, data-intensive computing, embedded systems and computer architecture, high-performance computing, grid and cloud computing, information visualization, knowledge representation and reasoning, medical image processing and applications, multimedia databases and information retrieval, pattern recognition and machine learning, pervasive computing, programming languages and software systems, VLSI circuits and systems, and wireless and sensor networks. (Web site: http://www.cse.buffalo.edu/)

Electrical Engineering
Dr. Chu Ryang Wie, Director of Graduate Study.

The Department of Electrical Engineering conducts research in the following areas: * signal processing, communications, and networking (adaptive signal processing, detection and estimation, coding and sequences, radar systems, communication theory and systems, secure communications, multimedia systems and video communications, digital data hiding, MIMO communications, cooperative communications, wireless networks, cognitive cross-layer networking, underwater communications, and networks); * electronics, optics, and photonics (bio-MEMS, computational and applied magnetics, computational electromagnetics/photonics, computational fluid dynamics, electromagnetic compatibility, MEMS, metamaterials, microfluidics, micromachined microwave systems, MIR and THz devices, molecular beam epitaxy, nanotechnology, optoelectronics, photonics, photovoltaics, plasmonics, superconductivity, and TFTs); and * energy systems (batteries, clean and renewable energy, electrochemical power, energy distribution and generation, energy storage, power electronics, power packaging, plasma processing, and smart grid power systems). (Web site: http://www.ee.buffalo.edu).

Industrial and Systems Engineering
Dr. Victor Paquet, Director of Graduate Study.

The Department of Industrial and Systems Engineering offers three areas of specialization for the Ph.D.: human factors (applications of engineering, psychology, computer science, and physical ergonomics to the modeling, analysis, and design of various environments and other systems), operations research (applies math and engineering principles to formulate models and solve problems in long range planning, energy and urban systems, and manufacturing), and production systems (focuses on production planning and scheduling, computer-integrated manufacturing, quality assurance, and related topics). In addition to the three areas of specialization mentioned above, there are two other programs (for a total of five) at the master's level: service systems engineering (applies industrial engineering principles to the growing service sector) and engineering management (focuses on leadership practices for a variety of engineering areas). (Web site: http://www.ise.buffalo.edu/index.shtml.)

Mechanical and Aerospace Engineering
Dr. John Crassidis, Director of Graduate Study.

Faculty members and students in the Department of Mechanical and Aerospace Engineering are involved in a wide range of research activities in the fluid and thermal sciences, dynamic systems and control, design, materials engineering, biomedical engineering, and applied mechanics. Faculty interests include computer and mathematical modeling as well as laboratory and experimental efforts in both basic and applied research. (Web site: http://www.mae.buffalo.edu/)

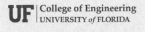

UNIVERSITY OF FLORIDA

College of Engineering
Online and On-Campus Programs

Programs of Study

UF EDGE (Electronic Delivery of Gator Engineering): The University of Florida (UF) College of Engineering offers master's degrees, graduate certificates, and individual courses from seven UF engineering departments for distance students worldwide through the UF EDGE program. Since its start in 1965, the UF College of Engineering distance learning program has evolved in media and delivery to the current UF EDGE model of complete online delivery of course lectures and materials to support engineering professionals and military members in continuing their engineering education from UF without requiring campus attendance.

UF EDGE master's degree programs consist of ten graduate courses, and students are free to take as many or few courses in a given semester as their work and family lives permit (as long as the master's degree is completed within the current UF grad school limit of seven years). UF EDGE students can begin any UF academic semester (fall, spring, or summer), for flexible rolling admissions. To obtain a master's degree, all admitted students must complete a minimum of 30 credit hours while maintaining a minimum grade point average of 3.0 on a 4.0 scale.

Courses are structured in a combined student population format, where on-campus students and UF EDGE distance learning students participate in the same courses. Lectures for on-campus students are held in studio classrooms, and those lecture videos are posted online for UF EDGE students the same day. UF EDGE program distance students view the same lectures, receive the same electronic supplemental materials, complete the same assignments, and take the same course exams as on-campus students complete. Exams are proctored local to the distance learning students, allowing for course and program completion without travel to the UF campus.

UF EDGE currently offers twenty master's degree tracks online for distance students, through seven engineering departments; each master's degree consists of ten courses. Departments participating in online delivered master's degrees include Civil & Coastal Engineering, Computer & Information Science & Engineering, Electrical & Computer Engineering, Environmental Engineering Sciences, Industrial & Systems Engineering, Materials Science & Engineering, and Mechanical & Aerospace Engineering. UF EDGE also offers online certificates in specialized engineering areas such as Sustainable Engineering, Solar Energy, Wind Turbines, Gas Turbines, Energy Management, Systems Engineering, Materials Characterization, Control Systems, Advanced Manufacturing, Environmental Policy & Management, and Engineering Entrepreneurship. All UF College of Engineering Online programs can be found at the UF EDGE Web site: www.ufedge.ufl.edu.

On Campus: The College of Engineering offers Master of Science, Master of Engineering, Engineer, and Doctor of Philosophy degrees in aerospace engineering, agricultural and biological engineering, biomedical engineering, chemical engineering, civil engineering, coastal and oceanographic engineering, computer and information science and engineering, electrical and computer engineering, environmental engineering sciences, industrial and systems engineering, materials science and engineering, mechanical engineering, and nuclear engineering sciences.

A minimum of 30 semester hours is required for the M.S. or M.E. with thesis, 6 of which represent work on the thesis. The nonthesis M.S. or M.E. requires 30 semester hours of course work. (An accredited bachelor's degree in engineering or its equivalent is a prerequisite for the M.E.) The Engineer degree requires 30 hours beyond the master's, with an optional thesis. The Ph.D. degree requires 90 credit hours (including dissertation) beyond the bachelor's; beyond the first 30 credits counted toward the Ph.D. degree, 30 must be completed while enrolled at the University of Florida campus or the Research and Engineering Education Facility. The language requirement for the Ph.D. degree varies by department. With ten engineering departments and many programs in cooperation with more than twenty other University colleges and schools, including the large on-campus health science center, the opportunities for interdisciplinary research are numerous. The College ranks among the top twenty public U.S. engineering colleges in research funding. For more information, visit www.eng.ufl.edu.

Research Facilities

The College currently has extensive research laboratories in a broad range of disciplines in modern buildings. The research arm of the College of Engineering is well recognized nationally and internationally for the quality and breadth of its programs, and faculty members are at the forefront of their fields. The College of Engineering and the University have extensive computational facilities, including parallel processing, computer graphics, and minicomputer and personal computer laboratories. The library system consists of several major units, including a modern science and engineering library.

Financial Aid

Nearly 1,200 graduate assistantships with competitive stipends are available in research and teaching for one-fourth to three-fourths-time work loads. There are also traineeships and fellowships that provide from $4000 to $30,000 and are supported by NSF, NIH, NDEA Title IV, NANT, USDOE, NASA, the University of Florida Graduate School, and the College of Engineering.

Cost of Study

The registration fee for graduate courses offered through the UF EDGE program (distance learning) for 2011–12 are $551.84 per credit hour for UF EDGE Florida residents and $670.47 per credit hour for UF EDGE non-Florida residents.

The registration fee for most on-campus graduate course work is $498.09 per credit hour for Florida residents and $1222.81 per credit hour for out-of-state students in 2011–12. Fee waivers are available for graduate assistantships.

Student Group

Students in the UF EDGE program consist of engineers from various undergraduate engineering fields wishing to pursue graduate education in engineering. Most UF EDGE graduate students are working professionals or military members wishing to continue their engineering education while maintaining their current career.

Student Outcomes

Employment opportunities for graduates are available in a variety of government agencies, consulting firms, and businesses in a variety of industries. A wide variety of employers recruit each year at the University of Florida. A sample of recent employers includes ABB, Accenture, Agilis, AMD, Bechtel, Boeing, Camp Dresser & McKee, Cargill, CH2M Hill, Citrix Systems, Dow Chemical, Entergy, ExxonMobil, Ford Motor Company, General Electric, Harris Corporation, Honeywell, IBM, Intel, Johnson & Johnson Company, Kimley-Horn, Lockheed Martin, Microsoft, Milliken & Company, Motorola, NASA, Naval Undersea Warfare, Nortel Networks, NSA, Oracle, Pratt & Whitney, Procter & Gamble, Raytheon, Sandia Laboratories, Schlumberger, Siemens and Siemens-Westinghouse, Southwestern Research Labs, and Texas Instruments.

Location

The University of Florida is located in Gainesville, a city of approximately 111,000, situated in north-central Florida. Gainesville lies midway between the Atlantic Ocean and the Gulf of Mexico, each of which is within a 2-hour drive. A University golf course is adjacent to the campus, and there are opportunities for swimming and boating at nearby lakes, springs, and rivers. Gainesville is served by several airlines and bus lines and is located along I-75, 1 hour south of I-10 and 2 hours north of Orlando.

The University

A combined state university and land-grant college, the University of Florida has sixteen colleges, including four professional colleges (Dentistry, Law, Medicine, and Veterinary Medicine). The College of Engineering consists of ten degree-granting departments occupying seventeen buildings and has 283 tenured or tenure-track, full-time faculty members. The University of Florida is a member of the Association of American Universities.

Applying

Program admission and graduation requirements for degree programs offered through UF EDGE online are the same as for on-campus engineering graduate students. All applicants for master's degree programs apply for admission to the UF graduate program of the specific department offering the graduate degree according to the same process and requirements as on-campus graduate degree students. Requirements for participation in master's degree programs generally include a bachelor's degree from a four-year accredited college or university, official test score for the Graduate Record Exam (or Fundamental of Engineering exam is accepted in some departments in substitution for GRE), official test scores on the Test of English as a Foreign Language (TOEFL) exam (international applicants only), and letters of recommendation.

Correspondence and Information

Chairman, Department of (specify)
College of Engineering
University of Florida
Gainesville, Florida 32611

Phone: 352-392-6000 (main college number)
      352-392-9670 (UF EDGE distance learning)
Fax: 352-392-9673
E-mail: academics@eng.ufl.edu
Web site: http://www.eng.ufl.edu
      http://ufedge.ufl.edu (distance learning and online programs)

University of Florida

THE FACULTY

The College of Engineering has 283 tenured or tenure-track, full-time faculty members. For more information about the faculty members, prospective students should visit http://www.eng.ufl.edu.

THE UNIVERSITY OF IOWA

College of Engineering

Programs of Study

The College of Engineering (http://www.engineering.uiowa.edu) at The University of Iowa (http://www.uiowa.edu) offers M.S. and Ph.D. programs in biomedical engineering, chemical and biochemical engineering, civil and environmental engineering, electrical and computer engineering, industrial engineering, and mechanical engineering. The College excels nationally and internationally in several specialty and interdisciplinary research areas, including computer-aided design and simulation, human factors, environmental health solutions, biotechnology, bioinformatics, medical imaging, photopolymerization, hydraulics and water/air resources, and nanotechnology. Master's candidates must maintain at least a 3.0 grade point average and may choose either a thesis or nonthesis program. Students must also successfully complete a minimum of 30 semester hours, 24 of which must be taken at The University of Iowa. Doctoral candidates must complete three years beyond the bachelor's degree, with a minimum of 72 semester hours. One academic year must be in residence. Research tools may be required as specified by the individual program. Those interested should contact the specific department for additional requirements. Graduate students often do interdisciplinary research work in a variety of programs and facilities noted in this description.

Research Facilities

The College of Engineering has twenty research locations in eastern Iowa, covering its six academic programs, four research centers reporting to the College, and interdisciplinary research efforts. IIHR–Hydroscience & Engineering (http://www.iihr.uiowa.edu) is unique for its state-of-the-art in-house capabilities in both computational simulations and laboratory modeling and for field observational research. Today IIHR pioneers high-speed computational analysis and simulation of complex flow phenomena while maintaining exceptional experimental laboratory capabilities and facilities. Observational facilities include a Mississippi River environmental research station (http://www.iihr.uiowa.edu/lacmrers) and a wide range of remote sensing equipment. Experimental facilities include hydraulic flumes, a hydraulic wave basin, air- and water-flow units, sediment labs, and advanced instruments for laboratory and field measurements. Engineers in IIHR's mechanical and electronic shops provide in-house expertise for construction of models and instruments. Active academic and research programs at IIHR are supported by a diverse set of computing resources and facilities. For high-performance computing (HPC) IIHR operates a parallel, distributed-memory computer cluster comprised of more than 3,500 2.66 GHz Intel Xeon X5650 cores, 9.5 TB memory, and 1.5 PB of scratch space running Linux, MPI, OpenMP, and the Intel and GNU compiler and tool suites. The computing nodes feature an InfiniBand quad data rate (fully unblocked at DDR) interconnect for high-speed, low-latency message passing. Three log in nodes provide access to the cluster for compiling and launching jobs.

Other engineering research-related facilities include the Engineering Research Facility, Iowa Advanced Technology Laboratories, Iowa Injury Prevention Research Center (http://www.public-health.uiowa.edu/IPRC), University of Iowa Hospitals and Clinics (http://www.uihealthcare.com/uihospitalsandclinics/index.html), National Advanced Driving Simulator (http://www.nads-sc.uiowa.edu), Center for Biocatalysis and Bioprocessing (http:/www.uiowa.edu/~biocat), and Chemistry Building, which support laboratories devoted to such areas as biomechanics, biotechnology, molecular and computational biology, bioinformatics, environmental contamination, and remote sensing.

The Center for Computer-Aided Design (http://www.ccad.uiowa.edu) is housed in the Engineering Research Facility and has 7,500 square feet of office space for staff researchers, student assistants, and program administration. The eight on-site laboratories house research facilities for two state-of-the-art motion capture research laboratories, one of which includes a 6-DOF shaker table motion platform, a fully immersive virtual reality environment, robotic systems, materials testing fixtures, and equipment for individual student research in various engineering disciplines. An off-site facility is maintained at the Iowa City Regional Airport that includes three flight simulation capabilities (a high-performance, functional Boeing 737-800 mockup for high-workload simulation and analysis as well as functional Boeing 777 and F-15 mock-ups). CCAD's Iowa City airport facility also houses three dedicated research aircraft, including a single-engine Beechcraft A-36 Bonanza aircraft, outfitted to create the CCAD Computerized Airborne Research Platform (CARP) in support of airborne human factors research for advanced flight deck technology, and two single-engine tandem seat L-29 jet trainer aircraft, to provide flight testing for additional avionics systems research programs. The Iowa City Airport facility also houses a fully instrumented automotive test platform and a recently acquired HMMWV vehicle platform supporting cognitive assessment testing related to ground vehicle human-machine interaction and operation activities at the Operator Performance Laboratory. The center's computer infrastructure incorporates high-performance workstations, servers, and PC network in support of intensive computation, geometric modeling and analysis, software development, and visualization and simulation. The National Advanced Driving Simulator (NADS) is located at the University of Iowa Research Park (http://enterprise.uiowa.edu/researchpark). The NADS conducts groundbreaking research and development in the field of driving simulation. Utilizing one of the world's most advanced driving simulator capabilities, researchers at the University have defined the state-of-the-art in driving simulation, vehicle performance, and cognitive systems engineering. The NADS houses the NADS-1 driving simulator as well as several lower-fidelity driving simulators primarily used to support development, testing, and refinement of experimental procedures at lower cost to the client. These include the NADS-2, a static-base simulator with a limited field of view, and several portable PC-based mini-simulators. All simulation platforms at the center share a common software architecture with the NADS-1, ensuring compatibility of scenarios and data across all NADS simulators.

Engineering Computer Systems Support (http://css.engineering.uiowa.edu) provides the curricular and research computing needs of the College through state-of-the-art hardware, the same commercial software used by engineers in the industry, and a dedicated professional support staff. All engineering students receive computer accounts and maintain those accounts throughout their college careers. Full Internet and Web access complement local educational resources, which include enhanced classroom instruction, online classes, engineering design and simulation packages, programming languages, and productivity software. There are twenty-eight Linux and approximately 300 Windows workstations, supported by more than $10 million worth of professional software dedicated for student use 24 hours a day. The H. William Lichtenberger Engineering Library provides Internet access to indexes and abstracts, more than 125,000 volumes, ANSI standards, and electronic access to thousands of engineering and science journals.

Financial Aid

Financial aid is available to graduate students in the form of research and teaching assistantships as well as fellowships from federal agencies and industry. Support includes a competitive stipend reduction in tuition and partial payment of tuition. Specific information is available from individual departments.

Cost of Study

For 2011–12, tuition per semester is $4593 for Iowa residents and $12,272 for nonresidents. There is a technology fee of $323 per semester, which allows students the use of Computer Systems Support. In addition there are, per semester, a mandatory student health fee of $117, a student activities fee of $33.50, a student services fee of $35.50, a student union fee of $58, a building fee of $59.50, an arts and cultural events fee of $12, recreation fee of $117.50, and a professional enhancement fee of $30.

Living and Housing Costs

Housing is available in apartments or private homes within walking distance of the campus.

Student Group

Total enrollment at the University for fall 2010 was 30,825 students. Students come from all fifty states, three U.S. possessions, and ninety-seven other countries. Engineering enrollment for fall 2010 was 1,573 undergraduate students and 411 graduate students.

Student Outcomes

Nearly half of the graduates accept positions in Iowa and Illinois, though companies and academic institutions from across the country present offers. Recent graduates have taken positions with companies such as 3M, Accenture, Cargill, Caterpillar, Deere & Company, General Mills, Hewlett-Packard, HNI, Monsanto, Motorola, Pella, and Rockwell Collins.

Location

The University is located in Iowa City, known as the "Athens of the Midwest" because of the many cultural, intellectual, and diverse opportunities available. The Iowa City metropolitan area is a community of 139,600 people, approximately 25 miles from Cedar Rapids, Iowa's second-largest city, with nearly 246,400 people.

The University

The University of Iowa, established in 1847, comprises eleven colleges. The University was the first state university to admit women on an equal basis with men. The University founded the first law school west of the Mississippi River, established one of the first university-based medical centers in the Midwest, and was the first state university in the nation to establish an interfaith school of religion. It was an innovator in accepting creative work—fine art, musical compositions, poetry, drama, and fiction—for academic credit. The University established Iowa City as a national college-prospect testing center. It was a leader in the development of actuarial science as an essential tool of business administration. As a pioneering participant in space exploration, it has become a center for education and research in astrophysical science.

Applying

The application fee is $60 ($100 for international students). Admission requirements differ in each department; students should contact the department in which they are interested for additional requirements.

Correspondence and Information

Admissions
107 Calvin Hall
The University of Iowa
Iowa City, Iowa 52242
Web site: http://www.grad.uiowa.edu/ (Graduate College)
http://www.engineering.uiowa.edu/research (College of Engineering)
http://www.engineering.uiowa.edu/future-students.html (College of Engineering)

The University of Iowa

DEPARTMENTS, CHAIRS, AND AREAS OF FACULTY RESEARCH

STUDIES BY ENGINEERING DISCIPLINE

Biomedical Engineering (http://www.bme.engineering.uiowa.edu). Joseph M. Reinhardt, Departmental Executive Officer. Biomechanics of the spine, low back pain and scoliosis, upper-extremity biomechanics, articular joint contact mechanics, total joint replacement, computational simulation of artificial heart valve dynamics, hemodynamics of arterial disease, mechanical properties of diseased arteries, biomechanics and rupture predication of abdominal aorta aneurysms, solution-perfused tubes for preventing blood-materials interaction, control and coordination of the cardiovascular and respiratory systems, controlled drug delivery, medical image acquisition, processing and quantitative analysis, wire coil–reinforced bone cement, models of cellular processes based on nonequilibrium thermodynamics, tissue engineered vascular grafts, bioinformatics and computational biology, drug/target discovery, gene therapy, development of genomic resources.

Chemical and Biochemical Engineering (http://www.cbe.engineering.uiowa.edu). David W. Murhammer, Departmental Executive Officer. Air pollution engineering, atmospheric aerosol particles, atmospheric chemistry, biocatalysis, biochemical engineering, biofilms, biofuels, biomaterials, biotechnological applications of extremophiles, controlled release, drug delivery, engineering education, fermentation, high-speed computing, insect and mammalian cell culture, medical aerosols, microlithography, nanotechnology, oxidative stress in cell culture, photopolymerization, polymer reaction engineering, polymer science, polymer/liquid crystal composites, process scale protein purification, protein crystallography, reversible emulsifiers, spectroscopy, supercritical fluids, surface science, vaccines, virus infection, chemicals from biomass, green chemistry, and sustainable energy.

Civil and Environmental Engineering (http://www.cee.engineering.uiowa.edu). Michelle M. Scherer, Departmental Executive Officer. Water sustainability, water quality, flood prediction and mitigation, environmental remediation, air pollution, drinking water quality, bioremediation, biogeochemistry, computational solid mechanics, digital human modeling, design of hydraulics structures, design simulation, hydropower, optimal control of nonlinear systems, optimal design of nonlinear structures, diverse aspects of water resources engineering, rainfall and flood forecasting, thermal pollution/power plant operation, transportation-infrastructure modeling, highway pavements, winter highway maintenance.

Electrical and Computer Engineering (http://www.ece.engineering.uiowa.edu). Milan Sonka, Departmental Executive Officer. Sustainable energy, quantitative medical image processing, communication systems and computer networks, sensors and sensor networks, wireless communication, controls, signal processing, parallel and distributed computing systems, large-scale intelligent systems, bioinformatics, photonics, plasma waves, software engineering, design and testing of very-large-scale integrated circuits, nanotechnology, materials, and devices.

Industrial Engineering (http://www.mie.engineering.uiowa.edu/IEProgram/IEMain.php). Andrew Kusiak, Departmental Executive Officer. Biomanufacturing, computational intelligence, informatics, engineering economics, engineering management, financial engineering, health-care systems, human factors and ergonomics, human-computer interfaces, flight simulation, driver behavior, manufacturing processes control and operations, operations research and applied statistics, optimization of energy systems, reliability, telerobotics, quality control, and wind energy.

Mechanical Engineering (http://www.mie.engineering.uiowa.edu/MEProgram/MEMain.php). Andrew Kusiak, Departmental Executive Officer. Biomechanics and biofluids, biology-based design, biorenewable and alternative fuels, bioengineering, casting and solidification, cloud computation, combustion, chemically reactive flows, computational mechanics, computer-aided analysis and design, dynamics, fatigue and fracture mechanics, fluid mechanics and ship hydrodynamics, fluid mechanics, human organ modeling, heat transfer, materials processing and behavior, multiscale modeling and simulation, reliability-based design, robotics, composite materials, nanotechnology, renewable energy, structural mechanics, system simulation, thermal systems, vehicle dynamics and simulation, virtual prototyping, and wind energy.

COLLEGE RESEARCH CENTERS, INSTITUTES, AND LABORATORIES

Center for Bioinformatics and Computational Biology (http://genome.uiowa.edu). Thomas L. Casavant, Director. A multidisciplinary research center dedicated to applying high-performance networking and computing to basic life science and applied biomedical research.

Center for Computer-Aided Design (http://www.ccad.uiowa.edu). Karim Abdel-Malek, Director. Virtual Soldier Research (musculoskeletal model, whole body vibration, validation, motion capture, intuitive interface, immersive virtual reality, physiology, standard ergonomic assessments, zone differentiation, posture and motion prediction, hand model, spine modeling, gait: walking and running, predictive dynamics, dynamic strength and fatigue, modeling of clothing, human performance, armor and soldier performance); Operator Performance Laboratory (optimal aircraft instrumentation configuration, rotorcraft, flight simulation supporting aircraft operation task analysis, warning-system effectiveness, roadway markings and illumination analysis, driver performance measurement, cognitive processing burden assessment/sensory and data input cognitive impact, human-vehicle interaction optimization for operational control and safety); Reliability and Sensor Prognostic Systems (mesh-free methods for structural analysis and design-sensitivity analysis, composite materials, probabilistic mechanics and reliability, reliability-based design optimization, topology optimization, multidisciplinary design optimization, sensor technologies, sensor-based process monitoring optimization); National Advanced Driving Simulator (highway safety and transportation efficiency, equipment product development effectiveness enhancement via virtual prototyping, vehicle dynamics and simulation, simulator technology and virtual reality environment and human factors); Musculoskeletal Imaging Modeling and Experimentation Program (computational modeling of anatomic structures, with emphasis on finite modeling); Biomechanics of Soft Tissue (soft tissue mechanics, biomechanics of the heart, cardiovascular system, aneurysm formation, CFD, nonlinear FEA).

IIHR–Hydroscience and Engineering (http://www.iihr.uiowa.edu). Larry J. Weber, Director. A leading institute in fluids-related fundamental and applied research. Cutting-edge research activities incorporate computational fluid dynamics with laboratory modeling and field observational studies. Research includes: fluid dynamics (ship hydrodynamics, turbulent flows, biological fluid flow); environmental hydraulics (structures, river and dam hydraulics, fish passage at dams, sediment management, heat dispersal in water bodies and power production, water-quality monitoring, air-water exchange processes); and water and air resources (atmospheric boundary layer, air pollution, hydrogeology, hydrology, hydrometeorology, remote sensing).

Iowa Institute for Biomedical Imaging (http://www.biomed-imaging.uiowa.edu). Milan Sonka, Director. Knowledge-based analysis of biomedical images from a variety of imaging modalities (e.g., CT, MR, and ultrasound). Current focus areas include development of computer-aided and automated techniques for quantitative analysis of human, animal, and cellular image data.

INTERDISCIPLINARY RESEARCH CENTERS AND INSTITUTES

Medicine and Bioengineering

Center for Biocatalysis and Bioprocessing (http://www.uiowa.edu/~biocat). Mani Subramanian, Director. Biocatalyst fundamental properties, bioremediation, bioprocessing, new biocatalyst discovery, novel biocatalyst applications, biosensing technology, reactive agent development.

Center for International Rural and Environmental Health (http://www.public-health.uiowa.edu/cireh). Tom Cook, Director. Rural and environmental health, with special emphasis on adverse health effects that threaten agricultural and other rural populations; promotes greater understanding and awareness of the causes, consequences, and prevention of communicable, chronic, environmental, and occupational diseases in all regions of the globe, focusing on nations with substantial agrarian economies.

Iowa Injury Prevention Research Center (http://www.public-health.uiowa.edu/IPRC). Corinne Peek-Asa, Director. Prevention, acute care, rehabilitation, surveillance, and biomechanics, including examining causes of delay in Iowa's trauma system, identifying risk factors for injuries to farmers and their families, domestic violence in rural populations, and studying the driving abilities of individuals with sleep disorders and epilepsy.

Orthopaedic Biomechanics Laboratory (http://poppy.obrl.uiowa.edu). Thomas D. Brown, Director. Application of advanced innovative computational formulations and novel experimental approaches to clinically-oriented problems across the diverse spectrum of musculoskeletal biomechanical research; total joint replacement (hip, spine, knee, ankle), posttraumatic arthritis, osteonecrosis of the hip, high-energy limb trauma, carpal tunnel syndrome, and articular contact stresses as they relate to joint degeneration.

Environmental and Hydroscience

NSF Center for Environmentally Beneficial Catalysis (http://www.erc-assoc.org/factsheets/09/09-Fact%20Sheet%202005.htm). Mani Subramanian, Director. A multidisciplinary, multi-university research center. Catalyst design, synthesis, and characterization; biocatalyst preparation and characterization; synthesis of catalyst supports with controlled pore structure; benign media, including carbon dioxide–based solvents and ionic liquids; probing reaction mechanisms with advanced analytical tools; advanced molecular modeling of chemical, physical, and thermodynamic properties involving reactions and media; multiphase reactor design and analysis; economic and environmental impact analysis; computational fluid dynamics.

Center for Global and Regional Environmental Research (http://www.cgrer.uiowa.edu). Gregory R. Carmichael and Jerald L. Schnoor, Co-directors. Multiple aspects of global environmental change, including the regional effects on natural ecosystems, environments, and resources and on human health, culture, and social systems.

Center for Health Effects of Environmental Contamination (http://www.cheec.uiowa.edu). Gene F. Parkin, Director. Conducts and supports research on the identification and measurement of environmental toxins, particularly water contaminants, and possible associations between exposure to environmental contaminants and adverse health effects. Provides environmental database design and development and systems support for environmental health research.

Environmental Health Sciences Research Center (http://www.ehsrc.uiowa.edu). Peter S. Thorne, Director. Agricultural and rural environmental exposures and health effects, agricultural chemical exposures and health effects.

Science and Technology

Iowa Alliance for Wind Innovation and Novel Development (http://www.iawind.org). P. Barry Butler, Principal Investigator. The Iowa Alliance for Wind Innovation and Novel Development (IAWIND) is a partnership with state and local governments, community colleges, Regents Universities, independent Iowa colleges, the private sector, and the federal government. It is designed to serve as a catalyst for the growth of wind energy and to support and to facilitate the research and training needs of wind energy companies.

Nanoscience and Nanotechnology Institute (http://research.uiowa.edu/nniui). Vicki Grassian, Director. Environment and health (air quality, natural environment, workplace environment, human and animal toxicity, environmental health, drug delivery, disease detection, imaging, bioanalytical assays, environmental remediation and decontamination, green chemistry, fuel cells, energy, sustainability, sensors); nanomaterials (quantum theory, understanding condensed-phase matter at the nanoscale, synthesis and characterization of nanomaterials, defense-related applications).

Optical Science and Technology Center (http://www.ostc.uiowa.edu). Michael Flatté, Director. Laser spectroscopy and photochemistry, photonics and optoelectronics, ultrafast laser development, condensed-matter physics, materials growth techniques, device physics/engineering, surface chemistry, chemical sensors, environmental chemistry, polymer science, plasma physics, nonlinear optics.

NSF IUCRC Photopolymerization Center (http://css.engineering.uiowa.edu/~cfap). Alec Scranton, Director. Kinetics and mechanisms of photopolymerizations and their impact on the structure and properties of photopolymerized materials.

Public Policy Center (http://ppc.uiowa.edu). Peter C. Damiano, Director. Transportation, environmental quality, health care, economic growth and development.

Water Sustainability Initiative (http://watersustainability.uiowa.edu). Jerald Schnoor, Chair, Steering Committee. The University of Iowa has expanded its existing strength in interdisciplinary research on water including its availability, quality, reuse, health impact, and its relationship to a changing climate. Economics, policy, and law, as well as the natural sciences and engineering, are all engaged to solve the problems of water. The faculty alliance on water sustainability encompasses the Colleges of Liberal Arts and Sciences, Public Health, Law, Engineering, the Graduate College, and the Public Policy Center. Among the various resources already developed to advance the initiative are the new Iowa Flood Center and the University of Iowa Office of Sustainability.

UNIVERSITY OF PENNSYLVANIA

School of Engineering and Applied Science

Programs of Study	Research and education form the creative graduate mission of Penn Engineering. The excitement and discovery of research is open to all students and is the keystone of the School's world-renowned Ph.D. programs. These programs are augmented by a diverse array of master's degree offerings.
	Penn Engineering's collaborative research and learning environment truly distinguish the School from its peers. Students work with and learn from faculty mentors within the core disciplinary programs as well as through scholarly interactions involving the School of Medicine, the School of Arts and Sciences, and the Wharton School, to note a few. This environment is further enriched by Penn's many institutes, centers, and laboratories. For more than 100 years, Penn Engineering has been at the forefront of innovation, just like the University's founder: America's first scientist and engineer—Benjamin Franklin.
	The six Doctor of Philosophy (Ph.D.) programs are research-oriented degree programs for students of superior caliber who will make original contributions to theory and practice in their fields of interest. The programs prepare them for a research career in academe, government, or industry. Curricula are purposely designed to develop the intellectual skills essential for the rapidly changing character of research.
	Penn Engineering's fifteen master's programs serve a wide range of highly qualified students such as working professionals seeking greater expertise to advance their careers and students expanding on their undergraduate training for professional engineering practice, preparing for doctoral studies, or pursuing an entirely new field of interest. The School's constantly evolving curricula, grounded in up-to-the-minute research findings and industrial priorities, and focused on practical applications of knowledge, are designed to be responsive to career and professional interests, as well as to the needs of today's high-tech society and economy.
Research Facilities	Shared research laboratories and facilities are an integral part of research and education at Penn Engineering. From nanotechnology to fluid mechanics to robotics to entrepreneurship, dedicated space exists for all forms of research in which students and faculty engage. The School's collection of labs and facilities include the Mechanical Engineering and Applied Mechanics Design and Prototyping Laboratories, SIG Center for Computer Graphics, Nano Probe Innovation Facility, Penn Regional Nanotechnology Facility, the Weiss Tech House, and Wolf Nanofabrication Facility.
	Interdisciplinary research centers and institutes span all departments within Penn Engineering and foster collaborations across different schools throughout the University. The physical connectivity of engineering buildings and the proximity to each of the other schools enables exciting collaborations with faculty, students, and postdoctoral scholars across Penn. From biotechnology and robotics to computer animation and nanotechnology, Penn Engineering's centers and institutes are at the forefront of research on each scientific and technological frontier. (http://www.seas.upenn.edu/research/centers-institutes.php)
Financial Aid	A number of fellowships, assistantships, and scholarships are available on a yearly competitive basis, mainly for doctoral candidates. Provisions of these awards vary; the maximum benefits include payment of tuition and the general and technology fees plus a stipend and health insurance.
Cost of Study	Tuition for five courses in the academic year 2010–11 was $24,020, and there was a general fee of $2152 and a technology fee of $646 for full-time study. For part-time study, the tuition was $4804 per course unit (one course), the general fee was $270, and the technology fee was $81.
Living and Housing Costs	On-campus housing is available for both single and married students. Students who choose to live on campus can expect to pay $712 to $1398 per month. There are numerous privately owned apartments for rent in the immediate area.
Student Group	There are approximately 21,000 students at the University, around 11,000 of whom are enrolled in graduate and professional schools. Of these, approximately 1,300 are in graduate engineering programs.
Location	The University of Pennsylvania is located in West Philadelphia, just a few blocks from the heart of the city. Philadelphia is a twenty-first-century city with seventeenth-century origins. Renowned museums, concert halls, theaters, and sports arenas provide cultural and recreational outlets for students. Fairmount Park extends through large sections of Philadelphia, occupying both banks of the Schuylkill River. Not far away are the Jersey shore to the east, Pennsylvania Dutch country to the west, and the Pocono Mountains to the north. Less than a 3-hour drive from New York City and Washington, D.C., the city of Philadelphia is a patchwork of distinctive neighborhoods ranging from colonial Society Hill to Chinatown.
The School	The School of Engineering and Applied Science has a distinguished reputation for the quality of its programs. Its alumni have achieved international distinction in research, higher education, management, entrepreneurship and industrial development, and government service. Its faculty leads a research program that is at the forefront of modern technology and has made major contributions in a wide variety of fields.
	The University of Pennsylvania was founded in 1740 by Benjamin Franklin. A member of the Ivy League and one of the world's leading universities, Penn is renowned for its graduate schools, faculty, research centers, and institutes. Conveniently situated on a compact and attractive campus, Penn offers an abundance of multidisciplinary and cross-school educational programs with exceptional opportunities for individually tailored graduate education. It also offers students all the amenities of a 21,000-student university.
Applying	Candidates may apply directly to the School of Engineering through an online application system. Visit http://www.seas.upenn.edu/prospective-students/graduate/admissions.php for detailed application requirements and access to the online application system. Ph.D. applications for fall admission must be received by December 15, January 2, or January 15 (varies by program) to ensure consideration for financial aid. Master's applications are considered on a rolling basis with a final deadline of June 1. Admission is based on the student's past record as well as on letters of recommendation. Scores on the Graduate Record Examinations (GRE) are required. All students whose native language is not English must arrange to take the Test of English as a Foreign Language (TOEFL) prior to the application process; the minimum score accepted on the Internet-based test is 100.
Correspondence and Information	Graduate Admissions School of Engineering and Applied Science 111 Towne Building 220 South 33rd Street University of Pennsylvania Philadelphia, Pennsylvania 19104-6391 Phone: 215-898-7246 E-mail: gradstudies@seas.upenn.edu Web site: http://www.seas.upenn.edu

University of Pennsylvania

AREAS OF RESEARCH

Bioengineering. The nation's first Ph.D. in bioengineering was granted at the University of Pennsylvania, and today the department consists of 16 primary faculty members and more than 80 secondary and associated faculty members. The Bioengineering Ph.D. Program is designed to train individuals for academic, government, or industrial research careers. Research interests include cellular biomechanics, bioactive biomaterials, cell and tissue engineering, neuroengineering, orthopedic bioengineering, neurorehabilitation, respiratory mechanics and transport, molecular and cellular aspects of bioengineering, and biomedical imaging. Penn's interdisciplinary research training laboratories are in the Department of Bioengineering, the School of Engineering and Applied Science, and the new Institute for Medicine and Engineering; the University's medical, dental, and veterinary schools; and four research-oriented hospitals, all of which are located on campus. Students are exposed to clinical applications of bioengineering. The department also offers an M.S.E. in bioengineering and a professional master's program as a medical engineering track in the master of biotechnology program. (http://www.be seas.upenn.edu/)

Biotechnology. The Master of Biotechnology program draws its faculty and courses from the School of Arts and Sciences and the School of Engineering and Applied Science. This interdisciplinary program prepares both full- and part-time students for productive and creative careers in the biotechnology and pharmaceutical industries. Students can specialize in one of the following tracks: bioinformatics/computational biology, biopharmaceutical/engineering biotechnology, biomedical technologies, or molecular biotechnology. These tracks, in combination with core courses, ensure that the students get a uniquely broad exposure to the entire field of biotechnology.

Chemical and Biomolecular Engineering. The department was one of the first in the United States to offer a degree in chemical engineering. Courses and research programs are offered in applied mathematics, adsorption, biochemical and biomedical engineering, computer-aided design, transport and interfacial phenomena, thermodynamics, polymer engineering, semiconductor and ceramic materials processing, reaction kinetics, catalysis, artificial intelligence, and process control. Many research projects are collaborative and take advantage of other strong programs in the University. Ongoing research includes joint projects with faculty members from the School of Medicine and Wistar Institute, from the Department of Biology, from the Department of Chemistry, from Computer Science and Engineering, and from Materials Science and Engineering. (http://www.seas.upenn.edu/cbe/)

Computer and Information Science. The program is intended for students from many disciplines and backgrounds who have had substantial course work in mathematics and computer science. Research and teaching covers a wide range of topics in theory and applications, including algorithms, architecture, programming languages, operating systems, logic and computation, software engineering, databases, parallel and distributed systems, real-time systems, high-speed networks, graphics, computational biology, artificial intelligence, natural language processing, machine learning, data-mining, vision, and robotics. Much of this research involves multidisciplinary collaborations with other graduate programs in the School of Engineering, as well as the Mathematics, Linguistics, Philosophy, Psychology, Biology, and Neuroscience departments. The department also has a number of ongoing research collaborations with national and international organizations and laboratories. The CIS faculty seeks students who, whether pursuing a master's degree or doctoral studies, will be actively involved at the leading edge of computer science research. (http://www.cis.upenn.edu)

Computer and Information Technology. The program is designed for candidates who have a strong academic background in areas other than computer science but who have a need for graduate education in computer science. Completion of the M.C.I.T. program gives the graduate a solid foundation in computer science, providing the advanced expertise needed to meet the demands of a fast-paced, high-tech global society. The program is also suitable for IT professionals who wish to augment their practical skills with an understanding of the foundations of computing. (http://www.cis.upenn.edu/mcit/index.shtml)

Computer Graphics and Game Technology. The goal of the program is to expose recent graduates, as well as students returning from industry, to state-of-the-art graphics and animation technologies, interactive media design principles, product development methodologies, and engineering entrepreneurship. This degree program prepares students for those positions that require multi-disciplinary skills, such as designers, technical animators, directors, and game programmers. Opportunities for specialization are provided in such core areas as art and animation, creative design, animation and simulation technology, human/computer interfaces, and production management. (http://www.cis.upenn.edu/grad/cggt/cggt-overview.shtml)

Electrical and Systems Engineering. The graduate group in electrical and systems engineering offers the following programs: Ph.D. in electrical and systems engineering (ESE), M.S.E. in Electrical Engineering (EE), and a M.S.E. in Systems Engineering (SE). The department is a leader in the areas of electroscience, systems science, network systems, and telecommunications. Electroscience includes electromagnetics and photonics, sensors and MEMS, LSI, and nanotechnology. Systems science covers signal processing, optimization, simulation, control and cybernetics, complex adaptive systems, stochastic processes, and decision sciences. Most of the research activities are interdisciplinary in nature and electrical and systems engineering faculty members and students typically interact or collaborate with professors and students from other departments within the School of Engineering and Applied Science, the School of Arts and Sciences, and the Wharton School. (http://www.ese.upenn.edu/grad)

Embedded Systems. The Master of Science in Engineering in Embedded Systems (E.M.B.S.) spans the core topics of embedded control, real-time operating systems, model-based design and verification, and implementation of embedded systems. This innovative and unique degree program is offered jointly by the departments of Computer and Information Science and Electrical and Systems Engineering and is integrated with the PRECISE Center for Research in Embedded Systems. The program is ideally suited for students with either computer science or electrical engineering academic backgrounds who wish to pursue industrial jobs within automotive, aerospace, defense, and consumer electronics, as well as for practicing engineers in the embedded systems industry who want to gain knowledge of state-of-the-art tools and theories. (http://www.cis.upenn.edu/grad/embedded.shtml)

Integrated Product Design. The IPD program is intended to cultivate design professionals who possess both a breadth of knowledge and a depth of expertise in a specialty to bridge the domains of technology, manufacturing, business, aesthetics, and human-product interaction. The guiding philosophy of the program is not only to teach students to create products but to understand and address the social, environmental, and experiential contexts of those products, so that product design can be harnessed as a force for the greater good. The program builds the skills to investigate, imagine, conceptualize, and model a wide range of products and their complementary business models. The program draws on the strengths of three internationally recognized schools within the University: the School of Engineering and Applied Science, the Wharton School, and the School of Design. The graduate courses that make up the program create an interdisciplinary point of view and are taught by professors from all three schools. Studio classes accompany classroom studies, providing creative and analytical approaches and shifting students between rigorous technical and explorative processes in the development of both experiential and theoretical knowledge. Collaborative team projects and student-driven independent projects complement the core courses to give students both a solid grasp of the fundamentals and a deep understanding of the nuances of these fields. (http://www.me.upenn.edu/ipd/)

Materials Science and Engineering. The department conducts an extensive program of graduate education and research aimed at understanding the physical origins of the behavior of ceramics, polymers, metals, and alloys in electronic, structural, magnetic, and interfacial applications. Students have access to a broad range of state-of-the-art instrumentation in the department and the Laboratory for Research on the Structure of Matter (LRSM), which is housed in the same building. The LRSM is one of the largest NSF-supported Materials Research Science and Engineering centers in the country and includes central facilities for surface studies, ion scattering, electron microscopy, X-ray diffraction, computer simulation, mechanical testing, and materials synthesis and processing. Access to synchrotron radiation (X-ray and UV) and neutron-scattering facilities is also available at nearby National Labs. Research within the department can be grouped under four general headings: surfaces and interfaces (polymer-polymer, metal-ceramic, and grain boundaries in metallic materials), complex materials (carbon-based nanotubes, copolymers, intermetallic alloys, and nanomaterials), failure mechanisms (plastic deformation, fatigue, embrittlement, corrosion, and predictive modeling), and novel electronic ceramics (ferroelectrics, microwave materials, batteries and fuel cells, superconductors, and catalysts). (http://www.seas.upenn.edu/mse/)

Mechanical Engineering and Applied Mechanics. The research in the department combines theory, computation, and experiments with applications. It is often interdisciplinary in nature and is done in collaboration with material sciences, computer sciences, electrical and systems engineering, chemical and biomolecular engineering, and the School of Medicine. The areas of focus are thermal and fluid sciences, mechanics of materials, computational science and engineering, mechanical systems and robotics, and biomechanics. Research in thermal fluids focuses on energy conversion, advanced power generation, Second-Law (energy) analysis, combustion, water desalination, microelectronic device fabrication and cooling, inorganic and organic (macromolecular) crystal growth, active control of flow patterns, transport processes associated with mesodevices and microdevices and with sensors, material processing, multiphase flows, computational fluid dynamics, and micro- and nano-scale thermofluid transport. The research in mechanics of materials focuses on crystal plasticity, effective properties of nonlinear composites, intermetallic compounds, localization studies, metal-forming processes, interfacial fracture, fatigue and high-temperature fracture, soft material, phase transitions in thermoelastic solids, nano-scale mechanics and tribology (friction, adhesion, and wear), and cell mechanics. Research in computational science and engineering focuses on parallel algorithms for the solution of differential and integral equations, inverse problems in nonlinear transport and wave propagation, and numerical study of systems with coupled multiple physics domains and multiple scales. Research in mechanical systems focuses on robotics, computational design, compliant mechanisms, optimization, computer vision, hybrid systems, dynamics, controls, virtual and rapid prototyping, and microelectromechanical systems (MEMS). Robotics research addresses control of multi-robot systems, active sensor networks, micromanipulation, and distributed control and sensing, flying robots, modular reconfigurable robots, robotic locomotion, haptic interfaces, teleoperation, and medical robotics. Biomechanics research spans scales from the tissue level through the molecular, with major efforts in cell mechanics, tendon and ligament properties, biomolecular network simulation, and gravity effects on cells and tissues. (http://www.me.upenn.edu)

Nanotechnology. The Master of Science in Engineering degree in nanotechnology prepares students for this profession with a solid foundation in the three technical core areas: nanofabrication, devices and fundamental properties, and biotechnology, as well as commercialization and societal impacts of technology. Courses are offered by the School of Engineering and Applied Science, the School of Arts and Sciences, and the Wharton School. (http://www.masters.nano.upenn.edu/)

Robotics. This new and unique program educates students in the interdisciplinary aspects of the science and technology of robotic and intelligent machines. The modern expert in robotics and intelligent systems must be proficient in artificial intelligence, computer vision, controls systems, dynamics, and machine learning as well as in design, programming, and prototyping of robotic systems. This multidepartmental, multidisciplinary program provides an ideal foundation for industrial jobs in robotics, defense, aerospace, and automotive industries and various government agencies. (https://www.grasp.upenn.edu/education/masters)

Telecommunications and Networking. This interdisciplinary program draws its faculty members and courses from two School of Engineering and Applied Science departments—electrical and systems engineering and computer and information science—from the Wharton School. Two required courses cover the theory and practice of modern data and voice networking as well as future broadband-integrated networking; five telecommunications electives provide breadth and depth in the field. Three additional free electives allow students to further deepen their technical proficiency or address the increasingly complex managerial and business demands placed on telecommunications professionals. The program's interdisciplinary nature offers full- and part-time students the flexibility to tailor the curriculum to their specific interests, backgrounds, and career goals. (http://www.seas.upenn.edu/profprog/tcom/index.html)

YALE UNIVERSITY

School of Engineering & Applied Science

Programs of Study	All research and instructional programs in engineering and applied science are coordinated by the School of Engineering & Applied Science, which consists of the Departments of Biomedical Engineering, Chemical & Environmental Engineering, Electrical Engineering, and Mechanical Engineering & Materials Science. These four units have autonomous faculty appointments and instructional programs, and students may obtain degrees designated according to different disciplines. A Director of Graduate Studies in each department oversees all graduate student matters. Students have considerable freedom in selecting programs to suit their interests and may choose programs of study that draw upon the resources of departments that are not within the School of Engineering & Applied Science, including the Departments of Applied Physics, Physics, Chemistry, Mathematics, Statistics, Astronomy, Geology and Geophysics, Molecular Biophysics and Biochemistry, and Computer Science, and departments of the School of Medicine and the School of Management.

The student plans his or her course of study in consultation with faculty advisers (the student's advisory committee). A minimum of ten term courses is required and they must be completed in the first two years. Mastery of the topics is expected, and the core courses, as identified by each department/program, should be taken in the first year. No more than two courses should be Special Investigations, and at least two should be outside the area of the dissertation. Periodically, the faculty reviews the overall performance of the student to determine whether he or she may continue working toward the Ph.D. degree. At the end of the first year, a faculty member typically agrees to accept the student as a research assistant. By December 5 of the third year, an area examination must be passed and a written prospectus submitted before dissertation research is begun. These events result in the student's admission to candidacy. Subsequently, students report orally each year to the full advisory committee on their progress. When the research is nearing completion, but before the thesis writing has commenced, the full advisory committee advises the student on the thesis plan. A final oral presentation of the dissertation research is required during term time. There is no foreign language requirement.

M.S. degrees are offered and require the successful completion of at least eight term courses, two of which may be special projects. Although this program can normally be completed in one year of full-time study, a part-time M.S. program is available for practicing engineers and others. Its requirements are the successful completion of eight term courses in a time period not to exceed four calendar years.

Research Facilities	Department facilities are equipped with state-of-the-art experimental and computational equipment in support of the research activity described above. They are centrally located on campus in Mason, Dunham, and Becton Laboratories and in the Malone Engineering Center, adjacent to the Departments of Mathematics and Computer Science and near the complex of facilities for physics, chemistry, and the biological sciences. The School of Engineering & Applied Science has a rich computing environment, including servers, UNIX workstations, and Macintosh and Microsoft Windows personal computers. High-speed data wired and wireless networks interconnect engineering and extends to the campus network. Yale has long been connected to the Internet and is now participating in vBNS and the emerging Internet2. In addition, advanced instrumentation, computing, and networking are combined in a number of laboratories.
Financial Aid	Almost all first-year Ph.D. students receive a University fellowship paying full tuition and an adjusted stipend. Support thereafter is generally provided by research assistantships, which pay $29,550 plus full tuition in 2011–12. Prize fellowships are available to exceptional students. Fellowship support is not available for master's degree students.
Cost of Study	Tuition was $33,500 for the 2010–11 academic year.
Living and Housing Costs	On-campus graduate dormitory housing units range from $4284 to $7300 per academic year. Graduate apartment units range from $810 to $1134 per month. Additional housing details can be found at http://www.yale.edu/gradhousing.
Student Group	Yale has 11,500 students—5,300 are undergraduates and the remainder are graduate and professional students. About 200 graduate students are in engineering, most of them working toward the Ph.D.
Location	Situated on Long Island Sound, among the scenic attractions of southern New England, New Haven provides outstanding cultural and recreational opportunities. The greater New Haven area has a population of more than 350,000 and is only 1½ hours from New York by train or car.
The University	Yale is the third-oldest university in the United States, and its engineering program is also one of the oldest. All programs at the University, including those in the School of Engineering & Applied Science, are structured to give students a high degree of flexibility in arranging their programs, with close interaction between individual students and faculty members.
Applying	Students with a bachelor's degree in any field of engineering or in mathematics, physics, or chemistry may apply for admission to graduate study, as may other students prepared to do graduate-level work in any of the study areas of the chosen department, regardless of their specific undergraduate field. Students are admitted only for the beginning of the fall term. Application should be initiated about a year in advance of desired admission, and the application should be submitted before December 25; the file, including letters of reference, should be completed before January 2. Notifications of admission and award of financial aid are sent by April 1. Applicants must take the General Test of the Graduate Record Examinations; the exam should be taken in October. International applicants must submit scores on the TOEFL unless the undergraduate degree is from an institution in which English is the primary language of instruction.
Correspondence and Information	Office of Graduate Studies School of Engineering & Applied Science Yale University P.O. Box 208267 New Haven, Connecticut 06520-8267 Phone: 203-432-4250 Fax: 203-432-7736 Web site: http://www.seas.yale.edu/

Yale University

THE FACULTY AND AREAS OF RESEARCH

APPLIED MECHANICS/MECHANICAL ENGINEERING/MATERIALS SCIENCE. A. Dollar, E. Dufresne, J. Fernández de la Mora, A. Gomez, M. B. Long, J. Morrell, C. S. O'Hern, N. Ouellette, A. G. Ramirez, J. Schroers, U. D. Schwarz, M. D. Smooke, H. Tang. Joint appointments (with primary appointment in another department): C. Ahn, D. Bercovici, S.-I. Karato, D. E. Rosner, R. B. Smith. Adjunct faculty: A. Liñan-Martinez, F. A. Williams. Emeritus faculty: I. B. Bernstein.

Mechanics of Fluids. Dynamics and stability of drops and bubbles; dynamics of thin liquid films; macroscopic and particle-scale dynamics of emulsions, foams, and colloidal suspensions; electrospray theory and applications; electrical propulsion applications; combustion and flames; computational methods for fluid dynamics and reacting flows; turbulence; particle tracking in fluid mechanics; laser diagnostics of reacting and nonreacting flows.

Mechanics of Solids/Material Science/Soft Matter. Characterization of crystallization and other phase transformations; studies of thin films, MEMS, smart materials such as shape memory alloys, amorphous metals, and nanomaterials including nanocomposites; jamming and slow dynamics in glasses and granular materials; mechanical properties of soft and biological materials; self assembly; dynamics of macromolecules; NEMS; nano-imprinting; classical and quantum optomechanics; atomic-scale investigations of surface interactions and properties; classical and quantum nanomechanics; and nanotribology.

Robotics/Mechatronics. Machine and mechanism design; dynamics and control; robotic grasping and manipulation; human-machine interface; rehabilitation robotics; haptics; electromechanical energy conversion; biomechanics of human movement; human powered vehicles.

BIOMEDICAL ENGINEERING. R. E. Carson, R. T. Constable, J. Duncan, T. Fahmy, R. Fan, A. Gonzalez, J. Humphrey, F. Hyder, T. Kyriakides, M. Levene, K. Miller-Jensen, D. Rothman, M. Saltzman, L. Staib, S. Zucker. Joint appointments (with primary appointment in another department): J. Bewersdorf, R. de Graaf, E. Morris, L. Niklason, X. Papademetris, S. Sampath, E. Shapiro, F. Sigworth, H. Tagare.

Biomedical Imaging and Biosignals. Formation of anatomical and functional medical images; magnetic resonance spectroscopy; analysis and processing of medical image data, including functional MRI (fMRI); diffusion tensor imaging; imaging of brain biochemical processes; image-guided neurosurgery; using biomechanical models to guide recovery of left ventricular strain from medical images; biomedical signal processing; relating EEG and fMRI information.

Biomechanics. Simulation and loading of the lumbar spine in regard to tissue loads during heavy lifting, low-back pain and mechanical instability of the spine, muscle mechanics and electromyography, mechanical performance of implants, microcirculation in skeletal muscle, mechanisms of blood-flow control, cell-to-cell communication in vascular resistance networks.

Biomolecular Engineering and Biotechnology. Drug delivery and tissue engineering, drug delivery systems, polymers as biomaterials, tissue engineering, spinal cord regeneration, drug delivery and repair in retina and optic nerve, new biomaterials for drug delivery and tissue engineering, bioseparations, chromatography and electrophoresis, electrical recording (patch clamp) and signal processing of ion channel currents, studies of structure and function of ion channel proteins, cryoelectron microscopy methods for macromolecular structure determination.

CHEMICAL & ENVIRONMENTAL ENGINEERING. E. I. Altman, M. Elimelech, G. L. Haller, M. Loewenberg, W. Mitch, C. Osuji, J. Peccia, L. D. Pfefferle, D. E. Rosner, M. Saltzman, A. D. Taylor, P. Van Tassel, T. K. Vanderlick, C. Wilson, J. Zimmerman. Adjunct faculty: A. Firoozabadi, Y. Khalil, R. McGraw, J. Pignatello. Joint appointments (with primary appointment in another department): M. Bell, G. Benoit, R. Blake, E. Dufresne, T. E. Graedel, E. Kaplan, J. Saiers, U. D. Schwarz, K. W. Zilm.

Nanomaterials. Carbon and inorganic nanotubes, nanoscale polymer films, nanoscale devices, nanomaterials and biomolecules in engineered and natural aquatic systems.

Soft Matter and Interfacial Phenomena. Colloidal and interfacial phenomena, surface science, physics of synthetic and biological macromolecules, microfluidic biosensors, self-assembled soft materials for biomedical applications.

Biomolecular Engineering. Biomolecules at interfaces, nanofilm biomaterials, bioaerosol detection and source tracking, microarrays and other high throughput measurements, production of functional binding biomolecules, biological production of sustainable fuels, transport and fate of microbial pathogens in aquatic environments, membrane separations for desalination and water quality control.

Energy. Biofuels, energy extraction from waste materials, efficient water treatment and delivery, integration of science and engineering with economics and policy.

Water. Sustainable and culturally appropriate technologies for low-quality-source water reclamation in the developing world.

Sustainability. Green solvents, bio-based materials, safer nanotechnology and systems optimization for reduced environmental impact and enhanced economic competitiveness.

ELECTRICAL ENGINEERING. E. Culurciello, J. Han, H. Koser, R. Kuc, M. Lee, T. P. Ma, A. S. Morse, K. S. Narendra, M. A. Reed, A. Savvides, H. Tang, S. Tatikonda, J. R. Vaisnys. Joint appointments (with primary appointment in another department): J. Duncan, L. Staib, H. D. Tagare, R. Yang. Adjunct faculty: P. J. Kindlmann, R. Lethin. Emeritus faculty: R. C. Barker, R. Chang, P. M. Schultheiss.

Signal Processing, Control, and Communications. Linear system models, automatic control systems, representation of information in signals, transmission and storage of information, processing information by computers, networking, communication theory. Applications include bioengineering, digital signal processing, image processing, neural networks, robotics, sensors, and telecommunication systems.

Computer Engineering, Sensor Networks, Circuits and Systems. Study and design of digital circuits and computer systems; computer architecture; sensor networks; very-large-scale integrated (VLSI) circuit design, implementation, and testing. Applications include computing networks, computer design, biomedical instrumentation, bio-inspired circuits and systems.

Electronics, Photonics, and Nanodevices. Design, fabrication, and characterization of novel electronic, photonic, and nano devices; study of structure-property relationships in electronic and photonic materials. Applications include chem./bio-sensing, solid-state lighting, solar cells, micro/nano-electromechanical systems, non-volatile memory, and ultrafast devices.

Section 2
Aerospace/Aeronautical Engineering

This section contains a directory of institutions offering graduate work in aerospace/aeronautical engineering. Additional information about programs listed in the directory may be obtained by writing directly to the dean of a graduate school or chair of a department at the address given in the directory.

For programs offering related work, see also in this book *Engineering and Applied Sciences* and *Mechanical Engineering and Mechanics.* In another guide in this series:

Graduate Programs in the Physical Sciences, Mathematics, Agricultural Sciences, the Environment & Natural Resources
See *Geosciences* and *Physics*

CONTENTS

Program Directories

Close-Up and Display

Aerospace/Aeronautical Engineering

Air Force Institute of Technology, Graduate School of Engineering and Management, Department of Aeronautics and Astronautics, Dayton, OH 45433-7765. Offers aeronautical engineering (MS, PhD); astronautical engineering (MS, PhD); materials science (MS, PhD); space operations (MS); systems engineering (MS, PhD). *Accreditation:* ABET (one or more programs are accredited). Part-time programs available. *Degree requirements:* For master's, thesis; for doctorate, thesis/dissertation. *Entrance requirements:* For master's and doctorate, GRE General Test, minimum GPA of 3.0, U.S. citizenship. *Faculty research:* Computational fluid dynamics, experimental aerodynamics, computational structural mechanics, experimental structural mechanics, aircraft and spacecraft stability and control.

Arizona State University, Ira A. Fulton School of Engineering, Department of Mechanical and Aerospace Engineering, Tempe, AZ 85281. Offers aerospace engineering (MS, MSE, PhD); chemical engineering (MS, MSE, PhD); materials science and engineering (MS, PhD); mechanical engineering (MS, MSE, PhD). Part-time and evening/weekend programs available. Postbaccalaureate distance learning degree programs offered (minimal on-campus study). *Faculty:* 50 full-time (10 women), 13 part-time/adjunct (3 women). *Students:* 258 full-time (47 women), 114 part-time (29 women); includes 48 minority (3 Black or African American, non-Hispanic/Latino; 2 American Indian or Alaska Native, non-Hispanic/Latino; 15 Asian, non-Hispanic/Latino; 27 Hispanic/Latino; 1 Two or more races, non-Hispanic/Latino), 164 international. Average age 28. 721 applicants, 58% accepted, 119 enrolled. In 2010, 55 master's, 29 doctorates awarded. Terminal master's awarded for partial completion of doctoral program. *Degree requirements:* For master's, thesis and oral defense (MS); applied project or comprehensive exam (MSE); interactive Program of Study (iPOS) submitted before completing 50 percent of required credit hours; for doctorate, comprehensive exam, thesis/dissertation, interactive Program of Study (iPOS) submitted before completing 50 percent of required credit hours. *Entrance requirements:* For master's, GRE, minimum GPA of 3.0 or equivalent in last 2 years of work leading to bachelor's degree; for doctorate, GRE, minimum GPA of 3.0 in last 2 years of work leading to bachelor's degree. Additional exam requirements/recommendations for international students: Required—TOEFL, IELTS, or Pearson Test of English. *Application deadline:* For fall admission, 1/31 for domestic and international students; for spring admission, 7/1 for domestic and international students. Application fee: $70 ($90 for international students). Electronic applications accepted. *Expenses:* Contact institution. *Financial support:* In 2010–11, 120 research assistantships with partial tuition reimbursements (averaging $15,353 per year), 34 teaching assistantships with partial tuition reimbursements (averaging $13,861 per year) were awarded; fellowships with full and partial tuition reimbursements, institutionally sponsored loans, scholarships/grants, and tuition waivers (full and partial) also available. Financial award application deadline: 3/1; financial award applicants required to submit FAFSA. *Faculty research:* Electronic materials and packaging, materials for energy (batteries), adaptive/intelligent materials and structures, multiscale fluid mechanics, membranes, therapeutics and bioseparations, flexible structures, nanostructured materials, and micro/nano transport. Total annual research expenditures: $17.5 million. *Unit head:* Dr. Kyle D. Squires, Director, 480-965-3957, E-mail: squires@asu.edu. *Application contact:* Graduate Admissions, 480-965-6113.

Auburn University, Graduate School, Ginn College of Engineering, Department of Aerospace Engineering, Auburn University, AL 36849. Offers MAE, MS, PhD. Part-time programs available. *Faculty:* 10 full-time (0 women), 3 part-time/adjunct (0 women). *Students:* 21 full-time (3 women), 16 part-time (2 women); includes 2 Asian, non-Hispanic/Latino; 1 Hispanic/Latino, 8 international. Average age 27. 76 applicants, 38% accepted, 10 enrolled. In 2010, 15 master's, 1 doctorate awarded. *Degree requirements:* For master's, thesis (MS), exam; for doctorate, thesis/dissertation, exams. *Entrance requirements:* For master's and doctorate, GRE General Test. *Application deadline:* For fall admission, 7/7 for domestic students; for spring admission, 11/24 for domestic students. Applications are processed on a rolling basis. Application fee: $50 ($60 for international students). Electronic applications accepted. *Expenses:* Tuition, state resident: full-time $7002. Tuition, nonresident: full-time $21,898. International tuition: $22,116 full-time. Required fees: $892. Tuition and fees vary according to course load and program. *Financial support:* Fellowships, research assistantships, teaching assistantships, Federal Work-Study available. Support available to part-time students. Financial award application deadline: 3/15; financial award applicants required to submit FAFSA. *Faculty research:* Aerodynamics, flight dynamics and simulation, propulsion, structures and aeroelasticity, aerospace smart structures. *Unit head:* Dr. John E. Cochran, Head, 334-844-6800. *Application contact:* Dr. George Flowers, Dean of the Graduate School, 334-844-2125.

California Institute of Technology, Division of Engineering and Applied Science, Option in Aeronautics, Pasadena, CA 91125-0001. Offers MS, PhD, Engr. *Faculty:* 12 full-time (2 women). *Students:* 49 full-time (14 women). 304 applicants, 9% accepted, 13 enrolled. In 2010, 6 master's, 7 doctorates awarded. Terminal master's awarded for partial completion of doctoral program. *Degree requirements:* For doctorate, thesis/dissertation. *Application deadline:* For fall admission, 1/15 for domestic students. Application fee: $0. *Financial support:* In 2010–11, 19 fellowships, 46 research assistantships, 14 teaching assistantships were awarded. *Faculty research:* Computational fluid dynamics, technical fluid dynamics, structural mechanics, mechanics of fracture, aeronautical engineering and propulsion. *Unit head:* Dr. Guruswami Ravichandran, Director, 626-395-4523, E-mail: ravi@aero.caltech.edu. *Application contact:* Natalie Gilmore, Assistant Dean of Graduate Studies, 626-395-3812, Fax: 626-577-9246, E-mail: ngilmore@caltech.edu.

California Polytechnic State University, San Luis Obispo, College of Engineering, Department of Aerospace Engineering, San Luis Obispo, CA 93407. Offers MS. Part-time programs available. *Faculty:* 2 full-time (0 women). *Students:* 15 full-time (2 women), 17 part-time (1 woman); includes 7 minority (all Asian, non-Hispanic/Latino). Average age 27. 36 applicants, 56% accepted, 14 enrolled. In 2010, 15 master's awarded. *Degree requirements:* For master's, thesis. *Entrance requirements:* For master's, GRE General Test, minimum GPA of 3.0 in last 90 quarter units. Additional exam requirements/recommendations for international students: Required—TOEFL (minimum score 550 paper-based; 213 computer-based) or IELTS (minimum score 6). *Application deadline:* For fall admission, 7/1 for domestic students, 11/30 for international students; for winter admission, 11/1 for domestic students, 6/30 for international students; for spring admission, 2/1 for domestic students. Applications are processed on a rolling basis. Application fee: $55. Electronic applications accepted. *Expenses:* Tuition, state resident: full-time $5386; part-time $3124 per year. Tuition, nonresident: full-time $11,160; part-time $248 per unit. Required fees: $2250; $614 per term. One-time fee: $2250 full-time; $1842 part-time. *Financial support:* Research assistantships, teaching assistantships, career-related internships or fieldwork, Federal Work-Study, scholarships/grants, and unspecified assistantships available. Support available to part-time students. Financial award application deadline: 3/2; financial award applicants required to submit FAFSA. *Faculty research:* Space systems engineering, space vehicle design, aerodynamics, aerospace propulsion, dynamics and control. *Unit head:* Dr. Jin Tso, Graduate Coordinator/Department Chair, 805-756-1391, Fax: 805-756-2376, E-mail: jtso@calpoly.edu. *Application contact:* Dr. Jin Tso, Graduate Coordinator/Department Chair, 805-756-1391, Fax: 805-756-2376, E-mail: jtso@calpoly.edu.

California State Polytechnic University, Pomona, Academic Affairs, College of Engineering, Program in Engineering, Pomona, CA 91768-2557. Offers aerospace engineering (MSE). *Students:* 17 part-time (3 women); includes 2 minority (1 Asian, non-Hispanic/Latino; 1 Hispanic/Latino). 15 applicants, 53% accepted, 8 enrolled. In 2010, 4 master's awarded. *Application deadline:* Applications are processed on a rolling basis. Application fee: $55. Electronic applications accepted. *Expenses:* Tuition, state resident: full-time $5386; part-time $2850 per year. Tuition, nonresident: full-time $12,082; part-time $248 per credit. Required fees: $577; $248 per credit. $577 per year. Tuition and fees vary according to course load and program. *Unit head:* Dr. Ali R. Ahmadi, Department Chair, 909-869-2470, E-mail: arahmadi@csupomona.edu. *Application contact:* Scott J. Duncan, Director, Admissions, 909-869-3258, E-mail: sjduncan@csupomona.edu.

California State University, Long Beach, Graduate Studies, College of Engineering, Department of Mechanical and Aerospace Engineering, Program in Aerospace Engineering, Long Beach, CA 90840. Offers MSAE. Part-time programs available. *Students:* 17 full-time (0 women), 24 part-time (4 women); includes 12 Asian, non-Hispanic/Latino; 3 Hispanic/Latino, 9 international. Average age 29. 70 applicants, 46% accepted, 13 enrolled. In 2010, 12 master's awarded. *Degree requirements:* For master's, thesis or alternative. *Entrance requirements:* Additional exam requirements/recommendations for international students: Required—TOEFL. *Application deadline:* For fall admission, 7/1 for domestic students. Application fee: $55. Electronic applications accepted. *Financial support:* Career-related internships or fieldwork, Federal Work-Study, institutionally sponsored loans, scholarships/grants, and unspecified assistantships available. Financial award application deadline: 3/2. *Faculty research:* Aerodynamic flows, ice accretion, stability and transition. *Unit head:* Dr. Hamid Hefazi, Chairman, 562-985-1563, Fax: 562-985-4408, E-mail: hefazi@csulb.edu. *Application contact:* Dr. Hsin-Piao Chen, Graduate Advisor, 562-985-1563.

Carleton University, Faculty of Graduate Studies, Faculty of Engineering and Design, Department of Mechanical and Aerospace Engineering, Ottawa, ON K1S 5B6, Canada. Offers aerospace engineering (M Eng, MA Sc, PhD); materials engineering (M Eng, MA Sc); mechanical engineering (M Eng, MA Sc, PhD). *Degree requirements:* For master's, thesis optional; for doctorate, thesis/dissertation. *Entrance requirements:* For master's, honors degree; for doctorate, MA Sc or M Eng. Additional exam requirements/recommendations for international students: Required—TOEFL. *Faculty research:* Thermal fluids engineering, heat transfer, vehicle engineering.

Case Western Reserve University, School of Graduate Studies, Case School of Engineering, Department of Mechanical and Aerospace Engineering, Cleveland, OH 44106. Offers MS, PhD, MD/PhD. Part-time programs available. Postbaccalaureate distance learning degree programs offered (no on-campus study). *Faculty:* 12 full-time (3 women). *Students:* 70 full-time (9 women), 20 part-time (4 women); includes 3 Black or African American, non-Hispanic/Latino; 2 American Indian or Alaska Native, non-Hispanic/Latino; 6 Asian, non-Hispanic/Latino; 1 Hispanic/Latino; 1 Two or more races, non-Hispanic/Latino, 33 international. In 2010, 22 master's, 1 doctorate awarded. *Degree requirements:* For master's, thesis (for some programs); for doctorate, thesis/dissertation, qualifying exam, teaching experience. *Entrance requirements:* For master's and doctorate, GRE General Test. Additional exam requirements/recommendations for international students: Required—TOEFL. *Application deadline:* For fall admission, 7/1 priority date for domestic students. Applications are processed on a rolling basis. Application fee: $50. *Financial support:* Fellowships with full and partial tuition reimbursements, research assistantships with full and partial tuition reimbursements, teaching assistantships, institutionally sponsored loans and tuition waivers (full and partial) available. Financial award application deadline: 3/1; financial award applicants required to submit FAFSA. *Faculty research:* Musculoskeletal biomechanics, combustion diagnostics and computation, mechanical behavior of advanced materials and nanostructures, biorobotics. Total annual research expenditures: $4.1 million. *Unit head:* Dr. Iwan Alexander, Department Chair, 216-368-6045, Fax: 216-368-6445, E-mail: ida2@case.edu. *Application contact:* Carla Wilson, Student Affairs Coordinator, 216-368-4580, Fax: 216-368-3007, E-mail: cxw75@case.edu.

Concordia University, School of Graduate Studies, Faculty of Engineering and Computer Science, Program in Aerospace Engineering, Montréal, QC H3G 1M8, Canada. Offers M Eng. Program offered jointly with École Polytechnique de Montréal and McGill University. *Degree requirements:* For master's, thesis or alternative. *Faculty research:* Aeronautics and propulsion avionics and control, structures and materials, space engineering.

Cornell University, Graduate School, Graduate Fields of Engineering, Field of Aerospace Engineering, Ithaca, NY 14853-0001. Offers M Eng, MS, PhD. *Faculty:* 34 full-time (5 women). *Students:* 44 full-time (9 women); includes 2 Asian, non-Hispanic/Latino; 4 Hispanic/Latino, 12 international. Average age 24. 156 applicants, 29% accepted, 27 enrolled. In 2010, 21 master's, 2 doctorates awarded. Terminal master's awarded for partial completion of doctoral program. *Degree requirements:* For master's, thesis (MS); for doctorate, one foreign language, comprehensive exam, thesis/dissertation. *Entrance requirements:* For master's and doctorate, GRE General Test, 3 letters of recommendation. Additional exam requirements/recommendations for international students: Required—TOEFL (minimum score 550 paper-based; 213 computer-based; 77 iBT). *Application deadline:* For fall admission, 1/15 for domestic students; for spring admission, 11/1 for domestic students. Application fee: $70. Electronic applications accepted. *Expenses:* Tuition: Full-time $29,500. Required fees: $76. Tuition and fees vary according to degree level and program. *Financial support:* In 2010–11, 22 students received support, including 11 fellowships with full tuition reimbursements available, 9 research assistantships with full tuition reimbursements available, 6 teaching assistantships with full tuition reimbursements available; institutionally sponsored loans, scholarships/grants, health care benefits, tuition waivers (full and partial), and unspecified assistantships also available. Financial award applicants required to submit FAFSA. *Faculty research:* Aerodynamics, fluid mechanics, turbulence, combustion/propulsion, aeroacoustics. *Unit head:* Director of Graduate Studies, 607-255-5250. *Application contact:* Graduate Field Assistant, 607-255-5250, E-mail: maegrad@cornell.edu.

École Polytechnique de Montréal, Graduate Programs, Department of Mechanical Engineering, Montréal, QC H3C 3A7, Canada. Offers aerothermics (M Eng, M Sc A, PhD); applied mechanics (M Eng, M Sc A, PhD); tool design (M Eng, M Sc A, PhD). Part-time and evening/weekend programs available. *Degree requirements:* For master's, one foreign language, thesis; for doctorate, one foreign language, thesis/dissertation. *Entrance requirements:* For master's, minimum GPA of 2.75; for doctorate, minimum GPA of 3.0. *Faculty research:* Noise control and vibration, fatigue and creep, aerodynamics, composite materials, biomechanics, robotics.

Embry-Riddle Aeronautical University–Daytona, Daytona Beach Campus Graduate Program, Department of Aerospace Engineering, Daytona Beach, FL 32114-3900. Offers aerospace engineering (MSAE); multidisciplinary engineering (MSE). Part-time programs available. *Faculty:* 8 full-time (0 women). *Students:* 110 full-time (17 women), 25 part-time (3 women); includes 19 minority (3 Black or African American, non-Hispanic/Latino; 7 Asian, non-Hispanic/Latino; 6 Hispanic/Latino; 3 Two or more races, non-Hispanic/Latino), 48 international. Average age 23. 110 applicants, 63% accepted, 37 enrolled. In 2010, 31 master's awarded. *Degree requirements:* For master's, thesis. *Entrance requirements:* For master's, BS in aeronautical engineering or equivalent; minimum GPA of 3.0 in last 2 undergraduate years, 2.5 overall. Additional exam requirements/recommendations for international students: Required—TOEFL (minimum score 550 paper-based; 213 computer-based; 79 iBT). *Application deadline:* For fall admission, 8/1 priority date for domestic students; for spring admission, 12/1 priority date for domestic students. Applications are processed on a rolling basis. Application fee: $50. Electronic applications accepted. *Expenses:* Tuition: Full-time $14,040; part-time $1170 per credit hour. *Financial support:* In 2010–11, 59 students received support, including 6 research assistantships with full and partial tuition reimbursements available (averaging $6,092 per year), 15 teaching assistantships with full and partial tuition reimbursements available (averaging $6,092 per year); career-related internships or fieldwork, Federal Work-Study, and unspecified assistantships also available. Support available to part-time students. Financial award application deadline: 4/15; financial award applicants required to submit FAFSA. *Faculty research:* Propulsion research: CFD research, composite torque research, establishing software engineering domain expertise, assessment of software tools for safety critical real-time systems, student NASA eagle eye satellite, structural blade testing support, remote airport lighting system (RALS). Total annual research expenditures: $377,487. *Unit head:* Dr. Y. Zhao, Graduate Program Coordinator, 386-226-6746, Fax: 386-226-6747, E-mail: yi.zhao@erau.edu. *Application contact:* Keith Deaton, Director, International and Graduate Admissions, 800-388-3728, Fax: 386-226-7070, E-mail: graduate.admissions@erau.edu.

Embry-Riddle Aeronautical University–Daytona, Daytona Beach Campus Graduate Program, Department of Applied Aviation Sciences, Daytona Beach, FL 32114-3900. Offers MSA. Part-time and evening/weekend programs available. *Faculty:* 8 full-time (0 women), 5 part-time/adjunct (0 women). *Students:* 118 full-time (34 women), 28 part-time (8 women); includes 29 minority (11 Black or African American, non-Hispanic/Latino; 8 Asian, non-Hispanic/Latino; 9 Hispanic/Latino; 1 Two or more races, non-Hispanic/Latino), 35 international. Average age 26. 97 applicants, 70% accepted, 46 enrolled. In 2010, 20 master's awarded. *Degree requirements:* For master's, thesis optional. *Entrance requirements:* For master's, minimum GPA of 2.5. Additional exam requirements/recommendations for international students: Required—TOEFL (minimum score 550 paper-based; 213 computer-based; 79 iBT). *Application deadline:* For fall admission, 8/1 priority date for domestic students; for spring admission, 12/1 priority date for domestic students. Applications are processed on a rolling basis. Application fee: $50. Electronic applications accepted. *Expenses:* Tuition: Full-time $14,040; part-time $1170 per credit hour. *Financial support:* In 2010–11, 26 students received support, including 11 research assistantships with full and partial tuition reimbursements available (averaging $5,460 per year), 1 teaching assistantship with full and partial tuition reimbursement available (averaging $5,256 per year); career-related internships or fieldwork, Federal Work-Study, and unspecified assistantships also available. Support available to part-time students. Financial award application deadline: 4/15; financial award applicants required to submit FAFSA. *Faculty research:* 4D flight management system trajectory-based operations, next-generation air transportation system weather research, agriculture in a changing climate, weather technology in the cockpit pilot training requirements, evolution of a companion website: an assessment of online ancillaries, environmental security research, east central Florida extreme weather events. *Unit head:* Dr. Marvin Smith, Program Coordinator, 386-226-6448, E-mail: smithm@erau.edu. *Application contact:* Keith Deaton, Director, International and Graduate Admissions, 800-388-3728, Fax: 386-226-7070, E-mail: graduate.admissions@erau.edu.

Embry-Riddle Aeronautical University–Worldwide, Worldwide Headquarters, Program in Aeronautics, Daytona Beach, FL 32114-3900. Offers MAS. Part-time and evening/weekend programs available. Postbaccalaureate distance learning degree programs offered (minimal on-campus study). *Faculty:* 2 full-time (0 women), 14 part-time/adjunct (4 women). *Students:* 1,712 full-time (252 women), 1,841 part-time (212 women); includes 620 minority (223 Black or African American, non-Hispanic/Latino; 19 American Indian or Alaska Native, non-Hispanic/Latino; 102 Asian, non-Hispanic/Latino; 233 Hispanic/Latino; 5 Native Hawaiian or other Pacific Islander, non-Hispanic/Latino; 38 Two or more races, non-Hispanic/Latino), 19 international. Average age 33. 867 applicants, 81% accepted, 554 enrolled. In 2010, 784 master's awarded. *Degree requirements:* For master's, thesis optional. *Application deadline:* Applications are processed on a rolling basis. Application fee: $50. Electronic applications accepted. *Financial support:* In 2010–11, 861 students received support. Available to part-time students. Applicants required to submit FAFSA. *Unit head:* Dr. Katherine A. Moran, Chair, 360-597-4560, E-mail: morank@erau.edu. *Application contact:* Linda Dammer, Director of Admissions, 386-226-6396 Ext. 1, Fax: 386-226-6984, E-mail: worldwide@erau.edu.

Florida Institute of Technology, Graduate Programs, College of Aeronautics, Melbourne, FL 32901-6975. Offers airport development and management (MSA); applied aviation safety option (MSA); aviation human factors (MS); human factors in aeronautics (MS). Part-time and evening/weekend programs available. *Faculty:* 9 full-time (0 women). *Students:* 23 full-time (3 women), 11 part-time (3 women); includes 3 minority (2 Asian, non-Hispanic/Latino; 1 Hispanic/Latino), 15 international. Average age 26. 36 applicants, 53% accepted, 9 enrolled. In 2010, 15 master's awarded. *Degree requirements:* For master's, thesis (for some programs). *Entrance requirements:* For master's, GRE, minimum GPA of 3.0, 3 letters of recommendation, resume, statement of objectives. Additional exam requirements/recommendations for international students: Required—TOEFL (minimum score 550 paper-based; 213 computer-based; 79 iBT). *Application deadline:* For fall admission, 4/1 for international students; for spring admission, 9/30 for international students. Applications are processed on a rolling basis. Application fee: $50. Electronic applications accepted. *Expenses:* Tuition: Part-time $1040 per credit hour. Tuition and fees vary according to campus/location. *Financial support:* Career-related internships or fieldwork, institutionally sponsored loans, tuition waivers (partial), and tuition remissions available. Support available to part-time students. Financial award application deadline: 3/1; financial award applicants required to submit FAFSA. *Faculty research:* Aircraft cockpit design, medical human factors, operating room human factors, hypobaric chamber operations and effects, aviation professional education. Total annual research expenditures: $98,763. *Unit head:* Dr. Winston E. Scott, Dean, 321-674-8971, Fax: 321-674-7368, E-mail: wscott@fit.edu. *Application contact:* Cheryl A. Brown, Associate Director of Graduate Admissions, 321-674-7581, Fax: 321-723-9468, E-mail: cbrown@fit.edu.

Florida Institute of Technology, Graduate Programs, College of Engineering, Mechanical and Aerospace Engineering Department, Melbourne, FL 32901-6975. Offers aerospace engineering (MS, PhD); mechanical engineering (MS, PhD). Part-time programs available. *Faculty:* 13 full-time (0 women). *Students:* 59 full-time (3 women), 30 part-time (5 women); includes 7 minority (1 Black or African American, non-Hispanic/Latino; 1 Asian, non-Hispanic/Latino; 4 Hispanic/Latino; 1 Two or more races, non-Hispanic/Latino), 47 international. Average age 26. 183 applicants, 47% accepted, 24 enrolled. In 2010, 24 master's awarded. Terminal master's awarded for partial completion of doctoral program. *Degree requirements:* For master's, comprehensive exam (for some programs), thesis optional; for doctorate, comprehensive exam, thesis/dissertation, oral section of written exam, complete program of significant original research. *Entrance requirements:* For master's, GRE General Test, minimum GPA of 3.0, bachelor's degree from an ABET-accredited program, transcripts; for doctorate, GRE General Test, 3 letters of recommendation, minimum GPA of 3.2, resume, statement of objectives. Additional exam requirements/recommendations for international students: Required—TOEFL (minimum score 550 paper-based; 213 computer-based; 79 iBT). *Application deadline:* For fall admission, 4/1 for international students; for spring admission, 9/30 for international students. Applications are processed on a rolling basis. Application fee: $50. Electronic applications accepted. *Expenses:* Tuition: Part-time $1040 per credit hour. Tuition and fees vary according to campus/location. *Financial support:* In 2010–11, 4 research assistantships with full and partial tuition reimbursements (averaging $3,310 per year), 14 teaching assistantships with full and partial tuition reimbursements (averaging $2,362 per year) were awarded; career-related internships or fieldwork, institutionally sponsored loans, tuition waivers (partial), unspecified assistantships, and tuition remissions also available. Support available to part-time students. Financial award application deadline: 3/1; financial award applicants required to submit FAFSA. *Faculty research:* Dynamic systems, robotics, and controls; structures, solid mechanics, and materials; thermal-fluid sciences, optical tomography, composite/recycled materials. Total annual research expenditures: $924,059. *Unit head:* Dr. Pei-feng Hsu, Department Head, 321-674-8092, Fax: 321-674-8813, E-mail: phsu@fit.edu. *Application contact:* Cheryl A. Brown, Associate Director of Graduate Admissions, 321-674-7581, Fax: 321-723-9468, E-mail: cbrown@fit.edu.

Florida Institute of Technology, Graduate Programs, Extended Studies Division, Melbourne, FL 32901-6975. Offers acquisition and contract management (MS); aerospace engineering (MS); business administration (MBA); computer information systems (MS); computer science (MS); electrical engineering (MS); engineering management (MS); human resources management (MS); logistics management (MS), including humanitarian and disaster relief logistics; management (MS), including acquisition and contract management, e-business, human resources management, information systems, logistics management, management, transportation management; material acquisition management (MS); mechanical engineering (MS); operations research (MS); project management (MS), including information systems, operations research; public administration (MPA); quality management (MS); software engineering (MS); space systems (MS); space systems management (MS); systems management (MS), including information systems, operations research. Part-time and evening/weekend programs available. Postbaccalaureate distance learning degree programs offered (no on-campus study). *Faculty:* 11 full-time (3 women), 118 part-time/adjunct (24 women). *Students:* 69 full-time (23 women), 907 part-time (369 women); includes 385 minority (242 Black or African American, non-Hispanic/Latino; 15 American Indian or Alaska Native, non-Hispanic/Latino; 44 Asian, non-Hispanic/Latino; 52 Hispanic/Latino; 3 Native Hawaiian or other Pacific Islander, non-Hispanic/Latino; 29 Two or more races, non-Hispanic/Latino), 17 international. 517 applicants, 49% accepted, 245 enrolled. In 2010, 430 degrees awarded. *Degree requirements:* For master's, comprehensive exam (for some programs), capstone course. *Entrance requirements:* For master's, GMAT or resume showing 8 years of supervised experience, minimum GPA of 3.0, 2 letters of recommendation, resume. Additional exam requirements/recommendations for international students: Required—TOEFL (minimum score 550 paper-based; 213 computer-based; 79 iBT). *Application deadline:* For fall admission, 4/1 for international students; for spring admission, 9/30 for international students. Applications are processed on a rolling basis. Application fee: $50. Electronic applications accepted. *Expenses:* Contact institution. *Financial support:* Application deadline: 3/1. *Unit head:* Dr. Theodore Richardson, Senior Associate Dean, 321-674-8123, Fax: 321-674-7597, E-mail: trichardson@fit.edu. *Application contact:* Carolyn Farrior, Director of Graduate Admissions, Online Learning and Off-Campus Programs, 321-674-7118, Fax: 321-674-8216, E-mail: cfarrior@fit.edu.

The George Washington University, School of Engineering and Applied Science, Department of Mechanical and Aerospace Engineering, Washington, DC 20052. Offers MS, D Sc, App Sc, Engr, Graduate Certificate. Part-time and evening/weekend programs available. *Faculty:* 13 full-time (1 woman), 14 part-time/adjunct (2 women). *Students:* 45 full-time (13 women), 28 part-time (3 women); includes 4 Black or African American, non-Hispanic/Latino; 1 American Indian or Alaska Native, non-Hispanic/Latino; 5 Asian, non-Hispanic/Latino; 3 Hispanic/Latino, 27 international. Average age 28. 95 applicants, 84% accepted, 19 enrolled. In 2010, 11 master's, 4 doctorates, 1 other advanced degree awarded. *Degree requirements:* For master's, thesis optional; for doctorate, thesis/dissertation, final and qualifying exams. *Entrance requirements:* For master's, appropriate bachelor's degree, minimum GPA of 3.0; for doctorate, appropriate bachelor's or master's degree, minimum GPA of 3.4, GRE if highest earned degree is BS; for other advanced degree, appropriate master's degree, minimum GPA of 3.0. Additional exam requirements/recommendations for international students: Required—TOEFL or The George Washington University English as a Foreign Language Test. *Application deadline:* For fall admission, 3/1 priority date for domestic students; for spring admission, 10/1 for domestic students. Applications are processed on a rolling basis. Application fee: $75. *Financial support:* In 2010–11, 51 students received support; fellowships with tuition reimbursements available, research assistantships, teaching assistantships with tuition reimbursements available, career-related internships or fieldwork and institutionally sponsored loans available. Financial award application deadline: 3/1; financial award applicants required to submit FAFSA. *Unit head:* Dr. Michael Plesniak, Chairman, 202-994-6749, E-mail: maeng@gwu.edu. *Application contact:* Adina Lav, Marketing, Recruiting and Admissions, 202-994-5827, Fax: 202-994-0909, E-mail: engineering@gwu.edu.

Georgia Institute of Technology, Graduate Studies and Research, College of Engineering, School of Aerospace Engineering, Atlanta, GA 30332-0001. Offers MS, MSAE, PhD. Part-time programs available. Terminal master's awarded for partial completion of doctoral program. *Degree requirements:* For master's, thesis optional; for doctorate, thesis/dissertation. *Entrance requirements:* For master's, GRE, minimum GPA of 3.0; for doctorate, GRE, minimum GPA of 3.25. Additional exam requirements/recommendations for international students: Required—TOEFL. *Faculty research:* Structural mechanics and dynamics, fluid mechanics, flight mechanics and controls, combustion and propulsion, system design and optimization.

Illinois Institute of Technology, Graduate College, Armour College of Engineering, Department of Mechanical, Materials and Aerospace Engineering, Chicago, IL 60616-3793. Offers manufacturing engineering (MME, MS); materials science and engineering (MMME, MS, PhD); mechanical and aerospace engineering (MMAE, MS, PhD), including economics (MS), energy (MS), environment (MS). Part-time and evening/weekend programs available. Postbaccalaureate distance learning degree programs offered (minimal on-campus study). *Faculty:* 26 full-time (1 woman), 6 part-time/adjunct (1 woman). *Students:* 135 full-time (22 women), 45 part-time (4 women); includes 11 minority (1 American Indian or Alaska Native, non-Hispanic/Latino; 9 Asian, non-Hispanic/Latino; 1 Hispanic/Latino), 117 international. Average age 27. 693 applicants, 41% accepted, 63 enrolled. In 2010, 58 master's, 4 doctorates awarded. Terminal master's awarded for partial completion of doctoral program. *Degree requirements:* For master's, comprehensive exam (for some programs), thesis (for some programs); for doctorate, comprehensive exam, thesis/dissertation. *Entrance requirements:* For master's and doctorate, GRE General Test (minimum score 1000 Quantitative and Verbal, 3.0 Analytical Writing), minimum undergraduate GPA of 3.0. Additional exam requirements/recommendations for international students: Required—TOEFL (minimum score 523 paper-based; 70 iBT); Recommended—IELTS (minimum score 5.5). *Application deadline:* For fall admission, 5/1 for domestic and international students; for spring admission, 10/15 for domestic and international students. Applications are processed on a rolling basis. Application fee: $50. Electronic applications accepted. *Expenses:* Tuition: Full-time $18,576; part-time $1032 per credit hour. Required fees: $583 per semester. One-time fee: $150. Tuition and fees vary according to program and student level. *Financial support:* In 2010–11, 7 fellowships with full and partial tuition reimbursements (averaging $7,673 per year), 33 research assistantships with full and partial tuition reimbursements (averaging $8,141 per year), 15 teaching assistantships with full and partial tuition reimbursements (averaging $6,930 per year) were awarded; Federal Work-Study, institutionally sponsored loans, scholarships/grants, health care benefits, tuition waivers, and unspecified assistantships also available. Support available to part-time students. Financial award applicants required to submit FAFSA. *Faculty research:* Fluid dynamics, metallurgical and materials engineering, solids and structures, computational mechanics, theoretical mechanics. Total annual research expenditures: $2.4 million. *Unit head:* Dr. Jamal Yagoobi, Professor and Chairman, 312-567-3239, Fax: 312-567-7230, E-mail: yagoobi@iit.edu. *Application contact:* Deborah Gibson, Director, Graduate Admission, 866-472-3448, Fax: 312-567-3138, E-mail: inquiry.grad@iit.edu.

Iowa State University of Science and Technology, Graduate College, College of Engineering, Department of Aerospace Engineering and Engineering Mechanics, Ames, IA 50011. Offers aerospace engineering (M Eng, MS, PhD); engineering mechanics (M Eng, MS, PhD). *Faculty:* 34 full-time (1 woman), 3 part-time/adjunct (0 women). *Students:* 47 full-time (8 women), 12 part-time (2 women); includes 2 Asian, non-Hispanic/Latino; 1 Hispanic/Latino, 31 international. 86 applicants, 12% accepted, 5 enrolled. In 2010, 9 master's, 3 doctorates awarded. *Degree requirements:* For master's, thesis (for some programs); for doctorate, thesis/dissertation. *Entrance requirements:* For master's and doctorate, GRE General Test, resume. Additional exam requirements/recommendations for international students: Required—TOEFL (minimum score 550 paper-based; 80 iBT), IELTS (minimum score 6.5). *Application deadline:* For fall admission, 1/1 priority date for domestic and international students; for spring admission, 9/1 priority date for domestic and international students. Application fee: $40 ($90 for international students). Electronic applications accepted. *Financial support:* In 2010–11, 26 research assistantships with full and partial tuition reimbursements (averaging $6,250 per year), 18 teaching assistantships with full and partial tuition reimbursements (averaging $6,164 per year) were awarded; fellowships, scholarships/grants, health care benefits, and unspecified assistantships also available. *Unit head:* Dr. Thomas Rudolphi, Interim Chair, 515-294-5666, E-mail: aere_@iastate.edu. *Application contact:* Dr. Alric Rothmayer, Director of Graduate Education, 515-294-8851, E-mail: aere_info@iastate.edu.

Massachusetts Institute of Technology, School of Engineering, Department of Aeronautics and Astronautics, Cambridge, MA 02139-4307. Offers aeronautics and astronautics (SM, PhD, Sc D, EAA); aerospace computational engineering (PhD, Sc D); air transportation systems (PhD, Sc D); air-breathing propulsion (PhD, Sc D); aircraft systems engineering (PhD, Sc D); autonomous systems (PhD, Sc D); communications and networks (PhD, Sc D); controls (PhD, Sc D); humans in aerospace (PhD, Sc D); materials and structures (PhD, Sc D); space propulsion (PhD, Sc D); space systems (PhD, Sc D); SM/MBA. *Faculty:* 33 full-time (7 women). *Students:* 225 full-time (42 women), 1 part-time (0 women); includes 39 minority (3 Black or African American, non-Hispanic/Latino; 21 Asian, non-Hispanic/Latino; 11 Hispanic/Latino; 4 Two or more races, non-Hispanic/Latino), 88 international. Average age 26. 485 applicants, 20% accepted, 70 enrolled. In 2010, 74 master's, 13 doctorates awarded. *Degree requirements:*

Aerospace/Aeronautical Engineering

Massachusetts Institute of Technology (continued)
For master's and EAA, thesis; for doctorate, comprehensive exam, thesis/dissertation. *Entrance requirements:* For master's and doctorate, GRE General Test. Additional exam requirements/recommendations for international students: Required—TOEFL (minimum score 600 paper-based; 250 computer-based; 100 iBT), IELTS (minimum score 7). *Application deadline:* For fall admission, 12/15 for domestic and international students. Application fee: $75. Electronic applications accepted. *Expenses:* Tuition: Full-time $38,940; part-time $605 per unit. Required fees: $272. *Financial support:* In 2010–11, 204 students received support, including 51 fellowships with tuition reimbursements available (averaging $26,412 per year), 151 research assistantships with tuition reimbursements available (averaging $27,483 per year), 18 teaching assistantships with tuition reimbursements available (averaging $30,117 per year); Federal Work-Study, institutionally sponsored loans, scholarships/grants, health care benefits, and unspecified assistantships also available. *Faculty research:* Aerospace information engineering, aerospace systems engineering, aerospace vehicles engineering. Total annual research expenditures: $24.4 million. *Unit head:* Prof. Jaime Peraire, Department Head, 617-258-7537, Fax: 617-258-7566. *Application contact:* Graduate Administrator, 617-253-0043, Fax: 617-253-0823, E-mail: aa-studentservices@mit.edu.

McGill University, Faculty of Graduate and Postdoctoral Studies, Faculty of Engineering, Department of Mechanical Engineering, Montréal, QC H3A 2T5, Canada. Offers aerospace (M Eng); manufacturing management (MMM); mechanical engineering (M Eng, M Sc, PhD).

Middle Tennessee State University, College of Graduate Studies, College of Basic and Applied Sciences, Department of Aerospace, Murfreesboro, TN 37132. Offers aerospace education (M Ed); aviation administration (MS). Part-time and evening/weekend programs available. Postbaccalaureate distance learning degree programs offered. *Faculty:* 4 full-time (1 woman). *Students:* 7 full-time (0 women), 25 part-time (5 women); includes 5 Black or African American, non-Hispanic/Latino; 2 Asian, non-Hispanic/Latino. Average age 29. 15 applicants, 67% accepted, 10 enrolled. In 2010, 5 master's awarded. *Degree requirements:* For master's, one foreign language, comprehensive exam. *Entrance requirements:* For master's, GRE General Test or MAT. Additional exam requirements/recommendations for international students: Required—TOEFL (minimum score 525 paper-based; 195 computer-based; 71 iBT) or IELTS (minimum score 6). *Application deadline:* For fall admission, 6/1 for domestic and international students. Applications are processed on a rolling basis. Application fee: $25 ($30 for international students). Electronic applications accepted. *Expenses:* Tuition, state resident: full-time $4632. Tuition, nonresident: full-time $11,520. *Financial support:* In 2010–11, 4 students received support. Institutionally sponsored loans available. Support available to part-time students. Financial award application deadline: 5/1. *Unit head:* Dr. Wayne Dornan, Chair, 615-898-2788, E-mail: wdornan@mtsu.edu. *Application contact:* Dr. Wayne Dornan, Chair, 615-898-2788, E-mail: wdornan@mtsu.edu.

Mississippi State University, Bagley College of Engineering, Department of Aerospace Engineering, Mississippi State, MS 39762. Offers aerospace engineering (MS); engineering (PhD), including aerospace engineering. Part-time programs available. *Faculty:* 13 full-time (2 women), 3 part-time/adjunct (0 women). *Students:* 30 full-time (4 women), 6 part-time (1 woman); includes 2 minority (both Black or African American, non-Hispanic/Latino), 11 international. Average age 26. 38 applicants, 47% accepted, 13 enrolled. In 2010, 7 master's, 1 doctorate awarded. *Degree requirements:* For master's, comprehensive exam, thesis; for doctorate, comprehensive exam, thesis/dissertation. *Entrance requirements:* For master's, GRE, bachelor's degree in engineering; for doctorate, GRE, bachelor's or master's degree in engineering. Additional exam requirements/recommendations for international students: Required—TOEFL (minimum score 550 paper-based; 213 computer-based; 79 iBT). Recommended—IELTS (minimum score 6.5). *Application deadline:* For fall admission, 7/1 for domestic students, 5/1 for international students; for spring admission, 11/1 for domestic students, 9/1 for international students. Applications are processed on a rolling basis. Application fee: $40. Electronic applications accepted. *Expenses:* Tuition, state resident: full-time $2730.50; part-time $304 per credit hour. Tuition, nonresident: full-time $6901; part-time $767 per credit hour. *Financial support:* In 2010–11, 17 research assistantships with partial tuition reimbursements (averaging $13,627 per year), 3 teaching assistantships with partial tuition reimbursements (averaging $12,106 per year) were awarded; Federal Work-Study, institutionally sponsored loans, and unspecified assistantships also available. Financial award application deadline: 4/1; financial award applicants required to submit FAFSA. *Faculty research:* Computational fluid dynamics, flight mechanics, aerodynamics, composite structures, prototype development. Total annual research expenditures: $4.1 million. *Unit head:* Dr. Pasquale J. Cinnella, Department Head, 662-325-3623, Fax: 662-325-7730, E-mail: cinnella@ae.msstate.edu. *Application contact:* Dr. Mark Janus, Professor and Graduate Coordinator, 662-325-2463, Fax: 662-325-7730, E-mail: mark@hpc.msstate.edu.

Missouri University of Science and Technology, Graduate School, Department of Mechanical and Aerospace Engineering, Rolla, MO 65409. Offers aerospace engineering (MS, PhD); mechanical engineering (MS, DE, PhD). Part-time and evening/weekend programs available. Terminal master's awarded for partial completion of doctoral program. *Degree requirements:* For master's, thesis optional; for doctorate, comprehensive exam, thesis/dissertation. *Entrance requirements:* For master's, GRE General Test (minimum score 1100 verbal and quantitative, writing 3.5), minimum GPA of 3.0; for doctorate, GRE General Test (minimum score: verbal and quantitative 1100, writing 3.5), minimum GPA of 3.5. Additional exam requirements/recommendations for international students: Required—TOEFL. Electronic applications accepted. *Faculty research:* Dynamics and controls, acoustics, computational fluid dynamics, space mechanics, hypersonics.

Naval Postgraduate School, Graduate Programs, Space Systems Academic Group, Monterey, CA 93943. Offers space systems operations (MS). Program only open to commissioned officers of the United States and friendly nations and selected United States federal civilian employees. Part-time programs available. *Degree requirements:* For master's, thesis.

North Carolina State University, Graduate School, College of Engineering, Department of Mechanical and Aerospace Engineering, Program in Aerospace Engineering, Raleigh, NC 27695. Offers MS, PhD. Postbaccalaureate distance learning degree programs offered (no on-campus study). *Degree requirements:* For master's, thesis (for some programs), oral exam; for doctorate, thesis/dissertation, oral and preliminary exams. *Entrance requirements:* For master's and doctorate, GRE General Test. Additional exam requirements/recommendations for international students: Required—TOEFL (minimum score 550 paper-based; 213 computer-based). Electronic applications accepted. *Faculty research:* Aerodynamics, computational fluid dynamics, flight research, smart structures, propulsion.

See Display on page 533 and Close-Up on page 555.

Old Dominion University, Frank Batten College of Engineering and Technology, Programs in Aerospace Engineering, Norfolk, VA 23529. Offers ME, MS, D Eng, PhD. Part-time and evening/weekend programs available. Postbaccalaureate distance learning degree programs offered (no on-campus study). *Faculty:* 22 full-time (0 women). *Students:* 34 full-time (4 women), 43 part-time (5 women); includes 7 minority (2 Black or African American, non-Hispanic/Latino; 3 Asian, non-Hispanic/Latino; 1 Hispanic/Latino; 1 Two or more races, non-Hispanic/Latino), 34 international. Average age 28. 50 applicants, 60% accepted; 10 enrolled. In 2010, 12 master's, 4 doctorates awarded. *Degree requirements:* For master's, comprehensive exam, thesis (MS), exam/project (ME); for doctorate, thesis/dissertation, candidacy exam, proposal, exam. *Entrance requirements:* For master's, GRE, minimum GPA of 3.0; for doctorate, GRE, minimum GPA of 3.5. Additional exam requirements/recommendations for international students: Required—TOEFL (minimum score 550 paper-based; 230 computer-based; 79 iBT). *Application deadline:* For fall admission, 7/1 priority date for domestic students, 5/1 priority date for international students; for spring admission, 10/1 priority date for domestic students, 9/1 priority date for international students. Applications are processed on a rolling basis. Application fee: $50. Electronic applications accepted. *Expenses:* Tuition, state resident: full-time $8592;

part-time $358 per credit. Tuition, nonresident: full-time $21,672; part-time $903 per credit. Required fees: $119 per semester. One-time fee: $50. *Financial support:* In 2010–11, 4 students received support, including 3 fellowships with full and partial tuition reimbursements available (averaging $17,000 per year), 30 research assistantships with full and partial tuition reimbursements available (averaging $17,000 per year); career-related internships or fieldwork, scholarships/grants, and unspecified assistantships also available. Financial award application deadline: 2/15; financial award applicants required to submit FAFSA. *Faculty research:* Computational fluid dynamics, experimental fluid dynamics, structural mechanics, dynamics and control, maglev, microfluidics. Total annual research expenditures: $1.6 million. *Unit head:* Dr. Colin Britcher, Chair, 757-683-4916, Fax: 757-683-3200, E-mail: britcher@aero.odu.edu. *Application contact:* Dr. Colin Britcher, Graduate Program Director, 757-683-4916, Fax: 757-683-3200, E-mail: britcher@aero.odu.edu.

Penn State University Park, Graduate School, College of Engineering, Department of Aerospace Engineering, State College, University Park, PA 16802-1503. Offers M Eng, MS, PhD.

Polytechnic Institute of NYU, Long Island Graduate Center, Graduate Programs, Department of Mechanical and Aerospace Engineering, Melville, NY 11747. Offers aeronautics and astronautics (MS); industrial engineering (MS); manufacturing engineering (MS); mechanical engineering (MS). Part-time and evening/weekend programs available. *Students:* 1 full-time (0 women), all international. Average age 28. *Degree requirements:* For master's, comprehensive exam (for some programs), thesis (for some programs). *Entrance requirements:* Additional exam requirements/recommendations for international students: Required—TOEFL (minimum score 550 paper-based; 213 computer-based; 80 iBT); Recommended—IELTS (minimum score 6.5). *Application deadline:* For fall admission, 7/31 priority date for domestic students, 4/30 priority date for international students; for spring admission, 12/31 priority date for domestic students, 11/30 priority date for international students. Applications are processed on a rolling basis. Application fee: $75. Electronic applications accepted. *Expenses:* Tuition: Full-time $21,492; part-time $1194 per credit. Required fees: $385 per semester. Tuition and fees vary according to course load. *Financial support:* In 2010–11, 16 fellowships with tuition reimbursements (averaging $1,394 per year) were awarded; research assistantships with tuition reimbursements, institutionally sponsored loans, scholarships/grants, and unspecified assistantships also available. Support available to part-time students. Financial award applicants required to submit FAFSA. *Faculty research:* UV filter, fuel efficient hydrodynamic containment for gas core fission, turbulent boundary layer research. *Unit head:* Dr. George Vradis, Department Head, 718-260-3875, E-mail: gvradis@duke.poly.edu. *Application contact:* JeanCarlo Bonilla, Director of Graduate Enrollment Management, 718-260-3182, Fax: 718-260-3624, E-mail: gradinfo@poly.edu.

Princeton University, Graduate School, School of Engineering and Applied Science, Department of Mechanical and Aerospace Engineering, Princeton, NJ 08544. Offers M Eng, MSE, PhD. Terminal master's awarded for partial completion of doctoral program. *Degree requirements:* For master's, thesis (MSE); for doctorate, thesis/dissertation, general exam. *Entrance requirements:* For master's, GRE General Test, 3 letters of recommendation; for doctorate, GRE General Test, official transcript(s), 3 letters of recommendation, personal statement. Additional exam requirements/recommendations for international students: Required—TOEFL. Electronic applications accepted. *Faculty research:* Bioengineering and bio-mechanics; combustion, energy conversion, and climate; fluid mechanics, dynamics, and control systems; lasers and applied physics; materials and mechanical systems.

Purdue University, College of Engineering, School of Aeronautics and Astronautics Engineering, West Lafayette, IN 47907. Offers MS, MSAAE, MSE, PhD. Part-time programs available. Postbaccalaureate distance learning degree programs offered (no on-campus study). Terminal master's awarded for partial completion of doctoral program. *Entrance requirements:* For master's, GRE General Test, minimum GPA of 3.2; for doctorate, GRE General Test, minimum GPA of 3.5. Additional exam requirements/recommendations for international students: Required—TOEFL (minimum score 550 paper-based; 213 computer-based; 77 iBT), IELTS (minimum score 6.5); Recommended—TWE. Electronic applications accepted. *Faculty research:* Structures and materials, propulsion, aerodynamics, dynamics and control.

Rensselaer Polytechnic Institute, Graduate School, School of Engineering, Program in Aerospace Engineering, Troy, NY 12180-3590. Offers M Eng, MS, PhD. Part-time programs available. *Faculty:* 10 full-time (0 women). *Students:* 17 full-time (2 women), 1 part-time (0 women); includes 1 Hispanic/Latino, 2 international. Average age 27. 35 applicants, 40% accepted, 6 enrolled. *Degree requirements:* For master's, thesis (for some programs); for doctorate, thesis/dissertation. *Entrance requirements:* For master's and doctorate, GRE. Additional exam requirements/recommendations for international students: Required—TOEFL (minimum score 600 paper-based; 250 computer-based; 100 iBT); Recommended—IELTS. *Application deadline:* For fall admission, 1/15 priority date for domestic and international students; for spring admission, 1/15 for domestic students, 1/15 priority date for international students. Applications are processed on a rolling basis. Application fee: $75. Electronic applications accepted. *Expenses:* Tuition: Full-time $39,600; part-time $1650 per credit. Required fees: $1896. *Financial support:* In 2010–11, 16 students received support, including 3 fellowships with full tuition reimbursements available (averaging $25,000 per year), 9 research assistantships with full tuition reimbursements available (averaging $17,500 per year), 6 teaching assistantships with full tuition reimbursements available (averaging $17,500 per year); unspecified assistantships also available. Financial award application deadline: 2/1. *Faculty research:* Vehicular performance and flight mechanics, gas dynamics, aerodynamics, structural dynamics, advanced propulsion, fluids. Total annual research expenditures: $3.4 million. *Unit head:* Dr. Timothy Wei, Head, 518-276-6351, Fax: 518-276-6025, E-mail: weit@rpi.edu. *Application contact:* Dr. Thierry A. Blanchet, Associate Chair for Graduate Studies, 518-276-8697, Fax: 518-276-2623, E-mail: blanct@rpi.edu.

Rutgers, The State University of New Jersey, New Brunswick, Graduate School-New Brunswick, Program in Mechanical and Aerospace Engineering, Piscataway, NJ 08854-8097. Offers design and control (MS, PhD); fluid mechanics (MS, PhD); solid mechanics (MS, PhD); thermal sciences (MS, PhD). Part-time and evening/weekend programs available. *Degree requirements:* For master's, thesis (for some programs); for doctorate, thesis/dissertation. *Entrance requirements:* For master's, GRE General Test, BS in mechanical/aerospace engineering or related field; for doctorate, GRE General Test, MS in mechanical/aerospace engineering or related field. Additional exam requirements/recommendations for international students: Required—TOEFL. Electronic applications accepted. *Expenses:* Tuition, state resident: full-time $7200; part-time $600 per credit. Tuition, nonresident: full-time $11,124; part-time $927 per credit. *Faculty research:* Combustion, propulsion, thermal transport, crystal plasticity, optimization, fabrication, nanoidentation.

San Diego State University, Graduate and Research Affairs, College of Engineering, Department of Aerospace Engineering and Engineering Mechanics, San Diego, CA 92182. Offers aerospace engineering (MS); engineering mechanics (MS); engineering sciences and applied mechanics (PhD); flight dynamics (MS); fluid dynamics (MS). PhD offered jointly with University of California, San Diego and Department of Mechanical Engineering. Terminal master's awarded for partial completion of doctoral program. *Degree requirements:* For master's, comprehensive exam (for some programs), thesis (for some programs); for doctorate, thesis/dissertation. *Entrance requirements:* For master's, GRE General Test; for doctorate, GRE, 3 letters of recommendation. Additional exam requirements/recommendations for international students: Required—TOEFL. Electronic applications accepted. *Faculty research:* Organized structures in post-stall flow over wings/three dimensional separated flow, airfoil growth effect, probabilities, structural mechanics.

San Jose State University, Graduate Studies and Research, Charles W. Davidson College of Engineering, Department of Mechanical and Aerospace Engineering, Program in Aerospace Engineering, San Jose, CA 95192-0001. Offers MS. *Entrance requirements:* For master's, GRE. Electronic applications accepted.

Stanford University, School of Engineering, Department of Aeronautics and Astronautics, Stanford, CA 94305-9991. Offers MS, PhD, Eng. Terminal master's awarded for partial completion of doctoral program. *Degree requirements:* For doctorate, thesis/dissertation; for Eng, thesis. *Entrance requirements:* For master's and Eng, GRE General Test, GRE Subject Test; for doctorate, GRE General Test, GRE Engineering Subject Test. Additional exam requirements/recommendations for international students: Required—TOEFL. Electronic applications accepted. *Expenses:* Tuition: Full-time $38,700; part-time $860 per unit. One-time fee: $200 full-time.

Stevens Institute of Technology, Graduate School, School of Systems and Enterprises, Program in Space Systems Engineering, Hoboken, NJ 07030. Offers M Eng, Certificate. *Students:* 1 full-time (0 women), 5 part-time (2 women); includes 1 Black or African American, non-Hispanic/Latino; 1 Asian, non-Hispanic/Latino. Average age 30. *Unit head:* Dr. Charles L. Suffel, Dean of the Graduate School, 201-216-5234, Fax: 201-216-8044, E-mail: csuffel@stevens-tech.edu. *Application contact:* Graduate Admissions, 800-496-4935, Fax: 201-216-8044, E-mail: gradadmissions@stevens.edu.

Syracuse University, L. C. Smith College of Engineering and Computer Science, Program in Mechanical and Aerospace Engineering, Syracuse, NY 13244. Offers MS, PhD. *Students:* 97 full-time (17 women), 15 part-time (2 women); includes 10 minority (1 Black or African American, non-Hispanic/Latino; 6 Asian, non-Hispanic/Latino; 3 Hispanic/Latino), 78 international. Average age 26. 155 applicants, 57% accepted, 43 enrolled. In 2010, 15 master's, 3 doctorates awarded. *Degree requirements:* For master's, project or thesis; for doctorate, thesis/dissertation. *Entrance requirements:* For master's and doctorate, GRE General Test. Additional exam requirements/recommendations for international students: Required—TOEFL (minimum score 100 iBT). *Application deadline:* For fall admission, 7/1 priority date for domestic students, 6/1 priority date for international students. Applications are processed on a rolling basis. Application fee: $75. Electronic applications accepted. *Expenses:* Tuition: Part-time $1162 per credit. *Financial support:* Fellowships with full tuition reimbursements, research assistantships with full and partial tuition reimbursements, teaching assistantships with full and partial tuition reimbursements, scholarships/grants and tuition waivers (partial) available. Financial award application deadline: 1/1. *Faculty research:* Solid mechanics and materials, fluid mechanics, thermal sciences, controls and robotics. *Unit head:* Dr. Alan Levy, Chair, 315-443-4311, Fax: 315-443-9099. *Application contact:* Kathy Datthyn-Madigan, Information Contact, 315-443-4367, E-mail: kjdatthy@syr.edu.

Texas A&M University, College of Engineering, Department of Aerospace Engineering, College Station, TX 77843. Offers M Eng, MS, PhD. *Faculty:* 29. *Students:* 131 full-time (20 women), 12 part-time (2 women); includes 15 minority (1 Black or African American, non-Hispanic/Latino; 5 Asian, non-Hispanic/Latino; 9 Hispanic/Latino), 50 international. Average age 27. In 2010, 26 master's, 10 doctorates awarded. *Degree requirements:* For master's, thesis (MS); for doctorate, thesis/dissertation. *Entrance requirements:* For master's and doctorate, GRE General Test. Additional exam requirements/recommendations for international students: Required—TOEFL. *Application deadline:* For fall admission, 1/15 priority date for domestic students; for spring admission, 9/15 for domestic students. Applications are processed on a rolling basis. Application fee: $50 ($75 for international students). Electronic applications accepted. *Financial support:* Fellowships, research assistantships, teaching assistantships available. Financial award application deadline: 3/1; financial award applicants required to submit FAFSA. *Faculty research:* Materials and structures, aerodynamics and CFD, flight dynamics and control. *Unit head:* Dr. Walter Haisler, Head, 979-854-1640, E-mail: haisler@tamu.edu. *Application contact:* Karen Knabe, Administrative Coordinator, Graduate Program, 979-845-5520, Fax: 979-845-6051.

Université Laval, Faculty of Sciences and Engineering, Department of Mechanical Engineering, Program in Aerospace Engineering, Québec, QC G1K 7P4, Canada. Offers M Sc. Program offered jointly with Concordia University, École Polytechnique de Montréal, McGill University, and Université de Sherbrooke. Part-time programs available. *Entrance requirements:* For master's, knowledge of French and English. Electronic applications accepted.

University at Buffalo, the State University of New York, Graduate School, School of Engineering and Applied Sciences, Department of Mechanical and Aerospace Engineering, Buffalo, NY 14260. Offers aerospace engineering (ME, MS, PhD); mechanical engineering (ME, MS, PhD). Part-time programs available. *Faculty:* 29 full-time (4 women), 10 part-time/adjunct (0 women). *Students:* 184 full-time (16 women), 63 part-time (4 women); includes 3 Black or African American, non-Hispanic/Latino; 11 Asian, non-Hispanic/Latino; 3 Hispanic/Latino, 128 international. Average age 26. 848 applicants, 17% accepted, 53 enrolled. In 2010, 52 master's, 9 doctorates awarded. Terminal master's awarded for partial completion of doctoral program. *Degree requirements:* For master's, comprehensive exam, project or thesis; for doctorate, thesis/dissertation. *Entrance requirements:* For master's and doctorate, GRE General Test, GRE Subject Test. Additional exam requirements/recommendations for international students: Required—TOEFL (minimum score 79 iBT). *Application deadline:* For fall admission, 1/15 for domestic and international students; for spring admission, 9/15 for domestic and international students. Applications are processed on a rolling basis. Application fee: $50. *Financial support:* In 2010–11, 73 students received support, including 4 fellowships with full tuition reimbursements available (averaging $28,900 per year), 17 research assistantships with full tuition reimbursements available (averaging $24,000 per year), 30 teaching assistantships with full tuition reimbursements available (averaging $20,900 per year); Federal Work-Study, institutionally sponsored loans, tuition waivers (partial), and unspecified assistantships also available. Financial award application deadline: 1/15; financial award applicants required to submit FAFSA. *Faculty research:* Fluid and thermal sciences, systems and design, mechanics and materials. Total annual research expenditures: $5.5 million. *Unit head:* Dr. Gary Dargush, Chair, 716-645-2593, Fax: 716-645-2883, E-mail: gdargush@buffalo.edu. *Application contact:* Dr. Susan Hua, Director of Graduate Studies, 716-645-1471, Fax: 716-645-3875, E-mail: zhua@.buffalo.edu.

The University of Alabama, Graduate School, College of Engineering, Department of Aerospace Engineering and Mechanics, Tuscaloosa, AL 35487. Offers aerospace engineering (MAE); engineering science and mechanics (MES, PhD). Part-time programs available. Post-baccalaureate distance learning degree programs offered (no on-campus study). *Faculty:* 14 full-time (1 woman). *Students:* 14 full-time (3 women), 35 part-time (5 women); includes 2 minority (both Hispanic/Latino), 17 international. Average age 29. 47 applicants, 72% accepted, 11 enrolled. In 2010, 10 master's, 4 doctorates awarded. Terminal master's awarded for partial completion of doctoral program. *Degree requirements:* For master's, comprehensive exam (for some programs), thesis (for some programs); for doctorate, comprehensive exam, thesis/dissertation, 1 year residency. *Entrance requirements:* For master's and doctorate, GRE, minimum undergraduate GPA of 3.0. Additional exam requirements/recommendations for international students: Required—TOEFL (minimum score 550 paper-based). *Application deadline:* For fall admission, 7/1 priority date for domestic students, 1/15 priority date for international students; for spring admission, 11/1 priority date for domestic students, 6/1 priority date for international students. Applications are processed on a rolling basis. Application fee: $50 ($60 for international students). Electronic applications accepted. *Expenses:* Tuition, state resident: full-time $7900. Tuition, nonresident: full-time $20,500. *Financial support:* In 2010–11, 18 students received support, including fellowships with full tuition reimbursements available (averaging $20,000 per year), research assistantships with full tuition reimbursements available (averaging $18,375 per year), teaching assistantships with full tuition reimbursements available (averaging $18,375 per year); Federal Work-Study, institutionally sponsored loans, scholarships/grants, health care benefits, and unspecified assistantships also available. Financial award application deadline: 2/15. *Faculty research:* Intelligent computer systems, genetic algorithms, neural networks, impact and penetration mechanics, spacecraft dynamics and controls. Total annual research expenditures: $959,591. *Unit head:* Dr. Stanley E. Jones, Interim Department Head and Cudworth Professor, 205-348-7242, Fax: 205-348-7240, E-mail: sejones@eng.ua.edu. *Application contact:* Dr. John E. Jackson, Professor, 205-348-7306, Fax: 208-348-7240, E-mail: johnjackson@eng.ua.edu.

The University of Alabama in Huntsville, School of Graduate Studies, College of Engineering, Department of Mechanical and Aerospace Engineering, Huntsville, AL 35899. Offers aerospace engineering (MSE), including missile systems engineering, rotorcraft systems engineering; aerospace systems engineering (MS, PhD); mechanical engineering (MSE, PhD). Part-time and evening/weekend programs available. *Faculty:* 19 full-time (1 woman), 4 part-time/adjunct (1 woman). *Students:* 50 full-time (10 women), 126 part-time (18 women); includes 15 minority (4 Black or African American, non-Hispanic/Latino; 2 American Indian or Alaska Native, non-Hispanic/Latino; 5 Asian, non-Hispanic/Latino; 4 Hispanic/Latino), 12 international. Average age 30. 134 applicants, 69% accepted, 59 enrolled. In 2010, 31 master's, 1 doctorate awarded. *Degree requirements:* For master's, comprehensive exam, thesis or alternative, oral and written exams; for doctorate, comprehensive exam, thesis/dissertation, oral and written exams. *Entrance requirements:* For master's, GRE General Test, BSE, minimum GPA of 3.0; for doctorate, GRE General Test, minimum GPA of 3.0. Additional exam requirements/recommendations for international students: Required—TOEFL (minimum score 500 paper-based; 173 computer-based; 62 iBT). *Application deadline:* For fall admission, 7/15 for domestic students, 4/1 for international students; for spring admission, 1/30 for domestic students, 9/1 for international students. Applications are processed on a rolling basis. Application fee: $40 ($50 for international students). Electronic applications accepted. *Expenses:* Tuition, state resident: full-time $7250; part-time $407.75 per credit hour. Tuition, nonresident: full-time $17,358; part-time $970.05 per credit hour. Required fees: $246.80 per semester. Tuition and fees vary according to course load and program. *Financial support:* In 2010–11, 34 students received support, including 19 research assistantships with full tuition reimbursements available (averaging $12,545 per year), 15 teaching assistantships with full tuition reimbursements available (averaging $10,840 per year); career-related internships or fieldwork, Federal Work-Study, institutionally sponsored loans, scholarships/grants, health care benefits, and unspecified assistantships also available. Support available to part-time students. Financial award application deadline: 4/1; financial award applicants required to submit FAFSA. *Faculty research:* Combustion, fluid dynamics, materials and structures, propulsion, laser diagnostics. Total annual research expenditures: $20.8 million. *Unit head:* Dr. Robert Frederick, Interim Chair, 256-824-7200, Fax: 256-824-6758, E-mail: robert.frederick@uah.edu. *Application contact:* Kathy Biggs, Graduate Studies Admissions Manager, 256-824-6199, Fax: 256-824-6405, E-mail: deangrad@uah.edu.

The University of Arizona, College of Engineering, Department of Aerospace and Mechanical Engineering, Program in Aerospace Engineering, Tucson, AZ 85721. Offers MS, PhD. Part-time programs available. *Students:* 26 full-time (2 women), 9 part-time (1 woman); includes 1 Black or African American, non-Hispanic/Latino; 1 Hispanic/Latino; 2 Two or more races, non-Hispanic/Latino, 11 international. Average age 27. 37 applicants, 68% accepted, 17 enrolled. In 2010, 6 master's, 1 doctorate awarded. *Degree requirements:* For master's, thesis or alternative; for doctorate, thesis/dissertation. *Entrance requirements:* For master's and doctorate, GRE General Test, minimum GPA of 3.25. Additional exam requirements/recommendations for international students: Required—TOEFL (minimum score 550 paper-based; 213 computer-based; 79 iBT). *Application deadline:* For fall admission, 6/1 for domestic students, 12/1 for international students; for spring admission, 10/1 for domestic students, 6/1 for international students. Applications are processed on a rolling basis. Application fee: $75. Electronic applications accepted. *Expenses:* Tuition, state resident: full-time $7692. *Financial support:* Research assistantships, teaching assistantships, unspecified assistantships available. *Faculty research:* Fluid mechanics, structures, computer-aided design, stability and control, combustion. *Unit head:* Dr. Ara Arabyan, Interim Department Head, 520-621-2116, Fax: 520-621-8191, E-mail: arabyan@email.arizona.edu. *Application contact:* Barbara Heefner, Graduate Secretary, 520-621-4692, Fax: 520-621-8191, E-mail: heefner@email.arizona.edu.

University of California, Davis, College of Engineering, Program in Mechanical and Aeronautical Engineering, Davis, CA 95616. Offers aeronautical engineering (M Engr, MS, D Engr, PhD, Certificate); mechanical engineering (M Engr, MS, D Engr, PhD, Certificate); M Engr/MBA. *Degree requirements:* For master's, comprehensive exam (for some programs), thesis (for some programs); for doctorate, thesis/dissertation. *Entrance requirements:* For master's and doctorate, GRE General Test, minimum GPA of 3.0. Additional exam requirements/recommendations for international students: Required—TOEFL (minimum score 550 paper-based; 213 computer-based). Electronic applications accepted.

University of California, Irvine, School of Engineering, Department of Mechanical and Aerospace Engineering, Irvine, CA 92697. Offers MS, PhD. Part-time programs available. *Students:* 125 full-time (19 women), 13 part-time (3 women); includes 38 minority (25 Asian, non-Hispanic/Latino; 12 Hispanic/Latino; 1 Two or more races, non-Hispanic/Latino), 57 international. Average age 28. 399 applicants, 35% accepted, 43 enrolled. In 2010, 31 master's, 11 doctorates awarded. Terminal master's awarded for partial completion of doctoral program. *Degree requirements:* For doctorate, thesis/dissertation. *Entrance requirements:* For master's and doctorate, GRE General Test, minimum GPA of 3.0, 3 letters of recommendation. Additional exam requirements/recommendations for international students: Required—TOEFL (minimum score 550 paper-based; 213 computer-based). *Application deadline:* For fall admission, 1/15 priority date for domestic students, 1/15 for international students. Applications are processed on a rolling basis. Application fee: $80 ($100 for international students). Electronic applications accepted. *Financial support:* Fellowships with tuition reimbursements, research assistantships with full tuition reimbursements, teaching assistantships with tuition reimbursements, institutionally sponsored loans, traineeships, health care benefits, and unspecified assistantships available. Financial award application deadline: 3/1; financial award applicants required to submit FAFSA. *Faculty research:* Thermal and fluid sciences, combustion and propulsion, control systems, robotics, lightweight structures. *Unit head:* Prof. Derek Dunn-Rankin, Chair, 949-824-8745, Fax: 949-824-8585, E-mail: ddunnran@uci.edu. *Application contact:* Lousie Yeager, Graduate Coordinator, 949-824-7984, Fax: 949-824-8585, E-mail: lyeager@uci.edu.

University of California, Los Angeles, Graduate Division, Henry Samueli School of Engineering and Applied Science, Department of Mechanical and Aerospace Engineering, Program in Aerospace Engineering, Los Angeles, CA 90095-1597. Offers MS, PhD. *Faculty:* 31 full-time (2 women). *Students:* 64 full-time (9 women); includes 1 Black or African American, non-Hispanic/Latino; 18 Asian, non-Hispanic/Latino; 5 Hispanic/Latino; 1 Native Hawaiian or other Pacific Islander, non-Hispanic/Latino, 5 international. 132 applicants, 58% accepted, 26 enrolled. In 2010, 13 master's, 5 doctorates awarded. *Degree requirements:* For master's, comprehensive exam or thesis; for doctorate, thesis/dissertation, qualifying exams. *Entrance requirements:* For master's, GRE General Test, minimum GPA of 3.0; for doctorate, GRE General Test, minimum GPA of 3.25. Additional exam requirements/recommendations for international students: Required—TOEFL (minimum score 560 paper-based; 87 iBT). *Application deadline:* For fall admission, 12/15 for domestic and international students; for winter admission, 10/1 for domestic students; for spring admission, 12/31 for domestic students. Application fee: $70 ($90 for international students). Electronic applications accepted. *Financial support:* Fellowships, research assistantships, teaching assistantships, Federal Work-Study, institutionally sponsored loans, and tuition waivers (full and partial) available. Financial award application deadline: 12/15; financial award applicants required to submit FAFSA. *Unit head:* Dr. Adrienne Lavine, Chair, 310-825-7468. *Application contact:* Angie Castillo, Student Affairs Officer, 310-825-7793, Fax: 310-206-4830, E-mail: angie@ea.ucla.edu.

University of California, San Diego, Office of Graduate Studies, Department of Mechanical and Aerospace Engineering, Program in Aerospace Engineering, La Jolla, CA 92093. Offers MS, PhD. Part-time programs available. *Degree requirements:* For master's, comprehensive exam or thesis; for doctorate, thesis/dissertation, qualifying exam. *Entrance requirements:* For master's and doctorate, GRE General Test, minimum GPA of 3.0. Additional exam requirements/recommendations for international students: Required—TOEFL. *Faculty research:* Aerospace structures, turbulence, gas dynamics and combustion.

University of Central Florida, College of Engineering and Computer Science, Department of Mechanical, Materials, and Aerospace Engineering, Program in Aerospace Engineering, Orlando, FL 32816. Offers MSAE. *Students:* 17 full-time (2 women), 10 part-time (1 woman); includes 2

Aerospace/Aeronautical Engineering

University of Central Florida (continued)
Black or African American, non-Hispanic/Latino; 4 Hispanic/Latino, 1 international. Average age 25. 31 applicants, 74% accepted, 10 enrolled. In 2010, 7 master's awarded. *Degree requirements:* For master's, thesis or alternative. *Application deadline:* For fall admission, 7/15 priority date for domestic students; for spring admission, 12/1 priority date for domestic students. Application fee: $30. Electronic applications accepted. *Expenses:* Tuition, state resident: part-time $256.56 per credit hour. Tuition, nonresident: part-time $1011.52 per credit hour. Part-time tuition and fees vary according to program. *Financial support:* In 2010–11, 8 students received support, including 1 fellowship (averaging $10,000 per year), 3 research assistantships (averaging $8,700 per year), 5 teaching assistantships (averaging $11,500 per year); career-related internships or fieldwork, institutionally sponsored loans, scholarships/grants, tuition waivers (partial), and unspecified assistantships also available.

University of Central Missouri, The Graduate School, College of Science and Technology, Warrensburg, MO 64093. Offers applied mathematics (MS); aviation safety (MS); biology (MS); computer science (MS); environmental studies (MA); industrial management (MS); mathematics (MS); technology (MS); technology management (PhD). PhD is offered jointly with Indiana State University. Part-time programs available. Postbaccalaureate distance learning degree programs offered. *Entrance requirements:* Additional exam requirements/recommendations for international students: Required—TOEFL (minimum score 550 paper-based; 79 computer-based). Electronic applications accepted.

University of Cincinnati, Graduate School, College of Engineering, Department of Aerospace Engineering and Engineering Mechanics, Cincinnati, OH 45221. Offers MS, PhD. Part-time programs available. Terminal master's awarded for partial completion of doctoral program. *Degree requirements:* For master's, project or thesis; for doctorate, thesis/dissertation. *Entrance requirements:* For master's and doctorate, GRE General Test. Additional exam requirements/recommendations for international students: Required—TOEFL (minimum score 550 paper-based; 213 computer-based). Electronic applications accepted. *Faculty research:* Computational fluid mechanics/propulsion, large space structures, dynamics and guidance of VTOL vehicles.

University of Colorado at Colorado Springs, College of Engineering and Applied Science, Department of Mechanical and Aerospace Engineering, Colorado Springs, CO 80933-7150. Offers engineering management (ME); information operations (ME); manufacturing (ME); mechanical engineering (MS); software engineering (ME); space operations (ME); space systems (MS). Part-time and evening/weekend programs available. *Faculty:* 10 full-time (2 women). *Students:* 56 full-time (11 women), 26 part-time (6 women); includes 3 Black or African American, non-Hispanic/Latino; 4 Asian, non-Hispanic/Latino; 3 Hispanic/Latino, 1 international. Average age 32. 33 applicants, 76% accepted, 19 enrolled. In 2010, 26 master's awarded. *Degree requirements:* For master's, thesis optional. *Entrance requirements:* For master's, GRE General Test, bachelor's degree in engineering or related degree, minimum GPA of 3.0. Additional exam requirements/recommendations for international students: Required—TOEFL. *Application deadline:* For fall admission, 5/1 for domestic students; for spring admission, 10/1 for domestic students. Applications are processed on a rolling basis. Application fee: $60 ($75 for international students). *Expenses:* Tuition, state resident: full-time $7916. Tuition, nonresident: full-time $16,610. Tuition and fees vary according to course load, degree level, program, reciprocity agreements and student level. *Financial support:* Federal Work-Study and scholarships/grants available. Support available to part-time students. Financial award application deadline: 3/1; financial award applicants required to submit FAFSA. *Faculty research:* Neural networks, artificial intelligence, robust control, space operations, space propulsion. Total annual research expenditures: $69,367. *Unit head:* Dr. James Stevens, Chair, 719-255-3581, Fax: 719-255-3042, E-mail: jstevens@uccs.edu. *Application contact:* Siew Nylund, Academic Adviser, 719-255-3243, Fax: 719-255-3589, E-mail: snylund@eas.uccs.edu.

University of Colorado Boulder, Graduate School, College of Engineering and Applied Science, Department of Aerospace Engineering Sciences, Boulder, CO 80309. Offers MS, PhD. Postbaccalaureate distance learning degree programs offered. *Faculty:* 28 full-time (3 women). *Students:* 206 full-time (29 women), 38 part-time (8 women); includes 21 minority (3 Black or African American, non-Hispanic/Latino; 1 American Indian or Alaska Native, non-Hispanic/Latino; 10 Asian, non-Hispanic/Latino; 6 Hispanic/Latino; 1 Two or more races, non-Hispanic/Latino), 31 international. Average age 26. 224 applicants, 54 enrolled. In 2010, 50 master's, 17 doctorates awarded. Terminal master's awarded for partial completion of doctoral program. *Degree requirements:* For master's, comprehensive exam, thesis or alternative; for doctorate, comprehensive exam, thesis/dissertation. *Entrance requirements:* For master's, GRE General Test, minimum undergraduate GPA of 3.0; for doctorate, minimum undergraduate GPA of 3.25. *Application deadline:* For fall admission, 2/1 priority date for domestic students, 12/1 for international students; for spring admission, 10/1 for domestic students, 8/1 for international students. Applications are processed on a rolling basis. Application fee: $50 ($60 for international students). *Financial support:* In 2010–11, 38 fellowships (averaging $14,348 per year), 71 research assistantships with full tuition reimbursements (averaging $15,952 per year), 13 teaching assistantships with full tuition reimbursements (averaging $17,431 per year) were awarded; career-related internships or fieldwork, Federal Work-Study, and scholarships/grants also available. Support available to part-time students. Financial award application deadline: 2/1. *Faculty research:* Aerodynamics, gas dynamics and fluid mechanics; astrodynamics; atmospheric and oceanic sciences; bioengineering; computational fluid dynamics; global positioning; guidance and control. Total annual research expenditures: $13 million.

University of Dayton, Graduate School, School of Engineering, Department of Mechanical and Aerospace Engineering, Dayton, OH 45469-1300. Offers aerospace engineering (MSAE, DE, PhD); mechanical engineering (MSME, DE, PhD); renewable and clean energy (MS). Part-time programs available. Postbaccalaureate distance learning degree programs offered (no on-campus study). *Faculty:* 16 full-time (2 women), 11 part-time/adjunct (1 woman). *Students:* 113 full-time (22 women), 26 part-time (6 women); includes 15 minority (6 Black or African American, non-Hispanic/Latino; 3 Asian, non-Hispanic/Latino; 6 Hispanic/Latino), 47 international. Average age 28. 113 applicants, 84% accepted, 50 enrolled. In 2010, 30 master's, 7 doctorates awarded. Terminal master's awarded for partial completion of doctoral program. *Degree requirements:* For master's, thesis optional; for doctorate, variable foreign language requirement, thesis/dissertation, departmental qualifying exam. *Entrance requirements:* Additional exam requirements/recommendations for international students: Required—TOEFL (minimum score 550 paper-based; 213 computer-based; 80 iBT). *Application deadline:* For fall admission, 8/1 priority date for domestic students, 6/1 priority date for international students; for winter admission, 9/1 priority date for international students; for spring admission, 3/1 priority date for international students. Applications are processed on a rolling basis. Application fee: $0. Electronic applications accepted. *Expenses:* Tuition: Full-time $7800; part-time $650 per credit hour. *Financial support:* In 2010–11, 25 students received support, including 29 research assistantships with full tuition reimbursements available (averaging $11,000 per year), 7 teaching assistantships with full tuition reimbursements available (averaging $9,100 per year). Financial award applicants required to submit FAFSA. *Faculty research:* Jet engine combustion, surface coating friction and wear, aircraft thermal management, aerospace fuels, energy efficient buildings, energy efficient manufacturing, renewable energy. Total annual research expenditures: $1.2 million. *Unit head:* Dr. Kelly Kissock, Chair, 937-229-2999, Fax: 937-229-4766, E-mail: kelly.kissock@udayton.edu. *Application contact:* Dr. Vinod Jain, Graduate Program Director, 937-229-2992, Fax: 937-229-4766, E-mail: vinod.jain@notes.udayton.edu.

University of Florida, Graduate School, College of Engineering, Department of Mechanical and Aerospace Engineering, Gainesville, FL 32611. Offers aerospace engineering (ME, MS, PhD, Engr); mechanical engineering (ME, MS, PhD, Engr). Part-time programs available. *Faculty:* 49 full-time (4 women). *Students:* 380 full-time (45 women), 76 part-time (7 women); includes 9 Black or African American, non-Hispanic/Latino; 20 Asian, non-Hispanic/Latino; 25 Hispanic/Latino, 210 international. Average age 26. 790 applicants, 32% accepted, 139 enrolled. In 2010, 102 master's, 28 doctorates awarded. *Degree requirements:* For master's, thesis (for some programs); for doctorate, comprehensive exam, thesis/dissertation; for Engr, thesis. *Entrance requirements:* For master's and doctorate, GRE General Test, minimum GPA of 3.0; for Engr, GRE General Test. Additional exam requirements/recommendations for international students: Required—TOEFL (minimum score 550 paper-based; 213 computer-based; 80 iBT), IELTS (minimum score 6). *Application deadline:* Applications are processed on a rolling basis. Application fee: $30. Electronic applications accepted. *Expenses:* Tuition, state resident: full-time $10,915.92. Tuition, nonresident: full-time $28,309. *Financial support:* In 2010–11, 203 students received support, including 5 fellowships, 197 research assistantships (averaging $21,150 per year), 1 teaching assistantship (averaging $18,540 per year); institutionally sponsored loans and unspecified assistantships also available. Support available to part-time students. Financial award applicants required to submit FAFSA. *Faculty research:* Thermal sciences, design, controls and robotics, manufacturing, energy transport and utilization. *Unit head:* David W. Hahn, PhD, Chair, 352-392-0807, Fax: 352-392-1071, E-mail: dwhahn@ufl.edu. *Application contact:* David W. Mikolaitis, PhD, Graduate Coordinator, 352-392-7632, Fax: 352-392-7303, E-mail: mollusk@ufl.edu.

University of Illinois at Urbana–Champaign, Graduate College, College of Engineering, Department of Aerospace Engineering, Champaign, IL 61820. Offers MS, PhD. *Faculty:* 18 full-time (2 women). *Students:* 125 full-time (15 women), 25 part-time (4 women); includes 3 Black or African American, non-Hispanic/Latino; 14 Asian, non-Hispanic/Latino; 1 Two or more races, non-Hispanic/Latino, 69 international. 278 applicants, 59% accepted, 53 enrolled. In 2010, 31 master's, 9 doctorates awarded. *Entrance requirements:* For master's and doctorate, GRE General Test. Additional exam requirements/recommendations for international students: Required—TOEFL (minimum score 613 paper-based; 257 computer-based; 103 iBT) or IELTS (minimum score 7). *Application deadline:* Applications are processed on a rolling basis. Application fee: $75 ($90 for international students). Electronic applications accepted. *Financial support:* In 2010–11, 19 fellowships, 76 research assistantships, 38 teaching assistantships were awarded; tuition waivers (full and partial) also available. *Unit head:* Dr. J. Craig Dutton, Head, 217-333-8580, Fax: 217-244-0720, E-mail: jcdutton@illinois.edu. *Application contact:* Staci L. Tankersley, Coordinator of Academic Programs, 217-333-3674, Fax: 217-244-0720, E-mail: tank@illinois.edu.

The University of Kansas, Graduate Studies, School of Engineering, Department of Aerospace Engineering, Lawrence, KS 66045. Offers ME, MS, DE, PhD. *Faculty:* 8 full-time (0 women), 1 part-time/adjunct (0 women). *Students:* 27 full-time (5 women), 13 part-time (1 woman); includes 2 minority (1 American Indian or Alaska Native, non-Hispanic/Latino; 1 Hispanic/Latino), 16 international. Average age 27. 37 applicants, 51% accepted, 5 enrolled. In 2010, 10 master's, 1 doctorate awarded. *Degree requirements:* For master's, comprehensive exam, thesis; for doctorate, comprehensive exam, thesis/dissertation, research and responsible scholarship skills, qualifying exam. *Entrance requirements:* For master's, GRE, minimum GPA of 3.0; for doctorate, GRE, minimum GPA of 3.5. Additional exam requirements/recommendations for international students: Required—TOEFL (minimum score 570 paper-based; 80 computer-based; 80 iBT). *Application deadline:* For fall admission, 3/1 for domestic students, 3/1 priority date for international students; for spring admission, 12/1 priority date for domestic and international students. Applications are processed on a rolling basis. Application fee: $55 ($65 for international students). Electronic applications accepted. *Expenses:* Tuition, state resident: full-time $7092; part-time $295.50 per credit hour. Tuition, nonresident: full-time $16,590; part-time $691.25 per credit hour. Required fees: $858; $71.49 per credit hour. Tuition and fees vary according to course load, campus/location and program. *Financial support:* Fellowships with full and partial tuition reimbursements, research assistantships with full and partial tuition reimbursements, teaching assistantships with full and partial tuition reimbursements, career-related internships or fieldwork, scholarships/grants, tuition waivers (full and partial), and unspecified assistantships available. Financial award application deadline: 1/1. *Faculty research:* Aerodynamics, propulsion, astronautics, fluid mechanics, flight dynamics and control, structures, flight vehicle design, flight testing, orbital mechanics, space craft attitude determination and control. *Unit head:* Dr. Mark Ewing, Chair and Associate Professor, 785-864-4267, Fax: 785-864-3597, E-mail: aerohawk@ku.edu. *Application contact:* Amy Borton, Graduate Secretary, 785-864-4267, Fax: 785-864-3597, E-mail: aerohawk@ku.edu.

The University of Manchester, School of Materials, Manchester, United Kingdom. Offers advanced aerospace materials engineering (M Sc); advanced metallic systems (PhD); biomedical materials (M Phil, M Sc, PhD); ceramics and glass (M Phil, M Sc, PhD); composite materials (M Sc, PhD); corrosion and protection (M Phil, M Sc, PhD); materials (M Phil, PhD); metallic materials (M Phil, M Sc, PhD); nanostructural materials (M Phil, M Sc, PhD); paper science (M Phil, M Sc, PhD); polymer science and engineering (M Phil, M Sc, PhD); technical textiles (M Sc); textile design, fashion and management (M Phil, M Sc, PhD); textile science and technology (M Phil, M Sc, PhD); textiles (M Phil, PhD); textiles and fashion (M Ent).

The University of Manchester, School of Mechanical, Aerospace and Civil Engineering, Manchester, United Kingdom. Offers advanced manufacturing technology (M Ent); aerospace engineering (M Phil, M Sc, PhD); civil engineering (M Phil, M Sc, PhD); environmental engineering (M Phil, PhD); management of projects (M Phil, M Sc, PhD); mechanical engineering (M Phil, M Sc, PhD); mechanical engineering design (M Ent); nuclear engineering (M Phil, D Eng, PhD).

University of Maryland, College Park, Academic Affairs, A. James Clark School of Engineering, Department of Aerospace Engineering, College Park, MD 20742. Offers M Eng, MS, PhD. Part-time and evening/weekend programs available. Postbaccalaureate distance learning degree programs offered. *Faculty:* 36 full-time (4 women), 11 part-time/adjunct (0 women). *Students:* 131 full-time (22 women), 49 part-time (11 women); includes 28 minority (5 Black or African American, non-Hispanic/Latino; 16 Asian, non-Hispanic/Latino; 5 Hispanic/Latino; 2 Two or more races, non-Hispanic/Latino), 40 international. 327 applicants, 33% accepted, 42 enrolled. In 2010, 17 master's, 6 doctorates awarded. *Degree requirements:* For master's, thesis optional; for doctorate, thesis/dissertation. *Entrance requirements:* For master's and doctorate, GRE General Test (recommended), 3 letters of recommendation. *Application deadline:* For fall admission, 5/15 for domestic students, 2/1 for international students; for spring admission, 10/31 for domestic students, 6/1 for international students. Applications are processed on a rolling basis. Application fee: $75. Electronic applications accepted. *Expenses:* Tuition, area resident: Part-time $471 per credit hour. Tuition, state resident: part-time $471 per credit hour. Tuition, nonresident: part-time $1016 per credit hour. Required fees: $337 per term. *Financial support:* In 2010–11, 14 fellowships with full and partial tuition reimbursements (averaging $13,369 per year), 104 research assistantships with tuition reimbursements (averaging $23,796 per year), 10 teaching assistantships with tuition reimbursements (averaging $17,965 per year) were awarded; Federal Work-Study and scholarships/grants also available. Support available to part-time students. Financial award applicants required to submit FAFSA. *Faculty research:* Aerodynamics and propulsion, structural mechanics, flight dynamics, rotor craft, space robotics. Total annual research expenditures: $16.4 million. *Unit head:* Mark Lewis, Chair, 301-405-0263, E-mail: lewis@umd.edu. *Application contact:* Dr. Charles A. Caramello, Dean of Graduate School, 301-405-0358, Fax: 301-314-9305.

University of Maryland, College Park, Academic Affairs, A. James Clark School of Engineering, Department of Continuing and Distance Learning in Engineering, College Park, MD 20742. Offers engineering (M Eng), including aerospace engineering, chemical engineering, civil engineering, electrical engineering, engineering, fire protection engineering, materials science and engineering, mechanical engineering, reliability engineering, systems engineering. *Faculty:* 4 full-time (1 woman), 11 part-time/adjunct (1 woman). *Students:* 56 full-time (15 women), 428 part-time (88 women); includes 153 minority (59 Black or African American, non-Hispanic/Latino; 63 Asian, non-Hispanic/Latino; 24 Hispanic/Latino; 7 Two or more races, non-Hispanic/Latino), 55 international. 551 applicants, 82% accepted, 360 enrolled. In 2010, 130 master's awarded. *Application deadline:* For fall admission, 8/15 for domestic students, 1/10 for international students; for spring admission, 12/15 for domestic students, 6/1 for international students. Applications are processed on a rolling basis. Application fee: $75. Electronic applications accepted. *Expenses:* Tuition, area resident: Part-time $471 per credit hour. Tuition, state resident: part-time $471 per credit hour. Tuition, nonresident: part-time $1016 per credit hour. Required fees: $337 per term. *Financial support:* In 2010–11, 2 research assistantships (averaging $20,285 per year), 7 teaching assistantships (averaging $16,962 per year) were awarded. *Unit head:* Dr. Darryll Pines, Dean, 301-405-0376, Fax: 301-314-5908, E-mail: pines@umd.edu. *Application contact:* Dr. Charles A. Caramello, Dean of the Graduate School, 301-405-0358, Fax: 301-314-9305, E-mail: ccaramel@umd.edu.

University of Miami, Graduate School, College of Engineering, Department of Mechanical and Aerospace Engineering, Coral Gables, FL 33124. Offers MSME, PhD. Part-time programs available. *Degree requirements:* For master's, thesis (for some programs); for doctorate, comprehensive exam, thesis/dissertation. *Entrance requirements:* For master's and doctorate, GRE General Test, minimum GPA of 3.0. Additional exam requirements/recommendations for international students: Required—TOEFL (minimum score 550 paper-based; 213 computer-based). Electronic applications accepted. *Faculty research:* Internal combustion engines, heat transfer, hydrogen energy, controls, fuel cells.

University of Michigan, Horace H. Rackham School of Graduate Studies, College of Engineering, Department of Aerospace Engineering, Ann Arbor, MI 48109. Offers M Eng, MS, MSE, PhD. Part-time programs available. *Students:* 189 full-time (21 women), 2 part-time (0 women). 436 applicants, 49% accepted, 97 enrolled. In 2010, 42 master's, 17 doctorates awarded. *Degree requirements:* For doctorate, thesis/dissertation, oral defense of dissertation, preliminary exams. *Entrance requirements:* For master's, GRE General Test; for doctorate, GRE General Test, master's degree. *Application deadline:* Applications are processed on a rolling basis. Application fee: $65 ($75 for international students). Electronic applications accepted. *Expenses:* Tuition, state resident: full-time $17,784; part-time $1116 per credit hour. Tuition, nonresident: full-time $35,944; part-time $2125 per credit hour. International tuition: $35,994 full-time. Required fees: $95 per semester. Tuition and fees vary according to course load, degree level and program. *Financial support:* Fellowships, research assistantships, teaching assistantships, Federal Work-Study and tuition waivers (full and partial) available. *Faculty research:* Turbulent flows and combustion, advanced spacecraft control, helicopter aeroelasticity, experimental fluid dynamics, space propulsion, optimal structural design, interactive materials, computational fluid and solid dynamics. *Unit head:* Dr. Kenneth Powell, Interim Chair, 734-764-1226, Fax: 734-763-0578, E-mail: powell@umich.edu. *Application contact:* Denise Phelps, Graduate Admissions Coordinator, 734-615-4406, Fax: 734-763-0578, E-mail: dphelps@umich.edu.

University of Michigan, Horace H. Rackham School of Graduate Studies, College of Engineering, Department of Atmospheric, Oceanic, and Space Sciences, Ann Arbor, MI 48109. Offers atmospheric and space sciences (MS, PhD); geoscience and remote sensing (PhD); space and planetary sciences (PhD); space engineering (M Eng). Part-time programs available. *Students:* 92 full-time (31 women), 1 part-time (0 women). 179 applicants, 60% accepted, 52 enrolled. In 2010, 29 master's, 6 doctorates awarded. Terminal master's awarded for partial completion of doctoral program. *Degree requirements:* For master's, thesis (for some programs); for doctorate, thesis/dissertation, oral defense of dissertation, preliminary exams. *Entrance requirements:* For master's and doctorate, GRE General Test. Additional exam requirements/recommendations for international students: Required—TOEFL. *Application deadline:* Applications are processed on a rolling basis. Application fee: $65 ($75 for international students). Electronic applications accepted. *Expenses:* Tuition, state resident: full-time $17,784; part-time $1116 per credit hour. Tuition, nonresident: full-time $35,944; part-time $2125 per credit hour. International tuition: $35,994 full-time. Required fees: $95 per semester. Tuition and fees vary according to course load, degree level and program. *Financial support:* Fellowships, research assistantships, teaching assistantships, career-related internships or fieldwork, Federal Work-Study, institutionally sponsored loans, and health care benefits available. Support available to part-time students. Financial award applicants required to submit FAFSA. *Faculty research:* Planetary environments, space instrumentation, air pollution meteorology, global climate change, sun-earth connection, space weather. *Unit head:* Tamas Gombosi, Chair, 734-764-7222, Fax: 734-615-4645, E-mail: tamas@umich.edu. *Application contact:* Margaret Reid, Student Services Associate, 734-936-0482, Fax: 734-763-0437, E-mail: aoss.um@umich.edu.

University of Minnesota, Twin Cities Campus, Institute of Technology, Department of Aerospace Engineering and Mechanics, Minneapolis, MN 55455-0213. Offers aerospace engineering (M Aero E); aerospace engineering and mechanics (MS, PhD). Part-time programs available. *Degree requirements:* For doctorate, thesis/dissertation. *Entrance requirements:* Additional exam requirements/recommendations for international students: Required—TOEFL (minimum score 550 paper-based; 213 computer-based). Electronic applications accepted. *Faculty research:* Fluid mechanics, solid and continuum fluid mechanics, computational mechanics, aerospace systems.

University of Missouri, Graduate School, College of Engineering, Department of Mechanical and Aerospace Engineering, Columbia, MO 65211. Offers MS, PhD. *Degree requirements:* For master's, thesis; for doctorate, one foreign language, thesis/dissertation. *Entrance requirements:* For master's and doctorate, GRE General Test, minimum GPA of 3.0. Additional exam requirements/recommendations for international students: Required—TOEFL (minimum score 500 paper-based; 173 computer-based; 61 iBT).

University of Nevada, Las Vegas, Graduate College, Howard R. Hughes College of Engineering, Department of Mechanical Engineering, Las Vegas, NV 89154-4027. Offers aerospace engineering (MS); biomedical engineering (MS); materials and nuclear engineering (MS); mechanical engineering (MSE, PhD). Part-time programs available. *Faculty:* 17 full-time (0 women), 10 part-time/adjunct (0 women). *Students:* 43 full-time (6 women), 24 part-time (6 women); includes 24 minority (1 Black or African American, non-Hispanic/Latino; 4 Asian, non-Hispanic/Latino; 1 Hispanic/Latino; 1 Native Hawaiian or other Pacific Islander, non-Hispanic/Latino; 17 Two or more races, non-Hispanic/Latino), 24 international. Average age 30. 32 applicants, 84% accepted, 15 enrolled. In 2010, 10 master's, 4 doctorates awarded. *Degree requirements:* For master's, comprehensive exam, thesis (for some programs), project; for doctorate, comprehensive exam, thesis/dissertation. *Entrance requirements:* For master's and doctorate, GRE General Test. Additional exam requirements/recommendations for international students: Required—TOEFL (minimum score 550 paper-based; 213 computer-based; 80 iBT), IELTS (minimum score 7). *Application deadline:* For fall admission, 5/1 priority date for domestic and international students; for spring admission, 10/1 priority date for domestic and international students. Applications are processed on a rolling basis. Application fee: $60 ($95 for international students). Electronic applications accepted. *Expenses:* Tuition, area resident: Part-time $239.50 per credit. Tuition, state resident: part-time $239.50 per credit. Tuition, nonresident: part-time $503 per credit. Required fees: $108 per semester. Tuition and fees vary according to course load, program and reciprocity agreements. *Financial support:* In 2010–11, 37 students received support, including 21 research assistantships with partial tuition reimbursements available (averaging $13,335 per year), 16 teaching assistantships with partial tuition reimbursements available (averaging $11,000 per year); institutionally sponsored loans, scholarships/grants, health care benefits, and unspecified assistantships also available. Financial award application deadline: 3/1. *Faculty research:* Dynamics and control systems; energy systems including renewable and nuclear; computational fluid and solid mechanics; structures, materials and manufacturing; vibrations and acoustics. Total annual research expenditures: $3 million. *Unit head:* Dr. Woosoon Yim, Chair/Professor, 702-895-0956, Fax: 702-895-3936, E-mail: wy@me.unlv.edu. *Application contact:* Graduate College Admissions Evaluator, 702-895-3320, Fax: 702-895-4180, E-mail: gradcollege@unlv.edu.

University of Notre Dame, Graduate School, College of Engineering, Department of Aerospace and Mechanical Engineering, Notre Dame, IN 46556. Offers aerospace and mechanical engineering (M Eng, PhD); aerospace engineering (MS Aero E); mechanical engineering (MEME, MSME). Terminal master's awarded for partial completion of doctoral program. *Degree requirements:* For master's, comprehensive exam, thesis or alternative; for doctorate, thesis/dissertation, candidacy exam. *Entrance requirements:* For master's and doctorate, GRE General Test. Additional exam requirements/recommendations for international students: Required—TOEFL (minimum score 600 paper-based; 250 computer-based; 80 iBT). Electronic applications accepted. *Faculty research:* Aerodynamics/fluid dynamics, design and manufacturing, controls/robotics, solid mechanics or biomechanics/biomaterials.

University of Oklahoma, College of Engineering, School of Aerospace and Mechanical Engineering, Program in Aerospace Engineering, Norman, OK 73019. Offers aerospace engineering (MS, PhD), including aerodynamics, composites, fluid mechanics, general, structures. Part-time programs available. *Students:* 9 full-time (1 woman), 13 part-time (0 women); includes 5 minority (1 Black or African American, non-Hispanic/Latino; 1 American Indian or Alaska Native, non-Hispanic/Latino; 2 Asian, non-Hispanic/Latino; 1 Hispanic/Latino), 4 international. Average age 27. 19 applicants, 68% accepted, 6 enrolled. In 2010, 6 master's, 2 doctorates awarded. *Degree requirements:* For master's, comprehensive exam, thesis or alternative; for doctorate, comprehensive exam, thesis/dissertation, combined general and qualifying exam. *Entrance requirements:* For master's, GRE General Test, BS in engineering or physical sciences; for doctorate, GRE General Test, MS in aerospace engineering or equivalent. Additional exam requirements/recommendations for international students: Required—TOEFL (minimum score 600 paper-based; 250 computer-based; 100 iBT). *Application deadline:* For fall admission, 6/1 priority date for domestic students, 4/1 for international students; for spring admission, 11/1 for domestic students, 9/1 for international students. Applications are processed on a rolling basis. Application fee: $40 ($90 for international students). Electronic applications accepted. *Expenses:* Tuition, state resident: full-time $3892.80; part-time $162.20 per credit hour. Tuition, nonresident: full-time $14,167; part-time $590.30 per credit hour. Required fees: $2523.40; $94.60 per credit hour. Tuition and fees vary according to course load and degree level. *Financial support:* In 2010–11, 16 students received support. Unspecified assistantships available. Financial award application deadline: 3/1; financial award applicants required to submit FAFSA. *Faculty research:* Dynamics; controls and robotics; materials, design and manufacturing; structures; thermal-fluid systems. *Unit head:* Farrokh Mistree, Director, 405-325-5011, Fax: 405-325-1088, E-mail: farrokh.mistree@ou.edu. *Application contact:* Dr. David P. Miller, Graduate Liaison, 405-325-1094, Fax: 405-325-1088, E-mail: dpmiller@ou.edu.

University of Ottawa, Faculty of Graduate and Postdoctoral Studies, Faculty of Engineering, Ottawa-Carleton Institute for Mechanical and Aerospace Engineering, Ottawa, ON K1N 6N5, Canada. Offers M Eng, MA Sc, PhD. MA Sc, M Eng, PhD offered jointly with Carleton University. *Degree requirements:* For master's, thesis or alternative; for doctorate, thesis/dissertation, seminar series, qualifying exam. *Entrance requirements:* For master's, honors degree or equivalent, minimum B average; for doctorate, master's degree, minimum B+ average. Electronic applications accepted. *Faculty research:* Fluid mechanics-heat transfer, solid mechanics, design, manufacturing and control.

University of Southern California, Graduate School, Viterbi School of Engineering, Department of Aerospace and Mechanical Engineering, Los Angeles, CA 90089. Offers aerospace and mechanical engineering: computational fluid and solid mechanics (MS); aerospace and mechanical engineering: dynamics and control (MS); aerospace engineering (MS, PhD, Engr), including aerospace engineering (PhD, Engr); green technologies (MS); mechanical engineering (MS, PhD, Engr), including mechanical engineering (PhD, Engr); product development engineering (MS). Part-time and evening/weekend programs available. Postbaccalaureate distance learning degree programs offered (no on-campus study). *Faculty:* 22 full-time (3 women), 19 part-time/adjunct (2 women). *Students:* 238 full-time (33 women), 214 part-time (30 women); includes 115 minority (10 Black or African American, non-Hispanic/Latino; 67 Asian, non-Hispanic/Latino; 32 Hispanic/Latino; 6 Two or more races, non-Hispanic/Latino), 151 international. 691 applicants, 43% accepted, 124 enrolled. In 2010, 107 master's, 11 doctorates, 1 other advanced degree awarded. Terminal master's awarded for partial completion of doctoral program. *Degree requirements:* For master's, thesis optional; for doctorate, thesis/dissertation. *Entrance requirements:* For master's, doctorate, and Engr, GRE General Test. *Application deadline:* For fall admission, 12/1 priority date for domestic and international students; for winter admission, 9/15 priority date for domestic and international students; for spring admission, 9/15 priority date for domestic and international students. Applications are processed on a rolling basis. Application fee: $85. Electronic applications accepted. *Expenses:* Tuition: Full-time $31,240; part-time $1420 per unit. Required fees: $600. One-time fee: $35 full-time. Full-time tuition and fees vary according to degree level and program. *Financial support:* In 2010–11, fellowships with full tuition reimbursements (averaging $30,000 per year), research assistantships with full tuition reimbursements (averaging $20,000 per year), teaching assistantships with full tuition reimbursements (averaging $20,000 per year) were awarded; career-related internships or fieldwork, scholarships/grants, health care benefits, and unspecified assistantships also available. Financial award application deadline: 12/1; financial award applicants required to submit CSS PROFILE or FAFSA. *Faculty research:* Mechanics and materials, aerodynamics of air/ground vehicles, gas dynamics, aerosols, astronautics and space science, geophysical and microgravity flows, planetary physics, power MEMs and MEMS vacuum pumps, heat transfer and combustion. Total annual research expenditures: $5 million. *Unit head:* Dr. Geoffrey Spedding, Chair, 213-740-5324, E-mail: ame@usc.edu. *Application contact:* Samantha Graves, Student Service Advisor, 213-740-1735, E-mail: smgraves@usc.edu.

University of Southern California, Graduate School, Viterbi School of Engineering, Division of Astronautics and Space Technology, Los Angeles, CA 90089. Offers astronautical engineering (MS, PhD, Engr, Graduate Certificate). Part-time and evening/weekend programs available. Postbaccalaureate distance learning degree programs offered (no on-campus study). *Faculty:* 4 full-time (0 women), 6 part-time/adjunct (0 women). *Students:* 28 full-time (5 women), 90 part-time (20 women); includes 25 minority (4 Black or African American, non-Hispanic/Latino; 12 Asian, non-Hispanic/Latino; 7 Hispanic/Latino; 2 Two or more races, non-Hispanic/Latino), 14 international. 87 applicants, 57% accepted, 35 enrolled. In 2010, 49 master's, 1 doctorate, 1 other advanced degree awarded. Terminal master's awarded for partial completion of doctoral program. *Degree requirements:* For master's, thesis optional; for doctorate, thesis/dissertation; for other advanced degree, comprehensive exam (for some programs). *Entrance requirements:* For master's, doctorate, and other advanced degree, GRE General Test. *Application deadline:* For fall admission, 12/1 priority date for domestic and international students; for spring admission, 9/15 priority date for domestic and international students. Applications are processed on a rolling basis. Application fee: $85. Electronic applications accepted. *Expenses:* Tuition: Full-time $31,240; part-time $1420 per unit. Required fees: $600. One-time fee: $35 full-time. Full-time tuition and fees vary according to degree level and program. *Financial support:* In 2010–11, fellowships with full tuition reimbursements (averaging $30,000 per year), research assistantships with full tuition reimbursements (averaging $19,250 per year), teaching assistantships with full tuition reimbursements (averaging $19,250 per year) were awarded; career-related internships or fieldwork, scholarships/grants, health care benefits, and unspecified assistantships also available. Financial award application deadline: 12/1; financial award applicants required to submit CSS PROFILE or FAFSA. *Faculty research:* Space technology, space science and applications, space instrumentation, advanced propulsion, fundamental processes in gases and plasmas. Total annual research expenditures: $660,973. *Unit head:* Dr. Daniel A. Erwin, Chair, 213-821-5817, E-mail: info@astronautics.usc.edu. *Application contact:* Marrietta Penoliar, Student Advisor, 213-821-4234, E-mail: marriett@usc.edu.

The University of Tennessee, Graduate School, College of Engineering, Department of Mechanical, Aerospace and Biomedical Engineering, Program in Aerospace Engineering, Knoxville, TN 37996. Offers MS, PhD, MS/MBA. Part-time programs available. Postbaccalaureate distance learning degree programs offered (minimal on-campus study). *Faculty:* 4 full-time (0 women). *Students:* 27 full-time (2 women), 12 part-time (0 women); includes 2 Hispanic/Latino, 8 international. Average age 26. 25 applicants, 44% accepted, 4 enrolled. In 2010, 7 master's, 1 doctorate awarded. *Degree requirements:* For master's, thesis or alternative; for doctorate, comprehensive exam, thesis/dissertation. *Entrance requirements:* For master's, GRE General Test, Minimum GPA of 2.7 (US degree holders); 3.0 (International degree holders); 3-References; Statement of purpose; for doctorate, GRE General Test, Minimum GPA of 3.0 (previous graduate course work); 3-References; Statement of purpose. Additional exam requirements/recommendations for international students: Required—TOEFL (minimum score 550 paper-

Aerospace/Aeronautical Engineering

The University of Tennessee (continued)

based; 213 computer-based). *Application deadline:* For fall admission, 2/1 priority date for domestic and international students; for spring admission, 6/15 for domestic and international students. Applications are processed on a rolling basis. Application fee: $35. Electronic applications accepted. *Expenses:* Tuition, state resident: full-time $7440; part-time $414 per credit hour. Tuition, nonresident: full-time $22,478; part-time $1250 per credit hour. Required fees: $922; $43 per credit hour. Tuition and fees vary according to program. *Financial support:* In 2010–11, 13 students received support, including 1 fellowship with full tuition reimbursement available (averaging $12,000 per year), 12 research assistantships with full tuition reimbursements available (averaging $15,480 per year), 6 teaching assistantships with full tuition reimbursements available (averaging $10,500 per year); career-related internships or fieldwork, Federal Work-Study, institutionally sponsored loans, health care benefits, and unspecified assistantships also available. Financial award application deadline: 2/1; financial award applicants required to submit FAFSA. *Faculty research:* Atmospheric re-entry mechanics; hybrid rocket propulsion; laser-induced plasma spectroscopy; unsteady aerodynamics and aeroelasticity. *Unit head:* Dr. William Hamel, Head, 865-974-5115, Fax: 865-974-5274, E-mail: whamel@utk.edu. *Application contact:* Dr. Gary V. Smith, Associate Head, 865-974-5271, Fax: 865-974-5274, E-mail: gvsmith@utk.edu.

The University of Tennessee Space Institute, Graduate Programs, Program in Aerospace Engineering, Tullahoma, TN 37388-9700. Offers MS, PhD. Part-time programs available. *Faculty:* 5 full-time (0 women), 11 part-time/adjunct (0 women). *Students:* 17 full-time (2 women), 14 part-time (0 women), 8 international. 6 applicants, 100% accepted, 3 enrolled. In 2010, 4 master's, 1 doctorate awarded. *Degree requirements:* For master's, thesis (for some programs); for doctorate, one foreign language, thesis/dissertation. *Entrance requirements:* For master's and doctorate, GRE General Test. Additional exam requirements/recommendations for international students: Required—TOEFL (minimum score 550 paper-based; 213 computer-based), IELTS (minimum score 6.5). *Application deadline:* For fall admission, 2/1 for international students; for spring admission, 6/15 for international students. Applications are processed on a rolling basis. Application fee: $35. Electronic applications accepted. *Financial support:* In 2010–11, 2 fellowships (averaging $1,425 per year), 13 research assistantships with full tuition reimbursements (averaging $17,791 per year) were awarded; career-related internships or fieldwork, Federal Work-Study, institutionally sponsored loans, health care benefits, tuition waivers (full and partial), and unspecified assistantships also available. Financial award applicants required to submit FAFSA. *Faculty research:* Air and space vehicles, flight mechanics, propulsion, fluid mechanics, gas dynamics, energy conversion, structure. *Unit head:* Dr. Trevor Moeller, Degree Program Chairman, 931-393-7351, Fax: 931-393-7437, E-mail: tmoeller@utsi.edu. *Application contact:* Dee Merriman, Coordinator III, 931-393-7213, Fax: 931-393-7211, E-mail: dmerrima@utsi.edu.

The University of Texas at Arlington, Graduate School, College of Engineering, Department of Mechanical and Aerospace Engineering, Program in Aerospace Engineering, Arlington, TX 76019. Offers M Engr, MS, PhD. Part-time and evening/weekend programs available. Postbaccalaureate distance learning degree programs offered (minimal on-campus study). *Faculty:* 11 full-time (0 women). *Students:* 54 full-time (9 women), 58 part-time (10 women); includes 26 minority (3 Black or African American, non-Hispanic/Latino; 15 Asian, non-Hispanic/Latino; 8 Hispanic/Latino), 44 international. 65 applicants, 94% accepted, 36 enrolled. In 2010, 18 master's, 1 doctorate awarded. *Degree requirements:* For master's, thesis optional; for doctorate, comprehensive exam, thesis/dissertation. *Entrance requirements:* For master's, GRE General Test, minimum GPA of 3.0; for doctorate, GRE General Test, minimum GPA of 3.3. Additional exam requirements/recommendations for international students: Required—TOEFL (minimum score 550 paper-based; 213 computer-based). *Application deadline:* For fall admission, 6/1 for domestic students, 4/1 for international students; for spring admission, 10/15 for domestic students, 9/15 for international students. Applications are processed on a rolling basis. Application fee: $25 ($50 for international students). *Expenses:* Tuition, state resident: full-time $7500. Tuition, nonresident: full-time $13,080. International tuition: $13,250 full-time. *Financial support:* In 2010–11, 7 fellowships with partial tuition reimbursements (averaging $1,000 per year), 7 research assistantships with partial tuition reimbursements (averaging $13,500 per year), 23 teaching assistantships with partial tuition reimbursements (averaging $14,000 per year) were awarded; institutionally sponsored loans, scholarships/grants, health care benefits, and unspecified assistantships also available. Financial award application deadline: 6/1; financial award applicants required to submit FAFSA. *Unit head:* Dr. Erian Armanios, Chair, 817-272-2603, Fax: 817-272-5010, E-mail: armanios@uta.edu. *Application contact:* Dr. Donald R. Wilson, Graduate Advisor, 817-272-2072, Fax: 817-272-5010, E-mail: wilson@uta.edu.

The University of Texas at Austin, Graduate School, Cockrell School of Engineering, Department of Aerospace Engineering and Engineering Mechanics, Program in Aerospace Engineering, Austin, TX 78712-1111. Offers MSE, PhD. *Entrance requirements:* For master's and doctorate, GRE General Test. Electronic applications accepted.

University of Toronto, School of Graduate Studies, Physical Sciences Division, Faculty of Applied Science and Engineering, Institute for Aerospace Science and Engineering, Toronto, ON M5S 1A1, Canada. Offers M Eng, MA Sc, PhD. Part-time programs available. *Degree requirements:* For master's, thesis (for some programs); for doctorate, thesis/dissertation, formal manuscript for publication. *Entrance requirements:* For master's, BA Sc degree or equivalent in engineering (M Eng); bachelor's degree in physics, mathematics, engineering or chemistry (MA Sc); 2 letters of reference; for doctorate, master's degree in applied science, engineering, mathematics, physics, or chemistry; demonstrated ability to perform advanced research, 2 letters of reference. Additional exam requirements/recommendations for international students: Required—TOEFL (minimum score 580 paper-based; 237 computer-based), TWE (minimum score 5), GRE.

University of Virginia, School of Engineering and Applied Science, Department of Mechanical and Aerospace Engineering, Charlottesville, VA 22903. Offers ME, MS, PhD. Postbaccalaureate distance learning degree programs offered (no on-campus study). *Faculty:* 20 full-time (3 women), 2 part-time/adjunct (0 women). *Students:* 80 full-time (8 women), 3 part-time (0 women); includes 4 Asian, non-Hispanic/Latino, 22 international. Average age 27. 167 applicants, 15% accepted, 16 enrolled. In 2010, 18 master's, 4 doctorates awarded. *Degree requirements:* For master's, thesis (MS); for doctorate, comprehensive exam, thesis/dissertation. *Entrance requirements:* For master's and doctorate, GRE General Test, 3 letters of recommendation. Additional exam requirements/recommendations for international students: Required—TOEFL (minimum score 650 paper-based; 250 computer-based; 90 iBT), IELTS (minimum score 7). *Application deadline:* For fall admission, 8/1 for domestic students, 4/1 for international students; for winter admission, 12/1 for domestic students, 8/1 for international students; for spring admission, 5/1 for domestic students, 1/1 for international students. Applications are processed on a rolling basis. Application fee: $60. Electronic applications accepted. *Financial support:* Fellowships, research assistantships, teaching assistantships available. Financial award application deadline: 1/15; financial award applicants required to submit FAFSA. *Faculty research:* Solid mechanics, dynamical systems and control, thermofluids. *Unit head:* Hossein Haj-Hariri, Chair, 434-924-7424, Fax: 434-982-2037, E-mail: mae-adm@virginia.edu. *Application contact:* Graduate Secretary, 434-924-7425, Fax: 434-982-2037, E-mail: mae-adm@virginia.edu.

University of Washington, Graduate School, College of Engineering, Department of Aeronautics and Astronautics, Seattle, WA 98195-2400. Offers aeronautics and astronautics (MS, PhD); composite materials and structures (MAE). Part-time programs available. Postbaccalaureate distance learning degree programs offered (no on-campus study). *Faculty:* 29 full-time (1 woman), 8 part-time/adjunct (0 women). *Students:* 76 full-time (15 women), 87 part-time (12 women); includes 5 Black or African American, non-Hispanic/Latino; 18 Asian, non-Hispanic/Latino; 13 Hispanic/Latino, 20 international. Average age 27. 251 applicants, 58% accepted, 63 enrolled. In 2010, 36 master's, 4 doctorates awarded. *Degree requirements:* For master's, thesis optional; for doctorate, comprehensive exam, thesis/dissertation, Qualifying, general & final exams. Complete all work toward doctoral degree (including applicable MS degree work, on-leave, & out-of-status) within 10 years. *Entrance requirements:* For master's and doctorate, GRE General Test, Minimum GPA of 3.0, letters of recommendation, statement of objectives, undergraduate degree in aerospace or mechanical engineering. Additional exam requirements/recommendations for international students: Required—TOEFL (minimum score 580 paper-based; 237 computer-based; 92 iBT); Recommended—IELTS (minimum score 7). *Application deadline:* For fall admission, 1/15 priority date for domestic and international students. Application fee: $75. Electronic applications accepted. *Financial support:* In 2010–11, 2 students received support, including 9 fellowships (averaging $5,787 per year), 33 research assistantships with full tuition reimbursements available (averaging $17,226 per year), 12 teaching assistantships with full tuition reimbursements available (averaging $13,725 per year); career-related internships or fieldwork, Federal Work-Study, health care benefits, tuition waivers (full), and unspecified assistantships also available. Financial award application deadline: 1/15; financial award applicants required to submit FAFSA. *Faculty research:* Space systems, aircraft systems, energy systems, composites/structures, fluid dynamics, controls. Total annual research expenditures: $8.4 million. *Unit head:* Dr. James Hermanson, Professor and Chair, 206-543-1950, Fax: 206-543-0217, E-mail: jherm@aa.washington.edu. *Application contact:* Wanda Frederick, Manager of Graduate Programs and External Relations, 206-616-1113, Fax: 206-543-0217, E-mail: wanda@aa.washington.edu.

Utah State University, School of Graduate Studies, College of Engineering, Department of Mechanical and Aerospace Engineering, Logan, UT 84322. Offers aerospace engineering (MS, PhD); mechanical engineering (ME, MS, PhD). Terminal master's awarded for partial completion of doctoral program. *Degree requirements:* For master's, thesis (for some programs); for doctorate, thesis/dissertation. *Entrance requirements:* For master's, GRE General Test, minimum GPA of 3.0; for doctorate, GRE General Test, minimum GPA of 3.3. Additional exam requirements/recommendations for international students: Required—TOEFL. *Faculty research:* In-space instruments, cryogenic cooling, thermal science, space structures, composite materials.

Virginia Polytechnic Institute and State University, Graduate School, College of Engineering, Department of Aerospace Engineering, Blacksburg, VA 24061. Offers M Eng, MS, PhD. *Faculty:* 18 full-time (1 woman). *Students:* 75 full-time (5 women), 29 part-time (3 women); includes 7 Asian, non-Hispanic/Latino; 1 Hispanic/Latino, 20 international. Average age 27. 172 applicants, 23% accepted, 21 enrolled. In 2010, 44 master's, 9 doctorates awarded. *Degree requirements:* For master's, comprehensive exam (for some programs), thesis (for some programs); for doctorate, comprehensive exam (for some programs), thesis/dissertation (for some programs). *Entrance requirements:* For master's and doctorate, GRE. Additional exam requirements/recommendations for international students: Required—TOEFL (minimum score 550 paper-based; 213 computer-based). *Application deadline:* For fall admission, 7/1 for domestic and international students; for spring admission, 12/1 for domestic and international students. Applications are processed on a rolling basis. Application fee: $65. Electronic applications accepted. *Expenses:* Tuition, area resident: Full-time $9399; part-time $488 per credit hour. Tuition, state resident: full-time $9399; part-time $488 per credit hour. Tuition, nonresident: full-time $17,854; part-time $957.75 per credit hour. International tuition: $17,854 full-time. Required fees: $1534. Full-time tuition and fees vary according to program. *Financial support:* In 2010–11, 3 fellowships with full tuition reimbursements (averaging $6,500 per year), 33 research assistantships with full tuition reimbursements (averaging $19,812 per year), 12 teaching assistantships with full tuition reimbursements (averaging $13,930 per year) were awarded; career-related internships or fieldwork, Federal Work-Study, scholarships/grants, health care benefits, and unspecified assistantships also available. Financial award application deadline: 1/15. *Faculty research:* Aerodynamics, flight mechanics, vehicle structures, space mechanics and design. Total annual research expenditures: $5.9 million. *Unit head:* Dr. Chris D. Hall, UNIT HEAD, 540-231-2314, Fax: 540-231-9632, E-mail: cdhall@vt.edu. *Application contact:* Craig Woolsey, Contact, 540-231-8117, Fax: 540-231-9632, E-mail: woolsey@vt.edu.

Virginia Polytechnic Institute and State University, VT Online, Blacksburg, VA 24061. Offers aerospace engineering (MS); business information systems (Graduate Certificate); career and technical education (MS); computer engineering (M Eng, MS); decision support systems (Graduate Certificate); eLearning leadership (MA); electrical engineering (M Eng, MS); engineering administration (MEA); environmental politics and policy (Graduate Certificate); foundations of political analysis (Graduate Certificate); health product risk management (Graduate Certificate); information policy and society (Graduate Certificate); information security (Graduate Certificate); instructional technology (MA); liberal arts (Graduate Certificate); life sciences: health product risk management (MS); natural resources (MNR, Graduate Certificate); networking (Graduate Certificate); nonprofit and nongovernmental organization management (Graduate Certificate); ocean engineering (MS); political science (MA); security studies (Graduate Certificate); software development (Graduate Certificate). *Expenses:* Tuition, area resident: Full-time $9399; part-time $488 per credit hour. Tuition, state resident: full-time $9399; part-time $488 per credit hour. Tuition, nonresident: full-time $17,854; part-time $957.75 per credit hour. International tuition: $17,854 full-time. Required fees: $1534. Full-time tuition and fees vary according to program.

Washington University in St. Louis, School of Engineering and Applied Science, Department of Mechanical, Aerospace and Structural Engineering, St. Louis, MO 63130-4899. Offers MS, D Sc, PhD. Part-time programs available. Terminal master's awarded for partial completion of doctoral program. *Degree requirements:* For master's, thesis optional; for doctorate, thesis/dissertation optional. *Entrance requirements:* For master's, GRE; for doctorate, GRE General Test, departmental qualifying exam. *Faculty research:* Aerosols science and technology, applied mechanics, biomechanics and biomedical engineering, design, dynamic systems, combustion science, composite materials, materials science.

Webster University, George Herbert Walker School of Business and Technology, Department of Management, St. Louis, MO 63119-3194. Offers business and organizational security management (MA); computer resources and information management (MA); environmental management (MS); government contracting (Certificate); health care management (MA); health services management (MA); human resources development (MA); human resources management (MA); management (DM); management and leadership (MA); marketing (MA); nonprofit management (Certificate); procurement and acquisitions management (MA); public administration (MA); quality management (MA); space systems operations management (MS); telecommunications management (MA). *Accreditation:* ACBSP. Part-time and evening/weekend programs available. Postbaccalaureate distance learning degree programs offered (no on-campus study). *Degree requirements:* For master's, thesis (for some programs); for doctorate, thesis/dissertation, written exam. *Entrance requirements:* For doctorate, GMAT, 3 years of work experience, MBA. Additional exam requirements/recommendations for international students: Required—TOEFL. *Expenses:* Tuition: Part-time $585 per credit hour. Tuition and fees vary according to degree level, campus/location and program.

West Virginia University, College of Engineering and Mineral Resources, Department of Mechanical and Aerospace Engineering, Program in Aerospace Engineering, Morgantown, WV 26506. Offers MSAE, PhD. Part-time programs available. Terminal master's awarded for partial completion of doctoral program. *Degree requirements:* For master's, thesis; for doctorate, comprehensive exam, thesis/dissertation, qualifying exams, proposal defense. *Entrance requirements:* For master's and doctorate, GRE General Test, minimum GPA of 3.0, 3 reference letters. Additional exam requirements/recommendations for international students: Required—TOEFL (minimum score 550 paper-based; 213 computer-based; 79 iBT). *Faculty research:* Transonic flight controls and simulations, thermal science, composite materials, aerospace design.

Wichita State University, Graduate School, College of Engineering, Department of Aerospace Engineering, Wichita, KS 67260. Offers MS, PhD. Part-time programs available. *Unit head:* Dr. L. Scott Miller, Chairperson, 316-978-3410, E-mail: scott.miller@wichita.edu. *Application contact:* Dr. Kamran Rokhsaz, Graduate Coordinator for MS Program, 316-978-3410, E-mail: kamran.rokhsaz@wichita.edu.

Aviation

Embry-Riddle Aeronautical University–Worldwide, Worldwide Headquarters, Program in Aviation, Daytona Beach, FL 32114-3900. Offers PhD. *Faculty:* 2 full-time (0 women), 3 part-time/adjunct (1 woman). *Students:* 10 full-time (1 woman), 13 part-time (2 women); includes 3 minority (1 Asian, non-Hispanic/Latino; 1 Hispanic/Latino; 1 Two or more races, non-Hispanic/Latino), 3 international. Average age 39. 55 applicants, 15% accepted, 7 enrolled. *Entrance requirements:* For doctorate, GRE. Additional exam requirements/recommendations for international students: Required—TOEFL (minimum score 600 paper-based; 250 computer-based; 105 iBT). *Application deadline:* For fall admission, 2/1 for domestic students. Applications are processed on a rolling basis. Application fee: $50. Electronic applications accepted. *Financial support:* In 2010–11, 1 student received support. Applicants required to submit FAFSA. *Faculty research:* Aviation safety informationanalysis and sharing for general aviation, design and manufacturing safety management systems, general aviation safety analysis adopting statistical approaches. *Unit head:* Dr. Tim Brady, Dean, College of Aviation, 386-226-6849, E-mail: tim.brady@erau.edu. *Application contact:* Linda Dammer, Director of Admissions, 386-226-6386 Ext. 1, Fax: 386-226-6984, E-mail: worldwide@erau.edu.

Everglades University, Graduate Programs, Program in Aviation Science, Boca Raton, FL 33431. Offers MSA. *Entrance requirements:* Additional exam requirements/recommendations for international students: Recommended—TOEFL (minimum score 500 paper-based; 173 computer-based). Electronic applications accepted.

Lewis University, College of Arts and Sciences, Program in Aviation and Transportation, Romeoville, IL 60446. Offers administration (MS); safety and security (MS). Part-time and evening/weekend programs available. Postbaccalaureate distance learning degree programs offered (minimal on-campus study). *Faculty:* 2 full-time (0 women), 1 part-time/adjunct (0 women). *Students:* 7 full-time (2 women), 13 part-time (1 woman); includes 3 Black or African American, non-Hispanic/Latino; 1 Hispanic/Latino, 1 international. Average age 37. In 2010, 4 master's awarded. *Entrance requirements:* For master's, bachelor's degree, minimum GPA of 3.0, personal statement, 3 letters of recommendation. Additional exam requirements/recommendations for international students: Required—TOEFL (minimum score 550 paper-based; 213 computer-based). *Application deadline:* For fall admission, 5/1 priority date for international students; for spring admission, 11/15 priority date for international students. Applications are processed on a rolling basis. Application fee: $40. Electronic applications accepted. *Expenses:* Tuition: Full-time $13,320; part-time $740 per credit hour. Tuition and fees vary according to program. *Financial support:* Application deadline: 5/1. *Unit head:* Dr. Randal DeMik, Head, 815-838-0500 Ext. 5559, E-mail: demikra@lewisu.edu. *Application contact:* Julie Nickel, Assistant Director, Graduate and Adult Admission, 815-836-5574, E-mail: nickelju@lewisu.edu.

Southeastern Oklahoma State University, Department of Aviation Science, Durant, OK 74701-0609. Offers aerospace administration and logistics (MS). Part-time and evening/weekend programs available. *Students:* 51 full-time (8 women), 65 part-time (12 women); includes 9 Black or African American, non-Hispanic/Latino; 6 American Indian or Alaska Native, non-Hispanic/Latino; 7 Asian, non-Hispanic/Latino; 12 Hispanic/Latino, 2 international. Average age 30. 117 applicants, 99% accepted, 116 enrolled. *Entrance requirements:* For master's, minimum GPA of 3.0 in last 60 hours or 2.75 overall. Additional exam requirements/recommendations for international students: Required—TOEFL (minimum score 550 paper-based; 213 computer-based). *Application deadline:* For fall admission, 8/1 for domestic students, 6/1 for international students; for spring admission, 1/5 for domestic students, 11/1 for international students. Application fee: $20 ($55 for international students). Electronic applications accepted. *Financial support:* Federal Work-Study and institutionally sponsored loans available. Support available to part-time students. Financial award application deadline: 6/15. *Unit head:* Dr. David Conway, Director, 580-745-3240, Fax: 580-924-0741, E-mail: dconway@se.edu. *Application contact:* Carrie Williamson, Administrative Assistant, Graduate Office, 580-745-2200, Fax: 580-745-7474, E-mail: cwilliamson@se.edu.

University of Illinois at Urbana–Champaign, Institute of Aviation, Champaign, IL 61820. Offers human factors (MS). *Students:* 11 full-time (8 women), 6 international. 18 applicants, 28% accepted, 4 enrolled. In 2010, 3 master's awarded. *Entrance requirements:* For master's, GRE, minimum undergraduate GPA of 3.0 for last 60 hours. Additional exam requirements/ recommendations for international students: Required—TOEFL. *Application deadline:* Applications are processed on a rolling basis. Application fee: $75 ($90 for international students). Electronic applications accepted. *Financial support:* In 2010–11, 5 research assistantships, 3 teaching assistantships were awarded; fellowships, tuition waivers (full and partial) also available. *Unit head:* Alex Kirlik, Acting Head, 217-244-8972, E-mail: kirlik@illinois.edu. *Application contact:* Peter Vlach, Information Systems Specialist, 217-265-9456, E-mail: pvlach@illinois.edu.

University of North Dakota, Graduate School, John D. Odegard School of Aerospace Sciences, Department of Aviation, Grand Forks, ND 58202. Offers MS. Part-time programs available. Postbaccalaureate distance learning degree programs offered (minimal on-campus study). *Faculty:* 5 full-time (2 women), 2 part-time/adjunct (0 women). *Students:* 5 full-time (2 women), 23 part-time (5 women); includes 2 minority (both Hispanic/Latino), 1 international. Average age 31. 14 applicants, 64% accepted, 8 enrolled. In 2010, 9 master's awarded. *Degree requirements:* For master's, comprehensive exam. *Entrance requirements:* For master's, GRE General Test, FAA private pilot certificate or foreign equivalent. Additional exam requirements/recommendations for international students: Required—TOEFL (minimum score 550 paper-based; 213 computer-based; 79 iBT), IELTS (minimum score 6.5). *Application deadline:* For fall admission, 8/1 priority date for domestic students, 5/1 priority date for international students; for spring admission, 12/1 priority date for domestic students, 9/1 priority date for international students. Applications are processed on a rolling basis. Application fee: $35. Electronic applications accepted. *Expenses:* Tuition, state resident: full-time $5857; part-time $306.74 per credit. Tuition, nonresident: full-time $15,666; part-time $729.77 per credit. Required fees: $53.42 per credit. Tuition and fees vary according to course load, program and reciprocity agreements. *Financial support:* Fellowships with full and partial tuition reimbursements, research assistantships with full and partial tuition reimbursements, teaching assistantships with full and partial tuition reimbursements, Federal Work-Study, institutionally sponsored loans, scholarships/grants, health care benefits, and unspecified assistantships available. Support available to part-time students. Financial award application deadline: 3/15; financial award applicants required to submit FAFSA. Total annual research expenditures: $3.6 million. *Unit head:* Dr. Kimberly Kenville, Graduate Director, 701-777-4964, E-mail: kimk@aero.und.edu. *Application contact:* Staci Wells, Admissions Specialist, 701-777-0748, Fax: 701-777-3619, E-mail: staci.wells@gradschool.und.edu.

The University of Tennessee, Graduate School, Intercollegiate Programs, Program in Aviation Systems, Knoxville, TN 37996. Offers MS. Part-time programs available. Postbaccalaureate distance learning degree programs offered (no on-campus study). *Degree requirements:* For master's, thesis optional. *Entrance requirements:* For master's, minimum GPA of 2.7. Additional exam requirements/recommendations for international students: Required—TOEFL. Electronic applications accepted. *Expenses:* Tuition, state resident: full-time $7440; part-time $414 per credit hour. Tuition, nonresident: full-time $22,478; part-time $1250 per credit hour. Required fees: $922; $43 per credit hour. Tuition and fees vary according to program.

The University of Tennessee Space Institute, Graduate Programs, Program in Aviation Systems, Tullahoma, TN 37388-9700. Offers MS. *Faculty:* 4 full-time (0 women), 3 part-time/adjunct (0 women). *Students:* 7 full-time (0 women), 13 part-time (3 women), 4 international. 10 applicants, 80% accepted, 8 enrolled. In 2010, 27 master's awarded. *Degree requirements:* For master's, thesis (for some programs). *Entrance requirements:* Additional exam requirements/recommendations for international students: Required—TOEFL (minimum score 550 paper-based; 213 computer-based), IELTS (minimum score 6.5). *Application deadline:* For fall admission, 2/1 for international students; for spring admission, 6/15 for international students. Applications are processed on a rolling basis. Application fee: $35. Electronic applications accepted. *Financial support:* In 2010–11, 4 research assistantships with full tuition reimbursements (averaging $17,791 per year) were awarded; fellowships, career-related internships or fieldwork, Federal Work-Study, institutionally sponsored loans, health care benefits, tuition waivers (full and partial), and unspecified assistantships also available. Financial award applicants required to submit FAFSA. *Faculty research:* Aircraft performance and flying qualities, atmospheric and earth/ocean science, flight systems and human factors, aircraft design, advanced flight test instrumentation. *Unit head:* Dr. Stephen Corda, Chairman, 931-393-7413, Fax: 931-393-7533, E-mail: scorda@utsi.edu. *Application contact:* Dee Merriman, Coordinator III, 931-393-7213, Fax: 931-393-7211, E-mail: dmerrima@utsi.edu.

Section 3
Agricultural Engineering and Bioengineering

This section contains a directory of institutions offering graduate work in agricultural engineering and bioengineering, followed by in-depth entries submitted by institutions that chose to prepare detailed program descriptions. Additional information about programs listed in the directory but not augmented by an in-depth entry may be obtained by writing directly to the dean of a graduate school or chair of a department at the address given in the directory.

For programs offering related work, see also in this book *Biomedical Engineering and Biotechnology; Civil and Environmental Engineering; Engineering and Applied Sciences;* and *Management of Engineering and Technology.* In the other guides in this series:

Graduate Programs in the Biological Sciences
See *Biological and Biomedical Sciences; Ecology, Environmental Biology, and Evolutionary Biology; Marine Biology; Nutrition;* and *Zoology*

Graduate Programs in the Physical Sciences, Mathematics, Agricultural Sciences, the Environment & Natural Resources
See *Agricultural and Food Sciences* and *Natural Resources*

CONTENTS

Agricultural Engineering

Cornell University, Graduate School, Graduate Fields of Agriculture and Life Sciences and Graduate Fields of Engineering, Field of Biological and Environmental Engineering, Ithaca, NY 14853-0001. Offers biological engineering (M Eng, MPS, MS, PhD); energy (M Eng, MPS, MS, PhD); environmental engineering (M Eng, MPS, MS, PhD); environmental management (MPS); food processing engineering (M Eng, MPS, MS, PhD); international agriculture (M Eng, MPS, MS, PhD); local roads (M Eng, MPS, MS, PhD); machine systems (M Eng, MPS, MS, PhD); soil and water engineering (M Eng, MPS, MS, PhD); structures and environment (M Eng, MPS, MS, PhD). *Faculty:* 33 full-time (6 women). *Students:* 75 full-time (36 women); includes 2 Black or African American, non-Hispanic/Latino; 7 Asian, non-Hispanic/Latino; 1 Hispanic/Latino, 25 international. Average age 26. 130 applicants, 39% accepted, 39 enrolled. In 2010, 14 master's, 11 doctorates awarded. Terminal master's awarded for partial completion of doctoral program. *Degree requirements:* For master's, thesis (MS); for doctorate, comprehensive exam, thesis/dissertation. *Entrance requirements:* For master's, letters of recommendation (3 for MS, 2 for M Eng and MPS); for doctorate, GRE General Test, 3 letters of recommendation. Additional exam requirements/recommendations for international students: Required—TOEFL (minimum score 550 paper-based; 213 computer-based; 77 iBT). *Application deadline:* For fall admission, 1/15 priority date for domestic students; for spring admission, 10/1 for domestic students. Applications are processed on a rolling basis. Application fee: $70. Electronic applications accepted. *Expenses:* Tuition: Full-time $29,500. Required fees: $76. Tuition and fees vary according to degree level and program. *Financial support:* In 2010–11, 7 fellowships with full tuition reimbursements, 31 research assistantships with full tuition reimbursements, 9 teaching assistantships with full tuition reimbursements were awarded; institutionally sponsored loans, scholarships/grants, health care benefits, tuition waivers (full and partial), and unspecified assistantships also available. Financial award applicants required to submit FAFSA. *Faculty research:* Biological and food engineering, environmental, soil and water engineering, international agricultural engineering, structures and controlled environments, machine systems and energy. *Unit head:* Director of Graduate Studies, 607-255-2173, Fax: 607-255-4080, E-mail: abengradfield@cornell.edu. *Application contact:* Graduate Field Assistant, 607-255-2173, Fax: 607-255-4080, E-mail: abengradfield@cornell.edu.

Dalhousie University, Faculty of Engineering, Department of Biological Engineering, Halifax, NS B3J 2X4, Canada. Offers M Eng, MA Sc, PhD. *Degree requirements:* For master's, thesis; for doctorate, thesis/dissertation. *Entrance requirements:* Additional exam requirements/recommendations for international students: Required—TOEFL, IELTS, CANTEST, CAEL, or Michigan English Language Assessment Battery. *Faculty research:* Waste management, energy and environment, bio-machinery and robotics, soil and water, aquacultural and food engineering.

Illinois Institute of Technology, Graduate College, Armour College of Engineering, Department of Chemical and Biological Engineering, Chicago, IL 60616-3793. Offers biological engineering (MBE); chemical engineering (M Ch E, MS, PhD); food process engineering (MFPE, MS). Part-time and evening/weekend programs available. Postbaccalaureate distance learning degree programs offered (minimal on-campus study). *Faculty:* 17 full-time (1 woman). *Students:* 156 full-time (63 women), 20 part-time (8 women); includes 11 minority (4 Black or African American, non-Hispanic/Latino; 4 Asian, non-Hispanic/Latino; 2 Hispanic/Latino; 1 Two or more races, non-Hispanic/Latino), 139 international. Average age 25. 413 applicants, 46% accepted, 63 enrolled. In 2010, 32 master's, 15 doctorates awarded. Terminal master's awarded for partial completion of doctoral program. *Degree requirements:* For master's, comprehensive exam (for some programs), thesis (for some programs); for doctorate, comprehensive exam, thesis/dissertation. *Entrance requirements:* For master's, GRE General Test (minimum score 900 Quantitative and Verbal, 2.5 Analytical Writing), minimum undergraduate GPA of 3.0; for doctorate, GRE General Test (minimum score 1000 Quantitative and Verbal, 3.0 Analytical Writing), minimum undergraduate GPA of 3.0. Additional exam requirements/recommendations for international students: Required—TOEFL (minimum score 523 paper-based; 70 iBT); Recommended—IELTS (minimum score 5.5). *Application deadline:* For fall admission, 5/1 for domestic and international students; for spring admission, 10/15 for domestic and international students. Applications are processed on a rolling basis. Application fee: $50. Electronic applications accepted. *Expenses:* Tuition: Full-time $18,576; part-time $1032 per credit hour. Required fees: $583 per semester. One-time fee: $150. Tuition and fees vary according to program and student level. *Financial support:* In 2010–11, 42 research assistantships with full and partial tuition reimbursements (averaging $7,975 per year), 7 teaching assistantships with full tuition reimbursements (averaging $5,107 per year) were awarded; fellowships with partial tuition reimbursements, Federal Work-Study, institutionally sponsored loans, scholarships/grants, health care benefits, and unspecified assistantships also available. Support available to part-time students. Financial award applicants required to submit FAFSA. *Faculty research:* Energy and sustainability, biological engineering, advanced materials, systems engineering. Total annual research expenditures: $2.6 million. *Unit head:* Dr. John Kallend, Acting Chair, 312-567-3054, Fax: 312-567-8875, E-mail: kallend@iit.edu. *Application contact:* Deborah Gibson, Director, Graduate Admission, 866-472-3448, Fax: 312-567-3138, E-mail: inquiry.grad@iit.edu.

Instituto Tecnológico y de Estudios Superiores de Monterrey, Campus Monterrey, Graduate and Research Division, Program in Agriculture, Monterrey, Mexico. Offers agricultural parasitology (PhD); agricultural sciences (MS); farming productivity (MS); food processing engineering (MS); phytopathology (MS). Part-time programs available. *Degree requirements:* For master's, one foreign language, thesis; for doctorate, one foreign language, thesis/dissertation. *Entrance requirements:* For master's, EXADEP; for doctorate, GMAT or GRE, master's degree in related field. Additional exam requirements/recommendations for international students: Required—TOEFL. *Faculty research:* Animal embryos and reproduction, crop entomology, tropical agriculture, agricultural productivity, induced mutation in oleaginous plants.

Iowa State University of Science and Technology, Graduate College, College of Engineering, Department of Agricultural and Biosystems Engineering, Ames, IA 50011. Offers M Eng, MS, PhD. *Faculty:* 30 full-time (2 women), 3 part-time/adjunct (0 women). *Students:* 55 full-time (21 women), 21 part-time (7 women); includes 3 Black or African American, non-Hispanic/Latino; 1 American Indian or Alaska Native, non-Hispanic/Latino; 2 Asian, non-Hispanic/Latino; 1 Hispanic/Latino, 29 international. 52 applicants, 31% accepted, 13 enrolled. In 2010, 9 master's, 5 doctorates awarded. *Degree requirements:* For master's, thesis (for some programs); for doctorate, thesis/dissertation. *Entrance requirements:* For master's and doctorate, GRE. Additional exam requirements/recommendations for international students: Required—TOEFL (minimum score 550 paper-based; 79 iBT), IELTS (minimum score 6.5). *Application deadline:* For fall admission, 2/1 priority date for domestic and international students; for spring admission, 7/1 priority date for domestic and international students. Applications are processed on a rolling basis. Application fee: $40 ($90 for international students). Electronic applications accepted. *Financial support:* In 2010–11, 51 research assistantships with full and partial tuition reimbursements (averaging $15,435 per year), 1 teaching assistantship with full and partial tuition reimbursement (averaging $9,613 per year) were awarded; fellowships, scholarships/grants, health care benefits, and unspecified assistantships also available. *Faculty research:* Grain processing and quality, tillage systems, simulation and controls, water management, environmental quality. *Unit head:* Dr. Ramesh Kanwar, Chair, 515-294-1434. *Application contact:* Dr. Steven Freeman, Director of Graduate Education, 515-294-9541, E-mail: sfreeman@iastate.edu.

Kansas State University, Graduate School, College of Agriculture, Department of Grain Science and Industry, Manhattan, KS 66506. Offers MS, PhD. Part-time programs available. Terminal master's awarded for partial completion of doctoral program. *Degree requirements:* For master's, thesis, oral exam; for doctorate, thesis/dissertation, preliminary exam. *Entrance requirements:* For master's and doctorate, GRE General Test, minimum undergraduate GPA of 3.0. Additional exam requirements/recommendations for international students: Required—TOEFL (minimum score 550 paper-based; 213 computer-based). Electronic applications accepted. *Faculty research:* Particle management, grain and cereal product research, industrial value added products from cereals and legumes, grain stored wheat and pest management, biosecurity and global tracing.

Kansas State University, Graduate School, College of Engineering, Department of Biological and Agricultural Engineering, Manhattan, KS 66506. Offers MS, PhD. Terminal master's awarded for partial completion of doctoral program. *Degree requirements:* For master's, thesis; for doctorate, thesis/dissertation. *Entrance requirements:* For master's, GRE (recommended), bachelor's degree in agricultural engineering; for doctorate, GRE (recommended). Additional exam requirements/recommendations for international students: Required—TOEFL (minimum score 600 paper-based; 250 computer-based). Electronic applications accepted. *Faculty research:* Ecological engineering, watershed modeling, air quality, bioprocessing, sensors and controls.

Louisiana State University and Agricultural and Mechanical College, Graduate School, College of Agriculture, Department of Biological and Agricultural Engineering, Baton Rouge, LA 70803. Offers biological and agricultural engineering (MSBAE); engineering science (MS, PhD). Part-time programs available. *Faculty:* 12 full-time (2 women). *Students:* 13 full-time (3 women), 3 part-time (0 women); includes 1 Black or African American, non-Hispanic/Latino; 3 Asian, non-Hispanic/Latino; 1 Hispanic/Latino, 6 international. Average age 26. 12 applicants, 58% accepted, 2 enrolled. In 2010, 8 master's awarded. Terminal master's awarded for partial completion of doctoral program. *Degree requirements:* For master's, thesis; for doctorate, thesis/dissertation. *Entrance requirements:* For master's and doctorate, GRE General Test, minimum GPA of 3.0. Additional exam requirements/recommendations for international students: Required—TOEFL (minimum score 550 paper-based; 213 computer-based; 79 iBT) or IELTS (minimum score 6.5). *Application deadline:* For fall admission, 1/25 priority date for domestic students, 5/15 for international students; for spring admission, 10/15 for international students. Applications are processed on a rolling basis. Application fee: $50 ($70 for international students). Electronic applications accepted. *Financial support:* In 2010–11, 14 students received support, including 1 fellowship (averaging $24,803 per year), 12 research assistantships with partial tuition reimbursements available (averaging $16,391 per year); teaching assistantships with partial tuition reimbursements available, career-related internships or fieldwork, Federal Work-Study, institutionally sponsored loans, scholarships/grants, health care benefits, and unspecified assistantships also available. Financial award application deadline: 7/1; financial award applicants required to submit FAFSA. *Faculty research:* Bioenergy, bioprocess engineering, cellular and molecular engineering, drug delivery using nanotechnology, environmental engineering. Total annual research expenditures: $37,654. *Unit head:* Dr. Dan Thomas, Head, 225-578-3153, Fax: 225-578-3492, E-mail: dthomas@agcenter.lsu.edu. *Application contact:* Dr. Steven Hall, Graduate Coordinator, 225-578-1058, Fax: 225-578-3492, E-mail: sghall@agcenter.lsu.edu.

McGill University, Faculty of Graduate and Postdoctoral Studies, Faculty of Agricultural and Environmental Sciences, Department of Bioresource Engineering, Montréal, QC H3A 2T5, Canada. Offers computer applications (M Sc, M Sc A, PhD); food engineering (M Sc, M Sc A, PhD); grain drying (M Sc, M Sc A, PhD); irrigation and drainage (M Sc, M Sc A, PhD); machinery (M Sc, M Sc A, PhD); pollution control (M Sc, M Sc A, PhD); post-harvest technology (M Sc, M Sc A, PhD); soil dynamics (M Sc, M Sc A, PhD); structure and environment (M Sc, M Sc A, PhD); vegetable and fruit storage (M Sc, M Sc A, PhD).

New York University, Graduate School of Arts and Science, Department of Environmental Medicine, New York, NY 10012-1019. Offers environmental health sciences (MS, PhD), including biostatistics (PhD), environmental hygiene (MS), epidemiology (PhD), ergonomics and biomechanics (PhD), exposure assessment and health effects (PhD), molecular toxicology/carcinogenesis (PhD), toxicology. Part-time programs available. *Faculty:* 26 full-time (7 women). *Students:* 53 full-time (38 women), 10 part-time (3 women); includes 3 Black or African American, non-Hispanic/Latino; 4 Asian, non-Hispanic/Latino; 5 Hispanic/Latino, 23 international. Average age 30. 60 applicants, 48% accepted, 14 enrolled. In 2010, 8 master's, 5 doctorates awarded. Terminal master's awarded for partial completion of doctoral program. *Degree requirements:* For master's, thesis or alternative; for doctorate, one foreign language, thesis/dissertation, oral and written exams. *Entrance requirements:* For master's and doctorate, GRE General Test, GRE Subject Test, minimum GPA of 3.0; bachelor's degree in biological, physical, or engineering science. Additional exam requirements/recommendations for international students: Required—TOEFL. *Application deadline:* For fall admission, 12/15 for domestic students. Application fee: $90. *Financial support:* Fellowships with tuition reimbursements, teaching assistantships with tuition reimbursements, career-related internships or fieldwork, Federal Work-Study, institutionally sponsored loans, and health care benefits available. Financial award application deadline: 12/15; financial award applicants required to submit FAFSA. *Unit head:* Dr. Max Costa, Chair, 845-731-3661, Fax: 845-351-4510, E-mail: ehs@env.med.nyu.edu. *Application contact:* Dr. Jerome J. Solomon, Director of Graduate Studies, 845-731-3661, Fax: 845-351-4510, E-mail: ehs@env.med.nyu.edu.

North Carolina State University, Graduate School, College of Agriculture and Life Sciences, Department of Biological and Agricultural Engineering, Raleigh, NC 27695. Offers MBAE, MS, PhD, Certificate. Part-time programs available. Postbaccalaureate distance learning degree programs offered. *Degree requirements:* For master's, thesis (for some programs); for doctorate, thesis/dissertation. *Entrance requirements:* For master's and doctorate, GRE. Additional exam requirements/recommendations for international students: Required—TOEFL. Electronic applications accepted. *Faculty research:* Bioinstrumentation, animal waste management, water quality engineering, machine systems, controlled environment agriculture.

North Dakota State University, College of Graduate and Interdisciplinary Studies, College of Engineering and Architecture, Department of Agricultural and Biosystems Engineering, Fargo, ND 58108. Offers agricultural and biosystems engineering (MS, PhD); engineering (PhD); natural resource management (MS); natural resources management (PhD). Part-time programs available. *Faculty:* 6 full-time (1 woman). *Students:* 8 full-time (2 women), 4 part-time (1 woman), 9 international. Average age 28. 19 applicants, 37% accepted, 4 enrolled. In 2010, 1 master's, 5 doctorates awarded. *Degree requirements:* For master's, thesis; for doctorate, thesis/dissertation. *Entrance requirements:* For master's and doctorate, BS in engineering or the equivalent, minimum undergraduate GPA of 3.0. Additional exam requirements/recommendations for international students: Required—TOEFL (minimum score 550 paper-based; 213 computer-based; 79 iBT). *Application deadline:* For fall admission, 7/1 priority date for domestic and international students; for spring admission, 10/1 priority date for domestic and international students. Applications are processed on a rolling basis. Application fee: $45 ($60 for international students). Electronic applications accepted. *Financial support:* In 2010–11, 9 research assistantships with full tuition reimbursements (averaging $15,000 per year) were awarded; career-related internships or fieldwork, Federal Work-Study, institutionally sponsored loans, and unspecified assistantships also available. Support available to part-time students. Financial award application deadline: 4/15. *Faculty research:* Irrigation, crop processing, food engineering, environmental resources, sensors and instrumentation. Total annual research expenditures: $158,309. *Unit head:* Leslie F. Backer, Chair, 701-231-7261, Fax: 701-231-1008, E-mail: leslie.backer@ndsu.edu. *Application contact:* Dr. David A. Wittrock, Dean, 701-231-7033, Fax: 701-231-6524.

The Ohio State University, Graduate School, College of Food, Agricultural, and Environmental Sciences, Department of Food, Agricultural, and Biological Engineering, Columbus, OH 43210. Offers MS, PhD. *Faculty:* 31. *Students:* 28 full-time (10 women), 10 part-time (3 women); includes 1 Black or African American, non-Hispanic/Latino; 1 Asian, non-Hispanic/Latino; 1 Hispanic/Latino, 19 international. Average age 28. In 2010, 11 master's awarded. *Degree requirements:* For master's, thesis optional; for doctorate, thesis/dissertation. *Entrance requirements:* For master's and doctorate, GRE General Test, GRE Subject Test in engineering (recommended). Additional exam requirements/recommendations for international students:

Required—TOEFL (minimum score 550 paper-based; 213 computer-based), IELTS (minimum score 7), or Michigan English Language Assessment Battery (minimum score 85). *Application deadline:* For fall admission, 8/15 priority date for domestic students, 7/1 priority date for international students; for winter admission, 12/1 priority date for domestic students, 11/1 priority date for international students; for spring admission, 3/1 priority date for domestic students, 2/1 priority date for international students. Applications are processed on a rolling basis. Application fee: $40 ($50 for international students). Electronic applications accepted. *Expenses:* Tuition, state resident: full-time $10,605. Tuition, nonresident: full-time $26,535. Tuition and fees vary according to course load and program. *Financial support:* Fellowships, research assistantships, teaching assistantships, career-related internships or fieldwork, Federal Work-Study, and institutionally sponsored loans available. Support available to part-time students. *Unit head:* Sudih Sastry, Chair, 614-292-9338, E-mail: bean.3@osu.edu. *Application contact:* Graduate Admissions, 614-292-9444, Fax: 614-292-3895, E-mail: domestic.grad@osu.edu.

Oklahoma State University, College of Agricultural Science and Natural Resources, Department of Biosystems and Agricultural Engineering, Stillwater, OK 74078. Offers biosystems engineering (MS, PhD); environmental and natural resources (MS, PhD). *Faculty:* 22 full-time (4 women), 4 part-time/adjunct (0 women). *Students:* 23 full-time (10 women), 45 part-time (16 women); includes 2 American Indian or Alaska Native, non-Hispanic/Latino; 1 Asian, non-Hispanic/Latino; 2 Hispanic/Latino, 36 international. Average age 30. 58 applicants, 40% accepted, 14 enrolled. In 2010, 4 master's, 3 doctorates awarded. *Degree requirements:* For master's, thesis; for doctorate, comprehensive exam, thesis/dissertation. *Entrance requirements:* For master's and doctorate, GRE or GMAT. Additional exam requirements/recommendations for international students: Required—TOEFL (minimum score 550 paper-based; 79 iBT). *Application deadline:* For fall admission, 3/1 priority date for international students; for spring admission, 8/1 priority date for international students. Applications are processed on a rolling basis. Application fee: $40 ($75 for international students). Electronic applications accepted. *Expenses:* Tuition, state resident: full-time $3716; part-time $154.85 per credit hour. Tuition, nonresident: full-time $14,892; part-time $621 per credit hour. Required fees: $2044; $85.20 per credit hour. One-time fee: $50. Tuition and fees vary according to course load and campus/location. *Financial support:* In 2010–11, 48 research assistantships (averaging $17,561 per year), 1 teaching assistantship (averaging $6,000 per year) were awarded; career-related internships or fieldwork, Federal Work-Study, scholarships/grants, health care benefits, tuition waivers (partial), and unspecified assistantships also available. Support available to part-time students. Financial award application deadline: 3/1; financial award applicants required to submit FAFSA. *Unit head:* Dr. Ronald L. Elliot, Head, 405-744-5431, Fax: 405-744-6059. *Application contact:* Dr. Gordon Emslie, Dean, 405-744-6368, Fax: 405-744-0355, E-mail: grad-i@okstate.edu.

Penn State University Park, Graduate School, College of Agricultural Sciences, Department of Agricultural and Biological Engineering, State College, University Park, PA 16802-1503. Offers MS, PhD.

Purdue University, College of Engineering, Department of Agricultural and Biological Engineering, West Lafayette, IN 47907-2093. Offers MS, MSABE, MSE, PhD. Part-time programs available. Terminal master's awarded for partial completion of doctoral program. *Degree requirements:* For master's, thesis (for some programs); for doctorate, thesis/dissertation. *Entrance requirements:* For master's and doctorate, GRE General Test. Additional exam requirements/recommendations for international students: Required—TOEFL (minimum score 550 paper-based; 213 computer-based; 77 iBT). Electronic applications accepted. *Faculty research:* Food and biological engineering, environmental engineering, machine systems, biotechnology, machine intelligence.

South Dakota State University, Graduate School, College of Engineering, Department of Agricultural and Biosystems Engineering, Brookings, SD 57007. Offers biological sciences (MS, PhD); engineering (MS). PhD offered jointly with Iowa State University of Science and Technology. Part-time programs available. *Degree requirements:* For master's, thesis (for some programs), oral exam; for doctorate, thesis/dissertation, preliminary oral and written exams. *Entrance requirements:* For master's and doctorate, engineering degree. Additional exam requirements/recommendations for international students: Required—TOEFL (minimum score 550 paper-based; 213 computer-based; 79 iBT). *Faculty research:* Water resources, food engineering, natural resources engineering, machine design, bioprocess engineering.

Texas A&M University, College of Agriculture and Life Sciences and College of Engineering, Department of Biological and Agricultural Engineering, College Station, TX 77843. Offers M Agr, M Eng, MS, DE, PhD. Part-time programs available. *Faculty:* 19. *Students:* 69 full-time (26 women), 17 part-time (2 women); includes 8 minority (3 Black or African American, non-Hispanic/Latino; 3 Asian, non-Hispanic/Latino; 2 Hispanic/Latino), 47 international. Average age 29. In 2010, 12 master's, 3 doctorates awarded. *Degree requirements:* For master's, thesis (MS), preliminary and final exams; for doctorate, thesis/dissertation, preliminary and final exams. *Entrance requirements:* For master's and doctorate, GRE General Test. Additional exam requirements/recommendations for international students: Required—TOEFL (minimum score 550 paper-based; 213 computer-based). *Application deadline:* For fall admission, 2/1 priority date for domestic students; for spring admission, 10/1 for domestic students. Applications are processed on a rolling basis. Application fee: $50 ($75 for international students). Electronic applications accepted. *Financial support:* In 2010–11, 3 fellowships with full and partial tuition reimbursements (averaging $15,000 per year), 17 research assistantships with full and partial tuition reimbursements (averaging $18,150 per year), 12 teaching assistantships with partial tuition reimbursements (averaging $19,590 per year) were awarded; career-related internships or fieldwork, institutionally sponsored loans, scholarships/grants, tuition waivers, and unspecified assistantships also available. Financial award application deadline: 3/1; financial award applicants required to submit FAFSA. *Faculty research:* Water quality and quantity; air quality; biological, food, ecological engineering; off-road equipment; mechatronics. *Unit head:* Dr. Steve Searcy, Interim Head, 979-845-3668, Fax: 979-862-3442, E-mail: s-searcy@tamu.edu. *Application contact:* Dr. Steve Searcy, Interim Head, 979-845-3668, Fax: 979-862-3442, E-mail: s-searcy@tamu.edu.

Université Laval, Faculty of Agricultural and Food Sciences, Department of Soils and Agricultural Engineering, Programs in Agri-Food Engineering, Québec, QC G1K 7P4, Canada. Offers agri-food engineering (M Sc); environmental technology (M Sc). *Degree requirements:* For master's, thesis (for some programs). *Entrance requirements:* For master's, knowledge of French. Electronic applications accepted.

The University of Arizona, College of Agriculture and Life Sciences, Department of Agricultural and Biosystems Engineering, Tucson, AZ 85721. Offers MS, PhD. *Faculty:* 10 full-time (1 woman). *Students:* 22 full-time (6 women), 8 part-time (3 women); includes 1 Asian, non-Hispanic/Latino; 1 Hispanic/Latino; 2 Two or more races, non-Hispanic/Latino, 18 international. Average age 32. 19 applicants, 74% accepted, 6 enrolled. In 2010, 6 master's, 5 doctorates awarded. Terminal master's awarded for partial completion of doctoral program. *Degree requirements:* For master's, thesis; for doctorate, thesis/dissertation. *Entrance requirements:* For master's, minimum GPA of 3.0 in last 2 years of undergraduate study, 3 letters of recommendation; for doctorate, minimum GPA of 3.0 in last 2 years of undergraduate study, 3 letters of recommendation, statement of purpose. Additional exam requirements/recommendations for international students: Required—TOEFL (minimum score 213 computer-based). *Application deadline:* For fall admission, 6/1 for domestic students, 2/1 for international students; for spring admission, 9/1 for domestic students, 8/1 for international students. Applications are processed on a rolling basis. Application fee: $75. Electronic applications accepted. *Expenses:* Tuition, state resident: full-time $7692. *Financial support:* In 2010–11, 13 research assistantships with full and partial tuition reimbursements (averaging $24,985 per year), 1 teaching assistantship with full and partial tuition reimbursement (averaging $24,435 per year) were awarded; fellowships, career-related internships or fieldwork, Federal Work-Study, institutionally sponsored loans, scholarships/grants, traineeships, health care benefits, tuition waivers (full and partial), and unspecified assistantships also available. Financial award application deadline: 5/1. *Faculty research:* Irrigation system design, energy-use management, equipment for alternative crops, food properties enhancement. Total annual research expenditures: $452,871. *Unit head:* Donald Slack, Head, 520-621-3691, Fax: 520-621-3963, E-mail: slackd@u.arizona.edu. *Application contact:* Daniela Ibarra, Senior Office Specialist, 520-621-1753, Fax: 520-621-3963, E-mail: dcastro@email.arizona.edu.

University of Arkansas, Graduate School, College of Engineering, Department of Biological and Agricultural Engineering, Fayetteville, AR 72701-1201. Offers biological and agricultural engineering (MSE, PhD); biological engineering (MSBE); biomedical engineering (MSBME). *Students:* 5 full-time (2 women), 17 part-time (2 women); includes 1 minority (Black or African American, non-Hispanic/Latino), 12 international. 23 applicants, 52% accepted. In 2010, 6 master's, 2 doctorates awarded. *Degree requirements:* For master's, thesis; for doctorate, one foreign language, thesis/dissertation. *Application deadline:* For fall admission, 4/1 for international students; for spring admission, 10/1 for international students. Applications are processed on a rolling basis. Application fee: $40 ($50 for international students). Electronic applications accepted. *Financial support:* In 2010–11, 2 fellowships with tuition reimbursements, 12 research assistantships, 4 teaching assistantships were awarded; career-related internships or fieldwork and Federal Work-Study also available. Support available to part-time students. Financial award application deadline: 4/1; financial award applicants required to submit FAFSA. *Unit head:* Dr. Lalit Verma, Department Head, 479-575-2351, Fax: 479-575-2846, E-mail: lverma@uark.edu. *Application contact:* Dr. Jin-Woo Kim, Program Coordinator, 479-575-2351, Fax: 479-575-2846, E-mail: jwkim@uark.edu.

University of Dayton, Graduate School, School of Engineering, Department of Civil and Environmental Engineering and Engineering Mechanics, Dayton, OH 45469-1300. Offers engineering mechanics (MSEM); environmental engineering (MSCE); geotechnical engineering (MSCE); structural engineering (MSCE); transportation engineering (MSCE); water resources engineering (MSCE). Part-time programs available. *Faculty:* 7 full-time (2 women), 2 part-time/adjunct (0 women). *Students:* 10 full-time (5 women), 7 part-time (2 women); includes 2 minority (both Black or African American, non-Hispanic/Latino), 6 international. Average age 27. 23 applicants, 43% accepted, 4 enrolled. In 2010, 5 master's awarded. *Degree requirements:* For master's, thesis optional. *Entrance requirements:* For master's, minimum GPA of 3.0 in undergraduate work. Additional exam requirements/recommendations for international students: Required—TOEFL (minimum score 550 paper-based; 213 computer-based; 80 iBT). *Application deadline:* For fall admission, 8/1 for domestic students, 3/1 priority date for international students; for winter admission, 7/1 priority date for international students; for spring admission, 1/1 priority date for international students. Applications are processed on a rolling basis. Application fee: $0 ($50 for international students). Electronic applications accepted. *Expenses:* Tuition: Full-time $7800; part-time $650 per credit hour. *Financial support:* In 2010–11, 2 research assistantships (averaging $10,600 per year) were awarded. Financial award applicants required to submit FAFSA. *Faculty research:* Physical modeling of hydraulic systems, finite element methods, mechanics of composite materials, transportation systems safety, biological treatment processes. Total annual research expenditures: $200,000. *Unit head:* Dr. Donald V. Chase, Chair, 937-229-3847, Fax: 937-229-3491, E-mail: donald.chase@notes.udayton.edu. *Application contact:* Alexander Popovski, Associate Director of International and Graduate Admissions, 937-229-2357, Fax: 937-229-4729, E-mail: alex.popovski@notes.udayton.edu.

University of Florida, Graduate School, College of Engineering and College of Agricultural and Life Sciences, Department of Agricultural and Biological Engineering, Gainesville, FL 32611. Offers ME, MS, PhD, Engr. Part-time programs available. *Students:* 81 full-time (28 women), 5 part-time (1 woman); includes 1 Black or African American, non-Hispanic/Latino; 2 Asian, non-Hispanic/Latino; 4 Hispanic/Latino, 49 international. Average age 29. 53 applicants, 43% accepted, 15 enrolled. In 2010, 19 master's, 16 doctorates awarded. Terminal master's awarded for partial completion of doctoral program. *Degree requirements:* For master's, comprehensive exam, thesis (for some programs), Thesis requirement depends on degree; for doctorate, comprehensive exam, thesis/dissertation. *Entrance requirements:* For master's and doctorate, GRE General Test, minimum GPA of 3.0; for Engr, GRE General Test. Additional exam requirements/recommendations for international students: Required—TOEFL (minimum score 550 paper-based; 213 computer-based; 80 iBT), IELTS (minimum score 6). *Application deadline:* For fall admission, 2/15 for domestic and international students; for spring admission, 7/1 for domestic and international students. Applications are processed on a rolling basis. Application fee: $30. Electronic applications accepted. *Expenses:* Tuition, state resident: full-time $10,915.92. Tuition, nonresident: full-time $28,309. *Financial support:* In 2010–11, 71 students received support, including 8 fellowships with full and partial tuition reimbursements available, 63 research assistantships with partial tuition reimbursements available (averaging $15,916 per year); unspecified assistantships also available. Financial award application deadline: 2/15; financial award applicants required to submit FAFSA. *Faculty research:* Biological processing, crop and climate modeling, land and water resources, robotic harvesting, food and packaging. *Unit head:* Dr. Dorota Z. Haman, Chair, 352-392-1864 Ext. 120, Fax: 352-392-4092, E-mail: dhaman@ufl.edu. *Application contact:* Dr. Ray A. Bucklin, Graduate Coordinator, 352-392-1864 Ext. 169, Fax: 352-392-4092, E-mail: bucklin@ufl.edu.

University of Georgia, College of Agricultural and Environmental Sciences, Department of Biological and Agricultural Engineering, Athens, GA 30602. Offers agricultural engineering (MS); biological and agricultural engineering (PhD); biological engineering (MS). *Faculty:* 29 full-time (3 women), 2 part-time/adjunct (0 women). *Students:* 38 full-time (11 women), 10 part-time (1 woman); includes 5 Black or African American, non-Hispanic/Latino; 2 Asian, non-Hispanic/Latino, 26 international. 43 applicants, 51% accepted, 12 enrolled. In 2010, 13 master's, 3 doctorates awarded. *Degree requirements:* For master's, thesis; for doctorate, one foreign language, thesis/dissertation. *Entrance requirements:* For master's and doctorate, GRE General Test. *Application deadline:* For fall admission, 7/1 priority date for domestic students; for spring admission, 11/15 for domestic students. Application fee: $50. Electronic applications accepted. *Expenses:* Tuition, state resident: full-time $7200; part-time $344 per credit hour. Tuition, nonresident: full-time $21,900; part-time $944 per credit hour. Tuition and fees vary according to course load and program. *Financial support:* Fellowships, research assistantships, teaching assistantships, unspecified assistantships available. *Unit head:* Dr. E. Dale Threadgill, Head, 706-542-1653, Fax: 706-542-8806, E-mail: tgill@engr.uga.edu. *Application contact:* Dr. William Tollner, Graduate Coordinator, 706-542-3047, Fax: 706-542-8806, E-mail: btollner@engr.uga.edu.

University of Idaho, College of Graduate Studies, College of Engineering, Department of Biological and Agricultural Engineering, Moscow, ID 83844-2282. Offers M Engr, MS, PhD. Program offered jointly with College of Agricultural and Life Sciences. *Faculty:* 5 full-time. *Students:* 5 full-time, 3 part-time. Average age 36. In 2010, 1 master's, 1 doctorate awarded. *Degree requirements:* For master's, thesis or alternative; for doctorate, one foreign language, thesis/dissertation. *Entrance requirements:* For master's, minimum GPA of 2.8; for doctorate, minimum undergraduate GPA of 2.8, 3.0 graduate. *Application deadline:* For fall admission, 8/1 for domestic students; for spring admission, 12/15 for domestic students. Applications are processed on a rolling basis. Application fee: $60. Electronic applications accepted. *Expenses:* Tuition, nonresident: part-time $580 per credit. Required fees: $306 per credit. *Financial support:* Research assistantships, teaching assistantships, career-related internships or fieldwork available. Financial award applicants required to submit FAFSA. *Faculty research:* Water and environmental research, alternative fuels/biodiesel, agricultural safety health, biological processes for agricultural/food waste. *Unit head:* Dr. Jon Harlan Van Gerpen, Department Head, 208-885-7891, E-mail: baengr@uidaho.edu. *Application contact:* Dr. Jon Harlan Van Gerpen, Department Head, 208-885-7891, E-mail: baengr@uidaho.edu.

University of Illinois at Urbana–Champaign, Graduate College, College of Agricultural, Consumer and Environmental Sciences, Department of Agricultural and Biological Engineering, Champaign, IL 61820. Offers agricultural and biological engineering (MS, PhD); technical systems management (MS, PSM). *Faculty:* 20 full-time (2 women). *Students:* 48 full-time (10 women), 3 part-time (1 woman); includes 2 Hispanic/Latino, 39 international. 57 applicants, 28% accepted, 11 enrolled. In 2010, 6 master's, 4 doctorates awarded. *Entrance requirements:* For master's and doctorate, minimum GPA of 3.0. Additional exam requirements/

Agricultural Engineering

University of Illinois at Urbana–Champaign *(continued)*
recommendations for international students: Required—TOEFL (minimum score 570 paper-based; 230 computer-based; 88 iBT) or IELTS (minimum score 6.5). *Application deadline:* Applications are processed on a rolling basis. Application fee: $75 ($90 for international students). Electronic applications accepted. *Financial support:* In 2010–11, 6 fellowships, 42 research assistantships, 3 teaching assistantships were awarded; tuition waivers (full and partial) also available. *Unit head:* Kuan Chong Ting, Head, 217-333-3570, Fax: 217-244-0323, E-mail: kcting@illinois.edu. *Application contact:* Ronda Sullivan, Assistant to the Head, 217-333-3570, Fax: 217-244-0323, E-mail: rsully@illinois.edu.

University of Kentucky, Graduate School, College of Agriculture, Program in Biosystems and Agricultural Engineering, Lexington, KY 40506-0032. Offers MS, PhD. Part-time programs available. *Degree requirements:* For master's, comprehensive exam, thesis optional; for doctorate, comprehensive exam, thesis/dissertation. *Entrance requirements:* For master's, GRE General Test, minimum undergraduate GPA of 2.75; for doctorate, GRE General Test, minimum graduate GPA of 3.0. Additional exam requirements/recommendations for international students: Required—TOEFL (minimum score 550 paper-based; 213 computer-based). Electronic applications accepted. *Faculty research:* Machine systems, food engineering, fermentation, hydrology, water quality.

University of Missouri, Graduate School, College of Engineering, Department of Biological Engineering, Columbia, MO 65211. Offers agricultural engineering (MS); biological engineering (MS, PhD). *Degree requirements:* For master's, thesis; for doctorate, thesis/dissertation. *Entrance requirements:* For master's and doctorate, GRE General Test, minimum GPA of 3.0. Additional exam requirements/recommendations for international students: Required—TOEFL (minimum score 550 paper-based; 213 computer-based; 80 iBT).

University of Nebraska–Lincoln, Graduate College, College of Engineering, Department of Biological Systems Engineering, Interdepartmental Area of Agricultural and Biological Systems Engineering, Lincoln, NE 68588. Offers MS, PhD. *Degree requirements:* For master's, thesis optional. *Entrance requirements:* Additional exam requirements/recommendations for international students: Required—TOEFL (minimum score 550 paper-based; 213 computer-based). Electronic applications accepted. *Faculty research:* Hydrological engineering, tractive performance, biomedical engineering, irrigation systems.

University of Saskatchewan, College of Graduate Studies and Research, College of Engineering, Department of Agricultural and Bioresource Engineering, Saskatoon, SK S7N 5A2, Canada. Offers M Eng, M Sc, PhD. *Degree requirements:* For master's, thesis (for some programs); for doctorate, thesis/dissertation. *Entrance requirements:* For master's and doctorate, GRE. Additional exam requirements/recommendations for international students: Required—TOEFL.

The University of Tennessee, Graduate School, College of Agricultural Sciences and Natural Resources, Department of Biosystems Engineering and Environmental Science, Program in Biosystems Engineering Technology, Knoxville, TN 37996. Offers MS. *Degree requirements:* For master's, thesis or alternative. *Entrance requirements:* For master's, GRE General Test, minimum GPA of 2.7. Additional exam requirements/recommendations for international students: Required—TOEFL. Electronic applications accepted. *Expenses:* Tuition, state resident: full-time $7440; part-time $414 per credit hour. Tuition, nonresident: full-time $22,478; part-time $1250 per credit hour. Required fees: $922; $43 per credit hour. Tuition and fees vary according to program.

University of Wisconsin–Madison, Graduate School, College of Agricultural and Life Sciences, Department of Biological Systems Engineering, Madison, WI 53706. Offers MS, PhD. Part-time programs available. *Students:* 26 full-time (5 women), 4 part-time (3 women); includes 11 Asian, non-Hispanic/Latino; 1 Hispanic/Latino, 12 international. Average age 30. 49 applicants, 16% accepted, 7 enrolled. In 2010, 6 master's awarded. Terminal master's awarded for partial completion of doctoral program. *Degree requirements:* For master's, thesis; for doctorate, thesis/dissertation. *Entrance requirements:* Additional exam requirements/recommendations for international students: Required—TOEFL. *Application deadline:* For fall admission, 7/15 for domestic students, 6/1 for international students; for spring admission, 12/15 for domestic students, 11/1 for international students. Applications are processed on a rolling basis. Application fee: $56. Electronic applications accepted. *Expenses:* Tuition, state resident: full-time $9887.36; part-time $617.96 per credit. Tuition, nonresident: full-time $24,054; part-time $1503.40 per credit. Required fees: $67.63 per credit. Tuition and fees vary according to reciprocity agreements. *Financial support:* In 2010–11, 1 fellowship with full tuition reimbursement (averaging $18,720 per year), 19 research assistantships with full tuition reimbursements (averaging

$17,430 per year) were awarded; Federal Work-Study and institutionally sponsored loans also available. Support available to part-time students. Financial award application deadline: 11/1; financial award applicants required to submit FAFSA. *Faculty research:* Biomaterials, biosensors, food safety, food engineering, bioprocessing, machinery systems, natural resources and environment, structures engineering. Total annual research expenditures: $20.9 million. *Unit head:* Richard Straub, Chair, 608-262-2757, Fax: 608-262-6055, E-mail: rjstraub@wisc.edu. *Application contact:* Debby Sumwalt, Graduate Admissions Coordinator, 608-262-3310, Fax: 608-262-1228, E-mail: dsumwalt@facstaff.wisc.edu.

Utah State University, School of Graduate Studies, College of Engineering, Department of Biological and Irrigation Engineering, Logan, UT 84322. Offers biological and agricultural engineering (MS, PhD); irrigation engineering (MS, PhD). Part-time programs available. Terminal master's awarded for partial completion of doctoral program. *Degree requirements:* For master's, thesis (for some programs); for doctorate, thesis/dissertation. *Entrance requirements:* For master's and doctorate, GRE General Test, minimum GPA of 3.0. Additional exam requirements/recommendations for international students: Required—TOEFL. *Faculty research:* On-farm water management, crop-water yield modeling, irrigation, biosensors, biological engineering.

Virginia Polytechnic Institute and State University, Graduate School, College of Engineering, Department of Biological Systems Engineering, Blacksburg, VA 24061. Offers M Eng, MS, PhD. *Faculty:* 17 full-time (2 women). *Students:* 57 full-time (17 women), 5 part-time (3 women); includes 1 Black or African American, non-Hispanic/Latino; 2 Asian, non-Hispanic/Latino; 2 Hispanic/Latino, 29 international. Average age 27. 65 applicants, 37% accepted, 18 enrolled. In 2010, 14 master's awarded. *Degree requirements:* For master's, comprehensive exam (for some programs), thesis (for some programs); for doctorate, comprehensive exam (for some programs), thesis/dissertation (for some programs). *Entrance requirements:* For master's and doctorate, GRE. Additional exam requirements/recommendations for international students: Required—TOEFL (minimum score 550 paper-based; 213 computer-based). *Application deadline:* For fall admission, 7/1 for domestic and international students; for spring admission, 12/1 for domestic and international students. Applications are processed on a rolling basis. Application fee: $65. Electronic applications accepted. *Expenses:* Tuition, area resident: Full-time $9399; part-time $488 per credit hour. Tuition, state resident: full-time $9399; part-time $488 per credit hour. Tuition, nonresident: full-time $17,854; part-time $957.75 per credit hour. International tuition: $17,854 full-time. Required fees: $1534. Full-time tuition and fees vary according to program. *Financial support:* In 2010–11, 1 fellowship with full tuition reimbursement (averaging $25,250 per year), 28 research assistantships with full tuition reimbursements (averaging $18,021 per year), 3 teaching assistantships with full tuition reimbursements (averaging $16,603 per year) were awarded; career-related internships or fieldwork, Federal Work-Study, scholarships/grants, health care benefits, and unspecified assistantships also available. Financial award application deadline: 1/15. *Faculty research:* Soil and water engineering, alternative energy sources for agriculture and agricultural mechanization. Total annual research expenditures: $3.2 million. *Unit head:* Dr. Mary Leigh Wolfe, UNIT HEAD, 540-231-6092, Fax: 540-231-3199, E-mail: mlwolfe@vt.edu. *Application contact:* Cully Hession, Contact, 540-231-9480, Fax: 540-231-3199, E-mail: chession@vt.edu.

Washington State University, Graduate School, College of Engineering and Architecture, Department of Biological Systems Engineering, Pullman, WA 99164. Offers biological and agricultural engineering (MS, PhD). *Faculty:* 10. *Students:* 48 full-time (14 women), 3 part-time (2 women); includes 1 minority (Asian, non-Hispanic/Latino), 40 international. Average age 30. 72 applicants, 24% accepted, 15 enrolled. In 2010, 2 master's awarded. *Degree requirements:* For master's, comprehensive exam; thesis (for some programs), written and oral exam; for doctorate, comprehensive exam, thesis/dissertation, written and oral exam. *Entrance requirements:* For master's, GRE General Test, GRE Subject Test, minimum GPA of 3.0, bachelor's degree in engineering or closely related subject; for doctorate, minimum GPA of 3.0, bachelor's degree in engineering or closely related subject. Additional exam requirements/recommendations for international students: Required—TOEFL. *Application deadline:* For fall admission, 2/1 priority date for domestic students, 3/1 for international students; for spring admission, 9/1 for domestic students, 7/1 for international students. Applications are processed on a rolling basis. Application fee: $50. *Expenses:* Tuition, state resident: full-time $8552; part-time $443 per credit. Tuition, nonresident: full-time $21,650; part-time $1083 per credit. Required fees: $846. *Financial support:* In 2010–11, 20 research assistantships (averaging $18,204 per year), 17 teaching assistantships (averaging $18,204 per year) were awarded. *Faculty research:* Social issues and engineering education, electronic instrument design, prediction, technology for dust from agricultural lands. Total annual research expenditures: $3.1 million. *Unit head:* Dr. Claudio Stockle, Chair, 509-335-1578, Fax: 509-335-2722, E-mail: stockle@wsu.edu. *Application contact:* Graduate School Admissions, 800-GRADWSU, Fax: 509-335-1949, E-mail: gradsch@wsu.edu.

Bioengineering

Alfred University, Graduate School, New York State College of Ceramics, School of Engineering, Alfred, NY 14802-1205. Offers biomedical materials engineering science (MS); ceramic engineering (MS); ceramics (PhD); electrical engineering (MS); glass science (MS, PhD); materials science and engineering (MS, PhD); mechanical engineering (MS). *Degree requirements:* For master's, thesis; for doctorate, thesis/dissertation. *Entrance requirements:* Additional exam requirements/recommendations for international students: Required—TOEFL (minimum score 590 paper-based; 243 computer-based). Electronic applications accepted. *Expenses:* Contact institution. *Faculty research:* Fine-particle technology, x-ray diffraction, superconductivity, electronic materials.

Baylor College of Medicine, Graduate School of Biomedical Sciences, Program in Translational Biology and Molecular Medicine, Houston, TX 77030-3498. Offers PhD. *Faculty:* 173 full-time (54 women). *Students:* 58 full-time (28 women); includes 6 Black or African American, non-Hispanic/Latino; 6 Hispanic/Latino, 16 international. Average age 27. 88 applicants, 32% accepted, 13 enrolled. In 2010, 1 doctorate awarded. *Degree requirements:* For doctorate, thesis/dissertation, public defense. *Entrance requirements:* For doctorate, GRE, minimum GPA of 3.0. Additional exam requirements/recommendations for international students: Required—TOEFL. *Application deadline:* For fall admission, 1/1 for domestic students. Application fee: $0. Electronic applications accepted. *Expenses:* Tuition: Full-time $11,000. Required fees: $4900. *Financial support:* In 2010–11, 58 students received support, including 24 fellowships with full tuition reimbursements available (averaging $26,000 per year), 34 research assistantships with full tuition reimbursements available (averaging $26,000 per year); career-related internships or fieldwork, Federal Work-Study, health care benefits, and students receive a scholarship unless there are grant funds available to pay tuition also available. Financial award applicants required to submit FAFSA. *Faculty research:* Molecular medicine, translational biology, human disease biology and therapy. *Unit head:* Dr. Mary Estes, Director, 713-798-3585, Fax: 713-798-3586, E-mail: tbmm@bcm.edu. *Application contact:* Wanda Waguespack, Graduate Program Administrator, 713-798-1077, Fax: 713-798-3586, E-mail: wandaw@bcm.edu.

California Institute of Technology, Division of Engineering and Applied Science, Option in Bioengineering, Pasadena, CA 91125-0001. Offers MS, PhD. *Faculty:* 4 full-time (0 women). *Students:* 32 full-time (4 women). 160 applicants, 11% accepted, 4 enrolled. In 2010, 2 master's, 13 doctorates awarded. *Degree requirements:* For master's, thesis; for doctorate, thesis/dissertation. *Application deadline:* For fall admission, 1/1 for domestic students. *Financial support:* In 2010–11, 8 fellowships, 20 research assistantships, 2 teaching assistantships were awarded. *Faculty research:* Biosynthesis and analysis, biometrics. *Unit head:* Dr. Niles Pierce, Executive Officer, 626-395-8086, E-mail: niles@caltech.edu. *Application contact:* Natalie Gilmore, Assistant Dean of Graduate Studies, 626-395-3812, Fax: 626-577-9246, E-mail: ngilmore@caltech.edu.

Carnegie Mellon University, Carnegie Institute of Technology, Biomedical and Health Engineering Program, Pittsburgh, PA 15213-3891. Offers bioengineering (MS, PhD); MD/PhD. *Degree requirements:* For master's, thesis; for doctorate, thesis/dissertation, qualifying exam. *Entrance requirements:* For master's and doctorate, GRE General Test. Additional exam requirements/recommendations for international students: Required—TOEFL. Electronic applications accepted. *Faculty research:* Cellular and molecular systematics, signal and image processing, materials and mechanics.

Clemson University, Graduate School, College of Engineering and Science, Department of Bioengineering, Clemson, SC 29634. Offers MS, PhD. Part-time programs available. *Faculty:* 16 full-time (4 women), 4 part-time/adjunct (3 women). *Students:* 94 full-time (27 women), 18 part-time (3 women); includes 2 Black or African American, non-Hispanic/Latino; 1 American Indian or Alaska Native, non-Hispanic/Latino; 8 Asian, non-Hispanic/Latino; 1 Hispanic/Latino; 1 Two or more races, non-Hispanic/Latino, 36 international. Average age 27. 155 applicants, 48% accepted, 29 enrolled. In 2010, 13 master's, 10 doctorates awarded. *Degree requirements:* For master's, thesis optional; for doctorate, thesis/dissertation. *Entrance requirements:* For master's and doctorate, GRE General Test. Additional exam requirements/recommendations for international students: Required—TOEFL. *Application deadline:* For fall admission, 6/1 for domestic students, 4/15 for international students; for spring admission, 11/1 for domestic students, 9/15 for international students. Applications are processed on a rolling basis. Application fee: $70 ($80 for international students). Electronic applications accepted. *Expenses:* Tuition, state resident: full-time $6492; part-time $400 per credit hour. Tuition, nonresident: full-time $13,634; part-time $800 per credit hour. Required fees: $262 per semester. Part-time tuition and fees vary according to course load and program. *Financial support:* In 2010–11, 82 students received support, including 6 fellowships with full and partial tuition reimbursements available (averaging $19,406 per year), 67 research assistantships with partial tuition reimbursements available (averaging $16,710 per year), 14 teaching assistantships with partial tuition reimbursements available (averaging $16,506 per year); career-related internships or fieldwork, institutionally sponsored loans, scholarships/grants, health care benefits, and unspecified assistantships also available. Support available to part-time students. Financial award application deadline: 2/15; financial award applicants required to submit FAFSA. *Faculty research:* Biomaterials, biomechanics, bioimaging, tissue engineering. Total annual research expenditures: $6.8 million. *Unit head:* Dr. Martine LaBerge, Interim Chair, 864-656-5556, Fax: 864-656-4466, E-mail: laberge@eng.clemson.edu. *Application contact:* Dr. Jiro Nagatomi, Graduate Student Coordinator, 864-656-5193, Fax: 864-656-4466, E-mail: jnagato@clemson.edu.

Cornell University, Graduate School, Graduate Fields of Agriculture and Life Sciences and Graduate Fields of Engineering, Field of Biological and Environmental Engineering, Ithaca, NY 14853-0001. Offers biological engineering (M Eng, MPS, MS, PhD); energy (M Eng, MPS, MS, PhD); environmental engineering (M Eng, MPS, MS, PhD); environmental management (MPS); food processing engineering (M Eng, MPS, MS, PhD); international agriculture (M Eng, MPS, MS, PhD); local roads (M Eng, MPS, MS, PhD); machine systems (M Eng, MPS, MS, PhD); soil and water engineering (M Eng, MPS, MS, PhD); structures and environment (M Eng, MPS, MS, PhD). *Faculty:* 33 full-time (6 women). *Students:* 75 full-time (36 women); includes 2 Black or African American, non-Hispanic/Latino; 7 Asian, non-Hispanic/Latino; 1 Hispanic/Latino, 25 international. Average age 26. 130 applicants, 39% accepted, 39 enrolled. In 2010, 14 master's, 11 doctorates awarded. Terminal master's awarded for partial completion of doctoral program. *Degree requirements:* For master's, thesis (MS); for doctorate, comprehensive exam, thesis/dissertation. *Entrance requirements:* For master's, letters of recommendation (3 for MS, 2 for M Eng and MPS); for doctorate, GRE General Test, 3 letters of recommendation. Additional exam requirements/recommendations for international students: Required—TOEFL (minimum score 550 paper-based; 213 computer-based; 77 iBT). *Application deadline:* For fall admission, 1/15 priority date for domestic students; for spring admission, 10/1 for domestic students. Applications are processed on a rolling basis. Application fee: $70. Electronic applications accepted. *Expenses:* Tuition: Full-time $29,500. Required fees: $76. Tuition and fees vary according to degree level and program. *Financial support:* In 2010–11, 7 fellowships with full tuition reimbursements, 31 research assistantships with full tuition reimbursements, 9 teaching assistantships with full tuition reimbursements were awarded; institutionally sponsored loans, scholarships/grants, health care benefits, tuition waivers (full and partial), and unspecified assistantships also available. Financial award applicants required to submit FAFSA. *Faculty research:* Biological and food engineering, environmental, soil and water engineering, international agricultural engineering, structures and controlled environments, machine systems and energy. *Unit head:* Director of Graduate Studies, 607-255-2173, Fax: 607-255-4080, E-mail: abengradfield@cornell.edu. *Application contact:* Graduate Field Assistant, 607-255-2173, Fax: 607-255-4080, E-mail: abengradfield@cornell.edu.

Dalhousie University, Faculty of Engineering, Department of Biological Engineering, Halifax, NS B3J 2X4, Canada. Offers M Eng, MA Sc, PhD. *Degree requirements:* For master's, thesis; for doctorate, thesis/dissertation. *Entrance requirements:* Additional exam requirements/recommendations for international students: Required—TOEFL, IELTS, CANTEST, CAEL, or Michigan English Language Assessment Battery. *Faculty research:* Waste management, energy and environment, bio-machinery and robotics, soil and water, aquacultural and food engineering.

Georgia Institute of Technology, Graduate Studies and Research, College of Engineering, School of Chemical and Biomolecular Engineering, Atlanta, GA 30332-0001. Offers bioengineering (MS Bio E, PhD); chemical engineering (MS Ch E, PhD); paper science and engineering (MS, PhD); polymers (MS Poly). *Degree requirements:* For master's, thesis; for doctorate, comprehensive exam, thesis/dissertation. *Entrance requirements:* For master's and doctorate, GRE, minimum GPA of 3.0. Additional exam requirements/recommendations for international students: Required—TOEFL (minimum score 550 paper-based; 213 computer-based). Electronic applications accepted. *Faculty research:* Biochemical engineering; process modeling, synthesis, and control; polymer science and engineering; thermodynamics and separations; surface and particle science.

Georgia Institute of Technology, Graduate Studies and Research, College of Engineering, The Wallace H. Coulter Department of Biomedical Engineering at Georgia Tech and Emory University, Atlanta, GA 30332-0001. Offers bioengineering (PhD); bioinformatics (PhD); biomedical engineering (PhD); MD/PhD. PhD in biomedical engineering program jointly offered with Emory University (Georgia) and Peking University (China). Terminal master's awarded for partial completion of doctoral program. *Degree requirements:* For doctorate, thesis/dissertation. *Entrance requirements:* Additional exam requirements/recommendations for international students: Required—TOEFL. *Faculty research:* Biomechanics and tissue engineering, bioinstrumentation and medical imaging.

Illinois Institute of Technology, Graduate College, Armour College of Engineering, Department of Chemical and Biological Engineering, Chicago, IL 60616-3793. Offers biological engineering (MBE); chemical engineering (M Ch E, MS, PhD); food process engineering (MFPE, MS). Part-time and evening/weekend programs available. Postbaccalaureate distance learning degree programs offered (minimal on-campus study). *Faculty:* 17 full-time (1 woman). *Students:* 156 full-time (63 women), 20 part-time (8 women); includes 11 minority (4 Black or African American, non-Hispanic/Latino; 4 Asian, non-Hispanic/Latino; 2 Hispanic/Latino; 1 Two or more races, non-Hispanic/Latino), 139 international. Average age 25. 413 applicants, 46% accepted, 63 enrolled. In 2010, 32 master's, 15 doctorates awarded. Terminal master's awarded for partial completion of doctoral program. *Degree requirements:* For master's, comprehensive exam (for some programs), thesis (for some programs); for doctorate, comprehensive exam, thesis/dissertation. *Entrance requirements:* For master's, GRE General Test (minimum score 900 Quantitative and Verbal, 2.5 Analytical Writing), minimum undergraduate GPA of 3.0; for doctorate, GRE General Test (minimum score 1000 Quantitative and Verbal, 3.0 Analytical Writing), minimum undergraduate GPA of 3.0. Additional exam requirements/recommendations for international students: Required—TOEFL (minimum score 523 paper-based; 70 iBT); Recommended—IELTS (minimum score 5.5). *Application deadline:* For fall admission, 5/1 for domestic and international students; for spring admission, 10/15 for domestic and international students. Applications are processed on a rolling basis. Application fee: $50. Electronic applications accepted. *Expenses:* Tuition: Full-time $18,576; part-time $1032 per credit hour. Required fees: $583 per semester. One-time fee: $150. Tuition and fees vary according to program and student level. *Financial support:* In 2010–11, 42 research assistantships with full and partial tuition reimbursements (averaging $7,975 per year), 7 teaching assistantships with full tuition reimbursements (averaging $5,107 per year) were awarded; fellowships with partial tuition reimbursements, Federal Work-Study, institutionally sponsored loans, scholarships/grants, health care benefits, and unspecified assistantships also available. Support available to part-time students. Financial award applicants required to submit FAFSA. *Faculty research:* Energy and sustainability, biological engineering, advanced materials, systems engineering. Total annual research expenditures: $2.6 million. *Unit head:* Dr. John Kallend, Acting Chair, 312-567-3054, Fax: 312-567-8875, E-mail: kallend@iit.edu. *Application contact:* Deborah Gibson, Director, Graduate Admission, 866-472-3448, Fax: 312-567-3138, E-mail: inquiry.grad@iit.edu.

Iowa State University of Science and Technology, Graduate College, College of Engineering, Department of Chemical and Biological Engineering, Ames, IA 50011. Offers M Eng, MS, PhD. *Faculty:* 23 full-time (5 women). *Students:* 56 full-time (21 women), 2 part-time (0 women); includes 2 Asian, non-Hispanic/Latino; 2 Hispanic/Latino, 32 international. 177 applicants, 15% accepted, 8 enrolled. In 2010, 3 master's, 8 doctorates awarded. *Degree requirements:* For master's, thesis (for some programs); for doctorate, thesis/dissertation. *Entrance requirements:* For master's and doctorate, GRE General Test. Additional exam requirements/recommendations for international students: Required—TOEFL (minimum score 587 paper-based; 94 iBT), IELTS (minimum score 7). *Application deadline:* For fall admission, 1/15 priority date for domestic and international students; for spring admission, 10/1 for domestic and international students. Application fee: $40 ($90 for international students). Electronic applications accepted. *Financial support:* In 2010–11, 41 research assistantships with full and partial tuition reimbursements (averaging $17,547 per year), 8 teaching assistantships with full and partial tuition reimbursements (averaging $8,772 per year) were awarded; scholarships/grants, health care benefits, and unspecified assistantships also available. *Unit head:* Dr. Surya Mallaragada, Chair, 515-294-8472, Fax: 515-294-2689, E-mail: suryakm@iastate.edu. *Application contact:* Dr. Monica Lamm, Director of Graduate Education, 515-294-7643, E-mail: chemengr@iastate.edu.

The Johns Hopkins University, G. W. C. Whiting School of Engineering and School of Medicine, Department of Biomedical Engineering, Baltimore, MD 21205. Offers bioengineering innovation and design (MSE); biomedical engineering (MSE, PhD). *Faculty:* 45 full-time (7 women). *Students:* 236 full-time (72 women); includes 11 minority (9 Asian, non-Hispanic/Latino; 1 Hispanic/Latino; 1 Two or more races, non-Hispanic/Latino), 23 international. Average age 23. 653 applicants, 20% accepted, 70 enrolled. In 2010, 33 master's, 17 doctorates awarded. Terminal master's awarded for partial completion of doctoral program. *Degree requirements:* For master's, thesis; for doctorate, comprehensive exam, thesis/dissertation, oral exam. *Entrance requirements:* For master's and doctorate, GRE General Test. Additional exam requirements/recommendations for international students: Required—TOEFL or IELTS. *Application deadline:* For fall admission, 1/15 for domestic and international students. Application fee: $75. Electronic applications accepted. *Financial support:* In 2010–11, 208 students received support, including 218 research assistantships with full tuition reimbursements available (averaging $27,532 per year), 37 teaching assistantships with full and partial tuition reimbursements available (averaging $10,000 per year); fellowships with partial tuition reimbursements available, Federal Work-Study, institutionally sponsored loans, scholarships/grants, tuition waivers (full), and unspecified assistantships also available. Support available to part-time students. *Faculty research:* Cell and tissue engineering, systems neuroscience, imaging, cardiovascular systems physiology, theoretical and computational biology. Total annual research expenditures: $15.6 million. *Unit head:* Dr. Elliot R. McVeigh, Director, 410-516-5282, Fax: 410-516-4771. *Application contact:* Samuel Bourne, Academic Master's Program Coordinator, 410-516-8482, Fax: 410-516-4771, E-mail: sbourne@jhu.edu.

The Johns Hopkins University, G. W. C. Whiting School of Engineering, Department of Chemical and Biomolecular Engineering, Baltimore, MD 21218. Offers MSE, PhD. Part-time programs available. *Faculty:* 21 full-time (6 women), 3 part-time/adjunct (0 women). *Students:* 83 full-time (26 women); includes 19 minority (4 Black or African American, non-Hispanic/Latino; 12 Asian, non-Hispanic/Latino; 3 Hispanic/Latino), 38 international. Average age 25. 231 applicants, 28% accepted, 29 enrolled. In 2010, 4 master's, 9 doctorates awarded. *Degree requirements:* For doctorate, thesis/dissertation, oral exam. *Entrance requirements:* For doctorate, GRE General Test. Additional exam requirements/recommendations for international students: Required—TOEFL (minimum score 600 paper-based; 250 computer-based; 100 iBT). *Application deadline:* For fall admission, 1/15 for domestic and international students. Applications are processed on a rolling basis. Application fee: $75. Electronic applications accepted. *Financial support:* In 2010–11, 25 fellowships with full and partial tuition reimbursements (averaging $30,000 per year), 70 research assistantships with full tuition reimbursements (averaging $26,496 per year) were awarded; teaching assistantships with full and partial tuition reimbursements, scholarships/grants, health care benefits, tuition waivers (partial), and unspecified assistantships also available. Financial award application deadline: 1/15. *Faculty research:* Polymers and complex fluids, nucleation, bioengineering and biotechnology, computational biology and genomics, cell and molecular biotechnology. Total annual research expenditures: $5.8 million. *Unit head:* Dr. Konstantinos Konstantopoulos, Chair and Professor, 410-516-7170, Fax: 410-516-5510, E-mail: kkonsta1@jhu.edu. *Application contact:* Lindsay Spivey, Academic Program Coordinator, 410-516-4166, Fax: 410-516-5510, E-mail: spivey@jhu.edu.

Kansas State University, Graduate School, College of Engineering, Department of Biological and Agricultural Engineering, Manhattan, KS 66506. Offers MS, PhD. Terminal master's awarded for partial completion of doctoral program. *Degree requirements:* For master's, thesis; for doctorate, thesis/dissertation. *Entrance requirements:* For master's, GRE (recommended), bachelor's degree in agricultural engineering; for doctorate, GRE (recommended). Additional exam requirements/recommendations for international students: Required—TOEFL (minimum score 600 paper-based; 250 computer-based). Electronic applications accepted. *Faculty research:* Ecological engineering, watershed modeling, air quality, bioprocessing, sensors and controls.

Lehigh University, P.C. Rossin College of Engineering and Applied Science, Department of Chemical Engineering, Bethlehem, PA 18015. Offers biological chemical engineering (M Eng); chemical engineering (M Eng, MS, PhD); MBA/E. Part-time programs available. Postbaccalaureate distance learning degree programs offered (no on-campus study). *Faculty:* 18 full-time (2 women), 1 part-time/adjunct (0 women). *Students:* 45 full-time (10 women), 31 part-time (11 women); includes 13 minority (4 Black or African American, non-Hispanic/Latino; 6 Asian, non-Hispanic/Latino; 3 Hispanic/Latino), 30 international. Average age 27. 198 applicants, 23% accepted, 26 enrolled. In 2010, 9 master's, 11 doctorates awarded. Terminal master's awarded for partial completion of doctoral program. *Degree requirements:* For master's, thesis (for some programs); for doctorate, comprehensive exam, thesis/dissertation. *Entrance requirements:* For master's and doctorate, GRE General Test. Additional exam requirements/recommendations for international students: Required—TOEFL (minimum score 570 paper-based; 230 computer-based; 79 iBT). *Application deadline:* For fall admission, 7/15 for domestic students, 1/15 priority date for international students; for spring admission, 12/1 for domestic and international students. Applications are processed on a rolling basis. Application fee: $75. Electronic applications accepted. *Financial support:* In 2010–11, 41 students received support, including 5 fellowships with full tuition reimbursements available (averaging $20,400 per year), 31 research assistantships with full tuition reimbursements available (averaging $20,400 per year), 8 teaching assistantships with full tuition reimbursements available (averaging $20,400 per year); career-related internships or fieldwork, institutionally sponsored loans, scholarships/grants, health care benefits, and unspecified assistantships also available. Financial award application deadline: 1/15. *Faculty research:* Emulsion polymers, process control, energy, biotechnology, catalysis. Total annual research expenditures: $2.7 million. *Unit head:* Dr. Anthony J. McHugh, Chairman, 610-758-4260, Fax: 610-758-5057, E-mail: ajm8@lehigh.edu. *Application contact:* Barbara A. Kessler, Graduate Coordinator, 610-758-4261, Fax: 610-758-5057, E-mail: inchegs@mail.lehigh.edu.

Louisiana State University and Agricultural and Mechanical College, Graduate School, College of Agriculture, Department of Biological and Agricultural Engineering, Baton Rouge, LA 70803. Offers biological and agricultural engineering (MSBAE); engineering science (MS, PhD). Part-time programs available. *Faculty:* 12 full-time (2 women). *Students:* 13 full-time (3 women), 3 part-time (0 women); includes 1 Black or African American, non-Hispanic/Latino; 3 Asian, non-Hispanic/Latino; 1 Hispanic/Latino, 6 international. Average age 26. 12 applicants, 58% accepted, 2 enrolled. In 2010, 8 master's awarded. Terminal master's awarded for partial completion of doctoral program. *Degree requirements:* For master's, thesis; for doctorate, thesis/dissertation. *Entrance requirements:* For master's and doctorate, GRE General Test, minimum GPA of 3.0. Additional exam requirements/recommendations for international students: Required—TOEFL (minimum score 550 paper-based; 213 computer-based; 79 iBT) or IELTS (minimum score 6.5). *Application deadline:* For fall admission, 1/25 priority date for domestic students, 5/15 for international students; for spring admission, 10/15 for international students. Applications are processed on a rolling basis. Application fee: $50 ($70 for international students). Electronic applications accepted. *Financial support:* In 2010–11, 14 students received support, including 1 fellowship (averaging $24,803 per year), 12 research assistantships with partial tuition reimbursements available (averaging $16,391 per year); teaching assistantships with partial tuition reimbursements available, career-related internships or fieldwork, Federal Work-Study, institutionally sponsored loans, scholarships/grants, health care benefits, and unspecified assistantships also available. Financial award application deadline: 7/1; financial award applicants required to submit FAFSA. *Faculty research:* Bioenergy, bioprocess engineering, cellular and molecular engineering, drug delivery using nanotechnology, environmental engineering. Total annual research expenditures: $37,654. *Unit head:* Dr. Dan Thomas, Head, 225-578-3153, Fax: 225-578-3492, E-mail: dthomas@agcenter.lsu.edu. *Application contact:* Dr. Steven Hall, Graduate Coordinator, 225-578-1058, Fax: 225-578-3492, E-mail: sghall@agcenter.lsu.edu.

Bioengineering

Massachusetts Institute of Technology, School of Engineering, Department of Biological Engineering, Cambridge, MA 02139-4307. Offers applied biosciences (PhD, Sc D); bioengineering (PhD, Sc D); biological engineering (PhD, Sc D); biomedical engineering (M Eng); toxicology (SM); SM/MBA. *Faculty:* 30 full-time (5 women). *Students:* 112 full-time (56 women); includes 32 minority (2 Black or African American, non-Hispanic/Latino; 20 Asian, non-Hispanic/Latino; 8 Hispanic/Latino; 2 Two or more races, non-Hispanic/Latino), 31 international. Average age 26. 441 applicants, 9% accepted, 24 enrolled. In 2010, 3 master's, 16 doctorates awarded. Terminal master's awarded for partial completion of doctoral program. *Degree requirements:* For master's, thesis; for doctorate, comprehensive exam, thesis/dissertation. *Entrance requirements:* For master's and doctorate, GRE General Test. Additional exam requirements/recommendations for international students: Required—TOEFL (minimum score 600 paper-based; 250 computer-based), IELTS (minimum score 7). *Application deadline:* For fall admission, 12/31 for domestic and international students. Application fee: $75. Electronic applications accepted. *Expenses:* Tuition: Full-time $38,940; part-time $605 per unit. Required fees: $272. *Financial support:* In 2010–11, 111 students received support, including 57 fellowships with tuition reimbursements available (averaging $35,847 per year), 51 research assistantships with tuition reimbursements available (averaging $32,873 per year), 3 teaching assistantships with tuition reimbursements available (averaging $31,681 per year); Federal Work-Study, institutionally sponsored loans, scholarships/grants, traineeships, health care benefits, and unspecified assistantships also available. *Faculty research:* Bioinformatics, computational, systems, and synthetic biology; biological materials, imaging, and transport phenomena; biomolecular and cell engineering; cancer initiation, progression, and therapeutics; genomics, proteomics, and glycomics; nanoscale engineering of biological systems; neurobiological systems; systems biology; macromolecular biochemistry and biophysics. Total annual research expenditures: $35.1 million. *Unit head:* Prof. Douglas A. Lauffenburger, Department Head, 617-253-1712, E-mail: be-acad@mit.edu. *Application contact:* Biological Engineering Academic Office, 617-253-1712, Fax: 617-258-8676, E-mail: be-acad@mit.edu.

McGill University, Faculty of Graduate and Postdoctoral Studies, Faculty of Agricultural and Environmental Sciences, Department of Bioresource Engineering, Montréal, QC H3A 2T5, Canada. Offers computer applications (M Sc, M Sc A, PhD); food engineering (M Sc, M Sc A, PhD); grain drying (M Sc, M Sc A, PhD); irrigation and drainage (M Sc, M Sc A, PhD); machinery (M Sc, M Sc A, PhD); pollution control (M Sc, M Sc A, PhD); post-harvest technology (M Sc, M Sc A, PhD); soil dynamics (M Sc, M Sc A, PhD); structure and environment (M Sc, M Sc A, PhD); vegetable and fruit storage (M Sc, M Sc A, PhD).

Mississippi State University, College of Agriculture and Life Sciences, Department of Agricultural and Biological Engineering, Mississippi State, MS 39762. Offers agricultural sciences (PhD), including engineering technology (MS, PhD); agriculture (MS), including engineering technology (MS, PhD); biological engineering (MS); biomedical engineering (MS, PhD); engineering (PhD), including biological engineering. PhD (agricultural sciences), MS (agriculture) are interdisciplinary. *Faculty:* 12 full-time (1 woman). *Students:* 39 full-time (14 women), 5 part-time (1 woman); includes 6 minority (3 Black or African American, non-Hispanic/Latino; 1 Asian, non-Hispanic/Latino; 1 Native Hawaiian or other Pacific Islander, non-Hispanic/Latino; 1 Two or more races, non-Hispanic/Latino), 11 international. Average age 27. 47 applicants, 43% accepted, 16 enrolled. In 2010, 5 master's, 3 doctorates awarded. *Degree requirements:* For master's, thesis; for doctorate, thesis/dissertation, preliminary exam. *Entrance requirements:* For master's, GRE General Test, minimum undergraduate GPA of 2.75 (3.0 for biomedical engineering); for doctorate, GRE General Test, minimum GPA of 3.0 (biomedical engineering). Additional exam requirements/recommendations for international students: Required—TOEFL (minimum score 550 paper-based; 213 computer-based; 79 iBT); Recommended—IELTS (minimum score 6.5). *Application deadline:* For fall admission, 7/1 for domestic students, 5/1 for international students; for spring admission, 11/1 for domestic students, 9/1 for international students. Applications are processed on a rolling basis. Application fee: $40. Electronic applications accepted. *Expenses:* Tuition, state resident: full-time $2730.50; part-time $304 per credit hour. Tuition, nonresident: full-time $6901; part-time $767 per credit hour. *Financial support:* In 2010–11, 32 research assistantships with partial tuition reimbursements (averaging $12,687 per year) were awarded; Federal Work-Study, institutionally sponsored loans, and unspecified assistantships also available. Financial award application deadline: 4/1; financial award applicants required to submit FAFSA. *Faculty research:* Bioenvironmental engineering, bioinstrumentation, biomechanics/biomaterials, precision agriculture, tissue engineering, ergonomics human factors, biosimulation and modeling. Total annual research expenditures: $1.1 million. *Unit head:* Dr. Jonathan Pote, Interim Department Head and Professor, 662-325-3280, Fax: 662-325-3853, E-mail: jpote@mafes.msstate.edu. *Application contact:* Dr. Steven Elder, Professor and Graduate Coordinator, 662-325-9107, Fax: 662-325-3853, E-mail: selder@abe.msstate.edu.

North Carolina State University, Graduate School, College of Agriculture and Life Sciences, Department of Biological and Agricultural Engineering, Raleigh, NC 27695. Offers MBAE, MS, PhD, Certificate. Part-time programs available. Postbaccalaureate distance learning degree programs offered. *Degree requirements:* For master's, thesis (for some programs); for doctorate, thesis/dissertation. *Entrance requirements:* For master's and doctorate, GRE. Additional exam requirements/recommendations for international students: Required—TOEFL. Electronic applications accepted. *Faculty research:* Bioinstrumentation, animal waste management, water quality engineering, machine systems, controlled environment agriculture.

The Ohio State University, Graduate School, College of Food, Agricultural, and Environmental Sciences, Department of Food, Agricultural, and Biological Engineering, Columbus, OH 43210. Offers MS, PhD. *Faculty:* 31. *Students:* 28 full-time (10 women), 10 part-time (3 women); includes 1 Black or African American, non-Hispanic/Latino; 1 Asian, non-Hispanic/Latino; 1 Hispanic/Latino, 19 international. Average age 28. In 2010, 11 master's awarded. *Degree requirements:* For master's, thesis optional; for doctorate, thesis/dissertation. *Entrance requirements:* For master's and doctorate, GRE General Test, GRE Subject Test in engineering (recommended). Additional exam requirements/recommendations for international students: Required—TOEFL (minimum score 550 paper-based; 213 computer-based), IELTS (minimum score 7), or Michigan English Language Assessment Battery (minimum score 85). *Application deadline:* For fall admission, 8/15 priority date for domestic students, 7/1 priority date for international students; for winter admission, 12/1 priority date for domestic students, 11/1 priority date for international students; for spring admission, 3/1 priority date for domestic students, 2/1 priority date for international students. Applications are processed on a rolling basis. Application fee: $40 ($50 for international students). Electronic applications accepted. *Expenses:* Tuition, state resident: full-time $10,605. Tuition, nonresident: full-time $26,535. Tuition and fees vary according to course load and program. *Financial support:* Fellowships, research assistantships, teaching assistantships, career-related internships or fieldwork, Federal Work-Study, and institutionally sponsored loans available. Support available to part-time students. *Unit head:* Sudih Sastry, Chair, 614-292-9338, E-mail: bean.3@osu.edu. *Application contact:* Graduate Admissions, 614-292-9444, Fax: 614-292-3895, E-mail: domestic.grad@osu.edu.

Oklahoma State University, College of Agricultural Science and Natural Resources, Department of Biosystems and Agricultural Engineering, Stillwater, OK 74078. Offers biosystems engineering (MS, PhD); environmental and natural resources (MS, PhD). *Faculty:* 22 full-time (4 women), 4 part-time/adjunct (0 women). *Students:* 23 full-time (10 women), 45 part-time (16 women); includes 2 American Indian or Alaska Native, non-Hispanic/Latino; 1 Asian, non-Hispanic/Latino; 2 Hispanic/Latino, 36 international. Average age 30. 58 applicants, 40% accepted, 14 enrolled. In 2010, 4 master's, 3 doctorates awarded. *Degree requirements:* For master's, thesis; for doctorate, comprehensive exam, thesis/dissertation. *Entrance requirements:* For master's and doctorate, GRE or GMAT. Additional exam requirements/recommendations for international students: Required—TOEFL (minimum score 550 paper-based; 79 iBT). *Application deadline:* For fall admission, 3/1 priority date for international students; for spring admission, 8/1 priority date for international students. Applications are processed on a rolling basis. Application fee: $40 ($75 for international students). Electronic applications accepted. *Expenses:* Tuition, state resident: full-time $3716; part-time $154.85 per credit hour. Tuition, nonresident: full-time $14,892; part-time $621 per credit hour. Required fees: $2044; $85.20 per credit hour.

One-time fee: $50. Tuition and fees vary according to course load and campus/location. *Financial support:* In 2010–11, 48 research assistantships (averaging $17,561 per year), 1 teaching assistantship (averaging $6,000 per year) were awarded; career-related internships or fieldwork, Federal Work-Study, scholarships/grants, health care benefits, tuition waivers (partial), and unspecified assistantships also available. Support available to part-time students. Financial award application deadline: 3/1; financial award applicants required to submit FAFSA. *Unit head:* Dr. Ronald L. Elliot, Head, 405-744-5431, Fax: 405-744-6059. *Application contact:* Dr. Gordon Emslie, Dean, 405-744-6368, Fax: 405-744-0355, E-mail: grad-i@okstate.edu.

Oregon State University, Graduate School, College of Engineering, Department of Biological and Ecological Engineering, Corvallis, OR 97331. Offers M Eng, MS, PhD. Terminal master's awarded for partial completion of doctoral program. *Degree requirements:* For master's, thesis or alternative; for doctorate, thesis/dissertation. *Entrance requirements:* For master's and doctorate, minimum GPA of 3.0 in last 90 hours. Additional exam requirements/recommendations for international students: Required—TOEFL (minimum score 550 paper-based; 213 computer-based). *Expenses:* Contact institution. *Faculty research:* Bioengineering, water resources engineering, food engineering, cell culture and fermentation, vadose zone transport.

Oregon State University, Graduate School, College of Engineering, School of Mechanical, Industrial, and Manufacturing Engineering, Corvallis, OR 97331. Offers human systems engineering (MS, PhD); industrial engineering (MS, PhD); information systems engineering (MS, PhD); manufacturing engineering (M Engr); manufacturing systems engineering (MS, PhD); materials science (MAIS, MS, PhD); mechanical engineering (MS, PhD); nano/micro fabrication (MS, PhD). Part-time programs available. Postbaccalaureate distance learning degree programs offered (minimal on-campus study). *Degree requirements:* For master's, thesis or alternative; for doctorate, thesis/dissertation. *Entrance requirements:* For master's, placement exam, minimum GPA of 3.0 in last 90 hours of course work; for doctorate, GRE, placement exam, minimum GPA of 3.0 in last 90 hours of course work. Additional exam requirements/recommendations for international students: Required—TOEFL (minimum score 550 paper-based; 213 computer-based). *Faculty research:* Computer-integrated manufacturing, human factors, robotics, decision support systems, simulation modeling and analysis.

Penn State Hershey Medical Center, College of Medicine, Graduate School Programs in the Biomedical Sciences, Intercollege Bioengineering Graduate Program, Hershey, PA 17033-2360. Offers MS, PhD, MD/PhD. Terminal master's awarded for partial completion of doctoral program. *Degree requirements:* For master's, thesis; for doctorate, comprehensive exam, thesis/dissertation, oral exam. *Entrance requirements:* For master's, GRE; for doctorate, GRE, minimum GPA of 3.0. Additional exam requirements/recommendations for international students: Required—TOEFL (minimum score 500 paper-based; 213 computer-based). *Application deadline:* Applications are processed on a rolling basis. Application fee: $65. Electronic applications accepted. *Financial support:* In 2010–11, 8 research assistantships with full tuition reimbursements were awarded; fellowships with full tuition reimbursements, scholarships/grants, health care benefits, and unspecified assistantships also available. Financial award applicants required to submit FAFSA. *Faculty research:* Artificial organs, cardiovascular and orthopedic biomaterials, magnetic resonance imaging, bio-degradable responsive polymers for drug delivery. *Unit head:* Program Director. *Application contact:* Program Director.

Penn State University Park, Graduate School, College of Agricultural Sciences, Department of Agricultural and Biological Engineering, State College, University Park, PA 16802-1503. Offers MS, PhD.

Penn State University Park, Graduate School, Intercollege Graduate Programs, Intercollege Graduate Program in Bioengineering, State College, University Park, PA 16802-1503. Offers MS, PhD. *Unit head:* Dr. Herbert H. Lipowsky, Head, 814-865-1407, Fax: 814-863-0490, E-mail: hhlbio@engr.psu.edu. *Application contact:* Dr. Herbert H. Lipowsky, Head, 814-865-1407, Fax: 814-863-0490, E-mail: hhlbio@engr.psu.edu.

Rensselaer Polytechnic Institute, Graduate School, School of Engineering, Program in Chemical Engineering, Troy, NY 12180-3590. Offers M Eng, MS, PhD. Part-time programs available. *Faculty:* 13 full-time (1 woman). *Students:* 67 full-time (15 women), 2 part-time (1 woman); includes 1 Black or African American, non-Hispanic/Latino; 5 Asian, non-Hispanic/Latino; 1 Hispanic/Latino, 39 international. Average age 24. 198 applicants, 24% accepted, 16 enrolled. In 2010, 6 master's, 9 doctorates awarded. Terminal master's awarded for partial completion of doctoral program. *Entrance requirements:* For master's, GRE (minimum score 550 verbal); for doctorate, GRE (Verbal minimum score of 550). Additional exam requirements/recommendations for international students: Required—TOEFL (minimum score 570 paper-based). *Application deadline:* For fall admission, 1/1 priority date for domestic students, 1/1 for international students; for spring admission, 8/15 for domestic and international students. Applications are processed on a rolling basis. Application fee: $75. Electronic applications accepted. *Expenses:* Tuition: Full-time $39,600; part-time $1650 per credit. Required fees: $1896. *Financial support:* In 2010–11, 65 students received support, including 5 fellowships with full tuition reimbursements available (averaging $30,000 per year), 54 research assistantships with full tuition reimbursements available (averaging $23,000 per year), 10 teaching assistantships with full tuition reimbursements available (averaging $17,500 per year); institutionally sponsored loans and scholarships/grants also available. Financial award application deadline: 1/1. *Faculty research:* Biocatalysis, bioseparations, biotechnology, molecular modeling and simulation, advanced materials, interfacial phenomena, systems biology. Total annual research expenditures: $4.9 million. *Unit head:* Dr. Shekhar Garde, Department Head, 518-276-2511, Fax: 518-276-4030, E-mail: gardes@rpi.edu. *Application contact:* Dr. B. Wayne Bequette, Chairman, Graduate Affairs Committee, 518-276-6929, Fax: 518-276-4030, E-mail: vilarl@rpi.edu.

Rice University, Graduate Programs, George R. Brown School of Engineering, Department of Bioengineering, Houston, TX 77251-1892. Offers MBE, MS, PhD, MD/PhD. Terminal master's awarded for partial completion of doctoral program. *Degree requirements:* For master's, thesis; for doctorate, thesis/dissertation, qualifying exam, internship. *Entrance requirements:* For master's and doctorate, GRE General Test. Additional exam requirements/recommendations for international students: Required—TOEFL (minimum score 600 paper-based; 250 computer-based; 90 iBT). Electronic applications accepted. *Faculty research:* Biomaterials, tissue engineering, laser-tissue interactions, biochemical engineering, gene therapy.

Rice University, Graduate Programs, George R. Brown School of Engineering, Department of Electrical and Computer Engineering, Houston, TX 77251-1892. Offers bioengineering (MS, PhD); circuits, controls, and communication systems (MS, PhD); computer science and engineering (MS, PhD); electrical engineering (MEE); lasers, microwaves, and solid-state electronics (MS, PhD); MBA/MEE. Part-time programs available. *Degree requirements:* For master's, thesis (for some programs); for doctorate, thesis/dissertation. *Entrance requirements:* For master's and doctorate, GRE General Test, GRE Subject Test, minimum GPA of 3.0. Additional exam requirements/recommendations for international students: Required—TOEFL (minimum score 600 paper-based; 250 computer-based; 90 iBT). Electronic applications accepted. *Faculty research:* Physical electronics, systems, computer engineering, bioengineering.

South Dakota School of Mines and Technology, Graduate Division, Program in Chemical and Biological Engineering, Rapid City, SD 57701-3995. Offers PhD.

Stanford University, School of Medicine, Department of Bioengineering, Stanford, CA 94305-9991. Offers MS, PhD. *Degree requirements:* For master's, thesis optional; for doctorate, comprehensive exam, thesis/dissertation. *Entrance requirements:* For master's and doctorate, GRE General Test. Additional exam requirements/recommendations for international students: Required—TOEFL. Electronic applications accepted. *Expenses:* Tuition: Full-time $38,700; part-time $860 per unit. One-time fee: $200 full-time. *Faculty research:* Biomedical computation, regenerative medicine/tissue engineering, molecular and cell bioengineering, biomedical imaging, biomedical devices.

Syracuse University, L. C. Smith College of Engineering and Computer Science, Program in Bioengineering, Syracuse, NY 13244. Offers MS, PhD. Part-time programs available. *Students:* 36 full-time (15 women), 2 part-time (1 woman); includes 5 minority (1 Black or African American, non-Hispanic/Latino; 3 Asian, non-Hispanic/Latino; 1 Hispanic/Latino), 19 international. Average age 25. 72 applicants, 36% accepted, 8 enrolled. In 2010, 9 master's, 2 doctorates awarded. *Entrance requirements:* For master's and doctorate, GRE General Test. Additional exam requirements/recommendations for international students: Required—TOEFL (minimum score 100 iBT). *Application deadline:* For fall admission, 7/1 priority date for domestic students, 6/1 priority date for international students. Applications are processed on a rolling basis. Application fee: $75. Electronic applications accepted. *Expenses:* Tuition: Part-time $1162 per credit. *Financial support:* Fellowships with full tuition reimbursements, research assistantships with full and partial tuition reimbursements, teaching assistantships with full and partial tuition reimbursements, tuition waivers (full and partial) available. Financial award application deadline: 1/1; financial award applicants required to submit FAFSA. *Unit head:* Dr. Radhakrishna Sureshkumar, Chair, 315-443-3194, Fax: 315-443-9175, E-mail: rsureshk@syr.edu. *Application contact:* Kathleen Joyce, Assistant Dean, 314-443-2219, E-mail: topgrads@syr.edu.

Texas A&M University, College of Agriculture and Life Sciences and College of Engineering, Department of Biological and Agricultural Engineering, College Station, TX 77843. Offers M Agr, M Eng, MS, DE, PhD. Part-time programs available. *Faculty:* 19. *Students:* 69 full-time (26 women), 17 part-time (2 women); includes 8 minority (3 Black or African American, non-Hispanic/Latino; 3 Asian, non-Hispanic/Latino; 2 Hispanic/Latino), 47 international. Average age 29. In 2010, 12 master's, 3 doctorates awarded. *Degree requirements:* For master's, thesis (MS), preliminary and final exams; for doctorate, thesis/dissertation, preliminary and final exams. *Entrance requirements:* For master's and doctorate, GRE General Test. Additional exam requirements/recommendations for international students: Required—TOEFL (minimum score 550 paper-based; 213 computer-based). *Application deadline:* For fall admission, 2/1 priority date for domestic students; for spring admission, 10/1 for domestic students. Applications are processed on a rolling basis. Application fee: $50 ($75 for international students). Electronic applications accepted. *Financial support:* In 2010–11, 3 fellowships with full and partial tuition reimbursements (averaging $15,000 per year), 17 research assistantships with full and partial tuition reimbursements (averaging $18,150 per year), 12 teaching assistantships with partial tuition reimbursements (averaging $19,590 per year) were awarded; career-related internships or fieldwork, institutionally sponsored loans, scholarships/grants, tuition waivers, and unspecified assistantships also available. Financial award application deadline: 3/1; financial award applicants required to submit FAFSA. *Faculty research:* Water quality and quantity; air quality; biological, food, ecological engineering; off-road equipment; mechatronics. *Unit head:* Dr. Steve Searcy, Interim Head, 979-845-3668, Fax: 979-862-3442, E-mail: s-searcy@tamu.edu. *Application contact:* Dr. Steve Searcy, Interim Head, 979-845-3668, Fax: 979-862-3442, E-mail: s-searcy@tamu.edu.

Tufts University, Graduate School of Arts and Sciences, Graduate Certificate Programs, Program in Bioengineering, Medford, MA 02155. Offers Certificate. Part-time and evening/weekend programs available. Electronic applications accepted. *Expenses:* Tuition: Full-time $39,624; part-time $3962 per course. Required fees: $40 per year. Full-time tuition and fees vary according to degree level, program and student level. Part-time tuition and fees vary according to course load.

Tufts University, School of Engineering, Department of Chemical and Biological Engineering, Medford, MA 02155. Offers ME, MS, PhD. Part-time programs available. Terminal master's awarded for partial completion of doctoral program. *Degree requirements:* For master's, thesis (for some programs); for doctorate, thesis/dissertation. *Entrance requirements:* For master's and doctorate, GRE General Test. Additional exam requirements/recommendations for international students: Required—TOEFL (minimum score 550 paper-based; 213 computer-based; 80 iBT). Electronic applications accepted. *Expenses:* Tuition: Full-time $39,624; part-time $3962 per course. Required fees: $40 per year. Full-time tuition and fees vary according to degree level, program and student level. Part-time tuition and fees vary according to course load.

University at Buffalo, the State University of New York, Graduate School, School of Engineering and Applied Sciences, Department of Chemical and Biological Engineering, Buffalo, NY 14260. Offers ME, MS, PhD. Part-time programs available. *Faculty:* 17 full-time (1 woman), 4 part-time/adjunct (1 woman). *Students:* 107 full-time (36 women), 9 part-time (4 women); includes 1 Black or African American, non-Hispanic/Latino; 2 Asian, non-Hispanic/Latino; 2 Hispanic/Latino, 85 international. Average age 26. 393 applicants, 12% accepted, 31 enrolled. In 2010, 13 master's, 5 doctorates awarded. *Degree requirements:* For master's, thesis (for some programs); for doctorate, comprehensive exam, thesis/dissertation. *Entrance requirements:* For master's and doctorate, GRE General Test. Additional exam requirements/recommendations for international students: Required—TOEFL (minimum score 550 paper-based; 213 computer-based; 79 iBT). *Application deadline:* For fall admission, 2/1 priority date for domestic and international students; for spring admission, 10/1 priority date for domestic and international students. Applications are processed on a rolling basis. Application fee: $50. Electronic applications accepted. *Financial support:* In 2010–11, 52 students received support, including 4 fellowships (averaging $30,000 per year), 33 research assistantships with full tuition reimbursements available (averaging $24,000 per year), 9 teaching assistantships with full tuition reimbursements available (averaging $20,900 per year); institutionally sponsored loans, scholarships/grants, health care benefits, tuition waivers (partial), and unspecified assistantships also available. Support available to part-time students. Financial award application deadline: 2/28; financial award applicants required to submit FAFSA. *Faculty research:* Transport, polymers, nanomaterials, biochemical engineering, catalysis. Total annual research expenditures: $11.2 million. *Unit head:* Dr. David A. Kofke, Chairman, 716-645-2911, Fax: 716-645-3822, E-mail: kofke@buffalo.edu. *Application contact:* Dr. Paschalis Alexandridis, Director of Graduate Studies, 716-645-1183, Fax: 716-645-3822, E-mail: palexand@buffalo.edu.

University of Arkansas, Graduate School, College of Engineering, Department of Biological and Agricultural Engineering, Program in Biological Engineering, Fayetteville, AR 72701-1201. Offers MSBE. *Accreditation:* ABET. *Students:* 4 full-time (1 woman), 12 part-time (1 woman); includes 1 minority (Black or African American, non-Hispanic/Latino), 9 international. 11 applicants, 64% accepted. In 2010, 3 master's awarded. *Application deadline:* For fall admission, 4/1 for international students; for spring admission, 10/1 for international students. Applications are processed on a rolling basis. Application fee: $40 ($50 for international students). Electronic applications accepted. *Financial support:* In 2010–11, 2 fellowships, 11 research assistantships, 2 teaching assistantships were awarded. *Unit head:* Dr. Lalit Verma, Department Head, 479-575-2351, Fax: 479-575-2846, E-mail: lverma@uark.edu. *Application contact:* Dr. Jin-Woo Kim, Program Coordinator, 479-575-2351, Fax: 479-575-2846, E-mail: jwkim@uark.edu.

University of California, Berkeley, Graduate Division, Bioengineering Graduate Program Berkeley/UCSF, Berkeley, CA 94720-1762. Offers PhD. Program offered jointly with University of California, San Francisco. *Faculty:* 91 full-time (22 women). *Students:* 169 full-time (58 women); includes 7 Black or African American, non-Hispanic/Latino; 1 American Indian or Alaska Native, non-Hispanic/Latino; 35 Asian, non-Hispanic/Latino; 11 Hispanic/Latino; 1 Native Hawaiian or other Pacific Islander, non-Hispanic/Latino, 23 international. Average age 27. 502 applicants, 11% accepted, 21 enrolled. In 2010, 24 doctorates awarded. *Degree requirements:* For doctorate, comprehensive exam, thesis/dissertation. *Entrance requirements:* For doctorate, GRE General Test, minimum GPA of 3.0. Additional exam requirements/recommendations for international students: Required—TOEFL (minimum score 570 paper-based; 230 computer-based; 68 iBT). *Application deadline:* For fall admission, 12/10 for domestic and international students. Application fee: $70 ($90 for international students). Electronic applications accepted. *Financial support:* In 2010–11, 149 students received support, including 15 fellowships with full tuition reimbursements available (averaging $28,000 per year), 105 research assistantships with full tuition reimbursements available (averaging $28,000 per year), 50 teaching assistantships with partial tuition reimbursements available (averaging $4,160 per year); Federal Work-Study, institutionally sponsored loans, scholarships/grants, traineeships, health care benefits, unspecified assistantships, and extramural fellowships/scholarships also available. Financial award application deadline: 1/3; financial award applicants required to submit FAFSA. *Faculty research:* Biomaterials, biomechanics, biomedical imaging and instrumentation, computational biology, drug delivery systems and pharmacogenomics, neural systems engineering and vision science, systems and synthetic biology, tissue engineering and regenerative medicine. Total annual research expenditures: $45 million. *Unit head:* Prof. Matthew Tirrell, Chair, 510-642-5833. *Application contact:* Rebecca Pauling, Graduate program administrator, 510-642-9931, Fax: 510-642-5835, E-mail: bioeng-admissions@lists.berkeley.edu.

University of California, Davis, College of Engineering, Program in Biological Systems Engineering, Davis, CA 95616. Offers M Engr, MS, D Engr, PhD, M Engr/MBA. Terminal master's awarded for partial completion of doctoral program. *Degree requirements:* For master's, thesis; for doctorate, thesis/dissertation. *Entrance requirements:* For master's, minimum GPA of 3.0; for doctorate, GRE, minimum graduate GPA of 3.25. Additional exam requirements/recommendations for international students: Required—TOEFL (minimum score 550 paper-based; 213 computer-based). Electronic applications accepted. *Faculty research:* Forestry, irrigation and drainage, power and machinery, structures and environment, information and energy technologies.

University of California, Merced, Division of Graduate Studies, School of Natural Sciences, Merced, CA 95343. Offers applied mathematics (MS, PhD); biological engineering and small-scale technologies (MS, PhD); environmental systems (MS, PhD); mechanical engineering and applied mechanics (MS, PhD); physics and chemistry (PhD); quantitative and systems biology (MS, PhD).

University of California, Riverside, Graduate Division, Department of Bioengineering, Riverside, CA 92521-0102. Offers MS, PhD. Part-time programs available. *Faculty:* 9 full-time (2 women). *Students:* 44 full-time (19 women). Average age 25. 100 applicants, 44% accepted, 26 enrolled. In 2010, 1 master's, 1 doctorate awarded. *Degree requirements:* For doctorate, thesis/dissertation, qualifying exams. *Entrance requirements:* Additional exam requirements/recommendations for international students: Required—TOEFL (minimum score 550 paper-based; 213 computer-based; 80 iBT). *Application deadline:* For fall admission, 5/1 for domestic students, 2/1 for international students; for winter admission, 9/1 for domestic students, 7/1 for international students; for spring admission, 12/1 for domestic students, 10/1 for international students. Application fee: $0 ($100 for international students). *Financial support:* In 2010–11, 24 students received support, including 21 fellowships with full tuition reimbursements (averaging $38,000 per year), research assistantships with tuition reimbursements available (averaging $18,000 per year), teaching assistantships with tuition reimbursements available (averaging $16,500 per year); health care benefits and unspecified assistantships also available. Financial award application deadline: 1/5. *Unit head:* Dr. Jerome S. Schultz, Unit Head, 951-827-2111, Fax: 951-827-5696, E-mail: jssbio@engr.ucr.edu. *Application contact:* Dr. Victor Rodgers, Graduate Adviser, 951-827-6241, E-mail: victor.rodgers@ucr.edu.

University of California, San Diego, Office of Graduate Studies, Department of Bioengineering, La Jolla, CA 92093. Offers M Eng, MS, PhD. *Entrance requirements:* For master's, GRE General Test, minimum GPA of 3.0 (for M Eng), 3.4 (for MS); for doctorate, GRE General Test, minimum GPA of 3.4. Additional exam requirements/recommendations for international students: Required—TOEFL. Electronic applications accepted.

See Display on next page and Close-Up on page 121.

University of California, San Francisco, Graduate Division, Program in Bioengineering, Berkeley, CA 94720-1762. Offers PhD. Program offered jointly with University of California, Berkeley. *Degree requirements:* For doctorate, thesis/dissertation, qualifying exam. *Entrance requirements:* For doctorate, GRE General Test, minimum GPA of 3.0. Additional exam requirements/recommendations for international students: Required—TOEFL (minimum score 570 paper-based). Electronic applications accepted. *Faculty research:* Bioengineering, biomaterials, biomedical imaging and instrumentation, biomechanics, microfluidics, computational biology, systems biology, drug delivery systems and pharmacogenomics, neural systems engineering and vision science, synthetic biology, tissue engineering, regenerative medicine.

University of California, Santa Barbara, Graduate Division, College of Letters and Sciences, Division of Mathematics, Life, and Physical Sciences, Interdepartmental Graduate Program in Biomolecular Science and Engineering, Santa Barbara, CA 93106-2014. Offers biochemistry and molecular biology (PhD), including biochemistry and molecular biology, biophysics and bioengineering. *Faculty:* 37 full-time (4 women), 1 (woman) part-time/adjunct. *Students:* 30 full-time (13 women); includes 4 Asian, non-Hispanic/Latino. Average age 28. 59 applicants, 22% accepted, 4 enrolled. In 2010, 5 doctorates awarded. Terminal master's awarded for partial completion of doctoral program. *Degree requirements:* For doctorate, thesis/dissertation. *Entrance requirements:* For doctorate, GRE General Test. Additional exam requirements/recommendations for international students: Required—TOEFL (minimum score 630 paper-based; 109 iBT), IELTS (minimum score 7). *Application deadline:* For fall admission, 12/15 for domestic and international students. Application fee: $70 ($90 for international students). Electronic applications accepted. *Financial support:* In 2010–11, 30 students received support, including 16 fellowships with full and partial tuition reimbursements available (averaging $11,321 per year), 31 research assistantships with full and partial tuition reimbursements available (averaging $14,777 per year), 16 teaching assistantships with full and partial tuition reimbursements available (averaging $6,307 per year); Federal Work-Study, traineeships, health care benefits, tuition waivers (full and partial), and unspecified assistantships also available. Financial award application deadline: 12/15; financial award applicants required to submit FAFSA. *Faculty research:* Biochemistry and molecular biology, biophysics, biomaterials, bioengineering, systems biology. *Unit head:* Prof. Philip A. Pincus, Director/Professor, 805-893-4685, E-mail: fyl@mrl.ucsb.edu. *Application contact:* Prof. Philip A. Pincus, Director/Professor, 805-893-4685, E-mail: fyl@mrl.ucsb.edu.

University of Colorado Denver, College of Engineering and Applied Science, Department of Bioengineering, Aurora, CO 80045-2560. Offers bioengineering (PhD); clinical imaging (MS); device design and entrepreneurship (MS); research (MS). Part-time programs available. *Faculty:* 3 full-time (1 woman). *Students:* 13 full-time (2 women), 1 part-time; includes 1 Black or African American, non-Hispanic/Latino; 1 Asian, non-Hispanic/Latino; 1 Hispanic/Latino. Average age 30. 15 applicants, 100% accepted, 12 enrolled. Terminal master's awarded for partial completion of doctoral program. *Degree requirements:* For master's, thesis or alternative, 30 credit hours; for doctorate, comprehensive exam, thesis/dissertation, 36 credit hours of classwork (18 core, 18 elective), additional 30 hours of thesis work, three formal examinations, approval of dissertations. *Entrance requirements:* For master's, GRE (recommended); for doctorate, GRE. Additional exam requirements/recommendations for international students: Required—TOEFL (minimum score 550 paper-based; 213 computer-based; 79 iBT), TOEFL (minimum 250 CBT/600 PBT/100IBT) for Ph D. *Application deadline:* For fall admission, 4/30 for domestic students. Application fee: $50. Electronic applications accepted. *Expenses:* Contact institution. *Financial support:* Fellowships, research assistantships, teaching assistantships, Federal Work-Study available. Financial award application deadline: 4/1; financial award applicants required to submit FAFSA. *Faculty research:* Imaging and biophotonics, cardiovascular biomechanics and hemodynamics, orthopedic biomechanics, ophthalmology, neuroscience engineering. *Unit head:* Dr. Robin Shandas, Chair, 303-724-4196, E-mail: robin.shandas@ucdenver.edu. *Application contact:* Dr. Robin Shandas, Chair, 303-724-4196, E-mail: robin.shandas@ucdenver.edu.

University of Dayton, Graduate School, School of Engineering, Department of Chemical Engineering, Dayton, OH 45469-1300. Offers bioengineering instrumentation (MS); bioprocess engineering (MS); biosystems engineering (MS). Part-time and evening/weekend programs available. *Faculty:* 10 full-time (1 woman), 4 part-time/adjunct (0 women). *Students:* 30 full-time (7 women), 5 part-time (1 woman); includes 7 minority (4 Black or African American, non-Hispanic/Latino; 3 Asian, non-Hispanic/Latino), 18 international. Average age 26. 43 applicants, 86% accepted, 17 enrolled. In 2010, 3 master's awarded. *Degree requirements:* For master's,

Bioengineering

BIOENGINEERING

Discovery

Innovation

Application

Change the World.

www.be.ucsd.edu

thesis optional. *Entrance requirements:* Additional exam requirements/recommendations for international students: Required—TOEFL (minimum score 550 paper-based; 213 computer-based; 80 iBT). *Application deadline:* For fall admission, 8/1 priority date for domestic students. Applications are processed on a rolling basis. Application fee: $0 ($50 for international students). Electronic applications accepted. *Expenses:* Tuition: Full-time $7800; part-time $650 per credit hour. *Financial support:* In 2010–11, 10 research assistantships with full tuition reimbursements (averaging $14,745 per year) were awarded; institutionally sponsored loans, health care benefits, and unspecified assistantships also available. Financial award applicants required to submit FAFSA. *Faculty research:* Vertically-aligned carbon nanotubes infiltrated with temperature-responsive polymers; smart nanocomposite films for self-cleaning and controlled release, bilayer and bulk heterojunction solar cells using liquid crystalline porphyrins as donors by solution processing, DNA damage induced by multiwalled carbon nanotubes in mouse embryonic stem cells. Total annual research expenditures: $1.5 million. *Unit head:* Dr. Robert Wilkins, Chair, 937-229-2627, E-mail: robert.wilkins@notes.udayton.edu. *Application contact:* Alexander Popovski, Associate Director of Graduate and International Admissions, 937-229-2357, Fax: 937-229-4729, E-mail: alex.popovski@notes.udayton.edu.

University of Denver, School of Engineering and Computer Science, Department of Mechanical and Materials Engineering, Denver, CO 80208. Offers bioengineering (MS); engineering (MS, PhD); interdisciplinary engineering (PhD); materials science (MS, PhD); mechanical engineering (MS, PhD); nanoscale science and engineering (PhD). Part-time programs available. *Faculty:* 8 full-time (1 woman), 5 part-time/adjunct (1 woman). *Students:* 3 full-time (1 woman), 21 part-time (5 women), 7 international. Average age 33. 63 applicants, 65% accepted, 5 enrolled. In 2010, 5 master's, 1 doctorate awarded. Terminal master's awarded for partial completion of doctoral program. *Degree requirements:* For master's, thesis or alternative; for doctorate, comprehensive exam, thesis/dissertation. *Entrance requirements:* For master's and doctorate, GRE General Test. Additional exam requirements/recommendations for international students: Required—TOEFL (minimum score 550 paper-based; 80 iBT). *Application deadline:* Applications are processed on a rolling basis. Application fee: $60. Electronic applications accepted. *Expenses:* Tuition: Full-time $35,604; part-time $29,670 per year. Required fees: $687 per year. Tuition and fees vary according to program. *Financial support:* In 2010–11, 7 research assistantships with full and partial tuition reimbursements (averaging $10,795 per year), 5 teaching assistantships with full and partial tuition reimbursements (averaging $13,230 per year) were awarded; Federal Work-Study, scholarships/grants, and unspecified assistantships also available. Financial award applicants required to submit FAFSA. *Faculty research:* Aerosols, biomechanics, composite materials, photo optics, drug delivery. *Unit head:* Dr. Daniel Armentrout, Chair, 303-871-3580, Fax: 303-871-4450, E-mail: darmentr@du.edu. *Application contact:* Renee Carvalho, Assistant to the Chair, 303-871-2107, Fax: 303-871-4450, E-mail: renee.carvalho@du.edu.

University of Florida, Graduate School, College of Engineering and College of Agricultural and Life Sciences, Department of Agricultural and Biological Engineering, Gainesville, FL 32611. Offers ME, MS, PhD, Engr. Part-time programs available. *Students:* 81 full-time (28 women), 5 part-time (1 woman); includes 1 Black or African American, non-Hispanic/Latino; 2 Asian, non-Hispanic/Latino; 4 Hispanic/Latino, 49 international. Average age 29. 53 applicants, 43% accepted, 15 enrolled. In 2010, 19 master's, 16 doctorates awarded. Terminal master's awarded for partial completion of doctoral program. *Degree requirements:* For master's, comprehensive exam, thesis (for some programs), Thesis requirement depends on degree; for doctorate, comprehensive exam, thesis/dissertation. *Entrance requirements:* For master's and doctorate, GRE General Test, minimum GPA of 3.0; for Engr, GRE General Test. Additional exam requirements/recommendations for international students: Required—TOEFL (minimum score 550 paper-based; 213 computer-based; 80 iBT), IELTS (minimum score 6). *Application deadline:* For fall admission, 2/15 for domestic and international students; for spring admission, 7/1 for domestic and international students. Applications are processed on a rolling basis. Application fee: $30. Electronic applications accepted. *Expenses:* Tuition, state resident: full-time $10,915.92. Tuition, nonresident: full-time $28,309. *Financial support:* In 2010–11, 71 students received support, including 8 fellowships with full and partial tuition reimbursements available, 63 research assistantships with partial tuition reimbursements available (averaging $15,916 per year); unspecified assistantships also available. Financial award application deadline: 2/15; financial award applicants required to submit FAFSA. *Faculty research:* Biological processing, crop and climate modeling, land and water resources, robotic harvesting, food and packaging. *Unit head:* Dr. Dorota Z. Haman, Chair, 352-392-1864 Ext. 120, Fax: 352-392-4092, E-mail: dhaman@ufl.edu. *Application contact:* Dr. Ray A. Bucklin, Graduate Coordinator, 352-392-1864 Ext. 169, Fax: 352-392-4092, E-mail: bucklin@ufl.edu.

University of Georgia, College of Agricultural and Environmental Sciences, Department of Biological and Agricultural Engineering, Athens, GA 30602. Offers agricultural engineering (MS); biological and agricultural engineering (PhD); biological engineering (MS). *Faculty:* 29 full-time (3 women), 2 part-time/adjunct (0 women). *Students:* 38 full-time (11 women), 10 part-time (1 woman); includes 5 Black or African American, non-Hispanic/Latino; 2 Asian, non-Hispanic/Latino, 26 international. 43 applicants, 51% accepted, 12 enrolled. In 2010, 13 master's, 3 doctorates awarded. *Degree requirements:* For master's, thesis; for doctorate, one foreign language, thesis/dissertation. *Entrance requirements:* For master's and doctorate, GRE General Test. *Application deadline:* For fall admission, 7/1 priority date for domestic students; for spring admission, 11/15 for domestic students. Application fee: $50. Electronic applications accepted. *Expenses:* Tuition, state resident: full-time $7200; part-time $344 per credit hour. Tuition, nonresident: full-time $21,900; part-time $944 per credit hour. Tuition and fees vary according to course load and program. *Financial support:* Fellowships, research assistantships, teaching assistantships, unspecified assistantships available. *Unit head:* Dr. E. Dale Threadgill, Head, 706-542-1653, Fax: 706-542-8806, E-mail: tgill@engr.uga.edu. *Application contact:* Dr. William Tollner, Graduate Coordinator, 706-542-3047, Fax: 706-542-8806, E-mail: btollner@engr.uga.edu.

University of Guelph, Graduate Studies, College of Physical and Engineering Science, School of Engineering, Guelph, ON N1G 2W1, Canada. Offers biological engineering (M Eng, M Sc, MA Sc, PhD); engineering systems and computing (M Eng, M Sc, MA Sc, PhD); environmental engineering (M Eng, M Sc, MA Sc, PhD); water resources engineering (M Eng, M Sc, MA Sc, PhD). Part-time programs available. *Degree requirements:* For master's, thesis (for some programs); for doctorate, comprehensive exam, thesis/dissertation. *Entrance requirements:* For master's, minimum B- average during previous 2 years of course work; for doctorate, minimum B average. Additional exam requirements/recommendations for international students: Required—TOEFL (minimum score 550 paper-based; 213 computer-based; 89 iBT), IELTS (minimum score 6.5). Electronic applications accepted. *Faculty research:* Water and food safety, environmental contaminant fates and mechanisms, computer systems, robotics and mechatronics, waste treatment.

University of Hawaii at Manoa, Graduate Division, College of Tropical Agriculture and Human Resources, Department of Molecular Biosciences and Bioengineering, Program in Bioengineering, Honolulu, HI 96822. Offers MS. Part-time programs available. *Faculty:* 6 full-time (0 women). *Students:* 3 full-time (1 woman), 2 part-time (both women); includes 1 Asian, non-Hispanic/Latino, 2 international. Average age 30. 20 applicants, 65% accepted, 7 enrolled. *Degree requirements:* For master's, thesis optional. *Entrance requirements:* For master's, GRE General Test. Additional exam requirements/recommendations for international students: Required—TOEFL (minimum score 500 paper-based; 173 computer-based; 61 iBT), IELTS (minimum score 5). *Application deadline:* For fall admission, 5/1 for domestic students, 3/1 for international students; for spring admission, 9/1 for domestic students, 8/1 for international students. Application fee: $50. *Financial support:* In 2010–11, 1 fellowship (averaging $6,200 per year), 3 research assistantships (averaging $18,770 per year) were awarded. *Application contact:* Dr. Samir Khanal, Graduate Chairperson, 808-956-8384, Fax: 808-956-3542, E-mail: khanal@hawaii.edu.

University of Idaho, College of Graduate Studies, College of Engineering, Department of Biological and Agricultural Engineering, Moscow, ID 83844-2282. Offers M Engr, MS, PhD.

Program offered jointly with College of Agricultural and Life Sciences. *Faculty:* 5 full-time. *Students:* 5 full-time, 3 part-time. Average age 36. In 2010, 1 master's, 1 doctorate awarded. *Degree requirements:* For master's, thesis or alternative; for doctorate, one foreign language, thesis/dissertation. *Entrance requirements:* For master's, minimum GPA of 2.8; for doctorate, minimum undergraduate GPA of 2.8, 3.0 graduate. *Application deadline:* For fall admission, 8/1 for domestic students; for spring admission, 12/15 for domestic students. Applications are processed on a rolling basis. Application fee: $60. Electronic applications accepted. *Expenses:* Tuition, nonresident: part-time $580 per credit. Required fees: $306 per credit. *Financial support:* Research assistantships, teaching assistantships, career-related internships or fieldwork available. Financial award applicants required to submit FAFSA. *Faculty research:* Water and environmental research, alternative fuels/biodiesel, agricultural safety health, biological processes for agricultural/food waste. *Unit head:* Dr. Jon Harlan Van Gerpen, Department Head, 208-885-7891, E-mail: baengr@uidaho.edu. *Application contact:* Dr. Jon Harlan Van Gerpen, Department Head, 208-885-7891, E-mail: baengr@uidaho.edu.

University of Illinois at Chicago, Graduate College, College of Engineering, Department of Bioengineering, Chicago, IL 60607-7128. Offers MS, PhD. Terminal master's awarded for partial completion of doctoral program. *Degree requirements:* For master's, thesis; for doctorate, thesis/dissertation. *Entrance requirements:* For master's and doctorate, GRE Subject Test, minimum GPA of 3.0. Additional exam requirements/recommendations for international students: Required—TOEFL. Electronic applications accepted. *Faculty research:* Imaging systems, bioinstrumentation, electrophysiology, biological control, laser scattering.

University of Illinois at Urbana–Champaign, Graduate College, College of Agricultural, Consumer and Environmental Sciences, Department of Agricultural and Biological Engineering, Champaign, IL 61820. Offers agricultural and biological engineering (MS, PhD); technical systems management (MS, PSM). *Faculty:* 20 full-time (2 women). *Students:* 48 full-time (10 women), 3 part-time (1 woman); includes 2 Hispanic/Latino, 39 international. 57 applicants, 28% accepted, 11 enrolled. In 2010, 6 master's, 4 doctorates awarded. *Entrance requirements:* For master's and doctorate, minimum GPA of 3.0. Additional exam requirements/recommendations for international students: Required—TOEFL (minimum score 570 paper-based; 230 computer-based; 88 iBT) or IELTS (minimum score 6.5). *Application deadline:* Applications are processed on a rolling basis. Application fee: $75 ($90 for international students). Electronic applications accepted. *Financial support:* In 2010–11, 6 fellowships, 42 research assistantships, 3 teaching assistantships were awarded; tuition waivers (full and partial) also available. *Unit head:* Kuan Chong Ting, Head, 217-333-3570, Fax: 217-244-0323, E-mail: kcting@illinois.edu. *Application contact:* Ronda Sullivan, Assistant to the Head, 217-333-3570, Fax: 217-244-0323, E-mail: rsully@illinois.edu.

University of Illinois at Urbana–Champaign, Graduate College, College of Engineering, Department of Bioengineering, Champaign, IL 61820. Offers MS, PhD. *Faculty:* 7 full-time (1 woman). *Students:* 44 full-time (16 women); includes 1 Black or African American, non-Hispanic/Latino; 9 Asian, non-Hispanic/Latino; 2 Two or more races, non-Hispanic/Latino, 18 international. 129 applicants, 9% accepted, 10 enrolled. In 2010, 13 master's, 1 doctorate awarded. *Entrance requirements:* For doctorate, GRE. Additional exam requirements/recommendations for international students: Required—TOEFL (minimum score 590 paper-based; 243 computer-based; 96 iBT) or IELTS (minimum score 6.5). *Application deadline:* Applications are processed on a rolling basis. Application fee: $75 ($90 for international students). Electronic applications accepted. *Financial support:* In 2010–11, 12 fellowships, 28 research assistantships, 7 teaching assistantships were awarded; tuition waivers (full and partial) also available. *Unit head:* Michael Insana, Interim Head, 217-244-0739, Fax: 217-265-0246, E-mail: mfi@illinois.edu. *Application contact:* Wendy Evans, Visiting Academic Programs Specialist, 217-333-1867, Fax: 217-265-0246, E-mail: wevans@illinois.edu.

University of Illinois at Urbana–Champaign, Graduate College, College of Liberal Arts and Sciences, School of Chemical Sciences, Department of Chemical and Biomolecular Engineering, Champaign, IL 61820. Offers bioinformatics: chemical and biomolecular engineering (MS); chemical engineering (MS, PhD). *Faculty:* 14 full-time (2 women). *Students:* 104 full-time (38 women), 3 part-time (2 women); includes 1 Black or African American, non-Hispanic/Latino; 8 Asian, non-Hispanic/Latino; 4 Hispanic/Latino; 1 Two or more races, non-Hispanic/Latino, 53 international. 375 applicants, 3% accepted, 12 enrolled. In 2010, 19 master's, 20 doctorates awarded. *Entrance requirements:* For master's and doctorate, GRE, minimum GPA of 3.0. Additional exam requirements/recommendations for international students: Required—TOEFL (minimum score 610 paper-based; 257 computer-based). *Application deadline:* Applications are processed on a rolling basis. Application fee: $75 ($90 for international students). Electronic applications accepted. *Financial support:* In 2010–11, 22 fellowships, 92 research assistantships, 39 teaching assistantships were awarded; tuition waivers (full and partial) also available. *Unit head:* Edmund Seebauer, Head, 217-244-9214, Fax: 217-333-5052, E-mail: eseebaue@illinois.edu. *Application contact:* Cathy Paceley, Office Manager, 217-333-3640, Fax: 217-333-5052, E-mail: paceley@illinois.edu.

The University of Kansas, Graduate Studies, School of Engineering, Program in Bioengineering, Lawrence, KS 66045. Offers MS, PhD. *Faculty:* 7. *Students:* 46 full-time (20 women); includes 2 minority (1 American Indian or Alaska Native, non-Hispanic/Latino; 1 Asian, non-Hispanic/Latino), 15 international. Average age 26. 39 applicants, 62% accepted, 11 enrolled. In 2010, 2 master's awarded. *Degree requirements:* For master's, thesis; for doctorate, comprehensive exam, thesis/dissertation. *Entrance requirements:* For master's and doctorate, GRE. Additional exam requirements/recommendations for international students: Required—TOEFL. *Application deadline:* For fall admission, 12/15 for domestic and international students; for spring admission, 10/31 for domestic students, 9/30 for international students. Application fee: $55 ($65 for international students). Electronic applications accepted. *Expenses:* Tuition, state resident: full-time $7092; part-time $295.50 per credit hour. Tuition, nonresident: full-time $16,590; part-time $691.25 per credit hour. Required fees: $858; $71.49 per credit hour. Tuition and fees vary according to course load, campus/location and program. *Financial support:* Fellowships, research assistantships with full and partial tuition reimbursements, teaching assistantships available. Financial award application deadline: 12/15. *Faculty research:* Bioimaging, bioinformatics, biomaterials and tissue engineering, biomechanics and neural engineering, biomedical product design and development, biomolecular engineering. *Unit head:* Dr. Sara E. Wilson, Director, 785-864-2103, Fax: 785-864-5445, E-mail: sewilson@ku.edu. *Application contact:* Administrative Associate, 785-864-5258, Fax: 785-864-5445, E-mail: bioe@ku.edu.

University of Maine, Graduate School, College of Engineering, Department of Chemical and Biological Engineering, Program in Biological Engineering, Orono, ME 04469. Offers MS. Part-time programs available. *Students:* 6 full-time (0 women), 1 (woman) part-time; includes 1 minority (American Indian or Alaska Native, non-Hispanic/Latino), 2 international. Average age 28. 6 applicants, 50% accepted, 3 enrolled. In 2010, 1 master's awarded. *Degree requirements:* For master's, thesis (for some programs). *Entrance requirements:* For master's, GRE General Test. Additional exam requirements/recommendations for international students: Required—TOEFL. *Application deadline:* For fall admission, 2/1 priority date for domestic students. Applications are processed on a rolling basis. Application fee: $65. Electronic applications accepted. *Expenses:* Tuition, state resident: full-time $400. Tuition, nonresident: full-time $1050. *Financial support:* Federal Work-Study available. Financial award application deadline: 3/1. *Unit head:* Dr. Douglas Bousfield, Coordinator, 207-581-2300, Fax: 207-581-2725. *Application contact:* Scott G. Delcourt, Associate Dean of the Graduate School, 207-581-3291, Fax: 207-581-3232, E-mail: graduate@maine.edu.

University of Maryland, College Park, Academic Affairs, A. James Clark School of Engineering, Department of Chemical and Biomolecular Engineering, College Park, MD 20742. Offers bioengineering (MS, PhD); chemical engineering (M Eng, MS, PhD). Part-time and evening/weekend programs available. *Faculty:* 25 full-time (2 women). *Students:* 50 full-time (15 women), 5 part-time (3 women); includes 9 minority (3 Black or African American, non-Hispanic/Latino; 5 Asian, non-Hispanic/Latino; 1 Hispanic/Latino), 31 international. 168 applicants, 19% accepted, 15 enrolled. In 2010, 8 master's, 7 doctorates awarded. *Degree requirements:* For master's, thesis optional; for doctorate, variable foreign language requirement, thesis/dissertation, exam, oral presentation. *Entrance requirements:* For master's and doctorate, GRE General Test, 3 letters of recommendation. Additional exam requirements/recommendations for international students: Required—TOEFL. *Application deadline:* For fall admission, 1/15 for domestic students, 2/1 for international students; for spring admission, 6/1 for domestic and international students. Applications are processed on a rolling basis. Application fee: $75. Electronic applications accepted. *Expenses:* Tuition, area resident: Part-time $471 per credit hour. Tuition, state resident: part-time $471 per credit hour. Tuition, nonresident: part-time $1016 per credit hour. Required fees: $337 per term. *Financial support:* In 2010–11, 3 fellowships with partial tuition reimbursements (averaging $11,490 per year), 27 research assistantships with tuition reimbursements (averaging $23,636 per year), 8 teaching assistantships with tuition reimbursements (averaging $22,731 per year) were awarded; Federal Work-Study and scholarships/grants also available. Support available to part-time students. Financial award applicants required to submit FAFSA. *Faculty research:* Applied polymer science, biochemical engineering, thermal properties, bioprocess monitoring. Total annual research expenditures: $1.7 million. *Unit head:* Sheryl Ehrman, Chair, 301-405-1074, E-mail: sehrman@umd.edu. *Application contact:* Dr. Charles A. Caramello, Dean of Graduate School, 301-405-0358, Fax: 301-314-9305, E-mail: ccaramel@umd.edu.

University of Maryland, College Park, Academic Affairs, A. James Clark School of Engineering, Fischell Department of Bioengineering, College Park, MD 20742. Offers MS, PhD. *Faculty:* 80 full-time (13 women), 4 part-time/adjunct (0 women). *Students:* 62 full-time (27 women), 3 part-time (2 women); includes 15 minority (1 Black or African American, non-Hispanic/Latino; 9 Asian, non-Hispanic/Latino; 1 Hispanic/Latino; 4 Two or more races, non-Hispanic/Latino), 8 international. 208 applicants, 13% accepted, 10 enrolled. In 2010, 1 master's, 3 doctorates awarded. *Degree requirements:* For master's, thesis optional; for doctorate, thesis/dissertation. *Entrance requirements:* For master's, GRE General Test, minimum GPA of 3.0, 3 letters of recommendation. *Application deadline:* For fall admission, 1/15 for domestic students, 2/1 for international students; for spring admission, 6/1 for international students. Applications are processed on a rolling basis. Application fee: $75. Electronic applications accepted. *Expenses:* Tuition, area resident: Part-time $471 per credit hour. Tuition, state resident: part-time $471 per credit hour. Tuition, nonresident: part-time $1016 per credit hour. Required fees: $337 per term. *Financial support:* In 2010–11, 8 fellowships with partial tuition reimbursements (averaging $11,456 per year), 46 research assistantships (averaging $23,096 per year), 4 teaching assistantships (averaging $22,603 per year) were awarded; career-related internships or fieldwork also available. Financial award applicants required to submit FAFSA. *Faculty research:* Bioengineering, bioenvironmental and water resources engineering, natural resources management. Total annual research expenditures: $2.2 million. *Unit head:* Dr. William Bentley, Chair, 301-405-4321, Fax: 301-405-9023, E-mail: bentley@umd.edu. *Application contact:* Dean of Graduate School, 301-405-0358, Fax: 301-314-9305.

University of Missouri, Graduate School, College of Engineering, Department of Biological Engineering, Columbia, MO 65211. Offers agricultural engineering (MS); biological engineering (MS, PhD). *Degree requirements:* For master's, thesis; for doctorate, thesis/dissertation. *Entrance requirements:* For master's and doctorate, GRE General Test, minimum GPA of 3.0. Additional exam requirements/recommendations for international students: Required—TOEFL (minimum score 550 paper-based; 213 computer-based; 80 iBT).

University of Nebraska–Lincoln, Graduate College, College of Engineering, Department of Biological Systems Engineering, Interdepartmental Area of Agricultural and Biological Systems Engineering, Lincoln, NE 68588. Offers MS, PhD. *Degree requirements:* For master's, thesis optional. *Entrance requirements:* Additional exam requirements/recommendations for international students: Required—TOEFL (minimum score 550 paper-based; 213 computer-based). Electronic applications accepted. *Faculty research:* Hydrological engineering, tractive performance, biomedical engineering, irrigation systems.

University of Nebraska–Lincoln, Graduate College, College of Engineering, Department of Chemical and Biomolecular Engineering, Lincoln, NE 68588. Offers MS, PhD. *Degree requirements:* For master's, thesis; for doctorate, comprehensive exam, thesis/dissertation. *Entrance requirements:* For master's and doctorate, GRE. Additional exam requirements/recommendations for international students: Required—TOEFL (minimum score 550 paper-based; 213 computer-based). Electronic applications accepted. *Faculty research:* Fermentation, radioactive waste remediation, chemical fuels from renewable feedstocks.

University of Notre Dame, Graduate School, College of Engineering, Department of Civil Engineering and Geological Sciences, Notre Dame, IN 46556. Offers bioengineering (MS Bio E); civil engineering (MSCE); civil engineering and geological sciences (PhD); environmental engineering (MS Env E); geological sciences (MS). Terminal master's awarded for partial completion of doctoral program. *Degree requirements:* For master's, comprehensive exam; for doctorate, thesis/dissertation, candidacy exam. *Entrance requirements:* For master's and doctorate, GRE General Test. Additional exam requirements/recommendations for international students: Required—TOEFL (minimum score 600 paper-based; 250 computer-based; 80 iBT). Electronic applications accepted. *Faculty research:* Environmental modeling, biological-waste treatment, petrology, environmental geology, geochemistry.

University of Oklahoma, College of Engineering, Center for Bioengineering, Norman, OK 73019. Offers MS, PhD. *Students:* 19 full-time (4 women), 10 part-time (2 women); includes 3 minority (1 Black or African American, non-Hispanic/Latino; 2 Asian, non-Hispanic/Latino), 15 international. Average age 29. 7 applicants, 86% accepted, 6 enrolled. In 2010, 8 master's, 2 doctorates awarded. Terminal master's awarded for partial completion of doctoral program. *Degree requirements:* For master's, thesis; for doctorate, thesis/dissertation, oral exam. *Entrance requirements:* For master's and doctorate, minimum GPA of 3.0. Additional exam requirements/recommendations for international students: Required—TOEFL (minimum score 600 paper-based; 250 computer-based; 100 iBT). *Application deadline:* For fall admission, 6/1 priority date for domestic students, 4/1 priority date for international students; for spring admission, 11/1 priority date for domestic students, 9/1 priority date for international students. Application fee: $40 ($90 for international students). Electronic applications accepted. *Expenses:* Tuition, state resident: full-time $3892.80; part-time $162.20 per credit hour. Tuition, nonresident: full-time $14,167; part-time $590.30 per credit hour. Required fees: $2523.40; $94.60 per credit hour. Tuition and fees vary according to course load and degree level. *Financial support:* Tuition waivers and unspecified assistantships available. Financial award applicants required to submit FAFSA. *Faculty research:* Bioengineering, biomaterials, biomechanics, biomedical nanomaterials, biosensors, cell adhesion, drug delivery/targeted therapeutics, medical implants, microfluidics, tissue engineering. *Unit head:* Dr. David Schmidtke, Director. *Application contact:* Dr. Ulli Nollert, Graduate Program Coordinator and Associate Professor, 405-325-4366, Fax: 405-325-5813, E-mail: nollert@ou.edu.

University of Pennsylvania, School of Engineering and Applied Science, Department of Bioengineering, Philadelphia, PA 19104. Offers MSE, PhD, MD/PhD, VMD/PhD. *Faculty:* 45 full-time (5 women), 11 part-time/adjunct (0 women). *Students:* 140 full-time (63 women), 11 part-time (6 women); includes 3 Black or African American, non-Hispanic/Latino; 1 American Indian or Alaska Native, non-Hispanic/Latino; 29 Asian, non-Hispanic/Latino; 5 Hispanic/Latino, 28 international. 480 applicants, 19% accepted, 43 enrolled. In 2010, 23 master's, 21 doctorates awarded. Terminal master's awarded for partial completion of doctoral program. *Degree requirements:* For master's, thesis optional; for doctorate, thesis/dissertation. *Entrance requirements:* For master's and doctorate, GRE General Test. Additional exam requirements/recommendations for international students: Required—TOEFL. *Application deadline:* For fall admission, 6/1 priority date for domestic students, 5/1 priority date for international students. Applications are processed on a rolling basis. Application fee: $70. Electronic applications accepted. *Expenses:* Tuition: Full-time $25,660; part-time $4758 per course. Required fees: $2152; $270 per course. Tuition and fees vary according to course load, degree level and program. *Financial support:* Fellowships, research assistantships, teaching assistantships, institutionally sponsored loans, scholarships/grants, traineeships, health care benefits, and

Bioengineering

University of Pennsylvania *(continued)*
unspecified assistantships available. *Faculty research:* Biomaterials and biomechanics, biofluid mechanics and transport, bioelectric phenomena, computational neuroscience. *Application contact:* Kathleen Venit, Graduate Coordinator, 215-746-8604, E-mail: kvenit@seas.upenn.edu.

University of Pittsburgh, School of Engineering, Department of Bioengineering, Pittsburgh, PA 15260. Offers MSBENG, PhD, MD/PhD. Part-time programs available. *Faculty:* 21 full-time (2 women), 83 part-time/adjunct (13 women). *Students:* 132 full-time (44 women), 15 part-time (3 women); includes 19 minority (3 Black or African American, non-Hispanic/Latino; 11 Asian, non-Hispanic/Latino; 5 Hispanic/Latino), 30 international. Average age 23. 305 applicants, 21% accepted, 33 enrolled. In 2010, 11 master's, 21 doctorates awarded. Terminal master's awarded for partial completion of doctoral program. *Degree requirements:* For master's, thesis; for doctorate, comprehensive exam, thesis/dissertation, final oral exams. *Entrance requirements:* For master's and doctorate, GRE General Test, minimum QPA of 3.0. Additional exam requirements/recommendations for international students: Required—TOEFL (minimum score 550 paper-based; 213 computer-based; 80 iBT). *Application deadline:* For fall admission, 3/1 priority date for domestic students; for spring admission, 7/1 for domestic students. Applications are processed on a rolling basis. Application fee: $50. Electronic applications accepted. *Expenses:* Tuition, state resident: full-time $17,304; part-time $701 per credit. Tuition, nonresident: full-time $29,554; part-time $1210 per credit. Required fees: $740; $214 per term. Tuition and fees vary according to program. *Financial support:* In 2010–11, 38 fellowships with full tuition reimbursements (averaging $26,000 per year), 72 research assistantships with full tuition reimbursements (averaging $25,000 per year), 18 teaching assistantships with full tuition reimbursements (averaging $24,000 per year) were awarded; scholarships/grants and traineeships also available. Financial award application deadline: 4/15. *Faculty research:* Artificial organs, biomechanics, biomaterials, signal processing, biotechnology. Total annual research expenditures: $40.8 million. *Unit head:* Harvey S. Borovetz, Chairman, 412-383-9713, Fax: 412-383-8788, E-mail: borovetzhs@msx.upmc.edu. *Application contact:* Harvey S. Borovetz, Chairman, 412-383-9713, Fax: 412-383-8788, E-mail: borovetzhs@msx.upmc.edu.

The University of Texas at Arlington, Graduate School, College of Engineering, Bioengineering Department, Arlington, TX 76019. Offers MS, PhD. Programs offered jointly with The University of Texas Southwestern Medical Center at Dallas. Part-time programs available. *Faculty:* 11 full-time (2 women). *Students:* 108 full-time (48 women), 47 part-time (15 women); includes 15 minority (4 Black or African American, non-Hispanic/Latino; 9 Asian, non-Hispanic/Latino; 2 Hispanic/Latino), 109 international. 98 applicants, 86% accepted, 45 enrolled. In 2010, 45 master's, 5 doctorates awarded. Terminal master's awarded for partial completion of doctoral program. *Degree requirements:* For master's, comprehensive exam (for some programs), thesis (for some programs); for doctorate, comprehensive exam, thesis/dissertation, qualifying exam. *Entrance requirements:* For master's, GRE General Test, Total of 1100 or greater with verbal score of 400 or greater, minimum GPA of 3.0 in last 60 hours of course work, 3 letters of recommendation; for doctorate, GRE General Test, total score of 1175 or greater with verbal score of 400 or greater, minimum GPA of 3.4 in last 60 hours of course work, 3 letters of recommendation. Additional exam requirements/recommendations for international students: Required—TOEFL. *Application deadline:* For fall admission, 6/6 for domestic students, 4/4 for international students; for spring admission, 10/15 for domestic students, 9/5 for international students. Applications are processed on a rolling basis. Application fee: $35 ($50 for international students). *Expenses:* Tuition, state resident: full-time $7500. Tuition, nonresident: full-time $13,080. International tuition: $13,250 full-time. *Financial support:* In 2010–11, 1 student received support, including 4 fellowships (averaging $1,000 per year), 5 research assistantships (averaging $10,000 per year), 9 teaching assistantships (averaging $18,000 per year); career-related internships or fieldwork, Federal Work-Study, institutionally sponsored loans, scholarships/grants, and tuition waivers (partial) also available. Financial award application deadline: 6/1; financial award applicants required to submit FAFSA. *Faculty research:* Instrumentation, mechanics, materials. *Unit head:* Dr. Khosrow Behbehani, Chair, 817-272-

2249, Fax: 817-272-2251, E-mail: kb@uta.edu. *Application contact:* Amanda Kerby, Academic Advisor, 817-272-0783, Fax: 817-272-5388, E-mail: akerby@uta.edu.

The University of Toledo, College of Graduate Studies, College of Engineering, Department of Bioengineering, Toledo, OH 43606-3390. Offers MS, PhD. Terminal master's awarded for partial completion of doctoral program. *Degree requirements:* For master's, thesis optional; for doctorate, thesis/dissertation, qualifying exam. *Entrance requirements:* For master's, GRE General Test, minimum GPA of 3.0; for doctorate, GRE General Test, minimum GPA of 3.3. Additional exam requirements/recommendations for international students: Required—TOEFL (minimum score 550 paper-based; 213 computer-based; 80 iBT). Electronic applications accepted. *Expenses:* Tuition, state resident: full-time $11,426; part-time $476 per credit hour. Tuition, nonresident: full-time $21,660; part-time $903 per credit hour. One-time fee: $62. *Faculty research:* Artificial organs, biochemical engineering, bioelectrical systems, biomechanics, cellular engineering.

University of Utah, Graduate School, College of Engineering, Department of Bioengineering, Salt Lake City, UT 84112-9202. Offers MS, PhD. *Faculty:* 20 full-time (2 women), 1 part-time/adjunct (0 women). *Students:* 116 full-time (24 women), 22 part-time (5 women); includes 8 minority (all Asian, non-Hispanic/Latino), 26 international. Average age 28. 57 applicants, 95% accepted, 43 enrolled. In 2010, 13 master's, 7 doctorates awarded. Terminal master's awarded for partial completion of doctoral program. *Degree requirements:* For master's, comprehensive exam, thesis, written project, oral presentation; for doctorate, thesis/dissertation. *Entrance requirements:* For master's and doctorate, GRE General Test, minimum GPA of 3.0. Additional exam requirements/recommendations for international students: Required—TOEFL (minimum score 500 paper-based; 173 computer-based; 61 iBT), IELTS. *Application deadline:* For fall admission, 4/1 for domestic and international students. Application fee: $55 ($65 for international students). Electronic applications accepted. *Expenses:* Contact institution. *Financial support:* In 2010–11, 8 fellowships with full tuition reimbursements (averaging $20,000 per year), 106 research assistantships with full tuition reimbursements (averaging $23,000 per year), 10 teaching assistantships with full tuition reimbursements (averaging $23,000 per year) were awarded; traineeships, health care benefits, tuition waivers (full), and unspecified assistantships also available. Financial award application deadline: 2/15; financial award applicants required to submit FAFSA. *Faculty research:* Ultrasonic bioinstrumentation, medical imaging, neuroprosthesis, biomaterials and tissue engineering, biomechanic biomedical computing/modeling. Total annual research expenditures: $7.9 million. *Unit head:* Dr. Patrick A. Tresco, Chair, 801-587-9263, Fax: 801-585-5151, E-mail: patrick.tresco@utah.edu. *Application contact:* Karen Lynn Terry, Graduate Program Advisor and Coordinator, 801-581-8559, Fax: 801-585-5151, E-mail: karen.terry@utah.edu.

See Display below and Close-Up on page 123.

University of Washington, Graduate School, College of Engineering and School of Medicine, Department of Bioengineering, Seattle, WA 98195-5061. Offers bioengineering (MS, PhD); bioengineering and nanotechnology (PhD); medical engineering (MME); pharmaceutical bioengineering (MS). Evening/weekend programs available. Postbaccalaureate distance learning degree programs offered (no on-campus study). *Faculty:* 30 full-time (10 women), 10 part-time/adjunct (2 women). *Students:* 109 full-time (47 women), 46 part-time (19 women); includes 3 Black or African American, non-Hispanic/Latino; 1 American Indian or Alaska Native, non-Hispanic/Latino; 33 Asian, non-Hispanic/Latino; 4 Hispanic/Latino, 28 international. Average age 26. 442 applicants, 19% accepted, 39 enrolled. In 2010, 19 master's, 16 doctorates awarded. *Degree requirements:* For master's, comprehensive exam, thesis; for doctorate, comprehensive exam, thesis/dissertation, qualifying exam, general exam, thesis defense. *Entrance requirements:* For master's and doctorate, GRE General Test, Minimum GPA of 3.0, transcripts, statement of purpose, letters of recommendation. Additional exam requirements/recommendations for international students: Required—TOEFL (minimum score 580 paper-based; 237 computer-based; 92 iBT); Recommended—IELTS (minimum score 7). *Application*

---

deadline: For fall admission, 12/15 priority date for domestic students, 12/1 priority date for international students. Application fee: $75. Electronic applications accepted. *Financial support:* In 2010–11, 2 students received support, including 25 fellowships with full tuition reimbursements available (averaging $19,098 per year), 111 research assistantships with full tuition reimbursements available (averaging $19,224 per year), 15 teaching assistantships with full tuition reimbursements available (averaging $19,224 per year); Federal Work-Study, institutionally sponsored loans, traineeships, health care benefits, and tuition waivers (full) also available. Support available to part-time students. Financial award application deadline: 12/15; financial award applicants required to submit FAFSA. *Faculty research:* Biomaterials and tissue engineering; global health, distributed diagnosis and home healthcare; bioinstrumentation; molecular bioengineering; imaging and image-guided therapy. Total annual research expenditures: $23.4 million. *Unit head:* Dr. Paul Yager, Professor and Chair, 206-685-2000, Fax: 206-685-3300, E-mail: yagerp@u.washington.edu. *Application contact:* Dorian Taylor, Senior Academic Counselor, 206-685-2000, Fax: 206-685-3300, E-mail: bioeng@u.washington.edu.

University of Wisconsin–Madison, Graduate School, College of Engineering, Department of Chemical and Biological Engineering, Madison, WI 53706-0607. Offers chemical engineering (MS, PhD). *Faculty:* 19 full-time (2 women), 1 part-time/adjunct (0 women). *Students:* 132 full-time (38 women); includes 1 American Indian or Alaska Native, non-Hispanic/Latino; 9 Asian, non-Hispanic/Latino; 7 Hispanic/Latino, 53 international. Average age 25. 428 applicants, 21% accepted, 28 enrolled. In 2010, 3 master's, 15 doctorates awarded. Terminal master's awarded for partial completion of doctoral program. *Degree requirements:* For master's, thesis or alternative; for doctorate, thesis/dissertation, 2 semesters of teaching assistantship. *Entrance requirements:* For master's and doctorate, GRE General Test. Additional exam requirements/recommendations for international students: Required—TOEFL (minimum score 550 paper-based; 213 computer-based; 80 iBT). *Application deadline:* For fall admission, 1/1 for domestic and international students; for spring admission, 10/15 for domestic and international students. Application fee: $56. Electronic applications accepted. *Expenses:* Tuition, state resident: full-time $9887.36; part-time $617.96 per credit. Tuition, nonresident: full-time $24,054; part-time $1503.40 per credit. Required fees: $67.63 per credit. Tuition and fees vary according to reciprocity agreements. *Financial support:* In 2010–11, 122 students received support, including 21 fellowships with full tuition reimbursements available (averaging $28,752 per year), 66 research assistantships with full tuition reimbursements available (averaging $24,000 per year), 45 teaching assistantships with full tuition reimbursements available (averaging $25,167 per year); traineeships and health care benefits also available. Financial award application deadline: 1/15. *Faculty research:* Biotechnology, nanotechnology, complex fluids, molecular and systems modeling, renewable energy and chemicals: materials and processes. Total annual research expenditures: $17.7 million. *Unit head:* Prof. Nicholas L. Abbott, Chair, 608-265-5278, Fax: 608-262-5434, E-mail: abbott@engr.wisc.edu. *Application contact:* Donna M. Bell, Graduate Coordinator, 608-263-3138, Fax: 608-262-5434, E-mail: gradoffice@che.wisc.edu.

Virginia Commonwealth University, Graduate School, School of Engineering, Department of Chemical and Life Science Engineering, Richmond, VA 23284-9005. Offers MS, PhD. *Faculty:* 7 full-time (0 women). *Entrance requirements:* For master's and doctorate, GRE. Additional exam requirements/recommendations for international students: Required—TOEFL (minimum score 600 paper-based; 250 computer-based; 100 iBT). *Application deadline:* For fall admission, 2/1 priority date for domestic students; for spring admission, 11/15 for domestic students. Application fee: $50. Electronic applications accepted. *Expenses:* Tuition, state resident: full-time $4308; part-time $479 per credit hour. Tuition, nonresident: full-time $8942; part-time $994 per credit hour. Required fees: $2000; $85 per credit hour. Tuition and fees vary according to course level, course load, degree level, campus/location and program. *Financial support:* Applicants required to submit FAFSA. *Faculty research:* Advanced polymers, including biopolymers and polymers in medicine; chemical and biochemical reactor analysis; the study of supercritical fluids for environmentally favorable processes; systems biological engineering; stem cell engineering; biosensors and biochips; computational bioinformatics and rational drug design. *Unit head:* Dr. Michael H. Peters, Chair, 804-828-7789, E-mail: mpeters@vcu.edu. *Application contact:* Dr. Kenneth J. Wynne, Director, Graduate Programs in Chemical and Life Science Engineering, 804-828-3925, E-mail: kjwynne@vcu.edu.

Virginia Polytechnic Institute and State University, Graduate School, College of Engineering, Department of Biological Systems Engineering, Blacksburg, VA 24061. Offers M Eng, MS, PhD. *Faculty:* 17 full-time (2 women). *Students:* 57 full-time (17 women), 5 part-time (3 women); includes 1 Black or African American, non-Hispanic/Latino; 2 Asian, non-Hispanic/Latino; 2 Hispanic/Latino, 29 international. Average age 27. 65 applicants, 37% accepted, 18 enrolled. In 2010, 14 master's awarded. *Degree requirements:* For master's, comprehensive exam (for some programs), thesis (for some programs); for doctorate, comprehensive exam (for some programs), thesis/dissertation (for some programs). *Entrance requirements:* For master's and doctorate, GRE. Additional exam requirements/recommendations for international students: Required—TOEFL (minimum score 550 paper-based; 213 computer-based). *Application deadline:* For fall admission, 7/1 for domestic and international students; for spring admission, 12/1 for domestic and international students. Applications are processed on a rolling basis. Application fee: $65. Electronic applications accepted. *Expenses:* Tuition, area resident: Full-time $9399; part-time $488 per credit hour. Tuition, state resident: full-time $9399; part-time $488 per credit hour. Tuition, nonresident: full-time $17,854; part-time $957.75 per credit hour. International tuition: $17,854 full-time. Required fees: $1534. Full-time tuition and fees vary according to program. *Financial support:* In 2010–11, 1 fellowship with full tuition reimbursement (averaging $25,250 per year), 28 research assistantships with full tuition reimbursements (averaging $18,021 per year), 3 teaching assistantships with full tuition reimbursements (averaging $16,603 per year) were awarded; career-related internships or fieldwork, Federal Work-Study, scholarships/grants, health care benefits, and unspecified assistantships also available. Financial award application deadline: 1/15. *Faculty research:* Soil and water engineering, alternative energy sources for agriculture and agricultural mechanization. Total annual research expenditures: $3.2 million. *Unit head:* Dr. Mary Leigh Wolfe, UNIT HEAD, 540-231-6092, Fax: 540-231-3199, E-mail: mlwolfe@vt.edu. *Application contact:* Cully Hession, Contact, 540-231-9480, Fax: 540-231-3199, E-mail: chession@vt.edu.

Washington State University, Graduate School, College of Engineering and Architecture, Department of Biological Systems Engineering, Pullman, WA 99164. Offers biological and agricultural engineering (MS, PhD). *Faculty:* 10. *Students:* 48 full-time (14 women), 3 part-time (2 women); includes 1 minority (Asian, non-Hispanic/Latino), 40 international. Average age 30. 72 applicants, 24% accepted, 15 enrolled. In 2010, 2 master's awarded. *Degree requirements:* For master's, comprehensive exam, thesis (for some programs), written and oral exam; for doctorate, comprehensive exam, thesis/dissertation, written and oral exam. *Entrance requirements:* For master's, GRE General Test, GRE Subject Test, minimum GPA of 3.0, bachelor's degree in engineering or closely related subject; for doctorate, minimum GPA of 3.0, bachelor's degree in engineering or closely related subject. Additional exam requirements/recommendations for international students: Required—TOEFL. *Application deadline:* For fall admission, 2/1 priority date for domestic students, 3/1 for international students; for spring admission, 9/1 for domestic students, 7/1 for international students. Applications are processed on a rolling basis. Application fee: $50. *Expenses:* Tuition, state resident: full-time $8552; part-time $443 per credit. Tuition, nonresident: full-time $21,650; part-time $1083 per credit. Required fees: $846. *Financial support:* In 2010–11, 20 research assistantships (averaging $18,204 per year), 17 teaching assistantships (averaging $18,204 per year) were awarded. *Faculty research:* Social issues and engineering education, electronic instrument design, prediction, technology for dust from agricultural lands. Total annual research expenditures: $3.1 million. *Unit head:* Dr. Claudio Stockle, Chair, 509-335-1578, Fax: 509-335-2722, E-mail: stockle@wsu.edu. *Application contact:* Graduate School Admissions, 800-GRADWSU, Fax: 509-335-1949, E-mail: gradsch@wsu.edu.

Biosystems Engineering

Clemson University, Graduate School, College of Engineering and Science, Department of Environmental Engineering and Earth Sciences and College of Engineering and Science, Program in Biosystems Engineering, Clemson, SC 29634. Offers MS, PhD. Part-time programs available. *Students:* 19 full-time (9 women), 4 part-time (1 woman); includes 1 Black or African American, non-Hispanic/Latino, 7 international. Average age 29. 29 applicants, 59% accepted, 11 enrolled. In 2010, 5 master's, 1 doctorate awarded. *Degree requirements:* For master's, thesis (for some programs); for doctorate, thesis/dissertation. *Entrance requirements:* For master's and doctorate, GRE General Test, minimum GPA of 3.0. Additional exam requirements/recommendations for international students: Required—TOEFL. *Application deadline:* For fall admission, 6/1 for domestic students, 4/15 for international students; for spring admission, 9/15 for international students. Applications are processed on a rolling basis. Application fee: $70 ($80 for international students). Electronic applications accepted. *Expenses:* Tuition, state resident: full-time $6492; part-time $400 per credit hour. Tuition, nonresident: full-time $13,634; part-time $800 per credit hour. Required fees: $262 per semester. Part-time tuition and fees vary according to course load and program. *Financial support:* In 2010–11, 20 students received support, including 4 fellowships with full and partial tuition reimbursements available (averaging $11,615 per year), 19 research assistantships with partial tuition reimbursements available (averaging $10,645 per year), 5 teaching assistantships with partial tuition reimbursements available (averaging $6,788 per year); career-related internships or fieldwork, institutionally sponsored loans, scholarships/grants, health care benefits, and unspecified assistantships also available. Support available to part-time students. *Unit head:* Dr. Tanju Karanfil, Chair, 864-653-1005, Fax: 864-656-5973, E-mail: tkaranf@clemson.edu. *Application contact:* Dr. Caye Drapcho, Graduate Coordinator, 864-656-0378, Fax: 864-656-0338, E-mail: cdrapch@clemson.edu.

Iowa State University of Science and Technology, Graduate College, College of Engineering, Department of Agricultural and Biosystems Engineering, Ames, IA 50011. Offers M Eng, MS, PhD. *Faculty:* 30 full-time (2 women), 3 part-time/adjunct (0 women). *Students:* 55 full-time (21 women), 21 part-time (7 women); includes 3 Black or African American, non-Hispanic/Latino; 1 American Indian or Alaska Native, non-Hispanic/Latino; 2 Asian, non-Hispanic/Latino; 1 Hispanic/Latino, 29 international. 52 applicants, 31% accepted, 13 enrolled. In 2010, 9 master's, 5 doctorates awarded. *Degree requirements:* For master's, thesis (for some programs); for doctorate, thesis/dissertation. *Entrance requirements:* For master's and doctorate, GRE. Additional exam requirements/recommendations for international students: Required—TOEFL (minimum score 550 paper-based; 79 iBT), IELTS (minimum score 6.5). *Application deadline:* For fall admission, 2/1 priority date for domestic and international students; for spring admission, 7/1 priority date for domestic and international students. Applications are processed on a rolling basis. Application fee: $40 ($90 for international students). Electronic applications accepted. *Financial support:* In 2010–11, 51 research assistantships with full and partial tuition reimbursements (averaging $15,435 per year), 1 teaching assistantship with full and partial tuition reimbursement (averaging $9,613 per year) were awarded; fellowships, scholarships/grants, health care benefits, and unspecified assistantships also available. *Faculty research:* Grain processing and quality, tillage systems, simulation and controls, water management, environmental quality. *Unit head:* Dr. Ramesh Kanwar, Chair, 515-294-1434. *Application contact:* Dr. Steven Freeman, Director of Graduate Education, 515-294-9541, E-mail: sfreeman@iastate.edu.

Michigan State University, The Graduate School, College of Agriculture and Natural Resources and College of Engineering, Department of Biosystems and Agricultural Engineering, East Lansing, MI 48824. Offers biosystems engineering (MS, PhD). *Entrance requirements:* Additional exam requirements/recommendations for international students: Required—TOEFL. Electronic applications accepted.

North Dakota State University, College of Graduate and Interdisciplinary Studies, College of Engineering and Architecture, Department of Agricultural and Biosystems Engineering, Fargo, ND 58108. Offers agricultural and biosystems engineering (MS, PhD); engineering (PhD); natural resource management (MS); natural resources management (PhD). Part-time programs available. *Faculty:* 6 full-time (1 woman). *Students:* 8 full-time (2 women), 4 part-time (1 woman), 9 international. Average age 28. 19 applicants, 37% accepted, 4 enrolled. In 2010, 1 master's, 5 doctorates awarded. *Degree requirements:* For master's, thesis; for doctorate, thesis/dissertation. *Entrance requirements:* For master's and doctorate, BS in engineering or the equivalent, minimum undergraduate GPA of 3.0. Additional exam requirements/recommendations for international students: Required—TOEFL (minimum score 550 paper-based; 213 computer-based; 79 iBT). *Application deadline:* For fall admission, 7/1 priority date for domestic and international students; for spring admission, 10/1 priority date for domestic and international students. Applications are processed on a rolling basis. Application fee: $45 ($60 for international students). Electronic applications accepted. *Financial support:* In 2010–11, 9 research assistantships with full tuition reimbursements (averaging $15,000 per year) were awarded; career-related internships or fieldwork, Federal Work-Study, institutionally sponsored loans, and unspecified assistantships also available. Support available to part-time students. Financial award application deadline: 4/15. *Faculty research:* Irrigation, crop processing, food engineering, environmental resources, sensors and instrumentation. Total annual research expenditures: $158,309. *Unit head:* Leslie F. Backer, Chair, 701-231-7261, Fax: 701-231-1008, E-mail: leslie.backer@ndsu.edu. *Application contact:* Dr. David A. Wittrock, Dean, 701-231-7033, Fax: 701-231-6524.

South Dakota State University, Graduate School, College of Agriculture and Biological Sciences, Department of Agriculture and Biosystems Engineering, Brookings, SD 57007. Offers MS, PhD. Part-time programs available. *Degree requirements:* For master's, thesis; for doctorate, comprehensive exam, thesis/dissertation, preliminary oral and written exams. *Entrance requirements:* Additional exam requirements/recommendations for international students: Required—TOEFL (minimum score 525 paper-based; 197 computer-based; 71 iBT).

South Dakota State University, Graduate School, College of Engineering, Department of Agricultural and Biosystems Engineering, Brookings, SD 57007. Offers biological sciences (MS, PhD); engineering (MS). PhD offered jointly with Iowa State University of Science and Technology. Part-time programs available. *Degree requirements:* For master's, thesis (for some programs), oral exam; for doctorate, thesis/dissertation, preliminary oral and written exams. *Entrance requirements:* For master's and doctorate, engineering degree. Additional exam requirements/recommendations for international students: Required—TOEFL (minimum score 550 paper-based; 213 computer-based; 79 iBT). *Faculty research:* Water resources, food engineering, natural resources engineering, machine design, bioprocess engineering.

The University of Arizona, College of Agriculture and Life Sciences, Department of Agricultural and Biosystems Engineering, Tucson, AZ 85721. Offers MS, PhD. *Faculty:* 10 full-time (1

Biosystems Engineering

The University of Arizona (continued)

woman). *Students:* 22 full-time (6 women), 8 part-time (3 women); includes 1 Asian, non-Hispanic/Latino; 1 Hispanic/Latino; 2 Two or more races, non-Hispanic/Latino, 18 international. Average age 32. 19 applicants, 74% accepted, 6 enrolled. In 2010, 6 master's, 5 doctorates awarded. Terminal master's awarded for partial completion of doctoral program. *Degree requirements:* For master's, thesis; for doctorate, thesis/dissertation. *Entrance requirements:* For master's, minimum GPA of 3.0 in last 2 years of undergraduate study, 3 letters of recommendation; for doctorate, minimum GPA of 3.0 in last 2 years of undergraduate study, 3 letters of recommendation, statement of purpose. Additional exam requirements/recommendations for international students: Required—TOEFL (minimum score 213 computer-based). *Application deadline:* For fall admission, 6/1 for domestic students, 2/1 for international students; for spring admission, 9/1 for domestic students, 8/1 for international students. Applications are processed on a rolling basis. Application fee: $75. Electronic applications accepted. *Expenses:* Tuition, state resident: full-time $7692. *Financial support:* In 2010–11, 13 research assistantships with full and partial tuition reimbursements (averaging $24,985 per year), 1 teaching assistantship with full and partial tuition reimbursement (averaging $24,435 per year) were awarded; fellowships, career-related internships or fieldwork, Federal Work-Study, institutionally sponsored loans, scholarships/grants, traineeships, health care benefits, tuition waivers (full and partial), and unspecified assistantships also available. Financial award application deadline: 5/1. *Faculty research:* Irrigation system design, energy-use management, equipment for alternative crops, food properties enhancement. Total annual research expenditures: $452,871. *Unit head:* Donald Slack, Head, 520-621-3691, Fax: 520-621-3963, E-mail: slackd@u.arizona.edu. *Application contact:* Daniela Ibarra, Senior Office Specialist, 520-621-1753, Fax: 520-621-3963, E-mail: dcastro@email.arizona.edu.

University of Dayton, Graduate School, School of Engineering, Department of Chemical Engineering, Dayton, OH 45469-1300. Offers bioengineering instrumentation (MS); bioprocess engineering (MS); biosystems engineering (MS). Part-time and evening/weekend programs available. *Faculty:* 10 full-time (1 woman), 4 part-time/adjunct (0 women). *Students:* 30 full-time (7 women), 5 part-time (1 woman); includes 7 minority (4 Black or African American, non-Hispanic/Latino; 3 Asian, non-Hispanic/Latino), 18 international. Average age 26. 43 applicants, 86% accepted, 17 enrolled. In 2010, 3 master's awarded. *Degree requirements:* For master's, thesis optional. *Entrance requirements:* Additional exam requirements/recommendations for international students: Required—TOEFL (minimum score 550 paper-based; 213 computer-based; 80 iBT). *Application deadline:* For fall admission, 8/1 priority date for domestic students. Applications are processed on a rolling basis. Application fee: $0 ($50 for international students). Electronic applications accepted. *Expenses:* Tuition: Full-time $7800; part-time $650 per credit hour. *Financial support:* In 2010–11, 10 research assistantships with full tuition reimbursements (averaging $14,745 per year) were awarded; institutionally sponsored loans, health care benefits, and unspecified assistantships also available. Financial award applicants required to submit FAFSA. *Faculty research:* Vertically-aligned carbon nanotubes infiltrated with temperature-responsive polymers: smart nanocomposite films for self-cleaning and controlled release, bilayer and bulk heterojunction solar cells using liquid crystalline porphyrins as donors by solution processing, DNA damage induced by multiwalled carbon nanotubes in mouse embryonic stem cells. Total annual research expenditures: $1.5 million. *Unit head:* Dr. Robert Wilkins, Chair, 937-229-2627, E-mail: robert.wilkins@notes.udayton.edu. *Application contact:* Alexander Popovski, Associate Director of Graduate and International Admissions, 937-229-2357, Fax: 937-229-4729, E-mail: alex.popovski@notes.udayton.edu.

University of Manitoba, Faculty of Graduate Studies, Faculty of Engineering, Department of Biosystems Engineering, Winnipeg, MB R3T 2N2, Canada. Offers M Eng, M Sc, PhD.

University of Minnesota, Twin Cities Campus, Graduate School, College of Food, Agricultural and Natural Resource Sciences, Bioproducts and Biosystems Science, Engineering and Management Graduate Program, Saint Paul, MN 55108. Offers MS, PhD. Part-time programs available. *Faculty:* 32 full-time (2 women). *Students:* 26 full-time (10 women), 2 part-time (0 women); includes 10 minority (9 Asian, non-Hispanic/Latino; 1 Hispanic/Latino), 17 international. Average age 30. 43 applicants, 35% accepted, 12 enrolled. In 2010, 1 master's awarded. Terminal master's awarded for partial completion of doctoral program. *Degree requirements:* For master's, comprehensive exam, thesis; for doctorate, comprehensive exam, thesis/dissertation. *Entrance requirements:* For master's and doctorate, GRE, BS in engineering, mathematics, physical or biological sciences, or related field. Additional exam requirements/recommendations for international students: Required—TOEFL (minimum score 550 paper-based; 213 computer-based; 79 iBT). *Application deadline:* For fall admission, 12/15 for domestic and international students; for spring admission, 10/15 for domestic and international students. Applications are processed on a rolling basis. Application fee: $75 ($95 for international students). Electronic applications accepted. *Financial support:* In 2010–11, fellowships with full tuition reimbursements (averaging $23,500 per year), research assistantships with full and partial tuition reimbursements (averaging $20,280 per year), teaching assistantships with full and partial tuition reimbursements (averaging $20,280 per year) were awarded; scholarships/grants, health care benefits, and unspecified assistantships also available. Support available to part-time students. Financial award application deadline: 12/15. *Faculty research:* Water quality, bioprocessing, food engineering, terramechanics, process and machine control. Total annual research expenditures: $6.2 million. *Unit head:* Dr. Gary Sands, Director of Graduate Studies, 612-625-4756, Fax: 612-624-3005, E-mail: grsands@umn.edu. *Application contact:* Sue Olsen, Graduate Coordinator, 612-625-7733, Fax: 612-624-3005, E-mail: olsen005@umn.edu.

The University of Tennessee, Graduate School, College of Agricultural Sciences and Natural Resources, Department of Biosystems Engineering and Environmental Science, Program in Biosystems Engineering, Knoxville, TN 37996. Offers MS, PhD. *Degree requirements:* For master's, thesis; for doctorate, thesis/dissertation. *Entrance requirements:* For master's and doctorate, GRE General Test, minimum GPA of 2.7. Additional exam requirements/recommendations for international students: Required—TOEFL. Electronic applications accepted. *Expenses:* Tuition, state resident: full-time $7440; part-time $414 per credit hour. Tuition, nonresident: full-time $22,478; part-time $1250 per credit hour. Required fees: $922; $43 per credit hour. Tuition and fees vary according to program.

The University of Tennessee, Graduate School, College of Agricultural Sciences and Natural Resources, Department of Biosystems Engineering and Environmental Science, Program in Biosystems Engineering Technology, Knoxville, TN 37996. Offers MS. *Degree requirements:* For master's, thesis or alternative. *Entrance requirements:* For master's, GRE General Test, minimum GPA of 2.7. Additional exam requirements/recommendations for international students: Required—TOEFL. Electronic applications accepted. *Expenses:* Tuition, state resident: full-time $7440; part-time $414 per credit hour. Tuition, nonresident: full-time $22,478; part-time $1250 per credit hour. Required fees: $922; $43 per credit hour. Tuition and fees vary according to program.

UNIVERSITY OF CALIFORNIA, SAN DIEGO

Department of Bioengineering

Programs of Study

The Department of Bioengineering at the University of California, San Diego (UCSD), offers graduate instruction leading to the Master of Engineering (M.Eng.), Master of Science (M.S.), and Doctor of Philosophy (Ph.D.) degrees. The bioengineering graduate program began in 1966, and the Department was established in the Jacobs School of Engineering in 1994. The graduate programs provide an excellent education, integrating the fields of engineering and biomedical sciences. Students with an undergraduate education in engineering learn how to use engineering concepts and methodology to analyze and solve biological problems associated with genes, molecules, cells, tissues, organs, and systems, with applications to clinical medicine and biology.

The M.S. program is intended to equip the student with fundamental knowledge in bioengineering. The degree may be terminal or obtained on the way to earning the Ph.D. degree. It requires successful completion of 48 quarter units of credit combining course work and research, culminating in a thesis. In addition to the M.S. degree, the Department offers the M.Eng. degree. This degree is intended to prepare design and project engineers for careers in the biomedical and biotechnology industries within the framework of the graduate program of the bioengineering department. It is a terminal professional degree in engineering.

The Ph.D. program is designed to prepare students for a career in research and/or teaching in bioengineering. Each student takes courses in engineering physics and the life sciences to prepare him or her for the Departmental Ph.D. qualifying examination, which tests students' capabilities and ascertains their potential for independent study and research. The degree requires the completion of a dissertation and defense of that research.

The Department of Bioengineering also participates in a new interdisciplinary graduate training program at the interfaces between the biological, medical, physical, and engineering sciences. UCSD is one of ten universities selected through the Howard Hughes Medical Institute (HHMI) to initiate this new program. To learn more about the UCSD Interfaces Training Program, students should visit http://interfaces.ucsd.edu/.

There is also an M.D./Ph.D. degree offered in conjunction with the UCSD Medical School, pending independent admission to the Medical School.

Research Facilities

The Department is housed in a modern research building constructed in 2003 with funds from the Whitaker and Powell Foundations. This building houses a majority of the bioengineering research laboratories in addition to premier core and instructional facilities. The research laboratories in the Department are fully equipped for modern bioengineering research. The Department houses several state-of-the-art core facilities, including biotechnology, microfabrication, cell engineering, and microscopy, and a vivarium. The state-of-the-art instrumentation includes access to high-throughput (Solexa) sequencers, mass spectrometry for proteomics and metabolomics, live-cell imaging, and new-generation cell-sorting/selection equipment. The Department maintains excellent computing and network facilities, including a graduate workstation lab, a multimedia laboratory, and two 105-node Linux clusters.

Financial Aid

The Department supports domestic full-time graduate students at the Ph.D. level. Financial support is available in the form of fellowships, traineeships, teaching assistantships, and research assistantships. Awarding of financial support is competitive, and stipends average $27,000 for the academic year, plus tuition and fees. Sources of funding include University fellowships and traineeships from an NIH training grant. Funds for support of international students are extremely limited, and the selection process is highly competitive. International students are encouraged to come with their own funding to gain admission.

Cost of Study

In 2011–12, full-time students who are California residents are expected to pay $4437.50 per quarter in registration and incidental fees. Nonresidents pay a total of $9471.50 per quarter in registration and incidental fees. There is a reduced fee structure for students enrolled on a half-time basis. Fees are subject to change.

Living and Housing Costs

UCSD provides 1,625 apartments for graduate students. Current monthly rates range from $417 for a single student to $1430 for a family. There is also a variety of off-campus housing in the surrounding communities. Prevailing rents range from $613 per month for a room in a private home to $1500 or more per month for a two-bedroom apartment. Information may be obtained from the UCSD Affiliated Housing Office.

Student Group

The current campus enrollment is 27,417 students, of whom 23,143 are undergraduates and 4,274 are graduate students. The Department of Bioengineering has an undergraduate enrollment of 843 and a graduate enrollment of 174.

Location

The 2,040-acre campus spreads from the coastline, where the Scripps Institution of Oceanography is located, across a large wooded portion of the Torrey Pines Mesa overlooking the Pacific Ocean. To the east and north lie mountains, and to the south are Mexico and the almost uninhabited seacoast of Baja California.

The University

One of ten campuses in the University of California System, UCSD comprises the general campus, the School of Medicine, and the Scripps Institution of Oceanography. Established in La Jolla in 1960, UCSD is one of the newer campuses, but in this short time, it has become one of the major universities in the country.

Applying

A minimum GPA of 3.4 (on a 4.0 scale) is required for Ph.D. and M.S. admission. For the M.Eng. degree, a minimum GPA of 3.0 (on a 4.0 scale) is required for admission. The average GPA for students offered support in 2010–11 was 3.80. All applicants are required to take the GRE General Test. International applicants whose native language is not English are required to take the TOEFL and obtain a minimum score of 80 on the Internet-based version. In addition to test scores, applicants must submit a completed Graduate Admission Application, all official transcripts (English translation must accompany official transcripts written in other languages), a statement of purpose, and three letters of recommendation. The deadline for filing applications for both international students and U.S. residents is December 1, 2011. Applicants are considered for admission for the fall quarter only.

Correspondence and Information

Department of Bioengineering 0419
University of California, San Diego
La Jolla, California 92093-0419
Phone: 858-822-0006
E-mail: be-gradinfo@bioeng.ucsd.edu
Web site: http://be.uscd.edu

University of California, San Diego

THE FACULTY AND THEIR RESEARCH

Shu Chien, M.D., Ph.D., University Professor of Bioengineering and Medicine. Effects of mechanical forces on endothelial gene expression and signal transduction, molecular bioengineering, DNA microarrays, nanotechnology, circulatory regulation in health and disease, energy balance and molecular basis of leukocyte-endothelial interactions, vascular tissue engineering.

Pedro Cabrales, Ph.D., Assistant Professor. Transport of biological gases and their ability to regulate or affect cardiovascular function and cellular metabolism in order to design novel therapeutic interventions to treat, manage, and ultimately prevent disease using an integrative analysis of physical and chemical phenomena, based on engineering sciences principles and methods.

Gert Cauwenberghs, Ph.D., Professor of Biological Sciences. Cross-cutting advances at the interface between in vivo and in silico neural information processing; silicon adaptive microsystems and emerging nanotechnologies as tools for basic neuroscience research and clinical biomedical applications, and the insights they provide regarding the inner workings of nervous systems; facilitating the development of sensory and neural prostheses and brain-machine interfaces.

Karen Christman, Ph.D., Assistant Professor. Regeneration of injured and diseased cardiovascular tissues in vivo, using polymer chemistry and nanotechnology methods to develop novel biomaterials for tissue implantation and cell delivery.

Adam Engler, Ph.D., Assistant Professor. Interactions between cells and their extracellular matrix (ECM), especially the role of mechanical properties of the matrix in regulating stem cell differentiation; applying basic studies of cell-matrix interactions and mechanobiology to design new models for studying cancer progress and new strategies for engineering nerve and muscle tissues.

David A. Gough, Ph.D., Professor. Implantable glucose sensor for diabetes; glucose and oxygen transport through tissues, sensor biocompatibility; dynamic models of the natural pancreas on based glucose input and insulin output; machine learning for prediction of protein-protein interactions.

Jeff M. Hasty, Ph.D., Professor. Computational genomics and the dynamics of gene regulatory networks: Dissection and analysis of the complex dynamical interactions involved in gene regulation using techniques from nonlinear dynamics, statistical physics, and molecular biology to model, design, and construct synthetic gene networks.

Michael J. Heller, Ph.D., Professor. Development of high-performance bioanalytical techniques and technologies for genomic, proteomic, and pharmacogenomic applications, including novel devices (DNA array/lab-on-a-chip) and systems for mutation scanning, ultrafast DNA sequencing, single molecule detection, and combinatorial selection processes; nanotechnology and research related to the development of biomolecular-based mechanisms for photonic/electronic energy transfer, chemical to mechanical energy conversions, and DNA-based self-organizing nanostructures for data storage and computation; development of nanofabrication processes for the assembly of highly integrated macroscopic 2-D and 3-D structures from molecular and nanoscale components.

Xiaohua Huang, Ph.D., Associate Professor. Genomics, molecular biotechnology, and bioinformatics, including chemistry and biophysics of protein and DNA molecules and technologies to uncover greater information regarding the human genome and genetics.

Trey Ideker, Ph.D., Professor. Development of large-scale, computer-aided models of cellular signaling and regulatory pathways; new types of models and statistical frameworks for integrating the enormous amount of data on gene expression, protein expression, and protein interactions arising in the wake of the Human Genome Project.

Marcos Intaglietta, Ph.D., Professor. Development of plasma expanders and artificial blood, theory of tissue oxygenation at the microvascular level, optical methods for the study of microcirculation.

Ratnesh Lal, Ph.D., Professor. Nano-bio-interface science and technology; atomic force microscopy-based multimodality imaging and functional mapping to study protein misfolding, cell-cell, and cell-surround interactions; design and application of biosensors and devices to study normal and pathophysiology, preventive strategies, and therapeutics.

Andrew D. McCulloch, Ph.D., Professor. In vivo, in vitro, and in silico studies of the normal and diseased heart in model organisms and humans; cardiac phenotyping in gene-targeted animal models; cardiac muscle tissue engineering; myocyte mechanotransduction and mechanoelectric feedback; computational modeling of cardiac electromechanics; excitation-contraction coupling; metabolism and cell signaling; systems biology of cardiac function in Drosophila.

Bernhard Palsson, Ph.D., Professor. Hematopoietic tissue engineering, stem cell technology, bioreactor design, metabolic dynamics and regulation, whole cell simulators, metabolic engineering, genetic circuits.

Robert L. Sah, M.D., Sc.D., Professor of Bioengineering and HHMI Professor. Bioengineering of cartilage tissue and synovial fluid at the molecular, cellular, tissue, and joint scales; cartilage growth, aging, degeneration, and repair; cartilage biophysics, biomechanics, and transport; chondrocyte and cartilage mechanoregulation.

Geert W. Schmid-Schönbein, Ph.D., Professor of Bioengineering and Medicine. Microcirculation, biomechanics, molecular, and cellular mechanisms for transport in living tissues; mechanisms for cell activation in cardiovascular disease with applications to shock, ischemia, inflammation, and hypertension.

Gabriel A. Silva, Ph.D., Associate Professor. Retinal and central nervous system neural engineering; use of microtechnology and nanotechnology applied to molecular neurobiology and cell biology for regeneration of the neural retina and central nervous system; theoretical and computational neuroscience applied to understanding the retinal neural code; focus on retinal neurophysiology and pathophysiology of degenerative retinal disorders, tissue engineering and cellular replacement theories, adult stem cell biology for neuroscience applications.

Shankar Subramaniam, Ph.D., Professor and Chair. Bioinformatics and systems biology and bioengineering; measurement and integration of cellular data to reconstruct context-specific metabolic, signaling, and regulatory pathways; development of quantitative systems models for deciphering phenotypes in mammalian cells.

Lanping Amy Sung, Ph.D., Professor. Molecular structure and control of gene expression of membrane skeletal proteins in relation to the mechanical properties of cells and tissues in differentiation, aging, and disease; molecular defects of membrane skeletal proteins in hereditary diseases; protein 4.2 as a pseudozyme in maintaining the stability and flexibility of erythrocyte membranes; mechanical function of tropomodulin (a tropomyosin-binding protein) in the heart, muscles, and erythrocytes.

Shyni Varghese, Ph.D., Associate Professor. Application of novel and rational biomaterial design and synthesis to the repair and regeneration of injured and diseased tissues, especially for developing embryonic stem cell–based therapies for cartilage defects and osteoarthritis; the interface between stem cell differentiation, cell-matrix interactions, and biopolymers with the translational science of orthopedic surgery.

John T. Watson, Ph.D., Professor-in-Residence of Bioengineering and Vice Chair, External Relations. Heart failure and mechanical circulatory support; biomaterials; medical implant design; bioimaging; creativity, innovation, and technology transfer.

Kun Zhang, Ph.D., Assistant Professor. Development and scientific application of new genomic technologies, with an emphasis on high-throughput genomic analyses of single DNA molecules.

Bioengineering Adjunct Faculty

Michael Berns, Professor. Application of lasers and associated optical technologies in biology, medicine, and biomedical engineering: Laser-tissue interactions, laser microbeam studies on cell structure and function, development of photonics-based biomedical instrumentation, and clinical research in oncology, fertility, and ophthalmology.

Lars M. Bjursten, M.D., Ph.D., Professor.

Charles Cantor, Ph.D., Professor. Genomics, biochemical assays, protein immobilization, and pharmacology; biophysical chemistry and bioassays.

Paul Citron, Professor.

J. S. Lee, Ph.D., Professor.

G. Paternostro, Ph.D., M.D., Professor. Cardiac imaging and noninvasive study of metabolism, applications to high-throughput screening, apoptosis, genetic and genomic analysis of cardiac aging, Drosophila melanogaster as a model of chronic heart dysfunction.

P. Tong, Ph.D., Professor.

Bioengineering Affiliate Faculty

Richard Buxton, Ph.D., Professor of Radiology. Recently developed functional MRI (fMRI) techniques to measure patterns of activation in the brain, including basic studies of the physiological mechanisms that underlie fMRI, novel approaches to the design and analysis of fMRI experiments, and development of new imaging techniques to directly measure tissue blood flow.

Pao C. Chau, Ph.D., Professor of Chemical Engineering. Biotechnology and cellular engineering; development of a hollow fiber bioreactor to produce human monoclonal antibodies or binding fragments specific to tumor-associated antigens; cell-cycle kinetics research to understand the basic phenomena of antibody synthesis, especially under serum-free conditions; uses of flow cytometry to measure cell-cycle parameters; molecular biology techniques to probe transcriptional and posttranscriptional regulations; complementation of data and system analyses by mathematical models.

James W. Covell, M.D., Professor Emeritus of Medicine. Cardiovascular physiology and pharmacology; biomedical computing; mechanisms of diseased cardiac muscle contraction in the intact animal, the function of ischemic and hypertrophied cardiac muscle, and the role of the extracellular matrix in hypertrophy and heart failure; high-resolution measurements of finite deformation and finite-element modeling to explore these relationships; role of the extracellular matrix linking adjacent myocardial laminae in ischemia and heart failure.

Mark H. Ellisman, Ph.D., Professor of Neurosciences. Development and application of advanced imaging technologies to obtain new information about cell structure and function, structural correlates of nerve impulse conduction and axonal transport, cellular interactions during nervous system regeneration, cellular mechanisms regulating transient changes in cytoplasmic calcium, aging in the central nervous system.

David Hall, Ph.D., Assistant Adjunct Professor of Radiology. Using optical imaging approaches to interrogate tissue in vivo.

Andrew Kummel, Ph.D., Professor of Chemistry and Biochemistry.

Juan Lasheras, Ph.D., Distinguished Professor of Mechanical and Aerospace Engineering. Turbulent flows, two-phase flows, biomedical fluid mechanics, biomechanics.

Richard L. Lieber, Ph.D., Professor of Orthopedics. Musculoskeletal system design and plasticity, skeletal muscle architecture and its relation to tendon transfer surgery, development of intraoperative and rehabilitative measuring devices, skeletal muscle mechanics, sarcomere length measurement in isolated fibers and whole muscles, myosin expression in skeletal muscle after exercise-induced injury, immobilization, spinal cord injury and electrical stimulation.

Thomas Liu, Ph.D., Associate Professor of Radiology. Design and analysis of experiments for functional MRI (fMRI), with emphasis on statistical optimization, nonlinear signal processing, and physiological noise reduction; characterization and modeling of hemodynamic response to neural activity, including effects of drugs such as caffeine; development of novel imaging methods to measure cerebral blood flow and volume; characterization of cerebral blood flow in Alzheimer's disease and glaucoma.

Thomas Nelson, Ph.D., Professor of Radiology.

Sanjay Nigam, M.D., Professor of Medicine.

Jeffrey H. Omens, Ph.D., Professor of Medicine. Regional mechanics of the normal and diseased heart; miniaturization of functional measurement techniques for rat and mouse hearts; role of mechanical factors in cardiac hypertrophy, remodeling and growth; residual stress in the heart; computer-assisted analysis of cardiac mechanics.

Michael Sailor, Ph.D., Professor of Chemistry and Biochemistry

Scott Thomson, M.D., Ph.D., Professor-in-Residence of Orthopedics. Kidney physiology, using animal models; studies of regulation of kidney function by the juxtaglomerular apparatus, using a variety of adaptations on the technique of renal micropuncture.

Peter D. Wagner, M.D., Professor of Medicine. Theoretical and experimental basis of oxygen transport in the lungs and skeletal muscles; muscle capillary growth regulation using molecular biological approaches in integrated systems—the role of oxygen, microvascular hemodynamics, physical factors, and inflammatory mediators; mechanisms of exercise limitation in health and disease, especially the role of muscle dysfunction in heart failure, emphysema, and renal failure.

Sam Ward, Ph.D., Assistant Professor of Radiology.

John B. West, M.D., Ph.D., D.Sc., Professor Emeritus of Medicine. Bioengineering aspects of the lung; stress failure and physiology of pulmonary capillaries when exposed to high transmural pressures; distribution of ventilation and blood flow in the lung; effect of gravity on the lung; measurements of pulmonary function during sustained weightlessness; distortion of the lung resulting from its weight; regulation of the structure of capillary walls, including changes of gene expression as the result of stress; high-altitude physiology, especially extreme altitude.

UNIVERSITY OF UTAH

Department of Bioengineering

Programs of Study	The Department of Bioengineering at the University of Utah prepares graduates to be leaders in the integration of engineering, biology, and medicine to detect and treat human disease and disability. The Department's programs are consistently ranked among the highest in the U.S. The students are among the highest achieving students entering any interdepartmental program on campus. Graduate instruction leads to the Master of Science (M.S.) and Doctor of Philosophy (Ph.D.) degrees. Research programs include biomechanics, biomaterials, biosensors, computation and modeling, drug and gene delivery, medical imaging, neural interfaces, tissue engineering, and other specialty areas. The graduate program draws more than 95 faculty members from over thirty departments across four colleges.
	Students in the M.S. program must complete the master's-level core curriculum and elective courses, including bioengineering-track courses in one of the following areas: biosensors, biomaterials, bioinstrumentation/imaging, biomechanics, or neural interfaces. In addition, all M.S. students are required to defend their thesis in a public forum.
	Students may be admitted directly to the Ph.D. program at the time of admission, depending upon the decision of the Graduate Admissions Committee. Ph.D. students must successfully complete the bioengineering graduate core curriculum or its equivalent and take additional advanced graduate courses. Students must also pass a written qualifying exam, write a research proposal on their dissertation topic, and publicly defend their dissertation.
	The Ph.D. degree program typically takes a minimum of five years to complete. It is strongly recommended that all graduate students select a research direction and begin thesis research as soon as they begin their studies. In addition, the program is individually tailored to meet the specific objectives of each candidate and may involve collaboration with faculty members in other departments.
Research Facilities	The Department of Bioengineering at the University of Utah is an internationally renowned center of interdisciplinary basic and applied medically related research. It has a rich history in artificial organs, biomaterials, and drug delivery. Research laboratories and offices are located on the Heath Sciences Campus with the University Hospital, Huntsman Cancer, Primary Children's and Orthopedic Specialty Hospitals, the School of Medicine, and the College of Pharmacy. Centers and institutes include the Institute for Biomedical Engineering; Brain Institute; Scientific Computing and Imaging Institute (SCI); Cardiovascular Research and Training Institute (CVRTI); Huntsman Cancer Institute (HCI); Utah Center for Advanced Imaging Research (UCAIR); NIH Center for Bioelectric Field Modeling, Simulation, and Visualization; Center for Controlled Chemical Delivery (CCCD); Keck Center for Tissue Engineering (KCTE); Center for Neural Interfaces; Center for Biopolymers at Interfaces; and Utah State Center of Excellence for Biomedical Microfluidics.
	The University has excellent libraries and state-of-the-art computing centers.
Financial Aid	Students making satisfactory progress in the Department typically receive stipend support and tuition waivers throughout their graduate studies, typically through their graduate adviser. A limited number of University and Department fellowships are offered on a competitive basis to exceptionally well-qualified applicants.
Cost of Study	Virtually all bioengineering graduate students receive full-time scholarships, fellowships, or assistantships. In addition, graduate students receiving financial support through the University of Utah are given full tuition waivers. Tuition and fees for 2010–11 for 11 credit hours were $3835 for state residents and $10,800 for nonresidents per semester.
Living and Housing Costs	On-campus housing for unmarried graduate students begins at approximately $539 per month. Unfurnished apartments for married students range from $468 to $828 per month at University Village and from $788 to $1041 per month at Shoreline Ridge. Medical Plaza housing costs for both married and single students range from approximately $611 to $1057 per month. Off-campus housing near the University is also available. For more specific information, students should visit http://www.apartments.utah.edu or http://www.orl.utah.edu.
Student Group	The University of Utah has a student population of 30,000, representing all fifty states and fifty other countries. The Department of Bioengineering welcomes approximately 35 to 40 new students each year and maintains an average total graduate enrollment of more than 130. Graduates are successful in industry, academics, medicine, government, and entrepreneurial pursuits.
Location	Salt Lake City is the center of a metropolitan area of nearly a million people. It lies in a valley with an elevation varying between 4,200 and 5,500 feet and is surrounded by mountain peaks reaching nearly 12,000 feet in elevation. The city is the cultural center of the intermountain area, with world-class ballet and modern dance companies, theater and opera companies, and a symphony orchestra. It also supports professional basketball, hockey, soccer, arena football, and baseball. Salt Lake City was the proud host of the 2002 Winter Olympics and is within 30 minutes of several world-class ski resorts. A major wilderness area is less than 2 hours away, and ten national parks are within a short drive of the city.
The University	The 1,500-acre University campus is nestled in the foothills of the Wasatch Mountains and is characterized by its modern buildings and attractive landscaping. Within a few minutes' walk of the University is Red Butte Gardens, which is a large, established garden and ecological center with an area of more than 400 miles, with display gardens and hiking trails. An international faculty of 3,600 members provides comprehensive instruction and research in disciplines ranging from medicine and law to fine arts and business.
Applying	Instructions for applying to the program can be obtained by writing to the Department or from the Department's home page at http://www.bioen.utah.edu. In addition to the application form and fee, students must submit three letters of recommendation, scores on the General Test of the Graduate Record Examinations, university transcripts, and a written statement of interests and goals.
	Detailed information on the various aspects of the Department of Bioengineering at the University of Utah can be obtained by accessing the Department's home page.
Correspondence and Information	Chair, Graduate Admissions Committee Department of Bioengineering University of Utah 20 South 2030 East, 108 BPRB Salt Lake City, Utah 84112-9458 Web site: http://www.bioen.utah.edu

University of Utah

THE FACULTY AND THEIR RESEARCH

Orly Alter, Ph.D., Stanford. Genomic signal processing and systems biology.

* B. Ambati, Ph.D., Medical College of Georgia. Computational biomechanics, biochemical analysis/molecular marker, characterization of hip osteoarthritis.

J. D. Andrade, Ph.D., Denver. Interfacial biochemistry, biochemical sensors, proteins engineering, integrated science education, bioluminescence.

* A. Angelucci, M.D., Rome (Italy); Ph.D., MIT. Mammalian visual system.

* H. E. Ayliffe, Ph.D., Utah. Microelectromechanical systems (MEMS), biophysics, biotechnology.

K. N. Bachus, Ph.D., Utah. Bone biomechanics, fracture analysis, implant failure mechanisms.

* You Han Bae, Ph.D., Utah, Pharmaceutical chemistry.

* K. Balagurunathan, Ph.D., Iowa. Biomaterials, chemical biology.

* Stacy Bamberg, Sc.D., Harvard-MIT, Bioinstrumentation, gait analysis, aging.

* D. Bearss, Ph.D., Texas at San Antonio. Pharmaceutics and drug/gene delivery.

* S. M. Blair, Ph.D., Colorado. Integrated-optics resonance biosensors.

R. D. Bloebaum, Ph.D., Western Australia. Orthopedic implants.

* D. Bloswick, Ph.D., Michigan. Biomechanics, ergonomics.

S. C. Bock, Ph.D., California, Irvine. Antithrombin III heparin cofactor, medically useful serpins, glycoprotein N-glycosylation.

J. H. B. Bridge, Ph.D., UCLA. Cardiac muscle biophysics.

* D. W. Britt, Ph.D., Utah. High-resolution microscopy, thin films, protein-surface interactions.

K. Broadhead, Ph.D., Utah. Tissue engineering.

* M. B. Bromberg, Ph.D., Vermont; M.D., Michigan. Bioelectric signals from nerve/muscle, neurophysiology.

* N. A. T. Brown, Ph.D., Texas at Austin. Biomechanics, musculoskeletal modeling.

* R. B. Brown, Ph.D., Utah. Medical applications for sensors, bioinstrumentation, implantable electronics.

* J. B. Bunnell, Sc.D., MIT. Medical device development.

* G. Burns, D.V.M., Colorado State; Ph.D., Washington State. Biomaterial implant pathology and immune response, artificial heart.

* K. D. Caldwell, Ph.D., Uppsala (Sweden). Separation and characterization of biopolymers, subcellular particles, and cells.

* T. E. Cheatham, Ph.D., California, San Francisco. Computer simulation of biological macromolecules.

* Elena Cherkaev, Ph.D., St. Petersburg. Mathematics.

D. A. Christensen, Ph.D., Utah. Optical/ultrasonic bioinstrumentation.

* E. B. Clark, M.D., Albany Medical College. Cardiovascular development in humans.

G. A. Clark, Ph.D., California, Irvine. Neurobiology, basis of behavior, cell neurophysiology and learning mechanisms, computational neuroscience.

Brittany Coats, Ph.D., Pennsylvania. Head and eye injury biomechanics.

* E. V. R. DiBella, Ph.D., Georgia Tech. Medical imaging, dynamic cardiac SPECT.

* Deborah Dixon, Ph.D., Rutgers. Cell culture, medical devices.

A. D. Dorval, Ph.D., Boston University. Neural engineering and interfaces.

* Derek Dosdall, Ph.D., Arizona State. Cardiac mapping and electrophysiology.

* R. O. Dull, Ph.D., Penn State; M.D., Illinois at Chicago. Microvascular endothelial cells, tissue/cell engineering.

* K. Dusek, Ph.D., Czechoslovak Academy of Sciences. Formation-structure-properties relations of polymers.

Peter Fitzgerald, Ph.D., Tissue remodeling.

* A. L. Fogelson, Ph.D., NYU. Physiological systems modeling.

* Darin Furgeson, Ph.D., Utah. Pharmaeutical chemistry.

* B. K. Gale, Ph.D., Utah. MEMS devices and their applications to biology and medicine.

* Guido Gerig, Ph.D., ETH Zurich (Switzerland). Medical imaging analysis.

* J. M. Gerton, Ph.D., Rice. Bioimaging techniques, biophysics.

H. Ghandehari, Ph.D., Utah. Pharmaceutics, drug/gene delivery.

D. W. Grainger, Ph.D., Utah. Biomaterials, drug delivery, biotechnology, fluorinated surface chemistry.

B. E. Greger, Ph.D., Washington (St. Louis). Neuroprosthetic technology, neural systems, sensory-motor processing/plasticity.

* J. M. Harris, Ph.D., Purdue. Laser-based bioinstrumentation, interfacial spectroscopy.

* T. G. Henderson, Ph.D., Texas at Austin. Artificial intelligence, computer vision, robotics.

J. N. Herron, Ph.D., Illinois. Protein engineering, molecular graphics, biosensors.

* R. W. Hitchcock, Ph.D., Utah. Medical product development.

V. Hlady, Ph.D., Zagreb. Biochemistry/biophysics at interfaces, solid-liquid interface of biomaterials, proteins as engineering.

K. W. Horch, D.Sc., Yale. Neuroprostheses, biomedical instrumentation, information processing in the somatosensory system, tactile aids.

* Harriet Hopf, Ph.D., Dartmouth Medical School, Genetics of health-care associated infection.

Eric Hunter, Ph.D., Vibration, exposure, and acoustics.

E. W. Hsu, Ph.D., Johns Hopkins. Magnetic resonance imaging and applications to bioengineering.

* D. T. Hutchinson, M.D., Jefferson Medical. Orthopedics implants for the hand.

S. C. Jacobsen, Ph.D., MIT. Prosthesis design, microelectromechanical systems, control theory, robotics.

C. R. Johnson, Ph.D., Utah. Theoretical/computational electrophysiology, inverse electrocardiography, dynamical systems theory.

Kenward Johnson, M.D., Tulane. Anesthesiology.

* E. M. Jorgensen, Ph.D., Washington (Seattle). Molecular biology, genetics, cellular neurophysiology.

S. C. Joshi, D.Sc., Washington (St. Louis). Computational anatomy, statistical shape analysis in medical imaging.

* D. J. Kadrmas, Ph.D., North Carolina. Molecular imaging, positron emission tomography (PET) of cancerous tissues.

* J. P. Keener, Ph.D., Caltech. Applied mathematics, nonlinear differential equations, chemical/biological dynamics.

S. E. Kern, Ph.D., Utah. Pharmacokinetics and pharmacodynamics modeling and control.

P. S. Khanwilkar, Ph.D., Utah. Artificial heart/assist devices, design, control, surgical implantation/physiologic interfaces.

* Hanseup Kim, Ph.D., Michigan. Bio nano- and micro-systems in moving fluids.

S. W. Kim, Ph.D., Utah. Blood compatibility, drug-delivery systems.

Richard Daniel King, Ph.D., Harvard. Alzheimer's image analysis.

* Mike Kirby, Ph.D., Brown. Large-scale scientific computation and visualization.

P. F. Kiser, Ph.D., Duke. Drug-delivery systems, biomimetic materials engineering, combinatorial materials engineering.

J. Kopecek, Ph.D., Czechoslovak Academy of Sciences. Biomaterials, chemistry/biochemistry of macromolecules, drug-delivery systems.

* Erik Kubiak, M.D., Washington (Seattle). Scientific computing and visualization, modeling, stimulation of ECG drug diffusion.

* Gianluca Lazzi, Ph.D., Utah. Computation, electromagnetics.

* Stephen Lessnick, M.D., Ph.D., UCLA. Pediatric hematology.

R. S. MacLeod, Ph.D., Dalhousie. Cardiac bioelectric modeling, body surface potential mapping, cardiac electrophysiology, scientific visualization.

* B. A. MacWilliams, Ph.D., Worcester Polytechnic. Vascular fluid dynamics, kinematic/kinetic biomechanics.

B. Mann, Ph.D., Iowa State. Tissue engineering.

* Carlos Mastrangelo, Ph.D., Berekley. Microfabricated systems, BioMEMS.

* E. M. Maynard, Ph.D., Utah. Application of microelectrode arrays restoring vision.

* James P. (Pat) McAllister, Ph.D., Purdue. Pathophysiology of hydrocephalus and brain injury, neural prosthesis, biocompatibility.

* J. C. McRea, Ph.D., Utah. Medical device development.

* S. G. Meek, Ph.D., Utah. Prosthetic design and control, EMG signal processing, biomechanics.

* Ken Monson, Ph.D., Berkeley. Traumatic brain injury, biomechanics.

Alonso P. Moreno, Ph.D., IPN (Mexico). Molecular and biophysical properties of gap junctions.

* C. J. Myers, Ph.D., Stanford. Modeling/analysis of biological networks.

* J. R. Nelson, Ph.D., Utah. Microbiology, immunology.

* F. Noo, Ph.D., Liege (Belgium). 3-D tomographic reconstruction.

R. A. Normann, Ph.D., Berkeley. Cell physiology, bioinstrumentation, neuroprosthetics.

D. B. Olsen, D.V.M., Colorado State. Artificial heart/assist devices, design, control, surgical implantation/physiologic interfaces.

* Agnes E. Ostafin, Ph.D., Minnesota, Twin Cities. Nanobiotechnology.

* D. L. Parker, Ph.D., Utah. Medical imaging, applications of physics in medicine.

* T. J. Petelenz, Ph.D., Utah. Medical instrumentation.

* W. G. Pitt, Ph.D., Wisconsin–Madison. Polymers and composite materials for biomedical applications, surface chemistry.

S. Poelzing, Ph.D., Case Western Reserve. Cardioelectrophysiology.

* Mark Porter, Ph.D., Ohio State. Discovery and rapid screening of therapeutic compounds.

* G. D. Prestwich, Ph.D., Stanford. Bioorganic chemistry.

* A. Pungor, Ph.D., Technical University (Hungary). Scanning-force microscopy, near-field optical microscopy, bioinstrumentation.

* B. B. Punske, Ph.D., North Carolina. Cardiovascular biomechanics.

R. D. Rabbitt, Ph.D., Rensselaer. Biomechanics, hearing/vestibular mechanisms, computational mechanics, computational neuroscience.

N. Rapoport, Ph.D., Moscow State; D.Sc., Academy of Sciences (USSR). Polymeric materials, biological magnetic resonance.

* R. B. Roemer, Ph.D., Stanford. Heat transfer, thermodynamics, design, optimization to biomedical problems.

F. B. Sachse, Dr.-Ing., Karlsruhe (Germany). Computational cardiac electrophysiology, cardiac electromechanics.

* Charles Saltzman, M.D., North Carolina at Chapel Hill. Orthopaedics.

* C. Shelton, M.D., Texas Southwestern Medical Center at Dallas. Hearing systems physiology.

Y.-T. Shiu, Ph.D., Rice. Cellular/tissue engineering of the cardiovascular system, biofluid dynamics, blood-material interactions.

* M. E. Smith, M.D., Illinois. Otolaryngology, neural interfaces.

* F. Solzbacher, Ph.D., Technical University (Germany). MEMS, micromachining.

* K. W. Spitzer, Ph.D., Buffalo, SUNY. Cardiac cellular electrophysiology, intracellular pH regulation.

R. J. Stewart, Ph.D., California, Santa Barbara. Protein engineering, energy transduction, protein structure-activities, molecular motors.

* Masood Tabib-Azar, Ph.D., Rensselaer. Advanced metrology and nano-device applications.

P. A. Tresco, Ph.D., Brown. Molecular delivery systems, synthetic membrane fabrication, neurodegenerative/neuroendocrine/endocrine disorders.

* P. Triolo, Ph.D., Utah. Development/regulatory approval of biomaterials/diagnostic devices, tissue-engineered products.

J. A. Weiss, Ph.D., Utah. Biomechanics, mechanics of normal/healing soft tissues, evaluation of injury mechanics/treatment regimens.

D. R. Westenskow, Ph.D., Utah. Bioinstrumentation, microprocessor applications in medicine.

* Ross Whitaker, Ph.D., North Carolina at Chapel Hill. Image processing, computer vision, visualization.

J. White, Ph.D., Johns Hopkins. Neural engineering and interfaces.

* J. W. Wiskin, Ph.D., Utah. Mathematical modeling/numerical techniques, inverse scattering.

* Carl Thomas Wittwer, Ph.D., Michigan. Real-time PCR and DNA analysis.

* M. Yoshigi, M.D., Kyoto (Japan); Ph.D., Tokyo Women's Medical College. Cardiovascular physiology and embryology.

* Darrin Young, Ph.D., Berkeley. Wireless micro- nano- systems.

A. V. Zaitsev, Ph.D., Moscow State (Russia). Cardioelectrophysiology.

* G. L. Zeng, Ph.D., New Mexico. Biomedical imaging.

---

* Adjunct faculty

Section 4
Architectural Engineering

This section contains a directory of institutions offering graduate work in architectural engineering. Additional information about programs listed in the directory may be obtained by writing directly to the dean of a graduate school or chair of a department at the address given in the directory.

For programs offering related work, see also in this book *Engineering and Applied Sciences* and *Management of Engineering and Technology.* In the other guides in this series:

Graduate Programs in the Humanities, Arts & Social Sciences
See *Applied Arts and Design (Industrial Design and Interior Design), Architecture (Environmental Design), Political Science and International Affairs,* and *Public, Regional, and Industrial Affairs (Urban and Regional Planning and Urban Studies)*

Graduate Programs in the Physical Sciences, Mathematics, Agricultural Sciences, the Environment & Natural Resources
See *Environmental Sciences* and *Management*

CONTENTS

Program Directory

Architectural Engineering

Carnegie Mellon University, College of Fine Arts, School of Architecture, Pittsburgh, PA 15213-3891. Offers architectural engineering construction management (M Sc); architecture (MSA); architecture, engineering, and construction management (PhD); building performance and diagnostics (M Sc, PhD); computational design (M Sc, PhD); sustainable design (M Sc); urban design (M Sc). Terminal master's awarded for partial completion of doctoral program. *Degree requirements:* For doctorate, thesis/dissertation. *Entrance requirements:* For master's and doctorate, GRE General Test. Additional exam requirements/recommendations for international students: Required—TOEFL.

Drexel University, College of Engineering, Department of Civil, Architectural, and Environmental Engineering, Philadelphia, PA 19104-2875. Offers architectural / building systems engineering (MS, PhD); civil engineering (MS, PhD); environmental engineering (MS, PhD); geotechnical, geoenvironmental and geosynthetics engineering (MS, PhD); hydraulics, hydrology and water resources engineering (MS, PhD); structures (MS). Part-time and evening/weekend programs available. *Degree requirements:* For master's, thesis optional; for doctorate, thesis/dissertation. *Entrance requirements:* For master's, minimum GPA of 3.0; for doctorate, minimum GPA of 3.5, MS in civil engineering. Additional exam requirements/recommendations for international students: Required—TOEFL. Electronic applications accepted. *Faculty research:* Structural dynamics, hazardous wastes, water resources, pavement materials, groundwater.

Illinois Institute of Technology, Graduate College, Armour College of Engineering, Department of Civil, Architectural and Environmental Engineering, Chicago, IL 60616-3793. Offers architectural engineering (M Arch E); civil engineering (MS, PhD), including architectural engineeering (MS), construction engineering and management (MS), geoenvironmental engineering (MS), geotechnical engineering (MS), structural engineering (MS), transportation engineering (MS); construction engineering and management (MCEM); environmental engineering (M Env E, PhD); geoenvironmental engineering (M Geoenv E); geotechnical engineering (MGE); public works (MPW); structural engineering (MSE); transportation engineering (M Trans E). Part-time and evening/weekend programs available. Postbaccalaureate distance learning degree programs offered (minimal on-campus study). *Faculty:* 15 full-time (1 woman), 13 part-time/adjunct (1 woman). *Students:* 159 full-time (63 women), 109 part-time (22 women); includes 30 minority (9 Black or African American, non-Hispanic/Latino; 16 Asian, non-Hispanic/Latino; 5 Hispanic/Latino), 126 international. Average age 27. 453 applicants, 66% accepted, 98 enrolled. In 2010, 76 master's, 1 doctorate awarded. Terminal master's awarded for partial completion of doctoral program. *Degree requirements:* For master's, thesis (for some programs); for doctorate, comprehensive exam, thesis/dissertation. *Entrance requirements:* For master's, GRE General Test (minimum score 900 Quantitative and Verbal, 2.5 Analytical Writing), minimum undergraduate GPA of 3.0; for doctorate, GRE General Test (minimum score 1000 Quantitative and Verbal, 3.0 Analytical Writing), minimum undergraduate GPA of 3.0. Additional exam requirements/recommendations for international students: Required—TOEFL (minimum score 523 paper-based; 70 iBT); Recommended—IELTS (minimum score 5.5). *Application deadline:* For fall admission, 5/1 for domestic and international students; for spring admission, 10/15 for domestic and international students. Applications are processed on a rolling basis. Application fee: $50. Electronic applications accepted. *Expenses:* Tuition: Full-time $18,576; part-time $1032 per credit hour. Required fees: $583 per semester. One-time fee: $150. Tuition and fees vary according to program and student level. *Financial support:* In 2010–11, 13 research assistantships with full and partial tuition reimbursements (averaging $9,453 per year), 19 teaching assistantships with full and partial tuition reimbursements (averaging $3,163 per year) were awarded; fellowships with full and partial tuition reimbursements, Federal Work-Study, institutionally sponsored loans, scholarships/grants, health care benefits, tuition waivers (partial), and unspecified assistantships also available. Support available to part-time students. Financial award applicants required to submit FAFSA. *Faculty research:* Structural, architectural, geotechnical and geoenvironmental engineering; construction engineering and management; transportation engineering; environmental engineering and public works. Total annual research expenditures: $763,042. *Unit head:* Dr. Jamshid Mohammadi, Professor and Chairman, 312-567-3629, Fax: 312-567-3519, E-mail: mohammadi@iit.edu. *Application contact:* Deborah Gibson, Director, Graduate Admission, 866-472-3448, Fax: 312-567-3138, E-mail: inquiry.grad@iit.edu.

Kansas State University, Graduate School, College of Engineering, Department of Architectural Engineering and Construction Science, Manhattan, KS 66506. Offers architectural engineering (MS). *Degree requirements:* For master's, thesis or alternative. *Entrance requirements:* For master's, GRE, minimum GPA of 3.25. Additional exam requirements/recommendations for international students: Required—TOEFL. Electronic applications accepted. *Faculty research:* Construction sciences, sustainable engineering, building electrical and lighting systems, building HVAC and plumbing systems, structural systems design and analysis.

Lawrence Technological University, College of Engineering, Southfield, MI 48075-1058. Offers architectural engineering (MS); automotive engineering (MS); civil engineering (MS); electrical and computer engineering (MS); engineering management (MEM); industrial engineering (MS); manufacturing systems (ME, DE); mechanical engineering (MS); mechatronic systems engineering (MS). Part-time and evening/weekend programs available. *Faculty:* 20 full-time (4 women), 12 part-time/adjunct (0 women). *Students:* 8 full-time (1 woman), 366 part-time (60 women); includes 29 Black or African American, non-Hispanic/Latino; 1 American Indian or Alaska Native, non-Hispanic/Latino; 36 Asian, non-Hispanic/Latino; 9 Hispanic/Latino; 4 Two or more races, non-Hispanic/Latino, 81 international. Average age 32. 398 applicants, 48% accepted, 87 enrolled. In 2010, 121 master's, 5 doctorates awarded. *Degree requirements:* For master's, thesis (for some programs). *Entrance requirements:* Additional exam requirements/recommendations for international students: Required—TOEFL (minimum score 550 paper-based; 213 computer-based; 79 iBT). *Application deadline:* For fall admission, 6/30 priority date for domestic students, 6/30 for international students; for spring admission, 11/15 priority date for domestic students, 11/15 for international students. Applications are processed on a rolling basis. Application fee: $50. Electronic applications accepted. *Financial support:* In 2010–11, 72 students received support. Federal Work-Study and institutionally sponsored loans available. Support available to part-time students. Financial award application deadline: 4/1; financial award applicants required to submit FAFSA. *Faculty research:* Advanced composite materials in bridges, strengthening existing bridges with carbon and glass fiber sheets, development of drive shafts using composite materials. *Unit head:* Dr. Nabil Grace, Interim Dean, 248-204-2500, Fax: 248-204-2509, E-mail: engrdean@ltu.edu. *Application contact:* Jane Rohrback, Director of Admissions, 248-204-3160, Fax: 248-204-2228, E-mail: admissions@ltu.edu.

Penn State University Park, Graduate School, College of Engineering, Department of Architectural Engineering, State College, University Park, PA 16802-1503. Offers M Eng, MAE, MS, PhD.

University of Colorado Boulder, Graduate School, College of Engineering and Applied Science, Department of Civil, Environmental, and Architectural Engineering, Boulder, CO 80309. Offers building systems (MS, PhD); construction engineering management (MS, PhD); environmental engineering (MS, PhD); geotechnical engineering and geomechanics (MS, PhD); hydrology, water resources and environmental fluid mechanics (MS, PhD); structural engineering and structural mechanics (MS, PhD). *Faculty:* 38 full-time (6 women). *Students:* 255 full-time (86 women), 40 part-time (11 women); includes 40 minority (1 Black or African American, non-Hispanic/Latino; 2 American Indian or Alaska Native, non-Hispanic/Latino; 15 Asian, non-Hispanic/Latino; 20 Hispanic/Latino; 2 Two or more races, non-Hispanic/Latino), 61 international. Average age 28. 420 applicants, 95 enrolled. In 2010, 56 master's, 18 doctorates awarded. *Degree requirements:* For master's, comprehensive exam, thesis or alternative; for doctorate, thesis/dissertation. *Entrance requirements:* For master's, GRE General Test, minimum undergraduate GPA of 3.0. *Application deadline:* For fall admission, 3/1 for domestic students, 12/1 for international students; for spring admission, 10/31 for domestic students, 10/1 for international students. Application fee: $50 ($60 for international students). *Financial support:* In 2010–11, 45 fellowships (averaging $7,876 per year), 68 research assistantships (averaging $15,204 per year) were awarded. Financial award application deadline: 1/15. *Faculty research:* Building systems engineering, construction engineering and management, environmental engineering, geoenvironmental engineering, geotechnical engineering, materials and mechanics, structural engineering, water resources engineering, life-cycle engineering. Total annual research expenditures: $8 million.

University of Detroit Mercy, School of Architecture, Detroit, MI 48221. Offers M Arch. *Entrance requirements:* For master's, BS in architecture, minimum GPA of 3.0, portfolio.

The University of Kansas, Graduate Studies, School of Engineering, Department of Civil, Environmental, and Architectural Engineering, Program in Architectural Engineering, Lawrence, KS 66045. Offers MS. Part-time programs available. *Faculty:* 11 full-time (2 women). *Students:* 5 full-time (2 women), 5 part-time (2 women); includes 1 minority (Black or African American, non-Hispanic/Latino), 2 international. Average age 28. 15 applicants, 87% accepted, 5 enrolled. In 2010, 2 master's awarded. *Degree requirements:* For master's, thesis or alternative, exam. *Entrance requirements:* For master's, GRE, BS in engineering. Additional exam requirements/recommendations for international students: Required—TOEFL. *Application deadline:* For fall admission, 7/1 priority date for domestic students, 3/1 priority date for international students; for spring admission, 12/1 priority date for domestic students, 8/15 priority date for international students. Applications are processed on a rolling basis. Application fee: $55 ($65 for international students). Electronic applications accepted. *Expenses:* Tuition, state resident: full-time $7092; part-time $295.50 per credit hour. Tuition, nonresident: full-time $16,590; part-time $691.25 per credit hour. Required fees: $858; $71.49 per credit hour. Tuition and fees vary according to course load, campus/location and program. *Financial support:* Fellowships with full tuition reimbursements, research assistantships with full tuition reimbursements, teaching assistantships with full tuition reimbursements, career-related internships or fieldwork available. Financial award application deadline: 2/7. *Faculty research:* Structural engineering, construction engineering, building mechanical systems, energy management. *Unit head:* Craig D. Adams, Chair, 785-864-2700, Fax: 785-864-5631, E-mail: adamscd@ku.edu. *Application contact:* Bruce M. McEnroe, Graduate Advisor, 785-864-2925, Fax: 785-864-2925, E-mail: mcenroe@ku.edu.

University of Louisiana at Lafayette, College of the Arts, School of Architecture, Lafayette, LA 70504. Offers M Arch. *Degree requirements:* For master's, thesis. *Entrance requirements:* For master's, GRE General Test. Additional exam requirements/recommendations for international students: Required—TOEFL (minimum score 550 paper-based; 213 computer-based). Electronic applications accepted.

University of Massachusetts Amherst, Graduate School, College of Natural Sciences, Department of Environmental Conservation, Amherst, MA 01003. Offers building systems (MS, PhD); environmental policy and human dimensions (MS, PhD); forest resources (MS, PhD); water, wetlands and watersheds (MS, PhD); wildlife and fisheries conservation (MS, PhD). Part-time programs available. *Faculty:* 51 full-time (7 women). *Students:* 55 full-time (30 women), 35 part-time (16 women); includes 5 minority (2 Black or African American, non-Hispanic/Latino; 3 Hispanic/Latino), 10 international. Average age 32. 73 applicants, 41% accepted, 23 enrolled. In 2010, 8 master's, 4 doctorates awarded. Terminal master's awarded for partial completion of doctoral program. *Degree requirements:* For master's, thesis or alternative; for doctorate, comprehensive exam, thesis/dissertation. *Entrance requirements:* For master's and doctorate, GRE General Test. Additional exam requirements/recommendations for international students: Required—TOEFL (minimum score 550 paper-based; 213 computer-based; 80 iBT), IELTS (minimum score 6.5). *Application deadline:* For fall admission, 2/1 for domestic and international students; for spring admission, 10/1 for domestic and international students. Applications are processed on a rolling basis. Application fee: $50 ($65 for international students). Electronic applications accepted. *Expenses:* Tuition, state resident: full-time $2640. Required fees: $8282. One-time fee: $357 full-time. *Financial support:* In 2010–11, 6 fellowships with full tuition reimbursements (averaging $14,507 per year), 62 research assistantships with full tuition reimbursements (averaging $9,977 per year), 33 teaching assistantships with full tuition reimbursements (averaging $6,243 per year) were awarded; career-related internships or fieldwork, Federal Work-Study, scholarships/grants, traineeships, health care benefits, tuition waivers (full), and unspecified assistantships also available. Support available to part-time students. Financial award application deadline: 2/1; financial award applicants required to submit FAFSA. *Unit head:* Dr. Matt Kelty, Graduate Program Director, 413-545-2666, Fax: 413-545-4358. *Application contact:* Jean M. Ames, Supervisor of Admissions, 413-545-0721, Fax: 413-577-0100, E-mail: gradadm@grad.umass.edu.

University of Miami, Graduate School, College of Engineering, Department of Civil, Architectural, and Environmental Engineering, Coral Gables, FL 33124. Offers architectural engineering (MSAE); civil engineering (MSCE, PhD). Part-time programs available. Terminal master's awarded for partial completion of doctoral program. *Degree requirements:* For master's, thesis (for some programs); for doctorate, comprehensive exam, thesis/dissertation. *Entrance requirements:* For master's, GRE General Test (minimum score 1000 verbal and quantitative), minimum GPA of 3.0; for doctorate, GRE General Test, minimum GPA of 3.5 in preceding degree. Additional exam requirements/recommendations for international students: Required—TOEFL (minimum score 550 paper-based; 213 computer-based). Electronic applications accepted. *Faculty research:* Structural assessment and wind engineering, sustainable construction and materials, moisture transport and management, wastewater and waste engineering, water management and risk analysis.

University of Nebraska–Lincoln, Graduate College, College of Engineering, Program in Architectural Engineering, Lincoln, NE 68588. Offers M Eng, MAE, MS, PhD. *Accreditation:* ABET. *Entrance requirements:* Additional exam requirements/recommendations for international students: Required—TOEFL (minimum score 550 paper-based; 213 computer-based), GRE.

The University of Texas at Austin, Graduate School, Cockrell School of Engineering, Department of Civil, Architectural and Environmental Engineering, Program in Architectural Engineering, Austin, TX 78712-1111. Offers MSE. Part-time programs available. *Degree requirements:* For master's, thesis. *Entrance requirements:* For master's, GRE General Test. Additional exam requirements/recommendations for international students: Required—TOEFL. Electronic applications accepted. *Faculty research:* Materials engineering, structural engineering, construction engineering, project management.

Section 5
Biomedical Engineering and Biotechnology

This section contains a directory of institutions offering graduate work in biomedical engineering and biotechnology, followed by in-depth entries submitted by institutions that chose to prepare detailed program descriptions. Additional information about programs listed in the directory but not augmented by an in-depth entry may be obtained by writing directly to the dean of a graduate school or chair of a department at the address given in the directory.

For programs offering related work, see also in this book *Aerospace/Aeronautical Engineering, Engineering and Applied Sciences, Engineering Design, Engineering Physics, Management of Engineering and Technology,* and *Mechanical Engineering and Mechanics.* In the other guides in this series:

Graduate Programs in the Biological Sciences
See *Biological and Biomedical Sciences and Physiology*
Graduate Programs in the Physical Sciences, Mathematics, Agricultural Sciences, the Environment & Natural Resources
See *Mathematical Sciences (Biometrics and Biostatistics)*
Graduate Programs in Business, Education, Health, Information Studies, Law & Social Work
See *Allied Health*

CONTENTS

Program Directories

Close-Ups and Displays

Biomedical Engineering

Arizona State University, Ira A. Fulton School of Engineering, School of Biological and Health Systems Engineering, Tempe, AZ 85287-9709. Offers biomedical engineering (MS, PhD). Part-time and evening/weekend programs available. *Faculty:* 21 full-time (2 women), 1 part-time/adjunct (0 women). *Students:* 71 full-time (25 women), 15 part-time (4 women); includes 18 minority (2 Black or African American, non-Hispanic/Latino; 10 Asian, non-Hispanic/Latino; 5 Hispanic/Latino; 1 Two or more races, non-Hispanic/Latino), 19 international. Average age 27. 188 applicants, 41% accepted, 40 enrolled. In 2010, 16 master's, 19 doctorates awarded. Terminal master's awarded for partial completion of doctoral program. *Degree requirements:* For master's, thesis and oral defense or applied project; interactive Program of Study (iPOS) submitted before completing 50 percent of required credit hours; for doctorate, comprehensive exam, thesis/dissertation, interactive Program of Study (iPOS) submitted before completing 50 percent of required credit hours. *Entrance requirements:* For master's and doctorate, GRE General Test, minimum GPA of 3.0 or equivalent in last 2 years of work leading to bachelor's degree, 3 letters of recommendation, one-page personal statement. Additional exam requirements/recommendations for international students: Required—TOEFL (minimum score 580 paper-based; 92 iBT). *Application deadline:* For fall admission, 12/31 priority date for domestic and international students; for spring admission, 8/31 priority date for domestic and international students. Applications are processed on a rolling basis. Application fee: $70 ($90 for international students). Electronic applications accepted. *Expenses:* Contact institution. *Financial support:* In 2010–11, 30 research assistantships with partial tuition reimbursements (averaging $18,265 per year), 3 teaching assistantships with partial tuition reimbursements (averaging $14,500 per year) were awarded; fellowships with full and partial tuition reimbursements, institutionally sponsored loans, scholarships/grants, and tuition waivers (full and partial) also available. Financial award application deadline: 3/1; financial award applicants required to submit FAFSA. *Faculty research:* Cardiovascular engineering; synthetic/computational biology; medical devices and diagnostics; neuroengineering; rehabilitation; regenerative medicine; imaging; molecular, cellular and tissue engineering; and virtual reality healthcare delivery systems. Total annual research expenditures: $5.9 million. *Unit head:* Dr. William Ditto, Director, 480-965-3676, E-mail: william.ditto@asu.edu. *Application contact:* Graduate Admissions, 480-965-6113.

Baylor College of Medicine, Graduate School of Biomedical Sciences, Program in Translational Biology and Molecular Medicine, Houston, TX 77030-3498. Offers PhD. *Faculty:* 173 full-time (54 women). *Students:* 58 full-time (28 women); includes 6 Black or African American, non-Hispanic/Latino; 6 Hispanic/Latino, 16 international. Average age 27. 88 applicants, 32% accepted, 13 enrolled. In 2010, 1 doctorate awarded. *Degree requirements:* For doctorate, thesis/dissertation, public defense. *Entrance requirements:* For doctorate, GRE, minimum GPA of 3.0. Additional exam requirements/recommendations for international students: Required—TOEFL. *Application deadline:* For fall admission, 1/1 for domestic students. Application fee: $0. Electronic applications accepted. *Expenses:* Tuition: Full-time $11,000. Required fees: $4900. *Financial support:* In 2010–11, 58 students received support, including 24 fellowships with full tuition reimbursements available (averaging $26,000 per year), 34 research assistantships with full tuition reimbursements available (averaging $26,000 per year); career-related internships or fieldwork, Federal Work-Study, health care benefits, and students receive a scholarship unless there are grant funds available to pay tuition also available. Financial award applicants required to submit FAFSA. *Faculty research:* Molecular medicine, translational biology, human disease biology and therapy. *Unit head:* Dr. Mary Estes, Director, 713-798-3585, Fax: 713-798-3586, E-mail: tbmm@bcm.edu. *Application contact:* Wanda Waguespack, Graduate Program Administrator, 713-798-1077, Fax: 713-798-3586, E-mail: wandaw@bcm.edu.

Baylor University, Graduate School, School of Engineering and Computer Science, Department of Engineering, Waco, TX 76798. Offers biomedical engineering (MSBE); electrical and computer engineering (MSECE, PhD); engineering (ME); mechanical engineering (MSME). *Faculty:* 14 full-time (1 woman). *Students:* 30 full-time (4 women), 6 part-time (0 women); includes 9 minority (3 Black or African American, non-Hispanic/Latino; 2 Asian, non-Hispanic/Latino; 1 Hispanic/Latino; 3 Two or more races, non-Hispanic/Latino), 7 international. In 2010, 7 master's awarded. *Unit head:* Dr. Mike Thompson, Graduate Director, 254-710-4188. *Application contact:* Linda Keer, Administrative Assistant, 254-710-4188, Fax: 254-710-3870, E-mail: linda_kerr@baylor.edu.

Boston University, College of Engineering, Department of Biomedical Engineering, Boston, MA 02215. Offers M Eng, MS, PhD, MD/PhD. Part-time programs available. *Faculty:* 34 full-time (4 women), 3 part-time/adjunct (1 woman). *Students:* 156 full-time (44 women), 7 part-time (1 woman); includes 29 minority (2 Black or African American, non-Hispanic/Latino; 18 Asian, non-Hispanic/Latino; 8 Hispanic/Latino; 1 Two or more races, non-Hispanic/Latino), 34 international. Average age 25. 550 applicants, 24% accepted, 50 enrolled. In 2010, 27 master's, 16 doctorates awarded. Terminal master's awarded for partial completion of doctoral program. *Degree requirements:* For master's, thesis (for some programs); for doctorate, comprehensive exam, thesis/dissertation. *Entrance requirements:* For master's and doctorate, GRE General Test. Additional exam requirements/recommendations for international students: Required—TOEFL (minimum score 550 paper-based; 213 computer-based; 84 iBT), IELTS (minimum score 6). *Application deadline:* For fall admission, 4/1 for domestic and international students; for spring admission, 10/1 for domestic and international students. Applications are processed on a rolling basis. Application fee: $70. Electronic applications accepted. *Expenses:* Tuition: Full-time $39,314; part-time $1228 per credit. Required fees: $40 per semester. *Financial support:* In 2010–11, 158 students received support, including 40 fellowships with full tuition reimbursements available (averaging $28,200 per year), 86 research assistantships with full tuition reimbursements available (averaging $18,800 per year), 18 teaching assistantships with full tuition reimbursements available (averaging $18,800 per year); career-related internships or fieldwork, Federal Work-Study, institutionally sponsored loans, scholarships/grants, traineeships, and health care benefits also available. Financial award application deadline: 1/15; financial award applicants required to submit FAFSA. *Faculty research:* Biomaterials, tissue engineering and drug delivery; modeling of biological systems; molecular bioengineering and biophysics; neuroscience and neural disease; synthetic biology and systems biology. Total annual research expenditures: $18.7 million. *Unit head:* Dr. Solomon Eisenberg, Chairman, 617-353-2805, Fax: 617-353-6766, E-mail: sre@bu.edu. *Application contact:* Stephen Doherty, Director of Graduate Programs, 617-353-9760, Fax: 617-353-0259, E-mail: enggrad@bu.edu.

Brown University, Graduate School, Division of Biology and Medicine, Program in Artificial Organs, Biomaterials, and Cell Technology, Providence, RI 02912. Offers MA, Sc M, PhD. Terminal master's awarded for partial completion of doctoral program. *Degree requirements:* For doctorate, thesis/dissertation, preliminary exam. *Entrance requirements:* For master's and doctorate, GRE General Test, GRE Subject Test. Additional exam requirements/recommendations for international students: Required—TOEFL. Electronic applications accepted.

Brown University, Graduate School, Division of Biology and Medicine and Division of Engineering, Program in Biomedical Engineering, Providence, RI 02912. Offers MS, PhD. *Entrance requirements:* For master's and doctorate, GRE General Test, interview. Additional exam requirements/recommendations for international students: Required—TOEFL.

Brown University, Graduate School, Division of Engineering and Division of Biology and Medicine, Center for Biomedical Engineering, Providence, RI 02912. Offers Sc M, PhD. *Degree requirements:* For master's, thesis.

Carleton University, Faculty of Graduate Studies, Faculty of Engineering and Design, Ottawa-Carleton Institute for Biomedical Engineering, Ottawa, ON K1S 5B6, Canada. Offers MA Sc. *Degree requirements:* For master's, thesis optional. *Entrance requirements:* For master's, honours degree. Additional exam requirements/recommendations for international students: Required—TOEFL.

Carnegie Mellon University, Carnegie Institute of Technology, Biomedical and Health Engineering Program, Pittsburgh, PA 15213-3891. Offers bioengineering (MS, PhD); MD/PhD. *Degree requirements:* For master's, thesis; for doctorate, thesis/dissertation, qualifying exam. *Entrance requirements:* For master's and doctorate, GRE General Test. Additional exam requirements/recommendations for international students: Required—TOEFL. Electronic applications accepted. *Faculty research:* Cellular and molecular systematics, signal and image processing, materials and mechanics.

Carnegie Mellon University, Carnegie Institute of Technology, Department of Electrical and Computer Engineering, Concentration in Biomedical Engineering, Pittsburgh, PA 15213-3891. Offers MS. Part-time programs available. *Degree requirements:* For master's, thesis. *Entrance requirements:* For master's, GRE General Test. Additional exam requirements/recommendations for international students: Required—TOEFL.

Case Western Reserve University, School of Graduate Studies, Case School of Engineering, Department of Biomedical Engineering, Cleveland, OH 44106. Offers MS, PhD, MD/MS, MD/PhD. *Faculty:* 20 full-time (3 women). *Students:* 116 full-time (33 women), 22 part-time (9 women); includes 4 Black or African American, non-Hispanic/Latino; 27 Asian, non-Hispanic/Latino; 6 Hispanic/Latino, 41 international. In 2010, 14 master's, 19 doctorates awarded. Terminal master's awarded for partial completion of doctoral program. *Degree requirements:* For master's, thesis (for some programs); for doctorate, thesis/dissertation, qualifying exam, teaching experience. *Entrance requirements:* For master's and doctorate, GRE General Test. Additional exam requirements/recommendations for international students: Required—TOEFL. *Application deadline:* For fall admission, 4/1 priority date for domestic students; for spring admission, 10/1 priority date for domestic students. Applications are processed on a rolling basis. Application fee: $50. *Financial support:* Fellowships with full tuition reimbursements, research assistantships with full and partial tuition reimbursements, traineeships available. Financial award application deadline: 2/15; financial award applicants required to submit FAFSA. *Faculty research:* Neuroengineering, biomaterials/tissue engineering, biomedical imaging, biomedical sensors/systems. Total annual research expenditures: $12.4 million. *Unit head:* Dr. Jeffrey Duerk, Department Chair, 216-368-6047, Fax: 216-368-4969, E-mail: duerk@case.edu. *Application contact:* Carol Adrine, Academic Operations Coordinator, 216-368-4094, Fax: 216-368-4969, E-mail: caa7@case.edu.

See Display on next page and Close-Up on page 147.

The Catholic University of America, School of Engineering, Department of Biomedical Engineering, Washington, DC 20064. Offers MBE, PhD. Part-time programs available. *Faculty:* 5 full-time (1 woman), 3 part-time/adjunct (0 women). *Students:* 6 full-time (2 women), 13 part-time (5 women); includes 4 Black or African American, non-Hispanic/Latino; 2 Hispanic/Latino, 5 international. Average age 31. 24 applicants, 71% accepted, 3 enrolled. In 2010, 7 master's, 1 doctorate awarded. *Degree requirements:* For master's, thesis or alternative; for doctorate, comprehensive exam, thesis/dissertation, oral exams. *Entrance requirements:* For master's, GRE (minimum score: 1250), minimum GPA of 3.0, statement of purpose, official copies of academic transcripts, three letters of recommendation; for doctorate, GRE (minimum score: 1300), minimum GPA of 3.4, statement of purpose, official copies of academic transcripts, three letters of recommendation. Additional exam requirements/recommendations for international students: Required—TOEFL (minimum score 580 paper-based; 237 computer-based). *Application deadline:* For fall admission, 8/1 priority date for domestic students, 7/15 for international students; for spring admission, 12/1 priority date for domestic students, 10/15 for international students. Applications are processed on a rolling basis. Application fee: $55. Electronic applications accepted. *Expenses:* Contact institution. *Financial support:* Fellowships, research assistantships, teaching assistantships, Federal Work-Study, scholarships/grants, tuition waivers (full and partial), and unspecified assistantships available. Financial award application deadline: 2/1; financial award applicants required to submit FAFSA. *Faculty research:* Cardiopulmonary biomechanics, robotics and human motor control, cell and tissue engineering, biomechanics, rehabilitation engineering. Total annual research expenditures: $780,403. *Unit head:* Dr. Binh Q. Tran, Chair, 202-319-5181, Fax: 202-319-4287, E-mail: tran@cua.edu. *Application contact:* Andrew Woodall, Director of Graduate Admissions, 202-319-5057, Fax: 202-319-6533, E-mail: cua-admissions@cua.edu.

City College of the City University of New York, Graduate School, Grove School of Engineering, Department of Biomedical Engineering, New York, NY 10031-9198. Offers ME, PhD. *Entrance requirements:* For master's, GRE. Additional exam requirements/recommendations for international students: Required—TOEFL (minimum score 550 paper-based; 213 computer-based).

Cleveland State University, College of Graduate Studies, Fenn College of Engineering, Department of Chemical and Biomedical Engineering, Program in Applied Biomedical Engineering, Cleveland, OH 44115. Offers D Eng. Part-time and evening/weekend programs available. *Faculty:* 11 full-time (1 woman), 24 part-time/adjunct (3 women). *Students:* 17 full-time (8 women), 6 part-time (1 woman); includes 1 Asian, non-Hispanic/Latino, 13 international. Average age 30. 15 applicants, 60% accepted, 3 enrolled. In 2010, 4 doctorates awarded. *Degree requirements:* For doctorate, thesis/dissertation. *Entrance requirements:* For doctorate, GRE, minimum undergraduate GPA of 2.75, minimum MS or MD GPA of 3.25, 1 degree in engineering. Additional exam requirements/recommendations for international students: Required—TOEFL (minimum score 525 paper-based; 197 computer-based). *Application deadline:* For fall admission, 4/15 for domestic and international students; for spring admission, 11/15 for domestic and international students. Applications are processed on a rolling basis. Application fee: $30. *Expenses:* Tuition, state resident: full-time $8447; part-time $469 per credit hour. Tuition, nonresident: full-time $16,020; part-time $890 per credit hour. Required fees: $50. *Financial support:* In 2010–11, research assistantships with full and partial tuition reimbursements (averaging $5,696 per year); career-related internships or fieldwork, scholarships/grants, and tuition waivers (full) also available. Financial award application deadline: 3/30. *Faculty research:* Biomechanics, drug delivery systems, medical imaging, tissue engineering, artificial heart valves. *Unit head:* Dr. Dhananjai B. Shah, Director, 216-687-3569, Fax: 216-687-9220, E-mail: d.shah@csuohio.edu. *Application contact:* Becky Laird, Administrative Coordinator, 216-687-2571, Fax: 216-687-9220, E-mail: b.laird@csuohio.edu.

Colorado State University, Graduate School, School of Biomedical Engineering, Fort Collins, CO 80523-1376. Offers ME, MS, PhD. Part-time and evening/weekend programs available. *Students:* 22 full-time (10 women), 12 part-time (4 women); includes 6 minority (2 Asian, non-Hispanic/Latino; 3 Hispanic/Latino; 1 Two or more races, non-Hispanic/Latino). Average age 28. 64 applicants, 55% accepted, 13 enrolled. *Degree requirements:* For master's, thesis; for doctorate, comprehensive exam, thesis/dissertation. *Entrance requirements:* For master's, GRE General Test, minimum GPA of 3.0, 3 letters of recommendation, resume; for doctorate, GRE General Test, minimum GPA of 3.0, 3 letters of recommendation, resume, official transcripts, statement of purpose. Additional exam requirements/recommendations for international students: Required—TOEFL (minimum score 550 paper-based; 213 computer-based; 95 iBT). *Application deadline:* For fall admission, 1/15 priority date for domestic and international students; for spring admission, 9/1 priority date for domestic students, 8/1 priority date for international students. Applications are processed on a rolling basis. Application fee: $50. Electronic applications accepted. *Expenses:* Tuition, state resident: full-time $7434; part-time $413 per credit. Tuition, nonresident: full-time $19,022; part-time $1057 per credit. Required fees: $1729; $88 per credit. *Financial support:* In 2010–11, 19 students received support, including 14 research assistantships with full tuition reimbursements available (averaging $12,764 per year), 5 teaching assistantships with full tuition reimbursements available (averaging $7,418 per year); fellowships, unspecified assistantships also available. Financial award application deadline:

2/15; financial award applicants required to submit FAFSA. *Faculty research:* Biomechanics and biomaterials; molecular, cellular and tissues engineering; medical diagnostics, devices and imaging. *Unit head:* Dr. Stuart Tobet, Director, 970-491-1672, Fax: 970-491-3827, E-mail: stuart.tobet@colostate.edu. *Application contact:* Sara Neys, Academic Advisor, 970-491-7157, E-mail: sara.neys@colostate.edu.

Columbia University, Fu Foundation School of Engineering and Applied Science, Department of Biomedical Engineering, New York, NY 10027. Offers MS, Eng Sc D, PhD. Part-time programs available. Postbaccalaureate distance learning degree programs offered (no on-campus study). *Faculty:* 24 full-time (5 women), 2 part-time/adjunct (0 women). *Students:* 104 full-time (41 women), 15 part-time (6 women); includes 25 minority (20 Asian, non-Hispanic/Latino; 4 Hispanic/Latino; 1 Two or more races, non-Hispanic/Latino), 41 international. Average age 28. 362 applicants, 19% accepted, 32 enrolled. In 2010, 35 master's, 19 doctorates awarded. *Degree requirements:* For doctorate, thesis/dissertation, qualifying exam. *Entrance requirements:* For master's and doctorate, GRE General Test. Additional exam requirements/recommendations for international students: Required—TOEFL, IELTS. *Application deadline:* For fall admission, 12/1 priority date for domestic and international students; for spring admission, 10/1 priority date for domestic and international students. Application fee: $95. Electronic applications accepted. *Financial support:* In 2010–11, 84 students received support, including 18 fellowships with full tuition reimbursements available (averaging $30,667 per year), 49 research assistantships with full tuition reimbursements available (averaging $30,667 per year), 17 teaching assistantships with full tuition reimbursements available (averaging $30,667 per year); traineeships and health care benefits also available. Financial award application deadline: 12/1; financial award applicants required to submit FAFSA. *Faculty research:* Orthopedic biomechanics and osteoarthritis research, biomedical optical and ultrasound imaging, neurocomputational modeling and neuroengineering including mechanical injury to brain tissue, cellular and tissue engineering and regenerative medicine, magnetic resonance imaging and spectroscopy. *Unit head:* Dr. Van C. Mow, Stanley Dicker Professor of Biomedical Engineering and Orthopedic Bioengineering and Department Chairman, 212-854-8462, Fax: 212-854-5117, E-mail: vcm1@columbia.edu. *Application contact:* Jarmaine Lomax, Assistant for Student Affairs, 212-854-4460, Fax: 212-854-8725, E-mail: jl432@columbia.edu.

Cornell University, Graduate School, Graduate Fields of Engineering, Field of Biomedical Engineering, Ithaca, NY 14853-0001. Offers M Eng, MS, PhD. *Faculty:* 47 full-time (11 women). *Students:* 165 full-time (63 women); includes 8 Black or African American, non-Hispanic/Latino; 34 Asian, non-Hispanic/Latino; 6 Hispanic/Latino, 41 international. Average age 24. 387 applicants, 45% accepted, 100 enrolled. In 2010, 83 master's, 9 doctorates awarded. *Degree requirements:* For master's, thesis; for doctorate, comprehensive exam, thesis/dissertation. *Entrance requirements:* For master's and doctorate, GRE General Test, GRE Subject Test (engineering), 3 letters of recommendation. Additional exam requirements/recommendations for international students: Required—TOEFL (minimum score 77 iBT). *Application deadline:* For fall admission, 1/15 priority date for domestic students. Application fee: $70. Electronic applications accepted. *Expenses:* Tuition: Full-time $29,500. Required fees: $76. Tuition and fees vary according to degree level and program. *Financial support:* In 2010–11, 57 students received support, including 32 fellowships with full tuition reimbursements available, 37 research assistantships with full tuition reimbursements available, 9 teaching assistantships; institutionally sponsored loans, scholarships/grants, health care benefits, tuition waivers (full and partial), and unspecified assistantships also available. *Faculty research:* Biomaterials; biomedical instrumentation and diagnostics; biomedical mechanics; drug delivery, design, and metabolism. *Unit head:* Director of Graduate Studies, 607-255-1003, Fax: 607-255-1136. *Application contact:* Graduate Field Assistant, 607-255-2573, Fax: 607-255-1136, E-mail: biomedgrad@cornell.edu.

Dalhousie University, Faculty of Engineering and Faculty of Medicine, Department of Biomedical Engineering, Halifax, NS B3H3J5, Canada. Offers MA Sc, PhD. *Entrance requirements:* Additional exam requirements/recommendations for international students:

Required—TOEFL, IELTS, CANTEST, CAEL, or Michigan English Language Assessment Battery. Electronic applications accepted.

Dartmouth College, Thayer School of Engineering, Program in Biomedical Engineering, Hanover, NH 03755. Offers MS, PhD. *Faculty research:* Imaging, physiological modeling, cancer hyperthermia and radiation therapy, bioelectromagnetics, biomedical optics and lasers. Total annual research expenditures: $6.7 million. *Unit head:* Dr. Joseph J. Helbie, Dean, 603-646-2238, Fax: 603-646-2580, E-mail: joseph.j.helbie@dartmouth.edu. *Application contact:* Candace S. Potter, Graduate Admissions Administrator, 603-646-3844, Fax: 603-646-1620, E-mail: candace.potter@dartmouth.edu.

Drexel University, School of Biomedical Engineering, Science and Health Systems, Program in Biomedical Engineering, Philadelphia, PA 19104-2875. Offers MS, PhD. *Degree requirements:* For master's, thesis (for some programs); for doctorate, thesis/dissertation. Electronic applications accepted.

Duke University, Graduate School, Pratt School of Engineering, Department of Biomedical Engineering, Durham, NC 27708. Offers MS, PhD. *Faculty:* 37 full-time. *Students:* 213 full-time (80 women); includes 3 Black or African American, non-Hispanic/Latino; 2 American Indian or Alaska Native, non-Hispanic/Latino; 33 Asian, non-Hispanic/Latino; 12 Hispanic/Latino, 68 international. 553 applicants, 24% accepted, 67 enrolled. In 2010, 42 master's, 24 doctorates awarded. *Degree requirements:* For doctorate, thesis/dissertation. *Entrance requirements:* For master's and doctorate, GRE General Test. Additional exam requirements/recommendations for international students: Required—TOEFL (minimum score 550 paper-based; 213 computer-based; 83 iBT), IELTS (minimum score 7). *Application deadline:* For fall admission, 12/8 priority date for domestic and international students; for spring admission, 11/1 for domestic students. Application fee: $75. *Financial support:* Fellowships, research assistantships, teaching assistantships, Federal Work-Study available. Financial award application deadline: 12/8. *Unit head:* Dr. Ashutosh Chilkoti, Director of Graduate Studies, 919-660-5143, Fax: 919-681-7432, E-mail: kwb@acpub.duke.edu. *Application contact:* Elizabeth Hutton, Director of Admissions, 919-684-3913, Fax: 919-684-2277, E-mail: grad-admissions@duke.edu.

Duke University, Graduate School, Pratt School of Engineering, Master of Engineering Program, Durham, NC 27708-0271. Offers biomedical engineering (M Eng); civil engineering (M Eng); electrical and computer engineering (M Eng); environmental engineering (M Eng); materials science and engineering (M Eng); mechanical engineering (M Eng); photonics and optical sciences (M Eng). Part-time programs available. *Faculty:* 123 full-time, 1 part-time/adjunct. *Students:* 9 full-time (4 women); includes 2 minority (both Asian, non-Hispanic/Latino), 3 international. Average age 24. *Entrance requirements:* For master's, GRE General Test, resume, 3 letters of recommendation, statement of purpose. Additional exam requirements/recommendations for international students: Required—TOEFL. *Application deadline:* For fall admission, 6/15 for domestic students, 2/15 for international students; for spring admission, 11/1 for domestic students, 9/1 for international students. Application fee: $75. *Financial support:* Merit scholarships/grants available. *Unit head:* Dr. Bradley A. Fox, Executive Director, 919-660-5455, Fax: 919-660-5456. *Application contact:* Erin Degerman, Admissions Coordinator, 919-668-6789, Fax: 919-660-5456, E-mail: erin.degerman@duke.edu.

École Polytechnique de Montréal, Graduate Programs, Institute of Biomedical Engineering, Montréal, QC H3C 3A7, Canada. Offers M Sc A, PhD, DESS. M Sc A and PhD programs offered jointly with Université de Montréal. Part-time programs available. *Degree requirements:* For master's, one foreign language, thesis; for doctorate, one foreign language, thesis/dissertation. *Entrance requirements:* For master's, minimum GPA of 2.75; for doctorate, minimum GPA of 3.0. *Faculty research:* Cardiac electrophysiology, biomedical instrumentation, biomechanics, biomaterials, medical imagery.

Florida Agricultural and Mechanical University, Division of Graduate Studies, Research, and Continuing Education, FAMU-FSU College of Engineering, Department of Biomedical

Biomedical Engineering

Florida Agricultural and Mechanical University (continued)
Engineering, Tallahassee, FL 32307-3200. Offers MS, PhD. *Degree requirements:* For master's, thesis optional; for doctorate, thesis/dissertation, paper presentation at professional meeting. *Entrance requirements:* For master's, GRE General Test, minimum GPA of 3.3, letters of recommendation (3); for doctorate, minimum GPA of 3.3. Additional exam requirements/recommendations for international students: Required—TOEFL (minimum score 550 paper-based; 213 computer-based). *Faculty research:* Cellular signaling, cancer therapy, drug delivery, cellular and tissue engineering, brain physiology.

Florida International University, College of Engineering and Computing, Department of Biomedical Engineering, Miami, FL 33175. Offers MS, PhD. Part-time and evening/weekend programs available. *Faculty:* 8 full-time (1 woman), 2 part-time/adjunct (0 women). *Students:* 48 full-time (18 women), 4 part-time (2 women); includes 3 Black or African American, non-Hispanic/Latino; 2 Asian, non-Hispanic/Latino; 9 Hispanic/Latino, 34 international. Average age 24. 130 applicants, 15% accepted, 19 enrolled. In 2010, 6 master's, 3 doctorates awarded. *Degree requirements:* For master's, thesis; for doctorate, comprehensive exam, thesis/dissertation. *Entrance requirements:* For master's, GRE General Test (minimum combined score 1000, verbal 350, quantitative 650), minimum GPA of 3.0; for doctorate, GRE General Test (minimum combined score 1150, verbal 450, quantitative 700), minimum GPA of 3.0, letter of intent, letters of recommendation. Additional exam requirements/recommendations for international students: Required—TOEFL (minimum score 550 paper-based; 80 iBT). *Application deadline:* For fall admission, 6/1 for domestic students, 4/1 for international students; for spring admission, 10/1 for domestic students, 9/1 for international students. Applications are processed on a rolling basis. Application fee: $30. Electronic applications accepted. *Financial support:* Institutionally sponsored loans, scholarships/grants, and unspecified assistantships available. Financial award application deadline: 3/1; financial award applicants required to submit FAFSA. *Faculty research:* Bio-imaging and bio-signal processing, bio-instrumentation, devices and sensors, biomaterials and bio-nano technology, cellular and tissue engineering. *Unit head:* Dr. Anthony McGoron, Acting Chair, Biomedical Engineering Department, 305-348-1352, Fax: 305-348-6954, E-mail: anthony.mcgoron@fiu.edu. *Application contact:* Maria Parrilla, Graduate Admissions Assistant, 305-348-1890, Fax: 305-348-6140, E-mail: grad_eng@fiu.edu.

Florida State University, The Graduate School, FAMU-FSU College of Engineering, Department of Chemical and Biomedical Engineering, Tallahassee, FL 32310-6046. Offers biomedical engineering (MS, PhD); chemical engineering (MS, PhD). Part-time programs available. *Faculty:* 13 full-time (1 woman). *Students:* 31 full-time (15 women); includes 3 Black or African American, non-Hispanic/Latino; 1 Asian, non-Hispanic/Latino; 1 Hispanic/Latino, 17 international. Average age 25. 78 applicants, 10% accepted, 8 enrolled. In 2010, 2 master's, 3 doctorates awarded. Terminal master's awarded for partial completion of doctoral program. *Degree requirements:* For master's, thesis (for some programs); for doctorate, comprehensive exam, thesis/dissertation, qualifying exam. *Entrance requirements:* For master's, GRE General Test (minimum score 1200), BS in chemical engineering or other physical science, minimum GPA of 3.0; for doctorate, GRE General Test (minimum score: 1200), BS in chemical engineering or other physical science, minimum GPA of 3.0, or MS in chemical or biomedical engineering. Additional exam requirements/recommendations for international students: Required—TOEFL (minimum score 550 paper-based; 213 computer-based). *Application deadline:* For fall admission, 3/1 priority date for domestic students, 3/1 for international students; for spring admission, 11/1 for domestic and international students. Applications are processed on a rolling basis. Application fee: $30. *Expenses:* Contact institution. *Financial support:* In 2010–11, 30 students received support, including 4 fellowships with full tuition reimbursements available (averaging $18,500 per year), 12 research assistantships with full tuition reimbursements available (averaging $18,500 per year), 10 teaching assistantships with full tuition reimbursements available (averaging $18,500 per year). Financial award application deadline: 3/1. *Faculty research:* Macromolecular transport, polymer processing, biochemical engineering, environmental engineering, transport and reaction, NMR-MRI, fuel cells. Total annual research expenditures: $1.2 million. *Unit head:* Dr. Bruce R. Locke, Chair and Professor, 850-410-6149, Fax: 850-410-6150, E-mail: locke@eng.fsu.edu. *Application contact:* Lisa Fowler, Office Administrator, 850-410-6151, Fax: 850-410-6150, E-mail: lfowler@fsu.edu.

Georgia Institute of Technology, Graduate Studies and Research, College of Engineering, The Wallace H. Coulter Department of Biomedical Engineering at Georgia Tech and Emory University, Atlanta, GA 30332-0001. Offers bioengineering (PhD); bioinformatics (PhD); biomedical engineering (PhD); MD/PhD. PhD in biomedical engineering program jointly offered with Emory University (Georgia) and Peking University (China). Terminal master's awarded for partial completion of doctoral program. *Degree requirements:* For doctorate, thesis/dissertation. *Entrance requirements:* Additional exam requirements/recommendations for international students: Required—TOEFL. *Faculty research:* Biomechanics and tissue engineering, bioinstrumentation and medical imaging.

Graduate School and University Center of the City University of New York, Graduate Studies, Program in Engineering, New York, NY 10016-4039. Offers biomedical engineering (PhD); chemical engineering (PhD); civil engineering (PhD); electrical engineering (PhD); mechanical engineering (PhD). *Degree requirements:* For doctorate, thesis/dissertation. *Entrance requirements:* For doctorate, GRE General Test. Additional exam requirements/recommendations for international students: Required—TOEFL. Electronic applications accepted.

Harvard University, Graduate School of Arts and Sciences, Department of Physics, Cambridge, MA 02138. Offers experimental physics (PhD); medical engineering/medical physics (PhD); including applied physics, engineering sciences, physics; theoretical physics (PhD). *Degree requirements:* For doctorate, thesis/dissertation, final exams, laboratory experience. *Entrance requirements:* For doctorate, GRE General Test, GRE Subject Test. Additional exam requirements/recommendations for international students: Required—TOEFL. *Expenses:* Tuition: Full-time $34,976. Required fees: $1166. Full-time tuition and fees vary according to program. *Faculty research:* Particle physics, condensed matter physics, atomic physics.

Harvard University, Harvard Medical School and Graduate School of Arts and Sciences, Division of Health Sciences and Technology, Program in Biomedical Engineering, Cambridge, MA 02138. Offers M Eng. *Students:* 3 applicants, 0% accepted, 0 enrolled. In 2010, 1 master's awarded. *Degree requirements:* For master's, thesis. *Entrance requirements:* For master's, status as current MIT undergraduate. *Application deadline:* For spring admission, 5/31 for domestic and international students. Application fee: $70. *Expenses:* Contact institution. *Financial support:* Health care benefits and unspecified assistantships available. Financial award application deadline: 12/15; financial award applicants required to submit FAFSA. *Unit head:* Dr. Roger G. Mark, Director, 617-495-1000. *Application contact:* Andrea Santp, Admissions Coordinator, 617-258-7084, E-mail: asanto@mit.edu.

Harvard University, Harvard Medical School and Graduate School of Arts and Sciences, Division of Health Sciences and Technology and Department of Physics and School of Engineering and Applied Sciences, Program in Medical Engineering/Medical Physics, Cambridge, MA 02138. Offers medical engineering (PhD); medical engineering/medical physics (Sc D); medical physics (PhD). Programs offered jointly with Massachusetts Institute of Technology. *Students:* 116 full-time (35 women); includes 3 Black or African American, non-Hispanic/Latino; 1 American Indian or Alaska Native, non-Hispanic/Latino; 19 Asian, non-Hispanic/Latino; 5 Hispanic/Latino; 6 Two or more races, non-Hispanic/Latino, 33 international. Average age 27. 236 applicants, 8% accepted, 17 enrolled. In 2010, 24 doctorates awarded. *Degree requirements:* For doctorate, comprehensive exam, thesis/dissertation, oral and written qualifying exams. *Entrance requirements:* For doctorate, GRE, bachelor's degree in engineering or science. Additional exam requirements/recommendations for international students: Required—TOEFL; Recommended—IELTS. *Application deadline:* For fall admission, 12/15 for domestic and international students. Application fee: $75. *Expenses:* Contact institution. *Financial support:* In 2010–11, 93 students received support, including 58 fellowships with full and partial tuition reimbursements available (averaging $57,010 per year), 37 research assistantships with full and partial tuition reimbursements available (averaging $54,720 per year), 7 teaching assistant-

ships with full and partial tuition reimbursements available (averaging $6,119 per year); career-related internships or fieldwork, institutionally sponsored loans, traineeships, health care benefits, and unspecified assistantships also available. Financial award application deadline: 12/15; financial award applicants required to submit FAFSA. *Faculty research:* Regenerative biomedical technologies, biomedical imaging and optics, biophysics, systems physiology, bioinstrumentation, biomedical informatics/integrative genomics. *Unit head:* Dr. Ram Sasisekharan, Director, 617-258-7282. *Application contact:* Laurie Ward, Graduate Administrator, 617-253-3609, Fax: 617-253-6692, E-mail: laurie@mit.edu.

Illinois Institute of Technology, Graduate College, Armour College of Engineering, Department of Biomedical Engineering, Chicago, IL 60616-3793. Offers PhD. Part-time programs available. *Faculty:* 9 full-time (2 women), 1 (woman) part-time/adjunct. *Students:* 25 full-time (6 women), 4 part-time (2 women); includes 1 minority (Black or African American, non-Hispanic/Latino), 14 international. Average age 26. 79 applicants, 44% accepted, 7 enrolled. *Degree requirements:* For doctorate, comprehensive exam, thesis/dissertation. *Entrance requirements:* For doctorate, GRE General Test (minimum score of 1200 Quantitative plus Verbal and 3.0 Analytical Writing), minimum cumulative undergraduate GPA of 3.2. Additional exam requirements/recommendations for international students: Required—TOEFL (minimum score 523 paper-based; 70 iBT); Recommended—IELTS (minimum score 5.5). *Application deadline:* For fall admission, 5/1 for domestic and international students; for spring admission, 10/15 for domestic and international students. Applications are processed on a rolling basis. Application fee: $50. Electronic applications accepted. *Expenses:* Tuition: Full-time $18,576; part-time $1032 per credit hour. Required fees: $583 per semester. One-time fee: $150. Tuition and fees vary according to program and student level. *Financial support:* In 2010–11, 20 research assistantships with partial tuition reimbursements (averaging $7,445 per year), 4 teaching assistantships with full and partial tuition reimbursements (averaging $7,125 per year) were awarded; fellowships with full tuition reimbursements, Federal Work-Study, institutionally sponsored loans, scholarships/grants, health care benefits, and unspecified assistantships also available. Support available to part-time students. Financial award applicants required to submit FAFSA. *Faculty research:* Medical imaging, cell and tissue engineering, neural engineering, diabetes research, bioinformatics. Total annual research expenditures: $1.7 million. *Unit head:* Dr. David Mogul, Interim Chair and Associate Professor, 312-567-3873, Fax: 312-567-5770, E-mail: mogul@iit.edu. *Application contact:* Deborah Gibson, Director, Graduate Admission, 866-472-3448, Fax: 312-567-3138, E-mail: inquiry.grad@iit.edu.

Indiana University–Purdue University Indianapolis, School of Engineering and Technology, Department of Electrical Engineering, Indianapolis, IN 46202-2896. Offers biomedical engineering (MS, PhD); electrical and computer engineering (MS, MSECE, PhD), including biomedical engineering (MSECE), control and automation (MSECE), signal processing (MSECE), engineering (interdisciplinary) (MSE). *Students:* 40 full-time (13 women), 35 part-time (7 women); includes 7 minority (1 Black or African American, non-Hispanic/Latino; 1 Asian, non-Hispanic/Latino; 3 Hispanic/Latino; 2 Two or more races, non-Hispanic/Latino), 45 international. Average age 27. 153 applicants, 53% accepted, 42 enrolled. In 2010, 37 master's awarded. Application fee: $55 ($65 for international students). *Unit head:* Yaobin Chen, Unit Head, 317-274-4032, Fax: 317-274-4493. *Application contact:* Valerie Diemer, Graduate Program, 317-278-4960, Fax: 317-278-1671, E-mail: grad@engr.iupui.edu.

Indiana University–Purdue University Indianapolis, School of Engineering and Technology, Department of Mechanical Engineering, Indianapolis, IN 46202-2896. Offers biomedical engineering (MS Bm E); computer-aided mechanical engineering (Certificate); mechanical engineering (MSME, PhD). Part-time programs available. *Students:* 22 full-time (6 women), 30 part-time (3 women); includes 4 minority (2 Black or African American, non-Hispanic/Latino; 2 Asian, non-Hispanic/Latino), 26 international. Average age 28. In 2010, 26 master's awarded. *Degree requirements:* For master's, thesis optional. *Entrance requirements:* For master's, GRE. Additional exam requirements/recommendations for international students: Required—TOEFL. *Application deadline:* For fall admission, 7/1 for domestic students. Application fee: $55 ($65 for international students). *Financial support:* Fellowships with tuition reimbursements, research assistantships with full and partial tuition reimbursements, tuition waivers (full and partial) available. Financial award application deadline: 3/1. *Faculty research:* Computational fluid dynamics, heat transfer, finite-element methods, composites, biomechanics. *Unit head:* Dr. Hasan Akay, Chairman, 317-274-9717, Fax: 317-274-9744. *Application contact:* Valerie Diemer, Graduate Program, 317-278-4960, Fax: 317-278-1671, E-mail: grad@engr.iupui.edu.

The Johns Hopkins University, Engineering for Professionals, Part-time Program in Applied Biomedical Engineering, Baltimore, MD 21218-2699. Offers MS, Post-Master's Certificate. Part-time and evening/weekend programs available. *Faculty:* 6 part-time/adjunct (0 women). *Students:* 3 full-time (0 women), 33 part-time (13 women); includes 10 minority (2 Black or African American, non-Hispanic/Latino; 1 American Indian or Alaska Native, non-Hispanic/Latino; 5 Asian, non-Hispanic/Latino; 1 Hispanic/Latino; 1 Two or more races, non-Hispanic/Latino), 1 international. Average age 29. 20 applicants, 75% accepted, 9 enrolled. In 2010, 11 master's awarded. *Application deadline:* Applications are processed on a rolling basis. Application fee: $75. Electronic applications accepted. *Financial support:* Institutionally sponsored loans available. *Unit head:* Dr. Eileen Haase, Program Chair, 443-778-6201, E-mail: ehaase1@jhu.edu. *Application contact:* Priyanka Dwivedi, Admissions Manager, 410-516-2300, Fax: 410-579-8049, E-mail: pdwived1@jhu.edu.

The Johns Hopkins University, G. W. C. Whiting School of Engineering and School of Medicine, Department of Biomedical Engineering, Baltimore, MD 21205. Offers bioengineering innovation and design (MSE); biomedical engineering (MSE, PhD). *Faculty:* 45 full-time (7 women). *Students:* 236 full-time (72 women); includes 11 minority (9 Asian, non-Hispanic/Latino; 1 Hispanic/Latino; 1 Two or more races, non-Hispanic/Latino), 23 international. Average age 23. 653 applicants, 20% accepted, 70 enrolled. In 2010, 33 master's, 17 doctorates awarded. Terminal master's awarded for partial completion of doctoral program. *Degree requirements:* For master's, thesis; for doctorate, comprehensive exam, thesis/dissertation, oral exam. *Entrance requirements:* For master's and doctorate, GRE General Test. Additional exam requirements/recommendations for international students: Required—TOEFL or IELTS. *Application deadline:* For fall admission, 1/15 for domestic and international students. Application fee: $75. Electronic applications accepted. *Financial support:* In 2010–11, 208 students received support, including 218 research assistantships with full tuition reimbursements available (averaging $27,532 per year), 37 teaching assistantships with full and partial tuition reimbursements available (averaging $10,000 per year); fellowships with partial tuition reimbursements available, Federal Work-Study, institutionally sponsored loans, scholarships/grants, tuition waivers (full), and unspecified assistantships also available. Support available to part-time students. *Faculty research:* Cell and tissue engineering, systems neuroscience, imaging, cardiovascular systems physiology, theoretical and computational biology. Total annual research expenditures: $15.6 million. *Unit head:* Dr. Elliot R. McVeigh, Director, 410-516-5282, Fax: 410-516-4771. *Application contact:* Samuel Bourne, Academic Master's Program Coordinator, 410-516-8482, Fax: 410-516-4771, E-mail: sbourne@jhu.edu.

Louisiana Tech University, Graduate School, College of Engineering and Science, Department of Biomedical Engineering, Ruston, LA 71272. Offers MS, PhD. Part-time programs available. Terminal master's awarded for partial completion of doctoral program. *Degree requirements:* For master's, thesis; for doctorate, thesis/dissertation. *Entrance requirements:* For master's, GRE General Test, minimum GPA of 3.0 in last 60 hours; for doctorate, minimum graduate GPA of 3.25 (MS) or GRE General Test. Additional exam requirements/recommendations for international students: Required—TOEFL. *Faculty research:* Microbiosensors and microcirculatory transport, speech recognition, artificial intelligence, rehabilitation engineering, bioelectromagnetics.

Marquette University, Graduate School, College of Engineering, Department of Biomedical Engineering, Milwaukee, WI 53201-1881. Offers biocomputing (ME); bioimaging (ME); bioinstrumentation (ME); bioinstrumentation/computers (MS, PhD); biomechanics (ME); biomechanics/biomaterials (MS, PhD); biorehabilitation (ME); functional imaging (PhD); healthcare technologies management (MS); rehabilitation bioengineering (PhD); systems physiology (MS, PhD). Part-time and evening/weekend programs available. *Faculty:* 15 full-time (5 women), 5 part-time/adjunct (2 women). *Students:* 59 full-time (18 women), 27 part-time (9 women); includes 8 minority (1 American Indian or Alaska Native, non-Hispanic/Latino; 5 Asian, non-Hispanic/Latino; 1 Hispanic/Latino; 1 Native Hawaiian or other Pacific Islander, non-Hispanic/Latino), 24 international. Average age 27. 128 applicants, 30% accepted, 14 enrolled. In 2010, 8 master's awarded. Terminal master's awarded for partial completion of doctoral program. *Degree requirements:* For master's, comprehensive exam, thesis; for doctorate, comprehensive exam, thesis/dissertation, dissertation defense, qualifying exam. *Entrance requirements:* For master's, GRE General Test, minimum GPA of 3.0, official transcripts from all current and previous colleges/universities except Marquette, three letters of recommendation, brief statement of purpose that includes proposed area of research specialization, interview with the M.E. program director, one year of post-baccalaureate professional work experience; for doctorate, GRE General Test, minimum GPA of 3.0, official transcripts from all current and previous colleges/universities except Marquette, three letters of recommendation, brief statement of purpose that includes proposed area of research specialization. Additional exam requirements/recommendations for international students: Required—TOEFL (minimum score 530 paper-based; 78 computer-based). *Application deadline:* For fall admission, 2/15 priority date for domestic students; for spring admission, 11/15 priority date for domestic students. Applications are processed on a rolling basis. Application fee: $50. Electronic applications accepted. *Expenses:* Tuition: Full-time $16,290; part-time $905 per credit hour. Tuition and fees vary according to program. *Financial support:* In 2010–11, 50 students received support, including 8 fellowships with full tuition reimbursements available, 4 research assistantships with full tuition reimbursements available, 7 teaching assistantships with full tuition reimbursements available; Federal Work-Study, institutionally sponsored loans, and scholarships/grants also available. Support available to part-time students. Financial award application deadline: 2/15. *Faculty research:* Cell and organ physiology, signal processing, gait analysis, orthopedic rehabilitation engineering, telemedicine. Total annual research expenditures: $1.8 million. *Unit head:* Dr. Kristina Ropella, Chair, 414-288-3375, Fax: 414-288-7938, E-mail: kristina.ropella@marquette.edu. *Application contact:* Erin Fox, Assistant Chair, 414-288-7182, Fax: 414-288-1902, E-mail: erin.fox@marquette.edu.

Massachusetts Institute of Technology, Harvard-MIT Division of Health Sciences and Technology, Medical Engineering/Medical Physics Program, Cambridge, MA 02139-4307. Offers medical engineering (PhD); medical engineering and medical physics (Sc D); medical physics (PhD). PhD, Sc D offered jointly with Harvard University. *Students:* 116 full-time (35 women); includes 3 Black or African American, non-Hispanic/Latino; 1 American Indian or Alaska Native, non-Hispanic/Latino; 19 Asian, non-Hispanic/Latino; 5 Hispanic/Latino; 6 Two or more races, non-Hispanic/Latino, 33 international. Average age 27. 236 applicants, 8% accepted, 17 enrolled. In 2010, 24 doctorates awarded. *Degree requirements:* For doctorate, comprehensive exam, thesis/dissertation, oral and written departmental qualifying exams. *Entrance requirements:* For doctorate, GRE, bachelor's degree in engineering or science. Additional exam requirements/recommendations for international students: Required—TOEFL; Recommended—IELTS. *Application deadline:* For fall admission, 12/15 for domestic and international students. Application fee: $75. Electronic applications accepted. *Expenses:* Contact institution. *Financial support:* In 2010–11, 93 students received support, including 58 fellowships with full and partial tuition reimbursements available (averaging $57,010 per year), 37 research assistantships with full and partial tuition reimbursements available (averaging $54,720 per year), 7 teaching assistantships with full and partial tuition reimbursements available (averaging $6,119 per year); career-related internships or fieldwork, institutionally sponsored loans, traineeships, health care benefits, and unspecified assistantships also available. Financial award application deadline: 12/15. *Faculty research:* Regenerative biomedical technologies, biomedical imaging and optics, biophysics, systems physiology, bioinstrumentation, biomedical informatics/integrative genomics. *Unit head:* Dr. Ram Sasisekharan, Director, 617-258-8974, E-mail: mgray@mit.edu. *Application contact:* Laurie Ward, Graduate Administrator, 617-253-3609, Fax: 617-253-6692, E-mail: laurie@mit.edu.

Massachusetts Institute of Technology, Harvard-MIT Division of Health Sciences and Technology, Program in Biomedical Engineering, Cambridge, MA 02139-4307. Offers M Eng. *Students:* 3 applicants, 0% accepted, 0 enrolled. In 2010, 1 master's awarded. *Degree requirements:* For master's, thesis. *Entrance requirements:* For master's, current status as MIT undergraduate. *Application deadline:* For spring admission, 5/31 for domestic and international students. Application fee: $70. *Expenses:* Contact institution. *Financial support:* Health care benefits and unspecified assistantships available. Financial award application deadline: 12/15. *Unit head:* Dr. Roger G. Mark, Director, 617-253-7818. *Application contact:* Andrea Santo, Admissions Coordinator, 617-258-7084, Fax: 617-253-6692, E-mail: asanto@mit.edu.

Massachusetts Institute of Technology, School of Engineering, Department of Biological Engineering, Cambridge, MA 02139-4307. Offers applied biosciences (PhD, Sc D); bioengineering (PhD, Sc D); biological engineering (PhD, Sc D); biomedical engineering (M Eng); toxicology (SM); SM/MBA. *Faculty:* 30 full-time (5 women). *Students:* 112 full-time (56 women); includes 32 minority (2 Black or African American, non-Hispanic/Latino; 20 Asian, non-Hispanic/Latino; 8 Hispanic/Latino; 2 Two or more races, non-Hispanic/Latino), 31 international. Average age 26. 441 applicants, 9% accepted, 24 enrolled. In 2010, 3 master's, 16 doctorates awarded. Terminal master's awarded for partial completion of doctoral program. *Degree requirements:* For master's, thesis; for doctorate, comprehensive exam, thesis/dissertation. *Entrance requirements:* For master's and doctorate, GRE General Test. Additional exam requirements/recommendations for international students: Required—TOEFL (minimum score 600 paper-based; 250 computer-based), IELTS (minimum score 7). *Application deadline:* For fall admission, 12/31 for domestic and international students. Application fee: $75. Electronic applications accepted. *Expenses:* Tuition: Full-time $38,940; part-time $605 per unit. Required fees: $272. *Financial support:* In 2010–11, 111 students received support, including 57 fellowships with tuition reimbursements available (averaging $35,847 per year), 51 research assistantships with tuition reimbursements available (averaging $32,873 per year), 3 teaching assistantships with tuition reimbursements available (averaging $31,681 per year); Federal Work-Study, institutionally sponsored loans, scholarships/grants, traineeships, health care benefits, and unspecified assistantships also available. *Faculty research:* Bioinformatics, computational, systems, and synthetic biology; biological materials, imaging, and transport phenomena; biomolecular and cell engineering; cancer initiation, progression, and therapeutics; genomics, proteomics, and glycomics; nanoscale engineering of biological systems; neurobiological systems; systems biology; macromolecular biochemistry and biophysics. Total annual research expenditures: $35.1 million. *Unit head:* Prof. Douglas A. Lauffenburger, Department Head, 617-253-1712, E-mail: be-acad@mit.edu. *Application contact:* Biological Engineering Academic Office, 617-253-1712, Fax: 617-258-8676, E-mail: be-acad@mit.edu.

Mayo Graduate School, Graduate Programs in Biomedical Sciences, Program in Biomedical Engineering, Rochester, MN 55905. Offers PhD. *Degree requirements:* For doctorate, oral defense of dissertation, qualifying oral and written exam. *Entrance requirements:* For doctorate, GRE, 1 year of chemistry, biology, calculus, and physics. Additional exam requirements/recommendations for international students: Required—TOEFL. Electronic applications accepted.

McGill University, Faculty of Graduate and Postdoctoral Studies, Faculty of Medicine, Department of Biomedical Engineering, Montréal, QC H3A 2T5, Canada. Offers M Eng, PhD.

Mercer University, Graduate Studies, Macon Campus, School of Engineering, Macon, GA 31207-0003. Offers biomedical engineering (MSE); computer engineering (MSE); electrical engineering (MSE); engineering management (MSE); environmental engineering (MSE); environmental systems (MS); mechanical engineering (MSE); software engineering (MSE); software systems (MS); technical communications management (MS); technical management (MS). Part-time and evening/weekend programs available. Postbaccalaureate distance learning degree programs offered (no on-campus study). *Faculty:* 18 full-time (4 women), 1 part-time/adjunct (0 women). *Students:* 11 full-time (2 women), 100 part-time (22 women); includes 26 minority (13 Black or African American, non-Hispanic/Latino; 12 Asian, non-Hispanic/Latino; 1 Hispanic/Latino), 3 international. Average age 32. In 2010, 46 master's awarded. *Degree requirements:* For master's, thesis or alternative. *Entrance requirements:* For master's, minimum undergraduate GPA of 3.0. Additional exam requirements/recommendations for international students: Required—TOEFL. *Application deadline:* For fall admission, 7/1 for domestic students; for spring admission, 11/15 for domestic students. Applications are processed on a rolling basis. Application fee: $35 ($50 for international students). Electronic applications accepted. *Expenses:* Contact institution. *Financial support:* Federal Work-Study available. *Unit head:* Dr. Wade H. Shaw, Dean, 478-301-2459, Fax: 478-301-5593, E-mail: shaw_wh@mercer.edu. *Application contact:* Greg Lofton, Graduate Program Coordinator, 478-301-5480, Fax: 478-301-5434, E-mail: lofton_g@mercer.edu.

Michigan Technological University, Graduate School, College of Engineering, Department of Biomedical Engineering, Houghton, MI 49931. Offers PhD. Part-time programs available. *Degree requirements:* For doctorate, comprehensive exam, thesis/dissertation. *Entrance requirements:* For doctorate, GRE. Additional exam requirements/recommendations for international students: Required—TOEFL (minimum score 550 paper-based; 213 computer-based). Electronic applications accepted. *Expenses:* Contact institution. *Faculty research:* Biomaterials/tissue engineering; physiology measurement; biomechanics; mechanotransduction; bone metabolism.

Mississippi State University, College of Agriculture and Life Sciences, Department of Agricultural and Biological Engineering, Mississippi State, MS 39762. Offers agricultural sciences (PhD), including engineering technology (MS, PhD); agriculture (MS), including engineering technology (MS, PhD); biological engineering (MS); biomedical engineering (MS, PhD); engineering (PhD), including biological engineering. PhD (agricultural sciences), MS (agriculture) are interdisciplinary. *Faculty:* 12 full-time (1 woman). *Students:* 39 full-time (14 women), 5 part-time (1 woman); includes 6 minority (3 Black or African American, non-Hispanic/Latino; 1 Asian, non-Hispanic/Latino; 1 Native Hawaiian or other Pacific Islander, non-Hispanic/Latino; 1 Two or more races, non-Hispanic/Latino), 11 international. Average age 27. 47 applicants, 43% accepted, 16 enrolled. In 2010, 5 master's, 3 doctorates awarded. *Degree requirements:* For master's, thesis; for doctorate, thesis/dissertation, preliminary exam. *Entrance requirements:* For master's, GRE General Test, minimum undergraduate GPA of 2.75 (3.0 for biomedical engineering); for doctorate, GRE General Test, minimum GPA of 3.0 (biomedical engineering). Additional exam requirements/recommendations for international students: Required—TOEFL (minimum score 550 paper-based; 213 computer-based; 79 iBT); Recommended—IELTS (minimum score 6.5). *Application deadline:* For fall admission, 7/1 for domestic students, 5/1 for international students; for spring admission, 11/1 for domestic students, 9/1 for international students. Applications are processed on a rolling basis. Application fee: $40. Electronic applications accepted. *Expenses:* Tuition, state resident: full-time $2730.50; part-time $304 per credit hour. Tuition, nonresident: full-time $6901; part-time $767 per credit hour. *Financial support:* In 2010–11, 32 research assistantships with partial tuition reimbursements (averaging $12,687 per year) were awarded; Federal Work-Study, institutionally sponsored loans, and unspecified assistantships also available. Financial award application deadline: 4/1; financial award applicants required to submit FAFSA. *Faculty research:* Bioenvironmental engineering, bioinstrumentation, biomechanics/biomaterials, precision agriculture, tissue engineering, ergonomics human factors, biosimulation and modeling. Total annual research expenditures: $1.1 million. *Unit head:* Dr. Jonathan Pote, Interim Department Head and Professor, 662-325-3280, Fax: 662-325-3853, E-mail: jpote@mafes.msstate.edu. *Application contact:* Dr. Steven Elder, Professor and Graduate Coordinator, 662-325-9107, Fax: 662-325-3853, E-mail: selder@abe.msstate.edu.

New Jersey Institute of Technology, Office of Graduate Studies, Newark College of Engineering, Department of Biomedical Engineering, Newark, NJ 07102. Offers MS, PhD. Part-time and evening/weekend programs available. *Faculty:* 14 full-time (3 women), 7 part-time/adjunct (1 woman). *Students:* 118 full-time (45 women), 38 part-time (19 women); includes 7 Black or African American, non-Hispanic/Latino; 2 American Indian or Alaska Native, non-Hispanic/Latino; 25 Asian, non-Hispanic/Latino; 8 Hispanic/Latino, 63 international. Average age 26. 205 applicants, 47% accepted, 46 enrolled. In 2010, 78 master's, 2 doctorates awarded. Terminal master's awarded for partial completion of doctoral program. *Degree requirements:* For master's, thesis optional; for doctorate, thesis/dissertation. *Entrance requirements:* For master's and doctorate, GRE General Test. Additional exam requirements/recommendations for international students: Required—TOEFL (minimum score 550 paper-based; 213 computer-based; 79 iBT). *Application deadline:* For fall admission, 6/5 priority date for domestic students, 4/1 for international students; for spring admission, 11/15 for domestic and international students. Applications are processed on a rolling basis. Application fee: $65. Electronic applications accepted. *Expenses:* Tuition, state resident: full-time $14,724; part-time $818 per credit. Tuition, nonresident: full-time $20,304; part-time $1128 per credit. Required fees: $2272; $209 per credit. $103 per semester. One-time fee: $312 full-time; $212 part-time. *Financial support:* Fellowships with full and partial tuition reimbursements, research assistantships with full and partial tuition reimbursements, teaching assistantships with full and partial tuition reimbursements, career-related internships or fieldwork, Federal Work-Study, institutionally sponsored loans, and unspecified assistantships available. Financial award application deadline: 3/15. Total annual research expenditures: $7.8 million. *Unit head:* Dr. William C. Van Buskirk, Chair, 973-596-8380, E-mail: vanb@njit.edu. *Application contact:* Kathryn Kelly, Director of Admissions, 973-596-3300, Fax: 973-596-3461, E-mail: admissions@njit.edu.

North Carolina State University, Graduate School, College of Engineering, Joint Department of Biomedical Engineering UNC-Chapel Hill and NC State, Raleigh, NC 27695. Offers MS, PhD. Programs offered jointly with the University of North Carolina at Chapel Hill. Terminal master's awarded for partial completion of doctoral program. *Degree requirements:* For master's, comprehensive exam, thesis, research laboratory experience; for doctorate, one foreign language, comprehensive exam, thesis/dissertation, written and oral examinations, dissertation defense, teaching experience, research laboratory experience. *Entrance requirements:* For master's and doctorate, GRE General Test. Additional exam requirements/recommendations for international students: Required—TOEFL. Electronic applications accepted.

Northwestern University, McCormick School of Engineering and Applied Science, Department of Biomedical Engineering, Evanston, IL 60208. Offers MS, PhD. Admissions and degrees offered through The Graduate School. Part-time programs available. *Faculty:* 17 full-time (3 women). *Students:* 142 full-time (60 women), 4 part-time (3 women); includes 3 Black or African American, non-Hispanic/Latino; 17 Asian, non-Hispanic/Latino; 9 Hispanic/Latino, 46 international. Average age 26. 252 applicants, 14% accepted, 16 enrolled. In 2010, 27 master's, 12 doctorates awarded. Terminal master's awarded for partial completion of doctoral program. *Degree requirements:* For master's, comprehensive exam, thesis (for some programs); for doctorate, comprehensive exam, thesis/dissertation. *Entrance requirements:* For master's and doctorate, General Exam of GRE. Additional exam requirements/recommendations for international students: Required—TOEFL (minimum score 577 paper-based; 233 computer-based; 90 iBT), IELTS (minimum score 7.5). *Application deadline:* For fall admission, 12/31 for domestic and international students. Application fee: $75. Electronic applications accepted. *Financial support:* Fellowships with full tuition reimbursements, research assistantships with full tuition reimbursements, teaching assistantships with full tuition reimbursements, career-related internships or fieldwork, institutionally sponsored loans, traineeships, health care benefits, and unspecified assistantships available. Financial award application deadline: 1/15; financial award applicants required to submit FAFSA. *Faculty research:* Biomechanics and transport, rehabilitation engineering, neuroscience, biomaterials, cellular engineering. Total annual research expenditures: $34.1 million. *Unit head:* Dr. John B. Troy, Chair, 847-491-3822, Fax: 847-491-4928, E-mail: j-troy@northwestern.edu. *Application contact:* Dr. Phillip Messersmith, Director of Graduate Admissions, 847-467-5273, Fax: 847-491-4928, E-mail: philm@northwestern.edu.

OGI School of Science & Engineering at Oregon Health & Science University, Graduate Studies, Department of Biomedical Engineering, Beaverton, OR 97006-8921. Offers MS, PhD. *Degree requirements:* For doctorate, comprehensive exam, thesis/dissertation. *Entrance requirements:* For master's and doctorate, GRE General Test, minimum GPA of 3.5, 3 letters of recommendation. Additional exam requirements/recommendations for international students:

Biomedical Engineering

OGI School of Science & Engineering at Oregon Health & Science University (continued)

Required—TOEFL (minimum score 620 paper-based; 250 computer-based). Electronic applications accepted. *Expenses:* Contact institution. *Faculty research:* Biomedical optics, genetic engineering, neuroengineering, tissue engineering and biomaterials.

The Ohio State University, Graduate School, College of Engineering, Program in Biomedical Engineering, Columbus, OH 43210. Offers MS, PhD. Evening/weekend programs available. *Faculty:* 86. *Students:* 30 full-time (14 women), 15 part-time (3 women); includes 1 Black or African American, non-Hispanic/Latino; 5 Asian, non-Hispanic/Latino; 1 Hispanic/Latino, 13 international. Average age 26. In 2010, 10 master's, 3 doctorates awarded. *Degree requirements:* For master's, thesis optional; for doctorate, thesis/dissertation. *Entrance requirements:* For master's and doctorate, GRE General Test. Additional exam requirements/recommendations for international students: Recommended—TOEFL (minimum score 600 paper-based; 250 computer-based). *Application deadline:* For fall admission, 8/15 priority date for domestic students, 7/1 priority date for international students; for winter admission, 12/1 priority date for domestic students, 11/1 priority date for international students; for spring admission, 3/1 priority date for domestic students, 2/1 priority date for international students. Applications are processed on a rolling basis. Application fee: $40 ($50 for international students). Electronic applications accepted. *Expenses:* Tuition, state resident: full-time $10,605. Tuition, nonresident: full-time $26,535. Tuition and fees vary according to course load and program. *Financial support:* Fellowships, research assistantships, career-related internships or fieldwork, Federal Work-Study, and institutionally sponsored loans available. Support available to part-time students. *Unit head:* Richard T. Hart, Chair, 614-292-1285, Fax: 614-292-7301, E-mail: hart.322@osu.edu. *Application contact:* 614-292-9444, Fax: 614-292-3895, E-mail: domestic.grad@osu.edu.

Ohio University, Graduate College, Russ College of Engineering and Technology, Department of Chemical and Biomolecular Engineering, Program in Biomedical Engineering, Athens, OH 45701-2979. Offers MS. Part-time programs available. *Students:* 9 full-time (3 women), 1 (woman) part-time, 4 international. Average age 27. 13 applicants, 38% accepted, 3 enrolled. In 2010, 3 master's awarded. *Degree requirements:* For master's, thesis. *Entrance requirements:* For master's, GRE General Test. Additional exam requirements/recommendations for international students: Required—TOEFL (minimum score 590 paper-based; 243 computer-based; 96 iBT), IELTS (minimum score 7). *Application deadline:* For fall admission, 2/1 priority date for domestic and international students. Applications are processed on a rolling basis. Application fee: $50 ($55 for international students). Electronic applications accepted. *Financial support:* In 2010–11, 1 fellowship with full tuition reimbursement (averaging $18,000 per year), 2 research assistantships with full tuition reimbursements (averaging $18,000 per year) were awarded; institutionally sponsored loans also available. Financial award application deadline: 2/1. *Faculty research:* Molecular mechanisms of human disease, molecular therapeutics, biomedical information analysis and management, image analysis, biomechanics. Total annual research expenditures: $1.5 million. *Unit head:* Dr. Douglas J. Goetz, Director, 740-593-1000. *Application contact:* Tom Riggs, Biomedical Engineering Assistant, 740-597-2797, Fax: 740-593-0873, E-mail: biomed@ohio.edu.

Ohio University, Graduate College, Russ College of Engineering and Technology, Department of Mechanical Engineering, Athens, OH 45701-2979. Offers biomedical engineering (MS); mechanical engineering (MS), including CAD/CAM, design, energy, manufacturing, materials, robotics, thermofluids. Part-time programs available. *Students:* 29 full-time (3 women), 4 part-time (1 woman); includes 3 minority (1 Black or African American, non-Hispanic/Latino; 1 Hispanic/Latino; 1 Two or more races, non-Hispanic/Latino), 12 international. 40 applicants, 73% accepted, 11 enrolled. In 2010, 4 master's awarded. *Degree requirements:* For master's, comprehensive exam (for some programs), thesis; for doctorate, comprehensive exam, thesis/dissertation. *Entrance requirements:* For master's, GRE, BS in engineering or science, minimum GPA of 2.8; for doctorate, GRE. Additional exam requirements/recommendations for international students: Required—TOEFL (minimum score 550 paper-based; 80 iBT) or IELTS (minimum score 6.5). *Application deadline:* For fall admission, 2/15 priority date for domestic and international students. Applications are processed on a rolling basis. Application fee: $50 ($55 for international students). Electronic applications accepted. *Financial support:* In 2010–11, research assistantships with tuition reimbursements (averaging $14,000 per year), teaching assistantships with tuition reimbursements (averaging $14,000 per year) were awarded; career-related internships or fieldwork, Federal Work-Study, institutionally sponsored loans, tuition waivers (full and partial), and unspecified assistantships also available. Financial award application deadline: 2/15; financial award applicants required to submit FAFSA. *Faculty research:* Biomedical, energy and the environment, materials and manufacturing, bioengineering. *Unit head:* Dr. Greg Kremer, Chairman, 740-593-1561, Fax: 740-593-0476, E-mail: kremer@bobcat.ent.ohiou.edu. *Application contact:* Dr. Frank F. Kraft, Graduate Chairman, 740-597-1478, Fax: 740-593-0476, E-mail: kraft@ohio.edu.

Oregon Health & Science University, School of Medicine, Graduate Programs in Medicine, Department of Biomedical Engineering, Portland, OR 97239-3098. Offers MS, PhD. *Faculty:* 12 full-time (5 women), 3 part-time/adjunct (0 women). *Students:* 20 full-time (10 women); includes 15 Black or African American, non-Hispanic/Latino, 5 international. Average age 25. 25 applicants, 88% accepted, 4 enrolled. In 2010, 1 master's, 5 doctorates awarded. *Degree requirements:* For doctorate, comprehensive exam, thesis/dissertation. *Entrance requirements:* For master's and doctorate, GRE. Additional exam requirements/recommendations for international students: Required—TOEFL. *Application deadline:* For fall admission, 7/15 for domestic students, 5/15 for international students; for winter admission, 10/15 for domestic students, 9/15 for international students; for spring admission, 1/15 for domestic students, 12/15 for international students. Applications are processed on a rolling basis. Application fee: $65. Electronic applications accepted. *Financial support:* Health care benefits, tuition waivers, and full tuition and stipends available. *Unit head:* Peter Heeman, PhD, Program Director, 503-418-9316, E-mail: info@bme.ogi.edu. *Application contact:* Virginia Howard, Administrative Coordinator, 503-418-9302, E-mail: info@bme.ogi.edu.

Polytechnic Institute of NYU, Department of Chemical and Biological Sciences, Major in Biomedical Engineering, Brooklyn, NY 11201-2990. Offers MS, PhD. *Students:* 52 full-time (20 women), 21 part-time (8 women); includes 2 Black or African American, non-Hispanic/Latino; 9 Asian, non-Hispanic/Latino; 3 Hispanic/Latino, 42 international. Average age 25. 124 applicants, 58% accepted, 29 enrolled. In 2010, 26 master's awarded. *Degree requirements:* For master's, comprehensive exam (for some programs), thesis (for some programs); for doctorate, comprehensive exam, thesis/dissertation. *Entrance requirements:* Additional exam requirements/recommendations for international students: Required—TOEFL (minimum score 550 paper-based; 213 computer-based; 80 iBT); Recommended—IELTS (minimum score 6.5). *Application deadline:* For fall admission, 7/31 priority date for domestic students, 4/30 priority date for international students; for spring admission, 12/31 priority date for domestic students, 10/30 priority date for international students. Applications are processed on a rolling basis. Application fee: $75. Electronic applications accepted. *Expenses:* Tuition: Full-time $21,492; part-time $1194 per credit. Required fees: $385 per semester. Tuition and fees vary according to course load. *Unit head:* Dr. Bruce Garetz, Department Head, 718-260-3287, E-mail: bgaretz@poly.edu. *Application contact:* JeanCarlo Bonilla, Director, Graduate Enrollment Management, 718-260-3182, Fax: 718-260-3624, E-mail: gradinfo@poly.edu.

Purdue University, College of Engineering, Weldon School of Biomedical Engineering, West Lafayette, IN 47907-2032. Offers MSBME, PhD, MD/PhD. Degree programs offered jointly with School of Mechanical Engineering, School of Electrical and Computer Engineering, and School of Chemical Engineering. *Entrance requirements:* For master's and doctorate, GRE General Test, minimum GPA of 3.25. Additional exam requirements/recommendations for international students: Required—TOEFL (minimum score 550 paper-based; 213 computer-based; 77 iBT); Recommended—TWE. Electronic applications accepted. *Faculty research:* Biomaterials, biomechanics, medical image and signal processing, medical instrumentation, tissue engineering.

Rensselaer Polytechnic Institute, Graduate School, School of Engineering, Program in Biomedical Engineering, Troy, NY 12180-3590. Offers MS, D Eng, PhD. *Faculty:* 11 full-time (1 woman), 2 part-time/adjunct (0 women). *Students:* 37 full-time (14 women), 1 (woman) part-time; includes 7 Asian, non-Hispanic/Latino. Average age 25. 130 applicants, 3% accepted, 3 enrolled. In 2010, 9 master's, 3 doctorates awarded. Terminal master's awarded for partial completion of doctoral program. *Degree requirements:* For master's, thesis optional; for doctorate, thesis/dissertation. *Entrance requirements:* For master's and doctorate, GRE, minimum GPA of 3.0. Additional exam requirements/recommendations for international students: Required—TOEFL (minimum score 620 paper-based; 260 computer-based; 106 iBT). *Application deadline:* For fall admission, 1/1 priority date for domestic students. Applications are processed on a rolling basis. Application fee: $75. Electronic applications accepted. *Expenses:* Tuition: Full-time $39,600; part-time $1650 per credit. Required fees: $1896. *Financial support:* In 2010–11, 33 students received support, including fellowships with full tuition reimbursements available (averaging $22,000 per year), 17 research assistantships with full tuition reimbursements available (averaging $16,500 per year), 16 teaching assistantships with full tuition reimbursements available (averaging $16,500 per year); career-related internships or fieldwork and institutionally sponsored loans also available. Financial award application deadline: 2/1. *Faculty research:* Computational biomechanics, cellular and tissue bioengineering, biofluids and cellular bioengineering, functional tissue engineering, orthopedic biomechanics. *Unit head:* Dr. Deepak Vashishth, Professor and Department Head, 518-276-6548, Fax: 518-276-3035, E-mail: vashid@rpi.edu. *Application contact:* Mary Foti, Administrative Coordinator, 518-276-6548, Fax: 518-276-3035, E-mail: fotim@rpi.edu.

Rice University, Graduate Programs, George R. Brown School of Engineering, Department of Chemical and Biomolecular Engineering, Houston, TX 77251-1892. Offers chemical and biomolecular engineering (MS, PhD); chemical engineering (M Ch E). Part-time programs available. *Degree requirements:* For master's, thesis (for some programs); for doctorate, thesis/dissertation. *Entrance requirements:* For master's and doctorate, GRE General Test, minimum GPA of 3.0. Additional exam requirements/recommendations for international students: Required—TOEFL (minimum score 600 paper-based; 250 computer-based; 90 iBT). Electronic applications accepted. *Faculty research:* Thermodynamics, phase equilibria, rheology, fluid mechanics, polymers, biomedical engineering, interfacial phenomena, process control, petroleum engineering, reaction engineering and catalysis, biomaterials, metabolic engineering.

Rose-Hulman Institute of Technology, Faculty of Engineering and Applied Sciences, Department of Applied Biology and Biomedical Engineering, Terre Haute, IN 47803-3999. Offers biomedical engineering (MD/MS); MD/MS. Part-time programs available. *Faculty:* 12 full-time (6 women). *Students:* 5 full-time (2 women), 1 international. Average age 23. 8 applicants, 75% accepted, 4 enrolled. In 2010, 2 master's awarded. *Degree requirements:* For master's, thesis. *Entrance requirements:* For master's, GRE, minimum GPA of 3.0. Additional exam requirements/recommendations for international students: Required—TOEFL (minimum score 580 paper-based; 237 computer-based; 92 iBT). *Application deadline:* For fall admission, 2/1 priority date for domestic students. Applications are processed on a rolling basis. Application fee: $0. *Expenses:* Tuition: Full-time $35,595; part-time $1038 per credit hour. *Financial support:* In 2010–11, 5 students received support; fellowships with full and partial tuition reimbursements available, research assistantships with full and partial tuition reimbursements available, institutionally sponsored loans, scholarships/grants, and tuition waivers (full and partial) available. *Faculty research:* Soft tissue biomechanics, tissue-biomaterial interaction, biomaterials, biomedical instrumentation, biomedical fluid mechanics. Total annual research expenditures: $28,703. *Unit head:* Dr. Lee Waite, Chairman, 812-877-8404, Fax: 812-877-3198, E-mail: lee.waite@rose-hulman.edu. *Application contact:* Dr. Daniel J. Moore, Associate Dean of the Faculty, 812-877-8110, Fax: 812-877-8061, E-mail: daniel.j.moore@rose-hulman.edu.

Rutgers, The State University of New Jersey, New Brunswick, Graduate School-New Brunswick, Program in Biomedical Engineering, Piscataway, NJ 08854-8097. Offers MS, PhD. MS, PhD offered jointly with University of Medicine and Dentistry of New Jersey. Part-time programs available. Terminal master's awarded for partial completion of doctoral program. *Degree requirements:* For master's, thesis optional; for doctorate, comprehensive exam, thesis/dissertation. *Entrance requirements:* For master's and doctorate, GRE General Test, minimum GPA of 3.0. Additional exam requirements/recommendations for international students: Required—TOEFL. Electronic applications accepted. *Expenses:* Tuition, state resident: full-time $7200; part-time $600 per credit. Tuition, nonresident: full-time $11,124; part-time $927 per credit. *Faculty research:* Molecular, cellular and nanosystems bioengineering; biomaterials and tissue engineering; biomechanics and rehabilitation engineering; integrative systems physiology and biomedical instrumentation; computational bioengineering and biomedical imaging.

St. Cloud State University, School of Graduate Studies, College of Science and Engineering, Academic Center for Regulatory Affairs and Services, St. Cloud, MN 56301-4498. Offers MS. Part-time programs available. *Degree requirements:* For master's, final paper. *Entrance requirements:* For master's, GRE General Test, minimum GPA of 2.75. *Expenses:* Contact institution.

Saint Louis University, Graduate Education, Parks College of Engineering, Aviation, and Technology and Graduate Education, Department of Biomedical Engineering, St. Louis, MO 63103-2097. Offers MS, MS-R, PhD. *Degree requirements:* For master's, thesis optional; for doctorate, thesis/dissertation. *Entrance requirements:* For master's, GRE General Test, letters of recommendation, resume, interview; for doctorate, GRE General Test, letters of recommendation, resumé, interview, transcripts, goal statement. Additional exam requirements/recommendations for international students: Required—TOEFL (minimum score 525 paper-based; 194 computer-based). *Faculty research:* Tissue engineering and biomaterialsûneural cardiovascular and orthopedic tissue engineering; tissue engineeringûairway remodeling, vasculopathy, and elastic, biodegradable scaffolds; biomechanicsûorthopedics, trauma biomechanics and biomechanical modeling; biosignalsûelectrophysiology, signal processing, and biomechanical instrumentation.

South Dakota School of Mines and Technology, Graduate Division, Program in Biomedical Engineering, Rapid City, SD 57701-3995. Offers MS, PhD. *Entrance requirements:* For doctorate, GRE General Test, 3 letters of recommendation, minimum GPA of 3.0. Additional exam requirements/recommendations for international students: Required—TOEFL.

Southern Illinois University Carbondale, Graduate School, College of Engineering, Program in Biomedical Engineering, Carbondale, IL 62901-4701. Offers ME, MS.

Stanford University, School of Engineering, Department of Mechanical Engineering, Program in Biomechanical Engineering, Stanford, CA 94305-9991. Offers MS. *Entrance requirements:* For master's, GRE General Test, undergraduate degree in engineering, math or sciences. Additional exam requirements/recommendations for international students: Required—TOEFL. *Expenses:* Tuition: Full-time $38,700; part-time $860 per unit. One-time fee: $200 full-time.

State University of New York at Binghamton, Graduate School, Thomas J. Watson School of Engineering and Applied Science, Department of Bioengineering, Binghamton, NY 13902-6000. Offers biomedical engineering (MS, PhD). *Faculty:* 7 full-time (1 woman), 1 part-time/adjunct (0 women). *Students:* 16 full-time (7 women); includes 2 Asian, non-Hispanic/Latino, 8 international. Average age 25. 28 applicants, 29% accepted, 4 enrolled. *Financial support:* In 2010–11, 7 students received support, including 2 fellowships with full tuition reimbursements available (averaging $16,500 per year), 3 teaching assistantships with full tuition reimbursements available (averaging $16,500 per year); career-related internships or fieldwork, Federal Work-Study, institutionally sponsored loans, scholarships/grants, health care benefits, tuition waivers (full and partial), and unspecified assistantships also available. Financial award application deadline: 2/15; financial award applicants required to submit FAFSA. *Unit head:* Dr. Jacques Beaumont, Director, 607-777-5280, Fax: 607-777-5780, E-mail: beaumont@binghamton.edu. *Application contact:* Catherine Smith, Recruiting and Admissions Coordinator, 607-777-2151, Fax: 607-777-2501, E-mail: cmsmith@binghamton.edu.

State University of New York Downstate Medical Center, School of Graduate Studies, Program in Biomedical Engineering, Brooklyn, NY 11203-2098. Offers bioimaging and neuroengineering (PhD); biomedical engineering (MS); MD/PhD. *Degree requirements:* For doctorate, comprehensive exam, thesis/dissertation.

Stevens Institute of Technology, Graduate School, Charles V. Schaefer Jr. School of Engineering, Department of Chemistry, Chemical Biology and Biomedical Engineering, Program in Biomedical Engineering, Hoboken, NJ 07030. Offers M Eng, Certificate. *Students:* 30 full-time (22 women), 13 part-time (0 women); includes 10 Asian, non-Hispanic/Latino; 4 Hispanic/Latino, 9 international. Average age 25. *Unit head:* Arthur Ritter, Director, 201-216-8290. *Application contact:* Graduate Admissions, 800-496-4935, Fax: 201-216-8044, E-mail: gradadmissions@stevens.edu.

Stony Brook University, State University of New York, Graduate School, College of Engineering and Applied Sciences, Department of Biomedical Engineering, Stony Brook, NY 11794. Offers biomedical engineering (MS, PhD, Certificate); medical physics (MS, PhD). *Faculty:* 14 full-time (3 women). *Students:* 76 full-time (28 women), 3 part-time (1 woman); includes 11 Asian, non-Hispanic/Latino; 2 Hispanic/Latino, 38 international. Average age 26. 252 applicants, 19% accepted, 18 enrolled. In 2010, 17 master's, 7 doctorates awarded. *Degree requirements:* For doctorate, thesis/dissertation, qualifying exams. *Entrance requirements:* For master's and doctorate, GRE General Test. Additional exam requirements/recommendations for international students: Required—TOEFL. *Application deadline:* For fall admission, 1/15 for domestic students. Application fee: $100. *Expenses:* Tuition, state resident: full-time $8370; part-time $349 per credit. Tuition, nonresident: full-time $13,780; part-time $574 per credit. Required fees: $994. *Financial support:* In 2010–11, 39 research assistantships, 15 teaching assistantships were awarded; fellowships also available. Total annual research expenditures: $5.7 million. *Unit head:* Dr. Helene Benveniste, Chair, 631-632-8521, Fax: 631-632-8577. *Application contact:* Graduate Director, 631-444-2303, Fax: 631-444-6646.

Texas A&M University, College of Engineering, Department of Biomedical Engineering, College Station, TX 77843. Offers M Eng, MS, D Eng, PhD. Part-time programs available. *Faculty:* 17. *Students:* 82 full-time (32 women), 6 part-time (2 women); includes 16 minority (2 Black or African American, non-Hispanic/Latino; 9 Asian, non-Hispanic/Latino; 5 Hispanic/Latino), 35 international. Average age 27. In 2010, 13 master's, 6 doctorates awarded. *Degree requirements:* For master's, thesis (MS); for doctorate, dissertation (PhD). *Entrance requirements:* For master's and doctorate, GRE General Test, leveling courses if non-engineering undergraduate major. Additional exam requirements/recommendations for international students: Required—TOEFL. *Application deadline:* For fall admission, 7/1 priority date for domestic students, 6/1 for international students; for winter admission, 11/1 priority date for domestic students, 3/1 for international students; for spring admission, 4/1 priority date for domestic students, 10/1 for international students. Applications are processed on a rolling basis. Application fee: $50 ($75 for international students). Electronic applications accepted. *Financial support:* In 2010–11, research assistantships with partial tuition reimbursements (averaging $12,600 per year), teaching assistantships (averaging $11,400 per year) were awarded; fellowships with partial tuition reimbursements, career-related internships or fieldwork, scholarships/grants, and unspecified assistantships also available. Financial award application deadline: 4/15; financial award applicants required to submit FAFSA. *Faculty research:* Medical lasers, optical biosensors, medical instrumentation, cardiovascular mechanics, orthopedic mechanics. *Unit head:* Gerard L. Cote, Head, 979-845-4196, Fax: 979-845-4450, E-mail: gcote@tamu.edu. *Application contact:* Dr. Fidel Fernandez, Academic Advisor, 979-845-5532, Fax: 979-845-4450, E-mail: fidel@tamu.edu.

Thomas Jefferson University, Jefferson College of Graduate Studies, PhD Program in Tissue Engineering and Regenerative Medicine, Philadelphia, PA 19107. Offers PhD. *Faculty:* 18 full-time (6 women). *Students:* 4 full-time (3 women); includes 1 Asian, non-Hispanic/Latino. 3 applicants, 0% accepted, 0 enrolled. In 2010, 2 doctorates awarded. *Degree requirements:* For doctorate, comprehensive exam, thesis/dissertation. *Entrance requirements:* For doctorate, GRE General Test, minimum GPA of 3.2. Additional exam requirements/recommendations for international students: Required—TOEFL (minimum score 250 computer-based; 100 iBT) or IELTS. *Application deadline:* For fall admission, 1/15 priority date for domestic and international students. Applications are processed on a rolling basis. Application fee: $50. Electronic applications accepted. *Financial support:* In 2010–11, 4 students received support, including 4 fellowships with full tuition reimbursements available (averaging $52,883 per year); Federal Work-Study, institutionally sponsored loans, traineeships, and stipend also available. Financial award application deadline: 5/1; financial award applicants required to submit FAFSA. *Faculty research:* Skeletal development, biomaterials, bone implant interaction, tissue engineering, high resolution imaging. Total annual research expenditures: $8 million. *Unit head:* Dr. Irving Shapiro, Program Director, 215-955-7217, Fax: 215-955-9159, E-mail: irving.shapiro@jefferson.edu. *Application contact:* Marc E. Stearns, Director of Admissions, 215-503-0155, Fax: 215-503-9920, E-mail: jcgs-info@jefferson.edu.

Tufts University, School of Engineering, Department of Biomedical Engineering, Medford, MA 02155. Offers ME, MS, PhD. Part-time programs available. Terminal master's awarded for partial completion of doctoral program. *Degree requirements:* For master's, thesis (for some programs); for doctorate, thesis/dissertation. *Entrance requirements:* For master's and doctorate, GRE General Test. Additional exam requirements/recommendations for international students: Required—TOEFL (minimum score 550 paper-based; 213 computer-based; 80 iBT). Electronic applications accepted. *Expenses:* Tuition: Full-time $39,624; part-time $3962 per course. Required fees: $40 per year. Full-time tuition and fees vary according to degree level, program and student level. Part-time tuition and fees vary according to course load.

Tulane University, School of Science and Engineering, Department of Biomedical Engineering, New Orleans, LA 70118-5669. Offers MS, PhD. MS and PhD offered through the Graduate School. Part-time programs available. Terminal master's awarded for partial completion of doctoral program. *Degree requirements:* For master's, thesis (for some programs); for doctorate, thesis/dissertation. *Entrance requirements:* For master's and doctorate, GRE General Test, minimum B average in undergraduate course work. Additional exam requirements/recommendations for international students: Required—TOEFL. Electronic applications accepted. *Faculty research:* Pulmonary and biofluid mechanics and biomechanics of bone, biomaterials science, finite element analysis, electric fields of the brain.

Université de Montréal, Faculty of Medicine, Institute of Biomedical Engineering, Montréal, QC H3C 3J7, Canada. Offers M Sc A, PhD, DESS. M Sc A and PhD programs offered jointly with École Polytechnique de Montréal. *Degree requirements:* For master's, thesis; for doctorate, thesis/dissertation, general exam. *Entrance requirements:* For master's and doctorate, proficiency in French, knowledge of English. Electronic applications accepted. *Faculty research:* Electrophysiology, biomechanics, instrumentation, imaging, simulation.

The University of Akron, Graduate School, College of Engineering, Department of Biomedical Engineering, Akron, OH 44325. Offers MS, PhD. Part-time and evening/weekend programs available. *Faculty:* 10 full-time (4 women). *Students:* 25 full-time (9 women), 8 part-time (4 women); includes 3 Asian, non-Hispanic/Latino; 1 Hispanic/Latino, 14 international. Average age 28. 52 applicants, 60% accepted, 11 enrolled. In 2010, 8 master's, 1 doctorate awarded. *Degree requirements:* For master's, thesis; for doctorate, one foreign language, thesis/dissertation, candidacy exam, qualifying exam. *Entrance requirements:* For master's, GRE, minimum GPA of 2.75, three letters of recommendation, statement of purpose, resume; for doctorate, GRE, minimum GPA of 3.0 with bachelor's degree, 3.5 with master's degree; three letters of recommendation; personal statement, resume. Additional exam requirements/recommendations for international students: Required—TOEFL (minimum score 590 paper-based; 243 computer-based; 96 iBT). *Application deadline:* Applications are processed on a rolling basis. Application fee: $30 ($40 for international students). Electronic applications accepted. *Expenses:* Tuition, state resident: full-time $6800; part-time $378 per credit hour. Tuition, nonresident: full-time $11,644; part-time $647 per credit hour. Required fees: $1265. One-time fee: $30 full-time. *Financial support:* In 2010–11, 7 research assistantships with full tuition reimbursements, 12 teaching assistantships with full tuition reimbursements were awarded; career-related internships or fieldwork, Federal Work-Study, and scholarships/grants also available. *Faculty research:* Signal and image processing, physiological controls and instrumentation, biomechanics—orthopaedic and hemodynamic, biomaterials for gene and drug delivery systems, telemedicine. Total annual research expenditures: $102,623. *Unit head:* Dr. Daniel Sheffer, Chair, 330-972-6977, E-mail: dsheffer@uakron.edu. *Application contact:* Dr. Daniel Sheffer, Chair, 330-972-6977, E-mail: dsheffer@uakron.edu.

The University of Akron, Graduate School, College of Engineering, Program in Engineering (Biomedical Engineering Specialization), Akron, OH 44325. Offers MS. *Students:* 1 applicant, 100% accepted. *Entrance requirements:* For master's, GRE, minimum GPA of 2.75, three letters of recommendation, statement of purpose, resume. Additional exam requirements/recommendations for international students: Required—TOEFL (minimum score 590 paper-based; 243 computer-based; 96 iBT). *Application deadline:* Applications are processed on a rolling basis. Application fee: $30 ($40 for international students). Electronic applications accepted. *Expenses:* Tuition, state resident: full-time $6800; part-time $378 per credit hour. Tuition, nonresident: full-time $11,644; part-time $647 per credit hour. Required fees: $1265. One-time fee: $30 full-time. *Unit head:* Dr. Daniel Sheffer, Chair, 330-972-6977, E-mail: sheffer@uakron.edu. *Application contact:* Director of Graduate Studies.

The University of Alabama at Birmingham, School of Engineering, Program in Biomedical Engineering, Birmingham, AL 35294. Offers MSBME, PhD. *Students:* 33 full-time (13 women), 4 part-time (0 women); includes 5 minority (3 Black or African American, non-Hispanic/Latino; 2 Asian, non-Hispanic/Latino), 13 international. Average age 26. 81 applicants, 27% accepted, 10 enrolled. In 2010, 6 master's, 1 doctorate awarded. *Degree requirements:* For master's, thesis or alternative, oral exam; for doctorate, comprehensive exam, thesis/dissertation. *Entrance requirements:* For master's and doctorate, GRE General Test. Additional exam requirements/recommendations for international students: Required—TOEFL. *Expenses:* Tuition, state resident: full-time $5482. Tuition, nonresident: full-time $12,430. Tuition and fees vary according to program. *Financial support:* Fellowships with full tuition reimbursements, research assistantships, career-related internships or fieldwork, Federal Work-Study, and institutionally sponsored loans available. *Unit head:* Dr. Timothy M. Wick, Chair, 205-934-8420, E-mail: macsmith@uab.edu. *Application contact:* Julie Bryant, Director of Graduate Admissions, 205-934-8227, Fax: 205-934-8413, E-mail: jbryant@uab.edu.

University of Alberta, Faculty of Medicine and Dentistry and Faculty of Graduate Studies and Research, Graduate Programs in Medicine, Department of Biomedical Engineering, Edmonton, AB T6G 2E1, Canada. Offers biomedical engineering (M Sc); medical sciences (PhD). *Degree requirements:* For master's, thesis; for doctorate, thesis/dissertation. Electronic applications accepted. *Faculty research:* Medical imaging, rehabilitation engineering, biomaterials and tissue engineering, biomechanics, cryobiology.

The University of Arizona, Graduate Interdisciplinary Programs, Graduate Interdisciplinary Program in Biomedical Engineering, Tucson, AZ 85721. Offers MS, PhD. *Faculty:* 5 full-time (1 woman). *Students:* 36 full-time (19 women), 3 part-time (0 women); includes 2 Asian, non-Hispanic/Latino; 4 Hispanic/Latino; 13 Two or more races, non-Hispanic/Latino. Average age 26. 46 applicants, 20% accepted, 7 enrolled. In 2010, 1 master's, 3 doctorates awarded. *Entrance requirements:* For master's, GRE, 3 letters of recommendation; for doctorate, GRE, 3 letters of recommendation, statement of purpose. Additional exam requirements/recommendations for international students: Required—TOEFL (minimum score 600 paper-based; 250 computer-based). *Application deadline:* For fall admission, 2/1 for domestic students, 12/1 for international students. Application fee: $65. Electronic applications accepted. *Expenses:* Tuition, state resident: full-time $7692. *Financial support:* In 2010–11, 6 research assistantships with full tuition reimbursements (averaging $18,773 per year) were awarded; institutionally sponsored loans, scholarships/grants, traineeships, health care benefits, tuition waivers (full), and unspecified assistantships also available. *Unit head:* Jennifer Barton, Chair, 520-621-4116, E-mail: barton@u.arizona.edu. *Application contact:* Debbi Howard, Program Coordinator, 520-626-8726, Fax: 520-626-8726, E-mail: dhoward@u.arizona.edu.

University of Arkansas, Graduate School, College of Engineering, Department of Biological and Agricultural Engineering, Program in Biomedical Engineering, Fayetteville, AR 72701-1201. Offers MSBME. *Students:* 1 (woman) full-time, 5 part-time (1 woman), 3 international. 12 applicants, 42% accepted. In 2010, 3 master's awarded. *Application deadline:* For fall admission, 4/1 for international students; for spring admission, 10/1 for international students. Applications are processed on a rolling basis. Application fee: $40 ($50 for international students). Electronic applications accepted. *Financial support:* In 2010–11, 1 research assistantship, 2 teaching assistantships were awarded; fellowships also available. *Unit head:* Dr. Lalit Verma, Department Head, 479-575-2351, Fax: 479-575-2846, E-mail: lverma@uark.edu. *Application contact:* Dr. Jin-Woo Kim, Program Coordinator, 479-575-2351, Fax: 479-575-2846, E-mail: jwkim@uark.edu.

University of Calgary, Faculty of Graduate Studies, Faculty of Kinesiology, Calgary, AB T2N 1N4, Canada. Offers biomedical engineering (M Sc, PhD); kinesiology (M Kin, M Sc, PhD), including biomechanics (PhD), health and exercise physiology (PhD). *Degree requirements:* For master's, thesis (M Sc); for doctorate, thesis/dissertation. *Entrance requirements:* Additional exam requirements/recommendations for international students: Required—TOEFL. Electronic applications accepted. *Faculty research:* Load acting on the human body, muscle mechanics and physiology, optimizing high performance athlete performance, eye movement in sports, analysis of body composition.

University of Calgary, Faculty of Graduate Studies, Schulich School of Engineering, Graduate Program in Biomedical Engineering, Calgary, AB T2N 1N4, Canada. Offers M Eng, M Sc, PhD. *Degree requirements:* For master's, thesis; for doctorate, comprehensive exam, thesis/dissertation. *Faculty research:* Bioinstrumentation and imaging, clinical engineering, biomechanics, biomaterials, systems physiology.

University of California, Davis, College of Engineering, Graduate Group in Biomedical Engineering, Davis, CA 95616. Offers MS, PhD. *Degree requirements:* For master's, thesis; for doctorate, thesis/dissertation. *Entrance requirements:* For master's and doctorate, GRE General Test, minimum GPA of 3.25. Additional exam requirements/recommendations for international students: Required—TOEFL (minimum score 550 paper-based; 213 computer-based), IELTS (minimum score 7). Electronic applications accepted. *Faculty research:* Orthopedic biomechanics, cell/molecular biomechanics and transport, biosensors and instrumentation, human movement, biomedical image analysis, spectroscopy.

University of California, Irvine, School of Engineering, Department of Biomedical Engineering, Irvine, CA 92697. Offers MS, PhD. Part-time programs available. *Students:* 109 full-time (32 women), 8 part-time (4 women); includes 41 minority (1 Black or African American, non-Hispanic/Latino; 1 American Indian or Alaska Native, non-Hispanic/Latino; 36 Asian, non-Hispanic/Latino; 2 Hispanic/Latino; 1 Two or more races, non-Hispanic/Latino), 30 international. Average age 28. 259 applicants, 32% accepted, 35 enrolled. In 2010, 5 master's, 10 doctorates awarded. Terminal master's awarded for partial completion of doctoral program. *Degree requirements:* For doctorate, thesis/dissertation. *Entrance requirements:* For master's and doctorate, GRE General Test, minimum GPA of 3.0, 3 letters of recommendation. Additional exam requirements/recommendations for international students: Required—TOEFL (minimum score 550 paper-based; 213 computer-based). *Application deadline:* For fall admission, 1/15 priority date for domestic students, 1/15 for international students. Applications are processed on a rolling basis. Application fee: $80 ($100 for international students). Electronic applications accepted. *Financial support:* Fellowships, research assistantships with full tuition reimburse-

Biomedical Engineering

University of California, Irvine (continued)

ments, teaching assistantships, institutionally sponsored loans, traineeships, health care benefits, and unspecified assistantships available. Financial award application deadline: 3/1; financial award applicants required to submit FAFSA. *Faculty research:* Biomedical photonics, biomedical imaging, biomedical nano- and micro-scale systems, biomedical computation/modeling, neuroengineering, tissue engineering. *Unit head:* Prof. Abraham P. Lee, Chair, 949-824-8155, Fax: 949-824-1727, E-mail: aplee@uci.edu. *Application contact:* Karen Stephens, Graduate Academic Counselor, 949-824-3494, Fax: 949-824-1727, E-mail: aplee@uci.edu.

University of California, Los Angeles, Graduate Division, Henry Samueli School of Engineering and Applied Science, Interdepartmental Graduate Program in Biomedical Engineering, Los Angeles, CA 90095-1600. Offers MS, PhD. *Faculty:* 8 full-time (1 woman). *Students:* 168 full-time (55 women); includes 1 Black or African American, non-Hispanic/Latino; 63 Asian, non-Hispanic/Latino; 6 Hispanic/Latino, 46 international. 305 applicants, 51% accepted, 57 enrolled. In 2010, 32 master's, 13 doctorates awarded. *Degree requirements:* For master's, comprehensive exam or thesis; for doctorate, thesis/dissertation, qualifying exams. *Entrance requirements:* For master's, GRE General Test, minimum GPA of 3.0; for doctorate, GRE General Test, minimum GPA of 3.25. Additional exam requirements/recommendations for international students: Required—TOEFL (minimum score 560 paper-based; 220 computer-based; 87 iBT). *Application deadline:* For fall admission, 12/15 for domestic and international students. Application fee: $70 ($90 for international students). Electronic applications accepted. *Financial support:* In 2010–11, 45 fellowships, 91 research assistantships, 26 teaching assistantships were awarded; career-related internships or fieldwork, Federal Work-Study, institutionally sponsored loans, and tuition waivers (full and partial) also available. Financial award application deadline: 1/15; financial award applicants required to submit FAFSA. Total annual research expenditures: $2.9 million. *Unit head:* Dr. James Dunn, Chair, 310-794-5945. *Application contact:* Larry Nadeau, Student Affairs Officer, 310-794-5945, Fax: 310-794-5956, E-mail: nadeau@ea.ucla.edu.

University of Cincinnati, Graduate School, College of Engineering, Department of Biomedical Engineering, Cincinnati, OH 45221. Offers bioinformatics (PhD); biomechanics (PhD); medical imaging (PhD); tissue engineering (PhD). Part-time programs available. *Degree requirements:* For doctorate, one foreign language, thesis/dissertation. *Entrance requirements:* For doctorate, GRE General Test. Additional exam requirements/recommendations for international students: Required—TOEFL (minimum score 600 paper-based; 250 computer-based).

University of Connecticut, Graduate School, School of Engineering, Department of Electrical and Computer Engineering, Field of Biomedical Engineering, Storrs, CT 06269. Offers MS, PhD. Terminal master's awarded for partial completion of doctoral program. *Degree requirements:* For master's, comprehensive exam, thesis or alternative; for doctorate, thesis/dissertation. *Entrance requirements:* For master's and doctorate, GRE General Test. Additional exam requirements/recommendations for international students: Required—TOEFL (minimum score 550 paper-based; 213 computer-based). Electronic applications accepted.

University of Florida, Graduate School, College of Engineering, Department of Biomedical Engineering, Gainesville, FL 32611. Offers ME, MS, PhD, Certificate. *Faculty:* 9 full-time (1 woman), 2 part-time/adjunct (1 woman). *Students:* 81 full-time (28 women), 5 part-time (3 women); includes 2 Black or African American, non-Hispanic/Latino; 7 Asian, non-Hispanic/Latino; 2 Hispanic/Latino, 47 international. Average age 26. 174 applicants, 24% accepted, 14 enrolled. In 2010, 19 master's, 9 doctorates awarded. Terminal master's awarded for partial completion of doctoral program. *Degree requirements:* For master's, comprehensive exam (for some programs), thesis (for some programs); for doctorate, comprehensive exam (for some programs), thesis/dissertation (for some programs). *Entrance requirements:* For master's, GRE General Test, minimum GPA of 3.1; for doctorate, GRE General Test, minimum GPA of 3.3. Additional exam requirements/recommendations for international students: Required—TOEFL (minimum score 550 paper-based; 213 computer-based; 80 iBT), IELTS (minimum score 6). *Application deadline:* For fall admission, 12/31 priority date for domestic students, 12/31 for international students; for spring admission, 6/30 for domestic and international students. Applications are processed on a rolling basis. Application fee: $30. Electronic applications accepted. *Expenses:* Tuition, state resident: full-time $10,915.92. Tuition, nonresident: full-time $28,309. *Financial support:* In 2010–11, 55 students received support, including 3 fellowships with full tuition reimbursements available, 49 research assistantships with full tuition reimbursements available (averaging $18,365 per year), 3 teaching assistantships (averaging $21,573 per year). Financial award application deadline: 12/31; financial award applicants required to submit FAFSA. *Faculty research:* Neural engineering, tissue engineering, biomedical imaging. *Unit head:* Dr. Bruce Wheeler, Chair, 352-273-9222, Fax: 352-392-9791, E-mail: bwheeler@ufl.edu. *Application contact:* Hans Van Oostrom, Graduate Coordinator, 352-273-9315, Fax: 352-392-9791, E-mail: oostrom@ufl.edu.

University of Houston, Cullen College of Engineering, Department of Biomedical Engineering, Houston, TX 77204. Offers PhD. Part-time programs available. *Students:* 4 full-time (3 women), 1 (woman) part-time; includes 1 Asian, non-Hispanic/Latino, 2 international. Average age 27. 1 applicant, 100% accepted, 0 enrolled. *Degree requirements:* For doctorate, seminar. *Entrance requirements:* For doctorate, GRE, BS or MS in biomedical engineering or related field, minimum GPA of 3.3 on last 60 hours. Additional exam requirements/recommendations for international students: Required—TOEFL (minimum score 580 paper-based; 237 computer-based; 92 iBT), IELTS (minimum score 6). *Application deadline:* For fall admission, 5/1 for domestic students, 4/1 for international students; for spring admission, 11/1 for domestic students, 10/1 for international students. Application fee: $25 ($75 for international students). Electronic applications accepted. *Expenses:* Tuition, state resident: full-time $8592; part-time $358 per credit hour. Tuition, nonresident: full-time $16,032; part-time $668 per credit hour. Required fees: $2889. Tuition and fees vary according to course load and program. *Financial support:* In 2010–11, 2 research assistantships with partial tuition reimbursements (averaging $13,136 per year), 1 teaching assistantship with partial tuition reimbursement (averaging $14,000 per year) were awarded. *Unit head:* Dr. Metin Akay, Chair, 832-842-8860, Fax: 713-743-2501, E-mail: makay@uh.edu. *Application contact:* Dr. Larry Witte, Associate Dean, Graduate Programs, 713-743-4205, Fax: 713-743-4214, E-mail: witte@uh.edu.

The University of Iowa, Graduate College, College of Engineering, Department of Biomedical Engineering, Iowa City, IA 52242-1316. Offers MS, PhD. Part-time programs available. *Faculty:* 15 full-time (2 women). *Students:* 99 full-time (39 women); includes 8 minority (1 Black or African American, non-Hispanic/Latino; 6 Asian, non-Hispanic/Latino; 1 Hispanic/Latino), 43 international. Average age 26. 60 applicants, 90% accepted, 30 enrolled. In 2010, 10 master's, 5 doctorates awarded. *Degree requirements:* For master's, thesis (for some programs), written and oral exam; for doctorate, comprehensive exam, thesis/dissertation, written and oral exam. *Entrance requirements:* For master's, GRE, minimum undergraduate GPA of 3.0; for doctorate, GRE. Additional exam requirements/recommendations for international students: Required—TOEFL (minimum score 600 paper-based; 250 computer-based; 100 iBT). *Application deadline:* For fall admission, 3/1 for domestic and international students; for spring admission, 8/1 for domestic and international students. Applications are processed on a rolling basis. Application fee: $60 ($100 for international students). Electronic applications accepted. *Financial support:* In 2010–11, 7 fellowships with partial tuition reimbursements (averaging $17,236 per year), 67 research assistantships with partial tuition reimbursements (averaging $23,776 per year), 8 teaching assistantships with partial tuition reimbursements (averaging $16,635 per year) were awarded; scholarships/grants, health care benefits, and unspecified assistantships also available. Support available to part-time students. Financial award application deadline: 3/1. *Faculty research:* Biomaterials, tissue engineering and cellular mechanics; cell motion analysis and modeling; spinal and joint biomechanics, digital human modeling, and biomedical imaging; bioinformatics and computational biology; fluid and cardiovascular biomechanics. Total annual research expenditures: $8.6 million. *Unit head:* Dr. Joseph M. Reinhardt, Departmental Executive Officer, 319-335-5634, Fax: 319-335-5631, E-mail: joe-reinhardt@uiowa.edu. *Application contact:* Lorena Lovetinsky, Secretary, 319-384-0671, Fax: 319-335-5631, E-mail: bme@engineering.uiowa.edu.

The University of Iowa, Roy J. and Lucille A. Carver College of Medicine and Graduate College, Biosciences Program, Iowa City, IA 52242-1316. Offers anatomy and biology (PhD); biochemistry (PhD); biology (PhD); biomedical engineering (PhD); chemistry (PhD); free radical and radiation biology (PhD); genetics (PhD); human toxicology (PhD); immunology (PhD); microbiology (PhD); molecular and cellular biology (PhD); molecular physiology and biophysics (PhD); neuroscience (PhD); pharmacology (PhD); physical therapy and rehabilitation science (PhD); speech and hearing (PhD). *Faculty:* 310 full-time. *Students:* 9 full-time (5 women); includes 4 minority (1 Black or African American, non-Hispanic/Latino; 2 Asian, non-Hispanic/Latino; 1 Hispanic/Latino), 3 international. 225 applicants. *Degree requirements:* For doctorate, thesis/dissertation. *Entrance requirements:* For doctorate, GRE General Test, minimum GPA of 3.0. Additional exam requirements/recommendations for international students: Required—TOEFL (minimum score 600 paper-based; 250 computer-based; 100 iBT). *Application deadline:* For fall admission, 1/15 priority date for domestic and international students. Applications are processed on a rolling basis. Application fee: $60 ($100 for international students). Electronic applications accepted. *Expenses:* Contact institution. *Financial support:* In 2010–11, 9 students received support, including 9 research assistantships with full tuition reimbursements available (averaging $25,000 per year); fellowships, teaching assistantships, health care benefits also available. *Unit head:* Dr. Andrew F. Russo, Director, 319-335-7872, Fax: 319-335-7656, E-mail: andrew-russo@uiowa.edu. *Application contact:* Jodi M. Graff, Program Associate, 319-335-8305, Fax: 319-335-7656, E-mail: biosciences-admissions@uiowa.edu.

University of Kentucky, Graduate School, Program in Biomedical Engineering, Lexington, KY 40506-0032. Offers MSBE, PBME, PhD. *Degree requirements:* For master's, comprehensive exam, thesis optional; for doctorate, comprehensive exam, thesis/dissertation. *Entrance requirements:* For master's, GRE General Test, minimum undergraduate GPA of 2.75; for doctorate, GRE General Test, minimum graduate GPA of 3.0. Additional exam requirements/recommendations for international students: Required—TOEFL (minimum score 550 paper-based; 213 computer-based). Electronic applications accepted. *Faculty research:* Signal processing and dynamical systems, cardiopulmonary mechanics and systems, bioelectromagnetics, neuromotor control and electrical stimulation, biomaterials and musculoskeletal biomechanics.

University of Maine, Graduate School, Program in Biomedical Sciences, Orono, ME 04469. Offers biomedical engineering (PhD); cell and molecular biology (PhD); neuroscience (PhD); toxicology (PhD). *Students:* 11 full-time (8 women), 13 part-time (6 women); includes 1 American Indian or Alaska Native, non-Hispanic/Latino, 5 international. Average age 29. 32 applicants, 19% accepted, 6 enrolled.Application fee: $60. *Expenses:* Tuition, state resident: full-time $400. Tuition, nonresident: full-time $1050. *Financial support:* In 2010–11, 8 research assistantships (averaging $25,625 per year) were awarded. *Unit head:* Dr. Carol Kim, Unit Head, 207-581-2803. *Application contact:* Dr. Carol Kim, Unit Head, 207-581-2803.

University of Massachusetts Dartmouth, Graduate School, Program in Biomedical Engineering and Biotechnology, North Dartmouth, MA 02747-2300. Offers PhD. Part-time programs available. *Students:* 18 full-time (12 women), 8 part-time (1 woman), 17 international. Average age 29. 19 applicants, 63% accepted, 3 enrolled. In 2010, 1 doctorate awarded. *Degree requirements:* For doctorate, comprehensive exam, thesis/dissertation. *Entrance requirements:* For doctorate, GRE, minimum GPA of 3.0, 3 letters of recommendation. Additional exam requirements/recommendations for international students: Required—TOEFL (minimum score 550 paper-based; 213 computer-based). *Application deadline:* For fall admission, 4/20 for domestic students, 2/20 for international students; for spring admission, 11/15 for domestic students, 9/15 for international students. Application fee: $40 ($60 for international students). Electronic applications accepted. *Expenses:* Tuition, state resident: full-time $2071; part-time $86 per credit. Tuition, nonresident: full-time $8099; part-time $337 per credit. Required fees: $9446; $394 per credit. One-time fee: $75. Part-time tuition and fees vary according to class time, course load, degree level and reciprocity agreements. *Financial support:* In 2010–11, 3 fellowships with full tuition reimbursements (averaging $10,512 per year), 10 research assistantships with full tuition reimbursements (averaging $10,868 per year), 1 teaching assistantship with full tuition reimbursement (averaging $3,000 per year) were awarded; unspecified assistantships also available. Financial award application deadline: 3/1; financial award applicants required to submit FAFSA. *Faculty research:* Tetracycline-encapsulated chitosan microspheres, artificial tissues, sensor arrays for orthopedic rehab, blue light cures, healing bandages. Total annual research expenditures; $1.4 million. *Unit head:* Dr. Vijay Chalivendra, Co-Director, 508-910-6572, E-mail: vchalivendra@umassd.edu. *Application contact:* Elan Turcotte-Shamski, Graduate Admissions Officer, 508-999-8604, Fax: 508-999-8183, E-mail: graduate@umassd.edu.

University of Medicine and Dentistry of New Jersey, Graduate School of Biomedical Sciences, Graduate Programs in Biomedical Sciences–Newark, Department of Biomedical Engineering, Newark, NJ 07107. Offers Certificate. *Entrance requirements:* Additional exam requirements/recommendations for international students: Required—TOEFL. Electronic applications accepted.

University of Medicine and Dentistry of New Jersey, Graduate School of Biomedical Sciences, Graduate Programs in Biomedical Sciences–Piscataway, Program in Biomedical Engineering, Piscataway, NJ 08854-5635. Offers MS, PhD, MD/PhD. MS, PhD offered jointly with Rutgers, The State University of New Jersey, New Brunswick. *Degree requirements:* For master's, thesis, qualifying exam; for doctorate, thesis/dissertation, qualifying exam. *Entrance requirements:* For master's and doctorate, GRE General Test. Additional exam requirements/recommendations for international students: Required—TOEFL. Electronic applications accepted.

University of Memphis, Graduate School, Herff College of Engineering, Program in Biomedical Engineering, Memphis, TN 38152. Offers MS, PhD. *Faculty:* 7 full-time (1 woman), 2 part-time/adjunct (1 woman). *Students:* 37 full-time (15 women), 13 part-time (3 women); includes 2 Black or African American, non-Hispanic/Latino; 1 Asian, non-Hispanic/Latino; 1 Hispanic/Latino, 11 international. Average age 29. 19 applicants, 68% accepted, 13 enrolled. In 2010, 6 master's awarded. *Degree requirements:* For master's, thesis or alternative, oral exam; for doctorate, thesis/dissertation, exams. *Entrance requirements:* For master's, GRE General Test or MAT, minimum undergraduate GPA of 3.0; for doctorate, GRE General Test, minimum undergraduate GPA of 3.25 or master's degree in biomedical engineering. *Application deadline:* For fall admission, 8/1 priority date for domestic students; for spring admission, 12/1 for domestic students. Applications are processed on a rolling basis. Application fee: $35 ($60 for international students). Electronic applications accepted. *Financial support:* In 2010–11, 8 students received support; fellowships with full tuition reimbursements available, research assistantships with full tuition reimbursements available, career-related internships or fieldwork, Federal Work-Study, scholarships/grants, and unspecified assistantships available. Financial award application deadline: 2/15; financial award applicants required to submit FAFSA. *Faculty research:* Biomaterials and cell/tissue engineering, especially for orthopedic applications; biosensors; biomechanics (hemodynamics, soft tissue, lung, gait); electrophysiology; novel medical image-acquisition devices. *Unit head:* Dr. Eugene C. Eckstein, Chairman, 901-678-3733, Fax: 901-678-5281, E-mail: eckstein@memphis.edu. *Application contact:* Dr. Steven M. Slack, Associate Dean, 901-678-4791, Fax: 901-678-5281, E-mail: sslack@memphis.edu.

University of Miami, Graduate School, College of Engineering, Department of Biomedical Engineering, Coral Gables, FL 33124. Offers MSBE, PhD. Part-time programs available. *Degree requirements:* For master's, thesis (for some programs); for doctorate, comprehensive exam, thesis/dissertation. *Entrance requirements:* For master's and doctorate, GRE General Test, minimum GPA of 3.0. Additional exam requirements/recommendations for international students: Required—TOEFL (minimum score 550 paper-based; 213 computer-based). Electronic applications accepted. *Faculty research:* Biomedical signal processing and instrumentation, cardiovascular engineering, optics and lasers, rehabilitation engineering, tissue mechanics.

University of Michigan, Horace H. Rackham School of Graduate Studies, College of Engineering, Department of Biomedical Engineering, Ann Arbor, MI 48109. Offers MS, MSE, PhD. Part-time programs available. *Students:* 213 full-time (87 women), 3 part-time (0 women). 454 applicants, 36% accepted, 82 enrolled. In 2010, 58 master's, 23 doctorates awarded. *Degree requirements:* For master's, thesis optional; for doctorate, comprehensive exam, oral defense of dissertation. *Entrance requirements:* For master's, GRE General Test; for doctorate, GRE General Test, master's degree. Additional exam requirements/recommendations for international students: Required—TOEFL. *Application deadline:* Applications are processed on a rolling basis. Application fee: $65 ($75 for international students). Electronic applications accepted. *Expenses:* Tuition, state resident: full-time $17,784; part-time $1116 per credit hour. Tuition, nonresident: full-time $35,944; part-time $2125 per credit hour. International tuition: $35,994 full-time. Required fees: $95 per semester. Tuition and fees vary according to course load, degree level and program. *Financial support:* Fellowships, research assistantships, teaching assistantships, Federal Work-Study, scholarships/grants, traineeships, and tuition waivers (partial) available. Financial award applicants required to submit FAFSA. *Faculty research:* Cellular and tissue engineering, biotechnology, biomedical materials, biomechanics, biomedical imaging, rehabilitation engineering. *Unit head:* Douglas Noll, Chair, Biomedical Engineering, 734-647-1091, Fax: 734-936-1905, E-mail: biomede@umich.edu. *Application contact:* Maria E. Steele, Senior Student Administration Assistant, 734-647-1091, Fax: 734-936-1905, E-mail: msteele@umich.edu.

University of Minnesota, Twin Cities Campus, Institute of Technology and Medical School, Department of Biomedical Engineering, Minneapolis, MN 55455-0213. Offers MS, PhD, MD/PhD. Part-time programs available. Terminal master's awarded for partial completion of doctoral program. *Degree requirements:* For master's, thesis optional; for doctorate, thesis/dissertation. *Entrance requirements:* For master's and doctorate, GRE General Test. *Faculty research:* Biomedical microelectromechanical systems, tissue engineering, biomechanics and blood/fluid dynamics, biomaterials, soft tissue mechanics, biomedical imaging.

University of Nevada, Las Vegas, Graduate College, Howard R. Hughes College of Engineering, Department of Mechanical Engineering, Las Vegas, NV 89154-4027. Offers aerospace engineering (MS); biomedical engineering (MS); materials and nuclear engineering (MS); mechanical engineering (MSE, PhD). Part-time programs available. *Faculty:* 17 full-time (0 women), 10 part-time/adjunct (0 women). *Students:* 43 full-time (6 women), 24 part-time (6 women); includes 24 minority (1 Black or African American, non-Hispanic/Latino; 4 Asian, non-Hispanic/Latino; 1 Hispanic/Latino; 1 Native Hawaiian or other Pacific Islander, non-Hispanic/Latino; 17 Two or more races, non-Hispanic/Latino), 24 international. Average age 30. 32 applicants, 84% accepted, 15 enrolled. In 2010, 10 master's, 4 doctorates awarded. *Degree requirements:* For master's, comprehensive exam, thesis (for some programs), project; for doctorate, comprehensive exam, thesis/dissertation. *Entrance requirements:* For master's and doctorate, GRE General Test. Additional exam requirements/recommendations for international students: Required—TOEFL (minimum score 550 paper-based; 213 computer-based; 80 iBT), IELTS (minimum score 7). *Application deadline:* For fall admission, 5/1 priority date for domestic and international students; for spring admission, 10/1 priority date for domestic and international students. Applications are processed on a rolling basis. Application fee: $60 ($95 for international students). Electronic applications accepted. *Expenses:* Tuition, area resident: Part-time $239.50 per credit. Tuition, state resident: part-time $239.50 per credit. Tuition, nonresident: part-time $503 per credit. Required fees: $108 per semester. Tuition and fees vary according to course load, program and reciprocity agreements. *Financial support:* In 2010–11, 37 students received support, including 21 research assistantships with partial tuition reimbursements available (averaging $13,335 per year), 16 teaching assistantships with partial tuition reimbursements available (averaging $11,000 per year); institutionally sponsored loans, scholarships/grants, health care benefits, and unspecified assistantships also available. Financial award application deadline: 3/1. *Faculty research:* Dynamics and control systems; energy systems including renewable and nuclear; computational fluid and solid mechanics; structures, materials and manufacturing; vibrations and acoustics. Total annual research expenditures: $3 million. *Unit head:* Dr. Woosoon Yim, Chair/Professor, 702-895-0956, Fax: 702-895-3936, E-mail: wy@me.unlv.edu. *Application contact:* Graduate College Admissions Evaluator, 702-895-3320, Fax: 702-895-4180, E-mail: gradcollege@unlv.edu.

University of Nevada, Reno, Graduate School, Interdisciplinary Program in Biomedical Engineering, Reno, NV 89557. Offers MS, PhD. Terminal master's awarded for partial completion of doctoral program. *Degree requirements:* For master's, thesis optional; for doctorate, thesis/dissertation. *Entrance requirements:* For master's, GRE General Test (recommended), minimum GPA of 2.75; for doctorate, GRE General Test (recommended), minimum GPA of 3.0. Additional exam requirements/recommendations for international students: Required—TOEFL (minimum score 500 paper-based; 173 computer-based; 61 iBT), IELTS (minimum score 6). Electronic applications accepted. *Expenses:* Tuition, state resident: full-time $2219; part-time $246 per credit. Tuition, nonresident: part-time $510 per credit. International tuition: $9009 full-time. Required fees: $59 per term. One-time fee: $101. Tuition and fees vary according to course load. *Faculty research:* Bioengineering, biophysics, biomedical instrumentation, biosensors.

University of New Mexico, Graduate School, School of Engineering, Program in Biomedical Engineering, Albuquerque, NM 87131-2039. Offers PhD. *Expenses:* Tuition, state resident: full-time $5991; part-time $251 per credit hour. Tuition, nonresident: full-time $14,405; part-time $800.20 per credit hour. Tuition and fees vary according to course level, course load, program and reciprocity agreements. *Unit head:* Dr. Steven Graves, Program Director, 505-277-5521. *Application contact:* Dr. Steven Graves, Program Director, 505-277-5521.

The University of North Carolina at Chapel Hill, School of Medicine and Graduate School, Graduate Programs in Medicine, Joint Department of Biomedical Engineering UNC-Chapel Hill and NC State, Chapel Hill, NC 27599. Offers MS, PhD. *Faculty:* 35 full-time (9 women), 77 part-time/adjunct (16 women). *Students:* 88 full-time (30 women); includes 4 Black or African American, non-Hispanic/Latino; 6 Asian, non-Hispanic/Latino; 3 Hispanic/Latino, 11 international. Average age 28. 300 applicants, 15% accepted, 22 enrolled. In 2010, 5 master's, 12 doctorates awarded. Terminal master's awarded for partial completion of doctoral program. *Degree requirements:* For master's, comprehensive exam, thesis, ethics seminar; for doctorate, comprehensive exam, thesis/dissertation, qualifying exam, teaching and ethics seminar. *Entrance requirements:* For master's, GRE General Test, minimum GPA of 3.0; for doctorate, GRE General Test, minimum GPA of 3.3. Additional exam requirements/recommendations for international students: Required—TOEFL. *Application deadline:* For fall admission, 1/15 for domestic and international students. Application fee: $77. Electronic applications accepted. *Financial support:* In 2010–11, 48 students received support, including 8 fellowships with full tuition reimbursements available (averaging $25,750 per year), 34 research assistantships with full tuition reimbursements available (averaging $23,400 per year), 12 teaching assistantships with full tuition reimbursements available (averaging $16,000 per year); Federal Work-Study, scholarships/grants, traineeships, health care benefits, and unspecified assistantships also available. Financial award application deadline: 12/15; financial award applicants required to submit FAFSA. *Faculty research:* Biomedical imaging, rehabilitation engineering, microsystems engineering. *Unit head:* Dr. Nancy L. Allbritton, Chair and Professor, 919-966-1175, Fax: 919-966-2963, E-mail: nlallbri@unc.edu. *Application contact:* Jennifer Allen, Graduate Programs coordinator/ Student Services manager, 919-966-8088, Fax: 919-966-2963, E-mail: jnallen@email.unc.edu.

University of Ottawa, Faculty of Graduate and Postdoctoral Studies, Ottawa—Carlton Joint Program in Biomedical Engineering, Ottawa, ON K1N 6N5, Canada. Offers MA Sc. *Degree requirements:* For master's, thesis or alternative. *Entrance requirements:* For master's, honors degree or equivalent, minimum B average.

University of Rhode Island, Graduate School, College of Engineering, Department of Electrical, Computer and Biomedical Engineering, Kingston, RI 02881. Offers MS, PhD, Graduate Certificate. Part-time programs available. *Faculty:* 18 full-time (3 women). *Students:* 28 full-time (6 women), 24 part-time (2 women); includes 10 minority (1 Black or African American, non-Hispanic/Latino; 6 Asian, non-Hispanic/Latino; 3 Hispanic/Latino), 12 international. In 2010, 12 master's, 1 doctorate awarded. *Degree requirements:* For master's, comprehensive exam (for some programs), thesis optional; for doctorate, comprehensive exam, thesis/dissertation. *Entrance requirements:* For master's and doctorate, 2 letters of recommendation.

Additional exam requirements/recommendations for international students: Required—TOEFL (minimum score 550 paper-based; 213 computer-based). *Application deadline:* For fall admission, 7/15 for domestic students, 2/1 for international students; for spring admission, 11/15 for domestic students, 7/15 for international students. Application fee: $65. Electronic applications accepted. *Expenses:* Tuition, state resident: full-time $9588; part-time $533 per credit hour. Tuition, nonresident: full-time $22,968; part-time $1276 per credit hour. Required fees: $1282; $68 per semester. Tuition and fees vary according to program. *Financial support:* In 2010–11, 8 research assistantships with full and partial tuition reimbursements (averaging $9,258 per year), 6 teaching assistantships with full and partial tuition reimbursements (averaging $9,889 per year) were awarded. Financial award application deadline: 7/15; financial award applicants required to submit FAFSA. *Faculty research:* Biomedical instrumentation, cardiac physiology and computational modeling, analog/digital CMOS circuits, neural-machine interface, digital circuit design and VLSI testing. Total annual research expenditures: $985,856. *Unit head:* Dr. G. Faye Boudreaux-Bartels, Chair, 401-874-5805, Fax: 401-782-6422, E-mail: boud@ele.uri.edu. *Application contact:* Dr. Godi Fischer, Director of Graduate Studies, 401-874-5879, Fax: 401-782-6422, E-mail: fischer@ele.uri.edu.

University of Rochester, Hajim School of Engineering and Applied Sciences, Department of Biomedical Engineering, Rochester, NY 14627. Offers biomedical engineering (MS, PhD). Part-time programs available. Terminal master's awarded for partial completion of doctoral program. *Degree requirements:* For master's, comprehensive exam; for doctorate, thesis/dissertation, qualifying exam. *Entrance requirements:* For doctorate, GRE General Test. Additional exam requirements/recommendations for international students: Required—TOEFL. *Faculty research:* Biomechanics, biomedical optics, cell and tissue engineering, medical imaging, neuroengineering.

University of Saskatchewan, College of Graduate Studies and Research, College of Engineering, Division of Biomedical Engineering, Saskatoon, SK S7N 5A2, Canada. Offers M Eng, M Sc, PhD. *Degree requirements:* For master's, thesis (for some programs); for doctorate, thesis/dissertation. *Entrance requirements:* For master's and doctorate, GRE. Additional exam requirements/recommendations for international students: Required—TOEFL.

University of Southern California, Graduate School, Viterbi School of Engineering, Department of Biomedical Engineering, Los Angeles, CA 90089. Offers biomedical engineering (PhD); medical device and diagnostic engineering (MS); medical imaging and imaging informatics (MS). Postbaccalaureate distance learning degree programs offered (minimal on-campus study). *Faculty:* 13 full-time (1 woman), 14 part-time/adjunct (3 women). *Students:* 177 full-time (63 women), 58 part-time (20 women); includes 63 minority (7 Black or African American, non-Hispanic/Latino; 41 Asian, non-Hispanic/Latino; 12 Hispanic/Latino; 3 Two or more races, non-Hispanic/Latino), 116 international. 402 applicants, 39% accepted, 68 enrolled. In 2010, 61 master's, 18 doctorates awarded. Terminal master's awarded for partial completion of doctoral program. *Degree requirements:* For master's, thesis optional; for doctorate, thesis/dissertation. *Entrance requirements:* For master's and doctorate, GRE General Test. *Application deadline:* For fall admission, 12/1 priority date for domestic and international students; for spring admission, 9/15 priority date for domestic and international students. Applications are processed on a rolling basis. Application fee: $85. Electronic applications accepted. *Expenses:* Tuition: Full-time $31,240; part-time $1420 per unit. Required fees: $600. One-time fee: $35 full-time. Full-time tuition and fees vary according to degree level and program. *Financial support:* In 2010–11, fellowships with full tuition reimbursements (averaging $30,000 per year), research assistantships with full tuition reimbursements (averaging $20,000 per year), teaching assistantships with full tuition reimbursements (averaging $20,000 per year) were awarded; career-related internships or fieldwork, scholarships/grants, health care benefits, and unspecified assistantships also available. Financial award application deadline: 12/1; financial award applicants required to submit CSS PROFILE or FAFSA. *Faculty research:* Medical ultrasound, BioMEMS, neural prosthetics, computational bioengineering, bioengineering of vision, medical devices. Total annual research expenditures: $13.9 million. *Unit head:* Dr. Norberto Grzywacz, Chair, 213-740-7237, E-mail: bmedept@usc.edu. *Application contact:* Mischal C. Diasanta, Student Advisor, 213-740-0344, E-mail: diasanta@usc.edu.

University of South Florida, Graduate School, College of Engineering, Department of Chemical and Biomedical Engineering, Tampa, FL 33620. Offers biomedical engineering (MSBE, PhD); chemical and biomedical engineering (MCH, ME, MSES, PhD); chemical engineering (PhD). Part-time programs available. *Faculty:* 11 full-time (1 woman). *Students:* 62 full-time (28 women), 15 part-time (6 women); includes 9 Black or African American, non-Hispanic/Latino; 7 Asian, non-Hispanic/Latino; 7 Hispanic/Latino, 26 international. Average age 29. 88 applicants, 44% accepted, 20 enrolled. In 2010, 15 master's, 11 doctorates awarded. Terminal master's awarded for partial completion of doctoral program. *Degree requirements:* For master's, comprehensive exam, thesis (for some programs); for doctorate, comprehensive exam, thesis/dissertation. *Entrance requirements:* For master's, GRE General Test, minimum GPA of 3.0 in last 60 hours of course work; for doctorate, GRE General Test. Additional exam requirements/recommendations for international students: Required—TOEFL (minimum score 550 paper-based; 213 computer-based; 79 iBT). *Application deadline:* For fall admission, 2/15 for domestic students, 1/2 priority date for international students; for spring admission, 10/15 for domestic students, 6/1 priority date for international students. Application fee: $30. Electronic applications accepted. *Financial support:* In 2010–11, 35 students received support, including 24 research assistantships with tuition reimbursements available (averaging $14,593 per year), 17 teaching assistantships with tuition reimbursements available (averaging $15,754 per year); unspecified assistantships also available. Financial award applicants required to submit FAFSA. *Faculty research:* Biomedical engineering, supercritical fluid technology, advanced materials, surface and interfacial science, alternative and renewable energy. Total annual research expenditures: $989,529. *Unit head:* Dr. Venkat R. Bhethanabotla, Chair, 813-974-3997. *Application contact:* Dr. Vinay Gupta, Graduate Admissions Coordinator for Chemical Engineering, 813-974-0851, Fax: 813-974-3651.

The University of Tennessee, Graduate School, College of Engineering, Department of Mechanical, Aerospace and Biomedical Engineering, Program in Biomedical Engineering, Knoxville, TN 37996. Offers MS, PhD, MS/PhD. Part-time programs available. Postbaccalaureate distance learning degree programs offered (minimal on-campus study). *Faculty:* 6 full-time (1 woman), 2 part-time/adjunct (0 women). *Students:* 34 full-time (7 women), 4 part-time (2 women); includes 2 Black or African American, non-Hispanic/Latino; 3 Asian, non-Hispanic/Latino, 11 international. Average age 27. 62 applicants, 45% accepted, 10 enrolled. In 2010, 8 master's, 1 doctorate awarded. *Degree requirements:* For master's, thesis or alternative; for doctorate, comprehensive exam, thesis/dissertation. *Entrance requirements:* For master's, GRE General Test, Minimum GPA of 2.7 (US degree holders); 3.0 (International degree holders); 3-References; Statement of purpose; for doctorate, GRE General Test, Minimum 3.0 (previous graduate course work); 3-References; Statement of purpose. Additional exam requirements/recommendations for international students: Required—TOEFL (minimum score 550 paper-based; 213 computer-based). *Application deadline:* For fall admission, 2/1 priority date for domestic and international students; for spring admission, 6/15 for domestic and international students. Applications are processed on a rolling basis. Application fee: $35. Electronic applications accepted. *Expenses:* Tuition, state resident: full-time $7440; part-time $414 per credit hour. Tuition, nonresident: full-time $22,478; part-time $1250 per credit hour. Required fees: $922; $43 per credit hour. Tuition and fees vary according to program. *Financial support:* In 2010–11, 12 students received support, including 1 fellowship with full tuition reimbursement available (averaging $12,000 per year), 12 research assistantships with full tuition reimbursements available (averaging $15,480 per year), 6 teaching assistantships with full tuition reimbursements available (averaging $10,500 per year); career-related internships or fieldwork, Federal Work-Study, institutionally sponsored loans, health care benefits, and unspecified assistantships also available. Financial award application deadline: 2/1; financial award applicants required to submit FAFSA. *Faculty research:* Bioimaging; biomechanics; biorobotics; biosensors; biomaterials. *Unit head:* Dr. William Hamel, Head, 865-974-5115, Fax: 865-974-5274, E-mail: whamel@utk.edu. *Application contact:* Dr. Gary V. Smith, Associate Head, 865-974-5271, Fax: 865-974-5274, E-mail: gvsmith@utk.edu.

Biomedical Engineering

MS IN BIOMEDICAL ENGINEERING

Program Overview

A Master of Science (M.S.)degree in Biomedical Engineering g (BME) at UTSA is offered through a joint graduate program with The University of Texas Health Science Center at San Antonio (UTHSCSA).

A matrix of academic tracks is offered based on segments of biomedical engineering and/or areas of clinical emphasis. Specifically, the program has emphases in the following areas: biomaterials, biomechanics, and bioimaging. The biological areas covered are orthopedics/dental tissues, cardiovascular systems, and neurological systems.

Focus Areas:

*Biomaterials *Biomechanics *Biomedical Imaging *Cellular Engineering *Nano-biotechnology *Tissue Engineering *Tissue Regeneration

Messages from our graduated students:

.. The great faculty in this program has made this the best experience in my life. – N. Torres

.. Outstanding academic experience for me and I've learned many skills that will help me as I continue my professional research career.- J. Wiemers

.. Very good institution for the people who want to excel in research. – M.Banka

Please visit us at
http://engineering.utsa.edu/BME or email to coegradinfo@utsa.edu

---

The University of Texas at Austin, Graduate School, Cockrell School of Engineering, Department of Biomedical Engineering, Austin, TX 78712-1111. Offers MS, PhD, MD/PhD. MD/PhD offered jointly with The University of Texas Medical Branch. Part-time programs available. *Degree requirements:* For master's, thesis optional; for doctorate, comprehensive exam, thesis/dissertation. *Entrance requirements:* For master's and doctorate, GRE General Test. Additional exam requirements/recommendations for international students: Required—TOEFL (minimum score 550 paper-based; 213 computer-based). Electronic applications accepted. *Faculty research:* Biomechanics, bioengineering, tissue engineering, tissue optics, biothermal studies.

The University of Texas at Dallas, Erik Jonsson School of Engineering and Computer Science, Department of Bioengineering, Richardson, TX 75080. Offers biomedical engineering (MS, PhD). *Faculty:* 3 full-time (2 women). *Students:* 12 full-time (5 women), 8 international. Average age 24. 42 applicants, 33% accepted, 8 enrolled. *Degree requirements:* For master's, thesis (for some programs); for doctorate, comprehensive exam, thesis/dissertation. *Entrance requirements:* For master's, GRE (minimum scores of 500 in verbal, 700 in quantitative and 4 in analytical writing), minimum GPA of 3.0 in upper-division quantitative course work; for doctorate, GRE (minimum scores of 500 in verbal, 700 in quantitative and 4 in analytical writing), minimum GPA of 3.5 in upper-division quantitative course work. Additional exam requirements/recommendations for international students: Required—TOEFL (minimum score 550 paper-based; 215 computer-based). *Application deadline:* For fall admission, 7/15 for domestic students, 5/1 priority date for international students; for spring admission, 11/15 for domestic students, 9/1 priority date for international students. Applications are processed on a rolling basis. Application fee: $50 ($100 for international students). Electronic applications accepted. *Expenses:* Tuition, state resident: full-time $10,248; part-time $569 per credit hour. Tuition, nonresident: full-time $18,544; part-time $1030 per credit hour. Tuition and fees vary according to course load. *Financial support:* In 2010–11, 7 students received support, including 5 research assistantships with partial tuition reimbursements available (averaging $13,890 per year); career-related internships or fieldwork, Federal Work-Study, institutionally sponsored loans, scholarships/grants, and unspecified assistantships also available. Support available to part-time students. Financial award application deadline: 4/30; financial award applicants required to submit FAFSA. *Faculty research:* Bio-nanotechnology, organic electronics, system-level design for medical devices, computational geometry and biomedical computing. *Unit head:* Dr. Mathukumalli Vidyasagar, Head, 972-883-4679, E-mail: m.vidyasagar@utdallas.edu. *Application contact:* Laranda D. Eakin, Administrative Services Officer, 972-883-4657, E-mail: laranda.eakin@utdallas.edu.

The University of Texas at San Antonio, College of Engineering, Department of Biomedical Engineering, San Antonio, TX 78249-0617. Offers MS, PhD. Part-time and evening/weekend programs available. *Faculty:* 7 full-time (2 women), 1 part-time/adjunct (0 women). *Students:* 14 full-time (9 women), 34 part-time (14 women); includes 16 minority (2 Black or African American, non-Hispanic/Latino; 2 Asian, non-Hispanic/Latino; 12 Hispanic/Latino), 11 international. Average age 28. 56 applicants, 61% accepted, 15 enrolled. In 2010, 7 master's, 3 doctorates awarded. *Degree requirements:* For master's, comprehensive exam (for some programs), thesis (for some programs); for doctorate, comprehensive exam, thesis/dissertation (for some programs). *Entrance requirements:* For master's, GRE, minimum GPA of 3.0 in last 60 hours; for doctorate, GRE. Additional exam requirements/recommendations for international students: Required—TOEFL (minimum score 500 paper-based; 173 computer-based; 61 iBT), IELTS (minimum score 5). *Application deadline:* For fall admission, 7/1 for domestic students, 4/1 for international students; for spring admission, 11/1 for domestic students, 9/1 for international students. Applications are processed on a rolling basis. Application fee: $45 ($80 for international students). Electronic applications accepted. *Expenses:* Tuition, state resident: full-time $4172; part-time $231.75 per credit hour. Tuition, nonresident: full-time $15,332; part-time $851.75 per credit hour. *Financial support:* In 2010–11, 21 students received support, including 10 research assistantships (averaging $20,295 per year), 2 teaching assistantships (averaging $10,800 per year); career-related internships or fieldwork, scholarships/grants, tuition waivers, and unspecified assistantships also available. Support available to part-time students. Total annual research expenditures: $115,470. *Unit head:* Dr. Joo L. Ong, Department Chair, 210-458-7084, Fax: 210-458-7007, E-mail: anson.ong@utsa.edu. *Application contact:* Veronica Flannagan, Assistant Dean of the Graduate School, 210-458-4330, Fax: 210-458-4332, E-mail: graduatestudies@utsa.edu.

See M.S. Close-Up on page 149 and Ph.D. Close-Up on page 151.

The University of Texas Southwestern Medical Center at Dallas, Southwestern Graduate School of Biomedical Sciences, Division of Basic Science, Biomedical Engineering Program, Dallas, TX 75390. Offers MS, PhD. Programs offered jointly with The University of Texas at Arlington. *Faculty:* 46 full-time (6 women), 22 part-time/adjunct (3 women). *Students:* 11 full-time (2 women), 11 part-time (2 women); includes 2 minority (both Asian, non-Hispanic/Latino), 13 international. Average age 26. 112 applicants, 0% accepted, 0 enrolled. In 2010, 1 doctorate awarded. *Degree requirements:* For master's, comprehensive exam or thesis; for doctorate, comprehensive exam, thesis/dissertation. *Entrance requirements:* For master's, GRE General Test, minimum GPA of 3.0; for doctorate, GRE General Test, minimum GPA of 3.4. Additional exam requirements/recommendations for international students: Required—TOEFL. *Application deadline:* For fall admission, 1/5 priority date for domestic students. Applications are processed on a rolling basis. Application fee: $0. Electronic applications accepted. *Financial support:* Fellowships with partial tuition reimbursements, research assistantships, career-related internships or fieldwork, institutionally sponsored loans, scholarships/grants, and tuition waivers (partial) available. Financial award application deadline: 3/1; financial award applicants required to submit FAFSA. *Faculty research:* Noninvasive image analysis, biomaterials development, rehabilitation engineering, biomechanics, bioinstrumentation. *Unit head:* Dr. Peter P. Antich, Chair, 214-648-2856, Fax: 214-648-2991, E-mail: peter.antich@utsouthwestern.edu. *Application contact:* Kay Emerson, Program Assistant, 214-648-2503, Fax: 214-648-2991, E-mail: kay.emerson@utsouthwestern.edu.

The University of Toledo, College of Graduate Studies, College of Engineering and College of Medicine and Life Sciences, PhD Program in Biomedical Engineering, Toledo, OH 43606-3390. Offers PhD. *Degree requirements:* For doctorate, thesis/dissertation, qualifying exam. *Entrance requirements:* For doctorate, GRE General Test, minimum GPA of 3.3. Additional exam requirements/recommendations for international students: Required—TOEFL (minimum score 550 paper-based; 213 computer-based; 80 iBT). Electronic applications accepted. *Expenses:* Tuition, state resident: full-time $11,426; part-time $476 per credit hour. Tuition, nonresident: full-time $21,660; part-time $903 per credit hour. One-time fee: $62. *Faculty research:* Biomechanics, biomaterials, tissue engineering, artificial organs, biosensors.

University of Toronto, School of Graduate Studies, Physical Sciences Division, Faculty of Applied Science and Engineering, Institute of Biomaterials and Biomedical Engineering, Toronto, ON M5S 1A1, Canada. Offers biomedical engineering (MA Sc, PhD); clinical biomedical engineering (MH Sc). Part-time programs available. *Degree requirements:* For master's, thesis (for some programs), research project (MH Sc), oral presentation (MA Sc); for doctorate, thesis/dissertation, qualifying exam. *Entrance requirements:* For master's, bachelor's degree or equivalent in engineering, physical or biological science (MA Sc), minimum A– average; bachelor's degree or equivalent in applied science or engineering (MH Sc); for doctorate, master's degree in engineering, engineering science, medicine, dentistry, or a physical or biological science. Additional exam requirements/recommendations for international students: Required—TOEFL (minimum score 600 paper-based; 260 computer-based), TWE (minimum score 4), Michigan English Language Assessment Battery, IELTS, or COPE.

University of Vermont, Graduate College, College of Engineering and Mathematics, Program in Biomedical Engineering, Burlington, VT 05405. Offers MS. *Students:* 4 (2 women). 22 applicants, 23% accepted, 3 enrolled. In 2010, 3 master's awarded. *Degree requirements:* For master's, thesis. *Entrance requirements:* For master's, GRE General Test. Additional exam requirements/recommendations for international students: Required—TOEFL (minimum score

550 paper-based; 213 computer-based; 80 iBT). *Application deadline:* For fall admission, 2/1 priority date for domestic students. Applications are processed on a rolling basis. Application fee: $40. Electronic applications accepted. *Expenses:* Tuition, state resident: part-time $537 per credit hour. Tuition, nonresident: part-time $1355 per credit hour. *Financial support:* Fellowships, research assistantships, teaching assistantships available. Financial award application deadline: 3/1. *Unit head:* Dr. J. Iatridis, Coordinator, 802-656-3343. *Application contact:* Dr. J. Iatridis, Coordinator, 802-656-3343.

University of Virginia, School of Engineering and Applied Science, Department of Biomedical Engineering, Charlottesville, VA 22903. Offers ME, MS, PhD. *Faculty:* 7 full-time (0 women). *Students:* 74 full-time (25 women), 1 part-time (0 women); includes 1 Black or African American, non-Hispanic/Latino; 9 Asian, non-Hispanic/Latino; 1 Hispanic/Latino; 1 Two or more races, non-Hispanic/Latino, 14 international. Average age 26. 267 applicants, 23% accepted, 12 enrolled. In 2010, 6 master's, 15 doctorates awarded. *Degree requirements:* For master's, project or thesis; for doctorate, thesis/dissertation. *Entrance requirements:* For master's, GRE General Test, 3 letters of recommendation; for doctorate, GRE General Test, 3 letters of recommendation, essay. Additional exam requirements/recommendations for international students: Required—TOEFL (minimum score 600 paper-based; 250 computer-based; 90 iBT), IELTS (minimum score 7). *Application deadline:* For fall admission, 8/1 for domestic students, 4/1 for international students; for winter admission, 12/1 for domestic students, 8/1 for international students; for spring admission, 5/1 for domestic students, 1/1 for international students. Applications are processed on a rolling basis. Application fee: $60. Electronic applications accepted. *Financial support:* Fellowships, research assistantships, teaching assistantships available. Financial award application deadline: 1/15; financial award applicants required to submit FAFSA. *Faculty research:* Cardiopulmonary and neural engineering, cellular engineering, image processing, orthopedics and rehabilitation engineering. *Unit head:* Michael B. Lawrence, Interim Chair, 434-924-5101, Fax: 434-982-3870, E-mail: bme-dept@virginia.edu. *Application contact:* Jeffrey Holmes, Director of Graduate Programs, 434-243-6906, E-mail: bmegrad@virginia.edu.

University of Washington, Graduate School, College of Engineering and School of Medicine, Department of Bioengineering, Seattle, WA 98195-5061. Offers bioengineering (MS, PhD); bioengineering and nanotechnology (PhD); medical engineering (MME); pharmaceutical bioengineering (MS). Evening/weekend programs available. Postbaccalaureate distance learning degree programs offered (no on-campus study). *Faculty:* 30 full-time (10 women), 10 part-time/ adjunct (2 women). *Students:* 109 full-time (47 women), 46 part-time (19 women); includes 3 Black or African American, non-Hispanic/Latino; 1 American Indian or Alaska Native, non-Hispanic/Latino; 33 Asian, non-Hispanic/Latino; 4 Hispanic/Latino, 28 international. Average age 26. 442 applicants, 19% accepted, 39 enrolled. In 2010, 19 master's, 16 doctorates awarded. *Degree requirements:* For master's, comprehensive exam, thesis; for doctorate, comprehensive exam, thesis/dissertation, qualifying exam, general exam, thesis defense. *Entrance requirements:* For master's and doctorate, GRE General Test, Minimum GPA of 3.0, transcripts, statement of purpose, letters of recommendation. Additional exam requirements/ recommendations for international students: Required—TOEFL (minimum score 580 paper-based; 237 computer-based; 92 iBT); Recommended—IELTS (minimum score 7). *Application deadline:* For fall admission, 12/15 priority date for domestic students, 12/1 priority date for international students. Application fee: $75. Electronic applications accepted. *Financial support:* In 2010–11, 2 students received support, including 25 fellowships with full tuition reimbursements available (averaging $19,098 per year), 111 research assistantships with full tuition reimbursements available (averaging $19,224 per year), 15 teaching assistantships with full tuition reimbursements available (averaging $19,224 per year); Federal Work-Study, institutionally sponsored loans, traineeships, health care benefits, and tuition waivers (full) also available. Support available to part-time students. Financial award application deadline: 12/15; financial award applicants required to submit FAFSA. *Faculty research:* Biomaterials and tissue engineering; global health, distributed diagnosis and home healthcare; bioinstrumentation; molecular bioengineering; imaging and image-guided therapy. Total annual research expenditures: $23.4 million. *Unit head:* Dr. Paul Yager, Professor and Chair, 206-685-2000, Fax: 206-685-3300, E-mail: yagerp@u.washington.edu. *Application contact:* Dorian Taylor, Senior Academic Counselor, 206-685-2000, Fax: 206-685-3300, E-mail: bioeng@u.washington.edu.

University of Wisconsin–Madison, Graduate School, College of Engineering, Department of Biomedical Engineering, Madison, WI 53706. Offers MS, PhD. Part-time programs available. *Faculty:* 23 full-time (7 women), 67 part-time/adjunct (14 women). *Students:* 93 full-time (37 women), 10 part-time (2 women); includes 2 Black or African American, non-Hispanic/Latino; 7 Asian, non-Hispanic/Latino; 6 Hispanic/Latino, 25 international. Average age 25. 358 applicants, 12% accepted, 17 enrolled. In 2010, 37 master's, 11 doctorates awarded. Terminal master's awarded for partial completion of doctoral program. *Degree requirements:* For master's, thesis optional; for doctorate, comprehensive exam, thesis/dissertation, 32 credits of coursework beyond MS. *Entrance requirements:* For master's and doctorate, GRE, bachelor's degree in engineering or a physical science (chemistry or physics). Additional exam requirements/ recommendations for international students: Recommended—TOEFL (minimum score 550 paper-based; 213 computer-based; 80 iBT), IELTS (minimum score 6). *Application deadline:* For fall admission, 12/31 for domestic and international students; for spring admission, 10/1 for domestic and international students. Application fee: $56. Electronic applications accepted. *Expenses:* Tuition, state resident: full-time $9887.36; part-time $617.96 per credit. Tuition, nonresident: full-time $24,054; part-time $1503.40 per credit. Required fees: $67.63 per credit. Tuition and fees vary according to reciprocity agreements. *Financial support:* In 2010–11, 77 students received support, including 2 fellowships with full tuition reimbursements available (averaging $22,260 per year), 71 research assistantships with full tuition reimbursements available (averaging $40,800 per year), 18 teaching assistantships with full tuition reimbursements available (averaging $28,175 per year); career-related internships or fieldwork, Federal Work-Study, scholarships/grants, traineeships, and health care benefits also available. *Faculty research:* Biomaterials; bioinstrumentation; cellular scale; biomechanics; biomedical imaging; ergonomics; design, fabrication, and testing of novel micro fabrication techniques; magnetic resonance; tissue engineering; biomedical optics. Total annual research expenditures: $10.2 million. *Unit head:* Dr. Elizabeth Meyerand, Professor and Chair, 608-263-1685, Fax: 608-263-1352, E-mail: bme@engr.wisce.du. *Application contact:* Anne Duchek, Graduate Admissions Coordinator, 608-890-2765, Fax: 608-890-2204, E-mail: amduchek@engr.wisc.edu.

Vanderbilt University, School of Engineering and Graduate School, Department of Biomedical Engineering, Nashville, TN 37240-1001. Offers M Eng, MS, PhD, MD/PhD. *Faculty:* 16 full-time (1 woman), 10 part-time/adjunct (0 women). *Students:* 19 full-time (6 women); includes 1 Asian, non-Hispanic/Latino, 5 international. Average age 26. 178 applicants, 10% accepted, 8 enrolled. In 2010, 15 master's, 4 doctorates awarded. *Degree requirements:* For master's, thesis (for some programs); for doctorate, thesis/dissertation. *Entrance requirements:* For master's, GRE General Test (for all except M Eng); for doctorate, GRE General Test. Additional exam requirements/recommendations for international students: Required—TOEFL. *Application deadline:* For fall admission, 1/15 for domestic and international students; for spring admission, 11/1 for domestic and international students. Application fee: $0. Electronic applications accepted. *Financial support:* In 2010–11, 2 fellowships with full tuition reimbursements (averaging $26,665 per year), 31 research assistantships with full tuition reimbursements (averaging $22,527 per year), 17 teaching assistantships with full tuition reimbursements (averaging $19,000 per year) were awarded; institutionally sponsored loans, scholarships/grants, traineeships, and tuition waivers (partial) also available. Support available to part-time students. Financial award application deadline: 1/15. *Faculty research:* Bio-medical imaging, cell bioengineering, biomedical optics, technology-guided therapy, laser-tissue interaction and spectroscopy. Total annual research expenditures: $10.5 million. *Unit head:* Dr. Todd D. Giorgio, Chair, 615-322-3756, Fax: 615-343-7919, E-mail: todd.d.giorgio@vanderbilt.edu. *Application contact:* Dr. E. Duco Jansen, Director of Graduate Studies, 615-343-1911, Fax: 615-343-7919, E-mail: duco.jansen@vanderbilt.edu.

Virginia Commonwealth University, Graduate School, School of Engineering, Department of Biomedical Engineering, Richmond, VA 23284-9005. Offers MS, PhD, MD/PhD. *Faculty:* 8

Biomedical Engineering

Virginia Commonwealth University (continued)
full-time (2 women). *Students:* 39 full-time (16 women), 16 part-time (6 women); includes 14 minority (4 Black or African American, non-Hispanic/Latino; 7 Asian, non-Hispanic/Latino; 3 Hispanic/Latino), 16 international. 72 applicants, 58% accepted, 20 enrolled. In 2010, 12 master's, 3 doctorates awarded. *Degree requirements:* For master's, thesis; for doctorate, thesis/dissertation, comprehensive oral and written exams. *Entrance requirements:* For master's and doctorate, GRE General Test. Additional exam requirements/recommendations for international students: Required—TOEFL (minimum score 600 paper-based; 250 computer-based; 100 iBT). *Application deadline:* For fall admission, 2/1 priority date for domestic students; for spring admission, 11/15 for domestic students. Application fee: $50. Electronic applications accepted. *Expenses:* Tuition, state resident: full-time $4308; part-time $479 per credit hour. Tuition, nonresident: full-time $8942; part-time $994 per credit hour. Required fees: $2000; $85 per credit hour. Tuition and fees vary according to course level, course load, degree level, campus/location and program. *Financial support:* Applicants required to submit FAFSA. *Faculty research:* Clinical instrumentation, mathematical modeling, neurosciences, radiation physics and rehabilitation. *Unit head:* Dr. Rosalyn S. Hobson, Associate Dean for Graduate Affairs, 804-828-3925, E-mail: rhobson@vcu.edu. *Application contact:* Dr. Gary L. Bowlin, Coordinator, 804-828-2592, E-mail: glbowlin@vcu.edu.

Wake Forest University, Virginia Tech-Wake Forest University School of Biomedical Engineering and Sciences, Winston-Salem, NC 27109. Offers biomedical engineering (MS, PhD); DVM/PhD; MD/PhD. Terminal master's awarded for partial completion of doctoral program. *Degree requirements:* For master's, comprehensive exam, thesis; for doctorate, comprehensive exam, thesis/dissertation. *Entrance requirements:* For master's and doctorate, GRE, 3 letters of recommendation. Additional exam requirements/recommendations for international students: Required—TOEFL (minimum score 603 paper-based; 250 computer-based). Electronic applications accepted. *Faculty research:* Biomechanics, cell and tissue engineering, medical imaging, medical physics.

Washington University in St. Louis, School of Engineering and Applied Science, Department of Biomedical Engineering, St. Louis, MO 63130-4899. Offers MS, D Sc, PhD. Terminal master's awarded for partial completion of doctoral program. *Degree requirements:* For master's, thesis optional; for doctorate, thesis/dissertation. *Entrance requirements:* For master's, GRE, minimum GPA of 3.0; for doctorate, GRE General Test, minimum GPA of 3.5. Additional exam requirements/recommendations for international students: Required—TOEFL. Electronic applications accepted. *Faculty research:* Cell and tissue engineering, molecular engineering, neural engineering.

Wayne State University, College of Engineering, Department of Biomedical Engineering, Detroit, MI 48202. Offers MS, PhD. *Faculty:* 13 full-time (3 women), 2 part-time/adjunct (1 woman). *Students:* 110 full-time (38 women), 71 part-time (33 women); includes 22 minority (6 Black or African American, non-Hispanic/Latino; 15 Asian, non-Hispanic/Latino; 1 Two or more races, non-Hispanic/Latino), 60 international. Average age 28. 125 applicants, 70% accepted, 40 enrolled. In 2010, 30 master's, 8 doctorates awarded. *Degree requirements:* For master's, thesis optional; for doctorate, thesis/dissertation. *Entrance requirements:* For master's, GRE (optional); for doctorate, GRE, personal statement. Additional exam requirements/recommendations for international students: Required—TOEFL (minimum score 550 paper-based; 213 computer-based); Recommended—TWE (minimum score 6). *Application deadline:* For fall admission, 7/1 priority date for domestic students, 6/1 for international students; for winter admission, 11/1 priority date for domestic students, 10/1 for international students; for

spring admission, 3/15 priority date for domestic students, 2/1 for international students). Applications are processed on a rolling basis. Application fee: $30 ($50 for international students). Electronic applications accepted. *Expenses:* Tuition, state resident: full-time $7662; part-time $478.85 per credit hour. Tuition, nonresident: full-time $16,920; part-time $1057.55 per credit hour. Required fees: $571.20; $35.70 per credit hour. $188.05 per semester. Tuition and fees vary according to course load and program. *Financial support:* In 2010–11, 4 fellowships (averaging $16,875 per year), 10 research assistantships (averaging $17,142 per year), 6 teaching assistantships (averaging $16,984 per year) were awarded. *Faculty research:* Injury and orthopedic biomechanics, neurophysiology of pain, smart sensors, biomaterials and imaging. *Unit head:* Albert King, Chair, 313-577-1347, Fax: 313-577-8333, E-mail: aa0003@wayne.edu. *Application contact:* Cynthia Bir, Graduate Director, 313-577-3830, E-mail: ac0451@wayne.edu.

Worcester Polytechnic Institute, Graduate Studies and Research, Department of Biomedical Engineering, Worcester, MA 01609-2280. Offers biomedical engineering (M Eng, MS, PhD, Graduate Certificate). Part-time and evening/weekend programs available. *Faculty:* 7 full-time (1 woman), 1 part-time/adjunct (0 women). *Students:* 41 full-time (18 women), 8 part-time (5 women); includes 1 Black or African American, non-Hispanic/Latino; 1 Hispanic/Latino; 4 Native Hawaiian or other Pacific Islander, non-Hispanic/Latino, 10 international. 126 applicants, 36% accepted, 20 enrolled. In 2010, 16 master's, 1 doctorate awarded. Terminal master's awarded for partial completion of doctoral program. *Degree requirements:* For master's, thesis optional; for doctorate, comprehensive exam, thesis/dissertation. *Entrance requirements:* For master's, GRE General Test, Statement of Purpose, 3 letters of recommendation; for doctorate, GRE General Test, Statement of Purpose, 3 letters of recommendation, statement of purpose. Additional exam requirements/recommendations for international students: Required—TOEFL (minimum score 550 paper-based; 213 computer-based; 79 iBT), IELTS (minimum score 6.5). *Application deadline:* For fall admission, 1/1 priority date for domestic and international students. Application fee: $70. Electronic applications accepted. *Expenses:* Tuition: Full-time $20,862; part-time $1159 per term. One-time fee: $15. *Financial support:* Career-related internships or fieldwork, institutionally sponsored loans, scholarships/grants, and unspecified assistantships available. Financial award application deadline: 1/1; financial award applicants required to submit FAFSA. *Faculty research:* Biomedical sensors and instrumentation, biomechanics, nuclear magnetic resonance image and spectroscopy, medical imaging, biomaterial/tissue interactions, engineering and regenerative medicine, biosignal processing. *Unit head:* Dr. Ki H Chon, Head, 508-831-5447, Fax: 508-831-5541, E-mail: kichon@wpi.edu. *Application contact:* Dr. Glenn Gaudette, Graduate Coordinator, 508-831-5447, Fax: 508-831-5541, E-mail: gaudette@wpi.edu.

Wright State University, School of Graduate Studies, College of Engineering and Computer Science, Programs in Engineering, Program in Biomedical and Human Factors Engineering, Dayton, OH 45435. Offers biomedical engineering (MSE); human factors engineering (MSE). Part-time programs available. *Degree requirements:* For master's, thesis or course option alternative. *Entrance requirements:* Additional exam requirements/recommendations for international students: Required—TOEFL. *Faculty research:* Medical imaging, functional electrical stimulation, implantable aids, man-machine interfaces, expert systems.

Yale University, Graduate School of Arts and Sciences, School of Engineering and Applied Science, Department of Biomedical Engineering, New Haven, CT 06520. Offers MS, PhD. *Faculty research:* Biomedical imaging and biosignals; biomechanics; biomolecular engineering and biotechnology.

Biotechnology

Albany College of Pharmacy and Health Sciences, Program in Pharmacy, Albany, NY 12208. Offers biotechnology (MS); cytotechnology (MS); health outcomes research (MS); pharmaceutical sciences (MS); pharmacy (Pharm D); pharmacy administration (MS). *Accreditation:* ACPE. *Faculty:* 59 full-time (25 women), 9 part-time/adjunct (3 women). *Students:* 467 full-time (251 women), 2 part-time (both women); includes 19 Black or African American, non-Hispanic/Latino; 60 Asian, non-Hispanic/Latino; 3 Hispanic/Latino; 6 Two or more races, non-Hispanic/Latino, 52 international. Average age 26. 1,648 applicants, 8% accepted, 76 enrolled. In 2010, 216 first professional degrees awarded. *Degree requirements:* For master's, thesis (for some programs); for Pharm D, comprehensive exam (for some programs), practice experience. *Entrance requirements:* For Pharm D, PCAT, minimum GPA of 3.0; for master's, GRE, minimum GPA of 3.0. Additional exam requirements/recommendations for international students: Required—TOEFL (minimum score 600 paper-based; 250 computer-based; 100 iBT). *Application deadline:* For fall admission, 3/1 for domestic and international students. Applications are processed on a rolling basis. Application fee: $75. Electronic applications accepted. *Expenses:* Tuition: Full-time $28,830; part-time $815 per credit hour. Required fees: $670. *Financial support:* Federal Work-Study and scholarships/grants available. Support available to part-time students. Financial award application deadline: 3/1; financial award applicants required to submit FAFSA. *Faculty research:* Therapeutic use of drugs, pharmacokinetics, drug delivery and design. *Unit head:* Dr. Mehdi Boroujerdi, Provost, 518-694-7212, Fax: 518-694-7063. *Application contact:* Donna Myers, Pharmacy and Graduate Admissions Counselor, 518-694-7149, Fax: 518-694-7063.

Arizona State University, Sandra Day O'Connor College of Law, Tempe, AZ 85287-7906. Offers biotechnology and genomics (LL M); global legal studies (LL M); law (JD); law (customized) (LL M); legal studies (MLS); tribal policy, law and government (LL M); JD/MBA; JD/MD; JD/PhD. JD/MD offered jointly with Mayo Medical School. *Accreditation:* ABA. *Faculty:* 63 full-time (20 women), 29 part-time/adjunct (4 women). *Students:* 643 full-time (286 women), 14 part-time (6 women); includes 161 minority (19 Black or African American, non-Hispanic/Latino; 36 American Indian or Alaska Native, non-Hispanic/Latino; 25 Asian, non-Hispanic/Latino; 70 Hispanic/Latino; 11 Two or more races, non-Hispanic/Latino), 8 international. Average age 28. 2,457 applicants, 24% accepted, 191 enrolled. In 2010, 167 first professional degrees awarded. *Degree requirements:* For JD, comprehensive exam, paper. *Entrance requirements:* For JD, LSAT, bachelor's degree; for master's, bachelor's degree; JD (for LL M). Additional exam requirements/recommendations for international students: Required—TOEFL (minimum score 550 paper-based; 80 iBT). *Application deadline:* For fall admission, 11/15 priority date for domestic and international students; for spring admission, 2/1 for domestic and international students. Applications are processed on a rolling basis. Application fee: $60. Electronic applications accepted. *Expenses:* Contact institution. *Financial support:* In 2010–11, 280 students received support; research assistantships, teaching assistantships, career-related internships or fieldwork, Federal Work-Study, institutionally sponsored loans, scholarships/grants, tuition waivers (full and partial), and unspecified assistantships available. Financial award application deadline: 3/15; financial award applicants required to submit FAFSA. *Faculty research:* Emerging technologies and the law, Indian law, law and philosophy, international law, intellectual property. Total annual research expenditures: $524,024. *Unit head:* Dean Paul Schiff Berman, Dean/Professor, 480-965-6188, Fax: 480-965-6521, E-mail: paul.berman@asu.edu. *Application contact:* Chitra Damania, Director of Operations, 480-965-1474, Fax: 480-727-7930, E-mail: law.admissions@asu.edu.

Arkansas State University, Graduate School, College of Sciences and Mathematics, Program in Molecular Biosciences, Jonesboro, State University, AR 72467. Offers biotechnology (Certificate); molecular biosciences (PhD). Part-time programs available. *Faculty:* 2 full-time (1

woman), 3 part-time/adjunct (1 woman). *Students:* 18 full-time (5 women), 1 (woman) part-time; includes 3 minority (1 American Indian or Alaska Native, non-Hispanic/Latino; 1 Asian, non-Hispanic/Latino; 1 Two or more races, non-Hispanic/Latino), 11 international. Average age 29. 4 applicants, 50% accepted, 2 enrolled. *Degree requirements:* For doctorate, comprehensive exam, thesis/dissertation. *Entrance requirements:* For doctorate, GRE, appropriate bachelor's or master's degree, interview, letters of reference, official transcripts, personal statement, immunization records. Additional exam requirements/recommendations for international students: Required—TOEFL (minimum score 550 paper-based; 213 computer-based; 79 iBT), IELTS (minimum score 6), PTE: Pearson Test of English Academic (56). *Application deadline:* For fall admission, 2/15 for domestic and international students; for spring admission, 11/15 for domestic students, 11/14 for international students. Applications are processed on a rolling basis. Application fee: $50. Electronic applications accepted. *Expenses:* Tuition, state resident: full-time $3888; part-time $216 per credit hour. Tuition, nonresident: full-time $9918; part-time $551 per credit hour. International tuition: $8376 full-time. Required fees: $932; $49 per credit hour. $25 per term. One-time fee: $30. Tuition and fees vary according to course load and program. *Financial support:* In 2010–11, 14 students received support; fellowships, research assistantships, teaching assistantships, career-related internships or fieldwork, scholarships/grants, and unspecified assistantships available. Financial award application deadline: 7/1; financial award applicants required to submit FAFSA. *Unit head:* Dr. Roger Buchanan, Director, 870-972-2007, Fax: 870-972-2008, E-mail: rbuck@astate.edu. *Application contact:* Dr. Andrew Sustich, Dean of the Graduate School, 870-972-3029, Fax: 870-972-3857, E-mail: sustich@astate.edu.

Brandeis University, Graduate School of Arts and Sciences, Program in Biotechnology, Waltham, MA 02454-9110. Offers MS. *Faculty:* 22 full-time (9 women), 2 part-time/adjunct (1 woman). *Students:* 6 full-time (5 women); includes 2 Black or African American, non-Hispanic/Latino, 3 international. 31 applicants, 65% accepted, 7 enrolled. *Degree requirements:* For master's, poster presentation. *Entrance requirements:* For master's, GRE, official transcript(s), 3 recommendation letters, curriculum vitae or resume, statement of purpose. Additional exam requirements/recommendations for international students: Required—TOEFL (minimum score 600 paper-based; 250 computer-based; 100 iBT); Recommended—IELTS (minimum score 7). *Application deadline:* Applications are processed on a rolling basis. Application fee: $75. Electronic applications accepted. *Financial support:* In 2010–11, teaching assistantships with partial tuition reimbursements (averaging $3,200 per year); career-related internships or fieldwork, scholarships/grants, and tuition waivers (partial) also available. Financial award application deadline: 4/15; financial award applicants required to submit FAFSA. *Faculty research:* Biosciences, business and biology, biotechnology, pharmaceutics. *Unit head:* Dr. Neil Simister, Director of Graduate Studies, 781-736-4952, Fax: 781-736-3107, E-mail: simister@brandeis.edu. *Application contact:* Marcia Cabral, Department Administrator, 781-736-3100, Fax: 781-736-3107, E-mail: cabral@brandeis.edu.

Brigham Young University, Graduate Studies, College of Life Sciences, Department of Plant and Wildlife Sciences, Provo, UT 84602-1001. Offers environmental science (MS); genetics and biotechnology (MS); wildlife and wildlands conservation (MS, PhD). *Faculty:* 26 full-time (2 women). *Students:* 63 full-time (23 women); includes 2 Asian, non-Hispanic/Latino; 1 Hispanic/Latino; 1 Native Hawaiian or other Pacific Islander, non-Hispanic/Latino, 5 international. Average age 25. 33 applicants, 55% accepted, 18 enrolled. *Degree requirements:* For master's, thesis; for doctorate, comprehensive exam, thesis/dissertation, minimum GPA of 3.2, 54 hours (18 dissertation, 36 coursework). *Entrance requirements:* For master's, GRE General Test, minimum GPA of 3.2 during last 60 hours of course work; for doctorate, GRE, minimum GPA of 3.2. Additional exam requirements/recommendations for international students: Required—TOEFL (minimum score 580 paper-based; 237 computer-based; 85 iBT). *Application deadline:* 2/1 for domestic and international students. Applications are processed on a rolling basis. Application fee: $0. Electronic applications accepted. *Expenses:* Tuition: Full-time $5580; part-time $310 per credit hour. Tuition and fees vary according to program and student's religious affiliation. *Financial support:* In 2010–11, 63 students received support, including 2 research assistantships with partial tuition reimbursements available (averaging $16,650 per year), 37 teaching assistantships with partial tuition reimbursements available (averaging $16,650 per year); scholarships/grants and tuition waivers (partial) also available. Financial award application deadline: 2/1. *Faculty research:* environmental science, plant genetics, plant ecology, plant nutrition and pathology, wildlife and wildlands conservation. *Unit head:* Dr. Val J. Anderson, Chair, 801-422-3527, Fax: 801-422-0008, E-mail: val_anderson@byu.edu. *Application contact:* Dr. Loreen Allphin, Graduate Coordinator, 801-422-5603, Fax: 801-422-0008, E-mail: loreen_allphin@byu.edu.

Brock University, Faculty of Graduate Studies, Faculty of Mathematics and Science, Program in Biotechnology, St. Catharines, ON L2S 3A1, Canada. Offers M Sc, PhD. Part-time programs available. *Degree requirements:* For master's, thesis; for doctorate, thesis/dissertation. *Entrance requirements:* For master's, honors B Sc; for doctorate, M Sc. Additional exam requirements/recommendations for international students: Required—TOEFL (minimum score 550 paper-based; 213 computer-based; 80 iBT), IELTS (minimum score 6.5), TWE (minimum score 4). Electronic applications accepted. *Faculty research:* Bioorganic chemistry, structural chemistry, electrochemistry, cell and molecular biology, plant sciences, oenology, and viticulture.

Brown University, Graduate School, Division of Biology and Medicine, Program in Artificial Organs, Biomaterials, and Cell Technology, Providence, RI 02912. Offers MA, Sc M, PhD. Terminal master's awarded for partial completion of doctoral program. *Degree requirements:* For doctorate, thesis/dissertation, preliminary exam. *Entrance requirements:* For master's and doctorate, GRE General Test, GRE Subject Test. Additional exam requirements/recommendations for international students: Required—TOEFL. Electronic applications accepted.

California State Polytechnic University, Pomona, Academic Affairs, College of Science, Program in Applied Biotechnology, Pomona, CA 91768-2557. Offers MBT. *Students:* 1 full-time (0 women), 11 part-time (4 women); includes 1 minority (Asian, non-Hispanic/Latino), 3 international. Average age 31. 18 applicants, 89% accepted, 10 enrolled. *Application deadline:* Applications are processed on a rolling basis. Application fee: $55. Electronic applications accepted. *Expenses:* Tuition, state resident: full-time $5386; part-time $2850 per year. Tuition, nonresident: full-time $12,082; part-time $248 per credit. Required fees: $577; $248 per credit. $577 per year. Tuition and fees vary according to course load and program. *Unit head:* Dr. Jill Adler-Moore, Liaison, 909-869-4047, E-mail: jadler@csupomona.edu.

California State University Channel Islands, Extended Education, Programs in Biotechnology, Camarillo, CA 93012. Offers biotechnology and bioinformatics (MS); MS/MBA. *Entrance requirements:* Additional exam requirements/recommendations for international students: Required—TOEFL (minimum score 550 paper-based).

Carnegie Mellon University, H. John Heinz III College, School of Public Policy and Management, Master of Science Program in Biotechnology and Management, Pittsburgh, PA 15213-3891. Offers MS. *Accreditation:* AACSB. *Entrance requirements:* For master's, GRE or GMAT, college-level course in advanced algebra/pre-calculus; college-level courses in economics and statistics (recommended). Additional exam requirements/recommendations for international students: Required—TOEFL or IELTS.

Carnegie Mellon University, Mellon College of Science, Department of Chemistry, Pittsburgh, PA 15213-3891. Offers biotechnology and management (MS); chemistry (PhD), including bioinorganic, bioorganic, organic and materials, biophysics and spectroscopy, computational and theoretical, polymer; colloids, polymers and surfaces (MS). Part-time programs available. Terminal master's awarded for partial completion of doctoral program. *Degree requirements:* For doctorate, thesis/dissertation, departmental qualifying and oral exams, teaching experience. *Entrance requirements:* For master's, GRE General Test; for doctorate, GRE General Test, GRE Subject Test. Additional exam requirements/recommendations for international students: Required—TOEFL. Electronic applications accepted. *Faculty research:* Physical and theoretical chemistry, chemical synthesis, biophysical/bioinorganic chemistry.

Claflin University, Graduate Programs, Orangeburg, SC 29115. Offers biotechnology (MS); business administration (MBA). Part-time programs available. *Students:* 71 full-time (48 women), 18 part-time (11 women); includes 72 minority (all Black or African American, non-Hispanic/Latino), 15 international. *Entrance requirements:* For master's, GRE, GMAT, baccalaureate degree, 3 letters of recommendation. Additional exam requirements/recommendations for international students: Recommended—TOEFL (minimum score 550 paper-based; 213 computer-based). *Application deadline:* For fall admission, 8/1 for domestic students; for spring admission, 12/1 for domestic students. Application fee: $40 ($55 for international students). *Expenses:* Tuition: Full-time $8532; part-time $474 per credit hour. Required fees: $312. *Financial support:* Research assistantships, teaching assistantships available. Financial award application deadline: 4/15; financial award applicants required to submit FAFSA. *Unit head:* Dr. Gloria Seabrook, Interim Executive Director of Professional and Continuing Studies, 803-535-5574, Fax: 803-535-5576, E-mail: gseabrook@claflin.edu. *Application contact:* Dr. Gloria Seabrook, Interim Executive Director of Professional and Continuing Studies, 803-535-5574, Fax: 803-535-5576, E-mail: gseabrook@claflin.edu.

Concordia University, School of Graduate Studies, Faculty of Arts and Science, Department of Biology, Montréal, QC H3G 1M8, Canada. Offers biology (M Sc, PhD); biotechnology and genomics (Diploma). *Degree requirements:* For master's, thesis; for doctorate, thesis/dissertation, pedagogical training. *Entrance requirements:* For master's, honors degree in biology; for doctorate, M Sc in life science. *Faculty research:* Cell biology, animal physiology, ecology, microbiology/molecular biology, plant physiology/biochemistry and biotechnology.

Dartmouth College, Thayer School of Engineering, Program in Biotechnology and Biochemical Engineering, Hanover, NH 03755. Offers MS, PhD. *Degree requirements:* For master's, thesis; for doctorate, thesis/dissertation, candidacy oral exam. *Entrance requirements:* For master's and doctorate, GRE General Test. *Application deadline:* For fall admission, 1/1 priority date for domestic students. Application fee: $45. *Financial support:* Fellowships, research assistantships, teaching assistantships, career-related internships or fieldwork, Federal Work-Study, institutionally sponsored loans, and tuition waivers (full and partial) available. Financial award application deadline: 1/15. *Faculty research:* Biomass processing, metabolic engineering, kinetics and reactor design, applied microbiology, resource and environmental analysis. Total annual research expenditures: $2.9 million. *Unit head:* Dr. Joseph J. Helbie, Dean, 603-646-2238, Fax: 603-646-2580, E-mail: joseph.j.helbie@dartmouth.edu. *Application contact:* Candace S. Potter, Graduate Admissions Administrator, 603-646-3844, Fax: 603-646-1620, E-mail: candace.potter@dartmouth.edu.

Duquesne University, Bayer School of Natural and Environmental Sciences, Program in Biotechnology, Pittsburgh, PA 15282-0001. Offers MS. Part-time programs available. *Faculty:* 1 full-time (0 women). *Students:* 8 full-time (4 women), 6 part-time (3 women), 2 international. Average age 23. 17 applicants, 65% accepted, 6 enrolled. In 2010, 2 master's awarded. *Entrance requirements:* For master's, GRE General Test, 3 letters of recommendation. Additional exam requirements/recommendations for international students: Required—TOEFL (minimum score 80 iBT). *Application deadline:* For fall admission, 5/1 priority date for domestic students, 5/1 for international students; for spring admission, 10/1 priority date for domestic students, 10/1 for international students. Applications are processed on a rolling basis. Application fee: $0 ($40 for international students). Electronic applications accepted. *Expenses:* Tuition: Part-time $884 per credit. Required fees: $84 per credit. Tuition and fees vary according to course load. *Financial support:* In 2010–11, 7 students received support. Career-related internships or fieldwork and tuition waivers (partial) available. *Unit head:* Dr. Alan W. Seadler, Director, 412-396-1568, E-mail: seadlera@duq.edu. *Application contact:* Heather Costello, Graduate Academic Advisor, 412-396-6339, Fax: 412-396-4881, E-mail: costelloh@duq.edu.

East Carolina University, Graduate School, Thomas Harriot College of Arts and Sciences, Department of Biology, Greenville, NC 27858-4353. Offers biology (MS); molecular biology/biotechnology (MS). Part-time programs available. *Degree requirements:* For master's, one foreign language, comprehensive exam, thesis. *Entrance requirements:* For master's, GRE General Test, GRE Subject Test. Additional exam requirements/recommendations for international students: Required—TOEFL. *Expenses:* Tuition, state resident: full-time $3130; part-time $391.25 per credit hour. Tuition, nonresident: full-time $13,817; part-time $1727.13 per credit hour. Required fees: $1916; $239.50 per credit hour. Tuition and fees vary according to campus/location and program. *Faculty research:* Biochemistry, microbiology, cell biology.

Florida Institute of Technology, Graduate Programs, College of Science, Department of Biological Sciences, Melbourne, FL 32901-6975. Offers biological sciences (PhD); biotechnology (MS); cell and molecular biology (MS); ecology (MS); marine biology (MS). Part-time programs available. *Faculty:* 15 full-time (2 women), 1 part-time/adjunct (0 women). *Students:* 72 full-time (40 women), 12 part-time (7 women); includes 6 minority (1 Asian, non-Hispanic/Latino; 4 Hispanic/Latino; 1 Two or more races, non-Hispanic/Latino), 37 international. Average age 26. 227 applicants, 36% accepted, 29 enrolled. In 2010, 15 master's, 5 doctorates awarded. *Degree requirements:* For master's, thesis (for some programs), Research, seminar, internship, or summer lab; for doctorate, comprehensive exam, thesis/dissertation, dissertations seminar, publications. *Entrance requirements:* For master's, GRE General Test, 3 letters of recommendation, minimum GPA of 3.0, resume, statement of objectives; for doctorate, GRE General Test, resume, 3 letters of recommendation, minimum GPA of 3.2, statement of objectives. Additional exam requirements/recommendations for international students: Required—TOEFL (minimum score 550 paper-based; 213 computer-based; 79 iBT). *Application deadline:* For fall admission, 3/1 for domestic students, 4/1 for international students; for spring admission, 9/1 for domestic and international students. Applications are processed on a rolling basis. Application fee: $50. Electronic applications accepted. *Expenses:* Tuition: Part-time $1040 per credit hour. Tuition and fees vary according to campus/location. *Financial support:* In 2010–11, 6 fellowships (averaging $20,737 per year), 15 research assistantships with full and partial tuition reimbursements (averaging $13,455 per year), 22 teaching assistantships with full and partial tuition reimbursements (averaging $13,353 per year) were awarded; career-related internships or fieldwork, institutionally sponsored loans, tuition waivers (partial), unspecified assistantships, and tuition remissions also available. Support available to part-time students. Financial award application deadline: 3/1; financial award applicants required to submit FAFSA. *Faculty research:* Initiation of protein synthesis in eukaryotic cells, fixation of radioactive carbon, changes in DNA molecule, endangered or threatened avian and mammalian species, hydroacoustics and feeding preference of the West Indian manatee. Total annual research expenditures: $1.3 million. *Unit head:* Dr. Richard B. Aronson, Department Head, 321-674-8034, Fax: 321-674-7238, E-mail: raronson@fit.edu. *Application contact:* Cheryl A. Brown, Associate Director of Graduate Admissions, 321-674-7581, Fax: 321-723-9468, E-mail: cbrown@fit.edu.

The George Washington University, College of Professional Studies, Program in Molecular Biotechnology, Washington, DC 20052. Offers MPS. *Students:* 4 full-time (2 women), 3 part-time (2 women); includes 4 Hispanic/Latino, 2 international. Average age 29. 14 applicants, 64% accepted, 2 enrolled. In 2010, 5 master's awarded. *Application deadline:* For fall admission, 4/1 for domestic and international students. Application fee: $25. Electronic applications accepted. *Financial support:* In 2010–11, 8 students received support. Tuition waivers available. *Unit head:* Dr. Mark Reeves, Director, 202-994-6279, Fax: 202-994-3001, E-mail: reevesme@gwu.edu. *Application contact:* Kristin Williams, Asst VP Grad&Spec Enrlmnt Mgmt, 202-994-0467, Fax: 202-994-0371, E-mail: ksw@gwu.edu.

Harvard University, Extension School, Cambridge, MA 02138-3722. Offers applied sciences (CAS); biotechnology (ALM); educational technologies (ALM); educational technology (CET); English for graduate and professional studies (DGP); environmental management (ALM, CEM); information technology (ALM); journalism (ALM); liberal arts (ALM); management (ALM, CM); mathematics for teaching (ALM); museum studies (ALM); premedical studies (Diploma); publication and communication (CPC). Part-time and evening/weekend programs available. *Degree requirements:* For master's, thesis. *Entrance requirements:* For master's, 3 completed graduate courses with grade of B or higher. Additional exam requirements/recommendations for international students: Required—TOEFL (minimum score 600 paper-based; 250 computer-based), TWE (minimum score 5). *Expenses:* Contact institution.

Hood College, Graduate School, Program in Biomedical Science, Frederick, MD 21701-8575. Offers biomedical science (MS), including biotechnology/molecular biology, microbiology/immunology/virology, regulatory compliance; regulatory compliance (Certificate). Part-time and evening/weekend programs available. *Faculty:* 3 full-time (1 woman), 7 part-time/adjunct (4 women). *Students:* 9 full-time (2 women), 87 part-time (55 women); includes 16 Black or African American, non-Hispanic/Latino; 9 Asian, non-Hispanic/Latino; 3 Hispanic/Latino; 1 Two or more races, non-Hispanic/Latino, 7 international. Average age 29. 61 applicants, 64% accepted, 21 enrolled. In 2010, 9 master's, 3 other advanced degrees awarded. *Degree requirements:* For master's, comprehensive exam, thesis or alternative. *Entrance requirements:* For master's, bachelor's degree in biology; minimum GPA of 2.75; undergraduate course work in cell biology, chemistry, organic chemistry, and genetics. Additional exam requirements/recommendations for international students: Required—TOEFL (minimum score 575 paper-based; 231 computer-based; 89 iBT). *Application deadline:* For fall admission, 7/15 for domestic and international students; for spring admission, 12/15 for domestic and international students. Applications are processed on a rolling basis. Application fee: $35. Electronic applications accepted. *Expenses:* Tuition: Full-time $6480; part-time $360 per credit. Required fees: $100; $50 per term. *Financial support:* In 2010–11, 3 research assistantships with full tuition reimbursements (averaging $10,609 per year) were awarded. Financial award applicants required to submit FAFSA. *Unit head:* Dr. Oney Smith, Director, 301-696-3653, Fax: 301-696-3597, E-mail: osmith@hood.edu. *Application contact:* Dr. Allen P. Flora, Dean of Graduate School, 301-696-3811, Fax: 301-696-3597, E-mail: gofurther@hood.edu.

Howard University, College of Medicine, Department of Biochemistry and Molecular Biology, Washington, DC 20059-0002. Offers biochemistry and molecular biology (PhD); biotechnology (MS); MD/PhD. Part-time programs available. *Degree requirements:* For master's, externship; for doctorate, comprehensive exam, thesis/dissertation. *Entrance requirements:* For master's and doctorate, GRE General Test, minimum GPA of 3.0. *Faculty research:* Cellular and molecular biology of olfaction, gene regulation and expression, enzymology, NMR spectroscopy of molecular structure, hormone regulation/metabolism.

Illinois Institute of Technology, Graduate College, College of Science and Letters, Department of Biological, Chemical and Physical Sciences, Biology Division, Chicago, IL 60616. Offers biochemistry (MBS, MS); biology (PhD); biotechnology (MBS, MS); cell and molecular biology (MBS, MS); microbiology (MB, MS); molecular biochemistry and biophysics (PhD); molecular biology and biophysics (MS). Part-time and evening/weekend programs available. Postbaccalaureate distance learning degree programs offered (minimal on-campus study). *Faculty:* 13 full-time (5 women), 5 part-time/adjunct (2 women). *Students:* 121 full-time (75 women), 56 part-time (37 women); includes 16 minority (5 Black or African American, non-Hispanic/Latino; 5 Asian, non-Hispanic/Latino; 5 Hispanic/Latino; 1 Two or more races, non-Hispanic/Latino), 104 international. Average age 27. 268 applicants, 76% accepted, 62 enrolled. In 2010, 74 master's, 4 doctorates awarded. Terminal master's awarded for partial completion of doctoral program. *Degree requirements:* For master's, comprehensive exam, thesis (for some programs); for doctorate, comprehensive exam, thesis/dissertation. *Entrance requirements:* For master's, GRE General Test (minimum score 1000 Quantitative and Verbal, 2.5 Analytical Writing), minimum undergraduate GPA of 3.0; for doctorate, GRE General Test (minimum score 1200 Quantitative and Verbal, 3.0 Analytical Writing), minimum undergraduate GPA of 3.0. Additional exam requirements/recommendations for international students: Required—TOEFL (minimum

Biotechnology

Illinois Institute of Technology (continued)

score 523 paper-based; 213 computer-based; 70 iBT); Recommended—IELTS (minimum score 5.5). *Application deadline:* For fall admission, 5/1 for domestic and international students; for spring admission, 10/15 for domestic and international students. Applications are processed on a rolling basis. Application fee: $40. Electronic applications accepted. *Expenses:* Tuition: Full-time $18,576; part-time $1032 per credit hour. Required fees: $583 per semester. One-time fee: $150. Tuition and fees vary according to program and student level. *Financial support:* In 2010–11, 15 research assistantships with full and partial tuition reimbursements (averaging $6,379 per year), 14 teaching assistantships with partial tuition reimbursements (averaging $6,296 per year) were awarded; fellowships with full and partial tuition reimbursements, career-related internships or fieldwork, Federal Work-Study, institutionally sponsored loans, scholarships/grants, traineeships, health care benefits, tuition waivers (partial), and unspecified assistantships also available. Support available to part-time students. Financial award applicants required to submit FAFSA. *Faculty research:* Structure and biophysics of macromolecular systems; efficacy and mechanism of action of chemopreventive agents in experimental carcinogenesis of breast, colon, lung and prostate; study of fundamental structural biochemistry problems that have direct links to the understanding and treatment of disease; spectroscopic techniques for the study of multi-domain proteins; molecular mechanisms of cancer and cancer gene therapy. Total annual research expenditures: $2.6 million. *Unit head:* Dr. Benjamin C. Stark, Professor and Associate Chair, 312-567-3488, Fax: 312-567-3494, E-mail: starkb@iit.edu. *Application contact:* Deborah Gibson, Director, Graduate Admissions, 866-472-3448, Fax: 312-567-3138, E-mail: inquiry.grad@iit.edu.

Illinois State University, Graduate School, College of Arts and Sciences, Department of Biological Sciences, Program in Biotechnology, Normal, IL 61790-2200. Offers MS. *Degree requirements:* For master's, thesis or alternative. *Entrance requirements:* For master's, GRE General Test, minimum GPA of 2.6 in last 60 hours of course work.

Indiana University Bloomington, University Graduate School, College of Arts and Sciences, Department of Biology, Bloomington, IN 47405. Offers biology teaching (MAT); biotechnology (MA); evolution, ecology, and behavior (MA, PhD); genetics (PhD); microbiology (MA, PhD); molecular, cellular, and developmental biology (PhD); plant sciences (MA, PhD); zoology (MA, PhD). *Faculty:* 58 full-time (15 women), 21 part-time/adjunct (6 women). *Students:* 163 full-time (98 women), 7 part-time (2 women); includes 17 minority (3 Black or African American, non-Hispanic/Latino; 1 American Indian or Alaska Native, non-Hispanic/Latino; 7 Asian, non-Hispanic/Latino; 5 Hispanic/Latino; 1 Native Hawaiian or other Pacific Islander, non-Hispanic/Latino), 52 international. Average age 27. 346 applicants, 15% accepted, 24 enrolled. In 2010, 17 master's, 24 doctorates awarded. Terminal master's awarded for partial completion of doctoral program. *Degree requirements:* For master's, thesis, oral defense; for doctorate, thesis/dissertation, oral defense. *Entrance requirements:* For master's and doctorate, GRE General Test. Additional exam requirements/recommendations for international students: Required—TOEFL (minimum score 100 iBT). *Application deadline:* For fall admission, 1/5 priority date for domestic students, 12/1 priority date for international students. Application fee: $55 ($65 for international students). Electronic applications accepted. *Financial support:* In 2010–11, 170 students received support, including 64 fellowships with tuition reimbursements available (averaging $19,484 per year), 44 research assistantships with tuition reimbursements available (averaging $20,300 per year), 62 teaching assistantships with tuition reimbursements available (averaging $20,521 per year); scholarships/grants, traineeships, health care benefits, and unspecified assistantships also available. Financial award application deadline: 1/5. *Faculty research:* Evolution, ecology and behavior; microbiology; molecular biology and genetics; plant biology. *Unit head:* Dr. Roger Innes, Chair, 812-855-2219, Fax: 812-855-6082, E-mail: rinnes@indiana.edu. *Application contact:* Tracey D. Stohr, Graduate Student Recruitment Coordinator, 812-856-6303, Fax: 812-855-6082, E-mail: gradbio@indiana.edu.

Instituto Tecnológico y de Estudios Superiores de Monterrey, Campus Monterrey, Graduate and Research Division, Program in Natural and Social Sciences, Monterrey, Mexico. Offers biotechnology (MS); chemistry (MS, PhD); communications (MS); education (MA). Part-time programs available. *Degree requirements:* For master's, one foreign language, thesis; for doctorate, one foreign language, thesis/dissertation. *Entrance requirements:* For master's, EXADEP; for doctorate, EXADEP, master's degree in related field. Additional exam requirements/recommendations for international students: Required—TOEFL. *Faculty research:* Cultural industries, mineral substances, bioremediation, food processing, CQ in industrial chemical processing.

Inter American University of Puerto Rico, Bayamón Campus, Graduate School, Bayamón, PR 00957. Offers biology (MS), including environmental sciences and ecology, molecular biotechnology; electronic commerce (MBA); human resources (MBA). Part-time and evening/weekend programs available. *Faculty:* 4 full-time (1 woman), 5 part-time/adjunct (4 women). *Students:* 115 part-time (84 women); includes 49 Hispanic/Latino. Average age 31. *Degree requirements:* For master's, comprehensive exam, research project. *Entrance requirements:* For master's, EXADEP, GRE General Test, letters of recommendation. *Application deadline:* For fall admission, 7/1 for domestic students, 5/1 priority date for international students; for winter admission, 11/15 priority date for domestic and international students; for spring admission, 2/15 priority date for domestic and international students. Application fee: $31. *Expenses:* Tuition: Full-time $4424; part-time $202 per credit. Required fees: $180 per trimester. *Unit head:* Prof. Juan F. Martinez, Chancellor, 787-279-1200 Ext. 2295, Fax: 787-279-2205, E-mail: jmartinez@bc.inter.edu. *Application contact:* Carlos Alicea, Director of Admission, 787-279-1200 Ext. 2017, Fax: 787-279-2205, E-mail: calicea@bc.inter.edu.

The Johns Hopkins University, G. W. C. Whiting School of Engineering, Program in Engineering Management, Baltimore, MD 21218-2699. Offers biomaterials (MSEM); communications science (MSEM); computer science (MSEM); fluid mechanics (MSEM); materials science and engineering (MSEM); mechanical engineering (MSEM); mechanics and materials (MSEM); nano-biotechnology (MSEM); nanomaterials and nanotechnology (MSEM); probability and statistics (MSEM); smart product and device design (MSEM); systems analysis, management and environmental policy (MSEM). *Students:* 32 full-time (5 women), 4 part-time (0 women); includes 7 minority (3 Black or African American, non-Hispanic/Latino; 3 Asian, non-Hispanic/Latino; 1 Hispanic/Latino), 11 international. Average age 23. 110 applicants, 60% accepted, 27 enrolled. In 2010, 6 master's awarded. *Entrance requirements:* For master's, GRE, 3 letters of recommendation, resume. Additional exam requirements/recommendations for international students: Required—TOEFL (minimum score 600 paper-based; 250 computer-based; 100 iBT) or IELTS (minimum score 7). *Application deadline:* For fall admission, 1/15 priority date for domestic students, 1/15 for international students; for spring admission, 9/15 priority date for domestic students, 9/15 for international students. Applications are processed on a rolling basis. Application fee: $75. Electronic applications accepted. *Financial support:* Fellowships, health care benefits available. *Unit head:* Dr. Edward R. Scheinerman, Interim Director/Vice Dean for Education, School of Engineering/Professor, Applied Mathematics and Statistics, 410-516-7395, Fax: 410-516-4880, E-mail: ers@jhu.edu. *Application contact:* Dennis McIver, Coordinator of Graduate Admissions, 410-516-8174, Fax: 410-516-0780, E-mail: graduateadmissions@jhu.edu.

The Johns Hopkins University, Zanvyl Krieger School of Arts and Sciences, Advanced Academic Programs, Program in Biotechnology, Baltimore, MD 21218-2699. Offers MS, MS/MBA. Part-time and evening/weekend programs available. Postbaccalaureate distance learning degree programs offered (minimal on-campus study). *Faculty:* 8 full-time (4 women), 99 part-time/adjunct (21 women). *Students:* 84 full-time (49 women), 458 part-time (274 women); includes 169 minority (37 Black or African American, non-Hispanic/Latino; 4 American Indian or Alaska Native, non-Hispanic/Latino; 87 Asian, non-Hispanic/Latino; 26 Hispanic/Latino; 3 Native Hawaiian or other Pacific Islander, non-Hispanic/Latino; 12 Two or more races, non-Hispanic/Latino), 64 international. Average age 30. 368 applicants, 57% accepted, 182 enrolled. In 2010, 195 master's awarded. *Degree requirements:* For master's, thesis (for some programs). *Entrance requirements:* For master's, minimum GPA of 3.0; coursework in biology and chemistry. Additional exam requirements/recommendations for international students: Required—TOEFL (minimum score 250 computer-based; 100 iBT). *Application deadline:* For fall admission, 5/31 priority date for domestic students, 4/30 priority date for international students; for spring admission, 10/31 priority date for domestic and international students. Applications are processed on a rolling basis. Application fee: $75. Electronic applications accepted. *Financial support:* Applicants required to submit FAFSA. *Unit head:* Dr. Lynn Johnson Langer, Senior Associate Program Chair, 301-294-7063, Fax: 301-294-7000. *Application contact:* Valana M. McMickens, Director of Admissions/Student Services, 202-452-1941, Fax: 202-452-1970, E-mail: aapadmissions@jhu.edu.

Kean University, New Jersey Center for Science, Technology and Mathematics, Program in Biotechnology, Union, NJ 07083. Offers MS. Part-time and evening/weekend programs available. *Faculty:* 8 full-time (4 women). *Students:* 16 full-time (8 women), 8 part-time (7 women); includes 1 Black or African American, non-Hispanic/Latino; 6 Asian, non-Hispanic/Latino; 3 Hispanic/Latino, 5 international. Average age 26. 21 applicants, 95% accepted, 14 enrolled. In 2010, 14 master's awarded. *Degree requirements:* For master's, written research project paper, presentation of research. *Entrance requirements:* For master's, GRE General Test, minimum GPA of 3.0 overall and in all science and math courses, 3 letters of recommendation, interview. *Application deadline:* For fall admission, 6/1 for domestic students; for spring admission, 11/1 for domestic students. Application fee: $75 ($150 for international students). Electronic applications accepted. *Expenses:* Tuition, state resident: full-time $10,872; part-time $500 per credit. Tuition, nonresident: full-time $14,736; part-time $614 per credit. Required fees: $2740.80; $125 per credit. Part-time tuition and fees vary according to course load and degree level. *Financial support:* In 2010–11, 3 research assistantships with full tuition reimbursements (averaging $3,263 per year) were awarded; unspecified assistantships also available. Financial award applicants required to submit FAFSA. *Unit head:* Dr. Dil Ramanathan, Program Coordinator, 908-737-7217, Fax: 908-737-3425, E-mail: ramanatd@kean.edu. *Application contact:* Reenat Hasan, Pre-Admissions Coordinator, 908-737-5923, Fax: 908-737-5925, E-mail: rhasan@exchange.kean.edu.

Marywood University, Academic Affairs, College of Liberal Arts and Sciences, Science Department, Program in Biotechnology, Scranton, PA 18509-1598. Offers MS. *Entrance requirements:* Additional exam requirements/recommendations for international students: Required—TOEFL (minimum score 550 paper-based; 213 computer-based; 79 iBT). Electronic applications accepted. *Expenses:* Tuition: Part-time $735 per credit. Required fees: $470 per semester. Tuition and fees vary according to degree level and campus/location. *Faculty research:* Microbiology, molecular biology, genetics.

McGill University, Faculty of Graduate and Postdoctoral Studies, Faculty of Agricultural and Environmental Sciences, Institute of Parasitology, Montréal, QC H3A 2T5, Canada. Offers biotechnology (M Sc A, Certificate); parasitology (M Sc, PhD).

New Mexico State University, Graduate School, College of Arts and Sciences, Department of Biology, Las Cruces, NM 88003-8001. Offers biology (MS, PhD); biotechnology and business (MS). Part-time programs available. *Faculty:* 25 full-time (10 women). *Students:* 70 full-time (46 women), 12 part-time (8 women); includes 20 minority (3 Black or African American, non-Hispanic/Latino; 1 American Indian or Alaska Native, non-Hispanic/Latino; 16 Hispanic/Latino), 24 international. Average age 30. 71 applicants, 86% accepted, 25 enrolled. In 2010, 13 master's, 10 doctorates awarded. *Degree requirements:* For master's, thesis (for some programs), defense or oral exam; for doctorate, comprehensive exam, thesis/dissertation, qualifying exam, defense. *Entrance requirements:* Additional exam requirements/recommendations for international students: Required—TOEFL. *Application deadline:* For fall admission, 1/15 priority date for domestic students, 1/15 for international students; for spring admission, 10/4 priority date for domestic students, 10/4 for international students. Applications are processed on a rolling basis. Application fee: $30 ($50 for international students). Electronic applications accepted. *Expenses:* Tuition, state resident: full-time $4536; part-time $242 per credit. Tuition, nonresident: full-time $15,816; part-time $712 per credit. Required fees: $636 per term. *Financial support:* In 2010–11, 21 research assistantships (averaging $16,987 per year), 33 teaching assistantships (averaging $10,202 per year) were awarded; fellowships, Federal Work-Study and health care benefits also available. Support available to part-time students. Financial award application deadline: 1/15. *Faculty research:* Microbiology, cell and organismal physiology, ecology and ethology, evolution, genetics, developmental biology. *Unit head:* Dr. Michele Nishiguchi, Head, 575-646-3611, Fax: 575-646-5665, E-mail: nish@nmsu.edu. *Application contact:* Gloria Valencia, Administration Assistant, 575-646-3611, Fax: 575-646-5665, E-mail: gvalenci@nmsu.edu.

North Carolina State University, Graduate School, College of Agriculture and Life Sciences, Department of Microbiology, Program in Microbial Biotechnology, Raleigh, NC 27695. Offers MMB. *Entrance requirements:* For master's, GRE. Electronic applications accepted.

Northeastern University, College of Science, Department of Biology and College of Arts and Sciences and College of Engineering, Program in Biotechnology, Boston, MA 02115-5096. Offers MS, PSM. Part-time and evening/weekend programs available. *Students:* 72 full-time (42 women), 28 part-time (14 women). 150 applicants, 73% accepted, 36 enrolled. In 2010, 21 master's awarded. *Entrance requirements:* For master's, GRE. Additional exam requirements/recommendations for international students: Required—TOEFL (minimum score 600 paper-based; 250 computer-based; 100 iBT). *Application deadline:* For fall admission, 4/1 for domestic students. Application fee: $50. Electronic applications accepted. *Expenses:* Contact institution. *Financial support:* Teaching assistantships, scholarships/grants available. *Faculty research:* Genomics, proteomics, gene expression analysis (molecular biotechnology), drug discovery, development, delivery (pharmaceutical biotechnology), bioprocess development and optimization (process development). *Unit head:* Prof. Thomas Gilbert, Professor, 617-373-4505, E-mail: t.gilbert@neu.edu. *Application contact:* Cynthia Bainton, Administrative Manager, 617-373-2627, Fax: 617-373-8795, E-mail: c.bainton@neu.edu.

Northwestern University, The Graduate School, Interdepartmental Biological Sciences Program (IBiS), Evanston, IL 60208. Offers biochemistry, molecular biology, and cell biology (PhD), including biochemistry, cell and molecular biology, molecular biophysics, structural biology; biotechnology (PhD); cell and molecular biology (PhD); developmental biology and genetics (PhD); hormone action and signal transduction (PhD); neuroscience (PhD); structural biology, biochemistry, and biophysics (PhD). Program participants include the Departments of Biochemistry, Molecular Biology, and Cell Biology; Chemistry; Neurobiology and Physiology; Chemical Engineering; Civil Engineering; and Evanston Hospital. *Degree requirements:* For doctorate, thesis/dissertation, qualifying exam. *Entrance requirements:* For doctorate, GRE General Test. Additional exam requirements/recommendations for international students: Required—TOEFL (minimum score 600 paper-based). Electronic applications accepted. *Faculty research:* Developmental genetics, gene regulation, DNA-protein interactions, biological clocks, bioremediation.

Polytechnic Institute of NYU, Department of Chemical and Biological Sciences, Major in Biotechnology, Brooklyn, NY 11201-2990. Offers MS. *Students:* 65 full-time (32 women), 19 part-time (5 women); includes 1 Black or African American, non-Hispanic/Latino; 4 Asian, non-Hispanic/Latino, 74 international. 132 applicants, 60% accepted, 26 enrolled. In 2010, 38 master's awarded. *Entrance requirements:* Additional exam requirements/recommendations for international students: Required—TOEFL (minimum score 550 paper-based; 213 computer-based; 80 iBT); Recommended—IELTS (minimum score 6.5). *Application deadline:* For fall admission, 7/31 priority date for domestic students, 4/30 priority date for international students; for spring admission, 12/31 priority date for domestic students, 10/30 priority date for international students. Applications are processed on a rolling basis. Application fee: $75. Electronic applications accepted. *Expenses:* Tuition: Full-time $21,492; part-time $1194 per credit. Required fees: $385 per semester. Tuition and fees vary according to course load. *Unit head:* Dr. Bruce Garetz, Department Head, 718-260-3287, E-mail: bgaretz@poly.edu. *Application contact:* JeanCarlo Bonilla, Director, Graduate Enrollment Management, 718-260-3182, Fax: 718-260-3624, E-mail: gradinfo@poly.edu.

Polytechnic Institute of NYU, Department of Chemical and Biological Sciences, Major in Biotechnology and Entrepreneurship, Brooklyn, NY 11201-2990. Offers MS. *Students:* 17 full-time (5 women), 5 part-time (0 women); includes 1 Asian, non-Hispanic/Latino, 18 international. Average age 24. 58 applicants, 43% accepted, 11 enrolled. In 2010, 17 master's awarded. *Entrance requirements:* Additional exam requirements/recommendations for international students: Required—TOEFL (minimum score 550 paper-based; 213 computer-based; 80 iBT); Recommended—IELTS (minimum score 6.5). *Application deadline:* For fall admission, 7/31 priority date for domestic students, 4/30 priority date for international students; for spring admission, 12/31 priority date for domestic students, 10/30 priority date for international students. Applications are processed on a rolling basis. Application fee: $75. Electronic applications accepted. *Expenses:* Tuition: Full-time $21,492; part-time $1194 per credit. Required fees: $385 per semester. Tuition and fees vary according to course load. *Financial support:* Institutionally sponsored loans, scholarships/grants, and unspecified assistantships available. Support available to part-time students. *Unit head:* Dr. Bruce Garetz, Department Head, 718-260-3287, E-mail: bgaretz@poly.edu. *Application contact:* JeanCarlo Bonilla, Director, Graduate Enrollment Management, 718-260-3182, Fax: 718-260-3624, E-mail: gradinfo@poly.edu.

Purdue University Calumet, Graduate Studies Office, School of Engineering, Mathematics, and Science, Department of Biological Sciences, Program in Biotechnology, Hammond, IN 46323-2094. Offers MS. *Degree requirements:* For master's, thesis (for some programs). *Entrance requirements:* For master's, GRE General Test, 3 letters of recommendation. Application fee: $55. *Expenses:* Tuition, state resident: full-time $6867. Tuition, nonresident: full-time $14,157. *Unit head:* Dr. Charles Tseng, Graduate Studies Advisor, Biological Sciences, 219-989-2404, Fax: 219-989-2130, E-mail: tseng@purduecal.edu. *Application contact:* Dr. Charles Tseng, Graduate Advisor, 219-989-2404, Fax: 219-989-2130, E-mail: tseng@purduecal.edu.

Regis College, Department of Health Product Regulation and Clinical Research, Weston, MA 02493. Offers MS. Part-time and evening/weekend programs available. *Degree requirements:* For master's, thesis optional, internship. *Entrance requirements:* For master's, GRE or MAT. Additional exam requirements/recommendations for international students: Required—TOEFL (minimum score 550 paper-based; 213 computer-based). *Expenses:* Contact institution. *Faculty research:* FDA regulatory affairs medical device.

Roosevelt University, Graduate Division, College of Arts and Sciences, Department of Biological, Chemical, and Physical Sciences, Chicago, IL 60605. Offers biotechnology and chemical science (MS). Part-time and evening/weekend programs available. *Degree requirements:* For master's, thesis optional. *Entrance requirements:* For master's, minimum GPA of 2.7, undergraduate course work in science and mathematics. *Faculty research:* Phase-transfer catalysts, bioinorganic chemistry, long chain dicarboxylic acids, organosilicon compounds, spectroscopic studies.

St. John's University, Institute for Biotechnology, Queens, NY 11439. Offers biological/pharmaceutical biotechnology (MS). *Students:* 8 full-time (4 women), 12 part-time (7 women); includes 6 minority (5 Asian, non-Hispanic/Latino; 1 Hispanic/Latino), 12 international. Average age 25. 65 applicants, 38% accepted, 5 enrolled. In 2010, 4 master's awarded. *Degree requirements:* For master's, comprehensive exam, thesis optional. *Entrance requirements:* For master's, GRE General and Subject Tests, minimum GPA of 3.0, 3 letters of recommendation, 1-page essay. Additional exam requirements/recommendations for international students: Required—TOEFL (minimum score 600 paper-based; 250 computer-based; 100 iBT), IELTS (minimum score 5.5). *Application deadline:* For fall admission, 5/1 priority date for domestic and international students; for spring admission, 11/1 priority date for domestic and international students. Applications are processed on a rolling basis. Application fee: $70. Electronic applications accepted. *Expenses:* Contact institution. *Financial support:* In 2010–11, 3 students received support, including 2 teaching assistantships with full tuition reimbursements available (averaging $7,612 per year). Financial award application deadline: 3/1; financial award applicants required to submit FAFSA. *Unit head:* Dr. Vijaya L. Korlipara, Director, Institute for Biotechnology, 718-990-5396, E-mail: korlipav@stjohns.edu. *Application contact:* Kathleen Davis, Director of Graduate Admission, 718-990-1601, E-mail: gradhelp@stjohns.edu.

San Francisco State University, Division of Graduate Studies, College of Science and Engineering, Department of Biology, Professional Science Master's Program, San Francisco, CA 94132-1722. Offers biotechnology (PSM); stem cell science (PSM). *Unit head:* Dr. Lily Chen, Director, 415-338-6763, E-mail: lilychen@sfsu.edu. *Application contact:* Dr. Linda H. Chen, Program Coordinator, 415-338-1696, E-mail: psm@sfsu.edu.

Simon Fraser University, Graduate Studies, Faculty of Business Administration, Burnaby, BC V5A 1S6, Canada. Offers business administration (EMBA, PhD); financial management (MA); general business (MBA); global asset and wealth management (MBA); management of technology/biotechnology (MBA); MBA/MRM. *Accreditation:* AACSB. Postbaccalaureate distance learning degree programs offered. *Degree requirements:* For master's, thesis or written project. *Entrance requirements:* For master's, minimum GPA of 3.0. Additional exam requirements/recommendations for international students: Required—TOEFL. *Expenses:* Contact institution. *Faculty research:* Leadership, marketing and technology, wealth management.

Southeastern Oklahoma State University, School of Arts and Sciences, Durant, OK 74701-0609. Offers biology (MT); computer information systems (MT). Part-time and evening/weekend programs available. *Faculty:* 12 full-time (4 women), 1 part-time/adjunct (0 women). *Students:* 19 full-time (4 women), 39 part-time (6 women); includes 13 American Indian or Alaska Native, non-Hispanic/Latino; 2 Hispanic/Latino. Average age 28. 10 applicants, 100% accepted, 10 enrolled. *Degree requirements:* For master's, thesis optional. *Entrance requirements:* For master's, minimum GPA of 3.0 in last 60 hours or 2.75 overall. Additional exam requirements/recommendations for international students: Required—TOEFL (minimum score 550 paper-based; 213 computer-based). *Application deadline:* For fall admission, 8/1 for domestic students, 6/1 for international students; for spring admission, 1/5 for domestic students, 11/1 for international students. Application fee: $20 ($55 for international students). Electronic applications accepted. *Financial support:* In 2010–11, 8 students received support; fellowships, research assistantships, teaching assistantships, Federal Work-Study and institutionally sponsored loans available. Support available to part-time students. Financial award application deadline: 6/15; financial award applicants required to submit FAFSA. *Unit head:* Dr. Teresa Golden, Graduate Coordinator, 580-745-2286, E-mail: tgolden@se.edu. *Application contact:* Carrie Williamson, Graduate Secretary, 580-745-2200, Fax: 580-745-7474, E-mail: cwilliamson@se.edu.

Southern Illinois University Edwardsville, Graduate School, College of Arts and Sciences, Department of Biological Sciences, Program in Biotechnology Management, Edwardsville, IL 62026-0001. Offers MS. Part-time programs available. *Students:* 4 full-time (3 women); includes 1 minority (Black or African American, non-Hispanic/Latino), 2 international. Average age 26. 32 applicants, 25% accepted. In 2010, 1 master's awarded. *Degree requirements:* For master's, thesis or alternative, internship, research paper. *Entrance requirements:* For master's, GRE. Additional exam requirements/recommendations for international students: Required—TOEFL (minimum score 550 paper-based; 213 computer-based; 79 iBT), IELTS (minimum score 6.5). *Application deadline:* For fall admission, 2/28 for domestic and international students. Application fee: $30. Electronic applications accepted. *Expenses:* Tuition, state resident: full-time $6012; part-time $1503 per semester. Tuition, nonresident: full-time $15,030; part-time $3758 per semester. Required fees: $1711; $675 per semester. *Financial support:* In 2010–11, 1 teaching assistantship with full tuition reimbursement (averaging $8,370 per year) was awarded; fellowships with full tuition reimbursements, research assistantships with full tuition reimbursements also available. Financial award application deadline: 3/1; financial award applicants required to submit FAFSA. *Unit head:* Dr. Steve McCommas, Director, 618-650-3406, E-mail: smccomm@siue.edu. *Application contact:* Michelle Robinson, Coordinator of Graduate Recruitment, 618-650-2811, Fax: 618-650-3523, E-mail: michero@siue.edu.

Stephen F. Austin State University, Graduate School, College of Sciences and Mathematics, Division of Biotechnology, Nacogdoches, TX 75962. Offers MS. *Degree requirements:* For master's, comprehensive exam, thesis. *Entrance requirements:* For master's, GRE General Test, minimum GPA of 2.8 in last 60 hours, 2.5 overall. Additional exam requirements/recommendations for international students: Required—TOEFL.

Texas Tech University, Center for Biotechnology and Genomics, Lubbock, TX 79409. Offers biotechnology (MS); JD/MS. Part-time programs available. *Faculty:* 1 full-time (0 women). *Students:* 26 full-time (16 women), 3 part-time (2 women); includes 1 Asian, non-Hispanic/Latino, 25 international. Average age 22. 90 applicants, 23% accepted, 9 enrolled. In 2010, 14 master's awarded. *Degree requirements:* For master's, thesis or alternative. *Entrance requirements:* For master's, GRE General Test. Additional exam requirements/recommendations for international students: Required—TOEFL (minimum score 550 paper-based; 213 computer-based; 79 iBT). *Application deadline:* For fall admission, 6/1 priority date for domestic students, 1/15 priority date for international students; for spring admission, 9/1 priority date for domestic students, 6/15 priority date for international students. Applications are processed on a rolling basis. Application fee: $50 ($75 for international students). Electronic applications accepted. *Expenses:* Tuition, state resident: full-time $5495.76; part-time $228.99 per credit hour. Tuition, nonresident: full-time $12,936; part-time $538.99 per credit hour. Required fees: $2674; $36 per credit hour. $905 per semester. *Financial support:* In 2010–11, 11 students received support, including 1 research assistantship with partial tuition reimbursement available (averaging $9,602 per year), 1 teaching assistantship with partial tuition reimbursement available (averaging $9,724 per year). Financial award application deadline: 4/15; financial award applicants required to submit FAFSA. *Faculty research:* Biotechnology and applied science. *Unit head:* Dr. David B. Knaff, Advisor, 806-742-0288, Fax: 806-742-1289, E-mail: david.knaff@ttu.edu. *Application contact:* Jatindra Tripathy, Senior Research Associate, 806-742-3722 Ext. 229, Fax: 806-742-3788, E-mail: jatindra.tripathy@ttu.edu.

Texas Tech University Health Sciences Center, Graduate School of Biomedical Sciences, Department of Cell Biology and Biochemistry, Program in Biotechnology, Lubbock, TX 79430. Offers MS. *Entrance requirements:* For master's, GRE General Test, minimum GPA of 3.0. Additional exam requirements/recommendations for international students: Required—TOEFL. *Faculty research:* Reproductive endocrinology, immunology, molecular biology and developmental biochemistry, biology of developing systems.

Thomas Jefferson University, Jefferson College of Graduate Studies, PhD Program in Tissue Engineering and Regenerative Medicine, Philadelphia, PA 19107. Offers PhD. *Faculty:* 18 full-time (6 women). *Students:* 4 full-time (3 women); includes 1 Asian, non-Hispanic/Latino. 3 applicants, 0% accepted, 0 enrolled. In 2010, 2 doctorates awarded. *Degree requirements:* For doctorate, comprehensive exam, thesis/dissertation. *Entrance requirements:* For doctorate, GRE General Test, minimum GPA of 3.2. Additional exam requirements/recommendations for international students: Required—TOEFL (minimum score 250 computer-based; 100 iBT) or IELTS. *Application deadline:* For fall admission, 1/15 priority date for domestic and international students. Applications are processed on a rolling basis. Application fee: $50. Electronic applications accepted. *Financial support:* In 2010–11, 4 students received support, including 4 fellowships with full tuition reimbursements available (averaging $52,883 per year); Federal Work-Study, institutionally sponsored loans, traineeships, and stipend also available. Financial award application deadline: 5/1; financial award applicants required to submit FAFSA. *Faculty research:* Skeletal development, biomaterials, bone implant interaction, tissue engineering, high resolution imaging. Total annual research expenditures: $8 million. *Unit head:* Dr. Irving Shapiro, Program Director, 215-955-7217, Fax: 215-955-9159, E-mail: irving.shapiro@jefferson.edu. *Application contact:* Marc E. Stearns, Director of Admissions, 215-503-0155, Fax: 215-503-9920, E-mail: jcgs-info@jefferson.edu.

Tufts University, Graduate School of Arts and Sciences, Graduate Certificate Programs, Biotechnology Engineering Program, Medford, MA 02155. Offers Certificate. Part-time and evening/weekend programs available. Electronic applications accepted. *Expenses:* Tuition: Full-time $39,624; part-time $3962 per course. Required fees: $40 per year. Full-time tuition and fees vary according to degree level, program and student level. Part-time tuition and fees vary according to course load.

Tufts University, Graduate School of Arts and Sciences, Graduate Certificate Programs, Biotechnology Program, Medford, MA 02155. Offers Certificate. Part-time and evening/weekend programs available. Electronic applications accepted. *Expenses:* Tuition: Full-time $39,624; part-time $3962 per course. Required fees: $40 per year. Full-time tuition and fees vary according to degree level, program and student level. Part-time tuition and fees vary according to course load.

Universidad de las Américas–Puebla, Division of Graduate Studies, School of Sciences, Program in Biotechnology, Puebla, Mexico. Offers MS. *Degree requirements:* For master's, one foreign language, thesis.

Université de Sherbrooke, Faculty of Law, Sherbrooke, QC J1K 2R1, Canada. Offers alternative dispute resolution (LL M, Diploma); biotechnology (LL B); business administration (LL B); business law (Diploma); health law (LL M, Diploma); law (LL B, LL D); legal management (Diploma); notarial law (DDN); transnational law (Diploma). Part-time and evening/weekend programs available. *Degree requirements:* For master's, thesis; for other advanced degree, one foreign language. *Entrance requirements:* For master's and other advanced degree, LL B. Electronic applications accepted.

University at Buffalo, the State University of New York, Graduate School, School of Medicine and Biomedical Sciences, Graduate Programs in Medicine and Biomedical Sciences, Department of Biotechnical and Clinical Laboratory Sciences, Buffalo, NY 14214. Offers biotechnology (MS). *Accreditation:* NAACLS. Part-time programs available. *Faculty:* 10 full-time (5 women). *Students:* 14 full-time (9 women), 1 (woman) part-time; includes 1 minority (Asian, non-Hispanic/Latino), 12 international. 151 applicants, 10% accepted, 4 enrolled. In 2010, 7 master's awarded. *Degree requirements:* For master's, thesis. *Entrance requirements:* For master's, GRE General Test, minimum GPA of 3.0 or equivalent, 4-year U.S. bachelor's degree or equivalent. Additional exam requirements/recommendations for international students: Required—TOEFL (minimum score 213 computer-based; 79 iBT), IELTS (minimum score 6). *Application deadline:* For fall admission, 3/1 priority date for domestic students, 2/1 priority date for international students. Applications are processed on a rolling basis. Application fee: $50. Electronic applications accepted. *Financial support:* In 2010–11, 5 teaching assistantships with full tuition reimbursements (averaging $9,000 per year) were awarded; health care benefits and unspecified assistantships also available. *Faculty research:* Tumor immunology, oxidative stress, breast cancer, erythropoiesis, toxicology. Total annual research expenditures: $1.2 million. *Unit head:* Dr. Stephen Thomas Koury, Director of Graduate Studies, 716-829-5188, Fax: 716-829-3601, E-mail: stvkoury@buffalo.edu. *Application contact:* Dr. Stephen Thomas Koury, Director of Graduate Studies, 716-829-5188, Fax: 716-829-3601, E-mail: stvkoury@buffalo.edu.

The University of Alabama in Huntsville, School of Graduate Studies, Interdisciplinary Studies, Interdisciplinary Program in Biotechnology Science and Engineering, Huntsville, AL 35899. Offers PhD. Part-time and evening/weekend programs available. *Faculty:* 18 full-time (4 women). *Students:* 23 full-time (12 women), 3 part-time (1 woman); includes 5 minority (4 Black or African American, non-Hispanic/Latino; 1 American Indian or Alaska Native, non-Hispanic/Latino), 11 international. Average age 30. 13 applicants, 31% accepted, 3 enrolled. In 2010, 2 doctorates awarded. *Degree requirements:* For doctorate, comprehensive exam, thesis/dissertation, oral and written exams. *Entrance requirements:* For doctorate, GRE General Test, bachelor's degree in science or engineering, minimum GPA of 3.0. Additional exam requirements/recommendations for international students: Required—TOEFL (minimum score 550 paper-based; 213 computer-based; 62 iBT). *Application deadline:* For fall admission, 7/15 for domestic students, 4/1 for international students; for spring admission, 11/30 for domestic students, 9/1 for international students. Applications are processed on a rolling basis. Application

Biotechnology

The University of Alabama in Huntsville (continued)

fee: $40 ($50 for international students). Electronic applications accepted. *Expenses:* Tuition, state resident: full-time $7250; part-time $407.75 per credit hour. Tuition, nonresident: full-time $17,358; part-time $970.05 per credit hour. Required fees: $246.80 per semester. Tuition and fees vary according to course load and program. *Financial support:* In 2010–11, 22 students received support, including 6 research assistantships with full tuition reimbursements available (averaging $13,465 per year), 16 teaching assistantships with full tuition reimbursements available (averaging $11,220 per year); career-related internships or fieldwork, Federal Work-Study, institutionally sponsored loans, scholarships/grants, health care benefits, and unspecified assistantships also available. Support available to part-time students. Financial award application deadline: 4/1; financial award applicants required to submit FAFSA. *Faculty research:* Protein structure and function, drug discovery, NMR spectroscopy, gene function and expression, molecular patterning. *Unit head:* Dr. Joseph Ng, Coordinator, 256-824-3715, Fax: 256-824-3469, E-mail: ngj@uah.edu. *Application contact:* Kathy Biggs, Graduate Studies Admissions Manager, 256-824-6199, Fax: 256-824-6405, E-mail: deangrad@uah.edu.

University of Alberta, Faculty of Graduate Studies and Research, Department of Biological Sciences, Edmonton, AB T6G 2E1, Canada. Offers environmental biology and ecology (M Sc, PhD); microbiology and biotechnology (M Sc, PhD); molecular biology and genetics (M Sc, PhD); physiology and cell biology (M Sc, PhD); plant biology (M Sc, PhD); systematics and evolution (M Sc, PhD). Terminal master's awarded for partial completion of doctoral program. *Degree requirements:* For master's, thesis; for doctorate, thesis/dissertation. *Entrance requirements:* Additional exam requirements/recommendations for international students: Required—TOEFL.

University of Calgary, Faculty of Medicine and Faculty of Graduate Studies, Program in Biomedical Technology, Calgary, AB T2N 1N4, Canada. Offers MBT. Part-time programs available. *Degree requirements:* For master's, comprehensive exam, practicum. *Entrance requirements:* For master's, minimum GPA of 3.2 in last 2 years, B Sc in biological science. Additional exam requirements/recommendations for international students: Required—TOEFL (minimum score 600 paper-based; 250 computer-based). Electronic applications accepted. *Expenses:* Contact institution. *Faculty research:* Patent law, intellectual proprietorship.

University of California, Irvine, School of Biological Sciences, Department of Molecular Biology and Biochemistry, Program in Biotechnology, Irvine, CA 92697. Offers MS. *Students:* 31 full-time (17 women); includes 9 minority (6 Asian, non-Hispanic/Latino; 1 Hispanic/Latino; 2 Two or more races, non-Hispanic/Latino), 10 international. Average age 28. 118 applicants, 22% accepted, 17 enrolled. In 2010, 13 master's awarded. *Entrance requirements:* For master's, GRE General Test, GRE Subject Test, minimum GPA of 3.0. *Application deadline:* For fall admission, 3/1 priority date for domestic and international students. Applications are processed on a rolling basis. Application fee: $80 ($100 for international students). Electronic applications accepted. *Financial support:* Application deadline: 3/1. *Unit head:* Renee Meria Frigo, Program Manager, 949-824-8145, Fax: 949-824-1965, E-mail: rfrigo@uci.edu. *Application contact:* Cathy A. Temple, Student Affairs Officer I, 949-824-6034, Fax: 949-824-8551, E-mail: catemple@uci.edu.

University of Central Florida, College of Medicine, Burnett School of Biomedical Sciences, Orlando, FL 32816. Offers biomedical sciences (MS); biotechnology (MS). *Faculty:* 27 full-time (7 women), 3 part-time/adjunct (1 woman). *Students:* 37 full-time (25 women), 7 part-time (5 women); includes 4 Asian, non-Hispanic/Latino; 4 Hispanic/Latino, 20 international. Average age 26. 105 applicants, 41% accepted, 19 enrolled. In 2010, 14 master's awarded. *Expenses:* Tuition, state resident: part-time $256.56 per credit hour. Tuition, nonresident: part-time $1011.52 per credit hour. Part-time tuition and fees vary according to program. *Financial support:* In 2010–11, 12 students received support, including 21 research assistantships (averaging $4,500 per year), 27 teaching assistantships (averaging $6,300 per year). *Unit head:* Dr. Pappachan E. Kolattukudy, Director, 407-823-1206, Fax: 407-823-0956, E-mail: pk@mail.ucf.edu. *Application contact:* Dr. Pappachan E. Kolattukudy, Director, 407-823-1206, Fax: 407-823-0956, E-mail: pk@mail.ucf.edu.

University of Delaware, College of Arts and Sciences, Department of Biological Sciences, Newark, DE 19716. Offers biotechnology (MS); cancer biology (MS, PhD); cell and extracellular matrix biology (MS, PhD); cell and systems physiology (MS, PhD); developmental biology (MS, PhD); ecology and evolution (MS, PhD); microbiology (MS, PhD); molecular biology and genetics (MS, PhD). Terminal master's awarded for partial completion of doctoral program. *Degree requirements:* For master's, thesis, preliminary exam; for doctorate, comprehensive exam, thesis/dissertation, preliminary exam. *Entrance requirements:* For master's and doctorate, GRE General Test. Additional exam requirements/recommendations for international students: Required—TOEFL (minimum score 600 paper-based; 250 computer-based); Recommended—TWE. Electronic applications accepted. *Faculty research:* Microorganisms, bone, cancer metastasis, developmental biology, cell biology, DNA.

University of Guelph, Graduate Studies, Ontario Agricultural College, Department of Environmental Biology, Guelph, ON N1G 2W1, Canada. Offers entomology (M Sc, PhD); environmental microbiology and biotechnology (M Sc, PhD); environmental toxicology (M Sc, PhD); plant and forest systems (M Sc, PhD); plant pathology (M Sc, PhD). Part-time programs available. *Degree requirements:* For master's, thesis; for doctorate, comprehensive exam, thesis/dissertation. *Entrance requirements:* For master's, minimum 75% average during previous 2 years of course work; for doctorate, minimum 75% average. Additional exam requirements/recommendations for international students: Required—TOEFL or IELTS. Electronic applications accepted. *Faculty research:* Entomology, environmental microbiology and biotechnology, environmental toxicology, forest ecology, plant pathology.

University of Houston–Clear Lake, School of Science and Computer Engineering, Program in Biotechnology, Houston, TX 77058-1098. Offers MS.

University of Illinois at Chicago, College of Pharmacy, Center for Pharmaceutical Biotechnology, Chicago, IL 60607-7173. Offers PhD.

The University of Kansas, University of Kansas Medical Center, School of Allied Health, Program in Molecular Biotechnology, Lawrence, KS 66045. Offers MS. *Faculty:* 5. *Students:* 2 full-time (0 women), 3 part-time (1 woman); includes 1 minority (American Indian or Alaska Native, non-Hispanic/Latino), 1 international. Average age 26. 15 applicants, 47% accepted, 3 enrolled. In 2010, 1 master's awarded. *Degree requirements:* For master's, comprehensive exam. *Entrance requirements:* For master's, GRE General Test. Additional exam requirements/recommendations for international students: Required—TOEFL. *Application deadline:* For fall admission, 2/1 priority date for domestic and international students. Application fee: $60. Electronic applications accepted. *Expenses:* Tuition, state resident: full-time $7092; part-time $295.50 per credit hour. Tuition, nonresident: full-time $16,590; part-time $691.25 per credit hour. Required fees: $858; $71.49 per credit hour. Tuition and fees vary according to course load, campus/location and program. *Financial support:* Career-related internships or fieldwork available. Financial award application deadline: 2/14; financial award applicants required to submit FAFSA. *Faculty research:* Diabetes, obesity, polycystic kidney disease, protein structure and function, cell signaling pathways. Total annual research expenditures: $220,000. *Unit head:* Dr. Eric Elsinghorst, Director of Graduate Studies, 913-588-1089, E-mail: eelsinghorst@kumc.edu. *Application contact:* Moffett Ferguson, Student Affairs Coordinator, 913-588-5275, Fax: 913-588-5254, E-mail: mfergus1@kumc.edu.

The University of Manchester, Faculty of Life Sciences, Manchester, United Kingdom. Offers adaptive organismal biology (M Phil, PhD); animal biology (M Phil, PhD); biochemistry (M Phil, PhD); bioinformatics (M Phil, PhD); biomolecular sciences (M Phil, PhD); biotechnology (M Phil, PhD); cell biology (M Phil, PhD); cell matrix research (M Phil, PhD); channels and transporters (M Phil, PhD); developmental biology (M Phil, PhD); Egyptology (M Phil, PhD); environmental biology (M Phil, PhD); evolutionary biology (M Phil, PhD); gene expression (M Phil, PhD); genetics (M Phil, PhD); history of science, technology and medicine (M Phil, PhD); immunology (M Phil, PhD); integrative neurobiology and behavior (M Phil, PhD); membrane trafficking (M Phil, PhD); microbiology (M Phil, PhD); molecular and cellular neuroscience (M Phil, PhD); molecular biology (M Phil, PhD); molecular cancer studies (M Phil, PhD); neuroscience (M Phil, PhD); ophthalmology (M Phil, PhD); optometry (M Phil, PhD); organelle function (M Phil, PhD); pharmacology (M Phil, PhD); physiology (M Phil, PhD); plant sciences (M Phil, PhD); stem cell research (M Phil, PhD); structural biology (M Phil, PhD); systems neuroscience (M Phil, PhD); toxicology (M Phil, PhD).

University of Maryland, Baltimore County, Graduate School, Continuing and Professional Studies, Program in Biotechnology Management, Baltimore, MD 21250. Offers Graduate Certificate. *Faculty:* 10 part-time/adjunct (4 women). *Students:* 8 full-time (7 women), 25 part-time (12 women); includes 2 Black or African American, non-Hispanic/Latino; 9 Asian, non-Hispanic/Latino; 1 Hispanic/Latino. 32 applicants, 50% accepted, 12 enrolled. *Entrance requirements:* Additional exam requirements/recommendations for international students: Required—TOEFL (minimum score 597 paper-based; 247 computer-based; 99 iBT). *Application deadline:* For fall admission, 8/15 for domestic students, 1/1 for international students; for spring admission, 12/15 for domestic students. Electronic applications accepted. *Financial support:* Career-related internships or fieldwork available. Financial award applicants required to submit FAFSA. *Unit head:* Dr. Chris Morris, Associate Vice Provost, CPS, 410-455-1570, E-mail: morrisc@umbc.edu. *Application contact:* Nancy Clements, Program Specialist, 410-455-5536, E-mail: nancyc@umbc.edu.

University of Maryland University College, Graduate School of Management and Technology, Program in Biotechnology Studies, Adelphi, MD 20783. Offers MS, Certificate. Part-time and evening/weekend programs available. Postbaccalaureate distance learning degree programs offered (no on-campus study). *Students:* 11 full-time (9 women), 432 part-time (249 women); includes 196 minority (116 Black or African American, non-Hispanic/Latino; 48 Asian, non-Hispanic/Latino; 27 Hispanic/Latino; 1 Native Hawaiian or other Pacific Islander, non-Hispanic/Latino; 4 Two or more races, non-Hispanic/Latino), 12 international. Average age 32. 123 applicants, 100% accepted, 81 enrolled. In 2010, 53 master's, 12 other advanced degrees awarded. *Degree requirements:* For master's, thesis or alternative, capstone course. *Application deadline:* Applications are processed on a rolling basis. Application fee: $50. Electronic applications accepted. *Financial support:* Federal Work-Study and scholarships/grants available. Support available to part-time students. Financial award application deadline: 6/1; financial award applicants required to submit FAFSA. *Unit head:* Dr. Rana Khan, Director, 240-684-2400, Fax: 240-684-2401, E-mail: rkhan@umuc.edu. *Application contact:* Coordinator, Graduate Admissions, 800-888-8682, Fax: 240-684-2151, E-mail: newgrad@umuc.edu.

University of Massachusetts Amherst, Graduate School, College of Natural Sciences, Department of Animal Biotechnology and Biomedical Sciences, Amherst, MA 01003. Offers MS, PhD. Part-time programs available. *Faculty:* 22 full-time (9 women). *Students:* 28 full-time (17 women), 1 (woman) part-time; includes 1 minority (Hispanic/Latino), 8 international. Average age 28. 52 applicants, 21% accepted, 10 enrolled. In 2010, 3 master's, 2 doctorates awarded. Terminal master's awarded for partial completion of doctoral program. *Degree requirements:* For master's, thesis or alternative; for doctorate, comprehensive exam, thesis/dissertation. *Entrance requirements:* For master's and doctorate, GRE General Test. Additional exam requirements/recommendations for international students: Required—TOEFL (minimum score 550 paper-based; 213 computer-based; 80 iBT), IELTS (minimum score 6.5). *Application deadline:* For fall admission, 2/1 for domestic and international students; for spring admission, 10/1 for domestic and international students. Applications are processed on a rolling basis. Application fee: $50 ($65 for international students). Electronic applications accepted. *Expenses:* Tuition, state resident: full-time $2640. Required fees: $8282. One-time fee: $357 full-time. *Financial support:* In 2010–11, 1 fellowship (averaging $1,731 per year), 40 research assistantships with full tuition reimbursements (averaging $12,032 per year), 13 teaching assistantships with full tuition reimbursements (averaging $9,586 per year) were awarded; career-related internships or fieldwork, Federal Work-Study, scholarships/grants, traineeships, health care benefits, tuition waivers (full), and unspecified assistantships also available. Support available to part-time students. Financial award application deadline: 2/1; financial award applicants required to submit FAFSA. *Unit head:* Dr. Pablo E. Visconti, Graduate Program Director, 413-577-1193, Fax: 413-577-1150. *Application contact:* Jean M. Ames, Supervisor of Admissions, 413-545-0722, Fax: 413-577-0010, E-mail: gradadm@grad.umass.edu.

University of Massachusetts Boston, Office of Graduate Studies, College of Science and Mathematics, Program in Biotechnology and Biomedical Science, Boston, MA 02125-3393. Offers MS. Part-time and evening/weekend programs available. *Degree requirements:* For master's, comprehensive exam, thesis optional, oral exams. *Entrance requirements:* For master's, GRE General Test, GRE Subject Test, minimum GPA of 2.75, 3.0 in science and math. *Faculty research:* Evolutionary and molecular immunology, molecular genetics, tissue culture, computerized laboratory technology.

University of Massachusetts Dartmouth, Graduate School, Program in Biomedical Engineering and Biotechnology, North Dartmouth, MA 02747-2300. Offers PhD. Part-time programs available. *Students:* 18 full-time (12 women), 8 part-time (1 woman), 17 international. Average age 29. 19 applicants, 63% accepted, 3 enrolled. In 2010, 1 doctorate awarded. *Degree requirements:* For doctorate, comprehensive exam, thesis/dissertation. *Entrance requirements:* For doctorate, GRE, minimum GPA of 3.0, 3 letters of recommendation. Additional exam requirements/recommendations for international students: Required—TOEFL (minimum score 550 paper-based; 213 computer-based). *Application deadline:* For fall admission, 4/20 for domestic students, 2/20 for international students; for spring admission, 11/15 for domestic students, 9/15 for international students. Application fee: $40 ($60 for international students). Electronic applications accepted. *Expenses:* Tuition, state resident: full-time $2071; part-time $86 per credit. Tuition, nonresident: full-time $8099; part-time $337 per credit. Required fees: $9446; $394 per credit. One-time fee: $75. Part-time tuition and fees vary according to class time, course load, degree level and reciprocity agreements. *Financial support:* In 2010–11, 3 fellowships with full tuition reimbursements (averaging $10,512 per year), 10 research assistantships with full tuition reimbursements (averaging $10,868 per year), 1 teaching assistantship with full tuition reimbursement (averaging $3,000 per year) were awarded; unspecified assistantships also available. Financial award application deadline: 3/1; financial award applicants required to submit FAFSA. *Faculty research:* Tetracycline-encapsulated chitosan microspheres, artificial tissues, sensor arrays for orthopedic rehab, blue light cures, healing bandages. Total annual research expenditures: $1.4 million. *Unit head:* Dr. Vijay Chalivendra, Co-Director, 508-910-6572, E-mail: vchalivendra@umassd.edu. *Application contact:* Elan Turcotte-Shamski, Graduate Admissions Officer, 508-999-8604, Fax: 508-999-8183, E-mail: graduate@umassd.edu.

University of Massachusetts Lowell, College of Arts and Sciences, Department of Biological Sciences, Lowell, MA 01854-2881. Offers biochemistry (PhD); biological sciences (MS); biotechnology (MS). Part-time programs available. *Degree requirements:* For master's, thesis; for doctorate, thesis/dissertation. *Entrance requirements:* For master's and doctorate, GRE General Test. Electronic applications accepted.

University of Minnesota, Twin Cities Campus, Graduate School, Program in Microbial Engineering, Minneapolis, MN 55455-0213. Offers MS. Part-time programs available. *Degree requirements:* For master's, thesis. *Entrance requirements:* For master's, GRE General Test. Additional exam requirements/recommendations for international students: Required—TOEFL. *Faculty research:* Microbial genetics, oncogenesis, gene transfer, fermentation, bioreactors, genetics of antibiotic biosynthesis.

University of Missouri–St. Louis, College of Arts and Sciences, Department of Biology, St. Louis, MO 63121. Offers biotechnology (Certificate); cell and molecular biology (MS, PhD); ecology, evolution and systematics (MS, PhD); tropical biology and conservation (Certificate). Part-time programs available. *Faculty:* 43 full-time (13 women), 2 part-time/adjunct (1 woman). *Students:* 73 full-time (36 women), 63 part-time (36 women); includes 17 minority (6 Black or African American, non-Hispanic/Latino; 9 Asian, non-Hispanic/Latino; 2 Hispanic/Latino), 45 international. Average age 29. 193 applicants, 44% accepted, 44 enrolled. In 2010, 35 master's,

11 doctorates, 6 other advanced degrees awarded. *Degree requirements:* For master's, thesis or alternative; for doctorate, thesis/dissertation, 1 semester of teaching experience. *Entrance requirements:* For master's, 3 letters of recommendation; for doctorate, GRE General Test, 3 letters of recommendation. Additional exam requirements/recommendations for international students: Required—TOEFL. *Application deadline:* For fall admission, 12/1 priority date for domestic and international students; for spring admission, 10/15 priority date for domestic and international students. Applications are processed on a rolling basis. Application fee: $35 ($40 for international students). Electronic applications accepted. *Expenses:* Tuition, state resident: full-time $5522; part-time $306.80 per credit hour. Tuition, nonresident: full-time $14,253; part-time $792.10 per credit hour. Required fees: $658; $49 per credit hour. One-time fee: $12. Tuition and fees vary according to program. *Financial support:* In 2010–11, 30 research assistantships with full and partial tuition reimbursements (averaging $18,113 per year), 15 teaching assistantships with full and partial tuition reimbursements (averaging $17,514 per year) were awarded; fellowships with full tuition reimbursements, career-related internships or fieldwork and Federal Work-Study also available. Support available to part-time students. Financial award application deadline: 2/1. *Faculty research:* Molecular biology, microbial genetics, animal behavior, tropical ecology, plant systematics. *Unit head:* Dr. Peter Stevens, Director of Graduate Studies, 314-516-6200, Fax: 314-516-6233, E-mail: stevensp@umsl.edu. *Application contact:* 314-516-5458, Fax: 314-516-6996, E-mail: gradadm@umsl.edu.

University of Nevada, Reno, Graduate School, College of Agriculture, Biotechnology and Natural Resources, Program in Biotechnology, Reno, NV 89557. Offers MS. 5 year degree; students are admitted to as undergraduates. *Degree requirements:* For master's, thesis. *Entrance requirements:* For master's, GRE, minimum GPA of 2.75. Additional exam requirements/recommendations for international students: Required—TOEFL (minimum score 500 paper-based; 173 computer-based; 61 iBT), IELTS (minimum score 6). Electronic applications accepted. *Expenses:* Tuition, state resident: full-time $2219; part-time $246 per credit. Tuition, nonresident: part-time $510 per credit. International tuition: $9009 full-time. Required fees: $59 per term. One-time fee: $101. Tuition and fees vary according to course load. *Faculty research:* Cancer biology, plant virology.

University of Northern Iowa, Graduate College, College of Natural Sciences, Department of Biology, Cedar Falls, IA 50614. Offers biology (MA, MS); biotechnology (PSM); ecosystem management (PSM). Part-time programs available. *Students:* 21 full-time (9 women), 7 part-time (2 women); includes 2 minority (1 Hispanic/Latino; 1 Two or more races, non-Hispanic/Latino), 1 international. 39 applicants, 49% accepted, 13 enrolled. In 2010, 17 master's awarded. *Degree requirements:* For master's, comprehensive exam (for some programs), thesis or alternative. *Entrance requirements:* For master's, minimum GPA of 3.0; 3 letters of recommendation. Additional exam requirements/recommendations for international students: Required—TOEFL (minimum score 500 paper-based; 180 computer-based; 61 iBT). *Application deadline:* For fall admission, 8/1 priority date for domestic students. Applications are processed on a rolling basis. Application fee: $50 ($70 for international students). Electronic applications accepted. *Financial support:* Scholarships/grants available. Financial award application deadline: 2/1. *Unit head:* Dr. David Saunders, Head, 319-273-2456, Fax: 319-273-7125, E-mail: david.saunders@uni.edu. *Application contact:* Laurie S. Russell, Record Analyst, 319-273-2623, Fax: 319-273-2885, E-mail: laurie.russell@uni.edu.

University of North Texas Health Science Center at Fort Worth, Graduate School of Biomedical Sciences, Fort Worth, TX 76107-2699. Offers anatomy and cell biology (MS, PhD); biochemistry and molecular biology (MS, PhD); biomedical sciences (MS, PhD); biotechnology (MS); forensic genetics (MS); integrative physiology (MS, PhD); medical science (MS); microbiology and immunology (MS, PhD); pharmacology (MS, PhD); science education (MS); DO/MS; DO/PhD. Terminal master's awarded for partial completion of doctoral program. *Degree requirements:* For master's, thesis; for doctorate, thesis/dissertation. *Entrance requirements:* For master's and doctorate, GRE General Test. Additional exam requirements/recommendations for international students: Required—TOEFL. *Expenses:* Contact institution. *Faculty research:* Alzheimer's disease, aging, eye diseases, cancer, cardiovascular disease.

University of Pennsylvania, School of Engineering and Applied Science, Program in Biotechnology, Philadelphia, PA 19104. Offers MS. Part-time programs available. *Students:* 78 full-time (44 women), 28 part-time (16 women); includes 2 Black or African American, non-Hispanic/Latino; 13 Asian, non-Hispanic/Latino; 2 Hispanic/Latino, 55 international. 167 applicants, 59% accepted, 69 enrolled. In 2010, 62 master's awarded. *Entrance requirements:* For master's, GRE General Test, bachelor's degree in science or undergraduate course work in molecular biology. Additional exam requirements/recommendations for international students: Required—TOEFL. *Application deadline:* For fall admission, 6/1 priority date for domestic students, 5/1 priority date for international students. Applications are processed on a rolling basis. Application fee: $70. Electronic applications accepted. *Expenses:* Tuition: Full-time $25,660; part-time $4758 per course. Required fees: $2152; $270 per course. Tuition and fees vary according to course load, degree level and program.

University of Rhode Island, Graduate School, College of the Environment and Life Sciences, Department of Cell and Molecular Biology, Kingston, RI 02881. Offers biochemistry (MS, PhD); clinical laboratory sciences (MS), including biotechnology, clinical laboratory science, cytopathology; microbiology (MS, PhD); molecular genetics (MS, PhD). Part-time programs available. *Faculty:* 13 full-time (5 women), 2 part-time/adjunct (1 woman). *Students:* 32 full-time (15 women), 37 part-time (23 women); includes 10 minority (5 Black or African American, non-Hispanic/Latino; 2 Asian, non-Hispanic/Latino; 3 Hispanic/Latino), 4 international. In 2010, 29 master's, 3 doctorates awarded. *Degree requirements:* For master's, comprehensive exam (for some programs); for doctorate, comprehensive exam. *Entrance requirements:* For master's and doctorate, GRE, 2 letters of recommendation. Additional exam requirements/recommendations for international students: Required—TOEFL (minimum score 550 paper-based; 213 computer-based). *Application deadline:* For fall admission, 7/15 for domestic students, 2/1 for international students; for spring admission, 11/15 for domestic students, 7/15 for international students. Application fee: $65. Electronic applications accepted. *Expenses:* Tuition, state resident: full-time $9588; part-time $533 per credit hour. Tuition, nonresident: full-time $22,968; part-time $1276 per credit hour. Required fees: $1282; $68 per semester. Tuition and fees vary according to program. *Financial support:* In 2010–11, 3 research assistantships with full and partial tuition reimbursements (averaging $11,653 per year), 12 teaching assistantships with full and partial tuition reimbursements (averaging $12,379 per year) were awarded. Financial award application deadline: 7/15; financial award applicants required to submit FAFSA. *Faculty research:* Genomics and Sequencing Center: an interdisciplinary genomics research and undergraduate and graduate student training program which provides researchers access to cutting-edge technologies in the field of genomics. Total annual research expenditures: $3.5 million. *Unit head:* Dr. Jay Sperry, Chairperson, 401-874-2201, Fax: 401-874-2202, E-mail: jsperry@mail.uri.edu. *Application contact:* Dr. Jay Sperry, Chairperson, 401-874-2201, Fax: 401-874-2202, E-mail: jsperry@mail.uri.edu.

University of Saskatchewan, College of Graduate Studies and Research, Edwards School of Business, Program in Business Administration, Saskatoon, SK S7N 5A2, Canada. Offers agribusiness management (MBA); biotechnology management (MBA); health services management (MBA); indigenous management (MBA); international business management (MBA).

The University of Texas at Dallas, School of Natural Sciences and Mathematics, Program in Biology, Richardson, TX 75080. Offers bioinformatics and computational biology (MS); biotechnology (MS); molecular and cell biology (MS, PhD). Part-time and evening/weekend programs available. *Faculty:* 18 full-time (3 women), 1 part-time/adjunct (0 women). *Students:* 109 full-time (61 women), 19 part-time (7 women); includes 22 minority (5 Black or African American, non-Hispanic/Latino; 14 Asian, non-Hispanic/Latino; 3 Hispanic/Latino), 82 international. Average age 26. 331 applicants, 37% accepted, 38 enrolled. In 2010, 36 master's, 5 doctorates awarded. *Degree requirements:* For master's, thesis optional; for doctorate, thesis/dissertation, publishable paper. *Entrance requirements:* For master's and doctorate, GRE (minimum combined score of 1000 on verbal and quantitative). Additional exam requirements/recommendations for international students: Required—TOEFL (minimum score 550 paper-based; 215 computer-based; 80 iBT). *Application deadline:* For fall admission, 7/15 for domestic students, 5/1 priority date for international students; for spring admission, 11/15 for domestic students, 9/1 priority date for international students. Applications are processed on a rolling basis. Application fee: $50 ($100 for international students). Electronic applications accepted. *Expenses:* Tuition, state resident: full-time $10,248; part-time $569 per credit hour. Tuition, nonresident: full-time $18,544; part-time $1030 per credit hour. Tuition and fees vary according to course load. *Financial support:* In 2010–11, 58 students received support, including 19 research assistantships with partial tuition reimbursements available (averaging $13,403 per year), 32 teaching assistantships with partial tuition reimbursements available (averaging $14,513 per year); career-related internships or fieldwork, Federal Work-Study, institutionally sponsored loans, scholarships/grants, and unspecified assistantships also available. Support available to part-time students. Financial award application deadline: 4/30; financial award applicants required to submit FAFSA. *Faculty research:* Role of mitochondria in neurodegenerative diseases, protein-DNA interactions in site-specific recombination, eukaryotic gene expression, bio-nanotechnology, sickle cell research. *Unit head:* Dr. Li Zhang, Department Head, 972-883-6032, Fax: 972-883-2502, E-mail: li.zhang@utdallas.edu. *Application contact:* Dr. Lawrence Reitzer, Graduate Advisor, 972-883-2502, Fax: 972-883-2402, E-mail: reitzer@utdallas.edu.

The University of Texas at San Antonio, College of Sciences, Department of Biology, San Antonio, TX 78249-0617. Offers biology (MS, PhD); biotechnology (MS); neurobiology (PhD). Part-time programs available. *Faculty:* 36 full-time (3 women), 7 part-time/adjunct (3 women). *Students:* 143 full-time (76 women), 65 part-time (37 women); includes 81 minority (10 Black or African American, non-Hispanic/Latino; 10 Asian, non-Hispanic/Latino; 48 Hispanic/Latino; 13 Two or more races, non-Hispanic/Latino), 73 international. Average age 27. 252 applicants, 50% accepted, 69 enrolled. In 2010, 42 master's, 17 doctorates awarded. *Degree requirements:* For master's, comprehensive exam, thesis; for doctorate, comprehensive exam, thesis/dissertation. *Entrance requirements:* For master's, GRE General Test, minimum GPA of 3.0; for doctorate, GRE General Test, minimum GPA of 3.3. Additional exam requirements/recommendations for international students: Required—TOEFL (minimum score 500 paper-based; 173 computer-based; 61 iBT), IELTS (minimum score 5). *Application deadline:* For fall admission, 7/1 for domestic students, 4/1 for international students; for spring admission, 11/1 for domestic students, 9/1 for international students. Applications are processed on a rolling basis. Application fee: $45 ($80 for international students). Electronic applications accepted. *Expenses:* Tuition, state resident: full-time $4172; part-time $231.75 per credit hour. Tuition, nonresident: full-time $15,332; part-time $851.75 per credit hour. *Financial support:* In 2010–11, 66 students received support, including 25 fellowships (averaging $24,632 per year), 162 research assistantships (averaging $19,317 per year), 73 teaching assistantships (averaging $10,841 per year); career-related internships or fieldwork, scholarships/grants, and unspecified assistantships also available. Support available to part-time students. *Faculty research:* Cell and molecular biology, neurobiology, microbiology, integrative biology, environmental science. Total annual research expenditures: $1.7 million. *Unit head:* Dr. Edwin J. Barea-Rodriguez, Interim Chair, 210-458-4511, Fax: 210-458-5658, E-mail: edwin.barea@utsa.edu. *Application contact:* Veronica Ramirez, Assistant Dean of the Graduate School, 210-458-4330, Fax: 210-458-4332, E-mail: graduatestudies@utsa.edu.

University of the Sciences in Philadelphia, College of Graduate Studies, Program in Cell Biology and Biotechnology, Philadelphia, PA 19104-4495. Offers cell and molecular biology (PhD); cell biology (MS). Part-time and evening/weekend programs available. *Degree requirements:* For master's, thesis (for some programs). *Entrance requirements:* For master's, GRE General Test. Additional exam requirements/recommendations for international students: Required—TOEFL, TWE. *Expenses:* Contact institution. *Faculty research:* Invertebrate cell adhesion, plant-microbe interactions, natural product mechanisms, cell signal transduction, gene regulation and organization.

University of Toronto, School of Graduate Studies, Life Sciences Division, Program in Biotechnology, Toronto, ON M5S 1A1, Canada. Offers MBiotech.

University of Utah, Graduate School, Professional Master of Science and Technology Program, Salt Lake City, UT 84112-1107. Offers biotechnology (PSM); computational science (PSM); environmental science (PSM); science instrumentation (PSM). Part-time programs available. *Faculty:* 2 full-time (0 women). *Students:* 32 full-time (17 women), 38 part-time (13 women); includes 1 Black or African American, non-Hispanic/Latino; 3 Asian, non-Hispanic/Latino; 1 Hispanic/Latino, 19 international. Average age 31. 66 applicants, 48% accepted, 16 enrolled. In 2010, 7 master's awarded. *Degree requirements:* For master's, internship. *Entrance requirements:* For master's, GRE (recommended), minimum undergraduate GPA of 3.0, bachelor's degree from accredited university or college. Additional exam requirements/recommendations for international students: Required—TOEFL (minimum score 500 paper-based; 173 computer-based; 61 iBT), IELTS (minimum score 6). *Application deadline:* For fall admission, 3/1 for domestic and international students. Application fee: $55 ($65 for international students). Electronic applications accepted. *Expenses:* Tuition, area resident: Part-time $179.19 per credit hour. Tuition, state resident: full-time $4384. Tuition, nonresident: full-time $16,684; part-time $630.67 per credit hour. Required fees: $350 per semester. Tuition and fees vary according to course load, degree level and program. *Financial support:* In 2010–11, 8 students received support, including 5 fellowships with full and partial tuition reimbursements available (averaging $16,800 per year), 2 research assistantships (averaging $6,200 per year); unspecified assistantships also available. Financial award applicants required to submit FAFSA. *Faculty research:* Drug delivery systems, in vitro erythroid expansion and HRE (Hypoxia responsive element). *Unit head:* Jennifer Schmidt, Program Director, 801-585-5630, E-mail: jennifer.schmidt@gradschool.utah.edu. *Application contact:* Amy Kimball, Project Coordinator, 801-585-3650, Fax: 801-585-6749, E-mail: amy.kimball@gradschool.utah.edu.

University of Washington, Graduate School, School of Medicine, Graduate Programs in Medicine, Department of Genome Sciences, Seattle, WA 98195. Offers PhD. *Degree requirements:* For doctorate, thesis/dissertation, general exam. *Entrance requirements:* For doctorate, GRE General Test, minimum GPA of 3.0. Additional exam requirements/recommendations for international students: Required—TOEFL. Electronic applications accepted. *Faculty research:* Model organism genetics, human and medical genetics, genomics and proteomics, computational biology.

University of West Florida, College of Arts and Sciences: Sciences, School of Allied Health and Life Sciences, Department of Biology, Pensacola, FL 32514-5750. Offers biological chemistry (MS); biology (MS); biology education (MST); biotechnology (MS); coastal zone studies (MS); environmental biology (MS). *Faculty:* 10 full-time (2 women). *Students:* 6 full-time (4 women), 32 part-time (18 women); includes 1 Black or African American, non-Hispanic/Latino; 1 Asian, non-Hispanic/Latino; 1 Hispanic/Latino, 1 international. Average age 28. 17 applicants, 53% accepted, 7 enrolled. In 2010, 3 master's awarded. *Degree requirements:* For master's, thesis. *Entrance requirements:* For master's, GRE General Test. Additional exam requirements/recommendations for international students: Required—TOEFL (minimum score 550 paper-based; 213 computer-based). *Application deadline:* For fall admission, 6/1 for domestic students, 5/15 for international students; for spring admission, 10/1 for domestic and international students. Applications are processed on a rolling basis. Application fee: $30. *Expenses:* Tuition, state resident: full-time $4982; part-time $208 per credit hour. Tuition, nonresident: full-time $20,059; part-time $836 per credit hour. Required fees: $1365; $57 per credit hour. *Financial support:* In 2010–11, 20 fellowships with partial tuition reimbursements (averaging $523 per year), 18 research assistantships with partial tuition reimbursements (averaging $5,700 per year), 12 teaching assistantships with partial tuition reimbursements (averaging $8,042 per year) were awarded; unspecified assistantships also available. Financial award application deadline: 4/15; financial award applicants required to submit FAFSA. *Unit head:* Dr. George L. Stewart, Chairperson, 850-474-2748. *Application contact:* Terry McCray, Assistant Director of Graduate Admissions, 850-473-7718, Fax: 850-473-7714, E-mail: gradadmissions@uwf.edu.

Biotechnology

University of Wyoming, Graduate Program in Molecular and Cellular Life Sciences, Laramie, WY 82070. Offers PhD. *Degree requirements:* For doctorate, thesis/dissertation, four eight-week laboratory rotations, comprehensive basic practical exam, two-part qualifying exam, seminars, symposium.

Virginia Polytechnic Institute and State University, Graduate School, College of Science, Program in Biomedical Technology Development and Management, Blacksburg, VA 24061. Offers MS. *Students:* 5 part-time (4 women); includes 3 Asian, non-Hispanic/Latino. Average age 25. 2 applicants, 100% accepted, 2 enrolled. *Degree requirements:* For master's, comprehensive exam (for some programs), thesis (for some programs). *Entrance requirements:* For master's, GRE. Additional exam requirements/recommendations for international students: Required—TOEFL (minimum score 550 paper-based; 213 computer-based). *Application deadline:* For fall admission, 7/1 for domestic and international students; for spring admission, 12/1 for domestic and international students. Applications are processed on a rolling basis. Application fee: $65. Electronic applications accepted. *Expenses:* Tuition, area resident: Full-time $9399; part-time $488 per credit hour. Tuition, state resident: full-time $9399; part-time $488 per credit hour. Tuition, nonresident: full-time $17,854; part-time $957.75 per credit hour. International tuition: $17,854 full-time. Required fees: $1534. Full-time tuition and fees vary according to program. *Financial support:* Career-related internships or fieldwork, Federal Work-Study, scholarships/grants, health care benefits, and unspecified assistantships available. Total annual research expenditures: $289,400. *Unit head:* Dr. Kenneth H. Wong, UNIT HEAD, 703-518-2978, Fax: 540-231-7511, E-mail: khwong@vt.edu. *Application contact:* Jennifer LeFurgy, Contact, 703-518-2710, Fax: 540-231-7511, E-mail: jlefurgy@vt.edu.

West Virginia State University, Graduate Programs, Institute, WV 25112-1000. Offers biotechnology (MA, MS); media studies (MA). *Entrance requirements:* For master's, GRE General Test, minimum GPA of 3.0, 3 letters of recommendation. Additional exam requirements/recommendations for international students: Required—TOEFL (minimum score 550 paper-based).

William Paterson University of New Jersey, College of Science and Health, Wayne, NJ 07470-8420. Offers biotechnology (MS); communication disorders (MS); general biology (MS); nursing (MSN). Part-time and evening/weekend programs available. *Entrance requirements:* For master's, GRE General Test, minimum GPA of 2.75. Electronic applications accepted. *Faculty research:* Plant tissue culture, DNA cloning, cellular structure, language development, speech and hearing science.

Worcester Polytechnic Institute, Graduate Studies and Research, Department of Biology and Biotechnology, Worcester, MA 01609-2280. Offers biology and biotechnology (MS); biotechnology (PhD). *Faculty:* 5 full-time (3 women). *Students:* 17 full-time (13 women); includes

1 Asian, non-Hispanic/Latino, 8 international. 103 applicants, 6% accepted, 4 enrolled. In 2010, 4 master's, 1 doctorate awarded. Terminal master's awarded for partial completion of doctoral program. *Degree requirements:* For master's, thesis; for doctorate, comprehensive exam, thesis/dissertation, qualifying exam. *Entrance requirements:* For master's, GRE General Test., 3 letters of recommendation, statement of purpose; for doctorate, GRE General Test, 3 letters of recommendation, statement of purpose. Additional exam requirements/recommendations for international students: Required—TOEFL (minimum score 550 paper-based; 213 computer-based; 79 iBT), IELTS (minimum score 6.5). *Application deadline:* For fall admission, 1/1 priority date for domestic and international students. Application fee: $70. Electronic applications accepted. *Expenses:* Tuition: Full-time $20,862; part-time $1159 per term. One-time fee: $15. *Financial support:* Teaching assistantships, career-related internships or fieldwork, institutionally sponsored loans, scholarships/grants, and unspecified assistantships available. Financial award application deadline: 1/1; financial award applicants required to submit FAFSA. *Faculty research:* Molecular and cellular biology, developmental, neuro- and regenerative biology, behavioral and environmental biology, plant biotechnology. *Unit head:* Dr. Joseph Duffy, Head, 508-831-5538, Fax: 508-831-5936, E-mail: jduffy@wpi.edu. *Application contact:* Dr. Reeta Prusty-Rao, Graduate Coordinator, 508-831-5538, Fax: 508-831-5936, E-mail: rpr@wpi.edu.

Worcester State University, Graduate Studies, Program in Biotechnology, Worcester, MA 01602-2597. Offers MS. Part-time and evening/weekend programs available. *Faculty:* 6 full-time (2 women). *Students:* 3 full-time (1 woman), 27 part-time (16 women); includes 3 Asian, non-Hispanic/Latino; 1 Hispanic/Latino; 1 Two or more races, non-Hispanic/Latino, 1 international. Average age 30. 29 applicants, 66% accepted, 9 enrolled. In 2010, 8 master's awarded. *Degree requirements:* For master's, comprehensive exam, thesis. *Entrance requirements:* For master's, GRE General Test or MAT, minimum undergraduate GPA of 3.0 in biology. Additional exam requirements/recommendations for international students: Required—TOEFL (minimum score 500 paper-based; 61 iBT). *Application deadline:* Applications are processed on a rolling basis. Application fee: $40. Electronic applications accepted. *Expenses:* Tuition, state resident: full-time $2700; part-time $150 per credit. Tuition, nonresident: full-time $2700; part-time $150 per credit. Required fees: $2016; $112 per credit. *Financial support:* In 2010–11, 2 students received support, including 2 research assistantships with full tuition reimbursements available (averaging $4,800 per year); career-related internships or fieldwork, scholarships/grants, and unspecified assistantships also available. Financial award application deadline: 3/1; financial award applicants required to submit FAFSA. *Faculty research:* Effects of insulin in invertebrates, ecology of freshwater turtles, symbiotic relations of plants and animals, *Unit head:* Dr. Peter Bradley, Coordinator, 508-929-8571, Fax: 508-929-8171, E-mail: pbradley@worcester.edu. *Application contact:* Sara Grady, Assistant Dean of Graduate and Continuing Education, 508-929-8787, Fax: 508-929-8100, E-mail: sara.grady@worcester.edu.

Nanotechnology

Arizona State University, College of Liberal Arts and Sciences, Department of Chemistry and Biochemistry, Tempe, AZ 85287-1604. Offers biochemistry (MS, PhD); chemistry (MS, PhD); nanoscience (PSM). *Faculty:* 68 full-time (16 women), 10 part-time/adjunct (6 women). *Students:* 180 full-time (59 women), 9 part-time (4 women); includes 13 minority (1 Black or African American, non-Hispanic/Latino; 10 Asian, non-Hispanic/Latino; 1 Hispanic/Latino; 1 Two or more races, non-Hispanic/Latino), 96 international. Average age 26. 505 applicants, 19% accepted, 45 enrolled. In 2010, 9 master's, 22 doctorates awarded. Terminal master's awarded for partial completion of doctoral program. *Degree requirements:* For master's, thesis, interactive Program of Study (iPOS) submitted before completing 50 percent of required credit hours; for doctorate, comprehensive exam, thesis/dissertation, interactive Program of Study (iPOS) submitted before completing 50 percent of required credit hours. *Entrance requirements:* For master's and doctorate, GRE, minimum GPA of 3.0 or equivalent in last 2 years of work leading to bachelor's degree. Additional exam requirements/recommendations for international students: Required—TOEFL, IELTS, or Pearson Test of English. *Application deadline:* For fall admission, 1/15 priority date for domestic and international students. Applications are processed on a rolling basis. Application fee: $70 ($90 for international students). Electronic applications accepted. *Expenses:* Tuition, state resident: full-time $8510; part-time $608 per credit. Tuition, nonresident: full-time $16,542; part-time $919 per credit. Required fees: $339; $110 per credit. Part-time tuition and fees vary according to course load. *Financial support:* In 2010–11, 77 research assistantships with full and partial tuition reimbursements (averaging $17,448 per year), 97 teaching assistantships with full and partial tuition reimbursements (averaging $17,637 per year) were awarded; fellowships with full tuition reimbursements, career-related internships or fieldwork, Federal Work-Study, institutionally sponsored loans, scholarships/grants, health care benefits, and tuition waivers (full and partial) also available. Financial award application deadline: 3/1. Total annual research expenditures: $18.2 million. *Unit head:* Dr. William Petuskey, Chair, 480-965-4430, Fax: 480-965-8607, E-mail: wpetuskey@asu.edu. *Application contact:* Graduate Admissions, 480-965-6113.

Arizona State University, College of Liberal Arts and Sciences, Department of Physics, Tempe, AZ 85287-1504. Offers nanoscience (PSM); physics (MNS, PhD). Part-time programs available. *Faculty:* 38 full-time (5 women), 1 part-time/adjunct (0 women). *Students:* 109 full-time (24 women), 21 part-time (9 women); includes 9 minority (5 Asian, non-Hispanic/Latino; 2 Hispanic/Latino; 2 Two or more races, non-Hispanic/Latino), 69 international. Average age 28. 166 applicants, 43% accepted, 29 enrolled. In 2010, 12 master's, 8 doctorates awarded. Terminal master's awarded for partial completion of doctoral program. *Degree requirements:* For master's, comprehensive exam, thesis or alternative, interactive Program of Study (iPOS) submitted before completing 50 percent of required credit hours; for doctorate, comprehensive exam, thesis/dissertation, interactive Program of Study (iPOS) submitted before completing 50 percent of required credit hours. *Entrance requirements:* For master's and doctorate, GRE, minimum GPA of 3.0 or equivalent in last 2 years of work leading to bachelor's degree. Additional exam requirements/recommendations for international students: Required—TOEFL, IELTS, or Pearson Test of English. *Application deadline:* For fall admission, 3/1 for domestic and international students; for spring admission, 9/1 for domestic and international students. Applications are processed on a rolling basis. Application fee: $70 ($90 for international students). Electronic applications accepted. *Expenses:* Contact institution. *Financial support:* In 2010–11, 49 research assistantships with tuition reimbursements (averaging $15,550 per year), 54 teaching assistantships with tuition reimbursements (averaging $15,486 per year) were awarded; fellowships with full tuition reimbursements, career-related internships or fieldwork, Federal Work-Study, institutionally sponsored loans, scholarships/grants, and tuition waivers (full and partial) also available. Financial award application deadline: 3/1; financial award applicants required to submit FAFSA. Total annual research expenditures: $5.5 million. *Unit head:* Dr. Robert J. Nemanich, Chair, 480-965-3561, E-mail: robert.nemanich@asu.edu. *Application contact:* Graduate Admissions, 480-965-6113.

The Johns Hopkins University, G. W. C. Whiting School of Engineering, Program in Engineering Management, Baltimore, MD 21218-2699. Offers biomaterials (MSEM); communications science (MSEM); computer science (MSEM); fluid mechanics (MSEM); materials science and engineering (MSEM); mechanical engineering (MSEM); mechanics and materials (MSEM); nano-biotechnology (MSEM); nanomaterials and nanotechnology (MSEM); probability and statistics (MSEM); smart product and device design (MSEM); systems analysis, management and environmental policy (MSEM). *Students:* 32 full-time (5 women), 4 part-time (0 women); includes 7 minority (3 Black or African American, non-Hispanic/Latino; 3 Asian,

non-Hispanic/Latino; 1 Hispanic/Latino), 11 international. Average age 23. 110 applicants, 60% accepted, 27 enrolled. In 2010, 6 master's awarded. *Entrance requirements:* For master's, GRE, 3 letters of recommendation, resume. Additional exam requirements/recommendations for international students: Required—TOEFL (minimum score 600 paper-based; 250 computer-based; 100 iBT) or IELTS (minimum score 7). *Application deadline:* For fall admission, 1/15 priority date for domestic students, 1/15 for international students; for spring admission, 9/15 priority date for domestic students, 9/15 for international students. Applications are processed on a rolling basis. Application fee: $75. Electronic applications accepted. *Financial support:* Fellowships, health care benefits available. *Unit head:* Dr. Edward R. Scheinerman, Interim Director/Vice Dean for Education, School of Engineering/Professor, Applied Mathematics and Statistics, 410-516-7395, Fax: 410-516-4880, E-mail: ers@jhu.edu. *Application contact:* Dennis McIver, Coordinator of Graduate Admissions, 410-516-8174, Fax: 410-516-0780, E-mail: graduateadmissions@jhu.edu.

North Dakota State University, College of Graduate and Interdisciplinary Studies, Interdisciplinary Program in Materials and Nanotechnology, Fargo, ND 58108. Offers PhD. *Students:* 11 full-time (2 women), 2 part-time (0 women), 7 international. 10 applicants, 50% accepted, 5 enrolled. In 2010, 1 doctorate awarded. *Entrance requirements:* For doctorate, GRE General Test. Additional exam requirements/recommendations for international students: Required—TOEFL (minimum score 525 paper-based; 197 computer-based; 71 iBT). *Application deadline:* For fall admission, 5/1 for international students; for spring admission, 8/1 for international students. Application fee: $45 ($60 for international students). *Unit head:* Dr. Erik Hobbe, Director, 701-231-7049, E-mail: erik.hobbie@ndsu.edu. *Application contact:* Dr. Erik Hobbe, Director, 701-231-7049, E-mail: erik.hobbie@ndsu.edu.

Oregon State University, Graduate School, College of Engineering, School of Mechanical, Industrial, and Manufacturing Engineering, Corvallis, OR 97331. Offers human systems engineering (MS, PhD); industrial engineering (MS, PhD); information systems engineering (MS, PhD); manufacturing engineering (M Engr); manufacturing systems engineering (MS, PhD); materials science (MAIS, MS, PhD); mechanical engineering (MS, PhD); nano/micro fabrication (MS, PhD). Part-time programs available. Postbaccalaureate distance learning degree programs offered (minimal on-campus study). *Degree requirements:* For master's, thesis or alternative; for doctorate, thesis/dissertation. *Entrance requirements:* For master's, placement exam, minimum GPA of 3.0 in last 90 hours of course work; for doctorate, GRE, placement exam, minimum GPA of 3.0 in last 90 hours of course work. Additional exam requirements/recommendations for international students: Required—TOEFL (minimum score 550 paper-based; 213 computer-based). *Faculty research:* Computer-integrated manufacturing, human factors, robotics, decision support systems, simulation modeling and analysis.

South Dakota School of Mines and Technology, Graduate Division, Program in Nanoscience and Nanoengineering, Rapid City, SD 57701-3995. Offers PhD.

University at Albany, State University of New York, College of Nanoscale Science and Engineering, Albany, NY 12222-0001. Offers MS, PhD. *Entrance requirements:* Additional exam requirements/recommendations for international students: Required—TOEFL (minimum score 550 paper-based; 213 computer-based). *Faculty research:* Thin film material structures, optoelectronic materials, design and fabrication of nano-mechanical systems, materials characterization.

University of Alberta, Faculty of Graduate Studies and Research, Department of Electrical and Computer Engineering, Edmonton, AB T6G 2E1, Canada. Offers communications (M Eng, M Sc, PhD); computer engineering (M Eng, M Sc, PhD); electromagnetics (M Eng, M Sc, PhD); nanotechnology and microdevices (M Eng, M Sc, PhD); power/power electronics (M Eng, M Sc, PhD); systems (M Eng, M Sc, PhD). Terminal master's awarded for partial completion of doctoral program. *Degree requirements:* For master's, thesis; for doctorate, thesis/dissertation. *Entrance requirements:* Additional exam requirements/recommendations for international students: Required—TOEFL. Electronic applications accepted. *Faculty research:* Controls, communications, microelectronics, electromagnetics.

University of California, Riverside, Graduate Division, Graduate Materials Science and Engineering Program, Riverside, CA 92521. Offers MS, PhD. *Faculty:* 40. *Students:* 15 full-time (5 women); includes 1 Black or African American, non-Hispanic/Latino; 6 Asian, non-Hispanic/Latino. Average age 27. 60 applicants, 30% accepted, 8 enrolled. *Entrance requirements:* For master's and doctorate, GRE. Additional exam requirements/recommendations for international students: Required—TOEFL (minimum score 550 paper-based; 213 computer-based; 80 iBT). *Application deadline:* For fall admission, 1/5 priority date for domestic students. Application fee: $0 ($100 for international students). Electronic applications accepted. *Financial support:* In 2010–11, 8 students received support; fellowships, research assistantships, teaching assistantships, scholarships/grants, health care benefits, and unspecified assistantships available. Financial award application deadline: 1/5. *Unit head:* MSE Program Office, 951-827-3392, Fax: 951-827-3188, E-mail: mse-program@engr.ucr.edu. *Application contact:* Graduate Admissions, 951-827-3392, Fax: 951-827-3188, E-mail: mse-program@engr.ucr.edu.

University of New Mexico, Graduate School, Program in Nanoscience and Microsystems, Albuquerque, NM 87131-2039. Offers MS, PhD. Part-time programs available. *Faculty:* 2 full-time (both women). *Students:* 31 full-time (12 women), 5 part-time (0 women); includes 11 minority (4 Asian, non-Hispanic/Latino; 7 Hispanic/Latino), 2 international. Average age 31. 18 applicants, 78% accepted, 11 enrolled. In 2010, 2 master's awarded. *Degree requirements:* For master's, comprehensive exam, thesis; for doctorate, comprehensive exam, thesis/dissertation. *Entrance requirements:* For master's and doctorate, GRE. Additional exam requirements/recommendations for international students: Required—TOEFL. *Application deadline:* For fall admission, 7/30 for domestic students, 2/1 for international students; for spring admission, 11/30 for domestic students, 6/1 for international students. Application fee: $50. Electronic applications accepted. *Expenses:* Tuition, state resident: full-time $5991; part-time $251 per credit hour. Tuition, nonresident: full-time $14,405; part-time $800.20 per credit hour. Tuition and fees vary according to course level, course load, program and reciprocity agreements. *Financial support:* In 2010–11, 31 students received support, including 30 research assistantships (averaging $17,556 per year), 7 teaching assistantships (averaging $7,505 per year). *Unit head:* Dr. Abhaya Datye, Distinguished Professor, 505-277-0477, Fax: 505-277-1024, E-mail: datye@unm.edu. *Application contact:* Heather Elizabeth Armstrong, Program Specialist, 505-277-6824, Fax: 505-277-1024, E-mail: heathera@unm.edu.

University of Washington, Graduate School, College of Engineering and School of Medicine, Department of Bioengineering, Seattle, WA 98195-5061. Offers bioengineering (MS, PhD); bioengineering and nanotechnology (PhD); medical engineering (MME); pharmaceutical bioengineering (MS). Evening/weekend programs available. Postbaccalaureate distance learning degree programs offered (no on-campus study). *Faculty:* 30 full-time (10 women), 10 part-time/adjunct (2 women). *Students:* 109 full-time (47 women), 46 part-time (19 women); includes 3 Black or African American, non-Hispanic/Latino; 1 American Indian or Alaska Native, non-Hispanic/Latino; 33 Asian, non-Hispanic/Latino; 4 Hispanic/Latino, 28 international. Average age 26. 442 applicants, 19% accepted, 39 enrolled. In 2010, 19 master's, 16 doctorates awarded. *Degree requirements:* For master's, comprehensive exam, thesis; for doctorate, comprehensive exam, thesis/dissertation, qualifying exam, general exam, thesis defense. *Entrance requirements:* For master's and doctorate, GRE General Test, Minimum GPA of 3.0, transcripts, statement of purpose, letters of recommendation. Additional exam requirements/recommendations for international students: Required—TOEFL (minimum score 580 paper-based; 237 computer-based; 92 iBT); Recommended—IELTS (minimum score 7). *Application deadline:* For fall admission, 12/15 priority date for domestic students, 12/1 priority date for international students. Application fee: $75. Electronic applications accepted. *Financial support:* In 2010–11, 2 students received support, including 25 fellowships with full tuition reimbursements available (averaging $19,098 per year), 111 research assistantships with full tuition reimbursements available (averaging $19,224 per year), 15 teaching assistantships with full tuition reimbursements available (averaging $19,224 per year); Federal Work-Study, institutionally sponsored loans, traineeships, health care benefits, and tuition waivers (full) also available. Support available to part-time students. Financial award application deadline: 12/15; financial award applicants required to submit FAFSA. *Faculty research:* Biomaterials and tissue engineering; global health, distributed diagnosis and home healthcare; bioinstrumentation; molecular bioengineering; imaging and image-guided therapy. Total annual research expenditures: $23.4 million. *Unit head:* Dr. Paul Yager, Professor and Chair, 206-685-2000, Fax: 206-685-3300, E-mail: yagerp@u.washington.edu. *Application contact:* Dorian Taylor, Senior Academic Counselor, 206-685-2000, Fax: 206-685-3300, E-mail: bioeng@u.washington.edu.

University of Washington, Graduate School, College of Engineering, Department of Chemical Engineering, Seattle, WA 98195-1750. Offers chemical engineering (MS, MSE, PhD); chemical engineering and nanotechnology (PhD). *Faculty:* 20 full-time (2 women), 6 part-time/adjunct (1 woman). *Students:* 72 full-time (24 women), 1 part-time (0 women); includes 2 Black or African American, non-Hispanic/Latino; 1 American Indian or Alaska Native, non-Hispanic/Latino; 10 Asian, non-Hispanic/Latino; 1 Hispanic/Latino, 18 international. Average age 25. 187 applicants, 25% accepted, 14 enrolled. In 2010, 17 master's, 5 doctorates awarded. Terminal master's awarded for partial completion of doctoral program. *Degree requirements:* For master's, thesis, Pass final exam, serve as TA for 1 quarter, research project; for doctorate, thesis/dissertation, Pass general & final exams, research project, complete all work for doctoral degree within 10 years.. *Entrance requirements:* For master's and doctorate, GRE General test (minimum Quantitative Score of 750), Minimum GPA of 3.0, official transcripts & degree statements, personal statement, confidential evaluations by 3 professors or other technical professional, highly ranked (top 5%) in respected chemical engineering program, optional: resume/cv, writing sample (journal articles only).. Additional exam requirements/recommendations for international students: Required—TOEFL (minimum score 580 paper-based; 237 computer-based; 92 iBT); Recommended—IELTS (minimum score 7). *Application deadline:* For fall admission, 1/15 priority date for domestic students, 12/15 priority date for international students. Applications are processed on a rolling basis. Application fee: $75. Electronic applications accepted. *Financial support:* In 2010–11, 4 students received support, including 24 fellowships with full tuition reimbursements available (averaging $22,500 per year), 40 research assistantships with full tuition reimbursements available (averaging $19,035 per year), 12 teaching assistantships with full tuition reimbursements available (averaging $19,035 per year); career-related internships or fieldwork, Federal Work-Study, health care benefits, and unspecified assistantships also available. Financial award application deadline: 1/15; financial award applicants required to submit FAFSA. *Faculty research:* Molecular energy processes, living systems and biomolecular processes, molecular aspects of materials and interfaces, molecular/organic electronics. Total annual research expenditures: $7 million. *Unit head:* Dr. Daniel T. Schwartz, Professor and Chair, 206-543-2250, Fax: 206-543-3778, E-mail: dts@uw.edu. *Application contact:* Dave Drischell, Lead Academic Counselor, 206-543-2252, Fax: 206-543-3778, E-mail: rdd@u.washington.edu.

University of Washington, Graduate School, College of Engineering, Department of Electrical Engineering, Seattle, WA 98195-2500. Offers electrical engineering (MS, PhD); electrical engineering and nanotechnology (PhD). Postbaccalaureate distance learning degree programs offered (no on-campus study). *Faculty:* 57 full-time (9 women), 12 part-time/adjunct (2 women). *Students:* 210 full-time (45 women), 134 part-time (11 women); includes 11 Black or African American, non-Hispanic/Latino; 1 American Indian or Alaska Native, non-Hispanic/Latino; 57 Asian, non-Hispanic/Latino; 11 Hispanic/Latino, 126 international. 903 applicants, 25% accepted, 101 enrolled. In 2010, 86 master's, 29 doctorates awarded. *Degree requirements:* For master's, thesis optional; for doctorate, thesis/dissertation, Qualifying, general, & final exams.. *Entrance requirements:* For master's and doctorate, GRE General Test: Recommend Verbal 500, Quantitative 720, Analytical 600 or Analytical Writing 5 or 6., Minimum GPA of 3.2, resume or cv, statement of purpose, 3 letters of recommendation, undergrad and grad transcripts, optional: personal statement.. Additional exam requirements/recommendations for international students: Required—TOEFL (minimum score 600 paper-based; 250 computer-based; 92 iBT); Recommended—IELTS (minimum score 7). *Application deadline:* For fall admission, 1/1 priority date for domestic students, 12/15 priority date for international students. Application fee: $75. Electronic applications accepted. *Financial support:* In 2010–11, 4 students received support, including 4 fellowships with full tuition reimbursements available (averaging $18,648 per year), 120 research assistantships with partial tuition reimbursements available (averaging $19,233 per year), 41 teaching assistantships with partial tuition reimbursements available (averaging $14,787 per year); career-related internships or fieldwork, Federal Work-Study, and institutionally sponsored loans also available. Financial award application deadline: 1/1; financial award applicants required to submit FAFSA. *Faculty research:* Controls and robotics, communications and signal processing, electromagnetics, optics and acoustics, electronic devices and photonics. Total annual research expenditures: $14.1 million. *Unit head:* Dr. Leung Tsang, Professor and Chair, 206-221-5270, Fax: 206-543-3842, E-mail: tsang@ee.washington.edu. *Application contact:* Scott Latiolais, Lead Graduate Program Academic Counselor, 206-221-7913, Fax: 206-543-3842, E-mail: latiolais@ee.washington.edu.

University of Washington, Graduate School, College of Engineering, Department of Materials Science and Engineering, Seattle, WA 98195-2120. Offers ceramic engineering (PhD); materials science and engineering (MS, MSE, PhD); materials science and engineering and nanotechnology (PhD). Part-time programs available. *Faculty:* 24 full-time (4 women). *Students:* 55 full-time (14 women), 9 part-time (2 women); includes 2 Black or African American, non-Hispanic/Latino; 7 Asian, non-Hispanic/Latino; 2 Hispanic/Latino, 22 international. Average age 30. 246 applicants, 11% accepted, 11 enrolled. In 2010, 3 master's, 9 doctorates awarded. *Degree requirements:* For master's, comprehensive exam, thesis optional; for doctorate, comprehensive exam, thesis/dissertation, Qualifying evaluation, general and final exams.. *Entrance requirements:* For master's and doctorate, GRE General Test, minimum GPA of 3.0. Additional exam requirements/recommendations for international students: Required—TOEFL (minimum score 580 paper-based; 237 computer-based; 92 iBT); Recommended—IELTS (minimum score 7). *Application deadline:* For fall admission, 1/15 priority date for domestic students, 12/15 priority date for international students. Application fee: $75. Electronic applications accepted. *Financial support:* In 2010–11, 3 students received support, including 7 fellowships with full tuition reimbursements available (averaging $22,500 per year), 39 research assistantships with full tuition reimbursements available (averaging $16,407 per year), 8 teaching assistantships with full tuition reimbursements available (averaging $16,362 per year); career-related internships or fieldwork, Federal Work-Study, institutionally sponsored loans, scholarships/grants, health care benefits, unspecified assistantships, and stipend supplements also available. Financial award application deadline: 1/15; financial award applicants required to submit FAFSA. *Faculty research:* Biomimetics and biomaterials; electronic, optical and magnetic materials; eco-materials and materials for energy applications; ceramics, metals, composites, and polymers. Total annual research expenditures: $8.8 million. *Unit head:* Dr. Alex Jen, Professor and Chair, 206-543-2600, Fax: 206-543-3100, E-mail: ajen@uw.edu. *Application contact:* Kathleen A. Elkins, Academic Counselor, 206-616-6581, Fax: 206-543-3100, E-mail: kelkins@uw.edu.

Virginia Commonwealth University, Graduate School, College of Humanities and Sciences, Department of Physics, Richmond, VA 23284-9005. Offers medical physics (MS, PhD); nanoscience and nanotechnology (PhD); physics and applied physics (MS). Part-time programs available. *Students:* 49 full-time (14 women), 3 part-time (0 women); includes 5 minority (2 Black or African American, non-Hispanic/Latino; 2 Asian, non-Hispanic/Latino; 1 Hispanic/Latino), 17 international. 58 applicants, 41% accepted, 16 enrolled. In 2010, 7 master's, 1 doctorate awarded. *Degree requirements:* For master's, comprehensive exam, thesis optional. *Entrance requirements:* For master's, GRE. Additional exam requirements/recommendations for international students: Required—TOEFL (minimum score 600 paper-based; 250 computer-based; 100 iBT); Recommended—IELTS (minimum score 6.5). *Application deadline:* For fall admission, 3/15 for domestic students; for spring admission, 11/15 for domestic students. Applications are processed on a rolling basis. Application fee: $50. Electronic applications accepted. *Expenses:* Tuition, state resident: full-time $4308; part-time $479 per credit hour. Tuition, nonresident: full-time $8942; part-time $994 per credit hour. Required fees: $2000; $85 per credit hour. Tuition and fees vary according to course level, course load, degree level, campus/location and program. *Financial support:* Fellowships, teaching assistantships, Federal Work-Study, institutionally sponsored loans, and tuition waivers (full and partial) available. Support available to part-time students. *Faculty research:* Condensed-matter theory and experimentation, electronic instrumentation, relativity. *Unit head:* Dr. Alison A. Baski, Chair, 804-828-8295, Fax: 804-828-7073, E-mail: aabaski@vcu.edu. *Application contact:* Dr. Shiv Khanna, Graduate Program Director, 804-828-1820, Fax: 804-828-7073, E-mail: snkhanna@vcu.edu.

Virginia Commonwealth University, Graduate School, College of Humanities and Sciences, Program in Nanosciences, Richmond, VA 23284-9005. Offers PhD. *Students:* 5 full-time (1 woman), 2 international. 5 applicants, 80% accepted, 3 enrolled. *Entrance requirements:* For doctorate, GRE General Test. Additional exam requirements/recommendations for international students: Required—TOEFL (minimum score 600 paper-based; 250 computer-based; 100 iBT); Recommended—IELTS (minimum score 6.5). *Application deadline:* For fall admission, 3/15 for domestic students; for spring admission, 11/15 for domestic students. Application fee: $50. Electronic applications accepted. *Expenses:* Tuition, state resident: full-time $4308; part-time $479 per credit hour. Tuition, nonresident: full-time $8942; part-time $994 per credit hour. Required fees: $2000; $85 per credit hour. Tuition and fees vary according to course level, course load, degree level, campus/location and program. *Faculty research:* Nanotechnology, nanoscience. *Unit head:* Dr. Everett E. Carpenter, Program Director, 804-828-7508, E-mail: ecarpenter2@vcu.edu. *Application contact:* Dr. Everett E. Carpenter, Program Director, 804-828-7508, E-mail: ecarpenter2@vcu.edu.

CASE WESTERN RESERVE UNIVERSITY

Department of Biomedical Engineering

Programs of Study	The Department offers many exceptional and innovative educational programs leading to career opportunities in biomedical engineering (BME) research, development, and design in industry, medical centers, and academic institutions. Graduate degrees offered include the M.S. and Ph.D. in BME, a combined M.D./M.S. degree offered to students admitted to the School of Medicine, and combined M.D./Ph.D. degrees in BME offered through the Physician Engineer Training Program or the Medical Scientist Training Program. Individualized BME programs of study allow students to develop strength in an engineering specialty and apply this expertise to an important biomedical problem under the supervision of a Faculty Guidance Committee. Students can choose from more than forty-three courses regularly taught in BME, as well as many courses in other departments. Typically, an M.S. program consists of seven to nine courses, and a Ph.D. program consists of about thirteen courses beyond the B.S. Students can select research projects from among the many strengths of the Department, including neural engineering and neural prostheses, biomaterials, tissue engineering, drug and gene delivery, biomedical imaging, sensors, optical imaging and diagnostics, the cardiovascular system, biomechanics, mass and heat transport, and metabolic systems. Collaborative research and training in basic biomedical sciences, as well as clinical and translational research, are available through primary faculty members, associated faculty members, and researchers in the nearby major medical centers.
Research Facilities	The primary faculty members have laboratories focusing on cardiovascular and skeletal biomaterials; cardiovascular, orthopaedic, and neural tissue engineering; materials and nanoparticles for drug and gene delivery, biomedical image processing, biomedical imaging in several modalities, cellular and tissue cardiac bioelectricity, ion channel function, electrochemical and fiber-optic sensors, neural engineering and brain electrophysiology, and neural prostheses. BME faculty members and students also make extensive use of campus research centers for special purposes such as microelectronic fabrication, biomedical imaging, and material analyses. Associated faculty members have labs devoted to eye movement control, gait analysis, implantable sensors/actuators, biomedical imaging, metabolism, and tissue pathology. These are located at four major medical centers and teaching hospitals that (with one exception) are within walking distance.
Financial Aid	Graduate students pursuing the Ph.D. may receive financial support from faculty members as research assistants, from training grants (NIH, NSF, DoE GAANN), or from the School of Medicine (M.D./Ph.D. only). These positions are awarded on a competitive basis. There are also opportunities for research assistantships in order to pursue the M.S.
Cost of Study	Tuition at Case in 2009–10 for graduate students was $1430 per credit hour. A full load for graduate students is a minimum of 9 credits per semester. Fees for health insurance and activities are estimated at $500 per semester.
Living and Housing Costs	Within a 2-mile radius of the campus, numerous apartments are available for married and single graduate students at rents ranging from $450 to $900 per month.
Student Group	The Department of Biomedical Engineering has 150 graduate students, of whom about 85 percent are advancing toward the Ph.D. At Case Western Reserve University, approximately 4,356 students are enrolled as undergraduates, 3,182 in graduate studies, and 2,276 in the professional schools.
Location	Case is located on the eastern boundary of Cleveland in University Circle, which is the city's cultural center. The area includes Severance Hall (home of the Cleveland Orchestra), the Museum of Art, the Museum of Natural History, the Garden Center, the Institute of Art, the Institute of Music, the Western Reserve Historical Society, and the Crawford Auto-Aviation Museum. Metropolitan Cleveland has a population of almost 2 million. The Cleveland Hopkins International Airport is 30 minutes away by rail transit. A network of parks encircles the greater Cleveland area. Opportunities are available for sailing on Lake Erie and for hiking and skiing nearby in Ohio, Pennsylvania, and New York. Major-league sports, theater, and all types of music provide a full range of entertainment.
The University and The Department	The Department of Biomedical Engineering at Case Western Reserve University is part of both the Case School of Engineering and the School of Medicine, which are located on the same campus. Established in 1967, the Department is one of the pioneers in biomedical engineering education and is currently among the nation's largest and highest rated (according to *U.S. News & World Report*). Case Western Reserve University was formed in 1967 by a federation of Western Reserve College and Case Institute of Technology. Numerous interdisciplinary programs exist with the professional Schools of Medicine, Dentistry, Nursing, Law, Social Work, and Management.
Applying	Applications that request financial aid should be submitted before February 1. The completed application requires official transcripts, scores on the GRE General Test, and three letters of reference. Application forms are available from the BME Admissions Coordinator or can be downloaded from the Case Web site (http://www.case.edu). Applicants for the M.D./M.S. and M.D./Ph.D. programs can apply through the School of Medicine.
Correspondence and Information	Admissions Coordinator Department of Biomedical Engineering Wickenden Building 310 Case Western Reserve University 10900 Euclid Avenue Cleveland, Ohio 44106-7207 Phone: 216-368-4094 Fax: 216-368-4969 Web site: http://bme.case.edu

Case Western Reserve University

THE FACULTY AND THEIR RESEARCH

Primary Faculty

Eben Alsberg, Ph.D., Assistant Professor. Biomimetic tissue engineering, innovative biomaterials and drug delivery vehicles for functional tissue regeneration and cancer therapy, control of stem cell differentiation, mechanotransduction and the influence of mechanics on cell and tissue function, cell-cell interactions.

James P. Basilion, Ph.D., Associate Professor of BME and Radiology. Molecular imaging, biomarkers, diagnosis and treatment of cancer.

Harihara Baskaran, Ph.D., Assistant Professor of BME and Chemical Engineering. Tissue engineering; cell/cellular transport processes in inflammation, wound healing, and cancer metastasis.

Patrick E. Crago, Ph.D., Professor. Control of neuroprostheses for motor function, neuromuscular control systems.

Jeffrey L. Duerk, Ph.D., Professor and Chairman. Radiology, MRI, fast MRI pulse sequence design, interventional MRI, MRI reconstruction.

Dominique M. Durand, Ph.D., Professor. Neural engineering, neuroprostheses, neural dynamics, magnetic and electric stimulation of the nervous system, neural interfaces with electronic devices, analysis and control of epilepsy.

Steven J. Eppell, Ph.D., Associate Professor. Nanoscale instrumentation for biomaterials, bone and cartilage structure and function.

Miklos Gratzl, Ph.D., Associate Professor. Fine chemical manipulation of microdroplets and single cells, cancer research and neurochemistry at the single-cell level, cost-effective biochemical diagnostics in microliter body fluids.

Kenneth Gustafson, Ph.D., Assistant Professor. Neural engineering, neural prostheses, neurophysiology and neural control of genitourinary function, devices to restore genitourinary function, functional neuromuscular stimulation.

Efstathios Karathanasis, Ph.D., Assistant Professor. Fabricating multifunctional agents that facilitate diagnosing, treating, and monitoring of therapies in a patient-specific manner.

J. Lawrence Katz, Ph.D., Professor Emeritus. Structure-property relationships in bone, osteophilic biomaterials, ultrasonic studies of tissue anisotropy, scanning acoustic microscopy.

Robert Kirsch, Ph.D., Professor. Functional neuromuscular stimulation, biomechanics and neural control of human movement, modeling and simulation of musculoskeletal systems, identification of physiological systems.

Melissa Knothe-Tate, Ph.D., Professor of BME and Mechanical and Aerospace Engineering. Etiology and innovative treatment modalities for osteoporosis, fracture healing, osteolysis, and osteonecrosis.

Erin Lavik, Sc.D., Associate Professor. Biomaterials and synthesis of new degradable polymers, tissue engineering, spinal cord repair, retinal regeneration, drug delivery for optic nerve preservation and repair.

Zheng-Rong Lu, Ph.D., Professor. Molecular imaging and drug delivery using novel nanotechnology.

Roger E. Marchant, Ph.D., Professor and Director of the Center for Cardiovascular Biomaterials. Surface modification of cardiovascular devices, molecular-level structure and function of plasma proteins, liposome drug delivery systems, mechanisms of bacterial adhesion to biomaterials.

J. Thomas Mortimer, Ph.D., Professor Emeritus. Neural prostheses, electrical activation of the nervous system, bowel and bladder assist device, respiratory assist device, selective stimulation and electrode development, electrochemical aspects of electrical stimulation.

P. Hunter Peckham, Ph.D., Professor and Director of the Functional Electrical Stimulation Center. Neural prostheses, implantable stimulation and control of movement, rehabilitation engineering.

Andrew M. Rollins, Ph.D., Assistant Professor. Biomedical diagnosis; novel optical methods for high-resolution, minimally invasive imaging; tissue characterization and analyte sensing; real-time microstructural and functional imaging using coherence tomography; endoscopy.

Gerald M. Saidel, Ph.D., Professor and Director of the Center for Modeling Integrated Metabolic Systems. Mass and heat transport and metabolic analysis in cells, tissues, and organs; mathematical modeling, simulation, and parameter estimation; optimal experimental design; metabolic dynamics; minimally invasive thermal tumor ablation; slow-release drug delivery.

Anirban Sen Gupta, Ph.D., Assistant Professor. Targeted drug delivery, targeted molecular imaging, image-guided therapy, platelet substitutes, novel polymeric biomaterials for tissue engineering scaffolds.

Dustin Tyler, Ph.D., Assistant Professor. Neuromimetic neuroprostheses, laryngeal neuroprostheses, clinical implementation of nerve electrodes, cortical neuroprostheses, minimally invasive implantation techniques, modeling of neural stimulation and neuroprostheses.

Horst von Recum, Ph.D., Assistant Professor. Tissue-engineered epithelia, prevascularized polymer scaffolds, directed stem cell differentiation, novel stimuli-responsive biomaterials for gene and drug delivery, systems biology approaches to the identification of angiogenic factors.

David L. Wilson, Ph.D., Professor. In vivo microscopic and molecular imaging; medical image processing; image segmentation, registration, and analysis; quantitative image quality of X-ray fluoroscopy and fast MRI; interventional MRI treatment of cancer.

Xin Yu, Sc.D., Associate Professor. Cardiovascular physiology, magnetic resonance imaging and spectroscopy, characterization of the structure-function and energy-function relationships in normal and diseased hearts, small-animal imaging and spectroscopy.

Associated Faculty (partial list)

Jay Alberts, Ph.D., Assistant Professor (BME, Cleveland Clinic Foundation). Neural basis of upper-extremity motor function and deep-brain stimulation in Parkinson's disease.

James M. Anderson, M.D./Ph.D., Professor (Pathology, University Hospitals). Biocompatibility of implants, human vascular grafts.

Richard C. Burgess, M.D./Ph.D., Adjunct Professor (Staff Physician, Neurology, Cleveland Clinic Foundation). Electrophysiological monitoring, EEG processing.

Arnold Caplan, Ph.D., Professor of Biology. Tissue engineering.

Peter R. Cavanagh, Ph.D., Adjunct Professor (Academic Director, Diabetic Foot Care Program, and Virginia Lois Kennedy Chairman of Biomedical Engineering, Cleveland Clinic Foundation). Foot complications of diabetes, bone biomechanics.

John Chae, M.D., Associate Professor (Neural Rehabilitation, MetroHealth Medical Center). Application of neuroprostheses in hemiplegia.

Yuanna Cheng, M.D./Ph.D., Adjunct Associate Professor (Cardiovascular Medicine, Cleveland Clinic Foundation). Cardiac imaging, mechanisms of arrhythmias, implantable defibrillators, cardiac remodeling, antiarrhythmic therapy.

Hillel J. Chiel, Ph.D., Professor. Biomechanical and neural basis of feeding behavior in *Aplysia californica*, neuromechanical system modeling.

Guy Chisolm, Ph.D., Adjunct Professor (Vice Chairman, Lerner Research Institute, and Staff, Cell Biology, Cleveland Clinic Foundation). Cell and molecular mechanisms in vascular disease and vascular biology; role of lipoprotein oxidation in atherosclerosis; lipoprotein transport into, accumulation in, and injury to arterial tissue.

Janis J. Daly, Ph.D., Adjunct Associate Professor (Neurology, VA Medical Center). Cognitive and motor processes involved in motor control.

Margot Damaser, Ph.D., Assistant Professor of Molecular Medicine (BME, Cleveland Clinic Foundation). Biomechanics as it relates to function and dysfunction of the lower urinary tract.

Brian Davis, Ph.D., Adjunct Associate Professor (BME, Cleveland Clinic Foundation). Human locomotion, diabetic foot pathology, space flight–induced osteoporosis, biomedical instrumentation.

David Dean, Ph.D., Assistant Professor (Neurological Surgery, University Hospitals). 3-D medical imaging and morphometrics; skull, brain, soft tissue face.

Louis F. Dell'Osso, Ph.D., Professor (Neurology, VA Medical Center). Neurophysiological control, ocular motor control and oscillations.

Kathleen Derwin, Ph.D., Assistant Professor (BME, Cleveland Clinic Foundation). Tendon mechanobiology and tissue engineering.

Isabelle Deschenes, Ph.D., Assistant Professor (Cardiology, MetroHealth Medical Center). Molecular imaging, ion channel structure and function, genetic regulation of ion channels, cellular and molecular mechanisms of cardiac arrhythmias.

Claire M. Doerschuk, M.D., Associate Professor (Pediatrics, RB&C, University Hospitals). Regulation of the inflammatory response in the lungs.

Agata Exner, Ph.D., Assistant Professor (Radiology, University Hospitals). Image-guided drug delivery, polymers for interventional radiology, models of cancer.

Baowei Fei, Ph.D., Assistant Professor (Radiology, University Hospitals). Quantitative image analysis, multimodality image registration, fusion visualization, image-guided minimally invasive therapy, prostate cancer, photodynamic therapy.

Elizabeth Fisher, Ph.D., Assistant Staff (BME, Cleveland Clinic Foundation). Quantitative image analysis for monitoring multiple sclerosis.

Marc Griswold, Ph.D., Associate Professor (Radiology, University Hospitals). Rapid magnetic resonance imaging, image reconstruction and processing, MRI hardware/instrumentation.

Elizabeth C. Hardin, Ph.D., Adjunct Assistant Professor (Rehabilitation Research and Development, VA Medical Center). Neural prostheses and gait mechanics, improving gait performance with neural prostheses using strategies developed in conjunction with forward dynamics musculoskeletal models.

Michael W. Keith, M.D., Professor (Orthopaedics, MetroHealth Medical Center). Restoration of motor function in hands.

Kevin Kilgore, Ph.D., Adjunct Assistant Professor (MetroHealth Medical Center). Functional electrical stimulation, restoration of hand function.

Kandice Kottke-Marchant, M.D./Ph.D., Adjunct Associate Professor (Staff, Clinical Pathology, Cleveland Clinic Foundation). Interaction of blood and materials, endothelial cell function on biomaterials.

Kenneth R. Laurita, Ph.D., Assistant Professor (Heart and Vascular Research Center, MetroHealth Medical Center). Cardiac electrophysiology, arrhythmia mechanisms, intracellular calcium homeostasis, fluorescence imaging, instrumentation and software for potential mapping.

Zhenghong Lee, Ph.D., Assistant Professor (Radiology, University Hospitals). Quantitative PET and SPECT imaging, multimodal image registration, 3-D visualization, molecular imaging, small-animal imaging systems.

R. John Leigh, M.D., Professor (Neurology, VA Medical Center). Normal and abnormal motor control, eye movements.

Cameron McIntyre, Ph.D., Adjunct Assistant Professor (BME, Cleveland Clinic Foundation). Electric field modeling in the nervous system, deep brain stimulation.

George Muschler, M.D., Professor (Staff, BME, Cleveland Clinic Foundation). Musculoskeletal oncology, adult reconstructive orthopaedic surgery, fracture nonunion, research in bone healing and bone-grafting materials.

Raymond Muzic, Ph.D., Assistant Professor (Radiology, University Hospitals). Modeling and experiment design for PET, image reconstruction.

Sherif G. Nour, M.D., Assistant Professor (Radiology, University Hospitals). Interventional MRI.

Marc Penn, M.D., Ph.D., Adjunct Assistant Professor (Assistant Staff, Cardiology and Cell Biology, Cleveland Clinic Foundation). Myocardial ischemia, remodeling, gene regulation and therapy.

Clare Rimnac, Ph.D., Associate Professor and Director of the Musculoskeletal Mechanics and Materials Laboratories, Mechanical and Aerospace Engineering. Orthopaedic implant performance and design, mechanical behavior of hand tissues.

David S. Rosenbaum, M.D., Associate Professor (Director, Heart and Vascular Research Center, MetroHealth Medical Center). High-resolution cardiac optical mapping, arrhythmia mechanisms, ECG signal processing.

Mark S. Rzeszotarski, Ph.D., Assistant Professor (Radiology, MetroHealth Medical Center). Computers in radiology: MRI/CT/nuclear medicine, ultrasound.

Dawn Taylor, Ph.D., Assistant Professor (BME, Cleveland Clinic Foundation). Brain-computer interfaces for control of computers, neural prostheses, and robotic devices; invasive and noninvasive brain signal acquisition; adaptive decoding algorithms for retraining the brain to control alternative devices after paralysis.

Ronald Triolo, Ph.D., Associate Professor (Orthopaedics, VA Medical Center). Rehabilitation engineering, neuroprostheses, orthopaedic biomechanics.

Antonie J. van den Bogert, Ph.D., Adjunct Assistant Professor (Assistant Staff, BME, Cleveland Clinic Foundation). Biomechanics of human movement.

D. Geoffrey Vince, Ph.D., Adjunct Assistant Professor (Assistant Staff, BME, Cleveland Clinic Foundation). Image and signal processing of intravascular ultrasound images, coronary plaque rupture, cellular aspects of atherosclerosis.

Albert L. Waldo, M.D., Professor (Medicine, University Hospitals). Cardiac electrophysiology, cardiac excitation mapping, mechanisms of cardiac arrhythmias and conduction.

Barry W. Wessels, Ph.D., Professor (Radiation Oncology, University Hospitals). Radio-labeled antibody therapy (dosimeter and clinical trials); image-guided radiotherapy; intensity-modulated radiation therapy; image fusion of CT, MR, SPECT, and PET for adaptive radiation therapy treatment planning.

Guang H. Yue, Ph.D., Adjunct Assistant Professor (Assistant Staff, BME, Cleveland Clinic Foundation). Neural control of movement, electrophysiology, MRI.

Marcie Zborowski, Ph.D., Adjunct Assistant Professor (Assistant Staff, BME, Cleveland Clinic Foundation). High-speed magnetic cell sorting.

Nicholas P. Ziats, Ph.D., Assistant Professor (Pathology, University Hospitals). Vascular grafts, cell-material interactions, extracellular matrix, tissue engineering, blood compatibility.

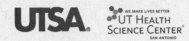

THE UNIVERSITY OF TEXAS AT SAN ANTONIO
THE UNIVERSITY OF TEXAS HEALTH SCIENCE CENTER AT SAN ANTONIO

Joint M.S. in Biomedical Engineering Program

Programs of Study

The University of Texas at San Antonio (UTSA) and the University of Texas Health Science Center at San Antonio (UTHSCSA) jointly offer a M.S. degree in biomedical engineering. The objective of the Program is to train students in the use of basic biomedical engineering approaches for the investigation of fundamental bioengineering questions associated with the diagnosis and treatment of human diseases. Engineers, basic scientists, and clinicians will participate in the education and training of each student, and new graduates from this program will be uniquely trained in the fundamental sciences and engineering related to medicine.

Students take core courses in the areas of biomaterials, biomechanics, bioelectronics/imaging, and biology (cell and molecular biology and either gross human anatomy or human physiology), as well as analytic techniques in engineering analysis, ethics in research, experimental design and data analysis, supervised teaching, and introduction to clinical practices. In addition to the basic core curriculum, students are required to take additional course work in their area of specialization and overall, students must complete a minimum of 30.5 hours (Thesis Option) or 34.5 hours (Non-thesis Option) of graduate work and must maintain an overall grade point average of at least 3.0. The required and selected courses are intended to focus and support the individual's mastery of his or her particular area of expertise. Throughout their graduate training, students have access to the bioengineering and biosciences laboratories at both UTHSCSA and UTSA. This provides a unique opportunity to have learning experiences in medical, dental, bioscience, and engineering environments.

Research Facilities

The University of Texas at San Antonio (UTSA) and the University of Texas Health Science Center at San Antonio (UTHSCSA) offer many resource facilities with biotechnology equipment and state-of-the art laboratories. The College of Engineering maintains laboratories and offices in three separate buildings. The newest building on the main campus is the Applied Engineering and Technology Building, which was completed in October 2009 and comprises 150,000 square feet of laboratories and classrooms for College of Engineering students as well as administrative offices.

At UTHSCSA, the new South Texas Research Facility (STRF) is slated to open in fall 2011 with over 190,000 square feet of research space. Research programs selected for the STRF include adult cancer, neurosciences, healthy aging, regenerative medicine, the Institute for the Integration of Medicine and Science, and South Texas Technology Management. Additional information regarding STRF is available at http://research.uthscsa.edu/STRF/index.shtml.

Financial Aid

Currently there is no Program funding for the master's degree program. Competitive scholarships are available for research in rehabilitation medicine with information requests to the Biomedical Engineering Program office. Teaching and research assistantships may also be available from research mentors. Other financial aid opportunities include the McNair and Valero scholarships and possible funding support on a principal investigator's grant. College of Engineering scholarships are also available and can be found at http://engineering.utsa.edu/scholarships/index.php.

Cost of Study

For the 2011–12 academic year, tuition and fees for a full-time graduate degree student (9 semester hours) are approximately $3149 per semester for Texas residents and $8783 per semester for nonresidents. Some courses and programs have additional fees. Please view the following Web sites for more information: http://www.utsa.edu/fiscalservices/tuition.html and http://www.graduateschool.utsa.edu/prospective_students/detail/graduate_tuition_and_fees.

Living and Housing Costs

University on-campus housing is available and includes apartment-style living at four complexes—Chisholm Hall, University Oaks, Laurel Village, and Chaparral Village. Off-campus housing is also available and includes many apartments adjacent to the University as well as a large number located within a 5-mile drive. Average costs for room and board are $4244 per semester.

Student Group

In the 2010 fall semester, the University enrolled more than 30,000 students, of whom more than 4,000 were graduate students. In spring 2011, 108 students were enrolled in the graduate-level Biomedical Engineering Programs. Admission into the Program is very competitive with only about 33 percent of the applicants being offered admission. The average GRE scores of all students matriculating into the Program were verbal 523 and quantitative 716; the average GPA was 3.46 on a 4.0 scale. The racial, ethnic, and gender diversity of the students is one of the strengths of the UTSA/UTHSCSA Joint Graduate Program in Biomedical Engineering, and continues the historic role of both UTSA and UTHSCSA as minority-serving institutions.

Location

San Antonio, with a population of 1.5 million, is one of the nation's major metropolitan areas. As the home of the Alamo and numerous other missions built by the Franciscans, the city is historically and culturally diverse. The Guadalupe Cultural Arts Center, McNay Art Museum, the San Antonio Museum of Art, and the Witte Museum enrich the city. The performing arts are represented by the San Antonio Symphony, the annual Tejano Music Festival and Tejano Music Awards, and performances by opera and ballet companies. Also notable are Sea World, Six Flags Fiesta Texas, Brackenridge Park, the Botanical Gardens, and the downtown Riverwalk. Numerous nearby lakes allow almost year-round outdoor activity, and the beaches of the Texas Gulf coast are within a 2-hour drive. San Antonio is home to numerous festivals throughout the year, including the Fiesta San Antonio and the Rodeo, with activities such as parades, fairs, and concerts.

The University

The University was founded in 1969 and has since become a comprehensive metropolitan institution. Its research expenditures place it in the top 25 percent of public universities in Texas. The University has entered a new building and recruitment phase with a view to greatly expand the research effort in the biosciences. UTSA has three campus locations in San Antonio (downtown campus, main campus, and the Institute of Texan Cultures); the Biomedical Engineering facilities are located on the main campus. Facilities are also available to the Joint Program students at the campus of the University of Texas Health Science Center (UTHSCSA), a premier health institution and medical school, dental school, and nursing school.

UTSA Roadrunners football is slated to compete as an NCAA Division I FCS independent in August 2011 and is expected to transition to the Division I FSB subdivision by 2013.

Applying

A completed application will include an online Graduate school application (http://www.graduateschool.utsa.edu/prospective_students/detail/on-line_application). All applications and required attachments are to be sent to the Graduate School (no documents will be accepted at the Biomedical Engineering office). The application fee is sent through the online system. Official transcripts from all institutions attended are required. GRE test scores (UTSA ETS code: 6919) and TOEFL scores for international applicants must be included in the application with supporting documentation. Three letters of recommendation must be included with the application. A Statement of Purpose describing prior experience, objectives, and subject area interests for research is required to be submitted with the admission application. The deadline for applications is February 1 for the fall semester and October 1 for the spring semester. All deadlines are determined by the Graduate School, and are firm, with no exceptions.

Correspondence and Information

For application information:
The Graduate School
The University of Texas at San Antonio
One UTSA Circle
San Antonio, Texas 78249

Phone: 210-458-4330
Web site: http://www.graduateschool.utsa.edu

For program information:
Department of Biomedical Engineering
The University of Texas at San Antonio
One UTSA Circle
San Antonio, Texas 78249

Phone: 210-458-5535
E-mail: Margaret.boullosa@utsa.edu
Web site:
http://engineering.utsa.edu/bme/BME_program/index.html

The University of Texas at San Antonio

THE FACULTY AND THEIR RESEARCH

There are core and associated faculty affiliated with the Biomedical Engineering Program, both with primary appointments at UTSA and UTHSCSA. They are at all academic ranks (Instructor through Professor/Chairman/Dean).

Faculty members at UTHSCSA are drawn from the Medical School (medicine/cardiology, orthopedics, radiology, rehabilitative medicine), Dental School (community dentistry, periodontics, restorative dentistry), and the Graduate School of Biomedical Sciences (physiology, radiological sciences, research imaging center).

Similarly, faculty members at UTSA are drawn from both the College of Engineering (biomedical engineering, electrical engineering, mechanical engineering) and the College of Sciences (biology, chemistry).

The Biomedical Engineering Program has a number of outstanding faculty members, several of whom are leaders in their respective fields and are internationally recognized. As a group, they generated over $80 million during the first four years of the Program's existence to support their research endeavors, published over 900 full-length manuscripts and abstracts, and filed 30 patent applications.

THE UNIVERSITY OF TEXAS AT SAN ANTONIO
THE UNIVERSITY OF TEXAS HEALTH SCIENCE CENTER AT SAN ANTONIO

Joint Ph.D. in Biomedical Engineering Program

Programs of Study

The University of Texas at San Antonio (UTSA) and The University of Texas Health Science Center at San Antonio (UTHSCSA) jointly offer a Ph.D. degree in biomedical engineering. The objective of the Program is to train students in the use of basic biomedical engineering approaches for the investigation of fundamental bioengineering questions associated with the diagnosis and treatment of human diseases. Engineers, basic scientists, and clinicians will participate in the education and training of each student, and new graduates from this program will be uniquely trained in the fundamental sciences and engineering related to medicine.

Students take core courses in the areas of biomaterials, biomechanics, bioelectronics/imaging, and biology (cell and molecular biology and either gross human anatomy or human physiology), as well as analytic techniques in engineering analysis, ethics in research, experimental design and data analysis, supervised teaching, and introduction to clinical practices. In addition to the basic core curriculum, students are required to take additional course work in their area of specialization and overall, students must complete a minimum of 81 hours of graduate work and must maintain an overall grade point average of at least 3.0. The required and selected courses are intended to focus and support the individual's mastery of his or her particular area of expertise. Throughout their graduate training, students have access to the bioengineering and biosciences laboratories at both UTHSCSA and UTSA. This provides a unique opportunity to have learning experiences in medical, dental, bioscience, and engineering environments.

Research Facilities

The University of Texas at San Antonio (UTSA) and the University of Texas Health Science Center at San Antonio (UTHSCSA) offer many resource facilities with biotechnology equipment and state-of-the art laboratories. The College of Engineering maintains laboratories and offices in three separate buildings. The newest building on the main campus is the Applied Engineering and Technology Building, which was completed in October 2009 and comprises 150,000 square feet of laboratories and classrooms for College of Engineering students as well as administrative offices.

At UTHSCSA, the new South Texas Research Facility (STRF) is slated to open in fall 2011 with over 190,000 square feet of research space. Research programs selected for the STRF include adult cancer, neurosciences, healthy aging, regenerative medicine, the Institute for the Integration of Medicine and Science, and South Texas Technology Management. Additional information regarding STRF is available at http://research.uthscsa.edu/STRF/index.shtml.

Financial Aid

All doctoral applicants applying for full-time status will automatically be considered for a stipend of $21,000 per year plus payment of full tuition and fees and student health insurance. The Program awards scholarships (stipend, tuition, fees, and student health insurance) to current Ph.D. students who maintain good academic standing and are in compliance with biomedical engineering policy requirements, ranging from $26,000 to $31,000 per year. Supplemental awards ($1000 to $5000) for outstanding students are also available. Teaching and research assistantships may also be available from research mentors. Other financial aid opportunities include the Beldon, Mcnair, Valero, and other scholarships. College of Engineering scholarships are also available; details can be found at http://engineering.utsa.edu/scholarships/index.php.

Cost of Study

For the 2011–12 academic year, tuition and fees for a full-time graduate degree student (9 semester hours) are approximately $3149 per semester for Texas residents and $8783 per semester for nonresidents. Some courses and programs have additional fees. Please view the following Web sites for more information: http://www.graduateschool.utsa.edu/prospective_students/detail/graduate_tuition_and_fees and http://www.utsa.edu/fiscalservices/tuition.html.

Living and Housing Costs

University on-campus housing is available and includes apartment-style living at four complexes—Chisholm Hall, University Oaks, Laurel Village, and Chaparral Village. Off-campus housing is also available and includes many apartments adjacent to the University as well as a large number located within a 5-mile drive. Average costs for room and board are $4244 per semester.

Student Group

In the 2010 fall semester, the University enrolled more than 30,000 students, of whom more than 4,000 were graduate students. Admission into the Program is very competitive with only about 33 percent of the applicants being offered admission. The average GRE scores of all students matriculating into the Program are verbal 523 and quantitative 716; the average GPA was 3.46 on a 4.0 scale. The racial, ethnic, and gender diversity of the students is one of the strengths of the UTSA/UTHSCSA Joint Graduate Program in Biomedical Engineering, and continues the historic role of both UTSA and UTHSCSA as minority-serving institutions.

Location

San Antonio, with a population of 1.5 million, is one of the nation's major metropolitan areas. As the home of the Alamo and numerous other missions built by the Franciscans, the city is historically and culturally diverse. The Guadalupe Cultural Arts Center, McNay Art Museum, the San Antonio Museum of Art, and the Witte Museum enrich the city. The performing arts are represented by the San Antonio Symphony, the annual Tejano Music Festival and Tejano Music Awards, and performances by opera and ballet companies. Also notable are Sea World, Six Flags Fiesta Texas, Brackenridge Park, the Botanical Gardens, and the downtown Riverwalk. Numerous nearby lakes allow almost year-round outdoor activity, and the beaches of the Texas Gulf coast are within a 2-hour drive. San Antonio is home to numerous festivals throughout the year, including the Fiesta San Antonio and the Rodeo with activities such as parades, fairs, and concerts.

The University

The University was founded in 1969 and has since become a comprehensive metropolitan institution. Its research expenditures place it in the top 25 percent of public universities in Texas. The University has entered a new building and recruitment phase with a view to greatly expand the research effort in the biosciences. UTSA has three campus locations in San Antonio (downtown campus, main campus, and the Institute of Texan Cultures); the Biomedical Engineering facilities are located on the main campus. Facilities are also available to the Joint Program students at the campus of the University of Texas Health Science Center (UTHSCSA), a premier health institution and medical school, dental school, and nursing school.

UTSA Roadrunners football is slated to compete as an NCAA Division I FCS independent in August 2011 and is expected to transition to the Division I FSB subdivision by 2013.

Applying

A completed application will include an online Graduate school application (http://www.graduateschool.utsa.edu/prospective_students/detail/on-line_application). All applications and required attachments are to be sent to the Graduate School (no documents will be accepted at the Biomedical Engineering office). The application fee is sent through the online system. Official transcripts from all institutions attended are required. GRE test scores (UTSA ETS code: 6919) and TOEFL scores for international applicants must be included in the application with supporting documentation. Three letters of recommendation must be included with the application. A Statement of Purpose describing prior experience, objectives, and subject area interests for research is required to be submitted with the admission application. The deadline for applications is February 1 for the fall semester and October 1 for the spring semester. All deadlines are determined by the Graduate School, and are firm, with no exceptions.

Correspondence and Information

For application information:
The Graduate School
The University of Texas at San Antonio
One UTSA Circle
San Antonio, Texas 78249
Phone: 210-458-4330
Web site: http://www.graduateschool.utsa.edu

For program information:
Department of Biomedical Engineering
The University of Texas at San Antonio
One UTSA Circle
San Antonio, Texas 78249
Phone: 210-458-5535
E-mail: Margaret.boullosa@utsa.edu
Web site:
http://engineering.utsa.edu/bme/BME_program/index.html

The University of Texas at San Antonio

THE FACULTY AND THEIR RESEARCH

There are core and associated faculty affiliated with the Biomedical Engineering Program, both with primary appointments at UTSA and UTHSCSA. They are at all academic ranks (Instructor through Professor/Chairman/Dean).

Faculty members at UTHSCSA are drawn from the Medical School (medicine/cardiology, orthopedics, radiology, rehabilitative medicine), Dental School (community dentistry, periodontics, restorative dentistry), and the Graduate School of Biomedical Sciences (physiology, radiological sciences, research imaging center).

Similarly, faculty members at UTSA are drawn from both the College of Engineering (biomedical engineering, electrical engineering, mechanical engineering) and the College of Sciences (biology, chemistry).

The Biomedical Engineering Program has a number of outstanding faculty members, several of whom are leaders in their respective fields and are internationally recognized. As a group, they generated over $80 million during the first four years of the Program's existence to support their research endeavors, published over 900 full-length manuscripts and abstracts, and filed 30 patent applications.

Section 6
Chemical Engineering

This section contains a directory of institutions offering graduate work in chemical engineering, followed by an in-depth entry submitted by an institution that chose to prepare a detailed program description. Additional information about programs listed in the directory but not augmented by an in-depth entry may be obtained by writing directly to the dean of a graduate school or chair of a department at the address given in the directory.

For programs offering related work, see also in this book *Engineering and Applied Sciences; Geological, Mineral/Mining, and Petroleum Engineering; Management of Engineering and Technology;* and *Materials Sciences and Engineering.* In the other guides in this series:

Graduate Programs in the Humanities, Arts & Social Sciences
See *Family and Consumer Sciences (Clothing and Textiles)*
Graduate Programs in the Biological Sciences
See *Biochemistry*
Graduate Programs in the Physical Sciences, Mathematics, Agricultural Sciences, the Environment & Natural Resources
See *Chemistry and Geosciences (Geochemistry and Geology)*

CONTENTS

Program Directories

Close-Ups and Displays

Biochemical Engineering

Cornell University, Graduate School, Graduate Fields of Engineering, Field of Chemical Engineering, Ithaca, NY 14853-0001. Offers advanced materials processing (M Eng, MS, PhD); applied mathematics and computational methods (M Eng, MS, PhD); biochemical engineering (M Eng, MS, PhD); chemical reaction engineering (M Eng, MS, PhD); classical and statistical thermodynamics (M Eng, MS, PhD); fluid dynamics, rheology and biorheology (M Eng, MS, PhD); heat and mass transfer (M Eng, MS, PhD); kinetics and catalysis (M Eng, MS, PhD); polymers (M Eng, MS, PhD); surface science (M Eng, MS, PhD). *Faculty:* 29 full-time (2 women). *Students:* 116 full-time (34 women); includes 1 Black or African American, non-Hispanic/Latino; 17 Asian, non-Hispanic/Latino; 5 Hispanic/Latino, 45 international. Average age 24. 392 applicants, 35% accepted, 70 enrolled. In 2010, 35 master's, 17 doctorates awarded. *Degree requirements:* For master's, thesis (MS); for doctorate, comprehensive exam, thesis/dissertation. *Entrance requirements:* For master's and doctorate, GRE General Test, 2 letters of recommendation. Additional exam requirements/recommendations for international students: Required—TOEFL (minimum score 600 paper-based; 237 computer-based; 77 iBT). *Application deadline:* For fall admission, 1/15 priority date for domestic students. Application fee: $70. Electronic applications accepted. *Expenses:* Tuition: Full-time $29,500. Required fees: $76. Tuition and fees vary according to degree level and program. *Financial support:* In 2010–11, 67 students received support, including 20 fellowships with full tuition reimbursements available, 40 research assistantships with full tuition reimbursements available, 13 teaching assistantships with full tuition reimbursements available; institutionally sponsored loans, scholarships/grants, health care benefits, tuition waivers (full and partial), and unspecified assistantships also available. Financial award applicants required to submit FAFSA. *Faculty research:* Biochemical, biomedical and metabolic engineering; fluid and polymer dynamics; surface science and chemical kinetics; electronics materials; microchemical systems and nanotechnology. *Unit head:* Director of Graduate Studies, 607-255-4550. *Application contact:* Graduate Field Assistant, 607-255-4550, E-mail: dgs@cheme.cornell.edu.

Dartmouth College, Thayer School of Engineering, Program in Biotechnology and Biochemical Engineering, Hanover, NH 03755. Offers MS, PhD. *Degree requirements:* For master's, thesis; for doctorate, thesis/dissertation, candidacy oral exam. *Entrance requirements:* For master's and doctorate, GRE General Test. *Application deadline:* For fall admission, 1/1 priority date for domestic students. Application fee: $45. *Financial support:* Fellowships, research assistantships, teaching assistantships, career-related internships or fieldwork, Federal Work-Study, institutionally sponsored loans, and tuition waivers (full and partial) available. Financial award application deadline: 1/15. *Faculty research:* Biomass processing, metabolic engineering, kinetics and reactor design, applied microbiology, resource and environmental analysis. Total annual research expenditures: $2.9 million. *Unit head:* Dr. Joseph J. Helbie, Dean, 603-646-2238, Fax: 603-646-2580, E-mail: joseph.j.helbie@dartmouth.edu. *Application contact:* Candace S. Potter, Graduate Admissions Administrator, 603-646-3844, Fax: 603-646-1620, E-mail: candace.potter@dartmouth.edu.

Drexel University, College of Engineering, Department of Chemical and Biological Engineering, Program in Biochemical Engineering, Philadelphia, PA 19104-2875. Offers MS. Part-time and evening/weekend programs available. *Degree requirements:* For master's, thesis. *Entrance requirements:* For master's, minimum GPA of 3.0 in chemical engineering or biological sciences. Additional exam requirements/recommendations for international students: Required—TOEFL. Electronic applications accepted. *Faculty research:* Monitoring and control of bioreactors, sensors for bioreactors, large-scale production of monoclonal antibodies.

Rutgers, The State University of New Jersey, New Brunswick, Graduate School-New Brunswick, Program in Chemical and Biochemical Engineering, Piscataway, NJ 08854-8097. Offers MS, PhD. Part-time and evening/weekend programs available. Terminal master's awarded for partial completion of doctoral program. *Degree requirements:* For master's, thesis or alternative; for doctorate, thesis/dissertation. *Entrance requirements:* For master's and doctorate, GRE General Test. Additional exam requirements/recommendations for international students: Required—TOEFL. *Expenses:* Tuition, state resident: full-time $7200; part-time $600 per credit. Tuition, nonresident: full-time $11,124; part-time $927 per credit. *Faculty research:* Biotechnology, pharmaceutical engineering, nanotechnology, process system engineering, materials and polymer science, chemical engineering sciences.

University of California, Irvine, School of Engineering, Department of Chemical Engineering and Materials Science, Irvine, CA 92697. Offers chemical and biochemical engineering (MS, PhD); materials science and engineering (MS, PhD). Part-time programs available. *Students:* 77 full-time (24 women), 3 part-time (1 woman); includes 22 minority (1 American Indian or Alaska Native, non-Hispanic/Latino; 16 Asian, non-Hispanic/Latino; 3 Hispanic/Latino; 1 Native Hawaiian or other Pacific Islander, non-Hispanic/Latino; 1 Two or more races, non-Hispanic/Latino), 32 international. Average age 28. 300 applicants, 27% accepted, 26 enrolled. In 2010, 24 master's, 8 doctorates awarded. Terminal master's awarded for partial completion of doctoral program. *Degree requirements:* For doctorate, thesis/dissertation. *Entrance requirements:* For master's and doctorate, GRE General Test, minimum GPA of 3.0, 3 letters of recommendation. Additional exam requirements/recommendations for international students: Required—TOEFL (minimum score 550 paper-based; 213 computer-based). *Application deadline:* For fall admission, 1/15 priority date for domestic students, 1/15 for international students. Applications are processed on a rolling basis. Application fee: $80 ($100 for international students). Electronic applications accepted. *Financial support:* Fellowships with tuition reimbursements, research assistantships with full tuition reimbursements, teaching assistantships with tuition reimbursements, institutionally sponsored loans, traineeships, health care benefits, and unspecified assistantships available. Financial award application deadline: 3/1; financial award applicants required to submit FAFSA. *Faculty research:* Molecular biotechnology, nano-bio-materials, biophotonics, synthesis, superplasticity and mechanical behavior, characterization of advanced and nanostructural materials. *Unit head:* Prof. Albert Yee, Chair, 949-824-7320, Fax: 949-824-2541, E-mail: albert.yee@uci.edu. *Application contact:* Grace Hai-Chin Chau, Academic Program/Graduate Admission Coordinator, 949-824-3887, Fax: 949-824-2541, E-mail: chaug@uci.edu.

University of Georgia, Faculty of Engineering, Program in Biochemical Engineering, Athens, GA 30602. Offers MS. *Students:* 4 full-time, 1 (woman) part-time, 4 international. 7 applicants, 43% accepted, 2 enrolled. In 2010, 1 master's awarded. *Entrance requirements:* For master's, GRE, baccalaureate degree in engineering or related field from accredited institution with minimum GPA of 3.0; undergraduate academic transcripts; statement of purpose; three letters of recommendation. Additional exam requirements/recommendations for international students: Required—TOEFL. *Expenses:* Tuition, state resident: full-time $7200; part-time $344 per credit hour. Tuition, nonresident: full-time $21,900; part-time $944 per credit hour. Tuition and fees vary according to course load and program. *Unit head:* Dr. E. Dale Threadgill. *Application contact:* Dr. Melissa Barry, Assistant Dean of The Graduate School, 706-425-2934, Fax: 706-425-3093, E-mail: mjb14@uga.edu.

The University of Iowa, Graduate College, College of Engineering, Department of Chemical and Biochemical Engineering, Iowa City, IA 52242-1316. Offers MS, PhD. Part-time programs available. *Faculty:* 11 full-time (3 women), 1 (woman) part-time/adjunct. *Students:* 39 full-time (13 women); includes 6 minority (4 Black or African American, non-Hispanic/Latino; 1 Asian, non-Hispanic/Latino; 1 Hispanic/Latino), 19 international. Average age 28. 44 applicants, 27% accepted, 6 enrolled. In 2010, 4 master's, 10 doctorates awarded. *Degree requirements:* For master's, comprehensive exam (for some programs), thesis (for some programs); for doctorate, comprehensive exam, thesis/dissertation. *Entrance requirements:* For master's and doctorate, GRE, minimum undergraduate GPA of 3.0. Additional exam requirements/recommendations for international students: Required—TOEFL (minimum score 550 paper-based; 213 computer-based). *Application deadline:* For fall admission, 2/1 for domestic and international students; for spring admission, 10/1 for domestic and international students. Applications are processed on a rolling basis. Application fee: $60 ($100 for international students). Electronic applications accepted. *Financial support:* In 2010–11, 3 fellowships with full tuition reimbursements (averaging $26,000 per year), 24 research assistantships with partial tuition reimbursements (averaging $24,500 per year), 2 teaching assistantships with partial tuition reimbursements (averaging $10,022 per year) were awarded; unspecified assistantships also available. Financial award applicants required to submit FAFSA. *Faculty research:* Polymeric materials; photopolymerization; atmospheric chemistry and air pollution; biochemical engineering; bioprocessing and biomedical engineering. Total annual research expenditures: $2.6 million. *Unit head:* Dr. David W. Murhammer, Department Executive Officer, 319-335-1228, Fax: 319-335-1415, E-mail: david-murhammer@uiowa.edu. *Application contact:* Natalie Potter, Secretary, 319-335-1215, Fax: 319-335-1415, E-mail: chemeng@engineering.uiowa.edu.

The University of Manchester, School of Chemical Engineering and Analytical Science, Manchester, United Kingdom. Offers biocatalysis (M Phil, PhD); chemical engineering (M Phil, PhD); chemical engineering and analytical science (M Phil, D Eng, PhD); colloids, crystals, interfaces and materials (M Phil, PhD); environment and sustainable technology (M Phil, PhD); instrumentation (M Phil, PhD); multi-scale modeling (M Phil, PhD); process integration (M Phil, PhD); systems biology (M Phil, PhD).

University of Maryland, Baltimore County, Graduate School, College of Engineering and Information Technology, Department of Chemical and Biochemical Engineering, Post Baccalaureate Certificate Program in Biochemical Regulatory Engineering, Baltimore, MD 21250. Offers Postbaccalaureate Certificate. Part-time programs available. *Students:* 3 part-time (2 women); includes 2 minority (1 Asian, non-Hispanic/Latino; 1 Hispanic/Latino), 1 international. Average age 44. 4 applicants, 75% accepted, 2 enrolled. In 2010, 3 Postbaccalaureate Certificates awarded. *Application deadline:* For fall admission, 7/1 for domestic and international students; for spring admission, 2/1 for domestic students, 12/1 for international students. Applications are processed on a rolling basis. Application fee: $50. Electronic applications accepted. *Unit head:* Dr. Antonio Moreira, Vice Provost for Academic Affairs, 410-455-6576, E-mail: moreira@umbc.edu. *Application contact:* Dr. Mark Marten, Professor and Graduate Program Director, 410-455-3439, Fax: 410-455-1049, E-mail: marten@umbc.edu.

University of Maryland, Baltimore County, Graduate School, College of Engineering and Information Technology, Department of Chemical and Biochemical Engineering, Program in Chemical and Biochemical Engineering, Baltimore, MD 21250. Offers MS, PhD. Part-time programs available. *Students:* 34 full-time (17 women), 3 part-time (2 women); includes 6 minority (3 Black or African American, non-Hispanic/Latino; 1 Asian, non-Hispanic/Latino; 1 Hispanic/Latino; 1 Two or more races, non-Hispanic/Latino), 22 international. Average age 26. 54 applicants, 41% accepted, 15 enrolled. In 2010, 5 master's, 1 doctorate awarded. *Degree requirements:* For master's, comprehensive exam (for some programs), thesis (for some programs); for doctorate, comprehensive exam, thesis/dissertation. *Entrance requirements:* For master's, GRE General Test, minimum GPA of 3.0; for doctorate, GRE General Test (within last 5 years), GRE Subject Test, minimum GPA of 3.0. Additional exam requirements/recommendations for international students: Required—TOEFL (minimum score 550 paper-based; 213 computer-based; 80 iBT). *Application deadline:* For fall admission, 6/1 for domestic students, 1/1 for international students; for spring admission, 11/1 for domestic students, 6/1 for international students. Applications are processed on a rolling basis. Application fee: $50. Electronic applications accepted. *Financial support:* In 2010–11, 3 students received support, including 1 fellowship with full tuition reimbursement available (averaging $30,000 per year), 20 research assistantships with full tuition reimbursements available (averaging $22,000 per year), 6 teaching assistantships with full tuition reimbursements available (averaging $17,000 per year); career-related internships or fieldwork, Federal Work-Study, scholarships/grants, health care benefits, tuition waivers (partial), and unspecified assistantships also available. Support available to part-time students. Financial award application deadline: 6/30; financial award applicants required to submit FAFSA. *Faculty research:* Biomaterials engineering, cellular engineering, sensor technology, systems biology and functional genomics, engineering education and outreach. *Unit head:* Dr. Julia M. Ross, Professor and Chair. *Application contact:* Dr. Mark Marten, Professor and Graduate Program Director, 410-455-3439, Fax: 410-455-1049, E-mail: marten@umbc.edu.

The University of Western Ontario, Faculty of Graduate Studies, Physical Sciences Division, Faculty of Engineering, London, ON N6A 5B8, Canada. Offers chemical and biochemical engineering (ME Sc, PhD); civil and environmental engineering (M Eng, ME Sc, PhD); electrical and computer engineering (M Eng, ME Sc, PhD); mechanical and materials engineering (M Eng, ME Sc, PhD). Part-time programs available. Terminal master's awarded for partial completion of doctoral program. *Degree requirements:* For master's, thesis; for doctorate, thesis/dissertation. *Entrance requirements:* For master's, minimum B average; for doctorate, minimum B+ average. *Faculty research:* Wind, geotechnical, chemical reactor engineering, applied electrostatics, biochemical engineering.

Villanova University, College of Engineering, Department of Chemical Engineering, Villanova, PA 19085-1699. Offers biochemical engineering (Certificate); chemical engineering (MSChE); environmental protection in the chemical process industries (Certificate). Part-time and evening/weekend programs available. *Faculty:* 10 full-time (1 woman), 1 (woman) part-time/adjunct. *Students:* 5 full-time (1 woman), 46 part-time (12 women); includes 3 Black or African American, non-Hispanic/Latino; 3 Asian, non-Hispanic/Latino; 1 Hispanic/Latino, 6 international. 12 applicants, 67% accepted, 5 enrolled. In 2010, 10 master's awarded. *Degree requirements:* For master's, comprehensive exam, thesis optional. *Entrance requirements:* For master's, GRE General Test (for applicants with degrees from foreign universities), B Ch E, minimum GPA of 3.0. Additional exam requirements/recommendations for international students: Required—TOEFL (minimum score 600 paper-based; 250 computer-based; 100 iBT). *Application deadline:* For fall admission, 8/1 priority date for domestic students, 3/15 priority date for international students; for spring admission, 12/1 priority date for domestic students, 10/1 priority date for international students. Applications are processed on a rolling basis. Application fee: $50. *Expenses:* Tuition: Part-time $700 per credit. Part-time tuition and fees vary according to degree level and program. *Financial support:* In 2010–11, research assistantships with full and partial tuition reimbursements (averaging $13,500 per year); Federal Work-Study, tuition waivers (full), and unspecified assistantships also available. Financial award application deadline: 1/15. *Faculty research:* Heat transfer, advanced materials, chemical vapor deposition, pyrolysis and combustion chemistry, industrial waste treatment. Total annual research expenditures: $31,111. *Unit head:* Dr. Randy Weinstein, Chairman, 610-519-4950, E-mail: randy.weinstein@villanova.edu. *Application contact:* College of Engineering, Graduate Programs Office, 610-519-5840, Fax: 610-519-5859, E-mail: engineering.grad@villanova.edu.

Chemical Engineering

American University of Sharjah, Graduate Programs, Sharjah, United Arab Emirates. Offers business (EMBA, GEMPA, MBA); chemical engineering (MS Ch E); civil engineering (MSCE); computer engineering (MS); electrical engineering (MSEE); mechanical engineering (MSME); mechatronics engineering (MS); public administration (MPA); teaching English to speakers of other languages (MA); translation and interpreting (MA); urban planning (MUP). Part-time and evening/weekend programs available. *Entrance requirements:* For master's, GMAT (MBA). Additional exam requirements/recommendations for international students: Required—TOEFL (minimum score 550 paper-based; 213 computer-based; 80 iBT), TWE (minimum score 5). Electronic applications accepted. *Faculty research:* Chemical engineering, civil engineering, computer engineering, electrical engineering, linguistics, translation.

Arizona State University, Ira A. Fulton School of Engineering, Department of Mechanical and Aerospace Engineering, Tempe, AZ 85281. Offers aerospace engineering (MS, MSE, PhD); chemical engineering (MS, MSE, PhD); materials science and engineering (MS, PhD); mechanical engineering (MS, MSE, PhD). Part-time and evening/weekend programs available. Postbaccalaureate distance learning degree programs offered (minimal on-campus study). *Faculty:* 50 full-time (10 women), 13 part-time/adjunct (3 women). *Students:* 258 full-time (47 women), 114 part-time (29 women); includes 48 minority (3 Black or African American, non-Hispanic/Latino; 2 American Indian or Alaska Native, non-Hispanic/Latino; 15 Asian, non-Hispanic/Latino; 27 Hispanic/Latino; 1 Two or more races, non-Hispanic/Latino), 164 international. Average age 28. 721 applicants, 58% accepted, 119 enrolled. In 2010, 55 master's, 29 doctorates awarded. Terminal master's awarded for partial completion of doctoral program. *Degree requirements:* For master's, thesis and oral defense (MS); applied project or comprehensive exam (MSE); interactive Program of Study (iPOS) submitted before completing 50 percent of required credit hours; for doctorate, comprehensive exam, thesis/dissertation, interactive Program of Study (iPOS) submitted before completing 50 percent of required credit hours. *Entrance requirements:* For master's, GRE, minimum GPA of 3.0 or equivalent in last 2 years of work leading to bachelor's degree; for doctorate, GRE, minimum GPA of 3.0 in last 2 years of work leading to bachelor's degree. Additional exam requirements/recommendations for international students: Required—TOEFL, IELTS, or Pearson Test of English. *Application deadline:* For fall admission, 1/31 for domestic and international students; for spring admission, 7/1 for domestic and international students. Application fee: $70 ($90 for international students). Electronic applications accepted. *Expenses:* Contact institution. *Financial support:* In 2010–11, 120 research assistantships with partial tuition reimbursements (averaging $15,353 per year), 34 teaching assistantships with partial tuition reimbursements (averaging $13,861 per year) were awarded; fellowships with full and partial tuition reimbursements, institutionally sponsored loans, scholarships/grants, and tuition waivers (full and partial) also available. Financial award application deadline: 3/1; financial award applicants required to submit FAFSA. *Faculty research:* Electronic materials and packaging, materials for energy (batteries), adaptive/intelligent materials and structures, multiscale fluid mechanics, membranes, therapeutics and bioseparations, flexible structures, nanostructured materials, and micro/nano transport. Total annual research expenditures: $17.5 million. *Unit head:* Dr. Kyle D. Squires, Director, 480-965-3957, E-mail: squires@asu.edu. *Application contact:* Graduate Admissions, 480-965-6113.

Auburn University, Graduate School, Ginn College of Engineering, Department of Chemical Engineering, Auburn University, AL 36849. Offers M Ch E, MS, PhD. Part-time programs available. *Faculty:* 17 full-time (3 women), 1 part-time/adjunct (0 women). *Students:* 47 full-time (17 women), 44 part-time (13 women); includes 4 Black or African American, non-Hispanic/Latino; 2 Asian, non-Hispanic/Latino; 2 Hispanic/Latino, 52 international. Average age 27. 216 applicants, 19% accepted, 16 enrolled. In 2010, 6 master's, 7 doctorates awarded. *Degree requirements:* For master's, thesis (for some programs); for doctorate, comprehensive exam, thesis/dissertation. *Entrance requirements:* For master's and doctorate, GRE General Test. *Application deadline:* For fall admission, 7/7 for domestic students; for spring admission, 11/24 for domestic students. Applications are processed on a rolling basis. Application fee: $50 ($60 for international students). Electronic applications accepted. *Expenses:* Tuition, state resident: full-time $7002. Tuition, nonresident: full-time $21,898. International tuition: $22,116 full-time. Required fees: $892. Tuition and fees vary according to course load and program. *Financial support:* Fellowships, research assistantships, teaching assistantships, Federal Work-Study available. Support available to part-time students. Financial award application deadline: 3/15; financial award applicants required to submit FAFSA. *Faculty research:* Coal liquefaction, asphalt research, pulp and paper engineering, surface science, biochemical engineering. *Unit head:* Dr. Christopher Roberts, Chair, 334-844-2036. *Application contact:* Dr. George Flowers, Dean of the Graduate School, 334-844-2125.

Brigham Young University, Graduate Studies, Ira A. Fulton College of Engineering and Technology, Department of Chemical Engineering, Provo, UT 84602. Offers MS, PhD. *Faculty:* 13 full-time (0 women), 6 part-time/adjunct (0 women). *Students:* 48 full-time (10 women); includes 21 Asian, non-Hispanic/Latino. Average age 25. 27 applicants, 78% accepted, 16 enrolled. In 2010, 2 master's, 1 doctorate awarded. *Degree requirements:* For master's, comprehensive exam, thesis; for doctorate, comprehensive exam, thesis/dissertation. *Entrance requirements:* For master's, GRE, minimum GPA of 3.0 in upper-division course work in major; for doctorate, GRE, minimum GPA of 3.3. Additional exam requirements/recommendations for international students: Required—TOEFL (minimum score 580 paper-based; 85 iBT), IELTS (minimum score 7). *Application deadline:* For fall admission, 2/15 for domestic and international students; for winter admission, 6/15 for domestic and international students; for spring admission, 10/15 for domestic and international students. Application fee: $50. Electronic applications accepted. *Expenses:* Tuition: Full-time $5580; part-time $310 per credit hour. Tuition and fees vary according to program and student's religious affiliation. *Financial support:* In 2010–11, 47 students received support, including 1 fellowship (averaging $22,000 per year), 31 research assistantships with full and partial tuition reimbursements available (averaging $22,000 per year), 17 teaching assistantships with full and partial tuition reimbursements available (averaging $21,000 per year); career-related internships or fieldwork and tuition scholarships for students receiving teaching or research assistantships also available. Financial award application deadline: 6/30. *Faculty research:* Biomedical engineering, oil reservoir simulation, electrochemical engineering, energy and combustion, molecular modeling, thermodynamics. Total annual research expenditures: $2.2 million. *Unit head:* Dr. Randy S. Lewis, Chair, 801-422-2586, Fax: 801-422-0151, E-mail: cheme@byu.edu. *Application contact:* Dr. Dean R. Wheeler, Graduate Coordinator, 801-422-2588, Fax: 801-422-0151, E-mail: dean_wheeler@byu.edu.

Brown University, Graduate School, Division of Engineering, Program in Fluid, Thermal and Chemical Processes, Providence, RI 02912. Offers Sc M, PhD. *Degree requirements:* For doctorate, thesis/dissertation, preliminary exam.

Bucknell University, Graduate Studies, College of Engineering, Department of Chemical Engineering, Lewisburg, PA 17837. Offers MS, MS Ch E. Part-time programs available. *Degree requirements:* For master's, thesis. *Entrance requirements:* For master's, GRE General Test, GRE Subject Test, minimum GPA of 2.8. Additional exam requirements/recommendations for international students: Required—TOEFL. *Expenses:* Tuition: Full-time $36,992; part-time $4624 per course. *Faculty research:* Computer-aided design, software engineering, applied mathematics and modeling, polymer science, digital process control.

California Institute of Technology, Division of Chemistry and Chemical Engineering, Program in Chemical Engineering, Pasadena, CA 91125-0001. Offers MS, PhD. *Faculty:* 11 full-time (3 women). *Students:* 57 full-time (22 women); includes 1 Black or African American, non-Hispanic/Latino; 1 Hispanic/Latino. Average age 25. 210 applicants, 18% accepted, 13 enrolled. In 2010, 6 master's, 13 doctorates awarded. Terminal master's awarded for partial completion of doctoral program. *Degree requirements:* For master's, thesis; for doctorate, thesis/dissertation. *Entrance requirements:* Additional exam requirements/recommendations for international students: Required—TOEFL; Recommended—IELTS, TWE. *Application deadline:* For fall admission, 1/15 for domestic and international students. Application fee: $80. Electronic applications accepted. *Financial support:* Fellowships, research assistantships, teaching assistantships, institutionally sponsored loans, scholarships/grants, traineeships, health care benefits, and unspecified assistantships available. Financial award application deadline: 1/15. *Faculty research:* Fluids, biomolecular engineering, atmospheric chemistry, polymers/materials, catalysis. *Unit head:* Prof. Jacqueline K. Barton, Chair, Chemistry and Chemical Engineering, 626-395-3646, Fax: 626-568-8824, E-mail: jkbarton@caltech.edu. *Application contact:* Kathy J. Bubash, Graduate Option Secretary, 626-395-4193, E-mail: kathy@cheme.caltech.edu.

California State University, Long Beach, Graduate Studies, College of Engineering, Department of Chemical Engineering, Long Beach, CA 90840. Offers MS. *Faculty:* 4 full-time (1 woman), 2 part-time/adjunct (0 women). *Unit head:* Dr. Larry Jang, Chair/Graduate Advisor, 562-985-7533, E-mail: jang@csulb.edu. *Application contact:* Dr. Sandra Cynar, Associate Dean for Instruction, 562-985-1512, Fax: 562-985-7561, E-mail: cynar@csulb.edu.

Carnegie Mellon University, Carnegie Institute of Technology, Department of Chemical Engineering, Pittsburgh, PA 15213-3891. Offers chemical engineering (M Ch E, MS, PhD); colloids, polymers and surfaces (MS). Part-time and evening/weekend programs available. Terminal master's awarded for partial completion of doctoral program. *Degree requirements:* For doctorate, thesis/dissertation, qualifying exam. *Entrance requirements:* For master's and doctorate, GRE General Test, GRE Subject Test. Additional exam requirements/recommendations for international students: Required—TOEFL. *Faculty research:* Computer-aided design in process engineering, biomedical engineering, biotechnology, complex fluids.

Case Western Reserve University, School of Graduate Studies, Case School of Engineering, Department of Chemical Engineering, Cleveland, OH 44106. Offers MS, PhD. Part-time and evening/weekend programs available. Postbaccalaureate distance learning degree programs offered. *Faculty:* 11 full-time (1 woman). *Students:* 38 full-time (12 women); includes 4 Asian, non-Hispanic/Latino; 2 Hispanic/Latino, 21 international. In 2010, 4 master's, 9 doctorates awarded. Terminal master's awarded for partial completion of doctoral program. *Degree requirements:* For master's, thesis (for some programs); for doctorate, thesis/dissertation, qualifying exam, research proposal, teaching experience. *Entrance requirements:* For master's and doctorate, GRE General Test. Additional exam requirements/recommendations for international students: Required—TOEFL. *Application deadline:* For fall admission, 2/15 priority date for domestic students; for spring admission, 11/1 for domestic students. Applications are processed on a rolling basis. Application fee: $50. *Financial support:* Fellowships with full and partial tuition reimbursements, research assistantships with full and partial tuition reimbursements, teaching assistantships, Federal Work-Study and institutionally sponsored loans available. Financial award application deadline: 3/1; financial award applicants required to submit FAFSA. *Faculty research:* Biotransport and bioprocessing, electrochemical engineering, materials engineering, energy storage and fuel cells. Total annual research expenditures: $3.3 million. *Unit head:* Uziel Landau, Department Chair, 216-368-4132, Fax: 216-368-3016. *Application contact:* Theresa Claytor, Student Affairs Coordinator, 216-368-8555, Fax: 216-368-8555, E-mail: theresa.claytor@case.edu.

City College of the City University of New York, Graduate School, Grove School of Engineering, Department of Chemical Engineering, New York, NY 10031-9198. Offers ME, MS, PhD. PhD program offered jointly with Graduate School and University Center of the City University of New York. Part-time programs available. *Degree requirements:* For master's, thesis optional; for doctorate, one foreign language, comprehensive exam, thesis/dissertation. *Entrance requirements:* For master's and doctorate, GRE General Test. Additional exam requirements/recommendations for international students: Required—TOEFL (minimum score 500 paper-based; 173 computer-based; 61 iBT). *Faculty research:* Theoretical turbulences, bio-fluid dynamics, polymers, fluidization, transport phenomena.

Clarkson University, Graduate School, Wallace H. Coulter School of Engineering, Department of Chemical and Biomolecular Engineering, Potsdam, NY 13699. Offers chemical engineering (ME, MS, PhD). Part-time programs available. *Faculty:* 16 full-time (7 women), 1 (woman) part-time/adjunct. *Students:* 23 full-time (5 women), 20 international. Average age 26. 72 applicants, 49% accepted, 7 enrolled. In 2010, 8 master's, 3 doctorates awarded. Terminal master's awarded for partial completion of doctoral program. *Degree requirements:* For master's, thesis; for doctorate, comprehensive exam, thesis/dissertation. *Entrance requirements:* For master's and doctorate, GRE, transcripts of all college coursework, resume, personal statement, three letters of recommendation. Additional exam requirements/recommendations for international students: Required—TOEFL (minimum score 550 paper-based; 213 computer-based; 80 iBT), IELTS (minimum score 6.5). *Application deadline:* For fall admission, 1/30 priority date for domestic and international students; for spring admission, 9/1 priority date for domestic and international students. Applications are processed on a rolling basis. Application fee: $25 ($35 for international students). Electronic applications accepted. *Expenses:* Tuition: Part-time $1136 per credit hour. *Financial support:* In 2010–11, 21 students received support, including fellowships with full tuition reimbursements available (averaging $21,580 per year), 10 research assistantships with full tuition reimbursements available (averaging $21,580 per year), 9 teaching assistantships with full tuition reimbursements available (averaging $21,580 per year); scholarships/grants, tuition waivers (partial), and unspecified assistantships also available. *Faculty research:* Emission testing, atmospheric species, diesel emissions, athletic enchancement, particle exposure. Total annual research expenditures: $2.1 million. *Unit head:* Dr. Ruth Baltus, Chair, 315-268-6650, Fax: 315-268-6654, E-mail: baltus@clarkson.edu. *Application contact:* Kelly Sharlow, Assistant to the Dean, 315-268-7929, Fax: 315-268-4494, E-mail: ksharlow@clarkson.edu.

Clemson University, Graduate School, College of Engineering and Science, Department of Chemical and Biomolecular Engineering, Clemson, SC 29634. Offers MS, PhD. *Faculty:* 10 full-time (1 woman). *Students:* 30 full-time (11 women); includes 1 Black or African American, non-Hispanic/Latino; 1 Asian, non-Hispanic/Latino, 20 international. Average age 27. 115 applicants, 8% accepted, 5 enrolled. In 2010, 1 master's, 6 doctorates awarded. *Degree requirements:* For master's, thesis; for doctorate, thesis/dissertation. *Entrance requirements:* For master's and doctorate, GRE General Test. Additional exam requirements/recommendations for international students: Required—TOEFL. *Application deadline:* For fall admission, 6/1 for domestic students, 4/15 for international students; for spring admission, 10/1 for domestic students, 9/15 for international students. Applications are processed on a rolling basis. Application fee: $70 ($80 for international students). Electronic applications accepted. *Expenses:* Tuition, state resident: full-time $6492; part-time $400 per credit hour. Tuition, nonresident: full-time $13,634; part-time $800 per credit hour. Required fees: $262 per semester. Part-time tuition and fees vary according to course load and program. *Financial support:* In 2010–11, 29 students received support, including 3 fellowships with full and partial tuition reimbursements available (averaging $10,667 per year), 23 research assistantships with partial tuition reimbursements available (averaging $20,806 per year), 7 teaching assistantships with partial tuition reimbursements available (averaging $24,000 per year); career-related internships or fieldwork, institutionally sponsored loans, scholarships/grants, health care benefits, and unspecified assistantships also available. Support available to part-time students. Financial award applicants required to submit FAFSA. *Faculty research:* Advanced materials, biotechnology, energy, molecular simulation, chemical and biochemical processing. Total annual research expenditures: $1.5 million. *Unit head:* Dr. Douglas E. Hirt, Chair, 864-656-0822, Fax: 864-656-0784, E-mail: hirtd@clemson.edu. *Application contact:* Dr. Scott M. Husson, Coordinator, 864-656-4502, Fax: 864-656-0784, E-mail: shusson@clemson.edu.

Cleveland State University, College of Graduate Studies, Fenn College of Engineering, Department of Chemical and Biomedical Engineering, Cleveland, OH 44115. Offers applied biomedical engineering (D Eng); chemical engineering (MS, D Eng). Part-time and evening/weekend programs available. *Faculty:* 7 full-time (1 woman), 5 part-time/adjunct (4 women).

Chemical Engineering

Cleveland State University (continued)

Students: 29 full-time (13 women), 32 part-time (6 women); includes 1 Black or African American, non-Hispanic/Latino; 1 Asian, non-Hispanic/Latino, 45 international. Average age 28. 72 applicants, 63% accepted, 18 enrolled. In 2010, 14 master's, 2 doctorates awarded. Degree requirements: For master's, project or thesis; for doctorate, thesis/dissertation, candidacy and qualifying exams. Entrance requirements: For master's, GRE General Test, minimum GPA of 2.75; for doctorate, GRE General Test, minimum GPA of 3.25. Additional exam requirements/recommendations for international students: Required—TOEFL (minimum score 550 paper-based; 213 computer-based; 78 iBT). Application deadline: For fall admission, 4/15 for domestic and international students; for spring admission, 10/15 for domestic and international students. Applications are processed on a rolling basis. Application fee: $30. Expenses: Tuition, state resident: full-time $8447; part-time $469 per credit hour. Tuition, nonresident: full-time $16,020; part-time $890 per credit hour. Required fees: $50. Financial support: In 2010–11, 19 research assistantships with full and partial tuition reimbursements (averaging $15,750 per year), 7 teaching assistantships with full and partial tuition reimbursements (averaging $15,000 per year) were awarded; fellowships, career-related internships or fieldwork, Federal Work-Study, institutionally sponsored loans, scholarships/grants, tuition waivers (full), and unspecified assistantships also available. Financial award application deadline: 3/30. Faculty research: Absorption equilibrium and dynamics, advanced materials processing, biomaterials surface characterization, bioprocessing, cardiovascular mechanics, magnetic resonance imaging, mechanics of biomolecules, metabolic modeling, molecular simulation, process systems engineering, statistical mechanics. Unit head: Dr. Dhananjai B. Shah, Chairperson, 216-687-3569, Fax: 216-687-9220, E-mail: d.shah@csuohio.edu. Application contact: Becky Laird, Administrative Coordinator, 216-687-2571, Fax: 216-687-9220, E-mail: b.laird@csuohio.edu.

Colorado School of Mines, Graduate School, Department of Chemical Engineering, Golden, CO 80401. Offers MS, PhD. Part-time programs available. Faculty: 39 full-time (9 women), 11 part-time/adjunct (4 women). Students: 63 full-time (15 women), 1 part-time (0 women); includes 2 Asian, non-Hispanic/Latino; 1 Native Hawaiian or other Pacific Islander, non-Hispanic/Latino, 29 international. Average age 28. 127 applicants, 43% accepted, 30 enrolled. In 2010, 14 master's, 6 doctorates awarded. Degree requirements: For master's, thesis (for some programs); for doctorate, comprehensive exam, thesis/dissertation. Entrance requirements: For master's and doctorate, GRE General Test. Additional exam requirements/recommendations for international students: Required—TOEFL (minimum score 550 paper-based; 213 computer-based; 80 iBT). Application deadline: For fall admission, 1/15 for domestic and international students; for spring admission, 10/15 for domestic and international students. Application fee: $50 ($70 for international students). Electronic applications accepted. Expenses: Tuition, state resident: full-time $11,550; part-time $641 per credit. Tuition, nonresident: full-time $25,980; part-time $1444 per credit. Required fees: $1874; $937 per semester. Financial support: In 2010–11, 62 students received support, including 2 fellowships with full tuition reimbursements available (averaging $20,000 per year), 34 research assistantships with full tuition reimbursements available (averaging $20,000 per year), 26 teaching assistantships with full tuition reimbursements available (averaging $20,000 per year); scholarships/grants, health care benefits, and unspecified assistantships also available. Financial award application deadline: 1/15; financial award applicants required to submit FAFSA. Faculty research: Liquid fuels for the future, responsible management of hazardous substances, surface and interfacial engineering, advanced computational methods and process control, gas hydrates. Total annual research expenditures: $3.9 million. Unit head: Dr. James F. Ely, Department Head, 303-273-3885, E-mail: jely@mines.edu. Application contact: Dr. Amadeu Sum, Professor, 303-273-3873, Fax: 303-273-3730, E-mail: asum@mines.edu.

Colorado State University, Graduate School, College of Engineering, Department of Chemical and Biological Engineering, Fort Collins, CO 80523-1370. Offers chemical engineering (MS, PhD); engineering (ME). Faculty: 11 full-time (1 woman). Students: 16 full-time (4 women), 11 part-time (1 woman); includes 2 minority (1 Hispanic/Latino; 1 Two or more races, non-Hispanic/Latino), 14 international. Average age 28. 81 applicants, 14% accepted, 10 enrolled. In 2010, 4 doctorates awarded. Terminal master's awarded for partial completion of doctoral program. Degree requirements: For master's, comprehensive exam, thesis (for some programs), preliminary exam (first year); for doctorate, comprehensive exam, thesis/dissertation, exams. Entrance requirements: For master's and doctorate, GRE General Test, minimum GPA of 3.0. Additional exam requirements/recommendations for international students: Required—TOEFL (minimum score 550 paper-based; 213 computer-based; 80 iBT). Application deadline: For fall admission, 1/15 priority date for domestic and international students; for spring admission, 9/15 priority date for domestic and international students. Applications are processed on a rolling basis. Application fee: $50. Electronic applications accepted. Expenses: Tuition, state resident: full-time $7434; part-time $413 per credit. Tuition, nonresident: full-time $19,022; part-time $1057 per credit. Required fees: $1729; $88 per credit. Financial support: In 2010–11, 19 students received support, including 8 fellowships (averaging $28,669 per year), 11 research assistantships with full tuition reimbursements available (averaging $18,578 per year); teaching assistantships with full tuition reimbursements available, scholarships/grants and unspecified assistantships also available. Financial award application deadline: 2/15; financial award applicants required to submit FAFSA. Faculty research: Biochemical and biomedical engineering, nanostructured materials, polymer science, transport phenomena, mathematical modeling. Total annual research expenditures: $2.6 million. Unit head: Dr. David S. Dandy, Department Head, 970-491-7437, Fax: 970-491-7369, E-mail: david.dandy@colostate.edu. Application contact: Marilyn Gross, Graduate Contact, 970-491-5252, Fax: 970-491-7369, E-mail: marilyn.gross@colostate.edu.

Columbia University, Fu Foundation School of Engineering and Applied Science, Department of Chemical Engineering, New York, NY 10027. Offers MS, Eng Sc D, PhD. PhD offered through the Graduate School of Arts and Sciences. Part-time programs available. Post-baccalaureate distance learning degree programs offered (no on-campus study). Faculty: 13 full-time (3 women), 7 part-time/adjunct (1 woman). Students: 50 full-time (19 women), 10 part-time (4 women); includes 9 minority (1 American Indian or Alaska Native, non-Hispanic/Latino; 8 Asian, non-Hispanic/Latino), 28 international. Average age 26. 155 applicants, 25% accepted, 15 enrolled. In 2010, 25 master's, 8 doctorates awarded. Degree requirements: For doctorate, thesis/dissertation, qualifying exam. Entrance requirements: For master's and doctorate, GRE General Test. Additional exam requirements/recommendations for international students: Required—TOEFL, IELTS. Application deadline: For fall admission, 12/1 priority date for domestic and international students; for spring admission, 10/1 priority date for domestic and international students. Application fee: $95. Electronic applications accepted. Financial support: In 2010–11, 42 students received support, including 1 fellowship with full tuition reimbursement available (averaging $30,000 per year), 31 research assistantships with full tuition reimbursements available (averaging $29,000 per year), 10 teaching assistantships with full tuition reimbursements available (averaging $29,000 per year); health care benefits also available. Financial award application deadline: 12/1; financial award applicants required to submit FAFSA. Faculty research: Polymer physics and science, genomics, colloids, protein, metabolic and biomedical engineering, electrochemical engineering. Unit head: Dr. Sanat K. Kumar, Professor of Chemical Engineering and Department Chairman, 212-854-2193, Fax: 212-854-3054, E-mail: sk2794@columbia.edu. Application contact: Teresa Colaizzo, Departmental Administrator, 212-854-4415, Fax: 212-854-3054, E-mail: tc16@columbia.edu.

Cooper Union for the Advancement of Science and Art, Albert Nerken School of Engineering, New York, NY 10003-7120. Offers chemical engineering (ME); civil engineering (ME); electrical engineering (ME); mechanical engineering (ME). Part-time programs available. Faculty: 27 full-time (1 woman), 15 part-time/adjunct (2 women). Students: 57 full-time (15 women), 25 part-time (1 woman); includes 2 Black or African American, non-Hispanic/Latino; 1 American Indian or Alaska Native, non-Hispanic/Latino; 22 Asian, non-Hispanic/Latino; 2 Hispanic/Latino, 16 international. Average age 24. 72 applicants, 39% accepted, 27 enrolled. In 2010, 25 master's awarded. Degree requirements: For master's, thesis. Entrance requirements: For master's, GRE, BE, minimum GPA of 3.5. Additional exam requirements/recommendations for international students: Required—TOEFL (minimum score 600 paper-based; 250 computer-based; 100 iBT). Application deadline: For fall admission, 2/15 for domestic and international students. Application fee: $65. Expenses: Tuition: Full-time $35,000; part-time $1100 per credit. Required fees: $825 per semester. Financial support: Fellowships with full tuition reimbursements, career-related internships or fieldwork, Federal Work-Study, tuition waivers (full), and all admitted students receive full-tuition scholarships available. Support available to part-time students. Financial award application deadline: 5/1; financial award applicants required to submit CSS PROFILE or FAFSA. Faculty research: Civil infrastructure, imaging and sensing technology, biomedical engineering, encryption technology, process engineering. Unit head: Dr. Simon Ben-Avi, Acting Dean, 212-353-4285, E-mail: benavi@cooper.edu. Application contact: Student Contact, 212-353-4120, E-mail: admissions@cooper.edu.

Cornell University, Graduate School, Graduate Fields of Engineering, Field of Chemical Engineering, Ithaca, NY 14853-0001. Offers advanced materials processing (M Eng, MS, PhD); applied mathematics and computational methods (M Eng, MS, PhD); biochemical engineering (M Eng, MS, PhD); chemical reaction engineering (M Eng, MS, PhD); classical and statistical thermodynamics (M Eng, MS, PhD); fluid dynamics, rheology and biorheology (M Eng, MS, PhD); heat and mass transfer (M Eng, MS, PhD); kinetics and catalysis (M Eng, MS, PhD); polymers (M Eng, MS, PhD); surface science (M Eng, MS, PhD). Faculty: 29 full-time (2 women). Students: 116 full-time (34 women); includes 1 Black or African American, non-Hispanic/Latino; 17 Asian, non-Hispanic/Latino; 5 Hispanic/Latino, 45 international. Average age 24. 392 applicants, 35% accepted, 70 enrolled. In 2010, 35 master's, 17 doctorates awarded. Degree requirements: For master's, thesis (MS); for doctorate, comprehensive exam, thesis/dissertation. Entrance requirements: For master's and doctorate, GRE General Test, 2 letters of recommendation. Additional exam requirements/recommendations for international students: Required—TOEFL (minimum score 600 paper-based; 237 computer-based; 77 iBT). Application deadline: For fall admission, 1/15 priority date for domestic students. Application fee: $70. Electronic applications accepted. Expenses: Tuition: Full-time $29,500. Required fees: $76. Tuition and fees vary according to degree level and program. Financial support: In 2010–11, 67 students received support, including 20 fellowships with full tuition reimbursements available, 40 research assistantships with full tuition reimbursements available, 13 teaching assistantships with full tuition reimbursements available; institutionally sponsored loans, scholarships/grants, health care benefits, tuition waivers (full and partial), and unspecified assistantships also available. Financial award applicants required to submit FAFSA. Faculty research: Biochemical, biomedical and metabolic engineering; fluid and polymer dynamics; surface science and chemical kinetics; electronics materials; microchemical systems and nanotechnology. Unit head: Director of Graduate Studies, 607-255-4550. Application contact: Graduate Field Assistant, 607-255-4550, E-mail: dgs@cheme.cornell.edu.

Dalhousie University, Faculty of Engineering, Department of Chemical Engineering, Halifax, NS B3J 1Z1, Canada. Offers M Eng, MA Sc, PhD. Degree requirements: For master's, thesis; for doctorate, thesis/dissertation. Entrance requirements: Additional exam requirements/recommendations for international students: Required—TOEFL, IELTS, CANTEST, CAEL, or Michigan English Language Assessment Battery. Electronic applications accepted. Faculty research: Explosions, process optimization, combustion synthesis of materials, waste minimization, treatment of industrial wastewater.

Drexel University, College of Engineering, Department of Chemical and Biological Engineering, Program in Chemical Engineering, Philadelphia, PA 19104-2875. Offers MS, PhD. Degree requirements: For doctorate, thesis/dissertation. Entrance requirements: For master's, minimum GPA of 3.0; for doctorate, minimum GPA of 3.5, MS in chemical engineering. Additional exam requirements/recommendations for international students: Required—TOEFL. Electronic applications accepted.

École Polytechnique de Montréal, Graduate Programs, Department of Chemical Engineering, Montréal, QC H3C 3A7, Canada. Offers M Eng, M Sc A, PhD, DESS. Part-time and evening/weekend programs available. Terminal master's awarded for partial completion of doctoral program. Degree requirements: For master's, one foreign language, thesis; for doctorate, one foreign language, thesis/dissertation. Entrance requirements: For master's, minimum GPA of 2.75; for doctorate, minimum GPA of 3.0. Electronic applications accepted. Faculty research: Polymer engineering, biochemical and food engineering, reactor engineering and industrial processes pollution control engineering, gas technology.

Fairleigh Dickinson University, College at Florham, Silberman College of Business, Program in Pharmaceutical Studies, Madison, NJ 07940-1099. Offers MBA, Certificate. Students: 8 full-time (4 women), 12 part-time (5 women), 7 international. Average age 30. 10 applicants, 70% accepted, 2 enrolled. In 2010, 14 master's awarded. Application deadline: Applications are processed on a rolling basis. Application fee: $40.

Florida Agricultural and Mechanical University, Division of Graduate Studies, Research, and Continuing Education, FAMU-FSU College of Engineering, Department of Chemical Engineering, Tallahassee, FL 32310-6046. Offers MS, PhD. Degree requirements: For master's, thesis (for some programs); for doctorate, thesis/dissertation, presentation of research topic at professional meeting. Entrance requirements: For master's, GRE General Test, minimum GPA of 3.0; for doctorate, GRE General Test, minimum GPA of 3.3. Additional exam requirements/recommendations for international students: Required—TOEFL (minimum score 550 paper-based; 213 computer-based). Expenses: Contact institution. Faculty research: Macromolecular transport, polymer processing, biochemical engineering, process control, environmental engineering.

Florida Institute of Technology, Graduate Programs, College of Engineering, Chemical Engineering Department, Melbourne, FL 32901-6975. Offers MS, PhD. Part-time programs available. Faculty: 4 full-time (1 woman). Students: 19 full-time (9 women), 4 part-time (1 woman); includes 1 minority (Black or African American, non-Hispanic/Latino), 14 international. Average age 25. 73 applicants, 58% accepted, 6 enrolled. In 2010, 3 master's, 1 doctorate awarded. Terminal master's awarded for partial completion of doctoral program. Degree requirements: For master's, thesis, seminar, independent research project; for doctorate, comprehensive exam, thesis/dissertation, oral exam, original research project, written exam. Entrance requirements: For master's, minimum GPA of 3.0; for doctorate, GRE General Test, GRE Subject Test, minimum GPA of 3.5, resume, 3 letters of recommendation, statement of objectives. Additional exam requirements/recommendations for international students: Required—TOEFL (minimum score 550 paper-based; 213 computer-based; 79 iBT). Application deadline: For fall admission, 4/1 for international students; for spring admission, 9/30 for international students. Applications are processed on a rolling basis. Application fee: $50. Electronic applications accepted. Expenses: Tuition: Part-time $1040 per credit hour. Tuition and fees vary according to campus/location. Financial support: In 2010–11, 3 teaching assistantships with full and partial tuition reimbursements (averaging $9,556 per year) were awarded; research assistantships with full and partial tuition reimbursements, career-related internships or fieldwork, institutionally sponsored loans, tuition waivers (partial), unspecified assistantships, and tuition remissions also available. Support available to part-time students. Financial award application deadline: 3/1; financial award applicants required to submit FAFSA. Faculty research: Space technology, biotechnology, materials synthesis and processing, supercritical fluids, water treatment, process control. Total annual research expenditures: $154,798. Unit head: Dr. Manolis M. Tomadakis, Department Head (interim), 321-674-7243, Fax: 321-674-7565, E-mail: tomadaki@fit.edu. Application contact: Cheryl A. Brown, Associate Director of Graduate Admissions, 321-674-7581, Fax: 321-723-9468, E-mail: cbrown@fit.edu.

Florida State University, The Graduate School, FAMU-FSU College of Engineering, Department of Chemical and Biomedical Engineering, Tallahassee, FL 32310-6046. Offers biomedical engineering (MS, PhD); chemical engineering (MS, PhD). Part-time programs available. Faculty: 13 full-time (1 woman). Students: 31 full-time (15 women); includes 3 Black or African American, non-Hispanic/Latino; 1 Asian, non-Hispanic/Latino; 1 Hispanic/Latino, 17 international. Average age 25. 78 applicants, 10% accepted, 8 enrolled. In 2010, 2 master's, 3 doctorates awarded. Terminal master's awarded for partial completion of doctoral program. Degree requirements: For master's, thesis (for some programs); for doctorate, comprehensive exam, thesis/

dissertation, qualifying exam. *Entrance requirements:* For master's, GRE General Test (minimum score 1200), BS in chemical engineering or other physical science, minimum GPA of 3.0; for doctorate, GRE General Test (minimum score: 1200), BS in chemical engineering or other physical science, minimum GPA of 3.0, or MS in chemical or biomedical engineering. Additional exam requirements/recommendations for international students: Required—TOEFL (minimum score 550 paper-based; 213 computer-based). *Application deadline:* For fall admission, 3/1 priority date for domestic students, 3/1 for international students; for spring admission, 11/1 for domestic and international students. Applications are processed on a rolling basis. Application fee: $30. *Expenses:* Contact institution. *Financial support:* In 2010–11, 30 students received support, including 4 fellowships with full tuition reimbursements available (averaging $18,500 per year), 12 research assistantships with full tuition reimbursements available (averaging $18,500 per year), 10 teaching assistantships with full tuition reimbursements available (averaging $18,500 per year). Financial award application deadline: 3/1. *Faculty research:* Macromolecular transport, polymer processing, biochemical engineering, environmental engineering, transport and reaction, NMR-MRI, fuel cells. Total annual research expenditures: $1.2 million. *Unit head:* Dr. Bruce R. Locke, Chair and Professor, 850-410-6149, Fax: 850-410-6150, E-mail: locke@eng.fsu.edu. *Application contact:* Lisa Fowler, Office Administrator, 850-410-6151, Fax: 850-410-6150, E-mail: lfowler@fsu.edu.

Georgia Institute of Technology, Graduate Studies and Research, College of Engineering, School of Chemical and Biomolecular Engineering, Atlanta, GA 30332-0001. Offers bioengineering (MS Bio E, PhD); chemical engineering (MS Ch E, PhD); paper science and engineering (MS, PhD); polymers (MS Poly). *Degree requirements:* For master's, thesis; for doctorate, comprehensive exam, thesis/dissertation. *Entrance requirements:* For master's and doctorate, GRE, minimum GPA of 3.0. Additional exam requirements/recommendations for international students: Required—TOEFL (minimum score 550 paper-based; 213 computer-based). Electronic applications accepted. *Faculty research:* Biochemical engineering; process modeling, synthesis, and control; polymer science and engineering; thermodynamics and separations; surface and particle science.

Graduate School and University Center of the City University of New York, Graduate Studies, Program in Engineering, New York, NY 10016-4039. Offers biomedical engineering (PhD); chemical engineering (PhD); civil engineering (PhD); electrical engineering (PhD); mechanical engineering (PhD). *Degree requirements:* For doctorate, thesis/dissertation. *Entrance requirements:* For doctorate, GRE General Test. Additional exam requirements/recommendations for international students: Required—TOEFL. Electronic applications accepted.

Howard University, College of Engineering, Architecture, and Computer Sciences, School of Engineering and Computer Science, Department of Chemical Engineering, Washington, DC 20059-0002. Offers MS. Offered through the Graduate School of Arts and Sciences. Part-time programs available. *Degree requirements:* For master's, thesis. *Entrance requirements:* For master's, GRE General Test, minimum GPA of 2.75. Additional exam requirements/recommendations for international students: Required—TOEFL. *Faculty research:* Bioengineering, reactor modeling, environmental engineering, nanotechnology, fuel cells.

Illinois Institute of Technology, Graduate College, Armour College of Engineering, Department of Chemical and Biological Engineering, Chicago, IL 60616-3793. Offers biological engineering (MBE); chemical engineering (M Ch E, MS, PhD); food process engineering (MFPE, MS). Part-time and evening/weekend programs available. Postbaccalaureate distance learning degree programs offered (minimal on-campus study). *Faculty:* 17 full-time (1 woman). *Students:* 156 full-time (63 women), 20 part-time (8 women); includes 11 minority (4 Black or African American, non-Hispanic/Latino; 4 Asian, non-Hispanic/Latino; 2 Hispanic/Latino; 1 Two or more races, non-Hispanic/Latino), 139 international. Average age 25. 413 applicants, 46% accepted, 63 enrolled. In 2010, 32 master's, 15 doctorates awarded. Terminal master's awarded for partial completion of doctoral program. *Degree requirements:* For master's, comprehensive exam (for some programs), thesis (for some programs); for doctorate, comprehensive exam, thesis/dissertation. *Entrance requirements:* For master's, GRE General Test (minimum score 900 Quantitative and Verbal, 2.5 Analytical Writing), minimum undergraduate GPA of 3.0; for doctorate, GRE General Test (minimum score 1000 Quantitative and Verbal, 3.0 Analytical Writing), minimum undergraduate GPA of 3.0. Additional exam requirements/recommendations for international students: Required—TOEFL (minimum score 523 paper-based; 70 iBT); Recommended—IELTS (minimum score 5.5). *Application deadline:* For fall admission, 5/1 for domestic and international students; for spring admission, 10/15 for domestic and international students. Applications are processed on a rolling basis. Application fee: $50. Electronic applications accepted. *Expenses:* Tuition: Full-time $18,576; part-time $1032 per credit hour. Required fees: $583 per semester. One-time fee: $150. Tuition and fees vary according to program and student level. *Financial support:* In 2010–11, 42 research assistantships with full and partial tuition reimbursements (averaging $7,975 per year), 7 teaching assistantships with full tuition reimbursements (averaging $5,107 per year) were awarded; fellowships with partial tuition reimbursements, Federal Work-Study, institutionally sponsored loans, scholarships/grants, health care benefits, and unspecified assistantships also available. Support available to part-time students. Financial award applicants required to submit FAFSA. *Faculty research:* Energy and sustainability, biological engineering, advanced materials, systems engineering. Total annual research expenditures: $2.6 million. *Unit head:* Dr. John Kallend, Acting Chair, 312-567-3054, Fax: 312-567-8875, E-mail: kallend@iit.edu. *Application contact:* Deborah Gibson, Director, Graduate Admission, 866-472-3448, Fax: 312-567-3138, E-mail: inquiry.grad@iit.edu.

Instituto Tecnológico y de Estudios Superiores de Monterrey, Campus Monterrey, Graduate and Research Division, Programs in Engineering, Monterrey, Mexico. Offers applied statistics (M Eng); artificial intelligence (PhD); automation engineering (M Eng); chemical engineering (M Eng); civil engineering (M Eng); electrical engineering (M Eng); electronic engineering (M Eng); environmental engineering (M Eng); industrial engineering (M Eng, PhD); manufacturing engineering (M Eng); mechanical engineering (M Eng); systems and quality engineering (M Eng). M Eng program offered jointly with University of Waterloo; PhD in industrial engineering with Texas A&M University. Part-time and evening/weekend programs available. Terminal master's awarded for partial completion of doctoral program. *Degree requirements:* For master's, one foreign language, thesis; for doctorate, one foreign language, thesis/dissertation. *Entrance requirements:* For master's, EXADEP; for doctorate, GRE, master's degree in related field. Additional exam requirements/recommendations for international students: Required—TOEFL. *Faculty research:* Flexible manufacturing cells, materials, statistical methods, environmental prevention, control and evaluation.

Iowa State University of Science and Technology, Graduate College, College of Engineering, Department of Chemical and Biological Engineering, Ames, IA 50011. Offers M Eng, MS, PhD. *Faculty:* 23 full-time (5 women). *Students:* 56 full-time (21 women), 2 part-time (0 women); includes 2 Asian, non-Hispanic/Latino; 2 Hispanic/Latino, 32 international. 177 applicants, 15% accepted, 8 enrolled. In 2010, 3 master's, 8 doctorates awarded. *Degree requirements:* For master's, thesis (for some programs); for doctorate, thesis/dissertation. *Entrance requirements:* For master's and doctorate, GRE General Test. Additional exam requirements/recommendations for international students: Required—TOEFL (minimum score 587 paper-based; 94 iBT), IELTS (minimum score 7). *Application deadline:* For fall admission, 1/15 priority date for domestic and international students; for spring admission, 10/1 for domestic and international students. Application fee: $40 ($90 for international students). Electronic applications accepted. *Financial support:* In 2010–11, 41 research assistantships with full and partial tuition reimbursements (averaging $17,547 per year), 8 teaching assistantships with full and partial tuition reimbursements (averaging $8,772 per year) were awarded; scholarships/grants, health care benefits, and unspecified assistantships also available. *Unit head:* Dr. Surya Mallaragada, Chair, 515-294-8472, Fax: 515-294-2689, E-mail: suryakm@iastate.edu. *Application contact:* Dr. Monica Lamm, Director of Graduate Education, 515-294-7643, E-mail: chemengr@iastate.edu.

The Johns Hopkins University, Engineering for Professionals, Part-time Program in Chemical and Biomolecular Engineering, Baltimore, MD 21218-2699. Offers M Ch E. Part-time and evening/weekend programs available. *Faculty:* 2 part-time/adjunct (both women). *Students:* 2 full-time (both women), 8 part-time (2 women); includes 4 minority (2 Black or African American, non-Hispanic/Latino; 2 Asian, non-Hispanic/Latino). Average age 26. 9 applicants, 67% accepted, 3 enrolled. *Application deadline:* Applications are processed on a rolling basis. Application fee: $75. Electronic applications accepted. *Financial support:* Institutionally sponsored loans available. *Unit head:* Dr. Dilip Asthagiri, Program Chair, 410-516-3475, E-mail: dilipa@jhu.edu. *Application contact:* Priyanka Dwivedi, Admissions Manager, 410-516-2300, Fax: 410-579-8049, E-mail: pdwived1@jhu.edu.

The Johns Hopkins University, G. W. C. Whiting School of Engineering, Department of Chemical and Biomolecular Engineering, Baltimore, MD 21218. Offers MSE, PhD. Part-time programs available. *Faculty:* 21 full-time (6 women), 3 part-time/adjunct (0 women). *Students:* 83 full-time (26 women); includes 19 minority (4 Black or African American, non-Hispanic/Latino; 12 Asian, non-Hispanic/Latino; 3 Hispanic/Latino), 38 international. Average age 25. 231 applicants, 28% accepted, 29 enrolled. In 2010, 4 master's, 9 doctorates awarded. *Degree requirements:* For doctorate, thesis/dissertation, oral exam. *Entrance requirements:* For doctorate, GRE General Test. Additional exam requirements/recommendations for international students: Required—TOEFL (minimum score 600 paper-based; 250 computer-based; 100 iBT). *Application deadline:* For fall admission, 1/15 for domestic and international students. Applications are processed on a rolling basis. Application fee: $75. Electronic applications accepted. *Financial support:* In 2010–11, 25 fellowships with full and partial tuition reimbursements (averaging $30,000 per year), 70 research assistantships with full tuition reimbursements (averaging $26,496 per year) were awarded; teaching assistantships with full and partial tuition reimbursements, scholarships/grants, health care benefits, tuition waivers (partial), and unspecified assistantships also available. Financial award application deadline: 1/15. *Faculty research:* Polymers and complex fluids, nucleation, bioengineering and biotechnology, computational biology and genomics, cell and molecular biotechnology. Total annual research expenditures: $5.8 million. *Unit head:* Dr. Konstantinos Konstantopoulos, Chair and Professor, 410-516-7170, Fax: 410-516-5510, E-mail: kkonsta1@jhu.edu. *Application contact:* Lindsay Spivey, Academic Program Coordinator, 410-516-4166, Fax: 410-516-5510, E-mail: spivey@jhu.edu.

Kansas State University, Graduate School, College of Engineering, Department of Chemical Engineering, Manhattan, KS 66506. Offers MS, PhD. Postbaccalaureate distance learning degree programs offered. *Degree requirements:* For master's, thesis or alternative; for doctorate, thesis/dissertation. *Entrance requirements:* For master's and doctorate, GRE. Additional exam requirements/recommendations for international students: Required—TOEFL. Electronic applications accepted. *Faculty research:* Renewable sustainable energy, molecular engineering, advanced materials.

Lamar University, College of Graduate Studies, College of Engineering, Department of Chemical Engineering, Beaumont, TX 77710. Offers ME, MES, DE, PhD. *Faculty:* 12 full-time (1 woman). *Students:* 60 full-time (11 women), 38 part-time (10 women); includes 2 Black or African American, non-Hispanic/Latino; 7 Asian, non-Hispanic/Latino; 1 Hispanic/Latino, 70 international. Average age 27. 70 applicants, 69% accepted, 16 enrolled. In 2010, 47 master's, 2 doctorates awarded. *Degree requirements:* For master's, comprehensive exam (for some programs), thesis (for some programs); for doctorate, comprehensive exam, thesis/dissertation. *Entrance requirements:* For master's and doctorate, GRE General Test. Additional exam requirements/recommendations for international students: Required—TOEFL. *Application deadline:* For fall admission, 5/15 priority date for domestic students; for spring admission, 10/1 priority date for domestic students. Applications are processed on a rolling basis. Application fee: $25 ($50 for international students). *Expenses:* Tuition, state resident: full-time $4160; part-time $208 per credit hour. Tuition, nonresident: full-time $10,360; part-time $518 per credit hour. *Financial support:* In 2010–11, 49 fellowships with partial tuition reimbursements (averaging $1,000 per year), 15 research assistantships with partial tuition reimbursements (averaging $6,000 per year), 8 teaching assistantships with partial tuition reimbursements (averaging $12,600 per year) were awarded; tuition waivers (full and partial) also available. Financial award application deadline: 4/1. *Faculty research:* Flare minimization, process optimization, process integration. *Unit head:* Dr. Kuyen Li, Chair, 409-880-8784, Fax: 409-880-2197, E-mail: che_dept@hal.lamar.edu. *Application contact:* Sandy Drane, Coordinator of Graduate Admissions, 409-880-8356, Fax: 409-880-8414, E-mail: gradmissions@hal.lamar.edu.

Lehigh University, P.C. Rossin College of Engineering and Applied Science, Department of Chemical Engineering, Bethlehem, PA 18015. Offers biological chemical engineering (M Eng); chemical engineering (M Eng, MS, PhD); MBA/E. Part-time programs available. Postbaccalaureate distance learning degree programs offered (no on-campus study). *Faculty:* 18 full-time (2 women), 1 part-time/adjunct (0 women). *Students:* 45 full-time (10 women), 31 part-time (11 women); includes 13 minority (4 Black or African American, non-Hispanic/Latino; 6 Asian, non-Hispanic/Latino; 3 Hispanic/Latino), 30 international. Average age 27. 198 applicants, 23% accepted, 26 enrolled. In 2010, 9 master's, 11 doctorates awarded. Terminal master's awarded for partial completion of doctoral program. *Degree requirements:* For master's, thesis (for some programs); for doctorate, comprehensive exam, thesis/dissertation. *Entrance requirements:* For master's and doctorate, GRE General Test. Additional exam requirements/recommendations for international students: Required—TOEFL (minimum score 570 paper-based; 230 computer-based; 79 iBT). *Application deadline:* For fall admission, 7/15 for domestic students, 1/15 priority date for international students; for spring admission, 12/1 for domestic and international students. Applications are processed on a rolling basis. Application fee: $75. Electronic applications accepted. *Financial support:* In 2010–11, 41 students received support, including 5 fellowships with full tuition reimbursements available (averaging $20,400 per year), 31 research assistantships with full tuition reimbursements available (averaging $20,400 per year), 8 teaching assistantships with full tuition reimbursements available (averaging $20,400 per year); career-related internships or fieldwork, institutionally sponsored loans, scholarships/grants, health care benefits, and unspecified assistantships also available. Financial award application deadline: 1/15. *Faculty research:* Emulsion polymers, process control, energy, biotechnology, catalysis. Total annual research expenditures: $2.7 million. *Unit head:* Dr. Anthony J. McHugh, Chairman, 610-758-4260, Fax: 610-758-5057, E-mail: ajm8@lehigh.edu. *Application contact:* Barbara A. Kessler, Graduate Coordinator, 610-758-4261, Fax: 610-758-5057, E-mail: inchegs@mail.lehigh.edu.

Louisiana State University and Agricultural and Mechanical College, Graduate School, College of Engineering, Cain Department of Chemical Engineering, Baton Rouge, LA 70803. Offers MS Ch E, PhD. Part-time and evening/weekend programs available. *Faculty:* 15 full-time (1 woman). *Students:* 67 full-time (19 women), 5 part-time (0 women); includes 4 Asian, non-Hispanic/Latino; 2 Hispanic/Latino, 45 international. Average age 26. 155 applicants, 19% accepted, 20 enrolled. In 2010, 5 master's, 7 doctorates awarded. Terminal master's awarded for partial completion of doctoral program. *Degree requirements:* For master's, comprehensive exam or thesis; for doctorate, thesis/dissertation, general exam, qualifying exam. *Entrance requirements:* For master's and doctorate, GRE General Test, minimum GPA of 3.0. Additional exam requirements/recommendations for international students: Required—TOEFL (minimum score 550 paper-based; 213 computer-based; 79 iBT) or IELTS (minimum score 6.5). *Application deadline:* For fall admission, 1/25 priority date for domestic students, 5/15 priority date for international students; for spring admission, 10/15 for international students. Applications are processed on a rolling basis. Application fee: $50 ($70 for international students). Electronic applications accepted. *Financial support:* In 2010–11, 66 students received support, including 3 fellowships (averaging $16,756 per year), 58 research assistantships with full and partial tuition reimbursements available (averaging $23,237 per year); teaching assistantships, Federal Work-Study, health care benefits, and tuition waivers (full and partial) also available. Financial award application deadline: 4/15; financial award applicants required to submit FAFSA. *Faculty research:* Reaction engineering, control, thermodynamic and transport phenomena, polymer processing and properties, biochemical engineering. Total annual research expenditures: $4.3 million. *Unit head:* Dr. K.T. Valsaraj, Chair, 225-578-1426, Fax: 225-578-1476, E-mail: valsaraj@lsu.edu. *Application contact:* Dr. Judy Wornat, Coordinator, 225-578-1426, Fax: 225-578-1476, E-mail: mjwornat@lsu.edu.

Chemical Engineering

Louisiana Tech University, Graduate School, College of Engineering and Science, Department of Chemical Engineering, Ruston, LA 71272. Offers MS, PhD. Part-time programs available. Terminal master's awarded for partial completion of doctoral program. *Degree requirements:* For master's, thesis; for doctorate, thesis/dissertation. *Entrance requirements:* For master's, GRE General Test, minimum GPA of 3.0 in last 60 hours; for doctorate, minimum graduate GPA of 3.25 (with MS) or GRE General Test. Additional exam requirements/recommendations for international students: Required—TOEFL. *Faculty research:* Artificial intelligence, biotechnology, hazardous waste process safety.

Manhattan College, Graduate Division, School of Engineering, Program in Chemical Engineering, Riverdale, NY 10471. Offers MS. Part-time programs available. *Faculty:* 4 full-time (1 woman), 2 part-time/adjunct (0 women). *Students:* 12 full-time (6 women), 7 part-time (3 women); includes 2 Black or African American, non-Hispanic/Latino; 1 Asian, non-Hispanic/Latino; 4 Hispanic/Latino. Average age 22. 19 applicants, 74% accepted, 14 enrolled. In 2010, 11 master's awarded. *Degree requirements:* For master's, thesis or alternative. *Entrance requirements:* For master's, GRE (recommended), minimum GPA of 3.0. Additional exam requirements/recommendations for international students: Required—TOEFL (minimum score 550 paper-based; 213 computer-based; 80 iBT), IELTS (minimum score 6). *Application deadline:* For fall admission, 8/10 priority date for domestic students, 8/10 for international students; for spring admission, 1/7 for domestic and international students. Applications are processed on a rolling basis. Application fee: $50. *Financial support:* In 2010–11, 8 students received support, including 8 fellowships with full and partial tuition reimbursements available; teaching assistantships, career-related internships or fieldwork, Federal Work-Study, scholarships/grants, and tuition waivers (partial) also available. Support available to part-time students. Financial award application deadline: 2/1. *Faculty research:* Advanced separation processes, environmental management, combustion, pollution prevention. *Unit head:* Dr. Ann Marie Flynn, Chairperson, 718-862-7286, Fax: 718-862-7819, E-mail: chmldept@manhattan.edu. *Application contact:* Kathy Ciarletta, Information Contact, 718-862-7185, Fax: 718-863-7819, E-mail: chmldept@manhattan.edu.

Massachusetts Institute of Technology, School of Engineering, Department of Chemical Engineering, Cambridge, MA 02139. Offers chemical engineering (SM, PhD, Sc D); chemical engineering practice (SM, PhD); SM/MBA. *Faculty:* 31 full-time (4 women). *Students:* 239 full-time (68 women); includes 31 minority (1 Black or African American, non-Hispanic/Latino; 24 Asian, non-Hispanic/Latino; 5 Hispanic/Latino; 1 Two or more races, non-Hispanic/Latino), 97 international. Average age 25. 440 applicants, 18% accepted, 55 enrolled. In 2010, 42 master's, 32 doctorates awarded. Terminal master's awarded for partial completion of doctoral program. *Degree requirements:* For master's, thesis (for some programs), 48 units of practice school experience for SM in chemical engineering practice; for doctorate, comprehensive exam, thesis/dissertation. *Entrance requirements:* For master's and doctorate, GRE General Test. Additional exam requirements/recommendations for international students: Required—TOEFL (minimum score 600 paper-based; 250 computer-based), IELTS (minimum score 7). *Application deadline:* For fall admission, 1/2 for domestic students, 1/3 for international students. Application fee: $75. Electronic applications accepted. *Expenses:* Tuition: Full-time $38,940; part-time $605 per unit. Required fees: $272. *Financial support:* In 2010–11, 214 students received support, including 97 fellowships with tuition reimbursements available (averaging $26,363 per year), 124 research assistantships with tuition reimbursements available (averaging $31,727 per year), 15 teaching assistantships with tuition reimbursements available (averaging $33,672 per year); career-related internships or fieldwork, Federal Work-Study, institutionally sponsored loans, scholarships/grants, traineeships, health care benefits, and unspecified assistantships also available. *Faculty research:* Catalysis and reaction engineering; biological engineering; materials and polymers; surfaces and nanostructures; thermodynamics and molecular computation. Total annual research expenditures: $41.9 million. *Unit head:* Prof. Klavs F. Jensen, Department Head, 617-253-4561, Fax: 617-258-8992. *Application contact:* Prof. Klavs F. Jensen, Department Head, 617-253-4561, Fax: 617-258-8992.

McGill University, Faculty of Graduate and Postdoctoral Studies, Faculty of Engineering, Department of Chemical Engineering, Montréal, QC H3A 2T5, Canada. Offers chemical engineering (M Eng, PhD); environmental engineering (M Eng).

McMaster University, School of Graduate Studies, Faculty of Engineering, Department of Chemical Engineering, Hamilton, ON L8S 4M2, Canada. Offers M Eng, MA Sc, PhD. *Degree requirements:* For master's, thesis; for doctorate, comprehensive exam, thesis/dissertation. *Entrance requirements:* For master's, minimum B average in the last two years. Additional exam requirements/recommendations for international students: Required—TOEFL (minimum score 550 paper-based; 213 computer-based). *Faculty research:* Biomaterials, computer process control, polymer processing, environmental biotechnology, reverse osmosis.

McNeese State University, Doré School of Graduate Studies, College of Engineering and Engineering Technology, Lake Charles, LA 70609. Offers chemical engineering (M Eng); civil engineering (M Eng); electrical engineering (M Eng); engineering management (M Eng); mechanical engineering (M Eng). Part-time and evening/weekend programs available. *Faculty:* 15 full-time (1 woman). *Students:* 37 full-time (10 women), 18 part-time (1 woman); includes 5 minority (3 Black or African American, non-Hispanic/Latino; 1 American Indian or Alaska Native, non-Hispanic/Latino; 1 Two or more races, non-Hispanic/Latino), 43 international. In 2010, 28 master's awarded. *Degree requirements:* For master's, thesis or alternative. *Entrance requirements:* For master's, GRE, minimum undergraduate GPA of 3.0. Additional exam requirements/recommendations for international students: Required—TOEFL (minimum score 560 paper-based; 220 computer-based; 83 iBT). *Application deadline:* For fall admission, 5/15 priority date for domestic and international students; for spring admission, 10/15 priority date for domestic and international students. Applications are processed on a rolling basis. Application fee: $20 ($30 for international students). Tuition and fees vary according to course load. *Financial support:* Federal Work-Study available. Support available to part-time students. Financial award application deadline: 5/1. *Unit head:* Dr. Nikos Kiritsis, Dean, 337-475-5875, Fax: 337-475-5237, E-mail: nikosk@mcneese.edu.

Michigan State University, The Graduate School, College of Engineering, Department of Chemical Engineering and Materials Science, East Lansing, MI 48824. Offers chemical engineering (MS, PhD); materials science and engineering (MS, PhD). *Entrance requirements:* Additional exam requirements/recommendations for international students: Required—TOEFL. Electronic applications accepted.

Michigan Technological University, Graduate School, College of Engineering, Department of Chemical Engineering, Houghton, MI 49931. Offers MS, PhD. Part-time programs available. Terminal master's awarded for partial completion of doctoral program. *Degree requirements:* For master's, comprehensive exam; for doctorate, comprehensive exam, thesis/dissertation. *Entrance requirements:* For master's, GRE. Additional exam requirements/recommendations for international students: Required—TOEFL (minimum score 575 paper-based; 230 computer-based). Electronic applications accepted. *Expenses:* Contact institution. *Faculty research:* Polymer engineering, thermodynamics, chemical process safety, surface science/catalysis, environmental chemical engineering.

Mississippi State University, Bagley College of Engineering, David C. Swalm School of Chemical Engineering, Mississippi State, MS 39762. Offers chemical engineering (MS); engineering (PhD), including chemical engineering. *Faculty:* 10 full-time (3 women), 1 part-time/adjunct (0 women). *Students:* 11 full-time (3 women), 16 part-time (4 women); includes 3 minority (2 Black or African American, non-Hispanic/Latino; 1 Asian, non-Hispanic/Latino), 11 international. Average age 29. 29 applicants, 21% accepted, 4 enrolled. In 2010, 3 master's, 4 doctorates awarded. *Degree requirements:* For master's, thesis optional, comprehensive oral or written exam; for doctorate, comprehensive exam, thesis/dissertation. *Entrance requirements:* For master's and doctorate, GRE, minimum GPA of 3.0. Additional exam requirements/recommendations for international students: Required—TOEFL (minimum score 550 paper-based; 213 computer-based; 79 iBT); Recommended—IELTS (minimum score 6.5). *Application deadline:* For fall admission, 4/1 priority date for domestic students, 5/1 for international

students; for spring admission, 8/1 priority date for domestic students, 9/1 for international students. Applications are processed on a rolling basis. Application fee: $40. Electronic applications accepted. *Expenses:* Tuition, state resident: full-time $2730.50; part-time $304 per credit hour. Tuition, nonresident: full-time $6901; part-time $767 per credit hour. *Financial support:* In 2010–11, 9 research assistantships with full tuition reimbursements (averaging $15,969 per year) were awarded; Federal Work-Study, institutionally sponsored loans, and unspecified assistantships also available. Financial award application deadline: 4/1; financial award applicants required to submit FAFSA. *Faculty research:* Thermodynamics, composite materials, catalysis, surface science, environmental engineering. Total annual research expenditures: $5.8 million. *Unit head:* Dr. Bill Elmore, Interim Director and Associate Professor, 662-325-7206, Fax: 662-325-2482, E-mail: elmore@che.msstate.edu. *Application contact:* Dr. Rafael Hernandez, Associate Professor and Graduate Coordinator, 662-325-0790, Fax: 662-325-2482, E-mail: rhernandez@che.msstate.edu.

Missouri University of Science and Technology, Graduate School, Department of Chemical and Biological Engineering, Rolla, MO 65409. Offers chemical engineering (MS, DE, PhD). *Degree requirements:* For master's, thesis optional; for doctorate, comprehensive exam. *Entrance requirements:* For master's, GRE (minimum score 1100 verbal and quantitative, 4 writing); for doctorate, GRE (minimum score: verbal and quantitative 1200, writing 4). Additional exam requirements/recommendations for international students: Required—TOEFL (minimum score 550 paper-based; 213 computer-based). *Faculty research:* Mixing, fluid mechanics, bioengineering, freeze-drying, extraction.

Montana State University, College of Graduate Studies, College of Engineering, Department of Chemical and Biological Engineering, Bozeman, MT 59717. Offers chemical engineering (MS); engineering (PhD), including chemical engineering option, environmental engineering option; environmental engineering (MS). Part-time programs available. *Faculty:* 9 full-time (2 women), 2 part-time/adjunct (0 women). *Students:* 6 full-time (2 women), 13 part-time (7 women); includes 3 minority (1 American Indian or Alaska Native, non-Hispanic/Latino; 1 Asian, non-Hispanic/Latino; 1 Two or more races, non-Hispanic/Latino), 4 international. Average age 27. 9 applicants, 33% accepted, 3 enrolled. In 2010, 2 master's, 6 doctorates awarded. *Degree requirements:* For master's, comprehensive exam, thesis (for some programs); for doctorate, comprehensive exam, thesis/dissertation. *Entrance requirements:* For master's and doctorate, GRE General Test. Additional exam requirements/recommendations for international students: Required—TOEFL (minimum score 550 paper-based; 213 computer-based). *Application deadline:* For fall admission, 7/15 priority date for domestic students, 5/15 priority date for international students; for spring admission, 12/1 priority date for domestic students, 10/1 priority date for international students. Applications are processed on a rolling basis. Application fee: $30. Electronic applications accepted. *Expenses:* Tuition, state resident: full-time $5553.90. Tuition, nonresident: full-time $14,646. Required fees: $1233. *Financial support:* In 2010–11, 1 fellowship with full tuition reimbursement (averaging $30,000 per year), 17 research assistantships with full tuition reimbursements (averaging $20,000 per year), 2 teaching assistantships with full tuition reimbursements (averaging $11,000 per year) were awarded; health care benefits also available. Financial award application deadline: 3/1; financial award applicants required to submit FAFSA. *Faculty research:* Biofuels, extremophilic bioprocessing, and situ biocatalyzed heavy metal transformations; metabolic network analysis and engineering; magnetic resonance microscopy; modeling of biological systems; the development of protective coatings on planar solid oxide fuel cell (SOFC) metallic interconnects; characterizing corrosion mechanisms of materials in precisely-controlled exposures; testing materials in poly-crystalline silicon production environments; environmental biotechnology and bioremediation. Total annual research expenditures: $1.3 million. *Unit head:* Dr. Ron W. Larson, Head, 406-994-2221, Fax: 406-994-5308, E-mail: ronl@coe.montana.edu. *Application contact:* Dr. Carl A. Fox, Vice Provost for Graduate Education, 406-994-4145, Fax: 406-994-7433, E-mail: gradstudy@montana.edu.

New Jersey Institute of Technology, Office of Graduate Studies, Newark College of Engineering, Department of Chemical Engineering, Program in Chemical Engineering, Newark, NJ 07102. Offers MS, PhD. Part-time and evening/weekend programs available. *Students:* 66 full-time (26 women), 15 part-time (6 women); includes 7 Black or African American, non-Hispanic/Latino; 14 Asian, non-Hispanic/Latino; 3 Hispanic/Latino, 40 international. Average age 30. 143 applicants, 26% accepted, 20 enrolled. In 2010, 25 master's, 4 doctorates awarded. Terminal master's awarded for partial completion of doctoral program. *Degree requirements:* For master's, thesis optional; for doctorate, thesis/dissertation, residency. *Entrance requirements:* For master's, GRE General Test; for doctorate, GRE General Test, minimum graduate GPA of 3.5. Additional exam requirements/recommendations for international students: Required—TOEFL (minimum score 550 paper-based; 213 computer-based; 79 iBT). *Application deadline:* For fall admission, 6/5 priority date for domestic students, 4/1 for international students; for spring admission, 11/15 for domestic and international students. Applications are processed on a rolling basis. Application fee: $65. Electronic applications accepted. *Expenses:* Tuition, state resident: full-time $14,724; part-time $818 per credit. Tuition, nonresident: full-time $20,304; part-time $1128 per credit. Required fees: $2272; $209 per credit. $103 per semester. One-time fee: $312 full-time; $212 part-time. *Financial support:* Fellowships with full and partial tuition reimbursements, research assistantships with full and partial tuition reimbursements, teaching assistantships with full and partial tuition reimbursements, career-related internships or fieldwork, Federal Work-Study, institutionally sponsored loans, and unspecified assistantships available. Financial award application deadline: 3/15. *Unit head:* Dr. Norman Loney, Chair, 973-596-6598, E-mail: norman.loney@njit.edu. *Application contact:* Kathryn Kelly, Director of Admissions, 973-596-3300, Fax: 973-596-3461, E-mail: admissions@njit.edu.

New Mexico State University, Graduate School, College of Engineering, Department of Chemical Engineering, Las Cruces, NM 88003-8001. Offers MS Ch E, PhD. Part-time programs available. *Faculty:* 7 full-time (3 women). *Students:* 22 full-time (6 women), 5 part-time (1 woman); includes 2 minority (both Hispanic/Latino), 21 international. Average age 26. 50 applicants, 84% accepted, 8 enrolled. In 2010, 7 master's, 1 doctorate awarded. Terminal master's awarded for partial completion of doctoral program. *Degree requirements:* For master's, thesis (for some programs); for doctorate, comprehensive exam, thesis/dissertation. *Entrance requirements:* For master's and doctorate, GRE General Test. Additional exam requirements/recommendations for international students: Required—TOEFL. *Application deadline:* For fall admission, 3/1 priority date for domestic and international students; for spring admission, 11/1 priority date for domestic and international students. Applications are processed on a rolling basis. Application fee: $30 ($50 for international students). Electronic applications accepted. *Expenses:* Tuition, state resident: full-time $4536; part-time $242 per credit. Tuition, nonresident: full-time $15,816; part-time $712 per credit. Required fees: $636 per term. *Financial support:* In 2010–11, 13 research assistantships with full and partial tuition reimbursements (averaging $7,265 per year), 7 teaching assistantships with full and partial tuition reimbursements (averaging $5,100 per year) were awarded; fellowships with full tuition reimbursements, career-related internships or fieldwork, Federal Work-Study, scholarships/grants, health care benefits, and unspecified assistantships also available. Support available to part-time students. Financial award application deadline: 3/1. *Faculty research:* Advanced materials separations, environmental engineering, computer-aided design, bioengineering, biofuels, biomedical engineering. *Unit head:* Dr. Martha C. Mitchell, Head, 575-646-2093, Fax: 575-646-7706, E-mail: martmitc@nmsu.edu. *Application contact:* Dr. David A. Rockstraw, Professor, 575-646-7705, Fax: 575-646-7706, E-mail: drockstr@nmsu.edu.

North Carolina Agricultural and Technical State University, Graduate School, College of Engineering, Department of Mechanical and Chemical Engineering, Greensboro, NC 27411. Offers chemical engineering (MS Ch E); mechanical engineering (MSME, PhD). Part-time programs available. *Degree requirements:* For master's, comprehensive exam, thesis optional, dual exam, qualifying exam, thesis defense; for doctorate, thesis/dissertation. *Entrance requirements:* For doctorate, GRE. *Faculty research:* Composites, smart materials and sensors, mechanical systems modeling and finite element analysis, computational fluid dynamics and engine research, design and manufacturing.

North Carolina State University, Graduate School, College of Engineering, Department of Chemical and Biomolecular Engineering, Raleigh, NC 27695. Offers chemical engineering (M Ch E, MS, PhD). Part-time programs available. Terminal master's awarded for partial completion of doctoral program. *Degree requirements:* For master's, thesis optional; for doctorate, thesis/dissertation. *Entrance requirements:* For master's and doctorate, GRE General Test. Additional exam requirements/recommendations for international students: Required—TOEFL. Electronic applications accepted. *Faculty research:* Molecular thermodynamics and computer simulation, catalysis, kinetics, electrochemical reaction engineering, biochemical engineering.

Northeastern University, College of Engineering, Department of Chemical Engineering, Boston, MA 02115-5096. Offers MS, PhD. Part-time programs available. *Faculty:* 8 full-time (5 women). *Students:* 40 full-time (19 women), 6 part-time (1 woman). 111 applicants, 15% accepted, 11 enrolled. In 2010, 2 master's, 4 doctorates awarded. *Degree requirements:* For master's, thesis optional; for doctorate, thesis/dissertation, departmental qualifying exam. *Entrance requirements:* For master's and doctorate, GRE General Test. Additional exam requirements/recommendations for international students: Required—TOEFL (minimum score 550 paper-based; 213 computer-based; 80 iBT). *Application deadline:* For fall admission, 1/15 priority date for domestic and international students. Applications are processed on a rolling basis. Application fee: $50. Electronic applications accepted. *Financial support:* In 2010–11, 21 students received support, including 1 fellowship with full tuition reimbursement available, 13 research assistantships with full tuition reimbursements available, 17 teaching assistantships with full tuition reimbursements available (averaging $18,320 per year); career-related internships or fieldwork, Federal Work-Study, scholarships/grants, tuition waivers (full), and unspecified assistantships also available. Support available to part-time students. Financial award application deadline: 1/15; financial award applicants required to submit FAFSA. *Faculty research:* Aerogel, catalysts, advanced microgravity materials processing, biomaterials, catalyst development, biochemical reactions. *Unit head:* Dr. Laura H. Lewis, Chair, 617-373-2989, Fax: 617-373-8504. *Application contact:* Jeffery Hengel, Admissions Specialist, 617-373-2711, Fax: 617-373-2501, E-mail: grad-eng@coe.neu.edu.

Northwestern University, McCormick School of Engineering and Applied Science, Department of Chemical and Biological Engineering, Evanston, IL 60208. Offers chemical engineering (MS, PhD). Admissions and degrees offered through The Graduate School. Part-time programs available. *Faculty:* 12 full-time (1 woman). *Students:* 97 full-time (39 women), 1 part-time (0 women); includes 25 minority (1 Black or African American, non-Hispanic/Latino; 1 American Indian or Alaska Native, non-Hispanic/Latino; 13 Asian, non-Hispanic/Latino; 8 Hispanic/Latino; 2 Two or more races, non-Hispanic/Latino), 22 international. Average age 26. 222 applicants, 27% accepted, 20 enrolled. In 2010, 6 master's, 18 doctorates awarded. Terminal master's awarded for partial completion of doctoral program. *Degree requirements:* For master's, comprehensive exam (for some programs), thesis optional; for doctorate, comprehensive exam, thesis/dissertation. *Entrance requirements:* For master's and doctorate, General Exam of GRE. Additional exam requirements/recommendations for international students: Required—TOEFL (minimum score 577 paper-based; 233 computer-based; 90 iBT), IELTS (minimum score 7.5). *Application deadline:* For fall admission, 12/31 for domestic and international students. Application fee: $75. Electronic applications accepted. *Financial support:* Fellowships with full tuition reimbursements, research assistantships with full tuition reimbursements, teaching assistantships with full tuition reimbursements, career-related internships or fieldwork, institutionally sponsored loans, traineeships, health care benefits, and unspecified assistantships available. Financial award application deadline: 1/15; financial award applicants required to submit FAFSA. *Faculty research:* Biotechnology and bioengineering; complex systems; environmental catalysis, kinetics and reaction engineering; modeling, theory, and simulation; polymer science and engineering; transport process. Total annual research expenditures: $10.3 million. *Unit head:* Dr. Linda Broadbelt, Chair, 847-491-2890, Fax: 847-491-3728, E-mail: broadbelt@northwestern.edu. *Application contact:* Dr. Luis Amaral, Admissions Officer, 847-491-7850, Fax: 847-491-3728, E-mail: amaral@northwestern.edu.

The Ohio State University, Graduate School, College of Engineering, Department of Chemical and Biomolecular Engineering, Columbus, OH 43210. Offers chemical engineering (MS, PhD). *Faculty:* 13. *Students:* 69 full-time (19 women), 17 part-time (10 women); includes 5 Asian, non-Hispanic/Latino; 2 Hispanic/Latino, 59 international. Average age 26. In 2010, 12 master's, 18 doctorates awarded. *Degree requirements:* For master's, thesis; for doctorate, thesis/dissertation. *Entrance requirements:* For master's and doctorate, GRE General Test. Additional exam requirements/recommendations for international students: Recommended—TOEFL (minimum score 600 paper-based; 250 computer-based). *Application deadline:* For fall admission, 8/15 priority date for domestic students, 7/1 priority date for international students; for winter admission, 12/1 priority date for domestic students, 11/1 priority date for international students; for spring admission, 3/1 priority date for domestic students, 2/1 priority date for international students. Applications are processed on a rolling basis. Application fee: $40 ($50 for international students). Electronic applications accepted. *Expenses:* Tuition, state resident: full-time $10,605. Tuition, nonresident: full-time $26,535. Tuition and fees vary according to course load and program. *Financial support:* Fellowships, research assistantships, teaching assistantships, career-related internships or fieldwork, Federal Work-Study, institutionally sponsored loans, and unspecified assistantships available. Support available to part-time students. *Unit head:* Stuart L. Cooper, Chair, 614-292-6591, Fax: 614-292-3769, E-mail: cooper.1682@osu.edu. *Application contact:* 614-292-9444, Fax: 614-292-3895, E-mail: domestic.grad@osu.edu.

Ohio University, Graduate College, Russ College of Engineering and Technology, Department of Chemical and Biomolecular Engineering, Athens, OH 45701-2979. Offers biomedical engineering (MS); chemical engineering (MS, PhD). Part-time programs available. *Students:* 51 full-time (20 women), 13 part-time (3 women), 49 international. 55 applicants, 38% accepted, 13 enrolled. In 2010, 9 master's, 5 doctorates awarded. *Degree requirements:* For master's, comprehensive exam (for some programs), thesis; for doctorate, comprehensive exam, thesis/dissertation, qualifying exams. *Entrance requirements:* For master's and doctorate, GRE General Test. Additional exam requirements/recommendations for international students: Required—TOEFL (minimum score 590 paper-based; 96 iBT) or IELTS (minimum score 7). *Application deadline:* For fall admission, 3/1 priority date for domestic and international students. Applications are processed on a rolling basis. Application fee: $50 ($55 for international students). Electronic applications accepted. *Financial support:* In 2010–11, fellowships with full tuition reimbursements (averaging $19,000 per year), research assistantships with full tuition reimbursements (averaging $17,000 per year), teaching assistantships with full tuition reimbursements (averaging $15,000 per year) were awarded; Federal Work-Study, institutionally sponsored loans, and unspecified assistantships also available. Financial award application deadline: 3/1; financial award applicants required to submit FAFSA. *Faculty research:* Corrosion and multiphase flow, biochemical engineering, thin film materials, air pollution modeling and control, biomedical engineering. Total annual research expenditures: $1.8 million. *Unit head:* Dr. Valerie L. Young, Chair, 740-593-1496, Fax: 740-593-0873, E-mail: youngv@ohio.edu. *Application contact:* Dr. Daniel A. Gulino, Assistant Chair for Graduate Studies, 740-593-1495, Fax: 740-593-0873, E-mail: gulino@ohio.edu.

Oklahoma State University, College of Engineering, Architecture and Technology, School of Chemical Engineering, Stillwater, OK 74078. Offers MS, PhD. *Faculty:* 14 full-time (2 women), 1 part-time/adjunct (0 women). *Students:* 27 full-time (8 women), 25 part-time (7 women); includes 2 American Indian or Alaska Native, non-Hispanic/Latino; 1 Asian, non-Hispanic/Latino, 47 international. Average age 27. 110 applicants, 23% accepted, 10 enrolled. In 2010, 13 master's, 8 doctorates awarded. *Degree requirements:* For master's, thesis or alternative; for doctorate, comprehensive exam, thesis/dissertation. *Entrance requirements:* For master's and doctorate, GRE or GMAT. Additional exam requirements/recommendations for international students: Required—TOEFL (minimum score 550 paper-based; 79 iBT). *Application deadline:* For fall admission, 3/1 priority date for international students; for spring admission, 8/1 priority date for international students. Applications are processed on a rolling basis. Application fee: $40 ($75 for international students). Electronic applications accepted. *Expenses:* Tuition, state resident: full-time $3716; part-time $154.85 per credit hour. Tuition, nonresident: full-time $14,892; part-time $621 per credit hour. Required fees: $2044; $85.20 per credit hour. One-time fee: $50. Tuition and fees vary according to course load and campus/location. *Financial support:* In 2010–11, 23 research assistantships (averaging $13,151 per year), 27 teaching assistantships (averaging $8,625 per year) were awarded; fellowships, career-related internships or fieldwork, Federal Work-Study, scholarships/grants, health care benefits, tuition waivers (partial), and unspecified assistantships also available. Support available to part-time students. Financial award application deadline: 3/1; financial award applicants required to submit FAFSA. *Unit head:* Dr. Khaled A.M. Gasem, Head, 405-744-5280, Fax: 405-744-6338. *Application contact:* Dr. Gordon Emslie, Dean, 405-744-6368, Fax: 405-744-0355, E-mail: grad-i@okstate.edu.

Oregon State University, Graduate School, College of Engineering, School of Chemical, Biological and Environmental Engineering, Department of Chemical Engineering, Corvallis, OR 97331. Offers M Eng, MS, PhD.

Penn State University Park, Graduate School, College of Engineering, Department of Chemical Engineering, State College, University Park, PA 16802-1503. Offers MS, PhD.

Polytechnic Institute of NYU, Department of Chemical and Biological Engineering, Major in Chemical Engineering, Brooklyn, NY 11201-2990. Offers MS, PhD. Part-time and evening/weekend programs available. *Students:* 24 full-time (11 women), 18 part-time (8 women); includes 6 Black or African American, non-Hispanic/Latino; 5 Asian, non-Hispanic/Latino; 1 Hispanic/Latino, 21 international. Average age 26. 106 applicants, 42% accepted, 16 enrolled. In 2010, 9 master's awarded. *Degree requirements:* For master's, comprehensive exam (for some programs), thesis (for some programs); for doctorate, comprehensive exam, thesis/dissertation. *Entrance requirements:* For master's, GRE General Test, BS in chemical engineering; for doctorate, GRE General Test. Additional exam requirements/recommendations for international students: Required—TOEFL (minimum score 550 paper-based; 213 computer-based; 80 iBT); Recommended—IELTS (minimum score 6.5). *Application deadline:* For fall admission, 7/31 priority date for domestic students, 4/30 priority date for international students; for spring admission, 12/31 priority date for domestic students, 11/30 priority date for international students. Applications are processed on a rolling basis. Application fee: $75. Electronic applications accepted. *Expenses:* Tuition: Full-time $21,492; part-time $1194 per credit. Required fees: $385 per semester. Tuition and fees vary according to course load. *Financial support:* Fellowships, research assistantships, teaching assistantships, institutionally sponsored loans, scholarships/grants, and unspecified assistantships available. Support available to part-time students. Financial award applicants required to submit FAFSA. *Faculty research:* Plasma polymerization, crystallization of organic compounds, dipolar relaxations in reactive polymers. *Unit head:* Dr. Walter Zurawsky, Head, 718-260-3725, Fax: 718-260-3125, E-mail: zurawsky@poly.edu. *Application contact:* JeanCarlo Bonilla, Dir. Graduate Enrollment Management, 718-260-3182, Fax: 718-260-3624, E-mail: gradinfo@poly.edu.

Polytechnic Institute of NYU, Long Island Graduate Center, Graduate Programs, Department of Chemical and Biological Engineering, Major in Chemical Engineering, Melville, NY 11747. Offers MS. *Degree requirements:* For master's, comprehensive exam (for some programs), thesis (for some programs). *Entrance requirements:* Additional exam requirements/recommendations for international students: Required—TOEFL (minimum score 550 paper-based; 213 computer-based; 80 iBT); Recommended—IELTS (minimum score 6.5). *Application deadline:* For fall admission, 7/31 priority date for domestic students, 4/30 priority date for international students; for spring admission, 12/31 priority date for domestic students, 11/30 priority date for international students. Applications are processed on a rolling basis. Application fee: $75. Electronic applications accepted. *Expenses:* Tuition: Full-time $21,492; part-time $1194 per credit. Required fees: $385 per semester. Tuition and fees vary according to course load. *Financial support:* Institutionally sponsored loans, scholarships/grants, and unspecified assistantships available. Support available to part-time students. *Unit head:* Dr. Walter Zurawsky, Department Head, 718-260-3725, E-mail: zurawsky@poly.edu. *Application contact:* JeanCarlo Bonilla, Director of Graduate Enrollment Management, 718-260-3182, Fax: 718-260-3624, E-mail: gradinfo@poly.edu.

Princeton University, Graduate School, School of Engineering and Applied Science, Department of Chemical Engineering, Princeton, NJ 08544-1019. Offers M Eng, MSE, PhD. Terminal master's awarded for partial completion of doctoral program. *Degree requirements:* For master's, thesis (MSE); for doctorate, thesis/dissertation, general exam. *Entrance requirements:* For master's, GRE General Test, 3 letters of recommendation; for doctorate, GRE General Test, official transcript(s), 3 letters of recommendation, personal statement. Additional exam requirements/recommendations for international students: Required—TOEFL. Electronic applications accepted. *Faculty research:* Applied and computational mathematics, bioengineering, environmental and energy science and technology, fluid mechanics and transport phenomena, materials science.

Purdue University, College of Engineering, School of Chemical Engineering, West Lafayette, IN 47907-2050. Offers MSChE, PhD. Terminal master's awarded for partial completion of doctoral program. *Entrance requirements:* For master's and doctorate, GRE, minimum GPA of 3.0. Additional exam requirements/recommendations for international students: Required—TOEFL (minimum score 550 paper-based; 213 computer-based); Recommended—TWE. Electronic applications accepted. *Faculty research:* Biochemical and biomedical processes, polymer materials, interfacial and surface phenomena, applied thermodynamics, process systems engineering.

Queen's University at Kingston, School of Graduate Studies and Research, Faculty of Applied Science, Department of Chemical Engineering, Kingston, ON K7L 3N6, Canada. Offers M Sc, PhD. Part-time programs available. *Degree requirements:* For master's, thesis or alternative; for doctorate, comprehensive exam, thesis/dissertation. *Entrance requirements:* Additional exam requirements/recommendations for international students: Required—TOEFL (minimum score 580 paper-based; 237 computer-based). Electronic applications accepted. *Faculty research:* Polymers and reaction engineering, process control and applied statistics, combustion, fermentation and bioremediation, biomaterials.

Rensselaer Polytechnic Institute, Graduate School, School of Engineering, Program in Chemical Engineering, Troy, NY 12180-3590. Offers M Eng, MS, PhD. Part-time programs available. *Faculty:* 13 full-time (1 woman). *Students:* 67 full-time (15 women), 2 part-time (1 woman); includes 1 Black or African American, non-Hispanic/Latino; 5 Asian, non-Hispanic/Latino; 1 Hispanic/Latino, 39 international. Average age 24. 198 applicants, 24% accepted, 16 enrolled. In 2010, 6 master's, 9 doctorates awarded. Terminal master's awarded for partial completion of doctoral program. *Entrance requirements:* For master's, GRE (minimum score 550 verbal); for doctorate, GRE (Verbal minimum score of 550). Additional exam requirements/recommendations for international students: Required—TOEFL (minimum score 570 paper-based). *Application deadline:* For fall admission, 1/1 priority date for domestic students, 1/1 for international students; for spring admission, 8/15 for domestic and international students. Applications are processed on a rolling basis. Application fee: $75. Electronic applications accepted. *Expenses:* Tuition: Full-time $39,600; part-time $1650 per credit. Required fees: $1896. *Financial support:* In 2010–11, 65 students received support, including 5 fellowships with full tuition reimbursements available (averaging $30,000 per year), 54 research assistantships with full tuition reimbursements available (averaging $23,000 per year), 10 teaching assistantships with full tuition reimbursements available (averaging $17,500 per year); institutionally sponsored loans and scholarships/grants also available. Financial award application deadline: 1/1. *Faculty research:* Biocatalysis, bioseparations, biotechnology, molecular modeling and simulation, advanced materials, interfacial phenomena, systems biology. Total annual research expenditures: $4.9 million. *Unit head:* Dr. Shekhar Garde, Department Head, 518-276-2511, Fax: 518-276-4030, E-mail: gardes@rpi.edu. *Application contact:* Dr. B. Wayne Bequette, Chairman, Graduate Affairs Committee, 518-276-6929, Fax: 518-276-4030, E-mail: vilarl@rpi.edu.

Chemical Engineering

Rice University, Graduate Programs, George R. Brown School of Engineering, Department of Chemical and Biomolecular Engineering, Houston, TX 77251-1892. Offers chemical and biomolecular engineering (MS, PhD); chemical engineering (M Ch E). Part-time programs available. *Degree requirements:* For master's, thesis (for some programs); for doctorate, thesis/dissertation. *Entrance requirements:* For master's and doctorate, GRE General Test, minimum GPA of 3.0. Additional exam requirements/recommendations for international students: Required—TOEFL (minimum score 600 paper-based; 250 computer-based; 90 iBT). Electronic applications accepted. *Faculty research:* Thermodynamics, phase equilibria, rheology, fluid mechanics, polymers, biomedical engineering, interfacial phenomena, process control, petroleum engineering, reaction engineering and catalysis, biomaterials, metabolic engineering.

Rose-Hulman Institute of Technology, Faculty of Engineering and Applied Sciences, Department of Chemical Engineering, Terre Haute, IN 47803-3999. Offers MS. Part-time programs available. *Faculty:* 9 full-time (2 women). *Students:* 3 full-time (0 women). Average age 22. 3 applicants, 67% accepted, 2 enrolled. *Degree requirements:* For master's, thesis. *Entrance requirements:* For master's, GRE, minimum GPA of 3.0. Additional exam requirements/recommendations for international students: Required—TOEFL (minimum score 580 paper-based; 237 computer-based; 92 iBT). *Application deadline:* For fall admission, 2/1 priority date for domestic students. Applications are processed on a rolling basis. Application fee: $0. *Expenses:* Tuition: Full-time $35,595; part-time $1038 per credit hour. *Financial support:* In 2010–11, 3 students received support; fellowships with full and partial tuition reimbursements available, research assistantships with full and partial tuition reimbursements available, institutionally sponsored loans, scholarships/grants, and tuition waivers (full and partial) available. *Faculty research:* Emulsification and emulsion stability, fermentation technology, adsorption and adsorption-based separations, process control. Total annual research expenditures: $19,743. *Unit head:* Dr. Mark Anklam, Chairman, 812-877-8098, Fax: 812-877-8992, E-mail: mark.r.anklam@rose-hulman.edu. *Application contact:* Dr. Daniel J. Moore, Associate Dean of the Faculty, 812-877-8110, Fax: 812-877-8061, E-mail: daniel.j.moore@rose-hulman.edu.

Rowan University, Graduate School, College of Engineering, Department of Chemical Engineering, Glassboro, NJ 08028-1701. Offers MS. Part-time and evening/weekend programs available. *Faculty:* 9 full-time (5 women), 2 part-time/adjunct (0 women). *Students:* 4 full-time. Average age 23. 7 applicants, 71% accepted, 3 enrolled. In 2010, 3 master's awarded. *Degree requirements:* For master's, thesis optional. *Entrance requirements:* For master's, GRE General Test. Additional exam requirements/recommendations for international students: Required—TOEFL. *Application deadline:* Applications are processed on a rolling basis. Application fee: $65 ($200 for international students). Electronic applications accepted. *Expenses:* Tuition, area resident: Part-time $602 per semester hour. Tuition, nonresident: part-time $602 per semester hour. Required fees: $100 per semester hour. One-time fee: $10 part-time. *Financial support:* Research assistantships, scholarships/grants available. *Unit head:* Robert Hesketh, Chair, 856-256-5313, E-mail: hesketh@rowan.edu. *Application contact:* Dr. Ralph Dusseau, Program Adviser, 856-256-5332.

Royal Military College of Canada, Division of Graduate Studies and Research, Science Division, Department of Chemistry and Chemical and Materials Engineering, Kingston, ON K7K 7B4, Canada. Offers chemical engineering (M Eng, MA Sc, PhD); chemistry (M Sc, PhD). *Degree requirements:* For master's, thesis; for doctorate, comprehensive exam, thesis/dissertation. *Entrance requirements:* For master's, honour's degree with second-class standing; for doctorate, master's degree. Electronic applications accepted.

Rutgers, The State University of New Jersey, New Brunswick, Graduate School-New Brunswick, Program in Chemical and Biochemical Engineering, Piscataway, NJ 08854-8097. Offers MS, PhD. Part-time and evening/weekend programs available. Terminal master's awarded for partial completion of doctoral program. *Degree requirements:* For master's, thesis or alternative; for doctorate, thesis/dissertation. *Entrance requirements:* For master's and doctorate, GRE General Test. Additional exam requirements/recommendations for international students: Required—TOEFL. *Expenses:* Tuition, state resident: full-time $7200; part-time $600 per credit. Tuition, nonresident: full-time $11,124; part-time $927 per credit. *Faculty research:* Biotechnology, pharmaceutical engineering, nanotechnology, process system engineering, materials and polymer science, chemical engineering sciences.

San Jose State University, Graduate Studies and Research, Charles W. Davidson College of Engineering, Department of Chemical and Materials Engineering, Program in Chemical Engineering, San Jose, CA 95192-0001. Offers MS. *Degree requirements:* For master's, thesis or alternative. Electronic applications accepted.

South Dakota School of Mines and Technology, Graduate Division, Program in Chemical and Biological Engineering, Rapid City, SD 57701-3995. Offers PhD.

South Dakota School of Mines and Technology, Graduate Division, Program in Chemical Engineering, Rapid City, SD 57701-3995. Offers MS. Part-time programs available. *Degree requirements:* For master's, thesis. *Entrance requirements:* For master's, GRE General Test. Additional exam requirements/recommendations for international students: Required—TOEFL, TWE. Electronic applications accepted. *Faculty research:* Incineration chemistry, environmental chemistry, polymer surface chemistry.

Stanford University, School of Engineering, Department of Chemical Engineering, Stanford, CA 94305-9991. Offers MS, PhD, Eng. Terminal master's awarded for partial completion of doctoral program. *Degree requirements:* For doctorate, thesis/dissertation; for Eng, thesis. *Entrance requirements:* For master's, doctorate, and Eng, GRE General Test. Additional exam requirements/recommendations for international students: Required—TOEFL. Electronic applications accepted. *Expenses:* Tuition: Full-time $38,700; part-time $860 per unit. One-time fee: $200 full-time.

Stevens Institute of Technology, Graduate School, Charles V. Schaefer Jr. School of Engineering, Department of Chemical Engineering and Materials Science, Program in Chemical Engineering, Hoboken, NJ 07030. Offers M Eng, PhD, Engr. *Students:* 28 full-time (14 women), 8 part-time (4 women); includes 2 Asian, non-Hispanic/Latino, 23 international. Average age 27. *Unit head:* Henry Du, Director, 201-216-5262, Fax: 201-216-8306, E-mail: hdu@stevens.edu. *Application contact:* Graduate Admissions, 800-496-4935, Fax: 201-216-8044, E-mail: gradadmissions@stevens.edu.

Syracuse University, L. C. Smith College of Engineering and Computer Science, Program in Chemical Engineering, Syracuse, NY 13244. Offers MS, PhD. Part-time programs available. *Students:* 28 full-time (16 women), 11 part-time (3 women); includes 2 minority (1 Black or African American, non-Hispanic/Latino; 1 Asian, non-Hispanic/Latino), 28 international. Average age 26. 57 applicants, 61% accepted, 17 enrolled. In 2010, 8 master's, 2 doctorates awarded. *Entrance requirements:* For master's, GRE General Test. Additional exam requirements/recommendations for international students: Required—TOEFL (minimum score 100 iBT). *Application deadline:* For fall admission, 7/1 priority date for domestic students, 6/1 priority date for international students. Applications are processed on a rolling basis. Application fee: $75. Electronic applications accepted. *Expenses:* Tuition: Part-time $1162 per credit. *Financial support:* Fellowships with full tuition reimbursements, research assistantships with full and partial tuition reimbursements, teaching assistantships with full and partial tuition reimbursements, tuition waivers (partial) available. Financial award application deadline: 1/1. *Unit head:* Dr. John Heydweiller, Interim Dean, 315-443-3064, E-mail: jcheydwe@syr.edu. *Application contact:* Kathleen Joyce, Assistant Dean, 314-443-2219, E-mail: topgrads@syr.edu.

Tennessee Technological University, Graduate School, College of Engineering, Department of Chemical Engineering, Cookeville, TN 38505. Offers MS, PhD. Part-time programs available. *Faculty:* 8 full-time (0 women). *Students:* 3 full-time (0 women), 5 part-time (2 women); includes 2 Black or African American, non-Hispanic/Latino; 4 Asian, non-Hispanic/Latino. Average age 26. 15 applicants, 53% accepted, 0 enrolled. In 2010, 4 master's awarded. *Degree requirements:* For master's, thesis. *Entrance requirements:* For master's, GRE General Test. Additional exam requirements/recommendations for international students: Required—

TOEFL (minimum score 550 paper-based; 79 iBT), IELTS (minimum score 5.5). *Application deadline:* For fall admission, 8/1 for domestic students, 5/1 for international students; for spring admission, 12/1 for domestic students, 10/1 for international students. Application fee: $25 ($30 for international students). Electronic applications accepted. *Expenses:* Tuition, state resident: full-time $7934; part-time $388 per credit hour. Tuition, nonresident: full-time $19,758; part-time $962 per credit hour. *Financial support:* In 2010–11, fellowships (averaging $8,000 per year), 7 research assistantships (averaging $7,000 per year), 5 teaching assistantships (averaging $5,433 per year) were awarded; career-related internships or fieldwork also available. Financial award application deadline: 4/1. *Faculty research:* Biochemical conversion, insulation, fuel reprocessing. *Unit head:* Dr. Pedro Arce, Chairperson, 931-372-3297, Fax: 931-372-6372. *Application contact:* Shelia K. Kendrick, Coordinator of Graduate Admissions, 931-372-3808, Fax: 931-372-3497, E-mail: skendrick@tntech.edu.

Texas A&M University, College of Engineering, Artie McFerrin Department of Chemical Engineering, College Station, TX 77843. Offers M Eng, MS, PhD. *Faculty:* 28. *Students:* 192 full-time (66 women), 5 part-time (1 woman); includes 15 minority (3 Black or African American, non-Hispanic/Latino; 1 American Indian or Alaska Native, non-Hispanic/Latino; 6 Asian, non-Hispanic/Latino; 5 Hispanic/Latino), 149 international. Average age 27. In 2010, 4 master's, 18 doctorates awarded. Terminal master's awarded for partial completion of doctoral program. *Degree requirements:* For master's, thesis (MS); for doctorate, thesis/dissertation. *Entrance requirements:* For master's and doctorate, GRE General Test. Additional exam requirements/recommendations for international students: Required—TOEFL. *Application deadline:* For fall admission, 3/1 priority date for domestic and international students; for spring admission, 10/1 priority date for domestic students, 10/1 for international students. Applications are processed on a rolling basis. Application fee: $50 ($75 for international students). Electronic applications accepted. *Financial support:* In 2010–11, fellowships with full tuition reimbursements (averaging $18,240 per year), research assistantships with full tuition reimbursements (averaging $17,000 per year), teaching assistantships with full tuition reimbursements (averaging $17,132 per year) were awarded; career-related internships or fieldwork, scholarships/grants, and tuition waivers (full) also available. Financial award application deadline: 3/31; financial award applicants required to submit FAFSA. *Faculty research:* Reaction engineering, interface phenomena, environmental applications, biochemical engineering, polymers. *Unit head:* Michael Pishko, Head, 979-845-3348, E-mail: mpishko@tamu.edu. *Application contact:* Towanna H. Arnold, Program Coordinator, 979-845-3364, Fax: 979-845-6446, E-mail: towanna@tamu.edu.

Texas A&M University–Kingsville, College of Graduate Studies, College of Engineering, Department of Chemical Engineering and Natural Gas Engineering, Program in Chemical Engineering, Kingsville, TX 78363. Offers ME, MS. Part-time and evening/weekend programs available. *Degree requirements:* For master's, comprehensive exam, thesis or alternative. *Entrance requirements:* For master's, GRE General Test, minimum GPA of 3.0. Additional exam requirements/recommendations for international students: Required—TOEFL. *Faculty research:* Process control, error detection and reconciliation, fluid mechanics, handling of solids.

Texas Tech University, Graduate School, Edward E. Whitacre Jr. College of Engineering, Department of Chemical Engineering, Lubbock, TX 79409. Offers MS Ch E, PhD. Part-time programs available. *Faculty:* 13 full-time (2 women). *Students:* 50 full-time (22 women), 4 part-time (3 women); includes 1 Black or African American, non-Hispanic/Latino; 1 Asian, non-Hispanic/Latino, 49 international. Average age 25. 102 applicants, 16% accepted, 8 enrolled. In 2010, 1 master's, 4 doctorates awarded. *Degree requirements:* For master's, thesis or alternative; for doctorate, thesis/dissertation. *Entrance requirements:* For master's and doctorate, GRE General Test, minimum GPA of 3.0. Additional exam requirements/recommendations for international students: Required—TOEFL (minimum score 550 paper-based; 213 computer-based; 79 iBT). *Application deadline:* For fall admission, 6/1 priority date for domestic students, 1/15 priority date for international students; for spring admission, 9/1 priority date for domestic students, 6/15 priority date for international students. Applications are processed on a rolling basis. Application fee: $50 ($75 for international students). Electronic applications accepted. *Expenses:* Tuition, state resident: full-time $5495.76; part-time $228.99 per credit hour. Tuition, nonresident: full-time $12,936; part-time $538.99 per credit hour. Required fees: $2674; $36 per credit hour. $905 per semester. *Financial support:* In 2010–11, 30 research assistantships with partial tuition reimbursements (averaging $5,504 per year) were awarded; fellowships also available. Financial award application deadline: 4/15; financial award applicants required to submit FAFSA. *Faculty research:* Chemical process control, polymers and materials science, computational methods, bioengineering, renewable resources. Total annual research expenditures: $2.4 million. *Unit head:* Dr. M. Nazmul Karim, Chair, 806-742-3553, Fax: 806-742-3552, E-mail: naz.karim@ttu.edu. *Application contact:* Dr. M. Nazmul Karim, Chair, 806-742-3553, Fax: 806-742-3552, E-mail: naz.karim@ttu.edu.

Tufts University, School of Engineering, Department of Chemical and Biological Engineering, Medford, MA 02155. Offers ME, MS, PhD. Part-time programs available. Terminal master's awarded for partial completion of doctoral program. *Degree requirements:* For master's, thesis (for some programs); for doctorate, thesis/dissertation. *Entrance requirements:* For master's and doctorate, GRE General Test. Additional exam requirements/recommendations for international students: Required—TOEFL (minimum score 550 paper-based; 213 computer-based; 80 iBT). Electronic applications accepted. *Expenses:* Tuition: Full-time $39,624; part-time $3962 per course. Required fees: $40 per year. Full-time tuition and fees vary according to degree level, program and student level. Part-time tuition and fees vary according to course load.

Tulane University, School of Science and Engineering, Department of Chemical and Biomolecular Engineering, New Orleans, LA 70118-5669. Offers PhD. Part-time programs available. Terminal master's awarded for partial completion of doctoral program. *Degree requirements:* For doctorate, thesis/dissertation. *Entrance requirements:* For doctorate, GRE General Test, minimum B average in undergraduate course work. Additional exam requirements/recommendations for international students: Required—TOEFL. Electronic applications accepted. *Faculty research:* Interfacial phenomena catalysis, electrochemical engineering, environmental science.

Universidad de las Américas–Puebla, Division of Graduate Studies, School of Engineering, Program in Chemical Engineering, Puebla, Mexico. Offers chemical engineering (MS); food technology (MS). Part-time and evening/weekend programs available. *Degree requirements:* For master's, one foreign language, thesis. *Faculty research:* Food science, reactors, oil industry, biotechnology.

Université de Sherbrooke, Faculty of Engineering, Department of Chemical Engineering, Sherbrooke, QC J1K 2R1, Canada. Offers M Sc A, PhD. *Degree requirements:* For master's, one foreign language, thesis; for doctorate, comprehensive exam, thesis/dissertation. *Entrance requirements:* For doctorate, master's degree in engineering or equivalent. Electronic applications accepted. *Faculty research:* Conversion processes, high-temperature plasma technologies, system engineering, environmental engineering, textile technologies.

Université Laval, Faculty of Sciences and Engineering, Department of Chemical Engineering, Programs in Chemical Engineering, Québec, QC G1K 7P4, Canada. Offers M Sc, PhD. Terminal master's awarded for partial completion of doctoral program. *Degree requirements:* For master's, thesis (for some programs); for doctorate, comprehensive exam, thesis/dissertation. *Entrance requirements:* Additional exam requirements/recommendations for international students: Required—TOEFL (minimum score 500 paper-based). Electronic applications accepted.

University at Buffalo, the State University of New York, Graduate School, School of Engineering and Applied Sciences, Department of Chemical and Biological Engineering, Buffalo, NY 14260. Offers ME, MS, PhD. Part-time programs available. *Faculty:* 17 full-time (1 woman), 4 part-time/adjunct (1 woman). *Students:* 107 full-time (36 women), 9 part-time (4 women); includes 1 Black or African American, non-Hispanic/Latino; 2 Asian, non-Hispanic/Latino; 2

Hispanic/Latino, 85 international. Average age 26. 393 applicants, 12% accepted, 31 enrolled. In 2010, 13 master's, 5 doctorates awarded. *Degree requirements:* For master's, thesis (for some programs); for doctorate, comprehensive exam, thesis/dissertation. *Entrance requirements:* For master's and doctorate, GRE General Test. Additional exam requirements/recommendations for international students: Required—TOEFL (minimum score 550 paper-based; 213 computer-based; 79 iBT). *Application deadline:* For fall admission, 2/1 priority date for domestic and international students; for spring admission, 10/1 priority date for domestic and international students. Applications are processed on a rolling basis. Application fee: $50. Electronic applications accepted. *Financial support:* In 2010–11, 52 students received support, including 4 fellowships (averaging $30,000 per year), 33 research assistantships with full tuition reimbursements available (averaging $24,000 per year), 9 teaching assistantships with full tuition reimbursements available (averaging $20,900 per year); institutionally sponsored loans, scholarships/grants, health care benefits, tuition waivers (partial), and unspecified assistantships also available. Support available to part-time students. Financial award application deadline: 2/28; financial award applicants required to submit FAFSA. *Faculty research:* Transport, polymers, nanomaterials, biochemical engineering, catalysis. Total annual research expenditures: $11.2 million. *Unit head:* Dr. David A. Kofke, Chairman, 716-645-2911, Fax: 716-645-3822, E-mail: kofke@buffalo.edu. *Application contact:* Dr. Paschalis Alexandridis, Director of Graduate Studies, 716-645-1183, Fax: 716-645-3822, E-mail: palexand@buffalo.edu.

The University of Akron, Graduate School, College of Engineering, Department of Chemical and Biomolecular Engineering, Akron, OH 44325. Offers MS, PhD. Part-time and evening/weekend programs available. *Faculty:* 13 full-time (3 women), 1 part-time/adjunct (0 women). *Students:* 63 full-time (16 women), 6 part-time (2 women); includes 4 Asian, non-Hispanic/Latino, 51 international. Average age 27. 60 applicants, 72% accepted, 17 enrolled. In 2010, 7 master's, 6 doctorates awarded. *Degree requirements:* For master's, thesis optional; for doctorate, one foreign language, thesis/dissertation, candidacy exam, qualifying exam. *Entrance requirements:* For master's, GRE, minimum GPA of 2.75, letter of recommendation; for doctorate, GRE, minimum GPA of 3.0 with bachelor's degree, 3.5 with master's degree; letters of recommendation; personal statement. Additional exam requirements/recommendations for international students: Required—TOEFL (minimum score 550 paper-based; 213 computer-based; 79 iBT). *Application deadline:* For fall admission, 5/1 for domestic and international students; for spring admission, 10/31 for domestic and international students. Application fee: $30 ($40 for international students). Electronic applications accepted. *Expenses:* Tuition, state resident: full-time $6800; part-time $378 per credit hour. Tuition, nonresident: full-time $11,644; part-time $647 per credit hour. Required fees: $1265. One-time fee: $30 full-time. *Financial support:* In 2010–11, 22 research assistantships with full tuition reimbursements, 40 teaching assistantships with full tuition reimbursements were awarded; career-related internships or fieldwork and scholarships/grants also available. *Faculty research:* Renewable energy, fuel cell and CO12 sequestration, nanofiber synthesis and applications, materials for biomedical applications, engineering, surface characterization and modification. Total annual research expenditures: $1.7 million. *Unit head:* Dr. Lu-Kwang Ju, Chair, 330-972-7252, E-mail: lukeju@uakron.edu. *Application contact:* Dr. Lu-Kwang Ju, Chair, 330-972-7252, E-mail: lukeju@uakron.edu.

The University of Alabama, Graduate School, College of Engineering, Department of Chemical and Biological Engineering, Tuscaloosa, AL 35487. Offers MS Ch E, PhD. *Faculty:* 12 full-time (2 women). *Students:* 19 full-time (3 women), 2 part-time (0 women); includes 1 minority (Asian, non-Hispanic/Latino), 16 international. Average age 27. 65 applicants, 29% accepted, 7 enrolled. In 2010, 2 master's, 3 doctorates awarded. Terminal master's awarded for partial completion of doctoral program. *Degree requirements:* For master's, comprehensive exam, thesis; for doctorate, comprehensive exam, thesis/dissertation. *Entrance requirements:* For master's, GRE, minimum GPA of 3.0 overall; for doctorate, GRE General Test or minimum GPA of 3.0. Additional exam requirements/recommendations for international students: Required—TOEFL (minimum score 550 paper-based; 213 computer-based); Recommended—IELTS (minimum score 6.5). *Application deadline:* Applications are processed on a rolling basis. Application fee: $50 ($60 for international students). Electronic applications accepted. *Expenses:* Tuition, state resident: full-time $7900. Tuition, nonresident: full-time $20,500. *Financial support:* In 2010–11, 2 fellowships with full tuition reimbursements (averaging $22,000 per year), 14 research assistantships with full tuition reimbursements, 4 teaching assistantships with full tuition reimbursements were awarded; Federal Work-Study also available. *Faculty research:* Nanostructured materials, catalysis, alternative energy. Total annual research expenditures: $2.2 million. *Unit head:* Dr. Viola L. Acoff, Interim Head, 205-348-2080, Fax: 205-348-6579, E-mail: vacoff@eng.ua.edu. *Application contact:* Dr. Stephen M.C. Ritchie, Associate Professor, 205-348-2712, Fax: 205-348-6579, E-mail: sritchie@eng.ua.edu.

The University of Alabama in Huntsville, School of Graduate Studies, College of Engineering, Department of Chemical and Materials Engineering, Huntsville, AL 35899. Offers chemical engineering (MSE). Part-time and evening/weekend programs available. *Faculty:* 5 full-time (0 women), 1 part-time/adjunct (0 women). *Students:* 7 full-time (3 women), 7 part-time (3 women); includes 2 minority (1 Asian, non-Hispanic/Latino; 1 Two or more races, non-Hispanic/Latino), 5 international. Average age 29. 15 applicants, 60% accepted, 7 enrolled. In 2010, 4 master's awarded. *Degree requirements:* For master's, comprehensive exam, thesis or alternative, oral and written exams. *Entrance requirements:* For master's, GRE General Test, appropriate bachelor's degree, minimum GPA of 3.0. Additional exam requirements/recommendations for international students: Required—TOEFL (minimum score 500 paper-based; 173 computer-based; 62 iBT). *Application deadline:* For fall admission, 7/15 for domestic students, 4/1 for international students; for spring admission, 11/30 for domestic students, 9/1 for international students. Applications are processed on a rolling basis. Application fee: $40 ($50 for international students). Electronic applications accepted. *Expenses:* Tuition, state resident: full-time $7250; part-time $407.75 per credit hour. Tuition, nonresident: full-time $17,358; part-time $970.05 per credit hour. Required fees: $246.80 per semester. Tuition and fees vary according to course load and program. *Financial support:* In 2010–11, 6 students received support, including 2 research assistantships with full and partial tuition reimbursements available (averaging $11,175 per year), 5 teaching assistantships with full and partial tuition reimbursements available (averaging $11,169 per year); career-related internships or fieldwork, Federal Work-Study, institutionally sponsored loans, scholarships/grants, health care benefits, and unspecified assistantships also available. Support available to part-time students. Financial award application deadline: 4/1; financial award applicants required to submit FAFSA. *Faculty research:* Ultrathin films for optical, sensor and biological applications; materials processing including low gravity; hypergolic reactants; computational fluid dynamics; biofuels and renewable resources. Total annual research expenditures: $108,210. *Unit head:* Dr. Chien Pin Chen, Chair, 256-824-7313, Fax: 256-824-6839, E-mail: chien-pin.chen@uah.edu. *Application contact:* Kathy Biggs, Graduate Studies Admissions Manager, 256-824-6199, Fax: 256-824-6405, E-mail: deangrad@uah.edu.

University of Alberta, Faculty of Graduate Studies and Research, Department of Chemical and Materials Engineering, Edmonton, AB T6G 2E1, Canada. Offers chemical engineering (M Eng, M Sc, PhD); materials engineering (M Eng, M Sc, PhD); process control (M Eng, M Sc, PhD); welding (M Eng). Part-time programs available. Postbaccalaureate distance learning degree programs offered (minimal on-campus study). Terminal master's awarded for partial completion of doctoral program. *Degree requirements:* For master's, thesis; for doctorate, thesis/dissertation. *Faculty research:* Advanced materials and polymers, catalytic and reaction engineering, mineral processing, physical metallurgy, fluid mechanics.

The University of Arizona, College of Engineering, Department of Chemical and Environmental Engineering, Program in Chemical Engineering, Tucson, AZ 85721. Offers MS, PhD. *Students:* 29 full-time (11 women), 5 part-time (1 woman); includes 7 minority (1 Black or African American, non-Hispanic/Latino; 1 Asian, non-Hispanic/Latino; 2 Hispanic/Latino; 3 Two or more races, non-Hispanic/Latino), 19 international. Average age 29. 72 applicants, 15% accepted, 8 enrolled. In 2010, 1 master's, 7 doctorates awarded. *Entrance requirements:* For master's and doctorate, GRE, 3 letters of recommendation, resume, statement of purpose. Additional exam requirements/recommendations for international students: Required—TOEFL

(minimum score 550 paper-based; 213 computer-based; 79 iBT). *Application deadline:* Applications are processed on a rolling basis. Application fee: $75. Electronic applications accepted. *Expenses:* Tuition, state resident: full-time $7692. *Financial support:* Unspecified assistantships available. *Unit head:* Dr. Glenn L. Schrader, Department Head, 520-621-2591, Fax: 520-621-6048, E-mail: schrader@email.arizona.edu. *Application contact:* Jo Leeming, Program Coordinator, 520-621-6044, Fax: 520-621-6048, E-mail: leeming@email.arizona.edu.

University of Arkansas, Graduate School, College of Engineering, Department of Chemical Engineering, Fayetteville, AR 72701-1201. Offers MS Ch E, MSE, PhD. Part-time programs available. *Students:* 9 full-time (4 women), 11 part-time (3 women); includes 1 minority (American Indian or Alaska Native, non-Hispanic/Latino), 7 international. 8 applicants, 50% accepted. In 2010, 4 master's, 2 doctorates awarded. *Degree requirements:* For master's, thesis optional; for doctorate, one foreign language, thesis/dissertation. *Entrance requirements:* For master's and doctorate, GRE General Test. *Application deadline:* For fall admission, 4/1 for international students; for spring admission, 10/1 for international students. Applications are processed on a rolling basis. Application fee: $40 ($50 for international students). Electronic applications accepted. *Financial support:* In 2010–11, 10 fellowships with tuition reimbursements, 14 research assistantships were awarded; teaching assistantships, career-related internships or fieldwork and Federal Work-Study also available. Support available to part-time students. Financial award application deadline: 4/1; financial award applicants required to submit FAFSA. *Unit head:* Dr. Tom Spicer, Department Chair, 479-575-4951, E-mail: tos@uark.edu. *Application contact:* Dr. Richard Ulrich, Graduate Coordinator, 479-575-5645, E-mail: rulrich@uark.edu.

The University of British Columbia, Faculty of Applied Science, Program in Chemical and Biological Engineering, Vancouver, BC V6T 1Z1, Canada. Offers chemical engineering (M Eng, M Sc, MA Sc, PhD). Part-time and evening/weekend programs available. *Degree requirements:* For master's, thesis (for some programs); for doctorate, thesis/dissertation. *Entrance requirements:* Additional exam requirements/recommendations for international students: Required—TOEFL, IELTS. Electronic applications accepted. Tuition charges are reported in Canadian dollars. *Expenses:* Tuition, area resident: Full-time $4179 Canadian dollars. International tuition: $7344 Canadian dollars full-time. *Faculty research:* Biotechnology, catalysis, polymers, fluidization, pulp and paper.

University of Calgary, Faculty of Graduate Studies, Schulich School of Engineering, Department of Chemical and Petroleum Engineering, Calgary, AB T2N 1N4, Canada. Offers M Eng, M Sc, PhD. Part-time programs available. *Degree requirements:* For master's, thesis (for some programs); for doctorate, comprehensive exam, thesis/dissertation, candidacy exam. *Entrance requirements:* For master's, minimum GPA of 3.0; for doctorate, minimum GPA of 3.5. Additional exam requirements/recommendations for international students: Required—TOEFL (minimum score 550 paper-based; 213 computer-based; 80 iBT), IELTS (minimum score 7). Electronic applications accepted. *Faculty research:* Environmental engineering, biomedical engineering modeling, simulation and control, petroleum recovery and reservoir engineering, phase equilibria and transport properties.

University of California, Berkeley, Graduate Division, College of Chemistry, Department of Chemical Engineering, Berkeley, CA 94720-1500. Offers MS, PhD. *Degree requirements:* For master's, thesis; for doctorate, thesis/dissertation, qualifying exam. *Entrance requirements:* For master's and doctorate, GRE General Test, minimum GPA of 3.0, 3 letters of recommendation. Additional exam requirements/recommendations for international students: Required—TOEFL. *Faculty research:* Biochemical engineering, electrochemical engineering, electronic materials, heterogeneous catalysis and reaction engineering, complex fluids.

University of California, Davis, College of Engineering, Program in Chemical Engineering, Davis, CA 95616. Offers MS, PhD. Terminal master's awarded for partial completion of doctoral program. *Degree requirements:* For master's, comprehensive exam (for some programs), thesis (for some programs); for doctorate, thesis/dissertation. *Entrance requirements:* For master's and doctorate, GRE General Test, minimum GPA of 3.0. Additional exam requirements/recommendations for international students: Required—TOEFL (minimum score 550 paper-based; 213 computer-based). Electronic applications accepted. *Faculty research:* Transport phenomena, colloid science, catalysis, biotechnology, materials.

University of California, Irvine, School of Engineering, Department of Chemical Engineering and Materials Science, Irvine, CA 92697. Offers chemical and biochemical engineering (MS, PhD); materials science and engineering (MS, PhD). Part-time programs available. *Students:* 77 full-time (24 women), 3 part-time (1 woman); includes 22 minority (1 American Indian or Alaska Native, non-Hispanic/Latino; 16 Asian, non-Hispanic/Latino; 3 Hispanic/Latino; 1 Native Hawaiian or other Pacific Islander, non-Hispanic/Latino; 1 Two or more races, non-Hispanic/Latino), 32 international. Average age 28. 300 applicants, 27% accepted, 26 enrolled. In 2010, 24 master's, 8 doctorates awarded. Terminal master's awarded for partial completion of doctoral program. *Degree requirements:* For doctorate, thesis/dissertation. *Entrance requirements:* For master's and doctorate, GRE General Test, minimum GPA of 3.0, 3 letters of recommendation. Additional exam requirements/recommendations for international students: Required—TOEFL (minimum score 550 paper-based; 213 computer-based). *Application deadline:* For fall admission, 1/15 priority date for domestic students, 1/15 for international students. Applications are processed on a rolling basis. Application fee: $80 ($100 for international students). Electronic applications accepted. *Financial support:* Fellowships with tuition reimbursements, research assistantships with full tuition reimbursements, teaching assistantships with tuition reimbursements, institutionally sponsored loans, traineeships, health care benefits, and unspecified assistantships available. Financial award application deadline: 3/1; financial award applicants required to submit FAFSA. *Faculty research:* Molecular biotechnology, nano-bio-materials, biophotonics, synthesis, superplasticity and mechanical behavior, characterization of advanced and nanostructural materials. *Unit head:* Prof. Albert Yee, Chair, 949-824-7320, Fax: 949-824-2541, E-mail: albert.yee@uci.edu. *Application contact:* Grace Hai-Chin Chau, Academic Program/Graduate Admission Coordinator, 949-824-3887, Fax: 949-824-2541, E-mail: chaug@uci.edu.

University of California, Los Angeles, Graduate Division, Henry Samueli School of Engineering and Applied Science, Department of Chemical and Biomolecular Engineering, Los Angeles, CA 90095-1592. Offers MS, PhD. *Faculty:* 12 full-time (2 women). *Students:* 81 full-time (30 women); includes 1 Black or African American, non-Hispanic/Latino; 22 Asian, non-Hispanic/Latino; 5 Hispanic/Latino, 34 international. 240 applicants, 18% accepted, 21 enrolled. In 2010, 11 master's, 14 doctorates awarded. *Degree requirements:* For master's, comprehensive exam (for some programs), thesis (for some programs); for doctorate, thesis/dissertation, qualifying exams. *Entrance requirements:* For master's, GRE General Test, minimum GPA of 3.0; for doctorate, GRE General Test, minimum GPA of 3.25. Additional exam requirements/recommendations for international students: Required—TOEFL (minimum score 560 paper-based; 220 computer-based; 87 iBT). *Application deadline:* For fall admission, 1/15 for domestic and international students; for winter admission, 10/1 for domestic and international students; for spring admission, 12/31 for domestic and international students. Application fee: $70 ($90 for international students). Electronic applications accepted. *Financial support:* In 2010–11, 20 fellowships, 151 research assistantships, 60 teaching assistantships were awarded; Federal Work-Study, institutionally sponsored loans, and tuition waivers (full and partial) also available. Financial award application deadline: 1/15; financial award applicants required to submit FAFSA. Total annual research expenditures: $4.9 million. *Unit head:* Dr. Harold G. Monbouquette, Chair, 310-825-8946. *Application contact:* John Berger, Student Affairs Officer, 310-825-9063, Fax: 310-206-4107, E-mail: jpberger@ea.ucla.edu.

University of California, Riverside, Graduate Division, Department of Chemical and Environmental Engineering, Riverside, CA 92521-0102. Offers MS, PhD. Part-time programs available. Terminal master's awarded for partial completion of doctoral program. *Degree requirements:* For master's, thesis (for some programs); for doctorate, comprehensive exam, thesis/dissertation. *Entrance requirements:* For master's and doctorate, GRE General Test, minimum GPA of 3.0. Additional exam requirements/recommendations for international students: Required—TOEFL (minimum score 550 paper-based; 213 computer-based; 80 iBT). Electronic

Chemical Engineering

University of California, Riverside (continued)
applications accepted. *Faculty research:* Air quality systems, water quality systems, advanced materials and nanotechnology, energy systems/alternative fuels, theory and molecular modeling.

University of California, San Diego, Office of Graduate Studies, Chemical Engineering Program, La Jolla, CA 92093. Offers MS, PhD. Part-time programs available. *Degree requirements:* For master's, thesis; for doctorate, thesis/dissertation. *Entrance requirements:* For master's and doctorate, GRE General Test. Additional exam requirements/recommendations for international students: Required—TOEFL (minimum score 550 paper-based). Electronic applications accepted. *Faculty research:* Semiconductor and composite materials processing, biochemical processing, electrochemistry and catalysis.

University of California, Santa Barbara, Graduate Division, College of Engineering, Department of Chemical Engineering, Santa Barbara, CA 93106-2014. Offers PhD. *Faculty:* 20 full-time (1 woman). *Students:* 81 full-time (19 women); includes 1 Black or African American, non-Hispanic/Latino; 24 Asian, non-Hispanic/Latino; 4 Hispanic/Latino. Average age 26. 351 applicants, 17% accepted, 15 enrolled. In 2010, 6 doctorates awarded. *Degree requirements:* For doctorate, thesis/dissertation, candidacy exam, thesis defense, seminar presentation. *Entrance requirements:* For doctorate, GRE. Additional exam requirements/recommendations for international students: Required—TOEFL (minimum score 560 paper-based; 83 iBT), IELTS (minimum score 7). *Application deadline:* For fall admission, 1/3 priority date for domestic and international students. Application fee: $70 ($90 for international students). Electronic applications accepted. *Financial support:* In 2010–11, 73 students received support, including 41 fellowships with full and partial tuition reimbursements available (averaging $7,652 per year), 69 research assistantships with full and partial tuition reimbursements available (averaging $14,947 per year), 37 teaching assistantships with full and partial tuition reimbursements available (averaging $3,897 per year); tuition waivers (full and partial) also available. Financial award application deadline: 1/3; financial award applicants required to submit FAFSA. *Faculty research:* Fluid transport, complex fluid and polymers, biomaterials/bioengineering, catalysis and reaction engineering, systems process design and control. Total annual research expenditures: $7.4 million. *Unit head:* Prof. Michael Doherty, Chair, 805-893-5309, Fax: 805-893-4731, E-mail: mfd@engineering.ucsb.edu. *Application contact:* Laura Crownover, Student Affairs Officer, 805-893-8671, Fax: 805-893-4731, E-mail: laura@engineering.ucsb.edu.

University of Cincinnati, Graduate School, College of Engineering, Department of Chemical and Materials Engineering, Program in Chemical Engineering, Cincinnati, OH 45221. Offers MS, PhD. Part-time and evening/weekend programs available. Terminal master's awarded for partial completion of doctoral program. *Degree requirements:* For master's, thesis; for doctorate, thesis/dissertation. *Entrance requirements:* For master's and doctorate, GRE General Test. Additional exam requirements/recommendations for international students: Required—TOEFL (minimum score 600 paper-based; 250 computer-based).

University of Colorado Boulder, Graduate School, College of Engineering and Applied Science, Department of Chemical and Biological Engineering, Boulder, CO 80309. Offers ME, MS, PhD. Part-time programs available. *Faculty:* 21 full-time (5 women). *Students:* 60 full-time (23 women), 56 part-time (24 women); includes 12 minority (1 Black or African American, non-Hispanic/Latino; 1 American Indian or Alaska Native, non-Hispanic/Latino; 3 Asian, non-Hispanic/Latino; 7 Hispanic/Latino), 17 international. Average age 26. 341 applicants, 22 enrolled. In 2010, 27 master's, 20 doctorates awarded. Terminal master's awarded for partial completion of doctoral program. *Degree requirements:* For master's, comprehensive exam, thesis; for doctorate, thesis/dissertation. *Entrance requirements:* For master's, minimum undergraduate GPA of 3.0. *Application deadline:* Applications are processed on a rolling basis. Application fee: $50 ($60 for international students). Electronic applications accepted. *Financial support:* In 2010–11, 49 fellowships (averaging $18,993 per year), 43 research assistantships (averaging $13,187 per year), 34 teaching assistantships (averaging $19,546 per year) were awarded; career-related internships or fieldwork, scholarships/grants, traineeships, and tuition waivers (full) also available. *Faculty research:* Bioengineering and biotechnology, ceramic materials, fluid dynamics and fluid-article technology, heterogeneous catalysis, interfacial and surface phenomena, low-gravity fluid mechanics and materials. Total annual research expenditures: $11.8 million.

University of Connecticut, Graduate School, School of Engineering, Department of Chemical, Materials and Biomolecular Engineering, Field of Chemical Engineering, Storrs, CT 06269. Offers MS, PhD. Terminal master's awarded for partial completion of doctoral program. *Degree requirements:* For master's, comprehensive exam, thesis or alternative; for doctorate, thesis/dissertation. *Entrance requirements:* For master's and doctorate, GRE General Test. Additional exam requirements/recommendations for international students: Required—TOEFL (minimum score 550 paper-based; 213 computer-based). Electronic applications accepted.

University of Dayton, Graduate School, School of Engineering, Department of Chemical Engineering, Dayton, OH 45469-1300. Offers bioengineering instrumentation (MS); bioprocess engineering (MS); biosystems engineering (MS). Part-time and evening/weekend programs available. *Faculty:* 10 full-time (1 woman), 4 part-time/adjunct (0 women). *Students:* 30 full-time (7 women), 5 part-time (1 woman); includes 7 minority (4 Black or African American, non-Hispanic/Latino; 3 Asian, non-Hispanic/Latino), 18 international. Average age 26. 43 applicants, 86% accepted, 17 enrolled. In 2010, 3 master's awarded. *Degree requirements:* For master's, thesis optional. *Entrance requirements:* Additional exam requirements/recommendations for international students: Required—TOEFL (minimum score 550 paper-based; 213 computer-based; 80 iBT). *Application deadline:* For fall admission, 8/1 priority date for domestic students. Applications are processed on a rolling basis. Application fee: $0 ($50 for international students). Electronic applications accepted. *Expenses:* Tuition: Full-time $7800; part-time $650 per credit hour. *Financial support:* In 2010–11, 10 research assistantships with full tuition reimbursements (averaging $14,745 per year) were awarded; institutionally sponsored loans, health care benefits, and unspecified assistantships also available. Financial award applicants required to submit FAFSA. *Faculty research:* Vertically-aligned carbon nanotubes infiltrated with temperature-responsive polymers; smart nanocomposite films for self-cleaning and controlled release, bilayer and bulk heterojunction solar cells using liquid crystalline porphyrins as donors by solution processing, DNA damage induced by multiwalled carbon nanotubes in mouse embryonic stem cells. Total annual research expenditures: $1.5 million. *Unit head:* Dr. Robert Wilkins, Chair, 937-229-2627, E-mail: robert.wilkins@notes.udayton.edu. *Application contact:* Alexander Popovski, Associate Director of Graduate and International Admissions, 937-229-2357, Fax: 937-229-4729, E-mail: alex.popovski@notes.udayton.edu.

University of Delaware, College of Engineering, Department of Chemical Engineering, Newark, DE 19716. Offers M Ch E, PhD. Part-time and evening/weekend programs available. Post-baccalaureate distance learning degree programs offered (minimal on-campus study). Terminal master's awarded for partial completion of doctoral program. *Degree requirements:* For master's, thesis (for some programs); for doctorate, thesis/dissertation. *Entrance requirements:* For master's and doctorate, GRE General Test. Additional exam requirements/recommendations for international students: Required—TOEFL. Electronic applications accepted. *Faculty research:* Biochemical/biomedical engineer, thermodynamics, polymers/composites, materials, catalysis/reactions, colloid/interfaces, expert systems/process control.

University of Florida, Graduate School, College of Engineering, Department of Chemical Engineering, Gainesville, FL 32611. Offers ME, MS, PhD. Part-time programs available. *Faculty:* 20 full-time (1 woman), 1 (woman) part-time/adjunct. *Students:* 121 full-time (30 women), 6 part-time (2 women); includes 1 Black or African American, non-Hispanic/Latino; 6 Asian, non-Hispanic/Latino; 8 Hispanic/Latino, 82 international. Average age 28. 348 applicants, 18% accepted, 51 enrolled. In 2010, 14 master's, 20 doctorates awarded. Terminal master's awarded for partial completion of doctoral program. *Degree requirements:* For master's, thesis (for some programs), Thesis required for Masters of Science; final report required for non-thesis program; for doctorate, comprehensive exam, thesis/dissertation. *Entrance requirements:* For master's and doctorate, GRE General Test, minimum GPA of 3.0. Additional exam

requirements/recommendations for international students: Required—TOEFL (minimum score 550 paper-based; 213 computer-based; 80 iBT), IELTS (minimum score 6). *Application deadline:* For fall admission, 2/28 priority date for domestic and international students; for spring admission, 11/1 for domestic and international students. Applications are processed on a rolling basis. Application fee: $30. Electronic applications accepted. *Expenses:* Tuition, state resident: full-time $10,915.92. Tuition, nonresident: full-time $28,309. *Financial support:* In 2010–11, 56 students received support, including 3 fellowships with full tuition reimbursements available, 53 research assistantships with full tuition reimbursements available (averaging $23,589 per year); Federal Work-Study, institutionally sponsored loans, scholarships/grants, and unspecified assistantships also available. Financial award application deadline: 1/28; financial award applicants required to submit FAFSA. *Faculty research:* Biomedical and microelectronic materials, complex fluids, interfacial and colloidal phenomena, electrochemistry, nanotechnology. Total annual research expenditures: $6.8 million. *Unit head:* Richard B. Dickinson, PhD, Chair, 352-392-0898, Fax: 352-392-9513, E-mail: dickinson@che.ufl.edu. *Application contact:* Anuj Chauhan, PhD, Graduate Coordinator, 352-392-2592, Fax: 352-392-9513, E-mail: chauhan@che.ufl.edu.

University of Houston, Cullen College of Engineering, Department of Chemical and Bio-molecular Engineering, Houston, TX 77204. Offers chemical engineering (MCHE, PhD); petroleum engineering (M Pet E). Part-time programs available. *Faculty:* 16 full-time (3 women), 12 part-time/adjunct (1 woman). *Students:* 99 full-time (26 women), 65 part-time (12 women); includes 6 Black or African American, non-Hispanic/Latino; 23 Asian, non-Hispanic/Latino; 11 Hispanic/Latino, 93 international. Average age 28. 382 applicants, 19% accepted, 45 enrolled. In 2010, 27 master's, 14 doctorates awarded. Terminal master's awarded for partial completion of doctoral program. *Entrance requirements:* For master's and doctorate, GRE General Test. Additional exam requirements/recommendations for international students: Required—TOEFL (minimum score 550 paper-based; 79 iBT), IELTS (minimum score 6.5). *Application deadline:* For fall admission, 2/15 for domestic and international students. Application fee: $25 ($75 for international students). *Expenses:* Tuition, state resident: full-time $8592; part-time $358 per credit hour. Tuition, nonresident: full-time $16,032; part-time $668 per credit hour. Required fees: $2889. Tuition and fees vary according to course load and program. *Financial support:* In 2010–11, 19 fellowships with partial tuition reimbursements (averaging $4,000 per year), 38 research assistantships with partial tuition reimbursements (averaging $15,120 per year), 10 teaching assistantships with partial tuition reimbursements (averaging $11,976 per year) were awarded; career-related internships or fieldwork, Federal Work-Study, institutionally sponsored loans, scholarships/grants, health care benefits, and unspecified assistantships also available. Support available to part-time students. Financial award application deadline: 2/1. *Faculty research:* Chemical engineering. *Unit head:* Dr. Ramanan Krishnamoorti, Chairperson, 713-743-4304, Fax: 713-743-4323, E-mail: ramanan@uh.edu. *Application contact:* Jane Geanangel, Graduate Program Academic Records Coordinator, 713-743-4219.

University of Idaho, College of Graduate Studies, College of Engineering, Department of Chemical and Materials Engineering, Moscow, ID 83844-2282. Offers chemical engineering (MS); materials science and engineering (MS, PhD), including materials science and engineering, metallurgical engineering (MS), mining engineering (PhD). *Faculty:* 10 full-time. *Students:* 17 full-time, 7 part-time. Average age 31. In 2010, 6 master's, 1 doctorate awarded. *Degree requirements:* For master's, thesis; for doctorate, one foreign language, thesis/dissertation. *Entrance requirements:* For master's, GRE, minimum GPA of 2.8; for doctorate, GRE, minimum undergraduate GPA of 2.8, 3.0 graduate. *Application deadline:* For fall admission, 8/1 for domestic students; for spring admission, 12/15 for domestic students. Applications are processed on a rolling basis. Application fee: $60. Electronic applications accepted. *Expenses:* Tuition, nonresident: part-time $580 per credit. Required fees: $306 per credit. *Financial support:* Fellowships, research assistantships, teaching assistantships available. Financial award applicants required to submit FAFSA. *Faculty research:* Geothermal energy utilization, alcohol production from agriculture waste material, energy conservation in pulp and paper mills. *Unit head:* Dr. Wudneh Admassu, 208-885-7572, E-mail: gailb@uidaho.edu. *Application contact:* Dr. Wudneh Admassu, 208-885-7572, E-mail: gailb@uidaho.edu.

University of Illinois at Chicago, Graduate College, College of Engineering, Department of Chemical Engineering, Chicago, IL 60607-7128. Offers MS, PhD. Part-time programs available. *Degree requirements:* For master's, thesis or project; for doctorate, thesis/dissertation, departmental qualifying exam. *Entrance requirements:* For master's and doctorate, GRE General Test, minimum GPA of 2.75. Additional exam requirements/recommendations for international students: Required—TOEFL. *Faculty research:* Multiphase flows, interfacial transport, heterogeneous catalysis, coal technology, molecular and static thermodynamics.

University of Illinois at Urbana–Champaign, Graduate College, College of Liberal Arts and Sciences, School of Chemical Sciences, Department of Chemical and Biomolecular Engineering, Champaign, IL 61820. Offers bioinformatics: chemical and biomolecular engineering (MS); chemical engineering (MS, PhD). *Faculty:* 14 full-time (2 women). *Students:* 104 full-time (38 women), 3 part-time (2 women); includes 1 Black or African American, non-Hispanic/Latino; 8 Asian, non-Hispanic/Latino; 4 Hispanic/Latino; 1 Two or more races, non-Hispanic/Latino, 53 international. 375 applicants, 3% accepted, 12 enrolled. In 2010, 19 master's, 20 doctorates awarded. *Entrance requirements:* For master's and doctorate, GRE, minimum GPA of 3.0. Additional exam requirements/recommendations for international students: Required—TOEFL (minimum score 610 paper-based; 257 computer-based). *Application deadline:* Applications are processed on a rolling basis. Application fee: $75 ($90 for international students). Electronic applications accepted. *Financial support:* In 2010–11, 22 fellowships, 92 research assistantships, 39 teaching assistantships were awarded; tuition waivers (full and partial) also available. *Unit head:* Edmund Seebauer, Head, 217-244-9214, Fax: 217-333-5052, E-mail: eseebaue@illinois.edu. *Application contact:* Cathy Paceley, Office Manager, 217-333-3640, Fax: 217-333-5052, E-mail: paceley@illinois.edu.

The University of Iowa, Graduate College, College of Engineering, Department of Chemical and Biochemical Engineering, Iowa City, IA 52242-1316. Offers MS, PhD. Part-time programs available. *Faculty:* 11 full-time (3 women), 1 (woman) part-time/adjunct. *Students:* 39 full-time (13 women); includes 6 minority (4 Black or African American, non-Hispanic/Latino; 1 Asian, non-Hispanic/Latino; 1 Hispanic/Latino), 19 international. Average age 28. 44 applicants, 27% accepted, 6 enrolled. In 2010, 4 master's, 10 doctorates awarded. *Degree requirements:* For master's, comprehensive exam (for some programs), thesis (for some programs); for doctorate, comprehensive exam, thesis/dissertation. *Entrance requirements:* For master's and doctorate, GRE, minimum undergraduate GPA of 3.0. Additional exam requirements/recommendations for international students: Required—TOEFL (minimum score 550 paper-based; 213 computer-based). *Application deadline:* For fall admission, 2/1 for domestic and international students; for spring admission, 10/1 for domestic and international students. Applications are processed on a rolling basis. Application fee: $60 ($100 for international students). Electronic applications accepted. *Financial support:* In 2010–11, 3 fellowships with full tuition reimbursements (averaging $26,000 per year), 24 research assistantships with partial tuition reimbursements (averaging $24,500 per year), 2 teaching assistantships with partial tuition reimbursements (averaging $10,022 per year) were awarded; unspecified assistantships also available. Financial award applicants required to submit FAFSA. *Faculty research:* Polymeric materials; photopolymerization; atmospheric chemistry and air pollution; biochemical engineering; bioprocessing and biomedical engineering. Total annual research expenditures: $2.6 million. *Unit head:* Dr. David W. Murhammer, Department Executive Officer, 319-335-1228, Fax: 319-335-1415, E-mail: david-murhammer@uiowa.edu. *Application contact:* Natalie Potter, Secretary, 319-335-1215, Fax: 319-335-1415, E-mail: chemeng@engineering.uiowa.edu.

The University of Kansas, Graduate Studies, School of Engineering, Department of Chemical and Petroleum Engineering, Lawrence, KS 66045. Offers chemical engineering (MS); chemical/petroleum engineering (PhD); petroleum engineering (MS). Part-time programs available. *Faculty:* 14 full-time (4 women). *Students:* 40 full-time (20 women), 3 part-time (0 women); includes 2 minority (1 American Indian or Alaska Native, non-Hispanic/Latino; 1 Asian, non-Hispanic/Latino), 31 international. Average age 27. 153 applicants, 10% accepted, 5 enrolled.

In 2010, 2 master's, 9 doctorates awarded. *Degree requirements:* For master's, thesis (for some programs), exam; for doctorate, comprehensive exam, thesis/dissertation, qualifying exams. *Entrance requirements:* For master's, GRE General Test, minimum GPA of 3.0; for doctorate, GRE General Test, minimum GPA of 3.5. Additional exam requirements/recommendations for international students: Required—TOEFL. *Application deadline:* For fall admission, 1/10 priority date for domestic students, 1/10 for international students; for spring admission, 6/10 priority date for domestic students, 6/10 for international students. Applications are processed on a rolling basis. Application fee: $55 ($65 for international students). Electronic applications accepted. *Expenses:* Tuition, state resident: full-time $7092; part-time $295.50 per credit hour. Tuition, nonresident: full-time $16,590; part-time $691.25 per credit hour. Required fees: $858; $71.49 per credit hour. Tuition and fees vary according to course load, campus/location and program. *Financial support:* Fellowships, research assistantships with full and partial tuition reimbursements, teaching assistantships with full and partial tuition reimbursements, career-related internships or fieldwork, Federal Work-Study, scholarships/grants, traineeships, and unspecified assistantships available. Financial award application deadline: 4/1; financial award applicants required to submit FAFSA. *Faculty research:* Enhanced oil recovery, catalysis and kinetics, electrochemical engineering, biomedical engineering, semiconductor materials processing. *Unit head:* Prof. Laurence Weatherley, Chairperson, 785-864-4965, Fax: 785-864-4967, E-mail: lweather@ku.edu. *Application contact:* Prof. Marylee Southard, Graduate Recruiting Officer, 785-864-4965, Fax: 785-864-4967, E-mail: marylee@ku.edu.

University of Kentucky, Graduate School, College of Engineering, Program in Chemical Engineering, Lexington, KY 40506-0032. Offers MS, PhD. *Degree requirements:* For master's, comprehensive exam, thesis optional; for doctorate, comprehensive exam, thesis/dissertation. *Entrance requirements:* For master's, GRE General Test, minimum undergraduate GPA of 2.75; for doctorate, GRE General Test, minimum undergraduate GPA of 3.0. Additional exam requirements/recommendations for international students: Required—TOEFL (minimum score 550 paper-based; 213 computer-based). Electronic applications accepted. *Faculty research:* Aerosol physics and chemistry, biocellular engineering fuel science, poly and membrane science.

University of Louisiana at Lafayette, College of Engineering, Department of Chemical Engineering, Lafayette, LA 70504. Offers MSE. Evening/weekend programs available. *Degree requirements:* For master's, comprehensive exam, thesis or alternative. *Entrance requirements:* For master's, GRE General Test, BS in chemical engineering, minimum GPA of 2.85. Additional exam requirements/recommendations for international students: Required—TOEFL (minimum score 550 paper-based; 213 computer-based). Electronic applications accepted. *Faculty research:* Corrosion, transport phenomena and thermodynamics in the oil and gas industry.

University of Louisville, J.B. Speed School of Engineering, Department of Chemical Engineering, Louisville, KY 40292-0001. Offers M Eng, MS, PhD. *Accreditation:* ABET (one or more programs are accredited). Part-time programs available. *Faculty:* 9 full-time (2 women). *Students:* 52 full-time (15 women), 12 part-time (5 women); includes 1 Black or African American, non-Hispanic/Latino; 2 Asian, non-Hispanic/Latino; 1 Hispanic/Latino, 20 international. Average age 25. 29 applicants, 55% accepted, 8 enrolled. In 2010, 12 master's, 3 doctorates awarded. Terminal master's awarded for partial completion of doctoral program. *Degree requirements:* For master's, comprehensive exam (for some programs), thesis or alternative; for doctorate, comprehensive exam, thesis/dissertation, minimum GPA of 3.0. *Entrance requirements:* For master's and doctorate, GRE General Test. Additional exam requirements/recommendations for international students: Required—TOEFL (minimum score 550 paper-based; 213 computer-based; 80 iBT), IELTS (minimum score 6.5). *Application deadline:* For fall admission, 5/1 priority date for domestic and international students; for spring admission, 11/1 priority date for domestic and international students. Applications are processed on a rolling basis. Application fee: $50. Electronic applications accepted. *Expenses:* Tuition, state resident: full-time $9144; part-time $508 per credit hour. Tuition, nonresident: full-time $19,026; part-time $1057 per credit hour. Tuition and fees vary according to program and reciprocity agreements. *Financial support:* In 2010–11, 11 students received support, including 3 fellowships with full tuition reimbursements available (averaging $20,000 per year), 3 research assistantships with full tuition reimbursements available (averaging $20,000 per year), 5 teaching assistantships with full tuition reimbursements available (averaging $20,000 per year). Financial award application deadline: 1/25; financial award applicants required to submit FAFSA. *Faculty research:* Mixing in chemical and biochemical systems; nanomaterials processing; nanoparticles; surface science; materials including polymers, thin films, and rapid prototyping. Total annual research expenditures: $1.4 million. *Unit head:* Dr. James C. Waters, Chair, 502-852-6347, Fax: 502-852-6355, E-mail: jcwatt01@louisville.edu. *Application contact:* Dr. Michael Day, Associate Dean, 502-852-6195, Fax: 502-852-7294, E-mail: day@louisville.edu.

University of Maine, Graduate School, College of Engineering, Department of Chemical and Biological Engineering, Program in Chemical Engineering, Orono, ME 04469. Offers MS, PhD. Part-time programs available. *Students:* 13 full-time (1 woman), 7 part-time (0 women); includes 2 minority (1 Black or African American, non-Hispanic/Latino; 1 Asian, non-Hispanic/Latino), 11 international. Average age 28. 27 applicants, 37% accepted, 9 enrolled. In 2010, 13 master's, 1 doctorate awarded. Terminal master's awarded for partial completion of doctoral program. *Degree requirements:* For master's, thesis; for doctorate, thesis/dissertation. *Entrance requirements:* For master's and doctorate, GRE General Test. Additional exam requirements/recommendations for international students: Required—TOEFL. *Application deadline:* For fall admission, 2/1 priority date for domestic students. Applications are processed on a rolling basis. Application fee: $65. Electronic applications accepted. *Expenses:* Tuition, state resident: full-time $400. Tuition, nonresident: full-time $1050. *Financial support:* Federal Work-Study and tuition waivers (full and partial) available. Financial award application deadline: 3/1. *Unit head:* Dr. Douglas Bousfield, Coordinator, 207-581-2300, Fax: 207-581-2725. *Application contact:* Scott G. Delcourt, Associate Dean of the Graduate School, 207-581-3291, Fax: 207-581-3232, E-mail: graduate@maine.edu.

The University of Manchester, School of Chemical Engineering and Analytical Science, Manchester, United Kingdom. Offers biocatalysis (M Phil, PhD); chemical engineering (M Phil, PhD); chemical engineering and analytical science (M Phil, D Eng, PhD); colloids, crystals, interfaces and materials (M Phil, PhD); environment and sustainable technology (M Phil, PhD); instrumentation (M Phil, PhD); multi-scale modeling (M Phil, PhD); process integration (M Phil, PhD); systems biology (M Phil, PhD).

University of Maryland, Baltimore County, Graduate School, College of Engineering and Information Technology, Department of Chemical and Biochemical Engineering, Program in Chemical and Biochemical Engineering, Baltimore, MD 21250. Offers MS, PhD. Part-time programs available. *Students:* 34 full-time (17 women), 3 part-time (2 women); includes 6 minority (3 Black or African American, non-Hispanic/Latino; 1 Asian, non-Hispanic/Latino; 1 Hispanic/Latino; 1 Two or more races, non-Hispanic/Latino), 22 international. Average age 26. 54 applicants, 41% accepted, 15 enrolled. In 2010, 5 master's, 1 doctorate awarded. *Degree requirements:* For master's, comprehensive exam (for some programs), thesis (for some programs); for doctorate, comprehensive exam, thesis/dissertation. *Entrance requirements:* For master's, GRE General Test, minimum GPA of 3.0; for doctorate, GRE General Test (within last 5 years), GRE Subject Test, minimum GPA of 3.0. Additional exam requirements/recommendations for international students: Required—TOEFL (minimum score 550 paper-based; 213 computer-based; 80 iBT). *Application deadline:* For fall admission, 6/1 for domestic students, 1/1 for international students; for spring admission, 11/1 for domestic students, 6/1 for international students. Applications are processed on a rolling basis. Application fee: $50. Electronic applications accepted. *Financial support:* In 2010–11, 3 students received support, including 1 fellowship with full tuition reimbursement available (averaging $30,000 per year), 20 research assistantships with full tuition reimbursements available (averaging $22,000 per year), 6 teaching assistantships with full tuition reimbursements available (averaging $17,000 per year); career-related internships or fieldwork, Federal Work-Study, scholarships/grants, health care benefits, tuition waivers (partial), and unspecified assistantships also available. Support available to part-time students. Financial award application deadline: 6/30; financial award applicants required to submit FAFSA. *Faculty research:* Biomaterials engineering, cellular engineering, sensor technology, systems biology and functional genomics, engineering education and outreach. *Unit head:* Dr. Julia M. Ross, Professor and Chair. *Application contact:* Dr. Mark Marten, Professor and Graduate Program Director, 410-455-3439, Fax: 410-455-1049, E-mail: marten@umbc.edu.

University of Maryland, College Park, Academic Affairs, A. James Clark School of Engineering, Department of Chemical and Biomolecular Engineering, College Park, MD 20742. Offers bioengineering (MS, PhD); chemical engineering (M Eng, MS, PhD). Part-time and evening/weekend programs available. *Faculty:* 25 full-time (2 women). *Students:* 50 full-time (15 women), 5 part-time (3 women); includes 9 minority (3 Black or African American, non-Hispanic/Latino; 5 Asian, non-Hispanic/Latino; 1 Hispanic/Latino), 31 international. 168 applicants, 19% accepted, 15 enrolled. In 2010, 8 master's, 7 doctorates awarded. *Degree requirements:* For master's, thesis optional; for doctorate, variable foreign language requirement, thesis/dissertation, exam, oral presentation. *Entrance requirements:* For master's and doctorate, GRE General Test, 3 letters of recommendation. Additional exam requirements/recommendations for international students: Required—TOEFL. *Application deadline:* For fall admission, 1/15 for domestic students, 2/1 for international students; for spring admission, 6/1 for domestic and international students. Applications are processed on a rolling basis. Application fee: $75. Electronic applications accepted. *Expenses:* Tuition, area resident: Part-time $471 per credit hour. Tuition, state resident: part-time $471 per credit hour. Tuition, nonresident: part-time $1016 per credit hour. Required fees: $337 per term. *Financial support:* In 2010–11, 3 fellowships with partial tuition reimbursements (averaging $11,490 per year), 27 research assistantships with tuition reimbursements (averaging $23,636 per year), 8 teaching assistantships with tuition reimbursements (averaging $22,731 per year) were awarded; Federal Work-Study and scholarships/grants also available. Support available to part-time students. Financial award applicants required to submit FAFSA. *Faculty research:* Applied polymer science, biochemical engineering, thermal properties, bioprocess monitoring. Total annual research expenditures: $1.7 million. *Unit head:* Sheryl Ehrman, Chair, 301-405-1074, E-mail: sehrman@umd.edu. *Application contact:* Dr. Charles A. Caramello, Dean of Graduate School, 301-405-0358, Fax: 301-314-9305, E-mail: ccaramel@umd.edu.

University of Maryland, College Park, Academic Affairs, A. James Clark School of Engineering, Department of Continuing and Distance Learning in Engineering, College Park, MD 20742. Offers engineering (M Eng), including aerospace engineering, chemical engineering, civil engineering, electrical engineering, engineering, fire protection engineering, materials science and engineering, mechanical engineering, reliability engineering, systems engineering. *Faculty:* 4 full-time (1 woman), 11 part-time/adjunct (1 woman). *Students:* 56 full-time (15 women), 428 part-time (88 women); includes 153 minority (59 Black or African American, non-Hispanic/Latino; 63 Asian, non-Hispanic/Latino; 24 Hispanic/Latino; 7 Two or more races, non-Hispanic/Latino), 55 international. 551 applicants, 82% accepted, 360 enrolled. In 2010, 130 master's awarded. *Application deadline:* For fall admission, 8/15 for domestic students, 1/10 for international students; for spring admission, 12/15 for domestic students, 6/1 for international students. Applications are processed on a rolling basis. Application fee: $75. Electronic applications accepted. *Expenses:* Tuition, area resident: Part-time $471 per credit hour. Tuition, state resident: part-time $471 per credit hour. Tuition, nonresident: part-time $1016 per credit hour. Required fees: $337 per term. *Financial support:* In 2010–11, 2 research assistantships (averaging $20,285 per year), 7 teaching assistantships (averaging $16,962 per year) were awarded. *Unit head:* Dr. Darryll Pines, Dean, 301-405-0376, Fax: 301-314-5908, E-mail: pines@umd.edu. *Application contact:* Dr. Charles A. Caramello, Dean of the Graduate School, 301-405-0358, Fax: 301-314-9305, E-mail: ccaramel@umd.edu.

University of Massachusetts Amherst, Graduate School, College of Engineering, Department of Chemical Engineering, Amherst, MA 01003. Offers MSChE, PhD. Part-time programs available. *Faculty:* 19 full-time (3 women). *Students:* 62 full-time (17 women), 10 part-time (2 women); includes 5 minority (1 Asian, non-Hispanic/Latino; 1 Hispanic/Latino; 3 Two or more races, non-Hispanic/Latino), 43 international. Average age 26. 224 applicants, 16% accepted, 13 enrolled. In 2010, 12 doctorates awarded. Terminal master's awarded for partial completion of doctoral program. *Degree requirements:* For master's, thesis; for doctorate, comprehensive exam, thesis/dissertation. *Entrance requirements:* For master's and doctorate, GRE General Test. Additional exam requirements/recommendations for international students: Required—TOEFL (minimum score 550 paper-based; 213 computer-based; 80 iBT), IELTS (minimum score 6.5). *Application deadline:* For fall admission, 1/15 for domestic and international students. Applications are processed on a rolling basis. Application fee: $50 ($65 for international students). Electronic applications accepted. *Expenses:* Tuition, state resident: full-time $2640. Required fees: $8282. One-time fee: $357 full-time. *Financial support:* In 2010–11, 15 fellowships with full tuition reimbursements (averaging $20,147 per year), 72 research assistantships with full tuition reimbursements (averaging $19,242 per year), 8 teaching assistantships with full tuition reimbursements (averaging $8,811 per year) were awarded; career-related internships or fieldwork, Federal Work-Study, scholarships/grants, traineeships, health care benefits, tuition waivers, and unspecified assistantships also available. Support available to part-time students. Financial award application deadline: 1/15; financial award applicants required to submit FAFSA. *Unit head:* Dr. Dimitrios Maroudas, Graduate Program Director, 413-545-6164, Fax: 413-545-1647. *Application contact:* Jean M. Ames, Supervisor of Admissions, 413-545-0722, Fax: 413-577-0010, E-mail: gradadm@grad.umass.edu.

University of Massachusetts Lowell, James B. Francis College of Engineering, Department of Chemical Engineering, Lowell, MA 01854-2881. Offers MS Eng, D Eng, PhD. Part-time programs available. *Degree requirements:* For master's, thesis; for doctorate, thesis/dissertation, seminar, qualifying examination. *Entrance requirements:* For master's, GRE General Test. Electronic applications accepted. *Faculty research:* Biotechnology/bioprocessing, nanomaterials, ceramic materials, materials characterization.

University of Michigan, Horace H. Rackham School of Graduate Studies, College of Engineering, Department of Chemical Engineering, Ann Arbor, MI 48109. Offers MSE, PhD, Ch E. Part-time programs available. Postbaccalaureate distance learning degree programs offered (no on-campus study). *Students:* 102 full-time (31 women), 3 part-time (0 women). 238 applicants, 34% accepted, 27 enrolled. In 2010, 17 master's, 9 doctorates awarded. Terminal master's awarded for partial completion of doctoral program. *Degree requirements:* For doctorate, thesis/dissertation, oral defense of dissertation, preliminary exams. *Entrance requirements:* For master's and doctorate, GRE General Test. Additional exam requirements/recommendations for international students: Required—TOEFL (minimum score 600 paper-based; 250 computer-based). *Application deadline:* Applications are processed on a rolling basis. Application fee: $65 ($75 for international students). Electronic applications accepted. *Expenses:* Tuition, state resident: full-time $17,784; part-time $1116 per credit hour. Tuition, nonresident: full-time $35,944; part-time $2125 per credit hour. International tuition: $35,994 full-time. Required fees: $95 per semester. Tuition and fees vary according to course load, degree level and program. *Financial support:* Fellowships, research assistantships, teaching assistantships, scholarships/grants, traineeships, health care benefits, tuition waivers (partial), and unspecified assistantships available. Financial award applicants required to submit FAFSA. *Faculty research:* Life sciences and biotechnology, energy and environment, complex fluids and nanostructured materials. *Unit head:* Mark Burns, Department Chair, 734-764-1516, E-mail: maburns@umich.edu. *Application contact:* Sue Hamlin, Department Office, 734-763-1148, Fax: 734-764-7453, E-mail: hamlins@umich.edu.

University of Minnesota, Twin Cities Campus, Institute of Technology, Department of Chemical Engineering and Materials Science, Program in Chemical Engineering, Minneapolis, MN 55455-0132. Offers M Ch E, MS Ch E, PhD. Part-time programs available. Terminal master's awarded for partial completion of doctoral program. *Degree requirements:* For master's, thesis; for doctorate, thesis/dissertation. *Entrance requirements:* For master's and doctorate, GRE General Test. *Faculty research:* Chemical kinetics, reaction engineering and modeling,

Chemical Engineering

University of Minnesota, Twin Cities Campus (continued)
gas and membrane separation processes, biochemical engineering, nonequilibrium statistical mechanics.

University of Missouri, Graduate School, College of Engineering, Department of Chemical Engineering, Columbia, MO 65211. Offers MS, PhD. *Degree requirements:* For master's, thesis; for doctorate, thesis/dissertation. *Entrance requirements:* For master's and doctorate, GRE General Test, minimum GPA of 3.0. Additional exam requirements/recommendations for international students: Required—TOEFL (minimum score 550 paper-based; 213 computer-based; 80 iBT).

University of Nebraska–Lincoln, Graduate College, College of Engineering, Department of Chemical and Biomolecular Engineering, Lincoln, NE 68588. Offers MS, PhD. *Degree requirements:* For master's, thesis; for doctorate, comprehensive exam, thesis/dissertation. *Entrance requirements:* For master's and doctorate, GRE. Additional exam requirements/recommendations for international students: Required—TOEFL (minimum score 550 paper-based; 213 computer-based). Electronic applications accepted. *Faculty research:* Fermentation, radioactive waste remediation, chemical fuels from renewable feedstocks.

University of Nebraska–Lincoln, Graduate College, College of Engineering, Department of Mechanical Engineering, Lincoln, NE 68588. Offers chemical and materials engineering (PhD); mechanical engineering (MS, PhD), including materials science engineering (MS), metallurgical engineering (MS). *Degree requirements:* For master's, thesis optional; for doctorate, comprehensive exam, thesis/dissertation. *Entrance requirements:* For master's and doctorate, GRE General Test. Additional exam requirements/recommendations for international students: Required—TOEFL (minimum score 550 paper-based; 213 computer-based). Electronic applications accepted. *Faculty research:* Robotics for planetary exploration, vehicle crashworthiness, transient heat conduction, laser beam/particle interactions.

See Display on page 543 and Close-Up on page 557.

University of Nevada, Reno, Graduate School, College of Engineering, Department of Chemical and Materials Engineering, Program in Chemical Engineering, Reno, NV 89557. Offers MS, PhD. Terminal master's awarded for partial completion of doctoral program. *Degree requirements:* For master's, comprehensive exam, thesis optional; for doctorate, thesis/dissertation. *Entrance requirements:* For master's, GRE General Test, minimum GPA of 2.75; for doctorate, GRE General Test, minimum GPA of 3.0. Additional exam requirements/recommendations for international students: Required—TOEFL (minimum score 500 paper-based; 173 computer-based; 61 iBT), IELTS (minimum score 6). Electronic applications accepted. *Expenses:* Tuition, state resident: full-time $2219; part-time $246 per credit. Tuition, nonresident: part-time $510 per credit. International tuition: $9009 full-time. Required fees: $59 per term. One-time fee: $101. Tuition and fees vary according to course load. *Faculty research:* Energy conservation, fuel efficiency, development and fabrication of new materials.

University of New Brunswick Fredericton, School of Graduate Studies, Faculty of Engineering, Department of Chemical Engineering, Fredericton, NB E3B 5A3, Canada. Offers chemical engineering (M Eng, M Sc E, PhD); environmental studies (M Eng). Part-time programs available. *Faculty:* 11 full-time (3 women), 1 part-time/adjunct (0 women). *Students:* 59 full-time (24 women), 6 part-time (0 women). In 2010, 10 master's, 3 doctorates awarded. *Degree requirements:* For master's, thesis; for doctorate, comprehensive exam, thesis/dissertation, qualifying exam. *Entrance requirements:* For master's and doctorate, minimum GPA of 3.0. Additional exam requirements/recommendations for international students: Required—TOEFL (minimum score 580 paper-based), TWE (minimum score 4). *Application deadline:* For fall admission, 3/1 priority date for domestic students. Application fee: $50 Canadian dollars. Electronic applications accepted. *Expenses:* Tuition, area resident: Full-time $3708; part-time $927 per term. International tuition: $6300 full-time. Required fees: $50 per term. *Financial support:* In 2010–11, 109 research assistantships with tuition reimbursements (averaging $18,000 per year), 51 teaching assistantships (averaging $1,500 per year) were awarded. *Faculty research:* Processing and characterizing nanoengineered composite materials based on carbon nanotubes, enhanced oil recovery processes and oil sweep strategies for conventional and heavy oils, pulp and paper, waste-water treatment, chemistry and corrosion of high and lower temperature water systems. *Unit head:* Dr. Kecheng Li, Director of Graduate Studies, 506-451-6861, Fax: 506-453-3591, E-mail: kecheng@unb.ca. *Application contact:* Sylvia Demerson, Graduate Secretary, 506-453-4520, Fax: 506-453-3591, E-mail: sdemerso@unb.ca.

University of New Hampshire, Graduate School, College of Engineering and Physical Sciences, Department of Chemical Engineering, Durham, NH 03824. Offers MS, PhD. *Faculty:* 7 full-time (1 woman). *Students:* 7 full-time (3 women), 7 part-time (1 woman), 7 international. Average age 25. 32 applicants, 56% accepted, 5 enrolled. In 2010, 1 master's, 1 doctorate awarded. *Degree requirements:* For master's, thesis; for doctorate, thesis/dissertation. *Entrance requirements:* For master's and doctorate, GRE. Additional exam requirements/recommendations for international students: Required—TOEFL (minimum score 550 paper-based; 213 computer-based). *Application deadline:* For fall admission, 6/1 priority date for domestic students, 4/1 for international students; for spring admission, 12/1 for domestic students. Applications are processed on a rolling basis. Application fee: $65. Electronic applications accepted. *Financial support:* In 2010–11, 12 students received support, including 3 research assistantships, 9 teaching assistantships; fellowships, Federal Work-Study, scholarships/grants, and tuition waivers (full and partial) also available. Support available to part-time students. Financial award application deadline: 2/15. *Unit head:* Dr. P. T. Vasudevan, Chairperson, 603-862-3654. *Application contact:* Nancy Littlefield, Administrative Assistant, 603-862-3654, E-mail: chemeng.grad@unh.edu.

University of New Mexico, Graduate School, School of Engineering, Department of Chemical and Nuclear Engineering, Program in Chemical Engineering, Albuquerque, NM 87131-2039. Offers MS, PhD. Part-time programs available. *Students:* 34 full-time (14 women), 10 part-time (3 women); includes 11 minority (1 Black or African American, non-Hispanic/Latino; 1 Asian, non-Hispanic/Latino; 8 Hispanic/Latino; 1 Two or more races, non-Hispanic/Latino), 7 international. Average age 29. 43 applicants, 33% accepted, 9 enrolled. In 2010, 3 master's awarded. Terminal master's awarded for partial completion of doctoral program. *Degree requirements:* For master's, thesis (for some programs); for doctorate, comprehensive exam, thesis/dissertation, qualifying exam. *Entrance requirements:* For master's, GRE General Test, minimum GPA of 3.0, 3 letters of reference, letter of intent; for doctorate, GRE General Test, 3 letters of reference, minimum GPA of 3.0, letter of intent. Additional exam requirements/recommendations for international students: Required—TOEFL. *Application deadline:* For fall admission, 1/15 priority date for domestic and international students; for spring admission, 7/15 priority date for domestic and international students. Application fee: $50. Electronic applications accepted. *Expenses:* Tuition, state resident: full-time $5991; part-time $251 per credit hour. Tuition, nonresident: full-time $14,405; part-time $800.20 per credit hour. Tuition and fees vary according to course level, course load, program and reciprocity agreements. *Financial support:* In 2010–11, 34 students received support, including 2 fellowships (averaging $19,909 per year), 30 research assistantships with full tuition reimbursements available (averaging $19,743 per year), 1 teaching assistantship (averaging $5,259 per year); scholarships/grants, traineeships, and health care benefits also available. Financial award application deadline: 1/15; financial award applicants required to submit FAFSA. *Faculty research:* Bioanalytical systems, ceramics, catalysis, colloidal science, bioengineering, biomaterials, fuel cells, protein engineering, semiconductors, tissue engineering. Total annual research expenditures: $7.6 million. *Unit head:* Dr. Timothy Ward, Chair, 505-277-5431, Fax: 505-277-5433, E-mail: tward@unm.edu. *Application contact:* Jocelyn White, Coordinator, Program Advisor, 505-277-5606, Fax: 505-277-5433, E-mail: jowhite@unm.edu.

University of North Dakota, Graduate School, School of Engineering and Mines, Department of Chemical Engineering, Grand Forks, ND 58202. Offers M Engr, MS. Part-time programs available. *Faculty:* 9 full-time (1 woman), 7 part-time/adjunct (0 women). *Students:* 18 full-time (2 women), 9 part-time (1 woman); includes 7 minority (2 Black or African American, non-Hispanic/Latino; 2 Asian, non-Hispanic/Latino; 3 Hispanic/Latino), 7 international. Average age 27. 28 applicants, 29% accepted, 5 enrolled. In 2010, 5 master's awarded. *Degree requirements:* For master's, comprehensive exam, thesis or alternative. *Entrance requirements:* For master's, GRE General Test, minimum GPA of 3.0 (MS), 2.5 (M Engr). Additional exam requirements/recommendations for international students: Required—TOEFL (minimum score 550 paper-based; 213 computer-based; 79 iBT), IELTS (minimum score 6.5). *Application deadline:* For fall admission, 8/1 priority date for domestic students, 5/1 priority date for international students; for spring admission, 12/1 priority date for domestic students, 9/1 priority date for international students. Applications are processed on a rolling basis. Application fee: $35. Electronic applications accepted. *Expenses:* Tuition, state resident: full-time $5857; part-time $306.74 per credit. Tuition, nonresident: full-time $15,666; part-time $729.77 per credit. Required fees: $53.42 per credit. Tuition and fees vary according to course load, program and reciprocity agreements. *Financial support:* In 2010–11, 22 students received support, including 16 research assistantships with full and partial tuition reimbursements available (averaging $6,688 per year), 6 teaching assistantships with full and partial tuition reimbursements available (averaging $6,074 per year); fellowships with full and partial tuition reimbursements available, career-related internships or fieldwork, Federal Work-Study, institutionally sponsored loans, scholarships/grants, health care benefits, tuition waivers (full and partial), and unspecified assistantships also available. Support available to part-time students. Financial award application deadline: 3/15; financial award applicants required to submit FAFSA. *Faculty research:* Catalysis, fluid flow and heat transfer, application of fractals, modeling and simulation, reaction engineering. Total annual research expenditures: $3 million. *Unit head:* Dr. Frank Burman, Graduate Director, 701-777-2958, Fax: 701-777-4838, E-mail: frank.burman@mail.und.nodak.edu. *Application contact:* Staci Wells, Admissions Associate, 701-777-2945, Fax: 701-777-3619, E-mail: staci.wells@gradschool.und.edu.

University of Notre Dame, Graduate School, College of Engineering, Department of Chemical and Biomolecular Engineering, Notre Dame, IN 46556. Offers MS Ch E, PhD. *Degree requirements:* For master's, comprehensive exam, thesis; for doctorate, comprehensive exam, thesis/dissertation, candidacy exam. *Entrance requirements:* For master's, GRE General Test; for doctorate, GRE General Test, GRE Subject Test (strongly recommended). Additional exam requirements/recommendations for international students: Required—TOEFL (minimum score 600 paper-based; 250 computer-based; 80 iBT). Electronic applications accepted. *Faculty research:* Biomolecular engineering, green chemistry and engineering for the environment, advanced materials, nanoengineering, catalysis and reaction engineering.

University of Oklahoma, College of Engineering, School of Chemical, Biological and Materials Engineering, Norman, OK 73019. Offers chemical engineering (MS, PhD). *Faculty:* 18 full-time (1 woman), 1 part-time/adjunct (0 women). *Students:* 55 full-time (20 women), 9 part-time (4 women), 52 international. Average age 25. 33 applicants, 55% accepted, 13 enrolled. In 2010, 5 master's, 7 doctorates awarded. Terminal master's awarded for partial completion of doctoral program. *Degree requirements:* For master's, thesis, oral exams; for doctorate, thesis/dissertation, oral exam, qualifying exams. *Entrance requirements:* For master's and doctorate, minimum GPA of 3.0. Additional exam requirements/recommendations for international students: Required—TOEFL (minimum score 600 paper-based; 213 computer-based; 100 iBT). *Application deadline:* For fall admission, 6/1 priority date for domestic students, 4/1 for international students; for spring admission, 11/1 for domestic students, 9/1 for international students. Applications are processed on a rolling basis. Application fee: $40 ($90 for international students). Electronic applications accepted. *Expenses:* Tuition, state resident: full-time $3892.80; part-time $162.20 per credit hour. Tuition, nonresident: full-time $14,167; part-time $590.30 per credit hour. Required fees: $2523.40; $94.60 per credit hour. Tuition and fees vary according to course load and degree level. *Financial support:* In 2010–11, 61 research assistantships with partial tuition reimbursements (averaging $16,485 per year) were awarded; tuition waivers and unspecified assistantships also available. Financial award application deadline: 3/1; financial award applicants required to submit FAFSA. *Faculty research:* Applied surfactant technologies, for remediation and recycling, biofuels and biorefining, catalytic production and utilization of carbon nanotubes, hydrocarbon conversion processes—catalytic and process modeling, polymer fiber production and characterization and tissue engineering. Total annual research expenditures: $4.4 million. *Unit head:* Dr. Lance Lobban, Director, 405-325-5811, Fax: 405-325-5813, E-mail: llobban@ou.edu. *Application contact:* Dr. Ulli Nollert, Graduate Program Coordinator and Associate Professor, 405-325-4366, Fax: 405-325-5813, E-mail: nollert@ou.edu.

University of Ottawa, Faculty of Graduate and Postdoctoral Studies, Faculty of Engineering, Department of Chemical Engineering, Ottawa, ON K1N 6N5, Canada. Offers M Eng, MA Sc, PhD. *Degree requirements:* For master's, thesis or alternative; for doctorate, comprehensive exam, thesis/dissertation. *Entrance requirements:* For master's, honors degree or equivalent, minimum B average; for doctorate, master's degree, minimum B+ average. Electronic applications accepted. *Faculty research:* Material development, process engineering, clean technologies.

University of Pennsylvania, School of Engineering and Applied Science, Department of Chemical Engineering, Philadelphia, PA 19104. Offers MSE, PhD, MSE/MBA. Part-time programs available. *Faculty:* 22 full-time (3 women), 2 part-time/adjunct (0 women). *Students:* 84 full-time (20 women), 4 part-time (0 women); includes 1 Black or African American, non-Hispanic/Latino; 12 Asian, non-Hispanic/Latino; 5 Hispanic/Latino, 36 international. 260 applicants, 29% accepted, 30 enrolled. In 2010, 27 master's, 10 doctorates awarded. Terminal master's awarded for partial completion of doctoral program. *Degree requirements:* For doctorate, thesis/dissertation. *Entrance requirements:* Additional exam requirements/recommendations for international students: Required—TOEFL. *Application deadline:* For fall admission, 6/1 priority date for domestic students. Applications are processed on a rolling basis. Application fee: $70. Electronic applications accepted. *Expenses:* Tuition: Full-time $25,660; part-time $4758 per course. Required fees: $2152; $270 per course. Tuition and fees vary according to course load, degree level and program. *Financial support:* Fellowships, research assistantships, teaching assistantships, institutionally sponsored loans, scholarships/grants, traineeships, health care benefits, and unspecified assistantships available. *Faculty research:* Biochemical engineering, surface and interfacial phenomena, process and design control, zeolites, molecular dynamics.

University of Pittsburgh, School of Engineering, Department of Chemical and Petroleum Engineering, Pittsburgh, PA 15260. Offers chemical engineering (MS Ch E, PhD); petroleum engineering (MSPE); MS Ch E/MSPE. Part-time programs available. Postbaccalaureate distance learning degree programs offered. *Faculty:* 18 full-time (3 women), 32 part-time/adjunct (5 women). *Students:* 51 full-time (13 women), 8 part-time (3 women); includes 5 minority (1 Black or African American, non-Hispanic/Latino; 2 Asian, non-Hispanic/Latino; 2 Hispanic/Latino), 34 international. 204 applicants, 31% accepted, 24 enrolled. In 2010, 2 master's, 5 doctorates awarded. *Degree requirements:* For master's, thesis; for doctorate, comprehensive exam, thesis/dissertation, final oral exams. *Entrance requirements:* For master's and doctorate, GRE General Test, minimum QPA of 3.2. Additional exam requirements/recommendations for international students: Required—TOEFL (minimum score 550 paper-based; 213 computer-based; 80 iBT). *Application deadline:* For fall admission, 3/1 priority date for domestic students; for spring admission, 7/1 priority date for domestic students. Applications are processed on a rolling basis. Application fee: $50. Electronic applications accepted. *Expenses:* Tuition, state resident: full-time $17,304; part-time $701 per credit. Tuition, nonresident: full-time $29,554; part-time $1210 per credit. Required fees: $740; $214 per term. Tuition and fees vary according to program. *Financial support:* In 2010–11, 38 students received support, including 6 fellowships with full tuition reimbursements available (averaging $26,000 per year), 25 research assistantships with full tuition reimbursements available (averaging $25,000 per year), 13 teaching assistantships with full tuition reimbursements available (averaging $24,000 per year); scholarships/grants, traineeships, and tuition waivers (full and partial) also available. Financial award application deadline: 4/15. *Faculty research:* Biotechnology, polymers, catalysis, energy and environment, computational modeling. Total annual research expenditures: $6.9 million. *Unit head:* Dr. J. Karl Johnson, Chairman, 412-624-5644, Fax: 412-624-9639, E-mail:

johnson@engr.pitt.edu. *Application contact:* William Federspiel, Associate Professor and Graduate Coordinator, 412-624-9499, Fax: 412-624-9639, E-mail: federspiel@engrng.pitt.edu.

University of Puerto Rico, Mayagüez Campus, Graduate Studies, College of Engineering, Department of Chemical Engineering, Mayagüez, PR 00681-9000. Offers ME, MS, PhD. Part-time programs available. *Students:* 54 full-time (25 women), 2 part-time (1 woman); includes 30 Hispanic/Latino, 26 international. 10 applicants, 70% accepted, 3 enrolled. In 2010, 6 master's, 1 doctorate awarded. *Degree requirements:* For master's, comprehensive exam, thesis; for doctorate, comprehensive exam, thesis/dissertation. *Entrance requirements:* For master's, BS in chemical engineering or its equivalent. Additional exam requirements/recommendations for international students: Required—TOEFL. *Application deadline:* For fall admission, 2/15 for domestic and international students; for spring admission, 9/15 for domestic and international students. Applications are processed on a rolling basis. Application fee: $25. *Expenses:* Tuition, state resident: full-time $1188. Tuition, nonresident: full-time $1188. International tuition: $6126 full-time. Tuition and fees vary according to course level and course load. *Financial support:* In 2010–11, 14 students received support, including fellowships (averaging $12,000 per year), 35 research assistantships (averaging $15,000 per year), 14 teaching assistantships (averaging $8,500 per year); Federal Work-Study and institutionally sponsored loans also available. *Faculty research:* Process simulation and optimization, air and water pollution control, mass transport, biochemical engineering. Total annual research expenditures: $2.4 million. *Unit head:* Dr. David Suleiman, Chairperson, 787-832-4040 Ext. 2568, Fax: 787-834-3655, E-mail: david.suleiman@upr.edu. *Application contact:* Dr. Aldo Acevedo, Graduate Coordinator, 787-832-4040 Ext. 2577, Fax: 787-834-3655, E-mail: aldacevedo@uprm.edu.

University of Rhode Island, Graduate School, College of Engineering, Department of Chemical Engineering, Kingston, RI 02881. Offers MS, PhD. Part-time programs available. *Faculty:* 10 full-time (1 woman), 1 part-time/adjunct (0 women). *Students:* 14 full-time (4 women), 4 part-time (0 women); includes 5 minority (2 Black or African American, non-Hispanic/Latino; 2 Asian, non-Hispanic/Latino; 1 Hispanic/Latino), 8 international. In 2010, 3 master's, 2 doctorates awarded. *Degree requirements:* For master's, comprehensive exam (for some programs), thesis optional; for doctorate, comprehensive exam, thesis/dissertation. *Entrance requirements:* For master's and doctorate, 3 letters of recommendation. Additional exam requirements/recommendations for international students: Required—TOEFL (minimum score 550 paper-based; 213 computer-based). *Application deadline:* For fall admission, 7/15 for domestic students, 2/1 for international students; for spring admission, 11/15 for domestic students, 7/15 for international students. Application fee: $65. Electronic applications accepted. *Expenses:* Tuition, state resident: full-time $9588; part-time $533 per credit hour. Tuition, nonresident: full-time $22,968; part-time $1276 per credit hour. Required fees: $1282; $68 per semester. Tuition and fees vary according to program. *Financial support:* In 2010–11, 7 research assistantships with full and partial tuition reimbursements (averaging $9,334 per year), 2 teaching assistantships with partial tuition reimbursements (averaging $6,164 per year) were awarded. Financial award application deadline: 7/15; financial award applicants required to submit FAFSA. *Faculty research:* Photobioreactors, colloidal and interfacial engineering, biomembrane thermodynamics and transport, degradation of materials, closed loop recycling systems. Total annual research expenditures: $1.3 million. *Unit head:* Dr. Arijit Bose, Chair, 401-874-2804, Fax: 401-874-4689, E-mail: bosea@egr.uri.edu. *Application contact:* Dr. Richard Brown, Director of Graduate Studies, 401-874-2707, Fax: 401-874-4689, E-mail: rbrown@uri.edu.

University of Rochester, Hajim School of Engineering and Applied Sciences, Department of Chemical Engineering, Programs in Chemical Engineering, Rochester, NY 14627.

See Display below and Close-Up on page 169.

University of Saskatchewan, College of Graduate Studies and Research, College of Engineering, Department of Chemical Engineering, Saskatoon, SK S7N 5A2, Canada. Offers M Eng, M Sc, PhD. *Degree requirements:* For master's, thesis (for some programs); for

doctorate, thesis/dissertation. *Entrance requirements:* For master's and doctorate, GRE. Additional exam requirements/recommendations for international students: Required—TOEFL.

University of South Africa, College of Science, Engineering and Technology, Pretoria, South Africa. Offers chemical engineering (M Tech); information technology (M Tech).

University of South Alabama, Graduate School, College of Engineering, Department of Chemical Engineering, Mobile, AL 36688-0002. Offers MS Ch E. *Faculty:* 5 full-time (0 women). *Students:* 11 full-time (4 women), 6 part-time (2 women); includes 1 minority (Black or African American, non-Hispanic/Latino), 9 international. 19 applicants, 42% accepted, 4 enrolled. In 2010, 5 master's awarded. *Degree requirements:* For master's, project or thesis. *Entrance requirements:* For master's, GRE General Test, BS in engineering, minimum GPA of 3.0. Additional exam requirements/recommendations for international students: Required—TOEFL. *Application deadline:* For fall admission, 7/15 priority date for domestic students, 6/15 priority date for international students; for spring admission, 12/1 priority date for domestic students, 11/1 priority date for international students. Applications are processed on a rolling basis. Application fee: $35. *Expenses:* Tuition, state resident: part-time $300 per credit hour. Tuition, nonresident: part-time $600 per credit hour. Required fees: $150 per semester. *Financial support:* Research assistantships, career-related internships or fieldwork and institutionally sponsored loans available. Support available to part-time students. Financial award application deadline: 4/1. *Unit head:* Dr. Srinivas Palanki, Chair, 251-460-6160. *Application contact:* Dr. Thomas Thomas, Director of Graduate Studies, 251-460-6160.

University of South Carolina, The Graduate School, College of Engineering and Computing, Department of Chemical Engineering, Columbia, SC 29208. Offers ME, MS, PhD. Part-time and evening/weekend programs available. Postbaccalaureate distance learning degree programs offered (minimal on-campus study). *Degree requirements:* For master's, comprehensive exam, thesis (for some programs); for doctorate, comprehensive exam, thesis/dissertation. *Entrance requirements:* For master's and doctorate, GRE General Test. Additional exam requirements/recommendations for international students: Required—TOEFL. Electronic applications accepted. *Faculty research:* Rheology, liquid and supercritical extractions, electrochemistry, corrosion, heterogeneous and homogeneous catalysis.

University of Southern California, Graduate School, Viterbi School of Engineering, Mork Family Department of Chemical Engineering and Materials Science, Los Angeles, CA 90089. Offers chemical engineering (MS, PhD, Engr); materials engineering (MS); materials science (MS, PhD, Engr); petroleum engineering (MS, PhD, Engr); smart oilfield technologies (MS, Graduate Certificate). *Faculty:* 19 full-time (3 women), 9 part-time/adjunct (1 woman). *Students:* 235 full-time (77 women), 77 part-time (25 women); includes 43 minority (6 Black or African American, non-Hispanic/Latino; 25 Asian, non-Hispanic/Latino; 11 Hispanic/Latino; 1 Two or more races, non-Hispanic/Latino), 213 international. 643 applicants, 36% accepted, 118 enrolled. In 2010, 37 master's, 19 doctorates, 4 other advanced degrees awarded. Terminal master's awarded for partial completion of doctoral program. *Degree requirements:* For master's, thesis optional; for doctorate, thesis/dissertation. *Entrance requirements:* For master's and doctorate, GRE General Test. *Application deadline:* For fall admission, 12/1 priority date for domestic and international students; for spring admission, 9/1 priority date for domestic and international students. Applications are processed on a rolling basis. Application fee: $85. Electronic applications accepted. *Expenses:* Contact institution. *Financial support:* In 2010–11, fellowships with full tuition reimbursements (averaging $30,000 per year), research assistantships with full tuition reimbursements (averaging $20,000 per year), teaching assistantships with full tuition reimbursements (averaging $20,000 per year) were awarded; career-related internships or fieldwork, scholarships/grants, health care benefits, and unspecified assistantships also available. Financial award application deadline: 12/1; financial award applicants required to submit CSS PROFILE or FAFSA. *Faculty research:* Heterogeneous materials and porous media, statistical mechanics, molecular simulation, polymer science and engineering, advanced materials, reaction engineering and catalysis, membrane processes and separation, biochemical engineering, cell

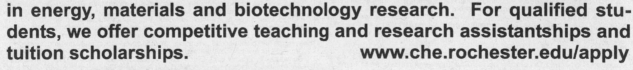

Chemical Engineering

University of Southern California (continued)
culture, bioreactor modeling, petroleum engineering. Total annual research expenditures: $11.6 million. *Unit head:* Dr. Theodore Tsotsis, Chair, 213-740-2227, E-mail: chedept@usc.edu. *Application contact:* Karen Woo, Student Services Advisor, 213-740-2227, E-mail: karenwoo@usc.edu.

University of South Florida, Graduate School, College of Engineering, Department of Chemical and Biomedical Engineering, Tampa, FL 33620. Offers biomedical engineering (MSBE, PhD); chemical and biomedical engineering (MCH, ME, MSES, PhD); chemical engineering (PhD). Part-time programs available. *Faculty:* 11 full-time (1 woman). *Students:* 62 full-time (28 women), 15 part-time (6 women); includes 9 Black or African American, non-Hispanic/Latino; 7 Asian, non-Hispanic/Latino; 7 Hispanic/Latino, 26 international. Average age 29. 88 applicants, 44% accepted, 20 enrolled. In 2010, 15 master's, 11 doctorates awarded. Terminal master's awarded for partial completion of doctoral program. *Degree requirements:* For master's, comprehensive exam, thesis (for some programs); for doctorate, comprehensive exam, thesis/dissertation. *Entrance requirements:* For master's, GRE General Test, minimum GPA of 3.0 in last 60 hours of course work; for doctorate, GRE General Test. Additional exam requirements/recommendations for international students: Required—TOEFL (minimum score 550 paper-based; 213 computer-based; 79 iBT). *Application deadline:* For fall admission, 2/15 for domestic students, 1/2 priority date for international students; for spring admission, 10/15 for domestic students, 6/1 priority date for international students. Application fee: $30. Electronic applications accepted. *Financial support:* In 2010–11, 35 students received support, including 24 research assistantships with tuition reimbursements available (averaging $14,593 per year), 17 teaching assistantships with tuition reimbursements available (averaging $15,754 per year); unspecified assistantships also available. Financial award applicants required to submit FAFSA. *Faculty research:* Biomedical engineering, supercritical fluid technology, advanced materials, surface and interfacial science, alternative and renewable energy. Total annual research expenditures: $989,529. *Unit head:* Dr. Venkat R. Bhethanabotla, Chair, 813-974-3997. *Application contact:* Dr. Vinay Gupta, Graduate Admissions Coordinator for Chemical Engineering, 813-974-0851, Fax: 813-974-3651.

The University of Tennessee, Graduate School, College of Engineering, Department of Chemical Engineering, Knoxville, TN 37996. Offers chemical engineering (MS, PhD); reliability and maintainability engineering (MS); MS/MBA. Part-time programs available. *Faculty:* 12 full-time (1 woman), 17 part-time/adjunct (0 women). *Students:* 35 full-time (12 women), 5 part-time (1 woman); includes 1 American Indian or Alaska Native, non-Hispanic/Latino; 2 Asian, non-Hispanic/Latino, 27 international. Average age 24. 73 applicants, 18% accepted, 8 enrolled. In 2010, 4 master's, 3 doctorates awarded. *Degree requirements:* For master's, thesis or alternative; for doctorate, comprehensive exam, thesis/dissertation. *Entrance requirements:* For master's, GRE General Test, Minimum GPA of 2.7 (US degree holders); 3.0 (International degree holders); for doctorate, GRE General Test, Minimum GPA of 3.0 (previous graduate course work). Additional exam requirements/recommendations for international students: Required—TOEFL (minimum score 550 paper-based; 213 computer-based). *Application deadline:* For fall admission, 2/1 priority date for domestic and international students; for spring admission, 6/15 for domestic and international students. Applications are processed on a rolling basis. Application fee: $35. Electronic applications accepted. *Expenses:* Tuition, state resident: full-time $7440; part-time $414 per credit hour. Tuition, nonresident: full-time $22,478; part-time $1250 per credit hour. Required fees: $922; $43 per credit hour. Tuition and fees vary according to program. *Financial support:* In 2010–11, 33 students received support, including 26 research assistantships with full tuition reimbursements available (averaging $22,020 per year), 11 teaching assistantships with full tuition reimbursements available (averaging $20,760 per year); career-related internships or fieldwork, Federal Work-Study, institutionally sponsored loans, health care benefits, and unspecified assistantships also available. Financial award application deadline: 2/1; financial award applicants required to submit FAFSA. *Faculty research:* Bio-fuels; engineering of soft, functional and structural materials; fuel cells and energy storage devices; molecular and cellular bioengineering; molecular modeling and simulations. Total annual research expenditures: $2.8 million. *Unit head:* Dr. Bamin Khomami, Head, 865-974-2421, Fax: 865-974-7076, E-mail: bkhomami@utk.edu. *Application contact:* Dr. Paul Frymier, Graduate Program Coordinator, 865-974-4961, Fax: 865-974-7076, E-mail: pdf@utk.edu.

The University of Tennessee at Chattanooga, Graduate School, College of Engineering and Computer Science, Program in Engineering, Chattanooga, TN 37403. Offers chemical engineering (MS Engr); civil engineering (MS Engr); computational engineering (MS Engr); electrical engineering (MS Engr); industrial engineering (MS Engr); mechanical engineering (MS Engr). Part-time and evening/weekend programs available. *Faculty:* 8 full-time (0 women). *Students:* 27 full-time (5 women), 31 part-time (6 women); includes 12 minority (7 Black or African American, non-Hispanic/Latino; 1 Asian, non-Hispanic/Latino; 4 Hispanic/Latino), 10 international. Average age 29. 43 applicants, 100% accepted, 26 enrolled. In 2010, 16 master's awarded. *Degree requirements:* For master's, comprehensive exam, thesis or alternative, engineering project. *Entrance requirements:* For master's, GRE General Test, minimum undergraduate GPA of 2.5 or 3.0 in last 30 hours of coursework. Additional exam requirements/recommendations for international students: Required—TOEFL (minimum score 550 paper-based; 213 computer-based; 79 iBT), IELTS (minimum score 6). *Application deadline:* For fall admission, 8/1 priority date for domestic students, 6/1 for international students; for spring admission, 12/1 priority date for domestic students, 10/1 for international students. Applications are processed on a rolling basis. Application fee: $35. Electronic applications accepted. *Financial support:* In 2010–11, 23 research assistantships with full and partial tuition reimbursements (averaging $5,500 per year) were awarded; career-related internships or fieldwork, scholarships/grants, and unspecified assistantships also available. Support available to part-time students. *Faculty research:* Quality control and reliability engineering, financial management, thermal science, energy conservation, structural analysis. Total annual research expenditures: $2.6 million. *Unit head:* Dr. Neslihan Alp, Director, 423-425-4032, Fax: 423-425-5229, E-mail: neslihan-alp@utc.edu. *Application contact:* Dr. Jerald Ainsworth, Dean of Graduate Studies, 423-425-4478, Fax: 423-425-5223, E-mail: jerald-ainsworth@utc.edu.

The University of Texas at Austin, Graduate School, Cockrell School of Engineering, Department of Chemical Engineering, Austin, TX 78712-1111. Offers MSE, PhD. Terminal master's awarded for partial completion of doctoral program. *Degree requirements:* For master's, thesis (for some programs); for doctorate, comprehensive exam, thesis/dissertation. *Entrance requirements:* For master's and doctorate, GRE General Test. Electronic applications accepted.

The University of Toledo, College of Graduate Studies, College of Engineering, Department of Chemical and Environmental Engineering, Toledo, OH 43606-3390. Offers chemical engineering (MS, PhD). Part-time and evening/weekend programs available. *Degree requirements:* For master's, thesis optional; for doctorate, thesis/dissertation, qualifying exam. *Entrance requirements:* For master's, GRE General Test, minimum GPA of 3.0; for doctorate, GRE General Test, minimum GPA of 3.3. Additional exam requirements/recommendations for international students: Required—TOEFL (minimum score 550 paper-based; 213 computer-based; 80 iBT). Electronic applications accepted. *Expenses:* Tuition, state resident: full-time $11,426; part-time $476 per credit hour. Tuition, nonresident: full-time $21,660; part-time $903 per credit hour. One-time fee: $62. *Faculty research:* Polymers, applied computing, membranes, alternative energy (fuel cells).

University of Toronto, School of Graduate Studies, Physical Sciences Division, Faculty of Applied Science and Engineering, Department of Chemical Engineering and Applied Chemistry, Toronto, ON M5S 1A1, Canada. Offers M Eng, MA Sc, PhD. Part-time programs available. *Degree requirements:* For master's, thesis (for some programs); for doctorate, thesis/dissertation. *Entrance requirements:* For master's, minimum B+ average in final 2 years, four-year degree in engineering (M Eng, MA Sc) or physical sciences (MA Sc), 2 letters of reference; for doctorate, research master's degree, minimum B+ average, 2 letters of reference.

Additional exam requirements/recommendations for international students: Required—TOEFL (minimum score 580 paper-based; 237 computer-based), TWE (minimum score 4).

University of Tulsa, Graduate School, College of Engineering and Natural Sciences, Department of Chemical Engineering, Tulsa, OK 74104-3189. Offers ME, MSE, PhD. Part-time programs available. *Faculty:* 9 full-time (3 women). *Students:* 27 full-time (10 women), 2 part-time (0 women); includes 1 minority (Hispanic/Latino), 19 international. Average age 25. 62 applicants, 55% accepted, 6 enrolled. In 2010, 2 master's, 1 doctorate awarded. *Degree requirements:* For master's, thesis (for some programs); for doctorate, comprehensive exam, thesis/dissertation. *Entrance requirements:* For master's and doctorate, GRE General Test. Additional exam requirements/recommendations for international students: Required—TOEFL (minimum score 550 paper-based; 213 computer-based; 80 iBT), IELTS (minimum score 6). *Application deadline:* Applications are processed on a rolling basis. Application fee: $40. Electronic applications accepted. *Expenses:* Tuition: Full-time $16,902; part-time $939 per credit hour. Required fees: $1020; $4 per credit hour. Tuition and fees vary according to course load. *Financial support:* In 2010–11, 24 students received support, including 4 fellowships (averaging $4,183 per year), 17 research assistantships with full and partial tuition reimbursements available (averaging $11,730 per year), 9 teaching assistantships with full and partial tuition reimbursements available (averaging $10,120 per year); career-related internships or fieldwork, Federal Work-Study, scholarships/grants, health care benefits, tuition waivers (full and partial), and unspecified assistantships also available. Support available to part-time students. Financial award application deadline: 2/1; financial award applicants required to submit FAFSA. *Faculty research:* Environment, surface science, catalysis, transport phenomena, process systems engineering, bioengineering, alternative energy, petrochemical processes. Total annual research expenditures: $3 million. *Unit head:* Dr. Geoffrey Price, Chairperson, 918-631-2575, Fax: 918-631-3268, E-mail: chegradadvisor@utulsa.edu. *Application contact:* Dr. Daniel Crunkleton, Advisor, 918-631-2644, Fax: 918-631-3268, E-mail: chegradadvisor@utulsa.edu.

University of Utah, Graduate School, College of Engineering, Department of Chemical Engineering, Salt Lake City, UT 84112-1107. Offers chemical engineering (ME, MS, PhD); environmental engineering (ME, MS, PhD). Part-time and evening/weekend programs available. Postbaccalaureate distance learning degree programs offered. *Faculty:* 15 full-time (1 woman), 1 part-time/adjunct (0 women). *Students:* 50 full-time (5 women), 20 part-time (7 women); includes 5 minority (2 Asian, non-Hispanic/Latino; 3 Hispanic/Latino), 22 international. Average age 28. 132 applicants, 13% accepted, 13 enrolled. In 2010, 8 master's, 7 doctorates awarded. Terminal master's awarded for partial completion of doctoral program. *Degree requirements:* For master's, comprehensive exam, thesis (for some programs); for doctorate, comprehensive exam, thesis/dissertation. *Entrance requirements:* For master's, GRE General Test; for doctorate, GRE General Test, minimum GPA of 3.0, degree or course work in chemical engineering. Additional exam requirements/recommendations for international students: Required—TOEFL (minimum score 500 paper-based; 173 computer-based). *Application deadline:* For fall admission, 4/1 priority date for domestic students, 2/1 for international students; for spring admission, 11/1 priority date for domestic students, 10/1 priority date for international students. Applications are processed on a rolling basis. Application fee: $55 ($65 for international students). Electronic applications accepted. *Expenses:* Contact institution. *Financial support:* In 2010–11, 7 fellowships with tuition reimbursements (averaging $26,750 per year), 53 research assistantships with tuition reimbursements (averaging $25,000 per year) were awarded; teaching assistantships with tuition reimbursements, Federal Work-Study, institutionally sponsored loans, scholarships/grants, health care benefits, and unspecified assistantships also available. Financial award application deadline: 4/1; financial award applicants required to submit FAFSA. *Faculty research:* Drug delivery, fossil fuel and biomass combustion and gasification, oil and gas reservoir characteristics and management, multi-scale simulation, micro-scale synthesis. Total annual research expenditures: $8.1 million. *Unit head:* Dr. JoAnn S. Lighty, Chair, 801-581-6715, Fax: 801-585-9291, E-mail: jlighty@utah.edu. *Application contact:* Jenny Jones, Academic Advisor, 801-581-6915, Fax: 801-585-9291, E-mail: jones.jenny@eng.utah.edu.

University of Virginia, School of Engineering and Applied Science, Department of Chemical Engineering, Charlottesville, VA 22903. Offers ME, MS, PhD. Postbaccalaureate distance learning degree programs offered (no on-campus study). *Faculty:* 11 full-time (1 woman). *Students:* 50 full-time (16 women), 1 part-time (0 women); includes 1 Black or African American, non-Hispanic/Latino; 2 Asian, non-Hispanic/Latino; 2 Hispanic/Latino, 27 international. Average age 25. 125 applicants, 22% accepted, 8 enrolled. In 2010, 9 master's, 5 doctorates awarded. *Degree requirements:* For master's, thesis (for some programs); for doctorate, thesis/dissertation. *Entrance requirements:* For master's, GRE General Test, 3 recommendations; for doctorate, GRE General Test, 3 recommendations, essay. Additional exam requirements/recommendations for international students: Required—TOEFL (minimum score 600 paper-based; 250 computer-based; 90 iBT), IELTS (minimum score 7). *Application deadline:* For fall admission, 8/1 for domestic students, 4/1 for international students; for winter admission, 12/1 for domestic students, 8/1 for international students; for spring admission, 5/1 for domestic students, 1/1 for international students. Applications are processed on a rolling basis. Application fee: $60. Electronic applications accepted. *Financial support:* Fellowships, research assistantships, teaching assistantships available. Financial award application deadline: 1/15; financial award applicants required to submit FAFSA. *Faculty research:* Fluid mechanics, heat and mass transfer, chemical reactor analysis and engineering, biochemical engineering and biotechnology. *Unit head:* Robert Davis, Chair, 434-924-7778, Fax: 434-982-2658, E-mail: cheadmis@virginia.edu. *Application contact:* David Green, Graduate Program Coordinator, 434-924-7778, Fax: 434-982-2658, E-mail: dlgreen@virginia.edu.

University of Washington, Graduate School, College of Engineering, Department of Chemical Engineering, Seattle, WA 98195-1750. Offers chemical engineering (MS, MSE, PhD); chemical engineering and nanotechnology (PhD). *Faculty:* 23 full-time (2 women), 6 part-time/adjunct (1 woman). *Students:* 72 full-time (24 women), 1 part-time (0 women); includes 2 Black or African American, non-Hispanic/Latino; 1 American Indian or Alaska Native, non-Hispanic/Latino; 10 Asian, non-Hispanic/Latino; 1 Hispanic/Latino, 18 international. Average age 25. 187 applicants, 25% accepted, 14 enrolled. In 2010, 17 master's, 5 doctorates awarded. Terminal master's awarded for partial completion of doctoral program. *Degree requirements:* For master's, thesis, Pass final exam, serve as TA for 1 quarter, research project; for doctorate, thesis/dissertation, Pass general & final exams, research project, complete all work for doctoral degree within 10 years. *Entrance requirements:* For master's and doctorate, GRE General test (minimum Quantitative Score of 750), Minimum GPA of 3.0, official transcripts & degree statements, personal statement, confidential evaluations by 3 professors or other technical professional, highly ranked (top 5%) in respected chemical engineering program, optional: resume/cv, writing sample (journal articles only). Additional exam requirements/recommendations for international students: Required—TOEFL (minimum score 580 paper-based; 237 computer-based; 92 iBT); Recommended—IELTS (minimum score 7). *Application deadline:* For fall admission, 1/15 priority date for domestic students, 12/15 priority date for international students. Applications are processed on a rolling basis. Application fee: $75. Electronic applications accepted. *Financial support:* In 2010–11, 4 students received support, including 24 fellowships with full tuition reimbursements available (averaging $22,500 per year), 40 research assistantships with full tuition reimbursements available (averaging $19,035 per year), 12 teaching assistantships with full tuition reimbursements available (averaging $19,035 per year); career-related internships or fieldwork, Federal Work-Study, health care benefits, and unspecified assistantships also available. Financial award application deadline: 1/15; financial award applicants required to submit FAFSA. *Faculty research:* Molecular energy processes, living systems and biomolecular processes, molecular aspects of materials and interfaces, molecular/organic electronics. Total annual research expenditures: $7 million. *Unit head:* Dr. Daniel T. Schwartz, Professor and Chair, 206-543-2250, Fax: 206-543-3778, E-mail: dts@uw.edu. *Application contact:* Dave Drischell, Lead Academic Counselor, 206-543-2252, Fax: 206-543-3778, E-mail: rdd@u.washington.edu.

University of Waterloo, Graduate Studies, Faculty of Engineering, Department of Chemical Engineering, Waterloo, ON N2L 3G1, Canada. Offers M Eng, MA Sc, PhD. Part-time programs available. *Degree requirements:* For master's, research project or thesis, seminar; for doctorate, comprehensive exam, thesis/dissertation. *Entrance requirements:* For master's, honors degree, minimum B average; for doctorate, master's degree, minimum A- average. Additional exam requirements/recommendations for international students: Required—TOEFL, TWE. Electronic applications accepted. *Faculty research:* Biotechnical and environmental engineering, mathematical analysis, statistics and control, polymer science and engineering.

The University of Western Ontario, Faculty of Graduate Studies, Physical Sciences Division, Faculty of Engineering, London, ON N6A 5B8, Canada. Offers chemical and biochemical engineering (ME Sc, PhD); civil and environmental engineering (M Eng, ME Sc, PhD); electrical and computer engineering (M Eng, ME Sc, PhD); mechanical and materials engineering (M Eng, ME Sc, PhD). Part-time programs available. Terminal master's awarded for partial completion of doctoral program. *Degree requirements:* For master's, thesis; for doctorate, thesis/dissertation. *Entrance requirements:* For master's, minimum B average; for doctorate, minimum B+ average. *Faculty research:* Wind, geotechnical, chemical reactor engineering, applied electrostatics, biochemical engineering.

University of Wisconsin–Madison, Graduate School, College of Engineering, Department of Chemical and Biological Engineering, Madison, WI 53706-0607. Offers chemical engineering (MS, PhD). *Faculty:* 19 full-time (2 women), 1 part-time/adjunct (0 women). *Students:* 132 full-time (38 women); includes 1 American Indian or Alaska Native, non-Hispanic/Latino; 9 Asian, non-Hispanic/Latino; 7 Hispanic/Latino, 53 international. Average age 25. 428 applicants, 21% accepted, 28 enrolled. In 2010, 3 master's, 15 doctorates awarded. Terminal master's awarded for partial completion of doctoral program. *Degree requirements:* For master's, thesis or alternative; for doctorate, thesis/dissertation, 2 semesters of teaching assistantship. *Entrance requirements:* For master's and doctorate, GRE General Test. Additional exam requirements/recommendations for international students: Required—TOEFL (minimum score 550 paper-based; 213 computer-based; 80 iBT). *Application deadline:* For fall admission, 1/1 for domestic and international students; for spring admission, 10/15 for domestic and international students. Application fee: $56. Electronic applications accepted. *Expenses:* Tuition, state resident: full-time $9887.36; part-time $617.96 per credit. Tuition, nonresident: full-time $24,054; part-time $1503.40 per credit. Required fees: $67.63 per credit. Tuition and fees vary according to reciprocity agreements. *Financial support:* In 2010–11, 122 students received support, including 21 fellowships with full tuition reimbursements available (averaging $28,752 per year), 66 research assistantships with full tuition reimbursements available (averaging $24,000 per year), 45 teaching assistantships with full tuition reimbursements available (averaging $25,167 per year); traineeships and health care benefits also available. Financial award application deadline: 1/15. *Faculty research:* Biotechnology, nanotechnology, complex fluids, molecular and systems modeling, renewable energy and chemicals: materials and processes. Total annual research expenditures: $17.7 million. *Unit head:* Prof. Nicholas L. Abbott, Chair, 608-265-5278, Fax: 608-262-5434, E-mail: abbott@engr.wisc.edu. *Application contact:* Donna M. Bell, Graduate Coordinator, 608-263-3138, Fax: 608-262-5434, E-mail: gradoffice@che.wisc.edu.

University of Wyoming, College of Engineering and Applied Sciences, Department of Chemical and Petroleum Engineering, Program in Chemical Engineering, Laramie, WY 82070. Offers MS, PhD. Part-time programs available. Terminal master's awarded for partial completion of doctoral program. *Degree requirements:* For master's, thesis; for doctorate, thesis/dissertation. *Entrance requirements:* For master's and doctorate, GRE General Test, minimum GPA of 3.0. Additional exam requirements/recommendations for international students: Required—TOEFL (minimum score 600 paper-based; 250 computer-based; 76 iBT). Electronic applications accepted. *Faculty research:* Microwave reactor systems, synthetic fuels, fluidization, coal combustion/gasification, flue-gas cleanup.

Vanderbilt University, School of Engineering, Department of Chemical and Biomolecular Engineering, Nashville, TN 37240-1001. Offers M Eng, MS, PhD. MS and PhD offered through the Graduate School. Part-time programs available. *Faculty:* 9 full-time (2 women), 6 part-time/adjunct (1 woman). *Students:* 41 full-time (13 women); includes 1 Black or African American, non-Hispanic/Latino; 1 Asian, non-Hispanic/Latino, 18 international. Average age 26. 142 applicants, 18% accepted, 11 enrolled. In 2010, 1 master's, 6 doctorates awarded. *Degree requirements:* For master's, thesis; for doctorate, thesis/dissertation. *Entrance requirements:* For master's and doctorate, GRE General Test. Additional exam requirements/recommendations for international students: Required—TOEFL. *Application deadline:* For fall admission, 1/15 for domestic students; for spring admission, 11/1 for domestic students. Application fee: $0. Electronic applications accepted. *Financial support:* In 2010–11, 8 fellowships with full tuition reimbursements (averaging $26,400 per year), 25 research assistantships with full tuition reimbursements (averaging $20,604 per year), 11 teaching assistantships with full tuition reimbursements (averaging $20,604 per year) were awarded; Federal Work-Study, institutionally sponsored loans, and tuition waivers (partial) also available. Support available to part-time students. Financial award application deadline: 1/15; financial award applicants required to submit CSS PROFILE or FAFSA. *Faculty research:* Adsorption and surface chemistry; biochemical engineering and biotechnology; chemical reaction engineering, environment, materials, process modeling and control; molecular modeling and thermodynamics. Total annual research expenditures: $2.9 million. *Unit head:* Dr. Peter N. Pintauro, Chair, 615-343-6918, Fax: 615-343-7951, E-mail: peter.n.pintauro@vanderbilt.edu. *Application contact:* Dr. G. Kane Jennings, Director of Graduate Studies, 615-322-2441, Fax: 615-343-7951, E-mail: jenningk@vuse.vanderbilt.edu.

Villanova University, College of Engineering, Department of Chemical Engineering, Villanova, PA 19085-1699. Offers biochemical engineering (Certificate); chemical engineering (MSChE); environmental protection in the chemical process industries (Certificate). Part-time and evening/weekend programs available. *Faculty:* 10 full-time (1 woman), 1 (woman) part-time/adjunct. *Students:* 5 full-time (1 woman), 46 part-time (12 women); includes 3 Black or African American, non-Hispanic/Latino; 3 Asian, non-Hispanic/Latino; 1 Hispanic/Latino, 6 international. 12 applicants, 67% accepted, 5 enrolled. In 2010, 10 master's awarded. *Degree requirements:* For master's, comprehensive exam, thesis optional. *Entrance requirements:* For master's, GRE General Test (for applicants with degrees from foreign universities), B Ch E, minimum GPA of 3.0. Additional exam requirements/recommendations for international students: Required—TOEFL (minimum score 600 paper-based; 250 computer-based; 100 iBT). *Application deadline:* For fall admission, 8/1 priority date for domestic students, 3/15 priority date for international students; for spring admission, 12/1 priority date for domestic students, 10/1 priority date for international students. Applications are processed on a rolling basis. Application fee: $50. *Expenses:* Tuition: Part-time $700 per credit. Part-time tuition and fees vary according to degree level and program. *Financial support:* In 2010–11, research assistantships with full and partial tuition reimbursements (averaging $13,500 per year); Federal Work-Study, tuition waivers (full), and unspecified assistantships also available. Financial award application deadline: 1/15. *Faculty research:* Heat transfer, advanced materials, chemical vapor deposition, pyrolysis and combustion chemistry, industrial waste treatment. Total annual research expenditures: $31,111. *Unit head:* Dr. Randy Weinstein, Chairman, 610-519-4950, E-mail: randy.weinstein@villanova.edu. *Application contact:* College of Engineering, Graduate Programs Office, 610-519-5840, Fax: 610-519-5859, E-mail: engineering.grad@villanova.edu.

Virginia Commonwealth University, Graduate School, School of Engineering, Department of Chemical and Life Science Engineering, Richmond, VA 23284-9005. Offers MS, PhD. *Faculty:* 7 full-time (0 women). *Entrance requirements:* For master's and doctorate, GRE. Additional exam requirements/recommendations for international students: Required—TOEFL (minimum score 600 paper-based; 250 computer-based; 100 iBT). *Application deadline:* For fall admission, 2/1 priority date for domestic students; for spring admission, 11/15 for domestic students. Application fee: $50. Electronic applications accepted. *Expenses:* Tuition, state resident: full-time $4308; part-time $479 per credit hour. Tuition, nonresident: full-time $8942; part-time $994 per credit hour. Required fees: $2000; $85 per credit hour. Tuition and fees vary according to course level, course load, degree level, campus/location and program. *Financial support:* Applicants required to submit FAFSA. *Faculty research:* Advanced polymers, including biopolymers and polymers in medicine; chemical and biochemical reactor analysis; the study of supercritical fluids for environmentally favorable processes; systems biological engineering; stem cell engineering; biosensors and biochips; computational bioinformatics and rational drug design. *Unit head:* Dr. Michael H. Peters, Chair, 804-828-7789, E-mail: mpeters@vcu.edu. *Application contact:* Dr. Kenneth J. Wynne, Director, Graduate Programs in Chemical and Life Science Engineering, 804-828-3925, E-mail: kjwynne@vcu.edu.

Virginia Polytechnic Institute and State University, Graduate School, College of Engineering, Department of Chemical Engineering, Blacksburg, VA 24061. Offers M Eng, MS, PhD. *Faculty:* 13 full-time (2 women). *Students:* 44 full-time (10 women), 5 part-time (1 woman); includes 1 Black or African American, non-Hispanic/Latino; 1 Asian, non-Hispanic/Latino, 30 international. Average age 27. 179 applicants, 6% accepted, 10 enrolled. In 2010, 7 master's, 5 doctorates awarded. *Degree requirements:* For master's, comprehensive exam (for some programs), thesis (for some programs); for doctorate, comprehensive exam (for some programs), thesis/dissertation (for some programs). *Entrance requirements:* For master's and doctorate, GRE. Additional exam requirements/recommendations for international students: Required—TOEFL (minimum score 550 paper-based; 213 computer-based). *Application deadline:* For fall admission, 7/1 for domestic and international students; for spring admission, 12/1 for domestic and international students. Applications are processed on a rolling basis. Application fee: $65. Electronic applications accepted. *Expenses:* Tuition, area resident: Full-time $9399; part-time $488 per credit hour. Tuition, state resident: full-time $9399; part-time $488 per credit hour. Tuition, nonresident: full-time $17,854; part-time $957.75 per credit hour. International tuition: $17,854 full-time. Required fees: $1534. Full-time tuition and fees vary according to program. *Financial support:* In 2010–11, 6 fellowships with full tuition reimbursements (averaging $4,778 per year), 38 research assistantships with full tuition reimbursements (averaging $20,368 per year), 7 teaching assistantships with full tuition reimbursements (averaging $11,914 per year) were awarded; career-related internships or fieldwork, Federal Work-Study, scholarships/grants, health care benefits, and unspecified assistantships also available. Financial award application deadline: 1/15. Total annual research expenditures: $2.8 million. *Unit head:* Dr. John Y. Walz, UNIT HEAD, 540-231-4213, Fax: 540-231-5022, E-mail: jywalz@vt.edu. *Application contact:* Luke Achenie, Contact, 540-231-4257, Fax: 540-231-5022, E-mail: achenie@vt.edu.

Washington State University, Graduate School, College of Engineering and Architecture, School of Chemical Engineering and Bioengineering, Program in Chemical Engineering, Pullman, WA 99164. Offers MS, PhD. *Faculty:* 13. *Students:* 33 full-time (10 women), 4 part-time (2 women); includes 3 minority (1 Black or African American, non-Hispanic/Latino; 1 Asian, non-Hispanic/Latino; 1 Two or more races, non-Hispanic/Latino), 21 international. Average age 28. 85 applicants, 22% accepted, 17 enrolled. In 2010, 5 master's, 5 doctorates awarded. Terminal master's awarded for partial completion of doctoral program. *Degree requirements:* For master's, comprehensive exam (for some programs), thesis, oral exam; for doctorate, one foreign language, comprehensive exam, thesis/dissertation, oral exam. *Entrance requirements:* For master's and doctorate, GRE, minimum GPA of 3.0, 3 letters of recommendation by faculty. Additional exam requirements/recommendations for international students: Required—TOEFL (minimum score 580 paper-based; 190 computer-based). *Application deadline:* For fall admission, 3/1 priority date for domestic students, 3/1 for international students; for spring admission, 7/1 priority date for domestic students, 7/1 for international students. Applications are processed on a rolling basis. Application fee: $50. *Expenses:* Tuition, state resident: full-time $8552; part-time $443 per credit. Tuition, nonresident: full-time $21,650; part-time $1083 per credit. Required fees: $846. *Financial support:* In 2010–11, 26 students received support, including 5 fellowships (averaging $4,991 per year), 7 research assistantships with full and partial tuition reimbursements available (averaging $18,204 per year), 4 teaching assistantships with full and partial tuition reimbursements available (averaging $18,204 per year); career-related internships or fieldwork, Federal Work-Study, institutionally sponsored loans, tuition waivers (partial), and teaching associateships also available. Financial award application deadline: 4/1; financial award applicants required to submit FAFSA. *Faculty research:* Bioprocessing, kinetics and catalysis, hazardous waste remediation. Total annual research expenditures: $2.3 million. *Unit head:* Dr. James Peterson, Interim Director, 509-335-4332, Fax: 509-335-4806, E-mail: jn_petersen@wsu.edu. *Application contact:* Graduate School Admissions, 800-GRADWSU, Fax: 509-335-1949, E-mail: gradsch@wsu.edu.

Washington University in St. Louis, School of Engineering and Applied Science, Department of Energy, Environmental and Chemical Engineering, St. Louis, MO 63130-4899. Offers chemical engineering (MS, D Sc); environmental engineering (MS, D Sc). Part-time programs available. Terminal master's awarded for partial completion of doctoral program. *Degree requirements:* For master's, thesis optional; for doctorate, thesis/dissertation, preliminary exam, qualifying exam. *Entrance requirements:* For master's and doctorate, GRE, minimum B average during final 2 years of course work. Additional exam requirements/recommendations for international students: Required—TOEFL, TWE. Electronic applications accepted. *Faculty research:* Reaction engineering, materials processing, catalysis, process control, air pollution control.

Wayne State University, College of Engineering, Department of Chemical Engineering and Materials Science, Program in Chemical Engineering, Detroit, MI 48202. Offers MS, PhD. *Faculty:* 8 full-time (2 women), 2 part-time/adjunct (0 women). *Students:* 18 full-time (7 women), 8 part-time (3 women); includes 4 minority (3 Asian, non-Hispanic/Latino; 1 Hispanic/Latino), 15 international. Average age 29. 28 applicants, 50% accepted, 5 enrolled. In 2010, 6 master's, 3 doctorates awarded. *Degree requirements:* For master's, thesis optional; for doctorate, thesis/dissertation. *Entrance requirements:* For master's, GRE (if applying for financial support), letter of recommendations, resume; for doctorate, GRE (if applying for financial support), recommendations; resume, personal statement. Additional exam requirements/recommendations for international students: Required—TOEFL (minimum score 550 paper-based; 213 computer-based), TWE (minimum score 6). *Application deadline:* For fall admission, 7/1 priority date for domestic students, 6/1 for international students; for winter admission, 10/1 for international students; for spring admission, 3/15 for domestic students, 2/1 for international students. Applications are processed on a rolling basis. Application fee: $30 ($50 for international students). Electronic applications accepted. *Expenses:* Tuition, state resident: full-time $7662; part-time $478.85 per credit hour. Tuition, nonresident: full-time $16,920; part-time $1057.55 per credit hour. Required fees: $571.20; $35.70 per credit hour. $188.05 per semester. Tuition and fees vary according to course load and program. *Financial support:* In 2010–11, 1 fellowship (averaging $15,750 per year), 8 research assistantships (averaging $17,752 per year), 5 teaching assistantships (averaging $16,984 per year) were awarded. *Faculty research:* Environmental management, biochemical engineering, supercritical technology, polymer process catalysis. *Unit head:* Charles Manke, Chair, 313-577-3849, Fax: 313-577-3810, E-mail: emanke@chem1.eng.wayne.edu. *Application contact:* Dr. Yinlun Huang, Graduate Director, 313-577-3800, E-mail: yhuang@wayne.edu.

Western Michigan University, Graduate College, College of Engineering and Applied Sciences, Department of Paper Engineering, Chemical Engineering, and Imaging, Kalamazoo, MI 49008. Offers paper and imaging science and engineering (MS, PhD). *Degree requirements:* For master's, thesis optional; for doctorate, one foreign language, comprehensive exam, thesis/dissertation. *Entrance requirements:* For master's, minimum GPA of 3.0. *Faculty research:* Fiber recycling, paper machine wet end operations, paper coating.

West Virginia University, College of Engineering and Mineral Resources, Department of Chemical Engineering, Morgantown, WV 26506. Offers MS Ch E, PhD. Part-time programs available. Terminal master's awarded for partial completion of doctoral program. *Degree requirements:* For master's, thesis; for doctorate, comprehensive exam, thesis/dissertation, original research proposal, dissertation research proposal. *Entrance requirements:* For master's and doctorate, minimum GPA of 3.0. Additional exam requirements/recommendations for international students: Required—TOEFL (minimum score 550 paper-based; 213 computer-based; 80 iBT). Electronic applications accepted. *Faculty research:* Biocatalysis and catalysis, fluid-particle systems, high-value non-fuel uses of coal, opto-electronic materials processing, polymer and polymer-composite nanotechnology.

Chemical Engineering

Widener University, Graduate Programs in Engineering, Program in Chemical Engineering, Chester, PA 19013-5792. Offers M Eng. Part-time and evening/weekend programs available. *Students:* 2 full-time (0 women), 4 part-time (0 women); includes 1 Black or African American, non-Hispanic/Latino. Average age 28. In 2010, 13 master's awarded. *Degree requirements:* For master's, thesis optional. *Application deadline:* For fall admission, 8/1 priority date for domestic students; for spring admission, 12/1 for domestic students. Applications are processed on a rolling basis. Application fee: $25 ($300 for international students). *Financial support:* Teaching assistantships with full tuition reimbursements, unspecified assistantships available. Financial award application deadline: 3/15. *Faculty research:* Biotechnology, environmental engineering, computational fluid mechanics, reaction kinetics, process design. *Unit head:* Dr. Charles R. Nippert, Chairman, 610-499-4050, Fax: 610-499-4059, E-mail: crnippert@widener.edu. *Application contact:* Dr. Charles R. Nippert, Chairman, 610-499-4050, Fax: 610-499-4059, E-mail: crnippert@widener.edu.

Worcester Polytechnic Institute, Graduate Studies and Research, Department of Chemical Engineering, Worcester, MA 01609-2280. Offers MS, PhD. Part-time and evening/weekend programs available. *Faculty:* 8 full-time (2 women). *Students:* 25 full-time (10 women), 2 part-time (1 woman); includes 1 Hispanic/Latino; 2 Native Hawaiian or other Pacific Islander, non-Hispanic/Latino, 14 international. 84 applicants, 33% accepted, 5 enrolled. In 2010, 3 master's, 2 doctorates awarded. Terminal master's awarded for partial completion of doctoral program. *Degree requirements:* For master's, thesis; for doctorate, comprehensive exam, thesis/dissertation. *Entrance requirements:* For master's and doctorate, GRE (recommended) Required for International Students, 3 letters of recommendation. Additional exam requirements/recommendations for international students: Required—TOEFL (minimum score 550 paper-based; 213 computer-based; 79 iBT), IELTS (minimum score 6.5). *Application deadline:* For fall admission, 1/1 priority date for domestic and international students; for spring admission, 10/1 priority date for domestic and international students. Applications are processed on a rolling basis. Application fee: $70. Electronic applications accepted. *Expenses:* Tuition: Full-time $20,862; part-time $1159 per term. One-time fee: $15. *Financial support:* Career-related internships or fieldwork, institutionally sponsored loans, scholarships/grants, and unspecified assistantships available. Financial award application deadline: 1/1; financial award applicants required to submit FAFSA. *Faculty research:* Process analysis in the presence of complexity, performance assessment of energy and environmental systems, process safety and risk analysis, economic assessment of energy technology options, regulation of chemicals. *Unit head:* Dr. David DiBiasio, Head, 508-831-5250, Fax: 508-831-5853, E-mail: dibiasio@wpi.edu. *Application contact:* Dr. Nikolaos Kazantzis, Graduate Coordinator, 508-831-5250, Fax: 508-831-5853, E-mail: nikolas@wp.edu.

Yale University, Graduate School of Arts and Sciences, School of Engineering and Applied Science, Department of Chemical Engineering, New Haven, CT 06520. Offers MS, PhD. Terminal master's awarded for partial completion of doctoral program. *Degree requirements:* For doctorate, thesis/dissertation, exam. *Entrance requirements:* For master's and doctorate, GRE General Test. Additional exam requirements/recommendations for international students: Required—TOEFL. *Faculty research:* Biochemical engineering, heterogeneous catalysis, high-temperature chemical reaction engineering, separation science and technology, colloids and complex fluids.

UNIVERSITY OF ROCHESTER

Edmund A. Hajim School of Engineering and Applied Sciences
Department of Chemical Engineering

Programs of Study

The interdisciplinary nature of the University of Rochester's chemical engineering program manifests itself in active collaborations with other departments at the school. The faculty enjoys generous research support from government agencies and private industries. The University's graduate programs are among the highest ranked in the nation according to the 2010 National Research Council survey report (www.nap.edu/rdp).

To earn a Ph.D., students must complete 90 credit hours. It typically takes five years to complete the program, which includes successful defense of a dissertation. The first two semesters are devoted to graduate courses in chemical engineering and other sciences. Students are expected to provide undergraduate teaching assistance during this time. At the end of this period, students take a first-year examination as a transition from classroom to full-time research.

Students without prior backgrounds in chemical engineering are encouraged to apply. The Department has a graduate curriculum devised for students with a background in science, such as chemistry, physics, and biology. The curriculum combines courses at the undergraduate and graduate levels and is designed to foster interdisciplinary research in advanced materials, nanotechnology, clean energy, and biotechnology.

The Master of Science degree may be obtained through either a full-time or a part-time program. Graduate students may complete a thesis (Plan A) or choose a nonthesis (Plan B) option. All students who pursue Plan A are expected to earn 30 hours of credit, of which a minimum of 18 and a maximum of 24 hours should be formal course work. The balance of credit hours required for the degree is earned through M.S. research and/or reading courses. Satisfactory completion of the master's thesis is also required. All students who pursue Plan B must earn a minimum of 32 credits of course work. At least 18 credits should be taken from courses within the Department. Overall, no more than 6 credits toward a degree may be earned by research and/or reading courses. Plan B students are required to pass a comprehensive oral exam toward the end of their program.

The Department's 3/2 B.S./M.S. program leads to both the B.S. and M.S. degrees in five years. Students are granted a 75 percent tuition scholarship for their fifth year of study and may earn a stipend in return for their research assistance.

The Department of Chemical Engineering also awards the Master of Science degree in alternative energy. Courses and research projects focus on the fundamentals and applications of the generation, storage, and utilization of various forms of alternative energy as well as their impact on sustainability and energy conservation. This program is designed for graduate students with a bachelor's degree in engineering or science who are interested in pursuing a technical career in alternative energy. As with the other M.S. programs, the M.S. degree in alternative energy is available as a full- or part-time program, with a thesis (Plan A) or nonthesis (Plan B) option. All students who pursue Plan A are expected to earn 30 hours of credit; at least 18 should be attributed to 400-level courses. The balance of the credit-hour requirement can be satisfied through independent reading (no more than 4 credit hours) and thesis research (at least 6 credit hours), culminating in a master's thesis. All students who pursue Plan B must earn a minimum of 32 credits of course work, with at least 18 credits from 400-level courses and no more than 4 through independent reading. Students may opt for industrial internship (1 credit hour), for which a final essay must be submitted as a part of their degree requirements. In addition to course work and the essay, all Plan B students must pass a comprehensive oral examination as part of the degree requirements.

Research Facilities

The River Campus Libraries hold approximately 2.5 million volumes and provide access to an extensive collection of electronic, multimedia, and interlibrary loan resources. Miner Library includes more than 230,000 volumes of journals, books, theses, and government documents for health-care and medical research. Located at the Medical Center, the library also maintains access to online databases and electronic resources.

The Laboratory for Laser Energetics and the Center for Optoelectronics and Imaging are two state-of-the-art facilities in which specialized material science research is conducted. The Laboratory for Laser Energetics was established in 1970 for the investigation of the interaction of intense radiation with matter, to conduct experiments in support of the National Inertial Confinement Fusion (ICF) program; develop new laser and materials technologies; provide education in electrooptics, high-power lasers, high-energy-density physics, plasma physics, and nuclear fusion technology; operate the National Laser User's Facility; and conduct research in advanced technology related to high-energy-density phenomena.

The renowned Medical Center, which is a few minutes' walk from the River Campus, houses the Peptide Sequencing/Mass Spectrometry Facilities, Cell Sorting Facility, Nucleic Acid Laboratory, Real-Time and Static Confocal Imaging Facility, Functional Genomics Center, and a network of nearly 1,000 investigators providing research, clinical trial, and education services. In addition, a recently founded research institute, the Aab Institute of Biomedical Sciences, is the centerpiece of a ten-year, $400 million strategic plan to expand the Medical Center's research programs in the basic sciences. It is headquartered in a 240,000-square-foot research building on the Medical Center campus.

Financial Aid

The University offers fellowships, scholarships, and assistantships for full-time graduate students, and individual departments provide support through research assistantships. Applicants are encouraged to apply for outside funding such as NSF or New York State fellowships. Full-time Ph.D. students receive an annual stipend of $24,000 plus full graduate tuition.

Cost of Study

In the 2011–12 academic year, tuition is $41,000. Students must also pay additional fees for health services ($504) and health insurance ($1776). These fee amounts are subject to change.

Living and Housing Costs

Students are eligible to lease a University apartment if enrolled as a full-time graduate student or postgraduate trainee. In the 2011–12 academic year, rent, utilities, food, and supplies are estimated at $12,600 per year; books at $1250; and personal expenses at $2475. These amounts are subject to change.

Student Group

The chemical engineering discipline appeals to students who are proficient at both analytical and descriptive sciences, and are intrigued by the prospect of investigating new phenomena, and devising new materials and devices for the technologies of the future. Students in the master's degree program should have acquired technical background in chemistry, mathematics, and physics. For students interested in biotechnology, a technical background in biology is desirable.

Student Outcomes

In addition to the traditional jobs in the chemical process and petrochemical industries, chemical engineers work in pharmaceuticals, health care, pulp and paper, food processing, polymers, biotechnology, and environmental health and safety industries. Their expertise is also applied in law, education, publishing, finance, and medicine. Chemical engineers also are well equipped to analyze environmental issues and develop solutions to environmental problems, such as pollution control and remediation.

Location

Located at a bend of the Genesee River, the 85-acre River Campus is about 2 miles south of downtown Rochester, New York. Recently ranked as one of the Northeast's ten "Best Places to Live in America" by *Money* magazine, Rochester has also been listed as one of the "Most Livable Cities" in America by the Partners for Livable Communities. Rochester claims more sites on the National Register of Historic Places than any other city its size. With Lake Ontario on its northern border and the scenic Finger Lakes to the south, the Rochester area of about 1 million people offers a wide variety of cultural and recreational opportunities through its museums, parks, orchestras, planetarium, theater companies, and professional sports teams.

The University

Founded in 1850, the University of Rochester ranks among the most highly regarded universities in the country, offering degree programs at the bachelor's, master's, and doctoral levels, as well as in several professional disciplines. In the last eighteen years, 27 faculty members have been named Guggenheim Fellows. Present faculty members include a MacArthur Foundation fellowship recipient and 6 National Endowment for the Humanities Senior Fellows. Past alumni have included 7 Nobel Prize winners and 11 Pulitzer Prize winners. The University's Eastman School of Music is consistently ranked as one of the top music schools in the nation.

Applying

The official graduate application can be found online at https://its-w2ks08.acs.rochester.edu/admgrad/. The entire application must be received by January 15 for fall admission. Late applications are considered for exceptional applicants only if scholarship slots are available. Applicants are required to send college transcripts, letters of recommendation, personal/research statement, curriculum vitae, and standardized test results to the Department of Chemical Engineering.

Correspondence and Information

Graduate Program Coordinator
Department of Chemical Engineering
206 Gavett Hall, Box 270166
University of Rochester
Rochester, New York 14627-0166

Phone: 585-275-4913
Fax: 585-273-1348
E-mail: chegradinfo@che.rochester.edu
Web site: http://www.che.rochester.edu

University of Rochester

THE FACULTY AND THEIR RESEARCH

Mitchell Anthamatten, Associate Professor and Scientist, LLE; Ph.D., MIT, 2001. Macromolecular self-assembly, associative and functional polymers, nanostructured materials, liquid crystals, interfacial phenomena, optoelectronic materials, vapor deposition polymerization, fuel cell membranes.

Danielle Benoit, Assistant Professor, Biomedical Engineering and Chemical Engineering; Ph.D., Colorado, 2006. The rational design, synthesis, characterization, and employment of materials to treat diseases or control cell behavior for applications in drug therapy, regenerative medicine, and tissue engineering.

Shaw H. Chen, Professor, Chair, and Senior Scientist, LLE; Ph.D., Minnesota, 1981. Organic semiconductors, glassy liquid crystals, photoalignment of conjugated molecules, bipolar hosts for phosphorescent OLEDs, geometric surfactancy for bulk heterojunction solar cells.

Eldred H. Chimowitz, Professor and Associate Chair; Ph.D., Connecticut, 1982. Critical phenomena, statistical mechanics of fluids, computer-aided design.

David Harding, Professor of Chemical Engineering and Senior Scientist, LLE; Ph.D., Cambridge, 1986. Thin-film deposition, properties of films and composite structures, and developing cryogenic fuel capsules for nuclear fusion experiments.

Stephen Jacobs, Professor of Optics and Chemical Engineering and Senior Scientist, LLE; Ph.D., Rochester, 1975. Optical materials for laser applications, liquid crystal optics, electrooptic devices, optics manufacturing processes, magnetorheological finishing, polishing abrasives and slurries, optical glass.

Jacob Jornè, Professor; Ph.D., Berkeley, 1972. Electrochemical engineering, microelectronics processing, fuel cells, polymer electrolyte membrane fuel cell.

F. Douglas Kelley, Associate Professor; Ph.D., Rochester, 1990. Ways to exploit the divergent transport properties of fluids near the critical point, energy storage technologies that can be useful in balancing energy demand with sustainable energy generation, polymer mixtures and composites.

H. Mukaibo, Assistant Professor, Ph.D., Waseda (Japan), 2006. Template synthesis, microstructured/nanostructured materials, electrochemistry, nanoporous thin film, cell/nanostructure interface, gene delivery, energy.

Lewis Rothberg, Professor of Chemistry and Chemical Engineering; Ph.D., Harvard, 1984. Polymer electronics, optoelectronic devices, light-emitting diodes, thin-film transistors, organic photovoltaics and solar cells, biomolecular sensors, plasmon-enhanced devices.

Yonathon Shapir, Professor of Physics and Chemical Engineering; Ph.D., Tel-Aviv, 1981. Critical phenomena in ordered and disordered systems, classical and quantum transport in dirty metals and the metal-insulator transition, statistical properties of different polymer configurations, fractal properties of percolation and other clusters, kinetic models of growth and aggregation.

Alexander A. Shestopalov, Assistant Professor; Ph.D., Duke, 2009. Development of new unconventional fabrication and patterning techniques and their use in preparation of functional micro- and nanostructured devices.

Ching Tang, Professor of Chemical Engineering, Chemistry, and Physics; Ph.D., Cornell, 1975. Applications of organic electronic devices—organic light-emitting diodes, solar cells, photoconductors, image sensors, photoreceptors; basic studies of organic thin-film devices: charge injection, transport, recombination and luminescence properties; metal-organic and organic-organic junction phenomena; development of flat-panel display technology based on organic light-emitting diodes.

J. H. David Wu, Professor of Chemical Engineering and Biomedical Engineering and Associate Professor of Microbiology and Immunology; Ph.D., MIT, 1987. Biofuels development, molecular enzymology, transcriptional network, genomics and systems biology of biomass degradation for bioenergy conversion, artificial bone marrow and lymphoid tissue engineering, molecular control of hematopoiesis and immune response, stem cell and lymphocyte culture, biochemical engineering, fermentation, molecular biology.

Hong Yang, Professor and Scientist, LLE; Ph.D., Toronto, 1998. Nanostructured materials, fuel cell catalysts, magnetic nanoparticles and nanocomposites, nanoparticles in ionic liquid, porous solids, microfabrication and nanofabrication, functional nanomaterials for biological applications.

Matthew Yates, Associate Professor and Scientist, LLE; Ph.D., Texas, 1999. Particle synthesis and assembly, crystallization, fuel cell membranes, microemulsions, supercritical fluids, microencapsulation.

Section 7
Civil and Environmental Engineering

This section contains a directory of institutions offering graduate work in civil and environmental engineering, followed by in-depth entries submitted by institutions that chose to prepare detailed program descriptions. Additional information about programs listed in the directory but not augmented by an in-depth entry may be obtained by writing directly to the dean of a graduate school or chair of a department at the address given in the directory.

For programs offering related work, see also in this book *Agricultural Engineering and Bioengineering, Biomedical Engineering and Biotechnology, Engineering and Applied Sciences, Management of Engineering and Technology,* and *Ocean Engineering.* In the other guides in this series:

Graduate Programs in the Humanities, Arts & Social Sciences
See *Public, Regional, and Industrial Affairs (Urban and Regional Planning and Urban Studies)*

Graduate Programs in the Biological Sciences
See *Ecology, Environmental Biology,* and *Evolutionary Biology*

Graduate Programs in the Physical Sciences, Mathematics, Agricultural Sciences, the Environment & Natural Resources
See *Agricultural and Food Sciences, Environmental Sciences and Management, Geosciences,* and *Marine Sciences and Oceanography*

CONTENTS

Civil Engineering

American University of Beirut, Graduate Programs, Faculty of Engineering and Architecture, Beirut, Lebanon. Offers applied energy (MME); civil engineering (ME, PhD); electrical and computer engineering (ME, PhD); engineering management (MEM); environmental and water resources (ME); environmental and water resources engineering (PhD); environmental technology (MSES); mechanical engineering (ME, PhD); urban design (MUD); urban planning and policy (MUP). Part-time programs available. *Faculty:* 57 full-time (12 women), 3 part-time/adjunct (0 women). *Students:* 261 full-time (92 women), 58 part-time (20 women). Average age 25. 272 applicants, 79% accepted, 108 enrolled. In 2010, 70 master's, 1 doctorate awarded. *Degree requirements:* For master's, one foreign language, comprehensive exam, thesis (for some programs); for doctorate, one foreign language, comprehensive exam, thesis/dissertation, publications. *Entrance requirements:* For master's, GRE (for electrical and computer engineering), letters of recommendation; for doctorate, GRE, letters of recommendation, master's degree, transcripts, curriculum vitae, interview. Additional exam requirements/recommendations for international students: Required—TOEFL (minimum score 600 paper-based; 250 computer-based; 100 iBT), IELTS (minimum score 7.5). *Application deadline:* For fall admission, 2/5 priority date for domestic and international students; for spring admission, 11/1 priority date for domestic students, 11/1 for international students. Applications are processed on a rolling basis. Application fee: $50. Electronic applications accepted. *Expenses:* Tuition: Full-time $12,294; part-time $683 per credit. Required fees: $499; $499 per credit. Tuition and fees vary according to course load and program. *Financial support:* In 2010–11, 10 fellowships with full tuition reimbursements (averaging $24,800 per year), 33 research assistantships with full tuition reimbursements (averaging $24,800 per year), 70 teaching assistantships with full tuition reimbursements (averaging $9,800 per year) were awarded; career-related internships or fieldwork, institutionally sponsored loans, scholarships/grants, health care benefits, and unspecified assistantships also available. Total annual research expenditures: $586,131. *Unit head:* Fadl H. Moukalled, Acting Dean, 961-135-0000 Ext. 3400, Fax: 961-174-4462, E-mail: memouk@aub.edu.lb. *Application contact:* Dr. Salim Kanaan, Director, Admissions Office, 961-135-0000 Ext. 2594, Fax: 961-175-0775, E-mail: sk00@aub.edu.lb.

American University of Sharjah, Graduate Programs, Sharjah, United Arab Emirates. Offers business (EMBA, GEMPA, MBA); chemical engineering (MS Ch E); civil engineering (MSCE); computer engineering (MS); electrical engineering (MSEE); mechanical engineering (MSME); mechatronics engineering (MS); public administration (MPA); teaching English to speakers of other languages (MA); translation and interpreting (MA); urban planning (MUP). Part-time and evening/weekend programs available. *Entrance requirements:* For master's, GMAT (MBA). Additional exam requirements/recommendations for international students: Required—TOEFL (minimum score 550 paper-based; 213 computer-based; 80 iBT), TWE (minimum score 5). Electronic applications accepted. *Faculty research:* Chemical engineering, civil engineering, computer engineering, electrical engineering, linguistics, translation.

Arizona State University, Ira A. Fulton School of Engineering, Del E. Webb School of Construction, Tempe, AZ 85287-5306. Offers civil, environmental and sustainable engineering (MS, MSE, PhD); construction (MS, MSE, PhD); construction engineering (MSE). Part-time and evening/weekend programs available. Postbaccalaureate distance learning degree programs offered (minimal on-campus study). *Faculty:* 40 full-time (4 women), 6 part-time/adjunct (1 woman). *Students:* 149 full-time (51 women), 85 part-time (17 women); includes 32 minority (6 Black or African American, non-Hispanic/Latino; 2 American Indian or Alaska Native, non-Hispanic/Latino; 13 Asian, non-Hispanic/Latino; 10 Hispanic/Latino; 1 Native Hawaiian or other Pacific Islander, non-Hispanic/Latino), 69 international. Average age 29. 379 applicants, 53% accepted, 77 enrolled. In 2010, 44 master's, 10 doctorates awarded. Terminal master's awarded for partial completion of doctoral program. *Degree requirements:* For master's, thesis optional, comprehensive exams (MSE); interactive Program of Study (iPOS) submitted before completing 50 percent of required credit hours; for doctorate, comprehensive exam, thesis/dissertation, interactive Program of Study (iPOS) submitted before completing 50 percent of required credit hours. *Entrance requirements:* For master's, GRE, minimum GPA of 3.0 or equivalent in last 2 years of work leading to bachelor's degree; for doctorate, GRE, minimum GPA of 3.0 in last 2 years of work leading to bachelor's degree, 3.2 in all graduate-level coursework with master's degree; 3 letters of recommendation; resume/curriculum vitae; letter of intent; thesis (if applicable); statement of research interests. Additional exam requirements/recommendations for international students: Required—TOEFL, IELTS, or Pearson Test of English. *Application deadline:* For fall admission, 1/1 for domestic and international students; for spring admission, 7/1 for domestic and international students. Application fee: $70 ($90 for international students). Electronic applications accepted. *Expenses:* Contact institution. *Financial support:* In 2010–11, 67 research assistantships with full and partial tuition reimbursements (averaging $16,393 per year), 17 teaching assistantships with full and partial tuition reimbursements (averaging $13,812 per year) were awarded; fellowships with full and partial tuition reimbursements, career-related internships or fieldwork, institutionally sponsored loans, scholarships/grants, traineeships, and tuition waivers (full and partial) also available. Financial award application deadline: 3/1; financial award applicants required to submit FAFSA. *Faculty research:* Water purification, transportation (safety and materials), construction management, environmental biotechnology, environmental nanotechnology, earth systems engineering and management, SMART innovations, project performance metrics, and underground infrastructure. Total annual research expenditures: $8.5 million. *Unit head:* Dr. G. Edward Gibson, Director, 480-965-7972, E-mail: edd.gibson@asu.edu. *Application contact:* Graduate Admissions, 480-965-6113.

Auburn University, Graduate School, Ginn College of Engineering, Department of Civil Engineering, Auburn University, AL 36849. Offers construction engineering and management (MCE, MS, PhD); environmental engineering (MCE, MS, PhD); geotechnical/materials engineering (MCE, MS, PhD); hydraulics/hydrology (MCE, MS, PhD); structural engineering (MCE, MS, PhD); transportation engineering (MCE, MS, PhD). Part-time programs available. *Faculty:* 21 full-time (1 woman), 3 part-time/adjunct (1 woman). *Students:* 46 full-time (15 women), 39 part-time (5 women); includes 3 Black or African American, non-Hispanic/Latino; 1 Asian, non-Hispanic/Latino, 29 international. Average age 26. 136 applicants, 43% accepted, 26 enrolled. In 2010, 19 master's, 4 doctorates awarded. *Degree requirements:* For master's, project (MCE), thesis (MS); for doctorate, comprehensive exam, thesis/dissertation. *Entrance requirements:* For master's and doctorate, GRE General Test. *Application deadline:* For fall admission, 7/7 for domestic students; for spring admission, 11/24 for domestic students. Applications are processed on a rolling basis. Application fee: $50 ($60 for international students). Electronic applications accepted. *Expenses:* Tuition, state resident: full-time $7002. Tuition, nonresident: full-time $21,898. International tuition: $22,116 full-time. Required fees: $892. Tuition and fees vary according to course load and program. *Financial support:* Fellowships, research assistantships, teaching assistantships, Federal Work-Study available. Support available to part-time students. Financial award application deadline: 3/15; financial award applicants required to submit FAFSA. *Unit head:* Dr. J. Michael Stallings, Head, 334-844-4320. *Application contact:* Dr. George Flowers, Dean of the Graduate School, 334-844-2125.

Boise State University, Graduate College, College of Engineering, Department of Civil Engineering, Boise, ID 83725-0399. Offers M Engr, MS. Part-time and evening/weekend programs available. *Degree requirements:* For master's, thesis. *Entrance requirements:* For master's, GRE General Test, minimum GPA of 3.0. Additional exam requirements/recommendations for international students: Required—TOEFL. Electronic applications accepted.

Bradley University, Graduate School, College of Engineering and Technology, Department of Civil Engineering and Construction, Peoria, IL 61625-0002. Offers MSCE. Part-time and evening/weekend programs available. *Degree requirements:* For master's, comprehensive exam. *Entrance requirements:* For master's, minimum GPA of 3.0, 2 letters of recommendation. Additional exam requirements/recommendations for international students: Required—TOEFL (minimum score 550 paper-based; 213 computer-based; 79 iBT).

Brigham Young University, Graduate Studies, Ira A. Fulton College of Engineering and Technology, Department of Civil and Environmental Engineering, Provo, UT 84602. Offers civil engineering (MS, PhD). Part-time programs available. *Faculty:* 16 full-time (0 women), 7 part-time/adjunct (0 women). *Students:* 86 full-time (5 women), 27 part-time (5 women); includes 25 minority (3 Black or African American, non-Hispanic/Latino; 8 Asian, non-Hispanic/Latino; 12 Hispanic/Latino; 2 Native Hawaiian or other Pacific Islander, non-Hispanic/Latino), 1 international. Average age 28. 56 applicants, 93% accepted, 48 enrolled. In 2010, 40 master's, 2 doctorates awarded. *Degree requirements:* For master's, thesis (for some programs), Fundamentals of Engineering (FE) Exam; for doctorate, comprehensive exam, thesis/dissertation. *Entrance requirements:* For master's, GRE General Test, minimum GPA of 3.0 in last 60 hours of course work; for doctorate, GRE General Test, minimum graduate GPA of 3.4. Additional exam requirements/recommendations for international students: Required—TOEFL (minimum score 580 paper-based; 237 computer-based; 85 iBT), IELTS (minimum score 7). *Application deadline:* For fall admission, 2/15 for domestic and international students; for winter admission, 8/15 for domestic students, 6/15 for international students; for spring admission, 2/15 for domestic students, 10/15 for international students. Applications are processed on a rolling basis. Application fee: $50. Electronic applications accepted. *Expenses:* Tuition: Full-time $5580; part-time $310 per credit hour. Tuition and fees vary according to program and student's religious affiliation. *Financial support:* In 2010–11, 43 students received support, including 57 research assistantships (averaging $3,117 per year), 41 teaching assistantships (averaging $2,044 per year); career-related internships or fieldwork and scholarships/grants also available. Support available to part-time students. Financial award application deadline: 3/1; financial award applicants required to submit FAFSA. *Faculty research:* Structural optimization, finite element modeling and earthquake resistant analysis, groundwater, surface water, watershed and hydrologic modeling and visualization, subsurface environmental issues including transport, remediation, monitoring and characterization, capacity of deep foundations under static and dynamic loading and the behavior and mitigation of liquefiable soils, traffic planning, operations, safety, pavements and materials. Total annual research expenditures: $2.2 million. *Unit head:* Dr. Steven E. Benzley, PhD, Department Chair, 801-422-2811, Fax: 801-422-0159, E-mail: seb@byu.edu. *Application contact:* Dr. E. James Nelson, Graduate Coordinator, 801-422-2811, Fax: 801-422-0159, E-mail: jimn@byu.edu.

Bucknell University, Graduate Studies, College of Engineering, Department of Civil and Environmental Engineering, Lewisburg, PA 17837. Offers MS, MSCE, MSEV. Part-time programs available. *Degree requirements:* For master's, thesis. *Entrance requirements:* For master's, GRE General Test, GRE Subject Test, minimum GPA of 2.8. Additional exam requirements/recommendations for international students: Required—TOEFL. *Expenses:* Tuition: Full-time $36,992; part-time $4624 per course. *Faculty research:* Pile foundations, rehabilitation of bridges, deep-shaft biological-waste treatment, pre-cast concrete structures.

California Institute of Technology, Division of Engineering and Applied Science, Option in Civil Engineering, Pasadena, CA 91125-0001. Offers MS, PhD, Engr. *Faculty:* 5 full-time (0 women). *Students:* 15 full-time (2 women). 67 applicants, 7% accepted, 2 enrolled. In 2010, 6 master's awarded. *Degree requirements:* For doctorate, thesis/dissertation. *Application deadline:* For fall admission, 1/1 for domestic students. Application fee: $0. *Financial support:* In 2010–11, 8 fellowships, 7 research assistantships, 4 teaching assistantships were awarded. *Faculty research:* Earthquake engineering, soil mechanics, finite-element analysis, hydraulics, coastal engineering. *Unit head:* Dr. Thomas H. Heaton, Option Representative, 626-395-4232, E-mail: heaton@caltech.edu. *Application contact:* Natalie Gilmore, Assistant Dean of Graduate Studies, 626-395-3812, Fax: 626-577-9246, E-mail: ngilmore@caltech.edu.

California Polytechnic State University, San Luis Obispo, College of Engineering, Department of Civil and Environmental Engineering, San Luis Obispo, CA 93407. Offers MS. Part-time programs available. *Faculty:* 3 full-time (0 women). *Students:* 33 full-time (7 women), 11 part-time (1 woman); includes 14 minority (1 Black or African American, non-Hispanic/Latino; 7 Asian, non-Hispanic/Latino; 6 Hispanic/Latino). Average age 23. 84 applicants, 39% accepted, 18 enrolled. In 2010, 29 master's awarded. *Degree requirements:* For master's, comprehensive exam (for some programs), thesis (for some programs). *Entrance requirements:* For master's, GRE General Test, minimum GPA of 3.0 in last 90 quarter units, 3 letters of recommendation. Additional exam requirements/recommendations for international students: Required—TOEFL (minimum score 550 paper-based; 213 computer-based). *Application deadline:* For fall admission, 3/1 for domestic students, 11/30 for international students; for winter admission, 10/1 for domestic students, 6/30 for international students; for spring admission, 1/1 for domestic students. Applications are processed on a rolling basis. Application fee: $55. Electronic applications accepted. *Expenses:* Tuition, state resident: full-time $5386; part-time $3124 per year. Tuition, nonresident: full-time $11,160; part-time $248 per unit. Required fees: $2250; $614 per term. One-time fee: $2250 full-time; $1842 part-time. *Financial support:* Fellowships, research assistantships, teaching assistantships, career-related internships or fieldwork, Federal Work-Study, and scholarships/grants available. Support available to part-time students. Financial award application deadline: 3/2; financial award applicants required to submit FAFSA. *Faculty research:* Soils, structures, transportation, traffic, environmental protection. *Unit head:* Dr. Robb Moss, Graduate Coordinator, 805-756-6427, Fax: 805-756-6330, E-mail: rmoss@calpoly.edu. *Application contact:* Dr. Robb Moss, Graduate Coordinator, 805-756-6427, Fax: 805-756-6330, E-mail: rmoss@calpoly.edu.

California State Polytechnic University, Pomona, Academic Affairs, College of Engineering, Program in Civil Engineering, Pomona, CA 91768-2557. Offers MS. *Students:* 17 full-time (1 woman), 67 part-time (9 women); includes 37 minority (1 Black or African American, non-Hispanic/Latino; 1 American Indian or Alaska Native, non-Hispanic/Latino; 20 Asian, non-Hispanic/Latino; 13 Hispanic/Latino; 2 Two or more races, non-Hispanic/Latino), 10 international. Average age 30. 140 applicants, 50% accepted, 43 enrolled. In 2010, 7 master's awarded. *Degree requirements:* For master's, project or thesis. *Application deadline:* Applications are processed on a rolling basis. Application fee: $55. Electronic applications accepted. *Expenses:* Tuition, state resident: full-time $5386; part-time $2850 per year. Tuition, nonresident: full-time $12,082; part-time $248 per credit. Required fees: $577; $248 per credit. $577 per year. Tuition and fees vary according to course load and program. *Unit head:* Francelina Neto, Interim Department Chair, 909-869-2488, E-mail: faneto@csupomona.edu. *Application contact:* Scott J. Duncan, Director, Admissions, 909-869-3258, E-mail: sjduncan@csupomona.edu.

California State University, Fresno, Division of Graduate Studies, College of Engineering and Computer Science, Department of Civil Engineering, Fresno, CA 93740-8027. Offers MS. Part-time and evening/weekend programs available. *Degree requirements:* For master's, thesis or alternative. *Entrance requirements:* For master's, GRE General Test, minimum GPA of 2.75. Additional exam requirements/recommendations for international students: Required—TOEFL. Electronic applications accepted. *Faculty research:* Surveying, water damage, instrumentation equipment, agricultural drainage, aerial triangulation, dairy manure particles.

California State University, Fullerton, Graduate Studies, College of Engineering and Computer Science, Department of Civil Engineering and Engineering Mechanics, Fullerton, CA 92834-9480. Offers MS. Part-time programs available. *Students:* 88 full-time (14 women), 82 part-time (22 women); includes 2 Black or African American, non-Hispanic/Latino; 60 Asian, non-Hispanic/Latino; 21 Hispanic/Latino; 3 Two or more races, non-Hispanic/Latino, 24 international. Average age 29. 238 applicants, 63% accepted, 91 enrolled. In 2010, 40 master's awarded. *Degree requirements:* For master's, comprehensive exam, project or thesis. *Entrance requirements:* For master's, minimum undergraduate GPA of 2.5. Application fee: $55. *Financial support:* Career-related internships or fieldwork, Federal Work-Study, institutionally sponsored loans, and scholarships/grants available. Support available to part-time students. Financial award application deadline: 3/1; financial award applicants required to submit FAFSA. *Faculty research:* Soil-structure interaction, finite-element analysis, computer-aided analysis and design. *Unit head:* Dr. Pinaki Chakrabarti, Chair, 657-278-3016. *Application contact:* Admissions/Applications, 657-278-2371.

California State University, Long Beach, Graduate Studies, College of Engineering, Department of Civil Engineering and Construction Engineering Management, Long Beach, CA 90840. Offers civil engineering (MSCE). Part-time programs available. *Faculty:* 5 full-time (1 woman), 4 part-time/adjunct (0 women). *Students:* 46 full-time (16 women), 82 part-time (20 women); includes 6 Black or African American, non-Hispanic/Latino; 1 American Indian or Alaska Native, non-Hispanic/Latino; 46 Asian, non-Hispanic/Latino; 21 Hispanic/Latino, 25 international. Average age 30. 200 applicants, 59% accepted, 60 enrolled. In 2010, 22 master's awarded. *Degree requirements:* For master's, comprehensive exam or thesis. *Entrance requirements:* Additional exam requirements/recommendations for international students: Required—TOEFL. *Application deadline:* For fall admission, 3/1 for domestic students. Application fee: $55. Electronic applications accepted. *Financial support:* Career-related internships or fieldwork, Federal Work-Study, institutionally sponsored loans, scholarships/grants, and unspecified assistantships available. Financial award application deadline: 3/2. *Faculty research:* Soils, hydraulics, seismic structures, composite metals, computer-aided manufacturing. *Unit head:* Dr. Emelinda Parentela, Chair, 562-985-4932, Fax: 562-985-2380, E-mail: parent@csulb.edu. *Application contact:* Dr. Jeremy Redman, Graduate Advisor, 562-985-5135, Fax: 562-985-2380, E-mail: jredman@csulb.edu.

California State University, Los Angeles, Graduate Studies, College of Engineering, Computer Science, and Technology, Department of Civil Engineering, Los Angeles, CA 90032-8530. Offers MS. Part-time and evening/weekend programs available. *Faculty:* 2 full-time (0 women), 2 part-time/adjunct (0 women). *Students:* 24 full-time (7 women), 35 part-time (8 women); includes 39 minority (5 Black or African American, non-Hispanic/Latino; 21 Asian, non-Hispanic/Latino; 13 Hispanic/Latino), 5 international. Average age 30. 47 applicants, 98% accepted, 17 enrolled. In 2010, 16 master's awarded. *Degree requirements:* For master's, comprehensive exam or thesis. *Entrance requirements:* For master's, GRE or minimum GPA of 2.4. Additional exam requirements/recommendations for international students: Required—TOEFL (minimum score 550 paper-based). *Application deadline:* For fall admission, 5/1 for domestic and international students. Applications are processed on a rolling basis. Application fee: $55. *Financial support:* Federal Work-Study available. Support available to part-time students. Financial award application deadline: 3/1. *Faculty research:* Structure, hydraulics, hydrology, soil mechanics. *Unit head:* Dr. Rupa Purasinghe, Chair, 323-343-4450, Fax: 323-343-6316, E-mail: rpurasi@calstatela.edu. *Application contact:* Dr. Alan Muchlinski, Dean of Graduate Studies, 323-343-3820, Fax: 323-343-5653, E-mail: amuchli@exchange.calstatela.edu.

California State University, Northridge, Graduate Studies, College of Engineering and Computer Science, Department of Civil Engineering and Applied Mechanics, Northridge, CA 91330. Offers engineering (MS), including structural engineering. Part-time and evening/weekend programs available. *Degree requirements:* For master's, thesis. *Entrance requirements:* Additional exam requirements/recommendations for international students: Required—TOEFL. *Faculty research:* Composite study.

California State University, Sacramento, Graduate Studies, College of Engineering and Computer Science, Department of Civil Engineering, Sacramento, CA 95819. Offers MS. Part-time and evening/weekend programs available. *Degree requirements:* For master's, thesis or alternative, writing proficiency exam. *Entrance requirements:* Additional exam requirements/recommendations for international students: Required—TOEFL. Electronic applications accepted.

Carleton University, Faculty of Graduate Studies, Faculty of Engineering and Design, Department of Civil and Environmental Engineering, Ottawa, ON K1S 5B6, Canada. Offers M Eng, MA Sc, PhD. *Degree requirements:* For master's, thesis optional; for doctorate, thesis/dissertation. *Entrance requirements:* For master's, honors degree; for doctorate, MA Sc or M Eng. Additional exam requirements/recommendations for international students: Required—TOEFL. *Faculty research:* Pollution and wastewater management, fire safety engineering, earthquake engineering, structural design, bridge engineering.

Carnegie Mellon University, Carnegie Institute of Technology, Department of Civil and Environmental Engineering, Pittsburgh, PA 15213. Offers advanced infrastructure systems (MS, PhD); civil and environmental engineering (MS, PhD); civil and environmental engineering/engineering and public policy (PhD); civil engineering (MS, PhD); computational mechanics (MS, PhD); computational science and engineering (MS, PhD); environmental engineering (MS, PhD); environmental management and science (MS, PhD). Part-time programs available. *Faculty:* 20 full-time (3 women), 15 part-time/adjunct (5 women). *Students:* 144 full-time (67 women), 8 part-time (2 women); includes 4 Black or African American, non-Hispanic/Latino; 1 American Indian or Alaska Native, non-Hispanic/Latino; 9 Asian, non-Hispanic/Latino, 99 international. Average age 26. 388 applicants, 66% accepted, 80 enrolled. In 2010, 62 master's, 8 doctorates awarded. Terminal master's awarded for partial completion of doctoral program. *Degree requirements:* For master's, thesis optional; for doctorate, comprehensive exam, thesis/dissertation, qualifying exam, public defense of dissertation. *Entrance requirements:* For master's and doctorate, GRE General Test. Additional exam requirements/recommendations for international students: Required—TOEFL (minimum score 84 iBT). *Application deadline:* For fall admission, 1/15 priority date for domestic and international students; for spring admission, 9/30 priority date for domestic and international students. Application fee: $65. Electronic applications accepted. *Financial support:* In 2010–11, 134 students received support, including 27 fellowships with full and partial tuition reimbursements available (averaging $21,708 per year), 42 research assistantships with full and partial tuition reimbursements available (averaging $24,474 per year); tuition waivers (partial) and unspecified assistantships also available. Financial award application deadline: 1/15. *Faculty research:* Advanced infrastructure systems; environmental engineering science and management; mechanics, materials, and computing; green design; global sustainable construction. Total annual research expenditures: $4.7 million. *Unit head:* Dr. James H. Garrett, Head, 412-268-2941, Fax: 412-268-7813, E-mail: garrett@cmu.edu. *Application contact:* Maxine A. Leffard, Director of the Graduate Program, 412-268-5673, Fax: 412-268-7813, E-mail: ce-admissions@andrew.cmu.edu.

Case Western Reserve University, School of Graduate Studies, Case School of Engineering, Department of Civil Engineering, Cleveland, OH 44106. Offers civil engineering (MS, PhD). Part-time programs available. Postbaccalaureate distance learning degree programs offered (minimal on-campus study). *Faculty:* 7 full-time (0 women). *Students:* 23 full-time (12 women); includes 1 Black or African American, non-Hispanic/Latino; 1 Asian, non-Hispanic/Latino, 13 international. In 2010, 7 master's, 2 doctorates awarded. *Degree requirements:* For master's, thesis (for some programs); for doctorate, thesis/dissertation, qualifying exam, teaching experience. *Entrance requirements:* For master's and doctorate, GRE General Test. Additional exam requirements/recommendations for international students: Required—TOEFL. *Application deadline:* For fall admission, 8/1 priority date for domestic students; for spring admission, 1/1 for domestic students. Application fee: $50. *Financial support:* Fellowships with full and partial tuition reimbursements, research assistantships with full and partial tuition reimbursements, teaching assistantships, institutionally sponsored loans available. Financial award application deadline: 8/1; financial award applicants required to submit FAFSA. *Faculty research:* Environmental, geotechnical, infrastructure reliability, mechanics, structures. Total annual research expenditures: $653,000. *Unit head:* Dr. David Zeng, Chairman and Frank H. Neff Professor, 216-368-2923, Fax: 216-368-5229, E-mail: xxz16@case.edu. *Application contact:* Carla Wilson, Student Affairs Coordinator, 216-368-4580, Fax: 216-368-3007, E-mail: cxw75@case.edu.

The Catholic University of America, School of Engineering, Department of Civil Engineering, Washington, DC 20064. Offers environmental engineering (PhD). Part-time programs available. *Faculty:* 6 full-time (0 women), 5 part-time/adjunct (0 women). *Students:* 8 full-time (3 women), 22 part-time (5 women); includes 6 Black or African American, non-Hispanic/Latino; 2 Asian, non-Hispanic/Latino; 2 Hispanic/Latino, 7 international. Average age 34. 46 applicants, 46% accepted, 8 enrolled. In 2010, 7 master's, 2 doctorates awarded. *Degree requirements:* For master's, thesis optional; for doctorate, comprehensive exam, thesis/dissertation. *Entrance requirements:* For master's and doctorate, statement of purpose, official copies of academic transcripts, three letters of recommendation. Additional exam requirements/recommendations for international students: Required—TOEFL (minimum score 580 paper-based; 237 computer-based). *Application deadline:* For fall admission, 8/1 priority date for domestic students, 7/15 for international students; for spring admission, 12/1 priority date for domestic students, 10/15 for international students. Applications are processed on a rolling basis. Application fee: $55. Electronic applications accepted. *Expenses:* Contact institution. *Financial support:* Fellowships, research assistantships, teaching assistantships, Federal Work-Study, scholarships/grants, tuition waivers (full and partial), and unspecified assistantships available. Financial award application deadline: 2/1; financial award applicants required to submit FAFSA. *Faculty research:* Geotechnical engineering, solid mechanics, construction engineering and management, environmental engineering, structural engineering. Total annual research expenditures: $438,834. *Unit head:* Dr. Lu Sun, Chair, 202-319-6671, Fax: 202-319-6677, E-mail: sunl@cua.edu. *Application contact:* Andrew Woodall, Director of Graduate Admissions, 202-319-5057, Fax: 202-319-6533, E-mail: cua-admissions@cua.edu.

City College of the City University of New York, Graduate School, Grove School of Engineering, Department of Civil Engineering, New York, NY 10031-9198. Offers ME, MS, PhD. PhD program offered jointly with Graduate School and University Center of the City University of New York. Part-time programs available. *Degree requirements:* For master's, thesis optional; for doctorate, one foreign language, comprehensive exam, thesis/dissertation. *Entrance requirements:* For master's and doctorate, GRE General Test. Additional exam requirements/recommendations for international students: Required—TOEFL (minimum score 500 paper-based; 173 computer-based; 61 iBT). *Faculty research:* Earthquake engineering, transportation systems, groundwater, environmental systems, highway systems.

Clarkson University, Graduate School, Wallace H. Coulter School of Engineering, Department of Civil and Environmental Engineering, Potsdam, NY 13699. Offers civil engineering (ME, MS). Part-time programs available. *Faculty:* 22 full-time (5 women), 3 part-time/adjunct (0 women). *Students:* 39 full-time (14 women); includes 2 minority (1 Asian, non-Hispanic/Latino; 1 Two or more races, non-Hispanic/Latino), 29 international. Average age 26. 104 applicants, 60% accepted, 10 enrolled. In 2010, 12 master's awarded. Terminal master's awarded for partial completion of doctoral program. *Degree requirements:* For master's, thesis. *Entrance requirements:* For master's, GRE, transcripts of all college coursework, resume, personal statement, three letters of recommendation. Additional exam requirements/recommendations for international students: Required—TOEFL (minimum score 550 paper-based; 213 computer-based; 80 iBT), IELTS (minimum score 6.5). *Application deadline:* For fall admission, 1/30 priority date for domestic and international students; for spring admission, 9/1 priority date for domestic and international students. Applications are processed on a rolling basis. Application fee: $25 ($35 for international students). Electronic applications accepted. *Expenses:* Tuition: Part-time $1136 per credit hour. *Financial support:* In 2010–11, 37 students received support, including 1 fellowship with full tuition reimbursement available (averaging $21,580 per year), 25 research assistantships with full tuition reimbursements available (averaging $21,580 per year), 10 teaching assistantships with full tuition reimbursements available (averaging $21,580 per year); scholarships/grants, tuition waivers (partial), and unspecified assistantships also available. *Faculty research:* Resuspended particles, methane digester, environmental systems, BCDSP measurements, CO2 bubbles, transverse cracking. Total annual research expenditures: $4.6 million. *Unit head:* Dr. Stefan Grimberg, Department Chair, 315-268-6529, Fax: 315-268-7985, E-mail: grimberg@clarkson.edu. *Application contact:* Kelly Sharlow, Assistant to the Dean, 315-268-7929, Fax: 315-268-4494, E-mail: ksharlow@clarkson.edu.

Clemson University, Graduate School, College of Engineering and Science, Department of Civil Engineering, Clemson, SC 29634. Offers MS, PhD. Part-time programs available. *Faculty:* 20 full-time (2 women), 1 part-time/adjunct (0 women). *Students:* 100 full-time (24 women), 10 part-time (3 women); includes 4 Black or African American, non-Hispanic/Latino; 2 Hispanic/Latino; 1 Two or more races, non-Hispanic/Latino, 49 international. Average age 27. 237 applicants, 68% accepted, 49 enrolled. In 2010, 41 master's, 3 doctorates awarded. *Degree requirements:* For master's, thesis or alternative, oral exam, seminar; for doctorate, thesis/dissertation, oral exam, seminar. *Entrance requirements:* For master's and doctorate, GRE General Test, minimum GPA of 3.0. Additional exam requirements/recommendations for international students: Required—TOEFL. *Application deadline:* For fall admission, 6/1 for domestic students, 4/15 for international students; for spring admission, 9/15 for international students. Applications are processed on a rolling basis. Application fee: $70 ($80 for international students). Electronic applications accepted. *Expenses:* Tuition, state resident: full-time $6492; part-time $400 per credit hour. Tuition, nonresident: full-time $13,634; part-time $800 per credit hour. Required fees: $262 per semester. Part-time tuition and fees vary according to course load and program. *Financial support:* In 2010–11, 85 students received support, including 15 fellowships with full and partial tuition reimbursements available (averaging $7,631 per year), 46 research assistantships with partial tuition reimbursements available (averaging $11,664 per year), 44 teaching assistantships with partial tuition reimbursements available (averaging $10,957 per year); career-related internships or fieldwork, institutionally sponsored loans, scholarships/grants, health care benefits, and unspecified assistantships also available. Support available to part-time students. Financial award application deadline: 2/15; financial award applicants required to submit FAFSA. *Faculty research:* Applied fluid mechanics, construction materials, project management, structural engineering. Total annual research expenditures: $2.5 million. *Unit head:* Dr. Nadim Aziz, Chair, 864-656-3300, Fax: 864-656-2670, E-mail: aziz@clemson.edu. *Application contact:* Dr. Ron D. Andrus, Graduate Program Coordinator, 864-656-0488, Fax: 864-656-2670, E-mail: randrus@clemson.edu.

Cleveland State University, College of Graduate Studies, Fenn College of Engineering, Department of Civil and Environmental Engineering, Cleveland, OH 44115. Offers accelerated program civil engineering (MS); accelerated program environmental engineering (MS); civil engineering (MS, D Eng); engineering mechanics (MS); environmental engineering (MS). Part-time and evening/weekend programs available. *Faculty:* 9 full-time (1 woman), 1 part-time/adjunct (0 women). *Students:* 8 full-time (0 women), 43 part-time (9 women); includes 2 Black or African American, non-Hispanic/Latino; 2 Asian, non-Hispanic/Latino; 1 Hispanic/Latino, 16 international. Average age 26. 67 applicants, 61% accepted, 14 enrolled. In 2010, 13 master's, 2 doctorates awarded. *Degree requirements:* For master's, project or thesis; for doctorate, comprehensive exam, thesis/dissertation, candidacy and qualifying exams. *Entrance requirements:* For master's, GRE General Test, GRE Subject Test, minimum GPA of 2.75; for doctorate, GRE General Test, GRE Subject Test, minimum GPA of 3.25. Additional exam requirements/recommendations for international students: Required—TOEFL (minimum score 525 paper-based; 197 computer-based). *Application deadline:* For fall admission, 7/15 priority date for domestic students. Applications are processed on a rolling basis. Application fee: $30. *Expenses:* Tuition, state resident: full-time $8447; part-time $469 per credit hour. Tuition, nonresident: full-time $16,020; part-time $890 per credit hour. Required fees: $50. *Financial support:* In 2010–11, 9 research assistantships with full and partial tuition reimbursements (averaging $3,920 per year) were awarded; teaching assistantships with tuition reimbursements, career-related internships or fieldwork, scholarships/grants, and unspecified assistantships also available. Financial award application deadline: 9/1. *Faculty research:* Solid-waste disposal, constitutive modeling, transportation, safety engineering. Total annual research expenditures: $800,000. *Unit head:* Dr. Stephen F. Duffy, Chairperson, 216-687-3874, Fax: 216-687-9280, E-mail: p.bosela@csuohio.edu. *Application contact:* Dr. Stephen F. Duffy, Chairperson, 216-687-3874, Fax: 216-687-9280, E-mail: p.bosela@csuohio.edu.

Colorado State University, Graduate School, College of Engineering, Department of Civil and Environmental Engineering, Fort Collins, CO 80523-1372. Offers civil engineering (ME, MS, PhD). Part-time programs available. Postbaccalaureate distance learning degree programs offered (no on-campus study). *Faculty:* 27 full-time (3 women), 4 part-time/adjunct (0 women). *Students:* 87 full-time (27 women), 98 part-time (21 women); includes 10 minority (2 Black or African American, non-Hispanic/Latino; 4 Asian, non-Hispanic/Latino; 2 Hispanic/Latino; 2 Two or more races, non-Hispanic/Latino), 63 international. Average age 31. 204 applicants, 78% accepted, 54 enrolled. In 2010, 35 master's, 15 doctorates awarded. Terminal master's awarded for partial completion of doctoral program. *Degree requirements:* For master's, comprehensive exam (for some programs), thesis with publication (required for some); for doctorate, comprehensive exam, thesis/dissertation, publication. *Entrance requirements:* For master's,

Civil Engineering

Colorado State University (continued)

GRE General Test, minimum GPA of 3.0, letters of recommendation, resume; for doctorate, GRE General Test, minimum GPA of 3.0, MS, letters of recommendation, statement of purpose, resume. Additional exam requirements/recommendations for international students: Required—TOEFL (minimum score 550 paper-based; 213 computer-based; 80 iBT); Recommended—IELTS (minimum score 6.5). *Application deadline:* For fall admission, 4/1 priority date for domestic and international students; for spring admission, 10/1 priority date for domestic and international students. Applications are processed on a rolling basis. Application fee: $50. Electronic applications accepted. *Expenses:* Tuition, state resident: full-time $7434; part-time $413 per credit. Tuition, nonresident: full-time $19,022; part-time $1057 per credit. Required fees: $1729; $88 per credit. *Financial support:* In 2010–11, 68 students received support, including 1 fellowship (averaging $37,500 per year), 53 research assistantships with tuition reimbursements available (averaging $13,596 per year), 14 teaching assistantships with tuition reimbursements available (averaging $10,612 per year); scholarships/grants and unspecified assistantships also available. Financial award application deadline: 2/15; financial award applicants required to submit FAFSA. *Faculty research:* Wind and fluid mechanics, structural engineering and mechanics, hydraulic engineering, geotechnical engineering, environmental and geoenvironmental engineering. Total annual research expenditures: $8.5 million. *Unit head:* Dr. Luis Garcia, Head, 970-491-5048, Fax: 970-491-7727, E-mail: luis.garcia@colostate.edu. *Application contact:* Laurie Alburn, Student Advisor, 970-491-5844, Fax: 970-491-7727, E-mail: laurie.alburn@colostate.edu.

Columbia University, Fu Foundation School of Engineering and Applied Science, Department of Civil Engineering and Engineering Mechanics, New York, NY 10027. Offers civil engineering (MS, Eng Sc D, PhD, Engr); construction engineering and management (MS); engineering mechanics (MS, Eng Sc D, PhD, Engr). Part-time programs available. Postbaccalaureate distance learning degree programs offered (no on-campus study). *Faculty:* 16 full-time (1 woman), 25 part-time/adjunct (3 women). *Students:* 96 full-time (19 women), 42 part-time (14 women); includes 25 minority (3 Black or African American, non-Hispanic/Latino; 11 Asian, non-Hispanic/Latino; 10 Hispanic/Latino; 1 Two or more races, non-Hispanic/Latino), 70 international. Average age 27. 265 applicants, 35% accepted, 59 enrolled. In 2010, 67 master's, 29 doctorates, 2 other advanced degrees awarded. Terminal master's awarded for partial completion of doctoral program. *Degree requirements:* For doctorate, thesis/dissertation, qualifying exam. *Entrance requirements:* For master's, doctorate, and Engr, GRE General Test. Additional exam requirements/recommendations for international students: Required—TOEFL, IELTS. *Application deadline:* For fall admission, 12/1 priority date for domestic and international students; for spring admission, 10/1 priority date for domestic and international students. Application fee: $95. Electronic applications accepted. *Financial support:* In 2010–11, 39 students received support, including 5 fellowships with full tuition reimbursements available (averaging $30,660 per year), 23 research assistantships with full tuition reimbursements available (averaging $30,660 per year), 11 teaching assistantships with full tuition reimbursements available (averaging $30,660 per year); traineeships and health care benefits also available. Financial award application deadline: 12/1; financial award applicants required to submit FAFSA. *Faculty research:* Motion monitoring of Manhattan Bridge, lightweight concrete panels, simulation of life of well sealant, intercultural knowledge system dynamics, corrosion monitoring of New York City bridges. *Unit head:* Dr. Raimondo Betti, Professor and Department Chairman, 212-854-6388, Fax: 212-854-7081, E-mail: betti@civil.columbia.edu. *Application contact:* Rene B. Testa, Professor, 212-854-3143, Fax: 212-854-6267, E-mail: testa@civil.columbia.edu.

Concordia University, School of Graduate Studies, Faculty of Engineering and Computer Science, Department of Building, Civil and Environmental Engineering, Montréal, QC H3G 1M8, Canada. Offers building engineering (M Eng, MA Sc, PhD, Certificate); civil engineering (M Eng, MA Sc, PhD); environmental engineering (Certificate). *Degree requirements:* For master's, thesis or alternative; for doctorate, comprehensive exam, thesis/dissertation. *Faculty research:* Structural engineering, geotechnical engineering, water resources and fluid engineering, transportation engineering, systems engineering.

Cooper Union for the Advancement of Science and Art, Albert Nerken School of Engineering, New York, NY 10003-7120. Offers chemical engineering (ME); civil engineering (ME); electrical engineering (ME); mechanical engineering (ME). Part-time programs available. *Faculty:* 27 full-time (1 woman), 15 part-time/adjunct (2 women). *Students:* 57 full-time (15 women), 25 part-time (1 woman); includes 2 Black or African American, non-Hispanic/Latino; 1 American Indian or Alaska Native, non-Hispanic/Latino; 22 Asian, non-Hispanic/Latino; 2 Hispanic/Latino, 16 international. Average age 24. 72 applicants, 39% accepted, 27 enrolled. In 2010, 25 master's awarded. *Degree requirements:* For master's, thesis. *Entrance requirements:* For master's, GRE, BE, minimum GPA of 3.5. Additional exam requirements/recommendations for international students: Required—TOEFL (minimum score 600 paper-based; 250 computer-based; 100 iBT). *Application deadline:* For fall admission, 2/15 for domestic and international students. Application fee: $65. *Expenses:* Tuition: Full-time $35,000; part-time $1100 per credit. Required fees: $825 per semester. *Financial support:* Fellowships with full tuition reimbursements, career-related internships or fieldwork, Federal Work-Study, tuition waivers (full), and all admitted students receive full-tuition scholarships available. Support available to part-time students. Financial award application deadline: 5/1; financial award applicants required to submit CSS PROFILE or FAFSA. *Faculty research:* Civil infrastructure, imaging and sensing technology, biomedical engineering, encryption technology, process engineering. *Unit head:* Dr. Simon Ben-Avi, Acting Dean, 212-353-4285, E-mail: benavi@cooper.edu. *Application contact:* Student Contact, 212-353-4120, E-mail: admissions@cooper.edu.

Cornell University, Graduate School, Graduate Fields of Engineering, Field of Civil and Environmental Engineering, Ithaca, NY 14853-0001. Offers engineering management (M Eng, MS, PhD); environmental engineering (M Eng, MS, PhD); environmental fluid mechanics and hydrology (M Eng, MS, PhD); environmental systems engineering (M Eng, MS, PhD); geotechnical engineering (M Eng, MS, PhD); remote sensing (M Eng, MS, PhD); structural engineering (M Eng, MS, PhD); structural mechanics (M Eng, MS); transportation engineering (MS, PhD); transportation systems engineering (M Eng); water resource systems (M Eng, MS, PhD). *Faculty:* 36 full-time (4 women). *Students:* 148 full-time (48 women); includes 3 Black or African American, non-Hispanic/Latino; 1 American Indian or Alaska Native, non-Hispanic/Latino; 16 Asian, non-Hispanic/Latino; 16 Hispanic/Latino, 60 international. Average age 24. 390 applicants, 56% accepted, 76 enrolled. In 2010, 93 master's, 5 doctorates awarded. Terminal master's awarded for partial completion of doctoral program. *Degree requirements:* For master's, thesis (MS); for doctorate, comprehensive exam, thesis/dissertation. *Entrance requirements:* For master's and doctorate, GRE General Test (recommended), 2 letters of recommendation. Additional exam requirements/recommendations for international students: Required—TOEFL (minimum score 600 paper-based; 250 computer-based; 77 iBT). *Application deadline:* For fall admission, 1/15 priority date for domestic students; for spring admission, 10/15 for domestic students. Application fee: $70. Electronic applications accepted. *Expenses:* Tuition: Full-time $29,500. Required fees: $76. Tuition and fees vary according to degree level and program. *Financial support:* In 2010–11, 50 students received support, including 17 fellowships with full tuition reimbursements available, 33 research assistantships with full tuition reimbursements available, 15 teaching assistantships with full tuition reimbursements available; institutionally sponsored loans, scholarships/grants, health care benefits, tuition waivers (full and partial), and unspecified assistantships also available. Financial award applicants required to submit FAFSA. *Faculty research:* Environmental engineering, geotechnical engineering, remote sensing, environmental fluid mechanics and hydrology, structural engineering. *Unit head:* Director of Graduate Studies, 607-255-7560, Fax: 607-255-9004. *Application contact:* Graduate Field Assistant, 607-255-7560, Fax: 607-255-9004, E-mail: cee_grad@cornell.edu.

Dalhousie University, Faculty of Engineering, Department of Civil and Resource Engineering, Halifax, NS B3J 2X4, Canada. Offers M Eng, MA Sc, PhD. *Degree requirements:* For master's, thesis; for doctorate, thesis/dissertation. *Entrance requirements:* Additional exam requirements/recommendations for international students: Required—TOEFL, IELTS, CANTEST, CAEL, or Michigan English Language Assessment Battery. Electronic applications accepted. *Faculty research:* Environmental/water resources, bridge engineering, geotechnical engineering, pavement design and management/highway materials, composite materials.

Drexel University, College of Engineering, Department of Civil, Architectural, and Environmental Engineering, Program in Civil Engineering, Philadelphia, PA 19104-2875. Offers MS, PhD. Part-time and evening/weekend programs available. *Degree requirements:* For master's, thesis optional; for doctorate, thesis/dissertation. *Entrance requirements:* For master's, minimum GPA of 3.0; for doctorate, minimum GPA of 3.5, MS in civil engineering. Additional exam requirements/recommendations for international students: Required—TOEFL. Electronic applications accepted.

Duke University, Graduate School, Pratt School of Engineering, Department of Civil and Environmental Engineering, Durham, NC 27708. Offers civil and environmental engineering (MS, PhD); environmental engineering (MS, PhD). Part-time programs available. *Faculty:* 21 full-time. *Students:* 55 full-time (18 women); includes 1 Black or African American, non-Hispanic/Latino; 1 Hispanic/Latino, 30 international. 149 applicants, 17% accepted, 15 enrolled. In 2010, 9 master's, 4 doctorates awarded. Terminal master's awarded for partial completion of doctoral program. *Degree requirements:* For doctorate, thesis/dissertation. *Entrance requirements:* For master's and doctorate, GRE General Test. Additional exam requirements/recommendations for international students: Required—TOEFL (minimum score 550 paper-based; 213 computer-based; 83 iBT), IELTS (minimum score 7). *Application deadline:* For fall admission, 12/8 priority date for domestic and international students; for spring admission, 11/1 for domestic students. Application fee: $75. Electronic applications accepted. *Financial support:* Fellowships, research assistantships, Federal Work-Study available. Financial award application deadline: 12/8. *Unit head:* Dolbow John, Director of Graduate Studies, 919-660-5200, Fax: 919-660-5219, E-mail: ruby.carpenter@duke.edu. *Application contact:* Elizabeth Hutton, Director of Admissions, 919-684-3913, Fax: 919-684-2277, E-mail: grad-admissions@duke.edu.

Duke University, Graduate School, Pratt School of Engineering, Master of Engineering Program, Durham, NC 27708-0271. Offers biomedical engineering (M Eng); civil engineering (M Eng); electrical and computer engineering (M Eng); environmental engineering (M Eng); materials science and engineering (M Eng); mechanical engineering (M Eng); photonics and optical sciences (M Eng). Part-time programs available. *Faculty:* 123 full-time, 1 part-time/adjunct. *Students:* 9 full-time (4 women); includes 2 minority (both Asian, non-Hispanic/Latino), 3 international. Average age 24. *Entrance requirements:* For master's, GRE General Test, resume, 3 letters of recommendation, statement of purpose. Additional exam requirements/recommendations for international students: Required—TOEFL. *Application deadline:* For fall admission, 6/15 for domestic students, 2/15 for international students; for spring admission, 11/1 for domestic students, 9/1 for international students. Application fee: $75. *Financial support:* Merit scholarships/grants available. *Unit head:* Dr. Bradley A. Fox, Executive Director, 919-660-5455, Fax: 919-660-5456. *Application contact:* Erin Degerman, Admissions Coordinator, 919-668-6789, Fax: 919-660-5456, E-mail: erin.degerman@duke.edu.

École Polytechnique de Montréal, Graduate Programs, Department of Civil, Geological and Mining Engineering, Montréal, QC H3C 3A7, Canada. Offers civil, geological and mining engineering (DESS); environmental engineering (M Eng, M Sc A, PhD); geotechnical engineering (M Eng, M Sc A, PhD); hydraulics engineering (M Eng, M Sc A, PhD); structural engineering (M Eng, M Sc A, PhD); transportation engineering (M Eng, M Sc A, PhD). Part-time programs available. *Degree requirements:* For master's, one foreign language, thesis; for doctorate, one foreign language, thesis/dissertation. *Entrance requirements:* For master's, minimum GPA of 2.75; for doctorate, minimum GPA of 3.0. *Faculty research:* Water resources management, characteristics of building materials, aging of dams, pollution control.

Florida Agricultural and Mechanical University, Division of Graduate Studies, Research, and Continuing Education, FAMU-FSU College of Engineering, Department of Civil and Environmental Engineering, Tallahassee, FL 32307-3200. Offers civil engineering (MS, PhD); environmental engineering (MS, PhD). *Degree requirements:* For master's, comprehensive exam, thesis optional; for doctorate, comprehensive exam, thesis/dissertation. *Entrance requirements:* For master's, GRE General Test, minimum GPA of 3.0; for doctorate, GRE General Test, minimum GPA of 3.0, letters of recommendation (3). Additional exam requirements/recommendations for international students: Required—TOEFL (minimum score 550 paper-based; 213 computer-based). *Faculty research:* Geotechnical, environmental, hydraulic, construction materials, and structures.

Florida Atlantic University, College of Engineering and Computer Science, Department of Civil, Environmental and Geomatics Engineering, Boca Raton, FL 33431-0991. Offers civil engineering (MS). Part-time and evening/weekend programs available. *Faculty:* 15 full-time (2 women), 2 part-time/adjunct (0 women). *Students:* 18 full-time (3 women), 14 part-time (3 women); includes 11 minority (5 Black or African American, non-Hispanic/Latino; 5 Hispanic/Latino; 1 Two or more races, non-Hispanic/Latino), 8 international. Average age 30. 53 applicants, 43% accepted, 13 enrolled. In 2010, 14 master's awarded. *Degree requirements:* For master's, thesis optional. *Entrance requirements:* For master's, GRE General Test, minimum GPA of 3.0 in last 60 hours of undergraduate course work. Additional exam requirements/recommendations for international students: Required—TOEFL (minimum score 550 paper-based; 213 computer-based). *Application deadline:* For fall admission, 7/1 priority date for domestic students, 2/15 for international students; for spring admission, 11/1 for domestic students, 7/15 for international students. Applications are processed on a rolling basis. Application fee: $30. *Expenses:* Tuition, area resident: Part-time $319.96 per credit. Tuition, state resident: part-time $319.96 per credit. Tuition, nonresident: part-time $926.42 per credit. *Financial support:* Research assistantships with full tuition reimbursements, teaching assistantships with full tuition reimbursements, career-related internships or fieldwork, Federal Work-Study, scholarships/grants, and unspecified assistantships available. Financial award applicants required to submit FAFSA. *Faculty research:* Structures, geotechnical engineering, environmental and water resources engineering, transportation engineering, materials. *Unit head:* Dr. Pete D. Scarlatos, Chair, 561-297-0466, Fax: 561-297-0493, E-mail: scarlatos@fau.edu. *Application contact:* Dr. Frederick Bloetscher, Assistant Professor, 561-297-0744, E-mail: fbloetscher@civil.fau.edu.

Florida Institute of Technology, Graduate Programs, College of Engineering, Civil Engineering Department, Melbourne, FL 32901-6975. Offers MS, PhD. Part-time programs available. *Faculty:* 6 full-time (0 women). *Students:* 15 full-time (1 woman), 5 part-time (2 women); includes 1 minority (Asian, non-Hispanic/Latino), 10 international. Average age 32. 67 applicants, 28% accepted, 4 enrolled. In 2010, 8 master's awarded. *Degree requirements:* For master's, comprehensive exam (for some programs), thesis optional, teaching or final examinations; for doctorate, comprehensive exam, thesis/dissertation, research project, Preliminary Examination. *Entrance requirements:* For master's, 2 letters of recommendation, minimum GPA of 3.0, statement of objectives; for doctorate, 3 letters of recommendation, minimum GPA of 3.2, resume, statement of objectives. Additional exam requirements/recommendations for international students: Required—TOEFL (minimum score 550 paper-based; 213 computer-based; 79 iBT). *Application deadline:* For fall admission, 4/1 for international students; for spring admission, 9/30 for international students. Applications are processed on a rolling basis. Application fee: $50. Electronic applications accepted. *Expenses:* Tuition: Part-time $1040 per credit hour. Tuition and fees vary according to campus/location. *Financial support:* In 2010–11, 8 research assistantships with full and partial tuition reimbursements (averaging $5,012 per year), 3 teaching assistantships with full and partial tuition reimbursements (averaging $5,300 per year) were awarded; career-related internships or fieldwork, institutionally sponsored loans, tuition waivers (partial), unspecified assistantships, and tuition remissions also available. Support available to part-time students. Financial award application deadline: 3/1; financial award applicants required to submit FAFSA. *Faculty research:* Groundwater and surface water modeling, pavements, waste materials, in situ soil testing, fiber optic sensors. Total annual research expenditures: $281,297. *Unit head:* Dr. Ashok Pandit, Department Head, 321-674-

7151, Fax: 321-768-7565; E-mail: apandit@fit.edu. *Application contact:* Cheryl A. Brown, Associate Director of Graduate Admissions, 321-674-7581, Fax: 321-723-9468, E-mail: cbrown@fit.edu.

Florida International University, College of Engineering and Computing, Department of Civil and Environmental Engineering, Program in Civil Engineering, Miami, FL 33175. Offers MS, PhD. Part-time and evening/weekend programs available. Postbaccalaureate distance learning degree programs offered (no on-campus study). *Students:* 54 full-time (12 women), 57 part-time (14 women); includes 12 Black or African American, non-Hispanic/Latino; 3 Asian, non-Hispanic/Latino; 37 Hispanic/Latino, 47 international. Average age 29. 180 applicants, 34% accepted, 50 enrolled. In 2010, 21 master's, 9 doctorates awarded. *Degree requirements:* For master's, thesis optional; for doctorate, comprehensive exam, thesis/dissertation. *Entrance requirements:* For master's, bachelor's degree in related field, minimum GPA of 3.0; for doctorate, GRE General Test, minimum graduate GPA of 3.3, master's degree, resume, letters of recommendation, statement of objectives. Additional exam requirements/recommendations for international students: Required—TOEFL (minimum score 550 paper-based; 80 iBT). *Application deadline:* For fall admission, 6/1 for domestic students, 4/1 for international students; for spring admission, 10/1 for domestic students, 9/1 for international students. Applications are processed on a rolling basis. Application fee: $30. Electronic applications accepted. *Financial support:* Federal Work-Study, institutionally sponsored loans, scholarships/grants, health care benefits, and unspecified assistantships available. Financial award application deadline: 3/1; financial award applicants required to submit FAFSA. *Faculty research:* Structural engineering, wind engineering, sustainable infrastructure engineering, water resources engineering, transportation engineering. *Unit head:* Dr. Atorod Azizinamini, Department Chair, 305-348-3821, Fax: 305-348-2802, E-mail: aazizina@fiu.edu. *Application contact:* Maria Parrilla, Graduate Admissions Assistant, 305-348-1890, Fax: 305-348-6142, E-mail: grad_eng@fiu.edu.

Florida State University, The Graduate School, FAMU-FSU College of Engineering, Department of Civil and Environmental Engineering, Tallahassee, FL 32306. Offers MS, PhD. Part-time programs available. *Faculty:* 16 full-time (3 women), 5 part-time/adjunct (1 woman). *Students:* 33 full-time (9 women), 13 part-time (6 women); includes 7 Black or African American, non-Hispanic/Latino; 4 Hispanic/Latino, 19 international. Average age 23. 72 applicants, 64% accepted, 14 enrolled. In 2010, 15 master's, 2 doctorates awarded. *Degree requirements:* For master's, thesis optional; for doctorate, thesis/dissertation. *Entrance requirements:* For master's, GRE General Test (minimum score 1000), BS in engineering or related field, minimum GPA of 3.0; for doctorate, GRE General Test (minimum score 1100), master's degree in engineering or related field, minimum GPA of 3.0. Additional exam requirements/recommendations for international students: Required—TOEFL (minimum score 550 paper-based; 213 computer-based; 80 iBT). *Application deadline:* For fall admission, 7/1 for domestic and international students; for spring admission, 11/1 for domestic and international students. Applications are processed on a rolling basis. Application fee: $30. *Expenses:* Tuition, state resident: full-time $8238.24. *Financial support:* In 2010–11, 25 students received support, including 2 fellowships (averaging $12,000 per year), 18 research assistantships with full tuition reimbursements available (averaging $15,000 per year), 26 teaching assistantships with full tuition reimbursements available (averaging $15,000 per year); Federal Work-Study, tuition waivers (full), and unspecified assistantships also available. Financial award application deadline: 6/15; financial award applicants required to submit FAFSA. *Faculty research:* Tidal hydraulics, temperature effects on bridge girders, codes for coastal construction, field performance of pine bridges, river basin management, transportation pavement design, soil dynamics, structural analysis. Total annual research expenditures: $1.3 million. *Unit head:* Dr. Kamal S. Tawfiq, Chair and Professor, 850-410-6143, Fax: 850-410-6142, E-mail: tawfiq@eng.fsu.edu. *Application contact:* Johnnye Belinda Morris, Office Manager, 850-410-6139, Fax: 850-410-6142, E-mail: bmorris@eng.fsu.edu.

George Mason University, Volgenau School of Engineering, Department of Civil, Environmental, and Infrastructure Engineering, Fairfax, VA 22030. Offers civil and infrastructure engineering (MS, PhD); civil infrastructure and security engineering (Certificate); leading technical enterprises (Certificate); sustainability and the environment (Certificate); water resources engineering (Certificate). Part-time and evening/weekend programs available. *Faculty:* 9 full-time (4 women), 18 part-time/adjunct (1 woman). *Students:* 15 full-time (4 women), 62 part-time (13 women); includes 7 Black or African American, non-Hispanic/Latino; 9 Asian, non-Hispanic/Latino; 4 Hispanic/Latino; 2 Two or more races, non-Hispanic/Latino, 6 international. Average age 32. 77 applicants, 70% accepted, 29 enrolled. In 2010, 13 master's, 1 doctorate, 2 other advanced degrees awarded. *Degree requirements:* For master's, thesis (for some programs), 30 credits, departmental seminars; for doctorate, thesis/dissertation, qualifying exams. *Entrance requirements:* For master's, GRE or GMAT. Additional exam requirements/recommendations for international students: Required—TOEFL (minimum score 570 paper-based; 230 computer-based; 88 iBT). *Application deadline:* For fall admission, 3/15 priority date for domestic students, 3/15 for international students; for spring admission, 11/1 for domestic students, 10/1 for international students. Application fee: $100. Electronic applications accepted. *Expenses:* Tuition, state resident: full-time $8192; part-time $440 per credit hour. Tuition, nonresident: full-time $22,952; part-time $1055 per credit hour. Required fees: $2364; $99 per credit hour. *Financial support:* In 2010–11, 13 students received support, including 1 fellowship (averaging $18,000 per year), 2 research assistantships with full and partial tuition reimbursements available (averaging $13,924 per year), 10 teaching assistantships with full and partial tuition reimbursements available (averaging $10,468 per year); career-related internships or fieldwork, Federal Work-Study, scholarships/grants, unspecified assistantships, and health care benefits (full-time research or teaching assistantship recipients) also available. Financial award application deadline: 3/1; financial award applicants required to submit FAFSA. *Faculty research:* Evolutionary design, infrastructure security, intelligent transportation systems, national transportation networks, water quality modeling. Total annual research expenditures: $177,807. *Unit head:* Dr. Michael Bronzini, Chair, 703-993-1504, Fax: 703-993-1521. *Application contact:* Lisa Nolder, Graduate Student Services Director, 703-993-1499, E-mail: snolder@gmu.edu.

The George Washington University, School of Engineering and Applied Science, Department of Civil and Environmental Engineering, Washington, DC 20052. Offers MS, D Sc, App Sc, Engr. Part-time and evening/weekend programs available. *Faculty:* 13 full-time (3 women), 7 part-time/adjunct (1 woman). *Students:* 22 full-time (6 women), 31 part-time (6 women); includes 3 Black or African American, non-Hispanic/Latino; 3 Hispanic/Latino, 30 international. Average age 30. 97 applicants, 53% accepted, 14 enrolled. In 2010, 8 master's, 4 doctorates awarded. *Degree requirements:* For master's, thesis optional; for doctorate, thesis/dissertation, final and qualifying exams. *Entrance requirements:* For master's, appropriate bachelor's degree, minimum GPA of 3.0; for doctorate, appropriate bachelor's or master's degree, minimum GPA of 3.4, GRE if highest earned degree is BS; for other advanced degree, appropriate master's degree, minimum GPA of 3.0. Additional exam requirements/recommendations for international students: Required—TOEFL or The George Washington University English as a Foreign Language Test. *Application deadline:* For fall admission, 3/1 priority date for domestic students; for spring admission, 10/1 for domestic students. Applications are processed on a rolling basis. Application fee: $75. *Financial support:* In 2010–11, 42 students received support; fellowships with tuition reimbursements available, research assistantships, teaching assistantships with tuition reimbursements available, career-related internships or fieldwork, Federal Work-Study, institutionally sponsored loans, and tuition waivers available. Financial award application deadline: 3/1; financial award applicants required to submit FAFSA. *Faculty research:* Computer-integrated manufacturing, materials engineering, electronic materials, fatigue and fracture, reliability. *Unit head:* Dr. Kim Roddis, Chair, 202-994-8515, Fax: 202-994-0127, E-mail: roddis@gwu.edu. *Application contact:* Adina Lav, Marketing, Recruiting and Admissions, 202-994-5827, Fax: 202-994-0909, E-mail: engineering@gwu.edu.

Georgia Institute of Technology, Graduate Studies and Research, College of Engineering, School of Civil and Environmental Engineering, Program in Civil Engineering, Atlanta, GA 30332-0001. Offers MS, MSCE, PhD. Part-time programs available. Terminal master's awarded for partial completion of doctoral program. *Degree requirements:* For doctorate, thesis/dissertation. *Entrance requirements:* For master's, GRE, minimum GPA of 3.0; for doctorate,

GRE, minimum GPA of 3.2. Additional exam requirements/recommendations for international students: Required—TOEFL. *Faculty research:* Structural analysis, fluid mechanics, geotechnical engineering, construction management, transportation engineering.

Graduate School and University Center of the City University of New York, Graduate Studies, Program in Engineering, New York, NY 10016-4039. Offers biomedical engineering (PhD); chemical engineering (PhD); civil engineering (PhD); electrical engineering (PhD); mechanical engineering (PhD). *Degree requirements:* For doctorate, thesis/dissertation. *Entrance requirements:* For doctorate, GRE General Test. Additional exam requirements/recommendations for international students: Required—TOEFL. Electronic applications accepted.

Howard University, College of Engineering, Architecture, and Computer Sciences, School of Engineering and Computer Science, Department of Civil Engineering, Washington, DC 20059-0002. Offers M Eng. Offered through the Graduate School of Arts and Sciences. *Degree requirements:* For master's, comprehensive exam, thesis. *Entrance requirements:* For master's, GRE General Test, minimum GPA of 3.0, bachelor's degree in engineering or related field. Additional exam requirements/recommendations for international students: Required—TOEFL. Electronic applications accepted. *Faculty research:* Modeling of concrete, structures, transportation planning, structural analysis, environmental and water resources.

Idaho State University, Office of Graduate Studies, College of Engineering, Civil and Environmental Engineering Department, Pocatello, ID 83209-8060. Offers civil engineering (MS); environmental engineering (MS); environmental science and management (MS). Part-time programs available. *Degree requirements:* For master's, comprehensive exam (for some programs), thesis optional, thesis project, 2 semesters of seminar. *Entrance requirements:* For master's, GRE. Additional exam requirements/recommendations for international students: Required—TOEFL (minimum score 550 paper-based; 213 computer-based; 80 iBT). Electronic applications accepted. *Faculty research:* Floor vibration investigations, earthquake engineering, base isolation systems and seismic risk assessment, infrastructure revitalization (building foundations and damage, bridge structures, highways, and dams), slope stability and soil erosion, pavement rehabilitation, computational fluid dynamics and flood control structures, microbial fuel cells, water treatment and water quality modeling, environmental risk assessment, biotechnology, nanotechnology.

Illinois Institute of Technology, Graduate College, Armour College of Engineering, Department of Civil, Architectural and Environmental Engineering, Chicago, IL 60616-3793. Offers architectural engineering (M Arch E); civil engineering (MS, PhD), including architectural engineering (MS), construction engineering and management (MS), geoenvironmental engineering (MS), geotechnical engineering (MS), structural engineering (MS), transportation engineering (MS); construction engineering and management (MCEM); environmental engineering (M Env E, PhD); geoenvironmental engineering (M Geoenv E); geotechnical engineering (MGE); public works (MPW); structural engineering (MSE); transportation engineering (M Trans E). Part-time and evening/weekend programs available. Postbaccalaureate distance learning degree programs offered (minimal on-campus study). *Faculty:* 15 full-time (1 woman), 13 part-time/adjunct (1 woman). *Students:* 159 full-time (63 women), 109 part-time (22 women); includes 30 minority (9 Black or African American, non-Hispanic/Latino; 16 Asian, non-Hispanic/Latino; 5 Hispanic/Latino), 126 international. Average age 27. 453 applicants, 66% accepted, 98 enrolled. In 2010, 76 master's, 1 doctorate awarded. Terminal master's awarded for partial completion of doctoral program. *Degree requirements:* For master's, thesis (for some programs); for doctorate, comprehensive exam, thesis/dissertation. *Entrance requirements:* For master's, GRE General Test (minimum score 900 Quantitative and Verbal, 2.5 Analytical Writing), minimum undergraduate GPA of 3.0; for doctorate, GRE General Test (minimum score 1000 Quantitative and Verbal, 3.0 Analytical Writing), minimum undergraduate GPA of 3.0. Additional exam requirements/recommendations for international students: Required—TOEFL (minimum score 523 paper-based; 70 iBT); Recommended—IELTS (minimum score 5.5). *Application deadline:* For fall admission, 5/1 for domestic and international students; for spring admission, 10/15 for domestic and international students. Applications are processed on a rolling basis. Application fee: $50. Electronic applications accepted. *Expenses:* Tuition: Full-time $18,576; part-time $1032 per credit hour. Required fees: $583 per semester. One-time fee: $150. Tuition and fees vary according to program and student level. *Financial support:* In 2010–11, 13 research assistantships with full and partial tuition reimbursements (averaging $9,453 per year), 19 teaching assistantships with full and partial tuition reimbursements (averaging $3,163 per year) were awarded; fellowships with full and partial tuition reimbursements, Federal Work-Study, institutionally sponsored loans, scholarships/grants, health care benefits, tuition waivers (partial), and unspecified assistantships also available. Support available to part-time students. Financial award applicants required to submit FAFSA. *Faculty research:* Structural, architectural, geotechnical and geoenvironmental engineering; construction engineering and management; transportation engineering; environmental engineering and public works. Total annual research expenditures: $763,042. *Unit head:* Dr. Jamshid Mohammadi, Professor and Chairman, 312-567-3629, Fax: 312-567-3519, E-mail: mohammadi@iit.edu. *Application contact:* Deborah Gibson, Director, Graduate Admission, 866-472-3448, Fax: 312-567-3138, E-mail: inquiry.grad@iit.edu.

Instituto Tecnológico y de Estudios Superiores de Monterrey, Campus Monterrey, Graduate and Research Division, Programs in Engineering, Monterrey, Mexico. Offers applied statistics (M Eng); artificial intelligence (PhD); automation engineering (M Eng); chemical engineering (M Eng); civil engineering (M Eng); electrical engineering (M Eng); electronic engineering (M Eng); environmental engineering (M Eng); industrial engineering (M Eng, PhD); manufacturing engineering (M Eng); mechanical engineering (M Eng); systems and quality engineering (M Eng). M Eng program offered jointly with University of Waterloo; PhD in industrial engineering with Texas A&M University. Part-time and evening/weekend programs available. Terminal master's awarded for partial completion of doctoral program. *Degree requirements:* For master's, one foreign language, thesis; for doctorate, one foreign language, thesis/dissertation. *Entrance requirements:* For master's, EXADEP; for doctorate, GRE, master's degree in related field. Additional exam requirements/recommendations for international students: Required—TOEFL. *Faculty research:* Flexible manufacturing cells, materials, statistical methods, environmental prevention, control and evaluation.

Iowa State University of Science and Technology, Graduate College, College of Engineering, Department of Civil and Construction Engineering, Ames, IA 50011. Offers civil engineering (MS, PhD), including civil engineering materials, construction engineering and management, environmental engineering, geometronics, geotechnical engineering, structural engineering, transportation engineering. *Faculty:* 35 full-time (6 women), 4 part-time/adjunct (0 women). *Students:* 93 full-time (31 women), 48 part-time (10 women); includes 1 Black or African American, non-Hispanic/Latino; 1 Asian, non-Hispanic/Latino; 4 Hispanic/Latino, 62 international. 179 applicants, 37% accepted, 35 enrolled. In 2010, 32 master's, 9 doctorates awarded. *Degree requirements:* For master's, thesis or alternative; for doctorate, thesis/dissertation. *Entrance requirements:* For master's and doctorate, GRE General Test. Additional exam requirements/recommendations for international students: Required—TOEFL (minimum score 550 paper-based; 82 iBT), IELTS (minimum score 6.5). *Application deadline:* For fall admission, 2/1 priority date for domestic students, 2/1 for international students; for spring admission, 8/1 priority date for domestic students, 8/1 for international students. Application fee: $40 ($90 for international students). Electronic applications accepted. *Financial support:* In 2010–11, 67 research assistantships with full and partial tuition reimbursements (averaging $7,654 per year), 4 teaching assistantships with full and partial tuition reimbursements (averaging $9,525 per year) were awarded; fellowships, scholarships/grants, health care benefits, and unspecified assistantships also available. *Unit head:* Dr. James Alleman, Chair, 515-294-3892, E-mail: ccee-grad-inquiry@iastate.edu. *Application contact:* Dr. Sri Srithanan, Director of Graduate Education, 515-294-5328, E-mail: ccee-grad-inquiry@iastate.edu.

The Johns Hopkins University, Engineering for Professionals, Part-time Program in Civil Engineering, Baltimore, MD 21218-2699. Offers MCE. Part-time and evening/weekend programs available. *Faculty:* 3 part-time/adjunct (1 woman). *Students:* 19 part-time (6 women); includes

Civil Engineering

The Johns Hopkins University (continued)
4 minority (2 Black or African American, non-Hispanic/Latino; 1 Asian, non-Hispanic/Latino; 1 Two or more races, non-Hispanic/Latino), 2 international. Average age 26. 5 applicants, 60% accepted, 1 enrolled. In 2010, 7 master's awarded. *Application deadline:* Applications are processed on a rolling basis. Application fee: $75. Electronic applications accepted. *Financial support:* Institutionally sponsored loans available. *Unit head:* Dr. A. Rajah Anandarajah, Chair, 410-516-8682, E-mail: rajah@jhu.edu. *Application contact:* Priyanka Dwivedi, Admissions Manager, 410-516-2300, Fax: 410-579-8049, E-mail: pdwived1@jhu.edu.

The Johns Hopkins University, G. W. C. Whiting School of Engineering, Department of Civil Engineering, Baltimore, MD 21218. Offers MCE, MSE, PhD. *Faculty:* 11 full-time (3 women), 3 part-time/adjunct (0 women). *Students:* 34 full-time (9 women); includes 2 minority (1 Asian, non-Hispanic/Latino; 1 Two or more races, non-Hispanic/Latino), 25 international. Average age 27. 90 applicants, 41% accepted, 10 enrolled. In 2010, 7 master's, 1 doctorate awarded. Terminal master's awarded for partial completion of doctoral program. *Degree requirements:* For master's, thesis (for some programs); for doctorate, comprehensive exam, thesis/dissertation, qualifying and oral exams. *Entrance requirements:* For master's and doctorate, GRE General Test. Additional exam requirements/recommendations for international students: Required—TOEFL. *Application deadline:* For fall admission, 2/15 for domestic and international students. Application fee: $25. Electronic applications accepted. *Financial support:* In 2010–11, 5 fellowships with full tuition reimbursements (averaging $25,272 per year), 20 research assistantships with full tuition reimbursements (averaging $21,456 per year) were awarded; teaching assistantships with tuition reimbursements, scholarships/grants, health care benefits, tuition waivers (partial), and unspecified assistantships also available. Financial award application deadline: 2/1. *Faculty research:* Geotechnical engineering, structural engineering, structural mechanics, geomechanics, probabilistic modeling. Total annual research expenditures: $1.4 million. *Unit head:* Prof. Benjamin Schafer, Chair, 410-516-6265, E-mail: schafer@jhu.edu. *Application contact:* Lisa Wetzelberger, Academic Coordinator, 410-516-8680, Fax: 410-516-7473, E-mail: lawetzel@jhu.edu.

Kansas State University, Graduate School, College of Engineering, Department of Civil Engineering, Manhattan, KS 66506. Offers MS, PhD. Postbaccalaureate distance learning degree programs offered (no on-campus study). *Degree requirements:* For master's, thesis or alternative; for doctorate, thesis/dissertation. *Entrance requirements:* For master's, GRE General Test, bachelor's degree or course work in civil engineering; for doctorate, GRE General Test. Additional exam requirements/recommendations for international students: Required—TOEFL. Electronic applications accepted. *Faculty research:* Transportation and materials engineering, water resources engineering, environmental engineering, geotechnical engineering, structural engineering.

Lamar University, College of Graduate Studies, College of Engineering, Department of Civil Engineering, Beaumont, TX 77710. Offers civil engineering (ME, MES, DE); environmental engineering (MS); environmental studies (MS). Part-time programs available. *Faculty:* 5 full-time (1 woman), 1 part-time/adjunct (0 women). *Students:* 31 full-time (6 women), 18 part-time (7 women); includes 1 Black or African American, non-Hispanic/Latino; 3 Asian, non-Hispanic/Latino, 28 international. Average age 29. 37 applicants, 65% accepted, 7 enrolled. In 2010, 42 master's, 1 doctorate awarded. *Degree requirements:* For master's, thesis optional; for doctorate, thesis/dissertation. *Entrance requirements:* For master's and doctorate, GRE General Test. Additional exam requirements/recommendations for international students: Required—TOEFL. *Application deadline:* For fall admission, 5/15 priority date for domestic students; for spring admission, 10/1 priority date for domestic students. Applications are processed on a rolling basis. Application fee: $25 ($50 for international students). *Expenses:* Tuition, state resident: full-time $4160; part-time $208 per credit hour. Tuition, nonresident: full-time $10,360; part-time $518 per credit hour. *Financial support:* In 2010–11, 45 fellowships with partial tuition reimbursements (averaging $1,000 per year), 10 research assistantships with partial tuition reimbursements (averaging $7,200 per year), 3 teaching assistantships with partial tuition reimbursements (averaging $7,200 per year) were awarded; scholarships/grants and tuition waivers (partial) also available. Financial award application deadline: 4/1. *Faculty research:* Environmental remediations, construction productivity, geotechnical soil stabilization, lake/reservoir hydrodynamics, air pollution. *Unit head:* Dr. Enno Koehn, Chair, 409-880-8759, Fax: 409-880-8121, E-mail: koehneu@hal.lamar.edu. *Application contact:* Sandy Drane, Coordinator of Graduate Admissions, 409-880-8356, Fax: 409-880-8414, E-mail: gradmissions@hal.lamar.edu.

Lawrence Technological University, College of Engineering, Southfield, MI 48075-1058. Offers architectural engineering (MS); automotive engineering (MS); civil engineering (MS); electrical and computer engineering (MS); engineering management (MEM); industrial engineering (MS); manufacturing systems (ME, DE); mechanical engineering (MS); mechatronic systems engineering (MS). Part-time and evening/weekend programs available. *Faculty:* 20 full-time (4 women), 12 part-time/adjunct (0 women). *Students:* 8 full-time (1 woman), 366 part-time (60 women); includes 29 Black or African American, non-Hispanic/Latino; 1 American Indian or Alaska Native, non-Hispanic/Latino; 36 Asian, non-Hispanic/Latino; 9 Hispanic/Latino; 4 Two or more races, non-Hispanic/Latino, 81 international. Average age 32. 398 applicants, 48% accepted, 87 enrolled. In 2010, 121 master's, 5 doctorates awarded. *Degree requirements:* For master's, thesis (for some programs). *Entrance requirements:* Additional exam requirements/recommendations for international students: Required—TOEFL (minimum score 550 paper-based; 213 computer-based; 79 iBT). *Application deadline:* For fall admission, 6/30 priority date for domestic students, 6/30 for international students; for spring admission, 11/15 priority date for domestic students, 11/15 for international students. Applications are processed on a rolling basis. Application fee: $50. Electronic applications accepted. *Financial support:* In 2010–11, 72 students received support. Federal Work-Study and institutionally sponsored loans available. Support available to part-time students. Financial award application deadline: 4/1; financial award applicants required to submit FAFSA. *Faculty research:* Advanced composite materials in bridges, strengthening existing bridges with carbon and glass fiber sheets, development of drive shafts using composite materials. *Unit head:* Dr. Nabil Grace, Interim Dean, 248-204-2500, Fax: 248-204-2509, E-mail: engrdean@ltu.edu. *Application contact:* Jane Rohrback, Director of Admissions, 248-204-3160, Fax: 248-204-2228, E-mail: admissions@ltu.edu.

Lehigh University, P.C. Rossin College of Engineering and Applied Science, Department of Civil and Environmental Engineering, Bethlehem, PA 18015. Offers civil engineering (M Eng, MS, PhD); environmental engineering (MS, PhD); structural engineering (M Eng, MS, PhD). Part-time programs available. *Faculty:* 15 full-time (3 women), 1 (woman) part-time/adjunct. *Students:* 107 full-time (33 women), 9 part-time (0 women); includes 8 minority (4 Black or African American, non-Hispanic/Latino; 1 Asian, non-Hispanic/Latino; 2 Hispanic/Latino; 1 Native Hawaiian or other Pacific Islander, non-Hispanic/Latino), 59 international. Average age 26. 270 applicants, 50% accepted, 65 enrolled. In 2010, 23 master's, 1 doctorate awarded. Terminal master's awarded for partial completion of doctoral program. *Median time to degree:* Of those who began their doctoral program in fall 2002, 100% received their degree in 8 years or less. *Degree requirements:* For master's, thesis (for some programs); for doctorate, comprehensive exam, thesis/dissertation. *Entrance requirements:* For master's and doctorate, GRE. Additional exam requirements/recommendations for international students: Required—TOEFL (minimum score 550 paper-based; 213 computer-based; 79 iBT). *Application deadline:* For fall admission, 7/15 priority date for domestic and international students; for spring admission, 12/1 priority date for domestic and international students. Applications are processed on a rolling basis. Application fee: $75. Electronic applications accepted. *Expenses:* Contact institution. *Financial support:* In 2010–11, 31 students received support, including 5 fellowships with full tuition reimbursements available (averaging $17,460 per year), 4 research assistantships with full tuition reimbursements available (averaging $22,350 per year), 7 teaching assistantships with full tuition reimbursements available (averaging $17,460 per year); institutionally sponsored loans, scholarships/grants, tuition waivers, and unspecified assistantships also available. Financial award application deadline: 1/15. *Faculty research:* Structural engineering, geotechnical engineering, water resources engineering, environmental engineering. Total annual research expenditures: $6.8 million. *Unit head:* Dr. Stephen Pessiki, Chairman, 610-758-3494, Fax: 610-758-6405, E-mail: pessiki@lehigh.edu. *Application contact:* Prisca Vidanage, Graduate Coordinator, 610-758-3530, Fax: 610-758-6405, E-mail: pmv1@lehigh.edu.

Louisiana State University and Agricultural and Mechanical College, Graduate School, College of Engineering, Department of Civil and Environmental Engineering, Baton Rouge, LA 70803. Offers environmental engineering (MSCE, PhD); geotechnical engineering (MSCE, PhD); structural engineering and mechanics (MSCE, PhD); transportation engineering (MSCE, PhD); water resources (MSCE, PhD). Part-time programs available. *Faculty:* 29 full-time (3 women). *Students:* 89 full-time (19 women), 35 part-time (8 women); includes 2 Black or African American, non-Hispanic/Latino; 1 American Indian or Alaska Native, non-Hispanic/Latino; 3 Asian, non-Hispanic/Latino; 3 Hispanic/Latino, 65 international. Average age 29. 96 applicants, 65% accepted, 16 enrolled. In 2010, 20 master's, 8 doctorates awarded. *Degree requirements:* For master's, thesis optional; for doctorate, one foreign language, thesis/dissertation. *Entrance requirements:* For master's and doctorate, GRE General Test, minimum GPA of 3.0. Additional exam requirements/recommendations for international students: Required—TOEFL (minimum score 550 paper-based; 213 computer-based; 79 iBT) or IELTS (minimum score 6.5). *Application deadline:* For fall admission, 1/25 priority date for domestic students, 5/15 for international students; for spring admission, 10/15 for international students. Applications are processed on a rolling basis. Application fee: $50 ($70 for international students). Electronic applications accepted. *Financial support:* In 2010–11, 89 students received support, including 2 fellowships with full and partial tuition reimbursements available (averaging $24,418 per year), 75 research assistantships with full and partial tuition reimbursements available (averaging $16,115 per year), 3 teaching assistantships with full and partial tuition reimbursements available (averaging $12,843 per year); career-related internships or fieldwork, institutionally sponsored loans, scholarships/grants, and health care benefits also available. Financial award application deadline: 3/1; financial award applicants required to submit FAFSA. *Faculty research:* Mechanics and structures, environmental, geotechnical transportation, water resources. Total annual research expenditures: $2.6 million. *Unit head:* Dr. George Z. Voyiadjis, Chair/Professor, 225-578-8668, Fax: 225-578-9176, E-mail: cegzv@lsu.edu. *Application contact:* Dr. Clinton Willson, Professor, 225-578-8652, E-mail: cwillson@lsu.edu.

Louisiana Tech University, Graduate School, College of Engineering and Science, Department of Civil Engineering, Ruston, LA 71272. Offers MS, PhD. Part-time programs available. Terminal master's awarded for partial completion of doctoral program. *Degree requirements:* For master's, thesis or alternative; for doctorate, thesis/dissertation. *Entrance requirements:* For master's, GRE General Test, minimum GPA of 3.0 in last 60 hours; for doctorate, minimum graduate GPA of 3.25 (with MS) or GRE General Test. Additional exam requirements/recommendations for international students: Required—TOEFL. *Faculty research:* Environmental engineering, trenchless excavation construction, structural mechanics, transportation materials and planning, water quality modeling.

Loyola Marymount University, College of Science and Engineering, Department of Civil Engineering and Environmental Science, Program in Civil Engineering, Los Angeles, CA 90045. Offers MSE. Part-time programs available. *Faculty:* 6 full-time (1 woman), 4 part-time/adjunct (0 women). *Students:* 5 full-time (2 women), 16 part-time (4 women); includes 3 Black or African American, non-Hispanic/Latino; 3 Asian, non-Hispanic/Latino; 7 Hispanic/Latino; 2 Two or more races, non-Hispanic/Latino, 2 international. Average age 31. 6 applicants, 83% accepted, 3 enrolled. In 2010, 4 master's awarded. *Degree requirements:* For master's, comprehensive exam. *Entrance requirements:* For master's, 2 letters of recommendation; BS or undergraduate engineering degree; 3 semester hours of general chemistry; course work in mathematics through one year of college calculus; 12 semester hours or 4 courses in science including biology, microbiology, chemistry, or physics. Additional exam requirements/recommendations for international students: Required—TOEFL (minimum score 550 paper-based; 213 computer-based; 80 iBT). *Application deadline:* Applications are processed on a rolling basis. Application fee: $50. Electronic applications accepted. *Financial support:* In 2010–11, 7 students received support. Scholarships/grants and laboratory assistantships available. Support available to part-time students. Financial award application deadline: 6/1; financial award applicants required to submit FAFSA. Total annual research expenditures: $6,004. *Unit head:* Prof. Joe Reichenberger, Graduate Director, 310-338-2830, E-mail: jreichenberger@lmu.edu. *Application contact:* Chake H. Kouyoumjian, Associate Dean of Graduate Studies, 310-338-2721, Fax: 310-338-6086, E-mail: ckouyoum@lmu.edu.

Manhattan College, Graduate Division, School of Engineering, Program in Civil Engineering, Riverdale, NY 10471. Offers MS. Part-time and evening/weekend programs available. *Faculty:* 6 full-time (0 women), 7 part-time/adjunct (0 women). *Students:* 5 full-time (2 women), 54 part-time (15 women); includes 3 Black or African American, non-Hispanic/Latino; 5 Hispanic/Latino; 2 Two or more races, non-Hispanic/Latino. Average age 25. 40 applicants, 80% accepted, 24 enrolled. In 2010, 10 master's awarded. *Degree requirements:* For master's, thesis or alternative. *Entrance requirements:* For master's, GRE (recommended), minimum GPA of 3.0. Additional exam requirements/recommendations for international students: Required—TOEFL (minimum score 550 paper-based; 213 computer-based; 80 iBT), IELTS (minimum score 6). *Application deadline:* For fall admission, 8/10 priority date for domestic students, 8/10 for international students; for spring admission, 1/7 for domestic and international students. Applications are processed on a rolling basis. Application fee: $50. Electronic applications accepted. *Financial support:* In 2010–11, 2 students received support; fellowships with partial tuition reimbursements available, research assistantships with full and partial tuition reimbursements available, career-related internships or fieldwork, Federal Work-Study, scholarships/grants, and laboratory assistantships available. Support available to part-time students. Financial award application deadline: 2/1. *Faculty research:* Compressible-inclusion function for geofoams used with rigid walls under static loading, validation of sediment criteria. *Unit head:* Dr. Moujalli Hourani, Chair, 718-862-7171, Fax: 718-862-8035, E-mail: moujalli.hourani@manhattan.edu. *Application contact:* Janet Horgan, Information Contact, 718-862-7171, Fax: 718-862-8035, E-mail: civildept@manhattan.edu.

Marquette University, Graduate School, College of Engineering, Department of Civil and Environmental Engineering, Milwaukee, WI 53201-1881. Offers construction and public works management (MS, PhD); construction engineering and management (Certificate); environmental/water resources engineering (MS, PhD); structural design (Certificate); structural/geotechnical engineering (MS, PhD); transportation planning and engineering (MS, PhD); waste and wastewater treatment processes (Certificate). Part-time and evening/weekend programs available. *Faculty:* 13 full-time (0 women), 3 part-time/adjunct (0 women). *Students:* 20 full-time (4 women), 12 part-time (1 woman); includes 1 minority (Black or African American, non-Hispanic/Latino), 12 international. Average age 27. 66 applicants, 64% accepted, 9 enrolled. In 2010, 8 master's, 1 doctorate awarded. Terminal master's awarded for partial completion of doctoral program. *Degree requirements:* For master's, comprehensive exam, thesis or alternative; for doctorate, thesis/dissertation. *Entrance requirements:* For master's, GRE General Test (recommended), minimum GPA of 3.0, official transcripts from all current and previous colleges/universities except Marquette, three letters of recommendation; for doctorate, GRE General Test, minimum GPA of 3.0, official transcripts from all current and previous colleges/universities except Marquette, three letters of recommendation, brief statement of purpose, submission of any English-language publications authored by applicant (strongly recommended). Additional exam requirements/recommendations for international students: Required—TOEFL (minimum score 530 paper-based; 78 computer-based). *Application deadline:* For fall admission, 6/1 priority date for domestic students. Applications are processed on a rolling basis. Application fee: $50. Electronic applications accepted. *Expenses:* Tuition: Full-time $16,290; part-time $905 per credit hour. Tuition and fees vary according to program. *Financial support:* In 2010–11, 13 students received support, including 4 fellowships with tuition reimbursements available, 4 research assistantships with tuition reimbursements available, 10 teaching assistantships with tuition reimbursements available; Federal Work-Study, institutionally sponsored loans, scholarships/grants, and tuition waivers (full and partial) also available. Support available to part-time students. Financial award application deadline: 2/15. *Faculty research:* Highway safety, highway performance, and intelligent transportation systems; surface mount technology;

watershed management. Total annual research expenditures: $662,392. *Unit head:* Dr. Thomas Wenzel, Chair, 414-288-7030, Fax: 414-288-7521, E-mail: thomas.wenzel@marquette.edu. *Application contact:* Dr. Stephen M. Heinrich, Director of Graduate Studies, 414-288-5466, E-mail: stephen.heinrich@marquette.edu.

Massachusetts Institute of Technology, School of Engineering, Department of Civil and Environmental Engineering, Cambridge, MA 02139. Offers biological oceanography (PhD, Sc D); chemical oceanography (PhD, Sc D); civil and environmental engineering (M Eng, SM, PhD, Sc D); civil and environmental systems (PhD, Sc D); civil engineering (PhD, Sc D, CE); coastal engineering (PhD, Sc D); construction engineering and management (PhD, Sc D); environmental biology (PhD, Sc D); environmental chemistry (PhD, Sc D); environmental engineering (PhD, Sc D); environmental fluid mechanics (PhD, Sc D); geotechnical and geoenvironmental engineering (PhD, Sc D); hydrology (PhD, Sc D); information technology (PhD, Sc D); oceanographic engineering (PhD, Sc D); structures and materials (PhD, Sc D); transportation (PhD, Sc D); SM/MBA. *Faculty:* 36 full-time (6 women). *Students:* 181 full-time (56 women); includes 27 minority (3 Black or African American, non-Hispanic/Latino; 10 Asian, non-Hispanic/Latino; 10 Hispanic/Latino; 4 Two or more races, non-Hispanic/Latino), 93 international. Average age 26. 525 applicants, 29% accepted, 74 enrolled. In 2010, 85 master's, 18 doctorates, 2 other advanced degrees awarded. *Degree requirements:* For master's and CE, thesis; for doctorate, comprehensive exam, thesis/dissertation. *Entrance requirements:* For master's and doctorate, GRE General Test. Additional exam requirements/recommendations for international students: Required—TOEFL (minimum score 577 paper-based; 233 computer-based; 90 iBT), IELTS (minimum score 7). *Application deadline:* For fall admission, 1/2 for domestic and international students. Application fee: $75. Electronic applications accepted. *Expenses:* Tuition: Full-time $38,940; part-time $605 per unit. Required fees: $272. *Financial support:* In 2010–11, 146 students received support, including 50 fellowships with tuition reimbursements available (averaging $21,808 per year), 90 research assistantships with tuition reimbursements available (averaging $28,452 per year), 20 teaching assistantships with tuition reimbursements available (averaging $27,842 per year); career-related internships or fieldwork, Federal Work-Study, institutionally sponsored loans, scholarships/grants, health care benefits, and unspecified assistantships also available. *Faculty research:* Environmental chemistry; environmental microbiology; environmental fluid mechanics and coastal engineering; geotechnical engineering and geomechanics; hydrology and hydroclimatology; mechanics of materials and structures; operations research/supply chain; transportation. Total annual research expenditures: $19.5 million. *Unit head:* Prof. Andrew Whittle, Department Head, 617-253-7101. *Application contact:* Patricia Glidden, Graduate Admissions Coordinator, 617-253-7119, Fax: 617-258-6775, E-mail: cee-admissions@mit.edu.

McGill University, Faculty of Graduate and Postdoctoral Studies, Faculty of Engineering, Department of Civil Engineering and Applied Mechanics, Montréal, QC H3A 2T5, Canada. Offers environmental engineering (M Eng, M Sc, PhD); fluid mechanics (M Sc); fluid mechanics and hydraulic engineering (M Eng, PhD); materials engineering (M Eng, PhD); rehabilitation of urban infrastructure (M Eng, PhD); soil behavior (M Eng, PhD); soil mechanics and foundations (M Eng, PhD); structures and structural mechanics (M Eng, PhD); water resources (M Sc); water resources engineering (M Eng, PhD).

McMaster University, School of Graduate Studies, Faculty of Engineering, Department of Civil Engineering, Hamilton, ON L8S 4M2, Canada. Offers M Eng, MA Sc, PhD. *Degree requirements:* For master's, thesis; for doctorate, comprehensive exam, thesis/dissertation. *Entrance requirements:* Additional exam requirements/recommendations for international students: Required—TOEFL (minimum score 550 paper-based; 213 computer-based). *Faculty research:* Building science, environmental hydrology, bolted steel connections, research on highway materials, earthquake engineering.

McNeese State University, Doré School of Graduate Studies, College of Engineering and Engineering Technology, Lake Charles, LA 70609. Offers chemical engineering (M Eng); civil engineering (M Eng); electrical engineering (M Eng); engineering management (M Eng); mechanical engineering (M Eng). Part-time and evening/weekend programs available. *Faculty:* 15 full-time (1 woman). *Students:* 37 full-time (10 women), 18 part-time (1 woman); includes 5 minority (3 Black or African American, non-Hispanic/Latino; 1 American Indian or Alaska Native, non-Hispanic/Latino; 1 Two or more races, non-Hispanic/Latino), 43 international. In 2010, 28 master's awarded. *Degree requirements:* For master's, thesis or alternative. *Entrance requirements:* For master's, GRE, minimum undergraduate GPA of 3.0. Additional exam requirements/recommendations for international students: Required—TOEFL (minimum score 560 paper-based; 220 computer-based; 83 iBT). *Application deadline:* For fall admission, 5/15 priority date for domestic and international students; for spring admission, 10/15 priority date for domestic and international students. Applications are processed on a rolling basis. Application fee: $20 ($30 for international students). Tuition and fees vary according to course load. *Financial support:* Federal Work-Study available. Support available to part-time students. Financial award application deadline: 5/1. *Unit head:* Dr. Nikos Kiritsis, Dean, 337-475-5875, Fax: 337-475-5237, E-mail: nikosk@mcneese.edu.

Memorial University of Newfoundland, School of Graduate Studies, Faculty of Engineering and Applied Science, St. John's, NL A1C 5S7, Canada. Offers civil engineering (M Eng, PhD); electrical and computer engineering (M Eng, PhD); mechanical engineering (M Eng, PhD); ocean and naval architecture engineering (M Eng, PhD). Part-time programs available. *Degree requirements:* For master's, thesis; for doctorate, comprehensive exam, thesis/dissertation, oral thesis defense. *Entrance requirements:* For master's, 2nd class degree; for doctorate, master's degree in engineering. Electronic applications accepted. *Faculty research:* Engineering analysis, environmental and hydrotechnical studies, manufacturing and robotics, mechanics, structures and materials.

Michigan State University, The Graduate School, College of Engineering, Department of Civil and Environmental Engineering, East Lansing, MI 48824. Offers civil engineering (MS, PhD); environmental engineering (MS, PhD); environmental engineering-environmental toxicology (PhD). Part-time programs available. *Entrance requirements:* Additional exam requirements/recommendations for international students: Required—TOEFL. Electronic applications accepted.

Michigan Technological University, Graduate School, College of Engineering, Department of Civil and Environmental Engineering, Program in Civil Engineering, Houghton, MI 49931. Offers ME, MS, PhD. Part-time programs available. Terminal master's awarded for partial completion of doctoral program. *Degree requirements:* For master's, comprehensive exam (for some programs), thesis (for some programs); for doctorate, comprehensive exam, thesis/dissertation. *Entrance requirements:* For master's, GRE (to be considered for university assistantship); for doctorate, GRE. Additional exam requirements/recommendations for international students: Required—TOEFL (minimum score 600 paper-based; 250 computer-based). Electronic applications accepted. *Expenses:* Contact institution.

Milwaukee School of Engineering, Civil and Architectural Engineering and Construction Management Department, Program in Civil Engineering, Milwaukee, WI 53202-3109. Offers MS. Five-year freshman-to-master's degree program. *Expenses:* Tuition: Full-time $17,550; part-time $650 per credit. One-time fee: $75. *Unit head:* Dr. Francis Mahuta, Director, 414-277-7599. *Application contact:* David E. Tietyen, Graduate Admissions Director, 800-332-6763, Fax: 414-277-7475, E-mail: wp@msoe.edu.

Mississippi State University, Bagley College of Engineering, Department of Civil and Environmental Engineering, Mississippi State, MS 39762. Offers civil engineering (MS); engineering (PhD), including civil engineering. Part-time programs available. Postbaccalaureate distance learning degree programs offered (no on-campus study). *Faculty:* 9 full-time (0 women), 2 part-time/adjunct (0 women). *Students:* 25 full-time (8 women), 39 part-time (6 women); includes 8 minority (4 Black or African American, non-Hispanic/Latino; 1 Asian, non-Hispanic/Latino; 3 Hispanic/Latino), 12 international. Average age 29. 40 applicants, 38% accepted, 10 enrolled. In 2010, 20 master's, 4 doctorates awarded. Terminal master's awarded for partial completion of doctoral program. *Degree requirements:* For master's, thesis (for some programs); for doctorate, thesis/dissertation, research on an approved topic. *Entrance requirements:* For master's and doctorate, GRE, minimum GPA of 3.0. Additional exam requirements/recommendations for international students: Required—TOEFL (minimum score 550 paper-based; 213 computer-based; 79 iBT); Recommended—IELTS (minimum score 6.5). *Application deadline:* For fall admission, 7/1 for domestic students, 5/1 for international students; for spring admission, 11/1 for domestic students, 9/1 for international students. Applications are processed on a rolling basis. Application fee: $40. Electronic applications accepted. *Expenses:* Tuition, state resident: full-time $2730.50; part-time $304 per credit hour. Tuition, nonresident: full-time $6901; part-time $767 per credit hour. *Financial support:* In 2010–11, 10 research assistantships with full tuition reimbursements (averaging $13,203 per year), 2 teaching assistantships with full tuition reimbursements (averaging $10,798 per year) were awarded; Federal Work-Study, institutionally sponsored loans, and unspecified assistantships also available. Financial award application deadline: 4/1; financial award applicants required to submit FAFSA. *Faculty research:* Transportation, water modeling, construction materials, structures. Total annual research expenditures: $5.8 million. *Unit head:* Dr. Dennis D. Truax, Department Head, 662-325-7187, Fax: 662-325-7189, E-mail: truax@cee.msstate.edu. *Application contact:* Dr. James L. Martin, Professor and Graduate Coordinator, 662-325-7194, Fax: 662-325-7189, E-mail: jmartin@cee.msstate.edu.

Missouri University of Science and Technology, Graduate School, Department of Civil, Architectural, and Environmental Engineering, Rolla, MO 65409. Offers civil engineering (MS, DE, PhD); construction engineering (MS, DE, PhD); environmental engineering (MS); fluid mechanics (MS, DE, PhD); geotechnical engineering (MS, DE, PhD); hydrology and hydraulic engineering (MS, DE, PhD). Part-time and evening/weekend programs available. Terminal master's awarded for partial completion of doctoral program. *Degree requirements:* For master's, thesis optional; for doctorate, comprehensive exam, thesis/dissertation. *Entrance requirements:* For master's, GRE General Test (minimum combined score 1100), minimum GPA of 3.0; for doctorate, GRE General Test (minimum score: verbal and quantitative 400, writing 3.5), minimum GPA of 3.0. Additional exam requirements/recommendations for international students: Required—TOEFL. Electronic applications accepted. *Faculty research:* Earthquake engineering, structural optimization and control systems, structural health monitoring/damage detection, soil-structure interaction, soil mechanics and foundation engineering.

Montana State University, College of Graduate Studies, College of Engineering, Department of Civil Engineering, Bozeman, MT 59717. Offers civil engineering (MS); construction engineering management (MCEM); engineering (PhD), including applied mechanics option, civil engineering option. Part-time programs available. *Faculty:* 19 full-time (2 women), 5 part-time/adjunct (1 woman). *Students:* 26 full-time (6 women), 21 part-time (6 women); includes 2 minority (1 American Indian or Alaska Native, non-Hispanic/Latino; 1 Two or more races, non-Hispanic/Latino), 1 international. Average age 27. 43 applicants, 44% accepted, 17 enrolled. In 2010, 15 master's, 1 doctorate awarded. *Degree requirements:* For master's, comprehensive exam, thesis (for some programs); for doctorate, comprehensive exam, thesis/dissertation. *Entrance requirements:* For master's and doctorate, GRE General Test. Additional exam requirements/recommendations for international students: Required—TOEFL (minimum score 550 paper-based; 213 computer-based). *Application deadline:* For fall admission, 7/15 priority date for domestic students, 5/15 priority date for international students; for spring admission, 12/1 priority date for domestic students, 10/1 priority date for international students. Applications are processed on a rolling basis. Application fee: $30. Electronic applications accepted. *Expenses:* Tuition, state resident: full-time $5553.90. Tuition, nonresident: full-time $14,646. Required fees: $1233. *Financial support:* In 2010–11, 20 students received support, including 1 fellowship (averaging $15,000 per year), 5 research assistantships with partial tuition reimbursements available (averaging $12,000 per year), 6 teaching assistantships with partial tuition reimbursements available (averaging $8,000 per year); scholarships/grants and tuition waivers (partial) also available. Financial award application deadline: 3/1; financial award applicants required to submit FAFSA. *Faculty research:* Snow and ice mechanics, biofilm engineering, transportation, structural and geo materials, water resources. Total annual research expenditures: $54,392. *Unit head:* Dr. Brett Gunnick, Head, 406-994-2111, Fax: 406-994-6105, E-mail: bgunnick@ce.montana.edu. *Application contact:* Dr. Carl A. Fox, Vice Provost for Graduate Education, 406-994-4145, Fax: 406-994-7433, E-mail: gradstudy@montana.edu.

Morgan State University, School of Graduate Studies, Clarence M. Mitchell, Jr. School of Engineering, Baltimore, MD 21251. Offers civil engineering (M Eng, D Eng); electrical engineering (M Eng, D Eng); industrial engineering (M Eng, D Eng); transportation (MS). Part-time and evening/weekend programs available. *Degree requirements:* For master's, thesis, comprehensive exam or equivalent; for doctorate, thesis/dissertation, comprehensive exam or equivalent. *Entrance requirements:* For master's, GRE, minimum undergraduate GPA of 2.5; for doctorate, GRE, minimum GPA of 3.0. Additional exam requirements/recommendations for international students: Required—TOEFL (minimum score 550 paper-based; 213 computer-based).

New Jersey Institute of Technology, Office of Graduate Studies, Newark College of Engineering, Department of Civil and Environmental Engineering, Program in Civil Engineering, Newark, NJ 07102. Offers MS, PhD. Part-time and evening/weekend programs available. *Students:* 62 full-time (18 women), 93 part-time (22 women); includes 16 Black or African American, non-Hispanic/Latino; 1 American Indian or Alaska Native, non-Hispanic/Latino; 23 Asian, non-Hispanic/Latino; 20 Hispanic/Latino, 28 international. Average age 29. 182 applicants, 43% accepted, 50 enrolled. In 2010, 39 master's, 4 doctorates awarded. Terminal master's awarded for partial completion of doctoral program. *Degree requirements:* For master's, thesis optional; for doctorate, thesis/dissertation. *Entrance requirements:* For master's and doctorate, GRE General Test. Additional exam requirements/recommendations for international students: Required—TOEFL (minimum score 550 paper-based; 213 computer-based; 79 iBT). *Application deadline:* For fall admission, 6/5 priority date for domestic students, 4/1 for international students; for spring admission, 11/15 for domestic and international students. Applications are processed on a rolling basis. Application fee: $65. Electronic applications accepted. *Expenses:* Tuition, state resident: full-time $14,724; part-time $818 per credit. Tuition, nonresident: full-time $20,304; part-time $1128 per credit. Required fees: $2272; $209 per credit. $103 per semester. One-time fee: $312 full-time; $212 part-time. *Financial support:* Fellowships with full and partial tuition reimbursements, research assistantships with full and partial tuition reimbursements, teaching assistantships with full and partial tuition reimbursements, career-related internships or fieldwork, Federal Work-Study, institutionally sponsored loans, and unspecified assistantships available. Financial award application deadline: 3/15. *Unit head:* Dr. Taha Marhaba, Chair, 973-642-4599, E-mail: taha.f.marhaba@njit.edu. *Application contact:* Kathryn Kelly, Director of Admissions, 973-596-3300, Fax: 973-596-3461, E-mail: admissions@njit.edu.

New Mexico State University, Graduate School, College of Engineering, Department of Civil Engineering, Las Cruces, NM 88003-8001. Offers civil engineering (MSCE, PhD); environmental engineering (MS Env E). Part-time programs available. Postbaccalaureate distance learning degree programs offered. *Faculty:* 13 full-time (2 women), 2 part-time/adjunct (1 woman). *Students:* 52 full-time (17 women), 16 part-time (4 women); includes 18 minority (1 American Indian or Alaska Native, non-Hispanic/Latino; 1 Asian, non-Hispanic/Latino; 16 Hispanic/Latino), 30 international. Average age 30. 52 applicants, 77% accepted, 15 enrolled. In 2010, 24 master's, 4 doctorates awarded. *Degree requirements:* For master's, thesis (for some programs); for doctorate, comprehensive exam (for some programs), thesis/dissertation. *Entrance requirements:* For master's, BS in engineering, minimum GPA of 3.0; for doctorate, qualifying exam, BS in engineering, minimum GPA of 3.0. Additional exam requirements/recommendations for international students: Required—TOEFL (minimum score 550 paper-based; 213 computer-based; 79 iBT), IELTS (minimum score 6). *Application deadline:* For fall admission, 4/1 priority date for domestic and international students; for spring admission, 9/1 priority date for domestic and international students. Applications are processed on a rolling basis. Application fee: $30 ($50 for international students). Electronic applications accepted. *Expenses:* Tuition, state resident: full-time $4536; part-time $242 per credit. Tuition, nonresident: full-time $15,816; part-time $712 per credit. Required fees: $636 per term. *Financial support:* In 2010–11, 13 research assistantships (averaging $12,766 per year), 32 teaching assistant-

Civil Engineering

New Mexico State University (continued)

ships (averaging $1,095 per year) were awarded; fellowships, career-related internships or fieldwork, Federal Work-Study, and health care benefits also available. Support available to part-time students. Financial award application deadline: 3/1. *Faculty research:* Structural engineering, water resources engineering, environmental engineering, geotechnical engineering, hydraulics/hydrology. *Unit head:* Dr. Adrian Hanson, Interim Head, 575-646-3801, E-mail: athanson@nmsu.edu. *Application contact:* Dr. Adrian Hanson, Interim Head, 575-646-3801, E-mail: athanson@nmsu.edu.

North Carolina Agricultural and Technical State University, Graduate School, College of Engineering, Department of Civil, Architectural, Agricultural, Environmental, and Geomatics Engineering, Greensboro, NC 27411. Offers civil engineering (MSCE). Part-time programs available. *Degree requirements:* For master's, thesis defense. *Entrance requirements:* For master's, GRE General Test, GRE Subject Test (recommended). Additional exam requirements/recommendations for international students: Required—TOEFL (MSCE). *Faculty research:* Lightning, indoor air quality, material behavior HVAC controls, structural masonry systems.

North Carolina State University, Graduate School, College of Engineering, Department of Civil, Construction, and Environmental Engineering, Raleigh, NC 27695. Offers civil engineering (MCE, MS, PhD). Part-time programs available. Postbaccalaureate distance learning degree programs offered. *Degree requirements:* For master's, thesis optional, oral exams; for doctorate, thesis/dissertation, oral exams. *Entrance requirements:* For master's, GRE General Test, minimum B average in major; for doctorate, GRE General Test. Additional exam requirements/recommendations for international students: Required—TOEFL. Electronic applications accepted. *Faculty research:* Materials; systems, environmental, geotechnical, structural, transportation and water rescue engineering.

North Dakota State University, College of Graduate and Interdisciplinary Studies, College of Engineering and Architecture, Department of Civil Engineering, Fargo, ND 58108. Offers civil engineering (MS, PhD); environmental engineering (MS, PhD); transportation and logistics (PhD). PhD in transportation and logistics offered jointly with Upper Great Plains Transportation Institute. Part-time programs available. Postbaccalaureate distance learning degree programs offered (minimal on-campus study). *Students:* 28 full-time (2 women), 19 part-time (3 women); includes 1 American Indian or Alaska Native, non-Hispanic/Latino, 24 international. 37 applicants, 57% accepted, 12 enrolled. In 2010, 1 master's, 3 doctorates awarded. *Degree requirements:* For master's, thesis; for doctorate, comprehensive exam, thesis/dissertation. *Entrance requirements:* Additional exam requirements/recommendations for international students: Required—TOEFL (minimum score 525 paper-based; 197 computer-based; 71 iBT). *Application deadline:* For fall admission, 7/1 priority date for domestic students, 1/15 priority date for international students; for spring admission, 5/1 priority date for international students. Applications are processed on a rolling basis. Application fee: $45 ($60 for international students). *Financial support:* Fellowships with full tuition reimbursements, research assistantships with full tuition reimbursements, teaching assistantships with full tuition reimbursements, career-related internships or fieldwork, Federal Work-Study, and institutionally sponsored loans available. Support available to part-time students. Financial award application deadline: 1/15. *Faculty research:* Wastewater, solid waste, composites, nanotechnology. Total annual research expenditures: $800,000. *Unit head:* Dr. Eakalak Khan, Chair, 701-231-7244, Fax: 701-231-6185, E-mail: eakalak.khan@ndsu.edu. *Application contact:* Dr. Kalpana Katti, Professor and Graduate Program Coordinator, 701-231-9504, Fax: 701-231-6185, E-mail: kalpana.katti@ndsu.edu.

Northeastern University, College of Engineering, Department of Civil and Environmental Engineering, Boston, MA 02115-5096. Offers MS, PhD. Part-time programs available. *Faculty:* 15 full-time (2 women), 2 part-time/adjunct (0 women). *Students:* 97 full-time (41 women), 38 part-time (14 women). 286 applicants, 67% accepted, 56 enrolled. In 2010, 23 master's, 3 doctorates awarded. *Degree requirements:* For master's, thesis optional; for doctorate, thesis/dissertation, departmental qualifying exam. *Entrance requirements:* For master's and doctorate, GRE General Test. Additional exam requirements/recommendations for international students: Required—TOEFL (minimum score 550 paper-based; 213 computer-based; 80 iBT). *Application deadline:* For fall admission, 1/15 priority date for domestic and international students. Applications are processed on a rolling basis. Application fee: $50. Electronic applications accepted. *Financial support:* In 2010–11, 33 students received support, including 21 research assistantships with full tuition reimbursements available (averaging $18,325 per year), 16 teaching assistantships with full tuition reimbursements available (averaging $18,325 per year); career-related internships or fieldwork, Federal Work-Study, scholarships/grants, tuition waivers (full), and unspecified assistantships also available. Support available to part-time students. Financial award application deadline: 1/15; financial award applicants required to submit FAFSA. *Faculty research:* Earthquake engineering, geotechnical and geoenvironmental engineering, structural engineering, transportation engineering, environmental engineering. *Unit head:* Dr. Jerome Jaffar, Chairman, 617-373-2444, Fax: 617-373-4419. *Application contact:* Jeffery Hengel, Admissions Specialist, 617-373-2711, Fax: 617-373-2501, E-mail: grad-eng@coe.neu.edu.

Northern Arizona University, Graduate College, College of Engineering, Forestry and Natural Sciences, Programs in Engineering, Flagstaff, AZ 86011. Offers civil and environmental engineering (M Eng); civil engineering (MSE); computer science (MSE); electrical engineering (M Eng, MSE); engineering (M Eng, MSE); environmental engineering (M Eng, MSE); mechanical engineering (M Eng, MSE). Part-time programs available. Postbaccalaureate distance learning degree programs offered (no on-campus study). *Faculty:* 42 full-time (12 women). *Students:* 19 full-time (3 women), 15 part-time (2 women); includes 6 minority (2 American Indian or Alaska Native, non-Hispanic/Latino; 3 Hispanic/Latino; 1 Two or more races, non-Hispanic/Latino), 7 international. Average age 28. 21 applicants, 48% accepted, 4 enrolled. In 2010, 15 master's awarded. *Degree requirements:* For master's, thesis. *Entrance requirements:* For master's, GRE General Test. Additional exam requirements/recommendations for international students: Required—TOEFL (minimum score 550 paper-based; 213 computer-based; 80 iBT), IELTS (minimum score 7). *Application deadline:* For fall admission, 3/1 priority date for domestic and international students; for spring admission, 9/15 priority date for domestic and international students. Applications are processed on a rolling basis. Application fee: $65. Electronic applications accepted. *Financial support:* In 2010–11, 3 research assistantships with partial tuition reimbursements (averaging $14,541 per year), 12 teaching assistantships with partial tuition reimbursements (averaging $12,863 per year) were awarded; career-related internships or fieldwork, Federal Work-Study, scholarships/grants, health care benefits, and unspecified assistantships also available. Financial award applicants required to submit FAFSA. *Unit head:* Dr. Ernesto Penado, Chair, 928-523-9453, Fax: 928-523-2300, E-mail: ernesto.penado@nau.edu. *Application contact:* Natasha Kypfer, Program Coordinator, 928-523-1447, Fax: 928-523-2300, E-mail: egrmasters@nau.edu.

Northwestern University, McCormick School of Engineering and Applied Science, Department of Civil and Environmental Engineering, Evanston, IL 60208-3109. Offers environmental engineering and science (MS, PhD); geotechnical engineering (MS, PhD); mechanics of materials and solids (MS, PhD); project management (MS, PhD); structural engineering and materials (MS, PhD); theoretical and applied mechanics (MS, PhD), including fluid mechanics, solid mechanics; transportation systems analysis and planning (MS, PhD). MS and PhD admissions and degrees offered through The Graduate School. Part-time programs available. Terminal master's awarded for partial completion of doctoral program. *Degree requirements:* For master's, thesis (for some programs); for doctorate, thesis/dissertation. *Entrance requirements:* For master's and doctorate, GRE General Test, minimum 2 letters of recommendation, transcripts from all academic institutions attended. Additional exam requirements/recommendations for international students: Required—TOEFL (minimum score 600 paper-based; 250 computer-based; 100 iBT), IELTS (minimum score 7). Electronic applications accepted. *Faculty research:* Environmental engineering and science, geotechnics, mechanics of materials and solids, structural engineering and materials, transportation systems analysis and planning.

Norwich University, School of Graduate and Continuing Studies, Program in Civil Engineering, Northfield, VT 05663. Offers construction management (MCE); geo-technical (MCE); structural (MCE); water/environmental (MCE). Evening/weekend programs available. *Faculty:* 20 full-time (3 women). *Students:* 78 full-time (19 women); includes 5 Black or African American, non-Hispanic/Latino; 4 Asian, non-Hispanic/Latino; 7 Hispanic/Latino. Average age 35. 107 applicants, 88% accepted, 90 enrolled. In 2010, 78 master's awarded. *Entrance requirements:* For master's, minimum GPA of 2.75. Additional exam requirements/recommendations for international students: Required—TOEFL (minimum score 550 paper-based; 213 computer-based; 83 iBT). *Application deadline:* For fall admission, 8/10 for domestic and international students; for spring admission, 2/6 for domestic and international students. Application fee: $50. *Expenses:* Tuition: Full-time $17,380; part-time $645 per credit. Tuition and fees vary according to program. *Financial support:* Scholarships/grants available. Financial award applicants required to submit FAFSA. *Unit head:* Dr. Thomas Descoteaux, Program Director, 802-485-2730, Fax: 802-485-2533, E-mail: tdescote@norwich.edu. *Application contact:* Shelley W. Brown, Director of Business Partnership, 802-485-2784, Fax: 802-485-2533, E-mail: sbrown@norwich.edu.

The Ohio State University, Graduate School, College of Engineering, Department of Civil and Environmental Engineering and Geodetic Science, Columbus, OH 43210. Offers civil engineering (MS, PhD); geodetic science and surveying (MS, PhD). *Students:* 78 full-time (18 women), 38 part-time (3 women); includes 2 Black or African American, non-Hispanic/Latino; 1 Asian, non-Hispanic/Latino; 1 Hispanic/Latino; 2 Two or more races, non-Hispanic/Latino, 66 international. Average age 28. In 2010, 29 master's, 8 doctorates awarded. *Expenses:* Tuition, state resident: full-time $10,605. Tuition, nonresident: full-time $26,535. Tuition and fees vary according to course load and program. *Unit head:* Dr. Carolyn J, Merry, Chair, 614-292-2771, Fax: 614-292-9379, E-mail: merry.1@osu.edu. *Application contact:* Dr. Carolyn J. Merry, Chair, 614-292-2771, Fax: 614-292-9379, E-mail: merry.1@osu.edu.

Ohio University, Graduate College, Russ College of Engineering and Technology, Department of Civil Engineering, Athens, OH 45701-2979. Offers civil engineering (PhD); construction (MS); environmental (MS); geotechnical and geoenvironmental (MS); mechanics (MS); structures (MS); transportation (MS); water resources and structures (MS). Part-time programs available. *Students:* 29 full-time (6 women), 5 part-time (1 woman); includes 2 minority (1 Hispanic/Latino; 1 Two or more races, non-Hispanic/Latino), 16 international. 52 applicants, 83% accepted, 14 enrolled. In 2010, 7 master's awarded. *Degree requirements:* For master's, comprehensive exam (for some programs), thesis or alternative; for doctorate, comprehensive exam, thesis/dissertation. *Entrance requirements:* For master's, GRE General Test, minimum GPA of 3.0, 3 letters of recommendation; for doctorate, GRE General Test. Additional exam requirements/recommendations for international students: Required—TOEFL (minimum score 550 paper-based; 80 iBT) or IELTS (minimum score 6.5). *Application deadline:* For fall admission, 5/1 priority date for domestic students, 2/1 priority date for international students; for winter admission, 8/1 priority date for domestic students, 4/1 priority date for international students; for spring admission, 2/1 priority date for domestic students, 7/1 priority date for international students. Applications are processed on a rolling basis. Application fee: $50 ($55 for inter-national students). Electronic applications accepted. *Financial support:* Research assistantships with full tuition reimbursements, teaching assistantships with full tuition reimbursements, Federal Work-Study, institutionally sponsored loans, scholarships/grants, and unspecified assistantships available. Financial award application deadline: 3/15; financial award applicants required to submit FAFSA. *Faculty research:* Noise abatement, materials and environment, highway infrastructure, subsurface investigation (pavements, pipes, bridges). *Unit head:* Dr. Gayle F. Mitchell, Chair, 740-593-0430, Fax: 740-593-0625, E-mail: mitchelg@ohio.edu. *Application contact:* Dr. Shad M. Sargand, Graduate Chair, 740-593-1465, Fax: 740-593-0625, E-mail: sargand@ohio.edu.

Oklahoma State University, College of Engineering, Architecture and Technology, School of Civil and Environmental Engineering, Stillwater, OK 74078. Offers civil engineering (MS); environmental engineering (PhD). *Faculty:* 15 full-time (1 woman), 3 part-time/adjunct (0 women). *Students:* 40 full-time (11 women), 45 part-time (7 women); includes 1 Black or African American, non-Hispanic/Latino; 3 American Indian or Alaska Native, non-Hispanic/Latino; 2 Asian, non-Hispanic/Latino; 1 Hispanic/Latino, 46 international. Average age 28. 100 applicants, 36% accepted, 15 enrolled. In 2010, 25 master's, 1 doctorate awarded. *Degree requirements:* For master's, thesis or alternative; for doctorate, comprehensive exam, thesis/dissertation. *Entrance requirements:* For master's and doctorate, GRE or GMAT. Additional exam requirements/recommendations for international students: Required—TOEFL (minimum score 550 paper-based; 79 iBT). *Application deadline:* For fall admission, 3/1 priority date for international students; for spring admission, 8/1 priority date for international students. Applications are processed on a rolling basis. Application fee: $40 ($75 for international students). Electronic applications accepted. *Expenses:* Tuition, state resident: full-time $3716; part-time $154.85 per credit hour. Tuition, nonresident: full-time $14,892; part-time $621 per credit hour. Required fees: $2044; $85.20 per credit hour. One-time fee: $50. Tuition and fees vary according to course load and campus/location. *Financial support:* In 2010–11, 24 research assistantships (averaging $13,245 per year), 16 teaching assistantships (averaging $10,681 per year) were awarded; career-related internships or fieldwork, Federal Work-Study, scholarships/grants, health care benefits, tuition waivers (partial), and unspecified assistantships also available. Support available to part-time students. Financial award application deadline: 3/1; financial award applicants required to submit FAFSA. *Unit head:* Dr. John Veenstra, Head, 405-744-5190, Fax: 405-744-7554. *Application contact:* Dr. Gordon Emslie, Dean, 405-744-6368, Fax: 405-744-0355, E-mail: grad-i@okstate.edu.

Old Dominion University, Frank Batten College of Engineering and Technology, Program in Civil and Environmental Engineering, Norfolk, VA 23529. Offers D Eng, PhD. Part-time and evening/weekend programs available. Postbaccalaureate distance learning degree programs offered (minimal on-campus study). *Faculty:* 11 full-time (1 woman), 10 part-time/adjunct (2 women). *Students:* 3 part-time (0 women). Average age 55. 15 applicants, 100% accepted. In 2010, 2 doctorates awarded. *Degree requirements:* For doctorate, thesis/dissertation, candidacy exam. *Entrance requirements:* For doctorate, GRE, minimum GPA of 3.5. Additional exam requirements/recommendations for international students: Required—TOEFL (minimum score 550 paper-based; 213 computer-based; 80 iBT). *Application deadline:* For fall admission, 6/1 priority date for domestic students, 4/15 priority date for international students; for spring admission, 11/1 priority date for domestic students, 10/1 priority date for international students. Applications are processed on a rolling basis. Application fee: $40. Electronic applications accepted. *Expenses:* Tuition, state resident: full-time $8592; part-time $358 per credit. Tuition, nonresident: full-time $21,672; part-time $903 per credit. Required fees: $119 per semester. One-time fee: $50. *Financial support:* In 2010–11, 5 research assistantships with full and partial tuition reimbursements (averaging $14,626 per year), 10 teaching assistantships with full and partial tuition reimbursements (averaging $15,622 per year) were awarded; scholarships/grants and unspecified assistantships also available. Support available to part-time students. Financial award application deadline: 4/1. *Faculty research:* Structural engineering, coastal engineering, environmental engineering, geotechnical engineering, water resources, transportation engineering. Total annual research expenditures: $597,143. *Unit head:* Dr. Isao Ishibashi, Graduate Program Director, 757-683-4641, Fax: 757-683-5354, E-mail: cegpd@odu.edu. *Application contact:* Dr. Isao Ishibashi, Graduate Program Director, 757-683-4641, Fax: 757-683-5354, E-mail: cegpd@odu.edu.

Old Dominion University, Frank Batten College of Engineering and Technology, Program in Civil Engineering, Norfolk, VA 23529. Offers ME, MS. Part-time and evening/weekend programs available. Postbaccalaureate distance learning degree programs offered (minimal on-campus study). *Faculty:* 11 full-time (1 woman), 10 part-time/adjunct (2 women). *Students:* 18 full-time (2 women), 56 part-time (11 women); includes 15 minority (5 Black or African American, non-Hispanic/Latino; 3 Asian, non-Hispanic/Latino; 5 Hispanic/Latino; 1 Native Hawaiian or other Pacific Islander, non-Hispanic/Latino; 1 Two or more races, non-Hispanic/Latino), 18 international. Average age 31. 19 applicants, 95% accepted, 6 enrolled. In 2010, 9 master's awarded. *Degree requirements:* For master's, comprehensive exam, thesis optional. *Entrance requirements:* For master's, GRE, minimum GPA of 3.0. Additional exam requirements/

recommendations for international students: Required—TOEFL (minimum score 550 paper-based; 213 computer-based; 80 iBT). *Application deadline:* For fall admission, 6/1 priority date for domestic students, 4/15 priority date for international students; for spring admission, 11/1 priority date for domestic students, 10/1 priority date for international students. Applications are processed on a rolling basis. Application fee: $40. Electronic applications accepted. *Expenses:* Tuition, state resident: full-time $8592; part-time $358 per credit. Tuition, nonresident: full-time $21,672; part-time $903 per credit. Required fees: $119 per semester. One-time fee: $50. *Financial support:* In 2010–11, 5 research assistantships with full and partial tuition reimbursements (averaging $6,160 per year) were awarded; scholarships/grants and unspecified assistantships also available. Support available to part-time students. Financial award application deadline: 4/1; financial award applicants required to submit FAFSA. *Faculty research:* Structural engineering, coastal engineering, environmental engineering, geotechnical engineering, water resources, transportation engineering. Total annual research expenditures: $597,143. *Unit head:* Dr. Isao Ishibashi, Graduate Program Director, 757-683-4641, Fax: 757-683-5354, E-mail: cegpd@odu.edu. *Application contact:* Dr. Isao Ishibashi, Graduate Program Director, 757-683-4641, Fax: 757-683-5354, E-mail: cegpd@odu.edu.

Oregon State University, Graduate School, College of Engineering, School of Civil and Construction Engineering, Corvallis, OR 97331. Offers civil engineering (MS, PhD); coastal and ocean engineering (M Oc E, PhD); coastal engineering (MS); construction engineering management (MBE, PhD); engineering (M Eng, MAIS); geotechnical engineering (MS, PhD); structural engineering (MS, PhD); transportation engineering (MS, PhD); water engineering (MS, PhD). Part-time programs available. Terminal master's awarded for partial completion of doctoral program. *Degree requirements:* For master's, thesis or alternative; for doctorate, one foreign language, thesis/dissertation. *Entrance requirements:* For master's, GRE General Test, minimum GPA of 3.0 in last 90 hours (3.5 for MS); for doctorate, GRE General Test, minimum GPA of 3.0 in last 90 hours of undergraduate course work. Additional exam requirements/recommendations for international students: Required—TOEFL (minimum score 580 paper-based; 237 computer-based). *Faculty research:* Hazardous waste management, carbon cycling, wave forces on structures, pavement design, seismic analysis.

Penn State University Park, Graduate School, College of Engineering, Department of Civil and Environmental Engineering, State College, University Park, PA 16802-1503. Offers M Eng, MS, PhD.

Polytechnic Institute of NYU, Department of Civil Engineering, Major in Civil Engineering, Brooklyn, NY 11201-2990. Offers MS, PhD. Part-time and evening/weekend programs available. *Students:* 51 full-time (13 women), 69 part-time (11 women); includes 13 Black or African American, non-Hispanic/Latino; 14 Asian, non-Hispanic/Latino; 5 Hispanic/Latino, 39 international. Average age 29. 131 applicants, 64% accepted, 45 enrolled. In 2010, 26 master's, 1 doctorate awarded. *Degree requirements:* For master's, comprehensive exam (for some programs), thesis (for some programs); for doctorate, comprehensive exam, thesis/dissertation. *Entrance requirements:* For doctorate, qualifying exam, MS in civil engineering. Additional exam requirements/recommendations for international students: Required—TOEFL (minimum score 550 paper-based; 213 computer-based; 80 iBT); Recommended—IELTS (minimum score 6.5). *Application deadline:* For fall admission, 7/31 priority date for domestic students, 4/30 priority date for international students; for spring admission, 12/31 priority date for domestic students, 10/30 priority date for international students. Applications are processed on a rolling basis. Application fee: $75. Electronic applications accepted. *Expenses:* Tuition: Full-time $21,492; part-time $1194 per credit. Required fees: $385 per semester. Tuition and fees vary according to course load. *Financial support:* Fellowships, research assistantships, teaching assistantships, institutionally sponsored loans, scholarships/grants, and unspecified assistantships available. Support available to part-time students. Financial award applicants required to submit FAFSA. *Unit head:* Dr. Lawrence Chiarelli, Department Head, 718-260-4040, Fax: 718-260-3433, E-mail: lchiarel@poly.edu. *Application contact:* JeanCarlo Bonilla, Director of Graduate Enrollment Management, 718-260-3182, Fax: 718-260-3624, E-mail: gradinfo@poly.edu.

Polytechnic Institute of NYU, Long Island Graduate Center, Graduate Programs, Department of Civil Engineering, Major in Civil Engineering, Melville, NY 11747. Offers MS. *Students:* 1 full-time (0 women). Average age 22. In 2010, 3 master's awarded. *Degree requirements:* For master's, comprehensive exam (for some programs), thesis (for some programs). *Entrance requirements:* Additional exam requirements/recommendations for international students: Required—TOEFL (minimum score 550 paper-based; 213 computer-based; 80 iBT); Recommended—IELTS (minimum score 6.5). *Application deadline:* For fall admission, 7/31 priority date for domestic students, 4/30 priority date for international students; for spring admission, 12/31 priority date for domestic students, 11/30 priority date for international students. Applications are processed on a rolling basis. Application fee: $75. Electronic applications accepted. *Expenses:* Tuition: Full-time $21,492; part-time $1194 per credit. Required fees: $385 per semester. Tuition and fees vary according to course load. *Financial support:* Institutionally sponsored loans, scholarships/grants, and unspecified assistantships available. Support available to part-time students. Financial award applicants required to submit FAFSA. *Unit head:* Dr. Roger Peter Roess, Department Head, 718-260-3018, E-mail: rroess@poly.edu. *Application contact:* JeanCarlo Bonilla, Director of Graduate Enrollment Management, 718-260-3182, Fax: 718-260-3624, E-mail: gradinfo@poly.edu.

Polytechnic University of Puerto Rico, Graduate School, Hato Rey, PR 00919. Offers business administration (MBA), including computer information systems, general management, management of information systems, management of international enterprises; civil engineering (ME, MS); computer engineering (ME, MS); computer science (MCS, MS); electrical engineering (ME, MS); engineering management (MEM); environmental management (MEM); landscape architecture (M Land Arch); manufacturing competitiveness (MMC, MS); manufacturing engineering (ME, MS); mechanical engineering (M Mech E). Part-time and evening/weekend programs available. *Entrance requirements:* For master's, 3 letters of recommendation.

Portland State University, Graduate Studies, Maseeh College of Engineering and Computer Science, Department of Civil and Environmental Engineering, Portland, OR 97207-0751. Offers civil and environmental engineering (M Eng, MS, PhD); civil and environmental engineering management (M Eng); environmental sciences and resources (PhD); systems science (PhD). Part-time and evening/weekend programs available. *Faculty:* 13 full-time (2 women), 3 part-time/adjunct (1 woman). *Students:* 48 full-time (17 women), 47 part-time (15 women); includes 1 Black or African American, non-Hispanic/Latino; 8 Asian, non-Hispanic/Latino; 5 Hispanic/Latino, 16 international. Average age 30. 98 applicants, 66% accepted, 32 enrolled. In 2010, 8 master's awarded. *Degree requirements:* For master's, thesis or alternative, oral exam; for doctorate, one foreign language, thesis/dissertation, oral and written exams. *Entrance requirements:* For master's, minimum GPA of 3.0 in upper-division course work, BS in civil engineering or allied field; for doctorate, GRE General Test, GRE Subject Test, minimum GPA of 3.0 in upper-division course work, master's in civil and environmental engineering, 2 years full-time graduate work beyond master's degree. Additional exam requirements/recommendations for international students: Required—TOEFL (minimum score 550 paper-based; 213 computer-based). *Application deadline:* For fall admission, 4/1 for domestic students, 4/11 for international students; for winter admission, 9/1 for domestic and international students; for spring admission, 11/1 for domestic and international students. Applications are processed on a rolling basis. Application fee: $50. *Expenses:* Tuition, state resident: full-time $8505; part-time $315 per credit. Tuition, nonresident: full-time $13,284; part-time $492 per credit. Required fees: $1482; $21 per credit. $99 per term. One-time fee: $120. Part-time tuition and fees vary according to course load and program. *Financial support:* In 2010–11, 15 research assistantships with tuition reimbursements (averaging $11,169 per year), 1 teaching assistantship with full tuition reimbursement (averaging $19,012 per year) were awarded; career-related internships or fieldwork, Federal Work-Study, scholarships/grants, and unspecified assistantships also available. Support available to part-time students. Financial award application deadline: 3/1; financial award applicants required to submit FAFSA. *Faculty research:* Structures, water resources, geotechnical engineering, environmental engineering, transportation. Total

annual research expenditures: $2.4 million. *Unit head:* Scott Wells, Chair, 503-725-4282, Fax: 503-725-4298, E-mail: wellss@pdx.edu. *Application contact:* Marianne Stupfel-Wallace, Information Contact, 503-725-4244, Fax: 503-725-4298, E-mail: ceedept@cecs.pdx.edu.

Portland State University, Graduate Studies, Systems Science Program, Portland, OR 97207-0751. Offers computational intelligence (Certificate); computer modeling and simulation (Certificate); systems science (MS); systems science/anthropology (PhD); systems science/business administration (PhD); systems science/civil engineering (PhD); systems science/economics (PhD); systems science/engineering management (PhD); systems science/general (PhD); systems science/mathematical sciences (PhD); systems science/mechanical engineering (PhD); systems science/psychology (PhD); systems science/sociology (PhD). *Faculty:* 4 full-time (0 women), 1 part-time/adjunct (0 women). *Students:* 15 full-time (4 women), 35 part-time (11 women); includes 1 American Indian or Alaska Native, non-Hispanic/Latino; 1 Asian, non-Hispanic/Latino; 1 Two or more races, non-Hispanic/Latino, 4 international. Average age 39. 8 applicants, 88% accepted, 5 enrolled. In 2010, 2 master's, 4 doctorates awarded. *Degree requirements:* For doctorate, variable foreign language requirement, thesis/dissertation. *Entrance requirements:* For master's, 2 letters of recommendation; for doctorate, GMAT, GRE General Test, minimum undergraduate GPA of 3.0. Additional exam requirements/recommendations for international students: Required—TOEFL. *Application deadline:* For fall admission, 2/1 for domestic students; for spring admission, 11/1 for domestic students. Application fee: $50. *Expenses:* Tuition, state resident: full-time $8505; part-time $315 per credit. Tuition, nonresident: full-time $13,284; part-time $492 per credit. Required fees: $1482; $21 per credit. $99 per term. One-time fee: $120. Part-time tuition and fees vary according to course load and program. *Financial support:* In 2010–11, 1 research assistantship with full tuition reimbursement (averaging $7,704 per year) was awarded; teaching assistantships with full tuition reimbursements, career-related internships or fieldwork, Federal Work-Study, scholarships/grants, and unspecified assistantships also available. Support available to part-time students. Financial award application deadline: 3/1; financial award applicants required to submit FAFSA. *Faculty research:* Systems theory and methodology, artificial intelligence neural networks, information theory, nonlinear dynamics/chaos, modeling and simulation. *Unit head:* George Lendaris, Acting Director, 503-725-4960. *Application contact:* Dawn Sharafi, Administrative Assistant, 503-725-4960, E-mail: dawn@sysc.pdx.edu.

Princeton University, Graduate School, School of Engineering and Applied Science, Department of Civil and Environmental Engineering, Princeton, NJ 08544-1019. Offers civil and environmental engineering (MSE). Terminal master's awarded for partial completion of doctoral program. *Degree requirements:* For master's, thesis (MSE); for doctorate, thesis/dissertation, general exam. *Entrance requirements:* For master's, GRE General Test, 3 letters of recommendation; for doctorate, GRE General Test, official transcript(s), 3 letters of recommendation, personal statement. Additional exam requirements/recommendations for international students: Required—TOEFL. Electronic applications accepted. *Faculty research:* Carbon mitigation; civil engineering materials and structures; climate and atmospheric dynamics; computational mechanics and risk assessment; hydrology, remote sensing, and sustainability.

Purdue University, College of Engineering, School of Civil Engineering, West Lafayette, IN 47907-2051. Offers MS, MSCE, MSE, PhD. Part-time programs available. Terminal master's awarded for partial completion of doctoral program. *Degree requirements:* For master's, thesis (for some programs); for doctorate, thesis/dissertation. *Entrance requirements:* For master's and doctorate, GRE General Test, minimum GPA of 3.0. Additional exam requirements/recommendations for international students: Required—TOEFL (minimum score 575 paper-based; 233 computer-based; 90 iBT); Recommended—TWE. Electronic applications accepted. *Faculty research:* Environmental and hydraulic engineering, geotechnical and materials engineering, structural engineering, construction engineering, infrastructure and transportation systems engineering.

Queen's University at Kingston, School of Graduate Studies and Research, Faculty of Applied Science, Department of Civil Engineering, Kingston, ON K7L 3N6, Canada. Offers M Eng, M Sc Eng, PhD. Part-time programs available. *Degree requirements:* For master's, thesis (for some programs); for doctorate, comprehensive exam, thesis/dissertation. *Entrance requirements:* Additional exam requirements/recommendations for international students: Required—TOEFL. *Faculty research:* Structural, geotechnical, transportation, hydrotechnical, and environmental engineering.

Rensselaer Polytechnic Institute, Graduate School, School of Engineering, Program in Civil Engineering, Troy, NY 12180-3590. Offers geotechnical engineering (M Eng, MS, PhD); mechanics of composite materials and structures (M Eng, MS, PhD); structural engineering (M Eng, MS, PhD); transportation engineering (M Eng, MS, PhD). Part-time programs available. *Faculty:* 13 full-time (1 woman), 3 part-time/adjunct (0 women). *Students:* 20 full-time (4 women); includes 1 Black or African American, non-Hispanic/Latino, 16 international. Average age 24. 65 applicants, 12% accepted, 5 enrolled. In 2010, 19 master's, 3 doctorates awarded. Terminal master's awarded for partial completion of doctoral program. *Degree requirements:* For master's, thesis (for some programs); for doctorate, thesis/dissertation. *Entrance requirements:* For master's and doctorate, GRE. Additional exam requirements/recommendations for international students: Required—TOEFL (minimum score 570 paper-based; 230 computer-based; 89 iBT), IELTS (minimum score 6.5). *Application deadline:* For fall admission, 1/15 priority date for domestic and international students; for spring admission, 8/15 priority date for domestic and international students. Applications are processed on a rolling basis. Application fee: $75. Electronic applications accepted. *Expenses:* Tuition: Full-time $39,600; part-time $1650 per credit. Required fees: $1896. *Financial support:* In 2010–11, 1 fellowship with full tuition reimbursement (averaging $16,500 per year), 3 research assistantships with full tuition reimbursements (averaging $16,500 per year), 4 teaching assistantships with full tuition reimbursements (averaging $16,500 per year) were awarded; career-related internships or fieldwork and institutionally sponsored loans also available. Financial award application deadline: 2/1. *Faculty research:* Computational mechanics, earthquake engineering, geo-environmental engineering. Total annual research expenditures: $2.7 million. *Unit head:* Dr. Chris Letchford, Head, 518-276-6362, Fax: 518-276-4833, E-mail: letchc@rpi.edu. *Application contact:* Kimberly Boyce, Administrative Assistant, 518-276-6941, Fax: 518-276-4833, E-mail: boycek@rpi.edu.

Rice University, Graduate Programs, George R. Brown School of Engineering, Department of Civil and Environmental Engineering, Houston, TX 77251-1892. Offers civil engineering (MCE, MS, PhD); environmental engineering (MEE, MES, MS, PhD); environmental science (MEE, MES, MS, PhD). Part-time programs available. *Degree requirements:* For master's, thesis (for some programs); for doctorate, thesis/dissertation. *Entrance requirements:* For master's and doctorate, GRE General Test, GRE Subject Test, minimum GPA of 3.25. Additional exam requirements/recommendations for international students: Required—TOEFL (minimum score 600 paper-based; 250 computer-based; 90 iBT). Electronic applications accepted. *Faculty research:* Biology and chemistry of groundwater, pollutant fate in groundwater systems, water quality monitoring, urban storm water runoff, urban air quality.

Rose-Hulman Institute of Technology, Faculty of Engineering and Applied Sciences, Department of Civil Engineering, Terre Haute, IN 47803-3999. Offers civil engineering (MS); environmental engineering (MS). Part-time programs available. *Faculty:* 7 full-time (2 women). *Students:* 1 (woman) part-time. Average age 22. 2 applicants, 50% accepted, 0 enrolled. *Degree requirements:* For master's, thesis. *Entrance requirements:* For master's, GRE, minimum GPA of 3.0. Additional exam requirements/recommendations for international students: Required—TOEFL (minimum score 580 paper-based; 237 computer-based; 92 iBT). *Application deadline:* For fall admission, 2/1 priority date for domestic students. Applications are processed on a rolling basis. Application fee: $0. *Expenses:* Tuition: Full-time $35,595; part-time $1038 per credit hour. *Financial support:* In 2010–11, 1 student received support; fellowships with full and partial tuition reimbursements available, research assistantships with full and partial tuition reimbursements available, institutionally sponsored loans, scholarships/grants, and tuition waivers (full and partial) available. Financial award application deadline: 2/1. *Faculty research:* Urban stormwater management, groundwater and surface water models, solid and hazardous

Civil Engineering

Rose-Hulman Institute of Technology (continued)
waste, risk and decision analysis. Total annual research expenditures: $16,578. *Unit head:* Dr. Kevin G. Sutterer, Chairman, 812-877-8959, Fax: 812-877-8440, E-mail: kevin.g.sutterer@rose-hulman.edu. *Application contact:* Dr. Daniel J. Moore, Associate Dean of the Faculty, 812-877-8110, Fax: 812-877-8061, E-mail: daniel.j.moore@rose-hulman.edu.

Rowan University, Graduate School, College of Engineering, Department of Civil and Environmental Engineering, Program in Civil Engineering, Glassboro, NJ 08028-1701. Offers MS. *Students:* 4 full-time, 7 part-time (1 woman); includes 1 Asian, non-Hispanic/Latino; 1 Hispanic/Latino. Average age 26. 7 applicants, 100% accepted, 3 enrolled. In 2010, 3 master's awarded. *Entrance requirements:* For master's, GRE General Test. Additional exam requirements/recommendations for international students: Required—TOEFL. *Application deadline:* Applications are processed on a rolling basis. Application fee: $65 ($200 for international students). Electronic applications accepted. *Expenses:* Tuition, area resident: Part-time $602 per semester hour. Tuition, nonresident: part-time $602 per semester hour. Required fees: $100 per semester hour. One-time fee: $10 part-time. *Unit head:* Kauser Jahan, Chair, 856-256-5323, E-mail: jahan@rowan.edu. *Application contact:* Dr. Ralph Dusseau, Program Adviser, 856-256-5332.

Royal Military College of Canada, Division of Graduate Studies and Research, Engineering Division, Department of Civil Engineering, Kingston, ON K7K 7B4, Canada. Offers M Eng, MA Sc, PhD. *Degree requirements:* For master's, thesis; for doctorate, comprehensive exam, thesis/dissertation. *Entrance requirements:* For master's, honours degree with second-class standing; for doctorate, master's degree. Electronic applications accepted.

Rutgers, The State University of New Jersey, New Brunswick, Graduate School-New Brunswick, Department of Civil and Environmental Engineering, Piscataway, NJ 08854-8097. Offers MS, PhD. Part-time and evening/weekend programs available. Terminal master's awarded for partial completion of doctoral program. *Degree requirements:* For master's, comprehensive exam, thesis or alternative; for doctorate, comprehensive exam, thesis/dissertation. *Entrance requirements:* For master's and doctorate, GRE General Test. Additional exam requirements/recommendations for international students: Required—TOEFL (minimum score 580 paper-based; 237 computer-based). Electronic applications accepted. *Expenses:* Tuition, state resident: full-time $7200; part-time $600 per credit. Tuition, nonresident: full-time $11,124; part-time $927 per credit. *Faculty research:* Civil engineering materials research, non-destructive evaluation of transportation infrastructure, transportation planning, intelligent transportation systems.

Saint Martin's University, Graduate Programs, Program in Civil Engineering, Lacey, WA 98503. Offers MCE. Part-time and evening/weekend programs available. *Faculty:* 4 full-time (0 women), 1 part-time/adjunct (0 women). *Students:* 3 full-time (0 women), 3 part-time (0 women); includes 2 Asian, non-Hispanic/Latino, 2 international. Average age 40. 1 applicant, 100% accepted, 1 enrolled. In 2010, 3 master's awarded. *Degree requirements:* For master's, thesis optional. *Entrance requirements:* For master's, minimum GPA of 2.8; BS in civil engineering or other engineering/science with completion of calculus, differential equations, physics, chemistry. Additional exam requirements/recommendations for international students: Required—TOEFL (minimum score 525 paper-based; 210 computer-based). *Application deadline:* For fall admission, 6/30 priority date for domestic students, 4/30 for international students; for spring admission, 9/30 priority date for domestic students, 6/30 for international students. Applications are processed on a rolling basis. Application fee: $35. *Financial support:* Scholarships/grants and tuition waivers (partial) available. Support available to part-time students. Financial award application deadline: 3/1; financial award applicants required to submit FAFSA. *Faculty research:* Transportation engineering, metal fatigue and fracture, environmental engineering. *Unit head:* Dr. Pius O. Igharo, Program Chair, 360-438-4322, Fax: 360-438-4548, E-mail: pigharo@stmartin.edu. *Application contact:* Hopie Lopez, Administrative Assistant, 360-438-4320, Fax: 360-438-4548, E-mail: hlopez@stmartin.edu.

San Diego State University, Graduate and Research Affairs, College of Engineering, Department of Civil and Environmental Engineering, San Diego, CA 92182. Offers civil engineering (MS). Part-time and evening/weekend programs available. *Degree requirements:* For master's, thesis optional. *Entrance requirements:* For master's, GRE General Test. Additional exam requirements/recommendations for international students: Required—TOEFL. Electronic applications accepted. *Faculty research:* Hydraulics, hydrology, transportation, smart material, concrete material.

San Jose State University, Graduate Studies and Research, Charles W. Davidson College of Engineering, Department of Civil and Environmental Engineering, San Jose, CA 95192-0001. Offers civil engineering (MS). *Degree requirements:* For master's, thesis or alternative. *Entrance requirements:* For master's, minimum GPA of 2.7. Electronic applications accepted.

Santa Clara University, School of Engineering, Department of Civil Engineering, Santa Clara, CA 95053. Offers MS. Part-time and evening/weekend programs available. *Students:* 15 full-time (6 women), 4 part-time (1 woman); includes 8 minority (1 Black or African American, non-Hispanic/Latino; 5 Asian, non-Hispanic/Latino; 1 Hispanic/Latino; 1 Native Hawaiian or other Pacific Islander, non-Hispanic/Latino), 4 international. Average age 26. 24 applicants, 75% accepted, 11 enrolled. In 2010, 1 master's awarded. *Degree requirements:* For master's, thesis (for some programs). *Entrance requirements:* For master's, GRE (waiver may be available), transcript. Additional exam requirements/recommendations for international students: Required—TOEFL (minimum score 550 paper-based; 213 computer-based; 79 iBT). *Application deadline:* For fall admission, 8/12 for domestic students, 7/15 for international students; for winter admission, 10/28 for domestic students, 9/23 for international students; for spring admission, 2/25 for domestic students, 1/21 for international students. Applications are processed on a rolling basis. Application fee: $60. Electronic applications accepted. *Expenses:* Contact institution. *Financial support:* Research assistantships, teaching assistantships available. Financial award application deadline: 3/2; financial award applicants required to submit FAFSA. *Unit head:* Dr. Alex Zecevic, PhD, Associate Dean for Graduate Studies, 408-554-2394, Fax: 408-554-4323, E-mail: azecevic@scu.edu. *Application contact:* Stacey Tinker, Director of Admissions, Graduate Engineering, 408-554-4748, Fax: 408-554-4323, E-mail: stinker@scu.edu.

South Carolina State University, School of Graduate Studies, Department of Civil and Mechanical Engineering Technology and Nuclear Engineering, Orangeburg, SC 29117-0001. Offers transportation (MS). Part-time and evening/weekend programs available. *Degree requirements:* For master's, comprehensive exam, thesis, departmental qualifying exam. *Entrance requirements:* For master's, GRE. Electronic applications accepted. *Faculty research:* Societal competence, relationship of parent-child interaction to adult, rehabilitation evaluation, vocation, language assessment of rural children.

South Dakota School of Mines and Technology, Graduate Division, Program in Civil Engineering, Rapid City, SD 57701-3995. Offers MS. Part-time programs available. *Entrance requirements:* Additional exam requirements/recommendations for international students: Required—TOEFL, TWE. Electronic applications accepted. *Faculty research:* Concrete technology, environmental and sanitation engineering, water resources engineering, composite materials, geotechnical engineering.

South Dakota State University, Graduate School, College of Engineering, Department of Civil and Environmental Engineering, Brookings, SD 57007. Offers engineering (MS). Part-time programs available. Postbaccalaureate distance learning degree programs offered (minimal on-campus study). *Degree requirements:* For master's, thesis (for some programs), oral exam. *Entrance requirements:* Additional exam requirements/recommendations for international students: Required—TOEFL (minimum score 525 paper-based). *Faculty research:* Structural, environmental, geotechnical, transportation engineering and water resources.

Southern Illinois University Carbondale, Graduate School, College of Engineering, Department of Civil and Environmental Engineering, Carbondale, IL 62901-4701. Offers civil engineering (MS). *Degree requirements:* For master's, comprehensive exam, thesis. *Entrance requirements:* For master's, minimum GPA of 2.7. Additional exam requirements/recommendations for international students: Required—TOEFL. *Faculty research:* Composite materials, wastewater treatment, solid waste disposal, slurry transport, geotechnical engineering.

Southern Illinois University Edwardsville, Graduate School, School of Engineering, Department of Civil Engineering, Edwardsville, IL 62026-0001. Offers MS. Part-time and evening/weekend programs available. *Faculty:* 8 full-time (1 woman). *Students:* 13 full-time (5 women), 43 part-time (7 women); includes 5 minority (1 Black or African American, non-Hispanic/Latino; 2 Asian, non-Hispanic/Latino; 1 Hispanic/Latino; 1 Two or more races, non-Hispanic/Latino), 15 international. Average age 26. 26 applicants, 62% accepted. In 2010, 17 master's awarded. *Degree requirements:* For master's, thesis (for some programs), research paper. *Entrance requirements:* For master's, minimum undergraduate GPA of 2.75 in science, math, and engineering courses. Additional exam requirements/recommendations for international students: Required—TOEFL (minimum score 550 paper-based; 213 computer-based; 79 iBT), IELTS (minimum score 6.5). *Application deadline:* For fall admission, 7/22 for domestic students, 6/1 for international students; for spring admission, 12/9 for domestic students, 10/1 for international students. Applications are processed on a rolling basis. Application fee: $30. Electronic applications accepted. *Expenses:* Tuition, state resident: full-time $6012; part-time $1503 per semester. Tuition, nonresident: full-time $15,030; part-time $3758 per semester. Required fees: $1711; $675 per semester. *Financial support:* In 2010–11, 2 fellowships with full tuition reimbursements (averaging $8,370 per year), 7 research assistantships with full tuition reimbursements (averaging $8,064 per year), 15 teaching assistantships with full tuition reimbursements (averaging $8,064 per year) were awarded; career-related internships or fieldwork, Federal Work-Study, institutionally sponsored loans, scholarships/grants, traineeships, and unspecified assistantships also available. Support available to part-time students. Financial award application deadline: 3/1; financial award applicants required to submit FAFSA. *Unit head:* Dr. Susan Morgan, Chair, 618-650-2533, E-mail: smorgan@siue.edu. *Application contact:* Dr. Jianpeng Zhou, Director, 618-650-3221, E-mail: jzhou@siue.edu.

Southern Methodist University, Bobby B. Lyle School of Engineering, Department of Environmental and Civil Engineering, Dallas, TX 75275-0340. Offers applied science (MS, PhD); civil and environmental engineering (PhD); civil engineering (MS); environmental engineering (MS); environmental science (MS), including environmental systems management. Part-time and evening/weekend programs available. Postbaccalaureate distance learning degree programs offered (no on-campus study). *Faculty:* 6 full-time (0 women), 11 part-time/adjunct (3 women). *Students:* 11 full-time (8 women), 47 part-time (21 women); includes 5 Black or African American, non-Hispanic/Latino; 2 Asian, non-Hispanic/Latino; 3 Hispanic/Latino, 6 international. Average age 37. 50 applicants, 86% accepted, 28 enrolled. In 2010, 26 master's awarded. Terminal master's awarded for partial completion of doctoral program. *Degree requirements:* For master's, thesis optional; for doctorate, thesis/dissertation, oral and written qualifying exams. *Entrance requirements:* For master's, GRE General Test, minimum GPA of 3.0 in last 2 years; bachelor's degree in engineering, mathematics, or sciences; for doctorate, GRE, BS and MS in related field, minimum GPA of 3.3. Additional exam requirements/recommendations for international students: Required—TOEFL. *Application deadline:* For fall admission, 7/1 for domestic students, 5/15 for international students; for spring admission, 11/15 for domestic students, 9/1 for international students. Applications are processed on a rolling basis. Application fee: $75. Electronic applications accepted. *Financial support:* In 2010–11, 9 students received support, including 2 research assistantships with full tuition reimbursements available (averaging $18,000 per year), 7 teaching assistantships with full tuition reimbursements available (averaging $18,000 per year); unspecified assistantships also available. *Faculty research:* Human and environmental health effects of endocrine disrupters, development of air pollution control systems for diesel engines, structural analysis and design, modeling and design of waste treatment systems. Total annual research expenditures: $100,000. *Unit head:* Prof. Khaled Abdelghany, Associate Chair, 214-768-3894, Fax: 214-768-2164, E-mail: khaled@lyle.smu.edu. *Application contact:* Marc Valerin, Director of Graduate and Executive Admissions, 214-768-3042, Fax: 214-768-3778, E-mail: valerin@lyle.smu.edu.

Stanford University, School of Engineering, Department of Civil and Environmental Engineering, Stanford, CA 94305-9991. Offers MS, PhD, Eng. Terminal master's awarded for partial completion of doctoral program. *Degree requirements:* For doctorate, thesis/dissertation, qualifying exam; for Eng, thesis. *Entrance requirements:* For master's, doctorate, and Eng, GRE General Test. Additional exam requirements/recommendations for international students: Required—TOEFL. Electronic applications accepted. *Expenses:* Tuition: Full-time $38,700; part-time $860 per unit. One-time fee: $200 full-time.

Stevens Institute of Technology, Graduate School, Charles V. Schaefer Jr. School of Engineering, Department of Civil, Environmental, and Ocean Engineering, Program in Civil Engineering, Hoboken, NJ 07030. Offers civil engineering (PhD); geotechnical engineering (Certificate); geotechnical/geoenvironmental engineering (M Eng, Engr); hydrologic modeling (M Eng); stormwater management (M Eng); structural engineering (M Eng, Engr); water resources engineering (M Eng). *Students:* 22 full-time (6 women), 36 part-time (11 women); includes 10 Asian, non-Hispanic/Latino; 3 Hispanic/Latino, 16 international. Average age 28. 37 applicants, 86% accepted. *Degree requirements:* For master's, thesis optional; for doctorate, variable foreign language requirement, thesis/dissertation; for other advanced degree, project or thesis. *Entrance requirements:* For doctorate, GRE. Additional exam requirements/recommendations for international students: Required—TOEFL. *Application deadline:* Applications are processed on a rolling basis. Application fee: $50. Electronic applications accepted. *Financial support:* Application deadline: 4/15. *Unit head:* Dr. David A. Vaccari, Director, 201-216-5570, Fax: 201-216-5352, E-mail: dvaccari@stevens.edu. *Application contact:* Dr. David A. Vaccari, Director, 201-216-5570, Fax: 201-216-5352, E-mail: dvaccari@stevens.edu.

Syracuse University, L. C. Smith College of Engineering and Computer Science, Program in Civil Engineering, Syracuse, NY 13244. Offers MS, PhD. Part-time programs available. *Students:* 44 full-time (12 women), 12 part-time (6 women); includes 5 minority (1 Black or African American, non-Hispanic/Latino; 4 Asian, non-Hispanic/Latino), 38 international. Average age 27. 457 applicants, 8% accepted, 17 enrolled. In 2010, 8 master's, 2 doctorates awarded. *Degree requirements:* For doctorate, thesis/dissertation. *Entrance requirements:* For master's and doctorate, GRE General Test. Additional exam requirements/recommendations for international students: Required—TOEFL (minimum score 100 iBT). *Application deadline:* For fall admission, 6/1 priority date for domestic and international students. Applications are processed on a rolling basis. Application fee: $75. Electronic applications accepted. *Expenses:* Tuition: Part-time $1162 per credit. *Financial support:* Fellowships with full tuition reimbursements, research assistantships with full and partial tuition reimbursements, teaching assistantships with full and partial tuition reimbursements, tuition waivers (partial) available. Financial award application deadline: 1/1. *Faculty research:* Fate and transport of pollutants, methods for characterization and remediation of hazardous wastes, response of eco-systems to disturbances, water quality and engineering. *Unit head:* Dr. Chris E. Johnson, Interim Chair, 315-443-2311, E-mail: cejohns@syr.edu. *Application contact:* Elizabeth Buchanan, Information Contact, 315-443-2558, E-mail: ebuchana@syr.edu.

Temple University, College of Engineering, Department of Civil and Environmental Engineering, Philadelphia, PA 19122-6096. Offers civil engineering (MSE). Part-time programs available. *Faculty:* 12 full-time (0 women). *Students:* 13 full-time (6 women), 4 part-time (2 women); includes 1 Black or African American, non-Hispanic/Latino; 4 Asian, non-Hispanic/Latino, 6 international. 25 applicants, 60% accepted, 6 enrolled. In 2010, 8 master's awarded. *Degree requirements:* For master's, thesis optional. *Entrance requirements:* For master's, GRE General Test, minimum GPA of 3.0. Additional exam requirements/recommendations for international students: Required—TOEFL (minimum score 550 paper-based; 213 computer-based; 79 iBT). *Application deadline:* For fall admission, 7/1 for domestic students, 12/15 for international students; for spring admission, 11/1 for domestic students, 8/1 for international students. Applications are processed on a rolling basis. Application fee: $50. *Financial support:* In 2010–11, 1 fellowship was awarded; research assistantships, teaching assistantships, Federal Work-Study also available. Financial award application deadline: 1/15; financial award applicants required to submit FAFSA. *Faculty research:* Prestressed masonry structure, recycling processes and products, finite element analysis of highways and runways. Total annual research expenditures: $118,428. *Unit head:* Dr. Michel Boufadel, Chair, 215-204-7871, Fax: 215-204-6936, E-mail: boufadel@temple.edu. *Application contact:* Dr. Michel Boufadel, Chair, 215-204-7871, Fax: 215-204-6936, E-mail: boufadel@temple.edu.

Tennessee Technological University, Graduate School, College of Engineering, Department of Civil Engineering, Cookeville, TN 38505. Offers MS, PhD. Part-time programs available. *Faculty:* 17 full-time (0 women). *Students:* 16 full-time (1 woman), 4 part-time (0 women); includes 1 Black or African American, non-Hispanic/Latino; 3 Asian, non-Hispanic/Latino. Average age 27. 25 applicants, 64% accepted, 5 enrolled. In 2010, 6 master's awarded. *Degree requirements:* For master's, thesis. *Entrance requirements:* For master's, GRE. Additional exam requirements/recommendations for international students: Required—TOEFL (minimum score 550 paper-based; 79 iBT), IELTS (minimum score 5.5). *Application deadline:* For fall admission, 8/1 for domestic students, 5/1 for international students; for spring admission, 12/1 for domestic students, 10/1 for international students. Application fee: $25 ($30 for international students). Electronic applications accepted. *Expenses:* Tuition, state resident: full-time $7934; part-time $388 per credit hour. Tuition, nonresident: full-time $19,758; part-time $962 per credit hour. *Financial support:* In 2010–11, 6 research assistantships (averaging $8,227 per year), 5 teaching assistantships (averaging $7,200 per year) were awarded; career-related internships or fieldwork also available. Financial award application deadline: 4/1. *Faculty research:* Environmental engineering, transportation, structural engineering, water resources. *Unit head:* Dr. Sharon Huo, Interim Chairperson, 931-372-3454, Fax: 931-372-6352. *Application contact:* Shelia K. Kendrick, Coordinator of Graduate Admissions, 931-372-3808, Fax: 931-372-3497, E-mail: skendrick@tntech.edu.

Texas A&M University, College of Engineering, Zachry Department of Civil Engineering, College Station, TX 77843. Offers coastal and ocean engineering (M Eng, MS, D Eng, PhD); construction engineering and management (M Eng, MS, D Eng, PhD); environmental engineering (M Eng, MS, D Eng, PhD); geotechnical engineering (M Eng, MS, D Eng, PhD); materials engineering (M Eng, MS, D Eng, PhD); structural engineering (M Eng, MS, D Eng, PhD); transportation engineering (M Eng, MS, D Eng, PhD); water resources engineering (M Eng, MS, D Eng, PhD). Part-time programs available. *Faculty:* 57. *Students:* 384 full-time (81 women), 35 part-time (7 women); includes 35 minority (3 Black or African American, non-Hispanic/Latino; 1 American Indian or Alaska Native, non-Hispanic/Latino; 14 Asian, non-Hispanic/Latino; 17 Hispanic/Latino), 263 international. Average age 29. In 2010, 136 master's, 26 doctorates awarded. *Degree requirements:* For master's, thesis (MS); for doctorate, dissertation (PhD), internship (D Eng). *Entrance requirements:* For master's and doctorate, GRE General Test. Additional exam requirements/recommendations for international students: Required—TOEFL. *Application deadline:* Applications are processed on a rolling basis. Application fee: $50 ($75 for international students). Electronic applications accepted. *Financial support:* In 2010–11, fellowships (averaging $4,500 per year), research assistantships (averaging $14,000 per year), teaching assistantships (averaging $14,400 per year) were awarded; career-related internships or fieldwork and institutionally sponsored loans also available. Financial award application deadline: 4/15; financial award applicants required to submit FAFSA. *Unit head:* Dr. Tony Cahill, Head, 979-845-3858, E-mail: tcahill@civil.tamu.edu. *Application contact:* Graduate Advisor, 979-845-7435, Fax: 979-845-6156, E-mail: info@civil.tamu.edu.

Texas A&M University–Kingsville, College of Graduate Studies, College of Engineering, Department of Civil Engineering, Kingsville, TX 78363. Offers ME, MS. Part-time and evening/weekend programs available. *Degree requirements:* For master's, comprehensive exam, thesis or alternative. *Entrance requirements:* For master's, GRE General Test. Additional exam requirements/recommendations for international students: Required—TOEFL. *Faculty research:* Geotechnical engineering, structural mechanics, structural design, transportation engineering.

Texas Tech University, Graduate School, Edward E. Whitacre Jr. College of Engineering, Department of Civil and Environmental Engineering, Lubbock, TX 79409. Offers civil engineering (MSCE, PhD); environmental engineering (MENVEGR). *Accreditation:* ABET. Part-time programs available. *Faculty:* 21 full-time (2 women), 1 part-time/adjunct (0 women). *Students:* 86 full-time (16 women), 14 part-time (3 women); includes 3 Black or African American, non-Hispanic/Latino; 1 Asian, non-Hispanic/Latino; 5 Hispanic/Latino, 44 international. Average age 26. 107 applicants, 63% accepted, 24 enrolled. In 2010, 23 master's, 6 doctorates awarded. *Degree requirements:* For master's, thesis or alternative; for doctorate, thesis/dissertation. *Entrance requirements:* For master's and doctorate, GRE General Test, minimum GPA of 3.0. Additional exam requirements/recommendations for international students: Required—TOEFL (minimum score 550 paper-based; 213 computer-based; 79 iBT). *Application deadline:* For fall admission, 6/1 priority date for domestic students, 1/15 priority date for international students; for spring admission, 9/1 priority date for domestic students, 6/15 priority date for international students. Applications are processed on a rolling basis. Application fee: $50 ($75 for international students). Electronic applications accepted. *Expenses:* Tuition, state resident: full-time $5495.76; part-time $228.99 per credit hour. Tuition, nonresident: full-time $12,936; part-time $538.99 per credit hour. Required fees: $2674; $36 per credit hour. $905 per semester. *Financial support:* In 2010–11, 65 students received support, including 25 research assistantships with partial tuition reimbursements available (averaging $5,431 per year), 10 teaching assistantships with partial tuition reimbursements available (averaging $5,535 per year). Financial award application deadline: 4/15; financial award applicants required to submit FAFSA. *Faculty research:* Wind load/engineering on structures, fluid mechanics, structural dynamics, water resource management, transportation engineering. Total annual research expenditures: $1.1 million. *Unit head:* Dr. H. Scott Norville, Chair, 806-742-3523, Fax: 806-742-3488, E-mail: scott.norville@ttu.edu. *Application contact:* Dr. Priyantha Jayawickrama, Graduate Adviser, 806-742-3523, Fax: 806-742-3488, E-mail: priyantha.jayawickrama@ttu.edu.

Trine University, Allen School of Engineering and Technology, Angola, IN 46703-1764. Offers civil engineering (ME); mechanical engineering (ME). Part-time and evening/weekend programs available. *Degree requirements:* For master's, comprehensive exam, thesis. *Faculty research:* CAD, computer aided MFG, computer numerical control, parametric modeling, megatronics.

Tufts University, School of Engineering, Department of Civil and Environmental Engineering, Medford, MA 02155. Offers civil engineering (ME, MS, PhD), including geotechnical engineering, structural engineering; environmental engineering (ME, MS, PhD), including environmental engineering and environmental sciences, environmental geotechnology, environmental health, environmental science and management, hazardous materials management, water resources engineering. Part-time programs available. Terminal master's awarded for partial completion of doctoral program. *Degree requirements:* For master's, thesis or alternative; for doctorate, thesis/dissertation. *Entrance requirements:* For master's and doctorate, GRE General Test. Additional exam requirements/recommendations for international students: Required—TOEFL (minimum score 550 paper-based; 213 computer-based; 80 iBT). Electronic applications accepted. *Expenses:* Tuition: Full-time $39,624; part-time $3962 per course. Required fees: $40 per year. Full-time tuition and fees vary according to degree level, program and student level. Part-time tuition and fees vary according to course load.

Université de Moncton, Faculty of Engineering, Program in Civil Engineering, Moncton, NB E1A 3E9, Canada. Offers M Sc A. *Degree requirements:* For master's, thesis, proficiency in French. *Faculty research:* Structures and materials, hydrology and water resources, soil mechanics and statistical analysis, environment, transportation.

Université de Sherbrooke, Faculty of Engineering, Department of Civil Engineering, Sherbrooke, QC J1K 2R1, Canada. Offers M Sc A, PhD. *Degree requirements:* For master's, one foreign language, thesis; for doctorate, comprehensive exam, thesis/dissertation. *Entrance requirements:* For master's, bachelor's degree in engineering or equivalent; for doctorate, master's degree in engineering or equivalent. Electronic applications accepted. *Faculty research:* High-strength concrete, dynamics of structures, solid mechanics, geotechnical engineering, wastewater treatment.

Université Laval, Faculty of Sciences and Engineering, Department of Civil Engineering, Program in Urban Infrastructure Engineering, Québec, QC G1K 7P4, Canada. Offers Diploma. Part-time and evening/weekend programs available. *Entrance requirements:* For degree, knowledge of French. Electronic applications accepted.

Université Laval, Faculty of Sciences and Engineering, Department of Civil Engineering, Programs in Civil Engineering, Québec, QC G1K 7P4, Canada. Offers civil engineering (M Sc, PhD); environmental technology (M Sc). Terminal master's awarded for partial completion of doctoral program. *Degree requirements:* For master's, thesis (for some programs); for doctorate, comprehensive exam, thesis/dissertation. *Entrance requirements:* For master's and doctorate, knowledge of French and English. Electronic applications accepted.

University at Buffalo, the State University of New York, Graduate School, School of Engineering and Applied Sciences, Department of Civil, Structural, and Environmental Engineering, Buffalo, NY 14260. Offers civil engineering (ME, MS, PhD); engineering science (MS). Part-time programs available. Postbaccalaureate distance learning degree programs offered (minimal on-campus study). *Faculty:* 25 full-time (3 women), 3 part-time/adjunct (1 woman). *Students:* 173 full-time (26 women), 21 part-time (7 women); includes 1 Black or African American, non-Hispanic/Latino; 1 American Indian or Alaska Native, non-Hispanic/Latino; 6 Asian, non-Hispanic/Latino; 4 Hispanic/Latino, 133 international. Average age 27. 542 applicants, 38% accepted, 71 enrolled. In 2010, 34 master's, 4 doctorates awarded. Terminal master's awarded for partial completion of doctoral program. *Degree requirements:* For master's, thesis optional, project, thesis, or comprehensive exam; for doctorate, thesis/dissertation. *Entrance requirements:* For master's and doctorate, GRE General Test, letters of reference. Additional exam requirements/recommendations for international students: Required—TOEFL (minimum score 550 paper-based; 213 computer-based; 79 iBT). *Application deadline:* For fall admission, 1/15 priority date for domestic and international students; for spring admission, 9/15 for domestic and international students. Applications are processed on a rolling basis. Application fee: $50. Electronic applications accepted. *Financial support:* In 2010–11, 115 students received support, including 15 fellowships with full tuition reimbursements available (averaging $17,200 per year), 59 research assistantships with full tuition reimbursements available (averaging $14,000 per year), 35 teaching assistantships with full tuition reimbursements available (averaging $14,700 per year); career-related internships or fieldwork, Federal Work-Study, institutionally sponsored loans, scholarships/grants, traineeships, health care benefits, tuition waivers (full and partial), and unspecified assistantships also available. Support available to part-time students. Financial award application deadline: 1/15; financial award applicants required to submit FAFSA. *Faculty research:* Environmental engineering and fluid mechanics, structural dynamics, geomechanics, earthquake engineering computational mechanics. Total annual research expenditures: $9.7 million. *Unit head:* Dr. Andrew S. Whittaker, Chairman, 716-645-2114, Fax: 716-645-3733, E-mail: awhittak@buffalo.edu. *Application contact:* Dr. Gilberto Mosqueda, Director of Graduate Studies, 716-645-4356, Fax: 716-645-3733, E-mail: mosqueda@buffalo.edu.

The University of Akron, Graduate School, College of Engineering, Department of Civil Engineering, Akron, OH 44325. Offers MS, PhD. Evening/weekend programs available. *Faculty:* 15 full-time (3 women), 5 part-time/adjunct (0 women). *Students:* 49 full-time (9 women), 16 part-time (6 women), 32 international. Average age 27. 62 applicants, 71% accepted, 18 enrolled. In 2010, 14 master's, 5 doctorates awarded. *Degree requirements:* For master's, thesis optional; for doctorate, thesis/dissertation, candidacy exam, qualifying exam. *Entrance requirements:* For master's, GRE, minimum GPA of 2.75, three statement of purpose, letters of recommendation, resume; for doctorate, GRE, minimum GPA of 3.0 with bachelor's degree, 3.5 with master's degree; three letters of recommendation; statement of purpose, resume. Additional exam requirements/recommendations for international students: Required—TOEFL (minimum score 550 paper-based; 213 computer-based; 79 iBT). *Application deadline:* Applications are processed on a rolling basis. Application fee: $30 ($40 for international students). Electronic applications accepted. *Expenses:* Tuition, state resident: full-time $6800; part-time $378 per credit hour. Tuition, nonresident: full-time $11,644; part-time $647 per credit hour. Required fees: $1265. One-time fee: $30 full-time. *Financial support:* In 2010–11, 2 fellowships with full tuition reimbursements, 7 research assistantships with full tuition reimbursements, 35 teaching assistantships with full tuition reimbursements were awarded; career-related internships or fieldwork and Federal Work-Study also available. *Faculty research:* Development of constitutive laws for numerical analysis of nonlinear problems in structural mechanics, multiscale modeling and simulation of novel materials, water quality and distribution system analysis, safety-related traffic control, dynamic pile testing and analysis. Total annual research expenditures: $1.8 million. *Unit head:* Dr. Wieslaw K. Binienda, Chair, 330-972-6693, E-mail: wbinienda@uakron.edu. *Application contact:* Dr. Wieslaw K. Binienda, Chair, 330-972-6693, E-mail: wbinienda@uakron.edu.

The University of Alabama, Graduate School, College of Engineering, Department of Civil, Construction and Environmental Engineering, Tuscaloosa, AL 35487-0205. Offers civil engineering (MSCE, PhD); environmental engineering (MS). Part-time programs available. *Faculty:* 20 full-time (2 women), 1 part-time/adjunct (0 women). *Students:* 40 full-time (12 women), 12 part-time (3 women); includes 9 minority (7 Black or African American, non-Hispanic/Latino; 1 Asian, non-Hispanic/Latino; 1 Two or more races, non-Hispanic/Latino), 15 international. Average age 29. 67 applicants, 51% accepted, 12 enrolled. In 2010, 21 master's, 2 doctorates awarded. Terminal master's awarded for partial completion of doctoral program. *Degree requirements:* For master's, thesis or alternative; for doctorate, one foreign language, thesis/dissertation. *Entrance requirements:* For master's and doctorate, GRE General Test, minimum GPA of 3.0 in last 60 hours of course work. Additional exam requirements/recommendations for international students: Required—TOEFL (minimum score 550 paper-based; 213 computer-based), IELTS (minimum score 6.5). *Application deadline:* For fall admission, 7/6 for domestic students, 1/15 for international students; for spring admission, 11/1 for domestic students, 6/1 for international students. Applications are processed on a rolling basis. Application fee: $50 ($60 for international students). Electronic applications accepted. *Expenses:* Tuition, state resident: full-time $7900. Tuition, nonresident: full-time $20,500. *Financial support:* In 2010–11, 40 students received support, including 32 research assistantships with full tuition reimbursements available (averaging $10,489 per year), 12 teaching assistantships with full tuition reimbursements available (averaging $10,489 per year); fellowships, scholarships/grants, tuition waivers (partial), and unspecified assistantships also available. Financial award application deadline: 3/15. *Faculty research:* Experimental structures, modeling of structures, bridge management systems, geotechnological engineering, environmental remediation. Total annual research expenditures: $1.9 million. *Unit head:* Dr. Kenneth J. Fridley, Head and Professor, 205-348-6550, Fax: 205-348-0783, E-mail: kfridley@coe.eng.ua.edu. *Application contact:* Dr. David A. Francko, Dean, 205-348-8280, Fax: 205-348-0400, E-mail: dfrancko@ua.edu.

The University of Alabama at Birmingham, School of Engineering, Program in Civil Engineering, Birmingham, AL 35294. Offers MSCE, PhD. *Students:* 23 full-time (9 women), 15 part-time (5 women); includes 6 minority (4 Black or African American, non-Hispanic/Latino; 2 Hispanic/Latino), 18 international. Average age 30. 19 applicants, 84% accepted, 8 enrolled. In 2010, 18 master's, 2 doctorates awarded. *Expenses:* Tuition, state resident: full-time $5482. Tuition, nonresident: full-time $12,430. Tuition and fees vary according to program. *Unit head:* Dr. Fouad H. Fouad, Chair, 205-934-8430, Fax: 205-934-9855, E-mail: ffouad@uab.edu. *Application contact:* Julie Bryant, Director of Graduate Admissions, 205-934-8227, Fax: 205-934-8413, E-mail: jbryant@uab.edu.

The University of Alabama in Huntsville, School of Graduate Studies, College of Engineering, Department of Civil and Environmental Engineering, Huntsville, AL 35899. Offers civil and environmental engineering (PhD); civil engineering (MSE), including environmental and water resource engineering, geotechnical engineering, structural engineering and structural mechanics, transportation engineering. PhD offered jointly with The University of Alabama at Birmingham. Part-time and evening/weekend programs available. *Faculty:* 6 full-time (1 woman), 1 part-time/adjunct (0 women). *Students:* 23 full-time (7 women), 11 part-time (4 women); includes 3 minority (2 Black or African American, non-Hispanic/Latino; 1 Asian, non-Hispanic/Latino), 12

Civil Engineering

The University of Alabama in Huntsville (continued)

international. Average age 30. 37 applicants, 57% accepted, 15 enrolled. In 2010, 1 master's, 3 doctorates awarded. *Degree requirements:* For master's, comprehensive exam, thesis or alternative, oral and written exams; for doctorate, comprehensive exam, thesis/dissertation, oral and written exams. *Entrance requirements:* For master's, GRE General Test, BSE, minimum GPA of 3.0; for doctorate, GRE General Test, minimum GPA of 3.0. Additional exam requirements/recommendations for international students: Required—TOEFL (minimum score 500 paper-based; 173 computer-based; 62 iBT). *Application deadline:* For fall admission, 7/15 for domestic students, 4/1 for international students; for spring admission, 11/30 for domestic students, 9/1 for international students. Applications are processed on a rolling basis. Application fee: $40 ($50 for international students). Electronic applications accepted. *Expenses:* Tuition, state resident: full-time $7250; part-time $407.75 per credit hour. Tuition, nonresident: full-time $17,358; part-time $970.05 per credit hour. Required fees: $246.80 per semester. Tuition and fees vary according to course load and program. *Financial support:* In 2010–11, 14 students received support, including 7 research assistantships with full and partial tuition reimbursements available (averaging $12,435 per year), 7 teaching assistantships with full and partial tuition reimbursements available (averaging $10,281 per year); career-related internships or fieldwork, Federal Work-Study, institutionally sponsored loans, scholarships/grants, health care benefits, and unspecified assistantships also available. Support available to part-time students. Financial award application deadline: 4/1; financial award applicants required to submit FAFSA. *Faculty research:* Hydrologic modeling, orbital debris impact, hydrogeology, environmental engineering, transportation engineering. Total annual research expenditures: $1.9 million. *Unit head:* Dr. Houssam Toutanji, Chair, 256-824-7361, Fax: 256-824-6724, E-mail: toutanji@cee.uah.edu. *Application contact:* Kathy Biggs, Graduate Studies Admissions Manager, 256-824-6199, Fax: 256-824-6405, E-mail: deangrad@uah.edu.

University of Alaska Anchorage, School of Engineering, Program in Civil Engineering, Anchorage, AK 99508. Offers civil engineering (MCE, MS); port and coastal engineering (Certificate). Part-time and evening/weekend programs available. *Degree requirements:* For master's, thesis (for some programs). *Entrance requirements:* For master's, bachelor's degree in engineering. Additional exam requirements/recommendations for international students: Required—TOEFL (minimum score 550 paper-based; 213 computer-based). *Faculty research:* Structural engineering, engineering education, astronomical observations related to engineering.

University of Alaska Fairbanks, College of Engineering and Mines, Department of Civil and Environmental Engineering, Fairbanks, AK 99775-5900. Offers arctic engineering (MS, PhD); civil engineering (MCE, MS, PhD); engineering (PhD); engineering and science management (MS, PhD), including engineering management, science management (MS); environmental engineering (MS, PhD), including engineering (PhD), environmental engineering (MS); environmental quality science (MS), including environmental contaminants, environmental quality science, environmental science and management, water supply and waste treatment. Part-time programs available. *Faculty:* 12 full-time (2 women). *Students:* 29 full-time (14 women), 8 part-time (1 woman); includes 3 minority (1 Black or African American, non-Hispanic/Latino; 1 American Indian or Alaska Native, non-Hispanic/Latino; 1 Two or more races, non-Hispanic/Latino), 12 international. Average age 29. 25 applicants, 56% accepted, 10 enrolled. In 2010, 11 master's, 2 doctorates awarded. Terminal master's awarded for partial completion of doctoral program. *Degree requirements:* For master's, comprehensive exam, thesis or alternative; for doctorate, comprehensive exam, thesis/dissertation, oral exam, oral defense. *Entrance requirements:* For doctorate, GRE General Test. Additional exam requirements/recommendations for international students: Required—TOEFL (minimum score 550 paper-based; 213 computer-based; 80 iBT). *Application deadline:* For fall admission, 6/1 for domestic students, 3/1 for international students; for spring admission, 10/15 for domestic students, 9/1 for international students. Applications are processed on a rolling basis. Application fee: $60. Electronic applications accepted. *Expenses:* Tuition, state resident: full-time $5688; part-time $316 per credit. Tuition, nonresident: full-time $11,628; part-time $646 per credit. Required fees: $289 per semester. Tuition and fees vary according to course load and reciprocity agreements. *Financial support:* In 2010–11, 19 research assistantships with tuition reimbursements (averaging $13,400 per year), 6 teaching assistantships with tuition reimbursements (averaging $6,694 per year) were awarded; fellowships with tuition reimbursements, career-related internships or fieldwork, Federal Work-Study, scholarships/grants, health care benefits, and unspecified assistantships also available. Support available to part-time students. Financial award application deadline: 7/1; financial award applicants required to submit FAFSA. *Faculty research:* Soils, structures, culvert thawing with solar power, pavement drainage, contaminant hydrogeology. *Unit head:* Dr. David Barnes, Department Chair, 907-474-7241, Fax: 907-474-6087, E-mail: fycee@uaf.edu. *Application contact:* Dr. David Barnes, Department Chair, 907-474-7241, Fax: 907-474-6087, E-mail: fycee@uaf.edu.

University of Alberta, Faculty of Graduate Studies and Research, Department of Civil and Environmental Engineering, Edmonton, AB T6G 2E1, Canada. Offers construction engineering and management (M Eng, M Sc, PhD); environmental engineering (M Eng, M Sc, PhD); environmental science (M Sc, PhD); geoenvironmental engineering (M Eng, M Sc, PhD); geotechnical engineering (M Eng, M Sc, PhD); mining engineering (M Eng, M Sc, PhD); petroleum engineering (M Eng, M Sc, PhD); structural engineering (M Eng, M Sc, PhD); water resources (M Eng, M Sc, PhD). Part-time programs available. Postbaccalaureate distance learning degree programs offered (minimal on-campus study). *Degree requirements:* For master's, thesis (for some programs); for doctorate, thesis/dissertation. *Entrance requirements:* For master's, minimum GPA of 3.0 in last 2 years of undergraduate studies; for doctorate, minimum GPA of 3.0. Additional exam requirements/recommendations for international students: Required—TOEFL (minimum score 550 paper-based; 213 computer-based). Electronic applications accepted. *Faculty research:* Mining.

The University of Arizona, College of Engineering, Department of Civil Engineering and Engineering Mechanics, Program in Civil Engineering, Tucson, AZ 85721. Offers MS, PhD. Part-time programs available. *Students:* 38 full-time (11 women), 23 part-time (3 women); includes 3 American Indian or Alaska Native, non-Hispanic/Latino; 3 Asian, non-Hispanic/Latino; 3 Hispanic/Latino, 33 international. Average age 30. 74 applicants, 46% accepted, 7 enrolled. In 2010, 7 master's, 6 doctorates awarded. *Degree requirements:* For master's, thesis; for doctorate, thesis/dissertation, departmental qualifying exam. *Entrance requirements:* For master's, GRE General Test, 3 letters of recommendation, statement of purpose; for doctorate, GRE General Test, minimum GPA of 3.5, 3 letters of recommendation, statement of purpose. Additional exam requirements/recommendations for international students: Required—TOEFL (minimum score 550 paper-based; 213 computer-based; 79 iBT). *Application deadline:* For fall admission, 6/1 for domestic students, 12/1 for international students; for spring admission, 10/1 for domestic students, 6/1 for international students. Applications are processed on a rolling basis. Application fee: $75. Electronic applications accepted. *Expenses:* Tuition, state resident: full-time $7692. *Financial support:* Institutionally sponsored loans and unspecified assistantships available. Financial award application deadline: 4/6. *Faculty research:* Soil-structure interaction, water resources, waste disposal, concrete and steel structures. *Unit head:* Kevin E. Lansey, Department Head, 520-621-6564, E-mail: lansey@engr.arizona.edu. *Application contact:* Graduate Coordinator, 520-621-2266, Fax: 520-621-2550, E-mail: ceem@engr.arizona.edu.

University of Arkansas, Graduate School, College of Engineering, Department of Civil Engineering, Program in Civil Engineering, Fayetteville, AR 72701-1201. Offers MSCE, MSE, PhD. *Students:* 25 full-time (3 women), 15 part-time (4 women); includes 2 minority (1 Black or African American, non-Hispanic/Latino; 1 Asian, non-Hispanic/Latino), 12 international. 23 applicants, 74% accepted. In 2010, 17 master's, 3 doctorates awarded. *Degree requirements:* For master's, thesis optional; for doctorate, one foreign language, thesis/dissertation. *Application deadline:* For fall admission, 4/1 for international students; for spring admission, 10/1 for international students. Applications are processed on a rolling basis. Application fee: $40 ($50 for international students). Electronic applications accepted. *Financial support:* In 2010–11, 4 fellowships, 29 research assistantships were awarded; teaching assistantships, career-related internships or fieldwork and Federal Work-Study also available. Support available to part-time students. Financial award application deadline: 4/1; financial award applicants required to submit FAFSA. *Unit head:* Dr. Kevin Hall, Department Chair, 479-575-4954, Fax: 479-575-7168, E-mail: kdhall@uark.edu. *Application contact:* Dr. Paneer Selvam, Graduate Coordinator, 479-575-4954, E-mail: rps@uark.edu.

The University of British Columbia, Faculty of Applied Science, Department of Civil Engineering, Vancouver, BC V6T 1Z1, Canada. Offers M Eng, MA Sc, PhD. Part-time programs available. *Degree requirements:* For master's, thesis; for doctorate, thesis/dissertation. *Entrance requirements:* Additional exam requirements/recommendations for international students: Required—TOEFL (minimum score 600 paper-based; 250 computer-based), IELTS (minimum score 7), TWE (minimum score 5). Electronic applications accepted. Tuition charges are reported in Canadian dollars. *Expenses:* Tuition, area resident: Full-time $4179 Canadian dollars. International tuition: $7344 Canadian dollars full-time. *Faculty research:* Geotechnology; structural, water, and environmental engineering; transportation; materials and construction engineering.

University of Calgary, Faculty of Graduate Studies, Schulich School of Engineering, Department of Civil Engineering, Calgary, AB T2N 1N4, Canada. Offers M Eng, M Sc, MPM, PhD. Part-time and evening/weekend programs available. *Degree requirements:* For master's, thesis (for some programs); for doctorate, thesis/dissertation, candidacy exam. *Entrance requirements:* For master's, minimum GPA of 3.0; for doctorate, minimum GPA of 3.5. Additional exam requirements/recommendations for international students: Required—TOEFL (minimum score 580 paper-based; 230 computer-based). *Faculty research:* Structures, including structural materials; transportation; project management and biomechanics; geotechnical engineering; environmental engineering.

University of California, Berkeley, Graduate Division, College of Engineering, Department of Civil and Environmental Engineering, Berkeley, CA 94720-1500. Offers engineering and project management (M Eng, MS, D Eng, PhD); environmental engineering (M Eng, MS, D Eng, PhD); geoengineering (M Eng, MS, D Eng, PhD); structural engineering, mechanics and materials (M Eng, MS, D Eng, PhD); transportation engineering (M Eng, MS, D Eng, PhD); M Arch/MS; MCP/MS; MPP/MS. *Degree requirements:* For master's, comprehensive exam or thesis (MS); for doctorate, thesis/dissertation, qualifying exam. *Entrance requirements:* For master's, GRE General Test, minimum GPA of 3.0, 3 letters of recommendation; for doctorate, GRE General Test, minimum GPA of 3.5, 3 letters of recommendation. Additional exam requirements/recommendations for international students: Required—TOEFL (minimum score 570 paper-based; 230 computer-based). Electronic applications accepted.

University of California, Davis, College of Engineering, Program in Civil and Environmental Engineering, Davis, CA 95616. Offers M Engr, MS, D Engr, PhD, Certificate, M Engr/MBA. *Degree requirements:* For master's, comprehensive exam (for some programs), thesis (for some programs); for doctorate, thesis/dissertation. *Entrance requirements:* For master's, GRE General Test, minimum GPA of 3.0; for doctorate, GRE, minimum graduate GPA of 3.5. Additional exam requirements/recommendations for international students: Required—TOEFL (minimum score 550 paper-based; 213 computer-based). Electronic applications accepted. *Faculty research:* Environmental water resources, transportation, structural mechanics, structural engineering, geotechnical engineering.

University of California, Irvine, School of Engineering, Department of Civil and Environmental Engineering, Irvine, CA 92697. Offers MS, PhD. Part-time programs available. *Students:* 115 full-time (30 women), 13 part-time (3 women); includes 27 minority (19 Asian, non-Hispanic/Latino; 8 Hispanic/Latino), 67 international. Average age 28. 333 applicants, 35% accepted, 42 enrolled. In 2010, 34 master's, 13 doctorates awarded. Terminal master's awarded for partial completion of doctoral program. *Degree requirements:* For doctorate, thesis/dissertation. *Entrance requirements:* For master's and doctorate, GRE General Test, minimum GPA of 3.0, 3 letters of recommendation. Additional exam requirements/recommendations for international students: Required—TOEFL (minimum score 550 paper-based; 213 computer-based). *Application deadline:* For fall admission, 1/15 priority date for domestic students, 1/15 for international students. Applications are processed on a rolling basis. Application fee: $80 ($100 for international students). Electronic applications accepted. *Financial support:* Fellowships, research assistantships with full tuition reimbursements, teaching assistantships, institutionally sponsored loans, traineeships, health care benefits, and unspecified assistantships available. Financial award application deadline: 3/1; financial award applicants required to submit FAFSA. *Faculty research:* Intelligent transportation systems and transportation economics, risk and reliability, fluid mechanics, environmental hydrodynamics, hydrological and climate systems, water resources. *Unit head:* Prof. Brett F. Sanders, Chair, 949-824-4327, Fax: 949-824-3672, E-mail: bsanders@uci.edu. *Application contact:* April M. Heath, Graduate Coordinator, 949-824-0584, Fax: 949-824-2117, E-mail: a.heath@uci.edu.

University of California, Los Angeles, Graduate Division, Henry Samueli School of Engineering and Applied Science, Department of Civil and Environmental Engineering, Los Angeles, CA 90095-1593. Offers MS, PhD. *Faculty:* 17 full-time (3 women). *Students:* 143 full-time (48 women); includes 39 Asian, non-Hispanic/Latino; 8 Hispanic/Latino, 45 international. 293 applicants, 56% accepted, 66 enrolled. In 2010, 53 master's, 21 doctorates awarded. *Degree requirements:* For master's, comprehensive exam or thesis; for doctorate, thesis/dissertation, qualifying exams. *Entrance requirements:* For master's, GRE General Test, minimum GPA of 3.0; for doctorate, GRE General Test, minimum GPA of 3.25. Additional exam requirements/recommendations for international students: Required—TOEFL (minimum score 560 paper-based; 220 computer-based; 87 iBT). *Application deadline:* For fall admission, 12/15 priority date for domestic and international students. Application fee: $70 ($90 for international students). Electronic applications accepted. *Financial support:* In 2010–11, 105 fellowships, 93 research assistantships, 48 teaching assistantships were awarded; Federal Work-Study, institutionally sponsored loans, and tuition waivers (full and partial) also available. Financial award application deadline: 12/15; financial award applicants required to submit FAFSA. Total annual research expenditures: $4 million. *Unit head:* Dr. Jiun-Shyan Chen, Chair, 310-267-4620. *Application contact:* Maida Bassili, Graduate Affairs Officer, 310-825-1851, Fax: 310-206-2222, E-mail: maida@ea.ucla.edu.

University of Central Florida, College of Engineering and Computer Science, Department of Civil, Environmental, and Construction Engineering, Program in Civil Engineering, Orlando, FL 32816. Offers civil engineering (MS, MSCE, PhD); construction engineering (Certificate); structural engineering (Certificate); transportation engineering (Certificate). Part-time and evening/weekend programs available. *Students:* 62 full-time (7 women), 77 part-time (15 women); includes 30 minority (4 Black or African American, non-Hispanic/Latino; 7 Asian, non-Hispanic/Latino; 17 Hispanic/Latino; 2 Two or more races, non-Hispanic/Latino), 35 international. Average age 30. 125 applicants, 73% accepted, 46 enrolled. In 2010, 26 master's, 8 doctorates awarded. *Degree requirements:* For master's, thesis or alternative; for doctorate, thesis/dissertation, departmental qualifying exam, candidacy exam. *Entrance requirements:* For master's, GRE General Test, minimum GPA of 3.0 in last 60 hours; for doctorate, GRE General Test, minimum GPA of 3.5 in last 60 hours. Additional exam requirements/recommendations for international students: Required—TOEFL. *Application deadline:* For fall admission, 7/15 priority date for domestic students; for spring admission, 12/15 priority date for domestic students. Application fee: $30. Electronic applications accepted. *Expenses:* Tuition, state resident: part-time $256.56 per credit hour. Tuition, nonresident: part-time $1011.52 per credit hour. Part-time tuition and fees vary according to program. *Financial support:* In 2010–11, 29 students received support, including 1 fellowship with partial tuition reimbursement available (averaging $10,000 per year), 22 research assistantships with partial tuition reimbursements available (averaging $11,000 per year), 18 teaching assistantships with partial tuition reimbursements available (averaging $7,900 per year); career-related internships or fieldwork, Federal Work-Study, institutionally sponsored loans, tuition waivers (partial), and unspecified assistantships also available. Financial award application deadline: 3/1; financial award applicants required to submit FAFSA.

University of Cincinnati, Graduate School, College of Engineering, Department of Civil and Environmental Engineering, Program in Civil Engineering, Cincinnati, OH 45221. Offers MS, PhD. Part-time programs available. Terminal master's awarded for partial completion of doctoral program. *Degree requirements:* For master's, project or thesis; for doctorate, one foreign language, thesis/dissertation. *Entrance requirements:* For master's and doctorate, GRE General Test. Additional exam requirements/recommendations for international students: Required—TOEFL (minimum score 580 paper-based; 237 computer-based; 92 iBT). Electronic applications accepted. *Faculty research:* Soil mechanics and foundations, structures, transportation, water resources systems and hydraulics.

University of Colorado Boulder, Graduate School, College of Engineering and Applied Science, Department of Civil, Environmental, and Architectural Engineering, Boulder, CO 80309. Offers building systems (MS, PhD); construction engineering management (MS, PhD); environmental engineering (MS, PhD); geotechnical engineering and geomechanics (MS, PhD); hydrology, water resources and environmental fluid mechanics (MS, PhD); structural engineering and structural mechanics (MS, PhD). *Faculty:* 38 full-time (6 women). *Students:* 255 full-time (86 women), 40 part-time (11 women); includes 40 minority (1 Black or African American, non-Hispanic/Latino; 2 American Indian or Alaska Native, non-Hispanic/Latino; 15 Asian, non-Hispanic/Latino; 20 Hispanic/Latino; 2 Two or more races, non-Hispanic/Latino), 61 international. Average age 28. 420 applicants, 95 enrolled. In 2010, 56 master's, 18 doctorates awarded. *Degree requirements:* For master's, comprehensive exam, thesis or alternative; for doctorate, thesis/dissertation. *Entrance requirements:* For master's, GRE General Test, minimum undergraduate GPA of 3.0. *Application deadline:* For fall admission, 3/1 for domestic students, 12/1 for international students; for spring admission, 10/31 for domestic students, 10/1 for international students. Application fee: $50 ($60 for international students). *Financial support:* In 2010–11, 45 fellowships (averaging $7,876 per year), 68 research assistantships (averaging $15,204 per year) were awarded. Financial award application deadline: 1/15. *Faculty research:* Building systems engineering, construction engineering and management, environmental engineering, geoenvironmental engineering, geotechnical engineering, materials and mechanics, structural engineering, water resources engineering, life-cycle engineering. Total annual research expenditures: $8 million.

University of Colorado Denver, College of Engineering and Applied Science, Department of Civil Engineering, Denver, CO 80217-3364. Offers civil engineering (PhD); environmental and sustainability engineering (MS); geographic information systems (MS); geotechnical engineering (MS); hydrology and hydraulics (MS); structural engineering (MS); transportation engineering (MS). Part-time and evening/weekend programs available. *Faculty:* 14 full-time (1 woman), 6 part-time/adjunct (0 women). *Students:* 66 full-time (13 women), 72 part-time (16 women); includes 9 Black or African American, non-Hispanic/Latino; 8 Asian, non-Hispanic/Latino; 11 Hispanic/Latino, 15 international. Average age 32. 72 applicants, 54% accepted, 29 enrolled. In 2010, 14 master's, 3 doctorates awarded. *Degree requirements:* For master's, comprehensive exam, thesis or alternative; for doctorate, comprehensive exam, thesis/dissertation. *Entrance requirements:* For master's, GRE, statement of purpose, transcripts, references; for doctorate, GRE, statement of purpose, transcripts, references, letter of support from faculty stating willingness to serve as dissertation advisor and outlining plan for financial support. Additional exam requirements/recommendations for international students: Required—TOEFL (minimum score 525 paper-based; 197 computer-based). *Application deadline:* For fall admission, 7/15 for domestic students, 6/15 for international students; for spring admission, 12/1 for domestic students, 11/1 for international students. Applications are processed on a rolling basis. Application fee: $50 ($75 for international students). Electronic applications accepted. *Expenses:* Contact institution. *Financial support:* Research assistantships, teaching assistantships, career-related internships or fieldwork and Federal Work-Study available. Financial award application deadline: 4/1; financial award applicants required to submit FAFSA. *Faculty research:* Environmental engineering and sustainable systems, geosynthetics, hydrologic andhydraulic engineering, structural engineering, transportation, transportation energy use and greenhouse gas emissions. *Unit head:* Dr. Nien-Yin Chang, Acting Chair, 303-556-2810, Fax: 303-556-2368, E-mail: nien.chang@ucdenver.edu. *Application contact:* Mindy Gewuerz, Program Assistant, 303-556-6712, Fax: 303-556-2368, E-mail: mindy.gewuerz@ucdenver.edu.

University of Colorado Denver, College of Engineering and Applied Science, Master of Engineering Program, Denver, CO 80217-3364. Offers civil engineering (M Eng); electrical engineering (M Eng); mechanical engineering (M Eng). Part-time programs available. *Students:* 26 full-time (9 women), 31 part-time (8 women); includes 1 Black or African American, non-Hispanic/Latino; 3 Asian, non-Hispanic/Latino; 1 Hispanic/Latino, 2 international. Average age 36. 22 applicants, 77% accepted, 14 enrolled. In 2010, 23 master's awarded. *Degree requirements:* For master's, comprehensive exam, thesis, 27 credit hours of course work, 3 credit hours of report or thesis work. *Entrance requirements:* For master's, GRE (required for those with GPA below 2.75), transcripts, references, statement of purpose. Additional exam requirements/recommendations for international students: Required—TOEFL (minimum score 525 paper-based; 71 iBT). *Application deadline:* For fall admission, 7/15 for domestic students, 6/15 for international students; for spring admission, 12/1 for domestic students, 11/1 for international students. Applications are processed on a rolling basis. Application fee: $50 ($75 for international students). Electronic applications accepted. *Expenses:* Contact institution. *Financial support:* Federal Work-Study and scholarships/grants available. Financial award application deadline: 4/1; financial award applicants required to submit FAFSA. *Faculty research:* Civil, electrical and mechanical engineering.

University of Connecticut, Graduate School, School of Engineering, Department of Civil and Environmental Engineering, Field of Civil Engineering, Storrs, CT 06269. Offers MS, PhD. Terminal master's awarded for partial completion of doctoral program. *Degree requirements:* For master's, comprehensive exam, thesis or alternative; for doctorate, thesis/dissertation. *Entrance requirements:* Additional exam requirements/recommendations for international students: Required—TOEFL (minimum score 550 paper-based; 213 computer-based). Electronic applications accepted.

University of Dayton, Graduate School, School of Engineering, Department of Civil and Environmental Engineering and Engineering Mechanics, Dayton, OH 45469-1300. Offers engineering mechanics (MSEM); environmental engineering (MSCE); geotechnical engineering (MSCE); structural engineering (MSCE); transportation engineering (MSCE); water resources engineering (MSCE). Part-time programs available. *Faculty:* 7 full-time (2 women), 2 part-time/adjunct (0 women). *Students:* 10 full-time (5 women), 7 part-time (2 women); includes 2 minority (both Black or African American, non-Hispanic/Latino), 6 international. Average age 27. 23 applicants, 43% accepted, 4 enrolled. In 2010, 5 master's awarded. *Degree requirements:* For master's, thesis optional. *Entrance requirements:* For master's, minimum GPA of 3.0 in undergraduate work. Additional exam requirements/recommendations for international students: Required—TOEFL (minimum score 550 paper-based; 213 computer-based; 80 iBT). *Application deadline:* For fall admission, 8/1 for domestic students, 3/1 priority date for international students; for winter admission, 7/1 priority date for international students; for spring admission, 1/1 priority date for international students. Applications are processed on a rolling basis. Application fee: $0 ($50 for international students). Electronic applications accepted. *Expenses:* Tuition: Full-time $7800; part-time $650 per credit hour. *Financial support:* In 2010–11, 2 research assistantships (averaging $10,600 per year) were awarded. Financial award applicants required to submit FAFSA. *Faculty research:* Physical modeling of hydraulic systems, finite element methods, mechanics of composite materials, transportation systems safety, biological treatment processes. Total annual research expenditures: $200,000. *Unit head:* Dr. Donald V. Chase, Chair, 937-229-3847, Fax: 937-229-3491, E-mail: donald.chase@notes.udayton.edu. *Application contact:* Alexander Popovski, Associate Director of International and Graduate Admissions, 937-229-2357, Fax: 937-229-4729, E-mail: alex.popovski@notes.udayton.edu.

University of Delaware, College of Engineering, Department of Civil and Environmental Engineering, Newark, DE 19716. Offers environmental engineering (MAS, MCE, PhD); geotechnical engineering (MAS, MCE, PhD); ocean engineering (MAS, MCE, PhD); structural engineering (MAS, MCE, PhD); transportation engineering (MAS, MCE, PhD); water resource engineering (MAS, MCE, PhD). Part-time programs available. Terminal master's awarded for partial completion of doctoral program. *Degree requirements:* For master's, thesis; for doctorate, thesis/dissertation. *Entrance requirements:* For master's and doctorate, GRE General Test. Additional exam requirements/recommendations for international students: Required—TOEFL. Electronic applications accepted. *Faculty research:* Structural engineering and mechanics; transportation engineering; ocean engineering; soil mechanics and foundation; water resources and environmental engineering.

University of Detroit Mercy, College of Engineering and Science, Department of Civil and Environmental Engineering, Detroit, MI 48221. Offers ME, DE. Evening/weekend programs available. *Faculty research:* Geotechnical engineering.

University of Florida, Graduate School, College of Engineering, Department of Civil and Coastal Engineering, Gainesville, FL 32611. Offers civil engineering (MCE, MS, PhD, Engr); coastal and oceanographic engineering (ME, MS, PhD, Engr). Part-time programs available. Postbaccalaureate distance learning degree programs offered (no on-campus study). *Faculty:* 29 full-time (2 women). *Students:* 238 full-time (55 women), 79 part-time (16 women); includes 12 Black or African American, non-Hispanic/Latino; 1 American Indian or Alaska Native, non-Hispanic/Latino; 11 Asian, non-Hispanic/Latino; 30 Hispanic/Latino, 115 international. Average age 27. 445 applicants, 60% accepted, 78 enrolled. In 2010, 115 master's, 23 doctorates awarded. Terminal master's awarded for partial completion of doctoral program. *Degree requirements:* For master's, thesis (for some programs); for doctorate, comprehensive exam, thesis/dissertation. *Entrance requirements:* For master's and doctorate, GRE General Test, minimum GPA of 3.0. Additional exam requirements/recommendations for international students: Required—TOEFL (minimum score 550 paper-based; 213 computer-based; 80 iBT), IELTS (minimum score 6). *Application deadline:* For fall admission, 8/1 priority date for domestic students, 1/31 for international students; for winter admission, 9/30 for international students; for spring admission, 12/1 for domestic students, 1/31 for international students. Applications are processed on a rolling basis. Application fee: $30. Electronic applications accepted. *Expenses:* Tuition, state resident: full-time $10,915.92. Tuition, nonresident: full-time $28,309. *Financial support:* In 2010–11, 118 students received support, including 14 fellowships, 85 research assistantships (averaging $20,326 per year), 19 teaching assistantships (averaging $14,158 per year); unspecified assistantships also available. Financial award application deadline: 1/31; financial award applicants required to submit FAFSA. *Faculty research:* Traffic congestion mitigation, wind mitigation, sustainable infrastructure materials, improved sensors for in situ measurements, storm surge modeling. Total annual research expenditures: $8.9 million. *Unit head:* Dr. Kirk Hatfield, Interim Department Chair, 352-392-9537 Ext. 1441, Fax: 352-392-3394, E-mail: khatf@ufl.edu. *Application contact:* Mange Tia, Graduate Coordinator, 352-392-9537 Ext. 1463, Fax: 352-392-3394, E-mail: tia@ce.ufl.edu.

University of Hawaii at Manoa, Graduate Division, College of Engineering, Department of Civil and Environmental Engineering, Honolulu, HI 96822. Offers MS, PhD. Part-time programs available. *Faculty:* 24 full-time (2 women). *Students:* 58 full-time (12 women), 22 part-time (6 women); includes 46 minority (32 Asian, non-Hispanic/Latino; 1 Hispanic/Latino; 7 Native Hawaiian or other Pacific Islander, non-Hispanic/Latino; 6 Two or more races, non-Hispanic/Latino), 24 international. Average age 29. 99 applicants, 64% accepted, 38 enrolled. In 2010, 17 master's, 2 doctorates awarded. *Degree requirements:* For master's, comprehensive exam, thesis; for doctorate, comprehensive exam, thesis/dissertation. *Entrance requirements:* For master's and doctorate, GRE General Test or EIT Exam. Additional exam requirements/recommendations for international students: Required—TOEFL (minimum score 540 paper-based; 207 computer-based; 76 iBT), IELTS (minimum score 5). *Application deadline:* For fall admission, 5/1 for domestic and international students; for spring admission, 9/1 for domestic and international students. Application fee: $60. *Financial support:* In 2010–11, 12 fellowships (averaging $1,277 per year), 30 research assistantships (averaging $18,171 per year), 6 teaching assistantships (averaging $15,293 per year) were awarded; career-related internships or fieldwork, Federal Work-Study, and tuition waivers (full and partial) also available. *Faculty research:* Structures, transportation, environmental engineering, geotechnical engineering, construction. Total annual research expenditures: $1.2 million. *Application contact:* Roger Babcock, Graduate Chair, 808-956-7449, Fax: 808-956-5014, E-mail: rbabcock@hawaii.edu.

University of Houston, Cullen College of Engineering, Department of Civil and Environmental Engineering, Houston, TX 77204. Offers civil engineering (MCE, PhD). Part-time programs available. *Faculty:* 13 full-time (2 women), 6 part-time/adjunct (1 woman). *Students:* 44 full-time (11 women), 37 part-time (10 women); includes 2 Black or African American, non-Hispanic/Latino; 11 Asian, non-Hispanic/Latino; 8 Hispanic/Latino, 34 international. Average age 30. 59 applicants, 66% accepted, 16 enrolled. In 2010, 24 master's, 1 doctorate awarded. Terminal master's awarded for partial completion of doctoral program. *Entrance requirements:* For master's and doctorate, GRE General Test. Additional exam requirements/recommendations for international students: Required—TOEFL (minimum score 550 paper-based; 213 computer-based; 79 iBT), IELTS (minimum score 6.5). *Application deadline:* For fall admission, 5/1 for domestic students, 4/1 for international students; for spring admission, 10/1 for domestic and international students. Applications are processed on a rolling basis. Application fee: $25 ($75 for international students). Electronic applications accepted. *Expenses:* Tuition, state resident: full-time $8592; part-time $358 per credit hour. Tuition, nonresident: full-time $16,032; part-time $668 per credit hour. Required fees: $2889. Tuition and fees vary according to course load and program. *Financial support:* In 2010–11, 11 research assistantships with partial tuition reimbursements (averaging $8,512 per year), 2 teaching assistantships with partial tuition reimbursements (averaging $12,000 per year) were awarded; career-related internships or fieldwork, Federal Work-Study, institutionally sponsored loans, scholarships/grants, health care benefits, and unspecified assistantships also available. Support available to part-time students. Financial award application deadline: 2/1. *Faculty research:* Civil engineering. *Unit head:* Dr. DJ Belarbi, Chairperson, 713-743-4266, Fax: 713-743-4260, E-mail: abelarbi@central.uh.edu. *Application contact:* Jane Geanangel, Graduate Program Academic Records Coordinator, 713-743-4219.

University of Idaho, College of Graduate Studies, College of Engineering, Department of Civil Engineering, Moscow, ID 83844-2282. Offers civil engineering (M Engr, MS, PhD); engineering management (M Engr); geological engineering (MS). *Faculty:* 20 full-time. *Students:* 35 full-time, 79 part-time. Average age 35. In 2010, 14 master's, 1 doctorate awarded. *Degree requirements:* For master's, thesis; for doctorate, thesis/dissertation. *Entrance requirements:* For master's, minimum GPA of 2.8; for doctorate, minimum undergraduate GPA of 2.8, 3.0 graduate. *Application deadline:* For fall admission, 8/1 for domestic students; for spring admission, 12/15 for domestic students. Applications are processed on a rolling basis. Application fee: $60. Electronic applications accepted. *Expenses:* Tuition, nonresident: part-time $580 per credit. Required fees: $306 per credit. *Financial support:* Fellowships, research assistantships, teaching assistantships, career-related internships or fieldwork available. Financial award applicants required to submit FAFSA. *Faculty research:* Water resources systems, structural analysis and design, soil mechanics, transportation technology. *Unit head:* Richard J. Nielsen, Chair, 208-885-8961, E-mail: civilengr@uidaho.edu. *Application contact:* Richard J. Nielsen, Chair, 208-885-8961, E-mail: civilengr@uidaho.edu.

University of Illinois at Chicago, Graduate College, College of Engineering, Department of Civil and Materials Engineering, Chicago, IL 60607-7128. Offers civil engineering (MS, PhD); materials engineering (MS, PhD). Evening/weekend programs available. *Degree requirements:* For master's, thesis (for some programs); for doctorate, thesis/dissertation, preliminary and qualifying exams. *Entrance requirements:* For master's and doctorate, GRE General Test, minimum GPA of 3.0. Additional exam requirements/recommendations for international students: Required—TOEFL. Electronic applications accepted. *Faculty research:* Transportation and geotechnical engineering, damage and anisotropic behavior, steel processing.

University of Illinois at Urbana–Champaign, Graduate College, College of Engineering, Department of Civil and Environmental Engineering, Champaign, IL 61820. Offers civil engineering (MS); environmental engineering in civil engineering (MS, PhD); environmental science in civil engineering (MS, PhD); M Arch/MS; MBA/MS. *Faculty:* 46 full-time (7 women),

Civil Engineering

University of Illinois at Urbana–Champaign (continued)
1 part-time/adjunct (0 women). *Students:* 380 full-time (103 women), 79 part-time (18 women); includes 2 Black or African American, non-Hispanic/Latino; 27 Asian, non-Hispanic/Latino; 15 Hispanic/Latino; 4 Two or more races, non-Hispanic/Latino, 248 international. 961 applicants, 38% accepted, 159 enrolled. In 2010, 119 master's, 45 doctorates awarded. *Entrance requirements:* For master's and doctorate, GRE. Additional exam requirements/recommendations for international students: Required—TOEFL (minimum score 550 paper-based; 213 computer-based; 79 iBT) or IELTS (minimum score 6.5). *Application deadline:* Applications are processed on a rolling basis. Application fee: $75 ($90 for international students). Electronic applications accepted. *Financial support:* In 2010–11, 60 fellowships, 260 research assistantships, 77 teaching assistantships were awarded; tuition waivers (full and partial) also available. *Unit head:* Amr S. Elnashai, Head, 217-265-5497, Fax: 217-265-8040, E-mail: aelnash@illinois.edu. *Application contact:* Mary Pearson, Administrative Secretary, 217-333-3811, Fax: 217-333-9464, E-mail: mkpearso@illinois.edu.

The University of Iowa, Graduate College, College of Engineering, Department of Civil and Environmental Engineering, Iowa City, IA 52242-1316. Offers MS, PhD. Part-time programs available. *Faculty:* 21 full-time (3 women). *Students:* 94 full-time (24 women); includes 3 minority (1 Black or African American, non-Hispanic/Latino; 1 Asian, non-Hispanic/Latino; 1 Hispanic/Latino), 39 international. Average age 27. 216 applicants, 30% accepted, 32 enrolled. In 2010, 24 master's, 11 doctorates awarded. Terminal master's awarded for partial completion of doctoral program. *Degree requirements:* For master's, thesis optional, exam; for doctorate, comprehensive exam, thesis/dissertation, exam. *Entrance requirements:* For master's, GRE, minimum undergraduate GPA of 3.0; for doctorate, GRE, master's degree or equivalent with minimum GPA of 3.2. Additional exam requirements/recommendations for international students: Required—TOEFL (minimum score 550 paper-based; 213 computer-based; 81 iBT). *Application deadline:* For fall admission, 2/1 priority date for domestic and international students; for spring admission, 12/1 for domestic students, 10/1 for international students. Applications are processed on a rolling basis. Application fee: $60 ($100 for international students). Electronic applications accepted. *Financial support:* In 2010–11, 7 fellowships with partial tuition reimbursements (averaging $23,480 per year), 74 research assistantships with partial tuition reimbursements (averaging $22,553 per year), 26 teaching assistantships with partial tuition reimbursements (averaging $16,575 per year) were awarded; career-related internships or fieldwork, Federal Work-Study, scholarships/grants, traineeships, and unspecified assistantships also available. Support available to part-time students. Financial award application deadline: 2/1; financial award applicants required to submit FAFSA. *Faculty research:* Water resources; environmental engineering and science; hydraulics and hydrology; structures, mechanics, and materials; transportation engineering. Total annual research expenditures: $16.4 million. *Unit head:* Dr. Michelle Scherer, Department Executive Officer, 319-335-5654, Fax: 319-335-5660, E-mail: michelle-scherer@uiowa.edu. *Application contact:* Judy Holland, Secretary, 319-335-5647, Fax: 319-335-5660, E-mail: cee@engineering.uiowa.edu.

The University of Kansas, Graduate Studies, School of Engineering, Department of Civil, Environmental, and Architectural Engineering, Program in Civil Engineering, Lawrence, KS 66045. Offers MCE, MS, DE, PhD. Part-time and evening/weekend programs available. *Faculty:* 25 full-time (3 women), 2 part-time/adjunct (0 women). *Students:* 50 full-time (11 women), 60 part-time (12 women); includes 12 minority (2 Black or African American, non-Hispanic/Latino; 2 Asian, non-Hispanic/Latino; 6 Hispanic/Latino; 2 Two or more races, non-Hispanic/Latino), 25 international. Average age 29. 71 applicants, 65% accepted, 26 enrolled. In 2010, 25 master's, 3 doctorates awarded. *Degree requirements:* For master's, thesis or alternative, exam; for doctorate, comprehensive exam, thesis/dissertation. *Entrance requirements:* For master's and doctorate, GRE, BS in engineering. Additional exam requirements/recommendations for international students: Required—TOEFL. *Application deadline:* For fall admission, 7/1 priority date for domestic students, 3/1 priority date for international students; for spring admission, 12/1 priority date for domestic students, 8/15 priority date for international students. Applications are processed on a rolling basis. Application fee: $55 ($65 for international students). Electronic applications accepted. *Expenses:* Tuition, state resident: full-time $7092; part-time $295.50 per credit hour. Tuition, nonresident: full-time $16,590; part-time $691.25 per credit hour. Required fees: $858; $71.49 per credit hour. Tuition and fees vary according to course load, campus/location and program. *Financial support:* Fellowships with full tuition reimbursements, research assistantships with full tuition reimbursements, teaching assistantships with full and partial tuition reimbursements, career-related internships or fieldwork available. Financial award application deadline: 2/7. *Faculty research:* Structural engineering, geotechnical engineering, transportation engineering, water resources engineering, construction engineering. *Unit head:* Craig D. Adams, Chair, 785-864-2700, Fax: 785-864-5631, E-mail: adamscd@ku.edu. *Application contact:* Bruce M. McEnroe, Graduate Advisor, 785-864-2925, Fax: 785-864-2925, E-mail: mcenroe@ku.edu.

University of Kentucky, Graduate School, College of Engineering, Program in Civil Engineering, Lexington, KY 40506-0032. Offers MCE, MSCE, PhD. *Degree requirements:* For master's, comprehensive exam, thesis optional; for doctorate, comprehensive exam, thesis/dissertation. *Entrance requirements:* For master's, GRE General Test, minimum undergraduate GPA of 2.75; for doctorate, GRE General Test, minimum undergraduate GPA of 3.0. Additional exam requirements/recommendations for international students: Required—TOEFL (minimum score 550 paper-based; 213 computer-based). Electronic applications accepted. *Faculty research:* Geotechnical engineering, structures, construction engineering and management, environmental engineering and water resources, transportation and materials.

University of Louisiana at Lafayette, College of Engineering, Department of Civil Engineering, Lafayette, LA 70504. Offers MSE. Evening/weekend programs available. *Degree requirements:* For master's, comprehensive exam, thesis or alternative. *Entrance requirements:* For master's, GRE General Test, BS in civil engineering, minimum GPA of 2.85. *Faculty research:* Structural mechanics, computer-aided design, environmental engineering.

University of Louisville, J.B. Speed School of Engineering, Department of Civil and Environmental Engineering, Louisville, KY 40292-0001. Offers civil engineering (M Eng, MS, PhD). *Accreditation:* ABET (one or more programs are accredited). Part-time programs available. Postbaccalaureate distance learning degree programs offered (no on-campus study). *Faculty:* 10 full-time (1 woman). *Students:* 36 full-time (5 women), 21 part-time (3 women); includes 1 Asian, non-Hispanic/Latino, 10 international. Average age 28. 24 applicants, 71% accepted, 12 enrolled. In 2010, 33 master's, 2 doctorates awarded. Terminal master's awarded for partial completion of doctoral program. *Degree requirements:* For master's, comprehensive exam (for some programs), thesis or alternative; for doctorate, comprehensive exam, thesis/dissertation, minimum GPA of 3.0. *Entrance requirements:* For master's and doctorate, GRE General Test. Additional exam requirements/recommendations for international students: Required—TOEFL (minimum score 550 paper-based; 213 computer-based; 80 iBT), IELTS (minimum score 6.5). *Application deadline:* For fall admission, 5/1 priority date for domestic and international students; for spring admission, 11/1 priority date for domestic and international students. Applications are processed on a rolling basis. Application fee: $50. Electronic applications accepted. *Expenses:* Tuition, state resident: full-time $9144; part-time $508 per credit hour. Tuition, nonresident: full-time $19,026; part-time $1057 per credit hour. Tuition and fees vary according to program and reciprocity agreements. *Financial support:* In 2010–11, 7 students received support, including 1 fellowship with full tuition reimbursement available (averaging $20,000 per year), 1 research assistantship with full tuition reimbursement available (averaging $20,000 per year), 5 teaching assistantships with full tuition reimbursements available (averaging $20,000 per year). Financial award application deadline: 1/25; financial award applicants required to submit FAFSA. *Faculty research:* Structures, hydraulics, transportation, environmental engineering, geomechanics. Total annual research expenditures: $1.8 million. *Unit head:* Dr. J. P. Mohsen, Chair, 502-852-6276, Fax: 502-852-8851, E-mail: jpmohs01@louisville.edu. *Application contact:* Dr. Michael Day, Associate Dean, 502-852-6195, Fax: 502-852-7294, E-mail: day@louisville.edu.

University of Maine, Graduate School, College of Engineering, Department of Civil and Environmental Engineering, Orono, ME 04469. Offers water resources (MS). *Faculty:* 10 full-time (2 women), 2 part-time/adjunct (1 woman). *Students:* 30 full-time (9 women), 13 part-time (3 women); includes 2 minority (1 American Indian or Alaska Native, non-Hispanic/Latino; 1 Two or more races, non-Hispanic/Latino), 4 international. Average age 28. 27 applicants, 37% accepted, 9 enrolled. In 2010, 13 master's, 1 doctorate awarded. *Degree requirements:* For doctorate, thesis/dissertation. *Entrance requirements:* For master's and doctorate, GRE General Test. Additional exam requirements/recommendations for international students: Required—TOEFL. *Application deadline:* For fall admission, 2/1 priority date for domestic students. Applications are processed on a rolling basis. Application fee: $65. Electronic applications accepted. *Expenses:* Tuition, state resident: full-time $400. Tuition, nonresident: full-time $1050. *Financial support:* In 2010–11, 15 research assistantships with tuition reimbursements (averaging $15,815 per year), 3 teaching assistantships with tuition reimbursements (averaging $12,790 per year) were awarded; Federal Work-Study, institutionally sponsored loans, scholarships/grants, and tuition waivers (full and partial) also available. Financial award application deadline: 3/1. *Unit head:* Dr. Eric Landis, Chair. *Application contact:* Scott G. Delcourt, Associate Dean of the Graduate School, 207-581-3291, Fax: 207-581-3232, E-mail: graduate@maine.edu.

University of Maine, Graduate School, College of Engineering, Department of Spatial Information Science and Engineering, Orono, ME 04469. Offers MS, PhD. *Faculty:* 7 full-time (1 woman). *Students:* 14 full-time (3 women), 12 part-time (1 woman), 8 international. Average age 34. 21 applicants, 48% accepted, 8 enrolled. In 2010, 4 master's awarded. *Degree requirements:* For master's, thesis (for some programs); for doctorate, thesis/dissertation. *Entrance requirements:* For master's and doctorate, GRE General Test. Additional exam requirements/recommendations for international students: Required—TOEFL. *Application deadline:* For fall admission, 2/1 priority date for domestic students. Applications are processed on a rolling basis. Application fee: $65. Electronic applications accepted. *Expenses:* Tuition, state resident: full-time $400. Tuition, nonresident: full-time $1050. *Financial support:* In 2010–11, 16 research assistantships with tuition reimbursements (averaging $26,470 per year) were awarded; Federal Work-Study, institutionally sponsored loans, and tuition waivers (full and partial) also available. Financial award application deadline: 3/1. *Faculty research:* Geographic information systems, analytical photogrammetry, geodesy, global positioning systems, remote sensing. *Unit head:* Dr. Michael Worboys, Chair, 207-581-3679. *Application contact:* Scott G. Delcourt, Associate Dean of the Graduate School, 207-581-3291, Fax: 207-581-3232, E-mail: graduate@maine.edu.

The University of Manchester, School of Mechanical, Aerospace and Civil Engineering, Manchester, United Kingdom. Offers advanced manufacturing technology (M Ent); aerospace engineering (M Phil, M Sc, PhD); civil engineering (M Phil, M Sc, PhD); environmental engineering (M Phil, PhD); management of projects (M Phil, M Sc, PhD); mechanical engineering (M Phil, M Sc, PhD); mechanical engineering design (M Ent); nuclear engineering (M Phil, D Eng, PhD).

University of Manitoba, Faculty of Graduate Studies, Faculty of Engineering, Department of Civil Engineering, Winnipeg, MB R3T 2N2, Canada. Offers M Eng, M Sc, PhD. *Degree requirements:* For master's, thesis.

University of Maryland, Baltimore County, Graduate School, College of Engineering and Information Technology, Department of Civil and Environmental Engineering, Program in Civil Engineering, Baltimore, MD 21250. Offers MS, PhD. Part-time programs available. *Faculty:* 2 full-time (0 women), 1 part-time/adjunct (0 women). *Students:* 8 full-time (5 women), 5 part-time (2 women); includes 2 minority (1 Asian, non-Hispanic/Latino; 1 Hispanic/Latino), 6 international. Average age 28. 8 applicants, 75% accepted, 1 enrolled. In 2010, 2 master's awarded. *Degree requirements:* For master's, comprehensive exam (for some programs), thesis (for some programs); for doctorate, comprehensive exam, thesis/dissertation. *Entrance requirements:* For master's and doctorate, GRE General Test, BS in civil and environmental engineering or related field of engineering. Additional exam requirements/recommendations for international students: Required—TOEFL (minimum score 550 paper-based; 213 computer-based; 80 iBT). *Application deadline:* For fall admission, 6/1 for domestic students, 1/1 for international students; for spring admission, 11/1 for domestic students, 6/1 for international students. Applications are processed on a rolling basis. Application fee: $50. Electronic applications accepted. *Financial support:* In 2010–11, 7 research assistantships with full tuition reimbursements (averaging $25,000 per year) were awarded; career-related internships or fieldwork, Federal Work-Study, scholarships/grants, health care benefits, tuition waivers (partial), and unspecified assistantships also available. Support available to part-time students. Financial award application deadline: 6/30; financial award applicants required to submit FAFSA. *Faculty research:* Environmental engineering, water resources engineering. *Unit head:* Dr. Brian Reed, Professor and Chair, 410-455-8646, Fax: 410-455-6500, E-mail: reedb@umbc.edu. *Application contact:* Dr. Upal Ghosh, Associate Professor and Graduate Program Director, 410-455-8665, Fax: 410-455-6500, E-mail: ughosh@umbc.edu.

University of Maryland, College Park, Academic Affairs, A. James Clark School of Engineering, Department of Civil and Environmental Engineering, College Park, MD 20742. Offers M Eng, MS, PhD. Part-time and evening/weekend programs available. Postbaccalaureate distance learning degree programs offered. *Faculty:* 65 full-time (12 women), 27 part-time/adjunct (8 women). *Students:* 170 full-time (57 women), 54 part-time (21 women); includes 41 minority (15 Black or African American, non-Hispanic/Latino; 15 Asian, non-Hispanic/Latino; 8 Hispanic/Latino; 3 Two or more races, non-Hispanic/Latino), 112 international. 376 applicants, 35% accepted, 58 enrolled. In 2010, 31 master's, 10 doctorates awarded. *Degree requirements:* For master's, thesis optional; for doctorate, thesis/dissertation, qualifying exam. *Entrance requirements:* For master's and doctorate, GRE General Test, 3 letters of recommendation. *Application deadline:* For fall admission, 5/1 for domestic students, 2/1 for international students; for spring admission, 10/15 for domestic students, 6/1 for international students. Applications are processed on a rolling basis. Application fee: $75. Electronic applications accepted. *Expenses:* Tuition, area resident: Part-time $471 per credit hour. Tuition, state resident: part-time $471 per credit hour. Tuition, nonresident: part-time $1016 per credit hour. Required fees: $337 per term. *Financial support:* In 2010–11, 19 fellowships with full and partial tuition reimbursements (averaging $14,546 per year), 67 research assistantships (averaging $19,189 per year), 29 teaching assistantships (averaging $19,575 per year) were awarded; Federal Work-Study and scholarships/grants also available. Support available to part-time students. Financial award applicants required to submit FAFSA. *Faculty research:* Transportation and urban systems, environmental engineering, geotechnical engineering, construction engineering and management, hydraulics. Total annual research expenditures: $22.6 million. *Unit head:* Dr. Ali Haghani, Chair, 301-405-1974, E-mail: haghani@umd.edu. *Application contact:* Dr. Charles A. Caramello, Dean of Graduate School, 301-405-0358, Fax: 301-314-9305, E-mail: ccaramel@umd.edu.

University of Maryland, College Park, Academic Affairs, A. James Clark School of Engineering, Department of Continuing and Distance Learning in Engineering, College Park, MD 20742. Offers engineering (M Eng), including aerospace engineering, chemical engineering, civil engineering, electrical engineering, engineering, fire protection engineering, materials science and engineering, mechanical engineering, reliability engineering, systems engineering. *Faculty:* 4 full-time (1 woman), 11 part-time/adjunct (1 woman). *Students:* 56 full-time (15 women), 428 part-time (88 women); includes 153 minority (59 Black or African American, non-Hispanic/Latino; 63 Asian, non-Hispanic/Latino; 24 Hispanic/Latino; 7 Two or more races, non-Hispanic/Latino), 55 international. 551 applicants, 82% accepted, 360 enrolled. In 2010, 130 master's awarded. *Application deadline:* For fall admission, 8/15 for domestic students, 1/10 for international students; for spring admission, 12/15 for domestic students, 6/1 for international students. Applications are processed on a rolling basis. Application fee: $75. Electronic applications accepted. *Expenses:* Tuition, area resident: Part-time $471 per credit hour. Tuition, state resident: part-time $471 per credit hour. Tuition, nonresident: part-time $1016 per credit hour. Required fees: $337 per term. *Financial support:* In 2010–11, 2 research assistantships (averaging $20,285 per year), 7 teaching assistantships (averaging $16,962 per year) were awarded. *Unit head:* Dr. Darryll Pines, Dean, 301-405-0376, Fax: 301-314-5908, E-mail: pines@umd.edu. *Application contact:* Dr. Charles A. Caramello, Dean of the Graduate School, 301-405-0358, Fax: 301-314-9305, E-mail: ccaramel@umd.edu.

University of Massachusetts Amherst, Graduate School, College of Engineering, Department of Civil and Environmental Engineering, Program in Civil Engineering, Amherst, MA 01003. Offers MSCE, PhD. Part-time programs available. *Faculty:* 25 full-time (5 women). *Students:* 71 full-time (24 women), 11 part-time (5 women); includes 6 minority (2 Asian, non-Hispanic/Latino; 4 Hispanic/Latino), 28 international. Average age 26. 322 applicants, 46% accepted, 46 enrolled. In 2010, 25 master's, 6 doctorates awarded. Terminal master's awarded for partial completion of doctoral program. *Degree requirements:* For master's, thesis or alternative; for doctorate, comprehensive exam, thesis/dissertation. *Entrance requirements:* For master's and doctorate, GRE General Test. Additional exam requirements/recommendations for international students: Required—TOEFL (minimum score 550 paper-based; 213 computer-based; 80 iBT), IELTS (minimum score 6.5). *Application deadline:* For fall admission, 2/1 for domestic and international students; for spring admission, 10/1 for domestic and international students. Applications are processed on a rolling basis. Application fee: $50 ($65 for international students). Electronic applications accepted. *Expenses:* Tuition, state resident: full-time $2640. Required fees: $8282. One-time fee: $357 full-time. *Financial support:* Fellowships with full tuition reimbursements, research assistantships with full tuition reimbursements, teaching assistantships with full tuition reimbursements, career-related internships or fieldwork, Federal Work-Study, scholarships/grants, traineeships, health care benefits, tuition waivers, and unspecified assistantships available. Support available to part-time students. Financial award application deadline: 2/1; financial award applicants required to submit FAFSA. *Unit head:* Dr. David Ahlfeld, Graduate Program Director, 413-545-0686, Fax: 413-545-2840. *Application contact:* Jean M. Ames, Supervisor of Admissions, 413-545-0722, Fax: 413-577-0100, E-mail: gradadm@grad.umass.edu.

University of Massachusetts Amherst, Graduate School, Interdisciplinary Programs, Program in Civil Engineering and Business Administration, Amherst, MA 01003. Offers MSCE/MBA. Part-time programs available. *Students:* 1 applicant, 0% accepted, 0 enrolled. *Entrance requirements:* Additional exam requirements/recommendations for international students: Required—TOEFL (minimum score 600 paper-based; 250 computer-based; 100 iBT), IELTS (minimum score 7). *Application deadline:* For fall admission, 2/1 for domestic and international students. Applications are processed on a rolling basis. Application fee: $50 ($65 for international students). Electronic applications accepted. *Expenses:* Tuition, state resident: full-time $2640. Required fees: $8282. One-time fee: $357 full-time. *Financial support:* Career-related internships or fieldwork, Federal Work-Study, scholarships/grants, traineeships, health care benefits, tuition waivers (full), and unspecified assistantships available. Support available to part-time students. Financial award application deadline: 2/1; financial award applicants required to submit FAFSA. *Unit head:* Dr. David Ahlfeld, Graduate Program Director, 413-545-0686, Fax: 413-545-2840. *Application contact:* Jean M. Ames, Supervisor of Admissions, 413-545-0722, Fax: 413-577-0010, E-mail: gradadm@grad.umass.edu.

University of Massachusetts Dartmouth, Graduate School, College of Engineering, Program in Civil and Environmental Engineering, North Dartmouth, MA 02747-2300. Offers MS. Part-time programs available. *Faculty:* 8 full-time (2 women), 3 part-time/adjunct (0 women). *Students:* 4 full-time (0 women), 13 part-time (2 women); includes 2 Hispanic/Latino. Average age 25. 28 applicants, 79% accepted, 8 enrolled. In 2010, 2 master's awarded. *Degree requirements:* For master's, thesis or alternative. *Entrance requirements:* For master's, GRE, minimum GPA of 3.0, 3 letters of recommendation. Additional exam requirements/recommendations for international students: Required—TOEFL (minimum score 550 paper-based). *Application deadline:* For fall admission, 4/20 priority date for domestic students, 2/20 priority date for international students; for spring admission, 11/15 priority date for domestic students, 9/15 priority date for international students. Application fee: $40 ($60 for international students). *Expenses:* Tuition, state resident: full-time $2071; part-time $86 per credit. Tuition, nonresident: full-time $8099; part-time $337 per credit. Required fees: $9446; $394 per credit. One-time fee: $75. Part-time tuition and fees vary according to class time, course load, degree level and reciprocity agreements. *Financial support:* In 2010–11, 5 teaching assistantships with full tuition reimbursements (averaging $12,500 per year) were awarded. Financial award application deadline: 3/1; financial award applicants required to submit FAFSA. *Faculty research:* Nutrient removal and recovery, water resources engineering, pavement design and management, waste water treatment systems, hydrology. Total annual research expenditures: $546,183. *Unit head:* Dr. Heather Miller, Graduate Director, 508-999-8481, E-mail: hmiller@umassd.edu. *Application contact:* Elan Turcotte-Shamski, Graduate Admissions Officer, 508-999-8604, Fax: 508-999-8183, E-mail: graduate@umassd.edu.

University of Massachusetts Lowell, James B. Francis College of Engineering, Department of Civil and Environmental Engineering, Lowell, MA 01854-2881. Offers civil and environmental engineering (MS Eng, Certificate); environmental engineering (D Eng); environmental studies (MSES, PhD, Certificate), including environmental engineering (MSES), environmental studies (PhD, Certificate); sustainable infrastructure for developing nations (Certificate). Part-time programs available. *Degree requirements:* For master's, thesis optional. *Entrance requirements:* For master's, GRE General Test. *Faculty research:* Bridge design, traffic control, groundwater remediation, pile capacity.

University of Memphis, Graduate School, Herff College of Engineering, Department of Civil Engineering, Memphis, TN 38152. Offers civil engineering (PhD); environmental engineering (MS); foundation engineering (MS); structural engineering (MS); transportation engineering (MS); water resources engineering (MS). *Faculty:* 12 full-time (1 woman), 1 part-time/adjunct (0 women). *Students:* 12 full-time (5 women), 13 part-time (3 women); includes 2 Black or African American, non-Hispanic/Latino; 2 Asian, non-Hispanic/Latino; 1 Two or more races, non-Hispanic/Latino, 7 international. Average age 28. 22 applicants, 55% accepted, 0 enrolled. In 2010, 11 master's awarded. Terminal master's awarded for partial completion of doctoral program. *Degree requirements:* For master's, comprehensive exam, thesis optional; for doctorate, comprehensive exam, thesis/dissertation. *Entrance requirements:* For master's, GRE General Test or MAT, minimum undergraduate GPA of 2.5; for doctorate, GRE, 3 letters of recommendation. Additional exam requirements/recommendations for international students: Required—TOEFL (minimum score 550 paper-based; 210 computer-based; 79 iBT). *Application deadline:* For fall admission, 1/7 for domestic students, 1/5 for international students; for spring admission, 12/1 for domestic students, 9/15 for international students. Application fee: $35 ($60 for international students). *Financial support:* In 2010–11, 6 students received support; fellowships with full tuition reimbursements available, research assistantships with full tuition reimbursements available, career-related internships or fieldwork, Federal Work-Study, scholarships/grants, and unspecified assistantships available. Financial award application deadline: 2/15; financial award applicants required to submit FAFSA. *Faculty research:* Structural response to earthquakes, pavement design, water quality, transportation safety, intermodal transportation. *Unit head:* Dr. Sharam Pezeshk, Interim Chair, 901-678-2746, Fax: 901-678-3026. *Application contact:* Dr. Roger Meier, Coordinator of Graduate Studies, 901-678-3284.

University of Miami, Graduate School, College of Engineering, Department of Civil, Architectural, and Environmental Engineering, Coral Gables, FL 33124. Offers architectural engineering (MSAE); civil engineering (MSCE, PhD). Part-time programs available. Terminal master's awarded for partial completion of doctoral program. *Degree requirements:* For master's, thesis (for some programs); for doctorate, comprehensive exam, thesis/dissertation. *Entrance requirements:* For master's, GRE General Test (minimum score 1000 verbal and quantitative), minimum GPA of 3.0; for doctorate, GRE General Test, minimum GPA of 3.5 in preceding degree. Additional exam requirements/recommendations for international students: Required—TOEFL (minimum score 550 paper-based; 213 computer-based). Electronic applications accepted. *Faculty research:* Structural assessment and wind engineering, sustainable construction and materials, moisture transport and management, wastewater and waste engineering, water management and risk analysis.

University of Michigan, Horace H. Rackham School of Graduate Studies, College of Engineering, Department of Civil and Environmental Engineering, Ann Arbor, MI 48109. Offers civil engineering (MSE, PhD, CE); construction engineering and management (M Eng, MSE); environmental engineering (MSE, PhD); structural engineering (M Eng); MBA/MSE. Part-time programs available. *Students:* 121 full-time (45 women), 5 part-time (2 women). 461 applicants, 30% accepted, 54 enrolled. In 2010, 36 master's, 13 doctorates awarded. *Degree requirements:* For master's, thesis optional; for doctorate, comprehensive exam, thesis/dissertation, oral defense of dissertation, preliminary and written exams. *Entrance requirements:* For master's and doctorate, GRE General Test. Additional exam requirements/recommendations for international students: Required—TOEFL (minimum score 560 paper-based; 220 computer-based). *Application deadline:* Applications are processed on a rolling basis. Application fee: $65 ($75 for international students). Electronic applications accepted. *Expenses:* Tuition, state resident: full-time $17,784; part-time $1116 per credit hour. Tuition, nonresident: full-time $35,944; part-time $2125 per credit hour. International tuition: $35,994 full-time. Required fees: $95 per semester. Tuition and fees vary according to course load, degree level and program. *Financial support:* Fellowships, research assistantships, teaching assistantships, institutionally sponsored loans and tuition waivers (partial) available. Financial award application deadline: 1/19. *Faculty research:* Construction engineering and management; geotechnical engineering; earthquake-resistant design of structures; environmental chemistry and microbiology; cost engineering; environmental and water resources engineering. *Unit head:* Nancy Love, Chair, 734-764-8405, Fax: 734-764-4292, E-mail: nglove@umich.edu. *Application contact:* Kimberly Smith, Student Advisor, 734-764-8405, Fax: 734-647-2127, E-mail: kansmith@umich.edu.

University of Michigan, Horace H. Rackham School of Graduate Studies, College of Engineering, Department of Naval Architecture and Marine Engineering, Ann Arbor, MI 48109. Offers concurrent marine design (M Eng); naval architecture and marine engineering (MS, MSE, PhD, Mar Eng, Nav Arch); MBA/MSE. Part-time programs available. *Students:* 88 full-time (15 women), 4 part-time (0 women). 110 applicants, 71% accepted, 52 enrolled. In 2010, 31 master's, 8 doctorates awarded. Terminal master's awarded for partial completion of doctoral program. *Degree requirements:* For master's, thesis (for some programs); for doctorate, comprehensive exam, thesis/dissertation, oral defense of dissertation, preliminary exams (written and oral); for other advanced degree, comprehensive exam, thesis, oral defense of thesis. *Entrance requirements:* For doctorate, GRE General Test, master's degree; for other advanced degree, GRE General Test. Additional exam requirements/recommendations for international students: Required—TOEFL (minimum score 560 paper-based; 220 computer-based). *Application deadline:* Applications are processed on a rolling basis. Application fee: $65 ($75 for international students). Electronic applications accepted. *Expenses:* Tuition, state resident: full-time $17,784; part-time $1116 per credit hour. Tuition, nonresident: full-time $35,944; part-time $2125 per credit hour. International tuition: $35,994 full-time. Required fees: $95 per semester. Tuition and fees vary according to course load, degree level and program. *Financial support:* Fellowships, research assistantships, teaching assistantships, career-related internships or fieldwork, Federal Work-Study, institutionally sponsored loans, scholarships/grants, and unspecified assistantships available. *Faculty research:* System and structural reliability, design and analysis of offshore structures and vehicles, marine systems design, remote sensing of ship wakes and sea surfaces, marine hydrodynamics, nonlinear seakeeping analysis. *Unit head:* Dr. Armin W. Troesch, Chair, 734-763-6644, Fax: 734-936-8820, E-mail: kdrake@engin.umich.edu. *Application contact:* Nathalie Fiveland, Unit Administrator, 734-936-0566, Fax: 734-936-8820, E-mail: fiveland@umich.edu.

University of Minnesota, Twin Cities Campus, Institute of Technology, Department of Civil Engineering, Minneapolis, MN 55455-0213. Offers civil engineering (MCE, MS, PhD); geological engineering (M Geo E, MS, PhD). Part-time programs available. *Degree requirements:* For master's, thesis optional; for doctorate, thesis/dissertation. *Entrance requirements:* For master's and doctorate, GRE General Test. Additional exam requirements/recommendations for international students: Required—TOEFL. *Faculty research:* Environmental engineering, rock mechanics, water resources, structural engineering, transportation.

University of Missouri, Graduate School, College of Engineering, Department of Civil and Environmental Engineering, Columbia, MO 65211. Offers civil engineering (MS, PhD); environmental engineering (MS, PhD); geotechnical engineering (MS, PhD); structural engineering (MS, PhD); transportation and highway engineering (MS); water resources (MS, PhD). *Degree requirements:* For master's, report or thesis; for doctorate, thesis/dissertation. *Entrance requirements:* For master's and doctorate, GRE General Test. Additional exam requirements/recommendations for international students: Required—TOEFL (minimum score 550 paper-based; 213 computer-based; 79 iBT).

University of Missouri–Kansas City, School of Computing and Engineering, Kansas City, MO 64110-2499. Offers civil engineering (MS); computer and electrical engineering (PhD); computer science (MS), including bioinformatics, software engineering, telecommunications networking; computer science and informatics (PhD); computing (PhD); electrical engineering (MS); engineering (PhD); mechanical engineering (MS); telecommunications (PhD). PhD (interdisciplinary) offered through the School of Graduate Studies. Part-time programs available. *Faculty:* 36 full-time (5 women), 21 part-time/adjunct (0 women). *Students:* 160 full-time (32 women), 194 part-time (41 women); includes 21 minority (5 Black or African American, non-Hispanic/Latino; 9 Asian, non-Hispanic/Latino; 6 Hispanic/Latino; 1 Two or more races, non-Hispanic/Latino), 273 international. Average age 25. 440 applicants, 55% accepted, 104 enrolled. In 2010, 135 master's awarded. *Degree requirements:* For doctorate, thesis/dissertation. *Entrance requirements:* For master's, GRE General Test, minimum GPA of 3.0, 3 letters of recommendation from professors; for doctorate, GRE General Test, minimum GPA of 3.5. Additional exam requirements/recommendations for international students: Required—TOEFL (minimum score 550 paper-based; 213 computer-based; 80 iBT). *Application deadline:* For fall admission, 1/15 priority date for domestic students, 1/15 for international students. Applications are processed on a rolling basis. Application fee: $45 ($50 for international students). *Expenses:* Tuition, state resident: full-time $5522.40; part-time $306.80 per credit hour. Tuition, nonresident: full-time $7128; part-time $792 per credit hour. Required fees: $261.15 per term. *Financial support:* In 2010–11, 35 research assistantships with partial tuition reimbursements (averaging $14,340 per year), 20 teaching assistantships with partial tuition reimbursements (averaging $13,351 per year) were awarded; career-related internships or fieldwork, Federal Work-Study, scholarships/grants, tuition waivers (partial), and unspecified assistantships also available. Support available to part-time students. Financial award application deadline: 3/1; financial award applicants required to submit FAFSA. *Faculty research:* Algorithms, bioinformatics and medical informatics, biomechanics/biomaterials, civil engineering materials, networking and telecommunications, thermal science. Total annual research expenditures: $1.1 million. *Unit head:* Dr. Kevin Z. Truman, Dean, 816-235-2399, Fax: 816-235-5159. *Application contact:* Dr. Kevin Z. Truman, Dean, 816-235-2399, Fax: 816-235-5159.

University of Nebraska–Lincoln, Graduate College, College of Engineering, Department of Civil Engineering, Lincoln, NE 68588. Offers MS, PhD. *Degree requirements:* For master's, thesis optional; for doctorate, comprehensive exam, thesis/dissertation. *Entrance requirements:* For master's and doctorate, GRE General Test. Additional exam requirements/recommendations for international students: Required—TOEFL (minimum score 550 paper-based; 213 computer-based). Electronic applications accepted. *Faculty research:* Water resources engineering, sediment transport, steel bridge systems, highway safety.

University of Nevada, Las Vegas, Graduate College, Howard R. Hughes College of Engineering, Department of Civil and Environmental Engineering, Las Vegas, NV 89154-4015. Offers civil and environmental engineering (PhD); transportation (MS). Part-time programs available. *Faculty:* 16 full-time (3 women), 4 part-time/adjunct (0 women). *Students:* 35 full-time (5 women), 20 part-time (7 women); includes 19 minority (1 Black or African American, non-Hispanic/Latino; 2 Asian, non-Hispanic/Latino; 5 Hispanic/Latino; 11 Two or more races, non-Hispanic/Latino), 19 international. Average age 32. 34 applicants, 82% accepted, 15 enrolled. In 2010, 17 master's, 8 doctorates awarded. *Degree requirements:* For master's,

Civil Engineering

University of Nevada, Las Vegas *(continued)*
comprehensive exam (for some programs), thesis (for some programs); for doctorate, comprehensive exam, thesis/dissertation. *Entrance requirements:* For master's and doctorate, GRE General Test. Additional exam requirements/recommendations for international students: Required—TOEFL (minimum score 550 paper-based; 213 computer-based; 80 iBT), IELTS (minimum score 7). *Application deadline:* For fall admission, 6/15 priority date for domestic students, 3/15 priority date for international students; for spring admission, 11/15 priority date for domestic students, 8/30 priority date for international students. Applications are processed on a rolling basis. Application fee: $60 ($95 for international students). Electronic applications accepted. *Expenses:* Tuition, area resident: Part-time $239.50 per credit. Tuition, state resident: part-time $239.50 per credit. Tuition, nonresident: part-time $503 per credit. Required fees: $108 per semester. Tuition and fees vary according to course load, program and reciprocity agreements. *Financial support:* In 2010–11, 38 students received support, including 23 research assistantships with partial tuition reimbursements available (averaging $13,595 per year), 15 teaching assistantships with partial tuition reimbursements available (averaging $11,200 per year); institutionally sponsored loans, scholarships/grants, health care benefits, and unspecified assistantships also available. Financial award application deadline: 3/1. Total annual research expenditures: $1.4 million. *Unit head:* Dr. David Ashley, Professor, 702-895-4040, Fax: 702-895-3936, E-mail: david.b.ashley@unlv.edu. *Application contact:* Graduate College Admissions Evaluator, 702-895-3320, Fax: 702-895-4180, E-mail: gradcollege@unlv.edu.

University of Nevada, Reno, Graduate School, College of Engineering, Department of Civil and Environmental Engineering, Reno, NV 89557. Offers MS, PhD. Terminal master's awarded for partial completion of doctoral program. *Degree requirements:* For master's, thesis optional; for doctorate, thesis/dissertation. *Entrance requirements:* For master's, GRE General Test, minimum GPA of 3.0; for doctorate, GRE General Test, minimum GPA of 3.25. Additional exam requirements/recommendations for international students: Required—TOEFL (minimum score 500 paper-based; 173 computer-based; 61 iBT), IELTS (minimum score 6). Electronic applications accepted. *Expenses:* Tuition, state resident: full-time $2219; part-time $246 per credit. Tuition, nonresident: part-time $510 per credit. International tuition: $9009 full-time. Required fees: $59 per term. One-time fee: $101. Tuition and fees vary according to course load. *Faculty research:* Structural and earthquake engineering, geotechnical engineering, environmental engineering, transportation, pavements/materials.

University of New Brunswick Fredericton, School of Graduate Studies, Faculty of Engineering, Department of Civil Engineering, Fredericton, NB E3B 5A3, Canada. Offers construction engineering and management (M Eng, M Sc E, PhD); environmental engineering (M Eng, M Sc E, PhD); environmental studies (M Eng); geotechnical engineering (M Eng, M Sc E, PhD); groundwater/hydrology (M Eng, M Sc E, PhD); materials (M Eng, M Sc E, PhD); pavements (M Eng, M Sc E, PhD); structures (M Eng, M Sc E, PhD); transportation (M Eng, M Sc E, PhD). Part-time programs available. *Faculty:* 13 full-time (1 woman), 7 part-time/adjunct (1 woman). *Students:* 34 full-time (8 women), 16 part-time (2 women). In 2010, 16 master's, 6 doctorates awarded. *Degree requirements:* For master's, thesis, proposal; for doctorate, comprehensive exam, thesis/dissertation, qualifying exam; proposal; 27 credit hours of courses. *Entrance requirements:* For master's, minimum GPA of 3.0; B Sc E in civil engineering or related engineering degree; for doctorate, minimum GPA of 3.0; graduate degree in engineering or applied science. Additional exam requirements/recommendations for international students: Required—TWE (minimum score 4), TOEFL (minimum score 580 paper-based; 237 computer-based) or IELTS (minimum score 7.5). *Application deadline:* For fall admission, 5/1 priority date for domestic students; for winter admission, 11/1 priority date for domestic students. Applications are processed on a rolling basis. Application fee: $50 Canadian dollars. *Expenses:* Tuition, area resident: Full-time $3708; part-time $927 per term. International tuition: $6300 full-time. Required fees: $50 per term. *Financial support:* In 2010–11, 52 research assistantships (averaging $7,000 per year), 46 teaching assistantships (averaging $2,000 per year) were awarded; career-related internships or fieldwork and scholarships/grants also available. *Faculty research:* Construction engineering and management; materials and infrastructure renewal; highway and pavement research; structures and solid mechanics; geotechnical, soil; structure interaction; transportation and planning; environment, solid waste management. *Unit head:* Dr. Eric Hildebrand, Director of Graduate Studies, 506-453-5113, Fax: 506-453-3568, E-mail: edh@unb.ca. *Application contact:* Joyce Moore, Graduate Secretary, 506-452-6127, Fax: 506-453-3568, E-mail: civil-grad@unb.ca.

University of New Hampshire, Graduate School, College of Engineering and Physical Sciences, Department of Civil Engineering, Durham, NH 03824. Offers MS, PhD. Part-time programs available. *Faculty:* 17 full-time (5 women). *Students:* 22 full-time (6 women), 37 part-time (11 women); includes 3 minority (1 American Indian or Alaska Native, non-Hispanic/Latino; 2 Two or more races, non-Hispanic/Latino), 7 international. Average age 33. 49 applicants, 84% accepted, 17 enrolled. In 2010, 20 master's awarded. *Degree requirements:* For master's, thesis or alternative; for doctorate, thesis/dissertation. *Entrance requirements:* For master's and doctorate, GRE. Additional exam requirements/recommendations for international students: Required—TOEFL (minimum score 550 paper-based; 213 computer-based; 80 iBT). *Application deadline:* For fall admission, 4/1 priority date for domestic students, 4/1 for international students; for spring admission, 12/1 for domestic students. Applications are processed on a rolling basis. Application fee: $65. *Financial support:* In 2010–11, 36 students received support, including 1 fellowship, 17 research assistantships, 16 teaching assistantships; Federal Work-Study, scholarships/grants, and tuition waivers (full and partial) also available. Support available to part-time students. Financial award application deadline: 2/15. *Faculty research:* Environmental, structural materials, geotechnical engineering, water resources, systems analysis. *Unit head:* Dr. Robin Collins, Chairperson, 603-862-1419. *Application contact:* Robin Collins, Administrative Assistant, 603-862-1353, E-mail: civil.engineering@unh.edu.

University of New Mexico, Graduate School, School of Engineering, Department of Civil Engineering, Albuquerque, NM 87131-0001. Offers civil engineering (MSCE); construction management (MCM); engineering (PhD). Part-time programs available. *Faculty:* 19 full-time (3 women), 1 part-time/adjunct (0 women). *Students:* 53 full-time (17 women), 21 part-time (8 women); includes 1 American Indian or Alaska Native, non-Hispanic/Latino; 2 Asian, non-Hispanic/Latino; 10 Hispanic/Latino; 1 Two or more races, non-Hispanic/Latino, 29 international. Average age 30. 80 applicants, 48% accepted, 13 enrolled. In 2010, 24 master's awarded. Terminal master's awarded for partial completion of doctoral program. *Degree requirements:* For master's, comprehensive exam, thesis (for some programs); for doctorate, comprehensive exam, thesis/dissertation. *Entrance requirements:* For master's, GRE General Test (for MSCE); GMAT (for MCM), minimum GPA of 3.0; for doctorate, GRE General Test, minimum GPA of 3.0. Additional exam requirements/recommendations for international students: Required—TOEFL (minimum score 550 paper-based; 213 computer-based; 79 iBT). *Application deadline:* For fall admission, 7/15 for domestic students, 3/1 for international students; for spring admission, 11/10 for domestic students, 8/1 for international students. Applications are processed on a rolling basis. Application fee: $50. Electronic applications accepted. *Expenses:* Tuition, state resident: full-time $5991; part-time $251 per credit hour. Tuition, nonresident: full-time $14,405; part-time $800.20 per credit hour. Tuition and fees vary according to course level, course load, program and reciprocity agreements. *Financial support:* In 2010–11, 58 students received support, including 6 fellowships (averaging $3,917 per year), 52 research assistantships with full and partial tuition reimbursements available (averaging $15,197 per year), 4 teaching assistantships with full and partial tuition reimbursements available (averaging $6,475 per year); scholarships/grants, health care benefits, and unspecified assistantships also available. Support available to part-time students. Financial award application deadline: 3/1; financial award applicants required to submit FAFSA. *Faculty research:* Integrating design and construction, project delivery methods, sustainable design and construction, leadership and management in construction, project management and project supervision, production management and improvement. Total annual research expenditures: $3 million. *Unit head:* Dr. John C. Stormont, Chair, 505-277-2722, Fax: 505-277-1988, E-mail: jcstorm@unm.edu. *Application contact:* Josie Gibson, Professional Academic Advisor, 505-277-2722, Fax: 505-277-1988, E-mail: civil@unm.edu.

The University of North Carolina at Charlotte, Graduate School, The William States Lee College of Engineering, Department of Civil and Environmental Engineering, Charlotte, NC 28223-0001. Offers civil engineering (MSCE); infrastructure and environmental systems (PhD), including infrastructure and environmental systems design. Part-time and evening/weekend programs available. *Faculty:* 20 full-time (2 women). *Students:* 44 full-time (13 women), 48 part-time (15 women); includes 11 minority (4 Black or African American, non-Hispanic/Latino; 1 American Indian or Alaska Native, non-Hispanic/Latino; 6 Hispanic/Latino), 29 international. Average age 29. 45 applicants, 69% accepted, 20 enrolled. In 2010, 10 master's, 3 doctorates awarded. Terminal master's awarded for partial completion of doctoral program. *Degree requirements:* For master's, thesis or alternative, thesis or project. *Entrance requirements:* For master's, GRE General Test, minimum GPA of 3.0 in undergraduate major, 2.75 overall. Additional exam requirements/recommendations for international students: Required—TOEFL (minimum score 550 paper-based; 220 computer-based; 83 iBT). *Application deadline:* For fall admission, 7/1 for domestic students, 5/1 for international students; for spring admission, 11/1 for domestic students, 10/1 for international students. Applications are processed on a rolling basis. Application fee: $55. Electronic applications accepted. *Expenses:* Tuition, state resident: full-time $3464. Tuition, nonresident: full-time $14,297. Required fees: $2094. Tuition and fees vary according to course load. *Financial support:* In 2010–11, 46 students received support, including 2 fellowships (averaging $28,347 per year), 19 research assistantships (averaging $5,352 per year), 25 teaching assistantships (averaging $6,166 per year); career-related internships or fieldwork, Federal Work-Study, institutionally sponsored loans, scholarships/grants, and administrative assistantship also available. Support available to part-time students. Financial award application deadline: 4/1; financial award applicants required to submit FAFSA. *Faculty research:* Structural composite materials, storm water systems, natural and man-made disaster reduction engineering, older drivers and nighttime driving, soil contamination and transport. Total annual research expenditures: $1.3 million. *Unit head:* Dr. David T. Young, Chair, 704-687-4175, Fax: 704-687-6953, E-mail: dyoung@uncc.edu. *Application contact:* Kathy B. Giddings, Director of Graduate Admissions, 704-687-5503, Fax: 704-687-3279, E-mail: gradadm@uncc.edu.

University of North Dakota, Graduate School, School of Engineering and Mines, Department of Civil Engineering, Grand Forks, ND 58202. Offers civil engineering (M Engr); sanitary engineering (M Engr), including soils and structures engineering, surface mining engineering. Part-time programs available. *Faculty:* 6 full-time (0 women). *Students:* 7 full-time (0 women), 4 part-time (0 women), 4 international. Average age 28. 6 applicants, 67% accepted, 4 enrolled. In 2010, 5 master's awarded. *Degree requirements:* For master's, comprehensive exam, thesis or alternative. *Entrance requirements:* For master's, GRE General Test, minimum GPA of 2.5. Additional exam requirements/recommendations for international students: Required—TOEFL (minimum score 550 paper-based; 213 computer-based; 79 iBT), IELTS (minimum score 6.5). *Application deadline:* For fall admission, 8/1 priority date for domestic students, 5/1 priority date for international students; for spring admission, 12/1 priority date for domestic students, 9/1 priority date for international students. Applications are processed on a rolling basis. Application fee: $35. Electronic applications accepted. *Expenses:* Tuition, state resident: full-time $5857; part-time $306.74 per credit. Tuition, nonresident: full-time $15,666; part-time $729.77 per credit. Required fees: $53.42 per credit. Tuition and fees vary according to course load, program and reciprocity agreements. *Financial support:* In 2010–11, 3 students received support, including 1 research assistantship with full and partial tuition reimbursement available (averaging $4,087 per year), 2 teaching assistantships with full and partial tuition reimbursements available (averaging $5,311 per year); fellowships with full and partial tuition reimbursements available, career-related internships or fieldwork, Federal Work-Study, scholarships/grants, health care benefits, tuition waivers (full and partial), and unspecified assistantships also available. Support available to part-time students. Financial award application deadline: 3/15; financial award applicants required to submit FAFSA. *Faculty research:* Soil-structures, environmental-water resources. Total annual research expenditures: $47,501. *Unit head:* Dr. Sukhvarsh Jerath, Graduate Director, 701-777-3564, Fax: 701-777-4838, E-mail: sukhvarshjerath@mail.und.edu. *Application contact:* Staci Wells, Admissions Associate, 701-777-2945, Fax: 701-777-3619, E-mail: staci.wells@gradschool.und.edu.

University of North Florida, College of Computing, Engineering, and Construction, School of Engineering, Jacksonville, FL 32224. Offers MSCE, MSEE, MSME. Part-time programs available. *Faculty:* 15 full-time (2 women). *Students:* 5 full-time (2 women), 41 part-time (5 women); includes 2 Black or African American, non-Hispanic/Latino; 1 Asian, non-Hispanic/Latino; 4 Hispanic/Latino; 1 Two or more races, non-Hispanic/Latino, 6 international. Average age 29. 45 applicants, 40% accepted, 13 enrolled. In 2010, 3 master's awarded. *Application deadline:* For fall admission, 7/1 for domestic students, 5/1 for international students; for spring admission, 11/1 for domestic students, 10/1 for international students. Application fee: $30. *Expenses:* Tuition, state resident: full-time $7646.40; part-time $318.60 per credit hour. Tuition, nonresident: full-time $23,502; part-time $979.24 per credit hour. Required fees: $1208.88; $50.37 per credit hour. Tuition and fees vary according to course load and program. *Financial support:* In 2010–11, 16 students received support, including research assistantships (averaging $2,669 per year), teaching assistantships (averaging $451 per year); Federal Work-Study, scholarships/grants, tuition waivers, and unspecified assistantships also available. Financial award application deadline: 4/1; financial award applicants required to submit FAFSA. Total annual research expenditures: $2.9 million. *Unit head:* Gerald Merckel, Associate Dean, 904-620-1390, E-mail: gmerckel@unf.edu. *Application contact:* Lillith Richardson, Assistant Director, The Graduate School, 904-320-1360, Fax: 904-620-1362, E-mail: graduateschool@unf.edu.

University of Notre Dame, Graduate School, College of Engineering, Department of Civil Engineering and Geological Sciences, Notre Dame, IN 46556. Offers bioengineering (MS Bio E); civil engineering (MSCE); civil engineering and geological sciences (PhD); environmental engineering (MS Env E); geological sciences (MS). Terminal master's awarded for partial completion of doctoral program. *Degree requirements:* For master's, comprehensive exam; for doctorate, thesis/dissertation, candidacy exam. *Entrance requirements:* For master's and doctorate, GRE General Test. Additional exam requirements/recommendations for international students: Required—TOEFL (minimum score 600 paper-based; 250 computer-based; 80 iBT). Electronic applications accepted. *Faculty research:* Environmental modeling, biological-waste treatment, petrology, environmental geology, geochemistry.

University of Oklahoma, College of Engineering, School of Civil Engineering and Environmental Science, Program in Civil Engineering, Norman, OK 73019-0390. Offers civil engineering (MS, PhD). Part-time programs available. *Students:* 43 full-time (10 women), 14 part-time (2 women); includes 6 minority (2 Black or African American, non-Hispanic/Latino; 2 American Indian or Alaska Native, non-Hispanic/Latino; 1 Asian, non-Hispanic/Latino; 1 Hispanic/Latino), 31 international. Average age 29. 25 applicants, 48% accepted, 8 enrolled. In 2010, 16 master's, 2 doctorates awarded. Terminal master's awarded for partial completion of doctoral program. *Degree requirements:* For master's, comprehensive exam, oral exams; for doctorate, thesis/dissertation, oral and qualifying exams. *Entrance requirements:* For master's, minimum GPA of 3.0; for doctorate, minimum graduate GPA of 3.5. Additional exam requirements/recommendations for international students: Required—TOEFL (minimum score 600 paper-based; 250 computer-based; 100 iBT). *Application deadline:* For fall admission, 4/1 priority date for domestic students, 4/1 for international students; for spring admission, 11/1 for domestic students, 9/1 for international students. Applications are processed on a rolling basis. Application fee: $40 ($90 for international students). Electronic applications accepted. *Expenses:* Tuition, state resident: full-time $3892.80; part-time $162.20 per credit hour. Tuition, nonresident: full-time $14,167; part-time $590.30 per credit hour. Required fees: $2523.40; $94.60 per credit hour. Tuition and fees vary according to course load and degree level. *Financial support:* Scholarships/grants available. Financial award application deadline: 3/1; financial award applicants required to submit FAFSA. *Faculty research:* Intelligent structures, composites, earthquake engineering, intelligent compaction, bridge engineering. *Unit head:* Robert C. Knox, Director, 405-325-5911, Fax: 405-325-4217, E-mail: rknox@ou.edu. *Application contact:* Susan Williams, Graduate Programs Assistant, 405-325-2344, Fax: 405-325-4147, E-mail: srwilliams@ou.edu.

University of Ottawa, Faculty of Graduate and Postdoctoral Studies, Faculty of Engineering, Ottawa-Carleton Institute for Civil Engineering, Ottawa, ON K1N 6N5, Canada. Offers M Eng, MA Sc, PhD. PhD, M Eng, MA Sc offered jointly with Carleton University. *Degree requirements:* For master's, thesis or alternative; for doctorate, comprehensive exam, thesis/dissertation, seminar series. *Entrance requirements:* For master's, honors degree or equivalent, minimum B average; for doctorate, master's degree, minimum B+ average. Electronic applications accepted. *Faculty research:* Environmental engineering, geotechnical engineering, structural engineering, transportation engineering, water resources engineering.

University of Pittsburgh, School of Engineering, Department of Civil and Environmental Engineering, Pittsburgh, PA 15260. Offers MSCEE, PhD. Part-time programs available. Postbaccalaureate distance learning degree programs offered. *Faculty:* 16 full-time (4 women), 20 part-time/adjunct (1 woman). *Students:* 88 full-time (25 women), 60 part-time (12 women); includes 7 minority (1 Black or African American, non-Hispanic/Latino; 3 Asian, non-Hispanic/Latino; 3 Hispanic/Latino), 54 international. 274 applicants, 75% accepted, 46 enrolled. In 2010, 17 master's, 1 doctorate awarded. Terminal master's awarded for partial completion of doctoral program. *Degree requirements:* For master's, thesis optional; for doctorate, comprehensive exam, thesis/dissertation, final oral exams. *Entrance requirements:* For master's and doctorate, minimum QPA of 3.0. Additional exam requirements/recommendations for international students: Required—TOEFL (minimum score 550 paper-based; 213 computer-based; 80 iBT). *Application deadline:* For fall admission, 3/1 priority date for domestic students; for spring admission, 7/1 priority date for domestic students. Applications are processed on a rolling basis. Application fee: $50. Electronic applications accepted. *Expenses:* Tuition, state resident: full-time $17,304; part-time $701 per credit. Tuition, nonresident: full-time $29,554; part-time $1210 per credit. Required fees: $740; $214 per term. Tuition and fees vary according to program. *Financial support:* In 2010–11, 44 students received support, including 16 fellowships with tuition reimbursements available (averaging $26,000 per year), 30 research assistantships with full tuition reimbursements available (averaging $25,000 per year), 15 teaching assistantships with full tuition reimbursements available (averaging $24,000 per year); scholarships/grants, traineeships, and tuition waivers (full and partial) also available. Financial award application deadline: 4/15. *Faculty research:* Environmental and water resources, structures and infrastructures, construction management. Total annual research expenditures: $4.5 million. *Unit head:* Dr. Radisav Vidic, Chairman, 412-624-9870, Fax: 412-624-0135. *Application contact:* Amir Kouboa, Academic Coordinator, 412-624-9869, Fax: 412-624-0135, E-mail: amk59@pitt.edu.

University of Puerto Rico, Mayagüez Campus, Graduate Studies, College of Engineering, Department of Civil Engineering and Surveying, Mayagüez, PR 00681-9000. Offers civil engineering (ME, MS, PhD). Part-time programs available. *Students:* 127 full-time (50 women), 18 part-time (7 women); includes 110 Hispanic/Latino, 34 international. 21 applicants, 71% accepted, 7 enrolled. In 2010, 15 master's, 1 doctorate awarded. *Degree requirements:* For master's, comprehensive exam, thesis (MS); for doctorate, one foreign language, thesis/dissertation. *Entrance requirements:* For master's, proficiency in English and Spanish, BS in civil engineering or its equivalent; for doctorate, proficiency in English and Spanish. *Application deadline:* For fall admission, 2/15 for domestic and international students; for spring admission, 9/15 for domestic and international students. Applications are processed on a rolling basis. Application fee: $25. *Expenses:* Tuition, state resident: full-time $1188. Tuition, nonresident: full-time $1188. International tuition: $6126 full-time. Tuition and fees vary according to course level and course load. *Financial support:* In 2010–11, 25 students received support, including fellowships (averaging $12,000 per year), 78 research assistantships (averaging $15,000 per year), 25 teaching assistantships (averaging $8,500 per year); Federal Work-Study and institutionally sponsored loans also available. *Faculty research:* Structural design, concrete structure, finite elements, dynamic analysis, transportation, soils. Total annual research expenditures: $2.6 million. *Unit head:* Prof. Ismael Pagan Trinidad, Chairperson, 787-832-4040 Ext. 3434, Fax: 787-833-8260, E-mail: ismael.pagan@upr.edu. *Application contact:* Dr. Ricardo Lopez, Associate Director, 787-832-4040 Ext. 2178, Fax: 787-833-8260, E-mail: rilopez@uprm.edu.

University of Rhode Island, Graduate School, College of Engineering, Department of Civil and Environmental Engineering, Kingston, RI 02881. Offers MS, PhD. Part-time programs available. *Faculty:* 8 full-time (3 women), 3 part-time/adjunct (0 women). *Students:* 22 full-time (6 women), 18 part-time (6 women); includes 5 minority (1 Asian, non-Hispanic/Latino; 2 Hispanic/Latino; 2 Two or more races, non-Hispanic/Latino), 9 international. In 2010, 13 master's awarded. *Degree requirements:* For master's, comprehensive exam (for some programs), thesis optional; for doctorate, comprehensive exam, thesis/dissertation. *Entrance requirements:* For master's and doctorate, 2 letters of recommendation. Additional exam requirements/recommendations for international students: Required—TOEFL (minimum score 550 paper-based; 213 computer-based). *Application deadline:* For fall admission, 7/15 for domestic students, 2/1 for international students; for spring admission, 11/15 for domestic students, 7/15 for international students. Application fee: $65. Electronic applications accepted. *Expenses:* Tuition, state resident: full-time $9588; part-time $533 per credit hour. Tuition, nonresident: full-time $22,968; part-time $1276 per credit hour. Required fees: $1282; $68 per semester. Tuition and fees vary according to program. *Financial support:* In 2010–11, 5 research assistantships with full and partial tuition reimbursements (averaging $7,871 per year), 3 teaching assistantships with full and partial tuition reimbursements (averaging $8,890 per year) were awarded. Financial award application deadline: 7/15; financial award applicants required to submit FAFSA. *Faculty research:* Industrial waste treatment, structural health monitoring, traffic and transit system operations, computational mechanics, engineering materials design. Total annual research expenditures: $460,423. *Unit head:* Dr. George E. Tsiatas, Chair, 401-874-5117, Fax: 401-874-2786, E-mail: gt@uri.edu. *Application contact:* Dr. Mayrai Gindy, Director of Graduate Studies, 401-874-5587, Fax: 401-874-2786, E-mail: gindy@egr.uri.edu.

University of Saskatchewan, College of Graduate Studies and Research, College of Engineering, Department of Civil and Geological Engineering, Saskatoon, SK S7N 5A2, Canada. Offers M Eng, M Sc, PhD. *Degree requirements:* For master's, thesis (for some programs); for doctorate, thesis/dissertation. *Entrance requirements:* For master's, GRE, minimum GPA of 5.0 on an 8.0 scale; for doctorate, GRE. Additional exam requirements/recommendations for international students: Required—TOEFL. *Faculty research:* Geotechnical engineering, structures, water sciences.

University of South Alabama, Graduate School, College of Engineering, Department of Civil Engineering, Mobile, AL 36688-0002. Offers MSCE. *Faculty:* 4 full-time (0 women). *Students:* 8 full-time (3 women), 6 part-time (3 women); includes 1 Hispanic/Latino, 4 international. 7 applicants, 57% accepted, 4 enrolled. In 2010, 2 master's awarded. *Entrance requirements:* Additional exam requirements/recommendations for international students: Required—TOEFL. *Application deadline:* For fall admission, 7/15 priority date for domestic students, 6/15 priority date for international students; for spring admission, 12/1 priority date for domestic students, 11/1 priority date for international students. Application fee: $35. *Expenses:* Tuition, state resident: part-time $300 per credit hour. Tuition, nonresident: part-time $600 per credit hour. Required fees: $150 per semester. *Unit head:* Dr. Kevin White, Chair, 251-460-6174. *Application contact:* Dr. B. Keith Harrison, Director of Graduate Studies, 251-460-6160.

University of South Carolina, The Graduate School, College of Engineering and Computing, Department of Civil and Environmental Engineering, Columbia, SC 29208. Offers civil engineering (ME, MS, PhD). Part-time and evening/weekend programs available. Postbaccalaureate distance learning degree programs offered (minimal on-campus study). *Degree requirements:* For master's, comprehensive exam, thesis (for some programs); for doctorate, thesis/dissertation. *Entrance requirements:* For master's and doctorate, GRE General Test, 2 letters of recommendation. Additional exam requirements/recommendations for international students: Required—TOEFL (minimum score 570 paper-based; 230 computer-based). Electronic applications accepted. *Faculty research:* Structures, Water Resources, Environmental, Geotechnical and Transportation.

University of Southern California, Graduate School, Viterbi School of Engineering, Sonny Astani Department of Civil Engineering, Los Angeles, CA 90089. Offers applied mechanics (MS); civil engineering (MS, PhD); computer-aided engineering (ME, Graduate Certificate); construction management (MCM); engineering technology commercialization (Graduate Certificate); environmental engineering (MS, PhD); environmental quality management (ME); structural design (ME); sustainable cities (Graduate Certificate); transportation systems (MS, Graduate Certificate); water and waste management (MS). Part-time and evening/weekend programs available. *Faculty:* 16 full-time (2 women), 35 part-time/adjunct (5 women). *Students:* 190 full-time (52 women), 81 part-time (20 women); includes 54 minority (2 Black or African American, non-Hispanic/Latino; 42 Asian, non-Hispanic/Latino; 9 Hispanic/Latino; 1 Two or more races, non-Hispanic/Latino), 149 international. 541 applicants, 43% accepted, 100 enrolled. In 2010, 74 master's, 10 doctorates awarded. Terminal master's awarded for partial completion of doctoral program. *Degree requirements:* For master's, thesis optional; for doctorate, thesis/dissertation. *Entrance requirements:* For master's and doctorate, GRE General Test. *Application deadline:* For fall admission, 12/1 priority date for domestic and international students; for spring admission, 9/15 for domestic students, 9/15 priority date for international students. Applications are processed on a rolling basis. Application fee: $85. Electronic applications accepted. *Expenses:* Tuition: Full-time $31,240; part-time $1420 per unit. Required fees: $600. One-time fee: $35 full-time. Full-time tuition and fees vary according to degree level and program. *Financial support:* In 2010–11, fellowships with full tuition reimbursements (averaging $30,000 per year), research assistantships with full tuition reimbursements (averaging $20,000 per year), teaching assistantships with full tuition reimbursements (averaging $20,000 per year) were awarded; career-related internships or fieldwork, scholarships/grants, health care benefits, and unspecified assistantships also available. Financial award application deadline: 12/1; financial award applicants required to submit CSS PROFILE or FAFSA. *Faculty research:* Geotechnical engineering, transportation engineering, structural engineering, construction management, environmental engineering, water resources. Total annual research expenditures: $5 million. *Unit head:* Dr. Jean-Pierre Bardet, Chair, 213-740-0603, Fax: 213-744-1426, E-mail: ceedept@usc.edu. *Application contact:* Jennifer A. Gerson, Director of Student Affairs, 213-740-0573, Fax: 213-740-8662, E-mail: jgerson@usc.edu.

University of South Florida, Graduate School, College of Engineering, Department of Civil and Environmental Engineering, Tampa, FL 33620-9951. Offers civil and environmental engineering (MSES); civil engineering (MCE, MSCE, PhD). Part-time programs available. *Faculty:* 18 full-time (4 women). *Students:* 109 full-time (42 women), 69 part-time (18 women); includes 29 minority (7 Black or African American, non-Hispanic/Latino; 6 Asian, non-Hispanic/Latino; 15 Hispanic/Latino; 1 Two or more races, non-Hispanic/Latino), 48 international. Average age 30. 208 applicants, 61% accepted, 66 enrolled. In 2010, 18 master's, 9 doctorates awarded. Terminal master's awarded for partial completion of doctoral program. *Degree requirements:* For master's, comprehensive exam, thesis (for some programs); for doctorate, comprehensive exam, thesis/dissertation. *Entrance requirements:* For master's, GRE General Test, minimum GPA of 3.0 in last 60 hours of coursework; for doctorate, GRE General Test, minimum GPA of 3.3 in last 60 hours of coursework. Additional exam requirements/recommendations for international students: Required—TOEFL (minimum score 550 paper-based; 213 computer-based; 79 iBT). *Application deadline:* For fall admission, 2/15 for domestic students, 1/2 priority date for international students; for spring admission, 10/15 for domestic students, 6/1 priority date for international students. Application fee: $30. Electronic applications accepted. *Financial support:* In 2010–11, 48 research assistantships (averaging $15,714 per year), 39 teaching assistantships with tuition reimbursements (averaging $14,402 per year) were awarded. *Faculty research:* Water resources, structures and materials, transportation, geotechnical engineering, mechanics. Total annual research expenditures: $2.3 million. *Application contact:* Dr. Sarina Ergas, Director, 813-974-1119, Fax: 813-974-2957, E-mail: sergas@usf.edu.

The University of Tennessee, Graduate School, College of Engineering, Department of Civil and Environmental Engineering, Program in Civil Engineering, Knoxville, TN 37996. Offers MS, PhD, MS/MBA. Part-time programs available. Postbaccalaureate distance learning degree programs offered (minimal on-campus study). *Faculty:* 20 full-time (2 women), 8 part-time/adjunct (0 women). *Students:* 70 full-time (12 women), 33 part-time (5 women); includes 4 Black or African American, non-Hispanic/Latino; 1 Asian, non-Hispanic/Latino; 1 Hispanic/Latino, 34 international. Average age 23. 115 applicants, 70% accepted, 30 enrolled. In 2010, 26 master's, 11 doctorates awarded. *Degree requirements:* For master's, thesis or alternative; for doctorate, comprehensive exam, thesis/dissertation. *Entrance requirements:* For master's, GRE General Test, Minimum GPA of 2.7 (US degree holders); 3.0 (International degree holders); 3-References; Statement of purpose; Resume; for doctorate, GRE General Test, Minimum GPA of 3.0 (previous graduate course work); 3-References; Statement of purpose; Resume. Additional exam requirements/recommendations for international students: Required—TOEFL (minimum score 550 paper-based; 213 computer-based). *Application deadline:* For fall admission, 2/1 priority date for domestic and international students; for spring admission, 6/15 for domestic and international students. Applications are processed on a rolling basis. Application fee: $35. Electronic applications accepted. *Expenses:* Tuition, state resident: full-time $7440; part-time $414 per credit hour. Tuition, nonresident: full-time $22,478; part-time $1250 per credit hour. Required fees: $922; $43 per credit hour. Tuition and fees vary according to program. *Financial support:* In 2010–11, 58 students received support, including 49 research assistantships with full tuition reimbursements available (averaging $14,028 per year), 21 teaching assistantships with full tuition reimbursements available (averaging $6,684 per year); career-related internships or fieldwork, Federal Work-Study, institutionally sponsored loans, health care benefits, and unspecified assistantships also available. Financial award application deadline: 2/1; financial award applicants required to submit FAFSA. *Faculty research:* Multi-functional composites and mechanics of materials; geohydrologic investigations and monitoring; structures and vibrations; geotechnical and earthquake engineering; transportation system planning and design. *Unit head:* Dr. Dayakar Penumadu, Head, 865-974-2355, Fax: 865-974-2355, E-mail: dpenumad@utk.edu. *Application contact:* Dr. Chris Cox, Associate Head, 865-974-7729, Fax: 865-974-2355, E-mail: ccox9@utk.edu.

The University of Tennessee at Chattanooga, Graduate School, College of Engineering and Computer Science, Program in Engineering, Chattanooga, TN 37403. Offers chemical engineering (MS Engr); civil engineering (MS Engr); computational engineering (MS Engr); electrical engineering (MS Engr); industrial engineering (MS Engr); mechanical engineering (MS Engr). Part-time and evening/weekend programs available. *Faculty:* 8 full-time (0 women). *Students:* 27 full-time (5 women), 31 part-time (6 women); includes 12 minority (7 Black or African American, non-Hispanic/Latino; 1 Asian, non-Hispanic/Latino; 4 Hispanic/Latino), 10 international. Average age 29. 43 applicants, 100% accepted, 26 enrolled. In 2010, 16 master's awarded. *Degree requirements:* For master's, comprehensive exam, thesis or alternative, engineering project. *Entrance requirements:* For master's, GRE General Test, minimum undergraduate GPA of 2.5 or 3.0 in last 30 hours of coursework. Additional exam requirements/recommendations for international students: Required—TOEFL (minimum score 550 paper-based; 213 computer-based; 79 iBT), IELTS (minimum score 6). *Application deadline:* For fall admission, 8/1 priority date for domestic students, 6/1 for international students; for spring admission, 12/1 priority date for domestic students, 10/1 for international students. Applications are processed on a rolling basis. Application fee: $35. Electronic applications accepted. *Financial support:* In 2010–11, 23 research assistantships with full and partial tuition reimbursements (averaging $5,500 per year) were awarded; career-related internships or fieldwork, scholarships/grants, and unspecified assistantships also available. Support available to part-time students. *Faculty research:* Quality control and reliability engineering, financial management, thermal science, energy conservation, structural analysis. Total annual research expenditures: $2.6 million. *Unit head:* Dr. Neslihan Alp, Director, 423-425-4032, Fax: 423-425-5229, E-mail: neslihan-alp@utc.edu. *Application contact:* Dr. Jerald Ainsworth, Dean of Graduate Studies, 423-425-4478, Fax: 423-425-5223, E-mail: jerald-ainsworth@utc.edu.

The University of Texas at Arlington, Graduate School, College of Engineering, Department of Civil Engineering, Arlington, TX 76019. Offers M Engr, MS, PhD. Part-time and evening/

Civil Engineering

The University of Texas at Arlington (continued)

weekend programs available. Postbaccalaureate distance learning degree programs offered (minimal on-campus study). *Faculty:* 18 full-time (1 woman). *Students:* 107 full-time (25 women), 100 part-time (34 women); includes 41 minority (13 Black or African American, non-Hispanic/Latino; 16 Asian, non-Hispanic/Latino; 9 Hispanic/Latino; 1 Native Hawaiian or other Pacific Islander, non-Hispanic/Latino; 2 Two or more races, non-Hispanic/Latino), 115 international. 104 applicants, 83% accepted, 48 enrolled. In 2010, 43 master's, 5 doctorates awarded. Terminal master's awarded for partial completion of doctoral program. *Degree requirements:* For master's, comprehensive exam, thesis (for some programs), oral and written exams; for doctorate, comprehensive exam, thesis/dissertation, oral and written defense of dissertation. *Entrance requirements:* For master's, GRE General Test = 600 verbal =450, total 1050, minimum GPA of 3.0 in last 60 hours of undergraduate course work; for doctorate, GRE General Test = 700, verbal = 500, total 1200. Additional exam requirements/recommendations for international students: Required—TOEFL. *Application deadline:* For fall admission, 6/6 for domestic students, 4/4 for international students; for spring admission, 10/15 for domestic students, 9/5 for international students. Applications are processed on a rolling basis. Application fee: $35 ($50 for international students). Electronic applications accepted. *Expenses:* Tuition, state resident: full-time $7500. Tuition, nonresident: full-time $13,080. International tuition: $13,250 full-time. *Financial support:* In 2010–11, 21 students received support, including 7 fellowships with partial tuition reimbursements available (averaging $1,000 per year), 18 research assistantships with partial tuition reimbursements available (averaging $14,850 per year), 25 teaching assistantships with partial tuition reimbursements available (averaging $16,300 per year); career-related internships or fieldwork, Federal Work-Study, scholarships/grants, tuition waivers (partial), and unspecified assistantships also available. Financial award application deadline: 6/1; financial award applicants required to submit FAFSA. *Faculty research:* Environmental and water resources structures, geotechnical, transportation. *Unit head:* Dr. Nur Yazdani, Chair, 817-272-5055, Fax: 817-272-2630, E-mail: yazdani@uta.edu. *Application contact:* Dr. Stephen Mattingly, Graduate Advisor, 817-272-2201, Fax: 817-272-2630, E-mail: mattingly@uta.edu.

The University of Texas at Austin, Graduate School, Cockrell School of Engineering, Department of Civil, Architectural and Environmental Engineering, Austin, TX 78712-1111. Offers architectural engineering (MSE); civil engineering (MS, PhD); environmental and water resources engineering (MS, PhD). *Accreditation:* ABET (one or more programs are accredited). Part-time programs available. *Degree requirements:* For master's, thesis or alternative; for doctorate, comprehensive exam, thesis/dissertation. *Entrance requirements:* For master's and doctorate, GRE General Test. Additional exam requirements/recommendations for international students: Required—TOEFL. Electronic applications accepted. *Faculty research:* Geotechnical structural engineering, transportation engineering, construction enginering/project management.

The University of Texas at El Paso, Graduate School, College of Engineering, Department of Civil Engineering, El Paso, TX 79968-0001. Offers civil engineering (MS, PhD); construction management (MS); construction mangement (Certificate); environmental engineering (MEENE, MSENE). Part-time and evening/weekend programs available. *Students:* 113 (36 women); includes 2 Asian, non-Hispanic/Latino; 62 Hispanic/Latino, 36 international. Average age 34. In 2010, 14 master's, 9 doctorates awarded. *Degree requirements:* For master's, thesis optional. *Entrance requirements:* For master's, GRE General Test, minimum GPA of 3.0. Additional exam requirements/recommendations for international students: Required—TOEFL. *Application deadline:* For fall admission, 7/1 priority date for domestic students, 3/1 for international students; for spring admission, 11/1 priority date for domestic students, 9/1 for international students. Applications are processed on a rolling basis. Application fee: $15 ($65 for international students). Electronic applications accepted. *Financial support:* In 2010–11, research assistantships with partial tuition reimbursements (averaging $21,125 per year), teaching assistantships with partial tuition reimbursements (averaging $16,900 per year) were awarded; fellowships with partial tuition reimbursements, career-related internships or fieldwork, Federal Work-Study, institutionally sponsored loans, scholarships/grants, tuition waivers (partial), and stipends also available. Financial award application deadline: 3/15; financial award applicants required to submit FAFSA. *Faculty research:* On-site wastewater treatment systems, wastewater reuse, disinfection by-product control, water resources, membrane filtration. *Unit head:* Wen-Whai Li, Chair, 915-747-5464, E-mail: wli@utep.edu. *Application contact:* Dr. Charles H. Ambler, Dean of the Graduate School, 915-747-5491 Ext. 7886, Fax: 915-747-5788, E-mail: cambler@utep.edu.

The University of Texas at San Antonio, College of Engineering, Department of Civil and Environmental Engineering, San Antonio, TX 78249-0617. Offers civil engineering (MS, MSCE); environmental science and engineering (PhD). Part-time and evening/weekend programs available. *Faculty:* 11 full-time (2 women). *Students:* 43 full-time (11 women), 34 part-time (8 women); includes 25 minority (5 Black or African American, non-Hispanic/Latino; 4 Asian, non-Hispanic/Latino; 15 Hispanic/Latino; 1 Two or more races, non-Hispanic/Latino), 24 international. Average age 32. 56 applicants, 50% accepted, 21 enrolled. In 2010, 12 master's, 4 doctorates awarded. *Degree requirements:* For master's, comprehensive exam (for some programs), thesis (for some programs); for doctorate, comprehensive exam, thesis/dissertation. *Entrance requirements:* For master's, GRE General Test, minimum GPA of 3.0 in last 60 hours of undergraduate degree. Additional exam requirements/recommendations for international students: Required—TOEFL (minimum score 500 paper-based; 173 computer-based; 61 iBT), IELTS (minimum score 5). *Application deadline:* For fall admission, 7/1 for domestic students, 4/1 for international students; for spring admission, 11/1 for domestic students, 9/1 for international students. Applications are processed on a rolling basis. Application fee: $45 ($80 for international students). Electronic applications accepted. *Expenses:* Tuition, state resident: full-time $4172; part-time $231.75 per credit hour. Tuition, nonresident: full-time $15,332; part-time $851.75 per credit hour. *Financial support:* In 2010–11, 29 students received support, including 20 research assistantships (averaging $15,462 per year); career-related internships or fieldwork, scholarships/grants, tuition waivers, and unspecified assistantships also available. Support available to part-time students. Financial award application deadline: 3/31. Total annual research expenditures: $475,434. *Unit head:* Dr. Athanassio T. Papagiannakis, Chair, 210-458-7517, Fax: 210-458-6475, E-mail: at.papagiannakis@utsa.edu. *Application contact:* Veronica Ramirez, Assistant Dean of the Graduate School, 210-458-4330, Fax: 210-458-4332, E-mail: graduatestudies@utsa.edu.

See Display on next page and Close-Up on page 227.

The University of Texas at Tyler, College of Engineering and Computer Science, Department of Civil Engineering, Tyler, TX 75799-0001. Offers environmental engineering (MS); industrial safety (MS); structural engineering (MS); transportation engineering (MS); water resources engineering (MS). Part-time and evening/weekend programs available. *Degree requirements:* For master's, thesis optional. *Entrance requirements:* For master's, GRE General Test, bachelor's degree in engineering, associated science degree. Additional exam requirements/recommendations for international students: Required—TOEFL (minimum score 79 computer-based). *Faculty research:* Non-destructive strength testing, indoor air quality, transportation routing and signaling, pavement replacement criteria, flood water routing, construction and long-term behavior of innovative geotechnical foundation and embankment construction used in highway construction, engineering education.

The University of Toledo, College of Graduate Studies, College of Engineering, Department of Civil Engineering, Toledo, OH 43606-3390. Offers MS, PhD. Part-time programs available. Terminal master's awarded for partial completion of doctoral program. *Degree requirements:* For master's, thesis or alternative; for doctorate, thesis/dissertation, qualifying exam. *Entrance requirements:* For master's, GRE General Test, minimum GPA of 3.0; for doctorate, GRE General Test, minimum GPA of 3.3. Additional exam requirements/recommendations for international students: Required—TOEFL (minimum score 550 paper-based; 213 computer-based; 80 iBT). Electronic applications accepted. *Expenses:* Tuition, state resident: full-time $11,426; part-time $476 per credit hour. Tuition, nonresident: full-time $21,660; part-time $903 per credit hour. One-time fee: $62. *Faculty research:* Environmental modeling, soil/pavement interaction, structural mechanics, earthquakes, transportation engineering.

University of Toronto, School of Graduate Studies, Physical Sciences Division, Faculty of Applied Science and Engineering, Department of Civil Engineering, Toronto, ON M5S 1A1, Canada. Offers M Eng, MA Sc, PhD. Part-time programs available. *Degree requirements:* For master's, thesis (for some programs), thesis and oral presentation (MA Sc); for doctorate, thesis/dissertation, oral presentation. *Entrance requirements:* For master's, bachelor's degree in civil engineering, proficiency in computer usage, minimum B average in final 2 years, 3 letters of reference; for doctorate, proficiency in computer usage, minimum B average in final 2 years, 3 letters of reference.

University of Utah, Graduate School, College of Engineering, Department of Civil and Environmental Engineering, Salt Lake City, UT 84112. Offers civil engineering (MS, PhD); environmental engineering (MS, PhD); nuclear engineering (MS, PhD). Part-time programs available. *Faculty:* 31 full-time (6 women), 2 part-time/adjunct (0 women). *Students:* 73 full-time (17 women), 44 part-time (4 women); includes 6 minority (2 Asian, non-Hispanic/Latino; 4 Hispanic/Latino), 32 international. Average age 31. 125 applicants, 58% accepted, 26 enrolled. In 2010, 34 master's, 7 doctorates awarded. Terminal master's awarded for partial completion of doctoral program. *Degree requirements:* For master's, comprehensive exam, thesis (for some programs); for doctorate, comprehensive exam, thesis/dissertation, departmental qualifying exam. *Entrance requirements:* For master's and doctorate, GRE General Test, minimum GPA of 3.0. Additional exam requirements/recommendations for international students: Required—TOEFL (minimum score 550 paper-based; 213 computer-based; 80 iBT). *Application deadline:* For fall admission, 12/31 for domestic students, 11/30 for international students; for spring admission, 10/1 for domestic and international students. Applications are processed on a rolling basis. Application fee: $55 ($65 for international students). Electronic applications accepted. *Expenses:* Contact institution. *Financial support:* In 2010–11, 55 students received support, including 1 fellowship with full tuition reimbursement available (averaging $22,000 per year), 29 research assistantships with full tuition reimbursements available (averaging $20,016 per year), 14 teaching assistantships with full tuition reimbursements available (averaging $19,200 per year); career-related internships or fieldwork, Federal Work-Study, institutionally sponsored loans, scholarships/grants, health care benefits, tuition waivers (full and partial), and unspecified assistantships also available. Support available to part-time students. Financial award application deadline: 11/30; financial award applicants required to submit FAFSA. *Faculty research:* Structural engineering, geotechnical engineering, transportation engineering, environmental engineering, water resources. Total annual research expenditures: $6.9 million. *Unit head:* Dr. Paul J. Tikalsky, Chair, 801-581-6931, Fax: 801-585-5477, E-mail: tikalsky@civil.utah.edu. *Application contact:* Amanda May, Academic Program Specialist, 801-581-6931, Fax: 801-585-5477, E-mail: amandam@civil.utah.edu.

See Display on page 190 and Close-Up on page 229.

University of Vermont, Graduate College, College of Engineering and Mathematics, Department of Civil and Environmental Engineering, Burlington, VT 05405. Offers MS, PhD. *Students:* 33 (12 women), 8 international. 53 applicants, 68% accepted, 9 enrolled. In 2010, 5 master's, 2 doctorates awarded. *Degree requirements:* For master's, thesis or alternative; for doctorate, thesis/dissertation. *Entrance requirements:* For master's and doctorate, GRE General Test. Additional exam requirements/recommendations for international students: Required—TOEFL (minimum score 550 paper-based; 213 computer-based; 80 iBT). *Application deadline:* For fall admission, 2/1 priority date for domestic students. Applications are processed on a rolling basis. Application fee: $40. Electronic applications accepted. *Expenses:* Tuition, state resident: part-time $537 per credit hour. Tuition, nonresident: part-time $1355 per credit hour. *Financial support:* Research assistantships, teaching assistantships available. Financial award application deadline: 3/1. *Unit head:* Dr. J. Marshall, Director, 802-656-3800. *Application contact:* Dr. Britt Holmen, Coordinator, 802-656-3800.

University of Virginia, School of Engineering and Applied Science, Department of Civil Engineering, Charlottesville, VA 22903. Offers ME, MS, PhD. Part-time programs available. Postbaccalaureate distance learning degree programs offered (no on-campus study). *Faculty:* 14 full-time (3 women), 1 part-time/adjunct (0 women). *Students:* 40 full-time (11 women), 3 part-time (1 woman); includes 3 Black or African American, non-Hispanic/Latino; 3 Asian, non-Hispanic/Latino, 15 international. Average age 28. 133 applicants, 30% accepted, 11 enrolled. In 2010, 26 master's, 3 doctorates awarded. Terminal master's awarded for partial completion of doctoral program. *Degree requirements:* For master's, thesis (for some programs); for doctorate, comprehensive exam, thesis/dissertation. *Entrance requirements:* For master's and doctorate, GRE General Test, 3 letters of recommendation. Additional exam requirements/recommendations for international students: Required—TOEFL (minimum score 600 paper-based; 250 computer-based; 90 iBT), IELTS (minimum score 7). *Application deadline:* For fall admission, 8/1 for domestic students, 4/1 for international students; for winter admission, 12/1 for domestic students, 8/1 for international students; for spring admission, 5/1 for domestic students, 1/1 for international students. Applications are processed on a rolling basis. Application fee: $60. Electronic applications accepted. *Financial support:* Fellowships with full tuition reimbursements, research assistantships with full tuition reimbursements, teaching assistantships with full tuition reimbursements available. Financial award application deadline: 1/15. *Faculty research:* Groundwater, surface water, traffic engineering, composite materials. *Unit head:* Bran L. Smith, Chair, 434-924-7464, Fax: 434-982-2951, E-mail: civil@virginia.edu. *Application contact:* Graduate Program Coordinator, 434-924-7464, Fax: 434-982-2951, E-mail: civil@virginia.edu.

University of Washington, Graduate School, College of Engineering, Department of Civil and Environmental Engineering, Seattle, WA 98195-2700. Offers construction engineering (MSCE); environmental engineering (MS, MSCE, MSE, PhD); hydrology, water resources, and environmental fluid mechanics (MS, MSCE, MSE, PhD); structural and geotechnical engineering and mechanics (MS, MSCE, MSE, PhD); transportation and construction engineering (MS, MSE, PhD); transportation engineering (MSCE). Part-time programs available. Postbaccalaureate distance learning degree programs offered (no on-campus study). *Faculty:* 44 full-time (10 women), 12 part-time/adjunct (1 woman). *Students:* 197 full-time (65 women), 65 part-time (15 women); includes 5 Black or African American, non-Hispanic/Latino; 28 Asian, non-Hispanic/Latino; 5 Hispanic/Latino, 55 international. 522 applicants, 51% accepted, 101 enrolled. In 2010, 68 master's, 5 doctorates awarded. Terminal master's awarded for partial completion of doctoral program. *Degree requirements:* For master's, thesis (for some programs); for doctorate, comprehensive exam, thesis/dissertation, General, qualifying, and final exams. Completion of doctoral degree within 10 years. *Entrance requirements:* For master's, GRE General Test, Minimum GPA of 3.0, statement of purpose, letters of recommendation, transcripts; for doctorate, GRE General Test, minimum GPA of 3.5, statement of purpose, letters of recommendation, transcripts. Additional exam requirements/recommendations for international students: Required—TOEFL (minimum score 580 paper-based; 237 computer-based; 92 iBT); Recommended—IELTS (minimum score 7). *Application deadline:* For fall admission, 1/10 priority date for domestic and international students. Application fee: $75. Electronic applications accepted. *Financial support:* In 2010–11, 2 students received support, including 25 fellowships with full and partial tuition reimbursements available (averaging $16,173 per year), 75 research assistantships with full tuition reimbursements available (averaging $16,515 per year), 11 teaching assistantships with full tuition reimbursements available (averaging $16,263 per year); scholarships/grants also available. Financial award application deadline: 1/10; financial award applicants required to submit FAFSA. *Faculty research:* Environmental/water resources, hydrology; construction/transportation; structures/ geotechnical. Total annual research expenditures: $14.4 million. *Unit head:* Dr. Gregory R. Miller, Professor and Chair, 206-543-0350, Fax: 206-543-1543, E-mail: gmiller@uw.edu. *Application contact:* Lorna Latal, Graduate Adviser, 206-543-2574, Fax: 206-543-1543, E-mail: llatal@u.washington.edu.

University of Waterloo, Graduate Studies, Faculty of Engineering, Department of Civil and Environmental Engineering, Waterloo, ON N2L 3G1, Canada. Offers M Eng, MA Sc, PhD.

Part-time programs available. *Degree requirements:* For master's, research paper or thesis; for doctorate, comprehensive exam, thesis/dissertation. *Entrance requirements:* For master's, honors degree, minimum B average; for doctorate, master's degree, minimum A- average. Additional exam requirements/recommendations for international students: Required—TOEFL, TWE. Electronic applications accepted. *Faculty research:* Water resources, structures, construction management, transportation, geotechnical engineering.

The University of Western Ontario, Faculty of Graduate Studies, Physical Sciences Division, Faculty of Engineering, London, ON N6A 5B8, Canada. Offers chemical and biochemical engineering (ME Sc, PhD); civil and environmental engineering (M Eng, ME Sc, PhD); electrical and computer engineering (M Eng, ME Sc, PhD); mechanical and materials engineering (M Eng, ME Sc, PhD). Part-time programs available. Terminal master's awarded for partial completion of doctoral program. *Degree requirements:* For master's, thesis; for doctorate, thesis/dissertation. *Entrance requirements:* For master's, minimum B average; for doctorate, minimum B+ average. *Faculty research:* Wind, geotechnical, chemical reactor engineering, applied electrostatics, biochemical engineering.

University of Windsor, Faculty of Graduate Studies, Faculty of Engineering, Department of Civil and Environmental Engineering, Windsor, ON N9B 3P4, Canada. Offers civil engineering (M Eng, MA Sc, PhD); environmental engineering (M Eng, MA Sc, PhD). Part-time programs available. *Degree requirements:* For master's, thesis; for doctorate, comprehensive exam, thesis/dissertation. *Entrance requirements:* For master's, minimum B average; for doctorate, master's degree, minimum A average. Additional exam requirements/recommendations for international students: Required—TOEFL (minimum score 580 paper-based; 237 computer-based). Electronic applications accepted. *Faculty research:* Odors: sampling, measurement, control; drinking water disinfection, hydrocarbon contaminated soil remediation, structural dynamics, numerical simulation of piezoelectric materials.

University of Wisconsin–Madison, Graduate School, College of Engineering, Department of Civil and Environmental Engineering, Madison, WI 53706-1380. Offers MS, PhD. Part-time programs available. *Faculty:* 31 full-time (3 women), 2 part-time/adjunct (0 women). *Students:* 164 full-time (36 women); includes 1 Black or African American, non-Hispanic/Latino; 5 Hispanic/Latino. Average age 29. 455 applicants, 8% accepted, 37 enrolled. In 2010, 41 master's, 9 doctorates awarded. Terminal master's awarded for partial completion of doctoral program. *Degree requirements:* For master's, thesis or alternative; for doctorate, thesis/dissertation, preliminary exam, qualifying exams. *Entrance requirements:* For master's and doctorate, GRE General Test, minimum GPA of 3.0 for last 60 credits of course work. Additional exam requirements/recommendations for international students: Required—TOEFL (minimum score 550 paper-based; 213 computer-based; 80 iBT). *Application deadline:* For fall admission, 3/15 for domestic and international students; for spring admission, 10/15 for domestic and international students. Applications are processed on a rolling basis. Application fee: $56. Electronic applications accepted. *Expenses:* Tuition, state resident: full-time $9887.36; part-time $617.96 per credit. Tuition, nonresident: full-time $24,054; part-time $1503.40 per credit. Required fees: $67.63 per credit. Tuition and fees vary according to reciprocity agreements. *Financial support:* In 2010–11, 63 students received support, including 9 fellowships with full tuition reimbursements available (averaging $22,224 per year), 76 research assistantships with full tuition reimbursements available (averaging $40,368 per year), 12 teaching assistantships with full tuition reimbursements available (averaging $28,175 per year); Federal Work-Study, scholarships/grants, health care benefits, and unspecified assistantships also available. Support available to part-time students. Financial award application deadline: 12/15. *Faculty research:* Environmental geotechnics and soil mechanics, design and analysis of structures, traffic engineering and intelligent transport systems, industrial pollution control, hydrological monitoring. Total annual research expenditures: $7.4 million. *Unit head:* Jeffrey S. Russell, Chair, 608-262-3542, Fax: 608-262-5199, E-mail: russell@engr.wisc.edu. *Application contact:* Cheryl Loschko, Student Status Examiner, 608-265-5570, Fax: 608-890-1174, E-mail: loschko@wisc.edu.

University of Wisconsin–Milwaukee, Graduate School, College of Engineering and Applied Science, Program in Engineering, Milwaukee, WI 53201-0413. Offers civil engineering (MS); electrical and computer engineering (MS); energy engineering (Certificate); engineering (PhD); engineering management (MS); engineering mechanics (MS); ergonomics (Certificate); industrial and management engineering (MS); manufacturing engineering (MS); materials engineering (MS); mechanical engineering (MS); MUP/MS. Part-time programs available. *Faculty:* 50 full-time (5 women). *Students:* 152 full-time (27 women), 115 part-time (23 women); includes 13 Black or African American, non-Hispanic/Latino; 3 American Indian or Alaska Native, non-Hispanic/Latino; 6 Asian, non-Hispanic/Latino; 10 Hispanic/Latino, 25 international. Average age 31. 236 applicants, 67% accepted, 55 enrolled. In 2010, 39 master's, 19 doctorates awarded. *Degree requirements:* For master's, comprehensive exam (for some programs), thesis or alternative; for doctorate, comprehensive exam, thesis/dissertation, internship. *Entrance requirements:* For master's, GRE, minimum GPA of 2.75; for doctorate, GRE, minimum GPA of 3.5. Additional exam requirements/recommendations for international students: Required—TOEFL (minimum score 550 paper-based; 79 iBT), IELTS (minimum score 6.5). *Application deadline:* For fall admission, 1/1 priority date for domestic students; for spring admission, 9/1 for domestic students. Applications are processed on a rolling basis. Application fee: $56 ($96 for international students). *Financial support:* In 2010–11, 3 fellowships, 55 research assistantships, 77 teaching assistantships were awarded; career-related internships or fieldwork, Federal Work-Study, unspecified assistantships, and project assistantships also available. Support available to part-time students. Financial award application deadline: 4/15. Total annual research expenditures: $6.2 million. *Unit head:* David Yu, Representative, 414-229-6169, E-mail: yu@uwm.edu. *Application contact:* Betty Warras, General Information Contact, 414-229-6169, Fax: 414-229-6967, E-mail: bwarras@uwm.edu.

University of Wyoming, College of Engineering and Applied Sciences, Department of Civil and Architectural Engineering, Program in Civil Engineering, Laramie, WY 82070. Offers MS, PhD. Part-time programs available. Terminal master's awarded for partial completion of doctoral program. *Degree requirements:* For master's, thesis (for some programs); for doctorate, variable foreign language requirement, comprehensive exam, thesis/dissertation. *Entrance requirements:* For master's, GRE General Test (minimum score 900), minimum GPA of 3.0; for doctorate, GRE General Test (minimum score: 1000), minimum GPA of 3.0. Additional exam requirements/recommendations for international students: Required—TOEFL. Electronic applications accepted. *Faculty research:* Structures, water, resources, geotechnical, transportation.

Utah State University, School of Graduate Studies, College of Engineering, Department of Civil and Environmental Engineering, Logan, UT 84322. Offers ME, MS, PhD, CE. *Degree requirements:* For master's, thesis (for some programs); for doctorate, thesis/dissertation. *Entrance requirements:* For master's and doctorate, GRE General Test, minimum GPA of 3.0. Additional exam requirements/recommendations for international students: Required—TOEFL. Electronic applications accepted. *Faculty research:* Hazardous waste treatment, large space structures, river basin management, earthquake engineering, environmental impact.

Vanderbilt University, School of Engineering, Department of Civil and Environmental Engineering, Program in Civil Engineering, Nashville, TN 37240-1001. Offers M Eng, MS, PhD. MS and PhD offered through the Graduate School. Part-time programs available. *Faculty:* 12 full-time (1 woman), 1 (woman) part-time/adjunct. *Students:* 27 full-time (4 women); includes 4 Black or African American, non-Hispanic/Latino, 12 international. Average age 28. 72 applicants, 17% accepted, 9 enrolled. In 2010, 18 master's, 5 doctorates awarded. Terminal master's awarded for partial completion of doctoral program. *Degree requirements:* For master's, thesis; for doctorate, thesis/dissertation. *Entrance requirements:* For master's and doctorate, GRE General Test. Additional exam requirements/recommendations for international students: Required—TOEFL. *Application deadline:* For fall admission, 1/15 for domestic students; for spring admission, 11/1 for domestic students. Applications are processed on a rolling basis. Application fee: $0. Electronic applications accepted. *Financial support:* In 2010–11, 12 fellowships with full tuition reimbursements (averaging $30,000 per year), 15 research assistantships with full tuition reimbursements (averaging $25,200 per year), 7 teaching assistantships

Civil Engineering

Vanderbilt University (continued)

with full tuition reimbursements (averaging $21,600 per year) were awarded; career-related internships or fieldwork, institutionally sponsored loans, scholarships/grants, traineeships, and tuition waivers (full and partial) also available. Financial award application deadline: 1/15. *Faculty research:* Structural mechanics, finite element analysis, urban transportation, hazardous material transport. *Unit head:* Dr. David S. Kosson, Chair, 615-322-2697, Fax: 615-322-3365, E-mail: david.kosson@vanderbilt.edu. *Application contact:* Dr. P. K. Basu, Director of Graduate Studies, 615-322-7477, Fax: 615-322-3365, E-mail: p.k.basu@vanderbilt.edu.

Villanova University, College of Engineering, Department of Civil and Environmental Engineering, Program in Civil Engineering, Villanova, PA 19085-1699. Offers MSCE. Part-time and evening/weekend programs available. *Students:* 8 full-time (0 women), 68 part-time (21 women); includes 1 Black or African American, non-Hispanic/Latino; 1 American Indian or Alaska Native, non-Hispanic/Latino; 3 Asian, non-Hispanic/Latino, 2 international. 29 applicants, 97% accepted, 15 enrolled. In 2010, 22 master's awarded. *Degree requirements:* For master's, thesis optional. *Entrance requirements:* For master's, GRE General Test (for applicants with degrees from foreign universities), minimum GPA of 3.0. Additional exam requirements/recommendations for international students: Required—TOEFL (minimum score 600 paper-based; 250 computer-based; 100 iBT). *Application deadline:* For fall admission, 8/1 priority date for domestic students, 4/1 priority date for international students; for spring admission, 12/1 for domestic students, 10/1 for international students. Applications are processed on a rolling basis. Application fee: $50. Electronic applications accepted. *Expenses:* Tuition: Part-time $700 per credit. Part-time tuition and fees vary according to degree level and program. *Financial support:* In 2010–11, research assistantships with full tuition reimbursements (averaging $13,100 per year); Federal Work-Study, scholarships/grants, tuition waivers (full and partial), and unspecified assistantships also available. Support available to part-time students. Financial award application deadline: 1/15. *Faculty research:* Bridge inspection, environment maintenance, economy and risk. *Unit head:* Dr. Ronald A. Chadderton, Chairman, 610-519-4960, Fax: 610-519-6754, E-mail: ronald.chadderton@villanova.edu. *Application contact:* College of Engineering Graduate Programs Office, 610-519-5840, Fax: 610-519-5859, E-mail: engineering.grad@villanova.edu.

Virginia Polytechnic Institute and State University, Graduate School, College of Engineering, Department of Civil and Environmental Engineering, Blacksburg, VA 24061. Offers civil engineering (M Eng, MS, PhD); civil infrastructure systems (Certificate); environmental engineering (MS); environmental sciences and engineering (MS); transportation systems engineering (Certificate); treatment process engineering (Certificate); urban hydrology and stormwater management (Certificate); water quality management (Certificate). *Accreditation:* ABET (one or more programs are accredited). *Faculty:* 44 full-time (8 women), 1 part-time/adjunct (0 women). *Students:* 320 full-time (108 women), 70 part-time (20 women); includes 9 Black or African American, non-Hispanic/Latino; 15 Asian, non-Hispanic/Latino; 13 Hispanic/Latino, 126 international. Average age 27. 639 applicants, 44% accepted, 121 enrolled. In 2010, 97 master's, 18 doctorates awarded. *Degree requirements:* For master's, comprehensive exam (for some programs), thesis (for some programs); for doctorate, comprehensive exam (for some programs), thesis/dissertation (for some programs). *Entrance requirements:* For master's and doctorate, GRE. Additional exam requirements/recommendations for international students: Required—TOEFL (minimum score 550 paper-based; 213 computer-based). *Application deadline:* For fall admission, 7/1 for domestic and international students; for spring admission, 12/1 for domestic and international students. Applications are processed on a rolling basis. Application fee: $65. Electronic applications accepted. *Expenses:* Tuition, area resident: Full-time $9399; part-time $488 per credit hour. Tuition, state resident: full-time $9399; part-time $488 per credit hour. Tuition, nonresident: full-time $17,854; part-time $957.75 per credit hour. International tuition: $17,854 full-time. Required fees: $1534. Full-time tuition and fees vary according to program. *Financial support:* In 2010–11, 35 fellowships with full tuition reimbursements (averaging $5,861 per year), 82 research assistantships with full tuition

reimbursements (averaging $20,397 per year), 33 teaching assistantships with full tuition reimbursements (averaging $14,542 per year) were awarded; career-related internships or fieldwork, Federal Work-Study, scholarships/grants, health care benefits, and unspecified assistantships also available. Financial award application deadline: 1/15. *Faculty research:* Construction, environmental geotechnical hydrosystems, structures and transportation engineering. Total annual research expenditures: $12.2 million. *Unit head:* Dr. Sam Easterling, UNIT HEAD, 540-231-5143, Fax: 540-231-7532, E-mail: seaster@vt.edu. *Application contact:* Marc Widdowson, Contact, 540-231-7153, Fax: 540-231-7532, E-mail: mwiddows@vt.edu.

Washington State University, Graduate School, College of Engineering and Architecture, Department of Civil and Environmental Engineering, Program in Civil Engineering, Pullman, WA 99164. Offers MS, PhD. *Students:* 67 full-time (17 women), 7 part-time (1 woman); includes 3 minority (1 American Indian or Alaska Native, non-Hispanic/Latino; 2 Asian, non-Hispanic/Latino), 32 international. Average age 29. 180 applicants, 26% accepted, 34 enrolled. In 2010, 25 master's, 4 doctorates awarded. Terminal master's awarded for partial completion of doctoral program. *Degree requirements:* For master's, comprehensive exam (for some programs), thesis (for some programs), oral exam; for doctorate, comprehensive exam, thesis/dissertation, oral exam, written exam. *Entrance requirements:* For master's and doctorate, GRE General Test, official transcripts from all colleges and universities attended; one-page statement of purpose; three letters of recommendation. Additional exam requirements/recommendations for international students: Required—TOEFL, IELTS. *Application deadline:* For fall admission, 1/10 priority date for domestic students, 1/10 for international students; for spring admission, 7/1 for domestic and international students. Applications are processed on a rolling basis. Application fee: $50. Electronic applications accepted. *Expenses:* Tuition, state resident: full-time $8552; part-time $443 per credit. Tuition, nonresident: full-time $21,650; part-time $1083 per credit. Required fees: $846. *Financial support:* In 2010–11, research assistantships with full and partial tuition reimbursements (averaging $18,204 per year), teaching assistantships with full and partial tuition reimbursements (averaging $18,204 per year) were awarded; career-related internships or fieldwork, Federal Work-Study, and institutionally sponsored loans also available. Financial award application deadline: 4/1; financial award applicants required to submit FAFSA. *Faculty research:* Environmental geotechnical, hydraulics transportation, structures, wood. Total annual research expenditures: $4.1 million. *Unit head:* Dr. David McLean, Chair, 509-335-9578, Fax: 509-335-7632, E-mail: mclean@wsu.edu. *Application contact:* Graduate School Admissions, 800-GRADWSU, Fax: 509-335-1949, E-mail: gradsch@wsu.edu.

Wayne State University, College of Engineering, Department of Civil and Environmental Engineering, Detroit, MI 48202. Offers MS, PhD. *Faculty:* 14 full-time (2 women), 7 part-time/adjunct (0 women). *Students:* 52 full-time (12 women), 35 part-time (9 women); includes 14 minority (4 Black or African American, non-Hispanic/Latino; 8 Asian, non-Hispanic/Latino; 2 Hispanic/Latino), 15 international. Average age 32. 41 applicants, 51% accepted, 14 enrolled. In 2010, 54 master's, 8 doctorates awarded. *Degree requirements:* For master's, thesis optional; for doctorate, thesis/dissertation. *Entrance requirements:* For master's, BS in civil engineering with minimum honor-point average of 2.8; for doctorate, GRE if BS in engineering is not from an ABET accredited institution in the US, MS in civil engineering with minimum honor-point average of 3.5, international: letters of recommendation. Additional exam requirements/recommendations for international students: Required—TOEFL (minimum score 550 paper-based; 213 computer-based); Recommended—TWE (minimum score 6). *Application deadline:* For fall admission, 7/1 priority date for domestic students, 6/1 for international students; for winter admission, 10/1 for international students; for spring admission, 3/15 for domestic students, 2/1 for international students. Applications are processed on a rolling basis. Application fee: $30 ($50 for international students). Electronic applications accepted. *Expenses:* Tuition, state resident: full-time $7662; part-time $478.85 per credit hour. Tuition, nonresident: full-time $16,920; part-time $1057.55 per credit hour. Required fees: $571.20; $35.70 per credit hour. $188.05 per semester. Tuition and fees vary according to course load and program. *Financial support:* In 2010–11, 1 fellowship (averaging $15,750 per year), 6 research

assistantships (averaging $15,667 per year), 5 teaching assistantships (averaging $16,984 per year) were awarded; career-related internships or fieldwork and tuition waivers (partial) also available. *Faculty research:* Environmental geotechnics, civil infrastructure systems and materials, seismic analysis of structures and foundations, traffic and construction safety, transportation planning and economics. *Unit head:* Dr. Carol Miller, Chair, 313-577-3789, Fax: 313-577-3881, E-mail: ab1421@wayne.edu. *Application contact:* Thomas Heidtke, Associate Professor, 313-577-3854, E-mail: theidtke@eng.wayne.edu.

Western Michigan University, Graduate College, College of Engineering and Applied Sciences, Department of Civil and Construction Engineering, Kalamazoo, MI 49008. Offers civil engineering (MS), including construction engineering and management, structural engineering, transportation engineering. *Entrance requirements:* For master's, minimum GPA of 3.0.

West Virginia University, College of Engineering and Mineral Resources, Department of Civil and Environmental Engineering, Morgantown, WV 26506. Offers civil engineering (MSCE, MSE, PhD). Part-time programs available. *Degree requirements:* For master's, thesis; for doctorate, comprehensive exam, thesis/dissertation. *Entrance requirements:* For master's and doctorate, minimum GPA of 3.0. Additional exam requirements/recommendations for international students: Required—TOEFL, GRE. *Faculty research:* Habitat restoration, advanced materials for civil infrastructure, pavement modeling, infrastructure condition assessment.

Widener University, Graduate Programs in Engineering, Program in Civil Engineering, Chester, PA 19013-5792. Offers M Eng. Part-time and evening/weekend programs available. *Students:* 2 full-time (0 women), 9 part-time (1 woman); includes 2 Black or African American, non-Hispanic/Latino, 2 international. Average age 30. In 2010, 1 master's awarded. *Degree requirements:* For master's, thesis optional. *Application deadline:* For fall admission, 8/1 priority date for domestic students; for spring admission, 12/1 for domestic students. Applications are processed on a rolling basis. Application fee: $25 ($300 for international students). *Financial support:* Teaching assistantships with full tuition reimbursements, unspecified assistantships available. Financial award application deadline: 3/15. *Faculty research:* Environmental engineering, laws and water supply, structural analysis and design. *Unit head:* Dr. Vicki L. Brown, Chairman, 610-499-4249, E-mail: vicki.l.brown@widener.edu. *Application contact:* Dr. Vicki L. Brown, Chairman, 610-499-4249, E-mail: vicki.l.brown@widener.edu.

Woods Hole Oceanographic Institution, MIT/WHOI Joint Program in Oceanography/Applied Ocean Science and Engineering, Woods Hole, MA 02543-1541. Offers applied ocean sciences (PhD); biological oceanography (PhD, Sc D); chemical oceanography (PhD, Sc D); civil and environmental and oceanographic engineering (PhD); electrical and oceanographic engineering (PhD); geochemistry (PhD); geophysics (PhD); marine biology (PhD); marine geochemistry (PhD, Sc D); marine geology (PhD, Sc D); marine geophysics (PhD); mechanical and oceanographic engineering (PhD); ocean engineering (PhD); oceanographic engineering (M Eng, MS, PhD, Sc D, Eng); paleoceanography (PhD); physical oceanography (PhD, Sc D). MS, PhD, Sc D offered jointly with Massachusetts Institute of Technology. Terminal master's awarded for partial completion of doctoral program. *Degree requirements:* For master's and Eng, thesis (for some programs); for doctorate, thesis/dissertation. *Entrance requirements:* For master's, GRE General Test; for doctorate, GRE General Test, GRE Subject Test. Additional exam requirements/recommendations for international students: Required—TOEFL. Electronic applications accepted.

Worcester Polytechnic Institute, Graduate Studies and Research, Department of Civil and Environmental Engineering, Worcester, MA 01609-2280. Offers civil and environmental engineering (Advanced Certificate, Graduate Certificate); civil engineering (ME, MS, PhD); construction project management (MS); environmental engineering (MS); master builder environmental engineering (M Eng). Part-time and evening/weekend programs available. Postbaccalaureate distance learning degree programs offered (no on-campus study). *Faculty:* 11 full-time (1 woman), 2 part-time/adjunct (1 woman). *Students:* 46 full-time (21 women), 42 part-time (10 women); includes 1 Black or African American, non-Hispanic/Latino; 5 Asian, non-Hispanic/Latino; 1 Hispanic/Latino; 4 Native Hawaiian or other Pacific Islander, non-Hispanic/Latino, 18 international. 135 applicants, 74% accepted, 36 enrolled. In 2010, 26 master's, 2 doctorates awarded. *Degree requirements:* For master's, thesis optional; for doctorate, comprehensive exam, thesis/dissertation. *Entrance requirements:* For master's and doctorate, GRE (recommended), 3 letters of recommendation. Additional exam requirements/recommendations for international students: Required—TOEFL (minimum score 550 paper-based; 213 computer-based; 79 iBT), IELTS (minimum score 6.5). *Application deadline:* For fall admission, 1/1 priority date for domestic and international students; for spring admission, 10/1 priority date for domestic and international students. Applications are processed on a rolling basis. Application fee: $70. Electronic applications accepted. *Expenses:* Tuition: Full-time $20,862; part-time $1159 per term. One-time fee: $15. *Financial support:* Career-related internships or fieldwork, institutionally sponsored loans, scholarships/grants, and unspecified assistantships available. Financial award application deadline: 1/1; financial award applicants required to submit FAFSA. *Faculty research:* Environmental engineering and sustainability, pavement engineering technology, impact mechanics and engineering. *Unit head:* Dr. Tahar El-Korchi, Interim Head, 508-831-5530, Fax: 508-831-5808, E-mail: tek@wpi.edu. *Application contact:* Dr. Paul Mathisen, Graduate Coordinator, 508-831-5530, Fax: 508-831-5808, E-mail: mathisen@wpi.edu.

Youngstown State University, Graduate School, College of Science, Technology, Engineering and Mathematics, Department of Civil and Environmental Engineering, Youngstown, OH 44555-0001. Offers MSE. Part-time and evening/weekend programs available. *Degree requirements:* For master's, thesis optional. *Entrance requirements:* For master's, minimum GPA of 2.75 in field. Additional exam requirements/recommendations for international students: Required—TOEFL. *Faculty research:* Structural mechanics, water quality modeling, surface and ground water hydrology, physical and chemical processes in aquatic systems.

Construction Engineering

The American University in Cairo, School of Sciences and Engineering, Department of Construction and Architectural Engineering, Cairo, Egypt. Offers construction engineering (M Eng, MS). *Degree requirements:* For master's, thesis. *Entrance requirements:* Additional exam requirements/recommendations for international students: Required—English entrance exam and/or TOEFL. *Faculty research:* Composite materials, superelasticity, expert systems, materials selection.

Arizona State University, Ira A. Fulton School of Engineering, Del E. Webb School of Construction, Tempe, AZ 85287-5306. Offers civil, environmental and sustainable engineering (MS, MSE, PhD); construction (MS, MSE, PhD); construction engineering (MSE). Part-time and evening/weekend programs available. Postbaccalaureate distance learning degree programs offered (minimal on-campus study). *Faculty:* 40 full-time (4 women), 6 part-time/adjunct (1 woman). *Students:* 149 full-time (51 women), 85 part-time (17 women); includes 32 minority (6 Black or African American, non-Hispanic/Latino; 2 American Indian or Alaska Native, non-Hispanic/Latino; 13 Asian, non-Hispanic/Latino; 10 Hispanic/Latino; 1 Native Hawaiian or other Pacific Islander, non-Hispanic/Latino), 69 international. Average age 29. 379 applicants, 53% accepted, 77 enrolled. In 2010, 44 master's, 10 doctorates awarded. Terminal master's awarded for partial completion of doctoral program. *Degree requirements:* For master's, thesis optional, comprehensive exams (MSE); interactive Program of Study (iPOS) submitted before completing 50 percent of required credit hours; for doctorate, comprehensive exam, thesis/dissertation, interactive Program of Study (iPOS) submitted before completing 50 percent of required credit hours. *Entrance requirements:* For master's, GRE, minimum GPA of 3.0 or equivalent in last 2 years of work leading to bachelor's degree; for doctorate, GRE, minimum GPA of 3.0 in last 2 years of work leading to bachelor's degree, 3.2 in all graduate-level coursework with master's degree; 3 letters of recommendation; resume/curriculum vitae; letter of intent; thesis (if applicable); statement of research interests. Additional exam requirements/recommendations for international students: Required—TOEFL, IELTS, or Pearson Test of English. *Application deadline:* For fall admission, 1/1 for domestic and international students; for spring admission, 7/1 for domestic and international students. Application fee: $70 ($90 for international students). Electronic applications accepted. *Expenses:* Contact institution. *Financial support:* In 2010–11, 67 research assistantships with full and partial tuition reimbursements (averaging $16,393 per year), 17 teaching assistantships with full and partial tuition reimbursements (averaging $13,812 per year) were awarded; fellowships with full and partial tuition reimbursements, career-related internships or fieldwork, institutionally sponsored loans, scholarships/grants, traineeships, and tuition waivers (full and partial) also available. Financial award application deadline: 3/1; financial award applicants required to submit FAFSA. *Faculty research:* Water purification, transportation (safety and materials), construction management, environmental biotechnology, environmental nanotechnology, earth systems engineering and management, SMART innovations, project performance metrics, and underground infrastructure. Total annual research expenditures: $8.5 million. *Unit head:* Dr. G. Edward Gibson, Director, 480-965-7972, E-mail: edd.gibson@asu.edu. *Application contact:* Graduate Admissions, 480-965-6113.

Auburn University, Graduate School, College of Architecture, Design, and Construction, Department of Building Science, Auburn University, AL 36849. Offers building science (MBS); construction management (MBS). *Faculty:* 18 full-time (1 woman), 3 part-time/adjunct (1 woman). *Students:* 23 full-time (6 women), 25 part-time (3 women); includes 1 Black or African American, non-Hispanic/Latino; 2 Hispanic/Latino, 4 international. Average age 27. 83 applicants, 60% accepted, 42 enrolled. In 2010, 7 master's awarded. *Entrance requirements:* For master's, GRE General Test. *Application deadline:* For fall admission, 7/7 for domestic students; for spring admission, 11/24 for domestic students. Applications are processed on a rolling basis. Application fee: $50 ($60 for international students). Electronic applications accepted. *Expenses:* Tuition, state resident: full-time $7002. Tuition, nonresident: full-time $21,898. International tuition: $22,116 full-time. Required fees: $892. Tuition and fees vary according to course load and program. *Financial support:* Application deadline: 3/15. *Unit head:* Dr. Richard Burt, Head, 334-844-5260. *Application contact:* Dr. George Flowers, Dean of the Graduate School, 334-844-2125.

Auburn University, Graduate School, Ginn College of Engineering, Department of Civil Engineering, Auburn University, AL 36849. Offers construction engineering and management (MCE, MS, PhD); environmental engineering (MCE, MS, PhD); geotechnical/materials engineering (MCE, MS, PhD); hydraulics/hydrology (MCE, MS, PhD); structural engineering (MCE, MS, PhD); transportation engineering (MCE, MS, PhD). Part-time programs available. *Faculty:* 21 full-time (1 woman), 3 part-time/adjunct (1 woman). *Students:* 46 full-time (15 women), 39 part-time (5 women); includes 3 Black or African American, non-Hispanic/Latino; 1 Asian, non-Hispanic/Latino, 29 international. Average age 26. 136 applicants, 43% accepted, 26 enrolled. In 2010, 19 master's, 4 doctorates awarded. *Degree requirements:* For master's, project (MCE), thesis (MS); for doctorate, comprehensive exam, thesis/dissertation. *Entrance requirements:* For master's and doctorate, GRE General Test. *Application deadline:* For fall admission, 7/7 for domestic students; for spring admission, 11/24 for domestic students. Applications are processed on a rolling basis. Application fee: $50 ($60 for international students). Electronic applications accepted. *Expenses:* Tuition, state resident: full-time $7002. Tuition, nonresident: full-time $21,898. International tuition: $22,116 full-time. Required fees: $892. Tuition and fees vary according to course load and program. *Financial support:* Fellowships, research assistantships, teaching assistantships, Federal Work-Study available. Support available to part-time students. Financial award application deadline: 3/15; financial award applicants required to submit FAFSA. *Unit head:* Dr. J. Michael Stallings, Head, 334-844-4320. *Application contact:* Dr. George Flowers, Dean of the Graduate School, 334-844-2125.

Bradley University, Graduate School, College of Engineering and Technology, Department of Civil Engineering and Construction, Peoria, IL 61625-0002. Offers MSCE. Part-time and evening/weekend programs available. *Degree requirements:* For master's, comprehensive exam. *Entrance requirements:* For master's, minimum GPA of 3.0, 2 letters of recommendation. Additional exam requirements/recommendations for international students: Required—TOEFL (minimum score 550 paper-based; 213 computer-based; 79 iBT).

Columbia University, Fu Foundation School of Engineering and Applied Science, Department of Civil Engineering and Engineering Mechanics, New York, NY 10027. Offers civil engineering (MS, Eng Sc D, PhD, Engr); construction engineering and management (MS); engineering mechanics (MS, Eng Sc D, PhD, Engr). Part-time programs available. Postbaccalaureate distance learning degree programs offered (no on-campus study). *Faculty:* 16 full-time (1 woman), 25 part-time/adjunct (3 women). *Students:* 96 full-time (19 women), 42 part-time (14 women); includes 25 minority (3 Black or African American, non-Hispanic/Latino; 11 Asian, non-Hispanic/Latino; 10 Hispanic/Latino; 1 Two or more races, non-Hispanic/Latino), 70 international. Average age 27. 265 applicants, 35% accepted, 59 enrolled. In 2010, 67 master's, 29 doctorates, 2 other advanced degrees awarded. Terminal master's awarded for partial completion of doctoral program. *Degree requirements:* For doctorate, thesis/dissertation, qualifying exam. *Entrance requirements:* For master's, doctorate, and Engr, GRE General Test. Additional exam requirements/recommendations for international students: Required—TOEFL, IELTS. *Application deadline:* For fall admission, 12/1 priority date for domestic and international students; for spring admission, 10/1 priority date for domestic and international students. Application fee: $95. Electronic applications accepted. *Financial support:* In 2010–11, 39 students received support, including 5 fellowships with full tuition reimbursements available (averaging $30,660 per year), 23 research assistantships with full tuition reimbursements available (averaging $30,660 per year), 11 teaching assistantships with full tuition reimbursements available (averaging $30,660 per year); traineeships and health care benefits also available. Financial award application deadline: 12/1; financial award applicants required to submit FAFSA. *Faculty research:* Motion monitoring of Manhattan Bridge, lightweight concrete panels, simulation of life of well sealant, intercultural knowledge system dynamics, corrosion monitoring of New York City bridges. *Unit head:* Dr. Raimondo Betti, Professor and Department Chairman, 212-854-6388, Fax: 212-854-7081, E-mail: betti@civil.columbia.edu. *Application contact:* Rene B. Testa, Professor, 212-854-3143, Fax: 212-854-6267, E-mail: testa@civil.columbia.edu.

Concordia University, School of Graduate Studies, Faculty of Engineering and Computer Science, Department of Building, Civil and Environmental Engineering, Montréal, QC H3G 1M8, Canada. Offers building engineering (M Eng, MA Sc, PhD, Certificate); civil engineering (M Eng, MA Sc, PhD); environmental engineering (Certificate). *Degree requirements:* For master's, thesis or alternative; for doctorate, comprehensive exam, thesis/dissertation. *Faculty research:* Structural engineering, geotechnical engineering, water resources and fluid engineering, transportation engineering, systems engineering.

Construction Engineering

Illinois Institute of Technology, Graduate College, Armour College of Engineering, Department of Civil, Architectural and Environmental Engineering, Chicago, IL 60616-3793. Offers architectural engineering (M Arch E); civil engineering (MS, PhD), including architectural engineering (MS), construction engineering and management (MS), geoenvironmental engineering (MS), geotechnical engineering (MS), structural engineering (MS), transportation engineering (MS); construction engineering and management (MCEM); environmental engineering (M Env E, PhD); geoenvironmental engineering (M Geoenv E); geotechnical engineering (MGE); public works (MPW); structural engineering (MSE); transportation engineering (M Trans E). Part-time and evening/weekend programs available. Postbaccalaureate distance learning degree programs offered (minimal on-campus study). *Faculty:* 15 full-time (1 woman), 13 part-time/adjunct (1 woman). *Students:* 159 full-time (63 women), 109 part-time (22 women); includes 30 minority (9 Black or African American, non-Hispanic/Latino; 16 Asian, non-Hispanic/Latino; 5 Hispanic/Latino), 126 international. Average age 27. 453 applicants, 66% accepted, 98 enrolled. In 2010, 76 master's, 1 doctorate awarded. Terminal master's awarded for partial completion of doctoral program. *Degree requirements:* For master's, thesis (for some programs); for doctorate, comprehensive exam, thesis/dissertation. *Entrance requirements:* For master's, GRE General Test (minimum score 900 Quantitative and Verbal, 2.5 Analytical Writing), minimum undergraduate GPA of 3.0; for doctorate, GRE General Test (minimum score 1000 Quantitative and Verbal, 3.0 Analytical Writing), minimum undergraduate GPA of 3.0. Additional exam requirements/recommendations for international students: Required—TOEFL (minimum score 523 paper-based; 70 iBT); Recommended—IELTS (minimum score 5.5). *Application deadline:* For fall admission, 5/1 for domestic and international students; for spring admission, 10/15 for domestic and international students. Applications are processed on a rolling basis. Application fee: $50. Electronic applications accepted. *Expenses:* Tuition: Full-time $18,576; part-time $1032 per credit hour. Required fees: $583 per semester. One-time fee: $150. Tuition and fees vary according to program and student level. *Financial support:* In 2010–11, 13 research assistantships with full and partial tuition reimbursements (averaging $9,453 per year), 19 teaching assistantships with full and partial tuition reimbursements (averaging $3,163 per year) were awarded; fellowships with full and partial tuition reimbursements, Federal Work-Study, institutionally sponsored loans, scholarships/grants, health care benefits, tuition waivers (partial), and unspecified assistantships also available. Support available to part-time students. Financial award applicants required to submit FAFSA. *Faculty research:* Structural, architectural, geotechnical and geoenvironmental engineering; construction engineering and management; transportation engineering; environmental engineering and public works. Total annual research expenditures: $763,042. *Unit head:* Dr. Jamshid Mohammadi, Professor and Chairman, 312-567-3629, Fax: 312-567-3519, E-mail: mohammadi@iit.edu. *Application contact:* Deborah Gibson, Director, Graduate Admission, 866-472-3448, Fax: 312-567-3138, E-mail: inquiry.grad@iit.edu.

Iowa State University of Science and Technology, Graduate College, College of Engineering, Department of Civil and Construction Engineering, Ames, IA 50011. Offers civil engineering (MS, PhD), including civil engineering materials, construction engineering and management, environmental engineering, geometronics, geotechnical engineering, structural engineering, transportation engineering. *Faculty:* 35 full-time (6 women), 4 part-time/adjunct (0 women). *Students:* 93 full-time (31 women), 48 part-time (10 women); includes 1 Black or African American, non-Hispanic/Latino; 1 Asian, non-Hispanic/Latino; 4 Hispanic/Latino, 62 international. 179 applicants, 37% accepted, 35 enrolled. In 2010, 32 master's, 9 doctorates awarded. *Degree requirements:* For master's, thesis or alternative; for doctorate, thesis/dissertation. *Entrance requirements:* For master's and doctorate, GRE General Test. Additional exam requirements/recommendations for international students: Required—TOEFL (minimum score 550 paper-based; 82 iBT), IELTS (minimum score 6.5). *Application deadline:* For fall admission, 2/1 priority date for domestic students, 2/1 for international students; for spring admission, 8/1 priority date for domestic students, 8/1 for international students. Application fee: $40 ($90 for international students). Electronic applications accepted. *Financial support:* In 2010–11, 67 research assistantships with full and partial tuition reimbursements (averaging $7,654 per year), 4 teaching assistantships with full and partial tuition reimbursements (averaging $9,525 per year) were awarded; fellowships, scholarships/grants, health care benefits, and unspecified assistantships also available. *Unit head:* Dr. James Alleman, Chair, 515-294-3892, E-mail: ccee-grad-inquiry@iastate.edu. *Application contact:* Dr. Sri Srithanan, Director of Graduate Education, 515-294-5328, E-mail: ccee-grad-inquiry@iastate.edu.

Marquette University, Graduate School, College of Engineering, Department of Civil and Environmental Engineering, Milwaukee, WI 53201-1881. Offers construction and public works management (MS, PhD); construction engineering and management (Certificate); environmental/water resources engineering (MS, PhD); structural design (Certificate); structural/geotechnical engineering (MS, PhD); transportation planning and engineering (MS, PhD); waste and wastewater treatment processes (Certificate). Part-time and evening/weekend programs available. *Faculty:* 13 full-time (0 women), 3 part-time/adjunct (0 women). *Students:* 20 full-time (4 women), 12 part-time (1 woman); includes 1 minority (Black or African American, non-Hispanic/Latino), 12 international. Average age 27. 66 applicants, 64% accepted, 9 enrolled. In 2010, 8 master's, 1 doctorate awarded. Terminal master's awarded for partial completion of doctoral program. *Degree requirements:* For master's, comprehensive exam, thesis or alternative; for doctorate, thesis/dissertation. *Entrance requirements:* For master's, GRE General Test (recommended), minimum GPA of 3.0, official transcripts from all current and previous colleges/universities except Marquette, three letters of recommendation; for doctorate, GRE General Test, minimum GPA of 3.0, official transcripts from all current and previous colleges/universities except Marquette, three letters of recommendation, brief statement of purpose, submission of any English-language publications authored by applicant (strongly recommended). Additional exam requirements/recommendations for international students: Required—TOEFL (minimum score 530 paper-based; 78 computer-based). *Application deadline:* For fall admission, 6/1 priority date for domestic students. Applications are processed on a rolling basis. Application fee: $50. Electronic applications accepted. *Expenses:* Tuition: Full-time $16,290; part-time $905 per credit hour. Tuition and fees vary according to program. *Financial support:* In 2010–11, 13 students received support, including 4 fellowships with tuition reimbursements available, 4 research assistantships with tuition reimbursements available, 10 teaching assistantships with tuition reimbursements available; Federal Work-Study, institutionally sponsored loans, scholarships/grants, and tuition waivers (full and partial) also available. Support available to part-time students. Financial award application deadline: 2/15. *Faculty research:* Highway safety, highway performance, and intelligent transportation systems; surface mount technology; watershed management. Total annual research expenditures: $662,392. *Unit head:* Dr. Thomas Wenzel, Chair, 414-288-7030, Fax: 414-288-7521, E-mail: thomas.wenzel@marquette.edu. *Application contact:* Dr. Stephen M. Heinrich, Director of Graduate Studies, 414-288-5466, E-mail: stephen.heinrich@marquette.edu.

Massachusetts Institute of Technology, School of Engineering, Department of Civil and Environmental Engineering, Cambridge, MA 02139. Offers biological oceanography (PhD, Sc D); chemical oceanography (PhD, Sc D); civil and environmental engineering (M Eng, SM, PhD, Sc D); civil and environmental systems (PhD, Sc D); civil engineering (PhD, Sc D, CE); coastal engineering (PhD, Sc D); construction engineering and management (PhD, Sc D); environmental biology (PhD, Sc D); environmental chemistry (PhD, Sc D); environmental engineering (PhD, Sc D); environmental fluid mechanics (PhD, Sc D); geotechnical and geoenvironmental engineering (PhD, Sc D); hydrology (PhD, Sc D); information technology (PhD, Sc D); oceanographic engineering (PhD, Sc D); structures and materials (PhD, Sc D); transportation (PhD, Sc D); SM/MBA. *Faculty:* 36 full-time (6 women). *Students:* 181 full-time (56 women); includes 27 minority (3 Black or African American, non-Hispanic/Latino; 10 Asian, non-Hispanic/Latino; 10 Hispanic/Latino; 4 Two or more races, non-Hispanic/Latino), 93 international. Average age 26. 525 applicants, 29% accepted, 74 enrolled. In 2010, 85 master's, 18 doctorates, 2 other advanced degrees awarded. *Degree requirements:* For master's and CE, thesis; for doctorate, comprehensive exam, thesis/dissertation. *Entrance requirements:* For master's and doctorate, GRE General Test. Additional exam requirements/recommendations for international students: Required—TOEFL (minimum score 577 paper-based; 233 computer-based; 90 iBT), IELTS (minimum score 7). *Application deadline:* For fall admission, 1/2 for domestic and international students. Application fee: $75. Electronic applications accepted. *Expenses:* Tuition: Full-time $38,940; part-time $605 per unit. Required fees: $272. *Financial support:* In 2010–11, 146 students received support, including 50 fellowships with tuition reimbursements available (averaging $21,808 per year), 90 research assistantships with tuition reimbursements available (averaging $28,452 per year), 20 teaching assistantships with tuition reimbursements available (averaging $27,842 per year); career-related internships or fieldwork, Federal Work-Study, institutionally sponsored loans, scholarships/grants, health care benefits, and unspecified assistantships also available. *Faculty research:* Environmental chemistry; environmental microbiology; environmental fluid mechanics and coastal engineering; geotechnical engineering and geomechanics; hydrology and hydroclimatology; mechanics of materials and structures; operations research/supply chain; transportation. Total annual research expenditures: $19.5 million. *Unit head:* Prof. Andrew Whittle, Department Head, 617-253-7101. *Application contact:* Patricia Glidden, Graduate Admissions Coordinator, 617-253-7119, Fax: 617-258-6775, E-mail: cee-admissions@mit.edu.

Missouri University of Science and Technology, Graduate School, Department of Civil, Architectural, and Environmental Engineering, Rolla, MO 65409. Offers civil engineering (MS, DE, PhD); construction engineering (MS, DE, PhD); environmental engineering (MS); fluid mechanics (MS, DE, PhD); geotechnical engineering (MS, DE, PhD); hydrology and hydraulic engineering (MS, DE, PhD). Part-time and evening/weekend programs available. Terminal master's awarded for partial completion of doctoral program. *Degree requirements:* For master's, thesis optional; for doctorate, comprehensive exam, thesis/dissertation. *Entrance requirements:* For master's, GRE General Test (minimum combined score 1100), minimum GPA of 3.0; for doctorate, GRE General Test (minimum score: verbal and quantitative 400, writing 3.5), minimum GPA of 3.0. Additional exam requirements/recommendations for international students: Required—TOEFL. Electronic applications accepted. *Faculty research:* Earthquake engineering, structural optimization and control systems, structural health monitoring/damage detection, soil-structure interaction, soil mechanics and foundation engineering.

Montana State University, College of Graduate Studies, College of Engineering, Department of Civil Engineering, Bozeman, MT 59717. Offers civil engineering (MS); construction engineering management (MCEM); engineering (PhD), including applied mechanics option, civil engineering option. Part-time programs available. *Faculty:* 19 full-time (2 women), 5 part-time/adjunct (1 woman). *Students:* 26 full-time (6 women), 21 part-time (6 women); includes 2 minority (1 American Indian or Alaska Native, non-Hispanic/Latino; 1 Two or more races, non-Hispanic/Latino), 1 international. Average age 27. 43 applicants, 44% accepted, 17 enrolled. In 2010, 15 master's, 1 doctorate awarded. *Degree requirements:* For master's, comprehensive exam, thesis (for some programs); for doctorate, comprehensive exam, thesis/dissertation. *Entrance requirements:* For master's and doctorate, GRE General Test. Additional exam requirements/recommendations for international students: Required—TOEFL (minimum score 550 paper-based; 213 computer-based). *Application deadline:* For fall admission, 7/15 priority date for domestic students, 5/15 priority date for international students; for spring admission, 12/1 priority date for domestic students, 10/1 priority date for international students. Applications are processed on a rolling basis. Application fee: $30. Electronic applications accepted. *Expenses:* Tuition, state resident: full-time $5553.90. Tuition, nonresident: full-time $14,646. Required fees: $1233. *Financial support:* In 2010–11, 20 students received support, including 1 fellowship (averaging $15,000 per year), 5 research assistantships with partial tuition reimbursements available (averaging $12,000 per year), 6 teaching assistantships with partial tuition reimbursements available (averaging $8,000 per year); scholarships/grants and tuition waivers (partial) also available. Financial award application deadline: 3/1; financial award applicants required to submit FAFSA. *Faculty research:* Snow and ice mechanics, biofilm engineering, transportation, structural and geo materials, water resources. Total annual research expenditures: $54,392. *Unit head:* Dr. Brett Gunnick, Head, 406-994-2111, Fax: 406-994-6105, E-mail: bgunnick@ce.montana.edu. *Application contact:* Dr. Carl A. Fox, Vice Provost for Graduate Education, 406-994-4145, Fax: 406-994-7433, E-mail: gradstudy@montana.edu.

Ohio University, Graduate College, Russ College of Engineering and Technology, Department of Civil Engineering, Athens, OH 45701-2979. Offers civil engineering (PhD); construction (MS); environmental (MS); geotechnical and geoenvironmental (MS); mechanics (MS); structures (MS); transportation (MS); water resources and structures (MS). Part-time programs available. *Students:* 29 full-time (6 women), 5 part-time (1 woman); includes 2 minority (1 Hispanic/Latino; 1 Two or more races, non-Hispanic/Latino), 16 international. 52 applicants, 83% accepted, 14 enrolled. In 2010, 7 master's awarded. *Degree requirements:* For master's, comprehensive exam (for some programs), thesis or alternative; for doctorate, comprehensive exam, thesis/dissertation. *Entrance requirements:* For master's, GRE General Test, minimum GPA of 3.0, 3 letters of recommendation; for doctorate, GRE General Test. Additional exam requirements/recommendations for international students: Required—TOEFL (minimum score 550 paper-based; 80 iBT) or IELTS (minimum score 6.5). *Application deadline:* For fall admission, 5/1 priority date for domestic students, 2/1 priority date for international students; for winter admission, 8/1 priority date for domestic students, 4/1 priority date for international students; for spring admission, 2/1 priority date for domestic students, 7/1 priority date for international students. Applications are processed on a rolling basis. Application fee: $50 ($55 for international students). Electronic applications accepted. *Financial support:* Research assistantships with full tuition reimbursements, teaching assistantships with full tuition reimbursements, Federal Work-Study, institutionally sponsored loans, scholarships/grants, and unspecified assistantships available. Financial award application deadline: 3/15; financial award applicants required to submit FAFSA. *Faculty research:* Noise abatement, materials and environment, highway infrastructure, subsurface investigation (pavements, pipes, bridges). *Unit head:* Dr. Gayle F. Mitchell, Chair, 740-593-0430, Fax: 740-593-0625, E-mail: mitchelg@ohio.edu. *Application contact:* Dr. Shad M. Sargand, Graduate Chair, 740-593-1465, Fax: 740-593-0625, E-mail: sargand@ohio.edu.

Oregon State University, Graduate School, College of Engineering, School of Civil and Construction Engineering, Corvallis, OR 97331. Offers civil engineering (MS, PhD); coastal and ocean engineering (M Oc E, PhD); coastal engineering (MS); construction engineering management (MBE, PhD); engineering (M Eng, MAIS); geotechnical engineering (MS, PhD); structural engineering (MS, PhD); transportation engineering (MS, PhD); water engineering (MS, PhD). Part-time programs available. Terminal master's awarded for partial completion of doctoral program. *Degree requirements:* For master's, thesis or alternative; for doctorate, one foreign language, thesis/dissertation. *Entrance requirements:* For master's, GRE General Test, minimum GPA of 3.0 in last 90 hours (3.5 for MS); for doctorate, GRE General Test, minimum GPA of 3.0 in last 90 hours of undergraduate course work. Additional exam requirements/recommendations for international students: Required—TOEFL (minimum score 580 paper-based; 237 computer-based). *Faculty research:* Hazardous waste management, carbon cycling, wave forces on structures, pavement design, seismic analysis.

Pittsburg State University, Graduate School, College of Technology, Department of Construction Management and Construction Engineering Technologies, Pittsburg, KS 66762. Offers construction (MET).

Stevens Institute of Technology, Graduate School, Charles V. Schaefer Jr. School of Engineering, Department of Civil, Environmental, and Ocean Engineering, Program in Construction Management, Hoboken, NJ 07030. Offers construction accounting/estimating (Certificate); construction engineering (Certificate); construction law/disputes (Certificate); construction management (MS); construction/quality management (Certificate). *Students:* 23 full-time (4 women), 29 part-time (3 women); includes 2 Black or African American, non-Hispanic/Latino; 6 Asian, non-Hispanic/Latino, 18 international. Average age 28. 21 applicants, 100% accepted. *Degree requirements:* For master's, thesis optional. *Entrance requirements:* For master's, GMAT, GRE General Test. Additional exam requirements/recommendations for international students: Required—TOEFL. *Application deadline:* Applications are processed on a rolling basis. Application fee: $50. Electronic applications accepted. *Unit head:* Henry Dobbelaar, Head, 201-216-5340. *Application contact:* Dr. David A. Vaccari, Director, 201-216-5570, Fax: 201-216-5352, E-mail: dvaccari@stevens.edu.

Texas A&M University, College of Architecture, Department of Construction Science, College Station, TX 77843. Offers construction management (MS). *Faculty:* 15. *Students:* 50 full-time (17 women), 5 part-time (0 women); includes 6 minority (2 Asian, non-Hispanic/Latino; 4 Hispanic/Latino), 38 international. Average age 30. In 2010, 52 master's awarded. *Degree requirements:* For master's, comprehensive exam. *Entrance requirements:* For master's, GRE General Test. Additional exam requirements/recommendations for international students: Required—TOEFL. *Application deadline:* For fall admission, 4/1 priority date for domestic students; for winter admission, 1/1 priority date for domestic students; for spring admission, 9/1 priority date for domestic students. Applications are processed on a rolling basis. Application fee: $50 ($75 for international students). Electronic applications accepted. *Financial support:* In 2010–11, fellowships with partial tuition reimbursements (averaging $1,000 per year), research assistantships with partial tuition reimbursements (averaging $9,000 per year), teaching assistantships with partial tuition reimbursements (averaging $9,000 per year) were awarded. Financial award application deadline: 4/1; financial award applicants required to submit FAFSA. *Faculty research:* Fire safety, housing foundations, construction project management, quality management. *Unit head:* Joe Horlen, JD, Head, 979-458-3477, E-mail: jhorlen@tamu.edu. *Application contact:* Joe Horlen, JD, Head, 979-458-3477, E-mail: jhorlen@tamu.edu.

Texas A&M University, College of Engineering, Zachry Department of Civil Engineering, College Station, TX 77843. Offers coastal and ocean engineering (M Eng, MS, D Eng, PhD); construction engineering and management (M Eng, MS, D Eng, PhD); environmental engineering (M Eng, MS, D Eng, PhD); geotechnical engineering (M Eng, MS, D Eng, PhD); materials engineering (M Eng, MS, D Eng, PhD); structural engineering (M Eng, MS, D Eng, PhD); transportation engineering (M Eng, MS, D Eng, PhD); water resources engineering (M Eng, MS, D Eng, PhD). Part-time programs available. *Faculty:* 57. *Students:* 384 full-time (81 women), 35 part-time (7 women); includes 35 minority (3 Black or African American, non-Hispanic/Latino; 1 American Indian or Alaska Native, non-Hispanic/Latino; 14 Asian, non-Hispanic/Latino; 17 Hispanic/Latino), 263 international. Average age 29. In 2010, 136 master's, 26 doctorates awarded. *Degree requirements:* For master's, thesis (MS); for doctorate, dissertation (PhD), internship (D Eng). *Entrance requirements:* For master's and doctorate, GRE General Test. Additional exam requirements/recommendations for international students: Required—TOEFL. *Application deadline:* Applications are processed on a rolling basis. Application fee: $50 ($75 for international students). Electronic applications accepted. *Financial support:* In 2010–11, fellowships (averaging $4,500 per year), research assistantships (averaging $14,000 per year), teaching assistantships (averaging $14,400 per year) were awarded; career-related internships or fieldwork and institutionally sponsored loans also available. Financial award application deadline: 4/15; financial award applicants required to submit FAFSA. *Unit head:* Dr. Tony Cahill, Head, 979-845-3858, E-mail: tcahill@civil.tamu.edu. *Application contact:* Graduate Advisor, 979-845-7435, Fax: 979-845-6156, E-mail: info@civil.tamu.edu.

The University of Alabama, Graduate School, College of Engineering, Department of Civil, Construction and Environmental Engineering, Tuscaloosa, AL 35487-0205. Offers civil engineering (MSCE, PhD); environmental engineering (MS). Part-time programs available. *Faculty:* 20 full-time (2 women), 1 part-time/adjunct (0 women). *Students:* 40 full-time (12 women), 12 part-time (3 women); includes 9 minority (7 Black or African American, non-Hispanic/Latino; 1 Asian, non-Hispanic/Latino; 1 Two or more races, non-Hispanic/Latino), 15 international. Average age 29. 67 applicants, 51% accepted, 12 enrolled. In 2010, 21 master's, 2 doctorates awarded. Terminal master's awarded for partial completion of doctoral program. *Degree requirements:* For master's, thesis or alternative; for doctorate, one foreign language, thesis/dissertation. *Entrance requirements:* For master's and doctorate, GRE General Test, minimum GPA of 3.0 in last 60 hours of course work. Additional exam requirements/recommendations for international students: Required—TOEFL (minimum score 550 paper-based; 213 computer-based), IELTS (minimum score 6.5). *Application deadline:* For fall admission, 7/6 for domestic students, 1/15 for international students; for spring admission, 11/1 for domestic students, 6/1 for international students. Applications are processed on a rolling basis. Application fee: $50 ($60 for international students). Electronic applications accepted. *Expenses:* Tuition, state resident: full-time $7900. Tuition, nonresident: full-time $20,500. *Financial support:* In 2010–11, 40 students received support, including 32 research assistantships with full tuition reimbursements available (averaging $10,489 per year), 12 teaching assistantships with full tuition reimbursements available (averaging $10,489 per year); fellowships, scholarships/grants, tuition waivers (partial), and unspecified assistantships also available. Financial award application deadline: 3/15. *Faculty research:* Experimental structures, modeling of structures, bridge management systems, geotechnological engineering, environmental remediation. Total annual research expenditures: $1.9 million. *Unit head:* Dr. Kenneth J. Fridley, Head and Professor, 205-348-6550, Fax: 205-348-0783, E-mail: kfridley@coe.eng.ua.edu. *Application contact:* Dr. David A. Francko, Dean, 205-348-8280, Fax: 205-348-0400, E-mail: dfrancko@ua.edu.

The University of Alabama at Birmingham, School of Engineering, Program in Engineering, Birmingham, AL 35294. Offers advanced safety engineering and management (M Eng); construction engineering management (M Eng); information engineering and management (M Eng). *Students:* 4 full-time (2 women), 170 part-time (42 women); includes 62 minority (46 Black or African American, non-Hispanic/Latino; 1 American Indian or Alaska Native, non-Hispanic/Latino; 8 Asian, non-Hispanic/Latino; 6 Hispanic/Latino; 1 Two or more races, non-Hispanic/Latino), 4 international. Average age 36. 99 applicants, 97% accepted, 81 enrolled. In 2010, 78 master's awarded. *Expenses:* Tuition, state resident: full-time $5482. Tuition, nonresident: full-time $12,430. Tuition and fees vary according to program. *Unit head:* Dr. Melinda Lalor, Dean, 205-934-8410. *Application contact:* Julie Bryant, Director of Graduate Admissions, 205-934-8227, Fax: 205-934-8413, E-mail: jbryant@uab.edu.

University of Alberta, Faculty of Graduate Studies and Research, Department of Civil and Environmental Engineering, Edmonton, AB T6G 2E1, Canada. Offers construction engineering and management (M Eng, M Sc, PhD); environmental engineering (M Eng, M Sc, PhD); environmental science (M Sc, PhD); geoenvironmental engineering (M Eng, M Sc, PhD); geotechnical engineering (M Eng, M Sc, PhD); mining engineering (M Eng, M Sc, PhD); petroleum engineering (M Eng, M Sc, PhD); structural engineering (M Eng, M Sc, PhD); water resources (M Eng, M Sc, PhD). Part-time programs available. Postbaccalaureate distance learning degree programs offered (minimal on-campus study). *Degree requirements:* For master's, thesis (for some programs); for doctorate, thesis/dissertation. *Entrance requirements:* For master's, minimum GPA of 3.0 in last 2 years of undergraduate studies; for doctorate, minimum GPA of 3.0. Additional exam requirements/recommendations for international students: Required—TOEFL (minimum score 550 paper-based; 213 computer-based). Electronic applications accepted. *Faculty research:* Mining.

University of Central Florida, College of Engineering and Computer Science, Department of Civil, Environmental, and Construction Engineering, Program in Civil Engineering, Orlando, FL 32816. Offers civil engineering (MS, MSCE, PhD); construction engineering (Certificate); structural engineering (Certificate); transportation engineering (Certificate). Part-time and evening/weekend programs available. *Students:* 62 full-time (7 women), 77 part-time (15 women); includes 30 minority (4 Black or African American, non-Hispanic/Latino; 7 Asian, non-Hispanic/Latino; 17 Hispanic/Latino; 2 Two or more races, non-Hispanic/Latino), 35 international. Average age 30. 125 applicants, 73% accepted, 46 enrolled. In 2010, 26 master's, 8 doctorates awarded. *Degree requirements:* For master's, thesis or alternative; for doctorate, thesis/dissertation, departmental qualifying exam, candidacy exam. *Entrance requirements:* For master's, GRE General Test, minimum GPA of 3.0 in last 60 hours; for doctorate, GRE General Test, minimum GPA of 3.5 in last 60 hours. Additional exam requirements/recommendations for international students: Required—TOEFL. *Application deadline:* For fall admission, 7/15 priority date for domestic students; for spring admission, 12/15 priority date for domestic students. Application fee: $30. Electronic applications accepted. *Expenses:* Tuition, state resident: part-time $256.56 per credit hour. Tuition, nonresident: part-time $1011.52 per credit hour. Part-time tuition and fees vary according to program. *Financial support:* In 2010–11, 29 students received support, including 1 fellowship with partial tuition reimbursement available (averaging $10,000 per year), 22 research assistantships with partial tuition reimbursements available (averaging $11,000 per year), 18 teaching assistantships with partial tuition reimbursements available (averaging $7,900 per year); career-related internships or fieldwork, Federal Work-Study, institutionally sponsored loans, tuition waivers (partial), and unspecified assistantships also available. Financial award application deadline: 3/1; financial award applicants required to submit FAFSA.

University of Colorado Boulder, Graduate School, College of Engineering and Applied Science, Department of Civil, Environmental, and Architectural Engineering, Boulder, CO 80309. Offers building systems (MS, PhD); construction engineering management (MS, PhD); environmental engineering (MS, PhD); geotechnical engineering and geomechanics (MS, PhD); hydrology, water resources and environmental fluid mechanics (MS, PhD); structural engineering and structural mechanics (MS, PhD). *Faculty:* 38 full-time (6 women). *Students:* 255 full-time (86 women), 40 part-time (11 women); includes 40 minority (1 Black or African American, non-Hispanic/Latino; 2 American Indian or Alaska Native, non-Hispanic/Latino; 15 Asian, non-Hispanic/Latino; 20 Hispanic/Latino; 2 Two or more races, non-Hispanic/Latino), 61 international. Average age 28. 420 applicants, 95 enrolled. In 2010, 56 master's, 18 doctorates awarded. *Degree requirements:* For master's, comprehensive exam, thesis or alternative; for doctorate, thesis/dissertation. *Entrance requirements:* For master's, GRE General Test, minimum undergraduate GPA of 3.0. *Application deadline:* For fall admission, 3/1 for domestic students, 12/1 for international students; for spring admission, 10/31 for domestic students, 10/1 for international students. Application fee: $50 ($60 for international students). *Financial support:* In 2010–11, 45 fellowships (averaging $7,876 per year), 68 research assistantships (averaging $15,204 per year) were awarded. Financial award application deadline: 1/15. *Faculty research:* Building systems engineering, construction engineering and management, environmental engineering, geoenvironmental engineering, geotechnical engineering, materials and mechanics, structural engineering, water resources engineering, life-cycle engineering. Total annual research expenditures: $8 million.

University of Florida, Graduate School, College of Design, Construction and Planning, M. E. Rinker, Sr. School of Building Construction, Gainesville, FL 32611. Offers MBC, MICM, MSBC, PhD. Part-time programs available. *Faculty:* 15 full-time (2 women). *Students:* 175 full-time (57 women), 45 part-time (16 women); includes 6 Black or African American, non-Hispanic/Latino; 9 Asian, non-Hispanic/Latino; 16 Hispanic/Latino, 60 international. Average age 26. 90 applicants, 70% accepted, 30 enrolled. In 2010, 64 master's, 6 doctorates awarded. *Degree requirements:* For master's, thesis; for doctorate, comprehensive exam, thesis/dissertation. *Entrance requirements:* For master's, GRE General Test, minimum GPA of 3.0; for doctorate, GRE General Test combined verbal and quantitative score of 1200, minimum GPA of 3.0. Additional exam requirements/recommendations for international students: Required—TOEFL (minimum score 550 paper-based; 213 computer-based; 80 iBT), IELTS (minimum score 6). *Application deadline:* Applications are processed on a rolling basis. Application fee: $30. Electronic applications accepted. *Expenses:* Tuition, state resident: full-time $10,915.92. Tuition, nonresident: full-time $28,309. *Financial support:* In 2010–11, 13 students received support, including 7 research assistantships with full tuition reimbursements available (averaging $8,836 per year), 6 teaching assistantships with full tuition reimbursements available (averaging $9,363 per year); career-related internships or fieldwork and unspecified assistantships also available. Financial award applicants required to submit FAFSA. *Faculty research:* Safety, affordable housing, construction management, environmental issues, sustainable construction. *Unit head:* Abdol R. Chini, PhD, Director, 352-273-1165, Fax: 352-392-9606, E-mail: chini@ufl.edu. *Application contact:* Ian Flood, PhD, Coordinator of PhD program, 352-273-1159, Fax: 352-392-7266, E-mail: flood@ufl.edu.

University of Michigan, Horace H. Rackham School of Graduate Studies, College of Engineering, Department of Civil and Environmental Engineering, Ann Arbor, MI 48109. Offers civil engineering (MSE, PhD, CE); construction engineering and management (M Eng, MSE); environmental engineering (MSE, PhD); structural engineering (M Eng); MBA/MSE. Part-time programs available. *Students:* 121 full-time (45 women), 5 part-time (2 women). 461 applicants, 30% accepted, 54 enrolled. In 2010, 36 master's, 13 doctorates awarded. *Degree requirements:* For master's, thesis optional; for doctorate, comprehensive exam, thesis/dissertation, oral defense of dissertation, preliminary and written exams. *Entrance requirements:* For master's and doctorate, GRE General Test. Additional exam requirements/recommendations for international students: Required—TOEFL (minimum score 560 paper-based; 220 computer-based). *Application deadline:* Applications are processed on a rolling basis. Application fee: $65 ($75 for international students). Electronic applications accepted. *Expenses:* Tuition, state resident: full-time $17,784; part-time $1116 per credit hour. Tuition, nonresident: full-time $35,944; part-time $2125 per credit hour. International tuition: $35,994 full-time. Required fees: $95 per semester. Tuition and fees vary according to course load, degree level and program. *Financial support:* Fellowships, research assistantships, teaching assistantships, institutionally sponsored loans and tuition waivers (partial) available. Financial award application deadline: 1/19. *Faculty research:* Construction engineering and management; geotechnical engineering; earthquake-resistant design of structures; environmental chemistry and microbiology; cost engineering; environmental and water resources engineering. *Unit head:* Nancy Love, Chair, 734-764-8405, Fax: 734-764-4292, E-mail: nglove@umich.edu. *Application contact:* Kimberly Smith, Student Advisor, 734-764-8405, Fax: 734-647-2127, E-mail: kansmith@umich.edu.

University of New Brunswick Fredericton, School of Graduate Studies, Faculty of Engineering, Department of Civil Engineering, Fredericton, NB E3B 5A3, Canada. Offers construction engineering and management (M Eng, M Sc E, PhD); environmental engineering (M Eng, M Sc E, PhD); environmental studies (M Eng); geotechnical engineering (M Eng, M Sc E, PhD); groundwater/hydrology (M Eng, M Sc E, PhD); materials (M Eng, M Sc E, PhD); pavements (M Eng, M Sc E, PhD); structures (M Eng, M Sc E, PhD); transportation (M Eng, M Sc E, PhD). Part-time programs available. *Faculty:* 13 full-time (1 woman), 7 part-time/adjunct (1 woman). *Students:* 34 full-time (8 women), 16 part-time (2 women). In 2010, 16 master's, 6 doctorates awarded. *Degree requirements:* For master's, thesis, proposal; for doctorate, comprehensive exam, thesis/dissertation, qualifying exam; proposal; 27 credit hours of courses. *Entrance requirements:* For master's, minimum GPA of 3.0; B Sc E in civil engineering or related engineering degree; for doctorate, minimum GPA of 3.0; graduate degree in engineering or applied science. Additional exam requirements/recommendations for international students: Required—TWE (minimum score 4), TOEFL (minimum score 580 paper-based; 237 computer-based) or IELTS (minimum score 7.5). *Application deadline:* For fall admission, 5/1 priority date for domestic students; for winter admission, 11/1 priority date for domestic students. Applications are processed on a rolling basis. Application fee: $50 Canadian dollars. *Expenses:* Tuition, area resident: Full-time $3708; part-time $927 per term. International tuition: $6300 full-time. Required fees: $50 per term. *Financial support:* In 2010–11, 52 research assistantships (averaging $7,000 per year), 46 teaching assistantships (averaging $2,000 per year) were awarded; career-related internships or fieldwork and scholarships/grants also available. *Faculty research:* Construction engineering and management; materials and infrastructure renewal; highway and pavement research; structures and solid mechanics; geotechnical, soil; structure interaction; transportation and planning; environment, solid waste management. *Unit head:* Dr. Eric Hildebrand, Director of Graduate Studies, 506-453-5113, Fax: 506-453-3568, E-mail: edh@unb.ca. *Application contact:* Joyce Moore, Graduate Secretary, 506-452-6127, Fax: 506-453-3568, E-mail: civil-grad@unb.ca.

University of Southern Mississippi, Graduate School, College of Science and Technology, School of Construction, Hattiesburg, MS 39406-0001. Offers logistics management and technology (MS). Part-time programs available. *Faculty:* 6 full-time (0 women). *Students:* 14 full-time (3 women), 5 part-time (2 women); includes 2 Black or African American, non-Hispanic/Latino, 2 international. Average age 31. 18 applicants, 67% accepted, 7 enrolled. In 2010, 8 master's awarded. *Degree requirements:* For master's, comprehensive exam, thesis optional. *Entrance requirements:* For master's, GMAT or GRE General Test, minimum GPA of 2.75 in last 60 hours. Additional exam requirements/recommendations for international students: Required—TOEFL, IELTS. *Application deadline:* For fall admission, 3/1 priority date for domestic students, 3/1 for international students. Applications are processed on a rolling basis. Application fee: $50. *Financial support:* In 2010–11, research assistantships with full tuition reimburse-

Construction Engineering

University of Southern Mississippi (continued)
ments (averaging $7,200 per year), 7 teaching assistantships with full tuition reimbursements (averaging $7,200 per year) were awarded; career-related internships or fieldwork, Federal Work-Study, scholarships/grants, health care benefits, and unspecified assistantships also available. Financial award application deadline: 3/15; financial award applicants required to submit FAFSA. *Faculty research:* Robotics; CAD/CAM; simulation; computer-integrated manufacturing processes; construction scheduling, estimating, and computer systems. *Unit head:* Dr. Desmond Fletcher, Director, 601-266-5185. *Application contact:* Dr. Tulio Sulbaran, Director, Graduate Studies, 601-266-5185.

University of Washington, Graduate School, College of Engineering, Department of Civil and Environmental Engineering, Seattle, WA 98195-2700. Offers construction engineering (MSCE); environmental engineering (MS, MSCE, MSE, PhD); hydrology, water resources, and environmental fluid mechanics (MS, MSCE, MSE, PhD); structural and geotechnical engineering and mechanics (MS, MSCE, MSE, PhD); transportation and construction engineering (MS, MSE, PhD); transportation engineering (MSCE). Part-time programs available. Postbaccalaureate distance learning degree programs offered (no on-campus study). *Faculty:* 44 full-time (10 women), 12 part-time/adjunct (1 woman). *Students:* 197 full-time (65 women), 65 part-time (15 women); includes 5 Black or African American, non-Hispanic/Latino; 28 Asian, non-Hispanic/Latino; 5 Hispanic/Latino, 55 international. 522 applicants, 51% accepted, 101 enrolled. In 2010, 68 master's, 5 doctorates awarded. Terminal master's awarded for partial completion of doctoral program. *Degree requirements:* For master's, thesis (for some programs); for doctorate, comprehensive exam, thesis/dissertation, General, qualifying, and final exams. Completion of doctoral degree within 10 years. *Entrance requirements:* For master's, GRE General Test, Minimum GPA of 3.0, statement of purpose, letters of recommendation, transcripts; for doctorate, GRE General Test, minimum GPA of 3.5, statement of purpose, letters of recommendation, transcripts. Additional exam requirements/recommendations for international students: Required—TOEFL (minimum score 580 paper-based; 237 computer-based; 92 iBT); Recommended—IELTS (minimum score 7). *Application deadline:* For fall admission, 1/10 priority date for domestic and international students. Application fee: $75. Electronic applications accepted. *Financial support:* In 2010–11, 2 students received support, including 25 fellowships with full and partial tuition reimbursements available (averaging $16,173 per year), 75 research assistantships with full tuition reimbursements available (averaging $16,515 per year), 11 teaching assistantships with full tuition reimbursements available (averaging $16,263 per year); scholarships/grants also available. Financial award application deadline: 1/10; financial award applicants required to submit FAFSA. *Faculty research:* Environmental/water resources, hydrology; construction/transportation; structures/ geotechnical. Total annual research expenditures: $14.4 million. *Unit head:* Dr. Gregory R. Miller, Professor and Chair, 206-543-0350, Fax: 206-543-1543, E-mail: gmiller@uw.edu. *Application contact:* Lorna Latal, Graduate Adviser, 206-543-2574, Fax: 206-543-1543, E-mail: llatal@u.washington.edu.

Virginia Polytechnic Institute and State University, Graduate School, College of Architecture and Urban Studies, Department of Building Construction, Blacksburg, VA 24061. Offers MS. *Faculty:* 8 full-time (2 women). *Students:* 12 full-time (0 women), 2 part-time (0 women); includes 1 Black or African American, non-Hispanic/Latino; 1 Hispanic/Latino. Average age 27. 24 applicants, 54% accepted, 3 enrolled. In 2010, 15 master's awarded. *Degree requirements:* For master's, comprehensive exam (for some programs), thesis (for some programs). *Entrance requirements:* For master's, GRE. Additional exam requirements/recommendations for international students: Required—TOEFL (minimum score 550 paper-based; 213 computer-based). *Application deadline:* For fall admission, 7/1 for domestic and international students; for spring admission, 12/1 for domestic and international students. Applications are processed on a rolling basis. Application fee: $65. Electronic applications accepted. *Expenses:* Tuition, area resident: Full-time $9399; part-time $488 per credit hour. Tuition, state resident: full-time $9399; part-time $488 per credit hour. Tuition, nonresident: full-time $17,854; part-time $957.75 per credit hour. International tuition: $17,854 full-time. Required fees: $1534. Full-time tuition and fees vary according to program. *Financial support:* In 2010–11, 11 fellowships with full tuition reimbursements (averaging $164 per year), 1 research assistantship with full tuition reimbursement (averaging $21,374 per year), 1 teaching assistantship with full tuition reimbursement (averaging $16,796 per year) were awarded; career-related internships or fieldwork, Federal Work-Study, scholarships/grants, health care benefits, and unspecified assistantships also available. Financial award application deadline: 1/15. Total annual research expenditures: $1.1 million. *Unit head:* Dr. Yvan J. Beliveau, UNIT HEAD, 540-818-4602, Fax: 540-231-7219, E-mail: yvan@vt.edu. *Application contact:* Walid Thabet, Contact, 703-818-4604, Fax: 540-231-7219, E-mail: thabet@vt.edu.

Western Michigan University, Graduate College, College of Engineering and Applied Sciences, Department of Civil and Construction Engineering, Kalamazoo, MI 49008. Offers civil engineering (MS), including construction engineering and management, structural engineering, transportation engineering. *Entrance requirements:* For master's, minimum GPA of 3.0.

Environmental Engineering

Air Force Institute of Technology, Graduate School of Engineering and Management, Department of Systems and Engineering Management, Dayton, OH 45433-7765. Offers cost analysis (MS); environmental and engineering management (MS); environmental engineering science (MS); information resource/systems management (MS). *Accreditation:* ABET. Part-time programs available. *Degree requirements:* For master's, thesis. *Entrance requirements:* For master's, GRE, GMAT, minimum GPA of 3.0.

Arizona State University, Ira A. Fulton School of Engineering, Del E. Webb School of Construction, Tempe, AZ 85287-5306. Offers civil, environmental and sustainable engineering (MS, MSE, PhD); construction (MS, MSE, PhD); construction engineering (MSE). Part-time and evening/weekend programs available. Postbaccalaureate distance learning degree programs offered (minimal on-campus study). *Faculty:* 40 full-time (4 women), 6 part-time/adjunct (1 woman). *Students:* 149 full-time (51 women), 85 part-time (17 women); includes 32 minority (6 Black or African American, non-Hispanic/Latino; 2 American Indian or Alaska Native, non-Hispanic/Latino; 13 Asian, non-Hispanic/Latino; 10 Hispanic/Latino; 1 Native Hawaiian or other Pacific Islander, non-Hispanic/Latino), 69 international. Average age 29. 379 applicants, 53% accepted, 77 enrolled. In 2010, 44 master's, 10 doctorates awarded. Terminal master's awarded for partial completion of doctoral program. *Degree requirements:* For master's, thesis optional, comprehensive exams (MSE); interactive Program of Study (iPOS) submitted before completing 50 percent of required credit hours; for doctorate, comprehensive exam, thesis/dissertation, interactive Program of Study (iPOS) submitted before completing 50 percent of required credit hours. *Entrance requirements:* For master's, GRE, minimum GPA of 3.0 or equivalent in last 2 years of work leading to bachelor's degree; for doctorate, GRE, minimum GPA of 3.0 in last 2 years of work leading to bachelor's degree, 3.2 in all graduate-level coursework with master's degree; 3 letters of recommendation; resume/curriculum vitae; letter of intent; thesis (if applicable); statement of research interests. Additional exam requirements/recommendations for international students: Required—TOEFL, IELTS, or Pearson Test of English. *Application deadline:* For fall admission, 1/1 for domestic and international students; for spring admission, 7/1 for domestic and international students. Application fee: $70 ($90 for international students). Electronic applications accepted. *Expenses:* Contact institution. *Financial support:* In 2010–11, 67 research assistantships with full and partial tuition reimbursements (averaging $16,393 per year), 17 teaching assistantships with full and partial tuition reimbursements (averaging $13,812 per year) were awarded; fellowships with full and partial tuition reimbursements, career-related internships or fieldwork, institutionally sponsored loans, scholarships/grants, traineeships, and tuition waivers (full and partial) also available. Financial award application deadline: 3/1; financial award applicants required to submit FAFSA. *Faculty research:* Water purification, transportation (safety and materials), construction management, environmental biotechnology, environmental nanotechnology, earth systems engineering and management, SMART innovations, project performance metrics, and underground infrastructure. Total annual research expenditures: $8.5 million. *Unit head:* Dr. G. Edward Gibson, Director, 480-965-7972, E-mail: edd.gibson@asu.edu. *Application contact:* Graduate Admissions, 480-965-6113.

Auburn University, Graduate School, Ginn College of Engineering, Department of Civil Engineering, Auburn University, AL 36849. Offers construction engineering and management (MCE, MS, PhD); environmental engineering (MCE, MS, PhD); geotechnical/materials engineering (MCE, MS, PhD); hydraulics/hydrology (MCE, MS, PhD); structural engineering (MCE, MS, PhD); transportation engineering (MCE, MS, PhD). Part-time programs available. *Faculty:* 21 full-time (1 woman), 3 part-time/adjunct (1 woman). *Students:* 46 full-time (15 women), 39 part-time (5 women); includes 3 Black or African American, non-Hispanic/Latino; 1 Asian, non-Hispanic/Latino, 29 international. Average age 26. 136 applicants, 43% accepted, 26 enrolled. In 2010, 19 master's, 4 doctorates awarded. *Degree requirements:* For master's, project (MCE), thesis (MS); for doctorate, comprehensive exam, thesis/dissertation. *Entrance requirements:* For master's and doctorate, GRE General Test. *Application deadline:* For fall admission, 7/7 for domestic students; for spring admission, 11/24 for domestic students. Applications are processed on a rolling basis. Application fee: $50 ($60 for international students). Electronic applications accepted. *Expenses:* Tuition, state resident: full-time $7002. Tuition, nonresident: full-time $21,898. International tuition: $22,116 full-time. Required fees: $892. Tuition and fees vary according to course load and program. *Financial support:* Fellowships, research assistantships, teaching assistantships, Federal Work-Study available. Support available to part-time students. Financial award application deadline: 3/15; financial award applicants required to submit FAFSA. *Unit head:* Dr. J. Michael Stallings, Head, 334-844-4320. *Application contact:* Dr. George Flowers, Dean of the Graduate School, 334-844-2125.

California Institute of Technology, Division of Engineering and Applied Science, Option in Environmental Science and Engineering, Pasadena, CA 91125-0001. Offers MS, PhD. *Faculty:* 5 full-time (1 woman). *Students:* 27 full-time (12 women). 77 applicants, 16% accepted, 4 enrolled. In 2010, 3 master's, 4 doctorates awarded. *Degree requirements:* For doctorate, thesis/dissertation. *Application deadline:* For fall admission, 1/1 for domestic students. Application fee: $0. Electronic applications accepted. *Financial support:* In 2010–11, 8 fellowships, 11 research assistantships, 3 teaching assistantships were awarded. *Faculty research:* Chemistry of natural waters, physics and chemistry of particulates, fluid mechanics of the natural environment, pollutant formation and control, environmental modeling systems. *Unit head:* Prof. Tapio Schneider, Executive Officer, 626-395-6143, E-mail: tapio@gps.caltech.edu. *Application contact:* Natalie Gilmore, Assistant Dean of Graduate Studies, 626-395-3812, Fax: 626-577-9246, E-mail: ngilmore@caltech.edu.

California Polytechnic State University, San Luis Obispo, College of Engineering, Department of Civil and Environmental Engineering, San Luis Obispo, CA 93407. Offers MS. Part-time programs available. *Faculty:* 3 full-time (0 women). *Students:* 33 full-time (7 women), 11 part-time (1 woman); includes 14 minority (1 Black or African American, non-Hispanic/Latino; 7 Asian, non-Hispanic/Latino; 6 Hispanic/Latino). Average age 23. 84 applicants, 39% accepted, 18 enrolled. In 2010, 29 master's awarded. *Degree requirements:* For master's, comprehensive exam (for some programs), thesis (for some programs). *Entrance requirements:* For master's, GRE General Test, minimum GPA of 3.0 in last 90 quarter units, 3 letters of recommendation. Additional exam requirements/recommendations for international students: Required—TOEFL (minimum score 550 paper-based; 213 computer-based). *Application deadline:* For fall admission, 3/1 for domestic students, 11/30 for international students; for winter admission, 10/1 for domestic students, 6/30 for international students; for spring admission, 1/1 for domestic students. Applications are processed on a rolling basis. Application fee: $55. Electronic applications accepted. *Expenses:* Tuition, state resident: full-time $5386; part-time $3124 per year. Tuition, nonresident: full-time $11,160; part-time $248 per unit. Required fees: $2250; $614 per term. One-time fee: $2250 full-time; $1842 part-time. *Financial support:* Fellowships, research assistantships, teaching assistantships, career-related internships or fieldwork, Federal Work-Study, and scholarships/grants available. Support available to part-time students. Financial award application deadline: 3/2; financial award applicants required to submit FAFSA. *Faculty research:* Soils, structures, transportation, traffic, environmental protection. *Unit head:* Dr. Robb Moss, Graduate Coordinator, 805-756-6427, Fax: 805-756-6330, E-mail: rmoss@calpoly.edu. *Application contact:* Dr. Robb Moss, Graduate Coordinator, 805-756-6427, Fax: 805-756-6330, E-mail: rmoss@calpoly.edu.

Carleton University, Faculty of Graduate Studies, Faculty of Engineering and Design, Department of Civil and Environmental Engineering, Ottawa, ON K1S 5B6, Canada. Offers M Eng, MA Sc, PhD. *Degree requirements:* For master's, thesis optional; for doctorate, thesis/dissertation. *Entrance requirements:* For master's, honors degree; for doctorate, MA Sc or M Eng. Additional exam requirements/recommendations for international students: Required—TOEFL. *Faculty research:* Pollution and wastewater management, fire safety engineering, earthquake engineering, structural design, bridge engineering.

Carnegie Mellon University, Carnegie Institute of Technology, Department of Civil and Environmental Engineering, Pittsburgh, PA 15213. Offers advanced infrastructure systems (MS, PhD); civil and environmental engineering (MS, PhD); civil and environmental engineering/engineering and public policy (PhD); civil engineering (MS, PhD); computational mechanics (MS, PhD); computational science and engineering (MS, PhD); environmental engineering (MS, PhD); environmental management and science (MS, PhD). Part-time programs available. *Faculty:* 20 full-time (3 women), 15 part-time/adjunct (5 women). *Students:* 144 full-time (67 women), 8 part-time (2 women); includes 4 Black or African American, non-Hispanic/Latino; 1 American Indian or Alaska Native, non-Hispanic/Latino; 9 Asian, non-Hispanic/Latino, 99 international. Average age 26. 388 applicants, 66% accepted, 80 enrolled. In 2010, 62 master's, 8 doctorates awarded. Terminal master's awarded for partial completion of doctoral program. *Degree requirements:* For master's, thesis optional; for doctorate, comprehensive exam, thesis/dissertation, qualifying exam, public defense of dissertation. *Entrance requirements:* For master's and doctorate, GRE General Test. Additional exam requirements/recommendations for international students: Required—TOEFL (minimum score 84 iBT). *Application deadline:* For fall admission, 1/15 priority date for domestic and international students; for spring admission, 9/30 priority date for domestic and international students. Application fee: $65. Electronic applications accepted. *Financial support:* In 2010–11, 134 students received support, including 27 fellowships with full and partial tuition reimbursements available (averaging $21,708 per year), 42 research assistantships with full and partial tuition reimbursements available (averaging $24,474 per year); tuition waivers (partial) and unspecified assistantships also available. Financial award application deadline: 1/15. *Faculty research:* Advanced infrastructure systems; environmental engineering science and management; mechanics, materials, and computing; green design; global sustainable construction. Total annual research expenditures: $4.7 million.

Unit head: Dr. James H. Garrett, Head, 412-268-2941, Fax: 412-268-7813, E-mail: garrett@cmu.edu. *Application contact:* Maxine A. Leffard, Director of the Graduate Program, 412-268-5673, Fax: 412-268-7813, E-mail: ce-admissions@andrew.cmu.edu.

Carnegie Mellon University, Tepper School of Business, Pittsburgh, PA 15213-3891. Offers accounting (PhD); algorithms, combinatorics, and optimization (MS, PhD); business management and software engineering (MBMSE); civil engineering and industrial management (MS); computational finance (MSCF); economics (MS, PhD); electronic commerce (MS); environmental engineering and management (MEEM); finance (PhD); financial economics (PhD); industrial administration (MBA), including administration and public management; information systems (PhD); management of manufacturing and automation (PhD); marketing (PhD); mathematical finance (PhD); operations research (PhD); organizational behavior and theory (PhD); political economy (PhD); production and operations management (PhD); public policy and management (MS, MSED); software engineering and business management (MS); JD/MS; JD/MSIA; M Div/MS; MOM/MSIA; MSCF/MSIA. JD/MSIA offered jointly with University of Pittsburgh. Part-time programs available. Terminal master's awarded for partial completion of doctoral program. *Degree requirements:* For doctorate, thesis/dissertation. *Entrance requirements:* For master's, GMAT. Additional exam requirements/recommendations for international students: Required—TOEFL. *Expenses:* Contact institution.

The Catholic University of America, School of Engineering, Department of Civil Engineering, Washington, DC 20064. Offers environmental engineering (PhD). Part-time programs available. *Faculty:* 6 full-time (0 women), 5 part-time/adjunct (0 women). *Students:* 8 full-time (3 women), 22 part-time (5 women); includes 6 Black or African American, non-Hispanic/Latino; 2 Asian, non-Hispanic/Latino; 2 Hispanic/Latino, 7 international. Average age 34. 46 applicants, 46% accepted, 8 enrolled. In 2010, 7 master's, 2 doctorates awarded. *Degree requirements:* For master's, thesis optional; for doctorate, comprehensive exam, thesis/dissertation. *Entrance requirements:* For master's and doctorate, statement of purpose, official copies of academic transcripts, three letters of recommendation. Additional exam requirements/recommendations for international students: Required—TOEFL (minimum score 580 paper-based; 237 computer-based). *Application deadline:* For fall admission, 8/1 priority date for domestic students, 7/15 for international students; for spring admission, 12/1 priority date for domestic students, 10/15 for international students. Applications are processed on a rolling basis. Application fee: $55. Electronic applications accepted. *Expenses:* Contact institution. *Financial support:* Fellowships, research assistantships, teaching assistantships, Federal Work-Study, scholarships/grants, tuition waivers (full and partial), and unspecified assistantships available. Financial award application deadline: 2/1; financial award applicants required to submit FAFSA. *Faculty research:* Geotechnical engineering, solid mechanics, construction engineering and management, environmental engineering, structural engineering. Total annual research expenditures: $438,834. *Unit head:* Dr. Lu Sun, Chair, 202-319-6671, Fax: 202-319-6677, E-mail: sunl@cua.edu. *Application contact:* Andrew Woodall, Director of Graduate Admissions, 202-319-5057, Fax: 202-319-6533, E-mail: cua-admissions@cua.edu.

Clarkson University, Graduate School, Institute for a Sustainable Environment, Program in Environmental Science and Engineering, Potsdam, NY 13699. Offers MS, PhD. Part-time programs available. *Students:* 30 full-time (16 women), 1 (woman) part-time, 16 international. Average age 27. 7 applicants, 100% accepted, 7 enrolled. In 2010, 5 master's, 2 doctorates awarded. Terminal master's awarded for partial completion of doctoral program. *Degree requirements:* For master's, thesis; for doctorate, comprehensive exam, thesis/dissertation, proposal/defense. *Entrance requirements:* For master's and doctorate, GRE, transcripts of all college coursework, resume, personal statement, three letters of recommendation. Additional exam requirements/recommendations for international students: Required—TOEFL (minimum score 550 paper-based; 213 computer-based; 80 iBT), IELTS (minimum score 6.5). *Application deadline:* For fall admission, 1/30 priority date for domestic and international students; for spring admission, 9/1 priority date for domestic and international students. Applications are processed on a rolling basis. Application fee: $25 ($35 for international students). Electronic applications accepted. *Expenses:* Tuition: Part-time $1136 per credit hour. *Financial support:* In 2010–11, 29 students received support, including fellowships with full tuition reimbursements available (averaging $21,580 per year), 17 research assistantships with full tuition reimbursements available (averaging $21,580 per year), 10 teaching assistantships with full tuition reimbursements available (averaging $21,580 per year); scholarships/grants, tuition waivers (partial), and unspecified assistantships also available. *Faculty research:* Biological, chemical, physical and social systems; renewable energy; environmental health. *Unit head:* Dr. Philip Hopke, Director, 315-268-3856, Fax: 315-268-4291, E-mail: hopkepk@clarkson.edu. *Application contact:* Suzann Cheney, Administrative Secretary, 315-268-3856, Fax: 315-268-4291, E-mail: scheney@clarkson.edu.

Clemson University, Graduate School, College of Engineering and Science, Department of Environmental Engineering and Earth Sciences, Programs in Environmental Engineering and Science, Clemson, SC 29634. Offers environmental engineering and science (M Engr, MS, PhD); environmental health physics (MS). *Accreditation:* ABET. *Students:* 62 full-time (27 women), 17 part-time (6 women); includes 3 Black or African American, non-Hispanic/Latino; 1 American Indian or Alaska Native, non-Hispanic/Latino; 2 Asian, non-Hispanic/Latino; 1 Hispanic/Latino; 1 Two or more races, non-Hispanic/Latino, 28 international. Average age 29. 138 applicants, 53% accepted, 32 enrolled. In 2010, 11 master's, 6 doctorates awarded. *Degree requirements:* For master's, thesis; for doctorate, thesis/dissertation. *Entrance requirements:* For master's and doctorate, GRE General Test, minimum GPA of 3.0. Additional exam requirements/recommendations for international students: Required—TOEFL. *Application deadline:* For fall admission, 3/1 priority date for domestic and international students; for spring admission, 9/15 for international students. Applications are processed on a rolling basis. Application fee: $70 ($80 for international students). Electronic applications accepted. *Expenses:* Tuition, state resident: full-time $6492; part-time $400 per credit hour. Tuition, nonresident: full-time $13,634; part-time $800 per credit hour. Required fees: $262 per semester. Part-time tuition and fees vary according to course load and program. *Financial support:* In 2010–11, 43 students received support, including 8 fellowships with full and partial tuition reimbursements available (averaging $7,885 per year), 24 research assistantships with partial tuition reimbursements available (averaging $16,407 per year), 16 teaching assistantships with partial tuition reimbursements available (averaging $13,995 per year); career-related internships or fieldwork, institutionally sponsored loans, scholarships/grants, health care benefits, and unspecified assistantships also available. Support available to part-time students. Financial award applicants required to submit FAFSA. *Faculty research:* Water and air pollution control, hazardous waste and environmental management, environmental chemistry and biology, containment transport modeling, risk assessment. *Unit head:* Dr. Tanju Karanfil, Chair, 864-656-1005, E-mail: tkaranf@clemson.edu. *Application contact:* Dr. Cindy Lee, Graduate Program Coordinator, 864-656-1006, Fax: 864-656-5973, E-mail: lc@clemson.edu.

Cleveland State University, College of Graduate Studies, Fenn College of Engineering, Department of Civil and Environmental Engineering, Cleveland, OH 44115. Offers accelerated program civil engineering (MS); accelerated program environmental engineering (MS); civil engineering (MS, D Eng); engineering mechanics (MS); environmental engineering (MS). Part-time and evening/weekend programs available. *Faculty:* 9 full-time (1 woman), 1 part-time/adjunct (0 women). *Students:* 8 full-time (0 women), 43 part-time (9 women); includes 2 Black or African American, non-Hispanic/Latino; 2 Asian, non-Hispanic/Latino; 1 Hispanic/Latino, 16 international. Average age 26. 67 applicants, 61% accepted, 14 enrolled. In 2010, 13 master's, 2 doctorates awarded. *Degree requirements:* For master's, project or thesis; for doctorate, comprehensive exam, thesis/dissertation, candidacy and qualifying exams. *Entrance requirements:* For master's, GRE General Test, GRE Subject Test, minimum GPA of 2.75; for doctorate, GRE General Test, GRE Subject Test, minimum GPA of 3.25. Additional exam requirements/recommendations for international students: Required—TOEFL (minimum score 525 paper-based; 197 computer-based). *Application deadline:* For fall admission, 7/15 priority date for domestic students. Applications are processed on a rolling basis. Application fee: $30. *Expenses:* Tuition, state resident: full-time $8447; part-time $469 per credit hour. Tuition, nonresident: full-time $16,020; part-time $890 per credit hour. Required fees: $50. *Financial support:* In 2010–11, 9 research assistantships with full and partial tuition reimbursements (averaging $3,920 per year) were awarded; teaching assistantships with tuition reimbursements, career-related internships or fieldwork, scholarships/grants, and unspecified assistantships also available. Financial award application deadline: 9/1. *Faculty research:* Solid-waste disposal, constitutive modeling, transportation, safety engineering. Total annual research expenditures: $800,000. *Unit head:* Dr. Stephen F. Duffy, Chairperson, 216-687-3874, Fax: 216-687-9280, E-mail: p.bosela@csuohio.edu. *Application contact:* Dr. Stephen F. Duffy, Chairperson, 216-687-3874, Fax: 216-687-9280, E-mail: p.bosela@csuohio.edu.

Colorado School of Mines, Graduate School, Division of Environmental Science and Engineering, Golden, CO 80401. Offers MS, PhD. Part-time programs available. *Faculty:* 22 full-time (5 women), 8 part-time/adjunct (3 women). *Students:* 90 full-time (45 women), 22 part-time (12 women); includes 3 Black or African American, non-Hispanic/Latino; 3 Asian, non-Hispanic/Latino; 8 Hispanic/Latino; 1 Two or more races, non-Hispanic/Latino, 9 international. Average age 28. 154 applicants, 54% accepted, 36 enrolled. In 2010, 37 master's, 4 doctorates awarded. *Degree requirements:* For master's, thesis (for some programs); for doctorate, comprehensive exam, thesis/dissertation. *Entrance requirements:* For master's and doctorate, GRE General Test. Additional exam requirements/recommendations for international students: Required—TOEFL (minimum score 550 paper-based; 213 computer-based; 80 iBT). *Application deadline:* For fall admission, 1/15 priority date for domestic and international students; for spring admission, 10/15 priority date for domestic and international students. Application fee: $50 ($70 for international students). Electronic applications accepted. *Expenses:* Tuition, state resident: full-time $11,550; part-time $641 per credit. Tuition, nonresident: full-time $25,980; part-time $1444 per credit. Required fees: $1874; $937 per semester. *Financial support:* In 2010–11, 41 students received support, including 1 fellowship with full tuition reimbursement available (averaging $20,000 per year), 38 research assistantships with full tuition reimbursements available (averaging $20,000 per year), 2 teaching assistantships with full tuition reimbursements available (averaging $20,000 per year); scholarships/grants, health care benefits, and unspecified assistantships also available. Financial award application deadline: 1/15; financial award applicants required to submit FAFSA. *Faculty research:* Treatment of water and wastes, environmental law: policy and practice, natural environment systems, hazardous waste management, environmental data analysis. Total annual research expenditures: $4.1 million. *Unit head:* Dr. John McCray, Division Director, 303-384-3490, Fax: 303-273-3413, E-mail: jmccray@mines.edu. *Application contact:* Tim VanHaverbeke, Research Faculty, 303-273-3467, Fax: 303-273-3413, E-mail: tvanhave@mines.edu.

Columbia University, Fu Foundation School of Engineering and Applied Science, Department of Earth and Environmental Engineering, New York, NY 10027. Offers earth and environmental engineering (MS, Eng Sc D, PhD); metallurgical engineering (Engr); mining engineering (Engr); MS/MBA. Part-time programs available. Postbaccalaureate distance learning degree programs offered (minimal on-campus study). *Faculty:* 12 full-time (1 woman), 6 part-time/adjunct (0 women). *Students:* 47 full-time (18 women), 14 part-time (9 women); includes 5 minority (1 American Indian or Alaska Native, non-Hispanic/Latino; 2 Asian, non-Hispanic/Latino; 1 Hispanic/Latino; 1 Two or more races, non-Hispanic/Latino), 30 international. Average age 29. 192 applicants, 14% accepted, 12 enrolled. In 2010, 28 master's, 8 doctorates awarded. Terminal master's awarded for partial completion of doctoral program. *Degree requirements:* For master's, thesis; for doctorate, thesis/dissertation, qualifying exam. *Entrance requirements:* For master's, doctorate, and Engr, GRE General Test. Additional exam requirements/recommendations for international students: Required—TOEFL, IELTS. *Application deadline:* For fall admission, 12/1 priority date for domestic and international students; for spring admission, 10/1 priority date for domestic and international students. Application fee: $95. Electronic applications accepted. *Financial support:* In 2010–11, 39 students received support, including 6 fellowships with full and partial tuition reimbursements available (averaging $16,478 per year), 26 research assistantships with full tuition reimbursements available (averaging $27,733 per year), 7 teaching assistantships with full tuition reimbursements available (averaging $22,500 per year); health care benefits and unspecified assistantships also available. Financial award application deadline: 12/1; financial award applicants required to submit FAFSA. *Faculty research:* Sustainable energy and materials, waste to energy, water resources and climate risks, environmental health engineering, life cycle analysis. *Unit head:* Dr. Klaus S. Lackner, Maurice Ewing and J. Lamar Worzel Professor of Geophysics and Department Chairman, 212-854-0304, Fax: 212-854-7081, E-mail: kl2010@columbia.edu. *Application contact:* Gary Hill, Administrative Assistant, 212-854-2905, Fax: 212-854-7081, E-mail: gh2206@columbia.edu.

Concordia University, School of Graduate Studies, Faculty of Engineering and Computer Science, Department of Building, Civil and Environmental Engineering, Montréal, QC H3G 1M8, Canada. Offers building engineering (M Eng, MA Sc, PhD, Certificate); civil engineering (M Eng, MA Sc, PhD); environmental engineering (Certificate). *Degree requirements:* For master's, thesis or alternative; for doctorate, comprehensive exam, thesis/dissertation. *Faculty research:* Structural engineering, geotechnical engineering, water resources and fluid engineering, transportation engineering, systems engineering.

Cornell University, Graduate School, Graduate Fields of Engineering, Field of Civil and Environmental Engineering, Ithaca, NY 14853-0001. Offers engineering management (M Eng, MS, PhD); environmental engineering (M Eng, MS, PhD); environmental fluid mechanics and hydrology (M Eng, MS, PhD); environmental systems engineering (M Eng, MS, PhD); geotechnical engineering (M Eng, MS, PhD); remote sensing (M Eng, MS, PhD); structural engineering (M Eng, MS, PhD); structural mechanics (M Eng, MS); transportation engineering (MS, PhD); transportation systems engineering (M Eng); water resource systems (M Eng, MS, PhD). *Faculty:* 36 full-time (4 women). *Students:* 148 full-time (48 women); includes 3 Black or African American, non-Hispanic/Latino; 1 American Indian or Alaska Native, non-Hispanic/Latino; 16 Asian, non-Hispanic/Latino; 16 Hispanic/Latino, 60 international. Average age 24. 390 applicants, 56% accepted, 76 enrolled. In 2010, 93 master's, 5 doctorates awarded. Terminal master's awarded for partial completion of doctoral program. *Degree requirements:* For master's, thesis (MS); for doctorate, comprehensive exam, thesis/dissertation. *Entrance requirements:* For master's and doctorate, GRE General Test (recommended), 2 letters of recommendation. Additional exam requirements/recommendations for international students: Required—TOEFL (minimum score 600 paper-based; 250 computer-based; 77 iBT). *Application deadline:* For fall admission, 1/15 priority date for domestic students; for spring admission, 10/15 for domestic students. Application fee: $70. Electronic applications accepted. *Expenses:* Tuition: Full-time $29,500. Required fees: $76. Tuition and fees vary according to degree level and program. *Financial support:* In 2010–11, 50 students received support, including 17 fellowships with full tuition reimbursements available, 33 research assistantships with full tuition reimbursements available, 15 teaching assistantships with full tuition reimbursements available; institutionally sponsored loans, scholarships/grants, health care benefits, tuition waivers (full and partial), and unspecified assistantships also available. Financial award applicants required to submit FAFSA. *Faculty research:* Environmental engineering, geotechnical engineering, remote sensing, environmental fluid mechanics and hydrology, structural engineering. *Unit head:* Director of Graduate Studies, 607-255-7560, Fax: 607-255-9004. *Application contact:* Graduate Field Assistant, 607-255-7560, Fax: 607-255-9004, E-mail: cee_grad@cornell.edu.

Dalhousie University, Faculty of Engineering, Department of Environmental Engineering, Halifax, NS B3J 2X4, Canada. Offers M Eng, MA Sc, PhD. *Entrance requirements:* Additional exam requirements/recommendations for international students: Required—TOEFL, IELTS, CANTEST, CAEL, or Michigan English Language Assessment Battery. Electronic applications accepted.

Dartmouth College, Thayer School of Engineering, Program in Environmental Engineering, Hanover, NH 03755. Offers MS, PhD. Application fee: $45. *Faculty research:* Resource and environmental analysis, decision theory, risk assessment and public policy, environmental fluid mechanics. Total annual research expenditures: $503,229. *Unit head:* Dr. Joseph J. Helbie, Dean, 603-646-2238, Fax: 603-646-2580, E-mail: joseph.j.helbie@dartmouth.edu. *Application*

Environmental Engineering

Dartmouth College (continued)

contact: Candace S. Potter, Graduate Admissions Administrator, 603-646-3844, Fax: 603-646-1620, E-mail: candace.potter@dartmouth.edu.

Drexel University, College of Engineering, Department of Civil, Architectural, and Environmental Engineering, Program in Environmental Engineering, Philadelphia, PA 19104-2875. Offers MS, PhD. Part-time and evening/weekend programs available. Terminal master's awarded for partial completion of doctoral program. *Degree requirements:* For master's, thesis optional; for doctorate, thesis/dissertation. Electronic applications accepted.

Drexel University, College of Engineering, Department of Civil, Architectural, and Environmental Engineering, Program in Geotechnical, Geoenvironmental and Geosynthetics Engineering, Philadelphia, PA 19104-2875. Offers MS, PhD.

Duke University, Graduate School, Pratt School of Engineering, Department of Civil and Environmental Engineering, Durham, NC 27708. Offers civil and environmental engineering (MS, PhD); environmental engineering (MS, PhD). Part-time programs available. *Faculty:* 21 full-time. *Students:* 55 full-time (18 women); includes 1 Black or African American, non-Hispanic/Latino; 1 Hispanic/Latino, 30 international. 149 applicants, 17% accepted, 15 enrolled. In 2010, 9 master's, 4 doctorates awarded. Terminal master's awarded for partial completion of doctoral program. *Degree requirements:* For doctorate, thesis/dissertation. *Entrance requirements:* For master's and doctorate, GRE General Test. Additional exam requirements/recommendations for international students: Required—TOEFL (minimum score 550 paper-based; 213 computer-based; 83 iBT), IELTS (minimum score 7). *Application deadline:* For fall admission, 12/8 priority date for domestic and international students; for spring admission, 11/1 for domestic students. Application fee: $75. Electronic applications accepted. *Financial support:* Fellowships, research assistantships, Federal Work-Study available. Financial award application deadline: 12/8. *Unit head:* Dolbow John, Director of Graduate Studies, 919-660-5200, Fax: 919-660-5219, E-mail: ruby.carpenter@duke.edu. *Application contact:* Elizabeth Hutton, Director of Admissions, 919-684-3913, Fax: 919-684-2277, E-mail: grad-admissions@duke.edu.

Duke University, Graduate School, Pratt School of Engineering, Master of Engineering Program, Durham, NC 27708-0271. Offers biomedical engineering (M Eng); civil engineering (M Eng); electrical and computer engineering (M Eng); environmental engineering (M Eng); materials science and engineering (M Eng); mechanical engineering (M Eng); photonics and optical sciences (M Eng). Part-time programs available. *Faculty:* 123 full-time, 1 part-time/adjunct. *Students:* 9 full-time (4 women); includes 2 minority (both Asian, non-Hispanic/Latino), 3 international. Average age 24. *Entrance requirements:* For master's, GRE General Test, resume, 3 letters of recommendation, statement of purpose. Additional exam requirements/recommendations for international students: Required—TOEFL. *Application deadline:* For fall admission, 6/15 for domestic students, 2/15 for international students; for spring admission, 11/1 for domestic students, 9/1 for international students. Application fee: $75. *Financial support:* Merit scholarships/grants available. *Unit head:* Dr. Bradley A. Fox, Executive Director, 919-660-5455, Fax: 919-660-5456. *Application contact:* Erin Degerman, Admissions Coordinator, 919-668-6789, Fax: 919-660-5456, E-mail: erin.degerman@duke.edu.

École Polytechnique de Montréal, Graduate Programs, Department of Civil, Geological and Mining Engineering, Montréal, QC H3C 3A7, Canada. Offers civil, geological and mining engineering (DESS); environmental engineering (M Eng, M Sc A, PhD); geotechnical engineering (M Eng, M Sc A, PhD); hydraulics engineering (M Eng, M Sc A, PhD); structural engineering (M Eng, M Sc A, PhD); transportation engineering (M Eng, M Sc A, PhD). Part-time programs available. *Degree requirements:* For master's, one foreign language, thesis; for doctorate, one foreign language, thesis/dissertation. *Entrance requirements:* For master's, minimum GPA of 2.75; for doctorate, minimum GPA of 3.0. *Faculty research:* Water resources management, characteristics of building materials, aging of dams, pollution control.

Florida Agricultural and Mechanical University, Division of Graduate Studies, Research, and Continuing Education, FAMU-FSU College of Engineering, Department of Civil and Environmental Engineering, Tallahassee, FL 32307-3200. Offers civil engineering (MS, PhD); environmental engineering (MS, PhD). *Degree requirements:* For master's, comprehensive exam, thesis optional; for doctorate, comprehensive exam, thesis/dissertation. *Entrance requirements:* For master's, GRE General Test, minimum GPA of 3.0; for doctorate, GRE General Test, minimum GPA of 3.0, letters of recommendation (3). Additional exam requirements/recommendations for international students: Required—TOEFL (minimum score 550 paper-based; 213 computer-based). *Faculty research:* Geotechnical, environmental, hydraulic, construction materials, and structures.

Florida International University, College of Engineering and Computing, Department of Civil and Environmental Engineering, Program in Environmental Engineering, Miami, FL 33175. Offers MS. Part-time and evening/weekend programs available. Postbaccalaureate distance learning degree programs offered (no on-campus study). *Students:* 11 full-time (4 women), 17 part-time (8 women); includes 2 Black or African American, non-Hispanic/Latino; 11 Hispanic/Latino, 10 international. Average age 28. 55 applicants, 24% accepted, 11 enrolled. In 2010, 11 master's awarded. *Degree requirements:* For master's, thesis optional. *Entrance requirements:* For master's, minimum GPA of 3.0; resume, 3 letters of recommendation. Additional exam requirements/recommendations for international students: Required—TOEFL (minimum score 550 paper-based; 80 iBT). *Application deadline:* For fall admission, 6/1 for domestic students, 4/1 for international students; for spring admission, 10/1 for domestic students, 9/1 for international students. Applications are processed on a rolling basis. Application fee: $30. Electronic applications accepted. *Financial support:* In 2010–11, 6 research assistantships (averaging $13,333 per year), 4 teaching assistantships (averaging $13,333 per year) were awarded; institutionally sponsored loans and scholarships/grants also available. Financial award application deadline: 3/1; financial award applicants required to submit FAFSA. *Faculty research:* Water and wastewater treatment, water quality, solid and hazardous waste, sustainability and green engineering, clean up, remediation and restoration. *Unit head:* Dr. Atorod Azizinamini, Department Chair, 305-348-3821, Fax: 305-348-2802, E-mail: aazizina@fiu.edu. *Application contact:* Maria Parrila, Graduate Admissions Assistant, 305-348-1890, Fax: 305-348-6142, E-mail: grad_eng@fiu.edu.

Florida State University, The Graduate School, FAMU-FSU College of Engineering, Department of Civil and Environmental Engineering, Tallahassee, FL 32306. Offers MS, PhD. Part-time programs available. *Faculty:* 16 full-time (3 women), 5 part-time/adjunct (1 woman). *Students:* 33 full-time (9 women), 13 part-time (6 women); includes 7 Black or African American, non-Hispanic/Latino; 4 Hispanic/Latino, 19 international. Average age 23. 72 applicants, 64% accepted, 14 enrolled. In 2010, 15 master's, 2 doctorates awarded. *Degree requirements:* For master's, thesis optional; for doctorate, thesis/dissertation. *Entrance requirements:* For master's, GRE General Test (minimum score 1000), BS in engineering or related field, minimum GPA of 3.0; for doctorate, GRE General Test (minimum score 1100), master's degree in engineering or related field, minimum GPA of 3.0. Additional exam requirements/recommendations for international students: Required—TOEFL (minimum score 550 paper-based; 213 computer-based; 80 iBT). *Application deadline:* For fall admission, 7/1 for domestic and international students; for spring admission, 11/1 for domestic and international students. Applications are processed on a rolling basis. Application fee: $30. *Expenses:* Tuition, state resident: full-time $8238.24. *Financial support:* In 2010–11, 25 students received support, including 2 fellowships (averaging $12,000 per year), 18 research assistantships with full tuition reimbursements available (averaging $15,000 per year), 26 teaching assistantships with full tuition reimbursements available (averaging $15,000 per year); Federal Work-Study, tuition waivers (full), and unspecified assistantships also available. Financial award application deadline: 6/15; financial award applicants required to submit FAFSA. *Faculty research:* Tidal hydraulics, temperature effects on bridge girders, codes for coastal construction, field performance of pine bridges, river basin management, transportation pavement design, soil dynamics, structural analysis. Total annual research expenditures: $1.3 million. *Unit head:* Dr. Kamal S. Tawfiq, Chair and Professor, 850-410-6143, Fax: 850-410-6142, E-mail: tawfiq@eng.fsu.edu. *Application contact:* Johnnye Belinda Morris, Office Manager, 850-410-6139, Fax: 850-410-6142, E-mail: bmorris@eng.fsu.edu.

Gannon University, School of Graduate Studies, College of Engineering and Business, School of Engineering and Computer Science, Program in Environmental Science and Engineering, Erie, PA 16541-0001. Offers MS. Part-time and evening/weekend programs available. *Students:* 12 full-time (5 women), 5 part-time (4 women), 3 international. Average age 28. 32 applicants, 63% accepted, 3 enrolled. In 2010, 4 master's awarded. *Degree requirements:* For master's, thesis, internship, research paper or project. *Entrance requirements:* For master's, GRE. Additional exam requirements/recommendations for international students: Required—TOEFL (minimum score 79 iBT). *Application deadline:* Applications are processed on a rolling basis. Application fee: $25. Electronic applications accepted. *Expenses:* Tuition: Full-time $14,670; part-time $815 per credit. Required fees: $430; $18 per credit. Tuition and fees vary according to class time, course load, degree level, campus/location and program. *Financial support:* Scholarships/grants and unspecified assistantships available. Financial award application deadline: 7/1; financial award applicants required to submit FAFSA. *Faculty research:* Water quality, air quality, biomass energy, industrial waste treatment, environmental risk assessment. *Unit head:* Dr. Harry Diz, Chair, 814-871-7633, E-mail: diz001@gannon.edu. *Application contact:* Kara Morgan, Assistant Director of Graduate Admissions, 814-871-5831, Fax: 814-871-5827, E-mail: graduate@gannon.edu.

The George Washington University, School of Engineering and Applied Science, Department of Civil and Environmental Engineering, Washington, DC 20052. Offers MS, D Sc, App Sc, Engr. Part-time and evening/weekend programs available. *Faculty:* 13 full-time (3 women), 7 part-time/adjunct (1 woman). *Students:* 22 full-time (6 women), 31 part-time (6 women); includes 3 Black or African American, non-Hispanic/Latino; 3 Hispanic/Latino, 30 international. Average age 30. 97 applicants, 53% accepted, 14 enrolled. In 2010, 8 master's, 4 doctorates awarded. *Degree requirements:* For master's, thesis optional; for doctorate, thesis/dissertation, final and qualifying exams. *Entrance requirements:* For master's, appropriate bachelor's degree, minimum GPA of 3.0; for doctorate, appropriate bachelor's or master's degree, minimum GPA of 3.4, GRE if highest earned degree is BS; for other advanced degree, appropriate master's degree, minimum GPA of 3.0. Additional exam requirements/recommendations for international students: Required—TOEFL or The George Washington University English as a Foreign Language Test. *Application deadline:* For fall admission, 3/1 priority date for domestic students; for spring admission, 10/1 for domestic students. Applications are processed on a rolling basis. Application fee: $75. *Financial support:* In 2010–11, 42 students received support; fellowships with tuition reimbursements available, research assistantships, teaching assistantships with tuition reimbursements available, career-related internships or fieldwork, Federal Work-Study, institutionally sponsored loans, and tuition waivers available. Financial award application deadline: 3/1; financial award applicants required to submit FAFSA. *Faculty research:* Computer-integrated manufacturing, materials engineering, electronic materials, fatigue and fracture, reliability. *Unit head:* Dr. Kim Roddis, Chair, 202-994-8515, Fax: 202-994-0127, E-mail: roddis@gwu.edu. *Application contact:* Adina Lav, Marketing, Recruiting and Admissions, 202-994-5827, Fax: 202-994-0909, E-mail: engineering@gwu.edu.

Georgia Institute of Technology, Graduate Studies and Research, College of Engineering, School of Civil and Environmental Engineering, Program in Environmental Engineering, Atlanta, GA 30332-0001. Offers MS, MS Env E, PhD. *Accreditation:* ABET (one or more programs are accredited). Part-time programs available. Postbaccalaureate distance learning degree programs offered (no on-campus study). *Degree requirements:* For master's, research report or thesis; for doctorate, thesis/dissertation. *Entrance requirements:* For master's and doctorate, GRE, minimum GPA of 3.2. Additional exam requirements/recommendations for international students: Required—TOEFL. *Faculty research:* Advanced microbiology of water and wastes, industrial waste treatment and disposal, air pollution measurements and control.

Idaho State University, Office of Graduate Studies, College of Engineering, Civil and Environmental Engineering Department, Pocatello, ID 83209-8060. Offers civil engineering (MS); environmental engineering (MS); environmental science and management (MS). Part-time programs available. *Degree requirements:* For master's, comprehensive exam (for some programs), thesis optional, thesis project, 2 semesters of seminar. *Entrance requirements:* For master's, GRE. Additional exam requirements/recommendations for international students: Required—TOEFL (minimum score 550 paper-based; 213 computer-based; 80 iBT). Electronic applications accepted. *Faculty research:* Floor vibration investigations, earthquake engineering, base isolation systems and seismic risk assessment, infrastructure revitalization (building foundations and damage, bridge structures, highways, and dams), slope stability and soil erosion, pavement rehabilitation, computational fluid dynamics and flood control structures, microbial fuel cells, water treatment and water quality modeling, environmental risk assessment, biotechnology, nanotechnology.

Illinois Institute of Technology, Graduate College, Armour College of Engineering, Department of Civil, Architectural and Environmental Engineering, Chicago, IL 60616-3793. Offers architectural engineering (M Arch E); civil engineering (MS, PhD), including architectural engineering (MS), construction engineering and management (MS), geoenvironmental engineering (MS), geotechnical engineering (MS), structural engineering (MS), transportation engineering (MS); construction engineering and management (MCEM); environmental engineering (M Env E, PhD); geoenvironmental engineering (M Geoenv E); geotechnical engineering (MGE); public works (MPW); structural engineering (MSE); transportation engineering (M Trans E). Part-time and evening/weekend programs available. Postbaccalaureate distance learning degree programs offered (minimal on-campus study). *Faculty:* 15 full-time (1 woman), 13 part-time/adjunct (1 woman). *Students:* 159 full-time (63 women), 109 part-time (22 women); includes 30 minority (9 Black or African American, non-Hispanic/Latino; 16 Asian, non-Hispanic/Latino; 5 Hispanic/Latino), 126 international. Average age 27. 453 applicants, 66% accepted, 98 enrolled. In 2010, 76 master's, 1 doctorate awarded. Terminal master's awarded for partial completion of doctoral program. *Degree requirements:* For master's, thesis (for some programs); for doctorate, comprehensive exam, thesis/dissertation. *Entrance requirements:* For master's, GRE General Test (minimum score 900 Quantitative and Verbal, 2.5 Analytical Writing), minimum undergraduate GPA of 3.0; for doctorate, GRE General Test (minimum score 1000 Quantitative and Verbal, 3.0 Analytical Writing), minimum undergraduate GPA of 3.0. Additional exam requirements/recommendations for international students: Required—TOEFL (minimum score 523 paper-based; 70 iBT); Recommended—IELTS (minimum score 5.5). *Application deadline:* For fall admission, 5/1 for domestic and international students; for spring admission, 10/15 for domestic and international students. Applications are processed on a rolling basis. Application fee: $50. Electronic applications accepted. *Expenses:* Tuition: Full-time $18,576; part-time $1032 per credit hour. Required fees: $583 per semester. One-time fee: $150. Tuition and fees vary according to program and student level. *Financial support:* In 2010–11, 13 research assistantships with full and partial tuition reimbursements (averaging $9,453 per year), 19 teaching assistantships with full and partial tuition reimbursements (averaging $3,163 per year) were awarded; fellowships with full and partial tuition reimbursements, Federal Work-Study, institutionally sponsored loans, scholarships/grants, health care benefits, tuition waivers (partial), and unspecified assistantships also available. Support available to part-time students. Financial award applicants required to submit FAFSA. *Faculty research:* Structural, architectural, geotechnical and geoenvironmental engineering; construction engineering and management; transportation engineering; environmental engineering and public works. Total annual research expenditures: $763,042. *Unit head:* Dr. Jamshid Mohammadi, Professor and Chairman, 312-567-3629, Fax: 312-567-3519, E-mail: mohammadi@iit.edu. *Application contact:* Deborah Gibson, Director, Graduate Admission, 866-472-3448, Fax: 312-567-3138, E-mail: inquiry.grad@iit.edu.

Instituto Tecnologico de Santo Domingo, Graduate School, Area of Engineering, Santo Domingo, Dominican Republic. Offers construction administration (MS, Certificate); data telecommunications (M Eng, MS, Certificate); industrial engineering (M Eng, Certificate); industrial management (M Mgmt); information technology (Certificate); maintenance engineering (M Eng);

occupational hazard prevention (M Mgmt); production management (Certificate); quantitative methods (Certificate); sanitary and environmental engineering (M Eng); structural engineering (M Eng); systems engineering and electronic data processing (Certificate); transportation (Certificate).

Instituto Tecnológico y de Estudios Superiores de Monterrey, Campus Ciudad de México, Virtual University Division, Ciudad de Mexico, Mexico. Offers administration of information technologies (MA); computer sciences (MA); education (MA, PhD); educational technology (MA); environmental engineering (MA); environmental systems (MA); humanistic studies (MA); industrial engineering (MA); international business for Latin America (MA); quality systems (MA); quality systems and productivity (MA). Part-time and evening/weekend programs available. Postbaccalaureate distance learning degree programs offered (minimal on-campus study). *Entrance requirements:* For master's and doctorate, Instituto entrance exam. Additional exam requirements/recommendations for international students: Required—TOEFL.

Instituto Tecnológico y de Estudios Superiores de Monterrey, Campus Monterrey, Graduate and Research Division, Programs in Engineering, Monterrey, Mexico. Offers applied statistics (M Eng); artificial intelligence (PhD); automation engineering (M Eng); chemical engineering (M Eng); civil engineering (M Eng); electrical engineering (M Eng); electronic engineering (M Eng); environmental engineering (M Eng); industrial engineering (M Eng, PhD); manufacturing engineering (M Eng); mechanical engineering (M Eng); systems and quality engineering (M Eng). M Eng program offered jointly with University of Waterloo; PhD in industrial engineering with Texas A&M University. Part-time and evening/weekend programs available. Terminal master's awarded for partial completion of doctoral program. *Degree requirements:* For master's, one foreign language, thesis; for doctorate, one foreign language, thesis/dissertation. *Entrance requirements:* For master's, EXADEP; for doctorate, GRE, master's degree in related field. Additional exam requirements/recommendations for international students: Required—TOEFL. *Faculty research:* Flexible manufacturing cells, materials, statistical methods, environmental prevention, control and evaluation.

Iowa State University of Science and Technology, Graduate College, College of Engineering, Department of Civil and Construction Engineering, Ames, IA 50011. Offers civil engineering (MS, PhD), including civil engineering materials, construction engineering and management, environmental engineering, geometronics, geotechnical engineering, structural engineering, transportation engineering. *Faculty:* 35 full-time (6 women), 4 part-time/adjunct (0 women). *Students:* 93 full-time (31 women), 48 part-time (10 women); includes 1 Black or African American, non-Hispanic/Latino; 1 Asian, non-Hispanic/Latino; 4 Hispanic/Latino, 62 international. 179 applicants, 37% accepted, 35 enrolled. In 2010, 32 master's, 9 doctorates awarded. *Degree requirements:* For master's, thesis or alternative; for doctorate, thesis/dissertation. *Entrance requirements:* For master's and doctorate, GRE General Test. Additional exam requirements/recommendations for international students: Required—TOEFL (minimum score 550 paper-based; 82 iBT), IELTS (minimum score 6.5). *Application deadline:* For fall admission, 2/1 priority date for domestic students, 2/1 for international students; for spring admission, 8/1 priority date for domestic students, 8/1 for international students. Application fee: $40 ($90 for international students). Electronic applications accepted. *Financial support:* In 2010–11, 67 research assistantships with full and partial tuition reimbursements (averaging $7,654 per year), 4 teaching assistantships with full and partial tuition reimbursements (averaging $9,525 per year) were awarded; fellowships, scholarships/grants, health care benefits, and unspecified assistantships also available. *Unit head:* Dr. James Alleman, Chair, 515-294-3892, E-mail: ccee-grad-inquiry@iastate.edu. *Application contact:* Dr. Sri Srithanan, Director of Graduate Education, 515-294-5328, E-mail: ccee-grad-inquiry@iastate.edu.

The Johns Hopkins University, Bloomberg School of Public Health, Department of Environmental Health Sciences, Baltimore, MD 21218-2699. Offers environmental health engineering (PhD); environmental health sciences (MHS, Dr PH); occupational and environmental health (PhD); occupational and environmental hygiene (MHS, MHS); physiology (PhD); toxicology (PhD). Postbaccalaureate distance learning degree programs offered (minimal on-campus study). *Faculty:* 71 full-time (27 women), 58 part-time/adjunct (26 women). *Students:* 66 full-time (38 women), 19 part-time (12 women); includes 25 minority (3 Black or African American, non-Hispanic/Latino; 13 Asian, non-Hispanic/Latino; 4 Hispanic/Latino; 5 Two or more races, non-Hispanic/Latino), 11 international. Average age 30. 101 applicants, 49% accepted, 31 enrolled. In 2010, 21 master's, 14 doctorates awarded. *Degree requirements:* For master's, essay, presentation; for doctorate, comprehensive exam, thesis/dissertation, 1 year full-time residency, oral and written exams. *Entrance requirements:* For master's, GRE General Test or MCAT, 3 letters of recommendation, transcripts; for doctorate, GRE General Test or MCAT, 3 letters of recommendation. Additional exam requirements/recommendations for international students: Required—TOEFL (minimum score 600 paper-based; 250 computer-based). *Application deadline:* For fall admission, 12/15 priority date for domestic and international students. Applications are processed on a rolling basis. Application fee: $45. Electronic applications accepted. *Financial support:* In 2010–11, 5 fellowships with full tuition reimbursements (averaging $26,500 per year) were awarded; Federal Work-Study, institutionally sponsored loans, scholarships/grants, traineeships, health care benefits, and stipends also available. Support available to part-time students. Financial award application deadline: 3/15; financial award applicants required to submit FAFSA. *Faculty research:* Chemical carcinogenesis/toxicology, lung disease, occupational and environmental health, nuclear imaging, molecular epidemiology. Total annual research expenditures: $23.7 million. *Unit head:* Dr. John Davis Groopman, Chair, 410-955-3720, Fax: 410-955-0617, E-mail: jgroopma@jhsph.edu. *Application contact:* Nina J. Kulacki, Academic Program Manager, 410-955-2212, Fax: 410-955-0617, E-mail: nkulacki@jhsph.edu.

The Johns Hopkins University, Engineering for Professionals, Part-Time Program in Environmental Engineering, Baltimore, MD 21218-2699. Offers MS, Graduate Certificate, Post-Master's Certificate. Part-time and evening/weekend programs available. *Faculty:* 9 part-time/adjunct (1 woman). *Students:* 20 part-time (12 women); includes 4 minority (2 Black or African American, non-Hispanic/Latino; 2 Hispanic/Latino), 1 international. Average age 27. 10 applicants, 40% accepted, 4 enrolled. In 2010, 10 master's awarded. Application fee: $75. *Unit head:* Dr. Hedy Alavi, Program Chair, 410-516-7091, Fax: 410-516-8996, E-mail: hedy.alavi@jhu.edu. *Application contact:* Priyanka Dwivedi, Admissions Manager, 410-516-2300, Fax: 410-579-8049, E-mail: dwived1@jhu.edu.

The Johns Hopkins University, Engineering for Professionals, Part-time Program in Environmental Engineering and Science, Baltimore, MD 21218-2699. Offers MEE, MS, Graduate Certificate, Post-Master's Certificate. Part-time and evening/weekend programs available. *Faculty:* 8 part-time/adjunct (2 women). *Students:* 3 full-time (all women), 32 part-time (13 women); includes 11 minority (3 Black or African American, non-Hispanic/Latino; 4 Asian, non-Hispanic/Latino; 2 Hispanic/Latino; 2 Two or more races, non-Hispanic/Latino). Average age 30. 7 applicants, 86% accepted, 4 enrolled. In 2010, 10 master's awarded. *Application deadline:* Applications are processed on a rolling basis. Application fee: $75. Electronic applications accepted. *Financial support:* Institutionally sponsored loans available. *Unit head:* Dr. Hedy Alavi, Program Chair, 410-516-7091, Fax: 410-516-8996, E-mail: hedy.alavi@jhu.edu. *Application contact:* Priyanka Dwivedi, Admissions Manager, 410-516-2300, Fax: 410-579-8049, E-mail: pdwived1@jhu.edu.

The Johns Hopkins University, G. W. C. Whiting School of Engineering, Department of Geography and Environmental Engineering, Baltimore, MD 21218-2699. Offers MA, MS, MSE, PhD. *Faculty:* 15 full-time (4 women), 4 part-time/adjunct (0 women). *Students:* 69 full-time (35 women), 7 part-time (4 women); includes 13 minority (2 Black or African American, non-Hispanic/Latino; 4 Asian, non-Hispanic/Latino; 6 Hispanic/Latino; 1 Two or more races, non-Hispanic/Latino), 37 international. Average age 25. 151 applicants, 74% accepted, 35 enrolled. In 2010, 19 master's, 5 doctorates awarded. Terminal master's awarded for partial completion of doctoral program. *Degree requirements:* For master's, thesis (for some programs), 1 year full-time residency; for doctorate, comprehensive exam, thesis/dissertation, oral exam, 2 year full-time residency. *Entrance requirements:* For master's and doctorate, GRE General Test.

Additional exam requirements/recommendations for international students: Required—TOEFL (minimum score 670 paper-based; 300 computer-based; 120 iBT); Recommended—IELTS. *Application deadline:* For fall admission, 1/15 priority date for domestic and international students. Applications are processed on a rolling basis. Application fee: $75. Electronic applications accepted. *Financial support:* In 2010–11, 12 fellowships with full tuition reimbursements (averaging $24,600 per year), 19 research assistantships with full tuition reimbursements (averaging $24,600 per year), 1 teaching assistantship with full tuition reimbursement (averaging $18,000 per year) were awarded; Federal Work-Study, institutionally sponsored loans, scholarships/grants, health care benefits, tuition waivers (partial), and unspecified assistantships also available. *Faculty research:* Environmental engineering; environmental chemistry; water resources engineering; systems analysis and economics for public decision-making; geomorphology, hydrology and ecology. Total annual research expenditures: $1.4 million. *Unit head:* Dr. Edward J. Bouwer, Chair, 410-516-7102, Fax: 410-516-8996, E-mail: bouwer@jhu.edu. *Application contact:* Dr. Edward J. Bouwer, Chair, 410-516-7102, Fax: 410-516-8996, E-mail: bouwer@jhu.edu.

Lakehead University, Graduate Studies, Faculty of Engineering, Thunder Bay, ON P7B 5E1, Canada. Offers control engineering (M Sc Engr); electrical/computer engineering (M Sc Engr); environmental engineering (M Sc Engr). Part-time programs available. *Degree requirements:* For master's, thesis. *Entrance requirements:* For master's, bachelor's degree in chemical, electrical or mechanical engineering, minimum B average. Additional exam requirements/recommendations for international students: Required—TOEFL. *Faculty research:* Pulp and paper, adaptive/process control, robust/interactive learning control, vibration control.

Lamar University, College of Graduate Studies, College of Engineering, Department of Civil Engineering, Beaumont, TX 77710. Offers civil engineering (ME, MES, DE); environmental engineering (MS); environmental studies (MS). Part-time programs available. *Faculty:* 5 full-time (1 woman), 1 part-time/adjunct (0 women). *Students:* 31 full-time (6 women), 18 part-time (7 women); includes 1 Black or African American, non-Hispanic/Latino; 3 Asian, non-Hispanic/Latino, 28 international. Average age 29. 37 applicants, 65% accepted, 7 enrolled. In 2010, 42 master's, 1 doctorate awarded. *Degree requirements:* For master's, thesis optional; for doctorate, thesis/dissertation. *Entrance requirements:* For master's and doctorate, GRE General Test. Additional exam requirements/recommendations for international students: Required—TOEFL. *Application deadline:* For fall admission, 5/15 priority date for domestic students; for spring admission, 10/1 priority date for domestic students. Applications are processed on a rolling basis. Application fee: $25 ($50 for international students). *Expenses:* Tuition, state resident: full-time $4160; part-time $208 per credit hour. Tuition, nonresident: full-time $10,360; part-time $518 per credit hour. *Financial support:* In 2010–11, 45 fellowships with partial tuition reimbursements (averaging $1,000 per year), 10 research assistantships with partial tuition reimbursements (averaging $7,200 per year), 3 teaching assistantships with partial tuition reimbursements (averaging $7,200 per year) were awarded; scholarships/grants and tuition waivers (partial) also available. Financial award application deadline: 4/1. *Faculty research:* Environmental remediations, construction productivity, geotechnical soil stabilization, lake/reservoir hydrodynamics, air pollution. *Unit head:* Dr. Enno Koehn, Chair, 409-880-8759, Fax: 409-880-8121, E-mail: koehneu@hal.lamar.edu. *Application contact:* Sandy Drane, Coordinator of Graduate Admissions, 409-880-8356, Fax: 409-880-8414, E-mail: gradmissions@hal.lamar.edu.

Lehigh University, P.C. Rossin College of Engineering and Applied Science, Department of Civil and Environmental Engineering, Bethlehem, PA 18015. Offers civil engineering (M Eng, MS, PhD); environmental engineering (MS, PhD); structural engineering (M Eng, MS, PhD). Part-time programs available. *Faculty:* 15 full-time (3 women), 1 (woman) part-time/adjunct. *Students:* 107 full-time (33 women), 9 part-time (0 women); includes 8 minority (4 Black or African American, non-Hispanic/Latino; 1 Asian, non-Hispanic/Latino; 2 Hispanic/Latino; 1 Native Hawaiian or other Pacific Islander, non-Hispanic/Latino), 59 international. Average age 26. 270 applicants, 50% accepted, 65 enrolled. In 2010, 23 master's, 1 doctorate awarded. Terminal master's awarded for partial completion of doctoral program. *Median time to degree:* Of those who began their doctoral program in fall 2002, 100% received their degree in 8 years or less. *Degree requirements:* For master's, thesis (for some programs); for doctorate, comprehensive exam, thesis/dissertation. *Entrance requirements:* For master's and doctorate, GRE. Additional exam requirements/recommendations for international students: Required—TOEFL (minimum score 550 paper-based; 213 computer-based; 79 iBT). *Application deadline:* For fall admission, 7/15 priority date for domestic and international students; for spring admission, 12/1 priority date for domestic and international students. Applications are processed on a rolling basis. Application fee: $75. Electronic applications accepted. *Expenses:* Contact institution. *Financial support:* In 2010–11, 31 students received support, including 5 fellowships with full tuition reimbursements available (averaging $17,460 per year), 4 research assistantships with full tuition reimbursements available (averaging $22,350 per year), 7 teaching assistantships with full tuition reimbursements available (averaging $17,460 per year); institutionally sponsored loans, scholarships/grants, tuition waivers, and unspecified assistantships also available. Financial award application deadline: 1/15. *Faculty research:* Structural engineering, geotechnical engineering, water resources engineering, environmental engineering. Total annual research expenditures: $6.8 million. *Unit head:* Dr. Stephen Pessiki, Chairman, 610-758-3494, Fax: 610-758-6405, E-mail: pessiki@lehigh.edu. *Application contact:* Prisca Vidanage, Graduate Coordinator, 610-758-3530, Fax: 610-758-6405, E-mail: pmv1@lehigh.edu.

Louisiana State University and Agricultural and Mechanical College, Graduate School, College of Engineering, Department of Civil and Environmental Engineering, Baton Rouge, LA 70803. Offers environmental engineering (MSCE, PhD); geotechnical engineering (MSCE, PhD); structural engineering and mechanics (MSCE, PhD); transportation engineering (MSCE, PhD); water resources (MSCE, PhD). Part-time programs available. *Faculty:* 29 full-time (3 women). *Students:* 89 full-time (19 women), 35 part-time (8 women); includes 2 Black or African American, non-Hispanic/Latino; 1 American Indian or Alaska Native, non-Hispanic/Latino; 3 Asian, non-Hispanic/Latino; 3 Hispanic/Latino, 65 international. Average age 29. 96 applicants, 65% accepted, 16 enrolled. In 2010, 20 master's, 8 doctorates awarded. *Degree requirements:* For master's, thesis optional; for doctorate, one foreign language, thesis/dissertation. *Entrance requirements:* For master's and doctorate, GRE General Test, minimum GPA of 3.0. Additional exam requirements/recommendations for international students: Required—TOEFL (minimum score 550 paper-based; 213 computer-based; 79 iBT) or IELTS (minimum score 6.5). *Application deadline:* For fall admission, 1/25 priority date for domestic students, 5/15 for international students; for spring admission, 10/15 for international students. Applications are processed on a rolling basis. Application fee: $50 ($70 for international students). Electronic applications accepted. *Financial support:* In 2010–11, 89 students received support, including 2 fellowships with full and partial tuition reimbursements available (averaging $24,418 per year), 75 research assistantships with full and partial tuition reimbursements available (averaging $16,115 per year), 3 teaching assistantships with full and partial tuition reimbursements available (averaging $12,843 per year); career-related internships or fieldwork, institutionally sponsored loans, scholarships/grants, and health care benefits also available. Financial award application deadline: 3/1; financial award applicants required to submit FAFSA. *Faculty research:* Mechanics and structures, environmental, geotechnical transportation, water resources. Total annual research expenditures: $2.6 million. *Unit head:* Dr. George Z. Voyiadjis, Chair/Professor, 225-578-8668, Fax: 225-578-9176, E-mail: cegzv@lsu.edu. *Application contact:* Dr. Clinton Willson, Professor, 225-578-8652, E-mail: cwillson@lsu.edu.

Manhattan College, Graduate Division, School of Engineering, Program in Environmental Engineering, Riverdale, NY 10471. Offers ME, MS. *Accreditation:* ABET. Part-time and evening/weekend programs available. *Faculty:* 4 full-time (0 women), 1 part-time/adjunct (0 women). *Students:* 12 full-time (3 women), 23 part-time (10 women); includes 1 Black or African American, non-Hispanic/Latino; 1 Asian, non-Hispanic/Latino; 3 Hispanic/Latino; 1 Two or more races, non-Hispanic/Latino. Average age 25. 19 applicants, 74% accepted, 9 enrolled. In 2010, 10 master's awarded. *Degree requirements:* For master's, thesis optional. *Entrance requirements:* For master's, GRE (recommended), minimum GPA of 3.0. Additional exam requirements/recommendations for international students: Required—TOEFL (minimum score 550 paper-based; 213 computer-based; 80 iBT), IELTS (minimum score 6). *Application deadline:*

Environmental Engineering

Manhattan College (continued)

For fall admission, 8/10 priority date for domestic students, 8/10 for international students; for spring admission, 1/7 for domestic and international students. Applications are processed on a rolling basis. Application fee: $50. *Financial support:* In 2010–11, 11 students received support, including 1 fellowship with full tuition reimbursement available (averaging $17,000 per year), 9 research assistantships with full tuition reimbursements available (averaging $17,000 per year), 1 teaching assistantship with full tuition reimbursement available (averaging $17,000 per year); career-related internships or fieldwork, scholarships/grants, tuition waivers (partial), unspecified assistantships, and laboratory assistantships also available. Support available to part-time students. Financial award application deadline: 3/1. *Faculty research:* Water quality modeling, environmental chemistry, air modeling, biological treatment, environmental chemistry. Total annual research expenditures: $400,000. *Unit head:* Dr. Kevin Farley, Graduate Program Director, 718-862-7171, Fax: 718-862-8035, E-mail: kevin.farley@manhattan.edu. *Application contact:* Janet Horgan, Information Contact, 718-862-7171, Fax: 718-862-8035, E-mail: janet.horgan@manhattan.edu.

Marquette University, Graduate School, College of Engineering, Department of Civil and Environmental Engineering, Milwaukee, WI 53201-1881. Offers construction and public works management (MS, PhD); construction engineering and management (Certificate); environmental/water resources engineering (MS, PhD); structural design (Certificate); structural/geotechnical engineering (MS, PhD); transportation planning and engineering (MS, PhD); waste and wastewater treatment processes (Certificate). Part-time and evening/weekend programs available. *Faculty:* 13 full-time (0 women), 3 part-time/adjunct (0 women). *Students:* 20 full-time (4 women), 12 part-time (1 woman); includes 1 minority (Black or African American, non-Hispanic/Latino), 12 international. Average age 27. 66 applicants, 64% accepted, 9 enrolled. In 2010, 8 master's, 1 doctorate awarded. Terminal master's awarded for partial completion of doctoral program. *Degree requirements:* For master's, comprehensive exam, thesis or alternative; for doctorate, thesis/dissertation. *Entrance requirements:* For master's, GRE General Test (recommended), minimum GPA of 3.0, official transcripts from all current and previous colleges/universities except Marquette, three letters of recommendation; for doctorate, GRE General Test, minimum GPA of 3.0, official transcripts from all current and previous colleges/universities except Marquette, three letters of recommendation, brief statement of purpose, submission of any English-language publications authored by applicant (strongly recommended). Additional exam requirements/recommendations for international students: Required—TOEFL (minimum score 530 paper-based; 78 computer-based). *Application deadline:* For fall admission, 6/1 priority date for domestic students. Applications are processed on a rolling basis. Application fee: $50. Electronic applications accepted. *Expenses:* Tuition: Full-time $16,290; part-time $905 per credit hour. Tuition and fees vary according to program. *Financial support:* In 2010–11, 13 students received support, including 4 fellowships with tuition reimbursements available, 4 research assistantships with tuition reimbursements available, 10 teaching assistantships with tuition reimbursements available; Federal Work-Study, institutionally sponsored loans, scholarships/grants, and tuition waivers (full and partial) also available. Support available to part-time students. Financial award application deadline: 2/15. *Faculty research:* Highway safety, highway performance, and intelligent transportation systems; surface mount technology; watershed management. Total annual research expenditures: $662,392. *Unit head:* Dr. Thomas Wenzel, Chair, 414-288-7030, Fax: 414-288-7521, E-mail: thomas.wenzel@marquette.edu. *Application contact:* Dr. Stephen M. Heinrich, Director of Graduate Studies, 414-288-5466, E-mail: stephen.heinrich@marquette.edu.

Marshall University, Academic Affairs Division, College of Information Technology and Engineering, Weisberg Division of Engineering and Computer Science, Huntington, WV 25755. Offers engineering (MSE); information systems (MS). Part-time and evening/weekend programs available. *Faculty:* 10 full-time (1 woman), 1 part-time/adjunct (0 women). *Students:* 21 full-time (2 women), 29 part-time (3 women); includes 3 Black or African American, non-Hispanic/Latino; 2 Asian, non-Hispanic/Latino, 16 international. Average age 29. In 2010, 15 master's awarded. *Degree requirements:* For master's, final project, oral exam. *Entrance requirements:* For master's, GMAT or GRE General Test, minimum undergraduate GPA of 2.75. Application fee: $40. *Financial support:* Tuition waivers (full) available. Support available to part-time students. Financial award application deadline: 8/1; financial award applicants required to submit FAFSA. *Unit head:* Dr. Bill Pierson, Chair, 304-696-2695, E-mail: pierson@marshall.edu. *Application contact:* Information Contact, 304-746-1900, Fax: 304-746-1902, E-mail: services@marshall.edu.

Massachusetts Institute of Technology, School of Engineering, Department of Civil and Environmental Engineering, Cambridge, MA 02139. Offers biological oceanography (PhD, Sc D); chemical oceanography (PhD, Sc D); civil and environmental engineering (M Eng, SM, PhD, Sc D); civil and environmental systems (PhD, Sc D); civil engineering (PhD, Sc D, CE); coastal engineering (PhD, Sc D); construction engineering and management (PhD, Sc D); environmental biology (PhD, Sc D); environmental chemistry (PhD, Sc D); environmental engineering (PhD, Sc D); environmental fluid mechanics (PhD, Sc D); geotechnical and geoenvironmental engineering (PhD, Sc D); hydrology (PhD, Sc D); information technology (PhD, Sc D); oceanographic engineering (PhD, Sc D); structures and materials (PhD, Sc D); transportation (PhD, Sc D); SM/MBA. *Faculty:* 36 full-time (6 women). *Students:* 181 full-time (56 women); includes 27 minority (3 Black or African American, non-Hispanic/Latino; 10 Asian, non-Hispanic/Latino; 10 Hispanic/Latino; 4 Two or more races, non-Hispanic/Latino), 93 international. Average age 26. 525 applicants, 29% accepted, 74 enrolled. In 2010, 85 master's, 18 doctorates, 2 other advanced degrees awarded. *Degree requirements:* For master's and CE, thesis; for doctorate, comprehensive exam, thesis/dissertation. *Entrance requirements:* For master's and doctorate, GRE General Test. Additional exam requirements/recommendations for international students: Required—TOEFL (minimum score 577 paper-based; 233 computer-based; 90 iBT), IELTS (minimum score 7). *Application deadline:* For fall admission, 1/2 for domestic and international students. Application fee: $75. Electronic applications accepted. *Expenses:* Tuition: Full-time $38,940; part-time $605 per unit. Required fees: $272. *Financial support:* In 2010–11, 146 students received support, including 50 fellowships with tuition reimbursements available (averaging $21,808 per year), 90 research assistantships with tuition reimbursements available (averaging $28,452 per year), 20 teaching assistantships with tuition reimbursements available (averaging $27,842 per year); career-related internships or fieldwork, Federal Work-Study, institutionally sponsored loans, scholarships/grants, health care benefits, and unspecified assistantships also available. *Faculty research:* Environmental chemistry; environmental microbiology; environmental fluid mechanics and coastal engineering; geotechnical engineering and geomechanics; hydrology and hydroclimatology; mechanics of materials and structures; operations research/supply chain; transportation. Total annual research expenditures: $19.5 million. *Unit head:* Prof. Andrew Whittle, Department Head, 617-253-7101. *Application contact:* Patricia Glidden, Graduate Admissions Coordinator, 617-253-7119, Fax: 617-258-6775, E-mail: cee-admissions@mit.edu.

McGill University, Faculty of Graduate and Postdoctoral Studies, Faculty of Engineering, Department of Chemical Engineering, Montréal, QC H3A 2T5, Canada. Offers chemical engineering (M Eng, PhD); environmental engineering (M Eng).

McGill University, Faculty of Graduate and Postdoctoral Studies, Faculty of Engineering, Department of Civil Engineering and Applied Mechanics, Montréal, QC H3A 2T5, Canada. Offers environmental engineering (M Eng, M Sc, PhD); fluid mechanics (M Sc); fluid mechanics and hydraulic engineering (M Eng, PhD); materials engineering (M Eng, PhD); rehabilitation of urban infrastructure (M Eng, PhD); soil behavior (M Eng, PhD); soil mechanics and foundations (M Eng, PhD); structures and structural mechanics (M Eng, PhD); water resources (M Sc); water resources engineering (M Eng, PhD).

Memorial University of Newfoundland, School of Graduate Studies, Interdisciplinary Program in Environmental Systems Engineering and Management, St. John's, NL A1C 5S7, Canada. Offers MA Sc. *Degree requirements:* For master's, project course. *Entrance requirements:* For master's, 2nd class engineering degree.

Mercer University, Graduate Studies, Macon Campus, School of Engineering, Macon, GA 31207-0003. Offers biomedical engineering (MSE); computer engineering (MSE); electrical engineering (MSE); engineering management (MSE); environmental engineering (MSE); environmental systems (MS); mechanical engineering (MSE); software engineering (MSE); software systems (MS); technical communications management (MS); technical management (MS). Part-time and evening/weekend programs available. Postbaccalaureate distance learning degree programs offered (no on-campus study). *Faculty:* 18 full-time (4 women), 1 part-time/adjunct (0 women). *Students:* 11 full-time (2 women), 100 part-time (22 women); includes 26 minority (13 Black or African American, non-Hispanic/Latino; 12 Asian, non-Hispanic/Latino; 1 Hispanic/Latino), 3 international. Average age 32. In 2010, 46 master's awarded. *Degree requirements:* For master's, thesis or alternative. *Entrance requirements:* For master's, minimum undergraduate GPA of 3.0. Additional exam requirements/recommendations for international students: Required—TOEFL. *Application deadline:* For fall admission, 7/1 for domestic students; for spring admission, 11/15 for domestic students. Applications are processed on a rolling basis. Application fee: $35 ($50 for international students). Electronic applications accepted. *Expenses:* Contact institution. *Financial support:* Federal Work-Study available. *Unit head:* Dr. Wade H. Shaw, Dean, 478-301-2459, Fax: 478-301-5593, E-mail: shaw_wh@mercer.edu. *Application contact:* Greg Lofton, Graduate Program Coordinator, 478-301-5480, Fax: 478-301-5434, E-mail: lofton_g@mercer.edu.

Michigan State University, The Graduate School, College of Engineering, Department of Civil and Environmental Engineering, East Lansing, MI 48824. Offers civil engineering (MS, PhD); environmental engineering (MS, PhD); environmental engineering-environmental toxicology (PhD). Part-time programs available. *Entrance requirements:* Additional exam requirements/recommendations for international students: Required—TOEFL. Electronic applications accepted.

Michigan Technological University, Graduate School, College of Engineering, Department of Civil and Environmental Engineering, Program in Environmental Engineering, Houghton, MI 49931. Offers ME, MS, PhD. Part-time programs available. Terminal master's awarded for partial completion of doctoral program. *Degree requirements:* For master's, comprehensive exam (for some programs), thesis (for some programs); for doctorate, comprehensive exam, thesis/dissertation. *Entrance requirements:* For master's, GRE (to be considered for university assistantship); for doctorate, GRE. Additional exam requirements/recommendations for international students: Required—TOEFL (minimum score 600 paper-based; 250 computer-based). Electronic applications accepted. *Expenses:* Contact institution.

Michigan Technological University, Graduate School, College of Engineering, Department of Civil and Environmental Engineering, Program in Environmental Engineering Science, Houghton, MI 49931. Offers MS. Part-time programs available. *Degree requirements:* For master's, comprehensive exam (for some programs), thesis (for some programs). *Entrance requirements:* For master's, GRE (to be considered for university assistantship). Additional exam requirements/recommendations for international students: Required—TOEFL (minimum score 600 paper-based; 250 computer-based). Electronic applications accepted. *Expenses:* Contact institution.

Milwaukee School of Engineering, Civil and Architectural Engineering and Construction Management Department, Program in Environmental Engineering, Milwaukee, WI 53202-3109. Offers MS. Part-time and evening/weekend programs available. *Faculty:* 2 full-time (1 woman), 7 part-time/adjunct (0 women). *Students:* 2 full-time (1 woman), 7 part-time (0 women). Average age 22. 11 applicants, 73% accepted, 3 enrolled. In 2010, 3 master's awarded. *Degree requirements:* For master's, design project. *Entrance requirements:* For master's, GRE General Test or GMAT, 2 letters of recommendation, BS in architectural, chemical, civil or mechanical engineering or a related field. Additional exam requirements/recommendations for international students: Required—TOEFL (minimum score 79 iBT). *Application deadline:* Applications are processed on a rolling basis. Application fee: $30. Electronic applications accepted. *Expenses:* Tuition: Full-time $17,550; part-time $650 per credit. One-time fee: $75. *Financial support:* In 2010–11, 4 students received support. Career-related internships or fieldwork available. Support available to part-time students. Financial award applicants required to submit FAFSA. *Faculty research:* Environmental systems. *Unit head:* Dr. Francis Manhuta, Director, 414-277-7599. *Application contact:* David E. Tietyen, Graduate Admissions Director, 800-332-6763, Fax: 414-277-7475, E-mail: wp@msoe.edu.

Missouri University of Science and Technology, Graduate School, Department of Civil, Architectural, and Environmental Engineering, Rolla, MO 65409. Offers civil engineering (MS, DE, PhD); construction engineering (MS, DE, PhD); environmental engineering (MS); fluid mechanics (MS, DE, PhD); geotechnical engineering (MS, DE, PhD); hydrology and hydraulic engineering (MS, DE, PhD). Part-time and evening/weekend programs available. Terminal master's awarded for partial completion of doctoral program. *Degree requirements:* For master's, thesis optional; for doctorate, comprehensive exam, thesis/dissertation. *Entrance requirements:* For master's, GRE General Test (minimum combined score 1100), minimum GPA of 3.0; for doctorate, GRE General Test (minimum score: verbal and quantitative 400, writing 3.5), minimum GPA of 3.0. Additional exam requirements/recommendations for international students: Required—TOEFL. Electronic applications accepted. *Faculty research:* Earthquake engineering, structural optimization and control systems, structural health monitoring/damage detection, soil-structure interaction, soil mechanics and foundation engineering.

Montana State University, College of Graduate Studies, College of Engineering, Department of Chemical and Biological Engineering, Bozeman, MT 59717. Offers chemical engineering (MS); engineering (PhD), including chemical engineering option, environmental engineering option; environmental engineering (MS). Part-time programs available. *Faculty:* 9 full-time (2 women), 2 part-time/adjunct (0 women). *Students:* 6 full-time (2 women), 13 part-time (7 women); includes 3 minority (1 American Indian or Alaska Native, non-Hispanic/Latino; 1 Asian, non-Hispanic/Latino; 1 Two or more races, non-Hispanic/Latino), 4 international. Average age 27. 9 applicants, 33% accepted, 3 enrolled. In 2010, 2 master's, 6 doctorates awarded. *Degree requirements:* For master's, comprehensive exam, thesis (for some programs); for doctorate, comprehensive exam, thesis/dissertation. *Entrance requirements:* For master's and doctorate, GRE General Test. Additional exam requirements/recommendations for international students: Required—TOEFL (minimum score 550 paper-based; 213 computer-based). *Application deadline:* For fall admission, 7/15 priority date for domestic students, 5/15 priority date for international students; for spring admission, 12/1 priority date for domestic students, 10/1 priority date for international students. Applications are processed on a rolling basis. Application fee: $30. Electronic applications accepted. *Expenses:* Tuition, state resident: full-time $5553.90. Tuition, nonresident: full-time $14,646. Required fees: $1233. *Financial support:* In 2010–11, 1 fellowship with full tuition reimbursement (averaging $30,000 per year), 17 research assistantships with full tuition reimbursements (averaging $20,000 per year), 2 teaching assistantships with full tuition reimbursements (averaging $11,000 per year) were awarded; health care benefits also available. Financial award application deadline: 3/1; financial award applicants required to submit FAFSA. *Faculty research:* Biofuels, extremophilic bioprocessing, and situ biocatalyzed heavy metal transformations; metabolic network analysis and engineering; magnetic resonance microscopy; modeling of biological systems; the development of protective coatings on planar solid oxide fuel cell (SOFC) metallic interconnects; characterizing corrosion mechanisms of materials in precisely-controlled exposures; testing materials in poly-crystalline silicon production environments; environmental biotechnology and bioremediation. Total annual research expenditures: $1.3 million. *Unit head:* Dr. Ron W. Larson, Head, 406-994-2221, Fax: 406-994-5308, E-mail: ronl@coe.montana.edu. *Application contact:* Dr. Carl A. Fox, Vice Provost for Graduate Education, 406-994-4145, Fax: 406-994-7433, E-mail: gradstudy@montana.edu.

Montana Tech of The University of Montana, Graduate School, Department of Environmental Engineering, Butte, MT 59701-8997. Offers MS. Part-time programs available. *Faculty:* 7 full-time (2 women), 1 part-time/adjunct (0 women). *Students:* 6 full-time (4 women). 5 applicants, 40% accepted, 2 enrolled. In 2010, 2 master's awarded. *Degree requirements:* For master's, thesis. *Entrance requirements:* For master's, GRE General Test, minimum GPA of 3.0. Additional exam requirements/recommendations for international students: Required—TOEFL (minimum score 525 paper-based; 195 computer-based; 71 iBT). *Application deadline:* For fall admission, 4/1 priority date for domestic students, 3/1 priority date for international students; for spring admission, 10/1 priority date for domestic students, 7/1 priority date for international students. Applications are processed on a rolling basis. Application fee: $30. Electronic applications accepted. *Expenses:* Tuition, state resident: full-time $5084. Tuition, nonresident: full-time $15,104. *Financial support:* In 2010–11, 5 students received support, including 4 teaching assistantships with partial tuition reimbursements available (averaging $4,500 per year); research assistantships with full tuition reimbursements available, career-related internships or fieldwork, tuition waivers (full and partial), and unspecified assistantships also available. Financial award application deadline: 4/1; financial award applicants required to submit FAFSA. *Faculty research:* Mine waste reclamation, modeling, air pollution control, wetlands, water pollution control. *Unit head:* Dr. Kumar Ganesan, Head, 406-496-4239, Fax: 406-496-4650, E-mail: kganesan@mtech.edu. *Application contact:* Fred Sullivan, Administrator, Graduate School, 406-496-4304, Fax: 406-496-4710, E-mail: fsullivan@mtech.edu.

National University, Academic Affairs, School of Engineering and Technology, Department of Applied Engineering, La Jolla, CA 92037-1011. Offers database administration (MS); engineering management (MS); environmental engineering (MS); homeland security and safety engineering (MS); system engineering (MS); wireless communications (MS). Part-time and evening/weekend programs available. Postbaccalaureate distance learning degree programs offered (no on-campus study). *Faculty:* 6 full-time (1 woman), 69 part-time/adjunct (12 women). *Students:* 82 full-time (16 women), 153 part-time (35 women); includes 87 minority (18 Black or African American, non-Hispanic/Latino; 1 American Indian or Alaska Native, non-Hispanic/Latino; 34 Asian, non-Hispanic/Latino; 28 Hispanic/Latino; 2 Native Hawaiian or other Pacific Islander, non-Hispanic/Latino; 4 Two or more races, non-Hispanic/Latino), 60 international. Average age 31. 166 applicants, 100% accepted, 106 enrolled. In 2010, 79 master's awarded. *Degree requirements:* For master's, thesis. *Entrance requirements:* For master's, interview, minimum GPA of 2.5. Additional exam requirements/recommendations for international students: Required—TOEFL (minimum score 550 paper-based; 213 computer-based; 79 iBT), IELTS (minimum score 6). *Application deadline:* Applications are processed on a rolling basis. Application fee: $60 ($65 for international students). Electronic applications accepted. *Expenses:* Tuition: Full-time $9450; part-time $350 per unit. Required fees: $350 per unit. One-time fee: $60. *Financial support:* Career-related internships or fieldwork, institutionally sponsored loans, scholarships/grants, and tuition waivers (partial) available. Support available to part-time students. Financial award application deadline: 6/30; financial award applicants required to submit FAFSA. *Unit head:* Dr. Shekar Viswanathan, Chair and Associate Professor, 858-309-8416, Fax: 858-309-3420, E-mail: sviswana@nu.edu. *Application contact:* Dominick Giovanniello, Associate Regional Dean—San Diego, 800-NAT-UNIV, Fax: 858-541-7792, E-mail: dgiovann@nu.edu.

New Jersey Institute of Technology, Office of Graduate Studies, Newark College of Engineering, Department of Civil and Environmental Engineering, Program in Environmental Engineering, Newark, NJ 07102. Offers MS, PhD. Part-time and evening/weekend programs available. *Students:* 27 full-time (11 women), 12 part-time (4 women); includes 2 Black or African American, non-Hispanic/Latino; 2 Asian, non-Hispanic/Latino; 4 Hispanic/Latino, 17 international. Average age 29. 94 applicants, 36% accepted, 13 enrolled. In 2010, 9 master's awarded. Terminal master's awarded for partial completion of doctoral program. *Degree requirements:* For master's, thesis or alternative; for doctorate, thesis/dissertation, residency. *Entrance requirements:* For master's, GRE General Test; for doctorate, GRE General Test, minimum graduate GPA of 3.5. Additional exam requirements/recommendations for international students: Required—TOEFL (minimum score 550 paper-based; 213 computer-based; 79 iBT). *Application deadline:* For fall admission, 6/5 priority date for domestic students, 4/1 for international students; for spring admission, 11/15 for domestic and international students. Applications are processed on a rolling basis. Application fee: $65. Electronic applications accepted. *Expenses:* Tuition, state resident: full-time $14,724; part-time $818 per credit. Tuition, nonresident: full-time $20,304; part-time $1128 per credit. Required fees: $2272; $209 per credit. $103 per semester. One-time fee: $312 full-time; $212 part-time. *Financial support:* Fellowships with full and partial tuition reimbursements, research assistantships with full and partial tuition reimbursements, teaching assistantships with full and partial tuition reimbursements, career-related internships or fieldwork, Federal Work-Study, institutionally sponsored loans, and unspecified assistantships available. Financial award application deadline: 3/15. *Faculty research:* Water resources engineering, solid and hazardous waste management. *Unit head:* Dr. Taha F. Marhaba, Chair, 973-642-4599, E-mail: taha.f.marhaba@njit.edu. *Application contact:* Kathryn Kelly, Director of Admissions, 973-596-3300, Fax: 973-596-3461, E-mail: admissions@njit.edu.

New Mexico Institute of Mining and Technology, Graduate Studies, Department of Environmental Engineering, Socorro, NM 87801. Offers environmental engineering (MS), including air quality engineering and science, hazardous waste engineering, water quality engineering and science. *Degree requirements:* For master's, thesis. *Entrance requirements:* For master's, GRE General Test. Additional exam requirements/recommendations for international students: Required—TOEFL (minimum score 540 paper-based; 207 computer-based). *Faculty research:* Air quality, hazardous waste management, wastewater management and treatment, site remediation.

New Mexico State University, Graduate School, College of Engineering, Department of Civil Engineering, Las Cruces, NM 88003-8001. Offers civil engineering (MSCE, PhD); environmental engineering (MS Env E). Part-time programs available. Postbaccalaureate distance learning degree programs offered. *Faculty:* 13 full-time (2 women), 2 part-time/adjunct (1 woman). *Students:* 52 full-time (17 women), 16 part-time (4 women); includes 18 minority (1 American Indian or Alaska Native, non-Hispanic/Latino; 1 Asian, non-Hispanic/Latino; 16 Hispanic/Latino), 30 international. Average age 30. 52 applicants, 77% accepted, 15 enrolled. In 2010, 24 master's, 4 doctorates awarded. *Degree requirements:* For master's, thesis (for some programs); for doctorate, comprehensive exam (for some programs), thesis/dissertation. *Entrance requirements:* For master's, BS in engineering, minimum GPA of 3.0; for doctorate, qualifying exam, BS in engineering, minimum GPA of 3.0. Additional exam requirements/recommendations for international students: Required—TOEFL (minimum score 550 paper-based; 213 computer-based; 79 iBT), IELTS (minimum score 6). *Application deadline:* For fall admission, 4/1 priority date for domestic and international students; for spring admission, 9/1 priority date for domestic and international students. Applications are processed on a rolling basis. Application fee: $30 ($50 for international students). Electronic applications accepted. *Expenses:* Tuition, state resident: full-time $4536; part-time $242 per credit. Tuition, nonresident: full-time $15,816; part-time $712 per credit. Required fees: $636 per term. *Financial support:* In 2010–11, 13 research assistantships (averaging $12,766 per year), 32 teaching assistantships (averaging $1,095 per year) were awarded; fellowships, career-related internships or fieldwork, Federal Work-Study, and health care benefits also available. Support available to part-time students. Financial award application deadline: 3/1. *Faculty research:* Structural engineering, water resources engineering, environmental engineering, geotechnical engineering, hydraulics/hydrology. *Unit head:* Dr. Adrian Hanson, Interim Head, 575-646-3801, E-mail: athanson@nmsu.edu. *Application contact:* Dr. Adrian Hanson, Interim Head, 575-646-3801, E-mail: athanson@nmsu.edu.

New York Institute of Technology, Graduate Division, School of Engineering and Computing Sciences, Program in Environmental Technology, Old Westbury, NY 11568-8000. Offers MS. Part-time and evening/weekend programs available. *Students:* 25 full-time (12 women), 27 part-time (10 women); includes 11 minority (7 Black or African American, non-Hispanic/Latino; 1 Asian, non-Hispanic/Latino; 3 Hispanic/Latino), 24 international. Average age 29. In 2010, 15 master's awarded. *Degree requirements:* For master's, thesis or alternative. *Entrance requirements:* For master's, minimum QPA of 2.85. Additional exam requirements/recommendations for international students: Required—TOEFL (minimum score 550 paper-based; 213 computer-based). *Application deadline:* For fall admission, 7/1 priority date for

domestic students; for spring admission, 12/1 priority date for domestic students. Applications are processed on a rolling basis. Application fee: $50. Electronic applications accepted. *Expenses:* Tuition: Part-time $835 per credit. *Financial support:* Fellowships, research assistantships with partial tuition reimbursements, career-related internships or fieldwork, institutionally sponsored loans, tuition waivers (full and partial), and unspecified assistantships available. Support available to part-time students. Financial award applicants required to submit FAFSA. *Faculty research:* Development and testing of methodology to assess health risks and environmental impacts from separate sanitary sewage, introduction of technology innovation (including geographical information systems). *Unit head:* Stanley Greenwald, Chair, 516-686-7717, Fax: 516-686-7919, E-mail: sgreenwa@nyit.edu. *Application contact:* Dr. Jacquelyn Nealon, Vice President for Enrollment Services, 516-686-7925, Fax: 516-686-7597, E-mail: jnealon@nyit.edu.

North Dakota State University, College of Graduate and Interdisciplinary Studies, College of Engineering and Architecture, Department of Civil Engineering, Fargo, ND 58108. Offers civil engineering (MS, PhD); environmental engineering (MS, PhD); transportation and logistics (PhD). PhD in transportation and logistics offered jointly with Upper Great Plains Transportation Institute. Part-time programs available. Postbaccalaureate distance learning degree programs offered (minimal on-campus study). *Students:* 28 full-time (2 women), 19 part-time (3 women); includes 1 American Indian or Alaska Native, non-Hispanic/Latino, 24 international. 37 applicants, 57% accepted, 12 enrolled. In 2010, 1 master's, 3 doctorates awarded. *Degree requirements:* For master's, thesis; for doctorate, comprehensive exam, thesis/dissertation. *Entrance requirements:* Additional exam requirements/recommendations for international students: Required—TOEFL (minimum score 525 paper-based; 197 computer-based; 71 iBT). *Application deadline:* For fall admission, 7/1 priority date for domestic students, 1/15 priority date for international students; for spring admission, 5/1 priority date for international students. Applications are processed on a rolling basis. Application fee: $45 ($60 for international students). *Financial support:* Fellowships with full tuition reimbursements, research assistantships with full tuition reimbursements, teaching assistantships with full tuition reimbursements, career-related internships or fieldwork, Federal Work-Study, and institutionally sponsored loans available. Support available to part-time students. Financial award application deadline: 1/15. *Faculty research:* Wastewater, solid waste, composites, nanotechnology. Total annual research expenditures: $800,000. *Unit head:* Dr. Eakalak Khan, Chair, 701-231-7244, Fax: 701-231-6185, E-mail: eakalak.khan@ndsu.edu. *Application contact:* Dr. Kalpana Katti, Professor and Graduate Program Coordinator, 701-231-9504, Fax: 701-231-6185, E-mail: kalpana.katti@ndsu.edu.

Northeastern University, College of Engineering, Department of Civil and Environmental Engineering, Boston, MA 02115-5096. Offers MS, PhD. Part-time programs available. *Faculty:* 15 full-time (2 women), 2 part-time/adjunct (0 women). *Students:* 97 full-time (41 women), 38 part-time (14 women). 286 applicants, 67% accepted, 56 enrolled. In 2010, 23 master's, 3 doctorates awarded. *Degree requirements:* For master's, thesis optional; for doctorate, thesis/dissertation, departmental qualifying exam. *Entrance requirements:* For master's and doctorate, GRE General Test. Additional exam requirements/recommendations for international students: Required—TOEFL (minimum score 550 paper-based; 213 computer-based; 80 iBT). *Application deadline:* For fall admission, 1/15 priority date for domestic and international students. Applications are processed on a rolling basis. Application fee: $50. Electronic applications accepted. *Financial support:* In 2010–11, 33 students received support, including 21 research assistantships with full tuition reimbursements available (averaging $18,325 per year), 16 teaching assistantships with full tuition reimbursements available (averaging $18,325 per year); career-related internships or fieldwork, Federal Work-Study, scholarships/grants, tuition waivers (full), and unspecified assistantships also available. Support available to part-time students. Financial award application deadline: 1/15; financial award applicants required to submit FAFSA. *Faculty research:* Earthquake engineering, geotechnical and geoenvironmental engineering, structural engineering, transportation engineering, environmental engineering. *Unit head:* Dr. Jerome Jaffar, Chairman, 617-373-2444, Fax: 617-373-4419. *Application contact:* Jeffery Hengel, Admissions Specialist, 617-373-2711, Fax: 617-373-2501, E-mail: grad-eng@coe.neu.edu.

Northern Arizona University, Graduate College, College of Engineering, Forestry and Natural Sciences, Programs in Engineering, Flagstaff, AZ 86011. Offers civil and environmental engineering (M Eng); civil engineering (MSE); computer science (MSE); electrical engineering (M Eng, MSE); engineering (M Eng, MSE); environmental engineering (M Eng, MSE); mechanical engineering (M Eng, MSE). Part-time programs available. Postbaccalaureate distance learning degree programs offered (no on-campus study). *Faculty:* 42 full-time (12 women). *Students:* 19 full-time (3 women), 15 part-time (2 women); includes 6 minority (2 American Indian or Alaska Native, non-Hispanic/Latino; 3 Hispanic/Latino; 1 Two or more races, non-Hispanic/Latino), 7 international. Average age 28. 21 applicants, 48% accepted, 4 enrolled. In 2010, 15 master's awarded. *Degree requirements:* For master's, thesis. *Entrance requirements:* For master's, GRE General Test. Additional exam requirements/recommendations for international students: Required—TOEFL (minimum score 550 paper-based; 213 computer-based; 80 iBT), IELTS (minimum score 7). *Application deadline:* For fall admission, 3/1 priority date for domestic and international students; for spring admission, 9/15 priority date for domestic and international students. Applications are processed on a rolling basis. Application fee: $65. Electronic applications accepted. *Financial support:* In 2010–11, 3 research assistantships with partial tuition reimbursements (averaging $14,541 per year), 12 teaching assistantships with partial tuition reimbursements (averaging $12,863 per year) were awarded; career-related internships or fieldwork, Federal Work-Study, scholarships/grants, health care benefits, and unspecified assistantships also available. Financial award applicants required to submit FAFSA. *Unit head:* Dr. Ernesto Penado, Chair, 928-523-9453, Fax: 928-523-2300, E-mail: ernesto.penado@nau.edu. *Application contact:* Natasha Kypfer, Program Coordinator, 928-523-1447, Fax: 928-523-2300, E-mail: egrmasters@nau.edu.

Northwestern University, McCormick School of Engineering and Applied Science, Department of Civil and Environmental Engineering, Evanston, IL 60208-3109. Offers environmental engineering and science (MS, PhD); geotechnical engineering (MS, PhD); mechanics of materials and solids (MS, PhD); project management (MS, PhD); structural engineering and materials (MS, PhD); theoretical and applied mechanics (MS, PhD), including fluid mechanics, solid mechanics; transportation systems analysis and planning (MS, PhD). MS and PhD admissions and degrees offered through The Graduate School. Part-time programs available. Terminal master's awarded for partial completion of doctoral program. *Degree requirements:* For master's, thesis (for some programs); for doctorate, thesis/dissertation. *Entrance requirements:* For master's and doctorate, GRE General Test, minimum 2 letters of recommendation, transcripts from all academic institutions attended. Additional exam requirements/recommendations for international students: Required—TOEFL (minimum score 600 paper-based; 250 computer-based; 100 iBT), IELTS (minimum score 7). Electronic applications accepted. *Faculty research:* Environmental engineering and science, geotechnics, mechanics of materials and solids, structural engineering and materials, transportation systems analysis and planning.

Norwich University, School of Graduate and Continuing Studies, Program in Civil Engineering, Northfield, VT 05663. Offers construction management (MCE); geo-technical (MCE); structural (MCE); water/environmental (MCE). Evening/weekend programs available. *Faculty:* 20 full-time (3 women). *Students:* 78 full-time (19 women); includes 5 Black or African American, non-Hispanic/Latino; 4 Asian, non-Hispanic/Latino; 7 Hispanic/Latino. Average age 35. 107 applicants, 88% accepted, 90 enrolled. In 2010, 78 master's awarded. *Entrance requirements:* For master's, minimum GPA of 2.75. Additional exam requirements/recommendations for international students: Required—TOEFL (minimum score 550 paper-based; 213 computer-based; 83 iBT). *Application deadline:* For fall admission, 8/10 for domestic and international students; for spring admission, 2/6 for domestic and international students. Application fee: $50. *Expenses:* Tuition: Full-time $17,380; part-time $645 per credit. Tuition and fees vary according to program. *Financial support:* Scholarships/grants available. Financial award applicants required to submit FAFSA. *Unit head:* Dr. Thomas Descoteaux, Program Director, 802-485-2730, Fax: 802-485-2533,

Environmental Engineering

Norwich University (continued)
E-mail: tdescote@norwich.edu. *Application contact:* Shelley W. Brown, Director of Business Partnership, 802-485-2784, Fax: 802-485-2533, E-mail: sbrown@norwich.edu.

OGI School of Science & Engineering at Oregon Health & Science University, Graduate Studies, Department of Environmental and Biomolecular Systems, Beaverton, OR 97006-8921. Offers biochemistry and molecular biology (MS, PhD); environmental health systems (MS); environmental information technology (MS, PhD); environmental science and engineering (MS, PhD). Part-time programs available. Terminal master's awarded for partial completion of doctoral program. *Degree requirements:* For master's, thesis optional; for doctorate, comprehensive exam, oral defense of dissertation. *Entrance requirements:* For master's and doctorate, GRE General Test. Additional exam requirements/recommendations for international students: Required—TOEFL. Electronic applications accepted. *Faculty research:* Air and water science, hydrogeology, estuarine and coastal modeling, environmental microbiology, contaminant transport, biochemistry, biomolecular systems.

Ohio University, Graduate College, Russ College of Engineering and Technology, Department of Civil Engineering, Athens, OH 45701-2979. Offers civil engineering (PhD); construction (MS); environmental (MS); geotechnical and geoenvironmental (MS); mechanics (MS); structures (MS); transportation (MS); water resources and structures (MS). Part-time programs available. *Students:* 29 full-time (6 women), 5 part-time (1 woman); includes 2 minority (1 Hispanic/Latino; 1 Two or more races, non-Hispanic/Latino), 16 international. 52 applicants, 83% accepted, 14 enrolled. In 2010, 7 master's awarded. *Degree requirements:* For master's, comprehensive exam (for some programs), thesis or alternative; for doctorate, comprehensive exam, thesis/dissertation. *Entrance requirements:* For master's, GRE General Test, minimum GPA of 3.0, 3 letters of recommendation; for doctorate, GRE General Test. Additional exam requirements/recommendations for international students: Required—TOEFL (minimum score 550 paper-based; 80 iBT) or IELTS (minimum score 6.5). *Application deadline:* For fall admission, 5/1 priority date for domestic students, 2/1 priority date for international students; for winter admission, 8/1 priority date for domestic students, 4/1 priority date for international students; for spring admission, 2/1 priority date for domestic students, 7/1 priority date for international students. Applications are processed on a rolling basis. Application fee: $50 ($55 for international students). Electronic applications accepted. *Financial support:* Research assistantships with full tuition reimbursements, teaching assistantships with full tuition reimbursements, Federal Work-Study, institutionally sponsored loans, scholarships/grants, and unspecified assistantships available. Financial award application deadline: 3/15; financial award applicants required to submit FAFSA. *Faculty research:* Noise abatement, materials and environment, highway infrastructure, subsurface investigation (pavements, pipes, bridges). *Unit head:* Dr. Gayle F. Mitchell, Chair, 740-593-0430, Fax: 740-593-0625, E-mail: mitchelg@ohio.edu. *Application contact:* Dr. Shad M. Sargand, Graduate Chair, 740-593-1465, Fax: 740-593-0625, E-mail: sargand@ohio.edu.

Oklahoma State University, College of Agricultural Science and Natural Resources, Department of Biosystems and Agricultural Engineering, Stillwater, OK 74078. Offers biosystems engineering (MS, PhD); environmental and natural resources (MS, PhD). *Faculty:* 22 full-time (4 women), 4 part-time/adjunct (0 women). *Students:* 23 full-time (10 women), 45 part-time (16 women); includes 2 American Indian or Alaska Native, non-Hispanic/Latino; 1 Asian, non-Hispanic/Latino; 2 Hispanic/Latino, 36 international. Average age 30. 58 applicants, 40% accepted, 14 enrolled. In 2010, 4 master's, 3 doctorates awarded. *Degree requirements:* For master's, thesis; for doctorate, comprehensive exam, thesis/dissertation. *Entrance requirements:* For master's and doctorate, GRE or GMAT. Additional exam requirements/recommendations for international students: Required—TOEFL (minimum score 550 paper-based; 79 iBT). *Application deadline:* For fall admission, 3/1 priority date for international students; for spring admission, 8/1 priority date for international students. Applications are processed on a rolling basis. Application fee: $40 ($75 for international students). Electronic applications accepted. *Expenses:* Tuition, state resident: full-time $3716; part-time $154.85 per credit hour. Tuition, nonresident: full-time $14,892; part-time $621 per credit hour. Required fees: $2044; $85.20 per credit hour. One-time fee: $50. Tuition and fees vary according to course load and campus/location. *Financial support:* In 2010–11, 48 research assistantships (averaging $17,561 per year), 1 teaching assistantship (averaging $6,000 per year) were awarded; career-related internships or fieldwork, Federal Work-Study, scholarships/grants, health care benefits, tuition waivers (partial), and unspecified assistantships also available. Support available to part-time students. Financial award application deadline: 3/1; financial award applicants required to submit FAFSA. *Unit head:* Dr. Ronald L. Elliot, Head, 405-744-5431, Fax: 405-744-6059. *Application contact:* Dr. Gordon Emslie, Dean, 405-744-6368, Fax: 405-744-0355, E-mail: grad-i@okstate.edu.

Oklahoma State University, College of Engineering, Architecture and Technology, School of Civil and Environmental Engineering, Stillwater, OK 74078. Offers civil engineering (MS); environmental engineering (PhD). *Faculty:* 15 full-time (1 woman), 3 part-time/adjunct (0 women). *Students:* 40 full-time (11 women), 45 part-time (7 women); includes 1 Black or African American, non-Hispanic/Latino; 3 American Indian or Alaska Native, non-Hispanic/Latino; 2 Asian, non-Hispanic/Latino; 1 Hispanic/Latino, 46 international. Average age 28. 100 applicants, 36% accepted, 15 enrolled. In 2010, 25 master's, 1 doctorate awarded. *Degree requirements:* For master's, thesis or alternative; for doctorate, comprehensive exam, thesis/dissertation. *Entrance requirements:* For master's and doctorate, GRE or GMAT. Additional exam requirements/recommendations for international students: Required—TOEFL (minimum score 550 paper-based; 79 iBT). *Application deadline:* For fall admission, 3/1 priority date for international students; for spring admission, 8/1 priority date for international students. Applications are processed on a rolling basis. Application fee: $40 ($75 for international students). Electronic applications accepted. *Expenses:* Tuition, state resident: full-time $3716; part-time $154.85 per credit hour. Tuition, nonresident: full-time $14,892; part-time $621 per credit hour. Required fees: $2044; $85.20 per credit hour. One-time fee: $50. Tuition and fees vary according to course load and campus/location. *Financial support:* In 2010–11, 24 research assistantships (averaging $13,245 per year), 16 teaching assistantships (averaging $10,681 per year) were awarded; career-related internships or fieldwork, Federal Work-Study, scholarships/grants, health care benefits, tuition waivers (partial), and unspecified assistantships also available. Support available to part-time students. Financial award application deadline: 3/1; financial award applicants required to submit FAFSA. *Unit head:* Dr. John Veenstra, Head, 405-744-5190, Fax: 405-744-7554. *Application contact:* Dr. Gordon Emslie, Dean, 405-744-6368, Fax: 405-744-0355, E-mail: grad-i@okstate.edu.

Old Dominion University, Frank Batten College of Engineering and Technology, Program in Civil and Environmental Engineering, Norfolk, VA 23529. Offers D Eng, PhD. Part-time and evening/weekend programs available. Postbaccalaureate distance learning degree programs offered (minimal on-campus study). *Faculty:* 11 full-time (1 woman), 10 part-time/adjunct (2 women). *Students:* 3 part-time (0 women). Average age 55. 15 applicants, 100% accepted. In 2010, 2 doctorates awarded. *Degree requirements:* For doctorate, thesis/dissertation, candidacy exam. *Entrance requirements:* For doctorate, GRE, minimum GPA of 3.5. Additional exam requirements/recommendations for international students: Required—TOEFL (minimum score 550 paper-based; 213 computer-based; 80 iBT). *Application deadline:* For fall admission, 6/1 priority date for domestic students, 4/15 priority date for international students; for spring admission, 11/1 priority date for domestic students, 10/1 priority date for international students. Applications are processed on a rolling basis. Application fee: $40. Electronic applications accepted. *Expenses:* Tuition, state resident: full-time $8592; part-time $358 per credit. Tuition, nonresident: full-time $21,672; part-time $903 per credit. Required fees: $119 per semester. One-time fee: $50. *Financial support:* In 2010–11, 5 research assistantships with full and partial tuition reimbursements (averaging $14,626 per year), 10 teaching assistantships with full and partial tuition reimbursements (averaging $15,622 per year) were awarded; scholarships/grants and unspecified assistantships also available. Support available to part-time students. Financial award application deadline: 4/1. *Faculty research:* Structural engineering, coastal engineering, environmental engineering, geotechnical engineering, water resources, transportation engineering. Total annual research expenditures: $597,143. *Unit head:* Dr. Isao Ishibashi, Graduate Program Director, 757-683-4641, Fax: 757-683-5354, E-mail: cegpd@odu.edu. *Application contact:* Dr. Isao Ishibashi, Graduate Program Director, 757-683-4641, Fax: 757-683-5354, E-mail: cegpd@odu.edu.

Old Dominion University, Frank Batten College of Engineering and Technology, Program in Environmental Engineering, Norfolk, VA 23529. Offers ME, MS. Part-time and evening/weekend programs available. Postbaccalaureate distance learning degree programs offered (minimal on-campus study). *Faculty:* 11 full-time (1 woman), 10 part-time/adjunct (2 women). *Students:* 9 full-time (3 women), 24 part-time (8 women); includes 6 minority (5 Black or African American, non-Hispanic/Latino; 1 American Indian or Alaska Native, non-Hispanic/Latino), 8 international. Average age 31. 19 applicants, 89% accepted, 7 enrolled. In 2010, 12 master's awarded. *Degree requirements:* For master's, comprehensive exam, thesis optional. *Entrance requirements:* For master's, GRE, minimum GPA of 3.0. Additional exam requirements/recommendations for international students: Required—TOEFL (minimum score 550 paper-based; 213 computer-based; 80 iBT). *Application deadline:* For fall admission, 6/1 priority date for domestic students, 4/15 priority date for international students; for spring admission, 11/1 priority date for domestic students, 10/1 priority date for international students. Applications are processed on a rolling basis. Application fee: $40. Electronic applications accepted. *Expenses:* Tuition, state resident: full-time $8592; part-time $358 per credit. Tuition, nonresident: full-time $21,672; part-time $903 per credit. Required fees: $119 per semester. One-time fee: $50. *Financial support:* In 2010–11, 1 research assistantship with partial tuition reimbursement (averaging $2,640 per year), 2 teaching assistantships with partial tuition reimbursements (averaging $1,800 per year) were awarded; scholarships/grants and unspecified assistantships also available. Support available to part-time students. Financial award application deadline: 4/1; financial award applicants required to submit FAFSA. *Faculty research:* Aquatic chemistry, physiochemical treatment, waste water treatment, hazardous waste treatment, environmental microbiology. Total annual research expenditures: $597,143. *Unit head:* Dr. Isao Ishibashi, Graduate Program Director, 757-683-4641, Fax: 757-683-5354, E-mail: cegpd@odu.edu. *Application contact:* Dr. Linda Vahala, Associate Dean, 757-683-3789, Fax: 757-683-4898, E-mail: lvahala@odu.edu.

Oregon Health & Science University, School of Medicine, Graduate Programs in Medicine, Department of Environmental and Biomolecular Systems, Portland, OR 97239-3098. Offers biochemistry and molecular biology (MS, PhD); environmental science and engineering (MS, PhD). Part-time programs available. *Faculty:* 14 full-time (4 women), 1 (woman) part-time/adjunct. *Students:* 21 full-time (12 women), 25 part-time (12 women); includes 1 Black or African American, non-Hispanic/Latino; 3 American Indian or Alaska Native, non-Hispanic/Latino; 5 Asian, non-Hispanic/Latino; 3 Hispanic/Latino, 8 international. Average age 33. 45 applicants, 60% accepted, 11 enrolled. In 2010, 8 master's, 2 doctorates awarded. Terminal master's awarded for partial completion of doctoral program. *Degree requirements:* For master's, thesis (for some programs); for doctorate, comprehensive exam, thesis/dissertation. *Entrance requirements:* For master's and doctorate, GRE General Test (minimum scores: 500 Verbal/600 Quantitative/4.5 Analytical) or MCAT (for some programs). Additional exam requirements/recommendations for international students: Required—TOEFL. *Application deadline:* For fall admission, 7/15 for domestic students, 5/15 for international students; for winter admission, 10/15 for domestic students, 9/15 for international students; for spring admission, 1/15 for domestic students, 12/15 for international students. Applications are processed on a rolling basis. Application fee: $65. Electronic applications accepted. *Financial support:* Health care benefits and full tuition and stipends available. *Unit head:* Paul Tratnyek, PhD, Program Director, 503-748-1070, E-mail: info@ebs.ogi.edu. *Application contact:* Nancy Christie, Program Coordinator, 503-748-1070, E-mail: info@ebs.ogi.edu.

Oregon State University, Graduate School, College of Engineering, School of Civil and Construction Engineering, Corvallis, OR 97331. Offers civil engineering (MS, PhD); coastal and ocean engineering (M Oc E, PhD); coastal engineering (MS); construction engineering management (MBE, PhD); engineering (M Eng, MAIS); geotechnical engineering (MS, PhD); structural engineering (MS, PhD); transportation engineering (MS, PhD); water engineering (MS, PhD). Part-time programs available. Terminal master's awarded for partial completion of doctoral program. *Degree requirements:* For master's, thesis or alternative; for doctorate, one foreign language, thesis/dissertation. *Entrance requirements:* For master's, GRE General Test, minimum GPA of 3.0 in last 90 hours (3.5 for MS); for doctorate, GRE General Test, minimum GPA of 3.0 in last 90 hours of undergraduate course work. Additional exam requirements/recommendations for international students: Required—TOEFL (minimum score 580 paper-based; 237 computer-based). *Faculty research:* Hazardous waste management, carbon cycling, wave forces on structures, pavement design, seismic analysis.

Penn State University Park, Graduate School, College of Engineering, Department of Civil and Environmental Engineering, State College, University Park, PA 16802-1503. Offers M Eng, MS, PhD.

Polytechnic Institute of NYU, Department of Civil Engineering, Major in Environmental Engineering, Brooklyn, NY 11201-2990. Offers MS. Part-time and evening/weekend programs available. *Students:* 12 full-time (5 women), 2 part-time (1 woman); includes 1 Black or African American, non-Hispanic/Latino; 1 Asian, non-Hispanic/Latino, 11 international. Average age 25. 28 applicants, 54% accepted, 6 enrolled. In 2010, 16 master's awarded. *Degree requirements:* For master's, comprehensive exam (for some programs), thesis (for some programs). *Entrance requirements:* Additional exam requirements/recommendations for international students: Required—TOEFL (minimum score 550 paper-based; 213 computer-based; 80 iBT); Recommended—IELTS (minimum score 6.5). *Application deadline:* For fall admission, 7/31 priority date for domestic students, 4/30 priority date for international students; for spring admission, 12/31 priority date for domestic students, 10/30 priority date for international students. Applications are processed on a rolling basis. Application fee: $75. Electronic applications accepted. *Expenses:* Tuition: Full-time $21,492; part-time $1194 per credit. Required fees: $385 per semester. Tuition and fees vary according to course load. *Financial support:* Fellowships, research assistantships, teaching assistantships, institutionally sponsored loans, scholarships/grants, and unspecified assistantships available. Support available to part-time students. Financial award applicants required to submit FAFSA. *Unit head:* Dr. Lawrence Chiarelli, Head, 718-260-4040, Fax: 718-260-3433, E-mail: lchiarel@poly.edu. *Application contact:* JeanCarlo Bonilla, Director, Graduate Enrollment Management, 718-260-3182, Fax: 718-260-3624, E-mail: gradinfo@poly.edu.

Polytechnic Institute of NYU, Long Island Graduate Center, Graduate Programs, Department of Civil Engineering, Major in Environmental Engineering, Melville, NY 11747. Offers MS. *Degree requirements:* For master's, comprehensive exam, thesis. *Entrance requirements:* Additional exam requirements/recommendations for international students: Required—TOEFL (minimum score 550 paper-based; 213 computer-based; 80 iBT); Recommended—IELTS (minimum score 6.5). *Application deadline:* For fall admission, 7/31 priority date for domestic students, 4/30 priority date for international students; for spring admission, 12/31 priority date for domestic students, 11/30 priority date for international students. Applications are processed on a rolling basis. Application fee: $75. Electronic applications accepted. *Expenses:* Tuition: Full-time $21,492; part-time $1194 per credit. Required fees: $385 per semester. Tuition and fees vary according to course load. *Financial support:* Institutionally sponsored loans, scholarships/grants, and unspecified assistantships available. Support available to part-time students. Financial award applicants required to submit FAFSA. *Unit head:* Dr. Roger Peter Roess, Department Head, 718-260-3018, E-mail: rroess@poly.edu. *Application contact:* JeanCarlo Bonilla, Director of Graduate Enrollment Management, 718-260-3182, Fax: 718-260-3624, E-mail: gradinfo@poly.edu.

Polytechnic University of Puerto Rico, Miami Campus, Graduate School, Miami, FL 33166. Offers accounting (MBA); business administration (MBA); construction management (MEM); environmental management (MEM); finance (MBA); human resources management (MBA); logistics and supply chain management (MBA); management of international enterprises (MBA); manufacturing management (MEM); marketing management (MBA); project management

(MBA). Part-time and evening/weekend programs available. Postbaccalaureate distance learning degree programs offered (no on-campus study). *Entrance requirements:* For master's, minimum GPA of 3.0. Electronic applications accepted.

Polytechnic University of Puerto Rico, Orlando Campus, Graduate School, Winter Park, FL 32792. Offers accounting (MBA); business administration (MBA); construction management (MEM); engineering management (MEM); environmental management (MEM); finance (MBA); human resources management (MBA); management of international enterprises (MBA); management of technology (MBA); manufacturing management (MEM). Part-time and evening/weekend programs available. Postbaccalaureate distance learning degree programs offered (no on-campus study). *Entrance requirements:* For master's, minimum GPA of 3.0. Electronic applications accepted.

Portland State University, Graduate Studies, Maseeh College of Engineering and Computer Science, Department of Civil and Environmental Engineering, Portland, OR 97207-0751. Offers civil and environmental engineering (M Eng, MS, PhD); civil and environmental engineering management (M Eng); environmental sciences and resources (PhD); systems science (PhD). Part-time and evening/weekend programs available. *Faculty:* 13 full-time (2 women), 3 part-time/adjunct (1 woman). *Students:* 48 full-time (17 women), 47 part-time (15 women); includes 1 Black or African American, non-Hispanic/Latino; 8 Asian, non-Hispanic/Latino; 5 Hispanic/Latino, 16 international. Average age 30. 98 applicants, 66% accepted, 32 enrolled. In 2010, 8 master's awarded. *Degree requirements:* For master's, thesis or alternative, oral exam; for doctorate, one foreign language, thesis/dissertation, oral and written exams. *Entrance requirements:* For master's, minimum GPA of 3.0 in upper-division course work, BS in civil engineering or allied field; for doctorate, GRE General Test, GRE Subject Test, minimum GPA of 3.0 in upper-division course work, master's in civil and environmental engineering, 2 years full-time graduate work beyond master's degree. Additional exam requirements/recommendations for international students: Required—TOEFL (minimum score 550 paper-based; 213 computer-based). *Application deadline:* For fall admission, 4/1 for domestic students, 4/11 for international students; for winter admission, 9/1 for domestic and international students; for spring admission, 11/1 for domestic and international students. Applications are processed on a rolling basis. Application fee: $50. *Expenses:* Tuition, state resident: full-time $8505; part-time $315 per credit. Tuition, nonresident: full-time $13,284; part-time $492 per credit. Required fees: $1482; $21 per credit. $99 per term. One-time fee: $120. Part-time tuition and fees vary according to course load and program. *Financial support:* In 2010–11, 15 research assistantships with tuition reimbursements (averaging $11,169 per year), 1 teaching assistantship with full tuition reimbursement (averaging $19,012 per year) were awarded; career-related internships or fieldwork, Federal Work-Study, scholarships/grants, and unspecified assistantships also available. Support available to part-time students. Financial award application deadline: 3/1; financial award applicants required to submit FAFSA. *Faculty research:* Structures, water resources, geotechnical engineering, environmental engineering, transportation. Total annual research expenditures: $2.4 million. *Unit head:* Scott Wells, Chair, 503-725-4282, Fax: 503-725-4298, E-mail: wellss@pdx.edu. *Application contact:* Marianne Stupfel-Wallace, Information Contact, 503-725-4244, Fax: 503-725-4298, E-mail: ceedept@cecs.pdx.edu.

Rensselaer Polytechnic Institute, Graduate School, School of Engineering, Program in Environmental Engineering, Troy, NY 12180-3590. Offers M Eng, MS, PhD. Part-time programs available. *Faculty:* 4 full-time (1 woman), 1 part-time/adjunct (0 women). *Students:* 10 full-time (4 women), 1 part-time (0 women), 1 international. Average age 25. 34 applicants, 12% accepted, 1 enrolled. In 2010, 5 master's, 3 doctorates awarded. Terminal master's awarded for partial completion of doctoral program. *Degree requirements:* For master's, thesis (for some programs); for doctorate, thesis/dissertation. *Entrance requirements:* For master's and doctorate, GRE. Additional exam requirements/recommendations for international students: Required—TOEFL (minimum score 570 paper-based; 230 computer-based; 89 iBT), IELTS (minimum score 6.5). *Application deadline:* For fall admission, 1/15 priority date for domestic students, 1/15 for international students; for spring admission, 8/15 for domestic and international students. Applications are processed on a rolling basis. Application fee: $75. Electronic applications accepted. *Expenses:* Tuition: Full-time $39,600; part-time $1650 per credit. Required fees: $1896. *Financial support:* In 2010–11, fellowships with full tuition reimbursements (averaging $16,500 per year), 1 research assistantship with full tuition reimbursement (averaging $16,500 per year), 2 teaching assistantships with full tuition reimbursements (averaging $16,500 per year) were awarded; career-related internships or fieldwork, institutionally sponsored loans, and tuition waivers (full and partial) also available. Financial award application deadline: 2/1. *Faculty research:* Water treatment, bioremediation of hazardous wastes, environmental systems. Total annual research expenditures: $44,940. *Unit head:* Dr. Chris Letchford, Head, 518-276-6362, Fax: 518-276-4833, E-mail: letchc@rpi.edu. *Application contact:* Kimberly Boyce, Administrator, 518-276-6941, Fax: 518-276-4833, E-mail: boycek@rpi.edu.

Rice University, Graduate Programs, George R. Brown School of Engineering, Department of Civil and Environmental Engineering, Houston, TX 77251-1892. Offers civil engineering (MCE, MS, PhD); environmental engineering (MEE, MES, MS, PhD); environmental science (MEE, MES, MS, PhD). Part-time programs available. *Degree requirements:* For master's, thesis (for some programs); for doctorate, thesis/dissertation. *Entrance requirements:* For master's and doctorate, GRE General Test, GRE Subject Test, minimum GPA of 3.25. Additional exam requirements/recommendations for international students: Required—TOEFL (minimum score 600 paper-based; 250 computer-based; 90 iBT). Electronic applications accepted. *Faculty research:* Biology and chemistry of groundwater, pollutant fate in groundwater systems, water quality monitoring, urban storm water runoff, urban air quality.

Rose-Hulman Institute of Technology, Faculty of Engineering and Applied Sciences, Department of Civil Engineering, Terre Haute, IN 47803-3999. Offers civil engineering (MS); environmental engineering (MS). Part-time programs available. *Faculty:* 7 full-time (2 women). *Students:* 1 (woman) part-time. Average age 22. 2 applicants, 50% accepted, 0 enrolled. *Degree requirements:* For master's, thesis. *Entrance requirements:* For master's, GRE, minimum GPA of 3.0. Additional exam requirements/recommendations for international students: Required—TOEFL (minimum score 580 paper-based; 237 computer-based; 92 iBT). *Application deadline:* For fall admission, 2/1 priority date for domestic students. Applications are processed on a rolling basis. Application fee: $0. *Expenses:* Tuition: Full-time $35,595; part-time $1038 per credit hour. *Financial support:* In 2010–11, 1 student received support; fellowships with full and partial tuition reimbursements available, research assistantships with full and partial tuition reimbursements available, institutionally sponsored loans, scholarships/grants, and tuition waivers (full and partial) available. Financial award application deadline: 2/1. *Faculty research:* Urban stormwater management, groundwater and surface water models, solid and hazardous waste, risk and decision analysis. Total annual research expenditures: $16,578. *Unit head:* Dr. Kevin G. Sutterer, Chairman, 812-877-8959, Fax: 812-877-8440, E-mail: kevin.g.sutterer@rose-hulman.edu. *Application contact:* Dr. Daniel J. Moore, Associate Dean of the Faculty, 812-877-8110, Fax: 812-877-8061, E-mail: daniel.j.moore@rose-hulman.edu.

Royal Military College of Canada, Division of Graduate Studies and Research, Engineering Division, Department of Chemistry and Chemical Engineering, Program in Environmental Engineering, Kingston, ON K7K 7B4, Canada. Offers chemical and materials (M Eng); chemistry (M Eng); environmental (PhD); nuclear (PhD). *Degree requirements:* For master's, thesis; for doctorate, comprehensive exam, thesis/dissertation. *Entrance requirements:* For master's, honours degree with second-class standing; for doctorate, master's degree. Electronic applications accepted.

Rutgers, The State University of New Jersey, New Brunswick, Graduate School-New Brunswick, Department of Civil and Environmental Engineering, Piscataway, NJ 08854-8097. Offers MS, PhD. Part-time and evening/weekend programs available. Terminal master's awarded for partial completion of doctoral program. *Degree requirements:* For master's, comprehensive exam, thesis or alternative; for doctorate, comprehensive exam, thesis/dissertation. *Entrance requirements:* For master's and doctorate, GRE General Test. Additional exam requirements/recommendations for international students: Required—TOEFL (minimum score 580 paper-

based; 237 computer-based). Electronic applications accepted. *Expenses:* Tuition, state resident: full-time $7200; part-time $600 per credit. Tuition, nonresident: full-time $11,124; part-time $927 per credit. *Faculty research:* Civil engineering materials research, non-destructive evaluation of transportation infrastructure, transportation planning, intelligent transportation systems.

Southern Methodist University, Bobby B. Lyle School of Engineering, Department of Environmental and Civil Engineering, Dallas, TX 75275-0340. Offers applied science (MS, PhD); civil and environmental engineering (PhD); civil engineering (MS); environmental engineering (MS); environmental science (MS), including environmental systems management. Part-time and evening/weekend programs available. Postbaccalaureate distance learning degree programs offered (no on-campus study). *Faculty:* 6 full-time (0 women), 11 part-time/adjunct (3 women). *Students:* 11 full-time (8 women), 47 part-time (21 women); includes 5 Black or African American, non-Hispanic/Latino; 2 Asian, non-Hispanic/Latino; 3 Hispanic/Latino, 6 international. Average age 37. 50 applicants, 86% accepted, 28 enrolled. In 2010, 26 master's awarded. Terminal master's awarded for partial completion of doctoral program. *Degree requirements:* For master's, thesis optional; for doctorate, thesis/dissertation, oral and written qualifying exams. *Entrance requirements:* For master's, GRE General Test, minimum GPA of 3.0 in last 2 years; bachelor's degree in engineering, mathematics, or sciences; for doctorate, GRE, BS and MS in related field, minimum GPA of 3.3. Additional exam requirements/recommendations for international students: Required—TOEFL. *Application deadline:* For fall admission, 7/1 for domestic students, 5/15 for international students; for spring admission, 11/15 for domestic students, 9/1 for international students. Applications are processed on a rolling basis. Application fee: $75. Electronic applications accepted. *Financial support:* In 2010–11, 9 students received support, including 2 research assistantships with full tuition reimbursements available (averaging $18,000 per year), 7 teaching assistantships with full tuition reimbursements available (averaging $18,000 per year); unspecified assistantships also available. *Faculty research:* Human and environmental health effects of endocrine disrupters, development of air pollution control systems for diesel engines, structural analysis and design, modeling and design of waste treatment systems. Total annual research expenditures: $100,000. *Unit head:* Prof. Khaled Abdelghany, Associate Chair, 214-768-3894, Fax: 214-768-2164, E-mail: khaled@lyle.smu.edu. *Application contact:* Marc Valerin, Director of Graduate and Executive Admissions, 214-768-3042, Fax: 214-768-3778, E-mail: valerin@lyle.smu.edu.

Stanford University, School of Engineering, Department of Civil and Environmental Engineering, Stanford, CA 94305-9991. Offers MS, PhD, Eng. Terminal master's awarded for partial completion of doctoral program. *Degree requirements:* For doctorate, thesis/dissertation, qualifying exam; for Eng, thesis. *Entrance requirements:* For master's, doctorate, and Eng, GRE General Test. Additional exam requirements/recommendations for international students: Required—TOEFL. Electronic applications accepted. *Expenses:* Tuition: Full-time $38,700; part-time $860 per unit. One-time fee: $200 full-time.

State University of New York College of Environmental Science and Forestry, Department of Environmental Resources Engineering, Syracuse, NY 13210-2779. Offers ecological engineering (MS, PhD); environmental and resources engineering (MPS, MS, PhD); environmental management (MPS); geospatial information science and engineering (MS, PhD); mapping sciences (MPS); water resources engineering (MS, PhD). *Degree requirements:* For master's, thesis (for some programs); for doctorate, comprehensive exam, thesis/dissertation. *Entrance requirements:* For master's and doctorate, GRE General Test, minimum GPA of 3.0. Additional exam requirements/recommendations for international students: Required—TOEFL (minimum score 550 paper-based; 213 computer-based; 80 iBT), IELTS (minimum score 6). *Expenses:* Tuition, state resident: full-time $8370; part-time $349 per credit hour. Tuition, nonresident: full-time $13,780. Required fees: $30.30 per credit hour. $20 per year. *Faculty research:* Forest engineering, paper science and engineering, wood products engineering.

State University of New York College of Environmental Science and Forestry, Department of Paper and Bioprocess Engineering, Syracuse, NY 13210-2779. Offers environmental and resource engineering (MPS, MS, PhD). *Degree requirements:* For master's, thesis; for doctorate, comprehensive exam, thesis/dissertation. *Entrance requirements:* For master's and doctorate, GRE General Test, minimum GPA of 3.0. Additional exam requirements/recommendations for international students: Required—TOEFL (minimum score 550 paper-based; 213 computer-based; 80 iBT), IELTS (minimum score 6). *Expenses:* Tuition, state resident: full-time $8370; part-time $349 per credit hour. Tuition, nonresident: full-time $13,780. Required fees: $30.30 per credit hour. $20 per year.

Stevens Institute of Technology, Graduate School, Charles V. Schaefer Jr. School of Engineering, Department of Civil, Environmental, and Ocean Engineering, Program in Environmental Engineering, Hoboken, NJ 07030. Offers environmental compatibility in engineering (Certificate); environmental engineering (PhD); environmental processes (M Eng, Certificate); groundwater and soil pollution control (M Eng, Certificate); inland and coastal environmental hydrodynamics (M Eng, Certificate); water quality control (Certificate). *Students:* 21 full-time (7 women), 9 part-time (5 women); includes 3 Asian, non-Hispanic/Latino; 1 Hispanic/Latino, 16 international. Average age 29. 24 applicants, 83% accepted. *Degree requirements:* For master's, thesis optional; for doctorate, variable foreign language requirement, thesis/dissertation; for Certificate, project or thesis. *Entrance requirements:* For doctorate, GRE. Additional exam requirements/recommendations for international students: Required—TOEFL. *Application deadline:* Applications are processed on a rolling basis. Application fee: $50. Electronic applications accepted. *Financial support:* Application deadline: 4/15. *Unit head:* Dr. Christos Christodoulatos, Director, 201-216-5675. *Application contact:* Dr. David A. Vaccari, Director, 201-216-5570, Fax: 201-216-5352, E-mail: dvaccari@stevens.edu.

Syracuse University, L. C. Smith College of Engineering and Computer Science, Program in Environmental Engineering, Syracuse, NY 13244. Offers environmental engineering (MS). Part-time programs available. *Students:* 9 full-time (5 women), 1 (woman) part-time; includes 1 minority (Hispanic/Latino), 7 international. Average age 24. 27 applicants, 41% accepted, 5 enrolled. In 2010, 3 master's awarded. *Entrance requirements:* For master's, GRE General Test. Additional exam requirements/recommendations for international students: Required—TOEFL (minimum score 100 iBT). *Application deadline:* For fall admission, 7/1 priority date for domestic students, 6/1 priority date for international students. Applications are processed on a rolling basis. Application fee: $75. Electronic applications accepted. *Expenses:* Tuition: Part-time $1162 per credit. *Financial support:* Fellowships with full tuition reimbursements, research assistantships with full and partial tuition reimbursements, teaching assistantships with full and partial tuition reimbursements, tuition waivers (partial) available. Financial award application deadline: 1/1. *Unit head:* Dr. Chris E. Johnson, Interim Chair, 315-443-4425, E-mail: cejohns@syr.edu. *Application contact:* Elizabeth Buchanan, Information Contact, 314-443-2558, E-mail: topgrads@syr.edu.

Syracuse University, L. C. Smith College of Engineering and Computer Science, Program in Environmental Engineering Science, Syracuse, NY 13244. Offers MS. Part-time programs available. *Students:* 2 full-time (0 women), 1 international. Average age 25. 14 applicants, 64% accepted, 0 enrolled. *Degree requirements:* For master's, thesis optional. *Entrance requirements:* For master's, GRE General. Additional exam requirements/recommendations for international students: Required—TOEFL (minimum score 100 iBT). *Application deadline:* For fall admission, 7/1 for domestic students, 6/1 priority date for international students. Applications are processed on a rolling basis. Application fee: $75. Electronic applications accepted. *Expenses:* Tuition: Part-time $1162 per credit. *Financial support:* Fellowships with full tuition reimbursements, research assistantships with full and partial tuition reimbursements, teaching assistantships with full and partial tuition reimbursements, tuition waivers (partial) available. *Unit head:* Dr. Laura J. Steinberg, Dean, 315-443-2545, E-mail: ljs@syr.edu. *Application contact:* Kathleen Joyce, Assistant Dean, 315-443-2219, E-mail: topgrads@syr.edu.

Texas A&M University, College of Engineering, Zachry Department of Civil Engineering, College Station, TX 77843. Offers coastal and ocean engineering (M Eng, MS, D Eng, PhD); construction engineering and management (M Eng, MS, D Eng, PhD); environmental engineering (M Eng, MS, D Eng, PhD); geotechnical engineering (M Eng, MS, D Eng, PhD); materials

Environmental Engineering

Texas A&M University (continued)
engineering (M Eng, MS, D Eng, PhD); structural engineering (M Eng, MS, D Eng, PhD); transportation engineering (M Eng, MS, D Eng, PhD); water resources engineering (M Eng, MS, D Eng, PhD). Part-time programs available. *Faculty:* 57. *Students:* 384 full-time (81 women), 35 part-time (7 women); includes 35 minority (3 Black or African American, non-Hispanic/Latino; 1 American Indian or Alaska Native, non-Hispanic/Latino; 14 Asian, non-Hispanic/Latino; 17 Hispanic/Latino), 263 international. Average age 29. In 2010, 136 master's, 26 doctorates awarded. *Degree requirements:* For master's, thesis (MS); for doctorate, dissertation (PhD), internship (D Eng). *Entrance requirements:* For master's and doctorate, GRE General Test. Additional exam requirements/recommendations for international students: Required—TOEFL. *Application deadline:* Applications are processed on a rolling basis. Application fee: $50 ($75 for international students). Electronic applications accepted. *Financial support:* In 2010–11, fellowships (averaging $4,500 per year), research assistantships (averaging $14,000 per year), teaching assistantships (averaging $14,400 per year) were awarded; career-related internships or fieldwork and institutionally sponsored loans also available. Financial award application deadline: 4/15; financial award applicants required to submit FAFSA. *Unit head:* Dr. Tony Cahill, Head, 979-845-3858, E-mail: tcahill@civil.tamu.edu. *Application contact:* Graduate Advisor, 979-845-7435, Fax: 979-845-6156, E-mail: info@civil.tamu.edu.

Texas A&M University–Kingsville, College of Graduate Studies, College of Engineering, Department of Environmental Engineering, Kingsville, TX 78363. Offers ME, MS, PhD. Part-time and evening/weekend programs available. *Degree requirements:* For master's, comprehensive exam, thesis. *Entrance requirements:* For master's, GRE General Test, bachelor's degree in engineering or physical science, minimum undergraduate GPA of 2.7. Additional exam requirements/recommendations for international students: Required—TOEFL. *Faculty research:* Biodegradation of hazardous waste, air modeling, toxicology and industrial hygiene, water waste treating.

Texas Tech University, Graduate School, Edward E. Whitacre Jr. College of Engineering, Department of Civil and Environmental Engineering, Lubbock, TX 79409. Offers civil engineering (MSCE, PhD); environmental engineering (MENVEGR). *Accreditation:* ABET. Part-time programs available. *Faculty:* 21 full-time (2 women), 1 part-time/adjunct (0 women). *Students:* 86 full-time (16 women), 14 part-time (3 women); includes 3 Black or African American, non-Hispanic/Latino; 1 Asian, non-Hispanic/Latino; 5 Hispanic/Latino, 44 international. Average age 26. 107 applicants, 63% accepted, 24 enrolled. In 2010, 23 master's, 6 doctorates awarded. *Degree requirements:* For master's, thesis or alternative; for doctorate, thesis/dissertation. *Entrance requirements:* For master's and doctorate, GRE General Test, minimum GPA of 3.0. Additional exam requirements/recommendations for international students: Required—TOEFL (minimum score 550 paper-based; 213 computer-based; 79 iBT). *Application deadline:* For fall admission, 6/1 priority date for domestic students, 1/15 priority date for international students; for spring admission, 9/1 priority date for domestic students, 6/15 priority date for international students. Applications are processed on a rolling basis. Application fee: $50 ($75 for international students). Electronic applications accepted. *Expenses:* Tuition, state resident: full-time $5495.76; part-time $228.99 per credit hour. Tuition, nonresident: full-time $12,936; part-time $538.99 per credit hour. Required fees: $2674; $36 per credit hour. $905 per semester. *Financial support:* In 2010–11, 65 students received support, including 25 research assistantships with partial tuition reimbursements available (averaging $5,431 per year), 10 teaching assistantships with partial tuition reimbursements available (averaging $5,535 per year). Financial award application deadline: 4/15; financial award applicants required to submit FAFSA. *Faculty research:* Wind load/engineering on structures, fluid mechanics, structural dynamics, water resource management, transportation engineering. Total annual research expenditures: $1.1 million. *Unit head:* Dr. H. Scott Norville, Chair, 806-742-3523, Fax: 806-742-3488, E-mail: scott.norville@ttu.edu. *Application contact:* Dr. Priyantha Jayawickrama, Graduate Adviser, 806-742-3523, Fax: 806-742-3488, E-mail: priyantha.jayawickrama@ttu.edu.

Tufts University, School of Engineering, Department of Civil and Environmental Engineering, Medford, MA 02155. Offers civil engineering (ME, MS, PhD), including geotechnical engineering, structural engineering; environmental engineering (ME, MS, PhD), including environmental engineering and environmental sciences, environmental geotechnology, environmental health, environmental science and management, hazardous materials management, water resources engineering. Part-time programs available. Terminal master's awarded for partial completion of doctoral program. *Degree requirements:* For master's, thesis or alternative; for doctorate, thesis/dissertation. *Entrance requirements:* For master's and doctorate, GRE General Test. Additional exam requirements/recommendations for international students: Required—TOEFL (minimum score 550 paper-based; 213 computer-based; 80 iBT). Electronic applications accepted. *Expenses:* Tuition: Full-time $39,624; part-time $3962 per course. Required fees: $40 per year. Full-time tuition and fees vary according to degree level, program and student level. Part-time tuition and fees vary according to course load.

Universidad Central del Este, Graduate School, San Pedro de Macoris, Dominican Republic. Offers environmental engineering (ME); financial management (M Ad); higher education (M Ed), including higher education management, higher education pedagogy; human resources (M Ad). *Entrance requirements:* For master's, letters of recommendation.

Universidad Nacional Pedro Henriquez Urena, Graduate School, Santo Domingo, Dominican Republic. Offers agricultural diversity (MS), including horticultural/fruit production, tropical animal production; conservation of monuments and cultural assets (M Arch); ecology and environment (MS); environmental engineering (MEE); international relations (MA); natural resource management (MS); political science (MA); project optimization (MPM); project feasibility (MPM); project management (MPM); sanitation engineering (ME); science for teachers (MS); tropical Caribbean architecture (M Arch).

Université de Sherbrooke, Faculty of Engineering, Program in the Environment, Sherbrooke, QC J1K 2R1, Canada. Offers M Env. *Degree requirements:* For master's, thesis.

Université Laval, Faculty of Sciences and Engineering, Department of Civil Engineering, Programs in Civil Engineering, Québec, QC G1K 7P4, Canada. Offers civil engineering (M Sc, PhD); environmental technology (M Sc). Terminal master's awarded for partial completion of doctoral program. *Degree requirements:* For master's, thesis (for some programs); for doctorate, comprehensive exam, thesis/dissertation. *Entrance requirements:* For master's and doctorate, knowledge of French and English. Electronic applications accepted.

University at Buffalo, the State University of New York, Graduate School, School of Engineering and Applied Sciences, Department of Civil, Structural, and Environmental Engineering, Buffalo, NY 14260. Offers civil engineering (ME, MS, PhD); engineering science (MS). Part-time programs available. Postbaccalaureate distance learning degree programs offered (minimal on-campus study). *Faculty:* 25 full-time (3 women), 3 part-time/adjunct (1 woman). *Students:* 173 full-time (26 women), 21 part-time (7 women); includes 1 Black or African American, non-Hispanic/Latino; 1 American Indian or Alaska Native, non-Hispanic/Latino; 6 Asian, non-Hispanic/Latino; 4 Hispanic/Latino, 133 international. Average age 27. 542 applicants, 38% accepted, 71 enrolled. In 2010, 34 master's, 4 doctorates awarded. Terminal master's awarded for partial completion of doctoral program. *Degree requirements:* For master's, thesis optional, project, thesis, or comprehensive exam; for doctorate, thesis/dissertation. *Entrance requirements:* For master's and doctorate, GRE General Test, letters of reference. Additional exam requirements/recommendations for international students: Required—TOEFL (minimum score 550 paper-based; 213 computer-based; 79 iBT). *Application deadline:* For fall admission, 1/15 priority date for domestic and international students; for spring admission, 9/15 for domestic and international students. Applications are processed on a rolling basis. Application fee: $50. Electronic applications accepted. *Financial support:* In 2010–11, 115 students received support, including 15 fellowships with full tuition reimbursements available (averaging $17,200 per year), 59 research assistantships with full tuition reimbursements available (averaging $14,000 per year), 35 teaching assistantships with full tuition reimbursements available (averaging $14,700 per year); career-related internships or fieldwork, Federal Work-Study, institutionally sponsored loans, scholarships/grants, traineeships, health care benefits, tuition waivers (full and partial), and unspecified assistantships also available. Support available to part-time students. Financial award application deadline: 1/15; financial award applicants required to submit FAFSA. *Faculty research:* Environmental engineering and fluid mechanics, structural dynamics, geomechanics, earthquake engineering computational mechanics. Total annual research expenditures: $9.7 million. *Unit head:* Dr. Andrew S. Whittaker, Chairman, 716-645-2114, Fax: 716-645-3733, E-mail: awhittak@buffalo.edu. *Application contact:* Dr. Gilberto Mosqueda, Director of Graduate Studies, 716-645-4356, Fax: 716-645-3733, E-mail: mosqueda@buffalo.edu.

The University of Alabama, Graduate School, College of Engineering, Department of Civil, Construction and Environmental Engineering, Tuscaloosa, AL 35487-0205. Offers civil engineering (MSCE, PhD); environmental engineering (MS). Part-time programs available. *Faculty:* 20 full-time (2 women), 1 part-time/adjunct (0 women). *Students:* 40 full-time (12 women), 12 part-time (3 women); includes 9 minority (7 Black or African American, non-Hispanic/Latino; 1 Asian, non-Hispanic/Latino; 1 Two or more races, non-Hispanic/Latino), 15 international. Average age 29. 67 applicants, 51% accepted, 12 enrolled. In 2010, 21 master's, 2 doctorates awarded. Terminal master's awarded for partial completion of doctoral program. *Degree requirements:* For master's, thesis or alternative; for doctorate, one foreign language, thesis/dissertation. *Entrance requirements:* For master's and doctorate, GRE General Test, minimum GPA of 3.0 in last 60 hours of course work. Additional exam requirements/recommendations for international students: Required—TOEFL (minimum score 550 paper-based; 213 computer-based), IELTS (minimum score 6.5). *Application deadline:* For fall admission, 7/6 for domestic students, 1/15 for international students; for spring admission, 11/1 for domestic students, 6/1 for international students. Applications are processed on a rolling basis. Application fee: $50 ($60 for international students). Electronic applications accepted. *Expenses:* Tuition, state resident: full-time $7900. Tuition, nonresident: full-time $20,500. *Financial support:* In 2010–11, 40 students received support, including 32 research assistantships with full tuition reimbursements available (averaging $10,489 per year), 12 teaching assistantships with full tuition reimbursements available (averaging $10,489 per year); fellowships, scholarships/grants, tuition waivers (partial), and unspecified assistantships also available. Financial award application deadline: 3/15. *Faculty research:* Experimental structures, modeling of structures, bridge management systems, geotechnological engineering, environmental remediation. Total annual research expenditures: $1.9 million. *Unit head:* Dr. Kenneth J. Fridley, Head and Professor, 205-348-6550, Fax: 205-348-0783, E-mail: kfridley@coe.eng.ua.edu. *Application contact:* Dr. David A. Francko, Dean, 205-348-8280, Fax: 205-348-0400, E-mail: dfrancko@ua.edu.

The University of Alabama in Huntsville, School of Graduate Studies, College of Engineering, Department of Civil and Environmental Engineering, Huntsville, AL 35899. Offers civil and environmental engineering (PhD); civil engineering (MSE), including environmental and water resource engineering, geotechnical engineering, structural engineering and structural mechanics, transportation engineering. PhD offered jointly with The University of Alabama at Birmingham. Part-time and evening/weekend programs available. *Faculty:* 6 full-time (1 woman), 1 part-time/adjunct (0 women). *Students:* 23 full-time (7 women), 11 part-time (4 women); includes 3 minority (2 Black or African American, non-Hispanic/Latino; 1 Asian, non-Hispanic/Latino), 12 international. Average age 30. 37 applicants, 57% accepted, 15 enrolled. In 2010, 1 master's, 3 doctorates awarded. *Degree requirements:* For master's, comprehensive exam, thesis or alternative, oral and written exams; for doctorate, comprehensive exam, thesis/dissertation, oral and written exams. *Entrance requirements:* For master's, GRE General Test, BSE, minimum GPA of 3.0; for doctorate, GRE General Test, minimum GPA of 3.0. Additional exam requirements/recommendations for international students: Required—TOEFL (minimum score 500 paper-based; 173 computer-based; 62 iBT). *Application deadline:* For fall admission, 7/15 for domestic students, 4/1 for international students; for spring admission, 11/30 for domestic students, 9/1 for international students. Applications are processed on a rolling basis. Application fee: $40 ($50 for international students). Electronic applications accepted. *Expenses:* Tuition, state resident: full-time $7250; part-time $407.75 per credit hour. Tuition, nonresident: full-time $17,358; part-time $970.05 per credit hour. Required fees: $246.80 per semester. Tuition and fees vary according to course load and program. *Financial support:* In 2010–11, 14 students received support, including 7 research assistantships with full and partial tuition reimbursements available (averaging $12,435 per year), 7 teaching assistantships with full and partial tuition reimbursements available (averaging $10,281 per year); career-related internships or fieldwork, Federal Work-Study, institutionally sponsored loans, scholarships/grants, health care benefits, and unspecified assistantships also available. Support available to part-time students. Financial award application deadline: 4/1; financial award applicants required to submit FAFSA. *Faculty research:* Hydrologic modeling, orbital debris impact, hydrogeology, environmental engineering, transportation engineering. Total annual research expenditures: $1.9 million. *Unit head:* Dr. Houssam Toutanji, Chair, 256-824-7361, Fax: 256-824-6724, E-mail: toutanji@cee.uah.edu. *Application contact:* Kathy Biggs, Graduate Studies Admissions Manager, 256-824-6199, Fax: 256-824-6405, E-mail: deangrad@uah.edu.

University of Alaska Anchorage, School of Engineering, Program in Applied Environmental Science and Technology, Anchorage, AK 99508. Offers M AEST, MS. Part-time and evening/weekend programs available. *Degree requirements:* For master's, comprehensive exam, thesis (for some programs). *Entrance requirements:* For master's, GRE General Test. Additional exam requirements/recommendations for international students: Required—TOEFL (minimum score 550 paper-based; 213 computer-based). *Faculty research:* Wastewater treatment, environmental regulations, water resources management, justification of public facilities, rural sanitation, biological treatment process.

University of Alaska Fairbanks, College of Engineering and Mines, Department of Civil and Environmental Engineering, Program in Environmental Engineering, Fairbanks, AK 99775-5900. Offers engineering (PhD), including environmental engineering; environmental engineering (MS), including environmental contaminants, environmental science and management, water supply and waste treatment. Part-time programs available. *Students:* 3 full-time (all women), 3 part-time (2 women). Average age 28. 5 applicants, 60% accepted, 1 enrolled. In 2010, 3 master's, 1 doctorate awarded. *Degree requirements:* For master's, comprehensive exam, thesis or alternative; for doctorate, comprehensive exam, thesis/dissertation, oral exam, oral defense. *Entrance requirements:* For master's, basic computer techniques; for doctorate, GRE General Test. Additional exam requirements/recommendations for international students: Required—TOEFL (minimum score 575 paper-based; 213 computer-based). *Application deadline:* For fall admission, 6/1 for domestic students, 3/1 for international students; for spring admission, 10/15 for domestic students, 9/1 for international students. Applications are processed on a rolling basis. Application fee: $60. Electronic applications accepted. *Expenses:* Tuition, state resident: full-time $5688; part-time $316 per credit. Tuition, nonresident: full-time $11,628; part-time $646 per credit. Required fees: $289 per semester. Tuition and fees vary according to course load and reciprocity agreements. *Financial support:* In 2010–11, 4 research assistantships (averaging $13,290 per year), 1 teaching assistantship (averaging $7,088 per year) were awarded; fellowships, career-related internships or fieldwork, Federal Work-Study, scholarships/grants, health care benefits, and unspecified assistantships also available. Support available to part-time students. Financial award application deadline: 7/1; financial award applicants required to submit FAFSA. *Unit head:* Dr. David Barnes, Department Chair, 907-474-7241, Fax: 907-474-6087, E-mail: fyeqe@uaf.edu. *Application contact:* Dr. David Barnes, Department Chair, 907-474-7241, Fax: 907-474-6087, E-mail: fyeqe@uaf.edu.

University of Alberta, Faculty of Graduate Studies and Research, Department of Civil and Environmental Engineering, Edmonton, AB T6G 2E1, Canada. Offers construction engineering and management (M Eng, M Sc, PhD); environmental engineering (M Eng, M Sc, PhD); environmental science (M Sc, PhD); geoenvironmental engineering (M Eng, M Sc, PhD); geotechnical engineering (M Eng, M Sc, PhD); mining engineering (M Eng, M Sc, PhD); petroleum engineering (M Eng, M Sc, PhD); structural engineering (M Eng, M Sc, PhD); water resources (M Eng, M Sc, PhD). Part-time programs available. Postbaccalaureate distance learning degree programs offered (minimal on-campus study). *Degree requirements:* For master's, thesis (for some programs); for doctorate, thesis/dissertation. *Entrance requirements:* For master's, minimum

GPA of 3.0 in last 2 years of undergraduate studies; for doctorate, minimum GPA of 3.0. Additional exam requirements/recommendations for international students: Required—TOEFL (minimum score 550 paper-based; 213 computer-based). Electronic applications accepted. *Faculty research:* Mining.

The University of Arizona, College of Engineering, Department of Chemical and Environmental Engineering, Program in Environmental Engineering, Tucson, AZ 85721. Offers MS, PhD. *Students:* 27 full-time (13 women), 7 part-time (2 women); includes 5 minority (1 Black or African American, non-Hispanic/Latino; 1 Asian, non-Hispanic/Latino; 3 Hispanic/Latino), 19 international. Average age 30. 54 applicants, 24% accepted, 5 enrolled. In 2010, 6 master's, 6 doctorates awarded. *Entrance requirements:* For master's and doctorate, GRE, 3 letters of recommendation, resume, statement of purpose. Additional exam requirements/recommendations for international students: Required—TOEFL (minimum score 550 paper-based; 213 computer-based; 79 iBT). *Application deadline:* Applications are processed on a rolling basis. Application fee: $75. Electronic applications accepted. *Expenses:* Tuition, state resident: full-time $7692. *Unit head:* Dr. Glenn L. Schrader, Department Head, 520-621-2591, Fax: 520-621-6048, E-mail: schrader@email.arizona.edu. *Application contact:* Jo Leeming, Program Coordinator, 520-621-6044, Fax: 520-621-6048, E-mail: leeming@email.arizona.edu.

University of Arkansas, Graduate School, College of Engineering, Department of Civil Engineering, Program in Environmental Engineering, Fayetteville, AR 72701-1201. Offers MS En E, MSE. *Accreditation:* ABET. *Students:* 1 (woman) full-time, 3 part-time (1 woman). 3 applicants, 33% accepted. *Degree requirements:* For master's, thesis optional. *Application deadline:* For fall admission, 4/1 for international students; for spring admission, 10/1 for international students. Applications are processed on a rolling basis. Application fee: $40 ($50 for international students). Electronic applications accepted. *Financial support:* In 2010–11, 4 research assistantships were awarded; fellowships, teaching assistantships, career-related internships or fieldwork and Federal Work-Study also available. Support available to part-time students. Financial award application deadline: 4/1; financial award applicants required to submit FAFSA. *Unit head:* Dr. Kevin Hall, Department Chair, 479-575-4954, Fax: 479-575-7168, E-mail: kdhall@uark.edu. *Application contact:* Dr. Paneer Selvam, Graduate Coordinator, 479-575-5356, E-mail: rps@uark.edu.

University of California, Berkeley, Graduate Division, College of Engineering, Department of Civil and Environmental Engineering, Berkeley, CA 94720-1500. Offers engineering and project management (M Eng, MS, D Eng, PhD); environmental engineering (M Eng, MS, D Eng, PhD); geoengineering (M Eng, MS, D Eng, PhD); structural engineering, mechanics and materials (M Eng, MS, D Eng, PhD); transportation engineering (M Eng, MS, D Eng, PhD); M Arch/MS; MCP/MS; MPP/MS. *Degree requirements:* For master's, comprehensive exam or thesis (MS); for doctorate, thesis/dissertation, qualifying exam. *Entrance requirements:* For master's, GRE General Test, minimum GPA of 3.0, 3 letters of recommendation; for doctorate, GRE General Test, minimum GPA of 3.5, 3 letters of recommendation. Additional exam requirements/recommendations for international students: Required—TOEFL (minimum score 570 paper-based; 230 computer-based). Electronic applications accepted.

University of California, Davis, College of Engineering, Program in Civil and Environmental Engineering, Davis, CA 95616. Offers M Engr, MS, D Engr, PhD, Certificate, M Engr/MBA. *Degree requirements:* For master's, comprehensive exam (for some programs), thesis (for some programs); for doctorate, thesis/dissertation. *Entrance requirements:* For master's, GRE General Test, minimum GPA of 3.0; for doctorate, GRE, minimum graduate GPA of 3.5. Additional exam requirements/recommendations for international students: Required—TOEFL (minimum score 550 paper-based; 213 computer-based). Electronic applications accepted. *Faculty research:* Environmental water resources, transportation, structural mechanics, structural engineering, geotechnical engineering.

University of California, Irvine, School of Engineering, Department of Civil and Environmental Engineering, Irvine, CA 92697. Offers MS, PhD. Part-time programs available. *Students:* 115 full-time (30 women), 13 part-time (3 women); includes 27 minority (19 Asian, non-Hispanic/Latino; 8 Hispanic/Latino), 67 international. Average age 28. 333 applicants, 35% accepted, 42 enrolled. In 2010, 34 master's, 13 doctorates awarded. Terminal master's awarded for partial completion of doctoral program. *Degree requirements:* For doctorate, thesis/dissertation. *Entrance requirements:* For master's and doctorate, GRE General Test, minimum GPA of 3.0, 3 letters of recommendation. Additional exam requirements/recommendations for international students: Required—TOEFL (minimum score 550 paper-based; 213 computer-based). *Application deadline:* For fall admission, 1/15 priority date for domestic students, 1/15 for international students. Applications are processed on a rolling basis. Application fee: $80 ($100 for international students). Electronic applications accepted. *Financial support:* Fellowships, research assistantships with full tuition reimbursements, teaching assistantships, institutionally sponsored loans, traineeships, health care benefits, and unspecified assistantships available. Financial award application deadline: 3/1; financial award applicants required to submit FAFSA. *Faculty research:* Intelligent transportation systems and transportation economics, risk and reliability, fluid mechanics, environmental hydrodynamics, hydrological and climate systems, water resources. *Unit head:* Prof. Brett F. Sanders, Chair, 949-824-4327, Fax: 949-824-3672, E-mail: bsanders@uci.edu. *Application contact:* April M. Heath, Graduate Coordinator, 949-824-0584, Fax: 949-824-2117, E-mail: a.heath@uci.edu.

University of California, Los Angeles, Graduate Division, Henry Samueli School of Engineering and Applied Science, Department of Civil and Environmental Engineering, Los Angeles, CA 90095-1593. Offers MS, PhD. *Faculty:* 17 full-time (3 women). *Students:* 143 full-time (48 women); includes 39 Asian, non-Hispanic/Latino; 8 Hispanic/Latino, 45 international. 293 applicants, 56% accepted, 66 enrolled. In 2010, 53 master's, 21 doctorates awarded. *Degree requirements:* For master's, comprehensive exam or thesis; for doctorate, thesis/dissertation, qualifying exams. *Entrance requirements:* For master's, GRE General Test, minimum GPA of 3.0; for doctorate, GRE General Test, minimum GPA of 3.25. Additional exam requirements/recommendations for international students: Required—TOEFL (minimum score 560 paper-based; 220 computer-based; 87 iBT). *Application deadline:* For fall admission, 12/15 priority date for domestic and international students. Application fee: $70 ($90 for international students). Electronic applications accepted. *Financial support:* In 2010–11, 105 fellowships, 93 research assistantships, 48 teaching assistantships were awarded; Federal Work-Study, institutionally sponsored loans, and tuition waivers (full and partial) also available. Financial award application deadline: 12/15; financial award applicants required to submit FAFSA. Total annual research expenditures: $4 million. *Unit head:* Dr. Jiun-Shyan Chen, Chair, 310-267-4620. *Application contact:* Maida Bassili, Graduate Affairs Officer, 310-825-1851, Fax: 310-206-2222, E-mail: maida@ea.ucla.edu.

University of California, Los Angeles, Graduate Division, School of Public Health, Department of Environmental Health Sciences, Los Angeles, CA 90095. Offers environmental health sciences (MS, PhD); environmental science and engineering (D Env); molecular toxicology (PhD); JD/MPH. *Accreditation:* ABET (one or more programs are accredited). *Degree requirements:* For master's, comprehensive exam or thesis; for doctorate, thesis/dissertation, oral and written qualifying exams. *Entrance requirements:* For master's, GRE General Test, minimum GPA of 3.0; for doctorate, GRE General Test, minimum undergraduate GPA of 3.0. Electronic applications accepted.

University of California, Los Angeles, Graduate Division, School of Public Health, Program in Environmental Science and Engineering, Los Angeles, CA 90095. Offers D Env. *Degree requirements:* For doctorate, thesis/dissertation, oral and written qualifying exams. *Entrance requirements:* For doctorate, GRE General Test, minimum undergraduate GPA of 3.0, master's degree or equivalent in a natural science, engineering, or public health. *Faculty research:* Toxic and hazardous substances, air and water pollution, risk assessment/management, water resources, marine science.

University of California, Riverside, Graduate Division, Department of Chemical and Environmental Engineering, Riverside, CA 92521-0102. Offers MS, PhD. Part-time programs available. Terminal master's awarded for partial completion of doctoral program. *Degree requirements:* For master's, thesis (for some programs); for doctorate, comprehensive exam, thesis/dissertation. *Entrance requirements:* For master's and doctorate, GRE General Test, minimum GPA of 3.0. Additional exam requirements/recommendations for international students: Required—TOEFL (minimum score 550 paper-based; 213 computer-based; 80 iBT). Electronic applications accepted. *Faculty research:* Air quality systems, water quality systems, advanced materials and nanotechnology, energy systems/alternative fuels, theory and molecular modeling.

University of Central Florida, College of Engineering and Computer Science, Department of Civil, Environmental, and Construction Engineering, Program in Environmental Engineering, Orlando, FL 32816. Offers MS, MS Env E, PhD. Part-time and evening/weekend programs available. *Students:* 27 full-time (9 women), 11 part-time (3 women); includes 2 Black or African American, non-Hispanic/Latino; 2 Asian, non-Hispanic/Latino; 3 Hispanic/Latino; 1 Two or more races, non-Hispanic/Latino, 7 international. Average age 29. 35 applicants, 86% accepted, 14 enrolled. In 2010, 5 master's awarded. *Degree requirements:* For master's, thesis or alternative; for doctorate, thesis/dissertation, departmental qualifying exam, candidacy exam. *Entrance requirements:* For master's, GRE General Test, minimum GPA of 3.0 in last 60 hours of course work; for doctorate, GRE General Test, minimum GPA of 3.5 in last 60 hours of course work, interview. Additional exam requirements/recommendations for international students: Required—TOEFL. *Application deadline:* For fall admission, 7/15 priority date for domestic students; for spring admission, 12/15 priority date for domestic students. Application fee: $30. Electronic applications accepted. *Expenses:* Tuition, state resident: part-time $256.56 per credit hour. Tuition, nonresident: part-time $1011.52 per credit hour. Part-time tuition and fees vary according to program. *Financial support:* In 2010–11, 18 students received support, including 2 fellowships with partial tuition reimbursements available (averaging $10,000 per year), 17 research assistantships with partial tuition reimbursements available (averaging $9,400 per year), 6 teaching assistantships with partial tuition reimbursements available (averaging $6,700 per year); career-related internships or fieldwork, Federal Work-Study, institutionally sponsored loans, tuition waivers (partial), and unspecified assistantships also available. Financial award application deadline: 3/1; financial award applicants required to submit FAFSA.

University of Cincinnati, Graduate School, College of Engineering, Department of Civil and Environmental Engineering, Program in Environmental Engineering, Cincinnati, OH 45221. Offers MS, PhD. *Accreditation:* ABET (one or more programs are accredited). Part-time programs available. *Degree requirements:* For master's, project or thesis; for doctorate, one foreign language, thesis/dissertation. *Entrance requirements:* For master's and doctorate, GRE General Test. Additional exam requirements/recommendations for international students: Required—TOEFL (minimum score 580 paper-based; 237 computer-based; 92 iBT). Electronic applications accepted. *Faculty research:* Environmental microbiology, solid-waste management, air pollution control, water pollution control, aerosols.

University of Colorado Boulder, Graduate School, College of Engineering and Applied Science, Department of Civil, Environmental, and Architectural Engineering, Boulder, CO 80309. Offers building systems (MS, PhD); construction engineering management (MS, PhD); environmental engineering (MS, PhD); geotechnical engineering and geomechanics (MS, PhD); hydrology, water resources and environmental fluid mechanics (MS, PhD); structural engineering and structural mechanics (MS, PhD). *Faculty:* 38 full-time (6 women). *Students:* 255 full-time (86 women), 40 part-time (11 women); includes 40 minority (1 Black or African American, non-Hispanic/Latino; 2 American Indian or Alaska Native, non-Hispanic/Latino; 15 Asian, non-Hispanic/Latino; 20 Hispanic/Latino; 2 Two or more races, non-Hispanic/Latino), 61 international. Average age 28. 420 applicants, 95 enrolled. In 2010, 56 master's, 18 doctorates awarded. *Degree requirements:* For master's, comprehensive exam, thesis or alternative; for doctorate, thesis/dissertation. *Entrance requirements:* For master's, GRE General Test, minimum undergraduate GPA of 3.0. *Application deadline:* For fall admission, 3/1 for domestic students, 12/1 for international students; for spring admission, 10/31 for domestic students, 10/1 for international students. Application fee: $50 ($60 for international students). *Financial support:* In 2010–11, 45 fellowships (averaging $7,876 per year), 68 research assistantships (averaging $15,204 per year) were awarded. Financial award application deadline: 1/15. *Faculty research:* Building systems engineering, construction engineering and management, environmental engineering, geoenvironmental engineering, geotechnical engineering, materials and mechanics, structural engineering, water resources engineering, life-cycle engineering. Total annual research expenditures: $8 million.

University of Colorado Denver, College of Engineering and Applied Science, Department of Civil Engineering, Denver, CO 80217-3364. Offers civil engineering (PhD); environmental and sustainability engineering (MS); geographic information systems (MS); geotechnical engineering (MS); hydrology and hydraulics (MS); structural engineering (MS); transportation engineering (MS). Part-time and evening/weekend programs available. *Faculty:* 14 full-time (1 woman), 6 part-time/adjunct (0 women). *Students:* 66 full-time (13 women), 72 part-time (16 women); includes 9 Black or African American, non-Hispanic/Latino; 8 Asian, non-Hispanic/Latino; 11 Hispanic/Latino, 15 international. Average age 32. 72 applicants, 54% accepted, 29 enrolled. In 2010, 14 master's, 3 doctorates awarded. *Degree requirements:* For master's, comprehensive exam, thesis or alternative; for doctorate, comprehensive exam, thesis/dissertation. *Entrance requirements:* For master's, GRE, statement of purpose, transcripts, references; for doctorate, GRE, statement of purpose, transcripts, references, letter of support from faculty stating willingness to serve as dissertation advisor and outlining plan for financial support. Additional exam requirements/recommendations for international students: Required—TOEFL (minimum score 525 paper-based; 197 computer-based). *Application deadline:* For fall admission, 7/15 for domestic students, 6/15 for international students; for spring admission, 12/1 for domestic students, 11/1 for international students. Applications are processed on a rolling basis. Application fee: $50 ($75 for international students). Electronic applications accepted. *Expenses:* Contact institution. *Financial support:* Research assistantships, teaching assistantships, career-related internships or fieldwork and Federal Work-Study available. Financial award application deadline: 4/1; financial award applicants required to submit FAFSA. *Faculty research:* Environmental engineering and sustainable systems, geosynthetics, hydrologic andhydraulic engineering, structural engineering, transportation, transportation energy use and greenhouse gas emissions. *Unit head:* Dr. Nien-Yin Chang, Acting Chair, 303-556-2810, Fax: 303-556-2368, E-mail: nien.chang@ucdenver.edu. *Application contact:* Mindy Gewuerz, Program Assistant, 303-556-6712, Fax: 303-556-2368, E-mail: mindy.gewuerz@ucdenver.edu.

University of Connecticut, Graduate School, School of Engineering, Department of Civil and Environmental Engineering, Field of Environmental Engineering, Storrs, CT 06269. Offers MS, PhD. *Degree requirements:* For master's, comprehensive exam; for doctorate, thesis/dissertation. *Entrance requirements:* For master's and doctorate, GRE General Test. Additional exam requirements/recommendations for international students: Required—TOEFL (minimum score 550 paper-based; 213 computer-based). Electronic applications accepted.

University of Dayton, Graduate School, School of Engineering, Department of Civil and Environmental Engineering and Engineering Mechanics, Dayton, OH 45469-1300. Offers engineering mechanics (MSEM); environmental engineering (MSCE); geotechnical engineering (MSCE); structural engineering (MSCE); transportation engineering (MSCE); water resources engineering (MSCE). Part-time programs available. *Faculty:* 7 full-time (2 women), 2 part-time/adjunct (0 women). *Students:* 10 full-time (5 women), 7 part-time (2 women); includes 2 minority (both Black or African American, non-Hispanic/Latino), 6 international. Average age 27. 23 applicants, 43% accepted, 4 enrolled. In 2010, 5 master's awarded. *Degree requirements:* For master's, thesis optional. *Entrance requirements:* For master's, minimum GPA of 3.0 in undergraduate work. Additional exam requirements/recommendations for international students: Required—TOEFL (minimum score 550 paper-based; 213 computer-based; 80 iBT). *Application deadline:* For fall admission, 8/1 for domestic students, 3/1 priority date for international students; for winter admission, 7/1 priority date for international students; for spring admission, 1/1 priority date for international students. Applications are processed on a rolling basis. Application fee: $0 ($50 for international students). Electronic applications accepted. *Expenses:*

Environmental Engineering

University of Dayton *(continued)*
Tuition: Full-time $7800; part-time $650 per credit hour. *Financial support:* In 2010–11, 2 research assistantships (averaging $10,600 per year) were awarded. Financial award applicants required to submit FAFSA. *Faculty research:* Physical modeling of hydraulic systems, finite element methods, mechanics of composite materials, transportation systems safety, biological treatment processes. Total annual research expenditures: $200,000. *Unit head:* Dr. Donald V. Chase, Chair, 937-229-3847, Fax: 937-229-3491, E-mail: donald.chase@notes.udayton.edu. *Application contact:* Alexander Popovski, Associate Director of International and Graduate Admissions, 937-229-2357, Fax: 937-229-4729, E-mail: alex.popovski@notes.udayton.edu.

University of Delaware, College of Engineering, Department of Civil and Environmental Engineering, Newark, DE 19716. Offers environmental engineering (MAS, MCE, PhD); geotechnical engineering (MAS, MCE, PhD); ocean engineering (MAS, MCE, PhD); structural engineering (MAS, MCE, PhD); transportation engineering (MAS, MCE, PhD); water resource engineering (MAS, MCE, PhD). Part-time programs available. Terminal master's awarded for partial completion of doctoral program. *Degree requirements:* For master's, thesis; for doctorate, thesis/dissertation. *Entrance requirements:* For master's and doctorate, GRE General Test. Additional exam requirements/recommendations for international students: Required—TOEFL. Electronic applications accepted. *Faculty research:* Structural engineering and mechanics; transportation engineering; ocean engineering; soil mechanics and foundation; water resources and environmental engineering.

University of Detroit Mercy, College of Engineering and Science, Department of Civil and Environmental Engineering, Detroit, MI 48221. Offers ME, DE. Evening/weekend programs available. *Faculty research:* Geotechnical engineering.

University of Florida, Graduate School, College of Engineering, Department of Environmental Engineering Sciences, Gainesville, FL 32611. Offers ME, MS, PhD, Engr, JD/MS. Part-time and evening/weekend programs available. Postbaccalaureate distance learning degree programs offered (no on-campus study). *Faculty:* 13 full-time (1 woman), 1 part-time/adjunct (0 women). *Students:* 83 full-time (39 women), 97 part-time (48 women); includes 5 Black or African American, non-Hispanic/Latino; 2 American Indian or Alaska Native, non-Hispanic/Latino; 9 Asian, non-Hispanic/Latino; 18 Hispanic/Latino, 36 international. Average age 31. 162 applicants, 22% accepted, 29 enrolled. In 2010, 49 master's, 6 doctorates awarded. Terminal master's awarded for partial completion of doctoral program. *Degree requirements:* For master's, comprehensive exam (for some programs), thesis (for some programs), project, thesis or coursework-only; for doctorate, comprehensive exam, thesis/dissertation; for Engr, project or thesis. *Entrance requirements:* For master's and doctorate, GRE General Test, minimum GPA of 3.0; for Engr, GRE General Test. Additional exam requirements/recommendations for international students: Required—TOEFL (minimum score 550 paper-based; 213 computer-based; 80 iBT), IELTS (minimum score 6). *Application deadline:* For fall admission, 6/1 priority date for domestic students, 2/1 for international students; for spring admission, 11/1 for domestic students, 10/1 for international students. Applications are processed on a rolling basis. Application fee: $30. Electronic applications accepted. *Expenses:* Tuition, state resident: full-time $10,915.92. Tuition, nonresident: full-time $28,309. *Financial support:* In 2010–11, 47 students received support, including 4 fellowships, 40 research assistantships (averaging $16,646 per year), 3 teaching assistantships (averaging $16,343 per year); career-related internships or fieldwork and unspecified assistantships also available. Financial award application deadline: 2/1; financial award applicants required to submit FAFSA. *Faculty research:* Air resources, ecological systems, solid and hazardous waste, sustainability and environmental nanotechnology, water and wastewater treatment. Total annual research expenditures: $3.9 million. *Unit head:* Dr. Paul A. Chadik, Chair, 352-392-0841, Fax: 352-392-3076, E-mail: pchadik@ufl.edu. *Application contact:* David Mazyck, Graduate Coordinator, 352-846-1039, Fax: 352-392-3076, E-mail: dmazyck@ufl.edu.

University of Georgia, Faculty of Engineering, Program in Environmental Engineering, Athens, GA 30602. Offers MS. *Students:* 7 full-time (2 women), 2 part-time (1 woman); includes 1 Hispanic/Latino; 1 Two or more races, non-Hispanic/Latino, 2 international. 10 applicants, 40% accepted, 3 enrolled. In 2010, 2 master's awarded. *Entrance requirements:* For master's, GRE, baccalaureate degree in engineering or related field from accredited institution with minimum GPA of 3.0; undergraduate academic transcripts; statement of purpose; three letters of recommendation. Additional exam requirements/recommendations for international students: Required—TOEFL. *Expenses:* Tuition, state resident: full-time $7200; part-time $344 per credit hour. Tuition, nonresident: full-time $21,900; part-time $944 per credit hour. Tuition and fees vary according to course load and program. *Unit head:* Dr. E. Dale Threadgill. *Application contact:* Dr. Melissa Barry, Assistant Dean of The Graduate School, 706-425-2934, Fax: 706-425-3093, E-mail: mjb14@uga.edu.

University of Guelph, Graduate Studies, College of Physical and Engineering Science, School of Engineering, Guelph, ON N1G 2W1, Canada. Offers biological engineering (M Eng, M Sc, MA Sc, PhD); engineering systems and computing (M Eng, M Sc, MA Sc, PhD); environmental engineering (M Eng, M Sc, MA Sc, PhD); water resources engineering (M Eng, M Sc, MA Sc, PhD). Part-time programs available. *Degree requirements:* For master's, thesis (for some programs); for doctorate, comprehensive exam, thesis/dissertation. *Entrance requirements:* For master's, minimum B- average during previous 2 years of course work; for doctorate, minimum B average. Additional exam requirements/recommendations for international students: Required—TOEFL (minimum score 550 paper-based; 213 computer-based; 89 iBT), IELTS (minimum score 6.5). Electronic applications accepted. *Faculty research:* Water and food safety, environmental contaminant fates and mechanisms, computer systems, robotics and mechatronics, waste treatment.

University of Hawaii at Manoa, Graduate Division, College of Engineering, Department of Civil and Environmental Engineering, Honolulu, HI 96822. Offers MS, PhD. Part-time programs available. *Faculty:* 24 full-time (2 women). *Students:* 58 full-time (12 women), 22 part-time (6 women); includes 46 minority (32 Asian, non-Hispanic/Latino; 1 Hispanic/Latino; 7 Native Hawaiian or other Pacific Islander, non-Hispanic/Latino; 6 Two or more races, non-Hispanic/Latino), 24 international. Average age 29. 99 applicants, 64% accepted, 38 enrolled. In 2010, 17 master's, 2 doctorates awarded. *Degree requirements:* For master's, comprehensive exam, thesis; for doctorate, comprehensive exam, thesis/dissertation. *Entrance requirements:* For master's and doctorate, GRE General Test or EIT Exam. Additional exam requirements/recommendations for international students: Required—TOEFL (minimum score 540 paper-based; 207 computer-based; 76 iBT), IELTS (minimum score 5). *Application deadline:* For fall admission, 5/1 for domestic and international students; for spring admission, 9/1 for domestic and international students. Application fee: $60. *Financial support:* In 2010–11, 12 fellowships (averaging $1,277 per year), 30 research assistantships (averaging $18,171 per year), 6 teaching assistantships (averaging $15,293 per year) were awarded; career-related internships or fieldwork, Federal Work-Study, and tuition waivers (full and partial) also available. *Faculty research:* Structures, transportation, environmental engineering, geotechnical engineering, construction. Total annual research expenditures: $1.2 million. *Application contact:* Roger Babcock, Graduate Chair, 808-956-7449, Fax: 808-956-5014, E-mail: rbabcock@hawaii.edu.

University of Idaho, College of Graduate Studies, College of Engineering, Department of Engineering, Program in Environmental Engineering, Moscow, ID 83844-2282. Offers M Engr, MS. *Students:* 2 full-time, 1 part-time. Average age 25. In 2010, 2 master's awarded. *Application deadline:* For fall admission, 8/1 for domestic students; for spring admission, 12/15 for domestic students. Applications are processed on a rolling basis. Application fee: $60. Electronic applications accepted. *Expenses:* Tuition, nonresident: part-time $580 per credit. Required fees: $306 per credit. *Financial support:* Applicants required to submit FAFSA. *Unit head:* Dr. Wudneh Admassu, Director, 208-885-7461, E-mail: enve@uidaho.edu. *Application contact:* Dr. Wudneh Admassu, Director, 208-885-7461, E-mail: enve@uidaho.edu.

University of Illinois at Urbana–Champaign, Graduate College, College of Engineering, Department of Civil and Environmental Engineering, Champaign, IL 61820. Offers civil engineering (MS); environmental engineering in civil engineering (MS, PhD); environmental science in civil engineering (MS, PhD); M Arch/MS; MBA/MS. *Faculty:* 46 full-time (7 women), 1 part-time/adjunct (0 women). *Students:* 380 full-time (103 women), 79 part-time (18 women); includes 2 Black or African American, non-Hispanic/Latino; 27 Asian, non-Hispanic/Latino; 15 Hispanic/Latino; 4 Two or more races, non-Hispanic/Latino, 248 international. 961 applicants, 38% accepted, 159 enrolled. In 2010, 119 master's, 45 doctorates awarded. *Entrance requirements:* For master's and doctorate, GRE. Additional exam requirements/recommendations for international students: Required—TOEFL (minimum score 550 paper-based; 213 computer-based; 79 iBT) or IELTS (minimum score 6.5). *Application deadline:* Applications are processed on a rolling basis. Application fee: $75 ($90 for international students). Electronic applications accepted. *Financial support:* In 2010–11, 60 fellowships, 260 research assistantships, 77 teaching assistantships were awarded; tuition waivers (full and partial) also available. *Unit head:* Amr S. Elnashai, Head, 217-265-5497, Fax: 217-265-8040, E-mail: aelnash@illinois.edu. *Application contact:* Mary Pearson, Administrative Secretary, 217-333-3811, Fax: 217-333-9464, E-mail: mkpearso@illinois.edu.

The University of Iowa, Graduate College, College of Engineering, Department of Civil and Environmental Engineering, Iowa City, IA 52242-1316. Offers MS, PhD. Part-time programs available. *Faculty:* 21 full-time (3 women). *Students:* 94 full-time (24 women); includes 3 minority (1 Black or African American, non-Hispanic/Latino; 1 Asian, non-Hispanic/Latino; 1 Hispanic/Latino), 39 international. Average age 27. 216 applicants, 30% accepted, 32 enrolled. In 2010, 24 master's, 11 doctorates awarded. Terminal master's awarded for partial completion of doctoral program. *Degree requirements:* For master's, thesis optional, exam; for doctorate, comprehensive exam, thesis/dissertation, exam. *Entrance requirements:* For master's, GRE, minimum undergraduate GPA of 3.0; for doctorate, GRE, master's degree or equivalent with minimum GPA of 3.2. Additional exam requirements/recommendations for international students: Required—TOEFL (minimum score 550 paper-based; 213 computer-based; 81 iBT). *Application deadline:* For fall admission, 2/1 priority date for domestic and international students; for spring admission, 12/1 for domestic students, 10/1 for international students. Applications are processed on a rolling basis. Application fee: $60 ($100 for international students). Electronic applications accepted. *Financial support:* In 2010–11, 7 fellowships with partial tuition reimbursements (averaging $23,480 per year), 74 research assistantships with partial tuition reimbursements (averaging $22,553 per year), 26 teaching assistantships with partial tuition reimbursements (averaging $16,575 per year) were awarded; career-related internships or fieldwork, Federal Work-Study, scholarships/grants, traineeships, and unspecified assistantships also available. Support available to part-time students. Financial award application deadline: 2/1; financial award applicants required to submit FAFSA. *Faculty research:* Water resources; environmental engineering and science; hydraulics and hydrology; structures, mechanics, and materials; transportation engineering. Total annual research expenditures: $16.4 million. *Unit head:* Dr. Michelle Scherer, Department Executive Officer, 319-335-5654, Fax: 319-335-5660, E-mail: michelle-scherer@uiowa.edu. *Application contact:* Judy Holland, Secretary, 319-335-5647, Fax: 319-335-5660, E-mail: cee@engineering.uiowa.edu.

The University of Kansas, Graduate Studies, School of Engineering, Department of Civil, Environmental, and Architectural Engineering, Program in Environmental Engineering, Lawrence, KS 66045. Offers MS, PhD. Part-time programs available. *Faculty:* 9 full-time (1 woman), 1 part-time/adjunct (0 women). *Students:* 11 full-time (6 women), 5 part-time (2 women), 5 international. Average age 30. 22 applicants, 68% accepted, 2 enrolled. In 2010, 3 master's awarded. *Degree requirements:* For master's, thesis or alternative, exam; for doctorate, comprehensive exam, thesis/dissertation. *Entrance requirements:* For master's and doctorate, GRE, BS in engineering. Additional exam requirements/recommendations for international students: Required—TOEFL. *Application deadline:* For fall admission, 3/1 priority date for domestic and international students; for spring admission, 12/1 priority date for domestic students, 8/15 priority date for international students. Applications are processed on a rolling basis. Application fee: $55 ($65 for international students). Electronic applications accepted. *Expenses:* Tuition, state resident: full-time $7092; part-time $295.50 per credit hour. Tuition, nonresident: full-time $16,590; part-time $691.25 per credit hour. Required fees: $858; $71.49 per credit hour. Tuition and fees vary according to course load, campus/location and program. *Financial support:* Fellowships with full tuition reimbursements, research assistantships with full tuition reimbursements, teaching assistantships with full and partial tuition reimbursements, career-related internships or fieldwork available. Financial award application deadline: 2/7. *Faculty research:* Water quality, water treatment, wastewater treatment, air quality, air pollution control, solid waste, hazardous waste, water resources engineering. *Unit head:* Craig D. Adams, Chair, 785-864-2700, Fax: 785-864-5631, E-mail: adamscd@ku.edu. *Application contact:* Bruce M. McEnroe, Graduate Advisor, 785-864-2925, Fax: 785-864-2925, E-mail: mcenroe@ku.edu.

University of Louisville, J.B. Speed School of Engineering, Department of Civil and Environmental Engineering, Louisville, KY 40292-0001. Offers civil engineering (M Eng, MS, PhD). *Accreditation:* ABET (one or more programs are accredited). Part-time programs available. Postbaccalaureate distance learning degree programs offered (no on-campus study). *Faculty:* 10 full-time (1 woman). *Students:* 36 full-time (5 women), 21 part-time (3 women); includes 1 Asian, non-Hispanic/Latino, 10 international. Average age 28. 24 applicants, 71% accepted, 12 enrolled. In 2010, 33 master's, 2 doctorates awarded. Terminal master's awarded for partial completion of doctoral program. *Degree requirements:* For master's, comprehensive exam (for some programs), thesis or alternative; for doctorate, comprehensive exam, thesis/dissertation, minimum GPA of 3.0. *Entrance requirements:* For master's and doctorate, GRE General Test. Additional exam requirements/recommendations for international students: Required—TOEFL (minimum score 550 paper-based; 213 computer-based; 80 iBT), IELTS (minimum score 6.5). *Application deadline:* For fall admission, 5/1 priority date for domestic and international students; for spring admission, 11/1 priority date for domestic and international students. Applications are processed on a rolling basis. Application fee: $50. Electronic applications accepted. *Expenses:* Tuition, state resident: full-time $9144; part-time $508 per credit hour. Tuition, nonresident: full-time $19,026; part-time $1057 per credit hour. Tuition and fees vary according to program and reciprocity agreements. *Financial support:* In 2010–11, 7 students received support, including 1 fellowship with full tuition reimbursement available (averaging $20,000 per year), 1 research assistantship with full tuition reimbursement available (averaging $20,000 per year), 5 teaching assistantships with full tuition reimbursements available (averaging $20,000 per year). Financial award application deadline: 1/25; financial award applicants required to submit FAFSA. *Faculty research:* Structures, hydraulics, transportation, environmental engineering, geomechanics. Total annual research expenditures: $1.8 million. *Unit head:* Dr. J. P. Mohsen, Chair, 502-852-6276, Fax: 502-852-8851, E-mail: jpmohs01@louisville.edu. *Application contact:* Dr. Michael Day, Associate Dean, 502-852-6195, Fax: 502-852-7294, E-mail: day@louisville.edu.

The University of Manchester, School of Mechanical, Aerospace and Civil Engineering, Manchester, United Kingdom. Offers advanced manufacturing technology (M Ent); aerospace engineering (M Phil, M Sc, PhD); civil engineering (M Phil, M Sc, PhD); environmental engineering (M Phil, PhD); management of projects (M Phil, M Sc, PhD); mechanical engineering (M Phil, M Sc, PhD); mechanical engineering design (M Ent); nuclear engineering (M Phil, D Eng, PhD).

University of Maryland, College Park, Academic Affairs, A. James Clark School of Engineering, Department of Civil and Environmental Engineering, College Park, MD 20742. Offers M Eng, MS, PhD. Part-time and evening/weekend programs available. Postbaccalaureate distance learning degree programs offered. *Faculty:* 65 full-time (12 women), 27 part-time/adjunct (8 women). *Students:* 170 full-time (57 women), 54 part-time (21 women); includes 41 minority (15 Black or African American, non-Hispanic/Latino; 15 Asian, non-Hispanic/Latino; 8 Hispanic/Latino; 3 Two or more races, non-Hispanic/Latino), 112 international. 376 applicants, 35% accepted, 58 enrolled. In 2010, 31 master's, 10 doctorates awarded. *Degree requirements:* For master's, thesis optional; for doctorate, thesis/dissertation, qualifying exam. *Entrance requirements:* For master's and doctorate, GRE General Test, 3 letters of recommendation. *Application deadline:* For fall admission, 5/1 for domestic students, 2/1 for international students;

for spring admission, 10/15 for domestic students, 6/1 for international students. Applications are processed on a rolling basis. Application fee: $75. Electronic applications accepted. *Expenses:* Tuition, area resident: Part-time $471 per credit hour. Tuition, state resident: part-time $471 per credit hour. Tuition, nonresident: part-time $1016 per credit hour. Required fees: $337 per term. *Financial support:* In 2010–11, 19 fellowships with full and partial tuition reimbursements (averaging $14,546 per year), 67 research assistantships (averaging $19,189 per year), 29 teaching assistantships (averaging $19,575 per year) were awarded; Federal Work-Study and scholarships/grants also available. Support available to part-time students. Financial award applicants required to submit FAFSA. *Faculty research:* Transportation and urban systems, environmental engineering, geotechnical engineering, construction engineering and management, hydraulics. Total annual research expenditures: $22.6 million. *Unit head:* Dr. Ali Haghani, Chair, 301-405-1974, E-mail: haghani@umd.edu. *Application contact:* Dr. Charles A. Caramello, Dean of Graduate School, 301-405-0358, Fax: 301-314-9305, E-mail: ccaramel@umd.edu.

University of Massachusetts Amherst, Graduate School, College of Engineering, Department of Civil and Environmental Engineering, Program in Environmental Engineering, Amherst, MA 01003. Offers MS. Part-time programs available. *Students:* 12 full-time (4 women), 1 part-time (0 women); includes 2 minority (1 Hispanic/Latino; 1 Two or more races, non-Hispanic/Latino), 1 international. Average age 25. 1 applicant, 0% accepted, 0 enrolled. In 2010, 3 master's awarded. *Degree requirements:* For master's, thesis or alternative. *Entrance requirements:* For master's, GRE General Test. Additional exam requirements/recommendations for international students: Required—TOEFL (minimum score 550 paper-based; 213 computer-based; 80 iBT), IELTS (minimum score 6.5). *Application deadline:* For fall admission, 2/1 for domestic and international students; for spring admission, 10/1 for domestic and international students. Applications are processed on a rolling basis. Application fee: $50 ($65 for international students). Electronic applications accepted. *Expenses:* Tuition, state resident: full-time $2640. Required fees: $8282. One-time fee: $357 full-time. *Financial support:* Fellowships with full tuition reimbursements, research assistantships with full tuition reimbursements, teaching assistantships with full tuition reimbursements, career-related internships or fieldwork, Federal Work-Study, scholarships/grants, traineeships, health care benefits, tuition waivers, and unspecified assistantships available. Support available to part-time students. Financial award application deadline: 2/1; financial award applicants required to submit FAFSA. *Unit head:* Dr. David Ahlfeld, Graduate Program Director, 413-545-0686, Fax: 413-545-2840. *Application contact:* Jean M. Ames, Supervisor of Admissions, 413-545-0722, Fax: 413-577-0100, E-mail: gradadm@grad.umass.edu.

University of Massachusetts Amherst, Graduate School, Interdisciplinary Programs, Program in Environmental Engineering and Business Administration, Amherst, MA 01003. Offers MS Envr E/MBA. Part-time programs available. *Students:* 1 applicant, 0% accepted, 0 enrolled. *Entrance requirements:* Additional exam requirements/recommendations for international students: Required—TOEFL (minimum score 600 paper-based; 250 computer-based; 100 iBT), IELTS (minimum score 7). *Application deadline:* For fall admission, 2/1 for domestic and international students. Applications are processed on a rolling basis. Application fee: $50 ($65 for international students). Electronic applications accepted. *Expenses:* Tuition, state resident: full-time $2640. Required fees: $8282. One-time fee: $357 full-time. *Financial support:* Career-related internships or fieldwork, Federal Work-Study, scholarships/grants, traineeships, health care benefits, tuition waivers (full), and unspecified assistantships available. Support available to part-time students. *Unit head:* Dr. David Ahlfeld, Graduate Program Director, 413-545-2681, Fax: 413-545-2840. *Application contact:* Jean M. Ames, Supervisor of Admissions, 413-545-0722, Fax: 413-577-0010, E-mail: gradadm@grad.umass.edu.

University of Massachusetts Dartmouth, Graduate School, College of Engineering, Program in Civil and Environmental Engineering, North Dartmouth, MA 02747-2300. Offers MS. Part-time programs available. *Faculty:* 8 full-time (2 women), 3 part-time/adjunct (0 women). *Students:* 4 full-time (0 women), 13 part-time (2 women); includes 2 Hispanic/Latino. Average age 25. 28 applicants, 79% accepted, 8 enrolled. In 2010, 2 master's awarded. *Degree requirements:* For master's, thesis or alternative. *Entrance requirements:* For master's, GRE, minimum GPA of 3.0, 3 letters of recommendation. Additional exam requirements/recommendations for international students: Required—TOEFL (minimum score 550 paper-based). *Application deadline:* For fall admission, 4/20 priority date for domestic students, 2/20 priority date for international students; for spring admission, 11/15 priority date for domestic students, 9/15 priority date for international students. Application fee: $40 ($60 for international students). *Expenses:* Tuition, state resident: full-time $2071; part-time $86 per credit. Tuition, nonresident: full-time $8099; part-time $337 per credit. Required fees: $9446; $394 per credit. One-time fee: $75. Part-time tuition and fees vary according to class time, course load, degree level and reciprocity agreements. *Financial support:* In 2010–11, 5 teaching assistantships with full tuition reimbursements (averaging $12,500 per year) were awarded. Financial award application deadline: 3/1; financial award applicants required to submit FAFSA. *Faculty research:* Nutrient removal and recovery, water resources engineering, pavement design and management, waste water treatment systems, hydrology. Total annual research expenditures: $546,183. *Unit head:* Dr. Heather Miller, Graduate Director, 508-999-8481, E-mail: hmiller@umassd.edu. *Application contact:* Elan Turcotte-Shamski, Graduate Admissions Officer, 508-999-8604, Fax: 508-999-8183, E-mail: graduate@umassd.edu.

University of Massachusetts Lowell, James B. Francis College of Engineering, Department of Civil and Environmental Engineering and College of Arts and Sciences, Program in Environmental Studies, Lowell, MA 01854-2881. Offers environmental engineering (MSES); environmental studies (PhD, Certificate). Part-time programs available. *Degree requirements:* For master's, thesis optional. *Entrance requirements:* For master's, GRE General Test. *Faculty research:* Remote sensing of air pollutants, atmospheric deposition of toxic metals, contaminant transport in groundwater, soil remediation.

University of Memphis, Graduate School, Herff College of Engineering, Department of Civil Engineering, Memphis, TN 38152. Offers civil engineering (PhD); environmental engineering (MS); foundation engineering (MS); structural engineering (MS); transportation engineering (MS); water resources engineering (MS). *Faculty:* 12 full-time (1 woman), 1 part-time/adjunct (0 women). *Students:* 12 full-time (5 women), 13 part-time (3 women); includes 2 Black or African American, non-Hispanic/Latino; 2 Asian, non-Hispanic/Latino; 1 Two or more races, non-Hispanic/Latino, 7 international. Average age 28. 22 applicants, 55% accepted, 0 enrolled. In 2010, 11 master's awarded. Terminal master's awarded for partial completion of doctoral program. *Degree requirements:* For master's, comprehensive exam, thesis optional; for doctorate, comprehensive exam, thesis/dissertation. *Entrance requirements:* For master's, GRE General Test or MAT, minimum undergraduate GPA of 2.5; for doctorate, GRE, 3 letters of recommendation. Additional exam requirements/recommendations for international students: Required—TOEFL (minimum score 550 paper-based; 210 computer-based; 79 iBT). *Application deadline:* For fall admission, 1/7 for domestic students, 1/5 for international students; for spring admission, 12/1 for domestic students, 9/15 for international students. Application fee: $35 ($60 for international students). *Financial support:* In 2010–11, 6 students received support; fellowships with full tuition reimbursements available, research assistantships with full tuition reimbursements available, career-related internships or fieldwork, Federal Work-Study, scholarships/grants, and unspecified assistantships available. Financial award application deadline: 2/15; financial award applicants required to submit FAFSA. *Faculty research:* Structural response to earthquakes, pavement design, water quality, transportation safety, intermodal transportation. *Unit head:* Dr. Sharam Pezeshk, Interim Chair, 901-678-2746, Fax: 901-678-3026. *Application contact:* Dr. Roger Meier, Coordinator of Graduate Studies, 901-678-3284.

University of Michigan, Horace H. Rackham School of Graduate Studies, College of Engineering, Department of Civil and Environmental Engineering, Ann Arbor, MI 48109. Offers civil engineering (MSE, PhD, CE); construction engineering and management (M Eng, MSE); environmental engineering (MSE, PhD); structural engineering (M Eng); MBA/MSE. Part-time programs available. *Students:* 121 full-time (45 women), 5 part-time (2 women). 461 applicants, 30% accepted, 54 enrolled. In 2010, 36 master's, 13 doctorates awarded. *Degree requirements:* For master's, thesis optional; for doctorate, comprehensive exam, thesis/dissertation, oral defense of dissertation, preliminary and written exams. *Entrance requirements:* For master's and doctorate, GRE General Test. Additional exam requirements/recommendations for international students: Required—TOEFL (minimum score 560 paper-based; 220 computer-based). *Application deadline:* Applications are processed on a rolling basis. Application fee: $65 ($75 for international students). Electronic applications accepted. *Expenses:* Tuition, state resident: full-time $17,784; part-time $1116 per credit hour. Tuition, nonresident: full-time $35,944; part-time $2125 per credit hour. International tuition: $35,994 full-time. Required fees: $95 per semester. Tuition and fees vary according to course load, degree level and program. *Financial support:* Fellowships, research assistantships, teaching assistantships, institutionally sponsored loans and tuition waivers (partial) available. Financial award application deadline: 1/19. *Faculty research:* Construction engineering and management; geotechnical engineering; earthquake-resistant design of structures; environmental chemistry and microbiology; cost engineering; environmental and water resources engineering. *Unit head:* Nancy Love, Chair, 734-764-8405, Fax: 734-764-4292, E-mail: nglove@umich.edu. *Application contact:* Kimberly Smith, Student Advisor, 734-764-8405, Fax: 734-647-2127, E-mail: kansmith@umich.edu.

University of Missouri, Graduate School, College of Engineering, Department of Civil and Environmental Engineering, Columbia, MO 65211. Offers civil engineering (MS, PhD); environmental engineering (MS, PhD); geotechnical engineering (MS, PhD); structural engineering (MS, PhD); transportation and highway engineering (MS); water resources (MS, PhD). *Degree requirements:* For master's, report or thesis; for doctorate, thesis/dissertation. *Entrance requirements:* For master's and doctorate, GRE General Test. Additional exam requirements/recommendations for international students: Required—TOEFL (minimum score 550 paper-based; 213 computer-based; 79 iBT).

University of Nebraska–Lincoln, Graduate College, College of Engineering, Interdepartmental Area of Environmental Engineering, Lincoln, NE 68588. Offers MS, PhD. *Degree requirements:* For master's, thesis optional; for doctorate, comprehensive exam, thesis/dissertation. *Entrance requirements:* For master's and doctorate, GRE General Test. Additional exam requirements/recommendations for international students: Required—TOEFL (minimum score 550 paper-based; 213 computer-based). Electronic applications accepted. *Faculty research:* Wastewater engineering, hazardous waste management, solid waste management, groundwater engineering.

University of Nevada, Las Vegas, Graduate College, Howard R. Hughes College of Engineering, Department of Civil and Environmental Engineering, Las Vegas, NV 89154-4015. Offers civil and environmental engineering (PhD); transportation (MS). Part-time programs available. *Faculty:* 16 full-time (3 women), 4 part-time/adjunct (0 women). *Students:* 35 full-time (5 women), 20 part-time (7 women); includes 19 minority (1 Black or African American, non-Hispanic/Latino; 2 Asian, non-Hispanic/Latino; 5 Hispanic/Latino; 11 Two or more races, non-Hispanic/Latino), 19 international. Average age 32. 34 applicants, 82% accepted, 15 enrolled. In 2010, 17 master's, 8 doctorates awarded. *Degree requirements:* For master's, comprehensive exam (for some programs), thesis (for some programs); for doctorate, comprehensive exam, thesis/dissertation. *Entrance requirements:* For master's and doctorate, GRE General Test. Additional exam requirements/recommendations for international students: Required—TOEFL (minimum score 550 paper-based; 213 computer-based; 80 iBT), IELTS (minimum score 7). *Application deadline:* For fall admission, 6/15 priority date for domestic students, 3/15 priority date for international students; for spring admission, 11/15 priority date for domestic students, 8/30 priority date for international students. Applications are processed on a rolling basis. Application fee: $60 ($95 for international students). Electronic applications accepted. *Expenses:* Tuition, area resident: Part-time $239.50 per credit. Tuition, state resident: part-time $239.50 per credit. Tuition, nonresident: part-time $503 per credit. Required fees: $108 per semester. Tuition and fees vary according to course load, program and reciprocity agreements. *Financial support:* In 2010–11, 38 students received support, including 23 research assistantships with partial tuition reimbursements available (averaging $13,595 per year), 15 teaching assistantships with partial tuition reimbursements available (averaging $11,200 per year); institutionally sponsored loans, scholarships/grants, health care benefits, and unspecified assistantships also available. Financial award application deadline: 3/1. Total annual research expenditures: $1.4 million. *Unit head:* Dr. David Ashley, Professor, 702-895-4040, Fax: 702-895-3936, E-mail: david.b.ashley@unlv.edu. *Application contact:* Graduate College Admissions Evaluator, 702-895-3320, Fax: 702-895-4180, E-mail: gradcollege@unlv.edu.

University of New Brunswick Fredericton, School of Graduate Studies, Faculty of Engineering, Department of Civil Engineering, Fredericton, NB E3B 5A3, Canada. Offers construction engineering and management (M Eng, M Sc E, PhD); environmental engineering (M Eng, M Sc E, PhD); environmental studies (M Eng); geotechnical engineering (M Eng, M Sc E, PhD); groundwater/hydrology (M Eng, M Sc E, PhD); materials (M Eng, M Sc E, PhD); pavements (M Eng, M Sc E, PhD); structures (M Eng, M Sc E, PhD); transportation (M Eng, M Sc E, PhD). Part-time programs available. *Faculty:* 13 full-time (1 woman), 7 part-time/adjunct (1 woman). *Students:* 34 full-time (8 women), 16 part-time (2 women). In 2010, 16 master's, 6 doctorates awarded. *Degree requirements:* For master's, thesis, proposal; for doctorate, comprehensive exam, thesis/dissertation, qualifying exam; proposal; 27 credit hours of courses. *Entrance requirements:* For master's, minimum GPA of 3.0; B Sc E in civil engineering or related engineering degree; for doctorate, minimum GPA of 3.0; graduate degree in engineering or applied science. Additional exam requirements/recommendations for international students: Required—TWE (minimum score 4), TOEFL (minimum score 580 paper-based; 237 computer-based) or IELTS (minimum score 7.5). *Application deadline:* For fall admission, 5/1 priority date for domestic students; for winter admission, 11/1 priority date for domestic students. Applications are processed on a rolling basis. Application fee: $50 Canadian dollars. *Expenses:* Tuition, area resident: Full-time $3708; part-time $927 per term. International tuition: $6300 full-time. Required fees: $50 per term. *Financial support:* In 2010–11, 52 research assistantships (averaging $7,000 per year), 46 teaching assistantships (averaging $2,000 per year) were awarded; career-related internships or fieldwork and scholarships/grants also available. *Faculty research:* Construction engineering and management; materials and infrastructure renewal; highway and pavement research; structures and solid mechanics; geotechnical, soil; structure interaction; transportation and planning; environment, solid waste management. *Unit head:* Dr. Eric Hildebrand, Director of Graduate Studies, 506-453-5113, Fax: 506-453-3568, E-mail: edh@unb.ca. *Application contact:* Joyce Moore, Graduate Secretary, 506-452-6127, Fax: 506-453-3568, E-mail: civil-grad@unb.ca.

University of New Haven, Graduate School, Tagliatela College of Engineering, Program in Environmental Engineering, West Haven, CT 06516-1916. Offers environmental engineering (MS); industrial and hazardous wastes (MS); water and wastewater treatment (MS); water resources (Certificate). Part-time and evening/weekend programs available. *Students:* 20 full-time (8 women), 5 part-time (2 women); includes 2 Black or African American, non-Hispanic/Latino, 20 international. Average age 31. 35 applicants, 97% accepted, 7 enrolled. In 2010, 10 master's awarded. *Degree requirements:* For master's, thesis or alternative. *Entrance requirements:* For master's, bachelor's degree in engineering. Additional exam requirements/recommendations for international students: Required—TOEFL (minimum score 520 paper-based; 190 computer-based; 70 iBT); Recommended—IELTS (minimum score 5.5). *Application deadline:* For fall admission, 5/31 for international students; for winter admission, 10/15 for international students; for spring admission, 1/15 for international students. Applications are processed on a rolling basis. Application fee: $50. Electronic applications accepted. *Financial support:* Research assistantships with partial tuition reimbursements, teaching assistantships with partial tuition reimbursements, career-related internships or fieldwork, Federal Work-Study, scholarships/grants, tuition waivers, and unspecified assistantships available. Support available to part-time students. Financial award application deadline: 5/1; financial award applicants required to submit FAFSA. *Unit head:* Dr. Agamemnon D. Koutsospyros, Coordinator, 203-932-7398. *Application contact:* Eloise Gormley, Director of Graduate Admissions, 203-932-7449, Fax: 203-932-7137, E-mail: gradinfo@newhaven.edu.

The University of North Carolina at Chapel Hill, Graduate School, School of Public Health, Department of Environmental Sciences and Engineering, Chapel Hill, NC 27599. Offers air,

Environmental Engineering

The University of North Carolina at Chapel Hill (continued)
radiation and industrial hygiene (MPH, MS, MSEE, MSPH, PhD); aquatic and atmospheric sciences (MPH, MS, MSPH, PhD); environmental engineering (MPH, MS, MSEE, MSPH, PhD); environmental health sciences (MPH, MS, MSPH, PhD); environmental management and policy (MPH, MS, MSPH, PhD). Terminal master's awarded for partial completion of doctoral program. *Degree requirements:* For master's, comprehensive exam, thesis (for some programs), research paper; for doctorate, comprehensive exam, thesis/dissertation. *Entrance requirements:* For master's and doctorate, GRE General Test, minimum GPA of 3.0. Additional exam requirements/recommendations for international students: Required—TOEFL. Electronic applications accepted. *Faculty research:* Air, radiation and industrial hygiene, aquatic and atmospheric sciences, environmental health sciences, environmental management and policy, water resources engineering.

The University of North Carolina at Charlotte, Graduate School, The William States Lee College of Engineering, Department of Civil and Environmental Engineering, Charlotte, NC 28223-0001. Offers civil engineering (MSCE); infrastructure and environmental systems (PhD), including infrastructure and environmental systems design. Part-time and evening/weekend programs available. *Faculty:* 20 full-time (2 women). *Students:* 44 full-time (13 women), 48 part-time (15 women); includes 11 minority (4 Black or African American, non-Hispanic/Latino; 1 American Indian or Alaska Native, non-Hispanic/Latino; 6 Hispanic/Latino), 29 international. Average age 29. 45 applicants, 69% accepted, 20 enrolled. In 2010, 10 master's, 3 doctorates awarded. Terminal master's awarded for partial completion of doctoral program. *Degree requirements:* For master's, thesis or alternative, thesis or project. *Entrance requirements:* For master's, GRE General Test, minimum GPA of 3.0 in undergraduate major, 2.75 overall. Additional exam requirements/recommendations for international students: Required—TOEFL (minimum score 550 paper-based; 220 computer-based; 83 iBT). *Application deadline:* For fall admission, 7/1 for domestic students, 5/1 for international students; for spring admission, 11/1 for domestic students, 10/1 for international students. Applications are processed on a rolling basis. Application fee: $55. Electronic applications accepted. *Expenses:* Tuition, state resident: full-time $3464. Tuition, nonresident: full-time $14,297. Required fees: $2094. Tuition and fees vary according to course load. *Financial support:* In 2010–11, 46 students received support, including 2 fellowships (averaging $28,347 per year), 19 research assistantships (averaging $5,352 per year), 25 teaching assistantships (averaging $6,166 per year); career-related internships or fieldwork, Federal Work-Study, institutionally sponsored loans, scholarships/grants, and administrative assistantship also available. Support available to part-time students. Financial award application deadline: 4/1; financial award applicants required to submit FAFSA. *Faculty research:* Structural composite materials, storm water systems, natural and man-made disaster reduction engineering, older drivers and nighttime driving, soil contamination and transport. Total annual research expenditures: $1.3 million. *Unit head:* Dr. David T. Young, Chair, 704-687-4175, Fax: 704-687-6953, E-mail: dyoung@.uncc.edu. *Application contact:* Kathy B. Giddings, Director of Graduate Admissions, 704-687-5503, Fax: 704-687-3279, E-mail: gradadm@uncc.edu.

University of North Dakota, Graduate School, School of Engineering and Mines, Department of Environmental Engineering, Grand Forks, ND 58202. Offers M Engr, MS. *Students:* 1 (woman) full-time, 2 part-time (0 women); includes 1 minority (Asian, non-Hispanic/Latino), 1 international. Average age 39. 6 applicants, 33% accepted, 2 enrolled. *Degree requirements:* For master's, thesis. *Entrance requirements:* For master's, GRE General Test, minimum GPA of 3.0. Additional exam requirements/recommendations for international students: Required—TOEFL (minimum score 550 paper-based; 213 computer-based; 79 iBT), IELTS (minimum score 6.5). *Application deadline:* For fall admission, 2/28 for domestic and international students; for spring admission, 9/15 for domestic and international students. Application fee: $35. Electronic applications accepted. *Expenses:* Tuition, state resident: full-time $5857; part-time $306.74 per credit. Tuition, nonresident: full-time $15,666; part-time $729.77 per credit. Required fees: $53.42 per credit. Tuition and fees vary according to course load, program and reciprocity agreements. *Financial support:* In 2010–11, 2 students received support, including 1 research assistantship with full and partial tuition reimbursement available (averaging $9,635 per year), 1 teaching assistantship with full and partial tuition reimbursement available; fellowships with full and partial tuition reimbursements available, Federal Work-Study, scholarships/grants, health care benefits, tuition waivers (full and partial), and unspecified assistantships also available. Support available to part-time students. Financial award applicants required to submit FAFSA. *Unit head:* Dr. Frank Bowman, Graduate Director, 701-777-4245, Fax: 701-777-4838, E-mail: frankbowman@mail.und.edu. *Application contact:* Staci Wells, Admissions Associate, 701-777-2945, Fax: 701-777-3619, E-mail: staci.wells@gradschool.und.edu.

University of Notre Dame, Graduate School, College of Engineering, Department of Civil Engineering and Geological Sciences, Notre Dame, IN 46556. Offers bioengineering (MS Bio E); civil engineering (MSCE); civil engineering and geological sciences (PhD); environmental engineering (MS Env E); geological sciences (MS). Terminal master's awarded for partial completion of doctoral program. *Degree requirements:* For master's, comprehensive exam; for doctorate, thesis/dissertation, candidacy exam. *Entrance requirements:* For master's and doctorate, GRE General Test. Additional exam requirements/recommendations for international students: Required—TOEFL (minimum score 600 paper-based; 250 computer-based; 80 iBT). Electronic applications accepted. *Faculty research:* Environmental modeling, biological-waste treatment, petrology, environmental geology, geochemistry.

University of Oklahoma, College of Earth and Energy, School of Petroleum and Geological Engineering, Program in Petroleum Engineering, Norman, OK 73019-0390. Offers natural gas engineering and management (MS); petroleum engineering (MS, PhD). Part-time programs available. *Students:* 83 full-time (16 women), 40 part-time (7 women); includes 5 minority (4 Black or African American, non-Hispanic/Latino; 1 Hispanic/Latino), 106 international. Average age 28. 143 applicants, 27% accepted, 26 enrolled. In 2010, 11 master's, 3 doctorates awarded. Terminal master's awarded for partial completion of doctoral program. *Degree requirements:* For master's, thesis optional, industrial team project or thesis; for doctorate, thesis/dissertation. *Entrance requirements:* For master's, GRE General Test, bachelor's degree in engineering, 3 letters of recommendation, minimum GPA of 3.0 during final 60 hours of undergraduate course work; for doctorate, GRE General Test, minimum GPA of 3.0, 3 letters of recommendation. Additional exam requirements/recommendations for international students: Required—TOEFL (minimum score 550 paper-based; 213 computer-based; 79 iBT). *Application deadline:* For fall admission, 6/1 priority date for domestic students, 4/1 for international students; for spring admission, 11/1 for domestic students, 9/1 for international students. Applications are processed on a rolling basis. Application fee: $40 ($90 for international students). Electronic applications accepted. *Expenses:* Tuition, state resident: full-time $3892.80; part-time $162.20 per credit hour. Tuition, nonresident: full-time $14,167; part-time $590.30 per credit hour. Required fees: $2523.40; $94.60 per credit hour. Tuition and fees vary according to course load and degree level. *Financial support:* In 2010–11, 96 students received support. Traineeships available. Financial award application deadline: 4/15; financial award applicants required to submit FAFSA. *Faculty research:* Petrophysics, shale gas, reservoir simulation coiled tubing, poro-mechanics, enhanced oil recovery. *Unit head:* Dr. Chandra Rai, Director, 405-325-2921, Fax: 405-325-7477, E-mail: crai@ou.edu. *Application contact:* Shalli Young, Executive Assistant to the Graduate Liaison, 405-325-2921, Fax: 405-325-7477, E-mail: syoung@ou.edu.

University of Oklahoma, College of Engineering, School of Civil Engineering and Environmental Science, Program in Environmental Engineering, Norman, OK 73019-0390. Offers MS, PhD. Part-time programs available. *Students:* 3 full-time (all women), 7 part-time (2 women); includes 1 minority (American Indian or Alaska Native, non-Hispanic/Latino), 3 international. Average age 30. 10 applicants, 40% accepted, 2 enrolled. In 2010, 3 master's, 2 doctorates awarded. *Entrance requirements:* For master's, undergraduate degree in a related engineering or science discipline. Additional exam requirements/recommendations for international students: Required—TOEFL (minimum score 600 paper-based; 250 computer-based; 100 iBT). *Application deadline:* For fall admission, 4/1 priority date for domestic students, 4/1 for international students; for spring admission, 11/1 for domestic students, 9/1 for international students. Applications are processed on a rolling basis. Application fee: $40 ($90 for international students). Electronic applications accepted. *Expenses:* Tuition, state resident: full-time $3892.80; part-time $162.20 per credit hour. Tuition, nonresident: full-time $14,167; part-time $590.30 per credit hour. Required fees: $2523.40; $94.60 per credit hour. Tuition and fees vary according to course load and degree level. *Financial support:* Scholarships/grants available. Financial award application deadline: 3/1. *Faculty research:* Coastal zone flood prediction, inland runoff modeling, flooding and drought due to climate change, water treatment. *Unit head:* Robert C. Knox, Director, 405-325-5911, Fax: 405-325-4217, E-mail: rknox@ou.edu. *Application contact:* Susan Williams, Graduate Programs Specialist, 405-325-2344, Fax: 405-325-4217, E-mail: srwilliams@ou.edu.

University of Pittsburgh, School of Engineering, Department of Civil and Environmental Engineering, Pittsburgh, PA 15260. Offers MSCEE, PhD. Part-time programs available. Post-baccalaureate distance learning degree programs offered. *Faculty:* 16 full-time (4 women), 20 part-time/adjunct (1 woman). *Students:* 88 full-time (25 women), 60 part-time (12 women); includes 7 minority (1 Black or African American, non-Hispanic/Latino; 3 Asian, non-Hispanic/Latino; 3 Hispanic/Latino), 54 international. 274 applicants, 75% accepted, 46 enrolled. In 2010, 17 master's, 1 doctorate awarded. Terminal master's awarded for partial completion of doctoral program. *Degree requirements:* For master's, thesis optional; for doctorate, comprehensive exam, thesis/dissertation, final oral exams. *Entrance requirements:* For master's and doctorate, minimum QPA of 3.0. Additional exam requirements/recommendations for international students: Required—TOEFL (minimum score 550 paper-based; 213 computer-based; 80 iBT). *Application deadline:* For fall admission, 3/1 priority date for domestic students; for spring admission, 7/1 priority date for domestic students. Applications are processed on a rolling basis. Application fee: $50. Electronic applications accepted. *Expenses:* Tuition, state resident: full-time $17,304; part-time $701 per credit. Tuition, nonresident: full-time $29,554; part-time $1210 per credit. Required fees: $740; $214 per term. Tuition and fees vary according to program. *Financial support:* In 2010–11, 44 students received support, including 16 fellowships with tuition reimbursements available (averaging $26,000 per year), 30 research assistantships with full tuition reimbursements available (averaging $25,000 per year), 15 teaching assistantships with full tuition reimbursements available (averaging $24,000 per year); scholarships/grants, traineeships, and tuition waivers (full and partial) also available. Financial award application deadline: 4/15. *Faculty research:* Environmental and water resources, structures and infrastructures, construction management. Total annual research expenditures: $4.5 million. *Unit head:* Dr. Radisav Vidic, Chairman, 412-624-9870, Fax: 412-624-0135. *Application contact:* Amir Kouboa, Academic Coordinator, 412-624-9869, Fax: 412-624-0135, E-mail: amk59@pitt.edu.

University of Regina, Faculty of Graduate Studies and Research, Faculty of Engineering and Applied Science, Program in Environmental Systems Engineering, Regina, SK S4S 0A2, Canada. Offers M Eng, MA Sc, PhD. Part-time programs available. *Faculty:* 10 full-time (3 women). *Students:* 51 full-time (16 women), 8 part-time (3 women). 51 applicants, 51% accepted. In 2010, 8 master's, 7 doctorates awarded. *Degree requirements:* For master's, thesis (for some programs); for doctorate, thesis/dissertation. *Entrance requirements:* For doctorate, master's degree. Additional exam requirements/recommendations for international students: Required—TOEFL (minimum score 550 paper-based; 80 iBT). *Application deadline:* For fall admission, 3/31 for domestic and international students; for winter admission, 7/31 for domestic and international students; for spring admission, 11/30 for domestic and international students. Application fee: $100. Electronic applications accepted. Tuition and fees charges are reported in Canadian dollars. *Expenses:* Tuition, area resident: Full-time $3244.50 Canadian dollars; part-time $180.25 Canadian dollars per credit hour. International tuition: $4744.50 Canadian dollars full-time. Required fees: $494 Canadian dollars; $115.25 Canadian dollars per credit hour. $115.25 Canadian dollars per semester. Tuition and fees vary according to program. *Financial support:* In 2010–11, 9 fellowships (averaging $19,000 per year), 3 research assistantships (averaging $17,500 per year), 12 teaching assistantships (averaging $6,924 per year) were awarded; career-related internships or fieldwork and scholarships/grants also available. Financial award application deadline: 6/15. *Faculty research:* Design of water and wastewater treatment systems, urban and regional transportation planning, environmental fluid mechanics, air quality management, environmental modeling and decision making. *Unit head:* Dr. Raphael Idem, Chair, 306-585-4770, Fax: 306-585-4855, E-mail: raphael.idem@uregina.ca. *Application contact:* Amy Veawab, Graduate Program Coordinator, 306-585-5665, Fax: 306-585-4855, E-mail: amy.veawab@uregina.ca.

University of Rhode Island, Graduate School, College of Engineering, Department of Civil and Environmental Engineering, Kingston, RI 02881. Offers MS, PhD. Part-time programs available. *Faculty:* 8 full-time (3 women), 3 part-time/adjunct (0 women). *Students:* 22 full-time (6 women), 18 part-time (6 women); includes 5 minority (1 Asian, non-Hispanic/Latino; 2 Hispanic/Latino; 2 Two or more races, non-Hispanic/Latino), 9 international. In 2010, 13 master's awarded. *Degree requirements:* For master's, comprehensive exam (for some programs), thesis optional; for doctorate, comprehensive exam, thesis/dissertation. *Entrance requirements:* For master's and doctorate, 2 letters of recommendation. Additional exam requirements/recommendations for international students: Required—TOEFL (minimum score 550 paper-based; 213 computer-based). *Application deadline:* For fall admission, 7/15 for domestic students, 2/1 for international students; for spring admission, 11/15 for domestic students, 7/15 for international students. Application fee: $65. Electronic applications accepted. *Expenses:* Tuition, state resident: full-time $9588; part-time $533 per credit hour. Tuition, nonresident: full-time $22,968; part-time $1276 per credit hour. Required fees: $1282; $68 per semester. Tuition and fees vary according to program. *Financial support:* In 2010–11, 5 research assistantships with full and partial tuition reimbursements (averaging $7,871 per year), 3 teaching assistantships with full and partial tuition reimbursements (averaging $8,890 per year) were awarded. Financial award application deadline: 7/15; financial award applicants required to submit FAFSA. *Faculty research:* Industrial waste treatment, structural health monitoring, traffic and transit system operations, computational mechanics, engineering materials design. Total annual research expenditures: $460,423. *Unit head:* Dr. George E. Tsiatas, Chair, 401-874-5117, Fax: 401-874-2786, E-mail: gt@uri.edu. *Application contact:* Dr. Mayrai Gindy, Director of Graduate Studies, 401-874-5587, Fax: 401-874-2786, E-mail: gindy@egr.uri.edu.

University of Saskatchewan, College of Graduate Studies and Research, College of Engineering, Division of Environmental Engineering, Saskatoon, SK S7N 5A2, Canada. Offers M Eng, M Sc, PhD, Diploma. *Degree requirements:* For master's, thesis (for some programs); for doctorate, thesis/dissertation. *Entrance requirements:* For master's and doctorate, GRE. Additional exam requirements/recommendations for international students: Required—TOEFL.

University of Southern California, Graduate School, Viterbi School of Engineering, Sonny Astani Department of Civil Engineering, Los Angeles, CA 90089. Offers applied mechanics (MS); civil engineering (MS, PhD); computer-aided engineering (ME, Graduate Certificate); construction management (MCM); engineering technology commercialization (Graduate Certificate); environmental engineering (MS, PhD); environmental quality management (ME); structural design (ME); sustainable cities (Graduate Certificate); transportation systems (MS, Graduate Certificate); water and waste management (MS). Part-time and evening/weekend programs available. *Faculty:* 16 full-time (2 women), 35 part-time/adjunct (5 women). *Students:* 190 full-time (52 women), 81 part-time (20 women); includes 54 minority (2 Black or African American, non-Hispanic/Latino; 42 Asian, non-Hispanic/Latino; 9 Hispanic/Latino; 1 Two or more races, non-Hispanic/Latino), 149 international. 541 applicants, 43% accepted, 100 enrolled. In 2010, 74 master's, 10 doctorates awarded. Terminal master's awarded for partial completion of doctoral program. *Degree requirements:* For master's, thesis optional; for doctorate, thesis/dissertation. *Entrance requirements:* For master's and doctorate, GRE General Test. *Application deadline:* For fall admission, 12/1 priority date for domestic and international students; for spring admission, 9/15 for domestic students, 9/15 priority date for international students. Applications are processed on a rolling basis. Application fee: $85. Electronic applications accepted. *Expenses:* Tuition: Full-time $31,240; part-time $1420 per unit. Required fees: $600. One-time fee: $35 full-time. Full-time tuition and fees vary according to degree level and program. *Financial support:* In 2010–11, fellowships with full tuition reimbursements (averaging $30,000 per year), research assistantships with full tuition reimbursements (averaging $20,000 per year), teaching assistantships with full tuition reimbursements (averaging $20,000 per year) were awarded; career-related internships or fieldwork, scholarships/grants, health care benefits, and unspecified assistantships also available. Financial award application deadline: 12/1; financial award applicants required to submit CSS PROFILE or FAFSA. *Faculty research:* Geotechnical engineering, transportation engineering, structural engineering, construction management, environmental engineering, water resources. Total annual research expenditures: $5 million. *Unit head:* Dr. Jean-Pierre Bardet, Chair, 213-740-0603, Fax: 213-744-1426, E-mail: ceedept@usc.edu. *Application contact:* Jennifer A. Gerson, Director of Student Affairs, 213-740-0573, Fax: 213-740-8662, E-mail: jgerson@usc.edu.

University of South Florida, Graduate School, College of Engineering, Department of Civil and Environmental Engineering, Tampa, FL 33620-9951. Offers civil and environmental engineering (MSES); civil engineering (MCE, MSCE, PhD). Part-time programs available. *Faculty:* 18 full-time (4 women). *Students:* 109 full-time (42 women), 69 part-time (18 women); includes 29 minority (7 Black or African American, non-Hispanic/Latino; 6 Asian, non-Hispanic/Latino; 15 Hispanic/Latino; 1 Two or more races, non-Hispanic/Latino), 48 international. Average age 30. 208 applicants, 61% accepted, 66 enrolled. In 2010, 18 master's, 9 doctorates awarded. Terminal master's awarded for partial completion of doctoral program. *Degree requirements:* For master's, comprehensive exam, thesis (for some programs); for doctorate, comprehensive exam, thesis/dissertation. *Entrance requirements:* For master's, GRE General Test, minimum GPA of 3.0 in last 60 hours of coursework; for doctorate, GRE General Test, minimum GPA of 3.3 in last 60 hours of coursework. Additional exam requirements/recommendations for international students: Required—TOEFL (minimum score 550 paper-based; 213 computer-based; 79 iBT). *Application deadline:* For fall admission, 2/15 for domestic students, 1/2 priority date for international students; for spring admission, 10/15 for domestic students, 6/1 priority date for international students. Application fee: $30. Electronic applications accepted. *Financial support:* In 2010–11, 48 research assistantships (averaging $15,714 per year), 39 teaching assistantships with tuition reimbursements (averaging $14,402 per year) were awarded. *Faculty research:* Water resources, structures and materials, transportation, geotechnical engineering, mechanics. Total annual research expenditures: $2.3 million. *Application contact:* Dr. Sarina Ergas, Director, 813-974-1119, Fax: 813-974-2957, E-mail: sergas@usf.edu.

The University of Tennessee, Graduate School, College of Engineering, Department of Civil and Environmental Engineering, Program in Environmental Engineering, Knoxville, TN 37996. Offers MS, MS/MBA. Part-time programs available. Postbaccalaureate distance learning degree programs offered (minimal on-campus study). *Faculty:* 7 full-time (0 women), 5 part-time/adjunct (0 women). *Students:* 15 full-time (6 women), 4 part-time (1 woman), 1 international. Average age 23. 42 applicants, 64% accepted, 14 enrolled. In 2010, 9 master's awarded. *Degree requirements:* For master's, thesis or alternative. *Entrance requirements:* For master's, GRE General Test, Minimum GPA of 2.7 (US degree holders); 3.0 (International degree holders); 3-References; Statement of purpose; Resume. Additional exam requirements/recommendations for international students: Required—TOEFL (minimum score 550 paper-based; 213 computer-based). *Application deadline:* For fall admission, 2/1 priority date for domestic and international students; for spring admission, 6/15 for domestic and international students. Applications are processed on a rolling basis. Application fee: $35. Electronic applications accepted. *Expenses:* Tuition, state resident: full-time $7440; part-time $414 per credit hour. Tuition, nonresident: full-time $22,478; part-time $1250 per credit hour. Required fees: $922; $43 per credit hour. Tuition and fees vary according to program. *Financial support:* In 2010–11, 11 students received support, including 9 research assistantships with full tuition reimbursements available (averaging $14,028 per year), 4 teaching assistantships with full tuition reimbursements available (averaging $6,684 per year); career-related internships or fieldwork, Federal Work-Study, institutionally sponsored loans, health care benefits, and unspecified assistantships also available. Financial award application deadline: 2/1; financial award applicants required to submit FAFSA. *Faculty research:* Air pollution control technologies; climate change and engineering impact on environment; environmental sampling, monitoring, and restoration; soil erosion prediction and control; waste management and utilization. *Unit head:* Dr. Dayakar Penumadu, Head, 865-974-2355, Fax: 865-974-2355, E-mail: dpenumad@utk.edu. *Application contact:* Dr. Chris Cox, Associate Head, 865-974-7729, Fax: 865-974-2355, E-mail: ccox9@utk.edu.

The University of Texas at Austin, Graduate School, Cockrell School of Engineering, Department of Civil, Architectural and Environmental Engineering, Program in Environmental and Water Resources Engineering, Austin, TX 78712-1111. Offers MS, PhD. *Accreditation:* ABET. Part-time programs available. *Degree requirements:* For master's, thesis or alternative. *Entrance requirements:* For master's, GRE General Test. Additional exam requirements/recommendations for international students: Required—TOEFL. Electronic applications accepted.

The University of Texas at El Paso, Graduate School, College of Engineering, Department of Civil Engineering, El Paso, TX 79968-0001. Offers civil engineering (MS, PhD); construction management (MS); construction mangement (Certificate); environmental engineering (MEENE, MSENE). Part-time and evening/weekend programs available. *Students:* 113 (36 women); includes 2 Asian, non-Hispanic/Latino; 62 Hispanic/Latino, 36 international. Average age 34. In 2010, 14 master's, 9 doctorates awarded. *Degree requirements:* For master's, thesis optional. *Entrance requirements:* For master's, GRE General Test, minimum GPA of 3.0. Additional exam requirements/recommendations for international students: Required—TOEFL. *Application deadline:* For fall admission, 7/1 priority date for domestic students, 3/1 for international students; for spring admission, 11/1 priority date for domestic students, 9/1 for international students. Applications are processed on a rolling basis. Application fee: $15 ($65 for international students). Electronic applications accepted. *Financial support:* In 2010–11, research assistantships with partial tuition reimbursements (averaging $21,125 per year), teaching assistantships with partial tuition reimbursements (averaging $16,900 per year) were awarded; fellowships with partial tuition reimbursements, career-related internships or fieldwork, Federal Work-Study, institutionally sponsored loans, scholarships/grants, tuition waivers (partial), and stipends also available. Financial award application deadline: 3/15; financial award applicants required to submit FAFSA. *Faculty research:* On-site wastewater treatment systems, wastewater reuse, disinfection by-product control, water resources, membrane filtration. *Unit head:* Wen-Whai Li, Chair, 915-747-5464, E-mail: wli@utep.edu. *Application contact:* Dr. Charles H. Ambler, Dean of the Graduate School, 915-747-5491 Ext. 7886, Fax: 915-747-5788, E-mail: cambler@utep.edu.

The University of Texas at El Paso, Graduate School, Interdisciplinary Program in Environmental Science and Engineering, El Paso, TX 79968-0001. Offers PhD. Part-time and evening/weekend programs available. *Students:* 41 (15 women); includes 3 Asian, non-Hispanic/Latino; 10 Hispanic/Latino, 21 international. Average age 34. In 2010, 4 doctorates awarded. *Degree requirements:* For doctorate, thesis/dissertation. *Entrance requirements:* For doctorate, GRE, letters of recommendation. Additional exam requirements/recommendations for international students: Required—TOEFL; Recommended—IELTS. *Application deadline:* For fall admission, 8/1 for domestic students, 3/1 for international students; for spring admission, 11/1 for domestic students, 9/1 for international students. Applications are processed on a rolling basis. Application fee: $45 ($80 for international students). Electronic applications accepted. *Financial support:* In 2010–11, research assistantships with partial tuition reimbursements (averaging $22,500 per year), teaching assistantships with partial tuition reimbursements (averaging $18,000 per year) were awarded; fellowships with partial tuition reimbursements, institutionally sponsored loans, scholarships/grants, health care benefits, tuition waivers (partial), and unspecified assistantships also available. Support available to part-time students. Financial award application deadline: 3/15; financial award applicants required to submit FAFSA. *Unit head:* Dr. Barry A. Benedict, Director, 915-747-5604, Fax: 915-747-5145, E-mail: babenedict@utep.edu. *Application contact:* Dr. Patricia D. Witherspoon, Dean of the Graduate School, 915-747-5491, Fax: 915-747-5788, E-mail: withersp@utep.edu.

The University of Texas at San Antonio, College of Engineering, Department of Civil and Environmental Engineering, San Antonio, TX 78249-0617. Offers civil engineering (MS, MSCE); environmental science and engineering (PhD). Part-time and evening/weekend programs available. *Faculty:* 11 full-time (2 women). *Students:* 43 full-time (11 women), 34 part-time (8 women); includes 25 minority (5 Black or African American, non-Hispanic/Latino; 4 Asian, non-Hispanic/Latino; 15 Hispanic/Latino; 1 Two or more races, non-Hispanic/Latino), 24 international. Average age 32. 56 applicants, 50% accepted, 21 enrolled. In 2010, 12 master's, 4 doctorates awarded. *Degree requirements:* For master's, comprehensive exam (for some programs), thesis (for some programs); for doctorate, comprehensive exam, thesis/dissertation. *Entrance requirements:* For master's, GRE General Test, minimum GPA of 3.0 in last 60 hours of undergraduate degree. Additional exam requirements/recommendations for international students: Required—TOEFL (minimum score 500 paper-based; 173 computer-based; 61 iBT), IELTS (minimum score 5). *Application deadline:* For fall admission, 7/1 for domestic students, 4/1 for international students; for spring admission, 11/1 for domestic students, 9/1 for international students. Applications are processed on a rolling basis. Application fee: $45 ($80 for international students). Electronic applications accepted. *Expenses:* Tuition, state resident: full-time $4172; part-time $231.75 per credit hour. Tuition, nonresident: full-time $15,332; part-time $851.75 per credit hour. *Financial support:* In 2010–11, 29 students received support, including 20 research assistantships (averaging $15,462 per year); career-related internships or fieldwork, scholarships/grants, tuition waivers, and unspecified assistantships also available. Support available to part-time students. Financial award application deadline: 3/31. Total annual research expenditures: $475,434. *Unit head:* Dr. Athanassio T. Papagiannakis, Chair, 210-458-7517, Fax: 210-458-6475, E-mail: at.papagiannakis@utsa.edu. *Application contact:* Veronica Ramirez, Assistant Dean of the Graduate School, 210-458-4330, Fax: 210-458-4332, E-mail: graduatestudies@utsa.edu.

See Display on page 189 and Close-Up on page 227.

The University of Texas at Tyler, College of Engineering and Computer Science, Department of Civil Engineering, Tyler, TX 75799-0001. Offers environmental engineering (MS); industrial safety (MS); structural engineering (MS); transportation engineering (MS); water resources engineering (MS). Part-time and evening/weekend programs available. *Degree requirements:* For master's, thesis optional. *Entrance requirements:* For master's, GRE General Test, bachelor's degree in engineering, associated science degree. Additional exam requirements/recommendations for international students: Required—TOEFL (minimum score 79 computer-based). *Faculty research:* Non-destructive strength testing, indoor air quality, transportation routing and signaling, pavement replacement criteria, flood water routing, construction and long-term behavior of innovative geotechnical foundation and embankment construction used in highway construction, engineering education.

University of Utah, Graduate School, College of Engineering, Department of Chemical Engineering, Salt Lake City, UT 84112-1107. Offers chemical engineering (ME, MS, PhD); environmental engineering (ME, MS, PhD). Part-time and evening/weekend programs available. Postbaccalaureate distance learning degree programs offered. *Faculty:* 15 full-time (1 woman), 1 part-time/adjunct (0 women). *Students:* 50 full-time (5 women), 20 part-time (7 women); includes 5 minority (2 Asian, non-Hispanic/Latino; 3 Hispanic/Latino), 22 international. Average age 28. 132 applicants, 13% accepted, 13 enrolled. In 2010, 8 master's, 7 doctorates awarded. Terminal master's awarded for partial completion of doctoral program. *Degree requirements:* For master's, comprehensive exam, thesis (for some programs); for doctorate, comprehensive exam, thesis/dissertation. *Entrance requirements:* For master's, GRE General Test; for doctorate, GRE General Test, minimum GPA of 3.0, degree or course work in chemical engineering. Additional exam requirements/recommendations for international students: Required—TOEFL (minimum score 500 paper-based; 173 computer-based). *Application deadline:* For fall admission, 4/1 priority date for domestic students, 2/1 for international students; for spring admission, 11/1 priority date for domestic students, 10/1 priority date for international students. Applications are processed on a rolling basis. Application fee: $55 ($65 for international students). Electronic applications accepted. *Expenses:* Contact institution. *Financial support:* In 2010–11, 7 fellowships with tuition reimbursements (averaging $26,750 per year), 53 research assistantships with tuition reimbursements (averaging $25,000 per year) were awarded; teaching assistantships with tuition reimbursements, Federal Work-Study, institutionally sponsored loans, scholarships/grants, health care benefits, and unspecified assistantships also available. Financial award application deadline: 4/1; financial award applicants required to submit FAFSA. *Faculty research:* Drug delivery, fossil fuel and biomass combustion and gasification, oil and gas reservoir characteristics and management, multi-scale simulation, micro-scale synthesis. Total annual research expenditures: $8.1 million. *Unit head:* Dr. JoAnn S. Lighty, Chair, 801-581-6715, Fax: 801-585-9291, E-mail: jlighty@utah.edu. *Application contact:* Jenny Jones, Academic Advisor, 801-581-6915, Fax: 801-585-9291, E-mail: jones.jenny@eng.utah.edu.

University of Utah, Graduate School, College of Engineering, Department of Civil and Environmental Engineering, Interdepartmental Program in Environmental Engineering, Salt Lake City, UT 84112-1107. Offers MS, PhD. Part-time programs available. *Students:* 1 (woman) full-time. Average age 44. 2 applicants, 0% accepted, 0 enrolled. In 2010, 2 master's awarded. Terminal master's awarded for partial completion of doctoral program. *Degree requirements:* For master's, comprehensive exam, thesis (for some programs); for doctorate, comprehensive exam, thesis/dissertation. *Entrance requirements:* For master's and doctorate, GRE, minimum undergraduate GPA of 3.0. Additional exam requirements/recommendations for international students: Required—TOEFL (minimum score 500 paper-based; 173 computer-based). *Application deadline:* For fall admission, 4/1 for domestic and international students; for spring admission, 11/1 for domestic and international students. Applications are processed on a rolling basis. Application fee: $55 ($65 for international students). Electronic applications accepted. *Expenses:* Contact institution. *Financial support:* Application deadline: 2/15. *Unit head:* Dr. Paul J. Tikalsky, Chair and Professor in Civil and Environmental Engineering, 801-581-6931, Fax: 801-585-5477, E-mail: tikalsky@civil.utah.edu. *Application contact:* Amanda May, Academic Program Specialist, 801-581-6931, Fax: 850-585-5477, E-mail: amandam@civil.utah.edu.

See Display on page 190 and Close-Up on page 229.

University of Utah, Graduate School, College of Mines and Earth Sciences, Department of Geology and Geophysics, Salt Lake City, UT 84112. Offers environmental engineering (ME, MS, PhD); geological engineering (ME, MS, PhD); geology (MS, PhD); geophysics (MS, PhD). *Faculty:* 21 full-time (4 women), 4 part-time/adjunct (1 woman). *Students:* 51 full-time (13 women), 19 part-time (6 women); includes 1 minority (Hispanic/Latino), 15 international. Average age 30. 128 applicants, 27% accepted, 23 enrolled. In 2010, 10 master's, 8 doctorates awarded. Terminal master's awarded for partial completion of doctoral program. *Degree requirements:* For master's, comprehensive exam, thesis; for doctorate, thesis/dissertation, qualifying exam (written and oral). *Entrance requirements:* For master's and doctorate, GRE General Test, minimum GPA of 3.25. Additional exam requirements/recommendations for international students: Required—TOEFL (minimum score 500 paper-based; 173 computer-based). *Application deadline:* For fall admission, 1/15 priority date for domestic and international students. Applications are processed on a rolling basis. Application fee: $55 ($65 for international students). Electronic applications accepted. *Expenses:* Tuition, area resident: Part-time $179.19 per credit hour. Tuition, state resident: full-time $4384. Tuition, nonresident: full-time $16,684; part-time $630.67 per credit hour. Required fees: $350 per semester. Tuition and fees vary according to course load, degree level and program. *Financial support:* In 2010–11, 22 students received support, including 11 fellowships with full tuition reimbursements available (averaging $13,450 per year), 45 research assistantships with full tuition reimbursements available (averaging $21,858 per year), 11 teaching assistantships with full tuition reimbursements available (averaging $13,450 per year); career-related internships or fieldwork, institutionally sponsored loans, scholarships/grants, unspecified assistantships, and stipends also available. Financial award application deadline: 1/15; financial award applicants required to submit FAFSA. *Faculty research:* Igneous, metamorphic, and sedimentary petrology; ore deposits; aqueous geochemistry; isotope geochemistry; heat flow. Total annual research expenditures: $2.2 million. *Unit head:* Dr. Kip Solomon, Chair, 801-581-7231, Fax: 801-581-

Environmental Engineering

University of Utah (continued)
7065, E-mail: kip.solomon@utah.edu. *Application contact:* Dr. Allan A. Ekdale, Director of Graduate Studies, 801-581-7266, Fax: 801-581-7065, E-mail: a.ekdale@utah.edu.

University of Vermont, Graduate College, College of Engineering and Mathematics, Department of Civil and Environmental Engineering, Burlington, VT 05405. Offers MS, PhD. *Students:* 33 (12 women), 8 international. 53 applicants, 68% accepted, 9 enrolled. In 2010, 5 master's, 2 doctorates awarded. *Degree requirements:* For master's, thesis or alternative; for doctorate, thesis/dissertation. *Entrance requirements:* For master's and doctorate, GRE General Test. Additional exam requirements/recommendations for international students: Required—TOEFL (minimum score 550 paper-based; 213 computer-based; 80 iBT). *Application deadline:* For fall admission, 2/1 priority date for domestic students. Applications are processed on a rolling basis. Application fee: $40. Electronic applications accepted. *Expenses:* Tuition, state resident: part-time $537 per credit hour. Tuition, nonresident: part-time $1355 per credit hour. *Financial support:* Research assistantships, teaching assistantships available. Financial award application deadline: 3/1. *Unit head:* Dr. J. Marshall, Director, 802-656-3800. *Application contact:* Dr. Britt Holmen, Coordinator, 802-656-3800.

University of Washington, Graduate School, College of Engineering, Department of Civil and Environmental Engineering, Seattle, WA 98195-2700. Offers construction engineering (MSCE); environmental engineering (MS, MSCE, MSE, PhD); hydrology, water resources, and environmental fluid mechanics (MS, MSCE, MSE, PhD); structural and geotechnical engineering and mechanics (MS, MSCE, MSE, PhD); transportation and construction engineering (MS, MSE, PhD); transportation engineering (MSCE). Part-time programs available. Postbaccalaureate distance learning degree programs offered (no on-campus study). *Faculty:* 44 full-time (10 women), 12 part-time/adjunct (1 woman). *Students:* 197 full-time (65 women), 65 part-time (15 women); includes 5 Black or African American, non-Hispanic/Latino; 28 Asian, non-Hispanic/Latino; 5 Hispanic/Latino, 55 international. 522 applicants, 51% accepted, 101 enrolled. In 2010, 68 master's, 5 doctorates awarded. Terminal master's awarded for partial completion of doctoral program. *Degree requirements:* For master's, thesis (for some programs); for doctorate, comprehensive exam, thesis/dissertation, General, qualifying, and final exams. Completion of doctoral degree within 10 years. *Entrance requirements:* For master's, GRE General Test, Minimum GPA of 3.0, statement of purpose, letters of recommendation, transcripts; for doctorate, GRE General Test, minimum GPA of 3.5, statement of purpose, letters of recommendation, transcripts. Additional exam requirements/recommendations for international students: Required—TOEFL (minimum score 580 paper-based; 237 computer-based; 92 iBT); Recommended—IELTS (minimum score 7). *Application deadline:* For fall admission, 1/10 priority date for domestic and international students. Application fee: $75. Electronic applications accepted. *Financial support:* In 2010–11, 2 students received support, including 25 fellowships with full and partial tuition reimbursements available (averaging $16,173 per year), 75 research assistantships with full tuition reimbursements available (averaging $16,515 per year), 11 teaching assistantships with full tuition reimbursements available (averaging $16,263 per year); scholarships/grants also available. Financial award application deadline: 1/10; financial award applicants required to submit FAFSA. *Faculty research:* Environmental/water resources, hydrology; construction/transportation; structures/ geotechnical. Total annual research expenditures: $14.4 million. *Unit head:* Dr. Gregory R. Miller, Professor and Chair, 206-543-0350, Fax: 206-543-1543, E-mail: gmiller@uw.edu. *Application contact:* Lorna Latal, Graduate Adviser, 206-543-2574, Fax: 206-543-1543, E-mail: llatal@u.washington.edu.

University of Waterloo, Graduate Studies, Faculty of Engineering, Department of Civil and Environmental Engineering, Waterloo, ON N2L 3G1, Canada. Offers M Eng, MA Sc, PhD. Part-time programs available. *Degree requirements:* For master's, research paper or thesis; for doctorate, comprehensive exam, thesis/dissertation. *Entrance requirements:* For master's, honors degree, minimum B average; for doctorate, master's degree, minimum A- average. Additional exam requirements/recommendations for international students: Required—TOEFL, TWE. Electronic applications accepted. *Faculty research:* Water resources, structures, construction management, transportation, geotechnical engineering.

The University of Western Ontario, Faculty of Graduate Studies, Physical Sciences Division, Faculty of Engineering, London, ON N6A 5B8, Canada. Offers chemical and biochemical engineering (ME Sc, PhD); civil and environmental engineering (M Eng, ME Sc, PhD); electrical and computer engineering (M Eng, ME Sc, PhD); mechanical and materials engineering (M Eng, ME Sc, PhD). Part-time programs available. Terminal master's awarded for partial completion of doctoral program. *Degree requirements:* For master's, thesis; for doctorate, thesis/ dissertation. *Entrance requirements:* For master's, minimum B average; for doctorate, minimum B+ average. *Faculty research:* Wind, geotechnical, chemical reactor engineering, applied electrostatics, biochemical engineering.

University of Windsor, Faculty of Graduate Studies, Faculty of Engineering, Department of Civil and Environmental Engineering, Windsor, ON N9B 3P4, Canada. Offers civil engineering (M Eng, MA Sc, PhD); environmental engineering (M Eng, MA Sc, PhD). Part-time programs available. *Degree requirements:* For master's, thesis; for doctorate, comprehensive exam, thesis/dissertation. *Entrance requirements:* For master's, minimum B average; for doctorate, master's degree, minimum A average. Additional exam requirements/recommendations for international students: Required—TOEFL (minimum score 580 paper-based; 237 computer-based). Electronic applications accepted. *Faculty research:* Odors: sampling, measurement, control; drinking water disinfection, hydrocarbon contaminated soil remediation, structural dynamics, numerical simulation of piezoelectric materials.

University of Wisconsin–Madison, Graduate School, College of Engineering, Department of Civil and Environmental Engineering, Madison, WI 53706-1380. Offers MS, PhD. Part-time programs available. *Faculty:* 31 full-time (3 women), 2 part-time/adjunct (0 women). *Students:* 164 full-time (36 women); includes 1 Black or African American, non-Hispanic/Latino; 5 Hispanic/Latino. Average age 29. 455 applicants, 8% accepted, 37 enrolled. In 2010, 41 master's, 9 doctorates awarded. Terminal master's awarded for partial completion of doctoral program. *Degree requirements:* For master's, thesis or alternative; for doctorate, thesis/dissertation, preliminary exam, qualifying exams. *Entrance requirements:* For master's and doctorate, GRE General Test, minimum GPA of 3.0 for last 60 credits of course work. Additional exam requirements/recommendations for international students: Required—TOEFL (minimum score 550 paper-based; 213 computer-based; 80 iBT). *Application deadline:* For fall admission, 3/15 for domestic and international students; for spring admission, 10/15 for domestic and international students. Applications are processed on a rolling basis. Application fee: $56. Electronic applications accepted. *Expenses:* Tuition, state resident: full-time $9887.36; part-time $617.96 per credit. Tuition, nonresident: full-time $24,054; part-time $1503.40 per credit. Required fees: $67.63 per credit. Tuition and fees vary according to reciprocity agreements. *Financial support:* In 2010–11, 63 students received support, including 9 fellowships with full tuition reimbursements available (averaging $22,224 per year), 76 research assistantships with full tuition reimbursements available (averaging $40,368 per year), 12 teaching assistantships with full tuition reimbursements available (averaging $28,175 per year); Federal Work-Study, scholarships/grants, health care benefits, and unspecified assistantships also available. Support available to part-time students. Financial award application deadline: 12/15. *Faculty research:* Environmental geotechnics and soil mechanics, design and analysis of structures, traffic engineering and intelligent transport systems, industrial pollution control, hydrological monitoring. Total annual research expenditures: $7.4 million. *Unit head:* Jeffrey S. Russell, Chair, 608-262-3542, Fax: 608-262-5199, E-mail: russell@engr.wisc.edu. *Application contact:* Cheryl Loschko, Student Status Examiner, 608-265-5570, Fax: 608-890-1174, E-mail: loschko@wisc.edu.

University of Wyoming, College of Engineering and Applied Sciences, Department of Civil and Architectural Engineering and Department of Chemical and Petroleum Engineering, Program in Environmental Engineering, Laramie, WY 82070. Offers MS. Part-time programs available. *Degree requirements:* For master's, thesis optional. *Entrance requirements:* For master's, GRE General Test, minimum GPA of 3.0. Additional exam requirements/recommendations for international students: Required—TOEFL (minimum score 550 paper-based; 213 computer-based). Electronic applications accepted. *Faculty research:* Water and waste water, solid and hazardous waste management, air pollution control, flue-gas cleanup.

Utah State University, School of Graduate Studies, College of Engineering, Department of Civil and Environmental Engineering, Logan, UT 84322. Offers ME, MS, PhD, CE. *Degree requirements:* For master's, thesis (for some programs); for doctorate, thesis/dissertation. *Entrance requirements:* For master's and doctorate, GRE General Test, minimum GPA of 3.0. Additional exam requirements/recommendations for international students: Required—TOEFL. Electronic applications accepted. *Faculty research:* Hazardous waste treatment, large space structures, river basin management, earthquake engineering, environmental impact.

Vanderbilt University, School of Engineering, Department of Civil and Environmental Engineering, Program in Environmental Engineering, Nashville, TN 37240-1001. Offers environmental engineering (M Eng); environmental management (MS, PhD). MS and PhD offered through the Graduate School. Part-time programs available. *Faculty:* 9 full-time (0 women), 1 (woman) part-time/adjunct. *Students:* 27 full-time (15 women); includes 2 Black or African American, non-Hispanic/Latino; 1 Asian, non-Hispanic/Latino, 4 international. Average age 30. 75 applicants, 17% accepted, 8 enrolled. In 2010, 10 master's, 3 doctorates awarded. Terminal master's awarded for partial completion of doctoral program. *Degree requirements:* For master's, thesis or alternative; for doctorate, thesis/dissertation. *Entrance requirements:* For master's and doctorate, GRE General Test. Additional exam requirements/recommendations for international students: Required—TOEFL. *Application deadline:* For fall admission, 1/15 for domestic students; for spring admission, 11/1 for domestic students. Applications are processed on a rolling basis. Application fee: $0. Electronic applications accepted. *Financial support:* In 2010–11, 5 fellowships with full tuition reimbursements (averaging $30,000 per year), 12 research assistantships with full tuition reimbursements (averaging $25,200 per year), 7 teaching assistantships with full tuition reimbursements (averaging $21,600 per year) were awarded; career-related internships or fieldwork, institutionally sponsored loans, scholarships/grants, traineeships, and tuition waivers (full and partial) also available. Financial award application deadline: 1/15. *Faculty research:* Waste treatment, hazardous waste management, chemical waste treatment, water quality. *Unit head:* Dr. David S. Kosson, Chair, 615-322-2697, Fax: 615-322-3365, E-mail: david.kosson@vanderbilt.edu. *Application contact:* Dr. James H. Clarke, Graduate Program Administrator, 615-322-3897, Fax: 615-322-3365.

Villanova University, College of Engineering, Department of Civil and Environmental Engineering, Program in Water Resources and Environmental Engineering, Villanova, PA 19085-1699. Offers urban water resources design (Certificate); water resources and environmental engineering (MSWREE). Part-time and evening/weekend programs available. Postbaccalaureate distance learning degree programs offered (no on-campus study). *Students:* 1 full-time (0 women), 25 part-time (7 women), 1 international. 11 applicants, 100% accepted, 4 enrolled. In 2010, 13 master's awarded. *Degree requirements:* For master's, thesis optional. *Entrance requirements:* For master's, GRE General Test (for applicants with degrees from foreign universities), BCE or bachelor's degree in science or related engineering field, minimum GPA of 3.0. Additional exam requirements/recommendations for international students: Required—TOEFL (minimum score 600 paper-based; 250 computer-based; 100 iBT). *Application deadline:* For fall admission, 8/1 priority date for domestic students, 4/1 priority date for international students; for spring admission, 12/1 for domestic students, 10/1 for international students. Applications are processed on a rolling basis. Application fee: $50. Electronic applications accepted. *Expenses:* Tuition: Part-time $700 per credit. Part-time tuition and fees vary according to degree level and program. *Financial support:* In 2010–11, research assistantships with full tuition reimbursements (averaging $13,500 per year); Federal Work-Study, tuition waivers (full and partial), and unspecified assistantships also available. Support available to part-time students. Financial award application deadline: 1/15. *Faculty research:* Photocatalytic decontamination and disinfection of water, urban storm water wetlands, economy and risk, removal and destruction of organic acids in water, sludge treatment. *Unit head:* Dr. Ronald A. Chadderton, Chairman, 610-519-4960, Fax: 610-519-6754, E-mail: ronald.chadderton@villanova.edu. *Application contact:* College of Engineering Graduate Programs Office, 610-519-5840, Fax: 610-519-5859, E-mail: engineering.grad@villanova.edu.

Virginia Polytechnic Institute and State University, Graduate School, College of Engineering, Department of Civil and Environmental Engineering, Blacksburg, VA 24061. Offers civil engineering (M Eng, MS, PhD); civil infrastructure systems (Certificate); environmental engineering (MS); environmental sciences and engineering (MS); transportation systems engineering (Certificate); treatment process engineering (Certificate); urban hydrology and stormwater management (Certificate); water quality management (Certificate). *Accreditation:* ABET (one or more programs are accredited). *Faculty:* 44 full-time (8 women), 1 part-time/adjunct (0 women). *Students:* 320 full-time (108 women), 70 part-time (20 women); includes 9 Black or African American, non-Hispanic/Latino; 15 Asian, non-Hispanic/Latino; 13 Hispanic/Latino, 126 international. Average age 27. 639 applicants, 44% accepted, 121 enrolled. In 2010, 97 master's, 18 doctorates awarded. *Degree requirements:* For master's, comprehensive exam (for some programs), thesis (for some programs); for doctorate, comprehensive exam (for some programs), thesis/dissertation (for some programs). *Entrance requirements:* For master's and doctorate, GRE. Additional exam requirements/recommendations for international students: Required—TOEFL (minimum score 550 paper-based; 213 computer-based). *Application deadline:* For fall admission, 7/1 for domestic and international students; for spring admission, 12/1 for domestic and international students. Applications are processed on a rolling basis. Application fee: $65. Electronic applications accepted. *Expenses:* Tuition, area resident: Full-time $9399; part-time $488 per credit hour. Tuition, state resident: full-time $9399; part-time $488 per credit hour. Tuition, nonresident: full-time $17,854; part-time $957.75 per credit hour. International tuition: $17,854 full-time. Required fees: $1534. Full-time tuition and fees vary according to program. *Financial support:* In 2010–11, 35 fellowships with full tuition reimbursements (averaging $5,861 per year), 82 research assistantships with full tuition reimbursements (averaging $20,397 per year), 33 teaching assistantships with full tuition reimbursements (averaging $14,542 per year) were awarded; career-related internships or fieldwork, Federal Work-Study, scholarships/grants, health care benefits, and unspecified assistantships also available. Financial award application deadline: 1/15. *Faculty research:* Construction, environmental geotechnical hydrosystems, structures and transportation engineering. Total annual research expenditures: $12.2 million. *Unit head:* Dr. Sam Easterling, UNIT HEAD, 540-231-5143, Fax: 540-231-7532, E-mail: seaster@vt.edu. *Application contact:* Marc Widdowson, Contact, 540-231-7153, Fax: 540-231-7532, E-mail: mwiddows@vt.edu.

Washington State University, Graduate School, College of Engineering and Architecture, Department of Civil and Environmental Engineering, Program in Environmental Engineering, Pullman, WA 99164. Offers MS. *Faculty:* 27. *Students:* 16 full-time (7 women), 8 part-time (2 women); includes 1 minority (Asian, non-Hispanic/Latino), 4 international. Average age 26. 50 applicants, 20% accepted, 10 enrolled. In 2010, 12 master's awarded. *Degree requirements:* For master's, comprehensive exam (for some programs), thesis (for some programs), oral exam. *Entrance requirements:* For master's, GRE General Test, official transcripts from all colleges and universities attended; one-page statement of purpose; three letters of recommendation. Additional exam requirements/recommendations for international students: Required—TOEFL, IELTS. *Application deadline:* For fall admission, 1/10 priority date for domestic students, 1/10 for international students; for spring admission, 7/1 for domestic and international students. Applications are processed on a rolling basis. Application fee: $50. Electronic applications accepted. *Expenses:* Tuition, state resident: full-time $8552; part-time $443 per credit. Tuition, nonresident: full-time $21,650; part-time $1083 per credit. Required fees: $846. *Financial support:* In 2010–11, research assistantships with full and partial tuition reimbursements (averaging $18,204 per year), teaching assistantships with full and partial tuition reimbursements (averaging $18,204 per year) were awarded; career-related internships or fieldwork, Federal Work-Study, and institutionally sponsored loans also available. Financial award application deadline: 4/1; financial award applicants required to submit FAFSA. *Faculty research:* Air quality, hazardous waste, soil and ground water contamination, acid precipitation, global climate. Total annual research expenditures: $4.1 million. *Unit head:* Dr. David McLean,

Chair, 509-335-9578, Fax: 509-335-7632, E-mail: mclean@wsu.edu. *Application contact:* Graduate School Admissions, 800-GRADWSU, Fax: 509-335-1949, E-mail: gradsch@wsu.edu.

Washington University in St. Louis, School of Engineering and Applied Science, Department of Energy, Environmental and Chemical Engineering, St. Louis, MO 63130-4899. Offers chemical engineering (MS, D Sc); environmental engineering (MS, D Sc). Part-time programs available. Terminal master's awarded for partial completion of doctoral program. *Degree requirements:* For master's, thesis optional; for doctorate, thesis/dissertation, preliminary exam, qualifying exam. *Entrance requirements:* For master's and doctorate, GRE, minimum B average during final 2 years of course work. Additional exam requirements/recommendations for international students: Required—TOEFL, TWE. Electronic applications accepted. *Faculty research:* Reaction engineering, materials processing, catalysis, process control, air pollution control.

West Virginia University, College of Engineering and Mineral Resources, Department of Civil and Environmental Engineering, Morgantown, WV 26506. Offers civil engineering (MSCE, MSE, PhD). Part-time programs available. *Degree requirements:* For master's, thesis; for doctorate, comprehensive exam, thesis/dissertation. *Entrance requirements:* For master's and doctorate, minimum GPA of 3.0. Additional exam requirements/recommendations for international students: Required—TOEFL, GRE. *Faculty research:* Habitat restoration, advanced materials for civil infrastructure, pavement modeling, infrastructure condition assessment.

Worcester Polytechnic Institute, Graduate Studies and Research, Department of Civil and Environmental Engineering, Worcester, MA 01609-2280. Offers civil and environmental engineering (Advanced Certificate, Graduate Certificate); civil engineering (ME, MS, PhD); construction project management (MS); environmental engineering (MS); master builder environmental engineering (M Eng). Part-time and evening/weekend programs available. Postbaccalaureate distance learning degree programs offered (no on-campus study). *Faculty:* 11 full-time (1 woman), 2 part-time/adjunct (1 woman). *Students:* 46 full-time (21 women), 42 part-time (10 women); includes 5 Black or African American, non-Hispanic/Latino; 5 Asian, non-Hispanic/Latino; 1 Hispanic/Latino; 4 Native Hawaiian or other Pacific Islander, non-Hispanic/Latino, 18 international. 135 applicants, 74% accepted, 36 enrolled. In 2010, 26 master's, 2 doctorates awarded. *Degree requirements:* For master's, thesis optional; for doctorate, comprehensive exam, thesis/dissertation. *Entrance requirements:* For master's and doctorate, GRE (recommended), 3 letters of recommendation. Additional exam requirements/recommendations for international students: Required—TOEFL (minimum score 550 paper-based; 213 computer-based; 79 iBT), IELTS (minimum score 6.5). *Application deadline:* For fall admission, 1/1 priority date for domestic and international students; for spring admission, 10/1 priority date for domestic and international students. Applications are processed on a rolling basis. Application fee: $70. Electronic applications accepted. *Expenses:* Tuition: Full-time $20,862; part-time $1159 per term. One-time fee: $15. *Financial support:* Career-related internships or fieldwork, institutionally sponsored loans, scholarships/grants, and unspecified assistantships available. Financial award application deadline: 1/1; financial award applicants required to submit FAFSA. *Faculty research:* Environmental engineering and sustainability, pavement engineering technology, impact mechanics and engineering. *Unit head:* Dr. Tahar El-Korchi, Interim Head, 508-831-5530, Fax: 508-831-5808, E-mail: tek@wpi.edu. *Application contact:* Dr. Paul Mathisen, Graduate Coordinator, 508-831-5530, Fax: 508-831-5808, E-mail: mathisen@wpi.edu.

Worcester Polytechnic Institute, Graduate Studies and Research, Programs in Interdisciplinary Studies, Worcester, MA 01609-2280. Offers bioscience administration (MS); impact engineering (MS); manufacturing engineering management (MS); power systems management (MS); social science (PhD); systems modeling (MS). Part-time and evening/weekend programs available. *Faculty:* 1 part-time/adjunct (0 women). *Students:* 6 full-time (1 woman), 146 part-time (25 women); includes 1 Black or African American, non-Hispanic/Latino; 6 Hispanic/Latino; 11 Native Hawaiian or other Pacific Islander, non-Hispanic/Latino, 1 international. 151 applicants, 76% accepted, 79 enrolled. In 2010, 47 master's awarded. *Degree requirements:* For master's, thesis; for doctorate, comprehensive exam, thesis/dissertation. *Entrance requirements:* For master's and doctorate, 3 letters of recommendation. Additional exam requirements/recommendations for international students: Required—TOEFL (minimum score 550 paper-based; 213 computer-based; 79 iBT), IELTS (minimum score 6.5). *Application deadline:* For fall admission, 1/1 priority date for domestic students, 1/1 for international students; for spring admission, 10/1 priority date for domestic students, 10/1 for international students. Application fee: $70. *Expenses:* Tuition: Full-time $20,862; part-time $1159 per term. One-time fee: $15. *Financial support:* Institutionally sponsored loans, scholarships/grants, and unspecified assistantships available. Financial award application deadline: 1/1; financial award applicants required to submit FAFSA. *Unit head:* Dr. Fred J. Looft, Head, 508-831-5231, Fax: 508-831-5491, E-mail: fjlooft@wpi.edu. *Application contact:* Lynne Dougherty, Administrative Assistant, 508-831-5301, Fax: 508-831-5717, E-mail: grad@wpi.edu.

Yale University, Graduate School of Arts and Sciences, School of Engineering and Applied Science, Program in Environmental Engineering, New Haven, CT 06520. Offers MS, PhD.

Youngstown State University, Graduate School, College of Science, Technology, Engineering and Mathematics, Department of Civil and Environmental Engineering, Youngstown, OH 44555-0001. Offers MSE. Part-time and evening/weekend programs available. *Degree requirements:* For master's, thesis optional. *Entrance requirements:* For master's, minimum GPA of 2.75 in field. Additional exam requirements/recommendations for international students: Required—TOEFL. *Faculty research:* Structural mechanics, water quality modeling, surface and ground water hydrology, physical and chemical processes in aquatic systems.

Fire Protection Engineering

Anna Maria College, Graduate Division, Program in Fire Science, Paxton, MA 01612. Offers MA. Part-time and evening/weekend programs available. *Degree requirements:* For master's, thesis, internship, research project. *Entrance requirements:* For master's, minimum GPA of 2.7, resume, bachelor's degree in fire science or employment in a fire science organization. Additional exam requirements/recommendations for international students: Required—TOEFL (minimum score 500 paper-based). Electronic applications accepted.

Oklahoma State University, College of Arts and Sciences, Department of Political Science, Stillwater, OK 74078. Offers fire and emergency management administration (MS, PhD); political science (MA). *Faculty:* 18 full-time (7 women), 7 part-time/adjunct (0 women). *Students:* 46 full-time (11 women), 86 part-time (20 women); includes 5 Black or African American, non-Hispanic/Latino; 5 American Indian or Alaska Native, non-Hispanic/Latino; 5 Hispanic/Latino, 24 international. Average age 35. 106 applicants, 45% accepted, 31 enrolled. In 2010, 23 master's awarded. *Degree requirements:* For master's, comprehensive exam, thesis or creative component; for doctorate, comprehensive exam, thesis/dissertation. *Entrance requirements:* For master's, GRE; for doctorate, GRE. Additional exam requirements/recommendations for international students: Required—TOEFL (minimum score 550 paper-based; 79 iBT). *Application deadline:* For fall admission, 3/1 priority date for international students; for spring admission, 8/1 priority date for international students. Applications are processed on a rolling basis. Application fee: $40 ($75 for international students). Electronic applications accepted. *Expenses:* Tuition, state resident: full-time $3716; part-time $154.85 per credit hour. Tuition, nonresident: full-time $14,892; part-time $621 per credit hour. Required fees: $2044; $85.20 per credit hour. One-time fee: $50. Tuition and fees vary according to course load and campus/location. *Financial support:* In 2010–11, 7 research assistantships (averaging $11,416 per year), 14 teaching assistantships (averaging $7,891 per year) were awarded; career-related internships or fieldwork, Federal Work-Study, scholarships/grants, health care benefits, tuition waivers (partial), and unspecified assistantships also available. Support available to part-time students. Financial award application deadline: 3/1; financial award applicants required to submit FAFSA. *Faculty research:* Fire and emergency management, environmental dispute resolution, voting and elections, women and politics, urban politics. *Unit head:* Dr. James Scott, Head, 405-744-5569, Fax: 405-744-6534. *Application contact:* Dr. Gordon Emslie, Dean, 405-744-6368, Fax: 405-744-0355, E-mail: grad-i@okstate.edu.

University of Maryland, College Park, Academic Affairs, A. James Clark School of Engineering, Department of Continuing and Distance Learning in Engineering, College Park, MD 20742. Offers engineering (M Eng), including aerospace engineering, chemical engineering, civil engineering, electrical engineering, engineering, fire protection engineering, materials science and engineering, mechanical engineering, reliability engineering, systems engineering. *Faculty:* 4 full-time (1 woman), 11 part-time/adjunct (1 woman). *Students:* 56 full-time (15 women), 428 part-time (88 women); includes 153 minority (59 Black or African American, non-Hispanic/Latino; 63 Asian, non-Hispanic/Latino; 24 Hispanic/Latino; 7 Two or more races, non-Hispanic/Latino), 55 international. 551 applicants, 82% accepted, 360 enrolled. In 2010, 130 master's awarded. *Application deadline:* For fall admission, 8/15 for domestic students, 1/10 for international students; for spring admission, 12/15 for domestic students, 6/1 for international students. Applications are processed on a rolling basis. Application fee: $75. Electronic applications accepted. *Expenses:* Tuition, area resident: Part-time $471 per credit hour. Tuition, state resident: part-time $471 per credit hour. Tuition, nonresident: part-time $1016 per credit hour. Required fees: $337 per term. *Financial support:* In 2010–11, 2 research assistantships (averaging $20,285 per year), 7 teaching assistantships (averaging $16,962 per year) were awarded. *Unit head:* Dr. Darryll Pines, Dean, 301-405-0376, Fax: 301-314-5908, E-mail: pines@umd.edu. *Application contact:* Dr. Charles A. Caramello, Dean of the Graduate School, 301-405-0358, Fax: 301-314-9305, E-mail: ccaramel@umd.edu.

University of Maryland, College Park, Academic Affairs, A. James Clark School of Engineering, Department of Fire Protection Engineering, College Park, MD 20742. Offers M Eng, MS. Part-time and evening/weekend programs available. *Faculty:* 9 full-time (0 women), 6 part-time/adjunct (0 women). *Students:* 16 full-time (0 women), 7 part-time (1 woman); includes 1 minority (Asian, non-Hispanic/Latino), 3 international. 25 applicants, 36% accepted, 8 enrolled. In 2010, 12 master's awarded. *Degree requirements:* For master's, thesis optional. *Entrance requirements:* For master's, GRE General Test, minimum GPA of 3.0, BS in any engineering or physical science area, 3 letters of recommendation. *Application deadline:* For fall admission, 5/31 for domestic students, 2/1 for international students; for spring admission, 10/31 for domestic students, 6/1 for international students. Applications are processed on a rolling basis. Application fee: $75. Electronic applications accepted. *Expenses:* Tuition, area resident: Part-time $471 per credit hour. Tuition, state resident: part-time $471 per credit hour. Tuition, nonresident: part-time $1016 per credit hour. Required fees: $337 per term. *Financial support:* In 2010–11, 11 research assistantships (averaging $21,543 per year), 2 teaching assistantships (averaging $22,570 per year) were awarded; fellowships, career-related internships or fieldwork, Federal Work-Study, institutionally sponsored loans, and scholarships/grants also available. Financial award application deadline: 2/1; financial award applicants required to submit FAFSA. *Faculty research:* Fire and thermal degradation of materials, fire modeling, fire dynamics, smoke detection and management, fire resistance. Total annual research expenditures: $1 million. *Unit head:* Dr. Marino Dimarzo, Chair, 301-405-5257, Fax: 301-314-9477, E-mail: marino@umd.edu. *Application contact:* Dr. Charles A. Caramello, Dean of Graduate School, 301-405-0358, Fax: 301-405-9305, E-mail: ccaramel@umd.edu.

University of New Haven, Graduate School, Henry C. Lee College of Criminal Justice and Forensic Sciences, Program in Fire Science, West Haven, CT 06516-1916. Offers emergency management (Certificate); fire administration (MS); fire science technology (Certificate); fire/arson investigation (MS, Certificate); forensic science/fire science (Certificate); public safety management (MS, Certificate). Part-time and evening/weekend programs available. *Students:* 3 full-time (0 women), 15 part-time (3 women); includes 1 Black or African American, non-Hispanic/Latino, 1 international. Average age 38. 6 applicants, 100% accepted, 4 enrolled. In 2010, 4 master's, 3 other advanced degrees awarded. *Degree requirements:* For master's, thesis or alternative. *Entrance requirements:* Additional exam requirements/recommendations for international students: Required—TOEFL (minimum score 520 paper-based; 190 computer-based; 70 iBT); Recommended—IELTS (minimum score 5.5). *Application deadline:* For fall admission, 5/31 for international students; for winter admission, 10/15 for international students; for spring admission, 1/15 for international students. Applications are processed on a rolling basis. Application fee: $50. Electronic applications accepted. *Financial support:* Research assistantships with partial tuition reimbursements, teaching assistantships with partial tuition reimbursements, career-related internships or fieldwork, Federal Work-Study, scholarships/grants, tuition waivers, and unspecified assistantships available. Support available to part-time students. Financial award applicants required to submit FAFSA. *Unit head:* Robert E. Massicotte, Director, 203-932-7424. *Application contact:* Eloise Gormley, Director of Graduate Admissions, 203-932-7449, Fax: 203-932-7137, E-mail: gradinfo@newhaven.edu.

Worcester Polytechnic Institute, Graduate Studies and Research, Department of Fire Protection Engineering, Worcester, MA 01609-2280. Offers MS, PhD, Advanced Certificate, Graduate Certificate. Part-time and evening/weekend programs available. Postbaccalaureate distance learning degree programs offered (no on-campus study). *Faculty:* 4 full-time (1 woman), 2 part-time/adjunct (0 women). *Students:* 56 full-time (6 women), 47 part-time (7 women); includes 2 Black or African American, non-Hispanic/Latino; 3 Hispanic/Latino; 5 Native Hawaiian or other Pacific Islander, non-Hispanic/Latino, 15 international. 91 applicants, 71% accepted, 47 enrolled. In 2010, 36 master's, 1 doctorate awarded. *Degree requirements:* For master's, thesis optional; for doctorate, comprehensive exam, thesis/dissertation. *Entrance requirements:* For master's, GRE General Test (recommended), BS in engineering or physical sciences, 3 letters of recommendation, work experience or statement of purpose; for doctorate, GRE General Test, 3 letters of recommendation, statement of purpose. Additional exam requirements/recommendations for international students: Required—TOEFL (minimum score 550 paper-based; 213 computer-based; 79 iBT), IELTS (minimum score 6.5). *Application deadline:* For fall admission, 1/1 priority date for domestic students, 1/1 for international students; for spring admission, 10/1 priority date for domestic students, 10/1 for international students. Applications are processed on a rolling basis. Electronic applications accepted. *Expenses:* Tuition: Full-time $20,862; part-time $1159 per term. One-time fee: $15. *Financial support:* Career-related internships or fieldwork, institutionally sponsored loans, scholarships/grants, and unspecified assistantships available. Financial award application deadline: 1/1; financial award applicants required to submit FAFSA. *Faculty research:* Computer fire modeling, fire dynamics and material evaluation, structural systems and fire safety, explosions, risk assessment and regulatory reform, forest fires. *Unit head:* Dr. Kathy Notarianni, Head, 508-831-5593, Fax: 508-831-5862, E-mail: kanfpe@wpi.edu. *Application contact:* Dr. Ali Rangwala, Graduate Coordinator, 508-831-5593, Fax: 508-831-5862, E-mail: rangwala@wpi.edu.

Geotechnical Engineering

Auburn University, Graduate School, Ginn College of Engineering, Department of Civil Engineering, Auburn University, AL 36849. Offers construction engineering and management (MCE, MS, PhD); environmental engineering (MCE, MS, PhD); geotechnical/materials engineering (MCE, MS, PhD); hydraulics/hydrology (MCE, MS, PhD); structural engineering (MCE, MS, PhD); transportation engineering (MCE, MS, PhD). Part-time programs available. *Faculty:* 21 full-time (1 woman), 3 part-time/adjunct (1 woman). *Students:* 46 full-time (15 women), 39 part-time (5 women); includes 3 Black or African American, non-Hispanic/Latino; 1 Asian, non-Hispanic/Latino, 29 international. Average age 26. 136 applicants, 43% accepted, 26 enrolled. In 2010, 19 master's, 4 doctorates awarded. *Degree requirements:* For master's, project (MCE), thesis (MS); for doctorate, comprehensive exam, thesis/dissertation. *Entrance requirements:* For master's and doctorate, GRE General Test. *Application deadline:* For fall admission, 7/7 for domestic students; for spring admission, 11/24 for domestic students. Applications are processed on a rolling basis. Application fee: $50 ($60 for international students). Electronic applications accepted. *Expenses:* Tuition, state resident: full-time $7002. Tuition, nonresident: full-time $21,898. International tuition: $22,116 full-time. Required fees: $892. Tuition and fees vary according to course load and program. *Financial support:* Fellowships, research assistantships, teaching assistantships, Federal Work-Study available. Support available to part-time students. Financial award application deadline: 3/15; financial award applicants required to submit FAFSA. *Unit head:* Dr. J. Michael Stallings, Head, 334-844-4320. *Application contact:* Dr. George Flowers, Dean of the Graduate School, 334-844-2125.

Cornell University, Graduate School, Graduate Fields of Engineering, Field of Civil and Environmental Engineering, Ithaca, NY 14853-0001. Offers engineering management (M Eng, MS, PhD); environmental engineering (M Eng, MS, PhD); environmental fluid mechanics and hydrology (M Eng, MS, PhD); environmental systems engineering (M Eng, MS, PhD); geotechnical engineering (M Eng, MS, PhD); remote sensing (M Eng, MS, PhD); structural engineering (M Eng, MS, PhD); structural mechanics (M Eng, MS); transportation engineering (MS, PhD); transportation systems engineering (M Eng); water resource systems (M Eng, MS, PhD). *Faculty:* 36 full-time (4 women). *Students:* 148 full-time (48 women); includes 3 Black or African American, non-Hispanic/Latino; 1 American Indian or Alaska Native, non-Hispanic/Latino; 16 Asian, non-Hispanic/Latino; 16 Hispanic/Latino, 60 international. Average age 24. 390 applicants, 56% accepted, 76 enrolled. In 2010, 93 master's, 5 doctorates awarded. Terminal master's awarded for partial completion of doctoral program. *Degree requirements:* For master's, thesis (MS); for doctorate, comprehensive exam, thesis/dissertation. *Entrance requirements:* For master's and doctorate, GRE General Test (recommended), 2 letters of recommendation. Additional exam requirements/recommendations for international students: Required—TOEFL (minimum score 600 paper-based; 250 computer-based; 77 iBT). *Application deadline:* For fall admission, 1/15 priority date for domestic students; for spring admission, 10/15 for domestic students. Application fee: $70. Electronic applications accepted. *Expenses:* Tuition: Full-time $29,500. Required fees: $76. Tuition and fees vary according to degree level and program. *Financial support:* In 2010–11, 50 students received support, including 17 fellowships with full tuition reimbursements available, 33 research assistantships with full tuition reimbursements available, 15 teaching assistantships with full tuition reimbursements available; institutionally sponsored loans, scholarships/grants, health care benefits, tuition waivers (full and partial), and unspecified assistantships also available. Financial award applicants required to submit FAFSA. *Faculty research:* Environmental engineering, geotechnical engineering, remote sensing, environmental fluid mechanics and hydrology, structural engineering. *Unit head:* Director of Graduate Studies, 607-255-7560, Fax: 607-255-9004. *Application contact:* Graduate Field Assistant, 607-255-7560, Fax: 607-255-9004, E-mail: cee_grad@cornell.edu.

Drexel University, College of Engineering, Department of Civil, Architectural, and Environmental Engineering, Program in Geotechnical, Geoenvironmental and Geosynthetics Engineering, Philadelphia, PA 19104-2875. Offers MS, PhD.

École Polytechnique de Montréal, Graduate Programs, Department of Civil, Geological and Mining Engineering, Montréal, QC H3C 3A7, Canada. Offers civil, geological and mining engineering (DESS); environmental engineering (M Eng, M Sc A, PhD); geotechnical engineering (M Eng, M Sc A, PhD); hydraulics engineering (M Eng, M Sc A, PhD); structural engineering (M Eng, M Sc A, PhD); transportation engineering (M Eng, M Sc A, PhD). Part-time programs available. *Degree requirements:* For master's, one foreign language, thesis; for doctorate, one foreign language, thesis/dissertation. *Entrance requirements:* For master's, minimum GPA of 2.75; for doctorate, minimum GPA of 3.0. *Faculty research:* Water resources management, characteristics of building materials, aging of dams, pollution control.

Illinois Institute of Technology, Graduate College, Armour College of Engineering, Department of Civil, Architectural and Environmental Engineering, Chicago, IL 60616-3793. Offers architectural engineering (M Arch E); civil engineering (MS, PhD), including architectural engineeering (MS), construction engineering and management (MS), geoenvironmental engineering (MS), geotechnical engineering (MS), structural engineering (MS), transportation engineering (MS); construction engineering and management (MCEM); environmental engineering (M Env E, PhD); geoenvironmental engineering (M Geoenv E); geotechnical engineering (MGE); public works (MPW); structural engineering (MSE); transportation engineering (M Trans E). Part-time and evening/weekend programs available. Postbaccalaureate distance learning degree programs offered (minimal on-campus study). *Faculty:* 15 full-time (1 woman), 13 part-time/adjunct (1 woman). *Students:* 159 full-time (63 women), 109 part-time (22 women); includes 30 minority (9 Black or African American, non-Hispanic/Latino; 16 Asian, non-Hispanic/Latino; 5 Hispanic/Latino), 126 international. Average age 27. 453 applicants, 66% accepted, 98 enrolled. In 2010, 76 master's, 1 doctorate awarded. Terminal master's awarded for partial completion of doctoral program. *Degree requirements:* For master's, thesis (for some programs); for doctorate, comprehensive exam, thesis/dissertation. *Entrance requirements:* For master's, GRE General Test (minimum score 900 Quantitative and Verbal, 2.5 Analytical Writing), minimum undergraduate GPA of 3.0; for doctorate, GRE General Test (minimum score 1000 Quantitative and Verbal, 3.0 Analytical Writing), minimum undergraduate GPA of 3.0. Additional exam requirements/recommendations for international students: Required—TOEFL (minimum score 523 paper-based; 70 iBT); Recommended—IELTS (minimum score 5.5). *Application deadline:* For fall admission, 5/1 for domestic and international students; for spring admission, 10/15 for domestic and international students. Applications are processed on a rolling basis. Application fee: $50. Electronic applications accepted. *Expenses:* Tuition: Full-time $18,576; part-time $1032 per credit hour. Required fees: $583 per semester. One-time fee: $150. Tuition and fees vary according to program and student level. *Financial support:* In 2010–11, 13 research assistantships with full and partial tuition reimbursements (averaging $9,453 per year), 19 teaching assistantships with full and partial tuition reimbursements (averaging $3,163 per year) were awarded; fellowships with full and partial tuition reimbursements, Federal Work-Study, institutionally sponsored loans, scholarships/grants, health care benefits, tuition waivers (partial), and unspecified assistantships also available. Support available to part-time students. Financial award applicants required to submit FAFSA. *Faculty research:* Structural, architectural, geotechnical and geoenvironmental engineering; construction engineering and management; transportation engineering; environmental engineering and public works. Total annual research expenditures: $763,042. *Unit head:* Dr. Jamshid Mohammadi, Professor and Chairman, 312-567-3629, Fax: 312-567-3519, E-mail: mohammadi@iit.edu. *Application contact:* Deborah Gibson, Director, Graduate Admission, 866-472-3448, Fax: 312-567-3138, E-mail: inquiry.grad@iit.edu.

Iowa State University of Science and Technology, Graduate College, College of Engineering, Department of Civil and Construction Engineering, Ames, IA 50011. Offers civil engineering (MS, PhD), including civil engineering materials, construction engineering and management, environmental engineering, geometronics, geotechnical engineering, structural engineering, transportation engineering. *Faculty:* 35 full-time (6 women), 4 part-time/adjunct (0 women). *Students:* 93 full-time (31 women), 48 part-time (10 women); includes 1 Black or African American, non-Hispanic/Latino; 1 Asian, non-Hispanic/Latino; 4 Hispanic/Latino, 62 international. 179 applicants, 37% accepted, 35 enrolled. In 2010, 32 master's, 9 doctorates awarded. *Degree requirements:* For master's, thesis or alternative; for doctorate, thesis/dissertation. *Entrance requirements:* For master's and doctorate, GRE General Test. Additional exam requirements/recommendations for international students: Required—TOEFL (minimum score 550 paper-based; 82 iBT), IELTS (minimum score 6.5). *Application deadline:* For fall admission, 2/1 priority date for domestic students, 2/1 for international students; for spring admission, 8/1 priority date for domestic students, 8/1 for international students. Application fee: $40 ($90 for international students). Electronic applications accepted. *Financial support:* In 2010–11, 67 research assistantships with full and partial tuition reimbursements (averaging $7,654 per year), 4 teaching assistantships with full and partial tuition reimbursements (averaging $9,525 per year) were awarded; fellowships, scholarships/grants, health care benefits, and unspecified assistantships also available. *Unit head:* Dr. James Alleman, Chair, 515-294-3892, E-mail: ccee-grad-inquiry@iastate.edu. *Application contact:* Dr. Sri Srithanan, Director of Graduate Education, 515-294-5328, E-mail: ccee-grad-inquiry@iastate.edu.

Louisiana State University and Agricultural and Mechanical College, Graduate School, College of Engineering, Department of Civil and Environmental Engineering, Baton Rouge, LA 70803. Offers environmental engineering (MSCE, PhD); geotechnical engineering (MSCE, PhD); structural engineering and mechanics (MSCE, PhD); transportation engineering (MSCE, PhD); water resources (MSCE, PhD). Part-time programs available. *Faculty:* 29 full-time (3 women). *Students:* 89 full-time (19 women), 35 part-time (8 women); includes 2 Black or African American, non-Hispanic/Latino; 1 American Indian or Alaska Native, non-Hispanic/Latino; 3 Asian, non-Hispanic/Latino; 3 Hispanic/Latino, 65 international. Average age 29. 96 applicants, 65% accepted, 16 enrolled. In 2010, 20 master's, 8 doctorates awarded. *Degree requirements:* For master's, thesis optional; for doctorate, one foreign language, thesis/dissertation. *Entrance requirements:* For master's and doctorate, GRE General Test, minimum GPA of 3.0. Additional exam requirements/recommendations for international students: Required—TOEFL (minimum score 550 paper-based; 213 computer-based; 79 iBT) or IELTS (minimum score 6.5). *Application deadline:* For fall admission, 1/25 priority date for domestic students, 5/15 for international students; for spring admission, 10/15 for international students. Applications are processed on a rolling basis. Application fee: $50 ($70 for international students). Electronic applications accepted. *Financial support:* In 2010–11, 89 students received support, including 2 fellowships with full and partial tuition reimbursements available (averaging $24,418 per year), 75 research assistantships with full and partial tuition reimbursements available (averaging $16,115 per year), 3 teaching assistantships with full and partial tuition reimbursements available (averaging $12,843 per year); career-related internships or fieldwork, institutionally sponsored loans, scholarships/grants, and health care benefits also available. Financial award application deadline: 3/1; financial award applicants required to submit FAFSA. *Faculty research:* Mechanics and structures, environmental, geotechnical transportation, water resources. Total annual research expenditures: $2.6 million. *Unit head:* Dr. George Z. Voyiadjis, Chair/Professor, 225-578-8668, Fax: 225-578-9176, E-mail: cegzv@lsu.edu. *Application contact:* Dr. Clinton Willson, Professor, 225-578-8652, E-mail: cwillson@lsu.edu.

Marquette University, Graduate School, College of Engineering, Department of Civil and Environmental Engineering, Milwaukee, WI 53201-1881. Offers construction and public works management (MS, PhD); construction engineering and management (Certificate); environmental/water resources engineering (MS, PhD); structural design (Certificate); structural/geotechnical engineering (MS, PhD); transportation planning and engineering (MS, PhD); waste and wastewater treatment processes (Certificate). Part-time and evening/weekend programs available. *Faculty:* 13 full-time (0 women), 3 part-time/adjunct (0 women). *Students:* 20 full-time (4 women), 12 part-time (1 woman); includes 1 minority (Black or African American, non-Hispanic/Latino), 12 international. Average age 27. 66 applicants, 64% accepted, 9 enrolled. In 2010, 8 master's, 1 doctorate awarded. Terminal master's awarded for partial completion of doctoral program. *Degree requirements:* For master's, comprehensive exam, thesis or alternative; for doctorate, thesis/dissertation. *Entrance requirements:* For master's, GRE General Test (recommended), minimum GPA of 3.0, official transcripts from all current and previous colleges/universities except Marquette, three letters of recommendation; for doctorate, GRE General Test, minimum GPA of 3.0, official transcripts from all current and previous colleges/universities except Marquette, three letters of recommendation, brief statement of purpose, submission of any English-language publications authored by applicant (strongly recommended). Additional exam requirements/recommendations for international students: Required—TOEFL (minimum score 530 paper-based; 78 computer-based). *Application deadline:* For fall admission, 6/1 priority date for domestic students. Applications are processed on a rolling basis. Application fee: $50. Electronic applications accepted. *Expenses:* Tuition: Full-time $16,290; part-time $905 per credit hour. Tuition and fees vary according to program. *Financial support:* In 2010–11, 13 students received support, including 4 fellowships with tuition reimbursements available, 4 research assistantships with tuition reimbursements available, 10 teaching assistantships with tuition reimbursements available; Federal Work-Study, institutionally sponsored loans, scholarships/grants, and tuition waivers (full and partial) also available. Support available to part-time students. Financial award application deadline: 2/15. *Faculty research:* Highway safety, highway performance, and intelligent transportation systems; surface mount technology; watershed management. Total annual research expenditures: $662,392. *Unit head:* Dr. Thomas Wenzel, Chair, 414-288-7030, Fax: 414-288-7521, E-mail: thomas.wenzel@marquette.edu. *Application contact:* Dr. Stephen M. Heinrich, Director of Graduate Studies, 414-288-5466, E-mail: stephen.heinrich@marquette.edu.

Massachusetts Institute of Technology, School of Engineering, Department of Civil and Environmental Engineering, Cambridge, MA 02139. Offers biological oceanography (PhD, Sc D); chemical oceanography (PhD, Sc D); civil and environmental engineering (M Eng, SM, PhD, Sc D); civil and environmental systems (PhD, Sc D); civil engineering (PhD, Sc D, CE); coastal engineering (PhD, Sc D); construction engineering and management (PhD, Sc D); environmental biology (PhD, Sc D); environmental chemistry (PhD, Sc D); environmental engineering (PhD, Sc D); environmental fluid mechanics (PhD, Sc D); geotechnical and geoenvironmental engineering (PhD, Sc D); hydrology (PhD, Sc D); information technology (PhD, Sc D); oceanographic engineering (PhD, Sc D); structures and materials (PhD, Sc D); transportation (PhD, Sc D); SM/MBA. *Faculty:* 36 full-time (6 women). *Students:* 181 full-time (56 women); includes 27 minority (3 Black or African American, non-Hispanic/Latino; 10 Asian, non-Hispanic/Latino; 10 Hispanic/Latino; 4 Two or more races, non-Hispanic/Latino), 93 international. Average age 26. 525 applicants, 29% accepted, 74 enrolled. In 2010, 85 master's, 18 doctorates, 2 other advanced degrees awarded. *Degree requirements:* For master's and CE, thesis; for doctorate, comprehensive exam, thesis/dissertation. *Entrance requirements:* For master's and doctorate, GRE General Test. Additional exam requirements/recommendations for international students: Required—TOEFL (minimum score 577 paper-based; 233 computer-based; 90 iBT), IELTS (minimum score 7). *Application deadline:* For fall admission, 1/2 for domestic and international students. Application fee: $75. Electronic applications accepted. *Expenses:* Tuition: Full-time $38,940; part-time $605 per unit. Required fees: $272. *Financial support:* In 2010–11, 146 students received support, including 50 fellowships with tuition reimbursements available (averaging $21,808 per year), 90 research assistantships with tuition reimbursements available (averaging $28,452 per year), 20 teaching assistantships with tuition reimbursements available (averaging $27,842 per year); career-related internships or fieldwork, Federal Work-Study, institutionally sponsored loans, scholarships/grants, health care benefits, and unspecified assistantships also available. *Faculty research:* Environmental chemistry; environmental microbiology; environmental fluid mechanics and coastal engineering; geotechnical engineering and geomechanics; hydrology and hydroclimatology; mechanics of materials and structures; operations research/supply chain; transportation. Total annual research expenditures: $19.5 million. *Unit head:* Prof. Andrew Whittle, Department Head, 617-253-7101. *Application contact:* Patricia Glidden, Graduate Admissions Coordinator, 617-253-7119, Fax: 617-258-6775, E-mail: cee-admissions@mit.edu.

McGill University, Faculty of Graduate and Postdoctoral Studies, Faculty of Engineering, Department of Civil Engineering and Applied Mechanics, Montréal, QC H3A 2T5, Canada. Offers environmental engineering (M Eng, M Sc, PhD); fluid mechanics (M Sc); fluid mechanics and hydraulic engineering (M Eng, PhD); materials engineering (M Eng, PhD); rehabilitation of urban infrastructure (M Eng, PhD); soil behavior (M Eng, PhD); soil mechanics and foundations (M Eng, PhD); structures and structural mechanics (M Eng, PhD); water resources (M Sc); water resources engineering (M Eng, PhD).

Missouri University of Science and Technology, Graduate School, Department of Civil, Architectural, and Environmental Engineering, Rolla, MO 65409. Offers civil engineering (MS, DE, PhD); construction engineering (MS, DE, PhD); environmental engineering (MS); fluid mechanics (MS, DE, PhD); geotechnical engineering (MS, DE, PhD); hydrology and hydraulic engineering (MS, DE, PhD). Part-time and evening/weekend programs available. Terminal master's awarded for partial completion of doctoral program. *Degree requirements:* For master's, thesis optional; for doctorate, comprehensive exam, thesis/dissertation. *Entrance requirements:* For master's, GRE General Test (minimum combined score 1100), minimum GPA of 3.0; for doctorate, GRE General Test (minimum score: verbal and quantitative 400, writing 3.5), minimum GPA of 3.0. Additional exam requirements/recommendations for international students: Required—TOEFL. Electronic applications accepted. *Faculty research:* Earthquake engineering, structural optimization and control systems, structural health monitoring/damage detection, soil-structure interaction, soil mechanics and foundation engineering.

Northwestern University, McCormick School of Engineering and Applied Science, Department of Civil and Environmental Engineering, Evanston, IL 60208-3109. Offers environmental engineering and science (MS, PhD); geotechnical engineering (MS, PhD); mechanics of materials and solids (MS, PhD); project management (MS, PhD); structural engineering and materials (MS, PhD); theoretical and applied mechanics (MS, PhD), including fluid mechanics, solid mechanics; transportation systems analysis and planning (MS, PhD). MS and PhD admissions and degrees offered through The Graduate School. Part-time programs available. Terminal master's awarded for partial completion of doctoral program. *Degree requirements:* For master's, thesis (for some programs); for doctorate, thesis/dissertation. *Entrance requirements:* For master's and doctorate, GRE General Test, minimum 2 letters of recommendation, transcripts from all academic institutions attended. Additional exam requirements/recommendations for international students: Required—TOEFL (minimum score 600 paper-based; 250 computer-based; 100 iBT), IELTS (minimum score 7). Electronic applications accepted. *Faculty research:* Environmental engineering and science, geotechnics, mechanics of materials and solids, structural engineering and materials, transportation systems analysis and planning.

Norwich University, School of Graduate and Continuing Studies, Program in Civil Engineering, Northfield, VT 05663. Offers construction management (MCE); geo-technical (MCE); structural (MCE); water/environmental (MCE). Evening/weekend programs available. *Faculty:* 20 full-time (3 women). *Students:* 78 full-time (19 women); includes 5 Black or African American, non-Hispanic/Latino; 4 Asian, non-Hispanic/Latino; 7 Hispanic/Latino. Average age 35. 107 applicants, 88% accepted, 90 enrolled. In 2010, 78 master's awarded. *Entrance requirements:* For master's, minimum GPA of 2.75. Additional exam requirements/recommendations for international students: Required—TOEFL (minimum score 550 paper-based; 213 computer-based; 83 iBT). *Application deadline:* For fall admission, 8/10 for domestic and international students; for spring admission, 2/6 for domestic and international students. Application fee: $50. *Expenses:* Tuition: Full-time $17,380; part-time $645 per credit. Tuition and fees vary according to program. *Financial support:* Scholarships/grants available. Financial award applicants required to submit FAFSA. *Unit head:* Dr. Thomas Descoteaux, Program Director, 802-485-2730, Fax: 802-485-2533, E-mail: tdescote@norwich.edu. *Application contact:* Shelley W. Brown, Director of Business Partnership, 802-485-2784, Fax: 802-485-2533, E-mail: sbrown@norwich.edu.

Ohio University, Graduate College, Russ College of Engineering and Technology, Department of Civil Engineering, Athens, OH 45701-2979. Offers civil engineering (PhD); construction (MS); environmental (MS); geotechnical and geoenvironmental (MS); mechanics (MS); structures (MS); transportation (MS); water resources and structures (MS). Part-time programs available. *Students:* 29 full-time (6 women), 5 part-time (1 woman); includes 2 minority (1 Hispanic/Latino; 1 Two or more races, non-Hispanic/Latino), 16 international. 52 applicants, 83% accepted, 14 enrolled. In 2010, 7 master's awarded. *Degree requirements:* For master's, comprehensive exam (for some programs), thesis or alternative; for doctorate, comprehensive exam, thesis/dissertation. *Entrance requirements:* For master's, GRE General Test, minimum GPA of 3.0, 3 letters of recommendation; for doctorate, GRE General Test. Additional exam requirements/recommendations for international students: Required—TOEFL (minimum score 550 paper-based; 80 iBT) or IELTS (minimum score 6.5). *Application deadline:* For fall admission, 5/1 priority date for domestic students, 2/1 priority date for international students; for winter admission, 8/1 priority date for domestic students, 4/1 priority date for international students; for spring admission, 2/1 priority date for domestic students, 7/1 priority date for international students. Applications are processed on a rolling basis. Application fee: $50 ($55 for international students). Electronic applications accepted. *Financial support:* Research assistantships with full tuition reimbursements, teaching assistantships with full tuition reimbursements, Federal Work-Study, institutionally sponsored loans, scholarships/grants, and unspecified assistantships available. Financial award application deadline: 3/15; financial award applicants required to submit FAFSA. *Faculty research:* Noise abatement, materials and environment, highway infrastructure, subsurface investigation (pavements, pipes, bridges). *Unit head:* Dr. Gayle F. Mitchell, Chair, 740-593-0430, Fax: 740-593-0625, E-mail: mitchelg@ohio.edu. *Application contact:* Dr. Shad M. Sargand, Graduate Chair, 740-593-1465, Fax: 740-593-0625, E-mail: sargand@ohio.edu.

Oregon State University, Graduate School, College of Engineering, School of Civil and Construction Engineering, Corvallis, OR 97331. Offers civil engineering (MS, PhD); coastal and ocean engineering (M Oc E, PhD); coastal engineering (MS); construction engineering management (MBE, PhD); engineering (M Eng, MAIS); geotechnical engineering (MS, PhD); structural engineering (MS, PhD); transportation engineering (MS, PhD); water engineering (MS, PhD). Part-time programs available. Terminal master's awarded for partial completion of doctoral program. *Degree requirements:* For master's, thesis or alternative; for doctorate, one foreign language, thesis/dissertation. *Entrance requirements:* For master's, GRE General Test, minimum GPA of 3.0 in last 90 hours (3.5 for MS); for doctorate, GRE General Test, minimum GPA of 3.0 in last 90 hours of undergraduate course work. Additional exam requirements/recommendations for international students: Required—TOEFL (minimum score 580 paper-based; 237 computer-based). *Faculty research:* Hazardous waste management, carbon cycling, wave forces on structures, pavement design, seismic analysis.

Penn State University Park, Graduate School, College of Earth and Mineral Sciences, Department of Energy and Mineral Engineering, State College, University Park, PA 16802-1503. Offers MS, PhD.

Rensselaer Polytechnic Institute, Graduate School, School of Engineering, Program in Civil Engineering, Troy, NY 12180-3590. Offers geotechnical engineering (M Eng, MS, PhD); mechanics of composite materials and structures (M Eng, MS, PhD); structural engineering (M Eng, MS, PhD); transportation engineering (M Eng, MS, PhD). Part-time programs available. *Faculty:* 13 full-time (1 woman), 3 part-time/adjunct (0 women). *Students:* 20 full-time (4 women); includes 1 Black or African American, non-Hispanic/Latino, 16 international. Average age 24. 65 applicants, 12% accepted, 5 enrolled. In 2010, 19 master's, 3 doctorates awarded. Terminal master's awarded for partial completion of doctoral program. *Degree requirements:* For master's, thesis (for some programs); for doctorate, thesis/dissertation. *Entrance requirements:* For master's and doctorate, GRE. Additional exam requirements/recommendations for international students: Required—TOEFL (minimum score 570 paper-based; 230 computer-based; 89 iBT), IELTS (minimum score 6.5). *Application deadline:* For fall admission, 1/15 priority date for domestic and international students; for spring admission, 8/15 priority date for domestic and international students. Applications are processed on a rolling basis. Application fee: $75. Electronic applications accepted. *Expenses:* Tuition: Full-time $39,600; part-time $1650 per credit. Required fees: $1896. *Financial support:* In 2010–11, 1 fellowship with full tuition reimbursement (averaging $16,500 per year), 3 research assistantships with full tuition reimbursements (averaging $16,500 per year), 4 teaching assistantships with full tuition reimbursements (averaging $16,500 per year) were awarded; career-related internships or fieldwork and institutionally sponsored loans also available. Financial award application deadline: 2/1. *Faculty research:* Computational mechanics, earthquake engineering, geo-environmental engineering. Total annual research expenditures: $2.7 million. *Unit head:* Dr. Chris Letchford, Head, 518-276-6362, Fax: 518-276-4833, E-mail: letchc@rpi.edu. *Application contact:* Kimberly Boyce, Administrative Assistant, 518-276-6941, Fax: 518-276-4833, E-mail: boycek@rpi.edu.

Texas A&M University, College of Engineering, Zachry Department of Civil Engineering, College Station, TX 77843. Offers coastal and ocean engineering (M Eng, MS, D Eng, PhD); construction engineering and management (M Eng, MS, D Eng, PhD); environmental engineering (M Eng, MS, D Eng, PhD); geotechnical engineering (M Eng, MS, D Eng, PhD); materials engineering (M Eng, MS, D Eng, PhD); structural engineering (M Eng, MS, D Eng, PhD); transportation engineering (M Eng, MS, D Eng, PhD); water resources engineering (M Eng, MS, D Eng, PhD). Part-time programs available. *Faculty:* 57. *Students:* 384 full-time (81 women), 35 part-time (7 women); includes 35 minority (3 Black or African American, non-Hispanic/Latino; 1 American Indian or Alaska Native, non-Hispanic/Latino; 14 Asian, non-Hispanic/Latino; 17 Hispanic/Latino), 263 international. Average age 29. In 2010, 136 master's, 26 doctorates awarded. *Degree requirements:* For master's, thesis (MS); for doctorate, dissertation (PhD), internship (D Eng). *Entrance requirements:* For master's and doctorate, GRE General Test. Additional exam requirements/recommendations for international students: Required—TOEFL. *Application deadline:* Applications are processed on a rolling basis. Application fee: $50 ($75 for international students). Electronic applications accepted. *Financial support:* In 2010–11, fellowships (averaging $4,500 per year), research assistantships (averaging $14,000 per year), teaching assistantships (averaging $14,400 per year) were awarded; career-related internships or fieldwork and institutionally sponsored loans also available. Financial award application deadline: 4/15; financial award applicants required to submit FAFSA. *Unit head:* Dr. Tony Cahill, Head, 979-845-3858, E-mail: tcahill@civil.tamu.edu. *Application contact:* Graduate Advisor, 979-845-7435, Fax: 979-845-6156, E-mail: info@civil.tamu.edu.

Tufts University, School of Engineering, Department of Civil and Environmental Engineering, Medford, MA 02155. Offers civil engineering (ME, MS, PhD), including geotechnical engineering, structural engineering; environmental engineering (ME, MS, PhD), including environmental engineering and environmental sciences, environmental geotechnology, environmental health, environmental science and management, hazardous materials management, water resources engineering. Part-time programs available. Terminal master's awarded for partial completion of doctoral program. *Degree requirements:* For master's, thesis or alternative; for doctorate, thesis/dissertation. *Entrance requirements:* For master's and doctorate, GRE General Test. Additional exam requirements/recommendations for international students: Required—TOEFL (minimum score 550 paper-based; 213 computer-based; 80 iBT). Electronic applications accepted. *Expenses:* Tuition: Full-time $39,624; part-time $3962 per course. Required fees: $40 per year. Full-time tuition and fees vary according to degree level, program and student level. Part-time tuition and fees vary according to course load.

The University of Alabama in Huntsville, School of Graduate Studies, College of Engineering, Department of Civil and Environmental Engineering, Huntsville, AL 35899. Offers civil and environmental engineering (PhD); civil engineering (MSE), including environmental and water resource engineering, geotechnical engineering, structural engineering and structural mechanics, transportation engineering. PhD offered jointly with The University of Alabama at Birmingham. Part-time and evening/weekend programs available. *Faculty:* 6 full-time (1 woman), 1 part-time/adjunct (0 women). *Students:* 23 full-time (7 women), 11 part-time (4 women); includes 3 minority (2 Black or African American, non-Hispanic/Latino; 1 Asian, non-Hispanic/Latino), 12 international. Average age 30. 37 applicants, 57% accepted, 15 enrolled. In 2010, 1 master's, 3 doctorates awarded. *Degree requirements:* For master's, comprehensive exam, thesis or alternative, oral and written exams; for doctorate, comprehensive exam, thesis/dissertation, oral and written exams. *Entrance requirements:* For master's, GRE General Test, BSE, minimum GPA of 3.0; for doctorate, GRE General Test, minimum GPA of 3.0. Additional exam requirements/recommendations for international students: Required—TOEFL (minimum score 500 paper-based; 173 computer-based; 62 iBT). *Application deadline:* For fall admission, 7/15 for domestic students, 4/1 for international students; for spring admission, 11/30 for domestic students, 9/1 for international students. Applications are processed on a rolling basis. Application fee: $40 ($50 for international students). Electronic applications accepted. *Expenses:* Tuition, state resident: full-time $7250; part-time $407.75 per credit hour. Tuition, nonresident: full-time $17,358; part-time $970.05 per credit hour. Required fees: $246.80 per semester. Tuition and fees vary according to course load and program. *Financial support:* In 2010–11, 14 students received support, including 7 research assistantships with full and partial tuition reimbursements available (averaging $12,435 per year), 7 teaching assistantships with full and partial tuition reimbursements available (averaging $10,281 per year); career-related internships or fieldwork, Federal Work-Study, institutionally sponsored loans, scholarships/grants, health care benefits, and unspecified assistantships also available. Support available to part-time students. Financial award application deadline: 4/1; financial award applicants required to submit FAFSA. *Faculty research:* Hydrologic modeling, orbital debris impact, hydrogeology, environmental engineering, transportation engineering. Total annual research expenditures: $1.9 million. *Unit head:* Dr. Houssam Toutanji, Chair, 256-824-7361, Fax: 256-824-6724, E-mail: toutanji@cee.uah.edu. *Application contact:* Kathy Biggs, Graduate Studies Admissions Manager, 256-824-6199, Fax: 256-824-6405, E-mail: deangrad@uah.edu.

University of Alberta, Faculty of Graduate Studies and Research, Department of Civil and Environmental Engineering, Edmonton, AB T6G 2E1, Canada. Offers construction engineering and management (M Eng, M Sc, PhD); environmental engineering (M Eng, M Sc, PhD); environmental science (M Sc, PhD); geoenvironmental engineering (M Eng, M Sc, PhD); geotechnical engineering (M Eng, M Sc, PhD); mining engineering (M Eng, M Sc, PhD); petroleum engineering (M Eng, M Sc, PhD); structural engineering (M Eng, M Sc, PhD); water resources (M Eng, M Sc, PhD). Part-time programs available. Postbaccalaureate distance learning degree programs offered (minimal on-campus study). *Degree requirements:* For master's, thesis (for some programs); for doctorate, thesis/dissertation. *Entrance requirements:* For master's, minimum GPA of 3.0 in last 2 years of undergraduate studies; for doctorate, minimum GPA of 3.0. Additional exam requirements/recommendations for international students: Required—TOEFL (minimum score 550 paper-based; 213 computer-based). Electronic applications accepted. *Faculty research:* Mining.

University of Calgary, Faculty of Graduate Studies, Schulich School of Engineering, Department of Geomatics Engineering, Calgary, AB T2N 1N4, Canada. Offers M Eng, M Sc, PhD. Part-time programs available. *Degree requirements:* For master's, thesis (for some programs); for doctorate, thesis/dissertation, candidacy exam. *Entrance requirements:* For master's, minimum GPA of 3.0; for doctorate, minimum GPA of 3.5. Additional exam requirements/recommendations for international students: Required—TOEFL (minimum score 550 paper-based; 213 computer-based). *Faculty research:* Gravity and geodynamics, digital imaging systems, engineering metrology, GIS and land tenure, positioning.

University of California, Berkeley, Graduate Division, College of Engineering, Department of Civil and Environmental Engineering, Berkeley, CA 94720-1500. Offers engineering and project management (M Eng, MS, D Eng, PhD); environmental engineering (M Eng, MS, D Eng, PhD); geoengineering (M Eng, MS, D Eng, PhD); structural engineering, mechanics and materials (M Eng, MS, D Eng, PhD); transportation engineering (M Eng, MS, D Eng, PhD); M Arch/MS; MCP/MS; MPP/MS. *Degree requirements:* For master's, comprehensive exam or thesis (MS); for doctorate, thesis/dissertation, qualifying exam. *Entrance requirements:* For master's, GRE General Test, minimum GPA of 3.0, 3 letters of recommendation; for doctorate, GRE General Test, minimum GPA of 3.5, 3 letters of recommendation. Additional exam

Geotechnical Engineering

University of California, Berkeley (continued)
requirements/recommendations for international students: Required—TOEFL (minimum score 570 paper-based; 230 computer-based). Electronic applications accepted.

University of Colorado Boulder, Graduate School, College of Engineering and Applied Science, Department of Civil, Environmental, and Architectural Engineering, Boulder, CO 80309. Offers building systems (MS, PhD); construction engineering management (MS, PhD); environmental engineering (MS, PhD); geotechnical engineering and geomechanics (MS, PhD); hydrology, water resources and environmental fluid mechanics (MS, PhD); structural engineering and structural mechanics (MS, PhD). *Faculty:* 38 full-time (6 women). *Students:* 255 full-time (86 women), 40 part-time (11 women); includes 40 minority (1 Black or African American, non-Hispanic/Latino; 2 American Indian or Alaska Native, non-Hispanic/Latino; 15 Asian, non-Hispanic/Latino; 20 Hispanic/Latino; 2 Two or more races, non-Hispanic/Latino), 61 international. Average age 28. 420 applicants, 95 enrolled. In 2010, 56 master's, 18 doctorates awarded. *Degree requirements:* For master's, comprehensive exam, thesis or alternative; for doctorate, thesis/dissertation. *Entrance requirements:* For master's, GRE General Test, minimum undergraduate GPA of 3.0. *Application deadline:* For fall admission, 3/1 for domestic students, 12/1 for international students; for spring admission, 10/31 for domestic students, 10/1 for international students. Application fee: $50 ($60 for international students). *Financial support:* In 2010–11, 45 fellowships (averaging $7,876 per year), 68 research assistantships (averaging $15,204 per year) were awarded. Financial award application deadline: 1/15. *Faculty research:* Building systems engineering, construction engineering and management, environmental engineering, geoenvironmental engineering, geotechnical engineering, materials and mechanics, structural engineering, water resources engineering, life-cycle engineering. Total annual research expenditures: $8 million.

University of Colorado Denver, College of Engineering and Applied Science, Department of Civil Engineering, Denver, CO 80217-3364. Offers civil engineering (PhD); environmental and sustainability engineering (MS); geographic information systems (MS); geotechnical engineering (MS); hydrology and hydraulics (MS); structural engineering (MS); transportation engineering (MS). Part-time and evening/weekend programs available. *Faculty:* 14 full-time (1 woman), 6 part-time/adjunct (0 women). *Students:* 66 full-time (13 women), 72 part-time (16 women); includes 9 Black or African American, non-Hispanic/Latino; 8 Asian, non-Hispanic/Latino; 11 Hispanic/Latino, 15 international. Average age 32. 72 applicants, 54% accepted, 29 enrolled. In 2010, 14 master's, 3 doctorates awarded. *Degree requirements:* For master's, comprehensive exam, thesis or alternative; for doctorate, comprehensive exam, thesis/dissertation. *Entrance requirements:* For master's, GRE, statement of purpose, transcripts, references; for doctorate, GRE, statement of purpose, transcripts, references, letter of support from faculty stating willingness to serve as dissertation advisor and outlining plan for financial support. Additional exam requirements/recommendations for international students: Required—TOEFL (minimum score 525 paper-based; 197 computer-based). *Application deadline:* For fall admission, 7/15 for domestic students, 6/15 for international students; for spring admission, 12/1 for domestic students, 11/1 for international students. Applications are processed on a rolling basis. Application fee: $50 ($75 for international students). Electronic applications accepted. *Expenses:* Contact institution. *Financial support:* Research assistantships, teaching assistantships, career-related internships or fieldwork and Federal Work-Study available. Financial award application deadline: 4/1; financial award applicants required to submit FAFSA. *Faculty research:* Environmental engineering and sustainable systems, geosynthetics, hydrologic andhydraulic engineering, structural engineering, transportation, transportation energy use and greenhouse gas emissions. *Unit head:* Dr. Nien-Yin Chang, Acting Chair, 303-556-2810, Fax: 303-556-2368, E-mail: nien.chang@ucdenver.edu. *Application contact:* Mindy Gewuerz, Program Assistant, 303-556-6712, Fax: 303-556-2368, E-mail: mindy.gewuerz@ucdenver.edu.

University of Delaware, College of Engineering, Department of Civil and Environmental Engineering, Newark, DE 19716. Offers environmental engineering (MAS, MCE, PhD); geotechnical engineering (MAS, MCE, PhD); ocean engineering (MAS, MCE, PhD); structural engineering (MAS, MCE, PhD); transportation engineering (MAS, MCE, PhD); water resource engineering (MAS, MCE, PhD). Part-time programs available. Terminal master's awarded for partial completion of doctoral program. *Degree requirements:* For master's, thesis; for doctorate, thesis/dissertation. *Entrance requirements:* For master's and doctorate, GRE General Test. Additional exam requirements/recommendations for international students: Required—TOEFL. Electronic applications accepted. *Faculty research:* Structural engineering and mechanics; transportation engineering; ocean engineering; soil mechanics and foundation; water resources and environmental engineering.

University of Missouri, Graduate School, College of Engineering, Department of Civil and Environmental Engineering, Columbia, MO 65211. Offers civil engineering (MS, PhD); environmental engineering (MS, PhD); geotechnical engineering (MS, PhD); structural engineering (MS, PhD); transportation and highway engineering (MS); water resources (MS, PhD). *Degree requirements:* For master's, report or thesis; for doctorate, thesis/dissertation. *Entrance requirements:* For master's and doctorate, GRE General Test. Additional exam requirements/recommendations for international students: Required—TOEFL (minimum score 550 paper-based; 213 computer-based; 79 iBT).

University of New Brunswick Fredericton, School of Graduate Studies, Faculty of Engineering, Department of Civil Engineering, Fredericton, NB E3B 5A3, Canada. Offers construction engineering and management (M Eng, M Sc E, PhD); environmental engineering (M Eng, M Sc E, PhD); environmental studies (M Eng); geotechnical engineering (M Eng, M Sc E, PhD); groundwater/hydrology (M Eng, M Sc E, PhD); materials (M Eng, M Sc E, PhD); pavements (M Eng, M Sc E, PhD); structures (M Eng, M Sc E, PhD); transportation (M Eng, M Sc E, PhD). Part-time programs available. *Faculty:* 13 full-time (1 woman), 7 part-time/adjunct (1 woman). *Students:* 34 full-time (8 women), 16 part-time (2 women). In 2010, 16 master's, 6 doctorates awarded. *Degree requirements:* For master's, thesis, proposal; for doctorate, comprehensive exam, thesis/dissertation, qualifying exam; proposal; 27 credit hours of courses. *Entrance requirements:* For master's, minimum GPA of 3.0; B Sc E in civil engineering or related engineering degree; for doctorate, minimum GPA of 3.0; graduate degree in engineering or applied science. Additional exam requirements/recommendations for international students: Required—TWE (minimum score 4), TOEFL (minimum score 580 paper-based; 237 computer-based) or IELTS (minimum score 7.5). *Application deadline:* For fall admission, 5/1 priority date for domestic students; for winter admission, 11/1 priority date for domestic students. Applications are processed on a rolling basis. Application fee: $50 Canadian dollars. *Expenses:* Tuition, area resident: Full-time $3708; part-time $927 per term. International tuition: $6300 full-time. Required fees: $50 per term. *Financial support:* In 2010–11, 52 research assistantships (averaging $7,000 per year), 46 teaching assistantships (averaging $2,000 per year) were awarded; career-related internships or fieldwork and scholarships/grants also available. *Faculty research:* Construction engineering and management; materials and infrastructure renewal; highway and pavement research; structures and solid mechanics; geotechnical, soil; structure interaction; transportation and planning; environment, solid waste management. *Unit head:* Dr. Eric Hildebrand, Director of Graduate Studies, 506-453-5113, Fax: 506-453-3568, E-mail: edh@unb.ca. *Application contact:* Joyce Moore, Graduate Secretary, 506-452-6127, Fax: 506-453-3568, E-mail: civil-grad@unb.ca.

The University of Texas at Austin, Graduate School, Cockrell School of Engineering, Department of Petroleum and Geosystems Engineering, Austin, TX 78712-1111. Offers energy and earth resources (MA); petroleum engineering (MS, PhD). Evening/weekend programs available. Postbaccalaureate distance learning degree programs offered (no on-campus study). *Entrance requirements:* For master's and doctorate, GRE General Test. Electronic applications accepted.

University of Washington, Graduate School, College of Engineering, Department of Civil and Environmental Engineering, Seattle, WA 98195-2700. Offers construction engineering (MSCE); environmental engineering (MS, MSCE, MSE, PhD); hydrology, water resources, and environmental fluid mechanics (MS, MSCE, MSE, PhD); structural and geotechnical engineering and mechanics (MS, MSCE, MSE, PhD); transportation and construction engineering (MS, MSE, PhD); transportation engineering (MSCE). Part-time programs available. Postbaccalaureate distance learning degree programs offered (no on-campus study). *Faculty:* 44 full-time (10 women), 12 part-time/adjunct (1 woman). *Students:* 197 full-time (65 women), 65 part-time (15 women); includes 5 Black or African American, non-Hispanic/Latino; 28 Asian, non-Hispanic/Latino; 5 Hispanic/Latino, 55 international. 522 applicants, 51% accepted, 101 enrolled. In 2010, 68 master's, 5 doctorates awarded. Terminal master's awarded for partial completion of doctoral program. *Degree requirements:* For master's, thesis (for some programs); for doctorate, comprehensive exam, thesis/dissertation, General, qualifying, and final exams. Completion of doctoral degree within 10 years. *Entrance requirements:* For master's, GRE General Test, Minimum GPA of 3.0, statement of purpose, letters of recommendation, transcripts; for doctorate, GRE General Test, minimum GPA of 3.5, statement of purpose, letters of recommendation, transcripts. Additional exam requirements/recommendations for international students: Required—TOEFL (minimum score 580 paper-based; 237 computer-based; 92 iBT); Recommended—IELTS (minimum score 7). *Application deadline:* For fall admission, 1/10 priority date for domestic and international students. Application fee: $75. Electronic applications accepted. *Financial support:* In 2010–11, 2 students received support, including 25 fellowships with full and partial tuition reimbursements available (averaging $16,173 per year), 75 research assistantships with full tuition reimbursements available (averaging $16,515 per year), 11 teaching assistantships with full tuition reimbursements available (averaging $16,263 per year); scholarships/grants also available. Financial award application deadline: 1/10; financial award applicants required to submit FAFSA. *Faculty research:* Environmental/water resources, hydrology; construction/transportation; structures/ geotechnical. Total annual research expenditures: $14.4 million. *Unit head:* Dr. Gregory R. Miller, Professor and Chair, 206-543-0350, Fax: 206-543-1543, E-mail: gmiller@uw.edu. *Application contact:* Lorna Latal, Graduate Adviser, 206-543-2574, Fax: 206-543-1543, E-mail: llatal@u.washington.edu.

Hazardous Materials Management

Humboldt State University, Academic Programs, College of Natural Resources and Sciences, Programs in Natural Resources, Arcata, CA 95521-8299. Offers natural resources (MS), including fisheries, forestry, natural resources planning and interpretation, rangeland resources and wildland soils, wastewater utilization, watershed management, wildlife. *Students:* 62 full-time (27 women), 21 part-time (7 women); includes 4 minority (1 Asian, non-Hispanic/Latino; 2 Hispanic/Latino; 1 Two or more races, non-Hispanic/Latino), 2 international. Average age 29. 117 applicants, 47% accepted, 33 enrolled. In 2010, 23 master's awarded. *Degree requirements:* For master's, thesis or alternative. *Entrance requirements:* For master's, GRE, appropriate bachelor's degree, minimum GPA of 2.5, 3 letters of recommendation, resume. Additional exam requirements/recommendations for international students: Required—TOEFL (minimum score 500 paper-based; 173 computer-based). *Application deadline:* For fall admission, 2/1 for domestic and international students; for spring admission, 9/30 for domestic and international students. Applications are processed on a rolling basis. Application fee: $55. Tuition and fees vary according to program. *Financial support:* Fellowships, career-related internships or fieldwork and Federal Work-Study available. Support available to part-time students. Financial award application deadline: 3/1; financial award applicants required to submit FAFSA. *Faculty research:* Spotted owl habitat, pre-settlement vegetation, hardwood utilization, tree physiology, fisheries. *Unit head:* Dr. Gary Hendrickson, Coordinator, 707-826-4233, E-mail: thiesfel@humboldt.edu. *Application contact:* Julie Tucker, Administrative Support Coordinator, 707-826-3256, E-mail: jlt7002@humboldt.edu.

Idaho State University, Office of Graduate Studies, Department of Interdisciplinary Studies, Pocatello, ID 83209. Offers general interdisciplinary (M Ed, MA, MNS); waste management and environmental science (MS). Part-time programs available. *Degree requirements:* For master's, comprehensive exam, thesis optional. *Entrance requirements:* For master's, GRE General Test or MAT, minimum GPA of 3.0. Additional exam requirements/recommendations for international students: Required—TOEFL (minimum score 550 paper-based; 213 computer-based; 80 iBT).

Marquette University, Graduate School, College of Engineering, Department of Civil and Environmental Engineering, Milwaukee, WI 53201-1881. Offers construction and public works management (MS, PhD); construction engineering and management (Certificate); environmental/water resources engineering (MS, PhD); structural design (Certificate); structural/geotechnical engineering (MS, PhD); transportation planning and engineering (MS, PhD); waste and wastewater treatment processes (Certificate). Part-time and evening/weekend programs available. *Faculty:* 13 full-time (0 women), 3 part-time/adjunct (0 women). *Students:* 20 full-time (4 women), 12 part-time (1 woman); includes 1 minority (Black or African American, non-Hispanic/Latino), 12 international. Average age 27. 66 applicants, 64% accepted, 9 enrolled. In 2010, 8 master's, 1 doctorate awarded. Terminal master's awarded for partial completion of doctoral program. *Degree requirements:* For master's, comprehensive exam, thesis or alternative; for doctorate, thesis/dissertation. *Entrance requirements:* For master's, GRE General Test (recommended), minimum GPA of 3.0, official transcripts from all current and previous colleges/universities except Marquette, three letters of recommendation; for doctorate, GRE General Test, minimum GPA of 3.0, official transcripts from all current and previous colleges/universities except Marquette, three letters of recommendation, brief statement of purpose, submission of any English-language publications authored by applicant (strongly recommended). Additional exam requirements/recommendations for international students: Required—TOEFL (minimum score 530 paper-based; 78 computer-based). *Application deadline:* For fall admission, 6/1 priority date for domestic students. Applications are processed on a rolling basis. Application fee: $50. Electronic applications accepted. *Expenses:* Tuition: Full-time $16,290; part-time $905 per credit hour. Tuition and fees vary according to program. *Financial support:* In 2010–11, 13 students received support, including 4 fellowships with tuition reimbursements available, 4 research assistantships with tuition reimbursements available, 10 teaching assistantships with tuition reimbursements available; Federal Work-Study, institutionally sponsored loans, scholarships/grants, and tuition waivers (full and partial) also available. Support available to part-time students. Financial award application deadline: 2/15. *Faculty research:* Highway safety, highway performance, and intelligent transportation systems; surface mount technology; watershed management. Total annual research expenditures: $662,392. *Unit head:* Dr. Thomas Wenzel, Chair, 414-288-7030, Fax: 414-288-7521, E-mail: thomas.wenzel@marquette.edu. *Application contact:* Dr. Stephen M. Heinrich, Director of Graduate Studies, 414-288-5466, E-mail: stephen.heinrich@marquette.edu.

New Mexico Institute of Mining and Technology, Graduate Studies, Department of Environmental Engineering, Socorro, NM 87801. Offers environmental engineering (MS), including air quality engineering and science, hazardous waste engineering, water quality engineering and science. *Degree requirements:* For master's, thesis. *Entrance requirements:* For master's, GRE General Test. Additional exam requirements/recommendations for international students: Required—TOEFL (minimum score 540 paper-based; 207 computer-based). *Faculty research:* Air quality, hazardous waste management, wastewater management and treatment, site remediation.

Rutgers, The State University of New Jersey, New Brunswick, Graduate School-New Brunswick, Department of Environmental Sciences, Piscataway, NJ 08854-8097. Offers air pollution and resources (MS, PhD); aquatic biology (MS, PhD); aquatic chemistry (MS, PhD); atmospheric science (MS, PhD); chemistry and physics of aerosol and hydrosol systems (MS, PhD); environmental chemistry (MS, PhD); environmental microbiology (MS, PhD); environmental toxicology (PhD); exposure assessment (PhD); fate and effects of pollutants (MS, PhD); pollution prevention and control (MS, PhD); water and wastewater treatment (MS, PhD); water resources (MS, PhD). Terminal master's awarded for partial completion of doctoral program. *Degree requirements:* For master's, comprehensive exam, thesis or alternative, oral final exam; for doctorate, comprehensive exam, thesis/dissertation, thesis defense, qualifying exam. *Entrance requirements:* For master's and doctorate, GRE General Test. Additional exam requirements/recommendations for international students: Required—TOEFL. Electronic applications accepted. *Expenses:* Tuition, state resident: full-time $7200; part-time $600 per credit. Tuition, nonresident: full-time $11,124; part-time $927 per credit. *Faculty research:* Biological waste treatment; contaminant fate and transport; air, soil and water quality.

Stony Brook University, State University of New York, School of Professional Development, Stony Brook, NY 11794. Offers biology-grade 7-12 (MAT); chemistry-grade 7-12 (MAT); coaching (Graduate Certificate); coaching online (Graduate Certificate); computer integrated engineering (Graduate Certificate); earth science-grade 7-12 (MAT); educational computing (Graduate Certificate); educational leadership (Advanced Certificate); English-grade 7-12 (MAT); environmental management (Graduate Certificate); environmental/occupational health and safety (Graduate Certificate); French-grade 7-12 (MAT); German-grade 7-12 (MAT); human resource management (Graduate Certificate); human resource management online (Graduate Certificate); information systems management (Graduate Certificate); Italian-grade 7-12 (MAT); liberal studies (MA); liberal studies online (MAT); mathematics-grade 7-12 (MAT); operation research (Graduate Certificate); physics-grade 7-12 (MAT); professional studies online (MPS); school administration and supervision (Graduate Certificate); school building leadership (Graduate Certificate); school district administration (Graduate Certificate); school district business leadership (Advanced Certificate); school district leadership (Graduate Certificate); social science and the professions (MPS), including environmental waste management, human resource management; social studies-grade 7-12 (MAT); Spanish-grade 7-12 (MAT); waste management (Graduate Certificate). Part-time and evening/weekend programs available. Post-baccalaureate distance learning degree programs offered. *Faculty:* 25 full-time (10 women), 105 part-time/adjunct (40 women). *Students:* 360 full-time (228 women), 1,097 part-time (729 women); includes 180 minority (65 Black or African American, non-Hispanic/Latino; 2 American Indian or Alaska Native, non-Hispanic/Latino; 30 Asian, non-Hispanic/Latino; 81 Hispanic/Latino; 1 Native Hawaiian or other Pacific Islander, non-Hispanic/Latino; 1 Two or more races, non-Hispanic/Latino), 10 international. Average age 28. In 2010, 505 master's, 187 other advanced degrees awarded. *Degree requirements:* For master's, one foreign language, thesis or alternative. *Application deadline:* Applications are processed on a rolling basis. Application fee: $100. *Expenses:* Tuition, state resident: full-time $8370; part-time $349 per credit. Tuition, nonresident: full-time $13,780; part-time $574 per credit. Required fees: $994. *Financial support:* In 2010–11, 1 teaching assistantship was awarded; fellowships, research assistantships, career-related internships or fieldwork also available. Support available to part-time students. *Unit head:* Dr. Paul J. Edelson, Dean, 631-632-7052, Fax: 631-632-9046, E-mail: paul.edelson@stonybrook.edu. *Application contact:* Dr. Paul J. Edelson, Dean, 631-632-7052, Fax: 631-632-9046, E-mail: paul.edelson@stonybrook.edu.

Tufts University, School of Engineering, Department of Civil and Environmental Engineering, Medford, MA 02155. Offers civil engineering (ME, MS, PhD), including geotechnical engineering, structural engineering; environmental engineering (ME, MS, PhD), including environmental engineering and environmental sciences, environmental geotechnology, environmental health, environmental science and management, hazardous materials management, water resources engineering. Part-time programs available. Terminal master's awarded for partial completion of doctoral program. *Degree requirements:* For master's, thesis or alternative; for doctorate, thesis/dissertation. *Entrance requirements:* For master's and doctorate, GRE General Test. Additional exam requirements/recommendations for international students: Required—TOEFL (minimum score 550 paper-based; 213 computer-based; 80 iBT). Electronic applications accepted. *Expenses:* Tuition: Full-time $39,624; part-time $3962 per course. Required fees: $40 per year. Full-time tuition and fees vary according to degree level, program and student level. Part-time tuition and fees vary according to course load.

University of Colorado Denver, College of Liberal Arts and Sciences, Department of Geography and Environmental Sciences, Denver, CO 80217. Offers environmental sciences (MS), including air quality, ecosystems, environmental health, environmental science education, environmental sciences, geo-spatial analysis, hazardous waste, water quality. Part-time and evening/weekend programs available. *Students:* 48 full-time (28 women), 4 part-time (3 women); includes 2 Black or African American, non-Hispanic/Latino; 2 Asian, non-Hispanic/Latino; 3 Hispanic/Latino, 8 international. Average age 29. 44 applicants, 52% accepted, 14 enrolled. In 2010, 17 master's awarded. *Degree requirements:* For master's, thesis or alternative. *Entrance requirements:* For master's, GRE General Test, BA in one of the natural/physical sciences or engineering (or equivalent background); prerequisite coursework in calculus and physics (one semester each), general chemistry with lab and general biology with lab (two semesters each). Additional exam requirements/recommendations for international students: Required—TOEFL (minimum score 525 paper-based; 197 computer-based). *Application deadline:* For fall admission, 4/1 for domestic students; for spring admission, 10/1 for domestic students. Application fee: $50 ($75 for international students). Electronic applications accepted. *Expenses:* Tuition, state resident: full-time $7332; part-time $355 per credit hour. Tuition, nonresident: full-time $18,990; part-time $1055 per credit hour. Required fees: $998. Tuition and fees vary according to course level, course load, degree level, campus/location, program, reciprocity agreements and student level. *Financial support:* Research assistantships, teaching assistantships, Federal Work-Study available. Financial award application deadline: 4/1; financial award applicants required to submit FAFSA. *Faculty research:* Air quality, environmental health, ecosystems, hazardous waste, water quality, geo-spatial analysis and environmental science education. *Unit head:* Dr. John Wyckoff, Director, 303-556-2590, Fax: 303-556-6197, E-mail: john.wyckoff@cudenver.edu. *Application contact:* Dr. John Wyckoff, Director, 303-556-2590, Fax: 303-556-6197, E-mail: john.wyckoff@cudenver.edu.

The University of Manchester, School of Materials, Manchester, United Kingdom. Offers advanced aerospace materials engineering (M Sc); advanced metallic systems (PhD); biomedical materials (M Phil, M Sc, PhD); ceramics and glass (M Phil, M Sc, PhD); composite materials (M Sc, PhD); corrosion and protection (M Phil, M Sc, PhD); materials (M Phil, PhD); metallic materials (M Phil, M Sc, PhD); nanostructural materials (M Phil, M Sc, PhD); paper science (M Phil, M Sc, PhD); polymer science and engineering (M Phil, M Sc, PhD); technical textiles (M Sc); textile design, fashion and management (M Phil, M Sc, PhD); textile science and technology (M Phil, M Sc, PhD); textiles (M Phil, PhD); textiles and fashion (M Ent).

University of New Haven, Graduate School, Tagliatela College of Engineering, Program in Environmental Engineering, West Haven, CT 06516-1916. Offers environmental engineering (MS); industrial and hazardous wastes (MS); water and wastewater treatment (MS); water resources (Certificate). Part-time and evening/weekend programs available. *Students:* 20 full-time (8 women), 5 part-time (2 women); includes 2 Black or African American, non-Hispanic/Latino, 20 international. Average age 31. 35 applicants, 97% accepted, 7 enrolled. In 2010, 10 master's awarded. *Degree requirements:* For master's, thesis or alternative. *Entrance requirements:* For master's, bachelor's degree in engineering. Additional exam requirements/recommendations for international students: Required—TOEFL (minimum score 520 paper-based; 190 computer-based; 70 iBT); Recommended—IELTS (minimum score 5.5). *Application deadline:* For fall admission, 5/31 for international students; for winter admission, 10/15 for international students; for spring admission, 1/15 for international students. Applications are processed on a rolling basis. Application fee: $50. Electronic applications accepted. *Financial support:* Research assistantships with partial tuition reimbursements, teaching assistantships with partial tuition reimbursements, career-related internships or fieldwork, Federal Work-Study, scholarships/grants, tuition waivers, and unspecified assistantships available. Support available to part-time students. Financial award application deadline: 5/1; financial award applicants required to submit FAFSA. *Unit head:* Dr. Agamemnon D. Koutsospyros, Coordinator, 203-932-7398. *Application contact:* Eloise Gormley, Director of Graduate Admissions, 203-932-7449, Fax: 203-932-7137, E-mail: gradinfo@newhaven.edu.

University of South Carolina, The Graduate School, Arnold School of Public Health, Department of Environmental Health Sciences, Program in Hazardous Materials Management, Columbia, SC 29208. Offers MPH, MSPH, PhD. *Degree requirements:* For master's, comprehensive exam, thesis (for some programs), practicum (MPH); for doctorate, one foreign language, comprehensive exam, thesis/dissertation. *Entrance requirements:* Additional exam requirements/recommendations for international students: Required—TOEFL (minimum score 570 paper-based; 230 computer-based). Electronic applications accepted. *Faculty research:* Environmental/human health protection; use and disposal of hazardous materials; site safety; exposure assessment; migration, fate and transformation of materials.

University of Southern California, Graduate School, Viterbi School of Engineering, Sonny Astani Department of Civil Engineering, Los Angeles, CA 90089. Offers applied mechanics (MS); civil engineering (MS, PhD); computer-aided engineering (ME, Graduate Certificate); construction management (MCM); engineering technology commercialization (Graduate Certificate); environmental engineering (MS, PhD); environmental quality management (ME); structural design (ME); sustainable cities (Graduate Certificate); transportation systems (MS, Graduate Certificate); water and waste management (MS). Part-time and evening/weekend programs available. *Faculty:* 16 full-time (2 women), 35 part-time/adjunct (5 women). *Students:* 190 full-time (52 women), 81 part-time (20 women); includes 54 minority (2 Black or African American, non-Hispanic/Latino; 42 Asian, non-Hispanic/Latino; 9 Hispanic/Latino; 1 Two or more races, non-Hispanic/Latino), 149 international. 541 applicants, 43% accepted, 100 enrolled. In 2010, 74 master's, 10 doctorates awarded. Terminal master's awarded for partial completion of doctoral program. *Degree requirements:* For master's, thesis optional; for doctorate, thesis/dissertation. *Entrance requirements:* For master's and doctorate, GRE General Test. *Application deadline:* For fall admission, 12/1 priority date for domestic and international students; for spring admission, 9/15 for domestic students, 9/15 priority date for international students. Applications are processed on a rolling basis. Application fee: $85. Electronic applications accepted. *Expenses:* Tuition: Full-time $31,240; part-time $1420 per unit. Required fees: $600. One-time fee: $35 full-time. Full-time tuition and fees vary according to degree level and program. *Financial support:* In 2010–11, fellowships with full tuition reimbursements (averaging $30,000 per year), research assistantships with full tuition reimbursements (averaging $20,000 per year), teaching assistantships with full tuition reimbursements (averaging $20,000 per year) were awarded; career-related internships or fieldwork, scholarships/grants, health care benefits, and unspecified assistantships also available. Financial award application deadline: 12/1; financial award applicants required to submit CSS PROFILE or FAFSA. *Faculty research:* Geotechnical engineering, transportation engineering, structural engineering, construction management, environmental engineering, water resources. Total annual research expenditures: $5 million. *Unit head:* Dr. Jean-Pierre Bardet, Chair, 213-740-0603, Fax: 213-744-1426, E-mail: ceedept@usc.edu. *Application contact:* Jennifer A. Gerson, Director of Student Affairs, 213-740-0573, Fax: 213-740-8662, E-mail: jgerson@usc.edu.

Virginia Polytechnic Institute and State University, Graduate School, College of Engineering, Department of Civil and Environmental Engineering, Blacksburg, VA 24061. Offers civil engineering (M Eng, MS, PhD); civil infrastructure systems (Certificate); environmental engineering (MS); environmental sciences and engineering (MS); transportation systems engineering (Certificate); treatment process engineering (Certificate); urban hydrology and stormwater management (Certificate); water quality management (Certificate). *Accreditation:* ABET (one or more programs are accredited). *Faculty:* 44 full-time (8 women), 1 part-time/adjunct (0 women). *Students:* 320 full-time (108 women), 70 part-time (20 women); includes 9 Black or African American, non-Hispanic/Latino; 15 Asian, non-Hispanic/Latino; 13 Hispanic/Latino, 126 international. Average age 27. 639 applicants, 44% accepted, 121 enrolled. In 2010, 97 master's, 18 doctorates awarded. *Degree requirements:* For master's, comprehensive exam (for some programs), thesis (for some programs); for doctorate, comprehensive exam (for some programs), thesis/dissertation (for some programs). *Entrance requirements:* For master's and doctorate, GRE. Additional exam requirements/recommendations for international students: Required—TOEFL (minimum score 550 paper-based; 213 computer-based). *Application deadline:* For fall admission, 7/1 for domestic and international students; for spring admission, 12/1 for domestic and international students. Applications are processed on a rolling basis. Application fee: $65. Electronic applications accepted. *Expenses:* Tuition, area resident: Full-time $9399; part-time $488 per credit hour. Tuition, state resident: full-time $9399; part-time $488 per credit hour. Tuition, nonresident: full-time $17,854; part-time $957.75 per credit hour. International tuition: $17,854 full-time. Required fees: $1534. Full-time tuition and fees vary according to program. *Financial support:* In 2010–11, 35 fellowships with full tuition reimbursements (averaging $5,861 per year), 82 research assistantships with full tuition reimbursements (averaging $20,397 per year), 33 teaching assistantships with full tuition reimbursements (averaging $14,542 per year) were awarded; career-related internships or fieldwork, Federal Work-Study, scholarships/grants, health care benefits, and unspecified assistantships also available. Financial award application deadline: 1/15. *Faculty research:* Construction, environmental geotechnical hydrosystems, structures and transportation engineering. Total annual research expenditures: $12.2 million. *Unit head:* Dr. Sam Easterling, UNIT HEAD, 540-231-5143, Fax: 540-231-7532, E-mail: seaster@vt.edu. *Application contact:* Marc Widdowson, Contact, 540-231-7153, Fax: 540-231-7532, E-mail: mwiddows@vt.edu.

Hydraulics

Auburn University, Graduate School, Ginn College of Engineering, Department of Civil Engineering, Auburn University, AL 36849. Offers construction engineering and management (MCE, MS, PhD); environmental engineering (MCE, MS, PhD); geotechnical/materials engineering (MCE, MS, PhD); hydraulics/hydrology (MCE, MS, PhD); structural engineering (MCE, MS, PhD); transportation engineering (MCE, MS, PhD). Part-time programs available. *Faculty:* 21 full-time (1 woman), 3 part-time/adjunct (1 woman). *Students:* 46 full-time (15 women), 39 part-time (5 women); includes 3 Black or African American, non-Hispanic/Latino; 1 Asian, non-Hispanic/Latino, 29 international. Average age 26. 136 applicants, 43% accepted, 26 enrolled. In 2010, 19 master's, 4 doctorates awarded. *Degree requirements:* For master's, project (MCE), thesis (MS); for doctorate, comprehensive exam, thesis/dissertation. *Entrance requirements:* For master's and doctorate, GRE General Test. *Application deadline:* For fall admission, 7/7 for domestic students; for spring admission, 11/24 for domestic students. Applications are processed on a rolling basis. Application fee: $50 ($60 for international students). Electronic applications accepted. *Expenses:* Tuition, state resident: full-time $7002. Tuition, nonresident: full-time $21,898. International tuition: $22,116 full-time. Required fees: $892. Tuition and fees vary according to course load and program. *Financial support:* Fellowships, research assistantships, teaching assistantships, Federal Work-Study available. Support available to part-time students. Financial award application deadline: 3/15; financial award applicants required to submit FAFSA. *Unit head:* Dr. J. Michael Stallings, Head, 334-844-4320. *Application contact:* Dr. George Flowers, Dean of the Graduate School, 334-844-2125.

Drexel University, College of Engineering, Department of Civil, Architectural, and Environmental Engineering, Philadelphia, PA 19104-2875. Offers architectural / building systems engineering (MS, PhD); civil engineering (MS, PhD); environmental engineering (MS, PhD); geotechnical, geoenvironmental and geosynthetics engineering (MS, PhD); hydraulics, hydrology and water resources engineering (MS, PhD); structures (MS). Part-time and evening/weekend programs available. *Degree requirements:* For master's, thesis optional; for doctorate, thesis/dissertation. *Entrance requirements:* For master's, minimum GPA of 3.0; for doctorate, minimum GPA of 3.5, MS in civil engineering. Additional exam requirements/recommendations for international students: Required—TOEFL. Electronic applications accepted. *Faculty research:* Structural dynamics, hazardous wastes, water resources, pavement materials, groundwater.

École Polytechnique de Montréal, Graduate Programs, Department of Civil, Geological and Mining Engineering, Montréal, QC H3C 3A7, Canada. Offers civil, geological and mining engineering (DESS); environmental engineering (M Eng, M Sc A, PhD); geotechnical engineering (M Eng, M Sc A, PhD); hydraulics engineering (M Eng, M Sc A, PhD); structural engineering (M Eng, M Sc A, PhD); transportation engineering (M Eng, M Sc A, PhD). Part-time programs available. *Degree requirements:* For master's, one foreign language, thesis; for doctorate, one foreign language, thesis/dissertation. *Entrance requirements:* For master's, minimum GPA of 2.75; for doctorate, minimum GPA of 3.0. *Faculty research:* Water resources management, characteristics of building materials, aging of dams, pollution control.

McGill University, Faculty of Graduate and Postdoctoral Studies, Faculty of Engineering, Department of Civil Engineering and Applied Mechanics, Montréal, QC H3A 2T5, Canada. Offers environmental engineering (M Eng, M Sc, PhD); fluid mechanics (M Sc); fluid mechanics and hydraulic engineering (M Eng, PhD); materials engineering (M Eng, PhD); rehabilitation of urban infrastructure (M Eng, PhD); soil behavior (M Eng, PhD); soil mechanics and foundations (M Eng, PhD); structures and structural mechanics (M Eng, PhD); water resources (M Sc); water resources engineering (M Eng, PhD).

Missouri University of Science and Technology, Graduate School, Department of Civil, Architectural, and Environmental Engineering, Rolla, MO 65409. Offers civil engineering (MS, DE, PhD); construction engineering (MS, DE, PhD); environmental engineering (MS); fluid mechanics (MS, DE, PhD); geotechnical engineering (MS, DE, PhD); hydrology and hydraulic engineering (MS, DE, PhD). Part-time and evening/weekend programs available. Terminal master's awarded for partial completion of doctoral program. *Degree requirements:* For master's, thesis optional; for doctorate, comprehensive exam, thesis/dissertation. *Entrance requirements:* For master's, GRE General Test (minimum combined score 1100), minimum GPA of 3.0; for doctorate, GRE General Test (minimum score: verbal and quantitative 400, writing 3.5), minimum GPA of 3.0. Additional exam requirements/recommendations for international students: Required—TOEFL. Electronic applications accepted. *Faculty research:* Earthquake engineering, structural optimization and control systems, structural health monitoring/damage detection, soil-structure interaction, soil mechanics and foundation engineering.

University of Colorado Denver, College of Engineering and Applied Science, Department of Civil Engineering, Denver, CO 80217-3364. Offers civil engineering (PhD); environmental and sustainability engineering (MS); geographic information systems (MS); geotechnical engineering (MS); hydrology and hydraulics (MS); structural engineering (MS); transportation engineering (MS). Part-time and evening/weekend programs available. *Faculty:* 14 full-time (1 woman), 6 part-time/adjunct (0 women). *Students:* 66 full-time (13 women), 72 part-time (16 women); includes 9 Black or African American, non-Hispanic/Latino; 8 Asian, non-Hispanic/Latino; 11 Hispanic/Latino, 15 international. Average age 32. 72 applicants, 54% accepted, 29 enrolled. In 2010, 14 master's, 3 doctorates awarded. *Degree requirements:* For master's, comprehensive exam, thesis or alternative; for doctorate, comprehensive exam, thesis/dissertation. *Entrance requirements:* For master's, GRE, statement of purpose, transcripts, references; for doctorate, GRE, statement of purpose, transcripts, references, letter of support from faculty stating willingness to serve as dissertation advisor and outlining plan for financial support. Additional exam requirements/recommendations for international students: Required—TOEFL (minimum score 525 paper-based; 197 computer-based). *Application deadline:* For fall admission, 7/15 for domestic students, 6/15 for international students; for spring admission, 12/1 for domestic students, 11/1 for international students. Applications are processed on a rolling basis. Application fee: $50 ($75 for international students). Electronic applications accepted. *Expenses:* Contact institution. *Financial support:* Research assistantships, teaching assistantships, career-related internships or fieldwork and Federal Work-Study available. Financial award application deadline: 4/1; financial award applicants required to submit FAFSA. *Faculty research:* Environmental engineering and sustainable systems, geosynthetics, hydrologic andhydraulic engineering, structural engineering, transportation, transportation energy use and greenhouse gas emissions. *Unit head:* Dr. Nien-Yin Chang, Acting Chair, 303-556-2810, Fax: 303-556-2368, E-mail: nien.chang@ucdenver.edu. *Application contact:* Mindy Gewuerz, Program Assistant, 303-556-6712, Fax: 303-556-2368, E-mail: mindy.gewuerz@ucdenver.edu.

Structural Engineering

Auburn University, Graduate School, Ginn College of Engineering, Department of Civil Engineering, Auburn University, AL 36849. Offers construction engineering and management (MCE, MS, PhD); environmental engineering (MCE, MS, PhD); geotechnical/materials engineering (MCE, MS, PhD); hydraulics/hydrology (MCE, MS, PhD); structural engineering (MCE, MS, PhD); transportation engineering (MCE, MS, PhD). Part-time programs available. *Faculty:* 21 full-time (1 woman), 3 part-time/adjunct (1 woman). *Students:* 46 full-time (15 women), 39 part-time (5 women); includes 3 Black or African American, non-Hispanic/Latino; 1 Asian, non-Hispanic/Latino, 29 international. Average age 26. 136 applicants, 43% accepted, 26 enrolled. In 2010, 19 master's, 4 doctorates awarded. *Degree requirements:* For master's, project (MCE), thesis (MS); for doctorate, comprehensive exam, thesis/dissertation. *Entrance requirements:* For master's and doctorate, GRE General Test. *Application deadline:* For fall admission, 7/7 for domestic students; for spring admission, 11/24 for domestic students. Applications are processed on a rolling basis. Application fee: $50 ($60 for international students). Electronic applications accepted. *Expenses:* Tuition, state resident: full-time $7002. Tuition, nonresident: full-time $21,898. International tuition: $22,116 full-time. Required fees: $892. Tuition and fees vary according to course load and program. *Financial support:* Fellowships, research assistantships, teaching assistantships, Federal Work-Study available. Support available to part-time students. Financial award application deadline: 3/15; financial award applicants required to submit FAFSA. *Unit head:* Dr. J. Michael Stallings, Head, 334-844-4320. *Application contact:* Dr. George Flowers, Dean of the Graduate School, 334-844-2125.

California State University, Northridge, Graduate Studies, College of Engineering and Computer Science, Department of Civil Engineering and Applied Mechanics, Northridge, CA 91330. Offers engineering (MS), including structural engineering. Part-time and evening/weekend programs available. *Degree requirements:* For master's, thesis. *Entrance requirements:* Additional exam requirements/recommendations for international students: Required—TOEFL. *Faculty research:* Composite study.

Cornell University, Graduate School, Graduate Fields of Engineering, Field of Civil and Environmental Engineering, Ithaca, NY 14853-0001. Offers engineering management (M Eng, MS, PhD); environmental engineering (M Eng, MS, PhD); environmental fluid mechanics and hydrology (M Eng, MS, PhD); environmental systems engineering (M Eng, MS, PhD); geotechnical engineering (M Eng, MS, PhD); remote sensing (M Eng, MS, PhD); structural engineering (M Eng, MS, PhD); structural mechanics (M Eng, MS); transportation engineering (MS, PhD); transportation systems engineering (M Eng); water resource systems (M Eng, MS, PhD). *Faculty:* 36 full-time (4 women). *Students:* 148 full-time (48 women); includes 3 Black or African American, non-Hispanic/Latino; 1 American Indian or Alaska Native, non-Hispanic/Latino; 16 Asian, non-Hispanic/Latino; 16 Hispanic/Latino, 60 international. Average age 24. 390 applicants, 56% accepted, 76 enrolled. In 2010, 93 master's, 5 doctorates awarded. Terminal master's awarded for partial completion of doctoral program. *Degree requirements:* For master's, thesis (MS); for doctorate, comprehensive exam, thesis/dissertation. *Entrance requirements:* For master's and doctorate, GRE General Test (recommended), 2 letters of recommendation. Additional exam requirements/recommendations for international students: Required—TOEFL (minimum score 600 paper-based; 250 computer-based; 77 iBT). *Application deadline:* For fall admission, 1/15 priority date for domestic students; for spring admission, 10/15 for domestic students. Application fee: $70. Electronic applications accepted. *Expenses:* Tuition: Full-time $29,500. Required fees: $76. Tuition and fees vary according to degree level and program. *Financial support:* In 2010–11, 50 students received support, including 17 fellowships with full tuition reimbursements available, 33 research assistantships with full tuition reimbursements available, 15 teaching assistantships with full tuition reimbursements available; institutionally sponsored loans, scholarships/grants, health care benefits, tuition waivers (full and partial), and unspecified assistantships also available. Financial award applicants required to submit FAFSA. *Faculty research:* Environmental engineering, geo-technical engineering, remote sensing, environmental fluid mechanics and hydrology, structural engineering. *Unit head:* Director of Graduate Studies, 607-255-7560, Fax: 607-255-9004. *Application contact:* Graduate Field Assistant, 607-255-7560, Fax: 607-255-9004, E-mail: cee_grad@cornell.edu.

Drexel University, College of Engineering, Department of Civil, Architectural, and Environmental Engineering, Philadelphia, PA 19104-2875. Offers architectural / building systems engineering (MS, PhD); civil engineering (MS, PhD); environmental engineering (MS, PhD); geotechnical, geoenvironmental and geosynthetics engineering (MS, PhD); hydraulics, hydrology and water resources engineering (MS, PhD); structures (MS). Part-time and evening/weekend programs available. *Degree requirements:* For master's, thesis optional; for doctorate, thesis/dissertation. *Entrance requirements:* For master's, minimum GPA of 3.0; for doctorate, minimum GPA of 3.5, MS in civil engineering. Additional exam requirements/recommendations for international students: Required—TOEFL. Electronic applications accepted. *Faculty research:* Structural dynamics, hazardous wastes, water resources, pavement materials, groundwater.

École Polytechnique de Montréal, Graduate Programs, Department of Civil, Geological and Mining Engineering, Montréal, QC H3C 3A7, Canada. Offers civil, geological and mining engineering (DESS); environmental engineering (M Eng, M Sc A, PhD); geotechnical engineering (M Eng, M Sc A, PhD); hydraulics engineering (M Eng, M Sc A, PhD); structural engineering (M Eng, M Sc A, PhD); transportation engineering (M Eng, M Sc A, PhD). Part-time programs available. *Degree requirements:* For master's, one foreign language, thesis; for doctorate, one foreign language, thesis/dissertation. *Entrance requirements:* For master's, minimum GPA of 2.75; for doctorate, minimum GPA of 3.0. *Faculty research:* Water resources management, characteristics of building materials, aging of dams, pollution control.

Illinois Institute of Technology, Graduate College, Armour College of Engineering, Department of Civil, Architectural and Environmental Engineering, Chicago, IL 60616-3793. Offers architectural engineering (M Arch E); civil engineering (MS, PhD), including architectural engineeering (MS), construction engineering and management (MS), geoenvironmental engineering (MS), geotechnical engineering (MS), structural engineering (MS), transportation engineering (MS); construction engineering and management (MCEM); environmental engineering (M Env E, PhD); geoenvironmental engineering (M Geoenv E); geotechnical engineering (MGE); public works (MPW); structural engineering (MSE); transportation engineering (M Trans E). Part-time and evening/weekend programs available. Postbaccalaureate distance learning degree programs offered (minimal on-campus study). *Faculty:* 15 full-time (1 woman), 13 part-time/adjunct (1 woman). *Students:* 159 full-time (63 women), 109 part-time (22 women); includes 30 minority (9 Black or African American, non-Hispanic/Latino; 16 Asian, non-Hispanic/Latino; 5 Hispanic/Latino), 126 international. Average age 27. 453 applicants, 66% accepted, 98 enrolled. In 2010, 76 master's, 1 doctorate awarded. Terminal master's awarded for partial completion of doctoral program. *Degree requirements:* For master's, thesis (for some programs); for doctorate, comprehensive exam, thesis/dissertation. *Entrance requirements:* For master's, GRE General Test (minimum score 900 Quantitative and Verbal, 2.5 Analytical Writing), minimum undergraduate GPA of 3.0; for doctorate, GRE General Test (minimum score 1000 Quantitative and Verbal, 3.0 Analytical Writing), minimum undergraduate GPA of 3.0. Additional exam requirements/recommendations for international students: Required—TOEFL (minimum score 523 paper-based; 70 iBT); Recommended—IELTS (minimum score 5.5). *Application deadline:* For fall admission, 5/1 for domestic and international students; for spring admission, 10/15 for domestic and international students. Applications are processed on a rolling basis. Application fee: $50. Electronic applications accepted. *Expenses:* Tuition: Full-time $18,576; part-time $1032 per credit hour. Required fees: $583 per semester. One-time fee: $150. Tuition and fees vary according to program and student level. *Financial support:* In 2010–11, 13 research assistantships with full and partial tuition reimbursements (averaging $9,453 per year), 19 teaching assistantships with full and partial tuition reimbursements (averaging $3,163 per year) were awarded; fellowships with full and partial tuition reimbursements, Federal Work-Study, institutionally sponsored loans, scholarships/grants, health care benefits, tuition waivers (partial), and unspecified assistantships also available. Support available to part-time students. Financial award applicants required to submit FAFSA. *Faculty research:* Structural, architectural, geotechnical and geoenvironmental engineering; construction engineering and management; transportation engineering; environmental engineering and public works. Total annual research expenditures: $763,042. *Unit head:* Dr. Jamshid Mohammadi, Professor and Chairman, 312-567-3629, Fax: 312-567-3519, E-mail: mohammadi@iit.edu. *Application contact:* Deborah Gibson, Director, Graduate Admission, 866-472-3448, Fax: 312-567-3138, E-mail: inquiry.grad@iit.edu.

Instituto Tecnologico de Santo Domingo, Graduate School, Area of Engineering, Santo Domingo, Dominican Republic. Offers construction administration (MS, Certificate); data telecommunications (M Eng, MS, Certificate); industrial engineering (M Eng, Certificate); industrial management (M Mgmt); information technology (Certificate); maintenance engineering (M Eng); occupational hazard prevention (M Mgmt); production management (Certificate); quantitative methods (Certificate); sanitary and environmental engineering (M Eng); structural engineering (M Eng); systems engineering and electronic data processing (Certificate); transportation (Certificate).

Iowa State University of Science and Technology, Graduate College, College of Engineering, Department of Civil and Construction Engineering, Ames, IA 50011. Offers civil engineering (MS, PhD), including civil engineering materials, construction engineering and management, environmental engineering, geometronics, geotechnical engineering, structural engineering, transportation engineering. *Faculty:* 35 full-time (6 women), 4 part-time/adjunct (0 women). *Students:* 93 full-time (31 women), 48 part-time (10 women); includes 1 Black or African American, non-Hispanic/Latino; 1 Asian, non-Hispanic/Latino; 4 Hispanic/Latino, 62 international. 179 applicants, 37% accepted, 35 enrolled. In 2010, 32 master's, 9 doctorates awarded. *Degree requirements:* For master's, thesis or alternative; for doctorate, thesis/dissertation. *Entrance requirements:* For master's and doctorate, GRE General Test. Additional exam requirements/recommendations for international students: Required—TOEFL (minimum score 550 paper-based; 82 iBT), IELTS (minimum score 6.5). *Application deadline:* For fall admission, 2/1 priority date for domestic students, 2/1 for international students; for spring admission, 8/1 priority date for domestic students, 8/1 for international students. Application fee: $40 ($90 for international students). Electronic applications accepted. *Financial support:* In 2010–11, 67 research assistantships with full and partial tuition reimbursements (averaging $7,654 per year), 4 teaching assistantships with full and partial tuition reimbursements (averaging $9,525 per year) were awarded; fellowships, scholarships/grants, health care benefits, and unspecified assistantships also available. *Unit head:* Dr. James Alleman, Chair, 515-294-3892, E-mail: ccee-grad-inquiry@iastate.edu. *Application contact:* Dr. Sri Srithanan, Director of Graduate Education, 515-294-5328, E-mail: ccee-grad-inquiry@iastate.edu.

Lehigh University, P.C. Rossin College of Engineering and Applied Science, Department of Civil and Environmental Engineering, Bethlehem, PA 18015. Offers civil engineering (M Eng, MS, PhD); environmental engineering (MS, PhD); structural engineering (M Eng, MS, PhD). Part-time programs available. *Faculty:* 15 full-time (3 women), 1 (woman) part-time/adjunct. *Students:* 107 full-time (33 women), 9 part-time (0 women); includes 8 minority (4 Black or African American, non-Hispanic/Latino; 1 Asian, non-Hispanic/Latino; 2 Hispanic/Latino; 1 Native Hawaiian or other Pacific Islander, non-Hispanic/Latino), 59 international. Average age 26. 270 applicants, 50% accepted, 65 enrolled. In 2010, 23 master's, 1 doctorate awarded. Terminal master's awarded for partial completion of doctoral program. *Median time to degree:* Of those who began their doctoral program in fall 2002, 100% received their degree in 8 years or less. *Degree requirements:* For master's, thesis (for some programs); for doctorate, comprehensive exam, thesis/dissertation. *Entrance requirements:* For master's and doctorate, GRE. Additional exam requirements/recommendations for international students: Required—TOEFL (minimum score 550 paper-based; 213 computer-based; 79 iBT). *Application deadline:* For fall admission, 7/15 priority date for domestic and international students; for spring admission, 12/1 priority date for domestic and international students. Applications are processed on a rolling basis. Application fee: $75. Electronic applications accepted. *Expenses:* Contact institution. *Financial support:* In 2010–11, 31 students received support, including 5 fellowships with full tuition reimbursements available (averaging $17,460 per year), 4 research assistantships with full tuition reimbursements available (averaging $22,350 per year), 7 teaching assistantships with full tuition reimbursements available (averaging $17,460 per year); institutionally sponsored loans, scholarships/grants, tuition waivers, and unspecified assistantships also available. Financial award application deadline: 1/15. *Faculty research:* Structural engineering, geotechnical engineering, water resources engineering, environmental engineering. Total annual research expenditures: $6.8 million. *Unit head:* Dr. Stephen Pessiki, Chairman, 610-758-3494, Fax: 610-758-6405, E-mail: pessiki@lehigh.edu. *Application contact:* Prisca Vidanage, Graduate Coordinator, 610-758-3530, Fax: 610-758-6405, E-mail: pmv1@lehigh.edu.

Louisiana State University and Agricultural and Mechanical College, Graduate School, College of Engineering, Department of Civil and Environmental Engineering, Baton Rouge, LA 70803. Offers environmental engineering (MSCE, PhD); geotechnical engineering (MSCE, PhD); structural engineering and mechanics (MSCE, PhD); transportation engineering (MSCE, PhD); water resources (MSCE, PhD). Part-time programs available. *Faculty:* 29 full-time (3 women). *Students:* 89 full-time (19 women), 35 part-time (8 women); includes 2 Black or African American, non-Hispanic/Latino; 1 American Indian or Alaska Native, non-Hispanic/Latino; 3 Asian, non-Hispanic/Latino; 3 Hispanic/Latino, 65 international. Average age 29. 96 applicants, 65% accepted, 16 enrolled. In 2010, 20 master's, 8 doctorates awarded. *Degree requirements:* For master's, thesis optional; for doctorate, one foreign language, thesis/dissertation. *Entrance requirements:* For master's and doctorate, GRE General Test, minimum GPA of 3.0. Additional exam requirements/recommendations for international students: Required—TOEFL (minimum score 550 paper-based; 213 computer-based; 79 iBT) or IELTS (minimum score 6.5). *Application deadline:* For fall admission, 1/25 priority date for domestic students, 5/15 for international students; for spring admission, 10/15 for international students. Applications are processed on a rolling basis. Application fee: $50 ($70 for international students). Electronic applications accepted. *Financial support:* In 2010–11, 89 students received support, including 2 fellowships with full and partial tuition reimbursements available (averaging $24,418 per year), 75 research assistantships with full and partial tuition reimbursements available (averaging $16,115 per year), 3 teaching assistantships with full and partial tuition reimbursements available (averaging $12,843 per year); career-related internships or fieldwork, institutionally sponsored loans, scholarships/grants, and health care benefits also available. Financial award application deadline: 3/1; financial award applicants required to submit FAFSA. *Faculty research:* Mechanics and structures, environmental, geotechnical transportation, water resources. Total annual research expenditures: $2.6 million. *Unit head:* Dr. George Z. Voyiadjis, Chair/Professor, 225-578-8668, Fax: 225-578-9176, E-mail: cegzv@lsu.edu. *Application contact:* Dr. Clinton Willson, Professor, 225-578-8652, E-mail: cwillson@lsu.edu.

Marquette University, Graduate School, College of Engineering, Department of Civil and Environmental Engineering, Milwaukee, WI 53201-1881. Offers construction and public works management (MS, PhD); construction engineering and management (Certificate); environmental/water resources engineering (MS, PhD); structural design (Certificate); structural/geotechnical engineering (MS, PhD); transportation planning and engineering (MS, PhD); waste and wastewater treatment processes (Certificate). Part-time and evening/weekend programs available. *Faculty:* 13 full-time (0 women), 3 part-time/adjunct (0 women). *Students:* 20 full-time (4 women), 12 part-time (1 woman); includes 1 minority (Black or African American, non-Hispanic/Latino), 12 international. Average age 27. 66 applicants, 64% accepted, 9 enrolled. In 2010, 8 master's, 1 doctorate awarded. Terminal master's awarded for partial completion of doctoral program. *Degree requirements:* For master's, comprehensive exam, thesis or alternative; for doctorate, thesis/dissertation. *Entrance requirements:* For master's, GRE General Test (recommended), minimum GPA of 3.0, official transcripts from all current and previous colleges/universities except Marquette, three letters of recommendation; for doctorate, GRE General Test, minimum GPA of 3.0, official transcripts from all current and previous colleges/universities except Marquette, three letters of recommendation, brief statement of purpose, submission of any English-language publications authored by applicant (strongly recommended). Additional exam requirements/recommendations for international students: Required—TOEFL (minimum score 530 paper-based; 78 computer-based). *Application deadline:* For fall admission, 6/1 priority date for domestic students. Applications are processed on a rolling basis. Application fee: $50. Electronic applications accepted. *Expenses:* Tuition: Full-time $16,290; part-time $905 per credit hour. Tuition and fees vary according to program. *Financial support:* In 2010–11, 13 students received support, including 4 fellowships with tuition reimbursements available, 4 research assistantships with tuition reimbursements available, 10 teaching assistantships with tuition reimbursements available; Federal Work-Study, institutionally sponsored loans, scholarships/grants, and tuition waivers (full and partial) also available. Support available to part-time students. Financial award application deadline: 2/15. *Faculty research:* Highway safety, highway performance, and intelligent transportation systems; surface mount technology; watershed management. Total annual research expenditures: $662,392. *Unit head:* Dr. Thomas Wenzel, Chair, 414-288-7030, Fax: 414-288-7521, E-mail: thomas.wenzel@marquette.edu. *Application contact:* Dr. Stephen M. Heinrich, Director of Graduate Studies, 414-288-5466, E-mail: stephen.heinrich@marquette.edu.

Massachusetts Institute of Technology, School of Engineering, Department of Civil and Environmental Engineering, Cambridge, MA 02139. Offers biological oceanography (PhD, Sc D); chemical oceanography (PhD, Sc D); civil and environmental engineering (M Eng, SM, PhD, Sc D); civil and environmental systems (PhD, Sc D); civil engineering (PhD, Sc D, CE); coastal engineering (PhD, Sc D); construction engineering and management (PhD, Sc D); environmental biology (PhD, Sc D); environmental chemistry (PhD, Sc D); environmental engineering (PhD, Sc D); environmental fluid mechanics (PhD, Sc D); geotechnical and geoenvironmental engineering (PhD, Sc D); hydrology (PhD, Sc D); information technology (PhD, Sc D); oceanographic engineering (PhD, Sc D); structures and materials (PhD, Sc D); transportation (PhD, Sc D); SM/MBA. *Faculty:* 36 full-time (6 women). *Students:* 181 full-time (56 women); includes 27 minority (3 Black or African American, non-Hispanic/Latino; 10 Asian, non-Hispanic/Latino; 10 Hispanic/Latino; 4 Two or more races, non-Hispanic/Latino), 93 international. Average age 26. 525 applicants, 29% accepted, 74 enrolled. In 2010, 85 master's, 18 doctorates, 2 other advanced degrees awarded. *Degree requirements:* For master's and CE, thesis; for doctorate, comprehensive exam, thesis/dissertation. *Entrance requirements:* For master's and doctorate, GRE General Test. Additional exam requirements/recommendations for international students: Required—TOEFL (minimum score 577 paper-based; 233 computer-based; 90 iBT), IELTS (minimum score 7). *Application deadline:* For fall admission, 1/2 for domestic and international students. Application fee: $75. Electronic applications accepted. *Expenses:* Tuition: Full-time $38,940; part-time $605 per unit. Required fees: $272. *Financial support:* In 2010–11, 146 students received support, including 50 fellowships with tuition reimbursements available (averaging $21,808 per year), 90 research assistantships with tuition reimbursements available (averaging $28,452 per year), 20 teaching assistantships with tuition reimbursements available (averaging $27,842 per year); career-related internships or fieldwork, Federal Work-Study, institutionally sponsored loans, scholarships/grants, health care benefits, and unspecified assistantships also available. *Faculty research:* Environmental chemistry; environmental microbiology; environmental fluid mechanics and coastal engineering; geotechnical engineering and geomechanics; hydrology and hydroclimatology; mechanics of materials and structures; operations research/supply chain; transportation. Total annual research expenditures: $19.5 million. *Unit head:* Prof. Andrew Whittle, Department Head, 617-253-7101. *Application contact:* Patricia Glidden, Graduate Admissions Coordinator, 617-253-7119, Fax: 617-258-6775, E-mail: cee-admissions@mit.edu.

Massachusetts Institute of Technology, School of Engineering, Department of Materials Science and Engineering, Cambridge, MA 02139. Offers archaeological materials (PhD, Sc D); bio- and polymeric materials (PhD, Sc D); electronic, photonic and magnetic materials (PhD, Sc D); emerging, fundamental and computational studies in materials science (Sc D); emerging, fundamental, and computational studies in materials science (PhD); materials engineering (Mat E); materials science and engineering (M Eng, SM, PhD, Sc D); metallurgical engineering (Met E); structural and environmental materials (PhD, Sc D); SM/MBA. *Faculty:* 34 full-time (8 women). *Students:* 196 full-time (52 women); includes 32 minority (2 Black or African American, non-Hispanic/Latino; 20 Asian, non-Hispanic/Latino; 7 Hispanic/Latino; 3 Two or more races, non-Hispanic/Latino), 113 international. Average age 26. 507 applicants, 15% accepted, 41 enrolled. In 2010, 22 master's, 38 doctorates awarded. Terminal master's awarded for partial completion of doctoral program. *Degree requirements:* For master's and other advanced degree, thesis; for doctorate, comprehensive exam, thesis/dissertation. *Entrance requirements:* For master's, doctorate, and other advanced degree, GRE General Test. Additional exam requirements/recommendations for international students: Required—IELTS (minimum score 7). *Application deadline:* For fall admission, 12/15 for domestic and international students. Application fee: $75. Electronic applications accepted. *Expenses:* Tuition: Full-time $38,940; part-time $605 per unit. Required fees: $272. *Financial support:* In 2010–11, 183 students received support, including 52 fellowships with tuition reimbursements available (averaging $32,695 per year), 124 research assistantships with tuition reimbursements available (averaging $27,409 per year), 8 teaching assistantships with tuition reimbursements available (averaging $31,861 per year); career-related internships or fieldwork, Federal Work-Study, institutionally sponsored loans, scholarships/grants, health care benefits, and unspecified assistantships also available. *Faculty research:* Thermodynamics and kinetics of phase transformations; structure of all materials classes: metals, ceramics, semiconductors, polymers, biomaterials; influence of processing on materials structure; structure ??? property relationships (electrical, magnetic, optical, mechanical); materials in extreme environments. Total annual research expenditures: $28.1 million. *Unit head:* Prof. Edwin L. Thomas, Department Head, 617-253-3300, Fax: 617-252-1775. *Application contact:* Angelita Mireles, Graduate Admissions, 617-253-3302, E-mail: dmse-admissions@mit.edu.

McGill University, Faculty of Graduate and Postdoctoral Studies, Faculty of Engineering, Department of Civil Engineering and Applied Mechanics, Montréal, QC H3A 2T5, Canada. Offers environmental engineering (M Eng, M Sc, PhD); fluid mechanics (M Sc); fluid mechanics and hydraulic engineering (M Eng, PhD); materials engineering (M Eng, PhD); rehabilitation of urban infrastructure (M Eng, PhD); soil behavior (M Eng, PhD); soil mechanics and foundations (M Eng, PhD); structures and structural mechanics (M Eng, PhD); water resources (M Sc); water resources engineering (M Eng, PhD).

Milwaukee School of Engineering, Civil and Architectural Engineering and Construction Management Department, Program in Structural Engineering, Milwaukee, WI 53202-3109. Offers MS. Part-time and evening/weekend programs available. *Faculty:* 4 full-time (0 women), 1 (woman) part-time/adjunct. *Students:* 8 part-time (2 women). Average age 22. 27 applicants, 74% accepted, 3 enrolled. In 2010, 23 master's awarded. *Degree requirements:* For master's, design project. *Entrance requirements:* For master's, GRE General Test or GMAT, 2 letters of recommendation, BS in architectural or structural engineering. Additional exam requirements/recommendations for international students: Required—TOEFL (minimum score 79 iBT). *Application deadline:* Applications are processed on a rolling basis. Application fee: $30. Electronic applications accepted. *Expenses:* Tuition: Full-time $17,550; part-time $650 per credit. One-time fee: $75. *Financial support:* In 2010–11, 5 students received support; research assistantships, career-related internships or fieldwork available. Support available to part-time students. *Faculty research:* Steel, materials. *Unit head:* Dr. Richard DeVries, Director, 414-277-7596. *Application contact:* David E. Tietyen, Graduate Admissions Director, 800-332-6763, Fax: 414-277-7475, E-mail: wp@msoe.edu.

Northwestern University, McCormick School of Engineering and Applied Science, Department of Civil and Environmental Engineering, Evanston, IL 60208-3109. Offers environmental engineering and science (MS, PhD); geotechnical engineering (MS, PhD); mechanics of materials and solids (MS, PhD); project management (MS, PhD); structural engineering and materials (MS, PhD); theoretical and applied mechanics (MS, PhD), including fluid mechanics, solid mechanics; transportation systems analysis and planning (MS, PhD). MS and PhD admissions and degrees offered through The Graduate School. Part-time programs available.

Structural Engineering

Northwestern University (continued)

Terminal master's awarded for partial completion of doctoral program. *Degree requirements:* For master's, thesis (for some programs); for doctorate, thesis/dissertation. *Entrance requirements:* For master's and doctorate, GRE General Test, minimum 2 letters of recommendation, transcripts from all academic institutions attended. Additional exam requirements/recommendations for international students: Required—TOEFL (minimum score 600 paper-based; 250 computer-based; 100 iBT), IELTS (minimum score 7). Electronic applications accepted. *Faculty research:* Environmental engineering and science, geotechnics, mechanics of materials and solids, structural engineering and materials, transportation systems analysis and planning.

Norwich University, School of Graduate and Continuing Studies, Program in Civil Engineering, Northfield, VT 05663. Offers construction management (MCE); geo-technical (MCE); structural (MCE); water/environmental (MCE). Evening/weekend programs available. *Faculty:* 20 full-time (3 women). *Students:* 78 full-time (19 women); includes 5 Black or African American, non-Hispanic/Latino; 4 Asian, non-Hispanic/Latino; 7 Hispanic/Latino. Average age 35. 107 applicants, 88% accepted, 90 enrolled. In 2010, 78 master's awarded. *Entrance requirements:* For master's, minimum GPA of 2.75. Additional exam requirements/recommendations for international students: Required—TOEFL (minimum score 550 paper-based; 213 computer-based; 83 iBT). *Application deadline:* For fall admission, 8/10 for domestic and international students; for spring admission, 2/6 for domestic and international students. Application fee: $50. *Expenses:* Tuition: Full-time $17,380; part-time $645 per credit. Tuition and fees vary according to program. *Financial support:* Scholarships/grants available. Financial award applicants required to submit FAFSA. *Unit head:* Dr. Thomas Descoteaux, Program Director, 802-485-2730, Fax: 802-485-2533, E-mail: tdescote@norwich.edu. *Application contact:* Shelley W. Brown, Director of Business Partnership, 802-485-2784, Fax: 802-485-2533, E-mail: sbrown@norwich.edu.

Ohio University, Graduate College, Russ College of Engineering and Technology, Department of Civil Engineering, Athens, OH 45701-2979. Offers civil engineering (PhD); construction (MS); environmental (MS); geotechnical and geoenvironmental (MS); mechanics (MS); structures (MS); transportation (MS); water resources and structures (MS). Part-time programs available. *Students:* 29 full-time (6 women), 5 part-time (1 woman); includes 2 minority (1 Hispanic/Latino; 1 Two or more races, non-Hispanic/Latino), 16 international. 52 applicants, 83% accepted, 14 enrolled. In 2010, 7 master's awarded. *Degree requirements:* For master's, comprehensive exam (for some programs), thesis or alternative; for doctorate, comprehensive exam, thesis/dissertation. *Entrance requirements:* For master's, GRE General Test, minimum GPA of 3.0, 3 letters of recommendation; for doctorate, GRE General Test. Additional exam requirements/recommendations for international students: Required—TOEFL (minimum score 550 paper-based; 80 iBT) or IELTS (minimum score 6.5). *Application deadline:* For fall admission, 5/1 priority date for domestic students, 2/1 priority date for international students; for winter admission, 8/1 priority date for domestic students, 4/1 priority date for international students; for spring admission, 2/1 priority date for domestic students, 7/1 priority date for international students. Applications are processed on a rolling basis. Application fee: $50 ($55 for international students). Electronic applications accepted. *Financial support:* Research assistantships with full tuition reimbursements, teaching assistantships with full tuition reimbursements, Federal Work-Study, institutionally sponsored loans, scholarships/grants, and unspecified assistantships available. Financial award application deadline: 3/15; financial award applicants required to submit FAFSA. *Faculty research:* Noise abatement, materials and environment, highway infrastructure, subsurface investigation (pavements, pipes, bridges). *Unit head:* Dr. Gayle F. Mitchell, Chair, 740-593-0430, Fax: 740-593-0625, E-mail: mitchelg@ohio.edu. *Application contact:* Dr. Shad M. Sargand, Graduate Chair, 740-593-1465, Fax: 740-593-0625, E-mail: sargand@ohio.edu.

Oregon State University, Graduate School, College of Engineering, School of Civil and Construction Engineering, Corvallis, OR 97331. Offers civil engineering (MS, PhD); coastal and ocean engineering (M Oc E, PhD); coastal engineering (MS); construction engineering management (MBE, PhD); engineering (M Eng, MAIS); geotechnical engineering (MS, PhD); structural engineering (MS, PhD); transportation engineering (MS, PhD); water engineering (MS, PhD). Part-time programs available. Terminal master's awarded for partial completion of doctoral program. *Degree requirements:* For master's, thesis or alternative; for doctorate, one foreign language, thesis/dissertation. *Entrance requirements:* For master's, GRE General Test, minimum GPA of 3.0 in last 90 hours (3.5 for MS); for doctorate, GRE General Test, minimum GPA of 3.0 in last 90 hours of undergraduate course work. Additional exam requirements/recommendations for international students: Required—TOEFL (minimum score 580 paper-based; 237 computer-based). *Faculty research:* Hazardous waste management, carbon cycling, wave forces on structures, pavement design, seismic analysis.

Pontificia Universidad Catolica Madre y Maestra, Graduate School, Faculty of Engineering Sciences, Santiago, Dominican Republic. Offers earthquake engineering (ME); logistics management (ME).

Rensselaer Polytechnic Institute, Graduate School, School of Engineering, Program in Civil Engineering, Troy, NY 12180-3590. Offers geotechnical engineering (M Eng, MS, PhD); mechanics of composite materials and structures (M Eng, MS, PhD); structural engineering (M Eng, MS, PhD); transportation engineering (M Eng, MS, PhD). Part-time programs available. *Faculty:* 13 full-time (1 woman), 3 part-time/adjunct (0 women). *Students:* 20 full-time (4 women); includes 1 Black or African American, non-Hispanic/Latino, 16 international. Average age 24. 65 applicants, 12% accepted, 5 enrolled. In 2010, 19 master's, 3 doctorates awarded. Terminal master's awarded for partial completion of doctoral program. *Degree requirements:* For master's, thesis (for some programs); for doctorate, thesis/dissertation. *Entrance requirements:* For master's and doctorate, GRE. Additional exam requirements/recommendations for international students: Required—TOEFL (minimum score 570 paper-based; 230 computer-based; 89 iBT), IELTS (minimum score 6.5). *Application deadline:* For fall admission, 1/15 priority date for domestic and international students; for spring admission, 8/15 priority date for domestic and international students. Applications are processed on a rolling basis. Application fee: $75. Electronic applications accepted. *Expenses:* Tuition: Full-time $39,600; part-time $1650 per credit. Required fees: $1896. *Financial support:* In 2010–11, 1 fellowship with full tuition reimbursement (averaging $16,500 per year), 3 research assistantships with full tuition reimbursements (averaging $16,500 per year), 4 teaching assistantships with full tuition reimbursements (averaging $16,500 per year) were awarded; career-related internships or fieldwork and institutionally sponsored loans also available. Financial award application deadline: 2/1. *Faculty research:* Computational mechanics, earthquake engineering, geo-environmental engineering. Total annual research expenditures: $2.7 million. *Unit head:* Dr. Chris Letchford, Head, 518-276-6362, Fax: 518-276-4833, E-mail: letchc@rpi.edu. *Application contact:* Kimberly Boyce, Administrative Assistant, 518-276-6941, Fax: 518-276-4833, E-mail: boycek@rpi.edu.

Stevens Institute of Technology, Graduate School, Charles V. Schaefer Jr. School of Engineering, Department of Civil, Environmental, and Ocean Engineering, Program in Civil Engineering, Hoboken, NJ 07030. Offers civil engineering (PhD); geotechnical engineering (Certificate); geotechnical/geoenvironmental engineering (M Eng, Engr); hydrologic modeling (M Eng); stormwater management (M Eng); structural engineering (M Eng, Engr); water resources engineering (M Eng). *Students:* 22 full-time (6 women), 36 part-time (11 women); includes 10 Asian, non-Hispanic/Latino; 3 Hispanic/Latino, 16 international. Average age 28. 37 applicants, 86% accepted. *Degree requirements:* For master's, thesis optional; for doctorate, variable foreign language requirement, thesis/dissertation; for other advanced degree, project or thesis. *Entrance requirements:* For doctorate, GRE. Additional exam requirements/recommendations for international students: Required—TOEFL. *Application deadline:* Applications are processed on a rolling basis. Application fee: $50. Electronic applications accepted. *Financial support:* Application deadline: 4/15. *Unit head:* Dr. David A. Vaccari, Director, 201-216-5570, Fax: 201-216-5352, E-mail: dvaccari@stevens.edu. *Application contact:* Dr. David A. Vaccari, Director, 201-216-5570, Fax: 201-216-5352, E-mail: dvaccari@stevens.edu.

Texas A&M University, College of Engineering, Zachry Department of Civil Engineering, College Station, TX 77843. Offers coastal and ocean engineering (M Eng, MS, D Eng, PhD); construction engineering and management (M Eng, MS, D Eng, PhD); environmental engineering (M Eng, MS, D Eng, PhD); geotechnical engineering (M Eng, MS, D Eng, PhD); materials engineering (M Eng, MS, D Eng, PhD); structural engineering (M Eng, MS, D Eng, PhD); transportation engineering (M Eng, MS, D Eng, PhD); water resources engineering (M Eng, MS, D Eng, PhD). Part-time programs available. *Faculty:* 57. *Students:* 384 full-time (81 women), 35 part-time (7 women); includes 35 minority (3 Black or African American, non-Hispanic/Latino; 1 American Indian or Alaska Native, non-Hispanic/Latino; 14 Asian, non-Hispanic/Latino; 17 Hispanic/Latino), 263 international. Average age 29. In 2010, 136 master's, 26 doctorates awarded. *Degree requirements:* For master's, thesis (MS); for doctorate, dissertation (PhD), internship (D Eng). *Entrance requirements:* For master's and doctorate, GRE General Test. Additional exam requirements/recommendations for international students: Required—TOEFL. *Application deadline:* Applications are processed on a rolling basis. Application fee: $50 ($75 for international students). Electronic applications accepted. *Financial support:* In 2010–11, fellowships (averaging $4,500 per year), research assistantships (averaging $14,000 per year), teaching assistantships (averaging $14,400 per year) were awarded; career-related internships or fieldwork and institutionally sponsored loans also available. Financial award application deadline: 4/15; financial award applicants required to submit FAFSA. *Unit head:* Dr. Tony Cahill, Head, 979-845-3858, E-mail: tcahill@civil.tamu.edu. *Application contact:* Graduate Advisor, 979-845-7435, Fax: 979-845-6156, E-mail: info@civil.tamu.edu.

Tufts University, School of Engineering, Department of Civil and Environmental Engineering, Medford, MA 02155. Offers civil engineering (ME, MS, PhD), including geotechnical engineering, structural engineering; environmental engineering (ME, MS, PhD), including environmental engineering and environmental sciences, environmental geotechnology, environmental health, environmental science and management, hazardous materials management, water resources engineering. Part-time programs available. Terminal master's awarded for partial completion of doctoral program. *Degree requirements:* For master's, thesis or alternative; for doctorate, thesis/dissertation. *Entrance requirements:* For master's and doctorate, GRE General Test. Additional exam requirements/recommendations for international students: Required—TOEFL (minimum score 550 paper-based; 213 computer-based; 80 iBT). Electronic applications accepted. *Expenses:* Tuition: Full-time $39,624; part-time $3962 per course. Required fees: $40 per year. Full-time tuition and fees vary according to degree level, program and student level. Part-time tuition and fees vary according to course load.

University at Buffalo, the State University of New York, Graduate School, School of Engineering and Applied Sciences, Department of Civil, Structural, and Environmental Engineering, Buffalo, NY 14260. Offers civil engineering (ME, MS, PhD); engineering science (MS). Part-time programs available. Postbaccalaureate distance learning degree programs offered (minimal on-campus study). *Faculty:* 25 full-time (3 women), 3 part-time/adjunct (1 woman). *Students:* 173 full-time (26 women), 21 part-time (7 women); includes 1 Black or African American, non-Hispanic/Latino; 1 American Indian or Alaska Native, non-Hispanic/Latino; 6 Asian, non-Hispanic/Latino; 4 Hispanic/Latino, 133 international. Average age 27. 542 applicants, 38% accepted, 71 enrolled. In 2010, 34 master's, 4 doctorates awarded. Terminal master's awarded for partial completion of doctoral program. *Degree requirements:* For master's, thesis optional, project, thesis, or comprehensive exam; for doctorate, thesis/dissertation. *Entrance requirements:* For master's and doctorate, GRE General Test, letters of reference. Additional exam requirements/recommendations for international students: Required—TOEFL (minimum score 550 paper-based; 213 computer-based; 79 iBT). *Application deadline:* For fall admission, 1/15 priority date for domestic and international students; for spring admission, 9/15 for domestic and international students. Applications are processed on a rolling basis. Application fee: $50. Electronic applications accepted. *Financial support:* In 2010–11, 115 students received support, including 15 fellowships with full tuition reimbursements available (averaging $17,200 per year), 59 research assistantships with full tuition reimbursements available (averaging $14,000 per year), 35 teaching assistantships with full tuition reimbursements available (averaging $14,700 per year); career-related internships or fieldwork, Federal Work-Study, institutionally sponsored loans, scholarships/grants, traineeships, health care benefits, tuition waivers (full and partial), and unspecified assistantships also available. Support available to part-time students. Financial award application deadline: 1/15; financial award applicants required to submit FAFSA. *Faculty research:* Environmental engineering and fluid mechanics, structural dynamics, geomechanics, earthquake engineering computational mechanics. Total annual research expenditures: $9.7 million. *Unit head:* Dr. Andrew S. Whittaker, Chairman, 716-645-2114, Fax: 716-645-3733, E-mail: awhittak@buffalo.edu. *Application contact:* Dr. Gilberto Mosqueda, Director of Graduate Studies, 716-645-4356, Fax: 716-645-3733, E-mail: mosqueda@buffalo.edu.

The University of Alabama in Huntsville, School of Graduate Studies, College of Engineering, Department of Civil and Environmental Engineering, Huntsville, AL 35899. Offers civil and environmental engineering (PhD); civil engineering (MSE), including environmental and water resource engineering, geotechnical engineering, structural engineering and structural mechanics, transportation engineering. PhD offered jointly with The University of Alabama at Birmingham. Part-time and evening/weekend programs available. *Faculty:* 6 full-time (1 woman), 1 part-time/adjunct (0 women). *Students:* 23 full-time (7 women), 11 part-time (4 women); includes 3 minority (2 Black or African American, non-Hispanic/Latino; 1 Asian, non-Hispanic/Latino), 12 international. Average age 30. 37 applicants, 57% accepted, 15 enrolled. In 2010, 1 master's, 3 doctorates awarded. *Degree requirements:* For master's, comprehensive exam, thesis or alternative, oral and written exams; for doctorate, comprehensive exam, thesis/dissertation, oral and written exams. *Entrance requirements:* For master's, GRE General Test, BSE, minimum GPA of 3.0; for doctorate, GRE General Test, minimum GPA of 3.0. Additional exam requirements/recommendations for international students: Required—TOEFL (minimum score 500 paper-based; 173 computer-based; 62 iBT). *Application deadline:* For fall admission, 7/15 for domestic students, 4/1 for international students; for spring admission, 11/30 for domestic students, 9/1 for international students. Applications are processed on a rolling basis. Application fee: $40 ($50 for international students). Electronic applications accepted. *Expenses:* Tuition, state resident: full-time $7250; part-time $407.75 per credit hour. Tuition, nonresident: full-time $17,358; part-time $970.05 per credit hour. Required fees: $246.80 per semester. Tuition and fees vary according to course load and program. *Financial support:* In 2010–11, 14 students received support, including 7 research assistantships with full and partial tuition reimbursements available (averaging $12,435 per year), 7 teaching assistantships with full and partial tuition reimbursements available (averaging $10,281 per year); career-related internships or fieldwork, Federal Work-Study, institutionally sponsored loans, scholarships/grants, health care benefits, and unspecified assistantships also available. Support available to part-time students. Financial award application deadline: 4/1; financial award applicants required to submit FAFSA. *Faculty research:* Hydrologic modeling, orbital debris impact, hydrogeology, environmental engineering, transportation engineering. Total annual research expenditures: $1.9 million. *Unit head:* Dr. Houssam Toutanji, Chair, 256-824-7361, Fax: 256-824-6724, E-mail: toutanji@cee.uah.edu. *Application contact:* Kathy Biggs, Graduate Studies Admissions Manager, 256-824-6199, Fax: 256-824-6405, E-mail: deangrad@uah.edu.

University of Alberta, Faculty of Graduate Studies and Research, Department of Civil and Environmental Engineering, Edmonton, AB T6G 2E1, Canada. Offers construction engineering and management (M Eng, M Sc, PhD); environmental engineering (M Eng, M Sc, PhD); environmental science (M Sc, PhD); geoenvironmental engineering (M Eng, M Sc, PhD); geotechnical engineering (M Eng, M Sc, PhD); mining engineering (M Eng, M Sc, PhD); petroleum engineering (M Eng, M Sc, PhD); structural engineering (M Eng, M Sc, PhD); water resources (M Eng, M Sc, PhD). Part-time programs available. Postbaccalaureate distance learning degree programs offered (minimal on-campus study). *Degree requirements:* For master's, thesis (for some programs); for doctorate, thesis/dissertation. *Entrance requirements:* For master's, minimum GPA of 3.0 in last 2 years of undergraduate studies; for doctorate, minimum GPA of 3.0. Additional exam requirements/recommendations for international students: Required—TOEFL (minimum score 550 paper-based; 213 computer-based). Electronic applications accepted. *Faculty research:* Mining.

University of California, Berkeley, Graduate Division, College of Engineering, Department of Civil and Environmental Engineering, Berkeley, CA 94720-1500. Offers engineering and project management (M Eng, MS, D Eng, PhD); environmental engineering (M Eng, MS, D Eng, PhD); geoengineering (M Eng, MS, D Eng, PhD); structural engineering, mechanics and materials (M Eng, MS, D Eng, PhD); transportation engineering (M Eng, MS, D Eng, PhD); M Arch/MS; MCP/MS; MPP/MS. *Degree requirements:* For master's, comprehensive exam or thesis (MS); for doctorate, thesis/dissertation, qualifying exam. *Entrance requirements:* For master's, GRE General Test, minimum GPA of 3.0, 3 letters of recommendation; for doctorate, GRE General Test, minimum GPA of 3.5, 3 letters of recommendation. Additional exam requirements/recommendations for international students: Required—TOEFL (minimum score 570 paper-based; 230 computer-based). Electronic applications accepted.

University of California, San Diego, Office of Graduate Studies, Department of Structural Engineering, La Jolla, CA 92093. Offers structural engineering (MS, PhD); structural health monitoring, prognosis, and validated simulations (MS). Applications accepted only for fall quarter. Part-time programs available. *Degree requirements:* For master's, comprehensive exam or thesis; for doctorate, comprehensive exam, thesis/dissertation, candidacy exam. *Entrance requirements:* For master's and doctorate, GRE General Test, minimum GPA of 3.0; BS in engineering, physical sciences, or mathematics; statement of purpose; three letters of recommendation; official transcripts from all institutions attended. Additional exam requirements/recommendations for international students: Required—TOEFL (minimum score 550 paper-based; 213 computer-based; 80 iBT). *Faculty research:* Advanced large-scale civil, mechanical, and aerospace structures.

University of Central Florida, College of Engineering and Computer Science, Department of Civil, Environmental, and Construction Engineering, Program in Civil Engineering, Orlando, FL 32816. Offers civil engineering (MS, MSCE, PhD); construction engineering (Certificate); structural engineering (Certificate); transportation engineering (Certificate). Part-time and evening/weekend programs available. *Students:* 62 full-time (7 women), 77 part-time (15 women); includes 30 minority (4 Black or African American, non-Hispanic/Latino; 7 Asian, non-Hispanic/Latino; 17 Hispanic/Latino; 2 Two or more races, non-Hispanic/Latino), 35 international. Average age 30. 125 applicants, 73% accepted, 46 enrolled. In 2010, 26 master's, 8 doctorates awarded. *Degree requirements:* For master's, thesis or alternative; for doctorate, thesis/dissertation, departmental qualifying exam, candidacy exam. *Entrance requirements:* For master's, GRE General Test, minimum GPA of 3.0 in last 60 hours; for doctorate, GRE General Test, minimum GPA of 3.5 in last 60 hours. Additional exam requirements/recommendations for international students: Required—TOEFL. *Application deadline:* For fall admission, 7/15 priority date for domestic students; for spring admission, 12/15 priority date for domestic students. Application fee: $30. Electronic applications accepted. *Expenses:* Tuition, state resident: part-time $256.56 per credit hour. Tuition, nonresident: part-time $1011.52 per credit hour. Part-time tuition and fees vary according to program. *Financial support:* In 2010–11, 29 students received support, including 1 fellowship with partial tuition reimbursement available (averaging $10,000 per year), 22 research assistantships with partial tuition reimbursements available (averaging $11,000 per year), 18 teaching assistantships with partial tuition reimbursements available (averaging $7,900 per year); career-related internships or fieldwork, Federal Work-Study, institutionally sponsored loans, tuition waivers (partial), and unspecified assistantships also available. Financial award application deadline: 3/1; financial award applicants required to submit FAFSA.

University of Colorado Boulder, Graduate School, College of Engineering and Applied Science, Department of Civil, Environmental, and Architectural Engineering, Boulder, CO 80309. Offers building systems (MS, PhD); construction engineering management (MS, PhD); environmental engineering (MS, PhD); geotechnical engineering and geomechanics (MS, PhD); hydrology, water resources and environmental fluid mechanics (MS, PhD); structural engineering and structural mechanics (MS, PhD). *Faculty:* 38 full-time (6 women). *Students:* 255 full-time (86 women), 40 part-time (11 women); includes 40 minority (1 Black or African American, non-Hispanic/Latino; 2 American Indian or Alaska Native, non-Hispanic/Latino; 15 Asian, non-Hispanic/Latino; 20 Hispanic/Latino; 2 Two or more races, non-Hispanic/Latino), 61 international. Average age 28. 420 applicants, 95 enrolled. In 2010, 56 master's, 18 doctorates awarded. *Degree requirements:* For master's, comprehensive exam, thesis or alternative; for doctorate, thesis/dissertation. *Entrance requirements:* For master's, GRE General Test, minimum undergraduate GPA of 3.0. *Application deadline:* For fall admission, 3/1 for domestic students, 12/1 for international students; for spring admission, 10/31 for domestic students, 10/1 for international students. Application fee: $50 ($60 for international students). *Financial support:* In 2010–11, 45 fellowships (averaging $7,876 per year), 68 research assistantships (averaging $15,204 per year) were awarded. Financial award application deadline: 1/15. *Faculty research:* Building systems engineering, construction engineering and management, environmental engineering, geoenvironmental engineering, geotechnical engineering, materials and mechanics, structural engineering, water resources engineering, life-cycle engineering. Total annual research expenditures: $8 million.

University of Colorado Denver, College of Engineering and Applied Science, Department of Civil Engineering, Denver, CO 80217-3364. Offers civil engineering (PhD); environmental and sustainability engineering (MS); geographic information systems (MS); geotechnical engineering (MS); hydrology and hydraulics (MS); structural engineering (MS); transportation engineering (MS). Part-time and evening/weekend programs available. *Faculty:* 14 full-time (1 woman), 6 part-time/adjunct (0 women). *Students:* 66 full-time (13 women), 72 part-time (16 women); includes 9 Black or African American, non-Hispanic/Latino; 8 Asian, non-Hispanic/Latino; 11 Hispanic/Latino, 15 international. Average age 32. 72 applicants, 54% accepted, 29 enrolled. In 2010, 14 master's, 3 doctorates awarded. *Degree requirements:* For master's, comprehensive exam, thesis or alternative; for doctorate, comprehensive exam, thesis/dissertation. *Entrance requirements:* For master's, GRE, statement of purpose, transcripts, references; for doctorate, GRE, statement of purpose, transcripts, references, letter of support from faculty stating willingness to serve as dissertation advisor and outlining plan for financial support. Additional exam requirements/recommendations for international students: Required—TOEFL (minimum score 525 paper-based; 197 computer-based). *Application deadline:* For fall admission, 7/15 for domestic students, 6/15 for international students; for spring admission, 12/1 for domestic students, 11/1 for international students. Applications are processed on a rolling basis. Application fee: $50 ($75 for international students). Electronic applications accepted. *Expenses:* Contact institution. *Financial support:* Research assistantships, teaching assistantships, career-related internships or fieldwork and Federal Work-Study available. Financial award application deadline: 4/1; financial award applicants required to submit FAFSA. *Faculty research:* Environmental engineering and sustainable systems, geosynthetics, hydrologic andhydraulic engineering, structural engineering, transportation, transportation energy use and greenhouse gas emissions. *Unit head:* Dr. Nien-Yin Chang, Acting Chair, 303-556-2810, Fax: 303-556-2368, E-mail: nien.chang@ucdenver.edu. *Application contact:* Mindy Gewuerz, Program Assistant, 303-556-6712, Fax: 303-556-2368, E-mail: mindy.gewuerz@ucdenver.edu.

University of Dayton, Graduate School, School of Engineering, Department of Civil and Environmental Engineering and Engineering Mechanics, Dayton, OH 45469-1300. Offers engineering mechanics (MSEM); environmental engineering (MSCE); geotechnical engineering (MSCE); structural engineering (MSCE); transportation engineering (MSCE); water resources engineering (MSCE). Part-time programs available. *Faculty:* 7 full-time (2 women), 2 part-time/adjunct (0 women). *Students:* 10 full-time (5 women), 7 part-time (2 women); includes 2 minority (both Black or African American, non-Hispanic/Latino), 6 international. Average age 27. 23 applicants, 43% accepted, 4 enrolled. In 2010, 5 master's awarded. *Degree requirements:* For master's, thesis optional. *Entrance requirements:* For master's, minimum GPA of 3.0 in undergraduate work. Additional exam requirements/recommendations for international students: Required—TOEFL (minimum score 550 paper-based; 213 computer-based; 80 iBT). *Application deadline:* For fall admission, 8/1 for domestic students, 3/1 priority date for international students; for winter admission, 7/1 priority date for international students; for spring admission, 1/1 priority date for international students. Applications are processed on a rolling basis. Application fee: $0 ($50 for international students). Electronic applications accepted. *Expenses:* Tuition: Full-time $7800; part-time $650 per credit hour. *Financial support:* In 2010–11, 2 research assistantships (averaging $10,600 per year) were awarded. Financial award applicants required to submit FAFSA. *Faculty research:* Physical modeling of hydraulic systems, finite element methods, mechanics of composite materials, transportation systems safety, biological treatment processes. Total annual research expenditures: $200,000. *Unit head:* Dr. Donald V. Chase, Chair, 937-229-3847, Fax: 937-229-3491, E-mail: donald.chase@notes.udayton.edu. *Application contact:* Alexander Popovski, Associate Director of International and Graduate Admissions, 937-229-2357, Fax: 937-229-4729, E-mail: alex.popovski@notes.udayton.edu.

University of Delaware, College of Engineering, Department of Civil and Environmental Engineering, Newark, DE 19716. Offers environmental engineering (MAS, MCE, PhD); geotechnical engineering (MAS, MCE, PhD); ocean engineering (MAS, MCE, PhD); structural engineering (MAS, MCE, PhD); transportation engineering (MAS, MCE, PhD); water resource engineering (MAS, MCE, PhD). Part-time programs available. Terminal master's awarded for partial completion of doctoral program. *Degree requirements:* For master's, thesis; for doctorate, thesis/dissertation. *Entrance requirements:* For master's and doctorate, GRE General Test. Additional exam requirements/recommendations for international students: Required—TOEFL. Electronic applications accepted. *Faculty research:* Structural engineering and mechanics; transportation engineering; ocean engineering; soil mechanics and foundation; water resources and environmental engineering.

The University of Manchester, School of Materials, Manchester, United Kingdom. Offers advanced aerospace materials engineering (M Sc); advanced metallic systems (PhD); biomedical materials (M Phil, M Sc, PhD); ceramics and glass (M Phil, M Sc, PhD); composite materials (M Sc, PhD); corrosion and protection (M Phil, M Sc, PhD); materials (M Phil, PhD); metallic materials (M Phil, M Sc, PhD); nanostructural materials (M Phil, M Sc, PhD); paper science (M Phil, M Sc, PhD); polymer science and engineering (M Phil, M Sc, PhD); technical textiles (M Sc); textile design, fashion and management (M Phil, M Sc, PhD); textile science and technology (M Phil, M Sc, PhD); textiles (M Phil, PhD); textiles and fashion (M Ent).

University of Memphis, Graduate School, Herff College of Engineering, Department of Civil Engineering, Memphis, TN 38152. Offers civil engineering (PhD); environmental engineering (MS); foundation engineering (MS); structural engineering (MS); transportation engineering (MS); water resources engineering (MS). *Faculty:* 12 full-time (1 woman), 1 part-time/adjunct (0 women). *Students:* 12 full-time (5 women), 13 part-time (3 women); includes 2 Black or African American, non-Hispanic/Latino; 2 Asian, non-Hispanic/Latino; 1 Two or more races, non-Hispanic/Latino, 7 international. Average age 28. 22 applicants, 55% accepted, 0 enrolled. In 2010, 11 master's awarded. Terminal master's awarded for partial completion of doctoral program. *Degree requirements:* For master's, comprehensive exam, thesis optional; for doctorate, comprehensive exam, thesis/dissertation. *Entrance requirements:* For master's, GRE General Test or MAT, minimum undergraduate GPA of 2.5; for doctorate, GRE, 3 letters of recommendation. Additional exam requirements/recommendations for international students: Required—TOEFL (minimum score 550 paper-based; 210 computer-based; 79 iBT). *Application deadline:* For fall admission, 1/7 for domestic students, 1/5 for international students; for spring admission, 12/1 for domestic students, 9/15 for international students. Application fee: $35 ($60 for international students). *Financial support:* In 2010–11, 6 students received support; fellowships with full tuition reimbursements available, research assistantships with full tuition reimbursements available, career-related internships or fieldwork, Federal Work-Study, scholarships/grants, and unspecified assistantships available. Financial award application deadline: 2/15; financial award applicants required to submit FAFSA. *Faculty research:* Structural response to earthquakes, pavement design, water quality, transportation safety, intermodal transportation. *Unit head:* Dr. Sharam Pezeshk, Interim Chair, 901-678-2746, Fax: 901-678-3026. *Application contact:* Dr. Roger Meier, Coordinator of Graduate Studies, 901-678-3284.

University of Michigan, Horace H. Rackham School of Graduate Studies, College of Engineering, Department of Civil and Environmental Engineering, Ann Arbor, MI 48109. Offers civil engineering (MSE, PhD, CE); construction engineering and management (M Eng, MSE); environmental engineering (MSE, PhD); structural engineering (M Eng); MBA/MSE. Part-time programs available. *Students:* 121 full-time (45 women), 5 part-time (2 women). 461 applicants, 30% accepted, 54 enrolled. In 2010, 36 master's, 13 doctorates awarded. *Degree requirements:* For master's, thesis optional; for doctorate, comprehensive exam, thesis/dissertation, oral defense of dissertation, preliminary and written exams. *Entrance requirements:* For master's and doctorate, GRE General Test. Additional exam requirements/recommendations for international students: Required—TOEFL (minimum score 560 paper-based; 220 computer-based). *Application deadline:* Applications are processed on a rolling basis. Application fee: $65 ($75 for international students). Electronic applications accepted. *Expenses:* Tuition, state resident: full-time $17,784; part-time $1116 per credit hour. Tuition, nonresident: full-time $35,944; part-time $2125 per credit hour. International tuition: $35,994 full-time. Required fees: $95 per semester. Tuition and fees vary according to course load, degree level and program. *Financial support:* Fellowships, research assistantships, teaching assistantships, institutionally sponsored loans and tuition waivers (partial) available. Financial award application deadline: 1/19. *Faculty research:* Construction engineering and management; geotechnical engineering; earthquake-resistant design of structures; environmental chemistry and microbiology; cost engineering; environmental and water resources engineering. *Unit head:* Nancy Love, Chair, 734-764-8405, Fax: 734-764-4292, E-mail: nglove@umich.edu. *Application contact:* Kimberly Smith, Student Advisor, 734-764-8405, Fax: 734-647-2127, E-mail: kansmith@umich.edu.

University of Missouri, Graduate School, College of Engineering, Department of Civil and Environmental Engineering, Columbia, MO 65211. Offers civil engineering (MS, PhD); environmental engineering (MS, PhD); geotechnical engineering (MS, PhD); structural engineering (MS, PhD); transportation and highway engineering (MS); water resources (MS, PhD). *Degree requirements:* For master's, report or thesis; for doctorate, thesis/dissertation. *Entrance requirements:* For master's and doctorate, GRE General Test. Additional exam requirements/recommendations for international students: Required—TOEFL (minimum score 550 paper-based; 213 computer-based; 79 iBT).

University of New Brunswick Fredericton, School of Graduate Studies, Faculty of Engineering, Department of Civil Engineering, Fredericton, NB E3B 5A3, Canada. Offers construction engineering and management (M Eng, M Sc E, PhD); environmental engineering (M Eng, M Sc E, PhD); environmental studies (M Eng); geotechnical engineering (M Eng, M Sc E, PhD); groundwater/hydrology (M Eng, M Sc E, PhD); materials (M Eng, M Sc E, PhD); pavements (M Eng, M Sc E, PhD); structures (M Eng, M Sc E, PhD); transportation (M Eng, M Sc E, PhD). Part-time programs available. *Faculty:* 13 full-time (1 woman), 7 part-time/adjunct (1 woman). *Students:* 34 full-time (8 women), 16 part-time (2 women). In 2010, 16 master's, 6 doctorates awarded. *Degree requirements:* For master's, thesis, proposal; for doctorate, comprehensive exam, thesis/dissertation, qualifying exam; proposal; 27 credit hours of courses. *Entrance requirements:* For master's, minimum GPA of 3.0; B Sc E in civil engineering or related engineering degree; for doctorate, minimum GPA of 3.0; graduate degree in engineering or applied science. Additional exam requirements/recommendations for international students: Required—TWE (minimum score 4), TOEFL (minimum score 580 paper-based; 237 computer-based) or IELTS (minimum score 7.5). *Application deadline:* For fall admission, 5/1 priority date for domestic students; for winter admission, 11/1 priority date for domestic students. Applications are processed on a rolling basis. Application fee: $50 Canadian dollars. *Expenses:* Tuition, area resident: Full-time $3708; part-time $927 per term. International tuition: $6300 full-time. Required fees: $50 per term. *Financial support:* In 2010–11, 52 research assistantships (averaging $7,000 per year), 46 teaching assistantships (averaging $2,000 per year) were awarded; career-related internships or fieldwork and scholarships/grants also available. *Faculty research:* Construction engineering and management; materials and infrastructure renewal; highway and pavement research; structures and solid mechanics; geotechnical, soil; structure interaction; transportation and planning; environment, solid waste management. *Unit head:* Dr. Eric Hildebrand, Director of Graduate Studies, 506-453-5113, Fax: 506-453-3568,

Structural Engineering

University of New Brunswick Fredericton (continued)
E-mail: edh@unb.ca. *Application contact:* Joyce Moore, Graduate Secretary, 506-452-6127, Fax: 506-453-3568, E-mail: civil-grad@unb.ca.

University of North Dakota, Graduate School, School of Engineering and Mines, Department of Civil Engineering, Grand Forks, ND 58202. Offers civil engineering (M Engr); sanitary engineering (M Engr), including soils and structures engineering, surface mining engineering. Part-time programs available. *Faculty:* 6 full-time (0 women). *Students:* 7 full-time (0 women), 4 part-time (0 women), 4 international. Average age 28. 6 applicants, 67% accepted, 4 enrolled. In 2010, 5 master's awarded. *Degree requirements:* For master's, comprehensive exam, thesis or alternative. *Entrance requirements:* For master's, GRE General Test, minimum GPA of 2.5. Additional exam requirements/recommendations for international students: Required—TOEFL (minimum score 550 paper-based; 213 computer-based; 79 iBT), IELTS (minimum score 6.5). *Application deadline:* For fall admission, 8/1 priority date for domestic students, 5/1 priority date for international students; for spring admission, 12/1 priority date for domestic students, 9/1 priority date for international students. Applications are processed on a rolling basis. Application fee: $35. Electronic applications accepted. *Expenses:* Tuition, state resident: full-time $5857; part-time $306.74 per credit. Tuition, nonresident: full-time $15,666; part-time $729.77 per credit. Required fees: $53.42 per credit. Tuition and fees vary according to course load, program and reciprocity agreements. *Financial support:* In 2010–11, 3 students received support, including 1 research assistantship with full and partial tuition reimbursement available (averaging $4,087 per year), 2 teaching assistantships with full and partial tuition reimbursements available (averaging $5,311 per year); fellowships with full and partial tuition reimbursements available, career-related internships or fieldwork, Federal Work-Study, scholarships/grants, health care benefits, tuition waivers (full and partial), and unspecified assistantships also available. Support available to part-time students. Financial award application deadline: 3/15; financial award applicants required to submit FAFSA. *Faculty research:* Soil-structures, environmental-water resources. Total annual research expenditures: $47,501. *Unit head:* Dr. Sukhvarsh Jerath, Graduate Director, 701-777-3564, Fax: 701-777-4838, E-mail: sukhvarshjerath@mail.und.edu. *Application contact:* Staci Wells, Admissions Associate, 701-777-2945, Fax: 701-777-3619, E-mail: staci.wells@gradschool.und.edu.

The University of Texas at Tyler, College of Engineering and Computer Science, Department of Civil Engineering, Tyler, TX 75799-0001. Offers environmental engineering (MS); industrial safety (MS); structural engineering (MS); transportation engineering (MS); water resources engineering (MS). Part-time and evening/weekend programs available. *Degree requirements:* For master's, thesis optional. *Entrance requirements:* For master's, GRE General Test, bachelor's degree in engineering, associated science degree. Additional exam requirements/recommendations for international students: Required—TOEFL (minimum score 79 computer-based). *Faculty research:* Non-destructive strength testing, indoor air quality, transportation routing and signaling, pavement replacement criteria, flood water routing, construction and long-term behavior of innovative geotechnical foundation and embankment construction used in highway construction, engineering education.

University of Washington, Graduate School, College of Engineering, Department of Civil and Environmental Engineering, Seattle, WA 98195-2700. Offers construction engineering (MSCE); environmental engineering (MS, MSCE, MSE, PhD); hydrology, water resources, and environmental fluid mechanics (MS, MSCE, MSE, PhD); structural and geotechnical engineering and mechanics (MS, MSCE, MSE, PhD); transportation and construction engineering (MS, MSE, PhD); transportation engineering (MSCE). Part-time programs available. Postbaccalaureate distance learning degree programs offered (no on-campus study). *Faculty:* 44 full-time (10 women), 12 part-time/adjunct (1 woman). *Students:* 197 full-time (65 women), 65 part-time (15 women); includes 5 Black or African American, non-Hispanic/Latino; 28 Asian, non-Hispanic/Latino; 5 Hispanic/Latino, 55 international. 522 applicants, 51% accepted, 101 enrolled. In 2010, 68 master's, 5 doctorates awarded. Terminal master's awarded for partial completion of doctoral program. *Degree requirements:* For master's, thesis (for some programs); for doctorate, comprehensive exam, thesis/dissertation, General, qualifying, and final exams. Completion of doctoral degree within 10 years. *Entrance requirements:* For master's, GRE General Test, Minimum GPA of 3.0, statement of purpose, letters of recommendation, transcripts; for doctorate, GRE General Test, minimum GPA of 3.5, statement of purpose, letters of recommendation, transcripts. Additional exam requirements/recommendations for international students: Required—TOEFL (minimum score 580 paper-based; 237 computer-based; 92 iBT); Recommended—IELTS (minimum score 7). *Application deadline:* For fall admission, 1/10 priority date for domestic and international students. Application fee: $75. Electronic applications accepted. *Financial support:* In 2010–11, 2 students received support, including 25 fellowships with full and partial tuition reimbursements available (averaging $16,173 per year), 75 research assistantships with full tuition reimbursements available (averaging $16,515 per year), 11 teaching assistantships with full tuition reimbursements available (averaging $16,263 per year); scholarships/grants also available. Financial award application deadline: 1/10; financial award applicants required to submit FAFSA. *Faculty research:* Environmental/water resources, hydrology; construction/transportation; structures/ geotechnical. Total annual research expenditures: $14.4 million. *Unit head:* Dr. Gregory R. Miller, Professor and Chair, 206-543-0350, Fax: 206-543-1543, E-mail: gmiller@uw.edu. *Application contact:* Lorna Latal, Graduate Adviser, 206-543-2574, Fax: 206-543-1543, E-mail: llatal@u.washington.edu.

Washington University in St. Louis, School of Engineering and Applied Science, Department of Mechanical, Aerospace and Structural Engineering, St. Louis, MO 63130-4899. Offers MS, D Sc, PhD. Part-time programs available. Terminal master's awarded for partial completion of doctoral program. *Degree requirements:* For master's, thesis optional; for doctorate, thesis/dissertation optional. *Entrance requirements:* For master's, GRE; for doctorate, GRE General Test, departmental qualifying exam. *Faculty research:* Aerosols science and technology, applied mechanics, biomechanics and biomedical engineering, design, dynamic systems, combustion science, composite materials, materials science.

Western Michigan University, Graduate College, College of Engineering and Applied Sciences, Department of Civil and Construction Engineering, Kalamazoo, MI 49008. Offers civil engineering (MS), including construction engineering and management, structural engineering, transportation engineering. *Entrance requirements:* For master's, minimum GPA of 3.0.

Surveying Science and Engineering

The Ohio State University, Graduate School, College of Engineering, Department of Civil and Environmental Engineering and Geodetic Science, Columbus, OH 43210. Offers civil engineering (MS, PhD); geodetic science and surveying (MS, PhD). *Students:* 78 full-time (18 women), 38 part-time (3 women); includes 2 Black or African American, non-Hispanic/Latino; 1 Asian, non-Hispanic/Latino; 1 Hispanic/Latino; 2 Two or more races, non-Hispanic/Latino, 66 international. Average age 28. In 2010, 29 master's, 8 doctorates awarded. *Expenses:* Tuition, state resident: full-time $10,605. Tuition, nonresident: full-time $26,535. Tuition and fees vary according to course load and program. *Unit head:* Dr. Carolyn J. Merry, Chair, 614-292-2771, Fax: 614-292-9379, E-mail: merry.1@osu.edu. *Application contact:* Dr. Carolyn J. Merry, Chair, 614-292-2771, Fax: 614-292-9379, E-mail: merry.1@osu.edu.

University of New Brunswick Fredericton, School of Graduate Studies, Faculty of Engineering, Department of Geodesy and Geomatics, Fredericton, NB E3B 5A3, Canada. Offers land information management (Diploma); mapping, charting and geodesy (Diploma); surveying engineering (M Eng, M Sc E, PhD). *Faculty:* 9 full-time (1 woman), 13 part-time/adjunct (1 woman). *Students:* 37 full-time (5 women), 4 part-time (0 women). In 2010, 9 master's, 3 doctorates awarded. *Degree requirements:* For master's, thesis; for doctorate, comprehensive exam, thesis/dissertation, qualifying exam. *Entrance requirements:* For master's and doctorate, minimum GPA of 3.0. Additional exam requirements/recommendations for international students: Required—TOEFL (minimum score 580 paper-based), TWE (minimum score 4). *Application deadline:* For fall admission, 3/1 priority date for domestic students. Applications are processed on a rolling basis. Application fee: $50 Canadian dollars. *Expenses:* Tuition, area resident: Full-time $3708; part-time $927 per term. International tuition: $6300 full-time. Required fees: $50 per term. *Financial support:* In 2010–11, 23 research assistantships, 22 teaching assistantships were awarded; fellowships also available. *Faculty research:* Remote sensing, ocean mapping, land administration. *Unit head:* Dr. Sue Nichols, Director of Graduate Studies, 506-453-5141, Fax: 506-453-4943, E-mail: nichols@unb.ca. *Application contact:* Sylvia Whitaker, Graduate Secretary, 506-458-7085, Fax: 506-453-4943, E-mail: swhitake@unb.ca.

Transportation and Highway Engineering

Arizona State University, College of Liberal Arts and Sciences, School of Geographical Sciences, Tempe, AZ 85287-5302. Offers atmospheric science (Graduate Certificate); geographic education (MAS); geographic information systems (MAS); geographical information science (Graduate Certificate); geography (MA, PhD); transportation systems (Graduate Certificate); urban and environmental planning (MUEP). *Faculty:* 34 full-time (9 women), 2 part-time/adjunct (both women). *Students:* 125 full-time (40 women), 47 part-time (25 women); includes 24 minority (4 Black or African American, non-Hispanic/Latino; 1 American Indian or Alaska Native, non-Hispanic/Latino; 1 Asian, non-Hispanic/Latino; 16 Hispanic/Latino; 2 Two or more races, non-Hispanic/Latino), 34 international. Average age 30. 261 applicants, 56% accepted, 79 enrolled. In 2010, 76 master's, 3 doctorates, 13 other advanced degrees awarded. Terminal master's awarded for partial completion of doctoral program. *Degree requirements:* For master's, thesis, interactive Program of Study (iPOS) submitted before completing 50 percent of required credit hours; for doctorate, comprehensive exam, thesis/dissertation, interactive Program of Study (iPOS) submitted before completing 50 percent of required credit hours. *Entrance requirements:* For master's and doctorate, GRE, minimum GPA of 3.0 or equivalent in last 2 years of work leading to bachelor's degree. Additional exam requirements/recommendations for international students: Required—TOEFL, IELTS, or Pearson Test of English. *Application deadline:* For fall admission, 1/15 for domestic and international students. Applications are processed on a rolling basis. Application fee: $70 ($90 for international students). Electronic applications accepted. *Expenses:* Contact institution. *Financial support:* In 2010–11, 25 research assistantships with full and partial tuition reimbursements (averaging $15,546 per year), 50 teaching assistantships with full and partial tuition reimbursements (averaging $10,686 per year) were awarded; fellowships with full tuition reimbursements, career-related internships or fieldwork, Federal Work-Study, institutionally sponsored loans, scholarships/grants, and tuition waivers (full and partial) also available. Financial award application deadline: 3/1; financial award applicants required to submit FAFSA. Total annual research expenditures: $2.6 million. *Unit head:* Dr. Luc Anselin, Chair and Director, 480-965-7533, E-mail: luc.anselin@asu.edu. *Application contact:* Graduate Admissions, 480-965-6113.

Auburn University, Graduate School, Ginn College of Engineering, Department of Civil Engineering, Auburn University, AL 36849. Offers construction engineering and management (MCE, MS, PhD); environmental engineering (MCE, MS, PhD); geotechnical/materials engineering (MCE, MS, PhD); hydraulics/hydrology (MCE, MS, PhD); structural engineering (MCE, MS, PhD); transportation engineering (MCE, MS, PhD). Part-time programs available. *Faculty:* 21 full-time (1 woman), 3 part-time/adjunct (1 woman). *Students:* 46 full-time (15 women), 39 part-time (5 women); includes 3 Black or African American, non-Hispanic/Latino; 1 Asian, non-Hispanic/Latino, 29 international. Average age 26. 136 applicants, 43% accepted, 26 enrolled. In 2010, 19 master's, 4 doctorates awarded. *Degree requirements:* For master's, project (MCE), thesis (MS); for doctorate, comprehensive exam, thesis/dissertation. *Entrance requirements:* For master's and doctorate, GRE General Test. *Application deadline:* For fall admission, 7/7 for domestic students; for spring admission, 11/24 for domestic students. Applications are processed on a rolling basis. Application fee: $50 ($60 for international students). Electronic applications accepted. *Expenses:* Tuition, state resident: full-time $7002. Tuition, nonresident: full-time $21,898. International tuition: $22,116 full-time. Required fees: $892. Tuition and fees vary according to course load and program. *Financial support:* Fellowships, research assistantships, teaching assistantships, Federal Work-Study available. Support available to part-time students. Financial award application deadline: 3/15; financial award applicants required to submit FAFSA. *Unit head:* Dr. J. Michael Stallings, Head, 334-844-4320. *Application contact:* Dr. George Flowers, Dean of the Graduate School, 334-844-2125.

Cornell University, Graduate School, Graduate Fields of Engineering, Field of Civil and Environmental Engineering, Ithaca, NY 14853-0001. Offers engineering management (M Eng, MS, PhD); environmental engineering (M Eng, MS, PhD); environmental fluid mechanics and hydrology (M Eng, MS, PhD); environmental systems engineering (M Eng, MS, PhD); geotechnical engineering (M Eng, MS, PhD); remote sensing (M Eng, MS, PhD); structural engineering (M Eng, MS, PhD); structural mechanics (M Eng, MS); transportation engineering (MS, PhD); transportation systems engineering (M Eng); water resource systems (M Eng, MS, PhD). *Faculty:* 36 full-time (4 women). *Students:* 148 full-time (48 women); includes 3 Black or African American, non-Hispanic/Latino; 1 American Indian or Alaska Native, non-Hispanic/Latino; 16 Asian, non-Hispanic/Latino; 16 Hispanic/Latino, 60 international. Average age 24. 390 applicants, 56% accepted, 76 enrolled. In 2010, 93 master's, 5 doctorates awarded. Terminal master's awarded for partial completion of doctoral program. *Degree requirements:* For master's, thesis (MS); for doctorate, comprehensive exam, thesis/dissertation. *Entrance requirements:* For master's and doctorate, GRE General Test (recommended), 2 letters of recommendation. Additional exam requirements/recommendations for international students: Required—TOEFL (minimum score 600 paper-based; 250 computer-based; 77 iBT). *Application deadline:* For fall admission, 1/15 priority date for domestic students; for spring admission, 10/15 for domestic students. Application fee: $70. Electronic applications accepted. *Expenses:* Tuition: Full-time $29,500. Required fees: $76. Tuition and fees vary according to degree level and program. *Financial support:* In 2010–11, 50 students received support, including 17 fellowships with full tuition reimbursements available, 33 research assistantships with full tuition reimbursements available, 15 teaching assistantships with full tuition reimbursements available; institutionally sponsored loans, scholarships/grants, health care benefits, tuition waivers (full and partial), and unspecified assistantships also available. Financial award applicants required to submit FAFSA. *Faculty research:* Environmental engineering, geotechnical engineering, remote sensing, environmental fluid mechanics and hydrology, structural engineering. *Unit head:* Director of Graduate Studies, 607-255-7560, Fax: 607-255-9004. *Application contact:* Graduate Field Assistant, 607-255-7560, Fax: 607-255-9004, E-mail: cee_grad@cornell.edu.

École Polytechnique de Montréal, Graduate Programs, Department of Civil, Geological and Mining Engineering, Montréal, QC H3C 3A7, Canada. Offers civil, geological and mining engineering (DESS); environmental engineering (M Eng, M Sc A, PhD); geotechnical engineering (M Eng, M Sc A, PhD); hydraulics engineering (M Eng, M Sc A, PhD); structural engineering (M Eng, M Sc A, PhD); transportation engineering (M Eng, M Sc A, PhD). Part-time programs available. *Degree requirements:* For master's, one foreign language, thesis; for doctorate, one foreign language, thesis/dissertation. *Entrance requirements:* For master's, minimum GPA of 2.75; for doctorate, minimum GPA of 3.0. *Faculty research:* Water resources management, characteristics of building materials, aging of dams, pollution control.

Illinois Institute of Technology, Graduate College, Armour College of Engineering, Department of Civil, Architectural and Environmental Engineering, Chicago, IL 60616-3793. Offers architectural engineering (M Arch E); civil engineering (MS, PhD), including architectural engineering (MS), construction engineering and management (MS), geoenvironmental engineering (MS), geotechnical engineering (MS), structural engineering (MS), transportation engineering (MS); construction engineering and management (MCEM); environmental engineering (M Env E, PhD); geoenvironmental engineering (M Geoenv E); geotechnical engineering (MGE); public works (MPW); structural engineering (MSE); transportation engineering (M Trans E). Part-time and evening/weekend programs available. Postbaccalaureate distance learning degree programs offered (minimal on-campus study). *Faculty:* 15 full-time (1 woman), 13 part-time/adjunct (1 woman). *Students:* 159 full-time (63 women), 109 part-time (22 women); includes 30 minority (9 Black or African American, non-Hispanic/Latino; 16 Asian, non-Hispanic/Latino; 5 Hispanic/Latino), 126 international. Average age 27. 453 applicants, 66% accepted, 98 enrolled. In 2010, 76 master's, 1 doctorate awarded. Terminal master's awarded for partial completion of doctoral program. *Degree requirements:* For master's, thesis (for some programs); for doctorate, comprehensive exam, thesis/dissertation. *Entrance requirements:* For master's, GRE General Test (minimum score 900 Quantitative and Verbal, 2.5 Analytical Writing), minimum undergraduate GPA of 3.0; for doctorate, GRE General Test (minimum score 1000 Quantitative and Verbal, 3.0 Analytical Writing), minimum undergraduate GPA of 3.0. Additional exam requirements/recommendations for international students: Required—TOEFL (minimum score 523 paper-based; 70 iBT); Recommended—IELTS (minimum score 5.5). *Application deadline:* For fall admission, 5/1 for domestic and international students; for spring admission, 10/15 for domestic and international students. Applications are processed on a rolling basis. Application fee: $50. Electronic applications accepted. *Expenses:* Tuition: Full-time $18,576; part-time $1032 per credit hour. Required fees: $583 per semester. One-time fee: $150. Tuition and fees vary according to program and student level. *Financial support:* In 2010–11, 13 research assistantships with full and partial tuition reimbursements (averaging $9,453 per year), 19 teaching assistantships with full and partial tuition reimbursements (averaging $3,163 per year) were awarded; fellowships with full and partial tuition reimbursements, Federal Work-Study, institutionally sponsored loans, scholarships/grants, health care benefits, tuition waivers (partial), and unspecified assistantships also available. Support available to part-time students. Financial award applicants required to submit FAFSA. *Faculty research:* Structural, architectural, geotechnical and geoenvironmental engineering; construction engineering and management; transportation engineering; environmental engineering and public works. Total annual research expenditures: $763,042. *Unit head:* Dr. Jamshid Mohammadi, Professor and Chairman, 312-567-3629, Fax: 312-567-3519, E-mail: mohammadi@iit.edu. *Application contact:* Deborah Gibson, Director, Graduate Admission, 866-472-3448, Fax: 312-567-3138, E-mail: inquiry.grad@iit.edu.

Iowa State University of Science and Technology, Graduate College, College of Engineering, Department of Civil and Construction Engineering, Ames, IA 50011. Offers civil engineering (MS, PhD), including civil engineering materials, construction engineering and management, environmental engineering, geometronics, geotechnical engineering, structural engineering, transportation engineering. *Faculty:* 35 full-time (6 women), 4 part-time/adjunct (0 women). *Students:* 93 full-time (31 women), 48 part-time (10 women); includes 1 Black or African American, non-Hispanic/Latino; 1 Asian, non-Hispanic/Latino; 4 Hispanic/Latino, 62 international. 179 applicants, 37% accepted, 35 enrolled. In 2010, 32 master's, 9 doctorates awarded. *Degree requirements:* For master's, thesis or alternative; for doctorate, thesis/dissertation. *Entrance requirements:* For master's and doctorate, GRE General Test. Additional exam requirements/recommendations for international students: Required—TOEFL (minimum score 550 paper-based; 82 iBT), IELTS (minimum score 6.5). *Application deadline:* For fall admission, 2/1 priority date for domestic students, 2/1 for international students; for spring admission, 8/1 priority date for domestic students, 8/1 for international students. Application fee: $40 ($90 for international students). Electronic applications accepted. *Financial support:* In 2010–11, 67 research assistantships with full and partial tuition reimbursements (averaging $7,654 per year), 4 teaching assistantships with full and partial tuition reimbursements (averaging $9,525 per year) were awarded; fellowships, scholarships/grants, health care benefits, and unspecified assistantships also available. *Unit head:* Dr. James Alleman, Chair, 515-294-3892, E-mail: ccee-grad-inquiry@iastate.edu. *Application contact:* Dr. Sri Srithanan, Director of Graduate Education, 515-294-5328, E-mail: ccee-grad-inquiry@iastate.edu.

Louisiana State University and Agricultural and Mechanical College, Graduate School, College of Engineering, Department of Civil and Environmental Engineering, Baton Rouge, LA 70803. Offers environmental engineering (MSCE, PhD); geotechnical engineering (MSCE, PhD); structural engineering and mechanics (MSCE, PhD); transportation engineering (MSCE, PhD); water resources (MSCE, PhD). Part-time programs available. *Faculty:* 29 full-time (3 women). *Students:* 89 full-time (19 women), 35 part-time (8 women); includes 2 Black or African American, non-Hispanic/Latino; 1 American Indian or Alaska Native, non-Hispanic/Latino; 3 Asian, non-Hispanic/Latino; 3 Hispanic/Latino, 65 international. Average age 29. 96 applicants, 65% accepted, 16 enrolled. In 2010, 20 master's, 8 doctorates awarded. *Degree requirements:* For master's, thesis optional; for doctorate, one foreign language, thesis/dissertation. *Entrance requirements:* For master's and doctorate, GRE General Test, minimum GPA of 3.0. Additional exam requirements/recommendations for international students: Required—TOEFL (minimum score 550 paper-based; 213 computer-based; 79 iBT) or IELTS (minimum score 6.5). *Application deadline:* For fall admission, 1/25 priority date for domestic students, 5/15 for international students; for spring admission, 10/15 for international students. Applications are processed on a rolling basis. Application fee: $50 ($70 for international students). Electronic applications accepted. *Financial support:* In 2010–11, 89 students received support, including 2 fellowships with full and partial tuition reimbursements available (averaging $24,418 per year), 75 research assistantships with full and partial tuition reimbursements available (averaging $16,115 per year), 3 teaching assistantships with full and partial tuition reimbursements available (averaging $12,843 per year); career-related internships or fieldwork, institutionally sponsored loans, scholarships/grants, and health care benefits also available. Financial award application deadline: 3/1; financial award applicants required to submit FAFSA. *Faculty research:* Mechanics and structures, environmental, geotechnical transportation, water resources. Total annual research expenditures: $2.6 million. *Unit head:* Dr. George Z. Voyiadjis, Chair/Professor, 225-578-8668, Fax: 225-578-9176, E-mail: cegzv@lsu.edu. *Application contact:* Dr. Clinton Willson, Professor, 225-578-8652, E-mail: cwillson@lsu.edu.

Marquette University, Graduate School, College of Engineering, Department of Civil and Environmental Engineering, Milwaukee, WI 53201-1881. Offers construction and public works management (MS, PhD); construction engineering and management (Certificate); environmental/water resources engineering (MS, PhD); structural design (Certificate); structural/geotechnical engineering (MS, PhD); transportation planning and engineering (MS, PhD); waste and wastewater treatment processes (Certificate). Part-time and evening/weekend programs available. *Faculty:* 13 full-time (0 women), 3 part-time/adjunct (0 women). *Students:* 20 full-time (4 women), 12 part-time (1 woman); includes 1 minority (Black or African American, non-Hispanic/Latino), 12 international. Average age 27. 66 applicants, 64% accepted, 9 enrolled. In 2010, 8 master's, 1 doctorate awarded. Terminal master's awarded for partial completion of doctoral program. *Degree requirements:* For master's, comprehensive exam, thesis or alternative; for doctorate, thesis/dissertation. *Entrance requirements:* For master's, GRE General Test (recommended), minimum GPA of 3.0, official transcripts from all current and previous colleges/universities except Marquette, three letters of recommendation; for doctorate, GRE General Test, minimum GPA of 3.0, official transcripts from all current and previous colleges/universities except Marquette, three letters of recommendation, brief statement of purpose, submission of any English-language publications authored by applicant (strongly recommended). Additional exam requirements/recommendations for international students: Required—TOEFL (minimum score 530 paper-based; 78 computer-based). *Application deadline:* For fall admission, 6/1 priority date for domestic students. Applications are processed on a rolling basis. Application fee: $50. Electronic applications accepted. *Expenses:* Tuition: Full-time $16,290; part-time $905 per credit hour. Tuition and fees vary according to program. *Financial support:* In 2010–11, 13 students received support, including 4 fellowships with tuition reimbursements available, 4 research assistantships with tuition reimbursements available, 10 teaching assistantships with tuition reimbursements available; Federal Work-Study, institutionally sponsored loans, scholarships/grants, and tuition waivers (full and partial) also available. Support available to part-time students. Financial award application deadline: 2/15. *Faculty research:* Highway safety, highway performance, and intelligent transportation systems; surface mount technology; watershed management. Total annual research expenditures: $662,392. *Unit head:* Dr. Thomas Wenzel, Chair, 414-288-7030, Fax: 414-288-7521, E-mail: thomas.wenzel@marquette.edu. *Application contact:* Dr. Stephen M. Heinrich, Director of Graduate Studies, 414-288-5466, E-mail: stephen.heinrich@marquette.edu.

Massachusetts Institute of Technology, School of Engineering, Department of Civil and Environmental Engineering, Cambridge, MA 02139. Offers biological oceanography (PhD, Sc D); chemical oceanography (PhD, Sc D); civil and environmental engineering (M Eng, SM, PhD, Sc D); civil and environmental systems (PhD, Sc D); civil engineering (PhD, Sc D, CE); coastal engineering (PhD, Sc D); construction engineering and management (PhD, Sc D); environmental biology (PhD, Sc D); environmental chemistry (PhD, Sc D); environmental engineering (PhD, Sc D); environmental fluid mechanics (PhD, Sc D); geotechnical and geoenvironmental engineering (PhD, Sc D); hydrology (PhD, Sc D); information technology (PhD, Sc D); oceanographic engineering (PhD, Sc D); structures and materials (PhD, Sc D); transportation (PhD, Sc D); SM/MBA. *Faculty:* 36 full-time (6 women). *Students:* 181 full-time (56 women); includes 27 minority (3 Black or African American, non-Hispanic/Latino; 10 Asian, non-Hispanic/Latino; 10 Hispanic/Latino; 4 Two or more races, non-Hispanic/Latino), 93 international. Average age 26. 525 applicants, 29% accepted, 74 enrolled. In 2010, 85 master's, 18 doctorates, 2 other advanced degrees awarded. *Degree requirements:* For master's and CE, thesis; for doctorate, comprehensive exam, thesis/dissertation. *Entrance requirements:* For master's and doctorate, GRE General Test. Additional exam requirements/recommendations for international students: Required—TOEFL (minimum score 577 paper-based; 233 computer-based; 90 iBT), IELTS (minimum score 7). *Application deadline:* For fall admission, 1/2 for domestic and international students. Application fee: $75. Electronic applications accepted. *Expenses:* Tuition: Full-time $38,940; part-time $605 per unit. Required fees: $272. *Financial support:* In 2010–11, 146 students received support, including 50 fellowships with tuition reimbursements available (averaging $21,808 per year), 90 research assistantships with tuition reimbursements available (averaging $28,452 per year), 20 teaching assistantships with tuition reimbursements available (averaging $27,842 per year); career-related internships or fieldwork, Federal Work-Study, institutionally sponsored loans, scholarships/grants, health care benefits, and unspecified assistantships also available. *Faculty research:* Environmental chemistry; environmental microbiology; environmental fluid mechanics and coastal engineering; geotechnical engineering and geomechanics; hydrology and hydroclimatology; mechanics of materials and structures; operations research/supply chain; transportation. Total annual research expenditures: $19.5 million. *Unit head:* Prof. Andrew Whittle, Department Head, 617-253-7101. *Application contact:* Patricia Glidden, Graduate Admissions Coordinator, 617-253-7119, Fax: 617-258-6775, E-mail: cee-admissions@mit.edu.

Morgan State University, School of Graduate Studies, Clarence M. Mitchell, Jr. School of Engineering, Department of Transportation, Baltimore, MD 21251. Offers MS. Part-time and evening/weekend programs available. *Degree requirements:* For master's, thesis optional, comprehensive exam or equivalent. *Entrance requirements:* For master's, minimum undergraduate GPA of 2.5. Additional exam requirements/recommendations for international students: Required—TOEFL (minimum score 550 paper-based; 213 computer-based). *Faculty research:* Distributional impacts of congestion, pricing education and training for intelligent vehicle highway systems.

New Jersey Institute of Technology, Office of Graduate Studies, Newark College of Engineering, Department of Civil and Environmental Engineering, Newark, NJ 07102. Offers civil engineering (MS, PhD); environmental engineering (MS, PhD); transportation (MS, PhD). Part-time and evening/weekend programs available. *Faculty:* 25 full-time (7 women), 17 part-time/adjunct (1 woman). *Students:* 112 full-time (33 women), 121 part-time (30 women); includes 22 Black or African American, non-Hispanic/Latino; 1 American Indian or Alaska Native, non-Hispanic/Latino; 33 Asian, non-Hispanic/Latino; 28 Hispanic/Latino, 57 international. Average age 30. 344 applicants, 41% accepted, 77 enrolled. In 2010, 54 master's, 6 doctorates awarded. Terminal master's awarded for partial completion of doctoral program. *Degree requirements:* For master's, thesis optional; for doctorate, thesis/dissertation, residency. *Entrance requirements:* For master's, GRE General Test; for doctorate, GRE General Test, minimum graduate GPA of 3.5. Additional exam requirements/recommendations for international students: Required—TOEFL (minimum score 550 paper-based; 213 computer-based; 79 iBT). *Application deadline:* For fall admission, 6/5 priority date for domestic students, 4/1 for international students; for spring admission, 11/15 for domestic and international students. Applications are processed on a rolling basis. Application fee: $65. Electronic applications accepted. *Expenses:* Tuition, state resident: full-time $14,724; part-time $818 per credit. Tuition, nonresident: full-time $20,304; part-time $1128 per credit. Required fees: $2272; $209 per credit. $103 per semester. One-time fee: $312 full-time; $212 part-time. *Financial support:* Fellowships with full and partial tuition reimbursements, research assistantships with full and partial tuition reimbursements, teaching assistantships with full and partial tuition reimbursements, career-related internships or fieldwork, Federal Work-Study, institutionally sponsored loans, and unspecified assistantships available. Financial award application deadline: 3/15. *Faculty research:* Geotechnical engineering, water resources engineering, construction engineering, transportation policy, traffic operations. Total annual research expenditures: $11.5 million. *Unit head:* Dr. Taha F. Marhaba, Chair, 973-642-4599, E-mail: marhaba@njit.edu. *Application contact:* Kathryn Kelly, Director of Admissions, 973-596-3300, Fax: 973-596-3461, E-mail: admissions@njit.edu.

New Jersey Institute of Technology, Office of Graduate Studies, Newark College of Engineering, Interdisciplinary Program in Transportation, Newark, NJ 07102. Offers MS, PhD. Part-time and evening/weekend programs available. *Students:* 24 full-time (4 women), 14 part-time (4 women); includes 4 Black or African American, non-Hispanic/Latino; 8 Asian, non-Hispanic/Latino; 4 Hispanic/Latino, 11 international. Average age 32. 63 applicants, 40% accepted, 13 enrolled. In 2010, 6 master's, 2 doctorates awarded. Terminal master's awarded for partial completion of doctoral program. *Degree requirements:* For master's, thesis or

Transportation and Highway Engineering

New Jersey Institute of Technology *(continued)*
alternative; for doctorate, thesis/dissertation, residency. *Entrance requirements:* For master's, GRE General Test; for doctorate, GRE General Test, minimum graduate GPA of 3.5. Additional exam requirements/recommendations for international students: Required—TOEFL (minimum score 550 paper-based; 213 computer-based; 79 iBT). *Application deadline:* For fall admission, 6/5 priority date for domestic students, 4/1 for international students; for spring admission, 11/15 for domestic and international students. Applications are processed on a rolling basis. Application fee: $65. Electronic applications accepted. *Expenses:* Tuition, state resident: full-time $14,724; part-time $818 per credit. Tuition, nonresident: full-time $20,304; part-time $1128 per credit. Required fees: $2272; $209 per credit. $103 per semester. One-time fee: $312 full-time; $212 part-time. *Financial support:* Fellowships with full and partial tuition reimbursements, research assistantships with full and partial tuition reimbursements, teaching assistantships with full and partial tuition reimbursements, career-related internships or fieldwork, Federal Work-Study, institutionally sponsored loans, and unspecified assistantships available. Financial award application deadline: 3/15. *Faculty research:* Transportation planning, administration, and policy; intelligent vehicle highway systems; bridge maintenance. *Unit head:* Dr. Athanassios Bladikas, Director, 973-596-3653, E-mail: athanassios.bladikas@njit.edu. *Application contact:* Kathryn Kelly, Director of Admissions, 973-596-3300, Fax: 973-596-3461, E-mail: admissions@njit.edu.

Northwestern University, McCormick School of Engineering and Applied Science, Department of Civil and Environmental Engineering, Evanston, IL 60208-3109. Offers environmental engineering and science (MS, PhD); geotechnical engineering (MS, PhD); mechanics of materials and solids (MS, PhD); project management (MS, PhD); structural engineering and materials (MS, PhD); theoretical and applied mechanics (MS, PhD), including fluid mechanics, solid mechanics; transportation systems analysis and planning (MS, PhD). MS and PhD admissions and degrees offered through The Graduate School. Part-time programs available. Terminal master's awarded for partial completion of doctoral program. *Degree requirements:* For master's, thesis (for some programs); for doctorate, thesis/dissertation. *Entrance requirements:* For master's and doctorate, GRE General Test, minimum 2 letters of recommendation, transcripts from all academic institutions attended. Additional exam requirements/recommendations for international students: Required—TOEFL (minimum score 600 paper-based; 250 computer-based; 100 iBT), IELTS (minimum score 7). Electronic applications accepted. *Faculty research:* Environmental engineering and science, geotechnics, mechanics of materials and solids, structural engineering and materials, transportation systems analysis and planning.

Ohio University, Graduate College, Russ College of Engineering and Technology, Department of Civil Engineering, Athens, OH 45701-2979. Offers civil engineering (PhD); construction (MS); environmental (MS); geotechnical and geoenvironmental (MS); mechanics (MS); structures (MS); transportation (MS); water resources and structures (MS). Part-time programs available. *Students:* 29 full-time (6 women), 5 part-time (1 woman); includes 2 minority (1 Hispanic/Latino; 1 Two or more races, non-Hispanic/Latino), 16 international. 52 applicants, 83% accepted, 14 enrolled. In 2010, 7 master's awarded. *Degree requirements:* For master's, comprehensive exam (for some programs), thesis or alternative; for doctorate, comprehensive exam, thesis/dissertation. *Entrance requirements:* For master's, GRE General Test, minimum GPA of 3.0, 3 letters of recommendation; for doctorate, GRE General Test. Additional exam requirements/recommendations for international students: Required—TOEFL (minimum score 550 paper-based; 80 iBT) or IELTS (minimum score 6.5). *Application deadline:* For fall admission, 5/1 priority date for domestic students, 2/1 priority date for international students; for winter admission, 8/1 priority date for domestic students, 4/1 priority date for international students; for spring admission, 2/1 priority date for domestic students, 7/1 priority date for international students. Applications are processed on a rolling basis. Application fee: $50 ($55 for international students). Electronic applications accepted. *Financial support:* Research assistantships with full tuition reimbursements, teaching assistantships with full tuition reimbursements, Federal Work-Study, institutionally sponsored loans, scholarships/grants, and unspecified assistantships available. Financial award application deadline: 3/15; financial award applicants required to submit FAFSA. *Faculty research:* Noise abatement, materials and environment, highway infrastructure, subsurface investigation (pavements, pipes, bridges). *Unit head:* Dr. Gayle F. Mitchell, Chair, 740-593-0430, Fax: 740-593-0625, E-mail: mitchelg@ohio.edu. *Application contact:* Dr. Shad M. Sargand, Graduate Chair, 740-593-1465, Fax: 740-593-0625, E-mail: sargand@ohio.edu.

Oregon State University, Graduate School, College of Engineering, School of Civil and Construction Engineering, Corvallis, OR 97331. Offers civil engineering (MS, PhD); coastal and ocean engineering (M Oc E, PhD); coastal engineering (MS); construction engineering management (MBE, PhD); engineering (M Eng, MAIS); geotechnical engineering (MS, PhD); structural engineering (MS, PhD); transportation engineering (MS, PhD); water engineering (MS, PhD). Part-time programs available. Terminal master's awarded for partial completion of doctoral program. *Degree requirements:* For master's, thesis or alternative; for doctorate, one foreign language, thesis/dissertation. *Entrance requirements:* For master's, GRE General Test, minimum GPA of 3.0 in last 90 hours (3.5 for MS); for doctorate, GRE General Test, minimum GPA of 3.0 in last 90 hours of undergraduate course work. Additional exam requirements/recommendations for international students: Required—TOEFL (minimum score 580 paper-based; 237 computer-based). *Faculty research:* Hazardous waste management, carbon cycling, wave forces on structures, pavement design, seismic analysis.

Polytechnic Institute of NYU, Department of Civil Engineering, Major in Transportation Planning and Engineering, Brooklyn, NY 11201-2990. Offers MS, PhD. Part-time and evening/weekend programs available. *Students:* 17 full-time (7 women), 22 part-time (6 women); includes 3 Black or African American, non-Hispanic/Latino; 7 Asian, non-Hispanic/Latino; 1 Hispanic/Latino, 11 international. Average age 30. 37 applicants, 62% accepted, 18 enrolled. In 2010, 13 master's, 1 doctorate awarded. *Degree requirements:* For master's, comprehensive exam (for some programs), thesis (for some programs); for doctorate, comprehensive exam, thesis/dissertation. *Entrance requirements:* Additional exam requirements/recommendations for international students: Required—TOEFL (minimum score 550 paper-based; 213 computer-based; 80 iBT); Recommended—IELTS (minimum score 6.5). *Application deadline:* For fall admission, 7/31 priority date for domestic students, 4/30 priority date for international students; for spring admission, 12/31 priority date for domestic students, 10/30 priority date for international students. Applications are processed on a rolling basis. Application fee: $75. Electronic applications accepted. *Expenses:* Tuition: Full-time $21,492; part-time $1194 per credit. Required fees: $385 per semester. Tuition and fees vary according to course load. *Financial support:* Fellowships, research assistantships, teaching assistantships, institutionally sponsored loans, scholarships/grants, and unspecified assistantships available. Support available to part-time students. Financial award applicants required to submit FAFSA. *Unit head:* Dr. Lawrence Chiarelli, Head, 718-260-4040, Fax: 718-260-3433, E-mail: lchiarel@poly.edu. *Application contact:* JeanCarlo Bonilla, Director of Graduate Enrollment Management, 718-260-3182, Fax: 718-260-3624, E-mail: gradinfo@gmail.com.

Polytechnic Institute of NYU, Long Island Graduate Center, Graduate Programs, Department of Civil Engineering, Major in Transportation Planning and Engineering, Melville, NY 11747. Offers MS. *Students:* 1 part-time (0 women). Average age 25. 1 applicant, 100% accepted, 1 enrolled. *Degree requirements:* For master's, comprehensive exam (for some programs), thesis (for some programs). *Entrance requirements:* Additional exam requirements/recommendations for international students: Required—TOEFL (minimum score 550 paper-based; 213 computer-based; 80 iBT); Recommended—IELTS (minimum score 6.5). *Application deadline:* For fall admission, 7/31 priority date for domestic students, 4/30 priority date for international students; for spring admission, 12/31 priority date for domestic students, 11/30 priority date for international students. Applications are processed on a rolling basis. Application fee: $75. Electronic applications accepted. *Expenses:* Tuition: Full-time $21,492; part-time $1194 per credit. Required fees: $385 per semester. Tuition and fees vary according to course load. *Financial support:* Institutionally sponsored loans, scholarships/grants, and unspecified

assistantships available. Support available to part-time students. Financial award applicants required to submit FAFSA. *Unit head:* Dr. Roger Peter Roess, Department Head, 718-260-3018, E-mail: rroess@poly.edu. *Application contact:* JeanCarlo Bonilla, Director of Graduate Enrollment Management, 718-260-3182, Fax: 718-260-3624, E-mail: gradinfo@poly.edu.

Rensselaer Polytechnic Institute, Graduate School, School of Engineering, Program in Civil Engineering, Troy, NY 12180-3590. Offers geotechnical engineering (M Eng, MS, PhD); mechanics of composite materials and structures (M Eng, MS, PhD); structural engineering (M Eng, MS, PhD); transportation engineering (M Eng, MS, PhD). Part-time programs available. *Faculty:* 13 full-time (1 woman), 3 part-time/adjunct (0 women). *Students:* 20 full-time (4 women); includes 1 Black or African American, non-Hispanic/Latino, 16 international. Average age 24. 65 applicants, 12% accepted, 5 enrolled. In 2010, 19 master's, 3 doctorates awarded. Terminal master's awarded for partial completion of doctoral program. *Degree requirements:* For master's, thesis (for some programs); for doctorate, thesis/dissertation. *Entrance requirements:* For master's and doctorate, GRE. Additional exam requirements/recommendations for international students: Required—TOEFL (minimum score 570 paper-based; 230 computer-based; 89 iBT), IELTS (minimum score 6.5). *Application deadline:* For fall admission, 1/15 priority date for domestic and international students; for spring admission, 8/15 priority date for domestic and international students. Applications are processed on a rolling basis. Application fee: $75. Electronic applications accepted. *Expenses:* Tuition: Full-time $39,600; part-time $1650 per credit. Required fees: $1896. *Financial support:* In 2010–11, 1 fellowship with full tuition reimbursement (averaging $16,500 per year), 3 research assistantships with full tuition reimbursements (averaging $16,500 per year), 4 teaching assistantships with full tuition reimbursements (averaging $16,500 per year) were awarded; career-related internships or fieldwork and institutionally sponsored loans also available. Financial award application deadline: 2/1. *Faculty research:* Computational mechanics, earthquake engineering, geo-environmental engineering. Total annual research expenditures: $2.7 million. *Unit head:* Dr. Chris Letchford, Head, 518-276-6362, Fax: 518-276-4833, E-mail: letchc@rpi.edu. *Application contact:* Kimberly Boyce, Administrative Assistant, 518-276-6941, Fax: 518-276-4833, E-mail: boycek@rpi.edu.

Rensselaer Polytechnic Institute, Graduate School, School of Engineering, Program in Transportation Engineering, Troy, NY 12180-3590. Offers M Eng, MS, PhD. Part-time programs available. *Faculty:* 3 full-time (0 women). *Students:* 7 full-time (1 woman), 6 international. Average age 25. 37 applicants, 5% accepted, 2 enrolled. In 2010, 4 master's awarded. Terminal master's awarded for partial completion of doctoral program. *Degree requirements:* For master's, thesis (for some programs); for doctorate, thesis/dissertation. *Entrance requirements:* For master's and doctorate, GRE. Additional exam requirements/recommendations for international students: Required—TOEFL (minimum score 570 paper-based; 230 computer-based; 89 iBT), IELTS (minimum score 6.5). *Application deadline:* For fall admission, 1/15 priority date for domestic and international students; for spring admission, 8/15 priority date for domestic and international students. Applications are processed on a rolling basis. Application fee: $75. Electronic applications accepted. *Expenses:* Tuition: Full-time $39,600; part-time $1650 per credit. Required fees: $1896. *Financial support:* In 2010–11, 1 fellowship with full tuition reimbursement (averaging $16,500 per year), 4 research assistantships with full tuition reimbursements (averaging $16,500 per year), 2 teaching assistantships (averaging $16,500 per year) were awarded; institutionally sponsored loans and unspecified assistantships also available. Financial award application deadline: 2/1. *Faculty research:* Intelligent transportation systems, routing algorithms, dynamic network management, user behavior. Total annual research expenditures: $919,337. *Unit head:* Dr. Chris Letchford, Head, 518-276-6362, Fax: 518-276-4833, E-mail: letchc@rpi.edu. *Application contact:* Kimberly Boyce, Assistant II, 518-276-6941, Fax: 518-276-4833, E-mail: boycek@rpi.edu.

South Carolina State University, School of Graduate Studies, Department of Civil and Mechanical Engineering Technology and Nuclear Engineering, Orangeburg, SC 29117-0001. Offers transportation (MS). Part-time and evening/weekend programs available. *Degree requirements:* For master's, comprehensive exam, thesis, departmental qualifying exam. *Entrance requirements:* For master's, GRE. Electronic applications accepted. *Faculty research:* Societal competence, relationship of parent-child interaction to adult, rehabilitation evaluation, vocation, language assessment of rural children.

Texas A&M University, College of Engineering, Zachry Department of Civil Engineering, College Station, TX 77843. Offers coastal and ocean engineering (M Eng, MS, D Eng, PhD); construction engineering and management (M Eng, MS, D Eng, PhD); environmental engineering (M Eng, MS, D Eng, PhD); geotechnical engineering (M Eng, MS, D Eng, PhD); materials engineering (M Eng, MS, D Eng, PhD); structural engineering (M Eng, MS, D Eng, PhD); transportation engineering (M Eng, MS, D Eng, PhD); water resources engineering (M Eng, MS, D Eng, PhD). Part-time programs available. *Faculty:* 57. *Students:* 384 full-time (81 women), 35 part-time (7 women); includes 35 minority (3 Black or African American, non-Hispanic/Latino; 1 American Indian or Alaska Native, non-Hispanic/Latino; 14 Asian, non-Hispanic/Latino; 17 Hispanic/Latino), 263 international. Average age 29. In 2010, 136 master's, 26 doctorates awarded. *Degree requirements:* For master's, thesis (MS); for doctorate, dissertation (PhD), internship (D Eng). *Entrance requirements:* For master's and doctorate, GRE General Test. Additional exam requirements/recommendations for international students: Required—TOEFL. *Application deadline:* Applications are processed on a rolling basis. Application fee: $50 ($75 for international students). Electronic applications accepted. *Financial support:* In 2010–11, fellowships (averaging $4,500 per year), research assistantships (averaging $14,000 per year), teaching assistantships (averaging $14,400 per year) were awarded; career-related internships or fieldwork and institutionally sponsored loans also available. Financial award application deadline: 4/15; financial award applicants required to submit FAFSA. *Unit head:* Dr. Tony Cahill, Head, 979-845-3858, E-mail: tcahill@civil.tamu.edu. *Application contact:* Graduate Advisor, 979-845-7435, Fax: 979-845-6156, E-mail: info@civil.tamu.edu.

Texas Southern University, School of Science and Technology, Program in Transportation, Planning and Management, Houston, TX 77004-4584. Offers MS. Part-time and evening/weekend programs available. *Faculty:* 4 full-time (2 women). *Students:* 36 full-time (15 women), 17 part-time (9 women); includes 24 Black or African American, non-Hispanic/Latino; 24 Asian, non-Hispanic/Latino; 2 Hispanic/Latino, 1 international. Average age 31. 17 applicants, 88% accepted, 11 enrolled. In 2010, 9 master's awarded. *Degree requirements:* For master's, comprehensive exam, thesis optional. *Entrance requirements:* For master's, GRE General Test, minimum GPA of 2.5. Additional exam requirements/recommendations for international students: Required—TOEFL. *Application deadline:* For fall admission, 7/1 for domestic and international students; for spring admission, 11/1 for domestic and international students. Applications are processed on a rolling basis. Application fee: $50 ($75 for international students). Electronic applications accepted. *Expenses:* Tuition, state resident: full-time $1875; part-time $100 per credit hour. Tuition, nonresident: full-time $6641; part-time $343 per credit hour. Tuition and fees vary according to course level, course load and degree level. *Financial support:* In 2010–11, 21 research assistantships (averaging $5,677 per year), 6 teaching assistantships (averaging $4,449 per year) were awarded; fellowships with partial tuition reimbursements, career-related internships or fieldwork, scholarships/grants, and unspecified assistantships also available. Financial award application deadline: 5/1. *Faculty research:* Highway traffic operations, transportation and policy planning, air quality in transportation, transportation modeling. Total annual research expenditures: $500,000. *Unit head:* Dr. Yi Qi, Interim Chair, 713-313-6809, E-mail: qiy@tsu.edu. *Application contact:* Paula Eakins, Administrative Assistant, 713-313-1841, E-mail: eakins_pl@tsu.edu.

The University of Alabama in Huntsville, School of Graduate Studies, College of Engineering, Department of Civil and Environmental Engineering, Huntsville, AL 35899. Offers civil and environmental engineering (PhD); civil engineering (MSE), including environmental and water resource engineering, geotechnical engineering, structural engineering and structural mechanics, transportation engineering. PhD offered jointly with The University of Alabama at Birmingham. Part-time and evening/weekend programs available. *Faculty:* 6 full-time (1 woman), 1 part-time/adjunct (0 women). *Students:* 23 full-time (7 women), 11 part-time (4 women); includes 3 minority (2 Black or African American, non-Hispanic/Latino; 1 Asian, non-Hispanic/Latino), 12 international. Average age 30. 37 applicants, 57% accepted, 15 enrolled. In 2010, 1 master's, 3 doctorates awarded. *Degree requirements:* For master's, comprehensive exam, thesis or alternative, oral and written exams; for doctorate, comprehensive exam, thesis/dissertation, oral and written exams. *Entrance requirements:* For master's, GRE General Test, BSE, minimum GPA of 3.0; for doctorate, GRE General Test, minimum GPA of 3.0. Additional exam requirements/recommendations for international students: Required—TOEFL (minimum score 500 paper-based; 173 computer-based; 62 iBT). *Application deadline:* For fall admission, 7/15 for domestic students, 4/1 for international students; for spring admission, 11/30 for domestic students, 9/1 for international students. Applications are processed on a rolling basis. Application fee: $40 ($50 for international students). Electronic applications accepted. *Expenses:* Tuition, state resident: full-time $7250; part-time $407.75 per credit hour. Tuition, nonresident: full-time $17,358; part-time $970.05 per credit hour. Required fees: $246.80 per semester. Tuition and fees vary according to course load and program. *Financial support:* In 2010–11, 14 students received support, including 7 research assistantships with full and partial tuition reimbursements available (averaging $12,435 per year), 7 teaching assistantships with full and partial tuition reimbursements available (averaging $10,281 per year); career-related internships or fieldwork, Federal Work-Study, institutionally sponsored loans, scholarships/grants, health care benefits, and unspecified assistantships also available. Support available to part-time students. Financial award application deadline: 4/1; financial award applicants required to submit FAFSA. *Faculty research:* Hydrologic modeling, orbital debris impact, hydrogeology, environmental engineering, transportation engineering. Total annual research expenditures: $1.9 million. *Unit head:* Dr. Houssam Toutanji, Chair, 256-824-7361, Fax: 256-824-6724, E-mail: toutanji@cee.uah.edu. *Application contact:* Kathy Biggs, Graduate Studies Admissions Manager, 256-824-6199, Fax: 256-824-6405, E-mail: deangrad@uah.edu.

University of Arkansas, Graduate School, College of Engineering, Department of Civil Engineering, Program in Transportation Engineering, Fayetteville, AR 72701-1201. Offers MSE, MSTE. *Students:* 2 full-time (1 woman); includes both Black or African American, non-Hispanic/Latino. *Degree requirements:* For master's, thesis optional. Application fee: $40 ($50 for international students). *Financial support:* Fellowships, research assistantships, teaching assistantships available. Financial award application deadline: 4/1. *Unit head:* Dr. Kevin Hall, Departmental Chair, 479-575-4954, Fax: 479-575-7168, E-mail: kdhall@uark.edu. *Application contact:* Dr. Kelvin Wang, Graduate Coordinator, 479-575-4954, Fax: 479-575-7168, E-mail: kcw@uark.edu.

University of California, Berkeley, Graduate Division, College of Engineering, Department of Civil and Environmental Engineering, Berkeley, CA 94720-1500. Offers engineering and project management (M Eng, MS, D Eng, PhD); environmental engineering (M Eng, MS, D Eng, PhD); geoengineering (M Eng, MS, D Eng, PhD); structural engineering, mechanics and materials (M Eng, MS, D Eng, PhD); transportation engineering (M Eng, MS, D Eng, PhD); M Arch/MS; MCP/MS; MPP/MS. *Degree requirements:* For master's, comprehensive exam or thesis (MS); for doctorate, thesis/dissertation, qualifying exam. *Entrance requirements:* For master's, GRE General Test, minimum GPA of 3.0, 3 letters of recommendation; for doctorate, GRE General Test, minimum GPA of 3.5, 3 letters of recommendation. Additional exam requirements/recommendations for international students: Required—TOEFL (minimum score 570 paper-based; 230 computer-based). Electronic applications accepted.

University of California, Davis, College of Engineering, Graduate Group in Transportation Technology and Policy, Davis, CA 95616. Offers MS, PhD. Terminal master's awarded for partial completion of doctoral program. *Degree requirements:* For master's, comprehensive exam (for some programs), thesis (for some programs); for doctorate, thesis/dissertation. *Entrance requirements:* For master's, GRE General Test, minimum GPA of 3.0; for doctorate, GRE General Test, minimum GPA of 3.5. Additional exam requirements/recommendations for international students: Required—TOEFL (minimum score 550 paper-based; 213 computer-based). Electronic applications accepted.

University of California, Irvine, School of Social Sciences, Program in Transportation Science, Irvine, CA 92697. Offers MA, PhD. *Students:* 12 full-time (6 women); includes 1 minority (Hispanic/Latino), 8 international. Average age 28. 15 applicants, 40% accepted, 3 enrolled. *Entrance requirements:* For master's and doctorate, GRE General Test, minimum GPA of 3.0. *Application deadline:* For fall admission, 1/15 for domestic and international students. Application fee: $80 ($100 for international students). *Financial support:* Fellowships, research assistantships with full tuition reimbursements, teaching assistantships, institutionally sponsored loans, traineeships, health care benefits, and unspecified assistantships available. Financial award application deadline: 3/1. *Unit head:* Dr. Jean-Daniel Saphores, Director, 949-824-7334, Fax: 949-824-8385, E-mail: saphores@uci.edu. *Application contact:* Anne Marie Defeo, Administrative Manager, 949-824-6564, Fax: 949-824-8385, E-mail: amdefeo@uci.edu.

University of Central Florida, College of Engineering and Computer Science, Department of Civil, Environmental, and Construction Engineering, Program in Civil Engineering, Orlando, FL 32816. Offers civil engineering (MS, MSCE, PhD); construction engineering (Certificate); structural engineering (Certificate); transportation engineering (Certificate). Part-time and evening/weekend programs available. *Students:* 62 full-time (7 women), 77 part-time (15 women); includes 30 minority (4 Black or African American, non-Hispanic/Latino; 7 Asian, non-Hispanic/Latino; 17 Hispanic/Latino; 2 Two or more races, non-Hispanic/Latino), 35 international. Average age 30. 125 applicants, 73% accepted, 46 enrolled. In 2010, 26 master's, 8 doctorates awarded. *Degree requirements:* For master's, thesis or alternative; for doctorate, thesis/dissertation, departmental qualifying exam, candidacy exam. *Entrance requirements:* For master's, GRE General Test, minimum GPA of 3.0 in last 60 hours; for doctorate, GRE General Test, minimum GPA of 3.5 in last 60 hours. Additional exam requirements/recommendations for international students: Required—TOEFL. *Application deadline:* For fall admission, 7/15 priority date for domestic students; for spring admission, 12/15 priority date for domestic students. Application fee: $30. Electronic applications accepted. *Expenses:* Tuition, state resident: part-time $256.56 per credit hour. Tuition, nonresident: part-time $1011.52 per credit hour. Part-time tuition and fees vary according to program. *Financial support:* In 2010–11, 29 students received support, including 1 fellowship with partial tuition reimbursement available (averaging $10,000 per year), 22 research assistantships with partial tuition reimbursements available (averaging $11,000 per year), 18 teaching assistantships with partial tuition reimbursements available (averaging $7,900 per year); career-related internships or fieldwork, Federal Work-Study, institutionally sponsored loans, tuition waivers (partial), and unspecified assistantships also available. Financial award application deadline: 3/1; financial award applicants required to submit FAFSA.

University of Colorado Denver, College of Engineering and Applied Science, Department of Civil Engineering, Denver, CO 80217-3364. Offers civil engineering (PhD); environmental and sustainability engineering (MS); geographic information systems (MS); geotechnical engineering (MS); hydrology and hydraulics (MS); structural engineering (MS); transportation engineering (MS). Part-time and evening/weekend programs available. *Faculty:* 14 full-time (1 woman), 6 part-time/adjunct (0 women). *Students:* 66 full-time (13 women), 72 part-time (16 women); includes 9 Black or African American, non-Hispanic/Latino; 8 Asian, non-Hispanic/Latino; 11 Hispanic/Latino, 15 international. Average age 32. 72 applicants, 54% accepted, 29 enrolled. In 2010, 14 master's, 3 doctorates awarded. *Degree requirements:* For master's, comprehensive exam, thesis or alternative; for doctorate, comprehensive exam, thesis/dissertation. *Entrance requirements:* For master's, GRE, statement of purpose, transcripts, references; for doctorate, GRE, statement of purpose, transcripts, references, letter of support from faculty stating willingness to serve as dissertation advisor and outlining plan for financial support. Additional exam requirements/recommendations for international students: Required—TOEFL (minimum score 525 paper-based; 197 computer-based). *Application deadline:* For fall admission, 7/15 for domestic students, 6/15 for international students; for spring admission, 12/1 for domestic students, 11/1 for international students. Applications are processed on a rolling basis. Application fee: $50 ($75 for international students). Electronic applications accepted. *Expenses:* Contact institution. *Financial support:* Research assistantships, teaching assistantships, career-related internships or fieldwork and Federal Work-Study available. Financial award application deadline: 4/1; financial award applicants required to submit FAFSA. *Faculty research:* Environmental engineering and sustainable systems, geosynthetics, hydrologic andhydraulic engineering, structural engineering, transportation, transportation energy use and greenhouse gas emissions. *Unit head:* Dr. Nien-Yin Chang, Acting Chair, 303-556-2810, Fax: 303-556-2368, E-mail: nien.chang@ucdenver.edu. *Application contact:* Mindy Gewuerz, Program Assistant, 303-556-6712, Fax: 303-556-2368, E-mail: mindy.gewuerz@ucdenver.edu.

University of Dayton, Graduate School, School of Engineering, Department of Civil and Environmental Engineering and Engineering Mechanics, Dayton, OH 45469-1300. Offers engineering mechanics (MSEM); environmental engineering (MSCE); geotechnical engineering (MSCE); structural engineering (MSCE); transportation engineering (MSCE); water resources engineering (MSCE). Part-time programs available. *Faculty:* 7 full-time (2 women), 2 part-time/adjunct (0 women). *Students:* 10 full-time (5 women), 7 part-time (2 women); includes 2 minority (both Black or African American, non-Hispanic/Latino), 6 international. Average age 27. 23 applicants, 43% accepted, 4 enrolled. In 2010, 5 master's awarded. *Degree requirements:* For master's, thesis optional. *Entrance requirements:* For master's, minimum GPA of 3.0 in undergraduate work. Additional exam requirements/recommendations for international students: Required—TOEFL (minimum score 550 paper-based; 213 computer-based; 80 iBT). *Application deadline:* For fall admission, 8/1 for domestic students, 3/1 priority date for international students; for winter admission, 7/1 priority date for international students; for spring admission, 1/1 priority date for international students. Applications are processed on a rolling basis. Application fee: $0 ($50 for international students). Electronic applications accepted. *Expenses:* Tuition: Full-time $7800; part-time $650 per credit hour. *Financial support:* In 2010–11, 2 research assistantships (averaging $10,600 per year) were awarded. Financial award applicants required to submit FAFSA. *Faculty research:* Physical modeling of hydraulic systems, finite element methods, mechanics of composite materials, transportation systems safety, biological treatment processes. Total annual research expenditures: $200,000. *Unit head:* Dr. Donald V. Chase, Chair, 937-229-3847, Fax: 937-229-3491, E-mail: donald.chase@notes.udayton.edu. *Application contact:* Alexander Popovski, Associate Director of International and Graduate Admissions, 937-229-2357, Fax: 937-229-4729, E-mail: alex.popovski@notes.udayton.edu.

University of Delaware, College of Engineering, Department of Civil and Environmental Engineering, Newark, DE 19716. Offers environmental engineering (MAS, MCE, PhD); geotechnical engineering (MAS, MCE, PhD); ocean engineering (MAS, MCE, PhD); structural engineering (MAS, MCE, PhD); transportation engineering (MAS, MCE, PhD); water resource engineering (MAS, MCE, PhD). Part-time programs available. Terminal master's awarded for partial completion of doctoral program. *Degree requirements:* For master's, thesis; for doctorate, thesis/dissertation. *Entrance requirements:* For master's and doctorate, GRE General Test. Additional exam requirements/recommendations for international students: Required—TOEFL. Electronic applications accepted. *Faculty research:* Structural engineering and mechanics; transportation engineering; ocean engineering; soil mechanics and foundation; water resources and environmental engineering.

University of Memphis, Graduate School, Herff College of Engineering, Department of Civil Engineering, Memphis, TN 38152. Offers civil engineering (PhD); environmental engineering (MS); foundation engineering (MS); structural engineering (MS); transportation engineering (MS); water resources engineering (MS). *Faculty:* 12 full-time (1 woman), 1 part-time/adjunct (0 women). *Students:* 12 full-time (5 women), 13 part-time (3 women); includes 2 Black or African American, non-Hispanic/Latino; 2 Asian, non-Hispanic/Latino; 1 Two or more races, non-Hispanic/Latino, 7 international. Average age 28. 22 applicants, 55% accepted, 0 enrolled. In 2010, 11 master's awarded. Terminal master's awarded for partial completion of doctoral program. *Degree requirements:* For master's, comprehensive exam, thesis optional; for doctorate, comprehensive exam, thesis/dissertation. *Entrance requirements:* For master's, GRE General Test or MAT, minimum undergraduate GPA of 2.5; for doctorate, GRE, 3 letters of recommendation. Additional exam requirements/recommendations for international students: Required—TOEFL (minimum score 550 paper-based; 210 computer-based; 79 iBT). *Application deadline:* For fall admission, 1/7 for domestic students, 1/5 for international students; for spring admission, 12/1 for domestic students, 9/15 for international students. Application fee: $35 ($60 for international students). *Financial support:* In 2010–11, 6 students received support; fellowships with full tuition reimbursements available, research assistantships with full tuition reimbursements available, career-related internships or fieldwork, Federal Work-Study, scholarships/grants, and unspecified assistantships available. Financial award application deadline: 2/15; financial award applicants required to submit FAFSA. *Faculty research:* Structural response to earthquakes, pavement design, water quality, transportation safety, intermodal transportation. *Unit head:* Dr. Sharam Pezeshk, Interim Chair, 901-678-2746, Fax: 901-678-3026. *Application contact:* Dr. Roger Meier, Coordinator of Graduate Studies, 901-678-3284.

University of Missouri, Graduate School, College of Engineering, Department of Civil and Environmental Engineering, Columbia, MO 65211. Offers civil engineering (MS, PhD); environmental engineering (MS, PhD); geotechnical engineering (MS, PhD); structural engineering (MS, PhD); transportation and highway engineering (MS); water resources (MS, PhD). *Degree requirements:* For master's, report or thesis; for doctorate, thesis/dissertation. *Entrance requirements:* For master's and doctorate, GRE General Test. Additional exam requirements/recommendations for international students: Required—TOEFL (minimum score 550 paper-based; 213 computer-based; 79 iBT).

University of Nevada, Las Vegas, Graduate College, Howard R. Hughes College of Engineering, Department of Civil and Environmental Engineering, Las Vegas, NV 89154-4015. Offers civil and environmental engineering (PhD); transportation (MS). Part-time programs available. *Faculty:* 16 full-time (3 women), 4 part-time/adjunct (0 women). *Students:* 35 full-time (5 women), 20 part-time (7 women); includes 19 minority (1 Black or African American, non-Hispanic/Latino; 2 Asian, non-Hispanic/Latino; 5 Hispanic/Latino; 11 Two or more races, non-Hispanic/Latino), 19 international. Average age 32. 34 applicants, 82% accepted, 15 enrolled. In 2010, 17 master's, 8 doctorates awarded. *Degree requirements:* For master's, comprehensive exam (for some programs), thesis (for some programs); for doctorate, comprehensive exam, thesis/dissertation. *Entrance requirements:* For master's and doctorate, GRE General Test. Additional exam requirements/recommendations for international students: Required—TOEFL (minimum score 550 paper-based; 213 computer-based; 80 iBT), IELTS (minimum score 7). *Application deadline:* For fall admission, 6/15 priority date for domestic students, 3/15 priority date for international students; for spring admission, 11/15 priority date for domestic students, 8/30 priority date for international students. Applications are processed on a rolling basis. Application fee: $60 ($95 for international students). Electronic applications accepted. *Expenses:* Tuition, area resident: Part-time $239.50 per credit. Tuition, state resident: part-time $239.50 per credit. Tuition, nonresident: part-time $503 per credit. Required fees: $108 per semester. Tuition and fees vary according to course load, program and reciprocity agreements. *Financial support:* In 2010–11, 38 students received support, including 23 research assistantships with partial tuition reimbursements available (averaging $13,595 per year), 15 teaching assistantships with partial tuition reimbursements available (averaging $11,200 per year); institutionally sponsored loans, scholarships/grants, health care benefits, and unspecified assistantships also available. Financial award application deadline: 3/1. Total annual research expenditures: $1.4 million. *Unit head:* Dr. David Ashley, Professor, 702-895-4040, Fax: 702-895-3936, E-mail: david.b.ashley@unlv.edu. *Application contact:* Graduate College Admissions Evaluator, 702-895-3320, Fax: 702-895-4180, E-mail: gradcollege@unlv.edu.

University of New Brunswick Fredericton, School of Graduate Studies, Faculty of Engineering, Department of Civil Engineering, Fredericton, NB E3B 5A3, Canada. Offers construction engineering and management (M Eng, M Sc E, PhD); environmental engineering (M Eng, M Sc E, PhD); environmental studies (M Eng); geotechnical engineering (M Eng, M Sc E, PhD); groundwater/hydrology (M Eng, M Sc E, PhD); materials (M Eng, M Sc E, PhD); pavements (M Eng, M Sc E, PhD); structures (M Eng, M Sc E, PhD); transportation (M Eng, M Sc E, PhD). Part-time programs available. *Faculty:* 13 full-time (1 woman), 7 part-time/adjunct (1 woman). *Students:* 34 full-time (8 women), 16 part-time (2 women). In 2010, 16 master's, 6 doctorates awarded. *Degree requirements:* For master's, thesis, proposal; for doctorate,

Transportation and Highway Engineering

University of New Brunswick Fredericton (continued)
comprehensive exam, thesis/dissertation, qualifying exam; proposal; 27 credit hours of courses. *Entrance requirements:* For master's, minimum GPA of 3.0; B Sc E in civil engineering or related engineering degree; for doctorate, minimum GPA of 3.0; graduate degree in engineering or applied science. Additional exam requirements/recommendations for international students: Required—TWE (minimum score 4), TOEFL (minimum score 580 paper-based; 237 computer-based) or IELTS (minimum score 7.5). *Application deadline:* For fall admission, 5/1 priority date for domestic students; for winter admission, 11/1 priority date for domestic students. Applications are processed on a rolling basis. Application fee: $50 Canadian dollars. *Expenses:* Tuition, area resident: Full-time $3708; part-time $927 per term. International tuition: $6300 full-time. Required fees: $50 per term. *Financial support:* In 2010–11, 52 research assistantships (averaging $7,000 per year), 46 teaching assistantships (averaging $2,000 per year) were awarded; career-related internships or fieldwork and scholarships/grants also available. *Faculty research:* Construction engineering and management; materials and infrastructure renewal; highway and pavement research; structures and solid mechanics; geotechnical, soil; structure interaction; transportation and planning; environment, solid waste management. *Unit head:* Dr. Eric Hildebrand, Director of Graduate Studies, 506-453-5113, Fax: 506-453-3568, E-mail: edh@unb.ca. *Application contact:* Joyce Moore, Graduate Secretary, 506-452-6127, Fax: 506-453-3568, E-mail: civil-grad@unb.ca.

University of Southern California, Graduate School, School of Policy, Planning, and Development, Master of Planning Program, Los Angeles, CA 90089. Offers sustainable cities (Graduate Certificate); transportation systems (Graduate Certificate); urban planning (M Pl); M Arch/M Pl; M Pl/MA; M Pl/MS; M Pl/MSW; MBA/M Pl; ML Arch/M Pl; MPA/M Pl. *Accreditation:* ACSP. Part-time programs available. *Faculty:* 51 full-time (12 women), 100 part-time/adjunct (30 women). *Students:* 114 full-time (63 women), 8 part-time (4 women); includes 45 minority (3 Black or African American, non-Hispanic/Latino; 23 Asian, non-Hispanic/Latino; 14 Hispanic/Latino; 5 Two or more races, non-Hispanic/Latino), 15 international. 259 applicants, 71% accepted, 74 enrolled. In 2010, 40 master's awarded. *Degree requirements:* For master's, comprehensive exam, internship. *Entrance requirements:* For master's, GRE, GMAT. Additional exam requirements/recommendations for international students: Required—TOEFL (minimum score 600 paper-based; 250 computer-based; 100 iBT). *Application deadline:* For fall admission, 12/15 priority date for domestic and international students; for spring admission, 11/1 for domestic students, 10/1 for international students. Applications are processed on a rolling basis. Application fee: $85. Electronic applications accepted. *Expenses:* Tuition: Full-time $31,240; part-time $1420 per unit. Required fees: $600. One-time fee: $35 full-time. Full-time tuition and fees vary according to degree level and program. *Financial support:* In 2010–11, 87 students received support, including 2 research assistantships with full tuition reimbursements available (averaging $9,806 per year); scholarships/grants and tuition waivers (full and partial) also available. Financial award application deadline: 12/15; financial award applicants required to submit CSS PROFILE or FAFSA. *Faculty research:* Transportation and infrastructure, comparative international development, healthy communities, socal economic development, sustainable community planning. Total annual research expenditures: $6.2 million. *Unit head:* Dr. Tridib Banerjee, Director, Graduate Programs in Urban Planning, 213-740-4724, Fax: 213-740-5379, E-mail: tbanerje@usc.edu. *Application contact:* Marisol R. Gonzalez, Director of Recruitment and Admission, 213-740-0550, Fax: 213-740-7573, E-mail: marisolr@usc.edu.

University of Southern California, Graduate School, Viterbi School of Engineering, Daniel J. Epstein Department of Industrial and Systems Engineering, Los Angeles, CA 90089. Offers digital supply chain management (MS); engineering management (MS); engineering technology communication (Graduate Certificate); health systems operations (Graduate Certificate); industrial and systems engineering (MS, PhD, Engr); manufacturing engineering (MS); operations research engineering (MS); optimization and supply chain management (Graduate Certificate); product development engineering (MS); safety systems and security (MS); systems architecting and engineering (MS, Graduate Certificate); systems safety and security (Graduate Certificate); transportation systems (Graduate Certificate); MS/MBA. Part-time and evening/weekend programs available. Postbaccalaureate distance learning degree programs offered (no on-campus study). *Faculty:* 12 full-time (2 women), 21 part-time/adjunct (2 women). *Students:* 224 full-time (69 women), 143 part-time (32 women); includes 63 minority (6 Black or African American, non-Hispanic/Latino; 35 Asian, non-Hispanic/Latino; 17 Hispanic/Latino; 5 Two or more races, non-Hispanic/Latino), 253 international. 669 applicants, 45% accepted, 155 enrolled. In 2010, 98 master's, 7 doctorates awarded. Terminal master's awarded for partial completion of doctoral program. *Degree requirements:* For master's, thesis optional; for doctorate, thesis/dissertation. *Entrance requirements:* For master's and doctorate, GRE General Test. *Application deadline:* For fall admission, 12/1 priority date for domestic students, 11/1 priority date for international students; for spring admission, 9/15 priority date for domestic and international students. Applications are processed on a rolling basis. Application fee: $85. Electronic applications accepted. *Expenses:* Tuition: Full-time $31,240; part-time $1420 per unit. Required fees: $600. One-time fee: $35 full-time. Full-time tuition and fees vary according to degree level and program. *Financial support:* In 2010–11, fellowships with full tuition reimbursements (averaging $30,000 per year), research assistantships with full tuition reimbursements (averaging $20,000 per year), teaching assistantships with full tuition reimbursements (averaging $20,000 per year) were awarded; career-related internships or fieldwork, scholarships/grants, health care benefits, and unspecified assistantships also available. Financial award application deadline: 12/1; financial award applicants required to submit CSS PROFILE or FAFSA. *Faculty research:* Health systems, music cognition and retrieval, transportation and logistics, manufacturing and automation, engineering systems design, risk and economic analysis. Total annual research expenditures: $1 million. *Unit head:* Dr. F. Stan Settles, Chair, 213-740-4893, E-mail: isedept@usc.edu. *Application contact:* Evelyn Felina, Director of Student Affairs, 213-740-7549, E-mail: efelina@usc.edu.

University of Southern California, Graduate School, Viterbi School of Engineering, Sonny Astani Department of Civil Engineering, Los Angeles, CA 90089. Offers applied mechanics (MS); civil engineering (MS, PhD); computer-aided engineering (ME, Graduate Certificate); construction management (MCM); engineering technology commercialization (Graduate Certificate); environmental engineering (MS, PhD); environmental quality management (ME); structural design (ME); sustainable cities (Graduate Certificate); transportation systems (MS, Graduate Certificate); water and waste management (MS). Part-time and evening/weekend programs available. *Faculty:* 16 full-time (2 women), 35 part-time/adjunct (5 women). *Students:* 190 full-time (52 women), 81 part-time (20 women); includes 54 minority (2 Black or African American, non-Hispanic/Latino; 42 Asian, non-Hispanic/Latino; 9 Hispanic/Latino; 1 Two or more races, non-Hispanic/Latino), 149 international. 541 applicants, 43% accepted, 100 enrolled. In 2010, 74 master's, 10 doctorates awarded. Terminal master's awarded for partial completion of doctoral program. *Degree requirements:* For master's, thesis optional; for doctorate, thesis/dissertation. *Entrance requirements:* For master's and doctorate, GRE General Test. *Application deadline:* For fall admission, 12/1 priority date for domestic and international students; for spring admission, 9/15 for domestic students, 9/15 priority date for international students. Applications are processed on a rolling basis. Application fee: $85. Electronic applications accepted. *Expenses:* Tuition: Full-time $31,240; part-time $1420 per unit. Required fees: $600. One-time fee: $35 full-time. Full-time tuition and fees vary according to degree level and program. *Financial support:* In 2010–11, fellowships with full tuition reimbursements (averaging $30,000 per year), research assistantships with full tuition reimbursements (averaging $20,000 per year), teaching assistantships with full tuition reimbursements (averaging $20,000 per year) were awarded; career-related internships or fieldwork, scholarships/grants, health care benefits, and unspecified assistantships also available. Financial award application deadline: 12/1; financial award applicants required to submit CSS PROFILE or FAFSA. *Faculty research:* Geotechnical engineering, transportation engineering, structural engineering, construction management, environmental engineering, water resources. Total annual research expenditures: $5 million. *Unit head:* Dr. Jean-Pierre Bardet, Chair, 213-740-0603, Fax: 213-744-1426, E-mail: ceedept@usc.edu. *Application contact:* Jennifer A. Gerson, Director of Student Affairs, 213-740-0573, Fax: 213-740-8662, E-mail: jgerson@usc.edu.

The University of Texas at Tyler, College of Engineering and Computer Science, Department of Civil Engineering, Tyler, TX 75799-0001. Offers environmental engineering (MS); industrial safety (MS); structural engineering (MS); transportation engineering (MS); water resources engineering (MS). Part-time and evening/weekend programs available. *Degree requirements:* For master's, thesis optional. *Entrance requirements:* For master's, GRE General Test, bachelor's degree in engineering, associated science degree. Additional exam requirements/recommendations for international students: Required—TOEFL (minimum score 79 computer-based). *Faculty research:* Non-destructive strength testing, indoor air quality, transportation routing and signaling, pavement replacement criteria, flood water routing, construction and long-term behavior of innovative geotechnical foundation and embankment construction used in highway construction, engineering education.

University of Washington, Graduate School, College of Engineering, Department of Civil and Environmental Engineering, Seattle, WA 98195-2700. Offers construction engineering (MSCE); environmental engineering (MS, MSCE, MSE, PhD); hydrology, water resources, and environmental fluid mechanics (MS, MSCE, MSE, PhD); structural and geotechnical engineering and mechanics (MS, MSCE, MSE, PhD); transportation and construction engineering (MS, MSE, PhD); transportation engineering (MSCE). Part-time programs available. Postbaccalaureate distance learning degree programs offered (no on-campus study). *Faculty:* 44 full-time (10 women), 12 part-time/adjunct (1 woman). *Students:* 197 full-time (65 women), 65 part-time (15 women); includes 5 Black or African American, non-Hispanic/Latino; 28 Asian, non-Hispanic/Latino; 5 Hispanic/Latino, 55 international. 522 applicants, 51% accepted, 101 enrolled. In 2010, 68 master's, 5 doctorates awarded. Terminal master's awarded for partial completion of doctoral program. *Degree requirements:* For master's, thesis (for some programs); for doctorate, comprehensive exam, thesis/dissertation, General, qualifying, and final exams. Completion of doctoral degree within 10 years. *Entrance requirements:* For master's, GRE General Test, Minimum GPA of 3.0, statement of purpose, letters of recommendation, transcripts; for doctorate, GRE General Test, minimum GPA of 3.5, statement of purpose, letters of recommendation, transcripts. Additional exam requirements/recommendations for international students: Required—TOEFL (minimum score 580 paper-based; 237 computer-based; 92 iBT); Recommended—IELTS (minimum score 7). *Application deadline:* For fall admission, 1/10 priority date for domestic and international students. Application fee: $75. Electronic applications accepted. *Financial support:* In 2010–11, 2 students received support, including 25 fellowships with full and partial tuition reimbursements available (averaging $16,173 per year), 75 research assistantships with full tuition reimbursements available (averaging $16,515 per year), 11 teaching assistantships with full tuition reimbursements available (averaging $16,263 per year); scholarships/grants also available. Financial award application deadline: 1/10; financial award applicants required to submit FAFSA. *Faculty research:* Environmental/water resources, hydrology; construction/transportation; structures/ geotechnical. Total annual research expenditures: $14.4 million. *Unit head:* Dr. Gregory R. Miller, Professor and Chair, 206-543-0350, Fax: 206-543-1543, E-mail: gmiller@uw.edu. *Application contact:* Lorna Latal, Graduate Adviser, 206-543-2574, Fax: 206-543-1543, E-mail: llatal@u.washington.edu.

Virginia Polytechnic Institute and State University, Graduate School, College of Engineering, Department of Civil and Environmental Engineering, Blacksburg, VA 24061. Offers civil engineering (M Eng, MS, PhD); civil infrastructure systems (Certificate); environmental engineering (MS); environmental sciences and engineering (MS); transportation systems engineering (Certificate); treatment process engineering (Certificate); urban hydrology and stormwater management (Certificate); water quality management (Certificate). *Accreditation:* ABET (one or more programs are accredited). *Faculty:* 44 full-time (8 women), 1 part-time/adjunct (0 women). *Students:* 320 full-time (108 women), 70 part-time (20 women); includes 9 Black or African American, non-Hispanic/Latino; 15 Asian, non-Hispanic/Latino; 13 Hispanic/Latino, 126 international. Average age 27. 639 applicants, 44% accepted, 121 enrolled. In 2010, 97 master's, 18 doctorates awarded. *Degree requirements:* For master's, comprehensive exam (for some programs), thesis (for some programs); for doctorate, comprehensive exam (for some programs), thesis/dissertation (for some programs). *Entrance requirements:* For master's and doctorate, GRE. Additional exam requirements/recommendations for international students: Required—TOEFL (minimum score 550 paper-based; 213 computer-based). *Application deadline:* For fall admission, 7/1 for domestic and international students; for spring admission, 12/1 for domestic and international students. Applications are processed on a rolling basis. Application fee: $65. Electronic applications accepted. *Expenses:* Tuition, area resident: Full-time $9399; part-time $488 per credit hour. Tuition, state resident: full-time $9399; part-time $488 per credit hour. Tuition, nonresident: full-time $17,854; part-time $957.75 per credit hour. International tuition: $17,854 full-time. Required fees: $1534. Full-time tuition and fees vary according to program. *Financial support:* In 2010–11, 35 fellowships with full tuition reimbursements (averaging $5,861 per year), 82 research assistantships with full tuition reimbursements (averaging $20,397 per year), 33 teaching assistantships with full tuition reimbursements (averaging $14,542 per year) were awarded; career-related internships or fieldwork, Federal Work-Study, scholarships/grants, health care benefits, and unspecified assistantships also available. Financial award application deadline: 1/15. *Faculty research:* Construction, environmental geotechnical hydrosystems, structures and transportation engineering. Total annual research expenditures: $12.2 million. *Unit head:* Dr. Sam Easterling, UNIT HEAD, 540-231-5143, Fax: 540-231-7532, E-mail: seaster@vt.edu. *Application contact:* Marc Widdowson, Contact, 540-231-7153, Fax: 540-231-7532, E-mail: mwiddows@vt.edu.

Western Michigan University, Graduate College, College of Engineering and Applied Sciences, Department of Civil and Construction Engineering, Kalamazoo, MI 49008. Offers civil engineering (MS), including construction engineering and management, structural engineering, transportation engineering. *Entrance requirements:* For master's, minimum GPA of 3.0.

Water Resources Engineering

American University of Beirut, Graduate Programs, Faculty of Engineering and Architecture, Beirut, Lebanon. Offers applied energy (MME); civil engineering (ME, PhD); electrical and computer engineering (ME, PhD); engineering management (MEM); environmental and water resources (ME); environmental and water resources engineering (PhD); environmental technology (MSES); mechanical engineering (ME, PhD); urban design (MUD); urban planning and policy (MUP). Part-time programs available. *Faculty:* 57 full-time (12 women), 3 part-time/adjunct (0 women). *Students:* 261 full-time (92 women), 58 part-time (20 women). Average age 25. 272 applicants, 79% accepted, 108 enrolled. In 2010, 70 master's, 1 doctorate awarded. *Degree requirements:* For master's, one foreign language, comprehensive exam, thesis (for some programs); for doctorate, one foreign language, comprehensive exam, thesis/dissertation, publications. *Entrance requirements:* For master's, GRE (for electrical and computer engineering), letters of recommendation; for doctorate, GRE, letters of recommendation, master's degree, transcripts, curriculum vitae, interview. Additional exam requirements/recommendations for international students: Required—TOEFL (minimum score 600 paper-based; 250 computer-based; 100 iBT), IELTS (minimum score 7.5). *Application deadline:* For fall admission, 2/5 priority date for domestic and international students; for spring admission, 11/1 priority date for domestic students, 11/1 for international students. Applications are processed on a rolling basis. Application fee: $50. Electronic applications accepted. *Expenses:* Tuition: Full-time $12,294; part-time $683 per credit. Required fees: $499; $499 per credit. Tuition and fees vary according to course load and program. *Financial support:* In 2010–11, 10 fellowships with full tuition reimbursements (averaging $24,800 per year), 33 research assistantships with full tuition reimbursements (averaging $24,800 per year), 70 teaching assistantships with full tuition reimbursements (averaging $9,800 per year) were awarded; career-related internships or fieldwork, institutionally sponsored loans, scholarships/grants, health care benefits, and unspecified assistantships also available. Total annual research expenditures: $586,131. *Unit head:* Fadl H. Moukalled, Acting Dean, 961-135-0000 Ext. 3400, Fax: 961-174-4462, E-mail: memouk@aub.edu.lb. *Application contact:* Dr. Salim Kanaan, Director, Admissions Office, 961-135-0000 Ext. 2594, Fax: 961-175-0775, E-mail: sk00@aub.edu.lb.

Cornell University, Graduate School, Graduate Fields of Engineering, Field of Civil and Environmental Engineering, Ithaca, NY 14853-0001. Offers engineering management (M Eng, MS, PhD); environmental engineering (M Eng, MS, PhD); environmental fluid mechanics and hydrology (M Eng, MS, PhD); environmental systems engineering (M Eng, MS, PhD); geotechnical engineering (M Eng, MS, PhD); remote sensing (M Eng, MS, PhD); structural engineering (M Eng, MS, PhD); structural mechanics (M Eng, MS); transportation engineering (MS, PhD); transportation systems engineering (M Eng); water resource systems (M Eng, MS, PhD). *Faculty:* 36 full-time (4 women). *Students:* 148 full-time (48 women); includes 3 Black or African American, non-Hispanic/Latino; 1 American Indian or Alaska Native, non-Hispanic/Latino; 16 Asian, non-Hispanic/Latino; 16 Hispanic/Latino, 60 international. Average age 24. 390 applicants, 56% accepted, 76 enrolled. In 2010, 93 master's, 5 doctorates awarded. Terminal master's awarded for partial completion of doctoral program. *Degree requirements:* For master's, thesis (MS); for doctorate, comprehensive exam, thesis/dissertation. *Entrance requirements:* For master's and doctorate, GRE General Test (recommended), 2 letters of recommendation. Additional exam requirements/recommendations for international students: Required—TOEFL (minimum score 600 paper-based; 250 computer-based; 77 iBT). *Application deadline:* For fall admission, 1/15 priority date for domestic students; for spring admission, 10/15 for domestic students. Application fee: $70. Electronic applications accepted. *Expenses:* Tuition: Full-time $29,500. Required fees: $76. Tuition and fees vary according to degree level and program. *Financial support:* In 2010–11, 50 students received support, including 17 fellowships with full tuition reimbursements available, 33 research assistantships with full tuition reimbursements available, 15 teaching assistantships with full tuition reimbursements available; institutionally sponsored loans, scholarships/grants, health care benefits, tuition waivers (full and partial), and unspecified assistantships also available. Financial award applicants required to submit FAFSA. *Faculty research:* Environmental engineering, geotechnical engineering, remote sensing, environmental fluid mechanics and hydrology, structural engineering. *Unit head:* Director of Graduate Studies, 607-255-7560, Fax: 607-255-9004. *Application contact:* Graduate Field Assistant, 607-255-7560, Fax: 607-255-9004, E-mail: cee_grad@cornell.edu.

George Mason University, Volgenau School of Engineering, Department of Civil, Environmental, and Infrastructure Engineering, Fairfax, VA 22030. Offers civil and infrastructure engineering (MS, PhD); civil infrastructure and security engineering (Certificate); leading technical enterprises (Certificate); sustainability and the environment (Certificate); water resources engineering (Certificate). Part-time and evening/weekend programs available. *Faculty:* 9 full-time (4 women), 18 part-time/adjunct (1 woman). *Students:* 15 full-time (4 women), 62 part-time (13 women); includes 7 Black or African American, non-Hispanic/Latino; 9 Asian, non-Hispanic/Latino; 4 Hispanic/Latino; 2 Two or more races, non-Hispanic/Latino, 6 international. Average age 32. 77 applicants, 70% accepted, 29 enrolled. In 2010, 13 master's, 1 doctorate, 2 other advanced degrees awarded. *Degree requirements:* For master's, thesis (for some programs), 30 credits, departmental seminars; for doctorate, thesis/dissertation, qualifying exams. *Entrance requirements:* For master's, GRE or GMAT. Additional exam requirements/recommendations for international students: Required—TOEFL (minimum score 570 paper-based; 230 computer-based; 88 iBT). *Application deadline:* For fall admission, 3/15 priority date for domestic students, 3/15 for international students; for spring admission, 11/1 for domestic students, 10/1 for international students. Application fee: $100. Electronic applications accepted. *Expenses:* Tuition, state resident: full-time $8192; part-time $440 per credit hour. Tuition, nonresident: full-time $22,952; part-time $1055 per credit hour. Required fees: $2364; $99 per credit hour. *Financial support:* In 2010–11, 13 students received support, including 1 fellowship (averaging $18,000 per year), 2 research assistantships with full and partial tuition reimbursements available (averaging $13,924 per year), 10 teaching assistantships with full and partial tuition reimbursements available (averaging $10,468 per year); career-related internships or fieldwork, Federal Work-Study, scholarships/grants, unspecified assistantships, and health care benefits (full-time research or teaching assistantship recipients) also available. Financial award application deadline: 3/1; financial award applicants required to submit FAFSA. *Faculty research:* Evolutionary design, infrastructure security, intelligent transportation systems, national transportation networks, water quality modeling. Total annual research expenditures: $177,807. *Unit head:* Dr. Michael Bronzini, Chair, 703-993-1504, Fax: 703-993-1521. *Application contact:* Lisa Nolder, Graduate Student Services Director, 703-993-1499, E-mail: snolder@gmu.edu.

Indiana University Bloomington, School of Public and Environmental Affairs, Environmental Science Programs, Bloomington, IN 47405-7000. Offers applied ecology (MSES); energy (MSES); environmental chemistry, toxicology, and risk assessment (MSES); environmental science (PhD); specialized environmental science (MSES); water resources (MSES); JD/MSES; MSES/MS. Part-time programs available. *Faculty:* 17 full-time, 8 part-time/adjunct. *Students:* 87 full-time (49 women), 2 part-time (1 woman); includes 1 Black or African American, non-Hispanic/Latino; 1 American Indian or Alaska Native, non-Hispanic/Latino; 10 Asian, non-Hispanic/Latino; 5 Hispanic/Latino, 11 international. Average age 26. 79 applicants, 29 enrolled. In 2010, 53 master's, 10 doctorates awarded. Terminal master's awarded for partial completion of doctoral program. *Degree requirements:* For master's, thesis optional; for doctorate, comprehensive exam, thesis/dissertation. *Entrance requirements:* For master's, GRE General Test or GMAT, official transcripts, 3 letters of recommendation, resume, personal statement, departmental questions; for doctorate, GRE General Test or LSAT and TOEFL (Intl.), official transcripts, 3 letters of recommendation, resume or curriculum vitae, statement of purpose, application, application fee, residence classification (Intl.). Additional exam requirements/recommendations for international students: Required—TOEFL (minimum score 600 paper-based; 96 iBT); Recommended—IELTS (minimum score 7). *Application deadline:* For fall admission, 5/1 for domestic students, 12/1 for international students; for spring admission, 11/1 for domestic and international students. Applications are processed on a rolling basis. Application fee: $55 ($65 for international students). Electronic applications accepted. *Financial support:* Fellowships with partial tuition reimbursements, research assistantships with partial tuition reimbursements, teaching assistantships with partial tuition reimbursements, career-related internships or fieldwork, Federal Work-Study, scholarships/grants, health care benefits, and unspecified assistantships available. Financial award application deadline: 2/1; financial award applicants required to submit FAFSA. *Faculty research:* Applied ecology, bio-geo chemistry, toxicology, wetlands ecology, environmental microbiology, forest ecology, environmental chemistry. *Unit head:* Jennifer J. Forney, Director, Graduate Student Servies, 812-855-9485, Fax: 812-856-3665, E-mail: speampo@indiana.edu. *Application contact:* Audrey Whittaker, Admissions Assistant, 812-855-2840, Fax: 812-856-3665, E-mail: speaapps@indiana.edu.

Louisiana State University and Agricultural and Mechanical College, Graduate School, College of Engineering, Department of Civil and Environmental Engineering, Baton Rouge, LA 70803. Offers environmental engineering (MSCE, PhD); geotechnical engineering (MSCE, PhD); structural engineering and mechanics (MSCE, PhD); transportation engineering (MSCE, PhD); water resources (MSCE, PhD). Part-time programs available. *Faculty:* 29 full-time (3 women). *Students:* 89 full-time (19 women), 35 part-time (8 women); includes 2 Black or African American, non-Hispanic/Latino; 1 American Indian or Alaska Native, non-Hispanic/Latino; 3 Asian, non-Hispanic/Latino; 3 Hispanic/Latino, 65 international. Average age 29. 96 applicants, 65% accepted, 16 enrolled. In 2010, 20 master's, 8 doctorates awarded. *Degree requirements:* For master's, thesis optional; for doctorate, one foreign language, thesis/dissertation. *Entrance requirements:* For master's and doctorate, GRE General Test, minimum GPA of 3.0. Additional exam requirements/recommendations for international students: Required—TOEFL (minimum score 550 paper-based; 213 computer-based; 79 iBT) or IELTS (minimum score 6.5). *Application deadline:* For fall admission, 1/25 priority date for domestic students, 5/15 for international students; for spring admission, 10/15 for international students. Applications are processed on a rolling basis. Application fee: $50 ($70 for international students). Electronic applications accepted. *Financial support:* In 2010–11, 89 students received support, including 2 fellowships with full and partial tuition reimbursements available (averaging $24,418 per year), 75 research assistantships with full and partial tuition reimbursements available (averaging $16,115 per year), 3 teaching assistantships with full and partial tuition reimbursements available (averaging $12,843 per year); career-related internships or fieldwork, institutionally sponsored loans, scholarships/grants, and health care benefits also available. Financial award application deadline: 3/1; financial award applicants required to submit FAFSA. *Faculty research:* Mechanics and structures, environmental, geotechnical transportation, water resources. Total annual research expenditures: $2.6 million. *Unit head:* Dr. George Z. Voyiadjis, Chair/Professor, 225-578-8668, Fax: 225-578-9176, E-mail: cegzv@lsu.edu. *Application contact:* Dr. Clinton Willson, Professor, 225-578-8652, E-mail: cwillson@lsu.edu.

Marquette University, Graduate School, College of Engineering, Department of Civil and Environmental Engineering, Milwaukee, WI 53201-1881. Offers construction and public works management (MS, PhD); construction engineering and management (Certificate); environmental/water resources engineering (MS, PhD); structural design (Certificate); structural/geotechnical engineering (MS, PhD); transportation planning and engineering (MS, PhD); waste and wastewater treatment processes (Certificate). Part-time and evening/weekend programs available. *Faculty:* 13 full-time (0 women), 3 part-time/adjunct (0 women). *Students:* 20 full-time (4 women), 12 part-time (1 woman); includes 1 minority (Black or African American, non-Hispanic/Latino), 12 international. Average age 27. 66 applicants, 64% accepted, 9 enrolled. In 2010, 8 master's, 1 doctorate awarded. Terminal master's awarded for partial completion of doctoral program. *Degree requirements:* For master's, comprehensive exam, thesis or alternative; for doctorate, thesis/dissertation. *Entrance requirements:* For master's, GRE General Test (recommended), minimum GPA of 3.0, official transcripts from all current and previous colleges/universities except Marquette, three letters of recommendation; for doctorate, GRE General Test, minimum GPA of 3.0, official transcripts from all current and previous colleges/universities except Marquette, three letters of recommendation, brief statement of purpose, submission of any English-language publications authored by applicant (strongly recommended). Additional exam requirements/recommendations for international students: Required—TOEFL (minimum score 530 paper-based; 78 computer-based). *Application deadline:* For fall admission, 6/1 priority date for domestic students. Applications are processed on a rolling basis. Application fee: $50. Electronic applications accepted. *Expenses:* Tuition: Full-time $16,290; part-time $905 per credit hour. Tuition and fees vary according to program. *Financial support:* In 2010–11, 13 students received support, including 4 fellowships with tuition reimbursements available, 4 research assistantships with tuition reimbursements available, 10 teaching assistantships with tuition reimbursements available; Federal Work-Study, institutionally sponsored loans, scholarships/grants, and tuition waivers (full and partial) also available. Support available to part-time students. Financial award application deadline: 2/15. *Faculty research:* Highway safety, highway performance, and intelligent transportation systems; surface mount technology; watershed management. Total annual research expenditures: $662,392. *Unit head:* Dr. Thomas Wenzel, Chair, 414-288-7030, Fax: 414-288-7521, E-mail: thomas.wenzel@marquette.edu. *Application contact:* Dr. Stephen M. Heinrich, Director of Graduate Studies, 414-288-5466, E-mail: stephen.heinrich@marquette.edu.

McGill University, Faculty of Graduate and Postdoctoral Studies, Faculty of Engineering, Department of Civil Engineering and Applied Mechanics, Montréal, QC H3A 2T5, Canada. Offers environmental engineering (M Eng, M Sc, PhD); fluid mechanics (M Sc); fluid mechanics and hydraulic engineering (M Eng, PhD); materials engineering (M Eng, PhD); rehabilitation of urban infrastructure (M Eng, PhD); soil behavior (M Eng, PhD); soil mechanics and foundations (M Eng, PhD); structures and structural mechanics (M Eng, PhD); water resources (M Sc); water resources engineering (M Eng, PhD).

New Mexico Institute of Mining and Technology, Graduate Studies, Department of Environmental Engineering, Socorro, NM 87801. Offers environmental engineering (MS), including air quality engineering and science, hazardous waste engineering, water quality engineering and science. *Degree requirements:* For master's, thesis. *Entrance requirements:* For master's, GRE General Test. Additional exam requirements/recommendations for international students: Required—TOEFL (minimum score 540 paper-based; 207 computer-based). *Faculty research:* Air quality, hazardous waste management, wastewater management and treatment, site remediation.

Norwich University, School of Graduate and Continuing Studies, Program in Civil Engineering, Northfield, VT 05663. Offers construction management (MCE); geo-technical (MCE); structural (MCE); water/environmental (MCE). Evening/weekend programs available. *Faculty:* 20 full-time (3 women). *Students:* 78 full-time (19 women); includes 5 Black or African American, non-Hispanic/Latino; 4 Asian, non-Hispanic/Latino; 7 Hispanic/Latino. Average age 35. 107 applicants, 88% accepted, 90 enrolled. In 2010, 78 master's awarded. *Entrance requirements:* For master's, minimum GPA of 2.75. Additional exam requirements/recommendations for international students: Required—TOEFL (minimum score 550 paper-based; 213 computer-based; 83 iBT). *Application deadline:* For fall admission, 8/10 for domestic and international students; for spring admission, 2/6 for domestic and international students. Application fee: $50. *Expenses:* Tuition: Full-time $17,380; part-time $645 per credit. Tuition and fees vary according to program. *Financial support:* Scholarships/grants available. Financial award applicants required to submit FAFSA. *Unit head:* Dr. Thomas Descoteaux, Program Director, 802-485-2730, Fax: 802-485-2533, E-mail: tdescote@norwich.edu. *Application contact:* Shelley W. Brown, Director of Business Partnership, 802-485-2784, Fax: 802-485-2533, E-mail: sbrown@norwich.edu.

Ohio University, Graduate College, Russ College of Engineering and Technology, Department of Civil Engineering, Athens, OH 45701-2979. Offers civil engineering (PhD); construction (MS); environmental (MS); geotechnical and geoenvironmental (MS); mechanics (MS); structures (MS); transportation (MS); water resources and structures (MS). Part-time programs available. *Students:* 29 full-time (6 women), 5 part-time (1 woman); includes 2 minority (1 Hispanic/Latino; 1 Two or more races, non-Hispanic/Latino), 16 international. 52 applicants, 83%

Water Resources Engineering

Ohio University (continued)

accepted, 14 enrolled. In 2010, 7 master's awarded. *Degree requirements:* For master's, comprehensive exam (for some programs), thesis or alternative; for doctorate, comprehensive exam, thesis/dissertation. *Entrance requirements:* For master's, GRE General Test, minimum GPA of 3.0, 3 letters of recommendation; for doctorate, GRE General Test. Additional exam requirements/recommendations for international students: Required—TOEFL (minimum score 550 paper-based; 80 iBT) or IELTS (minimum score 6.5). *Application deadline:* For fall admission, 5/1 priority date for domestic students, 2/1 priority date for international students; for winter admission, 8/1 priority date for domestic students, 4/1 priority date for international students; for spring admission, 2/1 priority date for domestic students, 7/1 priority date for international students. Applications are processed on a rolling basis. Application fee: $50 ($55 for international students). Electronic applications accepted. *Financial support:* Research assistantships with full tuition reimbursements, teaching assistantships with full tuition reimbursements, Federal Work-Study, institutionally sponsored loans, scholarships/grants, and unspecified assistantships available. Financial award application deadline: 3/15; financial award applicants required to submit FAFSA. *Faculty research:* Noise abatement, materials and environment, highway infrastructure, subsurface investigation (pavements, pipes, bridges). *Unit head:* Dr. Gayle F. Mitchell, Chair, 740-593-0430, Fax: 740-593-0625, E-mail: mitchelg@ohio.edu. *Application contact:* Dr. Shad M. Sargand, Graduate Chair, 740-593-1465, Fax: 740-593-0625, E-mail: sargand@ohio.edu.

Oregon State University, Graduate School, College of Engineering, Department of Biological and Ecological Engineering, Corvallis, OR 97331. Offers M Eng, MS, PhD. Terminal master's awarded for partial completion of doctoral program. *Degree requirements:* For master's, thesis or alternative; for doctorate, thesis/dissertation. *Entrance requirements:* For master's and doctorate, minimum GPA of 3.0 in last 90 hours. Additional exam requirements/recommendations for international students: Required—TOEFL (minimum score 550 paper-based; 213 computer-based). *Expenses:* Contact institution. *Faculty research:* Bioengineering, water resources engineering, food engineering, cell culture and fermentation, vadose zone transport.

Oregon State University, Graduate School, College of Engineering, School of Civil and Construction Engineering, Corvallis, OR 97331. Offers civil engineering (MS, PhD); coastal and ocean engineering (M Oc E, PhD); coastal engineering (MS); construction engineering management (MBE, PhD); engineering (M Eng, MAIS); geotechnical engineering (MS, PhD); structural engineering (MS, PhD); transportation engineering (MS, PhD); water engineering (MS, PhD). Part-time programs available. Terminal master's awarded for partial completion of doctoral program. *Degree requirements:* For master's, thesis or alternative; for doctorate, one foreign language, thesis/dissertation. *Entrance requirements:* For master's, GRE General Test, minimum GPA of 3.0 in last 90 hours (3.5 for MS); for doctorate, GRE General Test, minimum GPA of 3.0 in last 90 hours of undergraduate course work. Additional exam requirements/recommendations for international students: Required—TOEFL (minimum score 580 paper-based; 237 computer-based). *Faculty research:* Hazardous waste management, carbon cycling, wave forces on structures, pavement design, seismic analysis.

Oregon State University, Graduate School, Program in Water Resources Engineering, Corvallis, OR 97331. Offers MS, PhD.

State University of New York College of Environmental Science and Forestry, Department of Environmental Resources Engineering, Syracuse, NY 13210-2779. Offers ecological engineering (MS, PhD); environmental and resources engineering (MPS, MS, PhD); environmental management (MPS); geospatial information science and engineering (MS, PhD); mapping sciences (MPS); water resources engineering (MS, PhD). *Degree requirements:* For master's, thesis (for some programs); for doctorate, comprehensive exam, thesis/dissertation. *Entrance requirements:* For master's and doctorate, GRE General Test, minimum GPA of 3.0. Additional exam requirements/recommendations for international students: Required—TOEFL (minimum score 550 paper-based; 213 computer-based; 80 iBT), IELTS (minimum score 6). *Expenses:* Tuition, state resident: full-time $8370; part-time $349 per credit hour. Tuition, nonresident: full-time $13,780. Required fees: $30.30 per credit hour. $20 per year. *Faculty research:* Forest engineering, paper science and engineering, wood products engineering.

Stevens Institute of Technology, Graduate School, Charles V. Schaefer Jr. School of Engineering, Department of Civil, Environmental, and Ocean Engineering, Program in Civil Engineering, Hoboken, NJ 07030. Offers civil engineering (PhD); geotechnical engineering (Certificate); geotechnical/geoenvironmental engineering (M Eng, Engr); hydrologic modeling (M Eng); stormwater management (M Eng); structural engineering (M Eng, Engr); water resources engineering (M Eng). *Students:* 22 full-time (6 women), 36 part-time (11 women); includes 10 Asian, non-Hispanic/Latino; 3 Hispanic/Latino, 16 international. Average age 28. 37 applicants, 86% accepted. *Degree requirements:* For master's, thesis optional; for doctorate, variable foreign language requirement, thesis/dissertation; for other advanced degree, project or thesis. *Entrance requirements:* For doctorate, GRE. Additional exam requirements/recommendations for international students: Required—TOEFL. *Application deadline:* Applications are processed on a rolling basis. Application fee: $50. Electronic applications accepted. *Financial support:* Application deadline: 4/15. *Unit head:* Dr. David A. Vaccari, Director, 201-216-5570, Fax: 201-216-5352, E-mail: dvaccari@stevens.edu. *Application contact:* Dr. David A. Vaccari, Director, 201-216-5570, Fax: 201-216-5352, E-mail: dvaccari@stevens.edu.

Texas A&M University, College of Engineering, Zachry Department of Civil Engineering, College Station, TX 77843. Offers coastal and ocean engineering (M Eng, MS, D Eng, PhD); construction engineering and management (M Eng, MS, D Eng, PhD); environmental engineering (M Eng, MS, D Eng, PhD); geotechnical engineering (M Eng, MS, D Eng, PhD); materials engineering (M Eng, MS, D Eng, PhD); structural engineering (M Eng, MS, D Eng, PhD); transportation engineering (M Eng, MS, D Eng, PhD); water resources engineering (M Eng, MS, D Eng, PhD). Part-time programs available. *Faculty:* 57. *Students:* 384 full-time (81 women), 35 part-time (7 women); includes 35 minority (3 Black or African American, non-Hispanic/Latino; 1 American Indian or Alaska Native, non-Hispanic/Latino; 14 Asian, non-Hispanic/Latino; 17 Hispanic/Latino), 263 international. Average age 29. In 2010, 136 master's, 26 doctorates awarded. *Degree requirements:* For master's, thesis (MS); for doctorate, dissertation (PhD), internship (D Eng). *Entrance requirements:* For master's and doctorate, GRE General Test. Additional exam requirements/recommendations for international students: Required—TOEFL. *Application deadline:* Applications are processed on a rolling basis. Application fee: $50 ($75 for international students). Electronic applications accepted. *Financial support:* In 2010–11, fellowships (averaging $4,500 per year), research assistantships (averaging $14,000 per year), teaching assistantships (averaging $14,400 per year) were awarded; career-related internships or fieldwork and institutionally sponsored loans also available. Financial award application deadline: 4/15; financial award applicants required to submit FAFSA. *Unit head:* Dr. Tony Cahill, Head, 979-845-3858, E-mail: tcahill@civil.tamu.edu. *Application contact:* Graduate Advisor, 979-845-7435, Fax: 979-845-6156, E-mail: info@civil.tamu.edu.

Tufts University, School of Engineering, Department of Civil and Environmental Engineering, Medford, MA 02155. Offers civil engineering (ME, MS, PhD), including geotechnical engineering, structural engineering; environmental engineering (ME, MS, PhD), including environmental engineering and environmental sciences, environmental geotechnology, environmental health, environmental science and management, hazardous materials management, water resources engineering. Part-time programs available. Terminal master's awarded for partial completion of doctoral program. *Degree requirements:* For master's, thesis or alternative; for doctorate, thesis/dissertation. *Entrance requirements:* For master's and doctorate, GRE General Test. Additional exam requirements/recommendations for international students: Required—TOEFL (minimum score 550 paper-based; 213 computer-based; 80 iBT). Electronic applications accepted. *Expenses:* Tuition: Full-time $39,624; part-time $3962 per course. Required fees: $40 per year. Full-time tuition and fees vary according to degree level, program and student level. Part-time tuition and fees vary according to course load.

The University of Alabama in Huntsville, School of Graduate Studies, College of Engineering, Department of Civil and Environmental Engineering, Huntsville, AL 35899. Offers civil and environmental engineering (PhD); civil engineering (MSE), including environmental and water resource engineering, geotechnical engineering, structural engineering and structural mechanics, transportation engineering. PhD offered jointly with The University of Alabama at Birmingham. Part-time and evening/weekend programs available. *Faculty:* 6 full-time (1 woman), 1 part-time/adjunct (0 women). *Students:* 23 full-time (7 women), 11 part-time (4 women); includes 3 minority (2 Black or African American, non-Hispanic/Latino; 1 Asian, non-Hispanic/Latino), 12 international. Average age 30. 37 applicants, 57% accepted, 15 enrolled. In 2010, 1 master's, 3 doctorates awarded. *Degree requirements:* For master's, comprehensive exam, thesis or alternative, oral and written exams; for doctorate, comprehensive exam, thesis/dissertation, oral and written exams. *Entrance requirements:* For master's, GRE General Test, BSE, minimum GPA of 3.0; for doctorate, GRE General Test, minimum GPA of 3.0. Additional exam requirements/recommendations for international students: Required—TOEFL (minimum score 500 paper-based; 173 computer-based; 62 iBT). *Application deadline:* For fall admission, 7/15 for domestic students, 4/1 for international students; for spring admission, 11/30 for domestic students, 9/1 for international students. Applications are processed on a rolling basis. Application fee: $40 ($50 for international students). Electronic applications accepted. *Expenses:* Tuition, state resident: full-time $7250; part-time $407.75 per credit hour. Tuition, nonresident: full-time $17,358; part-time $970.05 per credit hour. Required fees: $246.80 per semester. Tuition and fees vary according to course load and program. *Financial support:* In 2010–11, 14 students received support, including 7 research assistantships with full and partial tuition reimbursements available (averaging $12,435 per year), 7 teaching assistantships with full and partial tuition reimbursements available (averaging $10,281 per year); career-related internships or fieldwork, Federal Work-Study, institutionally sponsored loans, scholarships/grants, health care benefits, and unspecified assistantships also available. Support available to part-time students. Financial award application deadline: 4/1; financial award applicants required to submit FAFSA. *Faculty research:* Hydrologic modeling, orbital debris impact, hydrogeology, environmental engineering, transportation engineering. Total annual research expenditures: $1.9 million. *Unit head:* Dr. Houssam Toutanji, Chair, 256-824-7361, Fax: 256-824-6724, E-mail: toutanji@cee.uah.edu. *Application contact:* Kathy Biggs, Graduate Studies Admissions Manager, 256-824-6199, Fax: 256-824-6405, E-mail: deangrad@uah.edu.

University of Alberta, Faculty of Graduate Studies and Research, Department of Civil and Environmental Engineering, Edmonton, AB T6G 2E1, Canada. Offers construction engineering and management (M Eng, M Sc, PhD); environmental engineering (M Eng, M Sc, PhD); environmental science (M Sc, PhD); geoenvironmental engineering (M Eng, M Sc, PhD); geotechnical engineering (M Eng, M Sc, PhD); mining engineering (M Eng, M Sc, PhD); petroleum engineering (M Eng, M Sc, PhD); structural engineering (M Eng, M Sc, PhD); water resources (M Eng, M Sc, PhD). Part-time programs available. Postbaccalaureate distance learning degree programs offered (minimal on-campus study). *Degree requirements:* For master's, thesis (for some programs); for doctorate, thesis/dissertation. *Entrance requirements:* For master's, minimum GPA of 3.0 in last 2 years of undergraduate studies; for doctorate, minimum GPA of 3.0. Additional exam requirements/recommendations for international students: Required—TOEFL (minimum score 550 paper-based; 213 computer-based). Electronic applications accepted. *Faculty research:* Mining.

University of California, Berkeley, Graduate Division, College of Engineering, Department of Civil and Environmental Engineering, Berkeley, CA 94720-1500. Offers engineering and project management (M Eng, MS, D Eng, PhD); environmental engineering (M Eng, MS, D Eng, PhD); geoengineering (M Eng, MS, D Eng, PhD); structural engineering, mechanics and materials (M Eng, MS, D Eng, PhD); transportation engineering (M Eng, MS, D Eng, PhD); M Arch/MS; MCP/MS; MPP/MS. *Degree requirements:* For master's, comprehensive exam or thesis (MS); for doctorate, thesis/dissertation, qualifying exam. *Entrance requirements:* For master's, GRE General Test, minimum GPA of 3.0, 3 letters of recommendation; for doctorate, GRE General Test, minimum GPA of 3.5, 3 letters of recommendation. Additional exam requirements/recommendations for international students: Required—TOEFL (minimum score 570 paper-based; 230 computer-based). Electronic applications accepted.

University of Colorado Boulder, Graduate School, College of Engineering and Applied Science, Department of Civil, Environmental, and Architectural Engineering, Boulder, CO 80309. Offers building systems (MS, PhD); construction engineering management (MS, PhD); environmental engineering (MS, PhD); geotechnical engineering and geomechanics (MS, PhD); hydrology, water resources and environmental fluid mechanics (MS, PhD); structural engineering and structural mechanics (MS, PhD). *Faculty:* 38 full-time (6 women). *Students:* 255 full-time (86 women), 40 part-time (11 women); includes 40 minority (1 Black or African American, non-Hispanic/Latino; 2 American Indian or Alaska Native, non-Hispanic/Latino; 15 Asian, non-Hispanic/Latino; 20 Hispanic/Latino; 2 Two or more races, non-Hispanic/Latino), 61 international. Average age 28. 420 applicants, 95 enrolled. In 2010, 56 master's, 18 doctorates awarded. *Degree requirements:* For master's, comprehensive exam, thesis or alternative; for doctorate, thesis/dissertation. *Entrance requirements:* For master's, GRE General Test, minimum undergraduate GPA of 3.0. *Application deadline:* For fall admission, 3/1 for domestic students, 12/1 for international students; for spring admission, 10/31 for domestic students, 10/1 for international students. Application fee: $50 ($60 for international students). *Financial support:* In 2010–11, 45 fellowships (averaging $7,876 per year), 68 research assistantships (averaging $15,204 per year) were awarded. Financial award application deadline: 1/15. *Faculty research:* Building systems engineering, construction engineering and management, environmental engineering, geoenvironmental engineering, geotechnical engineering, materials and mechanics, structural engineering, water resources engineering, life-cycle engineering. Total annual research expenditures: $8 million.

University of Dayton, Graduate School, School of Engineering, Department of Civil and Environmental Engineering and Engineering Mechanics, Dayton, OH 45469-1300. Offers engineering mechanics (MSEM); environmental engineering (MSCE); geotechnical engineering (MSCE); structural engineering (MSCE); transportation engineering (MSCE); water resources engineering (MSCE). Part-time programs available. *Faculty:* 7 full-time (2 women), 2 part-time/adjunct (0 women). *Students:* 10 full-time (5 women), 7 part-time (2 women); includes 2 minority (both Black or African American, non-Hispanic/Latino), 6 international. Average age 27. 23 applicants, 43% accepted, 4 enrolled. In 2010, 5 master's awarded. *Degree requirements:* For master's, thesis optional. *Entrance requirements:* For master's, minimum GPA of 3.0 in undergraduate work. Additional exam requirements/recommendations for international students: Required—TOEFL (minimum score 550 paper-based; 213 computer-based; 80 iBT). *Application deadline:* For fall admission, 8/1 for domestic students, 3/1 priority date for international students; for winter admission, 7/1 priority date for international students; for spring admission, 1/1 priority date for international students. Applications are processed on a rolling basis. Application fee: $0 ($50 for international students). Electronic applications accepted. *Expenses:* Tuition: Full-time $7800; part-time $650 per credit hour. *Financial support:* In 2010–11, 2 research assistantships (averaging $10,600 per year) were awarded. Financial award applicants required to submit FAFSA. *Faculty research:* Physical modeling of hydraulic systems, finite element methods, mechanics of composite materials, transportation systems safety, biological treatment processes. Total annual research expenditures: $200,000. *Unit head:* Dr. Donald V. Chase, Chair, 937-229-3847, Fax: 937-229-3491, E-mail: donald.chase@notes.udayton.edu. *Application contact:* Alexander Popovski, Associate Director of International and Graduate Admissions, 937-229-2357, Fax: 937-229-4729, E-mail: alex.popovski@notes.udayton.edu.

University of Delaware, College of Engineering, Department of Civil and Environmental Engineering, Newark, DE 19716. Offers environmental engineering (MAS, MCE, PhD); geotechnical engineering (MAS, MCE, PhD); ocean engineering (MAS, MCE, PhD); structural engineering (MAS, MCE, PhD); transportation engineering (MAS, MCE, PhD); water resource engineering (MAS, MCE, PhD). Part-time programs available. Terminal master's awarded for partial completion of doctoral program. *Degree requirements:* For master's, thesis; for doctorate, thesis/dissertation. *Entrance requirements:* For master's and doctorate, GRE General Test. Additional exam requirements/recommendations for international students: Required—TOEFL.

Electronic applications accepted. *Faculty research:* Structural engineering and mechanics; transportation engineering; ocean engineering; soil mechanics and foundation; water resources and environmental engineering.

University of Guelph, Graduate Studies, College of Physical and Engineering Science, School of Engineering, Guelph, ON N1G 2W1, Canada. Offers biological engineering (M Eng, M Sc, MA Sc, PhD); engineering systems and computing (M Eng, M Sc, MA Sc, PhD); environmental engineering (M Eng, M Sc, MA Sc, PhD); water resources engineering (M Eng, M Sc, MA Sc, PhD). Part-time programs available. *Degree requirements:* For master's, thesis (for some programs); for doctorate, comprehensive exam, thesis/dissertation. *Entrance requirements:* For master's, minimum B- average during previous 2 years of course work; for doctorate, minimum B average. Additional exam requirements/recommendations for international students: Required—TOEFL (minimum score 550 paper-based; 213 computer-based; 89 iBT), IELTS (minimum score 6.5). Electronic applications accepted. *Faculty research:* Water and food safety, environmental contaminant fates and mechanisms, computer systems, robotics and mechatronics, waste treatment.

University of Maine, Graduate School, College of Engineering, Department of Civil and Environmental Engineering, Orono, ME 04469. Offers water resources (MS). *Faculty:* 10 full-time (2 women), 2 part-time/adjunct (1 woman). *Students:* 30 full-time (9 women), 13 part-time (3 women); includes 2 minority (1 American Indian or Alaska Native, non-Hispanic/Latino; 1 Two or more races, non-Hispanic/Latino), 4 international. Average age 28. 27 applicants, 37% accepted, 9 enrolled. In 2010, 13 master's, 1 doctorate awarded. *Degree requirements:* For doctorate, thesis/dissertation. *Entrance requirements:* For master's and doctorate, GRE General Test. Additional exam requirements/recommendations for international students: Required—TOEFL. *Application deadline:* For fall admission, 2/1 priority date for domestic students. Applications are processed on a rolling basis. Application fee: $65. Electronic applications accepted. *Expenses:* Tuition, state resident: full-time $400. Tuition, nonresident: full-time $1050. *Financial support:* In 2010–11, 15 research assistantships with tuition reimbursements (averaging $15,815 per year), 3 teaching assistantships with tuition reimbursements (averaging $12,790 per year) were awarded; Federal Work-Study, institutionally sponsored loans, scholarships/grants, and tuition waivers (full and partial) also available. Financial award application deadline: 3/1. *Unit head:* Dr. Eric Landis, Chair. *Application contact:* Scott G. Delcourt, Associate Dean of the Graduate School, 207-581-3291, Fax: 207-581-3232, E-mail: graduate@maine.edu.

University of Memphis, Graduate School, Herff College of Engineering, Department of Civil Engineering, Memphis, TN 38152. Offers civil engineering (PhD); environmental engineering (MS); foundation engineering (MS); structural engineering (MS); transportation engineering (MS); water resources engineering (MS). *Faculty:* 12 full-time (1 woman), 1 part-time/adjunct (0 women). *Students:* 12 full-time (5 women), 13 part-time (3 women); includes 2 Black or African American, non-Hispanic/Latino; 2 Asian, non-Hispanic/Latino; 1 Two or more races, non-Hispanic/Latino, 7 international. Average age 28. 22 applicants, 55% accepted, 0 enrolled. In 2010, 11 master's awarded. Terminal master's awarded for partial completion of doctoral program. *Degree requirements:* For master's, comprehensive exam, thesis optional; for doctorate, comprehensive exam, thesis/dissertation. *Entrance requirements:* For master's, GRE General Test or MAT, minimum undergraduate GPA of 2.5; for doctorate, GRE, 3 letters of recommendation. Additional exam requirements/recommendations for international students: Required—TOEFL (minimum score 550 paper-based; 210 computer-based; 79 iBT). *Application deadline:* For fall admission, 1/7 for domestic students, 1/5 for international students; for spring admission, 12/1 for domestic students, 9/15 for international students. Application fee: $35 ($60 for international students). *Financial support:* In 2010–11, 6 students received support; fellowships with full tuition reimbursements available, research assistantships with full tuition reimbursements available, career-related internships or fieldwork, Federal Work-Study, scholarships/grants, and unspecified assistantships available. Financial award application deadline: 2/15; financial award applicants required to submit FAFSA. *Faculty research:* Structural response to earthquakes, pavement design, water quality, transportation safety, intermodal transportation. *Unit head:* Dr. Sharam Pezeshk, Interim Chair, 901-678-2746, Fax: 901-678-3026. *Application contact:* Dr. Roger Meier, Coordinator of Graduate Studies, 901-678-3284.

University of Missouri, Graduate School, College of Engineering, Department of Civil and Environmental Engineering, Columbia, MO 65211. Offers civil engineering (MS, PhD); environmental engineering (MS, PhD); geotechnical engineering (MS, PhD); structural engineering (MS, PhD); transportation and highway engineering (MS); water resources (MS, PhD). *Degree requirements:* For master's, report or thesis; for doctorate, thesis/dissertation. *Entrance requirements:* For master's and doctorate, GRE General Test. Additional exam requirements/recommendations for international students: Required—TOEFL (minimum score 550 paper-based; 213 computer-based; 79 iBT).

University of New Haven, Graduate School, Tagliatela College of Engineering, Program in Environmental Engineering, West Haven, CT 06516-1916. Offers environmental engineering (MS); industrial and hazardous wastes (MS); water and wastewater treatment (MS); water resources (Certificate). Part-time and evening/weekend programs available. *Students:* 20 full-time (8 women), 5 part-time (2 women); includes 2 Black or African American, non-Hispanic/Latino, 20 international. Average age 31. 35 applicants, 97% accepted, 7 enrolled. In 2010, 10 master's awarded. *Degree requirements:* For master's, thesis or alternative. *Entrance requirements:* For master's, bachelor's degree in engineering. Additional exam requirements/recommendations for international students: Required—TOEFL (minimum score 520 paper-based; 190 computer-based; 70 iBT); Recommended—IELTS (minimum score 5.5). *Application deadline:* For fall admission, 5/31 for international students; for winter admission, 10/15 for international students; for spring admission, 1/15 for international students. Applications are processed on a rolling basis. Application fee: $50. Electronic applications accepted. *Financial support:* Research assistantships with partial tuition reimbursements, teaching assistantships with partial tuition reimbursements, career-related internships or fieldwork, Federal Work-Study, scholarships/grants, tuition waivers, and unspecified assistantships available. Support available to part-time students. Financial award application deadline: 5/1; financial award applicants required to submit FAFSA. *Unit head:* Dr. Agamemnon D. Koutsospyros, Coordinator, 203-932-7398. *Application contact:* Eloise Gormley, Director of Graduate Admissions, 203-932-7449, Fax: 203-932-7137, E-mail: gradinfo@newhaven.edu.

The University of Texas at Austin, Graduate School, Cockrell School of Engineering, Department of Civil, Architectural and Environmental Engineering, Program in Environmental and Water Resources Engineering, Austin, TX 78712-1111. Offers MS, PhD. *Accreditation:* ABET. Part-time programs available. *Degree requirements:* For master's, thesis or alternative. *Entrance requirements:* For master's, GRE General Test. Additional exam requirements/recommendations for international students: Required—TOEFL. Electronic applications accepted.

The University of Texas at Tyler, College of Engineering and Computer Science, Department of Civil Engineering, Tyler, TX 75799-0001. Offers environmental engineering (MS); industrial safety (MS); structural engineering (MS); transportation engineering (MS); water resources engineering (MS). Part-time and evening/weekend programs available. *Degree requirements:* For master's, thesis optional. *Entrance requirements:* For master's, GRE General Test, bachelor's degree in engineering, associated science degree. Additional exam requirements/recommendations for international students: Required—TOEFL (minimum score 79 computer-based). *Faculty research:* Non-destructive strength testing, indoor air quality, transportation routing and signaling, pavement replacement criteria, flood water routing, construction and long-term behavior of innovative geotechnical foundation and embankment construction used in highway construction, engineering education.

University of Washington, Graduate School, College of Engineering, Department of Civil and Environmental Engineering, Seattle, WA 98195-2700. Offers construction engineering (MSCE); environmental engineering (MS, MSCE, MSE, PhD); hydrology, water resources, and environmental fluid mechanics (MS, MSCE, MSE, PhD); structural and geotechnical engineering and mechanics (MS, MSCE, MSE, PhD); transportation and construction engineering (MS, MSE, PhD); transportation engineering (MSCE). Part-time programs available. Postbaccalaureate distance learning degree programs offered (no on-campus study). *Faculty:* 44 full-time (10 women), 12 part-time/adjunct (1 woman). *Students:* 197 full-time (65 women), 65 part-time (15 women); includes 5 Black or African American, non-Hispanic/Latino; 28 Asian, non-Hispanic/Latino; 5 Hispanic/Latino, 55 international. 522 applicants, 51% accepted, 101 enrolled. In 2010, 68 master's, 5 doctorates awarded. Terminal master's awarded for partial completion of doctoral program. *Degree requirements:* For master's, thesis (for some programs); for doctorate, comprehensive exam, thesis/dissertation, General, qualifying, and final exams. Completion of doctoral degree within 10 years. *Entrance requirements:* For master's, GRE General Test, Minimum GPA of 3.0, statement of purpose, letters of recommendation, transcripts; for doctorate, GRE General Test, minimum GPA of 3.5, statement of purpose, letters of recommendation, transcripts. Additional exam requirements/recommendations for international students: Required—TOEFL (minimum score 580 paper-based; 237 computer-based; 92 iBT); Recommended—IELTS (minimum score 7). *Application deadline:* For fall admission, 1/10 priority date for domestic and international students. Application fee: $75. Electronic applications accepted. *Financial support:* In 2010–11, 2 students received support, including 25 fellowships with full and partial tuition reimbursements available (averaging $16,173 per year), 75 research assistantships with full tuition reimbursements available (averaging $16,515 per year), 11 teaching assistantships with full tuition reimbursements available (averaging $16,263 per year); scholarships/grants also available. Financial award application deadline: 1/10; financial award applicants required to submit FAFSA. *Faculty research:* Environmental/water resources, hydrology; construction/transportation; structures/ geotechnical. Total annual research expenditures: $14.4 million. *Unit head:* Dr. Gregory R. Miller, Professor and Chair, 206-543-0350, Fax: 206-543-1543, E-mail: gmiller@uw.edu. *Application contact:* Lorna Latal, Graduate Adviser, 206-543-2574, Fax: 206-543-1543, E-mail: llatal@u.washington.edu.

Utah State University, School of Graduate Studies, College of Engineering, Department of Biological and Irrigation Engineering, Logan, UT 84322. Offers biological and agricultural engineering (MS, PhD); irrigation engineering (MS, PhD). Part-time programs available. Terminal master's awarded for partial completion of doctoral program. *Degree requirements:* For master's, thesis (for some programs); for doctorate, thesis/dissertation. *Entrance requirements:* For master's and doctorate, GRE General Test, minimum GPA of 3.0. Additional exam requirements/recommendations for international students: Required—TOEFL. *Faculty research:* On-farm water management, crop-water yield modeling, irrigation, biosensors, biological engineering.

Villanova University, College of Engineering, Department of Civil and Environmental Engineering, Program in Water Resources and Environmental Engineering, Villanova, PA 19085-1699. Offers urban water resources design (Certificate); water resources and environmental engineering (MSWREE). Part-time and evening/weekend programs available. Postbaccalaureate distance learning degree programs offered (no on-campus study). *Students:* 1 full-time (0 women), 25 part-time (7 women), 1 international. 11 applicants, 100% accepted, 4 enrolled. In 2010, 13 master's awarded. *Degree requirements:* For master's, thesis optional. *Entrance requirements:* For master's, GRE General Test (for applicants with degrees from foreign universities), BCE or bachelor's degree in science or related engineering field, minimum GPA of 3.0. Additional exam requirements/recommendations for international students: Required—TOEFL (minimum score 600 paper-based; 250 computer-based; 100 iBT). *Application deadline:* For fall admission, 8/1 priority date for domestic students, 4/1 priority date for international students; for spring admission, 12/1 for domestic students, 10/1 for international students. Applications are processed on a rolling basis. Application fee: $50. Electronic applications accepted. *Expenses:* Tuition: Part-time $700 per credit. Part-time tuition and fees vary according to degree level and program. *Financial support:* In 2010–11, research assistantships with full tuition reimbursements (averaging $13,500 per year); Federal Work-Study, tuition waivers (full and partial), and unspecified assistantships also available. Support available to part-time students. Financial award application deadline: 1/15. *Faculty research:* Photocatalytic decontamination and disinfection of water, urban storm water wetlands, economy and risk, removal and destruction of organic acids in water, sludge treatment. *Unit head:* Dr. Ronald A. Chadderton, Chairman, 610-519-4960, Fax: 610-519-6754, E-mail: ronald.chadderton@villanova.edu. *Application contact:* College of Engineering Graduate Programs Office, 610-519-5840, Fax: 610-519-5859, E-mail: engineering.grad@villanova.edu.

Virginia Polytechnic Institute and State University, Graduate School, College of Engineering, Department of Civil and Environmental Engineering, Blacksburg, VA 24061. Offers civil engineering (M Eng, MS, PhD); civil infrastructure systems (Certificate); environmental engineering (MS); environmental sciences and engineering (MS); transportation systems engineering (Certificate); treatment process engineering (Certificate); urban hydrology and stormwater management (Certificate); water quality management (Certificate). *Accreditation:* ABET (one or more programs are accredited). *Faculty:* 44 full-time (8 women), 1 part-time/adjunct (0 women). *Students:* 320 full-time (108 women), 70 part-time (20 women); includes 9 Black or African American, non-Hispanic/Latino; 15 Asian, non-Hispanic/Latino; 13 Hispanic/Latino, 126 international. Average age 27. 639 applicants, 44% accepted, 121 enrolled. In 2010, 97 master's, 18 doctorates awarded. *Degree requirements:* For master's, comprehensive exam (for some programs), thesis (for some programs); for doctorate, comprehensive exam (for some programs), thesis/dissertation (for some programs). *Entrance requirements:* For master's and doctorate, GRE. Additional exam requirements/recommendations for international students: Required—TOEFL (minimum score 550 paper-based; 213 computer-based). *Application deadline:* For fall admission, 7/1 for domestic and international students; for spring admission, 12/1 for domestic and international students. Applications are processed on a rolling basis. Application fee: $65. Electronic applications accepted. *Expenses:* Tuition, area resident: Full-time $9399; part-time $488 per credit hour. Tuition, state resident: full-time $9399; part-time $488 per credit hour. Tuition, nonresident: full-time $17,854; part-time $957.75 per credit hour. International tuition: $17,854 full-time. Required fees: $1534. Full-time tuition and fees vary according to program. *Financial support:* In 2010–11, 35 fellowships with full tuition reimbursements (averaging $5,861 per year), 82 research assistantships with full tuition reimbursements (averaging $20,397 per year), 33 teaching assistantships with full tuition reimbursements (averaging $14,542 per year) were awarded; career-related internships or fieldwork, Federal Work-Study, scholarships/grants, health care benefits, and unspecified assistantships also available. Financial award application deadline: 1/15. *Faculty research:* Construction, environmental geotechnical hydrosystems, structures and transportation engineering. Total annual research expenditures: $12.2 million. *Unit head:* Dr. Sam Easterling, Unit Head, 540-231-5143, Fax: 540-231-7532, E-mail: seaster@vt.edu. *Application contact:* Marc Widdowson, Contact, 540-231-7153, Fax: 540-231-7532, E-mail: mwiddows@vt.edu.

THE UNIVERSITY OF TEXAS AT SAN ANTONIO

Department of Civil and Environmental Engineering

Programs of Study	The Department of Civil and Environmental Engineering (CEE Department) offers the Master of Science in Civil Engineering (M.S.C.E.) degree and the Master in Civil Engineering (M.C.E.) degree. The M.S.C.E. requires courses and a thesis, and provides specialized postbaccalaureate training and exposure to research. The M.C.E. requires courses only, and provides specialized training to practicing engineers. Specialization is in environmental, geotechnical, hydraulic, structural, and transportation engineering. More information on the curriculum can be found at http://engineering.utsa.edu/CE/curriculum.html.
Research Facilities	The CEE Department has state-of-the-art instructional and laboratory facilities including structural, environmental, bioenvironmental, GIS, and geomaterials. The geomaterials lab has full Superpave capabilities and is AASHTO-accredited. Additional information can be found at http://engineering.utsa.edu/CE/labs.html.
Financial Aid	Funding is available through teaching assistantships and research assistantships. A list of recent research projects is available at http://engineering.utsa.edu/CE/researchfunding.html. Students may also take advantage of scholarship opportunities listed at http://engineering.utsa.edu/scholarships/index.php.
Cost of Study	For the 2011–12 academic year, tuition and fees for a full-time graduate degree student (9 semester hours) are approximately $3149 per semester for Texas residents and $8783 per semester for nonresidents. Some courses and programs have additional fees. Please view the following Web sites for more information: http://www.utsa.edu/fiscalservices/tuition.html and http://www.graduateschool.utsa.edu/prospective_students/detail/graduate_tuition_and_fees.
Living and Housing Costs	University on-campus housing is available and includes apartment-style living at four complexes—Chisholm Hall, University Oaks, Laurel Village, and Chaparral Village. Off-campus housing is also available and includes many apartments adjacent to the University as well as a large number located within a 5-mile drive. The rate for a one-bedroom apartment is approximately $500 per month.
Student Group	In the 2010 fall semester, the University enrolled more than 30,000 students, of whom more than 4,000 were graduate students. The CEE Department enrolls over 75 full-time and part-time graduate students per year.
Location	San Antonio, with a population of 1.5 million, is one of the nation's major metropolitan areas. As the home of the Alamo and numerous other missions built by the Franciscans, the city is historically and culturally diverse. The Guadalupe Cultural Arts Center, McNay Art Museum, the San Antonio Museum of Art, and the Witte Museum enrich the city. The performing arts are represented by the San Antonio Symphony, the annual Tejano Music Festival and Tejano Music Awards, and performances by opera and ballet companies. Also notable are Sea World, Six Flags Fiesta Texas, Brackenridge Park, the Botanical Gardens, and the downtown Riverwalk. The San Antonio Zoo has the third-largest collection in North America. A city landmark is the Tower of the Americas, which was built for the 1968 World's Fair. San Antonio is home to the National Basketball Association's Spurs, league champions in 2000, 2003, 2005, and 2007. Numerous nearby lakes allow almost year-round outdoor activity, and the beaches of the Texas Gulf coast are within a 2-hour drive. San Antonio is home to numerous festivals throughout the year, including the Fiesta San Antonio and the Rodeo with activities such as parades, fairs, and concerts.
The University	The University was founded in 1969 and has since become a comprehensive metropolitan institution. Its research expenditures place it in the top 25 percent of public universities in Texas. The University has entered a new building and recruitment phase with a view to greatly expand the research effort in engineering and the sciences. UTSA Roadrunners football is slated to compete as an NCAA Division I FCS independent in August 2011 and is expected to transition to the Division I FBS subdivision by 2013.
Applying	Applicants for admission as master's degree-seeking, special, or nondegree-seeking students may apply for admission as early as nine months before the beginning of the semester in which they wish to begin graduate study. Because of the time needed to prepare graduate summaries, applicants are encouraged to have their admission file completed at least one month before the application deadline. Application forms and instructions are available on the Graduate School Web site at www.graduateschool.utsa.edu or from the Graduate School. The completed application form, a nonrefundable application fee, and all required supporting documents must be on file with the Graduate School by the appropriate application deadline.
Correspondence and Information	For application information: The Graduate School The University of Texas at San Antonio One UTSA Circle San Antonio, Texas 78249 Phone: 210-458-4330 Web site: http://www.graduateschool.utsa.edu For program information: Department of Civil and Environmental Engineering The University of Texas at San Antonio One UTSA Circle San Antonio, Texas 78249 Phone: 210-458-7571 E-mail: John.Strubelt@usta.edu Web site: http://engineering.utsa.edu/CE/deptinfo.html

The University of Texas at San Antonio

THE FACULTY AND THEIR RESEARCH

G. Alberto Arroyo, Professor. Structures/forensic analysis.

Sazzad Bin-Shafique, Associate Professor. Beneficial use of wastes and industrial byproducts, solidification and stabilization of soil and waste, waste geotechnics, remediation geotechnics, leachability testing and groundwater and contaminant transport modeling.

Samer Dessouky, Assistant Professor. Asphalt pavement materials.

Manuel Diaz, Associate Professor. Structures/bridges.

Richard French, Professor. Hydrology and hydraulics of semi-arid lands.

Jie Huang, Assistant Professor. Geotechnical engineering, full-scale instrumentation and numerical modeling.

Drew Johnson, Associate Professor. Research and development of novel membrane separation and transfer processes for air and water systems; research and development of biological, physical ,and chemical processes for water, wastewater, and waste treatment; water conveyance and conservation.

Xiaofeng Liu, Assistant Professor. Environmental fluid mechanics, sediment transport, multiphase flow, computational fluid dynamics (CFD), water quality modeling.

A. T. Papagiannakis, Professor and Department Chair. Pavement-vehicle interaction, pavement traffic loading, micromechanical analysis of asphalt concretes.

Ruoting Pei, Assistant Professor. Applied environmental microbiology, antibiotic resistance, microbial indicator, molecular microbial ecology, biological remediation, environmental toxicology.

Hatim Sharif, Associate Professor. Hydrologic analysis, modeling, and prediction; land-atmosphere interactions; remote-sensing application in hydrometeorology; application of geographic information systems (GIS) in water resources.

Les Shephard, Professor and Director of Sustainable Energy Research Institute (SERI). Energy and environmental quality.

Heather Shipley, Assistant Professor. Fate, transport, and reactivity of chemicals in natural systems, contaminant adsorption/desorption involving nanoparticles.

Jose Weismann, Professor. Transportation infrastructure management and pavement materials.

UNIVERSITY OF UTAH

Department of Civil and Environmental Engineering

Programs of Study

Civil and Environmental Engineers are pushing the envelopes of applied science to build a more sustainable future for the world. As engineers develop in their careers, they will be challenged to imagine new ways to support the needs of business, industry, public agencies, and their companies. Advanced degrees are essential for professional careers that require imagination, innovation, complex design solutions, and management knowledge. Graduate study at the Master of Science and Doctor of Philosophy levels or as a nonmatriculated professional improves one's depth of knowledge and provides exposure to the most recent technological advances.

At the University of Utah, the Department of Civil and Environmental Engineering (CvEEN) provides comprehensive degree programs in all areas of civil engineering and specialized programs in nuclear engineering. CvEEN boasts one of the most rapidly growing programs in the nation and a large experienced faculty. Graduate programs in civil and environmental engineering include an emphasis in environmental engineering, materials engineering, structural engineering, transportation engineering, water resource engineering, engineering management, and geotechnical engineering. Graduate students may choose to integrate several of these areas in both course work and research to develop the necessary expertise their careers demand. CvEEN graduates are trained to work in diverse teams with multiple disciplines and creative talents.

Research Facilities

CvEEN research facilities have had significant upgrades over the past five years. The improvements include a new building space, upgraded machines, new research technologies, and new specialized labs. The research labs within CvEEN include asphalt, biological hazard, biological systems, carbon sequestration, composites, concrete, environmental, environmental characterization, geotechnical, hydraulics, materials, structures, transportation computing, water chemistry, and water quality. For more information on the research areas within the Department, visit the research Web site: http://www.civil.utah.edu/research.html.

In addition, there are four research centers and labs associated with the CvEEN program. They include the Carbon Science and Engineering Center, Energy and Geosciences Institute, Nuclear Engineering Program, and the Utah Traffic Lab. Graduate students in CvEEN work in all of these labs to conduct their research. More information can be found on the Research Centers Web site: http://www.civil.utah.edu/centers.html.

Financial Aid

Financial assistance is available to students through fellowships, paid research and teaching assistantships, scholarships, and loans. Paid assistantships are offered to Master of Science–Thesis and Doctor of Philosophy students. Eligible students may also receive paid tuition if they meet the program requirements. Scholarships are awarded for an academic year, with applications due February 15 preceding the academic year the scholarship is needed. Domestic students are eligible for fellowships, which are offered by the College of Engineering on a competitive basis to exceptionally well-quailfied applicants. More information can be found at http://www.civil.utah.edu/grad.html.

Cost of Study

The University of Utah has one of the most affordable tution rates in the west. Tuition rates vary depending on residency and the number of enrolled credits. The College of Engineering also has a Differential Tution charge for each credit hour. More information can be found at http://fbs.admin.utah.edu/income.

Living and Housing Costs

Housing and Residential Education (HRE) primarily provides housing for single students. A wide range of options is available and the housing options, applications, and costs are all available on the HRE Web site: http://www.housing.utah.edu/.

University Student Apartments provides apartment housing for students and their families. Housing options, floor plans, rates, and applications are all available on the Web site: http://www.apartments.utah.edu/. Information for off-campus housing is available at http://offcampushousing.utah.edu/.

Student Group

CvEEN has student groups for most emphasis areas within the program. The groups that the Department currently recognizes are: American Concrete Institute (ACI), Associated General Contractors of America (AGC), American Society of Civil Engineers (ASCE), American Water Resources Association (AWRA), Chi Epsilon, Institute of Transportation Engineers (ITE), Student Advisory Committee (SAC), and Water Environment Federation (WEF). More information can be found at http://www.civil.utah.edu/student_group.html.

Location

Salt Lake City lies in a valley that is surrounded by mountain peaks reaching nearly 12,000 feet in elevation. The city is rich in cultural activities and professional sports. Salt Lake City is within minutes of eleven world-class ski resorts, and ten national parks are within a short drive of the city.

The University

The 1,500-acre University campus is nestled in the foothills of the Wasatch Mountains and is characterized by its diverse architecture and attractive landscaping. The Marriott Library is one of the centerpieces of campus and completed a major renovation in 2009. The libaray is five floors with over 29 miles of bookshelves. The University is ranked first in the nation for starting technology companies based on its research and is ranked third among America's most high-tech campuses.

Applying

To be considered for the graduate program, applicants must submit the University Application, along with a Personal Statement, resume, three letters of recommendation, and official GRE scores. International applicants must also submit a TOEFL/IELTS score. A minimum undergraduate GPA of 3.0 is required to apply to the program. For further information on GRE and TOEFL/IELTS exam requirements, how to submit an application and supporting materials, and how to apply for assistantships, prospective students should visit the Web site at www.civil.utah.edu.

Correspondence and Information

Amanda May, Academic Adviser
Department of Civil and Environmental Engineering
University of Utah
110 South Central Campus Drive, Suite 2000B
Salt Lake City, Utah 84112-9458
Phone: 801-581-6931
Fax: 801-585-5477
E-mail: amandam@civil.utah.edu
Web site: http://www.civil.utah.edu

Ramesh Goel, Director of Graduate Studies
Department of Civil and Environmental Engineering
University of Utah
110 South Central Campus Drive, Suite 2000
Salt Lake City, Utah 84112-9458
Phone: 801-581-6110
Fax: 801-585-5477
E-mail: rgoel@civil.utah.edu
Web site: http://www.civil.utah.edu

University of Utah

THE FACULTY AND THEIR RESEARCH

Steven Bartlett, Associate Professor, Ph.D., Brigham Young. Geotechnical and engineering management.

Amanda Bordelon, Assistant Professor, Ph.D., Illinois at Urbana-Champaign. Materials, transportation, sustainable infrastructure, and engineering management.

Steven Burian, Associate Professor, Ph.D., Alabama, Tuscaloosa. Environmental, water resources, and engineering management.

Janice Chambers, Associate Professor, Ph.D., Colorado at Boulder. Structures and engineering management.

Otakuye Conroy-Ben, Assistant Professor, Ph.D., Arizona. Environmental, water resources, and engineering management.

Ramesh Goel, Associate Professor, Ph.D., South Carolina, Columbia. Environmental and engineering management.

Andy Hong, Professor, Ph.D., Caltech. Environmental and engineering management.

Luis Ibarra, Assistant Professor, Ph.D., Stanford. Structural, nuclear, and engineering management.

Tatjana Jevremovic, Professor, Ph.D., Tokyo. Nuclear.

Evert Lawton, Professor, Ph.D., Washington State. Geotechnical and engineering management.

Peter Martin, Professor, Ph.D., Nottingham (Engand). Transportation and engineering management.

Brian McPherson, Associate Professor, Ph.D., Utah. Water resources, environmental, and engineering management.

Chris Pantelides, Professor, Ph.D., Missouri–Rolla. Structures, sustainable infrastructure, and engineering management.

Christine Pomeroy, Assistant Professor, Ph.D., Colorado State. Water resources, environmental, and engineering management..

Richard (R.J.) Porter, Assistant Professor, Ph.D., Penn State. Transportation and engineering management.

Lawrence Reaveley, Professor, Ph.D., New Mexico. Structural and engineering management.

Pedro Romero, Associate Professor, Ph.D., Penn State. Materials, transportation, and engineering management.

Paul Tikalsky, Professor and Chair, Ph.D., Texas at Austin. Materials, transportation, sustainable infrastructure, and engineering management.

Haori Yang, Assistant Professor, Ph.D., Michigan. Nuclear.

Xuesong Zhou, Assistant Professor, Ph.D., Maryland. Transportation and engineering management.

The University of Utah Legacy Bridge looking out onto the Salt Lake Valley.

Student researchers in the Utah Infrastructure Laboratory.

Section 8
Computer Science and Information Technology

This section contains a directory of institutions offering graduate work in computer science and information technology, followed by in-depth entries submitted by institutions that chose to prepare detailed program descriptions. Additional information about programs listed in the directory but not augmented by an in-depth entry may be obtained by writing directly to the dean of a graduate school or chair of a department at the address given in the directory.

For programs offering related work, see also in this book *Electrical and Computer Engineering, Engineering and Applied Sciences,* and *Industrial Engineering.* In the other guides in this series:

Graduate Programs in the Humanities, Arts & Social Sciences
See *Communication and Media*
Graduate Programs in the Physical Sciences, Mathematics, Agricultural Sciences, the Environment & Natural Resources
See *Mathematical Sciences*
Graduate Programs in Business, Education, Health, Information Studies, Law & Social Work, Allied Health
See *Business Administration and Management* and *Library and Information Studies*

CONTENTS

Program Directories

Close-Ups and Displays

Artificial Intelligence/Robotics

California State University, Northridge, Graduate Studies, College of Engineering and Computer Science, Department of Manufacturing Systems Engineering and Management, Northridge, CA 91330. Offers engineering automation (MS); engineering management (MS); manufacturing systems engineering (MS); materials engineering (MS). Postbaccalaureate distance learning degree programs offered. *Entrance requirements:* For master's, GRE (if cumulative undergraduate GPA less than 3.0).

Carnegie Mellon University, College of Humanities and Social Sciences, Department of Statistics, Pittsburgh, PA 15213-3891. Offers machine learning and statistics (PhD); mathematical finance (PhD); statistics (MS, PhD), including applied statistics (PhD), computational statistics (PhD), theoretical statistics (PhD); statistics and public policy (PhD). Terminal master's awarded for partial completion of doctoral program. *Degree requirements:* For doctorate, comprehensive exam, thesis/dissertation. *Entrance requirements:* For master's and doctorate, GRE General Test. Additional exam requirements/recommendations for international students: Required—TOEFL. *Faculty research:* Stochastic processes, Bayesian statistics, statistical computing, decision theory, psychiatric statistics.

Carnegie Mellon University, School of Computer Science, Department of Machine Learning, Pittsburgh, PA 15213-3891. Offers PhD.

Carnegie Mellon University, School of Computer Science and Carnegie Institute of Technology, Robotics Institute, Pittsburgh, PA 15213-3891. Offers robotic systems development (MS); robotics (MS, PhD); robotics technology (MS). *Degree requirements:* For doctorate, thesis/dissertation. *Entrance requirements:* For doctorate, GRE General Test, GRE Subject Test. Additional exam requirements/recommendations for international students: Required—TOEFL. *Faculty research:* Perception, cognition, manipulation, robot systems, manufacturing.

Cornell University, Graduate School, Graduate Fields of Engineering, Field of Computer Science, Ithaca, NY 14853-0001. Offers algorithms (M Eng, PhD); applied logic and automated reasoning (M Eng, PhD); artificial intelligence (M Eng, PhD); computer graphics (M Eng, PhD); computer science (M Eng, PhD); computer vision (M Eng, PhD); concurrency and distributed computing (M Eng, PhD); information organization and retrieval (M Eng, PhD); operating systems (M Eng, PhD); parallel computing (M Eng, PhD); programming environments (M Eng, PhD); programming languages and methodology (M Eng, PhD); robotics (M Eng, PhD); scientific computing (M Eng, PhD); theory of computation (M Eng, PhD). *Faculty:* 60 full-time (8 women). *Students:* 233 full-time (45 women); includes 1 Black or African American, non-Hispanic/Latino; 17 Asian, non-Hispanic/Latino; 1 Hispanic/Latino, 140 international. Average age 24. 1,026 applicants, 31% accepted, 163 enrolled. In 2010, 103 master's, 19 doctorates awarded. *Degree requirements:* For doctorate, comprehensive exam, thesis/dissertation. *Entrance requirements:* For master's, GRE General Test, 2 letters of recommendation; for doctorate, GRE General Test, GRE Subject Test (computer science or mathematics), 3 letters of recommendation. Additional exam requirements/recommendations for international students: Required—TOEFL (minimum score 505 paper-based; 213 computer-based; 77 iBT). *Application deadline:* For fall admission, 1/1 for domestic students. Application fee: $70. Electronic applications accepted. *Expenses:* Tuition: Full-time $29,500. Required fees: $76. Tuition and fees vary according to degree level and program. *Financial support:* In 2010–11, 100 students received support, including 25 fellowships with full tuition reimbursements available, 55 research assistantships with full tuition reimbursements available, 28 teaching assistantships with full tuition reimbursements available; institutionally sponsored loans, scholarships/grants, health care benefits, tuition waivers (full and partial), and unspecified assistantships also available. Financial award applicants required to submit FAFSA. *Faculty research:* Artificial intelligence, operating systems and databases, programming languages and security, scientific computing, theory of computing, computational biology and graphics. *Unit head:* Director of Graduate Studies, 607-255-8593, Fax: 607-255-4428. *Application contact:* Graduate Field Assistant, 607-255-8593, Fax: 607-255-4428, E-mail: phd@cs.cornell.edu.

Eastern Michigan University, Graduate School, College of Arts and Sciences, Department of Computer Science, Ypsilanti, MI 48197. Offers artificial intelligence (Graduate Certificate); computer science (MS). Part-time and evening/weekend programs available. Postbaccalaureate distance learning degree programs offered (no on-campus study). *Faculty:* 15 full-time (5 women). *Students:* 15 full-time (5 women), 27 part-time (2 women); includes 2 Black or African American, non-Hispanic/Latino; 1 American Indian or Alaska Native, non-Hispanic/Latino; 2 Asian, non-Hispanic/Latino, 17 international. Average age 30. 86 applicants, 59% accepted, 15 enrolled. In 2010, 7 master's, 1 other advanced degree awarded. *Degree requirements:* For master's, thesis or alternative. *Entrance requirements:* For master's, at least 18 credit hours of 200-level (or above) computer science courses including data structures, programming languages like java, C or C++, computer organization; courses in discrete mathematics, probability and statistics, linear algebra and calculus; minimum GPA of 2.75 in computer science. Additional exam requirements/recommendations for international students: Required—TOEFL. *Application deadline:* For fall admission, 8/1 for domestic students, 5/1 for international students; for winter admission, 12/1 for domestic students, 10/1 for international students; for spring admission, 4/1 for domestic students, 2/1 for international students. Application fee: $35. *Financial support:* Fellowships, research assistantships with full tuition reimbursements, teaching assistantships with full tuition reimbursements, career-related internships or fieldwork, Federal Work-Study, institutionally sponsored loans, scholarships/grants, tuition waivers (partial), and unspecified assistantships available. Support available to part-time students. Financial award applicants required to submit FAFSA. *Unit head:* Dr. William McMillan, Department Head, 734-487-1063, Fax: 734-487-6824, E-mail: wmcmillan@emich.edu. *Application contact:* Pamela Moore, Graduate Coordinator, 734-487-1063, Fax: 734-487-6824, E-mail: pmoore@emich.edu.

Eastern Michigan University, Graduate School, College of Arts and Sciences, Department of English Language and Literature, Program in Language Technology, Ypsilanti, MI 48197. Offers Graduate Certificate. Part-time and evening/weekend programs available. In 2010, 1 Graduate Certificate awarded. *Entrance requirements:* Additional exam requirements/recommendations for international students: Required—TOEFL. Application fee: $35. *Financial support:* Research assistantships with full tuition reimbursements, teaching assistantships with full tuition reimbursements, career-related internships or fieldwork, Federal Work-Study, institutionally sponsored loans, scholarships/grants, tuition waivers (full and partial), and unspecified assistantships available. Support available to part-time students. *Application contact:* Dr. Veronica Grondona, Program Advisor, 734-487-0145, Fax: 734-483-9744, E-mail: vgrondona@emich.edu.

Indiana University–Purdue University Indianapolis, School of Engineering and Technology, Department of Electrical Engineering, Indianapolis, IN 46202-2896. Offers biomedical engineering (MS, PhD); electrical and computer engineering (MS, MSECE, PhD), including biomedical engineering (MSECE), control and automation (MSECE), signal processing (MSECE); engineering (interdisciplinary) (MSE). *Students:* 40 full-time (13 women), 35 part-time (7 women); includes 7 minority (1 Black or African American, non-Hispanic/Latino; 1 Asian, non-Hispanic/Latino; 3 Hispanic/Latino; 2 Two or more races, non-Hispanic/Latino), 45 international. Average age 27. 153 applicants, 53% accepted, 42 enrolled. In 2010, 37 master's awarded. Application fee: $55 ($65 for international students). *Unit head:* Yaobin Chen, Unit Head, 317-274-4032, Fax: 317-274-4493. *Application contact:* Valerie Diemer, Graduate Program, 317-278-4960, Fax: 317-278-1671, E-mail: grad@engr.iupui.edu.

Instituto Tecnológico y de Estudios Superiores de Monterrey, Campus Monterrey, Graduate and Research Division, Program in Computer Science, Monterrey, Mexico. Offers artificial intelligence (PhD); computer science (MS); information systems (MS); information technology (MS). Part-time programs available. *Degree requirements:* For master's, one foreign language, thesis; for doctorate, one foreign language, thesis/dissertation. *Entrance requirements:* For master's, EXADEP; for doctorate, master's degree in related field. Additional exam

requirements/recommendations for international students: Required—TOEFL. *Faculty research:* Distributed systems, software engineering, decision support systems.

Instituto Tecnológico y de Estudios Superiores de Monterrey, Campus Monterrey, Graduate and Research Division, Programs in Engineering, Monterrey, Mexico. Offers applied statistics (M Eng); artificial intelligence (PhD); automation engineering (M Eng); chemical engineering (M Eng); civil engineering (M Eng); electrical engineering (M Eng); electronic engineering (M Eng); environmental engineering (M Eng); industrial engineering (M Eng, PhD); manufacturing engineering (M Eng); mechanical engineering (M Eng); systems and quality engineering (M Eng). M Eng program offered jointly with University of Waterloo; PhD in industrial engineering with Texas A&M University. Part-time and evening/weekend programs available. Terminal master's awarded for partial completion of doctoral program. *Degree requirements:* For master's, one foreign language, thesis; for doctorate, one foreign language, thesis/dissertation. *Entrance requirements:* For master's, EXADEP; for doctorate, GRE, master's degree in related field. Additional exam requirements/recommendations for international students: Required—TOEFL. *Faculty research:* Flexible manufacturing cells, materials, statistical methods, environmental prevention, control and evaluation.

Portland State University, Graduate Studies, Systems Science Program, Portland, OR 97207-0751. Offers computational intelligence (Certificate); computer modeling and simulation (Certificate); systems science (MS); systems science/anthropology (PhD); systems science/business administration (PhD); systems science/civil engineering (PhD); systems science/economics (PhD); systems science/engineering management (PhD); systems science/general (PhD); systems science/mathematical sciences (PhD); systems science/mechanical engineering (PhD); systems science/psychology (PhD); systems science/sociology (PhD). *Faculty:* 4 full-time (0 women), 1 part-time/adjunct (0 women). *Students:* 15 full-time (4 women), 35 part-time (11 women); includes 1 American Indian or Alaska Native, non-Hispanic/Latino; 1 Asian, non-Hispanic/Latino; 1 Two or more races, non-Hispanic/Latino, 4 international. Average age 39. 8 applicants, 88% accepted, 5 enrolled. In 2010, 2 master's, 4 doctorates awarded. *Degree requirements:* For doctorate, variable foreign language requirement, thesis/dissertation. *Entrance requirements:* For master's, 2 letters of recommendation; for doctorate, GMAT, GRE General Test, minimum undergraduate GPA of 3.0. Additional exam requirements/recommendations for international students: Required—TOEFL. *Application deadline:* For fall admission, 2/1 for domestic students; for spring admission, 11/1 for domestic students. Application fee: $50. *Expenses:* Tuition, state resident: full-time $8505; part-time $315 per credit. Tuition, nonresident: full-time $13,284; part-time $492 per credit. Required fees: $1482; $21 per credit. $99 per term. One-time fee: $120. Part-time tuition and fees vary according to course load and program. *Financial support:* In 2010–11, 1 research assistantship with full tuition reimbursement (averaging $7,704 per year) was awarded; teaching assistantships with full tuition reimbursements, career-related internships or fieldwork, Federal Work-Study, scholarships/grants, and unspecified assistantships also available. Support available to part-time students. Financial award application deadline: 3/1; financial award applicants required to submit FAFSA. *Faculty research:* Systems theory and methodology, artificial intelligence neural networks, information theory, nonlinear dynamics/chaos, modeling and simulation. *Unit head:* George Lendaris, Acting Director, 503-725-4960. *Application contact:* Dawn Sharafi, Administrative Assistant, 503-725-4960, E-mail: dawn@sysc.pdx.edu.

South Dakota School of Mines and Technology, Graduate Division, Program in Robotics and Intelligent Autonomous Systems, Rapid City, SD 57701-3995. Offers MS. Part-time programs available. *Entrance requirements:* Additional exam requirements/recommendations for international students: Required—TOEFL, TWE. Electronic applications accepted. *Faculty research:* Database systems, remote sensing, numerical modeling, artificial intelligence, neural networks.

University of California, Riverside, Graduate Division, Department of Electrical Engineering, Riverside, CA 92521-0102. Offers electrical engineering (MS, PhD), including computer engineering, control and robotics, intelligent systems, nano-materials, devices and circuits, signal processing and communications. Terminal master's awarded for partial completion of doctoral program. *Degree requirements:* For master's, thesis optional; for doctorate, thesis/dissertation, qualifying exams. *Entrance requirements:* For master's and doctorate, GRE General Test, minimum GPA of 3.25. Additional exam requirements/recommendations for international students: Required—TOEFL (minimum score 550 paper-based; 213 computer-based; 80 iBT). Electronic applications accepted. *Faculty research:* Solid state devices, integrated circuits, signal processing.

University of California, San Diego, Office of Graduate Studies, Department of Electrical and Computer Engineering, La Jolla, CA 92093. Offers applied ocean science (MS, PhD); applied physics (MS, PhD); communication theory and systems (MS, PhD); computer engineering (MS, PhD); electrical engineering (M Eng); electronic circuits and systems (MS, PhD); intelligent systems, robotics and control (MS, PhD); photonics (MS, PhD); signal and image processing (MS, PhD). MS only offered to students who have been admitted to the PhD program. *Entrance requirements:* For master's and doctorate, GRE General Test. Electronic applications accepted.

University of Georgia, College of Arts and Sciences, Artificial Intelligence Center, Athens, GA 30602. Offers MS. *Faculty:* 1 full-time (0 women). *Students:* 20 full-time (4 women), 6 part-time (2 women); includes 2 Black or African American, non-Hispanic/Latino; 1 Hispanic/Latino, 10 international. 17 applicants, 59% accepted, 10 enrolled. In 2010, 5 master's awarded. *Degree requirements:* For master's, thesis. *Entrance requirements:* For master's, GRE General Test. *Application deadline:* For fall admission, 7/1 priority date for domestic students; for spring admission, 11/15 for domestic students. Application fee: $50. Electronic applications accepted. *Expenses:* Tuition, state resident: full-time $7200; part-time $344 per credit hour. Tuition, nonresident: full-time $21,900; part-time $944 per credit hour. Tuition and fees vary according to course load and program. *Financial support:* Unspecified assistantships available. *Unit head:* Dr. Walter Don Potter, Director, 706-542-0361, E-mail: potter@uga.edu. *Application contact:* Dr. Khaled M. Rasheed, Graduate Coordinator, 706-542-3444, Fax: 706-542-8864, E-mail: khaled@cs.uga.edu.

University of Pittsburgh, Katz Graduate School of Business, Doctoral Program in Business Administration, Pittsburgh, PA 15260. Offers accounting (PhD); finance (PhD); information systems (PhD); marketing (PhD); operations/decision sciences/artificial intelligence (PhD); organizational behavior and human resource management (PhD); strategic planning (PhD). *Accreditation:* AACSB. *Faculty:* 50 full-time (15 women). *Students:* 51 full-time (22 women); includes 3 Black or African American, non-Hispanic/Latino; 4 Asian, non-Hispanic/Latino; 2 Hispanic/Latino, 18 international. 448 applicants, 5% accepted, 13 enrolled. In 2010, 4 doctorates awarded. *Degree requirements:* For doctorate, comprehensive exam, thesis/dissertation. *Entrance requirements:* For doctorate, GMAT or GRE, 0Bachelor's degree, references, 3.0 GPA. Additional exam requirements/recommendations for international students: Required—TOEFL, IELTS. *Application deadline:* For fall admission, 2/1 priority date for domestic and international students. Applications are processed on a rolling basis. Application fee: $50. Electronic applications accepted. *Expenses:* Tuition, state resident: full-time $17,304; part-time $701 per credit. Tuition, nonresident: full-time $29,554; part-time $1210 per credit. Required fees: $740; $214 per term. Tuition and fees vary according to program. *Financial support:* In 2010–11, 39 students received support, including 29 research assistantships with full tuition reimbursements available (averaging $1,900 per year), 10 teaching assistantships with full tuition reimbursements available (averaging $23,745 per year); fellowships, Federal Work-Study, scholarships/grants, health care benefits, and unspecified assistantships also available. Financial award application deadline: 2/1. *Faculty research:* Accounting statements and reporting, incentives and governance, corporate finance, mergers and acquisitions, information systems processes, structures and decision-making, organizational structure, knowledge management and corporate strategy, consumer behavior and marketing models. Total annual research expenditures: $362,777. *Unit head:* Dr. John E. Hulland, Director of Doctoral Program, 412-648-1534, Fax: 412-624-3633, E-mail: jhulland@katz.pitt.edu. *Application contact:* Carrie Woods, Assistant Director, Doctoral Office, 412-648-1525, Fax: 412-624-3633, E-mail: cawoods@katz.pitt.edu.

University of Pittsburgh, School of Arts and Sciences, Intelligent Systems Program, Pittsburgh, PA 15260. Offers MS, PhD. *Faculty:* 25 full-time (6 women). *Students:* 17 full-time (2 women), 9 international. Average age 30. 19 applicants, 26% accepted, 2 enrolled. In 2010, 4 master's, 3 doctorates awarded. Terminal master's awarded for partial completion of doctoral program. *Degree requirements:* For master's, thesis; for doctorate, comprehensive exam, thesis/dissertation. *Entrance requirements:* For master's and doctorate, GRE General Test. Additional exam requirements/recommendations for international students: Required—TOEFL. *Application deadline:* For fall admission, 2/1 priority date for domestic and international students. Applications are processed on a rolling basis. Application fee: $50. Electronic applications accepted. *Expenses:* Tuition, state resident: full-time $17,304; part-time $701 per credit. Tuition, nonresident: full-time $29,554; part-time $1210 per credit. Required fees: $740; $214 per term. Tuition and fees vary according to program. *Financial support:* In 2010–11, 14 students received support, including 5 fellowships with full tuition reimbursements available (averaging $20,630 per year), 9 research assistantships with full tuition reimbursements available (averaging $18,028 per year); Federal Work-Study, institutionally sponsored loans, scholarships/grants, traineeships, health care benefits, and unspecified assistantships also available. Financial award application deadline: 2/1. *Faculty research:* Medical artificial intelligence, expert systems, clinical decision support, plan generation and recognition, special cognition. *Unit head:* Diane Litman, Director, 412-624-8838, Fax: 412-624-8561, E-mail: litman@cs.pitt.edu. *Application contact:* Wendy Bergstein, Administrator, 412-624-5755, Fax: 412-624-8561, E-mail: wab23@pitt.edu.

See Display below and Close-Up on page 339.

University of Southern California, Graduate School, Viterbi School of Engineering, Department of Computer Science, Los Angeles, CA 90089. Offers computer networks (MS); computer science (MS, PhD); computer security (MS); game development (MS); high performance computing and simulations (MS); human language technology (MS); intelligent robotics (MS); multimedia and creative technologies (MS); software engineering (MS). Part-time and evening/weekend programs available. Postbaccalaureate distance learning degree programs offered (no on-campus study). *Faculty:* 28 full-time (3 women), 56 part-time/adjunct (7 women). *Students:* 710 full-time (115 women), 302 part-time (59 women); includes 76 minority (1 Black or African American, non-Hispanic/Latino; 55 Asian, non-Hispanic/Latino; 14 Hispanic/Latino; 6 Two or more races, non-Hispanic/Latino), 819 international. 2,379 applicants, 30% accepted, 319 enrolled. In 2010, 332 master's, 32 doctorates awarded. *Entrance requirements:* For master's and doctorate, GRE General Test. Additional exam requirements/recommendations for international students: Required—TOEFL. *Application deadline:* For fall admission, 12/1 priority date for domestic and international students; for spring admission, 9/15 priority date for domestic and international students. Applications are processed on a rolling basis. Application fee: $85. Electronic applications accepted. *Expenses:* Tuition: Full-time $31,240; part-time $1420 per unit. Required fees: $600. One-time fee: $35 full-time. Full-time tuition and fees vary according to degree level and program. *Financial support:* In 2010–11, fellowships with full tuition reimbursements (averaging $30,000 per year), research assistantships with full tuition reimbursements (averaging $20,000 per year), teaching assistantships with full tuition reimbursements (averaging $20,000 per year) were awarded; career-related internships or fieldwork, scholarships/grants, health care benefits, and unspecified assistantships also available. Financial award application deadline: 12/1; financial award applicants required to submit CSS PROFILE or FAFSA. *Faculty research:* Databases, computer graphics and computer vision, software engineering, networks and security, robotics, multimedia and virtual reality. Total annual research expenditures: $11.8 million. *Unit head:* Dr. Shanghua Teng, Chair, 213-740-4494, E-mail: csdept@usc.edu. *Application contact:* Lizsl DeLeon, Director of Student Affairs, 213-740-4496, E-mail: ldeleon@usc.edu.

Villanova University, College of Engineering, Department of Electrical and Computer Engineering, Program in Computer Engineering, Villanova, PA 19085-1699. Offers computer architectures (Certificate); computer engineering (MSCPE); intelligent control systems (Certificate). Part-time and evening/weekend programs available. *Students:* 3 full-time (0 women), 14 part-time (2 women); includes 1 Black or African American, non-Hispanic/Latino; 3 Hispanic/Latino, 3 international. 35 applicants, 54% accepted. In 2010, 13 master's awarded. *Degree requirements:* For master's, thesis optional. *Entrance requirements:* For master's, GRE General Test (for applicants with degrees from foreign universities), BEE, minimum GPA of 3.0. Additional exam requirements/recommendations for international students: Required—TOEFL (minimum score 600 paper-based; 250 computer-based; 100 iBT). *Application deadline:* For fall admission, 8/1 priority date for domestic students, 4/1 for international students; for spring admission, 12/1 for domestic students, 8/1 for international students. Applications are processed on a rolling basis. Application fee: $50. Electronic applications accepted. *Expenses:* Tuition: Part-time $700 per credit. Part-time tuition and fees vary according to degree level and program. *Financial support:* In 2010–11, research assistantships with full and partial tuition reimbursements (averaging $13,500 per year); Federal Work-Study, scholarships/grants, tuition waivers (full and partial), and unspecified assistantships also available. Support available to part-time students. Financial award application deadline: 1/15. *Faculty research:* Expert systems, computer vision, neural networks, image processing, computer architectures. *Unit head:* Dr. Pritpal Singh, Chairman, 610-519-4971, Fax: 610-519-4436. *Application contact:* College of Engineering, Graduate Programs Office, 610-519-5840, Fax: 610-519-5859, E-mail: engineering.grad@villanova.edu.

Villanova University, College of Engineering, Department of Electrical and Computer Engineering, Program in Electrical Engineering, Villanova, PA 19085-1699. Offers electric power systems (Certificate); electrical engineering (MSEE); electro mechanical systems (Certificate); high frequency systems (Certificate); intelligent control systems (Certificate); wireless and digital communications (Certificate). Part-time and evening/weekend programs available. *Students:* 9 full-time (1 woman), 55 part-time (11 women); includes 5 Black or African American, non-Hispanic/Latino; 6 Asian, non-Hispanic/Latino; 1 Hispanic/Latino, 16 international. 54 applicants, 63% accepted, 18 enrolled. In 2010, 16 master's awarded. *Degree requirements:* For master's, thesis optional. *Entrance requirements:* For master's, GRE General Test (for applicants with degrees from foreign universities), BEE, minimum GPA of 3.0. Additional exam requirements/recommendations for international students: Required—TOEFL (minimum score 600 paper-based; 250 computer-based; 100 iBT). *Application deadline:* For fall admission, 8/1 for domestic students, 4/1 for international students; for spring admission, 12/1 for domestic students, 8/1 for international students. Applications are processed on a rolling basis. Application fee: $50. *Expenses:* Tuition: Part-time $700 per credit. Part-time tuition and fees vary according to degree level and program. *Financial support:* In 2010–11, research assistantships with full and partial tuition reimbursements (averaging $13,500 per year); Federal Work-Study, scholarships/grants, tuition waivers (full and partial), and unspecified assistantships also available. Support available to part-time students. Financial award application deadline: 1/15. *Faculty research:* Signal processing, communications, antennas, devices. *Unit head:* Dr. Pritpal Singh, Chairman, 610-519-4971, Fax: 610-519-4436. *Application contact:* College of Engineering, Graduate Programs Office, 610-519-5840, Fax: 610-519-5859, E-mail: engineering.grad@villanova.edu.

Worcester Polytechnic Institute, Graduate Studies and Research, Department of Computer Science, Worcester, MA 01609-2280. Offers computer and communications networks (MS); computer science (MS, PhD, Advanced Certificate, Graduate Certificate); robotics engineering (MS, PhD). Part-time and evening/weekend programs available. *Faculty:* 19 full-time (3 women). *Students:* 84 full-time (16 women), 24 part-time (3 women); includes 3 Black or African American, non-Hispanic/Latino; 6 Native Hawaiian or other Pacific Islander, non-Hispanic/Latino, 50 international. 291 applicants, 48% accepted, 36 enrolled. In 2010, 25 master's, 4 doctorates awarded. Terminal master's awarded for partial completion of doctoral program. *Degree requirements:* For master's, thesis optional; for doctorate, comprehensive exam,

Peterson's Graduate Programs in Engineering & Applied Sciences 2012
www.facebook.com/petersonspublishing
233

Artificial Intelligence/Robotics

Worcester Polytechnic Institute (continued)
thesis/dissertation. *Entrance requirements:* For master's, GRE General Test, GRE Subject Test in computer science (recommended), 3 letters of recommendation; for doctorate, GRE General Test, GRE Subject Test in computer science (recommended), 3 letters of recommendation, statement of purpose. Additional exam requirements/recommendations for international students: Required—TOEFL (minimum score 550 paper-based; 213 computer-based; 79 iBT), IELTS (minimum score 6.5). *Application deadline:* For fall admission, 1/1 priority date for domestic and international students; for spring admission, 10/1 priority date for domestic and international students. Applications are processed on a rolling basis. Application fee: $70. Electronic applications accepted. *Expenses:* Tuition: Full-time $20,862; part-time $1159 per term. One-time fee: $15. *Financial support:* Career-related internships or fieldwork, institutionally sponsored loans, scholarships/grants, and unspecified assistantships available. Financial award application deadline: 1/1; financial award applicants required to submit FAFSA. *Faculty research:* Computer networks and distributed systems, databases and data mining, artificial intelligence, computer graphics and visualization, applied logic and security. *Unit head:* Dr. Michael Gennert, Interim Head, 508-831-5357, Fax: 508-831-5776, E-mail: michaelg@wpi.edu. *Application contact:* Dr. Carolina Ruiz, Graduate Coordinator, 508-831-5357, Fax: 508-831-5776, E-mail: ruiz@wpi.edu.

Worcester Polytechnic Institute, Graduate Studies and Research, Program in Robotics Engineering, Worcester, MA 01609-2280. Offers MS, PhD. Part-time and evening/weekend programs available. *Students:* 13 full-time (1 woman); includes 2 Black or African American, non-Hispanic/Latino; 1 Native Hawaiian or other Pacific Islander, non-Hispanic/Latino, 1 international. 40 applicants, 73% accepted, 10 enrolled. *Degree requirements:* For master's, thesis or capstone design project; for doctorate, thesis/dissertation. *Entrance requirements:* For master's and doctorate, GRE, 3 letters of recommendation, statement of purpose. Additional exam requirements/recommendations for international students: Required—TOEFL (minimum score 550 paper-based; 213 computer-based; 79 iBT), IELTS (minimum score 6.5). *Application deadline:* For fall admission, 1/1 priority date for domestic and international students; for spring admission, 10/1 priority date for domestic and international students. Applications are processed on a rolling basis. Electronic applications accepted. *Expenses:* Tuition: Full-time $20,862; part-time $1159 per term. One-time fee: $15. *Financial support:* Career-related internships or fieldwork, institutionally sponsored loans, scholarships/grants, and unspecified assistantships available. Financial award application deadline: 1/1; financial award applicants required to submit FAFSA. *Faculty research:* Medical robotics, human-robot interaction, robot learning, manipulation, adaptive control, multi-robot systems. *Unit head:* Dr. Michael Gennert, Director, Robotics Engineering Program, 508-831-5357, Fax: 508-831-5776, E-mail: michaelg@wpi.edu. *Application contact:* Tracey Coetzee, Administrative Assistant, 508-831-5357, Fax: 508-831-5776, E-mail: tcoetzee@wpi.edu.

Bioinformatics

Arizona State University, Graduate College, Department of Biomedical Informatics, Phoenix, AZ 85004. Offers MS, PhD. *Faculty:* 11 full-time (2 women). *Students:* 28 full-time (9 women), 7 part-time (0 women); includes 5 minority (1 American Indian or Alaska Native, non-Hispanic/Latino; 3 Asian, non-Hispanic/Latino; 1 Hispanic/Latino), 19 international. Average age 29. 60 applicants, 52% accepted, 10 enrolled. In 2010, 9 master's awarded. Terminal master's awarded for partial completion of doctoral program. *Degree requirements:* For master's, interactive Program of Study (iPOS) submitted before completing 50 percent of required credit hours; for doctorate, comprehensive exam, thesis/dissertation, interactive Program of Study (iPOS) submitted before completing 50 percent of required credit hours. *Entrance requirements:* For master's, GRE or MCAT, bachelor's degree with minimum GPA of 3.25 in computer science, biology, physiology, nursing, statistics, engineering, related fields, or unrelated fields with appropriate academic backgrounds; resume/curriculum vitae; statement of purpose; 3 letters of recommendation; all official transcripts; for doctorate, GRE or MCAT, bachelor's degree with minimum GPA of 3.5 in computer science, biology, physiology, nursing, statistics, engineering, related fields, or unrelated fields with appropriate academic backgrounds; resume/curriculum vitae; statement of purpose; 3 letters of recommendation; all official transcripts. Additional exam requirements/recommendations for international students: Required—TOEFL (minimum score 550 paper-based; 213 computer-based; 83 iBT), IELTS (minimum score 6.5). *Application deadline:* For fall admission, 1/15 for domestic students, 2/15 for international students. Applications are processed on a rolling basis. Application fee: $70 ($90 for international students). Electronic applications accepted. *Expenses:* Tuition, state resident: full-time $8510; part-time $608 per credit. Tuition, nonresident: full-time $16,542; part-time $919 per credit. Required fees: $339; $110 per credit. Part-time tuition and fees vary according to course load. *Financial support:* In 2010–11, 20 research assistantships with full and partial tuition reimbursements (averaging $13,356 per year) were awarded; fellowships with full and partial tuition reimbursements, teaching assistantships with full and partial tuition reimbursements, institutionally sponsored loans, scholarships/grants, and tuition waivers (partial) also available. Financial award application deadline: 3/1; financial award applicants required to submit FAFSA. Total annual research expenditures: $2 million. *Unit head:* Dr. Robert A. Greenes, Chair, 602-827-2548, E-mail: robert.greenes@asu.edu. *Application contact:* Graduate Admissions, 480-965-6113, Fax: 480-965-5158.

Boston University, Graduate School of Arts and Sciences and College of Engineering, Intercollegiate Program in Bioinformatics, Boston, MA 02215. Offers MS, PhD. *Students:* 77 full-time (21 women), 11 part-time (2 women); includes 13 minority (10 Asian, non-Hispanic/Latino; 3 Hispanic/Latino), 34 international. Average age 29. 145 applicants, 28% accepted, 22 enrolled. In 2010, 13 master's, 4 doctorates awarded. *Degree requirements:* For doctorate, thesis/dissertation. *Entrance requirements:* For master's and doctorate, GRE General Test, GRE Subject Test, 3 letters of recommendation, resume. Additional exam requirements/recommendations for international students: Required—TOEFL (minimum score 550 paper-based; 213 computer-based). *Application deadline:* For fall admission, 12/1 for domestic and international students; for spring admission, 10/1 for domestic and international students. Application fee: $70. Electronic applications accepted. *Expenses:* Tuition: Full-time $39,314; part-time $1228 per credit. Required fees: $40 per semester. *Financial support:* In 2010–11, 32 students received support, including 4 fellowships with full tuition reimbursements available (averaging $19,300 per year), 28 research assistantships with full tuition reimbursements available (averaging $18,800 per year); career-related internships or fieldwork, Federal Work-Study, scholarships/grants, traineeships, and unspecified assistantships also available. Financial award application deadline: 12/1; financial award applicants required to submit FAFSA. *Unit head:* Tom Tullius, Director, 617-353-2482, E-mail: tullius@bu.edu. *Application contact:* David King, Graduate Administrator, 617-358-0751, Fax: 617-353-5929, E-mail: dking@bu.edu.

Brandeis University, Rabb School of Continuing Studies, Division of Graduate Professional Studies, Bioinformatics Program, Waltham, MA 02454-9110. Offers MS, Graduate Certificate. Part-time and evening/weekend programs available. *Faculty:* 2 full-time (both women), 33 part-time/adjunct (5 women). *Students:* 16 part-time (7 women); includes 1 minority (Hispanic/Latino). Average age 35. 4 applicants, 100% accepted, 3 enrolled. In 2010, 9 master's awarded. *Entrance requirements:* For master's, resume, official transcripts, recommendations, goal statements; for Graduate Certificate, resume, official transcripts, letter of recommendation. Additional exam requirements/recommendations for international students: Recommended—TOEFL (minimum score 600 paper-based; 250 computer-based; 100 iBT). *Application deadline:* For fall admission, 6/15 priority date for domestic students; for winter admission, 10/15 priority date for domestic students; for spring admission, 2/15 priority date for domestic students. Applications are processed on a rolling basis. Application fee: $50. Electronic applications accepted. *Unit head:* Dr. Daniel Caffrey, Program Chair, 781-736-8787, Fax: 781-736-3420, E-mail: dcaffrey@brandeis.edu. *Application contact:* Frances Stearns, Associate Director of Admissions and Student Services, 781-736-8785, Fax: 781-736-3420, E-mail: fstearns@brandeis.edu.

California State University Channel Islands, Extended Education, Programs in Biotechnology, Camarillo, CA 93012. Offers biotechnology and bioinformatics (MS); MS/MBA. *Entrance requirements:* Additional exam requirements/recommendations for international students: Required—TOEFL (minimum score 550 paper-based).

California State University, Dominguez Hills, College of Natural and Behavioral Sciences, Department of Biology, Carson, CA 90747-0001. Offers MS. Part-time and evening/weekend programs available. *Faculty:* 10 full-time (3 women), 20 part-time/adjunct (6 women). *Students:* 9 full-time (5 women), 23 part-time (13 women); includes 6 Black or African American, non-Hispanic/Latino; 7 Asian, non-Hispanic/Latino; 6 Hispanic/Latino; 2 Two or more races, non-Hispanic/Latino. Average age 30. 21 applicants, 67% accepted, 12 enrolled. In 2010, 5 master's awarded. *Degree requirements:* For master's, thesis. *Entrance requirements:* For master's, minimum GPA of 2.75. Additional exam requirements/recommendations for international students: Required—TOEFL (minimum score 550 paper-based). *Application deadline:* For fall admission, 6/1 for domestic students, 5/1 for international students; for spring admission, 12/15 for domestic students, 10/1 for international students. Application fee: $55. Electronic applications accepted. *Faculty research:* Cancer biology, infectious diseases, ecology of native plants, remediation, community ecology. *Unit head:* Dr. John Thomlinson, Chair, 310-243-3381, Fax: 310-243-2350, E-mail: jthomlinson@csudh.edu. *Application contact:* Dr. Getachew Kidane, Graduate Program Coordinator, 310-243-3564, Fax: 310-243-2350, E-mail: gkidane@csudh.edu.

Dalhousie University, Faculty of Computer Science, Halifax, NS B3H 1W5, Canada. Offers computational biology and bioinformatics (M Sc); computer science (PhD); computer science (project-based) (MA Sc); computer science (thesis-based) (MC Sc); electronic commerce (MEC); health informatics (MHI). *Degree requirements:* For master's, thesis (for some programs); for doctorate, thesis/dissertation. *Entrance requirements:* Additional exam requirements/recommendations for international students: Required—1 of the following 5 approved tests: TOEFL, IELTS, CANTEST, CAEL, Michigan English Language Assessment Battery. Electronic applications accepted.

Duke University, Graduate School, Department of Computational Biology and Bioinformatics, Durham, NC 27705. Offers PhD, Certificate. *Faculty:* 39 full-time. *Students:* 34 full-time (10 women); includes 1 Black or African American, non-Hispanic/Latino; 1 Hispanic/Latino, 16 international. 112 applicants, 11% accepted, 7 enrolled. In 2010, 4 doctorates awarded. *Degree requirements:* For doctorate, thesis/dissertation. *Entrance requirements:* For doctorate, GRE General. Additional exam requirements/recommendations for international students: Required—TOEFL (minimum score 550 paper-based; 213 computer-based; 83 iBT), IELTS (minimum score 7). *Application deadline:* For fall admission, 12/8 priority date for domestic and international students. Application fee: $75. Electronic applications accepted. *Financial support:* Fellowships, research assistantships, teaching assistantships available. Financial award application deadline: 12/8. *Unit head:* Jeannette McCarthy, Director of Graduate Studies, 919-684-0881, Fax: 919-668-2465, E-mail: el81@duke.edu. *Application contact:* Elizabeth Hutton, Director, Graduate Admissions, 919-684-3913, Fax: 919-684-2277, E-mail: grad-admissions@duke.edu.

George Mason University, College of Science, Department of Bioinformatics and Computational Biology, Fairfax, VA 22030. Offers MS, PhD, Certificate. *Faculty:* 7 full-time (0 women), 2 part-time/adjunct (0 women). *Students:* 22 full-time (10 women), 38 part-time (18 women); includes 1 Black or African American, non-Hispanic/Latino; 12 Asian, non-Hispanic/Latino, 28 international. Average age 33. 92 applicants, 46% accepted, 11 enrolled. In 2010, 14 master's, 4 doctorates awarded. *Entrance requirements:* For master's, GRE General Test, Resume, Three letters of recommendation. Additional exam requirements/recommendations for international students: Required—TOEFL (minimum score 570 paper-based; 230 computer-based; 88 iBT). Application fee: $100. *Expenses:* Tuition, state resident: full-time $8192; part-time $440 per credit hour. Tuition, nonresident: full-time $22,952; part-time $1055 per credit hour. Required fees: $2364; $99 per credit hour. *Financial support:* In 2010–11, 15 students received support, including 3 fellowships (averaging $18,000 per year), 10 research assistantships (averaging $11,824 per year), 2 teaching assistantships (averaging $12,105 per year); career-related internships or fieldwork, Federal Work-Study, scholarships/grants, unspecified assistantships, and health care benefits (full-time research or teaching assistantship recipients) also available. Financial award applicants required to submit FAFSA. Total annual research expenditures: $824,761. *Unit head:* Dr. Saleer Jofri, Head, 703-993-8420. *Application contact:* Dr. Tim Born, Associate Dean for Graduate Programs, 703-993-4171, Fax: 703-993-9034, E-mail: tborn@gmu.edu.

George Mason University, College of Science, Department of Molecular and Microbiology, Fairfax, VA 22030. Offers biology (MS), including bioinformatics and computational biology, general biology, microbiology and infectious disease, molecular biology, systematics and evolutionary biology; biosciences (PhD). *Faculty:* 10 full-time (5 women). *Students:* 12 full-time (6 women), 63 part-time (36 women); includes 2 Black or African American, non-Hispanic/Latino; 1 American Indian or Alaska Native, non-Hispanic/Latino; 8 Asian, non-Hispanic/Latino; 1 Hispanic/Latino, 16 international. Average age 31. 98 applicants, 37% accepted, 19 enrolled. In 2010, 7 master's, 7 doctorates awarded. *Entrance requirements:* Additional exam requirements/recommendations for international students: Required—TOEFL (minimum score 570 paper-based; 230 computer-based; 88 iBT). Application fee: $100. *Expenses:* Tuition, state resident: full-time $8192; part-time $440 per credit hour. Tuition, nonresident: full-time $22,952; part-time $1055 per credit hour. Required fees: $2364; $99 per credit hour. *Financial support:* In 2010–11, 32 students received support, including 3 fellowships (averaging $18,000 per year), 6 research assistantships (averaging $14,073 per year), 23 teaching assistantships (averaging $12,194 per year); career-related internships or fieldwork, Federal Work-Study, scholarships/grants, unspecified assistantships, and health care benefits (full-time research or teaching assistantship recipients) also available. Financial award applicants required to submit FAFSA. Total annual research expenditures: $457,760. *Unit head:* Dr. James Willett, Director, 703-993-8311, Fax: 703-993-8976, E-mail: jwillett@gmu.edu. *Application contact:* Daniel Cox, Associate Dean for Graduate Programs, 703-993-4971, Fax: 703-993-4325, E-mail: dcox5@gmu.edu.

Georgetown University, Graduate School of Arts and Sciences, Programs in Biomedical Sciences, Department of Biostatistics, Bioinformatics and Biomathematics, Washington, DC 20057-1484. Offers biostatistics (MS), including bioinformatics, epidemiology. *Entrance requirements:* For master's, GRE General Test. Additional exam requirements/recommendations for international students: Required—TOEFL. *Faculty research:* Occupation epidemiology, cancer.

The George Washington University, School of Medicine and Health Sciences, Department of Biochemistry and Molecular Biology, Program in Molecular Biochemistry and Bioinformatics, Washington, DC 20052. Offers MS. Part-time programs available. *Students:* 4 full-time (2 women), 5 part-time (3 women), 5 international. Average age 26. In 2010, 6 master's awarded. *Entrance requirements:* For master's, GRE General Test, minimum GPA of 3.0. Additional exam requirements/recommendations for international students: Required—TOEFL (minimum score 550 paper-based; 213 computer-based). *Application deadline:* For fall admission, 4/1 priority date for domestic and international students; for spring admission, 10/1 priority date for domestic and international students. Applications are processed on a rolling basis. Application fee: $75. Electronic applications accepted. *Unit head:* Dr. Jack Vanderhoek, Director, 202-994-2929, E-mail: jyvdh@gwu.edu. *Application contact:* Dr. Fatah Kashanchi, Director, 202-994-1781, Fax: 202-994-6213, E-mail: bcmfxk@gwumc.edu.

Georgia Institute of Technology, Graduate Studies and Research, College of Engineering, The Wallace H. Coulter Department of Biomedical Engineering at Georgia Tech and Emory University, Atlanta, GA 30332-0001. Offers bioengineering (PhD); bioinformatics (PhD); biomedical engineering (PhD); MD/PhD. PhD in biomedical engineering program jointly offered with Emory University (Georgia) and Peking University (China). Terminal master's awarded for partial completion of doctoral program. *Degree requirements:* For doctorate, thesis/dissertation. *Entrance requirements:* Additional exam requirements/recommendations for international students: Required—TOEFL. *Faculty research:* Biomechanics and tissue engineering, bioinstrumentation and medical imaging.

Georgia Institute of Technology, Graduate Studies and Research, College of Sciences, School of Biology, Atlanta, GA 30332-0001. Offers applied biology (MS, PhD); bioinformatics (MS, PhD); biology (MS). Part-time programs available. Terminal master's awarded for partial completion of doctoral program. *Degree requirements:* For master's, thesis; for doctorate, thesis/dissertation, qualifying exam. *Entrance requirements:* For master's, GRE General Test, minimum GPA of 2.9; for doctorate, GRE General Test, minimum GPA of 3.0. Additional exam requirements/recommendations for international students: Required—TOEFL. Electronic applications accepted. *Faculty research:* Microbiology, molecular and cell biology, ecology.

Georgia Institute of Technology, Graduate Studies and Research, College of Sciences, School of Mathematics, Atlanta, GA 30332-0001. Offers algorithms, combinatorics, and optimization (PhD); applied mathematics (MS); bioinformatics (PhD); mathematics (PhD); quantitative and computational finance (MS); statistics (MS Stat). Terminal master's awarded for partial completion of doctoral program. *Degree requirements:* For master's, thesis or alternative; for doctorate, one foreign language, thesis/dissertation. *Entrance requirements:* For master's, GRE General Test, minimum GPA of 3.0; for doctorate, GRE General Test, GRE Subject Test, minimum GPA of 3.0. Additional exam requirements/recommendations for international students: Required—TOEFL. Electronic applications accepted. *Faculty research:* Dynamical systems, discrete mathematics, probability and statistics, mathematical physics.

Grand Valley State University, Padnos College of Engineering and Computing, Medical and Bioinformatics Program, Allendale, MI 49401-9403. Offers MS. Part-time and evening/weekend programs available. *Degree requirements:* For master's, thesis or alternative. *Faculty research:* Biomedical informatics, information visualization, data mining, high-performance computing, computational biology.

Indiana University Bloomington, School of Informatics, Bloomington, IN 47408. Offers bioinformatics (MS); chemical informatics (MS); computer science (MS, PhD); health informatics (MS); human computer interaction (MS); informatics (PhD); laboratory informatics (MS); media arts and science (MS); music informatics (MS); security informatics (MS); MS/PhD. PhD offered through University Graduate School. Part-time programs available. Postbaccalaureate distance learning degree programs offered (no on-campus study). *Faculty:* 63 full-time (12 women). *Students:* 372 full-time (88 women), 34 part-time (10 women); includes 7 Black or African American, non-Hispanic/Latino; 1 American Indian or Alaska Native, non-Hispanic/Latino; 10 Asian, non-Hispanic/Latino; 3 Hispanic/Latino; 3 Two or more races, non-Hispanic/Latino, 261 international. Average age 27. 746 applicants, 40% accepted, 131 enrolled. In 2010, 117 master's, 20 doctorates awarded. Terminal master's awarded for partial completion of doctoral program. *Degree requirements:* For master's, thesis optional; for doctorate, comprehensive exam, thesis/dissertation, oral and written exams. *Entrance requirements:* For master's and doctorate, GRE, letters of reference. Additional exam requirements/recommendations for international students: Required—TOEFL. *Application deadline:* For fall admission, 1/15 for domestic students, 12/1 for international students. Application fee: $55 ($65 for international students). Electronic applications accepted. *Financial support:* In 2010–11, fellowships with full and partial tuition reimbursements (averaging $20,000 per year), research assistantships (averaging $14,000 per year), teaching assistantships (averaging $13,000 per year) were awarded; Federal Work-Study, institutionally sponsored loans, scholarships/grants, health care benefits, tuition waivers (full and partial), and unspecified assistantships also available. Support available to part-time students. Total annual research expenditures: $2 million. *Unit head:* Dr. David Leake, Associate Dean for Graduate Studies, 812-855-9756, E-mail: leake@cs.indiana.edu. *Application contact:* Rachel Lawmaster, Manager of Graduate Admissions and Graduate Studies, 812-856-3622, Fax: 812-856-3825, E-mail: raclee@indiana.edu.

Iowa State University of Science and Technology, Graduate College, Interdisciplinary Programs, Bioinformatics and Computational Biology Program, Ames, IA 50011. Offers MS, PhD. *Students:* 54 full-time (22 women), 34 international. In 2010, 1 master's, 5 doctorates awarded. *Degree requirements:* For doctorate, thesis/dissertation. *Entrance requirements:* For master's and doctorate, GRE General Test. Additional exam requirements/recommendations for international students: Recommended—IELTS. *Application deadline:* For fall admission, 1/15 priority date for domestic students, 1/15 for international students; for spring admission, 10/15 for domestic and international students. Application fee: $40 ($90 for international students). Electronic applications accepted. *Financial support:* In 2010–11, 47 research assistantships with full and partial tuition reimbursements (averaging $22,000 per year), 3 teaching assistantships (averaging $20,000 per year) were awarded; fellowships with full tuition reimbursements, scholarships/grants, traineeships, health care benefits, and unspecified assistantships also available. *Faculty research:* Functional and structural genomics, genome evolution, macromolecular structure and function, mathematical biology and biological statistics, metabolic and developmental networks. *Unit head:* Dr. Julie Dickerson, Chair, Supervising Committee, 515-294-5122, Fax: 515-294-6790, E-mail: bcb@iastate.edu. *Application contact:* Dr. Julie Dickerson, Chair, Supervising Committee, 515-294-5122, Fax: 515-294-6790, E-mail: bcb@iastate.edu.

The Johns Hopkins University, Bloomberg School of Public Health, Department of Biostatistics, Baltimore, MD 21205-2179. Offers bioinformatics (MHS); biostatistics (MHS, Sc M, PhD). Part-time programs available. *Faculty:* 34 full-time (11 women), 16 part-time/adjunct (3 women). *Students:* 47 full-time (25 women), 3 part-time (0 women); includes 6 minority (1 Black or African American, non-Hispanic/Latino; 3 Asian, non-Hispanic/Latino; 1 Hispanic/Latino; 1 Two or more races, non-Hispanic/Latino), 25 international. Average age 26. 197 applicants, 22% accepted, 22 enrolled. In 2010, 15 master's, 6 doctorates awarded. *Degree requirements:* For master's, comprehensive exam (for some programs), thesis (for some programs), written exam, final project; for doctorate, comprehensive exam, thesis/dissertation, 1 year full-time residency, oral and written exams. *Entrance requirements:* For master's and doctorate, GRE General Test, course work in calculus and matrix algebra, 3 letters of recommendation, curriculum vitae. Additional exam requirements/recommendations for international students: Required—TOEFL (minimum score 600 paper-based; 250 computer-based). *Application deadline:* For fall admission, 1/15 for domestic and international students. Applications are processed on a rolling basis. Application fee: $45. Electronic applications accepted. *Financial support:* In 2010–11, 49 students received support, including 33 research assistantships (averaging $22,000 per year); fellowships, Federal Work-Study, institutionally sponsored loans, scholarships/grants, traineeships, health care benefits, and unspecified assistantships also available. Financial award application deadline: 3/15; financial award applicants required

to submit FAFSA. *Faculty research:* Statistical genetics, bioinformatics, statistical computing, statistical methods, environmental statistics. Total annual research expenditures: $4.2 million. *Unit head:* Dr. Karen Bandeen-Roche, Chair, 410-955-3067, Fax: 410-955-0958, E-mail: kbandeen@jhsph.edu. *Application contact:* Mary Joy Argo, Academic Administrator, 410-614-4454, Fax: 410-955-0958, E-mail: margo@jhsph.edu.

The Johns Hopkins University, Engineering for Professionals and Advanced Academic Programs, Part-time Program in Bioinformatics, Baltimore, MD 21218-2699. Offers MS, Post-Master's Certificate. Part-time and evening/weekend programs available. *Unit head:* Dr. Allan Bjerkaas, Associate Dean, 410-516-2300, Fax: 410-579-8049, E-mail: bjerkaas@jhu.edu. *Application contact:* Dr. Allan Bjerkaas, Associate Dean, 410-516-2300, Fax: 410-579-8049, E-mail: bjerkaas@jhu.edu.

The Johns Hopkins University, Engineering for Professionals, Part-Time Program in Computer Science, Baltimore, MD 21218-2699. Offers bioinformatics (MS); computer science (MS, Post-Master's Certificate); telecommunications and networking (MS). Part-time and evening/weekend programs available. Postbaccalaureate distance learning degree programs offered (no on-campus study). *Faculty:* 58 part-time/adjunct (5 women). *Students:* 16 full-time (5 women), 428 part-time (54 women); includes 131 minority (24 Black or African American, non-Hispanic/Latino; 81 Asian, non-Hispanic/Latino; 16 Hispanic/Latino; 1 Native Hawaiian or other Pacific Islander, non-Hispanic/Latino; 9 Two or more races, non-Hispanic/Latino), 16 international. Average age 29. 133 applicants, 87% accepted, 74 enrolled. In 2010, 153 master's, 2 other advanced degrees awarded. *Application deadline:* Applications are processed on a rolling basis. Application fee: $75. Electronic applications accepted. *Financial support:* Institutionally sponsored loans available. *Unit head:* Dr. Thomas A. Longstaff, Program Chair, 443-778-9389, E-mail: thomas.longstaff@jhuapl.edu. *Application contact:* Priyanka Dwivedi, Admissions Manager, 410-516-2300, Fax: 410-579-8049, E-mail: pdwived1@jhu.edu.

The Johns Hopkins University, Zanvyl Krieger School of Arts and Sciences, Advanced Academic Programs, Program in Bioinformatics, Baltimore, MD 21218-2699. Offers MS. Part-time and evening/weekend programs available. Postbaccalaureate distance learning degree programs offered (no on-campus study). *Faculty:* 8 full-time (4 women), 99 part-time/adjunct (21 women). *Students:* 10 full-time (2 women), 82 part-time (28 women); includes 26 minority (5 Black or African American, non-Hispanic/Latino; 15 Asian, non-Hispanic/Latino; 5 Hispanic/Latino; 1 Two or more races, non-Hispanic/Latino), 16 international. Average age 34. 56 applicants, 41% accepted, 23 enrolled. In 2010, 12 master's awarded. *Degree requirements:* For master's, thesis (for some programs). *Entrance requirements:* For master's, minimum GPA of 3.0; coursework in programming and data structures, biology, and chemistry. Additional exam requirements/recommendations for international students: Required—TOEFL (minimum score 250 computer-based; 100 iBT). *Application deadline:* For fall admission, 5/31 priority date for domestic students, 4/30 priority date for international students; for spring admission, 10/31 priority date for domestic and international students. Applications are processed on a rolling basis. Application fee: $75. Electronic applications accepted. *Financial support:* Applicants required to submit FAFSA. *Unit head:* Dr. Kristina Obom, Associate Program Chair, 301-294-7159, E-mail: bioinformatics@jhu.edu. *Application contact:* Valana M. McMickens, Admissions Manager, 202-452-1941, Fax: 202-452-1970, E-mail: aapadmissions@jhu.edu.

Marquette University, Graduate School, College of Arts and Sciences, Department of Mathematics, Statistics, and Computer Science, Milwaukee, WI 53201-1881. Offers bioinformatics (MS); computational sciences (MS, PhD); computing (MS); mathematics education (MS). Part-time and evening/weekend programs available. Postbaccalaureate distance learning degree programs offered (minimal on-campus study). *Faculty:* 27 full-time (9 women), 8 part-time/adjunct (3 women). *Students:* 13 full-time (2 women), 26 part-time (7 women); includes 2 minority (1 Black or African American, non-Hispanic/Latino; 1 Asian, non-Hispanic/Latino), 15 international. Average age 31. 57 applicants, 42% accepted, 10 enrolled. In 2010, 9 master's awarded. Terminal master's awarded for partial completion of doctoral program. *Degree requirements:* For master's, thesis or alternative, Master's essay with oral presentation; for doctorate, comprehensive exam, thesis/dissertation, Qualifying Examination. *Entrance requirements:* For master's, official transcripts from all current and previous colleges/universities except Marquette, three letters of recommendation; for doctorate, GRE General Test, official transcripts from all current and previous colleges/universities except Marquette, three letters of recommendation, English-language publications authored by applicant (if applicable, strongly recommended). Additional exam requirements/recommendations for international students: Required—TOEFL (minimum score 530 paper-based; 78 computer-based). *Application deadline:* For fall admission, 1/15 for domestic and international students. Applications are processed on a rolling basis. Application fee: $50. Electronic applications accepted. *Expenses:* Tuition: Full-time $16,290; part-time $905 per credit hour. Tuition and fees vary according to program. *Financial support:* In 2010–11, 4 fellowships, 6 research assistantships, 15 teaching assistantships were awarded; Federal Work-Study, institutionally sponsored loans, scholarships/grants, and tuition waivers (full and partial) also available. Support available to part-time students. Financial award application deadline: 2/15. *Faculty research:* Models of physiological systems, mathematical immunology, computational group theory, mathematical logic, computational science. Total annual research expenditures: $696,366. *Unit head:* Dr. Gary Krenz, Chair, 414-288-7573, Fax: 414-288-1578. *Application contact:* Dr. Francis Pastijn, Director of Graduate Studies, 414-288-5229.

Marquette University, Graduate School, College of Arts and Sciences, Program in Bioinformatics, Milwaukee, WI 53201-1881. Offers MS. Program offered jointly with Medical College of Wisconsin. Part-time and evening/weekend programs available. Postbaccalaureate distance learning degree programs offered (minimal on-campus study). *Students:* 3 full-time (1 woman), 7 part-time (4 women), 5 international. Average age 29. 14 applicants, 50% accepted, 3 enrolled. In 2010, 3 master's awarded. *Degree requirements:* For master's, thesis optional, Non Thesis option requires research practicum. *Entrance requirements:* For master's, Recent GRE score is strongly recommended, official transcripts from all current/previous colleges/universities except Marquette. An essay outlining relevant work experience or education, career goals, possible areas of interest, and reasons for seeking admission. Three letters of reference. Additional exam requirements/recommendations for international students: Required—TOEFL (minimum score 530 paper-based; 78 computer-based). *Application deadline:* Applications are processed on a rolling basis. Application fee: $50. Electronic applications accepted. *Expenses:* Tuition: Full-time $16,290; part-time $905 per credit hour. Tuition and fees vary according to program. *Financial support:* In 2010–11, 1 fellowship, 3 teaching assistantships were awarded; research assistantships. Financial award application deadline: 2/15. *Unit head:* Dr. Craig Stuble, Head, 414-288-3783, E-mail: clough@mscs.mu.edu. *Application contact:* Erin Fox, Assistant Director for Recruitment, 414-288-5319, Fax: 414-288-1902, E-mail: erin.fox@marquette.edu.

McGill University, Faculty of Graduate and Postdoctoral Studies, Faculty of Science, Department of Biology, Montréal, QC H3A 2T5, Canada. Offers bioinformatics (M Sc, PhD); environment (M Sc, PhD); neo-tropical environment (M Sc, PhD).

Medical College of Wisconsin, Graduate School of Biomedical Sciences, Program in Bioinformatics, Milwaukee, WI 53226-0509. Offers MS. *Expenses:* Tuition: Full-time $30,000; part-time $710 per credit. Required fees: $150.

Mississippi Valley State University, Department of Natural Science and Environmental Health, Itta Bena, MS 38941-1400. Offers bioinformatics (MS); environmental health (MS). Part-time and evening/weekend programs available. *Entrance requirements:* For master's, GRE, minimum GPA of 3.0. *Faculty research:* Toxicology, water equality, microbiology, ecology.

Morgan State University, School of Graduate Studies, School of Computer, Mathematical, and Natural Sciences, Department of Computer Science, Baltimore, MD 21251. Offers bioinformatics (MS). *Entrance requirements:* Additional exam requirements/recommendations for international students: Required—TOEFL (minimum score 550 paper-based; 213 computer-based).

Bioinformatics

New Jersey Institute of Technology, Office of Graduate Studies, College of Computing Science, Department of Computer Science, Newark, NJ 07102. Offers bioinformatics (MS); computer science (MS, PhD); computing and business (MS); software engineering (MS). Part-time and evening/weekend programs available. *Faculty:* 35 full-time (2 women), 5 part-time/adjunct (1 woman). *Students:* 212 full-time (66 women), 109 part-time (14 women); includes 13 Black or African American, non-Hispanic/Latino; 3 American Indian or Alaska Native, non-Hispanic/Latino; 36 Asian, non-Hispanic/Latino; 16 Hispanic/Latino, 196 international. Average age 28. 867 applicants, 39% accepted, 116 enrolled. In 2010, 152 master's, 5 doctorates awarded. Terminal master's awarded for partial completion of doctoral program. *Degree requirements:* For master's, thesis optional; for doctorate, thesis/dissertation. *Entrance requirements:* For master's, GRE General Test; for doctorate, GRE General Test, minimum graduate GPA of 3.5. Additional exam requirements/recommendations for international students: Required—TOEFL (minimum score 550 paper-based; 213 computer-based; 79 iBT). *Application deadline:* For fall admission, 6/5 priority date for domestic students, 4/1 for international students; for spring admission, 11/15 for domestic and international students. Applications are processed on a rolling basis. Application fee: $65. Electronic applications accepted. *Expenses:* Tuition, state resident: full-time $14,724; part-time $818 per credit. Tuition, nonresident: full-time $20,304; part-time $1128 per credit. Required fees: $2272; $209 per credit. $103 per semester. One-time fee: $312 full-time; $212 part-time. *Financial support:* Fellowships with full and partial tuition reimbursements, research assistantships with full and partial tuition reimbursements, teaching assistantships with full and partial tuition reimbursements, career-related internships or fieldwork, Federal Work-Study, institutionally sponsored loans, and unspecified assistantships available. Financial award application deadline: 3/15. Total annual research expenditures: $6.4 million. *Unit head:* Dr. Michael A. Baltrush, Interim Chair, 973-596-3386, E-mail: michael.a.baltrush@njit.edu. *Application contact:* Kathryn Kelly, Director of Admissions, 973-596-3300, Fax: 973-596-3461, E-mail: admissions@njit.edu.

New Mexico State University, Graduate School, College of Arts and Sciences, Department of Computer Science, Las Cruces, NM 88003-8001. Offers bioinformatics (MS); computer science (MS, PhD). PhD offered jointly with University of New Mexico. Part-time programs available. *Faculty:* 9 full-time (3 women). *Students:* 76 full-time (14 women), 23 part-time (7 women); includes 7 minority (2 Asian, non-Hispanic/Latino; 5 Hispanic/Latino), 78 international. Average age 27. 168 applicants, 89% accepted, 19 enrolled. In 2010, 28 master's, 1 doctorate awarded. Terminal master's awarded for partial completion of doctoral program. *Degree requirements:* For master's, comprehensive exam, thesis or alternative; for doctorate, comprehensive exam, thesis/dissertation, qualifying examination, thesis proposal. *Entrance requirements:* For master's and doctorate, BS in computer science. Additional exam requirements/recommendations for international students: Required—TOEFL. *Application deadline:* For fall admission, 3/1 priority date for domestic and international students; for spring admission, 11/1 priority date for domestic and international students. Applications are processed on a rolling basis. Application fee: $30 ($50 for international students). Electronic applications accepted. *Expenses:* Tuition, state resident: full-time $4536; part-time $242 per credit. Tuition, nonresident: full-time $15,816; part-time $712 per credit. Required fees: $636 per term. *Financial support:* In 2010–11, 6 fellowships with full tuition reimbursements (averaging $30,000 per year), 24 research assistantships (averaging $8,087 per year), 23 teaching assistantships (averaging $5,538 per year) were awarded; career-related internships or fieldwork, Federal Work-Study, scholarships/grants, health care benefits, and unspecified assistantships also available. Support available to part-time students. Financial award application deadline: 3/1; financial award applicants required to submit FAFSA. *Faculty research:* Programming languages, artificial intelligence, software engineering, bioinformatics, data mining, computer networks. *Unit head:* Dr. Enrico Pontelli, Head, 575-646-3723, Fax: 575-646-1002, E-mail: epontell@cs.nmsu.edu. *Application contact:* Dr. Son Tran, Chair, Admissions Committee, 575-646-1930, Fax: 575-646-1002, E-mail: tson@cs.nmsu.edu.

North Carolina State University, Graduate School, College of Agriculture and Life Sciences and College of Engineering, Program in Bioinformatics, Raleigh, NC 27695. Offers MB, PhD. *Degree requirements:* For master's, thesis optional; for doctorate, thesis/dissertation. *Entrance requirements:* For master's and doctorate, GRE, minimum B average. Additional exam requirements/recommendations for international students: Required—TOEFL. Electronic applications accepted. *Faculty research:* Statistical genetics, molecular evolution, pedigree analysis, quantitative genetics, protein structure.

North Dakota State University, College of Graduate and Interdisciplinary Studies, Interdisciplinary Program in Genomics and Bioinformatics, Fargo, ND 58108. Offers MS, PhD. Part-time programs available. *Faculty:* 21 full-time (3 women). *Students:* 5 full-time (3 women), 7 part-time (3 women), 10 international. 8 applicants, 38% accepted, 2 enrolled. In 2010, 1 doctorate awarded. *Degree requirements:* For master's, thesis; for doctorate, comprehensive exam, thesis/dissertation. *Entrance requirements:* For master's and doctorate, minimum GPA of 3.0. Additional exam requirements/recommendations for international students: Required—TOEFL (minimum score 525 paper-based; 197 computer-based; 71 iBT). *Application deadline:* For fall admission, 5/1 for international students; for spring admission, 8/1 for international students. Applications are processed on a rolling basis. Application fee: $45 ($60 for international students). Electronic applications accepted. *Financial support:* In 2010–11, 12 research assistantships with full tuition reimbursements (averaging $15,000 per year) were awarded; unspecified assistantships also available. *Faculty research:* Genome evolution, genome mapping, genome expression, bioinformatics, data mining. Total annual research expenditures: $300,000. *Unit head:* Dr. Phillip E. McClean, Director, 701-231-8443, Fax: 701-231-8474. *Application contact:* Dr. Phillip E. McClean, Director, 701-231-8443, Fax: 701-231-8474.

Northeastern University, College of Science, Department of Biology, Professional Program in Bioinformatics, Boston, MA 02115-5096. Offers PMS. Part-time programs available. *Faculty:* 6 full-time (0 women). *Students:* 25 full-time (15 women), 2 part-time. 31 applicants, 90% accepted, 5 enrolled. In 2010, 8 master's awarded. *Degree requirements:* For master's, internship. *Entrance requirements:* For master's, GRE General Test. *Application deadline:* For fall admission, 2/1 priority date for domestic and international students. Application fee: $50. *Expenses:* Contact institution. *Financial support:* In 2010–11, research assistantships (averaging $18,285 per year); Federal Work-Study, scholarships/grants, and tuition waivers (partial) also available. Support available to part-time students. Financial award application deadline: 3/1; financial award applicants required to submit FAFSA. *Unit head:* Dr. Jacqueline Piret, Program Coordinator, 617-373-2260, Fax: 617-373-3724, E-mail: j.piret@neu.edu. *Application contact:* Jo-Anne Dickinson, Admissions Contact, 617-373-5990, Fax: 617-373-7281, E-mail: gsas@neu.edu.

Nova Southeastern University, Health Professions Division, College of Osteopathic Medicine, Program in Biomedical Informatics, Fort Lauderdale, FL 33314-7796. Offers biomedical informatics (MS); clinical informatics (Graduate Certificate); public health informatics (Graduate Certificate). *Students:* 12 full-time (5 women), 55 part-time (34 women); includes 20 Black or African American, non-Hispanic/Latino; 5 Asian, non-Hispanic/Latino; 9 Hispanic/Latino, 6 international. Average age 36. In 2010, 5 master's awarded. *Unit head:* Dr. Jennie Q. Lou, Director, 954-262-1619, E-mail: jlou@nova.edu. *Application contact:* Ellen Rondino, College of Osteopathic Medicine Admissions Counselor, 866-817-4068.

Polytechnic Institute of NYU, Department of Interdisciplinary Studies, Major in Bioinformatics, Brooklyn, NY 11201-2990. Offers MS. *Students:* 14 full-time (9 women), 22 part-time (14 women); includes 1 Black or African American, non-Hispanic/Latino; 3 Asian, non-Hispanic/Latino, 11 international. Average age 33. 27 applicants, 41% accepted, 1 enrolled. In 2010, 18 master's awarded. *Degree requirements:* For master's, comprehensive exam (for some programs), thesis (for some programs). *Entrance requirements:* Additional exam requirements/recommendations for international students: Required—TOEFL (minimum score 550 paper-based; 213 computer-based; 80 iBT); Recommended—IELTS (minimum score 6.5). *Application deadline:* For fall admission, 7/31 for domestic students, 4/30 priority date for international students; for spring admission, 12/31 for domestic students, 10/30 priority date for international students. Applications are processed on a rolling basis. Application fee: $75. Electronic applications accepted. *Expenses:* Tuition: Full-time $21,492; part-time $1194 per credit. Required fees: $385 per semester. Tuition and fees vary according to course load. *Financial support:* Institutionally sponsored loans, scholarships/grants, and unspecified assistantships available. Support available to part-time students. *Unit head:* Prof. Michael Greenstein, Department Head, 718-260-3835, E-mail: mgreenst@poly.edu. *Application contact:* JeanCarlo Bonilla, Director, Graduate Enrollment Management, 718-260-3182, Fax: 718-260-3624, E-mail: gradinfo@poly.edu.

Polytechnic Institute of NYU, Long Island Graduate Center, Graduate Programs, Department of Interdisciplinary Studies, Major in Bioinformatics, Melville, NY 11747. Offers MS. Part-time and evening/weekend programs available. *Students:* 3 part-time (2 women); includes 1 minority (Black or African American, non-Hispanic/Latino). Average age 38. In 2010, 2 master's awarded. *Entrance requirements:* Additional exam requirements/recommendations for international students: Required—TOEFL (minimum score 550 paper-based; 213 computer-based; 80 iBT); Recommended—IELTS (minimum score 6.5). *Application deadline:* For fall admission, 7/31 priority date for domestic students, 4/30 priority date for international students; for spring admission, 12/31 priority date for domestic students, 11/30 priority date for international students. Applications are processed on a rolling basis. Application fee: $75. Electronic applications accepted. *Expenses:* Tuition: Full-time $21,492; part-time $1194 per credit. Required fees: $385 per semester. Tuition and fees vary according to course load. *Financial support:* Institutionally sponsored loans, scholarships/grants, and unspecified assistantships available. Support available to part-time students. *Application contact:* JeanCarlo Bonilla, Director of Graduate Enrollment Management, 718-260-3182, Fax: 718-260-3624, E-mail: gradinfo@poly.edu.

Polytechnic Institute of NYU, Westchester Graduate Center, Graduate Programs, Department of Interdisciplinary Studies, Major in Bioinformatics, Hawthorne, NY 10532-1507. Offers MS. *Entrance requirements:* Additional exam requirements/recommendations for international students: Required—TOEFL (minimum score 550 paper-based; 213 computer-based; 80 iBT); Recommended—IELTS (minimum score 6.5). *Application deadline:* For fall admission, 7/31 priority date for domestic students, 4/30 priority date for international students; for spring admission, 12/31 priority date for domestic students, 11/30 priority date for international students. Applications are processed on a rolling basis. Application fee: $75. Electronic applications accepted. *Expenses:* Tuition: Full-time $21,492; part-time $1194 per credit. Required fees: $385 per semester. Tuition and fees vary according to course load. *Financial support:* Institutionally sponsored loans, scholarships/grants, and unspecified assistantships available. Support available to part-time students. *Application contact:* JeanCarlo Bonilla, Director of Graduate Enrollment Management, 718-260-3182, Fax: 718-260-3624, E-mail: gradinfo@poly.edu.

Rice University, Graduate Programs, George R. Brown School of Engineering, Department of Statistics, Houston, TX 77251-1892. Offers bioinformatics (PhD); biostatistics (PhD); computational finance (PhD); general statistics (PhD); statistics (M Stat, MA); MBA/M Stat. Part-time programs available. *Degree requirements:* For master's, comprehensive exam; for doctorate, comprehensive exam, thesis/dissertation. *Entrance requirements:* For master's and doctorate, GRE General Test, minimum GPA of 3.0. Additional exam requirements/recommendations for international students: Required—TOEFL (minimum score 630 paper-based; 250 computer-based; 90 iBT). Electronic applications accepted. *Faculty research:* Statistical genetics, non parametric function estimation, computational statistics and visualization, stochastic processes.

Rochester Institute of Technology, Graduate Enrollment Services, College of Science, Health Sciences and Sustainability, Department of Biological Sciences, Program in Bioinformatics, Rochester, NY 14623-5603. Offers MS. Part-time programs available. *Students:* 14 full-time (4 women), 8 part-time (3 women); includes 1 Asian, non-Hispanic/Latino, 12 international. Average age 28. 68 applicants, 40% accepted, 9 enrolled. In 2010, 4 master's awarded. *Degree requirements:* For master's, thesis. *Entrance requirements:* For master's, GRE, minimum GPA of 3.2. Additional exam requirements/recommendations for international students: Required—TOEFL (minimum score 570 paper-based; 230 computer-based; 88 iBT) or IELTS (minimum score 6.5). *Application deadline:* For fall admission, 2/15 priority date for domestic and international students; for winter admission, 11/1 for domestic students; for spring admission, 2/1 for domestic students. Applications are processed on a rolling basis. Application fee: $50. Electronic applications accepted. *Expenses:* Tuition: Full-time $33,234; part-time $924 per credit hour. Required fees: $219. *Financial support:* In 2010–11, 17 students received support; fellowships with partial tuition reimbursements available, research assistantships with partial tuition reimbursements available, teaching assistantships with partial tuition reimbursements available, career-related internships or fieldwork, scholarships/grants, and unspecified assistantships also available. Support available to part-time students. Financial award applicants required to submit FAFSA. *Unit head:* Dr. Michael Osier, Director, 585-475-4392, Fax: 585-475-6970, E-mail: mvosd@rit.edu. *Application contact:* Diane Ellison, Assistant Vice President, Graduate Enrollment Services, 585-475-2229, Fax: 585-475-7164, E-mail: gradinfo@rit.edu.

Stevens Institute of Technology, Graduate School, Charles V. Schaefer Jr. School of Engineering, Department of Chemistry, Chemical Biology and Biomedical Engineering, Hoboken, NJ 07030. Offers analytical chemistry (PhD, Certificate); bioinformatics (PhD, Certificate); biomedical chemistry (Certificate); biomedical engineering (M Eng, Certificate); chemical biology (MS, PhD, Certificate); chemical physiology (Certificate); chemistry (MS, PhD); organic chemistry (PhD); physical chemistry (PhD); polymer chemistry (PhD, Certificate). Part-time and evening/weekend programs available. Postbaccalaureate distance learning degree programs offered (no on-campus study). *Students:* 66 full-time (35 women), 25 part-time (7 women); includes 2 Black or African American, non-Hispanic/Latino; 14 Asian, non-Hispanic/Latino; 8 Hispanic/Latino, 31 international. Average age 26. 109 applicants, 68% accepted.Terminal master's awarded for partial completion of doctoral program. *Degree requirements:* For master's, thesis or alternative; for doctorate, one foreign language, thesis/dissertation; for Certificate, project or thesis. *Entrance requirements:* Additional exam requirements/recommendations for international students: Required—TOEFL. *Application deadline:* Applications are processed on a rolling basis. Application fee: $50. Electronic applications accepted. *Financial support:* Fellowships, research assistantships, teaching assistantships available. Financial award application deadline: 4/1. *Faculty research:* Biochemical reaction engineering, polymerization engineering, reactor design, biochemical process control and synthesis. *Unit head:* Philip Leopold, Director, 201-216-8957, Fax: 201-216-8196, E-mail: pleopold@stevens.edu. *Application contact:* Graduate Admissions, 800-496-4935, Fax: 201-216-8044, E-mail: gradadmissions@stevens.edu.

Université de Montréal, Faculty of Medicine, Biochemistry Department, Montréal, QC H3C 3J7, Canada. Offers M Sc, PhD. Electronic applications accepted.

Université de Montréal, Faculty of Medicine, Program in Bioinformatics, Montréal, QC H3C 3J7, Canada. Offers M Sc, PhD.

University of Arkansas at Little Rock, Graduate School, George W. Donughey College of Engineering and Information Technology, Program in Bioinformatics, Little Rock, AR 72204-1099. Offers MS, PhD.

University of California, Los Angeles, Graduate Division, College of Letters and Science, Interdepartmental Program in Bioinformatics, Los Angeles, CA 90095. Offers MS, PhD. *Students:* 11 full-time (5 women); includes 2 minority (both Asian, non-Hispanic/Latino), 4 international. Average age 27. 40 applicants, 20% accepted, 4 enrolled.Application fee: $70 ($90 for international students). Electronic applications accepted. *Financial support:* In 2010–11, 5 fellowships, 1 teaching assistantship were awarded; research assistantships. *Unit head:* Dr. Christopher Lee, Chair, Interdepartmental Program in Bioinformatics, 310-825-7374, E-mail: leec@chem.ucla.edu. *Application contact:* Academic Services Manager, 310-825-7929, E-mail: nancyp@lifesci.ucla.edu.

University of California, Riverside, Graduate Division, Graduate Program in Genetics, Genomics, and Bioinformatics, Riverside, CA 92521-0102. Offers genomics and bioinformatics (PhD); molecular genetics (PhD); population and evolutionary genetics (PhD). *Degree requirements:* For doctorate, thesis/dissertation, qualifying exams, teaching experience. *Entrance requirements:* For doctorate, GRE General Test, minimum GPA of 3.2. Additional exam requirements/recommendations for international students: Required—TOEFL (minimum score 550 paper-based; 213 computer-based; 80 iBT). Electronic applications accepted. *Faculty research:* Molecular Genetics, Evolution and Population Genetics, Genomics and Bioinformatics.

University of California, San Diego, Office of Graduate Studies, Interdisciplinary Doctoral Program in Bioinformatics, La Jolla, CA 92093. Offers PhD. Offered through the Departments of Bioengineering, Biology, Biomedical Sciences, Chemistry and Biochemistry, Computer Sciences and Engineering, Mathematics, and Physics. *Entrance requirements:* For doctorate, GRE General Test. Electronic applications accepted.

University of California, San Diego, School of Medicine and Office of Graduate Studies, Molecular Pathology Program, La Jolla, CA 92093. Offers bioinformatics (PhD); cancer biology/oncology (PhD); cardiovascular sciences and disease (PhD); microbiology (PhD); molecular pathology (PhD); neurological disease (PhD); stem cell and developmental biology (PhD); structural biology/drug design (PhD). *Entrance requirements:* For doctorate, GRE General Test, GRE Subject Test. Additional exam requirements/recommendations for international students: Required—TOEFL. Electronic applications accepted.

University of California, San Francisco, School of Pharmacy and Graduate Division, Graduate Program in Biological and Medical Informatics, San Francisco, CA 94158-2517. Offers PhD. *Faculty:* 30 full-time (6 women). *Students:* 30 full-time (11 women); includes 1 Black or African American, non-Hispanic/Latino; 3 Asian, non-Hispanic/Latino; 4 Hispanic/Latino, 2 international. Average age 28. 140 applicants, 26% accepted, 8 enrolled. In 2010, 3 doctorates awarded. Terminal master's awarded for partial completion of doctoral program. *Degree requirements:* For doctorate, thesis/dissertation, cumulative qualifying exams, proposal defense. *Entrance requirements:* For doctorate, GRE General Test, minimum GPA of 3.0. Additional exam requirements/recommendations for international students: Required—TOEFL (minimum score 550 paper-based; 213 computer-based; 80 iBT). *Application deadline:* For fall admission, 12/1 for domestic and international students. Application fee: $70 ($90 for international students). *Financial support:* In 2010–11, 3 fellowships with full tuition reimbursements (averaging $28,000 per year), 26 research assistantships with full tuition reimbursements (averaging $28,000 per year) were awarded; career-related internships or fieldwork, scholarships/grants, traineeships, health care benefits, tuition waivers (full), and stipends also available. *Faculty research:* Bioinformatics, biomedical computing, decision science and engineering, imaging informatics, knowledge management/telehealth/health services research. *Unit head:* Thomas E. Ferrin, Director, 415-476-2299, Fax: 415-502-1755, E-mail: tef@cgl.ucsf.edu. *Application contact:* Julia Molla, Program Administrator, 415-514-0249, Fax: 415-514-0502, E-mail: jmolla@cgl.ucsf.edu.

University of California, Santa Cruz, Division of Graduate Studies, Jack Baskin School of Engineering, Program in Bioinformatics, Santa Cruz, CA 95064. Offers MS, PhD. *Students:* 36 full-time (8 women), 1 part-time (0 women); includes 12 minority (10 Asian, non-Hispanic/Latino; 1 Hispanic/Latino; 1 Two or more races, non-Hispanic/Latino), 2 international. Average age 32. 91 applicants, 26% accepted, 7 enrolled. In 2010, 11 master's, 8 doctorates awarded. *Degree requirements:* For master's, research project with written report; for doctorate, thesis/dissertation. *Entrance requirements:* For master's and doctorate, GRE General Test. Additional exam requirements/recommendations for international students: Required—TOEFL (minimum score 570 paper-based; 230 computer-based; 89 iBT); Recommended—IELTS (minimum score 8). *Application deadline:* For fall admission, 1/3 for domestic and international students. Application fee: $70 ($90 for international students). Electronic applications accepted. *Financial support:* Fellowships, research assistantships, teaching assistantships, institutionally sponsored loans and tuition waivers available. Financial award applicants required to submit FAFSA. *Faculty research:* Bioinformatics, genomics, nanopore, stem cell. *Unit head:* Carol Mullane, Graduate Program Coordinator, 831-459-2576, E-mail: mullane@soe.ucsc.edu. *Application contact:* Carol Mullane, Graduate Program Coordinator, 831-459-2576, E-mail: mullane@soe.ucsc.edu.

University of Cincinnati, Graduate School, College of Engineering, Department of Biomedical Engineering, Cincinnati, OH 45221. Offers bioinformatics (PhD); biomechanics (PhD); medical imaging (PhD); tissue engineering (PhD). Part-time programs available. *Degree requirements:* For doctorate, one foreign language, thesis/dissertation. *Entrance requirements:* For doctorate, GRE General Test. Additional exam requirements/recommendations for international students: Required—TOEFL (minimum score 600 paper-based; 250 computer-based).

University of Colorado Denver, School of Medicine, Program in Pharmacology, Denver, CO 80217-3364. Offers bioinformatics (PhD); biomolecular structure (PhD); pharmacology (PhD). *Students:* 25 full-time (13 women); includes 1 Black or African American, non-Hispanic/Latino; 2 Asian, non-Hispanic/Latino; 1 Hispanic/Latino. Average age 28. 31 applicants, 16% accepted, 5 enrolled. In 2010, 3 doctorates awarded. *Degree requirements:* For doctorate, comprehensive exam, thesis/dissertation, major seminar, 3 research rotations, 30 hours each of course work and thesis. *Entrance requirements:* For doctorate, GRE General Test. Additional exam requirements/recommendations for international students: Required—TOEFL (minimum score 550 paper-based; 213 computer-based; 80 iBT). *Application deadline:* For fall admission, 1/1 priority date for domestic students. Application fee: $50 ($75 for international students). Electronic applications accepted. *Expenses:* Contact institution. *Financial support:* Fellowships, research assistantships, teaching assistantships, health care benefits, tuition waivers (full), and stipend available. Financial award application deadline: 3/15; financial award applicants required to submit FAFSA. *Faculty research:* Cancer biology, drugs of abuse, neuroscience, signal transduction, structural biology. Total annual research expenditures: $16.7 million. *Unit head:* Dr. Andrew Thorburn, Interim Chair, 303-724-3290, Fax: 303-724-3663, E-mail: andrew.thorburn@ucdenver.edu. *Application contact:* Graduate Training Coordinator, 303-724-3565, E-mail: grad.pharm@ucdenver.edu.

University of Georgia, Institute of Bioinformatics, Athens, GA 30602. Offers MS, PhD, Graduate Certificate. *Students:* 46 full-time (21 women); includes 1 Black or African American, non-Hispanic/Latino; 3 Asian, non-Hispanic/Latino; 1 Hispanic/Latino, 35 international. 52 applicants, 23% accepted. In 2010, 2 master's awarded. *Expenses:* Tuition, state resident: full-time $7200; part-time $344 per credit hour. Tuition, nonresident: full-time $21,900; part-time $944 per credit hour. Tuition and fees vary according to course load and program. *Unit head:* Dr. Ying Xu, Director, 706-542-9779, E-mail: xyn@bmb.uga.edu. *Application contact:* Dr. Jeff Dean, Graduate Coordinator, 706-542-1710, E-mail: jeffdean@uga.edu.

University of Idaho, College of Graduate Studies, Program in Bioinformatics and Computational Biology, Moscow, ID 83844-2282. Offers MS, PhD. *Faculty:* 13 full-time. *Students:* 12 full-time, 1 part-time. Average age 28. In 2010, 4 doctorates awarded. *Entrance requirements:* For master's, GRE, minimum GPA of 2.8. *Application deadline:* For fall admission, 8/1 for domestic students; for spring admission, 12/15 for domestic students. Applications are processed on a rolling basis. Application fee: $60. Electronic applications accepted. *Expenses:* Tuition, nonresident: part-time $580 per credit. Required fees: $306 per credit. *Financial support:* Applicants required to submit FAFSA. *Unit head:* Dr. Paul Joyce, Director, 208-885-6010, E-mail: bcb@uidaho.edu. *Application contact:* Dr. Paul Joyce, Director, 208-885-6010, E-mail: bcb@uidaho.edu.

University of Illinois at Urbana–Champaign, Graduate College, College of Agricultural, Consumer and Environmental Sciences, Department of Crop Sciences, Champaign, IL 61820. Offers bioinformatics: crop sciences (MS); crop sciences (MS, PhD). Postbaccalaureate distance learning degree programs offered (no on-campus study). *Faculty:* 46 full-time (6 women), 1 (woman) part-time/adjunct. *Students:* 87 full-time (22 women), 39 part-time (10 women); includes 3 Asian, non-Hispanic/Latino; 2 Hispanic/Latino, 46 international. 101 applicants, 46% accepted, 34 enrolled. In 2010, 11 master's, 4 doctorates awarded. *Entrance requirements:* For master's and doctorate, GRE, minimum GPA of 3.0. Additional exam requirements/recommendations for international students: Required—TOEFL (minimum score 570 paper-based). *Application deadline:* Applications are processed on a rolling basis. Application fee: $75 ($90 for international students). Electronic applications accepted. *Financial support:* In 2010–11, 48 fellowships, 78 research assistantships, 17 teaching assistantships were awarded; tuition waivers (full and partial) also available. *Faculty research:* Plant breeding and genetics, molecular biology, crop production, plant physiology, weed science. *Unit head:* German A. Bollero, Head, 217-333-9475, Fax: 217-333-9817, E-mail: gbollero@illinois.edu. *Application contact:* S. Dianne Carson, Secretary, 217-244-0396, Fax: 217-333-9817, E-mail: sdcarson@illinois.edu.

University of Illinois at Urbana–Champaign, Graduate College, College of Engineering, Department of Computer Science, Champaign, IL 61820. Offers bioinformatics (MS); computer science (MCS, MS, PhD); MCS/JD; MCS/M Arch; MCS/MBA. Part-time programs available. Postbaccalaureate distance learning degree programs offered (no on-campus study). *Faculty:* 53 full-time (5 women), 2 part-time/adjunct (0 women). *Students:* 272 full-time (41 women), 179 part-time (26 women); includes 3 Black or African American, non-Hispanic/Latino; 36 Asian, non-Hispanic/Latino; 1 Hispanic/Latino; 1 Two or more races, non-Hispanic/Latino, 271 international. 1,324 applicants, 10% accepted, 64 enrolled. In 2010, 68 master's, 36 doctorates awarded. *Entrance requirements:* For master's and doctorate, minimum GPA of 3.0. Additional exam requirements/recommendations for international students: Required—TOEFL (minimum score 600 paper-based; 250 computer-based; 100 iBT) or IELTS (minimum score 6.5). *Application deadline:* Applications are processed on a rolling basis. Application fee: $75 ($90 for international students). Electronic applications accepted. *Financial support:* In 2010–11, 35 fellowships, 281 research assistantships, 87 teaching assistantships were awarded; tuition waivers (full and partial) also available. *Unit head:* Robin A. Rutenbar, Head, 217-333-3373, Fax: 217-333-3501, E-mail: rutenbar@illinois.edu. *Application contact:* Rhonda McElroy, Coordinator of Graduate Programs, 217-244-2745, Fax: 217-244-6073, E-mail: rmcelroy@illinois.edu.

University of Illinois at Urbana–Champaign, Graduate College, Graduate School of Library and Information Science, Champaign, IL 61820. Offers bioinformatics: library and information science (MS); library and information science (MS, PhD, CAS); library and information science: digital libraries (CAS). *Accreditation:* ALA (one or more programs are accredited). Postbaccalaureate distance learning degree programs offered. *Faculty:* 23 full-time (11 women), 10 part-time/adjunct (7 women). *Students:* 352 full-time (258 women), 367 part-time (270 women); includes 124 minority (38 Black or African American, non-Hispanic/Latino; 1 American Indian or Alaska Native, non-Hispanic/Latino; 34 Asian, non-Hispanic/Latino; 40 Hispanic/Latino; 11 Two or more races, non-Hispanic/Latino), 27 international. 737 applicants, 58% accepted, 242 enrolled. In 2010, 272 master's, 5 doctorates, 2 other advanced degrees awarded. *Entrance requirements:* For master's, GRE General Test, minimum GPA of 3.0; for doctorate, minimum GPA of 3.0; for CAS, master's degree in library and information science or related field with minimum GPA of 3.0. Additional exam requirements/recommendations for international students: Required—TOEFL (minimum score 620 paper-based; 260 computer-based; 105 iBT) or IELTS (minimum score 7). *Application deadline:* Applications are processed on a rolling basis. Application fee: $75 ($90 for international students). Electronic applications accepted. *Financial support:* In 2010–11, 37 fellowships, 37 research assistantships, 38 teaching assistantships were awarded; tuition waivers (full and partial) also available. *Unit head:* John Unsworth, Dean, 217-333-3281, Fax: 217-244-3302, E-mail: unsworth@illinois.edu. *Application contact:* Valerie Youngen, Admissions and Records Representative, 217-333-0734, Fax: 217-244-3302, E-mail: vyoungen@llinois.edu.

The University of Manchester, Faculty of Life Sciences, Manchester, United Kingdom. Offers adaptive organismal biology (M Phil, PhD); animal biology (M Phil, PhD); biochemistry (M Phil, PhD); bioinformatics (M Phil, PhD); biomolecular sciences (M Phil, PhD); biotechnology (M Phil, PhD); cell biology (M Phil, PhD); cell matrix research (M Phil, PhD); channels and transporters (M Phil, PhD); developmental biology (M Phil, PhD); Egyptology (M Phil, PhD); environmental biology (M Phil, PhD); evolutionary biology (M Phil, PhD); gene expression (M Phil, PhD); genetics (M Phil, PhD); history of science, technology and medicine (M Phil, PhD); immunology (M Phil, PhD); integrative neurobiology and behavior (M Phil, PhD); membrane trafficking (M Phil, PhD); microbiology (M Phil, PhD); molecular and cellular neuroscience (M Phil, PhD); molecular biology (M Phil, PhD); molecular cancer studies (M Phil, PhD); neuroscience (M Phil, PhD); ophthalmology (M Phil, PhD); optometry (M Phil, PhD); organelle function (M Phil, PhD); pharmacology (M Phil, PhD); physiology (M Phil, PhD); plant sciences (M Phil, PhD); stem cell research (M Phil, PhD); structural biology (M Phil, PhD); systems neuroscience (M Phil, PhD); toxicology (M Phil, PhD).

University of Massachusetts Worcester, Graduate School of Biomedical Sciences, Worcester, MA 01655-0115. Offers biochemistry and molecular pharmacology (PhD); bioinformatics and computational biology (PhD); cancer biology (PhD); cell biology (PhD); clinical and population health research (PhD); clinical investigation (MS); immunology and virology (PhD); interdisciplinary graduate program (PhD); molecular genetics and microbiology (PhD); neuroscience (PhD); DVM/PhD; MD/PhD. *Faculty:* 1,059 full-time (357 women), 145 part-time/adjunct (100 women). *Students:* 438 full-time (239 women), 1 (woman) part-time; includes 44 minority (9 Black or African American, non-Hispanic/Latino; 31 Asian, non-Hispanic/Latino; 4 Hispanic/Latino), 148 international. Average age 29. 687 applicants, 28% accepted, 116 enrolled. In 2010, 6 master's, 45 doctorates awarded. Terminal master's awarded for partial completion of doctoral program. *Degree requirements:* For master's, thesis; for doctorate, thesis/dissertation. *Entrance requirements:* For master's, bachelor's degree; for doctorate, GRE General Test, MS, MA, or MPH (for some programs). Additional exam requirements/recommendations for international students: Required—TOEFL (minimum score 600 paper-based; 250 computer-based). *Application deadline:* For fall admission, 12/15 for domestic and international students; for winter admission, 1/15 for domestic students, for spring admission, 5/15 for domestic students. Application fee: $35. Electronic applications accepted. *Expenses:* Contact institution. *Financial support:* In 2010–11, 439 students received support, including 439 research assistantships with full tuition reimbursements available (averaging $28,350 per year); scholarships/grants, health care benefits, tuition waivers (full), and unspecified assistantships also available. Financial award application deadline: 4/20. *Faculty research:* RNA interference, gene therapy, cell biology, bioinformatics, clinical research. Total annual research expenditures: $232 million. *Unit head:* Dr. Anthony Carruthers, Dean, 508-856-4135, E-mail: anthony.carruthers@umassmed.edu. *Application contact:* Dr. Kendall Knight, Associate Dean and Interim Director of Admissions and Recruitment, 508-856-5628, Fax: 508-856-3659, E-mail: kendall.knight@umassmed.edu.

University of Medicine and Dentistry of New Jersey, School of Health Related Professions, Department of Health Informatics, Program in Biomedical Informatics, Newark, NJ 07107-1709. Offers MS, PhD, DMD/MS, MD/MS. *Entrance requirements:* Additional exam requirements/recommendations for international students: Required—TOEFL. Electronic applications accepted.

University of Michigan, Horace H. Rackham School of Graduate Studies, Program in Biomedical Sciences (PIBS) and Horace H. Rackham School of Graduate Studies, Program in Bioinformatics, Ann Arbor, MI 48109. Offers MS, PhD. Part-time programs available. *Faculty:* 122 full-time (27 women). *Students:* 46 full-time (12 women), 1 part-time (0 women); includes 10 minority (1 Black or African American, non-Hispanic/Latino; 1 American Indian or Alaska Native, non-Hispanic/Latino; 4 Asian, non-Hispanic/Latino; 3 Hispanic/Latino; 1 Two or more races, non-Hispanic/Latino), 20 international. Average age 26. 39 applicants, 28% accepted, 6 enrolled. In 2010, 4 master's, 4 doctorates awarded. Terminal master's awarded for partial completion of doctoral program. *Degree requirements:* For master's, thesis optional, summer internship or rotation; for doctorate, thesis/dissertation, oral defense of dissertation, preliminary exam, two rotations. *Entrance requirements:* For master's and doctorate, GRE or MCAT. Additional exam requirements/recommendations for international students: Required—TOEFL (minimum score 100 iBT). *Application deadline:* For fall admission, 12/1 for domestic and

Bioinformatics

University of Michigan (continued)

international students. Application fee: $60 ($75 for international students). Electronic applications accepted. *Expenses:* Tuition, state resident: full-time $17,784; part-time $1116 per credit hour. Tuition, nonresident: full-time $35,944; part-time $2125 per credit hour. International tuition: $35,994 full-time. Required fees: $95 per semester. Tuition and fees vary according to course load, degree level and program. *Financial support:* In 2010–11, 44 students received support, including 22 fellowships with full tuition reimbursements available (averaging $26,500 per year), 18 research assistantships with full tuition reimbursements available (averaging $26,500 per year), 4 teaching assistantships with full tuition reimbursements available (averaging $26,500 per year); scholarships/grants, traineeships, health care benefits, and unspecified assistantships also available. Financial award application deadline: 12/1. *Faculty research:* Structural and chemical informatics, clinical informatics, databases and computing, genomics, proteomics, statistical applications, systemic modeling . *Unit head:* Dr. Dan Margit, Co-Director, 734-615-5510, Fax: 734-615-6553, E-mail: gradbioinfo@umich.edu. *Application contact:* Michelle S. Melis, Director of Student Life, 734-615-6538, Fax: 734-647-7022, E-mail: msmtegan@umich.edu.

University of Missouri, Graduate School, Informatics Institute, Columbia, MO 65211. Offers PhD. *Entrance requirements:* Additional exam requirements/recommendations for international students: Required—TOEFL (minimum score 577 paper-based; 233 computer-based; 90 iBT).

University of Missouri–Kansas City, School of Computing and Engineering, Kansas City, MO 64110-2499. Offers civil engineering (MS); computer and electrical engineering (PhD); computer science (MS), including bioinformatics, software engineering, telecommunications networking; computer science and informatics (PhD); computing (PhD); electrical engineering (MS); engineering (PhD); mechanical engineering (MS); telecommunications (PhD). PhD (interdisciplinary) offered through the School of Graduate Studies. Part-time programs available. *Faculty:* 36 full-time (5 women), 21 part-time/adjunct (0 women). *Students:* 160 full-time (32 women), 194 part-time (41 women); includes 21 minority (5 Black or African American, non-Hispanic/Latino; 9 Asian, non-Hispanic/Latino; 6 Hispanic/Latino; 1 Two or more races, non-Hispanic/Latino), 273 international. Average age 25. 440 applicants, 55% accepted, 104 enrolled. In 2010, 135 master's awarded. *Degree requirements:* For doctorate, thesis/dissertation. *Entrance requirements:* For master's, GRE General Test, minimum GPA of 3.0, 3 letters of recommendation from professors; for doctorate, GRE General Test, minimum GPA of 3.5. Additional exam requirements/recommendations for international students: Required—TOEFL (minimum score 550 paper-based; 213 computer-based; 80 iBT). *Application deadline:* For fall admission, 1/15 priority date for domestic students, 1/15 for international students. Applications are processed on a rolling basis. Application fee: $45 ($50 for international students). *Expenses:* Tuition, state resident: full-time $5522.40; part-time $306.80 per credit hour. Tuition, nonresident: full-time $7128; part-time $792 per credit hour. Required fees: $261.15 per term. *Financial support:* In 2010–11, 35 research assistantships with partial tuition reimbursements (averaging $14,340 per year), 20 teaching assistantships with partial tuition reimbursements (averaging $13,351 per year) were awarded; career-related internships or fieldwork, Federal Work-Study, scholarships/grants, tuition waivers (partial), and unspecified assistantships also available. Support available to part-time students. Financial award application deadline: 3/1; financial award applicants required to submit FAFSA. *Faculty research:* Algorithms, bioinformatics and medical informatics, biomechanics/biomaterials, civil engineering materials, networking and telecommunications, thermal science. Total annual research expenditures: $1.1 million. *Unit head:* Dr. Kevin Z. Truman, Dean, 816-235-2399, Fax: 816-235-5159. *Application contact:* Dr. Kevin Z. Truman, Dean, 816-235-2399, Fax: 816-235-5159.

University of Missouri–Kansas City, School of Medicine, Kansas City, MO 64110-2499. Offers anesthesia (MS); bioinformatics (MS); medicine (MD); MD/PhD. *Accreditation:* LCME/AMA. *Faculty:* 44 full-time (11 women), 15 part-time/adjunct (6 women). *Students:* 406 full-time (213 women), 4 part-time (2 women); includes 213 minority (24 Black or African American, non-Hispanic/Latino; 172 Asian, non-Hispanic/Latino; 16 Hispanic/Latino; 1 Two or more races, non-Hispanic/Latino), 1 international. Average age 23. 779 applicants, 13% accepted, 95 enrolled. In 2010, 92 first professional degrees, 4 master's awarded. *Degree requirements:* For MD, one foreign language, United States Medical Licensing Exam Step 1 and 2. *Entrance requirements:* Interview. *Application deadline:* For fall admission, 11/15 for domestic and international students. Application fee: $50. *Expenses:* Contact institution. *Financial support:* Career-related internships or fieldwork, Federal Work-Study, institutionally sponsored loans, scholarships/grants, and tuition waivers (partial) available. Financial award application deadline: 3/1; financial award applicants required to submit FAFSA. *Faculty research:* Cardiovascular disease, women's and children's health, trauma and infectious diseases, neurological, metabolic disease. Total annual research expenditures: $4.7 million. *Unit head:* Dr. Betty Drees, Dean, 816-235-1808, E-mail: dreesb@umkc.edu. *Application contact:* Kelly Kasper-Cushman, Selection Administrative Assistant, 816-235-1870, Fax: 816-235-6579, E-mail: kasperkm@umkc.edu.

University of Nebraska–Lincoln, Graduate College, College of Arts and Sciences and College of Engineering, Department of Computer Science and Engineering, Lincoln, NE 68588. Offers bioinformatics (MS, PhD); computer engineering (MS, PhD); computer science (MS, PhD); information technology (PhD). *Degree requirements:* For master's, thesis optional; for doctorate, comprehensive exam, thesis/dissertation. *Entrance requirements:* For master's and doctorate, GRE General Test. Additional exam requirements/recommendations for international students: Required—TOEFL (minimum score 600 paper-based; 250 computer-based). Electronic applications accepted. *Faculty research:* Software engineering, geo- and bio-informatics, scientific computation, secure communication.

The University of North Carolina at Chapel Hill, School of Medicine and Graduate School, Graduate Programs in Medicine, Curriculum in Bioinformatics and Computational Biology, Chapel Hill, NC 27599. Offers PhD. *Faculty:* 40 full-time (6 women). *Students:* 11 full-time (6 women); includes 1 Black or African American, non-Hispanic/Latino; 1 Asian, non-Hispanic/Latino, 3 international. Average age 27. In 2010, 1 doctorate awarded. *Degree requirements:* For doctorate, comprehensive exam, thesis/dissertation. *Entrance requirements:* For doctorate, GRE, minimum 3.0 GPA. Additional exam requirements/recommendations for international students: Required—TOEFL. *Application deadline:* For fall admission, 1/1 for domestic and international students. Applications are processed on a rolling basis. Application fee: $77. Electronic applications accepted. *Financial support:* In 2010–11, 2 fellowships with full tuition reimbursements (averaging $26,000 per year), 9 research assistantships with full tuition reimbursements (averaging $26,000 per year) were awarded; tuition waivers (full) also available. *Faculty research:* Protein folding, design and evolution and molecular biophysics of disease; mathematical modeling of signaling pathways and regulatory networks; bioinformatics, medical informatics, user interface design; statistical genetics and genetic epidemiologyp datamining, classification and clustering analysis of gene-expression data. *Unit head:* Dr. Tim C. Elston, Director, 919-843-7670, E-mail: telston@med.unc.edu. *Application contact:* Sausyty A. Hermreck, Graduate Student Coordinator, 919-966-2681, Fax: 919-966-0401, E-mail: sausytyh@med.unc.edu.

The University of North Carolina at Charlotte, Graduate School, College of Computing and Informatics, Department of Bioinformatics and Genomics, Charlotte, NC 28223-0001. Offers bioinformatics (MS). Part-time programs available. *Faculty:* 13 full-time (6 women). *Students:* 14 full-time (6 women), 4 part-time (2 women); includes 4 minority (1 Black or African American, non-Hispanic/Latino; 3 Asian, non-Hispanic/Latino), 6 international. Average age 28. 19 applicants, 53% accepted, 7 enrolled. In 2010, 5 master's awarded. Terminal master's awarded for partial completion of doctoral program. *Degree requirements:* For master's, internship, research project, or thesis. *Entrance requirements:* For master's, GRE, minimum undergraduate GPA of 3.0 overall and in undergraduate major. Additional exam requirements/recommendations for international students: Required—TOEFL (minimum score 557 paper-based; 220 computer-based; 83 iBT). *Application deadline:* For fall admission, 7/15 for domestic students, 5/1 for international students; for spring admission, 11/15 for domestic students, 10/1 for international students. Applications are processed on a rolling basis. Application fee: $55. Electronic applications accepted. *Expenses:* Tuition, state resident: full-time $3464. Tuition, nonresident: full-time $14,297. Required fees: $2094. Tuition and fees vary according to course load. *Financial support:* In 2010–11, 8 fellowships (averaging $25,083 per year), 4 research assistantships (averaging $14,375 per year), 14 teaching assistantships (averaging $11,481 per year) were awarded; career-related internships or fieldwork, institutionally sponsored loans, scholarships/grants, and unspecified assistantships also available. Support available to part-time students. *Faculty research:* High-throughput studies, computational biophysics, structural bioinformatics, metagenomics, computational mass spectrometry. Total annual research expenditures: $1.1 million. *Unit head:* Dr. Larry Mays, Chairman, 704-687-8555, E-mail: lemays@uncc.edu. *Application contact:* Kathy B. Giddings, Director of Graduate Admissions, 704-687-5503, Fax: 704-687-3279, E-mail: gradadm@uncc.edu.

University of Oklahoma, College of Arts and Sciences, Department of Chemistry and Biochemistry, Norman, OK 73019. Offers chemistry and biochemistry (MS, PhD), including bioinformatics, cellular and behavioral neurobiology (PhD), chemistry. Part-time programs available. *Faculty:* 27 full-time (6 women). *Students:* 72 full-time (27 women), 26 part-time (11 women); includes 12 minority (6 Black or African American, non-Hispanic/Latino; 1 American Indian or Alaska Native, non-Hispanic/Latino; 2 Asian, non-Hispanic/Latino; 1 Hispanic/Latino; 2 Two or more races, non-Hispanic/Latino), 50 international. Average age 28. 31 applicants, 61% accepted, 16 enrolled. In 2010, 17 master's, 17 doctorates awarded. Terminal master's awarded for partial completion of doctoral program. *Degree requirements:* For master's, thesis optional; for doctorate, thesis/dissertation. *Entrance requirements:* For master's, GRE, BS in chemistry; for doctorate, GRE. Additional exam requirements/recommendations for international students: Required—TOEFL (minimum score 550 paper-based; 213 computer-based; 79 iBT). *Application deadline:* For fall admission, 4/1 priority date for domestic students, 4/1 for international students; for spring admission, 9/1 priority date for domestic students, 9/1 for international students. Applications are processed on a rolling basis. Application fee: $40 ($90 for international students). Electronic applications accepted. *Expenses:* Tuition, state resident: full-time $3892.80; part-time $162.20 per credit hour. Tuition, nonresident: full-time $14,167; part-time $590.30 per credit hour. Required fees: $2523.40; $94.60 per credit hour. Tuition and fees vary according to course load and degree level. *Financial support:* In 2010–11, 1 fellowship with full tuition reimbursement (averaging $5,000 per year), 24 research assistantships with partial tuition reimbursements (averaging $14,788 per year), 62 teaching assistantships with partial tuition reimbursements (averaging $16,444 per year) were awarded; scholarships/grants and unspecified assistantships also available. Financial award application deadline: 4/1; financial award applicants required to submit FAFSA. *Faculty research:* Structural biology, synthesis and catalysis, biomaterials, membrane biochemistry, genomics. Total annual research expenditures: $6.8 million. *Unit head:* Dr. George Richter-Addo, Chair, 405-325-4811, Fax: 405-325-6111, E-mail: grichteraddo@ou.edu. *Application contact:* Angela Link-Perez, Graduate Program Assistant, 405-325-4811 Ext. 62946, Fax: 405-325-6111, E-mail: alperez@ou.edu.

University of Oklahoma, College of Engineering, School of Computer Science, Norman, OK 73019. Offers computer science (MS, PhD), including bioinformatics, general (MS), standard (PhD). *Faculty:* 17 full-time (3 women). *Students:* 63 full-time (12 women), 43 part-time (4 women); includes 4 minority (1 American Indian or Alaska Native, non-Hispanic/Latino; 3 Asian, non-Hispanic/Latino), 61 international. Average age 28. 64 applicants, 81% accepted, 15 enrolled. In 2010, 18 master's, 1 doctorate awarded. Terminal master's awarded for partial completion of doctoral program. *Degree requirements:* For master's, thesis optional, oral exams, qualifying exam; for doctorate, thesis/dissertation, general exam, qualifying exam. *Entrance requirements:* For master's and doctorate, GRE General Test. Additional exam requirements/recommendations for international students: Required—TOEFL (minimum score 550 paper-based; 250 computer-based; 79 iBT). *Application deadline:* For fall admission, 1/15 priority date for domestic students, 4/1 for international students; for spring admission, 11/1 for domestic students, 9/1 for international students. Applications are processed on a rolling basis. Application fee: $40 ($90 for international students). Electronic applications accepted. *Expenses:* Tuition, state resident: full-time $3892.80; part-time $162.20 per credit hour. Tuition, nonresident: full-time $14,167; part-time $590.30 per credit hour. Required fees: $2523.40; $94.60 per credit hour. Tuition and fees vary according to course load and degree level. *Financial support:* In 2010–11, 85 students received support, including 3 fellowships (averaging $3,000 per year), 16 research assistantships with partial tuition reimbursements available (averaging $15,006 per year), 16 teaching assistantships with partial tuition reimbursements available (averaging $14,116 per year); unspecified assistantships also available. Financial award application deadline: 3/1; financial award applicants required to submit FAFSA. *Faculty research:* Artificial intelligence and robotics, scientific computing, computer networks, high performance computing, computer architecture, database management, visual analytics, cryptography. Total annual research expenditures: $2.6 million. *Unit head:* Sridhar Radhakrishnan, Professor and Director, 405-325-4042, Fax: 405-325-4044, E-mail: sridhar@ou.edu. *Application contact:* Sridhar Radhakrishnan, Professor and Director, 405-325-4042, Fax: 405-325-4044, E-mail: sridhar@ou.edu.

University of Pittsburgh, School of Medicine, Biomedical Informatics Training Program, Pittsburgh, PA 15260. Offers MS, PhD, Certificate. Part-time programs available. *Faculty:* 16 full-time (4 women), 13 part-time/adjunct (7 women). *Students:* 28 full-time (13 women), 4 part-time (2 women); includes 1 Black or African American, non-Hispanic/Latino; 5 Asian, non-Hispanic/Latino, 12 international. Average age 32. 37 applicants, 46% accepted, 13 enrolled. In 2010, 5 master's, 2 doctorates, 2 other advanced degrees awarded. Terminal master's awarded for partial completion of doctoral program. *Degree requirements:* For master's, comprehensive exam, written research report or thesis; for doctorate, comprehensive exam, thesis/dissertation; for Certificate, written research report or thesis. *Entrance requirements:* For master's, doctorate, and Certificate, GRE. Additional exam requirements/recommendations for international students: Required—TOEFL. *Application deadline:* For fall admission, 12/15 priority date for domestic and international students. Application fee: $40. *Expenses:* Tuition, state resident: full-time $17,304; part-time $701 per credit. Tuition, nonresident: full-time $29,554; part-time $1210 per credit. Required fees: $740; $214 per term. Tuition and fees vary according to program. *Financial support:* In 2010–11, 20 students received support, including 11 fellowships with full tuition reimbursements available (averaging $25,500 per year), 9 research assistantships with full tuition reimbursements available (averaging $25,500 per year); health care benefits also available. Financial award application deadline: 12/15. *Faculty research:* Biomedical informatics; bioinformatics; global health informatics; artificial intelligence; probability theory; data mining; machine learning; evaluation methods; dental, radiology, and pathology imaging. *Unit head:* Dr. Rebecca Crowley, Program Director, 412-647-7176, Fax: 412-647-7190, E-mail: crowleyrs@upmc.edu. *Application contact:* Toni L. Porterfield, Training Program Coordinator, 412-647-7176, Fax: 412-647-7190, E-mail: tls18@pitt.edu.

University of Southern California, Graduate School, Dana and David Dornsife College of Letters, Arts and Sciences, Department of Biological Sciences, Program in Molecular and Computational Biology, Los Angeles, CA 90089. Offers computational biology and bioinformatics (PhD); molecular biology (PhD). *Faculty:* 40 full-time (7 women). *Students:* 100 full-time (48 women), 3 part-time (2 women); includes 19 minority (3 Black or African American, non-Hispanic/Latino; 10 Asian, non-Hispanic/Latino; 4 Hispanic/Latino; 2 Two or more races, non-Hispanic/Latino), 58 international. 178 applicants, 25% accepted, 24 enrolled. In 2010, 15 doctorates awarded. Terminal master's awarded for partial completion of doctoral program. *Degree requirements:* For doctorate, comprehensive exam, thesis/dissertation, course work, qualifying examination, dissertation defense. *Entrance requirements:* For doctorate, GRE, 3 letters of recommendation, personal statement, resume, minimum GPA of 3.0. Additional exam requirements/recommendations for international students: Required—TOEFL (minimum score 600 paper-based; 250 computer-based; 100 iBT). *Application deadline:* For fall admission, 12/1 priority date for domestic students, 11/1 priority date for international students. Application fee: $85. Electronic applications accepted. *Expenses:* Tuition: Full-time $31,240; part-time $1420 per unit. Required fees: $600. One-time fee: $35 full-time.

Full-time tuition and fees vary according to degree level and program. *Financial support:* In 2010–11, 100 students received support, including 31 fellowships with full tuition reimbursements available (averaging $29,000 per year), 48 research assistantships with full tuition reimbursements available (averaging $28,000 per year), 21 teaching assistantships with full tuition reimbursements available (averaging $28,000 per year); career-related internships or fieldwork, scholarships/grants, traineeships, health care benefits, and unspecified assistantships also available. Financial award application deadline: 12/1. *Faculty research:* Biochemistry and molecular biology; genomics; computational biology and bioinformatics; cell and developmental biology, and genetics; DNA replication and repair, and cancer biology. *Unit head:* Dr. Myron Goodman, Professor of Biological Sciences and Chemistry, Director of the MCB Research Section, 213-740-5190, E-mail: mgoodman@usc.edu. *Application contact:* Catherine Atienza, Student Services Advisor I, 213-740-5188, E-mail: catherine.atienza@usc.edu.

The University of Texas at El Paso, Graduate School, College of Science, Department of Biological Sciences, El Paso, TX 79968-0001. Offers bioinformatics (MS); biological sciences (MS, PhD). Part-time and evening/weekend programs available. *Students:* 71 (32 women); includes 4 Black or African American, non-Hispanic/Latino; 4 Asian, non-Hispanic/Latino; 31 Hispanic/Latino, 17 international. Average age 34. In 2010, 16 master's, 4 doctorates awarded. *Degree requirements:* For master's, thesis; for doctorate, thesis/dissertation. *Entrance requirements:* For master's, GRE, minimum GPA of 3.0, letters of recommendation; for doctorate, GRE, statement of purpose, letters of recommendation. Additional exam requirements/recommendations for international students: Required—TOEFL; Recommended—IELTS. *Application deadline:* For fall admission, 8/1 priority date for domestic students, 3/1 for international students; for spring admission, 11/1 priority date for domestic students, 9/1 for international students. Applications are processed on a rolling basis. Application fee: $45 ($80 for international students). Electronic applications accepted. *Financial support:* In 2010–11, research assistantships with partial tuition reimbursements (averaging $22,500 per year), teaching assistantships with partial tuition reimbursements (averaging $18,000 per year) were awarded; fellowships with partial tuition reimbursements, institutionally sponsored loans, scholarships/grants, health care benefits, tuition waivers (partial), and unspecified assistantships also available. Support available to part-time students. Financial award application deadline: 3/15; financial award applicants required to submit FAFSA. *Unit head:* Dr. Robert Kirken, Chair, 915-747-5844, Fax: 915-747-5808, E-mail: rkirken@utep.edu. *Application contact:* Dr. Patricia D. Witherspoon, Dean of Graduate School, 915-747-5491, Fax: 915-747-5788, E-mail: withersp@utep.edu.

The University of Texas at El Paso, Graduate School, College of Science, Program in Bioinformatics, El Paso, TX 79968-0001. Offers MS. *Students:* 14 (2 women); includes 3 Asian, non-Hispanic/Latino; 4 Hispanic/Latino, 6 international. 39 applicants, 38% accepted. *Entrance requirements:* For master's, GRE, minimum GPA of 3.0. Additional exam requirements/recommendations for international students: Required—TOEFL. *Application deadline:* For fall admission, 6/1 for domestic students, 3/1 for international students; for spring admission, 11/1 for domestic students, 9/1 for international students. Application fee: $15 ($65 for international students). *Unit head:* Dr. Ming-Ying Leung, Director, 915-747-8484, Fax: 915-747-6502, E-mail: bioinformatics@utep.edu. *Application contact:* Dr. Eppie D. Rael, Student Information Contact, 915-747-5844, E-mail: erael@miners.utep.edu.

The University of Texas Medical Branch, Graduate School of Biomedical Sciences, Program in Biochemistry and Molecular Biology, Galveston, TX 77555. Offers biochemistry (PhD); bioinformatics (PhD); biophysics (PhD); cell biology (PhD); computational biology (PhD); structural biology (PhD). *Degree requirements:* For doctorate, thesis/dissertation. *Entrance requirements:* Additional exam requirements/recommendations for international students: Required—TOEFL (minimum score 550 paper-based; 213 computer-based). Electronic applications accepted.

University of the Sciences in Philadelphia, College of Graduate Studies, Program in Bioinformatics, Philadelphia, PA 19104-4495. Offers MS. *Entrance requirements:* Additional exam requirements/recommendations for international students: Required—TOEFL, TWE. *Expenses:* Contact institution. *Faculty research:* Genomics, microarray analysis, computer aided drug design, molecular biophysics, cell structure, molecular dynamics, computational chemistry.

The University of Toledo, College of Graduate Studies, College of Medicine and Life Sciences, Interdepartmental Programs, Toledo, OH 43606-3390. Offers bioinformatics/proteomics/genomics (MSBS, Certificate); human donation sciences (MSBS). *Expenses:* Tuition, state resident: full-time $11,426; part-time $476 per credit hour. Tuition, nonresident: full-time $21,660; part-time $903 per credit hour. One-time fee: $62.

University of Utah, School of Medicine and Graduate School, Graduate Programs in Medicine, Department of Biomedical Informatics, Salt Lake City, UT 84112-1107. Offers MS, PhD, Certificate. Part-time programs available. Postbaccalaureate distance learning degree programs offered (minimal on-campus study). *Degree requirements:* For master's, comprehensive exam, thesis; for doctorate, comprehensive exam, thesis/dissertation, qualifying exam. *Entrance requirements:* For master's and doctorate, GRE General Test (minimum 60th percentile), minimum GPA of 3.3. Additional exam requirements/recommendations for international students: Required—TOEFL (minimum score 600 paper-based; 250 computer-based). Electronic applications accepted. *Expenses:* Tuition, area resident: Part-time $179.19 per credit hour. Tuition, state resident: full-time $4384. Tuition, nonresident: full-time $16,684; part-time $630.67 per credit hour. Required fees: $350 per semester. Tuition and fees vary according to course load, degree level and program. *Faculty research:* Health information systems and expert systems, genetic epidemiology, medical imaging, bioinformatics, public health informatics.

University of Washington, Graduate School, School of Medicine, Graduate Programs in Medicine, Department of Medical Education and Biomedical Informatics, Division of Biomedical and Health Informatics, Seattle, WA 98195. Offers MS, PhD. *Entrance requirements:* For master's and doctorate, GRE General Test, minimum GPA of 3.0; previous undergraduate course work in biology, computer programming, and mathematics. Additional exam requirements/recommendations for international students: Required—TOEFL (minimum score 580 paper-based; 237 computer-based; 70 iBT). Electronic applications accepted. *Faculty research:* Bio-clinical informatics, information retrieval, human-computer interaction, knowledge-based systems, telehealth.

University of Washington, Graduate School, School of Public Health, Department of Health Services, Seattle, WA 98195. Offers bioinformatics (PhD); cancer prevention and control (PhD); clinical research (MS); community oriented public health practice (MPH); economics or finance (PhD); evaluation sciences (PhD); executive program (MHA); health behavior and health promotion (PhD); health care and population health research (MPH); health policy analysis and process (PhD); health policy and analysis and process (MPH); health services (MS, PhD); health services administration (EMHA, MHA); in residence program (MHA); maternal and child health (MPH, PhD); occupational health (PhD); population health and social determinants (PhD); social and behavioral sciences (MPH); sociology and demography (PhD); JD/MHA; MHA/MBA; MHA/MD; MHA/MPA; MPH/JD; MPH/MD; MPH/MN; MPH/MPA; MPH/MS; MPH/MSD; MPH/MSW; MPH/PhD. Part-time and evening/weekend programs available. Postbaccalaureate distance learning degree programs offered (minimal on-campus study). *Faculty:* 36 full-time (18 women), 59 part-time/adjunct (26 women). *Students:* 107 full-time (82 women), 101 part-time (82 women); includes 1 Black or African American, non-Hispanic/Latino; 1 American Indian or Alaska Native, non-Hispanic/Latino; 27 Asian, non-Hispanic/Latino; 10 Hispanic/Latino, 4 international. Average age 34. 426 applicants, 41% accepted, 106 enrolled. In 2010, 37 master's, 11 doctorates awarded. Terminal master's awarded for partial completion of doctoral program. *Degree requirements:* For master's, thesis (for some programs), practicum (MPH); for doctorate, comprehensive exam, thesis/dissertation. *Entrance requirements:* For master's and doctorate, GRE General Test, minimum GPA of 3.0. Additional exam requirements/recommendations for international students: Required—TOEFL (minimum score 580 paper-based; 237 computer-based; 92 iBT), IELTS (minimum score 7). *Application deadline:* For fall admission, 1/1 for domestic students, 11/1 for international students. Application fee: 75 Albanian leks. Electronic applications accepted. *Financial support:* In 2010–11, 47 students received support, including 10 fellowships with full and partial tuition reimbursements available (averaging $22,000 per year), 10 research assistantships with full and partial tuition reimbursements available (averaging $18,700 per year), 3 teaching assistantships with full and partial tuition reimbursements available (averaging $4,575 per year); institutionally sponsored loans, traineeships, and health care benefits also available. Financial award application deadline: 2/28; financial award applicants required to submit FAFSA. *Faculty research:* Public health practice, health promotion and disease prevention, maternal and child health, organizational behavior and culture, health policy. *Unit head:* Dr. Larry Kessler, Chair, 206-543-2930. *Application contact:* Kitty A. Andert, MPH/MS/PhD Program Manager, 206-616-2926, Fax: 206-543-3964, E-mail: kitander@u.washington.edu.

Vanderbilt University, Graduate School, Department of Biomedical Informatics, Nashville, TN 37240-1001. Offers MS, PhD, MD/MS, MD/PhD. Part-time programs available. *Faculty:* 26 full-time (4 women). *Students:* 23 full-time (6 women), 1 (woman) part-time; includes 5 minority (4 Asian, non-Hispanic/Latino; 1 Two or more races, non-Hispanic/Latino). Average age 34. 33 applicants, 15% accepted, 3 enrolled. In 2010, 3 master's, 2 doctorates awarded. Terminal master's awarded for partial completion of doctoral program. *Degree requirements:* For master's, thesis; for doctorate, thesis/dissertation, final and qualifying exams. *Entrance requirements:* For master's and doctorate, GRE General Test. Additional exam requirements/recommendations for international students: Required—TOEFL (minimum score 600 paper-based; 230 computer-based; 88 iBT). *Application deadline:* For fall admission, 1/15 for domestic and international students. Application fee: $0. Electronic applications accepted. *Financial support:* Fellowships with full and partial tuition reimbursements, research assistantships with full and partial tuition reimbursements, teaching assistantships with full and partial tuition reimbursements, Federal Work-Study, institutionally sponsored loans, scholarships/grants, traineeships, and health care benefits available. Financial award application deadline: 1/15; financial award applicants required to submit CSS PROFILE or FAFSA. *Faculty research:* Organizational informatics; the application of informatics to the role of information technology in organizational change; clinical research and translational informatics; applications of informatics to facilitating 'bench to bedside" translational research. *Unit head:* Dr. Daniel R. Masys, Chair, 615-936-1556, Fax: 615-936-1427, E-mail: dan.masys@vanderbilt.edu. *Application contact:* Dr. Cynthia S. Gadd, Director of Graduate Studies, 615-936-1556, Fax: 615-936-1427, E-mail: cindy.gadd@vanderbilt.edu.

Virginia Commonwealth University, Graduate School, School of Life Sciences, Center for the Study of Biological Complexity, Richmond, VA 23284-9005. Offers bioinformatics (MS); integrative life sciences (PhD). *Faculty:* 9 full-time (3 women). *Students:* 39 full-time (22 women), 9 part-time (3 women); includes 5 minority (4 Black or African American, non-Hispanic/Latino; 1 American Indian or Alaska Native, non-Hispanic/Latino), 13 international. 59 applicants, 47% accepted, 12 enrolled. In 2010, 3 master's, 3 doctorates awarded. *Degree requirements:* For master's, thesis optional. *Entrance requirements:* For master's and doctorate, GRE. Additional exam requirements/recommendations for international students: Required—TOEFL (minimum score 600 paper-based; 250 computer-based; 100 iBT). Application fee: $50. Electronic applications accepted. *Expenses:* Tuition, state resident: full-time $4308; part-time $479 per credit hour. Tuition, nonresident: full-time $8942; part-time $994 per credit hour. Required fees: $2000; $85 per credit hour. Tuition and fees vary according to course level, course load, degree level, campus/location and program. *Financial support:* Applicants required to submit FAFSA. *Unit head:* Dr. Gregory A. Buck, Director, 804-827-0026, Fax: 804-828-1961, E-mail: gabuck@vcu.edu. *Application contact:* Dr. Herschell Emery, Coordinator of Bioinformatics Programs, 804-828-0559, Fax: 804-828-1961, E-mail: hsemery@vcu.edu.

Virginia Polytechnic Institute and State University, Graduate School, Intercollege, Program in Genetics, Bioinformatics and Computational Biology, Blacksburg, VA 24061. Offers PhD. *Students:* 42 full-time (18 women), 5 part-time (1 woman); includes 5 Black or African American, non-Hispanic/Latino; 2 Asian, non-Hispanic/Latino; 1 Hispanic/Latino, 27 international. Average age 30. 50 applicants, 22% accepted, 7 enrolled. In 2010, 4 doctorates awarded. *Degree requirements:* For doctorate, comprehensive exam (for some programs), thesis/dissertation (for some programs). *Entrance requirements:* For doctorate, GRE. Additional exam requirements/recommendations for international students: Required—TOEFL (minimum score 550 paper-based; 213 computer-based). *Application deadline:* For fall admission, 7/1 for domestic and international students; for spring admission, 12/1 for international students. Applications are processed on a rolling basis. Application fee: $65. Electronic applications accepted. *Expenses:* Tuition, area resident: Full-time $9399; part-time $488 per credit hour. Tuition, state resident: full-time $9399; part-time $488 per credit hour. Tuition, nonresident: full-time $17,854; part-time $957.75 per credit hour. International tuition: $17,854 full-time. Required fees: $1534. Full-time tuition and fees vary according to program. *Financial support:* Career-related internships or fieldwork, Federal Work-Study, scholarships/grants, health care benefits, and unspecified assistantships available. Financial award application deadline: 1/15. *Unit head:* Dr. David R. Bevan, UNIT HEAD, 540-231-5040, Fax: 540-231-3010, E-mail: drbevan@vt.edu. *Application contact:* Dennie Munson, Contact, 540-231-1928, Fax: 540-231-3010, E-mail: dennie@vt.edu.

Wesleyan University, Graduate Programs, Department of Biology, Middletown, CT 06459. Offers animal behavior (PhD); bioformatics/genomics (PhD); cell biology (PhD); developmental biology (PhD); evolution/ecology (PhD); genetics (PhD); neurobiology (PhD); population biology (PhD). *Faculty:* 12 full-time (4 women). *Students:* 20 full-time (12 women); includes 1 Black or African American, non-Hispanic/Latino; 3 Asian, non-Hispanic/Latino, 2 international. Average age 26. 24 applicants, 29% accepted, 2 enrolled. *Degree requirements:* For doctorate, variable foreign language requirement, thesis/dissertation. *Entrance requirements:* For doctorate, GRE. Additional exam requirements/recommendations for international students: Required—TOEFL. *Application deadline:* For fall admission, 1/15 for domestic and international students. Applications are processed on a rolling basis. Application fee: $0. *Expenses:* Tuition: Full-time $43,404. Required fees: $830. *Financial support:* In 2010–11, 5 research assistantships with full tuition reimbursements, 16 teaching assistantships with full tuition reimbursements were awarded; stipends also available. Financial award application deadline: 4/15; financial award applicants required to submit FAFSA. *Faculty research:* Microbial population genetics, genetic basis of evolutionary adaptation, genetic regulation of differentiation and pattern formation in *drosophila*. *Unit head:* Dr. Sonia E. Sultan, Chair and Professor of Biology, 860-685-3493, E-mail: jnaegele@wesleyan.edu. *Application contact:* Marjorie Fitzgibbons, Information Contact, 860-685-2140, E-mail: mfitzgibbons@wesleyan.edu.

Yale University, School of Medicine and Graduate School of Arts and Sciences, Combined Program in Biological and Biomedical Sciences (BBS), Computational Biology and Bioinformatics Track, New Haven, CT 06520. Offers PhD, MD/PhD. *Entrance requirements:* Additional exam requirements/recommendations for international students: Required—TOEFL.

Computer and Information Systems Security

American InterContinental University Online, Program in Information Technology, Hoffman Estates, IL 60192. Offers Internet security (MIT); IT project management (MIT). Evening/weekend programs available. Postbaccalaureate distance learning degree programs offered (no on-campus study). *Entrance requirements:* Additional exam requirements/recommendations for international students: Required—TOEFL (minimum score 550 paper-based; 213 computer-based). Electronic applications accepted.

American InterContinental University South Florida, Program in Information Technology, Weston, FL 33326. Offers Internet security (MIT); wireless computer forensics (MIT). Part-time and evening/weekend programs available. *Entrance requirements:* Additional exam requirements/recommendations for international students: Required—TOEFL (minimum score 670 paper-based). Electronic applications accepted.

Benedictine University, Graduate Programs, Program in Business Administration, Lisle, IL 60532-0900. Offers accounting (MBA); entrepreneurship and managing innovation (MBA); financial management (MBA); health administration (MBA); human resource management (MBA); information systems security (MBA); international business (MBA); management consulting (MBA); management information systems (MBA); marketing management (MBA); operations management and logistics (MBA); organizational leadership (MBA); MBA/MPH; MBA/MS. Part-time and evening/weekend programs available. Postbaccalaureate distance learning degree programs offered (minimal on-campus study). *Faculty:* 4 full-time (2 women), 24 part-time/adjunct (3 women). *Students:* 347 full-time (140 women), 672 part-time (360 women); includes 237 minority (155 Black or African American, non-Hispanic/Latino; 4 American Indian or Alaska Native, non-Hispanic/Latino; 43 Asian, non-Hispanic/Latino; 35 Hispanic/Latino), 21 international. Average age 34. 416 applicants, 88% accepted, 217 enrolled. In 2010, 355 master's awarded. *Entrance requirements:* For master's, GMAT. Additional exam requirements/recommendations for international students: Required—TOEFL (minimum score 550 paper-based; 213 computer-based). *Application deadline:* For fall admission, 9/1 for domestic students; for winter admission, 12/1 for domestic students; for spring admission, 2/15 for domestic students. Applications are processed on a rolling basis. Application fee: $40. Electronic applications accepted. *Financial support:* Career-related internships or fieldwork and health care benefits available. Support available to part-time students. *Faculty research:* Strategic leadership in professional organizations, sociology of professions, organizational change, social identity theory, applications to change management. *Unit head:* Dr. Sharon Borowicz, Director, 630-829-6219, E-mail: sborowicz@ben.edu. *Application contact:* Kari Gibbons, Director, Admissions, 630-829-6200, Fax: 630-829-6584, E-mail: kgibbons@ben.edu.

Boston University, Metropolitan College, Department of Computer Science, Boston, MA 02215. Offers computer information systems (MS), including computer networks, database management and business intelligence, health informatics, IT project management, security; computer science (MS), including computer networks, security; telecommunications (MS), including security. Part-time and evening/weekend programs available. Postbaccalaureate distance learning degree programs offered (no on-campus study). *Faculty:* 10 full-time (0 women), 30 part-time/adjunct (3 women). *Students:* 16 full-time (2 women), 681 part-time (155 women); includes 182 minority (44 Black or African American, non-Hispanic/Latino; 1 American Indian or Alaska Native, non-Hispanic/Latino; 88 Asian, non-Hispanic/Latino; 36 Hispanic/Latino; 2 Native Hawaiian or other Pacific Islander, non-Hispanic/Latino; 11 Two or more races, non-Hispanic/Latino), 66 international. Average age 35. 273 applicants, 78% accepted, 155 enrolled. In 2010, 143 master's awarded. *Degree requirements:* For master's, thesis optional. *Entrance requirements:* For master's, 3 letters of recommendation, professional resume. Additional exam requirements/recommendations for international students: Required—TOEFL (minimum score 550 paper-based; 213 computer-based; 80 iBT). *Application deadline:* For fall admission, 6/1 priority date for international students; for spring admission, 10/1 priority date for international students. Applications are processed on a rolling basis. Application fee: $70. Electronic applications accepted. *Expenses:* Tuition: Full-time $39,314; part-time $1228 per credit. Required fees: $40 per semester. *Financial support:* In 2010–11, 9 research assistantships with partial tuition reimbursements (averaging $5,000 per year) were awarded; career-related internships or fieldwork and unspecified assistantships also available. Support available to part-time students. Financial award applicants required to submit FAFSA. *Faculty research:* Medical informatics, Web technologies, telecom and networks, security and forensics, software engineering, programming languages, multimedia and AI, information systems and IT project management. *Unit head:* Dr. Lubomir Chitkushev, Chairman, 617-353-2566, Fax: 617-353-2367, E-mail: csinfo@bu.edu. *Application contact:* Kim Richards, Program Coordinator, 617-353-2566, Fax: 617-353-2367, E-mail: kimrich@bu.edu.

Brandeis University, Rabb School of Continuing Studies, Division of Graduate Professional Studies, Information Assurance Program, Waltham, MA 02454-9110. Offers MS, Graduate Certificate. Part-time programs available. Postbaccalaureate distance learning degree programs offered (no on-campus study). *Faculty:* 2 full-time (both women), 33 part-time/adjunct (5 women). *Students:* 1 full-time (0 women), 16 part-time (2 women); includes 1 Black or African American, non-Hispanic/Latino; 1 Asian, non-Hispanic/Latino; 2 Hispanic/Latino. Average age 35. 4 applicants, 100% accepted, 4 enrolled. *Entrance requirements:* For master's, resume, official transcripts, recommendations, goal statements; for Graduate Certificate, resume, official transcripts, recommendations. Additional exam requirements/recommendations for international students: Recommended—TOEFL (minimum score 600 paper-based; 250 computer-based; 100 iBT). *Application deadline:* For fall admission, 6/15 priority date for domestic students; for winter admission, 10/15 priority date for domestic students; for spring admission, 2/15 priority date for domestic students. Applications are processed on a rolling basis. Application fee: $50. Electronic applications accepted. *Unit head:* Dr. Cynthia Phillips, Program Chair, 781-736-8787, Fax: 781-736-3420, E-mail: cynthiap@brandeis.edu. *Application contact:* Frances Stearns, Associate Director of Admissions and Student Services, 781-736-8785, Fax: 781-736-3420, E-mail: fstearns@brandeis.edu.

Capella University, School of Business and Technology, Minneapolis, MN 55402. Offers accounting (MBA), including system design and programming; business (Certificate), including human resource management (MS, PhD, Certificate), information technology management (MS, PhD, Certificate), leadership (MBA, MS, PhD, Certificate); finance (MBA); general business (MBA); health care management (MBA); information technology (MS, Certificate), including general information technology (MS), information security, network architecture and design (MS), professional projects management (Certificate), project management and leadership (MS), system design and development (MS),); information technology management (MBA); marketing (MBA); organization and management (MBA, MS, PhD), including general business (PhD), general organization and management (MBA, MS), human resource management (MS, PhD, Certificate), information technology management (MS, PhD, Certificate), leadership (MBA, MS, PhD, Certificate); project management (MBA). Part-time and evening/weekend programs available. Postbaccalaureate distance learning degree programs offered (minimal on-campus study). Terminal master's awarded for partial completion of doctoral program. *Degree requirements:* For master's, thesis optional, integrative project; for doctorate, comprehensive exam, thesis/dissertation. *Entrance requirements:* Additional exam requirements/recommendations for international students: Required—TOEFL (minimum score 550 paper-based; 213 computer-based), TWE (minimum score 4). Electronic applications accepted. *Expenses:* Tuition: Full-time $11,880; part-time $440 per credit hour. *Faculty research:* Business policies: strategic, corporate, and financial management; interplay of technological, organizational and social change.

Capitol College, Graduate Programs, Laurel, MD 20708-9759. Offers business administration (MBA); computer science (MS); electrical engineering (MS); information and telecommunications systems management (MS); information architecture (MS); network security (MS). Part-time and evening/weekend programs available. Postbaccalaureate distance learning degree programs

offered (no on-campus study). *Entrance requirements:* For master's, minimum GPA of 3.0. Electronic applications accepted.

Carnegie Mellon University, Carnegie Institute of Technology, Information Networking Institute, Pittsburgh, PA 15213. Offers information networking (MS); information security technology and management (MS); information technology—information security (MS); information technology—mobility (MS); information technology—software management (MS). *Degree requirements:* For master's, thesis optional. *Entrance requirements:* For master's, GRE General Test, bachelor's degree in computer science, computer engineering, or electrical engineering, or related technology degree; programming skills (C/C++ fluency for some programs). Additional exam requirements/recommendations for international students: Required—TOEFL. *Faculty research:* Computer forensics and incident response; dependable systems, embedded systems, mobile systems, and sensor networks; computer and information networks, network and information security, human and socio-economic factors in secure system design; wireless sensor networks, survivable embedded systems, signal processing/compression; strategic management, international strategic management, group dynamics and decision-making structures, simulated competitive environments.

Carnegie Mellon University, H. John Heinz III College, School of Information Systems and Management, Master of Science in Information Security Policy and Management Program, Pittsburgh, PA 15213-3891. Offers MSISPM. *Entrance requirements:* For master's, GRE or GMAT, college-level course in advanced algebra/pre-calculus; college-level courses in economics and statistics (recommended). Additional exam requirements/recommendations for international students: Required—TOEFL or IELTS.

City University of Seattle, Graduate Division, School of Management, Bellevue, WA 98005. Offers accounting (Certificate); change leadership (MBA, Certificate); computer systems (MS); finance (Certificate); financial management (MBA); general management (MBA); general management-Europe (MBA); global marketing (MBA); human resources management (Certificate); individualized study (MBA); information security (MS); information systems (MBA); leadership (MA); marketing (MBA, Certificate); project management (MBA, MS, Certificate); sustainable business (Certificate); technology management (MBA, Certificate). Part-time and evening/weekend programs available. Postbaccalaureate distance learning degree programs offered (no on-campus study). *Entrance requirements:* Additional exam requirements/recommendations for international students: Required—TOEFL (minimum score 540 paper-based; 207 computer-based); Recommended—IELTS. Electronic applications accepted.

Colorado Christian University, Program in Business Administration, Lakewood, CO 80226. Offers corporate training (MBA); information security (MA); leadership (MBA); project management (MBA). Part-time and evening/weekend programs available. Postbaccalaureate distance learning degree programs offered (minimal on-campus study). *Faculty:* 10 full-time (7 women), 35 part-time/adjunct (17 women). *Students:* 65 full-time (33 women), 35 part-time (19 women); includes 6 Black or African American, non-Hispanic/Latino; 1 American Indian or Alaska Native, non-Hispanic/Latino; 2 Asian, non-Hispanic/Latino; 9 Hispanic/Latino. Average age 37. 25 applicants, 20% accepted. *Degree requirements:* For master's, thesis optional. *Entrance requirements:* For master's, GMAT, 2 letters of recommendation, resume. Additional exam requirements/recommendations for international students: Required—TOEFL. *Application deadline:* For fall admission, 8/25 priority date for domestic and international students; for spring admission, 1/12 priority date for domestic and international students. Applications are processed on a rolling basis. Application fee: $40. Electronic applications accepted. *Expenses:* Contact institution. *Financial support:* In 2010–11, 27 students received support. Scholarships/grants and tuition waivers (full and partial) available. Support available to part-time students. Financial award application deadline: 3/1; financial award applicants required to submit FAFSA. *Unit head:* Dr. Mellani Day, Dean of Business and Technology, 303-963-3300, Fax: 303-963-3301, E-mail: agsadmission@ccu.edu. *Application contact:* Dr. Mellani Day, Dean of Business and Technology, 303-963-3300, Fax: 303-963-3301, E-mail: agsadmission@ccu.edu.

Colorado Technical University Colorado Springs, Graduate Studies, Program in Computer Science, Colorado Springs, CO 80907-3896. Offers computer science (DCS); computer systems security (MSCS); database systems (MSCS); software engineering (MSCS). Part-time and evening/weekend programs available. Postbaccalaureate distance learning degree programs offered. *Degree requirements:* For master's, thesis or alternative; for doctorate, thesis/dissertation. *Entrance requirements:* For doctorate, minimum graduate GPA of 3.0, 5 years of related work experience. *Faculty research:* Software engineering, systems engineering.

Colorado Technical University Colorado Springs, Graduate Studies, Program in Information Science, Colorado Springs, CO 80907-3896. Offers information systems security (MSM). Postbaccalaureate distance learning degree programs offered.

Colorado Technical University Denver, Program in Computer Science, Greenwood Village, CO 80111. Offers computer systems security (MSCS); database systems (MSCS); software engineering (MSCS). Part-time and evening/weekend programs available. *Degree requirements:* For master's, thesis or alternative. *Entrance requirements:* For master's, minimum undergraduate GPA of 3.0, resume.

Colorado Technical University Denver, Program in Information Science, Greenwood Village, CO 80111. Offers information systems security (MSM).

Colorado Technical University Sioux Falls, Program in Computing, Sioux Falls, SD 57108. Offers computer systems security (MSCS); software engineering (MSCS).

Concordia University, School of Graduate Studies, Faculty of Engineering and Computer Science, Concordia Institute for Information Systems Engineering (CIISE), Montréal, QC H3G 1M8, Canada. Offers 3D graphics and game development (Certificate); information systems security (M Eng, MA Sc); quality systems engineering (M Eng, MA Sc); service engineering and network management (Certificate).

Concordia University College of Alberta, Program in Information Systems Security Management, Edmonton, AB T5B 4E4, Canada. Offers MA.

Davenport University, Sneden Graduate School, Grand Rapids, MI 49512. Offers accounting (MBA); business administration (EMBA); finance (MBA); health care management (MBA); human resources (MBA); information assurance (MS); public health (MPH); strategic management (MBA). Evening/weekend programs available. *Entrance requirements:* For master's, GMAT, minimum undergraduate GPA of 2.75. Additional exam requirements/recommendations for international students: Required—TOEFL. Electronic applications accepted. *Faculty research:* Leadership, management, marketing, organizational culture.

Davenport University, Sneden Graduate School, Warren, MI 48092-5209. Offers accounting (MBA); business administration (EMBA); finance (MBA); health care management (MBA); human resources management (MBA); information assurance (MS); public health (MPH); strategic management (MBA). *Entrance requirements:* For master's, minimum undergraduate GPA of 2.7.

Davenport University, Sneden Graduate School, Dearborn, MI 48126-3799. Offers accounting (MBA); business administration (EMBA); finance (MBA); health care management (MBA); human resources management (MBA); information assurance (MS); marketing (MBA); public health (MPH); strategic management (MBA). Part-time and evening/weekend programs available. Postbaccalaureate distance learning degree programs offered (no on-campus study). *Entrance requirements:* For master's, minimum GPA of 2.7, previous course work in accounting and statistics. *Faculty research:* Accounting, international accounting, social and environmental accounting, finance.

DePaul University, College of Computing and Digital Media, Chicago, IL 60604. Offers animation (MA, MFA); applied technology (MS); business information technology (MS); cinema (MFA); cinema production (MS); computational finance (MS); computer and information sciences (PhD); computer game development (MS); computer graphics and motion technology (MS); computer information and network security (MS); computer science (MS); e-commerce technology (MS); human-computer interaction (MS); information systems (MS); information technology (MA); information technology project management (MS); network engineering and management (MS); predictive analytics (MS); screenwriting (MFA); software engineering (MS); JD/MA; JD/MS. Part-time and evening/weekend programs available. Postbaccalaureate distance learning degree programs offered (no on-campus study). *Faculty:* 51 full-time (11 women), 50 part-time/adjunct (9 women). *Students:* 952 full-time (230 women), 927 part-time (226 women); includes 557 minority (205 Black or African American, non-Hispanic/Latino; 2 American Indian or Alaska Native, non-Hispanic/Latino; 167 Asian, non-Hispanic/Latino; 136 Hispanic/Latino; 7 Native Hawaiian or other Pacific Islander, non-Hispanic/Latino; 40 Two or more races, non-Hispanic/Latino), 292 international. Average age 31. 896 applicants, 70% accepted, 324 enrolled. In 2010, 417 master's, 6 doctorates awarded. *Degree requirements:* For master's, thesis (for some programs); for doctorate, comprehensive exam, thesis/dissertation. *Entrance requirements:* For master's, GRE or GMAT (MS in computational finance only), bachelor's degree, resume (MS in predictive analytics only), IT experience (MS in information technology project management only), portfolio review (MFA); for doctorate, GRE, master's degree in computer science. Additional exam requirements/recommendations for international students: Required—TOEFL (minimum score 550 paper-based; 213 computer-based; 80 iBT), IELTS (minimum score 6.5), Pearson Test of English (minimum score 53). *Application deadline:* For fall admission, 8/15 priority date for domestic students, 6/1 priority date for international students; for winter admission, 12/15 priority date for domestic students, 9/15 priority date for international students; for spring admission, 3/1 priority date for domestic students, 12/15 priority date for international students. Applications are processed on a rolling basis. Application fee: $25. Electronic applications accepted. *Expenses:* Contact institution. *Financial support:* In 2010–11, 102 students received support, including 4 fellowships with full tuition reimbursements available (averaging $24,435 per year), 6 research assistantships (averaging $21,100 per year), 92 teaching assistantships with full and partial tuition reimbursements available (averaging $6,904 per year); Federal Work-Study, scholarships/grants, tuition waivers (full and partial), and unspecified assistantships also available. Support available to part-time students. Financial award application deadline: 4/30; financial award applicants required to submit FAFSA. *Faculty research:* Bioinformatics, visual computing, graphics and animation, high performance and scientific computing, databases. Total annual research expenditures: $1.4 million. *Unit head:* Dr. David Miller, Dean, 312-362-8381, Fax: 312-362-5185. *Application contact:* Dr. Liz Friedman, Assistant Dean of Student Services, 312-362-8714, Fax: 312-362-5179, E-mail: efriedm2@cdm.depaul.edu.

Eastern Illinois University, Graduate School, Lumpkin College of Business and Applied Sciences, School of Technology, Charleston, IL 61920-3099. Offers computer technology (Certificate); quality systems (Certificate); technology (MS); technology security (Certificate); work performance improvement (Certificate). Part-time and evening/weekend programs available.

Eastern Michigan University, Graduate School, College of Technology, School of Technology Studies, Program in Information Assurance, Ypsilanti, MI 48197. Offers MLS, Graduate Certificate. Part-time and evening/weekend programs available. Postbaccalaureate distance learning degree programs offered (minimal on-campus study). *Students:* 3 part-time (0 women). Average age 44. In 2010, 1 other advanced degree awarded. *Entrance requirements:* Additional exam requirements/recommendations for international students: Required—TOEFL. *Application deadline:* Applications are processed on a rolling basis. Application fee: $35. *Financial support:* Fellowships, research assistantships with full tuition reimbursements, teaching assistantships with full tuition reimbursements, career-related internships or fieldwork, Federal Work-Study, institutionally sponsored loans, scholarships/grants, tuition waivers (partial), and unspecified assistantships available. Support available to part-time students. Financial award applicants required to submit FAFSA. *Unit head:* Prof. Gerald Lawver, Program Coordinator, 734-487-3170, Fax: 734-487-7690, E-mail: skip.lawver@emich.edu. *Application contact:* Prof. Gerald Lawver, Program Coordinator, 734-487-3170, Fax: 734-487-7690, E-mail: skip.lawver@emich.edu.

Florida State University, The Graduate School, College of Arts and Sciences, Department of Computer Science, Tallahassee, FL 32306. Offers computer science (MS, PhD); information security (MS). Part-time programs available. *Faculty:* 17 full-time (1 woman), 2 part-time/adjunct (0 women). *Students:* 111 full-time (14 women), 11 part-time (2 women); includes 3 Black or African American, non-Hispanic/Latino; 1 American Indian or Alaska Native, non-Hispanic/Latino; 3 Asian, non-Hispanic/Latino; 10 Hispanic/Latino, 58 international. Average age 28. 200 applicants, 61% accepted, 29 enrolled. In 2010, 34 master's, 6 doctorates awarded. Terminal master's awarded for partial completion of doctoral program. *Degree requirements:* For master's, thesis or alternative; for doctorate, comprehensive exam, thesis/dissertation. *Entrance requirements:* For master's, GRE General Test, minimum undergraduate GPA of 3.0; for doctorate, GRE General Test, minimum GPA of 3.0. Additional exam requirements/recommendations for international students: Required—TOEFL (minimum score 600 paper-based; 250 computer-based; 100 iBT). *Application deadline:* For fall admission, 3/1 priority date for domestic students, 3/1 for international students; for spring admission, 10/1 priority date for domestic students, 10/1 for international students. Application fee: $30. Electronic applications accepted. *Expenses:* Tuition, state resident: full-time $8238.24. *Financial support:* In 2010–11, 92 students received support, including 7 fellowships with full tuition reimbursements available (averaging $17,500 per year), 25 research assistantships with full tuition reimbursements available (averaging $17,000 per year), 53 teaching assistantships with full tuition reimbursements available (averaging $15,500 per year); career-related internships or fieldwork, scholarships/grants, health care benefits, tuition waivers (partial), and unspecified assistantships also available. Financial award application deadline: 3/1; financial award applicants required to submit FAFSA. *Faculty research:* Embedded systems, high performance computing, networking, operating systems, security, databases, algorithms. Total annual research expenditures: $1.3 million. *Unit head:* Dr. David Whalley, Chairman, 850-644-3506, Fax: 850-644-0058, E-mail: chair@cs.fsu.edu. *Application contact:* Kristan L. McAlpin, Graduate Coordinator, 850-645-4975, Fax: 850-644-0058, E-mail: mcalpin@cs.fsu.edu.

George Mason University, Volgenau School of Engineering, Department of Computer Science, Fairfax, VA 22030. Offers biometrics (Certificate); computer games technology (Certificate); computer networking (Certificate); computer science (MS, PhD); data mining (Certificate); database management (Certificate); electronic commerce (Certificate); foundations of information systems (Certificate); information engineering (Certificate); information security and assurance (MS, Certificate); information systems (MS); intelligent agents (Certificate); software architecture (Certificate); software engineering (MS, Certificate); systems engineering (MS); Web-based software engineering (Certificate). MS program offered jointly with Old Dominion University, University of Virginia, Virginia Commonwealth University, and Virginia Polytechnic Institute and State University. Part-time and evening/weekend programs available. Postbaccalaureate distance learning degree programs offered. *Faculty:* 42 full-time (9 women), 20 part-time/adjunct (1 woman). *Students:* 124 full-time (37 women), 453 part-time (103 women); includes 14 Black or African American, non-Hispanic/Latino; 66 Asian, non-Hispanic/Latino; 13 Hispanic/Latino; 3 Two or more races, non-Hispanic/Latino, 206 international. Average age 30. 904 applicants, 53% accepted, 150 enrolled. In 2010, 203 master's, 4 doctorates, 20 other advanced degrees awarded. *Degree requirements:* For master's, thesis optional; for doctorate, comprehensive exam, thesis/dissertation. *Entrance requirements:* For master's, GRE General Test, minimum GPA of 3.0 in last 60 hours, 3 letters of recommendation; for doctorate, GRE, 4-year BA, academic work in computer science, 3 letters of recommendation, statement of career goals and aspirations. Additional exam requirements/recommendations for international students: Required—TOEFL (minimum score 570 paper-based; 230 computer-based; 88 iBT). *Application deadline:* For fall admission, 4/15 priority date for domestic students, 1/15 for international students; for spring admission, 11/15 for domestic students. Application fee: $100. Electronic applications accepted. *Expenses:* Tuition, state resident: full-time $8192; part-time $440 per credit hour. Tuition, nonresident: full-time $22,952; part-time $1055 per credit hour. Required fees: $2364; $99 per credit hour. *Financial support:* In 2010–11, 101 students received support, including 3 fellowships (averaging $18,000 per year), 52 research assistantships (averaging $15,078 per year), 47 teaching assistantships (averaging $10,983 per year); career-related internships or fieldwork, Federal Work-Study, scholarships/grants, unspecified assistantships, and health care benefits (full-time research or teaching assistantship recipients) also available. Financial award application deadline: 3/1; financial award applicants required to submit FAFSA. *Faculty research:* Artificial intelligence, image processing/graphics, parallel/distributed systems, software engineering systems. Total annual research expenditures: $1.3 million. *Unit head:* Dr. Arun Sood, Director, 703-993-1524, Fax: 703-993-1710, E-mail: asood@gmu.edu. *Application contact:* Jay Shapiro, Professor, 703-993-1485, E-mail: jshapiro@gmu.edu.

Georgia Institute of Technology, Graduate Studies and Research, College of Computing, Atlanta, GA 30332-0001. Offers algorithms, combinatorics, and optimization (PhD); computational science and engineering (MS, PhD); computer science (MS, MSCS, PhD); human computer interaction (MSHCI); human-centered computing (PhD); information security (MS). Part-time programs available. Postbaccalaureate distance learning degree programs offered. Terminal master's awarded for partial completion of doctoral program. *Degree requirements:* For master's, thesis optional; for doctorate, comprehensive exam, thesis/dissertation. *Entrance requirements:* For master's, GRE General Test, GRE Subject Test, minimum GPA of 3.0; for doctorate, GRE General Test, GRE Subject Test, minimum GPA of 3.3. Additional exam requirements/recommendations for international students: Required—TOEFL. *Faculty research:* Computer systems, graphics, intelligent systems and artificial intelligence, networks and telecommunications, software engineering.

Henley-Putnam University, Program in Management of Personal Protection, San Jose, CA 95110. Offers MS. Part-time programs available. Postbaccalaureate distance learning degree programs offered.

Hood College, Graduate School, Programs in Computer and Information Sciences, Frederick, MD 21701-8575. Offers computer and information sciences (MS); computer science (MS); information security (Certificate). Part-time and evening/weekend programs available. *Faculty:* 5 full-time (1 woman), 4 part-time/adjunct (1 woman). *Students:* 18 full-time (4 women), 68 part-time (12 women); includes 5 Black or African American, non-Hispanic/Latino; 8 Asian, non-Hispanic/Latino; 4 Hispanic/Latino; 2 Two or more races, non-Hispanic/Latino, 14 international. Average age 33. 49 applicants, 65% accepted, 20 enrolled. In 2010, 14 master's awarded. *Degree requirements:* For master's, thesis. *Entrance requirements:* For master's, minimum GPA of 2.75. Additional exam requirements/recommendations for international students: Required—TOEFL (minimum score 575 paper-based; 231 computer-based; 89 iBT). *Application deadline:* For fall admission, 7/15 for domestic and international students; for spring admission, 12/15 for domestic and international students. Applications are processed on a rolling basis. Application fee: $35. Electronic applications accepted. *Expenses:* Tuition: Full-time $6480; part-time $360 per credit. Required fees: $100; $50 per term. *Financial support:* Applicants required to submit FAFSA. *Faculty research:* Systems engineering, natural language, processing, database design, artificial intelligence and parallel distributed computing. *Unit head:* Dr. Xinlian Liu, Director, 301-696-3981, E-mail: liu@hood.edu. *Application contact:* Dr. Allen P. Flora, Dean of Graduate School, 301-696-3811, Fax: 301-696-3597, E-mail: gofurther@hood.edu.

Inter American University of Puerto Rico, Guayama Campus, Department of Natural and Applied Sciences, Guayama, PR 00785. Offers computer security and networks (MS); networking and security (MCS).

The Johns Hopkins University, Carey Business School, Information Technology Programs, Baltimore, MD 21218-2699. Offers competitive intelligence (Certificate); information security management (Certificate); information systems (MS); MBA/MSIS. Part-time and evening/weekend programs available. *Faculty:* 29 full-time (6 women), 135 part-time/adjunct (29 women). *Students:* 11 full-time (3 women), 154 part-time (42 women); includes 62 minority (19 Black or African American, non-Hispanic/Latino; 1 American Indian or Alaska Native, non-Hispanic/Latino; 31 Asian, non-Hispanic/Latino; 7 Hispanic/Latino; 1 Native Hawaiian or other Pacific Islander, non-Hispanic/Latino; 3 Two or more races, non-Hispanic/Latino), 12 international. Average age 35. 53 applicants, 87% accepted, 30 enrolled. In 2010, 83 master's, 22 other advanced degrees awarded. *Degree requirements:* For master's, 36 credits including final project. *Entrance requirements:* For master's and Certificate, minimum GPA of 3.0, resume, work experience, two letters of recommendation. Additional exam requirements/recommendations for international students: Required—TOEFL (minimum score 600 paper-based; 250 computer-based; 100 iBT). *Application deadline:* For fall admission, 4/1 for international students; for spring admission, 9/15 for international students. Applications are processed on a rolling basis. Application fee: $100. Electronic applications accepted. *Financial support:* In 2010–11, 5 students received support. Scholarships/grants available. Support available to part-time students. Financial award application deadline: 4/15; financial award applicants required to submit FAFSA. *Faculty research:* Information security, healthcare information systems. Total annual research expenditures: $89,653. *Unit head:* Dr. Dipankar Chakravarti, Vice Dean of Programs, 410-234-9311, E-mail: dipankar.chakravarti@jhu.edu. *Application contact:* Robin Greenberg, Admissions Coordinator, 410-234-9227, Fax: 443-529-1554, E-mail: carey.admissions@jhu.edu.

The Johns Hopkins University, Engineering for Professionals, Part-Time Program in Information Assurance, Baltimore, MD 21218-2699. Offers MS. Part-time and evening/weekend programs available. *Faculty:* 4 part-time/adjunct (0 women). *Students:* 4 full-time (0 women), 26 part-time (5 women); includes 9 minority (3 Black or African American, non-Hispanic/Latino; 1 American Indian or Alaska Native, non-Hispanic/Latino; 3 Asian, non-Hispanic/Latino; 1 Hispanic/Latino; 1 Native Hawaiian or other Pacific Islander, non-Hispanic/Latino), 1 international. Average age 31. 21 applicants, 90% accepted, 10 enrolled. *Application deadline:* Applications are processed on a rolling basis. Application fee: $75. *Unit head:* Dr. Thomas A. Longstaff, Chair, 443-778-9389, E-mail: thomas.longstaff@jhuapl.edu. *Application contact:* Priyanka Dwivedi, Admissions Manager, 410-516-2300, Fax: 410-579-8049, E-mail: pdwived1@jhu.edu.

The Johns Hopkins University, G. W. C. Whiting School of Engineering, Information Security Institute, Baltimore, MD 21218-2699. Offers MSSI. Part-time programs available. *Faculty:* 6 part-time/adjunct (0 women). *Students:* 42 full-time (6 women), 6 part-time (2 women); includes 9 minority (2 Black or African American, non-Hispanic/Latino; 2 Asian, non-Hispanic/Latino; 4 Hispanic/Latino; 1 Two or more races, non-Hispanic/Latino), 28 international. Average age 25. 73 applicants, 92% accepted, 18 enrolled. In 2010, 24 master's awarded. *Degree requirements:* For master's, project. *Entrance requirements:* For master's, GRE, minimum GPA of 3.0. Additional exam requirements/recommendations for international students: Required—TOEFL (minimum score 600 paper-based; 250 computer-based). *Application deadline:* For fall admission, 6/15 priority date for domestic students, 3/15 for international students; for spring admission, 11/15 for domestic students, 11/1 for international students. Applications are processed on a rolling basis. Application fee: $25. Electronic applications accepted. *Financial support:* In 2010–11, 28 students received support, including 9 fellowships with full tuition reimbursements available (averaging $18,000 per year); career-related internships or fieldwork, Federal Work-Study, institutionally sponsored loans, scholarships/grants, traineeships, health care benefits, tuition waivers (partial), and unspecified assistantships also available. *Faculty research:* Critical infrastructure protection, insider/outsider cryptography and encryption methodologies, international policy protocols, Web-based intellectual property rights. Total annual research expenditures: $838,000. *Unit head:* Dr. Gerald M. Masson, Director, 410-516-7013, Fax: 410-516-3301, E-mail: masson@jhu.edu. *Application contact:* Deborah K. Higgins, Graduate Coordinator, 410-516-8521, Fax: 410-516-3301, E-mail: dhiggins@jhu.edu.

Jones International University, School of Business, Centennial, CO 80112. Offers accounting (MBA); business communication (MABC); entrepreneurship (MABC, MBA); finance (MBA);

Computer and Information Systems Security

Jones International University (continued)

global enterprise management (MBA); health care management (MBA); information security management (MBA); information technology management (MBA); leadership and influence (MABC); leading the customer-driven organization (MABC); negotiation and conflict management (MBA); project management (MABC, MBA). Program only offered online. Part-time and evening/weekend programs available. Postbaccalaureate distance learning degree programs offered (no on-campus study). *Degree requirements:* For master's, capstone project. *Entrance requirements:* For master's, minimum cumulative GPA of 2.5. Additional exam requirements/recommendations for international students: Recommended—TOEFL (minimum score 550 paper-based; 213 computer-based). Electronic applications accepted.

Kaplan University, Davenport Campus, School of Information Technology, Davenport, IA 52807-2095. Offers decision support systems (MS); information security and assurance (MS). Part-time and evening/weekend programs available. Postbaccalaureate distance learning degree programs offered (no on-campus study). *Entrance requirements:* Additional exam requirements/recommendations for international students: Required—TOEFL (minimum score 550 paper-based; 218 computer-based; 80 iBT).

Kentucky State University, College of Mathematics, Sciences, Technology and Health, Frankfort, KY 40601. Offers aquaculture (MS); computer science (MS), including computer science theory, information assurance, information technology; environmental science (MS). Part-time and evening/weekend programs available. *Faculty:* 10 full-time (1 woman), 1 part-time/adjunct (0 women). *Students:* 34 full-time (16 women), 32 part-time (6 women); includes 22 minority (15 Black or African American, non-Hispanic/Latino; 3 Asian, non-Hispanic/Latino; 1 Hispanic/Latino; 1 Native Hawaiian or other Pacific Islander, non-Hispanic/Latino; 2 Two or more races, non-Hispanic/Latino), 12 international. Average age 34. 55 applicants, 51% accepted, 18 enrolled. In 2010, 16 master's awarded. *Degree requirements:* For master's, comprehensive exam, thesis optional. *Entrance requirements:* For master's, GRE, GMAT. Additional exam requirements/recommendations for international students: Required—TOEFL (minimum score 525 paper-based; 173 computer-based). *Application deadline:* Applications are processed on a rolling basis. Application fee: $30 ($100 for international students). Electronic applications accepted. *Expenses:* Tuition, state resident: full-time $5886; part-time $352 per credit hour. Tuition, nonresident: full-time $9054; part-time $528 per credit hour. Required fees: $450; $26 per credit hour. *Financial support:* In 2010–11, 41 students received support, including 18 research assistantships (averaging $11,378 per year); career-related internships or fieldwork, scholarships/grants, tuition waivers (partial), and unspecified assistantships also available. Financial award application deadline: 4/15; financial award applicants required to submit FAFSA. *Unit head:* Dr. Charles Bennett, Dean, 502-597-6926, E-mail: charles.bennett@kysu.edu. *Application contact:* Dr. Titilayo Ufomata, Acting Director of Graduate Studies, 502-597-6443, E-mail: titilayo.ufomata@kysu.edu.

Lewis University, College of Business, Graduate School of Management, Program in Business Administration, Romeoville, IL 60446. Offers accounting (MBA); custom elective option (MBA); e-business (MBA); finance (MBA); healthcare management (MBA); human resources management (MBA); information security (MBA); international business (MBA); management information systems (MBA); marketing (MBA); project management (MBA); technology and operations management (MBA). Part-time and evening/weekend programs available. *Students:* 119 full-time (66 women), 204 part-time (104 women); includes 55 Black or African American, non-Hispanic/Latino; 9 Asian, non-Hispanic/Latino; 30 Hispanic/Latino; 1 Native Hawaiian or other Pacific Islander, non-Hispanic/Latino, 9 international. Average age 28. In 2010, 111 master's awarded. *Entrance requirements:* For master's, interview, bachelor's degree, resume, 2 recommendations. Additional exam requirements/recommendations for international students: Required—TOEFL (minimum score 550 paper-based; 213 computer-based). *Application deadline:* For fall admission, 8/15 priority date for domestic students, 5/1 priority date for international students; for spring admission, 11/15 priority date for international students. Applications are processed on a rolling basis. Application fee: $40. Electronic applications accepted. *Expenses:* Tuition: Full-time $13,320; part-time $740 per credit hour. Tuition and fees vary according to program. *Financial support:* Career-related internships or fieldwork, Federal Work-Study, scholarships/grants, and unspecified assistantships available. Financial award application deadline: 5/1; financial award applicants required to submit FAFSA. *Unit head:* Dr. Maureen Culleeney, Academic Program Director, 815-838-0500 Ext. 5631, E-mail: culleema@lewisu.edu. *Application contact:* Michele Ryan, Director of Admission, 815-838-0500 Ext. 5384, E-mail: gsm@lewisu.edu.

Lewis University, College of Business, Program in Information Security, Romeoville, IL 60446. Offers MS. Part-time and evening/weekend programs available. Postbaccalaureate distance learning degree programs offered (no on-campus study). *Students:* 19 full-time (1 woman), 59 part-time (10 women); includes 24 minority (12 Black or African American, non-Hispanic/Latino; 1 American Indian or Alaska Native, non-Hispanic/Latino; 4 Asian, non-Hispanic/Latino; 5 Hispanic/Latino; 1 Native Hawaiian or other Pacific Islander, non-Hispanic/Latino; 1 Two or more races, non-Hispanic/Latino), 7 international. Average age 35. In 2010, 8 master's awarded. *Entrance requirements:* For master's, bachelor's degree, minimum GPA of 3.0, resume, 2-page statement of purpose, 3 letters of recommendation. Additional exam requirements/recommendations for international students: Required—TOEFL (minimum score 550 paper-based; 213 computer-based). *Application deadline:* For fall admission, 5/1 priority date for international students; for spring admission, 11/15 priority date for international students. Applications are processed on a rolling basis. Application fee: $40. Electronic applications accepted. *Expenses:* Tuition: Full-time $13,320; part-time $740 per credit hour. Tuition and fees vary according to program. *Financial support:* Application deadline: 5/1. *Unit head:* Dr. Rami Khasawneh, Dean, 815-838-0500 Ext. 5360. *Application contact:* Michele Ryan, Director of Admission, Graduate School of Management, 800-897-9000, E-mail: gsm@lewisu.edu.

Marymount University, School of Business Administration, Program in Information Technology, Arlington, VA 22207-4299. Offers computer security and information assurance (Certificate); health care informatics (Certificate); information technology (MS, Certificate); information technology project management: technology leadership (Certificate). Part-time and evening/weekend programs available. *Degree requirements:* For master's, thesis or alternative. *Entrance requirements:* For master's, GMAT or GRE General Test, interview, resume, bachelor's degree in computer-related field or degree in another subject with a post-baccalaureate certificate in a computer-related field; for Certificate, resume. Additional exam requirements/recommendations for international students: Required—TOEFL (minimum score 600 paper-based; 250 computer-based; 96 iBT), IELTS (minimum score 6.5). Electronic applications accepted.

Mercy College, School of Liberal Arts, Program in Information Assurance and Security, Dobbs Ferry, NY 10522-1189. Offers cybersecurity (MS). Part-time and evening/weekend programs available. Postbaccalaureate distance learning degree programs offered (no on-campus study). *Students:* 8 full-time (0 women), 9 part-time (3 women); includes 5 Black or African American, non-Hispanic/Latino; 1 Asian, non-Hispanic/Latino; 2 Hispanic/Latino, 2 international. Average age 35. 20 applicants, 60% accepted, 9 enrolled. *Degree requirements:* For master's, project or thesis. *Entrance requirements:* For master's, two letters of recommendation; two-page written personal statement; completion of undergraduate prerequisites in local area networks, database management systems, cryptographgy and computer security, operating systems, and statistics. Additional exam requirements/recommendations for international students: Required—TOEFL (minimum score 600 paper-based; 250 computer-based; 100 iBT), IELTS (minimum score 8). *Application deadline:* For fall admission, 8/1 for international students. Applications are processed on a rolling basis. Application fee: $40. Electronic applications accepted. *Expenses:* Contact institution. *Financial support:* Career-related internships or fieldwork, Federal Work-Study, scholarships/grants, and unspecified assistantships available. Support available to part-time students. Financial award applicants required to submit FAFSA. *Faculty research:* Information security theory, assurance, technical and analytical abilities. *Unit head:* Dr. Nagaraj Rao, Professor, Mathematics and Computer Information Science, 914-674-7593, E-mail: nrao@mercy.edu. *Application contact:* Allison Gurdineer, 914-674-7601, E-mail: agurdineer@mercy.edu.

Metropolitan State University, College of Management, St. Paul, MN 55106-5000. Offers business administration (MBA, DBA); information assurance security (Graduate Certificate); management information systems (MMIS); MIS generalist (Graduate Certificate); MIS systems analysis and design (Graduate Certificate); nonprofit management (MPNA); project management (Graduate Certificate); public administration (MPNA). Part-time and evening/weekend programs available. *Students:* 158 full-time (74 women), 217 part-time (114 women); includes 31 Black or African American, non-Hispanic/Latino; 26 Asian, non-Hispanic/Latino; 10 Hispanic/Latino; 6 Two or more races, non-Hispanic/Latino, 47 international. Average age 35. In 2010, 100 master's, 7 other advanced degrees awarded. *Degree requirements:* For master's, thesis optional, computer language (MMIS). *Entrance requirements:* For master's, GMAT (MBA), resume. Additional exam requirements/recommendations for international students: Required—TOEFL (minimum score 550 paper-based; 213 computer-based). *Application deadline:* For fall admission, 7/15 for international students; for winter admission, 11/15 for international students; for spring admission, 3/15 for international students. Applications are processed on a rolling basis. Application fee: $20. Electronic applications accepted. *Expenses:* Tuition, state resident: full-time $5827; part-time $291 per credit hour. Tuition, nonresident: full-time $11,654; part-time $583 per credit hour. Required fees: $10 per credit hour. Tuition and fees vary according to degree level. *Financial support:* Research assistantships with partial tuition reimbursements, career-related internships or fieldwork and Federal Work-Study available. Support available to part-time students. Financial award applicants required to submit FAFSA. *Faculty research:* Yugoslav economic system, workers' cooperatives, participative management and job enrichment, global business systems. *Unit head:* Dr. Paul Huo, Graduate Director, 612-659-7271, Fax: 612-659-7268, E-mail: carol.bormann.young@metrostate.edu. *Application contact:* Gloria B. Marcus, Recruiter/Admissions Adviser, 612-659-7258, Fax: 612-659-7268, E-mail: gloria.marcus@metrostate.edu.

New York Institute of Technology, Graduate Division, School of Engineering and Computing Sciences, Program in Information, Network, and Computer Security, Old Westbury, NY 11568-8000. Offers MS. Part-time and evening/weekend programs available. Postbaccalaureate distance learning degree programs offered. *Students:* 65 full-time (12 women), 37 part-time (3 women); includes 16 minority (10 Black or African American, non-Hispanic/Latino; 4 Asian, non-Hispanic/Latino; 2 Hispanic/Latino), 38 international. Average age 28. In 2010, 35 master's awarded. *Entrance requirements:* Additional exam requirements/recommendations for international students: Required—TOEFL (minimum score 550 paper-based; 213 computer-based). *Application deadline:* For fall admission, 7/1 priority date for domestic students; for spring admission, 12/1 priority date for domestic students. Applications are processed on a rolling basis. Application fee: $50. Electronic applications accepted. *Expenses:* Tuition: Part-time $835 per credit. *Financial support:* Fellowships, research assistantships with partial tuition reimbursements, career-related internships or fieldwork, institutionally sponsored loans, tuition waivers (full and partial), and unspecified assistantships available. Support available to part-time students. Financial award applicants required to submit FAFSA. *Unit head:* Dr. Nada Anid, Dean, 516-686-7931, Fax: 516-625-7933, E-mail: nanid@nyit.edu. *Application contact:* Dr. Jacquelyn Nealon, Vice President for Enrollment Services, 516-686-7925, Fax: 516-686-7597, E-mail: jnealon@nyit.edu.

Northern Kentucky University, Office of Graduate Programs, College of Informatics, Department of Business Informatics, Highland Heights, KY 41099. Offers business informatics (MS, Certificate); corporate information security (Certificate); enterprise resource planning (Certificate). Part-time and evening/weekend programs available. Postbaccalaureate distance learning degree programs offered (no on-campus study). *Faculty:* 9 full-time (2 women), 1 part-time/adjunct (0 women). *Students:* 10 full-time (4 women), 36 part-time (15 women); includes 7 minority (3 Black or African American, non-Hispanic/Latino; 2 Asian, non-Hispanic/Latino; 2 Hispanic/Latino), 6 international. Average age 33. 40 applicants, 75% accepted, 19 enrolled. In 2010, 11 master's, 6 other advanced degrees awarded. *Degree requirements:* For master's, capstone and portfolio (some programs), internship. *Entrance requirements:* For master's, GMAT (minimum score 450), GRE General Test (minimum combined score 1000), resume, minimum GPA of 2.5. Additional exam requirements/recommendations for international students: Required—TOEFL (minimum score 550 paper-based; 213 computer-based; 79 iBT); Recommended—IELTS (minimum score 6.5). *Application deadline:* For fall admission, 8/1 for domestic students, 6/1 for international students; for spring admission, 12/1 for domestic students, 10/1 for international students. Applications are processed on a rolling basis. Application fee: $40. Electronic applications accepted. *Expenses:* Tuition, state resident: full-time $7254; part-time $403 per credit hour. Tuition, nonresident: full-time $12,492; part-time $694 per credit hour. Tuition and fees vary according to degree level and program. *Financial support:* Unspecified assistantships available. Financial award applicants required to submit FAFSA. *Faculty research:* Information systems implementation, information systems security, business analytics, healthcare informatics. Total annual research expenditures: $50,000. *Unit head:* Dr. Ben Martz, Department Chair, 859-572-6366, E-mail: matrzw1@nku.edu. *Application contact:* Dr. Peg Griffin, Director of Graduate Programs, 859-572-6934, Fax: 859-572-6670, E-mail: griffinp@nku.edu.

Northwestern University, School of Continuing Studies, Program in Information Systems, Evanston, IL 60208. Offers database and Internet technologies (MS); information systems management (MS); information systems security (MS); software project management and development (MS).

Norwich University, School of Graduate and Continuing Studies, Program in Information Assurance, Northfield, VT 05663. Offers business continuity management (MS); managing cyber crime and digital incidents (MS). Evening/weekend programs available. *Faculty:* 18 part-time/adjunct (3 women). *Students:* 166 full-time (8 women); includes 7 Black or African American, non-Hispanic/Latino; 2 Asian, non-Hispanic/Latino; 5 Hispanic/Latino. Average age 40. In 2010, 166 master's awarded. *Entrance requirements:* For master's, minimum undergraduate GPA of 2.75. Additional exam requirements/recommendations for international students: Required—TOEFL (minimum score 550 paper-based; 212 computer-based; 83 iBT). *Application deadline:* For fall admission, 8/10 for domestic and international students; for winter admission, 11/7 for domestic and international students; for spring admission, 2/6 for domestic and international students. Application fee: $50. *Expenses:* Tuition: Full-time $17,380; part-time $645 per credit. Tuition and fees vary according to program. *Financial support:* Scholarships/grants available. Financial award applicants required to submit FAFSA. *Unit head:* Dr. Thomas Desoteaux, Program Director, 802-485-2259, E-mail: tdescote@norwich.edu. *Application contact:* Elizabeth Templeton, Administrative Director, 802-485-2757, Fax: 802-485-2533, E-mail: etemplet@norwich.edu.

Nova Southeastern University, Graduate School of Computer and Information Sciences, Program in Computer Information Systems, Fort Lauderdale, FL 33314-7796. Offers information security (MS). *Students:* 14 full-time (4 women), 168 part-time (21 women); includes 22 Black or African American, non-Hispanic/Latino; 1 American Indian or Alaska Native, non-Hispanic/Latino; 13 Asian, non-Hispanic/Latino; 24 Hispanic/Latino, 2 international. Average age 42. 106 applicants, 38% accepted. In 2010, 21 master's, 10 doctorates awarded. *Degree requirements:* For master's, thesis optional; for doctorate, thesis/dissertation. *Entrance requirements:* Additional exam requirements/recommendations for international students: Required—TOEFL (minimum score 213 computer-based; 79 iBT), IELTS (minimum score 6). *Application deadline:* For fall admission, 8/22 for domestic students; for winter admission, 1/3 for domestic students. Applications are processed on a rolling basis. Electronic applications accepted. *Unit head:* Dr. Amon Seagull, Interim Dean, 954-262-7300. *Application contact:* 954-262-2000, Fax: 954-262-2752, E-mail: scisinfo@nova.edu.

Nova Southeastern University, Graduate School of Computer and Information Sciences, Program in Information Security, Fort Lauderdale, FL 33314-7796. Offers MS. *Students:* 6 full-time (1 woman), 56 part-time (9 women); includes 29 minority (8 Black or African American, non-Hispanic/Latino; 6 Asian, non-Hispanic/Latino; 15 Hispanic/Latino), 6 international. Average

age 34. 55 applicants, 45% accepted. In 2010, 19 master's awarded. *Degree requirements:* For master's, thesis optional. *Entrance requirements:* Additional exam requirements/ recommendations for international students: Required—TOEFL (minimum score 213 computer-based; 79 iBT), IELTS (minimum score 6). *Application deadline:* For fall admission, 8/22 for domestic students; for winter admission, 1/3 for domestic students. Applications are processed on a rolling basis. Electronic applications accepted. *Unit head:* Dr. Amon Seagull, Interim Dean, 954-262-7300. *Application contact:* 954-262-2000, Fax: 954-262-2752, E-mail: scisinfo@ nova.edu.

Nova Southeastern University, Graduate School of Computer and Information Sciences, Program in Management Information Systems, Fort Lauderdale, FL 33314-7796. Offers information security (MS); management information systems (MS). Part-time and evening/ weekend programs available. Postbaccalaureate distance learning degree programs offered (no on-campus study). *Students:* 27 full-time (6 women), 154 part-time (60 women); includes 47 Black or African American, non-Hispanic/Latino; 1 American Indian or Alaska Native, non-Hispanic/Latino; 15 Asian, non-Hispanic/Latino; 41 Hispanic/Latino; 3 Two or more races, non-Hispanic/Latino, 13 international. Average age 36. 87 applicants, 66% accepted. In 2010, 49 master's awarded. *Degree requirements:* For master's, thesis optional. *Entrance requirements:* Additional exam requirements/recommendations for international students: Required—TOEFL (minimum score 213 computer-based; 79 iBT), IELTS (minimum score 6). *Application deadline:* For fall admission, 8/22 for domestic students; for winter admission, 1/3 for domestic students. Applications are processed on a rolling basis. Application fee: $50. Electronic applications accepted. *Financial support:* Application deadline: 5/1. *Unit head:* Dr. Amon Seagull, Interim Dean. *Application contact:* 954-262-2000, Fax: 954-262-2752, E-mail: scisinfo@nova.edu.

Our Lady of the Lake University of San Antonio, School of Business and Leadership, Program in Information Systems and Security, San Antonio, TX 78207-4689. Offers MS. Postbaccalaureate distance learning degree programs offered. *Students:* 16 full-time (6 women), 28 part-time (13 women); includes 22 minority (4 Black or African American, non-Hispanic/ Latino; 1 American Indian or Alaska Native, non-Hispanic/Latino; 17 Hispanic/Latino). Average age 37. In 2010, 6 master's awarded. *Expenses:* Tuition: Full-time $13,500; part-time $750 per contact hour. Required fees: $330. Tuition and fees vary according to course level, degree level and campus/location. *Unit head:* Dr. Robert Bisking, Dean, 210-434-6711, Fax: 210-434-0821. *Application contact:* Dr. Robert Bisking, Dean, 210-434-6711, Fax: 210-434-0821.

Pace University, Seidenberg School of Computer Science and Information Systems, New York, NY 10038. Offers computer communications and networks (Certificate); computer science (MS); computing studies (DPS); information systems (MS); Internet technologies for e-commerce (MS); Internet technology (MS); object-oriented programming (Certificate); security and information assurance (Certificate); software development and engineering (MS); telecommunications (MS, Certificate). Part-time and evening/weekend programs available. *Entrance requirements:* For master's, GRE General Test. Additional exam requirements/recommendations for international students: Required—TOEFL. Electronic applications accepted. *Expenses:* Contact institution.

Polytechnic Institute of NYU, Department of Computer Science and Engineering, Major in Cyber Security, Brooklyn, NY 11201-2990. Offers Graduate Certificate. *Students:* 21 full-time (3 women), 59 part-time (5 women); includes 3 Black or African American, non-Hispanic/ Latino; 5 Asian, non-Hispanic/Latino; 3 Hispanic/Latino, 13 international. Average age 35. 92 applicants, 77% accepted, 58 enrolled. *Application deadline:* For fall admission, 7/31 priority date for domestic students, 4/30 priority date for international students; for spring admission, 12/31 priority date for domestic students, 11/30 priority date for international students. Applications are processed on a rolling basis. Application fee: $75. Electronic applications accepted. *Expenses:* Tuition: Full-time $21,492; part-time $1194 per credit. Required fees: $385 per semester. Tuition and fees vary according to course load. *Unit head:* Dr. Keith W. Ross, Head, 718-260-3859, Fax: 718-260-3609, E-mail: ross@poly.edu. *Application contact:* JeanCarlo Bonilla, Director, Graduate Enrollment Management, 718-260-3182, Fax: 718-260-3624, E-mail: gradinfo@poly.edu.

Purdue University, Graduate School, Center for Education and Research in Information Assurance and Security (CERIAS), Interdisciplinary Program in Information Security, West Lafayette, IN 47907. Offers MS. *Entrance requirements:* For master's, GRE. Additional exam requirements/recommendations for international students: Required—TOEFL. Electronic applications accepted.

Regis University, College for Professional Studies, School of Computer and Information Sciences, Denver, CO 80221-1099. Offers database administration with Oracle (Certificate); database development (Certificate); database technologies (M Sc); enterprise Java software development (Certificate); enterprise resource planning (Certificate); executive information technologies (Certificate); information assurance (M Sc, Certificate); information technology management (M Sc); software engineering (M Sc, Certificate); software engineering and database technologies (M Sc); storage area networks (Certificate); systems engineering (M Sc, Certificate). Offered at Boulder Campus, Northwest Denver Campus, Southeast Denver Campus, Fort Collins Campus, Colorado Springs Campus, and Broomfield Campus. Part-time and evening/weekend programs available. Postbaccalaureate distance learning degree programs offered (no on-campus study). *Degree requirements:* For master's, thesis, final research project. *Entrance requirements:* For master's, 2 years of related experience, resume, interview; for Certificate, 2 years of related experience, resumé. Additional exam requirements/ recommendations for international students: Required—TOEFL (minimum score 213 computer-based), TWE (minimum score 5), TOEFL or university-based test. Electronic applications accepted. *Expenses:* Contact institution. *Faculty research:* Secure Virtual Laboratory Architecture, Joint IA project with W2C06 Institute, Information Policy, OLTP and OLAP Technologies, knowledge management, software architectures.

Robert Morris University, Graduate Studies, School of Communications and Information Systems, Moon Township, PA 15108-1189. Offers communication and information systems (MS); competitive intelligence systems (MS); information security and assurance (MS); information systems and communications (D Sc); information systems management (MS); information technology project management (MS); Internet information systems (MS); organizational studies (MS). Part-time and evening/weekend programs available. *Degree requirements:* For doctorate, thesis/dissertation. *Entrance requirements:* For doctorate, employer letter of endorsement, interview. Additional exam requirements/recommendations for international students: Required—TOEFL (minimum score 550 paper-based; 213 computer-based; 79 iBT). Electronic applications accepted. *Expenses:* Contact institution.

Rochester Institute of Technology, Graduate Enrollment Services, B. Thomas Golisano College of Computing and Information Sciences, Department of Information Technology, Rochester, NY 14623-5603. Offers database administration (AC); human computer interaction (MS); information assurance (AC); information technology (MS); interactive multimedia development (AC); medical informatics (MS); software development and management (MS). Part-time and evening/weekend programs available. Postbaccalaureate distance learning degree programs offered (minimal on-campus study). *Students:* 84 full-time (23 women), 114 part-time (29 women); includes 8 Black or African American, non-Hispanic/Latino; 1 American Indian or Alaska Native, non-Hispanic/Latino; 4 Asian, non-Hispanic/Latino; 7 Hispanic/Latino, 77 international. Average age 30. 176 applicants, 64% accepted, 59 enrolled. In 2010, 53 master's, 5 other advanced degrees awarded. *Degree requirements:* For master's, thesis or project. *Entrance requirements:* For master's, GRE, minimum GPA of 3.0. Additional exam requirements/ recommendations for international students: Required—TOEFL (minimum score 570 paper-based; 230 computer-based; 99 iBT) or IELTS (minimum score 6.5). *Application deadline:* For fall admission, 8/1 for domestic students, 7/1 for international students; for spring admission, 2/1 for domestic students. Applications are processed on a rolling basis. Electronic applications accepted. *Expenses:* Tuition: Full-time $33,234; part-time $924 per credit hour. Required fees: $219. *Financial support:* In 2010–11, 137 students received support; research assistantships with partial tuition reimbursements available, teaching assistantships with partial tuition reimbursements available, career-related internships or fieldwork, scholarships/grants, and unspecified assistantships available. Support available to part-time students. Financial award applicants required to submit FAFSA. *Faculty research:* Human-computer interaction: eye tracking, usability engineering, usability testing, ubiquitous computing, interface design and development; platform-independent Multiuser Online Virtual Environments (MOVEs); simulation; service computing, query optimization, data mining and integration; applications programming, interface designs, needs assessment, data modeling, database administration. *Unit head:* Prof. Jeffrey Lasky, Department Chair, 585-475-2284, Fax: 585-475-6584, E-mail: jeffrey.lasky@ rit.edu. *Application contact:* Diane Ellison, Assistant Vice President, Graduate Enrollment Services, 585-475-2229, Fax: 585-475-7164, E-mail: gradinfo@rit.edu.

Rochester Institute of Technology, Graduate Enrollment Services, B. Thomas Golisano College of Computing and Information Sciences, Department of Networking, Security and Systems Administration, Program in Security and Information Assurance, Rochester, NY 14623-5603. Offers MS. Part-time and evening/weekend programs available. Postbaccalaureate distance learning degree programs offered (no on-campus study). *Students:* 12 full-time (1 woman), 15 part-time (3 women), 12 international. Average age 30. 29 applicants, 45% accepted, 6 enrolled. In 2010, 1 master's awarded. *Degree requirements:* For master's, thesis. *Entrance requirements:* For master's, GRE, minimum GPA of 3.0. Additional exam requirements/ recommendations for international students: Required—TOEFL (minimum score 570 paper-based; 230 computer-based; 88 iBT) or IELTS (minimum score 6.5). *Application deadline:* For fall admission, 8/1 for domestic students, 7/1 for international students; for spring admission, 2/1 for domestic students. Applications are processed on a rolling basis. Electronic applications accepted. *Expenses:* Tuition: Full-time $33,234; part-time $924 per credit hour. Required fees: $219. *Financial support:* In 2010–11, 19 students received support; research assistantships with partial tuition reimbursements available, teaching assistantships with partial tuition reimbursements available, career-related internships or fieldwork, scholarships/grants, and unspecified assistantships available. Support available to part-time students. Financial award applicants required to submit FAFSA. *Unit head:* Prof. Dianne Bills, Graduate Program Director, 585-475-2700, Fax: 585-475-6584, E-mail: informaticsgrad@rit.edu. *Application contact:* Diane Ellison, Assistant Vice President, Graduate Enrollment Services, 585-475-2229, Fax: 585-475-7164, E-mail: gradinfo@rit.edu.

Sacred Heart University, Graduate Programs, College of Arts and Sciences, Department of Computer Science and Information Technology, Fairfield, CT 06825-1000. Offers computer science (MS); database (CPS); information technology (MS, CPS); information technology and network security (CPS); interactive multimedia (CPS); Web development (CPS). Part-time and evening/weekend programs available. *Degree requirements:* For master's, thesis optional. *Entrance requirements:* Additional exam requirements/recommendations for international students: Required—TOEFL (minimum score 550 paper-based; 213 computer-based). Electronic applications accepted. *Faculty research:* Contemporary market software.

St. Cloud State University, School of Graduate Studies, College of Science and Engineering, Program in Information Assurance, St. Cloud, MN 56301-4498. Offers MS.

St. Cloud State University, School of Graduate Studies, G.R. Herberger College of Business, Program in Business Administration, St. Cloud, MN 56301-4498. Offers business administration (MBA); information assurance (MS). Part-time and evening/weekend programs available. *Degree requirements:* For master's, thesis or alternative. *Entrance requirements:* For master's, GMAT, minimum GPA of 2.75. Additional exam requirements/recommendations for international students: Required—Michigan English Language Assessment Battery; Recommended—TOEFL (minimum score 550 paper-based; 213 computer-based), IELTS (minimum score 6.5).

Saint Leo University, Graduate Business Studies, Saint Leo, FL 33574-6665. Offers accounting (MBA); business (MBA); health services management (MBA); human resource management (MBA); information security management (MBA); marketing (MBA); sport business (MBA). Part-time and evening/weekend programs available. Postbaccalaureate distance learning degree programs offered (no on-campus study). *Faculty:* 32 full-time (4 women), 53 part-time/adjunct (21 women). *Students:* 1,498 full-time (890 women), 10 part-time (6 women); includes 593 minority (465 Black or African American, non-Hispanic/Latino; 5 American Indian or Alaska Native, non-Hispanic/Latino; 23 Asian, non-Hispanic/Latino; 84 Hispanic/Latino; 2 Native Hawaiian or other Pacific Islander, non-Hispanic/Latino; 14 Two or more races, non-Hispanic/ Latino), 14 international. Average age 38. In 2010, 557 master's awarded. *Entrance requirements:* For master's, GMAT (minimum score 500 if applicant does not have 5 years of professional work experience), bachelor's degree from regionally-accredited college or university with minimum GPA of 3.0 in the last 60 hours of coursework; 5 years of professional work experience; resume; 2 letters of recommendation. Additional exam requirements/ recommendations for international students: Required—TOEFL (minimum score 550 paper-based; 213 computer-based; 80 iBT). *Application deadline:* For fall admission, 7/1 priority date for domestic and international students; for spring admission, 11/12 priority date for domestic students, 11/1 for international students. Applications are processed on a rolling basis. Application fee: $75. Electronic applications accepted. *Expenses:* Contact institution. *Financial support:* In 2010–11, 51 students received support. Career-related internships or fieldwork, Federal Work-Study, scholarships/grants, and health care benefits available. Financial award application deadline: 3/1; financial award applicants required to submit FAFSA. *Unit head:* Dr. Lorrie McGovern, Director, 352-588-7390, Fax: 352-588-8585, E-mail: mbaslu@saintleo.edu. *Application contact:* Jared Welling, Director, Graduate/Weekend and Evening Admission, 800-707-8846, Fax: 352-588-7873, E-mail: grad.admissions@saintleo.edu.

Salem International University, School of Business, Salem, WV 26426-0500. Offers information security (MBA); international business (MBA). Part-time programs available. Postbaccalaureate distance learning degree programs offered (no on-campus study). *Entrance requirements:* For master's, minimum undergraduate GPA of 2.5, course work in business, resume. Additional exam requirements/recommendations for international students: Recommended—TOEFL (minimum score 550 paper-based; 213 computer-based), IELTS (minimum score 6.5). Electronic applications accepted. *Expenses:* Contact institution. *Faculty research:* Organizational behavior strategy, marketing services.

Southern Polytechnic State University, School of Computing and Software Engineering, Department of Information Technology, Marietta, GA 30060-2896. Offers business continuity (Graduate Certificate); information security and assurance (Graduate Certificate); information technology (MSIT, Graduate Certificate, Graduate Transition Certificate). Part-time and evening/ weekend programs available. Postbaccalaureate distance learning degree programs offered (minimal on-campus study). *Faculty:* 6 full-time (3 women), 2 part-time/adjunct (1 woman). *Students:* 60 full-time (17 women), 71 part-time (26 women); includes 54 Black or African American, non-Hispanic/Latino; 11 Asian, non-Hispanic/Latino; 5 Hispanic/Latino; 2 Two or more races, non-Hispanic/Latino, 19 international. Average age 34. 67 applicants, 96% accepted, 41 enrolled. In 2010, 25 master's, 2 other advanced degrees awarded. *Degree requirements:* For master's, thesis or alternative. *Entrance requirements:* For master's, minimum GPA of 2.75; for other advanced degree, bachelor's degree. Additional exam requirements/ recommendations for international students: Required—TOEFL (minimum score 550 paper-based; 213 computer-based; 79 iBT), IELTS (minimum score 6.5). *Application deadline:* For fall admission, 7/1 priority date for domestic students, 5/1 priority date for international students; for spring admission, 11/1 priority date for domestic students, 9/1 priority date for international students. Applications are processed on a rolling basis. Application fee: $20. Electronic applications accepted. *Expenses:* Tuition, state resident: full-time $3690; part-time $205 per semester hour. Tuition, nonresident: full-time $13,428; part-time $746 per semester hour. Required fees: $598 per semester. *Financial support:* In 2010–11, 12 students received support, including 13 research assistantships with tuition reimbursements available (averaging $1,500 per year); career-related internships or fieldwork, scholarships/grants, and unspecified assistantships also available. Support available to part-time students. Financial award application deadline: 5/1; financial award applicants required to submit FAFSA. *Faculty research:* IT ethics, user

Computer and Information Systems Security

Southern Polytechnic State University (continued)
interface design, IT security, IT integration, IT management, health information technology. *Unit head:* Dr. Ju Au Wang, Chair, 678-915-3718, Fax: 678-915-5511, E-mail: jwang@spsu.edu. *Application contact:* Nikki Palamiotis, Director of Graduate Studies, 678-915-4276, Fax: 678-915-7292, E-mail: npalamio@spsu.edu.

Stevens Institute of Technology, Graduate School, Charles V. Schaefer Jr. School of Engineering, Department of Computer Science, Hoboken, NJ 07030. Offers computer graphics (Certificate); computer science (MS, PhD); computer systems (Certificate); database management systems (Certificate); distributed systems (Certificate); elements of computer science (Certificate); enterprise computing (Certificate); enterprise security and information assurance (Certificate); health informatics (Certificate); multimedia experience and management (Certificate); networks and systems administration (Certificate); security and privacy (Certificate); service oriented computing (Certificate); software design (Certificate); theoretical computer science (Certificate). Part-time and evening/weekend programs available. *Faculty:* 12 full-time (5 women). *Students:* 117 full-time (42 women), 88 part-time (17 women); includes 4 Black or African American, non-Hispanic/Latino; 21 Asian, non-Hispanic/Latino; 3 Hispanic/Latino, 99 international. Average age 28. 327 applicants, 57% accepted. In 2010, 72 master's, 2 doctorates awarded. Terminal master's awarded for partial completion of doctoral program. *Degree requirements:* For master's, thesis optional; for doctorate, variable foreign language requirement, comprehensive exam, thesis/dissertation. *Entrance requirements:* For master's and doctorate, GRE, minimum GPA of 3.0. Additional exam requirements/recommendations for international students: Required—TOEFL. *Application deadline:* Applications are processed on a rolling basis. Application fee: $50. Electronic applications accepted. *Financial support:* Fellowships, Federal Work-Study available. Financial award application deadline: 4/15. *Faculty research:* Semantics, reliability theory, programming language, cyber security. *Unit head:* Daniel Duchamp, Director, 201-216-5390, Fax: 201-216-8249, E-mail: djd@cs.stevens.edu. *Application contact:* Graduate Admissions, 800-496-4935, Fax: 201-216-8044, E-mail: gradadmissions@stevens.edu.

Stevens Institute of Technology, Graduate School, Wesley J. Howe School of Technology Management, Program in Information Systems, Hoboken, NJ 07030. Offers computer science (MS); e-commerce (MS); enterprise systems (MS); entrepreneurial information technology (MS); information architecture (MS); information management (MS, Certificate); information security (MS); information technology in financial services industry (MS); information technology in the pharmaceutical industry (MS); information technology outsourcing management (MS); project management (MS, Certificate); software engineering (MS); telecommunications (MS). *Degree requirements:* For master's, thesis optional. *Entrance requirements:* For master's, GMAT, GRE General Test. Additional exam requirements/recommendations for international students: Required—TOEFL. Electronic applications accepted.

Stratford University, School of Graduate Studies, Falls Church, VA 22043. Offers accounting (MS); business administration (IMBA, MBA); enterprise business management (MS); entrepreneurial management (MS); information assurance (MS); information systems (MS); software engineering (MS); telecommunications (MS). Part-time and evening/weekend programs available. Postbaccalaureate distance learning degree programs offered (no on-campus study). *Degree requirements:* For master's, comprehensive exam, capstone project. *Entrance requirements:* For master's, baccalaureate degree. Additional exam requirements/recommendations for international students: Required—TOEFL (minimum score 500 paper-based; 173 computer-based; 61 iBT). Electronic applications accepted.

Strayer University, Graduate Studies, Washington, DC 20005-2603. Offers accounting (MS); acquisition (MBA); business administration (MBA); communications technology (MS); educational management (M Ed); finance (MBA); health services administration (MHSA); hospitality and tourism management (MBA); human resource management (MBA); information systems (MS), including computer security management, decision support system management, enterprise resource management, network management, software engineering management, systems development management; management (MBA); management information systems (MS); marketing (MBA); professional accounting (MS), including accounting information systems, controllership, taxation; public administration (MPA); supply chain management (MBA); technology in education (M Ed). Programs also offered at campus locations in Birmingham, AL; Chamblee, GA; Cobb County, GA; Morrow, GA; White Marsh, MD; Charleston, SC; Columbia, SC; Greensboro, NC; Greenville, SC; Lexington, KY; Louisville, KY; Nashville, TN; North Raleigh, NC; Washington, DC. Part-time and evening/weekend programs available. Postbaccalaureate distance learning degree programs offered (minimal on-campus study). *Degree requirements:* For master's, thesis. *Entrance requirements:* For master's, GMAT, GRE General Test, bachelor's degree from an accredited college or university, minimum undergraduate GPA of 2.75. Electronic applications accepted.

Syracuse University, School of Information Studies, Program in Information Security Management, Syracuse, NY 13244. Offers CAS. Part-time and evening/weekend programs available. Postbaccalaureate distance learning degree programs offered. *Students:* 2 full-time (0 women), 11 part-time (1 woman); includes 5 minority (2 Black or African American, non-Hispanic/Latino; 2 Asian, non-Hispanic/Latino; 1 Hispanic/Latino). Average age 37. 41 applicants, 73% accepted, 3 enrolled. In 2010, 22 CASs awarded. *Entrance requirements:* Additional exam requirements/recommendations for international students: Required—TOEFL (minimum score 100 iBT). *Application deadline:* For fall admission, 2/1 priority date for domestic and international students; for spring admission, 10/15 priority date for domestic and international students. Applications are processed on a rolling basis. Application fee: $75. Electronic applications accepted. *Expenses:* Tuition: Part-time $1162 per credit. *Financial support:* Application deadline: 1/1. *Unit head:* Joon S. Park, Head, 315-443-2911, E-mail: ischool@syr.edu. *Application contact:* Susan Corieri, Director of Enrollment Management, 315-443-2575, E-mail: ischool@syr.edu.

Texas A&M University–San Antonio, School of Business, San Antonio, TX 78224. Offers business administration (MBA); enterprise resource planning systems (MBA); finance (MBA); healthcare management (MBA); human resources management (MBA); information assurance and security (MBA); international business (MBA); project management (MBA); supply chain management (MBA). Part-time and evening/weekend programs available. *Faculty:* 18 full-time (6 women), 1 part-time/adjunct (0 women). *Students:* 49 full-time (21 women), 195 part-time (107 women). In 2010, 20 master's awarded. *Entrance requirements:* For master's, GMAT. Additional exam requirements/recommendations for international students: Required—TOEFL (minimum score 550 paper-based; 213 computer-based; 80 iBT), IELTS (minimum score 6). *Application deadline:* For fall admission, 7/1 priority date for domestic students, 6/1 priority date for international students; for spring admission, 11/15 priority date for domestic students, 10/1 priority date for international students. Applications are processed on a rolling basis. Application fee: $35 ($50 for international students). Electronic applications accepted. *Expenses:* Tuition, state resident: full-time $2899; part-time $161 per credit hour. Tuition, nonresident: full-time $8479; part-time $471 per credit hour. Required fees: $1056; $61 per credit hour. $368 per semester. *Financial support:* Application deadline: 3/31. *Unit head:* Dr. Tracy Hurley, MBA Coordinator, 210-932-6200, E-mail: tracy.hurley@tamusa.tamus.edu. *Application contact:* Melissa A. Villanueva, Graduate Admissions Specialist, 210-932-6200, Fax: 210-932-6209, E-mail: melissa.villanueva@tamusa.tamus.edu.

Towson University, Master's Program in Applied Information Technology, Towson, MD 21252-0001. Offers applied information technology (MS, PhD); database management systems (Postbaccalaureate Certificate); information security and assurance (Postbaccalaureate Certificate); information systems management (Graduate Certificate); Internet applications development (Postbaccalaureate Certificate); networking technologies (Postbaccalaureate Certificate); software engineering (Postbaccalaureate Certificate). *Students:* 111 full-time (25 women), 232 part-time (62 women); includes 122 minority (75 Black or African American, non-Hispanic/Latino; 4 American Indian or Alaska Native, non-Hispanic/Latino; 31 Asian, non-Hispanic/Latino; 11 Hispanic/Latino; 1 Native Hawaiian or other Pacific Islander, non-Hispanic/Latino), 85 international. In 2010, 75 master's, 9 doctorates, 74 other advanced degrees awarded. *Expenses:* Tuition, state resident: part-time $324 per credit. Tuition, nonresident: part-time $681 per credit. Required fees: $95 per term. *Unit head:* Mike O'Leary, Graduate Program Director, 410-704-4757, E-mail: moleary@towson.edu. *Application contact:* Mike O'Leary, Graduate Program Director, 410-704-4757, E-mail: moleary@towson.edu.

TUI University, College of Business Administration, Program in Business Administration, Cypress, CA 90630. Offers business administration (PhD); conflict and negotiation management (MBA); criminal justice administration (MBA); entrepreneurship (MBA); finance (MBA); general management (MBA); government accounting (MBA); human resource management (MBA); information security and digital assurance management (MBA); information technology management (MBA); international business (MBA); logistics management (MBA); marketing (MBA); project management (MBA); public management (MBA); quality management (MBA); strategic leadership (MBA). Part-time and evening/weekend programs available. Postbaccalaureate distance learning degree programs offered (no on-campus study). *Students:* 741 full-time (200 women), 1,585 part-time (410 women). 379 applicants, 81% accepted, 300 enrolled. In 2010, 752 master's, 28 doctorates awarded. *Degree requirements:* For doctorate, comprehensive exam, thesis/dissertation, defense of dissertation. *Entrance requirements:* For master's, minimum GPA of 2.5 (students with GPA 3.0 or greater may transfer up to 30% of graduate level credits); for doctorate, minimum GPA of 3.4, curriculum vitae, course work in research methods or statistics. Additional exam requirements/recommendations for international students: Required—TOEFL. *Application deadline:* For fall admission, 10/3 for domestic and international students; for winter admission, 12/22 for domestic and international students; for spring admission, 4/3 for domestic and international students. Applications are processed on a rolling basis. Application fee: $75. Electronic applications accepted. *Expenses:* Tuition: Full-time $11,040; part-time $345 per semester hour. *Unit head:* Paul Watkins, Dean, College of Business Administration, 800-375-9878, E-mail: pwatkins@tuiu.edu. *Application contact:* Wei Ren-Finaly, Registrar, 800-375-9878, Fax: 714-827-7407, E-mail: registration@tuiu.edu.

Universidad del Este, Graduate School, Carolina, PR 00984. Offers accounting (MBA); adult education (M Ed); agribusiness (MBA); criminal justice and criminology (MA); curriculum and instruction—early education (M Ed); curriculum and instruction—elementary (M Ed); curriculum and instruction—English (M Ed); curriculum and instruction—Spanish (M Ed); human resources (MBA); information security management (MBA); information technology and Web business development (MBA); management (MBA); public policy (MPA); social work (MA), including clinical social work; special education (M Ed); strategic leadership (MBA).

Université de Sherbrooke, Faculty of Administration, Program in Governance, Audit and Security of Information Technology, Longueuil, QC J4K0A8, Canada. Offers M Adm. Part-time and evening/weekend programs available. Postbaccalaureate distance learning degree programs offered. *Faculty:* 1 full-time (0 women), 12 part-time/adjunct (2 women). *Students:* 13 part-time (2 women). Average age 40. 47 applicants, 36% accepted, 13 enrolled. In 2010, 14 master's awarded. *Degree requirements:* For master's, thesis. *Entrance requirements:* For master's, Related work experience. *Application deadline:* For fall admission, 4/30 priority date for domestic students. Applications are processed on a rolling basis. Application fee: $70. Electronic applications accepted. *Unit head:* Prof. Julien Bilodeau, Director, Graduate programs in business, 819-821-8000 Ext. 62355, E-mail: julien.bilodeau@usherbrooke.ca. *Application contact:* Lyne Cantin, assistant to the director, 450-463-1835 Ext. 61768, Fax: 450-670-1848, E-mail: lyne.cantin@usherbrooke.ca.

University of Advancing Technology, Master of Science Program in Technology, Tempe, AZ 85283-1042. Offers advancing computer science (MS); emerging technologies (MS); game production and management (MS); information assurance (MS); technology leadership (MS). *Faculty:* 9 full-time (3 women), 3 part-time/adjunct (1 woman). *Students:* 55 full-time (9 women), 4 part-time (1 woman). Average age 25. In 2010, 5 master's awarded. *Degree requirements:* For master's, project or thesis. *Entrance requirements:* Additional exam requirements/recommendations for international students: Required—TOEFL (minimum score 550 paper-based). *Application deadline:* For fall admission, 8/15 priority date for domestic students, 7/15 priority date for international students; for winter admission, 12/15 priority date for domestic students, 11/15 priority date for international students; for spring admission, 4/1 priority date for domestic students, 3/1 priority date for international students. Applications are processed on a rolling basis. Application fee: $100 ($250 for international students). Electronic applications accepted. *Expenses:* Tuition: Full-time $18,300. *Financial support:* Career-related internships or fieldwork, Federal Work-Study, and scholarships/grants available. Financial award applicants required to submit FAFSA. *Faculty research:* Artificial intelligence, fractals, organizational management. *Unit head:* Robert Marshall, Dean of Graduate Education, 602-383-8283, Fax: 602-383-8222, E-mail: rmarshall@uat.edu. *Application contact:* Information Contact, 800-658-5744, Fax: 602-383-8222.

The University of Alabama at Birmingham, College of Arts and Sciences, Program in Computer Forensics and Security Management, Birmingham, AL 35294. Offers MS. *Expenses:* Tuition, state resident: full-time $5482. Tuition, nonresident: full-time $12,430. Tuition and fees vary according to program. *Unit head:* Dr. John J. Sloan, 205-934-2069. *Application contact:* Julie Bryant, Director of Graduate Admissions, 205-934-8227, Fax: 205-934-8413, E-mail: jbryant@uab.edu.

University of Dayton, Graduate School, School of Business Administration, Dayton, OH 45469-1300. Offers accounting (MBA); business intelligence (MBA); cyber security (MBA); entrepreneurship (MBA); finance (MBA); international business (MBA); marketing (MBA); MIS (MBA); operations management (MBA); technology-enhanced business/e-commerce (MBA); JD/MBA. *Accreditation:* AACSB. Part-time and evening/weekend programs available. *Faculty:* 25 full-time (7 women), 14 part-time/adjunct (2 women). *Students:* 184 full-time (72 women), 110 part-time (34 women); includes 23 minority (7 Black or African American, non-Hispanic/Latino; 7 Asian, non-Hispanic/Latino; 8 Hispanic/Latino; 1 Two or more races, non-Hispanic/Latino), 31 international. Average age 28. 220 applicants, 85% accepted, 103 enrolled. In 2010, 113 master's awarded. *Entrance requirements:* For master's, GMAT or GRE. Additional exam requirements/recommendations for international students: Required—TOEFL (minimum score 550 paper-based; 213 computer-based; 79 iBT); Recommended—IELTS (minimum score 6.5). *Application deadline:* For fall admission, 3/1 priority date for international students; for winter admission, 7/1 priority date for international students; for spring admission, 1/1 priority date for international students. Applications are processed on a rolling basis. Application fee: $0 ($50 for international students). Electronic applications accepted. *Expenses:* Contact institution. *Financial support:* In 2010–11, 15 research assistantships with full and partial tuition reimbursements (averaging $7,020 per year) were awarded; career-related internships or fieldwork, institutionally sponsored loans, scholarships/grants, health care benefits, and unspecified assistantships also available. Support available to part-time students. Financial award application deadline: 3/15; financial award applicants required to submit FAFSA. *Faculty research:* Management information systems, economics, finance, entrepreneurship, marketing. *Unit head:* Janice M. Glynn, Director, MBA Program, 937-229-3733, Fax: 937-229-3882, E-mail: glynn@udayton.edu. *Application contact:* Jeffrey Carter, Assistant Director, MBA Program, 937-229-3733, Fax: 937-229-3882, E-mail: jeff.carter@notes.udayton.edu.

University of Denver, University College, Denver, CO 80208. Offers arts and culture (MLS, Certificate), including art, literature, and culture, arts development and program management (Certificate), creative writing; environmental policy and management (MAS, Certificate), including energy and sustainability (Certificate), environmental assessment of nuclear power (Certificate), environmental health and safety (Certificate), environmental management, natural resource management (Certificate); geographic information systems (MAS, Certificate); global affairs (MLS, Certificate), including translation studies, world history and culture; healthcare leadership (MPH, Certificate), including healthcare policy, law, and ethics, medical and healthcare information technologies, strategic management of healthcare; information and communications technology (MCIS, Certificate), including database design and administration (Certificate), geographic information systems (MCIS), information security systems security (Certificate), information systems security (MCIS), project management (MCIS, MPS, Certificate), software design and administration (Certificate), software design and programming (MCIS), technology management, telecommunications technology (MCIS), Web design and development; leadership and organizations (MPS, Certificate), including human capital in organizations, philanthropic leadership, project management (MCIS, MPS, Certificate), strategic innovation and change; organizational and professional communication (MPS, Certificate), including alternative dispute resolution, organizational communication, organizational development and training, public relations and marketing; security management (MAS, Certificate), including emergency planning and response, information security (MAS), organizational security; strategic human resource management (MPS, Certificate), including global human resources (MPS), human resource management and development (MPS). Part-time and evening/weekend programs available. Postbaccalaureate distance learning degree programs offered (no on-campus study). *Faculty:* 7 full-time (2 women), 212 part-time/adjunct (83 women). *Students:* 52 full-time (19 women), 1,044 part-time (625 women); includes 196 minority (81 Black or African American, non-Hispanic/Latino; 7 American Indian or Alaska Native, non-Hispanic/Latino; 30 Asian, non-Hispanic/Latino; 66 Hispanic/Latino; 3 Native Hawaiian or other Pacific Islander, non-Hispanic/Latino; 9 Two or more races, non-Hispanic/Latino), 76 international. Average age 36. 488 applicants, 91% accepted, 339 enrolled. In 2010, 286 master's, 130 other advanced degrees awarded. *Entrance requirements:* Additional exam requirements/recommendations for international students: Required—TOEFL (minimum score 550 paper-based; 80 iBT). *Application deadline:* For fall admission, 6/22 priority date for domestic students, 6/10 priority date for international students; for winter admission, 9/15 priority date for domestic students, 9/6 priority date for international students; for spring admission, 2/3 priority date for domestic students, 12/15 priority date for international students. Applications are processed on a rolling basis. Application fee: $75. Electronic applications accepted. *Expenses:* Contact institution. *Financial support:* Applicants required to submit FAFSA. *Unit head:* Dr. James Davis, Dean, 303-871-2291, Fax: 303-871-4047, E-mail: jdavis@du.edu. *Application contact:* Information Contact, 303-871-3155, Fax: 303-871-4047, E-mail: ucolinfo@du.edu.

University of Houston, College of Technology, Department of Information and Logistics Technology, Houston, TX 77204. Offers information security (MS); supply chain and logistics technology (MS); technology project management (MS). Part-time programs available. *Faculty:* 6 full-time (3 women), 6 part-time/adjunct (2 women). *Students:* 80 full-time (30 women), 75 part-time (29 women); includes 35 minority (12 Black or African American, non-Hispanic/Latino; 9 Asian, non-Hispanic/Latino; 11 Hispanic/Latino; 1 Native Hawaiian or other Pacific Islander, non-Hispanic/Latino; 2 Two or more races, non-Hispanic/Latino), 73 international. Average age 31. 60 applicants, 92% accepted, 35 enrolled. In 2010, 22 master's awarded. *Degree requirements:* For master's, project or thesis (most programs). *Entrance requirements:* For master's, GMAT. Additional exam requirements/recommendations for international students: Required—TOEFL (minimum score 550 paper-based; 79 iBT). *Application deadline:* For fall admission, 7/1 for domestic students, 4/1 for international students; for spring admission, 12/1 for domestic students, 10/1 for international students. Applications are processed on a rolling basis. Application fee: $75 ($150 for international students). Electronic applications accepted. *Expenses:* Tuition, state resident: full-time $8592; part-time $358 per credit hour. Tuition, nonresident: full-time $16,032; part-time $668 per credit hour. Required fees: $2889. Tuition and fees vary according to course load and program. *Financial support:* In 2010–11, 10 research assistantships with partial tuition reimbursements (averaging $8,380 per year), 15 teaching assistantships with partial tuition reimbursements (averaging $8,078 per year) were awarded. *Unit head:* Michael Gibson, Chairperson, 713-743-5116, E-mail: mlgibson@uh.edu. *Application contact:* Tiffany Roosa, Graduate Advisor, 713-743-4100, Fax: 713-743-4151, E-mail: troosa@uh.edu.

University of Louisville, J.B. Speed School of Engineering, Department of Computer Engineering and Computer Science, Louisville, KY 40292-0001. Offers computer engineering and computer science (M Eng, MS); computer science (MS); computer science and engineering (PhD); data mining (Certificate); network and information security (Certificate). *Accreditation:* ABET (one or more programs are accredited). Part-time programs available. Postbaccalaureate distance learning degree programs offered (no on-campus study). *Faculty:* 13 full-time (1 woman). *Students:* 74 full-time (15 women), 45 part-time (7 women); includes 8 Black or African American, non-Hispanic/Latino; 4 Asian, non-Hispanic/Latino; 1 Hispanic/Latino; 1 Two or more races, non-Hispanic/Latino, 40 international. Average age 29. 51 applicants, 41% accepted, 9 enrolled. In 2010, 22 master's, 11 doctorates awarded. Terminal master's awarded for partial completion of doctoral program. *Degree requirements:* For master's, comprehensive exam (for some programs), thesis or alternative; for doctorate, comprehensive exam, thesis/dissertation, minimum GPA of 3.0. *Entrance requirements:* For master's, doctorate, and Certificate, GRE General Test. Additional exam requirements/recommendations for international students: Required—TOEFL (minimum score 550 paper-based; 213 computer-based; 80 iBT), IELTS (minimum score 6.5). *Application deadline:* For fall admission, 5/1 priority date for domestic and international students; for spring admission, 11/1 priority date for domestic and international students. Applications are processed on a rolling basis. Application fee: $50. Electronic applications accepted. *Expenses:* Tuition, state resident: full-time $9144; part-time $508 per credit hour. Tuition, nonresident: full-time $19,026; part-time $1057 per credit hour. Tuition and fees vary according to program and reciprocity agreements. *Financial support:* In 2010–11, 22 students received support, including 1 fellowship with full tuition reimbursement available (averaging $20,000 per year), 15 research assistantships with full tuition reimbursements available (averaging $18,900 per year), 6 teaching assistantships with full tuition reimbursements available (averaging $20,000 per year). Financial award application deadline: 1/25; financial award applicants required to submit FAFSA. *Faculty research:* Software systems engineering, information security and forensics, multimedia and vision, mobile and distributed computing, intelligent systems. Total annual research expenditures: $1.3 million. *Unit head:* Dr. Adel S. Elmaghraby, Chair, 502-852-6304, Fax: 502-852-4713, E-mail: adel@louisville.edu. *Application contact:* Dr. Michael Day, Associate Dean, 502-852-6195, Fax: 502-852-6294, E-mail: day@louisville.edu.

University of Maryland University College, Graduate School of Management and Technology, Program in Cybersecurity, Adelphi, MD 20783. Offers MS, Certificate. Part-time and evening/weekend programs available. Postbaccalaureate distance learning degree programs offered (no on-campus study). *Students:* 2 full-time (both women), 508 part-time (149 women); includes 228 minority (150 Black or African American, non-Hispanic/Latino; 1 American Indian or Alaska Native, non-Hispanic/Latino; 37 Asian, non-Hispanic/Latino; 27 Hispanic/Latino; 1 Native Hawaiian or other Pacific Islander, non-Hispanic/Latino; 12 Two or more races, non-Hispanic/Latino), 2 international. Average age 36. 656 applicants, 100% accepted, 461 enrolled. *Degree requirements:* For master's, thesis or alternative, capstone course. *Application deadline:* Applications are processed on a rolling basis. Application fee: $50. Electronic applications accepted. *Financial support:* Federal Work-Study and scholarships/grants available. Support available to part-time students. Financial award application deadline: 6/1; financial award applicants required to submit FAFSA. *Unit head:* Dr. Moses Garuba, Vice Provost and Dean of Graduate Studies, 240-684-2400, Fax: 240-684-2401. *Application contact:* Coordinator, Graduate Admissions, 800-888-8682, Fax: 240-684-2151, E-mail: newgrad@umuc.edu.

University of Maryland University College, Graduate School of Management and Technology, Program in Cybersecurity Policy, Adelphi, MD 20783. Offers MS. Part-time and evening/weekend programs available. Postbaccalaureate distance learning degree programs offered (no on-campus study). *Students:* 87 part-time (27 women); includes 29 minority (20 Black or African American, non-Hispanic/Latino; 3 Asian, non-Hispanic/Latino; 4 Hispanic/Latino; 2 Two or more races, non-Hispanic/Latino), 1 international. Average age 39. 64 applicants, 100% accepted. *Degree requirements:* For master's, thesis or alternative, capstone course. *Application deadline:* Applications are processed on a rolling basis. Application fee: $50. Electronic applications accepted. *Financial support:* Federal Work-Study and scholarships/grants available. Support available to part-time students. Financial award application deadline: 6/1; financial award applicants required to submit FAFSA. *Unit head:* Dr. Clay Wilson, Director, 240-684-2400, Fax: 240-684-2401. *Application contact:* Coordinator, Graduate Admissions, 800-888-UMUC, Fax: 240-684-2151, E-mail: newgrad@umuc.edu.

University of Minnesota, Twin Cities Campus, Institute of Technology, Technological Leadership Institute, Program in Security Technologies, Minneapolis, MN 55455-0213. Offers MSST. Part-time programs available. *Degree requirements:* For master's, capstone project. *Entrance requirements:* Additional exam requirements/recommendations for international students: Required—TOEFL (minimum score 580 paper-based; 240 computer-based; 90 iBT). Electronic applications accepted.

University of New Haven, Graduate School, Henry C. Lee College of Criminal Justice and Forensic Sciences, National Security and Public Safety Program, West Haven, CT 06516-1916. Offers information protection and security (MS); national security (Certificate); national security administration (Certificate). Part-time and evening/weekend programs available. *Students:* 36 full-time (15 women), 38 part-time (17 women); includes 7 Black or African American, non-Hispanic/Latino; 2 American Indian or Alaska Native, non-Hispanic/Latino; 2 Asian, non-Hispanic/Latino; 10 Hispanic/Latino, 6 international. Average age 32. 27 applicants, 96% accepted, 19 enrolled. In 2010, 28 master's awarded. *Entrance requirements:* Additional exam requirements/recommendations for international students: Required—TOEFL (minimum score 520 paper-based; 190 computer-based; 70 iBT); Recommended—IELTS (minimum score 5.5). *Application deadline:* For fall admission, 5/31 for international students; for winter admission, 10/15 for international students; for spring admission, 1/15 for international students. Applications are processed on a rolling basis. Application fee: $50. Electronic applications accepted. *Financial support:* Research assistantships with partial tuition reimbursements, teaching assistantships with partial tuition reimbursements, career-related internships or fieldwork, Federal Work-Study, scholarships/grants, tuition waivers, and unspecified assistantships available. Support available to part-time students. Financial award applicants required to submit FAFSA. *Unit head:* Dr. William L. Tafoya, Dean, 203-932-7260. *Application contact:* Eloise Gormley, Director of Graduate Admissions, 203-932-7449, Fax: 203-932-7137, E-mail: gradinfo@newhaven.edu.

University of New Mexico, Robert O. Anderson Graduate School of Management, Department of Marketing, Information and Decision Sciences, Albuquerque, NM 87131. Offers information assurance (MBA); management information systems (MBA); marketing management (MBA); operations management (MBA). Part-time and evening/weekend programs available. *Entrance requirements:* For master's, GMAT or GRE (can be waived in some instances). Additional exam requirements/recommendations for international students: Required—TOEFL (minimum score 550 paper-based; 213 computer-based; 79 iBT). Electronic applications accepted. *Expenses:* Tuition, state resident: full-time $5991; part-time $251 per credit hour. Tuition, nonresident: full-time $14,405; part-time $800.20 per credit hour. Tuition and fees vary according to course level, course load, program and reciprocity agreements. *Faculty research:* Marketing, operations, information science.

The University of North Carolina at Charlotte, Graduate School, College of Computing and Informatics, Department of Information Technology, Charlotte, NC 28223-0001. Offers game design and development (Certificate); health care information (Certificate); information security/privacy (Certificate); information technology (MS, PhD, Certificate). Part-time programs available. *Faculty:* 15 full-time (3 women), 4 part-time/adjunct (0 women). *Students:* 143 full-time (42 women), 76 part-time (27 women); includes 37 minority (24 Black or African American, non-Hispanic/Latino; 1 American Indian or Alaska Native, non-Hispanic/Latino; 4 Asian, non-Hispanic/Latino; 7 Hispanic/Latino; 1 Two or more races, non-Hispanic/Latino), 93 international. Average age 29. 68 applicants, 94% accepted, 22 enrolled. In 2010, 37 master's, 19 doctorates awarded. Terminal master's awarded for partial completion of doctoral program. *Degree requirements:* For master's, thesis optional; for doctorate, comprehensive exam, thesis/dissertation. *Entrance requirements:* For master's, GRE or GMAT, minimum undergraduate GPA of 2.8 overall, 2.0 in last 2 years; for doctorate, GRE or GMAT, working knowledge of 2 high-level programming languages. Additional exam requirements/recommendations for international students: Required—TOEFL (minimum score 557 paper-based; 220 computer-based; 83 iBT). *Application deadline:* For fall admission, 7/1 for domestic students, 5/1 for international students; for spring admission, 11/1 for domestic students, 10/1 for international students. Applications are processed on a rolling basis. Application fee: $55. Electronic applications accepted. *Expenses:* Tuition, state resident: full-time $3464. Tuition, nonresident: full-time $14,297. Required fees: $2094. Tuition and fees vary according to course load. *Financial support:* In 2010–11, 24 students received support, including 2 fellowships (averaging $50,000 per year), 12 research assistantships (averaging $12,719 per year), 10 teaching assistantships (averaging $13,800 per year); career-related internships or fieldwork, institutionally sponsored loans, scholarships/grants, and unspecified assistantships also available. Support available to part-time students. Financial award application deadline: 4/1; financial award applicants required to submit FAFSA. *Faculty research:* Information security, information privacy, information assurance, cryptography, software engineering, enterprise integration, intelligent information systems, human computer interaction. Total annual research expenditures: $2.7 million. *Unit head:* Dr. Ken Chen, Program Director, 704-687-8545, Fax: 704-687-6065, E-mail: chen@uncc.edu. *Application contact:* Kathy B. Giddings, Director of Graduate Admissions, 704-687-5503, Fax: 704-687-3279, E-mail: gradadm@uncc.edu.

University of St. Thomas, Graduate Studies, Graduate Programs in Software, Saint Paul, MN 55105. Offers advanced studies in software engineering (Certificate); business analysis (Certificate); computer security (Certificate); information systems (Certificate); software design and development (Certificate); software engineering (MS); software management (MS); software systems (MSS); MS/MBA. Part-time and evening/weekend programs available. *Faculty:* 5 full-time (0 women), 16 part-time/adjunct (1 woman). *Students:* 26 full-time (9 women), 297 part-time (75 women); includes 31 Black or African American, non-Hispanic/Latino; 52 Asian, non-Hispanic/Latino; 6 Hispanic/Latino; 2 Two or more races, non-Hispanic/Latino, 69 international. Average age 34. 106 applicants, 96% accepted, 67 enrolled. In 2010, 40 master's, 4 other advanced degrees awarded. *Degree requirements:* For master's, thesis optional. *Entrance requirements:* For master's, Bachelor degree earned in US or equivalent earned international degree. Additional exam requirements/recommendations for international students: Required—TOEFL (minimum score 80 iBT). *Application deadline:* For fall admission, 8/1 priority date for domestic students, 5/1 priority date for international students; for spring admission, 1/1 priority date for domestic students, 10/1 priority date for international students. Applications are processed on a rolling basis. Application fee: $30. *Expenses:* Contact institution. *Financial support:* Federal Work-Study, institutionally sponsored loans, and scholarships/grants available. Financial award application deadline: 4/1. *Faculty research:* Data mining, distributed databases, computer security. *Unit head:* Dr. Bhabani Misra, Director, 651-962-5508, Fax: 651-962-5543, E-mail: bsmisra@stthomas.edu. *Application contact:* Douglas J. Stubeda, Assistant Director, 651-962-5503, Fax: 651-962-5543, E-mail: djstubeda@stthomas.edu.

University of Southern California, Graduate School, Viterbi School of Engineering, Department of Computer Science, Los Angeles, CA 90089. Offers computer networks (MS); computer science (MS, PhD); computer security (MS); game development (MS); high performance computing and simulations (MS); human language technology (MS); intelligent robotics (MS); multimedia and creative technologies (MS); software engineering (MS). Part-time and evening/weekend programs available. Postbaccalaureate distance learning degree programs offered (no on-campus study). *Faculty:* 28 full-time (3 women), 56 part-time/adjunct (7 women). *Students:* 710 full-time (115 women), 302 part-time (59 women); includes 76 minority (1 Black or African American, non-Hispanic/Latino; 55 Asian, non-Hispanic/Latino; 14 Hispanic/Latino; 6 Two or more races, non-Hispanic/Latino), 819 international. 2,379 applicants, 30% accepted, 319 enrolled. In 2010, 332 master's, 32 doctorates awarded. *Entrance requirements:* For master's and doctorate, GRE General Test. Additional exam requirements/recommendations for international students: Required—TOEFL. *Application deadline:* For fall admission, 12/1 priority date for domestic and international students; for spring admission, 9/15 priority date for domestic and international students. Applications are processed on a rolling basis. Application fee: $85. Electronic applications accepted. *Expenses:* Tuition: Full-time $31,240; part-time $1420 per unit. Required fees: $600. One-time fee: $35 full-time. Full-time tuition and fees vary according to degree level and program. *Financial support:* In 2010–11, fellowships with full tuition reimbursements (averaging $30,000 per year), research assistantships with full tuition reimbursements (averaging $20,000 per year), teaching assistantships with full tuition reimburse-

Computer and Information Systems Security

University of Southern California (continued)

ments (averaging $20,000 per year) were awarded; career-related internships or fieldwork, scholarships/grants, health care benefits, and unspecified assistantships also available. Financial award application deadline: 12/1; financial award applicants required to submit CSS PROFILE or FAFSA. *Faculty research:* Databases, computer graphics and computer vision, software engineering, networks and security, robotics, multimedia and virtual reality. Total annual research expenditures: $11.8 million. *Unit head:* Dr. Shanghua Teng, Chair, 213-740-4494, E-mail: csdept@usc.edu. *Application contact:* Lizsl DeLeon, Director of Student Affairs, 213-740-4496, E-mail: ldeleon@usc.edu.

The University of Texas at Dallas, School of Management, Program in Information Systems and Operations Management, Richardson, TX 75080. Offers information technology management (MS), including enterprise systems, health care systems, information security. Part-time and evening/weekend programs available. *Faculty:* 20 full-time (1 woman), 4 part-time/adjunct (1 woman). *Students:* 171 full-time (59 women), 109 part-time (37 women); includes 28 minority (2 Black or African American, non-Hispanic/Latino; 20 Asian, non-Hispanic/Latino; 6 Hispanic/Latino), 214 international. Average age 27. 404 applicants, 68% accepted, 103 enrolled. In 2010, 92 master's awarded. *Degree requirements:* For master's, thesis optional. *Entrance requirements:* For master's, GMAT. Additional exam requirements/recommendations for international students: Required—TOEFL (minimum score 550 paper-based; 215 computer-based). *Application deadline:* For fall admission, 7/15 for domestic students, 5/1 priority date for international students; for spring admission, 11/15 for domestic students, 9/1 priority date for international students. Applications are processed on a rolling basis. Application fee: $50 ($100 for international students). Electronic applications accepted. *Expenses:* Tuition, state resident: full-time $10,248; part-time $569 per credit hour. Tuition, nonresident: full-time $18,544; part-time $1030 per credit hour. Tuition and fees vary according to course load. *Financial support:* In 2010–11, 71 students received support, including 2 research assistantships with partial tuition reimbursements available (averaging $10,800 per year), 10 teaching assistantships with partial tuition reimbursements available (averaging $10,125 per year); career-related internships or fieldwork, Federal Work-Study, institutionally sponsored loans, scholarships/grants, and unspecified assistantships also available. Support available to part-time students. Financial award application deadline: 4/30; financial award applicants required to submit FAFSA. *Faculty research:* Technology marketing, measuring information work productivity, electronic commerce, decision support systems, data quality. *Unit head:* Dr. Mark Thouin, Director, 972-883-4011, E-mail: mark.thouin@utdallas.edu. *Application contact:* James Parker, Assistant Director, 972-883-5842, E-mail: jparker@utdallas.edu.

The University of Texas at San Antonio, College of Business, Department of Information Systems and Technology Management, San Antonio, TX 78249-0617. Offers information technology (MSIT); management technology (MSMOT), including information assurance. *Faculty:* 10 full-time (3 women), 1 part-time/adjunct (0 women). *Students:* 23 full-time (1 woman), 71 part-time (20 women); includes 33 minority (3 Black or African American, non-Hispanic/Latino; 3 Asian, non-Hispanic/Latino; 23 Hispanic/Latino; 1 Native Hawaiian or other Pacific Islander, non-Hispanic/Latino; 3 Two or more races, non-Hispanic/Latino), 7 international. Average age 32. 51 applicants, 61% accepted, 22 enrolled. In 2010, 48 master's awarded. *Degree requirements:* For master's, comprehensive exam (for some programs), thesis (for some programs). *Entrance requirements:* For master's, GMAT, minimum GPA of 3.0. Additional exam requirements/recommendations for international students: Required—TOEFL (minimum score 500 paper-based; 173 computer-based; 61 iBT), IELTS (minimum score 5). *Application deadline:* For fall admission, 7/1 for domestic students, 4/1 for international students; for spring admission, 11/1 for domestic students, 9/1 for international students. Applications are processed on a rolling basis. Application fee: $45 ($80 for international students). Electronic applications accepted. *Expenses:* Tuition, state resident: full-time $4172; part-time $231.75 per credit hour. Tuition, nonresident: full-time $15,332; part-time $851.75 per credit hour. *Financial support:* In 2010–11, 7 students received support, including 7 research assistantships (averaging $10,400 per year), 8 teaching assistantships (averaging $7,800 per year); scholarships/grants, tuition waivers (partial), and unspecified assistantships also available. Support available to part-time students. *Faculty research:* Infrastructure assurance, digital forensics, management of technology, e-commerce, technology transfer. Total annual research expenditures: $162,886. *Unit head:* Dr. Glenn Dietrich, PhD, Chair, 210-458-5354, Fax: 210-458-6305, E-mail: gdietrich@utsa.edu. *Application contact:* Veronica Ramirez, Assistant Dean of the Graduate School, 210-458-4330, Fax: 210-458-4332, E-mail: graduatestudies@utsa.edu.

The University of Texas at San Antonio, College of Sciences, Department of Computer Science, San Antonio, TX 78249-0617. Offers computer and information security (MS); computer science (MS, PhD); software engineering (MS). Part-time programs available. *Faculty:* 20 full-time (4 women), 2 part-time/adjunct (0 women). *Students:* 95 full-time (18 women), 49 part-time (9 women); includes 16 minority (2 Black or African American, non-Hispanic/Latino; 2 Asian, non-Hispanic/Latino; 11 Hispanic/Latino; 1 Two or more races, non-Hispanic/Latino), 89 international. Average age 28. 198 applicants, 58% accepted, 42 enrolled. In 2010, 10 master's, 4 doctorates awarded. *Degree requirements:* For master's, comprehensive exam, thesis (for some programs); for doctorate, comprehensive exam, thesis/dissertation. *Entrance requirements:* For master's, GRE General Test, minimum GPA of 3.0 in last 60 hours; for doctorate, GRE General Test, minimum GPA of 3.0. Additional exam requirements/recommendations for international students: Required—TOEFL (minimum score 500 paper-based; 173 computer-based; 61 iBT), IELTS (minimum score 5). *Application deadline:* For fall admission, 7/1 for domestic students, 4/1 for international students; for spring admission, 11/1 for domestic students, 9/1 for international students. Applications are processed on a rolling basis. Application fee: $45 ($80 for international students). Electronic applications accepted. *Expenses:* Tuition, state resident: full-time $4172; part-time $231.75 per credit hour. Tuition, nonresident: full-time $15,332; part-time $851.75 per credit hour. *Financial support:* In 2010–11, 69 students received support, including 6 fellowships (averaging $41,302 per year), 30 research assistantships (averaging $17,975 per year), 37 teaching assistantships (averaging $13,946 per year); career-related internships or fieldwork, scholarships/grants, tuition waivers, and unspecified assistantships also available. Support available to part-time students. *Faculty research:* Computer and information security, high performance computing, bioinformatics and computational biology, programming languages and compilers. Total annual research expenditures: $1.4 million. *Unit head:* Dr. Kleanthis Psarris, Department Chair, 210-458-4436, Fax: 210-458-4437, E-mail: kleanthis.psarris@utsa.edu. *Application contact:* Veronica Ramirez, Assistant Dean of the Graduate School, 210-458-4330, Fax: 210-458-4332, E-mail: graduatestudies@utsa.edu.

University of Wisconsin–Madison, Graduate School, Wisconsin School of Business, Wisconsin Full-Time MBA Program, Madison, WI 53706-1380. Offers applied security analysis (MBA); arts administration (MBA); brand and product management (MBA); corporate finance and investment banking (MBA); entrepreneurial management (MBA); marketing research (MBA); operations and technology management (MBA); real estate (MBA); risk management and insurance (MBA); strategic human resource management (MBA); strategic management in the life and engineering sciences (MBA); supply chain management (MBA). *Faculty:* 32 full-time (4 women), 17 part-time/adjunct (3 women). *Students:* 242 full-time (74 women); includes 16 Black or African American, non-Hispanic/Latino; 3 American Indian or Alaska Native, non-Hispanic/Latino; 16 Asian, non-Hispanic/Latino; 12 Hispanic/Latino, 29 international. Average age 28. 526 applicants, 32% accepted, 117 enrolled. In 2010, 106 master's awarded. *Entrance requirements:* For master's, GMAT, bachelor's or equivalent degree, 2 years of work experience, letters of recommendation. Additional exam requirements/recommendations for international students: Required—TOEFL (minimum score 600 paper-based; 250 computer-based; 100 iBT), IELTS. *Application deadline:* For fall admission, 11/4 for domestic students, 11/1 for international students; for winter admission, 2/5 for domestic and international students; for spring admission, 5/15 for domestic students, 4/5 for international students. Applications are processed on a rolling basis. Application fee: $56. Electronic applications accepted. *Expenses:* Tuition, state resident: full-time $9887.36; part-time $617.96 per credit. Tuition, nonresident: full-time $24,054; part-time $1503.40 per credit. Required fees: $67.63 per credit. Tuition and fees vary according to reciprocity agreements. *Financial support:* In 2010–11, 103 students received support, including 13 fellowships with full and partial tuition reimbursements available (averaging $15,000 per year), 53 research assistantships with full tuition reimbursements available (averaging $8,000 per year), 35 teaching assistantships with full tuition reimbursements available (averaging $11,000 per year); scholarships/grants, health care benefits, and unspecified assistantships also available. Financial award application deadline: 4/5; financial award applicants required to submit FAFSA. *Faculty research:* Market consequences of International Financial Reporting Standards (IFRS), inter-firm relationships and strategic partnerships, application of Bayesian statistical methods and applied probability models to understanding individuals' behaviors in the context of customer relationship management (CRM) applications, liquidity provision and the structure of financial markets, strategic management of global startups. *Unit head:* Prof. Kenneth A. Kavajecz, PhD, Associate Dean of Master's Programs, 608-265-3494, Fax: 608-265-4192, E-mail: kkavajecz@bus.wisc.edu. *Application contact:* Maria Reis, Assistant Director of MBA Marketing and Recruiting, 608-262-4000, Fax: 608-265-4192, E-mail: mreis@bus.wisc.edu.

Utica College, Program in Cybersecurity, Utica, NY 13502-4892. Offers MS. Part-time and evening/weekend programs available. Postbaccalaureate distance learning degree programs offered. *Students:* 58 part-time (19 women); includes 9 minority (4 Black or African American, non-Hispanic/Latino; 1 Asian, non-Hispanic/Latino; 4 Hispanic/Latino), 1 international. Average age 33. *Application deadline:* Applications are processed on a rolling basis. Electronic applications accepted. *Expenses:* Tuition: Full-time $26,100; part-time $700 per credit hour. Required fees: $400; $60 per course. Tuition and fees vary according to course load, degree level and program. *Financial support:* Applicants required to submit FAFSA. *Unit head:* Joseph Giordano, Chair, 315-792-2521. *Application contact:* John D. Rowe, Director of Graduate Admissions, 315-792-3824, Fax: 315-792-3003, E-mail: jrowe@utica.edu.

Virginia Polytechnic Institute and State University, Graduate School, College of Engineering, Department of Computer Science & Applications, Blacksburg, VA 24061. Offers computer science and applications (MS); human-computer interactions (Certificate); information assurance engineering (Certificate). *Faculty:* 42 full-time (7 women). *Students:* 186 full-time (45 women), 44 part-time (9 women); includes 6 Black or African American, non-Hispanic/Latino; 10 Asian, non-Hispanic/Latino; 6 Hispanic/Latino, 149 international. Average age 29. 784 applicants, 12% accepted, 34 enrolled. In 2010, 56 master's, 12 doctorates awarded. *Degree requirements:* For master's, comprehensive exam (for some programs), thesis (for some programs); for doctorate, comprehensive exam (for some programs), thesis/dissertation (for some programs). *Entrance requirements:* For master's and doctorate, GRE. Additional exam requirements/recommendations for international students: Required—TOEFL (minimum score 550 paper-based; 213 computer-based). *Application deadline:* For fall admission, 7/1 for domestic and international students; for spring admission, 12/1 for domestic and international students. Applications are processed on a rolling basis. Application fee: $65. Electronic applications accepted. *Expenses:* Tuition, area resident: Full-time $9399; part-time $488 per credit hour. Tuition, state resident: full-time $9399; part-time $488 per credit hour. Tuition, nonresident: full-time $17,854; part-time $957.75 per credit hour. International tuition: $17,854 full-time. Required fees: $1534. Full-time tuition and fees vary according to program. *Financial support:* In 2010–11, 39 research assistantships with full tuition reimbursements (averaging $18,060 per year), 18 teaching assistantships with full tuition reimbursements (averaging $17,706 per year) were awarded; career-related internships or fieldwork, Federal Work-Study, scholarships/grants, health care benefits, and unspecified assistantships also available. Financial award application deadline: 1/15. *Faculty research:* Bioinformatics, human-computer interaction, problem-solving environments, high performance computing, software engineering. Total annual research expenditures: $4.5 million. *Unit head:* Dr. Barbara G. Ryder, UNIT HEAD, 540-231-6931, Fax: 540-231-6075, E-mail: ryder@vt.edu. *Application contact:* Naren Ramakrishnan, Contact, 540-231-8451, Fax: 540-231-6075, E-mail: naren@vt.edu.

Virginia Polytechnic Institute and State University, VT Online, Blacksburg, VA 24061. Offers aerospace engineering (MS); business information systems (Graduate Certificate); career and technical education (MS); computer engineering (M Eng, MS); decision support systems (Graduate Certificate); eLearning leadership (MA); electrical engineering (M Eng, MS); engineering administration (MEA); environmental politics and policy (Graduate Certificate); foundations of political analysis (Graduate Certificate); health product risk management (Graduate Certificate); information policy and society (Graduate Certificate); information security (Graduate Certificate); instructional technology (MA); liberal arts (Graduate Certificate); life sciences: health product risk management (MS); natural resources (MNR, Graduate Certificate); networking (Graduate Certificate); nonprofit and nongovernmental organization management (Graduate Certificate); ocean engineering (MS); political science (MA); security studies (Graduate Certificate); software development (Graduate Certificate). *Expenses:* Tuition, area resident: Full-time $9399; part-time $488 per credit hour. Tuition, state resident: full-time $9399; part-time $488 per credit hour. Tuition, nonresident: full-time $17,854; part-time $957.75 per credit hour. International tuition: $17,854 full-time. Required fees: $1534. Full-time tuition and fees vary according to program.

Walden University, Graduate Programs, School of Management, Minneapolis, MN 55401. Offers accounting (MS), including cpa emphasis, professional track, self-designed; accounting and management (MS), including self-designed, strategic management; applied management and decision sciences (PhD), including accounting, engineering management, finance, general applied management and decision sciences, information systems management, knowledge management, leadership and organizational change, learning management, operations research, self-designed program in applied management and design sciences; business information management (MISM); enterprise information security (MISM); entrepreneurship (MBA, DBA); finance (MBA, DBA); global management (MS); global supply chain management (DBA); health informatics (MISM); healthcare management (MBA, MS); healthcare system improvement (MBA); human resource management (MBA, MS), including functional human resource management (MS), human resource management (MS), integrating functional and strategic human resource management (MS), organizational strategy (MS); information systems (MS); information systems management (DBA); information technology (MS), including information security, software engineering; international business (MBA, DBA); IT strategy and governance (MISM); leadership (MBA, MS, DBA), including entrepreneurship (MS), general management (MS), human resources leadership (MS), innovation and technology (MS), leader development (MS), leading sustainability (MS), project management (MS), self-designed (MS); managers as leaders (MS); managing global software and service supply chains (MISM); marketing (MBA, DBA); project management (MBA, MS); research strategies (MS); risk management (MBA); self-designed (MBA, DBA); social impact management (DBA); strategy and operations (MS); sustainable futures (MBA); sustainable management (MS); technology (MBA); technology entrepreneurship (DBA); technology management (MS). Part-time and evening/weekend programs available. Postbaccalaureate distance learning degree programs offered (minimal on-campus study). *Faculty:* 22 full-time (8 women), 291 part-time/adjunct (100 women). *Students:* 3,705 full-time (1,956 women), 976 part-time (549 women); includes 2,432 minority (2,021 Black or African American, non-Hispanic/Latino; 32 American Indian or Alaska Native, non-Hispanic/Latino; 137 Asian, non-Hispanic/Latino; 193 Hispanic/Latino; 5 Native Hawaiian or other Pacific Islander, non-Hispanic/Latino; 44 Two or more races, non-Hispanic/Latino), 302 international. Average age 40. In 2010, 658 master's, 86 doctorates awarded. *Degree requirements:* For doctorate, thesis/dissertation (for some programs), residency. *Entrance requirements:* For master's, bachelor's degree or equivalent in related field; minimum GPA of 2.5; official transcripts; goal statement; access to computer and Internet; for doctorate, master's degree or equivalent in related field; minimum GPA of 3.0; 3 years of related professional/academic experience (preferred). Additional exam requirements/recommendations for international students: Required—TOEFL (minimum score 550 paper-based; 213 computer-based), IELTS (minimum score 6.5), TOEFL, IELTS, or Michigan English Language Assessment Battery (minimum score 82). *Application deadline:* Applications are processed on a rolling basis. Application fee: $50. Electronic applications accepted. *Expenses:* Tuition: Full-time $10,274; part-time $445 per credit. Tuition and fees vary according to course load, degree level and program. *Financial support:* Fellowships, Federal Work-Study, scholarships/grants, unspecified assistantships, and family tuition reduction, active duty/veteran tuition reduction, group tuition reduction, interest-free payment plans available. Support available to part-time students. Financial award applicants required to submit FAFSA. *Unit head:* Dr. William Schulz, Associate Dean, 800-925-3368. *Application contact:* Jennifer Hall, Vice President of Enrollment Management, 866-4-WALDEN, E-mail: info@waldenu.edu.

West Chester University of Pennsylvania, Office of Graduate Studies, College of Arts and Sciences, Department of Computer Science, West Chester, PA 19383. Offers computer science (MS); computer security (Certificate); information systems (Certificate); Web technology (Certificate). Part-time and evening/weekend programs available. *Students:* 10 full-time (1 woman), 9 part-time (1 woman); includes 2 minority (1 Black or African American, non-Hispanic/Latino; 1 Hispanic/Latino), 6 international. Average age 29. 23 applicants, 57% accepted, 5 enrolled. In 2010, 11 master's, 1 other advanced degree awarded. *Degree requirements:* For master's, thesis optional. *Entrance requirements:* For master's, GRE, two letters of recommendation; for Certificate, BS. Additional exam requirements/recommendations for international students: Required—TOEFL (minimum score 550 paper-based; 213 computer-based; 80 iBT). *Application deadline:* For fall admission, 4/15 priority date for domestic students, 3/15 for international students; for spring admission, 10/15 for domestic students, 9/1 for international students. Applications are processed on a rolling basis. Application fee: $35. Electronic applications accepted. *Expenses:* Tuition, state resident: full-time $6966; part-time $387 per

credit. Tuition, nonresident: full-time $11,146; part-time $619 per credit. Required fees: $1614.40; $133.24 per credit. Part-time tuition and fees vary according to campus/location. *Financial support:* Unspecified assistantships available. Support available to part-time students. Financial award application deadline: 2/15; financial award applicants required to submit FAFSA. *Faculty research:* Automata theory, compilers, non well-founded sets, security in sensor and mobile ad-hoc networks, intrusion detection, security and trust in pervasive computing, economic modeling of security protocols. *Unit head:* Dr. James Fabrey, Chair, 610-436-2204, E-mail: jfabrey@wcupa.edu. *Application contact:* Dr. Afrand Agah, Graduate Coordinator, 610-436-4419, E-mail: aagah@wcupa.edu.

Western Governors University, Program in Information Security and Assurance, Salt Lake City, UT 84107. Offers MS. Postbaccalaureate distance learning degree programs offered. *Degree requirements:* For master's, capstone project.

Wilmington University, College of Technology, New Castle, DE 19720-6491. Offers corporate training (MS); information assurance (MS); information systems technologies (MS); Internet web design (MS); management information systems (MS). Part-time and evening/weekend programs available. *Entrance requirements:* Additional exam requirements/recommendations for international students: Required—TOEFL (minimum score 500 paper-based; 173 computer-based). Electronic applications accepted. *Expenses:* Tuition: Full-time $7110; part-time $395 per credit hour. Tuition and fees vary according to campus/location.

Computer Science

Acadia University, Faculty of Pure and Applied Science, Jodrey School of Computer Science, Wolfville, NS B4P 2R6, Canada. Offers M Sc. *Faculty:* 6 full-time (0 women), 5 part-time/adjunct (0 women). *Students:* 9 full-time (1 woman), 6 part-time (0 women). Average age 28. 40 applicants, 48% accepted, 11 enrolled. In 2010, 5 master's awarded. *Degree requirements:* For master's, thesis. *Entrance requirements:* For master's, honors degree in computer science. Additional exam requirements/recommendations for international students: Required—TOEFL (minimum score 580 paper-based; 237 computer-based; 93 iBT), IELTS (minimum score 6.5). *Application deadline:* For fall admission, 2/1 priority date for domestic and international students. Applications are processed on a rolling basis. Application fee: $50. *Financial support:* Research assistantships, teaching assistantships, career-related internships or fieldwork, scholarships/grants, and unspecified assistantships available. Financial award application deadline: 2/1. *Faculty research:* Visual and object-oriented programming, concurrency, artificial intelligence, hypertext and multimedia, algorithm analysis, xml. *Unit head:* Dr. Daniel L. Silver, Director, 902-585-1331, Fax: 902-585-1067, E-mail: cs@acadiau.ca. *Application contact:* Dr. Andre Trudel, Graduate Coordinator, 902-585-1136, E-mail: andre.trudel@acadiau.ca.

Air Force Institute of Technology, Graduate School of Engineering and Management, Department of Electrical and Computer Engineering, Dayton, OH 45433-7765. Offers computer engineering (MS, PhD); computer systems/science (MS); electrical engineering (MS, PhD); electro-optics (MS, PhD). *Accreditation:* ABET (one or more programs are accredited). Part-time programs available. *Degree requirements:* For master's, thesis; for doctorate, thesis/dissertation. *Entrance requirements:* For master's and doctorate, GRE General Test, minimum GPA of 3.0, U.S. citizenship. *Faculty research:* Remote sensing, information survivability, microelectronics, computer networks, artificial intelligence.

Alabama Agricultural and Mechanical University, School of Graduate Studies, School of Engineering and Technology, Department of Computer Science, Huntsville, AL 35811. Offers MS. Evening/weekend programs available. *Degree requirements:* For master's, comprehensive exam, thesis optional. *Entrance requirements:* For master's, GRE General Test. Additional exam requirements/recommendations for international students: Required—TOEFL (minimum score 500 paper-based; 173 computer-based; 61 iBT). Electronic applications accepted. *Faculty research:* Computer-assisted instruction, database management, software engineering, operating systems, neural networks.

Alcorn State University, School of Graduate Studies, School of Arts and Sciences, Department of Mathematical Sciences, Alcorn State, MS 39096-7500. Offers computer and information sciences (MS).

American Sentinel University, Graduate Programs, Aurora, CO 80014. Offers business administration (MBA); business intelligence (MS); computer science (MSCS); health information management (MS); healthcare (MBA); information systems (MSIS); nursing (MSN). Part-time and evening/weekend programs available. Postbaccalaureate distance learning degree programs offered (no on-campus study). *Entrance requirements:* Additional exam requirements/recommendations for international students: Required—TOEFL (minimum score 600 paper-based; 215 computer-based). Electronic applications accepted.

American University, College of Arts and Sciences, Program in Computer Science, Washington, DC 20016-8058. Offers MS, Certificate. Part-time and evening/weekend programs available. *Degree requirements:* For master's, comprehensive exam, thesis or alternative. *Entrance requirements:* For master's, GRE, minimum GPA of 3.0; for Certificate, bachelor's degree. Additional exam requirements/recommendations for international students: Required—TOEFL. *Faculty research:* Artificial intelligence, database systems, software engineering, expert systems.

The American University in Cairo, School of Sciences and Engineering, Department of Computer Science and Engineering, Cairo, Egypt. Offers M Comp. *Degree requirements:* For master's, thesis. *Entrance requirements:* Additional exam requirements/recommendations for international students: Required—English entrance exam and/or TOEFL. *Faculty research:* Software engineering, artificial intelligence, robotics, data and knowledge bases.

The American University of Athens, School of Graduate Studies, Athens, Greece. Offers biomedical sciences (MS); business (MBA); business communication (MA); computer sciences (MS); engineering and applied sciences (MS); politics and policy making (MA); systems engineering (MS); telecommunications (MS). *Entrance requirements:* For master's, resume, 2 recommendation letters. Additional exam requirements/recommendations for international students: Required—TOEFL (minimum score 550 paper-based; 213 computer-based). *Faculty research:* Nanotechnology, environmental sciences, rock mechanics, human skin studies, Monte Carlo algorithms and software.

American University of Beirut, Graduate Programs, Faculty of Arts and Sciences, Beirut, Lebanon. Offers anthropology (MA); Arabic language and literature (MA); archaeology (MA); biology (MS); chemistry (MS); computational science (MS); computer science (MS); economics (MA); education (MA); English language (MA); English literature (MA); environmental policy planning (MSES); financial economics (MAFE); geology (MS); history (MA); mathematics (MA, MS); Middle Eastern studies (MA); philosophy (MA); physics (MS); political studies (MA); psychology (MA); public administration (MA); sociology (MA); statistics (MA, MS). Part-time programs available. *Faculty:* 229 full-time (98 women), 136 part-time/adjunct (79 women). *Students:* 158 full-time (104 women), 263 part-time (171 women). Average age 25. 356 applicants, 59% accepted, 127 enrolled. In 2010, 57 master's awarded. *Degree requirements:* For master's, one foreign language, comprehensive exam, thesis (for some programs). *Entrance requirements:* For master's, GRE, letter of recommendation. Additional exam requirements/recommendations for international students: Required—TOEFL (minimum score 600 paper-based; 250 computer-based; 97 iBT), IELTS (minimum score 7). *Application deadline:* For fall

admission, 4/30 for domestic and international students; for spring admission, 11/1 for domestic and international students. Application fee: $50. *Expenses:* Tuition: Full-time $12,294; part-time $683 per credit. Required fees: $499; $499 per credit. Tuition and fees vary according to course load and program. *Financial support:* In 2010–11, 33 students received support. Career-related internships or fieldwork, institutionally sponsored loans, scholarships/grants, health care benefits, and unspecified assistantships available. Financial award application deadline: 2/4; financial award applicants required to submit FAFSA. *Faculty research:* Modern and contemporary world theatre; mineralogy, petrology, and geochemistry; cell differentiation and transformation; combinatorial technologies; philosophy of action; continental philosophy; Phoenician epigraphy; nascent complex societies and urbanism; the economies of the Arab world; environmental economics; tectonophysics; host-parasite interactions; innate immunity; insect-plant interactions; history of the Ottoman archives; decentralization; transparency and corruption. Total annual research expenditures: $622,243. *Unit head:* Dr. Patrick McGreevy, Dean, 961-137-4374 Ext. 3800, Fax: 961-174-4461, E-mail: pm07@aub.edu.lb. *Application contact:* Dr. Salim Kanaan, Director, Admissions Office, 961-135-0000 Ext. 2594, Fax: 961-175-0775, E-mail: sk00@aub.edu.lb.

Appalachian State University, Cratis D. Williams Graduate School, Department of Computer Science, Boone, NC 28608. Offers MS. Part-time programs available. *Faculty:* 9 full-time (3 women). *Students:* 18 full-time (2 women), 1 part-time (0 women), 1 international. 9 applicants, 100% accepted, 7 enrolled. In 2010, 5 master's awarded. *Degree requirements:* For master's, comprehensive exam, thesis. *Entrance requirements:* For master's, GRE General Test, 3 letters of recommendation. Additional exam requirements/recommendations for international students: Required—TOEFL (minimum score 570 paper-based; 230 computer-based; 79 iBT), IELTS (minimum score 6.5). *Application deadline:* For fall admission, 7/1 priority date for domestic students, 2/1 for international students; for spring admission, 11/1 for domestic students, 7/1 for international students. Applications are processed on a rolling basis. Application fee: $55. Electronic applications accepted. *Expenses:* Tuition, state resident: full-time $3428; part-time $428 per unit. Tuition, nonresident: full-time $14,518; part-time $1814 per unit. Required fees: $2320; $344 per unit. Tuition and fees vary according to campus/location. *Financial support:* In 2010–11, 8 teaching assistantships (averaging $9,500 per year) were awarded; fellowships, research assistantships, Federal Work-Study, scholarships/grants, and unspecified assistantships also available. Financial award application deadline: 4/1; financial award applicants required to submit FAFSA. *Faculty research:* Graph theory, compilers, parallel architecture, image processing. *Unit head:* Dr. James Wilkes, Chairperson, 828-262-2612. *Application contact:* Dr. Jay Fenwick, Advisor, 828-262-3050, Fax: 828-265-8617, E-mail: fenwickjb@appstate.edu.

Arizona State University, College of Technology and Innovation, Department of Engineering, Mesa, AZ 85212. Offers computing studies (MCST); simulation, modeling, and applied cognitive science (PhD). Part-time programs available. *Faculty:* 30 full-time (8 women). *Students:* 33 full-time (9 women), 12 part-time (10 women); includes 7 minority (1 Black or African American, non-Hispanic/Latino; 4 Asian, non-Hispanic/Latino; 2 Hispanic/Latino), 29 international. Average age 26. 208 applicants, 97% accepted, 15 enrolled. In 2010, 8 master's awarded. *Degree requirements:* For master's, thesis or applied project with oral defense; interactive Program of Study (iPOS) submitted before completing 50 percent of required credit hours; for doctorate, comprehensive exam, thesis/dissertation, interactive Program of Study (iPOS) submitted before completing 50 percent of required credit hours. *Entrance requirements:* For master's, GRE, minimum GPA of 3.0 or equivalent in last 2 years of work leading to bachelor's degree; for doctorate, GRE, master's degree in psychology, engineering, cognitive science, or computer science; 3 letters of recommendation; statement of research interests. Additional exam requirements/recommendations for international students: Required—TOEFL, IELTS, or Pearson Test of English. *Application deadline:* For fall admission, 1/31 for domestic and international students; for spring admission, 9/30 for domestic students, 8/30 for international students. Application fee: $70 ($90 for international students). Electronic applications accepted. *Expenses:* Tuition, state resident: full-time $8510; part-time $608 per credit. Tuition, nonresident: full-time $16,542; part-time $919 per credit. Required fees: $339; $110 per credit. Part-time tuition and fees vary according to course load. *Financial support:* In 2010–11, 3 research assistantships with full and partial tuition reimbursements (averaging $14,832 per year), 1 teaching assistantship with full and partial tuition reimbursement (averaging $10,400 per year) were awarded; fellowships with full and partial tuition reimbursements, career-related internships or fieldwork, Federal Work-Study, scholarships/grants, health care benefits, tuition waivers (full and partial), and unspecified assistantships also available. Support available to part-time students. Financial award application deadline: 3/1; financial award applicants required to submit FAFSA. *Faculty research:* Software process and automated workflow, software architecture, dotal technologies, relational database systems, embedded systems. Total annual research expenditures: $595,649. *Unit head:* Dr. Chell Roberts, Executive Dean, Chair, 480-727-1353, Fax: 480-727-1089, E-mail: chell.roberts@asu.edu. *Application contact:* Graduate Admissions, 480-965-6113.

Arizona State University, Ira A. Fulton School of Engineering, School of Computing, Informatics, and Decision Systems Engineering, Tempe, AZ 85287-8809. Offers computer science (MCS, MS, PhD); industrial engineering (MS, PhD). Part-time and evening/weekend programs available. Postbaccalaureate distance learning degree programs offered (minimal on-campus study). *Faculty:* 58 full-time (14 women), 5 part-time/adjunct (2 women). *Students:* 365 full-time (76 women), 168 part-time (36 women); includes 60 minority (10 Black or African American, non-Hispanic/Latino; 1 American Indian or Alaska Native, non-Hispanic/Latino; 29 Asian, non-Hispanic/Latino; 18 Hispanic/Latino; 2 Two or more races, non-Hispanic/Latino), 352 international. Average age 28. 1,016 applicants, 53% accepted, 152 enrolled. In 2010, 138 master's, 22 doctorates awarded. Terminal master's awarded for partial completion of doctoral program. *Degree requirements:* For master's, comprehensive exam (for some programs), portfolio (MCS); interactive Program of Study (iPOS) submitted before completing 50 percent

Computer Science

Arizona State University (continued)
of required credit hours; for doctorate, comprehensive exam, thesis/dissertation, interactive Program of Study (iPOS) submitted before completing 50 percent of required credit hours. *Entrance requirements:* For master's, GRE, minimum GPA of 3.0 or equivalent in last 2 years of work leading to bachelor's degree; for doctorate, GRE, minimum GPA of 3.0 in last 2 years of work leading to bachelor's degree. Additional exam requirements/recommendations for international students: Required—TOEFL, IELTS, or Pearson Test of English. *Application deadline:* For fall admission, 12/1 for domestic and international students; for spring admission, 8/1 for domestic and international students. Application fee: $70 ($90 for international students). Electronic applications accepted. *Expenses:* Contact institution. *Financial support:* In 2010–11, 156 research assistantships with full and partial tuition reimbursements (averaging $13,688 per year), 41 teaching assistantships with full and partial tuition reimbursements (averaging $10,940 per year) were awarded; fellowships with full and partial tuition reimbursements, institutionally sponsored loans, scholarships/grants, and tuition waivers (full and partial) also available. Financial award application deadline: 3/1; financial award applicants required to submit FAFSA. *Faculty research:* Artificial intelligence, cyberphysical and embedded systems, health informatics, information assurance and security, information management/multimedia/visualization, network science, personalized learning/educational games, production logistics, software and systems engineering, and statistical modeling and data mining. Total annual research expenditures: $11.2 million. *Unit head:* Dr. Ronald Askin, Director, 480-965-2567, E-mail: ron.askin@asu.edu. *Application contact:* Graduate Admissions, 480-965-6113.

Arkansas State University, Graduate School, College of Sciences and Mathematics, Department of Computer Science, Jonesboro, State University, AR 72467. Offers MS. Part-time programs available. *Faculty:* 5 full-time (1 woman). *Students:* 37 full-time (8 women), 13 part-time (3 women); includes 2 minority (both Black or African American, non-Hispanic/Latino), 46 international. Average age 26. 56 applicants, 91% accepted, 23 enrolled. In 2010, 4 master's awarded. *Degree requirements:* For master's, comprehensive exam, thesis or alternative. *Entrance requirements:* For master's, GRE General Test or MAT, appropriate bachelor's degree, official transcripts, immunization records. Additional exam requirements/recommendations for international students: Required—TOEFL (minimum score 550 paper-based; 213 computer-based; 79 iBT), IELTS (minimum score 6), PTE: Pearson Test of English Academic (56). *Application deadline:* For fall admission, 7/1 for domestic and international students; for spring admission, 11/15 for domestic students, 11/14 for international students. Applications are processed on a rolling basis. Application fee: $30 ($40 for international students). Electronic applications accepted. *Expenses:* Tuition, state resident: full-time $3888; part-time $216 per credit hour. Tuition, nonresident: full-time $9918; part-time $551 per credit hour. International tuition: $8376 full-time. Required fees: $932; $49 per credit hour. $25 per term. One-time fee: $30. Tuition and fees vary according to course load and program. *Financial support:* In 2010–11, 18 students received support. Career-related internships or fieldwork, scholarships/grants, and unspecified assistantships available. Financial award application deadline: 7/1; financial award applicants required to submit FAFSA. *Unit head:* Dr. Edward Hammerand, Chair, 870-972-3978, Fax: 870-972-3950, E-mail: hammerand@astate.edu. *Application contact:* Dr. Andrew Sustich, Dean of the Graduate School, 870-972-3029, Fax: 870-972-3857, E-mail: sustich@astate.edu.

Armstrong Atlantic State University, School of Graduate Studies, Program in Computer Science, Savannah, GA 31419-1997. Offers MS. Part-time programs available. *Degree requirements:* For master's, project. *Entrance requirements:* For master's, GRE, minimum GPA of 2.7, letters of recommendation, BS in computer science. Additional exam requirements/recommendations for international students: Required—TOEFL (minimum score 523 paper-based; 193 computer-based). Electronic applications accepted.

Auburn University, Graduate School, Ginn College of Engineering, Department of Computer Science and Software Engineering, Auburn University, AL 36849. Offers MS, MSWE, PhD. Part-time programs available. *Faculty:* 19 full-time (3 women). *Students:* 58 full-time (15 women), 65 part-time (17 women); includes 16 Black or African American, non-Hispanic/Latino; 1 Asian, non-Hispanic/Latino; 2 Hispanic/Latino, 59 international. Average age 30. 214 applicants, 33% accepted, 19 enrolled. In 2010, 21 master's, 11 doctorates awarded. *Degree requirements:* For master's, thesis (for some programs); for doctorate, thesis/dissertation. *Entrance requirements:* For master's and doctorate, GRE General Test, GRE Subject Test. *Application deadline:* For fall admission, 7/7 for domestic students; for spring admission, 11/24 for domestic students. Applications are processed on a rolling basis. Application fee: $50 ($60 for international students). Electronic applications accepted. *Expenses:* Tuition, state resident: full-time $7002. Tuition, nonresident: full-time $21,898. International tuition: $22,116 full-time. Required fees: $892. Tuition and fees vary according to course load and program. *Financial support:* Research assistantships, teaching assistantships, Federal Work-Study available. Support available to part-time students. Financial award application deadline: 3/15; financial award applicants required to submit FAFSA. *Faculty research:* Parallelizable, scalable software translations; graphical representations of algorithms, structures, and processes; graph drawing. Total annual research expenditures: $400,000. *Unit head:* Dr. Kai Chang, Chair, 334-844-6310. *Application contact:* Dr. George Flowers, Dean of the Graduate School, 334-844-2125.

Ball State University, Graduate School, College of Sciences and Humanities, Department of Computer Science, Muncie, IN 47306-1099. Offers MA, MS. *Faculty:* 12. *Students:* 22 full-time (5 women), 9 part-time (1 woman), 19 international. Average age 25. 45 applicants, 60% accepted, 8 enrolled. In 2010, 15 master's awarded. *Entrance requirements:* For master's, GRE General Test. Application fee: $50. *Expenses:* Tuition, state resident: full-time $6160; part-time $299 per credit hour. Tuition, nonresident: full-time $16,020; part-time $783 per credit hour. Required fees: $2278; $95 per credit hour. *Financial support:* In 2010–11, 2 research assistantships with full tuition reimbursements (averaging $10,815 per year), 7 teaching assistantships with full tuition reimbursements (averaging $11,214 per year) were awarded. Financial award application deadline: 3/1. *Faculty research:* Numerical methods, programmer productivity, graphics. *Unit head:* Dr. Paul Buis, Chairperson, 765-285-8641, Fax: 765-285-2614. *Application contact:* Dr. J. Michael McGrew, Graduate Program Director, 765-285-8641, Fax: 765-285-2614, E-mail: mmcgrew@bsu.edu.

Baylor University, Graduate School, School of Engineering and Computer Science, Department of Computer Science, Waco, TX 76798. Offers MS. Part-time programs available. *Faculty:* 10 full-time (1 woman). *Students:* 16 full-time (2 women), 2 part-time (both women); includes 5 minority (1 Asian, non-Hispanic/Latino; 4 Hispanic/Latino), 9 international. 27 applicants, 37% accepted, 10 enrolled. In 2010, 3 master's awarded. *Entrance requirements:* Additional exam requirements/recommendations for international students: Required—TOEFL (minimum score 550 paper-based; 213 computer-based). *Application deadline:* For fall admission, 2/15 priority date for domestic and international students; for spring admission, 9/1 priority date for domestic and international students. Applications are processed on a rolling basis. Application fee: $40. Electronic applications accepted. *Faculty research:* Bioinformatics, databases, machine learning, SWE, networking. *Unit head:* Dr. David Sturgill, Chair, 254-710-3876, E-mail: david_sturgill@baylor.edu. *Application contact:* Dr. Sharon Humphrey, Graduate Program Director, 254-710-6821, Fax: 254-710-3870, E-mail: sharon_humphrey@baylor.edu.

Boise State University, Graduate College, College of Engineering, Program in Computer Science, Boise, ID 83725-0399. Offers MS. Part-time programs available. *Degree requirements:* For master's, comprehensive exam, thesis. *Entrance requirements:* For master's, GRE General Test, minimum GPA of 3.0. Electronic applications accepted.

Boston University, Graduate School of Arts and Sciences, Department of Computer Science, Boston, MA 02215. Offers MA, PhD. *Students:* 55 full-time (11 women), 10 part-time (0 women); includes 1 minority (Hispanic/Latino), 38 international. Average age 28. 306 applicants, 20% accepted, 18 enrolled. In 2010, 62 master's, 8 doctorates awarded. *Degree requirements:* For master's, one foreign language, thesis optional, project; for doctorate, one foreign language, comprehensive exam, thesis/dissertation. *Entrance requirements:* For master's and doctorate, GRE General Test, 3 letters of recommendation. Additional exam requirements/recommendations for international students: Required—TOEFL (minimum score 550 paper-based; 213 computer-based). *Application deadline:* For fall admission, 12/15 for domestic and international students; for spring admission, 10/1 for domestic and international students. Application fee: $70. *Expenses:* Tuition: Full-time $39,314; part-time $1228 per credit. Required fees: $40 per semester. *Financial support:* In 2010–11, 1 fellowship with full tuition reimbursement (averaging $19,300 per year), 21 research assistantships with full tuition reimbursements (averaging $18,800 per year), 16 teaching assistantships with full tuition reimbursements (averaging $18,800 per year) were awarded; Federal Work-Study and scholarships/grants also available. Support available to part-time students. Financial award application deadline: 12/15; financial award applicants required to submit FAFSA. *Unit head:* Stan Sclaroff, Chairman, 617-353-8919, Fax: 617-353-6457, E-mail: sclaroff@bu.edu. *Application contact:* Jennifer Streubel, Program Coordinator, 617-353-8919, Fax: 617-353-6457, E-mail: jenn4@bu.edu.

Boston University, Metropolitan College, Department of Computer Science, Boston, MA 02215. Offers computer information systems (MS), including computer networks, database management and business intelligence, health informatics, IT project management, security; computer science (MS), including computer networks, security; telecommunications (MS), including security. Part-time and evening/weekend programs available. Postbaccalaureate distance learning degree programs offered (no on-campus study). *Faculty:* 10 full-time (0 women), 30 part-time/adjunct (3 women). *Students:* 16 full-time (2 women), 681 part-time (155 women); includes 182 minority (44 Black or African American, non-Hispanic/Latino; 1 American Indian or Alaska Native, non-Hispanic/Latino; 88 Asian, non-Hispanic/Latino; 36 Hispanic/Latino; 2 Native Hawaiian or other Pacific Islander, non-Hispanic/Latino; 11 Two or more races, non-Hispanic/Latino), 66 international. Average age 35. 273 applicants, 78% accepted, 155 enrolled. In 2010, 143 master's awarded. *Degree requirements:* For master's, thesis optional. *Entrance requirements:* For master's, 3 letters of recommendation, professional resume. Additional exam requirements/recommendations for international students: Required—TOEFL (minimum score 550 paper-based; 213 computer-based; 80 iBT). *Application deadline:* For fall admission, 6/1 priority date for international students; for spring admission, 10/1 priority date for international students. Applications are processed on a rolling basis. Application fee: $70. Electronic applications accepted. *Expenses:* Tuition: Full-time $39,314; part-time $1228 per credit. Required fees: $40 per semester. *Financial support:* In 2010–11, 9 research assistantships with partial tuition reimbursements (averaging $5,000 per year) were awarded; career-related internships or fieldwork and unspecified assistantships also available. Support available to part-time students. Financial award applicants required to submit FAFSA. *Faculty research:* Medical informatics, Web technologies, telecom and networks, security and forensics, software engineering, programming languages, multimedia and AI, information systems and IT project management. *Unit head:* Dr. Lubomir Chitkushev, Chairman, 617-353-2566, Fax: 617-353-2367, E-mail: csinfo@bu.edu. *Application contact:* Kim Richards, Program Coordinator, 617-353-2566, Fax: 617-353-2367, E-mail: kimrich@bu.edu.

Bowie State University, Graduate Programs, Department of Computer Science, Bowie, MD 20715-9465. Offers MS. Part-time and evening/weekend programs available. *Degree requirements:* For master's, comprehensive exam, thesis optional, research paper. *Entrance requirements:* For master's, minimum undergraduate GPA of 2.5. Electronic applications accepted. *Expenses:* Tuition, state resident: full-time $4080; part-time $340 per credit. Tuition, nonresident: full-time $7752; part-time $646 per credit. Required fees: $2128; $340 per credit. *Faculty research:* Holographics, launch vehicle ground truth ephemera.

Bowie State University, Graduate Programs, Program in Computer Science, Bowie, MD 20715-9465. Offers App Sc D. Part-time and evening/weekend programs available. Electronic applications accepted. *Expenses:* Tuition, state resident: full-time $4080; part-time $340 per credit. Tuition, nonresident: full-time $7752; part-time $646 per credit. Required fees: $2128; $340 per credit.

Bowling Green State University, Graduate College, College of Arts and Sciences, Department of Computer Science, Bowling Green, OH 43403. Offers computer science (MS), including operations research, parallel and distributed computing, software engineering. Part-time programs available. *Degree requirements:* For master's, thesis or alternative. *Entrance requirements:* For master's, GRE General Test. Additional exam requirements/recommendations for international students: Required—TOEFL. Electronic applications accepted. *Faculty research:* Artificial intelligence, real time and concurrent programming languages, behavioral aspects of computing, network protocols.

Bradley University, Graduate School, College of Liberal Arts and Sciences, Department of Computer Science and Information Systems, Peoria, IL 61625-0002. Offers computer information systems (MS); computer science (MS). Part-time and evening/weekend programs available. *Degree requirements:* For master's, comprehensive exam, thesis or alternative, programming test. *Entrance requirements:* For master's, 2 letters of recommendation. Additional exam requirements/recommendations for international students: Required—TOEFL (minimum score 550 paper-based; 213 computer-based; 79 iBT).

Brandeis University, Graduate School of Arts and Sciences, Department of Computer Science, Waltham, MA 02454-9110. Offers computational linguistics (MA); computer science (MA, PhD, Certificate); computer science and IT entrepreneurship (MA). Part-time programs available. *Faculty:* 13 full-time (3 women), 4 part-time/adjunct (2 women). *Students:* 41 full-time (10 women), 7 part-time (3 women); includes 2 Black or African American, non-Hispanic/Latino; 3 Asian, non-Hispanic/Latino, 20 international. 109 applicants, 52% accepted, 22 enrolled. In 2010, 9 master's, 5 doctorates, 3 other advanced degrees awarded. *Degree requirements:* For doctorate, thesis/dissertation, thesis proposal. *Entrance requirements:* For master's, GRE recommended, official transcript(s), statement of purpose, resume, 2 letters of recommendation; for doctorate, GRE required, official transcript(s), statement of purpose, resume, 3 letters of recommendation. Additional exam requirements/recommendations for international students: Required—TOEFL (minimum score 600 paper-based; 250 computer-based; 100 iBT); Recommended—IELTS (minimum score 7). *Application deadline:* For fall admission, 1/15 for domestic students. Applications are processed on a rolling basis. Application fee: $75. Electronic applications accepted. *Financial support:* In 2010–11, 23 students received support, including 8 fellowships with full tuition reimbursements available (averaging $20,000 per year), 10 research assistantships with full tuition reimbursements available (averaging $20,000 per year), teaching assistantships with partial tuition reimbursements available (averaging $3,200 per year); scholarships/grants, health care benefits, and tuition waivers (full and partial) also available. Support available to part-time students. Financial award application deadline: 4/15; financial award applicants required to submit FAFSA. *Faculty research:* Artificial intelligence, programming languages, parallel computing, computational linguistics, data compression, technology and IT entrepreneurship. *Unit head:* Dr. Jordan Pollack, Chair, 781-736-2700, Fax: 781-736-2741, E-mail: pollack@brandeis.edu. *Application contact:* Myrna Fox, Department Administrator, 781-736-2701, E-mail: maf@cs.brandeis.edu.

Brandeis University, Graduate School of Arts and Sciences, Program in Computational Linguistics, Waltham, MA 02454-9110. Offers MA. Part-time programs available. *Faculty:* 13 full-time (3 women), 4 part-time/adjunct (2 women). *Students:* 13 full-time (6 women), 1 part-time (0 women); includes 1 Asian, non-Hispanic/Latino; 1 Hispanic/Latino, 3 international. 25 applicants, 68% accepted, 11 enrolled. In 2010, 4 master's awarded. *Degree requirements:* For master's, thesis. *Entrance requirements:* For master's, statement of purpose, 2 letters of recommendation, official transcripts, resume or curriculum vitae. Additional exam requirements/recommendations for international students: Required—TOEFL (minimum score 650 paper-based; 250 computer-based; 100 iBT); Recommended—IELTS (minimum score 7). *Application deadline:* Applications are processed on a rolling basis. Application fee: $75. Electronic applications accepted. *Financial support:* In 2010–11, 3 teaching assistantships with partial tuition reimbursements (averaging $3,200 per year) were awarded; institutionally sponsored loans and scholarships/grants also available. Financial award application deadline: 4/15; financial award applicants required to submit FAFSA. *Faculty research:* Computer science (artificial intelligence, theory of computation, and programming methods), language and linguistics (phonology, syntax, semantics, and pragmatics). *Unit head:* Dr. James Pustejovsky, Program Chair, 781-736-2701, Fax: 781-736-2741, E-mail: jamesp@brandeis.edu. *Application contact:* David F. Cotter, Graduate School of Arts and Sciences, 781-736-3410, Fax: 781-736-3412, E-mail: gradschool@brandeis.edu.

Brandeis University, Graduate School of Arts and Sciences, Program in Computer Science and IT Entrepreneurship, Waltham, MA 02454-9110. Offers MA. Part-time programs available. *Faculty:* 13 full-time (3 women), 4 part-time/adjunct (2 women). *Students:* 11 full-time (6 women), 1 (woman) part-time; includes 1 Asian, non-Hispanic/Latino, 9 international. 26 applicants, 81% accepted, 12 enrolled. *Degree requirements:* For master's, practicum. *Entrance requirements:* For master's, official transcript(s), 2 letters of recommendation, curriculum vitae or resume, statement of purpose. Additional exam requirements/recommendations for international students: Required—TOEFL (minimum score 600 paper-based; 250 computer-based; 100 iBT); Recommended—IELTS (minimum score 7). *Application deadline:* Applications are processed on a rolling basis. Application fee: $75. Electronic applications accepted. *Financial support:* In 2010–11, teaching assistantships with partial tuition reimbursements (averaging $3,200 per year); institutionally sponsored loans, scholarships/grants, and tuition waivers (partial) also available. Financial award application deadline: 4/15; financial award applicants required to submit FAFSA. *Faculty research:* Software development, IT entrepreneurship, business, computer science, innovation. *Unit head:* Prof. Fernando Colon Osorio, Director of Graduate Studies, 781-736-4586, E-mail: fcco@brandeis.edu. *Application contact:* David F. Cotter, Assistant Dean, Graduate School of Arts and Sciences, 781-736-3410, Fax: 781-736-3412, E-mail: gradschool@brandeis.edu.

Bridgewater State University, School of Graduate Studies, School of Arts and Sciences, Department of Mathematics and Computer Science, Bridgewater, MA 02325-0001. Offers computer science (MS); mathematics (MAT). Part-time and evening/weekend programs available. *Entrance requirements:* For master's, GRE General Test.

Brigham Young University, Graduate Studies, College of Physical and Mathematical Sciences, Department of Computer Science, Provo, UT 84602-1001. Offers MS, PhD. *Faculty:* 27 full-time (0 women), 3 part-time/adjunct (0 women). *Students:* 98 full-time (5 women); includes 1 Black or African American, non-Hispanic/Latino; 12 Asian, non-Hispanic/Latino; 1 Hispanic/Latino, 17 international. Average age 29. 53 applicants, 66% accepted, 32 enrolled. In 2010, 21 master's, 5 doctorates awarded. Terminal master's awarded for partial completion of doctoral program. *Degree requirements:* For master's, thesis; for doctorate, comprehensive exam, thesis/dissertation, residency. *Entrance requirements:* For master's, GRE General Test, minimum GPA of 3.25 in last 60 hours; for doctorate, GRE General Test, minimum GPA of 3.5 in last 60 hours, undergraduate degree in computer science. Additional exam requirements/recommendations for international students: Required—TOEFL (minimum score 600 paper-based; 250 computer-based; 85 iBT). *Application deadline:* For fall admission, 1/15 for domestic and international students; for winter admission, 8/15 for domestic and international students. Application fee: $50. Electronic applications accepted. *Expenses:* Tuition: Full-time $5580; part-time $310 per credit hour. Tuition and fees vary according to program and student's religious affiliation. *Financial support:* In 2010–11, 78 students received support, including fellowships with full tuition reimbursements available (averaging $22,000 per year), 66 research assistantships with full and partial tuition reimbursements available (averaging $15,000 per year), 17 teaching assistantships with partial tuition reimbursements available (averaging $12,000 per year); scholarships/grants and health care benefits also available. Financial award application deadline: 4/4. *Faculty research:* Graphics, image processing, neural networks and machine learning, formal methods. Total annual research expenditures: $741,000. *Unit head:* Dr. Parris K. Egbert, Chair, 801-422-4029, Fax: 801-422-0169, E-mail: egbert@cs.byu.edu. *Application contact:* Dr. Kent E. Seamons, Graduate Coordinator, 801-422-3722, Fax: 801-422-0169, E-mail: graduate@cs.byu.edu.

Brock University, Faculty of Graduate Studies, Faculty of Mathematics and Science, Program in Computer Science, St. Catharines, ON L2S 3A1, Canada. Offers M Sc. Part-time programs available. *Degree requirements:* For master's, thesis. *Entrance requirements:* For master's, honors degree. Additional exam requirements/recommendations for international students: Required—TOEFL (minimum score 550 paper-based; 213 computer-based; 80 iBT), IELTS (minimum score 6.5), TWE (minimum score 4).

Brooklyn College of the City University of New York, Division of Graduate Studies, Department of Computer and Information Science, Brooklyn, NY 11210-2889. Offers computer science (MA, PhD); computer science and health science (MS); information systems (MS); parallel and distributed computing (Advanced Certificate). Part-time and evening/weekend programs available. *Students:* 11 full-time (2 women), 105 part-time (27 women); includes 60 minority (29 Black or African American, non-Hispanic/Latino; 25 Asian, non-Hispanic/Latino; 6 Hispanic/Latino), 28 international. Average age 32. 68 applicants, 78% accepted, 22 enrolled. In 2010, 26 master's awarded. *Degree requirements:* For master's, comprehensive exam, thesis or alternative. *Entrance requirements:* For master's, previous course work in computer science, 2 letters of recommendation. Additional exam requirements/recommendations for international students: Required—TOEFL (minimum score 525 paper-based; 195 computer-based; 70 iBT). *Application deadline:* For fall admission, 3/1 priority date for domestic students, 2/1 priority date for international students; for spring admission, 11/1 priority date for domestic students, 10/1 priority date for international students. Applications are processed on a rolling basis. Application fee: $125. Electronic applications accepted. *Expenses:* Tuition, state resident: full-time $7360; part-time $310 per credit hour. Tuition, nonresident: full-time $13,800; part-time $575 per credit hour. Required fees: $190 per semester. *Financial support:* Career-related internships or fieldwork, Federal Work-Study, institutionally sponsored loans, and scholarships/grants available. Support available to part-time students. Financial award application deadline: 5/1; financial award applicants required to submit FAFSA. *Faculty research:* Networks and distributed systems, programming languages, modeling and computer applications, algorithms, artificial intelligence, theoretical computer science. *Unit head:* Dr. Yedidyah Langsam, Chairperson, 718-951-5657, E-mail: langsam@sci.brooklyn.cuny.edu. *Application contact:* Hernan Sierra, Graduate Admissions Coordinator, 718-951-4536, Fax: 718-951-4506, E-mail: grads@brooklyn.cuny.edu.

Brown University, Graduate School, Department of Computer Science, Providence, RI 02912. Offers Sc M, PhD. *Degree requirements:* For master's, thesis or alternative; for doctorate, one foreign language, comprehensive exam, thesis/dissertation. *Entrance requirements:* For master's and doctorate, GRE General Test, GRE Subject Test.

California Institute of Technology, Division of Engineering and Applied Science, Option in Computer Science, Pasadena, CA 91125-0001. Offers MS, PhD. *Faculty:* 11 full-time (0 women). *Students:* 23 full-time (3 women). 310 applicants, 2% accepted, 3 enrolled. In 2010, 6 master's, 1 doctorate awarded. *Degree requirements:* For master's, thesis; for doctorate, thesis/dissertation. *Application deadline:* For fall admission, 1/1 for domestic students. Application fee: $0. Electronic applications accepted. *Financial support:* In 2010–11, 3 fellowships, 21 research assistantships, 2 teaching assistantships were awarded. *Faculty research:* VLSI systems, concurrent computation, high-level programming languages, signal and image processing, graphics. *Unit head:* Dr. Houman Owhadi, Academic Officer, 626-395-4547, E-mail: owhadi@caltech.edu. *Application contact:* Natalie Gilmore, Assistant Dean of Graduate Studies, 626-395-3812, Fax: 626-577-9246, E-mail: ngilmore@caltech.edu.

California Polytechnic State University, San Luis Obispo, College of Engineering, Department of Computer Science, San Luis Obispo, CA 93407. Offers MS. Part-time programs available. *Faculty:* 2 full-time (0 women). *Students:* 12 full-time (2 women), 14 part-time (3 women); includes 1 minority (Asian, non-Hispanic/Latino), 2 international. Average age 25. 39 applicants, 44% accepted, 11 enrolled. In 2010, 20 master's awarded. *Degree requirements:* For master's, thesis. *Entrance requirements:* For master's, GRE General Test, minimum GPA of 3.0 in last 90 quarter units. Additional exam requirements/recommendations for international students: Required—TOEFL (minimum score 550 paper-based; 213 computer-based) or IELTS (minimum score 6). *Application deadline:* For fall admission, 4/1 for domestic students, 11/30

for international students; for winter admission, 9/1 for domestic students, 6/30 for international students. Applications are processed on a rolling basis. Application fee: $55. Electronic applications accepted. *Expenses:* Tuition, state resident: full-time $5386; part-time $3124 per year. Tuition, nonresident: full-time $11,160; part-time $248 per unit. Required fees: $2250; $614 per term. One-time fee: $2250 full-time; $1842 part-time. *Financial support:* Teaching assistantships, career-related internships or fieldwork, Federal Work-Study, institutionally sponsored loans, scholarships/grants, and unspecified assistantships available. Support available to part-time students. Financial award application deadline: 3/2; financial award applicants required to submit FAFSA. *Faculty research:* Computer systems, software, graphics, hardware design, expert systems. *Unit head:* Dr. Gene Fisher, Graduate Coordinator, 805-756-2416, Fax: 805-756-2956, E-mail: gfisher@calpoly.edu. *Application contact:* Dr. Gene Fisher, Graduate Coordinator, 805-756-2416, Fax: 805-756-2956, E-mail: gfisher@calpoly.edu.

California State Polytechnic University, Pomona, Academic Affairs, College of Science, Program in Computer Science, Pomona, CA 91768-2557. Offers MS. Part-time programs available. *Students:* 12 full-time (1 woman), 54 part-time (7 women); includes 32 minority (1 Black or African American, non-Hispanic/Latino; 21 Asian, non-Hispanic/Latino; 7 Hispanic/Latino; 2 Native Hawaiian or other Pacific Islander, non-Hispanic/Latino; 1 Two or more races, non-Hispanic/Latino), 17 international. Average age 28. 92 applicants, 52% accepted, 30 enrolled. In 2010, 12 master's awarded. *Degree requirements:* For master's, thesis. *Entrance requirements:* For master's, GRE General Test. *Application deadline:* For fall admission, 5/1 priority date for domestic students; for winter admission, 10/15 priority date for domestic students; for spring admission, 1/20 priority date for domestic students. Applications are processed on a rolling basis. Application fee: $55. Electronic applications accepted. *Expenses:* Tuition, state resident: full-time $5386; part-time $2850 per year. Tuition, nonresident: full-time $12,082; part-time $248 per credit. Required fees: $577; $248 per credit. $577 per year. Tuition and fees vary according to course load and program. *Financial support:* Career-related internships or fieldwork, Federal Work-Study, and institutionally sponsored loans available. Support available to part-time students. Financial award application deadline: 3/2; financial award applicants required to submit FAFSA. *Unit head:* Dr. Salam Salloum, Graduate Coordinator, 909-869-5317, E-mail: mscs@csupomona.edu. *Application contact:* Scott J. Duncan, Director, Admissions, 909-869-3258, Fax: 909-869-4529, E-mail: sjduncan@csupomona.edu.

California State University Channel Islands, Extended Education, Program in Computer Science, Camarillo, CA 93012. Offers MS. Part-time and evening/weekend programs available. *Entrance requirements:* Additional exam requirements/recommendations for international students: Required—TOEFL (minimum score 550 paper-based).

California State University, Chico, Graduate School, College of Engineering, Computer Science, and Technology, Department of Computer Science, Chico, CA 95929-0722. Offers MS. Postbaccalaureate distance learning degree programs offered. *Students:* 11 full-time (1 woman), 8 part-time (0 women); includes 1 Asian, non-Hispanic/Latino, 13 international. Average age 27. 70 applicants, 54% accepted, 4 enrolled. In 2010, 28 master's awarded. *Entrance requirements:* For master's, GRE General Test, 2 letters of recommendation. Additional exam requirements/recommendations for international students: Required—TOEFL (minimum score 550 paper-based; 213 computer-based; 80 iBT), IELTS (minimum score 6.5). *Application deadline:* For fall admission, 3/1 priority date for domestic students, 3/1 for international students; for spring admission, 9/15 priority date for domestic students, 9/15 for international students. Applications are processed on a rolling basis. Application fee: $55. Electronic applications accepted. *Financial support:* Fellowships, research assistantships, teaching assistantships, career-related internships or fieldwork available. *Unit head:* Dr. Moaty Fayek, Graduate Coordinator, 530-898-4010. *Application contact:* Dr. Moaty Fayek, Graduate Coordinator, 530-898-4010.

California State University, Dominguez Hills, College of Natural and Behavioral Sciences, Department of Computer Science, Carson, CA 90747-0001. Offers MSCS. *Faculty:* 5 full-time (1 woman), 1 part-time/adjunct (0 women). *Students:* 9 full-time (3 women), 20 part-time (8 women); includes 1 Black or African American, non-Hispanic/Latino; 6 Asian, non-Hispanic/Latino; 9 Hispanic/Latino; 1 Two or more races, non-Hispanic/Latino, 8 international. Average age 33. 28 applicants, 100% accepted, 13 enrolled. *Degree requirements:* For master's, comprehensive exam (for some programs), thesis (for some programs). *Entrance requirements:* For master's, GRE (minimum score 900), minimum GPA of 2.75. Additional exam requirements/recommendations for international students: Required—TOEFL (minimum score 550 paper-based). Application fee: $55. Electronic applications accepted. *Unit head:* Dr. Mohsen Beheshti, Department Chair, 310-243-3398, E-mail: mbeheshti@csudh.edu. *Application contact:* Brandy McLelland, Interim Director, Student Information Services, 310-243-3654, E-mail: bmclelland@csudh.edu.

California State University, East Bay, Office of Academic Programs and Graduate Studies, College of Science, Department of Mathematics and Computer Science, Computer Science Program, Hayward, CA 94542-3000. Offers computer networks (MS); computer science (MS). Part-time programs available. *Faculty:* 15 full-time (4 women). *Students:* 61 full-time (30 women), 158 part-time (79 women); includes 3 Black or African American, non-Hispanic/Latino; 1 American Indian or Alaska Native, non-Hispanic/Latino; 28 Asian, non-Hispanic/Latino; 3 Hispanic/Latino, 147 international. Average age 27. 247 applicants, 70% accepted, 65 enrolled. In 2010, 67 master's awarded. *Degree requirements:* For master's, comprehensive exam or thesis. *Entrance requirements:* For master's, GRE, minimum GPA of 3.0 in field, 2.75 overall. Additional exam requirements/recommendations for international students: Required—TOEFL (minimum score 550 paper-based; 213 computer-based). *Application deadline:* For fall admission, 6/30 for domestic and international students. Application fee: $55. Electronic applications accepted. *Financial support:* Fellowships, career-related internships or fieldwork, Federal Work-Study, institutionally sponsored loans, and scholarships/grants available. Support available to part-time students. Financial award application deadline: 3/2; financial award applicants required to submit FAFSA. *Unit head:* Dr. Edna Reiter, Chair, 510-885-3414, Fax: 510-885-4169, E-mail: edna.reiter@csueastbay.edu. *Application contact:* Dr. Donna Wiley, Interim Associate Director, 510-885-2928, Fax: 510-885-4777, E-mail: donna.wiley@csueastbay.edu.

California State University, Fresno, Division of Graduate Studies, College of Science and Mathematics, Department of Computer Science, Fresno, CA 93740-8027. Offers MS. Part-time and evening/weekend programs available. *Degree requirements:* For master's, thesis or alternative. *Entrance requirements:* For master's, GRE General Test, minimum GPA of 2.75. Additional exam requirements/recommendations for international students: Required—TOEFL. Electronic applications accepted. *Faculty research:* Software design, parallel processing, computer engineering, autoline research.

California State University, Fullerton, Graduate Studies, College of Engineering and Computer Science, Department of Computer Science, Fullerton, CA 92834-9480. Offers computer science (MS); software engineering (MS). Part-time programs available. Postbaccalaureate distance learning degree programs offered. *Students:* 56 full-time (12 women), 280 part-time (74 women); includes 12 Black or African American, non-Hispanic/Latino; 76 Asian, non-Hispanic/Latino; 15 Hispanic/Latino; 5 Two or more races, non-Hispanic/Latino, 134 international. Average age 31. 238 applicants, 63% accepted, 91 enrolled. In 2010, 114 master's awarded. *Degree requirements:* For master's, comprehensive exam, project or thesis. *Entrance requirements:* For master's, GRE General Test, minimum undergraduate GPA of 2.5. Application fee: $55. *Financial support:* Career-related internships or fieldwork, Federal Work-Study, institutionally sponsored loans, and scholarships/grants available. Support available to part-time students. Financial award application deadline: 3/1; financial award applicants required to submit FAFSA. *Faculty research:* Software engineering, development of computer networks. *Unit head:* Dr. James Choi, Chair, 657-278-3700. *Application contact:* Admissions/Applications, 657-278-2371.

Computer Science

California State University, Long Beach, Graduate Studies, College of Engineering, Department of Computer Engineering and Computer Science, Long Beach, CA 90840. Offers computer engineering (MSCS); computer science (MSCS). Part-time programs available. *Faculty:* 13 full-time (3 women). *Students:* 120 full-time (30 women), 123 part-time (17 women); includes 4 Black or African American, non-Hispanic/Latino; 1 American Indian or Alaska Native, non-Hispanic/Latino; 46 Asian, non-Hispanic/Latino; 18 Hispanic/Latino, 102 international. Average age 29. 406 applicants, 65% accepted, 113 enrolled. In 2010, 43 master's awarded. *Degree requirements:* For master's, thesis or alternative. *Entrance requirements:* Additional exam requirements/recommendations for international students: Required—TOEFL. *Application deadline:* For fall admission, 3/1 for domestic students. Application fee: $55. Electronic applications accepted. *Financial support:* Teaching assistantships, Federal Work-Study, institutionally sponsored loans, scholarships/grants, and unspecified assistantships available. Financial award application deadline: 3/2. *Faculty research:* Artificial intelligence, software engineering, computer simulation and modeling, user-interface design, networking. *Unit head:* Dr. Kenneth James, Chair, 562-985-5105, Fax: 562-985-7823, E-mail: james@csulb.edu. *Application contact:* Dr. Burkhard Englert, Graduate Advisor, 562-985-7987, Fax: 562-985-7823, E-mail: benglert@.csulb.edu.

California State University, Los Angeles, Graduate Studies, College of Engineering, Computer Science, and Technology, Department of Computer Science, Los Angeles, CA 90032-8530. Offers MS. *Faculty:* 4 full-time (1 woman), 4 part-time/adjunct (0 women). *Students:* 59 full-time (24 women), 66 part-time (17 women); includes 25 minority (1 Black or African American, non-Hispanic/Latino; 17 Asian, non-Hispanic/Latino; 6 Hispanic/Latino; 1 Two or more races, non-Hispanic/Latino), 75 international. Average age 29. 90 applicants, 100% accepted, 21 enrolled. In 2010, 29 master's awarded. *Entrance requirements:* Additional exam requirements/recommendations for international students: Required—TOEFL (minimum score 550 paper-based). *Application deadline:* For fall admission, 5/1 for domestic and international students. Applications are processed on a rolling basis. Application fee: $55. Electronic applications accepted. *Unit head:* Dr. Raj Pamula, Chair, 323-343-6690, Fax: 323-343-6672, E-mail: rpamula@calstatela.edu. *Application contact:* Dr. Alan Muchlinski, Dean of Graduate Studies, 323-343-3820, Fax: 323-343-5653, E-mail: amuchli@exchange.calstatela.edu.

California State University, Northridge, Graduate Studies, College of Engineering and Computer Science, Department of Computer Science, Northridge, CA 91330. Offers computer science (MS); software engineering (MS). Part-time and evening/weekend programs available. *Degree requirements:* For master's, thesis. *Entrance requirements:* For master's, GRE General Test, minimum GPA of 2.5. Additional exam requirements/recommendations for international students: Required—TOEFL. *Faculty research:* Radar data processing.

California State University, Sacramento, Graduate Studies, College of Engineering and Computer Science, Department of Computer Science, Sacramento, CA 95819. Offers computer systems (MS); software engineering (MS). Part-time and evening/weekend programs available. *Degree requirements:* For master's, thesis or alternative, writing proficiency exam. *Entrance requirements:* Additional exam requirements/recommendations for international students: Required—TOEFL. Electronic applications accepted.

California State University, San Bernardino, Graduate Studies, College of Natural Sciences, Department of Computer Science, San Bernardino, CA 92407-2397. Offers MS. *Entrance requirements:* For master's, GRE.

California State University, San Marcos, College of Arts and Sciences, Program in Computer Science, San Marcos, CA 92096-0001. Offers MS. Part-time programs available. *Entrance requirements:* For master's, GRE General Test, GRE Subject Test (recommended). Additional exam requirements/recommendations for international students: Required—TOEFL. *Faculty research:* Networks, multimedia, parallel algorithms, software engineering, artificial intelligence.

Capitol College, Graduate Programs, Laurel, MD 20708-9759. Offers business administration (MBA); computer science (MS); electrical engineering (MS); information and telecommunications systems management (MS); information architecture (MS); network security (MS). Part-time and evening/weekend programs available. Postbaccalaureate distance learning degree programs offered (no on-campus study). *Entrance requirements:* For master's, minimum GPA of 3.0. Electronic applications accepted.

Carleton University, Faculty of Graduate Studies, Faculty of Science, School of Computer Science, Ottawa, ON K1S 5B6, Canada. Offers computer science (MCS, PhD); information and system science (M Sc). MCS and PhD programs offered jointly with University of Ottawa. Part-time programs available. *Degree requirements:* For master's, thesis optional, project; for doctorate, comprehensive exam, thesis/dissertation. *Entrance requirements:* For master's, honors degree. Additional exam requirements/recommendations for international students: Required—TOEFL. *Faculty research:* Programming systems, theory of computing, computer applications, computer systems.

Carnegie Mellon University, School of Computer Science, Department of Computer Science, Pittsburgh, PA 15213-3891. Offers algorithms, combinatorics, and optimization (PhD); computer science (MS, PhD); pure and applied logic (PhD). *Degree requirements:* For doctorate, thesis/dissertation. *Entrance requirements:* For doctorate, GRE General Test, GRE Subject Test, BS in computer science or equivalent. Additional exam requirements/recommendations for international students: Required—TOEFL. *Faculty research:* Software systems, theory of computations, artificial intelligence, computer systems, programming languages.

Carnegie Mellon University, School of Computer Science, Language Technologies Institute, Pittsburgh, PA 15213-3891. Offers MLT, PhD. Terminal master's awarded for partial completion of doctoral program. *Degree requirements:* For doctorate, thesis/dissertation. *Entrance requirements:* For master's and doctorate, GRE General Test, GRE Subject Test. Additional exam requirements/recommendations for international students: Required—TOEFL. *Faculty research:* Machine translation, natural language processing, speech and information retrieval, literacy.

Case Western Reserve University, School of Graduate Studies, Case School of Engineering, Department of Electrical Engineering and Computer Science, Cleveland, OH 44106. Offers computer engineering (MS, PhD); computing and information sciences (MS, PhD); electrical engineering (MS, PhD); systems and control engineering (MS, PhD). Part-time and evening/weekend programs available. Postbaccalaureate distance learning degree programs offered (minimal on-campus study). *Faculty:* 33 full-time (2 women). *Students:* 190 full-time (31 women), 26 part-time (4 women); includes 3 Black or African American, non-Hispanic/Latino; 6 Asian, non-Hispanic/Latino, 128 international. In 2010, 32 master's, 13 doctorates awarded. Terminal master's awarded for partial completion of doctoral program. *Degree requirements:* For master's, thesis; for doctorate, thesis/dissertation, qualifying exam, teaching experience. *Entrance requirements:* For master's and doctorate, GRE General Test. Additional exam requirements/recommendations for international students: Required—TOEFL. *Application deadline:* For fall admission, 2/1 for domestic students; for spring admission, 11/1 for domestic students. Applications are processed on a rolling basis. Application fee: $50. *Financial support:* Fellowships with full and partial tuition reimbursements, research assistantships with full and partial tuition reimbursements, teaching assistantships, career-related internships or fieldwork, Federal Work-Study, and institutionally sponsored loans available. Support available to part-time students. Financial award application deadline: 3/1; financial award applicants required to submit FAFSA. *Faculty research:* Applied artificial intelligence, automation, computer-aided design and testing of digital systems. Total annual research expenditures: $6.8 million. *Unit head:* Michael Branicky, Department Chair, 216-368-6888, E-mail: branicky@case.edu. *Application contact:* David Easler, Student Affairs Coordinator, 216-368-4080, Fax: 216-368-2801, E-mail: david.easler@case.edu.

The Catholic University of America, School of Engineering, Department of Electrical Engineering and Computer Science, Washington, DC 20064. Offers MEE, MSCS, D Engr, PhD. Part-time programs available. *Faculty:* 10 full-time (3 women), 13 part-time/adjunct (1

woman). *Students:* 15 full-time (3 women), 50 part-time (9 women); includes 2 Black or African American, non-Hispanic/Latino; 5 Asian, non-Hispanic/Latino; 3 Hispanic/Latino, 16 international. Average age 33. 58 applicants, 48% accepted, 16 enrolled. In 2010, 17 master's awarded. *Degree requirements:* For master's, thesis or alternative; for doctorate, comprehensive exam, thesis/dissertation, oral exams. *Entrance requirements:* For master's and doctorate, statement of purpose, official copies of academic transcripts, three letters of recommendation. Additional exam requirements/recommendations for international students: Required—TOEFL (minimum score 580 paper-based; 237 computer-based). *Application deadline:* For fall admission, 8/1 priority date for domestic students, 7/15 for international students; for spring admission, 12/1 priority date for domestic students, 10/15 for international students. Applications are processed on a rolling basis. Application fee: $55. Electronic applications accepted. *Expenses:* Contact institution. *Financial support:* Fellowships, research assistantships, teaching assistantships, Federal Work-Study, scholarships/grants, tuition waivers (full and partial), and unspecified assistantships available. Financial award application deadline: 2/1; financial award applicants required to submit FAFSA. *Faculty research:* Signal and image processing, computer communications, robotics, intelligent controls, bioelectromagnetics. Total annual research expenditures: $1.2 million. *Unit head:* Dr. Phillip Regalia, Chair, 202-319-5879, Fax: 202-319-5195, E-mail: regalia@cua.edu. *Application contact:* Andrew Woodall, Director of Graduate Admissions, 202-319-5057, Fax: 202-319-6533, E-mail: cua-admissions@cua.edu.

Central Connecticut State University, School of Graduate Studies, School of Arts and Sciences, Department of Computer Science, New Britain, CT 06050-4010. Offers computer information technology (MS). Part-time and evening/weekend programs available. *Faculty:* 8 full-time (5 women), 7 part-time/adjunct (0 women). *Students:* 10 full-time (3 women), 44 part-time (11 women); includes 17 minority (4 Black or African American, non-Hispanic/Latino; 7 Asian, non-Hispanic/Latino; 4 Hispanic/Latino; 2 Two or more races, non-Hispanic/Latino), 11 international. Average age 33. 28 applicants, 61% accepted, 8 enrolled. In 2010, 12 master's awarded. *Degree requirements:* For master's, comprehensive exam, thesis or alternative. *Entrance requirements:* For master's, minimum undergraduate GPA of 2.7. Additional exam requirements/recommendations for international students: Required—TOEFL. *Application deadline:* For fall admission, 7/1 for domestic students; for spring admission, 12/1 for domestic students. Applications are processed on a rolling basis. Application fee: $50. Electronic applications accepted. *Expenses:* Tuition, area resident: Full-time $5012; part-time $470 per credit. Tuition, state resident: full-time $7518; part-time $482 per credit. Tuition, nonresident: full-time $13,962; part-time $482 per credit. Required fees: $3772. One-time fee: $62 part-time. *Financial support:* In 2010–11, 1 student received support, including 1 research assistantship; career-related internships or fieldwork, Federal Work-Study, scholarships/grants, and unspecified assistantships also available. Support available to part-time students. Financial award application deadline: 2/15; financial award applicants required to submit FAFSA. *Unit head:* Dr. Bradley Kjell, Chair, 860-832-2710. *Application contact:* Dr. Bradley Kjell, Chair, 860-832-2710.

Central Connecticut State University, School of Graduate Studies, School of Arts and Sciences, Department of Mathematical Sciences, New Britain, CT 06050-4010. Offers data mining (MS, Certificate); mathematics (MA, MS, Certificate, Sixth Year Certificate), including actuarial science (MA), computer science (MA), statistics (MA). Part-time and evening/weekend programs available. *Faculty:* 33 full-time (10 women), 65 part-time/adjunct (28 women). *Students:* 20 full-time (10 women), 131 part-time (74 women); includes 18 minority (5 Black or African American, non-Hispanic/Latino; 5 Asian, non-Hispanic/Latino; 6 Hispanic/Latino; 2 Two or more races, non-Hispanic/Latino), 8 international. Average age 37. 76 applicants, 59% accepted, 28 enrolled. In 2010, 29 master's, 4 other advanced degrees awarded. *Degree requirements:* For master's, comprehensive exam, thesis or alternative; for other advanced degree, qualifying exam. *Entrance requirements:* For master's, minimum undergraduate GPA of 2.7. Additional exam requirements/recommendations for international students: Required—TOEFL. *Application deadline:* For fall admission, 7/1 for domestic students; for spring admission, 12/1 for domestic students. Applications are processed on a rolling basis. Application fee: $50. Electronic applications accepted. *Expenses:* Tuition, area resident: Full-time $5012; part-time $470 per credit. Tuition, state resident: full-time $7518; part-time $482 per credit. Tuition, nonresident: full-time $13,962; part-time $482 per credit. Required fees: $3772. One-time fee: $62 part-time. *Financial support:* In 2010–11, 6 students received support, including 2 research assistantships; career-related internships or fieldwork, Federal Work-Study, scholarships/grants, and unspecified assistantships also available. Support available to part-time students. Financial award application deadline: 2/15; financial award applicants required to submit FAFSA. *Faculty research:* Statistics, actuarial mathematics, computer systems and engineering, computer programming techniques, operations research. *Unit head:* Dr. Jeffrey McGowan, Chair, 860-832-2835. *Application contact:* Dr. Jeffrey McGowan, Chair, 860-832-2835.

Central Michigan University, College of Graduate Studies, College of Science and Technology, Department of Computer Science, Mount Pleasant, MI 48859. Offers MS. Part-time programs available. *Faculty:* 7 full-time (0 women). *Students:* 12 full-time (6 women), 6 part-time (2 women); includes 1 Asian, non-Hispanic/Latino, 9 international. Average age 24. *Degree requirements:* For master's, thesis or alternative. *Entrance requirements:* For master's, bachelor's degree from accredited institution with minimum GPA of 3.0 in last two years of study. *Application deadline:* For fall admission, 6/1 for international students; for spring admission, 10/1 for international students. Applications are processed on a rolling basis. Application fee: $35 ($45 for international students). Electronic applications accepted. *Expenses:* Tuition, state resident: full-time $8208; part-time $456 per credit hour. Tuition, nonresident: full-time $13,788; part-time $766 per credit hour. One-time fee: $25. *Financial support:* Fellowships with tuition reimbursements, research assistantships with tuition reimbursements, teaching assistantships with tuition reimbursements, career-related internships or fieldwork, Federal Work-Study, unspecified assistantships, and out-of-state merit awards, non-resident graduate awards available. *Faculty research:* Artificial intelligence, biocomputing, data mining, software engineering, operating systems. *Unit head:* Dr. Michael Stinson, Chairperson, 989-774-3774, Fax: 989-774-3728, E-mail: stins1m@cmich.edu. *Application contact:* Dr. Paul Albee, Graduate Program Coordinator, 989-774-3086, Fax: 989-774-3728, E-mail: albee1pb@cmich.edu.

Chicago State University, School of Graduate and Professional Studies, College of Arts and Sciences, Department of Mathematics and Computer Science, Chicago, IL 60628. Offers computer science (MS); mathematics (MS). *Degree requirements:* For master's, thesis optional, oral exam. *Entrance requirements:* For master's, minimum GPA of 2.75.

Christopher Newport University, Graduate Studies, Department of Physics, Computer Science, and Engineering, Newport News, VA 23606-2998. Offers applied physics and computer science (MS). Part-time and evening/weekend programs available. *Faculty:* 6 full-time (0 women), 2 part-time/adjunct (0 women). *Students:* 4 full-time (0 women), 15 part-time (2 women); includes 3 minority (2 Black or African American, non-Hispanic/Latino; 1 Two or more races, non-Hispanic/Latino). Average age 29. 10 applicants, 100% accepted, 2 enrolled. In 2010, 8 master's awarded. *Degree requirements:* For master's, comprehensive exam (for some programs), thesis optional. *Entrance requirements:* For master's, GRE General Test, minimum GPA of 3.0. Additional exam requirements/recommendations for international students: Required—TOEFL (minimum score 580 paper-based; 237 computer-based; 92 iBT). *Application deadline:* For fall admission, 8/15 priority date for domestic students, 4/1 for international students; for spring admission, 10/15 for domestic students, 10/1 for international students. Applications are processed on a rolling basis. Application fee: $50. Electronic applications accepted. *Expenses:* Tuition, state resident: part-time $418 per credit hour. Tuition, nonresident: part-time $769 per credit hour. *Financial support:* In 2010–11, 3 research assistantships with full and partial tuition reimbursements (averaging $2,000 per year) were awarded; fellowships with full tuition reimbursements, career-related internships or fieldwork, Federal Work-Study, and unspecified assistantships also available. Support available to part-time students. Financial award application deadline: 3/1; financial award applicants required to submit FAFSA. *Faculty research:* Advanced programming methodologies, experimental nuclear physics, computer architecture, semiconductor nanophysics, laser and optical fiber sensors. *Unit head:* Dr. Antonio Siochi, Coordinator, 757-594-7569, Fax: 757-594-7919, E-mail: siochi@cnu.edu. *Application* *contact:* Lyn Sawyer, Associate Director, Graduate Admissions and Records, 757-594-7544, Fax: 757-594-7649, E-mail: gradstdy@cnu.edu.

The Citadel, The Military College of South Carolina, Citadel Graduate College, Department of Mathematics and Computer Science, Charleston, SC 29409. Offers computer and information science (MS); mathematics education (MAE). *Accreditation:* NCATE (one or more programs are accredited). Part-time and evening/weekend programs available. *Faculty:* 3 full-time (0 women), 1 part-time/adjunct (0 women). *Students:* 1 (woman) full-time, 18 part-time (8 women); includes 1 Asian, non-Hispanic/Latino. Average age 35. In 2010, 3 master's awarded. *Degree requirements:* For master's, comprehensive exam (for some programs), thesis (for some programs). *Entrance requirements:* For master's, GRE (minimum score 1000 for MS; 900 verbal and quantitative for MAT, raw score of 396), minimum undergraduate GPA of 3.0 (MS) or 2.5 (MAT); competency, demonstrated through coursework, approved work experience, or a program-administrated competency exam, in the areas of basic computer architecture, object-oriented programming, discrete mathematics, and data structures (MS); successful completion of 7 courses (MAT). Additional exam requirements/recommendations for international students: Required—TOEFL (minimum score 550 paper-based; 213 computer-based; 79 iBT). *Application deadline:* Applications are processed on a rolling basis. Application fee: $30. Electronic applications accepted. *Expenses:* Tuition, state resident: part-time $460 per credit hour. Tuition, nonresident: part-time $756 per credit hour. Required fees: $40 per term. *Financial support:* Health care benefits and unspecified assistantships available. Support available to part-time students. Financial award application deadline: 7/1; financial award applicants required to submit FAFSA. *Unit head:* Dr. John I. Moore, Department Head, 843-953-5048, Fax: 843-953-7391, E-mail: john.moore@citadel.edu. *Application contact:* Dr. George L. Rudolph, Computer and Information Science Program Director, 843-953-5032, Fax: 843-953-7391, E-mail: george.rudolph@citadel.edu.

City College of the City University of New York, Graduate School, Grove School of Engineering, Department of Computer Sciences, New York, NY 10031-9198. Offers MS, PhD. PhD program offered jointly with Graduate School and University Center of the City University of New York. *Degree requirements:* For master's, thesis optional; for doctorate, one foreign language, comprehensive exam, thesis/dissertation. *Entrance requirements:* For master's and doctorate, GRE General Test. Additional exam requirements/recommendations for international students: Required—TOEFL (minimum score 500 paper-based; 173 computer-based; 61 iBT). *Faculty research:* Complexities of algebraic research, human issues in computer science, scientific computing, supercompilers, parallel algorithms.

City University of Seattle, Graduate Division, School of Management, Bellevue, WA 98005. Offers accounting (Certificate); change leadership (MBA, Certificate); computer systems (MS); finance (Certificate); financial management (MBA); general management (MBA); general management-Europe (MBA); global marketing (MBA); human resources management (Certificate); individualized study (MBA); information security (MS); information systems (MBA); leadership (MA); marketing (MBA, Certificate); project management (MBA, MS, Certificate); sustainable business (Certificate); technology management (MBA, Certificate). Part-time and evening/weekend programs available. Postbaccalaureate distance learning degree programs offered (no on-campus study). *Entrance requirements:* Additional exam requirements/recommendations for international students: Required—TOEFL (minimum score 540 paper-based; 207 computer-based); Recommended—IELTS. Electronic applications accepted.

Clark Atlanta University, School of Arts and Sciences, Department of Computer and Information Science, Atlanta, GA 30314. Offers MS. Part-time programs available. *Faculty:* 4 full-time (0 women), 1 part-time/adjunct (0 women). *Students:* 6 full-time (2 women), 3 part-time (2 women); includes 6 Black or African American, non-Hispanic/Latino, 2 international. Average age 31. 7 applicants, 100% accepted, 3 enrolled. In 2010, 5 master's awarded. *Degree requirements:* For master's, one foreign language, thesis. *Entrance requirements:* For master's, GRE General Test, minimum GPA of 2.5. Additional exam requirements/recommendations for international students: Required—TOEFL (minimum score 500 paper-based; 173 computer-based; 61 iBT). *Application deadline:* For fall admission, 4/1 for domestic and international students; for spring admission, 11/1 for domestic and international students. Applications are processed on a rolling basis. Application fee: $40 ($55 for international students). *Expenses:* Tuition: Full-time $12,942; part-time $719 per credit hour. Required fees: $710; $355 per semester. *Financial support:* In 2010–11, 4 fellowships were awarded; career-related internships or fieldwork, Federal Work-Study, scholarships/grants, and unspecified assistantships also available. Support available to part-time students. Financial award application deadline: 4/30; financial award applicants required to submit FAFSA. *Unit head:* Dr. Roy George, Chairperson, 404-880-6945, E-mail: rgeorge@cau.edu. *Application contact:* Michelle Clark-Davis, Graduate Program Admissions, 404-880-6605, E-mail: cauadmissions@cau.edu.

Clarkson University, Graduate School, School of Arts and Sciences, Program in Computer Science, Potsdam, NY 13699. Offers MS. Part-time programs available. *Faculty:* 7 full-time (2 women). *Students:* 19 full-time (3 women), 8 international. Average age 26. 29 applicants, 55% accepted, 6 enrolled. In 2010, 5 master's awarded. *Entrance requirements:* For master's, GRE, transcripts of all college coursework, three letters of recommendation; resume and personal statement (recommended). Additional exam requirements/recommendations for international students: Required—TOEFL, TSE recommended. *Application deadline:* For fall admission, 1/30 priority date for domestic and international students; for spring admission, 9/1 priority date for domestic and international students. Applications are processed on a rolling basis. Application fee: $25 ($35 for international students). Electronic applications accepted. *Expenses:* Tuition: Part-time $1136 per credit hour. *Financial support:* In 2010–11, 16 students received support, including 1 fellowship with full tuition reimbursement available (averaging $21,580 per year), 3 research assistantships with full tuition reimbursements available (averaging $21,580 per year), 3 teaching assistantships with full tuition reimbursements available (averaging $21,580 per year); scholarships/grants, tuition waivers (partial), and unspecified assistantships also available. *Faculty research:* Theoretical computer science cryptography. Total annual research expenditures: $76,063. *Unit head:* Dr. Peter Turner, Dean, 315-268-6544, Fax: 315-268-3989, E-mail: pturner@clarkson.edu. *Application contact:* Jennifer Reed, Graduate School Coordinator, School of Arts and Sciences, 315-268-3802, Fax: 315-268-3989, E-mail: sciencegrad@clarkson.edu.

Clemson University, Graduate School, College of Engineering and Science, School of Computing, Program in Computer Science, Clemson, SC 29634. Offers MS, PhD. *Students:* 121 full-time (28 women), 21 part-time (8 women); includes 10 Black or African American, non-Hispanic/Latino, 87 international. Average age 27. 274 applicants, 64% accepted, 56 enrolled. In 2010, 46 master's, 7 doctorates awarded. Terminal master's awarded for partial completion of doctoral program. *Degree requirements:* For master's, thesis optional; for doctorate, thesis/dissertation. *Entrance requirements:* For master's and doctorate, GRE General Test. Additional exam requirements/recommendations for international students: Required—TOEFL. *Application deadline:* Applications are processed on a rolling basis. Application fee: $70 ($80 for international students). Electronic applications accepted. *Expenses:* Tuition, state resident: full-time $6492; part-time $400 per credit hour. Tuition, nonresident: full-time $13,634; part-time $800 per credit hour. Required fees: $262 per semester. Part-time tuition and fees vary according to course load and program. *Financial support:* In 2010–11, 84 students received support, including 11 fellowships with full and partial tuition reimbursements available (averaging $9,207 per year), 33 research assistantships with partial tuition reimbursements available (averaging $14,695 per year), 29 teaching assistantships with partial tuition reimbursements available (averaging $15,113 per year); career-related internships or fieldwork, institutionally sponsored loans, scholarships/grants, health care benefits, and unspecified assistantships also available. Support available to part-time students. Financial award application deadline: 3/1; financial award applicants required to submit FAFSA. *Unit head:* Dr. Larry F. Hodges, Director, 864-656-7552, Fax: 864-656-0145, E-mail: lfh@clemson.edu. *Application contact:* Dr. Mark Smootherman, Director of Graduate Programs, 864-656-5878, Fax: 864-656-0145, E-mail: mark@clemson.edu.

Cleveland State University, College of Graduate Studies, Nance College of Business Administration, Department of Computer and Information Science, Cleveland, OH 44115. Offers computer and information science (MCIS); information systems (DBA). Part-time and evening/weekend programs available. *Faculty:* 11 full-time (1 woman), 6 part-time/adjunct (2 women). *Students:* 33 full-time (13 women), 60 part-time (45 women); includes 2 Asian, non-Hispanic/Latino, 64 international. Average age 26. 283 applicants, 60% accepted, 35 enrolled. In 2010, 27 master's, 1 doctorate awarded. Terminal master's awarded for partial completion of doctoral program. *Degree requirements:* For master's, thesis optional; for doctorate, comprehensive exam, thesis/dissertation. *Entrance requirements:* For master's, GRE or GMAT, minimum GPA of 2.75; for doctorate, GRE or GMAT, MBA, MCIS or equivalent. Additional exam requirements/recommendations for international students: Required—TOEFL (minimum score 525 paper-based; 197 computer-based; 78 iBT). *Application deadline:* For fall admission, 7/15 priority date for domestic students, 5/15 priority date for international students; for spring admission, 12/15 priority date for domestic students. Applications are processed on a rolling basis. Application fee: $30. Electronic applications accepted. *Expenses:* Tuition, state resident: full-time $8447; part-time $469 per credit hour. Tuition, nonresident: full-time $16,020; part-time $890 per credit hour. Required fees: $50. *Financial support:* In 2010–11, 21 students received support, including 7 research assistantships with full and partial tuition reimbursements available (averaging $7,800 per year), 2 teaching assistantships with full and partial tuition reimbursements available (averaging $16,000 per year); career-related internships or fieldwork, tuition waivers (full), and unspecified assistantships also available. *Faculty research:* Artificial intelligence, object-oriented analysis, database design, software efficiency, distributed system, geographical information systems. Total annual research expenditures: $7,500. *Unit head:* Dr. Santosh K. Misra, Chairman, 216-687-4760, Fax: 216-687-5448, E-mail: s.misra@csuohio.edu. *Application contact:* Dr. Santosh K. Misra, Chairman, 216-687-4760, Fax: 216-687-5448, E-mail: s.misra@csuohio.edu.

College of Charleston, Graduate School, School of Sciences and Mathematics, Program in Computer and Information Sciences, Charleston, SC 29424-0001. Offers MS. Program offered jointly with The Citadel, The Military College of South Carolina. Part-time and evening/weekend programs available. *Faculty:* 11 full-time (3 women), 3 part-time/adjunct (0 women). *Students:* 4 full-time (1 woman), 18 part-time (1 woman); includes 2 minority (1 Black or African American, non-Hispanic/Latino; 1 Asian, non-Hispanic/Latino), 1 international. Average age 29. 10 applicants, 60% accepted, 6 enrolled. In 2010, 9 master's awarded. *Degree requirements:* For master's, thesis optional. *Entrance requirements:* For master's, GRE. Additional exam requirements/recommendations for international students: Required—TOEFL (minimum score 81 iBT). *Application deadline:* For fall admission, 6/1 for domestic students; for spring admission, 11/1 for domestic students. Application fee: $45. Electronic applications accepted. *Financial support:* In 2010–11, research assistantships (averaging $12,400 per year); Federal Work-Study, scholarships/grants, and unspecified assistantships also available. Support available to part-time students. Financial award application deadline: 4/1; financial award applicants required to submit FAFSA. *Unit head:* Dr. Renee McCauley, Director, 843-953-3187, E-mail: mccauleyr@cofc.edu. *Application contact:* Susan Hallatt, Director of Graduate Admissions, 843-953-5614, Fax: 843-953-1434, E-mail: hallatts@cofc.edu.

The College of Saint Rose, Graduate Studies, School of Mathematics and Sciences, Program in Computer Information Systems, Albany, NY 12203-1419. Offers MS. Part-time and evening/weekend programs available. *Degree requirements:* For master's, comprehensive exam, research component. *Entrance requirements:* For master's, minimum GPA of 3.0, 9 undergraduate credits in math. Additional exam requirements/recommendations for international students: Required—TOEFL (minimum score 550 paper-based; 213 computer-based). Electronic applications accepted.

College of Staten Island of the City University of New York, Graduate Programs, Program in Computer Science, Staten Island, NY 10314-6600. Offers MS. Part-time and evening/weekend programs available. *Faculty:* 4 full-time (2 women), 2 part-time/adjunct (1 woman). *Students:* 7 full-time (3 women), 26 part-time (6 women); includes 2 Black or African American, non-Hispanic/Latino; 5 Asian, non-Hispanic/Latino, 12 international. Average age 27. 47 applicants, 64% accepted, 14 enrolled. In 2010, 18 master's awarded. *Degree requirements:* For master's, thesis optional. *Entrance requirements:* For master's, GRE General Test, previous undergraduate course work in computer science, minimum GPA of 3.0. Additional exam requirements/recommendations for international students: Required—TOEFL (minimum score 550 paper-based; 213 computer-based; 79 iBT), IELTS (minimum score 6.5). *Application deadline:* Applications are processed on a rolling basis. Application fee: $125. Electronic applications accepted. *Expenses:* Tuition, state resident: full-time $7730; part-time $325 per credit. Tuition, nonresident: full-time $14,520; part-time $605 per credit. Required fees: $378. *Financial support:* In 2010–11, 1 student received support; research assistantships, teaching assistantships, career-related internships or fieldwork, Federal Work-Study, and unspecified assistantships available. Support available to part-time students. Financial award applicants required to submit FAFSA. Total annual research expenditures: $53,000. *Unit head:* Dr. Anatoliy Gordonov, Coordinator, 718-982-2852, Fax: 718-982-2856, E-mail: anatoliy.gordonov@csi.cuny.edu. *Application contact:* Sasha Spence, Assistant Director of Graduate Recruitment and Admissions, 718-982-2699, Fax: 718-982-2500, E-mail: sasha.spence@csi.cuny.edu.

The College of William and Mary, Faculty of Arts and Sciences, Department of Computer Science, Williamsburg, VA 23187-8795. Offers computational operations research (MS), including computer science; computer science (MS, PhD), including computational science (PhD). Part-time programs available. *Faculty:* 13 full-time (3 women). *Students:* 73 full-time (17 women), 9 part-time (4 women); includes 4 minority (2 Black or African American, non-Hispanic/Latino; 1 Asian, non-Hispanic/Latino; 1 Hispanic/Latino), 41 international. Average age 28. 98 applicants, 68% accepted, 27 enrolled. In 2010, 16 master's, 6 doctorates awarded. *Degree requirements:* For master's, comprehensive exam, thesis optional, research project; for doctorate, comprehensive exam, thesis/dissertation. *Entrance requirements:* For master's, GRE General Test, minimum GPA of 2.5; for doctorate, GRE General Test, minimum GPA of 3.0. Additional exam requirements/recommendations for international students: Required—TOEFL, TWE. *Application deadline:* For fall admission, 3/1 priority date for domestic students, 3/1 for international students; for spring admission, 11/1 for domestic and international students. Applications are processed on a rolling basis. Application fee: $45. Electronic applications accepted. *Expenses:* Tuition, state resident: full-time $6400; part-time $345 per credit hour. Tuition, nonresident: full-time $19,720; part-time $920 per credit hour. Required fees: $4368. *Financial support:* In 2010–11, 2 fellowships with full tuition reimbursements (averaging $21,000 per year), 17 research assistantships with full tuition reimbursements (averaging $21,000 per year), 20 teaching assistantships with full tuition reimbursements (averaging $18,000 per year) were awarded; scholarships/grants and unspecified assistantships also available. Financial award application deadline: 3/1; financial award applicants required to submit FAFSA. *Faculty research:* High-performance computing, wireless computing, algorithms, computer systems and network computing, modeling and simulation. Total annual research expenditures: $1.3 million. *Unit head:* Dr. Virginia Torczon, Chair, 757-221-3460, Fax: 757-221-1717, E-mail: chair@cs.wm.edu. *Application contact:* Vanessa Godwin, Administrative Director, 757-221-3455, Fax: 757-221-1717, E-mail: gradinfo@cs.wm.edu.

Colorado School of Mines, Graduate School, Department of Mathematical and Computer Sciences, Golden, CO 80401. Offers MS, PhD. Part-time programs available. *Faculty:* 33 full-time (14 women), 6 part-time/adjunct (1 woman). *Students:* 54 full-time (16 women), 8 part-time (1 woman); includes 1 Black or African American, non-Hispanic/Latino; 1 American Indian or Alaska Native, non-Hispanic/Latino; 2 Asian, non-Hispanic/Latino; 1 Hispanic/Latino, 11 international. Average age 28. 80 applicants, 66% accepted, 24 enrolled. In 2010, 15 master's, 1 doctorate awarded. *Degree requirements:* For master's, thesis (for some programs); for doctorate, comprehensive exam, thesis/dissertation. *Entrance requirements:* For master's and doctorate, GRE General Test. Additional exam requirements/recommendations for international students: Required—TOEFL (minimum score 550 paper-based; 213 computer-based; 80 iBT). *Application deadline:* For fall admission, 1/15 priority date for domestic and international students; for spring admission, 10/15 priority date for domestic and international

Computer Science

Colorado School of Mines (continued)

students. Application fee: $50 ($70 for international students). Electronic applications accepted. *Expenses:* Tuition, state resident: full-time $11,550; part-time $641 per credit. Tuition, nonresident: full-time $25,980; part-time $1444 per credit. Required fees: $1874; $937 per semester. *Financial support:* In 2010–11, 38 students received support, including 6 fellowships with full tuition reimbursements available (averaging $20,000 per year), 19 research assistantships with full tuition reimbursements available (averaging $20,000 per year), 13 teaching assistantships with full tuition reimbursements available (averaging $20,000 per year); scholarships/grants, health care benefits, and unspecified assistantships also available. Financial award application deadline: 1/15; financial award applicants required to submit FAFSA. *Faculty research:* Applied statistics, numerical computation, artificial intelligence, linear optimization. Total annual research expenditures: $660,064. *Unit head:* Dr. Tracy Camp, Interim Department Head, 303-273-2184, Fax: 303-273-3875, E-mail: tcamp@mines.edu. *Application contact:* William Navidi, Professor, 303-273-3489, Fax: 303-273-3875, E-mail: wnavidi@mines.edu.

Colorado State University, Graduate School, College of Natural Sciences, Department of Computer Science, Fort Collins, CO 80523-1873. Offers MCS, MS, PhD. Postbaccalaureate distance learning degree programs offered (no on-campus study). *Faculty:* 19 full-time (3 women), 1 part-time/adjunct (0 women). *Students:* 48 full-time (13 women), 166 part-time (13 women); includes 27 minority (1 Black or African American, non-Hispanic/Latino; 12 Asian, non-Hispanic/Latino; 13 Hispanic/Latino; 1 Two or more races, non-Hispanic/Latino), 61 international. Average age 33. 216 applicants, 62% accepted, 60 enrolled. In 2010, 37 master's, 3 doctorates awarded. Terminal master's awarded for partial completion of doctoral program. *Degree requirements:* For master's, comprehensive exam (for some programs), thesis (MS); for doctorate, comprehensive exam, thesis/dissertation, qualifying, preliminary, and final exams. *Entrance requirements:* For master's, GRE, computer science background, minimum GPA of 3.0, 3 letters of recommendation, statement of purpose, transcripts; for doctorate, GRE General Test, BSC or master's degree in computer science, minimum GPA of 3.0. Additional exam requirements/recommendations for international students: Required—TOEFL (minimum score 550 paper-based; 213 computer-based; 80 iBT). *Application deadline:* For fall admission, 2/1 priority date for domestic and international students; for spring admission, 10/1 priority date for domestic and international students. Applications are processed on a rolling basis. Application fee: $50. Electronic applications accepted. *Expenses:* Tuition, state resident: full-time $7434; part-time $413 per credit. Tuition, nonresident: full-time $19,022; part-time $1057 per credit. Required fees: $1729; $88 per credit. *Financial support:* In 2010–11, 62 students received support, including 1 fellowship (averaging $13,400 per year), 27 research assistantships with full tuition reimbursements available (averaging $11,631 per year), 34 teaching assistantships with full tuition reimbursements available (averaging $11,325 per year); health care benefits also available. Financial award application deadline: 2/15; financial award applicants required to submit FAFSA. *Faculty research:* Artificial intelligence, parallel and distributed computing, software engineering, computer vision/graphics, security. Total annual research expenditures: $2.3 million. *Unit head:* Dr. L. Darrell Whitley, Chairman, 970-491-5373, Fax: 970-491-2466, E-mail: whitley@cs.colostate.edu. *Application contact:* James Peterson, Director of Graduate Admission, 970-491-7137, Fax: 970-491-2466, E-mail: peterson@cs.colostate.edu.

Colorado Technical University Colorado Springs, Graduate Studies, Program in Computer Science, Colorado Springs, CO 80907-3896. Offers computer science (DCS); computer systems security (MSCS); database systems (MSCS); software engineering (MSCS). Part-time and evening/weekend programs available. Postbaccalaureate distance learning degree programs offered. *Degree requirements:* For master's, thesis or alternative; for doctorate, thesis/dissertation. *Entrance requirements:* For doctorate, minimum graduate GPA of 3.0, 5 years of related work experience. *Faculty research:* Software engineering, systems engineering.

Colorado Technical University Denver, Program in Computer Science, Greenwood Village, CO 80111. Offers computer systems security (MSCS); database systems (MSCS); software engineering (MSCS). Part-time and evening/weekend programs available. *Degree requirements:* For master's, thesis or alternative. *Entrance requirements:* For master's, minimum undergraduate GPA of 3.0, resume.

Colorado Technical University Sioux Falls, Program in Computing, Sioux Falls, SD 57108. Offers computer systems security (MSCS); software engineering (MSCS).

Columbia University, Fu Foundation School of Engineering and Applied Science, Department of Computer Science, New York, NY 10027. Offers computer science (MS, Eng Sc D, PhD, Engr); computer science and journalism (MS). PhD offered through the Graduate School of Arts and Sciences. Part-time programs available. Postbaccalaureate distance learning degree programs offered (no on-campus study). *Faculty:* 43 full-time (5 women), 21 part-time/adjunct (2 women). *Students:* 283 full-time (65 women), 107 part-time (20 women); includes 13 minority (1 Black or African American, non-Hispanic/Latino; 11 Asian, non-Hispanic/Latino; 1 Two or more races, non-Hispanic/Latino), 289 international. Average age 27. 974 applicants, 31% accepted, 170 enrolled. In 2010, 155 master's, 18 doctorates, 1 other advanced degree awarded. Terminal master's awarded for partial completion of doctoral program. *Degree requirements:* For master's and Engr, thesis optional; for doctorate, comprehensive exam, thesis/dissertation, candidacy exam. *Entrance requirements:* For master's and Engr, GRE General Test; for doctorate, GRE General Test, GRE Subject Test (computer science). Additional exam requirements/recommendations for international students: Required—TOEFL, IELTS. *Application deadline:* For fall admission, 12/1 priority date for domestic and international students; for spring admission, 10/1 priority date for domestic and international students. Application fee: $95. Electronic applications accepted. *Financial support:* In 2010–11, 134 students received support, including 11 fellowships with full tuition reimbursements available (averaging $28,405 per year), 95 research assistantships with full tuition reimbursements available (averaging $24,894 per year), 28 teaching assistantships with full and partial tuition reimbursements available (averaging $6,000 per year); health care benefits also available. Financial award application deadline: 12/1; financial award applicants required to submit FAFSA. *Faculty research:* Robotics, network security, graphics and user interfaces, computer vision, computational learning theory. *Unit head:* Dr. Shree K. Nayar, T.C. Chang Professor of Computer Science and Department Chairman, 212-939-7092, E-mail: nayar@cs.columbia.edu. *Application contact:* Remiko O. Moss, Assistant Director, 212-939-7000, Fax: 212-666-0140, E-mail: ms-admissions@cs.columbia.edu.

See Display below and Close-Up on page 329.

Columbus State University, Graduate Studies, D. Abbott Turner College of Business and Computer Science, Columbus, GA 31907-5645. Offers applied computer science (MS); business administration (MBA); modeling and simulation (Certificate); organizational leadership (MS). *Accreditation:* AACSB. *Faculty:* 15 full-time (2 women). *Students:* 36 full-time (9 women), 145 part-time (54 women); includes 43 minority (19 Black or African American, non-Hispanic/Latino; 3 American Indian or Alaska Native, non-Hispanic/Latino; 12 Asian, non-Hispanic/Latino; 3 Hispanic/Latino; 6 Two or more races, non-Hispanic/Latino), 11 international. Average age 33. 133 applicants, 61% accepted, 58 enrolled. In 2010, 59 master's awarded. *Entrance requirements:* For master's, GMAT, GRE. Additional exam requirements/recommendations for international students: Required—TOEFL (minimum score 550 paper-based; 213 computer-based; 79 iBT). *Application deadline:* For fall admission, 6/30 for domestic students, 5/1 for international students; for spring admission, 11/1 for domestic and international students. Applications are processed on a rolling basis. Application fee: $30. Electronic applications accepted. *Expenses:* Tuition, state resident: full-time $5573; part-time $232 per semester hour. Tuition, nonresident: full-time $13,968; part-time $582 per semester hour. Required fees: $1300; $650 per semester. Tuition and fees vary according to degree level and program. *Financial support:* In 2010–11, 62 students received support, including 11 research assistantships (averaging $3,000 per year). Financial award application deadline: 5/1. *Unit head:* Dr. Linda U. Hadley, Dean, 706-568-2044, Fax: 706-568-2184, E-mail: hadley_linda@colstate.edu.

Application contact: Katie Thornton, Graduate Admissions Specialist, 706-568-2035, Fax: 706-568-2462, E-mail: thornton_katie@colstate.edu.

Concordia University, School of Graduate Studies, Faculty of Engineering and Computer Science, Department of Computer Science and Software Engineering, Montréal, QC H3G 1M8, Canada. Offers computer science (M App Comp Sc, M Comp Sc, PhD, Diploma); software engineering (MA Sc). *Degree requirements:* For master's, one foreign language, thesis optional; for doctorate, one foreign language, comprehensive exam, thesis/dissertation. *Faculty research:* Computer systems and applications, mathematics of computation, pattern recognition, artificial intelligence and robotics.

Cornell University, Graduate School, Graduate Fields of Engineering, Field of Computer Science, Ithaca, NY 14853-0001. Offers algorithms (M Eng, PhD); applied logic and automated reasoning (M Eng, PhD); artificial intelligence (M Eng, PhD); computer graphics (M Eng, PhD); computer science (M Eng, PhD); computer vision (M Eng, PhD); concurrency and distributed computing (M Eng, PhD); information organization and retrieval (M Eng, PhD); operating systems (M Eng, PhD); parallel computing (M Eng, PhD); programming environments (M Eng, PhD); programming languages and methodology (M Eng, PhD); robotics (M Eng, PhD); scientific computing (M Eng, PhD); theory of computation (M Eng, PhD). *Faculty:* 60 full-time (8 women). *Students:* 233 full-time (45 women); includes 1 Black or African American, non-Hispanic/Latino; 17 Asian, non-Hispanic/Latino; 1 Hispanic/Latino, 140 international. Average age 24. 1,026 applicants, 31% accepted, 163 enrolled. In 2010, 103 master's, 19 doctorates awarded. *Degree requirements:* For doctorate, comprehensive exam, thesis/dissertation. *Entrance requirements:* For master's, GRE General Test, 2 letters of recommendation; for doctorate, GRE General Test, GRE Subject Test (computer science or mathematics), 3 letters of recommendation. Additional exam requirements/recommendations for international students: Required—TOEFL (minimum score 505 paper-based; 213 computer-based; 77 iBT). *Application deadline:* For fall admission, 1/1 for domestic students. Application fee: $70. Electronic applications accepted. *Expenses:* Tuition: Full-time $29,500. Required fees: $76. Tuition and fees vary according to degree level and program. *Financial support:* In 2010–11, 100 students received support, including 25 fellowships with full tuition reimbursements available, 55 research assistantships with full tuition reimbursements available, 28 teaching assistantships with full tuition reimbursements available; institutionally sponsored loans, scholarships/grants, health care benefits, tuition waivers (full and partial), and unspecified assistantships also available. Financial award applicants required to submit FAFSA. *Faculty research:* Artificial intelligence, operating systems and databases, programming languages and security, scientific computing, theory of computing, computational biology and graphics. *Unit head:* Director of Graduate Studies, 607-255-8593, Fax: 607-255-4428. *Application contact:* Graduate Field Assistant, 607-255-8593, Fax: 607-255-4428, E-mail: phd@cs.cornell.edu.

Dalhousie University, Faculty of Computer Science, Halifax, NS B3H 1W5, Canada. Offers computational biology and bioinformatics (M Sc); computer science (PhD); computer science (project-based) (MA Sc); computer science (thesis-based) (MC Sc); electronic commerce (MEC); health informatics (MHI). *Degree requirements:* For master's, thesis (for some programs); for doctorate, thesis/dissertation. *Entrance requirements:* Additional exam requirements/recommendations for international students: Required—1 of the following 5 approved tests: TOEFL, IELTS, CANTEST, CAEL, Michigan English Language Assessment Battery. Electronic applications accepted.

Dartmouth College, Arts and Sciences Graduate Programs, Department of Computer Science, Hanover, NH 03755. Offers MS, PhD. Terminal master's awarded for partial completion of doctoral program. *Degree requirements:* For master's, thesis; for doctorate, thesis/dissertation. *Entrance requirements:* For master's and doctorate, GRE General Test, GRE Subject Test. *Faculty research:* Algorithms, computational geometry and learning, computer vision, information retrieval, robotics.

DePaul University, College of Computing and Digital Media, Chicago, IL 60604. Offers animation (MA, MFA); applied technology (MS); business information technology (MS); cinema (MFA); cinema production (MS); computational finance (MS); computer and information sciences (PhD); computer game development (MS); computer graphics and motion technology (MS); computer information and network security (MS); computer science (MS); e-commerce technology (MS); human-computer interaction (MS); information systems (MS); information technology (MA); information technology project management (MS); network engineering and management (MS); predictive analytics (MS); screenwriting (MFA); software engineering (MS); JD/MA; JD/MS. Part-time and evening/weekend programs available. Postbaccalaureate distance learning degree programs offered (no on-campus study). *Faculty:* 51 full-time (11 women), 50 part-time/adjunct (9 women). *Students:* 952 full-time (230 women), 927 part-time (226 women); includes 557 minority (205 Black or African American, non-Hispanic/Latino; 2 American Indian or Alaska Native, non-Hispanic/Latino; 167 Asian, non-Hispanic/Latino; 136 Hispanic/Latino; 7 Native Hawaiian or other Pacific Islander, non-Hispanic/Latino; 40 Two or more races, non-Hispanic/Latino), 292 international. Average age 31. 896 applicants, 70% accepted, 324 enrolled. In 2010, 417 master's, 6 doctorates awarded. *Degree requirements:* For master's, thesis (for some programs); for doctorate, comprehensive exam, thesis/dissertation. *Entrance requirements:* For master's, GRE or GMAT (MS in computational finance only), bachelor's degree, resume (MS in predictive analytics only), IT experience (MS in information technology project management only), portfolio review (MFA); for doctorate, GRE, master's degree in computer science. Additional exam requirements/recommendations for international students: Required—TOEFL (minimum score 550 paper-based; 213 computer-based; 80 iBT), IELTS (minimum score 6.5), Pearson Test of English (minimum score 53). *Application deadline:* For fall admission, 8/15 priority date for domestic students, 6/1 priority date for international students; for winter admission, 12/15 priority date for domestic students, 9/15 priority date for international students; for spring admission, 3/1 priority date for domestic students, 12/15 priority date for international students. Applications are processed on a rolling basis. Application fee: $25. Electronic applications accepted. *Expenses:* Contact institution. *Financial support:* In 2010–11, 102 students received support, including 4 fellowships with full tuition reimbursements available (averaging $24,435 per year), 6 research assistantships (averaging $21,100 per year), 92 teaching assistantships with full and partial tuition reimbursements available (averaging $6,904 per year); Federal Work-Study, scholarships/grants, tuition waivers (full and partial), and unspecified assistantships also available. Support available to part-time students. Financial award application deadline: 4/30; financial award applicants required to submit FAFSA. *Faculty research:* Bioinformatics, visual computing, graphics and animation, high performance and scientific computing, databases. Total annual research expenditures: $1.4 million. *Unit head:* Dr. David Miller, Dean, 312-362-8381, Fax: 312-362-5185. *Application contact:* Dr. Liz Friedman, Assistant Dean of Student Services, 312-362-8714, Fax: 312-362-5179, E-mail: efriedm2@cdm.depaul.edu.

DigiPen Institute of Technology, Master of Science in Computer Science Program, Redmond, WA 98052. Offers computer science (MS); computer science—part time program (MS). Part-time programs available. *Faculty:* 11 full-time (1 woman), 2 part-time/adjunct (0 women). *Students:* 26 full-time (5 women), 27 part-time (2 women); includes 15 minority (1 Black or African American, non-Hispanic/Latino; 5 Asian, non-Hispanic/Latino; 5 Hispanic/Latino; 1 Native Hawaiian or other Pacific Islander, non-Hispanic/Latino; 3 Two or more races, non-Hispanic/Latino), 9 international. Average age 25. 77 applicants, 53% accepted, 30 enrolled. In 2010, 9 master's awarded. *Degree requirements:* For master's, comprehensive exam (for some programs), thesis (for some programs). *Entrance requirements:* For master's, GRE General Test, GRE Subject Test in computer science (for students with non-computer science degrees). Additional exam requirements/recommendations for international students: Required—TOEFL (minimum score 550 paper-based; 213 computer-based; 80 iBT). *Application deadline:* For fall admission, 2/1 priority date for domestic students; for spring admission, 7/1 for domestic students. Applications are processed on a rolling basis. Application fee: $35. Electronic applications accepted. *Expenses:* Tuition: Full-time $12,004; part-time $8056 per semester. Required fees: $658 per credit. $80 per semester. One-time fee: $150. Tuition and fees vary according to course load. *Financial support:* In 2010–11, 2 students received support, including 1 fellowship with full and partial tuition reimbursement available (averaging $15,184 per year); career-related internships or fieldwork and scholarships/grants also available. Financial award application deadline: 5/1; financial award applicants required to submit FAFSA. *Faculty research:* Interactive Human Project (procedural facial animation), temporal planning for video games, Expressing Emotions through Actions (video game AI), strategies to solve 4x4x3 domineering game (combinatorial game theory), procedural music generation for video games. *Unit head:* Dr. Dmitri Volper, Associate Professor, 425-629-5018, E-mail: dvolper@digipen.edu. *Application contact:* Angela Kugler, Admissions Office, 425-558-0299, Fax: 425-558-0378, E-mail: admissions@digipen.edu.

Drexel University, College of Engineering, Department of Computer Science, Philadelphia, PA 19104-2875. Offers MS, PhD. *Entrance requirements:* For master's, GRE. Additional exam requirements/recommendations for international students: Required—TOEFL. Electronic applications accepted.

Duke University, Graduate School, Department of Computer Science, Durham, NC 27708. Offers MS, PhD. *Faculty:* 37 full-time. *Students:* 94 full-time (18 women); includes 3 Asian, non-Hispanic/Latino; 1 Hispanic/Latino, 73 international. 405 applicants, 21% accepted, 27 enrolled. In 2010, 16 master's, 5 doctorates awarded. *Degree requirements:* For doctorate, thesis/dissertation. *Entrance requirements:* For master's, GRE General Test; for doctorate, GRE General Test, GRE Subject Test (recommended for PhD. applicants). Additional exam requirements/recommendations for international students: Required—TOEFL (minimum score 550 paper-based; 213 computer-based; 83 iBT), IELTS (minimum score 7). *Application deadline:* For fall admission, 12/8 priority date for domestic and international students. Application fee: $75. Electronic applications accepted. *Financial support:* Fellowships, research assistantships, teaching assistantships, Federal Work-Study available. Financial award application deadline: 12/8. *Unit head:* Jun Yang, Director of Graduate Studies, 919-660-6538, Fax: 919-660-6519, E-mail: mkbutler@cs.duke.edu. *Application contact:* Elizabeth Hutton, Director, Graduate Admissions, 919-684-3913, Fax: 919-684-2277, E-mail: grad-admissions@duke.edu.

East Carolina University, Graduate School, College of Technology and Computer Science, Department of Computer Science, Greenville, NC 27858-4353. Offers MS. Part-time and evening/weekend programs available. *Degree requirements:* For master's, comprehensive exam, thesis or alternative. *Entrance requirements:* For master's, GRE General Test. Additional exam requirements/recommendations for international students: Required—TOEFL. Electronic applications accepted. *Expenses:* Tuition, state resident: full-time $3130; part-time $391.25 per credit hour. Tuition, nonresident: full-time $13,817; part-time $1727.13 per credit hour. Required fees: $1916; $239.50 per credit hour. Tuition and fees vary according to campus/location and program. *Faculty research:* Software development, software engineering, artificial intelligence, bioinformatics, cryptography.

East Carolina University, Graduate School, College of Technology and Computer Science, Department of Technology Systems, Greenville, NC 27858-4353. Offers computer network professional (Certificate); industrial technology (MS), including computer networking management, digital communications, industrial distribution and logistics, information security, manufacturing, performance improvement, planning; information assurance (Certificate); occupational safety (MS); technology management (PhD); Website developer (Certificate). *Entrance requirements:* For master's and Certificate, GRE General Test or MAT, minimum GPA of 2.5; for doctorate, GRE General Test, related work experience. *Expenses:* Tuition, state resident: full-time $3130; part-time $391.25 per credit hour. Tuition, nonresident: full-time $13,817; part-time $1727.13 per credit hour. Required fees: $1916; $239.50 per credit hour. Tuition and fees vary according to campus/location and program.

Eastern Illinois University, Graduate School, College of Sciences, Department of Mathematics and Computer Science, Charleston, IL 61920-3099. Offers mathematics (MA); mathematics education (MA). *Entrance requirements:* For master's, GRE General Test.

Eastern Illinois University, Graduate School, Lumpkin College of Business and Applied Sciences, School of Technology, Charleston, IL 61920-3099. Offers computer technology (Certificate); quality systems (Certificate); technology (MS); technology security (Certificate); work performance improvement (Certificate). Part-time and evening/weekend programs available.

Eastern Michigan University, Graduate School, College of Arts and Sciences, Department of Computer Science, Ypsilanti, MI 48197. Offers artificial intelligence (Graduate Certificate); computer science (MS). Part-time and evening/weekend programs available. Postbaccalaureate distance learning degree programs offered (no on-campus study). *Faculty:* 15 full-time (5 women). *Students:* 15 full-time (5 women), 27 part-time (2 women); includes 2 Black or African American, non-Hispanic/Latino; 1 American Indian or Alaska Native, non-Hispanic/Latino; 2 Asian, non-Hispanic/Latino, 17 international. Average age 30. 86 applicants, 59% accepted, 15 enrolled. In 2010, 7 master's, 1 other advanced degree awarded. *Degree requirements:* For master's, thesis or alternative. *Entrance requirements:* For master's, at least 18 credit hours of 200-level (or above) computer science courses including data structures, programming languages like java, C or C++, computer organization; courses in discrete mathematics, probability and statistics, linear algebra and calculus; minimum GPA of 2.75 in computer science. Additional exam requirements/recommendations for international students: Required—TOEFL. *Application deadline:* For fall admission, 8/1 for domestic students, 5/1 for international students; for winter admission, 12/1 for domestic students, 10/1 for international students; for spring admission, 4/1 for domestic students, 2/1 for international students. Application fee: $35. *Financial support:* Fellowships, research assistantships with full tuition reimbursements, teaching assistantships with full tuition reimbursements, career-related internships or fieldwork, Federal Work-Study, institutionally sponsored loans, scholarships/grants, tuition waivers (partial), and unspecified assistantships available. Support available to part-time students. Financial award applicants required to submit FAFSA. *Unit head:* Dr. William McMillan, Department Head, 734-487-1063, Fax: 734-487-6824, E-mail: wmcmillan@emich.edu. *Application contact:* Pamela Moore, Graduate Coordinator, 734-487-1063, Fax: 734-487-6824, E-mail: pmoore@emich.edu.

Eastern Michigan University, Graduate School, College of Arts and Sciences, Department of Mathematics, Ypsilanti, MI 48197. Offers applied statistics (MA); computer science (MA); mathematics (MA); mathematics education (MA). Part-time and evening/weekend programs available. Postbaccalaureate distance learning degree programs offered (minimal on-campus study). *Faculty:* 22 full-time (7 women). *Students:* 5 full-time (3 women), 50 part-time (26 women); includes 7 minority (4 Black or African American, non-Hispanic/Latino; 2 Asian, non-Hispanic/Latino; 1 Hispanic/Latino), 10 international. Average age 35. 35 applicants, 54% accepted, 15 enrolled. In 2010, 19 master's awarded. *Degree requirements:* For master's, thesis optional. *Entrance requirements:* Additional exam requirements/recommendations for international students: Required—TOEFL. *Application deadline:* Applications are processed on a rolling basis. Application fee: $35. *Financial support:* Fellowships, research assistantships with full tuition reimbursements, teaching assistantships with full tuition reimbursements, career-related internships or fieldwork, Federal Work-Study, institutionally sponsored loans, scholarships/grants, tuition waivers (partial), and unspecified assistantships available. Support available to part-time students. Financial award applicants required to submit FAFSA. *Unit head:* Dr. Christopher Gardiner, Department Head, 734-487-1444, Fax: 734-487-2489, E-mail: cgardiner@emich.edu. *Application contact:* Dr. Bingwu Wang, Graduate Coordinator, 734-487-5044, Fax: 734-487-2489, E-mail: bwang@emich.edu.

Eastern Washington University, Graduate Studies, College of Science, Health and Engineering, Department of Computer Science, Cheney, WA 99004-2431. Offers computer and technology-supported education (M Ed); computer science (MS). *Accreditation:* NCATE. Part-time programs available. *Degree requirements:* For master's, comprehensive exam, thesis or alternative. *Entrance requirements:* For master's, minimum GPA of 3.0.

East Stroudsburg University of Pennsylvania, Graduate School, College of Arts and Sciences, Department of Computer Science, East Stroudsburg, PA 18301-2999. Offers MS.

Computer Science

East Stroudsburg University of Pennsylvania (continued)

Part-time and evening/weekend programs available. *Degree requirements:* For master's, comprehensive exam, thesis or alternative. *Entrance requirements:* For master's, bachelor's degree in computer science or related field. Additional exam requirements/recommendations for international students: Required—TOEFL (minimum score 560 paper-based; 220 computer-based; 83 iBT).

East Tennessee State University, School of Graduate Studies, College of Business and Technology, Department of Computer and Information Sciences, Johnson City, TN 37614. Offers applied computer science (MS); information technology (MS). Part-time and evening/weekend programs available. *Faculty:* 15 full-time (3 women). *Students:* 31 full-time (4 women), 21 part-time (4 women); includes 2 minority (1 Asian, non-Hispanic/Latino; 1 Hispanic/Latino), 9 international. Average age 30. 42 applicants, 55% accepted, 15 enrolled. In 2010, 18 master's awarded. *Degree requirements:* For master's, comprehensive exam, thesis optional, capstone. *Entrance requirements:* For master's, GRE General Test, minimum GPA of 2.5. Additional exam requirements/recommendations for international students: Required—TOEFL (minimum score 550 paper-based; 213 computer-based; 79 iBT). *Application deadline:* For fall admission, 6/1 priority date for domestic students, 4/30 for international students; for spring admission, 11/1 for domestic students, 9/30 for international students. Application fee: $25 ($35 for international students). Electronic applications accepted. *Financial support:* In 2010–11, 13 research assistantships with full tuition reimbursements (averaging $9,000 per year), 10 teaching assistantships with full tuition reimbursements (averaging $9,000 per year) were awarded; career-related internships or fieldwork, institutionally sponsored loans, scholarships/grants, and unspecified assistantships also available. Financial award application deadline: 7/1; financial award applicants required to submit FAFSA. *Faculty research:* Operating systems, database design, artificial intelligence, simulation, parallel algorithms. Total annual research expenditures: $1,270. *Unit head:* Dr. Terry Countermine, Chair, 423-439-5332, Fax: 423-439-7119, E-mail: counter@etsu.edu. *Application contact:* Dr. Terry Countermine, Chair, 423-439-5332, Fax: 423-439-7119, E-mail: counter@etsu.edu.

École Polytechnique de Montréal, Graduate Programs, Department of Electrical and Computer Engineering, Montréal, QC H3C 3A7, Canada. Offers automation (M Eng, M Sc A, PhD); computer science (M Eng, M Sc A, PhD); electrical engineering (DESS); electrotechnology (M Eng, M Sc A, PhD); microelectronics (M Eng, M Sc A, PhD); microwave technology (M Eng, M Sc A, PhD). Part-time and evening/weekend programs available. *Degree requirements:* For master's, one foreign language, thesis; for doctorate, one foreign language, thesis/dissertation. *Entrance requirements:* For master's, minimum GPA of 2.75; for doctorate, minimum GPA of 3.0. *Faculty research:* Microwaves, telecommunications, software engineering.

Elmhurst College, Graduate Programs, Program in Computer Network Systems, Elmhurst, IL 60126-3296. Offers MS. Part-time and evening/weekend programs available. Postbaccalaureate distance learning degree programs offered (minimal on-campus study). *Faculty:* 2 full-time (1 woman), 1 part-time/adjunct (0 women). *Students:* 17 part-time (5 women); includes 5 minority (2 Black or African American, non-Hispanic/Latino; 2 Asian, non-Hispanic/Latino; 1 Hispanic/Latino). Average age 32. 18 applicants, 50% accepted, 9 enrolled. In 2010, 9 master's awarded. *Entrance requirements:* For master's, 3 recommendations, resume, statement of purpose. Additional exam requirements/recommendations for international students: Required—TOEFL (minimum score 550 paper-based; 213 computer-based). *Application deadline:* Applications are processed on a rolling basis. Application fee: $0. Electronic applications accepted. *Expenses:* Contact institution. *Financial support:* In 2010–11, 1 student received support. Federal Work-Study and scholarships/grants available. Support available to part-time students. Financial award application deadline: 6/1; financial award applicants required to submit FAFSA. *Unit head:* Elizabeth D. Kuebler, Director of Adult and Graduate Admission, 630-617-3300, Fax: 630-617-6415, E-mail: sal@elmhurst.edu. *Application contact:* Elizabeth D. Kuebler, Director of Adult and Graduate Admission, 630-617-3300, Fax: 630-617-6415, E-mail: sal@elmhurst.edu.

Emory University, Laney Graduate School, Department of Mathematics and Computer Science, Atlanta, GA 30322-1100. Offers computer science (MS, PhD); mathematics (MS, PhD). Terminal master's awarded for partial completion of doctoral program. *Degree requirements:* For master's, thesis; for doctorate, one foreign language, comprehensive exam, thesis/dissertation. *Entrance requirements:* For master's and doctorate, GRE General Test. Electronic applications accepted. *Expenses:* Tuition: Full-time $33,800. Required fees: $1300.

Fairleigh Dickinson University, College at Florham, Maxwell Becton College of Arts and Sciences, Department of Computer Science, Madison, NJ 07940-1099. Offers MS. *Students:* 1 (woman) full-time, 2 part-time (0 women). Average age 29. 3 applicants, 100% accepted, 2 enrolled. In 2010, 1 master's awarded. Application fee: $40. *Unit head:* Dean, 973-443-8500. *Application contact:* Susan Brooman, University Director, Graduate Admissions, 973-443-8905, Fax: 973-443-8088, E-mail: grad@fdu.edu.

Fairleigh Dickinson University, Metropolitan Campus, University College: Arts, Sciences, and Professional Studies, School of Computer Sciences and Engineering, Program in Computer Science, Teaneck, NJ 07666-1914. Offers MS. *Students:* 51 full-time (15 women), 10 part-time (4 women), 52 international. Average age 24. 205 applicants, 58% accepted, 30 enrolled. In 2010, 44 master's awarded. *Application deadline:* Applications are processed on a rolling basis. Application fee: $40. *Application contact:* Susan Brooman, University Director of Graduate Admissions, 201-692-2554, Fax: 201-692-2560, E-mail: globaleducation@fdu.edu.

Ferris State University, College of Business, Big Rapids, MI 49307. Offers application development (MSISM); business intelligence and informatics (MBA); database administration (MSISM); design and innovation management process (MBA); e-business (MSISM); networking (MSISM); quality management (MBA); security (MSISM). *Accreditation:* ACBSP. Part-time and evening/weekend programs available. *Faculty:* 10 full-time (3 women), 2 part-time/adjunct (both women). *Students:* 34 full-time (9 women), 112 part-time (55 women); includes 3 Black or African American, non-Hispanic/Latino; 4 American Indian or Alaska Native, non-Hispanic/Latino; 3 Asian, non-Hispanic/Latino; 3 Hispanic/Latino; 4 Two or more races, non-Hispanic/Latino, 16 international. Average age 32. 68 applicants, 35% accepted, 15 enrolled. In 2010, 62 master's awarded. *Degree requirements:* For master's, comprehensive exam, thesis (for MSISM). *Entrance requirements:* For master's, GRE or GMAT (waived if GPA is 3.5 or better), minimum GPA of 3.0 in junior/senior level classes, 2.75 overall; writing sample; 3 letters of reference; resume. Additional exam requirements/recommendations for international students: Required—TOEFL (minimum score 500 paper-based; 173 computer-based; 67 iBT). *Application deadline:* For fall admission, 7/1 priority date for domestic students, 6/15 for international students; for winter admission, 11/1 priority date for domestic students, 10/15 for international students; for spring admission, 3/1 priority date for domestic students, 2/15 for international students. Applications are processed on a rolling basis. Application fee: $30. Electronic applications accepted. *Financial support:* Career-related internships or fieldwork, Federal Work-Study, scholarships/grants, and unspecified assistantships available. Support available to part-time students. Financial award application deadline: 3/15; financial award applicants required to submit FAFSA. *Faculty research:* Quality improvement, client/server end-user computing, information management and policy, security, digital forensics. *Unit head:* Dr. David Steenstra, Department Chair, 231-591-2168, Fax: 231-591-3548, E-mail: yosts@ferris.edu. *Application contact:* Shannon Yost, Department Secretary, 231-591-2168, Fax: 231-591-3548, E-mail: yosts@ferris.edu.

Fitchburg State University, Division of Graduate and Continuing Education, Program in Computer Science, Fitchburg, MA 01420-2697. Offers MS. Part-time and evening/weekend programs available. *Students:* 31 full-time (10 women), 21 part-time (7 women); includes 2 Black or African American, non-Hispanic/Latino, 42 international. Average age 27. 16 applicants, 88% accepted, 9 enrolled. In 2010, 21 master's awarded. *Entrance requirements:* For master's, GRE General Test, appropriate bachelor's degree, letters of recommendation, resume. Additional exam requirements/recommendations for international students: Required—TOEFL (minimum score 550 paper-based; 213 computer-based; 79 iBT). *Application deadline:* Applications are processed on a rolling basis. Application fee: $25 ($50 for international students). *Expenses:* Tuition, area resident: Part-time $150 per credit. Tuition, state resident: part-time $150 per credit. Tuition, nonresident: part-time $150 per credit. Required fees: $127 per credit. *Financial support:* In 2010–11, research assistantships with partial tuition reimbursements (averaging $5,500 per year); Federal Work-Study, scholarships/grants, and unspecified assistantships also available. Support available to part-time students. Financial award application deadline: 3/1; financial award applicants required to submit FAFSA. *Unit head:* Dr. Stephen Taylor, Chair, 978-665-3704, Fax: 978-665-3658, E-mail: gce@fitchburgstate.edu. *Application contact:* Director of Admissions, 978-665-3144, Fax: 978-665-4540, E-mail: admissions@fitchburgstate.edu.

Florida Atlantic University, College of Engineering and Computer Science, Department of Computer and Electrical Engineering and Computer Science, Boca Raton, FL 33431-0991. Offers computer engineering (MS, PhD); computer science (MS, PhD); electrical engineering (MS, PhD). Part-time and evening/weekend programs available. *Faculty:* 35 full-time (6 women), 3 part-time/adjunct (1 woman). *Students:* 89 full-time (19 women), 101 part-time (25 women); includes 69 minority (14 Black or African American, non-Hispanic/Latino; 22 Asian, non-Hispanic/Latino; 32 Hispanic/Latino; 1 Two or more races, non-Hispanic/Latino), 55 international. Average age 32. 128 applicants, 48% accepted, 45 enrolled. In 2010, 41 master's, 8 doctorates awarded. Terminal master's awarded for partial completion of doctoral program. *Degree requirements:* For master's, thesis optional; for doctorate, thesis/dissertation, qualifying exam. *Entrance requirements:* For master's, GRE General Test, minimum GPA of 3.0; for doctorate, GRE General Test, master's degree, minimum GPA of 3.5. Additional exam requirements/recommendations for international students: Required—TOEFL. *Application deadline:* For fall admission, 7/1 priority date for domestic students, 2/15 for international students; for spring admission, 11/1 for domestic students, 7/15 for international students. Applications are processed on a rolling basis. Application fee: $30. *Expenses:* Tuition, area resident: Part-time $319.96 per credit. Tuition, state resident: part-time $319.96 per credit. Tuition, nonresident: part-time $926.42 per credit. *Financial support:* Fellowships, research assistantships with partial tuition reimbursements, teaching assistantships with full tuition reimbursements, career-related internships or fieldwork and Federal Work-Study available. Support available to part-time students. Financial award application deadline: 4/1; financial award applicants required to submit FAFSA. *Faculty research:* VLSI and neural networks, communication networks, software engineering, computer architecture, multimedia and video processing. *Unit head:* Dr. Borko Furht, Chairman, 561-297-3855, Fax: 561-297-2800. *Application contact:* Dr. Borko Furht, Chairman, 561-297-3855, Fax: 561-297-2800.

Florida Gulf Coast University, Lutgert College of Business, Program in Computer and Information Systems, Fort Myers, FL 33965-6565. Offers MS. *Faculty:* 64 full-time (21 women), 5 part-time/adjunct (1 woman). *Students:* 6 full-time (0 women), 6 part-time (3 women); includes 1 Hispanic/Latino. Average age 35. 10 applicants, 90% accepted, 5 enrolled. In 2010, 3 master's awarded. *Entrance requirements:* For master's, GMAT, minimum GPA of 3.0. Additional exam requirements/recommendations for international students: Required—TOEFL (minimum score 550 paper-based; 213 computer-based). *Application deadline:* For fall admission, 6/1 priority date for domestic students; for spring admission, 11/1 for domestic students. Applications are processed on a rolling basis. Application fee: $30. Electronic applications accepted. *Expenses:* Tuition, state resident: part-time $322.08 per credit hour. Tuition, nonresident: part-time $1117.08 per credit hour. *Faculty research:* Advanced distributed learning technologies, object-oriented systems analysis, database management systems, workgroup support systems, software engineering project management. *Unit head:* Dr. Judy Wynekoop, Chair, 239-590-7387, Fax: 239-590-7330, E-mail: jwynekoo@fgcu.edu. *Application contact:* Marisa Ouverson, Director of Enrollment Management, 239-590-7403, Fax: 239-590-7330, E-mail: mouverso@fgcu.edu.

Florida Institute of Technology, Graduate Programs, College of Engineering, Computer Science Department, Melbourne, FL 32901-6975. Offers computer science (MS, PhD); software engineering (MS). Part-time and evening/weekend programs available. *Faculty:* 11 full-time (0 women), 1 part-time/adjunct (0 women). *Students:* 70 full-time (17 women), 44 part-time (9 women); includes 8 minority (4 Black or African American, non-Hispanic/Latino; 2 Asian, non-Hispanic/Latino; 2 Hispanic/Latino), 73 international. Average age 28. 270 applicants, 60% accepted, 28 enrolled. In 2010, 21 master's, 2 doctorates awarded. *Degree requirements:* For master's, comprehensive exam (for some programs), thesis optional, non-thesis: final exam, seminar, or internship; for doctorate, comprehensive exam, thesis/dissertation, publication in journal, teaching experience (strongly encouraged), specialized research program. *Entrance requirements:* For master's, GRE General Test, minimum GPA of 3.0, 3 letters of recommendation; for doctorate, GRE General Test, GRE Subject Test in computer science (recommended), 3 letters of recommendation, minimum GPA of 3.5, resume, statement of objectives. Additional exam requirements/recommendations for international students: Required—TOEFL (minimum score 550 paper-based; 213 computer-based; 79 iBT). *Application deadline:* For fall admission, 4/1 for international students; for spring admission, 9/30 for international students. Applications are processed on a rolling basis. Application fee: $50. Electronic applications accepted. *Expenses:* Tuition: Part-time $1040 per credit hour. Tuition and fees vary according to campus/location. *Financial support:* In 2010–11, 1 research assistantship with full and partial tuition reimbursement (averaging $5,400 per year), 14 teaching assistantships with full and partial tuition reimbursements (averaging $12,239 per year) were awarded; career-related internships or fieldwork, institutionally sponsored loans, tuition waivers (partial), unspecified assistantships, and tuition remissions also available. Support available to part-time students. Financial award application deadline: 3/1; financial award applicants required to submit FAFSA. *Faculty research:* Artificial intelligence, software engineering, management and processes, programming languages, database systems. Total annual research expenditures: $1.2 million. *Unit head:* Dr. William D. Shoaff, Department Head, 321-674-8066, Fax: 321-674-7046, E-mail: wds@cs.fit.edu. *Application contact:* Cheryl A. Brown, Associate Director of Graduate Admissions, 321-674-7581, Fax: 321-723-9468, E-mail: cbrown@fit.edu.

Florida Institute of Technology, Graduate Programs, Extended Studies Division, Melbourne, FL 32901-6975. Offers acquisition and contract management (MS); aerospace engineering (MS); business administration (MBA); computer information systems (MS); computer science (MS); electrical engineering (MS); engineering management (MS); human resources management (MS); logistics management (MS), including humanitarian and disaster relief logistics; management (MS), including acquisition and contract management, e-business, human resources management, information systems, logistics management, management, transportation management; material acquisition management (MS); mechanical engineering (MS); operations research (MS); project management (MS), including information systems, operations research; public administration (MPA); quality management (MS); software engineering (MS); space systems (MS); space systems management (MS); systems management (MS), including information systems, operations research. Part-time and evening/weekend programs available. Postbaccalaureate distance learning degree programs offered (no on-campus study). *Faculty:* 11 full-time (3 women), 118 part-time/adjunct (24 women). *Students:* 69 full-time (23 women), 907 part-time (369 women); includes 385 minority (242 Black or African American, non-Hispanic/Latino; 15 American Indian or Alaska Native, non-Hispanic/Latino; 44 Asian, non-Hispanic/Latino; 52 Hispanic/Latino; 3 Native Hawaiian or other Pacific Islander, non-Hispanic/Latino; 29 Two or more races, non-Hispanic/Latino), 17 international. 517 applicants, 49% accepted, 245 enrolled. In 2010, 430 degrees awarded. *Degree requirements:* For master's, comprehensive exam (for some programs), capstone course. *Entrance requirements:* For master's, GMAT or resume showing 8 years of supervised experience, minimum GPA of 3.0, 2 letters of recommendation, resume. Additional exam requirements/recommendations for international students: Required—TOEFL (minimum score 550 paper-based; 213 computer-based; 79 iBT). *Application deadline:* For fall admission, 4/1 for international students; for spring admission, 9/30 for international students. Applications are processed on a rolling basis. Application fee: $50. Electronic applications accepted. *Expenses:* Contact institution. *Financial support:* Application deadline: 3/1. *Unit head:* Dr. Theodore Richardson, Senior Associate Dean, 321-674-8123, Fax: 321-674-7597, E-mail: trichardson@

fit.edu. *Application contact:* Carolyn Farrior, Director of Graduate Admissions, Online Learning and Off-Campus Programs, 321-674-7118, Fax: 321-674-8216, E-mail: cfarrior@fit.edu.

Florida International University, College of Engineering and Computing, School of Computing and Information Sciences, Miami, FL 33199. Offers computer science (MS, PhD); computing and information sciences (MS, PhD); telecommunications and networking (MS). Part-time and evening/weekend programs available. *Faculty:* 29 full-time (2 women), 5 part-time/adjunct (0 women). *Students:* 96 full-time (24 women), 67 part-time (12 women); includes 7 Black or African American, non-Hispanic/Latino; 4 Asian, non-Hispanic/Latino; 47 Hispanic/Latino, 84 international. Average age 31. 433 applicants, 21% accepted, 77 enrolled. In 2010, 25 master's, 5 doctorates awarded. *Degree requirements:* For master's, thesis or alternative; for doctorate, comprehensive exam, thesis/dissertation. *Entrance requirements:* For master's and doctorate, GRE General Test, 3 letters of recommendation, minimum GPA of 3.0. Additional exam requirements/recommendations for international students: Required—TOEFL (minimum score 550 paper-based; 80 iBT). *Application deadline:* For fall admission, 6/1 for domestic students, 4/1 for international students; for spring admission, 10/1 for domestic students, 9/1 for international students. Applications are processed on a rolling basis. Application fee: $30. Electronic applications accepted. *Financial support:* Research assistantships, teaching assistantships, institutionally sponsored loans, scholarships/grants, and unspecified assistantships available. Financial award application deadline: 3/1; financial award applicants required to submit FAFSA. *Faculty research:* Database systems, software engineering, operating systems, networks, bioinformatics and computational biology. *Unit head:* Dr. Jainendra Navlakha, Interim Director, School of Computing and Information Sciences, 305-348-2023, Fax: 305-348-3549, E-mail: navlakha@cis.fiu.edu. *Application contact:* Maria Parrilla, Graduate Admissions Assistant, 305-348-1890, Fax: 305-348-6142, E-mail: grad_eng@fiu.edu.

Florida State University, The Graduate School, College of Arts and Sciences, Department of Computer Science, Tallahassee, FL 32306. Offers computer science (MS, PhD); information security (MS). Part-time programs available. *Faculty:* 17 full-time (1 woman), 2 part-time/adjunct (0 women). *Students:* 111 full-time (14 women), 11 part-time (2 women); includes 3 Black or African American, non-Hispanic/Latino; 1 American Indian or Alaska Native, non-Hispanic/Latino; 3 Asian, non-Hispanic/Latino; 10 Hispanic/Latino, 58 international. Average age 28. 200 applicants, 61% accepted, 29 enrolled. In 2010, 34 master's, 6 doctorates awarded. Terminal master's awarded for partial completion of doctoral program. *Degree requirements:* For master's, thesis or alternative; for doctorate, comprehensive exam, thesis/dissertation. *Entrance requirements:* For master's, GRE General Test, minimum undergraduate GPA of 3.0; for doctorate, GRE General Test, minimum GPA of 3.0. Additional exam requirements/recommendations for international students: Required—TOEFL (minimum score 600 paper-based; 250 computer-based; 100 iBT). *Application deadline:* For fall admission, 3/1 priority date for domestic students, 3/1 for international students; for spring admission, 10/1 priority date for domestic students, 10/1 for international students. Application fee: $30. Electronic applications accepted. *Expenses:* Tuition, state resident: full-time $8238.24. *Financial support:* In 2010–11, 92 students received support, including 7 fellowships with full tuition reimbursements available (averaging $17,500 per year), 25 research assistantships with full tuition reimbursements available (averaging $17,000 per year), 53 teaching assistantships with full tuition reimbursements available (averaging $15,500 per year); career-related internships or fieldwork, scholarships/grants, health care benefits, tuition waivers (partial), and unspecified assistantships also available. Financial award application deadline: 3/1; financial award applicants required to submit FAFSA. *Faculty research:* Embedded systems, high performance computing, networking, operating systems, security, databases, algorithms. Total annual research expenditures: $1.3 million. *Unit head:* Dr. David Whalley, Chairman, 850-644-3506, Fax: 850-644-0058, E-mail: chair@cs.fsu.edu. *Application contact:* Kristan L. McAlpin, Graduate Coordinator, 850-645-4975, Fax: 850-644-0058, E-mail: mcalpin@cs.fsu.edu.

Fordham University, Graduate School of Arts and Sciences, Department of Computer and Information Sciences, New York, NY 10458. Offers computer science (MS). Part-time and evening/weekend programs available. *Faculty:* 11 full-time (1 woman). *Students:* 5 full-time (1 woman), 23 part-time (4 women); includes 1 Black or African American, non-Hispanic/Latino; 2 Asian, non-Hispanic/Latino; 5 Hispanic/Latino, 4 international. Average age 32. 27 applicants, 70% accepted, 9 enrolled. In 2010, 13 master's awarded. *Degree requirements:* For master's, thesis optional. *Entrance requirements:* For master's, GRE General Test. Additional exam requirements/recommendations for international students: Required—TOEFL (minimum score 550 paper-based; 213 computer-based). *Application deadline:* For fall admission, 1/4 priority date for domestic students; for spring admission, 11/1 for domestic students. Application fee: $70. Electronic applications accepted. *Financial support:* In 2010–11, 5 students received support, including 1 fellowship with tuition reimbursement available (averaging $21,800 per year), 4 research assistantships with tuition reimbursements available (averaging $18,400 per year); career-related internships or fieldwork, institutionally sponsored loans, tuition waivers (full and partial), and unspecified assistantships also available. Financial award application deadline: 1/4; financial award applicants required to submit CSS PROFILE or FAFSA. *Faculty research:* Robotics and computer vision, data mining and informatics, information and networking, computation and algorithms, biomedical informatics. Total annual research expenditures: $50,000. *Unit head:* Dr. Damian Lyons, Chair, 718-817-4480, Fax: 718-817-4488. *Application contact:* Charlene Dundie, Director of Graduate Admissions, 718-817-4420, Fax: 718-817-3566, E-mail: dundie@fordham.edu.

Franklin University, Computer Science Program, Columbus, OH 43215-5399. Offers MS. Part-time and evening/weekend programs available. *Students:* 22 full-time (6 women), 22 part-time (8 women); includes 8 minority (3 Black or African American, non-Hispanic/Latino; 5 Asian, non-Hispanic/Latino), 13 international. Average age 35. In 2010, 23 master's awarded. *Entrance requirements:* For master's, minimum undergraduate GPA of 2.75. Additional exam requirements/recommendations for international students: Required—TOEFL (minimum score 550 paper-based; 213 computer-based). *Application deadline:* For fall admission, 8/1 priority date for domestic students, 6/1 for international students; for winter admission, 12/1 priority date for domestic students, 10/1 for international students; for spring admission, 3/15 priority date for domestic students, 2/1 for international students. Applications are processed on a rolling basis. Application fee: $30. Electronic applications accepted. *Expenses:* Contact institution. *Financial support:* Application deadline: 6/15. *Unit head:* Dr. Ron Hartung, Program Chair, 614-947-6139, Fax: 614-224-4025, E-mail: hartung@franklin.edu. *Application contact:* 614-797-4700, Fax: 614-221-7723, E-mail: gradschl@franklin.edu.

Frostburg State University, Graduate School, College of Liberal Arts and Sciences, Department of Computer Science, Program in Applied Computer Science, Frostburg, MD 21532-1099. Offers MS. *Entrance requirements:* Additional exam requirements/recommendations for international students: Required—TOEFL. Electronic applications accepted.

Gannon University, School of Graduate Studies, College of Engineering and Business, School of Engineering and Computer Science, Program in Computer and Information Science, Erie, PA 16541-0001. Offers MCIS. Part-time and evening/weekend programs available. *Students:* 30 full-time (5 women), 12 part-time (7 women), 34 international. Average age 27. 340 applicants, 49% accepted, 16 enrolled. In 2010, 8 master's awarded. *Degree requirements:* For master's, research project or thesis. *Entrance requirements:* For master's, GRE or GMAT, letters of recommendation, resume. Additional exam requirements/recommendations for international students: Required—TOEFL (minimum score 79 iBT). *Application deadline:* Applications are processed on a rolling basis. Application fee: $25. Electronic applications accepted. *Expenses:* Tuition: Full-time $14,670; part-time $815 per credit. Required fees: $430; $18 per credit. Tuition and fees vary according to class time, course load, degree level, campus/location and program. *Financial support:* Career-related internships or fieldwork, Federal Work-Study, scholarships/grants, traineeships, and unspecified assistantships available. Financial award application deadline: 7/1; financial award applicants required to submit FAFSA. *Faculty research:* Refinement of software engineering processes, graph databases and bioinformatics, aspect-oriented programs and testing, software systems for healthcare applications, game programming. *Unit head:* Dr. Theresa Vitolo, Chair, 814-871-7126, E-mail: vitolo001@gannon.edu. *Application contact:* Kara Morgan, Assistant Director of Graduate Admissions, 814-871-5831, Fax: 814-871-5827, E-mail: graduate@gannon.edu.

George Mason University, Volgenau School of Engineering, Department of Computer Science, Fairfax, VA 22030. Offers biometrics (Certificate); computer games technology (Certificate); computer networking (Certificate); computer science (MS, PhD); data mining (Certificate); database management (Certificate); electronic commerce (Certificate); foundations of information systems (Certificate); information engineering (Certificate); information security and assurance (MS, Certificate); information systems (MS); intelligent agents (Certificate); software architecture (Certificate); software engineering (MS, Certificate); systems engineering (MS); Web-based software engineering (Certificate). MS program offered jointly with Old Dominion University, University of Virginia, Virginia Commonwealth University, and Virginia Polytechnic Institute and State University. Part-time and evening/weekend programs available. Postbaccalaureate distance learning degree programs offered. *Faculty:* 42 full-time (9 women), 20 part-time/adjunct (1 woman). *Students:* 124 full-time (37 women), 453 part-time (103 women); includes 14 Black or African American, non-Hispanic/Latino; 66 Asian, non-Hispanic/Latino; 13 Hispanic/Latino; 3 Two or more races, non-Hispanic/Latino, 206 international. Average age 30. 904 applicants, 53% accepted, 150 enrolled. In 2010, 203 master's, 4 doctorates, 20 other advanced degrees awarded. *Degree requirements:* For master's, thesis optional; for doctorate, comprehensive exam, thesis/dissertation. *Entrance requirements:* For master's, GRE General Test, minimum GPA of 3.0 in last 60 hours, 3 letters of recommendation; for doctorate, GRE, 4-year BA, academic work in computer science, 3 letters of recommendation, statement of career goals and aspirations. Additional exam requirements/recommendations for international students: Required—TOEFL (minimum score 570 paper-based; 230 computer-based; 88 iBT). *Application deadline:* For fall admission, 4/15 priority date for domestic students, 1/15 for international students; for spring admission, 11/15 for domestic students. Application fee: $100. Electronic applications accepted. *Expenses:* Tuition, state resident: full-time $8192; part-time $440 per credit hour. Tuition, nonresident: full-time $22,952; part-time $1055 per credit hour. Required fees: $2364; $99 per credit hour. *Financial support:* In 2010–11, 101 students received support, including 3 fellowships (averaging $18,000 per year), 52 research assistantships (averaging $15,078 per year), 47 teaching assistantships (averaging $10,983 per year); career-related internships or fieldwork, Federal Work-Study, scholarships/grants, unspecified assistantships, and health care benefits (full-time research or teaching assistantship recipients) also available. Financial award application deadline: 3/1; financial award applicants required to submit FAFSA. *Faculty research:* Artificial intelligence, image processing/graphics, parallel/distributed systems, software engineering systems. Total annual research expenditures: $1.3 million. *Unit head:* Dr. Arun Sood, Director, 703-993-1524, Fax: 703-993-1710, E-mail: asood@gmu.edu. *Application contact:* Jay Shapiro, Professor, 703-993-1485, E-mail: jshapiro@gmu.edu.

Georgetown University, Graduate School of Arts and Sciences, Department of Computer Science, Washington, DC 20057. Offers MS. Part-time and evening/weekend programs available. *Degree requirements:* For master's, thesis optional. *Entrance requirements:* For master's, GRE, basic course work in data structures, advanced math, and programming; 3 letters of recommendation. Additional exam requirements/recommendations for international students: Required—TOEFL. Electronic applications accepted. *Faculty research:* Data mining, artificial intelligence, software engineering, security.

The George Washington University, School of Engineering and Applied Science, Department of Computer Science, Washington, DC 20052. Offers MS, D Sc. Part-time and evening/weekend programs available. *Faculty:* 15 full-time (3 women), 19 part-time/adjunct (4 women). *Students:* 105 full-time (37 women), 195 part-time (50 women); includes 17 Black or African American, non-Hispanic/Latino; 2 American Indian or Alaska Native, non-Hispanic/Latino; 24 Asian, non-Hispanic/Latino; 3 Hispanic/Latino, 129 international. Average age 31. 369 applicants, 81% accepted, 79 enrolled. In 2010, 100 master's, 4 doctorates awarded. *Degree requirements:* For master's, thesis optional; for doctorate, thesis/dissertation, dissertation defense, qualifying exam. *Entrance requirements:* For master's, appropriate bachelor's degree, minimum GPA of 3.0; for doctorate, appropriate bachelor's or master's degree, minimum GPA of 3.3, GRE if highest earned degree is BS. Additional exam requirements/recommendations for international students: Required—TOEFL or The George Washington University English as a Foreign Language Test. *Application deadline:* For fall admission, 3/1 priority date for domestic students; for spring admission, 10/1 for domestic students. Applications are processed on a rolling basis. Application fee: $75. *Financial support:* In 2010–11, 49 students received support; fellowships with tuition reimbursements available, research assistantships, teaching assistantships with tuition reimbursements available, career-related internships or fieldwork, institutionally sponsored loans, and tuition waivers available. Financial award application deadline: 3/1; financial award applicants required to submit FAFSA. *Faculty research:* Computer graphics, multimedia, VLSI, parallel processing. *Unit head:* Abdou Youssef, Chair, 202-994-7181, E-mail: ayoussef@gwu.edu. *Application contact:* Adina Lav, Marketing, Recruiting and Admissions, 202-994-5827, Fax: 202-994-0909, E-mail: engineering@gwu.edu.

Georgia Institute of Technology, Graduate Studies and Research, College of Computing, Atlanta, GA 30332-0001. Offers algorithms, combinatorics, and optimization (PhD); computational science and engineering (MS, PhD); computer science (MS, MSCS, PhD); human computer interaction (MSHCI); human-centered computing (PhD); information security (MS). Part-time programs available. Postbaccalaureate distance learning degree programs offered. Terminal master's awarded for partial completion of doctoral program. *Degree requirements:* For master's, thesis optional; for doctorate, comprehensive exam, thesis/dissertation. *Entrance requirements:* For master's, GRE General Test, GRE Subject Test, minimum GPA of 3.0; for doctorate, GRE General Test, GRE Subject Test, minimum GPA of 3.3. Additional exam requirements/recommendations for international students: Required—TOEFL. *Faculty research:* Computer systems, graphics, intelligent systems and artificial intelligence, networks and telecommunications, software engineering.

Georgia Southern University, Jack N. Averitt College of Graduate Studies, College of Information Technology, Statesboro, GA 30460. Offers computer science (MS). Postbaccalaureate distance learning degree programs offered. *Faculty:* 21 full-time (4 women), 1 part-time/adjunct (0 women). *Students:* 2 full-time (1 woman), 11 part-time (2 women); includes 3 Black or African American, non-Hispanic/Latino; 1 Asian, non-Hispanic/Latino. Average age 30. 16 applicants, 100% accepted, 10 enrolled. *Expenses:* Tuition, state resident: full-time $6000; part-time $250 per semester hour. Tuition, nonresident: full-time $23,976; part-time $999 per semester hour. Required fees: $1644. *Financial support:* In 2010–11, 7 students received support. *Faculty research:* Game programming, software engineering, database, Internet technology, knowledge systems. Total annual research expenditures: $50,000. *Unit head:* Dr. Ron Shiffler, Interim Dean, 912-478-7454, E-mail: shiffler@georgiasouthern.edu. *Application contact:* Dr. Lixin Li, Graduate Director, 912-478-7646, Fax: 912-478-7672, E-mail: mscs@georgiasouthern.edu.

Georgia Southwestern State University, Graduate Studies, School of Computer and Information Sciences, Americus, GA 31709-4693. Offers computer information systems (MS); computer science (MS). Part-time programs available. *Degree requirements:* For master's, thesis (for some programs). *Entrance requirements:* For master's, GRE General Test, minimum GPA of 3.0. Electronic applications accepted. *Faculty research:* Database, Internet technologies, computational complexity, encryption.

Georgia State University, College of Arts and Sciences, Department of Computer Science, Atlanta, GA 30302-3083. Offers MS, PhD. Part-time and evening/weekend programs available. Terminal master's awarded for partial completion of doctoral program. *Degree requirements:* For master's, comprehensive exam, thesis or alternative; for doctorate, thesis/dissertation, qualifying exam. *Entrance requirements:* For master's, GRE General Test, 3 letters of recommendation; for doctorate, 3 letters of recommendation. Additional exam requirements/recommendations for international students: Required—TOEFL. Electronic applications accepted.

Computer Science

Georgia State University (continued)
Faculty research: Computer networks, databases, artificial intelligence, bioinformatics, parallel and distributed computing, graphics and visualization.

Governors State University, College of Arts and Sciences, Program in Computer Science, University Park, IL 60466-0975. Offers MS. Part-time and evening/weekend programs available. *Degree requirements:* For master's, thesis or alternative. *Entrance requirements:* For master's, minimum GPA of 2.75. *Expenses:* Tuition, state resident: full-time $5400; part-time $225 per credit hour. Tuition, nonresident: full-time $16,200; part-time $675 per credit hour. Required fees: $1358; $46 per credit hour. $126 per term. Tuition and fees vary according to degree level and program.

Graduate School and University Center of the City University of New York, Graduate Studies, Program in Computer Science, New York, NY 10016-4039. Offers PhD. Program offered jointly with College of Staten Island of the City University of New York. *Degree requirements:* For doctorate, one foreign language, thesis/dissertation. *Entrance requirements:* For doctorate, GRE General Test. Additional exam requirements/recommendations for international students: Required—TOEFL. Electronic applications accepted.

Grand Valley State University, Padnos College of Engineering and Computing, School of Computing and Information Systems, Allendale, MI 49401-9403. Offers computer information systems (MS), including databases, distributed systems, management of information systems, object-oriented systems, software engineering. Part-time and evening/weekend programs available. *Degree requirements:* For master's, thesis or alternative. *Entrance requirements:* For master's, GMAT or GRE General Test. Additional exam requirements/recommendations for international students: Required—TOEFL. Electronic applications accepted. *Faculty research:* Object technology, distributed computing, information systems management database, software engineering.

Hampton University, Graduate College, Department of Computer Science, Hampton, VA 23668. Offers MS. Part-time and evening/weekend programs available. *Degree requirements:* For master's, thesis or alternative. *Entrance requirements:* For master's, GRE General Test. *Faculty research:* Software testing, neural networks, parallel processing, computer graphics, natural language processing.

Harvard University, Graduate School of Arts and Sciences, School of Engineering and Applied Sciences, Cambridge, MA 02138. Offers applied mathematics (ME, SM, PhD); applied physics (ME, SM, PhD); computer science (ME, SM, PhD); engineering science (ME); engineering sciences (SM, PhD). Part-time programs available. Terminal master's awarded for partial completion of doctoral program. *Degree requirements:* For master's, thesis optional; for doctorate, comprehensive exam, thesis/dissertation. *Entrance requirements:* For master's and doctorate, GRE General Test, GRE Subject Test (recommended), 3 letters of recommendation. Additional exam requirements/recommendations for international students: Required—TOEFL (minimum score 80 iBT). Electronic applications accepted. *Expenses:* Tuition: Full-time $34,976. Required fees: $1166. Full-time tuition and fees vary according to program. *Faculty research:* Applied mathematics, applied physics, computer science and electrical engineering, environmental engineering, mechanical and biomedical engineering.

Hofstra University, College of Liberal Arts and Sciences, Department of Computer Science, Hempstead, NY 11549. Offers MA, MS. Part-time and evening/weekend programs available. Postbaccalaureate distance learning degree programs offered (minimal on-campus study). *Faculty:* 5 full-time (3 women), 5 part-time/adjunct (0 women). *Students:* 7 full-time (1 woman), 20 part-time (3 women); includes 5 minority (3 Black or African American, non-Hispanic/Latino; 2 Hispanic/Latino), 1 international. Average age 32. 23 applicants, 100% accepted, 14 enrolled. In 2010, 5 master's awarded. *Degree requirements:* For master's, thesis optional, 30 credits; 3.0 GPA. *Entrance requirements:* For master's, GRE, Minimum GPA of 3.0. Additional exam requirements/recommendations for international students: Required—TOEFL (minimum score 550 paper-based; 213 computer-based; 80 iBT). *Application deadline:* Applications are processed on a rolling basis. Application fee: $70 ($75 for international students). Electronic applications accepted. *Expenses:* Tuition: Full-time $18,000; part-time $1000 per credit hour. Required fees: $970; $145 per term. Tuition and fees vary according to program. *Financial support:* In 2010–11, 16 students received support, including 3 fellowships with full and partial tuition reimbursements available (averaging $2,983 per year); research assistantships with full and partial tuition reimbursements available, Federal Work-Study, institutionally sponsored loans, scholarships/grants, tuition waivers (full and partial), and unspecified assistantships also available. Support available to part-time students. Financial award applicants required to submit FAFSA. *Faculty research:* Computer vision, programming languages, data mining, software engineering, wireless sensor networks. Total annual research expenditures: $100,000. *Unit head:* Dr. Gerda Kamberova, Chairperson, 516-463-5775, Fax: 516-463-5790, E-mail: cscglk@hofstra.edu. *Application contact:* Carol Drummer, Dean of Graduate Admissions, 516-463-4876, Fax: 516-463-4664, E-mail: gradstudent@hofstra.edu.

Hood College, Graduate School, Programs in Computer and Information Sciences, Frederick, MD 21701-8575. Offers computer and information sciences (MS); computer science (MS); information security (Certificate). Part-time and evening/weekend programs available. *Faculty:* 5 full-time (1 woman), 4 part-time/adjunct (1 woman). *Students:* 18 full-time (4 women), 68 part-time (12 women); includes 5 Black or African American, non-Hispanic/Latino; 8 Asian, non-Hispanic/Latino; 4 Hispanic/Latino; 2 Two or more races, non-Hispanic/Latino, 14 international. Average age 33. 49 applicants, 65% accepted, 20 enrolled. In 2010, 14 master's awarded. *Degree requirements:* For master's, thesis. *Entrance requirements:* For master's, minimum GPA of 2.75. Additional exam requirements/recommendations for international students: Required—TOEFL (minimum score 575 paper-based; 231 computer-based; 89 iBT). *Application deadline:* For fall admission, 7/15 for domestic and international students; for spring admission, 12/15 for domestic and international students. Applications are processed on a rolling basis. Application fee: $35. Electronic applications accepted. *Expenses:* Tuition: Full-time $6480; part-time $360 per credit. Required fees: $100; $50 per term. *Financial support:* Applicants required to submit FAFSA. *Faculty research:* Systems engineering, natural language, processing, database design, artificial intelligence and parallel distributed computing. *Unit head:* Dr. Xinlian Liu, Director, 301-696-3981, E-mail: liu@hood.edu. *Application contact:* Dr. Allen P. Flora, Dean of Graduate School, 301-696-3811, Fax: 301-696-3597, E-mail: gofurther@hood.edu.

Howard University, College of Engineering, Architecture, and Computer Sciences, School of Engineering and Computer Science, Department of Systems and Computer Science, Washington, DC 20059-0002. Offers MCS. Offered through the Graduate School of Arts and Sciences. Part-time programs available. *Degree requirements:* For master's, thesis. *Entrance requirements:* For master's, GRE General Test, minimum GPA of 3.0. Additional exam requirements/recommendations for international students: Required—TOEFL (minimum score 213 computer-based). Electronic applications accepted. *Faculty research:* Software engineering, software fault-tolerance, software reliability, artificial intelligence.

Illinois Institute of Technology, Graduate College, College of Science and Letters, Department of Computer Science, Chicago, IL 60616-3793. Offers business (MCS); computer networking and telecommunications (MCS); computer science (MCS, MS, PhD); information systems (MCS); software engineering (MCS); teaching (MST). Part-time and evening/weekend programs available. Postbaccalaureate distance learning degree programs offered (no on-campus study). *Faculty:* 29 full-time (6 women), 3 part-time/adjunct (0 women). *Students:* 262 full-time (62 women), 132 part-time (27 women); includes 44 minority (3 Black or African American, non-Hispanic/Latino; 7 Asian, non-Hispanic/Latino; 34 Hispanic/Latino), 340 international. Average age 26. 974 applicants, 71% accepted, 148 enrolled. In 2010, 138 master's, 5 doctorates awarded. Terminal master's awarded for partial completion of doctoral program. *Degree requirements:* For master's, thesis optional; for doctorate, comprehensive exam, thesis/dissertation. *Entrance requirements:* For master's, GRE General Test (minimum scores: 1000 Quantitative and Verbal, 3.0 Analytical Writing), minimum undergraduate GPA of 3.0; for doctorate, GRE General Test (minimum scores: 1100 Quantitative and Verbal, 3.5 Analytical Writing), minimum undergraduate GPA of 3.0. Additional exam requirements/recommendations for international students: Required—TOEFL (minimum score 523 paper-based; 70 iBT). *Application deadline:* For fall admission, 5/1 for domestic and international students; for spring admission, 10/15 for domestic and international students. Applications are processed on a rolling basis. Application fee: $50. Electronic applications accepted. *Expenses:* Tuition: Full-time $18,576; part-time $1032 per credit hour. Required fees: $583 per semester. One-time fee: $150. Tuition and fees vary according to program and student level. *Financial support:* In 2010–11, 15 research assistantships with full and partial tuition reimbursements (averaging $10,380 per year), 21 teaching assistantships with full and partial tuition reimbursements (averaging $12,452 per year) were awarded; fellowships with partial tuition reimbursements, career-related internships or fieldwork, Federal Work-Study, institutionally sponsored loans, scholarships/grants, traineeships, health care benefits, tuition waivers (partial), and unspecified assistantships also available. Support available to part-time students. Financial award applicants required to submit FAFSA. *Faculty research:* Algorithms, data structures, artificial intelligences, computer architecture, computer graphics, computer networking and telecommunications. Total annual research expenditures: $1.8 million. *Unit head:* Dr. Xian-He Sun, Chair/Professor, 312-567-5260, Fax: 312-567-5067, E-mail: sun@cs.iit.edu. *Application contact:* Debbie Gibson, Director, Graduate Admission, 866-472-3448, Fax: 312-567-3138, E-mail: inquiry.grad@iit.edu.

Indiana State University, College of Graduate and Professional Studies, College of Arts and Sciences, Department of Mathematics and Computer Science, Terre Haute, IN 47809. Offers math teaching (MA, MS); mathematics and computer science (MA); mathematics and computer sciences (MS). Part-time programs available. *Degree requirements:* For master's, thesis or alternative. *Entrance requirements:* For master's, 24 semester hours of course work in undergraduate mathematics. Electronic applications accepted.

Indiana University Bloomington, School of Informatics, Program in Computer Science, Bloomington, IN 47405. Offers MS, PhD. *Faculty:* 33 full-time (6 women), 12 part-time/adjunct (1 woman). *Students:* 208 full-time (42 women), 7 part-time (3 women); includes 3 Black or African American, non-Hispanic/Latino; 3 Asian, non-Hispanic/Latino; 1 Two or more races, non-Hispanic/Latino, 165 international. Average age 27. 496 applicants, 36% accepted, 58 enrolled. In 2010, 64 master's, 18 doctorates awarded. Terminal master's awarded for partial completion of doctoral program. *Degree requirements:* For master's, thesis optional; for doctorate, comprehensive exam, thesis/dissertation, oral and written exams. *Entrance requirements:* For master's and doctorate, GRE General Test. Additional exam requirements/recommendations for international students: Required—TOEFL. *Application deadline:* For fall admission, 1/15 priority date for domestic students, 12/1 priority date for international students. Application fee: $55 ($65 for international students). Electronic applications accepted. *Financial support:* In 2010–11, fellowships with full tuition reimbursements (averaging $25,000 per year), research assistantships with full tuition reimbursements (averaging $14,000 per year), teaching assistantships with full tuition reimbursements (averaging $14,000 per year) were awarded; health care benefits and unspecified assistantships also available. *Faculty research:* Artificial intelligence, database and information systems, distributed and parallel systems, foundations, programming languages and compilers. *Unit head:* Dr. Andrew Lumsdaine, Chairman, 812-855-7071, E-mail: lums@cs.indiana.edu. *Application contact:* Debbie Canada, Graduate Administrator, 812-855-6487, Fax: 812-855-4829, E-mail: gradvise@cs.indiana.edu.

Indiana University–Purdue University Fort Wayne, College of Engineering, Technology, and Computer Science, Department of Computer Science, Fort Wayne, IN 46805-1499. Offers applied computer science (MS). Part-time programs available. *Faculty:* 10 full-time (1 woman), 1 part-time/adjunct (0 women). *Students:* 7 full-time (3 women), 23 part-time (7 women); includes 2 minority (1 Asian, non-Hispanic/Latino; 1 Hispanic/Latino), 4 international. Average age 30. 13 applicants, 85% accepted, 9 enrolled. In 2010, 6 master's awarded. *Entrance requirements:* For master's, GRE General Test, minimum GPA of 3.0. Additional exam requirements/recommendations for international students: Required—TOEFL (minimum score 550 paper-based; 213 computer-based; 77 iBT); Recommended—TWE. *Application deadline:* For fall admission, 7/15 for domestic students, 5/15 for international students; for spring admission, 12/1 for domestic students, 10/15 for international students. Applications are processed on a rolling basis. Application fee: $55 ($60 for international students). Electronic applications accepted. *Expenses:* Tuition, state resident: full-time $4824; part-time $268 per credit. Tuition, nonresident: full-time $11,625; part-time $646 per credit. Required fees: $555; $30.85 per credit. Tuition and fees vary according to course load. *Financial support:* In 2010–11, 1 research assistantship with partial tuition reimbursement (averaging $12,740 per year), 3 teaching assistantships with partial tuition reimbursements (averaging $12,740 per year) were awarded; career-related internships or fieldwork, scholarships/grants, and unspecified assistantships also available. Support available to part-time students. Financial award application deadline: 3/1; financial award applicants required to submit FAFSA. *Faculty research:* Congestion control and wireless networks, mining. Total annual research expenditures: $4,790. *Unit head:* Dr. Peter Ng, Chair, 260-481-6237, Fax: 260-481-5734, E-mail: ngp@ipfw.edu. *Application contact:* Dr. David Liu, Graduate Program Director, 260-481-0182, Fax: 260-481-5734, E-mail: liud@ipfw.edu.

Indiana University–Purdue University Indianapolis, School of Science, Department of Computer and Information Science, Indianapolis, IN 46202-5132. Offers computer science (MS, PhD). Part-time and evening/weekend programs available. *Faculty:* 3 full-time (0 women). *Students:* 43 full-time (12 women), 80 part-time (24 women); includes 15 minority (3 Black or African American, non-Hispanic/Latino; 10 Asian, non-Hispanic/Latino; 1 Hispanic/Latino; 1 Two or more races, non-Hispanic/Latino), 75 international. Average age 28. 128 applicants, 63% accepted, 43 enrolled. In 2010, 20 master's awarded. *Degree requirements:* For master's, thesis optional. *Entrance requirements:* For master's, GRE, BS in computer science or the equivalent. *Application deadline:* For fall admission, 1/15 priority date for domestic students; for spring admission, 9/15 for domestic students. Applications are processed on a rolling basis. Application fee: $55 ($65 for international students). Electronic applications accepted. *Financial support:* In 2010–11, 4 fellowships (averaging $13,125 per year), 18 teaching assistantships with tuition reimbursements (averaging $6,915 per year) were awarded; research assistantships with tuition reimbursements, career-related internships or fieldwork, institutionally sponsored loans, and tuition waivers (full and partial) also available. Support available to part-time students. Financial award application deadline: 1/15; financial award applicants required to submit FAFSA. *Faculty research:* Artificial intelligence, graphics and visualization, computational geometry, database systems, distributed computing. *Unit head:* Mathew J. Palakal, Chair, 317-274-9727, Fax: 317-274-9742, E-mail: grad_advisor@cs.iupui.edu. *Application contact:* 317-274-9727, Fax: 317-274-9742, E-mail: admissions@cs.iupui.edu.

Indiana University South Bend, College of Liberal Arts and Sciences, South Bend, IN 46634-7111. Offers applied mathematics and computer science (MS); applied psychology (MA); English (MA); liberal studies (MLS). Part-time and evening/weekend programs available. *Faculty:* 79 full-time (33 women). *Students:* 34 full-time (18 women), 100 part-time (69 women); includes 23 minority (15 Black or African American, non-Hispanic/Latino; 2 American Indian or Alaska Native, non-Hispanic/Latino; 3 Asian, non-Hispanic/Latino; 2 Hispanic/Latino; 1 Two or more races, non-Hispanic/Latino), 16 international. Average age 37. 44 applicants, 84% accepted, 27 enrolled. In 2010, 21 master's awarded. *Degree requirements:* For master's, thesis (for some programs). *Entrance requirements:* For master's, minimum GPA of 3.0. Additional exam requirements/recommendations for international students: Required—TOEFL. *Application deadline:* For fall admission, 7/31 priority date for domestic students, 7/1 priority date for international students; for spring admission, 3/31 priority date for domestic students, 11/1 priority date for international students. Applications are processed on a rolling basis. Application fee: $50 ($60 for international students). *Financial support:* In 2010–11, 5 students received support, including 5 teaching assistantships; Federal Work-Study also available. Support available to part-time students. *Faculty research:* Artificial intelligence, bioinformatics, English language and literature, creative writing, computer networks. Total annual research expenditures: $127,000. *Unit head:* Dr. Lynn R. Williams, Dean, 574-520-4322, Fax: 574-520-

4528, E-mail: lwilliam@iusb.edu. *Application contact:* Dr. Lynn R. Williams, Dean, 574-520-4322, Fax: 574-520-4528, E-mail: lwilliam@iusb.edu.

Instituto Tecnológico y de Estudios Superiores de Monterrey, Campus Central de Veracruz, Graduate Programs, Córdoba, Mexico. Offers administration (MA); administration of information technologies (MTI); computer sciences (MCC); education (MEE); educational institution administration (MAD); educational technology (MTE); electronic commerce (MCE); finance (MAF); humanistic studies (MEH); international business for Latin America (MNL); marketing (MMT); science (MCP); technology management (MTT). Part-time and evening/weekend programs available. Postbaccalaureate distance learning degree programs offered (minimal on-campus study). *Degree requirements:* For master's, thesis (for some programs). *Entrance requirements:* For master's, PAEP College Board. Electronic applications accepted.

Instituto Tecnológico y de Estudios Superiores de Monterrey, Campus Ciudad de México, Virtual University Division, Ciudad de Mexico, Mexico. Offers administration of information technologies (MA); computer sciences (MA); education (MA, PhD); educational technology (MA); environmental engineering (MA); environmental systems (MA); humanistic studies (MA); industrial engineering (MA); international business for Latin America (MA); quality systems (MA); quality systems and productivity (MA). Part-time and evening/weekend programs available. Postbaccalaureate distance learning degree programs offered (minimal on-campus study). *Entrance requirements:* For master's and doctorate, Instituto entrance exam. Additional exam requirements/recommendations for international students: Required—TOEFL.

Instituto Tecnológico y de Estudios Superiores de Monterrey, Campus Cuernavaca, Programs in Information Science, Temixco, Mexico. Offers administration of information technology (MATI); computer science (MCC, DCC); information technology (MTI).

Instituto Tecnológico y de Estudios Superiores de Monterrey, Campus Estado de México, Professional and Graduate Division, Estado de Mexico, Mexico. Offers administration of information technologies (MITA); architecture (M Arch); business administration (GMBA, MBA); computer sciences (MCS, PhD); education (M Ed); educational institution administration (MAD); educational technology and innovation (PhD); electronic commerce (MEC); environmental systems (MS); finance (MAF); humanistic studies (MHS); information sciences and knowledge management (MISKM); information systems (MS); manufacturing systems (MS); marketing (MEM); quality systems and productivity (MS); science and materials engineering (PhD); telecommunications management (MTM). Part-time programs available. Postbaccalaureate distance learning degree programs offered (minimal on-campus study). *Degree requirements:* For master's, one foreign language, thesis (for some programs); for doctorate, one foreign language, thesis/dissertation. *Entrance requirements:* For master's, E-PAEP 500, interview; for doctorate, E-PAEP 500, research proposal. Additional exam requirements/recommendations for international students: Required—TOEFL (minimum score 550 paper-based). *Faculty research:* Surface treatments by plasmas, mechanical properties, robotics, graphical computing, mechatronics security protocols.

Instituto Tecnológico y de Estudios Superiores de Monterrey, Campus Irapuato, Graduate Programs, Irapuato, Mexico. Offers administration (MBA); administration of information technology (MAIT); administration of telecommunications (MAT); architecture (M Arch); computer science (MCS); education (M Ed); educational administration (MEA); educational innovation and technology (DEIT); educational technology (MET); electronic commerce (MBA); environmental administration and planning (MEAP); environmental systems (MES); finances (MBA); humanistic studies (MHS); international management for Latin American executives (MIMLAE); library and information science (MLIS); manufacturing quality management (MMQM); marketing research (MBA).

Instituto Tecnológico y de Estudios Superiores de Monterrey, Campus Monterrey, Graduate and Research Division, Program in Computer Science, Monterrey, Mexico. Offers artificial intelligence (PhD); computer science (MS); information systems (MS); information technology (MS). Part-time programs available. *Degree requirements:* For master's, one foreign language, thesis; for doctorate, one foreign language, thesis/dissertation. *Entrance requirements:* For master's, EXADEP; for doctorate, master's degree in related field. Additional exam requirements/recommendations for international students: Required—TOEFL. *Faculty research:* Distributed systems, software engineering, decision support systems.

Inter American University of Puerto Rico, Guayama Campus, Department of Natural and Applied Sciences, Guayama, PR 00785. Offers computer security and networks (MS); networking and security (MCS).

Inter American University of Puerto Rico, Metropolitan Campus, Graduate Programs, Program in Open Information Systems, San Juan, PR 00919-1293. Offers MS. *Degree requirements:* For master's, 2 foreign languages.

International Technological University, Program in Computer Science, Santa Clara, CA 95050. Offers MS.

Iona College, School of Arts and Science, Program in Computer Science, New Rochelle, NY 10801-1890. Offers computer science (MS); telecommunications (MS). Part-time and evening/weekend programs available. *Faculty:* 8 full-time (3 women), 3 part-time/adjunct (0 women). *Students:* 1 full-time (0 women), 15 part-time (5 women); includes 3 minority (2 Black or African American, non-Hispanic/Latino; 1 Hispanic/Latino), 1 international. Average age 35. 6 applicants, 83% accepted, 5 enrolled. In 2010, 13 master's awarded. *Degree requirements:* For master's, thesis or alternative. *Entrance requirements:* For master's, minimum GPA of 3.0. Additional exam requirements/recommendations for international students: Required—TOEFL (minimum score 550 paper-based; 213 computer-based). *Application deadline:* Applications are processed on a rolling basis. Application fee: $50. Electronic applications accepted. *Expenses:* Contact institution. *Financial support:* Tuition waivers (partial) and unspecified assistantships available. Support available to part-time students. Financial award application deadline: 4/15; financial award applicants required to submit FAFSA. *Faculty research:* Telecommunications, expert systems, graph isomorphism, algorithms, formal verification of hardware. *Unit head:* Dr. Robert Schiaffino, Chair, 914-633-2338, E-mail: rschiaffino@iona.edu. *Application contact:* Veronica Jarek-Prinz, Director of Graduate Admissions, 914-633-2420, Fax: 914-633-2277, E-mail: vjarekprinz@iona.edu.

Iowa State University of Science and Technology, Graduate College, College of Liberal Arts and Sciences, Department of Computer Science, Ames, IA 50011. Offers MS, PhD. *Faculty:* 37 full-time (5 women), 4 part-time/adjunct (0 women). *Students:* 113 full-time (19 women), 35 part-time (7 women); includes 3 Black or African American, non-Hispanic/Latino; 2 Asian, non-Hispanic/Latino; 1 Hispanic/Latino, 116 international. 418 applicants, 13% accepted, 13 enrolled. In 2010, 21 master's, 15 doctorates awarded. *Degree requirements:* For master's, thesis; for doctorate, thesis/dissertation. *Entrance requirements:* For master's and doctorate, GRE General Test. Additional exam requirements/recommendations for international students: Recommended—TOEFL (minimum score 550 paper-based; 79 iBT), IELTS (minimum score 6.5). *Application deadline:* For fall admission, 1/1 priority date for domestic and international students; for spring admission, 9/1 priority date for domestic and international students. Application fee: $40 ($90 for international students). Electronic applications accepted. *Financial support:* In 2010–11, 67 research assistantships with full and partial tuition reimbursements (averaging $7,478 per year), 39 teaching assistantships with full and partial tuition reimbursements (averaging $9,682 per year) were awarded; fellowships, scholarships/grants, health care benefits, and unspecified assistantships also available. *Unit head:* Dr. Carl Chang, Chair, 515-294-4377, Fax: 515-294-0258, E-mail: grad_adm@cs.iastate.edu. *Application contact:* Samik Basu, Director of Graduate Education, 515-294-2987, E-mail: grad_adm@cs.iastate.edu.

Jackson State University, Graduate School, College of Science, Engineering and Technology, Department of Computer Science, Jackson, MS 39217. Offers MS. Part-time and evening/weekend programs available. *Faculty:* 6 full-time (2 women). *Students:* 16 full-time (8 women), 16 part-time (5 women); includes 16 Black or African American, non-Hispanic/Latino; 2 Asian, non-Hispanic/Latino; 1 Hispanic/Latino, 9 international. Average age 32. In 2010, 20 master's awarded. *Degree requirements:* For master's, comprehensive exam, thesis. *Entrance requirements:* For master's, GRE General Test. Additional exam requirements/recommendations for international students: Required—TOEFL (minimum score 520 paper-based; 195 computer-based; 67 iBT). *Application deadline:* For fall admission, 3/1 priority date for domestic students, 3/1 for international students; for spring admission, 10/1 for domestic and international students. Applications are processed on a rolling basis. Application fee: $25. *Expenses:* Tuition, state resident: full-time $5050; part-time $281 per credit hour. Tuition, nonresident: full-time $12,380; part-time $689 per credit hour. *Financial support:* Career-related internships or fieldwork, Federal Work-Study, scholarships/grants, and unspecified assistantships available. Support available to part-time students. Financial award application deadline: 3/1; financial award applicants required to submit FAFSA. *Unit head:* Dr. Loretta Moore, Chair, 601-979-2105, E-mail: loretta.a.moore@jsums.edu. *Application contact:* Sharlene Wilson, Director of Graduate Admissions, 601-979-2455, Fax: 601-979-4325, E-mail: sharlene.f.wilson@jsums.edu.

Jacksonville State University, College of Graduate Studies and Continuing Education, College of Arts and Sciences, Program in Computer Systems and Software Design, Jacksonville, AL 36265-1602. Offers MS. Part-time and evening/weekend programs available. *Degree requirements:* For master's, comprehensive exam, thesis (for some programs). Electronic applications accepted.

James Madison University, The Graduate School, College of Integrated Science and Technology, Department of Computer Science, Harrisonburg, VA 22807. Offers MS. Postbaccalaureate distance learning degree programs offered. *Faculty:* 8 full-time (0 women), 2 part-time/adjunct (0 women). *Students:* 11 full-time (0 women), 53 part-time (6 women); includes 7 minority (3 Black or African American, non-Hispanic/Latino; 1 American Indian or Alaska Native, non-Hispanic/Latino; 2 Asian, non-Hispanic/Latino; 1 Hispanic/Latino), 4 international. Average age 27. In 2010, 22 master's awarded. *Degree requirements:* For master's, thesis or alternative. *Entrance requirements:* For master's, GRE General Test. Additional exam requirements/recommendations for international students: Required—TOEFL. *Application deadline:* For fall admission, 5/1 priority date for domestic students; for spring admission, 9/1 priority date for domestic students. Applications are processed on a rolling basis. Application fee: $55. Electronic applications accepted. *Financial support:* In 2010–11, 9 students received support. Federal Work-Study and 9 graduate assistantships ($7382) available. Financial award application deadline: 3/1; financial award applicants required to submit FAFSA. *Unit head:* Dr. Sharon J. Simmons, Academic Unit Head, 540-568-4196. *Application contact:* Katherine R. Laycock, Graduate Coordinator, 540-568-8772.

The Johns Hopkins University, Engineering for Professionals, Part-Time Program in Computer Science, Baltimore, MD 21218-2699. Offers bioinformatics (MS); computer science (MS, Post-Master's Certificate); telecommunications and networking (MS). Part-time and evening/weekend programs available. Postbaccalaureate distance learning degree programs offered (no on-campus study). *Faculty:* 58 part-time/adjunct (5 women). *Students:* 16 full-time (5 women), 428 part-time (54 women); includes 131 minority (24 Black or African American, non-Hispanic/Latino; 81 Asian, non-Hispanic/Latino; 16 Hispanic/Latino; 1 Native Hawaiian or other Pacific Islander, non-Hispanic/Latino; 9 Two or more races, non-Hispanic/Latino), 16 international. Average age 29. 133 applicants, 87% accepted, 74 enrolled. In 2010, 153 master's, 2 other advanced degrees awarded. *Application deadline:* Applications are processed on a rolling basis. Application fee: $75. Electronic applications accepted. *Financial support:* Institutionally sponsored loans available. *Unit head:* Dr. Thomas A. Longstaff, Program Chair, 443-778-9389, E-mail: thomas.longstaff@jhuapl.edu. *Application contact:* Priyanka Dwivedi, Admissions Manager, 410-516-2300, Fax: 410-579-8049, E-mail: pdwived1@jhu.edu.

The Johns Hopkins University, G. W. C. Whiting School of Engineering, Department of Computer Science, Baltimore, MD 21218-2699. Offers MSE, PhD. *Faculty:* 21 full-time (2 women), 16 part-time/adjunct (2 women). *Students:* 136 full-time (28 women), 8 part-time (1 woman); includes 16 minority (1 Black or African American, non-Hispanic/Latino; 11 Asian, non-Hispanic/Latino; 1 Hispanic/Latino; 3 Two or more races, non-Hispanic/Latino), 83 international. Average age 27. 534 applicants, 26% accepted, 34 enrolled. In 2010, 39 master's, 3 doctorates awarded. Terminal master's awarded for partial completion of doctoral program. *Degree requirements:* For master's, thesis optional; for doctorate, comprehensive exam, thesis/dissertation, oral exam. *Entrance requirements:* For master's and doctorate, GRE General Test. Additional exam requirements/recommendations for international students: Required—TOEFL (minimum score 600 paper-based; 250 computer-based). *Application deadline:* For fall admission, 12/15 for domestic and international students; for spring admission, 12/15 for domestic students, 9/25 for international students. Application fee: $25. Electronic applications accepted. *Financial support:* In 2010–11, 13 fellowships with full and partial tuition reimbursements (averaging $21,600 per year), 62 research assistantships with full tuition reimbursements (averaging $27,720 per year), 11 teaching assistantships with full tuition reimbursements (averaging $10,359 per year) were awarded; scholarships/grants, health care benefits, tuition waivers (partial), and unspecified assistantships also available. Financial award application deadline: 12/15. *Faculty research:* Computer medical systems, networks/distributed systems, algorithms, security, natural language processing. Total annual research expenditures: $1.5 million. *Unit head:* Dr. Gregory Hager, Chair, 410-516-5521, Fax: 410-516-6134, E-mail: hager@cs.jhu.edu. *Application contact:* Cathy Thornton, Sr. Academic Program Coordinator, 410-516-8775, Fax: 410-516-6134, E-mail: cthornton@jhu.edu.

The Johns Hopkins University, G. W. C. Whiting School of Engineering, Program in Engineering Management, Baltimore, MD 21218-2699. Offers biomaterials (MSEM); communications science (MSEM); computer science (MSEM); fluid mechanics (MSEM); materials science and engineering (MSEM); mechanical engineering (MSEM); mechanics and materials (MSEM); nano-biotechnology (MSEM); nanomaterials and nanotechnology (MSEM); probability and statistics (MSEM); smart product and device design (MSEM); systems analysis, management and environmental policy (MSEM). *Students:* 32 full-time (5 women), 4 part-time (0 women); includes 7 minority (3 Black or African American, non-Hispanic/Latino; 3 Asian, non-Hispanic/Latino; 1 Hispanic/Latino), 11 international. Average age 23. 110 applicants, 60% accepted, 27 enrolled. In 2010, 6 master's awarded. *Entrance requirements:* For master's, GRE, 3 letters of recommendation, resume. Additional exam requirements/recommendations for international students: Required—TOEFL (minimum score 600 paper-based; 250 computer-based; 100 iBT) or IELTS (minimum score 7). *Application deadline:* For fall admission, 1/15 priority date for domestic students, 1/15 for international students; for spring admission, 9/15 priority date for domestic students, 9/15 for international students. Applications are processed on a rolling basis. Application fee: $75. Electronic applications accepted. *Financial support:* Fellowships, health care benefits available. *Unit head:* Dr. Edward R. Scheinerman, Interim Director/Vice Dean for Education, School of Engineering/Professor, Applied Mathematics and Statistics, 410-516-7395, Fax: 410-516-4880, E-mail: ers@jhu.edu. *Application contact:* Dennis McIver, Coordinator of Graduate Admissions, 410-516-8174, Fax: 410-516-0780, E-mail: graduateadmissions@jhu.edu.

Kansas State University, Graduate School, College of Engineering, Department of Computing and Information Sciences, Manhattan, KS 66506. Offers computer science (MS, PhD); software engineering (MSE). Part-time programs available. Postbaccalaureate distance learning degree programs offered (minimal on-campus study). Terminal master's awarded for partial completion of doctoral program. *Degree requirements:* For master's, thesis or alternative; for doctorate, thesis/dissertation, preliminary exams. *Entrance requirements:* For master's, GRE, bachelor's degree in computer science, minimum GPA of 3.0; for doctorate, GRE General Test, GRE Subject Test, master's degree in computer science or bachelor's degree and strong advanced computer knowledge. Additional exam requirements/recommendations for international students: Required—TOEFL (minimum score 575 paper-based; 233 computer-based). Electronic applications accepted. *Faculty research:* High-assurance software and programming languages, data mining, parallel and distributed computing, computer security, embedded systems.

Kennesaw State University, College of Science and Mathematics, Program in Applied Computer Science, Kennesaw, GA 30144-5591. Offers MSaCS. Part-time programs available.

Computer Science

Kennesaw State University (continued)
Postbaccalaureate distance learning degree programs offered (minimal on-campus study). *Students:* 19 full-time (6 women), 24 part-time (7 women); includes 15 minority (9 Black or African American, non-Hispanic/Latino; 2 Asian, non-Hispanic/Latino; 4 Hispanic/Latino), 11 international. Average age 31. 20 applicants, 85% accepted, 9 enrolled. In 2010, 9 master's awarded. *Entrance requirements:* For master's, GMAT or GRE, minimum GPA of 2.75. Additional exam requirements/recommendations for international students: Required—TOEFL (minimum score 550 paper-based; 213 computer-based; 80 iBT), IELTS (minimum score 6). *Application deadline:* For fall admission, 7/1 priority date for domestic students, 7/1 for international students; for spring admission, 12/1 priority date for domestic students, 12/1 for international students. Applications are processed on a rolling basis. Application fee: $60. Electronic applications accepted. *Expenses:* Contact institution. *Financial support:* In 2010–11, 2 research assistantships with full tuition reimbursements (averaging $4,000 per year) were awarded; Federal Work-Study and unspecified assistantships also available. Support available to part-time students. Financial award application deadline: 4/1; financial award applicants required to submit FAFSA. *Unit head:* Dr. Victor Clincy, Director, 770-420-4440, E-mail: vclincy@kennesaw.edu. *Application contact:* Tamara Hutto, Admissions Counselor, 770-420-4377, Fax: 770-423-6885, E-mail: ksugrad@kennesaw.edu.

Kent State University, College of Arts and Sciences, Department of Computer Science, Kent, OH 44242-0001. Offers MA, MS, PhD. Part-time and evening/weekend programs available. *Degree requirements:* For master's, thesis (for some programs); for doctorate, comprehensive exam, thesis/dissertation. *Entrance requirements:* Additional exam requirements/recommendations for international students: Required—TOEFL (minimum score 550 paper-based; 213 computer-based). Electronic applications accepted. *Expenses:* Tuition, state resident: full-time $7866; part-time $437 per credit hour. Tuition, nonresident: full-time $14,022; part-time $779 per credit hour. *Faculty research:* Distributed and parallel processing, networking, computational science, graphics and visualization, database and data mining.

Kentucky State University, College of Mathematics, Sciences, Technology and Health, Frankfort, KY 40601. Offers aquaculture (MS); computer science (MS), including computer science theory, information assurance, information technology; environmental science (MS). Part-time and evening/weekend programs available. *Faculty:* 10 full-time (1 woman), 1 part-time/adjunct (0 women). *Students:* 34 full-time (16 women), 32 part-time (6 women); includes 22 minority (15 Black or African American, non-Hispanic/Latino; 3 Asian, non-Hispanic/Latino; 1 Hispanic/Latino; 1 Native Hawaiian or other Pacific Islander, non-Hispanic/Latino; 2 Two or more races, non-Hispanic/Latino), 12 international. Average age 34. 55 applicants, 51% accepted, 18 enrolled. In 2010, 16 master's awarded. *Degree requirements:* For master's, comprehensive exam, thesis optional. *Entrance requirements:* For master's, GRE, GMAT. Additional exam requirements/recommendations for international students: Required—TOEFL (minimum score 525 paper-based; 173 computer-based). *Application deadline:* Applications are processed on a rolling basis. Application fee: $30 ($100 for international students). Electronic applications accepted. *Expenses:* Tuition, state resident: full-time $5886; part-time $352 per credit hour. Tuition, nonresident: full-time $9054; part-time $528 per credit hour. Required fees: $450; $26 per credit hour. *Financial support:* In 2010–11, 41 students received support, including 18 research assistantships (averaging $11,378 per year); career-related internships or fieldwork, scholarships/grants, tuition waivers (partial), and unspecified assistantships also available. Financial award application deadline: 4/15; financial award applicants required to submit FAFSA. *Unit head:* Dr. Charles Bennett, Dean, 502-597-6926, E-mail: charles.bennett@kysu.edu. *Application contact:* Dr. Titilayo Ufomata, Acting Director of Graduate Studies, 502-597-6443, E-mail: titilayo.ufomata@kysu.edu.

Knowledge Systems Institute, Program in Computer and Information Sciences, Skokie, IL 60076. Offers MS. Part-time and evening/weekend programs available. Postbaccalaureate distance learning degree programs offered (minimal on-campus study). *Degree requirements:* For master's, comprehensive exam, thesis. *Entrance requirements:* Additional exam requirements/recommendations for international students: Required—TOEFL (minimum score 550 paper-based; 213 computer-based; 79 iBT). Electronic applications accepted. *Faculty research:* Data mining, web development, database programming and administration.

Kutztown University of Pennsylvania, College of Liberal Arts and Sciences, Program in Computer Science, Kutztown, PA 19530-0730. Offers MS. Part-time and evening/weekend programs available. *Faculty:* 11 full-time (1 woman). *Students:* 12 full-time (6 women), 8 part-time (2 women); includes 2 minority (1 Black or African American, non-Hispanic/Latino; 1 Hispanic/Latino), 2 international. Average age 32. 22 applicants, 73% accepted, 9 enrolled. In 2010, 7 master's awarded. *Degree requirements:* For master's, comprehensive exam or thesis. *Entrance requirements:* For master's, GRE General Test. Additional exam requirements/recommendations for international students: Required—TOEFL (minimum score 550 paper-based; 79 iBT). *Application deadline:* For fall admission, 8/15 priority date for domestic and international students; for spring admission, 12/15 priority date for domestic and international students. Applications are processed on a rolling basis. Application fee: $35. Electronic applications accepted. *Expenses:* Tuition, state resident: full-time $6966; part-time $387 per credit. Tuition, nonresident: full-time $11,146; part-time $619 per credit hour. Required fees: $1499; $54 per credit. $68 per year. *Financial support:* Career-related internships or fieldwork, Federal Work-Study, scholarships/grants, and unspecified assistantships available. Financial award application deadline: 3/1; financial award applicants required to submit FAFSA. *Faculty research:* Artificial intelligence, expert systems, neural networks. *Unit head:* Linda L. Day, Chairperson, 610-683-4340, Fax: 610-683-4129, E-mail: day@kutztown.edu. *Application contact:* Kelly D. Burr, Associate Director, Graduate Admissions, 610-683-4200, Fax: 610-683-1393, E-mail: graduate@kutztown.edu.

Lakehead University, Graduate Studies, School of Mathematical Sciences, Thunder Bay, ON P7B 5E1, Canada. Offers computer science (M Sc); mathematical science (MA). Part-time and evening/weekend programs available. *Degree requirements:* For master's, thesis optional. *Entrance requirements:* For master's, minimum B average, honours degree in mathematics or computer science. Additional exam requirements/recommendations for international students: Required—TOEFL. *Faculty research:* Numerical analysis, classical analysis, theoretical computer science, abstract harmonic analysis, functional analysis.

Lamar University, College of Graduate Studies, College of Arts and Sciences, Department of Computer Science, Beaumont, TX 77710. Offers MS. Part-time programs available. *Faculty:* 7 full-time (2 women), 1 part-time/adjunct (0 women). *Students:* 32 full-time (5 women), 7 part-time (1 woman); includes 1 Black or African American, non-Hispanic/Latino; 4 Asian, non-Hispanic/Latino, 33 international. Average age 26. 104 applicants, 66% accepted, 12 enrolled. In 2010, 24 master's awarded. *Degree requirements:* For master's, comprehensive exams and project or thesis. *Entrance requirements:* For master's, GRE General Test, minimum GPA of 3.3 in last 60 hours of undergraduate course work or 3.0 overall. Additional exam requirements/recommendations for international students: Required—TOEFL (minimum score 550 paper-based; 213 computer-based). *Application deadline:* For fall admission, 5/15 priority date for domestic students; for spring admission, 10/1 priority date for domestic students. Applications are processed on a rolling basis. Application fee: $25 ($50 for international students). *Expenses:* Tuition, state resident: full-time $4160; part-time $208 per credit hour. Tuition, nonresident: full-time $10,360; part-time $518 per credit hour. *Financial support:* In 2010–11, 2 research assistantships with partial tuition reimbursements (averaging $6,000 per year), 4 teaching assistantships with partial tuition reimbursements (averaging $6,000 per year) were awarded; institutionally sponsored loans, scholarships/grants, and tuition waivers (partial) also available. Financial award application deadline: 4/1. *Faculty research:* Computer architecture, network security. *Unit head:* Dr. Lawrence J. Osborne, Chair, 409-880-8775, Fax: 409-880-2364, E-mail: osborne@hal.lamar.edu. *Application contact:* Daisy Estrella, Coordinator of Graduate Admissions, 409-880-8349, Fax: 409-880-8414, E-mail: gradmissions@hal.lamar.edu.

La Salle University, School of Arts and Sciences, Program in Computer Information Science, Philadelphia, PA 19141-1199. Offers MS. Part-time and evening/weekend programs available. *Entrance requirements:* For master's, GRE or MAT, 18 undergraduate credits in computer science, professional experience. *Expenses:* Contact institution. *Faculty research:* Human-computer interaction, networks, technology trends, databases, groupware.

Lawrence Technological University, College of Arts and Sciences, Southfield, MI 48075-1058. Offers computer science (MS); educational technology (MS); integrated science (MSE); science education (MSE); technical and professional communication (MS). Part-time and evening/weekend programs available. *Faculty:* 14 full-time (6 women), 14 part-time/adjunct (4 women). *Students:* 1 full-time (0 women), 93 part-time (54 women); includes 17 Black or African American, non-Hispanic/Latino; 7 Asian, non-Hispanic/Latino; 1 Hispanic/Latino; 4 Two or more races, non-Hispanic/Latino, 10 international. Average age 36. 116 applicants, 61% accepted, 23 enrolled. In 2010, 40 master's awarded. *Degree requirements:* For master's, thesis (for some programs). *Entrance requirements:* For master's, GRE. Additional exam requirements/recommendations for international students: Required—TOEFL (minimum score 550 paper-based; 213 computer-based; 79 iBT). *Application deadline:* For fall admission, 6/30 priority date for domestic students, 6/30 for international students; for spring admission, 11/15 priority date for domestic students, 11/15 for international students. Applications are processed on a rolling basis. Application fee: $50. Electronic applications accepted. *Financial support:* In 2010–11, 22 students received support. Federal Work-Study available. Financial award application deadline: 4/1; financial award applicants required to submit FAFSA. *Unit head:* Dr. Hsiao-Ping Moore, Dean, 248-204-3500, Fax: 248-204-3518, E-mail: scidean@ltu.edu. *Application contact:* Jane Rohrback, Director of Admissions, 248-204-3160, Fax: 248-204-2228, E-mail: admissions@ltu.edu.

Lebanese American University, School of Arts and Sciences, Beirut, Lebanon. Offers computer science (MS); international affairs (MA).

Lehigh University, P.C. Rossin College of Engineering and Applied Science, Department of Computer Science and Engineering, Bethlehem, PA 18015. Offers computer engineering (M Eng, MS, PhD); computer science (M Eng, MS, PhD, MBA/E); MBA/E. Part-time programs available. *Faculty:* 15 full-time (2 women). *Students:* 52 full-time (10 women), 18 part-time (4 women); includes 2 minority (both Asian, non-Hispanic/Latino), 52 international. Average age 27. 271 applicants, 21% accepted, 20 enrolled. In 2010, 17 master's, 4 doctorates awarded. *Degree requirements:* For master's, oral presentation of thesis; for doctorate, thesis/dissertation, qualifying, general, and oral exams. *Entrance requirements:* For master's, GRE General Test, minimum GPA of 3.0; for doctorate, GRE General Test, minimum GPA of 3.5. Additional exam requirements/recommendations for international students: Required—TOEFL (minimum score 550 paper-based; 213 computer-based; 79 iBT). *Application deadline:* For fall admission, 4/1 for domestic and international students; for spring admission, 11/1 for domestic and international students. Applications are processed on a rolling basis. Application fee: $75. Electronic applications accepted. *Expenses:* Contact institution. *Financial support:* In 2010–11, 2 fellowships with full tuition reimbursements (averaging $17,460 per year), 6 research assistantships with full tuition reimbursements (averaging $17,460 per year), 4 teaching assistantships with full tuition reimbursements (averaging $18,360 per year) were awarded. Financial award application deadline: 1/15. *Faculty research:* Artificial intelligence, networking-pattern recognition, multimedia e-learning/data mining/Web search, mobile robotics, bioinformatics, computervision. Total annual research expenditures: $2.6 million. *Unit head:* Dr. Daniel P. Lopresti, Chairman, 610-758-5782, Fax: 610-758-4096, E-mail: dal9@lehigh.edu. *Application contact:* Judy Frenick, Graduate Coordinator, 610-758-3605, Fax: 610-758-4096, E-mail: jlf2@lehigh.edu.

Lehman College of the City University of New York, Division of Natural and Social Sciences, Department of Mathematics and Computer Science, Program in Computer Science, Bronx, NY 10468-1589. Offers MS. *Degree requirements:* For master's, one foreign language, thesis or alternative.

Long Island University, Brooklyn Campus, School of Business, Public Administration and Information Sciences, Department of Computer Science, Brooklyn, NY 11201-8423. Offers MS. *Entrance requirements:* For master's, GMAT or GRE General Test, 2 letters of recommendation. Additional exam requirements/recommendations for international students: Required—TOEFL (minimum score 500 paper-based; 173 computer-based). Electronic applications accepted.

Long Island University, C.W. Post Campus, College of Information and Computer Science, Department of Computer Science/Management Engineering, Brookville, NY 11548-1300. Offers information systems (MS); information technology education (MS); management engineering (MS). Part-time and evening/weekend programs available. *Degree requirements:* For master's, comprehensive exam, thesis or alternative. *Entrance requirements:* For master's, bachelor's degree in science, mathematics, or engineering; minimum GPA of 2.5. Additional exam requirements/recommendations for international students: Required—TOEFL (minimum score 500 paper-based; 173 computer-based). Electronic applications accepted. *Faculty research:* Inductive music learning, re-engineering business process, technology and ethics.

Louisiana State University and Agricultural and Mechanical College, Graduate School, College of Basic Sciences, Department of Computer Science, Baton Rouge, LA 70803. Offers computer science (MSSS, PhD); systems science (MSSS). Part-time programs available. *Faculty:* 19 full-time (3 women). *Students:* 85 full-time (16 women), 19 part-time (6 women); includes 6 Black or African American, non-Hispanic/Latino; 1 American Indian or Alaska Native, non-Hispanic/Latino; 4 Asian, non-Hispanic/Latino, 76 international. Average age 28. 112 applicants, 74% accepted, 13 enrolled. In 2010, 27 master's, 6 doctorates awarded. Terminal master's awarded for partial completion of doctoral program. *Degree requirements:* For master's, thesis; for doctorate, thesis/dissertation. *Entrance requirements:* For master's and doctorate, GRE General Test, minimum GPA of 3.0. Additional exam requirements/recommendations for international students: Required—TOEFL (minimum score 550 paper-based; 213 computer-based; 79 iBT) or IELTS (minimum score 6.5). *Application deadline:* For fall admission, 2/1 for domestic students, 5/15 for international students; for spring admission, 10/1 for domestic students, 10/15 for international students. Applications are processed on a rolling basis. Application fee: $50 ($70 for international students). Electronic applications accepted. *Financial support:* In 2010–11, 80 students received support, including 7 fellowships with full tuition reimbursements available (averaging $13,182 per year), 44 research assistantships with full and partial tuition reimbursements available (averaging $16,480 per year), 22 teaching assistantships with full and partial tuition reimbursements available (averaging $14,432 per year); Federal Work-Study, institutionally sponsored loans, health care benefits, and unspecified assistantships also available. Financial award application deadline: 2/1; financial award applicants required to submit FAFSA. *Faculty research:* Robotics, artificial intelligence, algorithms, database software engineering, high-performance computing. Total annual research expenditures: $1.2 million. *Unit head:* Dr. Sitharama S. Iyengar, Chair, 225-578-1495, Fax: 225-578-1465, E-mail: iyengar@csc.lsu.edu. *Application contact:* Graduate Coordinator, 225-578-1495, Fax: 225-578-1465.

Louisiana State University in Shreveport, College of Sciences, Program in Computer Systems Technology, Shreveport, LA 71115-2399. Offers MS. *Students:* 3 full-time (1 woman), 14 part-time (3 women); includes 2 minority (1 Black or African American, non-Hispanic/Latino; 1 Asian, non-Hispanic/Latino), 3 international. Average age 33. 4 applicants, 75% accepted, 2 enrolled. In 2010, 5 master's awarded. *Degree requirements:* For master's, thesis or alternative. *Entrance requirements:* For master's, GRE, programming course in high-level language, interview. Additional exam requirements/recommendations for international students: Required—TOEFL (minimum score 500 paper-based; 173 computer-based; 61 iBT). *Application deadline:* For fall admission, 6/30 for domestic and international students; for spring admission, 11/30 for domestic and international students. Applications are processed on a rolling basis. Application fee: $10 ($20 for international students). *Expenses:* Tuition, state resident: full-time $3272; part-time $181.80 per credit hour. Tuition, nonresident: full-time $7902; part-time $471.19 per credit hour. Required fees: $850; $47 per credit hour. *Financial support:* In 2010–11, 2 research assistantships with partial tuition reimbursements (averaging $20,000 per year) were awarded. *Unit head:* Dr. Krishna Agarwal, Program Director, 318-795-4283, Fax: 318-795-2419, E-mail: krishna.agarwal@lsus.edu. *Application contact:* Yvonne Yarbrough, Secretary, Graduate Studies, 318-797-5247, Fax: 318-798-4120, E-mail: yyarbrou@lsus.edu.

Louisiana Tech University, Graduate School, College of Engineering and Science, Department of Computer Science, Ruston, LA 71272. Offers MS. Part-time programs available. *Degree requirements:* For master's, thesis or alternative. *Entrance requirements:* For master's, GRE General Test, minimum GPA of 3.0 in last 60 hours. Additional exam requirements/recommendations for international students: Required—TOEFL. *Faculty research:* Computer systems organization, artificial intelligence, expert systems, graphics, program language.

Loyola Marymount University, College of Science and Engineering, Department of Electrical Engineering and Computer Science, Program in Computer Science, Los Angeles, CA 90045. Offers MS. Part-time and evening/weekend programs available. *Faculty:* 9 full-time (3 women). *Students:* 3 part-time (1 woman), 1 international. Average age 42. In 2010, 4 master's awarded. *Degree requirements:* For master's, research seminar. *Entrance requirements:* Additional exam requirements/recommendations for international students: Required—TOEFL (minimum score 550 paper-based; 213 computer-based; 80 iBT). *Application deadline:* Applications are processed on a rolling basis. Application fee: $50. Electronic applications accepted. *Financial support:* In 2010–11, 4 students received support. Scholarships/grants available. Support available to part-time students. Financial award application deadline: 6/1; financial award applicants required to submit FAFSA. Total annual research expenditures: $22,929. *Unit head:* Dr. Raymond J. Toal, Program Director, 310-338-2773, E-mail: rtoal@lmu.edu. *Application contact:* Chake H. Kouyoumjian, Associate Dean of Graduate Studies, 310-338-2721, Fax: 310-338-6086, E-mail: ckouyoum@lmu.edu.

Loyola University Chicago, Graduate School, Department of Computer Science, Chicago, IL 60660. Offers computer science (MS); information technology (MS); software technology (MS). Part-time and evening/weekend programs available. *Faculty:* 9 full-time (1 woman), 10 part-time/adjunct (2 women). *Students:* 39 full-time (15 women), 46 part-time (11 women); includes 13 minority (3 Black or African American, non-Hispanic/Latino; 9 Asian, non-Hispanic/Latino; 1 Hispanic/Latino), 35 international. Average age 28. 87 applicants, 67% accepted, 30 enrolled. In 2010, 35 master's awarded. *Degree requirements:* For master's, thesis optional, Ten Graduate Courses. Prerequisites are additional if student does not have adequate CS background. *Entrance requirements:* For master's, 3 letters of recommendation, transcripts, statement of purpose. Additional exam requirements/recommendations for international students: Required—TOEFL (minimum score 550 paper-based, 213 computer-based, 79 iBT) or IELTS (6.5). *Application deadline:* For fall admission, 8/10 for domestic students, 5/15 priority date for international students; for spring admission, 12/20 for domestic students, 9/15 priority date for international students. Applications are processed on a rolling basis. Application fee: $0. Electronic applications accepted. *Expenses:* Tuition: Full-time $14,940; part-time $830 per credit hour. Required fees: $87 per semester. Part-time tuition and fees vary according to course load and program. *Financial support:* In 2010–11, 24 students received support, including 1 fellowship (averaging $3,000 per year), 16 teaching assistantships with partial tuition reimbursements available (averaging $2,900 per year); career-related internships or fieldwork, Federal Work-Study, scholarships/grants, tuition waivers (partial), and unspecified assistantships also available. Financial award application deadline: 3/15. *Faculty research:* Software engineering, high performance computing, algorithms and complexity, parallel and distributed computing, databases and computer networks. Total annual research expenditures: $22,000. *Unit head:* Dr. Chandra Sekharan, Chair, 312-915-7985, Fax: 312-915-7998, E-mail: csekhar@luc.edu. *Application contact:* Cecilia Murphy, Graduate Program Secretary, 312-915-7990, Fax: 312-915-7998, E-mail: gradinfo-cs@luc.edu.

Loyola University Maryland, Graduate Programs, Loyola College of Arts and Sciences, Department of Computer Science, Baltimore, MD 21210-2699. Offers computer science (MS); software engineering (MS). *Entrance requirements:* For master's, GRE General Test, GRE Subject Test (recommended). Additional exam requirements/recommendations for international students: Required—TOEFL (minimum score 550 paper-based; 213 computer-based).

Maharishi University of Management, Graduate Studies, Program in Computer Science, Fairfield, IA 52557. Offers MS. *Degree requirements:* For master's, thesis or alternative. *Entrance requirements:* For master's, GRE General Test, minimum GPA of 3.0. Additional exam requirements/recommendations for international students: Required—TOEFL. *Faculty research:* Parallel processing, computer systems in architecture.

Marist College, Graduate Programs, School of Computer Science and Mathematics, Poughkeepsie, NY 12601-1387. Offers computer science/software development (MS); information systems (MS, Adv C); technology management (MS). Part-time and evening/weekend programs available. Postbaccalaureate distance learning degree programs offered (minimal on-campus study). *Entrance requirements:* For master's, resume. Additional exam requirements/recommendations for international students: Required—TOEFL (minimum score 550 paper-based; 213 computer-based; 80 iBT); Recommended—IELTS (minimum score 6.5). Electronic applications accepted. *Faculty research:* Data quality, artificial intelligence, imaging, analysis of algorithms, distributed systems and applications.

Marquette University, Graduate School, College of Arts and Sciences, Department of Mathematics, Statistics, and Computer Science, Milwaukee, WI 53201-1881. Offers bioinformatics (MS); computational sciences (MS, PhD); computing (MS); mathematics education (MS). Part-time and evening/weekend programs available. Postbaccalaureate distance learning degree programs offered (minimal on-campus study). *Faculty:* 27 full-time (9 women), 8 part-time/adjunct (3 women). *Students:* 13 full-time (2 women), 26 part-time (7 women); includes 2 minority (1 Black or African American, non-Hispanic/Latino; 1 Asian, non-Hispanic/Latino), 15 international. Average age 31. 57 applicants, 42% accepted, 10 enrolled. In 2010, 9 master's awarded. Terminal master's awarded for partial completion of doctoral program. *Degree requirements:* For master's, thesis or alternative, Master's essay with oral presentation; for doctorate, comprehensive exam, thesis/dissertation, Qualifying Examination. *Entrance requirements:* For master's, official transcripts from all current and previous colleges/universities except Marquette, three letters of recommendation; for doctorate, GRE General Test, official transcripts from all current and previous colleges/universities except Marquette, three letters of recommendation, English-language publications authored by applicant (if applicable, strongly recommended). Additional exam requirements/recommendations for international students: Required—TOEFL (minimum score 530 paper-based; 78 computer-based). *Application deadline:* For fall admission, 1/15 for domestic and international students. Applications are processed on a rolling basis. Application fee: $50. Electronic applications accepted. *Expenses:* Tuition: Full-time $16,290; part-time $905 per credit hour. Tuition and fees vary according to program. *Financial support:* In 2010–11, 4 fellowships, 6 research assistantships, 15 teaching assistantships were awarded; Federal Work-Study, institutionally sponsored loans, scholarships/grants, and tuition waivers (full and partial) also available. Support available to part-time students. Financial award application deadline: 2/15. *Faculty research:* Models of physiological systems, mathematical immunology, computational group theory, mathematical logic, computational science. Total annual research expenditures: $696,366. *Unit head:* Dr. Gary Krenz, Chair, 414-288-7573, Fax: 414-288-1578. *Application contact:* Dr. Francis Pastijn, Director of Graduate Studies, 414-288-5229.

Marquette University, Graduate School, College of Arts and Sciences, Program in Computing, Milwaukee, WI 53201-1881. Offers MS. Part-time and evening/weekend programs available. Postbaccalaureate distance learning degree programs offered (minimal on-campus study). *Students:* 4 full-time (0 women), 23 part-time (4 women); includes 2 minority (1 Asian, non-Hispanic/Latino; 1 Hispanic/Latino), 9 international. Average age 31. 17 applicants, 88% accepted, 11 enrolled. In 2010, 1 master's awarded. *Degree requirements:* For master's, thesis optional, Enrollment in the Professional Seminar in Computing each term. *Entrance requirements:* For master's, official transcripts from all current and previous colleges/universities except Marquette, essay, three letters of reference. Additional exam requirements/recommendations for international students: Required—TOEFL (minimum score 530 paper-based; 78 computer-based). *Application deadline:* Applications are processed on a rolling basis. Application fee: $50. Electronic applications accepted. *Expenses:* Tuition: Full-time $16,290; part-time $905 per credit hour. Tuition and fees vary according to program. *Financial support:* In 2010–11, 1 teaching assistantship was awarded. Financial award application deadline: 2/15. *Unit head:* Dr. Thomas Kaczmarek, Director, 414-288-6734, E-mail: douglas.harris@marquette.edu. *Application contact:* Erin Fox, Assistant Director for Recruitment, 414-288-5319, Fax: 414-288-1902, E-mail: erin.fox@marquette.edu.

Massachusetts Institute of Technology, School of Engineering, Department of Electrical Engineering and Computer Science, Cambridge, MA 02139. Offers computer science (PhD, Sc D, ECS); computer science and engineering (PhD, Sc D); electrical engineering (PhD, Sc D, EE); electrical engineering and computer science (M Eng, SM, PhD, Sc D); SM/MBA. *Faculty:* 124 full-time (17 women), 1 part-time/adjunct (0 women). *Students:* 759 full-time (168 women), 4 part-time (1 woman); includes 165 minority (15 Black or African American, non-Hispanic/Latino; 3 American Indian or Alaska Native, non-Hispanic/Latino; 117 Asian, non-Hispanic/Latino; 27 Hispanic/Latino; 3 Two or more races, non-Hispanic/Latino), 341 international. Average age 26. 2,852 applicants, 11% accepted, 249 enrolled. In 2010, 199 master's, 103 doctorates, 4 other advanced degrees awarded. Terminal master's awarded for partial completion of doctoral program. *Degree requirements:* For master's and other advanced degree, thesis; for doctorate, comprehensive exam, thesis/dissertation. *Entrance requirements:* For master's, Leaders for Global Operations joint program requires GRE. Additional exam requirements/recommendations for international students: Required—TOEFL (minimum score 600 paper-based; 250 computer-based), IELTS (minimum score 7). *Application deadline:* For fall admission, 12/15 for domestic and international students. Application fee: $75. Electronic applications accepted. *Expenses:* Tuition: Full-time $38,940; part-time $605 per unit. Required fees: $272. *Financial support:* In 2010–11, 716 students received support, including 136 fellowships with tuition reimbursements available (averaging $28,627 per year), 470 research assistantships with tuition reimbursements available (averaging $29,178 per year), 116 teaching assistantships with tuition reimbursements available (averaging $30,108 per year); career-related internships or fieldwork, Federal Work-Study, institutionally sponsored loans, scholarships/grants, health care benefits, and unspecified assistantships also available. *Faculty research:* Artificial intelligence and applications; computer architecture, software, systems, and networks; communications, control, signal processing, and optimization; devices, electronics, electrodynamics, and photonics; bioelectrical engineering. Total annual research expenditures: $90.3 million. *Unit head:* Prof. Anantha P. Chandrakasan, Department Head, 617-253-4600, Fax: 617-258-7354. *Application contact:* Graduate Admissions, 617-253-4603, Fax: 617-258-7354, E-mail: grad-ap@eecs.mit.edu.

McGill University, Faculty of Graduate and Postdoctoral Studies, Faculty of Science, School of Computer Science, Montréal, QC H3A 2T5, Canada. Offers M Sc, PhD.

McMaster University, School of Graduate Studies, Faculty of Engineering, Department of Computing and Software, Hamilton, ON L8S 4M2, Canada. Offers computer science (M Sc, PhD); software engineering (M Eng, MA Sc, PhD). Part-time programs available. *Degree requirements:* For master's, thesis. *Entrance requirements:* Additional exam requirements/recommendations for international students: Required—TOEFL (minimum score 550 paper-based; 213 computer-based). *Faculty research:* Software engineering; theory of non-sequential systems; parallel and distributed computing; artificial intelligence; complexity, design, and analysis of algorithms; combinatorial computing, especially applications to molecular biology.

McNeese State University, Doré School of Graduate Studies, College of Science, Department of Mathematics, Computer Science, and Statistics, Lake Charles, LA 70609. Offers computer science (MS); mathematics (MS); statistics (MS). Evening/weekend programs available. *Faculty:* 11 full-time (3 women). *Students:* 25 full-time (9 women), 13 part-time (5 women); includes 3 minority (1 Black or African American, non-Hispanic/Latino; 1 Asian, non-Hispanic/Latino; 1 Hispanic/Latino), 27 international. In 2010, 17 master's awarded. *Degree requirements:* For master's, comprehensive exam, thesis or alternative, written exam. *Entrance requirements:* For master's, GRE. *Application deadline:* For fall admission, 5/15 priority date for domestic and international students; for spring admission, 10/15 priority date for domestic and international students. Applications are processed on a rolling basis. Application fee: $20 ($30 for international students). Tuition and fees vary according to course load. *Financial support:* Teaching assistantships available. Financial award application deadline: 5/1. *Unit head:* Sid Bradley, Head, 337-475-5788, Fax: 337-475-5799, E-mail: sbradley@mcneese.edu. *Application contact:* Dr. George F. Mead, Interim Dean of Dore' School of Graduate Studies, 337-475-5396, Fax: 337-475-5397, E-mail: admissions@mcneese.edu.

Memorial University of Newfoundland, School of Graduate Studies, Department of Computer Science, St. John's, NL A1C 5S7, Canada. Offers M Sc, PhD. Part-time programs available. *Degree requirements:* For master's, thesis; for doctorate, comprehensive exam, thesis/dissertation, oral thesis defense. *Entrance requirements:* For master's, GRE (strongly recommended), honors degree in computer science or related field; for doctorate, GRE (strongly recommended), master's degree in computer science. Additional exam requirements/recommendations for international students: Required—GRE. Electronic applications accepted. *Faculty research:* Theoretical computer science, parallel and distributed computing, scientific computing, software systems and artificial intelligence.

Metropolitan State University, College of Arts and Sciences, St. Paul, MN 55106-5000. Offers computer science (MS); liberal studies (MA); technical communication (MS). Part-time and evening/weekend programs available. *Students:* 38 full-time (16 women), 72 part-time (49 women); includes 4 Black or African American, non-Hispanic/Latino; 8 Asian, non-Hispanic/Latino; 3 Hispanic/Latino, 13 international. Average age 38. In 2010, 22 master's awarded. *Entrance requirements:* For master's, minimum GPA of 2.75, resume. Additional exam requirements/recommendations for international students: Required—TOEFL (minimum score 550 paper-based; 213 computer-based). *Application deadline:* For fall admission, 8/1 priority date for domestic students, 3/15 for international students; for winter admission, 10/15 for international students; for spring admission, 12/1 priority date for domestic students, 3/15 for international students. Applications are processed on a rolling basis. Application fee: $20. Electronic applications accepted. *Expenses:* Tuition, state resident: full-time $5827; part-time $291 per credit hour. Tuition, nonresident: full-time $11,654; part-time $583 per credit hour. Required fees: $10 per credit hour. Tuition and fees vary according to degree level. *Financial support:* Research assistantships available. Financial award applicants required to submit FAFSA. *Unit head:* Dr. Becky Omdahl, Dean, 651-793-1443, Fax: 651-793-1446, E-mail: becky.omdahl@metrostate.edu. *Application contact:* Lucille Maghrak, Graduate Studies Coordinator, 651-793-1932, E-mail: lucille.maghrak@metrostate.edu.

Michigan State University, The Graduate School, College of Engineering, Department of Computer Science and Engineering, East Lansing, MI 48824. Offers computer science (MS, PhD). *Entrance requirements:* Additional exam requirements/recommendations for international students: Required—TOEFL. Electronic applications accepted.

Michigan Technological University, Graduate School, College of Sciences and Arts, Department of Computer Science, Houghton, MI 49931. Offers computational science and engineering (PhD); computer science (MS, PhD). Part-time programs available. Terminal master's awarded for partial completion of doctoral program. *Degree requirements:* For master's, comprehensive exam, thesis optional; for doctorate, comprehensive exam, thesis/dissertation. *Entrance requirements:* Additional exam requirements/recommendations for international students: Required—TOEFL (minimum score 580 paper-based; 237 computer-based). Electronic applications accepted. *Expenses:* Contact institution. *Faculty research:* Artificial intelligence, graphics/visualization, software engineering, architecture and compiler optimization, human computing interaction.

Computer Science

Middle Tennessee State University, College of Graduate Studies, College of Basic and Applied Sciences, Department of Computer Science, Murfreesboro, TN 37132. Offers MS. Part-time and evening/weekend programs available. Postbaccalaureate distance learning degree programs offered. *Faculty:* 11 full-time (6 women). *Students:* 2 full-time (0 women), 27 part-time (10 women); includes 1 Black or African American, non-Hispanic/Latino; 7 Asian, non-Hispanic/Latino. Average age 29. 38 applicants, 26% accepted, 10 enrolled. In 2010, 11 master's awarded. *Degree requirements:* For master's, one foreign language, comprehensive exam, thesis. *Entrance requirements:* For master's, GRE. Additional exam requirements/recommendations for international students: Required—TOEFL (minimum score 525 paper-based; 195 computer-based; 71 iBT) or IELTS (minimum score 6). *Application deadline:* For fall admission, 6/1 for domestic and international students. Applications are processed on a rolling basis. Application fee: $25 ($30 for international students). Electronic applications accepted. *Expenses:* Tuition, state resident: full-time $4632. Tuition, nonresident: full-time $11,520. *Financial support:* In 2010–11, 10 students received support. Institutionally sponsored loans available. Support available to part-time students. Financial award application deadline: 5/1; financial award applicants required to submit FAFSA. *Unit head:* Dr. Chrisila C. Pettey, Chair, 615-898-2397, Fax: 615-898-5567, E-mail: cscbp@mtsu.edu. *Application contact:* Dr. Michael Allen, Dean and Vice Provost for Research, 615-898-2840, Fax: 615-904-8020, E-mail: mallen@mtsu.edu.

Midwestern State University, Graduate Studies, College of Science and Mathematics, Computer Science Program, Wichita Falls, TX 76308. Offers MS. Part-time and evening/weekend programs available. *Faculty:* 4 full-time (1 woman). *Students:* 13 full-time (3 women), 11 part-time (6 women); includes 2 Black or African American, non-Hispanic/Latino; 1 Asian, non-Hispanic/Latino, 14 international. Average age 28. In 2010, 14 master's awarded. *Degree requirements:* For master's, comprehensive exam, thesis. *Entrance requirements:* For master's, GRE General Test. Additional exam requirements/recommendations for international students: Required—TOEFL (minimum score 573 paper-based; 230 computer-based). *Application deadline:* For fall admission, 7/1 priority date for domestic students, 4/1 for international students; for spring admission, 11/1 priority date for domestic students, 8/1 for international students. Applications are processed on a rolling basis. Application fee: $35 ($50 for international students). Electronic applications accepted. *Expenses:* Tuition, state resident: full-time $1620; part-time $90 per credit hour. Tuition, nonresident: full-time $2160; part-time $120 per credit hour. International tuition: $7200 full-time. *Financial support:* In 2010–11, 18 students received support; teaching assistantships with partial tuition reimbursements available, career-related internships or fieldwork, Federal Work-Study, institutionally sponsored loans, scholarships/grants, tuition waivers (partial), and unspecified assistantships available. Support available to part-time students. Financial award application deadline: 3/1; financial award applicants required to submit FAFSA. *Faculty research:* Software engineering, genetic algorithms and graphics, ASIC design, computational epidemiology, new ways of GPS use. *Unit head:* Dr. Nelson Passos, Graduate Coordinator, 940-397-4129, E-mail: nelson.passos@mwsu.edu. *Application contact:* 800-842-1922, Fax: 940-397-4672, E-mail: admissions@mwsu.edu.

Mills College, Graduate Studies, Program in Computer Science, Oakland, CA 94613-1000. Offers computer science (Certificate); interdisciplinary computer science (MA). Part-time programs available. *Faculty:* 7 full-time (6 women), 1 (woman) part-time/adjunct. *Students:* 9 full-time (5 women), 3 part-time (2 women); includes 1 Black or African American, non-Hispanic/Latino; 2 Asian, non-Hispanic/Latino; 1 Hispanic/Latino. Average age 31. 13 applicants, 85% accepted, 7 enrolled. In 2010, 2 master's awarded. *Degree requirements:* For master's, thesis. *Entrance requirements:* Additional exam requirements/recommendations for international students: Required—TOEFL. *Application deadline:* For fall admission, 2/1 priority date for domestic students, 12/15 for international students; for spring admission, 11/1 priority date for domestic students, 10/1 for international students. Applications are processed on a rolling basis. Application fee: $50. Electronic applications accepted. *Expenses:* Tuition: Full-time $28,280; part-time $7070 per course. Required fees: $1058; $1058 per year. Tuition and fees vary according to program. *Financial support:* In 2010–11, 11 students received support, including 11 fellowships (averaging $2,614 per year), 11 teaching assistantships (averaging $2,614 per year); career-related internships or fieldwork and residence awards also available. Financial award application deadline: 2/1; financial award applicants required to submit FAFSA. *Faculty research:* Dynamical systems, linear programming, theory of computer viruses, interface design, intelligent tutoring systems. *Unit head:* Susan S. Wang, Department Head, 510-430-2138, E-mail: wang@mills.edu. *Application contact:* Jessica King, Graduate Admission Specialist, 510-430-3305, Fax: 510-430-2159, E-mail: rmcglaut@mills.edu.

Mississippi College, Graduate School, College of Arts and Sciences, School of Science and Mathematics, Department of Computer Science, Clinton, MS 39058. Offers M Ed, MS. Part-time programs available. *Degree requirements:* For master's, comprehensive exam, thesis or alternative. *Entrance requirements:* For master's, GRE. Additional exam requirements/recommendations for international students: Recommended—IELTS.

Mississippi State University, Bagley College of Engineering, Department of Computer Science and Engineering, Mississippi State, MS 39762. Offers computer science (MS, PhD). Part-time programs available. Postbaccalaureate distance learning degree programs offered (minimal on-campus study). *Faculty:* 15 full-time (3 women), 1 (woman) part-time/adjunct. *Students:* 54 full-time (9 women), 16 part-time (2 women); includes 13 minority (10 Black or African American, non-Hispanic/Latino; 3 Asian, non-Hispanic/Latino), 27 international. Average age 28. 154 applicants, 24% accepted, 25 enrolled. In 2010, 18 master's, 2 doctorates awarded. *Degree requirements:* For master's, thesis, comprehensive oral or written exam; for doctorate, thesis/dissertation, comprehensive oral or written exam. *Entrance requirements:* For master's, GRE, minimum GPA of 2.75; for doctorate, GRE. Additional exam requirements/recommendations for international students: Required—TOEFL (minimum score 550 paper-based; 213 computer-based; 79 iBT); Recommended—IELTS (minimum score 6.5). *Application deadline:* For fall admission, 7/1 for domestic students, 5/1 for international students; for spring admission, 11/1 for domestic students, 9/1 for international students. Applications are processed on a rolling basis. Application fee: $40. Electronic applications accepted. *Expenses:* Tuition, state resident: full-time $2730.50; part-time $304 per credit hour. Tuition, nonresident: full-time $6901; part-time $767 per credit hour. *Financial support:* In 2010–11, 20 research assistantships with full tuition reimbursements (averaging $13,659 per year), 9 teaching assistantships with full tuition reimbursements (averaging $12,150 per year) were awarded; Federal Work-Study, institutionally sponsored loans, and unspecified assistantships also available. Financial award application deadline: 4/1; financial award applicants required to submit FAFSA. *Faculty research:* Artificial intelligence, software engineering, visualization, high performance computing. Total annual research expenditures: $10.3 million. *Unit head:* Dr. Donna Reese, Professor and Interim Department Head, 662-325-0925, Fax: 662-325-8997, E-mail: dreese@bagley.msstate.edu. *Application contact:* Dr. Edward B. Allen, Associate Professor and Graduate Coordinator, 662-325-7449, Fax: 662-325-8997, E-mail: allen@cse.msstate.edu.

Missouri State University, Graduate College, College of Natural and Applied Sciences, Department of Computer Science, Springfield, MO 65897. Offers MNAS. Part-time programs available. *Degree requirements:* For master's, comprehensive exam, thesis or alternative. *Entrance requirements:* For master's, GRE, minimum GPA of 3.0. Additional exam requirements/recommendations for international students: Required—TOEFL (minimum score 550 paper-based; 213 computer-based; 79 iBT). Electronic applications accepted. *Expenses:* Tuition, state resident: full-time $3348; part-time $186 per credit hour. Tuition, nonresident: full-time $6696; part-time $372 per credit hour. Required fees: $238 per semester. Tuition and fees vary according to course level, course load and program. *Faculty research:* Floating point numbers, data compression, graph theory.

Missouri University of Science and Technology, Graduate School, Department of Computer Science, Rolla, MO 65409. Offers MS, PhD. Part-time programs available. Terminal master's awarded for partial completion of doctoral program. *Degree requirements:* For doctorate, thesis/dissertation, departmental qualifying exam. *Entrance requirements:* For master's, GRE General Test (minimum score 700 quantitative, 4 writing); for doctorate, GRE Subject Test (minimum score: quantitative 600, writing 3.5). Electronic applications accepted. *Faculty research:* Intelligent systems, artificial intelligence software engineering, distributed systems, database systems, computer systems.

Monmouth University, The Graduate School, Department of Computer Science, West Long Branch, NJ 07764-1898. Offers computer science (MS); software design and development (Certificate). Part-time and evening/weekend programs available. *Faculty:* 4 full-time (2 women), 3 part-time/adjunct (0 women). *Students:* 24 full-time (8 women), 20 part-time (7 women); includes 1 Hispanic/Latino; 1 Two or more races, non-Hispanic/Latino, 36 international. Average age 26. 55 applicants, 89% accepted, 21 enrolled. In 2010, 20 master's awarded. *Degree requirements:* For master's, thesis optional. *Entrance requirements:* For master's, minimum GPA of 3.0 in major, 2.75 overall. Additional exam requirements/recommendations for international students: Required—TOEFL (minimum score 550 paper-based; 213 computer-based; 79 iBT), IELTS (minimum score 5) or Michigan English Language Assessment Battery (minimum score 77), Cambridge A, B, C. *Application deadline:* For fall admission, 7/15 priority date for domestic students, 6/1 for international students; for spring admission, 11/15 priority date for domestic students, 11/1 for international students. Applications are processed on a rolling basis. Application fee: $50. Electronic applications accepted. *Expenses:* Tuition: Full-time $19,572; part-time $816 per credit. Required fees: $628; $157 per semester. *Financial support:* In 2010–11, 44 students received support, including 40 fellowships (averaging $1,718 per year), 19 research assistantships (averaging $4,941 per year); career-related internships or fieldwork, scholarships/grants, and unspecified assistantships also available. Support available to part-time students. Financial award application deadline: 3/1; financial award applicants required to submit FAFSA. *Faculty research:* Databases, natural language processing, protocols, performance analysis, communications networks (systems), telecommunications. *Unit head:* Dr. Cui Yu, Program Director, 732-571-4460, Fax: 732-263-5202, E-mail: cyu@monmouth.edu. *Application contact:* Kevin Roane, Director, Office of Graduate Admission, 732-571-3452, Fax: 732-263-5123, E-mail: gradadm@monmouth.edu.

Montana State University, College of Graduate Studies, College of Engineering, Department of Computer Science, Bozeman, MT 59717. Offers computer science (MS, PhD). Part-time programs available. *Faculty:* 8 full-time (0 women), 1 part-time/adjunct (0 women). *Students:* 13 full-time (1 woman), 25 part-time (1 woman); includes 4 minority (2 American Indian or Alaska Native, non-Hispanic/Latino; 2 Asian, non-Hispanic/Latino), 6 international. Average age 31. 28 applicants, 43% accepted, 8 enrolled. In 2010, 8 master's, 3 doctorates awarded. *Degree requirements:* For master's, comprehensive exam; for doctorate, comprehensive exam, thesis/dissertation. *Entrance requirements:* For master's and doctorate, GRE, TOEFL. Additional exam requirements/recommendations for international students: Required—TOEFL (minimum score 550 paper-based; 213 computer-based). *Application deadline:* For fall admission, 7/15 priority date for domestic students, 5/15 priority date for international students; for spring admission, 12/1 priority date for domestic students, 10/1 priority date for international students. Applications are processed on a rolling basis. Application fee: $30. Electronic applications accepted. *Expenses:* Tuition, state resident: full-time $5553.90. Tuition, nonresident: full-time $14,646. Required fees: $1233. *Financial support:* In 2010–11, 20 students received support, including 7 research assistantships with full and partial tuition reimbursements available (averaging $9,310 per year), 13 teaching assistantships with full and partial tuition reimbursements available (averaging $5,427 per year). Financial award application deadline: 3/1; financial award applicants required to submit FAFSA. *Faculty research:* Applied algorithms, artificial intelligence, data mining, software engineering, Web-based learning, wireless networking and robotics. Total annual research expenditures: $732,813. *Unit head:* Dr. John Paxton, Head, 406-994-4780, Fax: 406-994-4376, E-mail: paxton@cs.montana.edu. *Application contact:* Dr. Carl A. Fox, Vice Provost for Graduate Education, 406-994-4145, Fax: 406-994-7433, E-mail: gradstudy@montana.edu.

Montclair State University, The Graduate School, College of Science and Mathematics, Department of Computer Science, Montclair, NJ 07043-1624. Offers CISCO (Certificate); informatics (MS); object oriented computing (Certificate). Part-time and evening/weekend programs available. *Faculty:* 14 full-time (3 women), 16 part-time/adjunct (6 women). *Students:* 15 full-time (2 women), 18 part-time (7 women); includes 1 Asian, non-Hispanic/Latino; 1 Hispanic/Latino, 7 international. Average age 31. 16 applicants, 81% accepted, 5 enrolled. In 2010, 9 master's awarded. *Degree requirements:* For master's, comprehensive exam, thesis or alternative. *Entrance requirements:* For master's, GRE General Test, 2 letters of recommendation. Additional exam requirements/recommendations for international students: Required—TOEFL (minimum iBT score of 83) or IELTS. *Application deadline:* For fall admission, 6/1 for international students; for spring admission, 10/1 for international students. Applications are processed on a rolling basis. Application fee: $60. Electronic applications accepted. *Expenses:* Tuition, state resident: part-time $501.34 per credit. Tuition, nonresident: part-time $773.88 per credit. Required fees: $71.15 per credit. *Financial support:* In 2010–11, 4 research assistantships with full tuition reimbursements (averaging $7,000 per year) were awarded; Federal Work-Study, scholarships/grants, and unspecified assistantships also available. Support available to part-time students. Financial award application deadline: 3/1; financial award applicants required to submit FAFSA. Total annual research expenditures: $342,960. *Unit head:* Dr. Michael Oudshoorn, Chairperson, 973-655-4166. *Application contact:* Amy Aiello, Director of Graduate Admissions and Operations, 973-655-5147, Fax: 973-655-7869, E-mail: graduate.school@montclair.edu.

National University, Academic Affairs, School of Engineering and Technology, Department of Computer Science and Information Systems, La Jolla, CA 92037-1011. Offers computer science (MS); information systems (MS); software engineering (MS); technology management (MS). Part-time and evening/weekend programs available. Postbaccalaureate distance learning degree programs offered (no on-campus study). *Faculty:* 8 full-time (1 woman), 90 part-time/adjunct (13 women). *Students:* 60 full-time (12 women), 146 part-time (40 women); includes 365 minority (25 Black or African American, non-Hispanic/Latino; 21 Asian, non-Hispanic/Latino; 14 Hispanic/Latino; 2 Native Hawaiian or other Pacific Islander, non-Hispanic/Latino; 303 Two or more races, non-Hispanic/Latino), 54 international. Average age 32. 138 applicants, 100% accepted, 79 enrolled. In 2010, 79 master's awarded. *Degree requirements:* For master's, thesis. *Entrance requirements:* For master's, interview, minimum GPA of 2.5. Additional exam requirements/recommendations for international students: Required—TOEFL (minimum score 550 paper-based; 213 computer-based; 79 iBT), IELTS (minimum score 6). *Application deadline:* Applications are processed on a rolling basis. Application fee: $60 ($65 for international students). Electronic applications accepted. *Expenses:* Tuition: Full-time $9450; part-time $350 per unit. Required fees: $350 per unit. One-time fee: $60. *Financial support:* Career-related internships or fieldwork, institutionally sponsored loans, scholarships/grants, and tuition waivers (partial) available. Support available to part-time students. Financial award application deadline: 6/30; financial award applicants required to submit FAFSA. *Unit head:* Dr. Alireza M. Farahani, Chair and Instructor, 858-309-3438, Fax: 858-309-3420, E-mail: afarahan@nu.edu. *Application contact:* Dominick Giovanniello, Associate Regional Dean—San Diego, 800-NAT-UNIV, Fax: 858-541-7792, E-mail: dgiovann@nu.edu.

Naval Postgraduate School, Graduate Programs, Department of Computer Science, Monterey, CA 93943. Offers computer science (MS, PhD); modeling of virtual environments and simulations (MS, PhD); software engineering (MS, PhD). Program only open to commissioned officers of the United States and friendly nations and selected United States federal civilian employees. Part-time programs available. Postbaccalaureate distance learning degree programs offered (minimal on-campus study). *Degree requirements:* For master's, thesis; for doctorate, one foreign language, thesis/dissertation.

New Jersey Institute of Technology, Office of Graduate Studies, College of Computing Science, Department of Computer Science, Newark, NJ 07102. Offers bioinformatics (MS); computer science (MS, PhD); computing and business (MS); software engineering (MS). Part-time and evening/weekend programs available. *Faculty:* 35 full-time (2 women), 5 part-time/adjunct (1 woman). *Students:* 212 full-time (66 women), 109 part-time (14 women); includes 13 Black or African American, non-Hispanic/Latino; 3 American Indian or Alaska

Native, non-Hispanic/Latino; 36 Asian, non-Hispanic/Latino; 16 Hispanic/Latino, 196 international. Average age 28. 867 applicants, 39% accepted, 116 enrolled. In 2010, 152 master's, 5 doctorates awarded. Terminal master's awarded for partial completion of doctoral program. *Degree requirements:* For master's, thesis optional; for doctorate, thesis/dissertation. *Entrance requirements:* For master's, GRE General Test; for doctorate, GRE General Test, minimum graduate GPA of 3.5. Additional exam requirements/recommendations for international students: Required—TOEFL (minimum score 550 paper-based; 213 computer-based; 79 iBT). *Application deadline:* For fall admission, 6/5 priority date for domestic students, 4/1 for international students; for spring admission, 11/15 for domestic and international students. Applications are processed on a rolling basis. Application fee: $65. Electronic applications accepted. *Expenses:* Tuition, state resident: full-time $14,724; part-time $818 per credit. Tuition, nonresident: full-time $20,304; part-time $1128 per credit. Required fees: $2272; $209 per credit. $103 per semester. One-time fee: $312 full-time; $212 part-time. *Financial support:* Fellowships with full and partial tuition reimbursements, research assistantships with full and partial tuition reimbursements, teaching assistantships with full and partial tuition reimbursements, career-related internships or fieldwork, Federal Work-Study, institutionally sponsored loans, and unspecified assistantships available. Financial award application deadline: 3/15. Total annual research expenditures: $6.4 million. *Unit head:* Dr. Michael A. Baltrush, Interim Chair, 973-596-3386, E-mail: michael.a.baltrush@njit.edu. *Application contact:* Kathryn Kelly, Director of Admissions, 973-596-3300, Fax: 973-596-3461, E-mail: admissions@njit.edu.

New Mexico Highlands University, Graduate Studies, College of Arts and Sciences, Program in Media Arts and Computer Science, Las Vegas, NM 87701. Offers media arts and computer science (MS). *Faculty:* 7 full-time (2 women). *Students:* 9 full-time (5 women), 7 part-time (3 women); includes 7 Hispanic/Latino, 2 international. Average age 31. 17 applicants, 100% accepted, 4 enrolled. In 2010, 3 master's awarded. *Degree requirements:* For master's, comprehensive exam, thesis. *Entrance requirements:* For master's, minimum undergraduate GPA of 3.0. Additional exam requirements/recommendations for international students: Required—TOEFL (minimum score 540 paper-based; 270 computer-based). Application fee: $15. *Expenses:* Tuition, state resident: full-time $2544. Required fees: $624; $132 per credit hour. *Financial support:* In 2010–11, 7 students received support. Career-related internships or fieldwork, Federal Work-Study, institutionally sponsored loans, scholarships/grants, tuition waivers (full and partial), and unspecified assistantships available. Support available to part-time students. Financial award application deadline: 3/1; financial award applicants required to submit FAFSA. *Faculty research:* Advanced digital compositing, photographic installations and exhibition design, pattern recognition, parallel and distributed computing, computer security education. *Unit head:* Dr. Miriam Langer, Department Head, Visual and Performing Arts, 505-454-3390, E-mail: melanger@nmhu.edu. *Application contact:* Diane Trujillo, Administrative Assistant for Graduate Studies, 505-454-3266, Fax: 505-426-2117, E-mail: dtrujillo@nmhu.edu.

New Mexico Institute of Mining and Technology, Graduate Studies, Department of Computer Science, Socorro, NM 87801. Offers MS, PhD. Part-time programs available. *Degree requirements:* For master's, thesis optional; for doctorate, thesis/dissertation. *Entrance requirements:* For master's, GRE General Test; for doctorate, GRE General Test, GRE Subject Test. Additional exam requirements/recommendations for international students: Required—TOEFL. Electronic applications accepted.

New Mexico State University, Graduate School, College of Arts and Sciences, Department of Computer Science, Las Cruces, NM 88003-8001. Offers bioinformatics (MS); computer science (MS, PhD). PhD offered jointly with University of New Mexico. Part-time programs available. *Faculty:* 9 full-time (3 women). *Students:* 76 full-time (14 women), 23 part-time (7 women); includes 7 minority (2 Asian, non-Hispanic/Latino; 5 Hispanic/Latino), 78 international. Average age 27. 168 applicants, 89% accepted, 19 enrolled. In 2010, 28 master's, 1 doctorate awarded. Terminal master's awarded for partial completion of doctoral program. *Degree requirements:* For master's, comprehensive exam, thesis or alternative; for doctorate, comprehensive exam, thesis/dissertation, qualifying examination, thesis proposal. *Entrance requirements:* For master's and doctorate, BS in computer science. Additional exam requirements/recommendations for international students: Required—TOEFL. *Application deadline:* For fall admission, 3/1 priority date for domestic and international students; for spring admission, 11/1 priority date for domestic and international students. Applications are processed on a rolling basis. Application fee: $30 ($50 for international students). Electronic applications accepted. *Expenses:* Tuition, state resident: full-time $4536; part-time $242 per credit. Tuition, nonresident: full-time $15,816; part-time $712 per credit. Required fees: $636 per term. *Financial support:* In 2010–11, 6 fellowships with full tuition reimbursements (averaging $30,000 per year), 24 research assistantships (averaging $8,087 per year), 23 teaching assistantships (averaging $5,538 per year) were awarded; career-related internships or fieldwork, Federal Work-Study, scholarships/grants, health care benefits, and unspecified assistantships also available. Support available to part-time students. Financial award application deadline: 3/1; financial award applicants required to submit FAFSA. *Faculty research:* Programming languages, artificial intelligence, software engineering, bioinformatics, data mining, computer networks. *Unit head:* Dr. Enrico Pontelli, Head, 575-646-3723, Fax: 575-646-1002, E-mail: epontell@cs.nmsu.edu. *Application contact:* Dr. Son Tran, Chair, Admissions Committee, 575-646-1930, Fax: 575-646-1002, E-mail: tson@cs.nmsu.edu.

New York Institute of Technology, Graduate Division, School of Engineering and Computing Sciences, Program in Computer Science, Old Westbury, NY 11568-8000. Offers MS. Part-time and evening/weekend programs available. *Students:* 109 full-time (27 women), 55 part-time (15 women); includes 16 minority (4 Black or African American, non-Hispanic/Latino; 6 Asian, non-Hispanic/Latino; 5 Hispanic/Latino; 1 Two or more races, non-Hispanic/Latino), 129 international. Average age 26. In 2010, 83 master's awarded. *Degree requirements:* For master's, project. *Entrance requirements:* For master's, GRE General Test (if QPA less than 2.85), minimum QPA of 2.85, BS in computer science or related field. Additional exam requirements/recommendations for international students: Required—TOEFL (minimum score 550 paper-based; 213 computer-based). *Application deadline:* For fall admission, 7/1 priority date for domestic students; for spring admission, 12/1 priority date for domestic students. Applications are processed on a rolling basis. Application fee: $50. Electronic applications accepted. *Expenses:* Tuition: Part-time $835 per credit. *Financial support:* Fellowships, research assistantships with partial tuition reimbursements, institutionally sponsored loans, tuition waivers (partial), and unspecified assistantships available. Support available to part-time students. Financial award applicants required to submit FAFSA. *Faculty research:* Image processing, multimedia CD-ROM, prototype modules of the DTV application environment. *Unit head:* Dr. Ayat Jafari, Chair, 516-686-7569, Fax: 516-686-7439, E-mail: ajafari@nyit.edu. *Application contact:* Dr. Jacquelyn Nealon, Vice President for Enrollment Services, 516-686-7925, Fax: 516-686-7597, E-mail: jnealon@nyit.edu.

New York University, Graduate School of Arts and Science, Courant Institute of Mathematical Sciences, Department of Computer Science, New York, NY 10012-1019. Offers computer science (MS, PhD); information systems (MS); scientific computing (MS). Part-time and evening/weekend programs available. *Faculty:* 30 full-time (1 woman). *Students:* 237 full-time (54 women), 98 part-time (23 women); includes 2 Black or African American, non-Hispanic/Latino; 23 Asian, non-Hispanic/Latino; 3 Hispanic/Latino, 231 international. Average age 27. 836 applicants, 41% accepted, 136 enrolled. In 2010, 91 master's, 13 doctorates awarded. *Degree requirements:* For doctorate, thesis/dissertation, oral and written exams. *Entrance requirements:* For master's and doctorate, GRE General Test, GRE Subject Test. Additional exam requirements/recommendations for international students: Required—TOEFL. *Application deadline:* For fall admission, 12/15 for domestic students; for spring admission, 11/1 for domestic students. Application fee: $90. *Financial support:* Fellowships with tuition reimbursements, research assistantships with tuition reimbursements, teaching assistantships with tuition reimbursements, Federal Work-Study, institutionally sponsored loans, scholarships/grants, health care benefits, and unspecified assistantships available. Financial award application deadline: 12/15; financial award applicants required to submit FAFSA. *Faculty research:* Distributed parallel and secure computing, computer graphics and vision, algorithmic and theory of computation, natural language processing, computational biology. *Unit head:* Margaret Wright, Director of Graduate Studies, PhD Program, 212-998-3011, Fax: 212-995-4124, E-mail: admissions@cs.nyu.edu. *Application contact:* Benjamin Goldberg, Director of Graduate Studies, MS Program, 212-998-3011, Fax: 212-995-4124, E-mail: admissions@cs.nyu.edu.

Nicholls State University, Graduate Studies, College of Arts and Sciences, Department of Mathematics and Computer Science, Thibodaux, LA 70310. Offers community/technical college mathematics (MS). Part-time and evening/weekend programs available. *Degree requirements:* For master's, comprehensive exam. *Entrance requirements:* For master's, GRE General Test. Electronic applications accepted. *Faculty research:* Operations research, statistics, numerical analysis, algebra, topology.

Norfolk State University, School of Graduate Studies, School of Science and Technology, Department of Computer Science, Norfolk, VA 23504. Offers MS.

North Carolina Agricultural and Technical State University, Graduate School, College of Engineering, Department of Computer Science, Greensboro, NC 27411. Offers MSCS. Part-time programs available. *Degree requirements:* For master's, comprehensive exam, thesis (for some programs). *Faculty research:* Object-oriented analysis, artificial intelligence, distributed computing, societal implications of computing, testing.

North Carolina Agricultural and Technical State University, Graduate School, School of Technology, Department of Electronics, Computer, and Information Technology, Greensboro, NC 27411. Offers electronics and computer technology (MSIT).

North Carolina State University, Graduate School, College of Engineering, Department of Computer Science, Raleigh, NC 27695. Offers MC Sc, MS, PhD. Part-time programs available. Postbaccalaureate distance learning degree programs offered. *Degree requirements:* For master's, thesis optional; for doctorate, thesis/dissertation. *Entrance requirements:* For master's, GRE General Test, GRE Subject Test, minimum GPA of 3.0; for doctorate, GRE General Test, GRE Subject Test (recommended), minimum GPA of 3.5. Additional exam requirements/recommendations for international students: Required—TOEFL. Electronic applications accepted. *Faculty research:* Networking and performance analysis, theory and algorithms of computation, data mining, graphics and human computer interaction, software engineering and information security.

North Carolina State University, Graduate School, College of Engineering, Department of Electrical and Computer Engineering and Department of Computer Science, Program in Computer Networking, Raleigh, NC 27695. Offers MS. *Degree requirements:* For master's, thesis optional. *Entrance requirements:* For master's, GRE General Test, GRE Subject Test (recommended). Electronic applications accepted. *Faculty research:* High-speed networks, performance modelling, security, wireless and mobile.

North Central College, Graduate and Continuing Education Programs, Department of Computer Science, Naperville, IL 60566-7063. Offers Web and Internet applications (MS). Part-time and evening/weekend programs available. *Faculty:* 4 full-time (2 women). *Students:* 1 full-time (0 women), 10 part-time (3 women); includes 1 Black or African American, non-Hispanic/Latino, 1 international. Average age 30. In 2010, 4 master's awarded. *Degree requirements:* For master's, thesis optional, project. *Entrance requirements:* For master's, interview. Additional exam requirements/recommendations for international students: Required—TOEFL (minimum score 577 paper-based; 233 computer-based; 90 iBT). *Application deadline:* For fall admission, 8/15 for domestic students; for winter admission, 12/1 for domestic students; for spring admission, 2/1 for domestic students. Applications are processed on a rolling basis. Application fee: $25. *Expenses:* Contact institution. *Financial support:* Scholarships/grants available. Support available to part-time students. *Unit head:* Dr. Caroline St.Clair, Program Coordinator, 630-637-5171, Fax: 630-637-5172, E-mail: cstclair@noctrl.edu. *Application contact:* Wendy Kulpinski, Director and Graduate and Continuing Education Admission, 630-637-5808, Fax: 630-637-5819, E-mail: wekulpinski@noctrl.edu.

North Dakota State University, College of Graduate and Interdisciplinary Studies, College of Science and Mathematics, Department of Computer Science, Fargo, ND 58108. Offers computer science (MS, PhD); operations research (MS); software engineering (MS, PhD, Certificate). Part-time programs available. *Faculty:* 14 full-time (1 woman). *Students:* 100 full-time (19 women), 109 part-time (32 women); includes 3 Black or African American, non-Hispanic/Latino; 1 American Indian or Alaska Native, non-Hispanic/Latino; 8 Asian, non-Hispanic/Latino; 2 Hispanic/Latino, 161 international. Average age 24. 220 applicants, 34% accepted, 31 enrolled. In 2010, 30 master's, 2 doctorates awarded. *Degree requirements:* For master's, comprehensive exam, thesis optional; for doctorate, thesis/dissertation, qualifying exam. *Entrance requirements:* For master's, minimum GPA of 3.0, BS in computer science or related field; for doctorate, minimum GPA of 3.25, MS in computer science or related field. Additional exam requirements/recommendations for international students: Required—TOEFL (minimum score 550 paper-based; 213 computer-based; 79 iBT). *Application deadline:* For fall admission, 8/15 priority date for domestic students, 8/15 for international students; for spring admission, 12/15 priority date for domestic students, 12/15 for international students. Application fee: $45 ($60 for international students). *Financial support:* In 2010–11, 37 research assistantships with full tuition reimbursements (averaging $10,000 per year), 17 teaching assistantships with full tuition reimbursements (averaging $4,500 per year) were awarded; career-related internships or fieldwork, Federal Work-Study, institutionally sponsored loans, and tuition waivers (full) also available. Financial award application deadline: 4/15. *Faculty research:* Networking, software engineering, artificial intelligence, database, programming languages. Total annual research expenditures: $366,434. *Unit head:* Dr. Brian Slator, Head, 701-231-8562, Fax: 701-231-8255. *Application contact:* Dr. Ken R. Nygard, Graduate Coordinator, 701-231-9460, Fax: 701-231-8255, E-mail: kendall.nygard@ndsu.edu.

Northeastern Illinois University, Graduate College, College of Arts and Sciences, Department of Computer Science, Program in Computer Science, Chicago, IL 60625-4699. Offers MS. Part-time and evening/weekend programs available. *Faculty:* 11 full-time (3 women), 9 part-time/adjunct (3 women). *Students:* 36 full-time (11 women), 46 part-time (17 women); includes 17 minority (5 Black or African American, non-Hispanic/Latino; 11 Asian, non-Hispanic/Latino; 1 Hispanic/Latino), 27 international. Average age 33. 100 applicants, 65% accepted. In 2010, 29 master's awarded. *Degree requirements:* For master's, comprehensive exam, research project or thesis. *Entrance requirements:* For master's, minimum GPA of 2.75, proficiency in 2 higher-level computer languages, 1 course in discrete mathematics. Additional exam requirements/recommendations for international students: Required—TOEFL (minimum score 550 paper-based; 213 computer-based; 79 iBT). *Application deadline:* Applications are processed on a rolling basis. Application fee: $30. Electronic applications accepted. *Financial support:* In 2010–11, 22 students received support, including 3 research assistantships with full tuition reimbursements available (averaging $6,600 per year); career-related internships or fieldwork, Federal Work-Study, institutionally sponsored loans, scholarships/grants, tuition waivers (full and partial), and unspecified assistantships also available. Support available to part-time students. Financial award applicants required to submit FAFSA. *Faculty research:* Telecommunications, database inference problems, decision-making under uncertainty, belief networks, analysis of algorithms. *Unit head:* Dr. Rich E. Neapolitan, Chairperson, 773-442-4734, Fax: 773-442-4900, E-mail: re-neapolitan@neiu.edu. *Application contact:* Dr. Rich E. Neapolitan, Chairperson, 773-442-4734, Fax: 773-442-4900, E-mail: re-neapolitan@neiu.edu.

Northeastern University, College of Computer and Information Science, Boston, MA 02115-5096. Offers computer and information science (PhD); computer science (MS); health informatics (MS); information assurance (MS). Part-time and evening/weekend programs available. *Faculty:* 28 full-time (3 women), 3 part-time/adjunct (all women). *Students:* 337 full-time (91 women), 90 part-time (52 women). 1,045 applicants, 56% accepted, 150 enrolled. In 2010, 88 master's, 7 doctorates awarded. Terminal master's awarded for partial completion of doctoral program. *Degree requirements:* For master's, thesis optional; for doctorate, comprehensive exam, thesis/dissertation. *Entrance requirements:* For master's and doctorate, GRE General Test. Additional exam requirements/recommendations for international students: Required—TOEFL

Computer Science

Northeastern University (continued)

or IELTS. *Application deadline:* For fall admission, 7/15 for domestic students, 5/1 for international students; for spring admission, 10/15 for domestic students, 9/1 for international students. Applications are processed on a rolling basis. Application fee: $50. Electronic applications accepted. *Expenses:* Contact institution. *Financial support:* In 2010–11, 59 students received support, including 1 fellowship, 40 research assistantships with full tuition reimbursements available (averaging $18,260 per year), 33 teaching assistantships with full tuition reimbursements available (averaging $18,260 per year); career-related internships or fieldwork, Federal Work-Study, institutionally sponsored loans, scholarships/grants, and unspecified assistantships also available. Financial award application deadline: 1/15. *Faculty research:* Programming languages, artificial intelligence, human-computer interaction, database management, network security. *Unit head:* Dr. Larry A. Finkelstein, Dean, 617-373-2462, Fax: 617-373-5121. *Application contact:* Dr. Agnes Chan, Associate Dean and Director of Graduate Program, 617-373-2462, Fax: 617-373-5121, E-mail: gradschool@ccs.neu.edu.

Northern Arizona University, Graduate College, College of Engineering, Forestry and Natural Sciences, Programs in Engineering, Flagstaff, AZ 86011. Offers civil and environmental engineering (M Eng); civil engineering (MSE); computer science (MSE); electrical engineering (M Eng, MSE); engineering (M Eng, MSE); environmental engineering (M Eng, MSE); mechanical engineering (M Eng, MSE). Part-time programs available. Postbaccalaureate distance learning degree programs offered (no on-campus study). *Faculty:* 42 full-time (12 women). *Students:* 19 full-time (3 women), 15 part-time (2 women); includes 6 minority (2 American Indian or Alaska Native, non-Hispanic/Latino; 3 Hispanic/Latino; 1 Two or more races, non-Hispanic/Latino), 7 international. Average age 28. 21 applicants, 48% accepted, 4 enrolled. In 2010, 15 master's awarded. *Degree requirements:* For master's, thesis. *Entrance requirements:* For master's, GRE General Test. Additional exam requirements/recommendations for international students: Required—TOEFL (minimum score 550 paper-based; 213 computer-based; 80 iBT), IELTS (minimum score 7). *Application deadline:* For fall admission, 3/1 priority date for domestic and international students; for spring admission, 9/15 priority date for domestic and international students. Applications are processed on a rolling basis. Application fee: $65. Electronic applications accepted. *Financial support:* In 2010–11, 3 research assistantships with partial tuition reimbursements (averaging $14,541 per year), 12 teaching assistantships with partial tuition reimbursements (averaging $12,863 per year) were awarded; career-related internships or fieldwork, Federal Work-Study, scholarships/grants, health care benefits, and unspecified assistantships also available. Financial award applicants required to submit FAFSA. *Unit head:* Dr. Ernesto Penado, Chair, 928-523-9453, Fax: 928-523-2300, E-mail: ernesto.penado@nau.edu. *Application contact:* Natasha Kypfer, Program Coordinator, 928-523-1447, Fax: 928-523-2300, E-mail: egrmasters@nau.edu.

Northern Illinois University, Graduate School, College of Liberal Arts and Sciences, Department of Computer Science, De Kalb, IL 60115-2854. Offers MS. Part-time and evening/weekend programs available. *Faculty:* 14 full-time (3 women). *Students:* 78 full-time (16 women), 40 part-time (12 women); includes 1 Black or African American, non-Hispanic/Latino; 2 Asian, non-Hispanic/Latino; 2 Hispanic/Latino, 92 international. Average age 24. 261 applicants, 64% accepted, 79 enrolled. In 2010, 94 master's awarded. *Degree requirements:* For master's, comprehensive exam. *Entrance requirements:* For master's, GRE General Test, minimum GPA of 2.75. Additional exam requirements/recommendations for international students: Required—TOEFL (minimum score 550 paper-based; 213 computer-based). *Application deadline:* For fall admission, 6/1 for domestic students, 5/1 for international students; for spring admission, 11/1 for domestic students, 10/1 for international students. Applications are processed on a rolling basis. Application fee: $30. Electronic applications accepted. *Expenses:* Tuition, state resident: full-time $7200; part-time $300 per credit hour. Tuition, nonresident: full-time $14,400; part-time $600 per credit hour. Required fees: $79 per credit hour. *Financial support:* In 2010–11, 2 research assistantships with full tuition reimbursements, 28 teaching assistantships with full tuition reimbursements were awarded; fellowships with full tuition reimbursements, career-related internships or fieldwork, Federal Work-Study, scholarships/grants, tuition waivers (full), and unspecified assistantships also available. Support available to part-time students. Financial award applicants required to submit FAFSA. *Faculty research:* Databases, theorem proving, artificial intelligence, neural networks, computer ethics. *Unit head:* Dr. Nicholas Karonis, Chair, 815-753-0349, Fax: 815-753-0342, E-mail: karonis@niu.edu. *Application contact:* Graduate School Office, 815-753-0395, E-mail: gradsch@niu.edu.

Northern Kentucky University, Office of Graduate Programs, College of Informatics, Department of Computer Science, Highland Heights, KY 41099. Offers computer science (MSCS); geographic information systems (Certificate); secure software engineering (Certificate). Part-time and evening/weekend programs available. *Faculty:* 6 full-time (1 woman). *Students:* 3 full-time (1 woman), 18 part-time (3 women); includes 7 minority (3 Black or African American, non-Hispanic/Latino; 3 Asian, non-Hispanic/Latino; 1 Hispanic/Latino), 5 international. Average age 34. 23 applicants, 52% accepted, 7 enrolled. In 2010, 8 master's, 6 Certificates awarded. *Degree requirements:* For master's, thesis optional. *Entrance requirements:* For master's, minimum GPA of 3.0, at least 4 semesters of undergraduate study in computer science including intermediate computer programming and data structures, one year of calculus, one course in discrete mathematics. Additional exam requirements/recommendations for international students: Required—TOEFL (minimum score 550 paper-based; 213 computer-based; 79 iBT); Recommended—IELTS (minimum score 6.5). *Application deadline:* For fall admission, 8/1 for domestic students, 6/1 for international students; for spring admission, 12/1 for domestic students, 10/1 for international students. Applications are processed on a rolling basis. Application fee: $40. Electronic applications accepted. *Expenses:* Tuition, state resident: full-time $7254; part-time $403 per credit hour. Tuition, nonresident: full-time $12,492; part-time $694 per credit hour. Tuition and fees vary according to degree level and program. *Financial support:* Scholarships/grants and unspecified assistantships available. Financial award applicants required to submit FAFSA. *Faculty research:* Data privacy, data mining, wireless security, secure software engineering, secure networking. *Unit head:* Dr. Maureen Doyle, Program Director, 859-572-5468, Fax: 859-572-6097, E-mail: doylem3@nku.edu. *Application contact:* Dr. Peg Griffin, Director of Graduate Programs, 859-572-6934, Fax: 859-572-6670, E-mail: griffinp@nku.edu.

Northwestern Polytechnic University, School of Engineering, Fremont, CA 94539-7482. Offers computer science (MS); computer systems engineering (MS); electrical engineering (MS). Part-time and evening/weekend programs available. *Degree requirements:* For master's, thesis optional. *Entrance requirements:* For master's, minimum GPA of 3.0. Additional exam requirements/recommendations for international students: Required—TOEFL (minimum score 550 paper-based; 213 computer-based; 79 iBT). *Faculty research:* Computer networking, database design, Internet technology, software engineering, digital signal processing.

Northwestern University, McCormick School of Engineering and Applied Science, Department of Electrical Engineering and Computer Science, Evanston, IL 60208. Offers computer science (MS, PhD); electrical and computer engineering (MS, PhD); electronic materials (MS, PhD, Certificate); information technology (MS). MS and PhD admissions and degrees offered through The Graduate School. Part-time programs available. *Faculty:* 50 full-time (3 women). *Students:* 212 full-time (31 women), 18 part-time (2 women); includes 21 minority (15 Asian, non-Hispanic/Latino; 4 Hispanic/Latino; 2 Two or more races, non-Hispanic/Latino), 157 international. Average age 26. 588 applicants, 10% accepted, 30 enrolled. In 2010, 39 master's, 31 doctorates awarded. Terminal master's awarded for partial completion of doctoral program. *Degree requirements:* For master's, comprehensive exam (for some programs), thesis optional, Thesis or Project is optional; for doctorate, comprehensive exam (for some programs), thesis/dissertation. *Entrance requirements:* For master's and doctorate, General Exam of GRE. Additional exam requirements/recommendations for international students: Required—TOEFL (minimum score 577 paper-based, 233 computer-based, 90 iBT) or IELTS. *Application deadline:* For fall admission, 12/31 for domestic and international students. Application fee: $75. Electronic applications accepted. *Financial support:* Fellowships with full tuition reimbursements, research assistantships with full tuition reimbursements, teaching assistantships with full tuition reimbursements, career-related internships or fieldwork, institutionally sponsored loans, health care benefits, and unspecified assistantships available. Financial award application deadline: 1/15; financial award applicants required to submit FAFSA. *Faculty research:* Solid state and photonics; computing, algorithms, and applications; computer engineering and systems; cognitive systems; graphics and interactive media; signals and systems. Total annual research expenditures: $19.2 million. *Unit head:* Dr. Alan Sahakian, Chair, 847-491-7007, Fax: 847-491-4455, E-mail: sahakian@ece.northwestern.edu. *Application contact:* Dr. Thrasos Pappas, Admission Officer, 847-491-1243, Fax: 847-491-4455, E-mail: t-pappas@northwestern.edu.

Northwest Missouri State University, Graduate School, Melvin and Valorie Booth College of Business and Professional Studies, Department of Computer Science and Information Systems, Maryville, MO 64468-6001. Offers applied computer science (MS); instructional technology (Certificate); teaching instructional technology (MS Ed). Part-time programs available. *Faculty:* 12 full-time (5 women). *Students:* 106 full-time (31 women), 42 part-time (24 women); includes 2 Black or African American, non-Hispanic/Latino; 1 Asian, non-Hispanic/Latino, 112 international. 186 applicants, 74% accepted, 61 enrolled. In 2010, 53 master's awarded. *Degree requirements:* For master's, comprehensive exam. *Entrance requirements:* For master's, GRE General Test, minimum GPA of 3.0. Additional exam requirements/recommendations for international students: Required—TOEFL (minimum score 550 paper-based; 213 computer-based). *Application deadline:* Applications are processed on a rolling basis. Application fee: $0 ($50 for international students). *Financial support:* In 2010–11, 5 research assistantships (averaging $6,000 per year), 3 teaching assistantships with full tuition reimbursements (averaging $6,000 per year) were awarded; unspecified assistantships also available. Financial award application deadline: 4/1; financial award applicants required to submit FAFSA. *Unit head:* Dr. Phillip Heeler, Chairperson, 660-562-1200. *Application contact:* Dr. Gregory Haddock, Dean of Graduate School, 660-562-1145, Fax: 660-562-1096, E-mail: gradsch@nwmissouri.edu.

Nova Southeastern University, Graduate School of Computer and Information Sciences, Fort Lauderdale, FL 33314-7796. Offers computer information systems (MS, PhD), including information security; computer science (MS, PhD); computing technology in education (PhD); information security (MS); information systems (MS, PhD); management information systems (MS), including information security (MS, PhD), management information systems; JD/MS. Part-time and evening/weekend programs available. Postbaccalaureate distance learning degree programs offered (no on-campus study). *Faculty:* 20 full-time (5 women), 21 part-time/adjunct (3 women). *Students:* 142 full-time (35 women), 1,000 part-time (283 women); includes 219 Black or African American, non-Hispanic/Latino; 8 American Indian or Alaska Native, non-Hispanic/Latino; 88 Asian, non-Hispanic/Latino; 163 Hispanic/Latino; 8 Two or more races, non-Hispanic/Latino, 44 international. Average age 41. 486 applicants, 45% accepted. In 2010, 128 master's, 44 doctorates awarded. Terminal master's awarded for partial completion of doctoral program. *Degree requirements:* For master's, thesis optional; for doctorate, thesis/dissertation. *Entrance requirements:* For master's, minimum undergraduate GPA of 2.5; for doctorate, master's degree, minimum graduate GPA of 3.25. Additional exam requirements/recommendations for international students: Required—TOEFL (minimum score 213 computer-based; 79 iBT), IELTS (minimum score 6). *Application deadline:* Applications are processed on a rolling basis. Application fee: $50. Electronic applications accepted. *Expenses:* Contact institution. *Financial support:* Federal Work-Study, scholarships/grants, and unspecified assistantships available. Support available to part-time students. Financial award application deadline: 5/1. *Faculty research:* Artificial intelligence, database management, human-computer interaction, distance education, information security. *Unit head:* Dr. Amon Seagull, PhD, Interim Dean, 954-262-7300. *Application contact:* 954-262-2000, Fax: 954-262-2752, E-mail: scisinfo@nova.edu.

Oakland University, Graduate Study and Lifelong Learning, School of Engineering and Computer Science, Department of Computer Science and Engineering, Rochester, MI 48309-4401. Offers computer science (MS); embedded systems (MS); information systems engineering (MS); software engineering (MS). Part-time and evening/weekend programs available. *Entrance requirements:* For master's, minimum GPA of 3.0 for unconditional admission. Electronic applications accepted. *Expenses:* Contact institution. *Faculty research:* Cyber security, 3D imaging of neurochemicals in rat brains.

OGI School of Science & Engineering at Oregon Health & Science University, Graduate Studies, Department of Computer Science and Electrical Engineering, Beaverton, OR 97006-8921. Offers computer science (PhD); computer science and engineering (MS, PhD); electrical engineering (MS, PhD). Part-time and evening/weekend programs available. Terminal master's awarded for partial completion of doctoral program. *Degree requirements:* For master's, thesis optional; for doctorate, comprehensive exam, oral defense of dissertation. *Entrance requirements:* For master's and doctorate, GRE General Test. Additional exam requirements/recommendations for international students: Required—TOEFL (minimum score 650 paper-based; 280 computer-based). Electronic applications accepted. *Faculty research:* Computer systems architecture, intelligent and interactive systems, programming models and systems, theory of computation.

The Ohio State University, Graduate School, College of Engineering, Department of Computer Science and Engineering, Columbus, OH 43210. Offers computer and information science (MS, PhD); computer science and engineering (MS). *Faculty:* 40. *Students:* 244 full-time (45 women), 60 part-time (9 women); includes 2 Black or African American, non-Hispanic/Latino; 5 Asian, non-Hispanic/Latino; 1 Hispanic/Latino, 236 international. Average age 28. In 2010, 65 master's, 19 doctorates awarded. *Degree requirements:* For master's, thesis optional; for doctorate, thesis/dissertation. *Entrance requirements:* Additional exam requirements/recommendations for international students: Recommended—TOEFL (minimum score 600 paper-based; 250 computer-based). *Application deadline:* For fall admission, 8/15 priority date for domestic students, 7/1 priority date for international students; for winter admission, 12/1 priority date for domestic students, 11/1 priority date for international students; for spring admission, 3/1 priority date for domestic students, 2/1 priority date for international students. Applications are processed on a rolling basis. Application fee: $40 ($50 for international students). Electronic applications accepted. *Expenses:* Tuition, state resident: full-time $10,605. Tuition, nonresident: full-time $26,535. Tuition and fees vary according to course load and program. *Financial support:* Fellowships, teaching assistantships, career-related internships or fieldwork, Federal Work-Study, institutionally sponsored loans, and administrative assistantships available. Support available to part-time students. Financial award application deadline: 1/15. *Unit head:* Xiadong Zhang, Chair, 614-292-5813, E-mail: zhang.574@osu.edu. *Application contact:* 614-292-9444, Fax: 614-292-3895, E-mail: domestic.grad@osu.edu.

Ohio University, Graduate College, Russ College of Engineering and Technology, School of Electrical Engineering and Computer Science, Athens, OH 45701-2979. Offers computer science (MS); electrical engineering (MS); electrical engineering and computer science (PhD). *Students:* 88 full-time (19 women), 25 part-time (2 women); includes 3 minority (all Hispanic/Latino), 72 international. 121 applicants, 52% accepted, 18 enrolled. In 2010, 19 master's, 5 doctorates awarded. *Degree requirements:* For master's, comprehensive exam (for some programs), thesis; for doctorate, comprehensive exam, thesis/dissertation, qualifying exams. *Entrance requirements:* For master's, GRE, BSEE or BSCS, minimum GPA of 3.0; for doctorate, GRE, MSEE or MSCS, minimum GPA of 3.0. Additional exam requirements/recommendations for international students: Required—TOEFL (minimum score 550 paper-based; 80 iBT) or IELTS (minimum score 6.5). *Application deadline:* For fall admission, 2/1 priority date for domestic students, 1/1 priority date for international students; for winter admission, 6/1 priority date for domestic students, 5/1 priority date for international students; for spring admission, 8/15 priority date for domestic students, 7/15 priority date for international students. Applications are processed on a rolling basis. Application fee: $50 ($55 for international students). Electronic applications accepted. *Financial support:* In 2010–11, 54 research assistantships with full tuition reimbursements, 19 teaching assistantships with full tuition reimbursements were awarded; Federal Work-Study, institutionally sponsored loans, scholarships/grants, and unspecified assistantships also available. Financial award applicants required to submit FAFSA. *Faculty research:* Avionics, networking/communications, intelligent distribution, real-time computing, control systems, optical properties of semiconductors. *Unit head:* Dr. David Juedes, Chair, 740-593-1566, Fax: 740-593-0007, E-mail: juedes@ohio.edu. *Application contact:* Dr. David Matolak, Graduate Chair, 740-593-1241, Fax: 740-593-0007, E-mail: matolak@ohio.edu.

Oklahoma City University, Meinders School of Business, Division of Computer Science, Oklahoma City, OK 73106-1402. Offers). Part-time and evening/weekend programs available. *Degree requirements:* For master's, comprehensive exam, thesis optional. *Entrance requirements:* For master's, minimum GPA of 3.0. Additional exam requirements/recommendations for international students: Required—TOEFL. *Expenses:* Contact institution. *Faculty research:* Parallel processing, pedagogical techniques, databases, numerical analysis, gesture recognition.

Oklahoma State University, College of Arts and Sciences, Computer Science Department, Stillwater, OK 74078. Offers MS, PhD. *Faculty:* 13 full-time (0 women). *Students:* 49 full-time (11 women), 45 part-time (9 women); includes 1 Black or African American, non-Hispanic/Latino; 3 American Indian or Alaska Native, non-Hispanic/Latino; 1 Asian, non-Hispanic/Latino, 67 international. Average age 30. 281 applicants, 26% accepted, 14 enrolled. In 2010, 20 master's, 3 doctorates awarded. *Degree requirements:* For master's, thesis optional; for doctorate, comprehensive exam, thesis/dissertation. *Entrance requirements:* For master's, GRE; for doctorate, GRE General Test, GRE Subject Test in computer science (recommended), 3 letters of recommendation. Additional exam requirements/recommendations for international students: Required—TOEFL (minimum score 550 paper-based; 79 iBT). *Application deadline:* For fall admission, 3/1 priority date for international students; for spring admission, 8/1 priority date for international students. Applications are processed on a rolling basis. Application fee: $40 ($75 for international students). Electronic applications accepted. *Expenses:* Tuition, state resident: full-time $3716; part-time $154.85 per credit hour. Tuition, nonresident: full-time $14,892; part-time $621 per credit hour. Required fees: $2044; $85.20 per credit hour. One-time fee: $50. Tuition and fees vary according to course load and campus/location. *Financial support:* In 2010–11, 3 research assistantships (averaging $9,431 per year), 20 teaching assistantships (averaging $11,860 per year) were awarded; career-related internships or fieldwork, Federal Work-Study, scholarships/grants, health care benefits, tuition waivers (partial), and unspecified assistantships also available. Support available to part-time students. Financial award application deadline: 3/1; financial award applicants required to submit FAFSA. *Unit head:* Dr. Subhash Kak, Head, 405-744-5668, Fax: 405-774-9097. *Application contact:* Dr. Gordon Emslie, Dean, 405-744-6368, Fax: 405-744-0355, E-mail: grad-i@okstate.edu.

Old Dominion University, College of Sciences, Program in Computer Science, Norfolk, VA 23529. Offers MS, PhD. Part-time programs available. *Faculty:* 16 full-time (5 women). *Students:* 58 full-time (15 women), 64 part-time (12 women); includes 2 minority (1 Asian, non-Hispanic/Latino; 1 Native Hawaiian or other Pacific Islander, non-Hispanic/Latino), 93 international. Average age 28. 200 applicants, 60% accepted. In 2010, 44 master's, 1 doctorate awarded. Terminal master's awarded for partial completion of doctoral program. *Degree requirements:* For master's, thesis optional, comprehensive diagnostic exam; for doctorate, comprehensive exam, thesis/dissertation. *Entrance requirements:* For master's, GRE General Test, minimum GPA of 3.0; for doctorate, GRE General Test, MS in computer science. Additional exam requirements/recommendations for international students: Required—TOEFL. *Application deadline:* For fall admission, 7/1 for domestic students. Applications are processed on a rolling basis. Application fee: $40. *Expenses:* Tuition, state resident: full-time $8592; part-time $358 per credit. Tuition, nonresident: full-time $21,672; part-time $903 per credit. Required fees: $119 per semester. One-time fee: $50. *Financial support:* In 2010–11, 98 students received support, including 1 fellowship (averaging $2,021 per year), 27 research assistantships with tuition reimbursements available (averaging $8,736 per year), 28 teaching assistantships with tuition reimbursements available (averaging $7,926 per year); career-related internships or fieldwork, scholarships/grants, and tuition waivers (partial) also available. Support available to part-time students. Financial award application deadline: 2/15; financial award applicants required to submit FAFSA. *Faculty research:* Software engineering, foundations, high-performance computing, networking, mobile computer. Total annual research expenditures: $1.4 million. *Unit head:* Dr. Mohammed Zubair, Graduate Program Director—PhD, 757-683-3917, Fax: 757-683-4900, E-mail: csgpd@odu.edu. *Application contact:* Dr. Ravi Mukkamala, Graduate Program Director—MS, 757-683-6001, E-mail: rmukkama@odu.edu.

Oregon Health & Science University, School of Medicine, Graduate Programs in Medicine, Department of Computer Science and Engineering, Portland, OR 97239-3098. Offers computer science and engineering (MS, PhD); electrical engineering (MS, PhD). Part-time programs available. *Faculty:* 8 full-time (2 women), 3 part-time/adjunct (1 woman). *Students:* 26 full-time (10 women); includes 1 Asian, non-Hispanic/Latino, 2 international. Average age 34. 26 applicants, 92% accepted, 4 enrolled. In 2010, 2 master's, 2 doctorates awarded. Terminal master's awarded for partial completion of doctoral program. *Degree requirements:* For master's, thesis (for some programs); for doctorate, comprehensive exam, thesis/dissertation. *Entrance requirements:* For master's, GRE General Test (minimum scores: 500 Verbal/600 Quantitative/4.5 Analytical); for doctorate, GRE General Test (minimum scores: 500 Verbal/600 Quantitative/4.5 Analytical) or MCAT (for some programs). Additional exam requirements/recommendations for international students: Required—TOEFL. *Application deadline:* For fall admission, 7/15 for domestic students, 5/15 for international students; for winter admission, 10/15 for domestic students, 9/15 for international students; for spring admission, 1/15 for domestic students, 12/15 for international students. Applications are processed on a rolling basis. Application fee: $65. Electronic applications accepted. *Financial support:* Health care benefits, tuition waivers (full), and full tuition and stipends available. *Unit head:* Peter Heeman, PhD, Program Director, 503-748-1635, E-mail: cseedept@csee.ogi.edu. *Application contact:* Pat Dickerson, Administrative Coordinator, 503-748-1635, E-mail: cseedept@csee.ogi.edu.

Oregon State University, Graduate School, College of Engineering, School of Electrical Engineering and Computer Science, Corvallis, OR 97331. Offers computer science (M Eng, MAIS, MS, PhD); electrical and computer engineering (M Eng, MS, PhD). *Degree requirements:* For doctorate, thesis/dissertation, qualifying exam, preliminary exam. *Entrance requirements:* For master's and doctorate, minimum GPA of 3.0 in last 90 hours of course work. Additional exam requirements/recommendations for international students: Required—TOEFL (minimum score 600 paper-based; 250 computer-based; 80 iBT). Electronic applications accepted. *Faculty research:* Optical materials and devices, data security and cryptography, analog and mixed-signal integrated circuit design, algorithms, computer graphics and vision.

Pace University, Seidenberg School of Computer Science and Information Systems, New York, NY 10038. Offers computer communications and networks (Certificate); computer science (MS); computing studies (DPS); information systems (MS); Internet technologies for e-commerce (MS); Internet technology (MS); object-oriented programming (Certificate); security and information assurance (Certificate); software development and engineering (MS); telecommunications (MS, Certificate). Part-time and evening/weekend programs available. *Entrance requirements:* For master's, GRE General Test. Additional exam requirements/recommendations for international students: Required—TOEFL. Electronic applications accepted. *Expenses:* Contact institution.

Pacific States University, College of Computer Science, Los Angeles, CA 90006. Offers computer science (MSCS); information systems (MSCS). Part-time and evening/weekend programs available. *Faculty:* 4 part-time/adjunct (0 women). *Students:* 16 full-time (2 women); includes 1 Asian, non-Hispanic/Latino, 14 international. Average age 27. 9 applicants, 78% accepted, 6 enrolled. In 2010, 7 master's awarded. *Entrance requirements:* For master's, bachelor's degree in physics, engineering, computer science, or applied mathematics; minimum undergraduate GPA of 2.5 during last 90 hours of course work. Additional exam requirements/recommendations for international students: Required—TOEFL (minimum score 450 paper-based; 133 computer-based; 45 iBT), IELTS (minimum score 4.5). *Application deadline:* For fall admission, 8/15 priority date for domestic students; for winter admission, 10/15 priority date for domestic students; for spring admission, 1/15 priority date for domestic students. Applications are processed on a rolling basis. Application fee: $100. *Expenses:* Tuition: Full-time $8280; part-time $345 per credit hour. Required fees: $150 per quarter. *Financial support:*

Scholarships/grants available. Financial award applicants required to submit FAFSA. *Unit head:* John Ma, Director, 888-200-0383, Fax: 323-731-7276, E-mail: admission@psuca.edu. *Application contact:* Namyoung Chah, Registrar, 323-731-2383, Fax: 323-731-7276, E-mail: registrar@psuca.edu.

Penn State University Park, Graduate School, College of Engineering, Department of Computer Science and Engineering, State College, University Park, PA 16802-1503. Offers M Eng, MS, PhD.

Polytechnic Institute of NYU, Department of Computer Science and Engineering, Major in Computer Science, Brooklyn, NY 11201-2990. Offers MS, PhD. Part-time and evening/weekend programs available. *Students:* 250 full-time (53 women), 73 part-time (11 women); includes 7 Black or African American, non-Hispanic/Latino; 20 Asian, non-Hispanic/Latino; 7 Hispanic/Latino, 247 international. Average age 26. 725 applicants, 49% accepted, 132 enrolled. In 2010, 120 master's, 3 doctorates awarded. *Degree requirements:* For master's, comprehensive exam (for some programs), thesis (for some programs); for doctorate, comprehensive exam, thesis/dissertation. *Entrance requirements:* For master's, BA or BS in computer science, mathematics, science, or engineering; working knowledge of a high-level program; for doctorate, GRE General Test, GRE Subject Test, qualifying exam, BA or BS in science, engineering, or management; MS or 1 year of graduate course work. Additional exam requirements/recommendations for international students: Required—TOEFL (minimum score 550 paper-based; 213 computer-based; 80 iBT); Recommended—IELTS (minimum score 6.5). *Application deadline:* For fall admission, 7/31 priority date for domestic students, 4/30 priority date for international students; for spring admission, 12/31 priority date for domestic students, 11/30 priority date for international students. Applications are processed on a rolling basis. Application fee: $75. Electronic applications accepted. *Expenses:* Tuition: Full-time $21,492; part-time $1194 per credit. Required fees: $385 per semester. Tuition and fees vary according to course load. *Financial support:* Research assistantships, teaching assistantships, institutionally sponsored loans, scholarships/grants, and unspecified assistantships available. Support available to part-time students. Financial award applicants required to submit FAFSA. *Unit head:* Dr. Keith W. Ross, Head, 718-260-3859, Fax: 718-260-3609, E-mail: ross@poly.edu. *Application contact:* JeanCarlo Bonilla, Director of Graduate Enrollment Management, 718-260-3182, Fax: 718-260-3624, E-mail: gradinfo@poly.edu.

Polytechnic Institute of NYU, Long Island Graduate Center, Graduate Programs, Department of Computer Science and Engineering, Program in Computer Science, Melville, NY 11747. Offers MS. *Students:* 2 full-time (1 woman), 27 part-time (4 women); includes 2 Black or African American, non-Hispanic/Latino; 10 Asian, non-Hispanic/Latino; 2 Hispanic/Latino, 1 international. Average age 32. 22 applicants, 73% accepted, 10 enrolled. In 2010, 11 master's awarded. *Degree requirements:* For master's, comprehensive exam (for some programs), thesis (for some programs). *Entrance requirements:* Additional exam requirements/recommendations for international students: Required—TOEFL (minimum score 550 paper-based; 213 computer-based; 80 iBT); Recommended—IELTS (minimum score 6.5). *Application deadline:* For fall admission, 7/31 priority date for domestic students, 4/30 priority date for international students; for spring admission, 12/31 priority date for domestic students, 11/30 priority date for international students. Applications are processed on a rolling basis. Application fee: $75. Electronic applications accepted. *Expenses:* Tuition: Full-time $21,492; part-time $1194 per credit. Required fees: $385 per semester. Tuition and fees vary according to course load. *Financial support:* Institutionally sponsored loans, scholarships/grants, and unspecified assistantships available. Support available to part-time students. Financial award applicants required to submit FAFSA. *Unit head:* Dr. Keith W. Ross, Department Head, 718-260-3859, E-mail: ross@poly.edu. *Application contact:* JeanCarlo Bonilla, Director of Graduate Enrollment Management, 718-260-3182, Fax: 718-260-3624, E-mail: gradinfo@poly.edu.

Polytechnic Institute of NYU, Westchester Graduate Center, Graduate Programs, Department of Computer Science and Engineering, Major in Computer Science, Hawthorne, NY 10532-1507. Offers MS. *Students:* 3 full-time (1 woman), 8 part-time (1 woman); includes 1 Asian, non-Hispanic/Latino; 1 Hispanic/Latino, 2 international. Average age 35. 4 applicants, 75% accepted, 2 enrolled. In 2010, 9 master's awarded. *Degree requirements:* For master's, comprehensive exam (for some programs), thesis (for some programs). *Entrance requirements:* Additional exam requirements/recommendations for international students: Required—TOEFL (minimum score 550 paper-based; 213 computer-based; 80 iBT); Recommended—IELTS (minimum score 6.5). *Application deadline:* For fall admission, 7/31 priority date for domestic students, 4/30 priority date for international students; for spring admission, 12/31 priority date for domestic students, 11/30 priority date for international students. Applications are processed on a rolling basis. Application fee: $75. Electronic applications accepted. *Expenses:* Tuition: Full-time $21,492; part-time $1194 per credit. Required fees: $385 per semester. Tuition and fees vary according to course load. *Financial support:* Institutionally sponsored loans, scholarships/grants, and unspecified assistantships available. Support available to part-time students. *Unit head:* Dr. Keith W. Ross, Department Head, 718-260-3859, E-mail: ross@poly.edu. *Application contact:* JeanCarlo Bonilla, Director of Graduate Enrollment Management, 718-260-3182, Fax: 718-260-3624, E-mail: gradinfo@poly.edu.

Polytechnic University of Puerto Rico, Graduate School, Hato Rey, PR 00919. Offers business administration (MBA), including computer information systems, general management, management of information systems, management of international enterprises; civil engineering (ME, MS); computer engineering (ME, MS); computer science (MCS, MS); electrical engineering (ME, MS); engineering management (MEM); environmental management (MEM); landscape architecture (M Land Arch); manufacturing competitiveness (MMC, MS); manufacturing engineering (ME, MS); mechanical engineering (M Mech E). Part-time and evening/weekend programs available. *Entrance requirements:* For master's, 3 letters of recommendation.

Portland State University, Graduate Studies, Maseeh College of Engineering and Computer Science, Department of Computer Science, Portland, OR 97207-0751. Offers computer science (MS, PhD); software engineering (MSE). Part-time programs available. *Faculty:* 26 full-time (6 women), 4 part-time/adjunct (0 women). *Students:* 81 full-time (17 women), 78 part-time (18 women); includes 4 Black or African American, non-Hispanic/Latino; 5 Asian, non-Hispanic/Latino; 3 Hispanic/Latino; 1 Two or more races, non-Hispanic/Latino, 65 international. Average age 32. 106 applicants, 47% accepted, 26 enrolled. In 2010, 30 master's, 2 doctorates awarded. *Degree requirements:* For master's, thesis or alternative; for doctorate, thesis/dissertation. *Entrance requirements:* For master's, GRE General Test, minimum GPA of 3.0 in upper-division course work, 2 letters of recommendation, BS in computer science or allied field; for doctorate, MS in computer science or allied field. Additional exam requirements/recommendations for international students: Required—TOEFL (minimum score 550 paper-based; 213 computer-based). *Application deadline:* For fall admission, 3/1 for domestic students, 2/1 for international students; for spring admission, 11/1 for domestic students, 9/1 for international students. Applications are processed on a rolling basis. Application fee: $50. *Expenses:* Tuition, state resident: full-time $8505; part-time $315 per credit. Tuition, nonresident: full-time $13,284; part-time $492 per credit. Required fees: $1482; $21 per credit. $99 per term. One-time fee: $120. Part-time tuition and fees vary according to course load and program. *Financial support:* In 2010–11, 9 research assistantships with full tuition reimbursements (averaging $19,896 per year) were awarded; teaching assistantships with full tuition reimbursements, career-related internships or fieldwork, Federal Work-Study, scholarships/grants, tuition waivers (partial), and unspecified assistantships also available. Support available to part-time students. Financial award application deadline: 3/1; financial award applicants required to submit FAFSA. *Faculty research:* Formal methods, database systems, parallel programming environments, computer security, software tools. Total annual research expenditures: $2.6 million. *Unit head:* Dr. Warren Harrison, Chair, 503-725-3108, Fax: 503-725-3211, E-mail: warren@cs.pdx.edu. *Application contact:* Kelley Gardiner, Graduate Coordinator, 503-725-3218, Fax: 503-725-3211, E-mail: gc@cs.pdx.edu.

Prairie View A&M University, College of Engineering, Prairie View, TX 77446-0519. Offers computer information systems (MSCIS); computer science (MSCS); electrical engineering

Computer Science

Prairie View A&M University (continued)
(MSEE, PhDEE); engineering (MS Engr). Part-time and evening/weekend programs available. *Faculty:* 19 full-time (0 women). *Students:* 89 full-time (26 women), 34 part-time (5 women); includes 45 Black or African American, non-Hispanic/Latino; 1 American Indian or Alaska Native, non-Hispanic/Latino; 13 Asian, non-Hispanic/Latino; 3 Hispanic/Latino, 53 international. Average age 32. 50 applicants, 84% accepted, 33 enrolled. In 2010, 8 master's, 2 doctorates awarded. *Degree requirements:* For master's, thesis (for some programs); for doctorate, comprehensive exam, thesis/dissertation. *Entrance requirements:* For master's, GRE General Test, bachelor's degree in engineering from an ABET accredited institution; for doctorate, GRE. Additional exam requirements/recommendations for international students: Required—TOEFL (minimum score 550 paper-based). *Application deadline:* For fall admission, 7/1 priority date for domestic and international students; for spring admission, 11/1 priority date for domestic and international students. Application fee: $50. Electronic applications accepted. *Expenses:* Tuition, state resident: full-time $3586.14; part-time $119.06 per credit hour. Tuition, nonresident: part-time $511.23 per credit hour. *Financial support:* In 2010–11, 80 students received support, including 14 fellowships (averaging $1,050 per year), 16 research assistantships (averaging $16,150 per year), 13 teaching assistantships (averaging $14,000 per year); career-related internships or fieldwork, institutionally sponsored loans, scholarships/grants, health care benefits, tuition waivers (partial), and unspecified assistantships also available. Financial award application deadline: 3/1; financial award applicants required to submit FAFSA. *Faculty research:* Applied radiation research, thermal science, computational fluid dynamics, analog mixed signal, aerial space battlefield. Total annual research expenditures: $439,054. *Unit head:* Dr. Kendall T. Harris, Dean, 936-261-9956, Fax: 936-261-9869, E-mail: tharris@pvamu.edu. *Application contact:* Barbara A. Thompson, Administrative Assistant, 936-261-9896, Fax: 936-261-9869, E-mail: bathompson@pvamu.edu.

Princeton University, Graduate School, School of Engineering and Applied Science, Department of Computer Science, Princeton, NJ 08544-1019. Offers MSE, PhD. Terminal master's awarded for partial completion of doctoral program. *Degree requirements:* For master's, thesis; for doctorate, thesis/dissertation, general exam. *Entrance requirements:* For master's, GRE General Test, GRE Subject Test (recommended), 3 letters of recommendation; for doctorate, GRE General Test, GRE Subject Test (recommended), official transcript(s), 3 letters of recommendation, personal statement. Additional exam requirements/recommendations for international students: Required—TOEFL. Electronic applications accepted. *Faculty research:* Computational biology and bioinformatics; computer and network systems; graphics, vision, and sound; machine learning, programming languages and security; theory.

Purdue University, Graduate School, College of Science, Department of Computer Sciences, West Lafayette, IN 47907. Offers MS, PhD. Part-time programs available. Terminal master's awarded for partial completion of doctoral program. *Degree requirements:* For master's, thesis optional; for doctorate, thesis/dissertation. *Entrance requirements:* For master's and doctorate, minimum GPA of 3.5. Additional exam requirements/recommendations for international students: Required—TOEFL (minimum score 600 paper-based; 250 computer-based), TWE (minimum score 5). Electronic applications accepted. *Faculty research:* Geometric modeling, information security, software systems, theory and algorithms, databases, networking.

Purdue University Calumet, Graduate Studies Office, School of Engineering, Mathematics, and Science, Department of Mathematics, Computer Science, and Statistics, Hammond, IN 46323-2094. Offers computer science (MS); mathematics (MAT, MS). Part-time programs available. *Faculty:* 8 full-time (2 women). *Students:* 3 full-time (1 woman), 14 part-time (6 women); includes 2 Black or African American, non-Hispanic/Latino. Average age 29. 6 applicants, 100% accepted. *Entrance requirements:* Additional exam requirements/recommendations for international students: Required—TOEFL. *Application deadline:* For fall admission, 5/1 priority date for domestic students; for spring admission, 11/1 priority date for domestic students. Applications are processed on a rolling basis. Application fee: $30. *Expenses:* Tuition, state resident: full-time $6867. Tuition, nonresident: full-time $14,157. *Financial support:* In 2010–11, 5 students received support, including 1 research assistantship with partial tuition reimbursement available (averaging $7,000 per year), 4 teaching assistantships with partial tuition reimbursements available (averaging $7,000 per year). Financial award application deadline: 3/1. *Faculty research:* Topology, analysis, algebra, mathematics education. Total annual research expenditures: $55,000. *Unit head:* Dr. C. M. Murphy, Head, 219-989-2270, Fax: 219-989-2165, E-mail: cmmurphy@purduecal.edu. *Application contact:* Dr. Catherine M. Murphy, Graduate Advisor, 219-989-2270, E-mail: cmmurphy@purduecal.edu.

Queens College of the City University of New York, Division of Graduate Studies, Mathematics and Natural Sciences Division, Department of Computer Science, Flushing, NY 11367-1597. Offers MA. Part-time and evening/weekend programs available. *Faculty:* 22 full-time (5 women). *Students:* 10 full-time (1 woman), 65 part-time (15 women); includes 2 Black or African American, non-Hispanic/Latino; 26 Asian, non-Hispanic/Latino; 4 Hispanic/Latino, 27 international. 67 applicants, 64% accepted, 24 enrolled. In 2010, 24 master's awarded. *Degree requirements:* For master's, comprehensive exam, thesis optional. *Entrance requirements:* For master's, GRE, minimum GPA of 3.0. Additional exam requirements/recommendations for international students: Required—TOEFL. *Application deadline:* For fall admission, 4/1 for domestic students; for spring admission, 11/1 for domestic students. Applications are processed on a rolling basis. Application fee: $125. *Financial support:* Career-related internships or fieldwork, Federal Work-Study, institutionally sponsored loans, tuition waivers (partial), and unspecified assistantships available. Support available to part-time students. Financial award application deadline: 4/1; financial award applicants required to submit FAFSA. *Faculty research:* Fifth-generation computing, hardware/software development, analysis of algorithms and theoretical computer science. *Unit head:* Dr. Zhigang Xiang, Chairperson, 718-997-3500. *Application contact:* Dr. Keitaro Yukawa, Graduate Adviser, 718-997-3500, E-mail: keitaro_yukawa@qc.edu.

Queen's University at Kingston, School of Graduate Studies and Research, Faculty of Arts and Sciences, School of Computing, Kingston, ON K7L 3N6, Canada. Offers M Sc, PhD. *Degree requirements:* For master's, thesis; for doctorate, comprehensive exam, thesis/dissertation. *Entrance requirements:* For master's, honours B Sc in computer science; for doctorate, M Sc in computer science. Additional exam requirements/recommendations for international students: Required—TOEFL, TWE. *Faculty research:* Software engineering, human computer interaction, data base, networks, computational geometry.

Regis University, College for Professional Studies, School of Computer and Information Sciences, Denver, CO 80221-1099. Offers database administration with Oracle (Certificate); database development (Certificate); database technologies (M Sc); enterprise Java software development (Certificate); enterprise resource planning (Certificate); executive information technologies (Certificate); information assurance (M Sc, Certificate); information technology management (M Sc); software engineering (M Sc, Certificate); software engineering and database technologies (M Sc); storage area networks (Certificate); systems engineering (M Sc, Certificate). Offered at Boulder Campus, Northwest Denver Campus, Southeast Denver Campus, Fort Collins Campus, Colorado Springs Campus, and Broomfield Campus. Part-time and evening/weekend programs available. Postbaccalaureate distance learning degree programs offered (no on-campus study). *Degree requirements:* For master's, thesis, final research project. *Entrance requirements:* For master's, 2 years of related experience, resume, interview; for Certificate, 2 years of related experience, resumé. Additional exam requirements/recommendations for international students: Required—TOEFL (minimum score 213 computer-based), TWE (minimum score 5), TOEFL or university-based test. Electronic applications accepted. *Expenses:* Contact institution. *Faculty research:* Secure Virtual Laboratory Architecture, Joint IA project with W2C06 Institute, Information Policy, OLTP and OLAP Technologies, knowledge management, software architectures.

Rensselaer at Hartford, Department of Computer and Information Science, Hartford, CT 06120-2991. Offers computer science (MS); information technology (MS). Part-time and evening/weekend programs available. *Degree requirements:* For master's, thesis optional. *Entrance requirements:* For master's, GRE. Additional exam requirements/recommendations for international students: Required—TOEFL (minimum score 600 paper-based; 250 computer-based; 100 iBT). Electronic applications accepted.

Rensselaer Polytechnic Institute, Graduate School, School of Science, Program in Computer Science, Troy, NY 12180-3590. Offers MS, PhD. Part-time programs available. *Faculty:* 22 full-time (6 women). *Students:* 79 full-time (10 women), 3 part-time (0 women); includes 1 Asian, non-Hispanic/Latino, 43 international. 432 applicants, 13% accepted, 25 enrolled. In 2010, 15 master's, 4 doctorates awarded. Terminal master's awarded for partial completion of doctoral program. *Degree requirements:* For master's, thesis; for doctorate, comprehensive exam, thesis/dissertation. *Entrance requirements:* For master's and doctorate, GRE General Test. Additional exam requirements/recommendations for international students: Required—TOEFL (minimum score 570 paper-based; 230 computer-based; 89 iBT). *Application deadline:* For fall admission, 1/1 priority date for domestic and international students; for spring admission, 8/15 priority date for domestic and international students. Applications are processed on a rolling basis. Application fee: $75. Electronic applications accepted. *Expenses:* Tuition: Full-time $39,600; part-time $1650 per credit. Required fees: $1896. *Financial support:* In 2010–11, 68 students received support, including 2 fellowships with full tuition reimbursements available (averaging $23,500 per year), 42 research assistantships with full tuition reimbursements available (averaging $17,500 per year), 24 teaching assistantships with full tuition reimbursements available (averaging $17,500 per year). Financial award application deadline: 1/1. *Faculty research:* Computer vision and graphics, algorithms and theory, pervasive computing and networking, data mining and machine learning, semantic web. Total annual research expenditures: $1.8 million. *Unit head:* Prof. Martin Hardwick, Acting Department Head, 518-276-8291, Fax: 518-276-4033, E-mail: hardwick@cs.rpi.edu. *Application contact:* Terry Hayden, Coordinator of Graduate Admissions, 518-276-8419, Fax: 518-276-4033, E-mail: grad-adm@cs.rpi.edu.

Rice University, Graduate Programs, George R. Brown School of Engineering, Department of Computer Science, Houston, TX 77251-1892. Offers MCS, MS, PhD. Terminal master's awarded for partial completion of doctoral program. *Degree requirements:* For master's, comprehensive exam; for doctorate, comprehensive exam, thesis/dissertation. *Entrance requirements:* For master's and doctorate, bachelor's degree. Additional exam requirements/recommendations for international students: Required—TOEFL. Electronic applications accepted. *Faculty research:* Programming languages and compiler construction; robotics, bioinformatics, algorithms—motion planning with emphasis on high-dimensional systems; network protocols, distributed systems, and operating systems—adaptive protocols for wireless; computer architecture, aperating systems—virtual machine monitors; computer graphics—application of computers to geometric problems and centered around general problem of representing geometric shapes.

Rivier College, School of Graduate Studies, Department of Computer Science and Mathematics, Nashua, NH 03060. Offers computer science (MS); mathematics (MAT). Part-time and evening/weekend programs available. *Faculty:* 5 full-time (3 women), 3 part-time/adjunct (0 women). *Students:* 16 full-time (9 women), 36 part-time (17 women); includes 2 Black or African American, non-Hispanic/Latino; 20 Asian, non-Hispanic/Latino. Average age 36. 26 applicants, 50% accepted, 8 enrolled. In 2010, 16 master's awarded. *Entrance requirements:* For master's, GRE Subject Test. *Application deadline:* Applications are processed on a rolling basis. Application fee: $25. Electronic applications accepted. *Expenses:* Tuition: Part-time $456 per credit. *Financial support:* Available to part-time students. Application deadline: 2/1. *Unit head:* Dr. Paul Cunningham, Director, 603-897-8272, E-mail: pcunningham@rivier.edu. *Application contact:* Mathew Kittredge, Director of Graduate Admissions, 603-897-8229, Fax: 603-897-8810, E-mail: mkittredge@rivier.edu.

Rochester Institute of Technology, Graduate Enrollment Services, B. Thomas Golisano College of Computing and Information Sciences, Department of Computer Science, Rochester, NY 14623-5603. Offers MS. Part-time and evening/weekend programs available. *Students:* 206 full-time (35 women), 60 part-time (10 women); includes 1 Black or African American, non-Hispanic/Latino; 2 American Indian or Alaska Native, non-Hispanic/Latino; 7 Asian, non-Hispanic/Latino; 4 Hispanic/Latino, 195 international. Average age 26. 425 applicants, 73% accepted, 87 enrolled. In 2010, 56 master's awarded. *Degree requirements:* For master's, thesis or project. *Entrance requirements:* For master's, GRE, minimum GPA of 3.0. Additional exam requirements/recommendations for international students: Required—TOEFL (minimum score 550 paper-based; 213 computer-based; 80 iBT) or IELTS (minimum score 6.5). *Application deadline:* For fall admission, 2/15 priority date for domestic and international students; for winter admission, 11/1 for domestic and international students. Applications are processed on a rolling basis. Electronic applications accepted. *Expenses:* Tuition: Full-time $33,234; part-time $924 per credit hour. Required fees: $219. *Financial support:* In 2010–11, 149 students received support; research assistantships with partial tuition reimbursements available, teaching assistantships with partial tuition reimbursements available, career-related internships or fieldwork, scholarships/grants, and unspecified assistantships available. Support available to part-time students. Financial award applicants required to submit FAFSA. *Faculty research:* Computational vision and acoustics, computer graphics and visualization, data management, distributed systems, intelligent systems, language design, security. *Unit head:* Paul Tymann, Department Chair, 585-475-7908, Fax: 585-475-4935, E-mail: ptt@cs.rit.edu. *Application contact:* Diane Ellison, Assistant Vice President, Graduate Enrollment Services, 585-475-2229, Fax: 585-475-7164, E-mail: gradinfo@rit.edu.

Rochester Institute of Technology, Graduate Enrollment Services, B. Thomas Golisano College of Computing and Information Sciences, Department of Networking, Security and Systems Administration, Program in Networking and Systems Administration, Rochester, NY 14623-5603. Offers network planning and design (AC); networking and systems administration (MS, AC). Part-time programs available. Postbaccalaureate distance learning degree programs offered (no on-campus study). *Students:* 31 full-time, 58 part-time (7 women); includes 3 Black or African American, non-Hispanic/Latino; 3 Asian, non-Hispanic/Latino; 2 Hispanic/Latino, 26 international. Average age 28. 98 applicants, 50% accepted, 27 enrolled. In 2010, 30 master's awarded. *Degree requirements:* For master's, thesis (for some programs). *Entrance requirements:* For master's, GRE, minimum GPA of 3.0. Additional exam requirements/recommendations for international students: Required—TOEFL (minimum score 570 paper-based; 230 computer-based; 88 iBT) or IELTS (minimum score 6.5). *Application deadline:* For fall admission, 8/1 for domestic students, 7/1 for international students; for spring admission, 2/1 for domestic students. Applications are processed on a rolling basis. Electronic applications accepted. *Expenses:* Tuition: Full-time $33,234; part-time $924 per credit hour. Required fees: $219. *Financial support:* In 2010–11, 56 students received support; research assistantships with partial tuition reimbursements available, teaching assistantships with partial tuition reimbursements available, career-related internships or fieldwork, scholarships/grants, and unspecified assistantships available. Support available to part-time students. Financial award applicants required to submit FAFSA. *Unit head:* Prof. Dianne Bills, Graduate Program Director, 585-475-2700, Fax: 585-475-6584, E-mail: informaticsgrad@rit.edu. *Application contact:* Diane Ellison, Assistant Vice President, Graduate Enrollment Services, 585-475-2229, Fax: 585-475-7164, E-mail: gradinfo@rit.edu.

Rochester Institute of Technology, Graduate Enrollment Services, B. Thomas Golisano College of Computing and Information Sciences, PhD Program in Computing and Information Sciences, Rochester, NY 14623-5603. Offers PhD. *Students:* 19 full-time (5 women), 6 part-time; includes 3 Asian, non-Hispanic/Latino; 1 Hispanic/Latino, 15 international. Average age 31. 45 applicants, 27% accepted, 9 enrolled. *Degree requirements:* For doctorate, thesis/dissertation. *Entrance requirements:* For doctorate, GRE, minimum GPA of 3.0. Additional exam requirements/recommendations for international students: Required—TOEFL (minimum score 570 paper-based; 230 computer-based; 88 iBT) or IELTS (minimum score 6.5). *Application deadline:* For fall admission, 1/15 priority date for domestic and international students. Applications are processed on a rolling basis. Electronic applications accepted. *Expenses:* Tuition: Full-time $33,234; part-time $924 per credit hour. Required fees: $219. *Financial support:* In 2010–11, 16 students received support; research assistantships with full and partial tuition reimbursements available, teaching assistantships with full and partial tuition reimbursements available, career-related internships or fieldwork, scholarships/grants, health care benefits, and unspecified assistantships available. Financial award applicants required to submit FAFSA. *Faculty research:* The Center for Advancing the Study of Cyberinfrastructure (CASCI): the framework supporting science and engineering research, domain-specific informatics. *Unit head:* Dr. Pengcheng Shi, PhD Program Director, 585-475-6147, E-mail: pengcheng.shi@rit.edu. *Application contact:* Diane Ellison, Assistant Vice President, Graduate Enrollment Services, 585-475-2229, Fax: 585-475-7164, E-mail: gradinfo@rit.edu.

Roosevelt University, Graduate Division, College of Arts and Sciences, Department of Computer Science and Telecommunications, Program in Computer Science, Chicago, IL 60605. Offers MSC. Part-time and evening/weekend programs available. *Faculty research:* Artificial intelligence, software engineering, distributed databases, parallel processing.

Royal Military College of Canada, Division of Graduate Studies and Research, Science Division, Department of Mathematics and Computer Science, Kingston, ON K7K 7B4, Canada. Offers computer science (M Sc); mathematics (M Sc). *Degree requirements:* For master's, thesis. *Entrance requirements:* For master's, honours degree with second-class standing. Electronic applications accepted.

Rutgers, The State University of New Jersey, Camden, Graduate School of Arts and Sciences, Program in Computer Science, Camden, NJ 08102. Offers MS. Part-time and evening/weekend programs available. *Faculty:* 7 full-time (1 woman), 1 part-time/adjunct (0 women). *Students:* 2 full-time (0 women), 11 part-time (1 woman); includes 2 Black or African American, non-Hispanic/Latino, 3 international. Average age 32. 56 applicants, 59% accepted, 3 enrolled. *Degree requirements:* For master's, comprehensive exam, thesis (for some programs), 30 credits. *Entrance requirements:* For master's, GRE, 3 letters of recommendation; statement of personal, professional, and academic goals; computer science undergraduate degree (preferred). Additional exam requirements/recommendations for international students: Required—TOEFL, IELTS. *Application deadline:* For fall admission, 5/31 priority date for domestic students, 3/31 priority date for international students; for spring admission, 10/31 priority date for domestic students, 9/30 priority date for international students. Applications are processed on a rolling basis. Application fee: $65. Electronic applications accepted. *Expenses:* Tuition, state resident: full-time $4963; part-time $319 per credit. Tuition, nonresident: full-time $10,493; part-time $680 per credit. *Financial support:* In 2010–11, 8 students received support, including 4 fellowships with partial tuition reimbursements available (averaging $1,000 per year); Federal Work-Study and tuition waivers (partial) also available. Financial award application deadline: 3/15; financial award applicants required to submit FAFSA. *Faculty research:* Cryptography and computer security, approximation algorithms, optical networks and wireless communications, computational geometry, data compression and encoding. Total annual research expenditures: $496,992. *Unit head:* Dr. Jean-Camille Birget, Director, 856-225-6077, Fax: 856-225-6624, E-mail: birget@camden.rutgers.edu. *Application contact:* Dr. Jean-Camille Birget, Director, 856-225-6077, Fax: 856-225-6624, E-mail: birget@camden.rutgers.edu.

Rutgers, The State University of New Jersey, New Brunswick, Graduate School-New Brunswick, Program in Computer Science, Piscataway, NJ 08854-8097. Offers MS, PhD. Part-time programs available. Terminal master's awarded for partial completion of doctoral program. *Degree requirements:* For master's, comprehensive exam, thesis; for doctorate, comprehensive exam, thesis/dissertation. *Entrance requirements:* For master's and doctorate, GRE General Test, GRE Subject Test. Additional exam requirements/recommendations for international students: Required—TOEFL. *Expenses:* Tuition, state resident: full-time $7200; part-time $600 per credit. Tuition, nonresident: full-time $11,124; part-time $927 per credit. *Faculty research:* Artificial intelligence and machine learning, bioinformatics, algorithms and complexity, networking and operating systems, computational graphics and vision.

Sacred Heart University, Graduate Programs, College of Arts and Sciences, Department of Computer Science and Information Technology, Fairfield, CT 06825-1000. Offers computer science (MS); database (CPS); information technology (MS, CPS); information technology and network security (CPS); interactive multimedia (CPS); Web development (CPS). Part-time and evening/weekend programs available. *Degree requirements:* For master's, thesis optional. *Entrance requirements:* Additional exam requirements/recommendations for international students: Required—TOEFL (minimum score 550 paper-based; 213 computer-based). Electronic applications accepted. *Faculty research:* Contemporary market software.

St. Cloud State University, School of Graduate Studies, College of Science and Engineering, Department of Computer Science, St. Cloud, MN 56301-4498. Offers MS. *Degree requirements:* For master's, thesis or alternative. *Entrance requirements:* For master's, GRE General Test, minimum GPA of 2.75. Additional exam requirements/recommendations for international students: Required—Michigan English Language Assessment Battery; Recommended—TOEFL (minimum score 550 paper-based; 213 computer-based), IELTS (minimum score 6.5). Electronic applications accepted.

St. Francis Xavier University, Graduate Studies, Department of Mathematics, Statistics and Computer Science, Antigonish, NS B2G 2W5, Canada. Offers computer science (M Sc). *Degree requirements:* For master's, thesis. *Entrance requirements:* For master's, bachelor's degree or equivalent in computer science with minimum B average, 2 letters of recommendation. Additional exam requirements/recommendations for international students: Required—TOEFL (minimum score 580 paper-based; 237 computer-based).

St. John's University, St. John's College of Liberal Arts and Sciences, Department of Mathematics and Computer Science, Queens, NY 11439. Offers algebra (MA); analysis (MA); applied mathematics (MA); computer science (MA); geometry-topology (MA); logic and foundations (MA); probability and statistics (MA). Part-time and evening/weekend programs available. *Students:* 4 full-time (1 woman), 3 part-time (1 woman); includes 3 minority (1 Black or African American, non-Hispanic/Latino; 1 Asian, non-Hispanic/Latino; 1 Hispanic/Latino). Average age 25. 19 applicants, 42% accepted, 5 enrolled. In 2010, 3 master's awarded. *Degree requirements:* For master's, comprehensive exam, thesis optional. *Entrance requirements:* For master's, minimum GPA of 3.0. Additional exam requirements/recommendations for international students: Required—TOEFL (minimum score 600 paper-based; 250 computer-based; 100 iBT), IELTS (minimum score 5.5). *Application deadline:* For fall admission, 5/1 priority date for domestic and international students; for spring admission, 11/1 priority date for domestic and international students. Applications are processed on a rolling basis. Application fee: $70. Electronic applications accepted. *Expenses:* Tuition: Full-time $17,100; part-time $950 per credit. Required fees: $340; $170 per semester. Tuition and fees vary according to program. *Financial support:* Research assistantships, scholarships/grants available. Support available to part-time students. Financial award application deadline: 3/1; financial award applicants required to submit FAFSA. *Faculty research:* Functional analysis and operator theory, algebraic K-theory, applied mathematics, measure theory, differential geometry and mathematics education. *Unit head:* Dr. Charles Traina, Chair, 718-990-6166, E-mail: trainac@stjohns.edu. *Application contact:* Kathleen Davis, Director of Graduate Admission, 718-990-1601, Fax: 718-990-5686, E-mail: gradhelp@stjohns.edu.

Saint Joseph's University, College of Arts and Sciences, Department of Mathematics and Computer Science, Philadelphia, PA 19131-1395. Offers computer science (MS); mathematics and computer science (Post-Master's Certificate). Part-time and evening/weekend programs available. *Faculty:* 8 full-time (4 women), 2 part-time/adjunct (1 woman). *Students:* 45 full-time (12 women), 22 part-time (4 women); includes 3 Black or African American, non-Hispanic/Latino; 3 Asian, non-Hispanic/Latino, 54 international. Average age 27. 49 applicants, 61% accepted, 23 enrolled. In 2010, 25 master's awarded. *Entrance requirements:* For master's, 2 letters of recommendation. *Application deadline:* For fall admission, 7/15 priority date for domestic students, 4/15 for international students; for winter admission, 4/15 for domestic students, 1/15 for international students; for spring admission, 11/15 priority date for domestic students, 10/15 for international students. Applications are processed on a rolling basis.

Application fee: $35. Electronic applications accepted. *Expenses:* Tuition: Part-time $729 per credit. Tuition and fees vary according to course load, degree level and program. *Financial support:* Teaching assistantships with partial tuition reimbursements, unspecified assistantships available. Financial award applicants required to submit FAFSA. *Faculty research:* Computer vision, pathways to careers. Total annual research expenditures: $175,000. *Unit head:* Dr. Jonathan Hodgson, Director, Graduate Computer Science, 610-660-1517, Fax: 610-660-3082, E-mail: jhodgson@sju.edu. *Application contact:* Kate McConnell, Director, Graduate College of Arts and Sciences Admissions and Retention, 610-660-3184, Fax: 610-660-3230, E-mail: kate.mcconnell@sju.edu.

St. Mary's University, Graduate School, Department of Computer Science, Program in Computer Information Systems, San Antonio, TX 78228-8507. Offers MS. Part-time programs available. *Degree requirements:* For master's, comprehensive exam. *Entrance requirements:* For master's, GMAT or GRE General Test. Additional exam requirements/recommendations for international students: Required—TOEFL (minimum score 530 paper-based; 213 computer-based; 80 iBT). Electronic applications accepted. *Faculty research:* Artificial intelligence, database/knowledge base, software engineering, expert systems.

St. Mary's University, Graduate School, Department of Computer Science, Program in Computer Science, San Antonio, TX 78228-8507. Offers MS, JD/MS. Part-time programs available. *Degree requirements:* For master's, comprehensive exam, internship. *Entrance requirements:* For master's, GRE or GMAT. Additional exam requirements/recommendations for international students: Required—TOEFL (minimum score 550 paper-based; 213 computer-based; 80 iBT). Electronic applications accepted.

Saint Xavier University, Graduate Studies, School of Arts and Sciences, Department of Mathematics and Computer Science, Chicago, IL 60655-3105. Offers applied computer science in Internet information systems (MS); mathematics and computer science (MA); MBA/MS. *Degree requirements:* For master's, thesis optional.

Sam Houston State University, College of Arts and Sciences, Department of Computer Science, Huntsville, TX 77341. Offers computing and information science (MS). Part-time programs available. *Faculty:* 8 full-time (3 women). *Students:* 22 full-time (3 women), 30 part-time (9 women); includes 2 Black or African American, non-Hispanic/Latino; 1 Hispanic/Latino, 27 international. Average age 29. 29 applicants, 83% accepted, 15 enrolled. In 2010, 9 master's awarded. *Entrance requirements:* For master's, GRE General Test. Additional exam requirements/recommendations for international students: Required—TOEFL (minimum score 550 paper-based; 213 computer-based; 79 iBT). *Application deadline:* For fall admission, 8/1 for domestic and international students; for spring admission, 12/1 for domestic and international students. Application fee: $20. *Expenses:* Tuition, state resident: full-time $1363; part-time $163 per credit hour. Tuition, nonresident: full-time $3856; part-time $473 per credit hour. *Financial support:* Research assistantships, teaching assistantships, Federal Work-Study, institutionally sponsored loans, and tuition waivers (partial) available. Support available to part-time students. Financial award application deadline: 5/31; financial award applicants required to submit FAFSA. *Unit head:* Dr. Peter Cooper, Chair, 936-294-1569, Fax: 936-294-4312, E-mail: css_pac@shsu.edu. *Application contact:* Dr. Jiuhung Ji, Advisor, 936-294-1579, E-mail: csc_jxj@shsu.edu.

San Diego State University, Graduate and Research Affairs, College of Sciences, Program in Computer Science, San Diego, CA 92182. Offers MS. Part-time programs available. *Degree requirements:* For master's, comprehensive exam or thesis. *Entrance requirements:* For master's, GRE General Test. Additional exam requirements/recommendations for international students: Required—TOEFL. Electronic applications accepted.

San Francisco State University, Division of Graduate Studies, College of Science and Engineering, Department of Computer Science, San Francisco, CA 94132-1722. Offers computer science (MS); computer science: computing and business (MS); computer science: computing for life sciences (MS); computer science: software and engineering (MS). Part-time programs available. *Application deadline:* Applications are processed on a rolling basis. *Unit head:* Dr. Dragutin Petkovic, Chair, 415-338-1008, Fax: 415-338-6136, E-mail: csgrad@sfsu.edu. *Application contact:* Dr. Ilmi Yoon, Graduate Admissions, 415-338-1008, E-mail: csgrad@sfsu.edu.

San Jose State University, Graduate Studies and Research, College of Science, Department of Computer Science, San Jose, CA 95192-0001. Offers MS. Electronic applications accepted.

Santa Clara University, School of Engineering, Program in Computer Science and Engineering, Santa Clara, CA 95053. Offers computer science and engineering (MS, PhD, Engineer); information assurance (Certificate); networking (Certificate); software engineering (MS, Certificate). Part-time and evening/weekend programs available. *Students:* 139 full-time (46 women), 108 part-time (31 women); includes 58 minority (6 Black or African American, non-Hispanic/Latino; 47 Asian, non-Hispanic/Latino; 2 Hispanic/Latino; 3 Two or more races, non-Hispanic/Latino), 142 international. Average age 28. 242 applicants, 56% accepted, 73 enrolled. In 2010, 76 master's, 6 doctorates, 3 other advanced degrees awarded. *Degree requirements:* For master's, thesis (for some programs); for doctorate, thesis/dissertation; for other advanced degree, thesis. *Entrance requirements:* For master's, GRE (waiver may be available), transcript; for doctorate, GRE, master's degree or equivalent; for other advanced degree, master's degree, published paper. Additional exam requirements/recommendations for international students: Required—TOEFL (minimum score 550 paper-based; 213 computer-based; 79 iBT). *Application deadline:* For fall admission, 8/12 for domestic students, 7/15 for international students; for winter admission, 10/28 for domestic students, 9/23 for international students; for spring admission, 2/25 for domestic students, 1/21 for international students. Applications are processed on a rolling basis. Application fee: $60. Electronic applications accepted. *Expenses:* Contact institution. *Financial support:* Research assistantships, teaching assistantships available. Financial award application deadline: 3/2; financial award applicants required to submit FAFSA. *Unit head:* Dr. Alex Zecevic, Chair, 408-554-2394, E-mail: azecevic@scu.edu. *Application contact:* Stacey Tinker, Director of Enrollment Management, 408-554-4748, Fax: 408-554-4323, E-mail: stinker@scu.edu.

Shippensburg University of Pennsylvania, School of Graduate Studies, College of Arts and Sciences, Department of Computer Science, Shippensburg, PA 17257-2299. Offers computer science (MS). Part-time and evening/weekend programs available. *Faculty:* 6 full-time (3 women). *Students:* 12 full-time (6 women), 8 part-time (0 women); includes 3 minority (1 Black or African American, non-Hispanic/Latino; 2 Asian, non-Hispanic/Latino), 7 international. Average age 27. 22 applicants, 77% accepted, 5 enrolled. In 2010, 10 master's awarded. *Entrance requirements:* For master's, GRE (if GPA less than 2.75). Additional exam requirements/recommendations for international students: Required—TOEFL (minimum score 580 paper-based; 237 computer-based); Recommended—IELTS (minimum score 6). *Application deadline:* For fall admission, 3/1 for international students. Applications are processed on a rolling basis. Application fee: $30. Electronic applications accepted. *Expenses:* Tuition, state resident: full-time $6966. Tuition, nonresident: full-time $11,146. Required fees: $1802. *Financial support:* In 2010–11, 7 research assistantships with full tuition reimbursements (averaging $5,000 per year) were awarded; career-related internships or fieldwork, scholarships/grants, unspecified assistantships, and resident hall director and student payroll positions also available. Support available to part-time students. Financial award application deadline: 3/1; financial award applicants required to submit FAFSA. *Unit head:* Dr. Carol A. Wellington, Chairperson, 717-477-1178, Fax: 717-477-4002, E-mail: cawell@ship.edu. *Application contact:* Jeremy R. Goshorn, Associate Dean of Graduate Admissions, 717-477-1231, Fax: 717-477-4016, E-mail: jrgoshorn@ship.edu.

Silicon Valley University, Graduate Programs, San Jose, CA 95131. Offers business administration (MBA); computer engineering (MSCE); computer science (MSCS). *Degree requirements:* For master's, project (MSCS).

Computer Science

Simon Fraser University, Graduate Studies, Faculty of Applied Sciences, School of Computing Science, Burnaby, BC V5A 1S6, Canada. Offers M Sc, PhD. *Degree requirements:* For master's, comprehensive exam, thesis or alternative; for doctorate, comprehensive exam, thesis/dissertation, qualifying exams. *Entrance requirements:* For master's, minimum GPA of 3.0; for doctorate, minimum GPA of 3.5. Additional exam requirements/recommendations for international students: Required—GRE General Test, GRE Subject Test, or IELTS. Electronic applications accepted. *Faculty research:* Artificial intelligence, computer hardware, computer systems, database systems, theory.

Simon Fraser University, Graduate Studies, Faculty of Applied Sciences, School of Interactive Arts and Technology, Surrey, BC V3T 2W1, Canada. Offers information technology (M Sc, PhD); interactive arts (M Sc, PhD). *Degree requirements:* For master's, thesis; for doctorate, comprehensive exam, thesis/dissertation. *Entrance requirements:* For master's, 2 references, curriculum vitae; for doctorate, 3 references, curriculm vitae, minimum GPA of 3.0. Additional exam requirements/recommendations for international students: Required—TOEFL (minimum score 570 paper-based; 230 computer-based), TWE (minimum score 5). Electronic applications accepted.

Southeastern Louisiana University, College of Science and Technology, Program in Integrated Science and Technology, Hammond, LA 70402. Offers chemistry (MS); computer science (MS); information technology (MS); mathematics (MS); physics (MS). Part-time and evening/weekend programs available. *Faculty:* 11 full-time (3 women). *Students:* 13 full-time (5 women), 11 part-time (2 women); includes 1 minority (Asian, non-Hispanic/Latino), 8 international. Average age 32. 13 applicants, 46% accepted, 4 enrolled. In 2010, 5 master's awarded. *Degree requirements:* For master's, thesis (for some programs), 33-36 hours. *Entrance requirements:* For master's, GRE (minimum combined score 850), 2 letters of reference; minimum GPA of 2.75; 30 hours of course work including chemistry, physics, industrial technology, or mathematics. Additional exam requirements/recommendations for international students: Required—TOEFL (minimum score 500 paper-based; 173 computer-based; 61 iBT). *Application deadline:* For fall admission, 7/15 priority date for domestic students, 6/1 priority date for international students; for spring admission, 12/1 priority date for domestic students, 10/1 priority date for international students. Applications are processed on a rolling basis. Application fee: $20 ($30 for international students). Electronic applications accepted. *Expenses:* Tuition, state resident: full-time $3533. Tuition, nonresident: full-time $12,002. Required fees: $907. Tuition and fees vary according to degree level. *Financial support:* In 2010–11, 7 students received support, including 7 research assistantships (averaging $10,100 per year); career-related internships or fieldwork, Federal Work-Study, institutionally sponsored loans, and unspecified assistantships also available. Support available to part-time students. Financial award application deadline: 5/1; financial award applicants required to submit FAFSA. *Faculty research:* Computational statistics, medicinal chemistry, machine learning, optical interferometry,strength of materials and structure. *Unit head:* Dr. Ken Li, Coordinator, 985-549-3822, Fax: 985-549-2099, E-mail: kli@selu.edu. *Application contact:* Sandra Meyers, Graduate Admissions Analyst, 985-549-5620, Fax: 985-549-5632, E-mail: admissions@selu.edu.

Southern Arkansas University–Magnolia, Graduate Programs, Magnolia, AR 71753. Offers agriculture (MS); business administration (MBA); computer and information sciences (MS); education (M Ed), including counseling and development, curriculum and instruction emphasis, educational administration and supervision, elementary education, middle level emphasis, reading emphasis, secondary education, TESOL emphasis; kinesiology (M Ed); library media and information specialist (M Ed); mental health and clinical counseling (MS); public administration (MPA); school counseling (M Ed); teaching (MAT). *Accreditation:* NCATE. Part-time and evening/weekend programs available. *Faculty:* 32 full-time (16 women), 6 part-time/adjunct (5 women). *Students:* 71 full-time (43 women), 364 part-time (275 women); includes 109 Black or African American, non-Hispanic/Latino; 1 American Indian or Alaska Native, non-Hispanic/Latino; 3 Asian, non-Hispanic/Latino, 19 international. Average age 33. 107 applicants, 71% accepted, 69 enrolled. In 2010, 157 master's awarded. *Degree requirements:* For master's, comprehensive exam, thesis optional. *Entrance requirements:* For master's, GRE, MAT or GMAT, minimum GPA of 2.75. *Application deadline:* For fall admission, 7/31 for domestic students; for winter admission, 12/1 for domestic students; for spring admission, 12/1 for domestic students. Applications are processed on a rolling basis. Application fee: $25. *Expenses:* Tuition, state resident: part-time $221 per hour. Tuition, nonresident: part-time $325 per hour. *Financial support:* Career-related internships or fieldwork, Federal Work-Study, scholarships/grants, tuition waivers (full), and unspecified assistantships available. Financial award applicants required to submit FAFSA. *Faculty research:* Alternative certification for teachers, supervision of instruction, instructional leadership, counseling. *Unit head:* Dr. Kim Bloss, Dean, Graduate Studies, 870-235-4150, Fax: 870-235-5227, E-mail: kkbloss@saumag.edu. *Application contact:* Dr. Kim Bloss, Dean, Graduate Studies, 870-235-4150, Fax: 870-235-5227, E-mail: kkbloss@saumag.edu.

Southern Connecticut State University, School of Graduate Studies, School of Arts and Sciences, Department of Computer Science, New Haven, CT 06515-1355. Offers MS. *Faculty:* 11 full-time (4 women). *Students:* 8 full-time (1 woman), 10 part-time (1 woman); includes 1 Black or African American, non-Hispanic/Latino; 2 Asian, non-Hispanic/Latino, 3 international. 34 applicants, 21% accepted, 7 enrolled. In 2010, 6 master's awarded. *Entrance requirements:* For master's, GRE. *Application deadline:* Applications are processed on a rolling basis. Application fee: $50. Electronic applications accepted. *Expenses:* Tuition, state resident: full-time $5137; part-time $518 per credit. Tuition, nonresident: part-time $542 per credit. Required fees: $4008; $55 per semester. Tuition and fees vary according to program. *Unit head:* Dr. Winnie Yu, Chairperson, 203-392-5812, Fax: 203-392-5898, E-mail: yuw1@southernct.edu. *Application contact:* Dr. Lisa Lancor, Coordinator, 203-392-5890, Fax: 203-392-5898, E-mail: lancorl1@southernct.edu.

Southern Illinois University Carbondale, Graduate School, College of Science, Department of Computer Science, Carbondale, IL 62901-4701. Offers MS, PhD. *Degree requirements:* For master's, thesis. *Entrance requirements:* For master's, previous undergraduate course work in computer science, minimum GPA of 2.7. Additional exam requirements/recommendations for international students: Required—TOEFL. *Faculty research:* Analysis of algorithms, VLSI testing, database systems, artificial intelligence, computer architecture.

Southern Illinois University Edwardsville, Graduate School, School of Engineering, Department of Computer Science, Edwardsville, IL 62026-0001. Offers MS. Part-time programs available. *Faculty:* 9 full-time (1 woman). *Students:* 23 full-time (5 women), 17 part-time (7 women); includes 2 minority (1 Asian, non-Hispanic/Latino; 1 Two or more races, non-Hispanic/Latino), 27 international. Average age 26. 126 applicants, 71% accepted. In 2010, 18 master's awarded. *Degree requirements:* For master's, thesis (for some programs), final exam. *Entrance requirements:* Additional exam requirements/recommendations for international students: Required—TOEFL (minimum score 550 paper-based; 213 computer-based; 79 iBT), IELTS (minimum score 6.5). *Application deadline:* For fall admission, 7/22 for domestic students, 6/1 for international students; for spring admission, 12/9 for domestic students, 10/1 for international students. Applications are processed on a rolling basis. Application fee: $30. Electronic applications accepted. *Expenses:* Tuition, state resident: full-time $6012; part-time $1503 per semester. Tuition, nonresident: full-time $15,030; part-time $3758 per semester. Required fees: $1711; $675 per semester. *Financial support:* In 2010–11, fellowships with full tuition reimbursements (averaging $8,370 per year), 4 research assistantships with full tuition reimbursements (averaging $8,064 per year), 13 teaching assistantships with full tuition reimbursements (averaging $8,064 per year) were awarded; career-related internships or fieldwork, Federal Work-Study, institutionally sponsored loans, scholarships/grants, traineeships, and unspecified assistantships also available. Support available to part-time students. Financial award application deadline: 3/1; financial award applicants required to submit FAFSA. *Unit head:* Dr. Dennis Bouvier, Chair, 618-650-2369, E-mail: dbouvie@siue.edu. *Application contact:* Dr. Xudong Yu, Program Director, 618-650-2321, E-mail: xyu@siue.edu.

Southern Methodist University, Bobby B. Lyle School of Engineering, Department of Computer Science and Engineering, Dallas, TX 75275-0122. Offers computer engineering (MS Cp E, PhD); computer science (MS, PhD); security engineering (MS); software engineering (MS). Part-time and evening/weekend programs available. Postbaccalaureate distance learning degree programs offered (no on-campus study). *Faculty:* 13 full-time (3 women), 13 part-time/adjunct (0 women). *Students:* 35 full-time (16 women), 149 part-time (22 women); includes 13 Black or African American, non-Hispanic/Latino; 1 American Indian or Alaska Native, non-Hispanic/Latino; 24 Asian, non-Hispanic/Latino; 13 Hispanic/Latino, 39 international. Average age 34. 180 applicants, 73% accepted, 69 enrolled. In 2010, 77 master's, 4 doctorates awarded. Terminal master's awarded for partial completion of doctoral program. *Degree requirements:* For master's, thesis optional; for doctorate, thesis/dissertation, oral and written qualifying exams, oral final exam (PhD). *Entrance requirements:* For master's, GRE General Test, minimum GPA of 3.0 in last 2 years; bachelor's degree in engineering, mathematics, or sciences; for doctorate, preliminary counseling exam (PhD), minimum GPA of 3.0, bachelor's degree in related field, MA (DE). Additional exam requirements/recommendations for international students: Required—TOEFL (minimum score 550 paper-based; 213 computer-based). *Application deadline:* For fall admission, 7/1 priority date for domestic students, 5/15 for international students; for spring admission, 11/15 for domestic students, 9/1 for international students. Applications are processed on a rolling basis. Application fee: $75. *Financial support:* In 2010–11, 20 students received support, including 6 research assistantships with full tuition reimbursements available (averaging $14,400 per year), 14 teaching assistantships with full tuition reimbursements available (averaging $14,400 per year). Financial award application deadline: 3/31; financial award applicants required to submit FAFSA. *Faculty research:* Trusted and high performance network computing, software engineering and management, knowledge engineering and management, computer arithmetic, computer architecture and CAD. Total annual research expenditures: $366,537. *Unit head:* Dr. Suku Nair, Chair, 214-768-2856, Fax: 214-768-3085, E-mail: nair@lyle.smu.edu. *Application contact:* Marc Valerin, Director of Graduate and Executive Admissions, 214-768-3042, E-mail: valerin@engr.smu.edu.

Southern Oregon University, Graduate Studies, College of Arts and Sciences, Department of Computer Science, Ashland, OR 97520. Offers applied computer science (PSM). Part-time programs available. *Faculty:* 5 full-time (0 women), 1 part-time/adjunct (0 women). *Students:* 8 full-time (3 women), 1 (woman) part-time; includes 2 minority (1 Asian, non-Hispanic/Latino; 1 Hispanic/Latino), 1 international. Average age 35. 10 applicants, 60% accepted, 3 enrolled. *Entrance requirements:* For master's, GRE General Test, minimum GPA of 3.0. *Application deadline:* Applications are processed on a rolling basis. Application fee: $50. *Expenses:* Tuition, state resident: full-time $9450; part-time $350 per credit. Tuition, nonresident: full-time $15,000; part-time $350 per credit. Required fees: $400 per quarter. *Unit head:* Dr. Greg Pleva, Chair, 541-552-6973. *Application contact:* Mark Bottorff, Director of Admissions, 541-552-6411, Fax: 541-552-8403, E-mail: admissions@sou.edu.

Southern Polytechnic State University, School of Computing and Software Engineering, Department of Computer Science and Software Engineering, Marietta, GA 30060-2896. Offers computer science (MS, Graduate Certificate, Graduate Transition Certificate); software engineering (MSSWE, Graduate Certificate). Part-time and evening/weekend programs available. Postbaccalaureate distance learning degree programs offered (no on-campus study). *Faculty:* 13 full-time (1 woman), 4 part-time/adjunct (0 women). *Students:* 59 full-time (26 women), 63 part-time (11 women); includes 17 Black or African American, non-Hispanic/Latino; 13 Asian, non-Hispanic/Latino; 1 Hispanic/Latino, 46 international. Average age 32. 100 applicants, 88% accepted, 45 enrolled. In 2010, 34 master's, 4 other advanced degrees awarded. *Degree requirements:* For master's, thesis optional, capstone (software engineering). *Entrance requirements:* For master's, GRE (recommended). Additional exam requirements/recommendations for international students: Required—TOEFL (minimum score 550 paper-based; 213 computer-based; 79 iBT), IELTS (minimum score 6.5). *Application deadline:* For fall admission, 7/1 priority date for domestic students, 5/1 priority date for international students; for spring admission, 11/1 priority date for domestic students, 9/1 priority date for international students. Applications are processed on a rolling basis. Application fee: $20. Electronic applications accepted. *Expenses:* Tuition, state resident: full-time $3690; part-time $205 per semester hour. Tuition, nonresident: full-time $13,428; part-time $746 per semester hour. Required fees: $598 per semester. *Financial support:* Research assistantships with tuition reimbursements, teaching assistantships with tuition reimbursements, career-related internships or fieldwork, scholarships/grants, unspecified assistantships, and cooperative programs available. Financial award application deadline: 5/1; financial award applicants required to submit FAFSA. *Faculty research:* Image processing and artificial intelligence information retrieval, distributed computing, telemedicine applications, enterprise architectures, databases, software requirements engineering, software quality and metrics, usability, parallel and distributed computing, information security. *Unit head:* Dr. Venu Dasigi, Chair, 678-915-3571, Fax: 678-915-5511, E-mail: vdasigi@spsu.edu. *Application contact:* Nikki Palamiotis, Director of Graduate Studies, 678-915-4276, Fax: 678-915-7292, E-mail: npalamio@spsu.edu.

Southern University and Agricultural and Mechanical College, Graduate School, College of Sciences, Department of Computer Science, Baton Rouge, LA 70813. Offers information systems (MS); micro/minicomputer architecture (MS); operating systems (MS). Part-time programs available. Postbaccalaureate distance learning degree programs offered (minimal on-campus study). *Degree requirements:* For master's, thesis. *Entrance requirements:* For master's, GRE General Test, minimum GPA of 3.0, bachelor's degree in computer science or related field. Additional exam requirements/recommendations for international students: Required—TOEFL (minimum score 525 paper-based; 193 computer-based). *Faculty research:* Network theory, computational complexity, high speed computing, neural networking, data warehousing/mining.

Stanford University, School of Engineering, Department of Computer Science, Stanford, CA 94305-9991. Offers MS, PhD. Terminal master's awarded for partial completion of doctoral program. *Degree requirements:* For doctorate, thesis/dissertation. *Entrance requirements:* For master's, GRE General Test; for doctorate, GRE General Test, GRE Computer Science Subject Test. Additional exam requirements/recommendations for international students: Required—TOEFL. Electronic applications accepted. *Expenses:* Tuition: Full-time $38,700; part-time $860 per unit. One-time fee: $200 full-time.

Stanford University, School of Engineering, Program in Scientific Computing and Computational Mathematics, Stanford, CA 94305-9991. Offers MS, PhD. Terminal master's awarded for partial completion of doctoral program. *Degree requirements:* For doctorate, thesis/dissertation, qualifying exam. *Entrance requirements:* For master's, GRE General Test; for doctorate, GRE General Test, GRE Subject Test. Additional exam requirements/recommendations for international students: Required—TOEFL. Electronic applications accepted. *Expenses:* Tuition: Full-time $38,700; part-time $860 per unit. One-time fee: $200 full-time.

State University of New York at Binghamton, Graduate School, School of Arts and Sciences, Department of Mathematical Sciences, Binghamton, NY 13902-6000. Offers computer science (MA, PhD); probability and statistics (MA, PhD). Part-time programs available. *Faculty:* 26 full-time (5 women), 13 part-time/adjunct (5 women). *Students:* 42 full-time (13 women), 24 part-time (8 women); includes 3 Black or African American, non-Hispanic/Latino; 1 Asian, non-Hispanic/Latino; 2 Hispanic/Latino, 27 international. Average age 27. 82 applicants, 28% accepted, 16 enrolled. In 2010, 15 master's, 6 doctorates awarded. Terminal master's awarded for partial completion of doctoral program. *Degree requirements:* For master's, thesis or alternative; for doctorate, 2 foreign languages, thesis/dissertation. *Entrance requirements:* For master's and doctorate, GRE General Test, GRE Subject Test. Additional exam requirements/recommendations for international students: Required—TOEFL (minimum score 550 paper-based; 213 computer-based; 80 iBT). *Application deadline:* For fall admission, 4/15 priority date for domestic and international students; for spring admission, 11/30 priority date for domestic and international students. Applications are processed on a rolling basis. Application fee: $60. Electronic applications accepted. *Financial support:* In 2010–11, 51 students received support, including 4 fellowships with full tuition reimbursements available (averaging $16,500 per year), 1 research assistantship with full tuition reimbursement available (averaging $16,500 per year), 48 teaching assistantships with full tuition reimbursements available (averaging $16,500 per year); career-related internships or fieldwork, Federal Work-Study, institutionally sponsored loans, scholarships/grants, health care benefits, tuition waivers (full and partial), and unspecified assistantships also available. Financial award application deadline: 2/15; financial award applicants required to submit FAFSA. *Unit head:* Dr. Fernando Guzman, Chairperson, 607-777-2148, E-mail: fer@math.binghamton.edu. *Application contact:* Catherine Smith, Recruiting and Admissions Coordinator, 607-777-2151, Fax: 607-777-2501, E-mail: cmsmith@binghamton.edu.

State University of New York at Binghamton, Graduate School, Thomas J. Watson School of Engineering and Applied Science, Department of Computer Science, Binghamton, NY 13902-6000. Offers M Eng, MS, PhD. Part-time programs available. *Faculty:* 22 full-time (3 women), 7 part-time/adjunct (3 women). *Students:* 154 full-time (39 women), 138 part-time (22 women); includes 2 Black or African American, non-Hispanic/Latino; 10 Asian, non-Hispanic/Latino; 3 Hispanic/Latino, 227 international. Average age 26. 382 applicants, 59% accepted, 80 enrolled. In 2010, 93 master's, 3 doctorates awarded. *Degree requirements:* For master's, thesis or alternative; for doctorate, thesis/dissertation. *Entrance requirements:* For master's and doctorate, GRE General Test, GRE Subject Test. Additional exam requirements/recommendations for international students: Required—TOEFL. *Application deadline:* For fall admission, 4/15 priority date for domestic students, 1/15 priority date for international students; for spring admission, 11/1 for domestic students, 10/1 priority date for international students. Applications are processed on a rolling basis. Application fee: $60. Electronic applications accepted. *Financial support:* In 2010–11, 63 students received support, including 1 fellowship with full tuition reimbursement available (averaging $16,500 per year), 17 research assistantships with full tuition reimbursements available (averaging $16,500 per year), 28 teaching assistantships with full tuition reimbursements available (averaging $16,500 per year); career-related internships or fieldwork, Federal Work-Study, institutionally sponsored loans, scholarships/grants, health care benefits, and unspecified assistantships also available. Financial award application deadline: 2/15; financial award applicants required to submit FAFSA. *Unit head:* Dr. Kanad Ghose, Chair, 607-777-4803, E-mail: ghose@cs.binghamton.edu. *Application contact:* Catherien Smith, Recruiting and Admissions Coordinator, 607-777-2151, Fax: 607-777-2501, E-mail: cmsmith@binghamton.edu.

State University of New York at New Paltz, Graduate School, School of Science and Engineering, Department of Computer Science, New Paltz, NY 12561. Offers MS. Part-time and evening/weekend programs available. *Faculty:* 5 full-time (0 women), 1 part-time/adjunct (0 women). *Students:* 24 full-time (8 women), 18 part-time (4 women); includes 2 Black or African American, non-Hispanic/Latino; 1 American Indian or Alaska Native, non-Hispanic/Latino; 5 Hispanic/Latino, 26 international. Average age 26. 70 applicants, 63% accepted, 14 enrolled. In 2010, 26 master's awarded. *Degree requirements:* For master's, comprehensive exam, thesis. *Entrance requirements:* For master's, minimum GPA of 3.0, proficiency in program assembly. Additional exam requirements/recommendations for international students: Required—TOEFL (minimum score 550 paper-based; 213 computer-based; 80 iBT), IELTS (minimum score 6.5). *Application deadline:* For fall admission, 5/15 priority date for domestic and international students; for spring admission, 11/15 for domestic students, 11/15 priority date for international students. Applications are processed on a rolling basis. Application fee: $50. Electronic applications accepted. *Expenses:* Tuition, state resident: full-time $8370; part-time $349 per credit hour. Tuition, nonresident: full-time $13,780; part-time $574 per credit hour. Required fees: $1165; $33.80 per credit hour. $175 per term. Tuition and fees vary according to program. *Financial support:* In 2010–11, 3 students received support, including 3 teaching assistantships with partial tuition reimbursements available (averaging $5,000 per year); unspecified assistantships also available. Financial award application deadline: 8/1; financial award applicants required to submit FAFSA. *Unit head:* Dr. Andrew Pletch, Chair, 845-257-3990, Fax: 845-257-3996, E-mail: pletcha@newpaltz.edu. *Application contact:* Dr. Paul Zuckerman, Graduate Coordinator, 845-257-3516, E-mail: zuckerpr@newpaltz.edu.

State University of New York Institute of Technology, School of Information Systems and Engineering Technology, Program in Computer and Information Science, Utica, NY 13504-3050. Offers MS. Part-time and evening/weekend programs available. *Degree requirements:* For master's, thesis or project. *Entrance requirements:* For master's, GRE General Test, minimum GPA of 3.0, letter of recommendation. Additional exam requirements/recommendations for international students: Required—TOEFL (minimum score 550 paper-based; 213 computer-based). *Faculty research:* Cryptography, distributed systems, computer-aided system theory, reasoning with uncertainty, grid computing.

Stephen F. Austin State University, Graduate School, College of Business, Department of Computer Science, Nacogdoches, TX 75962. Offers MS. Part-time programs available. *Degree requirements:* For master's, comprehensive exam, thesis optional. *Entrance requirements:* For master's, GRE General Test. Additional exam requirements/recommendations for international students: Required—TOEFL.

Stevens Institute of Technology, Graduate School, Charles V. Schaefer Jr. School of Engineering, Department of Computer Science, Program in Computer Science, Hoboken, NJ 07030. Offers MS, PhD. *Students:* 109 full-time (37 women), 78 part-time (16 women); includes 3 Black or African American, non-Hispanic/Latino; 18 Asian, non-Hispanic/Latino; 2 Hispanic/Latino, 94 international. *Unit head:* Daniel Duchamp, Director, 201-216-5390, Fax: 201-216-8249, E-mail: djd@cs.stevens.edu. *Application contact:* Graduate Admissions, 800-496-4935, Fax: 201-216-8044, E-mail: gradadmissions@stevens.edu.

Stevens Institute of Technology, Graduate School, Wesley J. Howe School of Technology Management, Program in Information Systems, Hoboken, NJ 07030. Offers computer science (MS); e-commerce (MS); enterprise systems (MS); entrepreneurial information technology (MS); information architecture (MS); information management (MS, Certificate); information security (MS); information technology in financial services industry (MS); information technology in the pharmaceutical industry (MS); information technology outsourcing management (MS); project management (MS, Certificate); software engineering (MS); telecommunications (MS). *Degree requirements:* For master's, thesis optional. *Entrance requirements:* For master's, GMAT, GRE General Test. Additional exam requirements/recommendations for international students: Required—TOEFL. Electronic applications accepted.

Stony Brook University, State University of New York, Graduate School, College of Engineering and Applied Sciences, Department of Computer Science, Stony Brook, NY 11794. Offers computer science (MS, PhD); information systems (Certificate); information systems engineering (MS); software engineering (Certificate). *Faculty:* 38 full-time (6 women), 3 part-time/adjunct (1 woman). *Students:* 290 full-time (54 women), 44 part-time (11 women); includes 6 Black or African American, non-Hispanic/Latino; 17 Asian, non-Hispanic/Latino; 5 Hispanic/Latino; 1 Two or more races, non-Hispanic/Latino, 279 international. Average age 25. 1,619 applicants, 23% accepted, 118 enrolled. In 2010, 96 master's, 14 doctorates awarded. *Degree requirements:* For master's, thesis or alternative; for doctorate, comprehensive exam, thesis/dissertation. *Entrance requirements:* For master's and doctorate, GRE General Test. Additional exam requirements/recommendations for international students: Required—TOEFL. *Application deadline:* For fall admission, 1/15 for domestic students. Application fee: $100. *Expenses:* Tuition, state resident: full-time $8370; part-time $349 per credit. Tuition, nonresident: full-time $13,780; part-time $574 per credit. Required fees: $994. *Financial support:* In 2010–11, 95 research assistantships, 43 teaching assistantships were awarded; fellowships also available. *Faculty research:* Artificial intelligence, computer architecture, database management systems, VLSI, operating systems. Total annual research expenditures: $6.4 million. *Unit head:* Prof. Arie Kauffman, Chairman, 631-632-8428. *Application contact:* Graduate Director, 631-632-8462, Fax: 631-632-8334.

Suffolk University, College of Arts and Sciences, Department of Mathematics and Computer Science, Boston, MA 02108-2770. Offers software engineering and databases (MSCS). Part-time and evening/weekend programs available. *Faculty:* 6 full-time (0 women), 1 part-time/adjunct (0 women). *Students:* 22 full-time (7 women), 3 part-time (1 woman); includes 1 Asian, non-Hispanic/Latino, 21 international. Average age 26. 48 applicants, 73% accepted, 12 enrolled. In 2010, 10 master's awarded. *Degree requirements:* For master's, thesis optional. *Entrance requirements:* For master's, statement of professional goals, official transcripts, 2 letters of recommendation, resume. Additional exam requirements/recommendations for international students: Required—TOEFL (minimum score 550 paper-based; 213 computer-based; 80 iBT). *Application deadline:* For fall admission, 6/15 priority date for domestic students, 6/15 for international students; for spring admission, 11/1 priority date for domestic students, 11/1 for international students. Applications are processed on a rolling basis. Application fee: $50. Electronic applications accepted. *Expenses:* Contact institution. *Financial support:* In 2010–11, 21 students received support, including 21 fellowships with full and partial tuition reimbursements available (averaging $9,033 per year); career-related internships or fieldwork, Federal Work-Study, and institutionally sponsored loans also available. Financial award application deadline: 4/1; financial award applicants required to submit FAFSA. *Faculty research:* Peer-to-peer systems, grid cluster computing, human-computer interaction, large scale, IP networks, distributed load balancing. *Unit head:* Dr. Edith Cook, Chairperson, 617-573-8621, Fax: 617-573-8591, E-mail: ecook@mcs.suffolk.edu. *Application contact:* Judith Reynolds, Director of Graduate Admissions, 617-573-8302, Fax: 617-305-1733, E-mail: grad.admission@suffolk.edu.

Syracuse University, L. C. Smith College of Engineering and Computer Science, Program in Computer Science, Syracuse, NY 13244. Offers MS. Part-time programs available. *Students:* 110 full-time (22 women), 9 part-time (1 woman); includes 3 minority (1 Black or African American, non-Hispanic/Latino; 2 Asian, non-Hispanic/Latino), 108 international. Average age 24. 559 applicants, 39% accepted, 63 enrolled. In 2010, 43 master's awarded. *Entrance requirements:* For master's, GRE General Test. Additional exam requirements/recommendations for international students: Required—TOEFL (minimum score 100 iBT). *Application deadline:* For fall admission, 7/1 priority date for domestic students, 6/1 priority date for international students. Applications are processed on a rolling basis. Application fee: $75. Electronic applications accepted. *Expenses:* Tuition: Part-time $1162 per credit. *Financial support:* Fellowships with full tuition reimbursements, research assistantships with full and partial tuition reimbursements, teaching assistantships with full and partial tuition reimbursements, tuition waivers (partial) available. Financial award application deadline: 1/1; financial award applicants required to submit FAFSA. *Unit head:* Dr. Jae Oh, Program Director, 315-443-4740, Fax: 315-443-2583, E-mail: jcoh@syr.edu. *Application contact:* Barbara Decker, Information Contact, 315-443-2368, E-mail: badecker@syr.edu.

Télé-université, Graduate Programs, Québec, QC G1K 9H5, Canada. Offers computer science (PhD); corporate finance (MS); distance learning (MS). Part-time programs available.

Temple University, College of Science and Technology, Department of Computer and Information Sciences, Philadelphia, PA 19122-6096. Offers MS, PhD. Part-time and evening/weekend programs available. *Faculty:* 19 full-time (1 woman). *Students:* 48 full-time (11 women), 17 part-time (4 women); includes 3 Black or African American, non-Hispanic/Latino; 5 Asian, non-Hispanic/Latino, 48 international. 82 applicants, 70% accepted, 21 enrolled. In 2010, 5 master's, 1 doctorate awarded. Terminal master's awarded for partial completion of doctoral program. *Degree requirements:* For doctorate, thesis/dissertation. *Entrance requirements:* For master's and doctorate, GRE General Test, minimum GPA of 3.0. Additional exam requirements/recommendations for international students: Required—TOEFL (minimum score 550 paper-based; 213 computer-based; 79 iBT). *Application deadline:* For fall admission, 2/1 for domestic students, 12/15 for international students; for spring admission, 8/1 for domestic and international students. Applications are processed on a rolling basis. Application fee: $50. Electronic applications accepted. *Financial support:* Fellowships, research assistantships with tuition reimbursements, teaching assistantships with tuition reimbursements, career-related internships or fieldwork, institutionally sponsored loans, and unspecified assistantships available. Financial award application deadline: 1/15; financial award applicants required to submit FAFSA. *Faculty research:* Artificial intelligence, information systems, software engineering, network-distributed systems. *Unit head:* Dr. Jie Wu, Chair, 215-204-8450, Fax: 215-204-5082, E-mail: cis@temple.edu. *Application contact:* Dr. Jie Wu, Chair, 215-204-8450, Fax: 215-204-5082, E-mail: cis@temple.edu.

Tennessee Technological University, Graduate School, College of Engineering, Department of Computer Science, Cookeville, TN 38505. Offers MS. *Students:* 4 full-time (1 woman), 12 part-time (0 women); includes 2 Asian, non-Hispanic/Latino; 1 Hispanic/Latino. 34 applicants, 41% accepted, 5 enrolled. In 2010, 4 master's awarded. *Degree requirements:* For master's, thesis or alternative. *Entrance requirements:* For master's, GRE. Additional exam requirements/recommendations for international students: Required—TOEFL (minimum score 550 paper-based; 79 iBT), IELTS (minimum score 5.5). *Application deadline:* For fall admission, 8/1 for domestic students, 5/1 for international students; for spring admission, 12/1 for domestic and international students. Application fee: $25 ($30 for international students). *Expenses:* Tuition, state resident: full-time $7934; part-time $388 per credit hour. Tuition, nonresident: full-time $19,758; part-time $962 per credit hour. *Financial support:* In 2010–11, 4 research assistantships (averaging $7,500 per year), 3 teaching assistantships (averaging $7,500 per year) were awarded. Financial award application deadline: 4/1. *Unit head:* Dr. Doug Talbert, Interim Chairperson, 931-372-3691, Fax: 931-372-3686. *Application contact:* Shelia K. Kendrick, Coordinator of Graduate Admissions, 931-372-3808, Fax: 931-372-3497, E-mail: skendrick@tntech.edu.

Texas A&M University, College of Engineering, Department of Computer Science, College Station, TX 77843. Offers computer engineering (M En); computer science (MCS); computer science and engineering (MS, PhD). Part-time programs available. *Faculty:* 41. *Students:* 306 full-time (52 women), 42 part-time (6 women); includes 35 minority (7 Black or African American, non-Hispanic/Latino; 2 American Indian or Alaska Native, non-Hispanic/Latino; 17 Asian, non-Hispanic/Latino; 9 Hispanic/Latino), 240 international. Average age 28. In 2010, 36 master's, 22 doctorates awarded. *Degree requirements:* For master's, thesis (for some programs); for doctorate, thesis/dissertation. *Entrance requirements:* For master's and doctorate, GRE General Test. Additional exam requirements/recommendations for international students: Required—TOEFL (minimum score 213 computer-based). *Application deadline:* For fall admission, 3/1 priority date for domestic and international students; for spring admission, 8/1 priority date for domestic and international students. Applications are processed on a rolling basis. Application fee: $50 ($75 for international students). Electronic applications accepted. *Financial support:* In 2010–11, research assistantships with tuition reimbursements (averaging $15,478 per year), teaching assistantships (averaging $15,913 per year) were awarded; fellowships with full tuition reimbursements also available. Financial award application deadline: 3/1. *Faculty research:* Software, systems, informatics, human-centered systems, theory. *Unit head:* Valerie E. Taylor, Head, 979-845-5820, Fax: 979-847-8578, E-mail: taylor@cse.tamu.edu. *Application contact:* Dr. Jianer Chen, Head of Graduate Admissions, 979-845-4259, Fax: 979-862-3684, E-mail: chen@cse.tamu.edu.

Texas A&M University–Commerce, Graduate School, College of Arts and Sciences, Department of Computer Science and Information Systems, Commerce, TX 75429-3011. Offers computer science (MS). Part-time programs available. *Degree requirements:* For master's, comprehensive exam, thesis (for some programs). *Entrance requirements:* For master's, GMAT or GRE General Test. Electronic applications accepted. *Faculty research:* Programming.

Texas A&M University–Corpus Christi, Graduate Studies and Research, College of Science and Technology, Program in Computer Science, Corpus Christi, TX 78412-5503. Offers MS. Part-time and evening/weekend programs available. *Degree requirements:* For master's, comprehensive exam, thesis (for some programs). *Entrance requirements:* For master's, GRE General Test. Additional exam requirements/recommendations for international students: Required—TOEFL. Electronic applications accepted.

Texas A&M University–Kingsville, College of Graduate Studies, College of Engineering, Department of Electrical Engineering and Computer Science, Program in Computer Science, Kingsville, TX 78363. Offers MS. *Degree requirements:* For master's, comprehensive exam, thesis or alternative. *Entrance requirements:* For master's, GRE General Test, minimum GPA

Computer Science

Texas A&M University–Kingsville (continued)

of 3.0. Additional exam requirements/recommendations for international students: Required—TOEFL. *Faculty research:* Operating systems, programming languages, database systems, computer architecture, artificial intelligence.

Texas Southern University, School of Science and Technology, Department of Computer Science, Houston, TX 77004-4584. Offers MS. *Faculty:* 1 (woman) full-time, 1 part-time/adjunct (0 women). *Students:* 6 full-time (1 woman), 7 part-time (4 women); includes 8 Black or African American, non-Hispanic/Latino; 4 Asian, non-Hispanic/Latino; 1 Hispanic/Latino. Average age 32. 7 applicants, 100% accepted, 4 enrolled. In 2010, 5 master's awarded. *Application deadline:* For fall admission, 7/1 for domestic and international students; for spring admission, 11/1 for domestic and international students. Applications are processed on a rolling basis. Application fee: $50 ($75 for international students). Electronic applications accepted. *Expenses:* Tuition, state resident: full-time $1875; part-time $100 per credit hour. Tuition, nonresident: full-time $6641; part-time $343 per credit hour. Tuition and fees vary according to course level, course load and degree level. *Financial support:* In 2010–11, 5 teaching assistantships (averaging $3,900 per year) were awarded; fellowships, research assistantships, scholarships/grants and unspecified assistantships also available. *Unit head:* Dr. Wei Li, Chair, 713-313-1871, E-mail: liw@tsu.edu. *Application contact:* Nadereh Jahelmotlagh, Administrative Secretary, 713-313-7611, E-mail: Jahedmotlagh@tsu.edu.

Texas State University–San Marcos, Graduate School, College of Science, Department of Computer Science, San Marcos, TX 78666. Offers computer science (MA, MS); software engineering (MS). Part-time programs available. *Faculty:* 17 full-time (3 women). *Students:* 75 full-time (27 women), 53 part-time (14 women); includes 31 minority (3 Black or African American, non-Hispanic/Latino; 1 American Indian or Alaska Native, non-Hispanic/Latino; 13 Asian, non-Hispanic/Latino; 13 Hispanic/Latino; 1 Two or more races, non-Hispanic/Latino), 44 international. Average age 27. 71 applicants, 100% accepted, 25 enrolled. In 2010, 36 master's awarded. *Degree requirements:* For master's, comprehensive exam, thesis (for some programs). *Entrance requirements:* For master's, GRE General Test, minimum GPA of 2.75 in last 60 hours of course work. Additional exam requirements/recommendations for international students: Required—TOEFL (minimum score 550 paper-based; 213 computer-based; 78 iBT). *Application deadline:* For fall admission, 6/15 priority date for domestic students, 6/1 priority date for international students; for spring admission, 10/15 priority date for domestic students, 10/1 priority date for international students. Applications are processed on a rolling basis. Application fee: $40 ($90 for international students). Electronic applications accepted. *Expenses:* Tuition, state resident: full-time $6024; part-time $251 per credit hour. Tuition, nonresident: full-time $13,536; part-time $564 per credit hour. Required fees: $1776; $50 per credit hour. $306 per semester. *Financial support:* In 2010–11, 21 students received support, including 20 research assistantships (averaging $4,998 per year), 26 teaching assistantships (averaging $5,117 per year); career-related internships or fieldwork, Federal Work-Study, institutionally sponsored loans, scholarships/grants, health care benefits, and unspecified assistantships also available. Support available to part-time students. Financial award application deadline: 4/1; financial award applicants required to submit FAFSA. *Faculty research:* Software engineering, artificial intelligence, multimedia, distributed/parallel computing, database systems, operating systems. Total annual research expenditures: $206,162. *Unit head:* Dr. Hongchi Shi, Chair, 512-245-3409, Fax: 512-245-8750, E-mail: hs15@txstate.edu. *Application contact:* Dr. Khosrow Kaikhah, Head, 512-245-3409, Fax: 512-245-8750, E-mail: kk02@txstate.edu.

Texas Tech University, Graduate School, Edward E. Whitacre Jr. College of Engineering, Department of Computer Science, Lubbock, TX 79409. Offers computer science (MS, PhD); software engineering (MS). Part-time programs available. Postbaccalaureate distance learning degree programs offered (minimal on-campus study). *Faculty:* 14 full-time (3 women), 1 part-time/adjunct (0 women). *Students:* 109 full-time (18 women), 37 part-time (9 women); includes 3 Hispanic/Latino; 2 Two or more races, non-Hispanic/Latino, 122 international. Average age 25. 334 applicants, 57% accepted, 54 enrolled. In 2010, 47 master's, 9 doctorates awarded. *Degree requirements:* For master's, thesis or alternative; for doctorate, thesis/dissertation. *Entrance requirements:* For master's and doctorate, GRE General Test, minimum GPA of 3.0, statement of purpose, 3 letters of recommendation. Additional exam requirements/recommendations for international students: Required—TOEFL (minimum score 600 paper-based; 250 computer-based; 100 iBT). *Application deadline:* For fall admission, 6/1 priority date for domestic students, 1/15 priority date for international students; for spring admission, 9/1 priority date for domestic students, 6/15 priority date for international students. Applications are processed on a rolling basis. Application fee: $50 ($75 for international students). Electronic applications accepted. *Expenses:* Tuition, state resident: full-time $5495.76; part-time $228.99 per credit hour. Tuition, nonresident: full-time $12,936; part-time $538.99 per credit hour. Required fees: $2674; $36 per credit hour. $905 per semester. *Financial support:* In 2010–11, 59 students received support, including 34 research assistantships with partial tuition reimbursements available (averaging $3,927 per year), 1 teaching assistantship with partial tuition reimbursement available (averaging $4,952 per year). Financial award application deadline: 4/15; financial award applicants required to submit FAFSA. *Faculty research:* Artificial intelligence, software engineering and languages, high performance computing, logic programming, image processing. Total annual research expenditures: $937,133. *Unit head:* Dr. Joseph Urban, Chair, 806-742-3527, Fax: 806-742-3519, E-mail: joseph.urban@ttu.edu. *Application contact:* Dr. Susan Mengel, Graduate Advisor, 806-742-3527, Fax: 806-742-3519, E-mail: graduate_programs@cs.ttu.edu.

Towson University, Program in Computer Science, Towson, MD 21252-0001. Offers MS. Part-time and evening/weekend programs available. *Students:* 82 full-time (27 women), 51 part-time (9 women); includes 22 minority (15 Black or African American, non-Hispanic/Latino; 5 Asian, non-Hispanic/Latino; 1 Hispanic/Latino; 1 Two or more races, non-Hispanic/Latino), 63 international. Average age 28. In 2010, 36 master's awarded. *Degree requirements:* For master's, thesis optional, exam. *Entrance requirements:* For master's, minimum GPA of 3.0, bachelor's degree in computer science or completion of 1-3 preparatory courses. Additional exam requirements/recommendations for international students: Required—TOEFL (minimum score 550 paper-based). *Application deadline:* Applications are processed on a rolling basis. Application fee: $50. Electronic applications accepted. *Expenses:* Tuition, state resident: part-time $324 per credit. Tuition, nonresident: part-time $681 per credit. Required fees: $95 per term. *Financial support:* Federal Work-Study and unspecified assistantships available. Support available to part-time students. Financial award application deadline: 4/1; financial award applicants required to submit FAFSA. *Faculty research:* Deductive databases, neural nets, software engineering, data communications and networks. *Unit head:* Dr. Yanggon Kim, Graduate Program Director, 410-704-3782, E-mail: ykim@towson.edu. *Application contact:* 410-704-2501, Fax: 410-704-4675, E-mail: grads@towson.edu.

Toyota Technological Institute of Chicago, Program in Computer Science, Chicago, IL 60637. Offers PhD. *Degree requirements:* For doctorate, thesis/dissertation.

Trent University, Graduate Studies, Program in Applications of Modeling in the Natural and Social Sciences, Department of Computer Studies, Peterborough, ON K9J 7B8, Canada. Offers M Sc. *Degree requirements:* For master's, thesis. *Entrance requirements:* For master's, honours degree.

Troy University, Graduate School, College of Arts and Sciences, Program in Computer and Information Science, Troy, AL 36082. Offers computer science (MS). Part-time and evening/weekend programs available. *Students:* 15 full-time (5 women), 14 part-time (10 women); includes 15 minority (11 Black or African American, non-Hispanic/Latino; 4 Asian, non-Hispanic/Latino). Average age 35. 176 applicants, 61% accepted. In 2010, 10 master's awarded. *Degree requirements:* For master's, thesis or research project; minimum GPA of 3.0; admission to candidacy. *Entrance requirements:* For master's, GRE (minimum score of 800), BS in computer science; minimum GPA of 2.5. Additional exam requirements/recommendations for international students: Required—TOEFL (minimum score 523 paper-based; 193 computer-based; 70 iBT), IELTS (minimum score 6). *Application deadline:* For fall admission, 6/1 for international students; for spring admission, 10/15 for international students. Applications are processed on a rolling basis. Application fee: $50. Electronic applications accepted. *Expenses:* Tuition, state resident: full-time $4428; part-time $246 per credit hour. Tuition, nonresident: full-time $8856; part-time $492 per credit hour. Required fees: $432; $24 per credit hour. $50 per term. Tuition and fees vary according to program. *Unit head:* Dr. Irem Ozkarahan, Department Chairmen/Professor, 334-241-9589, Fax: 334-241-9734, E-mail: iozkarahan@troy.edu. *Application contact:* Brenda K. Campbell, Director of Graduate Admissions, 334-670-3178, Fax: 334-670-3733, E-mail: bcamp@troy.edu.

Tufts University, Graduate School of Arts and Sciences, Graduate Certificate Programs, Computer Science Program, Medford, MA 02155. Offers Certificate. Part-time and evening/weekend programs available. Electronic applications accepted. *Expenses:* Tuition: Full-time $39,624; part-time $3962 per course. Required fees: $40 per year. Full-time tuition and fees vary according to degree level, program and student level. Part-time tuition and fees vary according to course load.

Tufts University, Graduate School of Arts and Sciences, Graduate Certificate Programs, Post-Baccalaureate Minor Program in Computer Science, Medford, MA 02155. Offers Certificate. Part-time and evening/weekend programs available. Electronic applications accepted. *Expenses:* Tuition: Full-time $39,624; part-time $3962 per course. Required fees: $40 per year. Full-time tuition and fees vary according to degree level, program and student level. Part-time tuition and fees vary according to course load.

Tufts University, School of Engineering, Department of Computer Science, Medford, MA 02155. Offers MS, PhD. Part-time programs available. Terminal master's awarded for partial completion of doctoral program. *Degree requirements:* For master's, thesis (for some programs); for doctorate, thesis/dissertation. *Entrance requirements:* For master's and doctorate, GRE. Additional exam requirements/recommendations for international students: Required—TOEFL (minimum score 550 paper-based; 213 computer-based; 80 iBT). Electronic applications accepted. *Expenses:* Tuition: Full-time $39,624; part-time $3962 per course. Required fees: $40 per year. Full-time tuition and fees vary according to degree level, program and student level. Part-time tuition and fees vary according to course load.

Union Graduate College, School of Engineering and Computer Science, Schenectady, NY 12308-3107. Offers computer science (MS); electrical engineering (MS); engineering and management systems (MS); mechanical engineering (MS). Part-time and evening/weekend programs available. *Faculty:* 3 full-time (0 women), 9 part-time/adjunct (0 women). *Students:* 15 full-time (1 woman), 89 part-time (13 women); includes 1 Black or African American, non-Hispanic/Latino; 1 American Indian or Alaska Native, non-Hispanic/Latino; 7 Asian, non-Hispanic/Latino; 6 Hispanic/Latino, 2 international. Average age 27. 52 applicants, 79% accepted, 39 enrolled. In 2010, 24 master's awarded. *Degree requirements:* For master's, capstone course. *Entrance requirements:* For master's, minimum GPA of 3.0, letters of recommendation. Additional exam requirements/recommendations for international students: Required—TOEFL (minimum score 550 paper-based; 213 computer-based). *Application deadline:* Applications are processed on a rolling basis. Application fee: $60. Electronic applications accepted. *Expenses:* Contact institution. *Financial support:* Research assistantships, Federal Work-Study, scholarships/grants, health care benefits, tuition waivers (full and partial) available. Support available to part-time students. Financial award applicants required to submit FAFSA. *Unit head:* Robert Kozik, Dean, 515-631-9881, Fax: 518-631-9902, E-mail: kozikr@union.edu. *Application contact:* Diane Trzaskos, Coordinator, Admissions, 518-631-9837, Fax: 518-631-9901, E-mail: trzaskod@uniongraduatecollege.edu.

Universidad Autonoma de Guadalajara, Graduate Programs, Guadalajara, Mexico. Offers administrative law and justice (LL M); advertising and corporate communications (MA); architecture (M Arch); business (MBA); computational science (MCC); education (Ed M, Ed D); English-Spanish translation (MA); entrepreneurship and management (MBA); integrated management of digital animation (MA); international business (MIB); international corporate law (LL M); internet technologies (MS); manufacturing systems (MMS); occupational health (MS); philosophy (MA, PhD); power electronics (MS); quality systems (MQS); renewable energy (MS); social evaluation of projects (MBA); strategic market research (MBA); tax law (MA); teaching mathematics (MA).

Universidad de las Américas–Puebla, Division of Graduate Studies, School of Engineering, Program in Computer Engineering, Puebla, Mexico. Offers computer science (MS). Part-time and evening/weekend programs available. *Degree requirements:* For master's, one foreign language, thesis. *Faculty research:* Computers in education, robotics, artificial intelligence.

Universidad de las Américas–Puebla, Division of Graduate Studies, School of Engineering, Program in Computer Science, Puebla, Mexico. Offers PhD.

Université de Moncton, Faculty of Science, Information Technology Programs, Moncton, NB E1A 3E9, Canada. Offers M Sc, Certificate, Diploma. Part-time programs available. *Degree requirements:* For master's, thesis. Electronic applications accepted. *Faculty research:* Programming, databases, networks.

Université de Montréal, Faculty of Arts and Sciences, Department of Computer Science and Operational Research, Montréal, QC H3C 3J7, Canada. Offers computer systems (M Sc, PhD); electronic commerce (M Sc). Part-time programs available. Terminal master's awarded for partial completion of doctoral program. *Degree requirements:* For master's, one foreign language, thesis; for doctorate, one foreign language, thesis/dissertation, general exam. *Entrance requirements:* For master's, B Sc in related field; for doctorate, MA or M Sc in related field. Electronic applications accepted. *Faculty research:* Optimization statistics, programming languages, telecommunications, theoretical computer science, artificial intelligence.

Université du Québec à Trois-Rivières, Graduate Programs, Program in Mathematics and Computer Science, Trois-Rivières, QC G9A 5H7, Canada. Offers M Sc. *Faculty research:* Probability, statistics.

Université du Québec en Outaouais, Graduate Programs, Program in Computer Network, Gatineau, QC J8X 3X7, Canada. Offers computer science (M Sc, PhD). Part-time and evening/weekend programs available. *Students:* 25 full-time, 6 part-time, 13 international. *Degree requirements:* For master's, thesis; for doctorate, thesis/dissertation. *Application deadline:* For fall admission, 6/1 priority date for domestic students, 3/1 for international students; for winter admission, 11/1 priority date for domestic students, 10/1 for international students. Application fee: $30 Canadian dollars. *Unit head:* Luigi Logrippo, Director, 819-595-3900 Ext. 1885, Fax: 819-773-1638, E-mail: luigi.logrippo@uqo.ca. *Application contact:* Registrar's Office, 819-773-1850, Fax: 819-773-1835, E-mail: registraire@uqo.ca.

Université Laval, Faculty of Sciences and Engineering, Department of Computer Science, Programs in Computer Science, Québec, QC G1K 7P4, Canada. Offers M Sc, PhD. Terminal master's awarded for partial completion of doctoral program. *Degree requirements:* For master's, thesis; for doctorate, thesis/dissertation. *Entrance requirements:* For master's and doctorate, knowledge of French and English. Electronic applications accepted.

University at Albany, State University of New York, College of Computing and Information, Department of Computer Science, Albany, NY 12222-0001. Offers MS, PhD. *Degree requirements:* For master's, comprehensive exam, project or thesis; for doctorate, comprehensive exam, thesis/dissertation, area exams. *Entrance requirements:* For master's and doctorate, GRE General Test. Additional exam requirements/recommendations for international students: Required—TOEFL (minimum score 550 paper-based; 213 computer-based). Electronic applications accepted. *Faculty research:* Algorithm design and analysis, artificial intelligence, computational logic, databases, numerical analysis.

University at Buffalo, the State University of New York, Graduate School, School of Engineering and Applied Sciences, Department of Computer Science and Engineering, Buffalo, NY 14260. Offers MS, PhD. Part-time programs available. *Faculty:* 34 full-time (4 women).

Students: 309 full-time (61 women), 17 part-time (1 woman); includes 2 Black or African American, non-Hispanic/Latino; 3 Asian, non-Hispanic/Latino; 1 Hispanic/Latino, 275 international. Average age 25. 1,632 applicants, 40% accepted, 134 enrolled. In 2010, 100 master's, 16 doctorates awarded. Terminal master's awarded for partial completion of doctoral program. *Degree requirements:* For master's, thesis or alternative; for doctorate, thesis/dissertation, comprehensive qualifying exam. *Entrance requirements:* For master's and doctorate, GRE General Test. Additional exam requirements/recommendations for international students: Required—TOEFL (minimum score 550 paper-based; 213 computer-based; 79 iBT). *Application deadline:* For fall admission, 8/15 for domestic and international students. Application fee: $50. Electronic applications accepted. *Financial support:* In 2010–11, 86 students received support, including 5 fellowships with full tuition reimbursements available (averaging $28,900 per year), 43 research assistantships with full tuition reimbursements available (averaging $20,900 per year), 38 teaching assistantships with full tuition reimbursements available (averaging $24,000 per year); career-related internships or fieldwork, Federal Work-Study, institutionally sponsored loans, health care benefits, tuition waivers (partial), and unspecified assistantships also available. Financial award application deadline: 12/15; financial award applicants required to submit FAFSA. *Faculty research:* Bioinformatics, pattern recognition, computer networks and security, theory and algorithms, databases and data mining. Total annual research expenditures: $7.4 million. *Unit head:* Dr. Aidong Zhang, Chairman, 716-645-3180, Fax: 716-645-3464, E-mail: azhang@buffalo.edu. *Application contact:* Dr. Jan Chomicki, Director of Graduate Studies, 716-645-4735, Fax: 716-645-3464, E-mail: chomicki@buffalo.edu.

University of Advancing Technology, Master of Science Program in Technology, Tempe, AZ 85283-1042. Offers advancing computer science (MS); emerging technologies (MS); game production and management (MS); information assurance (MS); technology leadership (MS). *Faculty:* 9 full-time (3 women), 3 part-time/adjunct (1 woman). *Students:* 55 full-time (9 women), 4 part-time (1 woman). Average age 25. In 2010, 5 master's awarded. *Degree requirements:* For master's, project or thesis. *Entrance requirements:* Additional exam requirements/recommendations for international students: Required—TOEFL (minimum score 550 paper-based). *Application deadline:* For fall admission, 8/15 priority date for domestic students, 7/15 priority date for international students; for winter admission, 12/15 priority date for domestic students, 11/15 priority date for international students; for spring admission, 4/1 priority date for domestic students, 3/1 priority date for international students. Applications are processed on a rolling basis. Application fee: $100 ($250 for international students). Electronic applications accepted. *Expenses:* Tuition: Full-time $18,300. *Financial support:* Career-related internships or fieldwork, Federal Work-Study, and scholarships/grants available. Financial award applicants required to submit FAFSA. *Faculty research:* Artificial intelligence, fractals, organizational management. *Unit head:* Robert Marshall, Dean of Graduate Education, 602-383-8283, Fax: 602-383-8222, E-mail: rmarshall@uat.edu. *Application contact:* Information Contact, 800-658-5744, Fax: 602-383-8222.

The University of Akron, Graduate School, Buchtel College of Arts and Sciences, Department of Computer Science, Akron, OH 44325. Offers MS. *Faculty:* 7 full-time (2 women), 1 part-time/adjunct (0 women). *Students:* 41 full-time (13 women), 17 part-time (5 women); includes 2 Asian, non-Hispanic/Latino, 49 international. Average age 24. 68 applicants, 46% accepted, 9 enrolled. In 2010, 22 master's awarded. *Degree requirements:* For master's, comprehensive exam, thesis optional, seminar and comprehensive exam or thesis. *Entrance requirements:* For master's, baccalaureate degree in computer science or a related field, minimum GPA of 3.0, three letters of recommendation, statement of purpose, resume. Additional exam requirements/recommendations for international students: Required—TOEFL (minimum score 550 paper-based; 213 computer-based; 79 iBT). *Application deadline:* For fall admission, 3/15 for domestic and international students; for spring admission, 10/15 for domestic and international students. Application fee: $30 ($40 for international students). *Expenses:* Tuition, state resident: full-time $6800; part-time $378 per credit hour. Tuition, nonresident: full-time $11,644; part-time $647 per credit hour. Required fees: $1265. One-time fee: $30 full-time. *Financial support:* In 2010–11, 5 research assistantships with full tuition reimbursements, 22 teaching assistantships with full tuition reimbursements were awarded. *Faculty research:* Bioinformatics, database/data mining, networking, parallel computing, visualization. Total annual research expenditures: $101. *Unit head:* Dr. Chien-Chung Chan, Chair, 330-972-8805, E-mail: chan@uakron.edu. *Application contact:* Dr. Chien-Chung Chan, Chair, 330-972-8805, E-mail: chan@uakron.edu.

The University of Alabama, Graduate School, College of Engineering, Department of Computer Science, Tuscaloosa, AL 35487-0290. Offers MS, PhD. Part-time programs available. *Faculty:* 15 full-time (2 women). *Students:* 44 full-time (4 women), 25 part-time (6 women); includes 6 minority (5 Black or African American, non-Hispanic/Latino; 1 Two or more races, non-Hispanic/Latino), 34 international. Average age 28. 73 applicants, 45% accepted, 18 enrolled. In 2010, 16 master's, 4 doctorates awarded. Terminal master's awarded for partial completion of doctoral program. *Degree requirements:* For master's, comprehensive exam, thesis (for some programs); for doctorate, comprehensive exam, thesis/dissertation. *Entrance requirements:* For master's and doctorate, GRE, minimum undergraduate GPA of 3.0 from ABET-accredited program. Additional exam requirements/recommendations for international students: Required—TOEFL. *Application deadline:* For fall admission, 7/1 priority date for domestic students, 3/15 for international students; for spring admission, 11/1 priority date for domestic students, 7/1 for international students. Applications are processed on a rolling basis. Application fee: $50 ($60 for international students). Electronic applications accepted. *Expenses:* Tuition, state resident: full-time $7900. Tuition, nonresident: full-time $20,500. *Financial support:* In 2010–11, 28 students received support, including 2 fellowships with tuition reimbursements available (averaging $15,000 per year), 10 research assistantships with full tuition reimbursements available (averaging $15,750 per year), 18 teaching assistantships with full tuition reimbursements available (averaging $15,750 per year); health care benefits and unspecified assistantships also available. Financial award application deadline: 4/1. *Faculty research:* Software engineering, networking, database management, robotics, algorithms. Total annual research expenditures: $5.9 million. *Unit head:* Dr. David Cordes, Professor and Department Head, 205-348-6363, Fax: 205-348-0219, E-mail: david.cordes@ua.edu. *Application contact:* Dr. Susan Vrbsky, Associate Professor and Graduate Program Director, 205-348-6363, Fax: 205-348-0219, E-mail: vrbsky@cs.ua.edu.

The University of Alabama at Birmingham, College of Arts and Sciences, Program in Computer and Information Sciences, Birmingham, AL 35294. Offers MS, PhD. *Students:* 37 full-time (11 women), 11 part-time (2 women); includes 3 minority (2 Asian, non-Hispanic/Latino; 1 Hispanic/Latino), 28 international. Average age 28. 45 applicants, 60% accepted, 12 enrolled. In 2010, 16 master's, 5 doctorates awarded. Terminal master's awarded for partial completion of doctoral program. *Degree requirements:* For master's, thesis optional; for doctorate, thesis/dissertation. *Entrance requirements:* For master's and doctorate, GRE General Test. Additional exam requirements/recommendations for international students: Required—TOEFL. *Application deadline:* Applications are processed on a rolling basis. Electronic applications accepted. *Expenses:* Tuition, state resident: full-time $5482. Tuition, nonresident: full-time $12,430. Tuition and fees vary according to program. *Financial support:* In 2010–11, 30 students received support, including 7 fellowships with full tuition reimbursements available (averaging $16,450 per year), 2 research assistantships with full tuition reimbursements available (averaging $16,000 per year), 9 teaching assistantships with full tuition reimbursements available (averaging $14,500 per year); career-related internships or fieldwork, Federal Work-Study, institutionally sponsored loans, scholarships/grants, traineeships, health care benefits, and unspecified assistantships also available. Support available to part-time students. Financial award application deadline: 3/10. *Faculty research:* Theory and software systems, intelligent systems, systems architecture, high performance computing, computer architecture, computer graphics, data mining, software engineering. *Unit head:* Dr. Anthony Skjellum, Chair, 205-934-2213, Fax: 205-934-5473, E-mail: skjellum@uab.edu. *Application contact:* Dr. John Johnstone, Graduate Program Director/Associate Professor, 205-975-5633, Fax: 205-934-5473, E-mail: jkj@uab.edu.

The University of Alabama in Huntsville, School of Graduate Studies, College of Science, Department of Computer Science, Huntsville, AL 35899. Offers computer science (MS, PhD); software engineering (MSSE, Certificate). Part-time and evening/weekend programs available. *Faculty:* 12 full-time (3 women), 1 (woman) part-time/adjunct. *Students:* 53 full-time (19 women), 67 part-time (17 women); includes 9 minority (5 Black or African American, non-Hispanic/Latino; 4 Asian, non-Hispanic/Latino), 49 international. Average age 30. 180 applicants, 57% accepted, 39 enrolled. In 2010, 35 master's, 2 doctorates, 1 other advanced degree awarded. *Degree requirements:* For master's, comprehensive exam, thesis or alternative, oral and written exams; for doctorate, comprehensive exam, thesis/dissertation, oral and written exams. *Entrance requirements:* For master's, doctorate, and Certificate, GRE General Test, minimum GPA of 3.0. Additional exam requirements/recommendations for international students: Required—TOEFL (minimum score 550 paper-based; 213 computer-based; 62 iBT). *Application deadline:* For fall admission, 7/15 for domestic students, 4/1 for international students; for spring admission, 11/30 for domestic students, 9/1 for international students. Applications are processed on a rolling basis. Application fee: $40 ($50 for international students). Electronic applications accepted. *Expenses:* Tuition, state resident: full-time $7250; part-time $407.75 per credit hour. Tuition, nonresident: full-time $17,358; part-time $970.05 per credit hour. Required fees: $246.80 per semester. Tuition and fees vary according to course load and program. *Financial support:* In 2010–11, 32 students received support, including 12 research assistantships with full and partial tuition reimbursements available (averaging $9,201 per year), 23 teaching assistantships with full and partial tuition reimbursements available (averaging $9,129 per year); career-related internships or fieldwork, Federal Work-Study, institutionally sponsored loans, scholarships/grants, health care benefits, and unspecified assistantships also available. Support available to part-time students. Financial award application deadline: 4/1; financial award applicants required to submit FAFSA. *Faculty research:* Software engineering and systems, computer graphics and visualization, computer networking, artificial intelligence, modeling and simulation. Total annual research expenditures: $4.3 million. *Unit head:* Dr. Heggere Ranganath, Chair, 256-824-6088, Fax: 256-824-6239, E-mail: ranganat@uah.edu. *Application contact:* Kathy Biggs, Graduate Studies Admissions Manager, 256-824-6199, Fax: 256-824-6405, E-mail: deangrad@uah.edu.

University of Alaska Fairbanks, College of Engineering and Mines, Department of Computer Science, Fairbanks, AK 99775-6670. Offers computer science (MS); software engineering (MSE). Part-time programs available. *Faculty:* 7 full-time (1 woman). *Students:* 10 full-time (2 women), 3 part-time (0 women), 2 international. Average age 27. 20 applicants, 45% accepted, 6 enrolled. In 2010, 5 master's awarded. *Degree requirements:* For master's, comprehensive exam, thesis or alternative. *Entrance requirements:* For master's, GRE General Test. Additional exam requirements/recommendations for international students: Required—TOEFL (minimum score 550 paper-based; 213 computer-based; 80 iBT). *Application deadline:* For fall admission, 6/1 for domestic students, 3/1 for international students; for spring admission, 10/15 for domestic students, 9/1 for international students. Application fee: $60. *Expenses:* Tuition, state resident: full-time $5688; part-time $316 per credit. Tuition, nonresident: full-time $11,628; part-time $646 per credit. Required fees: $289 per semester. Tuition and fees vary according to course load and reciprocity agreements. *Financial support:* In 2010–11, 8 research assistantships with tuition reimbursements (averaging $11,138 per year), 2 teaching assistantships with tuition reimbursements (averaging $10,497 per year) were awarded; fellowships with tuition reimbursements, career-related internships or fieldwork, Federal Work-Study, scholarships/grants, health care benefits, and unspecified assistantships also available. Support available to part-time students. Financial award application deadline: 7/1; financial award applicants required to submit FAFSA. *Faculty research:* Interaction with a virtual reality environment, synthetic aperture radar interferometry software. *Unit head:* Dr. Kara Nance, Department Chair, 907-474-2777, Fax: 907-474-5030, E-mail: fycsci@uaf.edu. *Application contact:* Dr. Kara Nance, Department Chair, 907-474-2777, Fax: 907-474-5030, E-mail: fycsci@uaf.edu.

University of Alberta, Faculty of Graduate Studies and Research, Department of Computing Science, Edmonton, AB T6G 2E1, Canada. Offers M Sc, PhD. Part-time programs available. Terminal master's awarded for partial completion of doctoral program. *Degree requirements:* For master's, thesis (for some programs), oral exam, seminar; for doctorate, thesis/dissertation, oral exam, seminar. *Entrance requirements:* For master's and doctorate, GRE General Test. Additional exam requirements/recommendations for international students: Required—TOEFL. *Faculty research:* Artificial intelligence, multimedia, distributed computing, theory, software engineering.

The University of Arizona, College of Science, Department of Computer Science, Tucson, AZ 85721. Offers MS, PhD. Part-time programs available. *Faculty:* 15 full-time (0 women). *Students:* 71 full-time (15 women), 6 part-time (2 women); includes 1 Black or African American, non-Hispanic/Latino; 2 American Indian or Alaska Native, non-Hispanic/Latino; 6 Asian, non-Hispanic/Latino; 2 Hispanic/Latino, 44 international. Average age 29. 271 applicants, 13% accepted, 16 enrolled. In 2010, 17 master's, 4 doctorates awarded. Terminal master's awarded for partial completion of doctoral program. *Degree requirements:* For master's, thesis optional; for doctorate, comprehensive exam, thesis/dissertation. *Entrance requirements:* For master's, GRE General Test, minimum GPA of 3.2; for doctorate, GRE General Test, minimum undergraduate GPA of 3.5. Additional exam requirements/recommendations for international students: Required—TOEFL (minimum score 600 paper-based; 250 computer-based; 100 iBT). *Application deadline:* For fall admission, 1/15 for domestic and international students. Application fee: $75. Electronic applications accepted. *Expenses:* Tuition, state resident: full-time $7692. *Financial support:* In 2010–11, 44 students received support, including 5 fellowships with full tuition reimbursements available (averaging $25,000 per year), 32 research assistantships with full tuition reimbursements available (averaging $16,597 per year), 10 teaching assistantships with full tuition reimbursements available (averaging $14,858 per year); scholarships/grants, health care benefits, tuition waivers (full and partial), and unspecified assistantships also available. Financial award application deadline: 1/15. *Faculty research:* Operating systems, theory of computation, programming languages, databases, algorithms, networks, cloud computing, green computing, computational biology, machine learning, artificial intelligence. Total annual research expenditures: $3.5 million. *Unit head:* Dr. Saumya Debray, Department Head, 520-621-4527, Fax: 520-626-5997. *Application contact:* Cheryl L. Craddock, Program Coordinator, Senior, 520-621-4049, Fax: 520-626-5997, E-mail: gradadmissions@cs.arizona.edu.

University of Arkansas, Graduate School, College of Engineering, Department of Computer Science and Computer Engineering, Program in Computer Science, Fayetteville, AR 72701-1201. Offers MS, PhD. *Students:* 9 full-time (1 woman), 29 part-time (7 women); includes 3 minority (2 Asian, non-Hispanic/Latino; 1 Hispanic/Latino), 18 international. 48 applicants, 60% accepted. In 2010, 3 master's, 2 doctorates awarded. *Degree requirements:* For doctorate, thesis/dissertation. *Application deadline:* For fall admission, 4/1 for international students; for spring admission, 10/1 for international students. Applications are processed on a rolling basis. Application fee: $40 ($50 for international students). Electronic applications accepted. *Financial support:* In 2010–11, 5 fellowships with tuition reimbursements, 18 research assistantships, 3 teaching assistantships were awarded; career-related internships or fieldwork and Federal Work-Study also available. Support available to part-time students. Financial award application deadline: 4/1; financial award applicants required to submit FAFSA. *Unit head:* Dr. Susan Gauch, Departmental Chair, 479-575-6197, Fax: 479-575-5339, E-mail: sgauch@uark.edu. *Application contact:* Dr. Gordon Beavers, Graduate Coordinator, 479-575-6040, Fax: 479-575-5339, E-mail: gordonb@uark.edu.

University of Arkansas at Little Rock, Graduate School, George W. Donughey College of Engineering and Information Technology, Department of Computer Science, Little Rock, AR 72204-1099. Offers computer and information science (MS). Part-time and evening/weekend programs available. *Degree requirements:* For master's, thesis optional. *Entrance requirements:* For master's, GRE General Test, minimum GPA of 3.0; bachelor's degree in computer science, mathematics, or appropriate alternative.

University of Atlanta, Graduate Programs, Atlanta, GA 30360. Offers business (MS); business administration (Exec MBA, MBA); computer science (MS); educational leadership (MS, Ed D); healthcare administration (MS, D Sc, Graduate Certificate); information technology for

Computer Science

University of Atlanta (continued)
management (Graduate Certificate); international project management (Graduate Certificate); law (JD); managerial science (DBA); project management (Graduate Certificate); social science (MS). Postbaccalaureate distance learning degree programs offered. *Entrance requirements:* For master's, minimum cumulative GPA of 2.5.

University of Bridgeport, School of Engineering, Departments of Computer Science and Computer Engineering, Bridgeport, CT 06604. Offers computer engineering (MS); computer science (MS); computer science and engineering (PhD). *Degree requirements:* For master's, thesis optional; for doctorate, comprehensive exam, thesis/dissertation. *Entrance requirements:* Additional exam requirements/recommendations for international students: Recommended—TOEFL (minimum score 550 paper-based; 213 computer-based; 80 iBT), IELTS (minimum score 6.5). Electronic applications accepted. *Expenses:* Tuition: Full-time $22,000; part-time $575 per credit hour. Required fees: $90 per semester. Tuition and fees vary according to course level, course load and program.

The University of British Columbia, Faculty of Science, Department of Computer Science, Vancouver, BC V6T 1Z4, Canada. Offers M Sc, PhD. Part-time programs available. *Degree requirements:* For doctorate, comprehensive exam, thesis/dissertation. *Entrance requirements:* For master's and doctorate, GRE. Additional exam requirements/recommendations for international students: Required—TOEFL (minimum score 600 paper-based; 250 computer-based; 100 iBT). Electronic applications accepted. Tuition charges are reported in Canadian dollars. *Expenses:* Tuition, area resident: Full-time $4179 Canadian dollars. International tuition: $7344 Canadian dollars full-time. *Faculty research:* Computational intelligence, data management and mining, theory, graphics, network security and systems.

University of Calgary, Faculty of Graduate Studies, Faculty of Science, Department of Computer Science, Calgary, AB T2N 1N4, Canada. Offers computer science (M Sc, PhD); software engineering (M Sc). Part-time programs available. *Degree requirements:* For master's, comprehensive exam (for some programs), thesis (for some programs); for doctorate, thesis/dissertation, oral and written departmental exam. *Entrance requirements:* For master's, bachelor's degree in computer science; for doctorate, M Sc in computer science. Additional exam requirements/recommendations for international students: Required—TOEFL (minimum score 600 paper-based; 250 computer-based), GRE General Test recommended; Recommended—TWE. Electronic applications accepted. *Faculty research:* Visual and interactive computing, quantum computing and cryptography, evolutionary software engineering, distributed systems and algorithms.

University of California, Berkeley, Graduate Division, College of Engineering, Department of Electrical Engineering and Computer Sciences, Berkeley, CA 94720-1500. Offers computer science (MS, PhD); electrical engineering (MS, PhD). *Degree requirements:* For master's, comprehensive exam or thesis; for doctorate, thesis/dissertation, qualifying exam. *Entrance requirements:* For master's and doctorate, GRE General Test, minimum GPA of 3.0, 3 letters of recommendation. Additional exam requirements/recommendations for international students: Required—TOEFL. Electronic applications accepted.

University of California, Davis, College of Engineering, Graduate Group in Computer Science, Davis, CA 95616. Offers MS, PhD. Terminal master's awarded for partial completion of doctoral program. *Degree requirements:* For master's, comprehensive exam (for some programs), thesis optional; for doctorate, comprehensive exam, thesis/dissertation. *Entrance requirements:* For master's and doctorate, GRE General Test, GRE Subject Test, minimum GPA of 3.0. Additional exam requirements/recommendations for international students: Required—TOEFL (minimum score 550 paper-based; 213 computer-based). Electronic applications accepted. *Faculty research:* Intrusion detection, malicious code detection, next generation light wave computer networks, biological algorithms, parallel processing.

University of California, Irvine, Donald Bren School of Information and Computer Sciences, Department of Computer Science, Irvine, CA 92697. Offers MS, PhD. *Students:* 162 full-time (25 women), 13 part-time (1 woman); includes 26 minority (1 Black or African American, non-Hispanic/Latino; 21 Asian, non-Hispanic/Latino; 2 Hispanic/Latino; 2 Two or more races, non-Hispanic/Latino), 115 international. Average age 28. 1,015 applicants, 21% accepted, 76 enrolled. In 2010, 36 master's, 2 doctorates awarded. Application fee: $80 ($100 for international students). *Unit head:* Sandy Irani, Chair, 949-824-6346, Fax: 949-824-4056, E-mail: irani@ics.uci.edu. *Application contact:* Kris Bolcer, Assistant Director, Graduate Affairs, 949-824-5156, Fax: 949-824-4163, E-mail: kbolcer@uci.edu.

University of California, Irvine, Donald Bren School of Information and Computer Sciences, Program in Networked Systems, Irvine, CA 92697. Offers MS, PhD. *Students:* 23 full-time (3 women), 2 part-time (1 woman); includes 1 Asian, non-Hispanic/Latino, 23 international. Average age 28. 112 applicants, 26% accepted, 14 enrolled. In 2010, 4 master's, 4 doctorates awarded. *Application deadline:* For fall admission, 1/15 for domestic students. Application fee: $80 ($100 for international students). *Financial support:* Fellowships, research assistantships, teaching assistantships available. *Unit head:* Hamid Jafarkhani, Director, 949-824-1755, Fax: 949-824-2321, E-mail: hamidj@uci.edu. *Application contact:* Kris Bolcer, Assistant Director, Graduate Affairs, 949-824-5156, Fax: 949-824-4163, E-mail: kbolcer@uci.edu.

University of California, Irvine, School of Engineering, Department of Electrical Engineering and Computer Science, Irvine, CA 92697. Offers electrical engineering and computer science (MS, PhD); networked systems (MS, PhD). Part-time programs available. *Students:* 205 full-time (29 women), 29 part-time (6 women); includes 41 minority (1 Black or African American, non-Hispanic/Latino; 35 Asian, non-Hispanic/Latino; 1 Hispanic/Latino; 4 Two or more races, non-Hispanic/Latino), 161 international. Average age 28. 1,102 applicants, 16% accepted, 64 enrolled. In 2010, 53 master's, 26 doctorates awarded. Terminal master's awarded for partial completion of doctoral program. *Degree requirements:* For doctorate, thesis/dissertation. *Entrance requirements:* For master's and doctorate, GRE General Test, minimum GPA of 3.0, 3 letters of recommendation. Additional exam requirements/recommendations for international students: Required—TOEFL (minimum score 550 paper-based; 213 computer-based). *Application deadline:* For fall admission, 1/15 priority date for domestic students, 1/15 for international students. Applications are processed on a rolling basis. Application fee: $80 ($100 for international students). Electronic applications accepted. *Financial support:* Fellowships, research assistantships with full tuition reimbursements, teaching assistantships, institutionally sponsored loans, traineeships, health care benefits, and unspecified assistantships available. Financial award application deadline: 3/1; financial award applicants required to submit FAFSA. *Faculty research:* Optics and electronic devices and circuits, signal processing, communications, machine vision, power electronics. *Unit head:* Prof. Michael M. Green, Chair, 949-824-1656, Fax: 949-824-3203, E-mail: mgreen@uci.edu. *Application contact:* Ronnie A. Gran, Graduate Admissions Coordinator, 949-824-5489, Fax: 949-824-1853, E-mail: ragran@uci.edu.

University of California, Los Angeles, Graduate Division, Henry Samueli School of Engineering and Applied Science, Department of Computer Science, Los Angeles, CA 90095-1596. Offers MS, PhD, MBA/MS. *Faculty:* 30 full-time (3 women). *Students:* 353 full-time (56 women); includes 3 Black or African American, non-Hispanic/Latino; 68 Asian, non-Hispanic/Latino; 10 Hispanic/Latino; 3 Native Hawaiian or other Pacific Islander, non-Hispanic/Latino, 196 international. 1,020 applicants, 32% accepted, 119 enrolled. In 2010, 99 master's, 31 doctorates awarded. *Degree requirements:* For master's, comprehensive exam or thesis; for doctorate, thesis/dissertation, qualifying exams. *Entrance requirements:* For master's, GRE General Test, GRE Subject Test, minimum GPA of 3.0; for doctorate, GRE General Test, GRE Subject Test, minimum GPA of 3.25. Additional exam requirements/recommendations for international students: Required—TOEFL (minimum score 560 paper-based; 220 computer-based; 87 iBT). *Application deadline:* For fall admission, 12/1 for domestic and international students. Application fee: $70 ($90 for international students). Electronic applications accepted. *Financial support:* In 2010–11, 36 fellowships, 225 research assistantships, 107 teaching assistantships were awarded; Federal Work-Study, institutionally sponsored loans, and tuition waivers (full and partial) also available. Financial award application deadline: 1/15; financial award applicants required to submit FAFSA. Total annual research expenditures: $10 million. *Unit head:* Dr. Jens Palsberg, Chair, 310-825-3886. *Application contact:* Wenona Colinco, Student Affairs Officer, 310-825-0060, Fax: 310-825-2273, E-mail: wcolinco@cs.ucla.edu.

University of California, Merced, Division of Graduate Studies, School of Engineering, Merced, CA 95343. Offers electrical engineering and computer science (MS, PhD).

University of California, Riverside, Graduate Division, Department of Computer Science and Engineering, Riverside, CA 92521-0102. Offers computer science (MS, PhD). Part-time programs available. *Faculty:* 21 full-time (0 women), 1 (woman) part-time/adjunct. *Students:* 140 full-time (26 women), 5 part-time (0 women); includes 103 minority (6 Black or African American, non-Hispanic/Latino; 83 Asian, non-Hispanic/Latino; 3 Hispanic/Latino; 11 Two or more races, non-Hispanic/Latino), 87 international. Average age 28. 418 applicants, 27% accepted, 40 enrolled. In 2010, 22 master's, 13 doctorates awarded. Terminal master's awarded for partial completion of doctoral program. *Degree requirements:* For master's, thesis or project; for doctorate, thesis/dissertation, qualifying exams. *Entrance requirements:* For master's, GRE General Test (minimum score of 1100). GRE not required for 5 year BS+MS program, minimum GPA of 3.2; for doctorate, GRE General Test (minimum score of 1100), minimum GPA of 3.2. Additional exam requirements/recommendations for international students: Required—TOEFL (minimum score 550 paper-based; 213 computer-based; 80 iBT). *Application deadline:* For fall admission, 5/1 priority date for domestic students, 2/1 for international students. Application fee: $85 ($100 for international students). Electronic applications accepted. *Financial support:* In 2010–11, 76 students received support, including 20 fellowships with partial tuition reimbursements available (averaging $16,000 per year), 58 research assistantships with partial tuition reimbursements available (averaging $15,000 per year), 31 teaching assistantships with partial tuition reimbursements available (averaging $16,000 per year); institutionally sponsored loans, health care benefits, and unspecified assistantships also available. Financial award applicants required to submit FAFSA. *Faculty research:* Algorithms, bioinformatics, logic; architecture, compilers, embedded systems, verification; databases, data mining, artificial intelligence, graphics; systems, networks. Total annual research expenditures: $3.6 million. *Unit head:* Dr. Laxmi Bhuyan, Chair, 951-827-5639, Fax: 951-827-4643, E-mail: gradadmission@ucr.edu. *Application contact:* Amy S. Ricks, Graduate Student Affairs Officer, 951-827-5639, Fax: 951-827-4643, E-mail: amy@cs.ucr.edu.

University of California, San Diego, Office of Graduate Studies, Department of Computer Science and Engineering, La Jolla, CA 92093. Offers computer engineering (MS, PhD); computer science (MS, PhD). *Degree requirements:* For doctorate, thesis/dissertation. *Entrance requirements:* For master's and doctorate, GRE General Test. Electronic applications accepted. *Faculty research:* Analysis of algorithms, combinatorial algorithms, discrete optimization.

University of California, San Diego, Office of Graduate Studies, Interdisciplinary Program in Cognitive Science, La Jolla, CA 92093. Offers cognitive science/anthropology (PhD); cognitive science/communication (PhD); cognitive science/computer science and engineering (PhD); cognitive science/linguistics (PhD); cognitive science/neuroscience (PhD); cognitive science/philosophy (PhD); cognitive science/psychology (PhD); cognitive science/sociology (PhD). Admissions offered through affiliated departments. *Degree requirements:* For doctorate, thesis/dissertation. *Entrance requirements:* For doctorate, GRE General Test, acceptance into one of the eight participating departments. *Faculty research:* Language and cognition, philosophy of mind, visual perception, biological anthropology, sociolinguistics.

University of California, Santa Barbara, Graduate Division, College of Engineering, Department of Computer Science, Santa Barbara, CA 93106-5110. Offers cognitive science (PhD); computational science and engineering (PhD); computer science (MS, PhD); technology and society (PhD). *Faculty:* 33 full-time (5 women), 5 part-time/adjunct (0 women). *Students:* 135 full-time (31 women); includes 51 Asian, non-Hispanic/Latino; 4 Hispanic/Latino. Average age 27. 481 applicants, 20% accepted, 30 enrolled. In 2010, 33 master's, 12 doctorates awarded. Terminal master's awarded for partial completion of doctoral program. *Degree requirements:* For master's, comprehensive exam (for some programs), thesis (for some programs), project (for some programs); for doctorate, thesis/dissertation. *Entrance requirements:* For master's and doctorate, GRE. Additional exam requirements/recommendations for international students: Required—TOEFL (minimum score 600 paper-based; 100 iBT), IELTS (minimum score 7). *Application deadline:* For fall admission, 12/15 for domestic and international students. Application fee: $70 ($90 for international students). Electronic applications accepted. *Financial support:* In 2010–11, 117 students received support, including 36 fellowships with full and partial tuition reimbursements available (averaging $10,486 per year), 77 research assistantships with full and partial tuition reimbursements available (averaging $12,464 per year), 47 teaching assistantships with partial tuition reimbursements available (averaging $10,383 per year); career-related internships or fieldwork, Federal Work-Study, institutionally sponsored loans, scholarships/grants, health care benefits, tuition waivers (full and partial), and unspecified assistantships also available. Financial award application deadline: 12/15; financial award applicants required to submit FAFSA. *Faculty research:* Networking and security, database systems, computational science and engineering, programming languages and software engineering, human computer interaction. Total annual research expenditures: $8 million. *Unit head:* Subhash Suri, Chair, 805-893-5334, Fax: 805-893-8553, E-mail: suri@cs.ucsb.edu. *Application contact:* Morgan Marcos, Graduate Program Assistant, 805-893-4322, Fax: 805-893-8553, E-mail: mmarcos@cs.ucsb.edu.

University of California, Santa Cruz, Division of Graduate Studies, Jack Baskin School of Engineering, Department of Computer Science, Santa Cruz, CA 95064. Offers MS, PhD. *Students:* 97 full-time (21 women), 19 part-time (1 woman); includes 19 minority (1 Black or African American, non-Hispanic/Latino; 11 Asian, non-Hispanic/Latino; 6 Hispanic/Latino; 1 Two or more races, non-Hispanic/Latino), 28 international. Average age 29. 288 applicants, 33% accepted, 23 enrolled. In 2010, 23 master's, 8 doctorates awarded. Terminal master's awarded for partial completion of doctoral program. *Degree requirements:* For master's, thesis, project; for doctorate, one foreign language, thesis/dissertation, qualifying exam. *Entrance requirements:* For master's and doctorate, GRE General Test, GRE Subject Test. Additional exam requirements/recommendations for international students: Required—TOEFL (minimum score 570 paper-based; 230 computer-based; 89 iBT); Recommended—IELTS (minimum score 8). *Application deadline:* For fall admission, 1/3 for domestic and international students. Application fee: $70 ($90 for international students). Electronic applications accepted. *Financial support:* Fellowships, research assistantships, teaching assistantships, institutionally sponsored loans and tuition waivers available. Financial award applicants required to submit FAFSA. *Faculty research:* Algorithm analysis, artificial intelligence, scientific visualization, computer graphics and gaming, multimodal human-computer interaction. *Unit head:* Tracie Tucker, Graduate Program Coordinator, 831-459-5737, E-mail: ttucker@soe.ucsc.edu. *Application contact:* Tracie Tucker, Graduate Program Coordinator, 831-459-5737, E-mail: ttucker@soe.ucsc.edu.

University of Central Arkansas, Graduate School, College of Natural Sciences and Math, Department of Applied Computing, Conway, AR 72035-0001. Offers MS. *Faculty:* 5 full-time (0 women). *Students:* 11 full-time (2 women), 4 part-time (0 women), 11 international. Average age 25. 14 applicants, 100% accepted, 7 enrolled. In 2010, 2 master's awarded. *Entrance requirements:* For master's, GRE, minimum GPA of 2.7. Additional exam requirements/recommendations for international students: Required—TOEFL (minimum score 550 paper-based; 213 computer-based). *Application deadline:* For fall admission, 3/1 for domestic students. Application fee: $25 ($50 for international students). *Financial support:* Federal Work-Study, scholarships/grants, and unspecified assistantships available. Financial award applicants required to submit FAFSA. *Unit head:* Chenyi Hu, Department Chair, 501-450-3401, Fax: 501-450-5615, E-mail: chu@uca.edu. *Application contact:* Susan Wood, Admissions Assistant, 501-450-3124, Fax: 501-450-5678, E-mail: swood@uca.edu.

University of Central Florida, College of Engineering and Computer Science, Department of Electrical Engineering and Computer Science, Program in Computer Science, Orlando, FL 32816. Offers computer science (MS, PhD); digital forensics (MS). Part-time and evening/weekend programs available. *Students:* 118 full-time (34 women), 164 part-time (30 women); includes 43 minority (12 Black or African American, non-Hispanic/Latino; 1 American Indian or Alaska Native, non-Hispanic/Latino; 12 Asian, non-Hispanic/Latino; 12 Hispanic/Latino; 1 Native Hawaiian or other Pacific Islander, non-Hispanic/Latino; 5 Two or more races, non-Hispanic/Latino), 63 international. Average age 30. 312 applicants, 58% accepted, 84 enrolled. In 2010, 51 master's, 16 doctorates awarded. *Degree requirements:* For master's, thesis or alternative; for doctorate, thesis/dissertation, candidacy exam, departmental qualifying exam. *Entrance requirements:* For master's, GRE General Test, GRE Subject Test, minimum GPA of 3.0 in last 60 hours; for doctorate, GRE Subject Test, minimum GPA of 3.0 in last 60 hours. Additional exam requirements/recommendations for international students: Required—TOEFL. *Application deadline:* For fall admission, 7/15 priority date for domestic students; for spring admission, 12/1 priority date for domestic students. Application fee: $30. Electronic applications accepted. *Expenses:* Tuition, state resident: part-time $256.56 per credit hour. Tuition, nonresident: part-time $1011.52 per credit hour. Part-time tuition and fees vary according to program. *Financial support:* In 2010–11, 62 students received support, including 13 fellowships with partial tuition reimbursements available (averaging $5,800 per year), 55 research assistantships with partial tuition reimbursements available (averaging $9,400 per year), 30 teaching assistantships with partial tuition reimbursements available (averaging $6,200 per year); career-related internships or fieldwork, Federal Work-Study, institutionally sponsored loans, tuition waivers (partial), and unspecified assistantships also available. Financial award application deadline: 3/1; financial award applicants required to submit FAFSA. *Faculty research:* Parallel processing, databases, algorithms, virtual reality.

University of Central Missouri, The Graduate School, College of Science and Technology, Warrensburg, MO 64093. Offers applied mathematics (MS); aviation safety (MS); biology (MS); computer science (MS); environmental studies (MA); industrial management (MS); mathematics (MS); technology (MS); technology management (PhD). PhD is offered jointly with Indiana State University. Part-time programs available. Postbaccalaureate distance learning degree programs offered. *Entrance requirements:* Additional exam requirements/recommendations for international students: Required—TOEFL (minimum score 550 paper-based; 79 computer-based). Electronic applications accepted.

University of Central Oklahoma, College of Graduate Studies and Research, College of Mathematics and Science, Department of Mathematics and Statistics, Edmond, OK 73034-5209. Offers applied mathematical sciences (MS), including computer science, mathematics, mathematics/computer science teaching, statistics. Part-time programs available. *Degree requirements:* For master's, thesis. *Entrance requirements:* Additional exam requirements/recommendations for international students: Required—TOEFL (minimum score 550 paper-based; 213 computer-based). Electronic applications accepted. *Faculty research:* Curvature, FAA, math education.

University of Chicago, Division of the Physical Sciences, Department of Computer Science, Professional Master's Program in Computer Science, Chicago, IL 60637-1513. Offers SM. Part-time and evening/weekend programs available. *Faculty:* 1 full-time (0 women), 12 part-time/adjunct (3 women). *Students:* 12 full-time (2 women), 82 part-time (11 women); includes 2 Black or African American, non-Hispanic/Latino; 20 Asian, non-Hispanic/Latino, 14 international. Average age 33. 128 applicants, 66% accepted, 50 enrolled. In 2010, 31 master's awarded. *Entrance requirements:* For master's, GRE. Additional exam requirements/recommendations for international students: Required—TOEFL. *Application deadline:* For fall admission, 9/10 priority date for domestic students, 6/20 for international students; for winter admission, 12/1 priority date for domestic students, 10/1 for international students; for spring admission, 3/1 priority date for domestic students, 12/31 for international students. Applications are processed on a rolling basis. Application fee: $70. Electronic applications accepted. *Financial support:* Institutionally sponsored loans available. Financial award applicants required to submit FAFSA. *Unit head:* Dr. Janos Simon, Professor, Computer Science Program Director, 773-702-3488, Fax: 773-702-8487, E-mail: questions@masters.cs.uchicago.edu. *Application contact:* Karin M. Czaplewski, Student Support Representative, 773-834-8587, Fax: 773-702-8487, E-mail: questions@masters.cs.uchicago.edu.

University of Cincinnati, Graduate School, College of Engineering, Department of Electrical and Computer Engineering and Computer Science, Program in Computer Science, Cincinnati, OH 45221. Offers MS. *Degree requirements:* For master's, thesis. *Entrance requirements:* For master's, GRE General Test, GRE Subject Test or BS in computer science. Additional exam requirements/recommendations for international students: Required—TOEFL (minimum score 550 paper-based; 213 computer-based).

University of Cincinnati, Graduate School, College of Engineering, Department of Electrical and Computer Engineering and Computer Science, Program in Computer Science and Engineering, Cincinnati, OH 45221. Offers PhD. *Degree requirements:* For doctorate, thesis/dissertation. *Entrance requirements:* For doctorate, GRE General Test. Additional exam requirements/recommendations for international students: Required—TOEFL.

University of Colorado at Colorado Springs, College of Engineering and Applied Science, Department of Computer Science, Colorado Springs, CO 80933-7150. Offers computer science (MS); engineering (PhD). Part-time programs available. *Faculty:* 12 full-time (1 woman). *Students:* 33 full-time (5 women), 14 part-time (1 woman); includes 4 Asian, non-Hispanic/Latino; 1 Hispanic/Latino, 11 international. Average age 32. 13 applicants, 85% accepted, 6 enrolled. In 2010, 8 master's awarded. *Degree requirements:* For master's, thesis optional, oral final exam; for doctorate, comprehensive exam, thesis/dissertation, oral final exam. *Entrance requirements:* For master's, GRE General Test, minimum GPA of 3.0, 2 semesters of course work in calculus, 1 other math course, course work in computer science; for doctorate, GRE General Test, GRE Subject Test (computer science), bachelor's or master's degree in computer science; minimum GPA of 3.3 in all previous course work; 2 semesters of calculus and one course in discrete math, statistics, and linear algebra. Additional exam requirements/recommendations for international students: Required—TOEFL. *Application deadline:* For fall admission, 6/15 priority date for domestic students; for spring admission, 11/15 for domestic students. Applications are processed on a rolling basis. Application fee: $60 ($75 for international students). *Expenses:* Tuition, state resident: full-time $7916. Tuition, nonresident: full-time $16,610. Tuition and fees vary according to course load, degree level, program, reciprocity agreements and student level. *Financial support:* Teaching assistantships, Federal Work-Study and scholarships/grants available. Financial award application deadline: 3/1; financial award applicants required to submit FAFSA. Total annual research expenditures: $301,079. *Unit head:* Dr. Richard Wiener, Chair, 719-255-3325, Fax: 719-255-3369, E-mail: rsw@runbox.com. *Application contact:* Dr. Richard Wiener, Chair, 719-255-3325, Fax: 719-255-3369, E-mail: rsw@runbox.com.

University of Colorado Boulder, Graduate School, College of Engineering and Applied Science, Department of Computer Science, Boulder, CO 80309. Offers ME, MS, PhD. *Faculty:* 28 full-time (7 women). *Students:* 134 full-time (17 women), 59 part-time (7 women); includes 19 minority (3 Black or African American, non-Hispanic/Latino; 1 American Indian or Alaska Native, non-Hispanic/Latino; 12 Asian, non-Hispanic/Latino; 3 Hispanic/Latino), 56 international. Average age 30. 303 applicants, 46 enrolled. In 2010, 43 master's, 17 doctorates awarded. *Degree requirements:* For master's, comprehensive exam, thesis or alternative; for doctorate, one foreign language, thesis/dissertation. *Entrance requirements:* For master's, minimum undergraduate GPA of 3.0. *Application deadline:* For fall admission, 2/28 priority date for domestic students, 12/1 for international students; for spring admission, 10/15 for domestic students, 9/1 for international students. Applications are processed on a rolling basis. Application fee: $50 ($60 for international students). *Financial support:* In 2010–11, 31 fellowships (averaging $14,694 per year), 48 research assistantships (averaging $17,046 per year), 5 teaching assistantships (averaging $15,703 per year) were awarded; tuition waivers (full) also available. *Faculty research:* Artificial intelligence, databases, hardware systems, hypermedia, machine learning, networks, numerical analysis, parallel computation, program analysis, programming languages. Total annual research expenditures: $4.8 million.

University of Colorado Denver, Business School, Program in Computer Science and Information Systems, Denver, CO 80217-3364. Offers PhD. *Students:* 7 full-time (0 women), 6 part-time (2 women); includes 1 Black or African American, non-Hispanic/Latino; 1 Asian, non-Hispanic/Latino, 6 international. Average age 37. 23 applicants, 13% accepted, 2 enrolled. In 2010, 4 doctorates awarded. *Degree requirements:* For doctorate, comprehensive exam, thesis/dissertation, 30 hours of CSIS courses beyond the master's level for total of 90 semester hours. *Entrance requirements:* For doctorate, GMAT or GRE General Test, letters of recommendation, portfolio essay describing applicant's motivation and initial plan for doctoral study. Additional exam requirements/recommendations for international students: Required—TOEFL (minimum score 525 paper-based; 197 computer-based; 71 iBT). *Application deadline:* For fall admission, 6/1 for domestic students, 3/15 for international students; for spring admission, 11/1 for domestic students, 10/1 for international students. Application fee: $50 ($75 for international students). Electronic applications accepted. *Expenses:* Contact institution. *Financial support:* Research assistantships, teaching assistantships, Federal Work-Study, institutionally sponsored loans, and scholarships/grants available. Support available to part-time students. Financial award application deadline: 4/1; financial award applicants required to submit FAFSA. *Faculty research:* Design science of information systems, information system economics, organizational impacts of information technology, high performance parallel and distributed systems, performance measurement and prediction. *Unit head:* Dr. Michael Mannino, Associate Professor/Co-Director, 303-315-8427, E-mail: michael.mannino@ucdenver.edu. *Application contact:* Shelly Townley, Admissions Coordinator, 303-315-8202, Fax: 303-556-5904, E-mail: shelly.townley@ucdenver.edu.

University of Colorado Denver, College of Engineering and Applied Science, Department of Computer Science and Engineering, Denver, CO 80217. Offers computer science (MS); computer science and information systems (PhD). Part-time and evening/weekend programs available. *Faculty:* 8 full-time (2 women), 1 part-time/adjunct (0 women). *Students:* 61 full-time (31 women), 21 part-time (3 women); includes 1 Black or African American, non-Hispanic/Latino; 7 Asian, non-Hispanic/Latino; 1 Hispanic/Latino, 44 international. Average age 31. 93 applicants, 38% accepted, 19 enrolled. In 2010, 22 master's, 1 doctorate awarded. *Degree requirements:* For master's, thesis or alternative, at least 30 semester hours of computer science courses while maintaining minimum GPA of 3.0; for doctorate, comprehensive exam, thesis/dissertation. *Entrance requirements:* For master's, GRE, minimum GPA of 3.0, 10 semester hours of university-level calculus, at least one math course beyond calculus; for doctorate, GRE or GMAT. Additional exam requirements/recommendations for international students: Required—TOEFL (minimum score 500 paper-based; 172 computer-based). *Application deadline:* For fall admission, 4/1 for domestic students; for spring admission, 10/1 for domestic students. Applications are processed on a rolling basis. Application fee: $50 ($75 for international students). Electronic applications accepted. *Expenses:* Tuition, state resident: full-time $7332; part-time $355 per credit hour. Tuition, nonresident: full-time $18,990; part-time $1055 per credit hour. Required fees: $998. Tuition and fees vary according to course level, course load, degree level, campus/location, program, reciprocity agreements and student level. *Financial support:* Research assistantships, teaching assistantships, career-related internships or fieldwork and Federal Work-Study available. Financial award application deadline: 4/1; financial award applicants required to submit FAFSA. *Faculty research:* Algorithms, automata theory, artificial intelligence, communication networks, combinatorial geometry, computational geometry, computer architectures, computer graphics, distributed computing, high performance computing, graph theory, Internet, operating systems, parallel processing, simulation and software engineering. *Unit head:* Bogdan Chlebus, Chair, 303-556-8537, Fax: 303-556-8369, E-mail: bogdan.chlebus@ucdenver.edu. *Application contact:* Frances Moore, Program Assistant, 303-556-4083, Fax: 303-556-8369, E-mail: frances.moore@ucdenver.edu.

University of Colorado Denver, College of Liberal Arts and Sciences, Program in Integrated Sciences, Denver, CO 80217-3364. Offers applied science (MIS); computer science (MIS); mathematics (MIS). Part-time and evening/weekend programs available. *Students:* 4 full-time (1 woman), 3 part-time (1 woman); includes 1 Hispanic/Latino. Average age 41. 4 applicants, 100% accepted, 2 enrolled. In 2010, 1 master's awarded. *Degree requirements:* For master's, thesis or alternative, 30 credit hours; thesis or project. *Entrance requirements:* For master's, GRE if undergraduate GPA is 2.75 or less, minimum of 40 semester hours in mathematics, computer science, physics, biology, chemistry and/or geology. *Application deadline:* For fall admission, 4/15 for domestic students; for spring admission, 10/15 for domestic students. Application fee: $50 ($75 for international students). Electronic applications accepted. *Expenses:* Tuition, state resident: full-time $7332; part-time $355 per credit hour. Tuition, nonresident: full-time $18,990; part-time $1055 per credit hour. Required fees: $998. Tuition and fees vary according to course level, course load, degree level, campus/location, program, reciprocity agreements and student level. *Financial support:* Application deadline: 4/1. *Faculty research:* Computer science, applied science, mathematics.

University of Connecticut, Graduate School, School of Engineering, Department of Computer Science and Engineering, Storrs, CT 06269. Offers computer science (MS, PhD), including artificial intelligence, computer architecture, computer science, operating systems, robotics, software engineering. Terminal master's awarded for partial completion of doctoral program. *Degree requirements:* For master's, comprehensive exam, thesis or alternative; for doctorate, thesis/dissertation. *Entrance requirements:* For master's and doctorate, GRE General Test. Additional exam requirements/recommendations for international students: Required—TOEFL (minimum score 550 paper-based; 213 computer-based). Electronic applications accepted.

University of Dayton, Graduate School, College of Arts and Sciences, Department of Computer Science, Dayton, OH 45469-1300. Offers MCS. Part-time and evening/weekend programs available. *Faculty:* 8 full-time (3 women), 1 part-time/adjunct (0 women). *Students:* 18 full-time (5 women), 6 part-time (1 woman); includes 1 minority (Hispanic/Latino), 13 international. Average age 29. 70 applicants, 37% accepted, 5 enrolled. In 2010, 7 master's awarded. *Degree requirements:* For master's, software project, additional coursework, or thesis. *Entrance requirements:* For master's, GRE General Test, 3 specified undergraduate courses in computer science, minimum undergraduate GPA of 3.0, or performance on placement exam. Additional exam requirements/recommendations for international students: Required—TOEFL (minimum score 550 paper-based; 213 computer-based; 80 iBT), IELTS (minimum score 6.5). *Application deadline:* For fall admission, 8/1 for domestic students, 3/1 priority date for international students; for winter admission, 7/1 priority date for international students; for spring admission, 1/1 priority date for international students. Applications are processed on a rolling basis. Application fee: $0. Electronic applications accepted. *Expenses:* Tuition: Full-time $7800; part-time $650 per credit hour. *Financial support:* In 2010–11, 3 teaching assistantships with tuition reimbursements (averaging $10,000 per year) were awarded; institutionally sponsored loans, health care benefits, and unspecified assistantships also available. Financial award applicants required to submit FAFSA. Total annual research expenditures: $250,000. *Unit head:* Dr. Dale Courte, Chair, 937-229-3831, E-mail: dale.courte@notes.udayton.edu. *Application contact:* Alexander Popovski, Assistant Director of Graduate and International Admissions, 937-229-2357, Fax: 937-229-4729, E-mail: alex.popovski@notes.udayton.edu.

University of Delaware, College of Engineering, Department of Computer and Information Sciences, Newark, DE 19716. Offers MS, PhD. Part-time programs available. Terminal master's awarded for partial completion of doctoral program. *Degree requirements:* For master's, thesis optional; for doctorate, comprehensive exam, thesis/dissertation. *Entrance requirements:* For master's and doctorate, GRE General Test. Additional exam requirements/recommendations for international students: Required—TOEFL (minimum score 550 paper-based; 213 computer-based). Electronic applications accepted. *Faculty research:* Artificial intelligence, computational theory, graphics and computer vision, networks, systems.

University of Denver, School of Engineering and Computer Science, Department of Computer Science, Denver, CO 80208. Offers computer science (MS, PhD); computer science systems

Computer Science

University of Denver (continued)
engineering (MS). Part-time programs available. *Faculty:* 11 full-time (2 women), 2 part-time/adjunct (1 woman). *Students:* 2 full-time (1 woman), 80 part-time (12 women); includes 11 minority (2 Black or African American, non-Hispanic/Latino; 3 Asian, non-Hispanic/Latino; 6 Hispanic/Latino), 18 international. Average age 33. 43 applicants, 72% accepted, 7 enrolled. In 2010, 16 master's, 2 doctorates awarded. *Degree requirements:* For doctorate, variable foreign language requirement, comprehensive exam, thesis/dissertation, reading competency in two languages, modern typesetting system, or additional coursework. *Entrance requirements:* For master's and doctorate, GRE General Test. Additional exam requirements/recommendations for international students: Required—TOEFL (minimum score 550 paper-based; 80 iBT). *Application deadline:* Applications are processed on a rolling basis. Application fee: $60. Electronic applications accepted. *Expenses:* Tuition: Full-time $35,604; part-time $29,670 per year. Required fees: $687 per year. Tuition and fees vary according to program. *Financial support:* In 2010–11, 2 research assistantships with full and partial tuition reimbursements (averaging $18,297 per year), 8 teaching assistantships with full and partial tuition reimbursements (averaging $18,297 per year) were awarded; fellowships with full and partial tuition reimbursements, career-related internships or fieldwork, Federal Work-Study, institutionally sponsored loans, scholarships/grants, and unspecified assistantships also available. Financial award application deadline: 3/1; financial award applicants required to submit FAFSA. *Faculty research:* Gaming, UML designs, STAMP. *Unit head:* Dr. Kimon Valavanis, Chair, 303-871-2586, E-mail: kimon.valavanis@du.edu. *Application contact:* Information Contact, 303-871-2458, E-mail: info@cs.du.edu.

University of Denver, School of Engineering and Computer Science, Department of Electrical and Computer Engineering, Denver, CO 80208. Offers computer engineering (MS); computer science and engineering (MS); electrical and computer engineering (PhD); electrical engineering (MS); engineering (MS); mechatronic systems engineering (MS). Part-time and evening/weekend programs available. *Faculty:* 11 full-time (0 women), 1 part-time/adjunct (0 women). *Students:* 2 full-time (0 women), 104 part-time (20 women); includes 13 minority (1 Black or African American, non-Hispanic/Latino; 6 Asian, non-Hispanic/Latino; 5 Hispanic/Latino; 1 Two or more races, non-Hispanic/Latino), 18 international. Average age 30. 97 applicants, 67% accepted, 26 enrolled. In 2010, 28 master's, 4 doctorates awarded. Terminal master's awarded for partial completion of doctoral program. *Degree requirements:* For master's, thesis or alternative, proficiency in high- or low-level computer language; for doctorate, comprehensive exam, thesis/dissertation, proficiency in high- or low-level computer language. *Entrance requirements:* For master's and doctorate, GRE General Test. Additional exam requirements/recommendations for international students: Required—TOEFL (minimum score 550 paper-based; 80 iBT). *Application deadline:* Applications are processed on a rolling basis. Application fee: $60. Electronic applications accepted. *Expenses:* Tuition: Full-time $35,604; part-time $29,670 per year. Required fees: $687 per year. Tuition and fees vary according to program. *Financial support:* In 2010–11, 12 research assistantships with full and partial tuition reimbursements (averaging $12,166 per year), 5 teaching assistantships with full and partial tuition reimbursements (averaging $12,198 per year) were awarded; Federal Work-Study, scholarships/grants, and unspecified assistantships also available. Financial award application deadline: 3/1; financial award applicants required to submit FAFSA. *Unit head:* Dr. Kimon Valavanis, Chair, 303-871-2586, Fax: 303-871-2194, E-mail: kvalavan@du.ed. *Application contact:* Information Contact, 303-871-6618, Fax: 303-871-2194, E-mail: eceinfo@du.edu.

University of Detroit Mercy, College of Engineering and Science, Department of Mathematics and Computer Science, Program in Computer Science, Detroit, MI 48221. Offers computer systems applications (MSCS); software engineering (MSCS). Evening/weekend programs available. *Entrance requirements:* For master's, minimum GPA of 3.0.

University of Evansville, College of Engineering and Computer Science, Department of Electrical Engineering and Computer Science, Evansville, IN 47722. Offers MS. Part-time programs available. *Faculty:* 2 full-time (0 women). *Students:* 1 (woman) part-time. Average age 28. 1 applicant, 0% accepted, 0 enrolled. *Degree requirements:* For master's, thesis. *Entrance requirements:* For master's, GRE, minimum undergraduate GPA of 2.8, 2 letters of recommendation, BS in electrical engineering or computer science. Additional exam requirements/recommendations for international students: Required—TOEFL (minimum score 550 paper-based; 79 iBT), IELTS (minimum score 6.5). *Application deadline:* For fall admission, 5/1 priority date for domestic and international students. Applications are processed on a rolling basis. Application fee: $25 ($50 for international students). *Expenses:* Contact institution. *Financial support:* Scholarships/grants available. Financial award application deadline: 6/1; financial award applicants required to submit FAFSA. *Unit head:* Dr. Dick Blandford, Department Chair, 812-488-2570, Fax: 812-488-2662, E-mail: blandford@evansville.edu. *Application contact:* Dr. Dick Blandford, Department Chair, 812-488-2570, Fax: 812-488-2662, E-mail: blandford@evansville.edu.

University of Florida, Graduate School, College of Engineering and College of Liberal Arts and Sciences, Department of Computer and Information Science and Engineering, Gainesville, FL 32611. Offers computer engineering (ME, MS, PhD); computer science (MS); digital arts and sciences (MS). Part-time programs available. Postbaccalaureate distance learning degree programs offered (minimal on-campus study). *Faculty:* 32 full-time (4 women), 2 part-time/adjunct (0 women). *Students:* 439 full-time (104 women), 81 part-time (19 women); includes 4 Black or African American, non-Hispanic/Latino; 11 Asian, non-Hispanic/Latino; 7 Hispanic/Latino, 445 international. Average age 24. 816 applicants, 60% accepted, 224 enrolled. In 2010, 156 master's, 25 doctorates awarded. Terminal master's awarded for partial completion of doctoral program. *Degree requirements:* For master's, comprehensive exam, thesis optional; for doctorate, comprehensive exam, thesis/dissertation. *Entrance requirements:* For master's and doctorate, GRE General Test, minimum GPA of 3.0. Additional exam requirements/recommendations for international students: Required—TOEFL (minimum score 550 paper-based; 213 computer-based; 80 iBT), IELTS (minimum score 6). *Application deadline:* For fall admission, 6/1 priority date for domestic students, 2/1 for international students; for spring admission, 9/1 for domestic and international students. Applications are processed on a rolling basis. Application fee: $30. Electronic applications accepted. *Expenses:* Tuition, state resident: full-time $10,915.92. Tuition, nonresident: full-time $28,309. *Financial support:* In 2010–11, 164 students received support, including 5 fellowships, 90 research assistantships (averaging $15,999 per year), 69 teaching assistantships (averaging $10,640 per year); unspecified assistantships also available. Financial award application deadline: 2/1; financial award applicants required to submit FAFSA. *Faculty research:* Computer systems, database, computer networks, graphics and vision, algorithm and parallel processing. Total annual research expenditures: $5.7 million. *Unit head:* Dr. Sartaj Sahni, Chair, 352-392-1527, Fax: 352-392-1220, E-mail: sahni@cise.ufl.edu. *Application contact:* Dr. Jih-Kwon Peir, Graduate Coordinator, 352-450-3446, Fax: 352-392-1220, E-mail: peir@cise.ufl.edu.

University of Georgia, College of Arts and Sciences, Department of Computer Science, Athens, GA 30602. Offers applied mathematical science (MAMS); computer science (MS, PhD). *Faculty:* 19 full-time (3 women), 1 part-time/adjunct (0 women). *Students:* 98 full-time (15 women), 24 part-time (6 women); includes 1 Black or African American, non-Hispanic/Latino; 3 Asian, non-Hispanic/Latino, 89 international. 155 applicants, 52% accepted, 28 enrolled. In 2010, 23 master's, 3 doctorates awarded. *Degree requirements:* For doctorate, thesis/dissertation. *Entrance requirements:* For master's and doctorate, GRE General Test. *Application deadline:* For fall admission, 7/1 priority date for domestic students, 4/15 for international students; for spring admission, 11/15 for domestic and international students. Applications are processed on a rolling basis. Application fee: $50. Electronic applications accepted. *Expenses:* Tuition, state resident: full-time $7200; part-time $344 per credit hour. Tuition, nonresident: full-time $21,900; part-time $944 per credit hour. Tuition and fees vary according to course load and program. *Financial support:* In 2010–11, 55 students received support, including 20 research assistantships, 31 teaching assistantships; fellowships, tuition waivers (full) and unspecified assistantships also available. *Unit head:* Dr. Eileen T. Kraemer, Head, 706-542-3455, E-mail: eileen@cs.uga.edu. *Application contact:* Dr. Suchendra Bhandarkar, Graduate Coordinator, 706-542-1082, Fax: 706-542-2966, E-mail: gradadvisor@cs.uga.edu.

University of Guelph, Graduate Studies, College of Physical and Engineering Science, Department of Computing and Information Science, Guelph, ON N1G 2W1, Canada. Offers applied computer science (M Sc); computer science (PhD). *Degree requirements:* For master's, thesis; for doctorate, comprehensive exam, thesis/dissertation. *Entrance requirements:* For master's, major or minor in computer science, honors degree; for doctorate, M Sc in computer science or related discipline. Additional exam requirements/recommendations for international students: Required—TOEFL (minimum score 600 paper-based; 250 computer-based; 89 iBT), IELTS (minimum score 6.5). Electronic applications accepted. *Faculty research:* Modeling and theory, distributed computing, soft computing, software and information systems, data and knowledge management.

University of Hawaii at Manoa, Graduate Division, College of Natural Sciences, Department of Information and Computer Sciences, Honolulu, HI 96822. Offers computer science (MS, PhD); library and information science (MLI Sc, Graduate Certificate), including advanced library and information science (Graduate Certificate), library and information science (MLI Sc). Part-time programs available. *Faculty:* 22 full-time (8 women), 2 part-time/adjunct (0 women). *Students:* 25 full-time (5 women), 21 part-time (5 women); includes 17 minority (10 Asian, non-Hispanic/Latino; 2 Hispanic/Latino; 1 Native Hawaiian or other Pacific Islander, non-Hispanic/Latino; 4 Two or more races, non-Hispanic/Latino), 11 international. Average age 31. In 2010, 10 master's, 2 doctorates awarded. *Degree requirements:* For master's, thesis optional; for doctorate, comprehensive exam, thesis/dissertation. *Entrance requirements:* For master's and doctorate, GRE. Additional exam requirements/recommendations for international students: Required—TOEFL (minimum score 580 paper-based; 237 computer-based; 92 iBT), IELTS (minimum score 5). *Application deadline:* For fall admission, 3/15 for domestic students, 1/15 for international students; for spring admission, 9/1 for domestic students, 8/1 for international students. Application fee: $60. *Financial support:* In 2010–11, 8 fellowships (averaging $1,375 per year) were awarded; research assistantships, teaching assistantships, tuition waivers (full and partial) also available. *Faculty research:* Software engineering, telecommunications, artificial intelligence, multimedia. Total annual research expenditures: $235,000. *Application contact:* Henri Casanova, Graduate Chair, 808-956-3548, Fax: 808-956-3548, E-mail: henric@hawaii.edu.

University of Houston, College of Natural Sciences and Mathematics, Department of Computer Science, Houston, TX 77204. Offers MA, PhD. Part-time programs available. *Faculty:* 22 full-time (2 women), 5 part-time/adjunct (2 women). *Students:* 244 full-time (64 women), 42 part-time (16 women); includes 4 Black or African American, non-Hispanic/Latino; 21 Asian, non-Hispanic/Latino; 7 Hispanic/Latino; 1 Two or more races, non-Hispanic/Latino, 236 international. Average age 27. 357 applicants, 84% accepted, 67 enrolled. In 2010, 82 master's, 5 doctorates awarded. Terminal master's awarded for partial completion of doctoral program. *Degree requirements:* For master's, thesis or alternative; for doctorate, comprehensive exam, thesis/dissertation. *Entrance requirements:* For master's and doctorate, GRE. Additional exam requirements/recommendations for international students: Required—TOEFL (minimum score 550 paper-based; 213 computer-based; 79 iBT), IELTS (minimum score 6.5). *Application deadline:* For fall admission, 4/1 for domestic and international students; for spring admission, 10/1 for domestic and international students. Applications are processed on a rolling basis. Application fee: $0 ($75 for international students). Electronic applications accepted. *Expenses:* Tuition, state resident: full-time $8592; part-time $358 per credit hour. Tuition, nonresident: full-time $16,032; part-time $668 per credit hour. Required fees: $2889. Tuition and fees vary according to course load and program. *Financial support:* In 2010–11, 41 research assistantships with partial tuition reimbursements (averaging $11,184 per year), 23 teaching assistantships with partial tuition reimbursements (averaging $12,120 per year) were awarded; fellowships, career-related internships or fieldwork, Federal Work-Study, institutionally sponsored loans, scholarships/grants, health care benefits, and unspecified assistantships also available. Support available to part-time students. Financial award application deadline: 2/1; financial award applicants required to submit FAFSA. *Faculty research:* Databases, networks, image analysis, security, animation. *Unit head:* Dr. Jaspal Subhlok, Interim Chairperson, 713-743-3340, Fax: 713-743-3335, E-mail: jaspal@uh.edu. *Application contact:* Elizabeth Faig, Graduate Advisor, 713-743-3407, E-mail: ejfaig@central.uh.edu.

University of Houston–Clear Lake, School of Science and Computer Engineering, Program in Computer Science, Houston, TX 77058-1098. Offers MS. Part-time and evening/weekend programs available. *Entrance requirements:* For master's, GRE General Test. Additional exam requirements/recommendations for international students: Required—TOEFL (minimum score 550 paper-based; 213 computer-based).

University of Houston–Victoria, School of Arts and Sciences, Program in Computer Science, Victoria, TX 77901-4450. Offers computer information systems (MS). Part-time and evening/weekend programs available. Postbaccalaureate distance learning degree programs offered (no on-campus study). *Faculty:* 5 full-time, 7 part-time/adjunct. *Students:* 14 full-time (6 women), 58 part-time (23 women); includes 12 Black or African American, non-Hispanic/Latino; 15 Asian, non-Hispanic/Latino; 11 Hispanic/Latino; 1 Two or more races, non-Hispanic/Latino, 20 international. 37 applicants, 86% accepted, 14 enrolled. In 2010, 11 master's awarded. *Degree requirements:* For master's, comprehensive exam (for some programs), thesis (for some programs). *Entrance requirements:* For master's, GRE. Additional exam requirements/recommendations for international students: Required—TOEFL (minimum score 550 paper-based; 213 computer-based). *Application deadline:* Applications are processed on a rolling basis. Application fee: $0. *Expenses:* Tuition, state resident: full-time $4050; part-time $225 per credit hour. Tuition, nonresident: full-time $8730; part-time $485 per credit hour. Required fees: $810; $54 per credit hour. Tuition and fees vary according to course load. *Financial support:* In 2010–11, research assistantships (averaging $2,000 per year); career-related internships or fieldwork, scholarships/grants, and unspecified assistantships also available. Support available to part-time students. Financial award application deadline: 4/15. *Unit head:* Dr. Li Chao, Chair, Science, Technology and Mathematics Division, 281-275-8828, E-mail: chaol@uhv.edu. *Application contact:* Tracy Fox, School of Arts and Sciences, 361-570-4233, E-mail: foxt@uhv.edu.

University of Idaho, College of Graduate Studies, College of Engineering, Department of Computer Science, Moscow, ID 83844-2282. Offers MS, PhD. *Faculty:* 10 full-time. *Students:* 27 full-time, 24 part-time. Average age 35. In 2010, 8 master's, 4 doctorates awarded. *Degree requirements:* For master's, thesis; for doctorate, thesis/dissertation. *Entrance requirements:* For master's, GRE General Test, minimum GPA of 3.0; for doctorate, minimum undergraduate GPA of 2.8, 3.0 graduate. Additional exam requirements/recommendations for international students: Required—TOEFL. *Application deadline:* For fall admission, 8/1 for domestic students; for spring admission, 12/15 for domestic students. Applications are processed on a rolling basis. Application fee: $60. Electronic applications accepted. *Expenses:* Tuition, nonresident: part-time $580 per credit. Required fees: $306 per credit. *Financial support:* Research assistantships, teaching assistantships, career-related internships or fieldwork available. Financial award applicants required to submit FAFSA. *Faculty research:* Artificial intelligence, computer and network security, software engineering. *Unit head:* Dr. Greg Donahoe, Chair, 208-885-6589, E-mail: csinfo@uidaho.edu. *Application contact:* Dr. Greg Donahoe, Chair, 208-885-6589, E-mail: csinfo@uidaho.edu.

University of Illinois at Chicago, Graduate College, College of Engineering, Department of Computer Science, Chicago, IL 60607-7128. Offers MS, PhD. Part-time programs available. *Degree requirements:* For master's, thesis or alternative; for doctorate, thesis/dissertation, departmental qualifying exam. *Entrance requirements:* For master's, BS in related field, minimum GPA of 2.75; for doctorate, GRE General Test, minimum GPA of 2.75, MS in related field. Additional exam requirements/recommendations for international students: Required—TOEFL.

University of Illinois at Chicago, Graduate College, College of Liberal Arts and Sciences, Department of Mathematics, Statistics, and Computer Science, Chicago, IL 60607-7128. Offers applied mathematics (MS, PhD); computational finance (MS, PhD); computer science (MS, PhD); mathematics (DA); mathematics and information sciences for industry (MS); probability and statistics (PhD); pure mathematics (MS, PhD); statistics (MS); teaching of mathematics (MST), including elementary, secondary. Part-time programs available. *Faculty:* 36 full-time (3 women). *Students:* 150 full-time (54 women), 31 part-time (18 women); includes 3 Black or African American, non-Hispanic/Latino; 1 Asian, non-Hispanic/Latino; 8 Hispanic/Latino, 62 international. Average age 26. 224 applicants, 56% accepted, 43 enrolled. In 2010, 34 master's, 17 doctorates awarded. *Degree requirements:* For master's, comprehensive exam; for doctorate, one foreign language, thesis/dissertation. *Entrance requirements:* For master's and doctorate, GRE General Test, minimum GPA of 3.0. Additional exam requirements/recommendations for international students: Required—TOEFL (minimum score 100 iBT). *Application deadline:* For fall admission, 1/1 for domestic and international students; for spring admission, 10/1 for domestic students, 7/15 for international students. Applications are processed on a rolling basis. Application fee: $60. Electronic applications accepted. *Financial support:* In 2010–11, 109 students received support, including 2 fellowships with full tuition reimbursements available (averaging $20,000 per year), 8 research assistantships with full tuition reimbursements available (averaging $17,000 per year), 87 teaching assistantships with full tuition reimbursements available (averaging $17,000 per year); Federal Work-Study, scholarships/grants, and tuition waivers (full) also available. Financial award application deadline: 1/1. *Unit head:* Lawrence Ein, Head, 312-996-3044, E-mail: ein@math.uic.edu. *Application contact:* Brooke Shipley, Director of Graduate Studies, 312-996-5119, E-mail: dgs@math.uic.edu.

University of Illinois at Springfield, Graduate Programs, College of Liberal Arts and Sciences, Program in Computer Science, Springfield, IL 62703-5407. Offers MS. Part-time and evening/weekend programs available. Postbaccalaureate distance learning degree programs offered (no on-campus study). *Degree requirements:* For master's, research seminar. *Entrance requirements:* For master's, GRE General Test, minimum undergraduate GPA of 2.7. Additional exam requirements/recommendations for international students: Required—TOEFL (minimum score 550 paper-based; 213 computer-based; 79 iBT). Electronic applications accepted. *Expenses:* Tuition, state resident: full-time $6774; part-time $282.25 per credit hour. Tuition, nonresident: full-time $15,078; part-time $628.25 per credit hour. Required fees: $15.25 per credit hour. $492 per term.

University of Illinois at Urbana–Champaign, Graduate College, College of Engineering, Department of Computer Science, Champaign, IL 61820. Offers bioinformatics (MS); computer science (MCS, MS, PhD); MCS/JD; MCS/M Arch; MCS/MBA. Part-time programs available. Postbaccalaureate distance learning degree programs offered (no on-campus study). *Faculty:* 53 full-time (5 women), 2 part-time/adjunct (0 women). *Students:* 272 full-time (41 women), 179 part-time (26 women); includes 3 Black or African American, non-Hispanic/Latino; 36 Asian, non-Hispanic/Latino; 1 Hispanic/Latino; 1 Two or more races, non-Hispanic/Latino, 271 international. 1,324 applicants, 10% accepted, 64 enrolled. In 2010, 68 master's, 36 doctorates awarded. *Entrance requirements:* For master's and doctorate, minimum GPA of 3.0. Additional exam requirements/recommendations for international students: Required—TOEFL (minimum score 600 paper-based; 250 computer-based; 100 iBT) or IELTS (minimum score 6.5). *Application deadline:* Applications are processed on a rolling basis. Application fee: $75 ($90 for international students). Electronic applications accepted. *Financial support:* In 2010–11, 35 fellowships, 281 research assistantships, 87 teaching assistantships were awarded; tuition waivers (full and partial) also available. *Unit head:* Robin A. Rutenbar, Head, 217-333-3373, Fax: 217-333-3501, E-mail: rutenbar@illinois.edu. *Application contact:* Rhonda McElroy, Coordinator of Graduate Programs, 217-244-2745, Fax: 217-244-6073, E-mail: rmcelroy@illinois.edu.

The University of Iowa, Graduate College, College of Liberal Arts and Sciences, Department of Computer Science, Iowa City, IA 52242-1316. Offers MCS, MS, PhD. *Degree requirements:* For master's, thesis optional, exam; for doctorate, comprehensive exam, thesis/dissertation. *Entrance requirements:* For master's, minimum GPA of 3.0; for doctorate, GRE General Test, minimum GPA of 3.0. Additional exam requirements/recommendations for international students: Required—TOEFL (minimum score 550 paper-based; 213 computer-based; 81 iBT). Electronic applications accepted.

The University of Kansas, Graduate Studies, School of Engineering, Department of Electrical Engineering and Computer Science, Program in Computer Science, Lawrence, KS 66045. Offers MS, PhD. Part-time and evening/weekend programs available. *Faculty:* 35. *Students:* 46 full-time (11 women), 21 part-time (6 women); includes 8 minority (1 Black or African American, non-Hispanic/Latino; 6 Asian, non-Hispanic/Latino; 1 Hispanic/Latino), 34 international. Average age 28. 87 applicants, 33% accepted, 9 enrolled. In 2010, 14 master's, 3 doctorates awarded. Terminal master's awarded for partial completion of doctoral program. *Degree requirements:* For master's, thesis optional, exam; for doctorate, one foreign language, comprehensive exam, thesis/dissertation, qualifying exams. *Entrance requirements:* For master's, GRE, minimum GPA of 3.0; for doctorate, GRE, minimum GPA of 3.5. Additional exam requirements/recommendations for international students: Required—TOEFL (minimum score 600 paper-based; 250 computer-based; 100 iBT). *Application deadline:* For fall admission, 3/1 priority date for domestic students, 3/1 for international students; for spring admission, 10/1 priority date for domestic students, 10/1 for international students. Applications are processed on a rolling basis. Application fee: $55 ($65 for international students). Electronic applications accepted. *Expenses:* Tuition, state resident: full-time $7092; part-time $295.50 per credit hour. Tuition, nonresident: full-time $16,590; part-time $691.25 per credit hour. Required fees: $858; $71.49 per credit hour. Tuition and fees vary according to course load, campus/location and program. *Financial support:* Fellowships with full and partial tuition reimbursements, research assistantships with full and partial tuition reimbursements, teaching assistantships with full and partial tuition reimbursements, career-related internships or fieldwork, scholarships/grants, and unspecified assistantships available. Financial award application deadline: 1/1. *Faculty research:* Communication systems and networking, computer systems design, interactive intelligent systems, bioinformatics. *Unit head:* Glenn Prescott, Chairperson, 785-864-4620, Fax: 785-864-3226. *Application contact:* Pam Shadoin, Assistant to Graduate Director, 785-864-4487, Fax: 785-864-3226, E-mail: graduate@eecs.ku.edu.

University of Kentucky, Graduate School, College of Engineering, Program in Computer Science, Lexington, KY 40506-0032. Offers MS, PhD. *Degree requirements:* For master's, comprehensive exam, thesis optional; for doctorate, one foreign language, comprehensive exam, thesis/dissertation. *Entrance requirements:* For master's, GRE General Test, minimum undergraduate GPA of 2.75; for doctorate, GRE General Test, minimum undergraduate GPA of 3.0. Additional exam requirements/recommendations for international students: Required—TOEFL (minimum score 550 paper-based; 213 computer-based). Electronic applications accepted. *Faculty research:* Artificial intelligence and databases, communication networks and operating systems, graphics and vision, numerical analysis, theory.

University of Lethbridge, School of Graduate Studies, Lethbridge, AB T1K 3M4, Canada. Offers accounting (MScM); addictions counseling (M Sc); agricultural biotechnology (M Sc); agricultural studies (M Sc, MA); anthropology (MA); archaeology (MA); art (MA, MFA); biochemistry (M Sc); biological sciences (M Sc); biomolecular science (PhD); biosystems and biodiversity (PhD); Canadian studies (MA); chemistry (M Sc); computer science (M Sc); computer science and geographical information science (M Sc); counseling psychology (M Ed); dramatic arts (MA); earth, space, and physical science (PhD); economics (MA); educational leadership (M Ed); English (MA); environmental science (M Sc); evolution and behavior (PhD); exercise science (M Sc); finance (MScM); French (MA); French/German (MA); French/Spanish (MA); general education (M Ed); general management (MScM); geography (M Sc, MA); German (MA); health science (M Sc); history (MA); human resource management and labour relations (MScM); individualized multidisciplinary (M Sc, MA); information systems (MScM); international management (MScM); kinesiology (M Sc, MA); management (M Sc, MA); marketing (MScM); mathematics (M Sc); music (M Mus, MA); Native American studies (MA); neuroscience (M Sc, PhD); new media (MA); nursing (M Sc); philosophy (MA); physics (M Sc); policy and strategy (MScM); political science (MA); psychology (M Sc, MA); religious studies (MA); social sciences (MA); sociology (MA); theatre and dramatic arts (MFA); theoretical and computational science (PhD); urban and regional studies (MA); women's studies (MA). Part-time and evening/weekend programs available. *Degree requirements:* For doctorate, comprehensive exam, thesis/dissertation. *Entrance requirements:* For master's, GMAT (M Sc in management), bachelor's degree in related field, minimum GPA of 3.0 during previous 20 graded semester courses, 2 years teaching or related experience (M Ed); for doctorate, master's degree, minimum graduate GPA of 3.5. Additional exam requirements/recommendations for international students: Required—TOEFL. *Faculty research:* Movement and brain plasticity, gibberellin physiology, photosynthesis, carbon cycling, molecular properties of main-group ring components.

University of Louisiana at Lafayette, College of Engineering, Center for Advanced Computer Studies, Lafayette, LA 70504. Offers computer engineering (MS, PhD); computer science (MS, PhD). Part-time programs available. Terminal master's awarded for partial completion of doctoral program. *Degree requirements:* For master's, thesis or alternative; for doctorate, comprehensive exam, thesis/dissertation, final oral exam. *Entrance requirements:* For master's, GRE General Test, minimum GPA of 2.75; for doctorate, GRE General Test, minimum GPA of 3.0. Additional exam requirements/recommendations for international students: Required—TOEFL. Electronic applications accepted.

See Display on next page and Close-Up on page 333.

University of Louisville, J.B. Speed School of Engineering, Department of Computer Engineering and Computer Science, Louisville, KY 40292-0001. Offers computer engineering and computer science (M Eng, MS); computer science (MS); computer science and engineering (PhD); data mining (Certificate); network and information security (Certificate). *Accreditation:* ABET (one or more programs are accredited). Part-time programs available. Postbaccalaureate distance learning degree programs offered (no on-campus study). *Faculty:* 13 full-time (1 woman). *Students:* 74 full-time (15 women), 45 part-time (7 women); includes 8 Black or African American, non-Hispanic/Latino; 4 Asian, non-Hispanic/Latino; 1 Hispanic/Latino; 1 Two or more races, non-Hispanic/Latino, 40 international. Average age 29. 51 applicants, 41% accepted, 9 enrolled. In 2010, 22 master's, 11 doctorates awarded. Terminal master's awarded for partial completion of doctoral program. *Degree requirements:* For master's, comprehensive exam (for some programs), thesis or alternative; for doctorate, comprehensive exam, thesis/dissertation, minimum GPA of 3.0. *Entrance requirements:* For master's, doctorate, and Certificate, GRE General Test. Additional exam requirements/recommendations for international students: Required—TOEFL (minimum score 550 paper-based; 213 computer-based; 80 iBT), IELTS (minimum score 6.5). *Application deadline:* For fall admission, 5/1 priority date for domestic and international students; for spring admission, 11/1 priority date for domestic and international students. Applications are processed on a rolling basis. Application fee: $50. Electronic applications accepted. *Expenses:* Tuition, state resident: full-time $9144; part-time $508 per credit hour. Tuition, nonresident: full-time $19,026; part-time $1057 per credit hour. Tuition and fees vary according to program and reciprocity agreements. *Financial support:* In 2010–11, 22 students received support, including 1 fellowship with full tuition reimbursement available (averaging $20,000 per year), 15 research assistantships with full tuition reimbursements available (averaging $18,900 per year), 6 teaching assistantships with full tuition reimbursements available (averaging $20,000 per year). Financial award application deadline: 1/25; financial award applicants required to submit FAFSA. *Faculty research:* Software systems engineering, information security and forensics, multimedia and vision, mobile and distributed computing, intelligent systems. Total annual research expenditures: $1.3 million. *Unit head:* Dr. Adel S. Elmaghraby, Chair, 502-852-6304, Fax: 502-852-4713, E-mail: adel@louisville.edu. *Application contact:* Dr. Michael Day, Associate Dean, 502-852-6195, Fax: 502-852-6294, E-mail: day@louisville.edu.

University of Maine, Graduate School, College of Liberal Arts and Sciences, Department of Computer Science, Orono, ME 04469. Offers MS, PhD. Part-time programs available. *Faculty:* 8 full-time (1 woman), 1 part-time/adjunct (0 women). *Students:* 10 full-time (1 woman), 3 part-time (0 women), 1 international. Average age 32. 11 applicants, 45% accepted, 3 enrolled. In 2010, 4 master's, 1 doctorate awarded. *Degree requirements:* For master's, thesis optional; for doctorate, thesis/dissertation. *Entrance requirements:* For master's and doctorate, GRE General Test, GRE Subject Test. Additional exam requirements/recommendations for international students: Required—TOEFL. *Application deadline:* For fall admission, 2/1 priority date for domestic students. Applications are processed on a rolling basis. Application fee: $65. Electronic applications accepted. *Expenses:* Tuition, state resident: full-time $400. Tuition, nonresident: full-time $1050. *Financial support:* In 2010–11, 2 research assistantships with tuition reimbursements (averaging $22,554 per year), 9 teaching assistantships with tuition reimbursements (averaging $19,554 per year) were awarded; career-related internships or fieldwork, Federal Work-Study, institutionally sponsored loans, and tuition waivers (full) also available. Financial award application deadline: 3/1. *Faculty research:* Theory, software engineering, graphics, applications, artificial intelligence. *Unit head:* Dr. George Markowsky, Chair, 207-581-3912, Fax: 207-581-4977. *Application contact:* Scott G. Delcourt, Associate Dean of the Graduate School, 207-581-3291, Fax: 207-581-3232, E-mail: graduate@maine.edu.

University of Management and Technology, Program in Computer Science and Information Technology, Arlington, VA 22209. Offers computer science (MS); information technology (AC); information technology project management (MS); management information systems (MS); project management (AC); software engineering (MS). Part-time and evening/weekend programs available. Postbaccalaureate distance learning degree programs offered (no on-campus study). *Entrance requirements:* For master's, 3 recommendations, resume. Additional exam requirements/recommendations for international students: Required—TOEFL (minimum score 550 paper-based; 213 computer-based). Electronic applications accepted.

The University of Manchester, School of Computer Science, Manchester, United Kingdom. Offers M Phil, PhD.

University of Manitoba, Faculty of Graduate Studies, Faculty of Science, Department of Computer Science, Winnipeg, MB R3T 2N2, Canada. Offers M Sc, PhD. *Degree requirements:* For master's, thesis or alternative; for doctorate, thesis/dissertation.

University of Maryland, Baltimore County, Graduate School, College of Engineering and Information Technology, Department of Computer Science and Electrical Engineering, Program in Computer Science, Baltimore, MD 21250. Offers MS, PhD. Part-time programs available. *Students:* 108 full-time (22 women), 43 part-time (6 women); includes 20 minority (6 Black or African American, non-Hispanic/Latino; 9 Asian, non-Hispanic/Latino; 4 Hispanic/Latino; 1 Two or more races, non-Hispanic/Latino), 67 international. Average age 29. 309 applicants, 37% accepted, 37 enrolled. In 2010, 14 master's, 8 doctorates awarded. *Degree requirements:* For master's, comprehensive exam (for some programs), thesis (for some programs); for doctorate, comprehensive exam, thesis/dissertation. *Entrance requirements:* For master's, GRE General Test, strong background in computer science and math courses; for doctorate, GRE General Test, MS in computer science (strongly recommended). Additional exam requirements/recommendations for international students: Required—TOEFL (minimum score 550 paper-based; 213 computer-based; 80 iBT). *Application deadline:* For fall admission, 6/1 for domestic students, 1/1 for international students; for spring admission, 11/1 for domestic students, 6/1 for international students. Applications are processed on a rolling basis. Application fee: $50. Electronic applications accepted. *Financial support:* In 2010–11, 1 fellowship with full tuition reimbursement (averaging $21,500 per year), 36 research assistantships with full tuition reimbursements (averaging $17,000 per year), 31 teaching assistantships with full tuition reimbursements (averaging $17,000 per year) were awarded; career-related internships or fieldwork, Federal Work-Study, scholarships/grants, health care benefits, tuition waivers (partial), and unspecified assistantships also available. Support available to part-time students. Financial award application deadline: 6/30; financial award applicants required to submit FAFSA. *Faculty research:* Security and information assurance, intelligent agents and semantic web, wireless networking. *Unit head:* Dr. Gary Carter, Professor and Chair, 410-455-3500, Fax: 410-455-

Computer Science

University of Maryland, Baltimore County *(continued)*
3969, E-mail: carter@cs.umbc.edu. *Application contact:* Dr. Anupam Joshi, Professor and Graduate Program Coordinator, 410-455-2590, Fax: 410-455-3969, E-mail: joshi@cs.umbc.edu.

University of Maryland, Baltimore County, Graduate School, College of Engineering and Information Technology, Department of Information Systems, Program in Human-Centered Computing, Baltimore, MD 21250. Offers MS, PhD. Part-time and evening/weekend programs available. *Students:* 22 full-time (11 women), 29 part-time (14 women); includes 6 minority (5 Black or African American, non-Hispanic/Latino; 1 Asian, non-Hispanic/Latino), 11 international. Average age 30. 44 applicants, 75% accepted, 20 enrolled. In 2010, 5 master's awarded. Terminal master's awarded for partial completion of doctoral program. *Degree requirements:* For master's, comprehensive exam (for some programs), thesis optional; for doctorate, comprehensive exam, thesis/dissertation. *Entrance requirements:* For master's, minimum GPA of 3.0; for doctorate, GRE General Test or GMAT, minimum GPA of 3.0, competence in statistical analysis and experimental design (recommended). Additional exam requirements/recommendations for international students: Required—TOEFL (minimum score 550 paper-based; 213 computer-based; 80 iBT). *Application deadline:* For fall admission, 6/1 for domestic students, 1/1 for international students; for spring admission, 11/1 for domestic students, 6/1 for international students. Applications are processed on a rolling basis. Application fee: $50. Electronic applications accepted. *Financial support:* In 2010–11, 6 research assistantships with full tuition reimbursements (averaging $19,000 per year), 2 teaching assistantships with full tuition reimbursements (averaging $19,000 per year) were awarded; career-related internships or fieldwork, Federal Work-Study, scholarships/grants, health care benefits, tuition waivers (partial), and unspecified assistantships also available. Support available to part-time students. Financial award application deadline: 6/30; financial award applicants required to submit FAFSA. *Faculty research:* Human-centered computing, artificial intelligence, database/data mining, decision-making support systems, software engineering/systems analysis and design. *Unit head:* Dr. Andrew L. Sears, Professor and Chair, 410-455-3883, Fax: 410-455-1217, E-mail: asears@umbc.edu. *Application contact:* Dr. Anita Komlodi, Associate Professor and Graduate Program Director, 410-455-3212, Fax: 410-455-1217, E-mail: komlodi@umbc.edu.

University of Maryland, College Park, Academic Affairs, College of Computer, Mathematical and Natural Sciences, Department of Computer Science, College Park, MD 20742. Offers MS, PhD. Part-time and evening/weekend programs available. *Faculty:* 74 full-time (9 women), 3 part-time/adjunct (0 women). *Students:* 212 full-time (33 women), 29 part-time (5 women); includes 23 minority (3 Black or African American, non-Hispanic/Latino; 17 Asian, non-Hispanic/Latino; 2 Hispanic/Latino; 1 Two or more races, non-Hispanic/Latino), 129 international. 1,107 applicants, 13% accepted, 63 enrolled. In 2010, 33 master's, 26 doctorates awarded. Terminal master's awarded for partial completion of doctoral program. *Degree requirements:* For master's, thesis or scholarly paper and exam; for doctorate, thesis/dissertation. *Entrance requirements:* For master's and doctorate, GRE General Test, GRE Subject Test (recommended), minimum GPA of 3.0, 3 letters of recommendation. Additional exam requirements/recommendations for international students: Required—TOEFL; Recommended—TWE. *Application deadline:* For fall admission, 12/15 for domestic and international students; for spring admission, 10/15 for domestic students, 6/1 for international students. Applications are processed on a rolling basis. Application fee: $75. Electronic applications accepted. *Expenses:* Tuition, area resident: Part-time $471 per credit hour. Tuition, state resident: part-time $471 per credit hour. Tuition, nonresident: part-time $1016 per credit hour. Required fees: $337 per term. *Financial support:* In 2010–11, 2 fellowships with full and partial tuition reimbursements (averaging $22,522 per year), 128 research assistantships with tuition reimbursements (averaging $19,607 per year), 69 teaching assistantships with tuition reimbursements (averaging $18,385 per year) were awarded; career-related internships or fieldwork, Federal Work-Study, and scholarships/grants also available. Support available to part-time students. Financial award applicants required to submit FAFSA. *Faculty research:* Artificial intelligence, computer applications, information processing, bioinformatics and computational biology, human-computer interaction. Total annual research

expenditures: $4.3 million. *Unit head:* Dr. Larry S. Davis, Chairperson, 301-405-2662, Fax: 301-314-1353, E-mail: lsdavis@umd.edu. *Application contact:* Dr. Charles A. Caramello, Dean of Graduate School, 301-405-0358, Fax: 301-314-9305, E-mail: ccaramel@umd.edu.

University of Maryland Eastern Shore, Graduate Programs, Department of Mathematics and Computer Sciences, Princess Anne, MD 21853-1299. Offers applied computer science (MS). Part-time and evening/weekend programs available. *Degree requirements:* For master's, thesis or alternative, research project. *Entrance requirements:* For master's, GRE General Test, minimum GPA of 3.0. Additional exam requirements/recommendations for international students: Required—TOEFL (minimum score 213 computer-based; 80 iBT). Electronic applications accepted.

University of Massachusetts Amherst, Graduate School, College of Natural Sciences, Department of Computer Science, Amherst, MA 01003. Offers MS, PhD. Part-time programs available. *Faculty:* 46 full-time (7 women). *Students:* 129 full-time (31 women), 53 part-time (7 women); includes 8 minority (3 Black or African American, non-Hispanic/Latino; 3 Asian, non-Hispanic/Latino; 2 Two or more races, non-Hispanic/Latino), 100 international. Average age 28. 784 applicants, 8% accepted, 29 enrolled. In 2010, 21 master's, 18 doctorates awarded. Terminal master's awarded for partial completion of doctoral program. *Degree requirements:* For master's, thesis or alternative; for doctorate, comprehensive exam, thesis/dissertation. *Entrance requirements:* For master's and doctorate, GRE General Test. Additional exam requirements/recommendations for international students: Required—TOEFL (minimum score 550 paper-based; 213 computer-based; 80 iBT), IELTS (minimum score 6.5), TWE. *Application deadline:* For fall admission, 12/15 for domestic and international students. Applications are processed on a rolling basis. Application fee: $50 ($65 for international students). Electronic applications accepted. *Expenses:* Tuition, state resident: full-time $2640. Required fees: $8282. One-time fee: $357 full-time. *Financial support:* In 2010–11, 4 fellowships with full tuition reimbursements (averaging $11,024 per year), 167 research assistantships with full tuition reimbursements (averaging $17,669 per year), 54 teaching assistantships with full tuition reimbursements (averaging $9,475 per year) were awarded; career-related internships or fieldwork, Federal Work-Study, institutionally sponsored loans, scholarships/grants, traineeships, health care benefits, tuition waivers (full), and unspecified assistantships also available. Financial award applicants required to submit FAFSA. *Faculty research:* Artificial intelligence, robotics, computer vision, and wearable computing; autonomous and multiagent systems; information retrieval, data mining and machine learning; networking, distributed systems and security. *Unit head:* Dr. David Smith, Graduate Program Director, 413-545-3640, Fax: 413-545-1249. *Application contact:* Jean M. Ames, Supervisor of Admissions, 413-545-0721, Fax: 413-577-0010, E-mail: gradadm@grad.umass.edu.

University of Massachusetts Boston, Office of Graduate Studies, College of Science and Mathematics, Program in Computer Science, Boston, MA 02125-3393. Offers MS, PhD. Part-time and evening/weekend programs available. *Degree requirements:* For master's, comprehensive exam, thesis optional, capstone final project; for doctorate, comprehensive exam, thesis/dissertation, oral exams. *Entrance requirements:* For master's and doctorate, GRE General Test, minimum GPA of 3.0. *Faculty research:* Queuing theory, database design theory, computer networks, theory of database query languages, real-time systems.

University of Massachusetts Dartmouth, Graduate School, College of Engineering, Program in Computer Science, North Dartmouth, MA 02747-2300. Offers computer networks and distributed systems (Postbaccalaureate Certificate); computer science (MS); computer systems (Postbaccalaureate Certificate); software development and design (Postbaccalaureate Certificate). Part-time programs available. Postbaccalaureate distance learning degree programs offered. *Faculty:* 9 full-time (2 women), 2 part-time/adjunct (0 women). *Students:* 27 full-time (9 women), 32 part-time (5 women), 43 international. Average age 26. 90 applicants, 87% accepted, 16 enrolled. In 2010, 19 master's awarded. *Degree requirements:* For master's, thesis or alternative. *Entrance requirements:* For master's, GRE General Test, 3 letters of

CACS—THE CENTER FOR ADVANCED COMPUTER STUDIES
UNIVERSITY OF LOUISIANA AT LAFAYETTE

Contact:

Dr. Magdy A. Bayoumi, Director
Dr. Anthony Maida, Graduate Coordinator
The Center for Advanced Computer Studies (CACS)
University of Louisiana at Lafayette
301 East Lewis Street, OLVR 201D
Lafayette, LA 70503
E-mail: info@cacs.louisiana.edu
http://www.cacs.louisiana.edu

recommendation. Additional exam requirements/recommendations for international students: Required—TOEFL (minimum score 500 paper-based). *Application deadline:* For fall admission, 6/30 priority date for domestic students, 4/30 priority date for international students; for spring admission, 11/15 priority date for domestic students, 9/15 priority date for international students. Applications are processed on a rolling basis. Application fee: $35 ($55 for international students). Electronic applications accepted. *Expenses:* Tuition, state resident: full-time $2071; part-time $86 per credit. Tuition, nonresident: full-time $8099; part-time $337 per credit. Required fees: $9446; $394 per credit. One-time fee: $75. Part-time tuition and fees vary according to class time, course load, degree level and reciprocity agreements. *Financial support:* In 2010–11, 5 research assistantships with full tuition reimbursements (averaging $9,246 per year), 6 teaching assistantships with full tuition reimbursements (averaging $4,896 per year) were awarded; Federal Work-Study and unspecified assistantships also available. Support available to part-time students. Financial award application deadline: 3/1; financial award applicants required to submit FAFSA. *Faculty research:* Self-organizing feature maps, location-based services, brain modeling, software engineering, multi-agent systems. Total annual research expenditures: $387,292. *Unit head:* Dr. Shelley Zhang, Director, 508-999-8294, Fax: 508-999-9144, E-mail: x2zhang@umassd.edu. *Application contact:* Elan Turcotte-Shamski, Graduate Admissions Officer, 508-999-8604, Fax: 508-999-8183, E-mail: graduate@umassd.edu.

University of Massachusetts Lowell, College of Arts and Sciences, Department of Computer Science, Lowell, MA 01854-2881. Offers MS, PhD, Sc D. Part-time programs available. *Degree requirements:* For master's, thesis optional; for doctorate, thesis/dissertation. *Entrance requirements:* For master's and doctorate, GRE General Test. *Faculty research:* Networks, multimedia systems, human-computer interaction, graphics and visualization databases.

University of Memphis, Graduate School, College of Arts and Sciences, Department of Computer Science, Memphis, TN 38152. Offers applied computer science (MS); computer science (MS, PhD). *Faculty:* 15 full-time (3 women), 1 part-time/adjunct (0 women). *Students:* 62 full-time (20 women), 28 part-time (5 women); includes 11 minority (7 Black or African American, non-Hispanic/Latino; 1 Asian, non-Hispanic/Latino; 3 Two or more races, non-Hispanic/Latino), 67 international. Average age 28. 84 applicants, 40% accepted, 22 enrolled. In 2010, 10 master's, 1 doctorate awarded. *Degree requirements:* For master's, comprehensive exam, thesis; for doctorate, comprehensive exam, thesis/dissertation. *Entrance requirements:* For master's and doctorate, GRE, letters of recommendation. Additional exam requirements/recommendations for international students: Required—TOEFL (minimum score 550 paper-based; 210 computer-based; 80 iBT). Application fee: $35 ($60 for international students). *Financial support:* In 2010–11, 9 students received support; research assistantships with full tuition reimbursements available, teaching assistantships with full tuition reimbursements available, Federal Work-Study, scholarships/grants, and unspecified assistantships available. Financial award application deadline: 2/15; financial award applicants required to submit FAFSA. *Faculty research:* Network security, biomolecular and distributed computing, wireless sensor networks, artificial intelligence. *Unit head:* Dr. Sajjan Shiva, Chair, 901-678-5667, Fax: 901-678-2480, E-mail: info@cs.memphis.edu. *Application contact:* Dr. David Lin, Graduate Studies Coordinator, 901-678-3135, E-mail: davidlin@memphis.edu.

University of Memphis, Graduate School, College of Arts and Sciences, Department of Mathematical Sciences, Memphis, TN 38152. Offers applied mathematics (MS); applied statistics (PhD); bioinformatics (MS); computer science (PhD); computer sciences (MS); mathematics (MS, PhD); statistics (MS, PhD). Part-time programs available. *Faculty:* 19 full-time (4 women), 3 part-time/adjunct (0 women). *Students:* 38 full-time (12 women), 21 part-time (12 women); includes 8 minority (5 Black or African American, non-Hispanic/Latino; 2 Asian, non-Hispanic/Latino; 1 Hispanic/Latino), 25 international. Average age 34. 49 applicants, 55% accepted, 9 enrolled. In 2010, 6 master's, 5 doctorates awarded. Terminal master's awarded for partial completion of doctoral program. *Degree requirements:* For master's, comprehensive exam; for doctorate, one foreign language, thesis/dissertation, oral exams. *Entrance requirements:* For master's and doctorate, GRE General Test, minimum GPA of 2.5. Additional exam requirements/recommendations for international students: Required—TOEFL (minimum score 550 paper-based; 210 computer-based). *Application deadline:* For fall admission, 8/1 for domestic students, 5/1 priority date for international students; for spring admission, 12/1 for domestic students, 9/1 priority date for international students. Applications are processed on a rolling basis. Application fee: $35 ($60 for international students). Electronic applications accepted. *Financial support:* In 2010–11, 22 students received support; fellowships with full tuition reimbursements available, research assistantships with full tuition reimbursements available, teaching assistantships with full tuition reimbursements available, career-related internships or fieldwork, Federal Work-Study, scholarships/grants, and unspecified assistantships available. Financial award application deadline: 2/15; financial award applicants required to submit FAFSA. *Faculty research:* Combinatorics, ergodic theory, graph theory, Ramsey theory, applied statistics. *Unit head:* Dr. James E. Jamison, Chairman, 901-678-2482, Fax: 901-678-2480, E-mail: jjamison@memphis.edu. *Application contact:* Dr. Anna Kaminska, Coordinator of Graduate Studies, 901-678-2494, Fax: 901-678-2480.

University of Miami, Graduate School, College of Arts and Sciences, Department of Computer Science, Coral Gables, FL 33124. Offers MS, PhD. Part-time programs available. Postbaccalaureate distance learning degree programs offered (no on-campus study). *Degree requirements:* For master's, comprehensive exam (for some programs), thesis. *Entrance requirements:* For master's, GRE. Additional exam requirements/recommendations for international students: Required—TOEFL. Electronic applications accepted. *Faculty research:* Algorithm engineering, automated reasoning, computer graphics, cryptography, security network.

University of Michigan, Horace H. Rackham School of Graduate Studies, College of Engineering, Department of Computer Science and Engineering, Ann Arbor, MI 48109. Offers MS, MSE, PhD. *Students:* 237 full-time (29 women), 5 part-time (0 women). 977 applicants, 20% accepted, 81 enrolled. In 2010, 69 master's, 21 doctorates awarded. *Expenses:* Tuition, state resident: full-time $17,784; part-time $1116 per credit hour. Tuition, nonresident: full-time $35,944; part-time $2125 per credit hour. International tuition: $35,994 full-time. Required fees: $95 per semester. Tuition and fees vary according to course load, degree level and program. *Faculty research:* Solid state electronics and optics; communications, control, signal process; sensors and integrated circuitry, others; software systems; artificial intelligence; hardware systems. *Unit head:* Prof. John Laird, Interim Department Chair, 734-764-8504, Fax: 734-763-1503, E-mail: laird@umich.edu. *Application contact:* Dawn Freysinger, Graduate Programs Coordinator, 734-647-1807, Fax: 734-763-1503, E-mail: dawnf@umich.edu.

University of Michigan, Horace H. Rackham School of Graduate Studies, College of Engineering, Department of Electrical Engineering and Computer Science, Ann Arbor, MI 48109. Offers MS, MSE, PhD. *Students:* 480 full-time (59 women), 9 part-time (0 women). 1,551 applicants, 29% accepted, 213 enrolled. In 2010, 104 master's, 33 doctorates awarded. *Expenses:* Tuition, state resident: full-time $17,784; part-time $1116 per credit hour. Tuition, nonresident: full-time $35,944; part-time $2125 per credit hour. International tuition: $35,994 full-time. Required fees: $95 per semester. Tuition and fees vary according to course load, degree level and program. *Faculty research:* Solid state electronics and optics; communications, control, signal process; sensors and integrated circuitry, others; software systems; artificial intelligence; hardware systems. *Unit head:* Prof. Khalil Najafi, Chair, 734-647-7010, Fax: 734-647-7009, E-mail: najafi@umich.edu. *Application contact:* Beth Stalnaker, Graduate Coordinator, 734-647-1758, Fax: 734-763-1503, E-mail: beths@umich.edu.

University of Michigan–Dearborn, College of Engineering and Computer Science, Department of Computer and Information Science, Dearborn, MI 48128-1491. Offers MS. Part-time and evening/weekend programs available. Postbaccalaureate distance learning degree programs offered (minimal on-campus study). *Faculty:* 13 full-time (1 woman), 4 part-time/adjunct (0 women). *Students:* 16 full-time (9 women), 35 part-time (7 women); includes 11 minority (1 Black or African American, non-Hispanic/Latino; 9 Asian, non-Hispanic/Latino; 1 Hispanic/Latino), 11 international. Average age 33. 35 applicants, 26% accepted, 9 enrolled. In 2010, 14

master's awarded. *Degree requirements:* For master's, thesis optional. *Entrance requirements:* For master's, bachelor's degree in mathematics, computer science, or engineering; minimum GPA of 3.0. Additional exam requirements/recommendations for international students: Required—TOEFL (minimum score 560 paper-based; 220 computer-based; 84 iBT). *Application deadline:* For fall admission, 6/15 priority date for domestic students, 4/1 for international students; for winter admission, 10/15 priority date for domestic students, 8/1 for international students; for spring admission, 2/15 priority date for domestic students, 12/1 for international students. Application fee: $60 ($75 for international students). *Financial support:* In 2010–11, 3 research assistantships with full and partial tuition reimbursements (averaging $11,961 per year) were awarded; career-related internships or fieldwork also available. Financial award application deadline: 4/1; financial award applicants required to submit FAFSA. *Faculty research:* Information systems, geometric modeling, networks, databases. Total annual research expenditures: $54,056. *Unit head:* Dr. William I. Grosky, Chair, 313-583-6424, Fax: 313-593-4256, E-mail: wgrosky@umich.edu. *Application contact:* Katherine R. Markotan, Intermediate Academic Records Assistant, 313-436-9145, Fax: 313-593-4256, E-mail: tabatha@umd.umich.edu.

University of Michigan–Flint, College of Arts and Sciences, Program in Computer and Information Systems, Flint, MI 48502-1950. Offers computer science and information systems (MS). Part-time programs available. *Degree requirements:* For master's, thesis or alternative. *Entrance requirements:* For master's, minimum undergraduate GPA of 3.0. Additional exam requirements/recommendations for international students: Required—TOEFL (minimum score 560 paper-based; 220 computer-based; 84 iBT), IELTS (minimum score 6.5). *Expenses:* Contact institution.

University of Minnesota, Duluth, Graduate School, Swenson College of Science and Engineering, Department of Computer Science, Duluth, MN 55812-2496. Offers MS. Part-time programs available. *Entrance requirements:* For master's, GRE General Test, minimum GPA of 3.0. Additional exam requirements/recommendations for international students: Required—TOEFL (minimum score 550 paper-based; 213 computer-based). Electronic applications accepted. *Faculty research:* Information retrieval, artificial intelligence, machine learning, parallel/distributed computing, graphics.

University of Minnesota, Twin Cities Campus, Graduate School, Scientific Computation Program, Minneapolis, MN 55455-0213. Offers MS, PhD. Part-time programs available. *Degree requirements:* For master's, thesis; for doctorate, thesis/dissertation. *Entrance requirements:* For doctorate, GRE General Test. Additional exam requirements/recommendations for international students: Required—TOEFL (minimum score 550 paper-based; 213 computer-based; 79 iBT), IELTS (minimum score 6.5). Electronic applications accepted. *Faculty research:* Parallel computations, quantum mechanical dynamics, computational materials science, computational fluid dynamics, computational neuroscience.

University of Minnesota, Twin Cities Campus, Institute of Technology, Department of Computer Science and Engineering, Minneapolis, MN 55455-0213. Offers computer and information sciences (MCIS, MS, PhD). Part-time programs available. Terminal master's awarded for partial completion of doctoral program. *Degree requirements:* For doctorate, thesis/dissertation. *Entrance requirements:* For master's and doctorate, GRE General Test. *Faculty research:* Software systems, numerical analysis, theory, artificial intelligence.

University of Missouri, Graduate School, College of Engineering, Department of Computer Science, Columbia, MO 65211. Offers MS, PhD. Part-time programs available. *Degree requirements:* For doctorate, thesis/dissertation. *Entrance requirements:* For master's, GRE General Test, minimum GPA of 3.0; for doctorate, GRE General Test. Additional exam requirements/recommendations for international students: Required—TOEFL (minimum score 577 paper-based; 233 computer-based; 90 iBT).

See Display on next page and Close-Up on page 335.

University of Missouri–Kansas City, School of Computing and Engineering, Kansas City, MO 64110-2499. Offers civil engineering (MS); computer and electrical engineering (PhD); computer science (MS), including bioinformatics, software engineering, telecommunications networking; computer science and informatics (PhD); computing (PhD); electrical engineering (MS); engineering (PhD); mechanical engineering (MS); telecommunications (PhD). PhD (interdisciplinary) offered through the School of Graduate Studies. Part-time programs available. *Faculty:* 36 full-time (5 women), 21 part-time/adjunct (0 women). *Students:* 160 full-time (32 women), 194 part-time (41 women); includes 21 minority (5 Black or African American, non-Hispanic/Latino; 9 Asian, non-Hispanic/Latino; 6 Hispanic/Latino; 1 Two or more races, non-Hispanic/Latino), 273 international. Average age 25. 440 applicants, 55% accepted, 104 enrolled. In 2010, 135 master's awarded. *Degree requirements:* For doctorate, thesis/dissertation. *Entrance requirements:* For master's, GRE General Test, minimum GPA of 3.0, 3 letters of recommendation from professors; for doctorate, GRE General Test, minimum GPA of 3.5. Additional exam requirements/recommendations for international students: Required—TOEFL (minimum score 550 paper-based; 213 computer-based; 80 iBT). *Application deadline:* For fall admission, 1/15 priority date for domestic students, 1/15 for international students. Applications are processed on a rolling basis. Application fee: $45 ($50 for international students). *Expenses:* Tuition, state resident: full-time $5522.40; part-time $306.80 per credit hour. Tuition, nonresident: full-time $7128; part-time $792 per credit hour. Required fees: $261.15 per term. *Financial support:* In 2010–11, 35 research assistantships with partial tuition reimbursements (averaging $14,340 per year), 20 teaching assistantships with partial tuition reimbursements (averaging $13,351 per year) were awarded; career-related internships or fieldwork, Federal Work-Study, scholarships/grants, tuition waivers (partial), and unspecified assistantships also available. Support available to part-time students. Financial award application deadline: 3/1; financial award applicants required to submit FAFSA. *Faculty research:* Algorithms, bioinformatics and medical informatics, biomechanics/biomaterials, civil engineering materials, networking and telecommunications, thermal science. Total annual research expenditures: $1.1 million. *Unit head:* Dr. Kevin Z. Truman, Dean, 816-235-2399, Fax: 816-235-5159. *Application contact:* Dr. Kevin Z. Truman, Dean, 816-235-2399, Fax: 816-235-5159.

University of Missouri–St. Louis, College of Arts and Sciences, Department of Mathematics and Computer Science, St. Louis, MO 63121. Offers applied mathematics (PhD), including computer science, mathematics; computer science (MS); mathematics (MA). Part-time and evening/weekend programs available. *Faculty:* 16 full-time (2 women), 1 part-time/adjunct (0 women). *Students:* 21 full-time (8 women), 43 part-time (13 women); includes 9 minority (5 Black or African American, non-Hispanic/Latino; 2 American Indian or Alaska Native, non-Hispanic/Latino; 2 Asian, non-Hispanic/Latino), 17 international. Average age 32. 98 applicants, 49% accepted, 12 enrolled. In 2010, 18 master's awarded. *Degree requirements:* For master's, thesis optional; for doctorate, thesis/dissertation. *Entrance requirements:* For master's, GRE (for TA assistantships), 2 letters of recommendation; C programming, C++ or Java (for computer science); for doctorate, GRE General Test, 3 letters of recommendation. Additional exam requirements/recommendations for international students: Required—TOEFL (minimum score 550 paper-based; 213 computer-based). *Application deadline:* For fall admission, 7/1 priority date for domestic and international students; for spring admission, 12/1 priority date for domestic and international students. Applications are processed on a rolling basis. Application fee: $35 ($40 for international students). Electronic applications accepted. *Expenses:* Tuition, state resident: full-time $5522; part-time $306.80 per credit hour. Tuition, nonresident: full-time $14,253; part-time $792.10 per credit hour. Required fees: $658; $49 per credit hour. One-time fee: $12. Tuition and fees vary according to program. *Financial support:* In 2010–11, 5 research assistantships with full and partial tuition reimbursements (averaging $10,845 per year), 7 teaching assistantships with full and partial tuition reimbursements (averaging $13,285 per year) were awarded; fellowships with full tuition reimbursements also available. Financial award applicants required to submit FAFSA. *Faculty research:* Statistics, algebra, analysis. *Unit head:* Dr. Shiying Zhao, Director of Graduate Studies, 314-516-5741, Fax: 314-516-5400, E-mail: zhao@arch.cs.umsl.edu. *Application contact:* 314-516-5458, Fax: 314-516-6996, E-mail: gradadm@umsl.edu.

Computer Science

The University of Montana, Graduate School, College of Arts and Sciences, Department of Computer Science, Missoula, MT 59812-0002. Offers MS. Part-time programs available. *Degree requirements:* For master's, project or thesis. *Entrance requirements:* For master's, GRE General Test. Additional exam requirements/recommendations for international students: Required—TOEFL (minimum score 525 paper-based; 197 computer-based). *Faculty research:* Parallel and distributed systems, neural networks, genetic algorithms, machine learning, data visualization, artificial intelligence.

University of Nebraska at Omaha, Graduate Studies, College of Information Science and Technology, Department of Computer Science, Omaha, NE 68182. Offers MA, MS. Part-time and evening/weekend programs available. *Faculty:* 14 full-time (2 women). *Students:* 22 full-time (2 women), 51 part-time (6 women); includes 2 minority (1 Black or African American, non-Hispanic/Latino; 1 Asian, non-Hispanic/Latino), 28 international. Average age 38. 78 applicants, 51% accepted, 22 enrolled. In 2010, 22 master's awarded. *Degree requirements:* For master's, comprehensive exam, thesis (for some programs). *Entrance requirements:* For master's, GRE General Test, minimum GPA of 3.0, course work in computer science. Additional exam requirements/recommendations for international students: Required—TOEFL (minimum score 500 paper-based; 173 computer-based; 61 iBT). *Application deadline:* For fall admission, 7/1 priority date for domestic students; for spring admission, 11/15 priority date for domestic students. Applications are processed on a rolling basis. Application fee: $45. Electronic applications accepted. *Financial support:* In 2010–11, 31 students received support; research assistantships, teaching assistantships, Federal Work-Study, institutionally sponsored loans, scholarships/grants, tuition waivers (full), and unspecified assistantships available. Support available to part-time students. Financial award application deadline: 3/1; financial award applicants required to submit FAFSA. *Unit head:* Dr. Qiuming Zhu, Chairperson, 402-554-2423. *Application contact:* Carla Frakes, Information Contact, 402-554-2423.

University of Nebraska–Lincoln, Graduate College, College of Arts and Sciences and College of Engineering, Department of Computer Science and Engineering, Lincoln, NE 68588. Offers bioinformatics (MS, PhD); computer engineering (MS, PhD); computer science (MS, PhD); information technology (PhD). *Degree requirements:* For master's, thesis optional; for doctorate, comprehensive exam, thesis/dissertation. *Entrance requirements:* For master's and doctorate, GRE General Test. Additional exam requirements/recommendations for international students: Required—TOEFL (minimum score 600 paper-based; 250 computer-based). Electronic applications accepted. *Faculty research:* Software engineering, geo- and bio-informatics, scientific computation, secure communication.

University of Nevada, Las Vegas, Graduate College, Howard R. Hughes College of Engineering, School of Computer Science, Las Vegas, NV 89154-4019. Offers MS, PhD. Part-time programs available. *Faculty:* 13 full-time (2 women). *Students:* 22 full-time (9 women), 26 part-time (3 women); includes 9 minority (1 American Indian or Alaska Native, non-Hispanic/Latino; 4 Hispanic/Latino; 4 Two or more races, non-Hispanic/Latino), 24 international. Average age 27. 29 applicants, 93% accepted, 17 enrolled. In 2010, 14 master's awarded. *Degree requirements:* For master's, comprehensive exam, thesis optional, project; for doctorate, comprehensive exam, thesis/dissertation. *Entrance requirements:* For master's, GRE General Test; for doctorate, GRE General Test, GRE Subject Test (computer science). Additional exam requirements/recommendations for international students: Required—TOEFL (minimum score 550 paper-based; 213 computer-based; 80 iBT), IELTS (minimum score 7). *Application deadline:* For fall admission, 6/1 priority date for domestic and international students; for spring admission, 10/1 priority date for domestic and international students. Applications are processed on a rolling basis. Application fee: $60 ($95 for international students). Electronic applications accepted. *Expenses:* Tuition, area resident: Part-time $239.50 per credit. Tuition, state resident: part-time $239.50 per credit. Tuition, nonresident: part-time $503 per credit. Required fees: $108 per semester. Tuition and fees vary according to course load, program and reciprocity agreements. *Financial support:* In 2010–11, 15 students received support, including 15 teaching assistantships with partial tuition reimbursements available (averaging $10,000 per year); institutionally sponsored loans, scholarships/grants, health care benefits, and unspecified assistantships also available. Financial award application deadline: 3/1. *Faculty research:* Algorithms, computer graphics, databases and data mining, distributed systems and networks, parallel algorithms. Total annual research expenditures: $296,639. *Unit head:* Dr. John Minor, Director/ Associate Professor, 702-895-3715, Fax: 702-895-2639, E-mail: minor@cs.unlv.edu. *Application contact:* Graduate College Admissions Evaluator, 702-895-3320, Fax: 702-895-4180, E-mail: gradcollege@unlv.edu.

University of Nevada, Reno, Graduate School, College of Engineering, Department of Computer Science and Engineering, Program in Computer Science, Reno, NV 89557. Offers MS. *Degree requirements:* For master's, thesis optional. *Entrance requirements:* For master's, GRE General Test. Additional exam requirements/recommendations for international students: Required—TOEFL (minimum score 500 paper-based; 173 computer-based; 61 iBT), IELTS (minimum score 6). Electronic applications accepted. *Expenses:* Tuition, state resident: full-time $2219; part-time $246 per credit. Tuition, nonresident: part-time $510 per credit. International tuition: $9009 full-time. Required fees: $59 per term. One-time fee: $101. Tuition and fees vary according to course load. *Faculty research:* Evolutionary computing systems, computer vision/virtual reality, software engineering.

University of Nevada, Reno, Graduate School, College of Engineering, Department of Computer Science and Engineering, Program in Computer Science and Engineering, Reno, NV 89557. Offers PhD. *Degree requirements:* For doctorate, thesis/dissertation. *Entrance requirements:* For doctorate, GRE General Test. Additional exam requirements/recommendations for international students: Required—TOEFL (minimum score 500 paper-based; 173 computer-based; 61 iBT), IELTS (minimum score 6). Electronic applications accepted. *Expenses:* Tuition, state resident: full-time $2219; part-time $246 per credit. Tuition, nonresident: part-time $510 per credit. International tuition: $9009 full-time. Required fees: $59 per term. One-time fee: $101. Tuition and fees vary according to course load. *Faculty research:* Evolutionary computing systems, computer vision/virtual reality, software engineering.

University of New Brunswick Fredericton, School of Graduate Studies, Faculty of Computer Science, Fredericton, NB E3B 5A3, Canada. Offers M Sc CS, PhD. Part-time programs available. *Faculty:* 25 full-time (6 women), 10 part-time/adjunct (0 women). *Students:* 72 full-time (16 women), 18 part-time (4 women). In 2010, 13 master's, 3 doctorates awarded. *Degree requirements:* For master's, thesis; for doctorate, comprehensive exam, thesis/dissertation, qualifying exam. *Entrance requirements:* For master's, minimum GPA of 3.0; undergraduate degree with sufficient computer science background; for doctorate, research-based master's degree in computer science or related area. Additional exam requirements/recommendations for international students: Required—TWE (minimum score 4), TOEFL (minimum score 580 paper-based; 237 computer-based) or IELTS (minimum score 7). *Application deadline:* For fall admission, 3/1 priority date for domestic students. Application fee: $50 Canadian dollars. Electronic applications accepted. *Expenses:* Tuition, area resident: Full-time $3708; part-time $927 per term. International tuition: $6300 full-time. Required fees: $50 per term. *Financial support:* In 2010–11, 53 research assistantships, 27 teaching assistantships were awarded. *Faculty research:* Artificial consciousness and intelligence, automated reasoning, biomedical engineering, cloud computing, computer-aided drug design, cryptography, data structures, embedded systems, graph algorithms, health informatics, intelligent adaptive systems, legacy system modernization, machine learning and data mining, multicore computing, Net-centric computing, optimization, parallel and distributed computing, privacy and security, reconfigurable computing, sensor netwks, wireless communication. *Unit head:* Dr. Eric Aubanel, Director of Graduate Studies, 506-458-7268, Fax: 506-453-3566, E-mail: aubanel@unb.ca. *Application contact:* Jodi O'Neill, Graduate Secretary, 506-458-7285, Fax: 506-453-3566, E-mail: jodio@unb.ca.

University of New Hampshire, Graduate School, College of Engineering and Physical Sciences, Department of Computer Science, Durham, NH 03824. Offers computer science (MS,

PhD); software systems engineering (Postbaccalaureate Certificate). Part-time and evening/weekend programs available. *Faculty:* 10 full-time (2 women). *Students:* 41 full-time (12 women), 56 part-time (10 women); includes 5 minority (3 Asian, non-Hispanic/Latino; 2 Hispanic/Latino), 24 international. Average age 33. 93 applicants, 75% accepted, 45 enrolled. In 2010, 8 master's, 2 doctorates, 1 other advanced degree awarded. *Degree requirements:* For master's, thesis or alternative; for doctorate, thesis/dissertation. *Entrance requirements:* For master's and doctorate, GRE General Test. Additional exam requirements/recommendations for international students: Required—TOEFL (minimum score 550 paper-based; 213 computer-based; 80 iBT). *Application deadline:* For fall admission, 4/1 priority date for domestic students, 4/1 for international students; for spring admission, 12/1 for domestic students. Applications are processed on a rolling basis. Application fee: $65. Electronic applications accepted. *Financial support:* In 2010–11, 41 students received support, including 1 fellowship, 11 research assistantships, 10 teaching assistantships; career-related internships or fieldwork, Federal Work-Study, scholarships/grants, and tuition waivers (full and partial) also available. Support available to part-time students. *Faculty research:* Programming languages, compiler design, parallel algorithms, computer graphics, artificial intelligence. *Unit head:* Dr. Philip J. Hatcher, Chairperson, 603-862-2678. *Application contact:* Carolyn Kirkpatrick, Administrative Assistant, 603-862-3778, E-mail: office@cs.unh.edu.

University of New Haven, Graduate School, Henry C. Lee College of Criminal Justice and Forensic Sciences, Program in Criminal Justice, West Haven, CT 06516-1916. Offers crime analysis (MS); criminal justice (PhD); criminal justice management (MS); forensic computer investigation (MS, Certificate); forensic psychology (MS); victim advocacy and services management (Certificate); victimology (MS). Part-time and evening/weekend programs available. *Students:* 47 full-time (29 women), 42 part-time (25 women); includes 17 Black or African American, non-Hispanic/Latino; 5 Hispanic/Latino, 6 international. Average age 29. 95 applicants, 96% accepted, 54 enrolled. In 2010, 12 master's, 12 other advanced degrees awarded. *Degree requirements:* For master's, thesis or alternative. *Entrance requirements:* Additional exam requirements/recommendations for international students: Required—TOEFL (minimum score 520 paper-based; 190 computer-based; 70 iBT), IELTS (minimum score 5.5). *Application deadline:* For fall admission, 5/31 for international students; for winter admission, 10/15 for international students; for spring admission, 1/15 for international students. Applications are processed on a rolling basis. Application fee: $50. Electronic applications accepted. *Financial support:* Research assistantships with partial tuition reimbursements, teaching assistantships with partial tuition reimbursements, career-related internships or fieldwork, Federal Work-Study, scholarships/grants, tuition waivers, and unspecified assistantships available. Support available to part-time students. Financial award applicants required to submit FAFSA. *Unit head:* Dr. James J. Cassidy, Coordinator, 203-932-7374. *Application contact:* Eloise Gormley, Director of Graduate Admissions, 203-932-7449, Fax: 203-932-7137, E-mail: gradinfo@newhaven.edu.

University of New Haven, Graduate School, Tagliatela College of Engineering, Program in Computer and Information Science, West Haven, CT 06516-1916. Offers computer science (MS, Certificate), including advanced applications (MS), computer applications (Certificate), computer programming (Certificate), computer systems (MS), computing (Certificate), database and information systems (MS), network administration (Certificate), network systems (MS), software engineering and development (MS). Part-time and evening/weekend programs available. *Students:* 54 full-time (12 women), 25 part-time (4 women); includes 1 Black or African American, non-Hispanic/Latino; 3 Asian, non-Hispanic/Latino, 51 international. Average age 28. 204 applicants, 100% accepted, 40 enrolled. In 2010, 19 master's, 1 other advanced degree awarded. *Degree requirements:* For master's, thesis or alternative. *Entrance requirements:* Additional exam requirements/recommendations for international students: Required—TOEFL (minimum score 520 paper-based; 190 computer-based; 70 iBT); Recommended—IELTS (minimum score 5.5). *Application deadline:* For fall admission, 5/31 for international students; for winter admission, 10/15 for international students; for spring admission, 1/15 for international students. Applications are processed on a rolling basis. Application fee: $50. Electronic applications accepted. *Financial support:* Research assistantships with partial tuition reimbursements, teaching assistantships with partial tuition reimbursements, career-related internships or fieldwork, Federal Work-Study, scholarships/grants, tuition waivers, and unspecified assistantships available. Support available to part-time students. Financial award applicants required to submit FAFSA. *Unit head:* Dr. Tahany Fergany, Coordinator, 203-932-7067. *Application contact:* Eloise Gormley, Director of Graduate Admissions, 203-932-7449, Fax: 203-932-7137, E-mail: gradinfo@newhaven.edu.

University of New Mexico, Graduate School, School of Engineering, Department of Computer Science, Albuquerque, NM 87131-2039. Offers MS, PhD. Part-time programs available. *Faculty:* 28 full-time (5 women), 5 part-time/adjunct (2 women). *Students:* 77 full-time (18 women), 31 part-time (3 women); includes 1 Black or African American, non-Hispanic/Latino; 3 Asian, non-Hispanic/Latino; 3 Hispanic/Latino, 45 international. Average age 30. 105 applicants, 51% accepted, 27 enrolled. In 2010, 28 master's, 7 doctorates awarded. Terminal master's awarded for partial completion of doctoral program. *Degree requirements:* For master's, thesis or alternative; for doctorate, comprehensive exam, thesis/dissertation. *Entrance requirements:* For master's and doctorate, GRE General Test, minimum GPA of 3.0. Additional exam requirements/recommendations for international students: Required—TOEFL (minimum score 550 paper-based; 213 computer-based; 79 iBT), IELTS (minimum score 7). *Application deadline:* For fall admission, 1/15 for domestic students, 3/1 for international students; for spring admission, 8/1 for domestic and international students. Applications are processed on a rolling basis. Application fee: $50. Electronic applications accepted. *Expenses:* Tuition, state resident: full-time $5991; part-time $251 per credit hour. Tuition, nonresident: full-time $14,405; part-time $800.20 per credit hour. Tuition and fees vary according to course level, course load, program and reciprocity agreements. *Financial support:* In 2010–11, 67 students received support, including 1 fellowship with tuition reimbursement available (averaging $1,000 per year), 52 research assistantships with tuition reimbursements available (averaging $16,674 per year), 15 teaching assistantships with tuition reimbursements available (averaging $7,424 per year); career-related internships or fieldwork, scholarships/grants, and health care benefits also available. Financial award application deadline: 1/15; financial award applicants required to submit FAFSA. *Faculty research:* Artificial life, genetic algorithms, computer security, complexity theory, interactive computer graphics, operating systems and networking, biology and computation, machine learning, automated reasoning, quantum computation. Total annual research expenditures: $2.4 million. *Unit head:* Dr. Stephanie Forrest, Chairperson, 505-277-3112, Fax: 505-277-6927, E-mail: forrest@cs.unm.edu. *Application contact:* Lynne Jacobsen, Coordinator, Program Advisement, 505-277-3112, Fax: 505-277-6927, E-mail: ljake@cs.unm.edu.

University of New Orleans, Graduate School, College of Sciences, Department of Computer Science, New Orleans, LA 70148. Offers MS. *Entrance requirements:* For master's, GRE General Test. Additional exam requirements/recommendations for international students: Required—TOEFL (minimum score 550 paper-based; 213 computer-based; 79 iBT). Electronic applications accepted.

The University of North Carolina at Chapel Hill, Graduate School, College of Arts and Sciences, Department of Computer Science, Chapel Hill, NC 27599. Offers MS, PhD. Part-time programs available. Postbaccalaureate distance learning degree programs offered. Terminal master's awarded for partial completion of doctoral program. *Degree requirements:* For master's, comprehensive exam, thesis or alternative, programming product; for doctorate, comprehensive exam, thesis/dissertation, programming product, teaching requirement. *Entrance requirements:* For master's and doctorate, GRE General Test, minimum GPA of 3.0. Additional exam requirements/recommendations for international students: Required—TOEFL (minimum score 575 paper-based; 233 computer-based). Electronic applications accepted. *Faculty research:* Bioinformatics, graphics, hardware, systems, theory.

See Display on next page and Close-Up on page 337.

The University of North Carolina at Charlotte, Graduate School, College of Computing and Informatics, Department of Computer Science, Charlotte, NC 28223-0001. Offers advance databases and knowledge discovery (Certificate); computer science (MS). Part-time programs available. *Faculty:* 24 full-time (7 women), 1 part-time/adjunct (0 women). *Students:* 120 full-time (32 women), 31 part-time (8 women); includes 9 minority (2 Black or African American, non-Hispanic/Latino; 5 Asian, non-Hispanic/Latino; 1 Hispanic/Latino; 1 Two or more races, non-Hispanic/Latino), 112 international. Average age 24. 292 applicants, 85% accepted, 69 enrolled. In 2010, 66 master's awarded. *Degree requirements:* For master's, thesis or alternative. *Entrance requirements:* For master's, GRE General Test, minimum GPA of 3.0 during previous 2 years, 2.8 overall. Additional exam requirements/recommendations for international students: Required—TOEFL (minimum score 557 paper-based; 220 computer-based; 83 iBT). *Application deadline:* For fall admission, 7/1 for domestic students, 5/1 for international students; for spring admission, 11/1 for domestic students, 10/1 for international students. Applications are processed on a rolling basis. Application fee: $55. Electronic applications accepted. *Expenses:* Tuition, state resident: full-time $3464. Tuition, nonresident: full-time $14,297. Required fees: $2094. Tuition and fees vary according to course load. *Financial support:* In 2010–11, 57 students received support, including 1 fellowship (averaging $52,000 per year), 21 research assistantships (averaging $9,867 per year), 35 teaching assistantships (averaging $10,328 per year); career-related internships or fieldwork, Federal Work-Study, institutionally sponsored loans, scholarships/grants, and unspecified assistantships also available. Support available to part-time students. Financial award application deadline: 4/1; financial award applicants required to submit FAFSA. *Faculty research:* Visualization; visual analytics and computer graphics; intelligent and interactive systems; data mining theory, systems, and application; networked systems; computer game design. Total annual research expenditures: $3.1 million. *Unit head:* Dr. Larry F. Hodges, Chair, 704-687-8552, Fax: 704-687-3516, E-mail: lfhodges@uncc.edu. *Application contact:* Kathy B. Giddings, Director of Graduate Admissions, 704-687-3366, Fax: 704-687-3279, E-mail: gradadm@uncc.edu.

The University of North Carolina at Greensboro, Graduate School, College of Arts and Sciences, Department of Computer Science, Greensboro, NC 27412-5001. Offers MS.

The University of North Carolina Wilmington, College of Arts and Sciences, Program in Computer Science and Information Systems, Wilmington, NC 28403-3297. Offers MS. *Faculty:* 11 full-time (1 woman). *Students:* 18 full-time (3 women), 17 part-time (3 women); includes 1 Black or African American, non-Hispanic/Latino; 2 American Indian or Alaska Native, non-Hispanic/Latino; 3 Hispanic/Latino, 2 international. Average age 28. 17 applicants, 53% accepted, 7 enrolled. In 2010, 14 master's awarded. *Entrance requirements:* For master's, GMAT or GRE, 3 letters of recommendation, resume. *Application deadline:* For fall admission, 4/1 for domestic students; for spring admission, 11/1 for domestic students. Application fee: $45. *Financial support:* In 2010–11, 10 teaching assistantships were awarded. *Unit head:* Dr. Sridhar Narayan, Director, 910-962-3695, E-mail: narayans@uncw.edu. *Application contact:* Dr. Ron Vetter, Graduate Coordinator, 910-962-2160, Fax: 910-962-7457, E-mail: vetterv@uncw.edu.

University of North Dakota, Graduate School, John D. Odegard School of Aerospace Sciences, Department of Computer Science, Grand Forks, ND 58202. Offers MS, PhD. Part-time programs available. *Faculty:* 9 full-time (1 woman), 1 part-time/adjunct (0 women). *Students:* 19 full-time (7 women), 16 part-time (3 women); includes 5 minority (1 Black or African American, non-Hispanic/Latino; 3 Asian, non-Hispanic/Latino; 1 Hispanic/Latino), 20 international. Average age 28. 45 applicants, 60% accepted, 11 enrolled. In 2010, 1 master's awarded. *Degree requirements:* For master's, comprehensive exam, thesis or alternative. *Entrance requirements:* For master's, GRE General Test, minimum GPA of 3.0. Additional exam requirements/recommendations for international students: Required—TOEFL (minimum score 550 paper-based; 213 computer-based; 79 iBT), IELTS (minimum score 6.5). *Application deadline:* For fall admission, 8/1 priority date for domestic and international students; for spring admission, 12/1 priority date for domestic students, 9/1 priority date for international students. Applications are processed on a rolling basis. Application fee: $35. Electronic applications accepted. *Expenses:* Tuition, state resident: full-time $5857; part-time $306.74 per credit. Tuition, nonresident: full-time $15,666; part-time $729.77 per credit. Required fees: $53.42 per credit. Tuition and fees vary according to course load, program and reciprocity agreements. *Financial support:* In 2010–11, 19 students received support, including 7 research assistantships with full and partial tuition reimbursements available (averaging $6,654 per year), 9 teaching assistantships with full and partial tuition reimbursements available (averaging $8,367 per year); fellowships with full and partial tuition reimbursements available, Federal Work-Study, institutionally sponsored loans, scholarships/grants, health care benefits, tuition waivers (full and partial), and unspecified assistantships also available. Support available to part-time students. Financial award application deadline: 3/15; financial award applicants required to submit FAFSA. *Faculty research:* Operating systems, simulation, parallel computation, hypermedia, graph theory. Total annual research expenditures: $20,127. *Unit head:* Dr. Emanuel Grant, Graduate Director, 701-777-4133, Fax: 701-777-3330, E-mail: grante@cs.und.edu. *Application contact:* Staci Wells, Admissions Specialist, 701-777-0748, Fax: 701-777-3619, E-mail: staci.wells@gradschool.und.edu.

University of Northern British Columbia, Office of Graduate Studies, Prince George, BC V2N 4Z9, Canada. Offers business administration (Diploma); community health science (M Sc); disability management (MA); education (M Ed); first nations studies (MA); gender studies (MA); history (MA); interdisciplinary studies (MA); international studies (MA); mathematical, computer and physical sciences (M Sc); natural resources and environmental studies (M Sc, MA, MNRES, PhD); political science (MA); psychology (M Sc, PhD); social work (MSW). Part-time and evening/weekend programs available. Postbaccalaureate distance learning degree programs offered (no on-campus study). *Degree requirements:* For master's, thesis; for doctorate, thesis/dissertation. *Entrance requirements:* For master's, GRE, minimum B average in undergraduate course work; for doctorate, candidacy exam, minimum A average in graduate course work.

University of Northern Iowa, Graduate College, College of Natural Sciences, Department of Computer Science, Cedar Falls, IA 50614. Offers MS. *Students:* 9 full-time (1 woman), 7 part-time (2 women), 11 international. 23 applicants, 61% accepted, 4 enrolled. *Degree requirements:* For master's, comprehensive exam (for some programs), thesis (for some programs). *Entrance requirements:* For master's, GRE, minimum GPA of 3.0. Additional exam requirements/recommendations for international students: Required—TOEFL (minimum score 600 paper-based; 250 computer-based; 100 iBT). *Application deadline:* For fall admission, 8/1 priority date for domestic students. Applications are processed on a rolling basis. Application fee: $50 ($70 for international students). Electronic applications accepted. *Financial support:* Application deadline: 2/1. *Unit head:* Dr. Eugene Wallingford, Head, 319-273-2618, Fax: 319-273-7123, E-mail: wallingf@cs.uni.edu. *Application contact:* Laurie S. Russell, Record Analyst, 319-273-2623, Fax: 319-273-2885, E-mail: laurie.russell@uni.edu.

University of North Florida, College of Computing, Engineering, and Construction, School of Computing, Jacksonville, FL 32224. Offers computer science (MS); information systems (MS); software engineering (MS). Part-time programs available. *Faculty:* 15 full-time (4 women). *Students:* 12 full-time (4 women), 35 part-time (14 women); includes 5 Black or African American, non-Hispanic/Latino; 2 Asian, non-Hispanic/Latino; 2 Hispanic/Latino; 2 Two or more races, non-Hispanic/Latino, 14 international. Average age 32. 45 applicants, 58% accepted, 11 enrolled. In 2010, 5 master's awarded. *Degree requirements:* For master's, thesis. *Entrance requirements:* For master's, GRE General Test, minimum GPA of 3.0 in last 60 hours of course work. Additional exam requirements/recommendations for international students: Required—TOEFL (minimum score 500 paper-based; 173 computer-based; 61 iBT). *Application deadline:* For fall admission, 7/1 for domestic students, 5/1 for international students; for spring admission, 11/1 for domestic students, 10/1 for international students. Applications are processed on a rolling basis. Application fee: $30. Electronic applications accepted. *Expenses:* Tuition, state resident: full-time $7646.40; part-time $318.60 per credit hour. Tuition, nonresident: full-time $23,502; part-time $979.24 per credit hour. Required fees: $1208.88; $50.37 per credit hour.

Computer Science

Tuition and fees vary according to course load and program. *Financial support:* In 2010–11, 9 students received support, including 1 teaching assistantship (averaging $2,000 per year); Federal Work-Study, scholarships/grants, and unspecified assistantships also available. Financial award application deadline: 4/1; financial award applicants required to submit FAFSA. Total annual research expenditures: $62,830. *Unit head:* Dr. Neal Coulter, Dean, 904-620-1350, E-mail: ncoulter@unf.edu. *Application contact:* Lillith Richardson, Assistant Director, The Graduate School, 904-620-1360, Fax: 904-620-1362, E-mail: graduateschool@unf.edu.

University of North Texas, Toulouse Graduate School, College of Engineering, Department of Computer Science and Engineering, Denton, TX 76203-5017. Offers computer science (MS); computer science and engineering (PhD). Terminal master's awarded for partial completion of doctoral program. *Degree requirements:* For master's, comprehensive exam (for some programs), thesis (for some programs); for doctorate, comprehensive exam, thesis/dissertation. *Entrance requirements:* For master's, GRE General Test (minimum score 400 verbal, 700 quantitative, 600 analytical or 4.0), minimum GPA of 3.0; for doctorate, GRE General Test (minimum scores: Verbal 50th percentile, Quantitative 700, Analytical 600 or 4.5), minimum GPA of 3.5, 3 letters of recommendation. Additional exam requirements/recommendations for international students: Required—TOEFL (minimum score 550 paper-based; 213 computer-based; 79 iBT); Recommended—IELTS (minimum score 6.5). Electronic applications accepted. *Expenses:* Tuition, state resident: full-time $4298; part-time $239 per credit hour. Tuition, nonresident: full-time $10,782; part-time $549 per credit hour. Required fees: $1292; $270 per credit hour. *Financial support:* Fellowships with tuition reimbursements, research assistantships with tuition reimbursements, teaching assistantships with tuition reimbursements, career-related internships or fieldwork, Federal Work-Study, and institutionally sponsored loans available. Financial award application deadline: 4/1; financial award applicants required to submit FAFSA. *Faculty research:* Databases and data mining, computer architecture, cryptography, agent-oriented software engineering, graph theory, low power synthesis. *Application contact:* Graduate Program Coordinator, 940-565-2767, Fax: 940-565-2799, E-mail: armin.mikler@unt.edu.

University of Notre Dame, Graduate School, College of Engineering, Department of Computer Science and Engineering, Notre Dame, IN 46556. Offers MSCSE, PhD. Terminal master's awarded for partial completion of doctoral program. *Degree requirements:* For master's, comprehensive exam; for doctorate, thesis/dissertation, candidacy exam. *Entrance requirements:* For master's and doctorate, GRE General Test. Additional exam requirements/recommendations for international students: Required—TOEFL (minimum score 600 paper-based; 250 computer-based; 80 iBT). Electronic applications accepted. *Faculty research:* Algorithms and theory of computer science, artificial intelligence, behavior-based robotics, biometrics, computer vision.

University of Oklahoma, College of Engineering, School of Computer Science, Norman, OK 73019. Offers computer science (MS, PhD), including bioinformatics, general (MS), standard (PhD). *Faculty:* 17 full-time (3 women). *Students:* 63 full-time (12 women), 43 part-time (4 women); includes 4 minority (1 American Indian or Alaska Native, non-Hispanic/Latino; 3 Asian, non-Hispanic/Latino), 61 international. Average age 28. 64 applicants, 81% accepted, 15 enrolled. In 2010, 18 master's, 1 doctorate awarded. Terminal master's awarded for partial completion of doctoral program. *Degree requirements:* For master's, thesis optional, oral exams, qualifying exam; for doctorate, thesis/dissertation, general exam, qualifying exam. *Entrance requirements:* For master's and doctorate, GRE General Test. Additional exam requirements/recommendations for international students: Required—TOEFL (minimum score 550 paper-based; 250 computer-based; 79 iBT). *Application deadline:* For fall admission, 1/15 priority date for domestic students, 4/1 for international students; for spring admission, 11/1 for domestic students, 9/1 for international students. Applications are processed on a rolling basis. Application fee: $40 ($90 for international students). Electronic applications accepted. *Expenses:* Tuition, state resident: full-time $3892.80; part-time $162.20 per credit hour. Tuition, nonresident: full-time $14,167; part-time $590.30 per credit hour. Required fees: $2523.40; $94.60 per credit hour. Tuition and fees vary according to course load and degree level. *Financial support:* In 2010–11, 85 students received support, including 3 fellowships (averaging $3,000 per year), 16 research assistantships with partial tuition reimbursements available (averaging $15,006 per year), 16 teaching assistantships with partial tuition reimbursements available (averaging $14,116 per year); unspecified assistantships also available. Financial award application deadline: 3/1; financial award applicants required to submit FAFSA. *Faculty research:* Artificial intelligence and robotics, scientific computing, computer networks, high performance computing, computer architecture, database management, visual analytics, cryptography. Total annual research expenditures: $2.6 million. *Unit head:* Sridhar Radhakrishnan, Professor and Director, 405-325-4042, Fax: 405-325-4044, E-mail: sridhar@ou.edu. *Application contact:* Sridhar Radhakrishnan, Professor and Director, 405-325-4042, Fax: 405-325-4044, E-mail: sridhar@ou.edu.

University of Oregon, Graduate School, College of Arts and Sciences, Department of Computer and Information Science, Eugene, OR 97403. Offers MA, MS, PhD. Part-time programs available. Terminal master's awarded for partial completion of doctoral program. *Degree requirements:* For doctorate, thesis/dissertation. *Entrance requirements:* For master's and doctorate, GRE General Test, minimum GPA of 3.0. Additional exam requirements/recommendations for international students: Required—TOEFL. *Faculty research:* Artificial intelligence, graphics, natural-language processing, expert systems, operating systems.

University of Ottawa, Faculty of Graduate and Postdoctoral Studies, Faculty of Engineering, Ottawa-Carleton Institute for Computer Science, Ottawa, ON K1N 6N5, Canada. Offers MCS, PhD. MCS, PhD offered jointly with Carleton University. *Degree requirements:* For master's, thesis or alternative; for doctorate, comprehensive exam, thesis/dissertation, two seminars. *Entrance requirements:* For master's, honors degree or equivalent, minimum B average; for doctorate, minimum B+ average. Electronic applications accepted. *Faculty research:* Knowledge-based and intelligent systems, algorithms, parallel and distributed systems.

University of Pennsylvania, School of Engineering and Applied Science, Department of Computer and Information Science, Philadelphia, PA 19104. Offers MCIT, MSE, PhD. Part-time programs available. *Faculty:* 49 full-time (6 women), 7 part-time/adjunct (1 woman). *Students:* 260 full-time (55 women), 59 part-time (12 women); includes 3 Black or African American, non-Hispanic/Latino; 23 Asian, non-Hispanic/Latino; 3 Hispanic/Latino, 173 international. 1,148 applicants, 28% accepted, 145 enrolled. In 2010, 70 master's, 12 doctorates awarded. Terminal master's awarded for partial completion of doctoral program. *Degree requirements:* For master's, thesis optional; for doctorate, thesis/dissertation. *Entrance requirements:* For master's and doctorate, GRE General Test. Additional exam requirements/recommendations for international students: Required—TOEFL. *Application deadline:* For fall admission, 6/1 priority date for domestic students, 5/1 priority date for international students. Applications are processed on a rolling basis. Application fee: $70. Electronic applications accepted. *Expenses:* Tuition: Full-time $25,660; part-time $4758 per course. Required fees: $2152; $270 per course. Tuition and fees vary according to course load, degree level and program. *Financial support:* Fellowships with full tuition reimbursements, research assistantships with full tuition reimbursements, teaching assistantships, institutionally sponsored loans, scholarships/grants, traineeships, health care benefits, and unspecified assistantships available. *Faculty research:* AI, computer systems graphics, information management, robotics, software systems theory. *Application contact:* Mike Felker, Graduate Coordinator, 215-898-9672, E-mail: mfelker@cis.upenn.edu.

University of Pittsburgh, School of Arts and Sciences, Department of Computer Science, Pittsburgh, PA 15260. Offers MS, PhD. Part-time programs available. *Faculty:* 18 full-time (4 women). *Students:* 91 full-time (12 women), 3 part-time (2 women); includes 1 Black or African American, non-Hispanic/Latino; 21 Asian, non-Hispanic/Latino; 2 Hispanic/Latino, 34 international. Average age 27. 401 applicants, 6% accepted, 15 enrolled. In 2010, 10 master's, 8 doctorates awarded. Terminal master's awarded for partial completion of doctoral program. *Degree requirements:* For master's, thesis or alternative; for doctorate, comprehensive exam, thesis/dissertation, preliminary exams. *Entrance requirements:* For master's and doctorate, GRE General Test. Additional exam requirements/recommendations for international students: Required—TOEFL (minimum score 600 paper-based; 250 computer-based; 90 iBT). *Application* *deadline:* For fall admission, 1/15 for domestic and international students; for winter admission, 9/15 for domestic and international students. Applications are processed on a rolling basis. Application fee: $50. Electronic applications accepted. *Expenses:* Tuition, state resident: full-time $17,304; part-time $701 per credit. Tuition, nonresident: full-time $29,554; part-time $1210 per credit. Required fees: $740; $214 per term. Tuition and fees vary according to program. *Financial support:* In 2010–11, 60 students received support, including 7 fellowships with full tuition reimbursements available (averaging $17,972 per year), 24 research assistantships with full tuition reimbursements available (averaging $17,211 per year), 29 teaching assistantships with full tuition reimbursements available (averaging $15,520 per year); career-related internships or fieldwork, Federal Work-Study, scholarships/grants, health care benefits, and tuition waivers (partial) also available. Financial award application deadline: 1/15. *Faculty research:* Algorithms and theory, artificial intelligence, parallel and distributed systems, software systems and interfaces. Total annual research expenditures: $2.8 million. *Unit head:* Dr. Daniel Mosse, Chairman, 412-624-8493, Fax: 412-624-8854, E-mail: mosse@cs.pitt.edu. *Application contact:* Keena Walker, Graduate Secretary, 412-624-8495, Fax: 412-624-8854, E-mail: keena@cs.pitt.edu.

University of Puerto Rico, Mayagüez Campus, Graduate Studies, College of Engineering, Department of Electrical and Computer Engineering, Mayagüez, PR 00681-9000. Offers computer engineering (ME, MS); computing and information sciences and engineering (PhD); electrical engineering (ME, MS). Part-time programs available. *Students:* 97 full-time (23 women), 12 part-time (1 woman); includes 74 Hispanic/Latino, 35 international. 41 applicants, 54% accepted, 13 enrolled. In 2010, 19 master's, 1 doctorate awarded. *Degree requirements:* For master's, comprehensive exam, thesis; for doctorate, comprehensive exam, thesis/dissertation. *Entrance requirements:* For master's, proficiency in English and Spanish, BS in electrical or computer engineering or equivalent, minimum GPA of 3.0; for doctorate, GRE. Additional exam requirements/recommendations for international students: Required—TOEFL (minimum score 450 paper-based). *Application deadline:* For fall admission, 2/15 for domestic and international students; for spring admission, 9/15 for domestic and international students. Applications are processed on a rolling basis. Application fee: $25. *Expenses:* Tuition, state resident: full-time $1188. Tuition, nonresident: full-time $1188. International tuition: $6126 full-time. Tuition and fees vary according to course level and course load. *Financial support:* In 2010–11, 23 students received support, including fellowships (averaging $12,000 per year), 3 research assistantships (averaging $15,000 per year), 23 teaching assistantships (averaging $8,500 per year); Federal Work-Study and institutionally sponsored loans also available. *Faculty research:* Microcomputer interfacing, control systems, power systems, electronics. Total annual research expenditures: $3.8 million. *Unit head:* Dr. Erick Aponte-Diaz, Chairperson, 787-832-4040 Ext. 3821, E-mail: erick.aponte1@upr.edu. *Application contact:* Sandra Montalvo, Administrative Staff, 787-832-4040 Ext. 3094, Fax: 787-831-7564, E-mail: sandra@ece.uprm.edu.

University of Regina, Faculty of Graduate Studies and Research, Faculty of Science, Department of Computer Science, Regina, SK S4S 0A2, Canada. Offers M Sc, PhD. *Faculty:* 17 full-time (3 women). *Students:* 42 full-time (16 women), 13 part-time (0 women). 93 applicants, 34% accepted. In 2010, 13 master's, 3 doctorates awarded. *Degree requirements:* For master's, thesis; for doctorate, thesis/dissertation. *Entrance requirements:* Additional exam requirements/recommendations for international students: Required—TOEFL (minimum score 580 paper-based; 80 iBT). *Application deadline:* Applications are processed on a rolling basis. Application fee: $100. Electronic applications accepted. Tuition and fees charges are reported in Canadian dollars. *Expenses:* Tuition, area resident: Full-time $3244.50 Canadian dollars; part-time $180.25 Canadian dollars per credit hour. International tuition: $4744.50 Canadian dollars full-time. Required fees: $494 Canadian dollars; $115.25 Canadian dollars per credit hour. $115.25 Canadian dollars per semester. Tuition and fees vary according to program. *Financial support:* In 2010–11, 10 fellowships (averaging $20,700 per year), 4 research assistantships (averaging $18,000 per year), 15 teaching assistantships (averaging $6,978 per year) were awarded; career-related internships or fieldwork and scholarships/grants also available. Financial award application deadline: 6/15. *Faculty research:* Information retrieval, machine learning, computer visualization, theory and application of rough sets, human-computer interaction. *Unit head:* Dr. Xue Dong Yang, Head, 306-585-4692, Fax: 306-585-4745, E-mail: yang@cs.uregina.ca. *Application contact:* Dr. JingTao Yao, Graduate Program Coordinator, 306-585-4071, Fax: 306-585-4745, E-mail: jtyao@cs.uregina.ca.

University of Rhode Island, Graduate School, College of Arts and Sciences, Department of Computer Science and Statistics, Kingston, RI 02881. Offers applied mathematics (PhD), including computer science, statistics; computer science (MS, PhD); digital forensics (Graduate Certificate); statistics (MS). Part-time programs available. *Faculty:* 10 full-time (3 women), 2 part-time/adjunct (0 women). *Students:* 39 full-time (10 women), 44 part-time (11 women); includes 16 minority (2 Black or African American, non-Hispanic/Latino; 2 American Indian or Alaska Native, non-Hispanic/Latino; 2 Asian, non-Hispanic/Latino; 2 Hispanic/Latino; 8 Native Hawaiian or other Pacific Islander, non-Hispanic/Latino), 8 international. In 2010, 5 master's awarded. *Degree requirements:* For master's, comprehensive exam (for some programs), thesis optional; for doctorate, comprehensive exam, thesis/dissertation. *Entrance requirements:* For master's and doctorate, GRE, 2 letters of recommendation. Additional exam requirements/recommendations for international students: Required—TOEFL (minimum score 550 paper-based; 213 computer-based). *Application deadline:* For fall admission, 7/15 for domestic students, 2/1 for international students; for spring admission, 11/15 for domestic students, 7/15 for international students. Application fee: $65. Electronic applications accepted. *Expenses:* Tuition, state resident: full-time $9588; part-time $533 per credit hour. Tuition, nonresident: full-time $22,968; part-time $1276 per credit hour. Required fees: $1282; $68 per semester. Tuition and fees vary according to program. *Financial support:* In 2010–11, 1 research assistantship (averaging $5,210 per year), 10 teaching assistantships with full and partial tuition reimbursements (averaging $10,456 per year) were awarded. Financial award application deadline: 2/1; financial award applicants required to submit FAFSA. *Faculty research:* Bioinformatics, computer and digital forensics, behavioral model of pedestrian dynamics, real-time distributed object computing, cryptography. Total annual research expenditures: $962,948. *Unit head:* Dr. James G. Kowalski, Chair, 401-874-2510, Fax: 401-874-4617, E-mail: kowalski@cs.uri.edu. *Application contact:* Dr. Victor Fay-Wolfe, Director of Graduate Studies, 401-874-2701, Fax: 401-874-4617, E-mail: wolfe@cs.uri.edu.

University of Rochester, Hajim School of Engineering and Applied Sciences, Department of Computer Science, Rochester, NY 14627. Offers MS, PhD.

University of San Francisco, College of Arts and Sciences, Department of Computer Science, San Francisco, CA 94117-1080. Offers computer science (MS); Web science (MS). Part-time programs available. *Faculty:* 5 full-time (1 woman). *Students:* 62 full-time (13 women), 6 part-time (2 women); includes 7 minority (2 Black or African American, non-Hispanic/Latino; 3 Hispanic/Latino; 1 Native Hawaiian or other Pacific Islander, non-Hispanic/Latino; 1 Two or more races, non-Hispanic/Latino), 53 international. Average age 28. 142 applicants, 70% accepted, 32 enrolled. In 2010, 14 master's awarded. *Degree requirements:* For master's, thesis optional. *Entrance requirements:* For master's, GRE General Test, GRE Subject Test, BS in computer science or related field. Additional exam requirements/recommendations for international students: Required—TOEFL. *Application deadline:* For fall admission, 7/1 priority date for domestic students; for spring admission, 12/1 for domestic students. Applications are processed on a rolling basis. Application fee: $55 ($65 for international students). *Expenses:* Tuition: Full-time $20,070; part-time $1115 per credit hour. Tuition and fees vary according to course load, degree level and program. *Financial support:* In 2010–11, 25 students received support; fellowships, teaching assistantships, career-related internships or fieldwork and Federal Work-Study available. Financial award application deadline: 3/2; financial award applicants required to submit FAFSA. *Faculty research:* Software engineering, computer graphics, computer networks. *Unit head:* Dr. Terence Parr, Chairman, 415-422-6530. *Application contact:* Mark Landerghini, Graduate Adviser, 415-422-5135, E-mail: asgraduate@usfca.edu.

University of Saskatchewan, College of Graduate Studies and Research, College of Arts and Sciences, Department of Computer Science, Saskatoon, SK S7N 5A2, Canada. Offers M Sc, PhD. *Degree requirements:* For master's, thesis; for doctorate, comprehensive exam (for some programs), thesis/dissertation. *Entrance requirements:* For master's and doctorate, GRE. Additional exam requirements/recommendations for international students: Required—TOEFL (minimum score 80 iBT); Recommended—IELTS (minimum score 6.5). Electronic applications accepted.

University of South Alabama, Graduate School, School of Computer and Information Sciences, Mobile, AL 36688-0002. Offers computer science (MS); information systems (MS). Part-time and evening/weekend programs available. *Faculty:* 9 full-time (0 women). *Students:* 81 full-time (23 women), 20 part-time (4 women); includes 7 minority (4 Black or African American, non-Hispanic/Latino; 2 Asian, non-Hispanic/Latino; 1 Hispanic/Latino), 68 international. 164 applicants, 71% accepted, 31 enrolled. In 2010, 20 master's awarded. *Degree requirements:* For master's, thesis optional, project. *Entrance requirements:* For master's, GRE General Test. *Application deadline:* For fall admission, 7/15 priority date for domestic students, 6/15 priority date for international students; for spring admission, 12/1 for domestic students, 11/1 priority date for international students. Applications are processed on a rolling basis. Application fee: $35. *Expenses:* Tuition, state resident: part-time $300 per credit hour. Tuition, nonresident: part-time $600 per credit hour. Required fees: $150 per semester. *Financial support:* Research assistantships, career-related internships or fieldwork and institutionally sponsored loans available. Support available to part-time students. Financial award application deadline: 4/1. *Faculty research:* Numerical analysis, artificial intelligence, simulation, medical applications, software engineering. *Unit head:* Dr. Roy Daigle, Director of Graduate Studies, 251-460-6390. *Application contact:* Dr. B. Keith Harrison, Dean of the Graduate School, 251-460-6310, Fax: 251-461-1513, E-mail: kharriso@usouthal.edu.

University of South Carolina, The Graduate School, College of Engineering and Computing, Department of Computer Science and Engineering, Columbia, SC 29208. Offers computer science and engineering (ME, MS, PhD); software engineering (MS). Part-time and evening/weekend programs available. Postbaccalaureate distance learning degree programs offered (minimal on-campus study). *Degree requirements:* For master's, comprehensive exam, thesis (for some programs); for doctorate, comprehensive exam, thesis/dissertation. *Entrance requirements:* For master's and doctorate, GRE General Test. Additional exam requirements/recommendations for international students: Required—TOEFL (minimum score 570 paper-based; 230 computer-based). Electronic applications accepted. *Faculty research:* Computer security, computer vision, artificial intelligence, multiagent systems, bioinformatics.

The University of South Dakota, Graduate School, College of Arts and Sciences, Department of Computer Science, Vermillion, SD 57069-2390. Offers computational sciences and statistics (PhD); computer science (MS). Part-time programs available. *Degree requirements:* For master's, thesis optional. *Entrance requirements:* For master's, GRE General Test, GRE Subject Test (recommended), minimum GPA of 2.7. Additional exam requirements/recommendations for international students: Required—TOEFL (minimum score 550 paper-based; 213 computer-based; 79 iBT). Electronic applications accepted.

University of Southern California, Graduate School, Viterbi School of Engineering, Department of Computer Science, Los Angeles, CA 90089. Offers computer networks (MS); computer science (MS, PhD); computer security (MS); game development (MS); high performance computing and simulations (MS); human language technology (MS); intelligent robotics (MS); multimedia and creative technologies (MS); software engineering (MS). Part-time and evening/weekend programs available. Postbaccalaureate distance learning degree programs offered (no on-campus study). *Faculty:* 28 full-time (3 women), 56 part-time/adjunct (7 women). *Students:* 710 full-time (115 women), 302 part-time (59 women); includes 76 minority (1 Black or African American, non-Hispanic/Latino; 55 Asian, non-Hispanic/Latino; 14 Hispanic/Latino; 6 Two or more races, non-Hispanic/Latino), 819 international. 2,379 applicants, 30% accepted, 319 enrolled. In 2010, 332 master's, 32 doctorates awarded. *Entrance requirements:* For master's and doctorate, GRE General Test. Additional exam requirements/recommendations for international students: Required—TOEFL. *Application deadline:* For fall admission, 12/1 priority date for domestic and international students; for spring admission, 9/15 priority date for domestic and international students. Applications are processed on a rolling basis. Application fee: $85. Electronic applications accepted. *Expenses:* Tuition: Full-time $31,240; part-time $1420 per unit. Required fees: $600. One-time fee: $35 full-time. Full-time tuition and fees vary according to degree level and program. *Financial support:* In 2010–11, fellowships with full tuition reimbursements (averaging $30,000 per year), research assistantships with full tuition reimbursements (averaging $20,000 per year), teaching assistantships with full tuition reimbursements (averaging $20,000 per year) were awarded; career-related internships or fieldwork, scholarships/grants, health care benefits, and unspecified assistantships also available. Financial award application deadline: 12/1; financial award applicants required to submit CSS PROFILE or FAFSA. *Faculty research:* Databases, computer graphics and computer vision, software engineering, networks and security, robotics, multimedia and virtual reality. Total annual research expenditures: $11.8 million. *Unit head:* Dr. Shanghua Teng, Chair, 213-740-4494, E-mail: csdept@usc.edu. *Application contact:* Lizsl DeLeon, Director of Student Affairs, 213-740-4496, E-mail: ldeleon@usc.edu.

University of Southern Maine, School of Applied Science, Engineering, and Technology, Department of Computer Science, Portland, ME 04104-9300. Offers MS. Part-time programs available. *Degree requirements:* For master's, thesis. *Entrance requirements:* For master's, GRE General Test, minimum GPA of 3.0. Additional exam requirements/recommendations for international students: Required—TOEFL. Electronic applications accepted. *Faculty research:* Computer networks, database systems, software engineering, theory of computability, human factors.

University of Southern Mississippi, Graduate School, College of Science and Technology, School of Computing, Hattiesburg, MS 39406-0001. Offers computational science (MS, PhD); computer science (MS). *Faculty:* 18 full-time (3 women), 1 (woman) part-time/adjunct. *Students:* 58 full-time (11 women), 19 part-time (4 women); includes 5 Black or African American, non-Hispanic/Latino; 1 Asian, non-Hispanic/Latino; 1 Hispanic/Latino, 44 international. Average age 29. 66 applicants, 80% accepted, 16 enrolled. In 2010, 22 master's, 2 doctorates awarded. *Degree requirements:* For master's, comprehensive exam, thesis; for doctorate, comprehensive exam, thesis/dissertation. *Entrance requirements:* For master's, GRE General Test, minimum GPA of 2.75 in last 60 hours; for doctorate, GRE General Test, minimum GPA of 3.5. Additional exam requirements/recommendations for international students: Required—TOEFL, IELTS. *Application deadline:* For fall admission, 3/15 priority date for domestic students, 3/15 for international students; for spring admission, 1/10 priority date for domestic and international students. Applications are processed on a rolling basis. Application fee: $50. Electronic applications accepted. *Financial support:* In 2010–11, 29 research assistantships with full tuition reimbursements (averaging $8,800 per year), 7 teaching assistantships with full tuition reimbursements (averaging $10,000 per year) were awarded; Federal Work-Study, institutionally sponsored loans, scholarships/grants, health care benefits, and unspecified assistantships also available. Financial award application deadline: 3/15; financial award applicants required to submit FAFSA. *Faculty research:* Satellite telecommunications, advanced life-support systems, artificial intelligence. *Unit head:* Dr. Chaoyang Zhang, Chair, 601-266-4949, Fax: 601-266-6452. *Application contact:* Dr. Chaoyang Zhang, Manager of Graduate Admissions, 601-266-4949, Fax: 601-266-6452.

University of South Florida, Graduate School, College of Engineering, Department of Computer Science and Engineering, Tampa, FL 33620-9951. Offers computer engineering (MSCP); computer science (MSCS); computer science and engineering (PhD). Part-time programs available. *Faculty:* 14 full-time (1 woman). *Students:* 86 full-time (17 women), 27 part-time (5 women); includes 7 Black or African American, non-Hispanic/Latino; 2 Asian, non-Hispanic/Latino; 7 Hispanic/Latino, 54 international. Average age 29. 207 applicants, 44% accepted, 40 enrolled. In 2010, 24 master's, 13 doctorates awarded. Terminal master's awarded for partial completion of doctoral program. *Degree requirements:* For master's, comprehensive exam, thesis; for doctorate, comprehensive exam, thesis/dissertation, teaching of undergraduate

Computer Science

University of South Florida (continued)

computer science and engineering course. *Entrance requirements:* For master's, GRE General Test (minimum score 500 verbal, 700 quantitative), minimum GPA of 3.3 in last 60 hours of coursework; for doctorate, GRE General Test (minimum score: 500 Verbal, 700 Quantitative), minimum GPA of 3.3 in last 60 hours of coursework, MS (recommended). Additional exam requirements/recommendations for international students: Required—TOEFL (minimum score 550 paper-based; 213 computer-based). *Application deadline:* For fall admission, 2/15 for domestic students, 1/2 for international students; for spring admission, 10/15 for domestic students, 6/1 for international students. Application fee: $30. Electronic applications accepted. *Financial support:* In 2010–11, 67 students received support, including 27 research assistantships (averaging $15,168 per year), 33 teaching assistantships with tuition reimbursements available (averaging $15,018 per year); unspecified assistantships also available. Financial award application deadline: 1/1; financial award applicants required to submit FAFSA. *Faculty research:* Computer vision, networks, artificial intelligence, computer architecture, software security. Total annual research expenditures: $1.4 million. *Unit head:* Sudeep Sarkar, Director, 813-974-2113, Fax: 813-974-5094, E-mail: sarkar@cse.usf.edu. *Application contact:* Sudeep Sarkar, Director, 813-974-2113, Fax: 813-974-5094, E-mail: sarkar@cse.usf.edu.

The University of Tennessee, Graduate School, College of Arts and Sciences, Department of Computer Science, Knoxville, TN 37996. Offers MS, PhD. Part-time programs available. *Degree requirements:* For master's, thesis or alternative; for doctorate, thesis/dissertation. *Entrance requirements:* For master's and doctorate, GRE General Test, minimum GPA of 2.7. Additional exam requirements/recommendations for international students: Required—TOEFL. Electronic applications accepted. *Expenses:* Tuition, state resident: full-time $7440; part-time $414 per credit hour. Tuition, nonresident: full-time $22,478; part-time $1250 per credit hour. Required fees: $922; $43 per credit hour. Tuition and fees vary according to program.

The University of Tennessee, Graduate School, College of Engineering, Department of Electrical Engineering and Computer Science, Knoxville, TN 37996. Offers computer engineering (MS, PhD); computer science (MS, PhD); electrical engineering (MS, PhD); reliability and maintainability engineering (MS); MS/MBA. Part-time programs available. *Faculty:* 39 full-time (7 women), 14 part-time/adjunct (0 women). *Students:* 174 full-time (35 women), 43 part-time (6 women); includes 2 Black or African American, non-Hispanic/Latino; 3 Asian, non-Hispanic/Latino; 2 Hispanic/Latino, 114 international. Average age 29. 644 applicants, 12% accepted, 51 enrolled. In 2010, 42 master's, 21 doctorates awarded. *Degree requirements:* For master's, thesis or alternative; for doctorate, comprehensive exam, thesis/dissertation. *Entrance requirements:* For master's, GRE General Test, Minimum GPA of 2.7 (US degree holders); 3.0 (International degree holders); 3-References; Personal statement; for doctorate, GRE General Test, Minimum GPA of 3.0 (previous graduate degree); 3-References; Personal statement. Additional exam requirements/recommendations for international students: Required—TOEFL (minimum score 550 paper-based; 213 computer-based). *Application deadline:* For fall admission, 2/1 priority date for domestic and international students; for spring admission, 6/15 for domestic and international students. Applications are processed on a rolling basis. Application fee: $35. Electronic applications accepted. *Expenses:* Tuition, state resident: full-time $7440; part-time $414 per credit hour. Tuition, nonresident: full-time $22,478; part-time $1250 per credit hour. Required fees: $922; $43 per credit hour. Tuition and fees vary according to program. *Financial support:* In 2010–11, 148 students received support, including 13 fellowships with full tuition reimbursements available (averaging $12,312 per year), 100 research assistantships with full tuition reimbursements available (averaging $16,248 per year), 91 teaching assistantships with full tuition reimbursements available (averaging $12,996 per year); career-related internships or fieldwork, Federal Work-Study, institutionally sponsored loans, health care benefits, and unspecified assistantships also available. Financial award application deadline: 2/1; financial award applicants required to submit FAFSA. *Faculty research:* Artificial intelligence and visualization; microelectronics, mixed-signal electronics, VLSI, embedded systems; scientific and distributed computing; computer vision, robotics, and image processing; power electronics, power systems, communications. Total annual research expenditures: $10.7 million. *Unit head:* Dr. Kevin Tomsovic, Head, 865-974-3461, Fax: 865-974-5483, E-mail: tomsovic@eecs.utk.edu. *Application contact:* Dr. Lynne E. Parker, Associate Head, 865-974-4394, Fax: 865-974-5483, E-mail: parker@eecs.utk.edu.

The University of Tennessee at Chattanooga, Graduate School, College of Engineering and Computer Science, Program in Computer Science, Chattanooga, TN 37403. Offers MS, Graduate Certificate. Part-time and evening/weekend programs available. *Faculty:* 4 full-time (2 women), 2 part-time/adjunct (both women). *Students:* 11 full-time (1 woman), 10 part-time (2 women), 6 international. Average age 28. 12 applicants, 83% accepted, 6 enrolled. In 2010, 7 master's awarded. *Degree requirements:* For master's, comprehensive exam, thesis. *Entrance requirements:* For master's, GRE General Test. Additional exam requirements/recommendations for international students: Required—TOEFL (minimum score 550 paper-based; 213 computer-based; 79 iBT), IELTS (minimum score 6). *Application deadline:* For fall admission, 8/1 priority date for domestic students, 6/1 for international students; for spring admission, 12/1 priority date for domestic students, 10/1 for international students. Applications are processed on a rolling basis. Application fee: $35. Electronic applications accepted. *Financial support:* In 2010–11, 3 research assistantships with full and partial tuition reimbursements (averaging $5,500 per year), 1 teaching assistantship with full and partial tuition reimbursement (averaging $5,500 per year) were awarded; career-related internships or fieldwork, scholarships/grants, and unspecified assistantships also available. Support available to part-time students. *Faculty research:* Power systems, computer architecture, pattern recognition, artificial intelligence, statistical data analysis. Total annual research expenditures: $107,279. *Unit head:* Dr. Joseph Kizza, Department Head, 423-425-4349, Fax: 423-425-5442, E-mail: joseph-kizza@utc.edu. *Application contact:* Dr. Jerald Ainsworth, Dean of Graduate Studies, 423-425-4478, Fax: 423-425-5223, E-mail: jerald-ainsworth@utc.edu.

The University of Tennessee Space Institute, Graduate Programs, Program in Electrical Engineering and Computer Science, Tullahoma, TN 37388-9700. Offers MS, PhD. *Faculty:* 2 full-time (0 women), 2 part-time/adjunct (0 women). *Students:* 1 part-time (0 women). 1 applicant, 0% accepted, 0 enrolled. In 2010, 4 master's awarded. *Degree requirements:* For master's, thesis (for some programs); for doctorate, one foreign language, thesis/dissertation. *Entrance requirements:* Additional exam requirements/recommendations for international students: Required—TOEFL (minimum score 550 paper-based; 213 computer-based), IELTS (minimum score 6.5). *Application deadline:* For fall admission, 2/1 for international students; for spring admission, 6/15 for international students. Applications are processed on a rolling basis. Application fee: $35. Electronic applications accepted. *Financial support:* Fellowships, research assistantships with full tuition reimbursements, career-related internships or fieldwork, Federal Work-Study, institutionally sponsored loans, health care benefits, tuition waivers (full and partial), and unspecified assistantships available. Financial award applicants required to submit FAFSA. *Unit head:* Dr. Monty Smith, Degree Program Chairman, 931-393-7480, Fax: 931-393-7530, E-mail: msmith@utsi.edu. *Application contact:* Dee Merriman, Coordinator III, 931-393-7213, Fax: 931-393-7211, E-mail: dmerrima@utsi.edu.

The University of Texas at Arlington, Graduate School, College of Engineering, Department of Computer Science and Engineering, Arlington, TX 76019. Offers computer engineering (MS, PhD); computer science (MS, PhD); computer science and engineering (M Engr); software engineering (MS, PhD). Part-time programs available. Postbaccalaureate distance learning degree programs offered (minimal on-campus study). *Faculty:* 27 full-time (2 women), 1 part-time/adjunct (0 women). *Students:* 183 full-time (41 women), 89 part-time (18 women); includes 9 minority (3 Black or African American, non-Hispanic/Latino; 4 Asian, non-Hispanic/Latino; 1 Hispanic/Latino; 1 Two or more races, non-Hispanic/Latino), 219 international. 452 applicants, 62% accepted, 94 enrolled. In 2010, 82 master's, 10 doctorates awarded. Terminal master's awarded for partial completion of doctoral program. *Degree requirements:* For master's, comprehensive exam (for some programs), thesis; for doctorate, comprehensive exam, thesis/dissertation. *Entrance requirements:* For master's, GRE General Test, TTL 1150, minimum GPA of 3.0 (3.2 in computer science-related classes); for doctorate, GRE General Test, TTL 1250, minimum GPA of 3.5. Additional exam requirements/recommendations for international students: Required—TOEFL (minimum score 550 paper-based; 230 computer-based; 92 iBT). *Application deadline:* For fall admission, 6/1 for domestic students, 4/1 for international students; for spring admission, 10/15 for domestic students, 9/15 for international students. Applications are processed on a rolling basis. Application fee: $35 ($50 for international students). *Expenses:* Tuition, state resident: full-time $7500. Tuition, nonresident: full-time $13,080. International tuition: $13,250 full-time. *Financial support:* In 2010–11, 7 fellowships with full tuition reimbursements (averaging $24,000 per year), 57 research assistantships with partial tuition reimbursements (averaging $19,200 per year), 50 teaching assistantships with partial tuition reimbursements (averaging $16,200 per year) were awarded; career-related internships or fieldwork and scholarships/grants also available. Financial award application deadline: 6/1; financial award applicants required to submit FAFSA. *Faculty research:* Algorithms, homeland security, mobile pervasive computing, high performance computing bioinformation. *Unit head:* Dr. Fillia Makedon, Chairman, 817-272-3605, E-mail: makedon@uta.edu. *Application contact:* Dr. Bahram Khalili, Graduate Advisor, 817-272-5407, Fax: 817-272-3784, E-mail: khalili@uta.edu.

The University of Texas at Austin, Graduate School, College of Natural Sciences, Department of Computer Sciences, Austin, TX 78712-1111. Offers MA, MSCS, PhD. *Degree requirements:* For master's, thesis optional; for doctorate, thesis/dissertation, oral proposal, final defense. *Entrance requirements:* For master's and doctorate, GRE General Test, GRE Subject Test, bachelor's degree in computer sciences preferred. Additional exam requirements/recommendations for international students: Required—TOEFL. Electronic applications accepted. *Faculty research:* Artificial intelligence, distributed computing, networks, algorithms, experimental systems.

The University of Texas at Dallas, Erik Jonsson School of Engineering and Computer Science, Program in Computer Science, Richardson, TX 75080. Offers computer science (MS, PhD); software engineering (MS, PhD). Part-time and evening/weekend programs available. *Faculty:* 38 full-time (6 women), 3 part-time/adjunct (1 woman). *Students:* 389 full-time (97 women), 213 part-time (52 women); includes 40 minority (3 Black or African American, non-Hispanic/Latino; 1 American Indian or Alaska Native, non-Hispanic/Latino; 26 Asian, non-Hispanic/Latino; 8 Hispanic/Latino; 2 Two or more races, non-Hispanic/Latino), 452 international. Average age 26. 1,136 applicants, 59% accepted, 174 enrolled. In 2010, 222 master's, 23 doctorates awarded. *Degree requirements:* For master's, thesis optional; for doctorate, comprehensive exam, thesis/dissertation. *Entrance requirements:* For master's, GRE General Test, minimum GPA of 3.0 in undergraduate course work, 3.3 in quantitative course work; for doctorate, GRE General Test, minimum GPA of 3.5. Additional exam requirements/recommendations for international students: Required—TOEFL (minimum score 550 paper-based; 215 computer-based). *Application deadline:* For fall admission, 7/15 for domestic students, 5/1 priority date for international students; for spring admission, 11/15 for domestic students, 9/1 priority date for international students. Applications are processed on a rolling basis. Application fee: $50 ($100 for international students). Electronic applications accepted. *Expenses:* Tuition, state resident: full-time $10,248; part-time $569 per credit hour. Tuition, nonresident: full-time $18,544; part-time $1030 per credit hour. Tuition and fees vary according to course load. *Financial support:* In 2010–11, 160 students received support, including 1 fellowship with partial tuition reimbursement available (averaging $18,900 per year), 68 research assistantships with partial tuition reimbursements available (averaging $15,765 per year), 37 teaching assistantships with partial tuition reimbursements available (averaging $15,675 per year); career-related internships or fieldwork, Federal Work-Study, institutionally sponsored loans, and scholarships/grants also available. Support available to part-time students. Financial award application deadline: 4/30; financial award applicants required to submit FAFSA. *Faculty research:* AI-based automated software synthesis and testing, quality of service in computer networks, wireless networks, cloud computing and IT security, speech recognition. *Unit head:* Dr. Gopal Gupta, Department Head, 972-883-4107, Fax: 972-883-2349, E-mail: gupta@utdallas.edu. *Application contact:* Dr. Balaji Raghavachari, Associate Department Head and Director of Graduate Studies, 972-883-2136, Fax: 972-883-2813, E-mail: gradecs@utdallas.edu.

The University of Texas at El Paso, Graduate School, College of Engineering, Department of Computer Science, El Paso, TX 79968-0001. Offers computer science (MS, PhD); information technology (MSIT). Part-time and evening/weekend programs available. *Students:* 59 (15 women); includes 2 Asian, non-Hispanic/Latino; 23 Hispanic/Latino, 30 international. Average age 34. In 2010, 17 master's, 3 doctorates awarded. *Degree requirements:* For master's, thesis optional; for doctorate, thesis/dissertation. *Entrance requirements:* For master's, GRE, minimum GPA of 3.0; for doctorate, GRE, statement of purpose, letters of reference. Additional exam requirements/recommendations for international students: Required—TOEFL; Recommended—IELTS. *Application deadline:* For fall admission, 8/1 priority date for domestic students, 3/1 for international students; for spring admission, 11/1 priority date for domestic students, 9/1 for international students. Applications are processed on a rolling basis. Application fee: $45 ($80 for international students). Electronic applications accepted. *Financial support:* In 2010–11, research assistantships with partial tuition reimbursements (averaging $21,125 per year), teaching assistantships with partial tuition reimbursements (averaging $16,900 per year) were awarded; fellowships with partial tuition reimbursements, institutionally sponsored loans, scholarships/grants, health care benefits, tuition waivers (partial), and unspecified assistantships also available. Support available to part-time students. Financial award application deadline: 3/15; financial award applicants required to submit FAFSA. *Unit head:* Dr. Eunice E. Santos, Chair, 915-747-5480 Ext. 5480, Fax: 915-747-5030, E-mail: eesantos@utep.edu. *Application contact:* Dr. Patricia D. Witherspoon, Dean of the Graduate School, 915-747-5491, Fax: 915-747-5788, E-mail: withersp@utep.edu.

The University of Texas at San Antonio, College of Sciences, Department of Computer Science, San Antonio, TX 78249-0617. Offers computer and information security (MS); computer science (MS, PhD); software engineering (MS). Part-time programs available. *Faculty:* 20 full-time (4 women), 2 part-time/adjunct (0 women). *Students:* 95 full-time (18 women), 49 part-time (9 women); includes 16 minority (2 Black or African American, non-Hispanic/Latino; 2 Asian, non-Hispanic/Latino; 11 Hispanic/Latino; 1 Two or more races, non-Hispanic/Latino), 89 international. Average age 28. 198 applicants, 58% accepted, 42 enrolled. In 2010, 10 master's, 4 doctorates awarded. *Degree requirements:* For master's, comprehensive exam, thesis (for some programs); for doctorate, comprehensive exam, thesis/dissertation. *Entrance requirements:* For master's, GRE General Test, minimum GPA of 3.0 in last 60 hours; for doctorate, GRE General Test, minimum GPA of 3.0. Additional exam requirements/recommendations for international students: Required—TOEFL (minimum score 500 paper-based; 173 computer-based; 61 iBT), IELTS (minimum score 5). *Application deadline:* For fall admission, 7/1 for domestic students, 4/1 for international students; for spring admission, 11/1 for domestic students, 9/1 for international students. Applications are processed on a rolling basis. Application fee: $45 ($80 for international students). Electronic applications accepted. *Expenses:* Tuition, state resident: full-time $4172; part-time $231.75 per credit hour. Tuition, nonresident: full-time $15,332; part-time $851.75 per credit hour. *Financial support:* In 2010–11, 69 students received support, including 6 fellowships (averaging $41,302 per year), 30 research assistantships (averaging $17,975 per year), 37 teaching assistantships (averaging $13,946 per year); career-related internships or fieldwork, scholarships/grants, tuition waivers, and unspecified assistantships also available. Support available to part-time students. *Faculty research:* Computer and information security, high performance computing, bioinformatics and computational biology, programming languages and compilers. Total annual research expenditures: $1.4 million. *Unit head:* Dr. Kleanthis Psarris, Department Chair, 210-458-4436, Fax: 210-458-4437, E-mail: kleanthis.psarris@utsa.edu. *Application contact:* Veronica Ramirez, Assistant Dean of the Graduate School, 210-458-4330, Fax: 210-458-4332, E-mail: graduatestudies@utsa.edu.

The University of Texas at Tyler, College of Engineering and Computer Science, Department of Computer Science, Tyler, TX 75799-0001. Offers computer science (MS); interdisciplinary studies (MSIS). *Degree requirements:* For master's, comprehensive exam, thesis optional. *Entrance requirements:* For master's, GRE General Test, previous course work in data structures and computer organization, 6 hours of course work in calculus and statistics. Additional exam requirements/recommendations for international students: Required—TOEFL (minimum score 79 computer-based). Electronic applications accepted. *Faculty research:* Database design, software engineering, client-server architecture, visual programming, data mining, computer security, digital image processing, simulation and modeling, computer science education.

The University of Texas of the Permian Basin, Office of Graduate Studies, College of Arts and Sciences, Department of Math and Computer Science, Odessa, TX 79762-0001. Offers computer science (MS). Part-time and evening/weekend programs available. *Degree requirements:* For master's, comprehensive exam, thesis or alternative. *Entrance requirements:* For master's, GRE General Test. Additional exam requirements/recommendations for international students: Required—TOEFL (minimum score 550 paper-based; 213 computer-based).

The University of Texas–Pan American, College of Science and Engineering, Department of Computer Science, Edinburg, TX 78539. Offers MS. Part-time and evening/weekend programs available. Postbaccalaureate distance learning degree programs offered (minimal on-campus study). *Degree requirements:* For master's, final written exam, project. *Entrance requirements:* For master's, GRE General Test, minimum GPA of 3.0 in last 60 hours. Additional exam requirements/recommendations for international students: Required—TOEFL. *Faculty research:* Artificial intelligence, distributed systems internet computing, theoretical computer sciences, information visualization.

University of the District of Columbia, School of Engineering and Applied Science, Department of Computer Science and Information Technology, Program in Computer Science, Washington, DC 20008-1175. Offers MS. *Degree requirements:* For master's, thesis optional. *Expenses:* Tuition, state resident: full-time $7580; part-time $421 per credit. Tuition, nonresident: full-time $14,580; part-time $810 per credit. Required fees: $620; $30 per credit. One-time fee: $100 part-time.

The University of Toledo, College of Graduate Studies, College of Engineering, Department of Electrical Engineering and Computer Science, Toledo, OH 43606-3390. Offers computer science (MS, PhD); electrical engineering (MS, PhD). Part-time and evening/weekend programs available. *Degree requirements:* For master's, thesis or alternative; for doctorate, thesis/ dissertation, qualifying exam. *Entrance requirements:* For master's, GRE General Test, minimum GPA of 3.0; for doctorate, GRE General Test, minimum GPA of 3.3. Additional exam requirements/recommendations for international students: Required—TOEFL (minimum score 550 paper-based; 213 computer-based; 80 iBT). Electronic applications accepted. *Expenses:* Tuition, state resident: full-time $11,426; part-time $476 per credit hour. Tuition, nonresident: full-time $21,660; part-time $903 per credit hour. One-time fee: $62. *Faculty research:* Communication and signal processing, high performance computing systems, intelligent systems, power electronics and energy systems, RF and microwave systems, sensors and medical devices, solid state devices.

University of Toronto, School of Graduate Studies, Physical Sciences Division, Department of Computer Science, Toronto, ON M5S 1A1, Canada. Offers M Sc, PhD. Part-time programs available. *Degree requirements:* For master's, thesis; for doctorate, thesis/dissertation, thesis defense/oral exam. *Entrance requirements:* For master's, GRE (recommended), minimum B+ average overall and in final year; resume; 3 letters of reference; background in computer science and mathematics preferred; for doctorate, minimum B+ average overall and in final year; resumé; 3 letters of reference; background in computer science and mathematics preferred. Additional exam requirements/recommendations for international students: Required—TOEFL (minimum score 580 paper-based; 237 computer-based), TWE (minimum score 5).

University of Tulsa, Graduate School, College of Engineering and Natural Sciences, Department of Mathematical and Computer Sciences, Program in Computer Science, Tulsa, OK 74104-3189. Offers MS, PhD, JD/MS, MBA/MS. Part-time programs available. *Faculty:* 9 full-time (1 woman). *Students:* 46 full-time (10 women), 19 part-time (5 women); includes 8 minority (2 Black or African American, non-Hispanic/Latino; 4 American Indian or Alaska Native, non-Hispanic/Latino; 1 Asian, non-Hispanic/Latino; 1 Hispanic/Latino), 7 international. Average age 25. 47 applicants, 62% accepted, 17 enrolled. In 2010, 23 master's, 2 doctorates awarded. Terminal master's awarded for partial completion of doctoral program. *Degree requirements:* For master's, thesis (for some programs); for doctorate, comprehensive exam, thesis/ dissertation. *Entrance requirements:* For master's and doctorate, GRE General Test. Additional exam requirements/recommendations for international students: Required—TOEFL (minimum score 550 paper-based; 213 computer-based; 80 iBT), IELTS (minimum score 6). *Application deadline:* Applications are processed on a rolling basis. Application fee: $40. Electronic applications accepted. *Expenses:* Tuition: Full-time $16,902; part-time $939 per credit hour. Required fees: $1020; $4 per credit hour. Tuition and fees vary according to course load. *Financial support:* In 2010–11, 43 students received support, including 4 fellowships with full and partial tuition reimbursements available (averaging $12,086 per year), 32 research assistantships with full and partial tuition reimbursements available (averaging $11,581 per year), 12 teaching assistantships with full and partial tuition reimbursements available (averaging $10,110 per year); career-related internships or fieldwork, Federal Work-Study, scholarships/grants, health care benefits, tuition waivers (full and partial), and unspecified assistantships also available. Support available to part-time students. Financial award application deadline: 2/1; financial award applicants required to submit FAFSA. *Faculty research:* Robotics, human-computer interaction, systems security, information assurance, machine learning, intelligent systems, software engineering, distributed systems, evolutionary computation, computational biology, bioinformatics. *Application contact:* Dr. Rosanne Gamble, Advisor, 918-631-2988, Fax: 918-631-3077, E-mail: gamble@utulsa.edu.

University of Tulsa, Graduate School, Collins College of Business, Business Administration/ Computer Science Program, Tulsa, OK 74104-3189. Offers MBA/MS. Part-time programs available. *Students:* 1 full-time (0 women), 1 part-time (0 women). Average age 28. *Entrance requirements:* Additional exam requirements/recommendations for international students: Required—TOEFL (minimum score 575 paper-based; 231 computer-based; 79 iBT), IELTS (minimum score 6.5). *Application deadline:* Applications are processed on a rolling basis. Application fee: $40. Electronic applications accepted. *Expenses:* Tuition: Full-time $16,902; part-time $939 per credit hour. Required fees: $1020; $4 per credit hour. Tuition and fees vary according to course load. *Financial support:* In 2010–11, 1 student received support, including 1 teaching assistantship with full and partial tuition reimbursement available (averaging $11,594 per year); fellowships with full and partial tuition reimbursements available, research assistantships with full and partial tuition reimbursements available, career-related internships or fieldwork, Federal Work-Study, institutionally sponsored loans, scholarships/grants, health care benefits, tuition waivers, and unspecified assistantships also available. Support available to part-time students. Financial award application deadline: 2/1; financial award applicants required to submit FAFSA. *Unit head:* Dr. Linda Nichols, Associate Dean, 918-631-2242, Fax: 918-631-2142, E-mail: linda-nichols@utulsa.edu. *Application contact:* Information Contact, 918-631-2242, E-mail: graduate-business@utulsa.edu.

University of Utah, Graduate School, College of Engineering, School of Computing, Salt Lake City, UT 84112-9205. Offers computational engineering and science (MS); computer science (M Phil, MS, PhD); computing (MS, PhD). *Faculty:* 26 full-time (3 women), 2 part-time/adjunct (0 women). *Students:* 191 full-time (23 women), 63 part-time (5 women); includes 6 minority (1 Black or African American, non-Hispanic/Latino; 1 American Indian or Alaska Native, non-Hispanic/Latino; 3 Asian, non-Hispanic/Latino; 1 Hispanic/Latino), 145 international. Average age 28. 118 applicants, 96% accepted, 87 enrolled. In 2010, 44 master's, 16 doctorates awarded. Terminal master's awarded for partial completion of doctoral program. *Degree requirements:* For master's, comprehensive exam (for some programs), thesis (for some programs); for doctorate, comprehensive exam, thesis/dissertation. *Entrance requirements:* For master's and doctorate, GRE General Test, minimum GPA of 3.0. Additional exam requirements/recommendations for international students: Required—TOEFL (minimum score 500 paper-based; 173 computer-based; 61 iBT). *Application deadline:* For fall admission, 12/15 for domestic and international students. Application fee: $55 ($65 for international

students). Electronic applications accepted. *Expenses:* Contact institution. *Financial support:* In 2010–11, 1 student received support, including 4 fellowships with full tuition reimbursements available (averaging $20,000 per year), 102 research assistantships with full tuition reimbursements available (averaging $25,000 per year), 47 teaching assistantships with full tuition reimbursements available (averaging $12,000 per year); scholarships/grants, traineeships, health care benefits, and unspecified assistantships also available. Financial award application deadline: 12/15; financial award applicants required to submit FAFSA. *Faculty research:* Computer-aided graphic design, VLSI, information retrieval, portable artificial intelligence systems, functional programming. Total annual research expenditures: $5.9 million. *Unit head:* Dr. Alan Davis, Director, 801-581-8224, Fax: 801-581-5843, E-mail: ald@cs.utah.edu. *Application contact:* Ann Carlstrom, Graduate Advisor, 801-581-7631, Fax: 801-581-5843, E-mail: annc@cs.utah.edu.

University of Vermont, Graduate College, College of Engineering and Mathematics, Program in Computer Science, Burlington, VT 05405. Offers MS, PhD. *Students:* 24 (7 women); includes 1 Hispanic/Latino, 13 international. 46 applicants, 26% accepted, 2 enrolled. In 2010, 8 master's, 1 doctorate awarded. *Degree requirements:* For master's, thesis or alternative. *Entrance requirements:* For master's, GRE General Test. Additional exam requirements/ recommendations for international students: Required—TOEFL (minimum score 550 paper-based; 213 computer-based; 80 iBT). *Application deadline:* For fall admission, 4/1 priority date for domestic students. Applications are processed on a rolling basis. Application fee: $40. Electronic applications accepted. *Expenses:* Tuition, state resident: part-time $537 per credit hour. Tuition, nonresident: part-time $1355 per credit hour. *Financial support:* Research assistantships, teaching assistantships available. Financial award application deadline: 3/1. *Unit head:* Dr. Xindong Wu, Chair, 802-656-3330. *Application contact:* Prof. B. Lee, Coordinator, 802-656-3330.

University of Victoria, Faculty of Graduate Studies, Faculty of Engineering, Department of Computer Science, Victoria, BC V8W 2Y2, Canada. Offers M Sc, PhD. Part-time programs available. Terminal master's awarded for partial completion of doctoral program. *Degree requirements:* For master's, thesis or alternative; for doctorate, thesis/dissertation, candidacy exam. *Entrance requirements:* For master's, GRE (recommended), B Sc in computer science/ software engineering or the equivalent or bachelor's degree in mathematics with emphasis on computer science (recommended); for doctorate, GRE (recommended), MS in computer science or equivalent (recommended). Additional exam requirements/recommendations for international students: Required—TOEFL (minimum score 575 paper-based; 233 computer-based), IELTS (minimum score 7). Electronic applications accepted. *Faculty research:* Functional and logic programming, numerical analysis, parallel and distributed computing, software systems, theoretical computer science, VLSI design and testing.

University of Virginia, School of Engineering and Applied Science, Department of Computer Science, Charlottesville, VA 22903. Offers MCS, MS, PhD. *Faculty:* 24 full-time (2 women), 1 part-time/adjunct (0 women). *Students:* 77 full-time (12 women), 1 part-time (0 women); includes 1 Black or African American, non-Hispanic/Latino; 2 Asian, non-Hispanic/Latino; 1 Hispanic/Latino, 37 international. Average age 28. 322 applicants, 11% accepted, 11 enrolled. In 2010, 11 master's, 3 doctorates awarded. *Degree requirements:* For master's, thesis (for some programs); for doctorate, comprehensive exam, thesis/dissertation. *Entrance requirements:* For master's, GRE General Test, 3 letters of recommendation; for doctorate, GRE General Test, 3 letters of recommendation; essay. Additional exam requirements/recommendations for international students: Required—TOEFL (minimum score 650 paper-based; 250 computer-based; 90 iBT), IELTS (minimum score 7). *Application deadline:* For fall admission, 8/1 for domestic students, 4/1 for international students; for winter admission, 12/1 for domestic students, 8/1 for international students; for spring admission, 5/1 for domestic students, 1/1 for international students. Applications are processed on a rolling basis. Application fee: $60. Electronic applications accepted. *Financial support:* Fellowships available. Financial award application deadline: 10/15; financial award applicants required to submit FAFSA. *Faculty research:* Systems programming, operating systems, analysis of programs and computation theory, programming languages, software engineering. *Unit head:* Mary Lou Soffa, Chair, 434-982-2200, Fax: 434-982-2214, E-mail: inquiry@cs.virginia.edu. *Application contact:* Kathryn C. Thornton, Assistant Dean for Graduate Programs, 434-924-3897, Fax: 434-982-2214, E-mail: seas-grad-admission@cs.virginia.edu.

University of Washington, Graduate School, College of Engineering, Department of Computer Science and Engineering, Seattle, WA 98195-2350. Offers computer science (MS); computer science and engineering (PMS, PhD). Postbaccalaureate distance learning degree programs offered. *Faculty:* 56 full-time (7 women), 5 part-time/adjunct (2 women). *Students:* 168 full-time (41 women), 150 part-time (22 women); includes 1 Black or African American, non-Hispanic/ Latino; 34 Asian, non-Hispanic/Latino; 4 Hispanic/Latino, 108 international. Average age 28. 1,221 applicants, 9% accepted, 55 enrolled. In 2010, 77 master's, 23 doctorates awarded. *Degree requirements:* For doctorate, thesis/dissertation, Course work for qualifying evaluation, independent project, course work for breadth requirement. *Entrance requirements:* For doctorate, GRE General Test, Minimum GPA of 3.0, statement of purpose, curriculum vitae (academic life), letters of recommendation, transcript. Additional exam requirements/recommendations for international students: Required—TOEFL (minimum score 580 paper-based; 237 computer-based; 92 iBT); Recommended—IELTS (minimum score 7). *Application deadline:* For fall admission, 12/15 priority date for domestic and international students. Application fee: $75. Electronic applications accepted. *Financial support:* In 2010–11, 5 students received support, including 32 fellowships with full tuition reimbursements available (averaging $21,051 per year), 100 research assistantships with full tuition reimbursements available (averaging $18,216 per year), 13 teaching assistantships with full tuition reimbursements available (averaging $19,602 per year); career-related internships or fieldwork, traineeships, and health care benefits also available. Financial award application deadline: 12/15; financial award applicants required to submit FAFSA. *Faculty research:* Theory, systems, artificial intelligence, graphics, databases. Total annual research expenditures: $17.7 million. *Unit head:* Dr. Henry M. Levy, Professor and Chair, 206-543-9204, Fax: 206-543-2969, E-mail: levy@cs.washington.edu. *Application contact:* Lindsay Michimoto, Graduate Admissions Information Contact, 206-543-1695, Fax: 206-543-2969, E-mail: lindsaym@cs.washington.edu.

University of Waterloo, Graduate Studies, Faculty of Mathematics, David R. Cheriton School of Computer Science, Waterloo, ON N2L 3G1, Canada. Offers computer science (M Math, PhD); software engineering (M Math); statistics and computing (M Math). Part-time programs available. *Degree requirements:* For master's, research paper or thesis; for doctorate, comprehensive exam, thesis/dissertation. *Entrance requirements:* For master's, honors degree in field, minimum B+ average; for doctorate, master's degree, minimum B+ average. *Faculty research:* Computer graphics, artificial intelligence, algorithms and complexity, distributed computing and networks, software engineering.

The University of Western Ontario, Faculty of Graduate Studies, Physical Sciences Division, Department of Computer Science, London, ON N6A 5B8, Canada. Offers M Sc, PhD. Part-time programs available. *Degree requirements:* For master's, thesis, project or course work; for doctorate, thesis/dissertation. *Entrance requirements:* For master's, B Sc in computer science or comparable academic qualifications; for doctorate, M Sc in computer science or comparable academic qualifications. Additional exam requirements/recommendations for international students: Required—TOEFL. *Faculty research:* Artificial intelligence and logic programming, graphics and image processing, software and systems, theory of computing, symbolic mathematical computation.

University of West Florida, College of Arts and Sciences: Sciences, Department of Computer Science, Pensacola, FL 32514-5750. Offers computer science (MS); database systems (MS); software engineering (MS). Part-time and evening/weekend programs available. *Faculty:* 12 full-time (4 women), 4 part-time/adjunct (2 women). *Students:* 23 full-time (6 women), 123 part-time (26 women); includes 39 minority (6 Black or African American, non-Hispanic/Latino; 3 American Indian or Alaska Native, non-Hispanic/Latino; 12 Asian, non-Hispanic/Latino; 9

Computer Science

University of West Florida (continued)
Hispanic/Latino; 1 Native Hawaiian or other Pacific Islander, non-Hispanic/Latino; 8 Two or more races, non-Hispanic/Latino), 4 international. Average age 36. 62 applicants, 79% accepted, 38 enrolled. In 2010, 46 master's awarded. *Degree requirements:* For master's, thesis optional. *Entrance requirements:* For master's, GRE General Test: Additional exam requirements/recommendations for international students: Required—TOEFL (minimum score 550 paper-based; 213 computer-based). *Application deadline:* For fall admission, 6/1 for domestic students, 5/15 for international students; for spring admission, 10/1 for domestic and international students. Applications are processed on a rolling basis. Application fee: $30. *Expenses:* Tuition, state resident: full-time $4982; part-time $208 per credit hour. Tuition, nonresident: full-time $20,059; part-time $836 per credit hour. Required fees: $1365; $57 per credit hour. *Financial support:* In 2010–11, 16 fellowships with partial tuition reimbursements (averaging $453 per year), 8 research assistantships (averaging $3,280 per year), 3 teaching assistantships with partial tuition reimbursements (averaging $5,840 per year) were awarded; unspecified assistantships also available. Financial award application deadline: 4/15; financial award applicants required to submit FAFSA. *Unit head:* Dr. Leo Ter Haar, Chairperson, 850-474-2542. *Application contact:* Terry McCray, Assistant Director of Graduate Admissions, 850-473-7718, Fax: 850-473-7714, E-mail: gradadmissions@uwf.edu.

University of West Georgia, College of Arts and Sciences, Department of Computer Science, Carrollton, GA 30118. Offers applied computer science (MS); human centered computing (Certificate); software development (Certificate); system and network administration (Certificate); Web technologies (Certificate). Part-time and evening/weekend programs available. *Faculty:* 8 full-time (3 women). *Students:* 14 full-time (2 women), 8 part-time (3 women); includes 4 Black or African American, non-Hispanic/Latino; 1 Asian, non-Hispanic/Latino; 1 Two or more races, non-Hispanic/Latino, 2 international. Average age 30. 13 applicants, 46% accepted, 3 enrolled. In 2010, 9 master's awarded. *Degree requirements:* For master's, comprehensive exam, thesis optional. *Entrance requirements:* For master's, GRE, bachelor's degree, minimum overall undergraduate GPA of 2.5; for Certificate, bachelor's degree, minimum overall undergraduate GPA of 2.5. *Application deadline:* For fall admission, 7/17 priority date for domestic students; for spring admission, 11/20 for domestic students. Applications are processed on a rolling basis. Application fee: $30. Electronic applications accepted. *Expenses:* Tuition, state resident: full-time $4130; part-time $173 per semester hour. Tuition, nonresident: full-time $16,524; part-time $689 per semester hour. Required fees: $1586; $44.01 per semester hour. $397 per semester. Tuition and fees vary according to program. *Financial support:* In 2010–11, 7 research assistantships with full tuition reimbursements (averaging $6,000 per year) were awarded; unspecified assistantships also available. Financial award application deadline: 7/1; financial award applicants required to submit FAFSA. *Faculty research:* Artificial Intelligence, software engineering, Web technologies, database, networks. *Unit head:* Dr. Adel M. Abunawass, Chair, 678-839-6485, Fax: 678-839-6486, E-mail: adel@westga.edu. *Application contact:* Dr. Charles W. Clark, Dean, 678-839-6508, E-mail: cclark@westga.edu.

University of Windsor, Faculty of Graduate Studies, Faculty of Science, School of Computer Science, Windsor, ON N9B 3P4, Canada. Offers M Sc, PhD. Part-time programs available. *Degree requirements:* For master's, thesis; for doctorate, comprehensive exam, thesis/dissertation. *Entrance requirements:* For master's, GRE, minimum B average; for doctorate, master's degree in computer science, minimum B+ average. Additional exam requirements/recommendations for international students: Required—TOEFL (minimum score 580 paper-based; 237 computer-based). Electronic applications accepted. *Faculty research:* Data mining, distributed query optimization, distributed object based systems, grid computing, querying multimedia database systems.

University of Wisconsin–Madison, Graduate School, College of Letters and Science, Department of Computer Sciences, Madison, WI 53706-1380. Offers MS, PhD. Part-time programs available. Terminal master's awarded for partial completion of doctoral program. *Degree requirements:* For doctorate, thesis/dissertation. *Entrance requirements:* For master's and doctorate, GRE General Test, GRE Subject Test. Electronic applications accepted. *Expenses:* Tuition, state resident: full-time $9887.36; part-time $617.96 per credit. Tuition, nonresident: full-time $24,054; part-time $1503.40 per credit. Required fees: $67.63 per credit. Tuition and fees vary according to reciprocity agreements.

University of Wisconsin–Milwaukee, Graduate School, College of Engineering and Applied Science, Program in Computer Science, Milwaukee, WI 53201-0413. Offers computer science (MS, PhD). Part-time programs available. *Faculty:* 30 full-time (4 women). *Students:* 21 full-time (7 women), 23 part-time (1 woman); includes 2 Black or African American, non-Hispanic/Latino; 2 Asian, non-Hispanic/Latino, 4 international. Average age 31. 65 applicants, 55% accepted, 8 enrolled. In 2010, 16 master's awarded. *Degree requirements:* For master's, comprehensive exam (for some programs), thesis or alternative; for doctorate, comprehensive exam, thesis/dissertation, internship. *Entrance requirements:* For master's, GRE, minimum GPA of 2.75; for doctorate, GRE, minimum GPA of 3.5. Additional exam requirements/recommendations for international students: Required—TOEFL (minimum score 550 paper-based; 79 iBT), IELTS (minimum score 6.5). *Application deadline:* For fall admission, 1/1 priority date for domestic students; for spring admission, 9/1 for domestic students. Applications are processed on a rolling basis. Application fee: $56 ($96 for international students). *Financial support:* In 2010–11, 4 research assistantships, 10 teaching assistantships were awarded; fellowships, career-related internships or fieldwork, unspecified assistantships, and project assistantships also available. Support available to part-time students. Financial award application deadline: 4/15. Total annual research expenditures: $1 million. *Unit head:* Ichiro Suzuki, Representative, 414-229-4677, Fax: 414-229-6958, E-mail: csgpr@uwm.edu. *Application contact:* General Information Contact, 414-229-4982, Fax: 414-229-6967, E-mail: gradschool@uwm.edu.

University of Wisconsin–Parkside, School of Business and Technology, Program in Computer and Information Systems, Kenosha, WI 53141-2000. Offers MSCIS. *Entrance requirements:* For master's, GRE General Test or GMAT, 3 letters of recommendation, minimum GPA of 3.0. *Faculty research:* Distributed systems, data bases, natural language processing, event-driven systems.

University of Wisconsin–Platteville, School of Graduate Studies, College of Engineering, Mathematics and Science, Program in Computer Science, Platteville, WI 53818-3099. Offers MS. Part-time programs available. *Students:* 6 full-time (0 women), 3 part-time (0 women), 4 international. 6 applicants, 67% accepted. In 2010, 1 master's awarded. *Degree requirements:* For master's, comprehensive exam, thesis or alternative. *Entrance requirements:* Additional exam requirements/recommendations for international students: Required—TOEFL (minimum score 500 paper-based; 173 computer-based; 61 iBT). *Application deadline:* For fall admission, 7/1 priority date for domestic students; for spring admission, 11/1 for domestic students. Applications are processed on a rolling basis. Application fee: $56. Electronic applications accepted. *Expenses:* Tuition, state resident: full-time $7000. Tuition, nonresident: full-time $16,800. Required fees: $756. *Financial support:* Research assistantships with partial tuition reimbursements available. *Unit head:* Dr. Robert Hasker, Coordinator, 608-342-1561, Fax: 608-342-1965, E-mail: csse@uwplatt.edu. *Application contact:* Lisa Popp, School of Graduate Studies, 608-342-1322, Fax: 608-342-1389, E-mail: poppl@uwplatt.edu.

University of Wyoming, College of Engineering and Applied Sciences, Department of Computer Science, Laramie, WY 82070. Offers MS, PhD. Part-time programs available. Terminal master's awarded for partial completion of doctoral program. *Degree requirements:* For master's, thesis; for doctorate, thesis/dissertation. *Entrance requirements:* For master's and doctorate, GRE General Test, minimum GPA of 3.0. Additional exam requirements/recommendations for international students: Required—TOEFL (minimum score 550 paper-based; 213 computer-based), IELTS (minimum score 6). Electronic applications accepted. *Faculty research:* Fault-tolerant computing, distributed systems, knowledge representation, automated reasoning, parallel database access, formal methods.

Utah State University, School of Graduate Studies, College of Science, Department of Computer Science, Logan, UT 84322. Offers MCS, MS, PhD. Part-time and evening/weekend programs available. Postbaccalaureate distance learning degree programs offered. *Degree requirements:* For master's, thesis (for some programs), research project; for doctorate, thesis/dissertation. *Entrance requirements:* For master's, GRE General Test, GRE Subject Test, minimum GPA of 3.25, prerequisite coursework in math, 3 recommendation letters; for doctorate, GRE General Test, minimum GPA of 3.25, BS or MS. Additional exam requirements/recommendations for international students: Required—TOEFL. Electronic applications accepted. *Faculty research:* Artificial intelligence, software engineering, parallelism.

Vanderbilt University, School of Engineering, Department of Electrical Engineering and Computer Science, Program in Computer Science, Nashville, TN 37240-1001. Offers M Eng, MS, PhD. MS and PhD offered through the Graduate School. Part-time programs available. *Faculty:* 14 full-time (2 women). *Students:* 70 full-time (11 women); includes 1 Asian, non-Hispanic/Latino, 36 international. Average age 26. 236 applicants, 11% accepted, 14 enrolled. In 2010, 10 master's, 6 doctorates awarded. Terminal master's awarded for partial completion of doctoral program. *Degree requirements:* For master's, thesis (for some programs); for doctorate, comprehensive exam, thesis/dissertation. *Entrance requirements:* For master's and doctorate, GRE General Test, 3 letters of recommendation. Additional exam requirements/recommendations for international students: Required—TOEFL. *Application deadline:* For fall admission, 1/15 for domestic and international students; for spring admission, 11/1 for domestic and international students. Application fee: $0. Electronic applications accepted. *Financial support:* In 2010–11, fellowships with full tuition reimbursements (averaging $30,000 per year), research assistantships with full tuition reimbursements (averaging $21,600 per year), teaching assistantships with full tuition reimbursements (averaging $18,000 per year) were awarded; career-related internships or fieldwork, institutionally sponsored loans, scholarships/grants, health care benefits, tuition waivers (full and partial), and unspecified assistantships also available. Support available to part-time students. Financial award application deadline: 1/15. *Faculty research:* Artificial intelligence, performance evaluation, databases, software engineering, computational science. *Unit head:* Dr. Daniel M. Fleetwood, Chair, 615-322-2771, Fax: 615-343-6702, E-mail: dan.fleetwood@vanderbilt.edu. *Application contact:* Dr. Xenofan Koutsoukos, Director of Graduate Studies, 615-322-8283, Fax: 615-322-0677, E-mail: eecsinfo@eecsmail.vuse.vanderbilt.edu.

Villanova University, College of Engineering, Department of Electrical and Computer Engineering, Program in Computer Engineering, Villanova, PA 19085-1699. Offers computer architectures (Certificate); computer engineering (MSCPE); intelligent control systems (Certificate). Part-time and evening/weekend programs available. *Students:* 3 full-time (0 women), 14 part-time (2 women); includes 1 Black or African American, non-Hispanic/Latino; 3 Hispanic/Latino, 3 international. 35 applicants, 54% accepted. In 2010, 13 master's awarded. *Degree requirements:* For master's, thesis optional. *Entrance requirements:* For master's, GRE General Test (for applicants with degrees from foreign universities), BEE, minimum GPA of 3.0. Additional exam requirements/recommendations for international students: Required—TOEFL (minimum score 600 paper-based; 250 computer-based; 100 iBT). *Application deadline:* For fall admission, 8/1 priority date for domestic students, 4/1 for international students; for spring admission, 12/1 for domestic students, 8/1 for international students. Applications are processed on a rolling basis. Application fee: $50. Electronic applications accepted. *Expenses:* Tuition: Part-time $700 per credit. Part-time tuition and fees vary according to degree level and program. *Financial support:* In 2010–11, research assistantships with full and partial tuition reimbursements (averaging $13,500 per year); Federal Work-Study, scholarships/grants, tuition waivers (full and partial), and unspecified assistantships also available. Support available to part-time students. Financial award application deadline: 1/15. *Faculty research:* Expert systems, computer vision, neural networks, image processing, computer architectures. *Unit head:* Dr. Pritpal Singh, Chairman, 610-519-4971, Fax: 610-519-4436. *Application contact:* College of Engineering, Graduate Programs Office, 610-519-5840, Fax: 610-519-5859, E-mail: engineering.grad@villanova.edu.

Villanova University, Graduate School of Liberal Arts and Sciences, Department of Computing Sciences, Villanova, PA 19085-1699. Offers computer science (MS); software engineering (MS). Part-time and evening/weekend programs available. *Faculty:* 9 full-time (2 women), 3 part-time/adjunct (0 women). *Students:* 83 full-time (31 women), 27 part-time (4 women); includes 13 minority (2 Black or African American, non-Hispanic/Latino; 10 Asian, non-Hispanic/Latino; 1 Native Hawaiian or other Pacific Islander, non-Hispanic/Latino), 65 international. Average age 28. 72 applicants, 85% accepted, 27 enrolled. In 2010, 39 master's awarded. *Degree requirements:* For master's, thesis optional, independent study project. *Entrance requirements:* For master's, GRE, minimum GPA of 3.0. Additional exam requirements/recommendations for international students: Required—TOEFL. *Application deadline:* For fall admission, 3/1 priority date for domestic and international students; for spring admission, 11/15 priority date for domestic and international students. Applications are processed on a rolling basis. Application fee: $50. Electronic applications accepted. *Expenses:* Contact institution. *Financial support:* Research assistantships, Federal Work-Study and scholarships/grants available. Financial award applicants required to submit FAFSA. *Unit head:* Dr. Robert Beck, Chair, 610-519-7310. *Application contact:* Dr. Robert Beck, Chair, 610-519-7310.

Virginia Commonwealth University, Graduate School, School of Engineering, Department of Computer Science, Richmond, VA 23284-9005. Offers computer science (MS, PhD); engineering (PhD). *Faculty:* 9 full-time (2 women). *Students:* 12 full-time (6 women), 19 part-time (1 woman); includes 7 minority (1 Black or African American, non-Hispanic/Latino; 5 Asian, non-Hispanic/Latino; 1 Hispanic/Latino), 8 international. 51 applicants, 76% accepted, 20 enrolled. In 2010, 14 master's awarded. *Degree requirements:* For master's, thesis optional. *Entrance requirements:* For master's, GRE General Test; for doctorate, GRE. Additional exam requirements/recommendations for international students: Required—TOEFL (minimum score 600 paper-based; 250 computer-based; 100 iBT). *Application deadline:* For fall admission, 2/1 priority date for domestic students; for spring admission, 11/15 for domestic students. Application fee: $50. Electronic applications accepted. *Expenses:* Tuition, state resident: full-time $4308; part-time $479 per credit hour. Tuition, nonresident: full-time $8942; part-time $994 per credit hour. Required fees: $2000; $85 per credit hour. Tuition and fees vary according to course level, course load, degree level, campus/location and program. *Financial support:* Applicants required to submit FAFSA. *Unit head:* Dr. Rosalyn S. Hobson, Associate Dean for Graduate Studies, 804-828-8308, E-mail: rhobson@vcu.edu. *Application contact:* Dr. Vojislav Kecman, Director, Graduate Studies, Computer Science, 804-827-3608, E-mail: vkecman@vcu.edu.

Virginia International University, School of Computer Information Systems, Fairfax, VA 22030. Offers computer science (MS); information systems (MS). Part-time programs available. *Entrance requirements:* For master's, bachelor's degree. Additional exam requirements/recommendations for international students: Required—TOEFL (minimum score 550 paper-based; 213 computer-based; 80 iBT), IELTS. Electronic applications accepted.

Virginia Polytechnic Institute and State University, VT Online, Blacksburg, VA 24061. Offers aerospace engineering (MS); business information systems (Graduate Certificate); career and technical education (MS); computer engineering (M Eng, MS); decision support systems (Graduate Certificate); eLearning leadership (MA); electrical engineering (M Eng, MS); engineering administration (MEA); environmental politics and policy (Graduate Certificate); foundations of political analysis (Graduate Certificate); health product risk management (Graduate Certificate); information policy and society (Graduate Certificate); information security (Graduate Certificate); instructional technology (MA); liberal arts (Graduate Certificate); life sciences: health product risk management (MS); natural resources (MNR, Graduate Certificate); networking (Graduate Certificate); nonprofit and nongovernmental organization management (Graduate Certificate); ocean engineering (MS); political science (MA); security studies (Graduate Certificate); software development (Graduate Certificate). *Expenses:* Tuition, area resident: Full-time $9399; part-time $488 per credit hour. Tuition, state resident: full-time $9399; part-time $488 per credit hour. Tuition, nonresident: full-time $17,854; part-time $957.75 per credit hour.

International tuition: $17,854 full-time. Required fees: $1534. Full-time tuition and fees vary according to program.

Virginia State University, School of Graduate Studies, Research, and Outreach, School of Engineering, Science and Technology, Department of Mathematics and Computer Science, Petersburg, VA 23806-0001. Offers computer science (MS); mathematics (MS); mathematics education (M Ed). *Degree requirements:* For master's, thesis (for some programs). *Expenses:* Tuition, state resident: full-time $5576; part-time $335 per credit hour. Tuition, nonresident: full-time $13,402; part-time $670 per credit hour.

Wake Forest University, Graduate School of Arts and Sciences, Department of Computer Science, Winston-Salem, NC 27109. Offers MS. Part-time programs available. *Degree requirements:* For master's, one foreign language, thesis optional. *Entrance requirements:* For master's, GRE General Test. Additional exam requirements/recommendations for international students: Required—TOEFL (minimum score 213 computer-based; 79 iBT). Electronic applications accepted.

Washington State University, Graduate School, College of Engineering and Architecture, School of Electrical Engineering and Computer Science, Program in Computer Science, Pullman, WA 99164. Offers MS, PhD. *Faculty:* 24. *Students:* 50 full-time (12 women), 20 part-time (4 women); includes 4 minority (3 Asian, non-Hispanic/Latino; 1 Hispanic/Latino), 41 international. Average age 29. 195 applicants, 17% accepted, 17 enrolled. In 2010, 12 master's, 2 doctorates awarded. *Degree requirements:* For master's, comprehensive exam (for some programs), thesis optional, oral exam; for doctorate, comprehensive exam, thesis/dissertation, oral exam, qualifying exam. *Entrance requirements:* For master's and doctorate, GRE General Test, GRE Subject Test, statement of purpose giving qualifications, research interests, and goals; official college transcripts; three letters of recommendation. Additional exam requirements/recommendations for international students: Required—TOEFL (minimum score 520 paper-based; 190 computer-based), IELTS. *Application deadline:* For fall admission, 1/10 priority date for domestic students, 1/10 for international students; for spring admission, 7/1 for domestic and international students. Applications are processed on a rolling basis. Application fee: $50. *Expenses:* Tuition, state resident: full-time $8552; part-time $443 per credit. Tuition, nonresident: full-time $21,650; part-time $1083 per credit. Required fees: $846. *Financial support:* In 2010–11, 2 fellowships (averaging $2,500 per year), 18 research assistantships with full and partial tuition reimbursements (averaging $18,204 per year), 24 teaching assistantships with full and partial tuition reimbursements (averaging $18,204 per year) were awarded; career-related internships or fieldwork, Federal Work-Study, institutionally sponsored loans, tuition waivers (partial), and teaching associateships also available. Financial award application deadline: 2/10; financial award applicants required to submit FAFSA. *Faculty research:* Networks, software engineering; database systems, computer graphics, algorithmics. Total annual research expenditures: $3.9 million. *Unit head:* Dr. Anjan Bose, Director, 509-335-1147, Fax: 509-335-3818, E-mail: bose@wsu.edu. *Application contact:* Graduate School Admissions, 800-GRADWSU, Fax: 509-335-1949, E-mail: gradsch@wsu.edu.

Washington State University Tri-Cities, Graduate Programs, College of Engineering and Computer Science, Richland, WA 99352. Offers computer science (MS, PhD); electrical and computer engineering (PhD); electrical engineering (MS); mechanical engineering (MS, PhD). Part-time programs available. *Faculty:* 28. *Students:* 4 full-time (0 women), 25 part-time (8 women); includes 2 Black or African American, non-Hispanic/Latino, 1 international. *Degree requirements:* For master's, comprehensive exam, thesis (for some programs); for doctorate, comprehensive exam, thesis/dissertation, oral exam. *Entrance requirements:* For master's and doctorate, GRE, minimum GPA of 3.0, 3 letters of recommendation. Additional exam requirements/recommendations for international students: Required—TOEFL (minimum score 550 paper-based; 213 computer-based). *Application deadline:* For fall admission, 1/10 priority date for domestic students, 1/10 for international students; for spring admission, 7/1 priority date for domestic students, 7/1 for international students. Application fee: $50. *Financial*

support: Application deadline: 3/1. *Faculty research:* Positive ion track structure, biological systems computer simulations. *Unit head:* Dr. Ali Saberi, Chair, 509-372-7178, E-mail: sidra@eecs.wsu.edu. *Application contact:* Dr. Scott Hudson, Associate Director, 509-372-7254, Fax: 509-335-1949, E-mail: hudson@tricity.wsu.edu.

Washington State University Vancouver, Graduate Programs, School of Engineering and Computer Science, Vancouver, WA 98686. Offers computer science (MS); mechanical engineering (MS). Part-time programs available. *Faculty:* 9. *Students:* 14 full-time (1 woman), 5 part-time (1 woman); includes 1 Asian, non-Hispanic/Latino, 5 international. In 2010, 4 master's awarded. *Degree requirements:* For master's, comprehensive exam (for some programs), thesis, research project. *Entrance requirements:* For master's, minimum GPA of 3.0, 3 letters of recommendation with evaluation forms, resume. Additional exam requirements/recommendations for international students: Required—TOEFL (minimum score 550 paper-based). *Application deadline:* For fall admission, 1/10 priority date for domestic students, 1/10 for international students; for spring admission, 7/1 priority date for domestic students, 7/1 for international students. Applications are processed on a rolling basis. Application fee: $50. *Financial support:* In 2010–11, research assistantships with full tuition reimbursements (averaging $14,634 per year), teaching assistantships with full tuition reimbursements (averaging $13,383 per year) were awarded; health care benefits and unspecified assistantships also available. Financial award application deadline: 2/15. *Faculty research:* Software design, artificial intelligence, sensor networks, robotics, nanotechnology. Total annual research expenditures: $3.4 million. *Unit head:* Dr. Hakan Gurocak, Director, 360-546-9637, Fax: 360-546-9438, E-mail: hgurocak@vancouver.wsu.edu. *Application contact:* Peggy Moore, Academic Coordinator, 360-546-9638, Fax: 360-546-9438, E-mail: moorep@vancouver.wsu.edu.

Washington University in St. Louis, School of Engineering and Applied Science, Department of Computer Science and Engineering, St. Louis, MO 63130-4899. Offers computer engineering (MS, PhD); computer science (MS, PhD); computer science and engineering (M Eng). Part-time programs available. *Faculty:* 21 full-time (3 women), 4 part-time/adjunct (1 woman). *Students:* 85 full-time (11 women), 62 part-time (11 women); includes 5 Asian, non-Hispanic/Latino; 4 Hispanic/Latino; 3 Two or more races, non-Hispanic/Latino, 50 international. Average age 26. 423 applicants, 24% accepted, 50 enrolled. In 2010, 28 master's, 7 doctorates awarded. Terminal master's awarded for partial completion of doctoral program. *Degree requirements:* For master's, thesis optional; for doctorate, thesis/dissertation. *Entrance requirements:* For doctorate, GRE General Test. Additional exam requirements/recommendations for international students: Required—TOEFL. *Application deadline:* For fall admission, 1/15 for domestic and international students; for spring admission, 11/1 for domestic and international students. Applications are processed on a rolling basis. Application fee: $60. Electronic applications accepted. *Financial support:* In 2010–11, 4 fellowships with full tuition reimbursements (averaging $26,950 per year), 61 research assistantships with full tuition reimbursements (averaging $26,950 per year) were awarded; health care benefits, tuition waivers (partial), and unspecified assistantships also available. Financial award application deadline: 1/30. *Faculty research:* Artificial intelligence, computational genomics, computer and systems architecture, media and machines, networking and communication, software systems. Total annual research expenditures: $5.8 million. *Unit head:* Dr. Gruia-Catalin Roman, Chair, 314-935-6132, Fax: 314-935-7302, E-mail: roman@cse.wustl.edu. *Application contact:* Madeline Hawkins, Project Specialist, 314-935-6132, Fax: 314-935-7302, E-mail: admissions@cse.wustl.edu.

See Display below and Close-Up on page 341.

Wayne State University, College of Liberal Arts and Sciences, Department of Computer Science, Detroit, MI 48202. Offers computer science (MA, MS, PhD); scientific computing (Certificate). *Faculty:* 16 full-time (0 women), 1 part-time/adjunct (0 women). *Students:* 87 full-time (19 women), 35 part-time (6 women); includes 6 Black or African American, non-Hispanic/Latino; 1 American Indian or Alaska Native, non-Hispanic/Latino; 15 Asian, non-Hispanic/Latino, 75 international. Average age 30. 93 applicants, 48% accepted, 23 enrolled.

Computer Science

Wayne State University (continued)
In 2010, 26 master's, 10 doctorates awarded. *Degree requirements:* For master's, thesis (for some programs); for doctorate, thesis/dissertation. *Entrance requirements:* For master's, GRE General Test, minimum GPA of 3.0, letters of recommendation; for doctorate, GRE General Test, minimum GPA of 3.3; letters of recommendation; personal statement. Additional exam requirements/recommendations for international students: Required—TOEFL (minimum score 550 paper-based; 213 computer-based); Recommended—TWE (minimum score 6). *Application deadline:* For fall admission, 7/1 for domestic students, 6/1 for international students; for winter admission, 10/1 for international students; for spring admission, 2/1 for international students. Applications are processed on a rolling basis. Application fee: $30 ($50 for international students). Electronic applications accepted. *Expenses:* Tuition, state resident: full-time $7662; part-time $478.85 per credit hour. Tuition, nonresident: full-time $16,920; part-time $1057.55 per credit hour. Required fees: $571.20; $35.70 per credit hour. $188.05 per semester. Tuition and fees vary according to course load and program. *Financial support:* In 2010–11, 4 fellowships (averaging $23,995 per year), 22 research assistantships (averaging $17,676 per year), 30 teaching assistantships (averaging $16,984 per year) were awarded; career-related internships or fieldwork and Federal Work-Study also available. *Faculty research:* Software engineering, databases, bioinformatics, artificial intelligence, networking, distributed and parallel computing, security, graphics, visualizations. *Unit head:* Farshad Fotouhi, Chair, 313-577-2478, Fax: 313-577-6868, E-mail: aa2870@wayne.edu. *Application contact:* Loren Schwiebert, Associate Professor, 313-577-5474, E-mail: loren@cs.wayne.edu.

Webster University, George Herbert Walker School of Business and Technology, Department of Mathematics and Computer Science, St. Louis, MO 63119-3194. Offers computer science/ distributed systems (MS, Certificate); decision support systems (Certificate); web services (Certificate). Part-time and evening/weekend programs available. Postbaccalaureate distance learning degree programs offered (no on-campus study). *Entrance requirements:* For master's, 36 hours of graduate course work. Additional exam requirements/recommendations for international students: Required—TOEFL. *Expenses:* Tuition: Part-time $585 per credit hour. Tuition and fees vary according to degree level, campus/location and program. *Faculty research:* Databases, computer information systems networks, operating systems, computer architecture.

Wesleyan University, Graduate Programs, Department of Mathematics and Computer Science, Middletown, CT 06459. Offers MA, PhD. *Faculty:* 16 full-time (4 women). *Students:* 21 full-time (9 women); includes 1 Asian, non-Hispanic/Latino; 3 Hispanic/Latino, 4 international. Average age 28. 44 applicants, 9% accepted, 4 enrolled. In 2010, 2 master's, 1 doctorate awarded. Terminal master's awarded for partial completion of doctoral program. *Degree requirements:* For master's, one foreign language, thesis; for doctorate, 2 foreign languages, thesis/dissertation. *Entrance requirements:* For master's, GRE General Test, GRE Subject Test; for doctorate, GRE Subject Test. Additional exam requirements/recommendations for international students: Required—TOEFL. *Application deadline:* For fall admission, 2/15 for domestic and international students. Applications are processed on a rolling basis. Application fee: $0. Electronic applications accepted. *Expenses:* Tuition: Full-time $43,404. Required fees: $830. *Financial support:* In 2010–11, 18 teaching assistantships with full tuition reimbursements were awarded; tuition waivers (full and partial) also available. Financial award application deadline: 4/15; financial award applicants required to submit FAFSA. *Faculty research:* Topology, analysis. *Unit head:* Dr. Mark Hovey, Chair, 860-685-2169, E-mail: mhovey@wesleyan.edu. *Application contact:* Caryn Canalia, Administrative Assistant, 860-685-2182, Fax: 860-685-2571, E-mail: ccanalia@wesleyan.edu.

West Chester University of Pennsylvania, Office of Graduate Studies, College of Arts and Sciences, Department of Computer Science, West Chester, PA 19383. Offers computer science (MS); computer security (Certificate); information systems (Certificate); Web technology (Certificate). Part-time and evening/weekend programs available. *Students:* 10 full-time (1 woman), 9 part-time (1 woman); includes 2 minority (1 Black or African American, non-Hispanic/Latino; 1 Hispanic/Latino), 6 international. Average age 29. 23 applicants, 57% accepted, 5 enrolled. In 2010, 11 master's, 1 other advanced degree awarded. *Degree requirements:* For master's, thesis optional. *Entrance requirements:* For master's, GRE, two letters of recommendation; for Certificate, BS. Additional exam requirements/recommendations for international students: Required—TOEFL (minimum score 550 paper-based; 213 computer-based; 80 iBT). *Application deadline:* For fall admission, 4/15 priority date for domestic students, 3/15 for international students; for spring admission, 10/15 for domestic students, 9/1 for international students. Applications are processed on a rolling basis. Application fee: $35. Electronic applications accepted. *Expenses:* Tuition, state resident: full-time $6966; part-time $387 per credit. Tuition, nonresident: full-time $11,146; part-time $619 per credit. Required fees: $1614.40; $133.24 per credit. Part-time tuition and fees vary according to campus/location. *Financial support:* Unspecified assistantships available. Support available to part-time students. Financial award application deadline: 2/15; financial award applicants required to submit FAFSA. *Faculty research:* Automata theory, compilers, non well-founded sets, security in sensor and mobile ad-hoc networks, intrusion detection, security and trust in pervasive computing, economic modeling of security protocols. *Unit head:* Dr. James Fabrey, Chair, 610-436-2204, E-mail: jfabrey@wcupa.edu. *Application contact:* Dr. Afrand Agah, Graduate Coordinator, 610-436-4419, E-mail: aagah@wcupa.edu.

Western Carolina University, Graduate School, College of Arts and Sciences, Department of Mathematics and Computer Science, Cullowhee, NC 28723. Offers applied mathematics (MS). Part-time and evening/weekend programs available. *Degree requirements:* For master's, thesis or alternative. *Entrance requirements:* For master's, GRE General Test, appropriate undergraduate degree, 3 letters of recommendation. Additional exam requirements/recommendations for international students: Required—TOEFL (minimum score 550 paper-based; 270 computer-based; 79 iBT).

Western Illinois University, School of Graduate Studies, College of Business and Technology, Department of Computer Science, Macomb, IL 61455-1390. Offers MS. Part-time programs available. *Students:* 62 full-time (11 women), 16 part-time (4 women); includes 3 minority (all Black or African American, non-Hispanic/Latino), 59 international. Average age 25. 134 applicants, 74% accepted. In 2010, 43 master's awarded. *Degree requirements:* For master's, thesis or alternative. *Entrance requirements:* For master's, proficiency in Java. Additional exam requirements/recommendations for international students: Required—TOEFL (minimum score 550 paper-based; 213 computer-based; 80 iBT). *Application deadline:* Applications are processed on a rolling basis. Application fee: $30. Electronic applications accepted. *Expenses:* Tuition, state resident: full-time $6370; part-time $265.40 per credit hour. Tuition, nonresident: full-time $12,740; part-time $530.80 per credit hour. Required fees: $75.67 per credit hour. *Financial support:* In 2010–11, 17 students received support, including 8 research assistantships with full tuition reimbursements available (averaging $7,280 per year), 9 teaching assistantships with full tuition reimbursements available (averaging $8,400 per year). Financial award applicants required to submit FAFSA. *Unit head:* Dr. Kathleen Neumann, Program Director, 309-298-1452. *Application contact:* Evelyn Hoing, Assistant Director of Graduate Studies, 309-298-1806, Fax: 309-298-2345, E-mail: grad-office@wiu.edu.

Western Kentucky University, Graduate Studies, Ogden College of Science and Engineering, Department of Mathematics and Computer Science, Bowling Green, KY 42101. Offers computational mathematics (MS); computer science (MS); mathematics (MA, MS). *Degree requirements:* For master's, comprehensive exam, thesis optional, written exam. *Entrance*

requirements: For master's, GRE General Test, minimum GPA of 2.75. Additional exam requirements/recommendations for international students: Required—TOEFL (minimum score 555 paper-based; 213 computer-based; 79 iBT). *Faculty research:* Differential equations numerical analysis, probability statistics, algebra, typology, knot theory.

Western Michigan University, Graduate College, College of Engineering and Applied Sciences, Department of Computer Science, Kalamazoo, MI 49008. Offers MS, PhD. *Degree requirements:* For master's, thesis optional, oral exams; for doctorate, 2 foreign languages, thesis/dissertation. *Entrance requirements:* For master's and doctorate, GRE General Test.

Western Washington University, Graduate School, College of Sciences and Technology, Department of Computer Science, Bellingham, WA 98225-5996. Offers MS. Part-time programs available. *Degree requirements:* For master's, thesis optional, project. *Entrance requirements:* For master's, GRE General Test, minimum GPA of 3.0 in last 60 semester hours or last 90 quarter hours. Additional exam requirements/recommendations for international students: Required—TOEFL (minimum score 567 paper-based; 227 computer-based). Electronic applications accepted. *Faculty research:* Distributed operating systems, data mining, machine learning, robotics, information retrieval, graphics and visualization, parallel and distributed computing.

West Virginia University, College of Engineering and Mineral Resources, Lane Department of Computer Science and Electrical Engineering, Program in Computer Science, Morgantown, WV 26506. Offers MSCS, PhD. Part-time programs available. *Degree requirements:* For master's, thesis; for doctorate, comprehensive exam, thesis/dissertation. *Entrance requirements:* For master's, GRE General Test, letters of recommendation; for doctorate, GRE General Test, GRE Subject Test, MS in computer science, letters of recommendation. Additional exam requirements/recommendations for international students: Required—TOEFL. *Faculty research:* Artificial intelligence, knowledge-based simulation, data communications, mathematical computations, software engineering.

Wichita State University, Graduate School, College of Engineering, Department of Electrical Engineering and Computer Science, Wichita, KS 67260. Offers computer networking (MS); computer science (MS); electrical engineering (MS, PhD). Part-time and evening/weekend programs available. *Unit head:* Dr. John Watkins, Chair, 316-978-3156, Fax: 316-978-5408, E-mail: john.watkins@wichita.edu. *Application contact:* Dr. John Watkins, Chair, 316-978-3156, Fax: 316-978-5408, E-mail: john.watkins@wichita.edu.

Winston-Salem State University, Program in Computer Science and Information Technology, Winston-Salem, NC 27110-0003. Offers MS. Part-time programs available. *Degree requirements:* For master's, thesis optional. *Entrance requirements:* For master's, GRE, resume. Electronic applications accepted. *Faculty research:* Artificial intelligence, network protocols, software engineering.

Worcester Polytechnic Institute, Graduate Studies and Research, Department of Computer Science, Worcester, MA 01609-2280. Offers computer and communications networks (MS); computer science (MS, PhD, Advanced Certificate, Graduate Certificate); robotics engineering (MS, PhD). Part-time and evening/weekend programs available. *Faculty:* 19 full-time (3 women). *Students:* 84 full-time (16 women), 24 part-time (3 women); includes 3 Black or African American, non-Hispanic/Latino; 6 Native Hawaiian or other Pacific Islander, non-Hispanic/Latino, 50 international. 291 applicants, 48% accepted, 36 enrolled. In 2010, 25 master's, 4 doctorates awarded. Terminal master's awarded for partial completion of doctoral program. *Degree requirements:* For master's, thesis optional; for doctorate, comprehensive exam, thesis/dissertation. *Entrance requirements:* For master's, GRE General Test, GRE Subject Test in computer science (recommended), 3 letters of recommendation; for doctorate, GRE General Test, GRE Subject Test in computer science (recommended), 3 letters of recommendation, statement of purpose. Additional exam requirements/recommendations for international students: Required—TOEFL (minimum score 550 paper-based; 213 computer-based; 79 iBT), IELTS (minimum score 6.5). *Application deadline:* For fall admission, 1/1 priority date for domestic and international students; for spring admission, 10/1 priority date for domestic and international students. Applications are processed on a rolling basis. Application fee: $70. Electronic applications accepted. *Expenses:* Tuition: Full-time $20,862; part-time $1159 per term. One-time fee: $15. *Financial support:* Career-related internships or fieldwork, institutionally sponsored loans, scholarships/grants, and unspecified assistantships available. Financial award application deadline: 1/1; financial award applicants required to submit FAFSA. *Faculty research:* Computer networks and distributed systems, databases and data mining, artificial intelligence, computer graphics and visualization, applied logic and security. *Unit head:* Dr. Michael Gennert, Interim Head, 508-831-5357, Fax: 508-831-5776, E-mail: michaelg@wpi.edu. *Application contact:* Dr. Carolina Ruiz, Graduate Coordinator, 508-831-5357, Fax: 508-831-5776, E-mail: ruiz@wpi.edu.

Wright State University, School of Graduate Studies, College of Engineering and Computer Science, Department of Computer Science and Engineering, Computer Science Program, Dayton, OH 45435. Offers MS. *Degree requirements:* For master's, thesis optional. *Entrance requirements:* For master's, GRE General Test, minimum GPA of 3.0 in major, 2.7 overall. Additional exam requirements/recommendations for international students: Required—TOEFL.

Wright State University, School of Graduate Studies, College of Engineering and Computer Science, Department of Computer Science and Engineering, Program in Computer Science and Engineering, Dayton, OH 45435. Offers PhD. *Degree requirements:* For doctorate, thesis/dissertation, candidacy and general exams. *Entrance requirements:* For doctorate, GRE General Test, minimum GPA of 3.3. Additional exam requirements/recommendations for international students: Required—TOEFL.

Yale University, Graduate School of Arts and Sciences, Department of Computer Science, New Haven, CT 06520. Offers MS, PhD. *Degree requirements:* For doctorate, thesis/dissertation. *Entrance requirements:* For doctorate, GRE General Test, GRE Subject Test.

York University, Faculty of Graduate Studies, Faculty of Science and Engineering, Program in Computer Science, Toronto, ON M3J 1P3, Canada. Offers M Sc, PhD. *Degree requirements:* For master's, thesis or alternative; for doctorate, comprehensive exam, thesis/dissertation, internship or practicum. Electronic applications accepted.

Youngstown State University, Graduate School, College of Science, Technology, Engineering and Mathematics, Department of Computer Science and Information Systems, Youngstown, OH 44555-0001. Offers computing and information systems (MCIS). Part-time programs available. *Degree requirements:* For master's, thesis or capstone project. *Entrance requirements:* For master's, GRE or GMAT. Additional exam requirements/recommendations for international students: Required—TOEFL (minimum score 550 paper-based; 213 computer-based). *Faculty research:* Networking, computational science, graphics and visualization, database and data mining, biometrics, artificial intelligence, online learning environments.

Youngstown State University, Graduate School, College of Science, Technology, Engineering and Mathematics, Department of Mathematics and Statistics, Youngstown, OH 44555-0001. Offers applied mathematics (MS); computer science (MS); secondary mathematics (MS); statistics (MS). Part-time programs available. *Degree requirements:* For master's, comprehensive exam, thesis optional. *Entrance requirements:* For master's, minimum GPA of 2.7 in computer science and mathematics. Additional exam requirements/recommendations for international students: Required—TOEFL. *Faculty research:* Regression analysis, numerical analysis, statistics, Markov chain, topology and fuzzy sets.

Database Systems

Boston University, Metropolitan College, Department of Computer Science, Boston, MA 02215. Offers computer information systems (MS), including computer networks, database management and business intelligence, health informatics, IT project management, security; computer science (MS), including computer networks, security; telecommunications (MS), including security. Part-time and evening/weekend programs available. Postbaccalaureate distance learning degree programs offered (no on-campus study). *Faculty:* 10 full-time (0 women), 30 part-time/adjunct (3 women). *Students:* 16 full-time (2 women), 681 part-time (155 women); includes 182 minority (44 Black or African American, non-Hispanic/Latino; 1 American Indian or Alaska Native, non-Hispanic/Latino; 88 Asian, non-Hispanic/Latino; 36 Hispanic/Latino; 2 Native Hawaiian or other Pacific Islander, non-Hispanic/Latino; 11 Two or more races, non-Hispanic/Latino), 66 international. Average age 35. 273 applicants, 78% accepted, 155 enrolled. In 2010, 143 master's awarded. *Degree requirements:* For master's, thesis optional. *Entrance requirements:* For master's, 3 letters of recommendation, professional resume. Additional exam requirements/recommendations for international students: Required—TOEFL (minimum score 550 paper-based; 213 computer-based; 80 iBT). *Application deadline:* For fall admission, 6/1 priority date for international students; for spring admission, 10/1 priority date for international students. Applications are processed on a rolling basis. Application fee: $70. Electronic applications accepted. *Expenses:* Tuition: Full-time $39,314; part-time $1228 per credit. Required fees: $40 per semester. *Financial support:* In 2010–11, 9 research assistantships with partial tuition reimbursements (averaging $5,000 per year) were awarded; career-related internships or fieldwork and unspecified assistantships also available. Support available to part-time students. Financial award applicants required to submit FAFSA. *Faculty research:* Medical informatics, Web technologies, telecom and networks, security and forensics, software engineering, programming languages, multimedia and AI, information systems and IT project management. *Unit head:* Dr. Lubomir Chitkushev, Chairman, 617-353-2566, Fax: 617-353-2367, E-mail: csinfo@bu.edu. *Application contact:* Kim Richards, Program Coordinator, 617-353-2566, Fax: 617-353-2367, E-mail: kimrich@bu.edu.

Colorado Technical University Colorado Springs, Graduate Studies, Program in Computer Science, Colorado Springs, CO 80907-3896. Offers computer science (DCS); computer systems security (MSCS); database systems (MSCS); software engineering (MSCS). Part-time and evening/weekend programs available. Postbaccalaureate distance learning degree programs offered. *Degree requirements:* For master's, thesis or alternative; for doctorate, thesis/dissertation. *Entrance requirements:* For doctorate, minimum graduate GPA of 3.0, 5 years of related work experience. *Faculty research:* Software engineering, systems engineering.

Colorado Technical University Denver, Program in Computer Science, Greenwood Village, CO 80111. Offers computer systems security (MSCS); database systems (MSCS); software engineering (MSCS). Part-time and evening/weekend programs available. *Degree requirements:* For master's, thesis or alternative. *Entrance requirements:* For master's, minimum undergraduate GPA of 3.0, resume.

Ferris State University, College of Business, Big Rapids, MI 49307. Offers application development (MSISM); business intelligence and informatics (MBA); database administration (MSISM); design and innovation management process (MBA); e-business (MSISM); networking (MSISM); quality management (MBA); security (MSISM). *Accreditation:* ACBSP. Part-time and evening/weekend programs available. *Faculty:* 10 full-time (3 women), 2 part-time/adjunct (both women). *Students:* 34 full-time (9 women), 112 part-time (55 women); includes 3 Black or African American, non-Hispanic/Latino; 4 American Indian or Alaska Native, non-Hispanic/Latino; 3 Asian, non-Hispanic/Latino; 3 Hispanic/Latino; 4 Two or more races, non-Hispanic/Latino, 16 international. Average age 32. 68 applicants, 35% accepted, 15 enrolled. In 2010, 62 master's awarded. *Degree requirements:* For master's, comprehensive exam, thesis (for MSISM). *Entrance requirements:* For master's, GRE or GMAT (waived if GPA is 3.5 or better), minimum GPA of 3.0 in junior/senior level classes, 2.75 overall; writing sample; 3 letters of reference; resume. Additional exam requirements/recommendations for international students: Required—TOEFL (minimum score 500 paper-based; 173 computer-based; 67 iBT). *Application deadline:* For fall admission, 7/1 priority date for domestic students, 6/15 for international students; for winter admission, 11/1 priority date for domestic students, 10/15 for international students; for spring admission, 3/1 priority date for domestic students, 2/15 for international students. Applications are processed on a rolling basis. Application fee: $30. Electronic applications accepted. *Financial support:* Career-related internships or fieldwork, Federal Work-Study, scholarships/grants, and unspecified assistantships available. Support available to part-time students. Financial award application deadline: 3/15; financial award applicants required to submit FAFSA. *Faculty research:* Quality improvement, client/server end-user computing, information management and policy, security, digital forensics. *Unit head:* Dr. David Steenstra, Department Chair, 231-591-2168, Fax: 231-591-3548, E-mail: yosts@ferris.edu. *Application contact:* Shannon Yost, Department Secretary, 231-591-2168, Fax: 231-591-3548, E-mail: yosts@ferris.edu.

George Mason University, Volgenau School of Engineering, Department of Computer Science, Fairfax, VA 22030. Offers biometrics (Certificate); computer games technology (Certificate); computer networking (Certificate); computer science (MS, PhD); data mining (Certificate); database management (Certificate); electronic commerce (Certificate); foundations of information systems (Certificate); information engineering (Certificate); information security and assurance (MS, Certificate); information systems (MS); intelligent agents (Certificate); software architecture (Certificate); software engineering (MS, Certificate); systems engineering (MS); Web-based software engineering (Certificate). MS program offered jointly with Old Dominion University, University of Virginia, Virginia Commonwealth University, and Virginia Polytechnic Institute and State University. Part-time and evening/weekend programs available. Postbaccalaureate distance learning degree programs offered. *Faculty:* 42 full-time (9 women), 20 part-time/adjunct (1 woman). *Students:* 124 full-time (37 women), 453 part-time (103 women); includes 14 Black or African American, non-Hispanic/Latino; 66 Asian, non-Hispanic/Latino; 13 Hispanic/Latino; 3 Two or more races, non-Hispanic/Latino, 206 international. Average age 30. 904 applicants, 53% accepted, 150 enrolled. In 2010, 203 master's, 4 doctorates, 20 other advanced degrees awarded. *Degree requirements:* For master's, thesis optional; for doctorate, comprehensive exam, thesis/dissertation. *Entrance requirements:* For master's, GRE General Test, minimum GPA of 3.0 in last 60 hours, 3 letters of recommendation; for doctorate, GRE, 4-year BA, academic work in computer science, 3 letters of recommendation, statement of career goals and aspirations. Additional exam requirements/recommendations for international students: Required—TOEFL (minimum score 570 paper-based; 230 computer-based; 88 iBT). *Application deadline:* For fall admission, 4/15 priority date for domestic students, 1/15 for international students; for spring admission, 11/15 for domestic students. Application fee: $100. Electronic applications accepted. *Expenses:* Tuition, state resident: full-time $8192; part-time $440 per credit hour. Tuition, nonresident: full-time $22,952; part-time $1055 per credit hour. Required fees: $2364; $99 per credit hour. *Financial support:* In 2010–11, 101 students received support, including 3 fellowships (averaging $18,000 per year), 52 research assistantships (averaging $15,078 per year), 47 teaching assistantships (averaging $10,983 per year); career-related internships or fieldwork, Federal Work-Study, scholarships/grants, unspecified assistantships, and health care benefits (full-time research or teaching assistantship recipients) also available. Financial award application deadline: 3/1; financial award applicants required to submit FAFSA. *Faculty research:* Artificial intelligence, image processing/graphics, parallel/distributed systems, software engineering systems. Total annual research expenditures: $1.3 million. *Unit head:* Dr. Arun Sood, Director, 703-993-1524, Fax: 703-993-1710, E-mail: asood@gmu.edu. *Application contact:* Jay Shapiro, Professor, 703-993-1485, E-mail: jshapiro@gmu.edu.

Minnesota State University Mankato, College of Graduate Studies, College of Science, Engineering and Technology, Department of Information Systems and Technology, Mankato, MN 56001. Offers database technologies (Certificate); information technology (MS). *Students:* 13 full-time (2 women), 8 part-time (3 women). *Degree requirements:* For master's, comprehensive exam, thesis or alternative. *Entrance requirements:* For master's, GRE General Test, minimum GPA of 3.0 during previous 2 years. Additional exam requirements/recommendations for international students: Required—TOEFL (minimum score 550 paper-based; 213 computer-based; 80 iBT). *Application deadline:* For fall admission, 7/1 priority date for domestic students; for spring admission, 11/1 for domestic students. Applications are processed on a rolling basis. Electronic applications accepted. *Financial support:* Research assistantships with full tuition reimbursements, teaching assistantships with full tuition reimbursements, unspecified assistantships available. Financial award application deadline: 3/15; financial award applicants required to submit FAFSA. *Unit head:* Dr. Mahbubur Syed, Graduate Coordinator, 507-389-3226. *Application contact:* 507-389-2321, E-mail: grad@mnsu.edu.

National University, Academic Affairs, School of Engineering and Technology, Department of Applied Engineering, La Jolla, CA 92037-1011. Offers database administration (MS); engineering management (MS); environmental engineering (MS); homeland security and safety engineering (MS); system engineering (MS); wireless communications (MS). Part-time and evening/weekend programs available. Postbaccalaureate distance learning degree programs offered (no on-campus study). *Faculty:* 6 full-time (1 woman), 69 part-time/adjunct (12 women). *Students:* 82 full-time (16 women), 153 part-time (35 women); includes 87 minority (18 Black or African American, non-Hispanic/Latino; 1 American Indian or Alaska Native, non-Hispanic/Latino; 34 Asian, non-Hispanic/Latino; 28 Hispanic/Latino; 2 Native Hawaiian or other Pacific Islander, non-Hispanic/Latino; 4 Two or more races, non-Hispanic/Latino), 60 international. Average age 31. 166 applicants, 100% accepted, 106 enrolled. In 2010, 79 master's awarded. *Degree requirements:* For master's, thesis. *Entrance requirements:* For master's, interview, minimum GPA of 2.5. Additional exam requirements/recommendations for international students: Required—TOEFL (minimum score 550 paper-based; 213 computer-based; 79 iBT), IELTS (minimum score 6). *Application deadline:* Applications are processed on a rolling basis. Application fee: $60 ($65 for international students). Electronic applications accepted. *Expenses:* Tuition: Full-time $9450; part-time $350 per unit. Required fees: $350 per unit. One-time fee: $60. *Financial support:* Career-related internships or fieldwork, institutionally sponsored loans, scholarships/grants, and tuition waivers (partial) available. Support available to part-time students. Financial award application deadline: 6/30; financial award applicants required to submit FAFSA. *Unit head:* Dr. Shekar Viswanathan, Chair and Associate Professor, 858-309-8416, Fax: 858-309-3420, E-mail: sviswana@nu.edu. *Application contact:* Dominick Giovanniello, Associate Regional Dean—San Diego, 800-NAT-UNIV, Fax: 858-541-7792, E-mail: dgiovann@nu.edu.

New York University, School of Continuing and Professional Studies, Division of Programs in Business, Graduate Programs in Management and Systems, New York, NY 10012-1019. Offers core business competencies (Advanced Certificate); database technologies (MS); enterprise and risk management (Advanced Certificate); enterprise risk management (MS); information technologies (Advanced Certificate); strategy and leadership (MS, Advanced Certificate); systems management (MS). Part-time and evening/weekend programs available. Postbaccalaureate distance learning degree programs offered (no on-campus study). *Faculty:* 2 full-time (0 women), 27 part-time/adjunct (6 women). *Students:* 23 full-time (11 women), 166 part-time (56 women); includes 18 Black or African American, non-Hispanic/Latino; 29 Asian, non-Hispanic/Latino; 17 Hispanic/Latino, 34 international. Average age 33. 135 applicants, 52% accepted, 39 enrolled. In 2010, 61 master's, 15 other advanced degrees awarded. *Degree requirements:* For master's, thesis, capstone project. *Entrance requirements:* For master's, GMAT or GRE General Test (for recent graduates), resume, 2 letters of recommendation, essay, professional experience. Additional exam requirements/recommendations for international students: Required—TOEFL (minimum score 600 paper-based; 250 computer-based; 100 iBT). *Application deadline:* For fall admission, 2/1 priority date for domestic and international students; for spring admission, 10/15 priority date for domestic students, 8/15 priority date for international students. Applications are processed on a rolling basis. Application fee: $75. Electronic applications accepted. *Financial support:* In 2010–11, 73 students received support, including 73 fellowships (averaging $1,803 per year); scholarships/grants also available. Support available to part-time students. Financial award application deadline: 3/1; financial award applicants required to submit FAFSA. *Unit head:* Israel Moskowitz, Academic Director, 212-992-3600, Fax: 212-992-3650, E-mail: im36@nyu.edu. *Application contact:* Helen Sapp, Assistant Director, 212-992-3640, Fax: 212-992-3650, E-mail: helen.sapp@nyu.edu.

Northwestern University, School of Continuing Studies, Program in Information Systems, Evanston, IL 60208. Offers database and Internet technologies (MS); information systems management (MS); information systems security (MS); software project management and development (MS).

Regis University, College for Professional Studies, School of Computer and Information Sciences, Denver, CO 80221-1099. Offers database administration with Oracle (Certificate); database development (Certificate); database technologies (M Sc); enterprise Java software development (Certificate); enterprise resource planning (Certificate); executive information technologies (Certificate); information assurance (M Sc, Certificate); information technology management (M Sc); software engineering (M Sc, Certificate); software engineering and database technologies (M Sc); storage area networks (Certificate); systems engineering (M Sc, Certificate). Offered at Boulder Campus, Northwest Denver Campus, Southeast Denver Campus, Fort Collins Campus, Colorado Springs Campus, and Broomfield Campus. Part-time and evening/weekend programs available. Postbaccalaureate distance learning degree programs offered (no on-campus study). *Degree requirements:* For master's, thesis, final research project. *Entrance requirements:* For master's, 2 years of related experience, resume, interview; for Certificate, 2 years of related experience, resumé. Additional exam requirements/recommendations for international students: Required—TOEFL (minimum score 213 computer-based), TWE (minimum score 5), TOEFL or university-based test. Electronic applications accepted. *Expenses:* Contact institution. *Faculty research:* Secure Virtual Laboratory Architecture, Joint IA project with W2C06 Institute, Information Policy, OLTP and OLAP Technologies, knowledge management, software architectures.

Rochester Institute of Technology, Graduate Enrollment Services, B. Thomas Golisano College of Computing and Information Sciences, Department of Information Technology, Rochester, NY 14623-5603. Offers database administration (AC); human computer interaction (MS); information assurance (AC); information technology (MS); interactive multimedia development (AC); medical informatics (MS); software development and management (MS). Part-time and evening/weekend programs available. Postbaccalaureate distance learning degree programs offered (minimal on-campus study). *Students:* 84 full-time (23 women), 114 part-time (29 women); includes 8 Black or African American, non-Hispanic/Latino; 1 American Indian or Alaska Native, non-Hispanic/Latino; 4 Asian, non-Hispanic/Latino; 7 Hispanic/Latino, 77 international. Average age 30. 176 applicants, 64% accepted, 59 enrolled. In 2010, 53 master's, 5 other advanced degrees awarded. *Degree requirements:* For master's, thesis or project. *Entrance requirements:* For master's, GRE, minimum GPA of 3.0. Additional exam requirements/recommendations for international students: Required—TOEFL (minimum score 570 paper-based; 230 computer-based; 99 iBT) or IELTS (minimum score 6.5). *Application deadline:* For fall admission, 8/1 for domestic students, 7/1 for international students; for spring admission, 2/1 for domestic students. Applications are processed on a rolling basis. Electronic applications accepted. *Expenses:* Tuition: Full-time $33,234; part-time $924 per credit hour. Required fees: $219. *Financial support:* In 2010–11, 137 students received support; research assistantships with partial tuition reimbursements available, teaching assistantships with partial tuition reimbursements available, career-related internships or fieldwork, scholarships/grants, and unspecified assistantships available. Support available to part-time students. Financial award applicants required to submit FAFSA. *Faculty research:* Human-computer interaction: eye tracking, usability engineering, usability testing, ubiquitous computing, interface design and development; platform-independent Multiuser Online Virtual Environments (MOVEs); simulation; service computing, query optimization, data mining and integration; applications programming,

Database Systems

Rochester Institute of Technology (continued)
interface designs, needs assessment, data modeling, database administration. *Unit head:* Prof. Jeffrey Lasky, Department Chair, 585-475-2284, Fax: 585-475-6584, E-mail: jeffrey.lasky@rit.edu. *Application contact:* Diane Ellison, Assistant Vice President, Graduate Enrollment Services, 585-475-2229, Fax: 585-475-7164, E-mail: gradinfo@rit.edu.

Sacred Heart University, Graduate Programs, College of Arts and Sciences, Department of Computer Science and Information Technology, Fairfield, CT 06825-1000. Offers computer science (MS); database (CPS); information technology (MS, CPS); information technology and network security (CPS); interactive multimedia (CPS); Web development (CPS). Part-time and evening/weekend programs available. *Degree requirements:* For master's, thesis optional. *Entrance requirements:* Additional exam requirements/recommendations for international students: Required—TOEFL (minimum score 550 paper-based; 213 computer-based). Electronic applications accepted. *Faculty research:* Contemporary market software.

Stevens Institute of Technology, Graduate School, Charles V. Schaefer Jr. School of Engineering, Department of Computer Science, Hoboken, NJ 07030. Offers computer graphics (Certificate); computer science (MS, PhD); computer systems (Certificate); database management systems (Certificate); distributed systems (Certificate); elements of computer science (Certificate); enterprise computing (Certificate); enterprise security and information assurance (Certificate); health informatics (Certificate); multimedia experience and management (Certificate); networks and systems administration (Certificate); security and privacy (Certificate); service oriented computing (Certificate); software design (Certificate); theoretical computer science (Certificate). Part-time and evening/weekend programs available. *Faculty:* 12 full-time (5 women). *Students:* 117 full-time (42 women), 88 part-time (17 women); includes 4 Black or African American, non-Hispanic/Latino; 21 Asian, non-Hispanic/Latino; 3 Hispanic/Latino, 99 international. Average age 28. 327 applicants, 57% accepted. In 2010, 72 master's, 2 doctorates awarded. Terminal master's awarded for partial completion of doctoral program. *Degree requirements:* For master's, thesis optional; for doctorate, variable foreign language requirement, comprehensive exam, thesis/dissertation. *Entrance requirements:* For master's and doctorate, GRE, minimum GPA of 3.0. Additional exam requirements/recommendations for international students: Required—TOEFL. *Application deadline:* Applications are processed on a rolling basis. Application fee: $50. Electronic applications accepted. *Financial support:* Fellowships, Federal Work-Study available. Financial award application deadline: 4/15. *Faculty research:* Semantics, reliability theory, programming language, cyber security. *Unit head:* Daniel Duchamp, Director, 201-216-5390, Fax: 201-216-8249, E-mail: djd@cs.stevens.edu. *Application contact:* Graduate Admissions, 800-496-4935, Fax: 201-216-8044, E-mail: gradadmissions@stevens.edu.

Towson University, Master's Program in Applied Information Technology, Towson, MD 21252-0001. Offers applied information technology (MS, PhD); database management systems (Postbaccalaureate Certificate); information security and assurance (Postbaccalaureate Certificate); information systems management (Graduate Certificate); Internet applications development (Postbaccalaureate Certificate); networking technologies (Postbaccalaureate Certificate); software engineering (Postbaccalaureate Certificate). *Students:* 111 full-time (25 women), 232 part-time (62 women); includes 122 minority (75 Black or African American, non-Hispanic/Latino; 4 American Indian or Alaska Native, non-Hispanic/Latino; 31 Asian, non-Hispanic/Latino; 11 Hispanic/Latino; 1 Native Hawaiian or other Pacific Islander, non-Hispanic/Latino), 85 international. In 2010, 75 master's, 9 doctorates, 74 other advanced degrees awarded. *Expenses:* Tuition, state resident: part-time $324 per credit. Tuition, nonresident: part-time $681 per credit. Required fees: $95 per term. *Unit head:* Mike O'Leary, Graduate Program Director, 410-704-4757, E-mail: moleary@towson.edu. *Application contact:* Mike O'Leary, Graduate Program Director, 410-704-4757, E-mail: moleary@towson.edu.

University of Denver, University College, Denver, CO 80208. Offers arts and culture (MLS, Certificate), including art, literature, and culture, arts development and program management (Certificate), creative writing; environmental policy and management (MAS, Certificate), including energy and sustainability (Certificate), environmental assessment of nuclear power (Certificate), environmental health and safety (Certificate), environmental management, natural resource management (Certificate); geographic information systems (MAS, Certificate); global affairs (MLS, Certificate), including translation studies, world history and culture; healthcare leadership (MPH, Certificate), including healthcare policy, law, and ethics, medical and healthcare information technologies, strategic management of healthcare; information and communications technology (MCIS, Certificate), including database design and administration (Certificate), geographic information systems (MCIS), information security systems security (Certificate), information systems security (MCIS), project management (MCIS, MPS, Certificate), software design and administration (Certificate), software design and programming (MCIS), technology management, telecommunications technology (MCIS), Web design and development; leadership and organizations (MPS, Certificate), including human capital in organizations, philanthropic leadership, project management (MCIS, MPS, Certificate), strategic innovation and change; organizational and professional communication (MPS, Certificate), including alternative dispute resolution, organizational communication, organizational development and training, public relations and marketing; security management (MAS, Certificate), including emergency planning and response, information security (MAS), organizational security; strategic human resource management (MPS, Certificate), including global human resources (MPS), human resource management and development (MPS). Part-time and evening/weekend programs available. Postbaccalaureate distance learning degree programs offered (no on-campus study). *Faculty:* 7 full-time (2 women), 212 part-time/adjunct (83 women). *Students:* 52 full-time (19 women), 1,044 part-time (625 women); includes 196 minority (81 Black or African American, non-Hispanic/Latino; 7 American Indian or Alaska Native, non-Hispanic/Latino; 30 Asian, non-Hispanic/Latino; 66 Hispanic/Latino; 3 Native Hawaiian or other Pacific Islander, non-Hispanic/Latino; 9 Two or more races, non-Hispanic/Latino), 76 international. Average age 36. 488 applicants, 91% accepted, 339 enrolled. In 2010, 286 master's, 130 other advanced degrees awarded. *Entrance requirements:* Additional exam requirements/recommendations for international students: Required—TOEFL (minimum score 550 paper-based; 80 iBT). *Application deadline:* For fall admission, 6/22 priority date for domestic students, 6/10 priority date for international students; for winter admission, 9/15 priority date for domestic students, 9/6 priority date for international students; for spring admission, 2/3 priority date for domestic students, 12/15 priority date for international students. Applications are processed on a rolling basis. Application fee: $75. Electronic applications accepted. *Expenses:* Contact institution. *Financial support:* Applicants required to submit FAFSA. *Unit head:* Dr. James Davis, Dean, 303-871-2291, Fax: 303-871-4047, E-mail: jdavis@du.edu. *Application contact:* Information Contact, 303-871-3155, Fax: 303-871-4047, E-mail: ucolinfo@du.edu.

University of New Haven, Graduate School, Tagliatela College of Engineering, Program in Computer and Information Science, West Haven, CT 06516-1916. Offers computer science (MS, Certificate), including advanced applications (MS), computer applications (Certificate), computer programming (Certificate), computer systems (MS), computing (Certificate), database and information systems (MS), network administration (Certificate), network systems (MS), software engineering and development (MS). Part-time and evening/weekend programs available. *Students:* 54 full-time (12 women), 25 part-time (4 women); includes 1 Black or African American, non-Hispanic/Latino; 3 Asian, non-Hispanic/Latino, 51 international. Average age 28. 204 applicants, 100% accepted, 40 enrolled. In 2010, 19 master's, 1 other advanced degree awarded. *Degree requirements:* For master's, thesis or alternative. *Entrance requirements:* Additional exam requirements/recommendations for international students: Required—TOEFL (minimum score 520 paper-based; 190 computer-based; 70 iBT); Recommended—IELTS (minimum score 5.5). *Application deadline:* For fall admission, 5/31 for international students; for winter admission, 10/15 for international students; for spring admission, 1/15 for international students. Applications are processed on a rolling basis. Application fee: $50. Electronic applications accepted. *Financial support:* Research assistantships with partial tuition reimbursements, teaching assistantships with partial tuition reimbursements, career-related internships or fieldwork, Federal Work-Study, scholarships/grants, tuition waivers, and unspecified assistantships available. Support available to part-time students. Financial award applicants required to submit FAFSA. *Unit head:* Dr. Tahany Fergany, Coordinator, 203-932-7067. *Application contact:* Eloise Gormley, Director of Graduate Admissions, 203-932-7449, Fax: 203-932-7137, E-mail: gradinfo@newhaven.edu.

The University of North Carolina at Charlotte, Graduate School, College of Computing and Informatics, Department of Computer Science, Charlotte, NC 28223-0001. Offers advance databases and knowledge discovery (Certificate); computer science (MS). Part-time programs available. *Faculty:* 24 full-time (7 women), 1 part-time/adjunct (0 women). *Students:* 120 full-time (32 women), 31 part-time (8 women); includes 9 minority (2 Black or African American, non-Hispanic/Latino; 5 Asian, non-Hispanic/Latino; 1 Hispanic/Latino; 1 Two or more races, non-Hispanic/Latino), 112 international. Average age 24. 292 applicants, 85% accepted, 69 enrolled. In 2010, 66 master's awarded. *Degree requirements:* For master's, thesis or alternative. *Entrance requirements:* For master's, GRE General Test, minimum GPA of 3.0 during previous 2 years, 2.8 overall. Additional exam requirements/recommendations for international students: Required—TOEFL (minimum score 557 paper-based; 220 computer-based; 83 iBT). *Application deadline:* For fall admission, 7/1 for domestic students, 5/1 for international students; for spring admission, 11/1 for domestic students, 10/1 for international students. Applications are processed on a rolling basis. Application fee: $55. Electronic applications accepted. *Expenses:* Tuition, state resident: full-time $3464. Tuition, nonresident: full-time $14,297. Required fees: $2094. Tuition and fees vary according to course load. *Financial support:* In 2010–11, 57 students received support, including 1 fellowship (averaging $52,000 per year), 21 research assistantships (averaging $9,867 per year), 35 teaching assistantships (averaging $10,328 per year); career-related internships or fieldwork, Federal Work-Study, institutionally sponsored loans, scholarships/grants, and unspecified assistantships also available. Support available to part-time students. Financial award application deadline: 4/1; financial award applicants required to submit FAFSA. *Faculty research:* Visualization; visual analytics and computer graphics; intelligent and interactive systems; data mining theory, systems, and application; networked systems; computer game design. Total annual research expenditures: $3.1 million. *Unit head:* Dr. Larry F. Hodges, Chair, 704-687-8552, Fax: 704-687-3516, E-mail: lfhodges@uncc.edu. *Application contact:* Kathy B. Giddings, Director of Graduate Admissions, 704-687-3366, Fax: 704-687-3279, E-mail: gradadm@uncc.edu.

University of West Florida, College of Arts and Sciences: Sciences, Department of Computer Science, Pensacola, FL 32514-5750. Offers computer science (MS); database systems (MS); software engineering (MS). Part-time and evening/weekend programs available. *Faculty:* 12 full-time (4 women), 4 part-time/adjunct (2 women). *Students:* 23 full-time (6 women), 123 part-time (26 women); includes 39 minority (6 Black or African American, non-Hispanic/Latino; 3 American Indian or Alaska Native, non-Hispanic/Latino; 12 Asian, non-Hispanic/Latino; 9 Hispanic/Latino; 1 Native Hawaiian or other Pacific Islander, non-Hispanic/Latino; 8 Two or more races, non-Hispanic/Latino), 4 international. Average age 36. 62 applicants, 79% accepted, 38 enrolled. In 2010, 46 master's awarded. *Degree requirements:* For master's, thesis optional. *Entrance requirements:* For master's, GRE General Test. Additional exam requirements/recommendations for international students: Required—TOEFL (minimum score 550 paper-based; 213 computer-based). *Application deadline:* For fall admission, 6/1 for domestic students, 5/15 for international students; for spring admission, 10/1 for domestic and international students. Applications are processed on a rolling basis. Application fee: $30. *Expenses:* Tuition, state resident: full-time $4982; part-time $208 per credit hour. Tuition, nonresident: full-time $20,059; part-time $836 per credit hour. Required fees: $1365; $57 per credit hour. *Financial support:* In 2010–11, 16 fellowships with partial tuition reimbursements (averaging $453 per year), 8 research assistantships (averaging $3,280 per year), 3 teaching assistantships with partial tuition reimbursements (averaging $5,840 per year) were awarded; unspecified assistantships also available. Financial award application deadline: 4/15; financial award applicants required to submit FAFSA. *Unit head:* Dr. Leo Ter Haar, Chairperson, 850-474-2542. *Application contact:* Terry McCray, Assistant Director of Graduate Admissions, 850-473-7718, Fax: 850-473-7714, E-mail: gradadmissions@uwf.edu.

University of West Florida, College of Professional Studies, Department of Professional and Community Leadership, Program in Administration, Pensacola, FL 32514-5750. Offers acquisition and contract administration (MSA); biomedical/pharmaceutical (MSA); criminal justice administration (MSA); database administration (MSA); education leadership (MSA); healthcare administration (MSA); human performance technology (MSA); leadership (MSA); nursing administration (MSA); public administration (MSA); software engineering administration (MSA). Part-time and evening/weekend programs available. Postbaccalaureate distance learning degree programs offered (no on-campus study). *Students:* 26 full-time (24 women), 185 part-time (115 women); includes 30 Black or African American, non-Hispanic/Latino; 1 American Indian or Alaska Native, non-Hispanic/Latino; 5 Asian, non-Hispanic/Latino; 13 Hispanic/Latino; 1 Native Hawaiian or other Pacific Islander, non-Hispanic/Latino, 2 international. Average age 34. 139 applicants, 70% accepted, 80 enrolled. In 2010, 60 master's awarded. *Entrance requirements:* For master's, GRE General Test, letter of intent, names of references. Additional exam requirements/recommendations for international students: Required—TOEFL (minimum score 550 paper-based; 213 computer-based). *Application deadline:* For fall admission, 6/1 for domestic students, 5/15 for international students; for spring admission, 10/1 for domestic and international students. Applications are processed on a rolling basis. Application fee: $30. *Expenses:* Tuition, state resident: full-time $4982; part-time $208 per credit hour. Tuition, nonresident: full-time $20,059; part-time $836 per credit hour. Required fees: $1365; $57 per credit hour. *Financial support:* Unspecified assistantships available. Financial award application deadline: 4/15; financial award applicants required to submit FAFSA. *Unit head:* Dr. Karen Rasmussen, Chairperson, 850-474-2301, Fax: 850-474-2804, E-mail: krasmuss@uwf.edu. *Application contact:* Terry McCray, Assistant Director of Graduate Admissions, 850-473-7718, Fax: 850-473-7714, E-mail: gradadmissions@uwf.edu.

Financial Engineering

Claremont Graduate University, Graduate Programs, Financial Engineering Program, Claremont, CA 91711-6160. Offers MSFE, MS/EMBA, MS/MBA, MS/PhD. *Students:* 53 full-time (12 women), 2 part-time (both women); includes 2 Black or African American, non-Hispanic/Latino; 8 Asian, non-Hispanic/Latino; 2 Hispanic/Latino, 32 international. Average age 27. In 2010, 32 master's awarded. *Entrance requirements:* For master's, GRE General Test or GMAT. Additional exam requirements/recommendations for international students: Required—TOEFL (minimum score 550 paper-based; 213 computer-based; 80 iBT). *Application deadline:* For fall admission, 2/1 priority date for domestic students. Applications are processed on a rolling basis. Application fee: $60. Electronic applications accepted. *Expenses:* Tuition: Full-time $35,748; part-time $1554 per unit. Required fees: $215 per semester. *Financial support:* Fellowships, Federal Work-Study, institutionally sponsored loans, and scholarships/grants available. Support available to part-time students. Financial award application deadline: 2/15; financial award applicants required to submit FAFSA. *Unit head:* Jim Mills, Co-Director, 909-607-3310, E-mail: jim.mills@cgu.edu. *Application contact:* Christina Wassanaar, Administrative Director, 909-607-7812, E-mail: christina.wassenaar@cgu.edu.

Columbia University, Fu Foundation School of Engineering and Applied Science, Department of Industrial Engineering and Operations Research, New York, NY 10027. Offers financial engineering (MS); industrial engineering (Engr); industrial engineering and operations research (MS, Eng Sc D, PhD); MS/MBA. Part-time and evening/weekend programs available. Post-baccalaureate distance learning degree programs offered (no on-campus study). *Faculty:* 22 full-time (3 women), 23 part-time/adjunct (1 woman). *Students:* 295 full-time (81 women), 115 part-time (36 women); includes 23 minority (19 Asian, non-Hispanic/Latino; 3 Hispanic/Latino; 1 Two or more races, non-Hispanic/Latino), 352 international. Average age 26. 1,492 applicants, 21% accepted, 183 enrolled. In 2010, 258 master's, 7 doctorates, 1 other advanced degree awarded. *Degree requirements:* For doctorate, thesis/dissertation, oral and written qualifying exams. *Entrance requirements:* For master's, doctorate, and Engr, GRE General Test. Additional exam requirements/recommendations for international students: Required—TOEFL, IELTS. *Application deadline:* For fall admission, 12/1 priority date for domestic and international students; for spring admission, 10/1 priority date for domestic and international students. Application fee: $95. Electronic applications accepted. *Financial support:* In 2010–11, 59 students received support, including 12 fellowships (averaging $1,700 per year), 27 research assistantships with full tuition reimbursements available (averaging $30,765 per year), 20 teaching assistantships with full tuition reimbursements available (averaging $30,765 per year); career-related internships or fieldwork and health care benefits also available. Financial award application deadline: 12/1; financial award applicants required to submit FAFSA. *Faculty research:* Combinatorial optimization and mathematical programming; financial engineering; supply chain management and inventory theory; applied probability; queuing theory; scheduling, and simulation. *Unit head:* Dr. Cliff S. Stein, Professor and Department Chairman, 212-854-5238, Fax: 212-854-8103, E-mail: cliff@ieor.columbia.edu. *Application contact:* Adina Berrios Brooks, Student Affairs Manager, 212-854-1934, Fax: 212-854-8103, E-mail: admit@ieor.columbia.edu.

HEC Montreal, School of Business Administration, Master of Science Programs in Administration, Program in Financial Engineering, Montréal, QC H3T 2A7, Canada. Offers M Sc. All courses are given in French. Part-time programs available. *Students:* 50 full-time (6 women), 7 part-time (1 woman). 59 applicants, 59% accepted, 18 enrolled. In 2010, 15 master's awarded. *Degree requirements:* For master's, one foreign language, thesis. *Application deadline:* For fall admission, 3/15 for domestic and international students; for winter admission, 10/1 for domestic and international students. Application fee: $78 Canadian dollars. Electronic applications accepted. *Expenses:* Tuition, area resident: Part-time $68.93 per credit. Tuition, state resident: full-time $2481.48; part-time $188.92 per credit. Tuition, nonresident: full-time $6801; part-time $482.06 per course. International tuition: $17,354.16 full-time. Required fees: $1309.50; $30.28 per credit. $93.45 per term. Tuition and fees vary according to degree level and program. *Financial support:* Fellowships, research assistantships, teaching assistantships, scholarships/grants available. Financial award application deadline: 9/2. *Unit head:* Dr. Claude Laurin, Director, 514-340-6485, Fax: 514-340-6880, E-mail: claude.laurin@hec.ca. *Application contact:* Francine Blais, Administrative Director, 514-340-6112, Fax: 514-340-6411, E-mail: francine.blais@hec.ca.

The International University of Monaco, Graduate Programs, Monte Carlo, Monaco. Offers entrepreneurship (EMBA, MBA); financial engineering (M Sc); hedge fund and private equity (M Sc); international marketing (EMBA, MBA); international wealth management (M Sc); luxury goods and services (EMBA, M Sc, MBA); wealth and asset management (EMBA, MBA). Part-time programs available. *Degree requirements:* For master's, comprehensive exam (for some programs), applied research project. *Entrance requirements:* Additional exam requirements/recommendations for international students: Required—TOEFL (minimum score 550 paper-based; 213 computer-based), IELTS. Electronic applications accepted. *Faculty research:* Gaming, leadership, disintermediation.

Kent State University, Graduate School of Management, Program in Financial Engineering, Kent, OH 44242-0001. Offers MSFE. *Faculty:* 6 full-time (2 women). *Students:* 58 full-time (18 women); includes 1 Black or African American, non-Hispanic/Latino; 1 Asian, non-Hispanic/Latino; 1 Hispanic/Latino, 50 international. Average age 26. 221 applicants, 71% accepted, 49 enrolled. In 2010, 40 master's awarded. *Degree requirements:* For master's, capstone project. *Entrance requirements:* For master's, GMAT or GRE. Additional exam requirements/recommendations for international students: Required—TOEFL (minimum score 525 paper-based; 197 computer-based; 71 iBT). *Application deadline:* For fall admission, 2/1 priority date for domestic students, 2/1 for international students. Application fee: $30 ($60 for international students). Electronic applications accepted. *Expenses:* Tuition, state resident: full-time $7866; part-time $437 per credit hour. Tuition, nonresident: full-time $14,022; part-time $779 per credit hour. *Financial support:* In 2010–11, 2 students received support, including 2 research assistantships with full tuition reimbursements available (averaging $12,000 per year); Federal Work-Study also available. Financial award application deadline: 2/1; financial award applicants required to submit FAFSA. *Faculty research:* Stochastic models, financial derivatives. *Unit head:* Dr. Mark E. Holder, Associate Professor, 330-672-2426, Fax: 330-672-9806, E-mail: mholder@kent.edu. *Application contact:* Rebecca Evans, Program Administrator, 330-672-0190, Fax: 330-672-9806, E-mail: msfe@kent.edu.

North Carolina State University, Graduate School, College of Agriculture and Life Sciences and College of Engineering and College of Physical and Mathematical Sciences, Program in Financial Mathematics, Raleigh, NC 27695. Offers MFM. Part-time programs available. *Degree requirements:* For master's, thesis optional, project/internship. *Entrance requirements:* For master's, GRE General Test. Additional exam requirements/recommendations for international students: Required—TOEFL (minimum score 550 paper-based; 213 computer-based). Electronic applications accepted. *Faculty research:* Financial mathematics modeling and computation, futures, options and commodities markets, real options, credit risk, portfolio optimization.

Polytechnic Institute of NYU, Department of Finance and Risk Engineering, Brooklyn, NY 11201-2990. Offers financial engineering (MS, Advanced Certificate), including capital markets (MS), computational finance (MS); financial technology (MS); financial technology management (Advanced Certificate); organizational behavior (Advanced Certificate); risk management (Advanced Certificate); technology management (Advanced Certificate). Part-time and evening/weekend programs available. *Faculty:* 6 full-time (1 woman), 24 part-time/adjunct (5 women). *Students:* 126 full-time (45 women), 61 part-time (15 women); includes 4 Black or African American, non-Hispanic/Latino; 17 Asian, non-Hispanic/Latino; 1 Hispanic/Latino, 130 international. Average age 27. 528 applicants, 44% accepted, 67 enrolled. In 2010, 154 master's awarded. *Degree requirements:* For master's, comprehensive exam (for some programs), thesis (for some programs). *Entrance requirements:* For master's, GMAT, minimum B average in undergraduate course work. Additional exam requirements/recommendations for

international students: Required—TOEFL (minimum score 550 paper-based; 213 computer-based; 80 iBT); Recommended—IELTS (minimum score 6.5). *Application deadline:* For fall admission, 7/31 priority date for domestic students, 4/30 priority date for international students; for spring admission, 12/31 priority date for domestic students, 11/30 priority date for international students. Applications are processed on a rolling basis. Application fee: $75. Electronic applications accepted. *Expenses:* Tuition: Full-time $21,492; part-time $1194 per credit. Required fees: $385 per semester. Tuition and fees vary according to course load. *Financial support:* Institutionally sponsored loans, scholarships/grants, and unspecified assistantships available. Support available to part-time students. Financial award applicants required to submit FAFSA. *Unit head:* Prof. Charles S. Tapiero, Academic Director, 718-260-3653, Fax: 718-260-3874, E-mail: ctapiero@poly.edu. *Application contact:* JeanCarlo Bonilla, Director, Graduate Enrollment Management, 718-260-3182, Fax: 718-260-3624.

Polytechnic Institute of NYU, Long Island Graduate Center, Graduate Programs, Department of Finance and Risk Engineering, Major in Financial Engineering, Melville, NY 11747. Offers MS, AC. Part-time and evening/weekend programs available. *Students:* 1 part-time (0 women); minority (Asian, non-Hispanic/Latino). Average age 24. *Entrance requirements:* Additional exam requirements/recommendations for international students: Required—TOEFL (minimum score 550 paper-based; 213 computer-based; 80 iBT); Recommended—IELTS (minimum score 6.5). *Application deadline:* For fall admission, 7/31 priority date for domestic students, 4/30 priority date for international students; for spring admission, 12/31 priority date for domestic students, 11/30 priority date for international students. Applications are processed on a rolling basis. Application fee: $75. Electronic applications accepted. *Expenses:* Tuition: Full-time $21,492; part-time $1194 per credit. Required fees: $385 per semester. Tuition and fees vary according to course load. *Financial support:* Institutionally sponsored loans, scholarships/grants, and unspecified assistantships available. Support available to part-time students. *Unit head:* Dr. Charles S. Tapiero, Department Head, 718-260-3653, E-mail: ctapiero@poly.edu. *Application contact:* JeanCarlo Bonilla, Director of Graduate Enrollment Management, 718-260-3182, Fax: 718-260-3624, E-mail: gradinfo@poly.edu.

Polytechnic Institute of NYU, Westchester Graduate Center, Graduate Programs, Department of Finance and Risk Engineering, Major in Financial Engineering, Hawthorne, NY 10532-1507. Offers capital markets (MS); computational finance (MS); financial engineering (AC); financial technology (MS); financial technology management (AC); information management (AC). *Students:* 1 (woman) part-time, all international. Average age 25. In 2010, 8 master's awarded. *Degree requirements:* For master's, comprehensive exam (for some programs), thesis (for some programs). *Entrance requirements:* Additional exam requirements/recommendations for international students: Required—TOEFL (minimum score 550 paper-based; 213 computer-based; 80 iBT); Recommended—IELTS (minimum score 6.5). *Application deadline:* For fall admission, 7/31 priority date for domestic students, 4/30 priority date for international students; for spring admission, 12/31 priority date for domestic students, 11/30 priority date for international students. Applications are processed on a rolling basis. Application fee: $75. Electronic applications accepted. *Expenses:* Tuition: Full-time $21,492; part-time $1194 per credit. Required fees: $385 per semester. Tuition and fees vary according to course load. *Financial support:* Institutionally sponsored loans, scholarships/grants, and unspecified assistantships available. Support available to part-time students. *Unit head:* Dr. Charles S. Tapiero, Department Head, 718-260-3653, E-mail: ctapiero@poly.edu. *Application contact:* JeanCarlo Bonilla, Director of Graduate Enrollment Management, 718-260-3182, Fax: 718-260-3624, E-mail: gradinfo@poly.edu.

Princeton University, Graduate School, School of Engineering and Applied Science, Department of Operations Research and Financial Engineering, Princeton, NJ 08544-1019. Offers M Eng, MSE, PhD. Terminal master's awarded for partial completion of doctoral program. *Degree requirements:* For master's, thesis (MSE); for doctorate, thesis/dissertation, general exam. *Entrance requirements:* For master's and doctorate, GRE General Test, official transcript(s), 3 letters of recommendation, personal statement. Additional exam requirements/recommendations for international students: Required—TOEFL. Electronic applications accepted. *Faculty research:* Applied and computational mathematics; financial mathematics; optimization, queuing theory, and machine learning; statistics and stochastic analysis; transportation and logistics.

Rensselaer Polytechnic Institute, Graduate School, Lally School of Management and Technology, Troy, NY 12180-3590. Offers business (MBA); financial engineering and risk analysis (MS); management (MS, PhD); technology, commercialization, and entrepreneurship (MS). *Accreditation:* AACSB. Part-time and evening/weekend programs available. *Faculty:* 44 full-time (10 women), 19 part-time/adjunct (0 women). *Students:* 189 full-time (82 women), 162 part-time (40 women); includes 65 minority (22 Black or African American, non-Hispanic/Latino; 34 Asian, non-Hispanic/Latino; 9 Hispanic/Latino), 92 international. Average age 28. 507 applicants, 56% accepted, 150 enrolled. In 2010, 263 master's, 7 doctorates awarded. *Degree requirements:* For doctorate, thesis/dissertation. *Entrance requirements:* For master's, GMAT, 2 letters of recommendation, resume; for doctorate, GMAT or GRE General Test, 2 letters of recommendation. Additional exam requirements/recommendations for international students: Required—TOEFL (minimum score 600 paper-based; 250 computer-based; 100 iBT); Recommended—IELTS (minimum score 7). *Application deadline:* For fall admission, 3/15 priority date for domestic and international students. Applications are processed on a rolling basis. Application fee: $75. Electronic applications accepted. *Expenses:* Tuition: Full-time $39,600; part-time $1650 per credit. Required fees: $1896. *Financial support:* Fellowships with partial tuition reimbursements, career-related internships or fieldwork, institutionally sponsored loans, scholarships/grants, and assistantships are for Ph D students only available. Financial award application deadline: 3/15; financial award applicants required to submit FAFSA. *Faculty research:* Technological entrepreneurship, operations management, new product development and marketing, finance and financial engineering and risk analytics, information systems. *Unit head:* Dr. Iftekhar Hasan, Acting Dean/Professor, 518-276-6586, Fax: 518-276-2665, E-mail: lallymba@rpi.edu. *Application contact:* Michele M. Martens, Manager of Graduate Programs, 518-276-6586, Fax: 518-276-8190, E-mail: lallymba@rpi.edu.

Stevens Institute of Technology, Graduate School, School of Systems and Enterprises, Program in Financial Engineering, Hoboken, NJ 07030. Offers MS. *Students:* 69 full-time (23 women), 42 part-time (3 women); includes 8 Black or African American, non-Hispanic/Latino; 15 Asian, non-Hispanic/Latino; 4 Hispanic/Latino, 62 international. Average age 28. *Unit head:* Dr. Charles L. Suffel, Dean of the Graduate School, 201-216-5234, Fax: 201-216-8044, E-mail: csuffel@stevens-tech.edu. *Application contact:* Graduate Admissions, 800-496-4935, Fax: 201-216-8044, E-mail: gradadmissions@stevens.edu.

Temple University, Fox School of Business, Specialized Master's Programs, Philadelphia, PA 19122-6096. Offers accountancy (MS); actuarial science (MS); finance (MS); financial engineering (MS); human resource management (MS); marketing (MS); statistics (MS). *Accreditation:* AACSB. Part-time programs available. *Entrance requirements:* For master's, GRE General Test or GMAT, minimum undergraduate GPA of 3.0. Additional exam requirements/recommendations for international students: Required—TOEFL (minimum score 600 paper-based; 250 computer-based; 100 iBT), IELTS (minimum score 7.5).

University at Buffalo, the State University of New York, Graduate School, School of Management, Buffalo, NY 14260. Offers accounting (MS); business administration (EMBA, MBA, PMBA); finance (MS), including financial engineering, financial management; information assurance (Certificate); management (PhD); management information systems (MS); supply chains and operations management (MS); Au D/MBA; JD/MBA; M Arch/MBA; MA/MBA; MD/MBA; MPH/MBA; MSW/MBA; Pharm D/MBA. *Accreditation:* AACSB. Part-time and evening/weekend programs available. *Faculty:* 65 full-time (18 women), 32 part-time/adjunct (8 women). *Students:* 626 full-time (229 women), 202 part-time (69 women); includes 43 minority (18

Financial Engineering

University at Buffalo, the State University of New York (continued)
Black or African American, non-Hispanic/Latino; 2 American Indian or Alaska Native, non-Hispanic/Latino; 18 Asian, non-Hispanic/Latino; 5 Hispanic/Latino), 351 international. Average age 27. 1,553 applicants, 46% accepted, 400 enrolled. In 2010, 287 master's, 4 doctorates, 3 other advanced degrees awarded. *Degree requirements:* For master's, thesis (for some programs); for doctorate, comprehensive exam, thesis/dissertation. *Entrance requirements:* For master's, GMAT (MBA, MS in accounting), GRE or GMAT (for all other MS concentrations); for doctorate, GMAT or GRE. Additional exam requirements/recommendations for international students: Required—TOEFL (minimum score 230 computer-based; 95 iBT). *Application deadline:* For fall admission, 5/2 priority date for domestic students, 3/1 priority date for international students. Applications are processed on a rolling basis. Application fee: $100. Electronic applications accepted. *Expenses:* Contact institution. *Financial support:* In 2010–11, 91 students received support, including 5 fellowships with full and partial tuition reimbursements available (averaging $4,000 per year), 41 research assistantships with full and partial tuition reimbursements available (averaging $16,000 per year), 28 teaching assistantships with full and partial tuition reimbursements available (averaging $15,000 per year); career-related internships or fieldwork, Federal Work-Study, institutionally sponsored loans, scholarships/grants, health care benefits, and unspecified assistantships also available. Financial award application deadline: 2/15; financial award applicants required to submit FAFSA. *Faculty research:* Earnings management and electronic information assurance, supply chains and operations management, corporate financing and asset pricing, consumer behavior and quantitative modeling of marketing behavior, leadership and politics in organizations. Total annual research expenditures: $215,000. *Unit head:* David W. Frasier, Assistant Dean, 716-645-3204, Fax: 716-645-2341, E-mail: davidf@buffalo.edu. *Application contact:* David W. Frasier, Assistant Dean, 716-645-3204, Fax: 716-645-2341, E-mail: davidf@buffalo.edu.

University of California, Berkeley, Graduate Division, Haas School of Business, Master of Financial Engineering Program, Berkeley, CA 94720-1500. Offers MFE. *Students:* 67 full-time (11 women); includes 10 Asian, non-Hispanic/Latino; 1 Two or more races, non-Hispanic/Latino, 43 international. Average age 28. 333 applicants, 32% accepted, 67 enrolled. In 2010, 67 master's awarded. *Degree requirements:* For master's, comprehensive exam, internship/applied finance project. *Entrance requirements:* For master's, GMAT or GRE (waived if candidate holds PhD), bachelor's degree with minimum GPA of 3.0 or equivalent; two recommendation letters. Additional exam requirements/recommendations for international students: Required—TOEFL (minimum score 570 paper-based; 230 computer-based; 68 iBT). *Application deadline:* For winter admission, 12/1 for domestic students; for spring admission, 9/1 for international students. Applications are processed on a rolling basis. Application fee: $225. Electronic applications accepted. *Expenses:* Contact institution. *Financial support:* Teaching assistantships, scholarships/grants available. Financial award applicants required to submit FAFSA. *Faculty research:* Financial economics, modern portfolio theory, valuation of exotic options, mortgage markets. *Unit head:* Linda Kreitzman, Executive Director, 510-643-4329, Fax: 510-643-4345, E-mail: lindak@haas.berkeley.edu. *Application contact:* Christina Henri, Assistant Director, 510-642-4417, Fax: 510-643-4345, E-mail: mfe@haas.berkeley.edu.

University of California, Los Angeles, Graduate Division, UCLA Anderson School of Management, Los Angeles, CA 90095-1481. Offers accounting (PhD); business administration (MBA); decisions, operations and technology management (PhD); finance (PhD); financial engineering (MFE); global economics and management (PhD); human resources and organizational behavior (PhD); marketing (PhD); strategy and policy (PhD); DDS/MBA; MBA/JD; MBA/MD; MBA/MLAS; MBA/MLIS; MBA/MPH; MBA/MPP; MBA/MSCS; MBA/MSN; MBA/MUP. *Accreditation:* AACSB. Part-time programs available. *Faculty:* 102 full-time (17 women), 43 part-time/adjunct (6 women). *Students:* 833 full-time (270 women), 1,052 part-time (271 women); includes 592 minority (25 Black or African American, non-Hispanic/Latino; 3 American Indian or Alaska Native, non-Hispanic/Latino; 482 Asian, non-Hispanic/Latino; 60 Hispanic/Latino; 6 Native Hawaiian or other Pacific Islander, non-Hispanic/Latino; 16 Two or more races, non-Hispanic/Latino), 445 international. In 2010, 735 master's, 10 doctorates awarded. *Degree requirements:* For master's, comprehensive exam, Field Study Consulting Project (R) for all MBA programs. Thesis/Dissertation (A) for MFE program; for doctorate, comprehensive exam, thesis/dissertation, Oral and written qualifying exams. *Entrance requirements:* For master's, GMAT (Full-time, Part-time and Executive MBA), GMAT or GRE General Test (MFE), Minimum Undergraduate GPA of 3.0; for doctorate, GMAT or GRE General Test, Minimum Undergraduate GPA of 3.0. Additional exam requirements/recommendations for international students: Required—TOEFL (minimum score 560 paper-based; 220 computer-based; 87 iBT), IELTS (minimum score 7). *Application deadline:* For fall admission, 10/20 for domestic and international students; for winter admission, 1/5 for domestic and international students; for spring admission, 4/13 for domestic and international students. Application fee: $200. Electronic applications accepted. *Expenses:* Contact institution. *Financial support:* Fellowships, research assistantships, teaching assistantships, career-related internships or fieldwork, institutionally sponsored loans, scholarships/grants, health care benefits, and tuition waivers (partial) available. Financial award application deadline: 3/2; financial award applicants required to submit FAFSA. *Unit head:* Judy D. Olian, Dean, UCLA Anderson School of Management, 310-825-7982, Fax: 310-206-2073. *Application contact:* Mae Jennifer Shores, Assistant Dean and Director of Full-time MBA Admissions and Financial Aid, 310-825-6944, Fax: 310-825-8582, E-mail: mba.admissions@anderson.ucla.edu.

University of Hawaii at Manoa, Graduate Division, Shidler College of Business, Program in Financial Engineering, Honolulu, HI 96822. Offers MS. Part-time programs available. *Faculty:* 10 full-time (1 woman). *Students:* 15 full-time (5 women), 1 part-time (0 women); includes 5 minority (all Asian, non-Hispanic/Latino), 9 international. Average age 30. 61 applicants, 66% accepted, 32 enrolled. In 2010, 25 master's awarded. *Degree requirements:* For master's, thesis optional. *Entrance requirements:* For master's, GRE General Test. Additional exam requirements/recommendations for international students: Required—TOEFL (minimum score 600 paper-based; 250 computer-based; 100 iBT), IELTS (minimum score 7). *Application deadline:* For fall admission, 5/1 for domestic students. Application fee: $60. *Financial support:* In 2010–11, 2 fellowships (averaging $4,054 per year), 3 research assistantships (averaging $11,440 per year) were awarded; teaching assistantships. Total annual research expenditures: $20,000. *Unit head:* Gunter Eric Meissner, Gradiate Chair, Director, 808-956-2535, Fax: 808-956-9887, E-mail: meissner@hawaii.edu. *Application contact:* V. Vance Roley, Dean, 808-956-8377.

University of Illinois at Urbana–Champaign, Graduate College, College of Engineering, Joint Program in Financial Engineering, Champaign, IL 61820. Offers MS. Program offered jointly with College of Business. Part-time programs available. *Students:* 26 full-time (5 women); includes 3 Asian, non-Hispanic/Latino, 21 international. 147 applicants, 30% accepted, 22 enrolled. *Degree requirements:* For master's, thesis or alternative. *Entrance requirements:* For master's, one year of calculus, one semester each of linear algebra, differential equations, and programming (preferably in C/C++). Additional exam requirements/recommendations for international students: Required—TOEFL (minimum score 613 paper-based; 257 computer-based; 79 iBT) or IELTS (minimum score 7). *Application deadline:* Applications are processed on a rolling basis. Application fee: $75 ($90 for international students). Electronic applications accepted. *Financial support:* Scholarships/grants available. *Unit head:* Morton Lane, Director, 217-333-3284, Fax: 217-333-1486, E-mail: msfe@illinois.edu. *Application contact:* Morton Lane, Director, 217-333-3284, Fax: 217-333-1486, E-mail: msfe@illinois.edu.

The University of Texas at Dallas, School of Management, Program in Finance, Richardson, TX 75080. Offers finance (MS); financial analysis (MS); financial engineering and risk management (MS); investment management (MS). Part-time and evening/weekend programs available. *Faculty:* 14 full-time (3 women), 3 part-time/adjunct (1 woman). *Students:* 229 full-time (105 women), 55 part-time (18 women); includes 36 minority (4 Black or African American, non-Hispanic/Latino; 25 Asian, non-Hispanic/Latino; 7 Hispanic/Latino), 190 international. Average age 26. 447 applicants, 67% accepted, 158 enrolled. In 2010, 39 master's awarded. *Entrance requirements:* For master's, GMAT. Additional exam requirements/recommendations for international students: Required—TOEFL (minimum score 550 paper-based; 215 computer-based). *Application deadline:* For fall admission, 7/15 for domestic students, 5/1 priority date for international students; for spring admission, 11/15 for domestic students, 9/1 priority date for international students. Applications are processed on a rolling basis. Application fee: $50 ($100 for international students). Electronic applications accepted. *Expenses:* Tuition, state resident: full-time $10,248; part-time $569 per credit hour. Tuition, nonresident: full-time $18,544; part-time $1030 per credit hour. Tuition and fees vary according to course load. *Financial support:* In 2010–11, 101 students received support, including 3 teaching assistantships with partial tuition reimbursements available (averaging $10,050 per year); research assistantships with partial tuition reimbursements available, career-related internships or fieldwork, Federal Work-Study, institutionally sponsored loans, scholarships/grants, and unspecified assistantships also available. Support available to part-time students. Financial award application deadline: 4/30; financial award applicants required to submit FAFSA. *Faculty research:* Econometrics, industrial organization, auction theory, file-sharing copyrights and bundling, international financial management, entrepreneurial finance. *Unit head:* Dr. H. Joe Wells, Director, 972-883-4897, E-mail: hjoewells@utdallas.edu. *Application contact:* James Parker, Assistant Director, 972-883-5842, E-mail: jparker@utdallas.edu.

University of Tulsa, Graduate School, Collins College of Business, Program in Finance, Tulsa, OK 74104-3189. Offers corporate finance (MS); investments and portfolio management (MS); risk management (MS); JD/MSF; MBA/MSF; MSF/MSAM. Part-time and evening/weekend programs available. *Faculty:* 10 full-time (1 woman). *Students:* 21 full-time (10 women), 4 part-time (2 women), 12 international. Average age 25. 87 applicants, 51% accepted, 11 enrolled. In 2010, 16 master's awarded. *Degree requirements:* For master's, thesis optional. *Entrance requirements:* For master's, GMAT. Additional exam requirements/recommendations for international students: Required—TOEFL (minimum score 575 paper-based; 231 computer-based), IELTS (minimum score 6.5). *Application deadline:* Applications are processed on a rolling basis. Application fee: $40. Electronic applications accepted. *Expenses:* Tuition: Full-time $16,902; part-time $939 per credit hour. Required fees: $1020; $4 per credit hour. Tuition and fees vary according to course load. *Financial support:* In 2010–11, 9 students received support, including 2 fellowships with full and partial tuition reimbursements available (averaging $8,750 per year), 2 research assistantships with full and partial tuition reimbursements available (averaging $9,286 per year), 5 teaching assistantships with full and partial tuition reimbursements available (averaging $8,815 per year); career-related internships or fieldwork, Federal Work-Study, institutionally sponsored loans, scholarships/grants, health care benefits, tuition waivers (full and partial), and unspecified assistantships also available. Support available to part-time students. Financial award application deadline: 2/1; financial award applicants required to submit FAFSA. *Unit head:* Dr. Linda Nichols, Associate Dean, 918-631-2242, Fax: 918-631-2142, E-mail: linda-nichols@utulsa.edu. *Application contact:* Dr. Linda Nichols, Associate Dean, 918-631-2242, Fax: 918-631-2142, E-mail: linda-nichols@utulsa.edu.

Game Design and Development

Academy of Art University, Graduate Program, School of Game Design, San Francisco, CA 94105-3410. Offers MFA. Part-time programs available. Postbaccalaureate distance learning degree programs offered (no on-campus study). *Faculty:* 3 full-time (0 women), 8 part-time/adjunct (1 woman). *Students:* 58 full-time (13 women), 22 part-time (9 women); includes 5 Black or African American, non-Hispanic/Latino; 1 American Indian or Alaska Native, non-Hispanic/Latino; 7 Asian, non-Hispanic/Latino; 3 Hispanic/Latino; 1 Native Hawaiian or other Pacific Islander, non-Hispanic/Latino, 25 international. Average age 27. 80 applicants. *Degree requirements:* For master's, thesis, final review. *Application deadline:* For fall admission, 9/7 for domestic and international students; for spring admission, 2/2 for domestic and international students. Applications are processed on a rolling basis. Application fee: $100 ($500 for international students). Electronic applications accepted. *Expenses:* Tuition: Full-time $20,160; part-time $840 per semester hour. Required fees: $45 per semester. *Financial support:* Career-related internships or fieldwork and Federal Work-Study available. Support available to part-time students. Financial award application deadline: 8/10; financial award applicants required to submit FAFSA.

Concordia University, School of Graduate Studies, Faculty of Engineering and Computer Science, Concordia Institute for Information Systems Engineering (CIISE), Montréal, QC H3G 1M8, Canada. Offers 3D graphics and game development (Certificate); information systems security (M Eng, MA Sc); quality systems engineering (M Eng, MA Sc); service engineering and network management (Certificate).

DePaul University, College of Computing and Digital Media, Chicago, IL 60604. Offers animation (MA, MFA); applied technology (MS); business information technology (MS); cinema (MFA); cinema production (MS); computational finance (MS); computer and information sciences (PhD); computer game development (MS); computer graphics and motion technology (MS); computer information and network security (MS); computer science (MS); e-commerce technology (MS); human-computer interaction (MS); information systems (MS); information technology (MA); information technology project management (MS); network engineering and management (MS); predictive analytics (MS); screenwriting (MFA); software engineering (MS); JD/MA; JD/MS. Part-time and evening/weekend programs available. Postbaccalaureate distance learning degree programs offered (no on-campus study). *Faculty:* 51 full-time (11 women), 50 part-time/adjunct (9 women). *Students:* 952 full-time (230 women), 927 part-time (226 women); includes 557 minority (205 Black or African American, non-Hispanic/Latino; 2 American Indian or Alaska Native, non-Hispanic/Latino; 167 Asian, non-Hispanic/Latino; 136 Hispanic/Latino; 7 Native Hawaiian or other Pacific Islander, non-Hispanic/Latino; 40 Two or more races, non-Hispanic/Latino), 292 international. Average age 31. 896 applicants, 70% accepted, 324 enrolled. In 2010, 417 master's, 6 doctorates awarded. *Degree requirements:* For master's, thesis (for some programs); for doctorate, comprehensive exam, thesis/dissertation. *Entrance requirements:* For master's, GRE or GMAT (MS in computational finance only), bachelor's degree, resume (MS in predictive analytics only), IT experience (MS in information technology project management only), portfolio review (MFA); for doctorate, GRE, master's degree in computer science. Additional exam requirements/recommendations for international students: Required—TOEFL (minimum score 550 paper-based; 213 computer-based; 80 iBT), IELTS (minimum score 6.5), Pearson Test of English (minimum score 53). *Application deadline:* For fall admission, 8/15 priority date for domestic students, 6/1 priority date for international students; for winter admission, 12/15 priority date for domestic students, 9/15 priority date for international students; for spring admission, 3/1 priority date for domestic students, 12/15 priority date for international students. Applications are processed on a rolling basis. Application fee: $25. Electronic applications accepted. *Expenses:* Contact institution. *Financial support:* In 2010–11, 102 students received support, including 4 fellowships with full tuition reimbursements available (averaging $24,435 per year), 6 research assistantships (averaging $21,100 per year), 92 teaching assistantships with full and partial tuition reimbursements available (averaging $6,904 per year); Federal Work-Study, scholarships/grants, tuition waivers (full and partial), and unspecified assistantships also available. Support available to part-time students. Financial award application deadline: 4/30; financial award applicants required to submit FAFSA. *Faculty research:* Bioinformatics, visual computing, graphics and animation, high performance and scientific computing, databases. Total annual research expenditures: $1.4 million. *Unit head:* Dr. David Miller, Dean, 312-362-8381, Fax: 312-362-5185. *Application contact:* Dr. Liz Friedman, Assistant Dean of Student Services, 312-362-8714, Fax: 312-362-5179, E-mail: efriedm2@cdm.depaul.edu.

Full Sail University, Game Design Master of Science Program—Campus, Winter Park, FL 32792-7437. Offers MS.

George Mason University, Volgenau School of Engineering, Department of Computer Science, Fairfax, VA 22030. Offers biometrics (Certificate); computer games technology (Certificate); computer networking (Certificate); computer science (MS, PhD); data mining (Certificate); database management (Certificate); electronic commerce (Certificate); foundations of information systems (Certificate); information engineering (Certificate); information security and assurance (MS, Certificate); information systems (MS); intelligent agents (Certificate); software architecture (Certificate); software engineering (MS, Certificate); systems engineering (MS); Web-based software engineering (Certificate). MS program offered jointly with Old Dominion University, University of Virginia, Virginia Commonwealth University, and Virginia Polytechnic Institute and State University. Part-time and evening/weekend programs available. Postbaccalaureate distance learning degree programs offered. *Faculty:* 42 full-time (9 women), 20 part-time/adjunct (1 woman). *Students:* 124 full-time (37 women), 453 part-time (103 women); includes 14 Black or African American, non-Hispanic/Latino; 66 Asian, non-Hispanic/Latino; 13 Hispanic/Latino; 3 Two or more races, non-Hispanic/Latino, 206 international. Average age 30. 904 applicants, 53% accepted, 150 enrolled. In 2010, 203 master's, 4 doctorates, 20 other advanced degrees awarded. *Degree requirements:* For master's, thesis optional; for doctorate, comprehensive exam, thesis/dissertation. *Entrance requirements:* For master's, GRE General Test, minimum GPA of 3.0 in last 60 hours, 3 letters of recommendation; for doctorate, GRE, 4-year BA, academic work in computer science, 3 letters of recommendation, statement of career goals and aspirations. Additional exam requirements/recommendations for international students: Required—TOEFL (minimum score 570 paper-based; 230 computer-based; 88 iBT). *Application deadline:* For fall admission, 4/15 priority date for domestic students, 1/15 for international students; for spring admission, 11/15 for domestic students. Application fee: $100. Electronic applications accepted. *Expenses:* Tuition, state resident: full-time $8192; part-time $440 per credit hour. Tuition, nonresident: full-time $22,952; part-time $1055 per credit hour. Required fees: $2364; $99 per credit hour. *Financial support:* In 2010–11, 101 students received support, including 3 fellowships (averaging $18,000 per year), 52 research assistantships (averaging $15,078 per year), 47 teaching assistantships (averaging $10,983 per year); career-related internships or fieldwork, Federal Work-Study, scholarships/grants, unspecified assistantships, and health care benefits (full-time research or teaching assistantship recipients) also available. Financial award application deadline: 3/1; financial award applicants required to submit FAFSA. *Faculty research:* Artificial intelligence, image processing/graphics, parallel/distributed systems, software engineering systems. Total annual research expenditures: $1.3 million. *Unit head:* Dr. Arun Sood, Director, 703-993-1524, Fax: 703-993-1710, E-mail: asood@gmu.edu. *Application contact:* Jay Shapiro, Professor, 703-993-1485, E-mail: jshapiro@gmu.edu.

Michigan State University, The Graduate School, College of Communication Arts and Sciences, Department of Telecommunication, Information Studies, and Media, East Lansing, MI 48824. Offers digital media arts and technology (MA); information and telecommunication management (MA); information, policy and society (MA); serious game design (MA). *Entrance requirements:* Additional exam requirements/recommendations for international students: Required—TOEFL. Electronic applications accepted.

National University, Academic Affairs, School of Media and Communication, Department of Media, La Jolla, CA 92037-1011. Offers digital cinema (MFA); educational and instructional technology (MS); video game production and design (MFA). Part-time and evening/weekend programs available. Postbaccalaureate distance learning degree programs offered (no on-campus study). *Faculty:* 9 full-time (3 women), 61 part-time/adjunct (21 women). *Students:* 72 full-time (23 women), 131 part-time (63 women); includes 71 minority (31 Black or African American, non-Hispanic/Latino; 1 American Indian or Alaska Native, non-Hispanic/Latino; 7 Asian, non-Hispanic/Latino; 23 Hispanic/Latino; 1 Native Hawaiian or other Pacific Islander, non-Hispanic/Latino; 8 Two or more races, non-Hispanic/Latino), 10 international. Average age 39. 121 applicants, 100% accepted, 81 enrolled. In 2010, 47 master's awarded. *Degree requirements:* For master's, thesis. *Entrance requirements:* For master's, interview, minimum GPA of 2.5. Additional exam requirements/recommendations for international students: Required—TOEFL (minimum score 550 paper-based; 213 computer-based; 79 iBT), IELTS (minimum score 6). *Application deadline:* Applications are processed on a rolling basis. Application fee: $60 ($65 for international students). Electronic applications accepted. *Expenses:* Tuition: Full-time $9450; part-time $350 per unit. Required fees: $350 per unit. One-time fee: $60. *Financial support:* Career-related internships or fieldwork, institutionally sponsored loans, scholarships/grants, and tuition waivers (partial) available. Support available to part-time students. Financial award application deadline: 6/30; financial award applicants required to submit FAFSA. *Unit head:* Dr. Cynthia Sistek-Chandler, Department Chair, 858-309-3457, E-mail: cchandler@nu.edu. *Application contact:* Dominick Giovanniello, Associate Regional Dean—San Diego, 800-NAT-UNIV, Fax: 858-541-7792, E-mail: dgiovann@nu.edu.

Rochester Institute of Technology, Graduate Enrollment Services, B. Thomas Golisano College of Computing and Information Sciences, Department of Interactive Games and Media, Rochester, NY 14623-5603. Offers game design and development (MS). Part-time programs available. *Students:* 16 full-time (2 women), 1 part-time; includes 1 Black or African American, non-Hispanic/Latino; 2 Hispanic/Latino, 2 international. Average age 25. 26 applicants, 42% accepted, 7 enrolled. In 2010, 9 master's awarded. *Degree requirements:* For master's, thesis. *Entrance requirements:* For master's, GRE, minimum GPA of 3.25. Additional exam requirements/recommendations for international students: Required—TOEFL (minimum score 570 paper-based; 230 computer-based; 88 iBT) or IELTS (minimum score 6.5). *Application deadline:* For fall admission, 1/15 priority date for domestic students, 1/1 priority date for international students. Applications are processed on a rolling basis. Electronic applications accepted. *Expenses:* Tuition: Full-time $33,234; part-time $924 per credit hour. Required fees: $219. *Financial support:* Research assistantships with partial tuition reimbursements, teaching assistantships with partial tuition reimbursements, career-related internships or fieldwork, scholarships/grants, and unspecified assistantships available. Support available to part-time students. Financial award applicants required to submit FAFSA. *Faculty research:* Experimental game design and development; exploratory research in visualization environments and integrated media frameworks; outreach efforts that surround games and underlying technologies; support of STEM learning through games and interactive entertainment; the application of games and game technology to non-entertainment domains (Serious Games); small, discrete play experiences (Casual Games). *Unit head:* Andrew Phelps, Director, 585-475-6758, E-mail: andy@mail.rit.edu. *Application contact:* Diane Ellison, Assistant Vice President, Graduate Enrollment Services, 585-475-2229, Fax: 585-475-7164, E-mail: gradinfo@rit.edu.

Savannah College of Art and Design, Graduate School, Program in Interactive Design and Game Development, Savannah, GA 31402-3146. Offers MA, MFA, Graduate Certificate.

Part-time programs available. *Faculty:* 16 full-time (4 women), 4 part-time/adjunct (0 women). *Students:* 64 full-time (20 women), 34 part-time (15 women); includes 7 Black or African American, non-Hispanic/Latino; 3 Asian, non-Hispanic/Latino; 4 Hispanic/Latino, 19 international. Average age 29. In 2010, 19 master's, 1 other advanced degree awarded. *Degree requirements:* For master's, thesis, internships. *Entrance requirements:* For master's, interview, portfolio. Additional exam requirements/recommendations for international students: Required—TOEFL (minimum score 450 paper-based; 133 computer-based). *Application deadline:* For fall admission, 4/1 priority date for domestic and international students. Applications are processed on a rolling basis. Application fee: $35. Electronic applications accepted. *Expenses:* Tuition: Full-time $29,520; part-time $3280 per quarter. Tuition and fees vary according to campus/location. *Financial support:* Fellowships, career-related internships or fieldwork, Federal Work-Study, and scholarships/grants available. Financial award application deadline: 4/1; financial award applicants required to submit FAFSA. *Unit head:* Luis Cataldi, Chair, 912-525-8523, E-mail: lcataldi@scad.edu. *Application contact:* Elizabeth Mathis, Director of Graduate Recruitment, 912-525-5965, Fax: 912-525-5985, E-mail: emathis@scad.edu.

University of Advancing Technology, Master of Science Program in Technology, Tempe, AZ 85283-1042. Offers advancing computer science (MS); emerging technologies (MS); game production and management (MS); information assurance (MS); technology leadership (MS). *Faculty:* 9 full-time (3 women), 3 part-time/adjunct (1 woman). *Students:* 55 full-time (9 women), 4 part-time (1 woman). Average age 25. In 2010, 5 master's awarded. *Degree requirements:* For master's, project or thesis. *Entrance requirements:* Additional exam requirements/recommendations for international students: Required—TOEFL (minimum score 550 paper-based). *Application deadline:* For fall admission, 8/15 priority date for domestic students, 7/15 priority date for international students; for winter admission, 12/15 priority date for domestic students, 11/15 priority date for international students; for spring admission, 4/1 priority date for domestic students, 3/1 priority date for international students. Applications are processed on a rolling basis. Application fee: $100 ($250 for international students). Electronic applications accepted. *Expenses:* Tuition: Full-time $18,300. *Financial support:* Career-related internships or fieldwork, Federal Work-Study, and scholarships/grants available. Financial award applicants required to submit FAFSA. *Faculty research:* Artificial intelligence, fractals, organizational management. *Unit head:* Robert Marshall, Dean of Graduate Education, 602-383-8283, Fax: 602-383-8222, E-mail: rmarshall@uat.edu. *Application contact:* Information Contact, 800-658-5744, Fax: 602-383-8222.

University of Central Florida, College of Arts and Humanities, Florida Interactive Entertainment Academy, Orlando, FL 32816. Offers MS. *Students:* 60 full-time (11 women), 48 part-time (5 women); includes 2 Black or African American, non-Hispanic/Latino; 11 Asian, non-Hispanic/Latino; 17 Hispanic/Latino, 7 international. Average age 25. 133 applicants, 57% accepted, 59 enrolled. *Expenses:* Tuition, state resident: part-time $256.56 per credit hour. Tuition, nonresident: part-time $1011.52 per credit hour. Part-time tuition and fees vary according to program. *Unit head:* Ben Noel, Executive Director, 407-235-3612, Fax: 407-317-7094, E-mail: bnoel@fiea.ucf.edu. *Application contact:* Ben Noel, Executive Director, 407-235-3612, Fax: 407-317-7094, E-mail: bnoel@fiea.ucf.edu.

The University of North Carolina at Charlotte, Graduate School, College of Computing and Informatics, Department of Information Technology, Charlotte, NC 28223-0001. Offers game design and development (Certificate); health care information (Certificate); information security/privacy (Certificate); information technology (MS, PhD, Certificate). Part-time programs available. *Faculty:* 15 full-time (3 women), 4 part-time/adjunct (0 women). *Students:* 143 full-time (42 women), 76 part-time (27 women); includes 37 minority (24 Black or African American, non-Hispanic/Latino; 1 American Indian or Alaska Native, non-Hispanic/Latino; 4 Asian, non-Hispanic/Latino; 7 Hispanic/Latino; 1 Two or more races, non-Hispanic/Latino), 93 international. Average age 29. 68 applicants, 94% accepted, 22 enrolled. In 2010, 37 master's, 19 doctorates awarded. Terminal master's awarded for partial completion of doctoral program. *Degree requirements:* For master's, thesis optional; for doctorate, comprehensive exam, thesis/dissertation. *Entrance requirements:* For master's, GRE or GMAT, minimum undergraduate GPA of 2.8 overall, 2.0 In last 2 years; for doctorate, GRE or GMAT, working knowledge of 2 high-level programming languages. Additional exam requirements/recommendations for international students: Required—TOEFL (minimum score 557 paper-based; 220 computer-based; 83 iBT). *Application deadline:* For fall admission, 7/1 for domestic students, 5/1 for international students; for spring admission, 11/1 for domestic students, 10/1 for international students. Applications are processed on a rolling basis. Application fee: $55. Electronic applications accepted. *Expenses:* Tuition, state resident: full-time $3464. Tuition, nonresident: full-time $14,297. Required fees: $2094. Tuition and fees vary according to course load. *Financial support:* In 2010–11, 24 students received support, including 2 fellowships (averaging $50,000 per year), 12 research assistantships (averaging $12,719 per year), 10 teaching assistantships (averaging $13,800 per year); career-related internships or fieldwork, institutionally sponsored loans, scholarships/grants, and unspecified assistantships also available. Support available to part-time students. Financial award application deadline: 4/1; financial award applicants required to submit FAFSA. *Faculty research:* Information security, information privacy, information assurance, cryptography, software engineering, enterprise integration, intelligent information systems, human computer interaction. Total annual research expenditures: $2.7 million. *Unit head:* Dr. Ken Chen, Program Director, 704-687-8545, Fax: 704-687-6065, E-mail: chen@uncc.edu. *Application contact:* Kathy B. Giddings, Director of Graduate Admissions, 704-687-5503, Fax: 704-687-3279, E-mail: gradadm@uncc.edu.

University of Southern California, Graduate School, Viterbi School of Engineering, Department of Computer Science, Los Angeles, CA 90089. Offers computer networks (MS); computer science (MS, PhD); computer security (MS); game development (MS); high performance computing and simulations (MS); human language technology (MS); intelligent robotics (MS); multimedia and creative technologies (MS); software engineering (MS). Part-time and evening/weekend programs available. Postbaccalaureate distance learning degree programs offered (no on-campus study). *Faculty:* 28 full-time (3 women), 56 part-time/adjunct (7 women). *Students:* 710 full-time (115 women), 302 part-time (59 women); includes 76 minority (1 Black or African American, non-Hispanic/Latino; 55 Asian, non-Hispanic/Latino; 14 Hispanic/Latino; 6 Two or more races, non-Hispanic/Latino), 819 international. 2,379 applicants, 30% accepted, 319 enrolled. In 2010, 332 master's, 32 doctorates awarded. *Entrance requirements:* For master's and doctorate, GRE General Test. Additional exam requirements/recommendations for international students: Required—TOEFL. *Application deadline:* For fall admission, 12/1 priority date for domestic and international students; for spring admission, 9/15 priority date for domestic and international students. Applications are processed on a rolling basis. Application fee: $85. Electronic applications accepted. *Expenses:* Tuition: Full-time $31,240; part-time $1420 per unit. Required fees: $600. One-time fee: $35 full-time. Full-time tuition and fees vary according to degree level and program. *Financial support:* In 2010–11, fellowships with full tuition reimbursements (averaging $30,000 per year), research assistantships with full tuition reimbursements (averaging $20,000 per year), teaching assistantships with full tuition reimbursements (averaging $20,000 per year) were awarded; career-related internships or fieldwork, scholarships/grants, health care benefits, and unspecified assistantships also available. Financial award application deadline: 12/1; financial award applicants required to submit CSS PROFILE or FAFSA. *Faculty research:* Databases, computer graphics and computer vision, software engineering, networks and security, robotics, multimedia and virtual reality. Total annual research expenditures: $11.8 million. *Unit head:* Dr. Shanghua Teng, Chair, 213-740-4494, E-mail: csdept@usc.edu. *Application contact:* Lizsl DeLeon, Director of Student Affairs, 213-740-4496, E-mail: ldeleon@usc.edu.

Health Informatics

American Sentinel University, Graduate Programs, Aurora, CO 80014. Offers business administration (MBA); business intelligence (MS); computer science (MSCS); health information management (MS); healthcare (MBA); information systems (MSIS); nursing (MSN). Part-time and evening/weekend programs available. Postbaccalaureate distance learning degree programs offered (no on-campus study). *Entrance requirements:* Additional exam requirements/recommendations for international students: Required—TOEFL (minimum score 600 paper-based; 215 computer-based). Electronic applications accepted.

Arkansas Tech University, Graduate College, College of Natural and Health Sciences, Russellville, AR 72801. Offers fisheries and wildlife biology (MS); health informatics (MS); nursing (MSN). *Students:* 9 full-time (4 women), 25 part-time (21 women); includes 1 minority (Black or African American, non-Hispanic/Latino), 2 international. Average age 36. In 2010, 9 master's awarded. *Degree requirements:* For master's, thesis, project. *Entrance requirements:* For master's, GRE General Test. Additional exam requirements/recommendations for international students: Required—TOEFL (minimum score 550 paper-based; 213 computer-based; 79 iBT), IELTS (minimum score 6). *Application deadline:* For fall admission, 3/1 priority date for domestic students, 5/1 priority date for international students; for spring admission, 10/1 priority date for domestic and international students. Applications are processed on a rolling basis. Application fee: $0 ($30 for international students). Electronic applications accepted. *Expenses:* Tuition, state resident: full-time $4680; part-time $195 per credit hour. Tuition, nonresident: full-time $9360; part-time $390 per credit hour. Required fees: $714; $14 per credit hour. One-time fee: $326 part-time. Tuition and fees vary according to course load. *Financial support:* In 2010–11, teaching assistantships with full tuition reimbursements (averaging $4,000 per year); research assistantships, career-related internships or fieldwork, Federal Work-Study, scholarships/grants, health care benefits, and unspecified assistantships also available. Support available to part-time students. Financial award application deadline: 4/15; financial award applicants required to submit FAFSA. *Faculty research:* Fisheries, warblers, fish movement, darter populations, bob white studies. *Unit head:* Dr. Richard Cohoon, Dean, 479-964-0816, E-mail: richard.cohoon@atu.edu. *Application contact:* Dr. Mary B. Gunter, Dean of Graduate College, 479-968-0398, Fax: 479-964-0542, E-mail: graduate.school@atu.edu.

Barry University, College of Health Sciences, Graduate Certificate Programs, Miami Shores, FL 33161-6695. Offers health care leadership (Certificate); health care planning and informatics (Certificate); histotechnology (Certificate); long term care management (Certificate); medical group practice management (Certificate); quality improvement and outcomes management (Certificate).

Benedictine University, Graduate Programs, Program in Public Health, Lisle, IL 60532-0900. Offers administration of health care institutions (MPH); dietetics (MPH); disaster management (MPH); health education (MPH); health information systems (MPH); MBA/MPH; MPH/MS. Part-time and evening/weekend programs available. Postbaccalaureate distance learning degree programs offered. *Faculty:* 2 full-time (0 women), 8 part-time/adjunct (3 women). *Students:* 105 full-time (80 women), 401 part-time (313 women); includes 192 minority (121 Black or African American, non-Hispanic/Latino; 1 American Indian or Alaska Native, non-Hispanic/Latino; 48 Asian, non-Hispanic/Latino; 21 Hispanic/Latino; 1 Native Hawaiian or other Pacific Islander, non-Hispanic/Latino), 10 international. Average age 33. 293 applicants, 89% accepted, 145 enrolled. In 2010, 106 master's awarded. *Entrance requirements:* For master's, MAT, GRE, or GMAT. Additional exam requirements/recommendations for international students: Required—TOEFL (minimum score 550 paper-based; 213 computer-based). *Application deadline:* For fall admission, 9/1 for domestic students; for winter admission, 12/1 for domestic students; for spring admission, 2/15 for domestic students. Application fee: $40. *Financial support:* Career-related internships or fieldwork and health care benefits available. Support available to part-time students. *Unit head:* Dr. Alan Gorr, Director, 630-829-6566, Fax: 630-960-1126, E-mail: agorr@ben.edu. *Application contact:* Kari Gibbons, Director, Admissions, 630-829-6200, Fax: 630-829-6584, E-mail: kgibbons@ben.edu.

Boston University, Metropolitan College, Department of Computer Science, Boston, MA 02215. Offers computer information systems (MS), including computer networks, database management and business intelligence, health informatics, IT project management, security; computer science (MS), including computer networks, security; telecommunications (MS), including security. Part-time and evening/weekend programs available. Postbaccalaureate distance learning degree programs offered (no on-campus study). *Faculty:* 10 full-time (0 women), 30 part-time/adjunct (3 women). *Students:* 16 full-time (2 women), 681 part-time (155 women); includes 182 minority (44 Black or African American, non-Hispanic/Latino; 1 American Indian or Alaska Native, non-Hispanic/Latino; 88 Asian, non-Hispanic/Latino; 36 Hispanic/Latino; 2 Native Hawaiian or other Pacific Islander, non-Hispanic/Latino; 11 Two or more races, non-Hispanic/Latino), 66 international. Average age 35. 273 applicants, 78% accepted, 155 enrolled. In 2010, 143 master's awarded. *Degree requirements:* For master's, thesis optional. *Entrance requirements:* For master's, 3 letters of recommendation, professional resume. Additional exam requirements/recommendations for international students: Required—TOEFL (minimum score 550 paper-based; 213 computer-based; 80 iBT). *Application deadline:* For fall admission, 6/1 priority date for international students; for spring admission, 10/1 priority date for international students. Applications are processed on a rolling basis. Application fee: $70. Electronic applications accepted. *Expenses:* Tuition: Full-time $39,314; part-time $1228 per credit. Required fees: $40 per semester. *Financial support:* In 2010–11, 9 research assistantships with partial tuition reimbursements (averaging $5,000 per year) were awarded; career-related internships or fieldwork and unspecified assistantships also available. Support available to part-time students. Financial award applicants required to submit FAFSA. *Faculty research:* Medical informatics, Web technologies, telecom and networks, security and forensics, software engineering, programming languages, multimedia and AI, information systems and IT project management. *Unit head:* Dr. Lubomir Chitkushev, Chairman, 617-353-2566, Fax: 617-353-2367, E-mail: csinfo@bu.edu. *Application contact:* Kim Richards, Program Coordinator, 617-353-2566, Fax: 617-353-2367, E-mail: kimrich@bu.edu.

Brandeis University, Rabb School of Continuing Studies, Division of Graduate Professional Studies, Health and Medical Informatics Program, Waltham, MA 02454-9110. Offers MS, Graduate Certificate. Part-time programs available. Postbaccalaureate distance learning degree programs offered (no on-campus study). *Faculty:* 2 full-time (both women), 33 part-time/adjunct (5 women). *Students:* 2 part-time (1 woman). Average age 35. 1 applicant, 100% accepted, 1 enrolled. *Entrance requirements:* For master's, resume, official transcripts, recommendations, goal statements; for Graduate Certificate, resume, official transcripts, recommendations. Additional exam requirements/recommendations for international students: Recommended—TOEFL (minimum score 600 paper-based; 250 computer-based; 100 iBT). *Application deadline:* For fall admission, 6/15 priority date for domestic students; for winter admission, 10/15 for domestic students; for spring admission, 2/15 for domestic students. Application fee: $50. *Unit head:* Cynthia Phillips, Program Chair, 781-736-8787, Fax: 781-736-3420, E-mail: cynthiap@brandeis.edu. *Application contact:* Frances Stearns, Associate Director of Admissions and Student Services, 781-736-8785, Fax: 781-736-3420, E-mail: fstearns@brandeis.edu.

Claremont Graduate University, Graduate Programs, School of Information Systems and Technology, Claremont, CA 91711-6160. Offers electronic commerce (MS, PhD); health information management (MS); information systems (Certificate); knowledge management (MS, PhD); systems development (MS, PhD); telecommunications and networking (MS, PhD); MBA/MS. Part-time programs available. *Faculty:* 6 full-time (1 woman), 1 part-time/adjunct (0 women). *Students:* 87 full-time (24 women), 22 part-time (8 women); includes 31 minority (6 Black or African American, non-Hispanic/Latino; 1 American Indian or Alaska Native, non-Hispanic/Latino; 18 Asian, non-Hispanic/Latino; 3 Hispanic/Latino; 1 Native Hawaiian or other Pacific Islander, non-Hispanic/Latino; 2 Two or more races, non-Hispanic/Latino), 37 international. Average age 37. In 2010, 30 master's, 6 doctorates awarded. *Degree requirements:* For doctorate, comprehensive exam, thesis/dissertation, portfolio. *Entrance requirements:* For master's and doctorate, GMAT, GRE General Test. Additional exam requirements/recommendations for international students: Required—TOEFL (minimum score 550 paper-based; 213 computer-based; 80 iBT). *Application deadline:* For fall admission, 2/1 priority date for domestic students. Applications are processed on a rolling basis. Application fee: $60. Electronic applications accepted. *Expenses:* Tuition: Full-time $35,748; part-time $1554 per unit. Required fees: $215 per semester. *Financial support:* Fellowships, research assistantships, teaching assistantships, Federal Work-Study, institutionally sponsored loans, and scholarships/grants available. Support available to part-time students. Financial award application deadline: 2/15; financial award applicants required to submit FAFSA. *Faculty research:* GPSS, man-machine interaction, organizational aspects of computing, implementation of information systems, information systems practice. *Unit head:* Terry Ryan, Dean, 909-607-9591, Fax: 909-621-8564, E-mail: terry.ryan@cgu.edu. *Application contact:* Matt Hutter, Director of External Affairs, 909-621-3180, Fax: 909-621-8564, E-mail: matt.hutter@cgu.edu.

The College of St. Scholastica, Graduate Studies, Department of Health Information Management, Duluth, MN 55811-4199. Offers MA, Certificate. Part-time programs available. Postbaccalaureate distance learning degree programs offered (minimal on-campus study). *Faculty:* 4 full-time (all women), 12 part-time/adjunct (10 women). *Students:* 125 full-time (100 women), 44 part-time (38 women); includes 24 minority (13 Black or African American, non-Hispanic/Latino; 1 American Indian or Alaska Native, non-Hispanic/Latino; 7 Asian, non-Hispanic/Latino; 2 Hispanic/Latino; 1 Two or more races, non-Hispanic/Latino). Average age 41. 71 applicants, 59% accepted. In 2010, 20 master's awarded. *Degree requirements:* For master's, thesis. *Entrance requirements:* For master's, minimum GPA of 3.0. Additional exam requirements/recommendations for international students: Required—TOEFL (minimum score 550 paper-based; 213 computer-based; 79 iBT). *Application deadline:* For fall admission, 8/1 priority date for domestic students, 8/1 for international students; for spring admission, 11/1 priority date for domestic students, 11/1 for international students. Applications are processed on a rolling basis. Application fee: $50. Electronic applications accepted. *Expenses:* Contact institution. *Financial support:* In 2010–11, 55 students received support. Scholarships/grants available. Support available to part-time students. Financial award applicants required to submit FAFSA. *Faculty research:* Electronic health record implementation, personal health records, Athens project. *Unit head:* Amy Watters, Director, 218-723-7094, Fax: 218-733-2239, E-mail: awatters@css.edu. *Application contact:* Lindsay Lahti, Director of Graduate and Extended Studies Recruitment, 218-733-2240, Fax: 218-733-2275, E-mail: gradstudies@css.edu.

Emory University, Laney Graduate School, Department of Biostatistics, Atlanta, GA 30322-1100. Offers biostatistics (MPH, MSPH, PhD); public health informatics (MSPH). *Degree requirements:* For doctorate, comprehensive exam, thesis/dissertation. *Entrance requirements:* For doctorate, GRE General Test. Additional exam requirements/recommendations for international students: Required—TOEFL (minimum score 550 paper-based; 220 computer-based). Electronic applications accepted. *Expenses:* Tuition: Full-time $33,800. Required fees: $1300. *Faculty research:* Vaccine efficacy, clinical trials, spatial statistics, statistical genetics, neuroimaging.

Emory University, Rollins School of Public Health, Program in Public Health Informatics, Atlanta, GA 30322-1100. Offers MSPH. Part-time programs available. *Degree requirements:* For master's, thesis, practicum. *Entrance requirements:* For master's, GRE General Test. Additional exam requirements/recommendations for international students: Required—TOEFL (minimum score 550 paper-based; 213 computer-based; 80 iBT). Electronic applications accepted. *Expenses:* Contact institution.

George Mason University, College of Health and Human Services, Department of Health Administration and Policy, Fairfax, VA 22030. Offers health and medical policy (MS); health information systems (Certificate); health systems management (MS); quality improvement and outcomes management in health care systems (Certificate); risk management and patient safety (Certificate); senior housing administration (MS, Certificate). *Faculty:* 16 full-time (3 women), 11 part-time/adjunct (7 women). *Students:* 28 full-time (18 women), 111 part-time (85 women); includes 56 minority (15 Black or African American, non-Hispanic/Latino; 29 Asian, non-Hispanic/Latino; 9 Hispanic/Latino; 3 Two or more races, non-Hispanic/Latino), 9 international. Average age 32. 89 applicants, 67% accepted, 40 enrolled. In 2010, 28 master's, 7 other advanced degrees awarded. *Degree requirements:* For master's, comprehensive exam, internship. *Entrance requirements:* For master's, GRE, curriculum vitae, 2 letters of recommendation. Additional exam requirements/recommendations for international students: Required—TOEFL (minimum score 570 paper-based; 230 computer-based; 88 iBT). *Application deadline:* For fall admission, 3/1 priority date for domestic students; for spring admission, 11/1 for domestic students. Applications are processed on a rolling basis. Application fee: $100. Electronic applications accepted. *Expenses:* Tuition, state resident: full-time $8192; part-time $440 per credit hour. Tuition, nonresident: full-time $22,952; part-time $1055 per credit hour. Required fees: $2364; $99 per credit hour. *Financial support:* In 2010–11, 6 students received support, including 5 research assistantships with full and partial tuition reimbursements available (averaging $15,000 per year), 1 teaching assistantship (averaging $12,480 per year); career-related internships or fieldwork, Federal Work-Study, scholarships/grants, unspecified assistantships, and health care benefits (full-time research or teaching assistantship recipients) also available. Financial award application deadline: 3/1; financial award applicants required to submit FAFSA. *Faculty research:* Universal health care, publications, relationships between malpractice pressure and rates of cesarean section and VBAC, seniors and Wii gaming, relationships between changes in physician's incomes and practice settings and their care to Medicaid and charity patients. Total annual research expenditures: $838,668. *Unit head:* Dr. P. J. Maddox, Chair, 703-993-1982, E-mail: pmaddox@gmu.edu. *Application contact:* Adam McCutcheon, Office Manager, 703-993-1929, E-mail: amccutch@gmu.edu.

Georgia Health Sciences University, College of Graduate Studies, Program in Public Health–Informatics, Augusta, GA 30912. Offers MPH. Part-time programs available. *Faculty:* 9 full-time (6 women). *Students:* 18 full-time (11 women), 4 part-time (0 women); includes 3 Black or African American, non-Hispanic/Latino; 4 Asian, non-Hispanic/Latino; 1 Hispanic/Latino; 1 Two or more races, non-Hispanic/Latino, 1 international. Average age 32. 28 applicants, 39% accepted, 7 enrolled. In 2010, 5 master's awarded. *Degree requirements:* For master's, thesis (for some programs). *Entrance requirements:* For master's, GRE General Test. Additional exam requirements/recommendations for international students: Required—TOEFL. *Application deadline:* For fall admission, 6/1 for domestic and international students. Application fee: $30. Electronic applications accepted. *Expenses:* Tuition, state resident: full-time $7500; part-time $313 per semester hour. Tuition, nonresident: full-time $24,772; part-time $1033 per semester hour. Required fees: $1112. *Financial support:* Federal Work-Study available. Financial award application deadline: 5/31; financial award applicants required to submit FAFSA. *Unit head:* Dr. Douglas Keskula, Interim Dean, 706-721-2621, Fax: 706-721-7312, E-mail: dkeskula@georgiahealth.edu. *Application contact:* Lori Prince, Interim Chair, 706-721-3436, E-mail: lprince@georgiahealth.edu.

Golden Gate University, Ageno School of Business, San Francisco, CA 94105-2968. Offers accounting (MBA); business administration (EMBA, MBA, PMBA, DBA); finance (MBA, MS, Certificate); financial planning (MS, Certificate); healthcare information systems (Certificate); human resource management (MBA, MS); human resources management (Certificate); information systems (MS); information technology (MBA); information technology management (Certificate); integrated marketing and communications (MS, Certificate); international business (MBA); management (MBA); marketing (MBA, MS, Certificate); operations supply chain management (Certificate); psychology (MA, Certificate); public administration (EMPA); public relations (MS, Certificate); technical market analysis (Certificate); JD/MBA. Part-time and evening/weekend programs available. *Faculty:* 16 full-time (4 women), 241 part-time/adjunct (72 women). *Students:* 421 full-time (235 women), 744 part-time (425 women); includes 526 minority (114 Black or African American, non-Hispanic/Latino; 2 American Indian or Alaska

Native, non-Hispanic/Latino; 296 Asian, non-Hispanic/Latino; 73 Hispanic/Latino; 29 Native Hawaiian or other Pacific Islander, non-Hispanic/Latino; 12 Two or more races, non-Hispanic/Latino), 109 international. Average age 32. 681 applicants, 78% accepted, 270 enrolled. In 2010, 550 master's, 13 doctorates awarded. *Degree requirements:* For doctorate, thesis/dissertation. *Entrance requirements:* For master's, GMAT (MBA), minimum GPA of 2.5 (MS). Additional exam requirements/recommendations for international students: Required—TOEFL. *Application deadline:* For fall admission, 5/15 for domestic and international students; for winter admission, 1/15 for domestic and international students; for spring admission, 9/15 for domestic and international students. Applications are processed on a rolling basis. Application fee: $70 ($110 for international students). Electronic applications accepted. *Expenses:* Contact institution. *Financial support:* Career-related internships or fieldwork, Federal Work-Study, institutionally sponsored loans, and scholarships/grants available. Support available to part-time students. Financial award applicants required to submit FAFSA. *Unit head:* Dr. Paul Fouts, Dean, 415-442-7026, Fax: 415-442-6579. *Application contact:* Angela Melero, Enrollment Services, 415-442-7800, Fax: 415-442-7807, E-mail: info@ggu.edu.

Grand Canyon University, College of Nursing and Health Sciences, Phoenix, AZ 85017-1097. Offers addiction counseling (MS); health care administration (MS); health care informatics (MS); marriage and family therapy (MS); professional counseling (MS); public health (MS). Part-time and evening/weekend programs available. Postbaccalaureate distance learning degree programs offered (no on-campus study). *Faculty:* 2 full-time (1 woman), 54 part-time/adjunct (36 women). *Students:* 2 full-time (both women), 1,818 part-time (1,476 women); includes 414 minority (346 Black or African American, non-Hispanic/Latino; 14 American Indian or Alaska Native, non-Hispanic/Latino; 4 Asian, non-Hispanic/Latino; 29 Hispanic/Latino; 3 Native Hawaiian or other Pacific Islander, non-Hispanic/Latino; 18 Two or more races, non-Hispanic/Latino), 1 international. Average age 44. In 2010, 103 master's awarded. *Entrance requirements:* For master's, undergraduate degree with minimum GPA of 2.8. Additional exam requirements/recommendations for international students: Required—TOEFL (minimum score 575 paper-based; 233 computer-based; 90 iBT), IELTS (minimum score 7). *Application deadline:* For fall admission, 8/21 for domestic students, 7/2 for international students; for spring admission, 12/24 for domestic students, 11/1 for international students. Application fee: $0. *Financial support:* Federal Work-Study available. Support available to part-time students. Financial award applicants required to submit FAFSA. *Unit head:* Dr. Mark Wooden, Dean, 602-639-6815, E-mail: mark.wooden@gcu.edu. *Application contact:* Andrea Wolochuk, Information Contact, 602-639-6429, E-mail: awolochuk@gcu.edu.

Indiana University Bloomington, School of Informatics, Bloomington, IN 47408. Offers bioinformatics (MS); chemical informatics (MS); computer science (MS, PhD); health informatics (MS); human computer interaction (MS); informatics (PhD); laboratory informatics (MS); media arts and science (MS); music informatics (MS); security informatics (MS); MS/PhD. PhD offered through University Graduate School. Part-time programs available. Postbaccalaureate distance learning degree programs offered (no on-campus study). *Faculty:* 63 full-time (12 women). *Students:* 372 full-time (88 women), 34 part-time (10 women); includes 7 Black or African American, non-Hispanic/Latino; 1 American Indian or Alaska Native, non-Hispanic/Latino; 10 Asian, non-Hispanic/Latino; 3 Hispanic/Latino; 3 Two or more races, non-Hispanic/Latino, 261 international. Average age 27. 746 applicants, 40% accepted, 131 enrolled. In 2010, 117 master's, 20 doctorates awarded. Terminal master's awarded for partial completion of doctoral program. *Degree requirements:* For master's, thesis optional; for doctorate, comprehensive exam, thesis/dissertation, oral and written exams. *Entrance requirements:* For master's and doctorate, GRE, letters of reference. Additional exam requirements/recommendations for international students: Required—TOEFL. *Application deadline:* For fall admission, 1/15 for domestic students, 12/1 for international students. Application fee: $55 ($65 for international students). Electronic applications accepted. *Financial support:* In 2010–11, fellowships with full and partial tuition reimbursements (averaging $20,000 per year), research assistantships (averaging $14,000 per year), teaching assistantships (averaging $13,000 per year) were awarded; Federal Work-Study, institutionally sponsored loans, scholarships/grants, health care benefits, tuition waivers (full and partial), and unspecified assistantships also available. Support available to part-time students. Total annual research expenditures: $2 million. *Unit head:* Dr. David Leake, Associate Dean for Graduate Studies, 812-855-9756, E-mail: leake@cs.indiana.edu. *Application contact:* Rachel Lawmaster, Manager of Graduate Admissions and Graduate Studies, 812-856-3622, Fax: 812-856-3825, E-mail: raclee@indiana.edu.

The Johns Hopkins University, School of Medicine, Division of Health Sciences Informatics, Baltimore, MD 21218-2699. Offers applied health sciences informatics (MS); health sciences informatics research (MS). *Faculty:* 40 part-time/adjunct (10 women). *Students:* 9 full-time (0 women); includes 2 minority (1 Black or African American, non-Hispanic/Latino; 1 Asian, non-Hispanic/Latino), 5 international. 20 applicants, 15% accepted, 1 enrolled. In 2010, 6 master's awarded. *Degree requirements:* For master's, thesis, publications, practica. *Application deadline:* For spring admission, 2/15 priority date for domestic students, 2/15 for international students. Application fee: $85. Electronic applications accepted. *Financial support:* In 2010–11, 3 fellowships with full tuition reimbursements (averaging $42,750 per year) were awarded; career-related internships or fieldwork and health care benefits also available. *Faculty research:* Decision modeling, consumer health informatics, digital libraries, data standards, patient safety. Total annual research expenditures: $963,103. *Unit head:* Dr. Harold P. Lehmann, Director, Training Program, 410-502-2569, Fax: 410-614-2064, E-mail: lehmann@jhmi.edu. *Application contact:* Kersti Winny, Academic Program Administrator, 410-502-3768, Fax: 410-614-2064, E-mail: kwinny@jhmi.edu.

National University, Academic Affairs, School of Health and Human Services, Department of Community Health, La Jolla, CA 92037-1011. Offers health informatics (MS); healthcare administration (MHA); public health (MPH). Part-time and evening/weekend programs available. Postbaccalaureate distance learning degree programs offered. *Faculty:* 4 full-time (2 women), 19 part-time/adjunct (14 women). *Students:* 40 full-time (29 women), 28 part-time (16 women); includes 9 Black or African American, non-Hispanic/Latino; 11 Asian, non-Hispanic/Latino; 9 Hispanic/Latino; 2 Native Hawaiian or other Pacific Islander, non-Hispanic/Latino; 1 Two or more races, non-Hispanic/Latino, 21 international. Average age 31. 47 applicants, 100% accepted, 32 enrolled. In 2010, 9 master's awarded. *Degree requirements:* For master's, thesis. *Entrance requirements:* Additional exam requirements/recommendations for international students: Required—TOEFL (minimum score 550 paper-based; 213 computer-based; 79 iBT). Application fee: $60 ($65 for international students). *Expenses:* Tuition: Full-time $9450; part-time $350 per unit. Required fees: $350 per unit. One-time fee: $60. *Financial support:* Career-related internships or fieldwork, institutionally sponsored loans, and scholarships/grants available. Support available to part-time students. Financial award application deadline: 6/30; financial award applicants required to submit FAFSA. *Unit head:* Dr. Gina Piane, Head, 858-309-3474, E-mail: gpiane@nu.edu. *Application contact:* Dominick Giovanniello, Associate Regional Dean—San Diego, 800-NAT-UNIV, Fax: 858-541-7792, E-mail: dgiovann@nu.edu.

Northeastern University, College of Computer and Information Science, Boston, MA 02115-5096. Offers computer and information science (PhD); computer science (MS); health informatics (MS); information assurance (MS). Part-time and evening/weekend programs available. *Faculty:* 28 full-time (3 women), 3 part-time/adjunct (all women). *Students:* 337 full-time (91 women), 90 part-time (52 women). 1,045 applicants, 56% accepted, 150 enrolled. In 2010, 88 master's, 7 doctorates awarded. Terminal master's awarded for partial completion of doctoral program. *Degree requirements:* For master's, thesis optional; for doctorate, comprehensive exam, thesis/dissertation. *Entrance requirements:* For master's and doctorate, GRE General Test. Additional exam requirements/recommendations for international students: Required—TOEFL or IELTS. *Application deadline:* For fall admission, 7/15 for domestic students, 5/1 for international students; for spring admission, 10/15 for domestic students, 9/1 for international students. Applications are processed on a rolling basis. Application fee: $50. Electronic applications accepted. *Expenses:* Contact institution. *Financial support:* In 2010–11, 59 students received support, including 1 fellowship, 40 research assistantships with full tuition reimbursements available (averaging $18,260 per year), 33 teaching assistantships with full tuition reimbursements available (averaging $18,260 per year); career-related internships or fieldwork, Federal Work-Study, institutionally sponsored loans, scholarships/grants, and unspecified assistantships also available. Financial award application deadline: 1/15. *Faculty research:* Programming languages, artificial intelligence, human-computer interaction, database management, network security. *Unit head:* Dr. Larry A. Finkelstein, Dean, 617-373-2462, Fax: 617-373-5121. *Application contact:* Dr. Agnes Chan, Associate Dean and Director of Graduate Program, 617-373-2462, Fax: 617-373-5121, E-mail: gradschool@ccs.neu.edu.

Northern Kentucky University, Office of Graduate Programs, College of Informatics, Program in Health Informatics, Highland Heights, KY 41099. Offers MS, Certificate. Part-time and evening/weekend programs available. *Students:* 7 full-time (3 women), 63 part-time (41 women); includes 9 minority (6 Black or African American, non-Hispanic/Latino; 1 Asian, non-Hispanic/Latino; 2 Hispanic/Latino), 2 international. Average age 40. 57 applicants, 74% accepted, 25 enrolled. In 2010, 11 master's, 8 other advanced degrees awarded. *Degree requirements:* For master's, capstone. *Entrance requirements:* For master's, MAT, GRE, or GMAT, minimum GPA of 3.0. Additional exam requirements/recommendations for international students: Required—TOEFL (minimum score 550 paper-based; 213 computer-based; 79 iBT); Recommended—IELTS (minimum score 6.5). *Application deadline:* For fall admission, 8/1 for domestic students, 6/1 for international students; for spring admission, 12/1 for domestic students, 10/1 for international students. Applications are processed on a rolling basis. Application fee: $40. Electronic applications accepted. *Expenses:* Tuition, state resident: full-time $7254; part-time $403 per credit hour. Tuition, nonresident: full-time $12,492; part-time $694 per credit hour. Tuition and fees vary according to degree level and program. *Financial support:* Unspecified assistantships available. Financial award applicants required to submit FAFSA. *Unit head:* Dr. Gary Ozanich, Director, 859-572-1397, E-mail: ozanichg1@nku.edu. *Application contact:* Dr. Peg Griffin, Director of Graduate Programs, 859-572-6934, Fax: 859-572-6670, E-mail: griffinp@nku.edu.

Nova Southeastern University, Health Professions Division, College of Osteopathic Medicine, Program in Biomedical Informatics, Fort Lauderdale, FL 33314-7796. Offers biomedical informatics (MS); clinical informatics (Graduate Certificate); public health informatics (Graduate Certificate). *Students:* 12 full-time (5 women), 55 part-time (34 women); includes 20 Black or African American, non-Hispanic/Latino; 5 Asian, non-Hispanic/Latino; 9 Hispanic/Latino, 6 international. Average age 36. In 2010, 5 master's awarded. *Unit head:* Dr. Jennie Q. Lou, Director, 954-262-1619, E-mail: jlou@nova.edu. *Application contact:* Ellen Rondino, College of Osteopathic Medicine Admissions Counselor, 866-817-4068.

Oregon Health & Science University, School of Medicine, Graduate Programs in Medicine, Department of Medical Informatics and Clinical Epidemiology, Portland, OR 97239-3098. Offers clinical informatics (MS, PhD, Certificate); computational biology (MS, PhD); health information management (Certificate). Part-time programs available. Postbaccalaureate distance learning degree programs offered (minimal on-campus study). *Faculty:* 26. *Students:* 111 (34 women); includes 3 Black or African American, non-Hispanic/Latino; 1 American Indian or Alaska Native, non-Hispanic/Latino; 8 Asian, non-Hispanic/Latino; 4 Hispanic/Latino; 4 Native Hawaiian or other Pacific Islander, non-Hispanic/Latino, 12 international. Average age 42. 46 applicants, 70% accepted, 28 enrolled. In 2010, 11 master's, 1 doctorate awarded. Terminal master's awarded for partial completion of doctoral program. *Degree requirements:* For master's, thesis; for doctorate, comprehensive exam, thesis/dissertation. *Entrance requirements:* For master's and doctorate, GRE General Test, coursework in computer programming, human anatomy and physiology. Additional exam requirements/recommendations for international students: Required—TOEFL. *Application deadline:* For fall admission, 12/1 for domestic students; for winter admission, 11/1 for domestic students; for spring admission, 2/1 for domestic students. Applications are processed on a rolling basis. Application fee: $65. Electronic applications accepted. *Expenses:* Contact institution. *Financial support:* Fellowships with full tuition reimbursements, research assistantships, Federal Work-Study, institutionally sponsored loans, scholarships/grants, and full tuition and stipends available. Financial award application deadline: 3/1; financial award applicants required to submit FAFSA. *Faculty research:* Information retrieval, telemedicine, consumer health informatics, information needs assessment, healthcare quality. *Unit head:* Andrea Ilg, 503-494-2547, E-mail: informat@ohsu.edu. *Application contact:* Diane Doctor, 503-494-2547, E-mail: informat@ohsu.edu.

Saint Joseph's University, College of Arts and Sciences, Department of Health Services, Philadelphia, PA 19131-1395. Offers health administration (MS, Post-Master's Certificate); health care ethics (Post-Master's Certificate); health education (MS, Post-Master's Certificate); health informatics (Post-Master's Certificate); healthcare ethics (MS); nurse anesthesia (MS); school nurse certification (MS). Part-time and evening/weekend programs available. *Faculty:* 8 full-time (1 woman), 16 part-time/adjunct (8 women). *Students:* 28 full-time (19 women), 186 part-time (148 women); includes 62 Black or African American, non-Hispanic/Latino; 1 American Indian or Alaska Native, non-Hispanic/Latino; 9 Asian, non-Hispanic/Latino; 7 Hispanic/Latino; 1 Native Hawaiian or other Pacific Islander, non-Hispanic/Latino, 16 international. Average age 36. 89 applicants, 85% accepted, 66 enrolled. In 2010, 43 master's awarded. *Entrance requirements:* For master's, GRE (if GPA less than 2.75), 2 letters of recommendation, minimum GPA of 2.75, resume. Additional exam requirements/recommendations for international students: Required—TOEFL (minimum score 550 paper-based; 213 computer-based; 79 iBT). *Application deadline:* For fall admission, 7/15 priority date for domestic students, 4/15 for international students; for winter admission, 1/15 for international students; for spring admission, 11/15 priority date for domestic students, 10/15 for international students. Applications are processed on a rolling basis. Application fee: $35. Electronic applications accepted. *Expenses:* Tuition: Part-time $729 per credit. Tuition and fees vary according to course load, degree level and program. *Financial support:* Career-related internships or fieldwork and unspecified assistantships available. Financial award applicants required to submit FAFSA. *Unit head:* Nakia Henderson, Director, 610-660-2952, E-mail: nakia.henderson@sju.edu. *Application contact:* Kate McConnell, Director, Graduate College of Arts and Sciences Admissions and Retention, 610-660-3184, Fax: 610-660-3230, E-mail: kate.mcconnell@sju.edu.

Stephens College, Division of Graduate and Continuing Studies, Columbia, MO 65215-0002. Offers business (MBA, MSL); counseling (M Ed), including counseling; curriculum and instruction (M Ed); health information administration (Postbaccalaureate Certificate). Part-time and evening/weekend programs available. Postbaccalaureate distance learning degree programs offered (minimal on-campus study). *Faculty:* 2 full-time (both women), 27 part-time/adjunct (18 women). *Students:* 203 full-time (177 women), 60 part-time (54 women); includes 41 minority (25 Black or African American, non-Hispanic/Latino; 1 American Indian or Alaska Native, non-Hispanic/Latino; 7 Asian, non-Hispanic/Latino; 7 Hispanic/Latino; 1 Two or more races, non-Hispanic/Latino). Average age 35. 89 applicants, 46% accepted, 39 enrolled. In 2010, 94 master's awarded. *Entrance requirements:* For master's, minimum GPA of 3.0 in last 60 hours. Additional exam requirements/recommendations for international students: Required—TOEFL (minimum score 213 computer-based). *Application deadline:* For fall admission, 7/25 priority date for domestic and international students; for winter admission, 12/1 priority date for domestic and international students; for spring admission, 4/25 priority date for domestic and international students. Applications are processed on a rolling basis. Application fee: $40. Electronic applications accepted. *Financial support:* In 2010–11, 143 students received support, including 5 fellowships with full tuition reimbursements available (averaging $5,067 per year); scholarships/grants and unspecified assistantships also available. Financial award applicants required to submit FAFSA. *Faculty research:* Educational psychology, outcomes assessment. *Unit head:* Dean Suzanne Sharp, Dean of Graduate and Continuing Studies, 573-876-7123, Fax: 573-876-7237, E-mail: online@stephens.edu. *Application contact:* Jennifer Deaver, Director of Marketing and Recruitment, 800-388-7579, E-mail: online@stephens.edu.

Stevens Institute of Technology, Graduate School, Charles V. Schaefer Jr. School of Engineering, Department of Computer Science, Hoboken, NJ 07030. Offers computer graphics (Certificate); computer science (MS, PhD); computer systems (Certificate); database management systems (Certificate); distributed systems (Certificate); elements of computer science (Certificate); enterprise computing (Certificate); enterprise security and information

Health Informatics

Stevens Institute of Technology (continued)
assurance (Certificate); health informatics (Certificate); multimedia experience and management (Certificate); networks and systems administration (Certificate); security and privacy (Certificate); service oriented computing (Certificate); software design (Certificate); theoretical computer science (Certificate). Part-time and evening/weekend programs available. *Faculty:* 12 full-time (5 women). *Students:* 117 full-time (42 women), 88 part-time (17 women); includes 4 Black or African American, non-Hispanic/Latino; 21 Asian, non-Hispanic/Latino; 3 Hispanic/Latino, 99 international. Average age 28. 327 applicants, 57% accepted. In 2010, 72 master's, 2 doctorates awarded. Terminal master's awarded for partial completion of doctoral program. *Degree requirements:* For master's, thesis optional; for doctorate, variable foreign language requirement, comprehensive exam, thesis/dissertation. *Entrance requirements:* For master's and doctorate, GRE, minimum GPA of 3.0. Additional exam requirements/recommendations for international students: Required—TOEFL. *Application deadline:* Applications are processed on a rolling basis. Application fee: $50. Electronic applications accepted. *Financial support:* Fellowships, Federal Work-Study available. Financial award application deadline: 4/15. *Faculty research:* Semantics, reliability theory, programming language, cyber security. *Unit head:* Daniel Duchamp, Director, 201-216-5390, Fax: 201-216-8249, E-mail: djd@cs.stevens.edu. *Application contact:* Graduate Admissions, 800-496-4935, Fax: 201-216-8044, E-mail: gradadmissions@stevens.edu.

Temple University, Health Sciences Center and Graduate School, College of Health Professions, Department of Health Information Management, Philadelphia, PA 19122-6096. Offers health informatics (MS). Part-time and evening/weekend programs available. *Faculty:* 1 (woman) full-time. *Students:* 2 full-time (both women), 33 part-time (21 women); includes 9 Black or African American, non-Hispanic/Latino; 6 American Indian or Alaska Native, non-Hispanic/Latino, 1 international. 33 applicants, 48% accepted, 13 enrolled. *Entrance requirements:* Additional exam requirements/recommendations for international students: Required—TOEFL (minimum score 550 paper-based; 213 computer-based; 79 iBT). Application fee: $50. Electronic applications accepted. *Financial support:* Application deadline: 1/15. *Unit head:* Cindy Marselis, Interim Chair, 215-707-4811, Fax: 215-707-5852, E-mail: hlthinfo@temple.edu. *Application contact:* Tara Schumacher, Coordinator of Outreach, 215-204-6575, Fax: 215-204-8781, E-mail: tara.schumacher@temple.edu.

TUI University, College of Health Sciences, Program in Health Sciences, Cypress, CA 90630. Offers clinical research administration (MS, Certificate); emergency and disaster management (MS, Certificate); environmental health science (Certificate); health care administration (PhD); health care management (MS), including health informatics; health education (MS, Certificate); health informatics (Certificate); health sciences (PhD); international health (MS); international health: educator or researcher option (PhD); international health: practitioner option (PhD); law and expert witness studies (MS, Certificate); public health (MS); quality assurance (Certificate). Part-time and evening/weekend programs available. Postbaccalaureate distance learning degree programs offered (no on-campus study). *Students:* 322 full-time (170 women), 709 part-time (357 women). 227 applicants, 80% accepted, 164 enrolled. In 2010, 366 master's, 29 doctorates awarded. *Degree requirements:* For doctorate, comprehensive exam, thesis/dissertation, defense of dissertation. *Entrance requirements:* For master's, minimum GPA of 2.5 (students with GPA 3.0 or greater may transfer up to 30% of graduate level credits); for doctorate, minimum GPA of 3.4, curriculum vitae, course work in research methods or statistics. Additional exam requirements/recommendations for international students: Required—TOEFL. *Application deadline:* For fall admission, 10/3 for domestic and international students; for winter admission, 12/22 for domestic and international students; for spring admission, 4/3 for domestic and international students. Applications are processed on a rolling basis. Application fee: $75. Electronic applications accepted. *Expenses:* Tuition: Full-time $11,040; part-time $345 per semester hour. *Unit head:* Dr. Michaela Tanasescu, Dean, 714-816-0366, Fax: 714-226-9844, E-mail: infocoe@tuiu.edu. *Application contact:* Wei Ren-Finaly, Registrar, 800-375-9878, Fax: 714-827-7407, E-mail: registration@tuiu.edu.

The University of Alabama at Birmingham, School of Health Professions, Program in Health Informatics, Birmingham, AL 35294. Offers MSHI. *Students:* 50 part-time (27 women); includes 17 minority (13 Black or African American, non-Hispanic/Latino; 1 Asian, non-Hispanic/Latino; 2 Hispanic/Latino; 1 Two or more races, non-Hispanic/Latino), 4 international. Average age 37. 35 applicants, 86% accepted, 26 enrolled. In 2010, 12 master's awarded. *Degree requirements:* For master's, thesis or alternative. *Entrance requirements:* For master's, GRE General Test, MAT, minimum GPA of 3.0, course work in computing fundamentals and programming. Electronic applications accepted. *Expenses:* Tuition, state resident: full-time $5482. Tuition, nonresident: full-time $12,430. Tuition and fees vary according to program. *Financial support:* Career-related internships or fieldwork and Federal Work-Study available. *Faculty research:* Healthcare/medical informatics, natural language processing, application of expert systems, graphical user interface design. *Unit head:* Dr. Gerald Glandon, Director, 205-934-5665, Fax: 205-975-6608. *Application contact:* Julie Bryant, Director of Graduate Admissions, 205-934-8227, Fax: 205-934-8413, E-mail: jbryant@uab.edu.

University of Central Florida, College of Health and Public Affairs, Department of Health Management and Informatics, Orlando, FL 32816. Offers health care informatics (MS, Certificate); health sciences (MS). *Accreditation:* CAHME. Part-time and evening/weekend programs available. *Faculty:* 14 full-time (6 women), 15 part-time/adjunct (9 women). *Students:* 154 full-time (111 women), 162 part-time (116 women); includes 119 minority (65 Black or African American, non-Hispanic/Latino; 3 American Indian or Alaska Native, non-Hispanic/Latino; 24 Asian, non-Hispanic/Latino; 26 Hispanic/Latino; 1 Two or more races, non-Hispanic/Latino), 13 international. Average age 29. 255 applicants, 82% accepted, 142 enrolled. In 2010, 28 master's awarded. *Degree requirements:* For master's, comprehensive exam, thesis or alternative, research report. *Entrance requirements:* For master's, GRE General Test. Additional exam requirements/recommendations for international students: Required—TOEFL. *Application deadline:* For fall admission, 7/15 for domestic students; for spring admission, 10/1 for domestic students. Application fee: $30. Electronic applications accepted. *Expenses:* Tuition, state resident: part-time $256.56 per credit hour. Tuition, nonresident: part-time $1011.52 per credit hour. Part-time tuition and fees vary according to program. *Financial support:* In 2010–11, 3 students received support, including 1 fellowship with partial tuition reimbursement available (averaging $10,000 per year), 2 research assistantships (averaging $5,200 per year); career-related internships or fieldwork, Federal Work-Study, institutionally sponsored loans, and unspecified assistantships also available. Financial award application deadline: 3/1; financial award applicants required to submit FAFSA. *Unit head:* Dr. Aaron Liberman, Chair, 407-823-2359, Fax: 407-823-6138, E-mail: aliberma@mail.ucf.edu. *Application contact:* Dr. Aaron Liberman, Chair, 407-823-2359, Fax: 407-823-6138, E-mail: aliberma@mail.ucf.edu.

University of Illinois at Chicago, Graduate College, College of Applied Health Sciences, Program in Health Informatics, Chicago, IL 60607-7128. Offers MS. Postbaccalaureate distance learning degree programs offered (no on-campus study).

University of Illinois at Urbana–Champaign, Graduate College, Graduate School of Library and Information Science, Champaign, IL 61820. Offers bioinformatics: library and information science (MS); library and information science (MS, PhD, CAS); library and information science: digital libraries (CAS). *Accreditation:* ALA (one or more programs are accredited). Postbaccalaureate distance learning degree programs offered. *Faculty:* 23 full-time (11 women), 10 part-time/adjunct (7 women). *Students:* 352 full-time (258 women), 367 part-time (270 women); includes 124 minority (38 Black or African American, non-Hispanic/Latino; 1 American Indian or Alaska Native, non-Hispanic/Latino; 34 Asian, non-Hispanic/Latino; 40 Hispanic/Latino; 11 Two or more races, non-Hispanic/Latino), 27 international. 737 applicants, 58% accepted, 242 enrolled. In 2010, 272 master's, 5 doctorates, 2 other advanced degrees awarded. *Entrance requirements:* For master's, GRE General Test, minimum GPA of 3.0; for doctorate, minimum GPA of 3.0; for CAS, master's degree in library and information science or related field with minimum GPA of 3.0. Additional exam requirements/recommendations for international students: Required—TOEFL (minimum score 620 paper-based; 260 computer-based; 105 iBT) or IELTS (minimum score 7). *Application deadline:* Applications are processed on a rolling basis. Application fee: $75 ($90 for international students). Electronic applications accepted. *Financial support:* In 2010–11, 37 fellowships, 37 research assistantships, 38 teaching assistantships were awarded; tuition waivers (full and partial) also available. *Unit head:* John Unsworth, Dean, 217-333-3281, Fax: 217-244-3302, E-mail: unsworth@illinois.edu. *Application contact:* Valerie Youngen, Admissions and Records Representative, 217-333-0734, Fax: 217-244-3302, E-mail: vyoungen@llinois.edu.

The University of Iowa, Graduate College, Program in Informatics, Iowa City, IA 52242-1316. Offers bioinformatics and computational biology (Certificate); health informatics (MS, PhD, Certificate); information science (MS, PhD, Certificate). *Degree requirements:* For master's, thesis optional; for doctorate, comprehensive exam, thesis/dissertation. *Entrance requirements:* For master's and doctorate, GRE General Test, minimum GPA of 3.0. Additional exam requirements/recommendations for international students: Required—TOEFL (minimum score 550 paper-based; 213 computer-based; 81 iBT). Electronic applications accepted.

The University of Kansas, University of Kansas Medical Center, Program in Health Informatics, Lawrence, KS 66045. Offers MS. Part-time programs available. Postbaccalaureate distance learning degree programs offered (minimal on-campus study). *Faculty:* 6. *Students:* 3 part-time (1 woman); includes 1 minority (Black or African American, non-Hispanic/Latino). Average age 38. 8 applicants, 100% accepted. *Degree requirements:* For master's, comprehensive exam, thesis or alternative. *Entrance requirements:* Additional exam requirements/recommendations for international students: Required—TOEFL. *Application deadline:* For fall admission, 3/1 for domestic and international students; for spring admission, 9/1 for domestic and international students. Application fee: $60. *Expenses:* Tuition, state resident: full-time $7092; part-time $295.50 per credit hour. Tuition, nonresident: full-time $16,590; part-time $691.25 per credit hour. Required fees: $858; $71.49 per credit hour. Tuition and fees vary according to course load, campus/location and program. *Financial support:* Application deadline: 2/14. *Faculty research:* GIS in public health, symbolic representation of health data, smoking cessation. *Unit head:* Dr. Allen Rawitch, Vice Chancellor for Academic Affairs/Dean of Graduate Studies, 913-588-1258, E-mail: arawitch@kumc.edu. *Application contact:* Dr. Judith Warren, Director for Health Informatics Graduate Program, 913-588-4286, Fax: 913-588-1669, E-mail: jwarren2@kumc.edu.

University of La Verne, College of Business and Public Management, Program in Health Administration, La Verne, CA 91750-4443. Offers financial management (MHA); health administration (MHA); human resources (MHA); information management (MHA); leadership and management (MHA); managed care (MHA); marketing and business development (MHA). Part-time programs available. *Faculty:* 34 full-time (12 women), 36 part-time/adjunct (9 women). *Students:* 44 full-time (29 women), 27 part-time (18 women); includes 42 minority (15 Black or African American, non-Hispanic/Latino; 13 Asian, non-Hispanic/Latino; 14 Hispanic/Latino). Average age 31. In 2010, 27 master's awarded. *Entrance requirements:* For master's, minimum undergraduate GPA of 2.5, 3 letters of reference, curriculum vitae or resume, writing sample. Additional exam requirements/recommendations for international students: Required—TOEFL (minimum score 550 paper-based; 213 computer-based). *Application deadline:* Applications are processed on a rolling basis. Application fee: $50. *Expenses:* Contact institution. *Financial support:* Application deadline: 3/2. *Unit head:* Joan Branin, Chairperson, 909-593-3511 Ext. 4247, E-mail: jbranin@laverne.edu. *Application contact:* Barbara Cox, Program and Admissions Specialist, 909-593-3511 Ext. 4004, Fax: 909-392-2761, E-mail: bcox@laverne.edu.

University of Maryland University College, Graduate School of Management and Technology, Program in Health Administration Informatics, Adelphi, MD 20783. Offers MS, Certificate. Part-time and evening/weekend programs available. Postbaccalaureate distance learning degree programs offered (no on-campus study). *Students:* 3 full-time (2 women), 179 part-time (123 women); includes 105 minority (85 Black or African American, non-Hispanic/Latino; 1 American Indian or Alaska Native, non-Hispanic/Latino; 12 Asian, non-Hispanic/Latino; 4 Hispanic/Latino; 1 Native Hawaiian or other Pacific Islander, non-Hispanic/Latino; 2 Two or more races, non-Hispanic/Latino), 1 international. Average age 39. 75 applicants, 100% accepted, 42 enrolled. In 2010, 10 master's, 5 other advanced degrees awarded. *Degree requirements:* For master's, thesis or alternative, capstone course. *Application deadline:* Applications are processed on a rolling basis. Application fee: $40. Electronic applications accepted. *Financial support:* Federal Work-Study and scholarships/grants available. Support available to part-time students. Financial award application deadline: 6/1; financial award applicants required to submit FAFSA. *Unit head:* Dr. Kathrine Marconi, Director, 240-684-2400, Fax: 240-684-2401, E-mail: abouldin@umuc.edu. *Application contact:* Coordinator, Graduate Admissions, 800-888-8682, Fax: 240-684-2151, E-mail: newgrad@umuc.edu.

University of Massachusetts Lowell, School of Health and Environment, Department of Community Health and Sustainability, Lowell, MA 01854-2881. Offers health management and policy (MS, Graduate Certificate). Part-time programs available. *Degree requirements:* For master's, thesis optional. *Entrance requirements:* For master's, GRE General Test. *Faculty research:* Alzheimer's disease, total quality management systems, information systems, market analysis.

University of Michigan, Horace H. Rackham School of Graduate Studies, School of Information, Ann Arbor, MI 48109-1285. Offers archives and records management (MSI); community informatics (MSI); health informatics (MS); human computer interaction (MSI); information (PhD); information analysis and retrieval (MSI); information economics for management (MSI); information policy (MSI); library and information science (MSI); preservation of information (MSI); school library media (MSI); social computing (MSI). *Accreditation:* ALA (one or more programs are accredited). *Entrance requirements:* For master's and doctorate, GRE General Test. Additional exam requirements/recommendations for international students: Required—TOEFL (minimum score 600 paper-based; 100 iBT). Electronic applications accepted. *Expenses:* Tuition, state resident: full-time $17,784; part-time $1116 per credit hour. Tuition, nonresident: full-time $35,944; part-time $2125 per credit hour. International tuition: $35,994 full-time. Required fees: $95 per semester. Tuition and fees vary according to course load, degree level and program.

University of Minnesota, Twin Cities Campus, Graduate School, Program in Health Informatics, Minneapolis, MN 55455-0213. Offers MHI, MS, PhD, MD/MHI. Part-time programs available. *Degree requirements:* For master's, thesis or alternative; for doctorate, thesis/dissertation. *Entrance requirements:* For master's and doctorate, GRE General Test, previous course work in life sciences, programming, calculus. Additional exam requirements/recommendations for international students: Required—TOEFL (minimum score 550 paper-based; 237 computer-based). Electronic applications accepted. *Faculty research:* Medical decision making, physiological control systems, population studies, clinical information systems, telemedicine.

University of Missouri, Graduate School, Department of Health Management and Informatics, Columbia, MO 65211. Offers health administration (MHA); health informatics (MHA); health services management (MHA). *Accreditation:* CAHME. Part-time programs available. *Entrance requirements:* For master's, GRE General Test or GMAT, minimum GPA of 3.0. Additional exam requirements/recommendations for international students: Required—TOEFL (minimum score 500 paper-based; 173 computer-based; 61 iBT).

The University of North Carolina at Charlotte, Graduate School, College of Computing and Informatics, Department of Bioinformatics and Genomics, Charlotte, NC 28223-0001. Offers bioinformatics (MS). Part-time programs available. *Faculty:* 13 full-time (6 women). *Students:* 14 full-time (6 women), 4 part-time (2 women); includes 4 minority (1 Black or African American, non-Hispanic/Latino; 3 Asian, non-Hispanic/Latino), 6 international. Average age 28. 19 applicants, 53% accepted, 7 enrolled. In 2010, 5 master's awarded. Terminal master's awarded for partial completion of doctoral program. *Degree requirements:* For master's, internship, research project, or thesis. *Entrance requirements:* For master's, GRE, minimum undergraduate GPA of 3.0 overall and in undergraduate major. Additional exam requirements/recommendations for international students: Required—TOEFL (minimum score 557 paper-based; 220 computer-based; 83 iBT). *Application deadline:* For fall admission, 7/15 for domestic students, 5/1 for international students; for spring admission, 11/15 for domestic students, 10/1 for international students. Applications are processed on a rolling basis. Application fee: $55. Electronic applications accepted. *Expenses:* Tuition, state resident: full-time $3464. Tuition, nonresident: full-time $14,297. Required fees: $2094. Tuition and fees vary according to course load. *Financial support:* In 2010–11, 8 fellowships (averaging $25,083 per year), 4 research assistantships (averaging $14,375 per year), 14 teaching assistantships (averaging $11,481 per year) were awarded; career-related internships or fieldwork, institutionally sponsored loans, scholarships/grants, and unspecified assistantships also available. Support available to part-time students. *Faculty research:* High-throughput studies, computational biophysics, structural bioinformatics, metagenomics, computational mass spectrometry. Total annual research expenditures: $1.1 million. *Unit head:* Dr. Larry Mays, Chairman, 704-687-8555, E-mail: lemays@uncc.edu. *Application contact:* Kathy B. Giddings, Director of Graduate Admissions, 704-687-5503, Fax: 704-687-3279, E-mail: gradadm@uncc.edu.

The University of North Carolina at Charlotte, Graduate School, College of Computing and Informatics, Department of Information Technology, Charlotte, NC 28223-0001. Offers game design and development (Certificate); health care information (Certificate); information security/privacy (Certificate); information technology (MS, PhD, Certificate). Part-time programs available. *Faculty:* 15 full-time (3 women), 4 part-time/adjunct (0 women). *Students:* 143 full-time (42 women), 76 part-time (27 women); includes 37 minority (24 Black or African American, non-Hispanic/Latino; 1 American Indian or Alaska Native, non-Hispanic/Latino; 4 Asian, non-Hispanic/Latino; 7 Hispanic/Latino; 1 Two or more races, non-Hispanic/Latino), 93 international. Average age 29. 68 applicants, 94% accepted, 22 enrolled. In 2010, 37 master's, 19 doctorates awarded. Terminal master's awarded for partial completion of doctoral program. *Degree requirements:* For master's, thesis optional; for doctorate, comprehensive exam, thesis/dissertation. *Entrance requirements:* For master's, GRE or GMAT, minimum undergraduate GPA of 2.8 overall, 2.0 in last 2 years; for doctorate, GRE or GMAT, working knowledge of 2 high-level programming languages. Additional exam requirements/recommendations for international students: Required—TOEFL (minimum score 557 paper-based; 220 computer-based; 83 iBT). *Application deadline:* For fall admission, 7/1 for domestic students, 5/1 for international students; for spring admission, 11/1 for domestic students, 10/1 for international students. Applications are processed on a rolling basis. Application fee: $55. Electronic applications accepted. *Expenses:* Tuition, state resident: full-time $3464. Tuition, nonresident: full-time $14,297. Required fees: $2094. Tuition and fees vary according to course load. *Financial support:* In 2010–11, 24 students received support, including 2 fellowships (averaging $50,000 per year), 12 research assistantships (averaging $12,719 per year), 10 teaching assistantships (averaging $13,800 per year); career-related internships or fieldwork, institutionally sponsored loans, scholarships/grants, and unspecified assistantships also available. Support available to part-time students. Financial award application deadline: 4/1; financial award applicants required to submit FAFSA. *Faculty research:* Information security, information privacy, information assurance, cryptography, software engineering, enterprise integration, intelligent information systems, human computer interaction. Total annual research expenditures: $2.7 million. *Unit head:* Dr. Ken Chen, Program Director, 704-687-8545, Fax: 704-687-6065, E-mail: chen@uncc.edu. *Application contact:* Kathy B. Giddings, Director of Graduate Admissions, 704-687-5503, Fax: 704-687-3279, E-mail: gradadm@uncc.edu.

University of Phoenix, College of Natural Sciences, Phoenix, AZ 85034-7209. Offers gerontology (MHA); health administration (MHA); health administration education (MHA); informatics (MHA). Programs are offered at the online campus. Evening/weekend programs available. Postbaccalaureate distance learning degree programs offered. *Students:* 2,644 full-time (2,223 women); includes 947 minority (728 Black or African American, non-Hispanic/Latino; 20 American Indian or Alaska Native, non-Hispanic/Latino; 61 Asian, non-Hispanic/Latino; 119 Hispanic/Latino; 11 Native Hawaiian or other Pacific Islander, non-Hispanic/Latino; 8 Two or more races, non-Hispanic/Latino), 81 international. Average age 39. *Entrance requirements:* For master's, minimum undergraduate GPA of 2.5 from accredited university, 3 years of work experience, citizen of the United States or have valid visa. Additional exam requirements/recommendations for international students: Required—TOEFL (minimum paper score 550, computer score 213, iBT 79), Test of English for International Communication, or IELTS. *Application deadline:* Applications are processed on a rolling basis. Application fee: $45. Electronic applications accepted. *Expenses:* Tuition: Full-time $16,440. One-time fee: $45 full-time. Full-time tuition and fees vary according to course load, degree level, campus/location and program. *Financial support:* Scholarships/grants available. Financial award applicants required to submit FAFSA. *Unit head:* Dr. Hinrich Eylers, Dean/Executive Director, 602-557-7428, Fax: 602-794-8454, E-mail: hinrich.eylers@phoenix.edu. *Application contact:* Dr. Hinrich Eylers, Dean/Executive Director, 602-557-7428, Fax: 602-794-8454, E-mail: hinrich.eylers@phoenix.edu.

University of Phoenix–Birmingham Campus, College of Health and Human Services, Birmingham, AL 35244. Offers education (MHA); gerontology (MHA); health administration (MHA); health care management (MBA); informatics (MHA); nursing (MSN); nursing/health care education (MSN); MSN/MBA; MSN/MHA.

University of Phoenix–Charlotte Campus, College of Nursing, Charlotte, NC 28273-3409. Offers education (MHA); gerontology (MHA); health administration (MHA); informatics (MHA, MSN); nursing (MSN); nursing/health care education (MSN). Evening/weekend programs available. *Degree requirements:* For master's, thesis (for some programs). *Entrance requirements:* For master's, minimum undergraduate GPA of 2.5, 3 years work experience. Additional exam requirements/recommendations for international students: Required—TOEFL (minimum score 550 paper-based; 213 computer-based; 79 iBT). Electronic applications accepted.

University of Phoenix–Des Moines Campus, College of Nursing, Des Moines, IA 50266. Offers education (MHA); gerontology (MHA); health administration (MHA, DHA); informatics (MHA, MSN); nursing (MSN, PhD); nursing/health care education (MSN).

University of Phoenix–Louisville Campus, College of Nursing, Louisville, KY 40223-3839. Offers education (MHA); gerontology (MHA); health administration (MHA); informatics (MHA, MSN); nursing (MSN); nursing/health care education (MSN). Postbaccalaureate distance learning degree programs offered.

University of Phoenix–Milwaukee Campus, College of Nursing, Milwaukee, WI 53045. Offers education (MHA); gerontology (MHA); health administration (MHA, DHA); informatics (MHA, MSN); nursing (MSN, PhD); nursing/health care education (MSN); MSN/MBA; MSN/MHA.

University of Phoenix–Raleigh Campus, College of Nursing, Raleigh, NC 27606. Offers education (MHA); gerontology (MHA); health administration (MHA, DHA); informatics (MHA, MSN); nursing (MSN, PhD); nursing/health care education (MSN).

University of Phoenix–Washington D.C. Campus, College of Nursing, Washington, DC 20001. Offers education (MHA); gerontology (MHA); health administration (MHA, DHA); informatics (MHA, MSN); nursing (MSN, PhD); nursing/health care education (MSN); MSN/MBA; MSN/MHA.

University of Pittsburgh, School of Health and Rehabilitation Sciences, Master's Programs in Health and Rehabilitation Sciences, Pittsburgh, PA 15260. Offers health and rehabilitation sciences (MS), including clinical dietetics and nutrition, health care supervision and management, health information systems, occupational therapy, physical therapy, rehabilitation counseling, rehabilitation science and technology, sports medicine, wellness and human performance. *Accreditation:* APTA. Part-time and evening/weekend programs available. *Faculty:* 23 full-time (12 women), 4 part-time/adjunct (2 women). *Students:* 117 full-time (81 women), 41 part-time (27 women); includes 19 minority (8 Black or African American, non-Hispanic/Latino; 7 Asian, non-Hispanic/Latino; 1 Hispanic/Latino; 3 Two or more races, non-Hispanic/Latino), 67 international. Average age 28. 337 applicants, 64% accepted, 100 enrolled. In 2010, 110

master's awarded. *Degree requirements:* For master's, comprehensive exam (for some programs), thesis optional. *Entrance requirements:* For master's, NA, minimum GPA of 3.0. Additional exam requirements/recommendations for international students: Required—TOEFL, IELTS. *Application deadline:* For fall admission, 1/31 for international students; for spring admission, 7/31 for international students. Applications are processed on a rolling basis. Application fee: $50. Electronic applications accepted. *Expenses:* Contact institution. *Financial support:* Research assistantships, teaching assistantships, Federal Work-Study, institutionally sponsored loans, traineeships, and unspecified assistantships available. Financial award applicants required to submit FAFSA. *Faculty research:* Assistive technology, seating and wheeled mobility, cellular neurophysiology, low back syndrome, augmentative communication. Total annual research expenditures: $7.8 million. *Unit head:* Dr. Clifford E. Brubaker, Dean, 412-383-6560, Fax: 412-383-6535, E-mail: cliffb@pitt.edu. *Application contact:* Shameem Gangjee, Director of Admissions, 412-383-6558, Fax: 412-383-6535, E-mail: admissions@shrs.pitt.edu.

University of Puerto Rico, Medical Sciences Campus, School of Health Professions, Program in Health Information Administration, San Juan, PR 00936-5067. Offers MS. Part-time programs available. *Degree requirements:* For master's, one foreign language, thesis or alternative, internship. *Entrance requirements:* For master's, EXADEP or GRE General Test, minimum GPA of 2.5, interview, fluency in Spanish. *Faculty research:* Quality of medical records, health information data.

University of San Diego, Hahn School of Nursing and Health Science, San Diego, CA 92110-2492. Offers adult nurse practitioner/family nurse practitioner (MSN); adult-gerontology clinical nurse specialist (MSN); clinical nursing (MSN); entry-level nursing (for non-RNs) (MSN); executive nurse leader (MSN); family nurse practitioner (MSN); healthcare informatics (MS, MSN); nursing (PhD); nursing practice (DNP); pediatric nurse practitioner/family nurse practitioner (MSN); psychiatric-mental health nurse practitioner (MSN). *Accreditation:* AACN. Part-time and evening/weekend programs available. *Faculty:* 21 full-time (19 women), 38 part-time/adjunct (34 women). *Students:* 146 full-time (124 women), 173 part-time (151 women); includes 108 minority (14 Black or African American, non-Hispanic/Latino; 7 American Indian or Alaska Native, non-Hispanic/Latino; 37 Asian, non-Hispanic/Latino; 37 Hispanic/Latino; 1 Native Hawaiian or other Pacific Islander, non-Hispanic/Latino; 12 Two or more races, non-Hispanic/Latino), 7 international. Average age 38. 483 applicants, 45% accepted, 123 enrolled. In 2010, 116 master's, 10 doctorates awarded. *Degree requirements:* For doctorate, thesis/dissertation (for some programs), residency (DNP). *Entrance requirements:* For master's, GRE General Test (entry-level nursing), BSN, current California RN licensure (except for entry-level nursing); minimum GPA of 3.0; for doctorate, minimum GPA of 3.5, MSN, current California RN licensure. Additional exam requirements/recommendations for international students: Required—TOEFL (minimum score 580 paper-based; 237 computer-based; 83 iBT), TWE. *Application deadline:* For fall admission, 3/1 priority date for domestic students, 3/1 for international students; for spring admission, 11/1 priority date for domestic students, 11/1 for international students. Applications are processed on a rolling basis. Application fee: $45. Electronic applications accepted. *Expenses:* Tuition: Full-time $21,744; part-time $1208 per unit. Required fees: $224. Full-time tuition and fees vary according to course load and degree level. *Financial support:* In 2010–11, 270 students received support. Scholarships/grants and traineeships available. Support available to part-time students. Financial award application deadline: 4/1; financial award applicants required to submit FAFSA. *Faculty research:* Palliative and end of life care, maternal/child health, childhood obesity, health care disparities, cognitive functioning. *Unit head:* Dr. Sally Hardin, Dean, 619-260-4550, Fax: 619-260-6814. *Application contact:* Stephen Pultz, Director of Admissions and Enrollment, 619-260-4506, Fax: 619-260-6836, E-mail: admissions@sandiego.edu.

The University of Texas Health Science Center at Houston, School of Health Information Sciences, Houston, TX 77225-0036. Offers health informatics (MS, PhD, Certificate); MPH/MS; MPH/PhD. Part-time programs available. Postbaccalaureate distance learning degree programs offered (no on-campus study). *Degree requirements:* For master's, thesis; for doctorate, thesis/dissertation. *Entrance requirements:* For master's and doctorate, GRE or MAT. Additional exam requirements/recommendations for international students: Required—TOEFL (minimum score 550 paper-based; 213 computer-based; 87 iBT). Electronic applications accepted. *Faculty research:* Patient safety, human computer interface, artificial intelligence, decision support tools, 3-D visualization, biomedical engineering.

University of Toronto, School of Graduate Studies, Life Sciences Division, Program in Health Informatics, Toronto, ON M5S 1A1, Canada. Offers MHI.

University of Victoria, Faculty of Graduate Studies, Faculty of Human and Social Development, School of Health Information Science, Victoria, BC V8W 2Y2, Canada. Offers M Sc. *Degree requirements:* For master's, thesis or research project. *Entrance requirements:* Additional exam requirements/recommendations for international students: Required—TOEFL (minimum score 575 paper-based).

University of Virginia, School of Medicine, Department of Public Health Sciences, Program in Clinical Research, Charlottesville, VA 22903. Offers clinical investigation and patient-oriented research (MS); informatics in medicine (MS). Part-time programs available. *Students:* 8 full-time (3 women), 16 part-time (5 women); includes 1 Black or African American, non-Hispanic/Latino; 4 Asian, non-Hispanic/Latino; 1 Hispanic/Latino; 1 Two or more races, non-Hispanic/Latino, 1 international. Average age 35. 19 applicants, 68% accepted, 13 enrolled. In 2010, 7 master's awarded. *Degree requirements:* For master's, thesis (for some programs). *Entrance requirements:* For master's, 2 letters of recommendation. Additional exam requirements/recommendations for international students: Required—TOEFL (minimum score 600 paper-based; 250 computer-based; 90 iBT). *Application deadline:* For fall admission, 3/1 priority date for domestic and international students. Application fee: $60. Electronic applications accepted. *Financial support:* Career-related internships or fieldwork available. Financial award applicants required to submit FAFSA. *Unit head:* Dr. Ruth Gaare Bernheim, Chair, 434-924-8430, Fax: 434-924-8437. *Application contact:* Tracey L. Brookman, Academic Programs Administrator, 434-924-8430, Fax: 434-924-8437, E-mail: ms-hes@virginia.edu.

University of Washington, Graduate School, School of Medicine, Graduate Programs in Medicine, Department of Medical Education and Biomedical Informatics, Division of Biomedical and Health Informatics, Seattle, WA 98195. Offers MS, PhD. *Entrance requirements:* For master's and doctorate, GRE General Test, minimum GPA of 3.0; previous undergraduate course work in biology, computer programming, and mathematics. Additional exam requirements/recommendations for international students: Required—TOEFL (minimum score 580 paper-based; 237 computer-based; 70 iBT). Electronic applications accepted. *Faculty research:* Bio-clinical informatics, information retrieval, human-computer interaction, knowledge-based systems, telehealth.

University of Wisconsin–Milwaukee, Graduate School, College of Health Sciences, Interdepartmental Program in Healthcare Informatics, Milwaukee, WI 53201-0413. Offers MS, Certificate. *Faculty:* 7 full-time (3 women). *Students:* 4 full-time (2 women), 6 part-time (3 women), 3 international. Average age 36. 17 applicants, 53% accepted, 4 enrolled. In 2010, 6 master's awarded. *Degree requirements:* For master's, comprehensive exam, thesis optional. *Entrance requirements:* For master's, GRE General Test. Additional exam requirements/recommendations for international students: Required—TOEFL (minimum score 550 paper-based; 79 iBT), IELTS (minimum score 6.5). Application fee: $56 ($96 for international students). *Financial support:* Fellowships, research assistantships, teaching assistantships available. Total annual research expenditures: $710,931. *Unit head:* Timothy Patrick, Representative, 414-229-6849, Fax: 414-229-2619, E-mail: tp5@uwm.edu. *Application contact:* General Information Contact, 414-229-4982, Fax: 414-229-6967, E-mail: gradschool@uwm.edu.

Walden University, Graduate Programs, School of Health Sciences, Minneapolis, MN 55401. Offers clinical research administration (MS, Postbaccalaureate Certificate); health informatics (MS); health services (PhD), including community health promotion and education, general

Health Informatics

Walden University (continued)

program, health management and policy, healthcare administration, leadership, public health policy, self-designed; healthcare administration (MHA); public health (MPH, PhD), including community health promotion and education (PhD), epidemiology (PhD). Part-time and evening/weekend programs available. Postbaccalaureate distance learning degree programs offered (minimal on-campus study). *Faculty:* 15 full-time (11 women), 202 part-time/adjunct (94 women). *Students:* 2,651 full-time (2,079 women), 932 part-time (731 women); includes 1,624 Black or African American, non-Hispanic/Latino; 24 American Indian or Alaska Native, non-Hispanic/Latino; 132 Asian, non-Hispanic/Latino; 145 Hispanic/Latino; 28 Two or more races, non-Hispanic/Latino, 177 international. Average age 39. In 2010, 370 master's, 61 doctorates awarded. *Degree requirements:* For doctorate, thesis/dissertation, residency. *Entrance requirements:* For master's, bachelor's degree or equivalent in related field, minimum GPA of 2.5; for doctorate, master's degree or equivalent in related field; minimum GPA of 3.0; official transcripts; three years of related professional/academic experience (preferred); access to computer and Internet. Additional exam requirements/recommendations for international students: Required—TOEFL (minimum score 550 paper-based; 213 computer-based), IELTS (minimum score 6.5), TOEFL (minimum score 550 paper-based; 213 computer-based), IELTS (minimum score 6.5), or Michigan English Language Assessment Battery (minimum score 82). *Application deadline:* Applications are processed on a rolling basis. Application fee: $50. Electronic applications accepted. *Expenses:* Tuition: Full-time $10,274; part-time $445 per credit. Tuition and fees vary according to course load, degree level and program. *Financial support:* Fellowships, Federal Work-Study, scholarships/grants, unspecified assistantships, and family tuition reduction, active duty/veteran tuition reduction, group tuition reduction, interest-free payment plans available. Support available to part-time students. Financial award applicants required to submit FAFSA. *Unit head:* Dr. Jorg Westermann, Associate Dean, 800-925-3368. *Application contact:* Jennifer Hall, Vice President of Enrollment Management, 866-4-WALDEN, E-mail: info@waldenu.edu.

Walden University, Graduate Programs, School of Management, Minneapolis, MN 55401. Offers accounting (MS), including cpa emphasis, professional track, self-designed; accounting and management (MS), including self-designed, strategic management; applied management and decision sciences (PhD), including accounting, engineering management, finance, general applied management and decision sciences, information systems management, knowledge management, leadership and organizational change, learning management, operations research, self-designed program in applied management and design sciences; business information management (MISM); enterprise information security (MISM); entrepreneurship (MBA, DBA); finance (MBA, DBA); global management (MS); global supply chain management (DBA); health informatics (MISM); healthcare management (MBA, MS); healthcare system improvement (MBA); human resource management (MBA, MS), including functional human resource management (MS), human resource management (MS), integrating functional and strategic human resource management (MS), organizational strategy (MS); information systems (MS); information systems management (DBA); information technology (MS), including information security, software engineering; international business (MBA, DBA); IT strategy and governance (MISM); leadership (MBA, MS, DBA), including entrepreneurship (MS), general management (MS), human resources leadership (MS), innovation and technology (MS), leader development (MS), leading sustainability (MS), project management (MS), self-designed (MS); managers as leaders (MS); managing global software and service supply chains (MISM); marketing (MBA, DBA); project management (MBA, MS); research strategies (MS); risk management (MBA); self-designed (MBA, DBA); social impact management (DBA); strategy and operations (MS); sustainable futures (MBA); sustainable management (MS); technology (MBA); technology entrepreneurship (DBA); technology management (MS). Part-time and evening/weekend programs available. Postbaccalaureate distance learning degree programs offered (minimal on-campus study). *Faculty:* 22 full-time (8 women), 291 part-time/adjunct (100 women). *Students:* 3,705 full-time (1,956 women), 976 part-time (549 women); includes 2,432 minority (2,021 Black or African American, non-Hispanic/Latino; 32 American Indian or Alaska Native, non-Hispanic/Latino; 137 Asian, non-Hispanic/Latino; 193 Hispanic/Latino; 5 Native Hawaiian or other Pacific Islander, non-Hispanic/Latino; 44 Two or more races, non-Hispanic/Latino), 302 international. Average age 40. In 2010, 658 master's, 86 doctorates awarded. *Degree requirements:* For doctorate, thesis/dissertation (for some programs), residency. *Entrance requirements:* For master's, bachelor's degree or equivalent in related field; minimum GPA of 2.5; official transcripts; goal statement; access to computer and Internet; for doctorate, master's degree or equivalent in related field; minimum GPA of 3.0; 3 years of related professional/academic experience (preferred). Additional exam requirements/recommendations for international students: Required—TOEFL (minimum score 550 paper-based; 213 computer-based), IELTS (minimum score 6.5), TOEFL, IELTS, or Michigan English Language Assessment Battery (minimum score 82). *Application deadline:* Applications are processed on a rolling basis. Application fee: $50. Electronic applications accepted. *Expenses:* Tuition: Full-time $10,274; part-time $445 per credit. Tuition and fees vary according to course load, degree level and program. *Financial support:* Fellowships, Federal Work-Study, scholarships/grants, unspecified assistantships, and family tuition reduction, active duty/veteran tuition reduction, group tuition reduction, interest-free payment plans available. Support available to part-time students. Financial award applicants required to submit FAFSA. *Unit head:* Dr. William Schulz, Associate Dean, 800-925-3368. *Application contact:* Jennifer Hall, Vice President of Enrollment Management, 866-4-WALDEN, E-mail: info@waldenu.edu.

Human-Computer Interaction

Carnegie Mellon University, School of Computer Science, Department of Human-Computer Interaction, Pittsburgh, PA 15213-3891. Offers MHCI, PhD. *Entrance requirements:* For master's, GRE General Test, GRE Subject Test.

Cornell University, Graduate School, Graduate Fields of Arts and Sciences, Field of Information Science, Ithaca, NY 14853-0001. Offers cognition (PhD); human computer interaction (PhD); information systems (PhD); social aspects of information (PhD). *Faculty:* 33 full-time (10 women). *Students:* 23 full-time (9 women); includes 1 Black or African American, non-Hispanic/Latino; 2 Asian, non-Hispanic/Latino, 10 international. Average age 28. 98 applicants, 15% accepted, 8 enrolled. In 2010, 2 doctorates awarded. *Degree requirements:* For doctorate, comprehensive exam, thesis/dissertation. *Entrance requirements:* For doctorate, GRE General Test, 3 letters of recommendation. Additional exam requirements/recommendations for international students: Required—TOEFL (minimum score 550 paper-based; 213 computer-based; 77 iBT). *Application deadline:* For fall admission, 1/1 for domestic students. Application fee: $80. Electronic applications accepted. *Expenses:* Tuition: Full-time $29,500. Required fees: $76. Tuition and fees vary according to degree level and program. *Financial support:* In 2010–11, 5 fellowships with full tuition reimbursements, 10 research assistantships with full tuition reimbursements, 5 teaching assistantships with full tuition reimbursements were awarded; institutionally sponsored loans, scholarships/grants, tuition waivers (full and partial), and unspecified assistantships also available. Financial award applicants required to submit FAFSA. *Faculty research:* Digital libraries, game theory, data mining, human-computer interaction, computational linguistics. *Unit head:* Director of Graduate Studies, 607-255-5925. *Application contact:* Graduate Field Assistant, 607-255-5925, E-mail: info@infosci.cornell.edu.

Dalhousie University, Faculty of Engineering, Department of Internetworking, Halifax, NS B3J 1Z1, Canada. Offers M Eng. *Entrance requirements:* Additional exam requirements/recommendations for international students: Required—TOEFL, IELTS, CANTEST, CAEL, or Michigan English Language Assessment Battery. Electronic applications accepted.

DePaul University, College of Computing and Digital Media, Chicago, IL 60604. Offers animation (MA, MFA); applied technology (MS); business information technology (MS); cinema (MFA); cinema production (MS); computational finance (MS); computer and information sciences (PhD); computer game development (MS); computer graphics and motion technology (MS); computer information and network security (MS); computer science (MS); e-commerce technology (MS); human-computer interaction (MS); information systems (MS); information technology (MA); information technology project management (MS); network engineering and management (MS); predictive analytics (MS); screenwriting (MFA); software engineering (MS); JD/MA; JD/MS. Part-time and evening/weekend programs available. Postbaccalaureate distance learning degree programs offered (no on-campus study). *Faculty:* 51 full-time (11 women), 50 part-time/adjunct (9 women). *Students:* 952 full-time (230 women), 927 part-time (226 women); includes 557 minority (205 Black or African American, non-Hispanic/Latino; 2 American Indian or Alaska Native, non-Hispanic/Latino; 167 Asian, non-Hispanic/Latino; 136 Hispanic/Latino; 7 Native Hawaiian or other Pacific Islander, non-Hispanic/Latino; 40 Two or more races, non-Hispanic/Latino), 292 international. Average age 31. 896 applicants, 70% accepted, 324 enrolled. In 2010, 417 master's, 6 doctorates awarded. *Degree requirements:* For master's, thesis (for some programs); for doctorate, comprehensive exam, thesis/dissertation. *Entrance requirements:* For master's, GRE or GMAT (MS in computational finance only), bachelor's degree, resume (MS in predictive analytics only), IT experience (MS in information technology project management only), portfolio review (MFA); for doctorate, GRE, master's degree in computer science. Additional exam requirements/recommendations for international students: Required—TOEFL (minimum score 550 paper-based; 213 computer-based; 80 iBT), IELTS (minimum score 6.5), Pearson Test of English (minimum score 53). *Application deadline:* For fall admission, 8/15 priority date for domestic students, 6/1 priority date for international students; for winter admission, 12/15 priority date for domestic students, 9/15 priority date for international students; for spring admission, 3/1 priority date for domestic students, 12/15 priority date for international students. Applications are processed on a rolling basis. Application fee: $25. Electronic applications accepted. *Expenses:* Contact institution. *Financial support:* In 2010–11, 102 students received support, including 4 fellowships with full tuition reimbursements available (averaging $24,435 per year), 6 research assistantships (averaging $21,100 per year), 92 teaching assistantships with full and partial tuition reimbursements available (averaging $6,904 per year); Federal Work-Study, scholarships/grants, tuition waivers (full and partial), and unspecified assistantships also available. Support available to part-time students. Financial award application deadline: 4/30; financial award applicants required to submit FAFSA. *Faculty research:* Bioinformatics, visual computing, graphics and animation, high performance and scientific computing, databases. Total annual research expenditures: $1.4 million. *Unit head:* Dr. David Miller, Dean, 312-362-8381, Fax: 312-362-5185. *Application contact:* Dr. Liz Friedman, Assistant Dean of Student Services, 312-362-8714, Fax: 312-362-5179, E-mail: efriedm2@cdm.depaul.edu.

Georgia Institute of Technology, Graduate Studies and Research, College of Computing, Multidisciplinary Program in Human Computer Interaction, Atlanta, GA 30332-0001. Offers MSHCI. Part-time programs available. *Degree requirements:* For master's, project. *Entrance requirements:* For master's, GRE General Test. Additional exam requirements/recommendations for international students: Required—TOEFL (minimum score 600 paper-based; 250 computer-based). Electronic applications accepted.

Indiana University Bloomington, School of Informatics, Bloomington, IN 47408. Offers bioinformatics (MS); chemical informatics (MS); computer science (MS, PhD); health informatics (MS); human computer interaction (MS); informatics (PhD); laboratory informatics (MS); media arts and science (MS); music informatics (MS); security informatics (MS); MS/PhD. PhD offered through University Graduate School. Part-time programs available. Postbaccalaureate distance learning degree programs offered (no on-campus study). *Faculty:* 63 full-time (12 women). *Students:* 372 full-time (88 women), 34 part-time (10 women); includes 7 Black or African American, non-Hispanic/Latino; 1 American Indian or Alaska Native, non-Hispanic/Latino; 10 Asian, non-Hispanic/Latino; 3 Hispanic/Latino; 3 Two or more races, non-Hispanic/Latino, 261 international. Average age 27. 746 applicants, 40% accepted, 131 enrolled. In 2010, 117 master's, 20 doctorates awarded. Terminal master's awarded for partial completion of doctoral program. *Degree requirements:* For master's, thesis optional; for doctorate, comprehensive exam, thesis/dissertation, oral and written exams. *Entrance requirements:* For master's and doctorate, GRE, letters of reference. Additional exam requirements/recommendations for international students: Required—TOEFL. *Application deadline:* For fall admission, 1/15 for domestic students, 12/1 for international students. Application fee: $55 ($65 for international students). Electronic applications accepted. *Financial support:* In 2010–11, fellowships with full and partial tuition reimbursements (averaging $20,000 per year), research assistantships (averaging $14,000 per year), teaching assistantships (averaging $13,000 per year) were awarded; Federal Work-Study, institutionally sponsored loans, scholarships/grants, health care benefits, tuition waivers (full and partial), and unspecified assistantships also available. Support available to part-time students. Total annual research expenditures: $2 million. *Unit head:* Dr. David Leake, Associate Dean for Graduate Studies, 812-855-9756, E-mail: leake@cs.indiana.edu. *Application contact:* Rachel Lawmaster, Manager of Graduate Admissions and Graduate Studies, 812-856-3622, Fax: 812-856-3825, E-mail: raclee@indiana.edu.

Iowa State University of Science and Technology, Graduate College, Interdisciplinary Programs, Program in Human-Computer Interaction, Ames, IA 50011. Offers MS, PhD. *Students:* 65 full-time (19 women), 61 part-time (23 women); includes 6 Black or African American, non-Hispanic/Latino; 1 American Indian or Alaska Native, non-Hispanic/Latino; 6 Asian, non-Hispanic/Latino; 5 Hispanic/Latino, 25 international. In 2010, 11 master's, 4 doctorates awarded. *Degree requirements:* For master's, thesis; for doctorate, thesis/dissertation. *Entrance requirements:* For master's, GRE General Test; for doctorate, GRE General Test, e-portfolio of research. Additional exam requirements/recommendations for international students: Required—TOEFL (minimum score 580 paper-based; 95 iBT), IELTS (minimum score 7). *Application deadline:* For fall admission, 1/15 priority date for domestic and international students. Application fee: $40 ($90 for international students). *Financial support:* In 2010–11, 24 research assistantships with full and partial tuition reimbursements (averaging $12,640 per year), 1 teaching assistantship with full and partial tuition reimbursement (averaging $13,500 per year) were awarded. *Unit head:* Dr. James Oliver, Chair, Supervising Committee, 515-294-2089, E-mail: info@hci.iastate.edu. *Application contact:* Pam Shill, Information Contact, 515-294-5836, Fax: 515-294-2592, E-mail: grad_admissions@iastate.edu.

Old Dominion University, College of Arts and Letters, Graduate Program in International Studies, Norfolk, VA 23529. Offers modeling and simulation (MA); women's studies (PhD). Part-time programs available. *Faculty:* 14 full-time (3 women). *Students:* 54 full-time (23 women), 40 part-time (16 women); includes 11 minority (5 Black or African American, non-Hispanic/Latino; 3 Asian, non-Hispanic/Latino; 3 Hispanic/Latino), 28 international. Average age 31. 99 applicants, 54% accepted, 30 enrolled. In 2010, 14 master's, 7 doctorates awarded. Terminal master's awarded for partial completion of doctoral program. *Degree requirements:* For master's, one foreign language, comprehensive exam, thesis optional; for doctorate, one foreign language, comprehensive exam, thesis/dissertation. *Entrance requirements:* For master's, GRE General Test, sample of written work, 2 letters of recommendation; for doctorate, GRE General Test, sample of written work, 3 letters of recommendation. Additional exam requirements/recommendations for international students: Required—TOEFL (minimum score 570 paper-based; 230 computer-based). *Application deadline:* For fall admission, 1/15 for domestic and international students; for spring admission, 10/15 for domestic and international students. Application fee: $40. Electronic applications accepted. *Expenses:* Tuition, state resident: full-time $8592; part-time $358 per credit. Tuition, nonresident: full-time $21,672; part-time $903 per credit. Required fees: $119 per semester. One-time fee: $50. *Financial support:* In 2010–11, 20 students received support, including 2 fellowships (averaging $13,000 per year), 5 research assistantships with tuition reimbursements available (averaging $15,000 per year), 7 teaching assistantships with tuition reimbursements available (averaging $15,000 per year); career-related internships or fieldwork, institutionally sponsored loans, scholarships/grants, and unspecified assistantships also available. Support available to part-time students. Financial award application deadline: 2/15; financial award applicants required to submit FAFSA. *Faculty research:* U. S. foreign policy, international security, transatlantic and transpacific relations, transnational issues, IPE and development. Total annual research expenditures: $330,391. *Unit head:* Dr. Regina Karp, Graduate Program Director, 757-683-5700, Fax: 757-683-5701, E-mail: rkarp@odu.edu. *Application contact:* Dr. Regina Karp, Graduate Program Director, 757-683-5700, Fax: 757-683-5701, E-mail: rkarp@odu.edu.

Rensselaer Polytechnic Institute, Graduate School, School of Humanities, Arts, and Social Sciences, Program in Human-Computer Interaction, Troy, NY 12180-3590. Offers MS. Part-time programs available. *Faculty:* 14 full-time (8 women), 1 part-time/adjunct (0 women). *Students:* 11 full-time (3 women), 8 part-time (5 women); includes 1 Black or African American, non-Hispanic/Latino; 1 Asian, non-Hispanic/Latino; 1 Two or more races, non-Hispanic/Latino. 39 applicants, 51% accepted, 7 enrolled. In 2010, 18 master's awarded. *Degree requirements:* For master's, thesis optional. *Entrance requirements:* For master's, GRE General Test, resume. Additional exam requirements/recommendations for international students: Required—TOEFL (minimum score 570 paper-based; 230 computer-based; 89 iBT). *Application deadline:* For fall admission, 1/1 priority date for domestic and international students; for spring admission, 8/15 priority date for domestic students, 8/14 priority date for international students. Applications are processed on a rolling basis. Application fee: $75. Electronic applications accepted. *Expenses:* Tuition: Full-time $39,600; part-time $1650 per credit. Required fees: $1896. *Financial support:* Career-related internships or fieldwork and institutionally sponsored loans available. *Faculty research:* Usability testing and evaluation; games research and design; Web, interface, and interaction analysis and design; information architecture; human-media interaction. *Unit head:* Prof. James P. Zappen, Acting Department Head, 518-276-6468, Fax: 518-276-4092, E-mail: zappenj@rpi.edu. *Application contact:* Kathy A. Colman, Recruitment Coordinator, 518-276-6469, Fax: 518-276-4092, E-mail: colmak@rpi.edu.

Rochester Institute of Technology, Graduate Enrollment Services, B. Thomas Golisano College of Computing and Information Sciences, Department of Information Technology, Program in Human Computer Interaction, Rochester, NY 14623-5603. Offers MS. Part-time programs available. Postbaccalaureate distance learning degree programs offered (minimal on-campus study). *Students:* 17 full-time (9 women), 16 part-time (5 women); includes 3 Black or African American, non-Hispanic/Latino; 1 Asian, non-Hispanic/Latino; 1 Hispanic/Latino, 9 international. Average age 30. 49 applicants, 65% accepted, 15 enrolled. In 2010, 1 master's awarded. *Degree requirements:* For master's, thesis or project. *Entrance requirements:* For master's, GRE, minimum GPA of 3.0. Additional exam requirements/recommendations for international students: Required—TOEFL (minimum score 570 paper-based; 230 computer-based; 88 iBT) or IELTS (minimum score 6.5). *Application deadline:* For fall admission, 8/1 for domestic students, 7/1 for international students; for spring admission, 2/1 for domestic students. Applications are processed on a rolling basis. Electronic applications accepted. *Expenses:* Tuition: Full-time $33,234; part-time $924 per credit hour. Required fees: $219. *Financial support:* In 2010–11, 17 students received support; research assistantships with partial tuition reimbursements available, teaching assistantships with partial tuition reimbursements available, career-related internships or fieldwork, scholarships/grants, and unspecified assistantships available. Support available to part-time students. Financial award applicants required to submit FAFSA. *Unit head:* Prof. Dianne Bills, Graduate Program Director, 585-475-2700, Fax: 585-475-6584, E-mail: InformaticsGrad@rit.edu. *Application contact:* Diane Ellison, Assistant Vice President, Graduate Enrollment Services, 585-475-2229, Fax: 585-475-7164, E-mail: gradinfo@rit.edu.

State University of New York at Oswego, Graduate Studies, College of Liberal Arts and Sciences, Interdisciplinary Program in Human Computer Interaction, Oswego, NY 13126. Offers MA. Part-time programs available. *Faculty:* 3 full-time (1 woman). *Students:* 6 full-time (2 women), 1 (woman) part-time; includes 1 Hispanic/Latino, 1 international. Average age 29. 6 applicants, 100% accepted. *Entrance requirements:* For master's, GRE, minimum GPA of 3.0. Additional exam requirements/recommendations for international students: Required—TOEFL (minimum score 560 paper-based; 220 computer-based). *Application deadline:* For fall admission, 4/1 for domestic and international students; for spring admission, 10/1 for domestic and international students. Applications are processed on a rolling basis. Application fee: $50. *Expenses:* Tuition, state resident: full-time $8370; part-time $349 per credit hour. Tuition, nonresident: full-time $13,780; part-time $574 per credit hour. Required fees: $853; $22.59 per credit hour. *Financial support:* In 2010–11, 5 students received support, including fellowships with full tuition reimbursements available (averaging $5,100 per year), 5 teaching assistantships with partial tuition reimbursements available (averaging $3,800 per year). Financial award application deadline: 4/1. *Unit head:* Dr. Douglas Lea, Director, 315-312-2367, E-mail: douglas.lea@oswego.edu. *Application contact:* Dr. David W. King, Dean of Graduate Studies, 315-312-3152, Fax: 315-312-3228.

Tufts University, Graduate School of Arts and Sciences, Graduate Certificate Programs, Human-Computer Interaction Program, Medford, MA 02155. Offers Certificate. Part-time and evening/weekend programs available. Electronic applications accepted. *Expenses:* Tuition: Full-time $39,624; part-time $3962 per course. Required fees: $40 per year. Full-time tuition and fees vary according to degree level, program and student level. Part-time tuition and fees vary according to course load.

University of Baltimore, Graduate School, The Yale Gordon College of Liberal Arts, School of Information Arts and Technologies, Baltimore, MD 21201-5779. Offers communications design (DCD); human-computer interaction (MS); interaction design and information technology (MS). Part-time and evening/weekend programs available. *Entrance requirements:* For master's, GRE or MAT, minimum undergraduate GPA of 3.0. Additional exam requirements/recommendations for international students: Required—TOEFL (minimum score 550 paper-based; 213 computer-based).

University of Illinois at Urbana–Champaign, Graduate College, Graduate School of Library and Information Science, Champaign, IL 61820. Offers bioinformatics: library and information science (MS); library and information science (MS, PhD, CAS); library and information science: digital libraries (CAS). *Accreditation:* ALA (one or more programs are accredited). Postbaccalaureate distance learning degree programs offered. *Faculty:* 23 full-time (11 women), 10 part-time/adjunct (7 women). *Students:* 352 full-time (258 women), 367 part-time (270 women); includes 124 minority (38 Black or African American, non-Hispanic/Latino; 1 American Indian or Alaska Native, non-Hispanic/Latino; 34 Asian, non-Hispanic/Latino; 40 Hispanic/Latino; 11 Two or more races, non-Hispanic/Latino), 27 international. 737 applicants, 58% accepted, 242 enrolled. In 2010, 272 master's, 5 doctorates, 2 other advanced degrees awarded. *Entrance requirements:* For master's, GRE General Test, minimum GPA of 3.0; for doctorate, minimum GPA of 3.0; for CAS, master's degree in library and information science or related field with minimum GPA of 3.0. Additional exam requirements/recommendations for international students: Required—TOEFL (minimum score 620 paper-based; 260 computer-based; 105 iBT) or IELTS (minimum score 7). *Application deadline:* Applications are processed on a rolling basis. Application fee: $75 ($90 for international students). Electronic applications accepted. *Financial support:* In 2010–11, 37 fellowships, 37 research assistantships, 38 teaching assistantships were awarded; tuition waivers (full and partial) also available. *Unit head:* John Unsworth, Dean, 217-333-3281, Fax: 217-244-3302, E-mail: unsworth@illinois.edu. *Application contact:* Valerie Youngen, Admissions and Records Representative, 217-333-0734, Fax: 217-244-3302, E-mail: vyoungen@llinois.edu.

University of Michigan, Horace H. Rackham School of Graduate Studies, School of Information, Ann Arbor, MI 48109-1285. Offers archives and records management (MSI); community informatics (MSI); health informatics (MS); human computer interaction (MSI); information (PhD); information analysis and retrieval (MSI); information economics for management (MSI); information policy (MSI); library and information science (MSI); preservation of information (MSI); school library media (MSI); social computing (MSI). *Accreditation:* ALA (one or more programs are accredited). *Entrance requirements:* For master's and doctorate, GRE General Test. Additional exam requirements/recommendations for international students: Required—TOEFL (minimum score 600 paper-based; 100 iBT). Electronic applications accepted. *Expenses:* Tuition, state resident: full-time $17,784; part-time $1116 per credit hour. Tuition, nonresident: full-time $35,944; part-time $2125 per credit hour. International tuition: $35,994 full-time. Required fees: $95 per semester. Tuition and fees vary according to course load, degree level and program.

Virginia Polytechnic Institute and State University, Graduate School, College of Engineering, Department of Computer Science & Applications, Blacksburg, VA 24061. Offers computer science and applications (MS); human-computer interactions (Certificate); information assurance engineering (Certificate). *Faculty:* 42 full-time (7 women). *Students:* 186 full-time (45 women), 44 part-time (9 women); includes 6 Black or African American, non-Hispanic/Latino; 10 Asian, non-Hispanic/Latino; 6 Hispanic/Latino, 149 international. Average age 29. 784 applicants, 12% accepted, 34 enrolled. In 2010, 56 master's, 12 doctorates awarded. *Degree requirements:* For master's, comprehensive exam (for some programs), thesis (for some programs); for doctorate, comprehensive exam (for some programs), thesis/dissertation (for some programs). *Entrance requirements:* For master's and doctorate, GRE. Additional exam requirements/recommendations for international students: Required—TOEFL (minimum score 550 paper-based; 213 computer-based). *Application deadline:* For fall admission, 7/1 for domestic and international students; for spring admission, 12/1 for domestic and international students. Applications are processed on a rolling basis. Application fee: $65. Electronic applications accepted. *Expenses:* Tuition, area resident: Full-time $9399; part-time $488 per credit hour. Tuition, state resident: full-time $9399; part-time $488 per credit hour. Tuition, nonresident: full-time $17,854; part-time $957.75 per credit hour. International tuition: $17,854 full-time. Required fees: $1534. Full-time tuition and fees vary according to program. *Financial support:* In 2010–11, 39 research assistantships with full tuition reimbursements (averaging $18,060 per year), 18 teaching assistantships with full tuition reimbursements (averaging $17,706 per year) were awarded; career-related internships or fieldwork, Federal Work-Study, scholarships/grants, health care benefits, and unspecified assistantships also available. Financial award application deadline: 1/15. *Faculty research:* Bioinformatics, human-computer interaction, problem-solving environments, high performance computing, software engineering. Total annual research expenditures: $4.5 million. *Unit head:* Dr. Barbara G. Ryder, UNIT HEAD, 540-231-6931, Fax: 540-231-6075, E-mail: ryder@vt.edu. *Application contact:* Naren Ramakrishnan, Contact, 540-231-8451, Fax: 540-231-6075, E-mail: naren@vt.edu.

Virginia Polytechnic Institute and State University, Graduate School, College of Engineering, Department of Industrial and Systems Engineering, Blacksburg, VA 24061. Offers human-system integration (Certificate); industrial and systems engineering (MEA, PhD); systems engineering (MS). *Faculty:* 25 full-time (4 women). *Students:* 135 full-time (39 women), 48 part-time (10 women); includes 7 Black or African American, non-Hispanic/Latino; 7 Asian, non-Hispanic/Latino; 2 Hispanic/Latino, 92 international. Average age 29. 392 applicants, 25% accepted, 42 enrolled. In 2010, 64 master's, 15 doctorates awarded. *Degree requirements:* For master's, comprehensive exam (for some programs), thesis (for some programs); for doctorate, comprehensive exam (for some programs), thesis/dissertation (for some programs). *Entrance requirements:* For master's and doctorate, GRE. Additional exam requirements/recommendations for international students: Required—TOEFL (minimum score 550 paper-based; 213 computer-based). *Application deadline:* For fall admission, 7/1 for domestic and international students; for spring admission, 12/1 for domestic and international students. Applications are processed on a rolling basis. Application fee: $65. Electronic applications accepted. *Expenses:* Tuition, area resident: Full-time $9399; part-time $488 per credit hour. Tuition, state resident: full-time $9399; part-time $488 per credit hour. Tuition, nonresident: full-time $17,854; part-time $957.75 per credit hour. International tuition: $17,854 full-time. Required fees: $1534. Full-time tuition and fees vary according to program. *Financial support:* In 2010–11, 8 fellowships with full tuition reimbursements (averaging $13,216 per year), 26 research assistantships with full tuition reimbursements (averaging $19,107 per year), 17 teaching assistantships with full tuition reimbursements (averaging $18,060 per year) were awarded; career-related internships or fieldwork, Federal Work-Study, scholarships/grants, health care benefits, and unspecified assistantships also available. Financial award application deadline: 1/15. Total annual research expenditures: $3.3 million. *Unit head:* Dr. Gaylon D. Taylor, UNIT HEAD, 540-231-4771, Fax: 540-231-3322, E-mail: don.taylor@vt.edu. *Application contact:* Jaime Camelio, Contact, 540-231-8976, Fax: 540-231-3322, E-mail: jcamelio@vt.edu.

Information Science

Alcorn State University, School of Graduate Studies, School of Arts and Sciences, Department of Mathematical Sciences, Alcorn State, MS 39096-7500. Offers computer and information sciences (MS).

American InterContinental University Atlanta, Program in Information Technology, Atlanta, GA 30328. Offers MIT. Part-time and evening/weekend programs available. *Degree requirements:* For master's, technical proficiency demonstration. *Entrance requirements:* For master's, Computer Programmer Aptitude Battery Exam, interview. Electronic applications accepted. *Faculty research:* Operating systems, security issues, networks and routing, computer hardware.

American InterContinental University Online, Program in Information Technology, Hoffman Estates, IL 60192. Offers Internet security (MIT); IT project management (MIT). Evening/weekend programs available. Postbaccalaureate distance learning degree programs offered (no on-campus study). *Entrance requirements:* Additional exam requirements/recommendations

Information Science

American InterContinental University Online (continued)
for international students: Required—TOEFL (minimum score 550 paper-based; 213 computer-based). Electronic applications accepted.

American InterContinental University South Florida, Program in Information Technology, Weston, FL 33326. Offers Internet security (MIT); wireless computer forensics (MIT). Part-time and evening/weekend programs available. *Entrance requirements:* Additional exam requirements/recommendations for international students: Required—TOEFL (minimum score 670 paper-based). Electronic applications accepted.

Arizona State University, College of Technology and Innovation, Department of Technology Management, Mesa, AZ 85212. Offers technology (aviation management and human factors) (MS); technology (environmental technology management) (MS); technology (global technology and development) (MS); technology (graphic information technology) (MS); technology (management of technology) (MS). Part-time and evening/weekend programs available. Postbaccalaureate distance learning degree programs offered (minimal on-campus study). *Faculty:* 13 full-time (3 women), 6 part-time/adjunct (2 women). *Students:* 56 full-time (16 women), 212 part-time (95 women); includes 61 minority (14 Black or African American, non-Hispanic/Latino; 8 American Indian or Alaska Native, non-Hispanic/Latino; 14 Asian, non-Hispanic/Latino; 21 Hispanic/Latino; 4 Two or more races, non-Hispanic/Latino), 27 international. Average age 36. 124 applicants, 77% accepted, 58 enrolled. In 2010, 35 master's awarded. *Degree requirements:* For master's, thesis or applied project and oral defense; interactive Program of Study (iPOS) submitted before completing 50 percent of required credit hours. *Entrance requirements:* For master's, GRE, minimum GPA of 3.0 or equivalent in last 2 years of work leading to bachelor's degree. Additional exam requirements/recommendations for international students: Required—TOEFL, IELTS, or Pearson Test of English. *Application deadline:* For fall admission, 7/1 for domestic and international students; for spring admission, 12/1 for domestic and international students. Applications are processed on a rolling basis. Application fee: $70 ($90 for international students). Electronic applications accepted. *Expenses:* Tuition, state resident: full-time $8510; part-time $608 per credit. Tuition, nonresident: full-time $16,542; part-time $919 per credit. Required fees: $339; $110 per credit. Part-time tuition and fees vary according to course load. *Financial support:* In 2010–11, 3 research assistantships with full and partial tuition reimbursements (averaging $12,729 per year), 1 teaching assistantship with full and partial tuition reimbursement (averaging $14,125 per year) were awarded; career-related internships or fieldwork, Federal Work-Study, scholarships/grants, health care benefits, tuition waivers (full and partial), and unspecified assistantships also available. Support available to part-time students. Financial award application deadline: 3/1; financial award applicants required to submit FAFSA. *Faculty research:* Digital imaging, digital publishing, Internet development/e-commerce, information aviation human factors, pilot selection, databases, multimedia, commercial digital photography, digital workflow, computer graphics modeling and animation, information design, sociotechnology, visual and technical literacy, environmental management, quality management, project management, industrial ethics, hazardous materials, environmental chemistry. Total annual research expenditures: $755,686. *Unit head:* Dr. Mitzi Montoya, Vice Provost and Dean, 480-727-1955, Fax: 480-727-1538, E-mail: mitzi.montoya@asu.edu. *Application contact:* Graduate Admissions, 480-965-6113.

Arkansas Tech University, Graduate College, College of Applied Sciences, Russellville, AR 72801. Offers emergency management (MS); engineering (M Engr); information technology (MS). Part-time programs available. *Students:* 86 full-time (24 women), 53 part-time (21 women); includes 14 minority (5 Black or African American, non-Hispanic/Latino; 2 American Indian or Alaska Native, non-Hispanic/Latino; 1 Asian, non-Hispanic/Latino; 4 Hispanic/Latino; 2 Two or more races, non-Hispanic/Latino), 60 international. Average age 31. In 2010, 44 master's awarded. *Degree requirements:* For master's, comprehensive exam (for some programs), thesis (for some programs), internship. *Entrance requirements:* For master's, GRE General Test. Additional exam requirements/recommendations for international students: Required—TOEFL (minimum score 550 paper-based; 213 computer-based; 79 iBT), IELTS (minimum score 6). *Application deadline:* For fall admission, 3/1 priority date for domestic students, 5/1 priority date for international students; for spring admission, 10/1 priority date for domestic and international students. Applications are processed on a rolling basis. Application fee: $0 ($30 for international students). Electronic applications accepted. *Expenses:* Tuition, state resident: full-time $4680; part-time $195 per credit hour. Tuition, nonresident: full-time $9360; part-time $390 per credit hour. Required fees: $714; $14 per credit hour. One-time fee: $326 part-time. Tuition and fees vary according to course load. *Financial support:* In 2010–11, teaching assistantships with full tuition reimbursements (averaging $4,000 per year); research assistantships, career-related internships or fieldwork, Federal Work-Study, scholarships/grants, health care benefits, and unspecified assistantships also available. Support available to part-time students. Financial award application deadline: 4/15; financial award applicants required to submit FAFSA. *Unit head:* Dr. William Hoefler, Dean, 479-968-0353 Ext. 501, E-mail: whoeflerjr@atu.edu. *Application contact:* Dr. Mary B. Gunter, Dean of Graduate College, 479-968-0398, Fax: 479-964-0542, E-mail: graduate.school@atu.edu.

Aspen University, Program in Information Technology, Denver, CO 80246. Offers MS, Certificate. Part-time and evening/weekend programs available. Postbaccalaureate distance learning degree programs offered (no on-campus study). Electronic applications accepted.

Athabasca University, School of Computing and Information Systems, Athabasca, AB T9S 3A3, Canada. Offers information systems (M Sc). Part-time programs available. Postbaccalaureate distance learning degree programs offered (no on-campus study). *Degree requirements:* For master's, thesis optional. *Entrance requirements:* For master's, B Sc in computing or other bachelor's degree and IT experience. Electronic applications accepted. *Expenses:* Contact institution. *Faculty research:* Distributed systems multimedia, computer science education, e-services.

Ball State University, Graduate School, College of Communication, Information, and Media, Center for Information and Communication Sciences, Muncie, IN 47306-1099. Offers MS. *Faculty:* 7. *Students:* 59 full-time (19 women), 18 part-time (2 women); includes 5 minority (3 Black or African American, non-Hispanic/Latino; 1 American Indian or Alaska Native, non-Hispanic/Latino; 1 Asian, non-Hispanic/Latino), 10 international. Average age 25. 84 applicants, 70% accepted, 50 enrolled. In 2010, 44 master's awarded. Application fee: $50. *Expenses:* Tuition, state resident: full-time $6160; part-time $299 per credit hour. Tuition, nonresident: full-time $16,020; part-time $783 per credit hour. Required fees: $2278; $95 per credit hour. *Financial support:* In 2010–11, 25 teaching assistantships with full tuition reimbursements (averaging $6,668 per year) were awarded. Financial award application deadline: 3/1. *Unit head:* Dr. Stephan Jones, Director, 765-285-1889, Fax: 765-285-1516. *Application contact:* Dr. Robert Morris, Associate Provost for Research and Dean of the Graduate School, 765-285-4723, Fax: 765-285-1328, E-mail: rmorris@bsu.edu.

Barry University, School of Adult and Continuing Education, Program in Information Technology, Miami Shores, FL 33161-6695. Offers MS. Part-time and evening/weekend programs available. *Entrance requirements:* For master's, GMAT, GRE or MAT, bachelor's degree in information technology, related area or professional experience. Electronic applications accepted.

Bellevue University, Graduate School, Program in Computer Information Systems, Bellevue, NE 68005-3098. Offers MS.

Bentley University, McCallum Graduate School of Business, Program in Information Technology, Waltham, MA 02452-4705. Offers MSIT. Part-time and evening/weekend programs available. *Faculty:* 74 full-time (22 women), 21 part-time/adjunct (5 women). *Students:* 23 full-time (5 women), 42 part-time (10 women); includes 10 minority (8 Asian, non-Hispanic/Latino; 2 Hispanic/Latino), 19 international. Average age 31. 127 applicants, 73% accepted, 25 enrolled. *Entrance requirements:* For master's, GMAT or GRE General Test. Additional exam requirements/recommendations for international students: Required—TOEFL (minimum score 600 paper-based; 250 computer-based; 100 iBT) or IELTS (minimum score 7). *Application deadline:* For fall admission, 12/1 priority date for domestic and international students. Application fee: $50. Electronic applications accepted. *Expenses:* Tuition: Full-time $28,224; part-time $1176 per credit. Required fees: $404. Part-time tuition and fees vary according to course load. *Financial support:* In 2010–11, 15 students received support. Scholarships/grants available. Financial award application deadline: 6/1; financial award applicants required to submit CSS PROFILE or FAFSA. *Faculty research:* Business intelligence, enterprise networks and services, telemedicine, ERP usability, information visualization. *Unit head:* Dr. David J. Yates, Director, 781-891-2735, E-mail: dyates@bentley.edu. *Application contact:* Sharon Hill, Director of Graduate Admissions, 781-891-2108, Fax: 781-891-2464, E-mail: bentleygraduateadmissions@bentley.edu.

Bradley University, Graduate School, College of Liberal Arts and Sciences, Department of Computer Science and Information Systems, Peoria, IL 61625-0002. Offers computer information systems (MS); computer science (MS). Part-time and evening/weekend programs available. *Degree requirements:* For master's, comprehensive exam, thesis or alternative, programming test. *Entrance requirements:* For master's, 2 letters of recommendation. Additional exam requirements/recommendations for international students: Required—TOEFL (minimum score 550 paper-based; 213 computer-based; 79 iBT).

Brigham Young University, Graduate Studies, Ira A. Fulton College of Engineering and Technology, School of Technology, Provo, UT 84602-1001. Offers construction management (MS); information technology (MS); manufacturing systems (MS); technology and engineering education (MS). *Faculty:* 26 full-time (0 women). *Students:* 29 full-time (3 women), 6 part-time (0 women); includes 1 Black or African American, non-Hispanic/Latino; 7 American Indian or Alaska Native, non-Hispanic/Latino; 1 Asian, non-Hispanic/Latino; 3 Hispanic/Latino, 3 international. Average age 25. 14 applicants, 71% accepted, 6 enrolled. In 2010, 10 master's awarded. *Degree requirements:* For master's, thesis. *Entrance requirements:* For master's, GRE General Test, GMAT of GRE (Construction Management emphasis), minimum GPA of 3.0 in last 60 hours of course work. Additional exam requirements/recommendations for international students: Required—TOEFL (minimum score 580 paper-based; 237 computer-based; 85 iBT). *Application deadline:* For fall admission, 2/15 for domestic and international students; for winter admission, 9/15 for domestic and international students; for spring admission, 2/15 for domestic and international students. Application fee: $50. Electronic applications accepted. *Expenses:* Tuition: Full-time $5580; part-time $310 per credit hour. Tuition and fees vary according to program and student's religious affiliation. *Financial support:* In 2010–11, 34 students received support, including 13 research assistantships (averaging $3,498 per year), 6 teaching assistantships (averaging $3,000 per year); fellowships, career-related internships or fieldwork and scholarships/grants also available. Financial award application deadline: 2/1; financial award applicants required to submit FAFSA. *Faculty research:* Real time process control in IT, electronic physical design, processing and non-linear systems, networking, computerized systems in CM. Total annual research expenditures: $238,500. *Unit head:* Val D. Hawks, Director, 801-422-6300, Fax: 801-422-0490, E-mail: hawksv@byu.edu. *Application contact:* Ronald E. Terry, Graduate Coordinator, 801-422-4297, Fax: 801-422-0490, E-mail: ralowe@byu.edu.

Brooklyn College of the City University of New York, Division of Graduate Studies, Department of Computer and Information Science, Brooklyn, NY 11210-2889. Offers computer science (MA, PhD); computer science and health science (MS); information systems (MS); parallel and distributed computing (Advanced Certificate). Part-time and evening/weekend programs available. *Students:* 11 full-time (2 women), 105 part-time (27 women); includes 60 minority (29 Black or African American, non-Hispanic/Latino; 25 Asian, non-Hispanic/Latino; 6 Hispanic/Latino), 28 international. Average age 32. 68 applicants, 78% accepted, 22 enrolled. In 2010, 26 master's awarded. *Degree requirements:* For master's, comprehensive exam, thesis or alternative. *Entrance requirements:* For master's, previous course work in computer science, 2 letters of recommendation. Additional exam requirements/recommendations for international students: Required—TOEFL (minimum score 525 paper-based; 195 computer-based; 70 iBT). *Application deadline:* For fall admission, 3/1 priority date for domestic students, 2/1 priority date for international students; for spring admission, 11/1 priority date for domestic students, 10/1 priority date for international students. Applications are processed on a rolling basis. Application fee: $125. Electronic applications accepted. *Expenses:* Tuition, state resident: full-time $7360; part-time $310 per credit hour. Tuition, nonresident: full-time $13,800; part-time $575 per credit hour. Required fees: $190 per semester. *Financial support:* Career-related internships or fieldwork, Federal Work-Study, institutionally sponsored loans, and scholarships/grants available. Support available to part-time students. Financial award application deadline: 5/1; financial award applicants required to submit FAFSA. *Faculty research:* Networks and distributed systems, programming languages, modeling and computer applications, algorithms, artificial intelligence, theoretical computer science. *Unit head:* Dr. Yedidyah Langsam, Chairperson, 718-951-5657, E-mail: langsam@sci.brooklyn.cuny.edu. *Application contact:* Hernan Sierra, Graduate Admissions Coordinator, 718-951-4536, Fax: 718-951-4506, E-mail: grads@brooklyn.cuny.edu.

California State University, Fullerton, Graduate Studies, College of Business and Economics, Department of Information Systems and Decision Sciences, Fullerton, CA 92834-9480. Offers information systems (MS); information systems (decision sciences) (MS); information systems (e-commerce) (MS); information technology (MS); management science (MBA). Part-time programs available. *Students:* 13 full-time (2 women), 72 part-time (16 women); includes 2 Black or African American, non-Hispanic/Latino; 24 Asian, non-Hispanic/Latino; 6 Hispanic/Latino; 3 Two or more races, non-Hispanic/Latino, 10 international. Average age 35. 120 applicants, 34% accepted, 34 enrolled. In 2010, 23 master's awarded. *Degree requirements:* For master's, project or thesis. *Entrance requirements:* For master's, GMAT, minimum AACSB index of 950. Application fee: $55. *Financial support:* Career-related internships or fieldwork, Federal Work-Study, institutionally sponsored loans, and scholarships/grants available. Support available to part-time students. Financial award application deadline: 3/1; financial award applicants required to submit FAFSA. *Unit head:* Dr. Bhushan Kapoor, Chair, 657-278-2221. *Application contact:* Admissions/Applications, 657-278-2371.

Capitol College, Graduate Programs, Laurel, MD 20708-9759. Offers business administration (MBA); computer science (MS); electrical engineering (MS); information and telecommunications systems management (MS); information architecture (MS); network security (MS). Part-time and evening/weekend programs available. Postbaccalaureate distance learning degree programs offered (no on-campus study). *Entrance requirements:* For master's, minimum GPA of 3.0. Electronic applications accepted.

Carleton University, Faculty of Graduate Studies, Faculty of Engineering and Design, Ottawa-Carleton Institute for Electrical Engineering, Department of Systems and Computer Engineering, Program in Information and Systems Science, Ottawa, ON K1S 5B6, Canada. Offers M Sc.

Carleton University, Faculty of Graduate Studies, Faculty of Science, Information and Systems Science Program, Ottawa, ON K1S 5B6, Canada. Offers M Sc. *Degree requirements:* For master's, thesis optional. *Entrance requirements:* For master's, honors degree. Additional exam requirements/recommendations for international students: Required—TOEFL. *Faculty research:* Software engineering, real-time and microprocessor programming, computer communications.

Carleton University, Faculty of Graduate Studies, Faculty of Science, School of Computer Science, Ottawa, ON K1S 5B6, Canada. Offers computer science (MCS, PhD); information and system science (M Sc). MCS and PhD programs offered jointly with University of Ottawa. Part-time programs available. *Degree requirements:* For master's, thesis optional, project; for doctorate, comprehensive exam, thesis/dissertation. *Entrance requirements:* For master's, honors degree. Additional exam requirements/recommendations for international students: Required—TOEFL. *Faculty research:* Programming systems, theory of computing, computer applications, computer systems.

Carnegie Mellon University, Heinz College Australia, Master of Science in Information Technology Program (Adelaide, South Australia), Adelaide, PA 5000, Australia. Offers MSIT. *Entrance requirements:* For master's, GRE or GMAT, college-level course in advanced algebra/pre-calculus; college-level courses in economics and statistics (recommended). Additional exam requirements/recommendations for international students: Required—TOEFL or IELTS.

Carnegie Mellon University, H. John Heinz III College, School of Information Systems and Management, Master of Information Systems Management Program, Pittsburgh, PA 15213-3891. Offers MISM. *Entrance requirements:* For master's, GRE or GMAT, college-level course in advanced algebra/pre-calculus; college-level courses in economics and statistics (recommended). Additional exam requirements/recommendations for international students: Required—TOEFL or IELTS.

Carnegie Mellon University, School of Computer Science, Language Technologies Institute, Pittsburgh, PA 15213-3891. Offers MLT, PhD. Terminal master's awarded for partial completion of doctoral program. *Degree requirements:* For doctorate, thesis/dissertation. *Entrance requirements:* For master's and doctorate, GRE General Test, GRE Subject Test. Additional exam requirements/recommendations for international students: Required—TOEFL. *Faculty research:* Machine translation, natural language processing, speech and information retrieval, literacy.

Case Western Reserve University, School of Graduate Studies, Case School of Engineering, Department of Electrical Engineering and Computer Science, Cleveland, OH 44106. Offers computer engineering (MS, PhD); computing and information sciences (MS, PhD); electrical engineering (MS, PhD); systems and control engineering (MS, PhD). Part-time and evening/weekend programs available. Postbaccalaureate distance learning degree programs offered (minimal on-campus study). *Faculty:* 33 full-time (2 women). *Students:* 190 full-time (31 women), 26 part-time (4 women); includes 3 Black or African American, non-Hispanic/Latino; 6 Asian, non-Hispanic/Latino, 128 international. In 2010, 32 master's, 13 doctorates awarded. Terminal master's awarded for partial completion of doctoral program. *Degree requirements:* For master's, thesis; for doctorate, thesis/dissertation, qualifying exam, teaching experience. *Entrance requirements:* For master's and doctorate, GRE General Test. Additional exam requirements/recommendations for international students: Required—TOEFL. *Application deadline:* For fall admission, 2/1 for domestic students; for spring admission, 11/1 for domestic students. Applications are processed on a rolling basis. Application fee: $50. *Financial support:* Fellowships with full and partial tuition reimbursements, research assistantships with full and partial tuition reimbursements, teaching assistantships, career-related internships or fieldwork, Federal Work-Study, and institutionally sponsored loans available. Support available to part-time students. Financial award application deadline: 3/1; financial award applicants required to submit FAFSA. *Faculty research:* Applied artificial intelligence, automation, computer-aided design and testing of digital systems. Total annual research expenditures: $6.8 million. *Unit head:* Michael Branicky, Department Chair, 216-368-6888, E-mail: branicky@case.edu. *Application contact:* David Easler, Student Affairs Coordinator, 216-368-4080, Fax: 216-368-2801, E-mail: david.easler@case.edu.

The Citadel, The Military College of South Carolina, Citadel Graduate College, Department of Mathematics and Computer Science, Charleston, SC 29409. Offers computer and information science (MS); mathematics education (MAE). *Accreditation:* NCATE (one or more programs are accredited). Part-time and evening/weekend programs available. *Faculty:* 3 full-time (0 women), 1 part-time/adjunct (0 women). *Students:* 1 (woman) full-time, 18 part-time (8 women); includes 1 Asian, non-Hispanic/Latino. Average age 35. In 2010, 3 master's awarded. *Degree requirements:* For master's, comprehensive exam (for some programs), thesis (for some programs). *Entrance requirements:* For master's, GRE (minimum score 1000 for MS; 900 verbal and quantitative for MAT, raw score of 396), minimum undergraduate GPA of 3.0 (MS) or 2.5 (MAT); competency, demonstrated through coursework, approved work experience, or a program-administrated competency exam, in the areas of basic computer architecture, object-oriented programming, discrete mathematics, and data structures (MS); successful completion of 7 courses (MAT). Additional exam requirements/recommendations for international students: Required—TOEFL (minimum score 550 paper-based; 213 computer-based; 79 iBT). *Application deadline:* Applications are processed on a rolling basis. Application fee: $30. Electronic applications accepted. *Expenses:* Tuition, state resident: part-time $460 per credit hour. Tuition, nonresident: part-time $756 per credit hour. Required fees: $40 per term. *Financial support:* Health care benefits and unspecified assistantships available. Support available to part-time students. Financial award application deadline: 7/1; financial award applicants required to submit FAFSA. *Unit head:* Dr. John I. Moore, Department Head, 843-953-5048, Fax: 843-953-7391, E-mail: john.moore@citadel.edu. *Application contact:* Dr. George L. Rudolph, Computer and Information Science Program Director, 843-953-5032, Fax: 843-953-7391, E-mail: george.rudolph@citadel.edu.

Claremont Graduate University, Graduate Programs, School of Information Systems and Technology, Claremont, CA 91711-6160. Offers electronic commerce (MS, PhD); health information management (MS); information systems (Certificate); knowledge management (MS, PhD); systems development (MS, PhD); telecommunications and networking (MS, PhD); MBA/MS. Part-time programs available. *Faculty:* 6 full-time (1 woman), 1 part-time/adjunct (0 women). *Students:* 87 full-time (24 women), 22 part-time (8 women); includes 31 minority (6 Black or African American, non-Hispanic/Latino; 1 American Indian or Alaska Native, non-Hispanic/Latino; 18 Asian, non-Hispanic/Latino; 3 Hispanic/Latino; 1 Native Hawaiian or other Pacific Islander, non-Hispanic/Latino; 2 Two or more races, non-Hispanic/Latino), 37 international. Average age 37. In 2010, 30 master's, 6 doctorates awarded. *Degree requirements:* For doctorate, comprehensive exam, thesis/dissertation, portfolio. *Entrance requirements:* For master's and doctorate, GMAT, GRE General Test. Additional exam requirements/recommendations for international students: Required—TOEFL (minimum score 550 paper-based; 213 computer-based; 80 iBT). *Application deadline:* For fall admission, 2/1 priority date for domestic students. Applications are processed on a rolling basis. Application fee: $60. Electronic applications accepted. *Expenses:* Tuition: Full-time $35,748; part-time $1554 per unit. Required fees: $215 per semester. *Financial support:* Fellowships, research assistantships, teaching assistantships, Federal Work-Study, institutionally sponsored loans, and scholarships/grants available. Support available to part-time students. Financial award application deadline: 2/15; financial award applicants required to submit FAFSA. *Faculty research:* GPSS, man-machine interaction, organizational aspects of computing, implementation of information systems, information systems practice. *Unit head:* Terry Ryan, Dean, 909-607-9591, Fax: 909-621-8564, E-mail: terry.ryan@cgu.edu. *Application contact:* Matt Hutter, Director of External Affairs, 909-621-3180, Fax: 909-621-8564, E-mail: matt.hutter@cgu.edu.

Clark Atlanta University, School of Arts and Sciences, Department of Computer and Information Science, Atlanta, GA 30314. Offers MS. Part-time programs available. *Faculty:* 4 full-time (0 women), 1 part-time/adjunct (0 women). *Students:* 6 full-time (2 women), 3 part-time (2 women); includes 6 Black or African American, non-Hispanic/Latino, 2 international. Average age 31. 7 applicants, 100% accepted, 3 enrolled. In 2010, 5 master's awarded. *Degree requirements:* For master's, one foreign language, thesis. *Entrance requirements:* For master's, GRE General Test, minimum GPA of 2.5. Additional exam requirements/recommendations for international students: Required—TOEFL (minimum score 500 paper-based; 173 computer-based; 61 iBT). *Application deadline:* For fall admission, 4/1 for domestic and international students; for spring admission, 11/1 for domestic and international students. Applications are processed on a rolling basis. Application fee: $40 ($55 for international students). *Expenses:* Tuition: Full-time $12,942; part-time $719 per credit hour. Required fees: $710; $355 per semester. *Financial support:* In 2010–11, 4 fellowships were awarded; career-related internships or fieldwork, Federal Work-Study, scholarships/grants, and unspecified assistantships also available. Support available to part-time students. Financial award application deadline: 4/30; financial award applicants required to submit FAFSA. *Unit head:* Dr. Roy George, Chairperson, 404-880-6945, E-mail: rgeorge@cau.edu. *Application contact:* Michelle Clark-Davis, Graduate Program Admissions, 404-880-6605, E-mail: cauadmissions@cau.edu.

Clarkson University, Graduate School, School of Arts and Sciences, Program in Information Technology, Potsdam, NY 13699. Offers MS. Part-time programs available. *Students:* 8 full-time (2 women), 3 part-time (2 women), 4 international. Average age 29. 24 applicants, 75% accepted, 5 enrolled. In 2010, 4 master's awarded. *Entrance requirements:* For master's, GRE, transcripts of all college coursework, three letters of recommendation, resume and personal statement (recommended). Additional exam requirements/recommendations for international students: Required—TOEFL, TSE recommended. *Application deadline:* For fall admission, 1/30 priority date for domestic and international students; for spring admission, 9/1 priority date for domestic and international students. Applications are processed on a rolling basis. Application fee: $25 ($35 for international students). Electronic applications accepted. *Expenses:* Tuition: Part-time $1136 per credit hour. *Financial support:* In 2010–11, 8 students received support. Tuition waivers (partial) available. *Faculty research:* Information networks, technical communications, networking management information systems. Total annual research expenditures: $1,048. *Unit head:* Dr. William Horn, Director, 315-268-6420, Fax: 315-268-2335, E-mail: horn@clarkson.edu. *Application contact:* Jennifer Reed, Graduate School Coordinator, School of Arts and Sciences, 315-268-3802, Fax: 315-268-3989, E-mail: sciencegrad@clarkson.edu.

See Display on next page and Close-Up on page 327.

Clark University, Graduate School, College of Professional and Continuing Education, Program in Information Technology, Worcester, MA 01610-1477. Offers MSIT. *Students:* 6 full-time (4 women), 21 part-time (5 women); includes 1 Black or African American, non-Hispanic/Latino; 2 Asian, non-Hispanic/Latino; 1 Two or more races, non-Hispanic/Latino, 6 international. Average age 36. 10 applicants, 100% accepted, 3 enrolled. In 2010, 17 master's awarded. *Degree requirements:* For master's, thesis or alternative. *Application deadline:* Applications are processed on a rolling basis. Application fee: $50. Electronic applications accepted. *Expenses:* Tuition: Full-time $37,000; part-time $1156 per credit hour. Required fees: $30; $1156 per credit hour. *Financial support:* Tuition waivers (partial) available. *Unit head:* Max E. Hess, Director of Graduate Studies, 508-793-7217, Fax: 508-793-7232. *Application contact:* Julia Parent, Director of Marketing, Communications, and Admissions, 508-793-7217, Fax: 508-793-7232, E-mail: jparent@clarku.edu.

Cleveland State University, College of Graduate Studies, Nance College of Business Administration, Department of Computer and Information Science, Cleveland, OH 44115. Offers computer and information science (MCIS); information systems (DBA). Part-time and evening/weekend programs available. *Faculty:* 11 full-time (1 woman), 6 part-time/adjunct (2 women). *Students:* 33 full-time (13 women), 60 part-time (45 women); includes 2 Asian, non-Hispanic/Latino, 64 international. Average age 26. 283 applicants, 60% accepted, 35 enrolled. In 2010, 27 master's, 1 doctorate awarded. Terminal master's awarded for partial completion of doctoral program. *Degree requirements:* For master's, thesis optional; for doctorate, comprehensive exam, thesis/dissertation. *Entrance requirements:* For master's, GRE or GMAT, minimum GPA of 2.75; for doctorate, GRE or GMAT, MBA, MCIS or equivalent. Additional exam requirements/recommendations for international students: Required—TOEFL (minimum score 525 paper-based; 197 computer-based; 78 iBT). *Application deadline:* For fall admission, 7/15 priority date for domestic students, 5/15 priority date for international students; for spring admission, 12/15 priority date for domestic students. Applications are processed on a rolling basis. Application fee: $30. Electronic applications accepted. *Expenses:* Tuition, state resident: full-time $8447; part-time $469 per credit hour. Tuition, nonresident: full-time $16,020; part-time $890 per credit hour. Required fees: $50. *Financial support:* In 2010–11, 21 students received support, including 7 research assistantships with full and partial tuition reimbursements available (averaging $7,800 per year), 2 teaching assistantships with full and partial tuition reimbursements available (averaging $16,000 per year); career-related internships or fieldwork, tuition waivers (full), and unspecified assistantships also available. *Faculty research:* Artificial intelligence, object-oriented analysis, database design, software efficiency, distributed system, geographical information systems. Total annual research expenditures: $7,500. *Unit head:* Dr. Santosh K. Misra, Chairman, 216-687-4760, Fax: 216-687-5448, E-mail: s.misra@csuohio.edu. *Application contact:* Dr. Santosh K. Misra, Chairman, 216-687-4760, Fax: 216-687-5448, E-mail: s.misra@csuohio.edu.

Coleman University, Program in Information Technology, San Diego, CA 92123. Offers MSIT. Evening/weekend programs available. *Entrance requirements:* For master's, bachelor's degree in computer field, minimum GPA of 3.0. Additional exam requirements/recommendations for international students: Required—TOEFL (minimum score 500 paper-based).

The College of Saint Rose, Graduate Studies, School of Mathematics and Sciences, Program in Computer Information Systems, Albany, NY 12203-1419. Offers MS. Part-time and evening/weekend programs available. *Degree requirements:* For master's, comprehensive exam, research component. *Entrance requirements:* For master's, minimum GPA of 3.0, 9 undergraduate credits in math. Additional exam requirements/recommendations for international students: Required—TOEFL (minimum score 550 paper-based; 213 computer-based). Electronic applications accepted.

Cornell University, Graduate School, Graduate Fields of Arts and Sciences, Field of Information Science, Ithaca, NY 14853-0001. Offers cognition (PhD); human computer interaction (PhD); information systems (PhD); social aspects of information (PhD). *Faculty:* 33 full-time (10 women). *Students:* 23 full-time (9 women); includes 1 Black or African American, non-Hispanic/Latino; 2 Asian, non-Hispanic/Latino, 10 international. Average age 28. 98 applicants, 15% accepted, 8 enrolled. In 2010, 2 doctorates awarded. *Degree requirements:* For doctorate, comprehensive exam, thesis/dissertation. *Entrance requirements:* For doctorate, GRE General Test, 3 letters of recommendation. Additional exam requirements/recommendations for international students: Required—TOEFL (minimum score 550 paper-based; 213 computer-based; 77 iBT). *Application deadline:* For fall admission, 1/1 for domestic students. Application fee: $80. Electronic applications accepted. *Expenses:* Tuition: Full-time $29,500. Required fees: $76. Tuition and fees vary according to degree level and program. *Financial support:* In 2010–11, 5 fellowships with full tuition reimbursements, 10 research assistantships with full tuition reimbursements, 5 teaching assistantships with full tuition reimbursements were awarded; institutionally sponsored loans, scholarships/grants, tuition waivers (full and partial), and unspecified assistantships also available. Financial award applicants required to submit FAFSA. *Faculty research:* Digital libraries, game theory, data mining, human-computer interaction, computational linguistics. *Unit head:* Director of Graduate Studies, 607-255-5925. *Application contact:* Graduate Field Assistant, 607-255-5925, E-mail: info@infosci.cornell.edu.

Dakota State University, College of Business and Information Systems, Madison, SD 57042-1799. Offers MBA, MSHI, MSIA, MSIS, D Sc IS. *Accreditation:* ACBSP. Part-time and evening/weekend programs available. Postbaccalaureate distance learning degree programs offered (minimal on-campus study). *Faculty:* 28 full-time (7 women), 2 part-time/adjunct (1 woman). *Students:* 37 full-time (7 women), 164 part-time (41 women); includes 24 minority (7 Black or African American, non-Hispanic/Latino; 2 American Indian or Alaska Native, non-Hispanic/Latino; 5 Asian, non-Hispanic/Latino; 6 Hispanic/Latino; 1 Native Hawaiian or other Pacific Islander, non-Hispanic/Latino; 3 Two or more races, non-Hispanic/Latino), 49 international. Average age 36. 143 applicants, 60% accepted, 59 enrolled. In 2010, 49 master's, 3 doctorates awarded. *Degree requirements:* For master's, comprehensive exam, thesis optional, examination, integrative project; for doctorate, comprehensive exam, thesis/dissertation, portfolio. *Entrance requirements:* For master's, GRE General Test, demonstration of information systems skills, minimum GPA of 2.75 (MSIS); for doctorate, GRE General Test, demonstration of information systems skills. Additional exam requirements/recommendations for international students: Required—TOEFL (minimum score 550 paper-based; 213 computer-based; 78 iBT). *Application deadline:* For fall admission, 6/15 for domestic and international students; for spring admission, 11/15 for domestic and international students. Applications are processed on a rolling basis. Application fee: $35 ($85 for international students). *Financial support:* In 2010–11, 54 students received support, including 11 fellowships with partial tuition reimbursements available (averaging $31,837 per year), 15 research assistantships with partial tuition reimbursements available

Information Science

Dakota State University *(continued)*
(averaging $11,116 per year), 2 teaching assistantships with partial tuition reimbursements available (averaging $31,837 per year); Federal Work-Study, scholarships/grants, unspecified assistantships, and administrative assistantships also available. Support available to part-time students. Financial award applicants required to submit FAFSA. *Faculty research:* E-commerce, data mining and data warehousing, effectiveness of hybrid learning environments, biometrics and information assurance, decision support systems. *Unit head:* Dr. Tom Halverson, Dean, 605-256-5165, Fax: 605-256-5060, E-mail: tom.halverson@dsu.edu. *Application contact:* Pam Iverson, Secretary, Office of Graduate Studies and Research, 605-256-5799, Fax: 605-256-5093, E-mail: pamela.iverson@dsu.edu.

See Display on next page and Close-Up on page 331.

DePaul University, College of Computing and Digital Media, Chicago, IL 60604. Offers animation (MA, MFA); applied technology (MS); business information technology (MS); cinema (MFA); cinema production (MS); computational finance (MS); computer and information sciences (PhD); computer game development (MS); computer graphics and motion technology (MS); computer information and network security (MS); computer science (MS); e-commerce technology (MS); human-computer interaction (MS); information systems (MS); information technology (MA); information technology project management (MS); network engineering and management (MS); predictive analytics (MS); screenwriting (MFA); software engineering (MS); JD/MA; JD/MS. Part-time and evening/weekend programs available. Postbaccalaureate distance learning degree programs offered (no on-campus study). *Faculty:* 51 full-time (11 women), 50 part-time/adjunct (9 women). *Students:* 952 full-time (230 women), 927 part-time (226 women); includes 557 minority (205 Black or African American, non-Hispanic/Latino; 2 American Indian or Alaska Native, non-Hispanic/Latino; 167 Asian, non-Hispanic/Latino; 136 Hispanic/Latino; 7 Native Hawaiian or other Pacific Islander, non-Hispanic/Latino; 40 Two or more races, non-Hispanic/Latino), 292 international. Average age 31. 896 applicants, 70% accepted, 324 enrolled. In 2010, 417 master's, 6 doctorates awarded. *Degree requirements:* For master's, thesis (for some programs); for doctorate, comprehensive exam, thesis/dissertation. *Entrance requirements:* For master's, GRE or GMAT (MS in computational finance only), bachelor's degree, resume (MS in predictive analytics only), IT experience (MS in information technology project management only), portfolio review (MFA); for doctorate, GRE, master's degree in computer science. Additional exam requirements/recommendations for international students: Required—TOEFL (minimum score 550 paper-based; 213 computer-based; 80 iBT), IELTS (minimum score 6.5), Pearson Test of English (minimum score 53). *Application deadline:* For fall admission, 8/15 priority date for domestic students, 6/1 priority date for international students; for winter admission, 12/15 priority date for domestic students, 9/15 priority date for international students; for spring admission, 3/1 priority date for domestic students, 12/15 priority date for international students. Applications are processed on a rolling basis. Application fee: $25. Electronic applications accepted. *Expenses:* Contact institution. *Financial support:* In 2010–11, 102 students received support, including 4 fellowships with full tuition reimbursements available (averaging $24,435 per year), 6 research assistantships (averaging $21,100 per year), 92 teaching assistantships with full and partial tuition reimbursements available (averaging $6,904 per year); Federal Work-Study, scholarships/grants, tuition waivers (full and partial), and unspecified assistantships also available. Support available to part-time students. Financial award application deadline: 4/30; financial award applicants required to submit FAFSA. *Faculty research:* Bioinformatics, visual computing, graphics and animation, high performance and scientific computing, databases. Total annual research expenditures: $1.4 million. *Unit head:* Dr. David Miller, Dean, 312-362-8381, Fax: 312-362-5185. *Application contact:* Dr. Liz Friedman, Assistant Dean of Student Services, 312-362-8714, Fax: 312-362-5179, E-mail: efriedm2@cdm.depaul.edu.

DeSales University, Graduate Division, Program in Information Systems, Center Valley, PA 18034-9568. Offers MSIS. Part-time programs available. *Degree requirements:* For master's, comprehensive exam, thesis optional. *Entrance requirements:* Additional exam requirements/ recommendations for international students: Required—TOEFL. *Application deadline:* Applications are processed on a rolling basis. Application fee: $35. Electronic applications accepted. *Expenses:* Tuition: Full-time $18,200; part-time $690 per credit. Required fees: $1200. *Financial support:* Applicants required to submit FAFSA. *Faculty research:* Digital communication, numerical analysis, database design. *Unit head:* Bonita Moyer, Director, 610-282-1100 Ext. 1392, Fax: 610-282-2254, E-mail: bonita.moyer@desales.edu. *Application contact:* Caryn Stopper, Director of Graduate Admissions, 610-282-1100 Ext. 1768, Fax: 610-282-2254, E-mail: caryn.stopper@desales.edu.

Drexel University, The iSchool at Drexel, College of Information Science and Technology, Master of Science in Library and Information Science Program, Philadelphia, PA 19104-2875. Offers archival studies (MS); competitive intelligence and knowledge management (MS); digital libraries (MS); library and information services (MS); school library media (MS); youth services (MS). Part-time and evening/weekend programs available. Postbaccalaureate distance learning degree programs offered (no on-campus study). *Faculty:* 34 full-time (19 women), 24 part-time/adjunct (9 women). *Students:* 248 full-time (187 women), 363 part-time (289 women); includes 16 Black or African American, non-Hispanic/Latino; 1 American Indian or Alaska Native, non-Hispanic/Latino; 17 Asian, non-Hispanic/Latino; 13 Hispanic/Latino, 9 international. Average age 34. 465 applicants, 50% accepted, 224 enrolled. In 2010, 272 master's awarded. *Entrance requirements:* For master's, GRE General Test. Additional exam requirements/ recommendations for international students: Required—TOEFL (minimum score 600 paper-based; 250 computer-based; 100 iBT). *Application deadline:* For fall admission, 8/1 for domestic and international students; for spring admission, 2/1 for domestic and international students. Applications are processed on a rolling basis. Electronic applications accepted. *Expenses:* Contact institution. *Financial support:* In 2010–11, 217 students received support, including 237 fellowships with partial tuition reimbursements available (averaging $225 per year); institutionally sponsored loans and scholarships/grants also available. Support available to part-time students. Financial award applicants required to submit FAFSA. *Faculty research:* Library and information resources and services, knowledge organization and representation, information retrieval/information visualization/bibliometrics, information needs and behaviors, digital libraries. Total annual research expenditures: $2 million. *Unit head:* Dr. David E. Fenske, Dean and Isaac L. Auerbach Professor of Information Science, 215-895-2475, Fax: 215-895-6378, E-mail: fenske@drexel.edu. *Application contact:* Matthew Lechtenberg, Graduate Admissions Manager, 215-895-1951, Fax: 215-895-2303, E-mail: ml333@drexel.edu.

Drexel University, The iSchool at Drexel, College of Information Science and Technology, PhD in Information Studies Program, Philadelphia, PA 19104-2875. Offers PhD. Part-time and evening/weekend programs available. *Faculty:* 43 full-time (23 women). *Students:* 42 full-time (20 women), 14 part-time (5 women); includes 32 minority (5 Black or African American, non-Hispanic/Latino; 25 Asian, non-Hispanic/Latino; 2 Hispanic/Latino), 21 international. Average age 36. 66 applicants, 23% accepted, 9 enrolled. In 2010, 5 doctorates awarded. *Degree requirements:* For doctorate, thesis/dissertation. *Entrance requirements:* For doctorate, GRE General Test. Additional exam requirements/recommendations for international students: Required—TOEFL (minimum score 600 paper-based; 250 computer-based; 100 iBT). *Application deadline:* For fall admission, 2/1 for domestic and international students. Applications are processed on a rolling basis. Electronic applications accepted. *Financial support:* In 2010–11, 8 students received support, including 22 research assistantships with full tuition reimbursements available (averaging $22,500 per year), 8 teaching assistantships with full tuition reimbursements available (averaging $25,000 per year); career-related internships or fieldwork, institutionally sponsored loans, scholarships/grants, traineeships, health care benefits, tuition waivers (partial), and unspecified assistantships also available. Financial award application deadline: 2/1. *Faculty research:* Information retrieval/information visualization/bibliometrics, human-computer interaction, digital libraries, databases, text/data mining, healthcare informatics, school library media. Total annual research expenditures: $2 million. *Unit head:* Dr. David E. Fenske, Dean and Isaac L. Auerbach Professor of Information Science, 215-895-2475, Fax:

215-895-6378, E-mail: fenske@drexel.edu. *Application contact:* Matthew Lechtenberg, Graduate Admissions Manager, 215-895-1951, Fax: 215-895-2303, E-mail: ml333@drexel.edu.

East Carolina University, Graduate School, College of Education, Department of Business, Career, and Technical Education, Greenville, NC 27858-4353. Offers information technologies (MS); vocation education (MA Ed). *Accreditation:* NCATE. Part-time and evening/weekend programs available. Postbaccalaureate distance learning degree programs offered (no on-campus study). *Degree requirements:* For master's, comprehensive exam, thesis optional. *Entrance requirements:* For master's, GRE or MAT, minimum GPA of 2.5, bachelor's degree in related field, teaching license (MA Ed). Additional exam requirements/recommendations for international students: Required—TOEFL. *Expenses:* Tuition, state resident: full-time $3130; part-time $391.25 per credit hour. Tuition, nonresident: full-time $13,817; part-time $1727.13 per credit hour. Required fees: $1916; $239.50 per credit hour. Tuition and fees vary according to campus/location and program.

East Tennessee State University, School of Graduate Studies, College of Business and Technology, Department of Computer and Information Sciences, Johnson City, TN 37614. Offers applied computer science (MS); information technology (MS). Part-time and evening/weekend programs available. *Faculty:* 15 full-time (3 women). *Students:* 31 full-time (4 women), 21 part-time (4 women); includes 2 minority (1 Asian, non-Hispanic/Latino; 1 Hispanic/Latino), 9 international. Average age 30. 42 applicants, 55% accepted, 15 enrolled. In 2010, 18 master's awarded. *Degree requirements:* For master's, comprehensive exam, thesis optional, capstone. *Entrance requirements:* For master's, GRE General Test, minimum GPA of 2.5. Additional exam requirements/recommendations for international students: Required—TOEFL (minimum score 550 paper-based; 213 computer-based; 79 iBT). *Application deadline:* For fall admission, 6/1 priority date for domestic students, 4/30 for international students; for spring admission, 11/1 for domestic students, 9/30 for international students. Application fee: $25 ($35 for international students). Electronic applications accepted. *Financial support:* In 2010–11, 13 research assistantships with full tuition reimbursements (averaging $9,000 per year), 10 teaching assistantships with full tuition reimbursements (averaging $9,000 per year) were awarded; career-related internships or fieldwork, institutionally sponsored loans, scholarships/grants, and unspecified assistantships also available. Financial award application deadline: 7/1; financial award applicants required to submit FAFSA. *Faculty research:* Operating systems, database design, artificial intelligence, simulation, parallel algorithms. Total annual research expenditures: $1,270. *Unit head:* Dr. Terry Countermine, Chair, 423-439-5332, Fax: 423-439-7119, E-mail: counter@etsu.edu. *Application contact:* Dr. Terry Countermine, Chair, 423-439-5332, Fax: 423-439-7119, E-mail: counter@etsu.edu.

Everglades University, Graduate Programs, Program in Information Technology, Boca Raton, FL 33431. Offers MIT. *Entrance requirements:* Additional exam requirements/recommendations for international students: Recommended—TOEFL (minimum score 500 paper-based; 173 computer-based). Electronic applications accepted.

Florida Gulf Coast University, Lutgert College of Business, Program in Computer and Information Systems, Fort Myers, FL 33965-6565. Offers MS. *Faculty:* 64 full-time (21 women), 5 part-time/adjunct (1 woman). *Students:* 6 full-time (0 women), 6 part-time (3 women); includes 1 Hispanic/Latino. Average age 35. 10 applicants, 90% accepted, 9 enrolled. In 2010, 3 master's awarded. *Entrance requirements:* For master's, GMAT, minimum GPA of 3.0. Additional exam requirements/recommendations for international students: Required—TOEFL (minimum score 550 paper-based; 213 computer-based). *Application deadline:* For fall admission, 6/1 priority date for domestic students; for spring admission, 11/1 for domestic students. Applications are processed on a rolling basis. Application fee: $30. Electronic applications accepted. *Expenses:* Tuition, state resident: part-time $322.08 per credit hour. Tuition, nonresident: part-time $1117.08 per credit hour. *Faculty research:* Advanced distributed learning technologies, object-oriented systems analysis, database management systems, workgroup support systems, software engineering project management. *Unit head:* Dr. Judy Wynekoop,

Chair, 239-590-7387, Fax: 239-590-7330, E-mail: jwynekoo@fgcu.edu. *Application contact:* Marisa Ouverson, Director of Enrollment Management, 239-590-7403, Fax: 239-590-7330, E-mail: mouverso@fgcu.edu.

Florida International University, College of Engineering and Computing, School of Computing and Information Sciences, Miami, FL 33199. Offers computer science (MS, PhD); computing and information sciences (MS, PhD); telecommunications and networking (MS). Part-time and evening/weekend programs available. *Faculty:* 29 full-time (2 women), 5 part-time/adjunct (0 women). *Students:* 96 full-time (24 women), 67 part-time (12 women); includes 7 Black or African American, non-Hispanic/Latino; 4 Asian, non-Hispanic/Latino; 47 Hispanic/Latino, 84 international. Average age 31. 433 applicants, 21% accepted, 77 enrolled. In 2010, 25 master's, 5 doctorates awarded. *Degree requirements:* For master's, thesis or alternative; for doctorate, comprehensive exam, thesis/dissertation. *Entrance requirements:* For master's and doctorate, GRE General Test, 3 letters of recommendation, minimum GPA of 3.0. Additional exam requirements/recommendations for international students: Required—TOEFL (minimum score 550 paper-based; 80 iBT). *Application deadline:* For fall admission, 6/1 for domestic students, 4/1 for international students; for spring admission, 10/1 for domestic students, 9/1 for international students. Applications are processed on a rolling basis. Application fee: $30. Electronic applications accepted. *Financial support:* Research assistantships, teaching assistantships, institutionally sponsored loans, scholarships/grants, and unspecified assistantships available. Financial award application deadline: 3/1; financial award applicants required to submit FAFSA. *Faculty research:* Database systems, software engineering, operating systems, networks, bioinformatics and computational biology. *Unit head:* Dr. Jainendra Navlakha, Interim Director, School of Computing and Information Sciences, 305-348-2023, Fax: 305-348-3549, E-mail: navlakha@cis.fiu.edu. *Application contact:* Maria Parrilla, Graduate Admissions Assistant, 305-348-1890, Fax: 305-348-6142, E-mail: grad_eng@fiu.edu.

Gannon University, School of Graduate Studies, College of Engineering and Business, School of Engineering and Computer Science, Program in Computer and Information Science, Erie, PA 16541-0001. Offers MCIS. Part-time and evening/weekend programs available. *Students:* 30 full-time (5 women), 12 part-time (7 women), 34 international. Average age 27. 340 applicants, 49% accepted, 16 enrolled. In 2010, 8 master's awarded. *Degree requirements:* For master's, research project or thesis. *Entrance requirements:* For master's, GRE or GMAT, letters of recommendation, resume. Additional exam requirements/recommendations for international students: Required—TOEFL (minimum score 79 iBT). *Application deadline:* Applications are processed on a rolling basis. Application fee: $25. Electronic applications accepted. *Expenses:* Tuition: Full-time $14,670; part-time $815 per credit. Required fees: $430; $18 per credit. Tuition and fees vary according to class time, course load, degree level, campus/location and program. *Financial support:* Career-related internships or fieldwork, Federal Work-Study, scholarships/grants, traineeships, and unspecified assistantships available. Financial award application deadline: 7/1; financial award applicants required to submit FAFSA. *Faculty research:* Refinement of software engineering processes, graph databases and bioinformatics, aspect-oriented programs and testing, software systems for healthcare applications, game programming. *Unit head:* Dr. Theresa Vitolo, Chair, 814-871-7126, E-mail: vitolo001@gannon.edu. *Application contact:* Kara Morgan, Assistant Director of Graduate Admissions, 814-871-5831, Fax: 814-871-5827, E-mail: graduate@gannon.edu.

George Mason University, Volgenau School of Engineering, Department of Applied Information Technology, Fairfax, VA 22030. Offers MS. *Faculty:* 16 full-time (5 women), 37 part-time/adjunct (12 women). *Students:* 25 full-time (5 women), 62 part-time (11 women); includes 6 Black or African American, non-Hispanic/Latino; 18 Asian, non-Hispanic/Latino; 6 Hispanic/Latino, 6 international. Average age 29. 47 applicants, 83% accepted, 30 enrolled. In 2010, 22 master's awarded. *Degree requirements:* For master's, capstone course. *Entrance requirements:* Additional exam requirements/recommendations for international students: Required—TOEFL (minimum score 570 paper-based; 230 computer-based; 88 iBT). *Application deadline:* For fall admission, 3/1 priority date for domestic students; for spring admission, 10/15 for domestic

Information Science

George Mason University (continued)
students. Application fee: $100. *Expenses:* Tuition, state resident: full-time $8192; part-time $440 per credit hour. Tuition, nonresident: full-time $22,952; part-time $1055 per credit hour. Required fees: $2364; $99 per credit hour. *Financial support:* In 2010–11, 5 students received support, including 1 research assistantship (averaging $11,664 per year), 4 teaching assistantships (averaging $9,018 per year); career-related internships or fieldwork, Federal Work-Study, scholarships/grants, unspecified assistantships, and health care benefits (full-time research or teaching assistantship recipients) also available. Financial award application deadline: 3/1; financial award applicants required to submit FAFSA. Total annual research expenditures: $750,685. *Unit head:* Lloyd Griffiths, Dean, 703-993-1500, Fax: 703-993-1734, E-mail: lgriffiths@gmu.edu. *Application contact:* Nicole Sealey, Graduate Admission & Enrollment Services Director, 703-993-3932, E-mail: nsealey@gmu.edu.

George Mason University, Volgenau School of Engineering, Program in Information Technology, Fairfax, VA 22030. Offers PhD, Engr. *Faculty:* 16 full-time (5 women), 37 part-time/adjunct (12 women). *Students:* 17 full-time (3 women), 150 part-time (26 women); includes 12 Black or African American, non-Hispanic/Latino; 2 American Indian or Alaska Native, non-Hispanic/Latino; 15 Asian, non-Hispanic/Latino; 2 Hispanic/Latino; 1 Two or more races, non-Hispanic/Latino, 47 international. Average age 38. 84 applicants, 65% accepted, 18 enrolled. In 2010, 12 doctorates awarded. *Degree requirements:* For doctorate, comprehensive exam, thesis/dissertation, internship. *Entrance requirements:* For doctorate, GRE, 3 letters of recommendation, resume. Additional exam requirements/recommendations for international students: Required—TOEFL (minimum score 570 paper-based; 230 computer-based). *Application deadline:* For fall admission, 2/1 priority date for domestic students; for spring admission, 11/1 for domestic students. Application fee: $100. Electronic applications accepted. *Expenses:* Tuition, state resident: full-time $8192; part-time $440 per credit hour. Tuition, nonresident: full-time $22,952; part-time $1055 per credit hour. Required fees: $2364; $99 per credit hour. *Financial support:* In 2010–11, 31 students received support, including 1 fellowship with full tuition reimbursement available (averaging $18,000 per year), 13 research assistantships with full and partial tuition reimbursements available (averaging $17,721 per year), 17 teaching assistantships with full and partial tuition reimbursements available (averaging $12,982 per year); career-related internships or fieldwork, Federal Work-Study, scholarships/grants, unspecified assistantships, and health care benefits (full-time research or teaching assistantship recipients) also available. Financial award application deadline: 3/1; financial award applicants required to submit FAFSA. *Faculty research:* Rapid pace of technological innovation, need for efficient and effective technology development, unwavering interoperability challenges, the scope and complexity of major system design requirements. Total annual research expenditures: $750,685. *Unit head:* Dr. Donald Gantz, Professor and Chair, 703-993-3565, E-mail: dgantz@gmu.edu. *Application contact:* Stephanie Katavolos, Program Administrator, 703-993-2972, E-mail: skatavol@gmu.edu.

Georgia Southwestern State University, Graduate Studies, School of Computer and Information Sciences, Americus, GA 31709-4693. Offers computer information systems (MS); computer science (MS). Part-time programs available. *Degree requirements:* For master's, thesis (for some programs). *Entrance requirements:* For master's, GRE General Test, minimum GPA of 3.0. Electronic applications accepted. *Faculty research:* Database, Internet technologies, computational complexity, encryption.

Georgia State University, J. Mack Robinson College of Business, Program in General Business Administration, Atlanta, GA 30302-3083. Offers accounting/information systems (MBA); economics (MBA, MS); enterprise risk management (MBA); general business (MBA); general business administration (EMBA, PMBA); information systems consulting (MBA); information systems risk management (MBA); international business and information technology (MBA); international entrepreneurship (MBA); MBA/JD. *Accreditation:* AACSB. Part-time and evening/weekend programs available. *Entrance requirements:* For master's, GMAT. Additional exam requirements/recommendations for international students: Required—TOEFL (minimum score 610 paper-based; 255 computer-based; 101 iBT). Electronic applications accepted.

Grand Valley State University, Padnos College of Engineering and Computing, School of Computing and Information Systems, Allendale, MI 49401-9403. Offers computer information systems (MS), including databases, distributed systems, management of information systems, object-oriented systems, software engineering. Part-time and evening/weekend programs available. *Degree requirements:* For master's, thesis or alternative. *Entrance requirements:* For master's, GMAT or GRE General Test. Additional exam requirements/recommendations for international students: Required—TOEFL. Electronic applications accepted. *Faculty research:* Object technology, distributed computing, information systems management database, software engineering.

Harvard University, Extension School, Cambridge, MA 02138-3722. Offers applied sciences (CAS); biotechnology (ALM); educational technologies (ALM); educational technology (CET); English for graduate and professional studies (DGP); environmental management (ALM, CEM); information technology (ALM); journalism (ALM); liberal arts (ALM); management (ALM, CM); mathematics for teaching (ALM); museum studies (ALM); premedical studies (Diploma); publication and communication (CPC). Part-time and evening/weekend programs available. *Degree requirements:* For master's, thesis. *Entrance requirements:* For master's, 3 completed graduate courses with grade of B or higher. Additional exam requirements/recommendations for international students: Required—TOEFL (minimum score 600 paper-based; 250 computer-based), TWE (minimum score 5). *Expenses:* Contact institution.

Harvard University, Graduate School of Arts and Sciences, Program in Information, Technology and Management, Cambridge, MA 02138. Offers PhD. *Expenses:* Tuition: Full-time $34,976. Required fees: $1166. Full-time tuition and fees vary according to program.

Hood College, Graduate School, Program in Management of Information Technology, Frederick, MD 21701-8575. Offers MS. Part-time and evening/weekend programs available. *Faculty:* 1 (woman) full-time, 2 part-time/adjunct (1 woman). *Students:* 1 full-time (0 women), 14 part-time (5 women); includes 3 Black or African American, non-Hispanic/Latino, 1 international. Average age 40. 17 applicants, 65% accepted, 3 enrolled. In 2010, 2 master's awarded. *Degree requirements:* For master's, thesis. *Entrance requirements:* For master's, minimum GPA of 2.75. Additional exam requirements/recommendations for international students: Required—TOEFL (minimum score 575 paper-based; 231 computer-based; 89 iBT). *Application deadline:* For fall admission, 7/15 for domestic and international students; for spring admission, 12/15 for domestic and international students. Applications are processed on a rolling basis. Application fee: $35. Electronic applications accepted. *Expenses:* Tuition: Full-time $6480; part-time $360 per credit. Required fees: $100; $50 per term. *Financial support:* Applicants required to submit FAFSA. *Faculty research:* Systems engineering, parallel distributed computing, strategy, business ethics, entrepreneurship. *Unit head:* Dr. Elizabeth Chang, Director, 301-696-3724, E-mail: myers@hood.edu. *Application contact:* Dr. Allen P. Flora, Dean of Graduate School, 301-696-3811, Fax: 301-696-3597, E-mail: gofurther@hood.edu.

Hood College, Graduate School, Programs in Computer and Information Sciences, Frederick, MD 21701-8575. Offers computer and information sciences (MS); computer science (MS); information security (Certificate). Part-time and evening/weekend programs available. *Faculty:* 5 full-time (1 woman), 4 part-time/adjunct (1 woman). *Students:* 18 full-time (4 women), 68 part-time (12 women); includes 5 Black or African American, non-Hispanic/Latino; 8 Asian, non-Hispanic/Latino; 4 Hispanic/Latino; 2 Two or more races, non-Hispanic/Latino, 14 international. Average age 33. 49 applicants, 65% accepted, 20 enrolled. In 2010, 14 master's awarded. *Degree requirements:* For master's, thesis. *Entrance requirements:* For master's, minimum GPA of 2.75. Additional exam requirements/recommendations for international students: Required—TOEFL (minimum score 575 paper-based; 231 computer-based; 89 iBT). *Application deadline:* For fall admission, 7/15 for domestic and international students; for spring admission, 12/15 for domestic and international students. Applications are processed on a rolling basis. Application fee: $35. Electronic applications accepted. *Expenses:* Tuition: Full-time $6480; part-time $360 per credit. Required fees: $100; $50 per term. *Financial support:* Applicants required to submit FAFSA. *Faculty research:* Systems engineering, natural language, processing, database design, artificial intelligence and parallel distributed computing. *Unit head:* Dr. Xinlian Liu, Director, 301-696-3981, E-mail: liu@hood.edu. *Application contact:* Dr. Allen P. Flora, Dean of Graduate School, 301-696-3811, Fax: 301-696-3597, E-mail: gofurther@hood.edu.

Indiana University Bloomington, School of Informatics, Bloomington, IN 47408. Offers bioinformatics (MS); chemical informatics (MS); computer science (MS, PhD); health informatics (MS); human computer interaction (MS); informatics (PhD); laboratory informatics (MS); media arts and science (MS); music informatics (MS); security informatics (MS); MS/PhD. PhD offered through University Graduate School. Part-time programs available. Postbaccalaureate distance learning degree programs offered (no on-campus study). *Faculty:* 63 full-time (12 women). *Students:* 372 full-time (88 women), 34 part-time (10 women); includes 7 Black or African American, non-Hispanic/Latino; 1 American Indian or Alaska Native, non-Hispanic/Latino; 10 Asian, non-Hispanic/Latino; 3 Hispanic/Latino; 3 Two or more races, non-Hispanic/Latino, 261 international. Average age 27. 746 applicants, 40% accepted, 131 enrolled. In 2010, 117 master's, 20 doctorates awarded. Terminal master's awarded for partial completion of doctoral program. *Degree requirements:* For master's, thesis optional; for doctorate, comprehensive exam, thesis/dissertation, oral and written exams. *Entrance requirements:* For master's and doctorate, GRE, letters of reference. Additional exam requirements/recommendations for international students: Required—TOEFL. *Application deadline:* For fall admission, 1/15 for domestic students, 12/1 for international students. Application fee: $55 ($65 for international students). Electronic applications accepted. *Financial support:* In 2010–11, fellowships with full and partial tuition reimbursements (averaging $20,000 per year), research assistantships (averaging $14,000 per year), teaching assistantships (averaging $13,000 per year) were awarded; Federal Work-Study, institutionally sponsored loans, scholarships/grants, health care benefits, tuition waivers (full and partial), and unspecified assistantships also available. Support available to part-time students. Total annual research expenditures: $2 million. *Unit head:* Dr. David Leake, Associate Dean for Graduate Studies, 812-855-9756, E-mail: leake@cs.indiana.edu. *Application contact:* Rachel Lawmaster, Manager of Graduate Admissions and Graduate Studies, 812-856-3622, Fax: 812-856-3825, E-mail: raclee@indiana.edu.

Indiana University Bloomington, School of Library and Information Science, Bloomington, IN 47405-3907. Offers MIS, MLS, PhD, Sp LIS, JD/MLS, MIS/MA, MLS/MA, MPA/MIS, MPA/MLS. *Accreditation:* ALA (one or more programs are accredited). Part-time programs available. *Faculty:* 16 full-time (7 women). *Students:* Average age 29. 343 applicants, 86% accepted, 120 enrolled. In 2010, 149 master's, 4 doctorates, 3 other advanced degrees awarded. *Degree requirements:* For doctorate, thesis/dissertation. *Entrance requirements:* For master's and doctorate, GRE General Test, 3 letters of reference. Additional exam requirements/recommendations for international students: Required—TOEFL (minimum score 600 paper-based; 250 computer-based; 100 iBT). *Application deadline:* For fall admission, 5/15 priority date for domestic students, 12/1 priority date for international students; for spring admission, 10/15 priority date for domestic students, 9/1 priority date for international students. Applications are processed on a rolling basis. Application fee: $55 ($65 for international students). Electronic applications accepted. *Expenses:* Contact institution. *Financial support:* Fellowships with full and partial tuition reimbursements, research assistantships with full and partial tuition reimbursements, career-related internships or fieldwork, Federal Work-Study, institutionally sponsored loans, scholarships/grants, tuition waivers (partial), and unspecified assistantships available. Support available to part-time students. Financial award application deadline: 1/15. *Faculty research:* Scholarly communication, interface design, library and management policy, computer-mediated communication, information retrieval. *Application contact:* Rhonda Spencer, Director of Admissions, 812-855-2018, Fax: 812-855-6166, E-mail: slis@indiana.edu.

Indiana University–Purdue University Fort Wayne, College of Engineering, Technology, and Computer Science, Program in Technology, Fort Wayne, IN 46805-1499. Offers facilities and construction management (MS); industrial technology/manufacturing (MS); information technology/advanced computer applications (MS). Part-time programs available. *Faculty:* 12 full-time (6 women), 1 part-time/adjunct (0 women). *Students:* 4 full-time (2 women), 14 part-time (1 woman); includes 3 minority (2 Asian, non-Hispanic/Latino; 1 Hispanic/Latino), 2 international. Average age 32. 5 applicants, 100% accepted, 2 enrolled. In 2010, 4 master's awarded. *Entrance requirements:* For master's, minimum GPA of 3.0. Additional exam requirements/recommendations for international students: Required—TOEFL (minimum score 550 paper-based; 213 computer-based; 77 iBT), TWE. *Application deadline:* For fall admission, 7/15 for domestic students, 5/15 for international students; for spring admission, 12/1 for domestic students, 10/15 for international students. Applications are processed on a rolling basis. Application fee: $55 ($60 for international students). Electronic applications accepted. *Expenses:* Tuition, state resident: full-time $4824; part-time $268 per credit. Tuition, nonresident: full-time $11,625; part-time $646 per credit. Required fees: $555; $30.85 per credit. Tuition and fees vary according to course load. *Financial support:* Career-related internships or fieldwork, scholarships/grants, and unspecified assistantships available. Support available to part-time students. Financial award application deadline: 3/1; financial award applicants required to submit FAFSA. *Unit head:* Dr. Max Yen, Dean, 260-481-6839, Fax: 260-481-5734, E-mail: yens@ipfw.edu. *Application contact:* Dr. Gary Steffen, Chair, 260-481-6344, Fax: 260-481-5734, E-mail: steffen@ipfw.edu.

Indiana University–Purdue University Indianapolis, School of Informatics, Indianapolis, IN 46202-2896. Offers informatics (PhD); media arts and science (MS). Part-time and evening/weekend programs available. *Faculty:* 3 full-time (0 women). *Students:* 43 full-time (15 women), 83 part-time (29 women); includes 21 minority (13 Black or African American, non-Hispanic/Latino; 5 Asian, non-Hispanic/Latino; 3 Hispanic/Latino), 32 international. Average age 34. 87 applicants, 54% accepted, 26 enrolled. In 2010, 39 master's awarded. *Degree requirements:* For master's, multimedia project. *Entrance requirements:* For master's, minimum undergraduate GPA of 3.0, graduate 3.2; interview; portfolio; BA with demonstrated media arts skills. Additional exam requirements/recommendations for international students: Required—TOEFL. *Application deadline:* For fall admission, 3/15 for domestic students; for spring admission, 11/15 for domestic students. Application fee: $55 ($65 for international students). *Financial support:* In 2010–11, 6 fellowships (averaging $17,447 per year), 13 teaching assistantships (averaging $9,392 per year) were awarded; career-related internships or fieldwork, Federal Work-Study, institutionally sponsored loans, and scholarships/grants also available. Support available to part-time students. *Unit head:* Darrell L. Bailey, Executive Associate Dean, 317-278-4636, Fax: 317-278-7769. *Application contact:* Dr. Sherry Queener, Director, Graduate Studies and Associate Dean, 317-274-1577, Fax: 317-278-2380.

Indiana University–Purdue University Indianapolis, School of Library and Information Science, Indianapolis, IN 46202-2896. Offers MLS. Part-time and evening/weekend programs available. *Faculty:* 3 full-time (2 women). *Students:* 81 full-time (53 women), 211 part-time (161 women); includes 39 minority (23 Black or African American, non-Hispanic/Latino; 6 Asian, non-Hispanic/Latino; 7 Hispanic/Latino; 3 Two or more races, non-Hispanic/Latino). Average age 34. 67 applicants, 90% accepted, 40 enrolled. In 2010, 133 master's awarded. *Entrance requirements:* For master's, GRE General Test. Additional exam requirements/recommendations for international students: Required—TOEFL (minimum score 600 paper-based). *Application deadline:* For fall admission, 7/15 priority date for domestic students; for spring admission, 11/15 priority date for domestic students. Applications are processed on a rolling basis. Application fee: $55 ($65 for international students). *Financial support:* In 2010–11, 2 teaching assistantships (averaging $9,500 per year) were awarded; career-related internships or fieldwork, Federal Work-Study, institutionally sponsored loans, and scholarships/grants also available. Support available to part-time students. *Unit head:* Dr. Daniel Collison, Executive Associate Dean, 317-278-2375, Fax: 317-278-1807, E-mail: slisindy@iupui.edu. *Application contact:* Dr. Daniel Collison, Executive Associate Dean, 317-278-2375, Fax: 317-278-1807, E-mail: slisindy@iupui.edu.

Instituto Tecnologico de Santo Domingo, Graduate School, Area of Engineering, Santo Domingo, Dominican Republic. Offers construction administration (MS, Certificate); data telecommunications (M Eng, MS, Certificate); industrial engineering (M Eng, Certificate); industrial management (M Mgmt); information technology (Certificate); maintenance engineering (M Eng); occupational hazard prevention (M Mgmt); production management (Certificate); quantitative methods (Certificate); sanitary and environmental engineering (M Eng); structural engineering (M Eng); systems engineering and electronic data processing (Certificate); transportation (Certificate).

Instituto Tecnológico y de Estudios Superiores de Monterrey, Campus Cuernavaca, Programs in Information Science, Temixco, Mexico. Offers administration of information technology (MATI); computer science (MCC, DCC); information technology (MTI).

Instituto Tecnológico y de Estudios Superiores de Monterrey, Campus Estado de México, Professional and Graduate Division, Estado de Mexico, Mexico. Offers administration of information technologies (MITA); architecture (M Arch); business administration (GMBA, MBA); computer sciences (MCS, PhD); education (M Ed); educational institution administration (MAD); educational technology and innovation (PhD); electronic commerce (MEC); environmental systems (MS); finance (MAF); humanistic studies (MHS); information sciences and knowledge management (MISKM); information systems (MS); manufacturing systems (MS); marketing (MEM); quality systems and productivity (MS); science and materials engineering (PhD); telecommunications management (MTM). Part-time programs available. Postbaccalaureate distance learning degree programs offered (minimal on-campus study). *Degree requirements:* For master's, one foreign language, thesis (for some programs); for doctorate, one foreign language, thesis/dissertation. *Entrance requirements:* For master's, E-PAEP 500, interview; for doctorate, E-PAEP 500, research proposal. Additional exam requirements/recommendations for international students: Required—TOEFL (minimum score 550 paper-based). *Faculty research:* Surface treatments by plasmas, mechanical properties, robotics, graphical computing, mechatronics security protocols.

Instituto Tecnológico y de Estudios Superiores de Monterrey, Campus Irapuato, Graduate Programs, Irapuato, Mexico. Offers administration (MBA); administration of information technology (MAIT); administration of telecommunications (MAT); architecture (M Arch); computer science (MCS); education (M Ed); educational administration (MEA); educational innovation and technology (DEIT); educational technology (MET); electronic commerce (MBA); environmental administration and planning (MEAP); environmental systems (MES); finances (MBA); humanistic studies (MHS); international management for Latin American executives (MIMLAE); library and information science (MLIS); manufacturing quality management (MMQM); marketing research (MBA).

Instituto Tecnológico y de Estudios Superiores de Monterrey, Campus Monterrey, Graduate and Research Division, Program in Computer Science, Monterrey, Mexico. Offers artificial intelligence (PhD); computer science (MS); information systems (MS); information technology (MS). Part-time programs available. *Degree requirements:* For master's, one foreign language, thesis; for doctorate, one foreign language, thesis/dissertation. *Entrance requirements:* For master's, EXADEP; for doctorate, master's degree in related field. Additional exam requirements/recommendations for international students: Required—TOEFL. *Faculty research:* Distributed systems, software engineering, decision support systems.

Instituto Tecnológico y de Estudios Superiores de Monterrey, Campus Monterrey, Graduate and Research Division, Program in Informatics, Monterrey, Mexico. Offers PhD. Part-time programs available. *Degree requirements:* For doctorate, one foreign language, thesis/dissertation, technological project, arbitrated publication of articles. *Entrance requirements:* For doctorate, GRE General Test, GRE Subject Test, master's degree in related field. Additional exam requirements/recommendations for international students: Required—TOEFL. *Faculty research:* Artificial intelligence, distributed systems, software engineering, decision support systems.

Instituto Tecnológico y de Estudios Superiores de Monterrey, Campus Sonora Norte, Program in Technological Information Management, Hermosillo, Mexico. Offers MA.

Iowa State University of Science and Technology, Graduate College, Interdisciplinary Programs, Program in Information Assurance, Ames, IA 50011. Offers MS. *Students:* 18 full-time (3 women), 37 part-time (5 women); includes 3 Black or African American, non-Hispanic/Latino; 1 Asian, non-Hispanic/Latino; 1 Hispanic/Latino, 8 international. In 2010, 20 master's awarded. *Degree requirements:* For master's, thesis or alternative. *Entrance requirements:* For master's, GRE General Test. Additional exam requirements/recommendations for international students: Required—TOEFL (minimum score 570 paper-based; 79 iBT), IELTS (minimum score 6.5). *Application deadline:* For fall admission, 5/1 priority date for domestic and international students; for spring admission, 11/1 priority date for domestic and international students. Application fee: $40 ($90 for international students). *Financial support:* In 2010–11, 8 research assistantships with full and partial tuition reimbursements (averaging $6,711 per year) were awarded; teaching assistantships with full and partial tuition reimbursements, health care benefits and unspecified assistantships also available. *Unit head:* Dr. Doug Jacobson, Chair of Supervising Committee, 515-294-8307, E-mail: infas@iac.iastate.edu. *Application contact:* Information Contact, 515-294-5836, Fax: 515-294-2592, E-mail: grad_admissions@iastate.edu.

The Johns Hopkins University, G. W. C. Whiting School of Engineering, Information Security Institute, Baltimore, MD 21218-2699. Offers MSSI. Part-time programs available. *Faculty:* 6 part-time/adjunct (0 women). *Students:* 42 full-time (6 women), 6 part-time (2 women); includes 9 minority (2 Black or African American, non-Hispanic/Latino; 2 Asian, non-Hispanic/Latino; 4 Hispanic/Latino; 1 Two or more races, non-Hispanic/Latino), 28 international. Average age 25. 73 applicants, 92% accepted, 18 enrolled. In 2010, 24 master's awarded. *Degree requirements:* For master's, project. *Entrance requirements:* For master's, GRE, minimum GPA of 3.0. Additional exam requirements/recommendations for international students: Required—TOEFL (minimum score 600 paper-based; 250 computer-based). *Application deadline:* For fall admission, 6/15 priority date for domestic students, 3/15 for international students; for spring admission, 11/15 for domestic students, 11/1 for international students. Applications are processed on a rolling basis. Application fee: $25. Electronic applications accepted. *Financial support:* In 2010–11, 28 students received support, including 9 fellowships with full tuition reimbursements available (averaging $18,000 per year); career-related internships or fieldwork, Federal Work-Study, institutionally sponsored loans, scholarships/grants, traineeships, health care benefits, tuition waivers (partial), and unspecified assistantships also available. *Faculty research:* Critical infrastructure protection, insider/outsider cryptography and encryption methodologies, international policy protocols, Web-based intellectual property rights. Total annual research expenditures: $838,000. *Unit head:* Dr. Gerald M. Masson, Director, 410-516-7013, Fax: 410-516-3301, E-mail: masson@jhu.edu. *Application contact:* Deborah K. Higgins, Graduate Coordinator, 410-516-8521, Fax: 410-516-3301, E-mail: dhiggins@jhu.edu.

Kansas State University, Graduate School, College of Engineering, Department of Computing and Information Sciences, Manhattan, KS 66506. Offers computer science (MS, PhD); software engineering (MSE). Part-time programs available. Postbaccalaureate distance learning degree programs offered (minimal on-campus study). Terminal master's awarded for partial completion of doctoral program. *Degree requirements:* For master's, thesis or alternative; for doctorate, thesis/dissertation, preliminary exams. *Entrance requirements:* For master's, GRE, bachelor's degree in computer science, minimum GPA of 3.0; for doctorate, GRE General Test, GRE Subject Test, master's degree in computer science or bachelor's degree and strong advanced computer knowledge. Additional exam requirements/recommendations for international students: Required—TOEFL (minimum score 575 paper-based; 233 computer-based). Electronic applications accepted. *Faculty research:* High-assurance software and programming languages, data mining, parallel and distributed computing, computer security, embedded systems.

Kennesaw State University, College of Science and Mathematics, Program in Information Systems, Kennesaw, GA 30144-5591. Offers MSIS. Part-time programs available. *Students:* 29 full-time (10 women), 31 part-time (7 women); includes 20 minority (14 Black or African American, non-Hispanic/Latino; 4 Asian, non-Hispanic/Latino; 2 Hispanic/Latino), 8 international. Average age 33. 27 applicants, 85% accepted, 17 enrolled. In 2010, 25 master's awarded. *Entrance requirements:* For master's, GMAT or GRE General Test, minimum GPA of 2.75. Additional exam requirements/recommendations for international students: Required—TOEFL (minimum score 550 paper-based; 213 computer-based; 80 IBT), IELTS (minimum score 6). *Application deadline:* For fall admission, 7/1 for domestic and international students; for spring admission, 11/1 for domestic and international students. Applications are processed on a rolling basis. Application fee: $60. Electronic applications accepted. *Expenses:* Tuition, state resident: full-time $5500; part-time $225 per credit hour. Tuition, nonresident: full-time $16,100; part-time $813 per credit hour. Required fees: $673 per semester. *Financial support:* In 2010–11, 2 research assistantships with full tuition reimbursements (averaging $4,000 per year) were awarded; Federal Work-Study and unspecified assistantships also available. Support available to part-time students. Financial award application deadline: 4/1; financial award applicants required to submit FAFSA. *Unit head:* Dr. Amy Woszczynski, Director, 770-423-6005, Fax: 770-423-6731, E-mail: awoszczy@kennesaw.edu. *Application contact:* Tamara Hutto, Admissions Counselor, 770-420-4377, Fax: 770-423-6885, E-mail: ksugrad@kennesaw.edu.

Kent State University, College of Communication and Information, Interdisciplinary Program in Information Architecture and Knowledge Management, Kent, OH 44242-0001. Offers MS. Part-time and evening/weekend programs available. *Degree requirements:* For master's, capstone or thesis. *Entrance requirements:* For master's, GRE (recommended). *Expenses:* Tuition, state resident: full-time $7866; part-time $437 per credit hour. Tuition, nonresident: full-time $14,022; part-time $779 per credit hour. *Faculty research:* Information architecture, knowledge management, usability, organizational memory management, information design, user interface design.

Kentucky State University, College of Mathematics, Sciences, Technology and Health, Frankfort, KY 40601. Offers aquaculture (MS); computer science (MS), including computer science theory, information assurance, information technology; environmental science (MS). Part-time and evening/weekend programs available. *Faculty:* 10 full-time (1 woman), 1 part-time/adjunct (0 women). *Students:* 34 full-time (16 women), 32 part-time (6 women); includes 22 minority (15 Black or African American, non-Hispanic/Latino; 3 Asian, non-Hispanic/Latino; 1 Hispanic/Latino; 1 Native Hawaiian or other Pacific Islander, non-Hispanic/Latino; 2 Two or more races, non-Hispanic/Latino), 12 international. Average age 34. 55 applicants, 51% accepted, 18 enrolled. In 2010, 16 master's awarded. *Degree requirements:* For master's, comprehensive exam, thesis optional. *Entrance requirements:* For master's, GRE, GMAT. Additional exam requirements/recommendations for international students: Required—TOEFL (minimum score 525 paper-based; 173 computer-based). *Application deadline:* Applications are processed on a rolling basis. Application fee: $30 ($100 for international students). Electronic applications accepted. *Expenses:* Tuition, state resident: full-time $5886; part-time $352 per credit hour. Tuition, nonresident: full-time $9054; part-time $528 per credit hour. Required fees: $450; $26 per credit hour. *Financial support:* In 2010–11, 41 students received support, including 18 research assistantships (averaging $11,378 per year); career-related internships or fieldwork, scholarships/grants, tuition waivers (partial), and unspecified assistantships also available. Financial award application deadline: 4/15; financial award applicants required to submit FAFSA. *Unit head:* Dr. Charles Bennett, Dean, 502-597-6926, E-mail: charles.bennett@kysu.edu. *Application contact:* Dr. Titilayo Ufomata, Acting Director of Graduate Studies, 502-597-6443, E-mail: titilayo.ufomata@kysu.edu.

Knowledge Systems Institute, Program in Computer and Information Sciences, Skokie, IL 60076. Offers MS. Part-time and evening/weekend programs available. Postbaccalaureate distance learning degree programs offered (minimal on-campus study). *Degree requirements:* For master's, comprehensive exam, thesis. *Entrance requirements:* Additional exam requirements/recommendations for international students: Required—TOEFL (minimum score 550 paper-based; 213 computer-based; 79 iBT). Electronic applications accepted. *Faculty research:* Data mining, web development, database programming and administration.

Lamar University, College of Graduate Studies, College of Business, Beaumont, TX 77710. Offers accounting (MBA); experiential business and entrepreneurship (MBA); financial management (MBA); healthcare administration (MBA); information systems (MBA); management (MBA). *Accreditation:* AACSB. Part-time and evening/weekend programs available. *Faculty:* 17 full-time (4 women), 4 part-time/adjunct (0 women). *Students:* 79 full-time (37 women), 56 part-time (22 women); includes 14 Black or African American, non-Hispanic/Latino; 8 Asian, non-Hispanic/Latino; 12 Hispanic/Latino, 18 international. Average age 28. 103 applicants, 70% accepted, 40 enrolled. In 2010, 49 master's awarded. *Degree requirements:* For master's, comprehensive exam (for some programs), thesis optional. *Entrance requirements:* For master's, GMAT. Additional exam requirements/recommendations for international students: Required—TOEFL (minimum score 525 paper-based; 197 computer-based). *Application deadline:* For fall admission, 3/15 priority date for domestic students; for spring admission, 10/1 priority date for domestic students. Applications are processed on a rolling basis. Application fee: $25 ($50 for international students). *Expenses:* Tuition, state resident: full-time $4160; part-time $208 per credit hour. Tuition, nonresident: full-time $10,360; part-time $518 per credit hour. *Financial support:* In 2010–11, 12 students received support, including 4 research assistantships with partial tuition reimbursements available; fellowships with tuition reimbursements available, career-related internships or fieldwork, Federal Work-Study, institutionally sponsored loans, scholarships/grants, and tuition waivers (partial) also available. Support available to part-time students. Financial award application deadline: 4/1; financial award applicants required to submit FAFSA. *Faculty research:* Marketing, finance, quantitative methods, management information systems, legal, environmental. *Unit head:* Dr. Enrique R. Venta, Dean, 409-880-8604, Fax: 409-880-8088, E-mail: henry.venta@lamar.edu. *Application contact:* Dr. Brad Mayer, Professor and Associate Dean, 409-880-2383, Fax: 409-880-8605, E-mail: bradley.mayer@lamar.edu.

Lehigh University, College of Business and Economics, Department of Accounting, Bethlehem, PA 18015. Offers accounting and information analysis (MS). *Accreditation:* AACSB. *Faculty:* 8 full-time (0 women), 3 part-time/adjunct (1 woman). *Students:* 29 full-time (16 women), 6 part-time (4 women); includes 1 minority (Asian, non-Hispanic/Latino), 14 international. Average age 23. 162 applicants, 28% accepted, 31 enrolled. In 2010, 29 master's awarded. *Entrance requirements:* For master's, GMAT. Additional exam requirements/recommendations for international students: Required—TOEFL (minimum score 105 iBT). *Application deadline:* For fall admission, 5/1 for domestic and international students. Applications are processed on a rolling basis. Application fee: $100. Electronic applications accepted. *Expenses:* Contact institution. *Financial support:* In 2010–11, 6 research assistantships with partial tuition reimbursements (averaging $1,000 per year) were awarded; scholarships/grants and tuition waivers (partial) also available. Financial award application deadline: 1/15. *Faculty research:* Behavioral accounting, internal control, information systems, supply chain management, financial accounting. *Unit head:* Dr. Heibatollah Sami, Director, 610-758-3407, Fax: 610-758-6429, E-mail: hes205@lehigh.edu. *Application contact:* Corinn McBride, Director of Recruitment and Admissions, 610-758-3418, Fax: 610-758-5283, E-mail: com207@lehigh.edu.

Long Island University, C.W. Post Campus, College of Information and Computer Science, Department of Computer Science/Management Engineering, Brookville, NY 11548-1300. Offers information systems (MS); information technology education (MS); management engineering (MS). Part-time and evening/weekend programs available. *Degree requirements:* For master's, comprehensive exam, thesis or alternative. *Entrance requirements:* For master's, bachelor's degree in science, mathematics, or engineering; minimum GPA of 2.5. Additional exam requirements/recommendations for international students: Required—TOEFL (minimum score 500 paper-based; 173 computer-based). Electronic applications accepted. *Faculty research:* Inductive music learning, re-engineering business process, technology and ethics.

Loyola University Chicago, Graduate School, Department of Computer Science, Chicago, IL 60660. Offers computer science (MS); information technology (MS); software technology

Information Science

Loyola University Chicago (continued)
(MS). Part-time and evening/weekend programs available. *Faculty:* 9 full-time (1 woman), 10 part-time/adjunct (2 women). *Students:* 39 full-time (15 women), 46 part-time (11 women); includes 13 minority (3 Black or African American, non-Hispanic/Latino; 9 Asian, non-Hispanic/Latino; 1 Hispanic/Latino), 35 international. Average age 28. 87 applicants, 67% accepted, 30 enrolled. In 2010, 35 master's awarded. *Degree requirements:* For master's, thesis optional, Ten Graduate Courses. Prerequisites are additional if student does not have adequate CS background. *Entrance requirements:* For master's, 3 letters of recommendation, transcripts, statement of purpose. Additional exam requirements/recommendations for international students: Required—TOEFL (minimum score 550 paper-based, 213 computer-based, 79 iBT) or IELTS (6.5). *Application deadline:* For fall admission, 8/10 for domestic students, 5/15 priority date for international students; for spring admission, 12/20 for domestic students, 9/15 priority date for international students. Applications are processed on a rolling basis. Application fee: $0. Electronic applications accepted. *Expenses:* Tuition: Full-time $14,940; part-time $830 per credit hour. Required fees: $87 per semester. Part-time tuition and fees vary according to course load and program. *Financial support:* In 2010–11, 24 students received support, including 1 fellowship (averaging $3,000 per year), 16 teaching assistantships with partial tuition reimbursements available (averaging $2,900 per year); career-related internships or fieldwork, Federal Work-Study, scholarships/grants, tuition waivers (partial), and unspecified assistantships also available. Financial award application deadline: 3/15. *Faculty research:* Software engineering, high performance computing, algorithms and complexity, parallel and distributed computing, databases and computer networks. Total annual research expenditures: $22,000. *Unit head:* Dr. Chandra Sekharan, Chair, 312-915-7985, Fax: 312-915-7998, E-mail: csekhar@luc.edu. *Application contact:* Cecilia Murphy, Graduate Program Secretary, 312-915-7990, Fax: 312-915-7998, E-mail: gradinfo-cs@luc.edu.

Marlboro College, Graduate School, Program in Information Technologies, Marlboro, VT 05344. Offers information technologies (MS); open source Web development (Certificate); project management (Certificate). Part-time and evening/weekend programs available. Postbaccalaureate distance learning degree programs offered (minimal on-campus study). *Faculty:* 5 part-time/adjunct (4 women). *Students:* 4 full-time (2 women), 11 part-time (6 women); includes 1 Black or African American, non-Hispanic/Latino. Average age 40. 9 applicants, 100% accepted, 8 enrolled. In 2010, 12 master's awarded. *Degree requirements:* For master's, 30 credits including capstone project. *Entrance requirements:* For master's, letter of intent, 2 letters of recommendation, transcripts. *Application deadline:* For fall admission, 7/1 priority date for domestic students; for winter admission, 11/1 priority date for domestic students; for spring admission, 3/1 priority date for domestic students. Applications are processed on a rolling basis. Application fee: $0. Electronic applications accepted. *Expenses:* Tuition: Full-time $14,280; part-time $680 per credit. Tuition and fees vary according to course load and program. *Financial support:* Applicants required to submit FAFSA. *Unit head:* Sean Conley, Associate Dean of the Graduate School. *Application contact:* Joe Heslin, Associate Director of Admissions, 802-258-9209, Fax: 802-258-9201, E-mail: jheslin@gradschool.marlboro.edu.

Marshall University, Academic Affairs Division, College of Information Technology and Engineering, Weisberg Division of Engineering and Computer Science, Program in Information Systems, Huntington, WV 25755. Offers MS. Part-time and evening/weekend programs available. *Students:* 10 full-time (1 woman), 14 part-time (2 women); includes 2 Black or African American, non-Hispanic/Latino, 10 international. Average age 30. In 2010, 11 master's awarded. *Degree requirements:* For master's, final project, oral exam. *Entrance requirements:* For master's, GRE General Test or MAT, minimum undergraduate GPA of 2.5. Application fee: $40. *Financial support:* Tuition waivers (full) available. Support available to part-time students. Financial award application deadline: 8/1; financial award applicants required to submit FAFSA. *Unit head:* Dr. Thomas D. Hankins, Professor, 304-746-2044, E-mail: hankins@marshall.edu. *Application contact:* Information Contact, 304-746-1900, Fax: 304-746-1902, E-mail: services@marshall.edu.

Marywood University, Academic Affairs, Insalaco College of Creative and Performing Arts, Department of Communication Arts, Program in Information Sciences, Scranton, PA 18509-1598. Offers corporate communication (Certificate); e-business (Certificate); health communication (Certificate); information sciences (MS), including library science/information specialist; instructional technology (Certificate). *Entrance requirements:* Additional exam requirements/recommendations for international students: Required—TOEFL (minimum score 550 paper-based; 213 computer-based; 79 iBT). Electronic applications accepted. *Expenses:* Tuition: Part-time $735 per credit. Required fees: $470 per semester. Tuition and fees vary according to degree level and campus/location.

Massachusetts Institute of Technology, School of Engineering, Department of Civil and Environmental Engineering, Cambridge, MA 02139. Offers biological oceanography (PhD, Sc D); chemical oceanography (PhD, Sc D); civil and environmental engineering (M Eng, SM, PhD, Sc D); civil and environmental systems (PhD, Sc D); civil engineering (PhD, Sc D, CE); coastal engineering (PhD, Sc D); construction engineering and management (PhD, Sc D); environmental biology (PhD, Sc D); environmental chemistry (PhD, Sc D); environmental engineering (PhD, Sc D); environmental fluid mechanics (PhD, Sc D); geotechnical and geoenvironmental engineering (PhD, Sc D); hydrology (PhD, Sc D); information technology (PhD, Sc D); oceanographic engineering (PhD, Sc D); structures and materials (PhD, Sc D); transportation (PhD, Sc D); SM/MBA. *Faculty:* 36 full-time (6 women). *Students:* 181 full-time (56 women); includes 27 minority (3 Black or African American, non-Hispanic/Latino; 10 Asian, non-Hispanic/Latino; 10 Hispanic/Latino; 4 Two or more races, non-Hispanic/Latino), 93 international. Average age 26. 525 applicants, 29% accepted, 74 enrolled. In 2010, 85 master's, 18 doctorates, 2 other advanced degrees awarded. *Degree requirements:* For master's and CE, thesis; for doctorate, comprehensive exam, thesis/dissertation. *Entrance requirements:* For master's and doctorate, GRE General Test. Additional exam requirements/recommendations for international students: Required—TOEFL (minimum score 577 paper-based; 233 computer-based; 90 iBT), IELTS (minimum score 7). *Application deadline:* For fall admission, 1/2 for domestic and international students. Application fee: $75. Electronic applications accepted. *Expenses:* Tuition: Full-time $38,940; part-time $605 per unit. Required fees: $272. *Financial support:* In 2010–11, 146 students received support, including 50 fellowships with tuition reimbursements available (averaging $21,808 per year), 90 research assistantships with tuition reimbursements available (averaging $28,452 per year), 20 teaching assistantships with tuition reimbursements available (averaging $27,842 per year); career-related internships or fieldwork, Federal Work-Study, institutionally sponsored loans, scholarships/grants, health care benefits, and unspecified assistantships also available. *Faculty research:* Environmental chemistry; environmental microbiology; environmental fluid mechanics and coastal engineering; geotechnical engineering and geomechanics; hydrology and hydroclimatology; mechanics of materials and structures; operations research/supply chain; transportation. Total annual research expenditures: $19.5 million. *Unit head:* Prof. Andrew Whittle, Department Head, 617-253-7101. *Application contact:* Patricia Glidden, Graduate Admissions Coordinator, 617-253-7119, Fax: 617-258-6775, E-mail: cee-admissions@mit.edu.

Missouri University of Science and Technology, Graduate School, Department of Business and Information Technology, Rolla, MO 65409. Offers business and information technology (MBA); information science and technology (MS). *Degree requirements:* For master's, thesis or alternative. *Entrance requirements:* Additional exam requirements/recommendations for international students: Required—TOEFL (minimum score 600 paper-based; 250 computer-based).

Montclair State University, The Graduate School, College of Science and Mathematics, Department of Computer Science, Montclair, NJ 07043-1624. Offers CISCO (Certificate); informatics (MS); object oriented computing (Certificate). Part-time and evening/weekend programs available. *Faculty:* 14 full-time (3 women), 16 part-time/adjunct (6 women). *Students:* 15 full-time (2 women), 18 part-time (7 women); includes 1 Asian, non-Hispanic/Latino; 1 Hispanic/Latino, 7 international. Average age 31. 16 applicants, 81% accepted, 5 enrolled. In 2010, 9 master's awarded. *Degree requirements:* For master's, comprehensive exam, thesis or alternative. *Entrance requirements:* For master's, GRE General Test, 2 letters of recommendation. Additional exam requirements/recommendations for international students: Required—TOEFL (minimum iBT score of 83) or IELTS. *Application deadline:* For fall admission, 6/1 for international students; for spring admission, 10/1 for international students. Applications are processed on a rolling basis. Application fee: $60. Electronic applications accepted. *Expenses:* Tuition, state resident: part-time $501.34 per credit. Tuition, nonresident: part-time $773.88 per credit. Required fees: $71.15 per credit. *Financial support:* In 2010–11, 4 research assistantships with full tuition reimbursements (averaging $7,000 per year) were awarded; Federal Work-Study, scholarships/grants, and unspecified assistantships also available. Support available to part-time students. Financial award application deadline: 3/1; financial award applicants required to submit FAFSA. Total annual research expenditures: $342,960. *Unit head:* Dr. Michael Oudshoorn, Chairperson, 973-655-4166. *Application contact:* Amy Aiello, Director of Graduate Admissions and Operations, 973-655-5147, Fax: 973-655-7869, E-mail: graduate.school@montclair.edu.

National University, Academic Affairs, School of Engineering and Technology, Department of Computer Science and Information Systems, La Jolla, CA 92037-1011. Offers computer science (MS); information systems (MS); software engineering (MS); technology management (MS). Part-time and evening/weekend programs available. Postbaccalaureate distance learning degree programs offered (no on-campus study). *Faculty:* 8 full-time (1 woman), 90 part-time/adjunct (13 women). *Students:* 60 full-time (12 women), 146 part-time (40 women); includes 365 minority (25 Black or African American, non-Hispanic/Latino; 21 Asian, non-Hispanic/Latino; 14 Hispanic/Latino; 2 Native Hawaiian or other Pacific Islander, non-Hispanic/Latino; 303 Two or more races, non-Hispanic/Latino), 54 international. Average age 32. 138 applicants, 100% accepted, 79 enrolled. In 2010, 79 master's awarded. *Degree requirements:* For master's, thesis. *Entrance requirements:* For master's, interview, minimum GPA of 2.5. Additional exam requirements/recommendations for international students: Required—TOEFL (minimum score 550 paper-based; 213 computer-based; 79 iBT), IELTS (minimum score 6). *Application deadline:* Applications are processed on a rolling basis. Application fee: $60 ($65 for international students). Electronic applications accepted. *Expenses:* Tuition: Full-time $9450; part-time $350 per unit. Required fees: $350 per unit. One-time fee: $60. *Financial support:* Career-related internships or fieldwork, institutionally sponsored loans, scholarships/grants, and tuition waivers (partial) available. Support available to part-time students. Financial award application deadline: 6/30; financial award applicants required to submit FAFSA. *Unit head:* Dr. Alireza M. Farahani, Chair and Instructor, 858-309-3438, Fax: 858-309-3420, E-mail: afarahan@nu.edu. *Application contact:* Dominick Giovanniello, Associate Regional Dean—San Diego, 800-NAT-UNIV, Fax: 858-541-7792, E-mail: dgiovann@nu.edu.

Naval Postgraduate School, Graduate Programs, Department of Information Sciences, Monterey, CA 93943. Offers information sciences (MS); knowledge superiority (MS, Certificate). Program open only to commissioned officers of the United States and friendly nations and selected United States federal civilian employees. Part-time programs available. *Degree requirements:* For master's, thesis.

New Jersey Institute of Technology, Office of Graduate Studies, College of Computing Science, Program in Information Systems, Newark, NJ 07102. Offers business and information systems (MS); emergency management and business continuity (MS); information systems (MS, PhD). Part-time and evening/weekend programs available. *Students:* 86 full-time (26 women), 109 part-time (26 women); includes 23 Black or African American, non-Hispanic/Latino; 1 American Indian or Alaska Native, non-Hispanic/Latino; 30 Asian, non-Hispanic/Latino; 14 Hispanic/Latino, 53 international. Average age 31. 275 applicants, 55% accepted, 69 enrolled. In 2010, 94 master's, 6 doctorates awarded. Terminal master's awarded for partial completion of doctoral program. *Degree requirements:* For master's, thesis optional; for doctorate, thesis/dissertation. *Entrance requirements:* For master's, GRE General Test; for doctorate, GRE General Test, minimum graduate GPA of 3.5. Additional exam requirements/recommendations for international students: Required—TOEFL (minimum score 550 paper-based; 213 computer-based; 79 iBT). *Application deadline:* For fall admission, 6/5 priority date for domestic students, 4/1 for international students; for spring admission, 11/15 for domestic and international students. Applications are processed on a rolling basis. Application fee: $65. Electronic applications accepted. *Expenses:* Tuition, state resident: full-time $14,724; part-time $818 per credit. Tuition, nonresident: full-time $20,304; part-time $1128 per credit. Required fees: $2272; $209 per credit. $103 per semester. One-time fee: $312 full-time; $212 part-time. *Financial support:* Fellowships with full and partial tuition reimbursements, research assistantships with full and partial tuition reimbursements, teaching assistantships with full and partial tuition reimbursements, career-related internships or fieldwork, Federal Work-Study, institutionally sponsored loans, and unspecified assistantships available. Financial award application deadline: 3/15. *Unit head:* Dr. Michael P. Bieber, Associate Chair, 973-596-2681, Fax: 973-596-2986, E-mail: michael.p.bieber@njit.edu. *Application contact:* Kathryn Kelly, Director of Admissions, 973-596-3300, Fax: 973-596-3461, E-mail: admissions@njit.edu.

Northeastern University, College of Computer and Information Science, Boston, MA 02115-5096. Offers computer and information science (PhD); computer science (MS); health informatics (MS); information assurance (MS). Part-time and evening/weekend programs available. *Faculty:* 28 full-time (3 women), 3 part-time/adjunct (all women). *Students:* 337 full-time (91 women), 90 part-time (52 women). 1,045 applicants, 56% accepted, 150 enrolled. In 2010, 81 master's, 7 doctorates awarded. Terminal master's awarded for partial completion of doctoral program. *Degree requirements:* For master's, thesis optional; for doctorate, comprehensive exam, thesis/dissertation. *Entrance requirements:* For master's and doctorate, GRE General Test. Additional exam requirements/recommendations for international students: Required—TOEFL or IELTS. *Application deadline:* For fall admission, 7/15 for domestic students, 5/1 for international students; for spring admission, 10/15 for domestic students, 9/1 for international students. Applications are processed on a rolling basis. Application fee: $50. Electronic applications accepted. *Expenses:* Contact institution. *Financial support:* In 2010–11, 59 students received support, including 1 fellowship, 40 research assistantships with full tuition reimbursements available (averaging $18,260 per year), 33 teaching assistantships with full tuition reimbursements available (averaging $18,260 per year); career-related internships or fieldwork, Federal Work-Study, institutionally sponsored loans, scholarships/grants, and unspecified assistantships also available. Financial award application deadline: 1/15. *Faculty research:* Programming languages, artificial intelligence, human-computer interaction, database management, network security. *Unit head:* Dr. Larry A. Finkelstein, Dean, 617-373-2462, Fax: 617-373-5121. *Application contact:* Dr. Agnes Chan, Associate Dean and Director of Graduate Program, 617-373-2462, Fax: 617-373-5121, E-mail: gradschool@ccs.neu.edu.

Northeastern University, College of Engineering, Information Systems Program, Boston, MA 02115-5096. Offers MS, Certificate. Part-time programs available. Postbaccalaureate distance learning degree programs offered (no on-campus study). *Students:* 152 full-time (57 women), 11 part-time (2 women). Average age 26. 188 applicants, 91% accepted, 68 enrolled. In 2010, 58 master's awarded. *Degree requirements:* For master's, thesis optional. *Entrance requirements:* For master's, GRE General Test. Additional exam requirements/recommendations for international students: Required—TOEFL (minimum score 600 paper-based; 250 computer-based; 80 iBT). *Application deadline:* For fall admission, 1/15 priority date for domestic and international students. Applications are processed on a rolling basis. Application fee: $50. Electronic applications accepted. *Financial support:* In 2010–11, 18 students received support, including 1 fellowship with full tuition reimbursement available (averaging $18,325 per year), 1 research assistantship with full tuition reimbursement available, 12 teaching assistantships with full tuition reimbursements available; career-related internships or fieldwork, Federal Work-Study, scholarships/grants, tuition waivers (full), and unspecified assistantships also available. Support available to part-time students. Financial award application deadline: 1/15; financial award applicants required to submit FAFSA. *Faculty research:* Simulation analysis, software architecture. *Unit head:* Dr. Khaled Bugrara, Director, 617-373-3699. *Application contact:* Jeffrey Hengel, Admissions Specialist, 617-373-2711, Fax: 617-373-2501, E-mail: grad-eng@coe.neu.edu.

Northern Kentucky University, Office of Graduate Programs, College of Informatics, Department of Business Informatics, Highland Heights, KY 41099. Offers business informatics (MS, Certificate); corporate information security (Certificate); enterprise resource planning (Certificate). Part-time and evening/weekend programs available. Postbaccalaureate distance learning degree programs offered (no on-campus study). *Faculty:* 9 full-time (2 women), 1 part-time/adjunct (0 women). *Students:* 10 full-time (4 women), 36 part-time (15 women); includes 7 minority (3 Black or African American, non-Hispanic/Latino; 2 Asian, non-Hispanic/Latino; 2 Hispanic/Latino), 6 international. Average age 33. 40 applicants, 75% accepted, 19 enrolled. In 2010, 11 master's, 6 other advanced degrees awarded. *Degree requirements:* For master's, capstone and portfolio (some programs), internship. *Entrance requirements:* For master's, GMAT (minimum score 450), GRE General Test (minimum combined score 1000), resume, minimum GPA of 2.5. Additional exam requirements/recommendations for international students: Required—TOEFL (minimum score 550 paper-based; 213 computer-based; 79 iBT); Recommended—IELTS (minimum score 6.5). *Application deadline:* For fall admission, 8/1 for domestic students, 6/1 for international students; for spring admission, 12/1 for domestic students, 10/1 for international students. Applications are processed on a rolling basis. Application fee: $40. Electronic applications accepted. *Expenses:* Tuition, state resident: full-time $7254; part-time $403 per credit hour. Tuition, nonresident: full-time $12,492; part-time $694 per credit hour. Tuition and fees vary according to degree level and program. *Financial support:* Unspecified assistantships available. Financial award applicants required to submit FAFSA. *Faculty research:* Information systems implementation, information systems security, business analytics, healthcare informatics. Total annual research expenditures: $50,000. *Unit head:* Dr. Ben Martz, Department Chair, 859-572-6366, E-mail: matrzw1@nku.edu. *Application contact:* Dr. Peg Griffin, Director of Graduate Programs, 859-572-6934, Fax: 859-572-6670, E-mail: griffinp@nku.edu.

Northwestern University, McCormick School of Engineering and Applied Science, Department of Electrical Engineering and Computer Science, MS Program in Information Technology, Evanston, IL 60208. Offers MS. *Faculty:* 15 part-time/adjunct (0 women). *Students:* 1 (woman) full-time, 42 part-time (7 women); includes 16 minority (8 Black or African American, non-Hispanic/Latino; 5 Asian, non-Hispanic/Latino; 2 Hispanic/Latino; 1 Native Hawaiian or other Pacific Islander, non-Hispanic/Latino), 7 international. Average age 32. In 2010, 25 master's awarded. *Entrance requirements:* For master's, GRE General Test is required for some applicants. All applicants are required to have work experience in an IT-related position. Because IT positions exist in every industry and nearly every company, our students have a diverse professional background. Applicants may hold any type or level of position within their companies. *Application deadline:* For fall admission, 8/1 for domestic students, 6/1 for international students. Applications are processed on a rolling basis. Application fee: $50. Electronic applications accepted. *Financial support:* Institutionally sponsored loans and employers' reimbursement available. Financial award application deadline: 1/15; financial award applicants required to submit FAFSA. *Unit head:* Dr. Abraham Haddad, Director, 847-491-8175, Fax: 847-467-3550, E-mail: ahaddad@northwestern.edu. *Application contact:* Trista Wdziekonski, Associate Director, 847-467-6557, Fax: 847-467-3550, E-mail: trista@northwestern.edu.

Nova Southeastern University, Graduate School of Computer and Information Sciences, Fort Lauderdale, FL 33314-7796. Offers computer information systems (MS, PhD), including information security; computer science (MS, PhD); computing technology in education (PhD); information security (MS); information systems (MS, PhD); management information systems (MS), including information security (MS, PhD), management information systems; JD/MS. Part-time and evening/weekend programs available. Postbaccalaureate distance learning degree programs offered (no on-campus study). *Faculty:* 20 full-time (5 women), 21 part-time/adjunct (3 women). *Students:* 142 full-time (35 women), 1,000 part-time (283 women); includes 219 Black or African American, non-Hispanic/Latino; 8 American Indian or Alaska Native, non-Hispanic/Latino; 88 Asian, non-Hispanic/Latino; 163 Hispanic/Latino; 8 Two or more races, non-Hispanic/Latino, 44 international. Average age 41. 486 applicants, 45% accepted. In 2010, 128 master's, 44 doctorates awarded. Terminal master's awarded for partial completion of doctoral program. *Degree requirements:* For master's, thesis optional; for doctorate, thesis/dissertation. *Entrance requirements:* For master's, minimum undergraduate GPA of 2.5; for doctorate, master's degree, minimum graduate GPA of 3.25. Additional exam requirements/recommendations for international students: Required—TOEFL (minimum score 213 computer-based; 79 iBT), IELTS (minimum score 6). *Application deadline:* Applications are processed on a rolling basis. Application fee: $50. Electronic applications accepted. *Expenses:* Contact institution. *Financial support:* Federal Work-Study, scholarships/grants, and unspecified assistantships available. Support available to part-time students. Financial award application deadline: 5/1. *Faculty research:* Artificial intelligence, database management, human-computer interaction, distance education, information security. *Unit head:* Dr. Amon Seagull, PhD, Interim Dean, 954-262-7300. *Application contact:* 954-262-2000, Fax: 954-262-2752, E-mail: scisinfo@nova.edu.

The Ohio State University, Graduate School, College of Engineering, Department of Computer Science and Engineering, Columbus, OH 43210. Offers computer and information science (MS, PhD); computer science and engineering (MS). *Faculty:* 40. *Students:* 244 full-time (45 women), 60 part-time (9 women); includes 2 Black or African American, non-Hispanic/Latino; 5 Asian, non-Hispanic/Latino; 1 Hispanic/Latino, 236 international. Average age 28. In 2010, 65 master's, 19 doctorates awarded. *Degree requirements:* For master's, thesis optional; for doctorate, thesis/dissertation. *Entrance requirements:* Additional exam requirements/recommendations for international students: Recommended—TOEFL (minimum score 600 paper-based; 250 computer-based). *Application deadline:* For fall admission, 8/15 priority date for domestic students, 7/1 priority date for international students; for winter admission, 12/1 priority date for domestic students, 11/1 priority date for international students; for spring admission, 3/1 priority date for domestic students, 2/1 priority date for international students. Applications are processed on a rolling basis. Application fee: $40 ($50 for international students). Electronic applications accepted. *Expenses:* Tuition, state resident: full-time $10,605. Tuition, nonresident: full-time $26,535. Tuition and fees vary according to course load and program. *Financial support:* Fellowships, teaching assistantships, career-related internships or fieldwork, Federal Work-Study, institutionally sponsored loans, and administrative assistantships available. Support available to part-time students. Financial award application deadline: 1/15. *Unit head:* Xiadong Zhang, Chair, 614-292-5813, E-mail: zhang.574@osu.edu. *Application contact:* 614-292-9444, Fax: 614-292-3895, E-mail: domestic.grad@osu.edu.

Oklahoma State University, Spears School of Business, Department of Management Science and Information Systems, Stillwater, OK 74078. Offers management information systems (MS); management science and information systems (PhD); telecommunications management (MS). Part-time programs available. Postbaccalaureate distance learning degree programs offered. *Faculty:* 17 full-time (3 women), 2 part-time/adjunct (0 women). *Students:* 64 full-time (12 women), 75 part-time (15 women); includes 4 Black or African American, non-Hispanic/Latino; 4 American Indian or Alaska Native, non-Hispanic/Latino; 1 Asian, non-Hispanic/Latino, 74 international. Average age 29. 252 applicants, 36% accepted, 36 enrolled. In 2010, 68 master's, 1 doctorate awarded. *Degree requirements:* For master's, thesis or alternative; for doctorate, comprehensive exam, thesis/dissertation. *Entrance requirements:* For master's and doctorate, GRE or GMAT. Additional exam requirements/recommendations for international students: Required—TOEFL (minimum score 550 paper-based; 79 iBT). *Application deadline:* For fall admission, 3/1 priority date for international students; for spring admission, 8/1 priority date for international students. Applications are processed on a rolling basis. Application fee: $40 ($75 for international students). Electronic applications accepted. *Expenses:* Tuition, state resident: full-time $3716; part-time $154.85 per credit hour. Tuition, nonresident: full-time $14,892; part-time $621 per credit hour. Required fees: $2044; $85.20 per credit hour. One-time fee: $50. Tuition and fees vary according to course load and campus/location. *Financial support:* In 2010–11, 1 research assistantship (averaging $4,200 per year), 12 teaching assistantships (averaging $12,460 per year) were awarded; career-related internships or fieldwork, Federal Work-Study, scholarships/grants, health care benefits, tuition waivers (partial), and unspecified assistantships also available. Support available to part-time students. Financial award application deadline: 3/1; financial award applicants required to submit FAFSA. *Unit head:* Dr. Rick Wilson, Head, 405-744-3551, Fax: 405-744-5180. *Application contact:* Dr. Gordon Emslie, Dean, 405-744-6368, Fax: 405-744-0355, E-mail: grad-i@okstate.edu.

Old Dominion University, College of Business and Public Administration, Doctoral Program in Business Administration, Norfolk, VA 23529. Offers finance (PhD); information technology (PhD); marketing (PhD); strategic management (PhD). *Accreditation:* AACSB. *Faculty:* 21 full-time (2 women). *Students:* 36 full-time (13 women), 1 part-time (0 women); includes 6 minority (3 Black or African American, non-Hispanic/Latino; 2 Asian, non-Hispanic/Latino; 1 Native Hawaiian or other Pacific Islander, non-Hispanic/Latino), 28 international. Average age 35. 42 applicants, 69% accepted, 10 enrolled. In 2010, 5 doctorates awarded. *Degree requirements:* For doctorate, comprehensive exam, thesis/dissertation. *Entrance requirements:* For doctorate, GMAT. Additional exam requirements/recommendations for international students: Required—TOEFL (minimum score 550 paper-based; 213 computer-based; 79 iBT). *Application deadline:* For fall admission, 4/1 priority date for domestic and international students. Application fee: $50. Electronic applications accepted. *Expenses:* Tuition, state resident: full-time $8592; part-time $358 per credit. Tuition, nonresident: full-time $21,672; part-time $903 per credit. Required fees: $119 per semester. One-time fee: $50. *Financial support:* In 2010–11, 27 students received support, including 2 fellowships with full tuition reimbursements available (averaging $7,500 per year), 32 research assistantships with full tuition reimbursements available (averaging $7,500 per year), 12 teaching assistantships with full tuition reimbursements available (averaging $7,500 per year); scholarships/grants and unspecified assistantships also available. Financial award application deadline: 4/1; financial award applicants required to submit FAFSA. *Faculty research:* International business, buyer behavior, financial markets, strategy, operations research. *Unit head:* Dr. John B. Ford, Graduate Program Director, 757-683-3587, Fax: 757-683-4076, E-mail: jford@odu.edu. *Application contact:* Katrina Davenport, Program Coordinator, 757-683-5138, Fax: 757-683-4076, E-mail: kdavenpo@odu.edu.

Pace University, Seidenberg School of Computer Science and Information Systems, New York, NY 10038. Offers computer communications and networks (Certificate); computer science (MS); computing studies (DPS); information systems (MS); Internet technologies for e-commerce (MS); Internet technology (MS); object-oriented programming (Certificate); security and information assurance (Certificate); software development and engineering (MS); telecommunications (MS, Certificate). Part-time and evening/weekend programs available. *Entrance requirements:* For master's, GRE General Test. Additional exam requirements/recommendations for international students: Required—TOEFL. Electronic applications accepted. *Expenses:* Contact institution.

Penn State University Park, Graduate School, College of Information Sciences and Technology, State College, University Park, PA 16802-1503. Offers MPS, MS, PhD. *Students:* 95 full-time (39 women), 9 part-time (2 women). Average age 29. 183 applicants, 17% accepted, 24 enrolled. In 2010, 9 master's, 14 doctorates awarded. *Entrance requirements:* Additional exam requirements/recommendations for international students: Required—TOEFL (minimum score 550 paper-based; 213 computer-based; 80 iBT). *Application deadline:* Applications are processed on a rolling basis. Application fee: $65. Electronic applications accepted. *Financial support:* Fellowships, research assistantships, teaching assistantships available. Financial award applicants required to submit FAFSA. *Unit head:* Dr. David L. Hall, Dean (Interim), 814-863-3528, Fax: 814-865-5604, E-mail: dlh28@psu.edu. *Application contact:* Cynthia E Nicosia, Director, Graduate Enrollment Services, 814-865-1795, Fax: 814-865-4627, E-mail: cey1@psu.edu.

Polytechnic Institute of NYU, Westchester Graduate Center, Graduate Programs, Department of Computer Science and Engineering, Major in Information Systems Engineering, Hawthorne, NY 10532-1507. Offers MS. Evening/weekend programs available. *Students:* 3 full-time (0 women), 1 part-time (0 women); includes 1 Asian, non-Hispanic/Latino. Average age 40. 20 applicants, 55% accepted, 4 enrolled. In 2010, 6 master's awarded. *Degree requirements:* For master's, comprehensive exam (for some programs), thesis (for some programs). *Entrance requirements:* Additional exam requirements/recommendations for international students: Required—TOEFL (minimum score 550 paper-based; 213 computer-based; 80 iBT); Recommended—IELTS (minimum score 6.5). *Application deadline:* For fall admission, 7/31 priority date for domestic students, 4/30 priority date for international students; for spring admission, 12/31 priority date for domestic students, 11/30 priority date for international students. Applications are processed on a rolling basis. Application fee: $75. Electronic applications accepted. *Expenses:* Tuition: Full-time $21,492; part-time $1194 per credit. Required fees: $385 per semester. Tuition and fees vary according to course load. *Financial support:* Institutionally sponsored loans, scholarships/grants, and unspecified assistantships available. Support available to part-time students. *Unit head:* Dr. Keith W. Ross, Department Head, 718-260-3859, E-mail: ross@poly.edu. *Application contact:* JeanCarlo Bonilla, Director of Graduate Enrollment Management, 718-260-3182, Fax: 718-260-3624, E-mail: gradinfo@poly.edu.

Regis University, College for Professional Studies, School of Computer and Information Sciences, Denver, CO 80221-1099. Offers database administration with Oracle (Certificate); database development (Certificate); database technologies (M Sc); enterprise Java software development (Certificate); enterprise resource planning (Certificate); executive information technologies (Certificate); information assurance (M Sc, Certificate); information technology management (M Sc); software engineering (M Sc, Certificate); software engineering and database technologies (M Sc); storage area networks (Certificate); systems engineering (M Sc, Certificate). Offered at Boulder Campus, Northwest Denver Campus, Southeast Denver Campus, Fort Collins Campus, Colorado Springs Campus, and Broomfield Campus. Part-time and evening/weekend programs available. Postbaccalaureate distance learning degree programs offered (no on-campus study). *Degree requirements:* For master's, thesis, final research project. *Entrance requirements:* For master's, 2 years of related experience, resume, interview; for Certificate, 2 years of related experience, resumé. Additional exam requirements/recommendations for international students: Required—TOEFL (minimum score 213 computer-based), TWE (minimum score 5), TOEFL or university-based test. Electronic applications accepted. *Expenses:* Contact institution. *Faculty research:* Secure Virtual Laboratory Architecture, Joint IA project with W2C06 Institute, Information Policy, OLTP and OLAP Technologies, knowledge management, software architectures.

Rensselaer at Hartford, Department of Computer and Information Science, Program in Information Technology, Hartford, CT 06120-2991. Offers MS. Part-time and evening/weekend programs available. *Entrance requirements:* For master's, GRE. Additional exam requirements/recommendations for international students: Required—TOEFL (minimum score 600 paper-based; 250 computer-based; 100 iBT). Electronic applications accepted.

Rensselaer Polytechnic Institute, Graduate School, School of Science, Program in Information Technology and Web Science, Troy, NY 12180-3590. Offers MS. Part-time programs available. *Faculty:* 82 full-time (11 women). *Students:* 40 full-time (18 women), 3 part-time (0 women); includes 1 Black or African American, non-Hispanic/Latino; 8 Asian, non-Hispanic/Latino. 136 applicants, 59% accepted, 22 enrolled. In 2010, 34 master's awarded. *Degree requirements:* For master's, capstone course. *Entrance requirements:* For master's, GRE. Additional exam requirements/recommendations for international students: Required—TOEFL. *Application deadline:* For fall admission, 1/15 priority date for domestic and international students; for spring admission, 8/15 priority date for domestic students, 8/15 for international students. Applications are processed on a rolling basis. Application fee: $75. Electronic applications accepted. *Expenses:* Tuition: Full-time $39,600; part-time $1650 per credit. Required fees: $1896. *Financial support:* In 2010–11, 5 students received support, including 5 teaching assistantships with full tuition reimbursements available (averaging $17,500 per year); career-related internships or fieldwork, institutionally sponsored loans, scholarships/grants, health care benefits, tuition waivers (partial), and unspecified assistantships also available. Financial award application deadline: 3/15. *Faculty research:* Web science, database systems, software design, human-computer interaction, networking, information technology, financial engineering,

Information Science

Rensselaer Polytechnic Institute (continued)
electronic arts, management, information security. *Unit head:* Dr. James Hendler, Associate Dean, 518-276-2660, Fax: 518-276-6687, E-mail: hendler@cs.rpi.edu. *Application contact:* Linda Kramarchyk, Program Manager, 518-276-6304, Fax: 518-276-6687, E-mail: kramal@rpi.edu.

Robert Morris University, Graduate Studies, School of Communications and Information Systems, Moon Township, PA 15108-1189. Offers communication and information systems (MS); competitive intelligence systems (MS); information security and assurance (MS); information systems and communications (D Sc); information systems management (MS); information technology project management (MS); Internet information systems (MS); organizational studies (MS). Part-time and evening/weekend programs available. *Degree requirements:* For doctorate, thesis/dissertation. *Entrance requirements:* For doctorate, employer letter of endorsement, interview. Additional exam requirements/recommendations for international students: Required—TOEFL (minimum score 550 paper-based; 213 computer-based; 79 iBT). Electronic applications accepted. *Expenses:* Contact institution.

Rochester Institute of Technology, Graduate Enrollment Services, B. Thomas Golisano College of Computing and Information Sciences, Department of Information Technology, Program in Information Technology, Rochester, NY 14623-5603. Offers MS. Part-time and evening/weekend programs available. *Students:* 66 full-time (14 women), 63 part-time (16 women); includes 3 Black or African American, non-Hispanic/Latino; 1 American Indian or Alaska Native, non-Hispanic/Latino; 3 Asian, non-Hispanic/Latino; 2 Hispanic/Latino, 67 international. Average age 29. 112 applicants, 64% accepted, 36 enrolled. In 2010, 38 master's awarded. *Degree requirements:* For master's, thesis or project. *Entrance requirements:* For master's, GRE, minimum GPA of 3.0. Additional exam requirements/recommendations for international students: Required—TOEFL (minimum score 570 paper-based; 230 computer-based; 88 iBT) or IELTS (minimum score 6.5). *Application deadline:* For fall admission, 8/1 for domestic students, 7/1 for international students; for spring admission, 2/1 for domestic students. Applications are processed on a rolling basis. Electronic applications accepted. *Expenses:* Tuition: Full-time $33,234; part-time $924 per credit hour. Required fees: $219. *Financial support:* In 2010–11, 101 students received support; research assistantships with partial tuition reimbursements available, teaching assistantships with partial tuition reimbursements available, career-related internships or fieldwork, scholarships/grants, and unspecified assistantships available. Support available to part-time students. Financial award applicants required to submit FAFSA. *Unit head:* Prof. Dianne Bills, Graduate Program Director, 585-475-2700, Fax: 585-475-6584, E-mail: informaticsgrad@rit.edu. *Application contact:* Diane Ellison, Assistant Vice President, Graduate Enrollment Services, 585-475-2229, Fax: 585-475-7164, E-mail: gradinfo@rit.edu.

Rochester Institute of Technology, Graduate Enrollment Services, B. Thomas Golisano College of Computing and Information Sciences, PhD Program in Computing and Information Sciences, Rochester, NY 14623-5603. Offers PhD. *Students:* 19 full-time (5 women), 6 part-time; includes 3 Asian, non-Hispanic/Latino; 1 Hispanic/Latino, 15 international. Average age 31. 45 applicants, 27% accepted, 9 enrolled. *Degree requirements:* For doctorate, thesis/dissertation. *Entrance requirements:* For doctorate, GRE, minimum GPA of 3.0. Additional exam requirements/recommendations for international students: Required—TOEFL (minimum score 570 paper-based; 230 computer-based; 88 iBT) or IELTS (minimum score 6.5). *Application deadline:* For fall admission, 1/15 priority date for domestic and international students. Applications are processed on a rolling basis. Electronic applications accepted. *Expenses:* Tuition: Full-time $33,234; part-time $924 per credit hour. Required fees: $219. *Financial support:* In 2010–11, 16 students received support; research assistantships with full and partial tuition reimbursements available, teaching assistantships with full and partial tuition reimbursements available, career-related internships or fieldwork, scholarships/grants, health care benefits, and unspecified assistantships available. Financial award applicants required to submit FAFSA. *Faculty research:* The Center for Advancing the Study of Cyberinfrastructure (CASCI): the framework supporting science and engineering research, domain-specific informatics. *Unit head:* Dr. Pengcheng Shi, PhD Program Director, 585-475-6147, E-mail: pengcheng.shi@rit.edu. *Application contact:* Diane Ellison, Assistant Vice President, Graduate Enrollment Services, 585-475-2229, Fax: 585-475-7164, E-mail: gradinfo@rit.edu.

Sacred Heart University, Graduate Programs, College of Arts and Sciences, Department of Computer Science and Information Technology, Fairfield, CT 06825-1000. Offers computer science (MS); database (CPS); information technology (MS, CPS); information technology and network security (CPS); interactive multimedia (CPS); Web development (CPS). Part-time and evening/weekend programs available. *Degree requirements:* For master's, thesis optional. *Entrance requirements:* Additional exam requirements/recommendations for international students: Required—TOEFL (minimum score 550 paper-based; 213 computer-based). Electronic applications accepted. *Faculty research:* Contemporary market software.

St. Mary's University, Graduate School, Department of Computer Science, Program in Computer Information Systems, San Antonio, TX 78228-8507. Offers MS. Part-time programs available. *Degree requirements:* For master's, comprehensive exam. *Entrance requirements:* For master's, GMAT or GRE General Test. Additional exam requirements/recommendations for international students: Required—TOEFL (minimum score 530 paper-based; 213 computer-based; 80 iBT). Electronic applications accepted. *Faculty research:* Artificial intelligence, database/knowledge base, software engineering, expert systems.

Saint Xavier University, Graduate Studies, School of Arts and Sciences, Department of Mathematics and Computer Science, Chicago, IL 60655-3105. Offers applied computer science in Internet information systems (MS); mathematics and computer science (MA); MBA/MS. *Degree requirements:* For master's, thesis optional.

Sam Houston State University, College of Arts and Sciences, Department of Computer Science, Huntsville, TX 77341. Offers computing and information science (MS). Part-time programs available. *Faculty:* 8 full-time (3 women). *Students:* 22 full-time (3 women), 30 part-time (9 women); includes 2 Black or African American, non-Hispanic/Latino; 1 Hispanic/Latino, 27 international. Average age 29. 29 applicants, 83% accepted, 15 enrolled. In 2010, 9 master's awarded. *Entrance requirements:* For master's, GRE General Test. Additional exam requirements/recommendations for international students: Required—TOEFL (minimum score 550 paper-based; 213 computer-based; 79 iBT). *Application deadline:* For fall admission, 8/1 for domestic and international students; for spring admission, 12/1 for domestic and international students. Application fee: $20. *Expenses:* Tuition, state resident: full-time $1363; part-time $163 per credit hour. Tuition, nonresident: full-time $3856; part-time $473 per credit hour. *Financial support:* Research assistantships, teaching assistantships, Federal Work-Study, institutionally sponsored loans, and tuition waivers (partial) available. Support available to part-time students. Financial award application deadline: 5/31; financial award applicants required to submit FAFSA. *Unit head:* Dr. Peter Cooper, Chair, 936-294-1569, Fax: 936-294-4312, E-mail: css_pac@shsu.edu. *Application contact:* Dr. Jiuhung Ji, Advisor, 936-294-1579, E-mail: csc_jxj@shsu.edu.

Simon Fraser University, Graduate Studies, Faculty of Applied Sciences, School of Interactive Arts and Technology, Surrey, BC V3T 2W1, Canada. Offers information technology (M Sc, PhD); interactive arts (M Sc, PhD). *Degree requirements:* For master's, thesis; for doctorate, comprehensive exam, thesis/dissertation. *Entrance requirements:* For master's, 2 references, curriculum vitae; for doctorate, 3 references, curriculm vitae, minimum GPA of 3.0. Additional exam requirements/recommendations for international students: Required—TOEFL (minimum score 570 paper-based; 230 computer-based), TWE (minimum score 5). Electronic applications accepted.

Southern Methodist University, Bobby B. Lyle School of Engineering, Department of Engineering Management, Information, and Systems, Dallas, TX 75275. Offers applied science (MS); engineering management (MSEM, DE); information engineering and management (MSIEM); operations research (MS, PhD); systems engineering (MS, PhD). Part-time and evening/weekend programs available. Postbaccalaureate distance learning degree programs offered. *Faculty:* 8 full-time (1 woman), 22 part-time/adjunct (1 woman). *Students:* 47 full-time (12 women), 348 part-time (75 women); includes 114 minority (31 Black or African American, non-Hispanic/Latino; 2 American Indian or Alaska Native, non-Hispanic/Latino; 34 Asian, non-Hispanic/Latino; 44 Hispanic/Latino; 2 Native Hawaiian or other Pacific Islander, non-Hispanic/Latino; 1 Two or more races, non-Hispanic/Latino), 51 international. Average age 33. 208 applicants, 67% accepted, 92 enrolled. In 2010, 130 master's, 6 doctorates awarded. Terminal master's awarded for partial completion of doctoral program. *Degree requirements:* For master's, thesis optional; for doctorate, thesis/dissertation, oral and written qualifying exams. *Entrance requirements:* For master's, minimum GPA of 3.0 in last 2 years; bachelor's degree in engineering, mathematics, sciences, or technical area; for doctorate, GRE General Test (operations research, engineering management), bachelor's degree in related field. Additional exam requirements/recommendations for international students: Required—TOEFL. *Application deadline:* For fall admission, 7/1 for domestic students, 5/15 for international students; for spring admission, 11/15 for domestic students, 9/1 for international students. Applications are processed on a rolling basis. Application fee: $75. *Financial support:* In 2010–11, 6 students received support, including 4 research assistantships with full tuition reimbursements available (averaging $18,000 per year), 2 teaching assistantships with full tuition reimbursements available (averaging $18,000 per year); tuition waivers (full) also available. *Faculty research:* Telecommunications, decision systems, information engineering, operations research, software. Total annual research expenditures: $275,851. *Unit head:* Dr. Richard S. Barr, Chair, 214-768-1772, Fax: 214-768-1112, E-mail: emis@lyle.smu.edu. *Application contact:* Marc Valerin, Director of Graduate and Executive Admissions, 214-768-3042, E-mail: valerin@lyle.smu.edu.

Southern Polytechnic State University, School of Arts and Sciences, Department of English, Technical Communication, and Media Arts, Marietta, GA 30060-2896. Offers communications management (AGC); content development (AGC); information and instructional design (MSIID); information design and communication (MS); instructional design (AGC); technical communication (Graduate Certificate); visual communication and graphics (AGC). Part-time and evening/weekend programs available. Postbaccalaureate distance learning degree programs offered (no on-campus study). *Faculty:* 4 full-time (3 women), 1 (woman) part-time/adjunct. *Students:* 2 full-time (both women), 61 part-time (40 women); includes 19 Black or African American, non-Hispanic/Latino; 1 Two or more races, non-Hispanic/Latino, 3 international. Average age 38. 37 applicants, 100% accepted, 29 enrolled. In 2010, 6 master's, 5 other advanced degrees awarded. *Degree requirements:* For master's, thesis or internship; for other advanced degree, thesis optional, 18 hours completed through thesis option (6 hours), internship option (6 hours) or advanced coursework option (6 hours). *Entrance requirements:* For master's, GRE, statement of purpose, writing sample, professional recommendations, timed essay; for other advanced degree, writing sample, professional recommendations. Additional exam requirements/recommendations for international students: Required—TOEFL (minimum score 550 paper-based; 213 computer-based; 79 iBT), IELTS (minimum score 6.5). *Application deadline:* For fall admission, 5/1 priority date for domestic students, 7/1 priority date for international students; for spring admission, 9/1 priority date for domestic students, 11/1 priority date for international students. Applications are processed on a rolling basis. Application fee: $20. Electronic applications accepted. *Expenses:* Tuition, state resident: full-time $3690; part-time $205 per semester hour. Tuition, nonresident: full-time $13,428; part-time $746 per semester hour. Required fees: $598 per semester. *Financial support:* Research assistantships with tuition reimbursements, teaching assistantships with tuition reimbursements, career-related internships or fieldwork, Federal Work-Study, scholarships/grants, and unspecified assistantships available. Support available to part-time students. Financial award application deadline: 5/1; financial award applicants required to submit FAFSA. *Faculty research:* Usability, user-centered design, instructional design, information architecture, information design. *Unit head:* Dr. Mark Nunes, Chair, 678-915-7202, Fax: 678-915-7425, E-mail: mnunes@spsu.edu. *Application contact:* Nikki Palamiotis, Director of Graduate Studies, 678-915-4276, Fax: 678-915-7292, E-mail: npalamio@spsu.edu.

Southern Polytechnic State University, School of Computing and Software Engineering, Department of Information Technology, Marietta, GA 30060-2896. Offers business continuity (Graduate Certificate); information security and assurance (Graduate Certificate); information technology (MSIT, Graduate Certificate, Graduate Transition Certificate). Part-time and evening/weekend programs available. Postbaccalaureate distance learning degree programs offered (minimal on-campus study). *Faculty:* 6 full-time (3 women), 2 part-time/adjunct (1 woman). *Students:* 60 full-time (17 women), 71 part-time (26 women); includes 54 Black or African American, non-Hispanic/Latino; 11 Asian, non-Hispanic/Latino; 5 Hispanic/Latino; 2 Two or more races, non-Hispanic/Latino, 19 international. Average age 34. 67 applicants, 96% accepted, 41 enrolled. In 2010, 25 master's, 2 other advanced degrees awarded. *Degree requirements:* For master's, thesis or alternative. *Entrance requirements:* For master's, minimum GPA of 2.75; for other advanced degree, bachelor's degree. Additional exam requirements/recommendations for international students: Required—TOEFL (minimum score 550 paper-based; 213 computer-based; 79 iBT), IELTS (minimum score 6.5). *Application deadline:* For fall admission, 7/1 priority date for domestic students, 5/1 priority date for international students; for spring admission, 11/1 priority date for domestic students, 9/1 priority date for international students. Applications are processed on a rolling basis. Application fee: $20. Electronic applications accepted. *Expenses:* Tuition, state resident: full-time $3690; part-time $205 per semester hour. Tuition, nonresident: full-time $13,428; part-time $746 per semester hour. Required fees: $598 per semester. *Financial support:* In 2010–11, 12 students received support, including 13 research assistantships with tuition reimbursements available (averaging $1,500 per year); career-related internships or fieldwork, scholarships/grants, and unspecified assistantships also available. Support available to part-time students. Financial award application deadline: 5/1; financial award applicants required to submit FAFSA. *Faculty research:* IT ethics, user interface design, IT security, IT integration, IT management, health information technology. *Unit head:* Dr. Ju Au Wang, Chair, 678-915-3718, Fax: 678-915-5511, E-mail: jwang@spsu.edu. *Application contact:* Nikki Palamiotis, Director of Graduate Studies, 678-915-4276, Fax: 678-915-7292, E-mail: npalamio@spsu.edu.

State University of New York Institute of Technology, School of Arts and Sciences, Program in Information Design and Technology, Utica, NY 13504-3050. Offers MS. Part-time and evening/weekend programs available. *Degree requirements:* For master's, thesis or project. *Entrance requirements:* For master's, minimum GPA of 3.0; 2 letters of recommendation; portfolio; bachelor's degree in communication, rhetoric, journalism, English, or computer science, or 15 hours of communication. Additional exam requirements/recommendations for international students: Required—TOEFL (minimum score 550 paper-based; 213 computer-based). *Faculty research:* Textual-visualization, ethics and technology, behavioral information security.

State University of New York Institute of Technology, School of Information Systems and Engineering Technology, Program in Computer and Information Science, Utica, NY 13504-3050. Offers MS. Part-time and evening/weekend programs available. *Degree requirements:* For master's, thesis or project. *Entrance requirements:* For master's, GRE General Test, minimum GPA of 3.0, letter of recommendation. Additional exam requirements/recommendations for international students: Required—TOEFL (minimum score 550 paper-based; 213 computer-based). *Faculty research:* Cryptography, distributed systems, computer-aided system theory, reasoning with uncertainty, grid computing.

Stevens Institute of Technology, Graduate School, Wesley J. Howe School of Technology Management, Program in Information Systems, Hoboken, NJ 07030. Offers computer science (MS); e-commerce (MS); enterprise systems (MS); entrepreneurial information technology (MS); information architecture (MS); information management (MS, Certificate); information security (MS); information technology in financial services industry (MS); information technology in the pharmaceutical industry (MS); information technology outsourcing management (MS); project management (MS, Certificate); software engineering (MS); telecommunications (MS).

Degree requirements: For master's, thesis optional. *Entrance requirements:* For master's, GMAT, GRE General Test. Additional exam requirements/recommendations for international students: Required—TOEFL. Electronic applications accepted.

Strayer University, Graduate Studies, Washington, DC 20005-2603. Offers accounting (MS); acquisition (MBA); business administration (MBA); communications technology (MS); educational management (M Ed); finance (MBA); health services administration (MHSA); hospitality and tourism management (MBA); human resource management (MBA); information systems (MS), including computer security management, decision support system management, enterprise resource management, network management, software engineering management, systems development management; management (MBA); management information systems (MS); marketing (MBA); professional accounting (MS), including accounting information systems, controllership, taxation; public administration (MPA); supply chain management (MBA); technology in education (M Ed). Programs also offered at campus locations in Birmingham, AL; Chamblee, GA; Cobb County, GA; Morrow, GA; White Marsh, MD; Charleston, SC; Columbia, SC; Greensboro, NC; Greenville, SC; Lexington, KY; Louisville, KY; Nashville, TN; North Raleigh, NC; Washington, DC. Part-time and evening/weekend programs available. Postbaccalaureate distance learning degree programs offered (minimal on-campus study). *Degree requirements:* For master's, thesis. *Entrance requirements:* For master's, GMAT, GRE General Test, bachelor's degree from an accredited college or university, minimum undergraduate GPA of 2.75. Electronic applications accepted.

Syracuse University, L. C. Smith College of Engineering and Computer Science, Program in Computer and Information Science and Engineering, Syracuse, NY 13244. Offers PhD. *Students:* 21 full-time (4 women), 11 part-time (2 women); includes 2 minority (both Asian, non-Hispanic/Latino), 16 international. Average age 33. 67 applicants, 15% accepted, 7 enrolled. In 2010, 2 doctorates awarded. *Degree requirements:* For doctorate, thesis/dissertation. *Entrance requirements:* For doctorate, GRE General Test, GRE Subject Test (computer science). Additional exam requirements/recommendations for international students: Required—TOEFL (minimum score 100 iBT). *Application deadline:* For fall admission, 7/1 priority date for domestic students, 6/1 priority date for international students. Applications are processed on a rolling basis. Application fee: $75. Electronic applications accepted. *Expenses:* Tuition: Part-time $1162 per credit. *Financial support:* Fellowships with full tuition reimbursements, research assistantships with full and partial tuition reimbursements, teaching assistantships with full and partial tuition reimbursements, tuition waivers (partial) available. *Unit head:* Dr. Chilukuri Mohan, Department Chair, 315-443-2322, Fax: 315-443-2583, E-mail: ckmohan@syr.edu. *Application contact:* Barbara Decker, Information Contact, 315-443-2368, Fax: 315-443-2583, E-mail: badecker@syr.edu.

Syracuse University, School of Information Studies, Program in Information Innovation, Syracuse, NY 13244. Offers CAS. Part-time and evening/weekend programs available. Postbaccalaureate distance learning degree programs offered. *Entrance requirements:* Additional exam requirements/recommendations for international students: Required—TOEFL (minimum score 100 iBT). *Application deadline:* For fall admission, 2/1 priority date for domestic students, 1/1 priority date for international students. Applications are processed on a rolling basis. Application fee: $75. Electronic applications accepted. *Expenses:* Tuition: Part-time $1162 per credit. *Unit head:* Elizabeth Liddy, Dean, 315-443-2736. *Application contact:* Susan Corieri, Director of Enrollment Management, 315-443-2575, E-mail: ischool@syr.edu.

Syracuse University, School of Information Studies, Program in Information Science and Technology, Syracuse, NY 13244. Offers PhD. *Students:* 43 full-time (22 women), 10 part-time (3 women); includes 9 minority (5 Black or African American, non-Hispanic/Latino; 3 Asian, non-Hispanic/Latino; 1 Hispanic/Latino), 23 international. Average age 36. 49 applicants, 16% accepted, 8 enrolled. In 2010, 3 doctorates awarded. *Degree requirements:* For doctorate, thesis/dissertation. *Entrance requirements:* For doctorate, GRE General Test (recommended), interview. Additional exam requirements/recommendations for international students: Required—TOEFL (minimum score 100 iBT). *Application deadline:* For fall admission, 1/8 priority date for domestic and international students. Application fee: $75. Electronic applications accepted. *Expenses:* Tuition: Part-time $1162 per credit. *Financial support:* Fellowships with full tuition reimbursements, research assistantships with partial tuition reimbursements, teaching assistantships with partial tuition reimbursements available. Financial award application deadline: 1/1; financial award applicants required to submit FAFSA. *Unit head:* Ping Zang, Director, 315-443-5617, Fax: 315-443-6886, E-mail: pzhang@syr.edu. *Application contact:* Susan Corieri, Director of Enrollment Management, 315-443-2575, E-mail: ischool@syr.edu.

Temple University, College of Science and Technology, Department of Computer and Information Sciences, Philadelphia, PA 19122-6096. Offers MS, PhD. Part-time and evening/weekend programs available. *Faculty:* 19 full-time (1 woman). *Students:* 48 full-time (11 women), 17 part-time (4 women); includes 3 Black or African American, non-Hispanic/Latino; 5 Asian, non-Hispanic/Latino, 48 international. 82 applicants, 70% accepted, 21 enrolled. In 2010, 5 master's, 1 doctorate awarded. Terminal master's awarded for partial completion of doctoral program. *Degree requirements:* For doctorate, thesis/dissertation. *Entrance requirements:* For master's and doctorate, GRE General Test, minimum GPA of 3.0. Additional exam requirements/recommendations for international students: Required—TOEFL (minimum score 550 paper-based; 213 computer-based; 79 iBT). *Application deadline:* For fall admission, 2/1 for domestic students, 12/15 for international students; for spring admission, 8/1 for domestic and international students. Applications are processed on a rolling basis. Application fee: $50. Electronic applications accepted. *Financial support:* Fellowships, research assistantships with tuition reimbursements, teaching assistantships with tuition reimbursements, career-related internships or fieldwork, institutionally sponsored loans, and unspecified assistantships available. Financial award application deadline: 1/15; financial award applicants required to submit FAFSA. *Faculty research:* Artificial intelligence, information systems, software engineering, network-distributed systems. *Unit head:* Dr. Jie Wu, Chair, 215-204-8450, Fax: 215-204-5082, E-mail: cis@temple.edu. *Application contact:* Dr. Jie Wu, Chair, 215-204-8450, Fax: 215-204-5082, E-mail: cis@temple.edu.

Towson University, Master's Program in Applied Information Technology, Towson, MD 21252-0001. Offers applied information technology (MS, PhD); database management systems (Postbaccalaureate Certificate); information security and assurance (Postbaccalaureate Certificate); information systems management (Graduate Certificate); Internet applications development (Postbaccalaureate Certificate); networking technologies (Postbaccalaureate Certificate); software engineering (Postbaccalaureate Certificate). *Students:* 111 full-time (25 women), 232 part-time (62 women); includes 122 minority (75 Black or African American, non-Hispanic/Latino; 4 American Indian or Alaska Native, non-Hispanic/Latino; 31 Asian, non-Hispanic/Latino; 11 Hispanic/Latino; 1 Native Hawaiian or other Pacific Islander, non-Hispanic/Latino), 85 international. In 2010, 75 master's, 9 doctorates, 74 other advanced degrees awarded. *Expenses:* Tuition, state resident: part-time $324 per credit. Tuition, nonresident: part-time $681 per credit. Required fees: $95 per term. *Unit head:* Mike O'Leary, Graduate Program Director, 410-704-4757, E-mail: moleary@towson.edu. *Application contact:* Mike O'Leary, Graduate Program Director, 410-704-4757, E-mail: moleary@towson.edu.

Trevecca Nazarene University, Graduate Division, School of Education, Major in Library and Information Science, Nashville, TN 37210-2877. Offers MLI Sc. Evening/weekend programs available. *Students:* 28 full-time (26 women), 2 part-time (both women); includes 1 Black or African American, non-Hispanic/Latino. Average age 35. In 2010, 27 master's awarded. *Degree requirements:* For master's, exit assessment. *Entrance requirements:* For master's, GRE General Test, MAT, technology pre-assessment, minimum GPA of 2.7, 2 reference forms. Additional exam requirements/recommendations for international students: Required—TOEFL (minimum score 550 paper-based; 213 computer-based). *Application deadline:* Applications are processed on a rolling basis. Application fee: $25. *Expenses:* Contact institution. *Financial support:* Applicants required to submit FAFSA. *Unit head:* Dr. Esther Swink, Dean, School of Education/Director of Graduate Education Program, 615-248-1201, Fax: 615-248-1597, E-mail: admissions_ged@trevecca.edu. *Application contact:* Admissions Office, 615-248-1201, Fax: 615-248-1597, E-mail: admissions_ged@trevecca.edu.

Université de Sherbrooke, Faculty of Sciences, Department of Informatics, Sherbrooke, QC J1K 2R1, Canada. Offers M Sc, PhD. *Degree requirements:* For master's, thesis. Electronic applications accepted.

University at Albany, State University of New York, College of Computing and Information, Albany, NY 12222-0001. Offers computer science (MS, PhD); information science (PhD); information studies (MS, CAS), including information science. *Accreditation:* ALA (one or more programs are accredited). Part-time programs available. *Degree requirements:* For doctorate, thesis/dissertation. *Entrance requirements:* For doctorate, GRE General Test. Additional exam requirements/recommendations for international students: Required—TOEFL (minimum score 550 paper-based; 213 computer-based). Electronic applications accepted. *Faculty research:* Human-computer interaction, government information management, library information science, web development, social implications of technology.

The University of Alabama at Birmingham, College of Arts and Sciences, Program in Computer and Information Sciences, Birmingham, AL 35294. Offers MS, PhD. *Students:* 37 full-time (11 women), 11 part-time (2 women); includes 3 minority (2 Asian, non-Hispanic/Latino; 1 Hispanic/Latino), 28 international. Average age 28. 45 applicants, 60% accepted, 12 enrolled. In 2010, 16 master's, 5 doctorates awarded. Terminal master's awarded for partial completion of doctoral program. *Degree requirements:* For master's, thesis optional; for doctorate, thesis/dissertation. *Entrance requirements:* For master's and doctorate, GRE General Test. Additional exam requirements/recommendations for international students: Required—TOEFL. *Application deadline:* Applications are processed on a rolling basis. Electronic applications accepted. *Expenses:* Tuition, state resident: full-time $5482. Tuition, nonresident: full-time $12,430. Tuition and fees vary according to program. *Financial support:* In 2010–11, 30 students received support, including 7 fellowships with full tuition reimbursements available (averaging $16,450 per year), 2 research assistantships with full tuition reimbursements available (averaging $16,000 per year), 9 teaching assistantships with full tuition reimbursements available (averaging $14,500 per year); career-related internships or fieldwork, Federal Work-Study, institutionally sponsored loans, scholarships/grants, traineeships, health care benefits, and unspecified assistantships also available. Support available to part-time students. Financial award application deadline: 3/10. *Faculty research:* Theory and software systems, intelligent systems, systems architecture, high performance computing, computer architecture, computer graphics, data mining, software engineering. *Unit head:* Dr. Anthony Skjellum, Chair, 205-934-2213, Fax: 205-934-5473, E-mail: skjellum@uab.edu. *Application contact:* Dr. John Johnstone, Graduate Program Director/Associate Professor, 205-975-5633, Fax: 205-934-5473, E-mail: jkj@uab.edu.

University of Arkansas at Little Rock, Graduate School, George W. Donughey College of Engineering and Information Technology, Program in Information Quality, Little Rock, AR 72204-1099. Offers MS.

University of Baltimore, Graduate School, The Yale Gordon College of Liberal Arts, School of Information Arts and Technologies, Baltimore, MD 21201-5779. Offers communications design (DCD); human-computer interaction (MS); interaction design and information technology (MS). Part-time and evening/weekend programs available. *Entrance requirements:* For master's, GRE or MAT, minimum undergraduate GPA of 3.0. Additional exam requirements/recommendations for international students: Required—TOEFL (minimum score 550 paper-based; 213 computer-based).

University of California, Irvine, Donald Bren School of Information and Computer Sciences, Department of Informatics, Irvine, CA 92697. Offers information and computer science (MS, PhD). *Students:* 126 full-time (35 women), 12 part-time (2 women); includes 22 minority (1 Black or African American, non-Hispanic/Latino; 17 Asian, non-Hispanic/Latino; 4 Hispanic/Latino), 64 international. Average age 28. 227 applicants, 36% accepted, 30 enrolled. In 2010, 23 master's, 22 doctorates awarded. Application fee: $80 ($100 for international students). *Unit head:* Adriaan Van der Hoek, Chair, 949-824-6326, Fax: 949-824-4056, E-mail: andre@uci.edu. *Application contact:* Kris Bolcer, Assistant Director, Graduate Affairs, 949-824-5156, Fax: 949-824-4163, E-mail: kbolcer@uci.edu.

University of Central Missouri, The Graduate School, College of Education, Warrensburg, MO 64093. Offers career and technical education administration (MS); career and technical education industry training (MS); career and technical education leadership/teaching (MS); college student personnel administration (MS); counseling (MS); curriculum and instruction (Ed S); educational leadership (Ed D); educational technology (MS); elementary education/educational foundations and literacy (MSE); elementary school administration (MSE); elementary school principalship (Ed S); human services/learning resources (Ed S); human services/professional counseling (Ed S); human services/special education (Ed S); human services/technology and occupational education (Ed S); K-12 education/educational foundations and literacy (MSE); K-12 special education (MSE); library science and information services (MS); literacy education (MSE); secondary education/educational foundations & literacy (MSE); secondary school administration (MSE); secondary school principalship (Ed S); superintendency (Ed S); teaching (MAT). Ed D offered jointly with University of Missouri. Part-time programs available. Postbaccalaureate distance learning degree programs offered. *Entrance requirements:* Additional exam requirements/recommendations for international students: Required—TOEFL (minimum score 550 paper-based; 79 computer-based). Electronic applications accepted.

University of Colorado at Colorado Springs, College of Engineering and Applied Science, Department of Mechanical and Aerospace Engineering, Colorado Springs, CO 80933-7150. Offers engineering management (ME); information operations (ME); manufacturing (ME); mechanical engineering (MS); software engineering (ME); space operations (ME); space systems (MS). Part-time and evening/weekend programs available. *Faculty:* 10 full-time (2 women). *Students:* 56 full-time (11 women), 26 part-time (6 women); includes 3 Black or African American, non-Hispanic/Latino; 4 Asian, non-Hispanic/Latino; 3 Hispanic/Latino, 1 international. Average age 32. 33 applicants, 76% accepted, 19 enrolled. In 2010, 26 master's awarded. *Degree requirements:* For master's, thesis optional. *Entrance requirements:* For master's, GRE General Test, bachelor's degree in engineering or related degree, minimum GPA of 3.0. Additional exam requirements/recommendations for international students: Required—TOEFL. *Application deadline:* For fall admission, 5/1 for domestic students; for spring admission, 10/1 for domestic students. Applications are processed on a rolling basis. Application fee: $60 ($75 for international students). *Expenses:* Tuition, state resident: full-time $7916. Tuition, nonresident: full-time $16,610. Tuition and fees vary according to course load, degree level, program, reciprocity agreements and student level. *Financial support:* Federal Work-Study and scholarships/grants available. Support available to part-time students. Financial award application deadline: 3/1; financial award applicants required to submit FAFSA. *Faculty research:* Neural networks, artificial intelligence, robust control, space operations, space propulsion. Total annual research expenditures: $69,367. *Unit head:* Dr. James Stevens, Chair, 719-255-3581, Fax: 719-255-3042, E-mail: jstevens@uccs.edu. *Application contact:* Siew Nylund, Academic Adviser, 719-255-3243, Fax: 719-255-3589, E-mail: snylund@eas.uccs.edu.

University of Colorado Denver, College of Engineering and Applied Science, Department of Computer Science and Engineering, Denver, CO 80217. Offers computer science (MS); computer science and information systems (PhD). Part-time and evening/weekend programs available. *Faculty:* 8 full-time (2 women), 1 part-time/adjunct (0 women). *Students:* 61 full-time (31 women), 21 part-time (3 women); includes 1 Black or African American, non-Hispanic/Latino; 7 Asian, non-Hispanic/Latino; 1 Hispanic/Latino, 44 international. Average age 31. 93 applicants, 38% accepted, 19 enrolled. In 2010, 22 master's, 1 doctorate awarded. *Degree requirements:* For master's, thesis or alternative, at least 30 semester hours of computer science courses while maintaining minimum GPA of 3.0; for doctorate, comprehensive exam, thesis/dissertation. *Entrance requirements:* For master's, GRE, minimum GPA of 3.0, 10

Information Science

University of Colorado Denver (continued)
semester hours of university-level calculus, at least one math course beyond calculus; for doctorate, GRE or GMAT. Additional exam requirements/recommendations for international students: Required—TOEFL (minimum score 500 paper-based; 172 computer-based). *Application deadline:* For fall admission, 4/1 for domestic students; for spring admission, 10/1 for domestic students. Applications are processed on a rolling basis. Application fee: $50 ($75 for international students). Electronic applications accepted. *Expenses:* Tuition, state resident: full-time $7332; part-time $355 per credit hour. Tuition, nonresident: full-time $18,990; part-time $1055 per credit hour. Required fees: $998. Tuition and fees vary according to course level, course load, degree level, campus/location, program, reciprocity agreements and student level. *Financial support:* Research assistantships, teaching assistantships, career-related internships or fieldwork and Federal Work-Study available. Financial award application deadline: 4/1; financial award applicants required to submit FAFSA. *Faculty research:* Algorithms, automata theory, artificial intelligence, communication networks, combinatorial geometry, computational geometry, computer architectures, computer graphics, distributed computing, high performance computing, graph theory, Internet, operating systems, parallel processing, simulation and software engineering. *Unit head:* Bogdan Chlebus, Chair, 303-556-8537, Fax: 303-556-8369, E-mail: bogdan.chlebus@ucdenver.edu. *Application contact:* Frances Moore, Program Assistant, 303-556-4083, Fax: 303-556-8369, E-mail: frances.moore@ucdenver.edu.

University of Delaware, College of Engineering, Department of Computer and Information Sciences, Newark, DE 19716. Offers MS, PhD. Part-time programs available. Terminal master's awarded for partial completion of doctoral program. *Degree requirements:* For master's, thesis optional; for doctorate, comprehensive exam, thesis/dissertation. *Entrance requirements:* For master's and doctorate, GRE General Test. Additional exam requirements/recommendations for international students: Required—TOEFL (minimum score 550 paper-based; 213 computer-based). Electronic applications accepted. *Faculty research:* Artificial intelligence, computational theory, graphics and computer vision, networks, systems.

University of Detroit Mercy, College of Business Administration, Program in Information Assurance, Detroit, MI 48221. Offers MS.

University of Florida, Graduate School, College of Engineering and College of Liberal Arts and Sciences, Department of Computer and Information Science and Engineering, Gainesville, FL 32611. Offers computer engineering (ME, MS, PhD); computer science (MS); digital arts and sciences (MS). Part-time programs available. Postbaccalaureate distance learning degree programs offered (minimal on-campus study). *Faculty:* 32 full-time (4 women), 2 part-time/adjunct (0 women). *Students:* 439 full-time (104 women), 81 part-time (19 women); includes 4 Black or African American, non-Hispanic/Latino; 11 Asian, non-Hispanic/Latino; 7 Hispanic/Latino, 445 international. Average age 24. 816 applicants, 60% accepted, 224 enrolled. In 2010, 156 master's, 25 doctorates awarded. Terminal master's awarded for partial completion of doctoral program. *Degree requirements:* For master's, comprehensive exam, thesis optional; for doctorate, comprehensive exam, thesis/dissertation. *Entrance requirements:* For master's and doctorate, GRE General Test, minimum GPA of 3.0. Additional exam requirements/recommendations for international students: Required—TOEFL (minimum score 550 paper-based; 213 computer-based; 80 iBT), IELTS (minimum score 6). *Application deadline:* For fall admission, 6/1 priority date for domestic students, 2/1 for international students; for spring admission, 9/1 for domestic and international students. Applications are processed on a rolling basis. Application fee: $30. Electronic applications accepted. *Expenses:* Tuition, state resident: full-time $10,915.92. Tuition, nonresident: full-time $28,309. *Financial support:* In 2010–11, 164 students received support, including 5 fellowships, 90 research assistantships (averaging $15,999 per year), 69 teaching assistantships (averaging $10,640 per year); unspecified assistantships also available. Financial award application deadline: 2/1; financial award applicants required to submit FAFSA. *Faculty research:* Computer systems, database, computer networks, graphics and vision, algorithm and parallel processing. Total annual research expenditures: $5.7 million. *Unit head:* Dr. Sartaj Sahni, Chair, 352-392-1527, Fax: 352-392-1220, E-mail: sahni@cise.ufl.edu. *Application contact:* Dr. Jih-Kwon Peir, Graduate Coordinator, 352-450-3446, Fax: 352-392-1220, E-mail: peir@cise.ufl.edu.

University of Hawaii at Manoa, Graduate Division, Interdisciplinary Program in Communication and Information Sciences, Honolulu, HI 96822. Offers PhD. Part-time programs available. *Faculty:* 52 full-time (16 women). *Students:* 20 full-time (12 women), 12 part-time (8 women); includes 11 minority (7 Asian, non-Hispanic/Latino; 1 Hispanic/Latino; 2 Native Hawaiian or other Pacific Islander, non-Hispanic/Latino; 1 Two or more races, non-Hispanic/Latino), 9 international. Average age 40. 14 applicants, 29% accepted, 2 enrolled. In 2010, 4 doctorates awarded. *Degree requirements:* For doctorate, comprehensive exam, thesis/dissertation. *Entrance requirements:* For doctorate, GRE or GMAT. Additional exam requirements/recommendations for international students: Required—TOEFL (minimum score 600 paper-based; 250 computer-based; 100 iBT), IELTS (minimum score 7). *Application deadline:* For fall admission, 3/1 for domestic students, 1/15 for international students. Application fee: $60. *Financial support:* In 2010–11, 3 fellowships (averaging $5,417 per year), 4 research assistantships (averaging $18,246 per year), 6 teaching assistantships (averaging $15,980 per year) were awarded. *Application contact:* Richard Gazan, Graduate Chair, 808-956-5813, Fax: 808-956-5396, E-mail: gazan@hawaii.edu.

University of Hawaii at Manoa, Graduate Division, Shidler College of Business, Program in Business Administration, Honolulu, HI 96822. Offers Asian business studies (MBA); Chinese business studies (MBA); decision sciences (MBA); entrepreneurship (MBA); finance (MBA); finance and banking (MBA); human resources management (MBA); information management (MBA); information technology (MBA); international business (MBA); Japanese business studies (MBA); marketing (MBA); organizational behavior (MBA); organizational management (MBA); real estate (MBA); student-designed track (MBA). *Accreditation:* AACSB. Part-time and evening/weekend programs available. *Faculty:* 53 full-time (12 women). *Students:* 162 full-time (63 women), 102 part-time (43 women); includes 135 minority (1 Black or African American, non-Hispanic/Latino; 81 Asian, non-Hispanic/Latino; 5 Hispanic/Latino; 18 Native Hawaiian or other Pacific Islander, non-Hispanic/Latino; 30 Two or more races, non-Hispanic/Latino), 44 international. Average age 34. 361 applicants, 57% accepted, 172 enrolled. In 2010, 153 master's awarded. *Degree requirements:* For master's, thesis optional. *Entrance requirements:* For master's, GMAT, minimum GPA of 3.0. Additional exam requirements/recommendations for international students: Required—TOEFL (minimum score 600 paper-based; 250 computer-based; 100 iBT), IELTS (minimum score 7). *Application deadline:* For fall admission, 5/1 for domestic students, 3/1 for international students. Application fee: $60. *Expenses:* Contact institution. *Financial support:* In 2010–11, 83 fellowships (averaging $5,547 per year), 1 research assistantship (averaging $16,824 per year) were awarded. Total annual research expenditures: $427,000. *Application contact:* Daniel Port, Graduate Chair, 808-956-5565, Fax: 808-956-6889, E-mail: daniel.port@hawaii.edu.

University of Houston, Bauer College of Business, Decision and Information Sciences Program, Houston, TX 77204. Offers PhD. Evening/weekend programs available. *Faculty:* 9 full-time (0 women), 7 part-time/adjunct (0 women). *Expenses:* Tuition, state resident: full-time $8592; part-time $358 per credit hour. Tuition, nonresident: full-time $16,032; part-time $668 per credit hour. Required fees: $2889. Tuition and fees vary according to course load and program. *Financial support:* In 2010–11, 1 teaching assistantship with partial tuition reimbursement (averaging $18,128 per year) was awarded; career-related internships or fieldwork, Federal Work-Study, institutionally sponsored loans, scholarships/grants, health care benefits, and unspecified assistantships also available. Support available to part-time students. Financial award application deadline: 2/1; financial award applicants required to submit FAFSA. *Unit head:* Dr. Everette Gardner, Chairperson, 713-743-4747, Fax: 713-743-4940, E-mail: egardner@uh.edu.

University of Houston, College of Technology, Department of Information and Logistics Technology, Houston, TX 77204. Offers information security (MS); supply chain and logistics technology (MS); technology project management (MS). Part-time programs available. *Faculty:* 6 full-time (3 women), 6 part-time/adjunct (2 women). *Students:* 80 full-time (30 women), 75 part-time (29 women); includes 35 minority (12 Black or African American, non-Hispanic/Latino; 9 Asian, non-Hispanic/Latino; 11 Hispanic/Latino; 1 Native Hawaiian or other Pacific Islander, non-Hispanic/Latino; 2 Two or more races, non-Hispanic/Latino), 73 international. Average age 31. 60 applicants, 92% accepted, 35 enrolled. In 2010, 22 master's awarded. *Degree requirements:* For master's, project or thesis (most programs). *Entrance requirements:* For master's, GMAT. Additional exam requirements/recommendations for international students: Required—TOEFL (minimum score 550 paper-based; 79 iBT). *Application deadline:* For fall admission, 7/1 for domestic students, 4/1 for international students; for spring admission, 12/1 for domestic students, 10/1 for international students. Applications are processed on a rolling basis. Application fee: $75 ($150 for international students). Electronic applications accepted. *Expenses:* Tuition, state resident: full-time $8592; part-time $358 per credit hour. Tuition, nonresident: full-time $16,032; part-time $668 per credit hour. Required fees: $2889. Tuition and fees vary according to course load and program. *Financial support:* In 2010–11, 10 research assistantships with partial tuition reimbursements (averaging $8,380 per year), 15 teaching assistantships with partial tuition reimbursements (averaging $8,078 per year) were awarded. *Unit head:* Michael Gibson, Chairperson, 713-743-5116, E-mail: mlgibson@uh.edu. *Application contact:* Tiffany Roosa, Graduate Advisor, 713-743-4100, Fax: 713-743-4151, E-mail: troosa@uh.edu.

University of Houston–Clear Lake, School of Science and Computer Engineering, Program in Computer Information Systems, Houston, TX 77058-1098. Offers MS. Part-time and evening/weekend programs available. *Entrance requirements:* For master's, GRE General Test. Additional exam requirements/recommendations for international students: Required—TOEFL (minimum score 550 paper-based; 213 computer-based).

University of Illinois at Urbana–Champaign, Graduate College, Graduate School of Library and Information Science, Champaign, IL 61820. Offers bioinformatics: library and information science (MS); library and information science (MS, PhD, CAS); library and information science: digital libraries (CAS). *Accreditation:* ALA (one or more programs are accredited). Postbaccalaureate distance learning degree programs offered. *Faculty:* 23 full-time (11 women), 10 part-time/adjunct (7 women). *Students:* 352 full-time (258 women), 367 part-time (270 women); includes 124 minority (38 Black or African American, non-Hispanic/Latino; 1 American Indian or Alaska Native, non-Hispanic/Latino; 34 Asian, non-Hispanic/Latino; 40 Hispanic/Latino; 11 Two or more races, non-Hispanic/Latino), 27 international. 737 applicants, 58% accepted, 242 enrolled. In 2010, 272 master's, 5 doctorates, 2 other advanced degrees awarded. *Entrance requirements:* For master's, GRE General Test, minimum GPA of 3.0; for doctorate, minimum GPA of 3.0; for CAS, master's degree in library and information science or related field with minimum GPA of 3.0. Additional exam requirements/recommendations for international students: Required—TOEFL (minimum score 620 paper-based; 260 computer-based; 105 iBT) or IELTS (minimum score 7). *Application deadline:* Applications are processed on a rolling basis. Application fee: $75 ($90 for international students). Electronic applications accepted. *Financial support:* In 2010–11, 37 fellowships, 37 research assistantships, 38 teaching assistantships were awarded; tuition waivers (full and partial) also available. *Unit head:* John Unsworth, Dean, 217-333-3281, Fax: 217-244-3302, E-mail: unsworth@illinois.edu. *Application contact:* Valerie Youngen, Admissions and Records Representative, 217-333-0734, Fax: 217-244-3302, E-mail: vyoungen@llinois.edu.

University of Illinois at Urbana–Champaign, Informatics Institute, Champaign, IL 61820. Offers PhD. Part-time programs available. *Degree requirements:* For doctorate, thesis/dissertation. *Entrance requirements:* Additional exam requirements/recommendations for international students: Required—TOEFL (minimum score 600 paper-based; 250 computer-based; 100 iBT); Recommended—IELTS (minimum score 6.5). Application fee: $75 ($90 for international students). *Financial support:* Fellowships, research assistantships, teaching assistantships, tuition waivers (full and partial) available. *Unit head:* John Unsworth, Director, 217-333-3281, E-mail: unsworth@illinois.edu. *Application contact:* Judy Tolliver, Coordinator for Informatics Education Programs, 217-333-2322, E-mail: tolliver@illinois.edu.

The University of Iowa, Graduate College, Program in Informatics, Iowa City, IA 52242-1316. Offers bioinformatics and computational biology (Certificate); health informatics (MS, PhD, Certificate); information science (MS, PhD, Certificate). *Degree requirements:* For master's, thesis optional; for doctorate, comprehensive exam, thesis/dissertation. *Entrance requirements:* For master's and doctorate, GRE General Test, minimum GPA of 3.0. Additional exam requirements/recommendations for international students: Required—TOEFL (minimum score 550 paper-based; 213 computer-based; 81 iBT). Electronic applications accepted.

University of Management and Technology, Program in Computer Science and Information Technology, Arlington, VA 22209. Offers computer science (MS); information technology (AC); information technology project management (MS); management information systems (MS); project management (AC); software engineering (MS). Part-time and evening/weekend programs available. Postbaccalaureate distance learning degree programs offered (no on-campus study). *Entrance requirements:* For master's, 3 recommendations, resume. Additional exam requirements/recommendations for international students: Required—TOEFL (minimum score 550 paper-based; 213 computer-based). Electronic applications accepted.

University of Maryland, Baltimore County, Graduate School, College of Engineering and Information Technology, Department of Information Systems, Program in Information Systems, Baltimore, MD 21250. Offers MS, PhD. Part-time programs available. Postbaccalaureate distance learning degree programs offered (no on-campus study). *Students:* 91 full-time (39 women), 274 part-time (87 women); includes 101 minority (51 Black or African American, non-Hispanic/Latino; 42 Asian, non-Hispanic/Latino; 7 Hispanic/Latino; 1 Two or more races, non-Hispanic/Latino), 78 international. Average age 30. 253 applicants, 72% accepted, 79 enrolled. In 2010, 98 master's, 8 doctorates awarded. *Degree requirements:* For master's, comprehensive exam (for some programs), thesis optional; for doctorate, comprehensive exam, thesis/dissertation. *Entrance requirements:* For master's, minimum GPA of 3.0; for doctorate, GRE General Test or GMAT, minimum GPA of 3.0, competence in statistical analysis and experimental design (recommended). Additional exam requirements/recommendations for international students: Required—TOEFL (minimum score 550 paper-based; 213 computer-based; 80 iBT). *Application deadline:* For fall admission, 6/1 for domestic students, 1/1 for international students; for spring admission, 11/1 for domestic students, 6/1 for international students. Applications are processed on a rolling basis. Application fee: $50. Electronic applications accepted. *Financial support:* In 2010–11, 1 fellowship with full tuition reimbursement (averaging $30,000 per year), 14 research assistantships with full tuition reimbursements (averaging $19,000 per year), 15 teaching assistantships with full tuition reimbursements (averaging $17,000 per year) were awarded; career-related internships or fieldwork, Federal Work-Study, scholarships/grants, health care benefits, tuition waivers (partial), and unspecified assistantships also available. Support available to part-time students. Financial award application deadline: 6/30; financial award applicants required to submit FAFSA. *Faculty research:* Human-centered computing, artificial intelligence, database/data mining, decision-making support systems, software engineering/systems analysis and design. *Unit head:* Dr. Andrew L. Sears, Professor and Chair, 410-455-3883, Fax: 410-455-1217, E-mail: asears@umbc.edu. *Application contact:* Dr. George Karabatis, Associate Professor and Graduate Program Director, 410-455-3940, Fax: 410-455-1217, E-mail: georgek@umbc.edu.

University of Maryland University College, Graduate School of Management and Technology, Program in Accounting and Information Technology, Adelphi, MD 20783. Offers MS, Certificate. *Accreditation:* AACSB. Part-time and evening/weekend programs available. Postbaccalaureate distance learning degree programs offered (no on-campus study). *Students:* 7 full-time (4 women), 211 part-time (125 women); includes 125 minority (101 Black or African American, non-Hispanic/Latino; 15 Asian, non-Hispanic/Latino; 9 Hispanic/Latino), 3 international. Average age 35. 109 applicants, 100% accepted, 49 enrolled. In 2010, 36 master's, 6 other advanced degrees awarded. *Degree requirements:* For master's, thesis or alternative, capstone course. *Application deadline:* Applications are processed on a rolling basis. Application fee: $50.

Electronic applications accepted. *Financial support:* Federal Work-Study and scholarships/grants available. Support available to part-time students. Financial award application deadline: 6/1; financial award applicants required to submit FAFSA. *Unit head:* Dr. Kathryn Klose, Director, 240-684-2400, Fax: 240-684-2401, E-mail: kklose@umuc.edu. *Application contact:* Coordinator, Graduate Admissions, 800-888-8682, Fax: 240-684-2151, E-mail: newgrad@umuc.edu.

University of Maryland University College, Graduate School of Management and Technology, Program in Information Technology, Adelphi, MD 20783. Offers MS, Certificate. Part-time and evening/weekend programs available. Postbaccalaureate distance learning degree programs offered (no on-campus study). *Students:* 56 full-time (19 women), 2,239 part-time (715 women); includes 1,102 minority (799 Black or African American, non-Hispanic/Latino; 15 American Indian or Alaska Native, non-Hispanic/Latino; 169 Asian, non-Hispanic/Latino; 106 Hispanic/Latino; 3 Native Hawaiian or other Pacific Islander, non-Hispanic/Latino; 10 Two or more races, non-Hispanic/Latino), 60 international. Average age 43. 498 applicants, 100% accepted, 390 enrolled. In 2010, 365 master's, 103 other advanced degrees awarded. *Degree requirements:* For master's, thesis or alternative, capstone course. *Application deadline:* Applications are processed on a rolling basis. Application fee: $50. Electronic applications accepted. *Financial support:* Federal Work-Study and scholarships/grants available. Support available to part-time students. Financial award application deadline: 6/1; financial award applicants required to submit FAFSA. *Unit head:* Dr. Garth MacKenzie, Associate Chair and Program Director, ITEC Core, 240-684-2400, Fax: 240-684-2401, E-mail: gmackenzie@umuc.edu. *Application contact:* Coordinator, Graduate Admissions, 800-888-8682, Fax: 240-684-2151, E-mail: newgrad@umuc.edu.

University of Michigan, Horace H. Rackham School of Graduate Studies, School of Information, Ann Arbor, MI 48109-1285. Offers archives and records management (MSI); community informatics (MSI); health informatics (MS); human computer interaction (MSI); information (PhD); information analysis and retrieval (MSI); information economics for management (MSI); information policy (MSI); library and information science (MSI); preservation of information (MSI); school library media (MSI); social computing (MSI). *Accreditation:* ALA (one or more programs are accredited). *Entrance requirements:* For master's and doctorate, GRE General Test. Additional exam requirements/recommendations for international students: Required—TOEFL (minimum score 600 paper-based; 100 iBT). Electronic applications accepted. *Expenses:* Tuition, state resident: full-time $17,784; part-time $1116 per credit hour. Tuition, nonresident: full-time $35,944; part-time $2125 per credit hour. International tuition: $35,994 full-time. Required fees: $95 per semester. Tuition and fees vary according to course load, degree level and program.

University of Michigan–Dearborn, College of Engineering and Computer Science, Department of Computer and Information Science, Program in Computer and Information Science, Dearborn, MI 48128-1491. Offers MS. Part-time and evening/weekend programs available. Postbaccalaureate distance learning degree programs offered (minimal on-campus study). *Faculty:* 13 full-time (1 woman), 4 part-time/adjunct (0 women). *Students:* 16 full-time (9 women), 35 part-time (7 women); includes 11 minority (1 Black or African American, non-Hispanic/Latino; 9 Asian, non-Hispanic/Latino; 1 Hispanic/Latino), 11 international. Average age 33. 35 applicants, 26% accepted, 9 enrolled. In 2010, 14 master's awarded. *Degree requirements:* For master's, thesis optional. *Entrance requirements:* For master's, bachelor's degree in mathematics, computer science or engineering; minimum GPA of 3.0. Additional exam requirements/recommendations for international students: Required—TOEFL (minimum score 560 paper-based; 220 computer-based; 84 iBT). *Application deadline:* For fall admission, 6/15 priority date for domestic students, 4/1 for international students; for winter admission, 10/15 priority date for domestic students, 8/1 for international students; for spring admission, 2/15 priority date for domestic students, 12/1 for international students. Application fee: $60 ($75 for international students). *Financial support:* In 2010–11, 3 research assistantships with full and partial tuition reimbursements (averaging $11,961 per year) were awarded; career-related internships or fieldwork also available. Financial award application deadline: 4/1; financial award applicants required to submit FAFSA. *Faculty research:* Information systems, geometric modeling, networks, databases. Total annual research expenditures: $54,056. *Unit head:* Dr. William I. Grosky, Chair, 313-583-6424, Fax: 313-593-4256, E-mail: wgrosky@umich.edu. *Application contact:* Katherine R. Markotan, Intermediate Academic Records Assistant, 313-436-9145, Fax: 313-593-4256, E-mail: tabatha@umd.umich.edu.

University of Michigan–Dearborn, College of Engineering and Computer Science, Department of Industrial and Manufacturing Systems Engineering, Dearborn, MI 48128-1491. Offers engineering management (MS); industrial and systems engineering (MSE); information systems and technology (MS); information systems engineering (PhD); program and project management (MS); MBA/MSE. Part-time and evening/weekend programs available. *Faculty:* 13 full-time (0 women), 3 part-time/adjunct (0 women). *Students:* 23 full-time (8 women), 142 part-time (40 women); includes 14 Black or African American, non-Hispanic/Latino; 27 Asian, non-Hispanic/Latino; 8 Hispanic/Latino, 23 international. Average age 35. 81 applicants, 58% accepted, 47 enrolled. In 2010, 57 master's awarded. *Degree requirements:* For master's, thesis optional. *Entrance requirements:* For master's, bachelor's degree in applied mathematics, computer science, engineering, or physical science; minimum GPA of 3.0. Additional exam requirements/recommendations for international students: Required—TOEFL (minimum score 560 paper-based; 220 computer-based; 84 iBT). *Application deadline:* For fall admission, 8/1 priority date for domestic students, 4/1 for international students; for winter admission, 12/1 priority date for domestic students, 8/1 for international students; for spring admission, 4/1 for domestic students, 12/1 for international students. Applications are processed on a rolling basis. Application fee: $60. Electronic applications accepted. *Financial support:* Fellowships, research assistantships, teaching assistantships, Federal Work-Study available. Financial award application deadline: 4/1; financial award applicants required to submit FAFSA. *Faculty research:* Health care systems, data and knowledge management, human factors engineering, machine diagnostics, precision machining. *Unit head:* Dr. Armen Zakarian, Chair, 313-593-5361, Fax: 313-593-3692, E-mail: zakarian@umd.umich.edu. *Application contact:* Joey W. Woods, Graduate Program Assistant, 313-593-5361, Fax: 313-593-3692, E-mail: jwwoods@umd.umich.edu.

University of Michigan–Flint, College of Arts and Sciences, Program in Computer and Information Systems, Flint, MI 48502-1950. Offers computer science and information systems (MS). Part-time programs available. *Degree requirements:* For master's, thesis or alternative. *Entrance requirements:* For master's, minimum undergraduate GPA of 3.0. Additional exam requirements/recommendations for international students: Required—TOEFL (minimum score 560 paper-based; 220 computer-based; 84 iBT), IELTS (minimum score 6.5). *Expenses:* Contact institution.

University of Minnesota, Twin Cities Campus, Institute of Technology, Department of Computer Science and Engineering, Minneapolis, MN 55455-0213. Offers computer and information sciences (MCIS, MS, PhD). Part-time programs available. Terminal master's awarded for partial completion of doctoral program. *Degree requirements:* For doctorate, thesis/dissertation. *Entrance requirements:* For master's and doctorate, GRE General Test. *Faculty research:* Software systems, numerical analysis, theory, artificial intelligence.

University of Nebraska at Omaha, Graduate Studies, College of Information Science and Technology, Department of Information Systems and Quantitative Analysis, Omaha, NE 68182. Offers information systems and quantitative analysis (Certificate); information technology (PhD); management information systems (MS). Part-time and evening/weekend programs available. *Faculty:* 13 full-time (6 women). *Students:* 61 full-time (20 women), 87 part-time (32 women); includes 15 minority (6 Black or African American, non-Hispanic/Latino; 5 Asian, non-Hispanic/Latino; 3 Hispanic/Latino; 1 Two or more races, non-Hispanic/Latino), 75 international. Average age 37. 164 applicants, 35% accepted, 41 enrolled. In 2010, 36 master's, 5 doctorates, 21 other advanced degrees awarded. *Degree requirements:* For master's, comprehensive exam, thesis (for some programs); for doctorate, comprehensive exam, thesis/dissertation. *Entrance requirements:* For master's, GMAT or GRE General Test; for doctorate, GMAT or GRE General Test, letters of recommendation. Additional exam requirements/recommendations for international students: Required—TOEFL (minimum score 575 paper-based; 230 computer-based; 89 iBT). *Application deadline:* For fall admission, 3/15 for domestic students; for spring admission, 10/1 for domestic students. Applications are processed on a rolling basis. Application fee: $45. Electronic applications accepted. *Financial support:* In 2010–11, 80 students received support; fellowships, research assistantships with tuition reimbursements available, teaching assistantships with tuition reimbursements available, career-related internships or fieldwork, Federal Work-Study, scholarships/grants, tuition waivers (partial), and unspecified assistantships available. Financial award application deadline: 3/1; financial award applicants required to submit FAFSA. *Unit head:* Dr. Ilze Zigurs, Chairperson, 402-554-3770. *Application contact:* Carla Frakes, Information Contact, 402-554-2423.

University of Nebraska–Lincoln, Graduate College, College of Arts and Sciences and College of Engineering, Department of Computer Science and Engineering, Lincoln, NE 68588. Offers bioinformatics (MS, PhD); computer engineering (MS, PhD); computer science (MS, PhD); information technology (PhD). *Degree requirements:* For master's, thesis optional; for doctorate, comprehensive exam, thesis/dissertation. *Entrance requirements:* For master's and doctorate, GRE General Test. Additional exam requirements/recommendations for international students: Required—TOEFL (minimum score 600 paper-based; 250 computer-based). Electronic applications accepted. *Faculty research:* Software engineering, geo- and bio-informatics, scientific computation, secure communication.

University of Nevada, Las Vegas, Graduate College, Howard R. Hughes College of Engineering, School of Informatics, Las Vegas, NV 89154-4054. Offers MS, PhD. *Faculty:* 5 full-time (3 women), 1 part-time/adjunct (0 women). *Students:* 6 full-time (1 woman), 1 part-time (0 women); includes 4 minority (1 Asian, non-Hispanic/Latino; 1 Hispanic/Latino; 2 Two or more races, non-Hispanic/Latino), 1 international. Average age 31. 11 applicants, 3 enrolled. In 2010, 5 master's awarded. *Degree requirements:* For master's, project; for doctorate, comprehensive exam, thesis/dissertation. *Entrance requirements:* For master's, GRE General Test (verbal and quantitative), GMAT; for doctorate, GRE General Test (Verbal and Quantitative), GMAT. Additional exam requirements/recommendations for international students: Required—TOEFL (minimum score 550 paper-based; 213 computer-based; 80 iBT), IELTS (minimum score 7). Application fee: $60 ($95 for international students). *Expenses:* Tuition, area resident: Part-time $239.50 per credit. Tuition, state resident: part-time $239.50 per credit. Tuition, nonresident: part-time $503 per credit. Required fees: $108 per semester. Tuition and fees vary according to course load, program and reciprocity agreements. *Financial support:* In 2010–11, 3 students received support, including 1 research assistantship with partial tuition reimbursement available (averaging $10,000 per year), 2 teaching assistantships with partial tuition reimbursements available (averaging $12,000 per year); institutionally sponsored loans, scholarships/grants, health care benefits, and unspecified assistantships also available. Financial award application deadline: 3/1. *Faculty research:* Digital security, healthcare informatics, human computer interaction, ecology informatics, hospitality, gaming informatics. *Unit head:* Dr. Hal Berghel, Director/ Associate Dean, 702-895-2441, Fax: 702-895-0577, E-mail: hlb@berghel.net. *Application contact:* Graduate College Admissions Evaluator, 702-895-3320, Fax: 702-895-4180, E-mail: gradcollege@univ.edu.

University of New Haven, Graduate School, Tagliatela College of Engineering, Program in Computer and Information Science, West Haven, CT 06516-1916. Offers computer science (MS, Certificate), including advanced applications (MS), computer applications (Certificate), computer programming (Certificate), computer systems (MS), computing (Certificate), database and information systems (MS), network administration (Certificate), network systems (MS), software engineering and development (MS). Part-time and evening/weekend programs available. *Students:* 54 full-time (12 women), 25 part-time (4 women); includes 1 Black or African American, non-Hispanic/Latino; 3 Asian, non-Hispanic/Latino, 51 international. Average age 28. 204 applicants, 100% accepted, 40 enrolled. In 2010, 19 master's, 1 other advanced degree awarded. *Degree requirements:* For master's, thesis or alternative. *Entrance requirements:* Additional exam requirements/recommendations for international students: Required—TOEFL (minimum score 520 paper-based; 190 computer-based; 70 iBT); Recommended—IELTS (minimum score 5.5). *Application deadline:* For fall admission, 5/31 for international students; for winter admission, 10/15 for international students; for spring admission, 1/15 for international students. Applications are processed on a rolling basis. Application fee: $50. Electronic applications accepted. *Financial support:* Research assistantships with partial tuition reimbursements, teaching assistantships with partial tuition reimbursements, career-related internships or fieldwork, Federal Work-Study, scholarships/grants, tuition waivers, and unspecified assistantships available. Support available to part-time students. Financial award applicants required to submit FAFSA. *Unit head:* Dr. Tahany Fergany, Coordinator, 203-932-7067. *Application contact:* Eloise Gormley, Director of Graduate Admissions, 203-932-7449, Fax: 203-932-7137, E-mail: gradinfo@newhaven.edu.

The University of North Carolina at Charlotte, Graduate School, College of Computing and Informatics, Department of Information Technology, Charlotte, NC 28223-0001. Offers game design and development (Certificate); health care information (Certificate); information security/privacy (Certificate); information technology (MS, PhD, Certificate). Part-time programs available. *Faculty:* 15 full-time (3 women), 4 part-time/adjunct (0 women). *Students:* 143 full-time (42 women), 76 part-time (27 women); includes 37 minority (24 Black or African American, non-Hispanic/Latino; 1 American Indian or Alaska Native, non-Hispanic/Latino; 4 Asian, non-Hispanic/Latino; 7 Hispanic/Latino; 1 Two or more races, non-Hispanic/Latino), 93 international. Average age 29. 68 applicants, 94% accepted, 22 enrolled. In 2010, 37 master's, 19 doctorates awarded. Terminal master's awarded for partial completion of doctoral program. *Degree requirements:* For master's, thesis optional; for doctorate, comprehensive exam, thesis/dissertation. *Entrance requirements:* For master's, GRE or GMAT, minimum undergraduate GPA of 2.8 overall, 2.0 in last 2 years; for doctorate, GRE or GMAT, working knowledge of 2 high-level programming languages. Additional exam requirements/recommendations for international students: Required—TOEFL (minimum score 557 paper-based; 220 computer-based; 83 iBT). *Application deadline:* For fall admission, 7/1 for domestic students, 5/1 for international students; for spring admission, 11/1 for domestic students, 10/1 for international students. Applications are processed on a rolling basis. Application fee: $55. Electronic applications accepted. *Expenses:* Tuition, state resident: full-time $3464. Tuition, nonresident: full-time $14,297. Required fees: $2094. Tuition and fees vary according to course load. *Financial support:* In 2010–11, 24 students received support, including 2 fellowships (averaging $50,000 per year), 12 research assistantships (averaging $12,719 per year), 10 teaching assistantships (averaging $13,800 per year); career-related internships or fieldwork, institutionally sponsored loans, scholarships/grants, and unspecified assistantships also available. Support available to part-time students. Financial award application deadline: 4/1; financial award applicants required to submit FAFSA. *Faculty research:* Information security, information privacy, information assurance, cryptography, software engineering, enterprise integration, intelligent information systems, human computer interaction. Total annual research expenditures: $2.7 million. *Unit head:* Dr. Ken Chen, Program Director, 704-687-8545, Fax: 704-687-6065, E-mail: chen@uncc.edu. *Application contact:* Kathy B. Giddings, Director of Graduate Admissions, 704-687-5503, Fax: 704-687-3279, E-mail: gradadm@uncc.edu.

University of Oregon, Graduate School, College of Arts and Sciences, Department of Computer and Information Science, Eugene, OR 97403. Offers MA, MS, PhD. Part-time programs available. Terminal master's awarded for partial completion of doctoral program. *Degree requirements:* For doctorate, thesis/dissertation. *Entrance requirements:* For master's and doctorate, GRE General Test, minimum GPA of 3.0. Additional exam requirements/recommendations for international students: Required—TOEFL. *Faculty research:* Artificial intelligence, graphics, natural-language processing, expert systems, operating systems.

University of Ottawa, Faculty of Graduate and Postdoctoral Studies, Faculty of Engineering, Engineering Management Program, Ottawa, ON K1N 6N5, Canada. Offers engineering management (M Eng); information technology (Certificate); project management (Certificate).

Information Science

University of Ottawa (continued)
Degree requirements: For master's, thesis or alternative. *Entrance requirements:* For master's and Certificate, honors degree or equivalent, minimum B average. Electronic applications accepted.

University of Pennsylvania, School of Engineering and Applied Science, Department of Computer and Information Science, Philadelphia, PA 19104. Offers MCIT, MSE, PhD. Part-time programs available. *Faculty:* 49 full-time (6 women), 7 part-time/adjunct (1 woman). *Students:* 260 full-time (55 women), 59 part-time (12 women); includes 3 Black or African American, non-Hispanic/Latino; 23 Asian, non-Hispanic/Latino; 3 Hispanic/Latino, 173 international. 1,148 applicants, 28% accepted, 145 enrolled. In 2010, 70 master's, 12 doctorates awarded. Terminal master's awarded for partial completion of doctoral program. *Degree requirements:* For master's, thesis optional; for doctorate, thesis/dissertation. *Entrance requirements:* For master's and doctorate, GRE General Test. Additional exam requirements/recommendations for international students: Required—TOEFL. *Application deadline:* For fall admission, 6/1 priority date for domestic students, 5/1 priority date for international students. Applications are processed on a rolling basis. Application fee: $70. Electronic applications accepted. *Expenses:* Tuition: Full-time $25,660; part-time $4758 per course. Required fees: $2152; $270 per course. Tuition and fees vary according to course load, degree level and program. *Financial support:* Fellowships with full tuition reimbursements, research assistantships with full tuition reimbursements, teaching assistantships, institutionally sponsored loans, scholarships/grants, traineeships, health care benefits, and unspecified assistantships available. *Faculty research:* AI, computer systems graphics, information management, robotics, software systems theory. *Application contact:* Mike Felker, Graduate Coordinator, 215-898-9672, E-mail: mfelker@cis.upenn.edu.

University of Phoenix–Cincinnati Campus, College of Information Systems and Technology, West Chester, OH 45069-4875. Offers electronic business (MBA); information systems (MIS); technology management (MBA). Evening/weekend programs available. Postbaccalaureate distance learning degree programs offered. *Degree requirements:* For master's, thesis (for some programs). *Entrance requirements:* For master's, minimum undergraduate GPA of 2.5, 3 years of work experience. Additional exam requirements/recommendations for international students: Required—TOEFL (minimum score 550 paper-based; 213 computer-based; 79 iBT). Electronic applications accepted.

University of Pittsburgh, School of Information Sciences, Information Science and Technology Program, Pittsburgh, PA 15260. Offers MSIS, PhD, Certificate. Part-time and evening/weekend programs available. *Faculty:* 12 full-time (0 women), 2 part-time/adjunct (0 women). *Students:* 126 full-time (44 women), 51 part-time (13 women); includes 4 Black or African American, non-Hispanic/Latino; 7 Asian, non-Hispanic/Latino; 2 Hispanic/Latino, 105 international. 258 applicants, 79% accepted, 62 enrolled. In 2010, 55 master's, 9 doctorates awarded. *Degree requirements:* For master's, thesis optional; for doctorate, comprehensive exam, thesis/dissertation. *Entrance requirements:* For master's, GRE General Test, bachelor's degree with minimum GPA of 3.0; course work in structured programming language, statistics, mathematics; for doctorate, GRE General Test, master's degree; minimum QPA of 3.3; course work in statistics or mathematics, programming, cognitive psychology, systems analysis and design, data structures database management; for Certificate, master's degree in information science, telecommunications, or related field. Additional exam requirements/recommendations for international students: Required—TOEFL (minimum score 550 paper-based; 80 iBT). *Application deadline:* For fall admission, 7/15 priority date for domestic students, 1/15 for international students; for winter admission, 11/1 priority date for domestic students, 6/15 for international students; for spring admission, 3/15 priority date for domestic students, 12/15 for international students. Applications are processed on a rolling basis. Application fee: $50. Electronic applications accepted. *Expenses:* Contact institution. *Financial support:* Fellowships with full and partial tuition reimbursements, research assistantships with full and partial tuition reimbursements, teaching assistantships with full and partial tuition reimbursements, career-related internships or fieldwork, scholarships/grants, health care benefits, tuition waivers (full and partial), and unspecified assistantships available. Financial award application deadline: 1/15; financial award applicants required to submit FAFSA. *Faculty research:* Adaptive Web systems, systems analysis and design, geoinformatics, database and Web systems, information assurance and security. *Unit head:* Dr. Paul Munro, Program Chair, 412-624-4427, Fax: 421-624-2788, E-mail: pmunro@sis.pitt.edu. *Application contact:* Shabana Reza, Student Recruiting Coordinator, 412-624-3988, Fax: 412-624-5231, E-mail: isinq@sis.pitt.edu.

University of Puerto Rico, Mayagüez Campus, Graduate Studies, College of Engineering, Department of Electrical and Computer Engineering, Mayagüez, PR 00681-9000. Offers computer engineering (ME, MS); computing and information sciences and engineering (PhD); electrical engineering (ME, MS). Part-time programs available. *Students:* 97 full-time (23 women), 12 part-time (1 woman); includes 74 Hispanic/Latino, 35 international. 41 applicants, 54% accepted, 13 enrolled. In 2010, 19 master's, 1 doctorate awarded. *Degree requirements:* For master's, comprehensive exam, thesis; for doctorate, comprehensive exam, thesis/dissertation. *Entrance requirements:* For master's, proficiency in English and Spanish, BS in electrical or computer engineering or equivalent, minimum GPA of 3.0; for doctorate, GRE. Additional exam requirements/recommendations for international students: Required—TOEFL (minimum score 450 paper-based). *Application deadline:* For fall admission, 2/15 for domestic and international students; for spring admission, 9/15 for domestic and international students. Applications are processed on a rolling basis. Application fee: $25. *Expenses:* Tuition, state resident: full-time $1188. Tuition, nonresident: full-time $1188. International tuition: $6126 full-time. Tuition and fees vary according to course level and course load. *Financial support:* In 2010–11, 23 students received support, including fellowships (averaging $12,000 per year), 3 research assistantships (averaging $15,000 per year), 23 teaching assistantships (averaging $8,500 per year); Federal Work-Study and institutionally sponsored loans also available. *Faculty research:* Microcomputer interfacing, control systems, power systems, electronics. Total annual research expenditures: $3.8 million. *Unit head:* Dr. Erick Aponte-Diaz, Chairperson, 787-832-4040 Ext. 3821, E-mail: erick.aponte1@upr.edu. *Application contact:* Sandra Montalvo, Administrative Staff, 787-832-4040 Ext. 3094, Fax: 787-831-7564, E-mail: sandra@ece.uprm.edu.

University of Puerto Rico, Mayagüez Campus, Graduate Studies, College of Engineering, Program in Computer and Information Sciences and Engineering, Mayagüez, PR 00681-9000. Offers PhD. Part-time programs available. *Students:* 12 full-time (6 women), 4 part-time (0 women); includes 5 Hispanic/Latino, 10 international. 7 applicants, 71% accepted, 2 enrolled. In 2010, 1 doctorate awarded. *Degree requirements:* For doctorate, comprehensive exam, thesis/dissertation. *Entrance requirements:* For doctorate, GRE, BS in engineering or science; the equivalent of undergraduate courses in data structures, programming language, calculus III and linear algebra. *Application deadline:* For fall admission, 2/15 for domestic and international students; for spring admission, 9/15 for domestic and international students. Application fee: $25. *Expenses:* Tuition, state resident: full-time $1188. Tuition, nonresident: full-time $1188. International tuition: $6126 full-time. Tuition and fees vary according to course level and course load. *Financial support:* In 2010–11, fellowships (averaging $12,000 per year), research assistantships (averaging $15,000 per year), teaching assistantships (averaging $8,500 per year) were awarded. *Faculty research:* Algorithms, computer architectures. *Unit head:* Dr. Nestor Rodriguez, 787-832-4040 Ext. 5217, E-mail: nestor@ece.uprm.edu. *Application contact:* Dr. Nestor Rodriguez, 787-832-4040 Ext. 5217, E-mail: nestor@ece.uprm.edu.

University of Puerto Rico, Río Piedras, Graduate School of Information Sciences and Technologies, San Juan, PR 00931-3300. Offers administration of academic libraries (PMC); administration of public libraries (PMC); administration of special libraries (PMC); consultant in information services (PMC); documents and files administration (Post-Graduate Certificate); electronic information resources analyst (Post-Graduate Certificate); information science (MIS); librarianship and information services (MLS); school librarian (Post-Graduate Certificate); school librarian distance education mode (Post-Graduate Certificate); specialist in legal information (PMC). *Accreditation:* ALA. Part-time programs available. *Degree requirements:* For master's, comprehensive exam, thesis, portfolio. *Entrance requirements:* For master's, PAEG, GRE, interview, minimum GPA of 3.0, 3 letters of recommendation; for other advanced degree, PAEG, GRE, minimum GPA of 3.0, IST master's degree. *Faculty research:* Investigating the users needs and preferences for a specialized environmental library.

University of South Africa, College of Human Sciences, Pretoria, South Africa. Offers adult education (M Ed); African languages (MA, PhD); African politics (MA, PhD); Afrikaans (MA, PhD); ancient history (MA, PhD); ancient Near Eastern studies (MA, PhD); anthropology (MA, PhD); applied linguistics (MA); Arabic (MA, PhD); archaeology (MA); art history (MA); Biblical archaeology (MA); Biblical studies (M Th, D Th, PhD); Christian spirituality (M Th, D Th); church history (M Th, D Th); classical studies (MA, PhD); clinical psychology (MA); communication (MA, PhD); comparative education (M Ed, Ed D); consulting psychology (D Admin, D Com, PhD); curriculum studies (M Ed, Ed D); development studies (M Admin, MA, D Admin, PhD); didactics (M Ed, Ed D); education (M Tech); education management (M Ed, Ed D); educational psychology (M Ed); English (MA); environmental education (M Ed); French (MA, PhD); German (MA, PhD); Greek (MA); guidance and counseling (M Ed); health studies (MA, PhD), including health sciences education (MA), health services management (MA), medical and surgical nursing science (critical care general) (MA), midwifery and neonatal nursing science (MA), trauma and emergency care (MA); history (MA, PhD); history of education (Ed D); inclusive education (M Ed, Ed D); information and communications technology policy and regulation (MA); information science (MA, MIS, PhD); international politics (MA, PhD); Islamic studies (MA, PhD); Italian (MA, PhD); Judaica (MA, PhD); linguistics (MA, PhD); mathematical education (M Ed); mathematics education (MA); missiology (M Th, D Th); modern Hebrew (MA, PhD); musicology (MA, MMus, D Mus, PhD); natural science education (M Ed); New Testament (M Th, D Th); Old Testament (D Th); pastoral therapy (M Th, D Th); philosophy (MA); philosophy of education (M Ed, Ed D); politics (MA, PhD); Portuguese (MA, PhD); practical theology (M Th, D Th); psychology (MA, MS, PhD); psychology of education (M Ed, Ed D); public health (MA); religious studies (MA, D Th, PhD); Romance languages (MA); Russian (MA, PhD); Semitic languages (MA, PhD); social behavior studies in HIV/AIDS (MA); social science (mental health) (MA); social science in development studies (MA); social science in psychology (MA); social science in social work (MA); social science in sociology (MA); social work (MSW, DSW, PhD); socio-education (M Ed, Ed D); sociolinguistics (MA); sociology (MA, PhD); Spanish (MA, PhD); systematic theology (M Th, D Th); TESOL (teaching English to speakers of other languages) (MA); theological ethics (M Th, D Th); theory of literature (MA, PhD); urban ministries (D Th); urban ministry (M Th).

University of South Alabama, Graduate School, School of Computer and Information Sciences, Mobile, AL 36688-0002. Offers computer science (MS); information systems (MS). Part-time and evening/weekend programs available. *Faculty:* 9 full-time (0 women). *Students:* 81 full-time (23 women), 20 part-time (4 women); includes 7 minority (4 Black or African American, non-Hispanic/Latino; 2 Asian, non-Hispanic/Latino; 1 Hispanic/Latino), 68 international. 164 applicants, 71% accepted, 31 enrolled. In 2010, 20 master's awarded. *Degree requirements:* For master's, thesis optional, project. *Entrance requirements:* For master's, GRE General Test. *Application deadline:* For fall admission, 7/15 priority date for domestic students, 6/15 priority date for international students; for spring admission, 12/1 for domestic students, 11/1 priority date for international students. Applications are processed on a rolling basis. Application fee: $35. *Expenses:* Tuition, state resident: part-time $300 per credit hour. Tuition, nonresident: part-time $600 per credit hour. Required fees: $150 per semester. *Financial support:* Research assistantships, career-related internships or fieldwork and institutionally sponsored loans available. Support available to part-time students. Financial award application deadline: 4/1. *Faculty research:* Numerical analysis, artificial intelligence, simulation, medical applications, software engineering. *Unit head:* Dr. Roy Daigle, Director of Graduate Studies, 251-460-6390. *Application contact:* Dr. B. Keith Harrison, Dean of the Graduate School, 251-460-6310, Fax: 251-461-1513, E-mail: kharriso@usouthal.edu.

The University of Tennessee, Graduate School, College of Communication and Information, School of Information Sciences, Knoxville, TN 37996. Offers MS, PhD. *Accreditation:* ALA (one or more programs are accredited). Part-time programs available. Postbaccalaureate distance learning degree programs offered (no on-campus study). *Degree requirements:* For master's, thesis or alternative. *Entrance requirements:* For master's, GRE General Test, minimum GPA of 2.7. Additional exam requirements/recommendations for international students: Required—TOEFL. Electronic applications accepted. *Expenses:* Tuition, state resident: full-time $7440; part-time $414 per credit hour. Tuition, nonresident: full-time $22,478; part-time $1250 per credit hour. Required fees: $922; $43 per credit hour. Tuition and fees vary according to program.

The University of Texas at El Paso, Graduate School, College of Engineering, Department of Computer Science, El Paso, TX 79968-0001. Offers computer science (MS, PhD); information technology (MSIT). Part-time and evening/weekend programs available. *Students:* 59 (15 women); includes 2 Asian, non-Hispanic/Latino; 23 Hispanic/Latino, 30 international. Average age 34. In 2010, 17 master's, 3 doctorates awarded. *Degree requirements:* For master's, thesis optional; for doctorate, thesis/dissertation. *Entrance requirements:* For master's, GRE, minimum GPA of 3.0; for doctorate, GRE, statement of purpose, letters of reference. Additional exam requirements/recommendations for international students: Required—TOEFL; Recommended—IELTS. *Application deadline:* For fall admission, 8/1 priority date for domestic students, 3/1 for international students; for spring admission, 11/1 priority date for domestic students, 9/1 for international students. Applications are processed on a rolling basis. Application fee: $45 ($80 for international students). Electronic applications accepted. *Financial support:* In 2010–11, research assistantships with partial tuition reimbursements (averaging $21,125 per year), teaching assistantships with partial tuition reimbursements (averaging $16,900 per year) were awarded; fellowships with partial tuition reimbursements, institutionally sponsored loans, scholarships/grants, health care benefits, tuition waivers (partial), and unspecified assistantships also available. Support available to part-time students. Financial award application deadline: 3/15; financial award applicants required to submit FAFSA. *Unit head:* Dr. Eunice E. Santos, Chair, 915-747-5480 Ext. 5480, Fax: 915-747-5030, E-mail: eesantos@utep.edu. *Application contact:* Dr. Patricia D. Witherspoon, Dean of the Graduate School, 915-747-5491, Fax: 915-747-5788, E-mail: withersp@utep.edu.

The University of Texas at San Antonio, College of Business, Department of Information Systems and Technology Management, San Antonio, TX 78249-0617. Offers information technology (MSIT); management technology (MSMOT), including information assurance. *Faculty:* 10 full-time (3 women), 1 part-time/adjunct (0 women). *Students:* 23 full-time (1 woman), 71 part-time (20 women); includes 33 minority (3 Black or African American, non-Hispanic/Latino; 3 Asian, non-Hispanic/Latino; 23 Hispanic/Latino; 1 Native Hawaiian or other Pacific Islander, non-Hispanic/Latino; 3 Two or more races, non-Hispanic/Latino), 7 international. Average age 32. 51 applicants, 61% accepted, 22 enrolled. In 2010, 48 master's awarded. *Degree requirements:* For master's, comprehensive exam (for some programs), thesis (for some programs). *Entrance requirements:* For master's, GMAT, minimum GPA of 3.0. Additional exam requirements/recommendations for international students: Required—TOEFL (minimum score 500 paper-based; 173 computer-based; 61 iBT), IELTS (minimum score 5). *Application deadline:* For fall admission, 7/1 for domestic students, 4/1 for international students; for spring admission, 11/1 for domestic students, 9/1 for international students. Applications are processed on a rolling basis. Application fee: $45 ($80 for international students). Electronic applications accepted. *Expenses:* Tuition, state resident: full-time $4172; part-time $231.75 per credit hour. Tuition, nonresident: full-time $15,332; part-time $851.75 per credit hour. *Financial support:* In 2010–11, 7 students received support, including 7 research assistantships (averaging $10,400 per year), 8 teaching assistantships (averaging $7,800 per year); scholarships/grants, tuition waivers (partial), and unspecified assistantships also available. Support available to part-time students. *Faculty research:* Infrastructure assurance, digital forensics, management of technology, e-commerce, technology transfer. Total annual research expenditures: $162,886. *Unit head:* Dr. Glenn Dietrich, PhD, Chair, 210-458-5354, Fax: 210-458-6305, E-mail: gdietrich@utsa.edu. *Application contact:* Veronica Ramirez, Assistant Dean of the Graduate School, 210-458-4330, Fax: 210-458-4332, E-mail: graduatestudies@utsa.edu.

University of the Sacred Heart, Graduate Programs, Department of Business Administration, Program in Information Technology, San Juan, PR 00914-0383. Offers Certificate.

University of Washington, Graduate School, The Information School, Seattle, WA 98195. Offers information management (MSIM); information science (PhD); library and information science (MLIS). MSIS degree available within PhD program. *Accreditation:* ALA (one or more programs are accredited). Part-time and evening/weekend programs available. Postbaccalaureate distance learning degree programs offered (minimal on-campus study). *Faculty:* 36 full-time (15 women), 18 part-time/adjunct (11 women). *Students:* 275 full-time (178 women), 260 part-time (191 women); includes 12 Black or African American, non-Hispanic/Latino; 6 American Indian or Alaska Native, non-Hispanic/Latino; 51 Asian, non-Hispanic/Latino; 15 Hispanic/Latino, 67 international. Average age 32. 834 applicants, 47% accepted, 219 enrolled. In 2010, 200 master's, 1 doctorate awarded. Terminal master's awarded for partial completion of doctoral program. *Degree requirements:* For master's, comprehensive exam (for some programs), thesis optional, culminating experience project (thesis, capstone or portfolio), internship; for doctorate, comprehensive exam, thesis/dissertation. *Entrance requirements:* For master's, GRE General Test, GMAT, minimum GPA of 3.0; for doctorate, GRE General Test, minimum GPA of 3.0. Additional exam requirements/recommendations for international students: Required—TOEFL (minimum score 580 paper-based; 237 computer-based; 92 iBT), IELTS (minimum score 7), MLT (minimum score 90). *Application deadline:* For fall admission, 12/1 for domestic and international students. Application fee: $75. Electronic applications accepted. *Expenses:* Contact institution. *Financial support:* In 2010–11, 71 students received support, including 4 fellowships with full tuition reimbursements available (averaging $18,450 per year), 21 research assistantships with full and partial tuition reimbursements available (averaging $17,994 per year), 19 teaching assistantships with full and partial tuition reimbursements available (averaging $18,143 per year); career-related internships or fieldwork, Federal Work-Study, institutionally sponsored loans, scholarships/grants, health care benefits, tuition waivers (full and partial), and unspecified assistantships also available. Support available to part-time students. Financial award application deadline: 2/28; financial award applicants required to submit FAFSA. *Faculty research:* Human/computer interaction, information policy and ethics, knowledge organization, information literacy and access, information assurance and cyber security. Total annual research expenditures: $4.4 million. *Unit head:* Dr. Harry Bruce, Dean. *Application contact:* Kari Brothers, Admissions Counselor, 206-616-5541, Fax: 206-616-3152, E-mail: kari683@uw.edu.

University of Waterloo, Graduate Studies, Faculty of Engineering, Department of Management Sciences, Waterloo, ON N2L 3G1, Canada. Offers applied operations research (MA Sc, MMS, PhD); information systems (MA Sc, MMS, PhD); management of technology (MA Sc, MMS, PhD). Part-time programs available. Postbaccalaureate distance learning degree programs offered (no on-campus study). *Degree requirements:* For master's, research paper or thesis; for doctorate, comprehensive exam, thesis/dissertation. *Entrance requirements:* For master's, GMAT or GRE, honors degree, minimum B average, resume; for doctorate, GMAT or GRE, master's degree, minimum A- average, resumé. Additional exam requirements/recommendations for international students: Required—TOEFL, TWE. *Faculty research:* Operations research, manufacturing systems, scheduling, information systems.

University of Wisconsin–Parkside, School of Business and Technology, Program in Computer and Information Systems, Kenosha, WI 53141-2000. Offers MSCIS. *Entrance requirements:* For master's, GRE General Test or GMAT, 3 letters of recommendation, minimum GPA of 3.0. *Faculty research:* Distributed systems, data bases, natural language processing, event-driven systems.

University of Wisconsin–Stout, Graduate School, College of Technology, Engineering, and Management, Program in Information and Communication Technologies, Menomonie, WI 54751. Offers MS. Part-time programs available. Postbaccalaureate distance learning degree programs offered (minimal on-campus study). *Degree requirements:* For master's, thesis. *Entrance requirements:* For master's, minimum GPA of 2.75. Additional exam requirements/recommendations for international students: Required—TOEFL (minimum score 500 paper-based; 173 computer-based; 61 iBT). Electronic applications accepted.

Youngstown State University, Graduate School, College of Science, Technology, Engineering and Mathematics, Department of Computer Science and Information Systems, Youngstown, OH 44555-0001. Offers computing and information systems (MCIS). Part-time programs available. *Degree requirements:* For master's, thesis or capstone project. *Entrance requirements:* For master's, GRE or GMAT. Additional exam requirements/recommendations for international students: Required—TOEFL (minimum score 550 paper-based; 213 computer-based). *Faculty research:* Networking, computational science, graphics and visualization, database and data mining, biometrics, artificial intelligence, online learning environments.

Internet Engineering

New Jersey Institute of Technology, Office of Graduate Studies, Newark College of Engineering, Department of Electrical and Computer Engineering, Program in Internet Engineering, Newark, NJ 07102. Offers MS. Part-time and evening/weekend programs available. *Students:* 2 full-time (1 woman), 1 part-time (0 women), 2 international. Average age 33. 3 applicants, 33% accepted, 0 enrolled. In 2010, 3 master's awarded. *Degree requirements:* For master's, thesis optional. *Entrance requirements:* For master's, GRE General Test. Additional exam requirements/recommendations for international students: Required—TOEFL (minimum score 550 paper-based; 213 computer-based; 79 iBT). *Application deadline:* For fall admission, 6/5 priority date for domestic students, 4/1 for international students; for spring admission, 11/15 for domestic and international students. Applications are processed on a rolling basis. Application fee: $65. Electronic applications accepted. *Expenses:* Tuition, state resident: full-time $14,724; part-time $818 per credit. Tuition, nonresident: full-time $20,304; part-time $1128 per credit. Required fees: $2272; $209 per credit. $103 per semester. One-time fee: $312 full-time; $212 part-time. *Financial support:* Fellowships with full and partial tuition reimbursements, research assistantships with full and partial tuition reimbursements, teaching assistantships with full and partial tuition reimbursements, career-related internships or fieldwork, Federal Work-Study, institutionally sponsored loans, and unspecified assistantships available. Financial award application deadline: 3/15. *Unit head:* Dr. Leonid Tsybeskov, 973-596-6594, E-mail: leonid.tsybeskov@njit.edu. *Application contact:* Kathryn Kelly, Director of Admissions, 973-596-3300, Fax: 973-596-3461, E-mail: admissions@njit.edu.

University of Denver, University College, Denver, CO 80208. Offers arts and culture (MLS, Certificate), including art, literature, and culture, arts development and program management (Certificate), creative writing; environmental policy and management (MAS, Certificate), including energy and sustainability (Certificate), environmental assessment of nuclear power (Certificate), environmental health and safety (Certificate), environmental management, natural resource management (Certificate); geographic information systems (MAS, Certificate); global affairs (MLS, Certificate), including translation studies, world history and culture; healthcare leadership (MPH, Certificate), including healthcare policy, law, and ethics, medical and healthcare information technologies, strategic management of healthcare; information and communications technology (MCIS, Certificate), including database design and administration (Certificate), geographic information systems (MCIS), information security systems security (Certificate), information systems security (MCIS), project management (MCIS, MPS, Certificate), software design and administration (Certificate), software design and programming (MCIS), technology management, telecommunications technology (MCIS), Web design and development; leadership and organizations (MPS, Certificate), including human capital in organizations, philanthropic leadership, project management (MCIS, MPS, Certificate), strategic innovation and change; organizational and professional communication (MPS, Certificate), including alternative dispute resolution, organizational communication, organizational development and training, public relations and marketing; security management (MAS, Certificate), including emergency planning and response, information security (MAS), organizational security; strategic human resource management (MPS, Certificate), including global human resources (MPS), human resource management and development (MPS). Part-time and evening/weekend programs available. Postbaccalaureate distance learning degree programs offered (no on-campus study). *Faculty:* 7 full-time (2 women), 212 part-time/adjunct (83 women). *Students:* 52 full-time (19 women), 1,044 part-time (625 women); includes 196 minority (81 Black or African American, non-Hispanic/Latino; 7 American Indian or Alaska Native, non-Hispanic/Latino; 30 Asian, non-Hispanic/Latino; 66 Hispanic/Latino; 3 Native Hawaiian or other Pacific Islander, non-Hispanic/Latino; 9 Two or more races, non-Hispanic/Latino), 76 international. Average age 36. 488 applicants, 91% accepted, 339 enrolled. In 2010, 286 master's, 130 other advanced degrees awarded. *Entrance requirements:* Additional exam requirements/recommendations for international students: Required—TOEFL (minimum score 550 paper-based; 80 iBT). *Application deadline:* For fall admission, 6/22 priority date for domestic students, 6/10 priority date for international students; for winter admission, 9/15 priority date for domestic students, 9/6 priority date for international students; for spring admission, 2/3 priority date for domestic students, 12/15 priority date for international students. Applications are processed on a rolling basis. Application fee: $75. Electronic applications accepted. *Expenses:* Contact institution. *Financial support:* Applicants required to submit FAFSA. *Unit head:* Dr. James Davis, Dean, 303-871-2291, Fax: 303-871-4047, E-mail: jdavis@du.edu. *Application contact:* Information Contact, 303-871-3155, Fax: 303-871-4047, E-mail: ucolinfo@du.edu.

University of Georgia, Terry College of Business, Program in Internet Technology, Athens, GA 30602. Offers MIT. *Students:* 51 applicants, 61% accepted. *Application deadline:* For fall admission, 7/1 priority date for domestic students; for spring admission, 11/15 for domestic students. Application fee: $50. *Expenses:* Tuition, state resident: full-time $7200; part-time $344 per credit hour. Tuition, nonresident: full-time $21,900; part-time $944 per credit hour. Tuition and fees vary according to course load and program. *Unit head:* Director. *Application contact:* Dr. Craig A. Piercy, Graduate Coordinator, 706-542-3589, Fax: 706-543-0037, E-mail: cpiercy@terry.uga.edu.

University of San Francisco, College of Arts and Sciences, Department of Computer Science, Program in Web Science, San Francisco, CA 94117-1080. Offers MS. *Faculty:* 5 full-time (1 woman). *Students:* 15 full-time (3 women), 2 part-time (0 women); includes 2 minority (both Black or African American, non-Hispanic/Latino), 11 international. Average age 30. 20 applicants, 75% accepted, 5 enrolled. In 2010, 4 master's awarded. *Expenses:* Tuition: Full-time $20,070; part-time $1115 per credit hour. Tuition and fees vary according to course load, degree level and program. *Financial support:* In 2010–11, 7 students received support. *Unit head:* Terence Parr, Graduate Director, 415-422-6530, Fax: 415-422-5800. *Application contact:* Mark Landerghini, Graduate Adviser, 415-422-5135, E-mail: asgraduate@usfca.edu.

Wilmington University, College of Technology, New Castle, DE 19720-6491. Offers corporate training (MS); information assurance (MS); information systems technologies (MS); Internet web design (MS); management information systems (MS). Part-time and evening/weekend programs available. *Entrance requirements:* Additional exam requirements/recommendations for international students: Required—TOEFL (minimum score 500 paper-based; 173 computer-based). Electronic applications accepted. *Expenses:* Tuition: Full-time $7110; part-time $395 per credit hour. Tuition and fees vary according to campus/location.

Medical Informatics

Arizona State University, Graduate College, Department of Biomedical Informatics, Phoenix, AZ 85004. Offers MS, PhD. *Faculty:* 11 full-time (2 women). *Students:* 28 full-time (9 women), 7 part-time (0 women); includes 5 minority (1 American Indian or Alaska Native, non-Hispanic/Latino; 3 Asian, non-Hispanic/Latino; 1 Hispanic/Latino), 19 international. Average age 29. 60 applicants, 52% accepted, 10 enrolled. In 2010, 9 master's awarded. Terminal master's awarded for partial completion of doctoral program. *Degree requirements:* For master's, interactive Program of Study (iPOS) submitted before completing 50 percent of required credit hours; for doctorate, comprehensive exam, thesis/dissertation, interactive Program of Study (iPOS) submitted before completing 50 percent of required credit hours. *Entrance requirements:* For master's, GRE or MCAT, bachelor's degree with minimum GPA of 3.25 in computer science, biology, physiology, nursing, statistics, engineering, related fields, or unrelated fields with appropriate academic backgrounds; resume/curriculum vitae; statement of purpose; 3 letters of recommendation; all official transcripts; for doctorate, GRE or MCAT, bachelor's degree with minimum GPA of 3.5 in computer science, biology, physiology, nursing, statistics, engineering, related fields, or unrelated fields with appropriate academic backgrounds; resume/curriculum vitae; statement of purpose; 3 letters of recommendation; all official transcripts. Additional exam requirements/recommendations for international students: Required—TOEFL (minimum score 550 paper-based; 213 computer-based; 83 iBT), IELTS (minimum score 6.5). *Application deadline:* For fall admission, 1/15 for domestic students, 2/15 for international students. Applications are processed on a rolling basis. Application fee: $70 ($90 for international students). Electronic applications accepted. *Expenses:* Tuition, state resident: full-time $8510; part-time $608 per credit. Tuition, nonresident: full-time $16,542; part-time $919 per credit. Required fees: $339; $110 per credit. Part-time tuition and fees vary according to course load. *Financial support:* In 2010–11, 20 research assistantships with full and partial tuition reimbursements (averaging $13,356 per year) were awarded; fellowships with full and partial tuition reimbursements, teaching assistantships with full and partial tuition reimburse-

Medical Informatics

Arizona State University (continued)

ments, institutionally sponsored loans, scholarships/grants, and tuition waivers (partial) also available. Financial award application deadline: 3/1; financial award applicants required to submit FAFSA. Total annual research expenditures: $2 million. *Unit head:* Dr. Robert A. Greenes, Chair, 602-827-2548, E-mail: robert.greenes@asu.edu. *Application contact:* Graduate Admissions, 480-965-6113, Fax: 480-965-5158.

Cambridge College, School of Management, Cambridge, MA 02138-5304. Offers business negotiation and conflict resolution (M Mgt); general business (M Mgt); health care informatics (M Mgt); health care management (M Mgt); leadership in human and organizational dynamics (M Mgt); non-profit and public organization management (M Mgt); small business development (M Mgt); technology management (M Mgt). Part-time and evening/weekend programs available. *Faculty:* 6 full-time (3 women), 54 part-time/adjunct (26 women). *Students:* 222 full-time (121 women), 175 part-time (110 women); includes 127 minority (89 Black or African American, non-Hispanic/Latino; 2 American Indian or Alaska Native, non-Hispanic/Latino; 9 Asian, non-Hispanic/Latino; 25 Hispanic/Latino; 2 Two or more races, non-Hispanic/Latino), 125 international. Average age 37. In 2010, 221 master's awarded. *Degree requirements:* For master's, thesis, seminars. *Entrance requirements:* For master's, resume, 2 professional references. Additional exam requirements/recommendations for international students: Required—TOEFL (minimum score 550 paper-based; 213 computer-based; 79 iBT); Recommended—IELTS (minimum score 6). *Application deadline:* Applications are processed on a rolling basis. Application fee: $30. Electronic applications accepted. *Expenses:* Contact institution. *Financial support:* Career-related internships or fieldwork, Federal Work-Study, and scholarships/grants available. Financial award applicants required to submit FAFSA. *Faculty research:* Negotiation, mediation and conflict resolution; leadership; management of diverse organizations; case studies and simulation methodologies for management education, digital as a second language: social networking for digital immigrants, non-profit and public management. *Unit head:* Dr. Mary Ann Joseph, Acting Dean, 617-873-0227, E-mail: maryann.joseph@cambridgecollege.edu. *Application contact:* Elaine M. Lapomardo, Dean of Enrollment Management, 617-873-0274, Fax: 617-349-3561, E-mail: elaine.lapomardo@cambridgecollege.edu.

Columbia University, College of Dental Medicine and Graduate School of Arts and Sciences, Programs in Dental Specialties, New York, NY 10027. Offers advanced education in general dentistry (Certificate); biomedical informatics (MA, PhD); endodontics (Certificate); orthodontics (MS, Certificate); periodontics (MS, Certificate); prosthodontics (MS, Certificate); science education (MA). *Degree requirements:* For master's, thesis, presentation of seminar. *Entrance requirements:* For master's, GRE General Test, DDS or equivalent. *Expenses:* Contact institution. *Faculty research:* Analysis of growth/form, pulpal microcirculation, implants, microbiology of oral environment, calcified tissues.

Columbia University, College of Physicians and Surgeons, Department of Biomedical Informatics, New York, NY 10032. Offers M Phil, MA, PhD, MD/PhD. *Degree requirements:* For doctorate, thesis/dissertation. *Entrance requirements:* For master's and doctorate, GRE General Test, knowledge of computational techniques. Additional exam requirements/recommendations for international students: Required—TOEFL. Electronic applications accepted. *Faculty research:* Bioinformatics, bioimaging, clinical informatics, public health informatics.

Dalhousie University, Faculty of Computer Science, Halifax, NS B3H 1W5, Canada. Offers computational biology and bioinformatics (M Sc); computer science (PhD); computer science (project-based) (MA Sc); computer science (thesis-based) (MC Sc); electronic commerce (MEC); health informatics (MHI). *Degree requirements:* For master's, thesis (for some programs); for doctorate, thesis/dissertation. *Entrance requirements:* Additional exam requirements/recommendations for international students: Required—1 of the following 5 approved tests: TOEFL, IELTS, CANTEST, CAEL, Michigan English Language Assessment Battery. Electronic applications accepted.

Drexel University, The iSchool at Drexel, College of Information Science and Technology, Philadelphia, PA 19104-2875. Offers healthcare informatics (Certificate); information science and technology (PMC); information studies (PhD); information studies and technology (Advanced Certificate); information systems (MSIS); library and information science (MS), including archival studies, competitive intelligence and knowledge management, digital libraries, library and information services, school library media, youth services; software engineering (MSSE). *Accreditation:* ALA (one or more programs are accredited). Part-time and evening/weekend programs available. Postbaccalaureate distance learning degree programs offered (no on-campus study). *Faculty:* 33 full-time (21 women), 26 part-time/adjunct (12 women). *Students:* 278 full-time (187 women), 662 part-time (451 women); includes 123 minority (46 Black or African American, non-Hispanic/Latino; 7 American Indian or Alaska Native, non-Hispanic/Latino; 36 Asian, non-Hispanic/Latino; 34 Hispanic/Latino), 44 international. Average age 34. 674 applicants, 68% accepted, 343 enrolled. In 2010, 288 master's, 7 doctorates, 19 other advanced degrees awarded. *Degree requirements:* For doctorate, thesis/dissertation. *Entrance requirements:* For master's and doctorate, GRE General Test, TOEFL. Additional exam requirements/recommendations for international students: Required—TOEFL (minimum score 600 paper-based; 250 computer-based; 100 iBT). *Application deadline:* For fall admission, 9/1 for domestic and international students; for spring admission, 3/4 for domestic students, 2/15 for international students. Applications are processed on a rolling basis. Electronic applications accepted. *Expenses:* Contact institution. *Financial support:* In 2010–11, 250 students received support, including 264 fellowships with partial tuition reimbursements available (averaging $22,500 per year), 22 research assistantships with full tuition reimbursements available (averaging $22,500 per year), 8 teaching assistantships with full tuition reimbursements available (averaging $25,000 per year); institutionally sponsored loans, scholarships/grants, health care benefits, tuition waivers (partial), and unspecified assistantships also available. Support available to part-time students. Financial award applicants required to submit FAFSA. *Faculty research:* Information retrieval/information visualization/bibliometrics, human-computer interaction, digital libraries, databases, text/data mining. Total annual research expenditures: $2 million. *Unit head:* Dr. David E. Fenske, Dean and Isaac L. Auerbach Professor of Information Science, 215-895-2475, Fax: 215-895-6378, E-mail: fenske@drexel.edu. *Application contact:* Matthew Lechtenberg, Graduate Admissions Manager, 215-895-1951, Fax: 215-895-2303, E-mail: ml333@drexel.edu.

Excelsior College, School of Health Sciences, Albany, NY 12203-5159. Offers healthcare informatics (Certificate); hospice and palliative care (Certificate); nursing management (Certificate). Part-time and evening/weekend programs available. Postbaccalaureate distance learning degree programs offered (no on-campus study). *Entrance requirements:* For degree, bachelor's degree in applicable field. Electronic applications accepted. *Faculty research:* Use of technology in online learning.

Grand Valley State University, Padnos College of Engineering and Computing, Medical and Bioinformatics Program, Allendale, MI 49401-9403. Offers MS. Part-time and evening/weekend programs available. *Degree requirements:* For master's, thesis or alternative. *Faculty research:* Biomedical informatics, information visualization, data mining, high-performance computing, computational biology.

Harvard University, Harvard Medical School and Graduate School of Arts and Sciences, Division of Health Sciences and Technology, Program in Biomedical Informatics, Cambridge, MA 02138. Offers SM. Program offered jointly with Massachusetts Institute of Technology. *Students:* 5 full-time (1 woman); includes 1 American Indian or Alaska Native, non-Hispanic/Latino; 2 Asian, non-Hispanic/Latino; 1 Hispanic/Latino. Average age 36. 12 applicants, 25% accepted, 2 enrolled. In 2010, 5 master's awarded. *Degree requirements:* For master's, thesis. *Entrance requirements:* For master's, MD or doctoral degree in medically-relevant field. Additional exam requirements/recommendations for international students: Required—TOEFL. *Application deadline:* For fall admission, 12/15 for domestic and international students; for spring admission, 11/1 for domestic and international students. Application fee: $70. *Expenses:* Contact institution. *Financial support:* In 2010–11, 2 students received support, including 1 fellowship with full tuition reimbursement available (averaging $18,755 per year), 1 research assistantship with full tuition reimbursement available (averaging $58,498 per year); career-related internships or fieldwork, institutionally sponsored loans, traineeships, and unspecified assistantships also available. Financial award application deadline: 12/15; financial award applicants required to submit FAFSA. *Faculty research:* Bioinformatics, machine learning and predictive modeling, patents safety personal monitoring, clinical decision making, disaster response and public health. *Unit head:* Dr. Alexa McCray, Program Director, 617-432-2144, E-mail: alexa_mccray@hms.harvard.edu. *Application contact:* Traci Anderson, Academic Programs Administrator, 617-258-7470, E-mail: tanderso@mit.edu.

Marymount University, School of Business Administration, Program in Information Technology, Arlington, VA 22207-4299. Offers computer security and information assurance (Certificate); health care informatics (Certificate); information technology (MS, Certificate); information technology project management: technology leadership (Certificate). Part-time and evening/weekend programs available. *Degree requirements:* For master's, thesis or alternative. *Entrance requirements:* For master's, GMAT or GRE General Test, interview, resume, bachelor's degree in computer-related field or degree in another subject with a post-baccalaureate certificate in a computer-related field; for Certificate, resume. Additional exam requirements/recommendations for international students: Required—TOEFL (minimum score 600 paper-based; 250 computer-based; 96 iBT), IELTS (minimum score 6.5). Electronic applications accepted.

Massachusetts Institute of Technology, Harvard-MIT Division of Health Sciences and Technology, Program in Biomedical Informatics, Cambridge, MA 02139-4307. Offers SM. Program offered jointly with Harvard University. *Students:* 5 full-time (1 woman); includes 1 American Indian or Alaska Native, non-Hispanic/Latino; 2 Asian, non-Hispanic/Latino; 1 Hispanic/Latino. Average age 36. 12 applicants, 25% accepted, 2 enrolled. In 2010, 5 master's awarded. *Degree requirements:* For master's, thesis. *Entrance requirements:* For master's, MD, current enrollment in MD program, or doctoral degree in medically-relevant field. Additional exam requirements/recommendations for international students: Required—TOEFL. *Application deadline:* For fall admission, 12/15 for domestic and international students; for spring admission, 11/1 for domestic and international students. Application fee: $70. Electronic applications accepted. *Expenses:* Tuition: Full-time $38,940; part-time $605 per unit. Required fees: $272. *Financial support:* In 2010–11, 2 students received support, including 1 fellowship with full tuition reimbursement available (averaging $18,755 per year), 1 research assistantship with full tuition reimbursement available (averaging $58,498 per year); career-related internships or fieldwork, institutionally sponsored loans, traineeships, and unspecified assistantships also available. Financial award application deadline: 12/15. *Faculty research:* Bioinformatics, clinical decision-making, machine learning and predictive modeling, national safety, personal monitoring. *Unit head:* Dr. Alexa McCray, Program Director, 617-432-2144, E-mail: alexa_mccray@hms.harvard.edu. *Application contact:* Traci Anderson, Academic Programs Administrator, 617-253-7470, E-mail: tanderso@mit.edu.

Medical College of Wisconsin, Graduate School of Biomedical Sciences, Program in Medical Informatics, Milwaukee, WI 53226-0509. Offers MS. Program offered jointly with Milwaukee School of Engineering. Part-time and evening/weekend programs available. *Degree requirements:* For master's, thesis or alternative. *Entrance requirements:* For master's, GMAT or GRE General Test. Additional exam requirements/recommendations for international students: Required—TOEFL. *Expenses:* Tuition: Full-time $30,000; part-time $710 per credit. Required fees: $150. *Faculty research:* Computer science.

Middle Tennessee State University, College of Graduate Studies, College of Basic and Applied Sciences, Program in Professional Science, Murfreesboro, TN 37132. Offers biostatistics (MS); health care informatics (MS). Part-time and evening/weekend programs available. Postbaccalaureate distance learning degree programs offered. *Students:* 8 full-time (4 women), 65 part-time (44 women); includes 15 Black or African American, non-Hispanic/Latino; 17 Asian, non-Hispanic/Latino; 2 Hispanic/Latino; 1 Two or more races, non-Hispanic/Latino. Average age 28. 40 applicants, 55% accepted, 22 enrolled. In 2010, 25 master's awarded. *Degree requirements:* For master's, comprehensive exam. *Entrance requirements:* For master's, GRE. Additional exam requirements/recommendations for international students: Required—TOEFL (minimum score 525 paper-based; 195 computer-based; 71 iBT) or IELTS (minimum score 6). *Application deadline:* For fall admission, 6/1 for domestic and international students. Applications are processed on a rolling basis. Application fee: $25 ($30 for international students). *Expenses:* Tuition, state resident: full-time $4632. Tuition, nonresident: full-time $11,520. *Financial support:* In 2010–11, 7 students received support. Institutionally sponsored loans available. Support available to part-time students. Financial award application deadline: 5/1. *Unit head:* Dr. Thomas Cheatham, Dean, 615-898-5508, Fax: 615-898-2615. *Application contact:* Dr. Michael Allen, Dean and Vice Provost for Research, 615-898-2840, Fax: 615-904-8020, E-mail: mallen@mtsu.edu.

Milwaukee School of Engineering, Rader School of Business, Program in Medical Informatics, Milwaukee, WI 53202-3109. Offers MS. Part-time and evening/weekend programs available. *Faculty:* 1 full-time (0 women), 5 part-time/adjunct (1 woman). *Students:* 1 full-time (0 women), 10 part-time (7 women); includes 1 Asian, non-Hispanic/Latino. Average age 25. 8 applicants, 63% accepted, 4 enrolled. In 2010, 1 master's awarded. *Degree requirements:* For master's, thesis or alternative, capstone course, research project. *Entrance requirements:* For master's, GRE General Test or GMAT, 2 letters of recommendation. Additional exam requirements/recommendations for international students: Required—TOEFL (minimum score 79 iBT). *Application deadline:* Applications are processed on a rolling basis. Application fee: $30. Electronic applications accepted. *Expenses:* Tuition: Full-time $17,550; part-time $650 per credit. One-time fee: $75. *Financial support:* In 2010–11, 8 students received support. Career-related internships or fieldwork available. Support available to part-time students. Financial award applicants required to submit FAFSA. *Faculty research:* Information technology, databases. *Unit head:* Dr. John Traxler, Director, 414-277-2218, Fax: 414-277-7279, E-mail: traxler@msoe.edu. *Application contact:* Sarah K. Winchowky, Graduate Admissions Director, 800-321-6763, Fax: 414-277-7475, E-mail: wp@msoe.edu.

Northwestern University, School of Continuing Studies, Program in Medical Informatics, Evanston, IL 60208. Offers MS. Postbaccalaureate distance learning degree programs offered.

Nova Southeastern University, Health Professions Division, College of Osteopathic Medicine, Program in Biomedical Informatics, Fort Lauderdale, FL 33314-7796. Offers biomedical informatics (MS); clinical informatics (Graduate Certificate); public health informatics (Graduate Certificate). *Students:* 12 full-time (5 women), 55 part-time (34 women); includes 20 Black or African American, non-Hispanic/Latino; 5 Asian, non-Hispanic/Latino; 9 Hispanic/Latino, 6 international. Average age 36. In 2010, 5 master's awarded. *Unit head:* Dr. Jennie Q. Lou, Director, 954-262-1619, E-mail: jlou@nova.edu. *Application contact:* Ellen Rondino, College of Osteopathic Medicine Admissions Counselor, 866-817-4068.

Oregon Health & Science University, School of Medicine, Graduate Programs in Medicine, Department of Medical Informatics and Clinical Epidemiology, Portland, OR 97239-3098. Offers clinical informatics (MS, PhD, Certificate); computational biology (MS, PhD); health information management (Certificate). Part-time programs available. Postbaccalaureate distance learning degree programs offered (minimal on-campus study). *Faculty:* 26. *Students:* 111 (34 women); includes 3 Black or African American, non-Hispanic/Latino; 1 American Indian or Alaska Native, non-Hispanic/Latino; 8 Asian, non-Hispanic/Latino; 4 Hispanic/Latino; 4 Native Hawaiian or other Pacific Islander, non-Hispanic/Latino, 12 international. Average age 42. 46 applicants, 70% accepted, 28 enrolled. In 2010, 11 master's, 1 doctorate awarded. Terminal master's awarded for partial completion of doctoral program. *Degree requirements:* For master's, thesis; for doctorate, comprehensive exam, thesis/dissertation. *Entrance requirements:* For master's and doctorate, GRE General Test, coursework in computer programming, human anatomy and physiology. Additional exam requirements/recommendations for international students: Required—TOEFL. *Application deadline:* For fall admission, 12/1 for domestic students; for winter admission, 11/1 for domestic students; for spring admission, 2/1 for domestic students. Applications are processed on a rolling basis. Application fee: $65. Electronic applications accepted. *Expenses:* Contact institution. *Financial support:* Fellowships with full tuition reimbursements, research assistantships, Federal Work-Study, institutionally sponsored loans, scholarships/grants, and full tuition and stipends available. Financial award application deadline: 3/1; financial award applicants required to submit FAFSA. *Faculty research:* Information retrieval, telemedicine, consumer health informatics, information needs assessment, healthcare quality. *Unit head:* Andrea Ilg, 503-494-2547, E-mail: informat@ohsu.edu. *Application contact:* Diane Doctor, 503-494-2547, E-mail: informat@ohsu.edu.

Rochester Institute of Technology, Graduate Enrollment Services, B. Thomas Golisano College of Computing and Information Sciences, Department of Information Technology, Program in Medical Informatics, Rochester, NY 14623-5603. Offers MS. Part-time programs available. *Degree requirements:* For master's, thesis or alternative, capstone. *Entrance requirements:* Additional exam requirements/recommendations for international students: Required—TOEFL (minimum score 570 paper-based; 230 computer-based; 88 iBT). *Application deadline:* Applications are processed on a rolling basis. Application fee: $50. Electronic applications accepted. *Expenses:* Tuition: Full-time $33,234; part-time $924 per credit hour. Required fees: $219. *Financial support:* Applicants required to submit FAFSA. *Faculty research:* Electronic health record development, database systems, cinical systems integration, Web applications for medicine, management, public health. *Unit head:* Prof. Dianne Bills, Graduate Program Director, 585-475-2700, E-mail: informaticsgrad@rit.edu. *Application contact:* Diane Ellison, Assistant Vice President, Graduate Enrollment Services, 585-475-2229, Fax: 585-475-7164, E-mail: gradinfo@rit.edu.

Stanford University, School of Medicine, Graduate Programs in Medicine, Biomedical Informatics Program, Stanford, CA 94305-9991. Offers MS, PhD. Terminal master's awarded for partial completion of doctoral program. *Degree requirements:* For master's, thesis; for doctorate, thesis/dissertation. *Entrance requirements:* For doctorate, GRE or MCAT. Additional exam requirements/recommendations for international students: Required—TOEFL. Electronic applications accepted. *Expenses:* Tuition: Full-time $38,700; part-time $860 per unit. One-time fee: $200 full-time.

The University of Arizona, College of Nursing, Tucson, AZ 85721. Offers health care informatics (Certificate); nurse practitioner (MS, Certificate); nursing (DNP, PhD); rural health (Certificate). *Accreditation:* AACN. Part-time programs available. Postbaccalaureate distance learning degree programs offered (minimal on-campus study). *Faculty:* 19 full-time (18 women). *Students:* 119 full-time (107 women), 33 part-time (29 women); includes 44 minority (10 Black or African American, non-Hispanic/Latino; 4 American Indian or Alaska Native, non-Hispanic/Latino; 7 Asian, non-Hispanic/Latino; 16 Hispanic/Latino; 1 Native Hawaiian or other Pacific Islander, non-Hispanic/Latino; 6 Two or more races, non-Hispanic/Latino), 3 international. Average age 42. In 2010, 28 master's, 20 doctorates awarded. Terminal master's awarded for partial completion of doctoral program. *Degree requirements:* For master's, thesis optional; for doctorate, comprehensive exam, thesis/dissertation. *Entrance requirements:* For master's, BSN, eligibility for RN license; for doctorate, BSN; for Certificate, GRE General Test, Arizona RN license, BSN, minimum GPA of 3.0. Additional exam requirements/recommendations for international students: Required—TOEFL (minimum score 550 paper-based; 213 computer-based; 79 iBT). *Application deadline:* For fall admission, 1/15 for domestic and international students. Applications are processed on a rolling basis. Application fee: $75. Electronic applications accepted. *Expenses:* Contact institution. *Financial support:* In 2010–11, 9 research assistantships with full tuition reimbursements (averaging $18,220 per year), 1 teaching assistantship (averaging $18,327 per year) were awarded; career-related internships or fieldwork, institutionally sponsored loans, scholarships/grants, traineeships, health care benefits, tuition waivers (full), and unspecified assistantships also available. Financial award application deadline: 6/1. *Faculty research:* Vulnerable populations, injury mechanisms and biobehavioral responses, health care systems, informatics, rural health. Total annual research expenditures: $4.9 million. *Unit head:* Dr. Carolyn Murdaugh, Associate Dean, 520-626-7124, Fax: 520-626-6424, E-mail: cmurdaugh@nursing.arizona.edu. *Application contact:* Sally J. Reel, Assistant Dean, Student Affairs, 520-626-6767, Fax: 520-626-6424, E-mail: sreel@nursing.arizona.edu.

University of California, Davis, Graduate Studies, Graduate Group in Health Informatics, Davis, CA 95616. Offers MS. *Entrance requirements:* Additional exam requirements/recommendations for international students: Required—TOEFL (minimum score 550 paper-based; 213 computer-based).

University of California, San Francisco, School of Pharmacy and Graduate Division, Graduate Program in Biological and Medical Informatics, San Francisco, CA 94158-2517. Offers PhD. *Faculty:* 30 full-time (6 women). *Students:* 30 full-time (11 women); includes 1 Black or African American, non-Hispanic/Latino; 3 Asian, non-Hispanic/Latino; 4 Hispanic/Latino, 2 international. Average age 28. 140 applicants, 26% accepted, 8 enrolled. In 2010, 3 doctorates awarded. Terminal master's awarded for partial completion of doctoral program. *Degree requirements:* For doctorate, thesis/dissertation, cumulative qualifying exams, proposal defense. *Entrance requirements:* For doctorate, GRE General Test, minimum GPA of 3.0. Additional exam requirements/recommendations for international students: Required—TOEFL (minimum score 550 paper-based; 213 computer-based; 80 iBT). *Application deadline:* For fall admission, 12/1 for domestic and international students. Application fee: $70 ($90 for international students). *Financial support:* In 2010–11, 3 fellowships with full tuition reimbursements (averaging $28,000 per year), 26 research assistantships with full tuition reimbursements (averaging $28,000 per year) were awarded; career-related internships or fieldwork, scholarships/grants, traineeships, health care benefits, tuition waivers (full), and stipends also available. *Faculty research:* Bioinformatics, biomedical computing, decision science and engineering, imaging informatics, knowledge management/telehealth/health services research. *Unit head:* Thomas E. Ferrin, Director, 415-476-2299, Fax: 415-502-1755, E-mail: tef@cgl.ucsf.edu. *Application contact:* Julia Molla, Program Administrator, 415-514-0249, Fax: 415-514-0502, E-mail: jmolla@cgl.ucsf.edu.

University of Colorado Denver, College of Nursing, Aurora, CO 80045. Offers adult clinical nurse specialist (MS); adult nurse practitioner (MS); family nurse practitioner (MS); family psychiatric mental health nurse practitioner (MS); health care informatics (MS); nurse-midwifery (MS); nursing (DNP, PhD); nursing leadership and health care systems (MS); pediatric nurse practitioner (MS); pediatric nursing leadership (MS); special studies (MS); women's health care (MS); MS/DNP; MS/PhD. *Accreditation:* AACN; ACNM/DOA (one or more programs are accredited); NLN (one or more programs are accredited). Part-time and evening/weekend programs available. Postbaccalaureate distance learning degree programs offered (minimal on-campus study). *Faculty:* 69 full-time (65 women), 68 part-time/adjunct (64 women). *Students:* 269 full-time (248 women), 121 part-time (114 women); includes 9 Black or African American, non-Hispanic/Latino; 7 American Indian or Alaska Native, non-Hispanic/Latino; 8 Asian, non-Hispanic/Latino; 21 Hispanic/Latino; 1 Two or more races, non-Hispanic/Latino, 7 international. Average age 37. 242 applicants, 49% accepted, 108 enrolled. In 2010, 59 master's, 1 doctorate awarded. Terminal master's awarded for partial completion of doctoral program. *Degree requirements:* For master's, thesis optional; for doctorate, comprehensive exam, thesis/dissertation, 42 credits of coursework, 30 credits of dissertation. *Entrance requirements:* For master's, GRE if cumulative undergraduate GPA is less than 3.0, undergraduate nursing degree from NLNAC- or CCNE-accredited school or university; completion of research and statistics courses with grade of C or better; copy of current and unencumbered nursing license; for doctorate, GRE, bachelor's and/or master's degrees in nursing from NLN or CCNE accredited institution; portfolio; minimum undergraduate GPA of 3.0 and/or graduate GPA of 3.5; graduate-level intermediate statistics course with minimum B grade; master's-level nursing theory course with minimum B grade; interview. Additional exam requirements/recommendations for international students: Required—TOEFL (minimum score 560 paper-based; 220 computer-based; 83 iBT). *Application deadline:* For fall admission, 4/1 for domestic students; for spring admission, 9/1 for domestic students. Application fee: $65. Electronic applications accepted. *Expenses:* Contact institution. *Financial support:* In 2010–11, 40 students received support; fellowships, research assistantships, teaching assistantships, Federal Work-Study, scholarships/grants, and unspecified assistantships available. Support available to part-time students. Financial award application deadline: 3/15; financial award applicants required to submit FAFSA. *Faculty research:* Biological and behavioral phenomena in pregnancy and postpartum; patterns of glycemia during the insulin resistance of pregnancy; obesity, gestational diabetes, and relationship to neonatal adiposity; men's awareness and knowledge of male breast cancer; cognitive-behavioral therapy for chronic insomnia after breast cancer treatment; massage therapy for the treatment of tension-type headaches. Total annual research expenditures: $3.7 million. *Unit head:* Dr. Patricia Moritz, Dean, 303-724-1679, E-mail: pat.moritz@ucdenver.edu. *Application contact:* Judy Campbell, Graduate Programs Coordinator, 303-724-8503, E-mail: judy.campbell@ucdenver.edu.

University of Illinois at Urbana–Champaign, Graduate College, Graduate School of Library and Information Science, Champaign, IL 61820. Offers bioinformatics: library and information science (MS); library and information science (MS, PhD, CAS); library and information science: digital libraries (CAS). *Accreditation:* ALA (one or more programs are accredited). Postbaccalaureate distance learning degree programs offered. *Faculty:* 23 full-time (11 women), 10 part-time/adjunct (7 women). *Students:* 352 full-time (258 women), 367 part-time (270 women); includes 124 minority (38 Black or African American, non-Hispanic/Latino; 1 American Indian or Alaska Native, non-Hispanic/Latino; 34 Asian, non-Hispanic/Latino; 40 Hispanic/Latino; 11 Two or more races, non-Hispanic/Latino), 27 international. 737 applicants, 58% accepted, 242 enrolled. In 2010, 272 master's, 5 doctorates, 2 other advanced degrees awarded. *Entrance requirements:* For master's, GRE General Test, minimum GPA of 3.0; for doctorate, minimum GPA of 3.0; for CAS, master's degree in library and information science or related field with minimum GPA of 3.0. Additional exam requirements/recommendations for international students: Required—TOEFL (minimum score 620 paper-based; 260 computer-based; 105 iBT) or IELTS (minimum score 7). *Application deadline:* Applications are processed on a rolling basis. Application fee: $75 ($90 for international students). Electronic applications accepted. *Financial support:* In 2010–11, 37 fellowships, 37 research assistantships, 38 teaching assistantships were awarded; tuition waivers (full and partial) also available. *Unit head:* John Unsworth, Dean, 217-333-3281, Fax: 217-244-3302, E-mail: unsworth@illinois.edu. *Application contact:* Valerie Youngen, Admissions and Records Representative, 217-333-0734, Fax: 217-244-3302, E-mail: vyoungen@llinois.edu.

The University of Kansas, University of Kansas Medical Center, School of Nursing, Kansas City, KS 66160. Offers clinical research management (PMC); family nurse practitioner (PMC); health care informatics (PMC); health professions educator (PMC); nurse midwife (PMC); nursing (MS, DNP, PhD); organizational leadership (PMC); psychiatric/mental health nurse practitioner (PMC); public health nursing (PMC). *Accreditation:* AACN; ACNM/DOA. Part-time programs available. Postbaccalaureate distance learning degree programs offered (minimal on-campus study). *Faculty:* 77. *Students:* 54 full-time (51 women), 307 part-time (283 women); includes 49 minority (22 Black or African American, non-Hispanic/Latino; 3 American Indian or Alaska Native, non-Hispanic/Latino; 9 Asian, non-Hispanic/Latino; 11 Hispanic/Latino; 4 Two or more races, non-Hispanic/Latino), 6 international. Average age 38. 142 applicants, 45% accepted, 62 enrolled. In 2010, 78 master's, 7 doctorates, 17 other advanced degrees awarded. Terminal master's awarded for partial completion of doctoral program. *Degree requirements:* For master's, thesis optional, general oral exam; for doctorate, one foreign language, thesis/dissertation, comprehensive oral and written exam. *Entrance requirements:* For master's, bachelor's degree in nursing, minimum GPA of 3.0, RN license, 1 year of clinical experience; for doctorate, GRE General Test, master's degree in nursing, minimum GPA of 3.5. Additional exam requirements/recommendations for international students: Required—TOEFL. *Application deadline:* For fall admission, 4/1 for domestic and international students; for spring admission, 9/1 for domestic and international students. Application fee: $60. Electronic applications accepted. *Expenses:* Tuition, state resident: full-time $7092; part-time $295.50 per credit hour. Tuition, nonresident: full-time $16,590; part-time $691.25 per credit hour. Required fees: $858; $71.49 per credit hour. Tuition and fees vary according to course load, campus/location and program. *Financial support:* Research assistantships with full and partial tuition reimbursements, teaching assistantships with full and partial tuition reimbursements, traineeships available. Financial award application deadline: 2/14; financial award applicants required to submit FAFSA. *Faculty research:* Breastfeeding practices of teen mothers, national database of nursing quality indicators, caregiving of families of patients using technology in the home, self care talk intervention partnership between caregivers of stroke survivors and nurses, smoking cessation. Total annual research expenditures: $5.4 million. *Unit head:* Dr. Karen L. Miller, Dean, 913-588-1601, Fax: 913-588-1660, E-mail: kmiller@kumc.edu. *Application contact:* Dr. Rita K. Clifford, Associate Dean, Student Affairs, 913-588-1619, Fax: 913-588-1615, E-mail: rcliffor@kumc.edu.

University of Medicine and Dentistry of New Jersey, School of Health Related Professions, Department of Health Informatics, Program in Biomedical Informatics, Newark, NJ 07107-1709. Offers MS, PhD, DMD/MS, MD/MS. *Entrance requirements:* Additional exam requirements/recommendations for international students: Required—TOEFL. Electronic applications accepted.

University of Medicine and Dentistry of New Jersey, School of Health Related Professions, Department of Health Informatics, Program in Health Care Informatics, Newark, NJ 07107-1709. Offers Certificate. Part-time and evening/weekend programs available. Postbaccalaureate distance learning degree programs offered (minimal on-campus study). *Students:* 1 part-time (0 women). Average age 44. 1 applicant, 0% accepted, 0 enrolled. In 2010, 2 Certificates awarded. *Entrance requirements:* For degree, BS degree, all transcripts, 3 letters, basic proficiency in programming language. Additional exam requirements/recommendations for international students: Required—TOEFL (minimum score 500 paper-based; 79 iBT). *Application deadline:* For fall admission, 6/1 for domestic students, 3/1 for international students; for spring admission, 10/1 for domestic students, 7/1 for international students. Applications are processed on a rolling basis. Application fee: $75. Electronic applications accepted. *Unit head:* Dr. Syed Haque, Director, 973-972-6871, E-mail: haque@umdnj.edu. *Application contact:* Douglas Lomonaco, Assistant Dean, 973-972-5454, Fax: 973-972-7463, E-mail: shrpadm@umdnj.edu.

The University of Tennessee at Chattanooga, Graduate School, College of Health, Education and Professional Studies, School of Nursing, Chattanooga, TN 37403. Offers administration (MSN); certified nurse anesthetist (Post-Master's Certificate); education (MSN); family nurse practitioner (MSN, Post-Master's Certificate); health care informatics (Post-Master's Certificate); nurse anesthesia (MSN); nurse education (Post-Master's Certificate); nursing (DNP). *Accreditation:* AACN; AANA/CANAEP (one or more programs are accredited). *Faculty:* 4 full-time (all women). *Students:* 30 full-time (18 women), 49 part-time (40 women); includes 3 minority (all Black or African American, non-Hispanic/Latino). Average age 33. 15 applicants, 87% accepted, 11 enrolled. In 2010, 38 master's, 2 other advanced degrees awarded. *Degree requirements:* For master's, thesis optional, qualifying exams, professional project; for Post-Master's Certificate, thesis or alternative, practicum, seminar. *Entrance requirements:* For master's, GRE General Test, MAT, BSN, minimum GPA of 3.0, eligibility for Tennessee RN license, 1 year direct patient care experience; for Post-Master's Certificate, GRE General Test, MAT, MSN, minimum GPA of 3.0, eligibility for Tennessee RN license, one year of direct patient care experience. Additional exam requirements/recommendations for international students: Required—TOEFL (minimum score 550 paper-based; 213 computer-based; 79 iBT), IELTS (minimum score 6). *Application deadline:* For fall admission, 8/1 priority date for domestic students, 6/1 for international students; for spring admission, 12/1 priority date for domestic students, 10/1 for international students. Applications are processed on a rolling basis. Application fee: $35. Electronic applications accepted. *Financial support:* Career-related internships or fieldwork and scholarships/grants available. Support available to part-time students. *Faculty research:* Diabetes in women, health care for elderly, alternative medicine, hypertension, nurse anesthesia. Total annual research expenditures: $1.5 million. *Unit head:* Dr. Kay R. Lindgren, Head, 423-425-4646, Fax: 423-425-4668, E-mail: kay-lindgren@utc.edu. *Application contact:* Dr. Jerald Ainsworth, Dean of Graduate Studies, 423-425-4478, Fax: 423-425-5223, E-mail: jerald-ainsworth@utc.edu.

University of Washington, Graduate School, School of Medicine, Graduate Programs in Medicine, Department of Medical Education and Biomedical Informatics, Division of Biomedical and Health Informatics, Seattle, WA 98195. Offers MS, PhD. *Entrance requirements:* For

University of Washington (continued)
master's and doctorate, GRE General Test, minimum GPA of 3.0; previous undergraduate course work in biology, computer programming, and mathematics. Additional exam requirements/recommendations for international students: Required—TOEFL (minimum score 580 paper-based; 237 computer-based; 70 iBT). Electronic applications accepted. *Faculty research:* Bio-clinical informatics, information retrieval, human-computer interaction, knowledge-based systems, telehealth.

University of Wisconsin–Milwaukee, Graduate School, College of Engineering and Applied Science, Program in Medical Informatics, Milwaukee, WI 53201-0413. Offers PhD. *Students:* 13 full-time (3 women), 8 part-time (2 women); includes 1 Hispanic/Latino, 4 international. Average age 28. 8 applicants, 63% accepted, 1 enrolled. *Degree requirements:* For doctorate, comprehensive exam, thesis/dissertation. *Entrance requirements:* For doctorate, GRE, GMAT or MCAT. Additional exam requirements/recommendations for international students: Required—TOEFL (minimum score 600 paper-based; 250 computer-based; 79 iBT), IELTS (minimum score 6.5). Application fee: $56 ($96 for international students). *Financial support:* In 2010–11, 6 research assistantships, 4 teaching assistantships were awarded; fellowships, project assistantships also available. *Unit head:* Susan McRoy, Representative, 414-229-4677, Fax: 414-229-4677, E-mail: mcroy@uwm.edu. *Application contact:* General Information Contact, 414-229-4982, Fax: 414-229-6967, E-mail: gradschool@uwm.edu.

Modeling and Simulation

Academy of Art University, Graduate Program, School of Animation and Visual Effects, San Francisco, CA 94105-3410. Offers 2D animation (MFA); 3D animation (MFA); 3D modeling (MFA); visual effects (MFA). Part-time programs available. Postbaccalaureate distance learning degree programs offered (no on-campus study). *Faculty:* 20 full-time (4 women), 90 part-time/adjunct (17 women). *Students:* 613 full-time (224 women), 340 part-time (118 women); includes 41 Black or African American, non-Hispanic/Latino; 3 American Indian or Alaska Native, non-Hispanic/Latino; 70 Asian, non-Hispanic/Latino; 47 Hispanic/Latino; 1 Native Hawaiian or other Pacific Islander, non-Hispanic/Latino, 448 international. Average age 29. 244 applicants. In 2010, 109 master's awarded. *Degree requirements:* For master's, thesis, final review. *Entrance requirements:* For master's, portfolio. *Application deadline:* For fall admission, 9/7 for domestic and international students; for spring admission, 2/2 for domestic and international students. Applications are processed on a rolling basis. Application fee: $100 ($500 for international students). Electronic applications accepted. *Expenses:* Tuition: Full-time $20,160; part-time $840 per semester hour. Required fees: $45 per semester. *Financial support:* Career-related internships or fieldwork and Federal Work-Study available. Support available to part-time students. Financial award application deadline: 8/10; financial award applicants required to submit FAFSA.

Arizona State University, College of Technology and Innovation, Department of Engineering, Mesa, AZ 85212. Offers computing studies (MCST); simulation, modeling, and applied cognitive science (PhD). Part-time programs available. *Faculty:* 30 full-time (8 women). *Students:* 33 full-time (9 women), 12 part-time (10 women); includes 7 minority (1 Black or African American, non-Hispanic/Latino; 4 Asian, non-Hispanic/Latino; 2 Hispanic/Latino), 29 international. Average age 26. 208 applicants, 97% accepted, 15 enrolled. In 2010, 8 master's awarded. *Degree requirements:* For master's, thesis or applied project with oral defense; interactive Program of Study (iPOS) submitted before completing 50 percent of required credit hours; for doctorate, comprehensive exam, thesis/dissertation, interactive Program of Study (iPOS) submitted before completing 50 percent of required credit hours. *Entrance requirements:* For master's, GRE, minimum GPA of 3.0 or equivalent in last 2 years of work leading to bachelor's degree; for doctorate, GRE, master's degree in psychology, engineering, cognitive science, or computer science; 3 letters of recommendation; statement of research interests. Additional exam requirements/recommendations for international students: Required—TOEFL, IELTS, or Pearson Test of English. *Application deadline:* For fall admission, 1/31 for domestic and international students; for spring admission, 9/30 for domestic students, 8/30 for international students. Application fee: $70 ($90 for international students). Electronic applications accepted. *Expenses:* Tuition, state resident: full-time $8510; part-time $608 per credit. Tuition, nonresident: full-time $16,542; part-time $919 per credit. Required fees: $339; $110 per credit. Part-time tuition and fees vary according to course load. *Financial support:* In 2010–11, 3 research assistantships with full and partial tuition reimbursements (averaging $14,832 per year), 1 teaching assistantship with full and partial tuition reimbursement (averaging $10,400 per year) were awarded; fellowships with full and partial tuition reimbursements, career-related internships or fieldwork, Federal Work-Study, scholarships/grants, health care benefits, tuition waivers (full and partial), and unspecified assistantships also available. Support available to part-time students. Financial award application deadline: 3/1; financial award applicants required to submit FAFSA. *Faculty research:* Software process and automated workflow, software architecture, dotal technologies, relational database systems, embedded systems. Total annual research expenditures: $595,649. *Unit head:* Dr. Chell Roberts, Executive Dean, Chair, 480-727-1353, Fax: 480-727-1089, E-mail: chell.roberts@asu.edu. *Application contact:* Graduate Admissions, 480-965-6113.

Arizona State University, Ira A. Fulton School of Engineering, ASU Engineering Online Programs, Tempe, AZ 85287. Offers construction (MS); embedded systems (M Eng); enterprise systems innovation and management (MSE); modeling and simulation (M Eng); quality and reliability engineering (M Eng); software engineering (MSE); systems engineering (M Eng). *Expenses:* Tuition, state resident: full-time $8510; part-time $608 per credit. Tuition, nonresident: full-time $16,542; part-time $919 per credit. Required fees: $339; $110 per credit. Part-time tuition and fees vary according to course load.

California State University, Chico, Graduate School, Interdisciplinary Programs, Chico, CA 95929-0722. Offers interdisciplinary studies (MA, MS); science teaching (MS); simulation science (MS). Part-time programs available. *Students:* 22 full-time (18 women), 8 part-time (7 women); includes 1 Black or African American, non-Hispanic/Latino; 1 Asian, non-Hispanic/Latino; 5 Hispanic/Latino, 8 international. Average age 35. 22 applicants, 77% accepted, 8 enrolled. In 2010, 6 master's awarded. *Degree requirements:* For master's, thesis or alternative, oral exam. *Entrance requirements:* For master's, GRE General Test or MAT, 3 letters of recommendation. Additional exam requirements/recommendations for international students: Required—TOEFL (minimum score 550 paper-based; 213 computer-based; 80 iBT), IELTS (minimum score 6.5). *Application deadline:* For fall admission, 3/1 priority date for domestic students, 3/1 for international students; for spring admission, 9/15 priority date for domestic students, 9/15 for international students. Applications are processed on a rolling basis. Application fee: $55. *Financial support:* Fellowships, Federal Work-Study available. Support available to part-time students. *Unit head:* Dr. Sara Trechter, Graduate Coordinator, 530-898-5447. *Application contact:* School of Graduate, International, and Interdisciplinary Studies, 530-898-6880, Fax: 530-898-6889, E-mail: grin@csuchico.edu.

Columbus State University, Graduate Studies, D. Abbott Turner College of Business and Computer Science, Columbus, GA 31907-5645. Offers applied computer science (MS); business administration (MBA); modeling and simulation (Certificate); organizational leadership (MS). *Accreditation:* AACSB. *Faculty:* 15 full-time (2 women). *Students:* 36 full-time (9 women), 145 part-time (54 women); includes 43 minority (19 Black or African American, non-Hispanic/Latino; 3 American Indian or Alaska Native, non-Hispanic/Latino; 12 Asian, non-Hispanic/Latino; 3 Hispanic/Latino; 6 Two or more races, non-Hispanic/Latino), 11 international. Average age 33. 133 applicants, 61% accepted, 58 enrolled. In 2010, 59 master's awarded. *Entrance requirements:* For master's, GMAT, GRE. Additional exam requirements/recommendations for international students: Required—TOEFL (minimum score 550 paper-based; 213 computer-based; 79 iBT). *Application deadline:* For fall admission, 6/30 for domestic students, 5/1 for international students; for spring admission, 11/1 for domestic and international students. Applications are processed on a rolling basis. Application fee: $30. Electronic applications accepted. *Expenses:* Tuition, state resident: full-time $5573; part-time $232 per semester hour. Tuition, nonresident: full-time $13,968; part-time $582 per semester hour. Required fees: $1300; $650 per semester. Tuition and fees vary according to degree level and program. *Financial support:* In 2010–11, 62 students received support, including 11 research assistantships (averaging $3,000 per year). Financial award application deadline: 5/1. *Unit head:* Dr. Linda U. Hadley, Dean, 706-568-2044, Fax: 706-568-2184, E-mail: hadley_linda@colstate.edu. *Application contact:* Katie Thornton, Graduate Admissions Specialist, 706-568-2035, Fax: 706-568-2462, E-mail: thornton_katie@colstate.edu.

George Mason University, Volgenau School of Engineering, Department of Electrical and Computer Engineering, Fairfax, VA 22030. Offers advanced networking protocols for telecommunications (Certificate); communications and networking (Certificate); computer engineering (MS); computer forensics (MS); electrical and computer engineering (PhD); electrical engineering (MS); network technology and applications (Certificate); networks, system integration and testing (Certificate); signal processing (Certificate); telecom systems modeling (Certificate); telecommunications (MS); telecommunications forensics and security (Certificate); VLSI design/manufacturing (Certificate); wireless communication (Certificate). MS program offered jointly with Old Dominion University, University of Virginia, Virginia Commonwealth University, and Virginia Polytechnic Institute and State University. Part-time and evening/weekend programs available. *Faculty:* 33 full-time (4 women), 39 part-time/adjunct (4 women). *Students:* 106 full-time (27 women), 336 part-time (64 women); includes 24 Black or African American, non-Hispanic/Latino; 1 American Indian or Alaska Native, non-Hispanic/Latino; 54 Asian, non-Hispanic/Latino; 20 Hispanic/Latino; 1 Two or more races, non-Hispanic/Latino, 172 international. Average age 30. 506 applicants, 71% accepted, 142 enrolled. In 2010, 145 master's, 3 doctorates, 61 other advanced degrees awarded. *Degree requirements:* For master's, thesis optional; for doctorate, comprehensive exam, thesis or scholarly paper. *Entrance requirements:* For master's, GMAT or GRE General Test, letters of recommendation, resume; for doctorate, GRE/GMAT, personal goal statement, 2 transcripts, letter of recommendation. Additional exam requirements/recommendations for international students: Required—TOEFL (minimum score 570 paper-based; 230 computer-based; 88 iBT). *Application deadline:* For fall admission, 7/15 priority date for domestic and international students; for spring admission, 12/1 for domestic and international students. Applications are processed on a rolling basis. Application fee: $100. Electronic applications accepted. *Expenses:* Tuition, state resident: full-time $8192; part-time $440 per credit hour. Tuition, nonresident: full-time $22,952; part-time $1055 per credit hour. Required fees: $2364; $99 per credit hour. *Financial support:* In 2010–11, 74 students received support, including 2 fellowships with full tuition reimbursements available (averaging $18,000 per year), 26 research assistantships with full and partial tuition reimbursements available (averaging $14,648 per year), 46 teaching assistantships with full and partial tuition reimbursements available (averaging $10,946 per year); career-related internships or fieldwork, Federal Work-Study, scholarships/grants, unspecified assistantships, and health care benefits (full-time research or teaching assistantship recipients) also available. Financial award application deadline: 3/1; financial award applicants required to submit FAFSA. *Faculty research:* Communication networks, signal processing, system failure diagnosis, multiprocessors, material processing using microwave energy. Total annual research expenditures: $3.4 million. *Unit head:* Dr. Andre Manitius, Chairperson, 703-993-1569, Fax: 703-993-1601, E-mail: ece@gmu.edu. *Application contact:* Jessica Skinner, Associate Dean, 703-993-1569, E-mail: jskinne6@gmu.edu.

George Mason University, Volgenau School of Engineering, Department of Systems Engineering and Operations Research, Fairfax, VA 22030. Offers architecture-based systems integration (Certificate); command, control, communication, computing and intelligence (Certificate); computational modeling (Certificate); discovery, design and innovation (Certificate); military operations research (Certificate); operations research (MS); systems engineering (MS); systems engineering analysis and architecture (Certificate); systems engineering and operations research (PhD); systems engineering of software intensive systems (Certificate). MS programs offered jointly with Old Dominion University, University of Virginia, Virginia Commonwealth University, and Virginia Polytechnic Institute and State University. Part-time and evening/weekend programs available. *Faculty:* 16 full-time (4 women), 11 part-time/adjunct (4 women). *Students:* 27 full-time (2 women), 175 part-time (39 women); includes 10 Black or African American, non-Hispanic/Latino; 2 American Indian or Alaska Native, non-Hispanic/Latino; 19 Asian, non-Hispanic/Latino; 9 Hispanic/Latino, 17 international. Average age 33. 132 applicants, 72% accepted, 53 enrolled. In 2010, 76 master's, 1 doctorate, 25 other advanced degrees awarded. *Degree requirements:* For master's, thesis optional; for doctorate, comprehensive exam, thesis/dissertation, qualifying exams. *Entrance requirements:* For master's, GRE General Test, 3 letters of recommendation, resume; for doctorate, GRE, undergraduate and graduate transcripts, 3 letters of reference, resume, statement of career goals and aspirations, self assessment of background. Additional exam requirements/recommendations for international students: Required—TOEFL (minimum score 570 paper-based; 230 computer-based; 88 iBT). *Application deadline:* For fall admission, 3/15 priority date for domestic students, 2/15 priority date for international students; for spring admission, 10/1 for domestic and international students. Application fee: $100. Electronic applications accepted. *Expenses:* Tuition, state resident: full-time $8192; part-time $440 per credit hour. Tuition, nonresident: full-time $22,952; part-time $1055 per credit hour. Required fees: $2364; $99 per credit hour. *Financial support:* In 2010–11, 11 students received support, including 6 research assistantships with full and partial tuition reimbursements available (averaging $15,982 per year), 5 teaching assistantships with full and partial tuition reimbursements available (averaging $10,661 per year); career-related internships or fieldwork, Federal Work-Study, scholarships/grants, unspecified assistantships, and health care benefits (full-time research or teaching assistantship recipients) also available. Financial award application deadline: 3/1; financial award applicants required to submit FAFSA. *Faculty research:* Requirements engineering, signal processing, systems architecture, data fusion. Total annual research expenditures: $1.3 million. *Unit head:* Dr. Ariela Sofer, Chairman, 703-993-1692, Fax: 703-993-1521, E-mail: asofer@gmu.edu. *Application contact:* Dr. K. C. Chang, Graduate Coordinator, 703-993-1639, E-mail: kchang@gmu.edu.

Louisiana Tech University, Graduate School, College of Engineering and Science, Department of Physics, Ruston, LA 71272. Offers applied computational analysis and modeling (PhD); physics (MS). Part-time programs available. *Degree requirements:* For master's, thesis or alternative; for doctorate, thesis/dissertation. *Entrance requirements:* For master's, GRE General Test, minimum GPA of 3.0 in last 60 hours. Additional exam requirements/recommendations for international students: Required—TOEFL. *Faculty research:* Experimental high energy physics, laser/optics, computational physics, quantum gravity.

Naval Postgraduate School, Graduate Programs, Department of Computer Science, Program in Modeling of Virtual Environments and Simulations, Monterey, CA 93943. Offers MS, PhD.

Program only open to commissioned officers of the United States and friendly nations and selected United States federal civilian employees. Part-time programs available. *Degree requirements:* For master's, thesis; for doctorate, one foreign language, thesis/dissertation.

Old Dominion University, Frank Batten College of Engineering and Technology, Program in Modeling and Simulation, Norfolk, VA 23529. Offers ME, MS, D Eng, PhD. Part-time and evening/weekend programs available. Postbaccalaureate distance learning degree programs offered (no on-campus study). *Faculty:* 8 full-time (0 women), 3 part-time/adjunct (0 women). *Students:* 14 full-time (2 women), 38 part-time (6 women); includes 9 minority (2 Black or African American, non-Hispanic/Latino; 2 Asian, non-Hispanic/Latino; 2 Hispanic/Latino; 3 Two or more races, non-Hispanic/Latino), 11 international. Average age 36. 21 applicants, 57% accepted, 11 enrolled. In 2010, 7 master's, 2 doctorates awarded. Terminal master's awarded for partial completion of doctoral program. *Degree requirements:* For master's, comprehensive exam (for some programs), thesis (for some programs); for doctorate, comprehensive exam, thesis/dissertation, candidacy exam. *Entrance requirements:* For master's, GRE, proficiency in calculus, calculus-based statistics, and computer science; for doctorate, GRE, graduate-level proficiency in calculus, calculus-based statistics, and computer science. Additional exam requirements/recommendations for international students: Required—TOEFL (minimum score 550 paper-based; 213 computer-based; 79 iBT). *Application deadline:* For fall admission, 6/1 for domestic students, 2/15 priority date for international students; for spring admission, 11/1 for domestic students, 10/1 for international students. Applications are processed on a rolling basis. Application fee: $50. Electronic applications accepted. *Expenses:* Tuition, state resident: full-time $8592; part-time $358 per credit. Tuition, nonresident: full-time $21,672; part-time $903 per credit. Required fees: $119 per semester. One-time fee: $50. *Financial support:* In 2010–11, 17 students received support, including 2 fellowships with full tuition reimbursements available (averaging $16,100 per year), 10 research assistantships with full tuition reimbursements available (averaging $18,000 per year), 2 teaching assistantships with full tuition reimbursements available (averaging $15,000 per year); career-related internships or fieldwork, scholarships/grants, and unspecified assistantships also available. Financial award application deadline: 4/15; financial award applicants required to submit FAFSA. *Faculty research:* Distributed simulation and interoperability, medical modeling and simulation, transportation modeling and simulation, human factors, discrete event systems. Total annual research expenditures: $1.5 million. *Unit head:* Dr. Rick McKenzie, Graduate Program Director, 757-683-5590, Fax: 757-683-3200, E-mail: rdmckenz@odu.edu. *Application contact:* Dr. Rick McKenzie, Graduate Program Director, 757-683-5590, Fax: 757-683-3200, E-mail: rdmckenz@odu.edu.

Portland State University, Graduate Studies, Systems Science Program, Portland, OR 97207-0751. Offers computational intelligence (Certificate); computer modeling and simulation (Certificate); systems science (MS); systems science/anthropology (PhD); systems science/business administration (PhD); systems science/civil engineering (PhD); systems science/economics (PhD); systems science/engineering management (PhD); systems science/general (PhD); systems science/mathematical sciences (PhD); systems science/mechanical engineering (PhD); systems science/psychology (PhD); systems science/sociology (PhD). *Faculty:* 4 full-time (0 women), 1 part-time/adjunct (0 women). *Students:* 15 full-time (4 women), 35 part-time (11 women); includes 1 American Indian or Alaska Native, non-Hispanic/Latino; 1 Asian, non-Hispanic/Latino; 1 Two or more races, non-Hispanic/Latino, 4 international. Average age 39. 8 applicants, 88% accepted, 5 enrolled. In 2010, 2 master's, 4 doctorates awarded. *Degree requirements:* For doctorate, variable foreign language requirement, thesis/dissertation. *Entrance requirements:* For master's, 2 letters of recommendation; for doctorate, GMAT, GRE General Test, minimum undergraduate GPA of 3.0. Additional exam requirements/recommendations for international students: Required—TOEFL. *Application deadline:* For fall admission, 2/1 for domestic students; for spring admission, 11/1 for domestic students. Application fee: $50. *Expenses:* Tuition, state resident: full-time $8505; part-time $315 per credit. Tuition, nonresident: full-time $13,284; part-time $492 per credit. Required fees: $1482; $21 per credit. $99 per term. One-time fee: $120. Part-time tuition and fees vary according to course load and program. *Financial support:* In 2010–11, 1 research assistantship with full tuition reimbursement (averaging $7,704 per year) was awarded; teaching assistantships with full tuition reimbursements, career-related internships or fieldwork, Federal Work-Study, scholarships/grants, and unspecified assistantships also available. Support available to part-time students. Financial award application deadline: 3/1; financial award applicants required to submit FAFSA. *Faculty research:* Systems theory and methodology, artificial intelligence neural networks, information theory, nonlinear dynamics/chaos, modeling and simulation. *Unit head:* George Lendaris, Acting Director, 503-725-4960. *Application contact:* Dawn Sharafi, Administrative Assistant, 503-725-4960, E-mail: dawn@sysc.pdx.edu.

Stevens Institute of Technology, Graduate School, Charles V. Schaefer Jr. School of Engineering, Department of Civil, Environmental, and Ocean Engineering, Program in Civil Engineering, Hoboken, NJ 07030. Offers civil engineering (PhD); geotechnical engineering (Certificate); geotechnical/geoenvironmental engineering (M Eng, Engr); hydrologic modeling (M Eng); stormwater management (M Eng); structural engineering (M Eng, Engr); water resources engineering (M Eng). *Students:* 22 full-time (6 women), 36 part-time (11 women); includes 10 Asian, non-Hispanic/Latino; 3 Hispanic/Latino, 16 international. Average age 28. 37 applicants, 86% accepted. *Degree requirements:* For master's, thesis optional; for doctorate, variable foreign language requirement, thesis/dissertation; for other advanced degree, project or thesis. *Entrance requirements:* For doctorate, GRE. Additional exam requirements/recommendations for international students: Required—TOEFL. *Application deadline:* Applications are processed on a rolling basis. Application fee: $50. Electronic applications accepted. *Financial support:* Application deadline: 4/15. *Unit head:* Dr. David A. Vaccari, Director, 201-216-5570, Fax: 201-216-5352, E-mail: dvaccari@stevens.edu. *Application contact:* Dr. David A. Vaccari, Director, 201-216-5570, Fax: 201-216-5352, E-mail: dvaccari@stevens.edu.

Trent University, Graduate Studies, Program in Applications of Modeling in the Natural and Social Sciences, Peterborough, ON K9J 7B8, Canada. Offers applications of modeling in the natural and social sciences (MA); biology (M Sc, PhD); chemistry (M Sc); computer studies (M Sc); geography (M Sc, PhD); physics (M Sc). Part-time programs available. *Degree requirements:* For master's, thesis. *Entrance requirements:* For master's, honours degree. *Faculty research:* Computation of heat transfer, atmospheric physics, statistical mechanics, stress and coping, evolutionary ecology.

Université Laval, Faculty of Administrative Sciences, Programs in Business Administration, Québec, QC G1K 7P4, Canada. Offers accounting (MBA); agri-food management (MBA); electronic business (MBA, Diploma); factory management and logistics (MBA); finance (MBA); firm management (MBA); geomatic management (MBA); information technology management (MBA); international management (MBA); management (MBA); management accounting (MBA, Diploma); marketing (MBA); modeling and organizational decision (MBA); occupational health and safety management (MBA); pharmacy management (MBA); social and environmental responsibility (MBA); technological entrepreneurship (Diploma). *Accreditation:* AACSB. Part-time and evening/weekend programs available. Postbaccalaureate distance learning degree programs offered (no on-campus study). *Entrance requirements:* For master's and Diploma, knowledge of French and English. Electronic applications accepted.

University at Buffalo, the State University of New York, Graduate School, College of Arts and Sciences, Department of Geography, Buffalo, NY 14260. Offers earth systems science (MA); economic geography and international business and world trade (MA); environmental and earth systems science (MS); environmental modeling and analysis (MA); geographic information science (MA, Certificate); geographic information systems and science (MS); geography (MA, PhD); urban and regional geography (MA); MA/MBA. *Faculty:* 14 full-time (6 women), 1 part-time/adjunct (0 women). *Students:* 60 full-time (24 women), 49 part-time (13 women); includes 1 Black or African American, non-Hispanic/Latino; 46 Asian, non-Hispanic/Latino; 4 Hispanic/Latino, 1 international. 162 applicants, 46% accepted, 38 enrolled. In 2010, 21 master's, 5 doctorates awarded. Terminal master's awarded for partial completion of doctoral program. *Degree requirements:* For master's, thesis (for some programs), project; for doctorate, thesis/dissertation. *Entrance requirements:* For master's, GRE General Test, minimum GPA of 2.9; for doctorate, GRE General Test, minimum GPA of 3.0. Additional exam requirements/recommendations for international students: Required—TOEFL (minimum score 550 paper-based; 213 computer-based; 79 iBT). *Application deadline:* For fall admission, 7/1 priority date for domestic students, 1/10 priority date for international students; for spring admission, 12/1 priority date for domestic students, 10/1 priority date for international students. Applications are processed on a rolling basis. Application fee: $75. Electronic applications accepted. *Financial support:* In 2010–11, 19 students received support, including 7 fellowships with full tuition reimbursements available (averaging $5,714 per year), 14 teaching assistantships with full tuition reimbursements available (averaging $13,520 per year); research assistantships with full tuition reimbursements available, career-related internships or fieldwork, Federal Work-Study, institutionally sponsored loans, traineeships, health care benefits, and unspecified assistantships also available. Financial award application deadline: 1/10. *Faculty research:* International business and world trade, geographic information systems and cartography, transportation, urban and regional analysis, physical and environmental geography. Total annual research expenditures: $944,614. *Unit head:* Dr. Sharmistha Bagchi-Sen, Chairman, 716-645-0473, Fax: 716-645-2329, E-mail: geosbs@buffalo.edu. *Application contact:* Betsy Abraham, Graduate Secretary, 716-645-0471, Fax: 716-645-2329, E-mail: babraham@buffalo.edu.

The University of Alabama in Huntsville, School of Graduate Studies, Interdisciplinary Studies, Interdisciplinary Program of Modeling and Simulation, Huntsville, AL 35899. Offers MS, PhD, Certificate. Part-time and evening/weekend programs available. *Faculty:* 9 full-time (2 women). *Students:* 6 part-time (0 women). Average age 39. 8 applicants, 100% accepted, 6 enrolled. *Degree requirements:* For master's, comprehensive exam, thesis or alternative, 24 hours course work plus 6 hours thesis; for doctorate, comprehensive exam, thesis/dissertation, 54 hours course work plus 18 hours dissertation. *Entrance requirements:* For master's, doctorate, and Certificate, GRE General Test, minimum GPA of 3.0. Additional exam requirements/recommendations for international students: Required—TOEFL (minimum score 500 paper-based; 173 computer-based; 62 iBT). *Application deadline:* For fall admission, 7/15 for domestic students, 4/1 for international students; for spring admission, 11/30 for domestic students, 9/1 for international students. Applications are processed on a rolling basis. Application fee: $40 ($50 for international students). Electronic applications accepted. *Expenses:* Tuition, state resident: full-time $7250; part-time $407.75 per credit hour. Tuition, nonresident: full-time $17,358; part-time $970.05 per credit hour. Required fees: $246.80 per semester. Tuition and fees vary according to course load and program. *Financial support:* Career-related internships or fieldwork, Federal Work-Study, institutionally sponsored loans, scholarships/grants, health care benefits, and unspecified assistantships available. Support available to part-time students. Financial award application deadline: 4/1; financial award applicants required to submit FAFSA. *Faculty research:* Simulation interoperability and composability, discrete event simulation, mathematical modeling and analysis, system-level modeling, technical team performance. *Unit head:* Dr. Rhonda Kay Gaede, Dean of Graduate Studies, 256-824-6002, Fax: 256-824-6405, E-mail: deangrad@uah.edu. *Application contact:* Kathy Biggs, Graduate Studies Admissions Manager, 256-824-6199, Fax: 256-824-6405, E-mail: deangrad@uah.edu.

University of California, San Diego, Office of Graduate Studies, Department of Structural Engineering, La Jolla, CA 92093. Offers structural engineering (MS, PhD); structural health monitoring, prognosis, and validated simulations (MS). Applications accepted only for fall quarter. Part-time programs available. *Degree requirements:* For master's, comprehensive exam or thesis; for doctorate, comprehensive exam, thesis/dissertation, candidacy exam. *Entrance requirements:* For master's and doctorate, GRE General Test, minimum GPA of 3.0; BS in engineering, physical sciences, or mathematics; statement of purpose; three letters of recommendation; official transcripts from all institutions attended. Additional exam requirements/recommendations for international students: Required—TOEFL (minimum score 550 paper-based; 213 computer-based; 80 iBT). *Faculty research:* Advanced large-scale civil, mechanical, and aerospace structures.

University of Central Florida, College of Education, Department of Educational and Human Sciences, Program in Instructional Systems, Orlando, FL 32816. Offers instructional design for simulations (Certificate); instructional systems (MA); online educational media (Certificate). *Students:* 7 full-time (6 women), 36 part-time (23 women); includes 4 Black or African American, non-Hispanic/Latino; 4 Asian, non-Hispanic/Latino; 2 Hispanic/Latino, 3 international. Average age 36. 26 applicants, 100% accepted, 22 enrolled. In 2010, 10 master's, 14 other advanced degrees awarded. Application fee: $30. Electronic applications accepted. *Expenses:* Tuition, state resident: part-time $256.56 per credit hour. Tuition, nonresident: part-time $1011.52 per credit hour. Part-time tuition and fees vary according to program. *Financial support:* Fellowships with partial tuition reimbursements, research assistantships with partial tuition reimbursements, teaching assistantships with partial tuition reimbursements available.

University of Central Florida, College of Engineering and Computer Science, Department of Industrial Engineering and Management Systems, Orlando, FL 32816. Offers applied operations research (Certificate); design for usability (Certificate); industrial engineering (MSIE, PhD); industrial engineering and management systems (MS); industrial ergonomics and safety (Certificate); project engineering (Certificate); quality assurance (Certificate); systems engineering (Certificate); systems simulation for engineers (Certificate); training simulation (Certificate). Part-time and evening/weekend programs available. *Faculty:* 17 full-time (4 women), 6 part-time/adjunct (1 woman). *Students:* 112 full-time (31 women), 171 part-time (66 women); includes 79 minority (27 Black or African American, non-Hispanic/Latino; 17 Asian, non-Hispanic/Latino; 32 Hispanic/Latino; 1 Native Hawaiian or other Pacific Islander, non-Hispanic/Latino; 2 Two or more races, non-Hispanic/Latino), 72 international. Average age 33. 210 applicants, 74% accepted, 82 enrolled. In 2010, 65 master's, 7 doctorates, 34 other advanced degrees awarded. *Degree requirements:* For master's, thesis; for doctorate, thesis/dissertation, departmental qualifying exam, candidacy exam. *Entrance requirements:* For master's, GRE General Test, minimum GPA of 3.0 in last 60 hours of course work; for doctorate, minimum GPA of 3.5 in last 60 hours of course work. Additional exam requirements/recommendations for international students: Required—TOEFL. *Application deadline:* For fall admission, 7/15 priority date for domestic students; for spring admission, 12/1 priority date for domestic students. Application fee: $30. Electronic applications accepted. *Expenses:* Tuition, state resident: part-time $256.56 per credit hour. Tuition, nonresident: part-time $1011.52 per credit hour. Part-time tuition and fees vary according to program. *Financial support:* In 2010–11, 24 students received support, including 85 fellowships with partial tuition reimbursements available (averaging $7,300 per year), 19 research assistantships with partial tuition reimbursements available (averaging $8,500 per year), 6 teaching assistantships with partial tuition reimbursements available (averaging $12,200 per year); career-related internships or fieldwork, Federal Work-Study, institutionally sponsored loans, tuition waivers (partial), and unspecified assistantships also available. Financial award application deadline: 3/1; financial award applicants required to submit FAFSA. *Unit head:* Dr. Waldemar Karwowski, Chair, 407-823-2204, E-mail: wkar@mail.ucf.edu. *Application contact:* Dr. Waldemar Karwowski, Chair, 407-823-2204, E-mail: wkar@mail.ucf.edu.

University of Central Florida, College of Graduate Studies, Program in Modeling and Simulation, Orlando, FL 32816. Offers MS, PhD. *Students:* 54 full-time (15 women), 54 part-time (13 women); includes 4 Black or African American, non-Hispanic/Latino; 1 American Indian or Alaska Native, non-Hispanic/Latino; 6 Asian, non-Hispanic/Latino; 15 Hispanic/Latino, 8 international. Average age 35. 54 applicants, 72% accepted, 25 enrolled. In 2010, 16 master's, 5 doctorates awarded. *Expenses:* Tuition, state resident: part-time $256.56 per credit hour. Tuition, nonresident: part-time $1011.52 per credit hour. Part-time tuition and fees vary according to program. *Financial support:* In 2010–11, 20 students received support, including 4 fellowships (averaging $9,100 per year), 25 research assistantships (averaging $8,800 per year). *Unit head:* Dr. Peter Kincaid, Program Director, 407-882-1330, E-mail: pkincaid@ist.ucf.edu. *Application contact:* Dr. Peter Kincaid, Program Director, 407-882-1330, E-mail: pkincaid@ist.ucf.edu.

Modeling and Simulation

The University of Manchester, School of Chemical Engineering and Analytical Science, Manchester, United Kingdom. Offers biocatalysis (M Phil, PhD); chemical engineering (M Phil, PhD); chemical engineering and analytical science (M Phil, D Eng, PhD); colloids, crystals, interfaces and materials (M Phil, PhD); environment and sustainable technology (M Phil, PhD); instrumentation (M Phil, PhD); multi-scale modeling (M Phil, PhD); process integration (M Phil, PhD); systems biology (M Phil, PhD).

University of Northern Iowa, Graduate College, College of Natural Sciences, Department of Mathematics, Cedar Falls, IA 50614. Offers industrial mathematics (PSM), including actuarial science, continuous quality improvement, mathematical computing and modeling; mathematics (MA), including mathematics, secondary; mathematics for middle grades 4-8 (MA). Part-time programs available. *Students:* 19 full-time (13 women), 22 part-time (17 women); includes 2 minority (1 Asian, non-Hispanic/Latino; 1 Two or more races, non-Hispanic/Latino), 5 international. 20 applicants, 40% accepted, 6 enrolled. In 2010, 18 master's awarded. *Degree requirements:* For master's, comprehensive exam (for some programs), thesis or alternative. *Entrance requirements:* For master's, minimum GPA of 3.0. Additional exam requirements/recommendations for international students: Required—TOEFL (minimum score 600 paper-based; 250 computer-based; 100 iBT). *Application deadline:* For fall admission, 8/1 priority date for domestic students. Applications are processed on a rolling basis. Application fee: $50 ($70 for international students). Electronic applications accepted. *Financial support:* Career-related internships or fieldwork, Federal Work-Study, scholarships/grants, and tuition waivers (full and partial) available. Support available to part-time students. Financial award application deadline: 2/1. *Unit head:* Dr. Douglas Mupasiri, Interim Head, 319-273-2012, Fax: 319-273-2546, E-mail: douglas.mupasiri@uni.edu. *Application contact:* Laurie S. Russell, Record Analyst, 319-273-2623, Fax: 319-273-2885, E-mail: laurie.russell@uni.edu.

University of Southern California, Graduate School, Viterbi School of Engineering, Department of Computer Science, Los Angeles, CA 90089. Offers computer networks (MS); computer science (MS, PhD); computer security (MS); game development (MS); high performance computing and simulations (MS); human language technology (MS); intelligent robotics (MS); multimedia and creative technologies (MS); software engineering (MS). Part-time and evening/weekend programs available. Postbaccalaureate distance learning degree programs offered (no on-campus study). *Faculty:* 28 full-time (3 women), 56 part-time/adjunct (7 women). *Students:* 710 full-time (115 women), 302 part-time (59 women); includes 76 minority (1 Black or African American, non-Hispanic/Latino; 55 Asian, non-Hispanic/Latino; 14 Hispanic/Latino; 6 Two or more races, non-Hispanic/Latino), 819 international. 2,379 applicants, 30% accepted, 319 enrolled. In 2010, 332 master's, 32 doctorates awarded. *Entrance requirements:* For master's and doctorate, GRE General Test. Additional exam requirements/recommendations for international students: Required—TOEFL. *Application deadline:* For fall admission, 12/1 priority date for domestic and international students; for spring admission, 9/15 priority date for domestic and international students. Applications are processed on a rolling basis. Application fee: $85. Electronic applications accepted. *Expenses:* Tuition: Full-time $31,240; part-time $1420 per unit. Required fees: $600. One-time fee: $35 full-time. Full-time tuition and fees vary according to degree level and program. *Financial support:* In 2010–11, fellowships with full tuition reimbursements (averaging $30,000 per year), research assistantships with full tuition reimbursements (averaging $20,000 per year), teaching assistantships with full tuition reimbursements (averaging $20,000 per year) were awarded; career-related internships or fieldwork, scholarships/grants, health care benefits, and unspecified assistantships also available. Financial award application deadline: 12/1; financial award applicants required to submit CSS PROFILE or FAFSA. *Faculty research:* Databases, computer graphics and computer vision, software engineering, networks and security, robotics, multimedia and virtual reality. Total annual research expenditures: $11.8 million. *Unit head:* Dr. Shanghua Teng, Chair, 213-740-4494, E-mail: csdept@usc.edu. *Application contact:* Lizsl DeLeon, Director of Student Affairs, 213-740-4496, E-mail: ldeleon@usc.edu.

Worcester Polytechnic Institute, Graduate Studies and Research, Programs in Interdisciplinary Studies, Worcester, MA 01609-2280. Offers bioscience administration (MS); impact engineering (MS); manufacturing engineering management (MS); power systems management (MS); social science (PhD); systems modeling (MS). Part-time and evening/weekend programs available. *Faculty:* 1 part-time/adjunct (0 women). *Students:* 6 full-time (1 woman), 146 part-time (25 women); includes 1 Black or African American, non-Hispanic/Latino; 6 Hispanic/Latino; 11 Native Hawaiian or other Pacific Islander, non-Hispanic/Latino, 1 international. 151 applicants, 76% accepted, 79 enrolled. In 2010, 47 master's awarded. *Degree requirements:* For master's, thesis; for doctorate, comprehensive exam, thesis/dissertation. *Entrance requirements:* For master's and doctorate, 3 letters of recommendation. Additional exam requirements/recommendations for international students: Required—TOEFL (minimum score 550 paper-based; 213 computer-based; 79 iBT), IELTS (minimum score 6.5). *Application deadline:* For fall admission, 1/1 priority date for domestic students, 1/1 for international students; for spring admission, 10/1 priority date for domestic students, 10/1 for international students. Application fee: $70. *Expenses:* Tuition: Full-time $20,862; part-time $1159 per term. One-time fee: $15. *Financial support:* Institutionally sponsored loans, scholarships/grants, and unspecified assistantships available. Financial award application deadline: 1/1; financial award applicants required to submit FAFSA. *Unit head:* Dr. Fred J. Looft, Head, 508-831-5231, Fax: 508-831-5491, E-mail: fjlooft@wpi.edu. *Application contact:* Lynne Dougherty, Administrative Assistant, 508-831-5301, Fax: 508-831-5717, E-mail: grad@wpi.edu.

Software Engineering

Andrews University, School of Graduate Studies, College of Technology, Department of Engineering, Computer Science, and Engineering Technology, Berrien Springs, MI 49104. Offers software engineering (MS). *Entrance requirements:* For master's, GRE, minimum GPA of 2.6. Additional exam requirements/recommendations for international students: Required—TOEFL.

Arizona State University, Ira A. Fulton School of Engineering, ASU Engineering Online Programs, Tempe, AZ 85287. Offers construction (MS); embedded systems (M Eng); enterprise systems innovation and management (MSE); modeling and simulation (M Eng); quality and reliability engineering (M Eng); software engineering (MSE); systems engineering (M Eng). *Expenses:* Tuition, state resident: full-time $8510; part-time $608 per credit. Tuition, nonresident: full-time $16,542; part-time $919 per credit. Required fees: $339; $110 per credit. Part-time tuition and fees vary according to course load.

Auburn University, Graduate School, Ginn College of Engineering, Department of Computer Science and Software Engineering, Auburn University, AL 36849. Offers MS, MSWE, PhD. Part-time programs available. *Faculty:* 19 full-time (3 women). *Students:* 58 full-time (15 women), 65 part-time (17 women); includes 16 Black or African American, non-Hispanic/Latino; 1 Asian, non-Hispanic/Latino; 2 Hispanic/Latino, 59 international. Average age 30. 214 applicants, 33% accepted, 19 enrolled. In 2010, 21 master's, 11 doctorates awarded. *Degree requirements:* For master's, thesis (for some programs); for doctorate, thesis/dissertation. *Entrance requirements:* For master's and doctorate, GRE General Test, GRE Subject Test. *Application deadline:* For fall admission, 7/7 for domestic students; for spring admission, 11/24 for domestic students. Applications are processed on a rolling basis. Application fee: $50 ($60 for international students). Electronic applications accepted. *Expenses:* Tuition, state resident: full-time $7002. Tuition, nonresident: full-time $21,898. International tuition: $22,116 full-time. Required fees: $892. Tuition and fees vary according to course load and program. *Financial support:* Research assistantships, teaching assistantships, Federal Work-Study available. Support available to part-time students. Financial award application deadline: 3/15; financial award applicants required to submit FAFSA. *Faculty research:* Parallelizable, scalable software translations; graphical representations of algorithms, structures, and processes; graph drawing. Total annual research expenditures: $400,000. *Unit head:* Dr. Kai Chang, Chair, 334-844-6310. *Application contact:* Dr. George Flowers, Dean of the Graduate School, 334-844-2125.

Bowling Green State University, Graduate College, College of Arts and Sciences, Department of Computer Science, Bowling Green, OH 43403. Offers computer science (MS), including operations research, parallel and distributed computing, software engineering. Part-time programs available. *Degree requirements:* For master's, thesis or alternative. *Entrance requirements:* For master's, GRE General Test. Additional exam requirements/recommendations for international students: Required—TOEFL. Electronic applications accepted. *Faculty research:* Artificial intelligence, real time and concurrent programming languages, behavioral aspects of computing, network protocols.

Brandeis University, Rabb School of Continuing Studies, Division of Graduate Professional Studies, Software Engineering Program, Waltham, MA 02454-9110. Offers MSE, Graduate Certificate. Part-time programs available. Postbaccalaureate distance learning degree programs offered (no on-campus study). *Faculty:* 2 full-time (both women), 33 part-time/adjunct (5 women). *Students:* 1 full-time (0 women), 85 part-time (13 women); includes 2 Black or African American, non-Hispanic/Latino; 11 Asian, non-Hispanic/Latino; 6 Hispanic/Latino, 1 international. Average age 35. 16 applicants, 100% accepted, 14 enrolled. In 2010, 62 master's, 2 other advanced degrees awarded. *Entrance requirements:* For master's, resume, official transcripts, recommendations, goal statements; for Graduate Certificate, resume, official transcripts, recommendations. Additional exam requirements/recommendations for international students: Recommended—TOEFL (minimum score 600 paper-based; 250 computer-based; 100 iBT). *Application deadline:* For fall admission, 6/15 priority date for domestic students; for winter admission, 10/15 priority date for domestic students; for spring admission, 2/15 priority date for domestic students. Application fee: $50. *Unit head:* Erik Hemdal, Program Chair, 781-736-8787, Fax: 781-736-3420, E-mail: ehemdal@brandeis.edu. *Application contact:* Frances Stearns, Associate Director of Admissions and Student Services, 781-736-8785, Fax: 781-736-3420, E-mail: fstearns@brandeis.edu.

California State University, Fullerton, Graduate Studies, College of Engineering and Computer Science, Department of Computer Science, Fullerton, CA 92834-9480. Offers computer science (MS); software engineering (MS). Part-time programs available. Postbaccalaureate distance learning degree programs offered. *Students:* 56 full-time (12 women), 280 part-time (74 women); includes 12 Black or African American, non-Hispanic/Latino; 76 Asian, non-Hispanic/Latino; 15 Hispanic/Latino; 5 Two or more races, non-Hispanic/Latino, 134 international. Average age 31. 238 applicants, 63% accepted, 91 enrolled. In 2010, 114 master's awarded. *Degree requirements:* For master's, comprehensive exam, project or thesis. *Entrance requirements:* For master's, GRE General Test, minimum undergraduate GPA of 2.5. Application fee: $55. *Financial support:* Career-related internships or fieldwork, Federal Work-Study, institutionally sponsored loans, and scholarships/grants available. Support available to part-time students. Financial award application deadline: 3/1; financial award applicants required to submit FAFSA. *Faculty research:* Software engineering, development of computer networks. *Unit head:* Dr. James Choi, Chair, 657-278-3700. *Application contact:* Admissions/Applications, 657-278-2371.

California State University, Northridge, Graduate Studies, College of Engineering and Computer Science, Department of Computer Science, Northridge, CA 91330. Offers computer science (MS); software engineering (MS). Part-time and evening/weekend programs available. *Degree requirements:* For master's, thesis. *Entrance requirements:* For master's, GRE General Test, minimum GPA of 2.5. Additional exam requirements/recommendations for international students: Required—TOEFL. *Faculty research:* Radar data processing.

California State University, Sacramento, Graduate Studies, College of Engineering and Computer Science, Department of Computer Science, Sacramento, CA 95819. Offers computer systems (MS); software engineering (MS). Part-time and evening/weekend programs available. *Degree requirements:* For master's, thesis or alternative, writing proficiency exam. *Entrance requirements:* Additional exam requirements/recommendations for international students: Required—TOEFL. Electronic applications accepted.

Carnegie Mellon University, Carnegie Institute of Technology, Information Networking Institute, Pittsburgh, PA 15213. Offers information networking (MS); information security technology and management (MS); information technology—information security (MS); information technology—mobility (MS); information technology—software management (MS). *Degree requirements:* For master's, thesis optional. *Entrance requirements:* For master's, GRE General Test, bachelor's degree in computer science, computer engineering, or electrical engineering, or related technology degree; programming skills (C/C++ fluency for some programs). Additional exam requirements/recommendations for international students: Required—TOEFL. *Faculty research:* Computer forensics and incident response; dependable systems, embedded systems, mobile systems, and sensor networks; computer and information networks, network and information security, human and socio-economic factors in secure system design; wireless sensor networks, survivable embedded systems, signal processing/compression; strategic management, international strategic management, group dynamics and decision-making structures, simulated competitive environments.

Carnegie Mellon University, School of Computer Science, Software Engineering Program, Pittsburgh, PA 15213-3891. Offers MSE, PhD. *Entrance requirements:* For master's, GRE General Test, GRE Subject Test (computer science), 2 years of experience in large-scale software development project.

Carnegie Mellon University, Tepper School of Business, Pittsburgh, PA 15213-3891. Offers accounting (PhD); algorithms, combinatorics, and optimization (MS, PhD); business management and software engineering (MBMSE); civil engineering and industrial management (MS); computational finance (MSCF); economics (MS, PhD); electronic commerce (MS); environmental engineering and management (MEEM); finance (PhD); financial economics (PhD); industrial administration (MBA), including administration and public management; information systems (PhD); management of manufacturing and automation (PhD); marketing (PhD); mathematical finance (PhD); operations research (PhD); organizational behavior and theory (PhD); political economy (PhD); production and operations management (PhD); public policy and management (MS, MSED); software engineering and business management (MS); JD/MS; JD/MSIA; M Div/MS; MOM/MSIA; MSCF/MSIA. JD/MSIA offered jointly with University of Pittsburgh. Part-time programs available. Terminal master's awarded for partial completion of doctoral program. *Degree requirements:* For doctorate, thesis/dissertation. *Entrance requirements:* For master's, GMAT. Additional exam requirements/recommendations for international students: Required—TOEFL. *Expenses:* Contact institution.

Carroll University, Program in Software Engineering, Waukesha, WI 53186-5593. Offers MSE. Part-time and evening/weekend programs available. *Faculty:* 4 full-time (1 woman).

Students: 5 full-time (4 women), 27 part-time (5 women); includes 3 minority (1 Black or African American, non-Hispanic/Latino; 1 Asian, non-Hispanic/Latino; 1 Hispanic/Latino), 7 international. Average age 34. 29 applicants, 76% accepted, 8 enrolled. In 2010, 8 master's awarded. *Degree requirements:* For master's, professional experience, capstone project. *Entrance requirements:* For master's, BA or BS, 2 years professional experience. Additional exam requirements/recommendations for international students: Required—TOEFL. *Application deadline:* For fall admission, 9/15 priority date for domestic students. Applications are processed on a rolling basis. Application fee: $0. Electronic applications accepted. *Expenses:* Tuition: Full-time $24,749; part-time $440 per credit hour. Required fees: $550. *Financial support:* In 2010–11, 2 students received support. Institutionally sponsored loans available. Support available to part-time students. *Faculty research:* Networking, artificial intelligence, virtual reality, effective teaching of software design, computer science pedagogy. *Unit head:* Dr. Chenglie Hu, Associate Professor of Computer Science and Program Director, 262-524-7170, E-mail: chu@carrollu.edu. *Application contact:* Tami Bartunek, Graduate Admission Counselor, 262-524-7643, E-mail: tbartune@carrollu.edu.

Cleveland State University, College of Graduate Studies, Fenn College of Engineering, Department of Electrical and Computer Engineering, Cleveland, OH 44115. Offers electrical engineering (MS, D Eng); software engineering (MS). Part-time programs available. *Faculty:* 15 full-time (2 women), 2 part-time/adjunct (0 women). *Students:* 46 full-time (12 women), 160 part-time (26 women); includes 5 Black or African American, non-Hispanic/Latino; 9 Asian, non-Hispanic/Latino; 1 Hispanic/Latino, 140 international. Average age 27. 328 applicants, 48% accepted, 31 enrolled. In 2010, 59 master's, 1 doctorate awarded. *Degree requirements:* For master's, thesis optional; for doctorate, thesis/dissertation, qualifying and candidacy exams. *Entrance requirements:* For master's, GRE General Test (minimum score 650 quantitative), minimum GPA of 2.75; for doctorate, GRE General Test (quantitative score in 80th percentile), minimum GPA of 3.25. Additional exam requirements/recommendations for international students: Required—TOEFL (minimum score 535 paper-based; 197 computer-based; 65 iBT). *Application deadline:* For fall admission, 7/15 priority date for domestic students. Applications are processed on a rolling basis. Application fee: $30. *Expenses:* Tuition, state resident: full-time $8447; part-time $469 per credit hour. Tuition, nonresident: full-time $16,020; part-time $890 per credit hour. Required fees: $50. *Financial support:* In 2010–11, 31 students received support, including 23 research assistantships with full and partial tuition reimbursements available (averaging $4,242 per year), 8 teaching assistantships with full and partial tuition reimbursements available (averaging $4,242 per year); career-related internships or fieldwork also available. *Faculty research:* Computer networks, knowledge-based control systems, artificial intelligence, digital communications, MEMS, sensors, power systems, power electronics. *Unit head:* Dr. Fuqin Xiong, Chairperson, 216-687-2127, E-mail: f.xiong@csuohio.edu. *Application contact:* Dr. Fuqin Xiong, Chairperson, 216-687-2127, E-mail: f.xiong@csuohio.edu.

Colorado Technical University Colorado Springs, Graduate Studies, Program in Computer Science, Colorado Springs, CO 80907-3896. Offers computer science (DCS); computer systems security (MSCS); database systems (MSCS); software engineering (MSCS). Part-time and evening/weekend programs available. Postbaccalaureate distance learning degree programs offered. *Degree requirements:* For master's, thesis or alternative; for doctorate, thesis/dissertation. *Entrance requirements:* For doctorate, minimum graduate GPA of 3.0, 5 years of related work experience. *Faculty research:* Software engineering, systems engineering.

Colorado Technical University Denver, Program in Computer Science, Greenwood Village, CO 80111. Offers computer systems security (MSCS); database systems (MSCS); software engineering (MSCS). Part-time and evening/weekend programs available. *Degree requirements:* For master's, thesis or alternative. *Entrance requirements:* For master's, minimum undergraduate GPA of 3.0, resume.

Colorado Technical University Sioux Falls, Program in Computing, Sioux Falls, SD 57108. Offers computer systems security (MSCS); software engineering (MSCS).

Concordia University, School of Graduate Studies, Faculty of Engineering and Computer Science, Department of Computer Science and Software Engineering, Montréal, QC H3G 1M8, Canada. Offers computer science (M App Comp Sc, M Comp Sc, PhD, Diploma); software engineering (MA Sc). *Degree requirements:* For master's, one foreign language, thesis optional; for doctorate, one foreign language, comprehensive exam, thesis/dissertation. *Faculty research:* Computer systems and applications, mathematics of computation, pattern recognition, artificial intelligence and robotics.

Concordia University, School of Graduate Studies, Faculty of Engineering and Computer Science, Department of Mechanical and Industrial Engineering, Montréal, QC H3G 1M8, Canada. Offers composites (M Eng); industrial engineering (M Eng, MA Sc); mechanical engineering (M Eng, MA Sc, PhD, Certificate); software systems for industrial engineering (Certificate). M Eng in composites program offered jointly with École Polytechnique de Montréal. *Degree requirements:* For master's, variable foreign language requirement, thesis or alternative; for doctorate, comprehensive exam, thesis/dissertation. *Faculty research:* Mechanical systems, fluid control systems, thermofluids engineering and robotics, industrial control systems.

DePaul University, College of Computing and Digital Media, Chicago, IL 60604. Offers animation (MA, MFA); applied technology (MS); business information technology (MS); cinema (MFA); cinema production (MS); computational finance (MS); computer and information sciences (PhD); computer game development (MS); computer graphics and motion technology (MS); computer information and network security (MS); computer science (MS); e-commerce technology (MS); human-computer interaction (MS); information systems (MS); information technology (MA); information technology project management (MS); network engineering and management (MS); predictive analytics (MS); screenwriting (MFA); software engineering (MS); JD/MA; JD/MS. Part-time and evening/weekend programs available. Postbaccalaureate distance learning degree programs offered (no on-campus study). *Faculty:* 51 full-time (11 women), 50 part-time/adjunct (9 women). *Students:* 952 full-time (230 women), 927 part-time (226 women); includes 557 minority (205 Black or African American, non-Hispanic/Latino; 2 American Indian or Alaska Native, non-Hispanic/Latino; 167 Asian, non-Hispanic/Latino; 136 Hispanic/Latino; 7 Native Hawaiian or other Pacific Islander, non-Hispanic/Latino; 40 Two or more races, non-Hispanic/Latino), 292 international. Average age 31. 896 applicants, 70% accepted, 324 enrolled. In 2010, 417 master's, 6 doctorates awarded. *Degree requirements:* For master's, thesis (for some programs); for doctorate, comprehensive exam, thesis/dissertation. *Entrance requirements:* For master's, GRE or GMAT (MS in computational finance only), bachelor's degree, resume (MS in predictive analytics only), IT experience (MS in information technology project management only), portfolio review (MFA); for doctorate, GRE, master's degree in computer science. Additional exam requirements/recommendations for international students: Required—TOEFL (minimum score 550 paper-based; 213 computer-based; 80 iBT), IELTS (minimum score 6.5), Pearson Test of English (minimum score 53). *Application deadline:* For fall admission, 8/15 priority date for domestic students, 6/1 priority date for international students; for winter admission, 12/15 priority date for domestic students, 9/15 priority date for international students; for spring admission, 3/1 priority date for domestic students, 12/15 priority date for international students. Applications are processed on a rolling basis. Application fee: $25. Electronic applications accepted. *Expenses:* Contact institution. *Financial support:* In 2010–11, 102 students received support, including 4 fellowships with full tuition reimbursements available (averaging $24,435 per year), 6 research assistantships (averaging $21,100 per year), 92 teaching assistantships with full and partial tuition reimbursements available (averaging $6,904 per year); Federal Work-Study, scholarships/grants, tuition waivers (full and partial), and unspecified assistantships also available. Support available to part-time students. Financial award application deadline: 4/30; financial award applicants required to submit FAFSA. *Faculty research:* Bioinformatics, visual computing, graphics and animation, high performance and scientific computing, databases. Total annual research expenditures: $1.4 million. *Unit head:* Dr. David Miller, Dean, 312-362-8381, Fax: 312-362-5185. *Application contact:* Dr. Liz Friedman, Assistant Dean of Student Services, 312-362-8714, Fax: 312-362-5179, E-mail: efriedm2@cdm.depaul.edu.

Drexel University, College of Engineering, Department of Electrical and Computer Engineering, Program in Software Engineering, Philadelphia, PA 19104-2875. Offers MSSE. *Entrance requirements:* For master's, GRE. Additional exam requirements/recommendations for international students: Required—TOEFL. Electronic applications accepted.

Drexel University, The iSchool at Drexel, College of Information Science and Technology, Philadelphia, PA 19104-2875. Offers healthcare informatics (Certificate); information science and technology (PMC); information studies (PhD); information studies and technology (Advanced Certificate); information systems (MSIS); library and information science (MS), including archival studies, competitive intelligence and knowledge management, digital libraries, library and information services, school library media, youth services; software engineering (MSSE). *Accreditation:* ALA (one or more programs are accredited). Part-time and evening/weekend programs available. Postbaccalaureate distance learning degree programs offered (no on-campus study). *Faculty:* 33 full-time (21 women), 26 part-time/adjunct (12 women). *Students:* 278 full-time (187 women), 662 part-time (451 women); includes 123 minority (46 Black or African American, non-Hispanic/Latino; 7 American Indian or Alaska Native, non-Hispanic/Latino; 36 Asian, non-Hispanic/Latino; 34 Hispanic/Latino), 44 international. Average age 34. 674 applicants, 68% accepted, 343 enrolled. In 2010, 288 master's, 7 doctorates, 19 other advanced degrees awarded. *Degree requirements:* For doctorate, thesis/dissertation. *Entrance requirements:* For master's and doctorate, GRE General Test. Additional exam requirements/recommendations for international students: Required—TOEFL (minimum score 600 paper-based; 250 computer-based; 100 iBT). *Application deadline:* For fall admission, 9/1 for domestic and international students; for spring admission, 3/4 for domestic students, 2/15 for international students. Applications are processed on a rolling basis. Electronic applications accepted. *Expenses:* Contact institution. *Financial support:* In 2010–11, 250 students received support, including 264 fellowships with partial tuition reimbursements available (averaging $22,500 per year), 22 research assistantships with full tuition reimbursements available (averaging $22,500 per year), 8 teaching assistantships with full tuition reimbursements available (averaging $25,000 per year); institutionally sponsored loans, scholarships/grants, health care benefits, tuition waivers (partial), and unspecified assistantships also available. Support available to part-time students. Financial award applicants required to submit FAFSA. *Faculty research:* Information retrieval/information visualization/bibliometrics, human-computer interaction, digital libraries, databases, text/data mining. Total annual research expenditures: $2 million. *Unit head:* Dr. David E. Fenske, Dean and Isaac L. Auerbach Professor of Information Science, 215-895-2475, Fax: 215-895-6378, E-mail: fenske@drexel.edu. *Application contact:* Matthew Lechtenberg, Graduate Admissions Manager, 215-895-1951, Fax: 215-895-2303, E-mail: ml333@drexel.edu.

Embry-Riddle Aeronautical University–Daytona, Daytona Beach Campus Graduate Program, Department of Computer and Software Engineering, Daytona Beach, FL 32114-3900. Offers electrical/computer engineering (MSECE); software engineering (MSE). Part-time and evening/weekend programs available. *Faculty:* 6 full-time (0 women), 2 part-time/adjunct (1 woman). *Students:* 31 full-time (4 women), 3 part-time (0 women); includes 3 minority (1 Asian, non-Hispanic/Latino; 2 Hispanic/Latino), 10 international. Average age 26. 22 applicants, 64% accepted, 9 enrolled. In 2010, 10 master's awarded. *Degree requirements:* For master's, thesis or alternative. *Entrance requirements:* For master's, minimum GPA of 3.0 in senior year, 2.5 overall; course work in computer science. Additional exam requirements/recommendations for international students: Required—TOEFL (minimum score 550 paper-based; 213 computer-based; 79 iBT). *Application deadline:* For fall admission, 8/1 priority date for domestic students; for spring admission, 12/1 priority date for domestic students. Applications are processed on a rolling basis. Application fee: $50. *Expenses:* Tuition: Full-time $14,040; part-time $1170 per credit hour. *Financial support:* In 2010–11, 20 students received support, including 2 research assistantships with full and partial tuition reimbursements available (averaging $5,384 per year), 7 teaching assistantships with full and partial tuition reimbursements available (averaging $5,667 per year); career-related internships or fieldwork, Federal Work-Study, and unspecified assistantships also available. Financial award application deadline: 4/15; financial award applicants required to submit FAFSA. *Faculty research:* Evaluation of residual strength of Beechcraft Bonanza spar carry-through with fatigue cracks, Swift Fuel PA44-180, Scramjet engine simulation, marine turbines, wireless sensors for aircraft, bistatic radar, blind signal separation in dynamic environments, EcoCAR IDEA, FAA nextgen Task K demonstration of flight data object planning, NOAA UAS for in-situ tropical cyclone sensing, aeroelastic gust-airfoil interaction numerical studies. *Unit head:* Dr. Farahzad Behi, Program Coordinator, 386-226-6454, E-mail: farahzad.behi@erau.edu. *Application contact:* Keith Deaton, Director, International and Graduate Admissions, 800-388-3728, Fax: 386-226-7070, E-mail: graduate.admissions@erau.edu.

Fairfield University, School of Engineering, Fairfield, CT 06824-5195. Offers electrical and computer engineering (MS); management of technology (MS); mechanical engineering (MS); software engineering (MS). Part-time and evening/weekend programs available. *Faculty:* 8 full-time (1 woman), 11 part-time/adjunct (0 women). *Students:* 31 full-time (12 women), 98 part-time (20 women); includes 28 minority (5 Black or African American, non-Hispanic/Latino; 17 Asian, non-Hispanic/Latino; 4 Hispanic/Latino; 1 Native Hawaiian or other Pacific Islander, non-Hispanic/Latino; 1 Two or more races, non-Hispanic/Latino), 26 international. Average age 35. 120 applicants, 55% accepted, 15 enrolled. In 2010, 52 master's awarded. *Degree requirements:* For master's, thesis, capstone course. *Entrance requirements:* For master's, interview, minimum GPA of 2.8, resume, 2 recommendations. Additional exam requirements/recommendations for international students: Required—TOEFL (minimum score 550 paper-based; 213 computer-based; 80 iBT). *Application deadline:* For fall admission, 5/15 for international students; for spring admission, 10/15 for international students. Applications are processed on a rolling basis. Application fee: $60. Electronic applications accepted. *Expenses:* Contact institution. *Financial support:* In 2010–11, 25 students received support. Unspecified assistantships available. Financial award applicants required to submit FAFSA. *Faculty research:* Vehicle dynamics, image processing, multimedia in instruction, thermal packaging, character recognition, photovoltaics and nanotechnology, Web technology. *Unit head:* Dr. Jack Beal, Dean, 203-254-4000 Ext. 4147, Fax: 203-254-4013, E-mail: jwbeal@fairfield.edu. *Application contact:* Marianne Gumpper, Director of Graduate and Continuing Studies Admissions, 203-254-4184, Fax: 203-254-4073, E-mail: gradadmis@fairfield.edu.

Florida Agricultural and Mechanical University, Division of Graduate Studies, Research, and Continuing Education, College of Arts and Sciences, Department of Computer Information Sciences, Tallahassee, FL 32307-3200. Offers software engineering (MS). *Entrance requirements:* Additional exam requirements/recommendations for international students: Required—TOEFL.

Florida Institute of Technology, Graduate Programs, College of Engineering, Computer Science Department, Melbourne, FL 32901-6975. Offers computer science (MS, PhD); software engineering (MS). Part-time and evening/weekend programs available. *Faculty:* 11 full-time (0 women), 1 part-time/adjunct (0 women). *Students:* 70 full-time (17 women), 44 part-time (9 women); includes 8 minority (4 Black or African American, non-Hispanic/Latino; 2 Asian, non-Hispanic/Latino; 2 Hispanic/Latino), 73 international. Average age 28. 270 applicants, 60% accepted, 28 enrolled. In 2010, 21 master's, 2 doctorates awarded. *Degree requirements:* For master's, comprehensive exam (for some programs), thesis optional, non-thesis: final exam, seminar, or internship; for doctorate, comprehensive exam, thesis/dissertation, publication in journal, teaching experience (strongly encouraged), specialized research program. *Entrance requirements:* For master's, GRE General Test, minimum GPA of 3.0, 3 letters of recommendation; for doctorate, GRE General Test, GRE Subject Test in computer science (recommended), 3 letters of recommendation, minimum GPA of 3.5, resume, statement of objectives. Additional exam requirements/recommendations for international students: Required—TOEFL (minimum score 550 paper-based; 213 computer-based; 79 iBT). *Application deadline:* For fall admission, 4/1 for international students; for spring admission, 9/30 for international students. Applications are processed on a rolling basis. Application fee: $50. Electronic applications accepted. *Expenses:* Tuition: Part-time $1040 per credit hour. Tuition and fees vary according to campus/location. *Financial support:* In 2010–11, 1 research assistantship with full and partial tuition reimbursement (averaging $5,400 per year), 14 teaching assistantships with full

Software Engineering

Florida Institute of Technology (continued)

and partial tuition reimbursements (averaging $12,239 per year) were awarded; career-related internships or fieldwork, institutionally sponsored loans, tuition waivers (partial), unspecified assistantships, and tuition remissions also available. Support available to part-time students. Financial award application deadline: 3/1; financial award applicants required to submit FAFSA. *Faculty research:* Artificial intelligence, software engineering, management and processes, programming languages, database systems. Total annual research expenditures: $1.2 million. *Unit head:* Dr. William D. Shoaff, Department Head, 321-674-8066, Fax: 321-674-7046, E-mail: wds@cs.fit.edu. *Application contact:* Cheryl A. Brown, Associate Director of Graduate Admissions, 321-674-7581, Fax: 321-723-9468, E-mail: cbrown@fit.edu.

Florida Institute of Technology, Graduate Programs, Extended Studies Division, Melbourne, FL 32901-6975. Offers acquisition and contract management (MS); aerospace engineering (MS); business administration (MBA); computer information systems (MS); computer science (MS); electrical engineering (MS); engineering management (MS); human resources management (MS); logistics management (MS), including humanitarian and disaster relief logistics; management (MS), including acquisition and contract management, e-business, human resources management, information systems, logistics management, management, transportation management; material acquisition management (MS); mechanical engineering (MS); operations research (MS); project management (MS), including information systems, operations research; public administration (MPA); quality management (MS); software engineering (MS); space systems (MS); space systems management (MS); systems management (MS), including information systems, operations research. Part-time and evening/weekend programs available. Postbaccalaureate distance learning degree programs offered (no on-campus study). *Faculty:* 11 full-time (3 women), 118 part-time/adjunct (24 women). *Students:* 69 full-time (23 women), 907 part-time (369 women); includes 385 minority (242 Black or African American, non-Hispanic/Latino; 15 American Indian or Alaska Native, non-Hispanic/Latino; 44 Asian, non-Hispanic/Latino; 52 Hispanic/Latino; 3 Native Hawaiian or other Pacific Islander, non-Hispanic/Latino; 29 Two or more races, non-Hispanic/Latino), 17 international. 517 applicants, 49% accepted, 245 enrolled. In 2010, 430 degrees awarded. *Degree requirements:* For master's, comprehensive exam (for some programs), capstone course. *Entrance requirements:* For master's, GMAT or resume showing 8 years of supervised experience, minimum GPA of 3.0, 2 letters of recommendation, resume. Additional exam requirements/recommendations for international students: Required—TOEFL (minimum score 550 paper-based; 213 computer-based; 79 iBT). *Application deadline:* For fall admission, 4/1 for international students; for spring admission, 9/30 for international students. Applications are processed on a rolling basis. Application fee: $50. Electronic applications accepted. *Expenses:* Contact institution. *Financial support:* Application deadline: 3/1. *Unit head:* Dr. Theodore Richardson, Senior Associate Dean, 321-674-8123, Fax: 321-674-7597, E-mail: trichardson@fit.edu. *Application contact:* Carolyn Farrior, Director of Graduate Admissions, Online Learning and Off-Campus Programs, 321-674-7118, Fax: 321-674-8216, E-mail: cfarrior@fit.edu.

Gannon University, School of Graduate Studies, College of Engineering and Business, School of Engineering and Computer Science, Program in Embedded Software Engineering, Erie, PA 16541-0001. Offers MSES. Part-time and evening/weekend programs available. *Students:* 8 full-time (1 woman), 5 part-time (0 women), 10 international. Average age 25. 25 applicants, 80% accepted, 3 enrolled. In 2010, 23 master's awarded. *Degree requirements:* For master's, thesis or project. *Entrance requirements:* For master's, GRE or GMAT, bachelor's degree in engineering, minimum QPA of 2.5. Additional exam requirements/recommendations for international students: Required—TOEFL (minimum score 79 iBT). *Application deadline:* Applications are processed on a rolling basis. Application fee: $25. Electronic applications accepted. *Expenses:* Tuition: Full-time $14,670; part-time $815 per credit. Required fees: $430; $18 per credit. Tuition and fees vary according to class time, course load, degree level, campus/location and program. *Financial support:* Career-related internships or fieldwork, Federal Work-Study, scholarships/grants, traineeships, and unspecified assistantships available. Financial award application deadline: 7/1; financial award applicants required to submit FAFSA. *Unit head:* Dr. Fong Mak, Chair, 814-871-7625, E-mail: mak001@gannon.edu. *Application contact:* Kara Morgan, Assistant Director of Graduate Admissions, 814-871-5831, Fax: 814-871-5827, E-mail: graduate@gannon.edu.

George Mason University, Volgenau School of Engineering, Department of Computer Science, Fairfax, VA 22030. Offers biometrics (Certificate); computer games technology (Certificate); computer networking (Certificate); computer science (MS, PhD); data mining (Certificate); database management (Certificate); electronic commerce (Certificate); foundations of information systems (Certificate); information engineering (Certificate); information security and assurance (MS, Certificate); information systems (MS); intelligent agents (Certificate); software architecture (Certificate); software engineering (MS, Certificate); systems engineering (MS); Web-based software engineering (Certificate). MS program offered jointly with Old Dominion University, University of Virginia, Virginia Commonwealth University, and Virginia Polytechnic Institute and State University. Part-time and evening/weekend programs available. Postbaccalaureate distance learning degree programs offered. *Faculty:* 42 full-time (9 women), 20 part-time/adjunct (1 woman). *Students:* 124 full-time (37 women), 453 part-time (103 women); includes 14 Black or African American, non-Hispanic/Latino; 66 Asian, non-Hispanic/Latino; 13 Hispanic/Latino; 3 Two or more races, non-Hispanic/Latino, 206 international. Average age 30. 904 applicants, 53% accepted, 150 enrolled. In 2010, 203 master's, 4 doctorates, 20 other advanced degrees awarded. *Degree requirements:* For master's, thesis optional; for doctorate, comprehensive exam, thesis/dissertation. *Entrance requirements:* For master's, GRE General Test, minimum GPA of 3.0 in last 60 hours, 3 letters of recommendation; for doctorate, GRE, 4-year BA, academic work in computer science, 3 letters of recommendation, statement of career goals and aspirations. Additional exam requirements/recommendations for international students: Required—TOEFL (minimum score 570 paper-based; 230 computer-based; 88 iBT). *Application deadline:* For fall admission, 4/15 priority date for domestic students, 1/15 for international students; for spring admission, 11/15 for domestic students. Application fee: $100. Electronic applications accepted. *Expenses:* Tuition, state resident: full-time $8192; part-time $440 per credit hour. Tuition, nonresident: full-time $22,952; part-time $1055 per credit hour. Required fees: $2364; $99 per credit hour. *Financial support:* In 2010–11, 101 students received support, including 3 fellowships (averaging $18,000 per year), 52 research assistantships (averaging $15,078 per year), 47 teaching assistantships (averaging $10,983 per year); career-related internships or fieldwork, Federal Work-Study, scholarships/grants, unspecified assistantships, and health care benefits (full-time research or teaching assistantship recipients) also available. Financial award application deadline: 3/1; financial award applicants required to submit FAFSA. *Faculty research:* Artificial intelligence, image processing/graphics, parallel/distributed systems, software engineering systems. Total annual research expenditures: $1.3 million. *Unit head:* Dr. Arun Sood, Director, 703-993-1524, Fax: 703-993-1710, E-mail: asood@gmu.edu. *Application contact:* Jay Shapiro, Professor, 703-993-1485, E-mail: jshapiro@gmu.edu.

Grand Valley State University, Padnos College of Engineering and Computing, School of Computing and Information Systems, Allendale, MI 49401-9403. Offers computer information systems (MS), including databases, distributed systems, management of information systems, object-oriented systems, software engineering. Part-time and evening/weekend programs available. *Degree requirements:* For master's, thesis or alternative. *Entrance requirements:* For master's, GMAT or GRE General Test. Additional exam requirements/recommendations for international students: Required—TOEFL. Electronic applications accepted. *Faculty research:* Object technology, distributed computing, information systems management database, software engineering.

Hawai'i Pacific University, College of Business Administration, Program in Information Systems, Honolulu, HI 96813. Offers knowledge management (MSIS); software engineering (MSIS); telecommunications security (MSIS).

Illinois Institute of Technology, Graduate College, Armour College of Engineering, Department of Electrical and Computer Engineering, Chicago, IL 60616-3793. Offers biomedical imaging

and signals (MBMI); computer engineering (MS, PhD); electrical and computer engineering (MECE); electrical engineering (MS, PhD); electricity markets (MEM); network engineering (MNE); power engineering (MPE); telecommunications and software engineering (MTSE); VLSI and microelectronics (MVM). Part-time and evening/weekend programs available. Postbaccalaureate distance learning degree programs offered (minimal on-campus study). *Faculty:* 26 full-time (3 women), 2 part-time/adjunct (0 women). *Students:* 456 full-time (77 women), 140 part-time (17 women); includes 25 minority (4 Black or African American, non-Hispanic/Latino; 15 Asian, non-Hispanic/Latino; 4 Hispanic/Latino; 2 Two or more races, non-Hispanic/Latino), 488 international. Average age 26. 1,407 applicants, 68% accepted, 217 enrolled. In 2010, 214 master's, 17 doctorates awarded. Terminal master's awarded for partial completion of doctoral program. *Degree requirements:* For master's, comprehensive exam (for some programs), thesis (for some programs); for doctorate, comprehensive exam, thesis/dissertation. *Entrance requirements:* For master's and doctorate, GRE General Test (minimum score 1100 Quantitative and Verbal, 3.5 Analytical Writing), minimum undergraduate GPA of 3.0. Additional exam requirements/recommendations for international students: Required—TOEFL (minimum score 523 paper-based; 70 iBT); Recommended—IELTS (minimum score 5.5). *Application deadline:* For fall admission, 5/1 for domestic and international students; for spring admission, 10/15 for domestic and international students. Applications are processed on a rolling basis. Application fee: $50. Electronic applications accepted. *Expenses:* Tuition: Full-time $18,576; part-time $1032 per credit hour. Required fees: $583 per semester. One-time fee: $150. Tuition and fees vary according to program and student level. *Financial support:* In 2010–11, 1 fellowship with full and partial tuition reimbursement (averaging $1,090 per year), 52 research assistantships with full and partial tuition reimbursements (averaging $9,530 per year), 24 teaching assistantships with full and partial tuition reimbursements (averaging $9,092 per year) were awarded; career-related internships or fieldwork, Federal Work-Study, institutionally sponsored loans, scholarships/grants, health care benefits, tuition waivers (full), and unspecified assistantships also available. Support available to part-time students. Financial award applicants required to submit FAFSA. *Faculty research:* Communication systems, computer systems and micro-electronics, electromagnetics and electronics, power and control systems, signal and image processing. Total annual research expenditures: $5.6 million. *Unit head:* Dr. Geoffrey Williamson, Interim Chair, 312-567-5960, Fax: 312-567-8976, E-mail: williamson@iit.edu. *Application contact:* Deborah Gibson, Director, Graduate Admission, 866-472-3448, Fax: 312-567-3138, E-mail: inquiry.grad@iit.edu.

Illinois Institute of Technology, Graduate College, College of Science and Letters, Department of Computer Science, Chicago, IL 60616-3793. Offers business (MCS); computer networking and telecommunications (MCS); computer science (MCS, MS, PhD); information systems (MCS); software engineering (MCS); teaching (MST). Part-time and evening/weekend programs available. Postbaccalaureate distance learning degree programs offered (no on-campus study). *Faculty:* 29 full-time (6 women), 3 part-time/adjunct (0 women). *Students:* 262 full-time (62 women), 132 part-time (27 women); includes 44 minority (3 Black or African American, non-Hispanic/Latino; 7 Asian, non-Hispanic/Latino; 34 Hispanic/Latino), 340 international. Average age 26. 974 applicants, 71% accepted, 148 enrolled. In 2010, 138 master's, 5 doctorates awarded. Terminal master's awarded for partial completion of doctoral program. *Degree requirements:* For master's, thesis optional; for doctorate, comprehensive exam, thesis/dissertation. *Entrance requirements:* For master's, GRE General Test (minimum scores: 1000 Quantitative and Verbal, 3.0 Analytical Writing), minimum undergraduate GPA of 3.0; for doctorate, GRE General Test (minimum scores: 1100 Quantitative and Verbal, 3.5 Analytical Writing), minimum undergraduate GPA of 3.0. Additional exam requirements/recommendations for international students: Required—TOEFL (minimum score 523 paper-based; 70 iBT). *Application deadline:* For fall admission, 5/1 for domestic and international students; for spring admission, 10/15 for domestic and international students. Applications are processed on a rolling basis. Application fee: $50. Electronic applications accepted. *Expenses:* Tuition: Full-time $18,576; part-time $1032 per credit hour. Required fees: $583 per semester. One-time fee: $150. Tuition and fees vary according to program and student level. *Financial support:* In 2010–11, 15 research assistantships with full and partial tuition reimbursements (averaging $10,380 per year), 21 teaching assistantships with full and partial tuition reimbursements (averaging $12,452 per year) were awarded; fellowships with partial tuition reimbursements, career-related internships or fieldwork, Federal Work-Study, institutionally sponsored loans, scholarships/grants, traineeships, health care benefits, tuition waivers (partial), and unspecified assistantships also available. Support available to part-time students. Financial award applicants required to submit FAFSA. *Faculty research:* Algorithms, data structures, artificial intelligences, computer architecture, computer graphics, computer networking and telecommunications. Total annual research expenditures: $1.8 million. *Unit head:* Dr. Xian-He Sun, Chair/Professor, 312-567-5260, Fax: 312-567-5067, E-mail: sun@cs.iit.edu. *Application contact:* Debbie Gibson, Director, Graduate Admission, 866-472-3448, Fax: 312-567-3138, E-mail: inquiry.grad@iit.edu.

Instituto Tecnologico de Santo Domingo, Graduate School, Area of Engineering, Santo Domingo, Dominican Republic. Offers construction administration (MS, Certificate); data telecommunications (M Eng, MS, Certificate); industrial engineering (M Eng, Certificate); industrial management (M Mgmt); information technology (Certificate); maintenance engineering (M Eng); occupational hazard prevention (M Mgmt); production management (Certificate); quantitative methods (Certificate); sanitary and environmental engineering (M Eng); structural engineering (M Eng); systems engineering and electronic data processing (Certificate); transportation (Certificate).

International Technological University, Program in Software Engineering, Santa Clara, CA 95050. Offers MSSE, PhD. *Degree requirements:* For master's, thesis or alternative. *Entrance requirements:* For master's, 3 semesters of calculus, minimum GPA of 2.5. Additional exam requirements/recommendations for international students: Required—TOEFL. *Faculty research:* Software testing, web management, client service and the Internet.

Jacksonville State University, College of Graduate Studies and Continuing Education, College of Arts and Sciences, Program in Computer Systems and Software Design, Jacksonville, AL 36265-1602. Offers MS. Part-time and evening/weekend programs available. *Degree requirements:* For master's, comprehensive exam, thesis (for some programs). Electronic applications accepted.

Kansas State University, Graduate School, College of Engineering, Department of Computing and Information Sciences, Manhattan, KS 66506. Offers computer science (MS, PhD); software engineering (MSE). Part-time programs available. Postbaccalaureate distance learning degree programs offered (minimal on-campus study). Terminal master's awarded for partial completion of doctoral program. *Degree requirements:* For master's, thesis or alternative; for doctorate, thesis/dissertation, preliminary exams. *Entrance requirements:* For master's, GRE, bachelor's degree in computer science, minimum GPA of 3.0; for doctorate, GRE General Test, GRE Subject Test, master's degree in computer science or bachelor's degree and strong advanced computer knowledge. Additional exam requirements/recommendations for international students: Required—TOEFL (minimum score 575 paper-based; 233 computer-based). Electronic applications accepted. *Faculty research:* High-assurance software and programming languages, data mining, parallel and distributed computing, computer security, embedded systems.

Loyola University Chicago, Graduate School, Department of Computer Science, Chicago, IL 60660. Offers computer science (MS); information technology (MS); software technology (MS). Part-time and evening/weekend programs available. *Faculty:* 9 full-time (1 woman), 10 part-time/adjunct (2 women). *Students:* 39 full-time (15 women), 46 part-time (11 women); includes 13 minority (3 Black or African American, non-Hispanic/Latino; 9 Asian, non-Hispanic/Latino; 1 Hispanic/Latino), 35 international. Average age 28. 87 applicants, 67% accepted, 30 enrolled. In 2010, 35 master's awarded. *Degree requirements:* For master's, thesis optional, Ten Graduate Courses. Prerequisites are additional if student does not have adequate CS background. *Entrance requirements:* For master's, 3 letters of recommendation, transcripts, statement of purpose. Additional exam requirements/recommendations for international students: Required—TOEFL (minimum score 550 paper-based, 213 computer-based, 79 iBT) or IELTS

(6.5). *Application deadline:* For fall admission, 8/10 for domestic students, 5/15 priority date for international students; for spring admission, 12/20 for domestic students, 9/15 priority date for international students. Applications are processed on a rolling basis. Application fee: $0. Electronic applications accepted. *Expenses:* Tuition: Full-time $14,940; part-time $830 per credit hour. Required fees: $87 per semester. Part-time tuition and fees vary according to course load and program. *Financial support:* In 2010–11, 24 students received support, including 1 fellowship (averaging $3,000 per year), 16 teaching assistantships with partial tuition reimbursements available (averaging $2,900 per year); career-related internships or fieldwork, Federal Work-Study, scholarships/grants, tuition waivers (partial), and unspecified assistantships also available. Financial award application deadline: 3/15. *Faculty research:* Software engineering, high performance computing, algorithms and complexity, parallel and distributed computing, databases and computer networks. Total annual research expenditures: $22,000. *Unit head:* Dr. Chandra Sekharan, Chair, 312-915-7985, Fax: 312-915-7998, E-mail: csekhar@luc.edu. *Application contact:* Cecilia Murphy, Graduate Program Secretary, 312-915-7990, Fax: 312-915-7998, E-mail: gradinfo-cs@luc.edu.

Loyola University Maryland, Graduate Programs, Loyola College of Arts and Sciences, Department of Computer Science, Baltimore, MD 21210-2699. Offers computer science (MS); software engineering (MS). *Entrance requirements:* For master's, GRE General Test, GRE Subject Test (recommended). Additional exam requirements/recommendations for international students: Required—TOEFL (minimum score 550 paper-based; 213 computer-based).

Marist College, Graduate Programs, School of Computer Science and Mathematics, Poughkeepsie, NY 12601-1387. Offers computer science/software development (MS); information systems (MS, Adv C); technology management (MS). Part-time and evening/weekend programs available. Postbaccalaureate distance learning degree programs offered (minimal on-campus study). *Entrance requirements:* For master's, resume. Additional exam requirements/recommendations for international students: Required—TOEFL (minimum score 550 paper-based; 213 computer-based; 80 iBT); Recommended—IELTS (minimum score 6.5). Electronic applications accepted. *Faculty research:* Data quality, artificial intelligence, imaging, analysis of algorithms, distributed systems and applications.

McMaster University, School of Graduate Studies, Faculty of Engineering, Department of Computing and Software, Hamilton, ON L8S 4M2, Canada. Offers computer science (M Sc, PhD); software engineering (M Eng, MA Sc, PhD). Part-time programs available. *Degree requirements:* For master's, thesis. *Entrance requirements:* Additional exam requirements/recommendations for international students: Required—TOEFL (minimum score 550 paper-based; 213 computer-based). *Faculty research:* Software engineering; theory of non-sequential systems; parallel and distributed computing; artificial intelligence; complexity, design, and analysis of algorithms; combinatorial computing, especially applications to molecular biology.

Mercer University, Graduate Studies, Macon Campus, School of Engineering, Macon, GA 31207-0003. Offers biomedical engineering (MSE); computer engineering (MSE); electrical engineering (MSE); engineering management (MSE); environmental engineering (MSE); environmental systems (MS); mechanical engineering (MSE); software engineering (MSE); software systems (MS); technical communications management (MS); technical management (MS). Part-time and evening/weekend programs available. Postbaccalaureate distance learning degree programs offered (no on-campus study). *Faculty:* 18 full-time (4 women), 1 part-time/adjunct (0 women). *Students:* 11 full-time (2 women), 100 part-time (22 women); includes 26 minority (13 Black or African American, non-Hispanic/Latino; 12 Asian, non-Hispanic/Latino; 1 Hispanic/Latino), 3 international. Average age 32. In 2010, 46 master's awarded. *Degree requirements:* For master's, thesis or alternative. *Entrance requirements:* For master's, minimum undergraduate GPA of 3.0. Additional exam requirements/recommendations for international students: Required—TOEFL. *Application deadline:* For fall admission, 7/1 for domestic students; for spring admission, 11/15 for domestic students. Applications are processed on a rolling basis. Application fee: $35 ($50 for international students). Electronic applications accepted. *Expenses:* Contact institution. *Financial support:* Federal Work-Study available. *Unit head:* Dr. Wade H. Shaw, Dean, 478-301-2459, Fax: 478-301-5593, E-mail: shaw_wh@mercer.edu. *Application contact:* Greg Lofton, Graduate Program Coordinator, 478-301-5480, Fax: 478-301-5434, E-mail: lofton_g@mercer.edu.

Miami University, Graduate School, School of Engineering and Applied Science, Oxford, OH 45056. Offers chemical and paper engineering (MS); computational science and engineering (MS); computer science and software engineering (MCS), including computer science; software development (Certificate). *Students:* 40 full-time (11 women), 4 part-time (1 woman); includes 1 Black or African American, non-Hispanic/Latino; 1 Asian, non-Hispanic/Latino; 1 Hispanic/Latino, 23 international. Average age 25. In 2010, 14 master's awarded. *Entrance requirements:* For master's, GRE, minimum undergraduate GPA of 3.0 during previous 2 years or 2.75 overall. Additional exam requirements/recommendations for international students: Required—TOEFL. Application fee: $50. *Expenses:* Tuition, state resident: full-time $11,616; part-time $484 per credit hour. Tuition, nonresident: full-time $25,656; part-time $1069 per credit hour. Required fees: $528. *Financial support:* Fellowships with full tuition reimbursements, research assistantships, teaching assistantships, Federal Work-Study, health care benefits, tuition waivers (full), and unspecified assistantships available. Financial award application deadline: 3/1. *Unit head:* Dr. Marek Dollar, Dean, 513-529-0700, E-mail: seasfyi@muohio.edu. *Application contact:* Graduate Admission Coordinator, 513-529-3734, Fax: 513-529-3734, E-mail: gradschool@muohio.edu.

Monmouth University, The Graduate School, Department of Computer Science, West Long Branch, NJ 07764-1898. Offers computer science (MS); software design and development (Certificate). Part-time and evening/weekend programs available. *Faculty:* 4 full-time (2 women), 3 part-time/adjunct (0 women). *Students:* 24 full-time (8 women), 20 part-time (7 women); includes 1 Hispanic/Latino; 1 Two or more races, non-Hispanic/Latino, 36 international. Average age 26. 55 applicants, 89% accepted, 21 enrolled. In 2010, 20 master's awarded. *Degree requirements:* For master's, thesis optional. *Entrance requirements:* For master's, minimum GPA of 3.0 in major, 2.75 overall. Additional exam requirements/recommendations for international students: Required—TOEFL (minimum score 550 paper-based; 213 computer-based; 79 iBT), IELTS (minimum score 5) or Michigan English Language Assessment Battery (minimum score 77), Cambridge A, B, C. *Application deadline:* For fall admission, 7/15 priority date for domestic students, 6/1 for international students; for spring admission, 11/15 priority date for domestic students, 11/1 for international students. Applications are processed on a rolling basis. Application fee: $50. Electronic applications accepted. *Expenses:* Tuition: Full-time $19,572; part-time $816 per credit. Required fees: $628; $157 per semester. *Financial support:* In 2010–11, 44 students received support, including 40 fellowships (averaging $1,718 per year), 19 research assistantships (averaging $4,941 per year); career-related internships or fieldwork, scholarships/grants, and unspecified assistantships also available. Support available to part-time students. Financial award application deadline: 3/1; financial award applicants required to submit FAFSA. *Faculty research:* Databases, natural language processing, protocols, performance analysis, communications networks (systems), telecommunications. *Unit head:* Dr. Cui Yu, Program Director, 732-571-4460, Fax: 732-263-5202, E-mail: cyu@monmouth.edu. *Application contact:* Kevin Roane, Director, Office of Graduate Admission, 732-571-3452, Fax: 732-263-5123, E-mail: gradadm@monmouth.edu.

Monmouth University, The Graduate School, Department of Computer Science and Software Engineering, West Long Branch, NJ 07764-1898. Offers software development (Certificate); software engineering (MS, Certificate). Part-time and evening/weekend programs available. *Faculty:* 6 full-time (1 woman), 2 part-time/adjunct (0 women). *Students:* 13 full-time (1 woman), 15 part-time (3 women); includes 1 Black or African American, non-Hispanic/Latino; 4 Asian, non-Hispanic/Latino; 3 Hispanic/Latino; 1 Two or more races, non-Hispanic/Latino, 4 international. Average age 28. 31 applicants, 77% accepted, 12 enrolled. In 2010, 44 master's awarded. *Degree requirements:* For master's, thesis or alternative, practicum. *Entrance requirements:* For master's, bachelor's degree in computer science, engineering, mathematics,

or physics; minimum GPA of 3.0; 1 year of software development experience. Additional exam requirements/recommendations for international students: Required—TOEFL (minimum score 550 paper-based; 213 computer-based; 79 iBT), IELTS (minimum score 5) or Michigan English Language Assessment Battery (minimum score 77), Cambridge A, B, C. *Application deadline:* For fall admission, 7/15 priority date for domestic students, 6/1 for international students; for spring admission, 11/15 priority date for domestic students, 11/1 for international students. Applications are processed on a rolling basis. Application fee: $50. Electronic applications accepted. *Expenses:* Contact institution. *Financial support:* In 2010–11, 11 students received support, including 7 fellowships (averaging $1,857 per year), 7 research assistantships (averaging $5,843 per year); career-related internships or fieldwork, scholarships/grants, and unspecified assistantships also available. Support available to part-time students. Financial award applicants required to submit FAFSA. *Faculty research:* Conceptual structures, real time software, business rules, project management, software related to homeland security. *Unit head:* Dr. Daniela Rosca, Program Director, 732-571-4459, Fax: 732-263-5253, E-mail: drosca@monmouth.edu. *Application contact:* Kevin Roane, Director, Office of Graduate Admission, 732-571-3452, Fax: 732-263-5123, E-mail: gradadm@monmouth.edu.

National University, Academic Affairs, School of Engineering and Technology, Department of Computer Science and Information Systems, La Jolla, CA 92037-1011. Offers computer science (MS); information systems (MS); software engineering (MS); technology management (MS). Part-time and evening/weekend programs available. Postbaccalaureate distance learning degree programs offered (no on-campus study). *Faculty:* 8 full-time (1 woman), 90 part-time/adjunct (13 women). *Students:* 60 full-time (12 women), 146 part-time (40 women); includes 365 minority (25 Black or African American, non-Hispanic/Latino; 21 Asian, non-Hispanic/Latino; 14 Hispanic/Latino; 2 Native Hawaiian or other Pacific Islander, non-Hispanic/Latino; 303 Two or more races, non-Hispanic/Latino), 54 international. Average age 32. 138 applicants, 100% accepted, 79 enrolled. In 2010, 79 master's awarded. *Degree requirements:* For master's, thesis. *Entrance requirements:* For master's, interview, minimum GPA of 2.5. Additional exam requirements/recommendations for international students: Required—TOEFL (minimum score 550 paper-based; 213 computer-based; 79 iBT), IELTS (minimum score 6). *Application deadline:* Applications are processed on a rolling basis. Application fee: $60 ($65 for international students). Electronic applications accepted. *Expenses:* Tuition: Full-time $9450; part-time $350 per unit. Required fees: $350 per unit. One-time fee: $60. *Financial support:* Career-related internships or fieldwork, institutionally sponsored loans, scholarships/grants, and tuition waivers (partial) available. Support available to part-time students. Financial award application deadline: 6/30; financial award applicants required to submit FAFSA. *Unit head:* Dr. Alireza M. Farahani, Chair and Instructor, 858-309-3438, Fax: 858-309-3420, E-mail: afarahan@nu.edu. *Application contact:* Dominick Giovanniello, Associate Regional Dean—San Diego, 800-NAT-UNIV, Fax: 858-541-7792, E-mail: dgiovann@nu.edu.

Naval Postgraduate School, Graduate Programs, Department of Computer Science, Monterey, CA 93943. Offers computer science (MS, PhD); modeling of virtual environments and simulations (MS, PhD); software engineering (MS, PhD). Program only open to commissioned officers of the United States and friendly nations and selected United States federal civilian employees. Part-time programs available. Postbaccalaureate distance learning degree programs offered (minimal on-campus study). *Degree requirements:* For master's, thesis; for doctorate, one foreign language, thesis/dissertation.

New Jersey Institute of Technology, Office of Graduate Studies, College of Computing Science, Department of Computer Science, Newark, NJ 07102. Offers bioinformatics (MS); computer science (MS, PhD); computing and business (MS); software engineering (MS). Part-time and evening/weekend programs available. *Faculty:* 35 full-time (2 women), 5 part-time/adjunct (1 woman). *Students:* 212 full-time (66 women), 109 part-time (14 women); includes 13 Black or African American, non-Hispanic/Latino; 3 American Indian or Alaska Native, non-Hispanic/Latino; 36 Asian, non-Hispanic/Latino; 16 Hispanic/Latino, 196 international. Average age 28. 867 applicants, 39% accepted, 116 enrolled. In 2010, 152 master's, 5 doctorates awarded. Terminal master's awarded for partial completion of doctoral program. *Degree requirements:* For master's, thesis optional; for doctorate, thesis/dissertation. *Entrance requirements:* For master's, GRE General Test; for doctorate, GRE General Test, minimum graduate GPA of 3.5. Additional exam requirements/recommendations for international students: Required—TOEFL (minimum score 550 paper-based; 213 computer-based; 79 iBT). *Application deadline:* For fall admission, 6/5 priority date for domestic students, 4/1 for international students; for spring admission, 11/15 for domestic and international students. Applications are processed on a rolling basis. Application fee: $65. Electronic applications accepted. *Expenses:* Tuition, state resident: full-time $14,724; part-time $818 per credit. Tuition, nonresident: full-time $20,304; part-time $1128 per credit. Required fees: $2272; $209 per credit. $103 per semester. One-time fee: $312 full-time; $212 part-time. *Financial support:* Fellowships with full and partial tuition reimbursements, research assistantships with full and partial tuition reimbursements, teaching assistantships with full and partial tuition reimbursements, career-related internships or fieldwork, Federal Work-Study, institutionally sponsored loans, and unspecified assistantships available. Financial award application deadline: 3/15. Total annual research expenditures: $6.4 million. *Unit head:* Dr. Michael A. Baltrush, Interim Chair, 973-596-3386, E-mail: michael.a.baltrush@njit.edu. *Application contact:* Kathryn Kelly, Director of Admissions, 973-596-3300, Fax: 973-596-3461, E-mail: admissions@njit.edu.

North Dakota State University, College of Graduate and Interdisciplinary Studies, College of Science and Mathematics, Department of Computer Science, Program in Software Engineering, Fargo, ND 58108. Offers MS, PhD, Certificate. Part-time programs available. Postbaccalaureate distance learning degree programs offered (minimal on-campus study). *Students:* 38 full-time (9 women), 27 part-time (6 women); includes 3 Black or African American, non-Hispanic/Latino; 1 American Indian or Alaska Native, non-Hispanic/Latino; 5 Asian, non-Hispanic/Latino; 2 Hispanic/Latino, 41 international. 36 applicants, 56% accepted, 15 enrolled. In 2010, 6 master's, 1 doctorate awarded. Terminal master's awarded for partial completion of doctoral program. *Degree requirements:* For master's, comprehensive exam, thesis optional; for doctorate, thesis/dissertation, qualifying exam. *Entrance requirements:* For master's and doctorate, minimum GPA of 3.0 in software engineering or related field. Additional exam requirements/recommendations for international students: Required—TOEFL (minimum score 550 paper-based; 213 computer-based; 79 iBT). *Application deadline:* For fall admission, 8/15 priority date for domestic and international students; for spring admission, 12/15 priority date for domestic and international students. Application fee: $45 ($60 for international students). *Financial support:* Research assistantships with full tuition reimbursements, teaching assistantships with full tuition reimbursements, career-related internships or fieldwork, Federal Work-Study, institutionally sponsored loans, and tuition waivers (full) available. Financial award application deadline: 4/15. *Faculty research:* Data knowledge and engineering requirements, formal methods for software, software measurement and mobile agents, software development process. *Unit head:* Dr. Brian Slator, Head, 701-231-8562, Fax: 701-231-8255. *Application contact:* Dr. Ken R. Nygard, Graduate Coordinator, 701-231-9460, Fax: 701-231-8255, E-mail: kendall.nygard@ndsu.edu.

Northern Kentucky University, Office of Graduate Programs, College of Informatics, Department of Computer Science, Highland Heights, KY 41099. Offers computer science (MSCS); geographic information systems (Certificate); secure software engineering (Certificate). Part-time and evening/weekend programs available. *Faculty:* 6 full-time (1 woman). *Students:* 3 full-time (1 woman), 18 part-time (3 women); includes 7 minority (3 Black or African American, non-Hispanic/Latino; 3 Asian, non-Hispanic/Latino; 1 Hispanic/Latino), 5 international. Average age 34. 23 applicants, 52% accepted, 7 enrolled. In 2010, 8 master's, 6 Certificates awarded. *Degree requirements:* For master's, thesis optional. *Entrance requirements:* For master's, minimum GPA of 3.0, at least 4 semesters of undergraduate study in computer science including intermediate computer programming and data structures, one year of calculus, one course in discrete mathematics. Additional exam requirements/recommendations for international students: Required—TOEFL (minimum score 550 paper-based; 213 computer-based; 79 iBT); Recommended—IELTS (minimum score 6.5). *Application deadline:* For fall admission, 8/1 for domestic students, 6/1 for international students; for spring admission, 12/1 for domestic

Software Engineering

Northern Kentucky University (continued)

students, 10/1 for international students. Applications are processed on a rolling basis. Application fee: $40. Electronic applications accepted. *Expenses:* Tuition, state resident: full-time $7254; part-time $403 per credit hour. Tuition, nonresident: full-time $12,492; part-time $694 per credit hour. Tuition and fees vary according to degree level and program. *Financial support:* Scholarships/grants and unspecified assistantships available. Financial award applicants required to submit FAFSA. *Faculty research:* Data privacy, data mining, wireless security, secure software engineering, secure networking. *Unit head:* Dr. Maureen Doyle, Program Director, 859-572-5468, Fax: 859-572-6097, E-mail: doylem3@nku.edu. *Application contact:* Dr. Peg Griffin, Director of Graduate Programs, 859-572-6934, Fax: 859-572-6670, E-mail: griffinp@nku.edu.

Northwestern University, School of Continuing Studies, Program in Information Systems, Evanston, IL 60208. Offers database and Internet technologies (MS); information systems management (MS); information systems security (MS); software project management and development (MS).

Oakland University, Graduate Study and Lifelong Learning, School of Engineering and Computer Science, Department of Computer Science and Engineering, Rochester, MI 48309-4401. Offers computer science (MS); embedded systems (MS); information systems engineering (MS); software engineering (MS). Part-time and evening/weekend programs available. *Entrance requirements:* For master's, minimum GPA of 3.0 for unconditional admission. Electronic applications accepted. *Expenses:* Contact institution. *Faculty research:* Cyber security, 3D imaging of neurochemicals in rat brains.

Pace University, Seidenberg School of Computer Science and Information Systems, New York, NY 10038. Offers computer communications and networks (Certificate); computer science (MS); computing studies (DPS); information systems (MS); Internet technologies for e-commerce (MS); Internet technology (MS); object-oriented programming (Certificate); security and information assurance (Certificate); software development and engineering (MS); telecommunications (MS, Certificate). Part-time and evening/weekend programs available. *Entrance requirements:* For master's, GRE General Test. Additional exam requirements/recommendations for international students: Required—TOEFL. Electronic applications accepted. *Expenses:* Contact institution.

Polytechnic Institute of NYU, Department of Computer Science and Engineering, Major in Software Engineering, Brooklyn, NY 11201-2990. Offers Graduate Certificate. *Application deadline:* For fall admission, 7/31 priority date for domestic students, 4/30 priority date for international students; for spring admission, 12/31 priority date for domestic students, 11/30 priority date for international students. Applications are processed on a rolling basis. Application fee: $75. Electronic applications accepted. *Expenses:* Tuition: Full-time $21,492; part-time $1194 per credit. Required fees: $385 per semester. Tuition and fees vary according to course load. *Unit head:* Dr. Keith W. Ross, Head, 718-260-3859, Fax: 718-260-3609, E-mail: ross@poly.edu. *Application contact:* JeanCarlo Bonilla, Director, Graduate Enrollment Management, 718-260-3182, Fax: 718-260-3624, E-mail: gradinfo@poly.edu.

Portland State University, Graduate Studies, Maseeh College of Engineering and Computer Science, Department of Computer Science, Portland, OR 97207-0751. Offers computer science (MS, PhD); software engineering (MSE). Part-time programs available. *Faculty:* 26 full-time (6 women), 4 part-time/adjunct (0 women). *Students:* 81 full-time (17 women), 78 part-time (18 women); includes 4 Black or African American, non-Hispanic/Latino; 5 Asian, non-Hispanic/Latino; 3 Hispanic/Latino; 1 Two or more races, non-Hispanic/Latino, 65 international. Average age 32. 106 applicants, 47% accepted, 26 enrolled. In 2010, 30 master's, 2 doctorates awarded. *Degree requirements:* For master's, thesis or alternative; for doctorate, thesis/dissertation. *Entrance requirements:* For master's, GRE General Test, minimum GPA of 3.0 in upper-division course work, 2 letters of recommendation, BS in computer science or allied field; for doctorate, MS in computer science or allied field. Additional exam requirements/recommendations for international students: Required—TOEFL (minimum score 550 paper-based; 213 computer-based). *Application deadline:* For fall admission, 3/1 for domestic students, 2/1 for international students; for spring admission, 11/1 for domestic students, 9/1 for international students. Applications are processed on a rolling basis. Application fee: $50. *Expenses:* Tuition, state resident: full-time $8505; part-time $315 per credit. Tuition, nonresident: full-time $13,284; part-time $492 per credit. Required fees: $1482; $21 per credit. $99 per term. One-time fee: $120. Part-time tuition and fees vary according to course load and program. *Financial support:* In 2010–11, 9 research assistantships with full tuition reimbursements (averaging $19,896 per year) were awarded; teaching assistantships with full tuition reimbursements, career-related internships or fieldwork, Federal Work-Study, scholarships/grants, tuition waivers (partial), and unspecified assistantships also available. Support available to part-time students. Financial award application deadline: 3/1; financial award applicants required to submit FAFSA. *Faculty research:* Formal methods, database systems, parallel programming environments, computer security, software tools. Total annual research expenditures: $2.6 million. *Unit head:* Dr. Warren Harrison, Chair, 503-725-3108, Fax: 503-725-3211, E-mail: warren@cs.pdx.edu. *Application contact:* Kelley Gardiner, Graduate Coordinator, 503-725-3218, Fax: 503-725-3211, E-mail: gc@cs.pdx.edu.

Regis University, College for Professional Studies, School of Computer and Information Sciences, Denver, CO 80221-1099. Offers database administration with Oracle (Certificate); database development (Certificate); database technologies (M Sc); enterprise Java software development (Certificate); enterprise resource planning (Certificate); executive information technologies (Certificate); information assurance (M Sc, Certificate); information technology management (M Sc); software engineering (M Sc, Certificate); software engineering and database technologies (M Sc); storage area networks (Certificate); systems engineering (M Sc, Certificate). Offered at Boulder Campus, Northwest Denver Campus, Southeast Denver Campus, Fort Collins Campus, Colorado Springs Campus, and Broomfield Campus. Part-time and evening/weekend programs available. Postbaccalaureate distance learning degree programs offered (no on-campus study). *Degree requirements:* For master's, thesis, final research project. *Entrance requirements:* For master's, 2 years of related experience, resume, interview; for Certificate, 2 years of related experience, resumé. Additional exam requirements/recommendations for international students: Required—TOEFL (minimum score 213 computer-based), TWE (minimum score 5), TOEFL or university-based test. Electronic applications accepted. *Expenses:* Contact institution. *Faculty research:* Secure Virtual Laboratory Architecture, Joint IA project with W2C06 Institute, Information Policy, OLTP and OLAP Technologies, knowledge management, software architectures.

Rochester Institute of Technology, Graduate Enrollment Services, B. Thomas Golisano College of Computing and Information Sciences, Department of Information Technology, Program in Software Development and Management, Rochester, NY 14623-5603. Offers MS. Part-time and evening/weekend programs available. Postbaccalaureate distance learning degree programs offered (no on-campus study). *Students:* 1 full-time (0 women), 27 part-time (5 women); includes 2 Black or African American, non-Hispanic/Latino; 3 Hispanic/Latino, 1 international. Average age 35. 11 applicants, 55% accepted, 5 enrolled. In 2010, 12 master's awarded. *Degree requirements:* For master's, thesis or alternative, project. *Entrance requirements:* For master's, minimum GPA of 3.0. Additional exam requirements/recommendations for international students: Required—TOEFL (minimum score 570 paper-based; 230 computer-based; 88 iBT) or IELTS (minimum score 6.5). *Application deadline:* For fall admission, 8/1 for domestic students, 7/1 for international students; for spring admission, 2/1 for domestic students. Applications are processed on a rolling basis. Electronic applications accepted. *Expenses:* Tuition: Full-time $33,234; part-time $924 per credit hour. Required fees: $219. *Financial support:* In 2010–11, 13 students received support; research assistantships with partial tuition reimbursements available, teaching assistantships with partial tuition reimbursements available, career-related internships or fieldwork, scholarships/grants, and unspecified assistantships available. Support available to part-time students. Financial award applicants required to submit FAFSA. *Unit head:* Prof. Dianne Bills, Graduate Program Director, 585-475-

2700, Fax: 585-475-6584, E-mail: informaticsgrad@rit.edu. *Application contact:* Diane Ellison, Assistant Vice President, Graduate Enrollment Services, 585-475-2229, Fax: 585-475-7164, E-mail: gradinfo@rit.edu.

Rochester Institute of Technology, Graduate Enrollment Services, B. Thomas Golisano College of Computing and Information Sciences, Department of Software Engineering, Rochester, NY 14623-5603. Offers MS. Part-time programs available. *Students:* 8 full-time (1 woman), 5 part-time (1 woman), 9 international. Average age 27. 25 applicants, 68% accepted, 8 enrolled. In 2010, 11 master's awarded. *Degree requirements:* For master's, thesis or project. *Entrance requirements:* For master's, GRE, minimum GPA of 3.0. Additional exam requirements/recommendations for international students: Required—TOEFL (minimum score 570 paper-based; 230 computer-based; 88 iBT) or IELTS (minimum score 6.5). *Application deadline:* For fall admission, 2/15 priority date for domestic and international students; for winter admission, 11/1 for domestic and international students; for spring admission, 2/1 for domestic and international students. Applications are processed on a rolling basis. Electronic applications accepted. *Expenses:* Tuition: Full-time $33,234; part-time $924 per credit hour. Required fees: $219. *Financial support:* Research assistantships with partial tuition reimbursements, teaching assistantships with partial tuition reimbursements, career-related internships or fieldwork, scholarships/grants, and unspecified assistantships available. Support available to part-time students. Financial award applicants required to submit FAFSA. *Faculty research:* Software engineering education, software architecture and design, architectural styles and design patterns, mathematical foundations of software engineering, object-oriented software development, augmented and virtual reality systems, engineering of real-time and embedded software systems, concurrent systems, distributed systems, data communications and networking, programming environments and tools, computer graphics, computer vision. *Unit head:* Dr. Stephanie Ludi, Graduate Program Coordinator, 585-475-7407, E-mail: sal@se.rit.edu. *Application contact:* Diane Ellison, Assistant Vice President, Graduate Enrollment Services, 585-475-2229, Fax: 585-475-7164, E-mail: gradinfo@rit.edu.

Rose-Hulman Institute of Technology, Faculty of Engineering and Applied Sciences, Department of Computer Science and Software Engineering, Terre Haute, IN 47803-3999. Offers software engineering (MS). Part-time programs available. *Faculty:* 12 full-time (1 woman). *Students:* 1 full-time (0 women), 3 part-time (0 women). Average age 28. 4 applicants, 100% accepted, 4 enrolled. *Degree requirements:* For master's, thesis. *Entrance requirements:* For master's, GRE, minimum GPA of 3.0. Additional exam requirements/recommendations for international students: Required—TOEFL (minimum score 580 paper-based; 237 computer-based; 92 iBT). *Application deadline:* For fall admission, 2/1 priority date for domestic students. Applications are processed on a rolling basis. Application fee: $0. *Expenses:* Tuition: Full-time $35,595; part-time $1038 per credit hour. *Financial support:* Fellowships with full and partial tuition reimbursements, research assistantships with full and partial tuition reimbursements, tuition waivers (full and partial) available. Total annual research expenditures: $35,606. *Unit head:* Dr. Cary Laxer, Chairman, 812-877-8429, Fax: 812-872-6060, E-mail: laxer@rose-hulman.edu. *Application contact:* Dr. Daniel J. Moore, Associate Dean of the Faculty, 812-877-8110, Fax: 812-877-8061, E-mail: daniel.j.moore@rose-hulman.edu.

Royal Military College of Canada, Division of Graduate Studies and Research, Engineering Division, Department of Electrical and Computer Engineering, Kingston, ON K7K 7B4, Canada. Offers computer engineering (M Eng, PhD); electrical engineering (M Eng, PhD); software engineering (M Eng, PhD). *Degree requirements:* For master's, thesis; for doctorate, comprehensive exam, thesis/dissertation. *Entrance requirements:* For master's, honours degree with second-class standing in the appropriate field; for doctorate, master's degree. Electronic applications accepted.

St. Mary's University, Graduate School, Department of Engineering, Program in Software Engineering, San Antonio, TX 78228-8507. Offers MS. Part-time programs available. *Degree requirements:* For master's, comprehensive exam. *Entrance requirements:* For master's, GRE. Additional exam requirements/recommendations for international students: Required—TOEFL (minimum score 550 paper-based; 213 computer-based; 80 iBT). Electronic applications accepted.

San Francisco State University, Division of Graduate Studies, College of Science and Engineering, Department of Computer Science, San Francisco, CA 94132-1722. Offers computer science (MS); computer science: computing and business (MS); computer science: computing for life sciences (MS); computer science: software and engineering (MS). Part-time programs available. *Application deadline:* Applications are processed on a rolling basis. *Unit head:* Dr. Dragutin Petkovic, Chair, 415-338-1008, Fax: 415-338-6136, E-mail: csgrad@sfsu.edu. *Application contact:* Dr. Ilmi Yoon, Graduate Admissions, 415-338-1008, E-mail: csgrad@sfsu.edu.

San Jose State University, Graduate Studies and Research, Charles W. Davidson College of Engineering, Department of Computer Engineering, San Jose, CA 95192-0001. Offers computer engineering (MS); software engineering (MS). *Degree requirements:* For master's, comprehensive exam, thesis. *Entrance requirements:* For master's, GRE General Test. Electronic applications accepted. *Faculty research:* Robotics, database management systems, computer networks.

Santa Clara University, School of Engineering, Program in Computer Science and Engineering, Santa Clara, CA 95053. Offers computer science and engineering (MS, PhD, Engineer); information assurance (Certificate); networking (Certificate); software engineering (MS, Certificate). Part-time and evening/weekend programs available. *Students:* 139 full-time (46 women), 108 part-time (31 women); includes 58 minority (6 Black or African American, non-Hispanic/Latino; 47 Asian, non-Hispanic/Latino; 2 Hispanic/Latino; 3 Two or more races, non-Hispanic/Latino, 142 international. Average age 28. 242 applicants, 56% accepted, 73 enrolled. In 2010, 76 master's, 6 doctorates, 3 other advanced degrees awarded. *Degree requirements:* For master's, thesis (for some programs); for doctorate, thesis/dissertation; for other advanced degree, thesis. *Entrance requirements:* For master's, GRE (waiver may be available), transcript; for doctorate, GRE, master's degree or equivalent; for other advanced degree, master's degree, published paper. Additional exam requirements/recommendations for international students: Required—TOEFL (minimum score 550 paper-based; 213 computer-based; 79 iBT). *Application deadline:* For fall admission, 8/12 for domestic students, 7/15 for international students; for winter admission, 10/28 for domestic students, 9/23 for international students; for spring admission, 2/25 for domestic students, 1/21 for international students. Applications are processed on a rolling basis. Application fee: $60. Electronic applications accepted. *Expenses:* Contact institution. *Financial support:* Research assistantships, teaching assistantships available. Financial award application deadline: 3/2; financial award applicants required to submit FAFSA. *Unit head:* Dr. Alex Zecevic, Chair, 408-554-2394, E-mail: azecevic@scu.edu. *Application contact:* Stacey Tinker, Director of Enrollment Management, 408-554-4748, Fax: 408-554-4323, E-mail: stinker@scu.edu.

Seattle University, College of Science and Engineering, Program in Software Engineering, Seattle, WA 98122-1090. Offers MSE. Part-time and evening/weekend programs available. *Degree requirements:* For master's, thesis. *Entrance requirements:* For master's, GRE General Test, 2 years of related work experience.

Southern Methodist University, Bobby B. Lyle School of Engineering, Department of Computer Science and Engineering, Dallas, TX 75275-0122. Offers computer engineering (MS Cp E, PhD); computer science (MS, PhD); security engineering (MS); software engineering (MS). Part-time and evening/weekend programs available. Postbaccalaureate distance learning degree programs offered (no on-campus study). *Faculty:* 13 full-time (3 women), 13 part-time/adjunct (0 women). *Students:* 35 full-time (16 women), 149 part-time (22 women); includes 13 Black or African American, non-Hispanic/Latino; 1 American Indian or Alaska Native, non-Hispanic/Latino; 24 Asian, non-Hispanic/Latino; 13 Hispanic/Latino, 39 international. Average age 34. 180 applicants, 73% accepted, 69 enrolled. In 2010, 77 master's, 4 doctorates awarded. Terminal master's awarded for partial completion of doctoral program. *Degree requirements:* For master's, thesis optional; for doctorate, thesis/dissertation, oral and written qualifying exams, oral final exam (PhD). *Entrance requirements:* For master's, GRE General Test, minimum GPA of 3.0 in last 2 years; bachelor's degree in engineering, mathematics, or sciences; for doctorate, preliminary counseling exam (PhD), minimum GPA of 3.0, bachelor's degree in related field, MA (DE). Additional exam requirements/recommendations for international students: Required—TOEFL (minimum score 550 paper-based; 213 computer-based). *Application deadline:* For fall admission, 7/1 priority date for domestic students, 5/15 for international students; for spring admission, 11/15 for domestic students, 9/1 for international students. Applications are processed on a rolling basis. Application fee: $75. *Financial support:* In 2010–11, 20 students received support, including 6 research assistantships with full tuition reimbursements available (averaging $14,400 per year), 14 teaching assistantships with full tuition reimbursements available (averaging $14,400 per year). Financial award application deadline: 3/31; financial award applicants required to submit FAFSA. *Faculty research:* Trusted and high performance network computing, software engineering and management, knowledge engineering and management, computer arithmetic, computer architecture and CAD. Total annual research expenditures: $366,537. *Unit head:* Dr. Suku Nair, Chair, 214-768-2856, Fax: 214-768-3085, E-mail: nair@lyle.smu.edu. *Application contact:* Marc Valerin, Director of Graduate and Executive Admissions, 214-768-3042, E-mail: valerin@engr.smu.edu.

Southern Polytechnic State University, School of Computing and Software Engineering, Department of Computer Science and Software Engineering, Marietta, GA 30060-2896. Offers computer science (MS, Graduate Certificate, Graduate Transition Certificate); software engineering (MSSWE, Graduate Certificate). Part-time and evening/weekend programs available. Postbaccalaureate distance learning degree programs offered (no on-campus study). *Faculty:* 13 full-time (1 woman), 4 part-time/adjunct (0 women). *Students:* 59 full-time (26 women), 63 part-time (11 women); includes 17 Black or African American, non-Hispanic/Latino; 13 Asian, non-Hispanic/Latino; 1 Hispanic/Latino, 46 international. Average age 32. 100 applicants, 88% accepted, 45 enrolled. In 2010, 34 master's, 4 other advanced degrees awarded. *Degree requirements:* For master's, thesis optional, capstone (software engineering). *Entrance requirements:* For master's, GRE (recommended). Additional exam requirements/recommendations for international students: Required—TOEFL (minimum score 550 paper-based; 213 computer-based; 79 iBT), IELTS (minimum score 6.5). *Application deadline:* For fall admission, 7/1 priority date for domestic students, 5/1 priority date for international students; for spring admission, 11/1 priority date for domestic students, 9/1 priority date for international students. Applications are processed on a rolling basis. Application fee: $20. Electronic applications accepted. *Expenses:* Tuition, state resident: full-time $3690; part-time $205 per semester hour. Tuition, nonresident: full-time $13,428; part-time $746 per semester hour. Required fees: $598 per semester. *Financial support:* Research assistantships with tuition reimbursements, teaching assistantships with tuition reimbursements, career-related internships or fieldwork, scholarships/grants, unspecified assistantships, and cooperative programs available. Financial award application deadline: 5/1; financial award applicants required to submit FAFSA. *Faculty research:* Image processing and artificial intelligence information retrieval, distributed computing, telemedicine applications, enterprise architectures, databases, software requirements engineering, software quality and metrics, usability, parallel and distributed computing, information security. *Unit head:* Dr. Venu Dasigi, Chair, 678-915-3571, Fax: 678-915-5511, E-mail: vdasigi@spsu.edu. *Application contact:* Nikki Palamiotis, Director of Graduate Studies, 678-915-4276, Fax: 678-915-7292, E-mail: npalamio@spsu.edu.

Stevens Institute of Technology, Graduate School, Charles V. Schaefer Jr. School of Engineering, Department of Computer Science, Hoboken, NJ 07030. Offers computer graphics (Certificate); computer science (MS, PhD); computer systems (Certificate); database management systems (Certificate); distributed systems (Certificate); elements of computer science (Certificate); enterprise computing (Certificate); enterprise security and information assurance (Certificate); health informatics (Certificate); multimedia experience and management (Certificate); networks and systems administration (Certificate); security and privacy (Certificate); service oriented computing (Certificate); software design (Certificate); theoretical computer science (Certificate). Part-time and evening/weekend programs available. *Faculty:* 12 full-time (5 women). *Students:* 117 full-time (42 women), 88 part-time (17 women); includes 4 Black or African American, non-Hispanic/Latino; 21 Asian, non-Hispanic/Latino; 3 Hispanic/Latino, 99 international. Average age 28. 327 applicants, 57% accepted. In 2010, 72 master's, 2 doctorates awarded. Terminal master's awarded for partial completion of doctoral program. *Degree requirements:* For master's, thesis optional; for doctorate, variable foreign language requirement, comprehensive exam, thesis/dissertation. *Entrance requirements:* For master's and doctorate, GRE, minimum GPA of 3.0. Additional exam requirements/recommendations for international students: Required—TOEFL. *Application deadline:* Applications are processed on a rolling basis. Application fee: $50. Electronic applications accepted. *Financial support:* Fellowships, Federal Work-Study available. Financial award application deadline: 4/15. *Faculty research:* Semantics, reliability theory, programming language, cyber security. *Unit head:* Daniel Duchamp, Director, 201-216-5390, Fax: 201-216-8249, E-mail: djd@cs.stevens.edu. *Application contact:* Graduate Admissions, 800-496-4935, Fax: 201-216-8044, E-mail: gradadmissions@stevens.edu.

Stevens Institute of Technology, Graduate School, School of Systems and Enterprises, Program in Software Engineering, Hoboken, NJ 07030. Offers MS. *Students:* 9 full-time (3 women), 23 part-time (6 women); includes 1 Black or African American, non-Hispanic/Latino; 3 Asian, non-Hispanic/Latino; 2 Hispanic/Latino, 9 international. Average age 31. 17 applicants, 71% accepted. *Entrance requirements:* Additional exam requirements/recommendations for international students: Required—TOEFL. Application fee: $50. *Unit head:* Lawrence Bernstein, Head, 201-216-5442. *Application contact:* Graduate Admissions, 800-496-4935, Fax: 201-216-8044, E-mail: gradadmissions@stevens.edu.

Stony Brook University, State University of New York, Graduate School, College of Engineering and Applied Sciences, Department of Computer Science, Stony Brook, NY 11794. Offers computer science (MS, PhD); information systems (Certificate); information systems engineering (MS); software engineering (Certificate). *Faculty:* 38 full-time (6 women), 3 part-time/adjunct (1 woman). *Students:* 290 full-time (54 women), 44 part-time (11 women); includes 6 Black or African American, non-Hispanic/Latino; 17 Asian, non-Hispanic/Latino; 5 Hispanic/Latino; 1 Two or more races, non-Hispanic/Latino, 279 international. Average age 25. 1,619 applicants, 23% accepted, 118 enrolled. In 2010, 96 master's, 14 doctorates awarded. *Degree requirements:* For master's, thesis or alternative; for doctorate, comprehensive exam, thesis/dissertation. *Entrance requirements:* For master's and doctorate, GRE General Test. Additional exam requirements/recommendations for international students: Required—TOEFL. *Application deadline:* For fall admission, 1/15 for domestic students. Application fee: $100. *Expenses:* Tuition, state resident: full-time $8370; part-time $349 per credit. Tuition, nonresident: full-time $13,780; part-time $574 per credit. Required fees: $994. *Financial support:* In 2010–11, 95 research assistantships, 43 teaching assistantships were awarded; fellowships also available. *Faculty research:* Artificial intelligence, computer architecture, database management systems, VLSI, operating systems. Total annual research expenditures: $6.4 million. *Unit head:* Prof. Arie Kauffman, Chairman, 631-632-8428. *Application contact:* Graduate Director, 631-632-8462, Fax: 631-632-8334.

Stratford University, School of Graduate Studies, Falls Church, VA 22043. Offers accounting (MS); business administration (IMBA, MBA); enterprise business management (MS); entrepreneurial management (MS); information assurance (MS); information systems (MS); software engineering (MS); telecommunications (MS). Part-time and evening/weekend programs available. Postbaccalaureate distance learning degree programs offered (no on-campus study). *Degree requirements:* For master's, comprehensive exam, capstone project. *Entrance requirements:* For master's, baccalaureate degree. Additional exam requirements/recommendations for international students: Required—TOEFL (minimum score 500 paper-based; 173 computer-based; 61 iBT). Electronic applications accepted.

Strayer University, Graduate Studies, Washington, DC 20005-2603. Offers accounting (MS); acquisition (MBA); business administration (MBA); communications technology (MS); educational management (M Ed); finance (MBA); health services administration (MHSA); hospitality and tourism management (MBA); human resource management (MBA); information systems (MS), including computer security management, decision support system management, enterprise resource management, network management, software engineering management, systems development management; management (MBA); management information systems (MS); marketing (MBA); professional accounting (MS), including accounting information systems, controllership, taxation; public administration (MPA); supply chain management (MBA); technology in education (M Ed). Programs also offered at campus locations in Birmingham, AL; Chamblee, GA; Cobb County, GA; Morrow, GA; White Marsh, MD; Charleston, SC; Columbia, SC; Greensboro, NC; Greenville, SC; Lexington, KY; Louisville, KY; Nashville, TN; North Raleigh, NC; Washington, DC. Part-time and evening/weekend programs available. Postbaccalaureate distance learning degree programs offered (minimal on-campus study). *Degree requirements:* For master's, thesis. *Entrance requirements:* For master's, GMAT, GRE General Test, bachelor's degree from an accredited college or university, minimum undergraduate GPA of 2.75. Electronic applications accepted.

Texas State University–San Marcos, Graduate School, College of Science, Department of Computer Science, Program in Software Engineering, San Marcos, TX 78666. Offers MS. *Faculty:* 4 full-time (1 woman). *Students:* 9 full-time (2 women), 13 part-time (4 women); includes 7 minority (3 Black or African American, non-Hispanic/Latino; 2 Asian, non-Hispanic/Latino; 2 Hispanic/Latino), 3 international. Average age 33. 10 applicants, 100% accepted, 5 enrolled. In 2010, 8 master's awarded. *Degree requirements:* For master's, comprehensive exam, thesis (for some programs). *Entrance requirements:* For master's, GRE General Test, minimum GPA of 2.75 in last 60 hours of course work. Additional exam requirements/recommendations for international students: Required—TOEFL (minimum score 550 paper-based; 213 computer-based; 78 iBT). *Application deadline:* For fall admission, 6/15 priority date for domestic students, 6/1 priority date for international students; for spring admission, 10/15 priority date for domestic students, 10/1 priority date for international students. Applications are processed on a rolling basis. Application fee: $40 ($90 for international students). Electronic applications accepted. *Expenses:* Tuition, state resident: full-time $6024; part-time $251 per credit hour. Tuition, nonresident: full-time $13,536; part-time $564 per credit hour. Required fees: $1776; $50 per credit hour. $306 per semester. *Financial support:* In 2010–11, 4 students received support, including 1 research assistantship (averaging $5,053 per year), 3 teaching assistantships (averaging $5,301 per year); Federal Work-Study, institutionally sponsored loans, scholarships/grants, health care benefits, and unspecified assistantships also available. Support available to part-time students. Financial award application deadline: 4/1; financial award applicants required to submit FAFSA. *Unit head:* Dr. Khosrow Kaikhah, Head, 512-245-3409, Fax: 512-245-8750, E-mail: kk02@txstate.edu. *Application contact:* Dr. Khosrow Kaikhah, Head, 512-245-3409, Fax: 512-245-8750, E-mail: kk02@txstate.edu.

Texas Tech University, Graduate School, Edward E. Whitacre Jr. College of Engineering, Department of Computer Science, Lubbock, TX 79409. Offers computer science (MS, PhD); software engineering (MS). Part-time programs available. Postbaccalaureate distance learning degree programs offered (minimal on-campus study). *Faculty:* 14 full-time (3 women), 1 part-time/adjunct (0 women). *Students:* 109 full-time (18 women), 37 part-time (9 women); includes 3 Hispanic/Latino; 2 Two or more races, non-Hispanic/Latino, 122 international. Average age 25. 334 applicants, 57% accepted, 54 enrolled. In 2010, 47 master's, 9 doctorates awarded. *Degree requirements:* For master's, thesis or alternative; for doctorate, thesis/dissertation. *Entrance requirements:* For master's and doctorate, GRE General Test, minimum GPA of 3.0, statement of purpose, 3 letters of recommendation. Additional exam requirements/recommendations for international students: Required—TOEFL (minimum score 600 paper-based; 250 computer-based; 100 iBT). *Application deadline:* For fall admission, 6/1 priority date for domestic students, 1/15 priority date for international students; for spring admission, 9/1 priority date for domestic students, 6/15 priority date for international students. Applications are processed on a rolling basis. Application fee: $50 ($75 for international students). Electronic applications accepted. *Expenses:* Tuition, state resident: full-time $5495.76; part-time $228.99 per credit hour. Tuition, nonresident: full-time $12,936; part-time $538.99 per credit hour. Required fees: $2674; $36 per credit hour. $905 per semester. *Financial support:* In 2010–11, 59 students received support, including 34 research assistantships with partial tuition reimbursements available (averaging $3,927 per year), 1 teaching assistantship with partial tuition reimbursement available (averaging $4,952 per year). Financial award application deadline: 4/15; financial award applicants required to submit FAFSA. *Faculty research:* Artificial intelligence, software engineering and languages, high performance computing, logic programming, image processing. Total annual research expenditures: $937,133. *Unit head:* Dr. Joseph Urban, Chair, 806-742-3527, Fax: 806-742-3519, E-mail: joseph.urban@ttu.edu. *Application contact:* Dr. Susan Mengel, Graduate Advisor, 806-742-3527, Fax: 806-742-3519, E-mail: graduate_programs@cs.ttu.edu.

Towson University, Master's Program in Applied Information Technology, Towson, MD 21252-0001. Offers applied information technology (MS, PhD); database management systems (Postbaccalaureate Certificate); information security and assurance (Postbaccalaureate Certificate); information systems management (Graduate Certificate); Internet applications development (Postbaccalaureate Certificate); networking technologies (Postbaccalaureate Certificate); software engineering (Postbaccalaureate Certificate). *Students:* 111 full-time (25 women), 232 part-time (62 women); includes 122 minority (75 Black or African American, non-Hispanic/Latino; 4 American Indian or Alaska Native, non-Hispanic/Latino; 31 Asian, non-Hispanic/Latino; 11 Hispanic/Latino; 1 Native Hawaiian or other Pacific Islander, non-Hispanic/Latino), 85 international. In 2010, 75 master's, 9 doctorates, 74 other advanced degrees awarded. *Expenses:* Tuition, state resident: part-time $324 per credit. Tuition, nonresident: part-time $681 per credit. Required fees: $95 per term. *Unit head:* Mike O'Leary, Graduate Program Director, 410-704-4757, E-mail: moleary@towson.edu. *Application contact:* Mike O'Leary, Graduate Program Director, 410-704-4757, E-mail: moleary@towson.edu.

Université du Québec en Outaouais, Graduate Programs, Department of Language Studies, Gatineau, QC J8X 3X7, Canada. Offers localisation (DESS); second and foreign language teaching (Diploma). *Students:* 16 part-time. *Application deadline:* For fall admission, 6/1 priority date for domestic students, 3/1 for international students; for winter admission, 11/1 priority date for domestic students, 10/1 for international students. Application fee: $30. *Financial support:* Research assistantships available. *Unit head:* Natalia Dankova, Director, 819-595-3900 Ext. 4437, E-mail: natalia.dankova@uqo.ca. *Application contact:* Registrar's Office, 819-773-1850, Fax: 819-773-1835, E-mail: registraire@uqo.ca.

Université Laval, Faculty of Sciences and Engineering, Program in Software Engineering, Québec, QC G1K 7P4, Canada. Offers Diploma. Part-time programs available. *Entrance requirements:* For degree, knowledge of French. Electronic applications accepted.

The University of Alabama in Huntsville, School of Graduate Studies, College of Engineering, Department of Electrical and Computer Engineering, Huntsville, AL 35899. Offers computer engineering (MSE, PhD); electrical engineering (MSE, PhD); optical science and engineering (PhD); optics and photonics (MSE); software engineering (MSSE). Part-time and evening/weekend programs available. *Faculty:* 25 full-time (3 women), 4 part-time/adjunct (0 women). *Students:* 47 full-time (10 women), 145 part-time (21 women); includes 20 minority (7 Black or African American, non-Hispanic/Latino; 1 American Indian or Alaska Native, non-Hispanic/Latino; 9 Asian, non-Hispanic/Latino; 2 Hispanic/Latino; 1 Two or more races, non-Hispanic/Latino), 32 international. Average age 32. 190 applicants, 56% accepted, 57 enrolled. In 2010, 58 master's, 6 doctorates awarded. *Degree requirements:* For master's, comprehensive exam, thesis or alternative, oral and written exams; for doctorate, comprehensive exam, thesis/dissertation, oral and written exams. *Entrance requirements:* For master's, GRE General Test, appropriate bachelor's degree, minimum GPA of 3.0; for doctorate, GRE General Test, minimum GPA of 3.0. Additional exam requirements/recommendations for international students: Required—TOEFL (minimum score 500 paper-based; 173 computer-based; 62 iBT). *Application deadline:* For fall admission, 7/15 for domestic students, 4/1 for international students; for spring admission, 11/30 for domestic students, 9/1 for international students. Applications are processed on a rolling basis. Application fee: $40 ($50 for international students). Electronic

Software Engineering

The University of Alabama in Huntsville (continued)

applications accepted. *Expenses:* Tuition, state resident: full-time $7250; part-time $407.75 per credit hour. Tuition, nonresident: full-time $17,358; part-time $970.05 per credit hour. Required fees: $246.80 per semester. Tuition and fees vary according to course load and program. *Financial support:* In 2010–11, 42 students received support, including 16 research assistantships with full and partial tuition reimbursements available (averaging $10,649 per year), 21 teaching assistantships with full and partial tuition reimbursements available (averaging $10,593 per year); career-related internships or fieldwork, Federal Work-Study, institutionally sponsored loans, scholarships/grants, health care benefits, tuition waivers, and unspecified assistantships also available. Support available to part-time students. Financial award application deadline: 4/1; financial award applicants required to submit FAFSA. *Faculty research:* Optical signal processing, electromagnetics, photonics, nonlinear waves, computer architecture. Total annual research expenditures: $13.5 million. *Unit head:* Dr. Robert Lindquist, Chair, 256-824-6316, Fax: 256-824-6803, E-mail: lindquis@ece.uah.edu. *Application contact:* Kathy Biggs, Graduate Studies Admissions Manager, 256-824-6199, Fax: 256-824-6405, E-mail: deangrad@uah.edu.

The University of Alabama in Huntsville, School of Graduate Studies, College of Science, Department of Computer Science, Huntsville, AL 35899. Offers computer science (MS, PhD); software engineering (MSSE, Certificate). Part-time and evening/weekend programs available. *Faculty:* 12 full-time (3 women), 1 (woman) part-time/adjunct. *Students:* 53 full-time (19 women), 67 part-time (17 women); includes 9 minority (5 Black or African American, non-Hispanic/Latino; 4 Asian, non-Hispanic/Latino), 49 international. Average age 30. 180 applicants, 57% accepted, 39 enrolled. In 2010, 35 master's, 2 doctorates, 1 other advanced degree awarded. *Degree requirements:* For master's, comprehensive exam, thesis or alternative, oral and written exams; for doctorate, comprehensive exam, thesis/dissertation, oral and written exams. *Entrance requirements:* For master's, doctorate, and Certificate, GRE General Test, minimum GPA of 3.0. Additional exam requirements/recommendations for international students: Required—TOEFL (minimum score 550 paper-based; 213 computer-based; 62 iBT). *Application deadline:* For fall admission, 7/15 for domestic students, 4/1 for international students; for spring admission, 11/30 for domestic students, 9/1 for international students. Applications are processed on a rolling basis. Application fee: $40 ($50 for international students). Electronic applications accepted. *Expenses:* Tuition, state resident: full-time $7250; part-time $407.75 per credit hour. Tuition, nonresident: full-time $17,358; part-time $970.05 per credit hour. Required fees: $246.80 per semester. Tuition and fees vary according to course load and program. *Financial support:* In 2010–11, 32 students received support, including 12 research assistantships with full and partial tuition reimbursements available (averaging $9,201 per year), 23 teaching assistantships with full and partial tuition reimbursements available (averaging $9,129 per year); career-related internships or fieldwork, Federal Work-Study, institutionally sponsored loans, scholarships/grants, health care benefits, and unspecified assistantships also available. Support available to part-time students. Financial award application deadline: 4/1; financial award applicants required to submit FAFSA. *Faculty research:* Software engineering and systems, computer graphics and visualization, computer networking, artificial intelligence, modeling and simulation. Total annual research expenditures: $4.3 million. *Unit head:* Dr. Heggere Ranganath, Chair, 256-824-6088, Fax: 256-824-6239, E-mail: ranganat@uah.edu. *Application contact:* Kathy Biggs, Graduate Studies Admissions Manager, 256-824-6199, Fax: 256-824-6405, E-mail: deangrad@uah.edu.

University of Alaska Fairbanks, College of Engineering and Mines, Department of Computer Science, Fairbanks, AK 99775-6670. Offers computer science (MS); software engineering (MSE). Part-time programs available. *Faculty:* 7 full-time (1 woman). *Students:* 10 full-time (2 women), 3 part-time (0 women), 2 international. Average age 27. 20 applicants, 45% accepted, 6 enrolled. In 2010, 5 master's awarded. *Degree requirements:* For master's, comprehensive exam, thesis or alternative. *Entrance requirements:* For master's, GRE General Test. Additional exam requirements/recommendations for international students: Required—TOEFL (minimum score 550 paper-based; 213 computer-based; 80 iBT). *Application deadline:* For fall admission, 6/1 for domestic students, 3/1 for international students; for spring admission, 10/15 for domestic students, 9/1 for international students. Application fee: $60. *Expenses:* Tuition, state resident: full-time $5688; part-time $316 per credit. Tuition, nonresident: full-time $11,628; part-time $646 per credit. Required fees: $289 per semester. Tuition and fees vary according to course load and reciprocity agreements. *Financial support:* In 2010–11, 8 research assistantships with tuition reimbursements (averaging $11,138 per year), 2 teaching assistantships with tuition reimbursements (averaging $10,497 per year) were awarded; fellowships with tuition reimbursements, career-related internships or fieldwork, Federal Work-Study, scholarships/grants, health care benefits, and unspecified assistantships also available. Support available to part-time students. Financial award application deadline: 7/1; financial award applicants required to submit FAFSA. *Faculty research:* Interaction with a virtual reality environment, synthetic aperture radar interferometry software. *Unit head:* Dr. Kara Nance, Department Chair, 907-474-2777, Fax: 907-474-5030, E-mail: fycsci@uaf.edu. *Application contact:* Dr. Kara Nance, Department Chair, 907-474-2777, Fax: 907-474-5030, E-mail: fycsci@uaf.edu.

The University of British Columbia, Faculty of Applied Science, Program in Software Systems, Vancouver, BC V6T 1Z1, Canada. Offers MSS. *Degree requirements:* For master's, internship. *Entrance requirements:* For master's, bachelor's degree in science, engineering, business or technology (non-computer science). Additional exam requirements/recommendations for international students: Required—TOEFL (minimum score 600 paper-based; 250 computer-based; 100 iBT), IELTS (minimum score 6.5). Electronic applications accepted. *Expenses:* Contact institution.

University of Calgary, Faculty of Graduate Studies, Faculty of Science, Department of Computer Science, Calgary, AB T2N 1N4, Canada. Offers computer science (M Sc, PhD); software engineering (M Sc). Part-time programs available. *Degree requirements:* For master's, comprehensive exam (for some programs), thesis (for some programs); for doctorate, thesis/dissertation, oral and written departmental exam. *Entrance requirements:* For master's, bachelor's degree in computer science; for doctorate, M Sc in computer science. Additional exam requirements/recommendations for international students: Required—TOEFL (minimum score 600 paper-based; 250 computer-based), GRE General Test recommended; Recommended—TWE. Electronic applications accepted. *Faculty research:* Visual and interactive computing, quantum computing and cryptography, evolutionary software engineering, distributed systems and algorithms.

University of Colorado at Colorado Springs, College of Engineering and Applied Science, Department of Mechanical and Aerospace Engineering, Colorado Springs, CO 80933-7150. Offers engineering management (ME); information operations (ME); manufacturing (ME); mechanical engineering (MS); software engineering (ME); space operations (ME); space systems (MS). Part-time and evening/weekend programs available. *Faculty:* 10 full-time (2 women). *Students:* 56 full-time (11 women), 26 part-time (6 women); includes 3 Black or African American, non-Hispanic/Latino; 4 Asian, non-Hispanic/Latino; 3 Hispanic/Latino, 1 international. Average age 32. 33 applicants, 76% accepted, 19 enrolled. In 2010, 26 master's awarded. *Degree requirements:* For master's, thesis optional. *Entrance requirements:* For master's, GRE General Test, bachelor's degree in engineering or related degree, minimum GPA of 3.0. Additional exam requirements/recommendations for international students: Required—TOEFL. *Application deadline:* For fall admission, 5/1 for domestic students; for spring admission, 10/1 for domestic students. Applications are processed on a rolling basis. Application fee: $60 ($75 for international students). *Expenses:* Tuition, state resident: full-time $7916. Tuition, nonresident: full-time $16,610. Tuition and fees vary according to course load, degree level, program, reciprocity agreements and student level. *Financial support:* Federal Work-Study and scholarships/grants available. Support available to part-time students. Financial award application deadline: 3/1; financial award applicants required to submit FAFSA. *Faculty research:* Neural networks, artificial intelligence, robust control, space operations, space propulsion. Total annual research expenditures: $69,367. *Unit head:* Dr. James Stevens,

Chair, 719-255-3581, Fax: 719-255-3042, E-mail: jstevens@uccs.edu. *Application contact:* Siew Nylund, Academic Adviser, 719-255-3243, Fax: 719-255-3589, E-mail: snylund@eas.uccs.edu.

University of Connecticut, Graduate School, School of Engineering, Department of Computer Science and Engineering, Storrs, CT 06269. Offers computer science (MS, PhD), including artificial intelligence, computer architecture, computer science, operating systems, robotics, software engineering. Terminal master's awarded for partial completion of doctoral program. *Degree requirements:* For master's, comprehensive exam, thesis or alternative; for doctorate, thesis/dissertation. *Entrance requirements:* For master's and doctorate, GRE General Test. Additional exam requirements/recommendations for international students: Required—TOEFL (minimum score 550 paper-based; 213 computer-based). Electronic applications accepted.

University of Denver, University College, Denver, CO 80208. Offers arts and culture (MLS, Certificate), including art, literature, and culture, arts development and program management (Certificate), creative writing; environmental policy and management (MAS, Certificate), including energy and sustainability (Certificate), environmental assessment of nuclear power (Certificate), environmental health and safety (Certificate), environmental management, natural resource management (Certificate); geographic information systems (MAS, Certificate); global affairs (MLS, Certificate), including translation studies, world history and culture; healthcare leadership (MPH, Certificate), including healthcare policy, law, and ethics, medical and healthcare information technologies, strategic management of healthcare; information and communications technology (MCIS, Certificate), including database design and administration (Certificate), geographic information systems (MCIS), information security systems security (Certificate), information systems security (MCIS), project management (MCIS, MPS, Certificate), software design and administration (Certificate), software design and programming (MCIS), technology management, telecommunications technology (MCIS), Web design and development; leadership and organizations (MPS, Certificate), including human capital in organizations, philanthropic leadership, project management (MCIS, MPS, Certificate), strategic innovation and change; organizational and professional communication (MPS, Certificate), including alternative dispute resolution, organizational communication, organizational development and training, public relations and marketing; security management (MAS, Certificate), including emergency planning and response, information security (MAS), organizational security; strategic human resource management (MPS, Certificate), including global human resources (MPS), human resource management and development (MPS). Part-time and evening/weekend programs available. Postbaccalaureate distance learning degree programs offered (no on-campus study). *Faculty:* 7 full-time (2 women), 212 part-time/adjunct (83 women). *Students:* 52 full-time (19 women), 1,044 part-time (625 women); includes 196 minority (81 Black or African American, non-Hispanic/Latino; 7 American Indian or Alaska Native, non-Hispanic/Latino; 30 Asian, non-Hispanic/Latino; 66 Hispanic/Latino; 3 Native Hawaiian or other Pacific Islander, non-Hispanic/Latino; 9 Two or more races, non-Hispanic/Latino), 76 international. Average age 36. 488 applicants, 91% accepted, 339 enrolled. In 2010, 286 master's, 130 other advanced degrees awarded. *Entrance requirements:* Additional exam requirements/recommendations for international students: Required—TOEFL (minimum score 550 paper-based; 80 iBT). *Application deadline:* For fall admission, 6/22 priority date for domestic students, 6/10 priority date for international students; for winter admission, 9/15 priority date for domestic students, 9/6 priority date for international students; for spring admission, 2/3 priority date for domestic students, 12/15 priority date for international students. Applications are processed on a rolling basis. Application fee: $75. Electronic applications accepted. *Expenses:* Contact institution. *Financial support:* Applicants required to submit FAFSA. *Unit head:* Dr. James Davis, Dean, 303-871-2291, Fax: 303-871-4047, E-mail: jdavis@du.edu. *Application contact:* Information Contact, 303-871-3155, Fax: 303-871-4047, E-mail: ucolinfo@du.edu.

University of Detroit Mercy, College of Engineering and Science, Department of Mathematics and Computer Science, Program in Computer Science, Detroit, MI 48221. Offers computer systems applications (MSCS); software engineering (MSCS). Evening/weekend programs available. *Entrance requirements:* For master's, minimum GPA of 3.0.

University of Houston–Clear Lake, School of Science and Computer Engineering, Program in Software Engineering, Houston, TX 77058-1098. Offers MS. Part-time and evening/weekend programs available. *Entrance requirements:* For master's, GRE General Test. Additional exam requirements/recommendations for international students: Required—TOEFL (minimum score 550 paper-based; 213 computer-based).

University of Management and Technology, Program in Computer Science and Information Technology, Arlington, VA 22209. Offers computer science (MS); information technology (AC); information technology project management (MS); management information systems (MS); project management (AC); software engineering (MS). Part-time and evening/weekend programs available. Postbaccalaureate distance learning degree programs offered (no on-campus study). *Entrance requirements:* For master's, 3 recommendations, resume. Additional exam requirements/recommendations for international students: Required—TOEFL (minimum score 550 paper-based; 213 computer-based). Electronic applications accepted.

University of Massachusetts Dartmouth, Graduate School, College of Engineering, Program in Computer Science, North Dartmouth, MA 02747-2300. Offers computer networks and distributed systems (Postbaccalaureate Certificate); computer science (MS); computer systems (Postbaccalaureate Certificate); software development and design (Postbaccalaureate Certificate). Part-time programs available. Postbaccalaureate distance learning degree programs offered. *Faculty:* 9 full-time (2 women), 2 part-time/adjunct (0 women). *Students:* 27 full-time (9 women), 32 part-time (5 women), 43 international. Average age 26. 90 applicants, 87% accepted, 16 enrolled. In 2010, 19 master's awarded. *Degree requirements:* For master's, thesis or alternative. *Entrance requirements:* For master's, GRE General Test, 3 letters of recommendation. Additional exam requirements/recommendations for international students: Required—TOEFL (minimum score 500 paper-based). *Application deadline:* For fall admission, 6/30 priority date for domestic students, 4/30 priority date for international students; for spring admission, 11/15 priority date for domestic students, 9/15 priority date for international students. Applications are processed on a rolling basis. Application fee: $35 ($55 for international students). Electronic applications accepted. *Expenses:* Tuition, state resident: full-time $2071; part-time $86 per credit. Tuition, nonresident: full-time $8099; part-time $337 per credit. Required fees: $9446; $394 per credit. One-time fee: $75. Part-time tuition and fees vary according to class time, course load, degree level and reciprocity agreements. *Financial support:* In 2010–11, 5 research assistantships with full tuition reimbursements (averaging $9,246 per year), 6 teaching assistantships with full tuition reimbursements (averaging $4,896 per year) were awarded; Federal Work-Study and unspecified assistantships also available. Support available to part-time students. Financial award application deadline: 3/1; financial award applicants required to submit FAFSA. *Faculty research:* Self-organizing feature maps, location-based services, brain modeling, software engineering, multi-agent systems. Total annual research expenditures: $387,292. *Unit head:* Dr. Shelley Zhang, Director, 508-999-8294, Fax: 508-999-9144, E-mail: x2zhang@umassd.edu. *Application contact:* Elan Turcotte-Shamski, Graduate Admissions Officer, 508-999-8604, Fax: 508-999-8183, E-mail: graduate@umassd.edu.

University of Michigan–Dearborn, College of Engineering and Computer Science, Department of Electrical and Computer Engineering, Program in Software Engineering, Dearborn, MI 48128-1491. Offers MS. Part-time and evening/weekend programs available. *Faculty:* 14 full-time (0 women), 2 part-time/adjunct (1 woman). *Students:* 2 full-time (0 women), 23 part-time (3 women); includes 5 Asian, non-Hispanic/Latino; 1 Hispanic/Latino, 2 international. Average age 34. 9 applicants, 78% accepted, 6 enrolled. In 2010, 7 master's awarded. *Degree requirements:* For master's, thesis optional. *Entrance requirements:* For master's, bachelor's degree in mathematics, computer science or engineering, minimum GPA of 3.0. Additional exam requirements/recommendations for international students: Required—TOEFL (minimum score 560 paper-based; 220 computer-based; 84 iBT). *Application deadline:* For fall admission, 6/15 for domestic students, 4/1 for international students; for winter admission, 10/15 for domestic students, 8/1 for international students; for spring admission, 2/15 for domestic students, 12/1 for international students. Application fee: $60 ($75 for international students). *Financial support:* Research assistantships with full tuition reimbursements, career-related internships or fieldwork available. Financial award application deadline: 4/1; financial award applicants required to submit FAFSA. *Faculty research:* Information systems, geometric modeling, networks, databases. Total annual research expenditures: $54,056. *Unit head:* Dr. YiLu Murphey, Chair, 313-593-5028, Fax: 313-583-6336, E-mail: yilu@umich.edu. *Application contact:* Sandra Krzyskowski.

University of Missouri–Kansas City, School of Computing and Engineering, Kansas City, MO 64110-2499. Offers civil engineering (MS); computer and electrical engineering (PhD); computer science (MS), including bioinformatics, software engineering, telecommunications networking; computer science and informatics (PhD); computing (PhD); electrical engineering (MS); engineering (PhD); mechanical engineering (MS); telecommunications (PhD). PhD (interdisciplinary) offered through the School of Graduate Studies. Part-time programs available. *Faculty:* 36 full-time (5 women), 21 part-time/adjunct (0 women). *Students:* 160 full-time (32 women), 194 part-time (41 women); includes 21 minority (5 Black or African American, non-Hispanic/Latino; 9 Asian, non-Hispanic/Latino; 6 Hispanic/Latino; 1 Two or more races, non-Hispanic/Latino), 273 international. Average age 25. 440 applicants, 55% accepted, 104 enrolled. In 2010, 135 master's awarded. *Degree requirements:* For doctorate, thesis/ dissertation. *Entrance requirements:* For master's, GRE General Test, minimum GPA of 3.0, 3 letters of recommendation from professors; for doctorate, GRE General Test, minimum GPA of 3.5. Additional exam requirements/recommendations for international students: Required— TOEFL (minimum score 550 paper-based; 213 computer-based; 80 iBT). *Application deadline:* For fall admission, 1/15 priority date for domestic students, 1/15 for international students. Applications are processed on a rolling basis. Application fee: $45 ($50 for international students). *Expenses:* Tuition, state resident: full-time $5522.40; part-time $306.80 per credit hour. Tuition, nonresident: full-time $7128; part-time $792 per credit hour. Required fees: $261.15 per term. *Financial support:* In 2010–11, 35 research assistantships with partial tuition reimbursements (averaging $14,340 per year), 20 teaching assistantships with partial tuition reimbursements (averaging $13,351 per year) were awarded; career-related internships or fieldwork, Federal Work-Study, scholarships/grants, tuition waivers (partial), and unspecified assistantships also available. Support available to part-time students. Financial award application deadline: 3/1; financial award applicants required to submit FAFSA. *Faculty research:* Algorithms, bioinformatics and medical informatics, biomechanics/biomaterials, civil engineering materials, networking and telecommunications, thermal science. Total annual research expenditures: $1.1 million. *Unit head:* Dr. Kevin Z. Truman, Dean, 816-235-2399, Fax: 816-235-5159. *Application contact:* Dr. Kevin Z. Truman, Dean, 816-235-2399, Fax: 816-235-5159.

University of New Hampshire, Center for Graduate and Professional Studies, Manchester, NH 03101. Offers business administration (MBA); counseling (M Ed); education (M Ed, MAT); educational administration and supervision (M Ed, Ed S); industrial statistics (Certificate); public administration (MPA); public health (MPH, Certificate); social work (MSW); software systems engineering (Certificate). Part-time and evening/weekend programs available. *Students:* 97 full-time (65 women), 159 part-time (85 women); includes 20 minority (11 Black or African American, non-Hispanic/Latino; 1 American Indian or Alaska Native, non-Hispanic/Latino; 6 Asian, non-Hispanic/Latino; 2 Hispanic/Latino), 2 international. 119 applicants, 71% accepted, 61 enrolled. In 2010, 79 master's, 1 other advanced degree awarded. *Degree requirements:* For master's, thesis or alternative. *Entrance requirements:* Additional exam requirements/ recommendations for international students: Required—TOEFL (minimum score 550 paper-based; 213 computer-based; 80 iBT). *Application deadline:* For fall admission, 6/1 for domestic students, 4/1 for international students; for spring admission, 12/1 for domestic students. Applications are processed on a rolling basis. Application fee: $65. Electronic applications accepted. *Financial support:* In 2010–11, 21 students received support, including 1 fellowship, 1 teaching assistantship; research assistantships, Federal Work-Study, scholarships/grants, health care benefits, and unspecified assistantships also available. Support available to part-time students. Financial award application deadline: 3/1; financial award applicants required to submit FAFSA. *Unit head:* Kate Ferreira, Director, 603-641-4313, E-mail: unhm.gradcenter@ unh.edu. *Application contact:* Graduate Admissions Office, 603-862-3000, Fax: 603-862-0275, E-mail: grad.school@unh.edu.

University of New Hampshire, Graduate School, College of Engineering and Physical Sciences, Department of Computer Science, Durham, NH 03824. Offers computer science (MS, PhD); software systems engineering (Postbaccalaureate Certificate). Part-time and evening/ weekend programs available. *Faculty:* 10 full-time (2 women). *Students:* 41 full-time (12 women), 56 part-time (10 women); includes 5 minority (3 Asian, non-Hispanic/Latino; 2 Hispanic/ Latino), 24 international. Average age 33. 93 applicants, 75% accepted, 45 enrolled. In 2010, 8 master's, 2 doctorates, 1 other advanced degree awarded. *Degree requirements:* For master's, thesis or alternative; for doctorate, thesis/dissertation. *Entrance requirements:* For master's and doctorate, GRE General Test. Additional exam requirements/recommendations for international students: Required—TOEFL (minimum score 550 paper-based; 213 computer-based; 80 iBT). *Application deadline:* For fall admission, 4/1 priority date for domestic students, 4/1 for international students; for spring admission, 12/1 for domestic students. Applications are processed on a rolling basis. Application fee: $65. Electronic applications accepted. *Financial support:* In 2010–11, 41 students received support, including 1 fellowship, 11 research assistantships, 10 teaching assistantships; career-related internships or fieldwork, Federal Work-Study, scholarships/grants, and tuition waivers (full and partial) also available. Support available to part-time students. *Faculty research:* Programming languages, compiler design, parallel algorithms, computer graphics, artificial intelligence. *Unit head:* Dr. Philip J. Hatcher, Chairperson, 603-862-2678. *Application contact:* Carolyn Kirkpatrick, Administrative Assistant, 603-862-3778, E-mail: office@cs.unh.edu.

University of New Haven, Graduate School, Tagliatela College of Engineering, Program in Computer and Information Science, West Haven, CT 06516-1916. Offers computer science (MS, Certificate), including advanced applications (MS), computer applications (Certificate), computer programming (Certificate), computer systems (MS), computing (Certificate), database and information systems (MS), network administration (Certificate), network systems (MS), software engineering and development (MS). Part-time and evening/weekend programs available. *Students:* 54 full-time (12 women), 25 part-time (4 women); includes 1 Black or African American, non-Hispanic/Latino; 3 Asian, non-Hispanic/Latino, 51 international. Average age 28. 204 applicants, 100% accepted, 40 enrolled. In 2010, 19 master's, 1 other advanced degree awarded. *Degree requirements:* For master's, thesis or alternative. *Entrance requirements:* Additional exam requirements/recommendations for international students: Required—TOEFL (minimum score 520 paper-based; 190 computer-based; 70 iBT); Recommended—IELTS (minimum score 5.5). *Application deadline:* For fall admission, 5/31 for international students; for winter admission, 10/15 for international students; for spring admission, 1/15 for international students. Applications are processed on a rolling basis. Application fee: $50. Electronic applications accepted. *Financial support:* Research assistantships with partial tuition reimbursements, teaching assistantships with partial tuition reimbursements, career-related internships or fieldwork, Federal Work-Study, scholarships/grants, tuition waivers, and unspecified assistantships available. Support available to part-time students. Financial award applicants required to submit FAFSA. *Unit head:* Dr. Tahany Fergany, Coordinator, 203-932-7067. *Application contact:* Eloise Gormley, Director of Graduate Admissions, 203-932-7449, Fax: 203-932-7137, E-mail: gradinfo@newhaven.edu.

University of North Florida, College of Computing, Engineering, and Construction, School of Computing, Jacksonville, FL 32224. Offers computer science (MS); information systems (MS); software engineering (MS). Part-time programs available. *Faculty:* 15 full-time (4 women). *Students:* 12 full-time (4 women), 35 part-time (14 women); includes 5 Black or African American, non-Hispanic/Latino; 2 Asian, non-Hispanic/Latino; 2 Hispanic/Latino; 2 Two or more races, non-Hispanic/Latino, 14 international. Average age 32. 45 applicants, 58% accepted, 11 enrolled. In 2010, 5 master's awarded. *Degree requirements:* For master's, thesis. *Entrance requirements:* For master's, GRE General Test, minimum GPA of 3.0 in last 60 hours of course

work. Additional exam requirements/recommendations for international students: Required— TOEFL (minimum score 500 paper-based; 173 computer-based; 61 iBT). *Application deadline:* For fall admission, 7/1 for domestic students, 5/1 for international students; for spring admission, 11/1 for domestic students, 10/1 for international students. Applications are processed on a rolling basis. Application fee: $30. Electronic applications accepted. *Expenses:* Tuition, state resident: full-time $7646.40; part-time $318.60 per credit hour. Tuition, nonresident: full-time $23,502; part-time $979.24 per credit hour. Required fees: $1208.88; $50.37 per credit hour. Tuition and fees vary according to course load and program. *Financial support:* In 2010–11, 9 students received support, including 1 teaching assistantship (averaging $2,000 per year); Federal Work-Study, scholarships/grants, and unspecified assistantships also available. Financial award application deadline: 4/1; financial award applicants required to submit FAFSA. Total annual research expenditures: $62,830. *Unit head:* Dr. Neal Coulter, Dean, 904-620-1350, E-mail: ncoulter@unf.edu. *Application contact:* Lillith Richardson, Assistant Director, The Graduate School, 904-620-1360, Fax: 904-620-1362, E-mail: graduateschool@unf.edu.

University of Regina, Faculty of Graduate Studies and Research, Faculty of Engineering and Applied Science, Program in Software Systems Engineering, Regina, SK S4S 0A2, Canada. Offers M Eng, MA Sc, PhD. Part-time programs available. *Faculty:* 7 full-time (1 woman). *Students:* 14 full-time (1 woman), 4 part-time (2 women). 21 applicants, 33% accepted. In 2010, 6 master's awarded. *Degree requirements:* For master's, comprehensive exam, thesis. *Entrance requirements:* Additional exam requirements/recommendations for international students: Required—TOEFL (minimum score 550 paper-based; 80 iBT). *Application deadline:* For fall admission, 3/31 for domestic and international students; for winter admission, 7/31 for domestic and international students; for spring admission, 11/30 for domestic and international students. Application fee: $100. Electronic applications accepted. Tuition and fees charges are reported in Canadian dollars. *Expenses:* Tuition, area resident: Full-time $3244.50 Canadian dollars; part-time $180.25 Canadian dollars per credit hour. International tuition: $4744.50 Canadian dollars full-time. Required fees: $494 Canadian dollars; $115.25 Canadian dollars per credit hour. $115.25 Canadian dollars per semester. Tuition and fees vary according to program. *Financial support:* In 2010–11, 1 fellowship (averaging $18,000 per year), 1 research assistantship (averaging $16,500 per year), 3 teaching assistantships (averaging $6,759 per year) were awarded; career-related internships or fieldwork and scholarships/grants also available. Financial award application deadline: 6/15. *Faculty research:* Software design and development, network computing, multimedia communication, computational theories to real-life programming techniques, embedded systems construction. *Unit head:* Dr. Christine Chan, Chair, Graduate Program Coordinator, 306-585-5225, Fax: 306-585-4855, E-mail: christine. chan@uregina.ca. *Application contact:* Melissa Dyck, Administrative Contact, 306-337-2603, Fax: 306-585-4855, E-mail: melissa.dyck@uregina.ca.

University of St. Thomas, Graduate Studies, Graduate Programs in Software, Saint Paul, MN 55105. Offers advanced studies in software engineering (Certificate); business analysis (Certificate); computer security (Certificate); information systems (Certificate); software design and development (Certificate); software engineering (MS); software management (MS); software systems (MSS); MS/MBA. Part-time and evening/weekend programs available. *Faculty:* 5 full-time (0 women), 16 part-time/adjunct (1 woman). *Students:* 26 full-time (9 women), 297 part-time (75 women); includes 31 Black or African American, non-Hispanic/Latino; 52 Asian, non-Hispanic/Latino; 6 Hispanic/Latino; 2 Two or more races, non-Hispanic/Latino, 69 international. Average age 34. 106 applicants, 96% accepted, 67 enrolled. In 2010, 40 master's, 4 other advanced degrees awarded. *Degree requirements:* For master's, thesis optional. *Entrance requirements:* For master's, Bachelor degree earned in US or equivalent earned international degree. Additional exam requirements/recommendations for international students: Required—TOEFL (minimum score 80 iBT). *Application deadline:* For fall admission, 8/1 priority date for domestic students, 5/1 priority date for international students; for spring admission, 1/1 priority date for domestic students, 10/1 priority date for international students. Applications are processed on a rolling basis. Application fee: $30. *Expenses:* Contact institution. *Financial support:* Federal Work-Study, institutionally sponsored loans, and scholarships/ grants available. Financial award application deadline: 4/1. *Faculty research:* Data mining, distributed databases, computer security. *Unit head:* Dr. Bhabani Misra, Director, 651-962-5508, Fax: 651-962-5543, E-mail: bsmisra@stthomas.edu. *Application contact:* Douglas J. Stubeda, Assistant Director, 651-962-5503, Fax: 651-962-5543, E-mail: djstubeda@ stthomas.edu.

University of St. Thomas, Graduate Studies, School of Engineering, St. Paul, MN 55105-1096. Offers manufacturing engineering and operations (MS); mechanical engineering (MS); medical device development (Certificate); regulatory science (MS); software engineering (MS); software management (MS); software systems (MSS); systems engineering (MS); technology management (MS). *Accreditation:* ABET (one or more programs are accredited). *Entrance requirements:* For master's, resume, official transcripts. Additional exam requirements/ recommendations for international students: Required—TOEFL (minimum score 550 paper-based). *Application deadline:* For fall admission, 8/1 priority date for domestic students; for spring admission, 1/1 priority date for domestic students. Applications are processed on a rolling basis. Application fee: $30. Electronic applications accepted. *Expenses:* Contact institution. *Financial support:* Fellowships, research assistantships, institutionally sponsored loans and scholarships/grants available. Support available to part-time students. Financial award application deadline: 4/1; financial award applicants required to submit FAFSA. *Unit head:* Don Weinkauf, Dean, 651-962-5760, Fax: 651-962-6419, E-mail: dhweinkauf@stthomas.edu. *Application contact:* Joyce A. Taylor, Graduate Programs Coordinator, 651-962-5756, Fax: 651-962-6419, E-mail: jataylor1@stthomas.edu.

The University of Scranton, College of Graduate and Continuing Education, Program in Software Engineering, Scranton, PA 18510. Offers MS. Part-time and evening/weekend programs available. *Faculty:* 8 full-time (0 women). *Students:* 17 full-time (3 women), 3 part-time (0 women); includes 1 Asian, non-Hispanic/Latino, 3 international. Average age 27. 29 applicants, 41% accepted. In 2010, 3 master's awarded. *Degree requirements:* For master's, thesis, capstone experience. *Entrance requirements:* For master's, GMAT or GRE, minimum GPA of 3.0. Additional exam requirements/recommendations for international students: Required— TOEFL (minimum score 500 paper-based; 173 computer-based), IELTS (minimum score 5.5). *Application deadline:* For fall admission, 3/1 priority date for domestic students. Applications are processed on a rolling basis. Application fee: $0. *Financial support:* In 2010–11, 6 students received support, including 6 teaching assistantships with full tuition reimbursements available (averaging $8,800 per year); fellowships, career-related internships or fieldwork, Federal Work-Study, and unspecified assistantships also available. Support available to part-time students. Financial award application deadline: 3/1. *Faculty research:* Database, parallel and distributed systems, computer network, real time systems. *Unit head:* Dr. Yaodong Bi, Director, 570-941-6108, Fax: 570-941-4250, E-mail: biy1@scranton.edu. *Application contact:* Joseph M. Roback, Director of Admissions, 570-941-4385, Fax: 570-941-5928, E-mail: robackj2@ scranton.edu.

University of South Carolina, The Graduate School, College of Engineering and Computing, Department of Computer Science and Engineering, Columbia, SC 29208. Offers computer science and engineering (ME, MS, PhD); software engineering (MS). Part-time and evening/ weekend programs available. Postbaccalaureate distance learning degree programs offered (minimal on-campus study). *Degree requirements:* For master's, comprehensive exam, thesis (for some programs); for doctorate, comprehensive exam, thesis/dissertation. *Entrance requirements:* For master's and doctorate, GRE General Test. Additional exam requirements/ recommendations for international students: Required—TOEFL (minimum score 570 paper-based; 230 computer-based). Electronic applications accepted. *Faculty research:* Computer security, computer vision, artificial intelligence, multiagent systems, bioinformatics.

University of Southern California, Graduate School, Viterbi School of Engineering, Department of Computer Science, Los Angeles, CA 90089. Offers computer networks (MS); computer science (MS, PhD); computer security (MS); game development (MS); high performance computing and simulations (MS); human language technology (MS); intelligent robotics (MS);

Software Engineering

University of Southern California (continued)

multimedia and creative technologies (MS); software engineering (MS). Part-time and evening/weekend programs available. Postbaccalaureate distance learning degree programs offered (no on-campus study). *Faculty:* 28 full-time (3 women), 56 part-time/adjunct (7 women). *Students:* 710 full-time (115 women), 302 part-time (59 women); includes 76 minority (1 Black or African American, non-Hispanic/Latino; 55 Asian, non-Hispanic/Latino; 14 Hispanic/Latino; 6 Two or more races, non-Hispanic/Latino), 819 international. 2,379 applicants, 30% accepted, 319 enrolled. In 2010, 332 master's, 32 doctorates awarded. *Entrance requirements:* For master's and doctorate, GRE General Test. Additional exam requirements/recommendations for international students: Required—TOEFL. *Application deadline:* For fall admission, 12/1 priority date for domestic and international students; for spring admission, 9/15 priority date for domestic and international students. Applications are processed on a rolling basis. Application fee: $85. Electronic applications accepted. *Expenses:* Tuition: Full-time $31,240; part-time $1420 per unit. Required fees: $600. One-time fee: $35 full-time. Full-time tuition and fees vary according to degree level and program. *Financial support:* In 2010–11, fellowships with full tuition reimbursements (averaging $30,000 per year), research assistantships with full tuition reimbursements (averaging $20,000 per year), teaching assistantships with full tuition reimbursements (averaging $20,000 per year) were awarded; career-related internships or fieldwork, scholarships/grants, health care benefits, and unspecified assistantships also available. Financial award application deadline: 12/1; financial award applicants required to submit CSS PROFILE or FAFSA. *Faculty research:* Databases, computer graphics and computer vision, software engineering, networks and security, robotics, multimedia and virtual reality. Total annual research expenditures: $11.8 million. *Unit head:* Dr. Shanghua Teng, Chair, 213-740-4494, E-mail: csdept@usc.edu. *Application contact:* Lizsl DeLeon, Director of Student Affairs, 213-740-4496, E-mail: ldeleon@usc.edu.

The University of Texas at Arlington, Graduate School, College of Engineering, Department of Computer Science and Engineering, Arlington, TX 76019. Offers computer engineering (MS, PhD); computer science (MS, PhD); computer science and engineering (M Engr); software engineering (MS, PhD). Part-time programs available. Postbaccalaureate distance learning degree programs offered (minimal on-campus study). *Faculty:* 27 full-time (2 women), 1 part-time/adjunct (0 women). *Students:* 183 full-time (41 women), 89 part-time (18 women); includes 9 minority (3 Black or African American, non-Hispanic/Latino; 4 Asian, non-Hispanic/Latino; 1 Hispanic/Latino; 1 Two or more races, non-Hispanic/Latino), 219 international. 452 applicants, 62% accepted, 94 enrolled. In 2010, 82 master's, 10 doctorates awarded. Terminal master's awarded for partial completion of doctoral program. *Degree requirements:* For master's, comprehensive exam (for some programs), thesis; for doctorate, comprehensive exam, thesis/dissertation. *Entrance requirements:* For master's, GRE General Test, TTL 1150, minimum GPA of 3.0 (3.2 in computer science-related classes); for doctorate, GRE General Test, TTL 1250, minimum GPA of 3.5. Additional exam requirements/recommendations for international students: Required—TOEFL (minimum score 550 paper-based; 230 computer-based; 92 iBT). *Application deadline:* For fall admission, 6/1 for domestic students, 4/1 for international students; for spring admission, 10/15 for domestic students, 9/15 for international students. Applications are processed on a rolling basis. Application fee: $35 ($50 for international students). *Expenses:* Tuition, state resident: full-time $7500. Tuition, nonresident: full-time $13,080. International tuition: $13,250 full-time. *Financial support:* In 2010–11, 7 fellowships with full tuition reimbursements (averaging $24,000 per year), 57 research assistantships with partial tuition reimbursements (averaging $19,200 per year), 50 teaching assistantships with partial tuition reimbursements (averaging $16,200 per year) were awarded; career-related internships or fieldwork and scholarships/grants also available. Financial award application deadline: 6/1; financial award applicants required to submit FAFSA. *Faculty research:* Algorithms, homeland security, mobile pervasive computing, high performance computing bioinformation. *Unit head:* Dr. Fillia Makedon, Chairman, 817-272-3605, E-mail: makedon@uta.edu. *Application contact:* Dr. Bahram Khalili, Graduate Advisor, 817-272-5407, Fax: 817-272-3784, E-mail: khalili@uta.edu.

The University of Texas at Dallas, Erik Jonsson School of Engineering and Computer Science, Program in Computer Science, Richardson, TX 75080. Offers computer science (MS, PhD); software engineering (MS, PhD). Part-time and evening/weekend programs available. *Faculty:* 38 full-time (6 women), 3 part-time/adjunct (1 woman). *Students:* 389 full-time (97 women), 213 part-time (52 women); includes 40 minority (3 Black or African American, non-Hispanic/Latino; 1 American Indian or Alaska Native, non-Hispanic/Latino; 26 Asian, non-Hispanic/Latino; 8 Hispanic/Latino; 2 Two or more races, non-Hispanic/Latino), 452 international. Average age 26. 1,136 applicants, 59% accepted, 174 enrolled. In 2010, 222 master's, 23 doctorates awarded. *Degree requirements:* For master's, thesis optional; for doctorate, comprehensive exam, thesis/dissertation. *Entrance requirements:* For master's, GRE General Test, minimum GPA of 3.0 in undergraduate course work, 3.3 in quantitative course work; for doctorate, GRE General Test, minimum GPA of 3.5. Additional exam requirements/recommendations for international students: Required—TOEFL (minimum score 550 paper-based; 215 computer-based). *Application deadline:* For fall admission, 7/15 for domestic students, 5/1 priority date for international students; for spring admission, 11/15 for domestic students, 9/1 priority date for international students. Applications are processed on a rolling basis. Application fee: $50 ($100 for international students). Electronic applications accepted. *Expenses:* Tuition, state resident: full-time $10,248; part-time $569 per credit hour. Tuition, nonresident: full-time $18,544; part-time $1030 per credit hour. Tuition and fees vary according to course load. *Financial support:* In 2010–11, 160 students received support, including 1 fellowship with partial tuition reimbursement available (averaging $18,900 per year), 68 research assistantships with partial tuition reimbursements available (averaging $15,765 per year), 37 teaching assistantships with partial tuition reimbursements available (averaging $15,675 per year); career-related internships or fieldwork, Federal Work-Study, institutionally sponsored loans, and scholarships/grants also available. Support available to part-time students. Financial award application deadline: 4/30; financial award applicants required to submit FAFSA. *Faculty research:* AI-based automated software synthesis and testing, quality of service in computer networks, wireless networks, cloud computing and IT security, speech recognition. *Unit head:* Dr. Gopal Gupta, Department Head, 972-883-4107, Fax: 972-883-2349, E-mail: gupta@utdallas.edu. *Application contact:* Dr. Balaji Raghavachari, Associate Department Head and Director of Graduate Studies, 972-883-2136, Fax: 972-883-2813, E-mail: gradecs@utdallas.edu.

The University of Texas at San Antonio, College of Sciences, Department of Computer Science, San Antonio, TX 78249-0617. Offers computer and information security (MS); computer science (MS, PhD); software engineering (MS). Part-time programs available. *Faculty:* 20 full-time (4 women), 2 part-time/adjunct (0 women). *Students:* 95 full-time (18 women), 49 part-time (9 women); includes 16 minority (2 Black or African American, non-Hispanic/Latino; 2 Asian, non-Hispanic/Latino; 11 Hispanic/Latino; 1 Two or more races, non-Hispanic/Latino), 89 international. Average age 28. 198 applicants, 58% accepted, 42 enrolled. In 2010, 10 master's, 4 doctorates awarded. *Degree requirements:* For master's, comprehensive exam, thesis (for some programs); for doctorate, comprehensive exam, thesis/dissertation. *Entrance requirements:* For master's, GRE General Test, minimum GPA of 3.0 in last 60 hours; for doctorate, GRE General Test, minimum GPA of 3.0. Additional exam requirements/recommendations for international students: Required—TOEFL (minimum score 500 paper-based; 173 computer-based; 61 iBT), IELTS (minimum score 5). *Application deadline:* For fall admission, 7/1 for domestic students, 4/1 for international students; for spring admission, 11/1 for domestic students, 9/1 for international students. Applications are processed on a rolling basis. Application fee: $45 ($80 for international students). Electronic applications accepted. *Expenses:* Tuition, state resident: full-time $4172; part-time $231.75 per credit hour. Tuition, nonresident: full-time $15,332; part-time $851.75 per credit hour. *Financial support:* In 2010–11, 69 students received support, including 6 fellowships (averaging $41,302 per year), 30 research assistantships (averaging $17,975 per year), 37 teaching assistantships (averaging $13,946 per year); career-related internships or fieldwork, scholarships/grants, tuition waivers, and unspecified assistantships also available. Support available to part-time students. *Faculty research:* Computer and information security, high performance computing, bioinformatics and computational biology, programming languages and compilers. Total annual research expenditures: $1.4 million. *Unit head:* Dr. Kleanthis Psarris, Department Chair, 210-458-4436, Fax: 210-458-4437, E-mail: kleanthis.psarris@utsa.edu. *Application contact:* Veronica Ramirez, Assistant Dean of the Graduate School, 210-458-4330, Fax: 210-458-4332, E-mail: graduatestudies@utsa.edu.

University of Washington, Bothell, Program in Computing and Software Systems, Bothell, WA 98011-8246. Offers MS. Part-time and evening/weekend programs available. *Faculty:* 8 full-time (1 woman). *Students:* 6 full-time (3 women), 45 part-time (6 women); includes 2 Black or African American, non-Hispanic/Latino; 11 Asian, non-Hispanic/Latino; 1 Hispanic/Latino, 4 international. Average age 33. 31 applicants, 74% accepted, 19 enrolled. *Degree requirements:* For master's, comprehensive exam (for some programs), thesis optional. *Entrance requirements:* For master's, GRE. Additional exam requirements/recommendations for international students: Required—TOEFL (minimum score 580 paper-based; 237 computer-based; 92 iBT), IELTS (minimum score 7), TOEFL or IELTS. *Application deadline:* For fall admission, 7/1 for domestic students, 4/1 for international students; for winter admission, 11/1 for domestic students; for spring admission, 2/1 for domestic students. Application fee: $65. Electronic applications accepted. *Expenses:* Contact institution. *Financial support:* Applicants required to submit FAFSA. *Faculty research:* Computer vision, artificial intelligence, software engineering, computer graphics, parallel and distributed systems. *Unit head:* Dr. Michael Stiber, Professor and Director, 425-352-5279, E-mail: cssinfo@uwb.edu. *Application contact:* Megan Jewell, Graduate Advisor, 425-352-5279, E-mail: mjewell@uwb.edu.

University of Washington, Tacoma, Graduate Programs, Program in Computing and Software Systems, Tacoma, WA 98402-3100. Offers MS. Part-time programs available. *Faculty:* 15 full-time (4 women), 6 part-time/adjunct (1 woman). *Students:* 28 full-time (15 women), 11 part-time (1 woman); includes 1 Black or African American, non-Hispanic/Latino; 6 Asian, non-Hispanic/Latino; 2 Hispanic/Latino, 9 international. Average age 29. 32 applicants, 72% accepted, 16 enrolled. In 2010, 18 master's awarded. *Degree requirements:* For master's, capstone project/thesis or 15 credits elective coursework. *Entrance requirements:* For master's, GRE, personal statement, resume, transcripts, 3 recommendations. Additional exam requirements/recommendations for international students: Required—TOEFL (minimum score 580 paper-based; 237 computer-based; 92 iBT), IELTS (minimum score 7). *Application deadline:* For fall admission, 4/15 priority date for domestic students; for winter admission, 10/15 priority date for domestic students; for spring admission, 1/15 priority date for domestic students. Applications are processed on a rolling basis. Application fee: $65. Electronic applications accepted. *Financial support:* In 2010–11, 1 teaching assistantship with partial tuition reimbursement (averaging $14,000 per year) was awarded; career-related internships or fieldwork and scholarships/grants also available. *Faculty research:* Data stream analysis, formal methods, data mining, robotic systems, software development processes. Total annual research expenditures: $50,000. *Unit head:* Dr. Orlando Baiocchi, Director, 253-692-5860, Fax: 253-692-5862, E-mail: uwtech@u.washington.edu. *Application contact:* Dr. Larry Wear, Associate Director, 253-692-5860, Fax: 253-692-5862, E-mail: uwtech@u.washington.edu.

University of Waterloo, Graduate Studies, Faculty of Engineering, Department of Electrical and Computer Engineering, Waterloo, ON N2L 3G1, Canada. Offers electrical and computer engineering (M Eng, MA Sc, PhD); electrical and computer engineering (software engineering) (MA Sc). Part-time programs available. *Degree requirements:* For master's, research paper or thesis; for doctorate, comprehensive exam, thesis/dissertation. *Entrance requirements:* For master's, honors degree, minimum B+ average; for doctorate, master's degree, minimum A- average. Additional exam requirements/recommendations for international students: Required—TOEFL (minimum score 550 paper-based; 213 computer-based), TWE (minimum score 4). Electronic applications accepted. *Faculty research:* Communications, computers, systems and control, silicon devices, power engineering.

University of Waterloo, Graduate Studies, Faculty of Mathematics, David R. Cheriton School of Computer Science, Waterloo, ON N2L 3G1, Canada. Offers computer science (M Math, PhD); software engineering (M Math); statistics and computing (M Math). Part-time programs available. *Degree requirements:* For master's, research paper or thesis; for doctorate, comprehensive exam, thesis/dissertation. *Entrance requirements:* For master's, honors degree in field, minimum B+ average; for doctorate, master's degree, minimum B+ average. *Faculty research:* Computer graphics, artificial intelligence, algorithms and complexity, distributed computing and networks, software engineering.

University of West Florida, College of Arts and Sciences: Sciences, Department of Computer Science, Pensacola, FL 32514-5750. Offers computer science (MS); database systems (MS); software engineering (MS). Part-time and evening/weekend programs available. *Faculty:* 12 full-time (4 women), 4 part-time/adjunct (2 women). *Students:* 23 full-time (6 women), 123 part-time (26 women); includes 39 minority (6 Black or African American, non-Hispanic/Latino; 3 American Indian or Alaska Native, non-Hispanic/Latino; 12 Asian, non-Hispanic/Latino; 9 Hispanic/Latino; 1 Native Hawaiian or other Pacific Islander, non-Hispanic/Latino; 8 Two or more races, non-Hispanic/Latino), 4 international. Average age 36. 62 applicants, 79% accepted, 38 enrolled. In 2010, 46 master's awarded. *Degree requirements:* For master's, thesis optional. *Entrance requirements:* For master's, GRE General Test. Additional exam requirements/recommendations for international students: Required—TOEFL (minimum score 550 paper-based; 213 computer-based). *Application deadline:* For fall admission, 6/1 for domestic students, 5/15 for international students; for spring admission, 10/1 for domestic and international students. Applications are processed on a rolling basis. Application fee: $30. *Expenses:* Tuition, state resident: full-time $4982; part-time $208 per credit hour. Tuition, nonresident: full-time $20,059; part-time $836 per credit hour. Required fees: $1365; $57 per credit hour. *Financial support:* In 2010–11, 16 fellowships with partial tuition reimbursements (averaging $453 per year), 8 research assistantships (averaging $3,280 per year), 3 teaching assistantships with partial tuition reimbursements (averaging $5,840 per year) were awarded; unspecified assistantships also available. Financial award application deadline: 4/15; financial award applicants required to submit FAFSA. *Unit head:* Dr. Leo Ter Haar, Chairperson, 850-474-2542. *Application contact:* Terry McCray, Assistant Director of Graduate Admissions, 850-473-7718, Fax: 850-473-7714, E-mail: gradadmissions@uwf.edu.

University of West Florida, College of Professional Studies, Department of Professional and Community Leadership, Program in Administration, Pensacola, FL 32514-5750. Offers acquisition and contract administration (MSA); biomedical/pharmaceutical (MSA); criminal justice administration (MSA); database administration (MSA); education leadership (MSA); healthcare administration (MSA); human performance technology (MSA); leadership (MSA); nursing administration (MSA); public administration (MSA); software engineering administration (MSA). Part-time and evening/weekend programs available. Postbaccalaureate distance learning degree programs offered (no on-campus study). *Students:* 26 full-time (24 women), 185 part-time (115 women); includes 30 Black or African American, non-Hispanic/Latino; 1 American Indian or Alaska Native, non-Hispanic/Latino; 5 Asian, non-Hispanic/Latino; 13 Hispanic/Latino; 1 Native Hawaiian or other Pacific Islander, non-Hispanic/Latino, 2 international. Average age 34. 139 applicants, 70% accepted, 80 enrolled. In 2010, 60 master's awarded. *Entrance requirements:* For master's, GRE General Test, letter of intent, names of references. Additional exam requirements/recommendations for international students: Required—TOEFL (minimum score 550 paper-based; 213 computer-based). *Application deadline:* For fall admission, 6/1 for domestic students, 5/15 for international students; for spring admission, 10/1 for domestic and international students. Applications are processed on a rolling basis. Application fee: $30. *Expenses:* Tuition, state resident: full-time $4982; part-time $208 per credit hour. Tuition, nonresident: full-time $20,059; part-time $836 per credit hour. Required fees: $1365; $57 per credit hour. *Financial support:* Unspecified assistantships available. Financial award application deadline: 4/15; financial award applicants required to submit FAFSA. *Unit head:* Dr. Karen Rasmussen, Chairperson, 850-474-2301, Fax: 850-474-2804, E-mail: krasmuss@uwf.edu. *Application contact:* Terry McCray, Assistant Director of Graduate Admissions, 850-473-7718, Fax: 850-473-7714, E-mail: gradadmissions@uwf.edu.

University of West Georgia, College of Arts and Sciences, Department of Computer Science, Carrollton, GA 30118. Offers applied computer science (MS); human centered computing

(Certificate); software development (Certificate); system and network administration (Certificate); Web technologies (Certificate). Part-time and evening/weekend programs available. *Faculty:* 8 full-time (3 women). *Students:* 14 full-time (2 women), 8 part-time (3 women); includes 4 Black or African American, non-Hispanic/Latino; 1 Asian, non-Hispanic/Latino; 1 Two or more races, non-Hispanic/Latino, 2 international. Average age 30. 13 applicants, 46% accepted, 3 enrolled. In 2010, 9 master's awarded. *Degree requirements:* For master's, comprehensive exam, thesis optional. *Entrance requirements:* For master's, GRE, bachelor's degree, minimum overall undergraduate GPA of 2.5; for Certificate, bachelor's degree, minimum overall undergraduate GPA of 2.5. *Application deadline:* For fall admission, 7/17 priority date for domestic students; for spring admission, 11/20 for domestic students. Applications are processed on a rolling basis. Application fee: $30. Electronic applications accepted. *Expenses:* Tuition, state resident: full-time $4130; part-time $173 per semester hour. Tuition, nonresident: full-time $16,524; part-time $689 per semester hour. Required fees: $1586; $44.01 per semester hour. $397 per semester. Tuition and fees vary according to program. *Financial support:* In 2010–11, 7 research assistantships with full tuition reimbursements (averaging $6,000 per year) were awarded; unspecified assistantships also available. Financial award application deadline: 7/1; financial award applicants required to submit FAFSA. *Faculty research:* Artificial intelligence, software engineering, Web technologies, database, networks. *Unit head:* Dr. Adel M. Abunawass, Chair, 678-839-6485, Fax: 678-839-6486, E-mail: adel@westga.edu. *Application contact:* Dr. Charles W. Clark, Dean, 678-839-6508, E-mail: cclark@westga.edu.

University of Wisconsin–La Crosse, Office of University Graduate Studies, College of Science and Health, Department of Computer Science, La Crosse, WI 54601-3742. Offers software engineering (MSE). Part-time programs available. *Faculty:* 7 full-time (1 woman). *Students:* 30 full-time (6 women), 17 part-time (3 women); includes 2 minority (1 Asian, non-Hispanic/Latino; 1 Two or more races, non-Hispanic/Latino), 30 international. Average age 28. 35 applicants, 71% accepted, 10 enrolled. In 2010, 31 master's awarded. *Degree requirements:* For master's, thesis. *Entrance requirements:* Additional exam requirements/recommendations for international students: Required—TOEFL (minimum score 550 paper-based; 213 computer-based; 79 iBT). *Application deadline:* For fall admission, 5/1 priority date for domestic and international students; for spring admission, 11/1 priority date for domestic and international students. Applications are processed on a rolling basis. Application fee: $56. Electronic applications accepted. *Expenses:* Tuition, state resident: full-time $7121; part-time $395.61 per credit. Tuition, nonresident: full-time $16,891; part-time $938.41 per credit. Part-time tuition and fees vary according to course load, program and reciprocity agreements. *Financial support:* In 2010–11, 4 research assistantships with partial tuition reimbursements (averaging $7,542 per year) were awarded; Federal Work-Study, scholarships/grants, health care benefits, and tuition waivers (partial) also available. Support available to part-time students. *Unit head:* Dr. Kasi Periyasamy, Software Engineering Program Director, 608-785-6823, E-mail: periyasa.kas2@uwlax.edu. *Application contact:* Kathryn Kiefer, Director of Admissions, 608-785-8939, E-mail: admissions@uwlax.edu.

Villanova University, Graduate School of Liberal Arts and Sciences, Department of Computing Sciences, Villanova, PA 19085-1699. Offers computer science (MS); software engineering (MS). Part-time and evening/weekend programs available. *Faculty:* 9 full-time (2 women), 3 part-time/adjunct (0 women). *Students:* 83 full-time (31 women), 27 part-time (4 women); includes 13 minority (2 Black or African American, non-Hispanic/Latino; 10 Asian, non-Hispanic/Latino; 1 Native Hawaiian or other Pacific Islander, non-Hispanic/Latino), 65 international. Average age 28. 72 applicants, 85% accepted, 27 enrolled. In 2010, 39 master's awarded. *Degree requirements:* For master's, thesis optional, independent study project. *Entrance requirements:* For master's, GRE, minimum GPA of 3.0. Additional exam requirements/recommendations for international students: Required—TOEFL. *Application deadline:* For fall admission, 3/1 priority date for domestic and international students; for spring admission, 11/15 priority date for domestic and international students. Applications are processed on a rolling basis. Application fee: $50. Electronic applications accepted. *Expenses:* Contact institution. *Financial support:* Research assistantships, Federal Work-Study and scholarships/grants available. Financial award applicants required to submit FAFSA. *Unit head:* Dr. Robert Beck, Chair, 610-519-7310. *Application contact:* Dr. Robert Beck, Chair, 610-519-7310.

Virginia Polytechnic Institute and State University, VT Online, Blacksburg, VA 24061. Offers aerospace engineering (MS); business information systems (Graduate Certificate); career and technical education (MS); computer engineering (M Eng, MS); decision support systems (Graduate Certificate); eLearning leadership (MA); electrical engineering (M Eng, MS); engineering administration (MEA); environmental politics and policy (Graduate Certificate); foundations of political analysis (Graduate Certificate); health product risk management (Graduate Certificate); information policy and society (Graduate Certificate); information security (Graduate Certificate); instructional technology (MA); liberal arts (Graduate Certificate); life sciences: health product risk management (MS); natural resources (MNR, Graduate Certificate); networking (Graduate Certificate); nonprofit and nongovernmental organization management (Graduate Certificate); ocean engineering (MS); political science (MA); security studies (Graduate Certificate); software development (Graduate Certificate). *Expenses:* Tuition, area resident: Full-time $9399; part-time $488 per credit hour. Tuition, state resident: full-time $9399; part-time $488 per credit hour. Tuition, nonresident: full-time $17,854; part-time $957.75 per credit hour. International tuition: $17,854 full-time. Required fees: $1534. Full-time tuition and fees vary according to program.

Walden University, Graduate Programs, School of Management, Minneapolis, MN 55401. Offers accounting (MS), including cpa emphasis, professional track, self-designed; accounting and management (MS), including self-designed, strategic management; applied management and decision sciences (PhD), including accounting, engineering management, finance, general applied management and decision sciences, information systems management, knowledge management, leadership and organizational change, learning management, operations research, self-designed program in applied management and design sciences; business information management (MISM); enterprise information security (MISM); entrepreneurship (MBA, DBA); finance (MBA, DBA); global management (MS); global supply chain management (DBA); health informatics (MISM); healthcare management (MBA, MS); healthcare system improvement (MBA); human resource management (MBA, MS), including functional human resource management (MS), human resource management (MS), integrating functional and strategic human resource management (MS), organizational strategy (MS); information systems (MS); information systems management (DBA); information technology (MS), including information security, software engineering; international business (MBA, DBA); IT strategy and governance (MISM); leadership (MBA, MS, DBA), including entrepreneurship (MS), general management (MS), human resources leadership (MS), innovation and technology (MS), leader development (MS), leading sustainability (MS), project management (MS), self-designed (MS); managers as leaders (MS); managing global software and service supply chains (MISM); marketing (MBA, DBA); project management (MBA, MS); research strategies (MS); risk management (MBA); self-designed (MBA, DBA); social impact management (DBA); strategy and operations (MS); sustainable futures (MBA); sustainable management (MS); technology (MBA); technology entrepreneurship (DBA); technology management (MS). Part-time and evening/weekend programs available. Postbaccalaureate distance learning degree programs offered (minimal on-campus study). *Faculty:* 22 full-time (8 women), 291 part-time/adjunct (100 women). *Students:* 3,705 full-time (1,956 women), 976 part-time (549 women); includes 2,432 minority (2,021 Black or African American, non-Hispanic/Latino; 32 American Indian or Alaska Native, non-Hispanic/Latino; 137 Asian, non-Hispanic/Latino; 193 Hispanic/Latino; 5 Native Hawaiian or other Pacific Islander, non-Hispanic/Latino; 44 Two or more races, non-Hispanic/Latino), 302 international. Average age 40. In 2010, 658 master's, 86 doctorates awarded. *Degree requirements:* For doctorate, thesis/dissertation (for some programs), residency. *Entrance requirements:* For master's, bachelor's degree or equivalent in related field; minimum GPA of 2.5; official transcripts; goal statement; access to computer and Internet; for doctorate, master's degree or equivalent in related field; minimum GPA of 3.0; 3 years of related professional/academic experience (preferred). Additional exam requirements/recommendations for international students: Required—TOEFL (minimum score 550 paper-based; 213 computer-based), IELTS (minimum score 6.5), TOEFL, IELTS, or Michigan English Language Assessment Battery (minimum score 82). *Application deadline:* Applications are processed on a rolling basis. Application fee: $50. Electronic applications accepted. *Expenses:* Tuition: Full-time $10,274; part-time $445 per credit. Tuition and fees vary according to course load, degree level and program. *Financial support:* Fellowships, Federal Work-Study, scholarships/grants, unspecified assistantships, and family tuition reduction, active duty/veteran tuition reduction, group tuition reduction, interest-free payment plans available. Support available to part-time students. Financial award applicants required to submit FAFSA. *Unit head:* Dr. William Schulz, Associate Dean, 800-925-3368. *Application contact:* Jennifer Hall, Vice President of Enrollment Management, 866-4-WALDEN, E-mail: info@waldenu.edu.

West Virginia University, College of Engineering and Mineral Resources, Lane Department of Computer Science and Electrical Engineering, Program in Software Engineering, Morgantown, WV 26506. Offers MSSE. *Entrance requirements:* For master's, GRE or work experience.

Widener University, Graduate Programs in Engineering, Program in Computer and Software Engineering, Chester, PA 19013-5792. Offers M Eng. Part-time and evening/weekend programs available. *Students:* 1 full-time (0 women), 2 part-time (0 women), 2 international. Average age 28. In 2010, 5 master's awarded. *Degree requirements:* For master's, thesis optional. *Application deadline:* For fall admission, 8/1 priority date for domestic students; for spring admission, 12/1 for domestic students. Applications are processed on a rolling basis. Application fee: $25 ($300 for international students). *Financial support:* Research assistantships with full tuition reimbursements, unspecified assistantships available. Financial award application deadline: 3/15. *Faculty research:* Computer and software engineering, computer network fault-tolerant computing, optical computing. *Unit head:* Dr. Bryen E. Lorenz, Chairman, Department of Electrical/Telecommunication Engineering, 610-499-4064, Fax: 610-499-4059, E-mail: bryen.f.lorenz@widener.edu. *Application contact:* Dr. Bryen E. Lorenz, Chairman, Department of Electrical/Telecommunication Engineering, 610-499-4064, Fax: 610-499-4059, E-mail: bryen.f.lorenz@widener.edu.

Winthrop University, College of Business Administration, Program in Software Project Management, Rock Hill, SC 29733. Offers software development (MS); software project management (Certificate). *Entrance requirements:* For master's, GMAT.

Systems Science

Arizona State University, Ira A. Fulton School of Engineering, ASU Engineering Online Programs, Tempe, AZ 85287. Offers construction (MS); embedded systems (M Eng); enterprise systems innovation and management (MSE); modeling and simulation (M Eng); quality and reliability engineering (M Eng); software engineering (MSE); systems engineering (M Eng). *Expenses:* Tuition, state resident: full-time $8510; part-time $608 per credit. Tuition, nonresident: full-time $16,542; part-time $919 per credit. Required fees: $339; $110 per credit. Part-time tuition and fees vary according to course load.

Carleton University, Faculty of Graduate Studies, Faculty of Engineering and Design, Ottawa-Carleton Institute for Electrical Engineering, Department of Systems and Computer Engineering, Program in Information and Systems Science, Ottawa, ON K1S 5B6, Canada. Offers M Sc.

Carleton University, Faculty of Graduate Studies, Faculty of Science, Information and Systems Science Program, Ottawa, ON K1S 5B6, Canada. Offers M Sc. *Degree requirements:* For master's, thesis optional. *Entrance requirements:* For master's, honors degree. Additional exam requirements/recommendations for international students: Required—TOEFL. *Faculty research:* Software engineering, real-time and microprocessor programming, computer communications.

Carleton University, Faculty of Graduate Studies, Faculty of Science, School of Computer Science, Ottawa, ON K1S 5B6, Canada. Offers computer science (MCS, PhD); information and system science (M Sc). MCS and PhD programs offered jointly with University of Ottawa. Part-time programs available. *Degree requirements:* For master's, thesis optional, project; for doctorate, comprehensive exam, thesis/dissertation. *Entrance requirements:* For master's, honors degree. Additional exam requirements/recommendations for international students: Required—TOEFL. *Faculty research:* Programming systems, theory of computing, computer applications, computer systems.

Claremont Graduate University, Graduate Programs, School of Information Systems and Technology, Claremont, CA 91711-6160. Offers electronic commerce (MS, PhD); health information management (MS); information systems (Certificate); knowledge management (MS, PhD); systems development (MS, PhD); telecommunications and networking (MS, PhD); MBA/MS. Part-time programs available. *Faculty:* 6 full-time (1 woman), 1 part-time/adjunct (0 women). *Students:* 87 full-time (24 women), 22 part-time (8 women); includes 31 minority (6 Black or African American, non-Hispanic/Latino; 1 American Indian or Alaska Native, non-Hispanic/Latino; 18 Asian, non-Hispanic/Latino; 3 Hispanic/Latino; 1 Native Hawaiian or other Pacific Islander, non-Hispanic/Latino; 2 Two or more races, non-Hispanic/Latino), 37 international. Average age 37. In 2010, 30 master's, 6 doctorates awarded. *Degree requirements:* For doctorate, comprehensive exam, thesis/dissertation, portfolio. *Entrance requirements:* For master's and doctorate, GMAT, GRE General Test. Additional exam requirements/recommendations for international students: Required—TOEFL (minimum score 550 paper-based; 213 computer-based; 80 iBT). *Application deadline:* For fall admission, 2/1 priority date for domestic students. Applications are processed on a rolling basis. Application fee: $60. Electronic applications accepted. *Expenses:* Tuition: Full-time $35,748; part-time $1554 per unit. Required fees: $215 per semester. *Financial support:* Fellowships, research assistantships, teaching assistantships, Federal Work-Study, institutionally sponsored loans, and scholarships/grants available. Support available to part-time students. Financial award application deadline: 2/15; financial award applicants required to submit FAFSA. *Faculty research:* GPSS, man-machine interaction, organizational aspects of computing, implementation of information systems, information systems practice. *Unit head:* Terry Ryan, Dean, 909-607-9591, Fax: 909-621-8564, E-mail: terry.ryan@cgu.edu. *Application contact:* Matt Hutter, Director of External Affairs, 909-621-3180, Fax: 909-621-8564, E-mail: matt.hutter@cgu.edu.

Eastern Illinois University, Graduate School, Lumpkin College of Business and Applied Sciences, School of Technology, Charleston, IL 61920-3099. Offers computer technology (Certificate); quality systems (Certificate); technology (MS); technology security (Certificate); work performance improvement (Certificate). Part-time and evening/weekend programs available.

Fairleigh Dickinson University, Metropolitan Campus, University College: Arts, Sciences, and Professional Studies, Program in Systems Science, Teaneck, NJ 07666-1914. Offers MS.

Systems Science

Fairleigh Dickinson University, Metropolitan Campus (continued)
Students: 1 (woman) full-time, all international. Average age 24. 6 applicants, 50% accepted, 0 enrolled. *Entrance requirements:* For master's, GRE General Test. *Application deadline:* Applications are processed on a rolling basis. Application fee: $40. *Application contact:* Susan Brooman, University Director of Graduate Admissions, 201-692-2554, Fax: 201-692-2560, E-mail: globaleducation@fdu.edu.

Hood College, Graduate School, Program in Management of Information Technology, Frederick, MD 21701-8575. Offers MS. Part-time and evening/weekend programs available. *Faculty:* 1 (woman) full-time, 2 part-time/adjunct (1 woman). *Students:* 1 full-time (0 women), 14 part-time (5 women); includes 3 Black or African American, non-Hispanic/Latino, 1 international. Average age 40. 17 applicants, 65% accepted, 3 enrolled. In 2010, 2 master's awarded. *Degree requirements:* For master's, thesis. *Entrance requirements:* For master's, minimum GPA of 2.75. Additional exam requirements/recommendations for international students: Required—TOEFL (minimum score 575 paper-based; 231 computer-based; 89 iBT). *Application deadline:* For fall admission, 7/15 for domestic and international students; for spring admission, 12/15 for domestic and international students. Applications are processed on a rolling basis. Application fee: $35. Electronic applications accepted. *Expenses:* Tuition: Full-time $6480; part-time $360 per credit. Required fees: $100; $50 per term. *Financial support:* Applicants required to submit FAFSA. *Faculty research:* Systems engineering, parallel distributed computing, strategy, business ethics, entrepreneurship. *Unit head:* Dr. Elizabeth Chang, Director, 301-696-3724, E-mail: myers@hood.edu. *Application contact:* Dr. Allen P. Flora, Dean of Graduate School, 301-696-3811, Fax: 301-696-3597, E-mail: gofurther@hood.edu.

Louisiana State University and Agricultural and Mechanical College, Graduate School, College of Basic Sciences, Department of Computer Science, Baton Rouge, LA 70803. Offers computer science (MSSS, PhD); systems science (MSSS). Part-time programs available. *Faculty:* 19 full-time (3 women). *Students:* 85 full-time (16 women), 19 part-time (6 women); includes 6 Black or African American, non-Hispanic/Latino; 1 American Indian or Alaska Native, non-Hispanic/Latino; 4 Asian, non-Hispanic/Latino, 76 international. Average age 28. 112 applicants, 74% accepted, 13 enrolled. In 2010, 27 master's, 6 doctorates awarded. Terminal master's awarded for partial completion of doctoral program. *Degree requirements:* For master's, thesis; for doctorate, thesis/dissertation. *Entrance requirements:* For master's and doctorate, GRE General Test, minimum GPA of 3.0. Additional exam requirements/recommendations for international students: Required—TOEFL (minimum score 550 paper-based; 213 computer-based; 79 iBT) or IELTS (minimum score 6.5). *Application deadline:* For fall admission, 2/1 for domestic students, 5/15 for international students; for spring admission, 10/1 for domestic students, 10/15 for international students. Applications are processed on a rolling basis. Application fee: $50 ($70 for international students). Electronic applications accepted. *Financial support:* In 2010–11, 80 students received support, including 7 fellowships with full tuition reimbursements available (averaging $13,182 per year), 44 research assistantships with full and partial tuition reimbursements available (averaging $16,480 per year), 22 teaching assistantships with full and partial tuition reimbursements available (averaging $14,432 per year); Federal Work-Study, institutionally sponsored loans, health care benefits, and unspecified assistantships also available. Financial award application deadline: 2/1; financial award applicants required to submit FAFSA. *Faculty research:* Robotics, artificial intelligence, algorithms, database software engineering, high-performance computing. Total annual research expenditures: $1.2 million. *Unit head:* Dr. Sitharama S. Iyengar, Chair, 225-578-1495, Fax: 225-578-1465, E-mail: iyengar@csc.lsu.edu. *Application contact:* Graduate Coordinator, 225-578-1495, Fax: 225-578-1465.

Louisiana State University in Shreveport, College of Sciences, Program in Computer Systems Technology, Shreveport, LA 71115-2399. Offers MS. *Students:* 3 full-time (1 woman), 14 part-time (3 women); includes 2 minority (1 Black or African American, non-Hispanic/Latino; 1 Asian, non-Hispanic/Latino), 3 international. Average age 33. 4 applicants, 75% accepted, 2 enrolled. In 2010, 5 master's awarded. *Degree requirements:* For master's, thesis or alternative. *Entrance requirements:* For master's, GRE, programming course in high-level language, interview. Additional exam requirements/recommendations for international students: Required—TOEFL (minimum score 500 paper-based; 173 computer-based; 61 iBT). *Application deadline:* For fall admission, 6/30 for domestic and international students; for spring admission, 11/30 for domestic and international students. Applications are processed on a rolling basis. Application fee: $10 ($20 for international students). *Expenses:* Tuition, state resident: full-time $3272; part-time $181.80 per credit hour. Tuition, nonresident: full-time $7902; part-time $471.19 per credit hour. Required fees: $850; $47 per credit hour. *Financial support:* In 2010–11, 2 research assistantships with partial tuition reimbursements (averaging $20,000 per year) were awarded. *Unit head:* Dr. Krishna Agarwal, Program Director, 318-795-4283, Fax: 318-795-2419, E-mail: krishna.agarwal@lsus.edu. *Application contact:* Yvonne Yarbrough, Secretary, Graduate Studies, 318-797-5247, Fax: 318-798-4120, E-mail: yyarbrou@lsus.edu.

Miami University, Graduate School, School of Engineering and Applied Science, Department of Computer Science and Software Engineering, Oxford, OH 45056. Offers computer science (MCS). *Students:* 18 full-time (5 women), 3 part-time (1 woman); includes 2 minority (1 Black or African American, non-Hispanic/Latino; 1 Asian, non-Hispanic/Latino), 10 international. Average age 25. In 2010, 9 master's awarded. *Entrance requirements:* For master's, GRE, minimum cumulative undergraduate GPA of 3.0. Additional exam requirements/recommendations for international students: Required—TOEFL (minimum score 500 paper-based; 250 computer-based). *Application deadline:* For fall admission, 2/1 for domestic and international students. Application fee: $50. *Expenses:* Tuition, state resident: full-time $11,616; part-time $484 per credit hour. Tuition, nonresident: full-time $25,656; part-time $1069 per credit hour. Required fees: $528. *Financial support:* Fellowships, research assistantships, teaching assistantships, Federal Work-Study, health care benefits, tuition waivers (full), and unspecified assistantships available. Financial award application deadline: 3/1. *Unit head:* Dr. James Kiper, Chair, 513-529-0345, E-mail: kiperjd@muohio.edu. *Application contact:* Dr. James Kiper, Chair, 513-529-0345, E-mail: kiperjd@muohio.edu.

Oakland University, Graduate Study and Lifelong Learning, School of Engineering and Computer Science, Department of Computer Science and Engineering, Rochester, MI 48309-4401. Offers computer science (MS); embedded systems (MS); information systems engineering (MS); software engineering (MS). Part-time and evening/weekend programs available. *Entrance requirements:* For master's, minimum GPA of 3.0 for unconditional admission. Electronic applications accepted. *Expenses:* Contact institution. *Faculty research:* Cyber security, 3D imaging of neurochemicals in rat brains.

Portland State University, Graduate Studies, Maseeh College of Engineering and Computer Science, Department of Engineering and Technology Management, Portland, OR 97207-0751. Offers engineering and technology management (M Eng); engineering management (MS); manufacturing engineering (ME); manufacturing management (M Eng); systems science/engineering management (PhD); MS/MBA; MS/MS. Part-time and evening/weekend programs available. *Faculty:* 8 full-time (1 woman), 3 part-time/adjunct (2 women). *Students:* 50 full-time (13 women), 58 part-time (16 women); includes 13 Asian, non-Hispanic/Latino; 6 Hispanic/Latino, 51 international. Average age 35. 38 applicants, 76% accepted, 13 enrolled. In 2010, 42 master's awarded. *Degree requirements:* For master's, thesis optional; for doctorate, one foreign language, thesis/dissertation, oral and written exams. *Entrance requirements:* For master's, minimum GPA of 3.0 in upper-division course work, BS in civil engineering; for doctorate, GRE General Test, GRE Subject Test, minimum GPA of 3.0 in upper-division course work. Additional exam requirements/recommendations for international students: Required—TOEFL (minimum score 550 paper-based; 213 computer-based). *Application deadline:* For fall admission, 4/1 for domestic students, 3/1 for international students; for winter admission, 9/1 for domestic students, 7/1 for international students; for spring admission, 11/1 for domestic students, 9/1 for international students. Applications are processed on a rolling basis. Application fee: $50. *Expenses:* Tuition, state resident: full-time $8505; part-time $315 per credit. Tuition, nonresident: full-time $13,284; part-time $492 per credit. Required fees: $1482; $21 per credit. $99 per term. One-time fee: $120. Part-time tuition and fees vary according to course load and program. *Financial support:* In 2010–11, 3 teaching assistantships with full tuition reimbursements (averaging $8,916 per year) were awarded; research assistantships with full tuition reimbursements, career-related internships or fieldwork, Federal Work-Study, scholarships/grants, and unspecified assistantships also available. Support available to part-time students. Financial award application deadline: 3/1; financial award applicants required to submit FAFSA. *Faculty research:* Scheduling, hierarchical decision modeling, operations research, knowledge-based information systems. Total annual research expenditures: $1.1 million. *Unit head:* Dr. Dundar F. Kocaoglu, Chair, 503-725-4660, Fax: 503-725-4667, E-mail: kocaoglu@etm.pdx.edu. *Application contact:* Dr. Dundar F. Kocaoglu, Chair, 503-725-4660, Fax: 503-725-4667, E-mail: kocaoglu@etm.pdx.edu.

Portland State University, Graduate Studies, Systems Science Program, Portland, OR 97207-0751. Offers computational intelligence (Certificate); computer modeling and simulation (Certificate); systems science (MS); systems science/anthropology (PhD); systems science/business administration (PhD); systems science/civil engineering (PhD); systems science/economics (PhD); systems science/engineering management (PhD); systems science/general (PhD); systems science/mathematical sciences (PhD); systems science/mechanical engineering (PhD); systems science/psychology (PhD); systems science/sociology (PhD). *Faculty:* 4 full-time (0 women), 1 part-time/adjunct (0 women). *Students:* 15 full-time (4 women), 35 part-time (11 women); includes 1 American Indian or Alaska Native, non-Hispanic/Latino; 1 Asian, non-Hispanic/Latino; 1 Two or more races, non-Hispanic/Latino, 4 international. Average age 39. 8 applicants, 88% accepted, 5 enrolled. In 2010, 2 master's, 4 doctorates awarded. *Degree requirements:* For doctorate, variable foreign language requirement, thesis/dissertation. *Entrance requirements:* For master's, 2 letters of recommendation; for doctorate, GMAT, GRE General Test, minimum undergraduate GPA of 3.0. Additional exam requirements/recommendations for international students: Required—TOEFL. *Application deadline:* For fall admission, 2/1 for domestic students; for spring admission, 11/1 for domestic students. Application fee: $50. *Expenses:* Tuition, state resident: full-time $8505; part-time $315 per credit. Tuition, nonresident: full-time $13,284; part-time $492 per credit. Required fees: $1482; $21 per credit. $99 per term. One-time fee: $120. Part-time tuition and fees vary according to course load and program. *Financial support:* In 2010–11, 1 research assistantship with full tuition reimbursement (averaging $7,704 per year) was awarded; teaching assistantships with full tuition reimbursements, career-related internships or fieldwork, Federal Work-Study, scholarships/grants, and unspecified assistantships also available. Support available to part-time students. Financial award application deadline: 3/1; financial award applicants required to submit FAFSA. *Faculty research:* Systems theory and methodology, artificial intelligence neural networks, information theory, nonlinear dynamics/chaos, modeling and simulation. *Unit head:* George Lendaris, Acting Director, 503-725-4960. *Application contact:* Dawn Sharafi, Administrative Assistant, 503-725-4960, E-mail: dawn@sysc.pdx.edu.

Rensselaer at Hartford, Department of Engineering, Program in Computer and Systems Engineering, Hartford, CT 06120-2991. Offers ME. *Entrance requirements:* For master's, GRE.

Southern Methodist University, Bobby B. Lyle School of Engineering, Department of Engineering Management, Information, and Systems, Dallas, TX 75275. Offers applied science (MS); engineering management (MSEM, DE); information engineering and management (MSIEM); operations research (MS, PhD); systems engineering (MS, PhD). Part-time and evening/weekend programs available. Postbaccalaureate distance learning degree programs offered. *Faculty:* 8 full-time (1 woman), 22 part-time/adjunct (1 woman). *Students:* 47 full-time (12 women), 348 part-time (75 women); includes 114 minority (31 Black or African American, non-Hispanic/Latino; 2 American Indian or Alaska Native, non-Hispanic/Latino; 34 Asian, non-Hispanic/Latino; 44 Hispanic/Latino; 2 Native Hawaiian or other Pacific Islander, non-Hispanic/Latino; 1 Two or more races, non-Hispanic/Latino), 51 international. Average age 33. 208 applicants, 67% accepted, 92 enrolled. In 2010, 130 master's, 6 doctorates awarded. Terminal master's awarded for partial completion of doctoral program. *Degree requirements:* For master's, thesis optional; for doctorate, thesis/dissertation, oral and written qualifying exams. *Entrance requirements:* For master's, minimum GPA of 3.0 in last 2 years; bachelor's degree in engineering, mathematics, sciences, or technical area; for doctorate, GRE General Test (operations research, engineering management), bachelor's degree in related field. Additional exam requirements/recommendations for international students: Required—TOEFL. *Application deadline:* For fall admission, 7/1 for domestic students, 5/15 for international students; for spring admission, 11/15 for domestic students, 9/1 for international students. Applications are processed on a rolling basis. Application fee: $75. *Financial support:* In 2010–11, 6 students received support, including 4 research assistantships with full tuition reimbursements available (averaging $18,000 per year), 2 teaching assistantships with full tuition reimbursements available (averaging $18,000 per year); tuition waivers (full) also available. *Faculty research:* Telecommunications, decision systems, information engineering, operations research, software. Total annual research expenditures: $275,851. *Unit head:* Dr. Richard S. Barr, Chair, 214-768-1772, Fax: 214-768-1112, E-mail: emis@lyle.smu.edu. *Application contact:* Marc Valerin, Director of Graduate and Executive Admissions, 214-768-3042, E-mail: valerin@lyle.smu.edu.

State University of New York at Binghamton, Graduate School, Thomas J. Watson School of Engineering and Applied Science, Department of Systems Science and Industrial Engineering, Binghamton, NY 13902-6000. Offers M Eng, MS, MSAT, PhD. Part-time and evening/weekend programs available. *Faculty:* 10 full-time (3 women), 2 part-time/adjunct (0 women). *Students:* 77 full-time (17 women), 91 part-time (16 women); includes 6 Black or African American, non-Hispanic/Latino; 2 American Indian or Alaska Native, non-Hispanic/Latino; 10 Asian, non-Hispanic/Latino; 3 Hispanic/Latino, 97 international. Average age 29. 149 applicants, 56% accepted, 44 enrolled. In 2010, 41 master's, 10 doctorates awarded. Terminal master's awarded for partial completion of doctoral program. *Degree requirements:* For master's, thesis or alternative; for doctorate, thesis/dissertation. *Entrance requirements:* For master's and doctorate, GRE General Test, GRE Subject Test. Additional exam requirements/recommendations for international students: Required—TOEFL. *Application deadline:* For fall admission, 4/15 priority date for domestic students, 1/15 priority date for international students; for spring admission, 11/1 for domestic students, 10/1 priority date for international students. Applications are processed on a rolling basis. Application fee: $60. Electronic applications accepted. *Financial support:* In 2010–11, 73 students received support, including 2 fellowships with full tuition reimbursements available (averaging $16,500 per year), 51 research assistantships with full tuition reimbursements available (averaging $16,500 per year), 14 teaching assistantships with full tuition reimbursements available (averaging $16,500 per year); career-related internships or fieldwork, Federal Work-Study, institutionally sponsored loans, scholarships/grants, health care benefits, tuition waivers (full and partial), and unspecified assistantships also available. Financial award application deadline: 2/15; financial award applicants required to submit FAFSA. *Faculty research:* Problem restructuring, protein modeling. *Unit head:* Dr. Nagen Nagarur, Chair, 607-777-3027, E-mail: nnagarur@binghamton.edu. *Application contact:* Catherine Smith, Recruiting and Admissions Coordinator, 607-777-2151, Fax: 607-777-2501, E-mail: cmsmith@binghamton.edu.

Stevens Institute of Technology, Graduate School, Charles V. Schaefer Jr. School of Engineering, Department of Mechanical Engineering, Program in Integrated Product Development, Hoboken, NJ 07030. Offers armament engineering (M Eng); computer and electrical engineering (M Eng); manufacturing technologies (M Eng); systems reliability and design (M Eng). *Students:* 8 part-time (1 woman). Average age 26. *Unit head:* Dr. Constantin Chassapis, Director, 201-216-5564. *Application contact:* Graduate Admissions, 800-496-4935, Fax: 201-216-8044, E-mail: gradadmissions@stevens.edu.

Stevens Institute of Technology, Graduate School, School of Systems and Enterprises, Program in Enterprise Systems, Hoboken, NJ 07030. Offers MS, PhD. *Students:* 1 full-time (0 women), 6 part-time (5 women); includes 1 Black or African American, non-Hispanic/Latino; 1 Asian, non-Hispanic/Latino; 1 Hispanic/Latino, 1 international. Average age 30. *Unit head:* Dr.

Charles L. Suffel, Dean of the Graduate School, 201-216-5234, Fax: 201-216-8044, E-mail: csuffel@stevens-tech.edu. *Application contact:* Graduate Admissions, 800-496-4935, Fax: 201-216-8044, E-mail: gradadmissions@stevens.edu.

Strayer University, Graduate Studies, Washington, DC 20005-2603. Offers accounting (MS); acquisition (MBA); business administration (MBA); communications technology (MS); educational management (M Ed); finance (MBA); health services administration (MHSA); hospitality and tourism management (MBA); human resource management (MBA); information systems (MS), including computer security management, decision support system management, enterprise resource management, network management, software engineering management, systems development management; management (MBA); management information systems (MS); marketing (MBA); professional accounting (MS), including accounting information systems, controllership, taxation; public administration (MPA); supply chain management (MBA); technology in education (M Ed). Programs also offered at campus locations in Birmingham, AL; Chamblee, GA; Cobb County, GA; Morrow, GA; White Marsh, MD; Charleston, SC; Columbia, SC; Greensboro, NC; Greenville, SC; Lexington, KY; Louisville, KY; Nashville, TN; North Raleigh, NC; Washington, DC. Part-time and evening/weekend programs available. Postbaccalaureate distance learning degree programs offered (minimal on-campus study). *Degree requirements:* For master's, thesis. *Entrance requirements:* For master's, GMAT, GRE General Test, bachelor's degree from an accredited college or university, minimum undergraduate GPA of 2.75. Electronic applications accepted.

Universidad Autonoma de Guadalajara, Graduate Programs, Guadalajara, Mexico. Offers administrative law and justice (LL M); advertising and corporate communications (MA); architecture (M Arch); business (MBA); computational science (MCC); education (Ed M, Ed D); English-Spanish translation (MA); entrepreneurship and management (MBA); integrated management of digital animation (MA); international business (MIB); international corporate law (LL M); internet technologies (MS); manufacturing systems (MMS); occupational health (MS); philosophy (MA, PhD); power electronics (MS); quality systems (MQS); renewable energy (MS); social evaluation of projects (MBA); strategic market research (MBA); tax law (MA); teaching mathematics (MA).

University of Michigan–Dearborn, College of Engineering and Computer Science, Department of Industrial and Manufacturing Systems Engineering, Dearborn, MI 48128-1491. Offers engineering management (MS); industrial and systems engineering (MSE); information systems and technology (MS); information systems engineering (PhD); program and project management (MS); MBA/MSE. Part-time and evening/weekend programs available. *Faculty:* 13 full-time (0 women), 3 part-time/adjunct (0 women). *Students:* 23 full-time (8 women), 142 part-time (40 women); includes 14 Black or African American, non-Hispanic/Latino; 27 Asian, non-Hispanic/Latino; 8 Hispanic/Latino, 23 international. Average age 35. 81 applicants, 58% accepted, 47 enrolled. In 2010, 57 master's awarded. *Degree requirements:* For master's, thesis optional. *Entrance requirements:* For master's, bachelor's degree in applied mathematics, computer science, engineering, or physical science; minimum GPA of 3.0. Additional exam requirements/recommendations for international students: Required—TOEFL (minimum score 560 paper-based; 220 computer-based; 84 iBT). *Application deadline:* For fall admission, 8/1 priority date for domestic students, 4/1 for international students; for winter admission, 12/1 priority date for domestic students, 8/1 for international students; for spring admission, 4/1 for domestic students, 12/1 for international students. Applications are processed on a rolling basis. Application fee: $60. Electronic applications accepted. *Financial support:* Fellowships, research assistantships, teaching assistantships, Federal Work-Study available. Financial award application deadline: 4/1; financial award applicants required to submit FAFSA. *Faculty research:* Health care systems, data and knowledge management, human factors engineering, machine diagnostics, precision machining. *Unit head:* Dr. Armen Zakarian, Chair, 313-593-5361, Fax: 313-593-3692, E-mail: zakarian@umd.umich.edu. *Application contact:* Joey W. Woods, Graduate Program Assistant, 313-593-5361, Fax: 313-593-3692, E-mail: jwwoods@umd.umich.edu.

The University of North Carolina Wilmington, College of Arts and Sciences, Program in Computer Science and Information Systems, Wilmington, NC 28403-3297. Offers MS. *Faculty:* 11 full-time (1 woman). *Students:* 18 full-time (3 women), 17 part-time (3 women); includes 1 Black or African American, non-Hispanic/Latino; 2 American Indian or Alaska Native, non-Hispanic/Latino; 3 Hispanic/Latino, 2 international. Average age 28. 17 applicants, 53% accepted, 7 enrolled. In 2010, 14 master's awarded. *Entrance requirements:* For master's, GMAT or GRE, 3 letters of recommendation, resume. *Application deadline:* For fall admission, 4/1 for domestic students; for spring admission, 11/1 for domestic students. Application fee: $45. *Financial support:* In 2010–11, 10 teaching assistantships were awarded. *Unit head:* Dr.

Sridhar Narayan, Director, 910-962-3695, E-mail: narayans@uncw.edu. *Application contact:* Dr. Ron Vetter, Graduate Coordinator, 910-962-2160, Fax: 910-962-7457, E-mail: vetterv@uncw.edu.

University of Ottawa, Faculty of Graduate and Postdoctoral Studies, Interdisciplinary Programs, Ottawa, ON K1N 6N5, Canada. Offers e-business (Certificate); e-commerce (Certificate); finance (Certificate); health services and policies research (Diploma); population health (PhD); population health risk assessment and management (Certificate); public management and governance (Certificate); systems science (Certificate).

University of Ottawa, Faculty of Graduate and Postdoctoral Studies, Systems Science Program, Ottawa, ON K1N 6N5, Canada. Offers M Sc, M Sys Sc, Certificate. Part-time and evening/weekend programs available. *Degree requirements:* For master's and Certificate, thesis optional. *Entrance requirements:* For master's, bachelor's degree or equivalent, minimum B average; for Certificate, honors degree or equivalent, minimum B average. Additional exam requirements/recommendations for international students: Recommended—TOEFL (minimum score 237 computer-based). Electronic applications accepted. *Faculty research:* Software engineering, communication systems, information systems, production management, corporate managerial modeling.

Washington University in St. Louis, School of Engineering and Applied Science, Department of Electrical and Systems Engineering, St. Louis, MO 63130-4899. Offers electrical engineering (MS, D Sc, PhD); systems science and mathematics (MS, D Sc, PhD). Part-time programs available. *Faculty:* 16 full-time (2 women), 5 part-time/adjunct (0 women). *Students:* 63 full-time (12 women), 18 part-time (1 woman); includes 1 Black or African American, non-Hispanic/Latino; 15 Asian, non-Hispanic/Latino; 2 Hispanic/Latino, 45 international. Average age 23. 299 applicants, 18% accepted, 18 enrolled. In 2010, 21 master's, 6 doctorates awarded. Terminal master's awarded for partial completion of doctoral program. *Degree requirements:* For master's, thesis or alternative; for doctorate, comprehensive exam, thesis/dissertation. *Entrance requirements:* For master's, minimum GPA of 3.0 in the last 2 years of undergraduate course work; for doctorate, GRE. Additional exam requirements/recommendations for international students: Required—TOEFL (minimum score 550 paper-based; 213 computer-based; 80 iBT). *Application deadline:* For fall admission, 1/15 for domestic and international students. Applications are processed on a rolling basis. Application fee: $60. Electronic applications accepted. *Financial support:* In 2010–11, 12 fellowships with full tuition reimbursements (averaging $20,000 per year), 32 research assistantships with full tuition reimbursements (averaging $26,950 per year) were awarded; teaching assistantships with full tuition reimbursements, career-related internships or fieldwork, Federal Work-Study, institutionally sponsored loans, scholarships/grants, and unspecified assistantships also available. Financial award application deadline: 1/15; financial award applicants required to submit FAFSA. *Faculty research:* Applied physics and electronics, signal and image processing, systems analysis, biomedicine, and energy. Total annual research expenditures: $2 million. *Unit head:* Dr. Arye Nehorai, Chair, 314-935-5565, Fax: 314-935-7500, E-mail: nehorai@ese.wustl.edu. *Application contact:* Shauna Dollison, Director of Graduate Programs, 314-935-4830, Fax: 314-935-7500, E-mail: sdollison@ese.wustl.edu.

Worcester Polytechnic Institute, Graduate Studies and Research, Department of Social Science and Policy Studies, Worcester, MA 01609-2280. Offers interdisciplinary social science (PhD); system dynamics (MS, Graduate Certificate). Part-time and evening/weekend programs available. Postbaccalaureate distance learning degree programs offered (no on-campus study). *Faculty:* 4 full-time (1 woman), 3 part-time/adjunct (0 women). *Students:* 8 part-time (1 woman); includes 1 Hispanic/Latino; 1 Native Hawaiian or other Pacific Islander, non-Hispanic/Latino, 1 international. 23 applicants, 61% accepted, 2 enrolled. In 2010, 2 master's awarded. *Entrance requirements:* For master's, GRE General Test, 3 letters of recommendation. Additional exam requirements/recommendations for international students: Required—TOEFL (minimum score 550 paper-based; 213 computer-based; 79 iBT), IELTS (minimum score 6.5). *Application deadline:* For fall admission, 1/1 priority date for domestic students, 1/15 for international students; for spring admission, 10/1 priority date for domestic students, 10/1 for international students. Applications are processed on a rolling basis. Application fee: $70. Electronic applications accepted. *Expenses:* Tuition: Full-time $20,862; part-time $1159 per term. One-time fee: $15. *Financial support:* Career-related internships or fieldwork, institutionally sponsored loans, scholarships/grants, and unspecified assistantships available. Financial award application deadline: 1/1; financial award applicants required to submit FAFSA. *Faculty research:* Microeconomics, political economy, system dynamics, systems thinking, social simulation. *Unit head:* Dr. James K. Doyle, Head, 508-831-5296, Fax: 508-831-5896, E-mail: doyle@wpi.edu. *Application contact:* Dr. Oleg Pavlov, Graduate Coordinator, 508-831-5296, Fax: 508-831-5896, E-mail: opavlov@wpi.edu.

CLARKSON UNIVERSITY

Information Technology

Programs of Study	The Master of Science in information technology (IT) program offers an interdisciplinary, broad-based curriculum for this professional degree. Students take courses from a range of disciplines that include math and computer science, electrical and computer engineering, technical communications, and management information systems. The one-year program has a practical orientation that emphasizes hands-on learning and real-world experience in collaborative projects.
	The master's degree in IT program comprises a minimum of 30 credit hours, which include one course treating modern object-oriented design in a language such as C++, one course treating the principles of computing and telecommunication systems, one course in the management of technology, three courses in application of information technology, and 6 credits of project work. Additional credits can include course or project work. Through course selection and project work, students can focus on areas in IT they find compelling.
	Students in this program develop a broad base of competencies in hardware, operating systems, programming, computer applications, and the management of technology. At the same time, they can choose to explore specific application areas through elective classes and project work. Projects focus on real-world problems that provide experience directly applicable to IT in an organizational setting.
	Clarkson provides access to some of the latest equipment and software. Individuals can install and run multiple operating systems (UNIX/Linux, Microsoft Windows, VMware), manage Web servers, create storefront CGIs, and administer databases.
	The academic year consists of two semesters of fifteen weeks each. There is no formal summer session for graduate classes, but many students complete their projects during this time.
	Students can also opt to complete their degree in 1½ years, taking 10 credits each semester.
Financial Aid	Partial-tuition assistantships are available for all full-time students who are accepted. This includes up to 30 percent off the cost of tuition until degree requirements are met. This assistantship is merit-based.
Cost of Study	Tuition for graduate work is $1198 per credit hour for 2011–12. Fees are about $590 per year.
Living and Housing Costs	Estimated living expenses off campus are approximately $14,000 a year, which includes rent, food, books, clothing, recreation, and miscellaneous expenses. Most graduate students live off campus, as on-campus housing is very limited.
Student Group	There are approximately 400 total graduate students and 2,700 undergraduates.
Location	Clarkson is located in Potsdam, a quintessential college town, nestled in the foothills of the northern Adirondack region of New York. The beautiful northeast corner of the state is the home of the 6-million-acre Adirondack Park. Within 2 hours of the campus are Lake Placid and the cosmopolitan Canadian cities of Montreal and Ottawa.
The University	Founded in 1896, Clarkson stands out among America's private nationally ranked research institutions because of its dynamic collaborative learning environment, innovative degree and research programs, and unmatched track record for producing leaders and innovators.
	Clarkson is New York State's highest-ranked small research institution. The University attracts 3,000 enterprising students from diverse backgrounds (including some 400 graduate students) who thrive in rigorous programs in engineering, arts, sciences, business, and health sciences.
Applying	Although there is a rolling admission policy, the recommended application deadlines are May 15 for the fall semester and October 15 for the spring semester for U.S. applicants. International applicants are encouraged to apply by April 15 for the fall semester and October 1 for the spring semester. Students who apply by January 30 for the fall semester receive priority for assistantships and other financial aid. Prospective students may submit an online application using a credit card. Study may begin in August or January. Scores on the General Test of the GRE are required for all applications. TOEFL scores must be submitted by all applicants for whom English is a second language.
Correspondence and Information	Information Technology Graduate School Box 5802 Clarkson University Potsdam, New York 13699-5802 Phone: 315-268-3802 Fax: 315-268-3989 E-mail: sciencegrad@clarkson.edu horn@clarkson.edu Web site: http://www.clarkson.edu/graduate

Clarkson University

THE FACULTY

Fifteen full-time regular faculty members and 2 full-time regular instructors from the four departments participate in the graduate information technology program. The disciplines that compose the IT program include math and computer science, electrical and computer engineering, technical communications, and management information systems.

SAMPLE INFORMATION TECHNOLOGY PROJECTS

Virtual Computing Lab: Prototyping a Clarkson Cloud
Spring 2011

Adviser: Wm. Dennis Horn

This project implemented a virtual computing lab (VCL) that will replace the current PC labs on campus. The purpose of this project was to make it easier for the Office of Information Technology to manage the campus PC labs and eventually make VCL available to students using a PC from anywhere on the Internet. Software used was Citrix XenDesktop 4 on Windows Server 2008R2 and the Citrix XenServer, run on a Dell Equallogic PS6000XVS Storage Array which provides intelligent tiered storage among traditional SAS drives and solid state drives.

Academic Metric Management System
Fall 2010

Adviser: Boris Jukic

This project was the Web design and front-end development of the Clarkson Academic Metric Management system, designed to help the Clarkson University business faculty manage the data from the compliant standards of learning set forth by the AACSB (The Association to Advance Collegiate Schools of Business). Previously, MBA professors had to find a way to create and maintain metric data on their classes, but it was difficult to keep track of this data and remain organized. Written as an ITMS project, this web interface is essentially free to Clarkson and will allow the Clarkson University business faculty to maintain the necessary metric data with ease and in an organized fashion.

Online Voting System
Fall 2009

Adviser: Boris Jukic

The online voting system is an ASP.NET Web-based project. In this system there are two logins, one for the administrator who controls the entire working system and the second for the voter. The administrator has its own log-in ID and password. There can be more than one administrator. When an administrator logs in, the welcome page displays various links such as manage voters, manage candidates, check votes, and log out. Through this system the administrator can add candidates and voters. Each voter has their own log-in ID and password from which he or she can cast their vote from any system online. The administrator has all rights to check the number of votes for the respective candidates. The program can be reconfigured for new elections with different candidates and voters. The technology used here was .Net. The front-end language used was asp.net with JavaScript for validations and the back end was MS Access 2007 for the database.

Web Analysis Tools for TAD Study
Fall 2007

Adviser: Philip K. Hopke

This project analyzed the requirements, designed, implemented, and documented a Web interface for a TAD Study at Clarkson University to manage large volumes of data, maintain inventory, organize scheduling processes, etc. This project characterizes the efficiency of an air cleaner developed by a Syracuse company to reduce asthma attacks in children by providing a healthy environment. Different air quality instruments are installed in the subject's bedroom to determine the efficiency of the air cleaner in providing a healthy environment by reducing the levels of particles, VOCs, CO, etc. Subjects are tested for different biomarkers of inflammation such as nitrate levels and forced expiratory volume, using instruments such as RTubes and peak flow meters. Heart rate is also monitored during sleep.

Web-Based System for Teaching Controller Performance Assessment
Fall 2005

Adviser: Dr. Raghunathan Rengasamy

This project includes the development of a C++ interface for communicating, with an experiment for controlling the level of liquid in multiple tanks. Matlab is used to control the liquid level by opening and closing valves that regulate the flow into the various tanks. A module written in C++ is integrated with a Web server for displaying real time on the Web data from the experiment. The system allows for a two-way communication so that commands from the Web can be directly fed to the experimental system. The complete site contains a calendar, software for user registration, authentication, and other resources.

Automatic Web Survey Generator and Administrator
Fall 2005

Adviser: Dr. Wm. Dennis Horn

This system automates the process of creating surveys. The survey administrator enters questions for the survey. Multiple choices for the answers are generated by the software based on a predefined value. The survey generator is password protected to prevent unwanted people from creating or modifying surveys. When users take the survey, results are stored in a flat database. Additional software analyzes the data and presents results on the Web behind authentication. PHP is used for the survey generation and analytical processing. JavaScript is used for validation. HTML/CSS is used for the basic HTML page design.

E-mail Gateway
Spring 2004

Adviser: Professor Wm. Dennis Horn

This project created an e-mail gateway to handle all incoming and outgoing e-mail from Clarkson's campus. This gateway sits between the Internet and Clarkson's internal mail system and runs antivirus and antispam measures against all SMTP messages that it receives. The hardware for this project consists of an IBM xSeries 345 with dual hyperthreaded 3.2-GHz Xeon processors (four logical processors), 2 GB of RAM, and two 36-GB Ultra-360 SCSI disks in Raid 0. The software running on this box consists of a patched qmail (MTA), spamassassin (antispam), uvscan (antivirus), and a collection of custom Perl scripts to prevent blatant spam attacks. When fully operational, this box handles upwards of 100,000 messages per day and contains approximately 13,000 messages in its queue. The majority of these queued messages are bounces generated as the result of undeliverable mail.

Windmill Research Project
Fall 2002

Adviser: Professor Kenneth Visser

Every 10 seconds, sensors at the Windmill Site (Potsdam, New York, Airport) record data on wind speed at 18 meters, 12 meters, and 6 meters; wind direction at 18 meters and 6 meters; and the temperature, relative humidity, and pressure. This project reduces the massive amount of raw data to human-interpretable form by creating an HTML interface that allows researchers to select time intervals of minutes, hours, days, weeks, and months and graph changes over periods of days, months, and years. Perl/CGI is used to crunch the data in less than a second and graph it, using the Perl GD.pm module, in PNG format. Graphs are scaled to fit on the screen, and multiple graphs can be placed in a single display for comparison.

COLUMBIA UNIVERSITY

Department of Computer Science

Programs of Study

The doctoral program of the Department of Computer Science is geared toward the exceptional student. The faculty believes that the best way to learn how to do research is by doing it; therefore, starting in their first semester, students conduct joint research with faculty members. In addition to conducting research they also prepare themselves for the Ph.D. comprehensive examinations, which test breadth in computer science. The primary educational goal is to prepare students for research and teaching careers either in universities or in industry. The Department enjoys a low doctoral student–faculty ratio (about 4:1).

Current research areas include artificial intelligence, collaborative work, computational biology, computational complexity, computational learning theory, computer architecture, computer-aided design of digital systems, databases, digital libraries, distributed computing, graphics, HCI, logic synthesis, mobile and wearable computing, multimedia, natural-language processing, networking, network management, operating systems, parallel processing, robotics, security, software engineering, user interfaces, virtual and augmented reality, vision, and Web technologies.

The Department also offers the Master of Science degree in computer science. This program can be completed within three semesters of full-time classwork. Completing the optional thesis generally stretches the program to two years. The M.S. degree can also be earned through part-time study.

Research Facilities

The Department has well-equipped lab areas for research in computer graphics, computer-aided digital design, computer vision, databases and digital libraries, data mining and knowledge discovery, distributed systems, mobile and wearable computing, natural-language processing, networking, operating systems, programming systems, robotics, user interfaces, and real-time multimedia.

The computer facilities include a gigabit network with 3-GB uplink, NetApp file servers, two large disk backup servers, a student interactive teaching and research lab of high-end multimedia workstations, a large VMware system for teaching, a programming laboratory with eighteen Windows workstations and sixty-three Linux workstations, a large cluster of Linux servers for computational work, a cluster of Sun servers, and a compute cluster consisting of a Linux cloud that can support approximately 5,000 VMware instances. The research infrastructure includes hundreds of workstations and PCs running Solaris, Windows, Linux, and Mac OSX; terabytes of disk space are backed up by an LTO-5 tape library.

Research labs contain several large Linux and Solaris clusters, Puma 500 and IBM robotic arms, a UTAH-MIT dexterous hand, an Adept-1 robot, mobile research robots, a real-time defocus range sensor, interactive 3-D graphics workstations with 3-D position and orientation trackers, prototype wearable computers, wall-sized stereo projection systems, see-through head-mounted displays, a networking testbed with three Cisco 7500 backbone routers, traffic generators, Ethernet switches, and a 17-node (34CPU) IBM Netfinity cluster. The Department uses a 3COM SIP IP phone system. The protocol was developed in the Department.

The servers are connected on a gigabit network; all have remote consoles and remote power for easy maintenance after hours. The rest of the Department's computers are connected via a switched 100 Mb/s Ethernet network, which has direct connectivity to the campus OC-3 Internet and Internet2 gateways. The campus has 802.11 a/b wireless LAN coverage.

The research facility is supported by a full-time staff of professional system administrators and programmers aided by a number of part-time student system administrators.

Financial Aid

Most doctoral students and a few master's students receive graduate research assistantships. The stipend for 2010–11 was $2816 per month for the academic year. In addition, graduate research assistants receive full tuition exemption. A limited number of teaching assistantships are available to doctoral students.

Cost of Study

Tuition and fees totaled approximately $41,200 for the M.S. program and $36,500 for the Ph.D. program for the 2010–11 academic year.

Living and Housing Costs

In 2011–12, apartments in University-owned buildings cost $775–$1325 and up per month. Rooms are also available at International House; these cost $815–$1355 and up per month.

Student Group

There are 130 Ph.D. students in the Department. A large proportion of Columbia University's student body is at the graduate level; of the 25,459 students, 15,819 are in the graduate or professional schools.

Location

New York City is the intellectual, artistic, cultural, gastronomic, corporate, financial, and media center of the United States, and perhaps of the world. The city is renowned for its theaters, museums, libraries, restaurants, opera, and music. Inexpensive student tickets for cultural and sporting events are frequently available, and the museums are open to students at very modest cost or are free. The ethnic variety of the city adds to its appeal. The city is bordered by uncongested areas of great beauty that provide varied types of recreation, such as hiking, camping, skiing, and ocean and lake swimming. There are superb beaches on Long Island and in New Jersey, while to the north lie the Catskill, Green, Berkshire, and Adirondack mountains. Close at hand is the beautiful Hudson River valley.

The University

Columbia University was established as King's College in 1754. Today it consists of sixteen schools and faculties and is one of the leading universities in the world. The University draws students from many countries. The high caliber of the students and faculty makes it an intellectually stimulating place to be. Columbia University is located on Morningside Heights, close to Lincoln Center for the Performing Arts, Greenwich Village, Central Park, and midtown Manhattan. Columbia athletic teams compete in the Ivy League.

Applying

For maximum consideration for admission to the doctoral program, students should submit the required application materials before December 1 for the fall term and before October 1 for the spring term. Applicants must submit official applications, transcripts, at least three recommendation letters, and an application fee. The General and Subject Tests of the Graduate Record Examinations are required for all computer science graduate applicants. The deadlines for applications to the master's program are February 15 for fall admission and October 1 for spring admission.

Program information can be found at http://www.cs.columbia.edu. Further details on admission and online application for the M.S. program are on the Web at http://www.cs.columbia.edu/education/admissions#msadmissions and for the Ph.D. program at http://www.cs.columbia.edu/education/admissions#phd.

Correspondence and Information

Fu Foundation School of Engineering and Applied Science
Department of Computer Science
450 Computer Science Building
Mail Code 0401
Columbia University
1214 Amsterdam Avenue
New York, New York 10027-7003

Phone: 212-939-7000
Web site: http://www.cs.columbia.edu/education/admissions

Columbia University

THE FACULTY AND THEIR RESEARCH

Alfred V. Aho, Lawrence Gussman Professor. Programming languages, compilers, software, quantum computing.

Peter K. Allen, Professor. Robotics, computer vision, 3-D modeling.

Peter Belhumeur, Professor. Computer vision, biometrics, face recognition, computational photography, computer graphics, biological species identification.

Steven M. Bellovin, Professor. Internet security, computer security, privacy, information technology policy.

Adam H. Cannon, Lecturer in Discipline. Machine learning, statistical pattern recognition, computer science education.

Luca Carloni, Associate Professor. Computer-aided design, embedded systems, multi-core platform architectures, cyber-physical systems.

Augustin Chaintreau, Assistant Professor. Networked algorithms, social networks, mobile computing, stochastic networks.

Xi Chen, Assistant Professor. Algorithmic game theory and economics, computational complexity theory.

Michael Collins, Vikram S. Pandit Professor. Natural language processing and machine learning.

Stephen A. Edwards, Associate Professor. Embedded systems, domain-specific languages, compilers, hardware-software codesign, computer-aided design.

Steven K. Feiner, Professor. Human-computer interaction, augmented reality and virtual environments, 3-D user interfaces, knowledge-based design of graphics and multimedia, mobile and wearable computing, computer games, information visualization.

Luis Gravano, Associate Professor. Databases, digital libraries, distributed search over text databases, Web search, "top-k" query processing, information extraction, text mining.

Eitan Grinspun, Associate Professor. Computer graphics, scientific computing: computational mechanics, mathematical foundations of graphics, discrete differential geometry.

Jonathan L. Gross, Professor of Computer Science, Mathematics, and Mathematical Statistics. Computational aspects of topological graph theory and knot theory, enumerative analysis, and combinatorial models; applications to network layouts on higher-order surfaces and to interactive computer graphics of weaves and links.

Julia Hirschberg, Professor. Natural-language processing, spoken language processing, spoken dialogue systems, deceptive speech.

Tony Jebara, Associate Professor. Machine learning, social networks, graphs, vision, spatio-temporal modeling.

Gail E. Kaiser, Professor. Software testing, collaborative work, computer and network security, parallel computing and distributed systems, self-managing systems, Web technologies, information management, software development environments and tools.

John R. Kender, Professor. Computer vision, video understanding, visual user interfaces, medical imaging processing, artificial intelligence.

Angelos D. Keromytis, Associate Professor. Computer and network security.

Martha A. Kim, Assistant Professor. Computer architecture, hardware systems, hardware/software interaction, parallel hardware and software systems.

Tal G. Malkin, Associate Professor. Cryptography, information and network security, foundations of computer science, computational complexity, distributed computation, randomness in computation.

Kathleen R. McKeown, Henry and Gertrude Rothschild Professor. Artificial intelligence, natural-language processing, language generation, multimedia explanation, text summarization, user interfaces, user modeling, digital libraries.

Vishal Misra, Associate Professor. Networking, modeling and performance evaluation, Internet economics.

Shree K. Nayar, T. C. Chang Professor. Computer vision, computational imaging, computer graphics, robotics, human computer interfaces.

Jason Nieh, Associate Professor. Operating systems, distributed systems, mobile computing, thin-client computing, performance evaluation.

Steven M. Nowick, Professor. Asynchronous and mixed-timing digital circuits and systems, computer-aided design, networks-on-chip, interconnection networks for parallel processors, low-power digital design.

Itsik Pe'er, Assistant Professor. Computational biology, genomics, medical and population genetics, isolated and admixed populations, analysis of heritable variation in cancer.

Kenneth A. Ross, Professor. Databases, query optimization, declarative languages for database systems, logic programming, architecture-sensitive software design.

Dan Rubenstein, Associate Professor. Computer networks, network robustness and security, multimedia networking, performance evaluation, algorithms, low-power networking.

Henning G. Schulzrinne, Julian Clarence Levi Professor. Computer networks, multimedia systems, mobile and wireless systems, ubiquitous and pervasive computing.

Rocco A. Servedio, Associate Professor. Computational learning theory, computational complexity theory, randomness in computation, combinatorics, cryptography.

Simha Sethumadhavan, Assistant Professor. Computer architecture, hardware security.

Salvatore J. Stolfo, Professor. Computer security, intrusion detection systems, parallel computing, artificial intelligence, machine learning.

Joseph F. Traub, Edwin Howard Armstrong Professor. Quantum computing, computational complexity, information-based complexity, financial computations.

Henryk Woźniakowski, Professor. Computational complexity, information-based complexity, quantum computing, algorithmic analysis, numerical mathematics.

Junfeng Yang, Assistant Professor. Operating systems, software reliability, programming languages, security, distributed systems, software engineering.

Mihalis Yannakakis, Percy K. and Vida L. W. Hudson Professor. Algorithms, complexity theory, combinatorial optimization, databases, testing and verification.

Yechiam Yemini, Professor. Computer networks.

Associated Faculty/Research Scientists

Shih-Fu Chang, Professor, Electrical Engineering. Multimedia analysis, search, communication, and forensics with applications in next-generation media search engines; visual communication systems.

Mona T. Diab, Associate Research Scientist, Center for Computational Learning Systems. Computational linguistics, statistical natural language processing, machine learning, computational lexical semantics, multilinguality, social communication, Arabic natural language processing.

Haimonti Dutta, Associate Research Scientist, Center for Computational Learning Systems. Data mining and machine learning, data intensive computing, distributed data mining and optimization.

Nizar Habash, Research Scientist, Center for Computational Learning Systems. Natural-language processing, machine translation, multilingual processing, natural-language generation.

Claire Monteleoni, Associate Research Scientist, Center for Computational Learning Systems. Machine learning: theory and algorithms for active learning, online learning, and privacy- preserving machine learning; climate science.

Rebecca J. Passonneau, Research Scientist, Center for Computational Learning Systems. Natural language processing, spoken dialogue systems, text classification for real world problems, discourse and dialogue structure, reference and temporal reference, corpus design and annotation, evaluation.

Dana Pe'er, Assistant Professor (Biological Sciences). Computational biology, machine learning, biological networks, genomics and systems biology.

Owen Rambow, Research Scientist, Center for Computational Learning Systems. Natural-language processing, language in social networks, natural-language syntax, multilingual processing, natural-language generation.

Ansaf Salleb-Aouissi, Associate Research Scientist, Center for Computational Learning Systems. Machine learning, data mining: rule induction, frequent patterns, ranking, multi-relational learning, applications.

Clifford Stein, Professor. Algorithms, combinatorial optimization, scheduling, network algorithms.

Stephen H. Unger, Professor Emeritus of Computer Science and Electrical Engineering. Logic circuits theory, digital systems, self-timed systems, parallel processing, technology-society interface, engineering ethics.

Vladimir Vapnik, Professor, Computer Science and Center for Computational Learning Systems. Empirical inference, support vector machines, kernel methods, transductive inference.

David L. Waltz, Director, Center for Computational Learning Systems. Machine learning, cognitive modeling.

Arthur G. Werschulz, Adjunct Senior Research Scientist. Information-based complexity, especially that of partial differential equations, integral equations, and ill-posed problems.

DAKOTA STATE UNIVERSITY

Department of Information Systems and Technology

Programs of Study

Dakota State University (DSU) offers graduate degree programs in educational technology (M.S.E.T.), information assurance (M.S.I.A.), health informatics (M.S.H.I.), and information systems (M.S.I.S. and D.Sc.). The programs are available online or on campus. Educational technology requires a one-week residency on campus. There are no other required graduate program residencies.

The Master of Science in Educational Technology program (M.S.E.T) empowers educators and trainers to meet the increasing demands of integrating technology in curriculum and instruction. Specializations include distance education, technology systems, and a K–12 educational technology endorsement. Students take 36 credits in common core courses, which are shared between DSU and the University of South Dakota. GetEducated.com rates the program a best buy. For more information, students should visit http://www.dsu.edu/mset/index.aspx.

The Master of Science in Information Assurance program (M.S.I.A.) prepares graduates to protect an organization's information assets. Both the National Security Agency and the Department of Homeland Security have designated DSU as a National Center of Academic Excellence in Information Assurance Education (CAEIAE). The program requires 30 hours beyond the baccalaureate, including six core courses (18 credit hours) and a four-course sequence (12 credit hours) in a specialization. Specializations include banking and financial security, and cybersecurity. GetEducated.com rates the program a best buy. For more information, students should visit http://www.dsu.edu/msia/index.aspx.

The Master of Science in Health Informatics (M.S.H.I.) is intended to produce graduates who are expected to play a key role in the design, development, and management of health information systems in health-care related facilities, agencies, and organizations, in integrated delivery systems, and in interconnected, community-wide health data exchanges and regional networks. The program is intended to attract students with a variety of educational backgrounds and disciplines. The program requires 33 hours beyond the baccalaureate, including seven core courses (21 credit hours), three elective courses (9 credit hours), and a three-credit capstone experience. For more information, students should visit http://www.dsu.edu/mshi/index.aspx.

The Master of Science in Information Systems program (M.S.I.S.) focuses on the integration of information technology with business problems and opportunities. Specializations include data management, electronic commerce, network administration and security, and health-care information systems. GetEducated.com rates it a best buy. For more information, students should visit http://www.dsu.edu/msis/index.aspx.

The Doctor of Science (D.Sc.) in information systems program prepares students for careers in teaching, research, consulting, and corporate employment. Specializations include decision support, knowledge and data management, information assurance and computer security, and health-care information systems. The D.Sc. requires 88 semester credit hours. Students take 63 credit hours of graduate course work: 27 credit hours of master's-level information systems, which may be waived for students who have completed the M.S.I.S. program or equivalent; 9 credit hours of research methods; and 27 credit hours of research specialization, including research seminars and core and elective courses. D.Sc. students must also complete a screening examination, a qualifying portfolio, and 25 credit hours of dissertation. For more information, students should visit http://www.dsu.edu/doctor-of-science/index.aspx.

Research Facilities

The Karl E. Mundt Library provides access to an extensive collection of materials through its online library catalog, which includes more than 4.5 million holdings of more than seventy libraries in the South Dakota Library Network (SDLN). In addition to being an online catalog of library holdings, the SDLN has been enriched by the addition of a number of external databases, most notably, EBSCO's Academic Search Premier, Lexis-Nexis Academic, ProQuest Research Library, and ABI-Inform. Many of these databases provide the full text and images of articles and books. Web-based access to the information services provides students with access to databases critical to their disciplines. Materials held by other libraries are readily available through the electronic interlibrary loan system or full text. The library also provides online access to tutorials and other research aides.

DSU also offers an Advanced Informatics Research Lab (AIRL) which is a state-of-the-art computing lab supporting applied information systems research in the areas of decision support data and knowledge management, information assurance, and health care. It supports the information systems faculty, graduate assistants, and students (online and on-campus) involved in the D.Sc. in information systems program. The lab includes infrastructure to support development and deployment of prototypes and other research results and computing capacity for conducting statistical analysis and running and solving models. It allows distance students access to computing resources and specialized workstations and software. The AIRL also has a variety of decision support tools and technologies for building and deploying DSS. Its servers run Windows and Linux operating systems and the lab provides support for .NET, JAVA and other development environment/technologies, e.g., MS SQL, Visual Studio 2005, etc.

An excellent computer environment is found at DSU. Computer laboratories are available in every academic building on campus. To provide ample facilities for both instruction and outside course work, labs are used directly in teaching and for general access. For the convenience of students, microcomputers are located in the dorms, in the Trojan Center (student union), and the library. In addition to cabled connections, a wireless network also supports mobile computing devices in each academic building, the Trojan Center, and the library.

Financial Aid

Graduate students apply for federal financial aid with the Free Application for Federal Student Aid (FAFSA), either online or with a paper form. Graduate students may be eligible to receive Federal Stafford Loans and Federal Perkins Loans but not Federal Pell Grants or Federal Supplemental Education Opportunity Grants. In addition, graduate assistantships are available to qualified graduate students, based on need and/or merit and available funds. Recipients of an assistantship receive a reduced tuition rate (student pays one third the state-support tuition rate) and a stipend as established by the Board of Regents. More information is available online at http://www.dsu.edu/gradoffice/grad-assistantships.aspx or by telephone at 605-256-5799.

Cost of Study

For the academic year 2011–12, tuition per credit hour ranges from $173 to $367 depending on residency and delivery of the courses. Online courses are $368 per credit for both in-state and out-of-state students. Fees total around $116 per credit hour for all students in classes on the DSU campus. More information is available at http://www.dsu.edu/gradoffice/grad-tuition-fees.aspx.

Living and Housing Costs

On-campus housing is available. Local telephone service, cable TV, and Internet access are included in the semester room fee. Students are expected to provide their own phone. Each hall has one or more kitchens, TV lounges, and card/coin-operated washers and dryers. Residence hall rates range between $1351 and $1774 per semester, whereas apartments are $1635 per person per semester. Meal plans range from $1082 to $1233 per semester. The Madison community has several apartment complexes and other off-campus housing.

Location

DSU is in Madison, South Dakota, less than an hour northwest of Sioux Falls. Madison is in the state's southern lakes region, which offers great outdoor recreation. The University is minutes from Lake Herman State Park and Walker's Point Recreation Area. Madison offers a variety of options for dining, shopping, and entertainment. For fitness and other recreation, students can easily walk to Madison's excellent Community Center. Madison is a safe town, with little traffic and a high quality of life as well as job opportunities for students and spouses.

The University

Dakota State University (DSU) strives to be one of the best technological universities in the Midwest. *U.S. News & World Report* ranked DSU the number 1 Top Public Baccalaureate College in the Midwest five years in a row in 2007, 2008, 2009, 2010, and again in 2011. DSU is accredited by the North Central Association of Colleges and Schools, and GetEducated.com rates its online master's degree programs as best buys.

Applying

In general, students should have earned a baccalaureate degree from a regionally accredited college or university. Each applicant must provide a completed application form, the $35 application fee ($85 for international students), one official transcript for all college work, three forms of recommendation, and official scores on the standardized graduate admission test (see specific programs for what test is required). All international applicants must take the Test of English as a Foreign Language (TOEFL) and score at least 550 on the PBT (213 on the CBT or 79 on the iBT). Students should check online for program-specific requirements and deadlines.

Correspondence and Information

Office of Graduate Studies & Research
Dakota State University
Madison, South Dakota 57042-1799

Phone: 605-256-5799
Fax: 605-256-5093
E-mail: gradoffice@dsu.edu
Web site: http://www.dsu.edu/gradoffice/index.aspx

Dakota State University

THE FACULTY

Richard Avery, Associate Professor of Mathematics; Ph.D., Nebraska–Lincoln.
Richard Christoph, Professor of Computer Information Systems; Ph.D., Clemson.
Amit Deokar, Assistant Professor of Information Systems; Ph.D., Arizona.
Omar El-Gayar, Associate Professor and Dean of Graduate Studies and Research; Ph.D., Hawaii at Manoa.
William Figg, Associate Professor of Computer Information Systems; Ph.D., Capella.
Mark Geary, Assistant Professor of Education, Ph.D.
Steve Graham, Assistant Professor of Computer Science; Ph.D., Kansas.
Tom Halverson, Associate Professor of Computer Science and Dean of the College of Business and Information Systems; Ph.D., Iowa.
Mark Hawkes, Associate Professor of Instructional Technology and Program Coordinator of the Master of Science in Educational Technology; Ph.D., Syracuse.
Stephen Krebsbach, Associate Professor of Computer Science; Ph.D., North Dakota State.
Sreekanth Malladi, Assistant Professor of Information Assurance; Ph.D., Idaho.
Mark Moran, Assistant Professor of Information Systems; M.B.A., South Dakota; Ph.D., Capella.
Jeff Palmer, Professor of Mathematics; Ph.D., Washington State.
Josh Pauli, Assistant Professor of Information Systems; Ph.D., North Dakota State.
Wayne Pauli, Assistant Professor of Information Systems and Director of Center of Excellence in Computer Information Systems; Ph.D., Capella.
Ronghua Shan, Associate Professor of Computer Science/Information Systems; Ph.D., Nebraska–Lincoln.
Kevin Streff, Assistant Professor of Information Assurance, Director of Center of Excellence in Information Assurance, and MSIA Program Coordinator; Ph.D., Capella.
Daniel Talley, Associate Professor of Economics; Ph.D., Oregon.
Haomin Wang, Associate Professor of Instructional Technology and Webmaster; Ed.D., Northern Arizona.
Don Wiken, Associate Professor of Education; Ed.D., South Dakota.

UNIVERSITY OF LOUISIANA AT LAFAYETTE

The Center for Advanced Computer Studies

Programs of Study

The primary missions of The Center for Advanced Computer Studies (CACS) at the University of Louisiana at Lafayette (UL Lafayette) are to conduct research and provide graduate-level education in computer engineering and computer science. CACS offers four graduate degrees: the Ph.D. in computer engineering and the Ph.D. in computer science, the Master of Science in Computer Engineering (M.S.C.E.), and the Master of Science in Computer Science (M.S.C.S.). Areas of specialization are bioinformatics and biocomputing; computer and sensor networks; computer architecture and prototyping; computer visualization and graphics; cryptography and data security; entertainment computing and video game design; grid computing; image, video, and multimedia systems; information processing and data mining; intelligent systems and knowledge engineering; parallel and distributed systems; secure systems and networks; software engineering; software-hardware codesign and reconfigurable computing; virtual reality; VLSI and embedded systems; Web technologies and Internet computing; and wireless communications and mobile computing.

Research Facilities

CACS research computing facilities include over 300 mixed-base (Sun, Intel, and Mac) workstations, numerous laptops, several miniclusters, and about fifty servers. The computers run on multiple versions of Linux, Solaris, Microsoft Windows, and Apple operating systems supporting CACS's research diversity. To communicate with the world and within, CACS's extensive Ethernet network consists of more than twenty routers (five SuperStacks) capable of connecting up to 1,000 devices throughout the building. A wide variety of software is available and ranges from artificial intelligence to VLSI design and other well-known tools such as Cadence, Synopsys, QualNet, Mentor Graphics, Oracle, Maya, and MATLAB. CACS provides five miniclusters, including one in the making, for student research involving high performance, grid, and cloud computing.

CACS houses state-of-the-art research laboratories that specialize in a number of fields, including bioinformatics, CajunBot, computer architecture and networking (CAN), entertainment computing/video game design, FPGA and reconfigurable computing, integrated wireless information network (iWIN), Internet computing (LINC), neurocomputing and brain simulation, micro/nano-electronic embedded computing, software systems research, virtual reality, VLSI and SoC, and wireless systems and performance engineering research (WiSPER).

Financial Aid

Fellowships are available for entering students with superior academic records and strong GRE scores, valued at up to $15,775 for Ph.D. students and $9,500 for M.S. students. All fellowship application materials must be received by February 15 for consideration. CACS has a large number of teaching and research assistantships that include a waiver of tuition and most fees. Stipends range from about $7500 to more than $16,000 for the academic year.

Cost of Study

In spring 2011, Louisiana resident tuition totaled $2503.75 per semester. Nonresident students paid $6857.75 per semester. Tuition amounts are subject to change without notice.

Living and Housing Costs

Rooms and/or apartments are available on a first-come, first-served basis to single and married students. The typical cost is $3595 (including board) for married students. Room and board charges vary according to the board plan.

Student Group

Total University enrollment is more than 16,000 students. In fall 2010, there were approximately 200 students enrolled in CACS's graduate programs. UL Lafayette is known to attract international graduate students in the fields of computer science and engineering at both the master's and Ph.D. levels.

Student Outcomes

Among the universities employing/employed some of CACS's recent graduates are Penn State; Notre Dame; California, Davis; Arizona State; Alaska at Fairbanks; West Virginia Tech; Emory; George Mason; Columbia State; Alexandria (Egypt); Calgary (Canada); Arkansas; South Carolina; Houston; Stevens; South Alabama; Tulane; Louisiana Tech; Mississippi State; Haceteppe (Turkey); National Institute of Saudi Arabia; and Chungbuk National University (Korea). Some Ph.D. graduates have accepted employment in industry with Microsoft, IBM (Durham, Boca Raton), Schlumberger (Austin), Intel (San Jose, Portland), LSI Logic (Milpitas, California), Centigram Communication (San Jose), and the Stock Exchange of Thailand.

Location

The University of Louisiana is located in Lafayette, the central city of the geographic area known as Acadiana. The more than 500,000 inhabitants of this locale are mainly descendants of the exiled Acadians of Nova Scotia. Culturally, the region is characterized by a joie de vivre that has given it an international reputation. Lafayette is located approximately 52 miles from the state capital of Baton Rouge and 129 miles from New Orleans.

The University and The Center

The University has an impressive physical plant that is steadily being enlarged on all parts of the campus. It includes the administrative complex; Dupre Library; French House; academic buildings; athletic facilities; housing for men, women, and married students; an art museum; and a Student Union Complex situated on Cypress Lake. Located on the agricultural extension of the campus are Blackham Coliseum, Cajun Field, and the Cajun Dome, which seats approximately 12,000. Since its inception in 1984, The Center for Advanced Computer Studies has demonstrated a strong contribution to high-quality education and research in the fields of computer science and engineering. The University and CACS have created an environment unique in the nation. CACS is one of the first to merge the overlapping, yet disjointed, disciplines of computer science and computer engineering into a successful graduate program. CACS has 15 tenure-track faculty members, 2 research scientists, and 4 support staff members.

Applying

Applications for admission for the fall semester must be submitted to the Graduate School thirty days before classes begin. Applications for graduate assistantships for the fall semester must be submitted to the Graduate School by March 1 and for the spring semester by November 1. Students are notified by April 1 and December 1, respectively, of their acceptance. Requirements for admission include a baccalaureate degree from an accredited institution, an excellent GPA, GRE and TOEFL scores (if the degree is earned outside the United States), three letters of recommendation, and a fluent command of English. Application fees (nonrefundable) are $25 for U.S. citizens, permanent residents, and refugees and $30 for international students. Applications, inquiries, letters of recommendation, transcripts, and GRE and TOEFL scores should be sent to the Graduate School.

Correspondence and Information

Dr. Anthony S. Maida, Graduate Coordinator
The Center for Advanced Computer Studies
University of Louisiana at Lafayette
P.O. Box 44330
Lafayette, Louisiana 70504-4330
Phone: 337-482-6308
E-mail: info@louisiana.edu
Web site: http://www.cacs.louisiana.edu

University of Louisiana at Lafayette

THE FACULTY AND THEIR RESEARCH

Professors

Magdy A. Bayoumi, Director of CACS; Ph.D., Windsor, 1984. VLSI design, image and video signal processing, parallel processing, neural networks, wideband, multimedia network architectures.

Chee-Hung Henry Chu, Ph.D., Purdue, 1988. Computer vision, signal and image processing, pattern recognition.

Arun Lakhotia, Ph.D., Case Western Reserve, 1989. Computer security, malware analysis, robotics, autonomous ground vehicles.

Vijay V. Raghavan, Ph.D., Alberta, 1978. Information retrieval and extraction; conceptual categorization of text/images; knowledge discovery in databases; integration of unstructured, semi-structured, and structured data; bioinformatics.

Nian-Feng Tzeng, Ph.D., Illinois, 1986. Networked and distributed computer systems, wireless and sensor networks.

Associate Professors

Christoph Borst, Ph.D., Texas A&M, 2002. Virtual reality, computer graphics, visualization.

Kemal Efe, Ph.D., Leeds (England), 1985. Parallel and distributed systems, Internet computing, search engines, information retrieval.

Gui-Liang Feng, Ph.D., Lehigh, 1990. Error-correcting codes, data compression, fault-tolerant computing, cryptography, network coding, wireless network coding.

Rasiah Loganantharaj, Ph.D., Colorado State, 1985. Bioinformatics including gene regulation, functional annotations, microarray analysis, mining for interesting patterns from genomic sequences and databases.

Anthony S. Maida, Ph.D., SUNY at Buffalo, 1980. Neurocomputing, artificial intelligence, cognitive science.

Dmitri Perkins, Ph.D., Michigan State, 2002. Wireless networks, mobile computing, communication systems.

Hongyi Wu, Ph.D., SUNY at Buffalo, 2002. Computer networks.

Danella Zhao, Ph.D., SUNY at Buffalo, 2004. VLSI testing, embedded systems, wireless.

Assistant Professors

Miao Jin, Ph.D., Stony Brook, SUNY, 2008. Computer graphics, geometric modeling, medical imaging, computer vision, visualization, computational conformal geometry.

Dirk Reiners, Ph.D., Technical University Darmstadt (Germany), 2002. Software systems for interactive 3-D graphics, complex problem visualization, virtual reality, high-reality displays.

Research Scientists

Ryan Benton, Ph.D., Louisiana at Lafayette, 2001. Internet and grid computing.

Suresh Golconda, Ph.D., Louisiana at Lafayette, 2010. Robotics.

UNIVERSITY OF MISSOURI–COLUMBIA

Department of Computer Science

Programs of Study

The Department of Computer Science (http://engineering.missouri.edu/cs/) offers the Master of Science in Computer Science, the Master of Engineering in Computer Science, and the Doctor of Philosophy in Computer Science graduate programs of study. The graduate degree programs prepare prior recipients of four-year B.S. degrees in computer science or closely related areas for further study at the master's and doctoral levels or for successful careers as specialized computer professionals. The Ph.D. program is a professional research degree program designed to prepare students for advanced professional careers, including college teaching and research, as well as research and development in industrial, government, and nonprofit organizations. Specialized training is available through close interaction with the faculty members in their active research fields.

Research Facilities

Research facilities are well established around faculty members' expertise in artificial intelligence, bioinformatics and computational biology, biological and biomedical image analysis, graphics, human-computer interaction, information management systems, mobile computing, multimedia, networking, and computer science foundations. These facilities are clustered in core laboratories for multimedia and visualization, video processing, spoken-language processing, mobile networking and communications, wireless sensor networks, high-performance computing, cyber security, medical informatics, and bioinformatics.

In addition to online subscriptions to technical publications, the Ellis Library has over 3.2 million books, and the Engineering Library houses specialized collections in computer science. Students and faculty and staff members have access to a wide range of computing resources within the research laboratories and distributed throughout the campus, including a large-scale cluster computing environment. The educational computing environment includes student laboratories for programming and Web access comprising Windows, Mac OS, Linux, and UNIX systems.

Financial Aid

Teaching and research assistantships are available for qualified students in the graduate programs. The Department also offers fellowships (including Department of Education GAANN Fellowships and Shumaker Bioinformatics Fellowships) to a limited number of new Ph.D. students. In addition, there are other fellowships and scholarships available at the university level.

Teaching assistantships and research assistantships, with tuition waivers, are available in the Department. Applications for financial aid are examined at the same time as those for graduate admission, which are due before January 15 for fall semester and October 1 for spring semester.

Cost of Study

Tuition for full-time graduate study is $326.70 per credit hour for Missouri residents and $843.50 per credit hour for non-Missouri residents in 2011.

Living and Housing Costs

Graduate students may reside in any available housing they choose, whether it is University operated or off campus. Rooms and apartments are available on campus and in the area surrounding the University. More information can be acquired from the Residential Life Office at http://reslife.missouri.edu/. One- or two-bedroom apartments can be rented near the University starting around $400 per month.

Student Group

The Department's graduate enrollment is about 100, with approximately half enrolled in the Ph.D. program. Advised by the Director of Graduate Studies, the CS Graduate Student Council is an active body that works with the Department and provides social activities as well as student input for the continuous improvement of the graduate programs in computer science.

Location

Columbia has consistently been ranked by *Money* magazine as one of the nation's top places to live because of its excellent quality of life. As a college town with a growing population of more than 100,000, Columbia offers social and cultural attractions and entertainment possibilities that offer year-round activities through various community events. It is the hometown of the nationally ranked Mizzou Tigers, attracting numerous football fans from the entire state of Missouri during the football season every fall. Columbia is about 125 miles west of St. Louis and 150 miles east of Kansas City. Jefferson City, the state capital of Missouri, is about 40 miles south of Columbia, and the renowned Lake of the Ozarks recreation area is about 80 miles south of Columbia. Katy Trail, a major attraction to people who enjoy outdoor activities, winds through the city and has multiple exits and entrances. Movie theaters, stores, banks, snack shops, restaurants, and historic downtown Columbia are all within walking distance of the University.

The University

The University of Missouri, the first state university west of the Mississippi River, was established in Columbia in 1839. The University has 28,000 full-time students (32,000 students), of whom 7,514 are graduate students and professionals, and approximately 3,000 full-time faculty members. It is one of only six comprehensive universities across the nation that has a School of Veterinary Medicine, School of Medicine, College of Engineering, and College of Agriculture located on the same campus. In addition, the nuclear research reactor, Life Science Center, and teaching and research hospital facilities are unique assets that integrate research with education across several disciplines in graduate studies.

Applying

Applications for admission and financial aid are due twice a year: January 1 for the fall semester and October 1 for the spring semester. Applications for admission only for the fall semester are due March 1. GRE scores are required for all applicants. TOEFL scores are required for all applicants from countries where English is not the native language.

Correspondence and Information

Director of Graduate Studies
Department of Computer Science
201 Engineering Building West
University of Missouri–Columbia
Columbia, Missouri 65211
Web site: http://engineering.missouri.edu/cs/degree-programs/

University of Missouri-Columbia

THE FACULTY AND THEIR RESEARCH

The faculty members of the Department of Computer Science participate in the full spectrum of undergraduate and graduate education. Graduate education, in addition to direct involvement in projects funded by the federal government and industries, places equal emphasis on interdepartmental and cross-college research. The aim is to produce computer scientists who can function well in interdisciplinary research teams. Close integration of research with education is an invariant goal in the Department's graduate programs. It emphasizes in-depth studies that can also be tailored to fit graduate students' individual interests.

Jianlin Cheng, Assistant Professor; Ph.D., California, Irvine. Bioinformatics and computational biology, machine learning, data mining, systems biology.

Ye Duan, Associate Professor; Ph.D., SUNY at Stony Brook. Computer graphics and visualization, geometric and physics-based modeling, computer vision and biomedical imaging, virtual reality and human-computer interaction, computer animation and simulation.

William L. Harrison, Associate Professor; Ph.D., Illinois at Urbana-Champaign. Semantics of programming languages, formal verification and programming logic, semantic-based compilation and compiler correctness, language-based security, domain-specific languages for biology, cybersecurity.

Michael Jurczyk, Associate Professor and Director of Undergraduate Studies; Ph.D., Stuttgart. Cyber security, networked multimedia, networks for communication systems, parallel and distributed systems.

Toni Kazic, Associate Professor; Ph.D., Pennsylvania. Computational biology/bioinformatics, biological databases, database semantics and formal languages, analysis and inference of networks of biochemical reactions, graph algorithms, chemical informatics.

Dmitry Korkin, Assistant Professor; Ph.D., New Brunswick (Canada). Computational biology and bioinformatics, structural systems biology, machine learning, pattern recognition, computational systems neuroscience.

Dale Musser, Assistant Professor and Director of IT Program; Ph.D., Ohio State. Social computing, health informatics, performance support systems, Web and Internet applications, distributed applications, digital media systems, games and simulations.

Kannappan Palaniappan, Associate Professor; Ph.D., Illinois at Urbana-Champaign. Scientific visualization, computational remote sensing, parallel algorithms for image understanding, biological sequence analysis.

Markita Price, Teaching Associate Professor; Ph.D., Minnesota. Gender issues in mathematics and science, technical writing.

Youssef Saab, Associate Professor; Ph.D., Illinois at Urbana-Champaign. Combinatorial optimization, approximation algorithms, graph algorithms, computational geometry, design automation.

Yi Shang, Professor and Director of Graduate Studies; Ph.D., Illinois at Urbana-Champaign. Artificial intelligence, mobile computing, wireless sensor networks, bioinformatics, nonlinear and combinatorial optimization.

Chi-Ren Shyu, Professor and Director of MU Informatics Institute; Ph.D., Purdue. Digital libraries, content based access to multimedia database, biomedical informatics, database management, computer vision.

Gordon K. Springer, Associate Professor; Ph.D., Penn State. Internet2, distributed computing, animal genomics, biomedical informatics, computer networks, www, operating systems, computer graphics, supercomputer computation.

Jeffrey Uhlmann, Associate Professor; Ph.D., Oxford. Sensor and data fusion, dynamic data structures, large-scale simulation, Kalman filtering and related methods, autonomous vehicles and robotics, statistical algorithms, target tracking, least-cost routing.

Dong Xu, Professor and Chair; Ph.D., Illinois at Urbana-Champaign. Bioinformatics computational systems biology, high-throughput biological data analysis, protein structure prediction and modeling, gene function prediction, computational studies of cancers and plants.

Wenjun (Kevin) Zeng, Professor; Ph.D., Princeton. Wireless video streaming; joint source and network coding/optimization; multimedia content security and digital rights management; scalable and error-resilient video transmission; image and video coding, analysis, and processing; perceptual coding and modeling; multimedia system architecture.

Yunxin Zhao, Professor; Ph.D., Washington (Seattle). Automatic speech recognition, speech and signal processing, multimedia interface, multimodal human-computer interaction, statistical pattern recognition, statistical blind systems identification and estimation, biomedical applications of spoken-language technology and signal processing.

Xinhua Zhuang, Professor; Ph.D. equivalent, Peking (China). Scalable bandwidth-efficient reliable multimedia communications, error-resilient high-performance secured video coding, IP multimedia in next-generation mobile networks, bioinformatics and computational biology, computer vision and image processing, pattern recognition and neural networks.

AREAS OF RECENT RESEARCH ACTIVITIES

Bioinformatics and Computational Biology: High-throughput data analysis, intelligent information systems for physicians, protein structure modeling and prediction, semantic interoperability of biological information and computations, structure-function relationships, deconvolution of complex phenotypes.

Networks and Cybersecurity: Wireless networking, sensor networks, mobile computing, multimedia communication, distributed systems, cybersecurity, Internet technology, e-learning.

Human-Computer Interaction and Intelligent Systems: Spoken-language processing, multimedia, visualization, graphics, information fusion, intelligent health-care systems, artificial intelligence.

Information and Data Management Systems: Information retrieval; digital library; database; data mining and knowledge recovery from geospatial, medical, and biological databases.

UNIVERSITY OF NORTH CAROLINA AT CHAPEL HILL

Department of Computer Science

Programs of Study

The Department offers the Ph.D. and a professional M.S. degree. Study for the M.S. degree includes algorithms, programming languages, and hardware as well as important areas of application. The Ph.D. program includes courses in specialized areas and preparation for teaching and advanced research. Students pursue particular areas of their choice and are actively involved in research. The curricula emphasize the design and application of real computer systems and the portion of theory that guides and supports practice. The Department's orientation is experimental, with clusters of research in bioinformatics and computational biology, computer architecture, computer graphics, computer-supported collaborative work, computer vision, databases and data mining, geometric computing, high-performance computing, human-computer interaction, medical image analysis, networking, real-time systems, robotics, security, software engineering, and theory. Students holding an assistantship can typically expect to earn the M.S. degree in two academic years and the Ph.D. in four or five years.

Research Facilities

All of the Department's computing facilities are housed in two adjoining four-story computer science buildings that feature specialized research laboratories for graphics and image processing, telepresence and computer vision, computer building and design, robotics, computer security, and collaborative, distributed, and parallel systems. The labs, offices, conference areas, and classrooms are bound together by the Department's fully integrated distributed computing environment, which includes more than 1,000 computers, ranging from older systems used for generating network traffic for simulated Internet experiments to state-of-the-art workstations and clusters for graphics- and compute-intensive research. These systems are integrated by high-speed networks and by software that is consistent at the user level over the many architectural platforms. Each student is assigned a computer, with computer assignments based on the students' research or teaching responsibilities and their seniority within the Department. In addition to the Departmental servers and office systems, the research laboratories contain a wide variety of specialized equipment and facilities. The nearby Kenan Science Library has extensive holdings in mathematics, physics, statistics, operations research, and computer science.

Financial Aid

During the academic year, most students are supported by assistantships and fellowships. The stipend for research and teaching assistantships for the nine-month academic year in 2010–11 was $17,000 (20 hours per week). Full-time summer employment on a research project is normally available to students who would like to receive support. The rate for summer 2011 was $850 (40 hours per week) for ten to twelve weeks. This produces a combined annual financial package for graduate assistants of approximately $27,200. Students with assistantships qualify for a Graduate Student Tuition Grant and pay no tuition; they are responsible for paying student fees of $935 per semester. Graduate Student Tuition Grants typically cover M.S. students for four semesters of study and Ph.D. students for ten semesters of study. At no additional cost to them, students are also covered by a comprehensive major medical insurance program, underwritten by Blue Cross/Blue Shield of North Carolina. Each semester, the Department provides a $500 educational fund to any student who receives a competitive fellowship that is not granted by the University of North Carolina at Chapel Hill (UNC–Chapel Hill). The fund may be used for education-related expenses, including books, journals, travel, computer supplies and accessories, and professional memberships. The Department also awards a $1500 supplement each semester to nonservice fellowship holders who join a research team. To apply for an assistantship, the applicant should check the appropriate item on the admission application form. Applicants for assistantships are automatically considered for all available fellowships. Students can expect continued support, contingent upon satisfactory work performance and academic progress. Students are not assigned to specific research projects or teaching assistant positions immediately upon being admitted to the department. Assignments are made just prior to the start of each semester, after faculty members and students have had an opportunity to meet and to discuss their interests. Students are encouraged to gain professional experience through summer internships with companies in the Research Triangle area or in other parts of the country.

Cost of Study

For the 2011–12 academic year, tuition and fees for graduate students at the University of North Carolina at Chapel Hill are $8646 for state residents and $24,333 for nonresidents. Virtually all graduate students in computer science pay no tuition, as mentioned in the Financial Aid section.

Living and Housing Costs

Annual living costs for single graduate students in the Chapel Hill area are estimated by University staff members to be $18,000 or higher. On-campus housing is available for both married and single students attending the University.

Student Group

The Department of Computer Science enrolls approximately 160 graduate students, most of whom attend full-time.

Student Outcomes

A majority of the Department's master's graduates work in industry, in companies ranging from small start-up operations to government research labs and large research and development corporations. Ph.D. graduates work in both academia and industry. Academic employment ranges from positions in four-year colleges, where teaching is the primary focus, to positions at major research universities. Some graduates take postdoctoral positions at research laboratories prior to continuing in industry or joining academia.

Location

Chapel Hill (population 51,500) is a scenic college town located in the heart of North Carolina, where small-town charm mixes with a cosmopolitan atmosphere to provide students with a rich and varied living experience. The town and the surrounding area offer many cultural advantages, including excellent theater and music, museums, and a planetarium. There are also many opportunities to watch and to participate in sports. The Carolina beaches, the Outer Banks, Great Smoky Mountains National Park, and the Blue Ridge Mountains are only a few hours' drive away. The Research Triangle of North Carolina is formed by the University of North Carolina at Chapel Hill, Duke University in Durham, and North Carolina State University in Raleigh. The universities have a combined enrollment of more than 76,000 students, have libraries with more than 14 million volumes with interconnected catalogs and have national prominence in a variety of disciplines. Collectively, they conduct more than $1.5 billion in research each year.

The University and The Department

The 729-acre central campus of UNC–Chapel Hill is among the most beautiful in the country. Of the approximately 29,300 students enrolled, nearly 10,500 are graduate and professional students. The Department's primary missions are research and graduate and undergraduate teaching. It offers the B.S., M.S., and Ph.D. degrees. The Computer Science Students' Association sponsors both professional and social events and represents the students in Departmental matters. Its president is a voting member at faculty meetings. There is much interaction between students and faculty members, and students contribute to nearly every aspect of the Department's operation.

Applying

Applications for fall admission, complete with a personal statement, all transcripts, three letters of recommendation, and official GRE and/or TOEFL scores should be received by the Graduate School no later than January 1. Early submission is encouraged. International applicants should consider completing their applications earlier to allow time for processing financial and visa documents. Applicants should check the Department Web site for the latest information regarding application deadlines.

Correspondence and Information

For written information about graduate study:

Admissions and Graduate Studies
Department of Computer Science
Campus Box 3175, Brooks Computer Science Building
University of North Carolina
Chapel Hill, North Carolina 27599-3175

Phone: 919-962-1900
Fax: 919-962-1799
E-mail: admit@cs.unc.edu
Web site: http://www.cs.unc.edu

For applications and admissions information:

The Graduate School
Campus Box 4010, 200 Bynum Hall
University of North Carolina
Chapel Hill, North Carolina 27599-4010

Phone: 919-966-2611
E-mail: gradinfo@unc.edu
Web site: http://gradschool.unc.edu/

University of North Carolina at Chapel Hill

THE FACULTY AND THEIR RESEARCH

Stan Ahalt, Professor and Director of the Renaissance Computing Institute (RENCI); Ph.D., Clemson, 1986. Signal, image, and video processing; high-performance scientific and industrial computing; pattern recognition applied to national security problems; high-productivity, domain-specific languages.

Ron Alterovitz, Assistant Professor; Ph.D., Berkeley, 2006. Medical robotics, motion planning, physically-based simulation, optimization, medical image analysis.

James Anderson, Professor; Ph.D., Texas at Austin, 1990. Distributed and concurrent algorithms, real-time systems, Linux.

Sanjoy K. Baruah, Professor; Ph.D., Texas at Austin, 1993. Scheduling theory, real-time and safety-critical system design, computer networks, resource allocation and sharing in distributed computing environments.

Gary Bishop, Professor; Ph.D., North Carolina at Chapel Hill, 1984. Hardware and software for man-machine interaction, assistive technology, 3-D interactive computer graphics, virtual environments, tracking technologies, image-based rendering.

Frederick P. Brooks Jr., Kenan Professor; Ph.D., Harvard, 1956. 3-D interactive computer graphics, human-computer interaction, virtual worlds, computer architecture, the design process.

Peter Calingaert, Professor Emeritus; Ph.D., Harvard, 1955.

Prasun Dewan, Professor; Ph.D., Wisconsin–Madison, 1986. User interfaces, distributed collaboration, software engineering environments, mobile computing, access control.

Jan-Michael Frahm, Assistant Professor; Ph.D., Kiel (Germany), 2005. Structure from motion, camera self-calibration, camera sensor systems, multicamera systems, multiview stereo, robust estimation, fast-tracking of salient features in images and video, computer vision, active vision for model improvement, markerless augmented reality.

Henry Fuchs, Federico Gil Professor; Ph.D., Utah, 1975. Virtual environments, telepresence, future office environments, 3-D medical imaging, computer vision, robotics.

John H. Halton, Professor Emeritus; D.Phil., Oxford, 1960.

Kye S. Hedlund, Associate Professor; Ph.D., Purdue, 1982. Computer-aided design, computer architecture, algorithm design and analysis, parallel processing.

Kevin Jeffay, Gillian Cell Distinguished Professor and Associate Chairman for Academic Affairs; Ph.D., Washington (Seattle), 1989. Computer networking, operating systems, real-time systems, multimedia networking, performance evaluation.

Jasleen Kaur, Associate Professor; Ph.D., Texas at Austin, 2002. Design and analysis of networks and operating systems, specifically resource management for providing service guarantees, Internet measurements, transport protocols and congestion control.

Anselmo A. Lastra, Professor and Chairman; Ph.D., Duke, 1988. Interactive 3-D computer graphics, hardware architectures for computer graphics.

Svetlana Lazebnik, Assistant Professor; Ph.D., Illinois at Urbana-Champaign, 2006. Object recognition and scene interpretation, Internet photo collections, reconstruction of 3-D objects from photos/video, machine learning techniques for visual recognition problems, clustering and vector quantization, nonlinear dimensionality reduction and manifold learning.

Ming C. Lin, John R. and Louise S. Parker Distinguished Professor; Ph.D., Berkeley, 1993. Physically based and geometric modeling, applied computational geometry, robotics, distributed interactive simulation, virtual environments, algorithm analysis, many-core computing.

Gyula A. Magó, Professor Emeritus; Ph.D., Cambridge, 1970.

Dinesh Manocha, Phi Delta Theta/Matthew Mason Distinguished Professor; Ph.D., Berkeley, 1992. Interactive computer graphics, geometric and solid modeling, robotics, motion planning, many-core algorithms.

Ketan Mayer-Patel, Associate Professor and Director of Graduate Admissions; Ph.D., Berkeley, 1999. Multimedia systems, networking, multicast applications.

Leonard McMillan, Associate Professor; Ph.D., North Carolina at Chapel Hill, 1997. Computational biology, genetics, bioinformatics, information visualization, data-driven modeling, image processing, imaging technologies, computer graphics.

Fabian Monrose, Associate Professor; Ph.D., NYU, 1999. Computer and network security, biometrics and techniques for strong user authentication.

Tessa Joseph Nicholas, Lecturer; Ph.D., North Carolina at Chapel Hill, 2008. New media arts and poetics, digital communities, digital-age ethics.

Marc Niethammer, Assistant Professor; Ph.D., Georgia Tech, 2004. Quantitative image analysis, cellular imaging, shape analysis, visual tracking and estimation theory, diffusion-weighted magnetic resonance imaging, structural health monitoring.

Stephen M. Pizer, Kenan Professor; Ph.D., Harvard, 1967. Image analysis and display, human and computer vision, graphics, numerical computing, medical imaging.

David A. Plaisted, Professor; Ph.D., Stanford, 1976. Mechanical theorem proving, term rewriting systems, logic programming, algorithms.

Marc Pollefeys, Research Professor; Ph.D., Leuven (Belgium), 1999. Computer vision, image-based modeling and rendering, image and video analysis, multiview geometry.

Diane Pozefsky, Research Professor; Ph.D., North Carolina at Chapel Hill, 1979. Software engineering and environments; computer education; serious games design and development; social, legal, and ethical issues concerning information technology.

Jan F. Prins, Professor and Director of Graduate Studies; Ph.D., Cornell, 1987. High-performance computing: parallel algorithms, programming languages, compilers, and architectures; scientific computing with focus on computational biology and bioinformatics.

Timothy L. Quigg, Lecturer and Associate Chairman for Administration and Finance; M.P.A., North Carolina State, 1979. Intellectual property rights, industrial relations, contract management, research administration.

Michael K. Reiter, Lawrence M. Slifkin Distinguished Professor; Ph.D., Cornell, 1993. Computer and network security, distributed systems, applied cryptography.

Montek Singh, Associate Professor; Ph.D., Columbia, 2002. High-performance and low-power digital systems, asynchronous circuits and systems, VLSI CAD, graphics hardware.

F. Donelson Smith, Research Professor; Ph.D., North Carolina at Chapel Hill, 1978. Computer networks, operating systems, distributed systems, multimedia, computer-supported cooperative work.

John B. Smith, Professor Emeritus; Ph.D., North Carolina at Chapel Hill, 1970.

Jack S. Snoeyink, Professor; Ph.D., Stanford, 1990. Computational geometry, algorithms for geographical information systems and structural biology, geometric modeling and computation, algorithms and data structures, theory of computation.

Donald F. Stanat, Professor Emeritus; Ph.D., Michigan, 1966.

David Stotts, Professor; Ph.D., Virginia, 1985. Computer-supported cooperative work, especially collaborative user interfaces; software engineering, design patterns and formal methods; hypermedia and Web technology.

Martin Styner, Research Assistant Professor; Ph.D., North Carolina at Chapel Hill, 2001. Medical image processing and analysis including anatomical structure and tissue segmentation, morphometry using shape analysis, modeling and atlas building, intramodality and intermodality registration.

Russell M. Taylor II, Research Professor; Ph.D., North Carolina at Chapel Hill, 1994. 3-D interactive computer graphics, virtual worlds, distributed computing, scientific visualization, human-computer interaction.

Leandra Vicci, Lecturer and Director, Applied Engineering Laboratory; B.S., Antioch (Ohio), 1964. Information processing hardware: theory, practice, systems, and applications; computer-integrated magnetic force systems; wave optics; tracking and imaging; electricity and magnetism; low Reynolds number fluid dynamics; biophysical models of mitotic spindles; quantum theory.

Wei Wang, Associate Professor; Ph.D., UCLA, 1999. Data mining, database systems, bioinformatics.

Stephen F. Weiss, Professor Emeritus; Ph.D., Cornell, 1970.

Gregory F. Welch, Research Professor; Ph.D., North Carolina at Chapel Hill, 1997. Human motion tracking systems, 3-D telepresence, projector-based graphics, computer vision and view synthesis, medical applications of computers.

Mary C. Whitton, Research Associate Professor; M.S., North Carolina State, 1984. Developing and evaluating technology for virtual and augmented reality systems, virtual locomotion, tools for serious games.

William V. Wright, Research Professor Emeritus; Ph.D., North Carolina at Chapel Hill, 1972.

Adjunct Faculty

Stephen Aylward, Adjunct Associate Professor; Ph.D., North Carolina at Chapel Hill, 1997. Computer-aided diagnosis, computer-aided surgical planning, statistical pattern recognition, image processing, neural networks.

Larry Conrad, Professor of the Practice, Vice Chancellor for Information Technology, and Chief Information Officer; M.S., Arizona State.

Brad Davis, Adjunct Assistant Professor; Ph.D., North Carolina at Chapel Hill, 2008. Image analysis, shape analysis, image processing, statistical methods in nonlinear spaces, medical applications, visualization, software engineering.

Nick England, Adjunct Research Professor; E.E., North Carolina State, 1974. Systems architectures for graphics and imaging, scientific visualization, volume rendering, interactive surface modeling.

Mark Foskey, Adjunct Research Assistant Professor; Ph.D., California, San Diego, 1994. Medical image analysis, especially in cancer therapy; geometric computation.

Rob Fowler, Adjunct Professor; Ph.D., Washington (Seattle), 1985. High-performance computing.

Guido Gerig, Adjunct Professor; Ph.D., Swiss Federal Institute of Technology, 1987. Image analysis, shape-based object recognition, 3-D object representation and quantitative analysis, medical image processing.

Shawn Gomez, Adjunct Assistant Professor; Eng.Sc.D., Columbia. Bioinformatics, computational biology, systems biology.

Chris Healey, Adjunct Associate Professor; Ph.D., British Columbia, 1996. Computer graphics, scientific visualization, perception and cognitive vision, color, texture, databases, computational geometry.

M. Gail Jones, Adjunct Professor; Ph.D., North Carolina State, 1987. Science education, gender and science, high-stakes assessment nanotechnology education, haptics and learning.

Hye-Chung Kum, Adjunct Assistant Professor; Ph.D., North Carolina at Chapel Hill, 2004. Social welfare intelligence and informatics, health informatics, government informatics, data mining, KDD (Knowledge Discovery in Databases), government administrative data.

J. Stephen Marron, Adjunct Professor; Ph.D., UCLA, 1982. Smoothing methods for curve estimation.

Steven E. Molnar, Adjunct Associate Professor; Ph.D., North Carolina at Chapel Hill, 1991. Architectures for real-time computer graphics, VLSI-based system design, parallel rendering algorithms.

Frank Mueller, Adjunct Associate Professor; Ph.D., Florida State, 1994.

Andrew B. Nobel, Adjunct Professor; Ph.D., Stanford, 1992. Statistical analysis of microarrays, analysis of Internet traffic, nonparametric interference, pattern recognition: clustering and clarification.

Lars S. Nyland, Adjunct Research Associate Professor; Ph.D., Duke, 1991. High-performance computing, hardware systems, computer graphics and image analysis, geometric modeling and computation.

John Poulton, Adjunct Research Professor; Ph.D., North Carolina at Chapel Hill, 1980. Graphics architectures, VLSI-based system design, design tools, rapid system prototyping.

Julian Rosenman, Adjunct Professor; Ph.D., Texas at Austin, 1971; M.D., Texas Health Science Center at Dallas, 1977. Computer graphics for treatment of cancer patients, contrast enhancement for x-rays.

Dinggang Shen, Adjunct Associate Professor; Ph.D., Shanghai Jiao Tong (China), 1995. Medical image analysis, computer vision, pattern recognition.

Diane H. Sonnenwald, Adjunct Professor; Ph.D., Rutgers, 1993. Collaboration among multidisciplinary, cross-organizational teams, human information behavior, digital libraries.

Richard Superfine, Adjunct Professor; Ph.D., Berkeley, 1991. Condensed-matter physics, biophysics, microscopy.

Alexander Tropsha, Adjunct Professor; Ph.D., Moscow State (Russia), 1986. Computer-assisted drug design, computational toxicology, cheminformatics, structural bioinformatics.

Turner Whitted, Adjunct Research Professor; Ph.D., North Carolina State, 1978.

Sean Washburn, Adjunct Professor; Ph.D., Duke, 1982. Condensed-matter physics, materials science.

UNIVERSITY OF PITTSBURGH

Intelligent Systems Program

Programs of Study

The Intelligent Systems Program (ISP) at the University of Pittsburgh (Pitt) is devoted to artificial intelligence and enables graduate students to pursue a Master of Science or Ph.D. degree in a variety of areas and specializations. Through a broad interdisciplinary approach, the program allows students to collaborate with faculty members from many disciplines on research in computer science, biomedical informatics, cognitive psychology, information science, education, and law. The program utilizes a focused and customized curriculum. Graduate students design their own personalized curricula to enhance their knowledge, meet their interests, and prepare them for interdisciplinary research.

Faculty members and students present their research in regular program seminars, exposing students to a broad range of research topics and methods and affording them the opportunity to present their own research. Pitt's widely published ISP faculty members are leaders in their fields. Drawing on the strengths of diverse sectors of the University and participating in over thirty funded research projects, they support graduate students through collaborative research, personal mentoring, and external research funding.

The scope of the program is broad, but it also allows graduate students to explore concentrations in the specific areas that interest them the most. The program emphasizes research in four distinct and innovative areas: natural language processing and information retrieval, intelligent tutoring systems and educational technology, machine learning and decision making, and biomedical informatics. All four areas are led by highly regarded researchers with international reputations for excellence in their fields.

The natural language processing (NLP) and information retrieval research group focuses on areas ranging from spoken dialogue systems and subjectivity and sentiment analysis to statistical multilingual processing and information retrieval. Group members participate in extensive collaborations with several academic institutions to enhance real-world applications in areas such as automated tutoring, question answering, machine translation systems, and information extraction from medical records.

The intelligent tutoring systems and educational technology research group has created a number of well-known tutoring systems in several fields of science, and is exploring various areas of community-based systems such as digital libraries and adaptive Web systems. Researchers in this group work on a plethora of innovative and cutting-edge applications.

The machine learning and decision making research group is developing new methods and tools for solving complex learning and decision-making problems under conditions of uncertainty. Examples of applications include disease-outbreak surveillance, treatment-error detection, high-throughput genomic and proteomic data analysis, monitoring and analysis of traffic flows, diagnosis, and strategic financial planning within organizations.

The biomedical informatics research group is applying natural language processing, Bayesian modeling, and machine-learning methods to health-care tasks, including disease-outbreak detection and diagnosis, automated tutoring of medical trainees, and discovery of molecular-disease biomarkers.

Research Facilities

The Intelligent Systems Program is located in the University's Sennott Square Building. The ISP grad student lab offers 396 square feet of open space with workstations for 6 new students. The workstations have two monitors and new Dell desktop computers. The ISP Artifical Intelligence Seminars are held in Sennott Square 5317, an 810-square-foot facility with multimedia services available for presentations.

Once a student receives a Graduate Student Research (GSR) appointment, the student moves to the adviser's research lab, which is located in the ISP faculty member's primary appointed department. The ISP student has the opportunity to work with faculty members and students in the specific areas that interest him or her the most.

Financial Aid

ISP students may apply for financial aid through the program as well as financial assistance through the University's School of Arts and Sciences. Once a candidate is admitted to ISP, the ISP admissions committee makes every effort to identify a source of financial aid.

The competitive Mellon Predoctoral Fellowships are offered by the University. A limited number of Arts and Sciences Predoctoral Fellowships are offered by ISP for the fall and spring terms and incoming students are automatically considered. A number of graduate research awards are available through sponsored research projects and award decisions are usually made by the principal investigator.

Cost of Study

For the 2011–12 academic year, graduate tuition for the Univeristy of Pittsburgh's School of Arts and Sciences per semester is $9387 for Pennsylvania students and $15,368 for out-of-state students. The student activity fee; student health fee; computing and network fee; and security, safety, and transportation fees total $370 per semester.

Living and Housing Costs

Living and housing costs can vary depending on accommodations. Monthly costs are estimated at $920 for rent and utilities, $350 for food, and $140 for personal expenses.

Student Group

The ISP program has enrolled 24 students for the 2011–12 academic year, 18 men and 6 women. About two thirds are international students, coming from countries such as China, Germany, India, Iran, Korea, and Turkey. Approximately 80 percent receive some sort of financial support, such as Arts and Sciences predoctoral fellowships, Mellon Predoctoral Fellowships, National Library of Medicine Fellowships, or a Graduate Student Researcher (GSR) position with the principal investigator of a research grant.

Student Outcomes

ISP alumni have been rewarded with successful positions in academia, research labs, and industry. Former graduate students now work as professors and postdoctoral fellows abroad and in some of the nation's most prestigious universities and academic institutions, such as Arkansas, Boston University, British Columbia, Carnegie Mellon, Florida International, Mississippi State, North Carolina State, Pennsylvania, Pittsburgh ,Stanford, Texas Health Science Center at Houston, USC, and Vanderbilt. Some alumni are now research scientists at Georgia Tech, Johns Hopkins, NASA, the National Institutes of Health, and the U.S. National Library of Medicine. Many have also entered into industry positions at HRL Laboratories, Intel, SAS software, Amazon, IBM, Carnegie Learning, Inc., Microsoft, and the Institute for Defense Analyses, among others. Current graduate student summer internships are with Carnegie Mellon University, Microsoft, Intel, and Yahoo! Inc.

Location

Pittsburgh, with a population of 369,879, is part of a greater metropolitan area of 2.5 million people. The University occupies more than 120 acres of Oakland, the cultural hub of the city. Pittsburgh is of sufficient size to support a wide variety of cultural and athletics events, including performances of the Pittsburgh Symphony Orchestra, the Pittsburgh Ballet Theatre, the Pittsburgh Opera, the O'Reilly Theater, the Three Rivers Arts Festival, and the International Poetry Forum, as well as home games of the Pittsburgh Pirates, Steelers, and Penguins. The city also has an extensive system of large parks. Schenley Park, adjacent to the University and to Carnegie Mellon, is the site of the renowned Phipps Conservatory and Botanical Gardens, and Highland Park contains the Pittsburgh Zoo and PPG Aquarium. North of the downtown area are the Allegheny Observatory, the Carnegie Science Center, Andy Warhol Museum, and the National Aviary. Close to the campus are the Carnegie Museums of Natural History and Art and the Carnegie Library. Boating, camping, fishing, golf, hiking, ice-skating, and skiing are available in the area.

The University

The University of Pittsburgh, founded eleven years after the signing of the Declaration of Independence, is a nonsectarian, coeducational institution. As part of the Commonwealth System of Higher Education, it receives financial support from the state. The University has 17,246 undergraduate and 9,614 graduate students and 4,339 faculty members. The library system maintains excellent collections totaling more than 5.6 million volumes. Petersen Events Center, the University of Pittsburgh's athletic facility, is the venue for basketball games and concerts; it also houses exercise facilities and an Olympic-size swimming pool, which are open to all students. Intercollegiate athletics events with nationally ranked teams are frequent, and student tickets are available to many of these events.

Applying

Recognizing that people can come to this field from different paths, the program invites applicants from a wide variety of educational settings and disciplinary backgrounds. ISP looks for evidence of advanced standing and outstanding performance in some of the core areas relevant to the study of intelligent systems, including theoretical and applied computer science, cognitive psychology, other areas of cognitive science, and symbolic programming and software engineering. A B.A. or B.S. degree in one of these areas provides good preparation for entering the program.

Application to the Intelligent Systems Program can be completed online at https://app.applyyourself.com/?id=up-as. ISP requires the Graduate Record Examination (GRE), three letters of recommendation, and TOEFL scores for nonnative English speaking applicants. The deadline for receipt of applications with consideration for financial aid is on or around February 1 each year.

Correspondence and Information

Wendy Bergstein, Administrator
Intelligent Systems Program
5113 Sennott Square
University of Pittsburgh
210 South Bouquet Street
Pittsburgh, Pennsylvania 15260

Phone: 412-624-5755
E-mail: isp@pitt.edu
Web site: http://www.isp.pitt.edu

University of Pittsburgh

THE FACULTY AND THEIR RESEARCH

Many of Pitt's acclaimed schools are represented through associated faculty members from the School of Medicine, the School of Law, the School of Education, the School of Information Sciences, the Graduate School of Public Health, and the School of Arts and Sciences. There are especially strong connections to research groups in the Department of Computer Science, the Department of Biomedical Informatics, the Learning Research and Development Center, and the Department of Psychology.

Kevin Ashley, Professor. Case-based reasoning, intelligent tutoring systems, legal information management and retrieval.

Peter Brusilovsky, Associate Professor. Adaptive Web-based systems, adaptive hypermedia, adaptive interfaces, intelligent tutoring systems and shells.

Gregory Cooper, Professor. Application of probability theory and decision theory to medical informatics problems, Bayesian belief networks, causal discovery.

Rebecca Crowley, Associate Professor. Computer-based education, medical cognition, decision support, human-computer interaction.

Marek Druzdzel, Associate Professor. Decision making under uncertainty, decision-theoretic methods in intelligent systems, user interfaces to decision support systems.

Madhavi Ganapathiraju, Assistant Professor. Active machine learning, systems biology (protein interactions) and structural biology, genomics of diseases.

Vanathi Gopalakrishnan, Assistant Professor. Bioinformatics, gene expression analysis, machine learning, symbolic inductive learning from temporal data, data mining, scientific experiment design and planning.

John Grefenstette, Professor. Modeling and simulation of infectious diseases, bioinformatics, biological network analysis, machine learning, high-performance computing applications to public health.

Milos Hauskrecht, Associate Professor. Planning, reasoning, and optimization in the presence of uncertainty; machine learning and data mining; application of artificial intelligence in medicine and finance.

Daqing He, Associate Professor. Cross-media information retrieval, multilingual information retrieval.

Stephen Hirtle, Professor. Spacial cognition, classification, mathematical psychology.

Rebecca Hwa, Associate Professor. Statistical natural language processing, lifelike computer agents, artificial intelligence, human computer interfaces.

Alan Lesgold, Professor. Formal modeling; intelligent, computer-based instruction of complex skills.

Michael Lewis, Professor. Intelligent agents in human teams, visual information retrieval interfaces, ecological cognition in visualization.

Diane Litman, Professor and ISP Director. Computational linguistics, knowledge representation, plan recognition, spoken-language processing, user modeling.

Paul Munro, Associate Professor. Neural networks, neurobiological models, data compression and error correction.

John Rosenberg, Professor. Structural basis of sequence-specific DNA-protein interactions.

Christian Schunn, Associate Professor. Scientific reasoning and discovery learning, computational modeling of strategy choice, categorization and causal reasoning.

Richard Simpson, Associate Professor. Computer access, augmentative communication, rehabilitation robotics, adaptive interfaces.

Fu-Chiang Tsui, Research Assistant Professor. Biosurveillance/public health surveillance, grid computing, Bayesian networks, temporal and spatial algorithms for biosurveillance, clinical decision support systems, hospice information systems, database management systems.

Shyam Visweswaran, Assistant Professor. Data mining, patient-specific predictive modeling, medical anomaly detection, decision support systems.

Michael Wagner, Associate Professor. Construction of decision-theoretic reminder systems, computer-assisted medical decision making, data accuracy in computer-based medical records.

Jingtao Wang, Assistant Professor. Human-computer interaction, mobile interfaces, applications of machine learning in user interfaces, human-computer interaction in education.

Janyce Wiebe, Professor. Computational linguistics, discourse processing and word-sense disambiguation, statistical natural language processing.

WASHINGTON UNIVERSITY IN ST. LOUIS

Department of Computer Science and Engineering

Programs of Study

The Department of Computer Science and Engineering (CSE), in the School of Engineering and Applied Science at Washington University in St. Louis, offers several graduate degree programs tailored for students' specific interests and career goals.

The Doctor of Philosophy in Computer Science (PhDCS) program and the Doctor of Philosophy in Computer Engineering (PhDCoE) program are designed for students whose primary interest is a research career in academia or industry. Students must complete course work, conduct original research, and prepare and defend a high-quality doctoral dissertation on that research. Typically, four to six years are needed to complete the doctorate.

The Master of Science in Computer Science (M.S.C.S.) and the Master of Science in Computer Engineering (MSCoE) program are designed for students interested in launching an industry research career, or who wish to pursue an academic research career by eventually earning a Ph.D. The M.S.C.S. and MSCoE programs require 24 units of course work and an additional 6 units consisting of course work or a project or thesis under the supervision of a member of the CSE faculty. Both the M.S.C.S. and MSCoE are designed for completion within two years of full-time study, though both can be pursued part-time over a longer interval.

The Master of Engineering in Computer Science and Engineering (MEngCSE) program is designed to launch or enhance careers in professional practice, within a focused one year full-time degree program, or part-time over a longer time period. Students in the MEngCSE program have more flexibility to customize their course selections according to their specific interests than in our other graduate degree programs. Students complete 24 units of course work, and a 6 unit capstone project mentored by a member of the CSE faculty, to leverage and demonstrate the skills and knowledge each student has gained through his or her course work.

Research Facilities

Faculty and graduate student offices are housed across three connected modern research buildings. Most graduate students are in 2-person offices with individual workstations and have full access to a wide range of computing and communication resources. The Department has high-speed networks that reach across the campus and has dedicated laboratory facilities in networking and communications; graphics, vision, and robotics; mobile computing; computer engineering; parallel distributed computing; artificial intelligence; and computational science. Strong systems staff support is provided for the computing and network infrastructure.

Financial Aid

All students accepted into the Ph.D. program in the Department of Computer Science and Engineering receive graduate assistantships covering full tuition (generally 9 units per semester) and the cost of health insurance, with an annual salary of $27,000. The financial aid package is continued until graduation (up to five years), as long as the student continues to make satisfactory progress toward the degree with respect to both course work and research.

Cost of Study

For full-time students in the Department of Computer Science and Engineering, tuition is $20,475 per semester in 2011–12. For part-time students, tuition is $1450 per unit, and most courses are 3 units.

Living and Housing Costs

With a remarkably low cost of living for all of the comforts and attractions it affords, St. Louis has a small-town feel but offers all the amenities one would expect in a major metropolitan area. University-owned apartment buildings in neighborhoods adjacent to the campus offer affordable student housing. Many other options in attractive neighborhoods within walking or short driving distance of the campus are also available. The campus can also be reached by light rail, making it practical for students to live further away without having to drive to campus. Two-bedroom apartments range from $600 to $900 per month.

Student Group

Of approximately 200 graduate students in the Department of Computer Science and Engineering, about 70 are pursuing doctorates.

Student Outcomes

Doctoral graduates of the Department may be found on the faculty of many top universities, and graduates at all levels are highly sought after by major computer firms and by companies that make extensive use of computing capabilities in their business and products. Among recent doctoral graduates, a number chose to start their research careers at some of the national laboratories.

Location

The most visible symbol of St. Louis is its noted Gateway Arch, the nation's tallest monument, which represents its role as Gateway to the West. But St. Louis's location near the center of the country could just as well make it the Gateway to the East, North, or South. It is easy to get to any part of the continental U.S., and the Washington University campus is only about 15 minutes from Lambert–St. Louis International Airport.

St. Louis's metropolitan area has a population of more than 2.8 million people, and its many distinct neighborhoods mirror the city's cosmopolitan diversity. Food, music, and all the attributes of a culture are intact in the city's tightly knit communities. St. Louis is home to the world-renowned Missouri Botanical Garden, a first-rate zoo, art museum, history museum, and science center. Forest Park, one of the nation's largest urban parks, is adjacent to the campus and offers opportunities for walking, jogging, Rollerblading, and biking—along with golf, tennis, and boating. The Grand Center area is home to an excellent symphony, the palatial Fox Theatre, and dance and repertory theaters. The city has professional baseball, football, and hockey franchises. St. Louis is home to numerous Fortune 500 and Fortune 1000 companies.

The University and The Department

An independent institution founded in 1853, Washington University in St. Louis seeks excellence in everything that it does. With 13,500 students and more than 3,000 faculty members, the University is counted among the world's leaders in teaching and research and draws students from all fifty states and approximately 125 nations. The 169-acre campus is bordered on the east by St. Louis's famed Forest Park and on the north, west, and south by comfortable and attractive suburbs. Twenty-two Nobel Prize winners have been associated with the University.

The Department's size and collegial atmosphere provide a supportive and friendly environment. On average, each faculty member supervises 3 doctoral students. The Department has a history of strong ties to biomedical computing, and faculty members collaborate extensively with those from other departments. About 30 outside speakers arrive each year, and visiting researchers come from around the world.

Applying

A strong computing background is recommended regardless of undergraduate major. Students who wish to enter the computing field from other areas of science and engineering may need to take preparatory classes before enrolling in graduate-level courses. Electronic applications are available at http://cse.wustl.edu/graduateprograms/Pages/default.aspx. Applications for Ph.D. assistantships must be received by January 15. Applicants whose native language is not English must submit TOEFL or IELTS scores. Ph.D. applicants must submit GRE general test scores.

Correspondence and Information

Graduate Admissions
Washington University in St. Louis
Campus Box 1100
One Brookings Drive
St. Louis, Missouri 63130-4899

Phone: 314-935-7974
Fax: 314-935-6949
E-mail: admissions@cse.wustl.edu
Web site: http://cse.wustl.edu

Washington University in St. Louis

THE FACULTY AND THEIR RESEARCH

Kunal Agrawal, Assistant Professor; Ph.D., MIT, 2009. Parallel computing, adaptive scheduling, transactional memory.

Michael R. Brent, Henry Edwin Sever Professor; Ph.D., MIT, 1991. Computational genomics, mathematical modeling of biological sequences, algorithms for computational biology, integration of computational and experimental methods, bioinformatics.

Jeremy Buhler, Associate Professor; Ph.D., Washington (Seattle), 2001. Computational biology, genomics, algorithms for comparing and annotating large biosequences.

Roger D. Chamberlain, Associate Professor; D.Sc., Washington (St. Louis), 1989. Computer engineering, parallel computation, computer architecture, multiprocessor systems.

Yixin Chen, Associate Professor; Ph.D., Illinois at Urbana-Champaign, 2005. Mathematical optimization, artificial intelligence, planning and scheduling, data mining, learning data warehousing, operations research, data security.

Patrick Crowley, Associate Professor; Ph.D., Washington (Seattle), 2003. Computer and network systems architecture.

Ron K. Cytron, Professor and Associate Chair; Ph.D., Illinois at Urbana-Champaign, 1984. Programming languages, middleware, real-time systems.

Christopher D. Gill, Associate Professor; Ph.D., Washington (St. Louis), 2001. Distributed real-time embedded systems, middleware, formal models and analysis of concurrency and timing.

Viktor Gruev, Assistant Professor; Ph.D., Johns Hopkins, 2004. Low power integrated sensory systems, integrated polarization imaging.

Cindy M. Grimm, Associate Professor; Ph.D., Brown, 1996. Surface modeling, art-based rendering, user interfaces, texture generation.

Raj Jain, Professor; Ph.D., Harvard, 1978. Wireless networks, network security, next-generation Internet, sensor networks, telecommunications networks, performance analysis, traffic management, quality of service.

Tao Ju, Associate Professor; Ph.D., Rice, 2005. Computer graphics, visualization, mesh processing, medical imaging and modeling.

Caitlin Kelleher, Assistant Professor; Ph.D., Carnegie Mellon, 2006. Human-computer interaction, programming environments, learning environments.

Chenyang Lu, Associate Professor; Ph.D., Virginia, 2001. Real-time and embedded systems, wireless sensor networks, mobile computing.

Robert Pless, Associate Professor; Ph.D., Maryland, 2000. Computer vision, medical imaging, sensor network algorithms.

William D. Richard, Associate Professor; Ph.D., Missouri–Rolla, 1988. Ultrasonic imaging, medical instrumentation, computer engineering.

William D. Smart, Associate Professor; Ph.D., Brown, 2001. Machine learning, mobile robotics, human-robot interaction, brain-computer interfaces.

Jonathan S. Turner, Barbara J. and Jerome R. Cox Jr. Professor; Ph.D., Northwestern, 1982. Design and analysis of Internet routers and switching systems, networking and communications, algorithms.

Kilian Weinberger, Assistant Professor; Ph.D., Pennsylvania, 2007. Multitask learning, convex optimization, metric learning, dimensionality reduction, manifold learning, machine learned ranking.

Weixiong Zhang, Professor; Ph.D., UCLA, 1994. Computational biology, artificial intelligence, machine learning, heuristic search, combinatorial optimization, algorithms.

Senior Faculty

Jerome R. Cox Jr., Senior Professor; Sc.D., MIT, 1954. Computer system design, computer networking, biomedical computing.

Mark A. Franklin, Senior Professor; Ph.D., Carnegie Mellon, 1970. Computer architecture, systems analysis and parallel processing, storage systems design.

RESEARCH AREAS

Artificial Intelligence. Artificial intelligence (AI) research at Washington University, consists of a number of related research projects with both basic and applied research objectives. The research methodology covers a broad spectrum of theoretical work, prototype system building, and experimentation.

Computational Science. Computational science is the application of ideas and methods from computer science to the natural sciences. The current focus of the computational science group is on computational genomics and biological sequence analysis. Washington University's strength in the biomedical sciences provides an extraordinary intellectual environment for this work. The University houses one of four major genome sequencing centers in the United States. It is also home to world-class Departments of Genetics, Biochemistry, and other biological sciences, with special strengths in computational methods.

Computer Engineering and Systems Architecture. Research topics in this area cover a broad spectrum, from processor and multiprocessor architecture design to communications, Internet design, and storage hierarchies. Research places special emphasis on the characteristics and design of underlying hardware, on interactions with software and operating systems, and on overall system-level performance. Several key efforts exemplify this focus: optical interconnection network design in multiprocessors and communications switches; embedded and real-time computer systems (particularly on designs oriented toward multimedia and streaming data processing); and distributed data and mass storage systems, where system-level reliability and performance are critical.

Graphics, Vision, and Robotics. The multimedia industry is perhaps the most visible and dynamic part of the computing industry. Research in this area focuses on interactions between computers, humans, and the real world. This group focuses on developing and integrating advanced research in imaging and computer graphics, machine vision, robotics, and multimedia systems. The projects include developing teams that work together to explore new environments, robot systems that learn and interact with crowds of people, and video surveillance algorithms that detect patterns of motion. There is also extensive work with the Washington University medical school, working on real time 3-D analysis of MRI and PET data and developing models of heart dynamics and bone surface structure.

Networking and Communications. The networking and communications group at Washington University engages in fundamental research directed toward the development of flexible, high-performance networks. The work spans a wide range of activities, including the design of high-performance routers and switching systems, efficient IP packet processing, dynamically programmable networks, advanced multicast services, host-network interfacing, and optical networking. The group has a long track record of accomplishments in networking, including work that formed the basis for a successful startup company, Growth Networks, acquired by Cisco Systems.

Software Systems. Software systems research at Washington University is concerned with core issues in modern computing, including large-scale distribution, real-time embedded systems, sensor networks, and mobility. Formal studies set the stage for the development of new kinds of modeling and analysis tools. Many software research projects share a strong focus on middleware as an effective vehicle for rapid technology transfer. This focus underscores a pragmatic approach, and it has been an effective tool for building strong industrial collaborations. Software developed at Washington University is widely used by companies and research institutions.

Section 9
Electrical and Computer Engineering

This section contains a directory of institutions offering graduate work in electrical and computer engineering, followed by in-depth entries submitted by institutions that chose to prepare detailed program descriptions. Additional information about programs listed in the directory but not augmented by an in-depth entry may be obtained by writing directly to the dean of a graduate school or chair of a department at the address given in the directory.

For programs offering related work, see also in this book *Computer Science and Information Technology, Energy and Power Engineering, Engineering and Applied Sciences, Industrial Engineering,* and *Mechanical Engineering and Mechanics.* In another guide in this series: ***Graduate Programs in the Physical Sciences, Mathematics, Agricultural Sciences, the Environment & Natural Resources*** See *Mathematical Sciences* and *Physics*

CONTENTS

Program Directories

Close-Ups and Displays

Computer Engineering

Air Force Institute of Technology, Graduate School of Engineering and Management, Department of Electrical and Computer Engineering, Dayton, OH 45433-7765. Offers computer engineering (MS, PhD); computer systems/science (MS); electrical engineering (MS, PhD); electro-optics (MS, PhD). *Accreditation:* ABET (one or more programs are accredited). Part-time programs available. *Degree requirements:* For master's, thesis; for doctorate, thesis/dissertation. *Entrance requirements:* For master's and doctorate, GRE General Test, minimum GPA of 3.0, U.S. citizenship. *Faculty research:* Remote sensing, information survivability, microelectronics, computer networks, artificial intelligence.

American University of Beirut, Graduate Programs, Faculty of Engineering and Architecture, Beirut, Lebanon. Offers applied energy (MME); civil engineering (ME, PhD); electrical and computer engineering (ME, PhD); engineering management (MEM); environmental and water resources (ME); environmental and water resources engineering (PhD); environmental technology (MSES); mechanical engineering (ME, PhD); urban design (MUD); urban planning and policy (MUP). Part-time programs available. *Faculty:* 57 full-time (12 women), 3 part-time/adjunct (0 women). *Students:* 261 full-time (92 women), 58 part-time (20 women). Average age 25. 272 applicants, 79% accepted, 108 enrolled. In 2010, 70 master's, 1 doctorate awarded. *Degree requirements:* For master's, one foreign language, comprehensive exam, thesis (for some programs); for doctorate, one foreign language, comprehensive exam, thesis/dissertation, publications. *Entrance requirements:* For master's, GRE (for electrical and computer engineering), letters of recommendation; for doctorate, GRE, letters of recommendation, master's degree, transcripts, curriculum vitae, interview. Additional exam requirements/recommendations for international students: Required—TOEFL (minimum score 600 paper-based; 250 computer-based; 100 iBT), IELTS (minimum score 7.5). *Application deadline:* For fall admission, 2/5 priority date for domestic and international students; for spring admission, 11/1 priority date for domestic students, 11/1 for international students. Applications are processed on a rolling basis. Application fee: $50. Electronic applications accepted. *Expenses:* Tuition: Full-time $12,294; part-time $683 per credit. Required fees: $499; $499 per credit. Tuition and fees vary according to course load and program. *Financial support:* In 2010–11, 10 fellowships with full tuition reimbursements (averaging $24,800 per year), 33 research assistantships with full tuition reimbursements (averaging $24,800 per year), 70 teaching assistantships with full tuition reimbursements (averaging $9,800 per year) were awarded; career-related internships or fieldwork, institutionally sponsored loans, scholarships/grants, health care benefits, and unspecified assistantships also available. Total annual research expenditures: $586,131. *Unit head:* Fadl H. Moukalled, Acting Dean, 961-135-0000 Ext. 3400, Fax: 961-174-4462, E-mail: memouk@aub.edu.lb. *Application contact:* Dr. Salim Kanaan, Director, Admissions Office, 961-135-0000 Ext. 2594, Fax: 961-175-0775, E-mail: sk00@aub.edu.lb.

American University of Sharjah, Graduate Programs, Sharjah, United Arab Emirates. Offers business (EMBA, GEMPA, MBA); chemical engineering (MS Ch E); civil engineering (MSCE); computer engineering (MS); electrical engineering (MSEE); mechanical engineering (MSME); mechatronics engineering (MS); public administration (MPA); teaching English to speakers of other languages (MA); translation and interpreting (MA); urban planning (MUP). Part-time and evening/weekend programs available. *Entrance requirements:* For master's, GMAT (MBA). Additional exam requirements/recommendations for international students: Required—TOEFL (minimum score 550 paper-based; 213 computer-based; 80 iBT), TWE (minimum score 5). Electronic applications accepted. *Faculty research:* Chemical engineering, civil engineering, computer engineering, electrical engineering, linguistics, translation.

Auburn University, Graduate School, Ginn College of Engineering, Department of Electrical and Computer Engineering, Auburn University, AL 36849. Offers MEE, MS, PhD. Part-time programs available. *Faculty:* 27 full-time (2 women), 3 part-time/adjunct (1 woman). *Students:* 69 full-time (10 women), 48 part-time (10 women); includes 2 Black or African American, non-Hispanic/Latino; 1 American Indian or Alaska Native, non-Hispanic/Latino; 3 Asian, non-Hispanic/Latino; 1 Hispanic/Latino, 72 international. Average age 27. 355 applicants, 57% accepted, 16 enrolled. In 2010, 27 master's, 7 doctorates awarded. *Degree requirements:* For master's, comprehensive exam, thesis (for some programs); for doctorate, thesis/dissertation. *Entrance requirements:* For master's and doctorate, GRE General Test, GRE Subject Test. *Application deadline:* For fall admission, 7/7 for domestic students; for spring admission, 11/24 for domestic students. Applications are processed on a rolling basis. Application fee: $50 ($60 for international students). Electronic applications accepted. *Expenses:* Tuition, state resident: full-time $7002. Tuition, nonresident: full-time $21,898. International tuition: $22,116 full-time. Required fees: $892. Tuition and fees vary according to course load and program. *Financial support:* Fellowships, research assistantships, teaching assistantships, Federal Work-Study available. Support available to part-time students. Financial award application deadline: 3/15; financial award applicants required to submit FAFSA. *Faculty research:* Power systems, energy conversion, electronics, electromagnetics, digital systems. *Unit head:* Dr. J. David Irwin, Head, 334-844-1800. *Application contact:* Dr. George Flowers, Dean of the Graduate School, 334-844-2125.

Baylor University, Graduate School, School of Engineering and Computer Science, Department of Engineering, Waco, TX 76798. Offers biomedical engineering (MSBE); electrical and computer engineering (MSECE, PhD); engineering (ME); mechanical engineering (MSME). *Faculty:* 14 full-time (1 woman). *Students:* 30 full-time (4 women), 6 part-time (0 women); includes 9 minority (3 Black or African American, non-Hispanic/Latino; 2 Asian, non-Hispanic/Latino; 1 Hispanic/Latino; 3 Two or more races, non-Hispanic/Latino), 7 international. In 2010, 7 master's awarded. *Unit head:* Dr. Mike Thompson, Graduate Director, 254-710-4188. *Application contact:* Linda Keer, Administrative Assistant, 254-710-4188, Fax: 254-710-3870, E-mail: linda_kerr@baylor.edu.

Boise State University, Graduate College, College of Engineering, Department of Electrical and Computer Engineering, Boise, ID 83725-0399. Offers computer engineering (M Engr, MS); electrical and computer engineering (PhD); electrical engineering (M Engr, MS). Part-time and evening/weekend programs available. *Degree requirements:* For master's, thesis. *Entrance requirements:* For master's, GRE General Test, minimum GPA of 3.0. Additional exam requirements/recommendations for international students: Required—TOEFL. Electronic applications accepted.

Boston University, College of Engineering, Department of Electrical and Computer Engineering, Boston, MA 02215. Offers computer engineering (M Eng, MS, PhD); electrical engineering (M Eng, MS, PhD); photonics (M Eng, MS). Part-time programs available. *Faculty:* 40 full-time (3 women), 5 part-time/adjunct (0 women). *Students:* 205 full-time (34 women), 15 part-time (1 woman); includes 21 minority (1 Black or African American, non-Hispanic/Latino; 16 Asian, non-Hispanic/Latino; 4 Hispanic/Latino), 141 international. Average age 25. 810 applicants, 25% accepted, 112 enrolled. In 2010, 62 master's, 15 doctorates awarded. Terminal master's awarded for partial completion of doctoral program. *Degree requirements:* For master's, thesis (for some programs); for doctorate, comprehensive exam, thesis/dissertation. *Entrance requirements:* For master's and doctorate, GRE General Test. Additional exam requirements/recommendations for international students: Required—TOEFL (minimum score 550 paper-based; 213 computer-based; 84 iBT), IELTS (minimum score 6). *Application deadline:* For fall admission, 4/1 for domestic and international students; for spring admission, 10/1 for domestic and international students. Applications are processed on a rolling basis. Application fee: $70. Electronic applications accepted. *Expenses:* Tuition: Full-time $39,314; part-time $1228 per credit. Required fees: $40 per semester. *Financial support:* In 2010–11, 126 students received support, including 8 fellowships with full tuition reimbursements available (averaging $28,200 per year), 82 research assistantships with full tuition reimbursements available (averaging $18,800 per year), 18 teaching assistantships with full tuition reimbursements available (averaging $18,800 per year); career-related internships or fieldwork, Federal Work-Study, institutionally sponsored loans, scholarships/grants, traineeships, and health care benefits also available. Financial award application deadline: 1/15; financial award applicants required to submit FAFSA. *Faculty research:* Communications and computer networks; signal, image, video, and multimedia processing; solid-state materials, devices, and photonics; systems, control, and reliable computing; VLSI, computer engineering and high-performance computing. *Unit head:* Dr. David Castanon, Chairman, ad Interim, 617-353-9880, Fax: 617-353-6440, E-mail: dac@bu.edu. *Application contact:* Stephen Doherty, Director of Graduate Programs, 617-353-9760, Fax: 617-353-0259, E-mail: enggrad@bu.edu.

Boston University, Metropolitan College, Department of Computer Science, Boston, MA 02215. Offers computer information systems (MS), including computer networks, database management and business intelligence, health informatics, IT project management, security; computer science (MS), including computer networks, security; telecommunications (MS), including security. Part-time and evening/weekend programs available. Postbaccalaureate distance learning degree programs offered (no on-campus study). *Faculty:* 10 full-time (0 women), 30 part-time/adjunct (3 women). *Students:* 16 full-time (2 women), 681 part-time (155 women); includes 182 minority (44 Black or African American, non-Hispanic/Latino; 1 American Indian or Alaska Native, non-Hispanic/Latino; 88 Asian, non-Hispanic/Latino; 36 Hispanic/Latino; 2 Native Hawaiian or other Pacific Islander, non-Hispanic/Latino; 11 Two or more races, non-Hispanic/Latino), 66 international. Average age 35. 273 applicants, 78% accepted, 155 enrolled. In 2010, 143 master's awarded. *Degree requirements:* For master's, thesis optional. *Entrance requirements:* For master's, 3 letters of recommendation, professional resume. Additional exam requirements/recommendations for international students: Required—TOEFL (minimum score 550 paper-based; 213 computer-based; 80 iBT). *Application deadline:* For fall admission, 6/1 priority date for international students; for spring admission, 10/1 priority date for international students. Applications are processed on a rolling basis. Application fee: $70. Electronic applications accepted. *Expenses:* Tuition: Full-time $39,314; part-time $1228 per credit. Required fees: $40 per semester. *Financial support:* In 2010–11, 9 research assistantships with partial tuition reimbursements (averaging $5,000 per year) were awarded; career-related internships or fieldwork and unspecified assistantships also available. Support available to part-time students. Financial award applicants required to submit FAFSA. *Faculty research:* Medical informatics, Web technologies, telecom and networks, security and forensics, software engineering, programming languages, multimedia and AI, information systems and IT project management. *Unit head:* Dr. Lubomir Chitkushev, Chairman, 617-353-2566, Fax: 617-353-2367, E-mail: csinfo@bu.edu. *Application contact:* Kim Richards, Program Coordinator, 617-353-2566, Fax: 617-353-2367, E-mail: kimrich@bu.edu.

Brigham Young University, Graduate Studies, Ira A. Fulton College of Engineering and Technology, Department of Electrical and Computer Engineering, Provo, UT 84602. Offers MS, PhD. *Faculty:* 23 full-time (0 women). *Students:* 97 full-time (5 women); includes 1 Asian, non-Hispanic/Latino; 2 Hispanic/Latino, 24 international. Average age 28. 57 applicants, 68% accepted, 22 enrolled. In 2010, 15 master's, 9 doctorates awarded. *Degree requirements:* For master's, thesis optional; for doctorate, comprehensive exam, thesis/dissertation. *Entrance requirements:* For master's and doctorate, GRE General Test, minimum GPA of 3.2 in last 60 hours of course work. Additional exam requirements/recommendations for international students: Required—TOEFL (minimum score 580 paper-based; 237 computer-based; 85 iBT). *Application deadline:* For fall admission, 1/15 for domestic and international students; for winter admission, 8/15 for domestic and international students. Application fee: $50. Electronic applications accepted. *Expenses:* Tuition: Full-time $5580; part-time $310 per credit hour. Tuition and fees vary according to program and student's religious affiliation. *Financial support:* In 2010–11, 70 students received support, including 4 fellowships with full tuition reimbursements available (averaging $19,500 per year), 58 research assistantships with full tuition reimbursements available (averaging $19,500 per year), 8 teaching assistantships with full tuition reimbursements available (averaging $19,500 per year); scholarships/grants also available. Financial award application deadline: 5/15; financial award applicants required to submit FAFSA. *Faculty research:* Microwave remote sensing, reconfigurable computing, microelectronics, wireless communications, computer architecture, biomedical imaging, bio-chemical sensing. Total annual research expenditures: $3.1 million. *Unit head:* Dr. Michael A. Jensen, Chair, 801-422-4012, Fax: 801-422-0201, E-mail: jensen@ee.byu.edu. *Application contact:* Janalyn L. Mergist, Graduate Secretary, 801-422-4013, Fax: 801-422-0201, E-mail: janalyn@ee.byu.edu.

Brown University, Graduate School, Division of Engineering, Program in Electrical Sciences and Computer Engineering, Providence, RI 02912. Offers Sc M, PhD. *Degree requirements:* For doctorate, thesis/dissertation, preliminary exam.

California State University, Chico, Graduate School, College of Engineering, Computer Science, and Technology, Department of Electrical and Computer Engineering, Option in Computer Engineering, Chico, CA 95929-0722. Offers MS. *Students:* 1 part-time (0 women), all international. Average age 24. 12 applicants, 67% accepted, 1 enrolled. In 2010, 4 master's awarded. *Degree requirements:* For master's, thesis or alternative. *Entrance requirements:* For master's, GRE General Test, 2 letters of recommendation. Additional exam requirements/recommendations for international students: Required—TOEFL (minimum score 550 paper-based; 213 computer-based; 80 iBT), IELTS (minimum score 6.8). *Application deadline:* For fall admission, 3/1 priority date for domestic students, 3/1 for international students; for spring admission, 9/15 priority date for domestic students, 9/15 for international students. Applications are processed on a rolling basis. Application fee: $55. Electronic applications accepted. *Unit head:* Dr. Adel Ghandakly, Graduate Coordinator, 530-898-5343. *Application contact:* Dr. Adel Ghandakly, Graduate Coordinator, 530-898-5343.

California State University, Long Beach, Graduate Studies, College of Engineering, Department of Computer Engineering and Computer Science, Long Beach, CA 90840. Offers computer engineering (MSCS); computer science (MSCS). Part-time programs available. *Faculty:* 13 full-time (3 women). *Students:* 120 full-time (30 women), 123 part-time (17 women); includes 4 Black or African American, non-Hispanic/Latino; 1 American Indian or Alaska Native, non-Hispanic/Latino; 46 Asian, non-Hispanic/Latino; 18 Hispanic/Latino, 102 international. Average age 29. 406 applicants, 65% accepted, 113 enrolled. In 2010, 43 master's awarded. *Degree requirements:* For master's, thesis or alternative. *Entrance requirements:* Additional exam requirements/recommendations for international students: Required—TOEFL. *Application deadline:* For fall admission, 3/1 for domestic students. Application fee: $55. Electronic applications accepted. *Financial support:* Teaching assistantships, Federal Work-Study, institutionally sponsored loans, scholarships/grants, and unspecified assistantships available. Financial award application deadline: 3/2. *Faculty research:* Artificial intelligence, software engineering, computer simulation and modeling, user-interface design, networking. *Unit head:* Dr. Kenneth James, Chair, 562-985-5105, Fax: 562-985-7823, E-mail: james@csulb.edu. *Application contact:* Dr. Burkhard Englert, Graduate Advisor, 562-985-7987, Fax: 562-985-7823, E-mail: benglert@.csulb.edu.

Carnegie Mellon University, Carnegie Institute of Technology, Department of Electrical and Computer Engineering, Pittsburgh, PA 15213-3891. Offers biomedical engineering (MS); electrical and computer engineering (MS, PhD). Part-time programs available. *Degree requirements:* For master's, thesis; for doctorate, thesis/dissertation, qualifying exam, teaching experience. *Entrance requirements:* For master's and doctorate, GRE General Test. Additional exam requirements/recommendations for international students: Required—TOEFL. *Faculty research:* Computer-aided design, solid-state devices, VLSI, processing, robotics and controls, signal processing, data systems storage.

See Display on next page and Close-Up on page 389.

Carnegie Mellon University, Carnegie Institute of Technology, Information Networking Institute, Pittsburgh, PA 15213. Offers information networking (MS); information security technology and management (MS); information technology—information security (MS); information technology—mobility (MS); information technology—software management (MS). *Degree requirements:* For master's, thesis optional. *Entrance requirements:* For master's, GRE General Test, bachelor's degree in computer science, computer engineering, or electrical engineering, or related technology degree; programming skills (C/C++ fluency for some programs). Additional exam requirements/recommendations for international students: Required—TOEFL. *Faculty research:* Computer forensics and incident response; dependable systems, embedded systems, mobile systems, and sensor networks; computer and information networks, network and information security, human and socio-economic factors in secure system design; wireless sensor networks, survivable embedded systems, signal processing/compression; strategic management, international strategic management, group dynamics and decision-making structures, simulated competitive environments.

Case Western Reserve University, School of Graduate Studies, Case School of Engineering, Department of Electrical Engineering and Computer Science, Cleveland, OH 44106. Offers computer engineering (MS, PhD); computing and information sciences (MS, PhD); electrical engineering (MS, PhD); systems and control engineering (MS, PhD). Part-time and evening/weekend programs available. Postbaccalaureate distance learning degree programs offered (minimal on-campus study). *Faculty:* 33 full-time (2 women). *Students:* 190 full-time (31 women), 26 part-time (4 women); includes 3 Black or African American, non-Hispanic/Latino; 6 Asian, non-Hispanic/Latino, 128 international. In 2010, 32 master's, 13 doctorates awarded. Terminal master's awarded for partial completion of doctoral program. *Degree requirements:* For master's, thesis; for doctorate, thesis/dissertation, qualifying exam, teaching experience. *Entrance requirements:* For master's and doctorate, GRE General Test. Additional exam requirements/recommendations for international students: Required—TOEFL. *Application deadline:* For fall admission, 2/1 for domestic students; for spring admission, 11/1 for domestic students. Applications are processed on a rolling basis. Application fee: $50. *Financial support:* Fellowships with full and partial tuition reimbursements, research assistantships with full and partial tuition reimbursements, teaching assistantships, career-related internships or fieldwork, Federal Work-Study, and institutionally sponsored loans available. Support available to part-time students. Financial award application deadline: 3/1; financial award applicants required to submit FAFSA. *Faculty research:* Applied artificial intelligence, automation, computer-aided design and testing of digital systems. Total annual research expenditures: $6.8 million. *Unit head:* Michael Branicky, Department Chair, 216-368-6888, E-mail: branicky@case.edu. *Application contact:* David Easler, Student Affairs Coordinator, 216-368-4080, Fax: 216-368-2801, E-mail: david.easler@case.edu.

Clarkson University, Graduate School, Wallace H. Coulter School of Engineering, Department of Electrical and Computer Engineering, Potsdam, NY 13699. Offers electrical and computer engineering (PhD); electrical engineering (ME, MS). Part-time programs available. *Faculty:* 17 full-time (3 women), 3 part-time/adjunct (all women). *Students:* 41 full-time (7 women), 3 part-time (2 women); includes 3 minority (1 American Indian or Alaska Native, non-Hispanic/Latino; 1 Asian, non-Hispanic/Latino; 1 Hispanic/Latino), 16 international. Average age 28. 89 applicants, 39% accepted, 7 enrolled. In 2010, 8 master's, 3 doctorates awarded. Terminal master's awarded for partial completion of doctoral program. *Degree requirements:* For master's, thesis; for doctorate, comprehensive exam, thesis/dissertation, departmental qualifying exam. *Entrance requirements:* For master's and doctorate, GRE, transcripts of all college coursework, resume, personal statement, three letters of recommendation. Additional exam requirements/recommendations for international students: Required—TOEFL (minimum score 550 paper-based; 213 computer-based; 80 iBT), IELTS (minimum score 6.5). *Application deadline:* For fall admission, 1/30 priority date for domestic and international students; for spring admission, 9/1 priority date for domestic and international students. Applications are processed on a rolling basis. Application fee: $25 ($35 for international students). Electronic applications accepted. *Expenses:* Tuition: Part-time $1136 per credit hour. *Financial support:* In 2010–11, 29 students received support, including 7 fellowships with full tuition reimbursements available (averaging $21,580 per year), 10 research assistantships with full tuition reimbursements available (averaging $21,580 per year), 9 teaching assistantships with full tuition reimbursements available (averaging $21,580 per year); scholarships/grants, tuition waivers (partial), and unspecified assistantships also available. *Faculty research:* NEU nanotechnology, high

voltage insulator, biometric scanners, transdermal drug, eating patterns. Total annual research expenditures: $1.2 million. *Unit head:* Dr. William Jemison, Chair, 315-268-7648, Fax: 315-268-7600, E-mail: wjemison@clarkson.edu. *Application contact:* Kelly Sharlow, Assistant to the Dean, 315-268-7929, Fax: 315-268-4494, E-mail: ksharlow@clarkson.edu.

Clemson University, Graduate School, College of Engineering and Science, Department of Electrical and Computer Engineering, Program in Computer Engineering, Clemson, SC 29634. Offers MS, PhD. *Students:* 38 full-time (3 women), 6 part-time (0 women); includes 2 Black or African American, non-Hispanic/Latino; 2 Asian, non-Hispanic/Latino, 25 international. Average age 27. 95 applicants, 32% accepted, 12 enrolled. In 2010, 10 master's awarded. *Degree requirements:* For master's, thesis or alternative; for doctorate, thesis/dissertation, departmental qualifying exam. *Entrance requirements:* For master's and doctorate, GRE General Test. Additional exam requirements/recommendations for international students: Required—TOEFL. *Application deadline:* Applications are processed on a rolling basis. Application fee: $70 ($80 for international students). Electronic applications accepted. *Expenses:* Tuition, state resident: full-time $6492; part-time $400 per credit hour. Tuition, nonresident: full-time $13,634; part-time $800 per credit hour. Required fees: $262 per semester. Part-time tuition and fees vary according to course load and program. *Financial support:* In 2010–11, 32 students received support, including 4 fellowships with full and partial tuition reimbursements available (averaging $6,635 per year), 23 research assistantships with partial tuition reimbursements available (averaging $12,031 per year), 20 teaching assistantships with partial tuition reimbursements available (averaging $6,933 per year); career-related internships or fieldwork, institutionally sponsored loans, scholarships/grants, health care benefits, and unspecified assistantships also available. Support available to part-time students. Financial award applicants required to submit FAFSA. *Faculty research:* Interface applications, software development, multisystem communications, artificial intelligence, robotics. *Unit head:* Dr. Darren Dawson, Chair, 864-656-5249, Fax: 864-656-5917, E-mail: ddarren@clemson.edu. *Application contact:* Dr. Daniel Noneaker, 864-656-0100, Fax: 864-656-5917, E-mail: ece-grad-program@ces.clemson.edu.

Colorado Technical University Colorado Springs, Graduate Studies, Program in Computer Engineering, Colorado Springs, CO 80907-3896. Offers MSCE. Part-time and evening/weekend programs available. Postbaccalaureate distance learning degree programs offered. *Degree requirements:* For master's, thesis or alternative.

Colorado Technical University Denver, Program in Computer Engineering, Greenwood Village, CO 80111. Offers MS.

Columbia University, Fu Foundation School of Engineering and Applied Science, Department of Electrical Engineering, New York, NY 10027. Offers computer engineering (MS); electrical engineering (MS, Eng Sc D, PhD, Engr); solid state science and engineering (MS, Eng Sc D, PhD). PhD offered through the Graduate School of Arts and Sciences. Part-time programs available. Postbaccalaureate distance learning degree programs offered (no on-campus study). *Faculty:* 26 full-time (1 woman), 32 part-time/adjunct (1 woman). *Students:* 258 full-time (56 women), 95 part-time (19 women); includes 24 minority (2 Black or African American, non-Hispanic/Latino; 17 Asian, non-Hispanic/Latino; 4 Hispanic/Latino; 1 Two or more races, non-Hispanic/Latino), 259 international. Average age 26. 982 applicants, 34% accepted, 160 enrolled. In 2010, 121 master's, 17 doctorates, 2 other advanced degrees awarded. *Degree requirements:* For doctorate, thesis/dissertation, qualifying exam. *Entrance requirements:* For master's, doctorate, and Engr, GRE General Test. Additional exam requirements/recommendations for international students: Required—TOEFL, IELTS. *Application deadline:* For fall admission, 12/1 priority date for domestic and international students; for spring admission, 10/1 priority date for domestic and international students. Application fee: $95. Electronic applications accepted. *Financial support:* In 2010–11, 98 students received support, including 8 fellowships with full tuition reimbursements available (averaging $30,672 per year), 67 research assistantships with full tuition reimbursements available (averaging $30,672 per year), 23 teaching assistantships with full tuition reimbursements available (averaging $30,672

Computer Engineering

Columbia University (continued)

per year); health care benefits also available. Financial award application deadline: 12/1; financial award applicants required to submit FAFSA. *Faculty research:* Signal and information processing, networking and communications, integrated circuits and systems, systems biology, micro devices, electromagnetics, plasma physics, photonics, computer engineering. *Unit head:* Dr. Keren Bergman, Professor and Department Chair, 212-854-2280, Fax: 212-854-0300, E-mail: bergman@ee.columbia.edu. *Application contact:* Elsa Sanchez, Academic Program Officer, 212-854-3104, Fax: 212-932-9421, E-mail: elsa@ee.columbia.edu.

See Display on page 364 and Close-Up on page 391.

Concordia University, School of Graduate Studies, Faculty of Engineering and Computer Science, Department of Electrical and Computer Engineering, Montréal, QC H3G 1M8, Canada. Offers M Eng, MA Sc, PhD. *Degree requirements:* For master's, thesis optional; for doctorate, comprehensive exam, thesis/dissertation. *Faculty research:* Computer communications and protocols, circuits and systems, graph theory, VLSI systems, microelectronics.

Cornell University, Graduate School, Graduate Fields of Engineering, Field of Electrical and Computer Engineering, Ithaca, NY 14853. Offers computer engineering (M Eng, PhD); electrical engineering (M Eng, PhD); electrical systems (M Eng, PhD); electrophysics (M Eng, PhD). *Faculty:* 58 full-time (4 women). *Students:* 247 full-time (47 women); includes 1 Black or African American, non-Hispanic/Latino; 27 Asian, non-Hispanic/Latino; 9 Hispanic/Latino, 155 international. Average age 24. 935 applicants, 33% accepted, 135 enrolled. In 2010, 106 master's, 25 doctorates awarded. *Degree requirements:* For doctorate, comprehensive exam, thesis/dissertation. *Entrance requirements:* For master's, GRE General Test, 2 letters of recommendation; for doctorate, GRE General Test, 3 letters of recommendation. Additional exam requirements/recommendations for international students: Required—TOEFL (minimum score 600 paper-based; 250 computer-based; 77 iBT). *Application deadline:* For fall admission, 1/15 priority date for domestic students. Application fee: $70. Electronic applications accepted. *Expenses:* Tuition: Full-time $29,500. Required fees: $76. Tuition and fees vary according to degree level and program. *Financial support:* In 2010–11, 150 students received support, including 46 fellowships with full tuition reimbursements available, 94 research assistantships with full tuition reimbursements available, 18 teaching assistantships with full tuition reimbursements available; institutionally sponsored loans, scholarships/grants, health care benefits, tuition waivers (full and partial), and unspecified assistantships also available. Financial award applicants required to submit FAFSA. *Faculty research:* Communications, information theory, signal processing and power control, computer engineering, microelectromechanical systems and nanotechnology. *Unit head:* Director of Graduate Studies, 607-255-4304. *Application contact:* Graduate Field Assistant, 607-255-4304, E-mail: meng@ece.cornell.edu.

Dalhousie University, Faculty of Engineering, Department of Electrical and Computer Engineering, Halifax, NS B3J 1Z1, Canada. Offers M Eng, MA Sc, PhD. *Degree requirements:* For master's, thesis; for doctorate, thesis/dissertation. *Entrance requirements:* Additional exam requirements/recommendations for international students: Required—TOEFL, IELTS, CANTEST, CAEL, or Michigan English Language Assessment Battery. Electronic applications accepted. *Faculty research:* Communications, computer engineering, power engineering, electronics, systems engineering.

Dartmouth College, Thayer School of Engineering, Program in Computer Engineering, Hanover, NH 03755. Offers MS, PhD. *Degree requirements:* For master's, thesis; for doctorate, thesis/dissertation, candidacy oral exam. *Entrance requirements:* For master's and doctorate, GRE General Test. *Application deadline:* For fall admission, 1/1 priority date for domestic students. Application fee: $45. *Financial support:* Fellowships, research assistantships, teaching assistantships, career-related internships or fieldwork, Federal Work-Study, institutionally sponsored loans, and tuition waivers (full and partial) available. Financial award application deadline: 1/15. *Faculty research:* Analog VLSI, electromagnetic fields and waves, electronic instrumentation, microelectromechanical systems, optics, lasers and non-linear optics, power electronics and integrated power converters, networking, parallel and distributed computing, simulation, VLSI design and testing, wireless networking. Total annual research expenditures: $4 million. *Unit head:* Dr. Joseph J. Helbie, Dean, 603-646-2238, Fax: 603-646-2580, E-mail: joseph.j.helbie@dartmouth.edu. *Application contact:* Candace S. Potter, Graduate Admissions Administrator, 603-646-3844, Fax: 603-646-1620, E-mail: candace.potter@dartmouth.edu.

Drexel University, College of Engineering, Department of Electrical and Computer Engineering, Program in Computer Engineering, Philadelphia, PA 19104-2875. Offers MS. Part-time and evening/weekend programs available. *Degree requirements:* For master's, thesis (for some programs). Electronic applications accepted.

Duke University, Graduate School, Pratt School of Engineering, Department of Electrical and Computer Engineering, Durham, NC 27708. Offers MS, PhD, JD/MS. Part-time programs available. *Faculty:* 38 full-time. *Students:* 162 full-time (39 women); includes 4 Black or African American, non-Hispanic/Latino; 6 Asian, non-Hispanic/Latino; 2 Hispanic/Latino, 107 international. 554 applicants, 30% accepted, 41 enrolled. In 2010, 25 master's, 16 doctorates awarded. Terminal master's awarded for partial completion of doctoral program. *Degree requirements:* For doctorate, thesis/dissertation. *Entrance requirements:* For master's and doctorate, GRE General Test. Additional exam requirements/recommendations for international students: Required—TOEFL (minimum score 550 paper-based; 213 computer-based; 83 iBT), IELTS (minimum score 7). *Application deadline:* For fall admission, 12/8 priority date for domestic and international students; for spring admission, 11/1 for domestic students. Application fee: $75. Electronic applications accepted. *Financial support:* Fellowships, research assistantships, Federal Work-Study available. Financial award application deadline: 12/8. *Unit head:* Steve Cummer, Director of Graduate Studies, 919-660-5245, Fax: 919-660-5293, E-mail: samantha@ee.duke.edu. *Application contact:* Elizabeth Hutton, Associate Dean for Enrollment Services, 919-684-3913, Fax: 919-684-2277, E-mail: grad-admissions@duke.edu.

See Display on page 366 and Close-Up on page 393.

Duke University, Graduate School, Pratt School of Engineering, Master of Engineering Program, Durham, NC 27708-0271. Offers biomedical engineering (M Eng); civil engineering (M Eng); electrical and computer engineering (M Eng); environmental engineering (M Eng); materials science and engineering (M Eng); mechanical engineering (M Eng); photonics and optical sciences (M Eng). Part-time programs available. *Faculty:* 123 full-time, 1 part-time/adjunct. *Students:* 9 full-time (4 women); includes 2 minority (both Asian, non-Hispanic/Latino), 3 international. Average age 24. *Entrance requirements:* For master's, GRE General Test, resume, 3 letters of recommendation, statement of purpose. Additional exam requirements/recommendations for international students: Required—TOEFL. *Application deadline:* For fall admission, 6/15 for domestic students, 2/15 for international students; for spring admission, 11/1 for domestic students, 9/1 for international students. Application fee: $75. *Financial support:* Merit scholarships/grants available. *Unit head:* Dr. Bradley A. Fox, Executive Director, 919-660-5455, Fax: 919-660-5456. *Application contact:* Erin Degerman, Admissions Coordinator, 919-668-6789, Fax: 919-660-5456, E-mail: erin.degerman@duke.edu.

École Polytechnique de Montréal, Graduate Programs, Department of Electrical and Computer Engineering, Montréal, QC H3C 3A7, Canada. Offers automation (M Eng, M Sc A, PhD); computer science (M Eng, M Sc A, PhD); electrical engineering (DESS); electrotechnology (M Eng, M Sc A, PhD); microelectronics (M Eng, M Sc A, PhD); microwave technology (M Eng, M Sc A, PhD). Part-time and evening/weekend programs available. *Degree requirements:* For master's, one foreign language, thesis; for doctorate, one foreign language, thesis/dissertation. *Entrance requirements:* For master's, minimum GPA of 2.75; for doctorate, minimum GPA of 3.0. *Faculty research:* Microwaves, telecommunications, software engineering.

Embry-Riddle Aeronautical University–Daytona, Daytona Beach Campus Graduate Program, Department of Computer and Software Engineering, Daytona Beach, FL 32114-3900. Offers electrical/computer engineering (MSECE); software engineering (MSE). Part-time and evening/weekend programs available. *Faculty:* 6 full-time (0 women), 2 part-time/adjunct (1 woman). *Students:* 31 full-time (4 women), 3 part-time (0 women); includes 3 minority (1 Asian, non-Hispanic/Latino; 2 Hispanic/Latino), 10 international. Average age 26. 22 applicants, 64% accepted, 9 enrolled. In 2010, 10 master's awarded. *Degree requirements:* For master's, thesis or alternative. *Entrance requirements:* For master's, minimum GPA of 3.0 in senior year, 2.5 overall; course work in computer science. Additional exam requirements/recommendations for international students: Required—TOEFL (minimum score 550 paper-based; 213 computer-based; 79 iBT). *Application deadline:* For fall admission, 8/1 priority date for domestic students; for spring admission, 12/1 priority date for domestic students. Applications are processed on a rolling basis. Application fee: $50. *Expenses:* Tuition: Full-time $14,040; part-time $1170 per credit hour. *Financial support:* In 2010–11, 20 students received support, including 2 research assistantships with full and partial tuition reimbursements available (averaging $5,384 per year), 7 teaching assistantships with full and partial tuition reimbursements available (averaging $5,667 per year); career-related internships or fieldwork, Federal Work-Study, and unspecified assistantships also available. Financial award application deadline: 4/15; financial award applicants required to submit FAFSA. *Faculty research:* Evaluation of residual strength of Beechcraft Bonanza spar carry-through with fatigue cracks, Swift Fuel PA44-180, Scramjet engine simulation, marine turbines, wireless sensors for aircraft, bistatic radar, blind signal separation in dynamic environments, EcoCAR IDEA, FAA nextgen Task K demonstration of flight data object planning, NOAA UAS for in-situ tropical cyclone sensing, aeroelastic gust-airfoil interaction numerical studies. *Unit head:* Dr. Farahzad Behi, Program Coordinator, 386-226-6454, E-mail: farahzad.behi@erau.edu. *Application contact:* Keith Deaton, Director, International and Graduate Admissions, 800-388-3728, Fax: 386-226-7070, E-mail: graduate.admissions@erau.edu.

Fairfield University, School of Engineering, Fairfield, CT 06824-5195. Offers electrical and computer engineering (MS); management of technology (MS); mechanical engineering (MS); software engineering (MS). Part-time and evening/weekend programs available. *Faculty:* 8 full-time (1 woman), 11 part-time/adjunct (0 women). *Students:* 31 full-time (12 women), 98 part-time (20 women); includes 28 minority (5 Black or African American, non-Hispanic/Latino; 17 Asian, non-Hispanic/Latino; 4 Hispanic/Latino; 1 Native Hawaiian or other Pacific Islander, non-Hispanic/Latino; 1 Two or more races, non-Hispanic/Latino), 26 international. Average age 35. 120 applicants, 55% accepted, 15 enrolled. In 2010, 52 master's awarded. *Degree requirements:* For master's, thesis, capstone course. *Entrance requirements:* For master's, interview, minimum GPA of 2.8, resume, 2 recommendations. Additional exam requirements/recommendations for international students: Required—TOEFL (minimum score 550 paper-based; 213 computer-based; 80 iBT). *Application deadline:* For fall admission, 5/15 for international students; for spring admission, 10/15 for international students. Applications are processed on a rolling basis. Application fee: $60. Electronic applications accepted. *Expenses:* Contact institution. *Financial support:* In 2010–11, 25 students received support. Unspecified assistantships available. Financial award applicants required to submit FAFSA. *Faculty research:* Vehicle dynamics, image processing, multimedia in instruction, thermal packaging, character recognition, photovoltaics and nanotechnology, Web technology. *Unit head:* Dr. Jack Beal, Dean, 203-254-4000 Ext. 4147, Fax: 203-254-4013, E-mail: jwbeal@fairfield.edu. *Application contact:* Marianne Gumpper, Director of Graduate and Continuing Studies Admissions, 203-254-4184, Fax: 203-254-4073, E-mail: gradadmis@fairfield.edu.

Fairleigh Dickinson University, Metropolitan Campus, University College: Arts, Sciences, and Professional Studies, School of Computer Sciences and Engineering, Program in Computer Engineering, Teaneck, NJ 07666-1914. Offers MS. *Students:* 8 full-time (5 women), 1 part-time (0 women), 8 international. Average age 23. 21 applicants, 48% accepted, 1 enrolled. In 2010, 2 master's awarded. *Application deadline:* Applications are processed on a rolling basis. Application fee: $40. *Application contact:* Susan Brooman, University Director of Graduate Admissions, 201-692-2554, Fax: 201-692-2560, E-mail: globaleducation@fdu.edu.

Florida Atlantic University, College of Engineering and Computer Science, Department of Computer and Electrical Engineering and Computer Science, Boca Raton, FL 33431-0991. Offers computer engineering (MS, PhD); computer science (MS, PhD); electrical engineering (MS, PhD). Part-time and evening/weekend programs available. *Faculty:* 35 full-time (6 women), 3 part-time/adjunct (1 woman). *Students:* 89 full-time (19 women), 101 part-time (25 women); includes 69 minority (14 Black or African American, non-Hispanic/Latino; 22 Asian, non-Hispanic/Latino; 32 Hispanic/Latino; 1 Two or more races, non-Hispanic/Latino), 55 international. Average age 32. 128 applicants, 48% accepted, 45 enrolled. In 2010, 41 master's, 8 doctorates awarded. Terminal master's awarded for partial completion of doctoral program. *Degree requirements:* For master's, thesis optional; for doctorate, thesis/dissertation, qualifying exam. *Entrance requirements:* For master's, GRE General Test, minimum GPA of 3.0; for doctorate, GRE General Test, master's degree, minimum GPA of 3.5. Additional exam requirements/recommendations for international students: Required—TOEFL. *Application deadline:* For fall admission, 7/1 priority date for domestic students, 2/15 for international students; for spring admission, 11/1 for domestic students, 7/15 for international students. Applications are processed on a rolling basis. Application fee: $30. *Expenses:* Tuition, area resident: Part-time $319.96 per credit. Tuition, state resident: part-time $319.96 per credit. Tuition, nonresident: part-time $926.42 per credit. *Financial support:* Fellowships, research assistantships with partial tuition reimbursements, teaching assistantships with full tuition reimbursements, career-related internships or fieldwork and Federal Work-Study available. Support available to part-time students. Financial award application deadline: 4/1; financial award applicants required to submit FAFSA. *Faculty research:* VLSI and neural networks, communication networks, software engineering, computer architecture, multimedia and video processing. *Unit head:* Dr. Borko Furht, Chairman, 561-297-3855, Fax: 561-297-2800. *Application contact:* Dr. Borko Furht, Chairman, 561-297-3855, Fax: 561-297-2800.

Florida Institute of Technology, Graduate Programs, College of Engineering, Electrical and Computer Engineering Department, Melbourne, FL 32901-6975. Offers computer engineering (MS, PhD); electrical engineering (MS, PhD). Part-time and evening/weekend programs available. *Faculty:* 10 full-time (1 woman), 2 part-time/adjunct (0 women). *Students:* 88 full-time (20 women), 38 part-time (5 women); includes 8 minority (3 Black or African American, non-Hispanic/Latino; 3 Asian, non-Hispanic/Latino; 2 Hispanic/Latino), 91 international. Average age 28. 314 applicants, 54% accepted, 37 enrolled. In 2010, 21 master's, 8 doctorates awarded. *Degree requirements:* For master's, comprehensive exam (for some programs), thesis optional, final program exam, faculty-supervised specialized research; for doctorate, comprehensive exam (for some programs), thesis/dissertation, complete program of significant original research. *Entrance requirements:* For master's, GRE, minimum GPA of 3.0, bachelor's degree from an ABET-accredited program; for doctorate, 3 letters of recommendation, resume, minimum GPA of 3.2, statement of objectives, on campus interview (highly recommended). Additional exam requirements/recommendations for international students: Required—TOEFL (minimum score 550 paper-based; 213 computer-based; 79 iBT). *Application deadline:* For fall admission, 4/1 for international students; for spring admission, 9/30 for international students. Applications are processed on a rolling basis. Application fee: $50. Electronic applications accepted. *Expenses:* Tuition: Part-time $1040 per credit hour. Tuition and fees vary according to campus/location. *Financial support:* In 2010–11, 4 research assistantships with full and partial tuition reimbursements (averaging $5,250 per year), 7 teaching assistantships with full and partial tuition reimbursements (averaging $3,703 per year) were awarded; career-related internships or fieldwork, institutionally sponsored loans, tuition waivers (partial), unspecified assistantships, and tuition remissions also available. Support available to part-time students. Financial award application deadline: 3/1; financial award applicants required to submit FAFSA. *Faculty research:* Electro-optics, electromagnetics, microelectronics, communications, computer architecture, neural networks. Total annual research expenditures: $405,569. *Unit head:* Dr. Samuel P. Kozaitis, Department Head, 321-674-8060, Fax: 321-674-8192, E-mail: kozaitis@fit.edu. *Application contact:* Cheryl A. Brown, Associate Director of Graduate Admissions, 321-674-7581, Fax: 321-723-9468, E-mail: cbrown@fit.edu.

Florida International University, College of Engineering and Computing, Department of Electrical and Computer Engineering, Program in Computer Engineering, Miami, FL 33175.

Offers MS. Part-time and evening/weekend programs available. *Students:* 4 full-time (0 women), 4 part-time (1 woman); includes 1 Black or African American, non-Hispanic/Latino; 1 Asian, non-Hispanic/Latino; 3 Hispanic/Latino, 2 international. Average age 25. 40 applicants, 15% accepted, 5 enrolled. In 2010, 3 master's awarded. *Degree requirements:* For master's, thesis optional. *Entrance requirements:* For master's, minimum GPA of 3.0, resume, 3 letters of recommendation, letter of intent. Additional exam requirements/recommendations for international students: Required—TOEFL (minimum score 550 paper-based; 80 iBT). *Application deadline:* For fall admission, 6/1 for domestic students, 4/1 for international students; for spring admission, 10/1 for domestic students, 9/1 for international students. Applications are processed on a rolling basis. Application fee: $30. Electronic applications accepted. *Financial support:* Institutionally sponsored loans and scholarships/grants available. Financial award application deadline: 3/1; financial award applicants required to submit FAFSA. *Unit head:* Dr. Kang Yen, Chair, Electrical and Computer Engineering Department, 305-348-3037, Fax: 305-348-3707, E-mail: yenk@fiu.edu. *Application contact:* Maria Parrilla, Graduate Admissions Assistant, 305-348-1890, Fax: 305-348-6142, E-mail: grad_eng@fiu.edu.

George Mason University, Volgenau School of Engineering, Department of Electrical and Computer Engineering, Fairfax, VA 22030. Offers advanced networking protocols for telecommunications (Certificate); communications and networking (Certificate); computer engineering (MS); computer forensics (MS); electrical and computer engineering (PhD); electrical engineering (MS); network technology and applications (Certificate); networks, system integration and testing (Certificate); signal processing (Certificate); telecom systems modeling (Certificate); telecommunications (MS); telecommunications forensics and security (Certificate); VLSI design/manufacturing (Certificate); wireless communication (Certificate). MS program offered jointly with Old Dominion University, University of Virginia, Virginia Commonwealth University, and Virginia Polytechnic Institute and State University. Part-time and evening/weekend programs available. *Faculty:* 33 full-time (4 women), 39 part-time/adjunct (4 women). *Students:* 106 full-time (27 women), 336 part-time (64 women); includes 24 Black or African American, non-Hispanic/Latino; 1 American Indian or Alaska Native, non-Hispanic/Latino; 54 Asian, non-Hispanic/Latino; 20 Hispanic/Latino; 1 Two or more races, non-Hispanic/Latino, 172 international. Average age 30. 506 applicants, 71% accepted, 142 enrolled. In 2010, 145 master's, 3 doctorates, 61 other advanced degrees awarded. *Degree requirements:* For master's, thesis optional; for doctorate, comprehensive exam, thesis or scholarly paper. *Entrance requirements:* For master's, GMAT or GRE General Test, letters of recommendation, resume; for doctorate, GRE/GMAT, personal goal statement, 2 transcripts, letter of recommendation. Additional exam requirements/recommendations for international students: Required—TOEFL (minimum score 570 paper-based; 230 computer-based; 88 iBT). *Application deadline:* For fall admission, 7/15 priority date for domestic and international students; for spring admission, 12/1 for domestic and international students. Applications are processed on a rolling basis. Application fee: $100. Electronic applications accepted. *Expenses:* Tuition, state resident: full-time $8192; part-time $440 per credit hour. Tuition, nonresident: full-time $22,952; part-time $1055 per credit hour. Required fees: $2364; $99 per credit hour. *Financial support:* In 2010–11, 74 students received support, including 2 fellowships with full tuition reimbursements available (averaging $18,000 per year), 26 research assistantships with full and partial tuition reimbursements available (averaging $14,648 per year), 46 teaching assistantships with full and partial tuition reimbursements available (averaging $10,946 per year); career-related internships or fieldwork, Federal Work-Study, scholarships/grants, unspecified assistantships, and health care benefits (full-time research or teaching assistantship recipients) also available. Financial award application deadline: 3/1; financial award applicants required to submit FAFSA. *Faculty research:* Communication networks, signal processing, system failure diagnosis, multiprocessors, material processing using microwave energy. Total annual research expenditures: $3.4 million. *Unit head:* Dr. Andre Manitius, Chairperson, 703-993-1569, Fax: 703-993-1601, E-mail: ece@gmu.edu. *Application contact:* Jessica Skinner, Associate Dean, 703-993-1569, E-mail: jskinne6@gmu.edu.

The George Washington University, School of Engineering and Applied Science, Department of Electrical and Computer Engineering, Washington, DC 20052. Offers electrical and computer engineering (MS, D Sc); telecommunication and computers (MS). Part-time and evening/weekend programs available. *Faculty:* 24 full-time (2 women), 9 part-time/adjunct (0 women). *Students:* 101 full-time (19 women), 114 part-time (20 women); includes 12 Black or African American, non-Hispanic/Latino; 23 Asian, non-Hispanic/Latino; 2 Hispanic/Latino; 1 Native Hawaiian or other Pacific Islander, non-Hispanic/Latino, 112 international. Average age 29. 339 applicants, 81% accepted, 69 enrolled. In 2010, 65 master's, 14 doctorates awarded. *Degree requirements:* For master's, thesis optional; for doctorate, comprehensive exam, thesis/dissertation, dissertation defense, qualifying exam. *Entrance requirements:* For master's, appropriate bachelor's degree, minimum GPA of 3.0; for doctorate, appropriate bachelor's or master's degree, minimum GPA of 3.3, GRE if highest earned degree is BS. Additional exam requirements/recommendations for international students: Required—TOEFL or The George Washington University English as a Foreign Language Test. *Application deadline:* For fall admission, 3/1 priority date for domestic students; for spring admission, 10/1 for domestic students. Applications are processed on a rolling basis. Application fee: $75. *Financial support:* In 2010–11, 39 students received support; fellowships with tuition reimbursements available, research assistantships, teaching assistantships with tuition reimbursements available, career-related internships or fieldwork and institutionally sponsored loans available. Financial award application deadline: 3/1; financial award applicants required to submit FAFSA. *Faculty research:* Computer graphics, multimedia systems. *Unit head:* Can E. Korman, Chair, 202-994-4952, E-mail: korman@gwu.edu. *Application contact:* Adina Lav, Marketing, Recruiting and Admissions, 202-994-5827, Fax: 202-994-0909, E-mail: engineering@gwu.edu.

Georgia Institute of Technology, Graduate Studies and Research, College of Computing, Atlanta, GA 30332-0001. Offers algorithms, combinatorics, and optimization (PhD); computational science and engineering (MS, PhD); computer science (MS, MSCS, PhD); human computer interaction (MSHCI); human-centered computing (PhD); information security (MS). Part-time programs available. Postbaccalaureate distance learning degree programs offered. Terminal master's awarded for partial completion of doctoral program. *Degree requirements:* For master's, thesis optional; for doctorate, comprehensive exam, thesis/dissertation. *Entrance requirements:* For master's, GRE General Test, GRE Subject Test, minimum GPA of 3.0; for doctorate, GRE General Test, GRE Subject Test, minimum GPA of 3.3. Additional exam requirements/recommendations for international students: Required—TOEFL. *Faculty research:* Computer systems, graphics, intelligent systems and artificial intelligence, networks and telecommunications, software engineering.

Georgia Institute of Technology, Graduate Studies and Research, College of Engineering, School of Electrical and Computer Engineering, Atlanta, GA 30332-0001. Offers MS, MSEE, PhD. Part-time programs available. Postbaccalaureate distance learning degree programs offered (minimal on-campus study). Terminal master's awarded for partial completion of doctoral program. *Degree requirements:* For master's, thesis optional; for doctorate, thesis/dissertation. *Entrance requirements:* For master's, GRE General Test, minimum GPA of 3.0; for doctorate, GRE General Test, minimum GPA of 3.5. Additional exam requirements/recommendations for international students: Required—TOEFL. *Faculty research:* Telecommunications, computer systems, microelectronics, optical engineering, digital signal processing.

Grand Valley State University, Padnos College of Engineering and Computing, School of Engineering, Allendale, MI 49401-9403. Offers electrical and computer engineering (MSE); manufacturing operations (MSE); mechanical engineering (MSE); product design and manufacturing engineering (MSE). Part-time and evening/weekend programs available. *Degree requirements:* For master's, project or thesis. *Entrance requirements:* For master's, engineering degree, minimum GPA of 3.0. Additional exam requirements/recommendations for international students: Required—TOEFL. Electronic applications accepted. *Faculty research:* Digital signal processing, computer aided design, computer aided manufacturing, manufacturing simulation, biomechanics, product design.

Illinois Institute of Technology, Graduate College, Armour College of Engineering, Department of Electrical and Computer Engineering, Chicago, IL 60616-3793. Offers biomedical imaging and signals (MBMI); computer engineering (MS, PhD); electrical and computer engineering (MECE); electrical engineering (MS, PhD); electricity markets (MEM); network engineering (MNE); power engineering (MPE); telecommunications and software engineering (MTSE); VLSI and microelectronics (MVM). Part-time and evening/weekend programs available. Postbaccalaureate distance learning degree programs offered (minimal on-campus study). *Faculty:* 26 full-time (3 women), 2 part-time/adjunct (0 women). *Students:* 456 full-time (77 women), 140 part-time (17 women); includes 25 minority (4 Black or African American, non-Hispanic/Latino; 15 Asian, non-Hispanic/Latino; 4 Hispanic/Latino; 2 Two or more races, non-Hispanic/Latino), 488 international. Average age 26. 1,407 applicants, 68% accepted, 217 enrolled. In 2010, 214 master's, 17 doctorates awarded. Terminal master's awarded for partial completion of doctoral program. *Degree requirements:* For master's, comprehensive exam (for some programs), thesis (for some programs); for doctorate, comprehensive exam, thesis/dissertation. *Entrance requirements:* For master's and doctorate, GRE General Test (minimum score 1100 Quantitative and Verbal, 3.5 Analytical Writing), minimum undergraduate GPA of 3.0. Additional exam requirements/recommendations for international students: Required—TOEFL (minimum score 523 paper-based; 70 iBT); Recommended—IELTS (minimum score 5.5). *Application deadline:* For fall admission, 5/1 for domestic and international students; for spring admission, 10/15 for domestic and international students. Applications are processed on a rolling basis. Application fee: $50. Electronic applications accepted. *Expenses:* Tuition: Full-time $18,576; part-time $1032 per credit hour. Required fees: $583 per semester. One-time fee: $150. Tuition and fees vary according to program and student level. *Financial support:* In 2010–11, 1 fellowship with full and partial tuition reimbursement (averaging $1,090 per year), 52 research assistantships with full and partial tuition reimbursements (averaging $9,530 per year), 24 teaching assistantships with full and partial tuition reimbursements (averaging $9,092 per year) were awarded; career-related internships or fieldwork, Federal Work-Study, institutionally sponsored loans, scholarships/grants, health care benefits, tuition waivers (full), and unspecified assistantships also available. Support available to part-time students. Financial award applicants required to submit FAFSA. *Faculty research:* Communication systems, computer systems and micro-electronics, electromagnetics and electronics, power and control systems, signal and image processing. Total annual research expenditures: $5.6 million. *Unit head:* Dr. Geoffrey Williamson, Interim Chair, 312-567-5960, Fax: 312-567-8976, E-mail: williamson@iit.edu. *Application contact:* Deborah Gibson, Director, Graduate Admission, 866-472-3448, Fax: 312-567-3138, E-mail: inquiry.grad@iit.edu.

Indiana State University, College of Graduate and Professional Studies, College of Technology, Department of Electronics and Computer Technology, Terre Haute, IN 47809. Offers MS. *Degree requirements:* For master's, thesis or alternative. *Entrance requirements:* For master's, bachelor's degree in industrial technology or related field. Additional exam requirements/recommendations for international students: Required—TOEFL. Electronic applications accepted.

Indiana University–Purdue University Fort Wayne, College of Engineering, Technology, and Computer Science, Department of Engineering, Fort Wayne, IN 46805-1499. Offers computer engineering (MS); electrical engineering (MS); mechanical engineering (MS); systems engineering (MS). Part-time programs available. *Faculty:* 18 full-time (3 women). *Students:* 7 full-time (0 women), 31 part-time (7 women); includes 4 minority (1 Black or African American, non-Hispanic/Latino; 2 Asian, non-Hispanic/Latino; 1 Hispanic/Latino), 4 international. Average age 28. 21 applicants, 95% accepted, 18 enrolled. In 2010, 9 master's awarded. *Entrance requirements:* For master's, minimum GPA of 3.0, bachelor's degree in engineering discipline. Additional exam requirements/recommendations for international students: Required—TOEFL (minimum score 550 paper-based; 213 computer-based; 77 iBT); Recommended—TWE. *Application deadline:* For fall admission, 7/15 priority date for domestic students, 5/15 priority date for international students; for spring admission, 12/1 priority date for domestic students, 10/15 priority date for international students. Applications are processed on a rolling basis. Application fee: $55 ($60 for international students). Electronic applications accepted. *Expenses:* Tuition, state resident: full-time $4824; part-time $268 per credit. Tuition, nonresident: full-time $11,625; part-time $646 per credit. Required fees: $555; $30.85 per credit. Tuition and fees vary according to course load. *Financial support:* In 2010–11, 5 research assistantships with partial tuition reimbursements (averaging $12,740 per year), 3 teaching assistantships with partial tuition reimbursements (averaging $12,740 per year) were awarded. Financial award application deadline: 3/1; financial award applicants required to submit FAFSA. *Faculty research:* Worm-scanning strategies, measuring the acceleration of gravity. Total annual research expenditures: $129,186. *Unit head:* Dr. Donald Mueller, Chair, 260-481-5707, Fax: 260-481-6281, E-mail: mueller@engr.ipfw.edu. *Application contact:* Dr. Donald Mueller, Chair, 260-481-5707, Fax: 260-481-6281, E-mail: mueller@engr.ipfw.edu.

Indiana University–Purdue University Indianapolis, School of Engineering and Technology, Department of Electrical Engineering, Indianapolis, IN 46202-2896. Offers biomedical engineering (MS, PhD); electrical and computer engineering (MS, MSECE, PhD), including biomedical engineering (MSECE), control and automation (MSECE), signal processing (MSECE); engineering (interdisciplinary) (MSE). *Students:* 40 full-time (13 women), 35 part-time (7 women); includes 7 minority (1 Black or African American, non-Hispanic/Latino; 1 Asian, non-Hispanic/Latino; 3 Hispanic/Latino; 2 Two or more races, non-Hispanic/Latino), 45 international. Average age 27. 153 applicants, 53% accepted, 42 enrolled. In 2010, 37 master's awarded. Application fee: $55 ($65 for international students). *Unit head:* Yaobin Chen, Unit Head, 317-274-4032, Fax: 317-274-4493. *Application contact:* Valerie Diemer, Graduate Program, 317-278-4960, Fax: 317-278-1671, E-mail: grad@engr.iupui.edu.

Instituto Tecnológico y de Estudios Superiores de Monterrey, Campus Chihuahua, Graduate Programs, Chihuahua, Mexico. Offers computer systems engineering (Ingeniero); electrical engineering (Ingeniero); electromechanical engineering (Ingeniero); electronic engineering (Ingeniero); engineering administration (MEA); industrial engineering (MIE, Ingeniero); international trade (MIT); mechanical engineering (Ingeniero).

International Technological University, Program in Computer Engineering, Santa Clara, CA 95050. Offers MSCE. *Degree requirements:* For master's, thesis or alternative. *Entrance requirements:* For master's, 3 semesters of calculus, minimum GPA of 2.5. Additional exam requirements/recommendations for international students: Required—TOEFL. *Faculty research:* Computer networking management, digital systems, embedded system design.

Iowa State University of Science and Technology, Graduate College, College of Engineering, Department of Electrical and Computer Engineering, Ames, IA 50011. Offers computer engineering (M Eng, MS, PhD); electrical engineering (M Eng, MS, PhD). *Faculty:* 65 full-time (6 women), 4 part-time/adjunct (2 women). *Students:* 246 full-time (40 women), 170 part-time (32 women); includes 9 Black or African American, non-Hispanic/Latino; 14 Asian, non-Hispanic/Latino; 5 Hispanic/Latino, 256 international. 1,198 applicants, 9% accepted, 74 enrolled. In 2010, 58 master's, 15 doctorates awarded. *Degree requirements:* For master's, thesis or alternative; for doctorate, thesis/dissertation. *Entrance requirements:* For master's and doctorate, GRE General Test. Additional exam requirements/recommendations for international students: Required—TOEFL (minimum score 570 paper-based; 79 iBT), IELTS (minimum score 6.5). *Application deadline:* For fall admission, 1/15 priority date for domestic and international students; for spring admission, 9/15 for domestic and international students. Application fee: $40 ($90 for international students). Electronic applications accepted. *Financial support:* In 2010–11, 147 research assistantships with full and partial tuition reimbursements (averaging $10,227 per year), 40 teaching assistantships with full and partial tuition reimbursements (averaging $7,506 per year) were awarded; fellowships, scholarships/grants, health care benefits, and unspecified assistantships also available. *Unit head:* Dr. Arun Somani, Chair, 515-294-2664, E-mail: ecegrad@ee.iastate.edu. *Application contact:* Dr. Akhilesh Tyagi, Director of Graduate Education, 515-294-2667, E-mail: ecegrad@iastate.edu.

The Johns Hopkins University, Engineering for Professionals, Part-time Program in Electrical and Computer Engineering, Baltimore, MD 21218-2699. Offers MS, Post-Master's Certificate. Part-time and evening/weekend programs available. *Faculty:* 40 part-time/adjunct (1 woman). *Students:* 17 full-time (4 women), 324 part-time (49 women); includes 108 minority (31 Black

Computer Engineering

The Johns Hopkins University (continued)
or African American, non-Hispanic/Latino; 46 Asian, non-Hispanic/Latino; 22 Hispanic/Latino; 9 Two or more races, non-Hispanic/Latino), 1 international. Average age 28. 112 applicants, 92% accepted, 97 enrolled. In 2010, 101 master's, 1 other advanced degree awarded. *Application deadline:* Applications are processed on a rolling basis. Application fee: $75. Electronic applications accepted. *Financial support:* Institutionally sponsored loans available. *Unit head:* Dr. Brian Jennison, Program Chair, 443-778-6421, E-mail: brian.jennison@jhuapl.edu. *Application contact:* Priyanka Dwivedi, Admissions Manager, 410-516-2300, Fax: 410-579-8049, E-mail: pdwived1@jhu.edu.

The Johns Hopkins University, G. W. C. Whiting School of Engineering, Department of Electrical and Computer Engineering, Baltimore, MD 21218-2699. Offers MSE, PhD. *Faculty:* 18 full-time (3 women), 9 part-time/adjunct (0 women). *Students:* 122 full-time (23 women), 5 part-time (0 women); includes 10 minority (3 Black or African American, non-Hispanic/Latino; 5 Asian, non-Hispanic/Latino; 1 Hispanic/Latino; 1 Two or more races, non-Hispanic/Latino), 85 international. Average age 23. 345 applicants, 20% accepted, 22 enrolled. In 2010, 26 master's, 6 doctorates awarded. Terminal master's awarded for partial completion of doctoral program. *Degree requirements:* For master's, thesis optional; for doctorate, thesis/dissertation, qualifying and oral exams, seminar. *Entrance requirements:* For master's and doctorate, GRE General Test, transcripts, 3 letters of recommendation, statement of purpose. Additional exam requirements/recommendations for international students: Required—TOEFL (minimum score 600 paper-based; 250 computer-based; 100 iBT). *Application deadline:* For fall admission, 1/7 for domestic and international students. Application fee: $75. Electronic applications accepted. *Financial support:* In 2010–11, 13 fellowships with full tuition reimbursements (averaging $20,700 per year), 65 research assistantships with full tuition reimbursements (averaging $26,400 per year), 4 teaching assistantships with full tuition reimbursements (averaging $20,700 per year) were awarded; career-related internships or fieldwork, Federal Work-Study, institutionally sponsored loans, scholarships/grants, health care benefits, tuition waivers (partial), and unspecified assistantships also available. Financial award application deadline: 1/15. *Faculty research:* Computer engineering, systems and control, language and speech processing, photonics and optoelectronics, signal and image processing. Total annual research expenditures: $2.6 million. *Unit head:* Dr. Jin U. Kang, Chair, 410-516-7031, Fax: 410-516-5566, E-mail: jkang@jhu.edu. *Application contact:* Debbie Race, Graduate Program Coordinator, 410-516-4808, Fax: 410-516-5566, E-mail: eceinfo@jhu.edu.

Lakehead University, Graduate Studies, Faculty of Engineering, Thunder Bay, ON P7B 5E1, Canada. Offers control engineering (M Sc Engr); electrical/computer engineering (M Sc Engr); environmental engineering (M Sc Engr). Part-time programs available. *Degree requirements:* For master's, thesis. *Entrance requirements:* For master's, bachelor's degree in chemical, electrical or mechanical engineering, minimum B average. Additional exam requirements/recommendations for international students: Required—TOEFL. *Faculty research:* Pulp and paper, adaptive/process control, robust/interactive learning control, vibration control.

Lawrence Technological University, College of Engineering, Southfield, MI 48075-1058. Offers architectural engineering (MS); automotive engineering (MS); civil engineering (MS); electrical and computer engineering (MS); engineering management (MEM); industrial engineering (MS); manufacturing systems (ME, DE); mechanical engineering (MS); mechatronic systems engineering (MS). Part-time and evening/weekend programs available. *Faculty:* 20 full-time (4 women), 12 part-time/adjunct (0 women). *Students:* 8 full-time (1 woman), 366 part-time (60 women); includes 29 Black or African American, non-Hispanic/Latino; 1 American Indian or Alaska Native, non-Hispanic/Latino; 36 Asian, non-Hispanic/Latino; 9 Hispanic/Latino; 4 Two or more races, non-Hispanic/Latino, 81 international. Average age 32. 398 applicants, 48% accepted, 87 enrolled. In 2010, 121 master's, 5 doctorates awarded. *Degree requirements:* For master's, thesis (for some programs). *Entrance requirements:* Additional exam requirements/recommendations for international students: Required—TOEFL (minimum score 550 paper-based; 213 computer-based; 79 iBT). *Application deadline:* For fall admission, 6/30 priority date for domestic students, 6/30 for international students; for spring admission, 11/15 priority date for domestic students, 11/15 for international students. Applications are processed on a rolling basis. Application fee: $50. Electronic applications accepted. *Financial support:* In 2010–11, 72 students received support. Federal Work-Study and institutionally sponsored loans available. Support available to part-time students. Financial award application deadline: 4/1; financial award applicants required to submit FAFSA. *Faculty research:* Advanced composite materials in bridges, strengthening existing bridges with carbon and glass fiber sheets, development of drive shafts using composite materials. *Unit head:* Dr. Nabil Grace, Interim Dean, 248-204-2500, Fax: 248-204-2509, E-mail: engrdean@ltu.edu. *Application contact:* Jane Rohrback, Director of Admissions, 248-204-3160, Fax: 248-204-2228, E-mail: admissions@ltu.edu.

Lehigh University, P.C. Rossin College of Engineering and Applied Science, Department of Computer Science and Engineering, Bethlehem, PA 18015. Offers computer engineering (M Eng, MS, PhD); computer science (M Eng, MS, PhD, MBA/E); MBA/E. Part-time programs available. *Faculty:* 15 full-time (2 women). *Students:* 52 full-time (10 women), 18 part-time (4 women); includes 2 minority (both Asian, non-Hispanic/Latino), 52 international. Average age 27. 271 applicants, 21% accepted, 20 enrolled. In 2010, 17 master's, 4 doctorates awarded. *Degree requirements:* For master's, oral presentation of thesis; for doctorate, thesis/dissertation, qualifying, general, and oral exams. *Entrance requirements:* For master's, GRE General Test, minimum GPA of 3.0; for doctorate, GRE General Test, minimum GPA of 3.5. Additional exam requirements/recommendations for international students: Required—TOEFL (minimum score 550 paper-based; 213 computer-based; 79 iBT). *Application deadline:* For fall admission, 4/1 for domestic and international students; for spring admission, 11/1 for domestic and international students. Applications are processed on a rolling basis. Application fee: $75. Electronic applications accepted. *Expenses:* Contact institution. *Financial support:* In 2010–11, 2 fellowships with full tuition reimbursements (averaging $17,460 per year), 6 research assistantships with full tuition reimbursements (averaging $17,460 per year), 4 teaching assistantships with full tuition reimbursements (averaging $18,360 per year) were awarded. Financial award application deadline: 1/15. *Faculty research:* Artificial intelligence, networking-pattern recognition, multimedia e-learning/data mining/Web search, mobile robotics, bioinformatics, computervision. Total annual research expenditures: $2.6 million. *Unit head:* Dr. Daniel P. Lopresti, Chairman, 610-758-5782, Fax: 610-758-4096, E-mail: dal9@lehigh.edu. *Application contact:* Judy Frenick, Graduate Coordinator, 610-758-3605, Fax: 610-758-4096, E-mail: jlf2@lehigh.edu.

Louisiana State University and Agricultural and Mechanical College, Graduate School, College of Engineering, Department of Electrical and Computer Engineering, Baton Rouge, LA 70803. Offers MSEE, PhD. *Faculty:* 27 full-time (1 woman). *Students:* 116 full-time (16 women), 7 part-time (1 woman); includes 3 Black or African American, non-Hispanic/Latino; 2 Asian, non-Hispanic/Latino; 2 Hispanic/Latino, 104 international. Average age 26. 229 applicants, 72% accepted, 38 enrolled. In 2010, 19 master's, 2 doctorates awarded. Terminal master's awarded for partial completion of doctoral program. *Degree requirements:* For master's, thesis optional; for doctorate, thesis/dissertation. *Entrance requirements:* For master's, GRE General Test, minimum GPA of 3.0; for doctorate, GRE General Test, minimum GPA of 3.5. Additional exam requirements/recommendations for international students: Required—TOEFL (minimum score 550 paper-based; 213 computer-based; 79 iBT) or IELTS (minimum score 6.5). *Application deadline:* For fall admission, 1/25 priority date for domestic students, 5/15 for international students; for spring admission, 10/15 for international students. Applications are processed on a rolling basis. Application fee: $50 ($70 for international students). Electronic applications accepted. *Financial support:* In 2010–11, 85 students received support, including 4 fellowships with full and partial tuition reimbursements available (averaging $19,864 per year), 49 research assistantships with full and partial tuition reimbursements available (averaging $13,617 per year), 28 teaching assistantships with full and partial tuition reimbursements available (averaging $13,619 per year); Federal Work-Study, institutionally sponsored loans, health care benefits, tuition waivers (full and partial), and unspecified assistantships also available. Financial award application deadline: 2/28; financial award applicants required to submit FAFSA. *Faculty research:* Computer engineering, electronics, control systems and signal processing, communications. Total annual research expenditures: $1.2 million. *Unit head:* Dr. Pratul Ajmera, Interim Chair, 225-578-5534, Fax: 225-578-5200, E-mail: ajmera@lsu.edu. *Application contact:* Dr. Guoxiang GuU, Graduate Adviser, 225-578-5534, Fax: 225-578-5200, E-mail: ggu@lsu.edu.

Manhattan College, Graduate Division, School of Engineering, Program in Computer Engineering, Riverdale, NY 10471. Offers MS. Part-time and evening/weekend programs available. *Faculty:* 8 full-time (1 woman), 1 part-time/adjunct (0 women). *Students:* 2 full-time (0 women), 1 part-time (0 women), 2 international. Average age 24. 8 applicants, 63% accepted, 1 enrolled. In 2010, 4 master's awarded. *Degree requirements:* For master's, thesis or alternative. *Entrance requirements:* For master's, GRE (recommended), minimum GPA of 3.0. Additional exam requirements/recommendations for international students: Required—TOEFL (minimum score 550 paper-based; 213 computer-based; 80 iBT), IELTS (minimum score 6). *Application deadline:* For fall admission, 8/10 priority date for domestic students, 8/10 for international students; for spring admission, 1/7 for domestic and international students. Applications are processed on a rolling basis. Application fee: $50. *Financial support:* Fellowships, research assistantships, teaching assistantships, career-related internships or fieldwork, Federal Work-Study, scholarships/grants, and tuition waivers (partial) available. Support available to part-time students. Financial award application deadline: 5/15. *Unit head:* Dr. Robert Mauro, Chairperson, 718-862-7153, Fax: 718-862-7162, E-mail: robert.mauro@manhattan.edu. *Application contact:* Coralie Gale, 718-862-7153, Fax: 718-862-7162, E-mail: coralie.gale@manhattan.edu.

Marquette University, Graduate School, College of Engineering, Department of Electrical and Computer Engineering, Milwaukee, WI 53201-1881. Offers digital signal processing (Certificate); electric machines,drives, and controls (Certificate); electrical and computer engineering (MS, PhD); microwaves and antennas (Certificate); sensors and smart systems (Certificate). Part-time and evening/weekend programs available. *Faculty:* 14 full-time (2 women), 5 part-time/adjunct (0 women). *Students:* 24 full-time (4 women), 27 part-time (5 women); includes 4 minority (2 Black or African American, non-Hispanic/Latino; 2 Asian, non-Hispanic/Latino), 26 international. Average age 27. 68 applicants, 60% accepted, 14 enrolled. In 2010, 5 master's awarded. Terminal master's awarded for partial completion of doctoral program. *Degree requirements:* For master's, comprehensive exam (for some programs), thesis optional; for doctorate, thesis/dissertation, dissertation defense, qualifying exam. *Entrance requirements:* For master's, GRE General Test (recommended), official transcripts from all current and previous colleges/universities except Marquette, three letters of recommendation; for doctorate, GRE General Test, minimum GPA of 3.0, official transcripts from all current and previous colleges/universities except Marquette, three letters of recommendation, statement of purpose, submission of any English-language publications authored by applicant (strongly recommended). Additional exam requirements/recommendations for international students: Required—TOEFL (minimum score 530 paper-based; 78 computer-based). *Application deadline:* For fall admission, 7/15 priority date for domestic students; for spring admission, 11/15 for domestic students. Applications are processed on a rolling basis. Application fee: $50. Electronic applications accepted. *Expenses:* Tuition: Full-time $16,290; part-time $905 per credit hour. Tuition and fees vary according to program. *Financial support:* In 2010–11, 33 students received support, including 5 research assistantships with full tuition reimbursements available, 14 teaching assistantships with full tuition reimbursements available; fellowships with full tuition reimbursements available, Federal Work-Study, institutionally sponsored loans, and scholarships/grants also available. Support available to part-time students. Financial award application deadline: 2/15. *Faculty research:* Electric machines, drives, and controls; applied solid-state electronics; computers and signal processing; microwaves and antennas; solid state devices and acoustic wave sensors. Total annual research expenditures: $500,557. *Unit head:* Dr. Edwin E. Yaz, Chair, 414-288-6820, Fax: 414-288-5579, E-mail: edwin.yaz@marquette.edu. *Application contact:* Dr. Michael Johnson, Director of Graduate Studies, 414-288-0631, Fax: 414-288-5579, E-mail: michael.johnson@marquette.edu.

Massachusetts Institute of Technology, School of Engineering, Department of Electrical Engineering and Computer Science, Cambridge, MA 02139. Offers computer science (PhD, Sc D, ECS); computer science and engineering (PhD, Sc D); electrical engineering (PhD, Sc D, EE); electrical engineering and computer science (M Eng, SM, PhD, Sc D); SM/MBA. *Faculty:* 124 full-time (17 women), 1 part-time/adjunct (0 women). *Students:* 759 full-time (168 women), 4 part-time (1 woman); includes 165 minority (15 Black or African American, non-Hispanic/Latino; 3 American Indian or Alaska Native, non-Hispanic/Latino; 117 Asian, non-Hispanic/Latino; 27 Hispanic/Latino; 3 Two or more races, non-Hispanic/Latino), 341 international. Average age 26. 2,852 applicants, 11% accepted, 249 enrolled. In 2010, 199 master's, 103 doctorates, 4 other advanced degrees awarded. Terminal master's awarded for partial completion of doctoral program. *Degree requirements:* For master's and other advanced degree, thesis; for doctorate, comprehensive exam, thesis/dissertation. *Entrance requirements:* For master's, Leaders for Global Operations joint program requires GRE. Additional exam requirements/recommendations for international students: Required—TOEFL (minimum score 600 paper-based; 250 computer-based), IELTS (minimum score 7). *Application deadline:* For fall admission, 12/15 for domestic and international students. Application fee: $75. Electronic applications accepted. *Expenses:* Tuition: Full-time $38,940; part-time $605 per unit. Required fees: $272. *Financial support:* In 2010–11, 716 students received support, including 136 fellowships with tuition reimbursements available (averaging $28,627 per year), 470 research assistantships with tuition reimbursements available (averaging $29,178 per year), 116 teaching assistantships with tuition reimbursements available (averaging $30,108 per year); career-related internships or fieldwork, Federal Work-Study, institutionally sponsored loans, scholarships/grants, health care benefits, and unspecified assistantships also available. *Faculty research:* Artificial intelligence and applications; computer architecture, software, systems, and networks; communications, control, signal processing, and optimization; devices, electronics, electrodynamics, and photonics; bioelectrical engineering. Total annual research expenditures: $90.3 million. *Unit head:* Prof. Anantha P. Chandrakasan, Department Head, 617-253-4600, Fax: 617-258-7354. *Application contact:* Graduate Admissions, 617-253-4603, Fax: 617-258-7354, E-mail: grad-ap@eecs.mit.edu.

McGill University, Faculty of Graduate and Postdoctoral Studies, Faculty of Engineering, Department of Electrical and Computer Engineering, Montréal, QC H3A 2T5, Canada. Offers M Eng, PhD.

Memorial University of Newfoundland, School of Graduate Studies, Faculty of Engineering and Applied Science, St. John's, NL A1C 5S7, Canada. Offers civil engineering (M Eng, PhD); electrical and computer engineering (M Eng, PhD); mechanical engineering (M Eng, PhD); ocean and naval architecture engineering (M Eng, PhD). Part-time programs available. *Degree requirements:* For master's, thesis; for doctorate, comprehensive exam, thesis/dissertation, oral thesis defense. *Entrance requirements:* For master's, 2nd class degree; for doctorate, master's degree in engineering. Electronic applications accepted. *Faculty research:* Engineering analysis, environmental and hydrotechnical studies, manufacturing and robotics, mechanics, structures and materials.

Memorial University of Newfoundland, School of Graduate Studies, Interdisciplinary Program in Computer Engineering, St. John's, NL A1C 5S7, Canada. Offers MA Sc. *Degree requirements:* For master's, project course. *Entrance requirements:* For master's, 2nd class engineering degree.

Mercer University, Graduate Studies, Macon Campus, School of Engineering, Macon, GA 31207-0003. Offers biomedical engineering (MSE); computer engineering (MSE); electrical engineering (MSE); engineering management (MSE); environmental engineering (MSE); environmental systems (MS); mechanical engineering (MSE); software engineering (MSE); software systems (MS); technical communications management (MS); technical management (MS). Part-time and evening/weekend programs available. Postbaccalaureate distance learning degree programs offered (no on-campus study). *Faculty:* 18 full-time (4 women), 1 part-time/adjunct (0 women). *Students:* 11 full-time (2 women), 100 part-time (22 women); includes 26 minority (13 Black or African American, non-Hispanic/Latino; 12 Asian, non-Hispanic/Latino; 1 Hispanic/Latino), 3 international. Average age 32. In 2010, 46 master's awarded. *Degree requirements:* For master's, thesis or alternative. *Entrance requirements:* For master's, minimum undergraduate GPA of 3.0. Additional exam requirements/recommendations for international students: Required—TOEFL. *Application deadline:* For fall admission, 7/1 for domestic students; for spring admission, 11/15 for domestic students. Applications are processed on a rolling basis. Application fee: $35 ($50 for international students). Electronic applications accepted. *Expenses:* Contact institution. *Financial support:* Federal Work-Study available. *Unit head:* Dr. Wade H. Shaw, Dean, 478-301-2459, Fax: 478-301-5593, E-mail: shaw_wh@mercer.edu. *Application contact:* Greg Lofton, Graduate Program Coordinator, 478-301-5480, Fax: 478-301-5434, E-mail: lofton_g@mercer.edu.

Michigan Technological University, Graduate School, College of Engineering, Program in Computational Science and Engineering, Houghton, MI 49931. Offers PhD. Part-time programs available. *Degree requirements:* For doctorate, comprehensive exam, thesis/dissertation. *Entrance requirements:* For doctorate, MS in relevant discipline. Additional exam requirements/recommendations for international students: Required—TOEFL (minimum score 550 paper-based; 213 computer-based). Electronic applications accepted. *Expenses:* Contact institution.

Mississippi State University, Bagley College of Engineering, Department of Electrical and Computer Engineering, Mississippi State, MS 39762. Offers computer engineering (MS, PhD); electrical engineering (MS, PhD). Part-time programs available. Postbaccalaureate distance learning degree programs offered (minimal on-campus study). *Faculty:* 23 full-time (1 woman). *Students:* 87 full-time (13 women), 38 part-time (6 women); includes 9 minority (2 Black or African American, non-Hispanic/Latino; 4 Asian, non-Hispanic/Latino; 2 Hispanic/Latino; 1 Two or more races, non-Hispanic/Latino), 77 international. Average age 28. 260 applicants, 28% accepted, 34 enrolled. In 2010, 18 master's, 9 doctorates awarded. Terminal master's awarded for partial completion of doctoral program. *Degree requirements:* For master's, comprehensive exam, thesis optional; for doctorate, comprehensive exam, thesis/dissertation, written exam. *Entrance requirements:* For master's, GRE General Test, minimum undergraduate GPA of 3.0; for doctorate, GRE, minimum graduate GPA of 3.5. Additional exam requirements/recommendations for international students: Required—TOEFL (minimum score 550 paper-based; 213 computer-based; 79 iBT); Recommended—IELTS (minimum score 6.5). *Application deadline:* For fall admission, 7/1 for domestic students, 5/1 for international students; for spring admission, 11/1 for domestic students, 9/1 for international students. Applications are processed on a rolling basis. Application fee: $40. Electronic applications accepted. *Expenses:* Tuition, state resident: full-time $2730.50; part-time $304 per credit hour. Tuition, nonresident: full-time $6901; part-time $767 per credit hour. *Financial support:* In 2010–11, 26 research assistantships with full tuition reimbursements (averaging $15,687 per year), 18 teaching assistantships with full tuition reimbursements (averaging $14,650 per year) were awarded; Federal Work-Study, institutionally sponsored loans, scholarships/grants, and unspecified assistantships also available. Financial award application deadline: 4/1; financial award applicants required to submit FAFSA. *Faculty research:* Digital computing, power, controls, communication systems, microelectronics. Total annual research expenditures: $20.6 million. *Unit head:* Dr. Nicholas H. Younan, Professor and Department Head, 662-325-3721, Fax: 662-325-2298, E-mail: ece-head@ece.msstate.edu. *Application contact:* Dr. James E. Fowler, Professor and Interim Graduate Program Director, 662-325-3640, Fax: 662-325-2298, E-mail: fowler@ece.msstate.edu.

Missouri University of Science and Technology, Graduate School, School of Engineering, Department of Electrical and Computer Engineering, Rolla, MO 65409. Offers computer engineering (MS, DE, PhD); electrical engineering (MS, DE, PhD). Part-time and evening/weekend programs available. Terminal master's awarded for partial completion of doctoral program. *Degree requirements:* For master's, thesis optional; for doctorate, comprehensive exam, thesis/dissertation, departmental qualifying exam. *Entrance requirements:* For master's, GRE General Test (minimum score 1100 verbal and quantitative, writing 4.5); for doctorate, GRE General Test (minimum score: verbal and quantitative 1100, writing 3.5). Additional exam requirements/recommendations for international students: Required—TOEFL. Electronic applications accepted. *Faculty research:* Power systems, computer/communication networks, intelligent control/robotics, robust control, nanotechnologies.

Montana State University, College of Graduate Studies, College of Engineering, Department of Electrical and Computer Engineering, Bozeman, MT 59717. Offers electrical engineering (MS); engineering (PhD), including electrical and computer engineering option. Part-time programs available. *Faculty:* 14 full-time (0 women), 1 part-time/adjunct (0 women). *Students:* 13 full-time (1 woman), 25 part-time (5 women); includes 1 minority (Hispanic/Latino), 7 international. Average age 26. 34 applicants, 24% accepted, 8 enrolled. In 2010, 17 master's awarded. *Degree requirements:* For master's, comprehensive exam, thesis (for some programs); for doctorate, comprehensive exam, thesis/dissertation. *Entrance requirements:* For master's, GRE, BS in electrical or computer engineering or related field; for doctorate, GRE, MS in electrical or computer engineering or related field. Additional exam requirements/recommendations for international students: Required—TOEFL (minimum score 550 paper-based; 213 computer-based). *Application deadline:* For fall admission, 7/15 priority date for domestic students, 5/15 priority date for international students; for spring admission, 12/1 priority date for domestic students, 10/1 priority date for international students. Applications are processed on a rolling basis. Application fee: $30. Electronic applications accepted. *Expenses:* Tuition, state resident: full-time $5553.90. Tuition, nonresident: full-time $14,646. Required fees: $1233. *Financial support:* In 2010–11, 29 students received support, including 3 fellowships with full tuition reimbursements available (averaging $25,272 per year), 19 research assistantships with full tuition reimbursements available (averaging $18,456 per year), 7 teaching assistantships with partial tuition reimbursements available (averaging $15,120 per year); scholarships/grants, traineeships, health care benefits, and unspecified assistantships also available. Support available to part-time students. Financial award application deadline: 3/1; financial award applicants required to submit FAFSA. *Faculty research:* Optics and optoelectronics, communications and signal processing, microfabrication, complex systems and control, energy systems. Total annual research expenditures: $2.3 million. *Unit head:* Dr. Robert Maher, Head, 406-994-2505, Fax: 406-994-5958, E-mail: rmaher@ece.montana.edu. *Application contact:* Dr. Carl A. Fox, Vice Provost for Graduate Education, 406-994-4145, Fax: 406-994-7433, E-mail: gradstudy@montana.edu.

Naval Postgraduate School, Graduate Programs, Department of Electrical and Computer Engineering, Monterey, CA 93943. Offers MS, PhD, Eng. Program only open to commissioned officers of the United States and friendly nations and selected United States federal civilian employees. *Accreditation:* ABET (one or more programs are accredited). Part-time programs available. Postbaccalaureate distance learning degree programs offered (minimal on-campus study). *Degree requirements:* For master's and Eng, thesis; for doctorate, one foreign language, thesis/dissertation.

New Jersey Institute of Technology, Office of Graduate Studies, Newark College of Engineering, Department of Electrical and Computer Engineering, Program in Computer Engineering, Newark, NJ 07102. Offers MS, PhD. Part-time and evening/weekend programs available. *Students:* 23 full-time (3 women), 14 part-time (1 woman); includes 1 Black or African American, non-Hispanic/Latino; 6 Asian, non-Hispanic/Latino; 1 Hispanic/Latino, 24 international. Average age 27. 105 applicants, 34% accepted, 9 enrolled. In 2010, 16 master's, 2 doctorates awarded. Terminal master's awarded for partial completion of doctoral program. *Degree requirements:* For master's, thesis optional; for doctorate, thesis/dissertation, residency. *Entrance requirements:* For master's, GRE General Test; for doctorate, GRE General Test, minimum graduate GPA of 3.5. Additional exam requirements/recommendations for international students: Required—TOEFL (minimum score 550 paper-based; 213 computer-based; 79 iBT). *Application deadline:* For fall admission, 6/5 priority date for domestic students, 4/1 for international students; for spring admission, 11/15 for domestic and international students. Applications are processed on a rolling basis. Application fee: $65. Electronic applications accepted. *Expenses:* Tuition, state resident: full-time $14,724; part-time $818 per credit.

Tuition, nonresident: full-time $20,304; part-time $1128 per credit. Required fees: $2272; $209 per credit. $103 per semester. One-time fee: $312 full-time; $212 part-time. *Financial support:* Fellowships with full and partial tuition reimbursements, research assistantships with full and partial tuition reimbursements, teaching assistantships with full and partial tuition reimbursements, career-related internships or fieldwork, Federal Work-Study, institutionally sponsored loans, and unspecified assistantships available. Financial award application deadline: 3/15. *Unit head:* Dr. Leonid Tsybeskov, Interim Chair, 973-596-6594, E-mail: leonid.tsybeskov@njit.edu. *Application contact:* Kathryn Kelly, Director of Admissions, 973-596-3300, Fax: 973-596-3461, E-mail: admissions@njit.edu.

New Mexico State University, Graduate School, College of Engineering, Klipsch School of Electrical and Computer Engineering, Las Cruces, NM 88003-8001. Offers MSEE, PhD. Part-time and evening/weekend programs available. Postbaccalaureate distance learning degree programs offered (no on-campus study). *Faculty:* 18 full-time (1 woman). *Students:* 109 full-time (18 women), 52 part-time (5 women); includes 28 minority (1 Black or African American, non-Hispanic/Latino; 1 American Indian or Alaska Native, non-Hispanic/Latino; 1 Asian, non-Hispanic/Latino; 25 Hispanic/Latino), 101 international. Average age 28. 222 applicants, 78% accepted, 47 enrolled. In 2010, 39 master's, 4 doctorates awarded. Terminal master's awarded for partial completion of doctoral program. *Degree requirements:* For master's, thesis (for some programs), final oral or written exam; for doctorate, comprehensive exam, thesis/dissertation. *Entrance requirements:* For master's, GRE, minimum GPA of 3.0; for doctorate, departmental qualifying exam, minimum GPA of 3.0. Additional exam requirements/recommendations for international students: Required—TOEFL. *Application deadline:* For fall admission, 3/1 priority date for domestic and international students; for spring admission, 8/1 priority date for domestic and international students. Applications are processed on a rolling basis. Application fee: $30 ($50 for international students). Electronic applications accepted. *Expenses:* Tuition, state resident: full-time $4536; part-time $242 per credit. Tuition, nonresident: full-time $15,816; part-time $712 per credit. Required fees: $636 per term. *Financial support:* In 2010–11, 42 research assistantships (averaging $6,312 per year), 36 teaching assistantships (averaging $5,291 per year) were awarded; fellowships, career-related internships or fieldwork, Federal Work-Study, health care benefits, and unspecified assistantships also available. Support available to part-time students. Financial award application deadline: 3/1. *Faculty research:* Image and digital signal processing, energy systems, wireless communication, analog VLSI design, electro-optics. *Unit head:* Dr. Vojin Oklobdzija, Head, 575-646-3115, Fax: 575-646-1435, E-mail: vojin@nmsu.edu. *Application contact:* Sue Kord, Records Technician I, 575-646-6440, Fax: 575-646-1435, E-mail: kkord@nmsu.edu.

New York Institute of Technology, Graduate Division, School of Engineering and Computing Sciences, Program in Electrical Engineering and Computer Engineering, Old Westbury, NY 11568-8000. Offers MS. Part-time and evening/weekend programs available. *Students:* 100 full-time (24 women), 61 part-time (9 women); includes 23 minority (7 Black or African American, non-Hispanic/Latino; 1 American Indian or Alaska Native, non-Hispanic/Latino; 15 Asian, non-Hispanic/Latino), 102 international. Average age 26. In 2010, 63 master's awarded. *Degree requirements:* For master's, project. *Entrance requirements:* For master's, GRE General Test (if QPA less than 2.85), BS in electrical engineering or related field, minimum QPA of 2.85. Additional exam requirements/recommendations for international students: Required—TOEFL (minimum score 550 paper-based; 213 computer-based). *Application deadline:* For fall admission, 7/1 priority date for domestic students; for spring admission, 12/1 priority date for domestic students. Applications are processed on a rolling basis. Application fee: $50. Electronic applications accepted. *Expenses:* Tuition: Part-time $835 per credit. *Financial support:* Fellowships, research assistantships with partial tuition reimbursements, institutionally sponsored loans, tuition waivers (full and partial), and unspecified assistantships available. Support available to part-time students. Financial award applicants required to submit FAFSA. *Faculty research:* Computer networks, control theory, light waves and optics, robotics, signal processing. *Unit head:* Dr. Ayat Jafari, Chair, 516-686-7569, Fax: 516-686-7439, E-mail: ajafari@nyit.edu. *Application contact:* Dr. Jacquelyn Nealon, Vice President for Enrollment Services, 516-686-7925, Fax: 516-686-7597, E-mail: jnealon@nyit.edu.

Norfolk State University, School of Graduate Studies, School of Science and Technology, Program in Electronics Engineering, Norfolk, VA 23504. Offers MS.

North Carolina Agricultural and Technical State University, Graduate School, College of Engineering, Department of Electrical and Computer Engineering, Greensboro, NC 27411. Offers electrical engineering (MSEE, PhD), including communications and signal processing (MSEE), computer engineering (MSEE), electronic and optical materials and devices (MSEE), power systems and controls (MSEE). Part-time programs available. *Degree requirements:* For master's, project, thesis defense; for doctorate, thesis/dissertation. *Entrance requirements:* For master's, GRE General Test, GRE Subject Test, minimum GPA of 2.8; for doctorate, GRE General Test, minimum GPA of 3.0. *Faculty research:* Semiconductor compounds, VLSI design, image processing, optical systems and devices, fault-tolerant computing.

North Carolina State University, Graduate School, College of Engineering, Department of Electrical and Computer Engineering, Program in Computer Engineering, Raleigh, NC 27695. Offers MS, PhD. *Degree requirements:* For master's, thesis (for some programs); for doctorate, thesis/dissertation. *Entrance requirements:* For master's and doctorate, GRE. Additional exam requirements/recommendations for international students: Required—TOEFL (minimum score 575 paper-based). Electronic applications accepted. *Faculty research:* Computer architecture, parallel processing, embedded computer systems, VLSI design, computer networking performance and control.

North Dakota State University, College of Graduate and Interdisciplinary Studies, College of Engineering and Architecture, Department of Electrical and Computer Engineering, Fargo, ND 58108. Offers MS, PhD. Part-time programs available. *Students:* 30 full-time (13 women), 14 part-time (3 women), 31 international. Average age 28. 97 applicants, 31% accepted, 11 enrolled. In 2010, 5 master's, 1 doctorate awarded. Terminal master's awarded for partial completion of doctoral program. *Degree requirements:* For master's, comprehensive exam, thesis; for doctorate, comprehensive exam, thesis/dissertation. *Entrance requirements:* Additional exam requirements/recommendations for international students: Required—TOEFL (minimum score 525 paper-based; 197 computer-based; 71 iBT). *Application deadline:* For fall admission, 3/1 priority date for domestic and international students. Application fee: $45 ($60 for international students). Electronic applications accepted. *Financial support:* In 2010–11, 30 students received support, including 2 fellowships with full tuition reimbursements available (averaging $25,000 per year), 6 research assistantships with full tuition reimbursements available (averaging $8,100 per year), 10 teaching assistantships with full tuition reimbursements available (averaging $8,100 per year); career-related internships or fieldwork, Federal Work-Study, institutionally sponsored loans, and tuition waivers (full) also available. Financial award application deadline: 3/1. *Faculty research:* Computers, power and control systems, microwaves, communications and signal processing, bioengineering. Total annual research expenditures: $599,000. *Unit head:* Dr. Jacob Glower, Chair, 701-231-7608, Fax: 701-231-8677, E-mail: jacob.glower@ndsu.edu. *Application contact:* Dr. Rajesh Kavasseri, Associate Professor, 701-231-7019, E-mail: rajesh.kavasseri@ndsu.edu.

Northeastern University, College of Engineering, Department of Electrical and Computer Engineering, Boston, MA 02115-5096. Offers computer engineering (PhD); electrical engineering (MS, PhD); engineering leadership (MS). *Faculty:* 45 full-time (6 women), 2 part-time/adjunct (both women). *Students:* 257 full-time (49 women), 98 part-time (6 women), 1,054 applicants, 47% accepted, 122 enrolled. In 2010, 83 master's, 13 doctorates awarded. *Degree requirements:* For master's, thesis optional; for doctorate, thesis/dissertation, departmental qualifying exam. *Entrance requirements:* For master's and doctorate, GRE General Test. Additional exam requirements/recommendations for international students: Required—TOEFL (minimum score 550 paper-based; 213 computer-based). *Application deadline:* For fall admission, 1/15 priority date for domestic and international students. Applications are processed on a rolling basis. Application fee: $50. Electronic applications accepted. *Financial support:* In 2010–11, 136

Computer Engineering

Northeastern University (continued)
students received support, including 1 fellowship with full tuition reimbursement available, 102 research assistantships with full tuition reimbursements available (averaging $18,325 per year), 32 teaching assistantships with full tuition reimbursements available (averaging $18,325 per year); career-related internships or fieldwork, Federal Work-Study, scholarships/grants, tuition waivers (full), and unspecified assistantships also available. Support available to part-time students. Financial award application deadline: 1/15; financial award applicants required to submit FAFSA. *Faculty research:* Signal processing and sensor data fusion, plasma science, sensing and imaging, power electronics, computer engineering. *Unit head:* Dr. Ali Abur, Chairman, 617-373-4159, Fax: 617-373-8970. *Application contact:* Jeffery Hengel, Admissions Specialist, 617-373-2711, Fax: 617-373-2501, E-mail: grad-eng@coe.neu.edu.

Northwestern Polytechnic University, School of Engineering, Fremont, CA 94539-7482. Offers computer science (MS); computer systems engineering (MS); electrical engineering (MS). Part-time and evening/weekend programs available. *Degree requirements:* For master's, thesis optional. *Entrance requirements:* For master's, minimum GPA of 3.0. Additional exam requirements/recommendations for international students: Required—TOEFL (minimum score 550 paper-based; 213 computer-based; 79 iBT). *Faculty research:* Computer networking, database design, Internet technology, software engineering, digital signal processing.

Northwestern University, McCormick School of Engineering and Applied Science, Department of Electrical Engineering and Computer Science, Evanston, IL 60208. Offers computer science (MS, PhD); electrical and computer engineering (MS, PhD); electronic materials (MS, PhD, Certificate); information technology (MS). MS and PhD admissions and degrees offered through The Graduate School. Part-time programs available. *Faculty:* 50 full-time (3 women). *Students:* 212 full-time (31 women), 18 part-time (2 women); includes 21 minority (15 Asian, non-Hispanic/Latino; 4 Hispanic/Latino; 2 Two or more races, non-Hispanic/Latino), 157 international. Average age 26. 588 applicants, 10% accepted, 30 enrolled. In 2010, 39 master's, 31 doctorates awarded. Terminal master's awarded for partial completion of doctoral program. *Degree requirements:* For master's, comprehensive exam (for some programs), thesis optional, Thesis or Project is optional; for doctorate, comprehensive exam (for some programs), thesis/dissertation. *Entrance requirements:* For master's and doctorate, General Exam of GRE. Additional exam requirements/recommendations for international students: Required—TOEFL (minimum score 577 paper-based, 233 computer-based, 90 iBT) or IELTS. *Application deadline:* For fall admission, 12/31 for domestic and international students. Application fee: $75. Electronic applications accepted. *Financial support:* Fellowships with full tuition reimbursements, research assistantships with full tuition reimbursements, teaching assistantships with full tuition reimbursements, career-related internships or fieldwork, institutionally sponsored loans, health care benefits, and unspecified assistantships available. Financial award application deadline: 1/15; financial award applicants required to submit FAFSA. *Faculty research:* Solid state and photonics; computing, algorithms, and applications; computer engineering and systems; cognitive systems; graphics and interactive media; signals and systems. Total annual research expenditures: $19.2 million. *Unit head:* Dr. Alan Sahakian, Chair, 847-491-7007, Fax: 847-491-4455, E-mail: sahakian@ece.northwestern.edu. *Application contact:* Dr. Thrasos Pappas, Admission Officer, 847-491-1243, Fax: 847-491-4455, E-mail: t-pappas@northwestern.edu.

Oakland University, Graduate Study and Lifelong Learning, School of Engineering and Computer Science, Department of Computer Science and Engineering, Rochester, MI 48309-4401. Offers computer science (MS); embedded systems (MS); information systems engineering (MS); software engineering (MS). Part-time and evening/weekend programs available. *Entrance requirements:* For master's, minimum GPA of 3.0 for unconditional admission. Electronic applications accepted. *Expenses:* Contact institution. *Faculty research:* Cyber security, 3D imaging of neurochemicals in rat brains.

Oakland University, Graduate Study and Lifelong Learning, School of Engineering and Computer Science, Department of Electrical and Systems Engineering, Program in Electrical and Computer Engineering, Rochester, MI 48309-4401. Offers MS. Part-time and evening/weekend programs available. *Entrance requirements:* For master's, minimum GPA of 3.0 for unconditional admission. Additional exam requirements/recommendations for international students: Required—TOEFL (minimum score 550 paper-based; 213 computer-based). Electronic applications accepted. *Expenses:* Contact institution.

OGI School of Science & Engineering at Oregon Health & Science University, Graduate Studies, Department of Computer Science and Electrical Engineering, Beaverton, OR 97006-8921. Offers computer science (PhD); computer science and engineering (MS, PhD); electrical engineering (MS, PhD). Part-time and evening/weekend programs available. Terminal master's awarded for partial completion of doctoral program. *Degree requirements:* For master's, thesis optional; for doctorate, comprehensive exam, oral defense of dissertation. *Entrance requirements:* For master's and doctorate, GRE General Test. Additional exam requirements/recommendations for international students: Required—TOEFL (minimum score 650 paper-based; 280 computer-based). Electronic applications accepted. *Faculty research:* Computer systems architecture, intelligent and interactive systems, programming models and systems, theory of computation.

The Ohio State University, Graduate School, College of Engineering, Department of Computer Science and Engineering, Columbus, OH 43210. Offers computer and information science (MS, PhD); computer science and engineering (MS). *Faculty:* 40. *Students:* 244 full-time (45 women), 60 part-time (9 women); includes 2 Black or African American, non-Hispanic/Latino; 5 Asian, non-Hispanic/Latino; 1 Hispanic/Latino, 236 international. Average age 28. In 2010, 65 master's, 19 doctorates awarded. *Degree requirements:* For master's, thesis optional; for doctorate, thesis/dissertation. *Entrance requirements:* Additional exam requirements/recommendations for international students: Recommended—TOEFL (minimum score 600 paper-based; 250 computer-based). *Application deadline:* For fall admission, 8/15 priority date for domestic students, 7/1 priority date for international students; for winter admission, 12/1 priority date for domestic students, 11/1 priority date for international students; for spring admission, 3/1 priority date for domestic students, 2/1 priority date for international students. Applications are processed on a rolling basis. Application fee: $40 ($50 for international students). Electronic applications accepted. *Expenses:* Tuition, state resident: full-time $10,605. Tuition, nonresident: full-time $26,535. Tuition and fees vary according to course load and program. *Financial support:* Fellowships, teaching assistantships, career-related internships or fieldwork, Federal Work-Study, institutionally sponsored loans, and administrative assistantships available. Support available to part-time students. Financial award application deadline: 1/15. *Unit head:* Xiadong Zhang, Chair, 614-292-5813, E-mail: zhang.574@osu.edu. *Application contact:* 614-292-9444, Fax: 614-292-3895, E-mail: domestic.grad@osu.edu.

Oklahoma State University, College of Engineering, Architecture and Technology, School of Electrical and Computer Engineering, Stillwater, OK 74078. Offers MS, PhD. Postbaccalaureate distance learning degree programs offered. *Faculty:* 26 full-time (2 women). *Students:* 99 full-time (23 women), 107 part-time (20 women); includes 1 Black or African American, non-Hispanic/Latino; 2 American Indian or Alaska Native, non-Hispanic/Latino; 4 Asian, non-Hispanic/Latino; 3 Hispanic/Latino, 157 international. Average age 28. 393 applicants, 45% accepted, 48 enrolled. In 2010, 47 master's, 6 doctorates awarded. *Degree requirements:* For master's, thesis or alternative; for doctorate, comprehensive exam, thesis/dissertation. *Entrance requirements:* For master's and doctorate, GRE or GMAT. Additional exam requirements/recommendations for international students: Required—TOEFL (minimum score 550 paper-based; 79 iBT). *Application deadline:* For fall admission, 3/1 priority date for international students; for spring admission, 8/1 priority date for international students. Applications are processed on a rolling basis. Application fee: $40 ($75 for international students). Electronic applications accepted. *Expenses:* Tuition, state resident: full-time $3716; part-time $154.85 per credit hour. Tuition, nonresident: full-time $14,892; part-time $621 per credit hour. Required fees: $2044; $85.20 per credit hour. One-time fee: $50. Tuition and fees vary according to course load and campus/location. *Financial support:* In 2010–11, 70 research assistantships (averaging $12,214 per year), 30 teaching assistantships (averaging $8,654 per year) were awarded; career-related internships or fieldwork, Federal Work-Study, scholarships/grants, health care benefits, tuition waivers (partial), and unspecified assistantships also available. Support available to part-time students. Financial award application deadline: 3/1; financial award applicants required to submit FAFSA. *Unit head:* Dr. Keith Teague, Head, 405-744-5151, Fax: 405-744-9198. *Application contact:* Dr. Gordon Emslie, Dean, 405-744-6368, Fax: 405-744-0355, E-mail: grad-i@okstate.edu.

Old Dominion University, Frank Batten College of Engineering and Technology, Program in Electrical and Computer Engineering, Norfolk, VA 23529. Offers ME, MS, PhD. Part-time programs available. Postbaccalaureate distance learning degree programs offered (minimal on-campus study). *Faculty:* 21 full-time (1 woman), 2 part-time/adjunct (1 woman). *Students:* 93 full-time (14 women), 9 part-time (4 women); includes 65 minority (7 Black or African American, non-Hispanic/Latino; 58 Asian, non-Hispanic/Latino), 67 international. Average age 28. 107 applicants, 53% accepted, 14 enrolled. In 2010, 38 master's, 8 doctorates awarded. *Degree requirements:* For doctorate, thesis/dissertation, candidacy exam, diagnostic exam. *Entrance requirements:* For doctorate, GRE. Additional exam requirements/recommendations for international students: Required—TOEFL. *Application deadline:* For fall admission, 6/1 for domestic students, 4/15 for international students; for spring admission, 11/1 for domestic students, 10/1 for international students. Applications are processed on a rolling basis. Application fee: $40. Electronic applications accepted. *Expenses:* Tuition, state resident: full-time $8592; part-time $358 per credit. Tuition, nonresident: full-time $21,672; part-time $903 per credit. Required fees: $119 per semester. One-time fee: $50. *Financial support:* In 2010–11, 3 fellowships with full tuition reimbursements (averaging $15,000 per year), 38 research assistantships with full and partial tuition reimbursements (averaging $15,000 per year), 41 teaching assistantships with full and partial tuition reimbursements (averaging $15,000 per year) were awarded; career-related internships or fieldwork, Federal Work-Study, scholarships/grants, tuition waivers (partial), and unspecified assistantships also available. Support available to part-time students. Financial award application deadline: 2/15; financial award applicants required to submit FAFSA. *Faculty research:* Digital signal processing, control engineering, gaseous electronics, ultrafast (femtosecom) laser applications, interaction of fields with living organisms. Total annual research expenditures: $3 million. *Unit head:* Dr. Sach Albin, Graduate Program Director, 757-683-4967, Fax: 757-683-3220, E-mail: ecegpd@odu.edu. *Application contact:* Dr. Linda Vahala, Associate Dean, 757-683-3789, Fax: 757-683-4898, E-mail: lvahala@odu.edu.

Oregon Health & Science University, School of Medicine, Graduate Programs in Medicine, Department of Computer Science and Engineering, Portland, OR 97239-3098. Offers computer science and engineering (MS, PhD); electrical engineering (MS, PhD). Part-time programs available. *Faculty:* 8 full-time (2 women), 3 part-time/adjunct (1 woman). *Students:* 26 full-time (10 women); includes 1 Asian, non-Hispanic/Latino, 2 international. Average age 34. 26 applicants, 92% accepted, 4 enrolled. In 2010, 2 master's, 2 doctorates awarded. Terminal master's awarded for partial completion of doctoral program. *Degree requirements:* For master's, thesis (for some programs); for doctorate, comprehensive exam, thesis/dissertation. *Entrance requirements:* For master's, GRE General Test (minimum scores: 500 Verbal/600 Quantitative/4.5 Analytical); for doctorate, GRE General Test (minimum scores: 500 Verbal/600 Quantitative/4.5 Analytical) or MCAT (for some programs). Additional exam requirements/recommendations for international students: Required—TOEFL. *Application deadline:* For fall admission, 7/15 for domestic students, 5/15 for international students; for winter admission, 10/15 for domestic students, 9/15 for international students; for spring admission, 1/15 for domestic students, 12/15 for international students. Applications are processed on a rolling basis. Application fee: $65. Electronic applications accepted. *Financial support:* Health care benefits, tuition waivers (full), and full tuition and stipends available. *Unit head:* Peter Heeman, PhD, Program Director, 503-748-1635, E-mail: cseedept@csee.ogi.edu. *Application contact:* Pat Dickerson, Administrative Coordinator, 503-748-1635, E-mail: cseedept@csee.ogi.edu.

Oregon State University, Graduate School, College of Engineering, School of Electrical Engineering and Computer Science, Corvallis, OR 97331. Offers computer science (M Eng, MAIS, MS, PhD); electrical and computer engineering (M Eng, MS, PhD). *Degree requirements:* For doctorate, thesis/dissertation, qualifying exam, preliminary exam. *Entrance requirements:* For master's and doctorate, minimum GPA of 3.0 in last 90 hours of course work. Additional exam requirements/recommendations for international students: Required—TOEFL (minimum score 600 paper-based; 250 computer-based; 80 iBT). Electronic applications accepted. *Faculty research:* Optical materials and devices, data security and cryptography, analog and mixed-signal integrated circuit design, algorithms, computer graphics and vision.

Penn State University Park, Graduate School, College of Engineering, Department of Computer Science and Engineering, State College, University Park, PA 16802-1503. Offers M Eng, MS, PhD.

Polytechnic Institute of NYU, Department of Electrical and Computer Engineering, Major in Computer Engineering, Brooklyn, NY 11201-2990. Offers MS, Certificate. *Students:* 19 full-time (1 woman), 21 part-time (1 woman); includes 12 minority (2 Black or African American, non-Hispanic/Latino; 9 Asian, non-Hispanic/Latino; 1 Hispanic/Latino), 19 international. 73 applicants, 40% accepted, 10 enrolled. In 2010, 15 master's awarded. *Degree requirements:* For master's, comprehensive exam (for some programs), thesis (for some programs). *Entrance requirements:* For master's, BS in electrical engineering. Additional exam requirements/recommendations for international students: Required—TOEFL (minimum score 550 paper-based; 213 computer-based; 80 iBT); Recommended—IELTS (minimum score 6.5). *Application deadline:* For fall admission, 7/31 priority date for domestic students, 4/30 priority date for international students; for spring admission, 12/31 priority date for domestic students, 11/30 priority date for international students. Applications are processed on a rolling basis. Application fee: $75. Electronic applications accepted. *Expenses:* Tuition: Full-time $21,492; part-time $1194 per credit. Required fees: $385 per semester. Tuition and fees vary according to course load. *Financial support:* Applicants required to submit FAFSA. *Unit head:* Dr. Jonathan Chao, Head, 718-860-3478, Fax: 718-260-3302, E-mail: chao@poly.edu. *Application contact:* JeanCarlo Bonilla, Director, Graduate Enrollment Management, 718-260-3182, Fax: 718-260-3624.

Polytechnic Institute of NYU, Long Island Graduate Center, Graduate Programs, Department of Electrical and Computer Engineering, Major in Computer Engineering, Melville, NY 11747. Offers MS. *Students:* 2 full-time (1 woman), 8 part-time (0 women), 3 international. Average age 27. 7 applicants, 86% accepted, 5 enrolled. In 2010, 1 master's awarded. *Degree requirements:* For master's, comprehensive exam (for some programs), thesis (for some programs). *Entrance requirements:* Additional exam requirements/recommendations for international students: Required—TOEFL (minimum score 550 paper-based; 213 computer-based; 80 iBT); Recommended—IELTS (minimum score 6.5). *Application deadline:* For fall admission, 7/31 priority date for domestic students, 4/30 priority date for international students; for spring admission, 12/31 priority date for domestic students, 11/30 priority date for international students. Applications are processed on a rolling basis. Application fee: $75. Electronic applications accepted. *Expenses:* Tuition: Full-time $21,492; part-time $1194 per credit. Required fees: $385 per semester. Tuition and fees vary according to course load. *Financial support:* Institutionally sponsored loans, scholarships/grants, and unspecified assistantships available. Support available to part-time students. *Unit head:* Dr. Jonathan Chao, Department Head, 718-260-3302, E-mail: chao@poly.edu. *Application contact:* JeanCarlo Bonilla, Director of Graduate Enrollment Management, 718-260-3182, Fax: 718-260-3624, E-mail: gradinfo@poly.edu.

Polytechnic Institute of NYU, Westchester Graduate Center, Graduate Programs, Department of Electrical and Computer Engineering, Major in Computer Engineering, Hawthorne, NY 10532-1507. Offers MS. *Students:* 1 applicant, 100% accepted, 1 enrolled. *Degree requirements:* For master's, comprehensive exam (for some programs), thesis (for some programs). *Entrance requirements:* Additional exam requirements/recommendations for international students: Required—TOEFL (minimum score 550 paper-based; 213 computer-based; 80 iBT); Recommended—IELTS (minimum score 6.5). *Application deadline:* For fall admission,

7/31 priority date for domestic students, 4/30 priority date for international students; for spring admission, 12/31 priority date for domestic students, 11/30 priority date for international students. Applications are processed on a rolling basis. Application fee: $75. Electronic applications accepted. *Expenses:* Tuition: Full-time $21,492; part-time $1194 per credit. Required fees: $385 per semester. Tuition and fees vary according to course load. *Financial support:* Institutionally sponsored loans, scholarships/grants, and unspecified assistantships available. Support available to part-time students. Financial award applicants required to submit FAFSA. *Unit head:* Dr. Jonathan Chao, Department Head, 718-260-3302, E-mail: chao@poly.edu. *Application contact:* JeanCarlo Bonilla, Director of Graduate Enrollment Management, 718-260-3182, Fax: 718-260-3624, E-mail: gradinfo@poly.edu.

Polytechnic University of Puerto Rico, Graduate School, Hato Rey, PR 00919. Offers business administration (MBA), including computer information systems, general management, management of information systems, management of international enterprises; civil engineering (ME, MS); computer engineering (ME, MS); computer science (MCS, MS); electrical engineering (ME, MS); engineering management (MEM); environmental management (MEM); landscape architecture (M Land Arch); manufacturing competitiveness (MMC, MS); manufacturing engineering (ME, MS); mechanical engineering (M Mech E). Part-time and evening/weekend programs available. *Entrance requirements:* For master's, 3 letters of recommendation.

Portland State University, Graduate Studies, Maseeh College of Engineering and Computer Science, Department of Electrical and Computer Engineering, Portland, OR 97207-0751. Offers M Eng, MS, PhD. Part-time and evening/weekend programs available. *Faculty:* 18 full-time (3 women), 7 part-time/adjunct (2 women). *Students:* 93 full-time (21 women), 131 part-time (24 women); includes 31 minority (3 Black or African American, non-Hispanic/Latino; 22 Asian, non-Hispanic/Latino; 3 Hispanic/Latino; 2 Native Hawaiian or other Pacific Islander, non-Hispanic/Latino; 1 Two or more races, non-Hispanic/Latino), 130 international. Average age 29. 167 applicants, 65% accepted, 46 enrolled. In 2010, 48 master's, 3 doctorates awarded. *Degree requirements:* For master's, variable foreign language requirement, oral exam; for doctorate, one foreign language, comprehensive exam, thesis/dissertation, oral and written exams. *Entrance requirements:* For master's, minimum GPA of 3.0 in upper-division course work or 2.75 overall, BS in electrical or computer engineering or allied field; for doctorate, GRE General Test, GRE Subject Test, minimum GPA of 3.0 in upper-division course work, MS in electrical engineering or allied field. Additional exam requirements/recommendations for international students: Required—TOEFL (minimum score 550 paper-based; 213 computer-based). *Application deadline:* For fall admission, 4/1 for domestic students, 3/1 for international students; for winter admission, 9/1 for domestic and international students; for spring admission, 11/1 for domestic and international students. Applications are processed on a rolling basis. Application fee: $50. *Expenses:* Tuition, state resident: full-time $8505; part-time $315 per credit. Tuition, nonresident: full-time $13,284; part-time $492 per credit. Required fees: $1482; $21 per credit. $99 per term. One-time fee: $120. Part-time tuition and fees vary according to course load and program. *Financial support:* In 2010–11, 2 research assistantships with full tuition reimbursements (averaging $13,743 per year) were awarded; teaching assistantships with full tuition reimbursements, career-related internships or fieldwork, Federal Work-Study, scholarships/grants, and unspecified assistantships also available. Support available to part-time students. Financial award application deadline: 3/1; financial award applicants required to submit FAFSA. *Faculty research:* Optics and laser systems, design automation, VLSI design, computer systems, power electronics. Total annual research expenditures: $1.7 million. *Unit head:* Dr. James McNames, Chair, 503-725-5390, Fax: 503-725-3807, E-mail: mcnames@ece.pdx.edu. *Application contact:* Kelley Gardiner, Graduate Coordinator, 503-725-3002, Fax: 503-725-3807, E-mail: kelleyg@ece.pdx.edu.

Purdue University, College of Engineering, School of Electrical and Computer Engineering, West Lafayette, IN 47907-2035. Offers MS, MSE, MSECE, PhD. MS and PhD degree programs in biomedical engineering offered jointly with School of Mechanical Engineering and School of Chemical Engineering. Part-time programs available. Postbaccalaureate distance learning degree programs offered (no on-campus study). Terminal master's awarded for partial completion of doctoral program. *Entrance requirements:* For master's and doctorate, GRE General Test, minimum GPA of 3.25. Additional exam requirements/recommendations for international students: Required—TOEFL (minimum score 550 paper-based; 213 computer-based; 77 iBT). Electronic applications accepted. *Faculty research:* Automatic controls, biomedical imaging; computer engineering; communications, networking signal and image processing; fields and optics.

Purdue University Calumet, Graduate Studies Office, School of Engineering, Mathematics, and Science, Department of Engineering, Hammond, IN 46323-2094. Offers computer engineering (MSE); electrical engineering (MSE); engineering (MS); mechanical engineering (MSE). Evening/weekend programs available. *Entrance requirements:* Additional exam requirements/recommendations for international students: Required—TOEFL. Application fee: $30. *Expenses:* Tuition, state resident: full-time $6867. Tuition, nonresident: full-time $14,157. *Financial support:* Career-related internships or fieldwork available. Financial award application deadline: 3/1. *Unit head:* Dr. Kaliappan Gopalan, Head, 219-989-2685, E-mail: gopalan@purduecal.edu. *Application contact:* Janice Novosel, Engineering Graduate Program Secretary, 219-989-3106, E-mail: janice.novosel@purduecal.edu.

Queen's University at Kingston, School of Graduate Studies and Research, Faculty of Applied Science, Department of Electrical and Computer Engineering, Kingston, ON K7L 3N6, Canada. Offers M Eng, M Sc, M Sc Eng, PhD. Part-time programs available. *Degree requirements:* For master's, thesis optional; for doctorate, comprehensive exam, thesis/dissertation. *Entrance requirements:* Additional exam requirements/recommendations for international students: Required—TOEFL (minimum score 580 paper-based; 237 computer-based). *Faculty research:* Communications and signal processing systems, computer engineering systems.

Rensselaer at Hartford, Department of Engineering, Program in Computer and Systems Engineering, Hartford, CT 06120-2991. Offers ME. *Entrance requirements:* For master's, GRE.

Rensselaer Polytechnic Institute, Graduate School, School of Engineering, Program in Computer and Systems Engineering, Troy, NY 12180-3590. Offers M Eng, MS, PhD. Part-time programs available. *Faculty:* 40 full-time (5 women), 5 part-time/adjunct (2 women). *Students:* 11 full-time (0 women), 20 part-time (0 women), 7 international. 82 applicants, 23% accepted, 10 enrolled. In 2010, 11 master's, 4 doctorates awarded. Terminal master's awarded for partial completion of doctoral program. *Degree requirements:* For master's, thesis (for some programs); for doctorate, thesis/dissertation. *Entrance requirements:* For master's, GRE; for doctorate, GRE, qualifying exam, candidacy exam. Additional exam requirements/recommendations for international students: Required—TOEFL (minimum score 570 paper-based; 89 iBT). *Application deadline:* For fall admission, 1/15 priority date for domestic and international students; for spring admission, 8/15 priority date for domestic and international students. Applications are processed on a rolling basis. Application fee: $75. Electronic applications accepted. *Expenses:* Tuition: Full-time $39,600; part-time $1650 per credit. Required fees: $1896. *Financial support:* In 2010–11, 2 fellowships with full tuition reimbursements (averaging $22,000 per year), 7 research assistantships with full tuition reimbursements (averaging $21,000 per year), 2 teaching assistantships (averaging $17,500 per year) were awarded; career-related internships or fieldwork, institutionally sponsored loans, and unspecified assistantships also available. Financial award application deadline: 1/15. *Faculty research:* Multimedia via ATM, mobile robotics, thermophotovoltaic devices, microelectronic interconnections, agile manufacturing. Total annual research expenditures: $3.5 million. *Unit head:* Dr. Kim L. Boyer, Head, 518-276-2150, Fax: 518-276-6261, E-mail: kim@ecse.rpi.edu. *Application contact:* Ann Bruno, Manager of Student Services and Graduate Enrollment, 518-276-2554, Fax: 518-276-4403, E-mail: ann@ecse.rpi.edu.

Rice University, Graduate Programs, George R. Brown School of Engineering, Department of Electrical and Computer Engineering, Houston, TX 77251-1892. Offers bioengineering (MS, PhD); circuits, controls, and communication systems (MS, PhD); computer science and engineering (MS, PhD); electrical engineering (MEE); lasers, microwaves, and solid-state electronics (MS, PhD); MBA/MEE. Part-time programs available. *Degree requirements:* For master's, thesis (for some programs); for doctorate, thesis/dissertation. *Entrance requirements:* For master's and doctorate, GRE General Test, GRE Subject Test, minimum GPA of 3.0. Additional exam requirements/recommendations for international students: Required—TOEFL (minimum score 600 paper-based; 250 computer-based; 90 iBT). Electronic applications accepted. *Faculty research:* Physical electronics, systems, computer engineering, bioengineering.

Rice University, Graduate Programs, George R. Brown School of Engineering, Program in Computational Science and Engineering, Houston, TX 77251-1892. Offers MCSE.

Rochester Institute of Technology, Graduate Enrollment Services, Kate Gleason College of Engineering, Department of Computer Engineering, Rochester, NY 14623-5603. Offers MS. Part-time programs available. *Students:* 31 full-time (1 woman), 18 part-time (2 women); includes 5 Asian, non-Hispanic/Latino, 12 international. Average age 25. 98 applicants, 39% accepted, 7 enrolled. In 2010, 22 master's awarded. *Degree requirements:* For master's, thesis. *Entrance requirements:* For master's, GRE, minimum GPA of 3.0. Additional exam requirements/recommendations for international students: Required—TOEFL (minimum score 570 paper-based; 230 computer-based; 88 iBT) or IELTS (minimum score 6.5). *Application deadline:* For fall admission, 2/15 priority date for domestic and international students; for winter admission, 10/15 for domestic students, 10/15 priority date for international students. Applications are processed on a rolling basis. Application fee: $50. *Expenses:* Tuition: Full-time $33,234; part-time $924 per credit hour. Required fees: $219. *Financial support:* In 2010–11, 36 students received support; fellowships with partial tuition reimbursements available, research assistantships with partial tuition reimbursements available, teaching assistantships with partial tuition reimbursements available, career-related internships or fieldwork, institutionally sponsored loans, scholarships/grants, and unspecified assistantships available. Support available to part-time students. Financial award applicants required to submit FAFSA. *Faculty research:* Object detection and tracking using multiple cameras; face detection and recognition; pose and gaze estimation; activity recognition; power-constrained processing; lossless image compression; color forms processing; adaptive thresholding; automatic albuming; MPEG-7 color, shape and motion descriptors, Web printing. *Unit head:* Dr. Andreas Savakis, Department Head, 585-475-2987, Fax: 585-475-4084, E-mail: andreas.savakis@rit.edu. *Application contact:* Diane Ellison, Assistant Vice President, Graduate Enrollment Services, 585-475-2229, Fax: 585-475-7164, E-mail: gradinfo@rit.edu.

Rose-Hulman Institute of Technology, Faculty of Engineering and Applied Sciences, Department of Electrical and Computer Engineering, Terre Haute, IN 47803-3999. Offers electrical and computer engineering (M Eng); electrical engineering (MS). Part-time programs available. Postbaccalaureate distance learning degree programs offered (minimal on-campus study). *Faculty:* 18 full-time (4 women), 2 part-time/adjunct (1 woman). *Students:* 16 full-time (2 women), 2 part-time (1 women); includes 1 minority (Asian, non-Hispanic/Latino), 9 international. Average age 24. 12 applicants, 83% accepted, 4 enrolled. In 2010, 9 master's awarded. *Degree requirements:* For master's, thesis (for some programs). *Entrance requirements:* For master's, GRE, minimum GPA of 3.0. Additional exam requirements/recommendations for international students: Required—TOEFL (minimum score 580 paper-based; 237 computer-based; 92 iBT). *Application deadline:* For fall admission, 2/1 priority date for domestic students. Applications are processed on a rolling basis. Application fee: $0. *Expenses:* Tuition: Full-time $35,595; part-time $1038 per credit hour. *Financial support:* In 2010–11, 17 students received support; fellowships with full and partial tuition reimbursements available, research assistantships with full and partial tuition reimbursements available, institutionally sponsored loans, scholarships/grants, and tuition waivers (full and partial) available. *Faculty research:* Wireless systems, VLSI design, aerial robotics, power system dynamics and control, image and speech processing. Total annual research expenditures: $18,508. *Unit head:* Dr. Robert Throne, Interim Chairman, 812-877-8414, Fax: 812-877-8895, E-mail: robert.d.throne@rose-hulman.edu. *Application contact:* Dr. Daniel J. Moore, Associate Dean of the Faculty, 812-877-8110, Fax: 812-877-8061, E-mail: daniel.j.moore@rose-hulman.edu.

Royal Military College of Canada, Division of Graduate Studies and Research, Engineering Division, Department of Electrical and Computer Engineering, Kingston, ON K7K 7B4, Canada. Offers computer engineering (M Eng, PhD); electrical engineering (M Eng, PhD); software engineering (M Eng, PhD). *Degree requirements:* For master's, thesis; for doctorate, comprehensive exam, thesis/dissertation. *Entrance requirements:* For master's, honours degree with second-class standing in the appropriate field; for doctorate, master's degree. Electronic applications accepted.

Rutgers, The State University of New Jersey, New Brunswick, Graduate School-New Brunswick, Department of Electrical and Computer Engineering, Piscataway, NJ 08854-8097. Offers communications and solid-state electronics (MS, PhD); computer engineering (MS, PhD); control systems (MS, PhD); digital signal processing (MS, PhD). Part-time programs available. Terminal master's awarded for partial completion of doctoral program. *Degree requirements:* For master's, thesis or alternative; for doctorate, thesis/dissertation. *Entrance requirements:* For master's and doctorate, GRE General Test. Additional exam requirements/recommendations for international students: Required—TOEFL. Electronic applications accepted. *Expenses:* Tuition, state resident: full-time $7200; part-time $600 per credit. Tuition, nonresident: full-time $11,124; part-time $927 per credit. *Faculty research:* Communication and information processing, wireless information networks, micro-vacuum devices, machine vision, VLSI design.

St. Mary's University, Graduate School, Department of Engineering, Program in Electrical Engineering, San Antonio, TX 78228-8507. Offers electrical engineering (MS); electrical/computer engineering (MS). Part-time programs available. *Degree requirements:* For master's, comprehensive exam. *Entrance requirements:* For master's, GRE General Test. Additional exam requirements/recommendations for international students: Required—TOEFL (minimum score 550 paper-based; 213 computer-based; 80 iBT). Electronic applications accepted. *Faculty research:* Image processing, control, communication, artificial intelligence, robotics.

San Jose State University, Graduate Studies and Research, Charles W. Davidson College of Engineering, Department of Computer Engineering, San Jose, CA 95192-0001. Offers computer engineering (MS); software engineering (MS). *Degree requirements:* For master's, comprehensive exam, thesis. *Entrance requirements:* For master's, GRE General Test. Electronic applications accepted. *Faculty research:* Robotics, database management systems, computer networks.

Santa Clara University, School of Engineering, Program in Computer Science and Engineering, Santa Clara, CA 95053. Offers computer science and engineering (MS, PhD, Engineer); information assurance (Certificate); networking (Certificate); software engineering (MS, Certificate). Part-time and evening/weekend programs available. *Students:* 139 full-time (46 women), 108 part-time (31 women); includes 58 minority (6 Black or African American, non-Hispanic/Latino; 47 Asian, non-Hispanic/Latino; 2 Hispanic/Latino; 3 Two or more races, non-Hispanic/Latino), 142 international. Average age 28. 242 applicants, 56% accepted, 73 enrolled. In 2010, 76 master's, 6 doctorates, 3 other advanced degrees awarded. *Degree requirements:* For master's, thesis (for some programs); for doctorate, thesis/dissertation; for other advanced degree, thesis. *Entrance requirements:* For master's, GRE (waiver may be available), transcript; for doctorate, GRE, master's degree or equivalent; for other advanced degree, master's degree, published paper. Additional exam requirements/recommendations for international students: Required—TOEFL (minimum score 550 paper-based; 213 computer-based; 79 iBT). *Application deadline:* For fall admission, 8/12 for domestic students, 7/15 for international students; for winter admission, 10/28 for domestic students, 9/23 for international students; for spring admission, 2/25 for domestic students, 1/21 for international students. Applications are processed on a rolling basis. Application fee: $60. Electronic applications accepted. *Expenses:* Contact institution. *Financial support:* Research assistantships, teaching assistantships available. Financial award application deadline: 3/2; financial award applicants required to submit FAFSA. *Unit head:* Dr. Alex Zecevic, Chair, 408-554-2394, E-mail: azecevic@scu.edu. *Application contact:* Stacey Tinker, Director of Enrollment Management, 408-554-4748, Fax: 408-554-4323, E-mail: stinker@scu.edu.

Computer Engineering

Silicon Valley University, Graduate Programs, San Jose, CA 95131. Offers business administration (MBA); computer engineering (MSCE); computer science (MSCS). *Degree requirements:* For master's, project (MSCS).

Southern Illinois University Carbondale, Graduate School, College of Engineering, Department of Electrical and Computer Engineering, Carbondale, IL 62901-4701. Offers MS, PhD. *Degree requirements:* For master's, comprehensive exam, thesis. *Entrance requirements:* For master's, minimum GPA of 2.7. Additional exam requirements/recommendations for international students: Required—TOEFL. *Faculty research:* Circuits and power systems, communications and signal processing, controls and systems, electromagnetics and optics, electronics instrumentation and bioengineering.

Southern Methodist University, Bobby B. Lyle School of Engineering, Department of Computer Science and Engineering, Dallas, TX 75275-0122. Offers computer engineering (MS Cp E, PhD); computer science (MS, PhD); security engineering (MS); software engineering (MS). Part-time and evening/weekend programs available. Postbaccalaureate distance learning degree programs offered (no on-campus study). *Faculty:* 13 full-time (3 women), 13 part-time/adjunct (0 women). *Students:* 35 full-time (16 women), 149 part-time (22 women); includes 13 Black or African American, non-Hispanic/Latino; 1 American Indian or Alaska Native, non-Hispanic/Latino; 24 Asian, non-Hispanic/Latino; 13 Hispanic/Latino, 39 international. Average age 34. 180 applicants, 73% accepted, 69 enrolled. In 2010, 77 master's, 4 doctorates awarded. Terminal master's awarded for partial completion of doctoral program. *Degree requirements:* For master's, thesis optional; for doctorate, thesis/dissertation, oral and written qualifying exams, oral final exam (PhD). *Entrance requirements:* For master's, GRE General Test, minimum GPA of 3.0 in last 2 years; bachelor's degree in engineering, mathematics, or sciences; for doctorate, preliminary counseling exam (PhD), minimum GPA of 3.0, bachelor's degree in related field, MA (DE). Additional exam requirements/recommendations for international students: Required—TOEFL (minimum score 550 paper-based; 213 computer-based). *Application deadline:* For fall admission, 7/1 priority date for domestic students, 5/15 for international students; for spring admission, 11/15 for domestic students, 9/1 for international students. Applications are processed on a rolling basis. Application fee: $75. *Financial support:* In 2010–11, 20 students received support, including 6 research assistantships with full tuition reimbursements available (averaging $14,400 per year), 14 teaching assistantships with full tuition reimbursements available (averaging $14,400 per year). Financial award application deadline: 3/31; financial award applicants required to submit FAFSA. *Faculty research:* Trusted and high performance network computing, software engineering and management, knowledge engineering and management, computer arithmetic, computer architecture and CAD. Total annual research expenditures: $366,537. *Unit head:* Dr. Suku Nair, Chair, 214-768-2856, Fax: 214-768-3085, E-mail: nair@lyle.smu.edu. *Application contact:* Marc Valerin, Director of Graduate and Executive Admissions, 214-768-3042, E-mail: valerin@engr.smu.edu.

Southern Polytechnic State University, School of Engineering Technology and Management, Department of Electrical and Computer Engineering Technology, Marietta, GA 30060-2896. Offers engineering technology/electrical (MS). Part-time and evening/weekend programs available. *Faculty:* 7 full-time (1 woman), 3 part-time/adjunct (0 women). *Students:* 18 full-time (3 women), 9 part-time (1 woman); includes 6 Black or African American, non-Hispanic/Latino; 4 Asian, non-Hispanic/Latino, 11 international. Average age 30. 17 applicants, 71% accepted, 6 enrolled. In 2010, 8 master's awarded. *Degree requirements:* For master's, thesis. *Entrance requirements:* For master's, GRE (minimum score 500 quantitative/verbal/analytical), minimum GPA of 2.75. Additional exam requirements/recommendations for international students: Required—TOEFL (minimum score 550 paper-based; 213 computer-based; 79 iBT), IELTS (minimum score 6.5). *Application deadline:* For fall admission, 7/1 priority date for domestic students, 5/1 priority date for international students; for spring admission, 11/1 priority date for domestic students, 9/1 priority date for international students. Applications are processed on a rolling basis. Application fee: $20. Electronic applications accepted. *Expenses:* Tuition, state resident: full-time $3690; part-time $205 per semester hour. Tuition, nonresident: full-time $13,428; part-time $746 per semester hour. Required fees: $598 per semester. *Financial support:* In 2010–11, 5 students received support, including 4 teaching assistantships with partial tuition reimbursements available (averaging $3,000 per year); career-related internships or fieldwork, scholarships/grants, and unspecified assistantships also available. Support available to part-time students. Financial award application deadline: 5/1; financial award applicants required to submit FAFSA. *Faculty research:* Analog and digital communications, computer networking, analog and low power electronics design, control systems and digital signal processing, instrumentation (medical and industrial), biomedical signal analysis, biomedical imaging. *Unit head:* Dr. Austin Asgill, Chair, 678-915-7796, Fax: 678-915-7285, E-mail: aasgill@spsu.edu. *Application contact:* Nikki Palamiotis, Director of Graduate Studies, 678-915-4276, Fax: 678-915-7292, E-mail: npalamio@spsu.edu.

Stevens Institute of Technology, Graduate School, Charles V. Schaefer Jr. School of Engineering, Department of Electrical and Computer Engineering, Program in Computer Engineering, Hoboken, NJ 07030. Offers computer engineering (PhD); computer systems (M Eng); data communications and networks (M Eng); digital signal processing (Certificate); digital systems design (M Eng); engineered software systems (M Eng); image processing and multimedia (M Eng); information system security (M Eng); information systems (M Eng); real-time and embedded systems (Certificate). Part-time and evening/weekend programs available. *Students:* 41 full-time (5 women), 33 part-time (5 women); includes 3 Black or African American, non-Hispanic/Latino; 11 Asian, non-Hispanic/Latino; 2 Hispanic/Latino, 32 international. Average age 28. 91 applicants, 71% accepted.Terminal master's awarded for partial completion of doctoral program. *Degree requirements:* For doctorate, thesis/dissertation. *Entrance requirements:* For master's, doctorate, and Certificate, GRE. Additional exam requirements/recommendations for international students: Required—TOEFL. *Application deadline:* Applications are processed on a rolling basis. Application fee: $50. Electronic applications accepted. *Financial support:* Fellowships, research assistantships, teaching assistantships, Federal Work-Study and institutionally sponsored loans available. *Unit head:* Prof. R. Chandramouli, Head, 201-216-8642. *Application contact:* Graduate Admissions, 800-496-4935, Fax: 201-216-8044, E-mail: gradadmissions@stevens.edu.

Stevens Institute of Technology, Graduate School, Charles V. Schaefer Jr. School of Engineering, Department of Mechanical Engineering, Program in Integrated Product Development, Hoboken, NJ 07030. Offers armament engineering (M Eng); computer and electrical engineering (M Eng); manufacturing technologies (M Eng); systems reliability and design (M Eng). *Students:* 8 part-time (1 woman). Average age 26.*Unit head:* Dr. Constantin Chassapis, Director, 201-216-5564. *Application contact:* Graduate Admissions, 800-496-4935, Fax: 201-216-8044, E-mail: gradadmissions@stevens.edu.

Stony Brook University, State University of New York, Graduate School, College of Engineering and Applied Sciences, Department of Electrical and Computer Engineering, Program in Computer Engineering, Stony Brook, NY 11794. Offers MS, PhD. *Students:* 35 full-time (3 women), 6 part-time (3 women); includes 4 Asian, non-Hispanic/Latino, 34 international. In 2010, 5 master's awarded. Application fee: $100. *Expenses:* Tuition, state resident: full-time $8370; part-time $349 per credit. Tuition, nonresident: full-time $13,780; part-time $574 per credit. Required fees: $994. *Financial support:* In 2010–11, 11 research assistantships, 7 teaching assistantships were awarded. *Unit head:* Dr. Serge Luryi, Chairman, 631-632-8420. *Application contact:* Prof. Yuanyuan Yang, Graduate Program Director, 631-632-8474, Fax: 631-632-8494, E-mail: yang@ece.sunysb.edu.

Stony Brook University, State University of New York, School of Professional Development, Stony Brook, NY 11794. Offers biology-grade 7-12 (MAT); chemistry-grade 7-12 (MAT); coaching (Graduate Certificate); coaching online (Graduate Certificate); computer integrated engineering (Graduate Certificate); earth science-grade 7-12 (MAT); educational computing (Graduate Certificate); educational leadership (Advanced Certificate); English-grade 7-12 (MAT); environmental management (Graduate Certificate); environmental/occupational health and safety (Graduate Certificate); French-grade 7-12 (MAT); German-grade 7-12 (MAT); human resource management (Graduate Certificate); human resource management online (Graduate Certificate); information systems management (Graduate Certificate); Italian-grade 7-12 (MAT); liberal studies (MA); liberal studies online (MA); mathematics-grade 7-12 (MAT); operation research (Graduate Certificate); physics-grade 7-12 (MAT); professional studies online (MPS); school administration and supervision (Graduate Certificate); school building leadership (Graduate Certificate); school district administration (Graduate Certificate); school district business leadership (Advanced Certificate); school district leadership (Graduate Certificate); social science and the professions (MPS), including environmental waste management, human resource management; social studies-grade 7-12 (MAT); Spanish-grade 7-12 (MAT); waste management (Graduate Certificate). Part-time and evening/weekend programs available. Postbaccalaureate distance learning degree programs offered. *Faculty:* 25 full-time (10 women), 105 part-time/adjunct (40 women). *Students:* 360 full-time (228 women), 1,097 part-time (729 women); includes 180 minority (65 Black or African American, non-Hispanic/Latino; 2 American Indian or Alaska Native, non-Hispanic/Latino; 30 Asian, non-Hispanic/Latino; 81 Hispanic/Latino; 1 Native Hawaiian or other Pacific Islander, non-Hispanic/Latino; 1 Two or more races, non-Hispanic/Latino), 10 international. Average age 28. In 2010, 505 master's, 187 other advanced degrees awarded. *Degree requirements:* For master's, one foreign language, thesis or alternative. *Application deadline:* Applications are processed on a rolling basis. Application fee: $100. *Expenses:* Tuition, state resident: full-time $8370; part-time $349 per credit. Tuition, nonresident: full-time $13,780; part-time $574 per credit. Required fees: $994. *Financial support:* In 2010–11, 1 teaching assistantship was awarded; fellowships, research assistantships, career-related internships or fieldwork also available. Support available to part-time students. *Unit head:* Dr. Paul J. Edelson, Dean, 631-632-7052, Fax: 631-632-9046, E-mail: paul.edelson@stonybrook.edu. *Application contact:* Dr. Paul J. Edelson, Dean, 631-632-7052, Fax: 631-632-9046, E-mail: paul.edelson@stonybrook.edu.

Syracuse University, L. C. Smith College of Engineering and Computer Science, Program in Computer Engineering, Syracuse, NY 13244. Offers MS, CE. Part-time and evening/weekend programs available. *Students:* 121 full-time (27 women), 34 part-time (3 women); includes 3 minority (1 Black or African American, non-Hispanic/Latino; 2 Asian, non-Hispanic/Latino), 126 international. Average age 25. 117 applicants, 58% accepted, 28 enrolled. In 2010, 59 master's awarded. *Degree requirements:* For CE, thesis. *Entrance requirements:* For master's and CE, GRE General Test. Additional exam requirements/recommendations for international students: Required—TOEFL (minimum score 100 iBT). *Application deadline:* For fall admission, 6/1 priority date for domestic and international students. Applications are processed on a rolling basis. Application fee: $75. Electronic applications accepted. *Expenses:* Tuition: Part-time $1162 per credit. *Financial support:* Fellowships with full tuition reimbursements, research assistantships with full and partial tuition reimbursements, teaching assistantships with full and partial tuition reimbursements, tuition waivers (partial) available. Financial award application deadline: 1/1. *Faculty research:* Hardware, software, computer applications. *Unit head:* Dr. Roger Chen, Program Director, 315-443-4179, E-mail: crchen@syr.edu. *Application contact:* Barbara Decker, 315-443-2369, Fax: 315-443-2369, E-mail: badecker@syr.edu.

Syracuse University, L. C. Smith College of Engineering and Computer Science, Program in Electrical and Computer Engineering, Syracuse, NY 13244. Offers PhD. *Students:* 48 full-time (16 women), 6 part-time (0 women), 46 international. Average age 27. 130 applicants, 18% accepted, 15 enrolled. In 2010, 3 doctorates awarded. *Entrance requirements:* For doctorate, GRE General Test. Additional exam requirements/recommendations for international students: Required—TOEFL (minimum score 100 iBT). *Application deadline:* For fall admission, 7/1 priority date for domestic students, 6/1 priority date for international students. Application fee: $75. Electronic applications accepted. *Expenses:* Tuition: Part-time $1162 per credit. *Financial support:* Fellowships with full tuition reimbursements, research assistantships with full and partial tuition reimbursements, teaching assistantships with full and partial tuition reimbursements, tuition waivers (partial) available. Financial award application deadline: 1/1. *Unit head:* Prof. Chilukuri Mohan, Chair, 315-443-2583, E-mail: mohan@syr.edu. *Application contact:* Barbara Decker, Information Contact, 315-443-2368, Fax: 315-443-2583, E-mail: badecker@syr.edu.

Temple University, College of Engineering, Department of Electrical and Computer Engineering, Philadelphia, PA 19122-6096. Offers electrical engineering (MSE). Part-time and evening/weekend programs available. *Faculty:* 12 full-time (1 woman). *Students:* 25 full-time (3 women), 12 part-time (1 woman); includes 2 Asian, non-Hispanic/Latino, 25 international. 48 applicants, 40% accepted, 8 enrolled. In 2010, 27 master's awarded. *Degree requirements:* For master's, thesis optional. *Entrance requirements:* For master's, GRE General Test, minimum GPA of 3.0. Additional exam requirements/recommendations for international students: Required—TOEFL (minimum score 550 paper-based; 213 computer-based; 79 iBT). *Application deadline:* For fall admission, 7/1 for domestic students, 12/15 for international students; for spring admission, 11/1 for domestic students, 8/1 for international students. Applications are processed on a rolling basis. Application fee: $50. Electronic applications accepted. *Financial support:* In 2010–11; 1 fellowship with full tuition reimbursement, 1 research assistantship with full tuition reimbursement, 9 teaching assistantships with full tuition reimbursements were awarded; Federal Work-Study and institutionally sponsored loans also available. Financial award application deadline: 1/15; financial award applicants required to submit FAFSA. *Faculty research:* Computer engineering, intelligent control, microprocessors, digital processing, neutral networks. Total annual research expenditures: $425,000. *Unit head:* Dr. Joseph Picone, Chair, 215-204-7597, Fax: 215-204-5960, E-mail: picone@temple.edu. *Application contact:* Dr. Joseph Picone, Chair, 215-204-7597, Fax: 215-204-5960, E-mail: picone@temple.edu.

Texas A&M University, College of Engineering, Department of Computer Science, College Station, TX 77843. Offers computer engineering (M En); computer science (MCS); computer science and engineering (MS, PhD). Part-time programs available. *Faculty:* 41. *Students:* 306 full-time (52 women), 42 part-time (6 women); includes 35 minority (7 Black or African American, non-Hispanic/Latino; 2 American Indian or Alaska Native, non-Hispanic/Latino; 17 Asian, non-Hispanic/Latino; 9 Hispanic/Latino), 240 international. Average age 28. In 2010, 36 master's, 22 doctorates awarded. *Degree requirements:* For master's, thesis (for some programs); for doctorate, thesis/dissertation. *Entrance requirements:* For master's and doctorate, GRE General Test. Additional exam requirements/recommendations for international students: Required—TOEFL (minimum score 213 computer-based). *Application deadline:* For fall admission, 3/1 priority date for domestic and international students; for spring admission, 8/1 priority date for domestic and international students. Applications are processed on a rolling basis. Application fee: $50 ($75 for international students). Electronic applications accepted. *Financial support:* In 2010–11, research assistantships with tuition reimbursements (averaging $15,478 per year), teaching assistantships (averaging $15,913 per year) were awarded; fellowships with full tuition reimbursements also available. Financial award application deadline: 3/1. *Faculty research:* Software, systems, informatics, human-centered systems, theory. *Unit head:* Valerie E. Taylor, Head, 979-845-5820, Fax: 979-847-8578, E-mail: taylor@cse.tamu.edu. *Application contact:* Dr. Jianer Chen, Head of Graduate Admissions, 979-845-4259, Fax: 979-862-3684, E-mail: chen@cse.tamu.edu.

Texas A&M University, College of Engineering, Department of Electrical and Computer Engineering, College Station, TX 77843. Offers computer engineering (M Eng, MS, PhD); electrical engineering (MS, PhD). *Faculty:* 64. *Students:* 500 full-time (72 women), 45 part-time (8 women); includes 50 minority (9 Black or African American, non-Hispanic/Latino; 23 Asian, non-Hispanic/Latino; 18 Hispanic/Latino), 420 international. Average age 28. In 2010, 104 master's, 32 doctorates awarded. *Degree requirements:* For master's, thesis (MS); for doctorate, thesis/dissertation. *Entrance requirements:* For master's and doctorate, GRE General Test. Additional exam requirements/recommendations for international students: Required—TOEFL. Application fee: $50 ($75 for international students). *Financial support:* Fellowships, research assistantships, teaching assistantships, career-related internships or fieldwork available. Financial award application deadline: 4/1; financial award applicants required to submit FAFSA. *Faculty research:* Solid-state, electric power systems, and communications engineering. *Unit head:* Dr.

Scott Miller, Head, 979-845-7441, E-mail: smiller@ece.tamu.edu. *Application contact:* Graduate Advisor, 979-845-7441.

The University of Akron, Graduate School, College of Engineering, Department of Electrical and Computer Engineering, Akron, OH 44325. Offers MS, PhD. Evening/weekend programs available. *Faculty:* 17 full-time (1 woman), 2 part-time/adjunct (0 women). *Students:* 69 full-time (15 women), 16 part-time (1 woman); includes 1 Asian, non-Hispanic/Latino; 1 Native Hawaiian or other Pacific Islander, non-Hispanic/Latino, 65 international. Average age 26. 151 applicants, 42% accepted, 28 enrolled. In 2010, 11 master's, 5 doctorates awarded. *Degree requirements:* For master's, thesis optional, oral comprehensive exam or thesis; for doctorate, one foreign language, thesis/dissertation, candidacy exam, qualifying exam. *Entrance requirements:* For master's, GRE, minimum GPA of 2.75, three letters of recommendation, statement of purpose; for doctorate, GRE, minimum GPA of 3.0 with bachelor's degree, 3.5 with master's degree; three letters of recommendation; statement of purpose. Additional exam requirements/recommendations for international students: Required—TOEFL (minimum score 550 paper-based; 213 computer-based; 79 iBT). *Application deadline:* Applications are processed on a rolling basis. Application fee: $30 ($40 for international students). Electronic applications accepted. *Expenses:* Tuition, state resident: full-time $6800; part-time $378 per credit hour. Tuition, nonresident: full-time $11,644; part-time $647 per credit hour. Required fees: $1265. One-time fee: $30 full-time. *Financial support:* In 2010–11, 19 research assistantships with full tuition reimbursements, 14 teaching assistantships with full tuition reimbursements were awarded; career-related internships or fieldwork also available. *Faculty research:* Computational electromagnetics and nondestructive testing, control systems, sensors and actuators applications and networks, alternative energy systems and hybrid vehicles, analog IC design embedded systems. Total annual research expenditures: $308,566. *Unit head:* Dr. Jose De Abreu-Garcia, Chair, 330-972-6709, E-mail: jdeabreu-garcia@uakron.edu. *Application contact:* Dr. Jose De Abreu-Garcia, Chair, 330-972-6709, E-mail: jdeabreu-garcia@uakron.edu.

The University of Alabama, Graduate School, College of Engineering, Department of Electrical and Computer Engineering, Tuscaloosa, AL 35487-0286. Offers electrical engineering (MS, PhD). Part-time programs available. Postbaccalaureate distance learning degree programs offered (minimal on-campus study). *Faculty:* 16 full-time (4 women). *Students:* 34 full-time (5 women), 15 part-time (4 women); includes 3 minority (1 Black or African American, non-Hispanic/Latino; 1 Asian, non-Hispanic/Latino; 1 Hispanic/Latino), 28 international. Average age 27. 84 applicants, 50% accepted, 13 enrolled. In 2010, 11 master's, 2 doctorates awarded. *Degree requirements:* For master's, thesis or alternative; for doctorate, one foreign language, comprehensive exam, thesis/dissertation. *Entrance requirements:* For master's, GRE (for students from non ABET accredited schools), minimum GPA of 3.0 in last 60 hours of course work or overall; for doctorate, GRE (for students from non ABET-accredited schools), minimum GPA of 3.0 overall. Additional exam requirements/recommendations for international students: Required—TOEFL (minimum score 550 paper-based; 213 computer-based). *Application deadline:* For fall admission, 7/1 priority date for domestic students, 1/15 priority date for international students; for spring admission, 11/1 priority date for domestic students, 6/1 priority date for international students. Applications are processed on a rolling basis. Application fee: $50 ($60 for international students). Electronic applications accepted. *Expenses:* Tuition, state resident: full-time $7900. Tuition, nonresident: full-time $20,500. *Financial support:* In 2010–11, 1 fellowship with full tuition reimbursement (averaging $15,000 per year), 14 research assistantships with full tuition reimbursements (averaging $14,000 per year), 6 teaching assistantships with full tuition reimbursements (averaging $11,025 per year) were awarded; health care benefits and unspecified assistantships also available. *Faculty research:* Devices and materials, electromechanical systems, embedded systems. Total annual research expenditures: $1.3 million. *Unit head:* Dr. D. Jeff Jackson, Department Head, 205-348-2919, Fax: 205-348-6959, E-mail: jjackson@eng.ua.edu. *Application contact:* Dr. Tim Haskew, Graduate Program Director, 205-348-1766, Fax: 205-348-6959, E-mail: thaskew@eng.ua.edu.

The University of Alabama at Birmingham, School of Engineering, Program in Computer Engineering, Birmingham, AL 35294. Offers PhD. *Students:* 7 full-time (0 women), 6 part-time (2 women); includes 1 minority (Hispanic/Latino), 8 international. Average age 32. 5 applicants, 80% accepted, 3 enrolled. In 2010, 1 doctorate awarded. *Expenses:* Tuition, state resident: full-time $5482. Tuition, nonresident: full-time $12,430. Tuition and fees vary according to program. *Unit head:* Dr. Yehia Massoud, Chair, 205-934-8440. *Application contact:* Julie Bryant, Director of Graduate Admissions, 205-934-8227, Fax: 205-934-8413, E-mail: jbryant@uab.edu.

The University of Alabama in Huntsville, School of Graduate Studies, College of Engineering, Department of Electrical and Computer Engineering, Huntsville, AL 35899. Offers computer engineering (MSE, PhD); electrical engineering (MSE, PhD); optical science and engineering (PhD); optics and photonics (MSE); software engineering (MSSE). Part-time and evening/weekend programs available. *Faculty:* 25 full-time (3 women), 4 part-time/adjunct (0 women). *Students:* 47 full-time (10 women), 145 part-time (21 women); includes 20 minority (7 Black or African American, non-Hispanic/Latino; 1 American Indian or Alaska Native, non-Hispanic/Latino; 9 Asian, non-Hispanic/Latino; 2 Hispanic/Latino; 1 Two or more races, non-Hispanic/Latino), 32 international. Average age 32. 190 applicants, 56% accepted, 57 enrolled. In 2010, 58 master's, 6 doctorates awarded. *Degree requirements:* For master's, comprehensive exam, thesis or alternative, oral and written exams; for doctorate, comprehensive exam, thesis/dissertation, oral and written exams. *Entrance requirements:* For master's, GRE General Test, appropriate bachelor's degree, minimum GPA of 3.0; for doctorate, GRE General Test, minimum GPA of 3.0. Additional exam requirements/recommendations for international students: Required—TOEFL (minimum score 500 paper-based; 173 computer-based; 62 iBT). *Application deadline:* For fall admission, 7/15 for domestic students, 4/1 for international students; for spring admission, 11/30 for domestic students, 9/1 for international students. Applications are processed on a rolling basis. Application fee: $40 ($50 for international students). Electronic applications accepted. *Expenses:* Tuition, state resident: full-time $7250; part-time $407.75 per credit hour. Tuition, nonresident: full-time $17,358; part-time $970.05 per credit hour. Required fees: $246.80 per semester. Tuition and fees vary according to course load and program. *Financial support:* In 2010–11, 42 students received support, including 16 research assistantships with full and partial tuition reimbursements available (averaging $10,649 per year), 21 teaching assistantships with full and partial tuition reimbursements available (averaging $10,593 per year); career-related internships or fieldwork, Federal Work-Study, institutionally sponsored loans, scholarships/grants, health care benefits, tuition waivers, and unspecified assistantships also available. Support available to part-time students. Financial award application deadline: 4/1; financial award applicants required to submit FAFSA. *Faculty research:* Optical signal processing, electromagnetics, photonics, nonlinear waves, computer architecture. Total annual research expenditures: $13.5 million. *Unit head:* Dr. Robert Lindquist, Chair, 256-824-6316, Fax: 256-824-6803, E-mail: lindquis@ece.uah.edu. *Application contact:* Kathy Biggs, Graduate Studies Admissions Manager, 256-824-6199, Fax: 256-824-6405, E-mail: deangrad@uah.edu.

University of Alaska Fairbanks, College of Engineering and Mines, Department of Electrical and Computer Engineering, Fairbanks, AK 99775-5915. Offers electrical engineering (MEE, MS, PhD); engineering (PhD). Part-time programs available. *Faculty:* 8 full-time (1 woman). *Students:* 19 full-time (3 women), 1 part-time (0 women), 10 international. Average age 26. 20 applicants, 35% accepted, 6 enrolled. In 2010, 4 master's awarded. Terminal master's awarded for partial completion of doctoral program. *Degree requirements:* For master's, comprehensive exam, thesis or alternative; for doctorate, comprehensive exam, thesis/dissertation, oral exam, oral defense. *Entrance requirements:* For master's and doctorate, GRE General Test. Additional exam requirements/recommendations for international students: Required—TOEFL (minimum score 550 paper-based; 213 computer-based; 80 iBT). *Application deadline:* For fall admission, 6/1 for domestic students, 3/1 for international students; for spring admission, 10/15 for domestic students, 9/1 for international students. Applications are processed on a rolling basis. Application fee: $60. Electronic applications accepted. *Expenses:* Tuition, state resident: full-time $5688; part-time $316 per credit. Tuition, nonresident: full-time $11,628; part-time $646 per credit. Required fees: $289 per semester. Tuition and fees vary according to course

load and reciprocity agreements. *Financial support:* In 2010–11, 13 research assistantships with tuition reimbursements (averaging $11,876 per year), 10 teaching assistantships with tuition reimbursements (averaging $6,644 per year) were awarded; fellowships with tuition reimbursements, career-related internships or fieldwork, Federal Work-Study, scholarships/grants, health care benefits, and unspecified assistantships also available. Support available to part-time students. Financial award application deadline: 7/1; financial award applicants required to submit FAFSA. *Faculty research:* Geomagnetically-induced currents in power lines, electromagnetic wave propagation, laser radar systems, bioinformatics, distributed sensor networks. *Unit head:* Dr. Charles Mayer, Chair, 907-474-7137, Fax: 907-474-5135, E-mail: fyee@uaf.edu. *Application contact:* Dr. Charles Mayer, Chair, 907-474-7137, Fax: 907-474-5135, E-mail: fyee@uaf.edu.

University of Alberta, Faculty of Graduate Studies and Research, Department of Electrical and Computer Engineering, Edmonton, AB T6G 2E1, Canada. Offers communications (M Eng, M Sc, PhD); computer engineering (M Eng, M Sc, PhD); electromagnetics (M Eng, M Sc, PhD); nanotechnology and microdevices (M Eng, M Sc, PhD); power/power electronics (M Eng, M Sc, PhD); systems (M Eng, M Sc, PhD). Terminal master's awarded for partial completion of doctoral program. *Degree requirements:* For master's, thesis; for doctorate, thesis/dissertation. *Entrance requirements:* Additional exam requirements/recommendations for international students: Required—TOEFL. Electronic applications accepted. *Faculty research:* Controls, communications, microelectronics, electromagnetics.

The University of Arizona, College of Engineering, Department of Electrical and Computer Engineering, Tucson, AZ 85721. Offers M Eng, MS, PhD. Part-time programs available. *Faculty:* 27 full-time (4 women), 3 part-time/adjunct (1 woman). *Students:* 123 full-time (17 women), 33 part-time (5 women); includes 26 minority (1 Black or African American, non-Hispanic/Latino; 7 Asian, non-Hispanic/Latino; 11 Hispanic/Latino; 7 Two or more races, non-Hispanic/Latino), 95 international. Average age 31. 514 applicants, 23% accepted, 38 enrolled. In 2010, 19 master's, 16 doctorates awarded. *Degree requirements:* For master's, thesis (for some programs); for doctorate, thesis/dissertation. *Entrance requirements:* For master's, GRE General Test, 3 letters of recommendation, statement of purpose; for doctorate, GRE General Test, master's degree in related field, 3 letters of recommendation, statement of purpose. Additional exam requirements/recommendations for international students: Required—TOEFL (minimum score 550 paper-based; 213 computer-based; 79 iBT). *Application deadline:* For fall admission, 12/15 for domestic and international students; for spring admission, 7/15 for domestic and international students. Applications are processed on a rolling basis. Application fee: $75. Electronic applications accepted. *Expenses:* Tuition, state resident: full-time $7692. *Financial support:* In 2010–11, 73 research assistantships with full tuition reimbursements (averaging $23,715 per year), 14 teaching assistantships with full tuition reimbursements (averaging $23,585 per year) were awarded; institutionally sponsored loans, scholarships/grants, health care benefits, and unspecified assistantships also available. Financial award application deadline: 3/15. *Faculty research:* Communication systems, control systems, signal processing, computer-aided logic. Total annual research expenditures: $7.1 million. *Unit head:* Dr. Jerzy W. Rozenblit, Head, 520-621-6193, E-mail: head@ece.arizona.edu. *Application contact:* Tami J. Whelan, Senior Graduate Academic Adviser, 520-621-6195, Fax: 520-621-8076, E-mail: whelan@ece.arizona.edu.

University of Arkansas, Graduate School, College of Engineering, Department of Computer Science and Computer Engineering, Program in Computer Engineering, Fayetteville, AR 72701-1201. Offers MS Cmp E, MSE, PhD. *Students:* 4 full-time (0 women), 17 part-time (1 woman); includes 1 minority (Black or African American, non-Hispanic/Latino), 6 international. 4 applicants, 75% accepted. In 2010, 4 master's awarded. *Degree requirements:* For master's, thesis optional; for doctorate, one foreign language, thesis/dissertation. *Application deadline:* For fall admission, 4/1 for international students; for spring admission, 10/1 for international students. Applications are processed on a rolling basis. Application fee: $40 ($50 for international students). Electronic applications accepted. *Financial support:* In 2010–11, 4 research assistantships, 7 teaching assistantships were awarded; fellowships with tuition reimbursements, career-related internships or fieldwork and Federal Work-Study also available. Support available to part-time students. Financial award application deadline: 4/1; financial award applicants required to submit FAFSA. *Unit head:* Dr. Susan Gauch, Department Chair, 479-575-6197, Fax: 479-575-5339, E-mail: sgauch@uark.edu. *Application contact:* Dr. Gordon Beavers, Graduate Coordinator, 479-575-6040, Fax: 479-575-5339, E-mail: gordonb@uark.edu.

University of Bridgeport, School of Engineering, Departments of Computer Science and Computer Engineering, Bridgeport, CT 06604. Offers computer engineering (MS); computer science (MS); computer science and engineering (PhD). *Degree requirements:* For master's, thesis optional; for doctorate, comprehensive exam, thesis/dissertation. *Entrance requirements:* Additional exam requirements/recommendations for international students: Recommended—TOEFL (minimum score 550 paper-based; 213 computer-based; 80 iBT), IELTS (minimum score 6.5). Electronic applications accepted. *Expenses:* Tuition: Full-time $22,000; part-time $575 per credit hour. Required fees: $90 per semester. Tuition and fees vary according to course level, course load and program.

The University of British Columbia, Faculty of Applied Science, Program in Electrical and Computer Engineering, Vancouver, BC V6T 1Z1, Canada. Offers M Eng, MA Sc, PhD. Part-time programs available. *Degree requirements:* For master's, thesis (for some programs); for doctorate, thesis/dissertation. *Entrance requirements:* Additional exam requirements/recommendations for international students: Required—TOEFL (minimum score 600 paper-based; 250 computer-based; 100 iBT), TWE. Electronic applications accepted. Tuition charges are reported in Canadian dollars. *Expenses:* Tuition, area resident: Full-time $4179 Canadian dollars. International tuition: $7344 Canadian dollars full-time. *Faculty research:* Applied electromagnetics, biomedical engineering, communications and signal processing, computer and software engineering, power engineering, robotics, solid-state, systems and control.

University of Calgary, Faculty of Graduate Studies, Schulich School of Engineering, Department of Electrical and Computer Engineering, Calgary, AB T2N 1N4, Canada. Offers M Eng, M Sc, PhD. Part-time programs available. *Degree requirements:* For master's, thesis (M Sc); for doctorate, thesis/dissertation, candidacy exam. *Entrance requirements:* For master's and doctorate, minimum GPA of 3.0. Additional exam requirements/recommendations for international students: Required—TOEFL (minimum score 550 paper-based; 213 computer-based), IELTS (minimum score 7), TOEFL or IELTS. Electronic applications accepted. *Faculty research:* Biomedical and bioelectrics, telecommunications and signal processing, software and computer engineering, power and control, microelectronics and instrumentation.

University of California, Davis, College of Engineering, Program in Electrical and Computer Engineering, Davis, CA 95616. Offers MS, PhD. Terminal master's awarded for partial completion of doctoral program. *Degree requirements:* For master's, comprehensive exam (for some programs), thesis (for some programs); for doctorate, thesis/dissertation, preliminary and qualifying exams, thesis defense. *Entrance requirements:* For master's, GRE General Test, minimum GPA of 3.2; for doctorate, GRE, minimum graduate GPA of 3.5. Additional exam requirements/recommendations for international students: Required—TOEFL (minimum score 550 paper-based; 213 computer-based). Electronic applications accepted.

University of California, Riverside, Graduate Division, Department of Electrical Engineering, Riverside, CA 92521-0102. Offers electrical engineering (MS, PhD), including computer engineering, control and robotics, intelligent systems, nano-materials, devices and circuits, signal processing and communications. Terminal master's awarded for partial completion of doctoral program. *Degree requirements:* For master's, thesis optional; for doctorate, thesis/dissertation, qualifying exams. *Entrance requirements:* For master's and doctorate, GRE General Test, minimum GPA of 3.25. Additional exam requirements/recommendations for international students: Required—TOEFL (minimum score 550 paper-based; 213 computer-based; 80 iBT). Electronic applications accepted. *Faculty research:* Solid state devices, integrated circuits, signal processing.

Computer Engineering

University of California, San Diego, Office of Graduate Studies, Department of Computer Science and Engineering, La Jolla, CA 92093. Offers computer engineering (MS, PhD); computer science (MS, PhD). *Degree requirements:* For doctorate, thesis/dissertation. *Entrance requirements:* For master's and doctorate, GRE General Test. Electronic applications accepted. *Faculty research:* Analysis of algorithms, combinatorial algorithms, discrete optimization.

University of California, San Diego, Office of Graduate Studies, Department of Electrical and Computer Engineering, La Jolla, CA 92093. Offers applied ocean science (MS, PhD); applied physics (MS, PhD); communication theory and systems (MS, PhD); computer engineering (MS, PhD); electrical engineering (M Eng); electronic circuits and systems (MS, PhD); intelligent systems, robotics and control (MS, PhD); photonics (MS, PhD); signal and image processing (MS, PhD). MS only offered to students who have been admitted to the PhD program. *Entrance requirements:* For master's and doctorate, GRE General Test. Electronic applications accepted.

University of California, San Diego, Office of Graduate Studies, Interdisciplinary Program in Cognitive Science, La Jolla, CA 92093. Offers cognitive science/anthropology (PhD); cognitive science/communication (PhD); cognitive science/computer science and engineering (PhD); cognitive science/linguistics (PhD); cognitive science/neuroscience (PhD); cognitive science/philosophy (PhD); cognitive science/psychology (PhD); cognitive science/sociology (PhD). Admissions offered through affiliated departments. *Degree requirements:* For doctorate, thesis/dissertation. *Entrance requirements:* For doctorate, GRE General Test, acceptance into one of the eight participating departments. *Faculty research:* Language and cognition, philosophy of mind, visual perception, biological anthropology, sociolinguistics.

University of California, Santa Barbara, Graduate Division, College of Engineering, Department of Computer Science, Santa Barbara, CA 93106-5110. Offers cognitive science (PhD); computational science and engineering (PhD); computer science (MS, PhD); technology and society (PhD). *Faculty:* 33 full-time (5 women), 5 part-time/adjunct (0 women). *Students:* 135 full-time (31 women); includes 51 Asian, non-Hispanic/Latino; 4 Hispanic/Latino. Average age 27. 481 applicants, 20% accepted, 30 enrolled. In 2010, 33 master's, 12 doctorates awarded. Terminal master's awarded for partial completion of doctoral program. *Degree requirements:* For master's, comprehensive exam (for some programs), thesis (for some programs), project (for some programs); for doctorate, thesis/dissertation. *Entrance requirements:* For master's and doctorate, GRE. Additional exam requirements/recommendations for international students: Required—TOEFL (minimum score 600 paper-based; 100 iBT), IELTS (minimum score 7). *Application deadline:* For fall admission, 12/15 for domestic and international students. Application fee: $70 ($90 for international students). Electronic applications accepted. *Financial support:* In 2010–11, 117 students received support, including 36 fellowships with full and partial tuition reimbursements available (averaging $10,486 per year), 77 research assistantships with full and partial tuition reimbursements available (averaging $12,464 per year), 47 teaching assistantships with partial tuition reimbursements available (averaging $10,383 per year); career-related internships or fieldwork, Federal Work-Study, institutionally sponsored loans, scholarships/grants, health care benefits, tuition waivers (full and partial), and unspecified assistantships also available. Financial award application deadline: 12/15; financial award applicants required to submit FAFSA. *Faculty research:* Networking and security, database systems, computational science and engineering, programming languages and software engineering, human computer interaction. Total annual research expenditures: $8 million. *Unit head:* Subhash Suri, Chair, 805-893-5334, Fax: 805-893-8553, E-mail: suri@cs.ucsb.edu. *Application contact:* Morgan Marcos, Graduate Program Assistant, 805-893-4322, Fax: 805-893-8553, E-mail: mmarcos@cs.ucsb.edu.

University of California, Santa Barbara, Graduate Division, College of Engineering, Department of Electrical and Computer Engineering, Santa Barbara, CA 93106-2014. Offers communications, control and signal processing (PhD); computer engineering (MS); electronics and photonics (MS); MS/PhD. *Faculty:* 37 full-time (3 women), 1 part-time/adjunct (0 women). *Students:* 251 full-time (45 women); includes 2 Black or African American, non-Hispanic/Latino; 2 American Indian or Alaska Native, non-Hispanic/Latino; 123 Asian, non-Hispanic/Latino; 10 Hispanic/Latino; 1 Native Hawaiian or other Pacific Islander, non-Hispanic/Latino. Average age 26. 1,040 applicants, 27% accepted, 79 enrolled. In 2010, 47 master's, 31 doctorates awarded. Terminal master's awarded for partial completion of doctoral program. *Degree requirements:* For master's, comprehensive exam, thesis; for doctorate, thesis/dissertation. *Entrance requirements:* For master's and doctorate, GRE General Test. Additional exam requirements/recommendations for international students: Required—TOEFL (minimum score 550 paper-based; 80 iBT), IELTS (minimum score 7). *Application deadline:* For fall admission, 12/15 for domestic and international students; for winter admission, 11/1 for domestic and international students; for spring admission, 1/1 for domestic and international students. Application fee: $70 ($90 for international students). Electronic applications accepted. *Financial support:* In 2010–11, 196 students received support, including 70 fellowships with full and partial tuition reimbursements available (averaging $7,181 per year), 155 research assistantships with full and partial tuition reimbursements available (averaging $15,235 per year), 54 teaching assistantships with full and partial tuition reimbursements available (averaging $9,910 per year); tuition waivers (full and partial) also available. Financial award application deadline: 12/15; financial award applicants required to submit FAFSA. *Faculty research:* Communications, signal processing, computer engineering, control, electronics and photonics. Total annual research expenditures: $25.5 million. *Unit head:* Prof. Jerry Gibson, Chair, 805-893-3821, Fax: 805-893-6262, E-mail: gibson@ece.ucsb.edu. *Application contact:* Erika Raquel Klukovich, Graduate Admissions Coordinator, 805-893-3114, Fax: 805-893-5402, E-mail: erika@ece.ucsb.edu.

University of California, Santa Barbara, Graduate Division, College of Engineering, Department of Mechanical Engineering, Santa Barbara, CA 93106-5070. Offers computational science and engineering (MS, PhD); mechanical engineering (MS, PhD); MS/PhD. *Faculty:* 27 full-time (4 women), 7 part-time/adjunct (3 women). *Students:* 76 full-time (11 women); includes 1 Black or African American, non-Hispanic/Latino; 18 Asian, non-Hispanic/Latino; 2 Hispanic/Latino. Average age 27. 270 applicants, 11% accepted, 15 enrolled. In 2010, 7 master's, 8 doctorates awarded. *Degree requirements:* For master's, thesis; for doctorate, comprehensive exam, thesis/dissertation. *Entrance requirements:* For master's and doctorate, GRE. Additional exam requirements/recommendations for international students: Required—TOEFL (minimum score 550 paper-based; 80 iBT), IELTS (minimum score 7). *Application deadline:* For fall admission, 1/1 for domestic and international students. Application fee: $70 ($90 for international students). Electronic applications accepted. *Financial support:* In 2010–11, 72 students received support, including 18 fellowships with full and partial tuition reimbursements available (averaging $11,139 per year), 57 research assistantships with full and partial tuition reimbursements available (averaging $13,711 per year), 45 teaching assistantships with full and partial tuition reimbursements available (averaging $9,120 per year); scholarships/grants, health care benefits, tuition waivers (full and partial), and unspecified assistantships also available. Financial award application deadline: 1/1; financial award applicants required to submit FAFSA. *Faculty research:* Micro/nanoscale technology; computational science and engineering; dynamics systems, controls and robotics; thermofluid sciences, solid mechanics, materials, and structures. *Unit head:* Dr. Kimberly Turner, Chair, 805-893-8080, Fax: 805-893-8651, E-mail: turner@engineering.ucsb.edu. *Application contact:* Laura L. Reynolds, Staff Graduate Program Advisor, 805-893-2239, Fax: 805-893-8651, E-mail: megrad@engineering.ucsb.edu.

University of California, Santa Barbara, Graduate Division, College of Letters and Sciences, Division of Mathematics, Life, and Physical Sciences, Department of Ecology, Evolution, and Marine Biology, Santa Barbara, CA 93106-9620. Offers computational science and engineering (MA); computational sciences and engineering (PhD); ecology, evolution, and marine biology (MA, PhD); MA/PhD. *Faculty:* 27 full-time (7 women). *Students:* 59 full-time (38 women); includes 2 Black or African American, non-Hispanic/Latino; 5 Asian, non-Hispanic/Latino; 2 Hispanic/Latino. Average age 29. 119 applicants, 11% accepted, 8 enrolled. In 2010, 5 master's, 3 doctorates awarded. *Degree requirements:* For master's, comprehensive exam (for some programs), thesis (for some programs); for doctorate, comprehensive exam, thesis/ dissertation. *Entrance requirements:* For master's and doctorate, GRE General Test. Additional exam requirements/recommendations for international students: Required—TOEFL (minimum score 550 paper-based; 80 iBT), IELTS. *Application deadline:* For fall admission, 12/15 for domestic and international students. Application fee: $70 ($90 for international students). Electronic applications accepted. *Financial support:* In 2010–11, 54 students received support, including 35 fellowships with full and partial tuition reimbursements available (averaging $10,812 per year), 21 research assistantships with full and partial tuition reimbursements available (averaging $8,441 per year), 43 teaching assistantships with partial tuition reimbursements available (averaging $9,346 per year); Federal Work-Study, scholarships/grants, traineeships, health care benefits, and tuition waivers (full and partial) also available. Financial award application deadline: 12/15; financial award applicants required to submit FAFSA. *Faculty research:* Community ecology, evolution, marine biology, population genetics, stream ecology. *Unit head:* Dr. Cheryl Briggs, Chair, 805-893-2415, Fax: 805-893-5885. *Application contact:* Melanie Fujii, Staff Graduate Advisor, 805-893-2979, Fax: 805-893-5885, E-mail: eemb-info@lifesci.ucsb.edu.

University of California, Santa Cruz, Division of Graduate Studies, Jack Baskin School of Engineering, Program in Computer Engineering, Santa Cruz, CA 95064. Offers computer engineering (MS, PhD); network engineering (MS). Part-time programs available. *Students:* 77 full-time (15 women), 6 part-time (1 woman); includes 16 minority (1 Black or African American, non-Hispanic/Latino; 1 American Indian or Alaska Native, non-Hispanic/Latino; 9 Asian, non-Hispanic/Latino; 5 Hispanic/Latino), 23 international. Average age 31. 103 applicants, 24% accepted, 13 enrolled. In 2010, 8 master's, 8 doctorates awarded. Terminal master's awarded for partial completion of doctoral program. *Degree requirements:* For master's, thesis; for doctorate, comprehensive exam, thesis/dissertation, oral qualifying exams. *Entrance requirements:* For master's and doctorate, GRE General Test, GRE Subject Test. Additional exam requirements/ recommendations for international students: Required—TOEFL (minimum score 570 paper-based; 230 computer-based; 89 iBT); Recommended—IELTS (minimum score 8). *Application deadline:* For fall admission, 1/3 for domestic and international students. Application fee: $70 ($90 for international students). Electronic applications accepted. *Financial support:* Fellowships, research assistantships, teaching assistantships, institutionally sponsored loans and tuition waivers available. Financial award applicants required to submit FAFSA. *Faculty research:* Computer-aided design of digital systems, networks, robotics and control, sensing and interaction. *Unit head:* Carol Mullane, Graduate Program Coordinator, 831-459-2576, E-mail: mullane@soe.ucsc.edu. *Application contact:* Carol Mullane, Graduate Program Coordinator, 831-459-2576, E-mail: mullane@soe.ucsc.edu.

University of Central Florida, College of Engineering and Computer Science, Department of Electrical Engineering and Computer Science, Program in Computer Engineering, Orlando, FL 32816. Offers computer engineering (MS Cp E, PhD). Part-time and evening/weekend programs available. *Students:* 59 full-time (8 women), 49 part-time (9 women); includes 5 Black or African American, non-Hispanic/Latino; 5 Asian, non-Hispanic/Latino; 11 Hispanic/Latino; 1 Two or more races, non-Hispanic/Latino, 39 international. Average age 30. 67 applicants, 87% accepted, 27 enrolled. In 2010, 24 master's, 3 doctorates awarded. *Degree requirements:* For master's, thesis or alternative; for doctorate, thesis/dissertation, departmental qualifying exam, candidacy exam. *Entrance requirements:* For master's, GRE General Test, minimum GPA of 3.0 in last 60 hours; for doctorate, GRE General Test, minimum GPA of 3.5 in last 60 hours. Additional exam requirements/recommendations for international students: Required—TOEFL. *Application deadline:* For fall admission, 7/15 priority date for domestic students; for spring admission, 12/1 priority date for domestic students. Electronic applications accepted. *Expenses:* Tuition, state resident: part-time $256.56 per credit hour. Tuition, nonresident: part-time $1011.52 per credit hour. Part-time tuition and fees vary according to program. *Financial support:* In 2010–11, 33 students received support, including 10 fellowships (averaging $6,400 per year), 29 research assistantships (averaging $7,400 per year), 18 teaching assistantships (averaging $6,200 per year); tuition waivers (partial) also available.

University of Cincinnati, Graduate School, College of Engineering, Department of Electrical and Computer Engineering and Computer Science, Program in Computer Engineering, Cincinnati, OH 45221. Offers MS. *Degree requirements:* For master's, thesis. *Entrance requirements:* For master's, GRE General Test. Additional exam requirements/recommendations for international students: Required—TOEFL (minimum score 550 paper-based; 213 computer-based). Electronic applications accepted. *Faculty research:* Digital signal processing, large-scale systems, picture processing.

University of Cincinnati, Graduate School, College of Engineering, Department of Electrical and Computer Engineering and Computer Science, Program in Computer Science and Engineering, Cincinnati, OH 45221. Offers PhD. *Degree requirements:* For doctorate, thesis/dissertation. *Entrance requirements:* For doctorate, GRE General Test. Additional exam requirements/recommendations for international students: Required—TOEFL.

University of Colorado Boulder, Graduate School, College of Engineering and Applied Science, Department of Electrical, Computer and Energy Engineering, Boulder, CO 80309. Offers ME, MS, PhD. Part-time programs available. Postbaccalaureate distance learning degree programs offered (no on-campus study). *Faculty:* 37 full-time (5 women). *Students:* 243 full-time (41 women), 75 part-time (16 women); includes 22 minority (3 Black or African American, non-Hispanic/Latino; 15 Asian, non-Hispanic/Latino; 4 Hispanic/Latino), 150 international. Average age 27. 670 applicants, 85 enrolled. In 2010, 95 master's, 19 doctorates awarded. Terminal master's awarded for partial completion of doctoral program. *Degree requirements:* For master's, thesis or alternative; for doctorate, one foreign language, thesis/ dissertation, departmental qualifying exam. *Entrance requirements:* For master's, GRE General Test, minimum undergraduate GPA of 3.0; for doctorate, GRE General Test, minimum undergraduate GPA of 3.5. *Application deadline:* For fall admission, 1/15 priority date for domestic students, 12/1 for international students; for spring admission, 10/1 for domestic and international students. Applications are processed on a rolling basis. Application fee: $50 ($60 for international students). *Financial support:* In 2010–11, 31 fellowships (averaging $8,965 per year), 107 research assistantships (averaging $14,806 per year) were awarded; career-related internships or fieldwork, scholarships/grants, and tuition waivers (full) also available. Financial award application deadline: 1/15. *Faculty research:* Biomedical engineering and cognitive disabilities, computer engineering VLSI CAD, dynamics and control systems, digital signal processing communications, electromagnetics, RF and microwaves, nonostructures and devices, optics and optoelectronics, power electronics and renewable energy systems. Total annual research expenditures: $8.6 million.

University of Dayton, Graduate School, School of Engineering, Department of Electrical and Computer Engineering, Dayton, OH 45469-1300. Offers MSEE, DE, PhD. Part-time and evening/weekend programs available. *Faculty:* 15 full-time (0 women), 4 part-time/adjunct (1 woman). *Students:* 103 full-time (17 women), 23 part-time (5 women); includes 10 minority (2 Black or African American, non-Hispanic/Latino; 7 Asian, non-Hispanic/Latino; 1 Hispanic/Latino), 71 international. Average age 27. 118 applicants, 74% accepted, 25 enrolled. In 2010, 20 master's, 3 doctorates awarded. *Degree requirements:* For master's, thesis optional; for doctorate, variable foreign language requirement, thesis/dissertation, departmental qualifying exam. *Entrance requirements:* Additional exam requirements/recommendations for international students: Required—TOEFL (minimum score 550 paper-based; 213 computer-based; 80 iBT). *Application deadline:* For fall admission, 8/1 for domestic students, 3/1 priority date for international students; for winter admission, 7/1 priority date for international students; for spring admission, 1/1 priority date for international students. Applications are processed on a rolling basis. Application fee: $0 ($50 for international students). Electronic applications accepted. *Expenses:* Tuition: Full-time $7800; part-time $650 per credit hour. *Financial support:* In 2010–11, 1 fellowship (averaging $27,500 per year), 34 research assistantships with full tuition reimbursements (averaging $12,500 per year), 5 teaching assistantships with full tuition reimbursements (averaging $10,065 per year) were awarded. Financial award application deadline: 5/1; financial award applicants required to submit FAFSA. *Faculty research:* Electrical engineering, video processing, leaky wave antenna. Total annual research expenditures: $1.1

million. *Unit head:* Dr. Guru Subramanyam, Chair, 937-229-3611. *Application contact:* Alexander Popovski, Associate Director of Graduate and International Admissions, 937-229-2357, Fax: 937-229-4729, E-mail: alex.popovski@notes.udayton.edu.

University of Delaware, College of Engineering, Department of Electrical and Computer Engineering, Newark, DE 19716. Offers MSECE, PhD. Part-time programs available. Postbaccalaureate distance learning degree programs offered (no on-campus study). Terminal master's awarded for partial completion of doctoral program. *Degree requirements:* For master's, thesis optional; for doctorate, thesis/dissertation. *Entrance requirements:* For master's, GRE General Test; for doctorate, GRE General Test, qualifying exam. Additional exam requirements/recommendations for international students: Required—TOEFL. Electronic applications accepted. *Faculty research:* HIV Evolution During Dynamic Therapy, compressive sensing in imaging, sensor, networks, and UWB radios, computer network time synchronization, silicon spintronics, devices and imaging in the high-terahertz band.

University of Denver, School of Engineering and Computer Science, Department of Electrical and Computer Engineering, Denver, CO 80208. Offers computer engineering (MS); computer science and engineering (MS); electrical and computer engineering (PhD); electrical engineering (MS); engineering (MS); mechatronic systems engineering (MS). Part-time and evening/weekend programs available. *Faculty:* 11 full-time (0 women), 1 part-time/adjunct (0 women). *Students:* 2 full-time (0 women), 104 part-time (20 women); includes 13 minority (1 Black or African American, non-Hispanic/Latino; 6 Asian, non-Hispanic/Latino; 5 Hispanic/Latino; 1 Two or more races, non-Hispanic/Latino), 18 international. Average age 30. 97 applicants, 67% accepted, 26 enrolled. In 2010, 28 master's, 4 doctorates awarded. Terminal master's awarded for partial completion of doctoral program. *Degree requirements:* For master's, thesis or alternative, proficiency in high- or low-level computer language; for doctorate, comprehensive exam, thesis/dissertation, proficiency in high- or low-level computer language. *Entrance requirements:* For master's and doctorate, GRE General Test. Additional exam requirements/recommendations for international students: Required—TOEFL (minimum score 550 paper-based; 80 iBT). *Application deadline:* Applications are processed on a rolling basis. Application fee: $60. Electronic applications accepted. *Expenses:* Tuition: Full-time $35,604; part-time $29,670 per year. Required fees: $687 per year. Tuition and fees vary according to program. *Financial support:* In 2010–11, 12 research assistantships with full and partial tuition reimbursements (averaging $12,166 per year), 5 teaching assistantships with full and partial tuition reimbursements (averaging $12,198 per year) were awarded; Federal Work-Study, scholarships/grants, and unspecified assistantships also available. Financial award application deadline: 3/1; financial award applicants required to submit FAFSA. *Unit head:* Dr. Kimon Valavanis, Chair, 303-871-2586, Fax: 303-871-2194, E-mail: kvalavan@du.ed. *Application contact:* Information Contact, 303-871-6618, Fax: 303-871-2194, E-mail: eceinfo@du.edu.

University of Detroit Mercy, College of Engineering and Science, Department of Electrical and Computer Engineering, Detroit, MI 48221. Offers computer engineering (ME, DE); mechatronics systems (ME, DE); signals and systems (ME, DE). Evening/weekend programs available. *Degree requirements:* For doctorate, thesis/dissertation. *Faculty research:* Electromagnetics, computer architecture, systems.

University of Florida, Graduate School, College of Engineering and College of Liberal Arts and Sciences, Department of Computer and Information Science and Engineering, Gainesville, FL 32611. Offers computer engineering (ME, MS, PhD); computer science (MS); digital arts and sciences (MS). Part-time programs available. Postbaccalaureate distance learning degree programs offered (minimal on-campus study). *Faculty:* 32 full-time (4 women), 2 part-time/adjunct (0 women). *Students:* 439 full-time (104 women), 81 part-time (19 women); includes 4 Black or African American, non-Hispanic/Latino; 11 Asian, non-Hispanic/Latino; 7 Hispanic/Latino, 445 international. Average age 24. 816 applicants, 60% accepted, 224 enrolled. In 2010, 156 master's, 25 doctorates awarded. Terminal master's awarded for partial completion of doctoral program. *Degree requirements:* For master's, comprehensive exam, thesis optional; for doctorate, comprehensive exam, thesis/dissertation. *Entrance requirements:* For master's and doctorate, GRE General Test, minimum GPA of 3.0. Additional exam requirements/recommendations for international students: Required—TOEFL (minimum score 550 paper-based; 213 computer-based; 80 iBT), IELTS (minimum score 6). *Application deadline:* For fall admission, 6/1 priority date for domestic students, 2/1 for international students; for spring admission, 9/1 for domestic and international students. Applications are processed on a rolling basis. Application fee: $30. Electronic applications accepted. *Expenses:* Tuition, state resident: full-time $10,915.92. Tuition, nonresident: full-time $28,309. *Financial support:* In 2010–11, 164 students received support, including 5 fellowships, 90 research assistantships (averaging $15,999 per year), 69 teaching assistantships (averaging $10,640 per year); unspecified assistantships also available. Financial award application deadline: 2/1; financial award applicants required to submit FAFSA. *Faculty research:* Computer systems, database, computer networks, graphics and vision, algorithm and parallel processing. Total annual research expenditures: $5.7 million. *Unit head:* Dr. Sartaj Sahni, Chair, 352-392-1527, Fax: 352-392-1220, E-mail: sahni@cise.ufl.edu. *Application contact:* Dr. Jih-Kwon Peir, Graduate Coordinator, 352-450-3446, Fax: 352-392-1220, E-mail: peir@cise.ufl.edu.

University of Florida, Graduate School, College of Engineering, Department of Electrical and Computer Engineering, Gainesville, FL 32611. Offers ME, MS, PhD, Engr. Part-time programs available. Postbaccalaureate distance learning degree programs offered. *Faculty:* 38 full-time (5 women), 2 part-time/adjunct (0 women). *Students:* 535 full-time (98 women), 78 part-time (11 women); includes 8 Black or African American, non-Hispanic/Latino; 1 American Indian or Alaska Native, non-Hispanic/Latino; 21 Asian, non-Hispanic/Latino; 19 Hispanic/Latino, 441 international. Average age 23. 1,951 applicants, 39% accepted, 203 enrolled. In 2010, 233 master's, 46 doctorates awarded. Terminal master's awarded for partial completion of doctoral program. *Degree requirements:* For master's, comprehensive exam (for some programs), thesis (for some programs); for doctorate, comprehensive exam, thesis/dissertation; for Engr, thesis. *Entrance requirements:* For master's, GRE General Test, minimum GPA of 3.0; for doctorate, GRE General Test, minimum GPA of 3.5; for Engr, GRE General Test. Additional exam requirements/recommendations for international students: Required—TOEFL (minimum score 550 paper-based; 213 computer-based; 80 iBT), IELTS (minimum score 6). *Application deadline:* For fall admission, 1/15 priority date for domestic students, 1/15 for international students. Applications are processed on a rolling basis. Application fee: $30. Electronic applications accepted. *Expenses:* Tuition, state resident: full-time $10,915.92. Tuition, nonresident: full-time $28,309. *Financial support:* In 2010–11, 259 students received support, including 33 fellowships, 198 research assistantships (averaging $18,880 per year), 28 teaching assistantships (averaging $20,263 per year); unspecified assistantships also available. Financial award application deadline: 1/15; financial award applicants required to submit FAFSA. *Faculty research:* Computer engineering, devices, electromagnetics and energy systems, electronics and signals and systems. Total annual research expenditures: $12.5 million. *Unit head:* Dr. John G. Harris, Chair and Graduate Coordinator, 352-392-0913, Fax: 352-392-8671, E-mail: harris@cnel.ufl.edu. *Application contact:* Dr. John G. Harris, Chair and Graduate Coordinator, 352-392-0913, Fax: 352-392-8671, E-mail: harris@cnel.ufl.edu.

University of Houston–Clear Lake, School of Science and Computer Engineering, Program in Computer Engineering, Houston, TX 77058-1098. Offers MS. Part-time and evening/weekend programs available. *Entrance requirements:* For master's, GRE General Test. Additional exam requirements/recommendations for international students: Required—TOEFL (minimum score 550 paper-based; 213 computer-based).

University of Idaho, College of Graduate Studies, College of Engineering, Department of Electrical and Computer Engineering, Program in Computer Engineering, Moscow, ID 83844-2282. Offers M Engr, MS. *Students:* 2 full-time, 4 part-time. In 2010, 2 master's awarded. *Degree requirements:* For master's, thesis. *Entrance requirements:* For master's, minimum GPA of 2.8. *Application deadline:* For fall admission, 8/1 for domestic students; for spring admission, 12/15 for domestic students. Applications are processed on a rolling basis. Application fee: $60. Electronic applications accepted. *Expenses:* Tuition, nonresident: part-time $580 per

credit. Required fees: $306 per credit. *Financial support:* Federal Work-Study available. Financial award applicants required to submit FAFSA. *Unit head:* Dr. Brian Johnson, Chair, 208-885-6902. *Application contact:* Dr. Brian Johnson, Chair, 208-885-6902.

University of Illinois at Chicago, Graduate College, College of Engineering, Department of Electrical and Computer Engineering, Program in Electrical and Computer Engineering, Chicago, IL 60607-7128. Offers MS, PhD. Part-time programs available. *Degree requirements:* For master's, thesis or alternative; for doctorate, thesis/dissertation, departmental qualifying exam. *Entrance requirements:* For master's, minimum GPA of 2.75, BS in related field; for doctorate, GRE General Test, minimum GPA of 2.75, MS in related field. Additional exam requirements/recommendations for international students: Required—TOEFL.

University of Illinois at Urbana–Champaign, Graduate College, College of Engineering, Department of Electrical and Computer Engineering, Champaign, IL 61820. Offers electrical and computer engineering (MS, PhD); MS/MBA. *Faculty:* 80 full-time (6 women), 3 part-time/adjunct (0 women). *Students:* 490 full-time (65 women), 15 part-time (3 women); includes 6 Black or African American, non-Hispanic/Latino; 40 Asian, non-Hispanic/Latino; 13 Hispanic/Latino; 6 Two or more races, non-Hispanic/Latino, 283 international. 1,668 applicants, 13% accepted, 94 enrolled. In 2010, 112 master's, 46 doctorates awarded. *Entrance requirements:* For master's, GRE, minimum GPA of 3.0; for doctorate, GRE. Additional exam requirements/recommendations for international students: Required—TOEFL (minimum score 590 paper-based; 243 computer-based; 96 iBT) or IELTS (minimum score 6.5). *Application deadline:* Applications are processed on a rolling basis. Application fee: $75 ($90 for international students). Electronic applications accepted. *Financial support:* In 2010–11, 49 fellowships, 373 research assistantships, 165 teaching assistantships were awarded; tuition waivers (full and partial) also available. *Unit head:* Andreas C. Cangellaris, Head, 217-333-6037, Fax: 217-244-7075, E-mail: cangella@illinois.edu. *Application contact:* Laurie A. Fisher, Administrative Aide, 217-333-9709, Fax: 217-333-8582, E-mail: fisher2@illinois.edu.

The University of Iowa, Graduate College, College of Engineering, Department of Electrical and Computer Engineering, Iowa City, IA 52242-1316. Offers MS, PhD. Part-time programs available. *Faculty:* 17 full-time (1 woman), 1 part-time/adjunct (0 women). *Students:* 90 full-time (17 women); includes 7 minority (3 Black or African American, non-Hispanic/Latino; 2 Asian, non-Hispanic/Latino; 2 Hispanic/Latino), 51 international. Average age 28. 158 applicants, 24% accepted, 24 enrolled. In 2010, 5 master's, 3 doctorates awarded. *Degree requirements:* For master's, comprehensive exam, thesis optional; for doctorate, comprehensive exam, thesis/dissertation, qualifying exam. *Entrance requirements:* For master's and doctorate, GRE. Additional exam requirements/recommendations for international students: Required—TOEFL (minimum score 550 paper-based; 213 computer-based; 81 iBT). *Application deadline:* For fall admission, 2/1 priority date for domestic students, 2/1 for international students. Applications are processed on a rolling basis. Application fee: $60 ($100 for international students). Electronic applications accepted. *Financial support:* In 2010–11, 5 fellowships with partial tuition reimbursements (averaging $19,146 per year), 59 research assistantships with partial tuition reimbursements (averaging $18,073 per year), 21 teaching assistantships with partial tuition reimbursements (averaging $17,324 per year) were awarded; scholarships/grants and unspecified assistantships also available. Financial award application deadline: 2/1; financial award applicants required to submit FAFSA. *Faculty research:* Applied optics and nanotechnology; computational genomics; large-scale intelligent and control systems; medical image processing; VLSI design and test. Total annual research expenditures: $10.4 million. *Unit head:* Dr. Milan Sonka, Department Executive Officer, 319-335-6052, Fax: 319-335-6028, E-mail: milan-sonka@uiowa.edu. *Application contact:* Cathy Kern, Secretary, 319-335-5197, Fax: 319-335-6028, E-mail: ece@engineering.uiowa.edu.

The University of Kansas, Graduate Studies, School of Engineering, Department of Electrical Engineering and Computer Science, Program in Computer Engineering, Lawrence, KS 66045. Offers MS. Part-time programs available. *Faculty:* 35. *Students:* 9 full-time (4 women), 6 part-time (2 women), 13 international. Average age 25. 14 applicants, 21% accepted, 1 enrolled. In 2010, 9 master's awarded. *Degree requirements:* For master's, thesis optional, exam. *Entrance requirements:* For master's, GRE, minimum GPA of 3.0. Additional exam requirements/recommendations for international students: Required—TOEFL (minimum score 600 paper-based; 250 computer-based; 100 iBT). *Application deadline:* For fall admission, 3/1 priority date for domestic students, 3/1 for international students; for spring admission, 10/1 priority date for domestic students, 10/1 for international students. Applications are processed on a rolling basis. Application fee: $55 ($65 for international students). Electronic applications accepted. *Expenses:* Tuition, state resident: full-time $7092; part-time $295.50 per credit hour. Tuition, nonresident: full-time $16,590; part-time $691.25 per credit hour. Required fees: $858; $71.49 per credit hour. Tuition and fees vary according to course load, campus/location and program. *Financial support:* Fellowships with full and partial tuition reimbursements, research assistantships with full and partial tuition reimbursements, teaching assistantships with full and partial tuition reimbursements, career-related internships or fieldwork, scholarships/grants, and unspecified assistantships available. Financial award application deadline: 1/1. *Faculty research:* Communication systems and networking, computer systems design, interactive intelligent systems, radar systems and remote sensing, bioinformatics. *Unit head:* Glenn Prescott, Chairperson, 785-864-4620, Fax: 785-864-3226. *Application contact:* Pam Shadoin, Assistant to Graduate Director, 785-864-4487, Fax: 785-864-3226, E-mail: graduate@eecs.ku.edu.

University of Louisiana at Lafayette, College of Engineering, Center for Advanced Computer Studies, Lafayette, LA 70504. Offers computer engineering (MS, PhD); computer science (MS, PhD). Part-time programs available. Terminal master's awarded for partial completion of doctoral program. *Degree requirements:* For master's, thesis or alternative; for doctorate, comprehensive exam, thesis/dissertation, final oral exam. *Entrance requirements:* For master's, GRE General Test, minimum GPA of 2.75; for doctorate, GRE General Test, minimum GPA of 3.0. Additional exam requirements/recommendations for international students: Required—TOEFL. Electronic applications accepted.

See Display on page 274 and Close-Up on page 333.

University of Louisiana at Lafayette, College of Engineering, Department of Electrical and Computer Engineering, Lafayette, LA 70504. Offers computer engineering (MS, PhD); telecommunications (MSTC). *Degree requirements:* For master's, thesis or alternative; for doctorate, comprehensive exam, thesis/dissertation, final oral exam. *Entrance requirements:* For master's, GRE General Test, minimum GPA of 2.75. Additional exam requirements/recommendations for international students: Required—TOEFL (minimum score 550 paper-based; 213 computer-based). Electronic applications accepted.

University of Louisville, J.B. Speed School of Engineering, Department of Computer Engineering and Computer Science, Louisville, KY 40292-0001. Offers computer engineering and computer science (M Eng, MS); computer science (MS); computer science and engineering (PhD); data mining (Certificate); network and information security (Certificate). *Accreditation:* ABET (one or more programs are accredited). Part-time programs available. Postbaccalaureate distance learning degree programs offered (no on-campus study). *Faculty:* 13 full-time (1 woman). *Students:* 74 full-time (15 women), 45 part-time (7 women); includes 8 Black or African American, non-Hispanic/Latino; 4 Asian, non-Hispanic/Latino; 1 Hispanic/Latino; 1 Two or more races, non-Hispanic/Latino, 40 international. Average age 29. 51 applicants, 41% accepted, 9 enrolled. In 2010, 22 master's, 11 doctorates awarded. Terminal master's awarded for partial completion of doctoral program. *Degree requirements:* For master's, comprehensive exam (for some programs), thesis or alternative; for doctorate, comprehensive exam, thesis/dissertation, minimum GPA of 3.0. *Entrance requirements:* For master's, doctorate, and Certificate, GRE General Test. Additional exam requirements/recommendations for international students: Required—TOEFL (minimum score 550 paper-based; 213 computer-based; 80 iBT), IELTS (minimum score 6.5). *Application deadline:* For fall admission, 5/1 priority date for domestic and international students; for spring admission, 11/1 priority date for domestic and international students. Applications are processed on a rolling basis. Application fee: $50.

Computer Engineering

University of Louisville (continued)

Electronic applications accepted. *Expenses:* Tuition, state resident: full-time $9144; part-time $508 per credit hour. Tuition, nonresident: full-time $19,026; part-time $1057 per credit hour. Tuition and fees vary according to program and reciprocity agreements. *Financial support:* In 2010–11, 22 students received support, including 1 fellowship with full tuition reimbursement available (averaging $20,000 per year), 15 research assistantships with full tuition reimbursements available (averaging $18,900 per year), 6 teaching assistantships with full tuition reimbursements available (averaging $20,000 per year). Financial award application deadline: 1/25; financial award applicants required to submit FAFSA. *Faculty research:* Software systems engineering, information security and forensics, multimedia and vision, mobile and distributed computing, intelligent systems. Total annual research expenditures: $1.3 million. *Unit head:* Dr. Adel S. Elmaghraby, Chair, 502-852-6304, Fax: 502-852-4713, E-mail: adel@louisville.edu. *Application contact:* Dr. Michael Day, Associate Dean, 502-852-6195, Fax: 502-852-6294, E-mail: day@louisville.edu.

University of Louisville, J.B. Speed School of Engineering, Department of Electrical and Computer Engineering, Louisville, KY 40292-0001. Offers M Eng, MS, PhD. *Accreditation:* ABET (one or more programs are accredited). Part-time programs available. *Faculty:* 15 full-time (2 women). *Students:* 82 full-time (14 women), 19 part-time (4 women); includes 3 Black or African American, non-Hispanic/Latino; 2 Asian, non-Hispanic/Latino; 1 Hispanic/Latino; 2 Two or more races, non-Hispanic/Latino), 46 international. Average age 28. 50 applicants, 44% accepted, 14 enrolled. In 2010, 25 master's, 3 doctorates awarded. Terminal master's awarded for partial completion of doctoral program. *Degree requirements:* For master's, comprehensive exam (for some programs), thesis or alternative; for doctorate, comprehensive exam, thesis/dissertation, minimum GPA of 3.0. *Entrance requirements:* For master's and doctorate, GRE General Test. Additional exam requirements/recommendations for international students: Required—TOEFL (minimum score 550 paper-based; 213 computer-based; 80 iBT), IELTS (minimum score 6.5). *Application deadline:* For fall admission, 5/1 priority date for domestic and international students; for spring admission, 11/1 priority date for domestic and international students. Applications are processed on a rolling basis. Application fee: $50. Electronic applications accepted. *Expenses:* Tuition, state resident: full-time $9144; part-time $508 per credit hour. Tuition, nonresident: full-time $19,026; part-time $1057 per credit hour. Tuition and fees vary according to program and reciprocity agreements. *Financial support:* In 2010–11, 16 students received support, including 4 fellowships with full tuition reimbursements available (averaging $20,000 per year), 4 research assistantships with full tuition reimbursements available (averaging $21,000 per year), 8 teaching assistantships with full tuition reimbursements available (averaging $20,000 per year). Financial award application deadline: 1/25; financial award applicants required to submit FAFSA. *Faculty research:* Nanotechnology; microfabrication; computer engineering; control, communication and signal processing; electronic devices and systems. Total annual research expenditures: $5.8 million. *Unit head:* James H. Graham, Acting Chair, 502-852-6289, Fax: 502-852-6807, E-mail: jhgrah01@louisville.edu. *Application contact:* Dr. Michael Day, Associate Dean, 502-852-6195, Fax: 502-852-7294, E-mail: day@louisville.edu.

University of Maine, Graduate School, College of Engineering, Department of Electrical and Computer Engineering, Orono, ME 04469. Offers computer engineering (MS); electrical engineering (MS, PhD). Part-time programs available. *Faculty:* 12 full-time (1 woman). *Students:* 17 full-time (3 women), 14 part-time (2 women); includes 3 minority (all Asian, non-Hispanic/Latino), 14 international. Average age 27. 22 applicants, 18% accepted, 3 enrolled. In 2010, 14 master's, 1 doctorate awarded. *Degree requirements:* For master's, thesis (for some programs); for doctorate, thesis/dissertation. *Entrance requirements:* For master's and doctorate, GRE General Test. Additional exam requirements/recommendations for international students: Required—TOEFL. *Application deadline:* For fall admission, 2/1 priority date for domestic students. Applications are processed on a rolling basis. Application fee: $65. Electronic applications accepted. *Expenses:* Tuition, state resident: full-time $400. Tuition, nonresident: full-time $1050. *Financial support:* In 2010–11, 21 research assistantships with tuition reimbursements (averaging $21,737 per year), 2 teaching assistantships with tuition reimbursements (averaging $12,790 per year) were awarded; Federal Work-Study, institutionally sponsored loans, and tuition waivers (full and partial) also available. Financial award application deadline: 3/1. *Unit head:* Dr. Monamad Musavi, Chair, 207-581-2243. *Application contact:* Scott G. Delcourt, Associate Dean of the Graduate School, 207-581-3291, Fax: 207-581-3232, E-mail: graduate@maine.edu.

University of Manitoba, Faculty of Graduate Studies, Faculty of Engineering, Department of Electrical and Computer Engineering, Winnipeg, MB R3T 2N2, Canada. Offers M Eng, M Sc, PhD. *Degree requirements:* For master's, thesis; for doctorate, thesis/dissertation.

University of Maryland, Baltimore County, Graduate School, College of Engineering and Information Technology, Department of Computer Science and Electrical Engineering, Program in Computer Engineering, Baltimore, MD 21250. Offers MS, PhD. Part-time programs available. *Students:* 11 full-time (0 women), 12 part-time (3 women); includes 3 minority (1 Black or African American, non-Hispanic/Latino; 1 Asian, non-Hispanic/Latino; 1 Hispanic/Latino), 9 international. Average age 29. 24 applicants, 63% accepted, 5 enrolled. In 2010, 5 master's, 3 doctorates awarded. *Degree requirements:* For master's, comprehensive exam (for some programs), thesis or alternative; for doctorate, comprehensive exam, thesis/dissertation. *Entrance requirements:* For master's, GRE General Test, strong background in computer engineering, computer science, and math courses; for doctorate, GRE General Test, MS in computer science (strongly recommended). Additional exam requirements/recommendations for international students: Required—TOEFL (minimum score 550 paper-based; 213 computer-based; 80 iBT). *Application deadline:* For fall admission, 6/1 for domestic students, 1/1 for international students; for spring admission, 11/1 for domestic students, 6/1 for international students. Applications are processed on a rolling basis. Application fee: $50. Electronic applications accepted. *Financial support:* In 2010–11, 1 research assistantship with full tuition reimbursement (averaging $18,000 per year), 5 teaching assistantships with full tuition reimbursements (averaging $18,000 per year) were awarded; career-related internships or fieldwork, Federal Work-Study, scholarships/grants, health care benefits, tuition waivers (partial), and unspecified assistantships also available. Support available to part-time students. Financial award application deadline: 6/30; financial award applicants required to submit FAFSA. *Faculty research:* VLSI, signal processing and communication. *Unit head:* Dr. Gary Carter, Professor and Chair, 410-455-3500, Fax: 410-455-3969, E-mail: carter@cs.umbc.edu. *Application contact:* Dr. Joel Morris, Professor and Graduate Program Coordinator, 410-455-8416, Fax: 410-455-3969, E-mail: morris@cs.umbc.edu.

University of Maryland, College Park, Academic Affairs, A. James Clark School of Engineering, Department of Electrical and Computer Engineering, College Park, MD 20742. Offers electrical and computer engineering (M Eng, MS, PhD); electrical engineering (MS, PhD); telecommunications (MS). Part-time and evening/weekend programs available. Postbaccalaureate distance learning degree programs offered. *Faculty:* 106 full-time (10 women), 19 part-time/adjunct (3 women). *Students:* 397 full-time (92 women), 66 part-time (13 women); includes 62 minority (9 Black or African American, non-Hispanic/Latino; 43 Asian, non-Hispanic/Latino; 7 Hispanic/Latino; 3 Two or more races, non-Hispanic/Latino), 312 international. 1,588 applicants, 24% accepted, 132 enrolled. In 2010, 102 master's, 40 doctorates awarded. *Degree requirements:* For master's, thesis optional; for doctorate, thesis/dissertation, oral exam, qualifying exam. *Entrance requirements:* For master's and doctorate, GRE General Test, 3 letters of recommendation. *Application deadline:* For fall admission, 5/1 for domestic students, 2/1 for international students; for spring admission, 6/1 for international students. Applications are processed on a rolling basis. Application fee: $75. Electronic applications accepted. *Expenses:* Tuition, area resident: Part-time $471 per credit hour. Tuition, state resident: part-time $471 per credit hour. Tuition, nonresident: part-time $1016 per credit hour. Required fees: $337 per term. *Financial support:* In 2010–11, 11 fellowships with full and partial tuition reimbursements (averaging $19,987 per year), 170 research assistantships with tuition reimbursements (averaging $17,829 per year), 67 teaching assistantships with tuition reimbursements (averaging $17,042 per year) were awarded; career-related internships or fieldwork also available. Financial award applicants required to submit FAFSA. *Faculty research:* Communications and control, electrophysics, micro-electronics, robotics, computer engineering. Total annual research expenditures: $11.4 million. *Unit head:* Patrick O'Shea, Chair, 301-405-3683, E-mail: poshea@umd.edu. *Application contact:* Dr. Charles A. Caramello, Dean of Graduate School, 301-405-0358, Fax: 301-314-9305, E-mail: ccaramel@umd.edu.

University of Massachusetts Amherst, Graduate School, College of Engineering, Department of Electrical and Computer Engineering, Amherst, MA 01003. Offers MSECE, PhD. Part-time programs available. *Faculty:* 40 full-time (2 women). *Students:* 178 full-time (39 women), 24 part-time (4 women); includes 13 minority (3 Black or African American, non-Hispanic/Latino; 4 Asian, non-Hispanic/Latino; 5 Hispanic/Latino; 1 Two or more races, non-Hispanic/Latino), 160 international. Average age 26. 817 applicants, 25% accepted, 60 enrolled. In 2010, 25 master's, 10 doctorates awarded. Terminal master's awarded for partial completion of doctoral program. *Degree requirements:* For master's, thesis or alternative; for doctorate, comprehensive exam, thesis/dissertation. *Entrance requirements:* For master's and doctorate, GRE General Test. Additional exam requirements/recommendations for international students: Required—TOEFL (minimum score 550 paper-based; 213 computer-based; 80 iBT), IELTS (minimum score 6.5). *Application deadline:* For fall admission, 1/15 for domestic and international students; for spring admission, 10/1 for domestic and international students. Applications are processed on a rolling basis. Application fee: $50 ($65 for international students). Electronic applications accepted. *Expenses:* Tuition, state resident: full-time $2640. Required fees: $8282. One-time fee: $357 full-time. *Financial support:* In 2010–11, 8 fellowships with full tuition reimbursements (averaging $5,166 per year), 125 research assistantships with full tuition reimbursements (averaging $12,485 per year), 37 teaching assistantships with full tuition reimbursements (averaging $7,450 per year) were awarded; career-related internships or fieldwork, Federal Work-Study, scholarships/grants, traineeships, health care benefits, tuition waivers, and unspecified assistantships also available. Support available to part-time students. Financial award application deadline: 1/15; financial award applicants required to submit FAFSA. *Unit head:* Dr. C. Mani Krishna, Graduate Program Director, 413-545-4583, Fax: 413-545-4611, E-mail: ecegrad@ecs.umass.edu. *Application contact:* Jean M. Ames, Supervisor of Admissions, 413-545-0722, Fax: 413-577-0010, E-mail: gradadm@grad.umass.edu.

University of Massachusetts Dartmouth, Graduate School, College of Engineering, Department of Electrical and Computer Engineering, North Dartmouth, MA 02747-2300. Offers acoustics (Postbaccalaureate Certificate); communications (Postbaccalaureate Certificate); computer engineering (MS, PhD); computer systems engineering (Postbaccalaureate Certificate); digital signal processing (Postbaccalaureate Certificate); electrical engineering (MS, PhD); electrical engineering systems (Postbaccalaureate Certificate). Part-time programs available. *Faculty:* 17 full-time (3 women), 3 part-time/adjunct (0 women). *Students:* 32 full-time (6 women), 48 part-time (13 women); includes 2 Black or African American, non-Hispanic/Latino; 1 American Indian or Alaska Native, non-Hispanic/Latino; 4 Asian, non-Hispanic/Latino, 47 international. Average age 29. 97 applicants, 84% accepted, 19 enrolled. In 2010, 17 master's, 1 other advanced degree awarded. *Degree requirements:* For master's, culminating project or thesis; for doctorate, comprehensive exam, thesis/dissertation. *Entrance requirements:* For master's, GRE, minimum undergraduate GPA of 3.0, 3 letters of recommendation; for doctorate, GRE. Additional exam requirements/recommendations for international students: Required—TOEFL (minimum score 550 paper-based; 213 computer-based). *Application deadline:* For fall admission, 2/1 priority date for domestic students, 12/1 for international students; for spring admission, 11/1 priority date for domestic students, 9/1 for international students. Applications are processed on a rolling basis. Application fee: $40 ($60 for international students). Electronic applications accepted. *Expenses:* Tuition, state resident: full-time $2071; part-time $86 per credit. Tuition, nonresident: full-time $8099; part-time $337 per credit. Required fees: $9446; $394 per credit. One-time fee: $75. Part-time tuition and fees vary according to class time, course load, degree level and reciprocity agreements. *Financial support:* In 2010–11, 2 fellowships with full tuition reimbursements (averaging $16,000 per year), 14 research assistantships with full tuition reimbursements (averaging $11,096 per year), 9 teaching assistantships with full tuition reimbursements (averaging $12,500 per year) were awarded; Federal Work-Study and unspecified assistantships also available. Support available to part-time students. Financial award application deadline: 3/1; financial award applicants required to submit FAFSA. *Faculty research:* Speech acoustics, marine applications, signals and systems, applied electromagnetics, intelligent agency. Total annual research expenditures: $1.1 million. *Unit head:* Dr. Karen Payton, Director, 508-999-8434, Fax: 508-999-8489, E-mail: kpayton@umassd.edu. *Application contact:* Elan Turcotte-Shamski, Graduate Admissions Officer, 508-999-8604, Fax: 508-999-8183, E-mail: graduate@umassd.edu.

University of Massachusetts Lowell, James B. Francis College of Engineering, Department of Electrical and Computer Engineering, Program in Computer Engineering, Lowell, MA 01854-2881. Offers MS Eng. *Degree requirements:* For master's, thesis optional.

University of Memphis, Graduate School, Herff College of Engineering, Department of Electrical and Computer Engineering, Memphis, TN 38152. Offers automatic control systems (MS); biomedical systems (MS); communications and propagation systems (MS); computer engineering (PhD); electrical engineering (PhD); engineering computer systems (MS). *Faculty:* 8 full-time (1 woman), 2 part-time/adjunct (0 women). *Students:* 32 full-time (6 women), 4 part-time (1 woman); includes 3 Black or African American, non-Hispanic/Latino; 1 Asian, non-Hispanic/Latino, 25 international. Average age 26. 30 applicants, 87% accepted, 21 enrolled. In 2010, 10 master's awarded. *Degree requirements:* For master's, comprehensive exam, thesis or alternative. *Entrance requirements:* For master's, GRE General Test or MAT, minimum undergraduate GPA of 2.5. *Application deadline:* For fall admission, 8/1 for domestic students; for spring admission, 12/1 for domestic students. Application fee: $35 ($60 for international students). *Financial support:* In 2010–11, 4 students received support; research assistantships, teaching assistantships, career-related internships or fieldwork, Federal Work-Study, scholarships/grants, and unspecified assistantships available. Financial award application deadline: 2/15; financial award applicants required to submit FAFSA. *Faculty research:* Image processing, imaging sensors, biomedical systems, intelligent systems. *Unit head:* Dr. David J. Russomanno, Chair/Professor, 901-678-2175, Fax: 901-678-5469, E-mail: russmnn@memphis.edu. *Application contact:* Dr. Steven T. Griffin, Coordinator of Graduate Studies, 901-678-5268, Fax: 901-678-5469, E-mail: stgriffn@memphis.edu.

University of Memphis, Graduate School, Herff College of Engineering, Department of Engineering Technology, Memphis, TN 38152. Offers computer engineering technology (MS); electronics engineering technology (MS); manufacturing engineering technology (MS). Part-time and evening/weekend programs available. *Faculty:* 5 full-time (0 women). *Students:* 4 full-time (1 woman), 6 part-time (1 woman); includes 4 Black or African American, non-Hispanic/Latino, 2 international. Average age 38. 2 applicants, 50% accepted, 1 enrolled. *Degree requirements:* For master's, comprehensive exam, thesis optional. *Entrance requirements:* For master's, GRE General Test, minimum undergraduate GPA of 2.5. *Application deadline:* For fall admission, 8/1 for domestic students; for spring admission, 12/1 for domestic students. Applications are processed on a rolling basis. Application fee: $25 ($50 for international students). Electronic applications accepted. *Financial support:* In 2010–11, 5 students received support; research assistantships with full tuition reimbursements available, career-related internships or fieldwork, Federal Work-Study, scholarships/grants, and unspecified assistantships available. Financial award application deadline: 2/15; financial award applicants required to submit FAFSA. *Faculty research:* Teacher education services-technology education; flexible manufacturing control systems; embedded, dedicated, and real-time computer systems; network, Internet, and Web-based programming; analog and digital electronic communication systems. *Unit head:* Deborah J. Hochstein, Chairman, 901-678-2225, Fax: 901-678-5145, E-mail: dhochstn@memphis.edu. *Application contact:* Carl R. Williams, Coordinator of Graduate Studies, 901-678-3296, Fax: 901-678-5145, E-mail: crwillia@memphis.edu.

University of Miami, Graduate School, College of Engineering, Department of Electrical and Computer Engineering, Coral Gables, FL 33124. Offers MSECE, PhD. Part-time programs available. *Degree requirements:* For master's, thesis (for some programs); for doctorate, comprehensive exam, thesis/dissertation, dissertation proposal defense. *Entrance requirements:* For master's, GRE General Test, minimum GPA of 3.0; for doctorate, GRE General Test, minimum undergraduate GPA of 3.3, graduate 3.5. Additional exam requirements/recommendations for international students: Required—TOEFL (minimum score 550 paper-based; 213 computer-based; 59 iBT), IELTS (minimum score 7). Electronic applications accepted. *Faculty research:* Computer network, image processing, database systems, digital signal processing, machine intelligence.

University of Michigan, Horace H. Rackham School of Graduate Studies, College of Engineering, Department of Computer Science and Engineering, Ann Arbor, MI 48109. Offers MS, MSE, PhD. *Students:* 237 full-time (29 women), 5 part-time (0 women). 977 applicants, 20% accepted, 81 enrolled. In 2010, 69 master's, 21 doctorates awarded. *Expenses:* Tuition, state resident: full-time $17,784; part-time $1116 per credit hour. Tuition, nonresident: full-time $35,944; part-time $2125 per credit hour. International tuition: $35,994 full-time. Required fees: $95 per semester. Tuition and fees vary according to course load, degree level and program. *Faculty research:* Solid state electronics and optics; communications, control, signal process; sensors and integrated circuitry, others; software systems; artificial intelligence; hardware systems. *Unit head:* Prof. John Laird, Interim Department Chair, 734-764-8504, Fax: 734-763-1503, E-mail: laird@umich.edu. *Application contact:* Dawn Freysinger, Graduate Programs Coordinator, 734-647-1807, Fax: 734-763-1503, E-mail: dawnf@umich.edu.

University of Michigan–Dearborn, College of Engineering and Computer Science, Department of Electrical and Computer Engineering, Dearborn, MI 48128-1491. Offers computer engineering (MSE); electrical engineering (MSE); software engineering (MS). Part-time and evening/weekend programs available. *Faculty:* 5 full-time (1 woman). *Students:* 17 full-time (1 woman), 129 part-time (20 women); includes 49 minority (6 Black or African American, non-Hispanic/Latino; 37 Asian, non-Hispanic/Latino; 4 Hispanic/Latino; 2 Two or more races, non-Hispanic/Latino). Average age 32. 63 applicants, 56% accepted, 29 enrolled. In 2010, 57 master's awarded. *Degree requirements:* For master's, thesis optional. *Entrance requirements:* For master's, bachelor's degree in electrical and computer engineering or equivalent, minimum GPA of 3.0. Additional exam requirements/recommendations for international students: Required—TOEFL (minimum score 560 paper-based; 220 computer-based; 84 iBT). *Application deadline:* For fall admission, 8/1 priority date for domestic students, 4/1 for international students; for winter admission, 12/1 priority date for domestic students, 8/1 for international students; for spring admission, 4/1 priority date for domestic students, 2/1 for international students. Applications are processed on a rolling basis. Application fee: $60 ($75 for international students). *Financial support:* In 2010–11, 4 fellowships (averaging $26,340 per year), 1 research assistantship with partial tuition reimbursement (averaging $12,384 per year) were awarded; teaching assistantships, Federal Work-Study also available. Financial award application deadline: 4/1; financial award applicants required to submit FAFSA. *Faculty research:* Fuzzy systems and applications, machine vision, pattern recognition and machine intelligence, vehicle electronics, wireless communications. *Unit head:* Dr. YiLu Murphey, Chair, 313-593-5028, Fax: 313-583-6336, E-mail: yilu@umich.edu. *Application contact:* Sandra Marie Krzyskowski, Intermediate Academic Records Assistant, 313-593-5420, Fax: 313-583-6336, E-mail: ece-grad@umd.umich.edu.

University of Minnesota, Duluth, Graduate School, Swenson College of Science and Engineering, Department of Electrical and Computer Engineering, Duluth, MN 55812-2496. Offers MSECE. Part-time programs available. *Degree requirements:* For master's, thesis. *Entrance requirements:* Additional exam requirements/recommendations for international students: Recommended—IELTS, TWE. *Faculty research:* Biomedical instrumentation, transportation systems, computer hardware and software, signal processing, optical communications.

University of Minnesota, Twin Cities Campus, Institute of Technology, Department of Electrical and Computer Engineering, Minneapolis, MN 55455-0213. Offers MSEE, PhD. Part-time programs available. *Degree requirements:* For master's, thesis or alternative; for doctorate, thesis/dissertation. *Entrance requirements:* Additional exam requirements/recommendations for international students: Required—TOEFL (minimum score 550 paper-based; 213 computer-based), GRE. *Faculty research:* Signal processing, microelectronics, computers, controls, power electronics.

University of Minnesota, Twin Cities Campus, Institute of Technology, Program in Computer Engineering, Minneapolis, MN 55455-0213. Offers M Comp E, MS. Part-time programs available. Postbaccalaureate distance learning degree programs offered (no on-campus study). *Degree requirements:* For master's, thesis or alternative. *Entrance requirements:* Additional exam requirements/recommendations for international students: Required—TOEFL. *Faculty research:* Computer networks, parallel computing, software engineering, VLSI and CAI, databases.

University of Missouri–Kansas City, School of Computing and Engineering, Kansas City, MO 64110-2499. Offers civil engineering (MS); computer and electrical engineering (PhD); computer science (MS), including bioinformatics, software engineering, telecommunications networking; computer science and informatics (PhD); computing (PhD); electrical engineering (MS); engineering (PhD); mechanical engineering (MS); telecommunications (PhD). PhD (interdisciplinary) offered through the School of Graduate Studies. Part-time programs available. *Faculty:* 36 full-time (5 women), 21 part-time/adjunct (0 women). *Students:* 160 full-time (32 women), 194 part-time (41 women); includes 21 minority (5 Black or African American, non-Hispanic/Latino; 9 Asian, non-Hispanic/Latino; 6 Hispanic/Latino; 1 Two or more races, non-Hispanic/Latino), 273 international. Average age 25. 440 applicants, 55% accepted, 104 enrolled. In 2010, 135 master's awarded. *Degree requirements:* For doctorate, thesis/dissertation. *Entrance requirements:* For master's, GRE General Test, minimum GPA of 3.0, 3 letters of recommendation from professors; for doctorate, GRE General Test, minimum GPA of 3.5. Additional exam requirements/recommendations for international students: Required—TOEFL (minimum score 550 paper-based; 213 computer-based; 80 iBT). *Application deadline:* For fall admission, 1/15 priority date for domestic students, 1/15 for international students. Applications are processed on a rolling basis. Application fee: $45 ($50 for international students). *Expenses:* Tuition, state resident: full-time $5522.40; part-time $306.80 per credit hour. Tuition, nonresident: full-time $7128; part-time $792 per credit hour. Required fees: $261.15 per term. *Financial support:* In 2010–11, 35 research assistantships with partial tuition reimbursements (averaging $14,340 per year), 20 teaching assistantships with partial tuition reimbursements (averaging $13,351 per year) were awarded; career-related internships or fieldwork, Federal Work-Study, scholarships/grants, tuition waivers (partial), and unspecified assistantships also available. Support available to part-time students. Financial award application deadline: 3/1; financial award applicants required to submit FAFSA. *Faculty research:* Algorithms, bioinformatics and medical informatics, biomechanics/biomaterials, civil engineering materials, networking and telecommunications, thermal science. Total annual research expenditures: $1.1 million. *Unit head:* Dr. Kevin Z. Truman, Dean, 816-235-2399, Fax: 816-235-5159. *Application contact:* Dr. Kevin Z. Truman, Dean, 816-235-2399, Fax: 816-235-5159.

University of Nebraska–Lincoln, Graduate College, College of Arts and Sciences and College of Engineering, Department of Computer Science and Engineering, Lincoln, NE 68588. Offers bioinformatics (MS, PhD); computer engineering (MS, PhD); computer science (MS, PhD); information technology (PhD). *Degree requirements:* For master's, thesis optional; for doctorate, comprehensive exam, thesis/dissertation. *Entrance requirements:* For master's and doctorate, GRE General Test. Additional exam requirements/recommendations for international students: Required—TOEFL (minimum score 600 paper-based; 250 computer-based). Electronic applications accepted. *Faculty research:* Software engineering, geo- and bio-informatics, scientific computation, secure communication.

University of Nevada, Las Vegas, Graduate College, Howard R. Hughes College of Engineering, Department of Electrical and Computer Engineering, Las Vegas, NV 89154-4026. Offers MSE, PhD. Part-time programs available. *Faculty:* 14 full-time (1 woman), 3 part-time/adjunct (0 women). *Students:* 34 full-time (7 women), 13 part-time (1 woman); includes 9 minority (2 Black or African American, non-Hispanic/Latino; 1 American Indian or Alaska Native, non-Hispanic/Latino; 2 Asian, non-Hispanic/Latino; 1 Hispanic/Latino; 3 Two or more races, non-Hispanic/Latino), 29 international. Average age 28. 28 applicants, 75% accepted, 11 enrolled. In 2010, 10 master's, 4 doctorates awarded. *Degree requirements:* For master's, comprehensive exam, thesis, project; for doctorate, comprehensive exam, thesis/dissertation. *Entrance requirements:* Additional exam requirements/recommendations for international students: Required—TOEFL (minimum score 550 paper-based; 213 computer-based; 80 iBT), IELTS (minimum score 7). *Application deadline:* For fall admission, 6/1 priority date for domestic and international students; for spring admission, 10/1 priority date for domestic and international students. Applications are processed on a rolling basis. Application fee: $60 ($95 for international students). Electronic applications accepted. *Expenses:* Tuition, area resident: Part-time $239.50 per credit. Tuition, state resident: part-time $239.50 per credit. Tuition, nonresident: part-time $503 per credit. Required fees: $108 per semester. Tuition and fees vary according to course load, program and reciprocity agreements. *Financial support:* In 2010–11, 25 students received support, including 12 research assistantships with partial tuition reimbursements available (averaging $12,220 per year), 13 teaching assistantships with partial tuition reimbursements available (averaging $10,307 per year); institutionally sponsored loans, scholarships/grants, health care benefits, tuition waivers (full), and unspecified assistantships also available. Financial award application deadline: 3/1. *Faculty research:* Computer engineering, power engineering, semiconductor and nanotechnology, electronics and VLSI, telecommunications and control. Total annual research expenditures: $2.7 million. *Unit head:* Dr. Henry Selvaraj, Chair/ Professor, 702-895-4183, Fax: 702-895-4075, E-mail: ece.chair@unlv.edu. *Application contact:* Graduate College Admissions Evaluator, 702-895-3320, Fax: 702-895-4180, E-mail: gradcollege@unlv.edu.

University of Nevada, Reno, Graduate School, College of Engineering, Department of Computer Science and Engineering, Program in Computer Engineering, Reno, NV 89557. Offers MS. *Degree requirements:* For master's, thesis optional. *Entrance requirements:* For master's, GRE General Test, minimum GPA of 2.75. Additional exam requirements/recommendations for international students: Required—TOEFL (minimum score 500 paper-based; 173 computer-based; 61 iBT), IELTS (minimum score 6). Electronic applications accepted. *Expenses:* Tuition, state resident: full-time $2219; part-time $246 per credit. Tuition, nonresident: part-time $510 per credit. International tuition: $9009 full-time. Required fees: $59 per term. One-time fee: $101. Tuition and fees vary according to course load. *Faculty research:* Evolutionary computing systems, computer vision/virtual reality, software engineering.

University of Nevada, Reno, Graduate School, College of Engineering, Department of Computer Science and Engineering, Program in Computer Science and Engineering, Reno, NV 89557. Offers PhD. *Degree requirements:* For doctorate, thesis/dissertation. *Entrance requirements:* For doctorate, GRE General Test, minimum GPA of 3.0. Additional exam requirements/recommendations for international students: Required—TOEFL (minimum score 500 paper-based; 173 computer-based; 61 iBT), IELTS (minimum score 6). Electronic applications accepted. *Expenses:* Tuition, state resident: full-time $2219; part-time $246 per credit. Tuition, nonresident: part-time $510 per credit. International tuition: $9009 full-time. Required fees: $59 per term. One-time fee: $101. Tuition and fees vary according to course load. *Faculty research:* Evolutionary computing systems, computer vision/virtual reality, software engineering.

University of New Brunswick Fredericton, School of Graduate Studies, Faculty of Engineering, Department of Electrical and Computer Engineering, Fredericton, NB E3B 5A3, Canada. Offers M Eng, M Sc E, PhD. Part-time programs available. *Faculty:* 14 full-time (1 woman), 1 (woman) part-time/adjunct. *Students:* 60 full-time (4 women), 5 part-time (1 woman). 45 applicants, 44% accepted. In 2010, 10 master's, 5 doctorates awarded. *Degree requirements:* For master's, thesis, research proposal; 10 courses (for M Eng); for doctorate, comprehensive exam, thesis/dissertation, research proposal. *Entrance requirements:* For master's, minimum GPA of 3.0 or B average; references; for doctorate, M Sc; minimum GPA of 3.0 or B average; previous transcripts; references. Additional exam requirements/recommendations for international students: Required—TWE, TOEFL (minimum score 580 paper-based; 237 computer-based) or IELTS (minimum score 7). *Application deadline:* Applications are processed on a rolling basis. Application fee: $50 Canadian dollars. *Expenses:* Tuition, area resident: Full-time $3708; part-time $927 per term. International tuition: $6300 full-time. Required fees: $50 per term. *Financial support:* In 2010–11, 39 research assistantships (averaging $14,400 per year), 39 teaching assistantships were awarded; fellowships also available. *Faculty research:* Biomedical engineering, communications, robotics and control systems, electromagnetic systems, embedded systems, optical fiber systems, sustainable energy and power systems, signal processing, software systems. *Unit head:* Dr. Maryhelen Stevenson, Director of Graduate Studies, 504-447-3147, Fax: 504-453-3589, E-mail: stevenso@unb.ca. *Application contact:* Shelley Cormier, Graduate Secretary, 506-452-6142, Fax: 506-453-3589, E-mail: scormier@unb.ca.

University of New Haven, Graduate School, Tagliatela College of Engineering, Program in Electrical Engineering, West Haven, CT 06516-1916. Offers communications/digital signal processing (MS); control system (MS); electrical and computer engineering (MS); electrical engineering (MS). Part-time and evening/weekend programs available. *Students:* 42 full-time (7 women), 17 part-time (2 women); includes 4 Black or African American, non-Hispanic/Latino; 1 Asian, non-Hispanic/Latino, 46 international. Average age 27. 199 applicants, 99% accepted, 25 enrolled. In 2010, 18 master's awarded. *Degree requirements:* For master's, thesis or alternative. *Entrance requirements:* For master's, bachelor's degree in electrical engineering. Additional exam requirements/recommendations for international students: Required—TOEFL (minimum score 520 paper-based; 190 computer-based; 70 iBT); Recommended—IELTS (minimum score 5.5). *Application deadline:* For fall admission, 5/31 for international students; for winter admission, 10/15 for international students; for spring admission, 1/15 for international students. Applications are processed on a rolling basis. Application fee: $50. Electronic applications accepted. *Financial support:* Research assistantships with partial tuition reimbursements, teaching assistantships with partial tuition reimbursements, career-related internships or fieldwork, Federal Work-Study, scholarships/grants, tuition waivers, and unspecified assistantships available. Support available to part-time students. Financial award applicants required to submit FAFSA. *Unit head:* Dr. Ali Golbazi, Professor and Chair, 203-932-7164. *Application contact:* Eloise Gormley, Director of Graduate Admissions, 203-932-7449, Fax: 203-932-7137, E-mail: gradinfo@newhaven.edu.

University of New Haven, Graduate School, Tagliatela College of Engineering, Program in Network Systems, West Haven, CT 06516-1916. Offers MS. *Degree requirements:* For master's, project. *Unit head:* Dr. Barry Farbrother, Dean, 203-932-7167. *Application contact:* Eloise Gormley, Director of Graduate Admissions, 203-932-7449, Fax: 203-932-7137, E-mail: gradinfo@newhaven.edu.

University of New Mexico, Graduate School, School of Engineering, Department of Electrical and Computer Engineering, Albuquerque, NM 87131-2039. Offers computer engineering (MS, PhD); electrical engineering (MS, PhD). Part-time and evening/weekend programs available. Postbaccalaureate distance learning degree programs offered (no on-campus study). *Faculty:* 36 full-time (5 women), 8 part-time/adjunct (0 women). *Students:* 136 full-time (19 women), 72 part-time (10 women); includes 42 minority (4 Black or African American, non-Hispanic/Latino; 1 American Indian or Alaska Native, non-Hispanic/Latino; 7 Asian, non-Hispanic/Latino; 28 Hispanic/Latino; 2 Two or more races, non-Hispanic/Latino), 92 international. Average age 31. 245 applicants, 23% accepted, 40 enrolled. In 2010, 42 master's awarded. Terminal master's awarded for partial completion of doctoral program. *Degree requirements:* For master's, thesis; for doctorate, comprehensive exam, thesis/dissertation. *Entrance requirements:* For master's, GRE General Test, minimum GPA of 3.0; for doctorate, GRE General Test, minimum GPA of 3.5. Additional exam requirements/recommendations for international students: Required—TOEFL (minimum score 550 paper-based; 213 computer-based; 79 iBT). *Application deadline:* For fall admission, 7/15 for domestic students, 2/15 for international students; for spring admission, 11/1 for domestic students, 6/15 for international students. Application fee:

Computer Engineering

University of New Mexico (continued)

$50. Electronic applications accepted. *Expenses:* Tuition, state resident: full-time $5991; part-time $251 per credit hour. Tuition, nonresident: full-time $14,405; part-time $800.20 per credit hour. Tuition and fees vary according to course level, course load, program and reciprocity agreements. *Financial support:* In 2010–11, 124 students received support, including 2 fellowships with tuition reimbursements available (averaging $11,500 per year), 95 research assistantships with tuition reimbursements available (averaging $16,097 per year), 4 teaching assistantships with tuition reimbursements available (averaging $11,093 per year); scholarships/grants, health care benefits, and unspecified assistantships also available. Financial award application deadline: 2/15; financial award applicants required to submit FAFSA. *Faculty research:* Advanced graphics and visualization, biomedical engineering, communications and networking, networked control systems, photonics and microelectronics, pulsed power and high-power electromagnetics, reconfigurable systems. Total annual research expenditures: $3.2 million. *Unit head:* Dr. Chaouki T. Abdallah, Chair, 505-277-0298, Fax: 505-277-1439, E-mail: chaouki@ece.unm.edu. *Application contact:* Elmyra Grelle, Coordinator—Graduate Programs, 505-277-2600, Fax: 505-277-1439, E-mail: egrelle@ece.unm.edu.

See Display on page 381 and Close-Up on page 395.

The University of North Carolina at Charlotte, Graduate School, The William States Lee College of Engineering, Department of Electrical and Computer Engineering, Charlotte, NC 28223-0001. Offers electrical engineering (MSEE, PhD). Part-time and evening/weekend programs available. *Faculty:* 26 full-time (1 woman). *Students:* 99 full-time (20 women), 56 part-time (10 women); includes 10 minority (4 Black or African American, non-Hispanic/Latino; 1 American Indian or Alaska Native, non-Hispanic/Latino; 3 Asian, non-Hispanic/Latino; 2 Hispanic/Latino), 109 international. Average age 26. 336 applicants, 55% accepted, 34 enrolled. In 2010, 35 master's, 7 doctorates awarded. Terminal master's awarded for partial completion of doctoral program. *Degree requirements:* For master's, thesis optional, thesis or project; for doctorate, thesis/dissertation. *Entrance requirements:* For master's, GRE General Test, minimum GPA of 3.0 in undergraduate major, 2.75 overall; for doctorate, GRE General Test, 3 letters of reference. Additional exam requirements/recommendations for international students: Required—TOEFL (minimum score 557 paper-based; 220 computer-based; 83 iBT). *Application deadline:* For fall admission, 7/1 for domestic students, 5/1 for international students; for spring admission, 11/1 for domestic students, 10/1 for international students. Applications are processed on a rolling basis. Application fee: $55. Electronic applications accepted. *Expenses:* Tuition, state resident: full-time $3464. Tuition, nonresident: full-time $14,297. Required fees: $2094. Tuition and fees vary according to course load. *Financial support:* In 2010–11, 51 students received support, including 14 research assistantships (averaging $7,554 per year), 37 teaching assistantships (averaging $9,414 per year); career-related internships or fieldwork, institutionally sponsored loans, scholarships/grants, and unspecified assistantships also available. Support available to part-time students. Financial award application deadline: 4/1; financial award applicants required to submit FAFSA. *Faculty research:* Integrated circuits self test, control systems, optoelectronics/microelectronics devices and systems, communications, computer engineering. Total annual research expenditures: $1.2 million. *Unit head:* Dr. Ian Ferguson, Chair, 704-687-8404, Fax: 704-687-4762, E-mail: ianf@uncc.edu. *Application contact:* Kathy B. Giddings, Director of Graduate Admissions, 704-687-5503, Fax: 704-687-3279, E-mail: gradadm@uncc.edu.

University of North Texas, Toulouse Graduate School, College of Engineering, Department of Computer Science and Engineering, Denton, TX 76203-5017. Offers computer science (MS); computer science and engineering (PhD). Terminal master's awarded for partial completion of doctoral program. *Degree requirements:* For master's, comprehensive exam (for some programs), thesis (for some programs); for doctorate, comprehensive exam, thesis/dissertation. *Entrance requirements:* For master's, GRE General Test (minimum score 400 verbal, 700 quantitative, 600 analytical or 4.0), minimum GPA of 3.0; for doctorate, GRE General Test (minimum scores: Verbal 50th percentile, Quantitative 700, Analytical 600 or 4.5), minimum GPA of 3.5, 3 letters of recommendation. Additional exam requirements/recommendations for international students: Required—TOEFL (minimum score 550 paper-based; 213 computer-based; 79 iBT); Recommended—IELTS (minimum score 6.5). Electronic applications accepted. *Expenses:* Tuition, state resident: full-time $4298; part-time $239 per credit hour. Tuition, nonresident: full-time $10,782; part-time $549 per credit hour. Required fees: $1292; $270 per credit hour. *Financial support:* Fellowships with tuition reimbursements, research assistantships with tuition reimbursements, teaching assistantships with tuition reimbursements, career-related internships or fieldwork, Federal Work-Study, and institutionally sponsored loans available. Financial award application deadline: 4/1; financial award applicants required to submit FAFSA. *Faculty research:* Databases and data mining, computer architecture, cryptography, agent-oriented software engineering, graph theory, low power synthesis. *Application contact:* Graduate Program Coordinator, 940-565-2767, Fax: 940-565-2799, E-mail: armin.mikler@unt.edu.

University of Notre Dame, Graduate School, College of Engineering, Department of Computer Science and Engineering, Notre Dame, IN 46556. Offers MSCSE, PhD. Terminal master's awarded for partial completion of doctoral program. *Degree requirements:* For master's, comprehensive exam; for doctorate, thesis/dissertation, candidacy exam. *Entrance requirements:* For master's and doctorate, GRE General Test. Additional exam requirements/recommendations for international students: Required—TOEFL (minimum score 600 paper-based; 250 computer-based; 80 iBT). Electronic applications accepted. *Faculty research:* Algorithms and theory of computer science, artificial intelligence, behavior-based robotics, biometrics, computer vision.

University of Oklahoma, College of Engineering, Department of Electrical and Computer Engineering, Program in Electrical and Computer Engineering, Norman, OK 73019. Offers MS, PhD. Part-time programs available. *Students:* 100 full-time (21 women), 41 part-time (5 women); includes 12 minority (2 Black or African American, non-Hispanic/Latino; 1 American Indian or Alaska Native, non-Hispanic/Latino; 8 Asian, non-Hispanic/Latino; 1 Hispanic/Latino), 84 international. Average age 28. 46 applicants, 63% accepted, 14 enrolled. In 2010, 26 master's, 11 doctorates awarded. Terminal master's awarded for partial completion of doctoral program. *Degree requirements:* For master's, thesis, oral exam; for doctorate, thesis/dissertation, general exam, oral exam, qualifying exam. *Entrance requirements:* For master's and doctorate, GRE General Test. Additional exam requirements/recommendations for international students: Required—TOEFL (minimum score 550 paper-based; 213 computer-based; 79 iBT). *Application deadline:* For fall admission, 5/15 for domestic students, 4/1 for international students; for spring admission, 9/1 for domestic and international students. Applications are processed on a rolling basis. Application fee: $40 ($90 for international students). Electronic applications accepted. *Expenses:* Tuition, state resident: full-time $3892.80; part-time $162.20 per credit hour. Tuition, nonresident: full-time $14,167; part-time $590.30 per credit hour. Required fees: $2523.40; $94.60 per credit hour. Tuition and fees vary according to course load and degree level. *Financial support:* In 2010–11, 133 students received support. Career-related internships or fieldwork, scholarships/grants, health care benefits, and unspecified assistantships available. Financial award application deadline: 4/15; financial award applicants required to submit FAFSA. *Faculty research:* Signal/image processing, biomedical imaging, computer hardware design, weather radar, solid state electronics, intelligent transportation systems, navigation systems, power/electrical energy, control systems, communications. *Unit head:* Dr. James Sluss, Director, 405-325-4721, Fax: 405-325-7066, E-mail: sluss@ou.edu. *Application contact:* Lynn Hall, Graduate Program Assistant/Student Services Coordinator, 405-325-4285, Fax: 405-325-7066, E-mail: srg@ou.edu.

University of Ottawa, Faculty of Graduate and Postdoctoral Studies, Faculty of Engineering, Ottawa-Carleton Institute for Electrical and Computer Engineering, Ottawa, ON K1N 6N5, Canada. Offers M Eng, MA Sc, PhD. *Degree requirements:* For master's, thesis or alternative, project; for doctorate, comprehensive exam, thesis/dissertation. *Entrance requirements:* For master's, honors degree or equivalent, minimum B average; for doctorate, minimum A- average. Electronic applications accepted. *Faculty research:* CAD, CSE, distributed systems and BISDN, CCN, DOC.

University of Pittsburgh, School of Engineering, Computer Engineering Program, Pittsburgh, PA 15260. Offers MS, PhD. Program offered jointly with School of Arts and Sciences. *Faculty:* 14 full-time (1 woman). *Students:* 10 full-time (2 women), 1 part-time, 7 international. Average age 26. 100 applicants, 6% accepted, 6 enrolled. In 2010, 1 master's awarded. Terminal master's awarded for partial completion of doctoral program. *Degree requirements:* For master's, thesis; for doctorate, comprehensive exam, thesis/dissertation, Preliminary Exams. *Entrance requirements:* For master's and doctorate, GRE General Test. Additional exam requirements/recommendations for international students: Required—TOEFL. *Application deadline:* For fall admission, 1/15 priority date for domestic and international students. Applications are processed on a rolling basis. Application fee: $50. Electronic applications accepted. *Expenses:* Tuition, state resident: full-time $17,304; part-time $701 per credit. Tuition, nonresident: full-time $29,554; part-time $1210 per credit. Required fees: $740; $214 per term. Tuition and fees vary according to program. *Financial support:* In 2010–11, 8 research assistantships with full tuition reimbursements (averaging $17,211 per year), 3 teaching assistantships with full tuition reimbursements (averaging $15,520 per year) were awarded; health care benefits also available. Support available to part-time students. Financial award application deadline: 1/15. *Faculty research:* Computer architecture, high performance parallel and distributed systems, electronic design automation, reconfigurable computing systems and wireless networks. *Unit head:* Dr. Donald M. Chiarulli, Co-Director, 412-624-8839, Fax: 412-624-5249, E-mail: don@cs.pitt.edu. *Application contact:* Keena M. Walker, Graduate Secretary, 412-624-8495, Fax: 412-624-8854, E-mail: keena@cs.pitt.edu.

University of Puerto Rico, Mayagüez Campus, Graduate Studies, College of Engineering, Department of Electrical and Computer Engineering, Mayagüez, PR 00681-9000. Offers computer engineering (ME, MS); computing and information sciences and engineering (PhD); electrical engineering (ME, MS). Part-time programs available. *Students:* 97 full-time (23 women), 12 part-time (1 woman); includes 74 Hispanic/Latino, 35 international. 41 applicants, 54% accepted, 13 enrolled. In 2010, 19 master's, 1 doctorate awarded. *Degree requirements:* For master's, comprehensive exam, thesis; for doctorate, comprehensive exam, thesis/dissertation. *Entrance requirements:* For master's, proficiency in English and Spanish, BS in electrical or computer engineering or equivalent, minimum GPA of 3.0; for doctorate, GRE. Additional exam requirements/recommendations for international students: Required—TOEFL (minimum score 450 paper-based). *Application deadline:* For fall admission, 2/15 for domestic and international students; for spring admission, 9/15 for domestic and international students. Applications are processed on a rolling basis. Application fee: $25. *Expenses:* Tuition, state resident: full-time $1188. Tuition, nonresident: full-time $1188. International tuition: $6126 full-time. Tuition and fees vary according to course level and course load. *Financial support:* In 2010–11, 23 students received support, including fellowships (averaging $12,000 per year), 3 research assistantships (averaging $15,000 per year), 23 teaching assistantships (averaging $8,500 per year); Federal Work-Study and institutionally sponsored loans also available. *Faculty research:* Microcomputer interfacing, control systems, power systems, electronics. Total annual research expenditures: $3.8 million. *Unit head:* Dr. Erick Aponte-Diaz, Chairperson, 787-832-4040 Ext. 3821, E-mail: erick.aponte1@upr.edu. *Application contact:* Sandra Montalvo, Administrative Staff, 787-832-4040 Ext. 3094, Fax: 787-831-7564, E-mail: sandra@ece.uprm.edu.

University of Regina, Faculty of Graduate Studies and Research, Faculty of Engineering and Applied Science, Program in Electronic Systems Engineering, Regina, SK S4S 0A2, Canada. Offers M Eng, MA Sc, PhD. Part-time programs available. *Faculty:* 8 full-time (0 women), 2 part-time/adjunct (0 women). *Students:* 26 full-time (5 women), 3 part-time (0 women). 77 applicants, 56% accepted. In 2010, 5 master's, 1 doctorate awarded. *Degree requirements:* For master's, thesis (for some programs); for doctorate, thesis/dissertation. *Entrance requirements:* For doctorate, master's degree. Additional exam requirements/recommendations for international students: Required—TOEFL (minimum score 550 paper-based; 80 iBT). *Application deadline:* For fall admission, 3/31 for domestic and international students; for winter admission, 7/31 for domestic and international students; for spring admission, 11/30 for domestic and international students. Application fee: $100. Electronic applications accepted. Tuition and fees charges are reported in Canadian dollars. *Expenses:* Tuition, area resident: Full-time $3244.50 Canadian dollars; part-time $180.25 Canadian dollars per credit hour. International tuition: $4744.50 Canadian dollars full-time. Required fees: $494 Canadian dollars; $115.25 Canadian dollars per credit hour. $115.25 Canadian dollars per semester. Tuition and fees vary according to program. *Financial support:* In 2010–11, 2 fellowships (averaging $19,500 per year), 5 teaching assistantships (averaging $6,891 per year) were awarded; research assistantships, career-related internships or fieldwork and scholarships/grants also available. Financial award application deadline: 6/15. *Faculty research:* Local area networks, digital and data communications systems design, telecommunications and computer networks, image processing, RF and microwave engineering. *Unit head:* Dr. Raphael Idem, Associate Dean, Research and Graduate Studies, 306-585-4470, Fax: 306-585-4855, E-mail: raphael.idem@uregina.ca. *Application contact:* Dr. Thomas Conroy, Graduate Program Coordinator, 306-585-4397, Fax: 306-585-5855, E-mail: thomas.conroy@uregina.ca.

University of Rhode Island, Graduate School, College of Engineering, Department of Electrical, Computer and Biomedical Engineering, Kingston, RI 02881. Offers MS, PhD, Graduate Certificate. Part-time programs available. *Faculty:* 18 full-time (3 women). *Students:* 28 full-time (6 women), 24 part-time (2 women); includes 10 minority (1 Black or African American, non-Hispanic/Latino; 6 Asian, non-Hispanic/Latino; 3 Hispanic/Latino), 12 international. In 2010, 12 master's, 1 doctorate awarded. *Degree requirements:* For master's, comprehensive exam (for some programs), thesis optional; for doctorate, comprehensive exam, thesis/dissertation. *Entrance requirements:* For master's and doctorate, 2 letters of recommendation. Additional exam requirements/recommendations for international students: Required—TOEFL (minimum score 550 paper-based; 213 computer-based). *Application deadline:* For fall admission, 7/15 for domestic students, 2/1 for international students; for spring admission, 11/15 for domestic students, 7/15 for international students. Application fee: $65. Electronic applications accepted. *Expenses:* Tuition, state resident: full-time $9588; part-time $533 per credit hour. Tuition, nonresident: full-time $22,968; part-time $1276 per credit hour. Required fees: $1282; $68 per semester. Tuition and fees vary according to program. *Financial support:* In 2010–11, 8 research assistantships with full and partial tuition reimbursements (averaging $9,258 per year), 6 teaching assistantships with full and partial tuition reimbursements (averaging $9,889 per year) were awarded. Financial award application deadline: 7/15; financial award applicants required to submit FAFSA. *Faculty research:* Biomedical Instrumentation, cardiac physiology and computational modeling, analog/digital CMOS circuits, neural-machine interface, digital circuit design and VLSI testing. Total annual research expenditures: $985,856. *Unit head:* Dr. G. Faye Boudreaux-Bartels, Chair, 401-874-5805, Fax: 401-782-6422, E-mail: boud@ele.uri.edu. *Application contact:* Dr. Godi Fischer, Director of Graduate Studies, 401-874-5879, Fax: 401-782-6422, E-mail: fischer@ele.uri.edu.

University of Rochester, Hajim School of Engineering and Applied Sciences, Department of Electrical and Computer Engineering, Rochester, NY 14627. Offers MS, PhD. Terminal master's awarded for partial completion of doctoral program. *Degree requirements:* For master's, comprehensive exam; for doctorate, thesis/dissertation, preliminary and oral exams. *Entrance requirements:* For master's and doctorate, GRE. Additional exam requirements/recommendations for international students: Required—TOEFL.

University of South Carolina, The Graduate School, College of Engineering and Computing, Department of Computer Science and Engineering, Columbia, SC 29208. Offers computer science and engineering (ME, MS, PhD); software engineering (MS). Part-time and evening/weekend programs available. Postbaccalaureate distance learning degree programs offered (minimal on-campus study). *Degree requirements:* For master's, comprehensive exam, thesis (for some programs); for doctorate, comprehensive exam, thesis/dissertation. *Entrance requirements:* For master's and doctorate, GRE General Test. Additional exam requirements/recommendations for international students: Required—TOEFL (minimum score 570 paper-based; 230 computer-based). Electronic applications accepted. *Faculty research:* Computer security, computer vision, artificial intelligence, multiagent systems, bioinformatics.

University of Southern California, Graduate School, Viterbi School of Engineering, Department of Computer Science, Los Angeles, CA 90089. Offers computer networks (MS); computer science (MS, PhD); computer security (MS); game development (MS); high performance computing and simulations (MS); human language technology (MS); intelligent robotics (MS); multimedia and creative technologies (MS); software engineering (MS). Part-time and evening/weekend programs available. Postbaccalaureate distance learning degree programs offered (no on-campus study). *Faculty:* 28 full-time (3 women), 56 part-time/adjunct (7 women). *Students:* 710 full-time (115 women), 302 part-time (59 women); includes 76 minority (1 Black or African American, non-Hispanic/Latino; 55 Asian, non-Hispanic/Latino; 14 Hispanic/Latino; 6 Two or more races, non-Hispanic/Latino), 819 international. 2,379 applicants, 30% accepted, 319 enrolled. In 2010, 332 master's, 32 doctorates awarded. *Entrance requirements:* For master's and doctorate, GRE General Test. Additional exam requirements/recommendations for international students: Required—TOEFL. *Application deadline:* For fall admission, 12/1 priority date for domestic and international students; for spring admission, 9/15 priority date for domestic and international students. Applications are processed on a rolling basis. Application fee: $85. Electronic applications accepted. *Expenses:* Tuition: Full-time $31,240; part-time $1420 per unit. Required fees: $600. One-time fee: $35 full-time. Full-time tuition and fees vary according to degree level and program. *Financial support:* In 2010–11, fellowships with full tuition reimbursements (averaging $30,000 per year), research assistantships with full tuition reimbursements (averaging $20,000 per year), teaching assistantships with full tuition reimbursements (averaging $20,000 per year) were awarded; career-related internships or fieldwork, scholarships/grants, health care benefits, and unspecified assistantships also available. Financial award application deadline: 12/1; financial award applicants required to submit CSS PROFILE or FAFSA. *Faculty research:* Databases, computer graphics and computer vision, software engineering, networks and security, robotics, multimedia and virtual reality. Total annual research expenditures: $11.8 million. *Unit head:* Dr. Shanghua Teng, Chair, 213-740-4494, E-mail: csdept@usc.edu. *Application contact:* Lizsl DeLeon, Director of Student Affairs, 213-740-4496, E-mail: ldeleon@usc.edu.

University of Southern California, Graduate School, Viterbi School of Engineering, Ming Hsieh Department of Electrical Engineering, Los Angeles, CA 90089. Offers computer engineering (MS, PhD); electric power (MS); electrical engineering (MS, PhD, Engr); engineering technology commercialization (Graduate Certificate); multimedia and creative technologies (MS); telecommunications (MS); VLSI design (MS); wireless health technology (MS). Part-time programs available. Postbaccalaureate distance learning degree programs offered (no on-campus study). *Faculty:* 56 full-time (3 women), 31 part-time/adjunct (1 woman). *Students:* 886 full-time (171 women), 605 part-time (100 women); includes 209 minority (20 Black or African American, non-Hispanic/Latino; 145 Asian, non-Hispanic/Latino; 36 Hispanic/Latino; 8 Two or more races, non-Hispanic/Latino), 1,003 international. 2,986 applicants, 36% accepted, 461 enrolled. In 2010, 351 master's, 41 doctorates, 2 other advanced degrees awarded. Terminal master's awarded for partial completion of doctoral program. *Degree requirements:* For master's, thesis optional; for doctorate, thesis/dissertation. *Entrance requirements:* For master's and doctorate, GRE General Test. *Application deadline:* For fall admission, 12/1 priority date for domestic and international students; for spring admission, 9/15 priority date for domestic and international students. Applications are processed on a rolling basis. Application fee: $85. Electronic applications accepted. *Expenses:* Tuition: Full-time $31,240; part-time $1420 per unit. Required fees: $600. One-time fee: $35 full-time. Full-time tuition and fees vary according to degree level and program. *Financial support:* In 2010–11, fellowships with full tuition reimbursements (averaging $30,000 per year), research assistantships with full tuition reimbursements (averaging $20,000 per year), teaching assistantships with full tuition reimbursements (averaging $20,000 per year) were awarded; career-related internships or fieldwork, scholarships/grants, health care benefits, and unspecified assistantships also available. Financial award application deadline: 12/1; financial award applicants required to submit CSS PROFILE or FAFSA. *Faculty research:* Communications, computer engineering and networks, control systems, integrated circuits and systems, electromagnetics and energy conversion, micro electro-mechanical systems and nanotechnology, photonics and quantum electronics, plasma research, signal and image processing. Total annual research expenditures: $18 million. *Unit head:* Dr. Alexander A. Sawchuk, Chair, 213-740-4447, E-mail: studentinfo@ee.usc.edu. *Application contact:* Diane Demetras, Director of Student Affairs, 213-740-4447, E-mail: studentinfo@ee.usc.edu.

University of South Florida, Graduate School, College of Engineering, Department of Computer Science and Engineering, Tampa, FL 33620-9951. Offers computer engineering (MSCP); computer science (MSCS); computer science and engineering (PhD). Part-time programs available. *Faculty:* 14 full-time (1 woman). *Students:* 86 full-time (17 women), 27 part-time (5 women); includes 7 Black or African American, non-Hispanic/Latino; 2 Asian, non-Hispanic/Latino; 7 Hispanic/Latino, 54 international. Average age 29. 207 applicants, 44% accepted, 40 enrolled. In 2010, 24 master's, 13 doctorates awarded. Terminal master's awarded for partial completion of doctoral program. *Degree requirements:* For master's, comprehensive exam, thesis; for doctorate, comprehensive exam, thesis/dissertation, teaching of undergraduate computer science and engineering course. *Entrance requirements:* For master's, GRE General Test (minimum score 500 verbal, 700 quantitative), minimum GPA of 3.3 in last 60 hours of coursework; for doctorate, GRE General Test (minimum score: 500 Verbal, 700 Quantitative), minimum GPA of 3.3 in last 60 hours of coursework, MS (recommended). Additional exam requirements/recommendations for international students: Required—TOEFL (minimum score 550 paper-based; 213 computer-based). *Application deadline:* For fall admission, 2/15 for domestic students, 1/2 for international students; for spring admission, 10/15 for domestic students, 6/1 for international students. Application fee: $30. Electronic applications accepted. *Financial support:* In 2010–11, 67 students received support, including 27 research assistantships (averaging $15,168 per year), 33 teaching assistantships with tuition reimbursements available (averaging $15,018 per year); unspecified assistantships also available. Financial award application deadline: 1/1; financial award applicants required to submit FAFSA. *Faculty research:* Computer vision, networks, artificial intelligence, computer architecture, software security. Total annual research expenditures: $1.4 million. *Unit head:* Sudeep Sarkar, Director, 813-974-2113, Fax: 813-974-5094, E-mail: sarkar@cse.usf.edu. *Application contact:* Sudeep Sarkar, Director, 813-974-2113, Fax: 813-974-5094, E-mail: sarkar@cse.usf.edu.

The University of Tennessee, Graduate School, College of Engineering, Department of Electrical Engineering and Computer Science, Knoxville, TN 37996. Offers computer engineering (MS, PhD); computer science (MS, PhD); electrical engineering (MS, PhD); reliability and maintainability engineering (MS); MS/MBA. Part-time programs available. *Faculty:* 39 full-time (7 women), 14 part-time/adjunct (0 women). *Students:* 174 full-time (35 women), 43 part-time (6 women); includes 2 Black or African American, non-Hispanic/Latino; 3 Asian, non-Hispanic/Latino; 2 Hispanic/Latino, 114 international. Average age 29. 644 applicants, 12% accepted, 51 enrolled. In 2010, 42 master's, 21 doctorates awarded. *Degree requirements:* For master's, thesis or alternative; for doctorate, comprehensive exam, thesis/dissertation. *Entrance requirements:* For master's, GRE General Test, Minimum GPA of 2.7 (US degree holders); 3.0 (International degree holders); 3-References; Personal statement; for doctorate, GRE General Test, Minimum GPA of 3.0 (previous graduate degree); 3-References; Personal statement. Additional exam requirements/recommendations for international students: Required—TOEFL (minimum score 550 paper-based; 213 computer-based). *Application deadline:* For fall admission, 2/1 priority date for domestic and international students; for spring admission, 6/15 for domestic and international students. Applications are processed on a rolling basis. Application fee: $35. Electronic applications accepted. *Expenses:* Tuition, state resident: full-time $7440; part-time $414 per credit hour. Tuition, nonresident: full-time $22,478; part-time $1250 per credit hour. Required fees: $922; $43 per credit hour. Tuition and fees vary according to program. *Financial support:* In 2010–11, 148 students received support, including 13 fellowships with full tuition reimbursements available (averaging $12,312 per year), 100 research assistantships with full tuition reimbursements available (averaging $16,248 per year), 91 teaching assistantships with full tuition reimbursements available (averaging $12,996 per year); career-related internships or fieldwork, Federal Work-Study, institutionally sponsored loans, health care benefits, and unspecified assistantships also available. Financial award application deadline: 2/1; financial award applicants required to submit FAFSA. *Faculty research:* Artificial intelligence and visualization; microelectronics, mixed-signal electronics, VLSI, embedded systems; scientific and distributed computing; computer vision, robotics, and image processing; power electronics, power systems, communications. Total annual research expenditures: $10.7 million. *Unit head:* Dr. Kevin Tomsovic, Head, 865-974-3461, Fax: 865-974-5483, E-mail: tomsovic@eecs.utk.edu. *Application contact:* Dr. Lynne E. Parker, Associate Head, 865-974-4394, Fax: 865-974-5483, E-mail: parker@eecs.utk.edu.

The University of Texas at Arlington, Graduate School, College of Engineering, Department of Computer Science and Engineering, Arlington, TX 76019. Offers computer engineering (MS, PhD); computer science (MS, PhD); computer science and engineering (M Engr); software engineering (MS, PhD). Part-time programs available. Postbaccalaureate distance learning degree programs offered (minimal on-campus study). *Faculty:* 27 full-time (2 women), 1 part-time/adjunct (0 women). *Students:* 183 full-time (41 women), 89 part-time (18 women); includes 9 minority (3 Black or African American, non-Hispanic/Latino; 4 Asian, non-Hispanic/Latino; 1 Hispanic/Latino; 1 Two or more races, non-Hispanic/Latino), 219 international. 452 applicants, 62% accepted, 94 enrolled. In 2010, 82 master's, 10 doctorates awarded. Terminal master's awarded for partial completion of doctoral program. *Degree requirements:* For master's, comprehensive exam (for some programs), thesis; for doctorate, comprehensive exam, thesis/dissertation. *Entrance requirements:* For master's, GRE General Test, TTL 1150, minimum GPA of 3.0 (3.2 in computer science-related classes); for doctorate, GRE General Test, TTL 1250, minimum GPA of 3.5. Additional exam requirements/recommendations for international students: Required—TOEFL (minimum score 550 paper-based; 230 computer-based; 92 iBT). *Application deadline:* For fall admission, 6/1 for domestic students, 4/1 for international students; for spring admission, 10/15 for domestic students, 9/15 for international students. Applications are processed on a rolling basis. Application fee: $35 ($50 for international students). *Expenses:* Tuition, state resident: full-time $7500. Tuition, nonresident: full-time $13,080. International tuition: $13,250 full-time. *Financial support:* In 2010–11, 7 fellowships with full tuition reimbursements (averaging $24,000 per year), 57 research assistantships with partial tuition reimbursements (averaging $19,200 per year), 50 teaching assistantships with partial tuition reimbursements (averaging $16,200 per year) were awarded; career-related internships or fieldwork and scholarships/grants also available. Financial award application deadline: 6/1; financial award applicants required to submit FAFSA. *Faculty research:* Algorithms, homeland security, mobile pervasive computing, high performance computing bioinformation. *Unit head:* Dr. Fillia Makedon, Chairman, 817-272-3605, E-mail: makedon@uta.edu. *Application contact:* Dr. Bahram Khalili, Graduate Advisor, 817-272-5407, Fax: 817-272-3784, E-mail: khalili@uta.edu.

The University of Texas at Austin, Graduate School, Cockrell School of Engineering, Department of Electrical and Computer Engineering, Austin, TX 78712-1111. Offers MSE, PhD. Part-time programs available. *Entrance requirements:* For master's, GRE General Test, minimum GPA of 3.3 in upper-division course work; for doctorate, GRE General Test. Electronic applications accepted.

The University of Texas at Dallas, Erik Jonsson School of Engineering and Computer Science, Department of Electrical Engineering, Richardson, TX 75080. Offers computer engineering (MS, PhD); electrical engineering (MSEE, PhD); microelectronics (MSEE, PhD); telecommunications (MSEE, MSTE, PhD). Part-time and evening/weekend programs available. *Faculty:* 43 full-time (2 women). *Students:* 404 full-time (78 women), 186 part-time (32 women); includes 85 minority (11 Black or African American, non-Hispanic/Latino; 56 Asian, non-Hispanic/Latino; 17 Hispanic/Latino; 1 Two or more races, non-Hispanic/Latino), 406 international. Average age 27. 1,612 applicants, 44% accepted, 188 enrolled. In 2010, 152 master's, 31 doctorates awarded. *Degree requirements:* For master's, thesis or major design project; for doctorate, thesis/dissertation. *Entrance requirements:* For master's, GRE General Test, minimum GPA of 3.0 in related bachelor's degree; for doctorate, GRE General Test, minimum GPA of 3.5. Additional exam requirements/recommendations for international students: Required—TOEFL (minimum score 550 paper-based; 215 computer-based). *Application deadline:* For fall admission, 7/15 for domestic students, 5/1 priority date for international students; for spring admission, 11/15 for domestic students, 9/1 priority date for international students. Applications are processed on a rolling basis. Application fee: $50 ($100 for international students). Electronic applications accepted. *Expenses:* Tuition, state resident: full-time $10,248; part-time $569 per credit hour. Tuition, nonresident: full-time $18,544; part-time $1030 per credit hour. Tuition and fees vary according to course load. *Financial support:* In 2010–11, 211 students received support, including 5 fellowships with partial tuition reimbursements available (averaging $15,960 per year), 129 research assistantships with partial tuition reimbursements available (averaging $16,317 per year), 43 teaching assistantships with partial tuition reimbursements available (averaging $15,206 per year); Federal Work-Study, institutionally sponsored loans, scholarships/grants, unspecified assistantships, and cooperative positions also available. Support available to part-time students. Financial award application deadline: 4/30; financial award applicants required to submit FAFSA. *Faculty research:* Semiconductor device manufacturing, photonics devices and systems, signal processing and language technology, nano-fabrication, energy efficient digital systems. *Unit head:* Dr. John H.L. Hansen, Department Head, 972-883-6755, Fax: 972-883-2710, E-mail: john.hansen@utdallas.edu. *Application contact:* Kathy Gribble, Graduate Program Coordinator, 972-883-2649, Fax: 972-883-2710, E-mail: gradecs@utdallas.edu.

The University of Texas at El Paso, Graduate School, College of Engineering, Department of Electrical and Computer Engineering, El Paso, TX 79968-0001. Offers computer engineering (MS); electrical and computer engineering (PhD); electrical engineering (MS). Part-time and evening/weekend programs available. *Students:* 144 (38 women); includes 86 Hispanic/Latino, 53 international. Average age 34. In 2010, 38 master's, 2 doctorates awarded. *Degree requirements:* For master's, thesis optional; for doctorate, thesis/dissertation. *Entrance requirements:* For master's, GRE General Test, minimum GPA of 3.0; for doctorate, GRE General Test, qualifying exam, minimum graduate GPA of 3.0. Additional exam requirements/recommendations for international students: Required—TOEFL. *Application deadline:* For fall admission, 7/1 priority date for domestic students, 3/1 for international students; for spring admission, 11/1 priority date for domestic students, 9/1 for international students. Applications are processed on a rolling basis. Application fee: $15 ($65 for international students). Electronic applications accepted. *Financial support:* In 2010–11, 60 students received support, including research assistantships with partial tuition reimbursements available (averaging $22,375 per year), teaching assistantships with partial tuition reimbursements available (averaging $17,900 per year); fellowships with partial tuition reimbursements available, Federal Work-Study, institutionally sponsored loans, scholarships/grants, and tuition waivers (partial) also available. Financial award application deadline: 3/15; financial award applicants required to submit FAFSA. *Faculty research:* Signal and image processing, computer architecture, fiber optics, computational electromagnetics, electronic displays and thin films. *Unit head:* Patricia Nava, Chair, 915-747-5994, E-mail: pnava@utep.edu. *Application contact:* Dr. Charles H. Ambler, Dean of the Graduate School, 915-747-5491 Ext. 7886, Fax: 915-747-5788, E-mail: cambler@utep.edu.

The University of Texas at San Antonio, College of Engineering, Department of Electrical and Computer Engineering, San Antonio, TX 78249-0617. Offers computer engineering (MS); electrical engineering (MS, PhD). Part-time and evening/weekend programs available. *Faculty:* 20 full-time (2 women), 3 part-time/adjunct (1 woman). *Students:* 100 full-time (28 women), 69 part-time (10 women); includes 30 minority (3 Black or African American, non-Hispanic/Latino; 7 Asian, non-Hispanic/Latino; 18 Hispanic/Latino; 2 Two or more races, non-Hispanic/Latino), 103 international. Average age 28. 148 applicants, 82% accepted, 51 enrolled. In 2010, 56 master's, 7 doctorates awarded. *Degree requirements:* For master's, comprehensive exam (for some programs), thesis (for some programs); for doctorate, comprehensive exam, thesis/dissertation. *Entrance requirements:* For master's, GRE General Test, minimum GPA of 3.0 in last 60 hours of undergraduate degree; for doctorate, GRE General Test. Additional exam requirements/recommendations for international students: Required—TOEFL (minimum score 500 paper-based; 173 computer-based). *Application deadline:* For fall admission, 7/1 for domestic students, 4/1 for international students; for spring admission, 11/1 for domestic

Computer Engineering

The University of Texas at San Antonio (continued)
students, 9/1 for international students. Applications are processed on a rolling basis. Application fee: $45 ($80 for international students). Electronic applications accepted. *Expenses:* Tuition, state resident: full-time $4172; part-time $231.75 per credit hour. Tuition, nonresident: full-time $15,332; part-time $851.75 per credit hour. *Financial support:* In 2010–11, 60 students received support, including 10 fellowships (averaging $34,425 per year), 62 research assistantships (averaging $11,312 per year), 41 teaching assistantships (averaging $11,244 per year); career-related internships or fieldwork, scholarships/grants, and unspecified assistantships also available. Support available to part-time students. Financial award application deadline: 3/31. Total annual research expenditures: $873,745. *Unit head:* Dr. Ruyan Guo, Interim Chair, 210-458-7057, Fax: 210-458-5947, E-mail: ruyan.guo@utsa.edu. *Application contact:* Veronica Ramirez, Assistant Dean of the Graduate School, 210-458-4330, Fax: 210-458-4332, E-mail: graduatestudies@utsa.edu.

See M.S. Display on page 384 and Close-Up on page 399 and see Ph.D. Display on page 384 and Close-Up2 on page 401.

University of Toronto, School of Graduate Studies, Physical Sciences Division, Faculty of Applied Science and Engineering, Department of Electrical and Computer Engineering, Toronto, ON M5S 1A1, Canada. Offers M Eng, MA Sc, PhD. Part-time programs available. *Degree requirements:* For master's, thesis (for some programs), oral thesis defense (MA Sc); for doctorate, thesis/dissertation, qualifying exam, thesis defense. *Entrance requirements:* For master's, four-year degree in electrical or computer engineering, minimum B average, 2 letters of reference; for doctorate, minimum B+ average, MA Sc in electrical or computer engineering, 2 letters of reference.

University of Victoria, Faculty of Graduate Studies, Faculty of Engineering, Department of Electrical and Computer Engineering, Victoria, BC V8W 2Y2, Canada. Offers M Eng, MA Sc, PhD. *Degree requirements:* For master's, thesis; for doctorate, thesis/dissertation, candidacy exam. *Entrance requirements:* For master's, GRE (recommended), bachelor's degree in engineering; for doctorate, GRE (recommended), master's degree. Additional exam requirements/recommendations for international students: Required—TOEFL (minimum score 575 paper-based; 233 computer-based), IELTS (minimum score 7). Electronic applications accepted. *Faculty research:* Communications and computers; electromagnetics, microwaves, and optics; electronics; power systems, signal processing, and control.

University of Virginia, School of Engineering and Applied Science, Department of Electrical and Computer Engineering, Program in Computer Engineering, Charlottesville, VA 22903. Offers ME, MS, PhD. Postbaccalaureate distance learning degree programs offered (no on-campus study). *Students:* 22 full-time (2 women), 1 part-time (0 women), 20 international. Average age 27. 60 applicants, 8% accepted, 1 enrolled. In 2010, 10 master's, 2 doctorates awarded. Terminal master's awarded for partial completion of doctoral program. *Degree requirements:* For master's, thesis (for some programs); for doctorate, comprehensive exam, thesis/dissertation. *Entrance requirements:* For master's, GRE General Test, 3 letters of recommendation; for doctorate, GRE General Test, 3 letters of recommendation; essay. Additional exam requirements/recommendations for international students: Required—TOEFL (minimum score 650 paper-based; 250 computer-based; 90 iBT), IELTS (minimum score 7). *Application deadline:* For fall admission, 8/1 for domestic students, 4/1 for international students; for winter admission, 12/1 for domestic students, 8/1 for international students; for spring admission, 5/1 for domestic students, 1/1 for international students. Applications are processed on a rolling basis. Application fee: $60. Electronic applications accepted. *Financial support:* Fellowships, research assistantships, teaching assistantships available. Financial award application deadline: 1/15; financial award applicants required to submit FAFSA. *Faculty research:* Computer architecture, VLSI, switching theory, operating systems, real-time and embedded systems, compiler, software systems and software engineering, fault-tolerant computing and reliability engineering. *Unit head:* Joanne B. Dugan, Director, 434-924-3198, Fax: 434-924-8818, E-mail: compe@virginia.edu. *Application contact:* Joanne B. Dugan, Director, 434-924-3198, Fax: 434-924-8818, E-mail: compe@virginia.edu.

University of Washington, Bothell, Program in Computing and Software Systems, Bothell, WA 98011-8246. Offers MS. Part-time and evening/weekend programs available. *Faculty:* 8 full-time (1 woman). *Students:* 6 full-time (3 women), 45 part-time (6 women); includes 2 Black or African American, non-Hispanic/Latino; 11 Asian, non-Hispanic/Latino; 1 Hispanic/Latino, 4 international. Average age 33. 31 applicants, 74% accepted, 19 enrolled. *Degree requirements:* For master's, comprehensive exam (for some programs), thesis optional. *Entrance requirements:* For master's, GRE. Additional exam requirements/recommendations for international students: Required—TOEFL (minimum score 580 paper-based; 237 computer-based; 92 iBT), IELTS (minimum score 7), TOEFL or IELTS. *Application deadline:* For fall admission, 7/1 for domestic students, 4/1 for international students; for winter admission, 11/1 for domestic students; for spring admission, 2/1 for domestic students. Application fee: $65. Electronic applications accepted. *Expenses:* Contact institution. *Financial support:* Applicants required to submit FAFSA. *Faculty research:* Computer vision, artificial intelligence, software engineering, computer graphics, parallel and distributed systems. *Unit head:* Dr. Michael Stiber, Professor and Director, 425-352-5279, E-mail: cssinfo@uwb.edu. *Application contact:* Megan Jewell, Graduate Advisor, 425-352-5279, E-mail: mjewell@uwb.edu.

University of Washington, Tacoma, Graduate Programs, Program in Computing and Software Systems, Tacoma, WA 98402-3100. Offers MS. Part-time programs available. *Faculty:* 15 full-time (4 women), 6 part-time/adjunct (1 woman). *Students:* 28 full-time (15 women), 11 part-time (1 woman); includes 1 Black or African American, non-Hispanic/Latino; 6 Asian, non-Hispanic/Latino; 2 Hispanic/Latino, 9 international. Average age 29. 32 applicants, 72% accepted, 16 enrolled. In 2010, 18 master's awarded. *Degree requirements:* For master's, capstone project/thesis or 15 credits elective coursework. *Entrance requirements:* For master's, GRE, personal statement, resume, transcripts, 3 recommendations. Additional exam requirements/recommendations for international students: Required—TOEFL (minimum score 580 paper-based; 237 computer-based; 92 iBT), IELTS (minimum score 7). *Application deadline:* For fall admission, 4/15 priority date for domestic students; for winter admission, 10/15 priority date for domestic students; for spring admission, 1/15 priority date for domestic students. Applications are processed on a rolling basis. Application fee: $65. Electronic applications accepted. *Financial support:* In 2010–11, 1 teaching assistantship with partial tuition reimbursement (averaging $14,000 per year) was awarded; career-related internships or fieldwork and scholarships/grants also available. *Faculty research:* Data stream analysis, formal methods, data mining, robotic systems, software development processes. Total annual research expenditures: $50,000. *Unit head:* Dr. Orlando Baiocchi, Director, 253-692-5860, Fax: 253-692-5862, E-mail: uwtech@u.washington.edu. *Application contact:* Dr. Larry Wear, Associate Director, 253-692-5860, Fax: 253-692-5862, E-mail: uwtech@u.washington.edu.

University of Waterloo, Graduate Studies, Faculty of Engineering, Department of Electrical and Computer Engineering, Waterloo, ON N2L 3G1, Canada. Offers electrical and computer engineering (M Eng, MA Sc, PhD); electrical and computer engineering (software engineering) (MA Sc). Part-time programs available. *Degree requirements:* For master's, research paper or thesis; for doctorate, comprehensive exam, thesis/dissertation. *Entrance requirements:* For master's, honors degree, minimum B+ average; for doctorate, master's degree, minimum A-average. Additional exam requirements/recommendations for international students: Required—TOEFL (minimum score 550 paper-based; 213 computer-based), TWE (minimum score 4). Electronic applications accepted. *Faculty research:* Communications, computers, systems and control, silicon devices, power engineering.

The University of Western Ontario, Faculty of Graduate Studies, Physical Sciences Division, Faculty of Engineering, London, ON N6A 5B8, Canada. Offers chemical and biochemical engineering (ME Sc, PhD); civil and environmental engineering (M Eng, ME Sc, PhD); electrical and computer engineering (M Eng, ME Sc, PhD); mechanical and materials engineering (M Eng, ME Sc, PhD). Part-time programs available. Terminal master's awarded for partial completion of doctoral program. *Degree requirements:* For master's, thesis; for doctorate, thesis/dissertation. *Entrance requirements:* For master's, minimum B average; for doctorate, minimum B+ average. *Faculty research:* Wind, geotechnical, chemical reactor engineering, applied electrostatics, biochemical engineering.

University of Wisconsin–Milwaukee, Graduate School, College of Engineering and Applied Science, Program in Engineering, Milwaukee, WI 53201-0413. Offers civil engineering (MS); electrical and computer engineering (MS); energy engineering (Certificate); engineering (PhD); engineering management (MS); engineering mechanics (MS); ergonomics (Certificate); industrial and management engineering (MS); manufacturing engineering (MS); materials engineering (MS); mechanical engineering (MS); MUP/MS. Part-time programs available. *Faculty:* 50 full-time (5 women). *Students:* 152 full-time (27 women), 115 part-time (23 women); includes 13 Black or African American, non-Hispanic/Latino; 3 American Indian or Alaska Native, non-Hispanic/Latino; 6 Asian, non-Hispanic/Latino; 10 Hispanic/Latino, 25 international. Average age 31. 236 applicants, 67% accepted, 55 enrolled. In 2010, 39 master's, 19 doctorates awarded. *Degree requirements:* For master's, comprehensive exam (for some programs), thesis or alternative; for doctorate, comprehensive exam, thesis/dissertation, internship. *Entrance requirements:* For master's, GRE, minimum GPA of 2.75; for doctorate, GRE, minimum GPA of 3.5. Additional exam requirements/recommendations for international students: Required—TOEFL (minimum score 550 paper-based; 79 iBT), IELTS (minimum score 6.5). *Application deadline:* For fall admission, 1/1 priority date for domestic students; for spring admission, 9/1 for domestic students. Applications are processed on a rolling basis. Application fee: $56 ($96 for international students). *Financial support:* In 2010–11, 3 fellowships, 55 research assistantships, 77 teaching assistantships were awarded; career-related internships or fieldwork, Federal Work-Study, unspecified assistantships, and project assistantships also available. Support available to part-time students. Financial award application deadline: 4/15. Total annual research expenditures: $6.2 million. *Unit head:* David Yu, Representative, 414-229-6169, E-mail: yu@uwm.edu. *Application contact:* Betty Warras, General Information Contact, 414-229-6169, Fax: 414-229-6967, E-mail: bwarras@uwm.edu.

Villanova University, College of Engineering, Department of Electrical and Computer Engineering, Program in Computer Engineering, Villanova, PA 19085-1699. Offers computer architectures (Certificate); computer engineering (MSCPE); intelligent control systems (Certificate). Part-time and evening/weekend programs available. *Students:* 3 full-time (0 women), 14 part-time (2 women); includes 1 Black or African American, non-Hispanic/Latino; 3 Hispanic/Latino, 3 international. 35 applicants, 54% accepted. In 2010, 13 master's awarded. *Degree requirements:* For master's, thesis optional. *Entrance requirements:* For master's, GRE General Test (for applicants with degrees from foreign universities), BEE, minimum GPA of 3.0. Additional exam requirements/recommendations for international students: Required—TOEFL (minimum score 600 paper-based; 250 computer-based; 100 iBT). *Application deadline:* For fall admission, 8/1 priority date for domestic students, 4/1 for international students; for spring admission, 12/1 for domestic students, 8/1 for international students. Applications are processed on a rolling basis. Application fee: $50. Electronic applications accepted. *Expenses:* Tuition: Part-time $700 per credit. Part-time tuition and fees vary according to degree level and program. *Financial support:* In 2010–11, research assistantships with full and partial tuition reimbursements (averaging $13,500 per year); Federal Work-Study, scholarships/grants, tuition waivers (full and partial), and unspecified assistantships also available. Support available to part-time students. Financial award application deadline: 1/15. *Faculty research:* Expert systems, computer vision, neural networks, image processing, computer architectures. *Unit head:* Dr. Pritpal Singh, Chairman, 610-519-4971, Fax: 610-519-4436. *Application contact:* College of Engineering, Graduate Programs Office, 610-519-5840, Fax: 610-519-5859, E-mail: engineering.grad@villanova.edu.

Virginia Polytechnic Institute and State University, Graduate School, College of Engineering, Department of Electrical and Computer Engineering, Blacksburg, VA 24061. Offers air transportation systems (Certificate); computer engineering (M Eng, MS, PhD); electrical engineering (M Eng, MS, PhD); emerging devices technologies (Certificate); traffic control and operations (Certificate). *Faculty:* 67 full-time (6 women). *Students:* 386 full-time (62 women), 135 part-time (20 women); includes 8 Black or African American, non-Hispanic/Latino; 27 Asian, non-Hispanic/Latino; 8 Hispanic/Latino, 316 international. Average age 28. 1,444 applicants, 10% accepted, 89 enrolled. In 2010, 91 master's, 48 doctorates awarded. *Degree requirements:* For master's, comprehensive exam (for some programs), thesis (for some programs); for doctorate, comprehensive exam (for some programs), thesis/dissertation (for some programs). *Entrance requirements:* For master's and doctorate, GRE. Additional exam requirements/recommendations for international students: Required—TOEFL (minimum score 590 paper-based; 213 computer-based). *Application deadline:* For fall admission, 7/1 for domestic and international students; for spring admission, 12/1 for domestic and international students. Applications are processed on a rolling basis. Application fee: $65. Electronic applications accepted. *Expenses:* Tuition, area resident: Full-time $9399; part-time $488 per credit hour. Tuition, state resident: full-time $9399; part-time $488 per credit hour. Tuition, nonresident: full-time $17,854; part-time $957.75 per credit hour. International tuition: $17,854 full-time. Required fees: $1534. Full-time tuition and fees vary according to program. *Financial support:* In 2010–11, 10 fellowships with full tuition reimbursements (averaging $2,845 per year), 159 research assistantships with full tuition reimbursements (averaging $20,998 per year), 28 teaching assistantships with full tuition reimbursements (averaging $15,083 per year) were awarded; career-related internships or fieldwork, Federal Work-Study, scholarships/grants, health care benefits, and unspecified assistantships also available. Financial award application deadline: 1/15. *Faculty research:* Electromagnetics, controls, electronics, power, communications. *Unit head:* Dr. James S. Thorp, UNIT HEAD, 540-231-7494, Fax: 540-231-3362, E-mail: jsthorp@vt.edu. *Application contact:* Paul Plassmann, Contact, 540-231-5379, Fax: 540-231-3362, E-mail: plassmann@vt.edu.

Virginia Polytechnic Institute and State University, VT Online, Blacksburg, VA 24061. Offers aerospace engineering (MS); business information systems (Graduate Certificate); career and technical education (MS); computer engineering (M Eng, MS); decision support systems (Graduate Certificate); eLearning leadership (MA); electrical engineering (M Eng, MS); engineering administration (MEA); environmental politics and policy (Graduate Certificate); foundations of political analysis (Graduate Certificate); health product risk management (Graduate Certificate); information policy and society (Graduate Certificate); information security (Graduate Certificate); instructional technology (MA); liberal arts (Graduate Certificate); life sciences: health product risk management (MS); natural resources (MNR, Graduate Certificate); networking (Graduate Certificate); nonprofit and nongovernmental organization management (Graduate Certificate); ocean engineering (MS); political science (MA); security studies (Graduate Certificate); software development (Graduate Certificate). *Expenses:* Tuition, area resident: Full-time $9399; part-time $488 per credit hour. Tuition, state resident: full-time $9399; part-time $488 per credit hour. Tuition, nonresident: full-time $17,854; part-time $957.75 per credit hour. International tuition: $17,854 full-time. Required fees: $1534. Full-time tuition and fees vary according to program.

Washington State University, Graduate School, College of Engineering and Architecture, School of Electrical Engineering and Computer Science, Program in Computer Engineering, Pullman, WA 99164. Offers MS, PhD. *Faculty:* 24. *Students:* 67 full-time (17 women), 7 part-time (1 woman); includes 1 minority (Native Hawaiian or other Pacific Islander, non-Hispanic/Latino), 32 international. Average age 27. 180 applicants, 26% accepted, 34 enrolled. In 2010, 4 master's awarded. *Degree requirements:* For master's, comprehensive exam (for some programs), thesis optional, research project; for doctorate, comprehensive exam, thesis/dissertation. *Entrance requirements:* For master's, GRE, 3 letters of recommendation; for doctorate, 3 letters of recommendation. Additional exam requirements/recommendations for international students: Required—TOEFL. *Application deadline:* For fall admission, 3/1 for domestic and international students; for spring admission, 9/1 for domestic students, 7/1 for international students. Application fee: $50. *Expenses:* Tuition, state resident: full-time $8552; part-time $443 per credit. Tuition, nonresident: full-time $21,650; part-time $1083 per credit. Required fees: $846. *Financial support:* In 2010–11, research assistantships with tuition reimbursements (averaging $18,204 per year), teaching assistantships with tuition reimbursements (averaging $18,204 per year) were awarded. Total annual research expenditures: $3.9 million. *Unit head:* Behrooz Shirazi, Director, 509-335-8148, E-mail: shirazi@wsu.edu. *Application contact:* Graduate School Admissions, 800-GRADWSU, Fax: 509-335-1949, E-mail: gradsch@wsu.edu.

Washington State University Tri-Cities, Graduate Programs, College of Engineering and Computer Science, Richland, WA 99352. Offers computer science (MS, PhD); electrical and computer engineering (PhD); electrical engineering (MS); mechanical engineering (MS, PhD). Part-time programs available. *Faculty:* 28. *Students:* 4 full-time (0 women), 25 part-time (8 women); includes 2 Black or African American, non-Hispanic/Latino, 1 international. *Degree requirements:* For master's, comprehensive exam, thesis (for some programs); for doctorate, comprehensive exam, thesis/dissertation, oral exam. *Entrance requirements:* For master's and doctorate, GRE, minimum GPA of 3.0, 3 letters of recommendation. Additional exam requirements/recommendations for international students: Required—TOEFL (minimum score 550 paper-based; 213 computer-based). *Application deadline:* For fall admission, 1/10 priority date for domestic students, 1/10 for international students; for spring admission, 7/1 priority date for domestic students, 7/1 for international students. Application fee: $50. *Financial support:* Application deadline: 3/1. *Faculty research:* Positive ion track structure, biological systems computer simulations. *Unit head:* Dr. Ali Saberi, Chair, 509-372-7178, E-mail: sidra@eecs.wsu.edu. *Application contact:* Dr. Scott Hudson, Associate Director, 509-372-7254, Fax: 509-335-1949, E-mail: hudson@tricity.wsu.edu.

Washington University in St. Louis, School of Engineering and Applied Science, Department of Computer Science and Engineering, St. Louis, MO 63130-4899. Offers computer engineering (MS, PhD); computer science (MS, PhD); computer science and engineering (M Eng). Part-time programs available. *Faculty:* 21 full-time (3 women), 4 part-time/adjunct (1 woman). *Students:* 85 full-time (11 women), 62 part-time (11 women); includes 5 Asian, non-Hispanic/Latino; 4 Hispanic/Latino; 3 Two or more races, non-Hispanic/Latino, 50 international. Average age 26. 423 applicants, 24% accepted, 50 enrolled. In 2010, 28 master's, 7 doctorates awarded. Terminal master's awarded for partial completion of doctoral program. *Degree requirements:* For master's, thesis optional; for doctorate, thesis/dissertation. *Entrance requirements:* For doctorate, GRE General Test. Additional exam requirements/recommendations for international students: Required—TOEFL. *Application deadline:* For fall admission, 1/15 for domestic and international students; for spring admission, 11/1 for domestic and international students. Applications are processed on a rolling basis. Application fee: $60. Electronic applications accepted. *Financial support:* In 2010–11, 4 fellowships with full tuition reimbursements (averaging $26,950 per year), 61 research assistantships with full tuition reimbursements (averaging $26,950 per year) were awarded; health care benefits, tuition waivers (partial), and unspecified assistantships also available. Financial award application deadline: 1/30. *Faculty research:* Artificial intelligence, computational genomics, computer and systems architecture, media and machines, networking and communication, software systems. Total annual research expenditures: $5.8 million. *Unit head:* Dr. Gruia-Catalin Roman, Chair, 314-935-6132, Fax: 314-935-7302, E-mail: roman@cse.wustl.edu. *Application contact:* Madeline Hawkins, Project Specialist, 314-935-6132, Fax: 314-935-7302, E-mail: admissions@cse.wustl.edu.

See Display on page 283 and Close-Up on page 341.

Wayne State University, College of Engineering, Department of Electrical and Computer Engineering, Program in Computer Engineering, Detroit, MI 48202. Offers MS, PhD. *Faculty:* 17 full-time (1 woman). *Students:* 37 full-time (8 women), 4 part-time (1 woman); includes 3 minority (all Asian, non-Hispanic/Latino), 28 international. Average age 28. 46 applicants, 46% accepted, 9 enrolled. In 2010, 4 master's, 1 doctorate awarded. *Degree requirements:* For master's, thesis optional; for doctorate, thesis/dissertation. *Entrance requirements:* Additional exam requirements/recommendations for international students: Required—TOEFL (minimum score 550 paper-based; 213 computer-based), Michigan English Language Assessment Battery (minimum score: 85); Recommended—TWE (minimum score 6). *Application deadline:* For fall admission, 7/1 priority date for domestic students, 6/1 for international students; for winter admission, 10/1 for international students; for spring admission, 3/15 for domestic students, 2/1 for international students. Applications are processed on a rolling basis. Application fee: $30 ($50 for international students). Electronic applications accepted. *Expenses:* Tuition, state resident: full-time $7662; part-time $478.85 per credit hour. Tuition, nonresident: full-time $16,920; part-time $1057.55 per credit hour. Required fees: $571.20; $35.70 per credit hour. $188.05 per semester. Tuition and fees vary according to course load and program. *Financial support:* In 2010–11, 6 research assistantships (averaging $16,221 per year), 8 teaching assistantships (averaging $16,984 per year) were awarded. Financial award application deadline: 3/16. *Faculty research:* Neural networks, parallel processing, pattern recognition, VLSI, computer architecture. *Unit head:* Yang Zhao, Chair, 313-577-3920, Fax: 313-577-1101, E-mail: aa3606@wayne.edu. *Application contact:* Pepe Siy, Graduate Director, 313-577-3841, Fax: 313-577-1101, E-mail: psiy@ece.eng.wayne.edu.

Western Michigan University, Graduate College, College of Engineering and Applied Sciences, Department of Electrical and Computer Engineering, Kalamazoo, MI 49008. Offers computer engineering (MSE); electrical and computer engineering (PhD); electrical engineering (MSE). Part-time programs available. *Degree requirements:* For master's, thesis optional. *Entrance requirements:* For master's, minimum GPA of 3.0. *Faculty research:* Fiber optics, computer architecture, bioelectromagnetics, acoustics.

West Virginia University, College of Engineering and Mineral Resources, Lane Department of Computer Science and Electrical Engineering, Program in Computer Engineering, Morgantown, WV 26506. Offers PhD. *Degree requirements:* For doctorate, comprehensive exam, thesis/dissertation. *Entrance requirements:* For doctorate, GRE General Test, minimum GPA of 3.0, letters of recommendation. Additional exam requirements/recommendations for international students: Required—TOEFL. *Faculty research:* Software engineering, microprocessor applications, microelectronic systems, fault tolerance, advanced computer architectures and networks.

Wichita State University, Graduate School, College of Engineering, Department of Electrical Engineering and Computer Science, Wichita, KS 67260. Offers computer networking (MS); computer science (MS); electrical engineering (MS, PhD). Part-time and evening/weekend programs available. *Unit head:* Dr. John Watkins, Chair, 316-978-3156, Fax: 316-978-5408, E-mail: john.watkins@wichita.edu. *Application contact:* Dr. John Watkins, Chair, 316-978-3156, Fax: 316-978-5408, E-mail: john.watkins@wichita.edu.

Widener University, Graduate Programs in Engineering, Program in Computer and Software Engineering, Chester, PA 19013-5792. Offers M Eng. Part-time and evening/weekend programs available. *Students:* 1 full-time (0 women), 2 part-time (0 women), 2 international. Average age 28. In 2010, 5 master's awarded. *Degree requirements:* For master's, thesis optional. *Application deadline:* For fall admission, 8/1 priority date for domestic students; for spring admission, 12/1 for domestic students. Applications are processed on a rolling basis. Application fee: $25 ($300 for international students). *Financial support:* Research assistantships with full tuition reimbursements, unspecified assistantships available. Financial award application deadline: 3/15. *Faculty research:* Computer and software engineering, computer network fault-tolerant computing, optical computing. *Unit head:* Dr. Bryen E. Lorenz, Chairman, Department of Electrical/Telecommunication Engineering, 610-499-4064, Fax: 610-499-4059, E-mail: bryen.f.lorenz@widener.edu. *Application contact:* Dr. Bryen E. Lorenz, Chairman, Department of Electrical/Telecommunication Engineering, 610-499-4064, Fax: 610-499-4059, E-mail: bryen.f.lorenz@widener.edu.

Worcester Polytechnic Institute, Graduate Studies and Research, Department of Electrical and Computer Engineering, Worcester, MA 01609-2280. Offers electrical and computer engineering (Advanced Certificate, Graduate Certificate); electrical engineering (M Eng, MS, PhD). Part-time and evening/weekend programs available. *Faculty:* 17 full-time (1 woman), 3 part-time/adjunct (0 women). *Students:* 106 full-time (20 women), 103 part-time (14 women); includes 7 Black or African American, non-Hispanic/Latino; 10 Hispanic/Latino; 12 Native Hawaiian or other Pacific Islander, non-Hispanic/Latino, 72 international. 504 applicants, 53% accepted, 92 enrolled. In 2010, 46 master's, 8 doctorates awarded. Terminal master's awarded for partial completion of doctoral program. *Degree requirements:* For master's, thesis optional; for doctorate, comprehensive exam, thesis/dissertation. *Entrance requirements:* For master's, 3 letters of recommendation; for doctorate, 3 letters of recommendation, statement of purpose. Additional exam requirements/recommendations for international students: Required—TOEFL (minimum score 550 paper-based; 213 computer-based; 79 iBT), IELTS (minimum score 6.5). *Application deadline:* For fall admission, 1/1 priority date for domestic students, 1/1 for international students; for spring admission, 10/1 priority date for domestic students, 10/1 for international students. Applications are processed on a rolling basis. Application fee: $70. Electronic applications accepted. *Expenses:* Tuition: Full-time $20,862; part-time $1159 per term. One-time fee: $15. *Financial support:* Career-related internships or fieldwork, institutionally sponsored loans, scholarships/grants, and unspecified assistantships available. Financial award application deadline: 1/1; financial award applicants required to submit FAFSA. *Faculty research:* Analog and mixed signal IC design, cryptography, data and system security, networking and communication systems (including sw defined radios), biomedical signal processing and medical systems, indoor/outdoor localization and navigation systems. *Unit head:* Dr. Fred Looft, Department Head, 508-831-5231, Fax: 508-831-5491, E-mail: fjlooft@wpi.edu. *Application contact:* Dr. Donald Brown, Graduate Coordinator, 508-831-5231, Fax: 508-831-5491, E-mail: drb@wpi.edu.

Wright State University, School of Graduate Studies, College of Engineering and Computer Science, Department of Computer Science and Engineering, Computer Engineering Program, Dayton, OH 45435. Offers MSCE. *Degree requirements:* For master's, thesis optional. *Entrance requirements:* For master's, GRE General Test, minimum GPA of 3.0 in major, 2.7 overall. Additional exam requirements/recommendations for international students: Required—TOEFL. *Faculty research:* Networking and digital communications, parallel and concurrent computing, robotics and control, computer vision, optical computing.

Wright State University, School of Graduate Studies, College of Engineering and Computer Science, Department of Computer Science and Engineering, Program in Computer Science and Engineering, Dayton, OH 45435. Offers PhD. *Degree requirements:* For doctorate, thesis/dissertation, candidacy and general exams. *Entrance requirements:* For doctorate, GRE General Test, minimum GPA of 3.3. Additional exam requirements/recommendations for international students: Required—TOEFL.

Youngstown State University, Graduate School, College of Science, Technology, Engineering and Mathematics, Department of Electrical and Computer Engineering, Youngstown, OH 44555-0001. Offers computer engineering (MSE); electrical engineering (MSE). Part-time and evening/weekend programs available. *Degree requirements:* For master's, thesis optional. *Entrance requirements:* For master's, minimum GPA of 2.75 in field. Additional exam requirements/recommendations for international students: Required—TOEFL. *Faculty research:* Computer-aided design, power systems, electromagnetic energy conversion, sensors, control systems.

Electrical Engineering

Air Force Institute of Technology, Graduate School of Engineering and Management, Department of Electrical and Computer Engineering, Dayton, OH 45433-7765. Offers computer engineering (MS, PhD); computer systems/science (MS); electrical engineering (MS, PhD); electro-optics (MS, PhD). *Accreditation:* ABET (one or more programs are accredited). Part-time programs available. *Degree requirements:* For master's, thesis; for doctorate, thesis/dissertation. *Entrance requirements:* For master's and doctorate, GRE General Test, minimum GPA of 3.0, U.S. citizenship. *Faculty research:* Remote sensing, information survivability, microelectronics, computer networks, artificial intelligence.

Alfred University, Graduate School, New York State College of Ceramics, School of Engineering, Alfred, NY 14802-1205. Offers biomedical materials engineering science (MS); ceramic engineering (MS); ceramics (PhD); electrical engineering (MS); glass science (MS, PhD); materials science and engineering (MS, PhD); mechanical engineering (MS). *Degree requirements:* For master's, thesis; for doctorate, thesis/dissertation. *Entrance requirements:* Additional exam requirements/recommendations for international students: Required—TOEFL (minimum score 590 paper-based; 243 computer-based). Electronic applications accepted. *Expenses:* Contact institution. *Faculty research:* Fine-particle technology, x-ray diffraction, superconductivity, electronic materials.

The American University in Cairo, School of Sciences and Engineering, Department of Electronics Engineering, Cairo, Egypt. Offers electronics engineering (M Eng, MS); management of technology (M Eng).

American University of Beirut, Graduate Programs, Faculty of Engineering and Architecture, Beirut, Lebanon. Offers applied energy (MME); civil engineering (ME, PhD); electrical and computer engineering (ME, PhD); engineering management (MEM); environmental and water resources (ME); environmental and water resources engineering (PhD); environmental technology (MSES); mechanical engineering (ME, PhD); urban design (MUD); urban planning and policy (MUP). Part-time programs available. *Faculty:* 57 full-time (12 women), 3 part-time/adjunct (0 women). *Students:* 261 full-time (92 women), 58 part-time (20 women). Average age 25. 272 applicants, 79% accepted, 108 enrolled. In 2010, 70 master's, 1 doctorate awarded. *Degree requirements:* For master's, one foreign language, comprehensive exam, thesis (for some programs); for doctorate, one foreign language, comprehensive exam, thesis/dissertation, publications. *Entrance requirements:* For master's, GRE (for electrical and computer engineering), letters of recommendation; for doctorate, GRE, letters of recommendation, master's degree, transcripts, curriculum vitae, interview. Additional exam requirements/recommendations for international students: Required—TOEFL (minimum score 600 paper-based; 250 computer-based; 100 iBT), IELTS (minimum score 7.5). *Application deadline:* For fall admission, 2/5 priority date for domestic and international students; for spring admission, 11/1 priority date for domestic students, 11/1 for international students. Applications are processed on a rolling basis. Application fee: $50. Electronic applications accepted. *Expenses:* Tuition: Full-time $12,294; part-time $683 per credit. Required fees: $499; $499 per credit. Tuition and fees vary according to course load and program. *Financial support:* In 2010–11, 10 fellowships with full tuition reimbursements (averaging $24,800 per year), 33 research assistantships with full tuition reimbursements (averaging $24,800 per year), 70 teaching assistantships

Electrical Engineering

American University of Beirut (continued)
with full tuition reimbursements (averaging $9,800 per year) were awarded; career-related internships or fieldwork, institutionally sponsored loans, scholarships/grants, health care benefits, and unspecified assistantships also available. Total annual research expenditures: $586,131. *Unit head:* Fadl H. Moukalled, Acting Dean, 961-135-0000 Ext. 3400, Fax: 961-174-4462, E-mail: memouk@aub.edu.lb. *Application contact:* Dr. Salim Kanaan, Director, Admissions Office, 961-135-0000 Ext. 2594, Fax: 961-175-0775, E-mail: sk00@aub.edu.lb.

American University of Sharjah, Graduate Programs, Sharjah, United Arab Emirates. Offers business (EMBA, GEMPA, MBA); chemical engineering (MS Ch E); civil engineering (MSCE); computer engineering (MS); electrical engineering (MSEE); mechanical engineering (MSME); mechatronics engineering (MS); public administration (MPA); teaching English to speakers of other languages (MA); translation and interpreting (MA); urban planning (MUP). Part-time and evening/weekend programs available. *Entrance requirements:* For master's, GMAT (MBA). Additional exam requirements/recommendations for international students: Required—TOEFL (minimum score 550 paper-based; 213 computer-based; 80 iBT), TWE (minimum score 5). Electronic applications accepted. *Faculty research:* Chemical engineering, civil engineering, computer engineering, electrical engineering, linguistics, translation.

Arizona State University, Ira A. Fulton School of Engineering, Department of Electrical Engineering, Tempe, AZ 85287-5706. Offers electrical engineering (MS, MSE, PhD); nuclear power generation (Graduate Certificate). Part-time and evening/weekend programs available. Postbaccalaureate distance learning degree programs offered (minimal on-campus study). *Faculty:* 60 full-time (9 women), 8 part-time/adjunct (1 woman). *Students:* 521 full-time (92 women), 255 part-time (27 women); includes 82 minority (12 Black or African American, non-Hispanic/Latino; 2 American Indian or Alaska Native, non-Hispanic/Latino; 41 Asian, non-Hispanic/Latino; 26 Hispanic/Latino; 1 Two or more races, non-Hispanic/Latino), 531 international. Average age 27. 1,317 applicants, 69% accepted, 295 enrolled. In 2010, 212 master's, 35 doctorates awarded. Terminal master's awarded for partial completion of doctoral program. *Degree requirements:* For master's, thesis and defense (MS); comprehensive exams (MSE); interactive Program of Study (iPOS) submitted before completing 50 percent of required credit hours; for doctorate, comprehensive exam, thesis/dissertation, interactive Program of Study (iPOS) submitted before completing 50 percent of required credit hours. *Entrance requirements:* For master's, GRE, minimum GPA of 3.0 in last 2 years of work leading to bachelor's degree, 3.5 if from non-ABET accredited school; for doctorate, GRE, master's degree with minimum GPA of 3.5 or 3.6 in last 2 years of ABET-accredited undergraduate program. Additional exam requirements/recommendations for international students: Required—TOEFL, IELTS, or Pearson Test of English. *Application deadline:* For fall admission, 12/31 for domestic and international students; for spring admission, 7/31 for domestic and international students. Application fee: $70 ($90 for international students). Electronic applications accepted. *Expenses:* Contact institution. *Financial support:* In 2010–11, 165 research assistantships with partial tuition reimbursements (averaging $14,206 per year), 26 teaching assistantships with partial tuition reimbursements (averaging $13,854 per year) were awarded; fellowships with full and partial tuition reimbursements, career-related internships or fieldwork, institutionally sponsored loans, scholarships/grants, and tuition waivers (full and partial) also available. Financial award application deadline: 3/1; financial award applicants required to submit FAFSA. *Faculty research:* Power and energy systems, signal processing and communications, solid state devices and modeling, wireless communications and circuits, photovoltaics, biosignatures discovery automation, flexible electronics, and nanostructures. Total annual research expenditures: $27.1 million. *Unit head:* Dr. Stephen M. Phillips, Director, 480-965-6410, E-mail: stephen.phillips@asu.edu. *Application contact:* Dr. Stephen M. Phillips, Director, 480-965-6410, E-mail: stephen.phillips@asu.edu.

Auburn University, Graduate School, Ginn College of Engineering, Department of Electrical and Computer Engineering, Auburn University, AL 36849. Offers MEE, MS, PhD. Part-time programs available. *Faculty:* 27 full-time (2 women), 3 part-time/adjunct (1 woman). *Students:* 69 full-time (10 women), 48 part-time (10 women); includes 2 Black or African American, non-Hispanic/Latino; 1 American Indian or Alaska Native, non-Hispanic/Latino; 3 Asian, non-Hispanic/Latino; 1 Hispanic/Latino, 72 international. Average age 27. 355 applicants, 57% accepted, 16 enrolled. In 2010, 27 master's, 7 doctorates awarded. *Degree requirements:* For master's, comprehensive exam, thesis (for some programs); for doctorate, thesis/dissertation. *Entrance requirements:* For master's and doctorate, GRE General Test, GRE Subject Test. *Application deadline:* For fall admission, 7/7 for domestic students; for spring admission, 11/24 for domestic students. Applications are processed on a rolling basis. Application fee: $50 ($60 for international students). Electronic applications accepted. *Expenses:* Tuition, state resident: full-time $7002. Tuition, nonresident: full-time $21,898. International tuition: $22,116 full-time. Required fees: $892. Tuition and fees vary according to course load and program. *Financial support:* Fellowships, research assistantships, teaching assistantships, Federal Work-Study available. Support available to part-time students. Financial award application deadline: 3/15; financial award applicants required to submit FAFSA. *Faculty research:* Power systems, energy conversion, electronics, electromagnetics, digital systems. *Unit head:* Dr. J. David Irwin, Head, 334-844-1800. *Application contact:* Dr. George Flowers, Dean of the Graduate School, 334-844-2125.

Baylor University, Graduate School, School of Engineering and Computer Science, Department of Engineering, Waco, TX 76798. Offers biomedical engineering (MSBE); electrical and computer engineering (MSECE, PhD); engineering (ME); mechanical engineering (MSME). *Faculty:* 14 full-time (1 woman). *Students:* 30 full-time (4 women), 6 part-time (0 women); includes 9 minority (3 Black or African American, non-Hispanic/Latino; 2 Asian, non-Hispanic/Latino; 1 Hispanic/Latino; 3 Two or more races, non-Hispanic/Latino), 7 international. In 2010, 7 master's awarded. *Unit head:* Dr. Mike Thompson, Graduate Director, 254-710-4188. *Application contact:* Linda Keer, Administrative Assistant, 254-710-4188, Fax: 254-710-3870, E-mail: linda_kerr@baylor.edu.

Boise State University, Graduate College, College of Engineering, Department of Electrical and Computer Engineering, Boise, ID 83725-0399. Offers computer engineering (M Engr, MS); electrical and computer engineering (PhD); electrical engineering (M Engr, MS). Part-time and evening/weekend programs available. *Degree requirements:* For master's, thesis. *Entrance requirements:* For master's, GRE General Test, minimum GPA of 3.0. Additional exam requirements/recommendations for international students: Required—TOEFL. Electronic applications accepted.

Boston University, College of Engineering, Department of Electrical and Computer Engineering, Boston, MA 02215. Offers computer engineering (M Eng, MS, PhD); electrical engineering (M Eng, MS, PhD); photonics (M Eng, MS). Part-time programs available. *Faculty:* 40 full-time (3 women), 5 part-time/adjunct (0 women). *Students:* 205 full-time (34 women), 15 part-time (1 woman); includes 21 minority (1 Black or African American, non-Hispanic/Latino; 16 Asian, non-Hispanic/Latino; 4 Hispanic/Latino), 141 international. Average age 25. 810 applicants, 25% accepted, 112 enrolled. In 2010, 62 master's, 15 doctorates awarded. Terminal master's awarded for partial completion of doctoral program. *Degree requirements:* For master's, thesis (for some programs); for doctorate, comprehensive exam, thesis/dissertation. *Entrance requirements:* For master's and doctorate, GRE General Test. Additional exam requirements/recommendations for international students: Required—TOEFL (minimum score 550 paper-based; 213 computer-based; 84 iBT), IELTS (minimum score 6). *Application deadline:* For fall admission, 4/1 for domestic and international students; for spring admission, 10/1 for domestic and international students. Applications are processed on a rolling basis. Application fee: $70. Electronic applications accepted. *Expenses:* Tuition: Full-time $39,314; part-time $1228 per credit. Required fees: $40 per semester. *Financial support:* In 2010–11, 126 students received support, including 8 fellowships with full tuition reimbursements available (averaging $28,200 per year), 82 research assistantships with full tuition reimbursements available (averaging $18,800 per year), 18 teaching assistantships with full tuition reimbursements available (averaging $18,800 per year); career-related internships or fieldwork, Federal Work-Study,

institutionally sponsored loans, scholarships/grants, traineeships, and health care benefits also available. Financial award application deadline: 1/15; financial award applicants required to submit FAFSA. *Faculty research:* Communications and computer networks; signal, image, video, and multimedia processing; solid-state materials, devices, and photonics; systems, control, and reliable computing; VLSI, computer engineering and high-performance computing. *Unit head:* Dr. David Castanon, Chairman, ad Interim, 617-353-9880, Fax: 617-353-6440, E-mail: dac@bu.edu. *Application contact:* Stephen Doherty, Director of Graduate Programs, 617-353-9760, Fax: 617-353-0259, E-mail: enggrad@bu.edu.

Bradley University, Graduate School, College of Engineering and Technology, Department of Electrical Engineering, Peoria, IL 61625-0002. Offers MSEE. Part-time and evening/weekend programs available. *Degree requirements:* For master's, comprehensive exam. *Entrance requirements:* For master's, GRE, minimum GPA of 3.0. Additional exam requirements/recommendations for international students: Required—TOEFL (minimum score 550 paper-based; 213 computer-based; 79 iBT).

Brigham Young University, Graduate Studies, Ira A. Fulton College of Engineering and Technology, Department of Electrical and Computer Engineering, Provo, UT 84602. Offers MS, PhD. *Faculty:* 23 full-time (0 women). *Students:* 97 full-time (5 women); includes 1 Asian, non-Hispanic/Latino; 2 Hispanic/Latino, 24 international. Average age 28. 57 applicants, 68% accepted, 22 enrolled. In 2010, 15 master's, 9 doctorates awarded. *Degree requirements:* For master's, thesis optional; for doctorate, comprehensive exam, thesis/dissertation. *Entrance requirements:* For master's and doctorate, GRE General Test, minimum GPA of 3.2 in last 60 hours of course work. Additional exam requirements/recommendations for international students: Required—TOEFL (minimum score 580 paper-based; 237 computer-based; 85 iBT). *Application deadline:* For fall admission, 1/15 for domestic and international students; for winter admission, 8/15 for domestic and international students. Application fee: $50. Electronic applications accepted. *Expenses:* Tuition: Full-time $5580; part-time $310 per credit hour. Tuition and fees vary according to program and student's religious affiliation. *Financial support:* In 2010–11, 70 students received support, including 4 fellowships with full tuition reimbursements available (averaging $19,500 per year), 58 research assistantships with full tuition reimbursements available (averaging $19,500 per year), 8 teaching assistantships with full tuition reimbursements available (averaging $19,500 per year); scholarships/grants also available. Financial award application deadline: 5/15; financial award applicants required to submit FAFSA. *Faculty research:* Microwave remote sensing, reconfigurable computing, microelectronics, wireless communications, computer architecture, biomedical imaging, bio-chemical sensing. Total annual research expenditures: $3.1 million. *Unit head:* Dr. Michael A. Jensen, Chair, 801-422-4012, Fax: 801-422-0201, E-mail: jensen@ee.byu.edu. *Application contact:* Janalyn L. Mergist, Graduate Secretary, 801-422-4013, Fax: 801-422-0201, E-mail: janalyn@ee.byu.edu.

Brown University, Graduate School, Division of Engineering, Program in Electrical Sciences and Computer Engineering, Providence, RI 02912. Offers Sc M, PhD. *Degree requirements:* For doctorate, thesis/dissertation, preliminary exam.

Bucknell University, Graduate Studies, College of Engineering, Department of Electrical Engineering, Lewisburg, PA 17837. Offers MS, MSEE. Part-time programs available. *Degree requirements:* For master's, thesis. *Entrance requirements:* For master's, GRE General Test, GRE Subject Test, minimum GPA of 2.8. Additional exam requirements/recommendations for international students: Required—TOEFL. *Expenses:* Tuition: Full-time $36,992; part-time $4624 per course.

California Institute of Technology, Division of Engineering and Applied Science, Option in Electrical Engineering, Pasadena, CA 91125-0001. Offers MS, PhD, Engr. *Faculty:* 12 full-time (3 women). *Students:* 78 full-time (8 women). 724 applicants, 7% accepted, 15 enrolled. In 2010, 26 master's, 9 doctorates awarded. *Degree requirements:* For doctorate, thesis/dissertation. *Application deadline:* For fall admission, 1/15 for domestic students. Application fee: $0. Electronic applications accepted. *Financial support:* In 2010–11, 14 fellowships, 65 research assistantships, 32 teaching assistantships were awarded. *Faculty research:* Solid-state electronics, power electronics, communications, controls, submillimeter-wave integrated circuits. *Unit head:* Dr. Ali Hajimiri, Executive Officer, 626-395-2312, E-mail: hajimiri@caltech.edu. *Application contact:* Natalie Gilmore, Assistant Dean of Graduate Studies, 626-395-3812, Fax: 626-577-9246, E-mail: ngilmore@caltech.edu.

California Polytechnic State University, San Luis Obispo, College of Engineering, Department of Electrical Engineering, San Luis Obispo, CA 93407. Offers MS. Part-time programs available. *Faculty:* 1 (woman) full-time. *Students:* 50 full-time (1 woman), 13 part-time (1 woman); includes 26 minority (3 Black or African American, non-Hispanic/Latino; 21 Asian, non-Hispanic/Latino; 2 Hispanic/Latino), 7 international. Average age 25. 69 applicants, 54% accepted, 23 enrolled. In 2010, 33 master's awarded. *Degree requirements:* For master's, thesis. *Entrance requirements:* For master's, GRE General Test, minimum GPA of 3.0 in last 90 quarter units. Additional exam requirements/recommendations for international students: Required—TOEFL (minimum score 550 paper-based; 213 computer-based) or IELTS (minimum score 6). *Application deadline:* For fall admission, 7/1 for domestic students, 11/30 for international students; for winter admission, 11/1 for domestic students, 6/30 for international students; for spring admission, 2/1 for domestic students. Applications are processed on a rolling basis. Application fee: $55. Electronic applications accepted. *Expenses:* Tuition, state resident: full-time $5386; part-time $3124 per year. Tuition, nonresident: full-time $11,160; part-time $248 per unit. Required fees: $2250; $614 per term. One-time fee: $2250 full-time; $1842 part-time. *Financial support:* Fellowships, research assistantships, teaching assistantships, career-related internships or fieldwork, Federal Work-Study, scholarships/grants, and unspecified assistantships available. Support available to part-time students. Financial award application deadline: 3/2; financial award applicants required to submit FAFSA. *Faculty research:* Communications, systems analysis, control systems, electronic devices, microprocessors. *Unit head:* Dr. Dennis Derickson, Graduate Coordinator, 805-756-7584, Fax: 805-756-1456, E-mail: ddericks@calpoly.edu. *Application contact:* Dr. Dennis Derickson, Graduate Coordinator, 805-756-7584, Fax: 805-756-1456, E-mail: ddericks@calpoly.edu.

California State Polytechnic University, Pomona, Academic Affairs, College of Engineering, Program in Electrical Engineering, Pomona, CA 91768-2557. Offers MSEE. *Students:* 20 full-time (3 women), 69 part-time (8 women); includes 58 minority (1 Black or African American, non-Hispanic/Latino; 1 American Indian or Alaska Native, non-Hispanic/Latino; 38 Asian, non-Hispanic/Latino; 16 Hispanic/Latino; 2 Two or more races, non-Hispanic/Latino), 12 international. Average age 32. 126 applicants, 52% accepted, 33 enrolled. In 2010, 22 master's awarded. *Application deadline:* Applications are processed on a rolling basis. Application fee: $55. Electronic applications accepted. *Expenses:* Tuition, state resident: full-time $5386; part-time $2850 per year. Tuition, nonresident: full-time $12,082; part-time $248 per credit. Required fees: $577; $248 per credit. $577 per year. Tuition and fees vary according to course load and program. *Unit head:* Dr. Zekeriya Aliyazicioglu, Graduate Coordinator, 909-869-4609, E-mail: zaliyazici@csupomona.edu. *Application contact:* Scott J. Duncan, Director, Admissions, 909-869-3258, E-mail: sjduncan@csupomona.edu.

California State University, Chico, Graduate School, College of Engineering, Computer Science, and Technology, Department of Electrical and Computer Engineering, Option in Electronics Engineering, Chico, CA 95929-0722. Offers MS. *Students:* 12 full-time (1 woman), 9 part-time (1 woman), 16 international. Average age 25. 41 applicants, 76% accepted, 9 enrolled. In 2010, 19 master's awarded. *Degree requirements:* For master's, thesis or alternative. *Entrance requirements:* For master's, GRE General Test, 2 letters of recommendation. Additional exam requirements/recommendations for international students: Required—TOEFL (minimum score 550 paper-based; 213 computer-based; 80 iBT), IELTS (minimum score 6.5). *Application deadline:* For fall admission, 3/1 priority date for domestic students, 3/1 for international students; for spring admission, 9/15 priority date for domestic students, 9/15 for international students. Applications are processed on a rolling basis. Application fee: $55. Electronic applications accepted. *Unit head:* Dr. Adel Ghandakly, Graduate Coordinator, 530-898-5343. *Application contact:* Dr. Adel Ghandakly, Graduate Coordinator, 530-898-5343.

California State University, Fresno, Division of Graduate Studies, College of Engineering and Computer Science, Program in Electrical Engineering, Fresno, CA 93740-8027. Offers MS. Offered at Edwards Air Force Base. Part-time and evening/weekend programs available. *Degree requirements:* For master's, thesis or alternative. *Entrance requirements:* For master's, GRE General Test, minimum GPA of 2.7. Additional exam requirements/recommendations for international students: Required—TOEFL. Electronic applications accepted. *Faculty research:* Research in electromagnetic devices.

California State University, Fullerton, Graduate Studies, College of Engineering and Computer Science, Department of Electrical Engineering, Fullerton, CA 92834-9480. Offers electrical engineering (MS); systems engineering (MS). Part-time programs available. *Students:* 48 full-time (10 women), 120 part-time (26 women); includes 2 Black or African American, non-Hispanic/Latino; 35 Asian, non-Hispanic/Latino; 3 Hispanic/Latino; 1 Two or more races, non-Hispanic/Latino, 92 international. Average age 27. 238 applicants, 66% accepted, 54 enrolled. In 2010, 43 master's awarded. *Degree requirements:* For master's, comprehensive exam, project or thesis. *Entrance requirements:* For master's, GRE General Test, GRE Subject Test, minimum undergraduate GPA of 2.5, 3.0 graduate. Application fee: $55. *Financial support:* Career-related internships or fieldwork, Federal Work-Study, institutionally sponsored loans, and scholarships/grants available. Support available to part-time students. Financial award application deadline: 3/1; financial award applicants required to submit FAFSA. *Unit head:* Dr. Mostafa Shiva, Chair, 657-278-3013. *Application contact:* Admissions/Applications, 657-278-2371.

California State University, Long Beach, Graduate Studies, College of Engineering, Department of Electrical Engineering, Long Beach, CA 90840. Offers MSEE. Part-time programs available. *Faculty:* 16 full-time (2 women). *Students:* 84 full-time (7 women), 96 part-time (13 women); includes 6 Black or African American, non-Hispanic/Latino; 44 Asian, non-Hispanic/Latino; 14 Hispanic/Latino, 83 international. Average age 27. 298 applicants, 68% accepted, 65 enrolled. In 2010, 63 master's awarded. *Degree requirements:* For master's, comprehensive exam or thesis. *Entrance requirements:* Additional exam requirements/recommendations for international students: Required—TOEFL. *Application deadline:* For fall admission, 3/1 for domestic students. Application fee: $55. Electronic applications accepted. *Financial support:* Teaching assistantships, career-related internships or fieldwork, Federal Work-Study, institutionally sponsored loans, scholarships/grants, and unspecified assistantships available. Financial award application deadline: 3/2. *Faculty research:* Health care systems, VLSI, communications, CAD/CAM. *Unit head:* Dr. Bahram Shahian, Chair, 562-985-8041, Fax: 562-985-5327, E-mail: shahian@csulb.edu. *Application contact:* Dr. Fumio Hamano, Graduate Adviser, 562-985-7580, Fax: 562-985-5327, E-mail: fhamano@csulb.edu.

California State University, Los Angeles, Graduate Studies, College of Engineering, Computer Science, and Technology, Department of Electrical and Computer Engineering, Los Angeles, CA 90032-8530. Offers electrical engineering (MS). Part-time and evening/weekend programs available. *Faculty:* 4 full-time (2 women), 4 part-time/adjunct (2 women). *Students:* 54 full-time (15 women), 107 part-time (16 women); includes 58 minority (9 Black or African American, non-Hispanic/Latino; 31 Asian, non-Hispanic/Latino; 18 Hispanic/Latino), 85 international. Average age 28. 110 applicants, 99% accepted, 47 enrolled. In 2010, 86 master's awarded. *Degree requirements:* For master's, comprehensive exam or thesis. *Entrance requirements:* For master's, GRE General Test, GRE Subject Test. Additional exam requirements/recommendations for international students: Required—TOEFL (minimum score 550 paper-based). *Application deadline:* For fall admission, 5/1 for domestic and international students. Applications are processed on a rolling basis. Application fee: $55. Electronic applications accepted. *Financial support:* Federal Work-Study available. Support available to part-time students. Financial award application deadline: 3/1. *Unit head:* Dr. Fred Daneshgaran, Chair, 323-343-4470, Fax: 323-343-4547, E-mail: fdanesh@calstatela.edu. *Application contact:* Dr. Alan Muchlinski, Dean of Graduate Studies, 323-343-3820, Fax: 323-343-5653, E-mail: amuchli@exchange.calstatela.edu.

California State University, Northridge, Graduate Studies, College of Engineering and Computer Science, Department of Electrical and Computer Engineering, Northridge, CA 91330. Offers electrical engineering (MS). Part-time and evening/weekend programs available. *Degree requirements:* For master's, thesis or alternative. *Entrance requirements:* For master's, GRE General Test, minimum GPA of 2.75. Additional exam requirements/recommendations for international students: Required—TOEFL. *Faculty research:* Reflector antenna study.

California State University, Sacramento, Graduate Studies, College of Engineering and Computer Science, Department of Electrical and Electronic Engineering, Sacramento, CA 95819. Offers electrical engineering (MS). Part-time and evening/weekend programs available. *Degree requirements:* For master's, writing proficiency exam. *Entrance requirements:* Additional exam requirements/recommendations for international students: Required—TOEFL. Electronic applications accepted.

Capitol College, Graduate Programs, Laurel, MD 20708-9759. Offers business administration (MBA); computer science (MS); electrical engineering (MS); information and telecommunications systems management (MS); information architecture (MS); network security (MS). Part-time and evening/weekend programs available. Postbaccalaureate distance learning degree programs offered (no on-campus study). *Entrance requirements:* For master's, minimum GPA of 3.0. Electronic applications accepted.

Carleton University, Faculty of Graduate Studies, Faculty of Engineering and Design, Ottawa-Carleton Institute for Electrical Engineering, Department of Electronics, Ottawa, ON K1S 5B6, Canada. Offers electrical engineering (M Eng, MA Sc, PhD). *Degree requirements:* For master's, thesis optional; for doctorate, comprehensive exam, thesis/dissertation. *Entrance requirements:* For master's, honors degree; for doctorate, MA Sc or M Eng. Additional exam requirements/recommendations for international students: Required—TOEFL.

Carleton University, Faculty of Graduate Studies, Faculty of Engineering and Design, Ottawa-Carleton Institute for Electrical Engineering, Department of Systems and Computer Engineering, Ottawa, ON K1S 5B6, Canada. Offers electrical engineering (MA Sc, PhD); information and systems science (M Sc); technology innovation management (M Eng, MA Sc). PhD program offered jointly with University of Ottawa. *Degree requirements:* For master's, thesis optional. *Entrance requirements:* For master's, honors degree. Additional exam requirements/recommendations for international students: Required—TOEFL. *Faculty research:* Design manufacturing management; network design, protocols, and performance; software engineering; wireless and satellite communications.

Carnegie Mellon University, Carnegie Institute of Technology, Department of Electrical and Computer Engineering, Pittsburgh, PA 15213-3891. Offers biomedical engineering (MS); electrical and computer engineering (MS, PhD). Part-time programs available. *Degree requirements:* For master's, thesis; for doctorate, thesis/dissertation, qualifying exam, teaching experience. *Entrance requirements:* For master's and doctorate, GRE General Test. Additional exam requirements/recommendations for international students: Required—TOEFL. *Faculty research:* Computer-aided design, solid-state devices, VLSI, processing, robotics and controls, signal processing, data systems storage.

See Display on page 343 and Close-Up on page 389.

Case Western Reserve University, School of Graduate Studies, Case School of Engineering, Department of Electrical Engineering and Computer Science, Cleveland, OH 44106. Offers computer engineering (MS, PhD); computing and information sciences (MS, PhD); electrical engineering (MS, PhD); systems and control engineering (MS, PhD). Part-time and evening/weekend programs available. Postbaccalaureate distance learning degree programs offered (minimal on-campus study). *Faculty:* 33 full-time (2 women). *Students:* 190 full-time (31 women), 26 part-time (4 women); includes 3 Black or African American, non-Hispanic/Latino; 6 Asian, non-Hispanic/Latino, 128 international. In 2010, 32 master's, 13 doctorates awarded. Terminal master's awarded for partial completion of doctoral program. *Degree requirements:* For master's, thesis; for doctorate, thesis/dissertation, qualifying exam, teaching experience. *Entrance requirements:* For master's and doctorate, GRE General Test. Additional exam requirements/recommendations for international students: Required—TOEFL. *Application deadline:* For fall admission, 2/1 for domestic students; for spring admission, 11/1 for domestic students. Applications are processed on a rolling basis. Application fee: $50. *Financial support:* Fellowships with full and partial tuition reimbursements, research assistantships with full and partial tuition reimbursements, teaching assistantships, career-related internships or fieldwork, Federal Work-Study, and institutionally sponsored loans available. Support available to part-time students. Financial award application deadline: 3/1; financial award applicants required to submit FAFSA. *Faculty research:* Applied artificial intelligence, automation, computer-aided design and testing of digital systems. Total annual research expenditures: $6.8 million. *Unit head:* Michael Branicky, Department Chair, 216-368-6888, E-mail: branicky@case.edu. *Application contact:* David Easler, Student Affairs Coordinator, 216-368-4080, Fax: 216-368-2801, E-mail: david.easler@case.edu.

The Catholic University of America, School of Engineering, Department of Electrical Engineering and Computer Science, Washington, DC 20064. Offers MEE, MSCS, D Engr, PhD. Part-time programs available. *Faculty:* 10 full-time (3 women), 13 part-time/adjunct (1 woman). *Students:* 15 full-time (3 women), 50 part-time (9 women); includes 2 Black or African American, non-Hispanic/Latino; 5 Asian, non-Hispanic/Latino; 3 Hispanic/Latino, 16 international. Average age 33. 58 applicants, 48% accepted, 16 enrolled. In 2010, 17 master's awarded. *Degree requirements:* For master's, thesis or alternative; for doctorate, comprehensive exam, thesis/dissertation, oral exams. *Entrance requirements:* For master's and doctorate, statement of purpose, official copies of academic transcripts, three letters of recommendation. Additional exam requirements/recommendations for international students: Required—TOEFL (minimum score 580 paper-based; 237 computer-based). *Application deadline:* For fall admission, 8/1 priority date for domestic students, 7/15 for international students; for spring admission, 12/1 priority date for domestic students, 10/15 for international students. Applications are processed on a rolling basis. Application fee: $55. Electronic applications accepted. *Expenses:* Contact institution. *Financial support:* Fellowships, research assistantships, teaching assistantships, Federal Work-Study, scholarships/grants, tuition waivers (full and partial), and unspecified assistantships available. Financial award application deadline: 2/1; financial award applicants required to submit FAFSA. *Faculty research:* Signal and image processing, computer communications, robotics, intelligent controls, bioelectromagnetics. Total annual research expenditures: $1.2 million. *Unit head:* Dr. Phillip Regalia, Chair, 202-319-5879, Fax: 202-319-5195, E-mail: regalia@cua.edu. *Application contact:* Andrew Woodall, Director of Graduate Admissions, 202-319-5057, Fax: 202-319-6533, E-mail: cua-admissions@cua.edu.

City College of the City University of New York, Graduate School, Grove School of Engineering, Department of Electrical Engineering, New York, NY 10031-9198. Offers ME, MS, PhD. PhD program offered jointly with Graduate School and University Center of the City University of New York. Part-time programs available. *Degree requirements:* For master's, thesis optional; for doctorate, one foreign language, comprehensive exam, thesis/dissertation. *Entrance requirements:* For master's and doctorate, GRE General Test. Additional exam requirements/recommendations for international students: Required—TOEFL (minimum score 500 paper-based; 173 computer-based; 61 iBT). *Faculty research:* Optical electronics, microwaves, communication, signal processing, control systems.

Clarkson University, Graduate School, Wallace H. Coulter School of Engineering, Department of Electrical and Computer Engineering, Potsdam, NY 13699. Offers electrical and computer engineering (PhD); electrical engineering (ME, MS). Part-time programs available. *Faculty:* 17 full-time (3 women), 3 part-time/adjunct (all women). *Students:* 41 full-time (7 women), 3 part-time (2 women); includes 3 minority (1 American Indian or Alaska Native, non-Hispanic/Latino; 1 Asian, non-Hispanic/Latino; 1 Hispanic/Latino), 16 international. Average age 28. 89 applicants, 39% accepted, 7 enrolled. In 2010, 8 master's, 3 doctorates awarded. Terminal master's awarded for partial completion of doctoral program. *Degree requirements:* For master's, thesis; for doctorate, comprehensive exam, thesis/dissertation, departmental qualifying exam. *Entrance requirements:* For master's and doctorate, GRE, transcripts of all college coursework, resume, personal statement, three letters of recommendation. Additional exam requirements/recommendations for international students: Required—TOEFL (minimum score 550 paper-based; 213 computer-based; 80 iBT), IELTS (minimum score 6.5). *Application deadline:* For fall admission, 1/30 priority date for domestic and international students; for spring admission, 9/1 priority date for domestic and international students. Applications are processed on a rolling basis. Application fee: $25 ($35 for international students). Electronic applications accepted. *Expenses:* Tuition: Part-time $1136 per credit hour. *Financial support:* In 2010–11, 29 students received support, including 7 fellowships with full tuition reimbursements available (averaging $21,580 per year), 10 research assistantships with full tuition reimbursements available (averaging $21,580 per year), 9 teaching assistantships with full tuition reimbursements available (averaging $21,580 per year); scholarships/grants, tuition waivers (partial), and unspecified assistantships also available. *Faculty research:* NEU nanotechnology, high voltage insulator, biometric scanners, transdermal drug, eating patterns. Total annual research expenditures: $1.2 million. *Unit head:* Dr. William Jemison, Chair, 315-268-7648, Fax: 315-268-7600, E-mail: wjemison@clarkson.edu. *Application contact:* Kelly Sharlow, Assistant to the Dean, 315-268-7929, Fax: 315-268-4494, E-mail: ksharlow@clarkson.edu.

Clemson University, Graduate School, College of Engineering and Science, Department of Electrical and Computer Engineering, Program in Electrical Engineering, Clemson, SC 29634. Offers M Engr, MS, PhD. *Students:* 104 full-time (23 women), 6 part-time (0 women); includes 6 Black or African American, non-Hispanic/Latino; 4 Asian, non-Hispanic/Latino, 76 international. Average age 27. 556 applicants, 27% accepted, 37 enrolled. In 2010, 27 master's, 9 doctorates awarded. *Degree requirements:* For master's, thesis or alternative; for doctorate, thesis/dissertation, departmental qualifying exam. *Entrance requirements:* For master's, GRE General Test (MS); for doctorate, GRE General Test. Additional exam requirements/recommendations for international students: Required—TOEFL. *Application deadline:* For fall admission, 6/1 for domestic students, 4/15 for international students; for spring admission, 9/15 for international students. Applications are processed on a rolling basis. Application fee: $70 ($80 for international students). Electronic applications accepted. *Expenses:* Tuition, state resident: full-time $6492; part-time $400 per credit hour. Tuition, nonresident: full-time $13,634; part-time $800 per credit hour. Required fees: $262 per semester. Part-time tuition and fees vary according to course load and program. *Financial support:* In 2010–11, 88 students received support, including 15 fellowships with full and partial tuition reimbursements available (averaging $4,244 per year), 41 research assistantships with partial tuition reimbursements available (averaging $12,204 per year), 57 teaching assistantships with partial tuition reimbursements available (averaging $7,182 per year); career-related internships or fieldwork, institutionally sponsored loans, scholarships/grants, health care benefits, and unspecified assistantships also available. Support available to part-time students. Financial award applicants required to submit FAFSA. *Faculty research:* Microelectronics, robotics, signal processing/communications, power systems, control. *Unit head:* Dr. Darren Dawson, Chair, 864-656-5249, Fax: 864-656-5917, E-mail: ddarren@clemson.edu. *Application contact:* Dr. Daniel Noneaker, 864-656-0100, Fax: 864-656-5917, E-mail: ece-grad-program@ces.clemson.edu.

Cleveland State University, College of Graduate Studies, Fenn College of Engineering, Department of Electrical and Computer Engineering, Cleveland, OH 44115. Offers electrical engineering (MS, D Eng); software engineering (MS). Part-time programs available. *Faculty:* 15 full-time (2 women), 2 part-time/adjunct (0 women). *Students:* 46 full-time (12 women), 160 part-time (26 women); includes 5 Black or African American, non-Hispanic/Latino; 9 Asian, non-Hispanic/Latino; 1 Hispanic/Latino, 140 international. Average age 27. 328 applicants, 48% accepted, 31 enrolled. In 2010, 59 master's, 1 doctorate awarded. *Degree requirements:* For master's, thesis optional; for doctorate, thesis/dissertation, qualifying and candidacy exams. *Entrance requirements:* For master's, GRE General Test (minimum score 650 quantitative), minimum GPA of 2.75; for doctorate, GRE General Test (quantitative score in 80th percentile), minimum GPA of 3.25. Additional exam requirements/recommendations for international students: Required—TOEFL (minimum score 535 paper-based; 197 computer-based; 65 iBT). *Application*

Electrical Engineering

Cleveland State University (continued)

deadline: For fall admission, 7/15 priority date for domestic students. Applications are processed on a rolling basis. Application fee: $30. *Expenses:* Tuition, state resident: full-time $8447; part-time $469 per credit hour. Tuition, nonresident: full-time $16,020; part-time $890 per credit hour. Required fees: $50. *Financial support:* In 2010–11, 31 students received support, including 23 research assistantships with full and partial tuition reimbursements available (averaging $4,242 per year), 8 teaching assistantships with full and partial tuition reimbursements available (averaging $4,242 per year); career-related internships or fieldwork also available. *Faculty research:* Computer networks, knowledge-based control systems, artificial intelligence, digital communications, MEMS, sensors, power systems, power electronics. *Unit head:* Dr. Fuqin Xiong, Chairperson, 216-687-2127, E-mail: f.xiong@csuohio.edu. *Application contact:* Dr. Fuqin Xiong, Chairperson, 216-687-2127, E-mail: f.xiong@csuohio.edu.

Colorado State University, Graduate School, College of Engineering, Department of Electrical and Computer Engineering, Fort Collins, CO 80523-1373. Offers electrical engineering (MEE, MS, PhD). Part-time and evening/weekend programs available. Postbaccalaureate distance learning degree programs offered (no on-campus study). *Faculty:* 22 full-time (2 women), 2 part-time/adjunct (0 women). *Students:* 66 full-time (16 women), 64 part-time (6 women); includes 11 minority (3 Asian, non-Hispanic/Latino; 5 Hispanic/Latino; 3 Two or more races, non-Hispanic/Latino), 74 international. Average age 28. 157 applicants, 56% accepted, 35 enrolled. In 2010, 9 master's, 8 doctorates awarded. Terminal master's awarded for partial completion of doctoral program. *Degree requirements:* For master's, comprehensive exam (for some programs), thesis (for some programs), final exam; for doctorate, comprehensive exam, thesis/dissertation, qualifying, preliminary, and final exams. *Entrance requirements:* For master's, GRE General Test, minimum GPA of 3.5, BA/BS from ABET-accredited institution, 3 letters of recommendation; for doctorate, GRE General Test, minimum GPA of 3.5, transcripts, 3 letters of recommendation, statement of purpose. Additional exam requirements/recommendations for international students: Required—TOEFL (minimum score 550 paper-based; 213 computer-based; 80 iBT); Recommended—IELTS (minimum score 6). *Application deadline:* For fall admission, 2/1 priority date for domestic and international students; for spring admission, 9/1 priority date for domestic and international students. Applications are processed on a rolling basis. Application fee: $50. Electronic applications accepted. *Expenses:* Tuition, state resident: full-time $7434; part-time $413 per credit. Tuition, nonresident: full-time $19,022; part-time $1057 per credit. Required fees: $1729; $88 per credit. *Financial support:* In 2010–11, 91 students received support, including 8 fellowships (averaging $25,175 per year), 67 research assistantships with tuition reimbursements available (averaging $16,509 per year), 16 teaching assistantships with tuition reimbursements available (averaging $5,813 per year); unspecified assistantships also available. Financial award application deadline: 2/1; financial award applicants required to submit FAFSA. *Faculty research:* Communications, optoelectronics, controls and robotics, computer engineering, biomedical engineering. Total annual research expenditures: $11.2 million. *Unit head:* Dr. Anthony A. Maciejewski, Head, 970-491-6600, Fax: 970-491-2249, E-mail: aam@engr.colostate.edu. *Application contact:* Karen Ungerer, Academic Advisor, 970-491-0500, Fax: 970-491-2249, E-mail: karen.ungerer@colostate.edu.

Colorado Technical University Colorado Springs, Graduate Studies, Program in Electrical Engineering, Colorado Springs, CO 80907-3896. Offers MSEE. Part-time and evening/weekend programs available. Postbaccalaureate distance learning degree programs offered. *Degree requirements:* For master's, thesis or alternative. *Faculty research:* Electronic systems design, communication systems design.

Colorado Technical University Denver, Program in Electrical Engineering, Greenwood Village, CO 80111. Offers MS.

Columbia University, Fu Foundation School of Engineering and Applied Science, Department of Electrical Engineering, New York, NY 10027. Offers computer engineering (MS); electrical engineering (MS, Eng Sc D, PhD, Engr); solid state science and engineering (MS, Eng Sc D,

PhD). PhD offered through the Graduate School of Arts and Sciences. Part-time programs available. Postbaccalaureate distance learning degree programs offered (no on-campus study). *Faculty:* 26 full-time (1 woman), 32 part-time/adjunct (1 woman). *Students:* 258 full-time (56 women), 95 part-time (19 women); includes 24 minority (2 Black or African American, non-Hispanic/Latino; 17 Asian, non-Hispanic/Latino; 4 Hispanic/Latino; 1 Two or more races, non-Hispanic/Latino), 259 international. Average age 26. 982 applicants, 34% accepted, 160 enrolled. In 2010, 121 master's, 17 doctorates, 2 other advanced degrees awarded. *Degree requirements:* For doctorate, thesis/dissertation, qualifying exam. *Entrance requirements:* For master's, doctorate, and Engr, GRE General Test. Additional exam requirements/recommendations for international students: Required—TOEFL, IELTS. *Application deadline:* For fall admission, 12/1 priority date for domestic and international students; for spring admission, 10/1 priority date for domestic and international students. Application fee: $95. Electronic applications accepted. *Financial support:* In 2010–11, 98 students received support, including 8 fellowships with full tuition reimbursements available (averaging $30,672 per year), 67 research assistantships with full tuition reimbursements available (averaging $30,672 per year), 23 teaching assistantships with full tuition reimbursements available (averaging $30,672 per year); health care benefits also available. Financial award application deadline: 12/1; financial award applicants required to submit FAFSA. *Faculty research:* Signal and information processing, networking and communications, integrated circuits and systems, systems biology, micro devices, electromagnetics, plasma physics, photonics, computer engineering. *Unit head:* Dr. Keren Bergman, Professor and Department Chair, 212-854-2280, Fax: 212-854-0300, E-mail: bergman@ee.columbia.edu. *Application contact:* Elsa Sanchez, Academic Program Officer, 212-854-3104, Fax: 212-932-9421, E-mail: elsa@ee.columbia.edu.

See Display below and Close-Up on page 391.

Concordia University, School of Graduate Studies, Faculty of Engineering and Computer Science, Department of Electrical and Computer Engineering, Montréal, QC H3G 1M8, Canada. Offers M Eng, MA Sc, PhD. *Degree requirements:* For master's, thesis optional; for doctorate, comprehensive exam, thesis/dissertation. *Faculty research:* Computer communications and protocols, circuits and systems, graph theory, VLSI systems, microelectronics.

Cooper Union for the Advancement of Science and Art, Albert Nerken School of Engineering, New York, NY 10003-7120. Offers chemical engineering (ME); civil engineering (ME); electrical engineering (ME); mechanical engineering (ME). Part-time programs available. *Faculty:* 27 full-time (1 woman), 15 part-time/adjunct (2 women). *Students:* 57 full-time (15 women), 25 part-time (1 woman); includes 2 Black or African American, non-Hispanic/Latino; 1 American Indian or Alaska Native, non-Hispanic/Latino; 22 Asian, non-Hispanic/Latino; 2 Hispanic/Latino, 16 international. Average age 24. 72 applicants, 39% accepted, 27 enrolled. In 2010, 25 master's awarded. *Degree requirements:* For master's, thesis. *Entrance requirements:* For master's, GRE, BE, minimum GPA of 3.5. Additional exam requirements/recommendations for international students: Required—TOEFL (minimum score 600 paper-based; 250 computer-based; 100 iBT). *Application deadline:* For fall admission, 2/15 for domestic and international students. Application fee: $65. *Expenses:* Tuition: Full-time $35,000; part-time $1100 per credit. Required fees: $825 per semester. *Financial support:* Fellowships with full tuition reimbursements, career-related internships or fieldwork, Federal Work-Study, tuition waivers (full), and all admitted students receive full-tuition scholarships available. Support available to part-time students. Financial award application deadline: 5/1; financial award applicants required to submit CSS PROFILE or FAFSA. *Faculty research:* Civil infrastructure, imaging and sensing technology, biomedical engineering, encryption technology, process engineering. *Unit head:* Dr. Simon Ben-Avi, Acting Dean, 212-353-4285, E-mail: benavi@cooper.edu. *Application contact:* Student Contact, 212-353-4120, E-mail: admissions@cooper.edu.

Cornell University, Graduate School, Graduate Fields of Engineering, Field of Electrical and Computer Engineering, Ithaca, NY 14853. Offers computer engineering (M Eng, PhD); electrical engineering (M Eng, PhD); electrical systems (M Eng, PhD); electrophysics (M Eng, PhD).

Faculty: 58 full-time (4 women). *Students:* 247 full-time (47 women); includes 1 Black or African American, non-Hispanic/Latino; 27 Asian, non-Hispanic/Latino; 9 Hispanic/Latino, 155 international. Average age 24. 935 applicants, 33% accepted, 135 enrolled. In 2010, 106 master's, 25 doctorates awarded. *Degree requirements:* For doctorate, comprehensive exam, thesis/dissertation. *Entrance requirements:* For master's, GRE General Test, 2 letters of recommendation; for doctorate, GRE General Test, 3 letters of recommendation. Additional exam requirements/recommendations for international students: Required—TOEFL (minimum score 600 paper-based; 250 computer-based; 77 iBT). *Application deadline:* For fall admission, 1/15 priority date for domestic students. Application fee: $70. Electronic applications accepted. *Expenses:* Tuition: Full-time $29,500. Required fees: $76. Tuition and fees vary according to degree level and program. *Financial support:* In 2010–11, 150 students received support, including 46 fellowships with full tuition reimbursements available, 94 research assistantships with full tuition reimbursements available, 18 teaching assistantships with full tuition reimbursements available; institutionally sponsored loans, scholarships/grants, health care benefits, tuition waivers (full and partial), and unspecified assistantships also available. Financial award applicants required to submit FAFSA. *Faculty research:* Communications, information theory, signal processing and power control, computer engineering, microelectromechanical systems and nanotechnology. *Unit head:* Director of Graduate Studies, 607-255-4304. *Application contact:* Graduate Field Assistant, 607-255-4304, E-mail: meng@ece.cornell.edu.

Dalhousie University, Faculty of Engineering, Department of Electrical and Computer Engineering, Halifax, NS B3J 1Z1, Canada. Offers M Eng, MA Sc, PhD. *Degree requirements:* For master's, thesis; for doctorate, thesis/dissertation. *Entrance requirements:* Additional exam requirements/recommendations for international students: Required—TOEFL, IELTS, CANTEST, CAEL, or Michigan English Language Assessment Battery. Electronic applications accepted. *Faculty research:* Communications, computer engineering, power engineering, electronics, systems engineering.

Dartmouth College, Thayer School of Engineering, Program in Electrical Engineering, Hanover, NH 03755. Offers MS, PhD. *Degree requirements:* For master's, thesis; for doctorate, thesis/dissertation, candidacy oral exam. *Entrance requirements:* For master's and doctorate, GRE General Test. *Faculty research:* Power electronics and microengineering, signal/image processing and communications, optics, lasers and optoelectronics, electromagnetic fields and waves.

Drexel University, College of Engineering, Department of Electrical and Computer Engineering, Program in Electrical Engineering, Philadelphia, PA 19104-2875. Offers MSEE. Part-time and evening/weekend programs available. Terminal master's awarded for partial completion of doctoral program. *Degree requirements:* For master's, thesis (for some programs). Electronic applications accepted.

Duke University, Graduate School, Pratt School of Engineering, Department of Electrical and Computer Engineering, Durham, NC 27708. Offers MS, PhD, JD/MS. Part-time programs available. *Faculty:* 38 full-time. *Students:* 162 full-time (39 women); includes 4 Black or African American, non-Hispanic/Latino; 6 Asian, non-Hispanic/Latino; 2 Hispanic/Latino, 107 international. 554 applicants, 30% accepted, 41 enrolled. In 2010, 25 master's, 16 doctorates awarded. Terminal master's awarded for partial completion of doctoral program. *Degree requirements:* For doctorate, thesis/dissertation. *Entrance requirements:* For master's and doctorate, GRE General Test. Additional exam requirements/recommendations for international students: Required—TOEFL (minimum score 550 paper-based; 213 computer-based; 83 iBT), IELTS (minimum score 7). *Application deadline:* For fall admission, 12/8 priority date for domestic and international students; for spring admission, 11/1 for domestic students. Application fee: $75. Electronic applications accepted. *Financial support:* Fellowships, research assistantships, Federal Work-Study available. Financial award application deadline: 12/8. *Unit head:* Steve Cummer, Director of Graduate Studies, 919-660-5245, Fax: 919-660-5293, E-mail: samantha@ee.duke.edu. *Application contact:* Elizabeth Hutton, Associate Dean for Enrollment Services, 919-684-3913, Fax: 919-684-2277, E-mail: grad-admissions@duke.edu.

See Display on next page and Close-Up on page 393.

Duke University, Graduate School, Pratt School of Engineering, Master of Engineering Program, Durham, NC 27708-0271. Offers biomedical engineering (M Eng); civil engineering (M Eng); electrical and computer engineering (M Eng); environmental engineering (M Eng); materials science and engineering (M Eng); mechanical engineering (M Eng); photonics and optical sciences (M Eng). Part-time programs available. *Faculty:* 123 full-time, 1 part-time/adjunct. *Students:* 9 full-time (4 women); includes 2 minority (both Asian, non-Hispanic/Latino), 3 international. Average age 24. *Entrance requirements:* For master's, GRE General Test, resume, 3 letters of recommendation, statement of purpose. Additional exam requirements/recommendations for international students: Required—TOEFL. *Application deadline:* For fall admission, 6/15 for domestic students, 2/15 for international students; for spring admission, 11/1 for domestic students, 9/1 for international students. Application fee: $75. *Financial support:* Merit scholarships/grants available. *Unit head:* Dr. Bradley A. Fox, Executive Director, 919-660-5455, Fax: 919-660-5456. *Application contact:* Erin Degerman, Admissions Coordinator, 919-668-6789, Fax: 919-660-5456, E-mail: erin.degerman@duke.edu.

École Polytechnique de Montréal, Graduate Programs, Department of Electrical and Computer Engineering, Montréal, QC H3C 3A7, Canada. Offers automation (M Eng, M Sc A, PhD); computer science (M Eng, M Sc A, PhD); electrical engineering (DESS); electrotechnology (M Eng, M Sc A, PhD); microelectronics (M Eng, M Sc A, PhD); microwave technology (M Eng, M Sc A, PhD). Part-time and evening/weekend programs available. *Degree requirements:* For master's, one foreign language, thesis; for doctorate, one foreign language, thesis/dissertation. *Entrance requirements:* For master's, minimum GPA of 2.75; for doctorate, minimum GPA of 3.0. *Faculty research:* Microwaves, telecommunications, software engineering.

Embry-Riddle Aeronautical University–Daytona, Daytona Beach Campus Graduate Program, Department of Computer and Software Engineering, Daytona Beach, FL 32114-3900. Offers electrical/computer engineering (MSECE); software engineering (MSE). Part-time and evening/weekend programs available. *Faculty:* 6 full-time (0 women), 2 part-time/adjunct (1 woman). *Students:* 31 full-time (4 women), 3 part-time (0 women); includes 3 minority (1 Asian, non-Hispanic/Latino; 2 Hispanic/Latino), 10 international. Average age 26. 22 applicants, 64% accepted, 9 enrolled. In 2010, 10 master's awarded. *Degree requirements:* For master's, thesis or alternative. *Entrance requirements:* For master's, minimum GPA of 3.0 in senior year, 2.5 overall; course work in computer science. Additional exam requirements/recommendations for international students: Required—TOEFL (minimum score 550 paper-based; 213 computer-based; 79 iBT). *Application deadline:* For fall admission, 8/1 priority date for domestic students; for spring admission, 12/1 priority date for domestic students. Applications are processed on a rolling basis. Application fee: $50. *Expenses:* Tuition: Full-time $14,040; part-time $1170 per credit hour. *Financial support:* In 2010–11, 20 students received support, including 2 research assistantships with full and partial tuition reimbursements available (averaging $5,384 per year), 7 teaching assistantships with full and partial tuition reimbursements available (averaging $5,667 per year); career-related internships or fieldwork, Federal Work-Study, and unspecified assistantships also available. Financial award application deadline: 4/15; financial award applicants required to submit FAFSA. *Faculty research:* Evaluation of residual strength of Beechcraft Bonanza spar carry-through with fatigue cracks, Swift Fuel PA44-180, Scramjet engine simulation, marine turbines, wireless sensors for aircraft, bistatic radar, blind signal separation in dynamic environments, EcoCAR IDEA, FAA nextgen Task K demonstration of flight data object planning, NOAA UAS for in-situ tropical cyclone sensing, aeroelastic gust-airfoil interaction numerical studies. *Unit head:* Dr. Farahzad Behi, Program Coordinator, 386-226-6454, E-mail: farahzad.behi@erau.edu. *Application contact:* Keith Deaton, Director, International and Graduate Admissions, 800-388-3728, Fax: 386-226-7070, E-mail: graduate.admissions@erau.edu.

Fairfield University, School of Engineering, Fairfield, CT 06824-5195. Offers electrical and computer engineering (MS); management of technology (MS); mechanical engineering (MS); software engineering (MS). Part-time and evening/weekend programs available. *Faculty:* 8 full-time (1 woman), 11 part-time/adjunct (0 women). *Students:* 31 full-time (12 women), 98 part-time (20 women); includes 28 minority (5 Black or African American, non-Hispanic/Latino; 17 Asian, non-Hispanic/Latino; 4 Hispanic/Latino; 1 Native Hawaiian or other Pacific Islander, non-Hispanic/Latino; 1 Two or more races, non-Hispanic/Latino), 26 international. Average age 35. 120 applicants, 55% accepted, 15 enrolled. In 2010, 52 master's awarded. *Degree requirements:* For master's, thesis, capstone course. *Entrance requirements:* For master's, interview, minimum GPA of 2.8, resume, 2 recommendations. Additional exam requirements/recommendations for international students: Required—TOEFL (minimum score 550 paper-based; 213 computer-based; 80 iBT). *Application deadline:* For fall admission, 5/15 for international students; for spring admission, 10/15 for international students. Applications are processed on a rolling basis. Application fee: $60. Electronic applications accepted. *Expenses:* Contact institution. *Financial support:* In 2010–11, 25 students received support. Unspecified assistantships available. Financial award applicants required to submit FAFSA. *Faculty research:* Vehicle dynamics, image processing, multimedia in instruction, thermal packaging, character recognition, photovoltaics and nanotechnology, Web technology. *Unit head:* Dr. Jack Beal, Dean, 203-254-4000 Ext. 4147, Fax: 203-254-4013, E-mail: jwbeal@fairfield.edu. *Application contact:* Marianne Gumpper, Director of Graduate and Continuing Studies Admissions, 203-254-4184, Fax: 203-254-4073, E-mail: gradadmis@fairfield.edu.

Fairleigh Dickinson University, Metropolitan Campus, University College: Arts, Sciences, and Professional Studies, School of Computer Sciences and Engineering, Program in Electrical Engineering, Teaneck, NJ 07666-1914. Offers MSEE. *Students:* 37 full-time (8 women), 4 part-time (0 women), 34 international. Average age 24. 148 applicants, 56% accepted, 13 enrolled. In 2010, 36 master's awarded. *Entrance requirements:* For master's, GRE General Test. *Application deadline:* Applications are processed on a rolling basis. Application fee: $40. *Application contact:* Susan Brooman, University Director of Graduate Admissions, 201-692-2554, Fax: 201-692-2560, E-mail: globaleducation@fdu.edu.

Florida Agricultural and Mechanical University, Division of Graduate Studies, Research, and Continuing Education, FAMU-FSU College of Engineering, Department of Electrical Engineering, Tallahassee, FL 32307-3200. Offers MS, PhD. *Degree requirements:* For master's, comprehensive exam, thesis, conference paper; for doctorate, comprehensive exam, thesis/dissertation, publishable paper. *Entrance requirements:* For master's, GRE General Test, minimum GPA of 3.0; for doctorate, minimum GPA of 3.3. Additional exam requirements/recommendations for international students: Required—TOEFL (minimum score 550 paper-based; 213 computer-based). *Faculty research:* Electromagnetics, computer security, advanced power systems, sensor systems.

Florida Atlantic University, College of Engineering and Computer Science, Department of Computer and Electrical Engineering and Computer Science, Boca Raton, FL 33431-0991. Offers computer engineering (MS, PhD); computer science (MS, PhD); electrical engineering (MS, PhD). Part-time and evening/weekend programs available. *Faculty:* 35 full-time (6 women), 3 part-time/adjunct (1 woman). *Students:* 89 full-time (19 women), 101 part-time (25 women); includes 69 minority (14 Black or African American, non-Hispanic/Latino; 22 Asian, non-Hispanic/Latino; 32 Hispanic/Latino; 1 Two or more races, non-Hispanic/Latino), 55 international. Average age 32. 128 applicants, 48% accepted, 45 enrolled. In 2010, 41 master's, 8 doctorates awarded. Terminal master's awarded for partial completion of doctoral program. *Degree requirements:* For master's, thesis optional; for doctorate, thesis/dissertation, qualifying exam. *Entrance requirements:* For master's, GRE General Test, minimum GPA of 3.0; for doctorate, GRE General Test, master's degree, minimum GPA of 3.5. Additional exam requirements/recommendations for international students: Required—TOEFL. *Application deadline:* For fall admission, 7/1 priority date for domestic students, 2/15 for international students; for spring admission, 11/1 for domestic students, 7/15 for international students. Applications are processed on a rolling basis. Application fee: $30. *Expenses:* Tuition, area resident: Part-time $319.96 per credit. Tuition, state resident: part-time $319.96 per credit. Tuition, nonresident: part-time $926.42 per credit. *Financial support:* Fellowships, research assistantships with partial tuition reimbursements, teaching assistantships with full tuition reimbursements, career-related internships or fieldwork and Federal Work-Study available. Support available to part-time students. Financial award application deadline: 4/1; financial award applicants required to submit FAFSA. *Faculty research:* VLSI and neural networks, communication networks, software engineering, computer architecture, multimedia and video processing. *Unit head:* Dr. Borko Furht, Chairman, 561-297-3855, Fax: 561-297-2800. *Application contact:* Dr. Borko Furht, Chairman, 561-297-3855, Fax: 561-297-2800.

Florida Institute of Technology, Graduate Programs, College of Engineering, Electrical and Computer Engineering Department, Melbourne, FL 32901-6975. Offers computer engineering (MS, PhD); electrical engineering (MS, PhD). Part-time and evening/weekend programs available. *Faculty:* 10 full-time (1 woman), 2 part-time/adjunct (0 women). *Students:* 88 full-time (20 women), 38 part-time (5 women); includes 8 minority (3 Black or African American, non-Hispanic/Latino; 3 Asian, non-Hispanic/Latino; 2 Hispanic/Latino), 91 international. Average age 28. 314 applicants, 54% accepted, 37 enrolled. In 2010, 21 master's, 8 doctorates awarded. *Degree requirements:* For master's, comprehensive exam (for some programs), thesis optional, final program exam, faculty-supervised specialized research; for doctorate, comprehensive exam (for some programs), thesis/dissertation, complete program of significant original research. *Entrance requirements:* For master's, GRE, minimum GPA of 3.0, bachelor's degree from an ABET-accredited program; for doctorate, 3 letters of recommendation, resume, minimum GPA of 3.2, statement of objectives, on campus interview (highly recommended). Additional exam requirements/recommendations for international students: Required—TOEFL (minimum score 550 paper-based; 213 computer-based; 79 iBT). *Application deadline:* For fall admission, 4/1 for international students; for spring admission, 9/30 for international students. Applications are processed on a rolling basis. Application fee: $50. Electronic applications accepted. *Expenses:* Tuition: Part-time $1040 per credit hour. Tuition and fees vary according to campus/location. *Financial support:* In 2010–11, 4 research assistantships with full and partial tuition reimbursements (averaging $5,250 per year), 7 teaching assistantships with full and partial tuition reimbursements (averaging $3,703 per year) were awarded; career-related internships or fieldwork, institutionally sponsored loans, tuition waivers (partial), unspecified assistantships, and tuition remissions also available. Support available to part-time students. Financial award application deadline: 3/1; financial award applicants required to submit FAFSA. *Faculty research:* Electro-optics, electromagnetics, microelectronics, communications, computer architecture, neural networks. Total annual research expenditures: $405,569. *Unit head:* Dr. Samuel P. Kozaitis, Department Head, 321-674-8060, Fax: 321-674-8192, E-mail: kozaitis@fit.edu. *Application contact:* Cheryl A. Brown, Associate Director of Graduate Admissions, 321-674-7581, Fax: 321-723-9468, E-mail: cbrown@fit.edu.

Florida Institute of Technology, Graduate Programs, Extended Studies Division, Melbourne, FL 32901-6975. Offers acquisition and contract management (MS); aerospace engineering (MS); business administration (MBA); computer information systems (MS); computer science (MS); electrical engineering (MS); engineering management (MS); human resources management (MS); logistics management (MS), including humanitarian and disaster relief logistics; management (MS), including acquisition and contract management, e-business, human resources management, information systems, logistics management, management, transportation management; material acquisition management (MS); mechanical engineering (MS); operations research (MS); project management (MS), including information systems, operations research; public administration (MPA); quality management (MS); software engineering (MS); space systems (MS); space systems management (MS); systems management (MS), including information systems, operations research. Part-time and evening/weekend programs available. Postbaccalaureate distance learning degree programs offered (no on-campus study). *Faculty:* 11 full-time (3 women), 118 part-time/adjunct (24 women). *Students:* 69 full-time (23 women), 907 part-time (369 women); includes 385 minority (242 Black or African American, non-Hispanic/Latino; 15 American Indian or Alaska Native, non-Hispanic/Latino; 44 Asian, non-Hispanic/Latino; 52 Hispanic/Latino; 3 Native Hawaiian or other Pacific Islander, non-Hispanic/Latino; 29 Two or more races, non-Hispanic/Latino), 17

Electrical Engineering

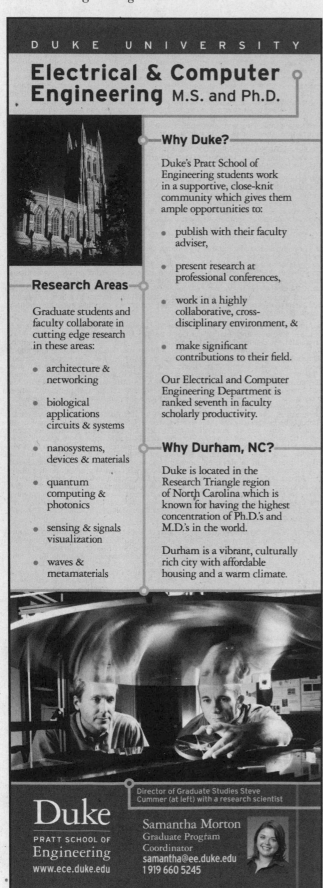

DUKE UNIVERSITY

Electrical & Computer Engineering M.S. and Ph.D.

Why Duke?

Duke's Pratt School of Engineering students work in a supportive, close-knit community which gives them ample opportunities to:

- publish with their faculty adviser,
- present research at professional conferences,
- work in a highly collaborative, cross-disciplinary environment, &
- make significant contributions to their field.

Our Electrical and Computer Engineering Department is ranked seventh in faculty scholarly productivity.

Research Areas

Graduate students and faculty collaborate in cutting edge research in these areas:

- architecture & networking
- biological applications circuits & systems
- nanosystems, devices & materials
- quantum computing & photonics
- sensing & signals visualization
- waves & metamaterials

Why Durham, NC?

Duke is located in the Research Triangle region of North Carolina which is known for having the highest concentration of Ph.D.'s and M.D.'s in the world.

Durham is a vibrant, culturally rich city with affordable housing and a warm climate.

Director of Graduate Studies Steve Cummer (at left) with a research scientist

Duke
PRATT SCHOOL OF
Engineering
www.ece.duke.edu

Samantha Morton
Graduate Program Coordinator
samantha@ee.duke.edu
1 919 660 5245

---

international. 517 applicants, 49% accepted, 245 enrolled. In 2010, 430 degrees awarded. *Degree requirements:* For master's, comprehensive exam (for some programs), capstone course. *Entrance requirements:* For master's, GMAT or resume showing 8 years of supervised experience, minimum GPA of 3.0, 2 letters of recommendation, resume. Additional exam requirements/recommendations for international students: Required—TOEFL (minimum score 550 paper-based; 213 computer-based; 79 iBT). *Application deadline:* For fall admission, 4/1 for international students; for spring admission, 9/30 for international students. Applications are processed on a rolling basis. Application fee: $50. Electronic applications accepted. *Expenses:* Contact institution. *Financial support:* Application deadline: 3/1. *Unit head:* Dr. Theodore Richardson, Senior Associate Dean, 321-674-8123, Fax: 321-674-7597, E-mail: trichardson@fit.edu. *Application contact:* Carolyn Farrior, Director of Graduate Admissions, Online Learning and Off-Campus Programs, 321-674-7118, Fax: 321-674-8216, E-mail: cfarrior@fit.edu.

Florida International University, College of Engineering and Computing, Department of Electrical and Computer Engineering, Program in Electrical Engineering, Miami, FL 33175. Offers MS, PhD. Part-time and evening/weekend programs available. *Students:* 91 full-time (17 women), 32 part-time (5 women); includes 4 Black or African American, non-Hispanic/Latino; 3 Asian, non-Hispanic/Latino; 24 Hispanic/Latino, 81 international. Average age 27. 311 applicants, 24% accepted, 60 enrolled. In 2010, 46 master's, 12 doctorates awarded. Terminal master's awarded for partial completion of doctoral program. *Degree requirements:* For master's, thesis optional; for doctorate, comprehensive exam, thesis/dissertation. *Entrance requirements:* For master's, minimum undergraduate GPA of 3.0 in upper-level coursework, resume, letters of recommendation, letter of intent; for doctorate, GRE General Test, minimum graduate GPA of 3.3, resume, master's degree, letters of recommendation, letter of intent. Additional exam requirements/recommendations for international students: Required—TOEFL (minimum score 550 paper-based; 80 iBT). *Application deadline:* For fall admission, 6/1 for domestic students, 4/1 for international students; for spring admission, 10/1 for domestic students, 9/1 for international students. Applications are processed on a rolling basis. Application fee: $30. Electronic applications accepted. *Financial support:* Institutionally sponsored loans and scholarships/grants available. Financial award application deadline: 3/1; financial award applicants required to submit FAFSA. *Unit head:* Dr. Kang Yen, Chair, Electrical and Computer Engineering Department, 305-348-3037, Fax: 305-348-3707, E-mail: yenk@fiu.edu. *Application contact:* Maria Parrilla, Graduate Admissions Assistant, 305-348-1890, Fax: 305-348-6142, E-mail: grad_eng@fiu.edu.

Florida State University, The Graduate School, FAMU-FSU College of Engineering, Department of Electrical and Computer Engineering, Tallahassee, FL 32306. Offers electrical engineering (MS, PhD). Part-time programs available. *Faculty:* 19 full-time (2 women), 1 part-time/adjunct (0 women). *Students:* 72 full-time (11 women), 13 part-time (2 women); includes 9 Black or African American, non-Hispanic/Latino; 1 American Indian or Alaska Native, non-Hispanic/Latino; 2 Asian, non-Hispanic/Latino; 5 Hispanic/Latino, 40 international. Average age 26. 129 applicants, 37% accepted, 12 enrolled. In 2010, 14 master's, 9 doctorates awarded. *Degree requirements:* For master's, thesis; for doctorate, comprehensive exam, thesis/dissertation, preliminary exam, qualifying exam. *Entrance requirements:* For master's, GRE General Test, minimum GPA of 3.0, BS in electrical engineering; for doctorate, GRE General Test, minimum graduate GPA of 3.3, MS in electrical engineering. Additional exam requirements/recommendations for international students: Required—TOEFL (minimum score 550 paper-based; 213 computer-based). *Application deadline:* For fall admission, 7/1 for domestic and international students; for spring admission, 11/1 for domestic and international students. Applications are processed on a rolling basis. Application fee: $30. *Expenses:* Tuition, state resident: full-time $8238.24. *Financial support:* In 2010–11, 80 students received support, including 1 fellowship with full tuition reimbursement available (averaging $12,000 per year), 11 research assistantships with full tuition reimbursements available (averaging $15,800 per year), 26 teaching assistantships with full tuition reimbursements available (averaging $15,800 per year); career-related internships or fieldwork, institutionally sponsored loans, scholarships/grants, and tuition waivers (full) also available. Financial award application deadline: 6/15. *Faculty research:* Electromagnetics, digital signal processing, computer systems, image processing, laser optics. Total annual research expenditures: $816,000. *Unit head:* Dr. Simon Foo, Chair and Professor, 850-410-6474, Fax: 850-410-6479, E-mail: foo@eng.fsu.edu. *Application contact:* Melissa Jackson, Graduate Program Assistant, 850-410-6454, Fax: 850-410-6479, E-mail: ecegrad@eng.fsu.edu.

Gannon University, School of Graduate Studies, College of Engineering and Business, School of Engineering and Computer Science, Program in Electrical Engineering, Erie, PA 16541-0001. Offers MSEE. Part-time and evening/weekend programs available. *Students:* 78 full-time (5 women), 14 part-time (3 women); includes 1 Asian, non-Hispanic/Latino, 85 international. Average age 24. 318 applicants, 94% accepted, 29 enrolled. In 2010, 40 master's awarded. *Degree requirements:* For master's, thesis or project. *Entrance requirements:* For master's, GRE or GMAT, bachelor's degree in engineering, minimum QPA of 2.5. Additional exam requirements/recommendations for international students: Required—TOEFL (minimum score 79 iBT). *Application deadline:* Applications are processed on a rolling basis. Application fee: $25. Electronic applications accepted. *Expenses:* Tuition: Full-time $14,670; part-time $815 per credit. Required fees: $430; $18 per credit. Tuition and fees vary according to class time, course load, degree level, campus/location and program. *Financial support:* Career-related internships or fieldwork, scholarships/grants, traineeships, and unspecified assistantships available. Financial award application deadline: 7/1; financial award applicants required to submit FAFSA. *Unit head:* Dr. Fong Mak, Chair, 814-871-7625, E-mail: mak001@gannon.edu. *Application contact:* Kara Morgan, Assistant Director of Graduate Admissions, 814-871-5831, Fax: 814-871-5827, E-mail: graduate@gannon.edu.

George Mason University, Volgenau School of Engineering, Department of Electrical and Computer Engineering, Fairfax, VA 22030. Offers advanced networking protocols for telecommunications (Certificate); communications and networking (Certificate); computer engineering (MS); computer forensics (MS); electrical and computer engineering (PhD); electrical engineering (MS); network technology and applications (Certificate); networks, system integration and testing (Certificate); signal processing (Certificate); telecom systems modeling (Certificate); telecommunications (MS); telecommunications forensics and security (Certificate); VLSI design/manufacturing (Certificate); wireless communication (Certificate). MS program offered jointly with Old Dominion University, University of Virginia, Virginia Commonwealth University, and Virginia Polytechnic Institute and State University. Part-time and evening/weekend programs available. *Faculty:* 33 full-time (4 women), 39 part-time/adjunct (4 women). *Students:* 106 full-time (27 women), 336 part-time (64 women); includes 24 Black or African American, non-Hispanic/Latino; 1 American Indian or Alaska Native, non-Hispanic/Latino; 54 Asian, non-Hispanic/Latino; 20 Hispanic/Latino; 1 Two or more races, non-Hispanic/Latino, 172 international. Average age 30. 506 applicants, 71% accepted, 142 enrolled. In 2010, 145 master's, 3 doctorates, 61 other advanced degrees awarded. *Degree requirements:* For master's, thesis optional; for doctorate, comprehensive exam, thesis or scholarly paper. *Entrance requirements:* For master's, GMAT or GRE General Test, letters of recommendation, resume; for doctorate, GRE/GMAT, personal goal statement, 2 transcripts, letter of recommendation. Additional exam requirements/recommendations for international students: Required—TOEFL (minimum score 570 paper-based; 230 computer-based; 88 iBT). *Application deadline:* For fall admission, 7/15 priority date for domestic and international students; for spring admission, 12/1 for domestic and international students. Applications are processed on a rolling basis. Application fee: $100. Electronic applications accepted. *Expenses:* Tuition, state resident: full-time $8192; part-time $440 per credit hour. Tuition, nonresident: full-time $22,952; part-time $1055 per credit hour. Required fees: $2364; $99 per credit hour. *Financial support:* In 2010–11, 74 students received support, including 2 fellowships with full tuition reimbursements available (averaging $18,000 per year), 26 research assistantships with full and partial tuition reimbursements available (averaging $14,648 per year), 46 teaching assistantships with full and partial tuition reimbursements available (averaging $10,946 per year); career-related internships or fieldwork, Federal Work-Study, scholarships/grants, unspecified assistantships, and health care benefits (full-time research or teaching assistantship recipients) also available.

Financial award application deadline: 3/1; financial award applicants required to submit FAFSA. *Faculty research:* Communication networks, signal processing, system failure diagnosis, multiprocessors, material processing using microwave energy. Total annual research expenditures: $3.4 million. *Unit head:* Dr. Andre Manitius, Chairperson, 703-993-1569, Fax: 703-993-1601, E-mail: ece@gmu.edu. *Application contact:* Jessica Skinner, Associate Dean, 703-993-1569, E-mail: jskinne6@gmu.edu.

The George Washington University, School of Engineering and Applied Science, Department of Electrical and Computer Engineering, Washington, DC 20052. Offers electrical and computer engineering (MS, D Sc); telecommunication and computers (MS). Part-time and evening/weekend programs available. *Faculty:* 24 full-time (2 women), 9 part-time/adjunct (0 women). *Students:* 101 full-time (19 women), 114 part-time (20 women); includes 12 Black or African American, non-Hispanic/Latino; 23 Asian, non-Hispanic/Latino; 2 Hispanic/Latino; 1 Native Hawaiian or other Pacific Islander, non-Hispanic/Latino, 112 international. Average age 29. 339 applicants, 81% accepted, 69 enrolled. In 2010, 65 master's, 14 doctorates awarded. *Degree requirements:* For master's, thesis optional; for doctorate, comprehensive exam, thesis/dissertation, dissertation defense, qualifying exam. *Entrance requirements:* For master's, appropriate bachelor's degree, minimum GPA of 3.0; for doctorate, appropriate bachelor's or master's degree, minimum GPA of 3.3, GRE if highest earned degree is BS. Additional exam requirements/recommendations for international students: Required—TOEFL or The George Washington University English as a Foreign Language Test. *Application deadline:* For fall admission, 3/1 priority date for domestic students; for spring admission, 10/1 for domestic students. Applications are processed on a rolling basis. Application fee: $75. *Financial support:* In 2010–11, 39 students received support; fellowships with tuition reimbursements available, research assistantships, teaching assistantships with tuition reimbursements available, career-related internships or fieldwork and institutionally sponsored loans available. Financial award application deadline: 3/1; financial award applicants required to submit FAFSA. *Faculty research:* Computer graphics, multimedia systems. *Unit head:* Can E. Korman, Chair, 202-994-4952, E-mail: korman@gwu.edu. *Application contact:* Adina Lav, Marketing, Recruiting and Admissions, 202-994-5827, Fax: 202-994-0909, E-mail: engineering@gwu.edu.

Georgia Institute of Technology, Graduate Studies and Research, College of Engineering, School of Electrical and Computer Engineering, Atlanta, GA 30332-0001. Offers MS, MSEE, PhD. Part-time programs available. Postbaccalaureate distance learning degree programs offered (minimal on-campus study). Terminal master's awarded for partial completion of doctoral program. *Degree requirements:* For master's, thesis optional; for doctorate, thesis/dissertation. *Entrance requirements:* For master's, GRE General Test, minimum GPA of 3.0; for doctorate, GRE General Test, minimum GPA of 3.5. Additional exam requirements/recommendations for international students: Required—TOEFL. *Faculty research:* Telecommunications, computer systems, microelectronics, optical engineering, digital signal processing.

Georgia Southern University, Jack N. Averitt College of Graduate Studies, Allen E. Paulson College of Science and Technology, Department of Mechanical and Electrical Engineering Technology, Statesboro, GA 30460. Offers M Tech, MSAE, Certificate. Part-time and evening/weekend programs available. *Students:* 33 full-time (8 women), 20 part-time (3 women); includes 14 Black or African American, non-Hispanic/Latino; 4 Hispanic/Latino; 4 Two or more races, non-Hispanic/Latino, 6 international. Average age 27. 11 applicants, 100% accepted, 6 enrolled. In 2010, 7 master's awarded. *Degree requirements:* For master's, comprehensive exam, thesis optional. *Entrance requirements:* For master's, GRE. Additional exam requirements/recommendations for international students: Required—TOEFL (minimum score 550 paper-based; 213 computer-based; 80 iBT). *Application deadline:* For fall admission, 3/1 priority date for domestic and international students; for spring admission, 10/1 priority date for domestic students, 10/1 for international students. Applications are processed on a rolling basis. Application fee: $50. Electronic applications accepted. *Expenses:* Tuition, state resident: full-time $6000; part-time $250 per semester hour. Tuition, nonresident: full-time $23,976; part-time $999 per semester hour. Required fees: $1644. *Financial support:* In 2010–11, 37 students received support, including 4 research assistantships with partial tuition reimbursements available (averaging $7,200 per year); tuition waivers (partial) and unspecified assistantships also available. Financial award application deadline: 4/15; financial award applicants required to submit FAFSA. *Faculty research:* Interdisciplinary research in computational mechanics, experimental and computational biofuel combustion and tribology, mechatronics and control, thermomechanical and thermofluid finite element modeling, information technology. Total annual research expenditures: $458,293. *Unit head:* Dr. Mohammad S. Davoud, Chair, 912-478-0540, Fax: 912-478-1455, E-mail: mdavoud@georgiasouthern.edu. *Application contact:* Dr. Charles Ziglar, Coordinator for Graduate Student Recruitment, 912-478-5635, Fax: 912-478-0740, E-mail: gradadmissions@georgiasouthern.edu.

Graduate School and University Center of the City University of New York, Graduate Studies, Program in Engineering, New York, NY 10016-4039. Offers biomedical engineering (PhD); chemical engineering (PhD); civil engineering (PhD); electrical engineering (PhD); mechanical engineering (PhD). *Degree requirements:* For doctorate, thesis/dissertation. *Entrance requirements:* For doctorate, GRE General Test. Additional exam requirements/recommendations for international students: Required—TOEFL. Electronic applications accepted.

Grand Valley State University, Padnos College of Engineering and Computing, School of Engineering, Allendale, MI 49401-9403. Offers electrical and computer engineering (MSE); manufacturing operations (MSE); mechanical engineering (MSE); product design and manufacturing engineering (MSE). Part-time and evening/weekend programs available. *Degree requirements:* For master's, project or thesis. *Entrance requirements:* For master's, engineering degree, minimum GPA of 3.0. Additional exam requirements/recommendations for international students: Required—TOEFL. Electronic applications accepted. *Faculty research:* Digital signal processing, computer aided design, computer aided manufacturing, manufacturing simulation, biomechanics, product design.

Howard University, College of Engineering, Architecture, and Computer Sciences, School of Engineering and Computer Science, Department of Electrical Engineering, Washington, DC 20059-0002. Offers M Eng, PhD. Offered through the Graduate School of Arts and Sciences. Part-time programs available. *Degree requirements:* For master's, thesis (for some programs), qualifying exam; for doctorate, thesis/dissertation, preliminary exam. *Entrance requirements:* For master's, GRE General Test, bachelor's degree in electrical engineering, minimum GPA of 3.0; for doctorate, GRE General Test, minimum GPA of 3.0. Additional exam requirements/recommendations for international students: Required—TOEFL. Electronic applications accepted. *Faculty research:* Solid-state electronics, antennas and microwaves, communications and signal processing, controls and power systems, nanotechnology.

Illinois Institute of Technology, Graduate College, Armour College of Engineering, Department of Electrical and Computer Engineering, Chicago, IL 60616-3793. Offers biomedical imaging and signals (MBMI); computer engineering (MS, PhD); electrical and computer engineering (MECE); electrical engineering (MS, PhD); electricity markets (MEM); network engineering (MNE); power engineering (MPE); telecommunications and software engineering (MTSE); VLSI and microelectronics (MVM). Part-time and evening/weekend programs available. Postbaccalaureate distance learning degree programs offered (minimal on-campus study). *Faculty:* 26 full-time (3 women), 2 part-time/adjunct (0 women). *Students:* 456 full-time (77 women), 140 part-time (17 women); includes 25 minority (4 Black or African American, non-Hispanic/Latino; 15 Asian, non-Hispanic/Latino; 4 Hispanic/Latino; 2 Two or more races, non-Hispanic/Latino), 488 international. Average age 26. 1,407 applicants, 68% accepted, 217 enrolled. In 2010, 214 master's, 17 doctorates awarded. Terminal master's awarded for partial completion of doctoral program. *Degree requirements:* For master's, comprehensive exam (for some programs), thesis (for some programs); for doctorate, comprehensive exam, thesis/dissertation. *Entrance requirements:* For master's and doctorate, GRE General Test (minimum score 1100 Quantitative and Verbal, 3.5 Analytical Writing), minimum undergraduate GPA of 3.0. Additional exam requirements/recommendations for international students: Required—TOEFL (minimum score 523 paper-based; 70 iBT); Recommended—IELTS (minimum score 5.5). *Application deadline:* For fall admission, 5/1 for domestic and international students; for spring admission, 10/15 for domestic and international students. Applications are processed on a rolling basis. Application fee: $50. Electronic applications accepted. *Expenses:* Tuition: Full-time $18,576; part-time $1032 per credit hour. Required fees: $583 per semester. One-time fee: $150. Tuition and fees vary according to program and student level. *Financial support:* In 2010–11, 1 fellowship with full and partial tuition reimbursement (averaging $1,090 per year), 52 research assistantships with full and partial tuition reimbursements (averaging $9,530 per year), 24 teaching assistantships with full and partial tuition reimbursements (averaging $9,092 per year) were awarded; career-related internships or fieldwork, Federal Work-Study, institutionally sponsored loans, scholarships/grants, health care benefits, tuition waivers (full), and unspecified assistantships also available. Support available to part-time students. Financial award applicants required to submit FAFSA. *Faculty research:* Communication systems, computer systems and micro-electronics, electromagnetics and electronics, power and control systems, signal and image processing. Total annual research expenditures: $5.6 million. *Unit head:* Dr. Geoffrey Williamson, Interim Chair, 312-567-5960, Fax: 312-567-8976, E-mail: williamson@iit.edu. *Application contact:* Deborah Gibson, Director, Graduate Admission, 866-472-3448, Fax: 312-567-3138, E-mail: inquiry.grad@iit.edu.

Indiana University–Purdue University Fort Wayne, College of Engineering, Technology, and Computer Science, Department of Engineering, Fort Wayne, IN 46805-1499. Offers computer engineering (MS); electrical engineering (MS); mechanical engineering (MS); systems engineering (MS). Part-time programs available. *Faculty:* 18 full-time (3 women). *Students:* 7 full-time (0 women), 31 part-time (7 women); includes 4 minority (1 Black or African American, non-Hispanic/Latino; 2 Asian, non-Hispanic/Latino; 1 Hispanic/Latino), 4 international. Average age 28. 21 applicants, 95% accepted, 18 enrolled. In 2010, 9 master's awarded. *Entrance requirements:* For master's, minimum GPA of 3.0, bachelor's degree in engineering discipline. Additional exam requirements/recommendations for international students: Required—TOEFL (minimum score 550 paper-based; 213 computer-based; 77 iBT); Recommended—TWE. *Application deadline:* For fall admission, 7/15 priority date for domestic students, 5/15 priority date for international students; for spring admission, 12/1 priority date for domestic students, 10/15 priority date for international students. Applications are processed on a rolling basis. Application fee: $55 ($60 for international students). Electronic applications accepted. *Expenses:* Tuition, state resident: full-time $4824; part-time $268 per credit. Tuition, nonresident: full-time $11,625; part-time $646 per credit. Required fees: $555; $30.85 per credit. Tuition and fees vary according to course load. *Financial support:* In 2010–11, 5 research assistantships with partial tuition reimbursements (averaging $12,740 per year), 3 teaching assistantships with partial tuition reimbursements (averaging $12,740 per year) were awarded. Financial award application deadline: 3/1; financial award applicants required to submit FAFSA. *Faculty research:* Worm-scanning strategies, measuring the acceleration of gravity. Total annual research expenditures: $129,186. *Unit head:* Dr. Donald Mueller, Chair, 260-481-5707, Fax: 260-481-6281, E-mail: mueller@engr.ipfw.edu. *Application contact:* Dr. Donald Mueller, Chair, 260-481-5707, Fax: 260-481-6281, E-mail: mueller@engr.ipfw.edu.

Indiana University–Purdue University Indianapolis, School of Engineering and Technology, Department of Electrical Engineering, Indianapolis, IN 46202-2896. Offers biomedical engineering (MS, PhD); electrical and computer engineering (MS, MSECE, PhD), including biomedical engineering (MSECE), control and automation (MSECE), signal processing (MSECE); engineering (interdisciplinary) (MSE). *Students:* 40 full-time (13 women), 35 part-time (7 women); includes 7 minority (1 Black or African American, non-Hispanic/Latino; 1 Asian, non-Hispanic/Latino; 3 Hispanic/Latino; 2 Two or more races, non-Hispanic/Latino), 45 international. Average age 27. 153 applicants, 53% accepted, 42 enrolled. In 2010, 37 master's awarded. Application fee: $55 ($65 for international students). *Unit head:* Yaobin Chen, Unit Head, 317-274-4032, Fax: 317-274-4493. *Application contact:* Valerie Diemer, Graduate Program, 317-278-4960, Fax: 317-278-1671, E-mail: grad@engr.iupui.edu.

Instituto Tecnológico y de Estudios Superiores de Monterrey, Campus Chihuahua, Graduate Programs, Chihuahua, Mexico. Offers computer systems engineering (Ingeniero); electrical engineering (Ingeniero); electromechanical engineering (Ingeniero); electronic engineering (Ingeniero); engineering administration (MEA); industrial engineering (MIE, Ingeniero); international trade (MIT); mechanical engineering (Ingeniero).

Instituto Tecnológico y de Estudios Superiores de Monterrey, Campus Monterrey, Graduate and Research Division, Programs in Engineering, Monterrey, Mexico. Offers applied statistics (M Eng); artificial intelligence (PhD); automation engineering (M Eng); chemical engineering (M Eng); civil engineering (M Eng); electrical engineering (M Eng); electronic engineering (M Eng); environmental engineering (M Eng); industrial engineering (M Eng, PhD); manufacturing engineering (M Eng); mechanical engineering (M Eng); systems and quality engineering (M Eng). M Eng program offered jointly with University of Waterloo; PhD in industrial engineering with Texas A&M University. Part-time and evening/weekend programs available. Terminal master's awarded for partial completion of doctoral program. *Degree requirements:* For master's, one foreign language, thesis; for doctorate, one foreign language, thesis/dissertation. *Entrance requirements:* For master's, EXADEP; for doctorate, GRE, master's degree in related field. Additional exam requirements/recommendations for international students: Required—TOEFL. *Faculty research:* Flexible manufacturing cells, materials, statistical methods, environmental prevention, control and evaluation.

International Technological University, Program in Electrical Engineering, Santa Clara, CA 95050. Offers MSEE, PhD. Part-time and evening/weekend programs available. *Degree requirements:* For master's, thesis or alternative. *Entrance requirements:* For master's, 3 semesters of calculus, minimum GPA of 2.5. Additional exam requirements/recommendations for international students: Required—TOEFL. *Faculty research:* VLSI design, digital systems, routing and optimization theory.

Iowa State University of Science and Technology, Graduate College, College of Engineering, Department of Electrical and Computer Engineering, Ames, IA 50011. Offers computer engineering (M Eng, MS, PhD); electrical engineering (M Eng, MS, PhD). *Faculty:* 65 full-time (6 women), 4 part-time/adjunct (2 women). *Students:* 246 full-time (40 women), 170 part-time (32 women); includes 9 Black or African American, non-Hispanic/Latino; 14 Asian, non-Hispanic/Latino; 5 Hispanic/Latino, 256 international. 1,198 applicants, 9% accepted, 74 enrolled. In 2010, 58 master's, 15 doctorates awarded. *Degree requirements:* For master's, thesis or alternative; for doctorate, thesis/dissertation. *Entrance requirements:* For master's and doctorate, GRE General Test. Additional exam requirements/recommendations for international students: Required—TOEFL (minimum score 570 paper-based; 79 iBT), IELTS (minimum score 6.5). *Application deadline:* For fall admission, 1/15 priority date for domestic and international students; for spring admission, 9/15 for domestic and international students. Application fee: $40 ($90 for international students). Electronic applications accepted. *Financial support:* In 2010–11, 147 research assistantships with full and partial tuition reimbursements (averaging $10,227 per year), 40 teaching assistantships with full and partial tuition reimbursements (averaging $7,506 per year) were awarded; fellowships, scholarships/grants, health care benefits, and unspecified assistantships also available. *Unit head:* Dr. Arun Somani, Chair, 515-294-2664, E-mail: ecegrad@ee.iastate.edu. *Application contact:* Dr. Akhilesh Tyagi, Director of Graduate Education, 515-294-2667, E-mail: ecegrad@iastate.edu.

The Johns Hopkins University, Engineering for Professionals, Part-time Program in Electrical and Computer Engineering, Baltimore, MD 21218-2699. Offers MS, Post-Master's Certificate. Part-time and evening/weekend programs available. *Faculty:* 40 part-time/adjunct (1 woman). *Students:* 17 full-time (4 women), 324 part-time (49 women); includes 108 minority (31 Black or African American, non-Hispanic/Latino; 46 Asian, non-Hispanic/Latino; 22 Hispanic/Latino; 9 Two or more races, non-Hispanic/Latino), 1 international. Average age 28. 112 applicants, 92% accepted, 97 enrolled. In 2010, 101 master's, 1 other advanced degree awarded. *Application deadline:* Applications are processed on a rolling basis. Application fee: $75. Electronic applications accepted. *Financial support:* Institutionally sponsored loans available. *Unit head:* Dr. Brian Jennison, Program Chair, 443-778-6421, E-mail: brian.jennison@

Electrical Engineering

The Johns Hopkins University (continued)
jhuapl.edu. *Application contact:* Priyanka Dwivedi, Admissions Manager, 410-516-2300, Fax: 410-579-8049, E-mail: pdwived1@jhu.edu.

The Johns Hopkins University, G. W. C. Whiting School of Engineering, Department of Electrical and Computer Engineering, Baltimore, MD 21218-2699. Offers MSE, PhD. *Faculty:* 18 full-time (3 women), 9 part-time/adjunct (0 women). *Students:* 122 full-time (23 women), 5 part-time (0 women); includes 10 minority (3 Black or African American, non-Hispanic/Latino; 5 Asian, non-Hispanic/Latino; 1 Hispanic/Latino; 1 Two or more races, non-Hispanic/Latino), 85 international. Average age 23. 345 applicants, 20% accepted, 22 enrolled. In 2010, 26 master's, 6 doctorates awarded. Terminal master's awarded for partial completion of doctoral program. *Degree requirements:* For master's, thesis optional; for doctorate, thesis/dissertation, qualifying and oral exams, seminar. *Entrance requirements:* For master's and doctorate, GRE General Test, transcripts, 3 letters of recommendation, statement of purpose. Additional exam requirements/recommendations for international students: Required—TOEFL (minimum score 600 paper-based; 250 computer-based; 100 iBT). *Application deadline:* For fall admission, 1/7 for domestic and international students. Application fee: $75. Electronic applications accepted. *Financial support:* In 2010–11, 13 fellowships with full tuition reimbursements (averaging $20,700 per year), 65 research assistantships with full tuition reimbursements (averaging $26,400 per year), 4 teaching assistantships with full tuition reimbursements (averaging $20,700 per year) were awarded; career-related internships or fieldwork, Federal Work-Study, institutionally sponsored loans, scholarships/grants, health care benefits, tuition waivers (partial), and unspecified assistantships also available. Financial award application deadline: 1/15. *Faculty research:* Computer engineering, systems and control, language and speech processing, photonics and optoelectronics, signal and image processing. Total annual research expenditures: $2.6 million. *Unit head:* Dr. Jin U. Kang, Chair, 410-516-7031, Fax: 410-516-5566, E-mail: jkang@jhu.edu. *Application contact:* Debbie Race, Graduate Program Coordinator, 410-516-4808, Fax: 410-516-5566, E-mail: eceinfo@jhu.edu.

Kansas State University, Graduate School, College of Engineering, Department of Electrical and Computer Engineering, Manhattan, KS 66506. Offers electrical engineering (MS, PhD). Postbaccalaureate distance learning degree programs offered (no on-campus study). *Degree requirements:* For master's, thesis or alternative, final exam; for doctorate, thesis/dissertation, preliminary exams. *Entrance requirements:* For master's, GRE General Test, bachelor's degree in electrical engineering or computer science, minimum GPA of 3.0; for doctorate, GRE General Test. Additional exam requirements/recommendations for international students: Required—TOEFL (minimum score 600 paper-based). Electronic applications accepted. *Faculty research:* Energy systems and renewable energy, computer systems and real time embedded systems, communication systems and signal processing, integrated circuits and devices, bioengineering.

Kettering University, Graduate School, Electrical and Computer Engineering Department, Flint, MI 48504. Offers engineering (MS). Part-time and evening/weekend programs available. Postbaccalaureate distance learning degree programs offered (no on-campus study). *Faculty:* 4 full-time (0 women). *Students:* 1 full-time (0 women), 11 part-time (4 women); includes 1 minority (Hispanic/Latino), 4 international. Average age 31. 19 applicants, 68% accepted, 4 enrolled. In 2010, 4 master's awarded. *Degree requirements:* For master's, thesis optional. *Entrance requirements:* Additional exam requirements/recommendations for international students: Required—TOEFL (minimum score 550 paper-based; 213 computer-based; 79 iBT). *Application deadline:* For fall admission, 9/15 for domestic students, 6/15 for international students; for winter admission, 12/15 for domestic students, 9/15 for international students; for spring admission, 3/15 for domestic students, 12/15 for international students. Applications are processed on a rolling basis. Application fee: $0. Electronic applications accepted. *Expenses:* Tuition: Full-time $11,120; part-time $695 per credit hour. *Financial support:* In 2010–11, 4 students received support, including fellowships with full tuition reimbursements available (averaging $13,000 per year), research assistantships with full tuition reimbursements available (averaging $13,000 per year), teaching assistantships with full tuition reimbursements available (averaging $13,000 per year); Federal Work-Study, scholarships/grants, and tuition waivers (partial) also available. Support available to part-time students. Financial award application deadline: 7/15; financial award applicants required to submit CSS PROFILE or FAFSA. *Faculty research:* Batteries, battery testing, robotics. Total annual research expenditures: $201,163. *Unit head:* Dr. James McDonald, Department Head, 810-762-9500 Ext. 5690, Fax: 810-762-9830, E-mail: jmcdonal@kettering.edu. *Application contact:* Bonnie Switzer, Admissions Representative, 810-762-7953, Fax: 810-762-9935, E-mail: bswitzer@kettering.edu.

Lakehead University, Graduate Studies, Faculty of Engineering, Thunder Bay, ON P7B 5E1, Canada. Offers control engineering (M Sc Engr); electrical/computer engineering (M Sc Engr); environmental engineering (M Sc Engr). Part-time programs available. *Degree requirements:* For master's, thesis. *Entrance requirements:* For master's, bachelor's degree in chemical, electrical or mechanical engineering, minimum B average. Additional exam requirements/recommendations for international students: Required—TOEFL. *Faculty research:* Pulp and paper, adaptive/process control, robust/interactive learning control, vibration control.

Lamar University, College of Graduate Studies, College of Engineering, Department of Electrical Engineering, Beaumont, TX 77710. Offers ME, MES, DE. Part-time programs available. *Faculty:* 3 full-time (0 women). *Students:* 57 full-time (11 women), 67 part-time (11 women); includes 3 Asian, non-Hispanic/Latino, 96 international. Average age 24. 137 applicants, 34% accepted, 3 enrolled. In 2010, 76 master's awarded. *Degree requirements:* For master's, thesis (for some programs); for doctorate, thesis/dissertation. *Entrance requirements:* For master's and doctorate, GRE General Test. Additional exam requirements/recommendations for international students: Required—TOEFL. *Application deadline:* For fall admission, 5/15 priority date for domestic students; for spring admission, 10/1 priority date for domestic students. Applications are processed on a rolling basis. Application fee: $25 ($50 for international students). *Expenses:* Tuition, state resident: full-time $4160; part-time $208 per credit hour. Tuition, nonresident: full-time $10,360; part-time $518 per credit hour. *Financial support:* In 2010–11, 2 fellowships with partial tuition reimbursements (averaging $6,000 per year), 20 research assistantships with partial tuition reimbursements (averaging $6,000 per year), 2 teaching assistantships with partial tuition reimbursements (averaging $4,500 per year) were awarded; tuition waivers (partial) also available. Financial award application deadline: 4/1. *Faculty research:* Video processing, photonics, VLSI design, computer networking. *Unit head:* Dr. Harley Ross Myler, Chair, 409-880-8746, Fax: 409-880-8121, E-mail: mylerhr@hal.lamar.edu. *Application contact:* Jane Stanley McCabe, Information Contact, 409-880-8746, Fax: 409-880-8121, E-mail: eece@hal.lamar.edu.

Lawrence Technological University, College of Engineering, Southfield, MI 48075-1058. Offers architectural engineering (MS); automotive engineering (MS); civil engineering (MS); electrical and computer engineering (MS); engineering management (MEM); industrial engineering (MS); manufacturing systems (ME, DE); mechanical engineering (MS); mechatronic systems engineering (MS). Part-time and evening/weekend programs available. *Faculty:* 20 full-time (4 women), 12 part-time/adjunct (0 women). *Students:* 8 full-time (1 woman), 366 part-time (60 women); includes 29 Black or African American, non-Hispanic/Latino; 1 American Indian or Alaska Native, non-Hispanic/Latino; 36 Asian, non-Hispanic/Latino; 9 Hispanic/Latino; 4 Two or more races, non-Hispanic/Latino, 81 international. Average age 32. 398 applicants, 48% accepted, 87 enrolled. In 2010, 121 master's, 5 doctorates awarded. *Degree requirements:* For master's, thesis (for some programs). *Entrance requirements:* Additional exam requirements/recommendations for international students: Required—TOEFL (minimum score 550 paper-based; 213 computer-based; 79 iBT). *Application deadline:* For fall admission, 6/30 priority date for domestic students, 6/30 for international students; for spring admission, 11/15 priority date for domestic students, 11/15 for international students. Applications are processed on a rolling basis. Application fee: $50. Electronic applications accepted. *Financial support:* In 2010–11, 72 students received support. Federal Work-Study and institutionally sponsored loans available. Support available to part-time students. Financial award application deadline: 4/1; financial award applicants required to submit FAFSA. *Faculty research:* Advanced composite materials in bridges, strengthening existing bridges with carbon and glass fiber sheets, development of drive shafts using composite materials. *Unit head:* Dr. Nabil Grace, Interim Dean, 248-204-2500, Fax: 248-204-2509, E-mail: engrdean@ltu.edu. *Application contact:* Jane Rohrback, Director of Admissions, 248-204-3160, Fax: 248-204-2228, E-mail: admissions@ltu.edu.

Lehigh University, P.C. Rossin College of Engineering and Applied Science, Department of Electrical and Computer Engineering, Bethlehem, PA 18015. Offers electrical engineering (M Eng, MS, PhD); photonics (MS); wireless network engineering (MS). Part-time programs available. *Faculty:* 20 full-time (3 women). *Students:* 58 full-time (12 women), 7 part-time (1 woman), 52 international. Average age 27. 258 applicants, 11% accepted, 20 enrolled. In 2010, 18 master's, 17 doctorates awarded. Terminal master's awarded for partial completion of doctoral program. *Degree requirements:* For master's, thesis optional; for doctorate, thesis/dissertation, qualifying or comprehensive exam for all 1st year PhD's; general exam 7 months or more prior to completion/dissertation defense. *Entrance requirements:* For master's and doctorate, GRE General Test, BS in field or related field. Additional exam requirements/recommendations for international students: Required—TOEFL (minimum score 79 iBT). *Application deadline:* For fall admission, 1/15 priority date for domestic and international students; for spring admission, 11/1 for domestic and international students. Application fee: $75. Electronic applications accepted. *Financial support:* In 2010–11, 4 fellowships with full tuition reimbursements (averaging $18,360 per year), 42 research assistantships with full tuition reimbursements (averaging $21,600 per year), 5 teaching assistantships with full tuition reimbursements (averaging $18,819 per year) were awarded; career-related internships or fieldwork, Federal Work-Study, institutionally sponsored loans, scholarships/grants, tuition waivers (full and partial), and unspecified assistantships also available. Support available to part-time students. Financial award application deadline: 1/15. *Faculty research:* Nanostructures/nanodevices, terahertz generation, analog devices, mixed mode design and signal circuits, optoelectronic sensors, micro-fabrication technology and design, packaging/reliability of microsensors, coding and networking information theory, radio frequency, wireless and optical wireless communication, wireless networks. Total annual research expenditures: $4.3 million. *Unit head:* Dr. Filbert J. Bartoli, Chair, 610-758-4069, Fax: 610-758-6279, E-mail: fjb205@lehigh.edu. *Application contact:* Coley B. Burke, Graduate Coordinator, 610-758-4072, Fax: 610-758-6279, E-mail: cbb310@lehigh.edu.

Louisiana State University and Agricultural and Mechanical College, Graduate School, College of Engineering, Department of Electrical and Computer Engineering, Baton Rouge, LA 70803. Offers MSEE, PhD. *Faculty:* 27 full-time (1 woman). *Students:* 116 full-time (16 women), 7 part-time (1 woman); includes 3 Black or African American, non-Hispanic/Latino; 2 Asian, non-Hispanic/Latino; 2 Hispanic/Latino, 104 international. Average age 26. 229 applicants, 72% accepted, 38 enrolled. In 2010, 19 master's, 2 doctorates awarded. Terminal master's awarded for partial completion of doctoral program. *Degree requirements:* For master's, thesis optional; for doctorate, thesis/dissertation. *Entrance requirements:* For master's, GRE General Test, minimum GPA of 3.0; for doctorate, GRE General Test, minimum GPA of 3.5. Additional exam requirements/recommendations for international students: Required—TOEFL (minimum score 550 paper-based; 213 computer-based; 79 iBT) or IELTS (minimum score 6.5). *Application deadline:* For fall admission, 1/25 priority date for domestic students, 5/15 for international students; for spring admission, 10/15 for international students. Applications are processed on a rolling basis. Application fee: $50 ($70 for international students). Electronic applications accepted. *Financial support:* In 2010–11, 85 students received support, including 4 fellowships with full and partial tuition reimbursements available (averaging $19,864 per year), 49 research assistantships with full and partial tuition reimbursements available (averaging $13,617 per year), 28 teaching assistantships with full and partial tuition reimbursements available (averaging $13,619 per year); Federal Work-Study, institutionally sponsored loans, health care benefits, tuition waivers (full and partial), and unspecified assistantships also available. Financial award application deadline: 2/28; financial award applicants required to submit FAFSA. *Faculty research:* Computer engineering, electronics, control systems and signal processing, communications. Total annual research expenditures: $1.2 million. *Unit head:* Dr. Pratul Ajmera, Interim Chair, 225-578-5534, Fax: 225-578-5200, E-mail: ajmera@lsu.edu. *Application contact:* Dr. Guoxiang GuU, Graduate Adviser, 225-578-5534, Fax: 225-578-5200, E-mail: ggu@lsu.edu.

Louisiana Tech University, Graduate School, College of Engineering and Science, Department of Electrical Engineering, Ruston, LA 71272. Offers MS, PhD. Part-time programs available. Terminal master's awarded for partial completion of doctoral program. *Degree requirements:* For master's, thesis; for doctorate, thesis/dissertation. *Entrance requirements:* For master's, GRE General Test, minimum GPA of 3.0 in last 60 hours; for doctorate, minimum graduate GPA of 3.25 (with MS) or GRE General Test. Additional exam requirements/recommendations for international students: Required—TOEFL. *Faculty research:* Communications, computers and microprocessors, electrical and power systems, pattern recognition, robotics.

Loyola Marymount University, College of Science and Engineering, Department of Electrical Engineering and Computer Science, Program in Electrical Engineering, Los Angeles, CA 90045. Offers MSE. Part-time and evening/weekend programs available. *Faculty:* 9 full-time (3 women). In 2010, 4 master's awarded. *Degree requirements:* For master's, research seminar. *Entrance requirements:* Additional exam requirements/recommendations for international students: Required—TOEFL (minimum score 550 paper-based; 213 computer-based; 80 iBT). *Application deadline:* Applications are processed on a rolling basis. Application fee: $50. Electronic applications accepted. *Financial support:* Scholarships/grants available. Support available to part-time students. Financial award application deadline: 6/1; financial award applicants required to submit FAFSA. Total annual research expenditures: $22,929. *Unit head:* Dr. Stephanie August, Graduate Director, 310-338-5973, Fax: 310-338-2872, E-mail: saugust@lmu.edu. *Application contact:* Chake H. Kouyoumjian, Associate Dean of Graduate Admissions, 310-338-2721, Fax: 310-338-6086, E-mail: ckouyoum@lmu.edu.

Manhattan College, Graduate Division, School of Engineering, Program in Electrical Engineering, Riverdale, NY 10471. Offers MS. Part-time and evening/weekend programs available. *Faculty:* 8 full-time (1 woman). *Students:* 9 full-time (0 women), 10 part-time (1 woman); includes 5 Black or African American, non-Hispanic/Latino; 7 Hispanic/Latino, 2 international. Average age 24. 12 applicants, 75% accepted, 7 enrolled. In 2010, 6 master's awarded. *Degree requirements:* For master's, thesis or alternative. *Entrance requirements:* For master's, GRE (recommended), minimum GPA of 3.0. Additional exam requirements/recommendations for international students: Required—TOEFL (minimum score 550 paper-based; 213 computer-based; 80 iBT), IELTS (minimum score 6). *Application deadline:* For fall admission, 8/10 priority date for domestic students, 8/10 for international students; for spring admission, 1/7 for domestic and international students. Applications are processed on a rolling basis. Application fee: $50. *Financial support:* In 2010–11, 3 students received support, including 2 teaching assistantships with partial tuition reimbursements available (averaging $8,000 per year); fellowships with partial tuition reimbursements available, research assistantships with partial tuition reimbursements available, career-related internships or fieldwork, Federal Work-Study, scholarships/grants, and laboratory assistantships also available. Support available to part-time students. Financial award application deadline: 5/15. *Faculty research:* Multimedia tools, neural networks, robotic control systems, magnetic resonance imaging, telemedicine, computer-based instruction. *Unit head:* Dr. Robert Mauro, Chairperson, 718-862-7153, Fax: 718-862-7162, E-mail: robert.mauro@manhattan.edu. *Application contact:* Coralie Gale, Chairperson, 718-862-7153, Fax: 718-862-7162, E-mail: coralie.gale@manhattan.edu.

Marquette University, Graduate School, College of Engineering, Department of Electrical and Computer Engineering, Milwaukee, WI 53201-1881. Offers digital signal processing (Certificate); electric machines,drives, and controls (Certificate); electrical and computer engineering (MS, PhD); microwaves and antennas (Certificate); sensors and smart systems (Certificate). Part-time and evening/weekend programs available. *Faculty:* 14 full-time (2 women), 5 part-time/adjunct (0 women). *Students:* 24 full-time (4 women), 27 part-time (5 women); includes 4 minority (2

Black or African American, non-Hispanic/Latino; 2 Asian, non-Hispanic/Latino), 26 international. Average age 27. 68 applicants, 60% accepted, 14 enrolled. In 2010, 5 master's awarded. Terminal master's awarded for partial completion of doctoral program. *Degree requirements:* For master's, comprehensive exam (for some programs), thesis optional; for doctorate, thesis/dissertation, dissertation defense, qualifying exam. *Entrance requirements:* For master's, GRE General Test (recommended), official transcripts from all current and previous colleges/universities except Marquette, three letters of recommendation; for doctorate, GRE General Test, minimum GPA of 3.0, official transcripts from all current and previous colleges/universities except Marquette, three letters of recommendation, statement of purpose, submission of any English-language publications authored by applicant (strongly recommended). Additional exam requirements/recommendations for international students: Required—TOEFL (minimum score 530 paper-based; 78 computer-based). *Application deadline:* For fall admission, 7/15 priority date for domestic students; for spring admission, 11/15 for domestic students. Applications are processed on a rolling basis. Application fee: $50. Electronic applications accepted. *Expenses:* Tuition: Full-time $16,290; part-time $905 per credit hour. Tuition and fees vary according to program. *Financial support:* In 2010–11, 33 students received support, including 5 research assistantships with full tuition reimbursements available, 14 teaching assistantships with full tuition reimbursements available; fellowships with full tuition reimbursements available, Federal Work-Study, institutionally sponsored loans, and scholarships/grants also available. Support available to part-time students. Financial award application deadline: 2/15. *Faculty research:* Electric machines, drives, and controls; applied solid-state electronics; computers and signal processing; microwaves and antennas; solid state devices and acoustic wave sensors. Total annual research expenditures: $500,557. *Unit head:* Dr. Edwin E. Yaz, Chair, 414-288-6820, Fax: 414-288-5579, E-mail: edwin.yaz@marquette.edu. *Application contact:* Dr. Michael Johnson, Director of Graduate Studies, 414-288-0631, Fax: 414-288-5579, E-mail: michael.johnson@marquette.edu.

Massachusetts Institute of Technology, School of Engineering, Department of Electrical Engineering and Computer Science, Cambridge, MA 02139. Offers computer science (PhD, Sc D, ECS); computer science and engineering (PhD, Sc D); electrical engineering (PhD, Sc D, EE); electrical engineering and computer science (M Eng, SM, PhD, Sc D); SM/MBA. *Faculty:* 124 full-time (17 women), 1 part-time/adjunct (0 women). *Students:* 759 full-time (168 women), 4 part-time (1 woman); includes 165 minority (15 Black or African American, non-Hispanic/Latino; 3 American Indian or Alaska Native, non-Hispanic/Latino; 117 Asian, non-Hispanic/Latino; 27 Hispanic/Latino; 3 Two or more races, non-Hispanic/Latino), 341 international. Average age 26. 2,852 applicants, 11% accepted, 249 enrolled. In 2010, 199 master's, 103 doctorates, 4 other advanced degrees awarded. Terminal master's awarded for partial completion of doctoral program. *Degree requirements:* For master's and other advanced degree, thesis; for doctorate, comprehensive exam, thesis/dissertation. *Entrance requirements:* For master's, Leaders for Global Operations joint program requires GRE. Additional exam requirements/recommendations for international students: Required—TOEFL (minimum score 600 paper-based; 250 computer-based), IELTS (minimum score 7). *Application deadline:* For fall admission, 12/15 for domestic and international students. Application fee: $75. Electronic applications accepted. *Expenses:* Tuition: Full-time $38,940; part-time $605 per unit. Required fees: $272. *Financial support:* In 2010–11, 716 students received support, including 136 fellowships with tuition reimbursements available (averaging $28,627 per year), 470 research assistantships with tuition reimbursements available (averaging $29,178 per year), 116 teaching assistantships with tuition reimbursements available (averaging $30,108 per year); career-related internships or fieldwork, Federal Work-Study, institutionally sponsored loans, scholarships/grants, health care benefits, and unspecified assistantships also available. *Faculty research:* Artificial intelligence and applications; computer architecture, software, systems, and networks; communications, control, signal processing, and optimization; devices, electronics, electrodynamics, and photonics; bioelectrical engineering. Total annual research expenditures: $90.3 million. *Unit head:* Prof. Anantha P. Chandrakasan, Department Head, 617-253-4600, Fax: 617-258-7354. *Application contact:* Graduate Admissions, 617-253-4603, Fax: 617-258-7354, E-mail: grad-ap@eecs.mit.edu.

McGill University, Faculty of Graduate and Postdoctoral Studies, Faculty of Engineering, Department of Electrical and Computer Engineering, Montréal, QC H3A 2T5, Canada. Offers M Eng, PhD.

McMaster University, School of Graduate Studies, Faculty of Engineering, Department of Electrical and Computer Engineering, Hamilton, ON L8S 4M2, Canada. Offers electrical engineering (M Eng, MA Sc, PhD). *Degree requirements:* For master's, thesis; for doctorate, comprehensive exam, thesis/dissertation. *Entrance requirements:* Additional exam requirements/recommendations for international students: Required—TOEFL (minimum score 550 paper-based; 213 computer-based). *Faculty research:* Robust and blind adaptive filtering, topics in statistical signal processing, local and metropolitan area networks, smart antennas, embedded wireless communications.

McNeese State University, Doré School of Graduate Studies, College of Engineering and Engineering Technology, Lake Charles, LA 70609. Offers chemical engineering (M Eng); civil engineering (M Eng); electrical engineering (M Eng); engineering management (M Eng); mechanical engineering (M Eng). Part-time and evening/weekend programs available. *Faculty:* 15 full-time (1 woman). *Students:* 37 full-time (10 women), 18 part-time (1 woman); includes 5 minority (3 Black or African American, non-Hispanic/Latino; 1 American Indian or Alaska Native, non-Hispanic/Latino; 1 Two or more races, non-Hispanic/Latino), 43 international. In 2010, 28 master's awarded. *Degree requirements:* For master's, thesis or alternative. *Entrance requirements:* For master's, GRE, minimum undergraduate GPA of 3.0. Additional exam requirements/recommendations for international students: Required—TOEFL (minimum score 560 paper-based; 220 computer-based; 83 iBT). *Application deadline:* For fall admission, 5/15 priority date for domestic and international students; for spring admission, 10/15 priority date for domestic and international students. Applications are processed on a rolling basis. Application fee: $20 ($30 for international students). Tuition and fees vary according to course load. *Financial support:* Federal Work-Study available. Support available to part-time students. Financial award application deadline: 5/1. *Unit head:* Dr. Nikos Kiritsis, Dean, 337-475-5875, Fax: 337-475-5237, E-mail: nikosk@mcneese.edu.

Memorial University of Newfoundland, School of Graduate Studies, Faculty of Engineering and Applied Science, St. John's, NL A1C 5S7, Canada. Offers civil engineering (M Eng, PhD); electrical and computer engineering (M Eng, PhD); mechanical engineering (M Eng, PhD); ocean and naval architecture engineering (M Eng, PhD). Part-time programs available. *Degree requirements:* For master's, thesis; for doctorate, comprehensive exam, thesis/dissertation, oral thesis defense. *Entrance requirements:* For master's, 2nd class degree; for doctorate, master's degree in engineering. Electronic applications accepted. *Faculty research:* Engineering analysis, environmental and hydrotechnical studies, manufacturing and robotics, mechanics, structures and materials.

Mercer University, Graduate Studies, Macon Campus, School of Engineering, Macon, GA 31207-0003. Offers biomedical engineering (MSE); computer engineering (MSE); electrical engineering (MSE); engineering management (MSE); environmental engineering (MSE); environmental systems (MS); mechanical engineering (MSE); software engineering (MSE); software systems (MS); technical communications management (MS); technical management (MS). Part-time and evening/weekend programs available. Postbaccalaureate distance learning degree programs offered (no on-campus study). *Faculty:* 18 full-time (4 women), 1 part-time/adjunct (0 women). *Students:* 11 full-time (2 women), 100 part-time (22 women); includes 26 minority (13 Black or African American, non-Hispanic/Latino; 12 Asian, non-Hispanic/Latino; 1 Hispanic/Latino), 3 international. Average age 32. In 2010, 46 master's awarded. *Degree requirements:* For master's, thesis or alternative. *Entrance requirements:* For master's, minimum undergraduate GPA of 3.0. Additional exam requirements/recommendations for international students: Required—TOEFL. *Application deadline:* For fall admission, 7/1 for domestic students; for spring admission, 11/15 for domestic students. Applications are processed on a rolling basis. Application fee: $35 ($50 for international students). Electronic applications accepted. *Expenses:* Contact institution. *Financial support:* Federal Work-Study available. *Unit head:* Dr. Wade H. Shaw, Dean, 478-301-2459, Fax: 478-301-5593, E-mail: shaw_wh@mercer.edu. *Application contact:* Greg Lofton, Graduate Program Coordinator, 478-301-5480, Fax: 478-301-5434, E-mail: lofton_g@mercer.edu.

Michigan State University, The Graduate School, College of Engineering, Department of Electrical and Computer Engineering, East Lansing, MI 48824. Offers electrical engineering (MS, PhD). *Entrance requirements:* Additional exam requirements/recommendations for international students: Required—TOEFL. Electronic applications accepted.

Michigan Technological University, Graduate School, College of Engineering, Department of Electrical and Computer Engineering, Houghton, MI 49931. Offers electrical engineering (MS, PhD). Part-time programs available. Postbaccalaureate distance learning degree programs offered (minimal on-campus study). Terminal master's awarded for partial completion of doctoral program. *Degree requirements:* For master's, comprehensive exam, thesis (for some programs); for doctorate, comprehensive exam, thesis/dissertation. *Entrance requirements:* Additional exam requirements/recommendations for international students: Required—TOEFL (minimum score 550 paper-based; 213 computer-based). Electronic applications accepted. *Expenses:* Contact institution. *Faculty research:* Information systems (signal processing and communications), solid-state electronics, power and energy systems, computer engineering.

Minnesota State University Mankato, College of Graduate Studies, College of Science, Engineering and Technology, Department of Electrical and Computer Engineering and Technology, Mankato, MN 56001. Offers MSE. *Students:* 7 full-time (0 women), 25 part-time (5 women). *Degree requirements:* For master's, comprehensive exam, thesis. *Entrance requirements:* For master's, GRE General Test, minimum GPA of 3.0 during previous 2 years. Additional exam requirements/recommendations for international students: Required—TOEFL (minimum score 550 paper-based; 213 computer-based; 80 iBT). *Application deadline:* For fall admission, 7/1 priority date for domestic students; for spring admission, 11/1 for domestic students. Applications are processed on a rolling basis. Application fee: $40. Electronic applications accepted. *Financial support:* Research assistantships with full tuition reimbursements, teaching assistantships with full tuition reimbursements, unspecified assistantships available. Financial award application deadline: 3/15. *Unit head:* Dr. Vince Winstead, Graduate Coordinator, 507-389-5747. *Application contact:* 507-389-2321, E-mail: grad@mnsu.edu.

Mississippi State University, Bagley College of Engineering, Department of Electrical and Computer Engineering, Mississippi State, MS 39762. Offers computer engineering (MS, PhD); electrical engineering (MS, PhD). Part-time programs available. Postbaccalaureate distance learning degree programs offered (minimal on-campus study). *Faculty:* 23 full-time (1 woman). *Students:* 87 full-time (13 women), 38 part-time (6 women); includes 9 minority (2 Black or African American, non-Hispanic/Latino; 4 Asian, non-Hispanic/Latino; 2 Hispanic/Latino; 1 Two or more races, non-Hispanic/Latino), 77 international. Average age 28. 260 applicants, 28% accepted, 34 enrolled. In 2010, 18 master's, 9 doctorates awarded. Terminal master's awarded for partial completion of doctoral program. *Degree requirements:* For master's, comprehensive exam, thesis optional; for doctorate, comprehensive exam, thesis/dissertation, written exam. *Entrance requirements:* For master's, GRE General Test, minimum undergraduate GPA of 3.0; for doctorate, GRE, minimum graduate GPA of 3.5. Additional exam requirements/recommendations for international students: Required—TOEFL (minimum score 550 paper-based; 213 computer-based; 79 iBT); Recommended—IELTS (minimum score 6.5). *Application deadline:* For fall admission, 7/1 for domestic students, 5/1 for international students; for spring admission, 11/1 for domestic students, 9/1 for international students. Applications are processed on a rolling basis. Application fee: $40. Electronic applications accepted. *Expenses:* Tuition, state resident: full-time $2730.50; part-time $304 per credit hour. Tuition, nonresident: full-time $6901; part-time $767 per credit hour. *Financial support:* In 2010–11, 26 research assistantships with full tuition reimbursements (averaging $15,687 per year), 18 teaching assistantships with full tuition reimbursements (averaging $14,650 per year) were awarded; Federal Work-Study, institutionally sponsored loans, scholarships/grants, and unspecified assistantships also available. Financial award application deadline: 4/1; financial award applicants required to submit FAFSA. *Faculty research:* Digital computing, power, controls, communication systems, microelectronics. Total annual research expenditures: $20.6 million. *Unit head:* Dr. Nicholas H. Younan, Professor and Department Head, 662-325-3721, Fax: 662-325-2298, E-mail: ece-head@ece.msstate.edu. *Application contact:* Dr. James E. Fowler, Professor and Interim Graduate Program Director, 662-325-3640, Fax: 662-325-2298, E-mail: fowler@ece.msstate.edu.

Missouri University of Science and Technology, Graduate School, School of Engineering, Department of Electrical and Computer Engineering, Rolla, MO 65409. Offers computer engineering (MS, DE, PhD); electrical engineering (MS, DE, PhD). Part-time and evening/weekend programs available. Terminal master's awarded for partial completion of doctoral program. *Degree requirements:* For master's, thesis optional; for doctorate, comprehensive exam, thesis/dissertation, departmental qualifying exam. *Entrance requirements:* For master's, GRE General Test (minimum score 1100 verbal and quantitative, writing 4.5); for doctorate, GRE General Test (minimum score: verbal and quantitative 1100, writing 3.5). Additional exam requirements/recommendations for international students: Required—TOEFL. Electronic applications accepted. *Faculty research:* Power systems, computer/communication networks, intelligent control/robotics, robust control, nanotechnologies.

Montana State University, College of Graduate Studies, College of Engineering, Department of Electrical and Computer Engineering, Bozeman, MT 59717. Offers electrical engineering (MS); engineering (PhD), including electrical and computer engineering option. Part-time programs available. *Faculty:* 14 full-time (0 women), 1 part-time/adjunct (0 women). *Students:* 13 full-time (1 woman), 25 part-time (5 women); includes 1 minority (Hispanic/Latino), 7 international. Average age 26. 34 applicants, 24% accepted, 8 enrolled. In 2010, 17 master's awarded. *Degree requirements:* For master's, comprehensive exam, thesis (for some programs); for doctorate, comprehensive exam, thesis/dissertation. *Entrance requirements:* For master's, GRE, BS in electrical or computer engineering or related field; for doctorate, GRE, MS in electrical or computer engineering or related field. Additional exam requirements/recommendations for international students: Required—TOEFL (minimum score 550 paper-based; 213 computer-based). *Application deadline:* For fall admission, 7/15 priority date for domestic students, 5/15 priority date for international students; for spring admission, 12/1 priority date for domestic students, 10/1 priority date for international students. Applications are processed on a rolling basis. Application fee: $30. Electronic applications accepted. *Expenses:* Tuition, state resident: full-time $5553.90. Tuition, nonresident: full-time $14,646. Required fees: $1233. *Financial support:* In 2010–11, 29 students received support, including 3 fellowships with full tuition reimbursements available (averaging $25,272 per year), 19 research assistantships with full tuition reimbursements available (averaging $18,456 per year), 7 teaching assistantships with partial tuition reimbursements available (averaging $15,120 per year); scholarships/grants, traineeships, health care benefits, and unspecified assistantships also available. Support available to part-time students. Financial award application deadline: 3/1; financial award applicants required to submit FAFSA. *Faculty research:* Optics and optoelectonics, communications and signal processing, microfabrication, complex systems and control, energy systems. Total annual research expenditures: $2.3 million. *Unit head:* Dr. Robert Maher, Head, 406-994-2505, Fax: 406-994-5958, E-mail: rmaher@ece.montana.edu. *Application contact:* Dr. Carl A. Fox, Vice Provost for Graduate Education, 406-994-4145, Fax: 406-994-7433, E-mail: gradstudy@montana.edu.

Montana Tech of The University of Montana, Graduate School, Electrical Engineering Program, Butte, MT 59701-8997. Offers MS. Part-time programs available. *Faculty:* 5 full-time (0 women). *Students:* 6 full-time (2 women), 1 part-time (0 women), 1 international. 6 applicants, 17% accepted, 1 enrolled. In 2010, 2 master's awarded. *Degree requirements:* For master's, comprehensive exam (for some programs), thesis optional. *Entrance requirements:* For master's, minimum GPA of 3.0. Additional exam requirements/recommendations for international students: Required—TOEFL (minimum score 525 paper-based; 195 computer-based; 71 iBT). *Application deadline:* For fall admission, 4/1 priority date for domestic students, 3/1 priority date for

Electrical Engineering

Montana Tech of The University of Montana *(continued)*
international students; for spring admission, 10/1 priority date for domestic students, 7/1 priority date for international students. Applications are processed on a rolling basis. Application fee: $30. Electronic applications accepted. *Expenses:* Tuition, state resident: full-time $5084. Tuition, nonresident: full-time $15,104. *Financial support:* In 2010–11, 5 students received support, including 5 teaching assistantships with partial tuition reimbursements available (averaging $6,600 per year); research assistantships with full tuition reimbursements available, career-related internships or fieldwork, tuition waivers (full and partial), and unspecified assistantships also available. Financial award application deadline: 4/1. *Faculty research:* Energy grid modernization, battery diagnostics instrumentation, wind turbine research, improving energy efficiency. *Unit head:* Dr. Daniel Trudnowski, Professor, 406-496-4681, Fax: 406-496-4849, E-mail: dtrudnowski@mtech.edu. *Application contact:* Fred Sullivan, Administrator, Graduate School, 406-496-4304, Fax: 406-496-4710, E-mail: fsullivan@mtech.edu.

Morgan State University, School of Graduate Studies, Clarence M. Mitchell, Jr. School of Engineering, Baltimore, MD 21251. Offers civil engineering (M Eng, D Eng); electrical engineering (M Eng, D Eng); industrial engineering (M Eng, D Eng); transportation (MS). Part-time and evening/weekend programs available. *Degree requirements:* For master's, thesis, comprehensive exam or equivalent; for doctorate, thesis/dissertation, comprehensive exam or equivalent. *Entrance requirements:* For master's, GRE, minimum undergraduate GPA of 2.5; for doctorate, GRE, minimum GPA of 3.0. Additional exam requirements/recommendations for international students: Required—TOEFL (minimum score 550 paper-based; 213 computer-based).

Naval Postgraduate School, Graduate Programs, Department of Electrical and Computer Engineering, Monterey, CA 93943. Offers MS, PhD, Eng. Program only open to commissioned officers of the United States and friendly nations and selected United States federal civilian employees. *Accreditation:* ABET (one or more programs are accredited). Part-time programs available. Postbaccalaureate distance learning degree programs offered (minimal on-campus study). *Degree requirements:* For master's and Eng, thesis; for doctorate, one foreign language, thesis/dissertation.

Naval Postgraduate School, Graduate Programs, Program in Undersea Warfare, Monterey, CA 93943. Offers applied science (MS); electrical engineering (MS); engineering acoustics (MS); operations research (MS); physical oceanography (MS). Program only open to commissioned officers of the United States and friendly nations and selected United States federal civilian employees. Part-time programs available. *Degree requirements:* For master's, thesis.

New Jersey Institute of Technology, Office of Graduate Studies, Newark College of Engineering, Department of Electrical and Computer Engineering, Program in Electrical Engineering, Newark, NJ 07102. Offers MS, PhD. Part-time and evening/weekend programs available. *Students:* 168 full-time (35 women), 44 part-time (8 women); includes 7 Black or African American, non-Hispanic/Latino; 18 Asian, non-Hispanic/Latino; 5 Hispanic/Latino, 161 international. Average age 26. 687 applicants, 42% accepted, 78 enrolled. In 2010, 102 master's, 10 doctorates awarded. Terminal master's awarded for partial completion of doctoral program. *Degree requirements:* For master's, thesis optional; for doctorate, thesis/dissertation, residency. *Entrance requirements:* For master's, GRE General Test; for doctorate, GRE General Test, minimum graduate GPA of 3.5. Additional exam requirements/recommendations for international students: Required—TOEFL (minimum score 550 paper-based; 213 computer-based; 79 iBT). *Application deadline:* For fall admission, 6/5 priority date for domestic students, 4/1 for international students; for spring admission, 11/15 for domestic and international students. Applications are processed on a rolling basis. Application fee: $65. Electronic applications accepted. *Expenses:* Tuition, state resident: full-time $14,724; part-time $818 per credit. Tuition, nonresident: full-time $20,304; part-time $1128 per credit. Required fees: $2272; $209 per credit. $103 per semester. One-time fee: $312 full-time; $212 part-time. *Financial support:* Fellowships with full and partial tuition reimbursements, research assistantships with full and partial tuition reimbursements, teaching assistantships with full and partial tuition reimbursements, career-related internships or fieldwork, Federal Work-Study, institutionally sponsored loans, and unspecified assistantships available. Financial award application deadline: 3/15. *Unit head:* Dr. Leonid Tsybeskov, Interim Chair, 973-596-6594, E-mail: leonid.tsybeskov@njit.edu. *Application contact:* Kathryn Kelly, Director of Admissions, 973-596-3300, Fax: 973-596-3461, E-mail: admissions@njit.edu.

New Mexico Institute of Mining and Technology, Graduate Studies, Department of Electrical Engineering, Socorro, NM 87801. Offers MS. *Entrance requirements:* Additional exam requirements/recommendations for international students: Required—TOEFL (minimum score 540 paper-based; 207 computer-based). Electronic applications accepted.

New Mexico State University, Graduate School, College of Engineering, Klipsch School of Electrical and Computer Engineering, Las Cruces, NM 88003-8001. Offers MSEE, PhD. Part-time and evening/weekend programs available. Postbaccalaureate distance learning degree programs offered (no on-campus study). *Faculty:* 18 full-time (1 woman). *Students:* 109 full-time (18 women), 52 part-time (5 women); includes 28 minority (1 Black or African American, non-Hispanic/Latino; 1 American Indian or Alaska Native, non-Hispanic/Latino; 1 Asian, non-Hispanic/Latino; 25 Hispanic/Latino), 101 international. Average age 28. 222 applicants, 78% accepted, 47 enrolled. In 2010, 39 master's, 4 doctorates awarded. Terminal master's awarded for partial completion of doctoral program. *Degree requirements:* For master's, thesis (for some programs), final oral or written exam; for doctorate, comprehensive exam, thesis/dissertation. *Entrance requirements:* For master's, GRE, minimum GPA of 3.0; for doctorate, departmental qualifying exam, minimum GPA of 3.0. Additional exam requirements/recommendations for international students: Required—TOEFL. *Application deadline:* For fall admission, 3/1 priority date for domestic and international students; for spring admission, 8/1 priority date for domestic and international students. Applications are processed on a rolling basis. Application fee: $30 ($50 for international students). Electronic applications accepted. *Expenses:* Tuition, state resident: full-time $4536; part-time $242 per credit. Tuition, nonresident: full-time $15,816; part-time $712 per credit. Required fees: $636 per term. *Financial support:* In 2010–11, 42 research assistantships (averaging $6,312 per year), 36 teaching assistantships (averaging $5,291 per year) were awarded; fellowships, career-related internships or fieldwork, Federal Work-Study, health care benefits, and unspecified assistantships also available. Support available to part-time students. Financial award application deadline: 3/1. *Faculty research:* Image and digital signal processing, energy systems, wireless communication, analog VLSI design, electro-optics. *Unit head:* Dr. Vojin Oklobdzija, Head, 575-646-3115, Fax: 575-646-1435, E-mail: vojin@nmsu.edu. *Application contact:* Sue Kord, Records Technician I, 575-646-6440, Fax: 575-646-1435, E-mail: kkord@nmsu.edu.

New York Institute of Technology, Graduate Division, School of Engineering and Computing Sciences, Program in Electrical Engineering and Computer Engineering, Old Westbury, NY 11568-8000. Offers MS. Part-time and evening/weekend programs available. *Students:* 100 full-time (24 women), 61 part-time (9 women); includes 23 minority (7 Black or African American, non-Hispanic/Latino; 1 American Indian or Alaska Native, non-Hispanic/Latino; 15 Asian, non-Hispanic/Latino), 102 international. Average age 26. In 2010, 63 master's awarded. *Degree requirements:* For master's, project. *Entrance requirements:* For master's, GRE General Test (if QPA less than 2.85), BS in electrical engineering or related field, minimum QPA of 2.85. Additional exam requirements/recommendations for international students: Required—TOEFL (minimum score 550 paper-based; 213 computer-based). *Application deadline:* For fall admission, 7/1 priority date for domestic students; for spring admission, 12/1 priority date for domestic students. Applications are processed on a rolling basis. Application fee: $50. Electronic applications accepted. *Expenses:* Tuition: Part-time $835 per credit. *Financial support:* Fellowships, research assistantships with partial tuition reimbursements, institutionally sponsored loans, tuition waivers (full and partial), and unspecified assistantships available. Support available to part-time students. Financial award applicants required to submit FAFSA. *Faculty research:* Computer networks, control theory, light waves and optics, robotics, signal processing. *Unit head:* Dr. Ayat Jafari, Chair, 516-686-7569, Fax: 516-686-7439, E-mail: ajafari@nyit.edu.

Application contact: Dr. Jacquelyn Nealon, Vice President for Enrollment Services, 516-686-7925, Fax: 516-686-7597, E-mail: jnealon@nyit.edu.

Norfolk State University, School of Graduate Studies, School of Science and Technology, Program in Electronics Engineering, Norfolk, VA 23504. Offers MS.

North Carolina Agricultural and Technical State University, Graduate School, College of Engineering, Department of Electrical and Computer Engineering, Greensboro, NC 27411. Offers electrical engineering (MSEE, PhD), including communications and signal processing (MSEE), computer engineering (MSEE), electronic and optical materials and devices (MSEE), power systems and controls (MSEE). Part-time programs available. *Degree requirements:* For master's, project, thesis defense; for doctorate, thesis/dissertation. *Entrance requirements:* For master's, GRE General Test, GRE Subject Test, minimum GPA of 2.8; for doctorate, GRE General Test, minimum GPA of 3.0. *Faculty research:* Semiconductor compounds, VLSI design, image processing, optical systems and devices, fault-tolerant computing.

North Carolina Agricultural and Technical State University, Graduate School, School of Technology, Department of Electronics, Computer, and Information Technology, Greensboro, NC 27411. Offers electronics and computer technology (MSIT).

North Carolina State University, Graduate School, College of Engineering, Department of Electrical and Computer Engineering, Program in Electrical Engineering, Raleigh, NC 27695. Offers MS, PhD. *Degree requirements:* For master's, thesis (for some programs); for doctorate, thesis/dissertation. *Entrance requirements:* For master's and doctorate, GRE. Additional exam requirements/recommendations for international students: Required—TOEFL (minimum score 575 paper-based). Electronic applications accepted. *Faculty research:* Microwave devices, wireless communications, nanoelectronics and photonics, robotic and mechatronics, power electronics.

North Dakota State University, College of Graduate and Interdisciplinary Studies, College of Engineering and Architecture, Department of Electrical and Computer Engineering, Fargo, ND 58108. Offers MS, PhD. Part-time programs available. *Students:* 30 full-time (13 women), 14 part-time (3 women), 31 international. Average age 28. 97 applicants, 31% accepted, 11 enrolled. In 2010, 5 master's, 1 doctorate awarded. Terminal master's awarded for partial completion of doctoral program. *Degree requirements:* For master's, comprehensive exam, thesis; for doctorate, comprehensive exam, thesis/dissertation. *Entrance requirements:* Additional exam requirements/recommendations for international students: Required—TOEFL (minimum score 525 paper-based; 197 computer-based; 71 iBT). *Application deadline:* For fall admission, 3/1 priority date for domestic and international students. Application fee: $45 ($60 for international students). Electronic applications accepted. *Financial support:* In 2010–11, 30 students received support, including 2 fellowships with full tuition reimbursements available (averaging $25,000 per year), 6 research assistantships with full tuition reimbursements available (averaging $8,100 per year), 10 teaching assistantships with full tuition reimbursements available (averaging $8,100 per year); career-related internships or fieldwork, Federal Work-Study, institutionally sponsored loans, and tuition waivers (full) also available. Financial award application deadline: 3/1. *Faculty research:* Computers, power and control systems, microwaves, communications and signal processing, bioengineering. Total annual research expenditures: $599,000. *Unit head:* Dr. Jacob Glower, Chair, 701-231-7608, Fax: 701-231-8677, E-mail: jacob.glower@ndsu.edu. *Application contact:* Dr. Rajesh Kavasseri, Associate Professor, 701-231-7019, E-mail: rajesh.kavasseri@ndsu.edu.

Northeastern University, College of Engineering, Department of Electrical and Computer Engineering, Boston, MA 02115-5096. Offers computer engineering (PhD); electrical engineering (MS, PhD); engineering leadership (MS). *Faculty:* 45 full-time (6 women), 2 part-time/adjunct (both women). *Students:* 257 full-time (49 women), 98 part-time (6 women). 1,054 applicants, 47% accepted, 122 enrolled. In 2010, 83 master's, 13 doctorates awarded. *Degree requirements:* For master's, thesis optional; for doctorate, thesis/dissertation, departmental qualifying exam. *Entrance requirements:* For master's and doctorate, GRE General Test. Additional exam requirements/recommendations for international students: Required—TOEFL (minimum score 550 paper-based; 213 computer-based). *Application deadline:* For fall admission, 1/15 priority date for domestic and international students. Applications are processed on a rolling basis. Application fee: $50. Electronic applications accepted. *Financial support:* In 2010–11, 136 students received support, including 1 fellowship with full tuition reimbursement available, 102 research assistantships with full tuition reimbursements available (averaging $18,325 per year), 32 teaching assistantships with full tuition reimbursements available (averaging $18,325 per year); career-related internships or fieldwork, Federal Work-Study, scholarships/grants, tuition waivers (full), and unspecified assistantships also available. Support available to part-time students. Financial award application deadline: 1/15; financial award applicants required to submit FAFSA. *Faculty research:* Signal processing and sensor data fusion, plasma science, sensing and imaging, power electronics, computer engineering. *Unit head:* Dr. Ali Abur, Chairman, 617-373-4159, Fax: 617-373-8970. *Application contact:* Jeffery Hengel, Admissions Specialist, 617-373-2711, Fax: 617-373-2501, E-mail: grad-eng@coe.neu.edu.

Northern Arizona University, Graduate College, College of Engineering, Forestry and Natural Sciences, Programs in Engineering, Flagstaff, AZ 86011. Offers civil and environmental engineering (M Eng); civil engineering (MSE); computer science (MSE); electrical engineering (M Eng, MSE); engineering (M Eng, MSE); environmental engineering (M Eng, MSE); mechanical engineering (M Eng, MSE). Part-time programs available. Postbaccalaureate distance learning degree programs offered (no on-campus study). *Faculty:* 42 full-time (12 women). *Students:* 19 full-time (3 women), 15 part-time (2 women); includes 6 minority (2 American Indian or Alaska Native, non-Hispanic/Latino; 3 Hispanic/Latino; 1 Two or more races, non-Hispanic/Latino), 7 international. Average age 28. 21 applicants, 48% accepted, 4 enrolled. In 2010, 15 master's awarded. *Degree requirements:* For master's, thesis. *Entrance requirements:* For master's, GRE General Test. Additional exam requirements/recommendations for international students: Required—TOEFL (minimum score 550 paper-based; 213 computer-based; 80 iBT), IELTS (minimum score 7). *Application deadline:* For fall admission, 3/1 priority date for domestic and international students; for spring admission, 9/15 priority date for domestic and international students. Applications are processed on a rolling basis. Application fee: $65. Electronic applications accepted. *Financial support:* In 2010–11, 3 research assistantships with partial tuition reimbursements (averaging $14,541 per year), 12 teaching assistantships with partial tuition reimbursements (averaging $12,863 per year) were awarded; career-related internships or fieldwork, Federal Work-Study, scholarships/grants, health care benefits, and unspecified assistantships also available. Financial award applicants required to submit FAFSA. *Unit head:* Dr. Ernesto Penado, Chair, 928-523-9453, Fax: 928-523-2300, E-mail: ernesto.penado@nau.edu. *Application contact:* Natasha Kypfer, Program Coordinator, 928-523-1447, Fax: 928-523-2300, E-mail: egrmasters@nau.edu.

Northern Illinois University, Graduate School, College of Engineering and Engineering Technology, Department of Electrical Engineering, De Kalb, IL 60115-2854. Offers MS. Part-time and evening/weekend programs available. *Faculty:* 9 full-time (0 women). *Students:* 32 full-time (7 women), 38 part-time (12 women); includes 3 Asian, non-Hispanic/Latino, 59 international. Average age 24. 225 applicants, 33% accepted, 31 enrolled. In 2010, 18 master's awarded. *Degree requirements:* For master's, comprehensive exam, thesis optional. *Entrance requirements:* For master's, GRE General Test, minimum GPA of 2.75. Additional exam requirements/recommendations for international students: Required—TOEFL (minimum score 550 paper-based; 213 computer-based). *Application deadline:* For fall admission, 6/1 for domestic students, 5/1 for international students; for spring admission, 11/1 for domestic students, 10/1 for international students. Applications are processed on a rolling basis. Application fee: $30. Electronic applications accepted. *Expenses:* Tuition, state resident: full-time $7200; part-time $300 per credit hour. Tuition, nonresident: full-time $14,400; part-time $600 per credit hour. Required fees: $79 per credit hour. *Financial support:* In 2010–11, 2 research assistantships with full tuition reimbursements, 15 teaching assistantships with full tuition reimbursements were awarded; fellowships with full tuition reimbursements, career-related internships or fieldwork, Federal Work-Study, scholarships/grants, tuition waivers (full), and staff assistantships also available. Support available to part-time students. Financial award applicants required to submit FAFSA. *Faculty research:* Digital signal processing, optics, nano-electronic devices, physion electronics, VLSI. *Unit head:* Dr. Ibrahim Abdel-motaleb, Chair, 815-753-1290, Fax: 815-753-1289, E-mail: ibrahim@niu.edu. *Application contact:* Graduate School Office, 815-753-0395, E-mail: gradsch@niu.edu.

Northwestern Polytechnic University, School of Engineering, Fremont, CA 94539-7482. Offers computer science (MS); computer systems engineering (MS); electrical engineering (MS). Part-time and evening/weekend programs available. *Degree requirements:* For master's, thesis optional. *Entrance requirements:* For master's, minimum GPA of 3.0. Additional exam requirements/recommendations for international students: Required—TOEFL (minimum score 550 paper-based; 213 computer-based; 79 iBT). *Faculty research:* Computer networking, database design, Internet technology, software engineering, digital signal processing.

Northwestern University, McCormick School of Engineering and Applied Science, Department of Electrical Engineering and Computer Science, Evanston, IL 60208. Offers computer science (MS, PhD); electrical and computer engineering (MS, PhD); electronic materials (MS, PhD, Certificate); information technology (MS). MS and PhD admissions and degrees offered through The Graduate School. Part-time programs available. *Faculty:* 50 full-time (3 women). *Students:* 212 full-time (31 women), 18 part-time (2 women); includes 21 minority (15 Asian, non-Hispanic/Latino; 4 Hispanic/Latino; 2 Two or more races, non-Hispanic/Latino), 157 international. Average age 26. 588 applicants, 10% accepted, 30 enrolled. In 2010, 39 master's, 31 doctorates awarded. Terminal master's awarded for partial completion of doctoral program. *Degree requirements:* For master's, comprehensive exam (for some programs), thesis optional, Thesis or Project is optional; for doctorate, comprehensive exam (for some programs), thesis/dissertation. *Entrance requirements:* For master's and doctorate, General Exam of GRE. Additional exam requirements/recommendations for international students: Required—TOEFL (minimum score 577 paper-based, 233 computer-based, 90 iBT) or IELTS. *Application deadline:* For fall admission, 12/31 for domestic and international students. Application fee: $75. Electronic applications accepted. *Financial support:* Fellowships with full tuition reimbursements, research assistantships with full tuition reimbursements, teaching assistantships with full tuition reimbursements, career-related internships or fieldwork, institutionally sponsored loans, health care benefits, and unspecified assistantships available. Financial award application deadline: 1/15; financial award applicants required to submit FAFSA. *Faculty research:* Solid state and photonics; computing, algorithms, and applications; computer engineering and systems; cognitive systems; graphics and interactive media; signals and systems. Total annual research expenditures: $19.2 million. *Unit head:* Dr. Alan Sahakian, Chair, 847-491-7007, Fax: 847-491-4455, E-mail: sahakian@ece.northwestern.edu. *Application contact:* Dr. Thrasos Pappas, Admission Officer, 847-491-1243, Fax: 847-491-4455, E-mail: t-pappas@northwestern.edu.

Oakland University, Graduate Study and Lifelong Learning, School of Engineering and Computer Science, Department of Electrical and Systems Engineering, Program in Electrical and Computer Engineering, Rochester, MI 48309-4401. Offers MS. Part-time and evening/weekend programs available. *Entrance requirements:* For master's, minimum GPA of 3.0 for unconditional admission. Additional exam requirements/recommendations for international students: Required—TOEFL (minimum score 550 paper-based; 213 computer-based). Electronic applications accepted. *Expenses:* Contact institution.

OGI School of Science & Engineering at Oregon Health & Science University, Graduate Studies, Department of Computer Science and Electrical Engineering, Beaverton, OR 97006-8921. Offers computer science (PhD); computer science and engineering (MS, PhD); electrical engineering (MS, PhD). Part-time and evening/weekend programs available. Terminal master's awarded for partial completion of doctoral program. *Degree requirements:* For master's, thesis optional; for doctorate, comprehensive exam, oral defense of dissertation. *Entrance requirements:* For master's and doctorate, GRE General Test. Additional exam requirements/recommendations for international students: Required—TOEFL (minimum score 650 paper-based; 280 computer-based). Electronic applications accepted. *Faculty research:* Computer systems architecture, intelligent and interactive systems, programming models and systems, theory of computation.

The Ohio State University, Graduate School, College of Engineering, Department of Electrical and Computer Engineering, Columbus, OH 43210. Offers electrical engineering (MS, PhD). Part-time programs available. *Faculty:* 68. *Students:* 287 full-time (46 women), 75 part-time (17 women); includes 4 Black or African American, non-Hispanic/Latino; 11 Asian, non-Hispanic/Latino; 6 Hispanic/Latino; 1 Two or more races, non-Hispanic/Latino, 248 international. Average age 27. In 2010, 64 master's, 28 doctorates awarded. Terminal master's awarded for partial completion of doctoral program. *Degree requirements:* For master's, thesis optional; for doctorate, thesis/dissertation. *Entrance requirements:* Additional exam requirements/recommendations for international students: Required—TOEFL (minimum score 580 paper-based; 237 computer-based). *Application deadline:* For fall admission, 8/15 priority date for domestic students, 7/1 priority date for international students; for winter admission, 12/1 priority date for domestic students, 11/1 priority date for international students; for spring admission, 3/1 priority date for domestic students, 2/1 priority date for international students. Applications are processed on a rolling basis. Application fee: $40 ($50 for international students). Electronic applications accepted. *Expenses:* Tuition, state resident: full-time $10,605. Tuition, nonresident: full-time $26,535. Tuition and fees vary according to course load and program. *Financial support:* In 2010–11, 25 fellowships with full tuition reimbursements (averaging $18,000 per year), 100 research assistantships with full tuition reimbursements (averaging $18,000 per year), 30 teaching assistantships with full tuition reimbursements (averaging $15,000 per year) were awarded; career-related internships or fieldwork, Federal Work-Study, institutionally sponsored loans, scholarships/grants, traineeships, health care benefits, and unspecified assistantships also available. Support available to part-time students. Total annual research expenditures: $13 million. *Unit head:* Robert Lee, Chair, 614-292-2572, Fax: 614-292-7596, E-mail: lee.146@osu.edu. *Application contact:* 614-292-9444, Fax: 614-292-3895, E-mail: domestic.grad@osu.edu.

Ohio University, Graduate College, Russ College of Engineering and Technology, School of Electrical Engineering and Computer Science, Athens, OH 45701-2979. Offers computer science (MS); electrical engineering (MS); electrical engineering and computer science (PhD). *Students:* 88 full-time (19 women), 25 part-time (2 women); includes 3 minority (all Hispanic/Latino), 72 international. 121 applicants, 52% accepted, 18 enrolled. In 2010, 19 master's, 5 doctorates awarded. *Degree requirements:* For master's, comprehensive exam (for some programs), thesis; for doctorate, comprehensive exam, thesis/dissertation, qualifying exams. *Entrance requirements:* For master's, GRE, BSEE or BSCS, minimum GPA of 3.0; for doctorate, GRE, MSEE or MSCS, minimum GPA of 3.0. Additional exam requirements/recommendations for international students: Required—TOEFL (minimum score 550 paper-based; 80 iBT) or IELTS (minimum score 6.5). *Application deadline:* For fall admission, 2/1 priority date for domestic students, 1/1 priority date for international students; for winter admission, 6/1 priority date for domestic students, 5/1 priority date for international students; for spring admission, 8/15 priority date for domestic students, 7/15 priority date for international students. Applications are processed on a rolling basis. Application fee: $50 ($55 for international students). Electronic applications accepted. *Financial support:* In 2010–11, 54 research assistantships with full tuition reimbursements, 19 teaching assistantships with full tuition reimbursements were awarded; Federal Work-Study, institutionally sponsored loans, scholarships/grants, and unspecified assistantships also available. Financial award applicants required to submit FAFSA. *Faculty research:* Avionics, networking/communications, intelligent distribution, real-time computing, control systems, optical properties of semiconductors. *Unit head:* Dr. David Juedes, Chair, 740-593-1566, Fax: 740-593-0007, E-mail: juedes@ohio.edu. *Application contact:* Dr. David Matolak, Graduate Chair, 740-593-1241, Fax: 740-593-0007, E-mail: matolak@ohio.edu.

Oklahoma State University, College of Engineering, Architecture and Technology, School of Electrical and Computer Engineering, Stillwater, OK 74078. Offers MS, PhD. Postbaccalaureate distance learning degree programs offered. *Faculty:* 26 full-time (2 women). *Students:* 99 full-time (23 women), 107 part-time (20 women); includes 1 Black or African American, non-Hispanic/Latino; 2 American Indian or Alaska Native, non-Hispanic/Latino; 4 Asian, non-Hispanic/Latino; 3 Hispanic/Latino, 157 international. Average age 28. 393 applicants, 45% accepted, 48 enrolled. In 2010, 47 master's, 6 doctorates awarded. *Degree requirements:* For master's, thesis or alternative; for doctorate, comprehensive exam, thesis/dissertation. *Entrance requirements:* For master's and doctorate, GRE or GMAT. Additional exam requirements/recommendations for international students: Required—TOEFL (minimum score 550 paper-based; 79 iBT). *Application deadline:* For fall admission, 3/1 priority date for international students; for spring admission, 8/1 priority date for international students. Applications are processed on a rolling basis. Application fee: $40 ($75 for international students). Electronic applications accepted. *Expenses:* Tuition, state resident: full-time $3716; part-time $154.85 per credit hour. Tuition, nonresident: full-time $14,892; part-time $621 per credit hour. Required fees: $2044; $85.20 per credit hour. One-time fee: $50. Tuition and fees vary according to course load and campus/location. *Financial support:* In 2010–11, 70 research assistantships (averaging $12,214 per year), 30 teaching assistantships (averaging $8,654 per year) were awarded; career-related internships or fieldwork, Federal Work-Study, scholarships/grants, health care benefits, tuition waivers (partial), and unspecified assistantships also available. Support available to part-time students. Financial award application deadline: 3/1; financial award applicants required to submit FAFSA. *Unit head:* Dr. Keith Teague, Head, 405-744-5151, Fax: 405-744-9198. *Application contact:* Dr. Gordon Emslie, Dean, 405-744-6368, Fax: 405-744-0355, E-mail: grad-i@okstate.edu.

Old Dominion University, Frank Batten College of Engineering and Technology, Program in Electrical and Computer Engineering, Norfolk, VA 23529. Offers ME, MS, PhD. Part-time programs available. Postbaccalaureate distance learning degree programs offered (minimal on-campus study). *Faculty:* 21 full-time (1 woman), 2 part-time/adjunct (1 woman). *Students:* 93 full-time (14 women), 9 part-time (4 women); includes 65 minority (7 Black or African American, non-Hispanic/Latino; 58 Asian, non-Hispanic/Latino), 67 international. Average age 28. 107 applicants, 53% accepted, 14 enrolled. In 2010, 38 master's, 8 doctorates awarded. *Degree requirements:* For doctorate, thesis/dissertation, candidacy exam, diagnostic exam. *Entrance requirements:* For doctorate, GRE. Additional exam requirements/recommendations for international students: Required—TOEFL. *Application deadline:* For fall admission, 6/1 for domestic students, 4/15 for international students; for spring admission, 11/1 for domestic students, 10/1 for international students. Applications are processed on a rolling basis. Application fee: $40. Electronic applications accepted. *Expenses:* Tuition, state resident: full-time $8592; part-time $358 per credit. Tuition, nonresident: full-time $21,672; part-time $903 per credit. Required fees: $119 per semester. One-time fee: $50. *Financial support:* In 2010–11, 3 fellowships with full tuition reimbursements (averaging $15,000 per year), 38 research assistantships with full and partial tuition reimbursements (averaging $15,000 per year), 41 teaching assistantships with full and partial tuition reimbursements (averaging $15,000 per year) were awarded; career-related internships or fieldwork, Federal Work-Study, scholarships/grants, tuition waivers (partial), and unspecified assistantships also available. Support available to part-time students. Financial award application deadline: 2/15; financial award applicants required to submit FAFSA. *Faculty research:* Digital signal processing, control engineering, gaseous electronics, ultrafast (femtosecom) laser applications, interaction of fields with living organisms. Total annual research expenditures: $3 million. *Unit head:* Dr. Sach Albin, Graduate Program Director, 757-683-4967, Fax: 757-683-3220, E-mail: ecegpd@odu.edu. *Application contact:* Dr. Linda Vahala, Associate Dean, 757-683-3789, Fax: 757-683-4898, E-mail: lvahala@odu.edu.

Oregon Health & Science University, School of Medicine, Graduate Programs in Medicine, Department of Computer Science and Engineering, Portland, OR 97239-3098. Offers computer science and engineering (MS, PhD); electrical engineering (MS, PhD). Part-time programs available. *Faculty:* 8 full-time (2 women), 3 part-time/adjunct (1 woman). *Students:* 26 full-time (10 women); includes 1 Asian, non-Hispanic/Latino, 2 international. Average age 34. 26 applicants, 92% accepted, 4 enrolled. In 2010, 2 master's, 2 doctorates awarded. Terminal master's awarded for partial completion of doctoral program. *Degree requirements:* For master's, thesis (for some programs); for doctorate, comprehensive exam, thesis/dissertation. *Entrance requirements:* For master's, GRE General Test (minimum scores: 500 Verbal/600 Quantitative/4.5 Analytical); for doctorate, GRE General Test (minimum scores: 500 Verbal/600 Quantitative/4.5 Analytical) or MCAT (for some programs). Additional exam requirements/recommendations for international students: Required—TOEFL. *Application deadline:* For fall admission, 7/15 for domestic students, 5/15 for international students; for winter admission, 10/15 for domestic students, 9/15 for international students; for spring admission, 1/15 for domestic students, 12/15 for international students. Applications are processed on a rolling basis. Application fee: $65. Electronic applications accepted. *Financial support:* Health care benefits, tuition waivers (full), and full tuition and stipends available. *Unit head:* Peter Heeman, PhD, Program Director, 503-748-1635, E-mail: cseedept@csee.ogi.edu. *Application contact:* Pat Dickerson, Administrative Coordinator, 503-748-1635, E-mail: cseedept@csee.ogi.edu.

Oregon State University, Graduate School, College of Engineering, School of Electrical Engineering and Computer Science, Corvallis, OR 97331. Offers computer science (M Eng, MAIS, MS, PhD); electrical and computer engineering (M Eng, MS, PhD). *Degree requirements:* For doctorate, thesis/dissertation, qualifying exam, preliminary exam. *Entrance requirements:* For master's and doctorate, minimum GPA of 3.0 in last 90 hours of course work. Additional exam requirements/recommendations for international students: Required—TOEFL (minimum score 600 paper-based; 250 computer-based; 80 iBT). Electronic applications accepted. *Faculty research:* Optical materials and devices, data security and cryptography, analog and mixed-signal integrated circuit design, algorithms, computer graphics and vision.

Penn State University Park, Graduate School, College of Engineering, Department of Electrical Engineering, State College, University Park, PA 16802-1503. Offers MS, PhD.

Polytechnic Institute of NYU, Department of Electrical and Computer Engineering, Major in Electrical Engineering, Brooklyn, NY 11201-2990. Offers MS, PhD. Part-time and evening/weekend programs available. *Students:* 393 full-time (84 women), 167 part-time (22 women); includes 16 Black or African American, non-Hispanic/Latino; 41 Asian, non-Hispanic/Latino; 12 Hispanic/Latino, 412 international. Average age 26. 992 applicants, 51% accepted, 216 enrolled. In 2010, 165 master's, 10 doctorates awarded. *Degree requirements:* For master's, comprehensive exam (for some programs), thesis (for some programs); for doctorate, comprehensive exam, thesis/dissertation. *Entrance requirements:* For master's, BS in electrical engineering; for doctorate, qualifying exam, MS in electrical engineering. Additional exam requirements/recommendations for international students: Required—TOEFL (minimum score 550 paper-based; 213 computer-based; 80 iBT); Recommended—IELTS (minimum score 6.5). *Application deadline:* For fall admission, 7/31 priority date for domestic students, 4/30 priority date for international students; for spring admission, 12/31 priority date for domestic students, 11/30 priority date for international students. Applications are processed on a rolling basis. Application fee: $75. Electronic applications accepted. *Expenses:* Tuition: Full-time $21,492; part-time $1194 per credit. Required fees: $385 per semester. Tuition and fees vary according to course load. *Financial support:* Fellowships, research assistantships, teaching assistantships, institutionally sponsored loans, scholarships/grants, and unspecified assistantships available. Support available to part-time students. Financial award applicants required to submit FAFSA. *Unit head:* Dr. Jonathan Chao, Head, 718-860-3478, Fax: 718-260-3302, E-mail: chao@poly.edu. *Application contact:* JeanCarlo Bonilla, Director of Graduate Enrollment Management, 718-260-3182, Fax: 718-260-3624, E-mail: gradinfo@poly.edu.

Polytechnic Institute of NYU, Long Island Graduate Center, Graduate Programs, Department of Electrical and Computer Engineering, Major in Electrical Engineering, Melville, NY 11747. Offers MS. Part-time and evening/weekend programs available. *Students:* 6 full-time (1 woman), 44 part-time (3 women); includes 5 Black or African American, non-Hispanic/Latino; 4 Asian, non-Hispanic/Latino; 3 Hispanic/Latino, 5 international. Average age 32. 35 applicants, 54% accepted, 12 enrolled. In 2010, 18 master's awarded. *Degree requirements:* For master's, comprehensive exam, thesis. *Entrance requirements:* Additional exam requirements/

Electrical Engineering

Polytechnic Institute of NYU, Long Island Graduate Center (continued)
recommendations for international students: Required—TOEFL (minimum score 550 paper-based; 213 computer-based; 80 iBT); Recommended—IELTS (minimum score 6.5). *Application deadline:* For fall admission, 7/31 priority date for domestic students, 4/30 priority date for international students; for spring admission, 12/31 priority date for domestic students, 11/30 priority date for international students. Applications are processed on a rolling basis. Application fee: $75. Electronic applications accepted. *Expenses:* Tuition: Full-time $21,492; part-time $1194 per credit. Required fees: $385 per semester. Tuition and fees vary according to course load. *Financial support:* Institutionally sponsored loans, scholarships/grants, and unspecified assistantships available. Support available to part-time students. Financial award applicants required to submit FAFSA. *Unit head:* Dr. Jonathan Chao, Department Head, 718-260-3302, E-mail: chao@poly.edu. *Application contact:* JeanCarlo Bonilla, Director of Graduate Enrollment Management, 718-260-3182, Fax: 718-260-3624, E-mail: gradinfo@poly.edu.

Polytechnic Institute of NYU, Westchester Graduate Center, Graduate Programs, Department of Electrical and Computer Engineering, Major in Electrical Engineering, Hawthorne, NY 10532-1507. Offers MS. *Students:* 3 full-time (0 women), 22 part-time (4 women); includes 4 Black or African American, non-Hispanic/Latino; 1 Asian, non-Hispanic/Latino, 5 international. Average age 32. 9 applicants, 67% accepted, 4 enrolled. In 2010, 2 master's awarded. *Degree requirements:* For master's, comprehensive exam (for some programs), thesis (for some programs). *Entrance requirements:* Additional exam requirements/recommendations for international students: Required—TOEFL (minimum score 550 paper-based; 213 computer-based; 80 iBT); Recommended—IELTS (minimum score 6.5). *Application deadline:* For fall admission, 7/31 priority date for domestic students, 4/30 priority date for international students; for spring admission, 12/31 priority date for domestic students, 11/30 priority date for international students. Applications are processed on a rolling basis. Application fee: $75. Electronic applications accepted. *Expenses:* Tuition: Full-time $21,492; part-time $1194 per credit. Required fees: $385 per semester. Tuition and fees vary according to course load. *Financial support:* Institutionally sponsored loans, scholarships/grants, and unspecified assistantships available. Support available to part-time students. *Unit head:* Dr. Jonathan Chao, Department Head, 718-260-3302, E-mail: chao@poly.edu. *Application contact:* JeanCarlo Bonilla, Director of Graduate Enrollment Management, 718-260-3182, Fax: 718-260-3624, E-mail: gradinfo@poly.edu.

Polytechnic University of Puerto Rico, Graduate School, Hato Rey, PR 00919. Offers business administration (MBA), including computer information systems, general management, management of information systems, management of international enterprises; civil engineering (ME, MS); computer engineering (ME, MS); computer science (MCS, MS); electrical engineering (ME, MS); engineering management (MEM); environmental management (MEM); landscape architecture (M Land Arch); manufacturing competitiveness (MMC, MS); manufacturing engineering (ME, MS); mechanical engineering (M Mech E). Part-time and evening/weekend programs available. *Entrance requirements:* For master's, 3 letters of recommendation.

Portland State University, Graduate Studies, Maseeh College of Engineering and Computer Science, Department of Electrical and Computer Engineering, Portland, OR 97207-0751. Offers M Eng, MS, PhD. Part-time and evening/weekend programs available. *Faculty:* 18 full-time (3 women), 7 part-time/adjunct (2 women). *Students:* 93 full-time (21 women), 131 part-time (24 women); includes 31 minority (3 Black or African American, non-Hispanic/Latino; 22 Asian, non-Hispanic/Latino; 3 Hispanic/Latino; 2 Native Hawaiian or other Pacific Islander, non-Hispanic/Latino; 1 Two or more races, non-Hispanic/Latino), 130 international. Average age 29. 167 applicants, 65% accepted, 46 enrolled. In 2010, 48 master's, 3 doctorates awarded. *Degree requirements:* For master's, variable foreign language requirement, oral exam; for doctorate, one foreign language, comprehensive exam, thesis/dissertation, oral and written exams. *Entrance requirements:* For master's, minimum GPA of 3.0 in upper-division course work or 2.75 overall, BS in electrical or computer engineering or allied field; for doctorate, GRE General Test, GRE Subject Test, minimum GPA of 3.0 in upper-division course work, MS in electrical engineering or allied field. Additional exam requirements/recommendations for international students: Required—TOEFL (minimum score 550 paper-based; 213 computer-based). *Application deadline:* For fall admission, 4/1 for domestic students, 3/1 for international students; for winter admission, 9/1 for domestic and international students; for spring admission, 11/1 for domestic and international students. Applications are processed on a rolling basis. Application fee: $50. *Expenses:* Tuition, state resident: full-time $8505; part-time $315 per credit. Tuition, nonresident: full-time $13,284; part-time $492 per credit. Required fees: $1482; $21 per credit. $99 per term. One-time fee: $120. Part-time tuition and fees vary according to course load and program. *Financial support:* In 2010–11, 2 research assistantships with full tuition reimbursements (averaging $13,743 per year) were awarded; teaching assistantships with full tuition reimbursements, career-related internships or fieldwork, Federal Work-Study, scholarships/grants, and unspecified assistantships also available. Support available to part-time students. Financial award application deadline: 3/1; financial award applicants required to submit FAFSA. *Faculty research:* Optics and laser systems, design automation, VLSI design, computer systems, power electronics. Total annual research expenditures: $1.7 million. *Unit head:* Dr. James McNames, Chair, 503-725-5390, Fax: 503-725-3807, E-mail: mcnames@ece.pdx.edu. *Application contact:* Kelley Gardiner, Graduate Coordinator, 503-725-3002, Fax: 503-725-3807, E-mail: kelleyg@ece.pdx.edu.

Prairie View A&M University, College of Engineering, Prairie View, TX 77446-0519. Offers computer information systems (MSCIS); computer science (MSCS); electrical engineering (MSEE, PhDEE); engineering (MS Engr). Part-time and evening/weekend programs available. *Faculty:* 19 full-time (0 women). *Students:* 89 full-time (26 women), 34 part-time (5 women); includes 45 Black or African American, non-Hispanic/Latino; 1 American Indian or Alaska Native, non-Hispanic/Latino; 13 Asian, non-Hispanic/Latino; 3 Hispanic/Latino, 53 international. Average age 32. 50 applicants, 84% accepted, 33 enrolled. In 2010, 8 master's, 2 doctorates awarded. *Degree requirements:* For master's, thesis (for some programs); for doctorate, comprehensive exam, thesis/dissertation. *Entrance requirements:* For master's, GRE General Test, bachelor's degree in engineering from an ABET accredited institution; for doctorate, GRE. Additional exam requirements/recommendations for international students: Required—TOEFL (minimum score 550 paper-based). *Application deadline:* For fall admission, 7/1 priority date for domestic and international students; for spring admission, 11/1 priority date for domestic and international students. Application fee: $50. Electronic applications accepted. *Expenses:* Tuition, state resident: full-time $3586.14; part-time $119.06 per credit hour. Tuition, nonresident: part-time $511.23 per credit hour. *Financial support:* In 2010–11, 80 students received support, including 14 fellowships (averaging $1,050 per year), 16 research assistantships (averaging $16,150 per year), 13 teaching assistantships (averaging $14,000 per year); career-related internships or fieldwork, institutionally sponsored loans, scholarships/grants, health care benefits, tuition waivers (partial), and unspecified assistantships also available. Financial award application deadline: 3/1; financial award applicants required to submit FAFSA. *Faculty research:* Applied radiation research, thermal science, computational fluid dynamics, analog mixed signal, aerial space battlefield. Total annual research expenditures: $439,054. *Unit head:* Dr. Kendall T. Harris, Dean, 936-261-9956, Fax: 936-261-9869, E-mail: tharris@pvamu.edu. *Application contact:* Barbara A. Thompson, Administrative Assistant, 936-261-9896, Fax: 936-261-9869, E-mail: bathompson@pvamu.edu.

Princeton University, Graduate School, School of Engineering and Applied Science, Department of Electrical Engineering, Princeton, NJ 08544-1019. Offers M Eng, PhD. Terminal master's awarded for partial completion of doctoral program. *Degree requirements:* For doctorate, thesis/dissertation, general exam. *Entrance requirements:* For master's, GRE General Test, 3 letters of recommendation; for doctorate, GRE General Test, official transcript(s), 3 letters of recommendation, personal statement. Additional exam requirements/recommendations for international students: Required—TOEFL. Electronic applications accepted. *Faculty research:* Computer engineering, electronic materials and devices, information sciences and systems, optics and optical electronics.

Purdue University, College of Engineering, School of Electrical and Computer Engineering, West Lafayette, IN 47907-2035. Offers MS, MSE, MSECE, PhD. MS and PhD degree programs in biomedical engineering offered jointly with School of Mechanical Engineering and School of Chemical Engineering. Part-time programs available. Postbaccalaureate distance learning degree programs offered (no on-campus study). Terminal master's awarded for partial completion of doctoral program. *Entrance requirements:* For master's and doctorate, GRE General Test, minimum GPA of 3.25. Additional exam requirements/recommendations for international students: Required—TOEFL (minimum score 550 paper-based; 213 computer-based; 77 iBT). Electronic applications accepted. *Faculty research:* Automatic controls; biomedical imaging; computer engineering; communications, networking signal and image processing; fields and optics.

Purdue University Calumet, Graduate Studies Office, School of Engineering, Mathematics, and Science, Department of Engineering, Hammond, IN 46323-2094. Offers computer engineering (MSE); electrical engineering (MSE); engineering (MS); mechanical engineering (MSE). Evening/weekend programs available. *Entrance requirements:* Additional exam requirements/recommendations for international students: Required—TOEFL. Application fee: $30. *Expenses:* Tuition, state resident: full-time $6867. Tuition, nonresident: full-time $14,157. *Financial support:* Career-related internships or fieldwork available. Financial award application deadline: 3/1. *Unit head:* Dr. Kaliappan Gopalan, Head, 219-989-2685, E-mail: gopalan@purduecal.edu. *Application contact:* Janice Novosel, Engineering Graduate Program Secretary, 219-989-3106, E-mail: janice.novosel@purduecal.edu.

Queen's University at Kingston, School of Graduate Studies and Research, Faculty of Applied Science, Department of Electrical and Computer Engineering, Kingston, ON K7L 3N6, Canada. Offers M Eng, M Sc, M Sc Eng, PhD. Part-time programs available. *Degree requirements:* For master's, thesis optional; for doctorate, comprehensive exam, thesis/dissertation. *Entrance requirements:* Additional exam requirements/recommendations for international students: Required—TOEFL (minimum score 580 paper-based; 237 computer-based). *Faculty research:* Communications and signal processing systems, computer engineering systems.

Rensselaer at Hartford, Department of Engineering, Program in Electrical Engineering, Hartford, CT 06120-2991. Offers ME, MS. Part-time and evening/weekend programs available. *Degree requirements:* For master's, thesis optional. *Entrance requirements:* For master's, GRE. Additional exam requirements/recommendations for international students: Required—TOEFL (minimum score 600 paper-based; 250 computer-based; 100 iBT).

Rensselaer Polytechnic Institute, Graduate School, School of Engineering, Program in Electrical Engineering, Troy, NY 12180-3590. Offers M Eng, MS, PhD. Part-time programs available. *Faculty:* 40 full-time (5 women), 5 part-time/adjunct (2 women). *Students:* 96 full-time (20 women), 11 part-time (1 woman); includes 3 Asian, non-Hispanic/Latino; 4 Hispanic/Latino, 66 international. 697 applicants, 15% accepted, 29 enrolled. In 2010, 31 master's, 20 doctorates awarded. Terminal master's awarded for partial completion of doctoral program. *Degree requirements:* For master's, thesis (for some programs); for doctorate, thesis/dissertation. *Entrance requirements:* For master's, GRE; for doctorate, GRE, qualifying exam, candidacy exam. Additional exam requirements/recommendations for international students: Required—TOEFL (minimum score 570 paper-based; 89 iBT). *Application deadline:* For fall admission, 1/15 priority date for domestic and international students; for spring admission, 8/15 priority date for domestic and international students. Applications are processed on a rolling basis. Application fee: $75. Electronic applications accepted. *Expenses:* Tuition: Full-time $39,600; part-time $1650 per credit. Required fees: $1896. *Financial support:* In 2010–11, 5 fellowships (averaging $22,000 per year), 60 research assistantships (averaging $21,000 per year), 28 teaching assistantships (averaging $17,500 per year) were awarded; career-related internships or fieldwork, institutionally sponsored loans, and unspecified assistantships also available. Financial award application deadline: 1/15. *Faculty research:* Networking and multimedia via ATM, thermophotovoltaic devices, microelectronic interconnections, agile manufacturing, mobile robotics. Total annual research expenditures: $3.5 million. *Unit head:* Dr. Kim L. Boyer, Head, 518-276-2150, Fax: 518-276-6261, E-mail: kim@ecse.rpi.edu. *Application contact:* Ann Bruno, Manager of Student Services and Graduate Enrollment, 518-276-2554, Fax: 518-276-4403, E-mail: ann@ecse.rpi.edu.

Rice University, Graduate Programs, George R. Brown School of Engineering, Department of Electrical and Computer Engineering, Houston, TX 77251-1892. Offers bioengineering (MS, PhD); circuits, controls, and communication systems (MS, PhD); computer science and engineering (MS, PhD); electrical engineering (MEE); lasers, microwaves, and solid-state electronics (MS, PhD); MBA/MEE. Part-time programs available. *Degree requirements:* For master's, thesis (for some programs); for doctorate, thesis/dissertation. *Entrance requirements:* For master's and doctorate, GRE General Test, GRE Subject Test, minimum GPA of 3.0. Additional exam requirements/recommendations for international students: Required—TOEFL (minimum score 600 paper-based; 250 computer-based; 90 iBT). Electronic applications accepted. *Faculty research:* Physical electronics, systems, computer engineering, bioengineering.

Rochester Institute of Technology, Graduate Enrollment Services, Kate Gleason College of Engineering, Department of Electrical Engineering, Rochester, NY 14623-5603. Offers MSEE. Part-time programs available. *Students:* 94 full-time (10 women), 68 part-time (3 women); includes 1 Black or African American, non-Hispanic/Latino; 3 Asian, non-Hispanic/Latino; 1 Hispanic/Latino, 92 international. Average age 26. 339 applicants, 67% accepted, 64 enrolled. In 2010, 47 master's awarded. *Degree requirements:* For master's, thesis optional. *Entrance requirements:* For master's, GRE, minimum GPA of 3.0. Additional exam requirements/recommendations for international students: Required—TOEFL (minimum score 570 paper-based; 230 computer-based; 88 iBT) or IELTS (minimum score 6.5). *Application deadline:* For fall admission, 2/15 priority date for domestic and international students; for winter admission, 10/15 for domestic and international students. Applications are processed on a rolling basis. Application fee: $50. Electronic applications accepted. *Expenses:* Tuition: Full-time $33,234; part-time $924 per credit hour. Required fees: $219. *Financial support:* In 2010–11, 64 students received support; research assistantships with partial tuition reimbursements available, teaching assistantships with partial tuition reimbursements available, career-related internships or fieldwork, institutionally sponsored loans, scholarships/grants, and unspecified assistantships available. Support available to part-time students. Financial award applicants required to submit FAFSA. *Faculty research:* Integrated optics, control systems, digital signal processing, robotic vision. *Unit head:* Dr. Eli Saber, Graduate Program Director, 585-475-6927, Fax: 585-475-5845, E-mail: ee@rit.edu. *Application contact:* Diane Ellison, Assistant Vice President, Graduate Enrollment Services, 585-475-2229, Fax: 585-475-7164, E-mail: gradinfo@rit.edu.

Rochester Institute of Technology, Graduate Enrollment Services, Kate Gleason College of Engineering, Department of Microelectronic Engineering, Program in Microelectronic Engineering, Rochester, NY 14623-5603. Offers MS. Part-time programs available. *Students:* 13 full-time (1 woman), 4 part-time (2 women); includes 1 Hispanic/Latino, 10 international. Average age 26. 22 applicants, 68% accepted, 8 enrolled. In 2010, 12 master's awarded. *Degree requirements:* For master's, thesis. *Entrance requirements:* Additional exam requirements/recommendations for international students: Required—TOEFL (minimum score 570 paper-based; 230 computer-based; 88 iBT) or IELTS (minimum score 6.5). *Application deadline:* For fall admission, 2/15 priority date for domestic and international students; for winter admission, 10/15 for domestic and international students. Applications are processed on a rolling basis. Application fee: $50. Electronic applications accepted. *Expenses:* Tuition: Full-time $33,234; part-time $924 per credit hour. Required fees: $219. *Financial support:* In 2010–11, 16 students received support; research assistantships with partial tuition reimbursements available, teaching assistantships with partial tuition reimbursements available, career-related internships or fieldwork, institutionally sponsored loans, scholarships/grants, and unspecified assistantships available. Support available to part-time students. Financial award applicants required to submit FAFSA. *Faculty research:* Electromagnetics, MEMs and Microfludics. *Unit head:* Dr. Robert Pearson, Director, 585-475-2923, Fax: 585-475-5845, E-mail: eme@rit.edu. *Application contact:* Diane Ellison, Assistant Vice President, Graduate Enrollment Services, 585-475-2229, Fax: 585-475-7164, E-mail: gradinfo@rit.edu.

Rose-Hulman Institute of Technology, Faculty of Engineering and Applied Sciences, Department of Electrical and Computer Engineering, Terre Haute, IN 47803-3999. Offers electrical and computer engineering (M Eng); electrical engineering (MS). Part-time programs available. Postbaccalaureate distance learning degree programs offered (minimal on-campus study). *Faculty:* 18 full-time (4 women), 2 part-time/adjunct (1 woman). *Students:* 16 full-time (2 women), 2 part-time (1 woman); includes 1 minority (Asian, non-Hispanic/Latino), 9 international. Average age 24. 12 applicants, 83% accepted, 4 enrolled. In 2010, 9 master's awarded. *Degree requirements:* For master's, thesis (for some programs). *Entrance requirements:* For master's, GRE, minimum GPA of 3.0. Additional exam requirements/recommendations for international students: Required—TOEFL (minimum score 580 paper-based; 237 computer-based; 92 iBT). *Application deadline:* For fall admission, 2/1 priority date for domestic students. Applications are processed on a rolling basis. Application fee: $0. *Expenses:* Tuition: Full-time $35,595; part-time $1038 per credit hour. *Financial support:* In 2010–11, 17 students received support; fellowships with full and partial tuition reimbursements available, research assistantships with full and partial tuition reimbursements available, institutionally sponsored loans, scholarships/grants, and tuition waivers (full and partial) available. *Faculty research:* Wireless systems, VLSI design, aerial robotics, power system dynamics and control, image and speech processing. Total annual research expenditures: $18,508. *Unit head:* Dr. Robert Throne, Interim Chairman, 812-877-8414, Fax: 812-877-8895, E-mail: robert.d.throne@rose-hulman.edu. *Application contact:* Dr. Daniel J. Moore, Associate Dean of the Faculty, 812-877-8110, Fax: 812-877-8061, E-mail: daniel.j.moore@rose-hulman.edu.

Rowan University, Graduate School, College of Engineering, Department of Electrical Engineering, Glassboro, NJ 08028-1701. Offers MS. Part-time and evening/weekend programs available. *Faculty:* 8 full-time (2 women), 3 part-time/adjunct (0 women). *Students:* 6 full-time (0 women), 5 part-time (0 women); includes 1 Black or African American, non-Hispanic/Latino; 2 Asian, non-Hispanic/Latino; 1 Hispanic/Latino. Average age 25. 4 applicants, 100% accepted, 3 enrolled. In 2010, 5 master's awarded. *Degree requirements:* For master's, thesis. *Entrance requirements:* For master's, GRE General Test. Additional exam requirements/recommendations for international students: Required—TOEFL. *Application deadline:* Applications are processed on a rolling basis. Application fee: $65 ($200 for international students). Electronic applications accepted. *Expenses:* Tuition, area resident: Part-time $602 per semester hour. Tuition, nonresident: part-time $602 per semester hour. Required fees: $100 per semester hour. One-time fee: $10 part-time. *Financial support:* Research assistantships available. *Unit head:* Dr. Shreekanth Mandayam, Graduate Studies Coordinator, 856-256-5333, Fax: 856-256-5241, E-mail: shreek@rowan.edu. *Application contact:* Dr. Ralph Dusseau, Program Adviser, 856-256-5332.

Royal Military College of Canada, Division of Graduate Studies and Research, Engineering Division, Department of Electrical and Computer Engineering, Kingston, ON K7K 7B4, Canada. Offers computer engineering (M Eng, PhD); electrical engineering (M Eng, PhD); software engineering (M Eng, PhD). *Degree requirements:* For master's, thesis; for doctorate, comprehensive exam, thesis/dissertation. *Entrance requirements:* For master's, honours degree with second-class standing in the appropriate field; for doctorate, master's degree. Electronic applications accepted.

Rutgers, The State University of New Jersey, New Brunswick, Graduate School-New Brunswick, Department of Electrical and Computer Engineering, Piscataway, NJ 08854-8097. Offers communications and solid-state electronics (MS, PhD); computer engineering (MS, PhD); control systems (MS, PhD); digital signal processing (MS, PhD). Part-time programs available. Terminal master's awarded for partial completion of doctoral program. *Degree requirements:* For master's, thesis or alternative; for doctorate, thesis/dissertation. *Entrance requirements:* For master's and doctorate, GRE General Test. Additional exam requirements/recommendations for international students: Required—TOEFL. Electronic applications accepted. *Expenses:* Tuition, state resident: full-time $7200; part-time $600 per credit. Tuition, nonresident: full-time $11,124; part-time $927 per credit. *Faculty research:* Communication and information processing, wireless information networks, micro-vacuum devices, machine vision, VLSI design.

St. Cloud State University, School of Graduate Studies, College of Science and Engineering, Department of Electrical and Computer Engineering, St. Cloud, MN 56301-4498. Offers electrical engineering (MS). *Degree requirements:* For master's, thesis or alternative. *Entrance requirements:* For master's, GRE General Test, minimum GPA of 2.75. Additional exam requirements/recommendations for international students: Required—Michigan English Language Assessment Battery; Recommended—TOEFL (minimum score 550 paper-based; 213 computer-based), IELTS (minimum score 6.5). Electronic applications accepted.

St. Mary's University, Graduate School, Department of Engineering, Program in Electrical Engineering, San Antonio, TX 78228-8507. Offers electrical engineering (MS); electrical/computer engineering (MS). Part-time programs available. *Degree requirements:* For master's, comprehensive exam. *Entrance requirements:* For master's, GRE General Test. Additional exam requirements/recommendations for international students: Required—TOEFL (minimum score 550 paper-based; 213 computer-based; 80 iBT). Electronic applications accepted. *Faculty research:* Image processing, control, communication, artificial intelligence, robotics.

San Diego State University, Graduate and Research Affairs, College of Engineering, Department of Electrical and Computer Engineering, San Diego, CA 92182. Offers electrical engineering (MS). Evening/weekend programs available. *Entrance requirements:* For master's, GRE General Test. Additional exam requirements/recommendations for international students: Required—TOEFL. Electronic applications accepted. *Faculty research:* Ultra-high speed integral circuits and systems, naval command control and ocean surveillance, signal processing and analysis.

San Jose State University, Graduate Studies and Research, Charles W. Davidson College of Engineering, Department of Electrical Engineering, San Jose, CA 95192-0001. Offers MS. *Degree requirements:* For master's, thesis. *Entrance requirements:* For master's, GRE General Test. Electronic applications accepted.

Santa Clara University, School of Engineering, Program in Electrical Engineering, Santa Clara, CA 95053. Offers analog circuit design (Certificate); ASIC design and test (Certificate); digital signal processing (Certificate); electrical engineering (MS, PhD, Engineer); fundamentals of electrical engineering (Certificate); microwave and antennas (Certificate); renewable energy (Certificate). Part-time and evening/weekend programs available. *Students:* 54 full-time (14 women), 123 part-time (20 women); includes 62 minority (1 Black or African American, non-Hispanic/Latino; 55 Asian, non-Hispanic/Latino; 5 Hispanic/Latino; 1 Two or more races, non-Hispanic/Latino), 61 international. Average age 31. 161 applicants, 60% accepted, 49 enrolled. In 2010, 51 master's, 2 doctorates, 3 other advanced degrees awarded. *Degree requirements:* For master's, thesis (for some programs); for doctorate, thesis/dissertation; for other advanced degree, thesis. *Entrance requirements:* For master's, GRE (waiver may be available), transcript; for doctorate, GRE, master's degree or equivalent; for other advanced degree, master's degree, published paper. Additional exam requirements/recommendations for international students: Required—TOEFL (minimum score 550 paper-based; 213 computer-based; 79 iBT). *Application deadline:* For fall admission, 8/12 for domestic students, 7/15 for international students; for winter admission, 10/28 for domestic students, 9/23 for international students; for spring admission, 2/25 for domestic students, 1/21 for international students. Applications are processed on a rolling basis. Application fee: $60. Electronic applications accepted. *Expenses:* Contact institution. *Financial support:* Research assistantships, teaching assistantships available. Financial award application deadline: 3/2; financial award applicants required to submit FAFSA. *Faculty research:* Thermal and electrical nanoscale transport (TENT). Total annual research expenditures: $1.3 million. *Unit head:* Dr. Alex Zecevic, Associate Dean for Graduate Studies, 408-554-2394, E-mail: azecevic@scu.edu. *Application contact:* Stacey Tinker, Director of Enrollment Management, 408-554-4748, Fax: 408-554-4323, E-mail: stinker@scu.edu.

South Dakota School of Mines and Technology, Graduate Division, Program in Electrical Engineering, Rapid City, SD 57701-3995. Offers MS. Part-time programs available. *Degree requirements:* For master's, thesis. *Entrance requirements:* Additional exam requirements/recommendations for international students: Required—TOEFL, TWE. Electronic applications accepted. *Faculty research:* Semiconductors, systems, digital systems, computers, superconductivity.

South Dakota State University, Graduate School, College of Engineering, Department of Electrical Engineering and Computer Science, Brookings, SD 57007. Offers electrical engineering (PhD); engineering (MS). Part-time programs available. *Degree requirements:* For master's, thesis (for some programs), oral exam; for doctorate, comprehensive exam, thesis/dissertation, oral exam. *Entrance requirements:* For master's and doctorate, GRE. Additional exam requirements/recommendations for international students: Required—TOEFL (minimum score 575 paper-based). *Faculty research:* Image processing, communications, power systems, electronic materials and devices, nanotechnology, photovoltaics.

Southern Illinois University Carbondale, Graduate School, College of Engineering, Department of Electrical and Computer Engineering, Carbondale, IL 62901-4701. Offers MS, PhD. *Degree requirements:* For master's, comprehensive exam, thesis. *Entrance requirements:* For master's, minimum GPA of 2.7. Additional exam requirements/recommendations for international students: Required—TOEFL. *Faculty research:* Circuits and power systems, communications and signal processing, controls and systems, electromagnetics and optics, electronics instrumentation and bioengineering.

Southern Illinois University Carbondale, Graduate School, College of Engineering, Program in Engineering Science, Carbondale, IL 62901-4701. Offers electrical systems (PhD); fossil energy (PhD); mechanics (PhD). *Degree requirements:* For doctorate, thesis/dissertation. *Entrance requirements:* For doctorate, GRE General Test, minimum GPA of 3.5. Additional exam requirements/recommendations for international students: Required—TOEFL.

Southern Illinois University Edwardsville, Graduate School, School of Engineering, Department of Electrical and Computer Engineering, Edwardsville, IL 62026-0001. Offers electrical engineering (MS). Part-time and evening/weekend programs available. *Faculty:* 10 full-time (0 women). *Students:* 48 full-time (10 women), 44 part-time (7 women); includes 7 minority (2 Black or African American, non-Hispanic/Latino; 1 American Indian or Alaska Native, non-Hispanic/Latino; 4 Asian, non-Hispanic/Latino), 61 international. Average age 26. 170 applicants, 56% accepted. In 2010, 40 master's awarded. *Degree requirements:* For master's, thesis (for some programs), research paper, final exam. *Entrance requirements:* For master's, minimum undergraduate GPA of 2.75 in engineering, mathematics, and science courses. Additional exam requirements/recommendations for international students: Required—TOEFL (minimum score 550 paper-based; 213 computer-based; 79 iBT), IELTS (minimum score 6.5). *Application deadline:* For fall admission, 7/22 for domestic students, 6/1 for international students; for spring admission, 12/9 for domestic students, 10/1 for international students. Applications are processed on a rolling basis. Application fee: $30. Electronic applications accepted. *Expenses:* Tuition, state resident: full-time $6012; part-time $1503 per semester. Tuition, nonresident: full-time $15,030; part-time $3758 per semester. Required fees: $1711; $675 per semester. *Financial support:* In 2010–11, 1 fellowship with full tuition reimbursement (averaging $8,370 per year), 11 research assistantships with full tuition reimbursements (averaging $8,064 per year), 31 teaching assistantships with full tuition reimbursements (averaging $8,064 per year) were awarded; career-related internships or fieldwork, Federal Work-Study, institutionally sponsored loans, scholarships/grants, traineeships, and unspecified assistantships also available. Support available to part-time students. Financial award application deadline: 3/1; financial award applicants required to submit FAFSA. *Unit head:* Dr. Luis Youn, Chair, 618-650-2524, E-mail: lyoun@siue.edu. *Application contact:* Dr. Scott Umbaugh, Program Director, 618-650-2948, E-mail: sumbaug@siue.edu.

Southern Methodist University, Bobby B. Lyle School of Engineering, Department of Electrical Engineering, Dallas, TX 75275-0338. Offers electrical engineering (MSEE, PhD); telecommunications (MS). Part-time and evening/weekend programs available. Postbaccalaureate distance learning degree programs offered (no on-campus study). *Faculty:* 12 full-time (1 woman), 9 part-time/adjunct (0 women). *Students:* 83 full-time (9 women), 61 part-time (10 women); includes 5 Black or African American, non-Hispanic/Latino; 10 Asian, non-Hispanic/Latino; 5 Hispanic/Latino, 97 international. Average age 28. 270 applicants, 49% accepted, 46 enrolled. In 2010, 60 master's, 3 doctorates awarded. Terminal master's awarded for partial completion of doctoral program. *Degree requirements:* For master's, thesis optional; for doctorate, thesis/dissertation, oral and written qualifying exams, oral final exam. *Entrance requirements:* For master's, GRE General Test, minimum GPA of 3.0 in last 2 years; bachelor's degree in engineering, mathematics, or sciences; for doctorate, preliminary counseling exam, minimum GPA of 3.0, bachelor's degree in related field. Additional exam requirements/recommendations for international students: Required—TOEFL. *Application deadline:* For fall admission, 7/1 priority date for domestic students, 5/15 for international students; for spring admission, 11/15 for domestic students, 9/1 for international students. Applications are processed on a rolling basis. Application fee: $75. Electronic applications accepted. *Financial support:* In 2010–11, 38 students received support, including 22 research assistantships with full tuition reimbursements available (averaging $19,200 per year), 16 teaching assistantships with full tuition reimbursements available (averaging $14,400 per year); unspecified assistantships also available. Financial award application deadline: 5/15; financial award applicants required to submit FAFSA. *Faculty research:* Mobile communications, optical communications, digital signal processing, photonics. *Unit head:* Dr. Marc P. Christensen, Chair, 214-768-3113, Fax: 214-768-3573, E-mail: mpc@lyle.smu.edu. *Application contact:* Marc Valerin, Director of Graduate and Executive Admissions, 214-768-3042, Fax: 214-768-3778, E-mail: valerin@lyle.smu.edu.

Southern Polytechnic State University, School of Engineering Technology and Management, Department of Electrical and Computer Engineering Technology, Marietta, GA 30060-2896. Offers engineering technology/electrical (MS). Part-time and evening/weekend programs available. *Faculty:* 7 full-time (1 woman), 3 part-time/adjunct (0 women). *Students:* 18 full-time (3 women), 9 part-time (1 woman); includes 6 Black or African American, non-Hispanic/Latino; 4 Asian, non-Hispanic/Latino, 11 international. Average age 30. 17 applicants, 71% accepted, 6 enrolled. In 2010, 8 master's awarded. *Degree requirements:* For master's, thesis. *Entrance requirements:* For master's, GRE (minimum score 500 quantitative/verbal/analytical), minimum GPA of 2.75. Additional exam requirements/recommendations for international students: Required—TOEFL (minimum score 550 paper-based; 213 computer-based; 79 iBT), IELTS (minimum score 6.5). *Application deadline:* For fall admission, 7/1 priority date for domestic students, 5/1 priority date for international students; for spring admission, 11/1 priority date for domestic students, 9/1 priority date for international students. Applications are processed on a rolling basis. Application fee: $20. Electronic applications accepted. *Expenses:* Tuition, state resident: full-time $3690; part-time $205 per semester hour. Tuition, nonresident: full-time $13,428; part-time $746 per semester hour. Required fees: $598 per semester. *Financial support:* In 2010–11, 5 students received support, including 4 teaching assistantships with partial tuition reimbursements available (averaging $3,000 per year); career-related internships or fieldwork, scholarships/grants, and unspecified assistantships also available. Support available to part-time students. Financial award application deadline: 5/1; financial award applicants required to submit FAFSA. *Faculty research:* Analog and digital communications, computer networking, analog and low power electronics design, control systems and digital signal processing, instrumentation (medical and industrial), biomedical signal analysis, biomedical imaging. *Unit head:* Dr. Austin Asgill, Chair, 678-915-7796, Fax: 678-915-7285, E-mail: aasgill@spsu.edu. *Application contact:* Nikki Palamiotis, Director of Graduate Studies, 678-915-4276, Fax: 678-915-7292, E-mail: npalamio@spsu.edu.

Stanford University, School of Engineering, Department of Electrical Engineering, Stanford, CA 94305-9991. Offers MS, PhD, Eng. Terminal master's awarded for partial completion of doctoral program. *Degree requirements:* For doctorate, thesis/dissertation; for Eng, thesis.

Electrical Engineering

Stanford University (continued)

Entrance requirements: For master's, doctorate, and Eng, GRE General Test. Additional exam requirements/recommendations for international students: Required—TOEFL. Electronic applications accepted. *Expenses:* Tuition: Full-time $38,700; part-time $860 per unit. One-time fee: $200 full-time.

State University of New York at Binghamton, Graduate School, Thomas J. Watson School of Engineering and Applied Science, Department of Electrical and Computer Engineering, Binghamton, NY 13902-6000. Offers M Eng, MS, PhD. Part-time and evening/weekend programs available. *Faculty:* 15 full-time (3 women), 2 part-time/adjunct (0 women). *Students:* 71 full-time (8 women), 97 part-time (10 women); includes 2 Black or African American, non-Hispanic/Latino; 17 Asian, non-Hispanic/Latino; 2 Hispanic/Latino, 76 international. Average age 28. 210 applicants, 47% accepted, 46 enrolled. In 2010, 58 master's, 8 doctorates awarded. *Degree requirements:* For master's, thesis or alternative; for doctorate, thesis/dissertation. *Entrance requirements:* For master's and doctorate, GRE General Test, GRE Subject Test. Additional exam requirements/recommendations for international students: Required—TOEFL. *Application deadline:* For fall admission, 4/15 priority date for domestic students, 1/15 priority date for international students; for spring admission, 11/1 for domestic students, 10/1 priority date for international students. Applications are processed on a rolling basis. Application fee: $60. Electronic applications accepted. *Financial support:* In 2010–11, 48 students received support, including 1 fellowship with full tuition reimbursement available (averaging $16,500 per year), 26 research assistantships with full tuition reimbursements available (averaging $16,500 per year), 15 teaching assistantships with full tuition reimbursements available (averaging $16,500 per year); career-related internships or fieldwork, Federal Work-Study, institutionally sponsored loans, scholarships/grants, health care benefits, tuition waivers (full and partial), and unspecified assistantships also available. Financial award application deadline: 2/15; financial award applicants required to submit FAFSA. *Unit head:* Dr. Stephen Zahorian, Chairperson, 607-777-4846, E-mail: zahorian@binghamton.edu. *Application contact:* Catherine Smith, Recruiting and Admissions Coordinator, 607-777-2151, Fax: 607-777-2501, E-mail: cmsmith@binghamton.edu.

State University of New York at New Paltz, Graduate School, School of Science and Engineering, Department of Electrical and Computer Engineering, New Paltz, NY 12561. Offers electrical engineering (MS). Part-time and evening/weekend programs available. *Faculty:* 9 full-time (1 woman), 3 part-time/adjunct (0 women). *Students:* 59 full-time (10 women), 38 part-time (6 women); includes 3 Asian, non-Hispanic/Latino, 87 international. Average age 24. 102 applicants, 70% accepted, 25 enrolled. In 2010, 57 master's awarded. *Degree requirements:* For master's, comprehensive exam, thesis optional. *Entrance requirements:* For master's, GRE General Test, minimum GPA of 3.0. Additional exam requirements/recommendations for international students: Required—TOEFL (minimum score 550 paper-based; 213 computer-based; 80 iBT), IELTS (minimum score 6.5). *Application deadline:* For fall admission, 5/15 priority date for domestic and international students; for spring admission, 11/15 for domestic students, 11/15 priority date for international students. Applications are processed on a rolling basis. Application fee: $50. Electronic applications accepted. *Expenses:* Tuition, state resident: full-time $8370; part-time $349 per credit hour. Tuition, nonresident: full-time $13,780; part-time $574 per credit hour. Required fees: $1165; $33.80 per credit hour. $175 per term. Tuition and fees vary according to program. *Financial support:* In 2010–11, 11 students received support. Tuition waivers (partial) available. *Unit head:* Dr. Baback Izadi, Chair, 845-257-3823, E-mail: bai@eng.newpaltz.edu. *Application contact:* Prof. Damodaran Radhakrishnan, Graduate Coordinator, 845-257-3772, E-mail: damu@newpaltz.edu.

Stevens Institute of Technology, Graduate School, Charles V. Schaefer Jr. School of Engineering, Department of Electrical and Computer Engineering, Program in Electrical Engineering, Hoboken, NJ 07030. Offers computer architecture and digital systems (M Eng); electrical engineering (PhD); microelectronics and photonics science and technology (M Eng); signal processing for communications (M Eng); telecommunications systems engineering (M Eng); wireless communications (M Eng, Certificate). *Students:* 161 full-time (20 women), 54 part-time (4 women); includes 1 Black or African American, non-Hispanic/Latino; 28 Asian, non-Hispanic/Latino; 2 Hispanic/Latino, 140 international. Average age 26. 177 applicants, 80% accepted. *Degree requirements:* For master's, thesis optional; for doctorate, variable foreign language requirement, thesis/dissertation. *Entrance requirements:* For master's, doctorate, and Certificate, GRE. Additional exam requirements/recommendations for international students: Required—TOEFL. *Application deadline:* Applications are processed on a rolling basis. Application fee: $50. Electronic applications accepted. *Unit head:* Prof. Yu-Dong Yao, Head, 201-216-5264. *Application contact:* Graduate Admissions, 800-496-4935, Fax: 201-216-8044, E-mail: gradadmissions@stevens.edu.

Stevens Institute of Technology, Graduate School, Charles V. Schaefer Jr. School of Engineering, Department of Mechanical Engineering, Program in Integrated Product Development, Hoboken, NJ 07030. Offers armament engineering (M Eng); computer and electrical engineering (M Eng); manufacturing technologies (M Eng); systems reliability and design (M Eng). *Students:* 8 part-time (1 woman). Average age 26. *Unit head:* Dr. Constantin Chassapis, Director, 201-216-5564. *Application contact:* Graduate Admissions, 800-496-4935, Fax: 201-216-8044, E-mail: gradadmissions@stevens.edu.

Stevens Institute of Technology, Graduate School, Charles V. Schaefer Jr. School of Engineering, Interdisciplinary Program in Microelectronics and Photonics, Hoboken, NJ 07030. Offers Certificate. *Unit head:* Dr. George Korfiatis, Dean, 201-216-5263. *Application contact:* Graduate Admissions, 800-496-4935, Fax: 201-216-8044, E-mail: gradadmissions@stevens.edu.

Stony Brook University, State University of New York, Graduate School, College of Engineering and Applied Sciences, Department of Electrical and Computer Engineering, Program in Electrical Engineering, Stony Brook, NY 11794. Offers MS, PhD. *Students:* 106 full-time (24 women), 17 part-time (4 women); includes 7 Asian, non-Hispanic/Latino; 3 Hispanic/Latino, 103 international. In 2010, 37 master's, 11 doctorates awarded. Application fee: $100. *Expenses:* Tuition, state resident: full-time $8370; part-time $349 per credit. Tuition, nonresident: full-time $13,780; part-time $574 per credit. Required fees: $994. *Financial support:* In 2010–11, 23 research assistantships, 24 teaching assistantships were awarded. Total annual research expenditures: $5.4 million. *Unit head:* Dr. Serge Luryi, Chairman, 631-632-8420. *Application contact:* Prof. Yuanyuan Yang, Graduate Program Director, 631-632-8474, Fax: 631-632-8494, E-mail: yang@ece.sunysb.edu.

Syracuse University, L. C. Smith College of Engineering and Computer Science, Program in Electrical and Computer Engineering, Syracuse, NY 13244. Offers PhD. *Students:* 48 full-time (16 women), 6 part-time (0 women), 46 international. Average age 27. 130 applicants, 18% accepted, 15 enrolled. In 2010, 3 doctorates awarded. *Entrance requirements:* For doctorate, GRE General Test. Additional exam requirements/recommendations for international students: Required—TOEFL (minimum score 100 iBT). *Application deadline:* For fall admission, 7/1 priority date for domestic students, 6/1 priority date for international students. Application fee: $75. Electronic applications accepted. *Expenses:* Tuition: Part-time $1162 per credit. *Financial support:* Fellowships with full tuition reimbursements, research assistantships with full and partial tuition reimbursements, teaching assistantships with full and partial tuition reimbursements, tuition waivers (partial) available. Financial award application deadline: 1/1. *Unit head:* Prof. Chilukuri Mohan, Chair, 315-443-2583, E-mail: mohan@syr.edu. *Application contact:* Barbara Decker, Information Contact, 315-443-2368, Fax: 315-443-2583, E-mail: badecker@syr.edu.

Syracuse University, L. C. Smith College of Engineering and Computer Science, Program in Electrical Engineering, Syracuse, NY 13244. Offers MS, EE. Part-time programs available. *Students:* 80 full-time (18 women), 32 part-time (2 women); includes 6 minority (2 Black or African American, non-Hispanic/Latino; 3 Asian, non-Hispanic/Latino; 1 Hispanic/Latino), 79 international. Average age 25. 445 applicants, 48% accepted, 41 enrolled. In 2010, 57 master's awarded. *Entrance requirements:* For master's, GRE General Test. Additional exam requirements/recommendations for international students: Required—TOEFL (minimum score 100 iBT). *Application deadline:* For fall admission, 7/1 priority date for domestic students, 6/1 priority date for international students. Applications are processed on a rolling basis. Application fee: $75. Electronic applications accepted. *Expenses:* Tuition: Part-time $1162 per credit. *Financial support:* Fellowships with full tuition reimbursements, research assistantships with full and partial tuition reimbursements, teaching assistantships with full and partial tuition reimbursements, scholarships/grants and tuition waivers (partial) available. Financial award application deadline: 1/1. *Faculty research:* Electromagnetics, electronic devices, systems. *Unit head:* Dr. Qi Wang Song, Program Director, 315-443-4395, Fax: 315-443-2583, E-mail: qwsong@syr.edu. *Application contact:* Heather Paris, 315-443-2368, Fax: 315-443-2583, E-mail: hdparis@syr.edu.

Syracuse University, L. C. Smith College of Engineering and Computer Science, Program in Microwave Engineering, Syracuse, NY 13244. Offers CAS. Part-time programs available. *Students:* 1 full-time (0 women), 1 part-time (0 women), 1 international. Average age 45. *Degree requirements:* For CAS, thesis. *Entrance requirements:* For degree, GRE General Test. Additional exam requirements/recommendations for international students: Required—TOEFL (minimum score 100 iBT). *Application deadline:* For fall admission, 7/1 priority date for domestic students, 6/1 priority date for international students. Applications are processed on a rolling basis. Application fee: $75. Electronic applications accepted. *Expenses:* Tuition: Part-time $1162 per credit. *Faculty research:* Software engineering, parallel and high-performance computing, computer aided design and architectures, coding theory, neural networks. *Application contact:* Barbara Decker, Information Contact, 315-443-2655, Fax: 315-443-2583, E-mail: badecker@syr.edu.

Temple University, College of Engineering, Department of Electrical and Computer Engineering, Philadelphia, PA 19122-6096. Offers electrical engineering (MSE). Part-time and evening/weekend programs available. *Faculty:* 12 full-time (1 woman). *Students:* 25 full-time (3 women), 12 part-time (1 woman); includes 2 Asian, non-Hispanic/Latino, 25 international. 48 applicants, 40% accepted, 8 enrolled. In 2010, 27 master's awarded. *Degree requirements:* For master's, thesis optional. *Entrance requirements:* For master's, GRE General Test, minimum GPA of 3.0. Additional exam requirements/recommendations for international students: Required—TOEFL (minimum score 550 paper-based; 213 computer-based; 79 iBT). *Application deadline:* For fall admission, 7/1 for domestic students, 12/15 for international students; for spring admission, 11/1 for domestic students, 8/1 for international students. Applications are processed on a rolling basis. Application fee: $50. Electronic applications accepted. *Financial support:* In 2010–11, 1 fellowship with full tuition reimbursement, 1 research assistantship with full tuition reimbursement, 9 teaching assistantships with full tuition reimbursements were awarded; Federal Work-Study and institutionally sponsored loans also available. Financial award application deadline: 1/15; financial award applicants required to submit FAFSA. *Faculty research:* Computer engineering, intelligent control, microprocessors, digital processing, neutral networks. Total annual research expenditures: $425,000. *Unit head:* Dr. Joseph Picone, Chair, 215-204-7597, Fax: 215-204-5960, E-mail: picone@temple.edu. *Application contact:* Dr. Joseph Picone, Chair, 215-204-7597, Fax: 215-204-5960, E-mail: picone@temple.edu.

Tennessee Technological University, Graduate School, College of Engineering, Department of Electrical Engineering, Cookeville, TN 38505. Offers MS, PhD. Part-time programs available. *Faculty:* 19 full-time (0 women). *Students:* 27 full-time (5 women), 9 part-time (1 woman); includes 5 Black or African American, non-Hispanic/Latino; 20 Asian, non-Hispanic/Latino. Average age 27. 87 applicants, 62% accepted, 10 enrolled. In 2010, 17 master's awarded. *Degree requirements:* For master's, thesis. *Entrance requirements:* For master's, GRE. Additional exam requirements/recommendations for international students: Required—TOEFL (minimum score 550 paper-based; 79 iBT), IELTS (minimum score 5.5). *Application deadline:* For fall admission, 8/1 for domestic students, 5/1 for international students; for spring admission, 12/1 for domestic students, 10/1 for international students. Application fee: $25 ($30 for international students). Electronic applications accepted. *Expenses:* Tuition, state resident: full-time $7934; part-time $388 per credit hour. Tuition, nonresident: full-time $19,758; part-time $962 per credit hour. *Financial support:* In 2010–11, 1 fellowship (averaging $8,000 per year), 9 research assistantships (averaging $7,650 per year), 15 teaching assistantships (averaging $7,500 per year) were awarded; career-related internships or fieldwork also available. Financial award application deadline: 4/1. *Faculty research:* Control, digital, and power systems. *Unit head:* Dr. Stephen Parke, Chairperson, 931-372-3397, Fax: 931-372-3436. *Application contact:* Shelia K. Kendrick, Coordinator of Graduate Admissions, 931-372-3808, Fax: 931-372-3497, E-mail: skendrick@tntech.edu.

Texas A&M University, College of Engineering, Department of Electrical and Computer Engineering, College Station, TX 77843. Offers computer engineering (M Eng, MS, PhD); electrical engineering (MS, PhD). *Faculty:* 64. *Students:* 500 full-time (72 women), 45 part-time (8 women); includes 50 minority (9 Black or African American, non-Hispanic/Latino; 23 Asian, non-Hispanic/Latino; 18 Hispanic/Latino), 420 international. Average age 28. In 2010, 104 master's, 32 doctorates awarded. *Degree requirements:* For master's, thesis (MS); for doctorate, thesis/dissertation. *Entrance requirements:* For master's and doctorate, GRE General Test. Additional exam requirements/recommendations for international students: Required—TOEFL. Application fee: $50 ($75 for international students). *Financial support:* Fellowships, research assistantships, teaching assistantships, career-related internships or fieldwork available. Financial award application deadline: 4/1; financial award applicants required to submit FAFSA. *Faculty research:* Solid-state, electric power systems, and communications engineering. *Unit head:* Dr. Scott Miller, Head, 979-845-7441, E-mail: smiller@ece.tamu.edu. *Application contact:* Graduate Advisor, 979-845-7441.

Texas A&M University–Kingsville, College of Graduate Studies, College of Engineering, Department of Electrical Engineering and Computer Science, Program in Electrical Engineering, Kingsville, TX 78363. Offers ME, MS. *Degree requirements:* For master's, comprehensive exam, thesis or alternative. *Entrance requirements:* For master's, GRE General Test, minimum GPA of 3.0. Additional exam requirements/recommendations for international students: Required—TOEFL.

Texas Tech University, Graduate School, Edward E. Whitacre Jr. College of Engineering, Department of Electrical and Computer Engineering, Lubbock, TX 79409. Offers electrical engineering (MSEE, PhD). Part-time programs available. *Faculty:* 18 full-time (4 women), 2 part-time/adjunct (0 women). *Students:* 145 full-time (27 women), 47 part-time (8 women); includes 2 Black or African American, non-Hispanic/Latino; 2 Asian, non-Hispanic/Latino; 9 Hispanic/Latino; 1 Two or more races, non-Hispanic/Latino, 121 international. Average age 24. 603 applicants, 16% accepted, 45 enrolled. In 2010, 55 master's, 6 doctorates awarded. *Degree requirements:* For master's, thesis or alternative; for doctorate, thesis/dissertation. *Entrance requirements:* For master's and doctorate, GRE General Test, minimum GPA of 3.0, statement of purpose, 3 letters of recommendation, resume. Additional exam requirements/recommendations for international students: Required—TOEFL (minimum score 550 paper-based; 213 computer-based; 79 iBT). *Application deadline:* For fall admission, 6/1 priority date for domestic students, 1/15 priority date for international students; for spring admission, 9/1 priority date for domestic students, 6/15 priority date for international students. Applications are processed on a rolling basis. Application fee: $50 ($75 for international students). Electronic applications accepted. *Expenses:* Tuition, state resident: full-time $5495.76; part-time $228.99 per credit hour. Tuition, nonresident: full-time $12,936; part-time $538.99 per credit hour. Required fees: $2674; $36 per credit hour. $905 per semester. *Financial support:* In 2010–11, 109 students received support, including 45 research assistantships with partial tuition reimbursements available (averaging $2,727 per year), 4 teaching assistantships with partial tuition reimbursements available (averaging $3,291 per year). Financial award application deadline: 4/15; financial award applicants required to submit FAFSA. *Faculty research:* Computer vision in image processing, pulsed power, power electronics, nanotechnology, advanced vehicle engineering. Total annual research expenditures: $1.9 million. *Unit head:* Dr. Vittal Rao, Chair, 806-742-3533, Fax: 806-742-1245, E-mail: vittal.rao@ttu.edu. *Application contact:* Dr. Vittal Rao, Chair, 806-742-3533, Fax: 806-742-1245, E-mail: vittal.rao@ttu.edu.

Tufts University, Graduate School of Arts and Sciences, Graduate Certificate Programs, Microwave and Wireless Engineering Program, Medford, MA 02155. Offers Certificate. Part-time and evening/weekend programs available. Electronic applications accepted. *Expenses:* Tuition: Full-time $39,624; part-time $3962 per course. Required fees: $40 per year. Full-time tuition and fees vary according to degree level, program and student level. Part-time tuition and fees vary according to course load.

Tufts University, School of Engineering, Department of Electrical and Computer Engineering, Medford, MA 02155. Offers electrical engineering (MS, PhD). Part-time programs available. Terminal master's awarded for partial completion of doctoral program. *Degree requirements:* For master's, thesis or alternative; for doctorate, thesis/dissertation. *Entrance requirements:* For master's and doctorate, GRE General Test. Additional exam requirements/recommendations for international students: Required—TOEFL (minimum score 550 paper-based; 213 computer-based; 80 iBT). Electronic applications accepted. *Expenses:* Tuition: Full-time $39,624; part-time $3962 per course. Required fees: $40 per year. Full-time tuition and fees vary according to degree level, program and student level. Part-time tuition and fees vary according to course load.

Tuskegee University, Graduate Programs, College of Engineering, Architecture and Physical Sciences, Department of Electrical Engineering, Tuskegee, AL 36088. Offers MSEE. *Faculty:* 8 full-time (10 women). *Students:* 29 full-time (10 women), 7 part-time (2 women); includes 22 Black or African American, non-Hispanic/Latino, 12 international. Average age 26. In 2010, 7 master's awarded. *Degree requirements:* For master's, thesis or alternative. *Entrance requirements:* For master's, GRE General Test, GRE Subject Test. Additional exam requirements/recommendations for international students: Required—TOEFL (minimum score 500 paper-based; 69 computer-based). *Application deadline:* For fall admission, 7/15 for domestic students. Applications are processed on a rolling basis. Application fee: $25 ($35 for international students). *Expenses:* Tuition: Full-time $16,100; part-time $665 per credit hour. Required fees: $650. *Financial support:* Fellowships, research assistantships, teaching assistantships, career-related internships or fieldwork, Federal Work-Study, and institutionally sponsored loans available. Support available to part-time students. Financial award application deadline: 4/15. *Faculty research:* Photovoltaic insulation, automatic guidance and control, wind energy. *Unit head:* Dr. Sammie Giles, Director, 334-727-8298. *Application contact:* Dr. Robert L. Laney, Vice President/ Director of Admissions and Enrollment Management, 334-727-8580, Fax: 334-727-5750, E-mail: planey@tuskegee.edu.

Union Graduate College, School of Engineering and Computer Science, Schenectady, NY 12308-3107. Offers computer science (MS); electrical engineering (MS); engineering and management systems (MS); mechanical engineering (MS). Part-time and evening/weekend programs available. *Faculty:* 3 full-time (0 women), 9 part-time/adjunct (0 women). *Students:* 15 full-time (1 woman), 89 part-time (13 women); includes 1 Black or African American, non-Hispanic/Latino; 1 American Indian or Alaska Native, non-Hispanic/Latino; 7 Asian, non-Hispanic/Latino; 6 Hispanic/Latino, 2 international. Average age 27. 52 applicants, 79% accepted, 39 enrolled. In 2010, 24 master's awarded. *Degree requirements:* For master's, capstone course. *Entrance requirements:* For master's, minimum GPA of 3.0, letters of recommendation. Additional exam requirements/recommendations for international students: Required—TOEFL (minimum score 550 paper-based; 213 computer-based). *Application deadline:* Applications are processed on a rolling basis. Application fee: $60. Electronic applications accepted. *Expenses:* Contact institution. *Financial support:* Research assistantships, Federal Work-Study, scholarships/grants, health care benefits, and tuition waivers (full and partial) available. Support available to part-time students. Financial award applicants required to submit FAFSA. *Unit head:* Robert Kozik, Dean, 515-631-9881, Fax: 518-631-9902, E-mail: kozikr@union.edu. *Application contact:* Diane Trzaskos, Coordinator, Admissions, 518-631-9837, Fax: 518-631-9901, E-mail: trzaskod@uniongraduatecollege.edu.

Universidad de las Américas–Puebla, Division of Graduate Studies, School of Engineering, Program in Electronic Engineering, Puebla, Mexico. Offers MS. Part-time and evening/ weekend programs available. *Faculty research:* Telecommunications, data processing, digital systems.

Université de Moncton, Faculty of Engineering, Program in Electrical Engineering, Moncton, NB E1A 3E9, Canada. Offers M Sc A. *Degree requirements:* For master's, thesis, proficiency in French. *Faculty research:* Telecommunications, electronics and instrumentation, analog and digital electronics, electronic control of machines, energy systems, electronic design.

Université de Sherbrooke, Faculty of Engineering, Department of Electrical Engineering and Computer Engineering, Sherbrooke, QC J1K 2R1, Canada. Offers electrical engineering (M Sc A, PhD). *Degree requirements:* For master's, one foreign language, thesis; for doctorate, comprehensive exam, thesis/dissertation. *Entrance requirements:* For master's, bachelor's degree in engineering or equivalent. Electronic applications accepted. *Faculty research:* Minielectronics, biomedical engineering, digital signal prolonging and telecommunications, software engineering and artificial intelligence.

Université du Québec à Trois-Rivières, Graduate Programs, Program in Electrical Engineering, Trois-Rivières, QC G9A 5H7, Canada. Offers M Sc A, PhD. Part-time programs available. *Degree requirements:* For master's, thesis; for doctorate, thesis/dissertation. *Entrance requirements:* For master's, appropriate bachelor's degree, proficiency in French; for doctorate, appropriate master's degree, proficiency in French. *Faculty research:* Industrial electronics.

Université Laval, Faculty of Sciences and Engineering, Department of Electrical and Computer Engineering, Programs in Electrical Engineering, Québec, QC G1K 7P4, Canada. Offers M Sc, PhD. Terminal master's awarded for partial completion of doctoral program. *Degree requirements:* For master's, thesis (for some programs); for doctorate, thesis/dissertation. *Entrance requirements:* For master's and doctorate, knowledge of French and English. Electronic applications accepted.

University at Buffalo, the State University of New York, Graduate School, School of Engineering and Applied Sciences, Department of Electrical Engineering, Buffalo, NY 14260. Offers ME, MS, PhD. Part-time programs available. *Faculty:* 26 full-time (5 women), 4 part-time/adjunct (0 women). *Students:* 212 full-time (50 women), 20 part-time (1 woman); includes 5 Black or African American, non-Hispanic/Latino; 4 Asian, non-Hispanic/Latino; 1 Hispanic/ Latino, 192 international. Average age 26. 1,075 applicants, 18% accepted, 52 enrolled. In 2010, 67 master's, 5 doctorates awarded. Terminal master's awarded for partial completion of doctoral program. *Degree requirements:* For master's, comprehensive exam (for some programs), thesis or exam; for doctorate, comprehensive exam, thesis/dissertation. *Entrance requirements:* For master's and doctorate, GRE General Test. Additional exam requirements/ recommendations for international students: Required—TOEFL (minimum score 550 paper-based; 213 computer-based; 79 iBT). *Application deadline:* For fall admission, 12/31 for domestic and international students; for spring admission, 8/31 for domestic and international students. Applications are processed on a rolling basis. Application fee: $50. Electronic applications accepted. *Financial support:* In 2010–11, 82 students received support, including 4 fellowships with full tuition reimbursements available (averaging $28,900 per year), 36 research assistantships with full tuition reimbursements available (averaging $24,000 per year), 36 teaching assistantships with full tuition reimbursements available (averaging $20,900 per year); career-related internships or fieldwork, Federal Work-Study, institutionally sponsored loans, tuition waivers (full and partial), and unspecified assistantships also available. Financial award application deadline: 2/1; financial award applicants required to submit FAFSA. *Faculty research:* High power electronics and plasmas, electronic materials signal and image processing, photonics and communications, optics, nanoelectronics. Total annual research expenditures: $3.9 million. *Unit head:* Dr. Stella N. Batalama, Chairman, 716-645-3115, Fax: 716-645-3656, E-mail: batalama@buffalo.edu. *Application contact:* Dr. Wayne A. Anderson, Director of Graduate Admissions, 716-645-1031, Fax: 716-645-3656, E-mail: eegradapply@buffalo.edu.

The University of Akron, Graduate School, College of Engineering, Department of Electrical and Computer Engineering, Akron, OH 44325. Offers MS, PhD. Evening/weekend programs available. *Faculty:* 17 full-time (1 woman), 2 part-time/adjunct (0 women). *Students:* 69 full-time (15 women), 16 part-time (1 woman); includes 1 Asian, non-Hispanic/Latino; 1 Native Hawaiian or other Pacific Islander, non-Hispanic/Latino, 65 international. Average age 26. 151 applicants, 42% accepted, 28 enrolled. In 2010, 11 master's, 5 doctorates awarded. *Degree requirements:* For master's, thesis optional, oral comprehensive exam or thesis; for doctorate, one foreign language, thesis/dissertation, candidacy exam, qualifying exam. *Entrance requirements:* For master's, GRE, minimum GPA of 2.75, three letters of recommendation, statement of purpose; for doctorate, GRE, minimum GPA of 3.0 with bachelor's degree, 3.5 with master's degree; three letters of recommendation; statement of purpose. Additional exam requirements/ recommendations for international students: Required—TOEFL (minimum score 550 paper-based; 213 computer-based; 79 iBT). *Application deadline:* Applications are processed on a rolling basis. Application fee: $30 ($40 for international students). Electronic applications accepted. *Expenses:* Tuition, state resident: full-time $6800; part-time $378 per credit hour. Tuition, nonresident: full-time $11,644; part-time $647 per credit hour. Required fees: $1265. One-time fee: $30 full-time. *Financial support:* In 2010–11, 19 research assistantships with full tuition reimbursements, 14 teaching assistantships with full tuition reimbursements were awarded; career-related internships or fieldwork also available. *Faculty research:* Computational electromagnetics and nondestructive testing, control systems, sensors and actuators applications and networks, alternative energy systems and hybrid vehicles, analog IC design embedded systems. Total annual research expenditures: $308,566. *Unit head:* Dr. Jose De Abreu-Garcia, Chair, 330-972-6709, E-mail: jdeabreu-garcia@uakron.edu. *Application contact:* Dr. Jose De Abreu-Garcia, Chair, 330-972-6709, E-mail: jdeabreu-garcia@uakron.edu.

The University of Alabama, Graduate School, College of Engineering, Department of Electrical and Computer Engineering, Tuscaloosa, AL 35487-0286. Offers electrical engineering (MS, PhD). Part-time programs available. Postbaccalaureate distance learning degree programs offered (minimal on-campus study). *Faculty:* 16 full-time (4 women). *Students:* 34 full-time (5 women), 15 part-time (4 women); includes 3 minority (1 Black or African American, non-Hispanic/ Latino; 1 Asian, non-Hispanic/Latino; 1 Hispanic/Latino), 28 international. Average age 27. 84 applicants, 50% accepted, 13 enrolled. In 2010, 11 master's, 2 doctorates awarded. *Degree requirements:* For master's, thesis or alternative; for doctorate, one foreign language, comprehensive exam, thesis/dissertation. *Entrance requirements:* For master's, GRE (for students from non ABET accredited schools), minimum GPA of 3.0 in last 60 hours of course work or overall; for doctorate, GRE (for students from non ABET-accredited schools), minimum GPA of 3.0 overall. Additional exam requirements/recommendations for international students: Required—TOEFL (minimum score 550 paper-based; 213 computer-based). *Application deadline:* For fall admission, 7/1 priority date for domestic students, 1/15 priority date for international students; for spring admission, 11/1 priority date for domestic students, 6/1 priority date for international students. Applications are processed on a rolling basis. Application fee: $50 ($60 for international students). Electronic applications accepted. *Expenses:* Tuition, state resident: full-time $7900. Tuition, nonresident: full-time $20,500. *Financial support:* In 2010–11, 1 fellowship with full tuition reimbursement (averaging $15,000 per year), 14 research assistantships with full tuition reimbursements (averaging $14,000 per year), 6 teaching assistantships with full tuition reimbursements (averaging $11,025 per year) were awarded; health care benefits and unspecified assistantships also available. *Faculty research:* Devices and materials, electromechanical systems, embedded systems. Total annual research expenditures: $1.3 million. *Unit head:* Dr. D. Jeff Jackson, Department Head, 205-348-2919, Fax: 205-348-6959, E-mail: jjackson@eng.ua.edu. *Application contact:* Dr. Tim Haskew, Graduate Program Director, 205-348-1766, Fax: 205-348-6959, E-mail: thaskew@eng.ua.edu.

The University of Alabama at Birmingham, School of Engineering, Program in Electrical Engineering, Birmingham, AL 35294. Offers MSEE. *Students:* 6 full-time (2 women), 27 part-time (3 women); includes 14 minority (3 Black or African American, non-Hispanic/Latino; 8 Asian, non-Hispanic/Latino; 2 Hispanic/Latino; 1 Two or more races, non-Hispanic/Latino), 5 international. Average age 31. 25 applicants, 60% accepted, 8 enrolled. In 2010, 15 master's awarded. *Expenses:* Tuition, state resident: full-time $5482. Tuition, nonresident: full-time $12,430. Tuition and fees vary according to program. *Unit head:* Dr. Yehia Massoud, Chair, 205-934-8440, Fax: 205-975-3337. *Application contact:* Julie Bryant, Director of Graduate Admissions, 205-934-8227, Fax: 205-934-8413, E-mail: jbryant@uab.edu.

The University of Alabama in Huntsville, School of Graduate Studies, College of Engineering, Department of Electrical and Computer Engineering, Huntsville, AL 35899. Offers computer engineering (MSE, PhD); electrical engineering (MSE, PhD); optical science and engineering (PhD); optics and photonics (MSE); software engineering (MSSE). Part-time and evening/ weekend programs available. *Faculty:* 25 full-time (3 women), 4 part-time/adjunct (0 women). *Students:* 47 full-time (10 women), 145 part-time (21 women); includes 20 minority (7 Black or African American, non-Hispanic/Latino; 1 American Indian or Alaska Native, non-Hispanic/ Latino; 9 Asian, non-Hispanic/Latino; 2 Hispanic/Latino; 1 Two or more races, non-Hispanic/ Latino), 32 international. Average age 32. 190 applicants, 56% accepted, 57 enrolled. In 2010, 58 master's, 6 doctorates awarded. *Degree requirements:* For master's, comprehensive exam, thesis or alternative, oral and written exams; for doctorate, comprehensive exam, thesis/ dissertation, oral and written exams. *Entrance requirements:* For master's, GRE General Test, appropriate bachelor's degree, minimum GPA of 3.0; for doctorate, GRE General Test, minimum GPA of 3.0. Additional exam requirements/recommendations for international students: Required—TOEFL (minimum score 500 paper-based; 173 computer-based; 62 iBT). *Application deadline:* For fall admission, 7/15 for domestic students, 4/1 for international students; for spring admission, 11/30 for domestic students, 9/1 for international students. Applications are processed on a rolling basis. Application fee: $40 ($50 for international students). Electronic applications accepted. *Expenses:* Tuition, state resident: full-time $7250; part-time $407.75 per credit hour. Tuition, nonresident: full-time $17,358; part-time $970.05 per credit hour. Required fees: $246.80 per semester. Tuition and fees vary according to course load and program. *Financial support:* In 2010–11, 42 students received support, including 16 research assistantships with full and partial tuition reimbursements available (averaging $10,649 per year), 21 teaching assistantships with full and partial tuition reimbursements available (averaging $10,593 per year); career-related internships or fieldwork, Federal Work-Study, institutionally sponsored loans, scholarships/grants, health care benefits, tuition waivers, and unspecified assistantships also available. Support available to part-time students. Financial award application deadline: 4/1; financial award applicants required to submit FAFSA. *Faculty research:* Optical signal processing, electromagnetics, photonics, nonlinear waves, computer architecture. Total annual research expenditures: $13.5 million. *Unit head:* Dr. Robert Lindquist, Chair, 256-824-6316, Fax: 256-824-6803, E-mail: lindquis@ece.uah.edu. *Application contact:* Kathy Biggs, Graduate Studies Admissions Manager, 256-824-6199, Fax: 256-824-6405, E-mail: deangrad@uah.edu.

University of Alaska Fairbanks, College of Engineering and Mines, Department of Electrical and Computer Engineering, Fairbanks, AK 99775-5915. Offers electrical engineering (MEE, MS, PhD); engineering (PhD). Part-time programs available. *Faculty:* 8 full-time (1 woman). *Students:* 19 full-time (3 women), 1 part-time (0 women), 10 international. Average age 26. 20 applicants, 35% accepted, 6 enrolled. In 2010, 4 master's awarded. Terminal master's awarded for partial completion of doctoral program. *Degree requirements:* For master's, comprehensive exam, thesis or alternative; for doctorate, comprehensive exam, thesis/dissertation, oral exam, oral defense. *Entrance requirements:* For master's and doctorate, GRE General Test. Additional exam requirements/recommendations for international students: Required—TOEFL (minimum score 550 paper-based; 213 computer-based; 80 iBT). *Application deadline:* For fall admission, 6/1 for domestic students, 3/1 for international students; for spring admission, 10/15 for domestic students, 9/1 for international students. Applications are processed on a rolling basis. Application fee: $60. Electronic applications accepted. *Expenses:* Tuition, state resident: full-time $5688; part-time $316 per credit. Tuition, nonresident: full-time $11,628; part-time $646 per credit. Required fees: $289 per semester. Tuition and fees vary according to course load and reciprocity agreements. *Financial support:* In 2010–11, 13 research assistantships

Electrical Engineering

University of Alaska Fairbanks (continued)
with tuition reimbursements (averaging $11,876 per year), 10 teaching assistantships with tuition reimbursements (averaging $6,644 per year) were awarded; fellowships with tuition reimbursements, career-related internships or fieldwork, Federal Work-Study, scholarships/grants, health care benefits, and unspecified assistantships also available. Support available to part-time students. Financial award application deadline: 7/1; financial award applicants required to submit FAFSA. *Faculty research:* Geomagnetically-induced currents in power lines, electromagnetic wave propagation, laser radar systems, bioinformatics, distributed sensor networks. *Unit head:* Dr. Charles Mayer, Chair, 907-474-7137, Fax: 907-474-5135, E-mail: fyee@uaf.edu. *Application contact:* Dr. Charles Mayer, Chair, 907-474-7137, Fax: 907-474-5135, E-mail: fyee@uaf.edu.

University of Alberta, Faculty of Graduate Studies and Research, Department of Electrical and Computer Engineering, Edmonton, AB T6G 2E1, Canada. Offers communications (M Eng, M Sc, PhD); computer engineering (M Eng, M Sc, PhD); electromagnetics (M Eng, M Sc, PhD); nanotechnology and microdevices (M Eng, M Sc, PhD); power/power electronics (M Eng, M Sc, PhD); systems (M Eng, M Sc, PhD). Terminal master's awarded for partial completion of doctoral program. *Degree requirements:* For master's, thesis; for doctorate, thesis/dissertation. *Entrance requirements:* Additional exam requirements/recommendations for international students: Required—TOEFL. Electronic applications accepted. *Faculty research:* Controls, communications, microelectronics, electromagnetics.

The University of Arizona, College of Engineering, Department of Electrical and Computer Engineering, Tucson, AZ 85721. Offers M Eng, MS, PhD. Part-time programs available. *Faculty:* 27 full-time (4 women), 3 part-time/adjunct (1 woman). *Students:* 123 full-time (17 women), 33 part-time (5 women); includes 26 minority (1 Black or African American, non-Hispanic/Latino; 7 Asian, non-Hispanic/Latino; 11 Hispanic/Latino; 7 Two or more races, non-Hispanic/Latino), 95 international. Average age 31. 514 applicants, 23% accepted, 38 enrolled. In 2010, 19 master's, 16 doctorates awarded. *Degree requirements:* For master's, thesis (for some programs); for doctorate, thesis/dissertation. *Entrance requirements:* For master's, GRE General Test, 3 letters of recommendation, statement of purpose; for doctorate, GRE General Test, master's degree in related field, 3 letters of recommendation, statement of purpose. Additional exam requirements/recommendations for international students: Required—TOEFL (minimum score 550 paper-based; 213 computer-based; 79 iBT). *Application deadline:* For fall admission, 12/15 for domestic and international students; for spring admission, 7/15 for domestic and international students. Applications are processed on a rolling basis. Application fee: $75. Electronic applications accepted. *Expenses:* Tuition, state resident: full-time $7692. *Financial support:* In 2010–11, 73 research assistantships with full tuition reimbursements (averaging $23,715 per year), 14 teaching assistantships with full tuition reimbursements (averaging $23,585 per year) were awarded; institutionally sponsored loans, scholarships/grants, health care benefits, and unspecified assistantships also available. Financial award application deadline: 3/15. *Faculty research:* Communication systems, control systems, signal processing, computer-aided logic. Total annual research expenditures: $7.1 million. *Unit head:* Dr. Jerzy W. Rozenblit, Head, 520-621-6193, E-mail: head@ece.arizona.edu. *Application contact:* Tami J. Whelan, Senior Graduate Academic Adviser, 520-621-6195, Fax: 520-621-8076, E-mail: whelan@ece.arizona.edu.

University of Arkansas, Graduate School, College of Engineering, Department of Electrical Engineering, Program in Electrical Engineering, Fayetteville, AR 72701-1201. Offers MSEE, PhD. *Students:* 24 full-time (0 women), 58 part-time (5 women); includes 2 Black or African American, non-Hispanic/Latino, 56 international. In 2010, 15 master's, 5 doctorates awarded. *Entrance requirements:* For master's and doctorate, GRE General Test. Application fee: $40 ($50 for international students). *Financial support:* In 2010–11, 10 fellowships with tuition reimbursements, 52 research assistantships, 4 teaching assistantships were awarded. Financial award application deadline: 4/1. *Unit head:* Dr. Juan Balda, Department Chair, 479-575-3005, E-mail: jbalda@uark.edu. *Application contact:* Dr. Randy Brown, Graduate Coordinator, 479-575-6581, E-mail: rlb02@uark.edu.

University of Bridgeport, School of Engineering, Department of Electrical Engineering, Bridgeport, CT 06604. Offers MS. Part-time and evening/weekend programs available. *Degree requirements:* For master's, thesis optional. *Entrance requirements:* Additional exam requirements/recommendations for international students: Recommended—TOEFL (minimum score 550 paper-based; 213 computer-based; 80 iBT), IELTS (minimum score 6.5). Electronic applications accepted. *Expenses:* Tuition: Full-time $22,000; part-time $575 per credit hour. Required fees: $90 per semester. Tuition and fees vary according to course level, course load and program.

The University of British Columbia, Faculty of Applied Science, Program in Electrical and Computer Engineering, Vancouver, BC V6T 1Z1, Canada. Offers M Eng, MA Sc, PhD. Part-time programs available. *Degree requirements:* For master's, thesis (for some programs); for doctorate, thesis/dissertation. *Entrance requirements:* Additional exam requirements/recommendations for international students: Required—TOEFL (minimum score 600 paper-based; 250 computer-based; 100 iBT), TWE. Electronic applications accepted. Tuition charges are reported in Canadian dollars. *Expenses:* Tuition, area resident: Full-time $4179 Canadian dollars. International tuition: $7344 Canadian dollars full-time. *Faculty research:* Applied electromagnetics, biomedical engineering, communications and signal processing, computer and software engineering, power engineering, robotics, solid-state, systems and control.

University of Calgary, Faculty of Graduate Studies, Schulich School of Engineering, Department of Electrical and Computer Engineering, Calgary, AB T2N 1N4, Canada. Offers M Eng, M Sc, PhD. Part-time programs available. *Degree requirements:* For master's, thesis (M Sc); for doctorate, thesis/dissertation, candidacy exam. *Entrance requirements:* For master's and doctorate, minimum GPA of 3.0. Additional exam requirements/recommendations for international students: Required—TOEFL (minimum score 550 paper-based; 213 computer-based), IELTS (minimum score 7), TOEFL or IELTS. Electronic applications accepted. *Faculty research:* Biomedical and bioelectrics, telecommunications and signal processing, software and computer engineering, power and control, microelectronics and instrumentation.

University of California, Berkeley, Graduate Division, College of Engineering, Department of Electrical Engineering and Computer Sciences, Berkeley, CA 94720-1500. Offers computer science (MS, PhD); electrical engineering (MS, PhD). *Degree requirements:* For master's, comprehensive exam or thesis; for doctorate, thesis/dissertation, qualifying exam. *Entrance requirements:* For master's and doctorate, GRE General Test, minimum GPA of 3.0, 3 letters of recommendation. Additional exam requirements/recommendations for international students: Required—TOEFL. Electronic applications accepted.

University of California, Davis, College of Engineering, Program in Electrical and Computer Engineering, Davis, CA 95616. Offers MS, PhD. Terminal master's awarded for partial completion of doctoral program. *Degree requirements:* For master's, comprehensive exam (for some programs), thesis (for some programs); for doctorate, thesis/dissertation, preliminary and qualifying exams, thesis defense. *Entrance requirements:* For master's, GRE General Test, minimum GPA of 3.2; for doctorate, GRE, minimum graduate GPA of 3.5. Additional exam requirements/recommendations for international students: Required—TOEFL (minimum score 550 paper-based; 213 computer-based). Electronic applications accepted.

University of California, Irvine, School of Engineering, Department of Electrical Engineering and Computer Science, Irvine, CA 92697. Offers electrical engineering and computer science (MS, PhD); networked systems (MS, PhD). Part-time programs available. *Students:* 205 full-time (29 women), 29 part-time (6 women); includes 41 minority (1 Black or African American, non-Hispanic/Latino; 35 Asian, non-Hispanic/Latino; 1 Hispanic/Latino; 4 Two or more races, non-Hispanic/Latino), 161 international. Average age 28. 1,102 applicants, 16% accepted, 64 enrolled. In 2010, 53 master's, 26 doctorates awarded. Terminal master's awarded for partial completion of doctoral program. *Degree requirements:* For doctorate, thesis/dissertation. *Entrance requirements:* For master's and doctorate, GRE General Test, minimum GPA of 3.0, 3 letters of recommendation. Additional exam requirements/recommendations for international students: Required—TOEFL (minimum score 550 paper-based; 213 computer-based). *Application deadline:* For fall admission, 1/15 priority date for domestic students, 1/15 for international students. Applications are processed on a rolling basis. Application fee: $80 ($100 for international students). Electronic applications accepted. *Financial support:* Fellowships, research assistantships with full tuition reimbursements, teaching assistantships, institutionally sponsored loans, traineeships, health care benefits, and unspecified assistantships available. Financial award application deadline: 3/1; financial award applicants required to submit FAFSA. *Faculty research:* Optics and electronic devices and circuits, signal processing, communications, machine vision, power electronics. *Unit head:* Prof. Michael M. Green, Chair, 949-824-1656, Fax: 949-824-3203, E-mail: mgreen@uci.edu. *Application contact:* Ronnie A. Gran, Graduate Admissions Coordinator, 949-824-5489, Fax: 949-824-1853, E-mail: ragran@uci.edu.

University of California, Los Angeles, Graduate Division, Henry Samueli School of Engineering and Applied Science, Department of Electrical Engineering, Los Angeles, CA 90095-1594. Offers electrical engineering (MS, PhD). *Faculty:* 45 full-time (5 women). *Students:* 397 full-time (57 women); includes 3 Black or African American, non-Hispanic/Latino; 1 American Indian or Alaska Native, non-Hispanic/Latino; 65 Asian, non-Hispanic/Latino; 5 Hispanic/Latino; 2 Native Hawaiian or other Pacific Islander, non-Hispanic/Latino, 259 international. 1,250 applicants, 32% accepted, 151 enrolled. In 2010, 89 master's, 42 doctorates awarded. *Degree requirements:* For master's, comprehensive exam or thesis; for doctorate, thesis/dissertation, qualifying exams. *Entrance requirements:* For master's, GRE General Test, minimum GPA of 3.0; for doctorate, GRE General Test, minimum GPA of 3.25. Additional exam requirements/recommendations for international students: Required—TOEFL (minimum score 560 paper-based; 220 computer-based; 87 iBT). *Application deadline:* For fall admission, 12/15 for domestic and international students. Application fee: $70 ($90 for international students). Electronic applications accepted. *Financial support:* In 2010–11, 148 fellowships, 457 research assistantships, 111 teaching assistantships were awarded; career-related internships or fieldwork, Federal Work-Study, institutionally sponsored loans, and tuition waivers (full and partial) also available. Financial award application deadline: 12/15; financial award applicants required to submit FAFSA. Total annual research expenditures: $20.5 million. *Unit head:* Dr. M.C. Frank Chang, Chair, 310-825-2647. *Application contact:* Deeona Columbia, Student Affairs Officer, 310-825-7574, E-mail: deeona@ea.ucla.edu.

University of California, Merced, Division of Graduate Studies, School of Engineering, Merced, CA 95343. Offers electrical engineering and computer science (MS, PhD).

University of California, Riverside, Graduate Division, Department of Electrical Engineering, Riverside, CA 92521-0102. Offers electrical engineering (MS, PhD), including computer engineering, control and robotics, intelligent systems, nano-materials, devices and circuits, signal processing and communications. Terminal master's awarded for partial completion of doctoral program. *Degree requirements:* For master's, thesis optional; for doctorate, thesis/dissertation, qualifying exams. *Entrance requirements:* For master's and doctorate, GRE General Test, minimum GPA of 3.25. Additional exam requirements/recommendations for international students: Required—TOEFL (minimum score 550 paper-based; 213 computer-based; 80 iBT). Electronic applications accepted. *Faculty research:* Solid state devices, integrated circuits, signal processing.

University of California, San Diego, Office of Graduate Studies, Department of Electrical and Computer Engineering, La Jolla, CA 92093. Offers applied ocean science (MS, PhD); applied physics (MS, PhD); communication theory and systems (MS, PhD); computer engineering (MS, PhD); electrical engineering (M Eng); electronic circuits and systems (MS, PhD); intelligent systems, robotics and control (MS, PhD); photonics (MS, PhD); signal and image processing (MS, PhD). MS only offered to students who have been admitted to the PhD program. *Entrance requirements:* For master's and doctorate, GRE General Test. Electronic applications accepted.

University of California, Santa Barbara, Graduate Division, College of Engineering, Department of Electrical and Computer Engineering, Santa Barbara, CA 93106-2014. Offers communications, control and signal processing (PhD); computer engineering (MS); electronics and photonics (MS); MS/PhD. *Faculty:* 37 full-time (3 women), 1 part-time/adjunct (0 women). *Students:* 251 full-time (45 women); includes 2 Black or African American, non-Hispanic/Latino; 2 American Indian or Alaska Native, non-Hispanic/Latino; 123 Asian, non-Hispanic/Latino; 10 Hispanic/Latino; 1 Native Hawaiian or other Pacific Islander, non-Hispanic/Latino. Average age 26. 1,040 applicants, 27% accepted, 79 enrolled. In 2010, 47 master's, 31 doctorates awarded. Terminal master's awarded for partial completion of doctoral program. *Degree requirements:* For master's, comprehensive exam, thesis; for doctorate, thesis/dissertation. *Entrance requirements:* For master's and doctorate, GRE General Test. Additional exam requirements/recommendations for international students: Required—TOEFL (minimum score 550 paper-based; 80 iBT), IELTS (minimum score 7). *Application deadline:* For fall admission, 12/15 for domestic and international students; for winter admission, 11/1 for domestic and international students; for spring admission, 1/1 for domestic and international students. Application fee: $70 ($90 for international students). Electronic applications accepted. *Financial support:* In 2010–11, 196 students received support, including 70 fellowships with full and partial tuition reimbursements available (averaging $7,181 per year), 155 research assistantships with full and partial tuition reimbursements available (averaging $15,235 per year), 54 teaching assistantships with full and partial tuition reimbursements available (averaging $9,910 per year); tuition waivers (full and partial) also available. Financial award application deadline: 12/15; financial award applicants required to submit FAFSA. *Faculty research:* Communications, signal processing, computer engineering, control, electronics and photonics. Total annual research expenditures: $25.5 million. *Unit head:* Prof. Jerry Gibson, Chair, 805-893-3821, Fax: 805-893-6262, E-mail: gibson@ece.ucsb.edu. *Application contact:* Erika Raquel Klukovich, Graduate Admissions Coordinator, 805-893-3114, Fax: 805-893-5402, E-mail: erika@ece.ucsb.edu.

University of California, Santa Cruz, Division of Graduate Studies, Jack Baskin School of Engineering, Department of Electrical Engineering, Santa Cruz, CA 95064. Offers MS, PhD. *Students:* 59 full-time (14 women), 15 part-time (0 women); includes 16 minority (1 Black or African American, non-Hispanic/Latino; 10 Asian, non-Hispanic/Latino; 5 Hispanic/Latino), 29 international. Average age 33. 155 applicants, 26% accepted, 9 enrolled. In 2010, 3 master's, 8 doctorates awarded. *Degree requirements:* For master's, thesis; for doctorate, thesis/dissertation, qualifying exam. *Entrance requirements:* For master's and doctorate, GRE General Test. Additional exam requirements/recommendations for international students: Required—TOEFL (minimum score 570 paper-based; 230 computer-based; 89 iBT); Recommended—IELTS (minimum score 8). *Application deadline:* For fall admission, 1/3 for domestic and international students. Application fee: $70 ($90 for international students). Electronic applications accepted. *Financial support:* Fellowships, research assistantships, teaching assistantships, institutionally sponsored loans and tuition waivers available. Financial award applicants required to submit FAFSA. *Faculty research:* Photonics and electronics, signal processing and communications, remote sensing, nanotechnology. *Unit head:* Carol Mullane, Graduate Program Coordinator, 831-459-2576, E-mail: mullane@soe.ucsc.edu. *Application contact:* Carol Mullane, Graduate Program Coordinator, 831-459-2576, E-mail: mullane@soe.ucsc.edu.

University of Central Florida, College of Engineering and Computer Science, Department of Electrical Engineering and Computer Science, Program in Electrical Engineering, Orlando, FL 32816. Offers electrical engineering (MSEE, PhD); electronic circuits (Certificate). Part-time and evening/weekend programs available. *Students:* 122 full-time (28 women), 87 part-time (11 women); includes 47 minority (11 Black or African American, non-Hispanic/Latino; 14 Asian, non-Hispanic/Latino; 21 Hispanic/Latino; 1 Two or more races, non-Hispanic/Latino), 89 international. Average age 28. 294 applicants, 77% accepted, 46 enrolled. In 2010, 29 master's, 17 doctorates, 1 other advanced degree awarded. *Degree requirements:* For master's, thesis or alternative; for doctorate, thesis/dissertation, departmental qualifying exam, candidacy exam. *Entrance requirements:* For master's, GRE General Test, minimum GPA of 3.0 in last 60 hours; for doctorate, GRE General Test, minimum GPA of 3.5 in last 60 hours. Additional exam requirements/recommendations for international students: Required—TOEFL. *Application deadline:* For fall admission, 7/15 priority date for domestic students; for spring admission, 12/1 priority date for domestic students. Application fee: $30. Electronic applications accepted. *Expenses:* Tuition, state resident: part-time $256.56 per credit hour. Tuition, nonresident: part-time $1011.52 per credit hour. Part-time tuition and fees vary according to program. *Financial support:* In 2010–11, 65 students received support, including 12 fellowships (averaging $10,700 per year), 72 research assistantships (averaging $7,100 per year), 23 teaching assistantships (averaging $6,000 per year); tuition waivers (partial) also available.

University of Cincinnati, Graduate School, College of Engineering, Department of Electrical and Computer Engineering and Computer Science, Program in Electrical Engineering, Cincinnati, OH 45221. Offers MS, PhD. *Degree requirements:* For master's, thesis; for doctorate, thesis/dissertation. *Entrance requirements:* For master's and doctorate, GRE General Test. Additional exam requirements/recommendations for international students: Required—TOEFL (minimum score 550 paper-based; 213 computer-based). *Faculty research:* Integrated circuits and optical devices, charge-coupled devices, photosensitive devices.

University of Colorado at Colorado Springs, College of Engineering and Applied Science, Department of Electrical and Computer Engineering, Colorado Springs, CO 80933-7150. Offers electrical engineering (ME, MS, PhD). Part-time and evening/weekend programs available. *Faculty:* 7 full-time (2 women), 1 part-time/adjunct (0 women). *Students:* 19 full-time (4 women), 21 part-time (0 women); includes 1 Asian, non-Hispanic/Latino; 2 Hispanic/Latino, 5 international. Average age 34. 37 applicants, 81% accepted, 25 enrolled. In 2010, 25 master's awarded. *Degree requirements:* For master's, thesis (for some programs), final oral exam (for non-thesis option); for doctorate, comprehensive exam, thesis/dissertation, preliminary exam. *Entrance requirements:* For master's, GRE General Test, minimum GPA of 3.0, BS or course work in electrical engineering; for doctorate, GRE General Test, minimum GPA of 3.3. Additional exam requirements/recommendations for international students: Required—TOEFL. *Application deadline:* Applications are processed on a rolling basis. Application fee: $60 ($75 for international students). *Expenses:* Tuition, state resident: full-time $7916. Tuition, nonresident: full-time $16,610. Tuition and fees vary according to course load, degree level, program, reciprocity agreements and student level. *Financial support:* Fellowships, research assistantships, teaching assistantships, career-related internships or fieldwork, Federal Work-Study, and scholarships/grants available. Support available to part-time students. Financial award application deadline: 3/1; financial award applicants required to submit FAFSA. *Faculty research:* Integrated ferroelectric devices; applied electromagnetics; digital/mixed-signal circuit design, test and design for testability; signal processing for communications and controls. Total annual research expenditures: $481,671. *Unit head:* Dr. T. S. Kalkur, Chair, 719-255-3147, Fax: 719-255-3589. *Application contact:* Laura Baur, Academic Adviser, 719-255-3351, Fax: 719-255-3589, E-mail: lbaur@uccs.edu.

University of Colorado Boulder, Graduate School, College of Engineering and Applied Science, Department of Electrical, Computer and Energy Engineering, Boulder, CO 80309. Offers ME, MS, PhD. Part-time programs available. Postbaccalaureate distance learning degree programs offered (no on-campus study). *Faculty:* 37 full-time (5 women). *Students:* 243 full-time (41 women), 75 part-time (16 women); includes 22 minority (3 Black or African American, non-Hispanic/Latino; 15 Asian, non-Hispanic/Latino; 4 Hispanic/Latino), 150 international. Average age 27. 670 applicants, 85 enrolled. In 2010, 95 master's, 19 doctorates awarded. Terminal master's awarded for partial completion of doctoral program. *Degree requirements:* For master's, thesis or alternative; for doctorate, one foreign language, thesis/dissertation, departmental qualifying exam. *Entrance requirements:* For master's, GRE General Test, minimum undergraduate GPA of 3.0; for doctorate, GRE General Test, minimum undergraduate GPA of 3.5. *Application deadline:* For fall admission, 1/15 priority date for domestic students, 12/1 for international students; for spring admission, 10/1 for domestic and international students. Applications are processed on a rolling basis. Application fee: $50 ($60 for international students). *Financial support:* In 2010–11, 31 fellowships (averaging $8,965 per year), 107 research assistantships (averaging $14,806 per year) were awarded; career-related internships or fieldwork, scholarships/grants, and tuition waivers (full) also available. Financial award application deadline: 1/15. *Faculty research:* Biomedical engineering and cognitive disabilities, computer engineering VLSI CAD, dynamics and control systems, digital signal processing communications, electromagnetics, RF and microwaves, nonostructures and devices, optics and optoelectronics, power electronics and renewable energy systems. Total annual research expenditures: $8.6 million.

University of Colorado Denver, College of Engineering and Applied Science, Department of Electrical Engineering, Denver, CO 80217. Offers MS. Part-time and evening/weekend programs available. *Faculty:* 11 full-time (1 woman), 3 part-time/adjunct (1 woman). *Students:* 58 full-time (11 women), 24 part-time (2 women); includes 3 Black or African American, non-Hispanic/Latino; 2 Asian, non-Hispanic/Latino; 3 Hispanic/Latino, 49 international. Average age 30. 86 applicants, 44% accepted, 16 enrolled. In 2010, 16 master's awarded. *Degree requirements:* For master's, thesis or alternative, thesis or project, 30 credit hours. *Entrance requirements:* For master's, GRE. Additional exam requirements/recommendations for international students: Required—TOEFL (minimum score 525 paper-based; 193 computer-based). *Application deadline:* For fall admission, 4/1 for domestic students; for spring admission, 10/1 for domestic students. Applications are processed on a rolling basis. Application fee: $50 ($75 for international students). Electronic applications accepted. *Expenses:* Contact institution. *Financial support:* Research assistantships, teaching assistantships, career-related internships or fieldwork and Federal Work-Study available. Financial award application deadline: 4/1; financial award applicants required to submit FAFSA. *Faculty research:* Communication and signal processing, embedded systems, electromagnetic fields and matter, energy and power systems, photonics and biomedical imaging. *Unit head:* Dr. Mike Radenkovic, Professor/Chair, 303-556-3616, E-mail: miloje.radenkovic@ucdenver.edu. *Application contact:* Janiece Hockaday, Administrative Assistant, 303-556-4718, E-mail: janiece.hockaday@ucdenver.edu.

University of Colorado Denver, College of Engineering and Applied Science, Master of Engineering Program, Denver, CO 80217-3364. Offers civil engineering (M Eng); electrical engineering (M Eng); mechanical engineering (M Eng). Part-time programs available. *Students:* 26 full-time (9 women), 31 part-time (8 women); includes 1 Black or African American, non-Hispanic/Latino; 3 Asian, non-Hispanic/Latino; 1 Hispanic/Latino, 2 international. Average age 36. 22 applicants, 77% accepted, 14 enrolled. In 2010, 23 master's awarded. *Degree requirements:* For master's, comprehensive exam, thesis, 27 credit hours of course work, 3 credit hours of report or thesis work. *Entrance requirements:* For master's, GRE (required for those with GPA below 2.75), transcripts, references, statement of purpose. Additional exam requirements/recommendations for international students: Required—TOEFL (minimum score 525 paper-based; 71 iBT). *Application deadline:* For fall admission, 7/15 for domestic students, 6/15 for international students; for spring admission, 12/1 for domestic students, 11/1 for international students. Applications are processed on a rolling basis. Application fee: $50 ($75 for international students). Electronic applications accepted. *Expenses:* Contact institution. *Financial support:* Federal Work-Study and scholarships/grants available. Financial award application deadline: 4/1; financial award applicants required to submit FAFSA. *Faculty research:* Civil, electrical and mechanical engineering.

University of Connecticut, Graduate School, School of Engineering, Department of Electrical and Computer Engineering, Field of Electrical Engineering, Storrs, CT 06269. Offers MS, PhD. Terminal master's awarded for partial completion of doctoral program. *Degree requirements:* For master's, comprehensive exam; for doctorate, thesis/dissertation. *Entrance requirements:* For master's and doctorate, GRE General Test. Additional exam requirements/recommendations for international students: Required—TOEFL (minimum score 550 paper-based; 213 computer-based). Electronic applications accepted.

University of Dayton, Graduate School, School of Engineering, Department of Electrical and Computer Engineering, Dayton, OH 45469-1300. Offers MSEE, DE, PhD. Part-time and evening/weekend programs available. *Faculty:* 15 full-time (0 women), 4 part-time/adjunct (1 woman). *Students:* 103 full-time (17 women), 23 part-time (5 women); includes 10 minority (2 Black or African American, non-Hispanic/Latino; 7 Asian, non-Hispanic/Latino; 1 Hispanic/Latino), 71 international. Average age 27. 118 applicants, 74% accepted, 25 enrolled. In 2010, 20 master's, 3 doctorates awarded. *Degree requirements:* For master's, thesis optional; for doctorate, variable foreign language requirement, thesis/dissertation, departmental qualifying exam. *Entrance requirements:* Additional exam requirements/recommendations for international students: Required—TOEFL (minimum score 550 paper-based; 213 computer-based; 80 iBT). *Application deadline:* For fall admission, 8/1 for domestic students, 3/1 priority date for international students; for winter admission, 7/1 priority date for international students; for spring admission, 1/1 priority date for international students. Applications are processed on a rolling basis. Application fee: $0 ($50 for international students). Electronic applications accepted. *Expenses:* Tuition: Full-time $7800; part-time $650 per credit hour. *Financial support:* In 2010–11, 1 fellowship (averaging $27,500 per year), 34 research assistantships with full tuition reimbursements (averaging $12,500 per year), 5 teaching assistantships with full tuition reimbursements (averaging $10,065 per year) were awarded. Financial award application deadline: 5/1; financial award applicants required to submit FAFSA. *Faculty research:* Electrical engineering, video processing, leaky wave antenna. Total annual research expenditures: $1.1 million. *Unit head:* Dr. Guru Subramanyam, Chair, 937-229-3611. *Application contact:* Alexander Popovski, Associate Director of Graduate and International Admissions, 937-229-2357, Fax: 937-229-4729, E-mail: alex.popovski@notes.udayton.edu.

University of Delaware, College of Engineering, Department of Electrical and Computer Engineering, Newark, DE 19716. Offers MSECE, PhD. Part-time programs available. Postbaccalaureate distance learning degree programs offered (no on-campus study). Terminal master's awarded for partial completion of doctoral program. *Degree requirements:* For master's, thesis optional; for doctorate, thesis/dissertation. *Entrance requirements:* For master's, GRE General Test; for doctorate, GRE General Test, qualifying exam. Additional exam requirements/recommendations for international students: Required—TOEFL. Electronic applications accepted. *Faculty research:* HIV Evolution During Dynamic Therapy, compressive sensing in imaging, sensor, networks, and UWB radios, computer network time synchronization, silicon spintronics, devices and imaging in the high-terahertz band.

University of Denver, School of Engineering and Computer Science, Department of Electrical and Computer Engineering, Denver, CO 80208. Offers computer engineering (MS); computer science and engineering (MS); electrical and computer engineering (PhD); electrical engineering (MS); engineering (MS); mechatronic systems engineering (MS). Part-time and evening/weekend programs available. *Faculty:* 11 full-time (0 women), 1 part-time/adjunct (0 women). *Students:* 2 full-time (0 women), 104 part-time (20 women); includes 13 minority (1 Black or African American, non-Hispanic/Latino; 6 Asian, non-Hispanic/Latino; 5 Hispanic/Latino; 1 Two or more races, non-Hispanic/Latino), 18 international. Average age 30. 97 applicants, 67% accepted, 26 enrolled. In 2010, 28 master's, 4 doctorates awarded. Terminal master's awarded for partial completion of doctoral program. *Degree requirements:* For master's, thesis or alternative, proficiency in high- or low-level computer language; for doctorate, comprehensive exam, thesis/dissertation, proficiency in high- or low-level computer language. *Entrance requirements:* For master's and doctorate, GRE General Test. Additional exam requirements/recommendations for international students: Required—TOEFL (minimum score 550 paper-based; 80 iBT). *Application deadline:* Applications are processed on a rolling basis. Application fee: $60. Electronic applications accepted. *Expenses:* Tuition: Full-time $35,604; part-time $29,670 per year. Required fees: $687 per year. Tuition and fees vary according to program. *Financial support:* In 2010–11, 12 research assistantships with full and partial tuition reimbursements (averaging $12,166 per year), 5 teaching assistantships with full and partial tuition reimbursements (averaging $12,198 per year) were awarded; Federal Work-Study, scholarships/grants, and unspecified assistantships also available. Financial award application deadline: 3/1; financial award applicants required to submit FAFSA. *Unit head:* Dr. Kimon Valavanis, Chair, 303-871-2586, Fax: 303-871-2194, E-mail: kvalavan@du.ed. *Application contact:* Information Contact, 303-871-6618, Fax: 303-871-2194, E-mail: eceinfo@du.edu.

University of Detroit Mercy, College of Engineering and Science, Department of Electrical and Computer Engineering, Detroit, MI 48221. Offers computer engineering (ME, DE); mechatronics systems (ME, DE); signals and systems (ME, DE). Evening/weekend programs available. *Degree requirements:* For doctorate, thesis/dissertation. *Faculty research:* Electromagnetics, computer architecture, systems.

University of Evansville, College of Engineering and Computer Science, Department of Electrical Engineering and Computer Science, Evansville, IN 47722. Offers MS. Part-time programs available. *Faculty:* 2 full-time (0 women). *Students:* 1 (woman) part-time. Average age 28. 1 applicant, 0% accepted, 0 enrolled. *Degree requirements:* For master's, thesis. *Entrance requirements:* For master's, GRE, minimum undergraduate GPA of 2.8, 2 letters of recommendation, BS in electrical engineering or computer science. Additional exam requirements/recommendations for international students: Required—TOEFL (minimum score 550 paper-based; 79 iBT), IELTS (minimum score 6.5). *Application deadline:* For fall admission, 5/1 priority date for domestic and international students. Applications are processed on a rolling basis. Application fee: $25 ($50 for international students). *Expenses:* Contact institution. *Financial support:* Scholarships/grants available. Financial award application deadline: 6/1; financial award applicants required to submit FAFSA. *Unit head:* Dr. Dick Blandford, Department Chair, 812-488-2570, Fax: 812-488-2662, E-mail: blandford@evansville.edu. *Application contact:* Dr. Dick Blandford, Department Chair, 812-488-2570, Fax: 812-488-2662, E-mail: blandford@evansville.edu.

University of Florida, Graduate School, College of Engineering, Department of Electrical and Computer Engineering, Gainesville, FL 32611. Offers ME, MS, PhD, Engr. Part-time programs available. Postbaccalaureate distance learning degree programs offered. *Faculty:* 38 full-time (5 women), 2 part-time/adjunct (0 women). *Students:* 535 full-time (98 women), 78 part-time (11 women); includes 8 Black or African American, non-Hispanic/Latino; 1 American Indian or Alaska Native, non-Hispanic/Latino; 21 Asian, non-Hispanic/Latino; 19 Hispanic/Latino, 441 international. Average age 23. 1,951 applicants, 39% accepted, 203 enrolled. In 2010, 233 master's, 46 doctorates awarded. Terminal master's awarded for partial completion of doctoral program. *Degree requirements:* For master's, comprehensive exam (for some programs), thesis (for some programs); for doctorate, comprehensive exam, thesis/dissertation; for Engr, thesis. *Entrance requirements:* For master's, GRE General Test, minimum GPA of 3.0; for doctorate, GRE General Test, minimum GPA of 3.5; for Engr, GRE General Test. Additional exam requirements/recommendations for international students: Required—TOEFL (minimum score 550 paper-based; 213 computer-based; 80 iBT), IELTS (minimum score 6). *Application deadline:* For fall admission, 1/15 priority date for domestic students, 1/15 for international students. Applications are processed on a rolling basis. Application fee: $30. Electronic applications accepted. *Expenses:* Tuition, state resident: full-time $10,915.92. Tuition, nonresident: full-time $28,309. *Financial support:* In 2010–11, 259 students received support, including 33 fellowships, 198 research assistantships (averaging $18,880 per year), 28 teaching assistantships (averaging $20,263 per year); unspecified assistantships also available. Financial award application deadline: 1/15; financial award applicants required to submit FAFSA. *Faculty research:* Computer engineering, devices, electromagnetics and energy systems, electronics and signals and systems. Total annual research expenditures: $12.5 million. *Unit head:* Dr. John G. Harris, Chair and Graduate Coordinator, 352-392-0913, Fax: 352-392-8671, E-mail: harris@cnel.ufl.edu. *Application contact:* Dr. John G. Harris, Chair and Graduate Coordinator, 352-392-0913, Fax: 352-392-8671, E-mail: harris@cnel.ufl.edu.

University of Hawaii at Manoa, Graduate Division, College of Engineering, Department of Electrical Engineering, Honolulu, HI 96822. Offers MS, PhD. Part-time programs available. *Faculty:* 32 full-time (1 woman). *Students:* 59 full-time (16 women), 15 part-time (4 women); includes 38 minority (1 Black or African American, non-Hispanic/Latino; 27 Asian, non-Hispanic/

Electrical Engineering

University of Hawaii at Manoa (continued)

Latino; 2 Hispanic/Latino; 2 Native Hawaiian or other Pacific Islander, non-Hispanic/Latino; 6 Two or more races, non-Hispanic/Latino), 26 international. Average age 30. 59 applicants, 80% accepted, 25 enrolled. In 2010, 8 master's, 5 doctorates awarded. *Degree requirements:* For master's, comprehensive exam, thesis; for doctorate, comprehensive exam, thesis/dissertation. *Entrance requirements:* For master's and doctorate, GRE General Test. Additional exam requirements/recommendations for international students: Required—TOEFL (minimum score 540 paper-based; 207 computer-based; 76 iBT), IELTS (minimum score 5). *Application deadline:* For fall admission, 3/1 for domestic students, 1/15 for international students; for spring admission, 9/1 for domestic students, 8/1 for international students. Applications are processed on a rolling basis. Application fee: $50. *Financial support:* In 2010–11, 9 fellowships (averaging $889 per year), 42 research assistantships (averaging $18,920 per year), 11 teaching assistantships (averaging $14,969 per year) were awarded; tuition waivers (full and partial) also available. *Faculty research:* Computers and artificial intelligence, communication and networking, control theory, physical electronics, VLSI design, micromillimeter waves. Total annual research expenditures: $735,000. *Application contact:* Aleksander Kavcic, Chairperson, 808-956-7568, Fax: 808-956-3427, E-mail: kavcic@hawaii.edu.

University of Houston, Cullen College of Engineering, Department of Electrical and Computer Engineering, Houston, TX 77204. Offers electrical engineering (MEE, MSEE, PhD). Part-time programs available. *Faculty:* 28 full-time (3 women), 1 part-time/adjunct (0 women). *Students:* 199 full-time (54 women), 44 part-time (10 women); includes 6 Black or African American, non-Hispanic/Latino; 16 Asian, non-Hispanic/Latino; 4 Hispanic/Latino; 1 Two or more races, non-Hispanic/Latino, 196 international. Average age 25. 378 applicants, 42% accepted, 50 enrolled. In 2010, 54 master's, 14 doctorates awarded. Terminal master's awarded for partial completion of doctoral program. *Degree requirements:* For master's, thesis (for some programs); for doctorate, comprehensive exam, thesis/dissertation. *Entrance requirements:* For master's and doctorate, GRE General Test. Additional exam requirements/recommendations for international students: Required—TOEFL (minimum score 580 paper-based; 237 computer-based; 92 iBT). *Application deadline:* For fall admission, 2/1 for domestic and international students; for spring admission, 8/1 for domestic and international students. Application fee: $25 ($75 for international students). Electronic applications accepted. *Expenses:* Tuition, state resident: full-time $8592; part-time $358 per credit hour. Tuition, nonresident: full-time $16,032; part-time $668 per credit hour. Required fees: $2889. Tuition and fees vary according to course load and program. *Financial support:* In 2010–11, 2 fellowships with partial tuition reimbursements (averaging $2,700 per year), 56 research assistantships with partial tuition reimbursements (averaging $10,944 per year), 47 teaching assistantships with partial tuition reimbursements (averaging $9,371 per year) were awarded; career-related internships or fieldwork, Federal Work-Study, institutionally sponsored loans, scholarships/grants, health care benefits, and unspecified assistantships also available. Support available to part-time students. Financial award application deadline: 2/1. *Faculty research:* Applied electromagnetics and microelectronics, signal and image processing, biomedical engineering, geophysical applications, control engineering. *Unit head:* Dr. Badri Roysam, Chairperson, 713-743-1773, Fax: 713-743-4444, E-mail: broysam@central.uh.edu. *Application contact:* MyTrang Baccam, Graduate Academic Advisor, 713-743-4403, Fax: 713-743-4402, E-mail: mytrang.baccam@mail.uh.edu.

University of Idaho, College of Graduate Studies, College of Engineering, Department of Electrical and Computer Engineering, Program in Electrical Engineering, Moscow, ID 83844-2282. Offers M Engr, MS, PhD. *Students:* 43 full-time, 84 part-time. Average age 33. In 2010, 31 master's, 1 doctorate awarded. *Application deadline:* Applications are processed on a rolling basis. Application fee: $60. Electronic applications accepted. *Expenses:* Tuition, nonresident: part-time $580 per credit. Required fees: $306 per credit. *Financial support:* Applicants required to submit FAFSA. *Unit head:* Dr. Brian Johnson, Chair, 208-885-6902. *Application contact:* Dr. Brian Johnson, Chair, 208-885-6902.

University of Illinois at Chicago, Graduate College, College of Engineering, Department of Electrical and Computer Engineering, Program in Electrical and Computer Engineering, Chicago, IL 60607-7128. Offers MS, PhD. Part-time programs available. *Degree requirements:* For master's, thesis or alternative; for doctorate, thesis/dissertation, departmental qualifying exam. *Entrance requirements:* For master's, minimum GPA of 2.75, BS in related field; for doctorate, GRE General Test, minimum GPA of 2.75, MS in related field. Additional exam requirements/recommendations for international students: Required—TOEFL.

University of Illinois at Urbana–Champaign, Graduate College, College of Engineering, Department of Electrical and Computer Engineering, Champaign, IL 61820. Offers electrical and computer engineering (MS, PhD); MS/MBA. *Faculty:* 80 full-time (6 women), 3 part-time/adjunct (0 women). *Students:* 490 full-time (65 women), 15 part-time (3 women); includes 6 Black or African American, non-Hispanic/Latino; 40 Asian, non-Hispanic/Latino; 13 Hispanic/Latino; 6 Two or more races, non-Hispanic/Latino, 283 international. 1,668 applicants, 13% accepted, 94 enrolled. In 2010, 112 master's, 46 doctorates awarded. *Entrance requirements:* For master's, GRE, minimum GPA of 3.0; for doctorate, GRE. Additional exam requirements/recommendations for international students: Required—TOEFL (minimum score 590 paper-based; 243 computer-based; 96 iBT) or IELTS (minimum score 6.5). *Application deadline:* Applications are processed on a rolling basis. Application fee: $75 ($90 for international students). Electronic applications accepted. *Financial support:* In 2010–11, 49 fellowships, 373 research assistantships, 165 teaching assistantships were awarded; tuition waivers (full and partial) also available. *Unit head:* Andreas C. Cangellaris, Head, 217-333-6037, Fax: 217-244-7075, E-mail: cangella@illinois.edu. *Application contact:* Laurie A. Fisher, Administrative Aide, 217-333-9709, Fax: 217-333-8582, E-mail: fisher2@illinois.edu.

The University of Iowa, Graduate College, College of Engineering, Department of Electrical and Computer Engineering, Iowa City, IA 52242-1316. Offers MS, PhD. Part-time programs available. *Faculty:* 17 full-time (1 woman), 1 part-time/adjunct (0 women). *Students:* 90 full-time (17 women); includes 7 minority (3 Black or African American, non-Hispanic/Latino; 2 Asian, non-Hispanic/Latino; 2 Hispanic/Latino), 51 international. Average age 28. 158 applicants, 24% accepted, 24 enrolled. In 2010, 5 master's, 3 doctorates awarded. *Degree requirements:* For master's, comprehensive exam, thesis optional; for doctorate, comprehensive exam, thesis/dissertation, qualifying exam. *Entrance requirements:* For master's and doctorate, GRE. Additional exam requirements/recommendations for international students: Required—TOEFL (minimum score 550 paper-based; 213 computer-based; 81 iBT). *Application deadline:* For fall admission, 2/1 priority date for domestic students, 2/1 for international students. Applications are processed on a rolling basis. Application fee: $60 ($100 for international students). Electronic applications accepted. *Financial support:* In 2010–11, 5 fellowships with partial tuition reimbursements (averaging $19,146 per year), 59 research assistantships with partial tuition reimbursements (averaging $18,073 per year), 21 teaching assistantships with partial tuition reimbursements (averaging $17,324 per year) were awarded; scholarships/grants and unspecified assistantships also available. Financial award application deadline: 2/1; financial award applicants required to submit FAFSA. *Faculty research:* Applied optics and nanotechnology; computational genomics; large-scale intelligent and control systems; medical image processing; VLSI design and test. Total annual research expenditures: $10.4 million. *Unit head:* Dr. Milan Sonka, Department Executive Officer, 319-335-6052, Fax: 319-335-6028, E-mail: milan-sonka@uiowa.edu. *Application contact:* Cathy Kern, Secretary, 319-335-5197, Fax: 319-335-6028, E-mail: ece@engineering.uiowa.edu.

The University of Kansas, Graduate Studies, School of Engineering, Department of Electrical Engineering and Computer Science, Program in Electrical Engineering, Lawrence, KS 66045. Offers MS, DE, PhD. Part-time programs available. *Faculty:* 35. *Students:* 52 full-time (10 women), 13 part-time (1 woman); includes 5 minority (1 American Indian or Alaska Native, non-Hispanic/Latino; 1 Asian, non-Hispanic/Latino; 2 Hispanic/Latino; 1 Native Hawaiian or other Pacific Islander, non-Hispanic/Latino), 30 international. Average age 27. 124 applicants, 39% accepted, 12 enrolled. In 2010, 14 master's, 5 doctorates awarded. Terminal master's awarded for partial completion of doctoral program. *Degree requirements:* For master's, thesis optional, exam; for doctorate, one foreign language, comprehensive exam, thesis/dissertation, qualifying exams. *Entrance requirements:* For master's, GRE, minimum GPA of 3.0; for doctorate, GRE, minimum GPA of 3.5. Additional exam requirements/recommendations for international students: Required—TOEFL (minimum score 600 paper-based; 250 computer-based; 100 iBT). *Application deadline:* For fall admission, 3/1 priority date for domestic students, 3/1 for international students; for spring admission, 10/1 priority date for domestic students, 10/1 for international students. Applications are processed on a rolling basis. Application fee: $55 ($65 for international students). Electronic applications accepted. *Expenses:* Tuition, state resident: full-time $7092; part-time $295.50 per credit hour. Tuition, nonresident: full-time $16,590; part-time $691.25 per credit hour. Required fees: $858; $71.49 per credit hour. Tuition and fees vary according to course load, campus/location and program. *Financial support:* Fellowships with full and partial tuition reimbursements, research assistantships with full and partial tuition reimbursements, teaching assistantships with full and partial tuition reimbursements, career-related internships or fieldwork, scholarships/grants, and unspecified assistantships available. Financial award application deadline: 1/1. *Faculty research:* Communication systems and networking, computer systems design, radar systems and remote sensing. *Unit head:* Glenn Prescott, Chairperson, 785-864-4620, Fax: 785-864-3226. *Application contact:* Pam Shadoin, Assistant to Graduate Director, 785-864-4487, Fax: 785-864-3226, E-mail: graduate@eecs.ku.edu.

University of Kentucky, Graduate School, College of Engineering, Program in Electrical Engineering, Lexington, KY 40506-0032. Offers MSEE, PhD. *Degree requirements:* For master's, comprehensive exam, thesis optional; for doctorate, one foreign language, comprehensive exam, thesis/dissertation. *Entrance requirements:* For master's, GRE General Test, minimum undergraduate GPA of 2.75; for doctorate, GRE General Test, minimum undergraduate GPA of 3.0. Additional exam requirements/recommendations for international students: Required—TOEFL (minimum score 550 paper-based; 213 computer-based). Electronic applications accepted. *Faculty research:* Signal processing, systems, and control; electromagnetic field theory; power electronics and machines; computer engineering and VLSI; materials and devices.

University of Louisville, J.B. Speed School of Engineering, Department of Electrical and Computer Engineering, Louisville, KY 40292-0001. Offers M Eng, MS, PhD. *Accreditation:* ABET (one or more programs are accredited). Part-time programs available. *Faculty:* 15 full-time (2 women). *Students:* 82 full-time (14 women), 19 part-time (4 women); includes 3 Black or African American, non-Hispanic/Latino; 2 Asian, non-Hispanic/Latino; 1 Hispanic/Latino; 2 Two or more races, non-Hispanic/Latino, 46 international. Average age 28. 50 applicants, 44% accepted, 14 enrolled. In 2010, 25 master's, 3 doctorates awarded. Terminal master's awarded for partial completion of doctoral program. *Degree requirements:* For master's, comprehensive exam (for some programs), thesis or alternative; for doctorate, comprehensive exam, thesis/dissertation, minimum GPA of 3.0. *Entrance requirements:* For master's and doctorate, GRE General Test. Additional exam requirements/recommendations for international students: Required—TOEFL (minimum score 550 paper-based; 213 computer-based; 80 iBT), IELTS (minimum score 6.5). *Application deadline:* For fall admission, 5/1 priority date for domestic and international students; for spring admission, 11/1 priority date for domestic and international students. Applications are processed on a rolling basis. Application fee: $50. Electronic applications accepted. *Expenses:* Tuition, state resident: full-time $9144; part-time $508 per credit hour. Tuition, nonresident: full-time $19,026; part-time $1057 per credit hour. Tuition and fees vary according to program and reciprocity agreements. *Financial support:* In 2010–11, 16 students received support, including 4 fellowships with full tuition reimbursements available (averaging $20,000 per year), 4 research assistantships with full tuition reimbursements available (averaging $21,000 per year), 8 teaching assistantships with full tuition reimbursements available (averaging $20,000 per year). Financial award application deadline: 1/25; financial award applicants required to submit FAFSA. *Faculty research:* Nanotechnology; microfabrication; computer engineering; control, communication and signal processing; electronic devices and systems. Total annual research expenditures: $5.8 million. *Unit head:* James H. Graham, Acting Chair, 502-852-6289, Fax: 502-852-6807, E-mail: jhgrah01@louisville.edu. *Application contact:* Dr. Michael Day, Associate Dean, 502-852-6195, Fax: 502-852-7294, E-mail: day@louisville.edu.

University of Maine, Graduate School, College of Engineering, Department of Electrical and Computer Engineering, Orono, ME 04469. Offers computer engineering (MS); electrical engineering (MS, PhD). Part-time programs available. *Faculty:* 12 full-time (1 woman). *Students:* 17 full-time (3 women), 14 part-time (2 women); includes 3 minority (all Asian, non-Hispanic/Latino), 14 international. Average age 27. 22 applicants, 18% accepted, 3 enrolled. In 2010, 14 master's, 1 doctorate awarded. *Degree requirements:* For master's, thesis (for some programs); for doctorate, thesis/dissertation. *Entrance requirements:* For master's and doctorate, GRE General Test. Additional exam requirements/recommendations for international students: Required—TOEFL. *Application deadline:* For fall admission, 2/1 priority date for domestic students. Applications are processed on a rolling basis. Application fee: $65. Electronic applications accepted. *Expenses:* Tuition, state resident: full-time $400. Tuition, nonresident: full-time $1050. *Financial support:* In 2010–11, 21 research assistantships with tuition reimbursements (averaging $21,737 per year), 2 teaching assistantships with tuition reimbursements (averaging $12,790 per year) were awarded; Federal Work-Study, institutionally sponsored loans, and tuition waivers (full and partial) also available. Financial award application deadline: 3/1. *Unit head:* Dr. Monamad Musavi, Chair, 207-581-2243. *Application contact:* Scott G. Delcourt, Associate Dean of the Graduate School, 207-581-3291, Fax: 207-581-3232, E-mail: graduate@maine.edu.

The University of Manchester, School of Electrical and Electronic Engineering, Manchester, United Kingdom. Offers M Phil, PhD.

University of Manitoba, Faculty of Graduate Studies, Faculty of Engineering, Department of Electrical and Computer Engineering, Winnipeg, MB R3T 2N2, Canada. Offers M Eng, M Sc, PhD. *Degree requirements:* For master's, thesis; for doctorate, thesis/dissertation.

University of Maryland, Baltimore County, Graduate School, College of Engineering and Information Technology, Department of Computer Science and Electrical Engineering, Program in Electrical Engineering, Baltimore, MD 21250. Offers MS, PhD. Part-time programs available. *Students:* 33 full-time (6 women), 21 part-time (3 women); includes 9 minority (3 Black or African American, non-Hispanic/Latino; 4 Asian, non-Hispanic/Latino; 2 Hispanic/Latino), 25 international. Average age 31. 75 applicants, 61% accepted, 16 enrolled. In 2010, 5 master's, 3 doctorates awarded. *Degree requirements:* For master's, thesis optional; for doctorate, comprehensive exam, thesis/dissertation. *Entrance requirements:* For master's, GRE General Test, BS from ABET-accredited undergraduate program in electrical engineering or strong background in computer science, math, physics, or other engineering science; for doctorate, GRE General Test, BS from ABET-accredited undergraduate program in electrical engineering or strong background in computer science. Additional exam requirements/recommendations for international students: Required—TOEFL (minimum score 550 paper-based; 213 computer-based; 80 iBT). *Application deadline:* For fall admission, 6/1 for domestic students, 1/1 for international students; for spring admission, 11/1 for domestic students, 6/1 for international students. Applications are processed on a rolling basis. Application fee: $50. Electronic applications accepted. *Financial support:* In 2010–11, 10 research assistantships with full tuition reimbursements (averaging $22,000 per year), 4 teaching assistantships with partial tuition reimbursements (averaging $17,000 per year) were awarded; fellowships, career-related internships or fieldwork, Federal Work-Study, scholarships/grants, health care benefits, tuition waivers (partial), and unspecified assistantships also available. Support available to part-time students. Financial award application deadline: 6/30; financial award applicants required to submit FAFSA. *Unit head:* Dr. Gary Carter, Professor and Chair, 410-455-3500, Fax: 410-455-3969, E-mail: carter@cs.umbc.edu. *Application contact:* Dr. Joel Morris, Professor and Graduate Program Coordinator, 410-455-8416, Fax: 410-455-3969, E-mail: morris@cs.umbc.edu.

University of Maryland, College Park, Academic Affairs, A. James Clark School of Engineering, Department of Continuing and Distance Learning in Engineering, College Park, MD 20742.

Offers engineering (M Eng), including aerospace engineering, chemical engineering, civil engineering, electrical engineering, engineering, fire protection engineering, materials science and engineering, mechanical engineering, reliability engineering, systems engineering. *Faculty:* 4 full-time (1 woman), 11 part-time/adjunct (1 woman). *Students:* 56 full-time (15 women), 428 part-time (88 women); includes 153 minority (59 Black or African American, non-Hispanic/Latino; 63 Asian, non-Hispanic/Latino; 24 Hispanic/Latino; 7 Two or more races, non-Hispanic/Latino), 55 international. 551 applicants, 82% accepted, 360 enrolled. In 2010, 130 master's awarded. *Application deadline:* For fall admission, 8/15 for domestic students, 1/10 for international students; for spring admission, 12/15 for domestic students, 6/1 for international students. Applications are processed on a rolling basis. Application fee: $75. Electronic applications accepted. *Expenses:* Tuition, area resident: Part-time $471 per credit hour. Tuition, state resident: part-time $471 per credit hour. Tuition, nonresident: part-time $1016 per credit hour. Required fees: $337 per term. *Financial support:* In 2010–11, 2 research assistantships (averaging $20,285 per year), 7 teaching assistantships (averaging $16,962 per year) were awarded. *Unit head:* Dr. Darryll Pines, Dean, 301-405-0376, Fax: 301-314-5908, E-mail: pines@umd.edu. *Application contact:* Dr. Charles A. Caramello, Dean of the Graduate School, 301-405-0358, Fax: 301-314-9305, E-mail: ccaramel@umd.edu.

University of Maryland, College Park, Academic Affairs, A. James Clark School of Engineering, Department of Electrical and Computer Engineering, College Park, MD 20742. Offers electrical and computer engineering (M Eng, MS, PhD); electrical engineering (MS, PhD); telecommunications (MS). Part-time and evening/weekend programs available. Postbaccalaureate distance learning degree programs offered. *Faculty:* 106 full-time (10 women), 19 part-time/adjunct (3 women). *Students:* 397 full-time (92 women), 66 part-time (13 women); includes 62 minority (9 Black or African American, non-Hispanic/Latino; 43 Asian, non-Hispanic/Latino; 7 Hispanic/Latino; 3 Two or more races, non-Hispanic/Latino), 312 international. 1,588 applicants, 24% accepted, 132 enrolled. In 2010, 102 master's, 40 doctorates awarded. *Degree requirements:* For master's, thesis optional; for doctorate, thesis/dissertation, oral exam, qualifying exam. *Entrance requirements:* For master's and doctorate, GRE General Test, 3 letters of recommendation. *Application deadline:* For fall admission, 5/1 for domestic students, 2/1 for international students; for spring admission, 6/1 for international students. Applications are processed on a rolling basis. Application fee: $75. Electronic applications accepted. *Expenses:* Tuition, area resident: Part-time $471 per credit hour. Tuition, state resident: part-time $471 per credit hour. Tuition, nonresident: part-time $1016 per credit hour. Required fees: $337 per term. *Financial support:* In 2010–11, 11 fellowships with full and partial tuition reimbursements (averaging $19,987 per year), 170 research assistantships with tuition reimbursements (averaging $17,829 per year), 67 teaching assistantships with tuition reimbursements (averaging $17,042 per year) were awarded; career-related internships or fieldwork also available. Financial award applicants required to submit FAFSA. *Faculty research:* Communications and control, electrophysics, micro-electronics, robotics, computer engineering. Total annual research expenditures: $11.4 million. *Unit head:* Patrick O'Shea, Chair, 301-405-3683, E-mail: poshea@umd.edu. *Application contact:* Dr. Charles A. Caramello, Dean of Graduate School, 301-405-0358, Fax: 301-314-9305, E-mail: ccaramel@umd.edu.

University of Massachusetts Amherst, Graduate School, College of Engineering, Department of Electrical and Computer Engineering, Amherst, MA 01003. Offers MSECE, PhD. Part-time programs available. *Faculty:* 40 full-time (2 women). *Students:* 178 full-time (39 women), 24 part-time (4 women); includes 13 minority (3 Black or African American, non-Hispanic/Latino; 4 Asian, non-Hispanic/Latino; 5 Hispanic/Latino; 1 Two or more races, non-Hispanic/Latino), 160 international. Average age 26. 817 applicants, 25% accepted, 60 enrolled. In 2010, 25 master's, 10 doctorates awarded. Terminal master's awarded for partial completion of doctoral program. *Degree requirements:* For master's, thesis or alternative; for doctorate, comprehensive exam, thesis/dissertation. *Entrance requirements:* For master's and doctorate, GRE General Test. Additional exam requirements/recommendations for international students: Required—TOEFL (minimum score 550 paper-based; 213 computer-based; 80 iBT), IELTS (minimum score 6.5). *Application deadline:* For fall admission, 1/15 for domestic and international students; for spring admission, 10/1 for domestic and international students. Applications are processed on a rolling basis. Application fee: $50 ($65 for international students). Electronic applications accepted. *Expenses:* Tuition, state resident: full-time $2640. Required fees: $8282. One-time fee: $357 full-time. *Financial support:* In 2010–11, 8 fellowships with full tuition reimbursements (averaging $5,166 per year), 125 research assistantships with full tuition reimbursements (averaging $12,485 per year), 37 teaching assistantships with full tuition reimbursements (averaging $7,450 per year) were awarded; career-related internships or fieldwork, Federal Work-Study, scholarships/grants, traineeships, health care benefits, tuition waivers, and unspecified assistantships also available. Support available to part-time students. Financial award application deadline: 1/15; financial award applicants required to submit FAFSA. *Unit head:* Dr. C. Mani Krishna, Graduate Program Director, 413-545-4583, Fax: 413-545-4611, E-mail: ecegrad@ecs.umass.edu. *Application contact:* Jean M. Ames, Supervisor of Admissions, 413-545-0722, Fax: 413-577-0010, E-mail: gradadm@grad.umass.edu.

University of Massachusetts Dartmouth, Graduate School, College of Engineering, Department of Electrical and Computer Engineering, North Dartmouth, MA 02747-2300. Offers acoustics (Postbaccalaureate Certificate); communications (Postbaccalaureate Certificate); computer engineering (MS, PhD); computer systems engineering (Postbaccalaureate Certificate); digital signal processing (Postbaccalaureate Certificate); electrical engineering (MS, PhD); electrical engineering systems (Postbaccalaureate Certificate). Part-time programs available. *Faculty:* 17 full-time (3 women), 3 part-time/adjunct (0 women). *Students:* 32 full-time (6 women), 48 part-time (13 women); includes 2 Black or African American, non-Hispanic/Latino; 1 American Indian or Alaska Native, non-Hispanic/Latino; 4 Asian, non-Hispanic/Latino, 47 international. Average age 29. 97 applicants, 84% accepted, 19 enrolled. In 2010, 17 master's, 1 other advanced degree awarded. *Degree requirements:* For master's, culminating project or thesis; for doctorate, comprehensive exam, thesis/dissertation. *Entrance requirements:* For master's, GRE, minimum undergraduate GPA of 3.0, 3 letters of recommendation; for doctorate, GRE. Additional exam requirements/recommendations for international students: Required—TOEFL (minimum score 550 paper-based; 213 computer-based). *Application deadline:* For fall admission, 2/1 priority date for domestic students, 12/1 for international students; for spring admission, 11/1 priority date for domestic students, 9/1 for international students. Applications are processed on a rolling basis. Application fee: $40 ($60 for international students). Electronic applications accepted. *Expenses:* Tuition, state resident: full-time $2071; part-time $86 per credit. Tuition, nonresident: full-time $8099; part-time $337 per credit. Required fees: $9446; $394 per credit. One-time fee: $75. Part-time tuition and fees vary according to class time, course load, degree level and reciprocity agreements. *Financial support:* In 2010–11, 2 fellowships with full tuition reimbursements (averaging $16,000 per year), 14 research assistantships with full tuition reimbursements (averaging $11,096 per year), 9 teaching assistantships with full tuition reimbursements (averaging $12,500 per year) were awarded; Federal Work-Study and unspecified assistantships also available. Support available to part-time students. Financial award application deadline: 3/1; financial award applicants required to submit FAFSA. *Faculty research:* Speech acoustics, marine applications, signals and systems, applied electromagnetics, intelligent agency. Total annual research expenditures: $1.1 million. *Unit head:* Dr. Karen Payton, Director, 508-999-8434, Fax: 508-999-8489, E-mail: kpayton@umassd.edu. *Application contact:* Elan Turcotte-Shamski, Graduate Admissions Officer, 508-999-8604, Fax: 508-999-8183, E-mail: graduate@umassd.edu.

University of Massachusetts Lowell, James B. Francis College of Engineering, Department of Electrical and Computer Engineering, Program in Electrical Engineering, Lowell, MA 01854-2881. Offers MS Eng, D Eng. Part-time and evening/weekend programs available. Terminal master's awarded for partial completion of doctoral program. *Degree requirements:* For master's, thesis; for doctorate, 2 foreign languages, thesis/dissertation. *Entrance requirements:* For master's and doctorate, GRE General Test.

University of Memphis, Graduate School, Herff College of Engineering, Department of Electrical and Computer Engineering, Memphis, TN 38152. Offers automatic control systems (MS); biomedical systems (MS); communications and propagation systems (MS); computer engineering (PhD); electrical engineering (PhD); engineering computer systems (MS). *Faculty:* 8 full-time (1 woman), 2 part-time/adjunct (0 women). *Students:* 32 full-time (6 women), 4 part-time (1 woman); includes 3 Black or African American, non-Hispanic/Latino; 1 Asian, non-Hispanic/Latino, 25 international. Average age 26. 30 applicants, 87% accepted, 21 enrolled. In 2010, 10 master's awarded. *Degree requirements:* For master's, comprehensive exam, thesis or alternative. *Entrance requirements:* For master's, GRE General Test or MAT, minimum undergraduate GPA of 2.5. *Application deadline:* For fall admission, 8/1 for domestic students; for spring admission, 12/1 for domestic students. Application fee: $35 ($60 for international students). *Financial support:* In 2010–11, 4 students received support; research assistantships, teaching assistantships, career-related internships or fieldwork, Federal Work-Study, scholarships/grants, and unspecified assistantships available. Financial award application deadline: 2/15; financial award applicants required to submit FAFSA. *Faculty research:* Image processing, imaging sensors, biomedical systems, intelligent systems. *Unit head:* Dr. David J. Russomanno, Chair/Professor, 901-678-2175, Fax: 901-678-5469, E-mail: russmnn@memphis.edu. *Application contact:* Dr. Steven T. Griffin, Coordinator of Graduate Studies, 901-678-5268, Fax: 901-678-5469, E-mail: stgriffn@memphis.edu.

University of Miami, Graduate School, College of Engineering, Department of Electrical and Computer Engineering, Coral Gables, FL 33124. Offers MSECE, PhD. Part-time programs available. *Degree requirements:* For master's, thesis (for some programs); for doctorate, comprehensive exam, thesis/dissertation, dissertation proposal defense. *Entrance requirements:* For master's, GRE General Test, minimum GPA of 3.0; for doctorate, GRE General Test, minimum undergraduate GPA of 3.3, graduate 3.5. Additional exam requirements/recommendations for international students: Required—TOEFL (minimum score 550 paper-based; 213 computer-based; 59 iBT), IELTS (minimum score 7). Electronic applications accepted. *Faculty research:* Computer network, image processing, database systems, digital signal processing, machine intelligence.

University of Michigan, Horace H. Rackham School of Graduate Studies, College of Engineering, Department of Electrical Engineering and Computer Science, Ann Arbor, MI 48109. Offers MS, MSE, PhD. *Students:* 480 full-time (59 women), 9 part-time (0 women). 1,551 applicants, 29% accepted, 213 enrolled. In 2010, 104 master's, 33 doctorates awarded. *Expenses:* Tuition, state resident: full-time $17,784; part-time $1116 per credit hour. Tuition, nonresident: full-time $35,944; part-time $2125 per credit hour. International tuition: $35,994 full-time. Required fees: $95 per semester. Tuition and fees vary according to course load, degree level and program. *Faculty research:* Solid state electronics and optics; communications, control, signal process; sensors and integrated circuitry, others; software systems; artificial intelligence; hardware systems. *Unit head:* Prof. Khalil Najafi, Chair, 734-647-7010, Fax: 734-647-7009, E-mail: najafi@umich.edu. *Application contact:* Beth Stalnaker, Graduate Coordinator, 734-647-1758, Fax: 734-763-1503, E-mail: beths@umich.edu.

University of Michigan–Dearborn, College of Engineering and Computer Science, Department of Electrical and Computer Engineering, Dearborn, MI 48128-1491. Offers computer engineering (MSE); electrical engineering (MSE); software engineering (MS). Part-time and evening/weekend programs available. *Faculty:* 5 full-time (1 woman). *Students:* 17 full-time (1 woman), 129 part-time (20 women); includes 49 minority (6 Black or African American, non-Hispanic/Latino; 37 Asian, non-Hispanic/Latino; 4 Hispanic/Latino; 2 Two or more races, non-Hispanic/Latino). Average age 32. 63 applicants, 56% accepted, 29 enrolled. In 2010, 57 master's awarded. *Degree requirements:* For master's, thesis optional. *Entrance requirements:* For master's, bachelor's degree in electrical and computer engineering or equivalent, minimum GPA of 3.0. Additional exam requirements/recommendations for international students: Required—TOEFL (minimum score 560 paper-based; 220 computer-based; 84 iBT). *Application deadline:* For fall admission, 8/1 priority date for domestic students, 4/1 for international students; for winter admission, 12/1 priority date for domestic students, 8/1 for international students; for spring admission, 4/1 priority date for domestic students, 2/1 for international students. Applications are processed on a rolling basis. Application fee: $60 ($75 for international students). *Financial support:* In 2010–11, 4 fellowships (averaging $26,340 per year), 1 research assistantship with partial tuition reimbursement (averaging $12,384 per year) were awarded; teaching assistantships, Federal Work-Study also available. Financial award application deadline: 4/1; financial award applicants required to submit FAFSA. *Faculty research:* Fuzzy systems and applications, machine vision, pattern recognition and machine intelligence, vehicle electronics, wireless communications. *Unit head:* Dr. YiLu Murphey, Chair, 313-593-5028, Fax: 313-583-6336, E-mail: yilu@umich.edu. *Application contact:* Sandra Marie Krzyskowski, Intermediate Academic Records Assistant, 313-593-5420, Fax: 313-583-6336, E-mail: ece-grad@umd.umich.edu.

University of Minnesota, Duluth, Graduate School, Swenson College of Science and Engineering, Department of Electrical and Computer Engineering, Duluth, MN 55812-2496. Offers MSECE. Part-time programs available. *Degree requirements:* For master's, thesis. *Entrance requirements:* Additional exam requirements/recommendations for international students: Recommended—IELTS, TWE. *Faculty research:* Biomedical instrumentation, transportation systems, computer hardware and software, signal processing, optical communications.

University of Minnesota, Twin Cities Campus, Institute of Technology, Department of Electrical and Computer Engineering, Minneapolis, MN 55455-0213. Offers MSEE, PhD. Part-time programs available. *Degree requirements:* For master's, thesis or alternative; for doctorate, thesis/dissertation. *Entrance requirements:* Additional exam requirements/recommendations for international students: Required—TOEFL (minimum score 550 paper-based; 213 computer-based), GRE. *Faculty research:* Signal processing, microelectronics, computers, controls, power electronics.

University of Missouri, Graduate School, College of Engineering, Department of Electrical and Computer Engineering, Columbia, MO 65211. Offers MS, PhD. *Degree requirements:* For master's, thesis or alternative; for doctorate, thesis/dissertation. *Entrance requirements:* For master's, GRE General Test, minimum GPA of 3.0; for doctorate, GRE General Test, GRE Subject Test, minimum GPA of 3.0. Additional exam requirements/recommendations for international students: Required—TOEFL (minimum score 550 paper-based; 213 computer-based; 80 iBT).

University of Missouri–Kansas City, School of Computing and Engineering, Kansas City, MO 64110-2499. Offers civil engineering (MS); computer and electrical engineering (PhD); computer science (MS), including bioinformatics, software engineering, telecommunications networking; computer science and informatics (PhD); computing (PhD); electrical engineering (MS); engineering (PhD); mechanical engineering (MS); telecommunications (PhD). PhD (interdisciplinary) offered through the School of Graduate Studies. Part-time programs available. *Faculty:* 36 full-time (5 women), 21 part-time/adjunct (0 women). *Students:* 160 full-time (32 women), 194 part-time (41 women); includes 21 minority (5 Black or African American, non-Hispanic/Latino; 9 Asian, non-Hispanic/Latino; 6 Hispanic/Latino; 1 Two or more races, non-Hispanic/Latino), 273 international. Average age 25. 440 applicants, 55% accepted, 104 enrolled. In 2010, 135 master's awarded. *Degree requirements:* For doctorate, thesis/dissertation. *Entrance requirements:* For master's, GRE General Test, minimum GPA of 3.0, 3 letters of recommendation from professors; for doctorate, GRE General Test, minimum GPA of 3.5. Additional exam requirements/recommendations for international students: Required—TOEFL (minimum score 550 paper-based; 213 computer-based; 80 iBT). *Application deadline:* For fall admission, 1/15 priority date for domestic students, 1/15 for international students. Applications are processed on a rolling basis. Application fee: $45 ($50 for international students). *Expenses:* Tuition, state resident: full-time $5522.40; part-time $306.80 per credit hour. Tuition, nonresident: full-time $7128; part-time $792 per credit hour. Required fees: $261.15 per term. *Financial support:* In 2010–11, 35 research assistantships with partial tuition reimbursements (averaging $14,340 per year), 20 teaching assistantships with partial tuition reimbursements (averaging $13,351 per year) were awarded; career-related internships or fieldwork, Federal Work-Study, scholarships/grants, tuition waivers (partial), and unspecified

Electrical Engineering

University of Missouri–Kansas City (continued)
assistantships also available. Support available to part-time students. Financial award application deadline: 3/1; financial award applicants required to submit FAFSA. *Faculty research:* Algorithms, bioinformatics and medical informatics, biomechanics/biomaterials, civil engineering materials, networking and telecommunications, thermal science. Total annual research expenditures: $1.1 million. *Unit head:* Dr. Kevin Z. Truman, Dean, 816-235-2399, Fax: 816-235-5159. *Application contact:* Dr. Kevin Z. Truman, Dean, 816-235-2399, Fax: 816-235-5159.

University of Nebraska–Lincoln, Graduate College, College of Engineering, Department of Electrical Engineering, Lincoln, NE 68588. Offers MS, PhD. *Degree requirements:* For master's, thesis optional; for doctorate, comprehensive exam, thesis/dissertation. *Entrance requirements:* For master's and doctorate, GRE General Test. Additional exam requirements/recommendations for international students: Required—TOEFL (minimum score 550 paper-based; 213 computer-based). Electronic applications accepted. *Faculty research:* Electromagnetics, communications, biomedical digital signal processing, electrical breakdown of gases, optical properties of microelectronic materials.

University of Nevada, Las Vegas, Graduate College, Howard R. Hughes College of Engineering, Department of Electrical and Computer Engineering, Las Vegas, NV 89154-4026. Offers MSE, PhD. Part-time programs available. *Faculty:* 14 full-time (1 woman), 3 part-time/adjunct (0 women). *Students:* 34 full-time (7 women), 13 part-time (1 woman); includes 9 minority (2 Black or African American, non-Hispanic/Latino; 1 American Indian or Alaska Native, non-Hispanic/Latino; 2 Asian, non-Hispanic/Latino; 1 Hispanic/Latino; 3 Two or more races, non-Hispanic/Latino), 29 international. Average age 28. 28 applicants, 75% accepted, 11 enrolled. In 2010, 10 master's, 4 doctorates awarded. *Degree requirements:* For master's, comprehensive exam, thesis, project; for doctorate, comprehensive exam, thesis/dissertation. *Entrance requirements:* Additional exam requirements/recommendations for international students: Required—TOEFL (minimum score 550 paper-based; 213 computer-based; 80 iBT), IELTS (minimum score 7). *Application deadline:* For fall admission, 6/1 priority date for domestic and international students; for spring admission, 10/1 priority date for domestic and international students. Applications are processed on a rolling basis. Application fee: $60 ($95 for international students). Electronic applications accepted. *Expenses:* Tuition, area resident: Part-time $239.50 per credit. Tuition, state resident: part-time $239.50 per credit. Tuition, nonresident: part-time $503 per credit. Required fees: $108 per semester. Tuition and fees vary according to course load, program and reciprocity agreements. *Financial support:* In 2010–11, 25 students received support, including 12 research assistantships with partial tuition reimbursements available (averaging $12,220 per year), 13 teaching assistantships with partial tuition reimbursements available (averaging $10,307 per year); institutionally sponsored loans, scholarships/grants, health care benefits, tuition waivers (full), and unspecified assistantships also available. Financial award application deadline: 3/1. *Faculty research:* Computer engineering, power engineering, semiconductor and nanotechnology, electronics and VLSI, telecommunications and control. Total annual research expenditures: $2.7 million. *Unit head:* Dr. Henry Selvaraj, Chair/ Professor, 702-895-4183, Fax: 702-895-4075, E-mail: ece.chair@unlv.edu. *Application contact:* Graduate College Admissions Evaluator, 702-895-3320, Fax: 702-895-4180, E-mail: gradcollege@unlv.edu.

University of Nevada, Reno, Graduate School, College of Engineering, Department of Electrical Engineering, Reno, NV 89557. Offers MS, PhD. Terminal master's awarded for partial completion of doctoral program. *Degree requirements:* For master's, thesis optional; for doctorate, thesis/dissertation. *Entrance requirements:* For master's, GRE General Test, minimum GPA of 2.75; for doctorate, GRE General Test, minimum GPA of 3.0. Additional exam requirements/recommendations for international students: Required—TOEFL (minimum score 500 paper-based; 173 computer-based; 61 iBT), IELTS (minimum score 6). Electronic applications accepted. *Expenses:* Tuition, state resident: full-time $2219; part-time $246 per credit. Tuition, nonresident: part-time $510 per credit. International tuition: $9009 full-time. Required fees: $59 per term. One-time fee: $101. Tuition and fees vary according to course load. *Faculty research:* Acoustics, neural networking, synthetic aperture radar simulation, optical fiber communications and sensors.

University of New Brunswick Fredericton, School of Graduate Studies, Faculty of Engineering, Department of Electrical and Computer Engineering, Fredericton, NB E3B 5A3, Canada. Offers M Eng, M Sc E, PhD. Part-time programs available. *Faculty:* 14 full-time (1 woman), 1 (woman) part-time/adjunct. *Students:* 60 full-time (4 women), 5 part-time (1 woman). 45 applicants, 44% accepted. In 2010, 10 master's, 5 doctorates awarded. *Degree requirements:* For master's, thesis, research proposal; 10 courses (for M Eng); for doctorate, comprehensive exam, thesis/dissertation, research proposal. *Entrance requirements:* For master's, minimum GPA of 3.0 or B average; references; for doctorate, M Sc; minimum GPA of 3.0 or B average; previous transcripts; references. Additional exam requirements/recommendations for international students: Required—TWE, TOEFL (minimum score 580 paper-based; 237 computer-based) or IELTS (minimum score 7). *Application deadline:* Applications are processed on a rolling basis. Application fee: $50 Canadian dollars. *Expenses:* Tuition, area resident: Full-time $3708; part-time $927 per term. International tuition: $6300 full-time. Required fees: $50 per term. *Financial support:* In 2010–11, 39 research assistantships (averaging $14,400 per year), 39 teaching assistantships were awarded; fellowships also available. *Faculty research:* Biomedical engineering, communications, robotics and control systems, electromagnetic systems, embedded systems, optical fiber systems, sustainable energy and power systems, signal processing, software systems. *Unit head:* Dr. Maryhelen Stevenson, Director of Graduate Studies, 504-447-3147, Fax: 504-453-3589, E-mail: stevenso@unb.ca. *Application contact:* Shelley Cormier, Graduate Secretary, 506-452-6142, Fax: 506-453-3589, E-mail: scormier@unb.ca.

University of New Hampshire, Graduate School, College of Engineering and Physical Sciences, Department of Electrical and Computer Engineering, Durham, NH 03824. Offers electrical engineering (MS, PhD). Part-time and evening/weekend programs available. *Faculty:* 11 full-time (0 women). *Students:* 8 full-time (0 women), 24 part-time (1 woman); includes 3 minority (1 Asian, non-Hispanic/Latino; 1 Hispanic/Latino; 1 Two or more races, non-Hispanic/Latino), 5 international. Average age 28. 54 applicants, 54% accepted, 5 enrolled. In 2010, 11 master's, 2 doctorates awarded. *Degree requirements:* For master's, thesis or alternative; for doctorate, thesis/dissertation. *Entrance requirements:* For master's, GRE (for non-U. S. university bachelor's degree holders); for doctorate, GRE (for non-US university bachelor's degree holders). Additional exam requirements/recommendations for international students: Required—TOEFL (minimum score 550 paper-based; 213 computer-based; 80 iBT). *Application deadline:* For fall admission, 4/1 priority date for domestic students, 4/1 for international students; for spring admission, 12/1 for domestic students. Applications are processed on a rolling basis. Application fee: $65. Electronic applications accepted. *Financial support:* In 2010–11, 15 students received support, including 8 research assistantships, 6 teaching assistantships; fellowships, Federal Work-Study, scholarships/grants, and tuition waivers (full and partial) also available. Support available to part-time students. Financial award application deadline: 2/15. *Faculty research:* Biomedical engineering, communications systems and information theory, digital systems, illumination engineering. *Unit head:* John LaCourse, Chairperson, 603-862-1324. *Application contact:* Kathryn Reynolds, Administrative Assistant, 603-862-1358, E-mail: ece.dept@unh.edu.

University of New Haven, Graduate School, Tagliatela College of Engineering, Program in Electrical Engineering, West Haven, CT 06516-1916. Offers communications/digital signal processing (MS); control system (MS); electrical and computer engineering (MS); electrical engineering (MS). Part-time and evening/weekend programs available. *Students:* 42 full-time (7 women), 17 part-time (2 women); includes 4 Black or African American, non-Hispanic/Latino; 1 Asian, non-Hispanic/Latino, 46 international. Average age 27. 199 applicants, 99% accepted, 25 enrolled. In 2010, 18 master's awarded. *Degree requirements:* For master's, thesis or alternative. *Entrance requirements:* For master's, bachelor's degree in electrical engineering. Additional exam requirements/recommendations for international students: Required—TOEFL (minimum score 520 paper-based; 190 computer-based; 70 iBT); Recommended—IELTS (minimum score 5.5). *Application deadline:* For fall admission, 5/31 for

international students; for winter admission, 10/15 for international students; for spring admission, 1/15 for international students. Applications are processed on a rolling basis. Application fee: $50. Electronic applications accepted. *Financial support:* Research assistantships with partial tuition reimbursements, teaching assistantships with partial tuition reimbursements, career-related internships or fieldwork, Federal Work-Study, scholarships/grants, tuition waivers, and unspecified assistantships available. Support available to part-time students. Financial award applicants required to submit FAFSA. *Unit head:* Dr. Ali Golbazi, Professor and Chair, 203-932-7164. *Application contact:* Eloise Gormley, Director of Graduate Admissions, 203-932-7449, Fax: 203-932-7137, E-mail: gradinfo@newhaven.edu.

University of New Mexico, Graduate School, School of Engineering, Department of Electrical and Computer Engineering, Albuquerque, NM 87131-2039. Offers computer engineering (MS, PhD); electrical engineering (MS, PhD). Part-time and evening/weekend programs available. Postbaccalaureate distance learning degree programs offered (no on-campus study). *Faculty:* 36 full-time (5 women), 8 part-time/adjunct (0 women). *Students:* 136 full-time (19 women), 72 part-time (10 women); includes 42 minority (4 Black or African American, non-Hispanic/Latino; 1 American Indian or Alaska Native, non-Hispanic/Latino; 7 Asian, non-Hispanic/Latino; 28 Hispanic/Latino; 2 Two or more races, non-Hispanic/Latino), 92 international. Average age 31. 245 applicants, 23% accepted, 40 enrolled. In 2010, 42 master's awarded. Terminal master's awarded for partial completion of doctoral program. *Degree requirements:* For master's, thesis; for doctorate, comprehensive exam, thesis/dissertation. *Entrance requirements:* For master's, GRE General Test, minimum GPA of 3.0; for doctorate, GRE General Test, minimum GPA of 3.5. Additional exam requirements/recommendations for international students: Required—TOEFL (minimum score 550 paper-based; 213 computer-based; 79 iBT). *Application deadline:* For fall admission, 7/15 for domestic students, 2/15 for international students; for spring admission, 11/1 for domestic students, 6/15 for international students. Application fee: $50. Electronic applications accepted. *Expenses:* Tuition, state resident: full-time $5991; part-time $251 per credit hour. Tuition, nonresident: full-time $14,405; part-time $800.20 per credit hour. Tuition and fees vary according to course level, course load, program and reciprocity agreements. *Financial support:* In 2010–11, 124 students received support, including 2 fellowships with tuition reimbursements available (averaging $11,500 per year), 95 research assistantships with tuition reimbursements available (averaging $16,097 per year), 4 teaching assistantships with tuition reimbursements available (averaging $11,093 per year); scholarships/grants, health care benefits, and unspecified assistantships also available. Financial award application deadline: 2/15; financial award applicants required to submit FAFSA. *Faculty research:* Advanced graphics and visualization, biomedical engineering, communications and networking, networked control systems, photonics and microelectronics, pulsed power and high-power electromagnetics, reconfigurable systems. Total annual research expenditures: $3.2 million. *Unit head:* Dr. Chaouki T. Abdallah, Chair, 505-277-0298, Fax: 505-277-1439, E-mail: chaouki@ece.unm.edu. *Application contact:* Elmyra Grelle, Coordinator—Graduate Programs, 505-277-2600, Fax: 505-277-1439, E-mail: egrelle@ece.unm.edu.

See Display on next page and Close-Up on page 395.

The University of North Carolina at Charlotte, Graduate School, The William States Lee College of Engineering, Department of Electrical and Computer Engineering, Charlotte, NC 28223-0001. Offers electrical engineering (MSEE, PhD). Part-time and evening/weekend programs available. *Faculty:* 26 full-time (1 woman). *Students:* 99 full-time (20 women), 56 part-time (10 women); includes 10 minority (4 Black or African American, non-Hispanic/Latino; 1 American Indian or Alaska Native, non-Hispanic/Latino; 3 Asian, non-Hispanic/Latino; 2 Hispanic/Latino), 109 international. Average age 26. 336 applicants, 55% accepted, 34 enrolled. In 2010, 35 master's, 7 doctorates awarded. Terminal master's awarded for partial completion of doctoral program. *Degree requirements:* For master's, thesis optional, thesis or project; for doctorate, thesis/dissertation. *Entrance requirements:* For master's, GRE General Test, minimum GPA of 3.0 in undergraduate major, 2.75 overall; for doctorate, GRE General Test, 3 letters of reference. Additional exam requirements/recommendations for international students: Required—TOEFL (minimum score 557 paper-based; 220 computer-based; 83 iBT). *Application deadline:* For fall admission, 7/1 for domestic students, 5/1 for international students; for spring admission, 11/1 for domestic students, 10/1 for international students. Applications are processed on a rolling basis. Application fee: $55. Electronic applications accepted. *Expenses:* Tuition, state resident: full-time $3464. Tuition, nonresident: full-time $14,297. Required fees: $2094. Tuition and fees vary according to course load. *Financial support:* In 2010–11, 51 students received support, including 14 research assistantships (averaging $7,554 per year), 37 teaching assistantships (averaging $9,414 per year); career-related internships or fieldwork, institutionally sponsored loans, scholarships/grants, and unspecified assistantships also available. Support available to part-time students. Financial award application deadline: 4/1; financial award applicants required to submit FAFSA. *Faculty research:* Integrated circuits self test, control systems, optoelectronics/microelectronics devices and systems, communications, computer engineering. Total annual research expenditures: $1.2 million. *Unit head:* Dr. Ian Ferguson, Chair, 704-687-8404, Fax: 704-687-4762, E-mail: ianf@uncc.edu. *Application contact:* Kathy B. Giddings, Director of Graduate Admissions, 704-687-5503, Fax: 704-687-3279, E-mail: gradadm@uncc.edu.

University of North Dakota, Graduate School, School of Engineering and Mines, Department of Electrical Engineering, Grand Forks, ND 58202. Offers M Engr, MS. Part-time programs available. *Faculty:* 7 full-time (2 women). *Students:* 19 full-time (3 women), 3 part-time (0 women); includes 3 minority (2 Black or African American, non-Hispanic/Latino; 1 Asian, non-Hispanic/Latino), 3 international. Average age 26. 34 applicants, 44% accepted, 8 enrolled. In 2010, 4 master's awarded. *Degree requirements:* For master's, comprehensive exam, thesis or alternative. *Entrance requirements:* For master's, GRE General Test, minimum GPA of 3.0 (MS), 2.5 (M Engr). Additional exam requirements/recommendations for international students: Required—TOEFL (minimum score 550 paper-based; 213 computer-based; 79 iBT), IELTS (minimum score 6.5). *Application deadline:* For fall admission, 8/1 priority date for domestic students, 5/1 priority date for international students; for spring admission, 12/1 priority date for domestic students, 9/1 priority date for international students. Applications are processed on a rolling basis. Application fee: $35. Electronic applications accepted. *Expenses:* Tuition, state resident: full-time $5857; part-time $306.74 per credit. Tuition, nonresident: full-time $15,666; part-time $729.77 per credit. Required fees: $53.42 per credit. Tuition and fees vary according to course load, program and reciprocity agreements. *Financial support:* In 2010–11, 9 students received support, including 7 research assistantships with full and partial tuition reimbursements available (averaging $6,402 per year), 1 teaching assistantship with full and partial tuition reimbursement available (averaging $5,727 per year); fellowships with full and partial tuition reimbursements available, Federal Work-Study, institutionally sponsored loans, scholarships/grants, health care benefits, tuition waivers (full and partial), and unspecified assistantships also available. Support available to part-time students. Financial award application deadline: 3/15; financial award applicants required to submit FAFSA. *Faculty research:* Controls and robotics, signal processing, energy conversion, microwaves, computer engineering. Total annual research expenditures: $903,377. *Unit head:* Dr. Naima Kaabouch, Graduate Director, 701-777-4460, Fax: 701-777-4838, E-mail: naimakaabouch@mail.und.edu. *Application contact:* Staci Wells, Admissions Associate, 701-777-2945, Fax: 701-777-3619, E-mail: staci.wells@gradschool.und.edu.

University of North Florida, College of Computing, Engineering, and Construction, School of Engineering, Jacksonville, FL 32224. Offers MSCE, MSEE, MSME. Part-time programs available. *Faculty:* 15 full-time (2 women). *Students:* 5 full-time (2 women), 41 part-time (5 women); includes 2 Black or African American, non-Hispanic/Latino; 1 Asian, non-Hispanic/Latino; 4 Hispanic/Latino; 1 Two or more races, non-Hispanic/Latino, 6 international. Average age 29. 45 applicants, 40% accepted, 13 enrolled. In 2010, 3 master's awarded. *Application deadline:* For fall admission, 7/1 for domestic students, 5/1 for international students; for spring admission, 11/1 for domestic students, 10/1 for international students. Application fee: $30. *Expenses:* Tuition, state resident: full-time $7646.40; part-time $318.60 per credit hour. Tuition, nonresident: full-time $23,502; part-time $979.24 per credit hour. Required fees: $1208.88; $50.37 per credit hour. Tuition and fees vary according to course load and program. *Financial support:* In

2010–11, 16 students received support, including research assistantships (averaging $2,669 per year), teaching assistantships (averaging $451 per year); Federal Work-Study, scholarships/grants, tuition waivers, and unspecified assistantships also available. Financial award application deadline: 4/1; financial award applicants required to submit FAFSA. Total annual research expenditures: $2.9 million. *Unit head:* Gerald Merckel, Associate Dean, 904-620-1390, E-mail: gmerckel@unf.edu. *Application contact:* Lillith Richardson, Assistant Director, The Graduate School, 904-320-1360, Fax: 904-620-1362, E-mail: graduateschool@unf.edu.

University of North Texas, Toulouse Graduate School, College of Engineering, Department of Electrical Engineering, Denton, TX 76203. Offers MS. Part-time programs available. *Degree requirements:* For master's, thesis optional. *Entrance requirements:* For master's, GRE, minimum GPA of 3.0. Additional exam requirements/recommendations for international students: Required—TOEFL (minimum score 550 paper-based; 213 computer-based; 79 iBT). *Expenses:* Tuition, state resident: full-time $4298; part-time $239 per credit hour. Tuition, nonresident: full-time $10,782; part-time $549 per credit hour. Required fees: $1292; $270 per credit hour. *Financial support:* Fellowships with tuition reimbursements, research assistantships with tuition reimbursements, teaching assistantships with tuition reimbursements, career-related internships or fieldwork, scholarships/grants, health care benefits, tuition waivers (full), and unspecified assistantships available. Financial award application deadline: 4/1. *Faculty research:* Ecological and environmental modeling, radar systems, wireless communication, human-computer interaction, computer vision, signal processing, information assurance, VISI design. *Application contact:* Graduate Advisor, 940-891-6942, Fax: 940-891-6881, E-mail: fu@unt.edu.

University of Notre Dame, Graduate School, College of Engineering, Department of Electrical Engineering, Notre Dame, IN 46556. Offers MSEE, PhD. Terminal master's awarded for partial completion of doctoral program. *Degree requirements:* For master's, comprehensive exam; for doctorate, thesis/dissertation, candidacy exam. *Entrance requirements:* For master's and doctorate, GRE General Test. Additional exam requirements/recommendations for international students: Required—TOEFL (minimum score 600 paper-based; 250 computer-based; 80 iBT). Electronic applications accepted. *Faculty research:* Electronic properties of materials and devices, signal and imaging processing, communication theory, control theory and applications, optoelectronics.

See Display on next page and Close-Up on page 397.

University of Oklahoma, College of Engineering, Department of Electrical and Computer Engineering, Program in Electrical and Computer Engineering, Norman, OK 73019. Offers MS, PhD. Part-time programs available. *Students:* 100 full-time (21 women), 41 part-time (5 women); includes 12 minority (2 Black or African American, non-Hispanic/Latino; 1 American Indian or Alaska Native, non-Hispanic/Latino; 8 Asian, non-Hispanic/Latino; 1 Hispanic/Latino), 84 international. Average age 28. 46 applicants, 63% accepted, 14 enrolled. In 2010, 26 master's, 11 doctorates awarded. Terminal master's awarded for partial completion of doctoral program. *Degree requirements:* For master's, thesis; for doctorate, thesis/dissertation, general exam, oral exam, qualifying exam. *Entrance requirements:* For master's and doctorate, GRE General Test. Additional exam requirements/recommendations for international students: Required—TOEFL (minimum score 550 paper-based; 213 computer-based; 79 iBT). *Application deadline:* For fall admission, 5/15 for domestic students, 4/1 for international students; for spring admission, 9/1 for domestic and international students. Applications are processed on a rolling basis. Application fee: $40 ($90 for international students). Electronic applications accepted. *Expenses:* Tuition, state resident: full-time $3892.80; part-time $162.20 per credit hour. Tuition, nonresident: full-time $14,167; part-time $590.30 per credit hour. Required fees: $2523.40; $94.60 per credit hour. Tuition and fees vary according to course load and degree level. *Financial support:* In 2010–11, 133 students received support. Career-related internships or fieldwork, scholarships/grants, health care benefits, and unspecified assistantships available. Financial award application deadline: 4/15; financial award applicants required to submit FAFSA. *Faculty research:* Signal/image processing, biomedical imaging, computer hardware design, weather radar, solid state electronics, intelligent transportation systems, navigation systems, power/electrical energy, control systems, communications. *Unit head:* Dr. James Sluss, Director, 405-325-4721, Fax: 405-325-7066, E-mail: sluss@ou.edu. *Application contact:* Lynn Hall, Graduate Program Assistant/Student Services Coordinator, 405-325-4285, Fax: 405-325-7066, E-mail: srg@ou.edu.

University of Ottawa, Faculty of Graduate and Postdoctoral Studies, Faculty of Engineering, Ottawa-Carleton Institute for Electrical and Computer Engineering, Ottawa, ON K1N 6N5, Canada. Offers M Eng, MA Sc, PhD. *Degree requirements:* For master's, thesis or alternative, project; for doctorate, comprehensive exam, thesis/dissertation. *Entrance requirements:* For master's, honors degree or equivalent, minimum B average; for doctorate, minimum A- average. Electronic applications accepted. *Faculty research:* CAD, CSE, distributed systems and BISDN, CCN, DOC.

University of Pennsylvania, School of Engineering and Applied Science, Department of Electrical and Systems Engineering, Philadelphia, PA 19104. Offers MSE, PhD. Part-time programs available. *Faculty:* 27 full-time (2 women), 9 part-time/adjunct (0 women). *Students:* 155 full-time (37 women), 42 part-time (4 women); includes 2 Black or African American, non-Hispanic/Latino; 15 Asian, non-Hispanic/Latino; 1 Hispanic/Latino, 137 international. 724 applicants, 33% accepted, 111 enrolled. In 2010, 59 master's, 1 doctorate awarded. Terminal master's awarded for partial completion of doctoral program. *Degree requirements:* For master's, thesis optional; for doctorate, comprehensive exam, thesis/dissertation. *Entrance requirements:* For master's and doctorate, GRE General Test. Additional exam requirements/recommendations for international students: Required—TOEFL. *Application deadline:* For fall admission, 6/1 priority date for domestic students, 5/1 priority date for international students; for spring admission, 11/1 priority date for domestic students, 10/1 priority date for international students. Applications are processed on a rolling basis. Application fee: $70. Electronic applications accepted. *Expenses:* Tuition: Full-time $25,660; part-time $4758 per course. Required fees: $2152; $270 per course. Tuition and fees vary according to course load, degree level and program. *Financial support:* Fellowships, research assistantships, teaching assistantships, institutionally sponsored loans, scholarships/grants, traineeships, health care benefits, and unspecified assistantships available. *Faculty research:* Electro-optics, microwave and millimeter-wave optics, solid-state and chemical electronics, electromagnetic propagation, telecommunications. *Application contact:* Nichole Wood, Graduate Coordinator, 215-898-9390, E-mail: woodn@seas.upenn.edu.

University of Pittsburgh, School of Engineering, Department of Electrical Engineering, Pittsburgh, PA 15260. Offers MSEE, PhD. Part-time programs available. Postbaccalaureate distance learning degree programs offered. *Faculty:* 17 full-time (1 woman), 15 part-time/adjunct (1 woman). *Students:* 80 full-time (19 women), 48 part-time (3 women); includes 8 minority (6 Black or African American, non-Hispanic/Latino; 2 Asian, non-Hispanic/Latino), 61 international. 661 applicants, 18% accepted, 46 enrolled. In 2010, 30 master's, 11 doctorates awarded. Terminal master's awarded for partial completion of doctoral program. *Degree requirements:* For master's, thesis optional; for doctorate, comprehensive exam, thesis/dissertation, final oral exams. *Entrance requirements:* For master's and doctorate, GRE General Test, minimum QPA of 3.0. Additional exam requirements/recommendations for international students: Required—TOEFL (minimum score 550 paper-based; 213 computer-based; 80 iBT). *Application deadline:* For fall admission, 3/1 priority date for domestic students; for spring admission, 7/1 priority date for domestic students. Applications are processed on a rolling basis. Application fee: $50. Electronic applications accepted. *Expenses:* Tuition, state resident: full-time $17,304; part-time $701 per credit. Tuition, nonresident: full-time $29,554; part-time $1210 per credit. Required fees: $740; $214 per term. Tuition and fees vary according to program. *Financial support:* In 2010–11, 53 students received support, including 7 fellowships with full tuition reimbursements available (averaging $26,000 per year), 23 research assistantships with full tuition reimbursements available (averaging $25,000 per year), 18 teaching assistantships with full tuition reimbursements available (averaging $24,000 per year);

Electrical Engineering

Graduate Studies in Electrical Engineering

UNIVERSITY OF NOTRE DAME

The Department of Electrical Engineering offers programs of study and research leading to M.S. and Ph.D. degrees. These programs are designed to prepare students for careers in academia and research as well as industrial or governmental research and advanced development.

Areas of specialization include:

Communication systems

Control systems

Digital signal and image processing

Nanoelectronics

Optical and microwave electronics

Solid-state materials and devices

Nano-biotechnology

Department URL: www.ee.nd.edu

Graduate School URL: graduateschool.nd.edu

E-mail: eegrad@nd.edu

scholarships/grants and tuition waivers (full and partial) also available. Financial award application deadline: 4/15. *Faculty research:* Computer engineering, image processing, signal processing, electro-optic devices, controls/power. Total annual research expenditures: $5.6 million. *Unit head:* Dr. William Stanchina, Chairman, 412-624-8000, Fax: 412-624-8003, E-mail: wstasnchina@engr.bitt.edu. *Application contact:* Steven Levitan, Graduate Coordinator, 412-624-8001, Fax: 412-624-8003, E-mail: levitan@engr.pitt.edu.

University of Puerto Rico, Mayagüez Campus, Graduate Studies, College of Engineering, Department of Electrical and Computer Engineering, Mayagüez, PR 00681-9000. Offers computer engineering (ME, MS); computing and information sciences and engineering (PhD); electrical engineering (ME, MS). Part-time programs available. *Students:* 97 full-time (23 women), 12 part-time (1 woman); includes 74 Hispanic/Latino, 35 international. 41 applicants, 54% accepted, 13 enrolled. In 2010, 19 master's, 1 doctorate awarded. *Degree requirements:* For master's, comprehensive exam, thesis; for doctorate, comprehensive exam, thesis/dissertation. *Entrance requirements:* For master's, proficiency in English and Spanish, BS in electrical or computer engineering or equivalent, minimum GPA of 3.0; for doctorate, GRE. Additional exam requirements/recommendations for international students: Required—TOEFL (minimum score 450 paper-based). *Application deadline:* For fall admission, 2/15 for domestic and international students; for spring admission, 9/15 for domestic and international students. Applications are processed on a rolling basis. Application fee: $25. *Expenses:* Tuition, state resident: full-time $1188. Tuition, nonresident: full-time $1188. International tuition: $6126 full-time. Tuition and fees vary according to course level and course load. *Financial support:* In 2010–11, 23 students received support, including fellowships (averaging $12,000 per year), 3 research assistantships (averaging $15,000 per year), 23 teaching assistantships (averaging $8,500 per year); Federal Work-Study and institutionally sponsored loans also available. *Faculty research:* Microcomputer interfacing, control systems, power systems, electronics. Total annual research expenditures: $3.8 million. *Unit head:* Dr. Erick Aponte-Diaz, Chairperson, 787-832-4040 Ext. 3821, E-mail: erick.aponte1@upr.edu. *Application contact:* Sandra Montalvo, Administrative Staff, 787-832-4040 Ext. 3094, Fax: 787-831-7564, E-mail: sandra@ece.uprm.edu.

University of Rhode Island, Graduate School, College of Engineering, Department of Electrical, Computer and Biomedical Engineering, Kingston, RI 02881. Offers MS, PhD, Graduate Certificate. Part-time programs available. *Faculty:* 18 full-time (3 women). *Students:* 28 full-time (6 women), 24 part-time (2 women); includes 10 minority (1 Black or African American, non-Hispanic/Latino; 6 Asian, non-Hispanic/Latino; 3 Hispanic/Latino), 12 international. In 2010, 12 master's, 1 doctorate awarded. *Degree requirements:* For master's, comprehensive exam (for some programs), thesis optional; for doctorate, comprehensive exam, thesis/dissertation. *Entrance requirements:* For master's and doctorate, 2 letters of recommendation. Additional exam requirements/recommendations for international students: Required—TOEFL (minimum score 550 paper-based; 213 computer-based). *Application deadline:* For fall admission, 7/15 for domestic students, 2/1 for international students; for spring admission, 11/15 for domestic students, 7/15 for international students. Application fee: $65. Electronic applications accepted. *Expenses:* Tuition, state resident: full-time $9588; part-time $533 per credit hour. Tuition, nonresident: full-time $22,968; part-time $1276 per credit hour. Required fees: $1282; $68 per semester. Tuition and fees vary according to program. *Financial support:* In 2010–11, 8 research assistantships with full and partial tuition reimbursements (averaging $9,258 per year), 6 teaching assistantships with full and partial tuition reimbursements (averaging $9,889 per year) were awarded. Financial award application deadline: 7/15; financial award applicants required to submit FAFSA. *Faculty research:* Biomedical Instrumentation, cardiac physiology and computational modeling, analog/digital CMOS circuits, neural-machine interface, digital circuit design and VLSI testing. Total annual research expenditures: $985,856. *Unit head:* Dr. G. Faye Boudreaux-Bartels, Chair, 401-874-5805, Fax: 401-782-6422, E-mail: boud@ele.uri.edu. *Application contact:* Dr. Godi Fischer, Director of Graduate Studies, 401-874-5879, Fax: 401-782-6422, E-mail: fischer@ele.uri.edu.

University of Rochester, Hajim School of Engineering and Applied Sciences, Department of Electrical and Computer Engineering, Programs in Electrical Engineering, Rochester, NY 14627.

University of Saskatchewan, College of Graduate Studies and Research, College of Engineering, Department of Electrical Engineering, Saskatoon, SK S7N 5A2, Canada. Offers M Eng, M Sc, PhD. *Degree requirements:* For master's, thesis (for some programs); for doctorate, thesis/dissertation. *Entrance requirements:* For master's and doctorate, GRE. Additional exam requirements/recommendations for international students: Required—TOEFL.

University of South Alabama, Graduate School, College of Engineering, Department of Electrical and Computer Engineering, Mobile, AL 36688-0002. Offers electrical engineering (MSEE). Part-time programs available. *Faculty:* 12 full-time (0 women). *Students:* 83 full-time (8 women), 29 part-time (5 women); includes 3 Asian, non-Hispanic/Latino, 105 international. 114 applicants, 55% accepted, 25 enrolled. In 2010, 51 master's awarded. *Degree requirements:* For master's, project or thesis. *Entrance requirements:* For master's, GRE General Test, BS in engineering, minimum GPA of 3.0. *Application deadline:* For fall admission, 7/15 priority date for domestic students, 6/15 priority date for international students; for spring admission, 12/1 priority date for domestic students, 11/1 priority date for international students. Applications are processed on a rolling basis. Application fee: $35. *Expenses:* Tuition, state resident: part-time $300 per credit hour. Tuition, nonresident: part-time $600 per credit hour. Required fees: $150 per semester. *Financial support:* Research assistantships, career-related internships or fieldwork and institutionally sponsored loans available. Support available to part-time students. Financial award application deadline: 4/1. *Unit head:* Dr. Mohammed Alam, Chair, 251-460-6117. *Application contact:* Dr. B. Keith Harrison, Director of Graduate Studies, 251-460-6160.

University of South Carolina, The Graduate School, College of Engineering and Computing, Department of Electrical Engineering, Columbia, SC 29208. Offers ME, MS, PhD. Part-time and evening/weekend programs available. Postbaccalaureate distance learning degree programs offered (minimal on-campus study). *Degree requirements:* For master's, comprehensive exam, thesis (for some programs); for doctorate, comprehensive exam, thesis/dissertation, qualifying exam. *Entrance requirements:* For master's and doctorate, GRE General Test. Additional exam requirements/recommendations for international students: Required—TOEFL (minimum score 570 paper-based; 230 computer-based; 88 iBT). Electronic applications accepted. *Faculty research:* Microelectronics, photonics, wireless communications, signal integrity, energy and control systems.

University of Southern California, Graduate School, Viterbi School of Engineering, Ming Hsieh Department of Electrical Engineering, Los Angeles, CA 90089. Offers computer engineering (MS, PhD); electric power (MS); electrical engineering (MS, PhD, Engr); engineering technology commercialization (Graduate Certificate); multimedia and creative technologies (MS); telecommunications (MS); VLSI design (MS); wireless health technology (MS). Part-time programs available. Postbaccalaureate distance learning degree programs offered (no on-campus study). *Faculty:* 56 full-time (3 women), 31 part-time/adjunct (1 woman). *Students:* 886 full-time (171 women), 605 part-time (100 women); includes 209 minority (20 Black or African American, non-Hispanic/Latino; 145 Asian, non-Hispanic/Latino; 36 Hispanic/Latino; 8 Two or more races, non-Hispanic/Latino), 1,003 international. 2,986 applicants, 36% accepted, 461 enrolled. In 2010, 351 master's, 41 doctorates, 2 other advanced degrees awarded. Terminal master's awarded for partial completion of doctoral program. *Degree requirements:* For master's, thesis optional; for doctorate, thesis/dissertation. *Entrance requirements:* For master's and doctorate, GRE General Test. *Application deadline:* For fall admission, 12/1 priority date for domestic and international students; for spring admission, 9/15 priority date for domestic and international students. Applications are processed on a rolling basis. Application fee: $85. Electronic applications accepted. *Expenses:* Tuition: Full-time $31,240; part-time $1420 per unit. Required fees: $600. One-time fee: $35 full-time. Full-time tuition and fees vary according to degree level and program. *Financial support:* In 2010–11, fellowships with full tuition reimbursements (averaging $30,000 per year), research assistantships with full tuition reimbursements (averaging $20,000 per year), teaching assistantships with full tuition reimbursements (averaging $20,000 per year) were awarded; career-related internships or fieldwork, scholarships/grants, health care benefits, and unspecified assistantships also available. Financial award application deadline: 12/1; financial award applicants required to submit CSS PROFILE or FAFSA. *Faculty research:* Communications, computer engineering and networks, control systems, integrated circuits and systems, electromagnetics and energy conversion, micro electro-mechanical systems and nanotechnology, photonics and quantum electronics, plasma research, signal and image processing. Total annual research expenditures: $18 million. *Unit head:* Dr. Alexander A. Sawchuk, Chair, 213-740-4447, E-mail: studentinfo@ee.usc.edu. *Application contact:* Diane Demetras, Director of Student Affairs, 213-740-4447, E-mail: studentinfo@ee.usc.edu.

University of South Florida, Graduate School, College of Engineering, Department of Electrical Engineering, Tampa, FL 33620-9951. Offers ME, MSEE, MSES, PhD. Part-time programs available. Postbaccalaureate distance learning degree programs offered (no on-campus study). *Faculty:* 21 full-time (3 women), 1 part-time/adjunct (0 women). *Students:* 125 full-time (27 women), 85 part-time (12 women); includes 7 Black or African American, non-Hispanic/Latino; 6 Asian, non-Hispanic/Latino; 15 Hispanic/Latino; 1 Two or more races, non-Hispanic/Latino, 48 international. Average age 31. 173 applicants, 59% accepted, 49 enrolled. In 2010, 56 master's, 13 doctorates awarded. Terminal master's awarded for partial completion of doctoral program. *Degree requirements:* For master's, comprehensive exam, thesis or alternative; for doctorate, comprehensive exam, thesis/dissertation. *Entrance requirements:* For master's, GRE General Test (minimum score 1000 verbal and quantitative, 700 quantitative), minimum GPA of 3.0 in last 60 hours of coursework; for doctorate, GRE General Test (Quantitative 700, combined Verbal and Quantitative 1100). Additional exam requirements/recommendations for international students: Required—TOEFL (minimum score 550 paper-based; 213 computer-based; 79 iBT). *Application deadline:* For fall admission, 2/15 for domestic students, 1/2 for international students; for spring admission, 10/15 for domestic students, 6/1 for international students. Application fee: $30. Electronic applications accepted. *Financial support:* In 2010–11, 48 research assistantships (averaging $13,068 per year), 36 teaching assistantships with tuition reimbursements (averaging $13,022 per year) were awarded. Financial award applicants required to submit FAFSA. *Faculty research:* Silicon processing, micro/millimeter waves, communication and signal processing, clean energy and sustainability, bioengineering. Total annual research expenditures: $3.1 million. *Unit head:* Dr. Sal Morgera, Department Chair, 813-974-1004, E-mail: morgera@usf.edu. *Application contact:* Dr. Kenneth A. Buckle, Director, 813-974-4772, Fax: 813-974-5250, E-mail: buckle@usf.edu.

The University of Tennessee, Graduate School, College of Engineering, Department of Electrical Engineering and Computer Science, Knoxville, TN 37996. Offers computer engineering (MS, PhD); computer science (MS, PhD); electrical engineering (MS, PhD); reliability and maintainability engineering (MS); MS/MBA. Part-time programs available. *Faculty:* 39 full-time (7 women), 14 part-time/adjunct (0 women). *Students:* 174 full-time (35 women), 43 part-time (6 women); includes 2 Black or African American, non-Hispanic/Latino; 3 Asian, non-Hispanic/Latino; 2 Hispanic/Latino, 114 international. Average age 29. 644 applicants, 12% accepted, 51 enrolled. In 2010, 42 master's, 21 doctorates awarded. *Degree requirements:* For master's, thesis or alternative; for doctorate, comprehensive exam, thesis/dissertation. *Entrance requirements:* For master's, GRE General Test, Minimum GPA of 2.7 (US degree holders); 3.0 (International degree holders); 3-References; Personal statement; for doctorate, GRE General Test, Minimum GPA of 3.0 (previous graduate degree); 3-References; Personal statement. Additional exam requirements/recommendations for international students: Required—TOEFL (minimum score 550 paper-based; 213 computer-based). *Application deadline:* For fall admission, 2/1 priority date for domestic and international students; for spring admission, 6/15 for domestic and international students. Applications are processed on a rolling basis. Application fee: $35. Electronic applications accepted. *Expenses:* Tuition, state resident: full-time $7440; part-time $414 per credit hour. Tuition, nonresident: full-time $22,478; part-time $1250 per credit hour. Required fees: $922; $43 per credit hour. Tuition and fees vary according to program. *Financial support:* In 2010–11, 148 students received support, including 13 fellowships with full tuition reimbursements available (averaging $12,312 per year), 100 research assistantships with full tuition reimbursements available (averaging $16,248 per year), 91 teaching assistantships with full tuition reimbursements available (averaging $12,996 per year); career-related internships or fieldwork, Federal Work-Study, institutionally sponsored loans, health care benefits, and unspecified assistantships also available. Financial award application deadline: 2/1; financial award applicants required to submit FAFSA. *Faculty research:* Artificial intelligence and visualization; microelectronics, mixed-signal electronics, VLSI, embedded systems; scientific and distributed computing; computer vision, robotics, and image processing; power electronics, power systems, communications. Total annual research expenditures: $10.7 million. *Unit head:* Dr. Kevin Tomsovic, Head, 865-974-3461, Fax: 865-974-5483, E-mail: tomsovic@eecs.utk.edu. *Application contact:* Dr. Lynne E. Parker, Associate Head, 865-974-4394, Fax: 865-974-5483, E-mail: parker@eecs.utk.edu.

The University of Tennessee at Chattanooga, Graduate School, College of Engineering and Computer Science, Program in Engineering, Chattanooga, TN 37403. Offers chemical engineering (MS Engr); civil engineering (MS Engr); computational engineering (MS Engr); electrical engineering (MS Engr); industrial engineering (MS Engr); mechanical engineering (MS Engr). Part-time and evening/weekend programs available. *Faculty:* 8 full-time (0 women). *Students:* 27 full-time (5 women), 31 part-time (6 women); includes 12 minority (7 Black or African American, non-Hispanic/Latino; 1 Asian, non-Hispanic/Latino; 4 Hispanic/Latino), 10 international. Average age 29. 43 applicants, 100% accepted, 26 enrolled. In 2010, 16 master's awarded. *Degree requirements:* For master's, comprehensive exam, thesis or alternative, engineering project. *Entrance requirements:* For master's, GRE General Test, minimum undergraduate GPA of 2.5 or 3.0 in last 30 hours of coursework. Additional exam requirements/recommendations for international students: Required—TOEFL (minimum score 550 paper-based; 213 computer-based; 79 iBT), IELTS (minimum score 6). *Application deadline:* For fall admission, 8/1 priority date for domestic students, 6/1 for international students; for spring admission, 12/1 priority date for domestic students, 10/1 for international students. Applications are processed on a rolling basis. Application fee: $35. Electronic applications accepted. *Financial support:* In 2010–11, 23 research assistantships with full and partial tuition reimbursements (averaging $5,500 per year) were awarded; career-related internships or fieldwork, scholarships/grants, and unspecified assistantships also available. Support available to part-time students. *Faculty research:* Quality control and reliability engineering, financial management, thermal science, energy conservation, structural analysis. Total annual research expenditures: $2.6 million. *Unit head:* Dr. Neslihan Alp, Director, 423-425-4032, Fax: 423-425-5229, E-mail: neslihan-alp@utc.edu. *Application contact:* Dr. Jerald Ainsworth, Dean of Graduate Studies, 423-425-4478, Fax: 423-425-5223, E-mail: jerald-ainsworth@utc.edu.

The University of Tennessee Space Institute, Graduate Programs, Program in Electrical Engineering and Computer Science, Tullahoma, TN 37388-9700. Offers MS, PhD. *Faculty:* 2 full-time (0 women), 2 part-time/adjunct (0 women). *Students:* 1 part-time (0 women). 1 applicant, 0% accepted, 0 enrolled. In 2010, 4 master's awarded. *Degree requirements:* For master's, thesis (for some programs); for doctorate, one foreign language, thesis/dissertation. *Entrance requirements:* Additional exam requirements/recommendations for international students: Required—TOEFL (minimum score 550 paper-based; 213 computer-based), IELTS (minimum score 6.5). *Application deadline:* For fall admission, 2/1 for international students; for spring admission, 6/15 for international students. Applications are processed on a rolling basis. Application fee: $35. Electronic applications accepted. *Financial support:* Fellowships, research assistantships with full tuition reimbursements, career-related internships or fieldwork, Federal Work-Study, institutionally sponsored loans, health care benefits, tuition waivers (full and partial), and unspecified assistantships available. Financial award applicants required to submit FAFSA. *Unit head:* Dr. Monty Smith, Degree Program Chairman, 931-393-7480, Fax: 931-393-7530, E-mail: msmith@utsi.edu. *Application contact:* Dee Merriman, Coordinator III, 931-393-7213, Fax: 931-393-7211, E-mail: dmerrima@utsi.edu.

The University of Texas at Arlington, Graduate School, College of Engineering, Department of Electrical Engineering, Arlington, TX 76019. Offers M Engr, MS, PhD. Part-time and evening/weekend programs available. Postbaccalaureate distance learning degree programs offered (no on-campus study). *Faculty:* 27 full-time (1 woman). *Students:* 245 full-time (49 women), 143 part-time (19 women); includes 22 minority (6 Black or African American, non-Hispanic/Latino; 13 Asian, non-Hispanic/Latino; 3 Hispanic/Latino), 329 international. 409 applicants, 63% accepted, 90 enrolled. In 2010, 209 master's, 22 doctorates awarded. Terminal master's awarded for partial completion of doctoral program. *Degree requirements:* For master's, thesis optional; for doctorate, comprehensive exam, thesis/dissertation, written diagnostic exam. *Entrance requirements:* For master's, GRE General Test, minimum GPA of 3.25; for doctorate, GRE General Test, minimum GPA of 3.5. Additional exam requirements/recommendations for international students: Required—TOEFL (minimum score 560 paper-based; 220 computer-based); Recommended—TWE (minimum score 4). *Application deadline:* For fall admission, 6/1 for domestic students, 4/4 for international students; for spring admission, 10/15 for domestic students, 9/5 for international students. Applications are processed on a rolling basis. Application fee: $35 ($50 for international students). *Expenses:* Tuition, state resident: full-time $7500. Tuition, nonresident: full-time $13,080. International tuition: $13,250 full-time. *Financial support:* In 2010–11, 202 students received support, including 23 fellowships (averaging $1,000 per year), 60 research assistantships (averaging $14,400 per year), 40 teaching assistantships (averaging $10,800 per year); Federal Work-Study, institutionally sponsored loans, scholarships/grants, and unspecified assistantships also available. Financial award application deadline: 6/1; financial award applicants required to submit FAFSA. *Faculty research:* Nanotech and MEMS, digital image processing, telecommunications and optics, energy systems and power electronics, VLSI and semiconductors. Total annual research expenditures: $1 million. *Unit head:* Dr. Jonathan Bredow, Chair, 817-272-3497, Fax: 817-272-2253, E-mail: jbredow@uta.edu. *Application contact:* Dr. William E. Dillon, Graduate Adviser, 817-272-2671, Fax: 817-272-1509, E-mail: eedept@uta.edu.

The University of Texas at Austin, Graduate School, Cockrell School of Engineering, Department of Electrical and Computer Engineering, Austin, TX 78712-1111. Offers MSE, PhD. Part-time programs available. *Entrance requirements:* For master's, GRE General Test, minimum GPA of 3.3 in upper-division course work; for doctorate, GRE General Test. Electronic applications accepted.

The University of Texas at Dallas, Erik Jonsson School of Engineering and Computer Science, Department of Electrical Engineering, Richardson, TX 75080. Offers computer engineering (MS, PhD); electrical engineering (MSEE, PhD); microelectronics (MSEE, PhD); telecommunications (MSEE, MSTE, PhD). Part-time and evening/weekend programs available. *Faculty:* 43 full-time (2 women). *Students:* 404 full-time (78 women), 186 part-time (32 women); includes 85 minority (11 Black or African American, non-Hispanic/Latino; 56 Asian, non-Hispanic/Latino; 17 Hispanic/Latino; 1 Two or more races, non-Hispanic/Latino), 406 international. Average age 27. 1,612 applicants, 44% accepted, 188 enrolled. In 2010, 152 master's, 31 doctorates awarded. *Degree requirements:* For master's, thesis or major design project; for doctorate, thesis/dissertation. *Entrance requirements:* For master's, GRE General Test, minimum GPA of 3.0 in related bachelor's degree; for doctorate, GRE General Test, minimum GPA of 3.5. Additional exam requirements/recommendations for international students: Required—TOEFL (minimum score 550 paper-based; 215 computer-based). *Application deadline:* For fall admission, 7/15 for domestic students, 5/1 priority date for international students; for spring admission, 11/15 for domestic students, 9/1 priority date for international students. Applications are processed on a rolling basis. Application fee: $50 ($100 for international students). Electronic applications accepted. *Expenses:* Tuition, state resident: full-time $10,248; part-time $569 per credit hour. Tuition, nonresident: full-time $18,544; part-time $1030 per credit hour. Tuition and fees vary according to course load. *Financial support:* In 2010–11, 211 students received support, including 5 fellowships with partial tuition reimbursements available (averaging $15,960 per year), 129 research assistantships with partial tuition reimbursements available (averaging $16,317 per year), 43 teaching assistantships with partial tuition reimbursements available (averaging $15,206 per year); Federal Work-Study, institutionally sponsored loans, scholarships/grants, unspecified assistantships, and cooperative positions also available. Support available to part-time students. Financial award application deadline: 4/30; financial award applicants required to submit FAFSA. *Faculty research:* Semiconductor device manufacturing, photonics devices and systems, signal processing and language technology, nano-fabrication, energy efficient digital systems. *Unit head:* Dr. John H.L. Hansen, Department Head, 972-883-6755, Fax: 972-883-2710, E-mail: john.hansen@utdallas.edu. *Application contact:* Kathy Gribble, Graduate Program Coordinator, 972-883-2649, Fax: 972-883-2710, E-mail: gradecs@utdallas.edu.

The University of Texas at El Paso, Graduate School, College of Engineering, Department of Electrical and Computer Engineering, El Paso, TX 79968-0001. Offers computer engineering (MS); electrical and computer engineering (PhD); electrical engineering (MS). Part-time and evening/weekend programs available. *Students:* 144 (38 women); includes 86 Hispanic/Latino, 53 international. Average age 34. In 2010, 38 master's, 2 doctorates awarded. *Degree requirements:* For master's, thesis optional; for doctorate, thesis/dissertation. *Entrance requirements:* For master's, GRE General Test, minimum GPA of 3.0; for doctorate, GRE General Test, qualifying exam, minimum graduate GPA of 3.0. Additional exam requirements/recommendations for international students: Required—TOEFL. *Application deadline:* For fall admission, 7/1 priority date for domestic students, 3/1 for international students; for spring admission, 11/1 priority date for domestic students, 9/1 for international students. Applications are processed on a rolling basis. Application fee: $15 ($65 for international students). Electronic applications accepted. *Financial support:* In 2010–11, 60 students received support, including research assistantships with partial tuition reimbursements available (averaging $22,375 per year), teaching assistantships with partial tuition reimbursements available (averaging $17,900 per year); fellowships with partial tuition reimbursements available, Federal Work-Study, institutionally sponsored loans, scholarships/grants, and tuition waivers (partial) also available. Financial award application deadline: 3/15; financial award applicants required to submit FAFSA. *Faculty research:* Signal and image processing, computer architecture, fiber optics, computational electromagnetics, electronic displays and thin films. *Unit head:* Patricia Nava, Chair, 915-747-5994, E-mail: pnava@utep.edu. *Application contact:* Dr. Charles H. Ambler, Dean of the Graduate School, 915-747-5491 Ext. 7886, Fax: 915-747-5788, E-mail: cambler@utep.edu.

The University of Texas at San Antonio, College of Engineering, Department of Electrical and Computer Engineering, San Antonio, TX 78249-0617. Offers computer engineering (MS); electrical engineering (MS, PhD). Part-time and evening/weekend programs available. *Faculty:* 20 full-time (2 women), 3 part-time/adjunct (1 woman). *Students:* 100 full-time (28 women), 69 part-time (10 women); includes 30 minority (3 Black or African American, non-Hispanic/Latino; 7 Asian, non-Hispanic/Latino; 18 Hispanic/Latino; 2 Two or more races, non-Hispanic/Latino), 103 international. Average age 28. 148 applicants, 82% accepted, 51 enrolled. In 2010, 56 master's, 7 doctorates awarded. *Degree requirements:* For master's, comprehensive exam (for some programs), thesis (for some programs); for doctorate, comprehensive exam, thesis/dissertation. *Entrance requirements:* For master's, GRE General Test, minimum GPA of 3.0 in last 60 hours of undergraduate degree; for doctorate, GRE General Test. Additional exam requirements/recommendations for international students: Required—TOEFL (minimum score 500 paper-based; 173 computer-based). *Application deadline:* For fall admission, 7/1 for domestic students, 4/1 for international students; for spring admission, 11/1 for domestic students, 9/1 for international students. Applications are processed on a rolling basis. Application fee: $45 ($80 for international students). Electronic applications accepted. *Expenses:* Tuition, state resident: full-time $4172; part-time $231.75 per credit hour. Tuition, nonresident: full-time $15,332; part-time $851.75 per credit hour. *Financial support:* In 2010–11, 60 students received support, including 10 fellowships (averaging $34,425 per year), 62 research assistantships (averaging $11,312 per year), 41 teaching assistantships (averaging $11,244 per year); career-related internships or fieldwork, scholarships/grants, and unspecified assistantships also available. Support available to part-time students. Financial award application deadline: 3/31. Total annual research expenditures: $873,745. *Unit head:* Dr. Ruyan Guo, Interim Chair, 210-458-7057, Fax: 210-458-5947, E-mail: ruyan.guo@utsa.edu. *Application contact:* Veronica

Ramirez, Assistant Dean of the Graduate School, 210-458-4330, Fax: 210-458-4332, E-mail: graduatestudies@utsa.edu.

See M.S. Display on page 384 and Close-Up on page 399 and see Ph.D. Display on page 384 and Close-Up on page 401.

The University of Texas at Tyler, College of Engineering and Computer Science, Department of Electrical Engineering, Tyler, TX 75799-0001. Offers MS. Part-time and evening/weekend programs available. *Degree requirements:* For master's, comprehensive exam (for some programs). *Entrance requirements:* For master's, GRE General Test, bachelor's degree in electrical engineering. Additional exam requirements/recommendations for international students: Required—TOEFL (minimum score 79 computer-based). *Faculty research:* Electronics, digital sign processing, real time systems electromagnetic fields, semiconductor modeling.

The University of Texas–Pan American, College of Science and Engineering, Department of Electrical Engineering, Edinburg, TX 78539. Offers MS.

University of the District of Columbia, School of Engineering and Applied Science, Department of Electrical and Computer Engineering, Washington, DC 20008-1175. Offers electrical engineering (MS). *Expenses:* Tuition, state resident: full-time $7580; part-time $421 per credit. Tuition, nonresident: full-time $14,580; part-time $810 per credit. Required fees: $620; $30 per credit. One-time fee: $100 part-time.

The University of Toledo, College of Graduate Studies, College of Engineering, Department of Electrical Engineering and Computer Science, Toledo, OH 43606-3390. Offers computer science (MS, PhD); electrical engineering (MS, PhD). Part-time and evening/weekend programs available. *Degree requirements:* For master's, thesis or alternative; for doctorate, thesis, dissertation, qualifying exam. *Entrance requirements:* For master's, GRE General Test, minimum GPA of 3.0; for doctorate, GRE General Test, minimum GPA of 3.3. Additional exam requirements/recommendations for international students: Required—TOEFL (minimum score 550 paper-based; 213 computer-based; 80 iBT). Electronic applications accepted. *Expenses:* Tuition, state resident: full-time $11,426; part-time $476 per credit hour. Tuition, nonresident: full-time $21,660; part-time $903 per credit hour. One-time fee: $62. *Faculty research:* Communication and signal processing, high performance computing systems, intelligent systems, power electronics and energy systems, RF and microwave systems, sensors and medical devices, solid state devices.

University of Toronto, School of Graduate Studies, Physical Sciences Division, Faculty of Applied Science and Engineering, Department of Electrical and Computer Engineering, Toronto, ON M5S 1A1, Canada. Offers M Eng, MA Sc, PhD. Part-time programs available. *Degree requirements:* For master's, thesis (for some programs), oral thesis defense (MA Sc); for doctorate, thesis/dissertation, qualifying exam, thesis defense. *Entrance requirements:* For master's, four-year degree in electrical or computer engineering, minimum B average, 2 letters of reference; for doctorate, minimum B+ average, MA Sc in electrical or computer engineering, 2 letters of reference.

University of Tulsa, Graduate School, College of Engineering and Natural Sciences, Department of Electrical Engineering, Tulsa, OK 74104-3189. Offers ME, MSE. Part-time programs available. *Faculty:* 7 full-time (0 women). *Students:* 12 full-time (2 women), 4 part-time (0 women); includes 1 minority (American Indian or Alaska Native, non-Hispanic/Latino), 6 international. Average age 24. 17 applicants, 53% accepted, 4 enrolled. In 2010, 7 master's awarded. *Degree requirements:* For master's, comprehensive exam (for some programs), design report (ME), thesis (MS). *Entrance requirements:* For master's, GRE General Test. Additional exam requirements/recommendations for international students: Required—TOEFL (minimum score 550 paper-based; 213 computer-based; 80 iBT), IELTS (minimum score 6). *Application deadline:* Applications are processed on a rolling basis. Application fee: $40. Electronic applications accepted. *Expenses:* Tuition: Full-time $16,902; part-time $939 per credit hour. Required fees: $1020; $4 per credit hour. Tuition and fees vary according to course load. *Financial support:* In 2010–11, 10 students received support, including 5 research assistantships with full and partial tuition reimbursements available (averaging $10,393 per year), 6 teaching assistantships with full and partial tuition reimbursements available (averaging $11,942 per year); fellowships with full and partial tuition reimbursements available, career-related internships or fieldwork, Federal Work-Study, scholarships/grants, health care benefits, tuition waivers (full and partial), and unspecified assistantships also available. Support available to part-time students. Financial award application deadline: 2/1; financial award applicants required to submit FAFSA. *Faculty research:* VLSI microprocessors, intelligent systems, electromagnetics, intrusion detection systems, digital electronics. Total annual research expenditures: $772,107. *Unit head:* Dr. Gerald R. Kane, Chairperson, 918-631-3280. *Application contact:* Dr. Heng-Ming Tai, Adviser, 918-631-3271, Fax: 918-631-3344, E-mail: tai@utulsa.edu.

University of Utah, Graduate School, College of Engineering, Department of Electrical and Computer Engineering, Salt Lake City, UT 84112. Offers electrical engineering (ME, MS, PhD). Part-time programs available. *Faculty:* 27 full-time (2 women), 3 part-time/adjunct (0 women). *Students:* 86 full-time (11 women), 33 part-time (1 woman); includes 10 minority (1 Black or African American, non-Hispanic/Latino; 5 Asian, non-Hispanic/Latino; 4 Hispanic/Latino), 57 international. Average age 29. 40 applicants, 93% accepted, 23 enrolled. In 2010, 35 master's, 12 doctorates awarded. Terminal master's awarded for partial completion of doctoral program. *Degree requirements:* For master's, comprehensive exam (for some programs), thesis (for some programs); for doctorate, comprehensive exam, thesis/dissertation. *Entrance requirements:* For master's, GRE General Test, minimum GPA of 3.2; for doctorate, GRE General Test, minimum GPA of 3.5. Additional exam requirements/recommendations for international students: Required—TOEFL (minimum score 600 paper-based; 250 computer-based; 100 iBT). *Application deadline:* For fall admission, 4/1 priority date for domestic students, 1/15 priority date for international students; for spring admission, 10/1 for domestic students. Application fee: $55 ($65 for international students). *Expenses:* Contact institution. *Financial support:* In 2010–11, 2 students received support, including 3 fellowships with full tuition reimbursements available (averaging $20,000 per year), 40 research assistantships with full tuition reimbursements available (averaging $13,900 per year), 14 teaching assistantships with full tuition reimbursements available (averaging $11,000 per year); Federal Work-Study, institutionally sponsored loans, health care benefits, and unspecified assistantships also available. Financial award application deadline: 2/15; financial award applicants required to submit FAFSA. *Faculty research:* Semiconductors, VLSI design, control systems, electromagnetics and applied optics, communication theory and digital signal processing, power systems. Total annual research expenditures: $8.3 million. *Unit head:* Dr. Gianluca Lazzi, Chair, 801-581-6941, Fax: 801-581-5281, E-mail: lazzi@utah.edu. *Application contact:* Lori Sather, Graduate Coordinator, 801-581-6943, Fax: 801-581-5281, E-mail: sather@ece.utah.edu.

University of Vermont, Graduate College, College of Engineering and Mathematics, Department of Electrical Engineering, Burlington, VT 05405. Offers MS, PhD. *Students:* 33 (4 women); includes 1 Black or African American, non-Hispanic/Latino; 3 Asian, non-Hispanic/Latino, 9 international. 41 applicants, 54% accepted, 4 enrolled. In 2010, 5 master's awarded. *Degree requirements:* For master's, thesis or alternative; for doctorate, one foreign language, thesis/dissertation. *Entrance requirements:* For master's, GRE General Test. Additional exam requirements/recommendations for international students: Required—TOEFL (minimum score 550 paper-based; 213 computer-based; 80 iBT). *Application deadline:* For fall admission, 2/1 priority date for domestic students. Applications are processed on a rolling basis. Application fee: $40. Electronic applications accepted. *Expenses:* Tuition, state resident: part-time $537 per credit hour. Tuition, nonresident: part-time $1355 per credit hour. *Financial support:* Fellowships, research assistantships, teaching assistantships available. Financial award application deadline: 3/1. *Unit head:* Dr. Jeff Marshall, Director, 802-656-3331. *Application contact:* Prof. Kurt Oughstun, Coordinator, 802-656-3331.

University of Victoria, Faculty of Graduate Studies, Faculty of Engineering, Department of Electrical and Computer Engineering, Victoria, BC V8W 2Y2, Canada. Offers M Eng, MA Sc,

PhD. *Degree requirements:* For master's, thesis; for doctorate, thesis/dissertation, candidacy exam. *Entrance requirements:* For master's, GRE (recommended), bachelor's degree in engineering; for doctorate, GRE (recommended), master's degree. Additional exam requirements/recommendations for international students: Required—TOEFL (minimum score 575 paper-based; 233 computer-based), IELTS (minimum score 7). Electronic applications accepted. *Faculty research:* Communications and computers; electromagnetics, microwaves, and optics; electronics; power systems, signal processing, and control.

University of Virginia, School of Engineering and Applied Science, Department of Electrical and Computer Engineering, Program in Electrical Engineering, Charlottesville, VA 22903. Offers ME, MS, PhD. *Students:* 107 full-time (25 women), 9 part-time (1 woman); includes 5 Black or African American, non-Hispanic/Latino; 8 Asian, non-Hispanic/Latino; 1 Hispanic/Latino, 59 international. Average age 27. 237 applicants, 14% accepted, 20 enrolled. In 2010, 18 master's, 12 doctorates awarded. *Degree requirements:* For doctorate, thesis/dissertation. *Entrance requirements:* For master's, GRE General Test, 3 letters of recommendation; for doctorate, GRE General Test, 3 letters of recommendation; essay. Additional exam requirements/recommendations for international students: Required—TOEFL (minimum score 650 paper-based; 250 computer-based; 100 iBT), IELTS (minimum score 7). *Application deadline:* For fall admission, 8/1 for domestic students, 1/15 for international students; for winter admission, 12/1 for domestic students, 8/1 for international students; for spring admission, 5/1 for domestic students. Applications are processed on a rolling basis. Application fee: $60. Electronic applications accepted. *Financial support:* Fellowships, research assistantships, teaching assistantships available. Financial award application deadline: 1/15; financial award applicants required to submit FAFSA. *Unit head:* Chair. *Application contact:* Nathan Swami, Graduate Program Director, 434-924-3960, Fax: 434-924-8818, E-mail: nathanswami@virginia.edu.

University of Washington, Graduate School, College of Engineering, Department of Electrical Engineering, Seattle, WA 98195-2500. Offers electrical engineering (MS, PhD); electrical engineering and nanotechnology (PhD). Postbaccalaureate distance learning degree programs offered (no on-campus study). *Faculty:* 57 full-time (9 women), 12 part-time/adjunct (2 women). *Students:* 210 full-time (45 women), 134 part-time (11 women); includes 11 Black or African American, non-Hispanic/Latino; 1 American Indian or Alaska Native, non-Hispanic/Latino; 57 Asian, non-Hispanic/Latino; 11 Hispanic/Latino, 126 international. 903 applicants, 25% accepted, 101 enrolled. In 2010, 86 master's, 29 doctorates awarded. *Degree requirements:* For master's, thesis optional; for doctorate, thesis/dissertation, Qualifying, general, & final exams.. *Entrance requirements:* For master's and doctorate, GRE General Test: Recommend Verbal 500, Quantitative 720, Analytical 600 or Analytical Writing 5 or 6., Minimum GPA of 3.2, resume or cv, statement of purpose, 3 letters of recommendation, undergrad and grad transcripts, optional: personal statement.. Additional exam requirements/recommendations for international students: Required—TOEFL (minimum score 600 paper-based; 250 computer-based; 92 iBT); Recommended—IELTS (minimum score 7). *Application deadline:* For fall admission, 1/1 priority date for domestic students, 12/15 priority date for international students. Application fee: $75. Electronic applications accepted. *Financial support:* In 2010–11, 4 students received support, including 4 fellowships with full tuition reimbursements available (averaging $18,648 per year), 120 research assistantships with partial tuition reimbursements available (averaging $19,233 per year), 41 teaching assistantships with partial tuition reimbursements available (averaging $14,787 per year); career-related internships or fieldwork, Federal Work-Study, and institutionally sponsored loans also available. Financial award application deadline: 1/1; financial award applicants required to submit FAFSA. *Faculty research:* Controls and robotics, communications and signal processing, electromagnetics, optics and acoustics, electronic devices and photonics. Total annual research expenditures: $14.1 million. *Unit head:* Dr. Leung Tsang, Professor and Chair, 206-221-5270, Fax: 206-543-3842, E-mail: tsang@ee.washington.edu. *Application contact:* Scott Latiolais, Lead Graduate Program Academic Counselor, 206-221-7913, Fax: 206-543-3842, E-mail: latiolais@ee.washington.edu.

University of Waterloo, Graduate Studies, Faculty of Engineering, Department of Electrical and Computer Engineering, Waterloo, ON N2L 3G1, Canada. Offers electrical and computer engineering (M Eng, MA Sc, PhD); electrical and computer engineering (software engineering) (MA Sc). Part-time programs available. *Degree requirements:* For master's, research paper or thesis; for doctorate, comprehensive exam, thesis/dissertation. *Entrance requirements:* For master's, honors degree, minimum B+ average; for doctorate, master's degree, minimum A-average. Additional exam requirements/recommendations for international students: Required—TOEFL (minimum score 550 paper-based; 213 computer-based), TWE (minimum score 4). Electronic applications accepted. *Faculty research:* Communications, computers, systems and control, silicon devices, power engineering.

The University of Western Ontario, Faculty of Graduate Studies, Physical Sciences Division, Faculty of Engineering, London, ON N6A 5B8, Canada. Offers chemical and biochemical engineering (ME Sc, PhD); civil and environmental engineering (M Eng, ME Sc, PhD); electrical and computer engineering (M Eng, ME Sc, PhD); mechanical and materials engineering (M Eng, ME Sc, PhD). Part-time programs available. Terminal master's awarded for partial completion of doctoral program. *Degree requirements:* For master's, thesis; for doctorate, thesis/dissertation. *Entrance requirements:* For master's, minimum B average; for doctorate, minimum B+ average. *Faculty research:* Wind, geotechnical, chemical reactor engineering, applied electrostatics, biochemical engineering.

University of Windsor, Faculty of Graduate Studies, Faculty of Engineering, Department of Electrical and Computer Engineering, Windsor, ON N9B 3P4, Canada. Offers electrical engineering (M Eng, MA Sc, PhD). Part-time programs available. *Degree requirements:* For master's, thesis; for doctorate, comprehensive exam, thesis/dissertation. *Entrance requirements:* For master's, minimum B average; for doctorate, master's degree, minimum B+ average. Additional exam requirements/recommendations for international students: Required—TOEFL (minimum score 600 paper-based; 250 computer-based). Electronic applications accepted. *Faculty research:* Systems, signals, power.

University of Wisconsin–Madison, Graduate School, College of Engineering, Department of Electrical and Computer Engineering, Madison, WI 53706-1380. Offers electrical engineering (MS, PhD). Part-time programs available. Postbaccalaureate distance learning degree programs offered (minimal on-campus study). *Faculty:* 39 full-time (5 women), 2 part-time/adjunct (0 women). *Students:* 343 full-time (43 women); includes 4 Black or African American, non-Hispanic/Latino; 1 American Indian or Alaska Native, non-Hispanic/Latino; 16 Asian, non-Hispanic/Latino; 3 Hispanic/Latino. Average age 27. 1,128 applicants, 32% accepted, 71 enrolled. In 2010, 67 master's, 21 doctorates awarded. Terminal master's awarded for partial completion of doctoral program. *Degree requirements:* For master's, thesis or alternative; for doctorate, thesis/dissertation, exam. *Entrance requirements:* For master's and doctorate, GRE General Test. Additional exam requirements/recommendations for international students: Required—TOEFL (minimum score 550 paper-based; 213 computer-based; 80 iBT). *Application deadline:* For fall admission, 3/15 for domestic students, 11/15 for international students; for spring admission, 9/30 for domestic and international students. Applications are processed on a rolling basis. Application fee: $56. Electronic applications accepted. *Expenses:* Tuition, state resident: full-time $9887.36; part-time $617.96 per credit. Tuition, nonresident: full-time $24,054; part-time $1503.40 per credit. Required fees: $67.63 per credit. Tuition and fees vary according to reciprocity agreements. *Financial support:* In 2010–11, 260 students received support, including 13 fellowships with full tuition reimbursements available (averaging $13,000 per year), 154 research assistantships with full tuition reimbursements available (averaging $20,400 per year), 93 teaching assistantships with full tuition reimbursements available (averaging $9,392 per year); career-related internships or fieldwork, Federal Work-Study, institutionally sponsored loans, health care benefits, and unspecified assistantships also available. Support available to part-time students. Financial award application deadline: 1/5. *Faculty research:* Microelectronics, computer architecture, power electronics and systems, communications, signal processing. Total annual research expenditures: $13.9 million. *Unit head:* John Booske, Chair, 608-262-3840, Fax: 608-262-1267, E-mail: ecechair@engr.wisc.edu. *Application contact:*

Electrical Engineering

University of Wisconsin–Madison (continued)
Marc Nowak, Graduate Admissions Coordinator, 608-265-5570, Fax: 608-890-1174, E-mail: ece.gradadmissions@uwalumni.com.

University of Wisconsin–Milwaukee, Graduate School, College of Engineering and Applied Science, Program in Engineering, Milwaukee, WI 53201-0413. Offers civil engineering (MS); electrical and computer engineering (MS); energy engineering (Certificate); engineering (PhD); engineering management (MS); engineering mechanics (MS); ergonomics (Certificate); industrial and management engineering (MS); manufacturing engineering (MS); materials engineering (MS); mechanical engineering (MS); MUP/MS. Part-time programs available. *Faculty:* 50 full-time (5 women). *Students:* 152 full-time (27 women), 115 part-time (23 women); includes 13 Black or African American, non-Hispanic/Latino; 3 American Indian or Alaska Native, non-Hispanic/Latino; 6 Asian, non-Hispanic/Latino; 10 Hispanic/Latino, 25 international. Average age 31. 236 applicants, 67% accepted, 55 enrolled. In 2010, 39 master's, 19 doctorates awarded. *Degree requirements:* For master's, comprehensive exam (for some programs), thesis or alternative; for doctorate, comprehensive exam, thesis/dissertation, internship. *Entrance requirements:* For master's, GRE, minimum GPA of 2.75; for doctorate, GRE, minimum GPA of 3.5. Additional exam requirements/recommendations for international students: Required—TOEFL (minimum score 550 paper-based; 79 iBT), IELTS (minimum score 6.5). *Application deadline:* For fall admission, 1/1 priority date for domestic students; for spring admission, 9/1 for domestic students. Applications are processed on a rolling basis. Application fee: $56 ($96 for international students). *Financial support:* In 2010–11, 3 fellowships, 55 research assistantships, 77 teaching assistantships were awarded; career-related internships or fieldwork, Federal Work-Study, unspecified assistantships, and project assistantships also available. Support available to part-time students. Financial award application deadline: 4/15. Total annual research expenditures: $6.2 million. *Unit head:* David Yu, Representative, 414-229-6169, E-mail: yu@uwm.edu. *Application contact:* Betty Warras, General Information Contact, 414-229-6169, Fax: 414-229-6967, E-mail: bwarras@uwm.edu.

University of Wyoming, College of Engineering and Applied Sciences, Department of Electrical and Computer Engineering, Laramie, WY 82070. Offers electrical engineering (MS, PhD). Part-time programs available. *Degree requirements:* For master's, thesis (for some programs); for doctorate, comprehensive exam, thesis/dissertation, dissertation proposal/presentation. *Entrance requirements:* For master's, GRE General Test, minimum undergraduate GPA of 3.0; for doctorate, GRE General Test, minimum GPA of 3.0. Additional exam requirements/recommendations for international students: Required—TOEFL (minimum score 550 paper-based; 213 computer-based; 79 iBT). Electronic applications accepted. *Faculty research:* Robotics and controls, signal and image processing, power electronics, power systems, computer networks, wind energy.

Utah State University, School of Graduate Studies, College of Engineering, Department of Electrical and Computer Engineering, Logan, UT 84322. Offers electrical engineering (ME, MS, PhD). Part-time programs available. *Degree requirements:* For master's, thesis (for some programs); for doctorate, comprehensive exam, thesis/dissertation. *Entrance requirements:* For master's, GRE General Test, minimum GPA of 3.0, BS in electrical engineering, 3 recommendation letters; for doctorate, GRE General Test, minimum GPA of 3.0, MS in electrical engineering, 3 recommendation letters. Additional exam requirements/recommendations for international students: Required—TOEFL. Electronic applications accepted. *Faculty research:* Parallel processing, networking, control systems, digital signal processing, communications.

Vanderbilt University, School of Engineering, Department of Electrical Engineering and Computer Science, Program in Electrical Engineering, Nashville, TN 37240-1001. Offers M Eng, MS, PhD. MS and PhD offered through the Graduate School. Part-time programs available. *Faculty:* 22 full-time (1 woman). *Students:* 103 full-time (27 women); includes 2 Black or African American, non-Hispanic/Latino; 3 Asian, non-Hispanic/Latino; 3 Hispanic/Latino, 59 international. Average age 27. 283 applicants, 11% accepted, 21 enrolled. In 2010, 14 master's, 9 doctorates awarded. Terminal master's awarded for partial completion of doctoral program. *Degree requirements:* For master's, thesis; for doctorate, comprehensive exam, thesis/dissertation. *Entrance requirements:* For master's and doctorate, GRE General Test, 3 letters of recommendation. Additional exam requirements/recommendations for international students: Required—TOEFL. *Application deadline:* For fall admission, 1/15 for domestic and international students; for spring admission, 11/1 for domestic and international students. Application fee: $0. Electronic applications accepted. *Financial support:* In 2010–11, 85 students received support, including fellowships with full and partial tuition reimbursements available (averaging $30,000 per year), research assistantships with full tuition reimbursements available (averaging $21,600 per year), teaching assistantships with full tuition reimbursements available (averaging $18,000 per year); career-related internships or fieldwork, institutionally sponsored loans, scholarships/grants, health care benefits, tuition waivers (full and partial), and unspecified assistantships also available. Support available to part-time students. Financial award application deadline: 1/15. *Faculty research:* Robotics, microelectronics, signal and image processing, VLSI, solid-state sensors, radiation effects and reliability. *Unit head:* Dr. Daniel M. Fleetwood, Chair, 615-322-2771, Fax: 615-343-6702, E-mail: dan.fleetwood@vanderbilt.edu. *Application contact:* Dr. Bharat Bhuva, Director of Graduate Studies, 615-343-3184, Fax: 615-343-6614, E-mail: bharat.bhuva@vanderbilt.edu.

Villanova University, College of Engineering, Department of Electrical and Computer Engineering, Program in Electrical Engineering, Villanova, PA 19085-1699. Offers electric power systems (Certificate); electrical engineering (MSEE); electro mechanical systems (Certificate); high frequency systems (Certificate); intelligent control systems (Certificate); wireless and digital communications (Certificate). Part-time and evening/weekend programs available. *Students:* 9 full-time (1 woman), 55 part-time (11 women); includes 5 Black or African American, non-Hispanic/Latino; 6 Asian, non-Hispanic/Latino; 1 Hispanic/Latino, 16 international. 54 applicants, 63% accepted, 18 enrolled. In 2010, 16 master's awarded. *Degree requirements:* For master's, thesis optional. *Entrance requirements:* For master's, GRE General Test (for applicants with degrees from foreign universities), BEE, minimum GPA of 3.0. Additional exam requirements/recommendations for international students: Required—TOEFL (minimum score 600 paper-based; 250 computer-based; 100 iBT). *Application deadline:* For fall admission, 8/1 for domestic students, 4/1 for international students; for spring admission, 12/1 for domestic students, 8/1 for international students. Applications are processed on a rolling basis. Application fee: $50. *Expenses:* Tuition: Part-time $700 per credit. Part-time tuition and fees vary according to degree level and program. *Financial support:* In 2010–11, research assistantships with full and partial tuition reimbursements (averaging $13,500 per year); Federal Work-Study, scholarships/grants, tuition waivers (full and partial), and unspecified assistantships also available. Support available to part-time students. Financial award application deadline: 1/15. *Faculty research:* Signal processing, communications, antennas, devices. *Unit head:* Dr. Pritpal Singh, Chairman, 610-519-4971, Fax: 610-519-4436. *Application contact:* College of Engineering, Graduate Programs Office, 610-519-5840, Fax: 610-519-5859, E-mail: engineering.grad@villanova.edu.

Virginia Commonwealth University, Graduate School, School of Engineering, Department of Electrical and Computer Engineering, Richmond, VA 23284-9005. Offers electrical engineering (MS, PhD). *Faculty:* 12 full-time (3 women). *Entrance requirements:* For master's and doctorate, GRE. Additional exam requirements/recommendations for international students: Required—TOEFL (minimum score 600 paper-based; 250 computer-based; 100 iBT). *Application deadline:* For fall admission, 2/1 priority date for domestic students; for spring admission, 11/15 for domestic students. Application fee: $50. Electronic applications accepted. *Expenses:* Tuition, state resident: full-time $4308; part-time $479 per credit hour. Tuition, nonresident: full-time $8942; part-time $994 per credit hour. Required fees: $2000; $85 per credit hour. Tuition and fees vary according to course level, course load, degree level, campus/location and program. *Financial support:* Applicants required to submit FAFSA. *Unit head:* Dr. Rosalyn S. Hobson, Associate Dean for Graduate Studies, 804-828-8308, E-mail: rhobson@vcu.edu. *Application contact:* Dr. Supriyio Bandyopadhyay, Director, Graduate Programs, 804-827-6275, E-mail: sbandy@vcu.edu.

Virginia Polytechnic Institute and State University, Graduate School, College of Engineering, Department of Electrical and Computer Engineering, Blacksburg, VA 24061. Offers air transportation systems (Certificate); computer engineering (M Eng, MS, PhD); electrical engineering (M Eng, MS, PhD); emerging devices technologies (Certificate); traffic control and operations (Certificate). *Faculty:* 67 full-time (6 women). *Students:* 386 full-time (62 women), 135 part-time (20 women); includes 8 Black or African American, non-Hispanic/Latino; 27 Asian, non-Hispanic/Latino; 8 Hispanic/Latino, 316 international. Average age 28. 1,444 applicants, 10% accepted, 89 enrolled. In 2010, 91 master's, 48 doctorates awarded. *Degree requirements:* For master's, comprehensive exam (for some programs), thesis (for some programs); for doctorate, comprehensive exam (for some programs), thesis/dissertation (for some programs). *Entrance requirements:* For master's and doctorate, GRE. Additional exam requirements/recommendations for international students: Required—TOEFL (minimum score 590 paper-based; 213 computer-based). *Application deadline:* For fall admission, 7/1 for domestic and international students; for spring admission, 12/1 for domestic and international students. Applications are processed on a rolling basis. Application fee: $65. Electronic applications accepted. *Expenses:* Tuition, area resident: Full-time $9399; part-time $488 per credit hour. Tuition, state resident: full-time $9399; part-time $488 per credit hour. Tuition, nonresident: full-time $17,854; part-time $957.75 per credit hour. International tuition: $17,854 full-time. Required fees: $1534. Full-time tuition and fees vary according to program. *Financial support:* In 2010–11, 10 fellowships with full tuition reimbursements (averaging $2,845 per year), 159 research assistantships with full tuition reimbursements (averaging $20,998 per year), 28 teaching assistantships with full tuition reimbursements (averaging $15,083 per year) were awarded; career-related internships or fieldwork, Federal Work-Study, scholarships/grants, health care benefits, and unspecified assistantships also available. Financial award application deadline: 1/15. *Faculty research:* Electromagnetics, controls, electronics, power, communications. *Unit head:* Dr. James S. Thorp, UNIT HEAD, 540-231-7494, Fax: 540-231-3362, E-mail: jsthorp@vt.edu. *Application contact:* Paul Plassmann, Contact, 540-231-5379, Fax: 540-231-3362, E-mail: plassmann@vt.edu.

Virginia Polytechnic Institute and State University, VT Online, Blacksburg, VA 24061. Offers aerospace engineering (MS); business information systems (Graduate Certificate); career and technical education (MS); computer engineering (M Eng, MS); decision support systems (Graduate Certificate); eLearning leadership (MA); electrical engineering (M Eng, MS); engineering administration (MEA); environmental politics and policy (Graduate Certificate); foundations of political analysis (Graduate Certificate); health product risk management (Graduate Certificate); information policy and society (Graduate Certificate); information security (Graduate Certificate); instructional technology (MA); liberal arts (Graduate Certificate); life sciences: health product risk management (MS); natural resources (MNR, Graduate Certificate); networking (Graduate Certificate); nonprofit and nongovernmental organization management (Graduate Certificate); ocean engineering (MS); political science (MA); security studies (Graduate Certificate); software development (Graduate Certificate). *Expenses:* Tuition, area resident: Full-time $9399; part-time $488 per credit hour. Tuition, state resident: full-time $9399; part-time $488 per credit hour. Tuition, nonresident: full-time $17,854; part-time $957.75 per credit hour. International tuition: $17,854 full-time. Required fees: $1534. Full-time tuition and fees vary according to program.

Washington State University, Graduate School, College of Engineering and Architecture, School of Electrical Engineering and Computer Science, Program in Electrical Engineering, Pullman, WA 99164. Offers MS, PhD. *Faculty:* 30. *Students:* 61 full-time (5 women), 12 part-time (2 women); includes 1 Black or African American, non-Hispanic/Latino, 51 international. Average age 29. 307 applicants, 12% accepted, 17 enrolled. In 2010, 5 master's, 5 doctorates awarded. *Degree requirements:* For master's, comprehensive exam (for some programs), thesis, oral exam; for doctorate, comprehensive exam, thesis/dissertation, oral exam, qualifying exam, preliminary exam, oral defense of dissertation. *Entrance requirements:* For master's and doctorate, GRE General Test, major in computer engineering, electrical engineering, or computer science; statement of purpose giving qualifications, research interests, and goals; official college transcripts; three letters of recommendation. Additional exam requirements/recommendations for international students: Required—TOEFL (minimum score 520 paper-based; 190 computer-based), IELTS. *Application deadline:* For fall admission, 1/10 priority date for domestic students, 1/10 for international students; for spring admission, 7/1 for domestic and international students. Applications are processed on a rolling basis. Application fee: $50. *Expenses:* Tuition, state resident: full-time $8552; part-time $443 per credit. Tuition, nonresident: full-time $21,650; part-time $1083 per credit. Required fees: $846. *Financial support:* In 2010–11, 3 fellowships with full tuition reimbursements (averaging $2,500 per year), 18 research assistantships with full tuition reimbursements (averaging $13,917 per year), 24 teaching assistantships with full tuition reimbursements (averaging $13,056 per year) were awarded; career-related internships or fieldwork, Federal Work-Study, and institutionally sponsored loans also available. Financial award application deadline: 2/10; financial award applicants required to submit FAFSA. *Faculty research:* Energy and power systems, microelectronics, electrophysics controls, systems telecommunications. *Unit head:* Dr. Anjan Bose, Chair, 509-335-1147, Fax: 509-335-3818, E-mail: bose@wsu.edu. *Application contact:* Graduate School Admissions, 800-GRADWSU, Fax: 509-335-1949, E-mail: gradsch@wsu.edu.

Washington State University Tri-Cities, Graduate Programs, College of Engineering and Computer Science, Richland, WA 99352. Offers computer science (MS, PhD); electrical and computer engineering (PhD); electrical engineering (MS); mechanical engineering (MS, PhD). Part-time programs available. *Faculty:* 28. *Students:* 4 full-time (0 women), 25 part-time (8 women); includes 2 Black or African American, non-Hispanic/Latino, 1 international. *Degree requirements:* For master's, comprehensive exam, thesis (for some programs); for doctorate, comprehensive exam, thesis/dissertation, oral exam. *Entrance requirements:* For master's and doctorate, GRE, minimum GPA of 3.0, 3 letters of recommendation. Additional exam requirements/recommendations for international students: Required—TOEFL (minimum score 550 paper-based; 213 computer-based). *Application deadline:* For fall admission, 1/10 priority date for domestic students, 1/10 for international students; for spring admission, 7/1 priority date for domestic students, 7/1 for international students. Application fee: $50. *Financial support:* Application deadline: 3/1. *Faculty research:* Positive ion track structure, biological systems computer simulations. *Unit head:* Dr. Ali Saberi, Chair, 509-372-7178, E-mail: sidra@eecs.wsu.edu. *Application contact:* Dr. Scott Hudson, Associate Director, 509-372-7254, Fax: 509-335-1949, E-mail: hudson@tricity.wsu.edu.

Washington University in St. Louis, School of Engineering and Applied Science, Department of Electrical and Systems Engineering, St. Louis, MO 63130-4899. Offers electrical engineering (MS, D Sc, PhD); systems science and mathematics (MS, D Sc, PhD). Part-time programs available. *Faculty:* 16 full-time (2 women), 5 part-time/adjunct (0 women). *Students:* 63 full-time (12 women), 18 part-time (1 woman); includes 1 Black or African American, non-Hispanic/Latino; 15 Asian, non-Hispanic/Latino; 2 Hispanic/Latino, 45 international. Average age 23. 299 applicants, 18% accepted, 18 enrolled. In 2010, 21 master's, 6 doctorates awarded. Terminal master's awarded for partial completion of doctoral program. *Degree requirements:* For master's, thesis or alternative; for doctorate, comprehensive exam, thesis/dissertation. *Entrance requirements:* For master's, minimum GPA of 3.0 in the last 2 years of undergraduate course work; for doctorate, GRE. Additional exam requirements/recommendations for international students: Required—TOEFL (minimum score 550 paper-based; 213 computer-based; 80 iBT). *Application deadline:* For fall admission, 1/15 for domestic and international students. Applications are processed on a rolling basis. Application fee: $60. Electronic applications accepted. *Financial support:* In 2010–11, 12 fellowships with full tuition reimbursements (averaging $20,000 per year), 32 research assistantships with full tuition reimbursements (averaging $26,950 per year) were awarded; teaching assistantships with full tuition reimbursements, career-related internships or fieldwork, Federal Work-Study, institutionally sponsored loans, scholarships/grants, and unspecified assistantships also available. Financial award application deadline: 1/15; financial award applicants required to submit FAFSA. *Faculty research:* Applied physics and electronics, signal and image processing, systems analysis, biomedicine, and energy. Total annual research expenditures: $2 million. *Unit head:* Dr. Arye

Electrical Engineering

Nehorai, Chair, 314-935-5565, Fax: 314-935-7500, E-mail: nehorai@ese.wustl.edu. *Application contact:* Shauna Dollison, Director of Graduate Programs, 314-935-4830, Fax: 314-935-7500, E-mail: sdollison@ese.wustl.edu.

Wayne State University, College of Engineering, Department of Electrical and Computer Engineering, Program in Electrical Engineering, Detroit, MI 48202. Offers MS, PhD. *Faculty:* 17 full-time (1 woman). *Students:* 66 full-time (5 women), 29 part-time (5 women); includes 20 minority (5 Black or African American, non-Hispanic/Latino; 14 Asian, non-Hispanic/Latino; 1 Hispanic/Latino), 50 international. Average age 29. 109 applicants, 59% accepted, 16 enrolled. In 2010, 18 master's, 1 doctorate awarded. *Degree requirements:* For master's, thesis optional; for doctorate, thesis/dissertation. *Entrance requirements:* Additional exam requirements/recommendations for international students: Required—TOEFL (minimum score 550 paper-based; 213 computer-based), Michigan English Language Assessment Battery (minimum score: 85); Recommended—TWE (minimum score 6). *Application deadline:* For fall admission, 7/1 priority date for domestic students, 6/1 for international students; for winter admission, 10/1 for international students; for spring admission, 3/15 for domestic students, 2/1 for international students. Applications are processed on a rolling basis. Application fee: $30 ($50 for international students). Electronic applications accepted. *Expenses:* Tuition, state resident: full-time $7662; part-time $478.85 per credit hour. Tuition, nonresident: full-time $16,920; part-time $1057.55 per credit hour. Required fees: $571.20; $35.70 per credit hour. $188.05 per semester. Tuition and fees vary according to course load and program. *Financial support:* In 2010–11, 3 fellowships (averaging $18,560 per year), 10 research assistantships (averaging $17,974 per year), 7 teaching assistantships (averaging $16,984 per year) were awarded. Financial award application deadline: 3/16. *Faculty research:* Biomedical systems, control systems, solid state materials, optical materials, hybrid vehicle. *Unit head:* Yang Zhao, Chair, 313-577-3920, Fax: 313-577-1101, E-mail: aa3606@wayne.edu. *Application contact:* Pepe Siy, Graduate Director, 313-577-3841, Fax: 313-577-1101, E-mail: psiy@ece.eng.wayne.edu.

Western Michigan University, Graduate College, College of Engineering and Applied Sciences, Department of Electrical and Computer Engineering, Kalamazoo, MI 49008. Offers computer engineering (MSE); electrical and computer engineering (PhD); electrical engineering (MSE). Part-time programs available. *Degree requirements:* For master's, thesis optional. *Entrance requirements:* For master's, minimum GPA of 3.0. *Faculty research:* Fiber optics, computer architecture, bioelectromagnetics, acoustics.

Western New England University, School of Engineering, Department of Electrical Engineering, Springfield, MA 01119. Offers MSEE. Part-time and evening/weekend programs available. *Students:* 4 part-time (1 woman); includes 1 Asian, non-Hispanic/Latino. In 2010, 3 master's awarded. *Degree requirements:* For master's, comprehensive exam, thesis optional. *Entrance requirements:* For master's, GRE, bachelor's degree in engineering or related field, two recommendations, resume. *Application deadline:* Applications are processed on a rolling basis. Application fee: $30. *Expenses:* Tuition: Full-time $35,582. *Financial support:* Available to part-time students. Applicants required to submit FAFSA. *Faculty research:* Superconductors, microwave cooking, computer voice output, digital filters, computer engineering. *Unit head:* Dr. James J. Moriarty, Chair, 413-782-1272, E-mail: jmoriart@wnec.edu. *Application contact:* Matt Fox, Director of Recruiting and Marketing for Adult Learners, 413-782-1249, Fax: 413-782-1779, E-mail: study@wnec.edu.

West Virginia University, College of Engineering and Mineral Resources, Lane Department of Computer Science and Electrical Engineering, Program in Electrical Engineering, Morgantown, WV 26506. Offers MSEE, PhD. Terminal master's awarded for partial completion of doctoral program. *Degree requirements:* For master's, thesis or alternative; for doctorate, comprehensive exam, thesis/dissertation. *Entrance requirements:* For master's and doctorate, GRE General Test, minimum GPA of 3.0, letters of recommendation. Additional exam requirements/recommendations for international students: Required—TOEFL. *Faculty research:* Power and control systems, communications and signal processing, electromechanical systems, microelectronics and photonics.

Wichita State University, Graduate School, College of Engineering, Department of Electrical Engineering and Computer Science, Wichita, KS 67260. Offers computer networking (MS); computer science (MS); electrical engineering (MS, PhD). Part-time and evening/weekend programs available. *Unit head:* Dr. John Watkins, Chair, 316-978-3156, Fax: 316-978-5408, E-mail: john.watkins@wichita.edu. *Application contact:* Dr. John Watkins, Chair, 316-978-3156, Fax: 316-978-5408, E-mail: john.watkins@wichita.edu.

Wilkes University, College of Graduate and Professional Studies, College of Science and Engineering, Division of Engineering and Physics, Wilkes-Barre, PA 18766-0002. Offers electrical engineering (MSEE); engineering management (MS); mechanical engineering (MS). Part-time programs available. *Students:* 13 full-time (1 woman), 15 part-time (2 women); includes 1 Asian, non-Hispanic/Latino; 1 Two or more races, non-Hispanic/Latino, 8 international. Average age 28. In 2010, 25 master's awarded. *Entrance requirements:* For master's, GRE General Test. Additional exam requirements/recommendations for international students: Required—TOEFL (minimum score 550 paper-based; 213 computer-based; 79 iBT). *Application deadline:* Applications are processed on a rolling basis. Application fee: $45 ($65 for international

students). Electronic applications accepted. Tuition and fees vary according to degree level and program. *Financial support:* Federal Work-Study and unspecified assistantships available. Financial award application deadline: 3/1; financial award applicants required to submit FAFSA. *Unit head:* Dr. Rodney Ridley, Director, 570-408-4824, Fax: 570-408-7846, E-mail: rodney.ridley@wilkes.edu. *Application contact:* Kathleen Houlihan, Director of Graduate Studies, 570-408-3235, Fax: 570-408-7846, E-mail: kathleen.houlihan@wilkes.edu.

Woods Hole Oceanographic Institution, MIT/WHOI Joint Program in Oceanography/Applied Ocean Science and Engineering, Woods Hole, MA 02543-1541. Offers applied ocean sciences (PhD); biological oceanography (PhD, Sc D); chemical oceanography (PhD, Sc D); civil and environmental and oceanographic engineering (PhD); electrical and oceanographic engineering (PhD); geochemistry (PhD); geophysics (PhD); marine biology (PhD); marine geochemistry (PhD, Sc D); marine geology (PhD, Sc D); marine geophysics (PhD); mechanical and oceanographic engineering (PhD); ocean engineering (PhD); oceanographic engineering (M Eng, MS, PhD, Sc D, Eng); paleoceanography (PhD); physical oceanography (PhD, Sc D). MS, PhD, Sc D offered jointly with Massachusetts Institute of Technology. Terminal master's awarded for partial completion of doctoral program. *Degree requirements:* For master's and Eng, thesis (for some programs); for doctorate, thesis/dissertation. *Entrance requirements:* For master's, GRE General Test; for doctorate, GRE General Test, GRE Subject Test. Additional exam requirements/recommendations for international students: Required—TOEFL. Electronic applications accepted.

Worcester Polytechnic Institute, Graduate Studies and Research, Department of Electrical and Computer Engineering, Worcester, MA 01609-2280. Offers electrical and computer engineering (Advanced Certificate, Graduate Certificate); electrical engineering (M Eng, MS, PhD). Part-time and evening/weekend programs available. *Faculty:* 17 full-time (1 woman), 3 part-time/adjunct (0 women). *Students:* 106 full-time (20 women), 103 part-time (14 women); includes 7 Black or African American, non-Hispanic/Latino; 10 Hispanic/Latino; 12 Native Hawaiian or other Pacific Islander, non-Hispanic/Latino, 72 international. 504 applicants, 53% accepted, 92 enrolled. In 2010, 46 master's, 8 doctorates awarded. Terminal master's awarded for partial completion of doctoral program. *Degree requirements:* For master's, thesis optional; for doctorate, comprehensive exam, thesis/dissertation. *Entrance requirements:* For master's, 3 letters of recommendation; for doctorate, 3 letters of recommendation, statement of purpose. Additional exam requirements/recommendations for international students: Required—TOEFL (minimum score 550 paper-based; 213 computer-based; 79 iBT), IELTS (minimum score 6.5). *Application deadline:* For fall admission, 1/1 priority date for domestic students, 1/1 for international students; for spring admission, 10/1 priority date for domestic students, 10/1 for international students. Applications are processed on a rolling basis. Application fee: $70. Electronic applications accepted. *Expenses:* Tuition: Full-time $20,862; part-time $1159 per term. One-time fee: $15. *Financial support:* Career-related internships or fieldwork, institutionally sponsored loans, scholarships/grants, and unspecified assistantships available. Financial award application deadline: 1/1; financial award applicants required to submit FAFSA. *Faculty research:* Analog and mixed signal IC design, cryptography, data and system security, networking and communication systems (including sw defined radios), biomedical signal processing and medical systems, indoor/outdoor localization and navigation systems. *Unit head:* Dr. Fred Looft, Department Head, 508-831-5231, Fax: 508-831-5491, E-mail: fjlooft@wpi.edu. *Application contact:* Dr. Donald Brown, Graduate Coordinator, 508-831-5231, Fax: 508-831-5491, E-mail: drb@wpi.edu.

Wright State University, School of Graduate Studies, College of Engineering and Computer Science, Programs in Engineering, Program in Electrical Engineering, Dayton, OH 45435. Offers MSE. Part-time and evening/weekend programs available. *Degree requirements:* For master's, thesis or course option alternative. *Entrance requirements:* Additional exam requirements/recommendations for international students: Required—TOEFL. *Faculty research:* Robotics, circuit design, power electronics, image processing, communication systems.

Yale University, Graduate School of Arts and Sciences, School of Engineering and Applied Science, Department of Electrical Engineering, New Haven, CT 06520. Offers MS, PhD. Terminal master's awarded for partial completion of doctoral program. *Degree requirements:* For doctorate, thesis/dissertation, exam. *Entrance requirements:* For master's and doctorate, GRE General Test. Additional exam requirements/recommendations for international students: Required—TOEFL. *Faculty research:* Signal processing, control, and communications; digital systems and computer engineering; microelectronics and photonics; nanotechnology; computers, sensors, and networking.

Youngstown State University, Graduate School, College of Science, Technology, Engineering and Mathematics, Department of Electrical and Computer Engineering, Youngstown, OH 44555-0001. Offers computer engineering (MSE); electrical engineering (MSE). Part-time and evening/weekend programs available. *Degree requirements:* For master's, thesis optional. *Entrance requirements:* For master's, minimum GPA of 2.75 in field. Additional exam requirements/recommendations for international students: Required—TOEFL. *Faculty research:* Computer-aided design, power systems, electromagnetic energy conversion, sensors, control systems.

Carnegie Mellon

CARNEGIE MELLON UNIVERSITY

Department of Electrical and Computer Engineering

Programs of Study

Graduate study in the Department of Electrical and Computer Engineering (ECE) prepares students for roles in research, development, design, and leadership positions. The Department offers two graduate degree programs that lead to an M.S. or a Ph.D. degree in electrical and computer engineering.

Students who have earned a B.S. or M.S. and whose intention is to obtain a Ph.D. degree may apply to the Ph.D. program. The Ph.D. program is a research-oriented degree. Those students in the Ph.D. program who do not already have an M.S. degree are required to complete an academic course of study that usually results in the awarding of an M.S. degree prior to the Ph.D.

The Professional M.S. program is more course intensive than the research-oriented Ph.D. program. This program is for students who have a B.S. degree and are interested in further professional development. Students in this program study the fundamentals of electrical and computer engineering and have the opportunity for in-depth specialization in a particular aspect of this field. Upon enrollment in the Department, students are given the opportunity, with the help of a faculty adviser, to choose an educational program that is consistent with their background and is best suited to their own academic goals.

Fulfillment of the Ph.D. requirements takes three to four years beyond an M.S. degree and requires passing a qualifying examination, completing two internships in university teaching, writing a thesis that describes the results of independent research, and passing an oral defense of the research.

The Department is home to several internationally recognized research centers and laboratories, including the Data Storage Systems Center (DSSC), Center for Silicon Systems Implementation (CSSI), Center for Circuit and System Solutions (C2S2), Computer Architecture Laboratory at Carnegie Mellon (CALCM), Advanced Mechatronics Laboratory (AML), Micro Electro-Mechanical Systems (MEMS) Laboratory, Parallel Data Laboratory (PDL), Multimedia Laboratory, General Motors Collaborative Laboratory at Carnegie Mellon, and Center for Memory Intensive Self Configuring ICs.

Faculty members hold joint appointments with other departments, and most of them also have close ties with various interdisciplinary research centers in the University, such as the Institute for Complex Engineered Systems (ICES), Robotics Institute (RI), Information Networking Institute (INI), Institute for Software Research (ISRI), Human Computer Interaction Institute (HCII), Center for Nano-Enabled Devices and Energy Technology, and Carnegie Mellon CyLab in Network and Computer Security, including CyLabs Mobility Research Center at Carnegie Mellon's West Coast campus.

Major areas of research include agent-based systems; communications, wireless, and broadband networking; biomedical engineering; communications/information systems and engineering; computer system and network architecture; computer-aided design of VLSI circuits, systems, and technology, including synthesis, verification, simulation, test, manufacturing, custom analog and digital IC design, and semiconductor fabrication; information storage technology and systems, including magnetic and optical recording; design, fabrication, and characterization of microelectromechanical systems; design optimization; distributed and real-time/multimedia systems; distributed computer systems; electronic, magnetic, and optical materials and processing; embedded systems; fault tolerance and affordable dependable computing; high-performance I/O systems; high-speed processor architectures and design; information security; intelligent and hybrid control; intelligent robotics; manufacturing systems and automatic assembly; mobile and wireless computing; nanotechnology; neural networks; operating systems; parallel processing; rapid prototyping; sensory-based and supervisory control; signal processing in optical, video, image, speech, storage, and mobility systems; and technology and public policy.

Research Facilities

The Department has extensive computational facilities that include more than 2,000 networked workstations supporting research and education. Many of these are deployed in a cluster configuration to accommodate large and/or time-intensive batch computations. Research projects also make frequent use of supercomputers, which are available to the Department through the Pittsburgh Supercomputing Center. These systems are all connected to the CMU campuswide computer network via gigabit or faster Ethernet networking as well as via the Andrew Wireless Network. The centers and laboratories within the Department use advanced hardware and software infrastructure and experimental facilities that are conducive to building systems in all areas of research within the Department. A fully equipped 4,000-square-foot, class 100 clean room supports research in MEMS, nanotechnology, semiconductors, and magnetic and optical device research and can be used to produce state-of-the-art solid-state and recording devices.

Since most of the research is multidisciplinary and collaborative, students and faculty members have access to experimental and laboratory facilities housed in several multidisciplinary institutes.

Financial Aid

Graduate research assistantships are available to U.S. and international students admitted to the graduate Ph.D. program and include a typical stipend of about $2310 per month plus tuition. In the award of financial aid, consideration is given to the student's undergraduate and graduate academic records, GRE and TOEFL scores, and letters of reference indicating outstanding academic potential.

Virtually all students in the research-intensive Ph.D. program receive financial aid, which covers tuition, fees, and reasonable living expenses for the entire year. All applicants are considered for financial aid, and no special form is required.

Students in the Professional M.S. program are ineligible to receive Departmental fellowships that cover tuition and living expenses. Students in this program are self-supported and must complete at least two academic semesters before they are eligible to apply to the Ph.D. program, if they so choose.

Cost of Study

Tuition for graduate students enrolled in the Department of Electrical and Computer Engineering is set at $37,800 for the 2011–12 academic year. Books and supplies cost about $2300 per year.

Living and Housing Costs

Graduate accommodations are not provided, although there are various board plans available in nearby rooms or apartments. Approximate living expenses, including room and board, insurance, transportation, and miscellaneous expenses, average $22,000 per academic year, exclusive of tuition.

Student Group

The campus enrollment averages 10,402 students; 4,644 are graduate students. The University has 1,426 full-time faculty members. Within the Department of Electrical and Computer Engineering, there are 341 full-time graduate students in the master's program and in the Ph.D. program

Location

The greater Pittsburgh metropolitan area has more than 2 million residents. The Carnegie Mellon campus encompasses approximately 100 acres and adjoins a 500-acre city park and quiet residential communities with abundant student housing.

The University

The University is composed of the Carnegie Institute of Technology (the Engineering School), Mellon College of Science, the College of Fine Arts, the Graduate School of Industrial Administration, the Heinz School, the College of Humanities and Social Sciences, and the School of Computer Sciences.

Applying

All applicants are required to take the GRE (General Test) at least six weeks prior to the application deadline. All students whose native language is not English are required to take the Test of English as a Foreign Language (TOEFL). Applications for the fall semester must be received by December 15. Applications for spring semester must be received by October 1. Official transcripts, three letters of recommendation, and official GRE and TOEFL scores must be provided. Additional information about the graduate programs, faculty and research initiatives, and application procedures are located on the ECE Web site: www.ece.cmu.edu.

Correspondence and Information

Graduate Admissions Office, HH B204
Department of Electrical and Computer Engineering
Carnegie Mellon University
Pittsburgh, Pennsylvania 15213

Phone: 412-268-6327
Fax: 412-268-3155
E-mail: apps@ece.cmu.edu
Web site: http://www.ece.cmu.edu

Carnegie Mellon University

THE FACULTY AND THEIR RESEARCH

J. Bain, Professor and Associate Director, DSSC; Ph.D., Stanford, 1993: magnetic materials, thin-film magnetic devices, magnetic disk and tape recording. V. Bhagavatula, Professor; Ph.D., Carnegie Mellon, 1980: coding and signal processing for data storage, biometrics, pattern recognition. R. Blanton, Professor and Director, CSSI; Ph.D., Michigan, 1985: test and verification of VLSI circuits and systems. D. J. Brumley, Professor. L. R. Carley, ST Microelectronics Professor; Ph.D., MIT, 1984: CAD and design of analog signal processing circuits and MEMS systems. D. P. Casasent, George Westinghouse Professor and Director, Optics Lab; Ph.D., Illinois, 1969: pattern recognition, neural nets, ATR image processing and product inspection. S. H. Charap, Professor Emeritus; Ph.D., Rutgers, 1959: applied magnetism, with particular emphasis on magnetic recording. T. Chen, Professor; Ph.D., Caltech, 1993: multimedia coding and streaming, computer vision, pattern recognition, computer graphics, multimodal biometrics. A. Davidson, Senior Systems Scientist; Ph.D., Harvard, 1976: device physics, nonlinear dynamics, MEMS-based mass storage. G. K. Fedder, Howard M. Wilkoff Professor of ECE and Robotics and Director, Institute for Complex Engineered Systems; Ph.D., Berkeley, 1994: MEMS, MEMS CAD, microrobotics. F. Franchetti, Systems Scientist; Ph.D., Vienna Technical, 2003: automatic performance tuning, digital signal-processing transforms, advanced architectures. R. Gandhi, Systems Engineer; Ph.D., California, Santa Barbara, 2000: wireless systems and signal/video compression. G. Ganger, Professor of ECE and CS and Director, Parallel Data Lab; Ph.D., Michigan, 1995: operating systems, security, distributed systems, storage/file systems, networking. V. Gligor, Professor; Ph.D., Berkeley, 1976. D. W. Greve, Professor; Ph.D., Lehigh, 1979: semiconductor device physics, semiconductor process technology, sensors. J. F. Hoburg, Professor; Ph.D., MIT, 1975: electromagnetics, electromechanics, magnetic shielding, applied electrostatics, electrohydrodynamics, microfluidics. J. C. Hoe, Associate Professor of ECE and CS; Ph.D., MIT, 2000: computer architecture, high-level hardware description and synthesis. M. Ilic, Professor of ECE and EPP; Ph.D., Washington (St. Louis), 1980: large-scale systems modeling and simulation, power systems control and pricing algorithms, critical infrastructures/interdependencies. A. G. Jordan, Keithley University Professor Emeritus of ECE and Robotics; Ph.D., Carnegie Tech, 1959: advanced video systems, robotics. P. K. Khosla, Dowd Professor of Engineering and Robotics; Dean, Carnegie Institute of Technology; and Director, Carnegie Mellon CyLab; Ph.D., Carnegie Mellon, 1986. H. S. Kim, Drew D. Perkins Professor and Director, CyLab Korea; Ph.D., Toronto, 1990: advanced switch and network architectures, fault-tolerant network architectures, network management and control. P. J. Koopman, Associate Professor of ECE and CS; Ph.D., Carnegie Mellon, 1989: distributed embedded systems, survivable system architecture, dependability. B. H. Krogh, Professor; Ph.D., Illinois at Urbana-Champaign, 1982: Synthesis and verification of embedded control software, distributed control strategies, distributed supervisory control, information and control in wireless sensor networks, discrete event and hybrid dynamic systems. M. H. Kryder, University Professor; Ph.D., Caltech, 1970: magnetic recording, optical recording, ferroelectric materials. D. N. Lambeth, Professor of ECE and MSE; Ph.D., MIT, 1973: physical and chemical sensors, transducers, MEMS, magnetism, materials, thin films, data storage, RF devices. X. Li, Systems Scientist; Ph.D., Carnegie Mellon, 2005: integrated circuits, computer-aided design. Y. Luo, Assistant Professor; Ph.D., Columbia, 2000: nanoelectronic devices, molecular electronics, nanoscale materials and fabrication techniques. K. Mai, Assistant Professor; Ph.D., Stanford, 2005: digital circuit design, computer architecture, memory design, reconfigurable computing. W. Maly, U. A. and Helen Whitaker Professor; Ph.D., Polish Academy of Sciences, 1975: computer-aided design and manufacturing of VLSICs. D. Marculescu, Associate Professor; Ph.D., USC, 1998: VLSI/computer architecture, energy-aware computing. R. Marculescu, Professor; Ph.D., USC, 1998: computer-aided design of digital systems, low-power design, embedded systems. M. G. Morgan, Lord Professor of ECE and EPP and Department Head, EPP; Ph.D., California, San Diego, 1969: technology and policy, including climate change and electric power. J. M. F. Moura, Professor; D.Sc., MIT, 1975: communications; statistical signal/image, video, and multimedia processing; wavelet transforms. T. Mukherjee, Professor; Ph.D., Carnegie Mellon, 1995: methodologies for microelectromechanical systems (MEMS) and biofluidic microsystems. O. Mutulu, Professor. W. Nace, Lecturer. P. Narasimhan, Associate Professor of ECE and CS; Ph.D., California, Santa Barbara, 1999: fault tolerance, survivability, real time, distributed systems, middleware. R. Negi, Associate Professor; Ph.D., Stanford, 2000: wireless systems, networking, signal processing, coding for communications, information theory. C. P. Neuman, Professor; Ph.D., Harvard, 1968: control engineering and robotics. D. O'Hallaron, Associate Professor of ECE and CS; Ph.D., Virginia, 1986: scientific computing, parallel computing, computational database systems, virtualization. J. Paramesh, Assistant Professor; Ph.D., Washington (Seattle), 2006. A. Perrig, Associate Professor of ECE, EPP, and CS and Director of CyLab; Ph.D., Carnegie Mellon, 2001: information systems security, focusing on network security (Internet, mobile computing, and sensor networks) and trusted computing. L. T. Pileggi, Tanoto Professor; Ph.D., Carnegie Mellon, 1989: design, implementation, and modeling of integrated circuits and systems. M. Püschel, Associate Research Professor; Ph.D., Karlsruhe (Germany), 1998: signal processing (theory, algorithms, implementations), scientific computing, compilers, applied mathematics. R. Rajkumar, Professor and Director, GM Collaborative Laboratory; Ph.D., Carnegie Mellon, 1989: multimedia and real-time systems. D. Ricketts, Assistant Professor; Ph.D., Harvard, 2006: nanoscale electronics, nanoscale devices, nonlinear dynamics, analog circuits. R. A. Rohrer, Professor Emeritus; Ph.D., Berkeley, 1963: electronic circuits, systems design automation. R. A. Rutenbar, Jatras Professor of ECE and CS; Ph.D., Michigan, 1984: VLSI CAD, algorithms, analog and digital circuits, automatic speech recognition. T. E. Schlesinger, Professor and Head of ECE; Ph.D., Caltech, 1985: optoelectronics, information storage, nanotechnology. D. P. Siewiorek, Buhl University Professor of ECE and CS and Director, HCI Institute; Ph.D., Stanford, 1972: computer architecture, reliability, context-aware mobile computing. B. Sinopoli, Assistant Professor; Ph.D., Berkeley, 2005: networked embedded control systems, sensory/actuator networks, control theory. D. D. Stancil, Professor; Ph.D., MIT, 1981: wireless communication, nanophotonics, spin-wave devices. P. A. Steenkiste, Professor of ECE and CS; Ph.D., Stanford, 1987: computer networks, distributed systems, pervasive computing. R. M. Stern Jr., Professor of ECE, CS, and BME; Ph.D., MIT, 1976: automatic speech recognition, auditory perception, signal processing. A. J. Strojwas, Keithley Professor; Ph.D., Carnegie Mellon, 1982: statistically based CAD/CAM of VLSI circuits. T. Sullivan, Associate Teaching Professor; Ph.D., Carnegie Mellon, 1996: audio signal processing, music and sound recording applications. S. N. Talukdar, Professor Emeritus; Ph.D., Purdue, 1970: agent-based systems, distributed problem solving, power systems, organization design. D. E. Thomas Jr., Professor; Ph.D., Carnegie Mellon, 1977: computer-aided design of single-chip heterogeneous multiprocessing systems. O. Tonguz, Professor; Ph.D., Rutgers, 1990: optical networks, wireless communications and high-speed networking. E. Towe, Grobstein Professor of ECE and MSE; Ph.D., MIT, 1997: photonics, optical networks, biophotonics, sensors, quantum phenomena in optical materials. R. M. White, University Professor Emeritus; Ph.D., Stanford, 1964: magnetic device phenomena, technology policy. J. G. Zhu, ABB Professor and Director, DSSC; Ph.D., California, San Diego, 1989: micromagnetics, magnetoelectronic devices, magnetic recording.

COLUMBIA UNIVERSITY

Department of Electrical Engineering

Programs of Study	The Department of Electrical Engineering offers programs of study leading to the degrees of Master of Science (M.S.), Electrical Engineer (E.E.), Doctor of Engineering Science (Eng.Sc.D.), and Doctor of Philosophy (Ph.D.). Registration as a nondegree candidate (special student) is also permitted.
	There are no prescribed course requirements for these degrees. Students, in consultation with their faculty advisers, design their own programs, focusing on particular fields. Among them are semiconductor physics materials and devices; telecommunication systems and computer networks; high-speed analog, RF analog, and mixed analog/digital integrated circuits and systems; image, video, audio, and speech processing; electromagnetic theory and applications; plasma physics; quantum electronics; photonics; and sensory perception.
	Graduate studies are closely associated with research. Faculty members are engaged in theoretical and experimental research in various areas of their disciplines.
	Access also exists to a number of interdisciplinary programs, such as Computer Engineering, Solid-State Science and Engineering, and Bioengineering. In addition, substantial research interactions occur with the Departments of Applied Physics, Computer Science, and Industrial Engineering and Operations Research and with the College of Physicians and Surgeons.
	The requirements for the Ph.D. and Eng.Sc.D. degrees are essentially identical. Both require a dissertation based on the candidate's original research, conducted under the supervision of a faculty member. The work may be theoretical or experimental or both. The E.E. professional degree program does not require a thesis. It provides specialization beyond the M.S. degree in a field chosen by the student and is particularly suited to those who wish to advance their professional development after a period of industrial employment.
Research Facilities	Every phase of current research activities is fully supported and carried out in one of more than a dozen well-equipped research laboratories run by the Department. Specifically, laboratory research is conducted in the following laboratories: Multimedia Networking Laboratory, Ultrafast Opto-Electronics Laboratory, Photonics Laboratory, Microelectronics Device Fabrication Laboratory, Digital Video and Multimedia Laboratory, Molecular Beam Epitaxy Laboratory, Laser Processing and Quantum Physics Laboratory, Integrated Systems Laboratory, Laboratory for Recognition and Organization of Speech and Audio, Lightwave Communications Laboratory, Bioelectronic Systems Laboratory, Columbia Laboratory for Unconventional Electronics, and Plasma Physics Laboratory (in conjunction with the Department of Applied Physics).
Financial Aid	Teaching assistantships and graduate research assistantships are available. For the 2011–12 academic year, stipends are $2595 per month plus tuition exemption.
Cost of Study	The annual tuition for 2010–11 was about $41,580, plus fees.
Living and Housing Costs	The University provides limited housing for graduate men and women who are registered either for an approved program of full-time academic study or for doctoral dissertation research. University residence halls include traditional dormitory facilities as well as suites and apartments for single and married students; furnishings and utilities may be included. An estimated minimum of $20,000 should be allowed for board, room, and personal expenses for the academic year.
	University Real Estate properties include apartments owned and managed by the University in the immediate vicinity of the Morningside Heights campus. These are leased yearly, as they become available, to single and married students at rates that reflect the size and location of each apartment as well as whether furnishings or utilities are included.
	Requests for additional information and application forms should be directed to the Assignments Office, 111 Wallach Hall, Columbia University, New York, New York 10027.
Student Group	In 2010–12, enrollment in the Department of Electrical Engineering is projected to be 605 students and included 73 undergraduates (46 electrical engineering juniors and seniors and 27 computer engineering juniors and seniors), 307 electrical engineering master's degree candidates, 37 computer engineering master's candidates, 137 doctoral candidates with master's degrees, and 5 professional candidates. The student population has a diverse and international character.
Location	The proximity of many local industries provides strong student-industry contact and excellent job opportunities. Cooperative research projects are available in neighboring industrial laboratories, which are engaged in research and development in computers, telecommunications, electronics, defense, and health care. Adjunct faculty members from industry provide courses in areas of current professional interest. Frequent colloquia are given on current research by distinguished speakers from industry and neighboring universities.
The University	Since its founding in 1754, Columbia University has attracted students interested in the issues of their times. Opened as King's College under charter of King George II to "prevent the growth of republican principles which prevail already too much in the colonies," it instead educated founders of a new and powerful nation: Alexander Hamilton, John Jay, Robert Livingston, and Gouverneur Morris. Since then such notable figures as Michael Pupin, Edwin Armstrong, and Jacob Millman have served as professors of electrical engineering at Columbia.
Applying	The Department of Electrical Engineering uses an online application that can be found at http://www.engineering.columbia.edu/admissions. October 1 is the priority deadline for all spring applicants. December 1 is the priority deadline for fall doctoral applicants. February 15 is the priority deadline for fall M.S. and professional degree applicants. Notification of admission decisions are mailed beginning March 1.
Correspondence and Information	Office of Engineering Admissions Department of Electrical Engineering 524 S.W. Mudd, Mail Code 4708 Columbia University 500 West 120th Street New York, New York 10027 Phone: 212-854-6438 E-mail: seasgradmit@columbia.edu Web site: http://www.engineering.columbia.edu/admissions (admissions home page) 　　　　　http://www.ee.columbia.edu (Department home page)

Columbia University

THE FACULTY AND THEIR RESEARCH

Dimitris Anastassiou, Professor; Ph.D., Berkeley, 1979. Computational biology, with emphasis on systems-based gene expression analysis and comparative genomics. (phone: 212-854-3113; e-mail: anastas@ee.columbia.edu)

Keren Bergman, Professor; Ph.D., MIT, 1994. Optical interconnection networks for high-performance data centers, photonic networks-on-chip, silicon photonics, optically interconnected memory, WDM optical networking, cross-layer networking, multiwavelength optical packet switching. (phone: 212-854-2280; e-mail: bergman@ee.columbia.edu)

Shih-Fu Chang, Professor; Ph.D., Berkeley, 1993. Multimedia search, digital video analysis, statistical pattern recognition, machine learning, multimedia forensics and security. (phone: 212-854-6894; e-mail: sfchang@ee.columbia.edu)

Edward Coffman, Professor; Ph.D., UCLA, 1966. Performance evaluation and optimization of computer communication systems and networks, scheduling theory, bin-packing theory, probabilistic analysis of algorithms, random structures in nanotechnology. (phone: 212-854-2152; e-mail: egc@ee.columbia.edu)

Paul Diament, Professor; Ph.D., Columbia, 1963. Electromagnetics, microwaves, antennas, biological and medical applications of electromagnetics, mutual coupling in arrays, fiber optics, wave interactions. (phone: 212-854-3111; e-mail: diament@ee.columbia.edu)

Dan Ellis, Associate Professor; Ph.D., MIT, 1996. Audio information extraction, speech recognition, source separation, music informat retrieval, computational hearing, sound visualization. (phone: 212-854-8928; e-mail: dpwe@ee.columbia.edu)

Dirk Englund, Assistant Professor; Ph.D., Stanford, 2008. Quantum information and metrology, nanophotonics, advanced optoelectronic devices, nuclear spin dynamics in semiconductors. (phone: 212 851-5958; email: englund@columbia.edu)

Tony F. Heinz, David M. Rickey Professor; Ph.D., Berkeley, 1982. Ultrafast optics and spectroscopy, nonlinear optics, properties of nanostructures and interfaces. (phone: 212-854-6564; e-mail: tony.heinz@columbia.edu)

Predrag Jelenkovic, Associate Professor; Ph.D., Columbia, 1996. Mathematical modeling and analysis of resource control and management in multimedia communication networks. (phone: 212-854-8174; e-mail: predrag@ee.columbia.edu)

Peter Kinget, Associate Professor; Ph.D., Leuven (Belgium), 1996. Design of analog, radio-frequency (RF) and power integrated circuits for applications in communications, sensing, and power management. (e-mail: kinget@ee.columbia.edu)

Harish Krishnaswamy, Assistant Professor, Ph. D., USC, 2009. Radio-frequency (RF), millimeter-wave (mm-Wave) and sub-mmWave integrated circuits, with an emphasis on multiple-antenna systems, efficient, high-power transmitters, sub-mmWave signal sources, and low-phase-noise oscillators. (phone: 212-854-8196; email: harish@ee.columbia.edu)

Ioannis Kymissis, Assistant Professor; Ph.D., MIT, 2003. Organic semiconductors, OFETs, photodetectors, OLEDs, large-area thin-film electronics, hybrid device integration. (phone: 212-854-4023; e-mail: johnkym@ee.columbia.edu)

Aurel A. Lazar, Professor; Ph.D., Princeton, 1980. Time encoding and information representation in sensory systems, spike processing and neural computation in the cortex. (phone: 212-854-1747; e-mail: aurel@ee.columbia.edu)

Nicholas Maxemchuk, Professor; Ph.D., Pennsylvania, 1975. Communications networks: protocols, topological design, applications. (phone: 212-854-0580; e-mail: nick@ee.columbia.edu)

Vishal Misra, Associate Professor; Ph.D., Massachusetts Amherst, 2000. Networking, modeling and performance evaluation, information theory. (phone: 212-939-7061; e-mail: misra@cs.columbia.edu)

Steven M. Nowick, Associate Professor; Ph.D., Stanford, 1993. Asynchronous and mixed-timing circuits, computer-aided digital design, low-power and high-performance digital systems. (phone: 212-939-7056; e-mail: nowick@cs.columbia.edu)

Richard M. Osgood Jr., Higgins Professor; Ph.D., MIT, 1973. Integrated and guided-wave SI and other optoelectronic devices and their design, semiconductor and nanoscale surface physics and chemistry, ultrafast laser sources, quantum size studies. (phone: 212-854-4462; e-mail: osgood@columbia.edu)

Henning Schulzrinne, Professor; Ph.D., Massachusetts Amherst. Internet real-time and multimedia services and protocols, wireless networks, modeling and analysis of computer communication networks, network security. (phone: 212-939-7004; e-mail: hgs@cs.columbia.edu)

Amiya K. Sen, Professor; Ph.D., Columbia, 1963. Plasma instabilities and their feedback control, plasma turbulence and anomalous transport. (phone: 212-854-3124; e-mail: amiya@ee.columbia.edu)

Mingoo Seok, Assistant Professor; Ph.D., Michigan, 2011. Low-power integrated circuit and digital VLSI design, robust and high-performance circuit and system design, computer-aided design for VLSI, power electronics and circuits design, implantable medical devices and cyber physical systems applications (phone: 212-854-3105)

Kenneth Shepard, Associate Professor; Ph.D., Stanford, 1992. Design and analysis of mixed-signal CMOS integrated circuits, bioelectronics, application of CMOS circuit design to biological applications, carbon-based electronics integrated with CMOS. (phone: 212-854-2529; e-mail: shepard@ee.columbia.edu)

Yannis Tsividis, Charles Batchelor Professor; Ph.D., Berkeley, 1976. Analog and mixed-signal integrated circuits, RF integrated circuits, circuit theory, analog and mixed signal processing. (phone: 212-854-4229; e-mail: tsividis@ee.columbia.edu)

Wen I. Wang, Thayer Lindsley Professor; Ph.D., Cornell, 1981. Quantum and heterostructure optoelectronics, materials and devices, photovoltaics, molecular beam epitaxy. (phone: 212-854-1748; e-mail: wen@ee.columbia.edu)

Xiaodong Wang, Associate Professor; Ph.D., Princeton, 1998. Statistical signal processing, multiuser communication theory, wireless communications. (phone: 212-854-6592; e-mail: wangx@ee.columbia.edu)

John Wright, Assistant Professor; Ph.D., Illinois at Urbana-Champaign, 2009. Signal processing, sparse signal representation, robust estimation, computer vision. (phone: 212-854-3105; e-mail: johnwright@ee.columbia.edu)

Charles A. Zukowski, Professor; Ph.D., MIT, 1985. Design and analysis of digital VLSI circuits, simulation of circuits and biological networks, communication circuits. (phone: 212-854-2073; e-mail: caz@columbia.edu)

Gil Zussman, Assistant Professor; Ph.D., Technion–Israel Institute of Technology, 2004. Wireless and mobile networks, including ad hoc, mesh, sensor, vehicular, and cognitive radio networks. (phone: 212-854-8670; e-mail: gil@ee.columbia.edu)

DUKE UNIVERSITY

Department of Electrical and Computer Engineering

Programs of Study	Graduate study in the Department of Electrical and Computer Engineering (ECE) is intended to prepare students for leadership roles in academia, industry, and government that require creative technical problem-solving skills. The Department offers both Ph.D. and M.S. degree programs, with opportunities for study in a broad spectrum of areas within the disciplines of electrical and computer engineering. Research and course offerings in the Department are organized into six areas of specialization: computer engineering, imaging and information physics, microsystems and nanosystems, photonics, sensing and waves, and signal processing and communications. Interdisciplinary programs are also available that connect the above programs with those in other engineering departments and computer science, the natural sciences, and the Medical School. Students in the Department may also be involved in research conducted in one of the Duke centers, e.g., the Fitzpatrick Institute for Photonics. Under a reciprocal agreement with neighboring universities, a student may elect to enroll in some courses offered at the University of North Carolina at Chapel Hill and North Carolina State University in Raleigh. Since an important criterion for admitting new students is the match between student and faculty research interests, prospective students are encouraged to indicate in which Departmental specialization areas they are interested when applying.
Research Facilities	The ECE department currently occupies approximately 47,000 square feet in two buildings: the Fitzpatrick Center for Interdisciplinary Engineering, Medicine and Applied Sciences (FCIEMAS) and Hudson Hall. CIEMAS houses cross-disciplinary activities involving the Pratt School and its partners in the fields of bioengineering, photonics, microsystems integration, sensing and simulation, and materials science and materials engineering. This comprehensive facility provides extensive fabrication and test laboratories, Departmental offices, teaching labs, and other lab support spaces as well as direct access to a café. In addition, the Shared Materials Instrumentation Facility (SMiF), a state-of-the-art clean room for nanotechnology research, is housed on its main floor. Hudson Hall is the oldest of the buildings in the engineering complex. It was built in 1948 when the Engineering School moved to Duke's West Campus and was known as Old Red. An annex was built onto the back of the building in 1972, and in 1992, the building was expanded again and renamed Hudson Hall to honor Fitzgerald S. (Jerry) Hudson E'46. Hudson Hall is home to all four departments in the Pratt School of Engineering, as well as the school's laboratories, computing facilities, offices, and classrooms.
Financial Aid	Financial support is available for the majority of Ph.D. students. Graduate fellowships for the first two semesters of study provide a stipend, registration fees, and full tuition. Beyond this initial period, most students receive research assistantships funded by faculty research grants, which, together with financial aid, cover their full registration fees, tuition, and stipend until completion of the Ph.D. degree.
Cost of Study	For the 2011–12 academic year, tuition for doctoral students is $40,720. Tuition for terminal master's students is $15,405 per semester.
Living and Housing Costs	Duke has residential apartment facilities available to graduate students through an application process. These furnished apartments are available for continuous occupancy throughout the calendar year. Academic-year rates in central campus apartments range from $7300 per occupant for 2 students in a two-bedroom apartment to $14,600 for family housing for an efficiency apartment. There are also a wide variety of options for off-campus housing near campus and in the greater Durham area.
Student Group	In the academic year 2011–12, a total of 185 students are enrolled, of whom 130 are doctoral students and 55 are master's students.
Location	Located in the rolling central Piedmont area of North Carolina, the Duke University campus is widely regarded as one of the most beautiful in the nation. The four-season climate is mild, but winter skiing is available in the North Carolina mountains a few hours' drive to the west, and ocean recreation is a similar distance away to the east. Duke is readily accessible by Interstates 85 and 40 and from Raleigh-Durham International Airport, which is about a 20-minute drive from the campus via Interstate 40 and the Durham expressway.
The University and The Department	Trinity College, founded in 1859, was selected by James B. Duke as the major recipient of a 1924 endowment that enabled a university to be organized around the college and to be named for Washington B. Duke, the family patriarch. A department of engineering was established at Trinity College in 1910, and the Department of Electrical Engineering was formed in 1920. Its name changed to the Department of Electrical and Computer Engineering in 1996. Duke University remains a privately supported university, with more than 11,000 students in degree programs.
Applying	Admission to the Department is based on a review of previous education and experience, the applicant's statement of intent, letters of evaluation, standardized test scores (GRE and TOEFL), and grade point average. The application deadline for spring admission is October 15. December 8 is the priority deadline for submission of Ph.D. applications for admission and financial award for the fall semester. January 30 is the priority deadline for submission of M.S. applications for admission.
Correspondence and Information	Steven A. Cummer Professor and Director of Graduate Studies Department of Electrical and Computer Engineering Pratt School of Engineering, Box 90291 Duke University Durham, North Carolina 27708-0291 Phone: 919-660-5245 E-mail: dgs@ee.duke.edu Web site: http://www.ee.duke.edu

Duke University

THE FACULTY AND THEIR RESEARCH

John A. Board, Associate Professor of ECE and Computer Science; D.Phil., Oxford. High performance scientific computing and simulation, novel computer architectures, cluster computing and parallel processing, ubiquitous computing.

David J. Brady, Professor; Ph.D., Caltech. Computational optical sensor systems, hyperspectral microscopy, Raman spectroscopy for tissue chemometrics, optical coherence sensors and infrared spectral filters.

Martin A. Brooke, Associate Professor; Ph.D., USC. Integrated analog CMOS circuit design, integrated nanoscale systems, mixed signal VLSI design, sensing and sensor systems, optical imaging and communications, analog and power electronics, electronic circuit assembly and testing.

April S. Brown, John Cocke Professor and Sr. Associate Dean for Research; D.Sc., Cornell. Nanomaterial manufacturing and characterization, sensing and sensor systems, nanoscale/microscale computing systems, integrated nanoscale systems.

Robert Calderbank, Dean of Natural Sciences and Professor of ECE, Math, and Computer Science; Ph.D., Caltech. Computer engineering, computer architecture, information theory.

Lawrence Carin, William H. Younger Professor; Ph.D., Maryland, College Park, Homeland security, sensing and sensor systems, signal processing, land mine detection.

Krishnendu Chakrabarty, Professor; Ph.D., Michigan. Computer engineering, nanoscale/microscale computing systems, self-assembled computer architecture, micro-electronic mechanical machines, failure analysis, integrated nanoscale systems, microsystems.

Leslie M. Collins, Professor and Chair; Ph.D., Michigan. Sensing and sensor systems, homeland security, land mine detection, neural prosthesis, geophysics, signal processing.

Steven A. Cummer, Jeffrey N. Vinik Associate Professor and Director of Graduate Studies; Ph.D., Stanford. Geophysics, photonics, atmospheric science, metamaterials, electromagnetics.

Chris Dwyer, Assistant Professor; Ph.D., North Carolina at Chapel Hill. Self-assembled computer architecture, nanoscale/microscale computing systems, nanomaterial manufacturing and characterization, computer engineering, biological computing, computer architecture, nanoscience, materials.

Richard B. Fair, Lord-Chandran Professor; Ph.D., Duke. Computer engineering, sensing and sensor systems, electronic devices, integrated nanoscale systems, medical diagnostics, microsystems, semiconductors.

Jeffrey T. Glass, Professor and Hogg Family Director, Engineering Management and Entrepreneurship; Ph.D., Virginia. Micro-electronic mechanical machines, engineering management, entrepreneurship, social entrepreneurship, sensing and sensor systems, materials.

Michael R. Gustafson, Associate Professor of the Practice; Ph.D., Duke. Engineering education, electronic circuit assembly and testing, electronic devices.

Lisa G. Huettel, Associate Professor of the Practice and Director of Undergraduate Studies; Ph.D., Duke. Sensing and sensor systems, engineering education, signal processing, distributed systems.

William T. Joines, Professor; Ph.D., Duke. Photonics and electromagnetics.

Nan M. Jokerst, J. A. Jones Professor; Ph.D., USC. Photonics, sensing and sensor systems, nanomaterial manufacturing and characterization, semiconductors, integrated nanoscale systems, microsystems.

Tom Katsouleas, Professor and Dean; Ph.D., Physics, UCLA. Use of plasmas as novel particle accelerators and light sources.

Jungsang Kim, Associate Professor; Ph.D., Stanford. Photonics, micro-electronic mechanical machines, sensing and sensor systems, semiconductors, quantum information, integrated nanoscale systems.

Jeffrey L. Krolik, Professor; Ph.D., Toronto (Canada). Sensing and sensor systems, signal processing, acoustics, medical imaging, homeland security, electromagnetics, antennas.

Benjamin C. Lee, Assistant Professor; Ph.D., Harvard. Scalable technologies, power-efficient computer architectures, high-performance applications.

Xuejun Liao, Assistant Research Professor; Ph.D., Xidian University, Xi'an (China). Pattern recognition and machine learning, bioinformatics, signal processing.

Qing H. Liu, Professor; Ph.D., Illinois at Urbana-Champaign. Electromagnetics, antennas, medical imaging, photonics, acoustics, computational electromagnetics.

Daniel L. Marks, Assistant Research Professor; Ph.D., Illinois at Urbana-Champaign: Imaging and spectroscopy.

Hisham Z. Massoud, Professor; Ph.D., Stanford. Nanomaterial manufacturing and characterization, nanoscale/microscale computing systems, computer engineering, engineering education, electronic devices, manufacturing, semiconductors, microsystems.

Peter Maunz, Assistant Research Professor; Ph.D., TU München (Germany). Multifunctional integrated systems, atomic physics, cavity quantum electrodynamics, trapped-ion quantum information processing.

James Morizio, Assistant Research Professor; Ph.D., Duke. Computer engineering, nanoscale/microscale computing systems, biological computing, mixed signal VLSI design, integrated analog CMOS circuit design.

Kenneth D. Morton Jr., Assistant Research Professor; Ph.D., Duke. Statistical signal processing, sensing and sensor systems, machine learning, land mine detection, acoustics.

Loren W. Nolte, Professor; Ph.D., Michigan. Sensing and sensor systems, medical imaging, signal processing.

Douglas P. Nowacek, Repass-Rodgers University Associate Professor of Conservation Technology and Associate Professor of ECE; Ph.D., MIT/Woods Hole Oceanographic Institution. Acoustics, micro-electronic mechanical machines.

Ekaterina Poutrina, Assistant Research Professor; Ph.D., Rochester. Theory of active and nonlinear metamaterials.

Maxim Raginsky, Assistant Research Professor; Ph.D., Northwestern. Signal processing, sensing and sensor systems, information theory, statistical learning theory, optimization and games, stochastic adaptive control.

Matthew S. Reynolds, Assistant Professor; Ph.D., MIT. RFID and its applications to robotics and human-computer interaction, ultra-low power sensing and computation, parasitic power and smart materials, surfaces, spaces.

Romit Roy Choudhury, Nortel Networks Assistant Professor; Ph.D., Illinois at Urbana-Champaign. Computer engineering, antennas, electronic devices, wireless networking, mobile computing, distributed systems.

David R. Smith, William Bevan Professor; Ph.D., California, San Diego. Photonics, metamaterials, electromagnetic, plasmonics.

Daniel J. Sorin, Associate Professor; Ph.D., Wisconsin–Madison. Computer engineering, computer architecture, fault tolerance, reliability.

Adrienne D. Stiff-Roberts, Assistant Professor; Ph.D., Michigan. Nanomaterial manufacturing and characterization, semiconductor photonic devices, photonics, nanoscience.

Peter A. Torrione; Assistant Research Professor; Ph.D., Duke. Statistical signal processing, machine learning, pattern recognition, buried threat detection.

Kishor S. Trivedi; Hudson Professor (joint with Computer Science); Ph.D., Illinois at Urbana-Champaign. Computer engineering, failure analysis, fault tolerance, reliability, computer architecture.

Yaroslav A. Urzhumov, Assistant Research Professor; Ph.D., Texas at Austin. Numerical simulation of metamaterials and plasmonic nanosystems.

Rebecca Willett, Assistant Professor; Ph.D., Rice. Sensing and sensor systems, homeland security, medical imaging, K–12 education in science and mathematics, signal processing, photonics, distributed systems.

Gary A. Ybarra, Professor of the Practice; Ph.D., North Carolina State. Engineering education, K–12 education in science and mathematics, medical imaging.

Tomoyuki Yoshie, Assistant Professor; Ph.D., Caltech. Photonics, semiconductor photonic devices, nanoscale/microscale computing systems, quantum information, integrated nanoscale systems.

The University of New Mexico

UNIVERSITY OF NEW MEXICO

Department of Electrical and Computer Engineering

Programs of Study

Graduate work leading to the M.S. and Ph.D. degrees is offered by the Department in the areas of bioengineering, communications, computational intelligence, computer architecture, computer networks and systems, control systems, electromagnetics, image processing, microelectronics and optoelectronics, plasma science, and signal processing. The M.S. degree is also offered in optical science and engineering. The master's degree program requires 30 semester credit hours for a thesis option and 33 semester credit hours for a nonthesis option. The Ph.D. program requires that a minimum of 24 graduate credit hours beyond the master's degree be completed at the University of New Mexico (UNM). Additional course work and research leading to the dissertation are geared to the individual student's needs and interests. As a potential candidate for the Ph.D. program, each student must pass the Ph.D. qualifying examination to establish levels and areas of scholastic competence.

Research Facilities

The Department maintains state-of-the-art laboratories for computer vision and image processing, wireless communications, high-performance computing and networking, laser and electrooptics, microprocessors (including advanced DSP platforms and emerging architectures), microwaves and antennas, pulsed power and plasma science, real-time computing and embedded systems (including a number of mobile robots and advanced real-time development systems), solid-state fabrication, and virtual reality/advanced human-computer interfaces. In addition, the Department has a close affiliation with world-class research laboratories and terascale supercomputing platforms at the Albuquerque Center for High Performance Computing, the Sandia National Laboratories, the Air Force Research Laboratory, and the Los Alamos National Laboratory. Sponsored research expenditures for the past three years were approximately $13 million each year.

Financial Aid

Support is available in the form of teaching, graduate, and research assistantships. Graduate internship programs are conducted with local industries, such as Sandia National Laboratories and the Air Force Research Laboratories. Annual stipends for full-time assistantships require no more than 20 hours of service per week for the academic year and include a tuition waiver of up to 12 credit hours per semester. Assistants are paid on a scale of $1250 to $2400 per month.

Cost of Study

In 2010–12, tuition for students carrying 12 or more credit hours is $3166 for state residents and $10,210 for nonresidents per semester. All residents carrying 11 or fewer credit hours paid $266 per semester credit hour. Domestic students can meet the requirements for resident status by living continuously in New Mexico for at least one year prior to registration for the following semester and by providing satisfactory evidence of their intent to retain residency in New Mexico. International students must provide proof of financial support prior to admission to UNM.

Living and Housing Costs

Living costs in Albuquerque are somewhat lower than those in other cities of comparable size. In addition to tuition and fees, a single domestic student's expenses are estimated at $16,000 per year; expenses for a single international student are approximately $24,000 per year, including tuition and fees.

Student Group

Students come from all parts of the United States as well as from many other countries around the world. The graduate enrollment in the Department, including part-time students, is about 275, of whom 150 are post-M.S. or Ph.D. candidates. During the past two years, the Department has awarded seventy master's degrees and thirty-nine Ph.D. degrees.

Student Outcomes

The current demand for graduate engineers is excellent, and the employment rate for electrical engineering and computer engineering graduates has been almost 100 percent. Graduates of the Department have been employed in various positions, such as senior engineer, vice president, manufacturing, electronics engineer, and systems engineer. Examples of companies that hire the Department's graduates include Intel, Motorola, IBM, Ford, Agilent, Xilinx, Northrop Grumman, Boeing, ATK Mission Research, Microsoft, and Honeywell in addition to small entrepreneurial companies and the National Labs (Sandia, Los Alamos, etc.).

Location

Albuquerque's metropolitan population is more than 670,000 and is the largest city in New Mexico. The city offers a delightful and interesting blend of several cultures; a wide variety of cultural, artistic, and aesthetic events are available year-round. Many of these take place on the campus, while others are located in the city and neighboring pueblos. The Indian Pueblo Cultural Center, the National Atomic Museum, and the UNM Maxwell Museum of Anthropology are facilities of particular interest. Albuquerque lies between the low land of the Rio Grande and the towering 11,000-foot Sandia Mountains. In this "Land of Enchantment" environment, the climate is dry and warm, and sunny days are followed by cool nights. Hiking, fishing, ballooning, mountain climbing, and skiing are only a few of the recreational activities that are readily available.

The University and The Department

The University of New Mexico was established in 1889 and is situated on 600 acres in the center of metropolitan Albuquerque. It is the largest university in the state, with more than 30,000 students. UNM is a Carnegie-designated Doctoral/Research-Extensive University, one of only three in the U.S. In the most recent *U.S. News & World Report*, the electrical engineering program was ranked fifty-third in the nation and twenty-eighth among all public universities, while the computer engineering program was ranked seventy-second in the nation and forty-eighth among all public universities.

The resources of the University and its proximity to Sandia National Laboratories, Kirtland Air Force Base, and the Los Alamos National Laboratory provide an excellent environment for advanced studies and research.

Applying

Prospective domestic applicants should contact the Office of Graduate Studies as well as the Department of Electrical and Computer Engineering for the latest information and dates. The GRE General Test is required for admission to both the M.S. and Ph.D. programs. Applications, fees, and transcripts should be on file with the Office of Graduate Studies by July 1 for domestic students and February 15 for international students for the fall semester, by November 1 for domestic students and June 15 for international students for the spring semester, and by April 30 for the summer session.

Correspondence and Information

Graduate Office
Department of Electrical and Computer Engineering
MSC01 1100
1 University of New Mexico
Albuquerque, New Mexico 87131-0001

Phone: 505-277-2600
Fax: 505-277-1439
E-mail: gradinfo@ece.unm.edu
Web site: http://www.ece.unm.edu

University of New Mexico

THE FACULTY AND THEIR RESEARCH

Chaouki T. Abdallah, Professor and Chair; Ph.D., Georgia Tech. Control systems, control of computing systems, reconfigurable systems and networks.

Ganesh Balakrishnan, Assistant Professor; Ph.D., New Mexico. Semiconductor device development including epitaxy and characterization, high-power vertical-external-cavity surface-emitting lasers, novel semiconductor material development for mid-infrared lasers.

Steven R. J. Brueck, Distinguished Professor and Director, Center for High Technology Materials (CHTM); Ph.D., MIT. Nanoscale lithography and nanofabrication with applications to nanophotonics, nanofluidics, and nanoscale epitaxial growth and sources/detectors; tunable infrared lasers; ultrahigh resolution optical microscopy.

Vince D. Calhoun, Professor and Chief Technology Officer, The Research Network; Ph.D., Maryland, Baltimore County. Biomedical engineering, psychiatric neuroimaging, functional and structural magnetic resonance imaging (MRI), multimodal data fusion, neuroimaging genetics, medical image analysis.

Thomas P. Caudell, Professor; Ph.D., Arizona. Computational cognitive neurosciences, neural networks theory and simulation, virtual reality and visualization, art/science collaborations, evolutionary computation, high-performance computing, autonomous robotics.

Christos G. Christodoulou, Professor and Director, UNM Aerospace Institute; Ph.D., North Carolina State. Modeling of electromagnetic systems, smart antennas, reconfigurable antennas, machine learning applications in electromagnetics, RF/photonics.

Rafael Fierro, Associate Professor; Ph.D., Texas at Arlington. Cooperative control of multi-agent systems, cyber-physical systems, mobile sensor and robotic networks, motion planning under sensing/communication constraints, optimization-based multivehicle coordination.

Charles B. Fleddermann, Professor; Associate Dean (Academic Affairs), School of Engineering; Ph.D., Illinois at Urbana-Champaign. Plasma processing, physical electronics, photovoltaics.

Nasir Ghani, Associate Professor; Ph.D., Waterloo. High-speed networking, cyber-infrastructures, protocols and architectures, traffic engineering, routing, network virtualization, optical and access networks, TCP/IP enhancements, performance evaluation, survivability, network simulation, stochastic modeling.

Mark A. Gilmore, Associate Professor; Ph.D., UCLA. Plasma physics, plasma diagnostics, magnetic confinement fusion, microwave engineering.

Majeed M. Hayat, Professor; Ph.D., Wisconsin–Madison. Statistical communication theory, signal and image processing, algorithms for infrared spectral sensors and imagers, novel avalanche photodiodes, optical communication, cooperative distributed sensing and computing, algorithms for synthetic aperture radar, applied probability and stochastic processes.

Gregory L. Heileman, Professor, Associate Chair, and Director, Undergraduate Program; Ph.D., Central Florida. Data structures and algorithmic analysis; theory of information, security and computing; machine learning and pattern recognition.

Stephen D. Hersee, Professor; Ph.D., Brighton Polytechnic (England). GaN-based nanowire devices and nanostructures, advanced semiconductor materials and devices.

Mani Hossein-Zadeh, Assistant Professor; Ph.D., USC. Electrooptics, microwave-photonic devices and systems, ultra-high-Q optical microresonators, optomechanical interaction in UH-Q optical resonators, optical communication, photonic sensors, optofluidics and plasmonics.

Ravinder K. Jain, Professor; Ph.D., Berkeley. Quantum electronics, optoelectronics, electrooptics, experimental solid-state physics.

Sudharman K. Jayaweera, Assistant Professor; Ph.D., Princeton. Wireless communications, statistical signal processing, network information theory, cognitive radios, cooperative communications, information theoretic aspects of networked control systems, smart-grid communications and control, wireless mobile sensor networks.

Ramiro Jordan, Associate Professor, Founder and Executive VP, Ibero American Science and Technology Consortium (ISTEC); Ph.D., Kansas State. Communications, wireless sensor networks, multidimensional signal processing and embedded systems.

Sanjay Krishna, Professor and Associate Director, CHTM; Ph.D., Michigan. Investigation of nanostructured semiconductor materials for mid infrared lasers, detectors, and thermophotovoltaic cells; nanoscale materials consisting of self-assembled quantum dots, strain-layer superlattices for next generation bio-inspired sensors.

Olga Lavrova, Assistant Professor; Ph.D., California, Santa Barbara. Photovoltaics and nanoscale semiconductor structures for photovoltaic applications; smart-grid and emerging energy generation, distribution, and storage technologies.

Luke F. Lester, Professor and General Chair, Optical Science in Engineering; Ph.D., Cornell. RF photonics, solar cells, semiconductor lasers, and quantum dot devices.

Yasamin Mostofi, Assistant Professor; Ph.D., Stanford. Cooperative/sensor networks, wireless communication networks, networked control systems, control and dynamical systems.

Meeko Mitsuko Oishi, Assistant Professor, Ph.D., Stanford. Cyber-physical systems, hybrid control theory, nonlinear dynamical systems, verification of human-automation interaction, assistive technologies, control-based modeling of Parkinson's disease.

Marek Osinski, Professor; Ph.D., Institute of Physics, Polish Academy of Sciences. Magnetic nanoparticles, nanotechnology, colloidal nanocrystals, nuclear radiation detectors, semiconductor lasers, optoelectronic devices and materials, integrated optoelectronic circuits, group-III nitrides, degradation mechanisms and reliability, computer simulation, biomedical applications of nanocrystals.

Marios S. Pattichis, Associate Professor; Ph.D., Texas at Austin. Biomedical image and video processing and communications, medical imaging, dynamically reconfigurable systems, general methods for image and video analysis.

Fernando Perez-Gonzalez, Professor, Prince of Asturias Endowed Chair; Ph.D., Vigo (Spain). Information forensics and security, digital watermarking, cognitive radio, digital communications, adaptive algorithms.

James F. Plusquellic, Associate Professor; Ph.D., Pittsburgh. IC Trust, design for manufacturability, defect-based and data-driven VLSI test, small delay faulty test, model-to-hardware correlation and IC fabrication process monitors.

L. Howard Pollard, Assistant Professor; Ph.D., Illinois at Urbana-Champaign. Computer architecture, digital design, fault tolerance, microprocessors, FPGA systems, space electronics.

Balu Santhanam, Associate Professor; Ph.D., Georgia Tech. Digital signal processing, statistical communication theory, adaptive filtering, time-frequency analysis and representations, multicomponent AM-FM signal modeling, SAR-based vibrometry and related nonstationary signal analysis, ICA-related signal separation and classification.

Edl Schamiloglu, Professor; Ph.D., Cornell. Physics and technology of charged particle beam generation and propagation, high-power microwave sources and effects, pulsed-power science and technologies, plasma physics and diagnostics, electromagnetics and wave propagation, neurosystems engineering.

Pradeep Sen, Assistant Professor; Ph.D., Stanford. Computer graphics, real-time rendering, computational photography, computer vision, image processing.

Wei Wennie Shu, Associate Professor, Associate Chair, and Director, Graduate Program; Ph.D., Illinois at Urbana-Champaign. Distributed systems, high performance computing, wireless networking, mobile ad-hoc and sensor networks, biomed modeling and simulation.

Jamesina J. Simpson, Assistant Professor; Ph.D., Northwestern. Computational electromagnetics theory and applications, especially finite-difference time-domain (FDTD) solutions of Maxwell's equations; research topics range from near-DC to light and include wave propagation in the Earth-ionosphere system and optical interactions with living tissues.

Payman Zarkesh-Ha, Assistant Professor; Ph.D., Georgia Tech. Statistical modeling of VLSI systems, design for manufacturability, low-power and high-performance VLSI design.

Joint Appointees

Edward S. Angel, Professor; Ph.D., USC. Computer graphics, scientific visualization.

Jean-Claude M. Diels, Professor; Ph.D., Brussels (Belgium). Laser physics and nonlinear optics, ultrafast phenomena.

Frank L. Gilfeather, Professor; Ph.D., California, Irvine. High-performance computing applications, intelligence analysis, functional analysis.

Sang M. Han, Associate Professor; Ph.D., California, Santa Barbara. Selective growth of Ge quantum structures/high-quality heteroepitaxial films on Si for III-V compound semiconductor integration; integration of semiconductor nanocrystals (NCs) in usable matrices for photovoltaic, nonlinear optical, and biological applications; synthetic modification of semiconductor surfaces using self-assembled monolayers of polyfunctional organic molecules; micro/nanofluidic separation of functionalized NCs; hybrid micro/nanofluidic systems for advanced bioseparation and analysis.

Terran D. R. Lane, Associate Professor; Ph.D., Purdue. Machine learning, including applications to bioinformatics, information security, user and cognitive modeling, and neuroimaging; reinforcement learning, behavior, and control; artificial intelligence in general.

Zayd Chad Leseman, Assistant Professor; Ph.D., Illinois at Urbana-Champaign. MEMS, NEMS, photonic and phononic crystals, thin film growth and characterization, carbon nanostructures.

Ronald Lumia, Professor; Ph.D., Virginia. Robotics, automation, image processing.

Stefan Posse, Professor; Ph.D., Berne (Switzerland). Biomedical MR imaging and spectroscopy.

Timothy J. Ross, Professor; Ph.D., Stanford. Structural system reliability, structural dynamics, autonomous control, fuzzy logic, fuzzy set theory, risk assessment.

Wolfgang G. Rudolph, Professor; Ph.D., Jena (Germany). Laser physics, ultrashort light pulses, time-resolved spectroscopy and imaging.

Monsoor Sheik-Bahae, Associate Professor; Ph.D., SUNY at Buffalo. Lasers and photonics, coherent and ultrafast processes in semiconductors, laser cooling of solids, nonlinear optics.

Gregory P. Starr, Professor; Ph.D., Stanford. Robotics and dynamic systems and controls.

Mahmoud Reda Taha, Assistant Professor; Ph.D., Calgary (Canada). Structural health monitoring, application of artificial intelligence in structural engineering and biomechanics.

Research Professors

Ladan Arissian, Research Assistant Professor; Ph.D., New Mexico.
Simon Barriga, Research Assistant Professor; Ph.D., New Mexico.
Jerald C. Buchenauer, Research Professor; Ph.D., Cornell.
Larry Ralph Dawson, Research Professor; Ph.D., USC.
David Dietz, Research Professor; Ph.D., Indiana.
Abdel-Rahman A. El-Emawy, Research Associate Professor; Ph.D., Colorado State.
Ihab El-Kady, Research Associate Professor; Ph.D., Iowa State.
Mikhail Isaakovich Fuks, Research Professor; Ph.D., Gorky State (Russia).
John A. Gaudet, Research Professor; Ph.D., Air Force Tech.
Edward D. Graham, Lecturer and Research Professor; Ph.D., North Carolina State.
Michael John Healy, Research Scholar; M.S., Idaho.
Sameer D. Hemmady, Research Assistant Professor; Ph.D., Maryland, College Park.
Craig Kief, Research Scholar; M.S., New Mexico.
Alan G. Lynn, Research Assistant Professor; Ph.D., Texas at Austin.
Victor Murray Herrera, Research Assistant Professor; Ph.D., New Mexico.
Asal Naseri-Kouzehgarani, Research Assistant Professor; Ph.D., Illinois at Urbana-Champaign.
Mikhail N. Naydenkov, Post-Doctoral Fellow; Ph.D., Academy of Sciences (Russia).
Matthew P. Pepin, Post-Doctoral Fellow; Ph.D., Air Force Tech.
Andrew C. Pineda, Senior Research Scientist; Ph.D., Harvard.
Elena A. Plis, Research Assistant Professor; Ph.D., New Mexico.
John Rasure, Research Associate Professor; Ph.D., Kansas State.
Thomas J. Rotter, Research Assistant Professor; Ph.D., New Mexico.
Yagyadeva D. Sharma, Research Assistant Professor; Ph.D., New Delhi (India).
Gennady Smolyakov, Research Assistant Professor; Ph.D., Saratov State (Russia).
Samuel D. Stearns, Research Professor; D.Sc., New Mexico.
Mehmet F. Su, Research Assistant Professor; Ph.D., New Mexico.
Steven C. Suddarth, Research Professor; Ph.D., Washington (Seattle).
Victor M. Vergara, Research Assistant Professor; Ph.D., New Mexico.

RESEARCH CENTERS ASSOCIATED WITH THE DEPARTMENT

Center for High Technology Materials (CHTM). Creating a leading optoelectronics and nanotechnology research center is the primary goal of the CHTM, an interdisciplinary organization that sponsors and encourages research efforts in the Departments of Electrical and Computer Engineering, Physics and Astronomy, Chemistry, and Chemical and Nuclear Engineering. CHTM's multilateral mission involves both research and education. It is dedicated to encouraging and strengthening interactions and the flow of technology among the University, government laboratories, and private industry, while promoting economic development in the state.

UNIVERSITY OF NOTRE DAME

College of Engineering
Department of Electrical Engineering

Programs of Study	The Department offers programs leading to the M.S. and Ph.D. degrees in electrical engineering. Research areas include communications systems, control systems, signal and image processing, solid-state nanoelectronics, microwave electronics, optoelectronic materials and devices, and ultrahigh-speed and microwave-integrated circuits. A research M.S. degree requires a total of 30 credit hours beyond the B.S., with at least 6 credit hours coming from thesis research, and the completion and defense of an M.S. thesis. A nonresearch M.S. degree requires 30 course credit hours of course work. All students must take a qualifying examination at the end of their second semester of graduate study; successful completion of the exam is required to receive an M.S. degree and to continue to the Ph.D. program. Doctoral students must accumulate a minimum of 36 course credits beyond the B.S. degree, pass the qualifying and candidacy examinations, spend at least two years in resident study, and write and defend a Ph.D. dissertation.
Research Facilities	There are several major research laboratories in the Department to support the study of electronic and photonic materials and devices and the analysis and design of communication systems, control systems, and signal and image processing algorithms.
	The Notre Dame Nanofabrication Facility allows fabrication of ICs and devices with geometries as small as 6 nm. The 9,000-square-foot clean room is divided into areas of class 100, 1,000, and 10,000 cleanliness areas. The facility contains a broad range of fabrication equipment for processing a variety of materials for circuits and devices. Lithography tools include an i-line stepper, two contact lithography systems, and Elionix 7700 and Vistec EPG500 plus electron-beam lithography systems. Etching systems include an Oerlikon ShuttleLock ICP, Alcatel ICP deep RIE, MemStar XeF2 etcher, and PlasmaTherm 790 RIE, and two plasma etchers. Deposition systems include a FirstNano LPCVD, Unaxis PECVD, atmospheric CVD, six evaporators, and three sputtering systems. Thermal processing capabilities include eight furnace tubes and two rapid thermal processing systems. Inspection systems include ISI and Elionix SEMs, Hitachi FESEM, a prism coupler, an interferometer, an ellipsometer, a variable-angle spectroscopic ellipsometer, two surface profilers, a four-point probe, and two Zeiss optical microscopes. Postprocessing equipment includes a wafer-dicing saw, two wire bonders, and a die bonder. In addition, the clean room houses facilities for molecular-beam epitaxial (MBE) growth of III-V nitride materials and growth of graphene.
	The Low-Temperature Nanoelectronics Lab houses equipment such as a ^{3}He cryostat capable of 300 mK and magnetic fields of 8T, a ^{3}He system for RF measurements, and a dilution refrigerator capable of 10mK, with fields up to 8T.
	The High-Speed Circuits and Devices Laboratory houses a state-of-the-art microwave and high-speed digital device and circuits characterization facility. Full on-wafer testing capability, including analog characterization to 220 GHz and digital testing to 12.5 Gb/s, allow for comprehensive characterization of both analog and digital high-speed microelectronic circuits. In addition, facilities for high-speed optoelectronic characterization of detectors and photoreceiver subsystems for fiber-optic telecommunications are available. State-of-the-art microwave CAD, data collection, and data analysis facilities are also in place for rapid circuit design and characterization.
	The Semiconductor Optics Lab includes a 15-watt Argon-ion laser, a tunable, mode-locked Ti:sapphire laser delivering femtosecond pulses, an He-Cd laser, and He cryostats with high spatial resolution and magnetic fields up to 12 Tesla.
	The Laboratory for Image and Signal Analysis (LISA) features state-of-the-art workstations for the development and analysis of digital signal, image, and video processing algorithms in addition to equipment for the acquisition, processing, and real-time display of HDTV sequences; cameras; frame grabbers; several high-definition, 24-bit color monitors; and specialized printers.
	The Control Systems Research Laboratory contains several workstations networked to a set of dSpace miniboxes (microcontrollers) and a network of personal computers (PCs) running QNX (a real-time version of UNIX).
	The Wireless Institute and the associated Wireless At Notre Dame (WAND) Lab have a full complement of RF measurement equipment, wide-band digitizers, and connections to roof antennas as well as a full complement of supporting workstations. WAND also offers an environment for software radio development and testing.
	The Network Communications and Information Processing (NCIP) Lab provides a test bed for sensor network technology, network protocol design, and distributed signal processing.
	The Department has its own electronics shop run by a full-time technician, and the solid-state laboratories are overseen by a full-time professional specialist and two full-time technicians; similarly, the WAND lab has a full-time engineer available for hardware prototype design and development. Another full-time professional specialist manages the Department's undergraduate laboratories.
Financial Aid	Several prestigious fellowships are available to highly qualified first-time applicants, women, and students from groups that are underrepresented in engineering. Also available are about twenty-five teaching assistantships and several research assistantships that provide stipends of at least $2300 per month. All appointments include full remission of academic-year tuition.
Cost of Study	Tuition in 2011–12 for graduate students is $20,600 per semester for full-time study. Tuition is waived for fellowship and assistantship recipients.
Living and Housing Costs	Two large modern apartment complexes are available on campus for single graduate students. Married student housing and apartments adjacent to the campus in South Bend are also available, renting for $470 to $600 per month. The cost of living is below the national average. More information is available at http://www.nd.edu/~orlh.
Student Group	The Department has 95 undergraduates and 110 graduate students. It awards about nineteen M.S. degrees and fifteen Ph.D. degrees per year.
Location	The University is the cultural center of the northern Indiana–southwestern Michigan area and offers extensive cultural, social, and sports events throughout the year. Its 2,150-acre campus is just north of South Bend, a city of about 130,000 people, and approximately 90 miles east of Chicago (a 2-hour trip by car or train). South Bend's Morris Civic Auditorium hosts performances of Broadway plays and is the home of a first-rate symphony orchestra.
The University and The College	The University was founded in 1842 by the Reverend Edward Frederick Sorin and 6 brothers of the Congregation of Holy Cross. It was chartered as a university in 1844, and engineering studies were begun in 1873. The campus's twin lakes and many wooded areas provide a setting of natural beauty for more than 102 University buildings. The engineering buildings, Cushing and Fitzpatrick Halls, were erected in 1931 and 1979, respectively, and a new building, Stinson-Remick Hall, was completed in January 2010.
Applying	GRE General Test scores, TOEFL scores for international students, two transcripts showing academic credits and degrees, and letters of recommendation from 3 or 4 college faculty members are required. The application process is carried out online, starting at the Web site http://graduateschool.nd.edu. The GRE should be taken no later than January preceding the academic year of enrollment, particularly if financial aid is desired. The application deadline is February 1 for fall admission and November 1 for spring. The application fee for fall admission is $35 for applications submitted by December 1 and $50 for applications submitted after this date.
Correspondence and Information	Graduate Admissions Department of Electrical Engineering University of Notre Dame Notre Dame, Indiana 46556-5637 Phone: 574-631-8264 E-mail: eegrad@nd.edu Web site: http://ee.nd.edu

University of Notre Dame

THE FACULTY AND THEIR RESEARCH

Panos J. Antsaklis, H. C. and E. A. Brosey Professor of Electrical Engineering; Ph.D., Brown, 1977. Distributed sensor/actuator networks, network congestion control, networked control systems, system theory, digital signal processing, stability theory, multidimensional systems.

Peter H. Bauer, Professor; Ph.D., Miami (Florida), 1988. Digital filters, multidimensional systems and filtering, robust stability.

Gary H. Bernstein, Frank M. Freimann Professor of Electrical Engineering; Ph.D., Arizona State, 1987. Nanostructure fabrication, electron beam lithography, high-speed circuits.

William B. Berry, Professor Emeritus; Ph.D., Purdue, 1964. Solid-state energy conversion, thermoelectrics, photovoltaics.

Kevin W. Bowyer, Concurrent Professor; Ph.D., Duke, 1980. Computer vision and image processing, pattern recognition, medical image analysis.

Jay B. Brockman, Concurrent Associate Professor; Ph.D., Carnegie Mellon, 1992. Computer architecture, VLSI, processing-in-memory architecture, multidisciplinary design methodologies.

Daniel J. Costello, Leonard Bettex Professor of Electrical Engineering, Emeritus; Ph.D., Notre Dame, 1969. Information theory, channel coding, digital communications, wireless communications.

Patrick J. Fay, Professor; Ph.D., Illinois at Urbana-Champaign, 1996. Microwave device characterization; monolithic microwave integrated circuit (MMIC) and optoelectronic integrated circuit (OEIC) design, fabrication, and characterization; device technologies for ultrahigh-speed digital circuits.

Thomas E. Fuja, Professor and Chair; Ph.D., Cornell, 1987. Digital communications, error control coding, joint source-channel coding, information theory.

Vijay Gupta, Assistant Professor; Ph.D., Caltech, 2007. Cyberphysical systems, sensor-actuator networks, distributed estimation and control, networked and embedded control.

Martin Haenggi, Associate Professor; Ph.D., Swiss Federal Institute of Technology, 1999. Wireless communications and networks, nonlinear dynamics.

Douglas C. Hall, Associate Professor; Ph.D., Illinois at Urbana-Champaign, 1991. Optoelectronics device characterization, fabrication, semi-conductor lasers, materials studies.

Bertrand Hochwald, Professor; Ph.D., Yale, 1995. Wireless communications, mobile devices and antennas, next-generation standards.

Scott Howard, Assistant Professor; Ph.D., Princeton, 2008. Optoelectronic devices, biological imaging and diagnostics.

Yih-Fang Huang, Professor; Ph.D., Princeton, 1982. Statistical signal processing and communications image source coding, adaptive systems, neural networks.

Debdeep Jena, Assistant Professor; Ph.D., California, Santa Barbara, 2003. Semiconductor growth, physics and device applications, epitaxial nanostructures, charge, heat and spin transport.

Thomas H. Kosel, Associate Professor; Ph.D., Berkeley, 1975. Wear, erosion, electron microscopy, abrasion, tribology, crystal defects.

J. Nicholas Laneman, Associate Professor; Ph.D., MIT, 2002. Multiuser and wireless communications, signal processing, information theory.

Michael D. Lemmon, Professor; Ph.D., Carnegie Mellon, 1990. Real-time embedded control systems, networked control systems, sensor networks, mathematical systems theory.

Craig S. Lent, Frank M. Freimann Professor of Electrical Engineering; Ph.D., Minnesota, 1984. Solid-state physics and devices, quantum transport, quantum cellular automata.

Christine M. Maziar, Professor, Vice President, and Associate Provost of the University; Ph.D., Purdue, 1986. Device modeling and simulation for transport in ultrasmall semiconductor materials and structures.

James L. Merz, Frank M. Freimann Professor of Electrical Engineering, Emeritus; Ph.D., Harvard, 1967. Optical properties of nanostructures; quantum wells, wires and dots; optoelectronic materials.

Anthony N. Michel, Frank M. Freimann Professor of Electrical Engineering, Emeritus; Ph.D., Marquette, 1968; D.Sc., Graz (Austria), 1973. Circuit and system theory, large-scale systems.

Paolo Minero, Assistant Professor; Ph.D., California, San Diego, 2011. Communication networks.

Alexander Mintairov, Research Professor; Ph.D., Ioffe (Russia), 1987. Nanophotonics and nanoplasmonics, near-field optical spectroscopy, solid-state optoelectronic devices and materials, physics of nanostructures.

Alexei Orlov, Research Professor; Ph.D., Russian Academy of Science (Moscow), 1990. Design fabrication and testing on nanoelectronic and cryoelectronic devices.

Wolfgang Porod, Frank M. Freimann Professor of Electrical Engineering; Ph.D., Graz (Austria), 1981. Solid-state devices, computational electronics, nanoelectronics.

Thomas G. Pratt, Research Associate Professor; Ph.D., Georgia Tech, 1999. Communications and signal processing.

Ken D. Sauer, Associate Professor and Associate Chair for Undergraduate Studies; Ph.D., Princeton, 1989. Tomographic imaging, multivariate detection and estimation, image compression.

R. Michael Schafer, Professional Specialist; Ph.D., Notre Dame, 1980 (1996). Data networks, quality of service in data networks, multiprotocol label switching (MPLS).

Alan C. Seabaugh, Professor; Ph.D., Virginia, 1985. High-speed devices and circuits, nanoelectronics, nanofabrication, electromechanical devices, bioagent detection.

Gregory L. Snider, Professor and Associate Chair for Graduate Studies; Ph.D., California, Santa Barbara, 1991. Design and fabrication of nanoelectronic devices.

Robert L. Stevenson, Professor; Ph.D., Purdue, 1990. Statistical and multidimensional signal and image processing, computer vision.

Greg Timp, Keough-Hesburgh Chair in Electrical Engineering and Biological Sciences; Ph.D., MIT, 1984. Nanobiotechnology and cell biology.

Mark Wistey, Assistant Professor; Ph.D., Stanford, 2005. Group IV photonics, III-V devices, molecular beam epitaxy.

Grace Xing, Assistant Professor; Ph.D., California, Santa Barbara, 2003. Semiconductor growth, physics, processing and devices, nanostructures and nanotechnologies.

RESEARCH AREAS

Electronic Circuits and Systems. Approximately half of the faculty members have research interests in this area, which includes communications, systems and control, and signal and image processing. Ongoing projects include work in these areas: communications (sensor networks, graph-based channel coding and iterative decoding, software radio, network analysis via random graphs, capacity-approaching performance on fading channels, cooperative communications, and novel transceiver architectures), systems and control (networked control systems, design and scaling of cyber-physical systems, statistical control, and supervisory control of hybrid systems), and signal and image processing (tomographic image reconstruction, restoration, and enhancement, detection, and estimation and their applications).

Electronic Materials and Devices. The other half of the faculty members have research interests in the area that includes solid-state, nanoelectronic, and optoelectronic materials and devices. Ongoing projects include work in these areas: materials and nanostructures (Si/Ge, III-V, and II-VI semiconductors, including nitride-based semiconductors; complex oxides; molecular beam epitaxy; nanomagnetics; nanowires and tubes; quantum dots; molecular and magnetic quantum-dot cellular automata; and grapheme), nanoelectronics and energy-efficient electronics (quantum devices, quantum-dot cellular automata, silicon-based single-electron devices, and integrated CMOS and nanoelectronics), photonics and optoelectronics (semiconductor lasers; photonic integration; photodetectors, ranging from the IR to the UV; Er-doped waveguide amplifiers; and high-speed optoelectronics), nanobioelectronics (nanofabrication and sensor technologies, cell-semiconductor communication, and fluidics), advanced electronics (high-performance compound-semiconductor electronic devices, microwave/millimeter-wave integrated circuit (MMIC) design and fabrication, millimeter-wave detectors and imaging, wafer bonding, and advanced packaging and interconnects), and energy harvesting (thermal and photovoltaic energy converters, acoustic and rf energy extraction technology, and autonomous micro/nanosystems).

THE UNIVERSITY OF TEXAS AT SAN ANTONIO

Department of Electrical and Computer Engineering
Master of Science in Electrical Engineering
Master of Science in Computer Engineering

Programs of Study

The Department of Electrical and Computer Engineering (ECE) at the University of Texas at San Antonio (USTA) offers the Master of Science degree in electrical engineering and the Master of Science degree in computer engineering. These programs are designed to offer students the opportunity to prepare for careers and leadership roles in industry, government, or educational institutions. The programs have emphases in five major concentration areas: computer engineering, systems and control, digital signal processing, communications, and electronic materials and devices. Students have the opportunity to participate in active research in both traditional and emerging fields of electrical and computer engineering including security, electronic sensors and actuators, bioinformatics, power electronics, smart electric grid, and others. Department faculty members also have ongoing collaborations involving local academic and research institutions such as the University of Texas Health Science Center at San Antonio and Southwest Research Institute.

M.S. thesis and non-thesis (project) degree options are available for students. The thesis option requires 30 semester credit hours consisting of 24 technical course credits including 2 credits for research seminar and 6 thesis credits. The project option requires 33 semester credit hours consisting of 27 technical course credits including 1 credit for research seminar and 3 project credits. Core courses both inside and outside the selected concentration area are required. More information on the programs can be found at http://engineering.utsa.edu/graduate/ms-electrical-engineering.php (electrical engineering) and http://engineering.utsa.edu/graduate/ms-computer-engineering.php (computer engineering).

Research Facilities

Students in the Department of Electrical and Computer Engineering have access to a wide range of equipment and resources. Teaching labs include the dielectric, optoelectronic, and communications lab and the power electronics and mixed signals lab. Faculty research is conducted in the autonomous control engineering lab; computational systems biology lab; control, computation, and cybernetics lab; multifunctional electronic materials and devices research lab; multimedia and mobile signal processing lab; and photonics and telecommunications lab.

The Department is also affiliated with several research centers including the NSF Center for Simulation, Visualization, and Real Time Prediction (SiViRT–imaging group) and Texas Sustainable Energy Research Institute (TSERI–smart grid and electric energy). State-of-the-art research facilities are well established and maintained at the ECE Department for graduate students. Fabrication equipment includes processing and sintering furnaces, ceramics and single crystal growth stations, and RF and DC magnetron sputter. Test and measurement equipment includes optical tables, lasers and OSA, ellipsometer, LCR meter, impedance and network analyzers, source meters, DC/AC/magnetic power sources, and lock-in amplifiers. Characterization equipment includes x-ray powder diffractometer with ICDD and Jade II+, and Multimode V Scanning Force microscope. Computational resources include Dell PowerEdge R910 128GB 1066MHz Quad RDIMMs high performance computers, and an extensive array of simulation and design software. The Advanced Visualization Lab also provides a unique capability for simulation and visualization research. More information can be found at http://ece.utsa.edu/research/html.

Financial Aid

Funding is available through teaching assistantships and research assistantships. The ECE Department also offers grader positions with out-of-state tuition waiver. Students have access to other financial support such as the College of Engineering Valero Scholarship and Fellowships, faculty-established research fellowships, and various donor-established scholarships. More information on updated research stipends and scholarships can be found at http://engineering.utsa.edu/scholarships/index.php and http://www.graduateschool.utsa.edu/prospective_students/detail/financing_your_future.

Cost of Study

For the 2011–12 academic year, tuition and fees for a full-time graduate degree student (9 semester hours) are approximately $3149 per semester for Texas residents and $8783 per semester for nonresidents. Some courses and programs have additional fees. Please view the following Web sites for more information: http://www.graduateschool.utsa.edu/prospective_students/detail/graduate_tuition_and_fees and http://www.utsa.edu/fiscalservices/tuition.html.

Living and Housing Costs

University on-campus housing is available and includes apartment-style living at four complexes—Chisholm Hall, University Oaks, Laurel Village, and Chaparral Village. Off-campus housing is also available and includes many apartments adjacent to the University as well as a large number located within a 5-mile drive. The rate for a one-bedroom apartment is approximately $500 per month.

Student Group

In the 2010 fall semester, the University enrolled more than 30,000 students, of whom more than 4,000 were graduate students. The Department of ECE enrolled more than 700 students, of whom about 170 were graduate students (30 percent Ph.D.); of those, 21% were women, 18% minority, and 59% international. ECE students are active in chapters of several professional organizations at UTSA including IEEE, National Society of Black Engineers (NSBE), Society of Women Engineers (SWE), Society of Hispanic Professional Engineers (SHPE), Tau Beta Pi, and Eta Kappa Nu.

Location

San Antonio, with a population of 1.5 million, is one of the nation's major metropolitan areas. As the home of the Alamo and numerous other missions built by the Franciscans, the city is historically and culturally diverse. The Guadalupe Cultural Arts Center, McNay Art Museum, the San Antonio Museum of Art, and the Witte Museum enrich the city. The performing arts are represented by the San Antonio Symphony, the annual Tejano Music Festival and Tejano Music Awards, and performances by opera and ballet companies. Also notable are Sea World, Six Flags Fiesta Texas, Brackenridge Park, the Botanical Gardens, and the downtown Riverwalk. The San Antonio Zoo has the third-largest collection in North America. A city landmark is the Tower of the Americas, which was built for the 1968 World's Fair. San Antonio is home to the National Basketball Association's Spurs, league champions in 2000, 2003, 2005, and 2007. Numerous nearby lakes allow almost year-round outdoor activity, and the beaches of the Texas Gulf coast are within a 2-hour drive. San Antonio is home to numerous festivals throughout the year, including the Fiesta San Antonio and the Rodeo with activities such as parades, fairs, and concerts.

The University

The University was founded in 1969 and has since become a comprehensive metropolitan institution. Its research expenditures place it in the top 25 percent of public universities in Texas. UTSA prides itself on providing access and opportunity to historically underserved students and is ranked among top 10 in the nation in diversity, in the number of undergraduate degrees awarded to Hispanic students, and in the number of engineering master's degrees awarded to Hispanics. UTSA is also striving toward national recognition as a premier research university. UTSA Roadrunners football is slated to compete as an NCAA Division I FCS independent in August 2011 and is expected to transition to the Division I FBS subdivision by 2013.

Applying

In addition to the University-wide graduate admission requirements, entrance requirements for doctoral programs of the ECE Department include the GRE General Test and a minimum GPA of 3.3. Additional exam requirements/recommendations for international students include TOEFL (minimum score 500, paper-based), iBT (minimum score 61), or IELTS (minimum score 5). Prospective students may apply online at http://www.utsa.edu/admissions/index.html; there is an application fee of $45 ($80 for international students).

The application deadlines for the fall term are July 1 for domestic applicants and April 1 for international applicants. Deadlines for the spring term are November 1 for domestic applicants and September 1 for international applicants.

Correspondence and Information

For application information:
The Graduate School
The University of Texas at San Antonio
One UTSA Circle
San Antonio, Texas 78249
Phone: 210-458-4330
Web site: http://www.graduateschool.utsa.edu

For program information:
Department of Electrical and Computer Engineering
The University of Texas at San Antonio
One UTSA Circle
San Antonio, Texas 78249
Phone: 210-458-7928
E-mail: electrical.engineering@usta.edu
Web site: http://engineering.utsa.edu/graduate/index.php

The University of Texas at San Antonio

THE FACULTY AND THEIR RESEARCH

Further details on teaching/research interests and academic credentials of ECE graduate faculty can be found at http://ece.utsa.edu/people/faculty.php.

Sos Agaian, Peter Flawn Professor; Ph.D., Steklov Institute of Mathematics (Moscow). Signal/image processing, multimedia security and privacy system, sensor-imaging network, biometric, bioinformatics, medical imaging, pattern recognition and machine vision.

David Akopian, Associate Professor; Ph.D., Tampere (Finland). Communication and navigation systems, global positioning systems, location technologies, wireless applications for education and health care.

Amar Bhalla, Distinguished Research Professor; Ph.D., Penn State. Nonlinear ferroic tunable sensors, multifunctional materials and applications, nanomaterials and nanotech.

Artyom Grigoryan, Associate Professor; Ph.D., Yerevan State (Armenia). Signal and image processing/programming, applied mathematics, network theory, signals and systems, biomedical image processing, digital image processing.

Ruyan Guo, Robert E. Clarke Endowed Professor; Ph.D., Penn State. Electronic and optoelectronic materials and devices; ferroelectric, piezoelectric, and pyroelectric oxides; crystal chemistry and structure-composition-property relationships.

Yufei Huang, Associate Professor; Ph.D., Stony Brook, SUNY. Statistical signal processing and its applications to wireless communications, array processing, frequency estimation, parameter estimation, image processing, model section.

Fred Hudson, Associate Professor; Ph.D., Texas at Austin. C++ and data structures, microcomputer systems, computer graphics, programming languages, computer graphics hardware and software parallelism, visualization techniques, information science, optimization and forecasting.

Mo Jamshidi, Lutcher Brown Endowed Chair Professor; Ph.D., Illinois at Urbana-Champaign. System of systems, intelligent robotics, large-scale systems, computational intelligence, mobile robotics.

Yufang Jin, Associate Professor; Ph.D., Central Florida. Analysis and design of control systems, embedded control systems, embedded controls for mobile robotics, adaptive control systems, control systems: advanced mobile robotics.

Eugene John, Professor; Ph.D., Penn State. VLSI design, super scalar processor design, low power circuits and systems, power estimation and optimization, multimedia and network processors, computer architecture, performance evaluation, biometrics.

Youngjoong Joo, Assistant Professor; Ph.D., Georgia Tech. Circuits, microelectronics, analog and mixed-signal integrated circuits, advanced integrated circuits, CMOS image sensors, RFID, smart sensor systems.

Brian Kelley, Assistant Professor; Ph.D., Georgia Tech. 4G cellular communications, signal processing algorithms for wireless communications, application specific DSP processors, system-level design, high-speed computer arithmetic.

Ram Krishnan, Assistant Professor; Ph.D., George Mason. Computer security/access control, secure information sharing, trusted computing, security issues in emerging applications and technologies such as cloud computing and smart grid.

Hariharan Krishnaswami, Assistant Professor; Ph.D., Minnesota. Power electronics, power converter topologies and control, soft-switching, power electronic applications to renewable energy power conversion and distribution.

Byeong Lee, Assistant Professor; Ph.D., Texas at Austin. Digital system design, high-performance computer architecture, processor performance evaluation, computer architecture, low-power design, application-specific embedded systems.

Wei-Ming Lin, Professor; Ph.D., USC. Computer architecture, parallel and distributed computing, computer networks, real-time performance optimization methodologies, network intrusion detection.

Bao Liu, Assistant Professor; Ph.D., California, San Diego. Advanced VLSI design, digital integrated circuits, reconfigurable computing, low-power design, VLSI testing, multi-core chip design, nanoelectronics, biosystems, adaptive, resilient and alternative design.

Chunjiang Qian, Associate Professor; Ph.D., Case Western Reserve. Analysis and design of control systems, discrete time control systems, intelligent controls, robust nonlinear controls, robust and adaptive control of nonlinear systems, communication network, robotics.

G. V. S. Raju, Peter Flawn Professor; Ph.D., Polytechnic of Brooklyn. Analysis and design of control systems, data communications and networks, computer networks, communications networks, wireless network security.

Mehdi Shadaram, Briscoe Distinguished Professor; Ph.D., Oklahoma, PE. Fiber-optic communications, coding and error correction, communications.

Bruce Smith, Associate Professor; Ph.D., Rhode Island. Signal processing, numerical methods, high-performance computing, tomographic imaging.

Shuo Wang, Assistant Professor; Ph.D., Virginia Tech. Power electronics; electromagnetic integration for power electronics systems; EMI/EMC and power quality in power conversion systems; motor drive, generator control, and power systems.

J. Michelle Zhang, Assistant Professor; Ph.D., Stony Brook, SUNY. Signal processing for bioinformatics and biomedical applications, information theory and applications in genomics, wireless communications.

THE UNIVERSITY OF TEXAS AT SAN ANTONIO

Department of Electrical and Computer Engineering
Ph.D. in Electrical Engineering

Programs of Study

The Department of Electrical and Computer Engineering (ECE) offers advanced course work integrated with research leading to the Doctor of Philosophy (Ph.D.) degree in electrical engineering. The program has emphases in five key concentration areas: computer engineering, systems and control, digital signal processing, communications, and electronic materials and micro devices. The University of Texas at San Antonio (UTSA) Ph.D. in electrical engineering degrees are awarded to candidates who have displayed an in-depth understanding of the subject matter and demonstrated the ability to make an original contribution to knowledge in their field of specialty. Students have the opportunity to participate in active research in both traditional and emerging fields of electrical and computer engineering including security, electronic sensors and actuators, bioinformatics, power electronics, smart electric grid, and others. Department faculty members also have ongoing collaborations involving local academic and research institutions such as the University of Texas Health Science Center at San Antonio and Southwest Research Institute.

The degree requirement consists of 90 semester credit hours beyond the bachelor's degree (or 60 semester credit hours beyond the master's degree), qualifying and comprehensive examinations, thesis defense, and acceptance of the Ph.D. dissertation. Core courses within and outside of the selected concentration are required. Interdisciplinary training is emphasized with research seminar and graduate elective courses outside of the ECE Department. Prospective students can find more information at http://engineering.utsa.edu/graduate/degree-reg-phd.php.

Research Facilities

Students in the Department of Electrical and Computer Engineering have access to a wide range of equipment and resources. Teaching labs include the dielectric, optoelectronic, and communications lab and the power electronics and mixed signals lab. Faculty research is conducted in the autonomous control engineering lab; computational systems biology lab; control, computation, and cybernetics lab; multifunctional electronic materials and devices research lab; multimedia and mobile signal processing lab; and photonics and telecommunications lab.

The Department is also affiliated with several research centers including the NSF Center for Simulation, Visualization, and Real Time Prediction (SiViRT–imaging group) and Texas Sustainable Energy Research Institute (TSERI–smart grid and electric energy). State-of-the-art research facilities are well established and maintained at the ECE Department for graduate students. Fabrication equipment includes processing and sintering furnaces, ceramics and single crystal growth stations, and RF and DC magnetron sputter. Test and measurement equipment includes optical tables, lasers and OSA, ellipsometer, LCR meter, impedance and network analyzers, source meters, DC/AC/magnetic power sources, and lock-in amplifiers. Characterization equipment includes x-ray powder diffractometer with ICDD and Jade II+, and Multimode V Scanning Force microscope. Computational resources include Dell PowerEdge R910 128GB 1066MHz Quad RDIMMs high performance computers, and an extensive array of simulation and design software. The Advanced Visualization Lab also provides a unique capability for simulation and visualization research. More information can be found at http://ece.utsa.edu/research/html.

Financial Aid

The ECE Department offers doctoral fellowships, teaching assistantships, and research assistantships (through faculty research). Those financial supports are awarded based on merits, predetermined criteria, and availability. All full-time students who apply are automatically considered for a doctoral fellowship. All full-time doctoral students with good academic standing qualify for teaching assistantships or research assistantships. Ph.D. students also have access to other financial support such as the Presidential Dissertation Fellowships, College of Engineering Valero Scholarship and Fellowships, faculty-established research fellowships, and various donor-established scholarships. More information on updated research stipends and scholarships can be found at http://engineering.utsa.edu/scholarships/index.php and http://www.graduateschool.utsa.edu/prospective_students/detail/financing_your_future.

Cost of Study

For the 2011–12 academic year, tuition and fees for a full-time graduate degree student (9 semester hours) are approximately $3149 per semester for Texas residents and $8783 per semester for nonresidents. Some courses and programs have additional fees. Please view the following Web sites for more information: http://www.graduateschool.utsa.edu/prospective_students/detail/graduate_tuition_and_fees and http://www.utsa.edu/fiscalservices/tuition.html.

Living and Housing Costs

University on-campus housing is available and includes apartment-style living at four complexes—Chisholm Hall, University Oaks, Laurel Village, and Chaparral Village. Off-campus housing is also available and includes many apartments adjacent to the University as well as a large number located within a 5-mile drive. The rate for a one-bedroom apartment is approximately $500 per month.

Student Group

In the 2010 fall semester, the University enrolled more than 30,000 students, of whom more than 4,000 were graduate students. The Department of ECE enrolled more than 700 students, of whom about 170 were graduate students (30 percent Ph.D.); of those, 21 percent were women, 18 percent minority, and 59 percent international. ECE students are active in chapters of several professional organizations at UTSA including IEEE, National Society of Black Engineers (NSBE), Society of Hispanic Professional Engineers (SHPE), Society of Women Engineers (SWE), Tau Beta Pi, and Eta Kappa Nu.

Location

San Antonio, with a population of 1.5 million, is one of the nation's major metropolitan areas. As the home of the Alamo and numerous other missions built by the Franciscans, the city is historically and culturally diverse. The Guadalupe Cultural Arts Center, McNay Art Museum, the San Antonio Museum of Art, and the Witte Museum enrich the city. The performing arts are represented by the San Antonio Symphony, the annual Tejano Music Festival and Tejano Music Awards, and performances by opera and ballet companies. Also notable are Sea World, Six Flags Fiesta Texas, Brackenridge Park, the Botanical Gardens, and the downtown Riverwalk. The San Antonio Zoo has the third-largest collection in North America. A city landmark is the Tower of the Americas, which was built for the 1968 World's Fair. San Antonio is home to the National Basketball Association's Spurs, league champions in 2000, 2003, 2005, and 2007. Numerous nearby lakes allow almost year-round outdoor activity, and the beaches of the Texas Gulf coast are within a 2-hour drive. San Antonio is home to numerous festivals throughout the year, including the Fiesta San Antonio and the Rodeo with activities such as parades, fairs, and concerts.

The University

The University was founded in 1969 and has since become a comprehensive metropolitan institution. Its research expenditures place it in the top 25 percent of public universities in Texas. UTSA prides itself on providing access and opportunity to historically underserved students and is ranked among top 10 in the nation in diversity, in the number of undergraduate degrees awarded to Hispanic students, and in the number of engineering master's degrees awarded to Hispanic students. UTSA is also striving toward national recognition as a premier research university. UTSA Roadrunners football is slated to compete as an NCAA Division I FCS independent in August 2011 and is expected to transition to the Division I FBS subdivision by 2013.

Applying

In addition to the University-wide graduate admission requirements, entrance requirements for doctoral programs of the ECE Department include the GRE General Test and a minimum GPA of 3.3. Additional exam requirements/recommendations for international students include TOEFL (minimum score 550, paper-based), iBT (minimum score 79), or IELTS (minimum score 6.5). Prospective students may apply online at http://www.utsa.edu/admissions/index.html; there is an application fee of $45 ($80 for international students).

The application deadline is February 1 for the fall term and October 1 for the spring term.

Correspondence and Information

For application information:
The Graduate School
The University of Texas at San Antonio
One UTSA Circle
San Antonio, Texas 78249
Phone: 210-458-4330
Web site: http://www.graduateschool.utsa.edu

For program information:
Department of Electrical and Computer Engineering
The University of Texas at San Antonio
One UTSA Circle
San Antonio, Texas 78249
Phone: 210-458-7928
E-mail: electrical.engineering@utsa.edu
Web site: http://engineering.utsa.edu/graduate/phd-electrical-engineering.php

The University of Texas at San Antonio

THE FACULTY AND THEIR RESEARCH

Further details on teaching/research interests and academic credentials of ECE graduate faculty can be found at http://ece.utsa.edu/people/faculty.php.

Sos Agaian, Peter Flawn Professor; Ph.D., Steklov Institute of Mathematics (Moscow). Signal/image processing, multimedia security and privacy system, sensor-imaging network, biometric, bioinformatics, medical imaging, pattern recognition and machine vision.

David Akopian, Associate Professor; Ph.D., Tampere (Finland). Communication and navigation systems, global positioning systems, location technologies, wireless applications for education and health care.

Amar Bhalla, Distinguished Research Professor; Ph.D., Penn State. Nonlinear ferroic tunable sensors, multifunctional materials and applications, nanomaterials and nanotech.

Artyom Grigoryan, Associate Professor; Ph.D., Yerevan State (Armenia). Signal and image processing/programming, applied mathematics, network theory, signals and systems, biomedical image processing, digital image processing.

Ruyan Guo, Robert E. Clarke Endowed Professor; Ph.D., Penn State. Electronic and optoelectronic materials and devices; ferroelectric, piezoelectric, and pyroelectric oxides; crystal chemistry and structure-composition-property relationships.

Yufei Huang, Associate Professor; Ph.D., Stony Brook, SUNY. Statistical signal processing and its applications to wireless communications, array processing, frequency estimation, parameter estimation, image processing, model section.

Fred Hudson, Associate Professor; Ph.D., Texas at Austin. C++ and data structures, microcomputer systems, computer graphics, programming languages, computer graphics hardware and software parallelism, visualization techniques, information science, optimization and forecasting.

Mo Jamshidi, Lutcher Brown Endowed Chair Professor; Ph.D., Illinois at Urbana-Champaign. System of systems, intelligent robotics, large-scale systems, computational intelligence, mobile robotics.

Yufang Jin, Associate Professor; Ph.D., Central Florida. Analysis and design of control systems, embedded control systems, embedded controls for mobile robotics, adaptive control systems, control systems: advanced mobile robotics.

Eugene John, Professor; Ph.D., Penn State. VLSI design, super scalar processor design, low power circuits and systems, power estimation and optimization, multimedia and network processors, computer architecture, performance evaluation, biometrics.

Youngjoong Joo, Assistant Professor; Ph.D., Georgia Tech. Circuits, microelectronics, analog and mixed-signal integrated circuits, advanced integrated circuits, CMOS image sensors, RFID, smart sensor systems.

Brian Kelley, Assistant Professor; Ph.D., Georgia Tech. 4G cellular communications, signal processing algorithms for wireless communications, application specific DSP processors; system-level design, high-speed computer arithmetic.

Ram Krishnan, Assistant Professor; Ph.D., George Mason. Computer security/access control, secure information sharing, trusted computing, security issues in emerging applications and technologies such as cloud computing and smart grid.

Hariharan Krishnaswami, Assistant Professor; Ph.D., Minnesota. Power electronics, power converter topologies and control, soft-switching, power electronic applications to renewable energy power conversion and distribution.

Byeong Lee, Assistant Professor; Ph.D., Texas at Austin. Digital system design, high-performance computer architecture, processor performance evaluation, computer architecture, low-power design, application-specific embedded systems.

Wei-Ming Lin, Professor; Ph.D., USC. Computer architecture, parallel and distributed computing, computer networks, real-time performance optimization methodologies, network intrusion detection.

Bao Liu, Assistant Professor; Ph.D., California, San Diego. Advanced VLSI design, digital integrated circuits, reconfigurable computing, low-power design, VLSI testing, multi-core chip design, nanoelectronics, biosystems, adaptive, resilient and alternative design.

Chunjiang Qian, Associate Professor; Ph.D., Case Western Reserve. Analysis and design of control systems, discrete time control systems, intelligent controls, robust nonlinear controls, robust and adaptive control of nonlinear systems, communication network, robotics.

G.V.S. Raju, Peter Flawn Professor; Ph.D., Polytechnic of Brooklyn. Analysis and design of control systems, data communications and networks, computer networks, communications networks, wireless network security.

Mehdi Shadaram, Briscoe Distinguished Professor; Ph.D., Oklahoma, PE. Fiber-optic communications, coding and error correction, communications.

Bruce Smith, Associate Professor; Ph.D., Rhode Island. Signal processing, numerical methods, high-performance computing, tomographic imaging.

Shuo Wang, Assistant Professor; Ph.D., Virginia Tech. Power electronics; electromagnetic integration for power electronics systems; EMI/EMC and power quality in power conversion systems; motor drive, generator control, and power systems.

J. Michelle Zhang, Assistant Professor; Ph.D., Stony Brook, SUNY. Signal processing for bioinformatics and biomedical applications, information theory and applications in genomics, wireless communications.

Section 10
Energy and Power Engineering

This section contains a directory of institutions offering graduate work in energy and power engineering. Additional information about programs listed in the directory may be obtained by writing directly to the dean of a graduate school or chair of a department at the address given in the directory.

For programs offering related work, see also in this book *Computer Science and Information Technology, Engineering and Applied Sciences, Industrial Engineering,* and *Mechanical Engineering and Mechanics.* In another guide in this series:

Graduate Programs in the Physical Sciences, Mathematics, Agricultural Sciences, the Environment & Natural Resources
See *Physics and Mathematical Sciences*

CONTENTS

Program Directories

Close-Up and Display

Energy and Power Engineering

Florida State University, The Graduate School, FAMU-FSU College of Engineering, Department of Mechanical Engineering, Tallahassee, FL 32310-6046. Offers mechanical engineering (MS, PhD); sustainable energy (MS). Part-time programs available. *Faculty:* 18 full-time (2 women), 4 part-time/adjunct (0 women). *Students:* 72 full-time (12 women); includes 12 Black or African American, non-Hispanic/Latino; 3 Hispanic/Latino, 26 international. 92 applicants, 52% accepted, 16 enrolled. In 2010, 11 master's, 6 doctorates awarded. Terminal master's awarded for partial completion of doctoral program. *Degree requirements:* For master's, thesis optional, 30 credit hours (27 course, 6 research) or 33 credit hours (for non-thesis); for doctorate, thesis/dissertation, 45 credit hours (21 course, 24 research). *Entrance requirements:* For master's and doctorate, GRE General Test, minimum GPA of 3.0, official transcripts, resume, personal statement, 3 letters of recommendation. Additional exam requirements/recommendations for international students: Required—TOEFL (minimum score 550 paper-based; 213 computer-based; 80 iBT), IELTS (minimum score 6.5), Michigan English Language Assessment Battery (minimum score 77). *Application deadline:* For fall admission, 5/1 for domestic and international students; for spring admission, 10/1 for domestic and international students. Applications are processed on a rolling basis. Application fee: $30. Electronic applications accepted. *Expenses:* Tuition, state resident: full-time $8238.24. *Financial support:* In 2010–11, 1 fellowship with full tuition reimbursement (averaging $30,000 per year), 50 research assistantships with full tuition reimbursements (averaging $20,000 per year), 10 teaching assistantships with full tuition reimbursements (averaging $20,000 per year) were awarded; career-related internships or fieldwork, institutionally sponsored loans, scholarships/grants, health care benefits, tuition waivers (partial), and unspecified assistantships also available. Support available to part-time students. Financial award applicants required to submit FAFSA. *Faculty research:* Aero-propulsion, superconductivity, smart materials, nano-materials, intelligent robotic systems, robotic locomotion, sustainable energy. Total annual research expenditures: $5 million. *Unit head:* Dr. Chiang Shih, Chair, 850-410-6321, Fax: 850-410-6337, E-mail: shih@eng.fsu.edu. *Application contact:* George Green, Coordinator of Graduate Studies, 850-410-6196, Fax: 850-410-6337, E-mail: ggreen@eng.fsu.edu.

Instituto Tecnologico de Santo Domingo, Graduate School, Area of Basic And Environmental Sciences, Santo Domingo, Dominican Republic. Offers environmental science (M En S), including environmental education, environmental management, marine resources, natural resources management; mathematics (MS, PhD); renewable energy technology (MS, Certificate).

Lehigh University, P.C. Rossin College of Engineering and Applied Science, Program in Energy Systems Engineering, Bethlehem, PA 18015. Offers M Eng. *Faculty:* 1 part-time/adjunct (0 women). *Students:* 22 full-time (5 women), 2 part-time (0 women); includes 4 minority (1 Asian, non-Hispanic/Latino; 3 Hispanic/Latino), 3 international. Average age 24. 155 applicants, 17% accepted, 23 enrolled. In 2010, 21 master's awarded. *Entrance requirements:* For master's, GRE. Additional exam requirements/recommendations for international students: Required—TOEFL (minimum score 79 iBT). *Application deadline:* For fall admission, 5/15 for domestic and international students. Applications are processed on a rolling basis. Application fee: $75. Electronic applications accepted. *Financial support:* In 2010–11, 14 students received support. Scholarships/grants available. Financial award application deadline: 1/15. *Unit head:* Dr. John P. Coulter, Director, 610-758-6311, E-mail: jc0i@lehigh.edu. *Application contact:* Shaku Jain-Cocks, Graduate Coordinator, 610-758-6311, Fax: 610-758-5623, E-mail: shj208@lehigh.edu.

Marylhurst University, Department of Business Administration, Marylhurst, OR 97036-0261. Offers finance (MBA); general management (MBA); government policy and administration (MBA); green development (MBA); health care management (MBA); marketing (MBA); natural and organic resources (MBA); nonprofit management (MBA); organizational behavior (MBA); real estate (MBA); renewable energy (MBA); sustainable business (MBA). Part-time and evening/weekend programs available. Postbaccalaureate distance learning degree programs offered (no on-campus study). *Faculty:* 3 full-time (0 women), 36 part-time/adjunct (6 women). *Students:* 27 full-time (13 women), 727 part-time (373 women); includes 167 minority (47 Black or African American, non-Hispanic/Latino; 6 American Indian or Alaska Native, non-Hispanic/Latino; 36 Asian, non-Hispanic/Latino; 51 Hispanic/Latino; 6 Native Hawaiian or other Pacific Islander, non-Hispanic/Latino; 21 Two or more races, non-Hispanic/Latino), 7 international. Average age 38. 262 applicants, 91% accepted, 194 enrolled. In 2010, 289 master's awarded. *Degree requirements:* For master's, comprehensive exam, capstone course. *Entrance requirements:* For master's, GMAT (if GPA less than 3.0 and fewer than 5 years of work experience), interview, resume, 2 letters of recommendation. Additional exam requirements/recommendations for international students: Recommended—TOEFL (minimum score 550 paper-based; 213 computer-based; 80 iBT). *Application deadline:* For fall admission, 9/11 priority date for domestic and international students; for winter admission, 12/15 priority date for domestic and international students; for spring admission, 3/15 priority date for domestic students, 3/17 priority date for international students. Applications are processed on a rolling basis. Application fee: $50. Electronic applications accepted. *Expenses:* Tuition: Full-time $13,932; part-time $516 per credit. Tuition and fees vary according to course load and program. *Financial support:* Scholarships/grants available. Support available to part-time students. Financial award applicants required to submit FAFSA. *Unit head:* Bob Hanks, Director of Business and Real Estate Programs, 503-636-8141, Fax: 503-697-5597, E-mail: mba@marylhurst.edu. *Application contact:* Maruska Lynch, Graduate Admissions Specialist, 800-634-9982 Ext. 6322, Fax: 503-699-6320, E-mail: admissions@marylhurst.edu.

New Jersey Institute of Technology, Office of Graduate Studies, Newark College of Engineering, Department of Electrical and Computer Engineering, Program in Power and Energy Systems, Newark, NJ 07102. Offers MS. Part-time and evening/weekend programs available. Postbaccalaureate distance learning degree programs offered. *Students:* 12 full-time (2 women), 14 part-time (2 women); includes 3 Black or African American, non-Hispanic/Latino; 3 Asian, non-Hispanic/Latino; 2 Hispanic/Latino, 12 international. Average age 29. 37 applicants, 46% accepted, 10 enrolled. *Degree requirements:* For master's, thesis optional. *Entrance requirements:* For master's, GRE General Test. Additional exam requirements/recommendations for international students: Required—TOEFL (minimum score 550 paper-based; 213 computer-based; 79 iBT). *Application deadline:* For fall admission, 6/5 for domestic students, 4/1 for international students; for spring admission, 11/15 for domestic and international students. Applications are processed on a rolling basis. Application fee: $65. Electronic applications accepted. *Expenses:* Tuition, state resident: full-time $14,724; part-time $818 per credit. Tuition, nonresident: full-time $20,304; part-time $1128 per credit. Required fees: $2272; $209 per credit. $103 per semester. One-time fee: $312 full-time; $212 part-time. *Financial support:* Application deadline: 3/15. *Unit head:* Dr. Nirwan Ansari, Director, 973-596-3670, E-mail: nirwan.ansari@njit.edu. *Application contact:* Kathryn Kelly, Director of Admissions, 973-596-3300, Fax: 973-596-3461, E-mail: admissions@njit.edu.

New York Institute of Technology, Graduate Division, School of Engineering and Computing Sciences, Program in Energy Management, Old Westbury, NY 11568-8000. Offers energy management (MS); energy technology (Advanced Certificate); environmental management (Advanced Certificate); facilities management (Advanced Certificate). Part-time and evening/weekend programs available. Postbaccalaureate distance learning degree programs offered. *Students:* 57 full-time (12 women), 104 part-time (17 women); includes 31 minority (12 Black or African American, non-Hispanic/Latino; 2 American Indian or Alaska Native, non-Hispanic/Latino; 6 Asian, non-Hispanic/Latino; 11 Hispanic/Latino), 38 international. Average age 32. In 2010, 48 master's, 34 other advanced degrees awarded. *Degree requirements:* For master's, comprehensive exam, thesis or alternative. *Entrance requirements:* For master's, minimum QPA of 2.85. Additional exam requirements/recommendations for international students: Required—TOEFL (minimum score 550 paper-based; 213 computer-based). *Application deadline:* For fall admission, 7/1 priority date for domestic students; for spring admission, 12/1 priority date for domestic students. Applications are processed on a rolling basis. Application fee: $50. Electronic applications accepted. *Expenses:* Tuition: Part-time $835 per credit. *Financial support:* Fellowships, research assistantships with partial tuition reimbursements, institutionally sponsored loans, tuition waivers (full and partial), and unspecified assistantships available. Support available to part-time students. Financial award applicants required to submit FAFSA. *Unit head:* Dr. Robert Amundsen, Director, 516-686-7578, E-mail: ramundse@nyit.edu. *Application contact:* Dr. Jacquelyn Nealon, Vice President for Enrollment Services, 516-686-7925, Fax: 516-686-7597, E-mail: jnealon@nyit.edu.

North Carolina Agricultural and Technical State University, Graduate School, College of Engineering, Department of Electrical and Computer Engineering, Greensboro, NC 27411. Offers electrical engineering (MSEE, PhD), including communications and signal processing (MSEE), computer engineering (MSEE), electronic and optical materials and devices (MSEE), power systems and controls (MSEE). Part-time programs available. *Degree requirements:* For master's, project, thesis defense; for doctorate, thesis/dissertation. *Entrance requirements:* For master's, GRE General Test, GRE Subject Test, minimum GPA of 2.8; for doctorate, GRE General Test, minimum GPA of 3.0. *Faculty research:* Semiconductor compounds, VLSI design, image processing, optical systems and devices, fault-tolerant computing.

Northeastern University, College of Engineering, Program in Energy Systems, Boston, MA 02115-5096. Offers MS. Part-time programs available. *Students:* 31 full-time (7 women), 7 part-time (1 woman). Average age 25. 58 applicants, 76% accepted, 26 enrolled. *Entrance requirements:* For master's, GRE General Test. Additional exam requirements/recommendations for international students: Required—TOEFL (minimum score 550 paper-based; 213 computer-based). *Application deadline:* For fall admission, 1/15 for domestic and international students. Applications are processed on a rolling basis. Application fee: $50. Electronic applications accepted. *Financial support:* Career-related internships or fieldwork, Federal Work-Study, scholarships/grants, tuition waivers (full), and unspecified assistantships available. Support available to part-time students. Financial award application deadline: 1/15; financial award applicants required to submit FAFSA. *Unit head:* Dr. Yaman Yener, Associate Dean of Engineering for Research and Graduate Studies, 617-373-2711, Fax: 617-373-2501. *Application contact:* Jeffrey Hengel, Admissions Specialist, 617-373-2711, Fax: 617-373-2501, E-mail: grad-eng@coe.neu.edu.

Santa Clara University, School of Engineering, Program in Electrical Engineering, Santa Clara, CA 95053. Offers analog circuit design (Certificate); ASIC design and test (Certificate); digital signal processing (Certificate); electrical engineering (MS, PhD, Engineer); fundamentals of electrical engineering (Certificate); microwave and antennas (Certificate); renewable energy (Certificate). Part-time and evening/weekend programs available. *Students:* 54 full-time (14 women), 123 part-time (20 women); includes 62 minority (1 Black or African American, non-Hispanic/Latino; 55 Asian, non-Hispanic/Latino; 5 Hispanic/Latino; 1 Two or more races, non-Hispanic/Latino), 61 international. Average age 31. 161 applicants, 60% accepted, 49 enrolled. In 2010, 51 master's, 2 doctorates, 3 other advanced degrees awarded. *Degree requirements:* For master's, thesis (for some programs); for doctorate, thesis/dissertation; for other advanced degree, thesis. *Entrance requirements:* For master's, GRE (waiver may be available), transcript; for doctorate, GRE, master's degree or equivalent; for other advanced degree, master's degree, published paper. Additional exam requirements/recommendations for international students: Required—TOEFL (minimum score 550 paper-based; 213 computer-based; 79 iBT). *Application deadline:* For fall admission, 8/12 for domestic students, 7/15 for international students; for winter admission, 10/28 for domestic students, 9/23 for international students; for spring admission, 2/25 for domestic students, 1/21 for international students. Applications are processed on a rolling basis. Application fee: $60. Electronic applications accepted. *Expenses:* Contact institution. *Financial support:* Research assistantships, teaching assistantships available. Financial award application deadline: 3/2; financial award applicants required to submit FAFSA. *Faculty research:* Thermal and electrical nanoscale transport (TENT). Total annual research expenditures: $1.3 million. *Unit head:* Dr. Alex Zecevic, Associate Dean for Graduate Studies, 408-554-2394, E-mail: azecevic@scu.edu. *Application contact:* Stacey Tinker, Director of Enrollment Management, 408-554-4748, Fax: 408-554-4323, E-mail: stinker@scu.edu.

Southern Illinois University Carbondale, Graduate School, College of Engineering, Program in Engineering Science, Carbondale, IL 62901-4701. Offers electrical systems (PhD); fossil energy (PhD); mechanics (PhD). *Degree requirements:* For doctorate, thesis/dissertation. *Entrance requirements:* For doctorate, GRE General Test, minimum GPA of 3.5. Additional exam requirements/recommendations for international students: Required—TOEFL.

Universidad Autonoma de Guadalajara, Graduate Programs, Guadalajara, Mexico. Offers administrative law and justice (LL M); advertising and corporate communications (MA); architecture (M Arch); business (MBA); computational science (MCC); education (Ed M, Ed D); English-Spanish translation (MA); entrepreneurship and management (MBA); integrated management of digital animation (MA); international business (MIB); international corporate law (LL M); internet technologies (MS); manufacturing systems (MMS); occupational health (MS); philosophy (MA, PhD); power electronics (MS); quality systems (MQS); renewable energy (MS); social evaluation of projects (MBA); strategic market research (MBA); tax law (MA); teaching mathematics (MA).

University of Alberta, Faculty of Graduate Studies and Research, Department of Electrical and Computer Engineering, Edmonton, AB T6G 2E1, Canada. Offers communications (M Eng, M Sc, PhD); computer engineering (M Eng, M Sc, PhD); electromagnetics (M Eng, M Sc, PhD); nanotechnology and microdevices (M Eng, M Sc, PhD); power/power electronics (M Eng, M Sc, PhD); systems (M Eng, M Sc, PhD). Terminal master's awarded for partial completion of doctoral program. *Degree requirements:* For master's, thesis; for doctorate, thesis/dissertation. *Entrance requirements:* Additional exam requirements/recommendations for international students: Required—TOEFL. Electronic applications accepted. *Faculty research:* Controls, communications, microelectronics, electromagnetics.

University of Massachusetts Lowell, James B. Francis College of Engineering, Program in Energy Engineering, Lowell, MA 01854-2881. Offers MS Eng, D Eng, PhD. *Degree requirements:* For master's, thesis optional. *Entrance requirements:* For master's, GRE General Test. Additional exam requirements/recommendations for international students: Required—TOEFL.

University of Memphis, Graduate School, Herff College of Engineering, Department of Mechanical Engineering, Memphis, TN 38152. Offers design and mechanical engineering (MS); energy systems (MS); industrial engineering (MS); mechanical engineering (PhD); mechanical systems (MS); power systems (MS). Part-time programs available. *Faculty:* 8 full-time (0 women). *Students:* 3 full-time (1 woman), 8 part-time (0 women); includes 2 Black or African American, non-Hispanic/Latino, 5 international. Average age 30. 11 applicants, 64% accepted, 3 enrolled. In 2010, 5 master's awarded. Terminal master's awarded for partial completion of doctoral program. *Degree requirements:* For master's, comprehensive exam, thesis; for doctorate, comprehensive exam, thesis/dissertation. *Entrance requirements:* For master's, GRE General Test, BS in mechanical engineering, minimum undergraduate GPA of 3.0. *Application deadline:* For fall admission, 8/1 for domestic students; for spring admission, 12/1 for domestic students. Application fee: $35 ($60 for international students). *Financial support:* In 2010–11, 6 students received support; fellowships with full tuition reimbursements available, research assistantships with full tuition reimbursements available, teaching assistantships with full tuition reimbursements available, career-related internships or fieldwork, Federal Work-Study, scholarships/grants, and unspecified assistantships available. Financial award application deadline: 2/15; financial award applicants required to submit FAFSA. *Faculty research:* Computational fluid dynamics, computational mechanics, integrated design, nondestructive testing, operations research. *Unit head:* Dr. John I. Hochstein, Chair, 901-678-2173, Fax: 901-678-5459, E-mail: jhochste@memphis.edu. *Application contact:* Dr. Teong Tan, Graduate Studies Coordinator, 901-678-3264, Fax: 901-678-5459, E-mail: ttan@memphis.edu.

University of Rochester, Hajim School of Engineering and Applied Sciences, Department of Chemical Engineering, Program in Alternative Energy, Rochester, NY 14627.

The University of Tennessee at Chattanooga, Graduate School, College of Engineering and Computer Science, Program in Engineering Management, Chattanooga, TN 37403. Offers engineering management (MS), fundamentals of engineering management (Graduate Certificate); power systems management (Graduate Certificate); project and value management (Graduate Certificate); quality management (Graduate Certificate). Postbaccalaureate distance learning degree programs offered (no on-campus study). *Faculty:* 4 full-time (1 woman). *Students:* 15 full-time (4 women), 77 part-time (13 women); includes 8 Black or African American, non-Hispanic/Latino; 1 Asian, non-Hispanic/Latino; 1 Hispanic/Latino, 11 international. Average age 32. 29 applicants, 100% accepted, 20 enrolled. In 2010, 23 master's, 20 other advanced degrees awarded. *Degree requirements:* For master's, thesis. *Entrance requirements:* For master's, GRE General Test, letters of recommendation; minimum undergraduate GPA of 2.5 overall or 3.0 in senior year. Additional exam requirements/recommendations for international students: Required—TOEFL (minimum score 550 paper-based; 213 computer-based; 79 iBT), IELTS (minimum score 6). *Application deadline:* For fall admission, 8/1 priority date for domestic students, 6/1 for international students; for spring admission, 12/1 priority date for domestic students, 10/1 for international students. Applications are processed on a rolling basis. Application fee: $35. Electronic applications accepted. *Financial support:* In 2010–11, 5 research assistantships with full and partial tuition reimbursements (averaging $5,500 per year) were awarded; career-related internships or fieldwork, scholarships/grants, and unspecified assistantships also available. Support available to part-time students. *Faculty research:* Plant layout design, lean manufacturing, six sigma, value management, product development. *Unit head:* Dr. Neslihan Alp, Director, 423-425-4032, Fax: 423-425-5229, E-mail: neslihan-alp@utc.edu. *Application contact:* Dr. Jerald Ainsworth, Dean of Graduate Studies, 423-425-4478, Fax: 423-425-5223, E-mail: jerald-ainsworth@utc.edu.

University of Wisconsin–Madison, Graduate School, College of Engineering, Department of Mechanical Engineering, Madison, WI 53706-1380. Offers energy systems (ME); engine systems (ME); mechanical engineering (MS, PhD); polymers (ME). Part-time programs available. Postbaccalaureate distance learning degree programs offered (no on-campus study). *Faculty:* 33 full-time (3 women), 1 part-time/adjunct (0 women). *Students:* 181 full-time (17 women), 54 part-time (6 women); includes 3 Black or African American, non-Hispanic/Latino; 9 Asian, non-Hispanic/Latino; 8 Hispanic/Latino. Average age 25. 652 applicants, 19% accepted, 68 enrolled. In 2010, 62 master's, 14 doctorates awarded. Terminal master's awarded for partial completion of doctoral program. *Degree requirements:* For master's, thesis optional; for doctorate, thesis/dissertation, qualifying exam, preliminary exam. *Entrance requirements:* For master's, GRE, BS in mechanical engineering or related field, minimum GPA of 3.0 in last 60 hours of course work; for doctorate, GRE, BS in mechanical engineering or related field, minimum undergraduate GPA of 3.0 in last 60 hours of course work. Additional exam requirements/recommendations for international students: Required—TOEFL (minimum score 550 paper-based; 213 computer-based; 80 iBT). *Application deadline:* For fall admission, 5/1 for domestic students, 6/1 for international students; for spring admission, 11/30 for domestic students, 10/1 for international students. Applications are processed on a rolling basis. Application fee: $56. Electronic applications accepted. *Expenses:* Tuition, state resident: full-time $9887.36; part-time $617.96 per credit. Tuition, nonresident: full-time $24,054; part-time $1503.40 per credit. Required fees: $67.63 per credit. Tuition and fees vary according to reciprocity agreements. *Financial support:* In 2010–11, 14 fellowships with full tuition reimbursements (averaging $22,224 per year), 148 research assistantships with full tuition reimbursements (averaging $19,596 per year), 45 teaching assistantships with full tuition reimbursements (averaging $8,595 per year) were awarded; career-related internships or fieldwork, institutionally sponsored loans, scholarships/grants, traineeships, health care benefits, and unspecified assistantships also available. *Faculty research:* Design and manufacturing, materials processing, combustion, energy systems nanotechnology. Total annual research expenditures: $10 million. *Unit head:* Roxann L. Engelstad, Chair, 608-262-5745, Fax: 608-265-2316, E-mail: engelsta@engr.wisc.edu. *Application contact:* Roxann L. Engelstad, Chair, 608-262-5745, Fax: 608-265-2316, E-mail: engelsta@engr.wisc.edu.

Worcester Polytechnic Institute, Graduate Studies and Research, Programs in Interdisciplinary Studies, Worcester, MA 01609-2280. Offers bioscience administration (MS); impact engineering (MS); manufacturing engineering management (MS); power systems management (MS); social science (PhD); systems modeling (MS). Part-time and evening/weekend programs available. *Faculty:* 1 part-time/adjunct (0 women). *Students:* 6 full-time (1 woman), 146 part-time (25 women); includes 1 Black or African American, non-Hispanic/Latino; 6 Hispanic/Latino; 11 Native Hawaiian or other Pacific Islander, non-Hispanic/Latino, 1 international. 151 applicants, 76% accepted, 79 enrolled. In 2010, 47 master's awarded. *Degree requirements:* For master's, thesis; for doctorate, comprehensive exam, thesis/dissertation. *Entrance requirements:* For master's and doctorate, 3 letters of recommendation. Additional exam requirements/recommendations for international students: Required—TOEFL (minimum score 550 paper-based; 213 computer-based; 79 iBT), IELTS (minimum score 6.5). *Application deadline:* For fall admission, 1/1 priority date for domestic students, 1/1 for international students; for spring admission, 10/1 priority date for domestic students, 10/1 for international students. Application fee: $70. *Expenses:* Tuition: Full-time $20,862; part-time $1159 per term. One-time fee: $15. *Financial support:* Institutionally sponsored loans, scholarships/grants, and unspecified assistantships available. Financial award application deadline: 1/1; financial award applicants required to submit FAFSA. *Unit head:* Dr. Fred J. Looft, Head, 508-831-5231, Fax: 508-831-5491, E-mail: fjlooft@wpi.edu. *Application contact:* Lynne Dougherty, Administrative Assistant, 508-831-5301, Fax: 508-831-5717, E-mail: grad@wpi.edu.

Nuclear Engineering

Air Force Institute of Technology, Graduate School of Engineering and Management, Department of Engineering Physics, Dayton, OH 45433-7765. Offers applied physics (MS, PhD); electro-optics (MS, PhD); materials science (PhD); nuclear engineering (MS, PhD); space physics (MS). Part-time programs available. *Degree requirements:* For master's, thesis; for doctorate, thesis/dissertation. *Entrance requirements:* For master's and doctorate, GRE General Test, minimum GPA of 3.0, U.S. citizenship. *Faculty research:* High-energy lasers, space physics, nuclear weapon effects, semiconductor physics.

Arizona State University, Ira A. Fulton School of Engineering, Department of Electrical Engineering, Tempe, AZ 85287-5706. Offers electrical engineering (MS, MSE, PhD); nuclear power generation (Graduate Certificate). Part-time and evening/weekend programs available. Postbaccalaureate distance learning degree programs offered (minimal on-campus study). *Faculty:* 60 full-time (9 women), 8 part-time/adjunct (1 woman). *Students:* 521 full-time (92 women), 255 part-time (27 women); includes 82 minority (12 Black or African American, non-Hispanic/Latino; 2 American Indian or Alaska Native, non-Hispanic/Latino; 41 Asian, non-Hispanic/Latino; 26 Hispanic/Latino; 1 Two or more races, non-Hispanic/Latino), 531 international. Average age 27. 1,317 applicants, 69% accepted, 295 enrolled. In 2010, 212 master's, 35 doctorates awarded. Terminal master's awarded for partial completion of doctoral program. *Degree requirements:* For master's, thesis and defense (MS); comprehensive exams (MSE); interactive Program of Study (iPOS) submitted before completing 50 percent of required credit hours; for doctorate, comprehensive exam, thesis/dissertation, interactive Program of Study (iPOS) submitted before completing 50 percent of required credit hours. *Entrance requirements:* For master's, GRE, minimum GPA of 3.0 in last 2 years of work leading to bachelor's degree, 3.5 if from non-ABET accredited school; for doctorate, GRE, master's degree with minimum GPA of 3.5 or 3.6 in last 2 years of ABET-accredited undergraduate program. Additional exam requirements/recommendations for international students: Required—TOEFL, IELTS, or Pearson Test of English. *Application deadline:* For fall admission, 12/31 for domestic and international students; for spring admission, 7/31 for domestic and international students. Application fee: $70 ($90 for international students). Electronic applications accepted. *Expenses:* Contact institution. *Financial support:* In 2010–11, 165 research assistantships with partial tuition reimbursements (averaging $14,206 per year), 26 teaching assistantships with partial tuition reimbursements (averaging $13,854 per year) were awarded; fellowships with full and partial tuition reimbursements, career-related internships or fieldwork, institutionally sponsored loans, scholarships/grants, and tuition waivers (full and partial) also available. Financial award application deadline: 3/1; financial award applicants required to submit FAFSA. *Faculty research:* Power and energy systems, signal processing and communications, solid state devices and modeling, wireless communications and circuits, photovoltaics, biosignatures discovery automation, flexible electronics, and nanostructures. Total annual research expenditures: $27.1 million. *Unit head:* Dr. Stephen M. Phillips, Director, 480-965-6410, E-mail: stephen.phillips@asu.edu. *Application contact:* Dr. Stephen M. Phillips, Director, 480-965-6410, E-mail: stephen.phillips@asu.edu.

Colorado School of Mines, Graduate School, Program in Nuclear Engineering, Golden, CO 80401. Offers MS, PhD. Part-time programs available. *Students:* 20 full-time (3 women), 1 part-time (0 women); includes 2 Hispanic/Latino, 4 international. Average age 29. 21 applicants, 62% accepted, 8 enrolled. In 2010, 1 master's awarded. *Degree requirements:* For master's, thesis (for some programs); for doctorate, comprehensive exam, thesis/dissertation. *Entrance requirements:* For master's and doctorate, GRE General Test. Additional exam requirements/recommendations for international students: Required—TOEFL (minimum score 550 paper-based; 213 computer-based; 80 iBT). *Application deadline:* For fall admission, 1/15 priority date for domestic and international students; for spring admission, 10/15 priority date for domestic and international students. Electronic applications accepted. *Expenses:* Tuition, state resident: full-time $11,550; part-time $641 per credit. Tuition, nonresident: full-time $25,980; part-time $1444 per credit. Required fees: $1874; $937 per semester. *Financial support:* In 2010–11, 15 students received support, including 1 fellowship with full tuition reimbursement available (averaging $20,000 per year), 12 research assistantships with full tuition reimbursements available (averaging $20,000 per year), 2 teaching assistantships with full tuition reimbursements available (averaging $20,000 per year); career-related internships or fieldwork, Federal Work-Study, institutionally sponsored loans, scholarships/grants, health care benefits, and unspecified assistantships also available. Financial award application deadline: 1/15; financial award applicants required to submit FAFSA. *Faculty research:* Nuclear materials and nuclear fuel cycle. *Unit head:* Dr. Jeff King, Program Director, 303-384-2133, Fax: 303-279-3919, E-mail: kingjc@mines.edu. *Application contact:* Dr. Jeff King, Program Director, 303-384-2133, Fax: 303-273-3919, E-mail: ukingjc@mines.edu.

École Polytechnique de Montréal, Graduate Programs, Institute of Nuclear Engineering, Montréal, QC H3C 3A7, Canada. Offers nuclear engineering (M Eng, PhD, DESS); nuclear engineering, socio-economics of energy (M Sc A). *Degree requirements:* For master's, one foreign language, thesis; for doctorate, one foreign language, thesis/dissertation. *Entrance requirements:* For master's, minimum GPA of 2.75; for doctorate, minimum GPA of 3.0. *Faculty research:* Nuclear technology, thermohydraulics.

Georgia Institute of Technology, Graduate Studies and Research, College of Engineering, George W. Woodruff School of Mechanical Engineering, Nuclear and Radiological Engineering and Medical Physics Programs, Atlanta, GA 30332-0001. Offers medical physics (MS); nuclear and radiological engineering (MSNE, PhD). Part-time programs available. Postbaccalaureate distance learning degree programs offered (no on-campus study). Terminal master's awarded for partial completion of doctoral program. *Degree requirements:* For master's, thesis optional; for doctorate, comprehensive exam, thesis/dissertation. *Entrance requirements:* For master's and doctorate, GRE General Test, minimum GPA of 3.0. Additional exam requirements/recommendations for international students: Required—TOEFL (minimum score 580 paper-based; 240 computer-based). *Faculty research:* Reactor physics, nuclear materials, plasma physics, radiation detection, radiological assessment.

Idaho State University, Office of Graduate Studies, College of Engineering, Nuclear Engineering Department, Pocatello, ID 83209. Offers engineering and applied science (PhD); nuclear science and engineering (MS, PhD, Postbaccalaureate Certificate). Part-time programs available. *Degree requirements:* For master's, comprehensive exam (for some programs), thesis, seminar; for doctorate, comprehensive exam, thesis/dissertation, oral and written exams at the end of 1st year; for Postbaccalaureate Certificate, comprehensive exam (for some programs), thesis optional, seminar. *Entrance requirements:* For master's, GRE; for doctorate, master's degree in engineering, physics, geosciences, math, etc.; 3 letters of recommendation; for Postbaccalaureate Certificate, GRE if GPA is between 2.0 and 3.0, bachelor's degree, minimum GPA of 3.0 in upper division courses. Additional exam requirements/recommendations for international students: Required—TOEFL (minimum score 550 paper-based; 213 computer-based; 80 iBT). Electronic applications accepted.

Kansas State University, Graduate School, College of Engineering, Department of Mechanical and Nuclear Engineering, Manhattan, KS 66506. Offers mechanical engineering (MS, PhD); nuclear engineering (MS, PhD). *Degree requirements:* For master's, thesis or alternative; for doctorate, comprehensive exam, thesis/dissertation. *Entrance requirements:* For master's, GRE General Test, minimum GPA of 3.0 in physics, mathematics, and chemistry; for doctorate, GRE General Test, master's degree in mechanical engineering. Additional exam requirements/recommendations for international students: Required—TOEFL. Electronic applications accepted. *Faculty research:* Radiation detection and protection, heat and mass transfer, machine design, control systems, nuclear reactor physics and engineering.

Massachusetts Institute of Technology, School of Engineering, Department of Nuclear Science and Engineering, Cambridge, MA 02139. Offers SM, PhD, Sc D, NE. *Faculty:* 13 full-time (3 women). *Students:* 119 full-time (17 women); includes 12 minority (2 Black or African American, non-Hispanic/Latino; 1 American Indian or Alaska Native, non-Hispanic/Latino; 5 Asian, non-Hispanic/Latino; 2 Hispanic/Latino; 2 Two or more races, non-Hispanic/Latino), 39 international. Average age 26. 157 applicants, 36% accepted, 40 enrolled. In 2010, 23 master's, 15 doctorates, 1 other advanced degree awarded. Terminal master's awarded for partial completion of doctoral program. *Degree requirements:* For master's and NE, thesis; for doctorate, comprehensive exam, thesis/dissertation. *Entrance requirements:* For master's, doctorate, and NE, GRE General Test. Additional exam requirements/recommendations for international students: Required—TOEFL (minimum score 577 paper-based; 233 computer-based; 90 iBT), IELTS (minimum score 7). *Application deadline:* For fall admission, 1/2 for domestic students, 1/7 for international students. Application fee: $75. Electronic applications accepted. *Expenses:* Tuition: Full-time $38,940; part-time $605 per unit. Required fees: $272. *Financial support:* In 2010–11, 104 students received support, including 37 fellowships with tuition reimbursements available (averaging $25,977 per year), 72 research assistantships with tuition reimbursements available (averaging $28,557 per year), 6 teaching assistantships

Nuclear Engineering

Massachusetts Institute of Technology (continued)
with tuition reimbursements available (averaging $30,963 per year); career-related internships or fieldwork, Federal Work-Study, institutionally sponsored loans, scholarships/grants, health care benefits, and unspecified assistantships also available. *Faculty research:* Advanced reactor design and innovation; nuclear fuel cycle technology and economics; plasma physics and fusion engineering; materials in extreme environments; radiation science, nuclear imaging and quantum information; nuclear systems engineering, management and policy. Total annual research expenditures: $10.7 million. *Unit head:* Prof. Richard Lester, Department Head, 617-253-7704, E-mail: nse-info@mit.edu. *Application contact:* Academic Programs Administrator, 617-253-3814, Fax: 617-258-7437, E-mail: applynse@mit.edu.

McMaster University, School of Graduate Studies, Faculty of Engineering, Department of Engineering Physics, Hamilton, ON L8S 4M2, Canada. Offers engineering physics (M Eng, MA Sc, PhD); nuclear engineering (PhD). *Degree requirements:* For master's, thesis or alternative; for doctorate, comprehensive exam, thesis/dissertation. *Entrance requirements:* For master's, minimum B average in engineering, mathematics, or physical sciences. Additional exam requirements/recommendations for international students: Required—TOEFL (minimum score 550 paper-based; 213 computer-based). *Faculty research:* Non-thermal plasmas for pollution control and electrostatic precipitation, bulk and thin film luminescent materials, devices and systems for optical fiber communications, physics and applications of III-V materials and devices, defect spectroscopy in semiconductors.

Missouri University of Science and Technology, Graduate School, Department of Mining and Nuclear Engineering, Rolla, MO 65409. Offers mining engineering (MS, DE, PhD); nuclear engineering (MS, DE, PhD). *Degree requirements:* For master's, thesis optional; for doctorate, comprehensive exam. *Entrance requirements:* For master's, GRE (minimum score 600 quantitative, 3 writing); for doctorate, GRE (minimum score: quantitative 600, writing 3.5). Additional exam requirements/recommendations for international students: Required—TOEFL (minimum score 550 paper-based; 213 computer-based). *Faculty research:* Mine health and safety, nuclear radiation transport, modeling of mining operations, radiation effects, blasting.

North Carolina State University, Graduate School, College of Engineering, Department of Nuclear Engineering, Raleigh, NC 27695. Offers MNE, MS, PhD. *Degree requirements:* For master's, thesis (for some programs); for doctorate, thesis/dissertation. *Entrance requirements:* For master's, bachelor's degree in engineering or GRE; for doctorate, engineering degree or GRE. Electronic applications accepted. *Faculty research:* Computational reactor engineering, plasma applications, waste management, materials, radiation applications and measurement.

The Ohio State University, Graduate School, College of Engineering, Department of Mechanical and Aerospace Engineering, Program in Nuclear Engineering, Columbus, OH 43210. Offers MS, PhD. *Faculty:* 12. *Students:* 22 full-time (4 women), 8 part-time (1 woman); includes 1 Asian, non-Hispanic/Latino; 1 Hispanic/Latino, 8 international. Average age 27. In 2010, 4 master's, 4 doctorates awarded. *Degree requirements:* For master's, thesis optional; for doctorate, thesis/dissertation. *Entrance requirements:* Additional exam requirements/recommendations for international students: Recommended—TOEFL (minimum score 600 paper-based; 250 computer-based). *Application deadline:* For fall admission, 8/15 priority date for domestic students, 7/1 priority date for international students; for winter admission, 12/1 priority date for domestic students, 11/1 priority date for international students; for spring admission, 3/1 priority date for domestic students, 2/1 priority date for international students. Applications are processed on a rolling basis. Application fee: $40 ($50 for international students). Electronic applications accepted. *Expenses:* Tuition, state resident: full-time $10,605. Tuition, nonresident: full-time $26,535. Tuition and fees vary according to course load and program. *Financial support:* Fellowships, research assistantships, teaching assistantships, career-related internships or fieldwork, Federal Work-Study, and institutionally sponsored loans available. Support available to part-time students. *Unit head:* Tunc Aldemir, Graduate Studies Committee Chair, 614-292-7930, Fax: 614-292-3163, E-mail: aldemir.1@osu.edu. *Application contact:* 614-292-9444, Fax: 614-292-3895, E-mail: domestic.grad@osu.edu.

Oregon State University, Graduate School, College of Engineering, Department of Nuclear Engineering and Radiation Health Physics, Corvallis, OR 97331. Offers nuclear engineering (M Eng, MS, PhD); radiation health physics (MA, MHP, MS, PhD). Part-time programs available. Terminal master's awarded for partial completion of doctoral program. *Degree requirements:* For master's, thesis; for doctorate, thesis/dissertation. *Entrance requirements:* For master's and doctorate, GRE General Test, minimum GPA of 3.0 in last 90 hours. Additional exam requirements/recommendations for international students: Required—TOEFL (minimum score 550 paper-based; 213 computer-based). *Faculty research:* Reactor thermal hydraulics and safety, applications of radiation and nuclear techniques, computational methods development, environmental transport of radioactive materials.

Penn State University Park, Graduate School, College of Engineering, Department of Mechanical and Nuclear Engineering, State College, University Park, PA 16802-1503. Offers M Eng, MS, PhD. *Faculty research:* Reactor safety, radiation damage, advanced controls, radiation instrumentation, computational methods.

Purdue University, College of Engineering, School of Nuclear Engineering, West Lafayette, IN 47907-2017. Offers MS, MSNE, PhD. Part-time programs available. Terminal master's awarded for partial completion of doctoral program. *Entrance requirements:* For master's and doctorate, GRE General Test, minimum GPA of 3.0. Additional exam requirements/recommendations for international students: Required—TOEFL (minimum score 550 paper-based; 213 computer-based; 77 iBT); Recommended—TWE. Electronic applications accepted. *Faculty research:* Nuclear reactor safety, thermal hydraulics, fusion technology, reactor materials, reactor physics.

Rensselaer Polytechnic Institute, Graduate School, School of Engineering, Program in Nuclear Engineering, Troy, NY 12180-3590. Offers nuclear engineering (M Eng, MS); nuclear engineering and science (PhD). Part-time programs available. *Faculty:* 7 full-time (1 woman), 2 part-time/adjunct (0 women). *Students:* 20 full-time (0 women), 4 part-time (1 woman); includes 1 Black or African American, non-Hispanic/Latino, 12 international. Average age 27. 26 applicants, 38% accepted, 3 enrolled. In 2010, 1 doctorate awarded. *Degree requirements:* For master's, thesis (for some programs); for doctorate, thesis/dissertation. *Entrance requirements:* For master's and doctorate, GRE. Additional exam requirements/recommendations for international students: Required—TOEFL (minimum score 600 paper-based; 250 computer-based; 100 iBT). *Application deadline:* For fall admission, 1/15 priority date for domestic and international students; for spring admission, 1/15 for domestic students, 1/15 priority date for international students. Applications are processed on a rolling basis. Application fee: $75. Electronic applications accepted. *Expenses:* Tuition: Full-time $39,600; part-time $1650 per credit. Required fees: $1896. *Financial support:* In 2010–11, 20 students received support, including 5 fellowships with full tuition reimbursements available (averaging $25,000 per year), 13 research assistantships with full tuition reimbursements available (averaging $17,500 per year), 2 teaching assistantships with full tuition reimbursements available (averaging $17,500 per year); unspecified assistantships also available. Financial award application deadline: 2/1. *Faculty research:* Nuclear data measurement, multiphase flow and heat transfer, environmental and operational health physics, fusion reactor engineering and safety. Total annual research expenditures: $2.9 million. *Unit head:* Dr. Timothy Wei, Head, 518-276-6351, Fax: 518-276-6025, E-mail: weit@rpi.edu. *Application contact:* Prof. Thierry A. Blanchet, Associate Chair of Graduate Studies, 518-276-8697, Fax: 518-276-2623, E-mail: blanct@rpi.edu.

Royal Military College of Canada, Division of Graduate Studies and Research, Engineering Division, Program in Nuclear Engineering, Kingston, ON K7K 7B4, Canada. Offers M Eng, MA Sc, PhD. *Degree requirements:* For master's, thesis; for doctorate, comprehensive exam, thesis/dissertation. *Entrance requirements:* For master's, honours degree with second-class standing; for doctorate, master's degree. Electronic applications accepted.

Royal Military College of Canada, Division of Graduate Studies and Research, Engineering Division, Program in Nuclear Science, Kingston, ON K7K 7B4, Canada. Offers M Sc, PhD. *Degree requirements:* For master's, thesis; for doctorate, comprehensive exam, thesis/dissertation. *Entrance requirements:* For master's, honour's degree with second-class standing; for doctorate, master's degree. Electronic applications accepted.

Texas A&M University, College of Engineering, Department of Nuclear Engineering, College Station, TX 77843. Offers health physics (MS, PhD); nuclear engineering (M Eng, MS, PhD). *Faculty:* 21. *Students:* 113 full-time (19 women), 18 part-time (3 women); includes 18 minority (3 Black or African American, non-Hispanic/Latino; 6 Asian, non-Hispanic/Latino; 9 Hispanic/Latino), 36 international. Average age 28. In 2010, 26 master's, 7 doctorates awarded. *Degree requirements:* For master's, thesis or alternative; for doctorate, thesis/dissertation, departmental qualifying exams. *Entrance requirements:* For master's and doctorate, GRE General Test, 3 letters of recommendation. Additional exam requirements/recommendations for international students: Required—TOEFL. *Application deadline:* For fall admission, 3/1 for domestic and international students; for spring admission, 8/1 for domestic and international students. Applications are processed on a rolling basis. Application fee: $50 ($75 for international students). Electronic applications accepted. *Financial support:* Fellowships, research assistantships, career-related internships or fieldwork, scholarships/grants, and unspecified assistantships available. Financial award application deadline: 4/1; financial award applicants required to submit FAFSA. *Faculty research:* Accelerators, aerosols, computational transport, fission, fusion. Total annual research expenditures: $4.2 million. *Unit head:* Raymond Juzaitis, Head, 979-845-1956, E-mail: rjuzaitis@tamu.edu. *Application contact:* Graduate Coordinator, 979-845-7090.

University of California, Berkeley, Graduate Division, College of Engineering, Department of Nuclear Engineering, Berkeley, CA 94720-1730. Offers M Eng, MS, D Eng, PhD. *Degree requirements:* For master's, project or thesis; for doctorate, thesis/dissertation, oral exam. *Entrance requirements:* For master's and doctorate, GRE General Test, minimum GPA of 3.0, 3 letters of recommendation. Additional exam requirements/recommendations for international students: Required—TOEFL. *Faculty research:* Applied nuclear reactions and instrumentation, fission reactor engineering, fusion reactor technology, nuclear waste and materials management, radiation protection and environmental effects.

University of Cincinnati, Graduate School, College of Engineering, Department of Mechanical, Industrial and Nuclear Engineering, Program in Nuclear Engineering, Cincinnati, OH 45221. Offers MS, PhD. Part-time programs available. Terminal master's awarded for partial completion of doctoral program. *Degree requirements:* For master's, project or thesis; for doctorate, thesis/dissertation. *Entrance requirements:* For master's and doctorate, GRE General Test. Additional exam requirements/recommendations for international students: Required—TOEFL (minimum score 575 paper-based; 233 computer-based). Electronic applications accepted. *Faculty research:* Nuclear fission reactor engineering, reduction and fusion effects, health and medical physics, radiological assessment.

University of Florida, Graduate School, College of Engineering, Department of Nuclear and Radiological Engineering, Gainesville, FL 32611. Offers nuclear engineering sciences (ME, MS, PhD, Engr). Part-time programs available. *Faculty:* 5 full-time (0 women). *Students:* 45 full-time (18 women), 15 part-time (3 women); includes 1 Black or African American, non-Hispanic/Latino; 1 American Indian or Alaska Native, non-Hispanic/Latino; 7 Asian, non-Hispanic/Latino; 4 Hispanic/Latino, 8 international. Average age 28. 161 applicants, 29% accepted, 16 enrolled. In 2010, 9 master's, 9 doctorates awarded. Terminal master's awarded for partial completion of doctoral program. *Degree requirements:* For master's, comprehensive exam, thesis; for doctorate, comprehensive exam, thesis/dissertation; for Engr, thesis. *Entrance requirements:* For master's and doctorate, GRE General Test, minimum GPA of 3.0; for Engr, GRE General Test. Additional exam requirements/recommendations for international students: Required—TOEFL (minimum score 550 paper-based; 213 computer-based; 80 iBT), IELTS (minimum score 6). *Application deadline:* For fall admission, 7/1 priority date for domestic students, 5/1 for international students; for spring admission, 11/1 for domestic students, 9/1 for international students. Applications are processed on a rolling basis. Application fee: $30. Electronic applications accepted. *Expenses:* Tuition, state resident: full-time $10,915.92. Tuition, nonresident: full-time $28,309. *Financial support:* In 2010–11, 32 students received support, including 1 fellowship, 31 research assistantships (averaging $20,698 per year); institutionally sponsored loans and unspecified assistantships also available. Financial award application deadline: 3/1; financial award applicants required to submit FAFSA. *Faculty research:* Nuclear materials, radiation detection, thermal hydraulics, reactor physics and transport, generation 4 reactor technology. Total annual research expenditures: $2.4 million. *Unit head:* Dr. David E. Hintenlang, Chair, 352-392-8112, Fax: 352-392-3380, E-mail: dhinten@ufl.edu. *Application contact:* Terri Sparks, Graduate Coordinator, 352-392-1401 Ext. 304, Fax: 352-392-3380, E-mail: terria@ufl.edu.

University of Idaho, College of Graduate Studies, College of Engineering, Department of Engineering, Program in Nuclear Engineering, Moscow, ID 83844-2282. Offers M Engr, MS, PhD. *Faculty:* 6 full-time, 1 part-time/adjunct. *Students:* 14 full-time, 26 part-time. Average age 34. In 2010, 4 master's awarded. *Degree requirements:* For master's, thesis or alternative; for doctorate, thesis/dissertation. *Entrance requirements:* For master's, minimum GPA of 2.8; for doctorate, minimum undergraduate GPA of 2.8, 3.0 graduate. Additional exam requirements/recommendations for international students: Required—TOEFL. *Application deadline:* For fall admission, 8/1 for domestic students; for spring admission, 12/15 for domestic students. Applications are processed on a rolling basis. Application fee: $60. Electronic applications accepted. *Expenses:* Tuition, nonresident: part-time $580 per credit. Required fees: $306 per credit. *Financial support:* Applicants required to submit FAFSA. *Unit head:* Dr. Wudneh Admassu, Director, 208-282-7962, E-mail: wadmassu@uidaho.edu. *Application contact:* Dr. Wudneh Admassu, Director, 208-282-7962, E-mail: wadmassu@uidaho.edu.

University of Illinois at Urbana–Champaign, Graduate College, College of Engineering, Department of Nuclear, Plasma, and Radiological Engineering, Champaign, IL 61820. Offers nuclear engineering (MS, PhD). *Faculty:* 9 full-time (0 women). *Students:* 63 full-time (11 women), 3 part-time (0 women); includes 3 Asian, non-Hispanic/Latino; 2 Hispanic/Latino, 41 international. 69 applicants, 46% accepted, 14 enrolled. In 2010, 8 master's, 10 doctorates awarded. *Entrance requirements:* For master's and doctorate, minimum GPA of 3.0. Additional exam requirements/recommendations for international students: Required—TOEFL (minimum score 550 paper-based; 213 computer-based; 79 iBT) or IELTS. *Application deadline:* Applications are processed on a rolling basis. Application fee: $75 ($90 for international students). Electronic applications accepted. *Financial support:* In 2010–11, 10 fellowships, 35 research assistantships, 25 teaching assistantships were awarded; tuition waivers (full and partial) also available. *Unit head:* James F. Stubbins, Head, 217-333-6474, Fax: 217-333-3906, E-mail: jstubbin@illinois.edu. *Application contact:* Becky Meline, Admissions and Records Officer, 217-333-3598, Fax: 217-333-3906, E-mail: bmeline@illinois.edu.

The University of Manchester, School of Mechanical, Aerospace and Civil Engineering, Manchester, United Kingdom. Offers advanced manufacturing technology (M Ent); aerospace engineering (M Phil, M Sc, PhD); civil engineering (M Phil, M Sc, PhD); environmental engineering (M Phil, PhD); management of projects (M Phil, M Sc, PhD); mechanical engineering (M Phil, M Sc, PhD); mechanical engineering design (M Ent); nuclear engineering (M Phil, D Eng, PhD).

University of Maryland, College Park, Academic Affairs, A. James Clark School of Engineering, Department of Materials and Nuclear Engineering, Nuclear Engineering Program, College Park, MD 20742. Offers ME, MS, PhD. Part-time and evening/weekend programs available. Postbaccalaureate distance learning degree programs offered. *Students:* 13 full-time (5 women), 1 (woman) part-time; includes 4 minority (1 Asian, non-Hispanic/Latino; 2 Hispanic/Latino; 1 Two or more races, non-Hispanic/Latino), 1 international. 30 applicants, 37% accepted, 4 enrolled. In 2010, 5 master's, 2 doctorates awarded. *Degree requirements:* For master's, thesis optional; for doctorate, variable foreign language requirement, thesis/dissertation, oral exam. *Entrance requirements:* For master's and doctorate, GRE General Test, minimum GPA of 3.0. Additional exam requirements/recommendations for international students: Required—TOEFL. *Application deadline:* For fall admission, 1/15 for domestic and international students; for spring admission, 6/1 for domestic and international students. Applications are processed on a rolling basis. Application fee: $75. Electronic applications accepted. *Expenses:* Tuition, area resident: Part-time $471 per credit hour. Tuition, state resident: part-time $471 per credit hour. Tuition, nonresident: part-time $1016 per credit hour. Required fees: $337 per term. *Financial support:* In 2010–11, 4 research assistantships (averaging $23,924 per year) were awarded; fellowships, teaching assistantships, tuition waivers (full) also available. Financial award applicants required to submit FAFSA. *Faculty research:* Reliability and risk assessment, heat transfer and two-phase flow, reactor safety analysis, nuclear reactor, radiation/polymers. *Unit head:* Robert M. Briber, Head, 301-405-7313, Fax: 301-314-2029, E-mail: rbriber@umd.edu. *Application contact:* Dr. Charles A. Caramello, Dean of Graduate School, 301-405-0358, Fax: 301-314-9305, E-mail: ccaramel@umd.edu.

University of Massachusetts Lowell, James B. Francis College of Engineering, Program in Energy Engineering, Lowell, MA 01854-2881. Offers MS Eng, D Eng, PhD. *Degree requirements:* For master's, thesis optional. *Entrance requirements:* For master's, GRE General Test. Additional exam requirements/recommendations for international students: Required—TOEFL.

University of Michigan, Horace H. Rackham School of Graduate Studies, College of Engineering, Department of Nuclear Engineering and Radiological Sciences, Ann Arbor, MI 48109. Offers nuclear engineering (Nuc E); nuclear engineering and radiological sciences (MSE, PhD); nuclear science (MS, PhD). *Students:* 122 full-time (22 women), 2 part-time (1 woman). 147 applicants, 53% accepted, 45 enrolled. In 2010, 39 master's, 12 doctorates awarded. Terminal master's awarded for partial completion of doctoral program. *Degree requirements:* For master's, thesis optional; for doctorate, thesis/dissertation, oral defense of dissertation, preliminary exams. *Entrance requirements:* For master's and doctorate, GRE General Test. Additional exam requirements/recommendations for international students: Required—TOEFL (minimum score 560 paper-based; 220 computer-based). *Application deadline:* Applications are processed on a rolling basis. Application fee: $65 ($75 for international students). Electronic applications accepted. *Expenses:* Tuition, state resident: full-time $17,784; part-time $1116 per credit hour. Tuition, nonresident: full-time $35,944; part-time $2125 per credit hour. International tuition: $35,994 full-time. Required fees: $95 per semester. Tuition and fees vary according to course load, degree level and program. *Financial support:* Fellowships, research assistantships, teaching assistantships, career-related internships or fieldwork, institutionally sponsored loans, scholarships/grants, traineeships, health care benefits, and unspecified assistantships available. *Faculty research:* Radiation safety, environmental sciences, medical physics, fission systems and radiation transport, materials, plasmas and fusion, radiation measurements and imaging. *Unit head:* Dr. Ronald Gilgenbach, Chair, 734-936-0122, Fax: 734-763-4540, E-mail: rongilg@umich.edu. *Application contact:* Peggy Jo Gramer, Graduate Program Coordinator, 734-615-8810, Fax: 734-763-4540, E-mail: pjgramer@umich.edu.

University of Missouri, Graduate School, Nuclear Science and Engineering Institute, Columbia, MO 65211. Offers nuclear power engineering (MS, PhD), including health physics (MS), medical physics (MS), nuclear power engineering (MS). *Degree requirements:* For master's, research project; for doctorate, thesis/dissertation. *Entrance requirements:* For master's and doctorate, GRE General Test. Additional exam requirements/recommendations for international students: Required—TOEFL (minimum score 500 paper-based; 173 computer-based; 61 iBT).

University of Nevada, Las Vegas, Graduate College, Howard R. Hughes College of Engineering, Department of Mechanical Engineering, Las Vegas, NV 89154-4027. Offers aerospace engineering (MS); biomedical engineering (MS); materials and nuclear engineering (MS); mechanical engineering (MSE, PhD). Part-time programs available. *Faculty:* 17 full-time (0 women), 10 part-time/adjunct (0 women). *Students:* 43 full-time (6 women), 24 part-time (6 women); includes 24 minority (1 Black or African American, non-Hispanic/Latino; 4 Asian, non-Hispanic/Latino; 1 Hispanic/Latino; 1 Native Hawaiian or other Pacific Islander, non-Hispanic/Latino; 17 Two or more races, non-Hispanic/Latino), 24 international. Average age 30. 32 applicants, 84% accepted, 15 enrolled. In 2010, 10 master's, 4 doctorates awarded. *Degree requirements:* For master's, comprehensive exam, thesis (for some programs), project; for doctorate, comprehensive exam, thesis/dissertation. *Entrance requirements:* For master's and doctorate, GRE General Test. Additional exam requirements/recommendations for international students: Required—TOEFL (minimum score 550 paper-based; 213 computer-based; 80 iBT), IELTS (minimum score 7). *Application deadline:* For fall admission, 5/1 priority date for domestic and international students; for spring admission, 10/1 priority date for domestic and international students. Applications are processed on a rolling basis. Application fee: $60 ($95 for international students). Electronic applications accepted. *Expenses:* Tuition, area resident: Part-time $239.50 per credit. Tuition, state resident: part-time $239.50 per credit. Tuition, nonresident: part-time $503 per credit. Required fees: $108 per semester. Tuition and fees vary according to course load, program and reciprocity agreements. *Financial support:* In 2010–11, 37 students received support, including 21 research assistantships with partial tuition reimbursements available (averaging $13,335 per year), 16 teaching assistantships with partial tuition reimbursements available (averaging $11,000 per year); institutionally sponsored loans, scholarships/grants, health care benefits, and unspecified assistantships also available. Financial award application deadline: 3/1. *Faculty research:* Dynamics and control systems; energy systems including renewable and nuclear; computational fluid and solid mechanics; structures, materials and manufacturing; vibrations and acoustics. Total annual research expenditures: $3 million. *Unit head:* Dr. Woosoon Yim, Chair/Professor, 702-895-0956, Fax: 702-895-3936, E-mail: wy@me.unlv.edu. *Application contact:* Graduate College Admissions Evaluator, 702-895-3320, Fax: 702-895-4180, E-mail: gradcollege@unlv.edu.

University of New Mexico, Graduate School, School of Engineering, Department of Chemical and Nuclear Engineering, Program in Nuclear Engineering, Albuquerque, NM 87131-2039. Offers MS, PhD. Part-time programs available. Postbaccalaureate distance learning degree programs offered (no on-campus study). *Students:* 23 full-time (5 women), 17 part-time (3 women); includes 8 minority (1 Asian, non-Hispanic/Latino; 6 Hispanic/Latino; 1 Native Hawaiian or other Pacific Islander, non-Hispanic/Latino), 1 international. Average age 34. 62 applicants, 24% accepted, 7 enrolled. In 2010, 6 master's awarded. Terminal master's awarded for partial completion of doctoral program. *Degree requirements:* For master's, thesis (for some programs); for doctorate, comprehensive exam, thesis/dissertation. *Entrance requirements:* For master's, GRE General Test, minimum GPA of 3.0, 3 letters of recommendation, letter of intent; for doctorate, GRE General Test, 3 letters of recommendation, letter of intent. Additional exam requirements/recommendations for international students: Required—TOEFL. *Application deadline:* For fall admission, 1/15 priority date for domestic students, 3/1 for international students; for spring admission, 7/15 priority date for domestic students, 8/1 for international students. Application fee: $50. Electronic applications accepted. *Expenses:* Tuition, state resident: full-time $5991; part-time $251 per credit hour. Tuition, nonresident: full-time $14,405; part-time $800.20 per credit hour. Tuition and fees vary according to course level, course load, program and reciprocity agreements. *Financial support:* In 2010–11, 21 students received support, including 4 fellowships (averaging $4,875 per year), 15 research assistantships with full tuition reimbursements available (averaging $17,613 per year); teaching assistantships, scholarships/grants, health care benefits, and tuition waivers (full) also available. Financial award application deadline: 3/1; financial award applicants required to submit FAFSA. *Faculty research:* Plasma science, space power, thermal hydraulics, radiation measurement and protection, fusion plasma measurements, medical physics, nuclear criticality safety, radiation measurements and protection, radiation transport modeling and simulation, Monte Carlo methods. Total annual research expenditures: $1 million. *Unit head:* Dr. Timothy Ward, Chair, 505-277-5431, Fax: 505-277-5433, E-mail: tward@unm.edu. *Application contact:* Jocelyn White, Coordinator, Program Advisor, 505-277-5606, Fax: 505-277-5433, E-mail: jowhite@unm.edu.

University of South Carolina, The Graduate School, College of Engineering and Computing, Department of Nuclear Engineering, Columbia, SC 29208. Offers ME, MS, PhD. Part-time and evening/weekend programs available. Postbaccalaureate distance learning degree programs offered. *Degree requirements:* For master's, thesis (for some programs); for doctorate, thesis/dissertation. *Entrance requirements:* For master's and doctorate, GRE General Test. Additional exam requirements/recommendations for international students: Required—TOEFL (minimum score 600 paper-based; 250 computer-based; 100 iBT). Electronic applications accepted.

The University of Tennessee, Graduate School, College of Engineering, Department of Nuclear and Radiological Engineering, Knoxville, TN 37996. Offers nuclear engineering (MS, PhD); reliability and maintainability engineering (MS); MS/MBA. Part-time programs available. Postbaccalaureate distance learning degree programs offered (minimal on-campus study). *Faculty:* 14 full-time (1 woman), 54 part-time/adjunct (2 women). *Students:* 68 full-time (7 women), 30 part-time (4 women); includes 3 Black or African American, non-Hispanic/Latino; 2 Asian, non-Hispanic/Latino; 1 Hispanic/Latino, 9 international. Average age 30. 108 applicants, 56% accepted, 35 enrolled. In 2010, 11 master's, 5 doctorates awarded. *Degree requirements:* For master's, thesis or alternative; for doctorate, comprehensive exam, thesis/dissertation. *Entrance requirements:* For master's, GRE General Test, Minimum GPA of 2.7 (US degree holders); 3.0 (International degree holders); for doctorate, GRE General Test, Minimum GPA of 3.0 (previous graduate course work). Additional exam requirements/recommendations for international students: Required—TOEFL (minimum score 550 paper-based; 213 computer-based). *Application deadline:* For fall admission, 2/1 priority date for domestic and international students; for spring admission, 6/15 for domestic and international students. Applications are processed on a rolling basis. Application fee: $35. Electronic applications accepted. *Expenses:* Tuition, state resident: full-time $7440; part-time $414 per credit hour. Tuition, nonresident: full-time $22,478; part-time $1250 per credit hour. Required fees: $922; $43 per credit hour. Tuition and fees vary according to program. *Financial support:* In 2010–11, 63 students received support, including 16 fellowships with full tuition reimbursements available (averaging $25,200 per year), 46 research assistantships with full tuition reimbursements available (averaging $25,200 per year), 12 teaching assistantships with full tuition reimbursements available (averaging $25,200 per year); career-related internships or fieldwork, Federal Work-Study, institutionally sponsored loans, health care benefits, and unspecified assistantships also available. Financial award application deadline: 2/1; financial award applicants required to submit FAFSA. *Faculty research:* Heat transfer and fluid dynamics; instrumentation, sensors and controls; nuclear materials and nuclear security; radiological engineering; reactor system design and safety. Total annual research expenditures: $4.5 million. *Unit head:* Dr. Harold L. Dodds, Head, 865-974-2525, Fax: 865-974-0668, E-mail: hdj@utk.edu. *Application contact:* Dr. Masood Parang, Associate Dean of Student Affairs, 865-974-2454, Fax: 865-974-9871, E-mail: mparang@utk.edu.

University of Utah, Graduate School, College of Engineering, Department of Civil and Environmental Engineering, Program in Nuclear Engineering, Salt Lake City, UT 84112. Offers MS, PhD. Part-time programs available. *Faculty:* 2 full-time (1 woman), 1 part-time/adjunct (0 women). *Students:* 4 full-time (0 women), 5 part-time (0 women). Average age 31. 10 applicants, 60% accepted, 1 enrolled. In 2010, 1 master's awarded. Terminal master's awarded for partial completion of doctoral program. *Degree requirements:* For master's, comprehensive exam, thesis, thesis (MS); for doctorate, comprehensive exam, thesis/dissertation, qualifying exam. *Entrance requirements:* For master's and doctorate, GRE General Test, minimum GPA of 3.0. Additional exam requirements/recommendations for international students: Required—TOEFL (minimum score 580 paper-based; 237 computer-based; 93 iBT). *Application deadline:* For fall admission, 12/31 for domestic students, 11/30 for international students; for spring admission, 10/1 for domestic and international students. Applications are processed on a rolling basis. Application fee: $55 ($65 for international students). Electronic applications accepted. *Expenses:* Contact institution. *Financial support:* In 2010–11, 2 students received support, including 1 research assistantship with full tuition reimbursement available (averaging $20,016 per year), 1 teaching assistantship with full tuition reimbursement available (averaging $19,200 per year); fellowships, career-related internships or fieldwork, institutionally sponsored loans, scholarships/grants, traineeships, health care benefits, and unspecified assistantships also available. Support available to part-time students. Financial award application deadline: 11/30; financial award applicants required to submit FAFSA. *Faculty research:* Dosimetry, material damage, energy. Total annual research expenditures: $350,542. *Unit head:* Dr. Paul J. Tikalsky, Department Chair—Civil and Environmental Engineering, 801-581-6931, Fax: 801-585-5477, E-mail: tikalsky@civil.utah.edu. *Application contact:* Amanda May, Academic Program Specialist, 801-581-6931, Fax: 801-585-5477, E-mail: amandam@civil.utah.edu.

See Display on page 190 and Close-Up on page 229.

University of Wisconsin–Madison, Graduate School, College of Engineering, Department of Engineering Physics, Madison, WI 53706-1380. Offers engineering mechanics (MS, PhD); nuclear engineering and engineering physics (MS, PhD). Part-time programs available. Postbaccalaureate distance learning degree programs offered (minimal on-campus study). Terminal master's awarded for partial completion of doctoral program. *Degree requirements:* For master's, thesis optional; for doctorate, thesis/dissertation. *Entrance requirements:* For master's and doctorate, GRE General Test, minimum GPA of 3.0 in last 60 hours, appropriate bachelor's degree. Additional exam requirements/recommendations for international students: Required—TOEFL (minimum score 600 paper-based; 245 computer-based). Electronic applications accepted. *Expenses:* Tuition, state resident: full-time $9887.36; part-time $617.96 per credit. Tuition, nonresident: full-time $24,054; part-time $1503.40 per credit. Required fees: $67.63 per credit. Tuition and fees vary according to reciprocity agreements. *Faculty research:* Fission reactor engineering and safety, plasma physics and fusion technology, plasma processing and ion implantation, nanotechnology, engineering mechanics and astronautics.

Section 11
Engineering Design

This section contains a directory of institutions offering graduate work in engineering design. Additional information about programs listed in the directory may be obtained by writing directly to the dean of a graduate school or chair of a department at the address given in the directory.

For programs offering related work, see also in this book *Aerospace/ Aeronautical Engineering; Agricultural Engineering and Bioengineering; Biomedical Engineering and Biotechnology; Computer Science and Information Technology; Electrical and Computer Engineering; Energy and Power Engineering; Engineering and Applied Sciences; Industrial Engineering; Management of Engineering and Technology;* and *Mechanical Engineering and Mechanics.* In another guide in this series:

Graduate Programs in the Biological Sciences
See *Biological and Biomedical Sciences*

CONTENTS

Program Directory

Engineering Design

Northwestern University, McCormick School of Engineering and Applied Science, Segal Design Institute, Program in Engineering Design and Innovation, Evanston, IL 60208. Offers MS. *Faculty:* 9 full-time (4 women). *Students:* 17 full-time (4 women); includes 2 minority (both Asian, non-Hispanic/Latino), 5 international. Average age 23. 42 applicants, 69% accepted, 16 enrolled. In 2010, 18 master's awarded. *Entrance requirements:* For master's, General Exam of GRE, 2 letters of recommendation. Additional exam requirements/recommendations for international students: Required—TOEFL (minimum score 550 paper-based, 233 computer-based, 90 iBT) or IELTS (7). *Application deadline:* For fall admission, 7/15 for domestic students, 7/1 for international students. Applications are processed on a rolling basis. Application fee: $75. Electronic applications accepted. *Financial support:* Career-related internships or fieldwork, health care benefits, and unspecified assistantships available. Financial award application deadline: 1/15; financial award applicants required to submit FAFSA. *Unit head:* Kim Hoffmann, Associate Program Director, 847-467-3534, Fax: 847-491-2603, E-mail: kimhoffmann@northwestern.edu. *Application contact:* Kim Hoffmann, Admission Officer, 847-491-5434, Fax: 847-491-2603, E-mail: kimhoffmann@northwestern.edu.

Polytechnic Institute of NYU, Long Island Graduate Center, Graduate Programs, Department of Electrical and Computer Engineering, Interdisciplinary Major in Wireless Innovations, Melville, NY 11747. Offers M Engr. Part-time and evening/weekend programs available. *Students:* 4 full-time (1 woman), 6 part-time (1 woman); includes 1 Black or African American, non-Hispanic/Latino; 1 Hispanic/Latino, 5 international. Average age 29. 100 applicants, 51% accepted, 6 enrolled. In 2010, 2 master's awarded. *Degree requirements:* For master's, comprehensive exam (for some programs), thesis (for some programs). *Entrance requirements:* Additional exam requirements/recommendations for international students: Required—TOEFL (minimum score 550 paper-based; 213 computer-based; 80 iBT); Recommended—IELTS (minimum score 6.5). *Application deadline:* For fall admission, 7/31 priority date for domestic students, 4/30 priority date for international students; for spring admission, 12/31 priority date for domestic students, 11/30 priority date for international students. Applications are processed on a rolling basis. Application fee: $75. Electronic applications accepted. *Expenses:* Tuition: Full-time $21,492; part-time $1194 per credit. Required fees: $385 per semester. Tuition and fees vary according to course load. *Financial support:* Institutionally sponsored loans, scholarships/grants, and unspecified assistantships available. Support available to part-time students. *Unit head:* Dr. Jonathan Chao, Department Head, 718-260-3302, Fax: 718-260-3906, E-mail: chao@poly.edu. *Application contact:* JeanCarlo Bonilla, Director of Graduate Enrollment Management, 718-260-3182, Fax: 718-260-3624, E-mail: gradinfo@poly.edu.

Rochester Institute of Technology, Graduate Enrollment Services, Kate Gleason College of Engineering, Department of Design, Development and Manufacturing, Rochester, NY 14623-5603. Offers manufacturing leadership (MS); product development (MS). Part-time and evening/weekend programs available. *Students:* 3 full-time (all women), 62 part-time (6 women); includes 2 Black or African American, non-Hispanic/Latino; 2 Asian, non-Hispanic/Latino; 3 Hispanic/Latino, 4 international. Average age 37. 12 applicants, 83% accepted, 9 enrolled. In 2010, 24 master's awarded. *Degree requirements:* For master's, capstone. *Entrance requirements:* For master's, minimum GPA of 2.5. Additional exam requirements/recommendations for international students: Required—TOEFL (minimum score 570 paper-based; 230 computer-based; 88 iBT) or IELTS (minimum score 6.5). *Application deadline:* For fall admission, 2/15 priority date for domestic and international students. Applications are processed on a rolling basis. Application fee: $50. Electronic applications accepted. *Expenses:* Tuition: Full-time $33,234; part-time $924 per credit hour. Required fees: $219. *Financial support:* In 2010–11, 7 students received support. *Faculty research:* Computer-integrated manufacturing, industrial ergonomics, optics and photonics, micromachines, electrochemical heating, signal and image processing, cardiovascular biomechanics, robotics and control, VLSI design, electron beam lithography, computer architecture, multimedia information systems, object-oriented software development. *Unit head:* Mark Smith, Director, 585-475-7971, Fax: 585-475-7955, E-mail: mpdmail@rit.edu. *Application contact:* Diane Ellison, Assistant Vice President, Graduate Enrollment Services, 585-475-2229, Fax: 585-475-7164, E-mail: gradinfo@rit.edu.

San Diego State University, Graduate and Research Affairs, College of Engineering, Department of Mechanical Engineering, San Diego, CA 92182. Offers engineering sciences and applied mechanics (PhD); manufacture and design (MS); mechanical engineering (MS). PhD offered jointly with University of California, San Diego and Department of Aerospace Engineering and Engineering Mechanics. Evening/weekend programs available. *Degree requirements:* For master's, comprehensive exam (for some programs), thesis (for some programs); for doctorate, thesis/dissertation. *Entrance requirements:* For master's, GRE General Test; for doctorate, GRE, 3 letters of recommendation. Additional exam requirements/recommendations for international students: Required—TOEFL. Electronic applications accepted. *Faculty research:* Energy analysis and diagnosis, seawater pump design, space-related research.

Santa Clara University, School of Engineering, Program in Mechanical Engineering, Santa Clara, CA 95053. Offers controls (Certificate); dynamics (Certificate); materials engineering (Certificate); mechanical design analysis (Certificate); mechanical engineering (MS, PhD, Engineer); mechatronics systems engineering (Certificate); technology jump-start (Certificate); thermofluids (Certificate). Part-time and evening/weekend programs available. *Students:* 33 full-time (4 women), 55 part-time (6 women); includes 30 minority (21 Asian, non-Hispanic/Latino; 6 Hispanic/Latino; 1 Native Hawaiian or other Pacific Islander, non-Hispanic/Latino; 2 Two or more races, non-Hispanic/Latino), 15 international. Average age 28. 82 applicants, 71% accepted, 29 enrolled. In 2010, 19 master's awarded. *Degree requirements:* For master's, thesis (for some programs); for doctorate, thesis/dissertation; for other advanced degree, thesis. *Entrance requirements:* For master's, GRE (waiver may be available), transcript; for doctorate, GRE, master's degree or equivalent; for other advanced degree, master's degree, published paper. Additional exam requirements/recommendations for international students: Required—TOEFL (minimum score 550 paper-based; 213 computer-based; 79 iBT). *Application deadline:* For fall admission, 8/12 for domestic students, 7/15 for international students; for winter admission, 10/28 for domestic students, 9/23 for international students; for spring admission, 2/25 for domestic students, 1/21 for international students. Applications are processed on a rolling basis. Application fee: $60. Electronic applications accepted. *Expenses:* Contact institution. *Financial support:* Research assistantships, teaching assistantships available. Financial award application deadline: 3/2; financial award applicants required to submit FAFSA. *Faculty research:* Development of small satellite design, tests and operations technology. Total annual research expenditures: $585,448. *Unit head:* Dr. Alex Zecevic, Associate Dean for Graduate Studies, 408-554-2394, E-mail: azecevic@scu.edu. *Application contact:* Stacey Tinker, Director of Admissions, Graduate Engineering, 408-554-4748, Fax: 408-554-4323, E-mail: stinker@scu.edu.

Stanford University, School of Engineering, Department of Mechanical Engineering, Program in Product Design, Stanford, CA 94305-9991. Offers MS. *Entrance requirements:* For master's, GRE General Test, undergraduate degree in engineering, math or sciences. Additional exam requirements/recommendations for international students: Required—TOEFL. *Expenses:* Tuition: Full-time $38,700; part-time $860 per unit. One-time fee: $200 full-time.

Stevens Institute of Technology, Graduate School, Charles V. Schaefer Jr. School of Engineering, Department of Mechanical Engineering, Program in Product Architecture and Engineering, Hoboken, NJ 07030. Offers M Eng. *Students:* 12 full-time (1 woman), 6 part-time (0 women); includes 1 Black or African American, non-Hispanic/Latino; 1 Hispanic/Latino, 1 international. Average age 26. *Unit head:* Dr. Constantin Chassapis, Director, 201-216-5564. *Application contact:* Graduate Admissions, 800-496-4935, Fax: 201-216-8044, E-mail: gradadmissions@stevens.edu.

University of Central Florida, College of Engineering and Computer Science, Department of Industrial Engineering and Management Systems, Orlando, FL 32816. Offers applied operations research (Certificate); design for usability (Certificate); industrial engineering (MSIE, PhD); industrial engineering and management systems (MS); industrial ergonomics and safety (Certificate); project engineering (Certificate); quality assurance (Certificate); systems engineering (Certificate); systems simulation for engineers (Certificate); training simulation (Certificate). Part-time and evening/weekend programs available. *Faculty:* 17 full-time (4 women), 6 part-time/adjunct (1 woman). *Students:* 112 full-time (31 women), 171 part-time (66 women); includes 79 minority (27 Black or African American, non-Hispanic/Latino; 17 Asian, non-Hispanic/Latino; 32 Hispanic/Latino; 1 Native Hawaiian or other Pacific Islander, non-Hispanic/Latino; 2 Two or more races, non-Hispanic/Latino), 72 international. Average age 33. 210 applicants, 74% accepted, 82 enrolled. In 2010, 65 master's, 7 doctorates, 34 other advanced degrees awarded. *Degree requirements:* For master's, thesis; for doctorate, thesis/dissertation, departmental qualifying exam, candidacy exam. *Entrance requirements:* For master's, GRE General Test, minimum GPA of 3.0 in last 60 hours of course work; for doctorate, minimum GPA of 3.5 in last 60 hours of course work. Additional exam requirements/recommendations for international students: Required—TOEFL. *Application deadline:* For fall admission, 7/15 priority date for domestic students; for spring admission, 12/1 priority date for domestic students. Application fee: $30. Electronic applications accepted. *Expenses:* Tuition, state resident: part-time $256.56 per credit hour. Tuition, nonresident: part-time $1011.52 per credit hour. Part-time tuition and fees vary according to program. *Financial support:* In 2010–11, 24 students received support, including 85 fellowships with partial tuition reimbursements available (averaging $7,300 per year), 19 research assistantships with partial tuition reimbursements available (averaging $8,500 per year), 6 teaching assistantships with partial tuition reimbursements available (averaging $12,200 per year); career-related internships or fieldwork, Federal Work-Study, institutionally sponsored loans, tuition waivers (partial), and unspecified assistantships also available. Financial award application deadline: 3/1; financial award applicants required to submit FAFSA. *Unit head:* Dr. Waldemar Karwowski, Chair, 407-823-2204, E-mail: wkar@mail.ucf.edu. *Application contact:* Dr. Waldemar Karwowski, Chair, 407-823-2204, E-mail: wkar@mail.ucf.edu.

Worcester Polytechnic Institute, Graduate Studies and Research, School of Business, Worcester, MA 01609-2280. Offers information technology (MS), including information security management; management (Graduate Certificate); marketing and technological innovation (MS); operations design and leadership (MS); technology (MBA). *Accreditation:* AACSB. Part-time and evening/weekend programs available. Postbaccalaureate distance learning degree programs offered (minimal on-campus study). *Faculty:* 13 full-time (7 women), 9 part-time/adjunct (2 women). *Students:* 112 full-time (53 women), 135 part-time (33 women); includes 5 Black or African American, non-Hispanic/Latino; 1 Hispanic/Latino; 15 Native Hawaiian or other Pacific Islander, non-Hispanic/Latino, 105 international. 396 applicants, 67% accepted, 79 enrolled. In 2010, 69 master's awarded. *Degree requirements:* For master's, thesis optional. *Entrance requirements:* For master's, GMAT (MBA), GMAT or GRE General Test (MS), resume; for Graduate Certificate, GMAT or GRE General Test, statement of purpose, 3 letters of recommendation. Additional exam requirements/recommendations for international students: Required—TOEFL (minimum score 550 paper-based; 213 computer-based; 79 iBT), IELTS (minimum score 6.5). *Application deadline:* For fall admission, 6/1 priority date for domestic and international students; for spring admission, 11/1 priority date for domestic students, 10/1 priority date for international students. Applications are processed on a rolling basis. Application fee: $70. Electronic applications accepted. *Expenses:* Tuition: Full-time $20,862; part-time $1159 per term. One-time fee: $15. *Financial support:* Career-related internships or fieldwork, institutionally sponsored loans, scholarships/grants, and unspecified assistantships available. Financial award application deadline: 6/1; financial award applicants required to submit FAFSA. *Faculty research:* Organizational aesthetics, resistance in organizations, dynamics of product innovation, economic approaches to productivity, corporate earnings forecasts and value relevance, ERP implementation, improving Web accessibility, information quality assessment, measuring strategic and transactional IT, website quality, service operations modeling, healthcare operations and performance analysis, loan process design. *Unit head:* Dr. Mark Rice, Dean, 508-831-4665, Fax: 508-831-5218, E-mail: rice@wpi.edu. *Application contact:* Alyssa Bates, Director, Graduate Management Programs, 508-831-4665, Fax: 508-831-5720, E-mail: ajbates@wpi.edu.

Section 12
Engineering Physics

This section contains a directory of institutions offering graduate work in engineering physics. Additional information about programs listed in the directory may be obtained by writing directly to the dean of a graduate school or chair of a department at the address given in the directory.

For programs offering related work, see also in this book *Electrical and Computer Engineering, Energy and Power Engineering (Nuclear Engineering), Engineering and Applied Sciences,* and *Materials Sciences and Engineering.* In the other guides in this series:
Graduate Programs in the Biological Sciences
See *Biophysics*

Graduate Programs in the Physical Sciences, Mathematics, Agricultural Sciences, the Environment & Natural Resources
See *Physics*
Graduate Programs in Business, Education, Health, Information Studies, Law & Social Work
See *Health Sciences (Medical Physics)*

CONTENTS

Program Directory

Engineering Physics

Air Force Institute of Technology, Graduate School of Engineering and Management, Department of Engineering Physics, Dayton, OH 45433-7765. Offers applied physics (MS, PhD); electro-optics (MS, PhD); materials science (PhD); nuclear engineering (MS, PhD); space physics (MS). Part-time programs available. *Degree requirements:* For master's, thesis; for doctorate, thesis/dissertation. *Entrance requirements:* For master's and doctorate, GRE General Test, minimum GPA of 3.0, U.S. citizenship. *Faculty research:* High-energy lasers, space physics, nuclear weapon effects, semiconductor physics.

Appalachian State University, Cratis D. Williams Graduate School, Department of Physics and Astronomy, Boone, NC 28608. Offers engineering physics (MS). Part-time programs available. *Faculty:* 13 full-time (3 women), 4 part-time/adjunct (1 woman). *Students:* 13 full-time (5 women), 4 part-time (0 women). 9 applicants, 89% accepted, 6 enrolled. In 2010, 8 master's awarded. *Degree requirements:* For master's, comprehensive exam, thesis optional. *Entrance requirements:* For master's, GRE General Test, 3 letters of recommendation. Additional exam requirements/recommendations for international students: Required—TOEFL (minimum score 570 paper-based; 230 computer-based; 79 iBT), IELTS (minimum score 6.5). *Application deadline:* For fall admission, 7/1 for domestic students, 2/1 for international students; for spring admission, 11/1 for domestic students, 7/1 for international students. Applications are processed on a rolling basis. Application fee: $55. Electronic applications accepted. *Expenses:* Tuition, state resident: full-time $3428; part-time $428 per unit. Tuition, nonresident: full-time $14,518; part-time $1814 per unit. Required fees: $2320; $344 per unit. Tuition and fees vary according to campus/location. *Financial support:* In 2010–11, 1 research assistantship with tuition reimbursement (averaging $10,000 per year), 7 teaching assistantships with tuition reimbursements (averaging $9,500 per year) were awarded; fellowships, career-related internships or fieldwork, Federal Work-Study, scholarships/grants, and unspecified assistantships also available. Financial award application deadline: 4/1. *Faculty research:* Raman spectroscopy, applied electrostatics, scanning tunneling microscope/atomic force microscope (STM/AFM), stellar spectroscopy and photometry, surface physics, remote sensing. Total annual research expenditures: $352,000. *Unit head:* Dr. Leon Ginsberg, Chairperson, 828-262-3090, E-mail: ginsberglh@appstate.edu. *Application contact:* Dr. Sid Clements, Director, 828-262-2447, E-mail: clementsjs@appstate.edu.

Cornell University, Graduate School, Graduate Fields of Engineering, Field of Applied Physics, Ithaca, NY 14853-0001. Offers applied physics (PhD); engineering physics (M Eng). *Faculty:* 39 full-time (4 women). *Students:* 83 full-time (15 women); includes 8 Asian, non-Hispanic/Latino; 3 Hispanic/Latino, 39 international. Average age 25. 170 applicants, 35% accepted, 30 enrolled. In 2010, 11 master's, 16 doctorates awarded. *Degree requirements:* For doctorate, comprehensive exam, thesis/dissertation, written exams. *Entrance requirements:* For master's, GRE General Test, 3 letters of recommendation; for doctorate, GRE General Test, GRE Subject Test (physics), GRE Writing Assessment, 3 letters of recommendation. Additional exam requirements/recommendations for international students: Required—TOEFL (minimum score 600 paper-based; 250 computer-based; 77 iBT). *Application deadline:* For fall admission, 1/15 for domestic students. Application fee: $70. Electronic applications accepted. *Expenses:* Tuition: Full-time $29,500. Required fees: $76. Tuition and fees vary according to degree level and program. *Financial support:* In 2010–11, 70 students received support, including 7 fellowships with full tuition reimbursements available, 48 research assistantships with full tuition reimbursements available, 9 teaching assistantships with full tuition reimbursements available; institutionally sponsored loans, scholarships/grants, health care benefits, tuition waivers (full and partial), and unspecified assistantships also available. *Faculty research:* Quantum and nonlinear optics, plasma physics, solid state physics, condensed matter physics and nanotechnology, electron and x-ray spectroscopy. *Unit head:* Graduate Faculty Representative, 607-255-0638. *Application contact:* Graduate Field Assistant, 607-255-0638, E-mail: aep_info@cornell.edu.

Dartmouth College, Thayer School of Engineering, Program in Engineering Physics, Hanover, NH 03755. Offers MS, PhD. *Faculty research:* Computational physics, medical physics, radiation physics, plasma science and magneto hydro-dynamics, magnetospheric and ionospheric physics.

École Polytechnique de Montréal, Graduate Programs, Department of Engineering Physics, Montréal, QC H3C 3A7, Canada. Offers optical engineering (M Eng, M Sc A, PhD); solid-state physics and engineering (M Eng, M Sc A, PhD). Part-time programs available. *Degree requirements:* For master's, one foreign language, thesis; for doctorate, one foreign language, thesis/dissertation. *Entrance requirements:* For master's, minimum GPA of 2.75; for doctorate, minimum GPA of 3.0. *Faculty research:* Optics, thin-film physics, laser spectroscopy, plasmas, photonic devices.

Embry-Riddle Aeronautical University–Daytona, Daytona Beach Campus Graduate Program, Department of Physical Sciences, Daytona Beach, FL 32114-3900. Offers engineering physics (PhD). Part-time and evening/weekend programs available. *Faculty:* 6 full-time (0 women). *Students:* 21 full-time (5 women), 1 part-time (0 women); includes 7 minority (1 Black or African American, non-Hispanic/Latino; 1 American Indian or Alaska Native, non-Hispanic/Latino; 3 Asian, non-Hispanic/Latino; 1 Hispanic/Latino; 1 Two or more races, non-Hispanic/Latino), 5 international. Average age 26. 37 applicants, 41% accepted, 9 enrolled. *Degree requirements:* For doctorate, comprehensive exam, thesis/dissertation. *Entrance requirements:* For doctorate, GRE (minimum score verbal plus quantitative of 1200 obtained within previous two years of application), master's degree in physics or engineering, minimum GPA of 3.2, statement of goals, 3 letters of recommendation. Additional exam requirements/recommendations for international students: Required—TOEFL. *Application deadline:* For fall admission, 3/15 for domestic students, 2/15 for international students. Applications are processed on a rolling basis. Application fee: $50. Electronic applications accepted. *Expenses:* Tuition: Full-time $14,040; part-time $1170 per credit hour. *Financial support:* In 2010–11, 18 students received support, including 2 research assistantships with full and partial tuition reimbursements available (averaging $5,972 per year), 10 teaching assistantships with full and partial tuition reimbursements available (averaging $5,972 per year); career-related internships or fieldwork also available. Financial award application deadline: 4/15; financial award applicants required to submit FAFSA. *Unit head:* Dr. Michael Hickey, Interim Department Chair, 386-226-7059, E-mail: michael.hickey@erau.edu. *Application contact:* Keith Deaton, Director, International and Graduate Admissions, 800-388-3728, Fax: 386-226-7070, E-mail: graduate.admissions@erau.edu.

George Mason University, College of Science, Department of Physics and Astronomy, Fairfax, VA 22030. Offers applied and engineering physics (MS); physics (PhD). *Faculty:* 30 full-time (9 women), 6 part-time/adjunct (1 woman). *Students:* 11 full-time (0 women), 48 part-time (16 women); includes 12 minority (1 Black or African American, non-Hispanic/Latino; 7 Asian, non-Hispanic/Latino; 4 Hispanic/Latino), 9 international. Average age 33. 41 applicants, 68% accepted, 15 enrolled. In 2010, 5 master's, 3 doctorates awarded. *Degree requirements:* For master's, thesis optional. *Entrance requirements:* For master's, minimum GPA of 2.75 in last 60 hours of course work. Additional exam requirements/recommendations for international students: Required—TOEFL (minimum score 570 paper-based; 230 computer-based; 88 iBT). *Application deadline:* For fall admission, 5/1 for domestic students; for spring admission, 11/1 for domestic students. Application fee: $100. Electronic applications accepted. *Expenses:* Tuition, state resident: full-time $8192; part-time $440 per credit hour. Tuition, nonresident: full-time $22,952; part-time $1055 per credit hour. Required fees: $2364; $99 per credit hour. *Financial support:* In 2010–11, 25 students received support, including 3 fellowships with full tuition reimbursements available (averaging $18,000 per year), 12 research assistantships with full and partial tuition reimbursements available (averaging $15,945 per year), 11 teaching assistantships with full and partial tuition reimbursements available (averaging $11,298 per year); career-related internships or fieldwork, Federal Work-Study, scholarships/grants, unspecified assistantships, and health care benefits (full-time research or teaching assistantship recipients) also available. Support available to part-time students. Financial award application deadline: 3/1; financial award applicants required to submit FAFSA. *Faculty research:* Astronomy, astrophysics, and space and planetary science; astronomy and physics education; atomic physics; biophysics and neuroscience. Total annual research expenditures: $2.4 million. *Unit head:* Dr. Michael Summers, Chairman, 703-993-3971, Fax: 703-993-1269, E-mail: msummers@gmu.edu. *Application contact:* Dr. Paul So, Information Contact, 703-993-4377, E-mail: paso@gmu.edu.

McMaster University, School of Graduate Studies, Faculty of Engineering, Department of Engineering Physics, Hamilton, ON L8S 4M2, Canada. Offers engineering physics (M Eng, MA Sc, PhD); nuclear engineering (PhD). *Degree requirements:* For master's, thesis or alternative; for doctorate, comprehensive exam, thesis/dissertation. *Entrance requirements:* For master's, minimum B average in engineering, mathematics, or physical sciences. Additional exam requirements/recommendations for international students: Required—TOEFL (minimum score 550 paper-based; 213 computer-based). *Faculty research:* Non-thermal plasmas for pollution control and electrostatic precipitation, bulk and thin film luminescent materials, devices and systems for optical fiber communications, physics and applications of III-V materials and devices, defect spectroscopy in semiconductors.

Michigan Technological University, Graduate School, College of Sciences and Arts, Department of Physics, Program in Engineering Physics, Houghton, MI 49931. Offers PhD. Part-time programs available. *Degree requirements:* For doctorate, comprehensive exam, thesis/dissertation. *Entrance requirements:* For doctorate, BS in physics or related discipline. Additional exam requirements/recommendations for international students: Required—TOEFL (minimum score 570 paper-based; 230 computer-based). Electronic applications accepted.

Polytechnic Institute of NYU, Department of Electrical and Computer Engineering, Major in Electrophysics, Brooklyn, NY 11201-2990. Offers MS. Part-time and evening/weekend programs available. *Students:* 9 full-time (3 women), 2 part-time (0 women); includes 2 Black or African American, non-Hispanic/Latino; 2 Asian, non-Hispanic/Latino, 5 international. Average age 27. 11 applicants, 55% accepted, 4 enrolled. In 2010, 1 master's awarded. *Degree requirements:* For master's, comprehensive exam (for some programs), thesis (for some programs). *Entrance requirements:* For master's, BS in electrical engineering. Additional exam requirements/recommendations for international students: Required—TOEFL (minimum score 550 paper-based; 213 computer-based; 80 iBT); Recommended—IELTS (minimum score 6.5). *Application deadline:* For fall admission, 7/31 priority date for domestic students, 4/30 priority date for international students; for spring admission, 12/31 priority date for domestic students, 11/30 priority date for international students. Applications are processed on a rolling basis. Application fee: $75. Electronic applications accepted. *Expenses:* Tuition: Full-time $21,492; part-time $1194 per credit. Required fees: $385 per semester. Tuition and fees vary according to course load. *Financial support:* Fellowships, research assistantships, teaching assistantships, institutionally sponsored loans, scholarships/grants, and unspecified assistantships available. Support available to part-time students. Financial award applicants required to submit FAFSA. *Unit head:* Dr. Jonathan Chao, Head, 718-860-3478, Fax: 718-260-3302, E-mail: chao@poly.edu. *Application contact:* JeanCarlo Bonilla, Director of Graduate Enrollment Management, 718-260-3182, Fax: 718-260-3624.

Polytechnic Institute of NYU, Long Island Graduate Center, Graduate Programs, Department of Electrical and Computer Engineering, Major in Electrophysics, Melville, NY 11747. Offers MS. Part-time and evening/weekend programs available. In 2010, 1 master's awarded. *Degree requirements:* For master's, comprehensive exam (for some programs), thesis (for some programs). *Entrance requirements:* Additional exam requirements/recommendations for international students: Required—TOEFL (minimum score 550 paper-based; 213 computer-based; 80 iBT); Recommended—IELTS (minimum score 6.5). *Application deadline:* For fall admission, 7/31 priority date for domestic students, 4/30 priority date for international students; for spring admission, 12/31 priority date for domestic students, 11/30 priority date for international students. Applications are processed on a rolling basis. Application fee: $75. Electronic applications accepted. *Expenses:* Tuition: Full-time $21,492; part-time $1194 per credit. Required fees: $385 per semester. Tuition and fees vary according to course load. *Financial support:* Institutionally sponsored loans, scholarships/grants, and unspecified assistantships available. Support available to part-time students. Financial award applicants required to submit FAFSA. *Unit head:* Dr. Jonathan Chao, Department Head, 718-260-3302, E-mail: chao@poly.edu. *Application contact:* JeanCarlo Bonilla, Director of Graduate Enrollment Management, 718-260-3182, Fax: 718-260-3624, E-mail: gradinfo@poly.edu.

Rensselaer Polytechnic Institute, Graduate School, School of Engineering, Program in Engineering Physics, Troy, NY 12180-3590. Offers MS, PhD. Part-time programs available. *Faculty:* 1 full-time (0 women). *Students:* 1 full-time (0 women). Average age 27. 8 applicants, 38% accepted, 1 enrolled. In 2010, 1 doctorate awarded. Terminal master's awarded for partial completion of doctoral program. *Degree requirements:* For master's, thesis (for some programs); for doctorate, thesis/dissertation. *Entrance requirements:* For master's and doctorate, GRE. Additional exam requirements/recommendations for international students: Required—TOEFL (minimum score 600 paper-based; 250 computer-based; 100 iBT). *Application deadline:* For fall admission, 1/15 priority date for domestic and international students; for spring admission, 10/15 for domestic students, 1/15 priority date for international students. Applications are processed on a rolling basis. Application fee: $75. Electronic applications accepted. *Expenses:* Tuition: Full-time $39,600; part-time $1650 per credit. Required fees: $1896. *Financial support:* In 2010–11, 1 student received support, including 1 fellowship (averaging $25,000 per year); unspecified assistantships also available. Financial award application deadline: 2/1. *Faculty research:* Nuclear data management, multiphase flow and heat transfer, environmental and operational health physics, fusion reactor engineering and safety, radiation destruction of hazardous chemicals. *Unit head:* Dr. Timothy Wei, Head, 518-276-6351, Fax: 518-276-6025, E-mail: weit@rpi.edu. *Application contact:* Dr. Thierry A. Blanchet, Associate Chair of Graduate Studies, 518-276-8697, Fax: 518-276-2623, E-mail: blanct@rpi.edu.

Stevens Institute of Technology, Graduate School, Charles V. Schaefer Jr. School of Engineering, Department of Physics and Engineering Physics, Hoboken, NJ 07030. Offers applied optics (Certificate); engineering physics (M Eng); microdevices and microsystems (Certificate); physics (MS, PhD); plasma and surface physics (Certificate). Part-time and evening/weekend programs available. *Students:* 46 full-time (6 women), 8 part-time (0 women); includes 1 Black or African American, non-Hispanic/Latino; 4 Asian, non-Hispanic/Latino; 4 Hispanic/Latino, 23 international. Average age 30. 44 applicants, 100% accepted.Terminal master's awarded for partial completion of doctoral program. *Degree requirements:* For master's, thesis optional; for doctorate, thesis/dissertation. *Entrance requirements:* For master's and doctorate, GRE. Additional exam requirements/recommendations for international students: Required—TOEFL. *Application deadline:* Applications are processed on a rolling basis. Application fee: $50. Electronic applications accepted. *Financial support:* Fellowships, research assistantships, teaching assistantships, Federal Work-Study, and institutionally sponsored loans available. *Faculty research:* Laser spectroscopy, physical kinetics, semiconductor-device physics, condensed-matter theory. *Unit head:* Knut Stamnes, Director, 201-216-8194, Fax: 201-216-5638, E-mail: kstamnes@stevens.edu. *Application contact:* H. L. Cui, Chairman, Graduate Committee, 201-216-5637, Fax: 201-216-5638, E-mail: hcui@stevens-tech.edu.

University of California, San Diego, Office of Graduate Studies, Department of Mechanical and Aerospace Engineering, Program in Engineering Physics, La Jolla, CA 92093. Offers MS, PhD. Part-time programs available. *Degree requirements:* For master's, comprehensive exam or thesis; for doctorate, thesis/dissertation, qualifying exam. *Entrance requirements:* For master's and doctorate, GRE General Test, minimum GPA of 3.0. Additional exam requirements/recommendations for international students: Required—TOEFL. Electronic applications accepted.

Faculty research: Combustion engineering, environmental mechanics, magnetic recording, materials processing, computational fluid dynamics.

University of Maine, Graduate School, College of Liberal Arts and Sciences, Department of Physics and Astronomy, Program in Engineering Physics, Orono, ME 04469. Offers M Eng. *Students:* 2 full-time (0 women). Average age 25. In 2010, 1 master's awarded. *Degree requirements:* For master's, thesis or alternative. *Entrance requirements:* For master's, GRE General Test, GRE Subject Test. Additional exam requirements/recommendations for international students: Required—TOEFL. *Application deadline:* For fall admission, 2/1 priority date for domestic students; for spring admission, 10/15 for domestic students. Applications are processed on a rolling basis. Application fee: $65. *Expenses:* Tuition, state resident: full-time $400. Tuition, nonresident: full-time $1050. *Financial support:* In 2010–11, 1 teaching assistantship with tuition reimbursement (averaging $12,790 per year) was awarded. Financial award application deadline: 3/1. *Unit head:* Dr. Susan McKay, Chair, 207-581-1015, Fax: 207-581-3410. *Application contact:* Scott G. Delcourt, Associate Dean of the Graduate School, 207-581-3291, Fax: 207-581-3232, E-mail: graduate@maine.edu.

University of Oklahoma, College of Engineering, Program in Engineering Physics, Norman, OK 73019-0390. Offers MS, PhD. Terminal master's awarded for partial completion of doctoral program. *Degree requirements:* For master's, thesis or alternative, departmental qualifying exam; for doctorate, thesis/dissertation, comprehensive, departmental qualifying, oral, and written exams. *Entrance requirements:* For master's and doctorate, GRE General Test, GRE Subject Test (physics), previous course work in physics. Additional exam requirements/recommendations for international students: Required—TOEFL (minimum score 550 paper-based; 213 computer-based; 79 iBT). *Application deadline:* For fall admission, 3/1 priority date for domestic students, 4/1 for international students; for spring admission, 10/1 for domestic students, 9/1 for international students. Applications are processed on a rolling basis. Application fee: $40 ($90 for international students). Electronic applications accepted. *Expenses:* Tuition, state resident: full-time $3892.80; part-time $162.20 per credit hour. Tuition, nonresident: full-time $14,167; part-time $590.30 per credit hour. Required fees: $2523.40; $94.60 per credit hour. Tuition and fees vary according to course load and degree level. *Financial support:* Scholarships/grants, health care benefits, tuition waivers (full), and unspecified assistantships available. Financial award application deadline: 3/1; financial award applicants required to submit FAFSA. *Faculty research:* Nanoscience, ultra cold atoms, high energy physics. *Unit head:* Mike Santos, Director, 405-325-3961, Fax: 405-325-7557, E-mail: msantos@ou.edu. *Application contact:* Mike Santos, Director, 405-325-3961, Fax: 405-325-7557, E-mail: msantos@ou.edu.

University of Saskatchewan, College of Graduate Studies and Research, College of Arts and Sciences, Department of Physics and Engineering Physics, Saskatoon, SK S7N 5A2, Canada. Offers M Sc, PhD. *Degree requirements:* For master's, thesis; for doctorate, comprehensive exam (for some programs), thesis/dissertation. *Entrance requirements:* Additional exam requirements/recommendations for international students: Required—TOEFL (minimum score 80 iBT); Recommended—IELTS (minimum score 6.5). Electronic applications accepted.

University of Tulsa, Graduate School, College of Engineering and Natural Sciences, Department of Physics and Engineering Physics, Program in Engineering Physics, Tulsa, OK 74104-3189. Offers MS. Part-time programs available. *Students:* 2 full-time (0 women), 1 (woman) part-time, 2 international. Average age 26. 3 applicants, 100% accepted, 2 enrolled. *Degree requirements:* For master's, thesis. *Entrance requirements:* For master's, GRE General Test. Additional exam requirements/recommendations for international students: Required—TOEFL (minimum score 550 paper-based; 213 computer-based; 80 iBT), IELTS (minimum score 6). *Application deadline:* Applications are processed on a rolling basis. Application fee: $40.

Electronic applications accepted. *Expenses:* Tuition: Full-time $16,902; part-time $939 per credit hour. Required fees: $1020; $4 per credit hour. Tuition and fees vary according to course load. *Financial support:* In 2010–11, 3 students received support, including 2 research assistantships (averaging $5,951 per year), 2 teaching assistantships (averaging $8,956 per year); fellowships, career-related internships or fieldwork, Federal Work-Study, scholarships/grants, health care benefits, tuition waivers (full and partial), and unspecified assistantships also available. Support available to part-time students. *Faculty research:* Nanotechnology, theoretical plasma physics/fusion, condensed matter, laser spectroscopy, optics and optical applications for environmental applications. *Unit head:* Dr. George Miller, Advisor and Program Chair, 918-631-3021, Fax: 918-631-2995, E-mail: george-miller@utulsa.edu. *Application contact:* Dr. George Miller, Advisor and Program Chair, 918-631-3021, Fax: 918-631-2995, E-mail: george-miller@utulsa.edu.

University of Virginia, School of Engineering and Applied Science, Program in Engineering Physics, Charlottesville, VA 22903. Offers MEP, MS, PhD. Postbaccalaureate distance learning degree programs offered (no on-campus study). *Students:* 30 full-time (8 women); includes 2 Black or African American, non-Hispanic/Latino; 2 Asian, non-Hispanic/Latino, 7 international. Average age 28. 34 applicants, 21% accepted, 2 enrolled. In 2010, 1 master's, 1 doctorate awarded. *Degree requirements:* For master's, comprehensive exam; for doctorate, comprehensive exam, thesis/dissertation. *Entrance requirements:* For master's and doctorate, GRE General Test, 3 recommendations. Additional exam requirements/recommendations for international students: Required—TOEFL. *Application deadline:* For fall admission, 1/15 for domestic and international students. Applications are processed on a rolling basis. Application fee: $60. Electronic applications accepted. *Financial support:* Fellowships, research assistantships, teaching assistantships available. Financial award application deadline: 2/1; financial award applicants required to submit FAFSA. *Faculty research:* Continuum and rarefied gas dynamics, ultracentrifuge isotope enrichment, solid-state physics, atmospheric physics, atomic collisions. *Unit head:* Petra Reinke, Co-Chair, 434-924-7237, Fax: 434-982-5660, E-mail: pr6e@virginia.edu. *Application contact:* Kathryn C. Thornton, Assistant Dean for Graduate Programs, 434-924-3897, Fax: 434-982-2214, E-mail: seas-grad-admission@cs.virginia.edu.

University of Wisconsin–Madison, Graduate School, College of Engineering, Department of Engineering Physics, Madison, WI 53706-1380. Offers engineering mechanics (MS, PhD); nuclear engineering and engineering physics (MS, PhD). Part-time programs available. Postbaccalaureate distance learning degree programs offered (minimal on-campus study). Terminal master's awarded for partial completion of doctoral program. *Degree requirements:* For master's, thesis optional; for doctorate, thesis/dissertation. *Entrance requirements:* For master's and doctorate, GRE General Test, minimum GPA of 3.0 in last 60 hours, appropriate bachelor's degree. Additional exam requirements/recommendations for international students: Required—TOEFL (minimum score 600 paper-based; 245 computer-based). Electronic applications accepted. *Expenses:* Tuition, state resident: full-time $9887.36; part-time $617.96 per credit. Tuition, nonresident: full-time $24,054; part-time $1503.40 per credit. Required fees: $67.63 per credit. Tuition and fees vary according to reciprocity agreements. *Faculty research:* Fission reactor engineering and safety, plasma physics and fusion technology, plasma processing and ion implantation, nanotechnology, engineering mechanics and astronautics.

Yale University, Graduate School of Arts and Sciences, School of Engineering and Applied Science, Department of Applied Physics, New Haven, CT 06520. Offers MS, PhD. Terminal master's awarded for partial completion of doctoral program. *Degree requirements:* For doctorate, thesis/dissertation, area exam. *Entrance requirements:* For master's and doctorate, GRE General Test. Additional exam requirements/recommendations for international students: Required—TOEFL. *Faculty research:* Condensed-matter physics, optical physics, materials science.

Section 13
Geological, Mineral/Mining, and Petroleum Engineering

This section contains a directory of institutions offering graduate work in geological, mineral/mining, and petroleum engineering. Additional information about programs listed in the directory may be obtained by writing directly to the dean of a graduate school or chair of a department at the address given in the directory.

For programs offering related work, see also in this book *Chemical Engineering, Civil and Environmental Engineering, Electrical and Computer Engineering, Energy and Power Engineering, Engineering and Applied Sciences, Management of Engineering and Technology,* and *Materials Sciences and Engineering.* In another guide in this series:

Graduate Programs in the Physical Sciences, Mathematics, Agricultural Sciences, the Environment & Natural Resources
See *Geosciences* and *Marine Sciences and Oceanography*

CONTENTS

Program Directories

Geological Engineering

Arizona State University, College of Liberal Arts and Sciences, School of Earth and Space Exploration, Tempe, AZ 85287-1404. Offers astrophysics (MS, PhD); exploration systems design (PhD); geological sciences (MS, PhD). PhD in exploration systems design is offered in collaboration with the Fulton Schools of Engineering. *Faculty:* 43 full-time (4 women), 2 part-time/adjunct (1 woman). *Students:* 89 full-time (32 women), 16 part-time (8 women); includes 12 minority (2 American Indian or Alaska Native, non-Hispanic/Latino; 4 Asian, non-Hispanic/Latino; 6 Hispanic/Latino), 18 international. Average age 30. 181 applicants, 28% accepted, 28 enrolled. In 2010, 6 master's, 7 doctorates awarded. Terminal master's awarded for partial completion of doctoral program. *Degree requirements:* For master's, thesis, interactive Program of Study (iPOS) submitted before completing 50 percent of required credit hours; for doctorate, thesis/dissertation, interactive Program of Study (iPOS) submitted before completing 50 percent of required credit hours. *Entrance requirements:* For master's and doctorate, GRE, minimum GPA of 3.0 or equivalent in last 2 years of work leading to bachelor's degree. Additional exam requirements/recommendations for international students: Required—TOEFL, IELTS, or Pearson Test of English. *Application deadline:* For fall admission, 1/15 for domestic and international students; for spring admission, 10/1 for domestic and international students. Applications are processed on a rolling basis. Application fee: $70 ($90 for international students). Electronic applications accepted. *Expenses:* Tuition, state resident: full-time $8510; part-time $608 per credit. Tuition, nonresident: full-time $16,542; part-time $919 per credit. Required fees: $339; $110 per credit. Part-time tuition and fees vary according to course load. *Financial support:* In 2010–11, 52 research assistantships with full and partial tuition reimbursements (averaging $15,804 per year), 42 teaching assistantships with full and partial tuition reimbursements (averaging $15,169 per year) were awarded; fellowships with full tuition reimbursements, career-related internships or fieldwork, Federal Work-Study, institutionally sponsored loans, scholarships/grants, and tuition waivers (full and partial) also available. Financial award application deadline: 3/1; financial award applicants required to submit FAFSA. Total annual research expenditures: $18.8 million. *Unit head:* Dr. Kip Hodges, Director, 480-965-5331, Fax: 480-965-8102, E-mail: kvhodges@asu.edu. *Application contact:* Graduate Admissions, 480-965-6113.

Colorado School of Mines, Graduate School, Department of Geology and Geological Engineering, Golden, CO 80401. Offers geochemistry (MS, PMS, PhD); geological engineering (ME, MS, PhD); geology (MS, PhD). Part-time programs available. *Faculty:* 23 full-time (7 women), 4 part-time/adjunct (2 women). *Students:* 122 full-time (49 women), 24 part-time (9 women); includes 2 Black or African American, non-Hispanic/Latino; 3 American Indian or Alaska Native, non-Hispanic/Latino; 1 Asian, non-Hispanic/Latino; 3 Hispanic/Latino, 20 international. Average age 29. 206 applicants, 48% accepted, 44 enrolled. In 2010, 40 master's, 3 doctorates awarded. *Degree requirements:* For master's, thesis (for some programs); for doctorate, comprehensive exam, thesis/dissertation. *Entrance requirements:* For master's and doctorate, GRE General Test. Additional exam requirements/recommendations for international students: Required—TOEFL (minimum score 550 paper-based; 213 computer-based; 80 iBT). *Application deadline:* For fall admission, 1/15 for domestic and international students; for spring admission, 10/15 for domestic and international students. Application fee: $50 ($70 for international students). Electronic applications accepted. *Expenses:* Tuition, state resident: full-time $11,550; part-time $641 per credit. Tuition, nonresident: full-time $25,980; part-time $1444 per credit. Required fees: $1874; $937 per semester. *Financial support:* In 2010–11, 74 students received support, including 14 fellowships with full tuition reimbursements available (averaging $20,000 per year), 44 research assistantships with full tuition reimbursements available (averaging $20,000 per year), 16 teaching assistantships with full tuition reimbursements available (averaging $20,000 per year); scholarships/grants, health care benefits, and unspecified assistantships also available. Financial award application deadline: 1/15; financial award applicants required to submit FAFSA. *Faculty research:* Predictive sediment modeling, petrophysics, aquifer-contaminant flow modeling, water-rock interactions, geotechnical engineering. Total annual research expenditures: $3 million. *Unit head:* Dr. John Humphrey, Department Head, 303-273-3819, Fax: 303-273-3859, E-mail: jhumphre@mines.edu. *Application contact:* Dr. Christian Shorey, Lecturer, 303-273-3556, Fax: 303-273-3859, E-mail: cshorey@mines.edu.

Colorado School of Mines, Graduate School, Department of Geophysics, Golden, CO 80401. Offers geophysical engineering (ME, MS, PhD); geophysics (MS, PhD); mineral exploration and mining geosciences (PMS). Part-time programs available. *Faculty:* 16 full-time (1 woman), 4 part-time/adjunct (0 women). *Students:* 79 full-time (20 women), 5 part-time (3 women); includes 1 American Indian or Alaska Native, non-Hispanic/Latino; 2 Asian, non-Hispanic/Latino; 3 Hispanic/Latino, 48 international. Average age 30. 127 applicants, 33% accepted, 24 enrolled. In 2010, 13 master's, 6 doctorates awarded. *Degree requirements:* For master's, thesis (for some programs); for doctorate, one foreign language, comprehensive exam, thesis/dissertation, oral exams. *Entrance requirements:* For master's and doctorate, GRE General Test. Additional exam requirements/recommendations for international students: Required—TOEFL (minimum score 550 paper-based; 213 computer-based; 80 iBT). *Application deadline:* For fall admission, 1/15 for domestic and international students; for spring admission, 10/15 for domestic and international students. Application fee: $50 ($70 for international students). Electronic applications accepted. *Expenses:* Tuition, state resident: full-time $11,550; part-time $641 per credit. Tuition, nonresident: full-time $25,980; part-time $1444 per credit. Required fees: $1874; $937 per semester. *Financial support:* In 2010–11, 50 students received support, including 6 fellowships with full tuition reimbursements available (averaging $20,000 per year), 42 research assistantships with full tuition reimbursements available (averaging $20,000 per year), 2 teaching assistantships with full tuition reimbursements available (averaging $20,000 per year); scholarships/grants, health care benefits, and unspecified assistantships also available. Financial award application deadline: 1/15; financial award applicants required to submit FAFSA. *Faculty research:* Seismic exploration, gravity and geomagnetic fields, electrical mapping and sounding, bore hole measurements, environmental physics. Total annual research expenditures: $4.5 million. *Unit head:* Dr. Terence K. Young, Department Head, 303-273-3454, Fax: 303-273-3478, E-mail: tkyoung@mines.edu. *Application contact:* Michelle Szobody, Office Manager, 303-273-3935, Fax: 303-273-3478, E-mail: mszobody@mines.edu.

Michigan Technological University, Graduate School, College of Engineering, Department of Geological and Mining Engineering and Sciences, Program in Geological Engineering, Houghton, MI 49931. Offers MS, PhD. Part-time programs available. Terminal master's awarded for partial completion of doctoral program. *Degree requirements:* For master's, comprehensive exam; for doctorate, comprehensive exam, thesis/dissertation. *Entrance requirements:* Additional exam requirements/recommendations for international students: Required—TOEFL (minimum score 550 paper-based; 213 computer-based). Electronic applications accepted. *Expenses:* Contact institution.

Missouri University of Science and Technology, Graduate School, Department of Geological Sciences and Engineering, Rolla, MO 65409. Offers geological engineering (MS, DE, PhD); geology and geophysics (MS, PhD), including geochemistry, geology, geophysics, groundwater and environmental geology; petroleum engineering (MS, DE, PhD). Part-time programs available. *Degree requirements:* For master's, thesis optional; for doctorate, comprehensive exam, thesis/dissertation. *Entrance requirements:* For master's, GRE General Test (minimum score 600 quantitative, writing 3.5), minimum GPA of 3.0 in last 4 semesters; for doctorate, GRE General Test (minimum: Q 600, GRE WR 3.5). Additional exam requirements/recommendations for international students: Required—TOEFL. Electronic applications accepted. *Faculty research:* Digital image processing and geographic information systems, mineralogy, igneous and sedimentary petrology-geochemistry, sedimentology groundwater hydrology and contaminant transport.

Montana Tech of The University of Montana, Graduate School, Geosciences Programs, Butte, MT 59701-8997. Offers geochemistry (MS); geological engineering (MS); geology (MS); geophysical engineering (MS); hydrogeological engineering (MS); hydrogeology (MS). Part-time programs available. *Faculty:* 16 full-time (4 women), 4 part-time/adjunct (0 women). *Students:* 15 full-time (6 women), 10 part-time (5 women); includes 1 Black or African American, non-Hispanic/Latino; 1 American Indian or Alaska Native, non-Hispanic/Latino, 2 international. 9 applicants, 89% accepted, 8 enrolled. In 2010, 4 master's awarded. *Degree requirements:* For master's, comprehensive exam (for some programs), thesis (for some programs). *Entrance requirements:* For master's, GRE General Test, minimum GPA of 3.0. Additional exam requirements/recommendations for international students: Required—TOEFL (minimum score 525 paper-based; 195 computer-based; 71 iBT). *Application deadline:* For fall admission, 4/1 priority date for domestic students, 3/1 priority date for international students; for spring admission, 10/1 priority date for domestic students, 7/1 priority date for international students. Applications are processed on a rolling basis. Application fee: $30. Electronic applications accepted. *Expenses:* Tuition, state resident: full-time $5084. Tuition, nonresident: full-time $15,104. *Financial support:* In 2010–11, 17 students received support, including 10 teaching assistantships with partial tuition reimbursements available (averaging $5,200 per year); research assistantships with partial tuition reimbursements available, career-related internships or fieldwork, tuition waivers (full and partial), and unspecified assistantships also available. Financial award application deadline: 4/1; financial award applicants required to submit FAFSA. *Faculty research:* Water resource development, seismic processing, petroleum reservoir characterization, environmental geochemistry, geologic mapping. *Unit head:* Dr. Mary MacLaughlin, Department Head, 406-496-4655, Fax: 406-496-4260, E-mail: mmaclaughlin@mtech.edu. *Application contact:* Fred Sullivan, Administrator, Graduate School, 406-496-4304, Fax: 406-496-4710, E-mail: fsullivan@mtech.edu.

South Dakota School of Mines and Technology, Graduate Division, Department of Geology and Geological Engineering, Rapid City, SD 57701-3995. Offers geology and geological engineering (MS, PhD); paleontology (MS). Part-time programs available. *Degree requirements:* For master's, thesis; for doctorate, thesis/dissertation. *Entrance requirements:* For master's and doctorate, GRE General Test, GRE Subject Test. Additional exam requirements/recommendations for international students: Required—TOEFL, TWE. Electronic applications accepted. *Faculty research:* Contaminants in soil, nitrate leaching, environmental changes, fracture formations, greenhouse effect.

University of Alaska Anchorage, School of Engineering, Program in Arctic Engineering, Anchorage, AK 99508. Offers MS. Part-time and evening/weekend programs available. *Degree requirements:* For master's, thesis or alternative, engineering project report. *Entrance requirements:* For master's, bachelor's degree in engineering. Additional exam requirements/recommendations for international students: Required—TOEFL (minimum score 550 paper-based; 213 computer-based). *Faculty research:* Load-bearing ice, control of drifting snow, permafrost and foundations, frozen ground engineering.

University of Alaska Fairbanks, College of Engineering and Mines, Department of Mining and Geological Engineering, Fairbanks, AK 99775-5800. Offers geological engineering (MS, PhD); mineral preparation engineering (MS); mining engineering (MS, PhD). Part-time programs available. *Faculty:* 8 full-time (1 woman). *Students:* 11 full-time (2 women), 5 part-time (2 women); includes 2 minority (1 Asian, non-Hispanic/Latino; 1 Two or more races, non-Hispanic/Latino), 4 international. Average age 31. 10 applicants, 40% accepted, 3 enrolled.Terminal master's awarded for partial completion of doctoral program. *Degree requirements:* For master's, comprehensive exam, thesis or alternative; for doctorate, comprehensive exam, thesis/dissertation, oral exam, oral defense. *Entrance requirements:* For doctorate, GRE General Test. Additional exam requirements/recommendations for international students: Required—TOEFL (minimum score 550 paper-based; 213 computer-based; 80 iBT). *Application deadline:* For fall admission, 6/1 for domestic students, 3/1 for international students; for spring admission, 10/15 for domestic students, 9/1 for international students. Applications are processed on a rolling basis. Application fee: $60. Electronic applications accepted. *Expenses:* Tuition, state resident: full-time $5688; part-time $316 per credit. Tuition, nonresident: full-time $11,628; part-time $646 per credit. Required fees: $289 per semester. Tuition and fees vary according to course load and reciprocity agreements. *Financial support:* In 2010–11, 6 research assistantships with tuition reimbursements (averaging $13,677 per year), 4 teaching assistantships with tuition reimbursements (averaging $7,302 per year) were awarded; fellowships with tuition reimbursements, career-related internships or fieldwork, Federal Work-Study, scholarships/grants, health care benefits, and unspecified assistantships also available. Support available to part-time students. Financial award application deadline: 7/1; financial award applicants required to submit FAFSA. *Faculty research:* Underground mining in permafrost, testing of ultra clean diesel, slope stability, fractal and mathematical morphology, soil and rock mechanics. *Unit head:* Dr. Rajive Ganguli, Chair, 907-474-7388, Fax: 907-474-6635, E-mail: fyminge@uaf.edu. *Application contact:* Dr. Rajive Ganguli, Chair, 907-474-7388, Fax: 907-474-6635, E-mail: fyminge@uaf.edu.

The University of Arizona, College of Engineering, Department of Mining, Geological and Geophysical Engineering, Tucson, AZ 85721. Offers geological engineering (MS, PhD); mining engineering (M Eng, Certificate), including mine health and safety (Certificate), mine information and production technology (Certificate), mining engineering (M Eng), rock mechanics (Certificate). Part-time programs available. Postbaccalaureate distance learning degree programs offered (minimal on-campus study). *Faculty:* 7 full-time (0 women), 1 part-time/adjunct (0 women). *Students:* 17 full-time (1 woman), 7 part-time (1 woman); includes 1 minority (Asian, non-Hispanic/Latino), 11 international. Average age 36. 28 applicants, 32% accepted, 4 enrolled. In 2010, 5 master's, 2 doctorates awarded. *Degree requirements:* For master's, thesis; for doctorate, thesis/dissertation. *Entrance requirements:* For master's, GRE General Test, 3 letters of recommendation; for doctorate, GRE General Test, 3 letters of recommendation, statements of purpose. Additional exam requirements/recommendations for international students: Required—TOEFL (minimum score 550 paper-based; 213 computer-based; 79 iBT). *Application deadline:* For fall admission, 6/1 for domestic students, 12/1 for international students; for spring admission, 10/1 for domestic students, 6/1 for international students. Applications are processed on a rolling basis. Application fee: $75. *Expenses:* Tuition, state resident: full-time $7692. *Financial support:* In 2010–11, 16 research assistantships with full tuition reimbursements (averaging $25,063 per year), 1 teaching assistantship with full tuition reimbursement (averaging $23,586 per year) were awarded; institutionally sponsored loans, scholarships/grants, health care benefits, tuition waivers (partial), and unspecified assistantships also available. Financial award application deadline: 4/1. *Faculty research:* Geomechanics, mineral processing, information technology, automation, geosensing. Total annual research expenditures: $420,172. *Unit head:* Dr. Mary M. Poulton, Head, 520-621-6063, Fax: 520-621-8330, E-mail: mpoulton@u.arizona.edu. *Application contact:* Olivia Hanson, Graduate Advisor, 520-621-6063, Fax: 520-621-8330, E-mail: ohanson@engr.arizona.edu.

The University of British Columbia, Faculty of Science, Department of Earth and Ocean Sciences, Vancouver, BC V6T 1Z4, Canada. Offers atmospheric science (M Sc, PhD); geological engineering (M Eng, MA Sc, PhD); geological sciences (M Sc, PhD); geophysics (M Sc, MA Sc, PhD); oceanography (M Sc, PhD). *Degree requirements:* For master's, thesis (for some programs); for doctorate, comprehensive exam, thesis/dissertation. *Entrance requirements:* Additional exam requirements/recommendations for international students: Required—TOEFL (minimum score 600 paper-based; 250 computer-based; 100 iBT). Electronic applications accepted. Tuition charges are reported in Canadian dollars. *Expenses:* Tuition, area resident: Full-time $4179 Canadian dollars. International tuition: $7344 Canadian dollars full-time. *Faculty research:* Oceans and atmosphere, environmental earth science, hydro geology, mineral deposits, geophysics.

University of Hawaii at Manoa, Graduate Division, School of Ocean and Earth Science and Technology, Department of Geology and Geophysics, Honolulu, HI 96822. Offers high-pressure geophysics and geochemistry (MS, PhD); hydrogeology and engineering geology (MS, PhD); marine geology and geophysics (MS, PhD); planetary geosciences and remote sensing (MS, PhD); seismology and solid-earth geophysics (MS, PhD); volcanology, petrology, and geochemistry (MS, PhD). Part-time programs available. *Faculty:* 72 full-time (15 women), 6 part-time/adjunct (3 women). *Students:* 38 full-time (20 women), 5 part-time (3 women); includes 8 minority (1 Black or African American, non-Hispanic/Latino; 2 Asian, non-Hispanic/Latino; 1 Hispanic/Latino; 1 Native Hawaiian or other Pacific Islander, non-Hispanic/Latino; 3 Two or more races, non-Hispanic/Latino), 6 international. Average age 31. 64 applicants, 23% accepted, 7 enrolled. In 2010, 7 master's, 8 doctorates awarded. Terminal master's awarded for partial completion of doctoral program. *Degree requirements:* For master's, thesis optional; for doctorate, comprehensive exam, thesis/dissertation. *Entrance requirements:* For master's and doctorate, GRE General Test, minimum GPA of 3.0. Additional exam requirements/recommendations for international students: Required—TOEFL (minimum score 580 paper-based; 237 computer-based; 92 iBT), IELTS (minimum score 5). *Application deadline:* For fall admission, 1/15 for domestic students, 1/1 for international students; for spring admission, 9/1 for domestic students, 8/15 for international students. Application fee: $60. *Financial support:* In 2010–11, 7 fellowships (averaging $1,359 per year), 30 research assistantships (averaging $23,988 per year), 4 teaching assistantships (averaging $15,350 per year) were awarded. Total annual research expenditures: $3.8 million. *Application contact:* Dr. Gregory Moore, Chair, 808-956-7640, Fax: 808-956-5512, E-mail: gg-dept@soest.hawaii.edu.

University of Idaho, College of Graduate Studies, College of Engineering, Department of Civil Engineering, Program in Geological Engineering, Moscow, ID 83844-2282. Offers MS. *Students:* 8 part-time. Average age 39. In 2010, 1 master's awarded. *Degree requirements:* For master's, one foreign language, thesis. *Entrance requirements:* For master's, minimum GPA of 2.8. *Application deadline:* For fall admission, 8/1 for domestic students; for spring admission, 12/15 for domestic students. Applications are processed on a rolling basis. Application fee: $60. Electronic applications accepted. *Expenses:* Tuition, nonresident: part-time $580 per credit. Required fees: $306 per credit. *Financial support:* Applicants required to submit FAFSA. *Faculty research:* Slope stability and landslide mitigation, erosion and sediment control for construction sites, rock engineering and rock reinforcement, underground natural gas storage. *Unit head:* Dr. Richard Nielsen, Chair, 208-885-6782. *Application contact:* Dr. Richard Nielsen, Chair, 208-885-6782.

University of Minnesota, Twin Cities Campus, Institute of Technology, Department of Civil Engineering, Minneapolis, MN 55455-0213. Offers civil engineering (MCE, MS, PhD); geological engineering (M Geo E, MS, PhD). Part-time programs available. *Degree requirements:* For master's, thesis optional; for doctorate, thesis/dissertation. *Entrance requirements:* For master's and doctorate, GRE General Test. Additional exam requirements/recommendations for international students: Required—TOEFL. *Faculty research:* Environmental engineering, rock mechanics, water resources, structural engineering, transportation.

University of Nevada, Reno, Graduate School, College of Science, Mackay School of Earth Sciences and Engineering, Department of Geological Sciences, Program in Geological Engineering, Reno, NV 89557. Offers MS, PhD. Terminal master's awarded for partial completion of doctoral program. *Degree requirements:* For master's, thesis optional; for doctorate, thesis/dissertation. *Entrance requirements:* For master's and doctorate, GRE General Test, minimum GPA of 2.75. Additional exam requirements/recommendations for international students: Required—TOEFL (minimum score 500 paper-based; 173 computer-based; 61 iBT), IELTS (minimum score 6). Electronic applications accepted. *Expenses:* Tuition, state resident: full-time $2219; part-time $246 per credit. Tuition, nonresident: part-time $510 per credit. International tuition: $9009 full-time. Required fees: $59 per term. One-time fee: $101. Tuition and fees vary according to course load. *Faculty research:* Reclamation, remediation, restoration.

University of North Dakota, Graduate School, School of Engineering and Mines, Department of Geological Engineering, Grand Forks, ND 58202. Offers M Engr, MS. *Faculty:* 4 full-time (0 women), 2 part-time/adjunct (0 women). *Students:* 2 full-time (0 women). Average age 23. 4 applicants, 25% accepted, 1 enrolled. *Degree requirements:* For master's, thesis. *Entrance requirements:* For master's, GRE General Test. Additional exam requirements/recommendations for international students: Required—TOEFL (minimum score 550 paper-based; 213 computer-based; 79 iBT), IELTS (minimum score 6.5). *Application deadline:* For fall admission, 8/1 priority date for domestic and international students; for spring admission, 12/1 priority date for domestic and international students. Applications are processed on a rolling basis. Application fee: $35. Electronic applications accepted. *Expenses:* Tuition, state resident: full-time $5857; part-time $306.74 per credit. Tuition, nonresident: full-time $15,666; part-time $729.77 per credit. Required fees: $53.42 per credit. Tuition and fees vary according to course load, program and reciprocity agreements. *Financial support:* In 2010–11, 1 student received support, including 1 research assistantship with full and partial tuition reimbursement available (averaging $9,635 per year), teaching assistantships with full and partial tuition reimbursements available (averaging $9,635 per year); fellowships with full and partial tuition reimbursements available, Federal Work-Study, scholarships/grants, health care benefits, tuition waivers (full and partial), and unspecified assistantships also available. Support available to part-time students. Financial award applicants required to submit FAFSA. Total annual research expenditures: $1.7 million. *Unit head:* Dr. Scott Korom, Graduate Director, 701-777-6156, E-mail: scottkorom@mail.nodak.edu. *Application contact:* Staci Wells, Admissions Associate, 701-777-2945, Fax: 701-777-3619, E-mail: staci.wells@gradschool.und.edu.

University of Oklahoma, College of Earth and Energy, School of Petroleum and Geological Engineering, Program in Geological Engineering, Norman, OK 73019-0390. Offers MS, PhD. Part-time programs available. *Students:* 2 full-time (both women), 1 part-time (0 women), all international. Average age 23. 1 applicant, 0% accepted, 0 enrolled. *Entrance requirements:* Additional exam requirements/recommendations for international students: Required—TOEFL (minimum score 550 paper-based; 213 computer-based; 79 iBT). *Application deadline:* For fall admission, 6/1 for domestic students, 4/1 for international students; for spring admission, 11/1 for domestic students, 9/1 for international students. Applications are processed on a rolling basis. Application fee: $40 ($90 for international students). Electronic applications accepted. *Expenses:* Tuition, state resident: full-time $3892.80; part-time $162.20 per credit hour. Tuition, nonresident: full-time $14,167; part-time $590.30 per credit hour. Required fees: $2523.40; $94.60 per credit hour. Tuition and fees vary according to course load and degree level. *Financial support:* Traineeships available. *Faculty research:* Hydraulic fracturing, geothermal energy. *Unit head:* Dr. Chandra Rai, Director, 405-325-2921, Fax: 405-325-7477, E-mail: crai@ou.edu. *Application contact:* Shalli Young, Executive Assistant to Graduate Liaison, 405-325-2921, Fax: 405-325-7477, E-mail: syoung@ou.edu.

University of Utah, Graduate School, College of Mines and Earth Sciences, Department of Geology and Geophysics, Salt Lake City, UT 84112. Offers environmental engineering (ME, MS, PhD); geological engineering (ME, MS, PhD); geology (MS, PhD); geophysics (MS, PhD). *Faculty:* 21 full-time (4 women), 4 part-time/adjunct (1 woman). *Students:* 51 full-time (13 women), 19 part-time (6 women); includes 1 minority (Hispanic/Latino), 15 international. Average age 30. 128 applicants, 27% accepted, 23 enrolled. In 2010, 10 master's, 8 doctorates awarded. Terminal master's awarded for partial completion of doctoral program. *Degree requirements:* For master's, comprehensive exam, thesis; for doctorate, thesis/dissertation, qualifying exam (written and oral). *Entrance requirements:* For master's and doctorate, GRE General Test, minimum GPA of 3.25. Additional exam requirements/recommendations for international students: Required—TOEFL (minimum score 500 paper-based; 173 computer-based). *Application deadline:* For fall admission, 1/15 priority date for domestic and international students. Applications are processed on a rolling basis. Application fee: $55 ($65 for international students). Electronic applications accepted. *Expenses:* Tuition, area resident: Part-time $179.19 per credit hour. Tuition, state resident: full-time $4384. Tuition, nonresident: full-time $16,684; part-time $630.67 per credit hour. Required fees: $350 per semester. Tuition and fees vary according to course load, degree level and program. *Financial support:* In 2010–11, 22 students received support, including 11 fellowships with full tuition reimbursements available (averaging $13,450 per year), 45 research assistantships with full tuition reimbursements available (averaging $21,858 per year), 11 teaching assistantships with full tuition reimbursements available (averaging $13,450 per year); career-related internships or fieldwork, institutionally sponsored loans, scholarships/grants, unspecified assistantships, and stipends also available. Financial award application deadline: 1/15; financial award applicants required to submit FAFSA. *Faculty research:* Igneous, metamorphic, and sedimentary petrology; ore deposits; aqueous geochemistry; isotope geochemistry; heat flow. Total annual research expenditures: $2.2 million. *Unit head:* Dr. Kip Solomon, Chair, 801-581-7231, Fax: 801-581-7065, E-mail: kip.solomon@utah.edu. *Application contact:* Dr. Allan A. Ekdale, Director of Graduate Studies, 801-581-7266, Fax: 801-581-7065, E-mail: a.ekdale@utah.edu.

University of Wisconsin–Madison, Graduate School, College of Engineering, Geological Engineering Program, Madison, WI 53706-1380. Offers MS, PhD. Part-time programs available. *Faculty:* 17 full-time (3 women). *Students:* 11 full-time (3 women), 4 part-time (0 women); includes 1 Hispanic/Latino. Average age 25. 15 applicants, 147% accepted, 2 enrolled. In 2010, 1 master's, 1 doctorate awarded. *Degree requirements:* For doctorate, thesis/dissertation. *Entrance requirements:* For master's and doctorate, GRE. Additional exam requirements/recommendations for international students: Required—TOEFL (minimum score 550 paper-based; 213 computer-based; 80 iBT). *Application deadline:* For fall admission, 3/15 priority date for domestic and international students; for spring admission, 10/15 priority date for domestic and international students. Applications are processed on a rolling basis. Application fee: $56. Electronic applications accepted. *Expenses:* Tuition, state resident: full-time $9887.36; part-time $617.96 per credit. Tuition, nonresident: full-time $24,054; part-time $1503.40 per credit. Required fees: $67.63 per credit. Tuition and fees vary according to reciprocity agreements. *Financial support:* In 2010–11, 9 students received support, including fellowships with full tuition reimbursements available (averaging $22,224 per year), 12 research assistantships with full tuition reimbursements available (averaging $40,368 per year), 1 teaching assistantship with full tuition reimbursement available (averaging $28,175 per year); Federal Work-Study, scholarships/grants, and unspecified assistantships also available. Support available to part-time students. Financial award application deadline: 1/2. *Faculty research:* Constitute models for geomaterials, rock fracture, in situ stress determination, environmental geotechnics, site remediation. Total annual research expenditures: $1.2 million. *Unit head:* Craig H. Benson, Chair, 608-262-3491, Fax: 608-263-2453, E-mail: benson@engr.wisc.edu. *Application contact:* Cheryl Loschko, Program Coordinator, 608-265-5570, Fax: 608-890-1174, E-mail: loschko@wisc.edu.

Mineral/Mining Engineering

Colorado School of Mines, Graduate School, Department of Geophysics, Golden, CO 80401. Offers geophysical engineering (ME, MS, PhD); geophysics (MS, PhD); mineral exploration and mining geosciences (PMS). Part-time programs available. *Faculty:* 16 full-time (1 woman), 4 part-time/adjunct (0 women). *Students:* 79 full-time (20 women), 5 part-time (3 women); includes 1 American Indian or Alaska Native, non-Hispanic/Latino; 2 Asian, non-Hispanic/Latino; 3 Hispanic/Latino, 48 international. Average age 30. 127 applicants, 33% accepted, 24 enrolled. In 2010, 13 master's, 6 doctorates awarded. *Degree requirements:* For master's, thesis (for some programs); for doctorate, one foreign language, comprehensive exam, thesis/dissertation, oral exams. *Entrance requirements:* For master's and doctorate, GRE General Test. Additional exam requirements/recommendations for international students: Required—TOEFL (minimum score 550 paper-based; 213 computer-based; 80 iBT). *Application deadline:* For fall admission, 1/15 for domestic and international students, for spring admission, 10/15 for domestic and international students. Application fee: $50 ($70 for international students). Electronic applications accepted. *Expenses:* Tuition, state resident: full-time $11,550; part-time $641 per credit. Tuition, nonresident: full-time $25,980; part-time $1444 per credit. Required fees: $1874; $937 per semester. *Financial support:* In 2010–11, 50 students received support, including 6 fellowships with full tuition reimbursements available (averaging $20,000 per year), 42 research assistantships with full tuition reimbursements available (averaging $20,000 per year), 2 teaching assistantships with full tuition reimbursements available (averaging $20,000 per year); scholarships/grants, health care benefits, and unspecified assistantships also available. Financial award application deadline: 1/15; financial award applicants required to submit FAFSA. *Faculty research:* Seismic exploration, gravity and geomagnetic fields, electrical mapping and sounding, bore hole measurements, environmental physics. Total annual research expenditures: $4.5 million. *Unit head:* Dr. Terence K. Young, Department Head, 303-273-3454, Fax: 303-273-3478, E-mail: tkyoung@mines.edu. *Application contact:* Michelle Szobody, Office Manager, 303-273-3935, Fax: 303-273-3478, E-mail: mszobody@mines.edu.

Colorado School of Mines, Graduate School, Department of Mining Engineering, Golden, CO 80401. Offers engineer of mines (ME); mining and earth systems engineering (MS); mining engineering (PhD). Part-time programs available. *Faculty:* 9 full-time (0 women), 5 part-time/adjunct (0 women). *Students:* 18 full-time (3 women), 7 part-time (0 women); includes 1 Black or African American, non-Hispanic/Latino; 1 Asian, non-Hispanic/Latino; 1 Hispanic/Latino, 11 international. Average age 27. 40 applicants, 83% accepted, 7 enrolled. In 2010, 8 master's awarded. *Degree requirements:* For master's, thesis (for some programs); for doctorate, one foreign language, comprehensive exam, thesis/dissertation. *Entrance requirements:* For master's and doctorate, GRE General Test. Additional exam requirements/recommendations for international students: Required—TOEFL (minimum score 550 paper-based; 213 computer-based; 80 iBT). *Application deadline:* For fall admission, 1/15 priority date for domestic and international students; for spring admission, 10/15 priority date for domestic and international students. Application fee: $50 ($70 for international students). Electronic applications accepted. *Expenses:* Tuition, state resident: full-time $11,550; part-time $641 per credit. Tuition, nonresident: full-time $25,980; part-time $1444 per credit. Required fees: $1874; $937 per semester. *Financial support:* In 2010–11, 14 students received support, including 2 fellowships with full tuition reimbursements available (averaging $20,000 per year), 6 research assistantships with full tuition reimbursements available (averaging $20,000 per year), 6 teaching assistantships with full tuition reimbursements available (averaging $20,000 per year); scholarships/grants, health care benefits, and unspecified assistantships also available. Financial award application deadline: 1/15; financial award applicants required to submit FAFSA. *Faculty research:* Mine evaluation and planning, geostatistics, mining robotics, water jet cutting, rock mechanics. Total annual research expenditures: $735,884. *Unit head:* Dr. Kadri Dagdelen, Department Head, 303-273-3711, Fax: 303-273-3719, E-mail: kdagdele@mines.edu. *Application contact:* Christine Monroe, Administrative Assistant, 303-273-3992, Fax: 303-273-3719, E-mail: cmonroe@mines.edu.

Columbia University, Fu Foundation School of Engineering and Applied Science, Department of Earth and Environmental Engineering, New York, NY 10027. Offers earth and environmental engineering (MS, Eng Sc D, PhD); metallurgical engineering (Engr); mining engineering (Engr); MS/MBA. Part-time programs available. Postbaccalaureate distance learning degree programs

Mineral/Mining Engineering

Columbia University (continued)
offered (minimal on-campus study). *Faculty:* 12 full-time (1 woman), 6 part-time/adjunct (0 women). *Students:* 47 full-time (18 women), 14 part-time (9 women); includes 5 minority (1 American Indian or Alaska Native, non-Hispanic/Latino; 2 Asian, non-Hispanic/Latino; 1 Hispanic/ Latino; 1 Two or more races, non-Hispanic/Latino), 30 international. Average age 29. 192 applicants, 14% accepted, 12 enrolled. In 2010, 28 master's, 8 doctorates awarded. Terminal master's awarded for partial completion of doctoral program. *Degree requirements:* For master's, thesis; for doctorate, thesis/dissertation, qualifying exam. *Entrance requirements:* For master's, doctorate, and Engr, GRE General Test. Additional exam requirements/recommendations for international students: Required—TOEFL, IELTS. *Application deadline:* For fall admission, 12/1 priority date for domestic and international students; for spring admission, 10/1 priority date for domestic and international students. Application fee: $95. Electronic applications accepted. *Financial support:* In 2010–11, 39 students received support, including 6 fellowships with full and partial tuition reimbursements available (averaging $16,478 per year), 26 research assistantships with full tuition reimbursements available (averaging $27,733 per year), 7 teaching assistantships with full tuition reimbursements available (averaging $22,500 per year); health care benefits and unspecified assistantships also available. Financial award application deadline: 12/1; financial award applicants required to submit FAFSA. *Faculty research:* Sustainable energy and materials, waste to energy, water resources and climate risks, environmental health engineering, life cycle analysis. *Unit head:* Dr. Klaus S. Lackner, Maurice Ewing and J. Lamar Worzel Professor of Geophysics and Department Chairman, 212-854-0304, Fax: 212-854-7081, E-mail: kl2010@columbia.edu. *Application contact:* Gary Hill, Administrative Assistant, 212-854-2905, Fax: 212-854-7081, E-mail: gh2206@columbia.edu.

Dalhousie University, Faculty of Engineering, Department of Mineral Resource Engineering, Halifax, NS B3J 1Z1, Canada. Offers mineral resource engineering (M Eng, MA Sc, PhD). *Degree requirements:* For master's, thesis; for doctorate, thesis/dissertation. *Entrance requirements:* Additional exam requirements/recommendations for international students: Required—TOEFL, IELTS, CANTEST, CAEL, or Michigan English Language Assessment Battery. Electronic applications accepted. *Faculty research:* Mining technology, environmental impact, petroleum engineering, mine waste management, rock mechanics.

Laurentian University, School of Graduate Studies and Research, Programme in Geology (Earth Sciences), Sudbury, ON P3E 2C6, Canada. Offers geology (M Sc); mineral deposits and precambrian geology (PhD); mineral exploration (M Sc). Part-time programs available. *Degree requirements:* For master's, thesis. *Entrance requirements:* For master's, honors degree with second class or better. *Faculty research:* Localization and metallogenesis of Ni-Cu-(PGE) sulfide mineralization in the Thompson Nickel Belt, mapping lithology and ore-grade and monitoring dissolved organic carbon in lakes using remote sensing, global reefs, volcanic effects on VMS deposits.

Laurentian University, School of Graduate Studies and Research, School of Engineering, Sudbury, ON P3E 2C6, Canada. Offers mineral resources engineering (M Eng, MA Sc); natural resources engineering (PhD). Part-time programs available. *Faculty research:* Mining engineering, rock mechanics (tunneling, rockbursts, rock support), metallurgy (mineral processing, hydro and pyrometallurgy), simulations and remote mining, simulations and scheduling.

McGill University, Faculty of Graduate and Postdoctoral Studies, Faculty of Engineering, Department of Mining and Materials Engineering, Montréal, QC H3A 2T5, Canada. Offers materials engineering (M Eng, PhD); mining engineering (M Eng, M Sc, PhD, Diploma).

Michigan Technological University, Graduate School, College of Engineering, Department of Geological and Mining Engineering and Sciences, Program in Mining Engineering, Houghton, MI 49931. Offers MS, PhD. Part-time programs available. Terminal master's awarded for partial completion of doctoral program. *Degree requirements:* For master's, comprehensive exam; for doctorate, comprehensive exam, thesis/dissertation. *Entrance requirements:* Additional exam requirements/recommendations for international students: Required—TOEFL (minimum score 550 paper-based; 213 computer-based). Electronic applications accepted. *Expenses:* Contact institution.

Missouri University of Science and Technology, Graduate School, Department of Mining and Nuclear Engineering, Rolla, MO 65409. Offers mining engineering (MS, DE, PhD); nuclear engineering (MS, DE, PhD). *Degree requirements:* For master's, thesis optional; for doctorate, comprehensive exam. *Entrance requirements:* For master's, GRE (minimum score 600 quantitative, 3 writing); for doctorate, GRE (minimum score: quantitative 600, writing 3.5). Additional exam requirements/recommendations for international students: Required—TOEFL (minimum score 550 paper-based; 213 computer-based). *Faculty research:* Mine health and safety, nuclear radiation transport, modeling of mining operations, radiation effects, blasting.

Montana Tech of The University of Montana, Graduate School, Metallurgical/Mineral Processing Engineering Programs, Butte, MT 59701-8997. Offers MS. Part-time programs available. *Faculty:* 6 full-time (0 women). *Students:* 5 full-time (3 women), 2 part-time (0 women). 3 applicants, 67% accepted, 2 enrolled. In 2010, 2 master's awarded. *Degree requirements:* For master's, comprehensive exam (for some programs), thesis optional. *Entrance requirements:* For master's, GRE General Test, minimum GPA of 3.0. Additional exam requirements/recommendations for international students: Required—TOEFL (minimum score 525 paper-based; 195 computer-based; 71 iBT). *Application deadline:* For fall admission, 4/1 priority date for domestic students, 3/1 priority date for international students; for spring admission, 10/1 priority date for domestic students, 7/1 priority date for international students. Applications are processed on a rolling basis. Application fee: $30. Electronic applications accepted. *Expenses:* Tuition, state resident: full-time $5084. Tuition, nonresident: full-time $15,104. *Financial support:* In 2010–11, 5 students received support, including 5 teaching assistantships with partial tuition reimbursements available (averaging $5,000 per year); research assistantships with partial tuition reimbursements available, career-related internships or fieldwork, tuition waivers (full and partial), and unspecified assistantships also available. Financial award application deadline: 4/1; financial award applicants required to submit FAFSA. *Faculty research:* Stabilizing hazardous waste, decontamination of metals by melt refining, ultraviolet enhancement of stabilization reactions, extractive metallurgy, fuel cells. *Unit head:* Dr. Courtney Young, Department Head, 406-496-4158, Fax: 406-496-4664, E-mail: cyoung@mtech.edu. *Application contact:* Fred Sullivan, Administrator, Graduate School, 406-496-4304, Fax: 406-496-4710, E-mail: fsullivan@mtech.edu.

Montana Tech of The University of Montana, Graduate School, Mining Engineering Program, Butte, MT 59701-8997. Offers MS. Part-time programs available. *Faculty:* 4 full-time (0 women). *Students:* 3 full-time (0 women), 1 part-time (0 women); includes 1 American Indian or Alaska Native, non-Hispanic/Latino. 5 applicants, 20% accepted, 1 enrolled. *Degree requirements:* For master's, thesis optional. *Entrance requirements:* For master's, minimum GPA of 3.0. Additional exam requirements/recommendations for international students: Required—TOEFL (minimum score 525 paper-based; 195 computer-based; 71 iBT). *Application deadline:* For fall admission, 4/1 priority date for domestic students, 3/1 priority date for international students; for spring admission, 10/1 priority date for domestic students, 7/1 priority date for international students. Applications are processed on a rolling basis. Application fee: $30. Electronic applications accepted. *Expenses:* Tuition, state resident: full-time $5084. Tuition, nonresident: full-time $15,104. *Financial support:* In 2010–11, 2 students received support, including 2 teaching assistantships with partial tuition reimbursements available (averaging $4,000 per year); research assistantships, career-related internships or fieldwork, tuition waivers (full and partial), and unspecified assistantships also available. Financial award application deadline: 4/1; financial award applicants required to submit FAFSA. *Faculty research:* Geostatistics, geomechanics, mine planning, economic models, equipment selection. *Unit head:* Dr. David Armstrong, Department Head, 406-496-4867, Fax: 406-496-4260, E-mail: darmstrong@mtech.edu. *Application contact:* Fred Sullivan, Administrator, Graduate School, 406-496-4304, Fax: 406-496-4710, E-mail: fsullivan@mtech.edu.

New Mexico Institute of Mining and Technology, Graduate Studies, Department of Mining and Mineral Engineering, Socorro, NM 87801. Offers MS. *Degree requirements:* For master's, thesis. *Entrance requirements:* Additional exam requirements/recommendations for international students: Required—TOEFL (minimum score 540 paper-based; 207 computer-based). *Faculty research:* Drilling and blasting, geological engineering, mine design, applied mineral exploration, rock mechanics.

Penn State University Park, Graduate School, College of Earth and Mineral Sciences, Department of Energy and Mineral Engineering, State College, University Park, PA 16802-1503. Offers MS, PhD.

Queen's University at Kingston, School of Graduate Studies and Research, Faculty of Applied Science, Department of Mining Engineering, Kingston, ON K7L 3N6, Canada. Offers M Eng, M Sc, M Sc Eng, PhD. Part-time programs available. *Degree requirements:* For master's, thesis optional; for doctorate, comprehensive exam, thesis/dissertation. *Entrance requirements:* Additional exam requirements/recommendations for international students: Required—TOEFL (minimum score 550 paper-based; 213 computer-based). Electronic applications accepted. *Faculty research:* Rock mechanics, drilling, ventilation/environmental control, gold extraction.

Southern Illinois University Carbondale, Graduate School, College of Engineering, Department of Mining and Mineral Resources Engineering, Carbondale, IL 62901-4701. Offers mining engineering (MS). *Degree requirements:* For master's, comprehensive exam, thesis. *Entrance requirements:* For master's, minimum GPA of 2.7. Additional exam requirements/ recommendations for international students: Required—TOEFL. *Faculty research:* Rock mechanics and ground control, mine subsidence, mine systems analysis, fine coal cleaning, surface mine reclamation.

Université du Québec en Abitibi-Témiscamingue, Graduate Programs, Program in Engineering, Rouyn-Noranda, QC J9X 5E4, Canada. Offers engineering (ME); mineral engineering (ME); mining engineering (DESS).

Université Laval, Faculty of Sciences and Engineering, Department of Mining, Metallurgical and Materials Engineering, Programs in Mining Engineering, Québec, QC G1K 7P4, Canada. Offers M Sc, PhD. Terminal master's awarded for partial completion of doctoral program. *Degree requirements:* For master's, thesis; for doctorate, comprehensive exam, thesis/ dissertation. *Entrance requirements:* For master's and doctorate, knowledge of French and English. Electronic applications accepted.

University of Alaska Fairbanks, College of Engineering and Mines, Department of Mining and Geological Engineering, Program in Mineral Preparation Engineering, Fairbanks, AK 99775. Offers MS. Part-time programs available. *Students:* 1 part-time (0 women). Average age 39. *Degree requirements:* For master's, comprehensive exam, thesis or alternative. *Entrance requirements:* For master's, GRE General Test. Additional exam requirements/ recommendations for international students: Required—TOEFL (minimum score 550 paper-based; 213 computer-based; 80 iBT). *Application deadline:* For fall admission, 6/1 for domestic students, 3/1 for international students; for spring admission, 10/15 for domestic students, 9/1 for international students. Applications are processed on a rolling basis. Application fee: $60. Electronic applications accepted. *Expenses:* Tuition, state resident: full-time $5688; part-time $316 per credit. Tuition, nonresident: full-time $11,628; part-time $646 per credit. Required fees: $289 per semester. Tuition and fees vary according to course load and reciprocity agreements. *Financial support:* Fellowships, research assistantships, teaching assistantships, career-related internships or fieldwork, Federal Work-Study, scholarships/grants, health care benefits, and unspecified assistantships available. Support available to part-time students. Financial award application deadline: 7/1; financial award applicants required to submit FAFSA. *Faculty research:* Washability of coal, microbial mining, mineral leaching, pollution control technology, concentration of target minerals. *Unit head:* Dr. Rajive Ganguli, Department Chair, 907-474-7388, Fax: 907-474-6635, E-mail: fyminge@uaf.edu. *Application contact:* Dr. Rajive Ganguli, Department Chair, 907-474-7388, Fax: 907-474-6635, E-mail: fyminge@uaf.edu.

University of Alberta, Faculty of Graduate Studies and Research, Department of Civil and Environmental Engineering, Edmonton, AB T6G 2E1, Canada. Offers construction engineering and management (M Eng, M Sc, PhD); environmental engineering (M Eng, M Sc, PhD); environmental science (M Sc, PhD); geoenvironmental engineering (M Eng, M Sc, PhD); geotechnical engineering (M Eng, M Sc, PhD); mining engineering (M Eng, M Sc, PhD); petroleum engineering (M Eng, M Sc, PhD); structural engineering (M Eng, M Sc, PhD); water resources (M Eng, M Sc, PhD). Part-time programs available. Postbaccalaureate distance learning degree programs offered (minimal on-campus study). *Degree requirements:* For master's, thesis (for some programs); for doctorate, thesis/dissertation. *Entrance requirements:* For master's, minimum GPA of 3.0 in last 2 years of undergraduate studies; for doctorate, minimum GPA of 3.0. Additional exam requirements/recommendations for international students: Required—TOEFL (minimum score 550 paper-based; 213 computer-based). Electronic applications accepted. *Faculty research:* Mining.

The University of Arizona, College of Engineering, Department of Mining, Geological and Geophysical Engineering, Program in Mining Engineering, Tucson, AZ 85721. Offers mine health and safety (Certificate); mine information and production technology (Certificate); mining engineering (M Eng); rock mechanics (Certificate). Part-time programs available. Postbaccalaureate distance learning degree programs offered (minimal on-campus study). *Students:* 1 part-time (0 women), all international. Average age 40. *Degree requirements:* For master's, thesis. *Entrance requirements:* For master's, GRE General Test, 3 letters of recommendation, statement of purpose. Additional exam requirements/recommendations for international students: Required—TOEFL (minimum score 550 paper-based; 213 computer-based; 79 iBT). *Application deadline:* For fall admission, 6/1 for domestic students, 12/1 for international students; for spring admission, 10/1 for domestic students, 6/1 for international students. Applications are processed on a rolling basis. Application fee: $75. Electronic applications accepted. *Expenses:* Tuition, state resident: full-time $7692. *Financial support:* Institutionally sponsored loans, scholarships/grants, health care benefits, tuition waivers (partial), and unspecified assistantships available. Financial award application deadline: 4/1. *Faculty research:* Mine system design, in-site leaching, fluid flow in rocks, geostatistics, rock mechanics. *Unit head:* Dr. Mary M. Poulton, Head, 520-621-6063, Fax: 520-621-8330, E-mail: mpoulton@u.arizona.edu. *Application contact:* Olivia Hanson, Graduate Advisor, 520-621-6063, Fax: 520-621-8330, E-mail: ohanson@engr.arizona.edu.

The University of British Columbia, Faculty of Applied Science, Program in Mining Engineering, Vancouver, BC V6T 1Z4, Canada. Offers M Eng, MA Sc, PhD. *Degree requirements:* For master's, thesis; for doctorate, thesis/dissertation. *Entrance requirements:* Additional exam requirements/recommendations for international students: Required—TOEFL (minimum score 213 computer-based; 80 iBT), IELTS. Tuition charges are reported in Canadian dollars. *Expenses:* Tuition, area resident: Full-time $4179 Canadian dollars. International tuition: $7344 Canadian dollars full-time. *Faculty research:* Advanced mining methods and automation, rock mechanics, mine economics, operations research, mine waste management, environmental aspects of mining, process control, fine particle processing, surface chemistry.

University of Idaho, College of Graduate Studies, College of Engineering, Department of Chemical and Materials Engineering, Program in Materials Science and Engineering, Moscow, ID 83844-2282. Offers materials science and engineering (MS, PhD); metallurgical engineering (MS); mining engineering (PhD). *Students:* 8 full-time. Average age 30. In 2010, 2 master's, 1 doctorate awarded. *Application deadline:* Applications are processed on a rolling basis. Application fee: $60. Electronic applications accepted. *Expenses:* Tuition, nonresident: part-time $580 per credit. Required fees: $306 per credit. *Financial support:* Applicants required to submit FAFSA. *Unit head:* Dr. Wudneh Admassu, Chair, 208-885-6376. *Application contact:* Dr. Wudneh Admassu, Chair, 208-885-6376.

University of Kentucky, Graduate School, College of Engineering, Program in Mining Engineering, Lexington, KY 40506-0032. Offers MME, MS Min, PhD. *Degree requirements:*

For master's, comprehensive exam, thesis optional; for doctorate, one foreign language, comprehensive exam, thesis/dissertation. *Entrance requirements:* For master's, GRE General Test, minimum undergraduate GPA of 2.75; for doctorate, GRE General Test, minimum undergraduate GPA of 3.0. Additional exam requirements/recommendations for international students: Required—TOEFL (minimum score 550 paper-based; 213 computer-based). Electronic applications accepted. *Faculty research:* Benefication of fine and ultrafine particles, operation research in mining and mineral processing, land reclamation.

University of Nevada, Reno, Graduate School, College of Science, Mackay School of Earth Sciences and Engineering, Department of Mining Engineering, Reno, NV 89557. Offers MS. *Degree requirements:* For master's, thesis optional. *Entrance requirements:* For master's, GRE, minimum GPA of 2.75. Additional exam requirements/recommendations for international students: Required—TOEFL (minimum score 500 paper-based; 173 computer-based; 61 iBT), IELTS (minimum score 6). Electronic applications accepted. *Expenses:* Tuition, state resident: full-time $2219; part-time $246 per credit. Tuition, nonresident: part-time $510 per credit. International tuition: $9009 full-time. Required fees: $59 per term. One-time fee: $101. Tuition and fees vary according to course load. *Faculty research:* Mine ventilation, rock mechanics, mine design.

University of North Dakota, Graduate School, School of Engineering and Mines, Department of Civil Engineering, Grand Forks, ND 58202. Offers civil engineering (M Engr); sanitary engineering (M Engr), including soils and structures engineering, surface mining engineering. Part-time programs available. *Faculty:* 6 full-time (0 women). *Students:* 7 full-time (0 women), 4 part-time (0 women), 4 international. Average age 28. 6 applicants, 67% accepted, 4 enrolled. In 2010, 5 master's awarded. *Degree requirements:* For master's, comprehensive exam, thesis or alternative. *Entrance requirements:* For master's, GRE General Test, minimum GPA of 2.5. Additional exam requirements/recommendations for international students: Required—TOEFL (minimum score 550 paper-based; 213 computer-based; 79 iBT), IELTS (minimum score 6.5). *Application deadline:* For fall admission, 8/1 priority date for domestic students, 5/1 priority date for international students; for spring admission, 12/1 priority date for domestic students, 9/1 priority date for international students. Applications are processed on a rolling basis. Application fee: $35. Electronic applications accepted. *Expenses:* Tuition, state resident: full-time $5857; part-time $306.74 per credit. Tuition, nonresident: full-time $15,666; part-time $729.77 per credit. Required fees: $53.42 per credit. Tuition and fees vary according to course load, program and reciprocity agreements. *Financial support:* In 2010–11, 3 students received support, including 1 research assistantship with full and partial tuition reimbursement available (averaging $4,087 per year), 2 teaching assistantships with full and partial tuition reimbursements available (averaging $5,311 per year); fellowships with full and partial tuition reimbursements available, career-related internships or fieldwork, Federal Work-Study, scholarships/grants, health care benefits, tuition waivers (full and partial), and unspecified assistantships also available. Support available to part-time students. Financial award application deadline: 3/15; financial award applicants required to submit FAFSA. *Faculty research:* Soil-structures, environmental-water resources. Total annual research expenditures: $47,501. *Unit head:* Dr. Sukhvarsh Jerath, Graduate Director, 701-777-3564, Fax: 701-777-4838, E-mail: sukhvarshjerath@mail.und.edu. *Application contact:* Staci Wells, Admissions Associate, 701-777-2945, Fax: 701-777-3619, E-mail: staci.wells@gradschool.und.edu.

The University of Texas at Austin, Graduate School, Cockrell School of Engineering, Department of Petroleum and Geosystems Engineering, Program in Energy and Earth Resources, Austin, TX 78712-1111. Offers MA. *Degree requirements:* For master's, thesis, seminar. *Entrance requirements:* For master's, GRE General Test. Additional exam requirements/recommendations for international students: Required—TOEFL. Electronic applications accepted.

University of Utah, Graduate School, College of Mines and Earth Sciences, Department of Mining Engineering, Salt Lake City, UT 84112. Offers ME, MS, PhD. Part-time programs available. *Faculty:* 4 full-time (0 women). *Students:* 7 full-time (1 woman), 1 part-time (0 women); includes 2 minority (1 Asian, non-Hispanic/Latino; 1 Hispanic/Latino), 3 international. Average age 36. 15 applicants, 53% accepted, 1 enrolled. In 2010, 1 doctorate awarded. *Degree requirements:* For master's, comprehensive exam (ME), thesis (MS); for doctorate, one foreign language, thesis/dissertation. *Entrance requirements:* For master's, minimum undergraduate GPA of 3.0; for doctorate, GRE General Test. Additional exam requirements/recommendations for international students: Required—TOEFL (minimum score 550 paper-based; 173 computer-based; 60 iBT). *Application deadline:* For fall admission, 4/1 for domestic and international students; for spring admission, 11/1 priority date for domestic students, 11/1 for international students. Application fee: $55 ($65 for international students). Electronic applications accepted. *Expenses:* Tuition, area resident: Part-time $179.19 per credit hour. Tuition, state resident: full-time $4384. Tuition, nonresident: full-time $16,684; part-time $630.67 per credit hour. Required fees: $350 per semester. Tuition and fees vary according to course load, degree level and program. *Financial support:* In 2010–11, 3 students received support, including 5 fellowships with tuition reimbursements available (averaging $16,000 per year), 2 research assistantships with tuition reimbursements available (averaging $17,000 per year); career-related internships or fieldwork and institutionally sponsored loans also available. Support available to part-time students. Financial award application deadline: 2/15. *Faculty research:* Blasting, underground coal mine design and operations, rock mechanics, mine ventilation, 2-D and 3-D visualization, mine automation, mine safety. Total annual research expenditures: $379,186. *Unit head:* Dr. Michael Gordon Nelson, Chair, 801-585-3064, Fax: 801-585-5410, E-mail: nelsonelson@aol.com. *Application contact:* Pam Hofmann, Administrative Assistant, 801-581-7198, Fax: 801-585-5410, E-mail: pamhofmann@utah.edu.

Virginia Polytechnic Institute and State University, Graduate School, College of Engineering, Department of Mining and Minerals Engineering, Blacksburg, VA 24061. Offers M Eng, MS, PhD. *Faculty:* 8 full-time (1 woman). *Students:* 28 full-time (6 women), 3 part-time (0 women); includes 1 Asian, non-Hispanic/Latino, 10 international. Average age 29. 15 applicants, 60% accepted, 8 enrolled. In 2010, 3 master's, 3 doctorates awarded. *Degree requirements:* For master's, comprehensive exam (for some programs), thesis (for some programs); for doctorate, comprehensive exam (for some programs), thesis/dissertation (for some programs). *Entrance requirements:* For master's and doctorate, GRE. Additional exam requirements/recommendations for international students: Required—TOEFL (minimum score 550 paper-based; 213 computer-based). *Application deadline:* For fall admission, 7/1 for domestic and international students; for spring admission, 12/1 for domestic and international students. Applications are processed on a rolling basis. Application fee: $65. Electronic applications accepted. *Expenses:* Tuition, area resident: Full-time $9399; part-time $488 per credit hour. Tuition, state resident: full-time $9399; part-time $488 per credit hour. Tuition, nonresident: full-time $17,854; part-time $957.75 per credit hour. International tuition: $17,854 full-time. Required fees: $1534. Full-time tuition and fees vary according to program. *Financial support:* In 2010–11, 16 research assistantships with full tuition reimbursements (averaging $22,134 per year), 2 teaching assistantships with full tuition reimbursements (averaging $16,097 per year) were awarded; career-related internships or fieldwork, Federal Work-Study, scholarships/grants, health care benefits, and unspecified assistantships also available. Financial award application deadline: 1/15. *Faculty research:* Sensor development, slope stability, rock fracture, mechanics, ground control, environmental remediation. Total annual research expenditures: $3.5 million. *Unit head:* Dr. Tom Novak, UNIT HEAD, 540-231-7057, Fax: 540-231-4070, E-mail: tomnovak@vt.edu. *Application contact:* Gerald Luttrell, Contact, 540-231-6314, Fax: 540-231-4070, E-mail: luttrell@vt.edu.

West Virginia University, College of Engineering and Mineral Resources, Department of Mining Engineering, Morgantown, WV 26506. Offers MS Min E, PhD. Part-time programs available. *Degree requirements:* For master's, thesis; for doctorate, comprehensive exam, thesis/dissertation. *Entrance requirements:* For master's, minimum GPA of 3.0; for doctorate, GRE General Test, MS in mineral engineering, minimum GPA of 3.5. Additional exam requirements/recommendations for international students: Required—TOEFL. *Faculty research:* Mine safety.

Petroleum Engineering

Colorado School of Mines, Graduate School, Department of Petroleum Engineering, Golden, CO 80401. Offers petroleum engineering (ME, MS, PhD); petroleum reservoir systems (PMS). Part-time programs available. *Faculty:* 15 full-time (4 women), 5 part-time/adjunct (3 women). *Students:* 71 full-time (15 women), 3 part-time (2 women); includes 1 Black or African American, non-Hispanic/Latino, 59 international. Average age 29. 244 applicants, 26% accepted, 17 enrolled. In 2010, 21 master's, 4 doctorates awarded. *Degree requirements:* For master's, thesis (for some programs); for doctorate, comprehensive exam, thesis/dissertation. *Entrance requirements:* For master's and doctorate, GRE General Test. Additional exam requirements/recommendations for international students: Required—TOEFL (minimum score 550 paper-based; 213 computer-based; 80 iBT). *Application deadline:* For fall admission, 1/15 priority date for domestic and international students; for spring admission, 10/15 priority date for domestic and international students. Application fee: $50 ($70 for international students). Electronic applications accepted. *Expenses:* Tuition, state resident: full-time $11,550; part-time $641 per credit. Tuition, nonresident: full-time $25,980; part-time $1444 per credit. Required fees: $1874; $937 per semester. *Financial support:* In 2010–11, 42 students received support, including 2 fellowships with full tuition reimbursements available (averaging $20,000 per year), 21 research assistantships with full tuition reimbursements available (averaging $20,000 per year), 19 teaching assistantships with full tuition reimbursements available (averaging $20,000 per year); career-related internships or fieldwork, scholarships/grants, health care benefits, and unspecified assistantships also available. Financial award application deadline: 1/15; financial award applicants required to submit FAFSA. *Faculty research:* Dynamic rock mechanics, deflagration theory, geostatistics, geochemistry, petrophysics. Total annual research expenditures: $1.9 million. *Unit head:* Dr. Ramona Graves, Department Head, 303-273-3746, Fax: 303-273-3189, E-mail: rgraves@mines.edu. *Application contact:* Denise Winn-Bower, Administrative Assistant, 303-273-3740, Fax: 303-273-3189, E-mail: dwinnbow@mines.edu.

Louisiana State University and Agricultural and Mechanical College, Graduate School, College of Engineering, Department of Petroleum Engineering, Baton Rouge, LA 70803. Offers MS Pet E, PhD. *Faculty:* 10 full-time (1 woman). *Students:* 42 full-time (10 women), 3 part-time (0 women); includes 1 Black or African American, non-Hispanic/Latino, 36 international. Average age 29. 201 applicants, 7% accepted, 4 enrolled. In 2010, 5 master's awarded. *Degree requirements:* For master's, thesis or alternative; for doctorate, thesis/dissertation, exam. *Entrance requirements:* For master's and doctorate, GRE General Test, minimum GPA of 3.0. Additional exam requirements/recommendations for international students: Required—TOEFL (minimum score 550 paper-based; 213 computer-based; 79 iBT) or IELTS (minimum score 6.5). *Application deadline:* For fall admission, 1/25 priority date for domestic students, 5/15 for international students; for spring admission, 10/15 for international students. Applications are processed on a rolling basis. Application fee: $50 ($70 for international students). Electronic applications accepted. *Financial support:* In 2010–11, 33 students received support, including 29 research assistantships with full and partial tuition reimbursements available (averaging $13,561 per year), 3 teaching assistantships with full and partial tuition reimbursements available (averaging $8,083 per year); fellowships, Federal Work-Study, institutionally sponsored loans, health care benefits, and unspecified assistantships also available. Financial award applicants required to submit FAFSA. *Faculty research:* Rock properties, well logging, production engineering, drilling, reservoir engineering. Total annual research expenditures: $851,144. *Unit head:* Dr. Stephen O. Sears, Chair, 225-578-6055, Fax: 225-578-6039, E-mail: sosears@lsu.edu. *Application contact:* Dr. Andrew Wojtanowicz, Graduate Adviser, 225-578-6049, Fax: 225-578-6039, E-mail: awojtan@lsu.edu.

Missouri University of Science and Technology, Graduate School, Department of Geological Sciences and Engineering, Rolla, MO 65409. Offers geological engineering (MS, DE, PhD); geology and geophysics (MS, PhD), including geochemistry, geology, geophysics, groundwater and environmental geology; petroleum engineering (MS, DE, PhD). Part-time programs available. *Degree requirements:* For master's, thesis optional; for doctorate, comprehensive exam, thesis/dissertation. *Entrance requirements:* For master's, GRE General Test (minimum score 600 quantitative, writing 3.5), minimum GPA of 3.0 in last 4 semesters; for doctorate, GRE General Test (minimum: Q 600, GRE WR 3.5). Additional exam requirements/recommendations for international students: Required—TOEFL. Electronic applications accepted. *Faculty research:* Digital image processing and geographic information systems, mineralogy, igneous and sedimentary petrology-geochemistry, sedimentology groundwater hydrology and contaminant transport.

Montana Tech of The University of Montana, Graduate School, Department of Petroleum Engineering, Butte, MT 59701-8997. Offers MS. Part-time and evening/weekend programs available. *Faculty:* 7 full-time (2 women), 1 part-time/adjunct (0 women). *Students:* 5 full-time (0 women), 1 part-time (0 women); includes 1 Black or African American, non-Hispanic/Latino, 2 international. 39 applicants, 5% accepted, 2 enrolled. *Degree requirements:* For master's, thesis optional. *Entrance requirements:* For master's, minimum GPA of 3.0. Additional exam requirements/recommendations for international students: Required—TOEFL (minimum score 525 paper-based; 195 computer-based; 71 iBT). *Application deadline:* For fall admission, 4/1 priority date for domestic students, 3/1 priority date for international students; for spring admission, 10/1 priority date for domestic students, 7/1 priority date for international students. Applications are processed on a rolling basis. Application fee: $30. Electronic applications accepted. *Expenses:* Tuition, state resident: full-time $5084. Tuition, nonresident: full-time $15,104. *Financial support:* In 2010–11, 6 students received support, including 5 teaching assistantships with partial tuition reimbursements available (averaging $4,800 per year); research assistantships, career-related internships or fieldwork, institutionally sponsored loans, and tuition waivers (full and partial) also available. Financial award application deadline: 4/1; financial award applicants required to submit FAFSA. *Faculty research:* Reservoir characterization, simulations, near well bore problems, PVT, environmental waste. *Unit head:* Leo Heath, Head, 406-496-4507, Fax: 406-496-4417, E-mail: lheath@mtech.edu. *Application contact:* Fred Sullivan, Administrator, Graduate School, 406-496-4304, Fax: 406-496-4710, E-mail: fsullivan@mtech.edu.

New Mexico Institute of Mining and Technology, Graduate Studies, Program in Petroleum Engineering, Socorro, NM 87801. Offers MS, PhD. *Degree requirements:* For master's, thesis optional; for doctorate, thesis/dissertation. *Entrance requirements:* For master's, GRE General Test; for doctorate, GRE General Test, GRE Subject Test. Additional exam requirements/recommendations for international students: Required—TOEFL (minimum score 540 paper-based; 207 computer-based). *Faculty research:* Enhanced recovery processes, drilling and production, reservoir evaluation, produced water management, wettability and phase behavior.

Stanford University, School of Earth Sciences, Department of Petroleum Engineering, Stanford, CA 94305-9991. Offers MS, PhD, Eng. Terminal master's awarded for partial completion of

Petroleum Engineering

Stanford University (continued)
doctoral program. *Degree requirements:* For doctorate, thesis/dissertation; for Eng, thesis. *Entrance requirements:* For master's, doctorate, and Eng, GRE General Test. Additional exam requirements/recommendations for international students: Required—TOEFL. Electronic applications accepted. *Expenses:* Tuition: Full-time $38,700; part-time $860 per unit. One-time fee: $200 full-time.

Texas A&M University, College of Engineering, Department of Petroleum Engineering, College Station, TX 77843. Offers M Eng, MS, PhD. Part-time programs available. Postbaccalaureate distance learning degree programs offered (no on-campus study). *Faculty:* 28. *Students:* 224 full-time (42 women), 78 part-time (8 women); includes 38 minority (9 Black or African American, non-Hispanic/Latino; 14 Asian, non-Hispanic/Latino; 15 Hispanic/Latino), 204 international. Average age 25. In 2010, 69 master's, 5 doctorates awarded. *Degree requirements:* For master's, comprehensive exam, thesis (MS); for doctorate, comprehensive exam, thesis/dissertation. *Entrance requirements:* For master's and doctorate, GRE General Test. Additional exam requirements/recommendations for international students: Required—TOEFL (minimum score 550 paper-based; 213 computer-based). *Application deadline:* Applications are processed on a rolling basis. Application fee: $50 ($75 for international students). Electronic applications accepted. *Financial support:* In 2010–11, fellowships (averaging $1,000 per year), research assistantships (averaging $15,000 per year), teaching assistantships (averaging $15,000 per year) were awarded; career-related internships or fieldwork and tuition waivers (partial) also available. Financial award application deadline: 3/1; financial award applicants required to submit FAFSA. *Faculty research:* Drilling and well stimulation, well completions and well performance, reservoir modeling and reservoir description, reservoir simulation, improved/enhanced recovery. *Unit head:* Steve Holditch, Head, 979-845-2255, E-mail: steve.holditch@pe.tamu.edu. *Application contact:* Dr. Thomas A. Blasingame, Graduate Advisor, 979-845-2292, Fax: 979-845-1307, E-mail: t-blasingame@pe.tamu.edu.

Texas A&M University–Kingsville, College of Graduate Studies, College of Engineering, Department of Chemical Engineering and Natural Gas Engineering, Program in Natural Gas Engineering, Kingsville, TX 78363. Offers ME, MS. *Degree requirements:* For master's, comprehensive exam, thesis or alternative. *Entrance requirements:* For master's, GRE General Test, minimum GPA of 3.0. Additional exam requirements/recommendations for international students: Required—TOEFL. *Faculty research:* Gas processing, coal gasification and liquefaction, enhanced oil recovery, gas measurement, unconventional gas recovery.

Texas Tech University, Graduate School, Edward E. Whitacre Jr. College of Engineering, Department of Petroleum Engineering, Lubbock, TX 79409. Offers MSPE, PhD. Part-time programs available. *Faculty:* 6 full-time (1 woman). *Students:* 31 full-time (5 women), 9 part-time (1 woman), 38 international. Average age 27. 176 applicants, 26% accepted, 16 enrolled. In 2010, 13 master's, 2 doctorates awarded. Terminal master's awarded for partial completion of doctoral program. *Degree requirements:* For master's, thesis or alternative; for doctorate, thesis/dissertation. *Entrance requirements:* For master's and doctorate, GRE General Test, minimum GPA of 3.0. Additional exam requirements/recommendations for international students: Required—TOEFL (minimum score 550 paper-based; 213 computer-based; 79 iBT). *Application deadline:* For fall admission, 6/1 priority date for domestic students, 1/15 priority date for international students; for spring admission, 9/1 priority date for domestic students, 6/15 priority date for international students. Applications are processed on a rolling basis. Application fee: $50 ($75 for international students). Electronic applications accepted. *Expenses:* Tuition, state resident: full-time $5495.76; part-time $228.99 per credit hour. Tuition, nonresident: full-time $12,936; part-time $538.99 per credit hour. Required fees: $2674; $36 per credit hour. $905 per semester. *Financial support:* In 2010–11, 5 students received support, including 1 research assistantship with partial tuition reimbursement available (averaging $127 per year), 1 teaching assistantship with partial tuition reimbursement available (averaging $4,852 per year). Financial award application deadline: 4/15; financial award applicants required to submit FAFSA. *Faculty research:* New artificial lift optimization, fatigue failure in tubular, pore to reservoir scale porous media model, transport and thermodynamic fluid property measurements, geologic carbon dioxide storage in gas hydrate and reservoir. Total annual research expenditures: $333,327. *Unit head:* Dr. Lloyd R. Heinze, Chair, 806-742-3573, Fax: 806-742-3502, E-mail: lloyd.heinze@ttu.edu. *Application contact:* Jamie L. Perez, Advisor, 806-742-3573 Ext. 223, Fax: 806-742-3502, E-mail: jamie.l.perez@ttu.edu.

University of Alaska Fairbanks, College of Engineering and Mines, Department of Petroleum Engineering, Fairbanks, AK 99775. Offers MS, PhD. Part-time programs available. *Faculty:* 5 full-time (2 women). *Students:* 19 full-time (2 women), 9 part-time (3 women); includes 2 minority (1 Black or African American, non-Hispanic/Latino; 1 Asian, non-Hispanic/Latino), 19 international. Average age 26. 48 applicants, 29% accepted, 9 enrolled. In 2010, 4 master's awarded. Terminal master's awarded for partial completion of doctoral program. *Degree requirements:* For master's, comprehensive exam, thesis or alternative; for doctorate, comprehensive exam, thesis/dissertation, oral exam, oral defense. *Entrance requirements:* For doctorate, GRE General Test. Additional exam requirements/recommendations for international students: Required—TOEFL (minimum score 550 paper-based; 213 computer-based; 80 iBT). *Application deadline:* For fall admission, 6/1 for domestic students, 3/1 for international students; for spring admission, 10/15 for domestic students, 9/1 for international students. Applications are processed on a rolling basis. Application fee: $60. Electronic applications accepted. *Expenses:* Tuition, state resident: full-time $5688; part-time $316 per credit. Tuition, nonresident: full-time $11,628; part-time $646 per credit. Required fees: $289 per semester. Tuition and fees vary according to course load and reciprocity agreements. *Financial support:* In 2010–11, 7 research assistantships with tuition reimbursements (averaging $11,265 per year), 7 teaching assistantships with tuition reimbursements (averaging $6,791 per year) were awarded; fellowships with tuition reimbursements, career-related internships or fieldwork, Federal Work-Study, scholarships/grants, health care benefits, and unspecified assistantships also available. Support available to part-time students. Financial award application deadline: 7/1; financial award applicants required to submit FAFSA. *Faculty research:* Gas-to-liquid transportation hydraulics and issues, carbon sequestration, enhanced oil recovery, reservoir engineering, coalbed methane. *Unit head:* Dr. Catherine Hanks, Chair, 907-474-7734, Fax: 907-474-5912, E-mail: fyipete@uaf.edu. *Application contact:* Dr. Catherine Hanks, Chair, 907-474-7734, Fax: 907-474-5912, E-mail: fyipete@uaf.edu.

University of Alberta, Faculty of Graduate Studies and Research, Department of Civil and Environmental Engineering, Edmonton, AB T6G 2E1, Canada. Offers construction engineering and management (M Eng, M Sc, PhD); environmental engineering (M Eng, M Sc, PhD); environmental science (M Sc, PhD); geoenvironmental engineering (M Eng, M Sc, PhD); geotechnical engineering (M Eng, M Sc, PhD); mining engineering (M Eng, M Sc, PhD); petroleum engineering (M Eng, M Sc, PhD); structural engineering (M Eng, M Sc, PhD); water resources (M Eng, M Sc, PhD). Part-time programs available. Postbaccalaureate distance learning degree programs offered (minimal on-campus study). *Degree requirements:* For master's, thesis (for some programs); for doctorate, thesis/dissertation. *Entrance requirements:* For master's, minimum GPA of 3.0 in last 2 years of undergraduate studies; for doctorate, minimum GPA of 3.0. Additional exam requirements/recommendations for international students: Required—TOEFL (minimum score 550 paper-based; 213 computer-based). Electronic applications accepted. *Faculty research:* Mining.

University of Calgary, Faculty of Graduate Studies, Schulich School of Engineering, Department of Chemical and Petroleum Engineering, Calgary, AB T2N 1N4, Canada. Offers M Eng, M Sc, PhD. Part-time programs available. *Degree requirements:* For master's, thesis (for some programs); for doctorate, comprehensive exam, thesis/dissertation, candidacy exam. *Entrance requirements:* For master's, minimum GPA of 3.0; for doctorate, minimum GPA of 3.5. Additional exam requirements/recommendations for international students: Required—TOEFL (minimum score 550 paper-based; 213 computer-based; 80 iBT), IELTS (minimum score 7). Electronic applications accepted. *Faculty research:* Environmental engineering, biomedical engineering

modeling, simulation and control, petroleum recovery and reservoir engineering, phase equilibria and transport properties.

University of Houston, Cullen College of Engineering, Department of Chemical and Biomolecular Engineering, Houston, TX 77204. Offers chemical engineering (MChE, PhD); petroleum engineering (M Pet E). Part-time programs available. *Faculty:* 16 full-time (3 women), 12 part-time/adjunct (1 woman). *Students:* 99 full-time (26 women), 65 part-time (12 women); includes 6 Black or African American, non-Hispanic/Latino; 23 Asian, non-Hispanic/Latino; 11 Hispanic/Latino, 93 international. Average age 28. 382 applicants, 19% accepted, 45 enrolled. In 2010, 27 master's, 14 doctorates awarded. Terminal master's awarded for partial completion of doctoral program. *Entrance requirements:* For master's and doctorate, GRE General Test. Additional exam requirements/recommendations for international students: Required—TOEFL (minimum score 550 paper-based; 79 iBT), IELTS (minimum score 6.5). *Application deadline:* For fall admission, 2/15 for domestic and international students. Application fee: $25 ($75 for international students). *Expenses:* Tuition, state resident: full-time $8592; part-time $358 per credit hour. Tuition, nonresident: full-time $16,032; part-time $668 per credit hour. Required fees: $2889. Tuition and fees vary according to course load and program. *Financial support:* In 2010–11, 19 fellowships with partial tuition reimbursements (averaging $4,000 per year), 38 research assistantships with partial tuition reimbursements (averaging $15,120 per year), 10 teaching assistantships with partial tuition reimbursements (averaging $11,976 per year) were awarded; career-related internships or fieldwork, Federal Work-Study, institutionally sponsored loans, scholarships/grants, health care benefits, and unspecified assistantships also available. Support available to part-time students. Financial award application deadline: 2/1. *Faculty research:* Chemical engineering. *Unit head:* Dr. Ramanan Krishnamoorti, Chairperson, 713-743-4304, Fax: 713-743-4323, E-mail: ramanan@uh.edu. *Application contact:* Jane Geanangel, Graduate Program Academic Records Coordinator, 713-743-4219.

The University of Kansas, Graduate Studies, School of Engineering, Department of Chemical and Petroleum Engineering, Lawrence, KS 66045. Offers chemical engineering (MS); chemical/petroleum engineering (PhD); petroleum engineering (MS). Part-time programs available. *Faculty:* 14 full-time (4 women). *Students:* 40 full-time (20 women), 3 part-time (0 women); includes 2 minority (1 American Indian or Alaska Native, non-Hispanic/Latino; 1 Asian, non-Hispanic/Latino), 31 international. Average age 27. 153 applicants, 10% accepted, 5 enrolled. In 2010, 2 master's, 9 doctorates awarded. *Degree requirements:* For master's, thesis (for some programs), exam; for doctorate, comprehensive exam, thesis/dissertation, qualifying exams. *Entrance requirements:* For master's, GRE General Test, minimum GPA of 3.0; for doctorate, GRE General Test, minimum GPA of 3.5. Additional exam requirements/recommendations for international students: Required—TOEFL. *Application deadline:* For fall admission, 1/10 priority date for domestic students, 1/10 for international students; for spring admission, 6/10 priority date for domestic students, 6/10 for international students. Applications are processed on a rolling basis. Application fee: $55 ($65 for international students). Electronic applications accepted. *Expenses:* Tuition, state resident: full-time $7092; part-time $295.50 per credit hour. Tuition, nonresident: full-time $16,590; part-time $691.25 per credit hour. Required fees: $858; $71.49 per credit hour. Tuition and fees vary according to course load, campus/location and program. *Financial support:* Fellowships, research assistantships with full and partial tuition reimbursements, teaching assistantships with full and partial tuition reimbursements, career-related internships or fieldwork, Federal Work-Study, scholarships/grants, traineeships, and unspecified assistantships available. Financial award application deadline: 4/1; financial award applicants required to submit FAFSA. *Faculty research:* Enhanced oil recovery, catalysis and kinetics, electrochemical engineering, biomedical engineering, semiconductor materials processing. *Unit head:* Prof. Laurence Weatherley, Chairperson, 785-864-4965, Fax: 785-864-4967, E-mail: lweather@ku.edu. *Application contact:* Prof. Marylee Southard, Graduate Recruiting Officer, 785-864-4965, Fax: 785-864-4967, E-mail: marylee@ku.edu.

University of Louisiana at Lafayette, College of Engineering, Department of Petroleum Engineering, Lafayette, LA 70504. Offers MSE. Evening/weekend programs available. *Degree requirements:* For master's, comprehensive exam, thesis or alternative. *Entrance requirements:* For master's, GRE General Test, minimum GPA of 2.85. Electronic applications accepted.

University of Oklahoma, College of Earth and Energy, School of Petroleum and Geological Engineering, Program in Petroleum Engineering, Norman, OK 73019-0390. Offers natural gas engineering and management (MS); petroleum engineering (MS, PhD). Part-time programs available. *Students:* 83 full-time (16 women), 40 part-time (7 women); includes 5 minority (4 Black or African American, non-Hispanic/Latino; 1 Hispanic/Latino), 106 international. Average age 28. 143 applicants, 27% accepted, 26 enrolled. In 2010, 11 master's, 3 doctorates awarded. Terminal master's awarded for partial completion of doctoral program. *Degree requirements:* For master's, thesis optional, industrial team project or thesis; for doctorate, thesis/dissertation. *Entrance requirements:* For master's, GRE General Test, bachelor's degree in engineering, 3 letters of recommendation, minimum GPA of 3.0 during final 60 hours of undergraduate course work; for doctorate, GRE General Test, minimum GPA of 3.0, 3 letters of recommendation. Additional exam requirements/recommendations for international students: Required—TOEFL (minimum score 550 paper-based; 213 computer-based; 79 iBT). *Application deadline:* For fall admission, 6/1 priority date for domestic students, 4/1 for international students; for spring admission, 11/1 for domestic students, 9/1 for international students. Applications are processed on a rolling basis. Application fee: $40 ($90 for international students). Electronic applications accepted. *Expenses:* Tuition, state resident: full-time $3892.80; part-time $162.20 per credit hour. Tuition, nonresident: full-time $14,167; part-time $590.30 per credit hour. Required fees: $2523.40; $94.60 per credit hour. Tuition and fees vary according to course load and degree level. *Financial support:* In 2010–11, 96 students received support. Traineeships available. Financial award application deadline: 4/15; financial award applicants required to submit FAFSA. *Faculty research:* Petrophysics, shale gas, reservoir simulation coiled tubing, poro-mechanics, enhanced oil recovery. *Unit head:* Dr. Chandra Rai, Director, 405-325-2921, Fax: 405-325-7477, E-mail: crai@ou.edu. *Application contact:* Shalli Young, Executive Assistant to the Graduate Liaison, 405-325-2921, Fax: 405-325-7477, E-mail: syoung@ou.edu.

University of Pittsburgh, School of Engineering, Department of Chemical and Petroleum Engineering, Pittsburgh, PA 15260. Offers chemical engineering (MS Ch E, PhD); petroleum engineering (MSPE); MS Ch E/MSPE. Part-time programs available. Postbaccalaureate distance learning degree programs offered. *Faculty:* 18 full-time (3 women), 32 part-time/adjunct (5 women). *Students:* 51 full-time (13 women), 8 part-time (3 women); includes 5 minority (1 Black or African American, non-Hispanic/Latino; 2 Asian, non-Hispanic/Latino; 2 Hispanic/Latino), 34 international. 204 applicants, 31% accepted, 24 enrolled. In 2010, 2 master's, 5 doctorates awarded. *Degree requirements:* For master's, thesis; for doctorate, comprehensive exam, thesis/dissertation, final oral exams. *Entrance requirements:* For master's and doctorate, GRE General Test, minimum QPA of 3.2. Additional exam requirements/recommendations for international students: Required—TOEFL (minimum score 550 paper-based; 213 computer-based; 80 iBT). *Application deadline:* For fall admission, 3/1 priority date for domestic students; for spring admission, 7/1 priority date for domestic students. Applications are processed on a rolling basis. Application fee: $50. Electronic applications accepted. *Expenses:* Tuition, state resident: full-time $17,304; part-time $701 per credit. Tuition, nonresident: full-time $29,554; part-time $1210 per credit. Required fees: $740; $214 per term. Tuition and fees vary according to program. *Financial support:* In 2010–11, 38 students received support, including 6 fellowships with full tuition reimbursements available (averaging $26,000 per year), 25 research assistantships with full tuition reimbursements available (averaging $25,000 per year), 13 teaching assistantships with full tuition reimbursements available (averaging $24,000 per year); scholarships/grants, traineeships, and tuition waivers (full and partial) also available. Financial award application deadline: 4/15. *Faculty research:* Biotechnology, polymers, catalysis, energy and environment, computational modeling. Total annual research expenditures: $6.9 million. *Unit head:* Dr. J. Karl Johnson, Chairman, 412-624-5644, Fax: 412-624-9639, E-mail: johnson@engr.pitt.edu. *Application contact:* William Federspiel, Associate Professor and Graduate Coordinator, 412-624-9499, Fax: 412-624-9639, E-mail: federspiel@engrng.pitt.edu.

University of Regina, Faculty of Graduate Studies and Research, Faculty of Engineering and Applied Science, Program in Petroleum Systems Engineering, Regina, SK S4S 0A2, Canada. Offers M Eng, MA Sc, PhD. Part-time programs available. *Faculty:* 7 full-time (1 woman). *Students:* 32 full-time (5 women), 6 part-time (1 woman). 91 applicants, 30% accepted. In 2010, 8 master's, 2 doctorates awarded. *Degree requirements:* For master's, thesis; for doctorate, thesis/dissertation. *Entrance requirements:* Additional exam requirements/recommendations for international students: Required—TOEFL (minimum score 550 paper-based; 80 iBT). *Application deadline:* For fall admission, 3/31 for domestic and international students; for winter admission, 7/31 for domestic and international students; for spring admission, 11/30 for domestic and international students. Application fee: $100. Electronic applications accepted. Tuition and fees charges are reported in Canadian dollars. *Expenses:* Tuition, area resident: Full-time $3244.50 Canadian dollars; part-time $180.25 Canadian dollars per credit hour. International tuition: $4744.50 Canadian dollars full-time. Required fees: $494 Canadian dollars; $115.25 Canadian dollars per credit hour. $115.25 Canadian dollars per semester. Tuition and fees vary according to program. *Financial support:* In 2010–11, 3 fellowships (averaging $19,000 per year), 2 research assistantships (averaging $17,250 per year), 7 teaching assistantships (averaging $6,853 per year) were awarded; career-related internships or fieldwork and scholarships/grants also available. Financial award application deadline: 6/15. *Faculty research:* Enhanced oil recovery, production engineering, reservoir engineering, surface thermodynamics, geostatistics. *Unit head:* Dr. Raphael Idem, Associate Dean, Research and Graduate Studies, 306-337-3287, Fax: 306-585-4855, E-mail: raphael.idem@uregina.ca. *Application contact:* Dr. Farshid Torabi, Chair, Graduate Program Coordinator, 306-337-3287, Fax: 306-585-4855, E-mail: farshid.torabi@uregina.ca.

University of Southern California, Graduate School, Viterbi School of Engineering, Mork Family Department of Chemical Engineering and Materials Science, Los Angeles, CA 90089. Offers chemical engineering (MS, PhD, Engr); materials engineering (MS); materials science (MS, PhD, Engr); petroleum engineering (MS, PhD, Engr); smart oilfield technologies (MS, Graduate Certificate). *Faculty:* 19 full-time (3 women), 9 part-time/adjunct (1 woman). *Students:* 235 full-time (77 women), 77 part-time (25 women); includes 43 minority (6 Black or African American, non-Hispanic/Latino; 25 Asian, non-Hispanic/Latino; 11 Hispanic/Latino; 1 Two or more races, non-Hispanic/Latino), 213 international. 643 applicants, 36% accepted, 118 enrolled. In 2010, 37 master's, 19 doctorates, 4 other advanced degrees awarded. Terminal master's awarded for partial completion of doctoral program. *Degree requirements:* For master's, thesis optional; for doctorate, thesis/dissertation. *Entrance requirements:* For master's and doctorate, GRE General Test. *Application deadline:* For fall admission, 12/1 priority date for domestic and international students; for spring admission, 9/1 priority date for domestic and international students. Applications are processed on a rolling basis. Application fee: $85. Electronic applications accepted. *Expenses:* Contact institution. *Financial support:* In 2010–11, fellowships with full tuition reimbursements (averaging $30,000 per year), research assistantships with full tuition reimbursements (averaging $20,000 per year), teaching assistantships with full tuition reimbursements (averaging $20,000 per year) were awarded; career-related internships or fieldwork, scholarships/grants, health care benefits, and unspecified assistantships also available. Financial award application deadline: 12/1; financial award applicants required to submit CSS PROFILE or FAFSA. *Faculty research:* Heterogeneous materials and porous media, statistical mechanics, molecular simulation, polymer science and engineering, advanced materials, reaction engineering and catalysis, membrane processes and separation, biochemical engineering, cell culture, bioreactor modeling, petroleum engineering. Total annual research expenditures: $11.6 million. *Unit head:* Dr. Theodore Tsotsis, Chair, 213-740-2227, E-mail: chedept@usc.edu. *Application contact:* Karen Woo, Student Services Advisor, 213-740-2227, E-mail: karenwoo@usc.edu.

The University of Texas at Austin, Graduate School, Cockrell School of Engineering, Department of Petroleum and Geosystems Engineering, Austin, TX 78712-1111. Offers energy and earth resources (MA); petroleum engineering (MS, PhD). Evening/weekend programs available. Postbaccalaureate distance learning degree programs offered (no on-campus study). *Entrance requirements:* For master's and doctorate, GRE General Test. Electronic applications accepted.

University of Tulsa, Graduate School, College of Engineering and Natural Sciences, Department of Petroleum Engineering, Tulsa, OK 74104-3189. Offers ME, MSE, PhD. Part-time programs available. *Faculty:* 11 full-time (0 women). *Students:* 66 full-time (12 women), 26 part-time (5 women), 86 international. Average age 26. 280 applicants, 16% accepted, 23 enrolled. In 2010, 22 master's, 3 doctorates awarded. *Degree requirements:* For master's, thesis (MSE); for doctorate, one foreign language, comprehensive exam, thesis/dissertation. *Entrance requirements:* For master's and doctorate, GRE General Test. Additional exam requirements/recommendations for international students: Required—TOEFL (minimum score 550 paper-based; 213 computer-based; 80 iBT), IELTS (minimum score 6). *Application deadline:* Applications are processed on a rolling basis. Application fee: $40. Electronic applications accepted. *Expenses:* Tuition: Full-time $16,902; part-time $939 per credit hour. Required fees: $1020; $4 per credit hour. Tuition and fees vary according to course load. *Financial support:* In 2010–11, 69 students received support, including 6 fellowships with partial tuition reimbursements available (averaging $5,209 per year), 56 research assistantships with full and partial tuition reimbursements available (averaging $11,168 per year), 18 teaching assistantships with full and partial tuition reimbursements available (averaging $7,886 per year); career-related internships or fieldwork, Federal Work-Study, scholarships/grants, health care benefits, tuition waivers (full and partial), and unspecified assistantships also available. Support available to part-time students. Financial award application deadline: 2/1; financial award applicants required to submit FAFSA. *Faculty research:* Artificial lift, drilling, multiphase flow in pipes, separation technology, horizontal well technology, reservoir characterization, well testing, reservoir simulation, unconventional natural gas. Total annual research expenditures: $8.5 million. *Unit head:* Dr. Mohan Kelkar, Chairperson, 918-631-3036, Fax: 915-631-2059, E-mail: mohan@utulsa.edu. *Application contact:* Dr. Jagan Mahadevan, Adviser, 918-631-3906, Fax: 918-631-5142, E-mail: jmahadevan@utulsa.edu.

University of Wyoming, College of Engineering and Applied Sciences, Department of Chemical and Petroleum Engineering, Program in Petroleum Engineering, Laramie, WY 82070. Offers MS, PhD. Part-time programs available. Terminal master's awarded for partial completion of doctoral program. *Degree requirements:* For master's, thesis; for doctorate, thesis/dissertation. *Entrance requirements:* For master's and doctorate, GRE General Test, minimum GPA of 3.0. Additional exam requirements/recommendations for international students: Required—TOEFL (minimum score 600 paper-based; 250 computer-based). Electronic applications accepted. *Faculty research:* Oil recovery methods, oil production, coal bed methane.

West Virginia University, College of Engineering and Mineral Resources, Department of Petroleum and Natural Gas Engineering, Morgantown, WV 26506. Offers MSPNGE, PhD. Part-time programs available. *Degree requirements:* For master's, thesis; for doctorate, thesis/dissertation. *Entrance requirements:* For master's, minimum GPA of 3.0, BS or equivalent in petroleum or natural gas engineering; for doctorate, minimum GPA of 3.0, BS or MS in petroleum engineering from an ABET accredited or an internationally recognized petroleum engineering program or equivalent. Additional exam requirements/recommendations for international students: Required—TOEFL. *Faculty research:* Gas reservoir engineering, well logging, environment artificial intelligence.

Section 14
Industrial Engineering

This section contains a directory of institutions offering graduate work in industrial engineering, followed by an in-depth entry submitted by an institution that chose to prepare a detailed program description. Additional information about programs listed in the directory but not augmented by an in-depth entry may be obtained by writing directly to the dean of a graduate school or chair of a department at the address given in the directory.

For programs offering related work, see also in this book *Computer Science and Information Technology, Electrical and Computer Engineering, Energy and Power Engineering, Engineering and Applied Sciences,* and *Management of Engineering and Technology.* In the other guides in this series:

Graduate Programs in the Physical Sciences, Mathematics, Agricultural Sciences, the Environment & Natural Resources
See *Mathematical Sciences*
Graduate Programs in Business, Education, Health, Information Studies, Law & Social Work
See *Business Administration and Management*

CONTENTS

Program Directories

Close-Ups and Displays

Automotive Engineering

Central Michigan University, Central Michigan University Off-Campus Programs, Program in Administration, Mount Pleasant, MI 48859. Offers acquisitions administration (MSA, Certificate); general administration (MSA, Certificate); health services administration (MSA, Certificate); human resources administration (MSA, Certificate); information resource management (MSA, Certificate); international administration (MSA, Certificate); leadership (MSA, Certificate); public administration (MSA, Certificate); vehicle design and manufacturing administration (Certificate). Part-time and evening/weekend programs available. Postbaccalaureate distance learning degree programs offered (no on-campus study). *Students:* Average age 38. *Entrance requirements:* For master's, minimum GPA of 2.7 in major. *Application deadline:* Applications are processed on a rolling basis. Application fee: $50. Electronic applications accepted. *Expenses:* Tuition, state resident: full-time $8208; part-time $456 per credit hour. Tuition, nonresident: full-time $13,788; part-time $766 per credit hour. One-time fee: $25. *Financial support:* Scholarships/grants available. Support available to part-time students. Financial award applicants required to submit FAFSA. *Unit head:* Dr. Nana Korsah, Director, MSA Programs, 989-774-6525, E-mail: korsa1na@cmich.edu. *Application contact:* 877-268-4636, E-mail: cmuoffcampus@cmich.edu.

Clemson University, Graduate School, College of Engineering and Science, Department of Automotive Engineering, Clemson, SC 29634. Offers MS, PhD. *Faculty:* 11 full-time (0 women), 9 part-time/adjunct (0 women). *Students:* 101 full-time (7 women), 6 part-time (1 woman); includes 1 Black or African American, non-Hispanic/Latino; 2 Asian, non-Hispanic/Latino; 1 Hispanic/Latino; 2 Two or more races, non-Hispanic/Latino, 63 international. Average age 27. 158 applicants, 85% accepted, 54 enrolled. In 2010, 14 master's, 3 doctorates awarded. *Degree requirements:* For master's, one foreign language, industrial internship; for doctorate, one foreign language, thesis/dissertation. *Entrance requirements:* For master's, GRE; for doctorate, GRE, MS or 2 years post-bachelor's experience. Additional exam requirements/recommendations for international students: Required—TOEFL. *Application deadline:* Applications are processed on a rolling basis. Application fee: $70 ($80 for international students). Electronic applications accepted. *Expenses:* Contact institution. *Financial support:* In 2010–11, 46 students received support, including 4 fellowships with partial tuition reimbursements available (averaging $20,000 per year), 33 research assistantships with partial tuition reimbursements available (averaging $16,153 per year), 4 teaching assistantships with partial tuition reimbursements available (averaging $12,330 per year); career-related internships or fieldwork, institutionally sponsored loans, scholarships/grants, traineeships, health care benefits, and unspecified assistantships also available. Support available to part-time students. Financial award application deadline: 2/1. *Faculty research:* Systems integration, manufacturing product design/development/vehicle electronics. Total annual research expenditures: $1.5 million. *Unit head:* Dr. Donald Beasley, ME Department Chair, 864-656-5622, Fax: 864-656-4435, E-mail: debsl@exchange.clemson.edu. *Application contact:* Dr. Mohammed Omar, Coordinator, 864-656-5537, Fax: 864-656-4435, E-mail: momar@clemson.edu.

Lawrence Technological University, College of Engineering, Southfield, MI 48075-1058. Offers architectural engineering (MS); automotive engineering (MS); civil engineering (MS); electrical and computer engineering (MS); engineering management (MEM); industrial engineering (MS); manufacturing systems (ME, DE); mechanical engineering (MS); mechatronic systems engineering (MS). Part-time and evening/weekend programs available. *Faculty:* 20 full-time (4 women), 12 part-time/adjunct (0 women). *Students:* 8 full-time (1 woman), 366 part-time (60 women); includes 29 Black or African American, non-Hispanic/Latino; 1 American Indian or Alaska Native, non-Hispanic/Latino; 36 Asian, non-Hispanic/Latino; 9 Hispanic/Latino; 4 Two or more races, non-Hispanic/Latino, 81 international. Average age 32. 398 applicants, 48% accepted, 87 enrolled. In 2010, 121 master's, 5 doctorates awarded. *Degree requirements:* For master's, thesis (for some programs). *Entrance requirements:* Additional exam requirements/recommendations for international students: Required—TOEFL (minimum score 550 paper-based; 213 computer-based; 79 iBT). *Application deadline:* For fall admission, 6/30 priority date for domestic students, 6/30 for international students; for spring admission, 11/15 priority date for domestic students, 11/15 for international students. Applications are processed on a rolling basis. Application fee: $50. Electronic applications accepted. *Financial support:* In 2010–11, 72 students received support. Federal Work-Study and institutionally sponsored loans available. Support available to part-time students. Financial award application deadline: 4/1; financial award applicants required to submit FAFSA. *Faculty research:* Advanced composite materials in bridges, strengthening existing bridges with carbon and glass fiber sheets, development of drive shafts using composite materials. *Unit head:* Dr. Nabil Grace, Interim Dean, 248-204-2500, Fax: 248-204-2509, E-mail: engrdean@ltu.edu. *Application contact:* Jane Rohrback, Director of Admissions, 248-204-3160, Fax: 248-204-2228, E-mail: admissions@ltu.edu.

Minnesota State University Mankato, College of Graduate Studies, College of Science, Engineering and Technology, Department of Automotive and Manufacturing Engineering Technology, Mankato, MN 56001. Offers manufacturing engineering technology (MS). *Students:* 9 full-time (0 women), 10 part-time (1 woman). *Degree requirements:* For master's, comprehensive exam, thesis. *Entrance requirements:* For master's, GRE General Test (if GPA less than 3.0), minimum GPA of 3.0 during previous 2 years. Additional exam requirements/recommendations for international students: Required—TOEFL. *Application deadline:* For fall admission, 7/1 priority date for domestic students; for spring admission, 11/1 for domestic students. Applications are processed on a rolling basis. Application fee: $40. Electronic applications accepted. *Financial support:* Research assistantships with full tuition reimbursements, teaching assistantships with full tuition reimbursements, unspecified assistantships available. Financial award application deadline: 3/15; financial award applicants required to submit FAFSA. *Unit head:* Dr. Bruce Jones, Graduate Coordinator, 507-389-6700. *Application contact:* 507-389-2321, E-mail: grad@mnsu.edu.

University of Michigan–Dearborn, College of Engineering and Computer Science, Interdisciplinary Programs, MSE Program in Automotive Systems Engineering, Dearborn, MI 48128-1491. Offers MSE. Part-time and evening/weekend programs available. Postbaccalaureate distance learning degree programs offered. *Faculty:* 1 full-time (0 women). *Students:* 13 full-time (2 women), 24 part-time (3 women); includes 4 minority (1 Black or African American, non-Hispanic/Latino; 3 Hispanic/Latino), 15 international. Average age 30. 23 applicants, 70% accepted, 10 enrolled. In 2010, 12 master's awarded. *Degree requirements:* For master's, thesis optional. *Entrance requirements:* For master's, bachelor's degree in applied mathematics, computer science, engineering, or physical science; minimum GPA of 3.0. Additional exam requirements/recommendations for international students: Required—TOEFL (minimum score 560 paper-based; 220 computer-based; 84 iBT). *Application deadline:* For fall admission, 8/1 priority date for domestic students, 4/1 for international students; for winter admission, 12/1 priority date for domestic students, 8/1 for international students; for spring admission, 4/1 priority date for domestic students, 12/1 for international students. Applications are processed on a rolling basis. Application fee: $60 ($75 for international students). Electronic applications accepted. *Financial support:* In 2010–11, 3 research assistantships with full tuition reimbursements (averaging $19,000 per year) were awarded; scholarships/grants and unspecified assistantships also available. Financial award application deadline: 4/1; financial award applicants required to submit FAFSA. *Faculty research:* Performance of lightweight automotive materials, stamping, hydroforming, tailor-welded blanking, automotive composites processing and design, thermoplastic matrix composites, injection molding. *Unit head:* Dr. Pankaj K. Mallick, Director/Professor, 313-593-5119, Fax: 313-593-5386, E-mail: pkm@umich.edu. *Application contact:* Sherry Boyd, Intermediate Administrative Assistant, 313-593-5582, Fax: 313-593-5386, E-mail: idpgrad@umd.umich.edu.

University of Michigan–Dearborn, College of Engineering and Computer Science, Interdisciplinary Programs, PhD Program in Automotive Systems Engineering, Dearborn, MI 48128-1491. Offers PhD. Part-time and evening/weekend programs available. *Faculty:* 1 full-time (0 women). *Students:* 8 full-time (0 women), 10 part-time (0 women); includes 1 Asian, non-Hispanic/Latino; 1 Hispanic/Latino, 10 international. Average age 29. 22 applicants, 41% accepted, 4 enrolled. *Degree requirements:* For doctorate, thesis/dissertation. *Entrance requirements:* For doctorate, GRE. Additional exam requirements/recommendations for international students: Required—TOEFL (minimum score 560 paper-based; 220 computer-based; 84 iBT). *Application deadline:* For fall admission, 8/1 priority date for domestic students, 4/1 for international students; for winter admission, 12/1 priority date for domestic students, 8/1 for international students; for spring admission, 4/1 priority date for domestic students, 12/1 for international students. Applications are processed on a rolling basis. Application fee: $60 ($75 for international students). Electronic applications accepted. *Financial support:* In 2010–11, 4 research assistantships with full tuition reimbursements (averaging $19,000 per year) were awarded; scholarships/grants and unspecified assistantships also available. Financial award applicants required to submit FAFSA. *Unit head:* Dr. Pankaj K. Mallick, Director/Professor, 313-593-5119, Fax: 313-593-5386, E-mail: pkm@umich.edu. *Application contact:* Sherry Boyd, Intermediate Administrative Assistant, 313-593-5582, Fax: 313-593-5386, E-mail: idpgrad@umd.umich.edu.

Wayne State University, College of Engineering, Department of Electric-drive Vehicle Engineering, Detroit, MI 48202. Offers MS, Graduate Certificate. *Faculty:* 5 full-time (0 women), 3 part-time/adjunct (1 woman). *Students:* 3 full-time (0 women), 7 part-time (0 women). Average age 45. 9 applicants, 67% accepted, 5 enrolled. *Expenses:* Tuition, state resident: full-time $7662; part-time $478.85 per credit hour. Tuition, nonresident: full-time $16,920; part-time $1057.55 per credit hour. Required fees: $571.20; $35.70 per credit hour. $188.05 per semester. Tuition and fees vary according to course load and program. *Unit head:* Dr. Ralph Kummler, Dean, 313-577-3861, Fax: 313-577-5300, E-mail: rkummler@eng.wayne.edu. *Application contact:* Dr. Gerald O. Thompkins, Associate Dean, 313-577-3780.

Industrial/Management Engineering

Arizona State University, Ira A. Fulton School of Engineering, School of Computing, Informatics, and Decision Systems Engineering, Tempe, AZ 85287-8809. Offers computer science (MCS, MS, PhD); industrial engineering (MS, PhD). Part-time and evening/weekend programs available. Postbaccalaureate distance learning degree programs offered (minimal on-campus study). *Faculty:* 58 full-time (14 women), 5 part-time/adjunct (2 women). *Students:* 365 full-time (76 women), 168 part-time (36 women); includes 60 minority (10 Black or African American, non-Hispanic/Latino; 1 American Indian or Alaska Native, non-Hispanic/Latino; 29 Asian, non-Hispanic/Latino; 18 Hispanic/Latino; 2 Two or more races, non-Hispanic/Latino), 352 international. Average age 28. 1,016 applicants, 53% accepted, 152 enrolled. In 2010, 138 master's, 22 doctorates awarded. Terminal master's awarded for partial completion of doctoral program. *Degree requirements:* For master's, comprehensive exam (for some programs), portfolio (MCS); interactive Program of Study (iPOS) submitted before completing 50 percent of required credit hours; for doctorate, comprehensive exam, thesis/dissertation, interactive Program of Study (iPOS) submitted before completing 50 percent of required credit hours. *Entrance requirements:* For master's, GRE, minimum GPA of 3.0 or equivalent in last 2 years of work leading to bachelor's degree; for doctorate, GRE, minimum GPA of 3.0 in last 2 years of work leading to bachelor's degree. Additional exam requirements/recommendations for international students: Required—TOEFL, IELTS, or Pearson Test of English. *Application deadline:* For fall admission, 12/1 for domestic and international students; for spring admission, 8/1 for domestic and international students. Application fee: $70 ($90 for international students). Electronic applications accepted. *Expenses:* Contact institution. *Financial support:* In 2010–11, 156 research assistantships with full and partial tuition reimbursements (averaging $13,688 per year), 41 teaching assistantships with full and partial tuition reimbursements (averaging $10,940 per year) were awarded; fellowships with full and partial tuition reimbursements, institutionally sponsored loans, scholarships/grants, and tuition waivers (full and partial) also available. Financial award application deadline: 3/1; financial award applicants required to submit FAFSA. *Faculty research:* Artificial intelligence, cyberphysical and embedded systems, health informatics, information assurance and security, information management/multimedia/visualization, network science, personalized learning/educational games, production logistics, software and systems engineering, and statistical modeling and data mining. Total annual research expenditures: $11.2 million. *Unit head:* Dr. Ronald Askin, Director, 480-965-2567, E-mail: ron.askin@asu.edu. *Application contact:* Graduate Admissions, 480-965-6113.

Auburn University, Graduate School, Ginn College of Engineering, Department of Industrial and Systems Engineering, Auburn University, AL 36849. Offers MISE, MS, PhD. Part-time programs available. *Faculty:* 10 full-time (1 woman), 4 part-time/adjunct (0 women). *Students:* 89 full-time (21 women), 49 part-time (13 women); includes 12 Black or African American, non-Hispanic/Latino; 3 Asian, non-Hispanic/Latino; 1 Hispanic/Latino, 66 international. Average age 29. 252 applicants, 62% accepted, 50 enrolled. In 2010, 20 master's, 7 doctorates awarded. *Degree requirements:* For master's, thesis (MS); for doctorate, thesis/dissertation. *Entrance requirements:* For master's and doctorate, GRE General Test. *Application deadline:* For fall admission, 7/7 for domestic students; for spring admission, 11/24 for domestic students. Applications are processed on a rolling basis. Application fee: $50 ($60 for international students). *Expenses:* Tuition, state resident: full-time $7002. Tuition, nonresident: full-time $21,898. International tuition: $22,116 full-time. Required fees: $892. Tuition and fees vary according to course load and program. *Financial support:* Fellowships, research assistantships, teaching assistantships, Federal Work-Study available. Support available to part-time students. Financial award application deadline: 3/15; financial award applicants required to submit FAFSA. *Unit head:* Dr. Alice E. Smith, Chair, 334-844-1401. *Application contact:* Dr. George Flowers, Dean of the Graduate School, 334-844-2125.

Bradley University, Graduate School, College of Engineering and Technology, Department of Industrial and Manufacturing Engineering and Technology, Peoria, IL 61625-0002. Offers industrial engineering (MSIE); manufacturing engineering (MSIE). Part-time and evening/weekend programs available. *Degree requirements:* For master's, comprehensive exam, project. *Entrance requirements:* For master's, minimum GPA of 3.0. Additional exam requirements/recommendations for international students: Required—TOEFL (minimum score 550 paper-based; 213 computer-based; 79 iBT).

Buffalo State College, State University of New York, The Graduate School, Faculty of Applied Science and Education, Department of Technology, Program in Industrial Technology, Buffalo, NY 14222-1095. Offers MS. *Degree requirements:* For master's, thesis or project.

Entrance requirements: For master's, minimum GPA of 2.5. Additional exam requirements/recommendations for international students: Required—TOEFL (minimum score 550 paper-based; 213 computer-based).

California Polytechnic State University, San Luis Obispo, College of Engineering, Department of Industrial Engineering, San Luis Obispo, CA 93407. Offers MS. Part-time programs available. *Faculty:* 1 (woman) part-time/adjunct. *Students:* 9 full-time (0 women), 6 part-time (1 woman); includes 5 minority (2 Asian, non-Hispanic/Latino; 3 Hispanic/Latino). Average age 23. 5 applicants, 40% accepted, 2 enrolled. In 2010, 4 master's awarded. *Degree requirements:* For master's, comprehensive exam (for some programs), thesis (for some programs). *Entrance requirements:* For master's, GRE General Test, minimum GPA of 3.0 in last 90 quarter units of course work. Additional exam requirements/recommendations for international students: Required—TOEFL (minimum score 550 paper-based; 213 computer-based) or IELTS (minimum score 6). *Application deadline:* For fall admission, 7/1 for domestic students, 11/30 for international students; for winter admission, 11/1 for domestic students, 6/30 for international students; for spring admission, 2/1 for domestic students. Applications are processed on a rolling basis. Application fee: $55. Electronic applications accepted. *Expenses:* Tuition, state resident: full-time $5386; part-time $3124 per year. Tuition, nonresident: full-time $11,160; part-time $248 per unit. Required fees: $2250; $614 per term. One-time fee: $2250 full-time; $1842 part-time. *Financial support:* Fellowships, research assistantships, teaching assistantships, career-related internships or fieldwork, Federal Work-Study, institutionally sponsored loans, and scholarships/grants available. Support available to part-time students. Financial award application deadline: 3/2; financial award applicants required to submit FAFSA. *Faculty research:* Operations research, simulation, project management, supply chain and logistics, quality engineering. *Unit head:* Dr. Liz Schlemer, Graduate Coordinator, 805-756-2183, Fax: 805-756-5439, E-mail: lschleme@calpoly.edu. *Application contact:* Dr. Liz Schlemer, Graduate Coordinator, 805-756-2183, Fax: 805-756-5439, E-mail: lschleme@calpoly.edu.

California State University, Fresno, Division of Graduate Studies, College of Agricultural Sciences and Technology, Department of Industrial Technology, Fresno, CA 93740-8027. Offers MS. Part-time and evening/weekend programs available. *Degree requirements:* For master's, comprehensive exam (for some programs), thesis (for some programs). *Entrance requirements:* For master's, GRE General Test, minimum GPA of 2.5. Additional exam requirements/recommendations for international students: Required—TOEFL. Electronic applications accepted. *Faculty research:* Fuels/pollution, energy, outdoor storage methods.

California State University, Northridge, Graduate Studies, College of Engineering and Computer Science, Department of Manufacturing Systems Engineering and Management, Northridge, CA 91330. Offers engineering automation (MS); engineering management (MS); manufacturing systems engineering (MS); materials engineering (MS). Postbaccalaureate distance learning degree programs offered. *Entrance requirements:* For master's, GRE (if cumulative undergraduate GPA less than 3.0).

Central Washington University, Graduate Studies and Research, College of Education and Professional Studies, Department of Industrial and Engineering Technology, Ellensburg, WA 98926. Offers engineering technology (MS). Part-time programs available. *Degree requirements:* For master's, thesis or alternative. *Entrance requirements:* For master's, minimum GPA of 3.0. Additional exam requirements/recommendations for international students: Required—TOEFL (minimum score 550 paper-based; 213 computer-based; 79 iBT). Electronic applications accepted.

Clemson University, Graduate School, College of Engineering and Science, Department of Industrial Engineering, Clemson, SC 29634. Offers M Eng, MS, PhD. Part-time programs available. Postbaccalaureate distance learning degree programs offered (no on-campus study). *Faculty:* 11 full-time (3 women), 2 part-time/adjunct (both women). *Students:* 65 full-time (22 women), 86 part-time (34 women); includes 5 Black or African American, non-Hispanic/Latino; 2 American Indian or Alaska Native, non-Hispanic/Latino; 5 Asian, non-Hispanic/Latino; 4 Hispanic/Latino; 2 Two or more races, non-Hispanic/Latino, 62 international. Average age 32. 175 applicants, 74% accepted, 46 enrolled. In 2010, 18 master's, 5 doctorates awarded. Terminal master's awarded for partial completion of doctoral program. *Degree requirements:* For master's, thesis or alternative; for doctorate, thesis/dissertation. *Entrance requirements:* For master's and doctorate, GRE General Test. Additional exam requirements/recommendations for international students: Required—TOEFL. *Application deadline:* For fall admission, 6/1 for domestic students, 11/31 for international students. Applications are processed on a rolling basis. Application fee: $70 ($80 for international students). Electronic applications accepted. *Expenses:* Tuition, state resident: full-time $6492; part-time $400 per credit hour. Tuition, nonresident: full-time $13,634; part-time $800 per credit hour. Required fees: $262 per semester. Part-time tuition and fees vary according to course load and program. *Financial support:* In 2010–11, 45 students received support, including 1 fellowship with full and partial tuition reimbursement available (averaging $2,000 per year), 22 research assistantships with partial tuition reimbursements available (averaging $10,231 per year), 25 teaching assistantships with partial tuition reimbursements available (averaging $6,035 per year); career-related internships or fieldwork, institutionally sponsored loans, scholarships/grants, health care benefits, and unspecified assistantships also available. Support available to part-time students. Financial award applicants required to submit FAFSA. *Faculty research:* System optimization, health care engineering, human factors and safety, human-computer interaction, quality. Total annual research expenditures: $1.1 million. *Unit head:* Dr. Anand Gramopadhye, Head, 864-656-4716, E-mail: agramop@ces.clemson.edu. *Application contact:* Kevin M. Taaffe, Graduate Coordinator, 864-656-0291, E-mail: taaffe@clemson.edu.

Cleveland State University, College of Graduate Studies, Fenn College of Engineering, Department of Industrial and Manufacturing Engineering, Cleveland, OH 44115. Offers industrial engineering (MS, D Eng). Part-time programs available. *Faculty:* 5 full-time (0 women), 2 part-time/adjunct (0 women). *Students:* 16 full-time (3 women), 12 part-time (2 women); includes 2 Black or African American, non-Hispanic/Latino; 1 American Indian or Alaska Native, non-Hispanic/Latino; 1 Asian, non-Hispanic/Latino, 17 international. Average age 28. 84 applicants, 49% accepted, 8 enrolled. In 2010, 19 master's, 1 doctorate awarded. Terminal master's awarded for partial completion of doctoral program. *Degree requirements:* For master's, thesis or alternative; for doctorate, thesis/dissertation, candidacy and qualifying exams. *Entrance requirements:* For master's, GRE General Test, minimum GPA of 2.75; for doctorate, GRE General Test, minimum GPA of 3.25. Additional exam requirements/recommendations for international students: Required—TOEFL (minimum score 525 paper-based; 197 computer-based). *Application deadline:* For fall admission, 7/15 priority date for domestic students, 6/1 priority date for international students; for spring admission, 11/1 priority date for international students. Applications are processed on a rolling basis. Application fee: $30. *Expenses:* Tuition, state resident: full-time $8447; part-time $469 per credit hour. Tuition, nonresident: full-time $16,020; part-time $890 per credit hour. Required fees: $50. *Financial support:* In 2010–11, 4 research assistantships with full and partial tuition reimbursements (averaging $3,550 per year), 2 teaching assistantships with tuition reimbursements (averaging $3,725 per year) were awarded; fellowships, career-related internships or fieldwork, institutionally sponsored loans, tuition waivers (partial), and unspecified assistantships also available. Support available to part-time students. *Faculty research:* Modeling of manufacturing systems, statistical process control, computerized production planning and facilities design, cellular manufacturing, artificial intelligence and sensors. *Unit head:* Dr. Joseph A. Svestka, Chairperson, 216-687-4662, Fax: 216-687-9330, E-mail: j.svestka@csuohio.edu. *Application contact:* Shirley A. Love, Administrative Services Coordinator, 216-687-2044, Fax: 216-687-9330, E-mail: s.love@csuohio.edu.

Colorado State University–Pueblo, College of Education, Engineering and Professional Studies, Department of Engineering, Pueblo, CO 81001-4901. Offers industrial and systems engineering (MS). *Degree requirements:* For master's, thesis optional. *Entrance requirements:* For master's, GRE General Test. Additional exam requirements/recommendations for international students: Required—TOEFL (minimum score 500 paper-based). *Faculty research:* Nanotechnology, applied operations, research transportation, decision analysis.

Columbia University, Fu Foundation School of Engineering and Applied Science, Department of Industrial Engineering and Operations Research, New York, NY 10027. Offers financial engineering (MS); industrial engineering (Engr); industrial engineering and operations research (MS, Eng Sc D, PhD); MS/MBA. Part-time and evening/weekend programs available. Postbaccalaureate distance learning degree programs offered (no on-campus study). *Faculty:* 22 full-time (3 women), 23 part-time/adjunct (1 woman). *Students:* 295 full-time (81 women), 115 part-time (36 women); includes 23 minority (19 Asian, non-Hispanic/Latino; 3 Hispanic/Latino; 1 Two or more races, non-Hispanic/Latino), 352 international. Average age 26. 1,492 applicants, 21% accepted, 183 enrolled. In 2010, 258 master's, 7 doctorates, 1 other advanced degree awarded. *Degree requirements:* For doctorate, thesis/dissertation, oral and written qualifying exams. *Entrance requirements:* For master's, doctorate, and Engr, GRE General Test. Additional exam requirements/recommendations for international students: Required—TOEFL, IELTS. *Application deadline:* For fall admission, 12/1 priority date for domestic and international students; for spring admission, 10/1 priority date for domestic and international students. Application fee: $95. Electronic applications accepted. *Financial support:* In 2010–11, 59 students received support, including 12 fellowships (averaging $1,700 per year), 27 research assistantships with full tuition reimbursements available (averaging $30,765 per year), 20 teaching assistantships with full tuition reimbursements available (averaging $30,765 per year); career-related internships or fieldwork and health care benefits also available. Financial award application deadline: 12/1; financial award applicants required to submit FAFSA. *Faculty research:* Combinatorial optimization and mathematical programming; financial engineering; supply chain management and inventory theory; applied probability; queuing theory; scheduling, and simulation. *Unit head:* Dr. Cliff S. Stein, Professor and Department Chairman, 212-854-5238, Fax: 212-854-8103, E-mail: cliff@ieor.columbia.edu. *Application contact:* Adina Berrios Brooks, Student Affairs Manager, 212-854-1934, Fax: 212-854-8103, E-mail: admit@ieor.columbia.edu.

Concordia University, School of Graduate Studies, Faculty of Engineering and Computer Science, Department of Mechanical and Industrial Engineering, Montréal, QC H3G 1M8, Canada. Offers composites (M Eng); industrial engineering (M Eng, MA Sc); mechanical engineering (M Eng, MA Sc, PhD, Certificate); software systems for industrial engineering (Certificate). M Eng in composites program offered jointly with École Polytechnique de Montréal. *Degree requirements:* For master's, variable foreign language requirement, thesis or alternative; for doctorate, comprehensive exam, thesis/dissertation. *Faculty research:* Mechanical systems, fluid control systems, thermofluids engineering and robotics, industrial control systems.

Cornell University, Graduate School, Graduate Fields of Engineering, Field of Operations Research and Information Engineering, Ithaca, NY 14853. Offers applied probability and statistics (PhD); manufacturing systems engineering (PhD); mathematical programming (PhD); operations research and industrial engineering (M Eng). *Faculty:* 35 full-time (5 women). *Students:* 162 full-time (46 women); includes 3 Black or African American, non-Hispanic/Latino; 14 Asian, non-Hispanic/Latino; 3 Hispanic/Latino, 117 international. Average age 23. 1,076 applicants, 34% accepted, 139 enrolled. In 2010, 85 master's, 6 doctorates awarded. *Degree requirements:* For doctorate, comprehensive exam, thesis/dissertation. *Entrance requirements:* For master's and doctorate, GRE General Test, 3 letters of recommendation. Additional exam requirements/recommendations for international students: Required—TOEFL (minimum score 600 paper-based; 250 computer-based; 100 iBT). *Application deadline:* For fall admission, 12/15 for domestic students. Application fee: $70. Electronic applications accepted. *Expenses:* Tuition: Full-time $29,500. Required fees: $76. Tuition and fees vary according to degree level and program. *Financial support:* In 2010–11, 44 students received support, including 12 fellowships with full tuition reimbursements available, 9 research assistantships with full tuition reimbursements available, 24 teaching assistantships with full tuition reimbursements available; institutionally sponsored loans, scholarships/grants, health care benefits, tuition waivers (full and partial), and unspecified assistantships also available. Financial award applicants required to submit FAFSA. *Faculty research:* Mathematical programming and combinatorial optimization, statistics, stochastic processes, mathematical finance, simulation, manufacturing, e-commerce. *Unit head:* Director of Graduate Studies, 607-255-9128, Fax: 607-255-9129. *Application contact:* Graduate Field Assistant, 607-255-9128, Fax: 607-255-9129, E-mail: orie@cornell.edu.

Dalhousie University, Faculty of Engineering, Department of Industrial Engineering, Halifax, NS B3J 2X4, Canada. Offers M Eng, MA Sc, PhD. *Degree requirements:* For master's, thesis; for doctorate, thesis/dissertation. *Entrance requirements:* Additional exam requirements/recommendations for international students: Required—TOEFL, IELTS, CANTEST, CAEL, or Michigan English Language Assessment Battery. Electronic applications accepted. *Faculty research:* Industrial ergonomics, operations research, production manufacturing systems, scheduling stochastic models.

East Carolina University, Graduate School, College of Technology and Computer Science, Department of Technology Systems, Greenville, NC 27858-4353. Offers computer network professional (Certificate); industrial technology (MS), including computer networking management, digital communications, industrial distribution and logistics, information security, manufacturing, performance improvement, planning; information assurance (Certificate); occupational safety (MS); technology management (PhD); Website developer (Certificate). *Entrance requirements:* For master's and Certificate, GRE General Test or MAT, minimum GPA of 2.5; for doctorate, GRE General Test, related work experience. *Expenses:* Tuition, state resident: full-time $3130; part-time $391.25 per credit hour. Tuition, nonresident: full-time $13,817; part-time $1727.13 per credit hour. Required fees: $1916; $239.50 per credit hour. Tuition and fees vary according to campus/location and program.

Eastern Kentucky University, The Graduate School, College of Business and Technology, Department of Technology, Program in Industrial Technology, Richmond, KY 40475-3102. Offers MS. Part-time programs available. *Entrance requirements:* For master's, GRE General Test, minimum GPA of 2.5. *Faculty research:* Quality control, dental implants, manufacturing technology.

École Polytechnique de Montréal, Graduate Programs, Department of Mathematics and Industrial Engineering, Montréal, QC H3C 3A7, Canada. Offers ergonomy (M Eng, M Sc A, DESS); mathematical method in CA engineering (M Eng, M Sc A, PhD); operational research (M Eng, M Sc A, PhD); production (M Eng, M Sc A); technology management (M Eng, M Sc A). DESS program offered jointly with HEC Montreal and Université de Montréal. Part-time programs available. *Degree requirements:* For master's, one foreign language, thesis. *Entrance requirements:* For master's, minimum GPA of 2.75. *Faculty research:* Use of computers in organizations.

Florida Agricultural and Mechanical University, Division of Graduate Studies, Research, and Continuing Education, FAMU-FSU College of Engineering, Department of Industrial Engineering, Tallahassee, FL 32307-3200. Offers MS, PhD. *Degree requirements:* For master's, thesis optional. *Entrance requirements:* For master's, GRE General Test, minimum GPA of 3.0. Additional exam requirements/recommendations for international students: Required—TOEFL (minimum score 550 paper-based; 213 computer-based). *Faculty research:* Design for environmentally conscious manufacturing, affordable composite manufacturing, integrated product and process design, precision machining research.

Florida State University, The Graduate School, FAMU-FSU College of Engineering, Department of Industrial and Manufacturing Engineering, Tallahassee, FL 32306. Offers industrial engineering (MS, PhD). *Faculty:* 10 full-time (1 woman), 1 (woman) part-time/adjunct. *Students:* 43 full-time (7 women), 2 part-time (1 woman); includes 10 Black or African American, non-Hispanic/Latino; 2 Asian, non-Hispanic/Latino; 2 Hispanic/Latino, 22 international. Average age 24. 84 applicants, 54% accepted, 13 enrolled. In 2010, 11 master's, 3 doctorates awarded. *Degree requirements:* For master's, thesis; for doctorate, thesis/dissertation, preliminary exam, qualifying exam. *Entrance requirements:* For master's, GRE General Test (minimum score of 400 Verbal and 650 Quantitative), minimum GPA of 3.0; for doctorate, GRE General Test (minimum score of 450 Verbal and 700 Quantitative), minimum GPA of 3.0 (without MS in industrial engineering),

Industrial/Management Engineering

Florida State University *(continued)*
3.4 (with MS in industrial engineering). Additional exam requirements/recommendations for international students: Required—TOEFL (minimum score 550 paper-based; 213 computer-based; 80 iBT). *Application deadline:* For fall admission, 7/1 for domestic and international students; for spring admission, 11/1 for domestic and international students. Applications are processed on a rolling basis. Application fee: $30. *Expenses:* Tuition, state resident: full-time $8238.24. *Financial support:* In 2010–11, 31 students received support, including fellowships with full tuition reimbursements available (averaging $18,000 per year), 22 research assistantships with full tuition reimbursements available (averaging $15,000 per year), 1 teaching assistantship with full tuition reimbursement available (averaging $15,000 per year); tuition waivers (full) also available. Financial award application deadline: 6/15. *Faculty research:* Precision manufacturing, composite manufacturing, green manufacturing, applied optimization, simulation. Total annual research expenditures: $3.7 million. *Unit head:* Dr. Chun Zhang, Chair and Professor, 850-410-6355, Fax: 850-410-6342, E-mail: chzhang@eng.fsu.edu. *Application contact:* Stephanie Salters, Office Manager, 850-410-6345, Fax: 850-410-6342, E-mail: salters@eng.fsu.edu.

Georgia Institute of Technology, Graduate Studies and Research, College of Engineering, School of Industrial and Systems Engineering, Program in Industrial and Systems Engineering, Atlanta, GA 30332-0001. Offers algorithms, combinatorics, and optimization (PhD); industrial and systems engineering (PhD); industrial engineering (MS, MSIE); statistics (MS Stat). Part-time programs available. Terminal master's awarded for partial completion of doctoral program. *Degree requirements:* For master's, thesis optional; for doctorate, thesis/dissertation. *Entrance requirements:* For master's and doctorate, GRE General Test, minimum GPA of 3.0. Additional exam requirements/recommendations for international students: Required—TOEFL. Electronic applications accepted. *Faculty research:* Computer-integrated manufacturing systems, materials handling systems, production and distribution.

Illinois State University, Graduate School, College of Applied Science and Technology, Department of Technology, Normal, IL 61790-2200. Offers MS. *Degree requirements:* For master's, thesis or alternative. *Entrance requirements:* For master's, GRE General Test, minimum GPA of 2.8. *Faculty research:* National Center for Engineering and Technology Education, Illinois Manufacturing Extension Center Field Office hosting, model for the professional development of K-12 technology education teachers, Illinois State University Illinois Mathematics and Science Partnership, Illinois University council for career and technical education.

Indiana State University, College of Graduate and Professional Studies, College of Technology, Program in Industrial Technology, Terre Haute, IN 47809. Offers MS. *Entrance requirements:* For master's, bachelor's degree in industrial technology or related field. Additional exam requirements/recommendations for international students: Required—TOEFL. Electronic applications accepted.

Indiana University–Purdue University Fort Wayne, College of Engineering, Technology, and Computer Science, Program in Technology, Fort Wayne, IN 46805-1499. Offers facilities and construction management (MS); industrial technology/manufacturing (MS); information technology/advanced computer applications (MS). Part-time programs available. *Faculty:* 12 full-time (6 women), 1 part-time/adjunct (0 women). *Students:* 4 full-time (2 women), 14 part-time (1 woman); includes 3 minority (2 Asian, non-Hispanic/Latino; 1 Hispanic/Latino), 2 international. Average age 32. 5 applicants, 100% accepted, 2 enrolled. In 2010, 4 master's awarded. *Entrance requirements:* For master's, minimum GPA of 3.0. Additional exam requirements/recommendations for international students: Required—TOEFL (minimum score 550 paper-based; 213 computer-based; 77 iBT), TWE. *Application deadline:* For fall admission, 7/15 for domestic students, 5/15 for international students; for spring admission, 12/1 for domestic students, 10/15 for international students. Applications are processed on a rolling basis. Application fee: $55 ($60 for international students). Electronic applications accepted. *Expenses:* Tuition, state resident: full-time $4824; part-time $268 per credit. Tuition, nonresident: full-time $11,625; part-time $646 per credit. Required fees: $555; $30.85 per credit. Tuition and fees vary according to course load. *Financial support:* Career-related internships or fieldwork, scholarships/grants, and unspecified assistantships available. Support available to part-time students. Financial award application deadline: 3/1; financial award applicants required to submit FAFSA. *Unit head:* Dr. Max Yen, Dean, 260-481-6839, Fax: 260-481-5734, E-mail: yens@ipfw.edu. *Application contact:* Dr. Gary Steffen, Chair, 260-481-6344, Fax: 260-481-5734, E-mail: steffen@ipfw.edu.

Instituto Tecnologico de Santo Domingo, Graduate School, Area of Engineering, Santo Domingo, Dominican Republic. Offers construction administration (MS, Certificate); data telecommunications (M Eng, MS, Certificate); industrial engineering (M Eng, Certificate); industrial management (M Mgmt); information technology (Certificate); maintenance engineering (M Eng); occupational hazard prevention (M Mgmt); production management (Certificate); quantitative methods (Certificate); sanitary and environmental engineering (M Eng); structural engineering (M Eng); systems engineering and electronic data processing (Certificate); transportation (Certificate).

Instituto Tecnológico y de Estudios Superiores de Monterrey, Campus Chihuahua, Graduate Programs, Chihuahua, Mexico. Offers computer systems engineering (Ingeniero); electrical engineering (Ingeniero); electromechanical engineering (Ingeniero); electronic engineering (Ingeniero); engineering administration (MEA); industrial engineering (MIE, Ingeniero); international trade (MIT); mechanical engineering (Ingeniero).

Instituto Tecnológico y de Estudios Superiores de Monterrey, Campus Ciudad de México, Virtual University Division, Ciudad de Mexico, Mexico. Offers administration of information technologies (MA); computer sciences (MA); education (MA, PhD); educational technology (MA); environmental engineering (MA); environmental systems (MA); humanistic studies (MA); industrial engineering (MA); international business for Latin America (MA); quality systems (MA); quality systems and productivity (MA). Part-time and evening/weekend programs available. Postbaccalaureate distance learning degree programs offered (minimal on-campus study). *Entrance requirements:* For master's and doctorate, Instituto entrance exam. Additional exam requirements/recommendations for international students: Required—TOEFL.

Instituto Tecnológico y de Estudios Superiores de Monterrey, Campus Laguna, Graduate School, Torreón, Mexico. Offers business administration (MBA); industrial engineering (MIE); management information systems (MS). Part-time programs available. *Entrance requirements:* For master's, GMAT. *Faculty research:* Computer communications from home to the university.

Instituto Tecnológico y de Estudios Superiores de Monterrey, Campus Monterrey, Graduate and Research Division, Programs in Engineering, Monterrey, Mexico. Offers applied statistics (M Eng); artificial intelligence (PhD); automation engineering (M Eng); chemical engineering (M Eng); civil engineering (M Eng); electrical engineering (M Eng); electronic engineering (M Eng); environmental engineering (M Eng); industrial engineering (M Eng, PhD); manufacturing engineering (M Eng); mechanical engineering (M Eng); systems and quality engineering (M Eng). M Eng program offered jointly with University of Waterloo; PhD in industrial engineering with Texas A&M University. Part-time and evening/weekend programs available. Terminal master's awarded for partial completion of doctoral program. *Degree requirements:* For master's, one foreign language, thesis; for doctorate, one foreign language, thesis/dissertation. *Entrance requirements:* For master's, EXADEP; for doctorate, GRE, master's degree in related field. Additional exam requirements/recommendations for international students: Required—TOEFL. *Faculty research:* Flexible manufacturing cells, materials, statistical methods, environmental prevention, control and evaluation.

Iowa State University of Science and Technology, Graduate College, College of Engineering, Department of Industrial and Manufacturing Systems Engineering, Ames, IA 50011. Offers industrial engineering (M Eng, MS, PhD); operations research (MS); systems engineering (M Eng). *Faculty:* 14 full-time (2 women). *Students:* 50 full-time (12 women), 54 part-time (9 women); includes 3 Black or African American, non-Hispanic/Latino; 1 Asian, non-Hispanic/Latino; 1 Hispanic/Latino, 50 international. 142 applicants, 22% accepted, 10 enrolled. In 2010, 6 master's, 4 doctorates awarded. *Degree requirements:* For master's, thesis or alternative; for doctorate, thesis/dissertation. *Entrance requirements:* For master's and doctorate, GRE General Test. Additional exam requirements/recommendations for international students: Required—TOEFL (minimum score 550 paper-based; 79 iBT), IELTS (minimum score 6.5). *Application deadline:* For fall admission, 1/15 priority date for international students; for spring admission, 7/15 priority date for international students. Application fee: $40 ($90 for international students). Electronic applications accepted. *Financial support:* In 2010–11, 23 research assistantships with full and partial tuition reimbursements (averaging $6,292 per year), 6 teaching assistantships with full and partial tuition reimbursements (averaging $4,298 per year) were awarded; fellowships, scholarships/grants, health care benefits, and unspecified assistantships also available. *Faculty research:* Economic modeling, valuation techniques, robotics, digital controls, systems reliability. *Unit head:* Dr. Gary Mirka, Chair, 515-294-8661, Fax: 515-294-3524. *Application contact:* Dr. Sarah Ryan, Director of Graduate Studies, 515-294-4347, E-mail: smryan@iastate.edu.

Kansas State University, Graduate School, College of Engineering, Department of Industrial and Manufacturing Systems Engineering, Manhattan, KS 66506. Offers engineering management (MEM); industrial engineering (MS, PhD); operations research (MS). Part-time programs available. Postbaccalaureate distance learning degree programs offered. *Degree requirements:* For master's, thesis or alternative; for doctorate, thesis/dissertation. *Entrance requirements:* For master's, GRE General Test, bachelor's degree in engineering, mathematics, or physical science; for doctorate, GRE General Test, master's degree in engineering or industrial manufacturing. Additional exam requirements/recommendations for international students: Required—TOEFL. Electronic applications accepted. *Faculty research:* Ergonomics, healthcare systems engineering, manufacturing processes, operations research, engineering management.

Lamar University, College of Graduate Studies, College of Engineering, Department of Industrial Engineering, Beaumont, TX 77710. Offers engineering management (MEM); industrial engineering (ME, MES, DE). *Faculty:* 4 full-time (0 women). *Students:* 43 full-time (7 women), 8 part-time (1 woman); includes 3 Black or African American, non-Hispanic/Latino; 4 Asian, non-Hispanic/Latino; 3 Hispanic/Latino, 28 international. Average age 29. 61 applicants, 66% accepted, 9 enrolled. In 2010, 10 master's awarded. *Degree requirements:* For doctorate, thesis/dissertation. *Entrance requirements:* For master's and doctorate, GRE General Test. Additional exam requirements/recommendations for international students: Required—TOEFL. *Application deadline:* For fall admission, 5/15 priority date for domestic students; for spring admission, 10/1 priority date for domestic students. Applications are processed on a rolling basis. Application fee: $25 ($50 for international students). *Expenses:* Tuition, state resident: full-time $4160; part-time $208 per credit hour. Tuition, nonresident: full-time $10,360; part-time $518 per credit hour. *Financial support:* In 2010–11, 2 fellowships (averaging $6,000 per year), 4 research assistantships (averaging $1,000 per year), 2 teaching assistantships (averaging $4,500 per year) were awarded. Financial award application deadline: 4/1. *Faculty research:* Process simulation, total quality management, ergonomics and safety, scheduling. *Unit head:* Dr. Victor Zaloom, Chair, 409-880-8804, Fax: 409-880-8121. *Application contact:* Dr. Hsing-Wei Chu, Professor, 409-880-8804, Fax: 409-880-8121.

Lawrence Technological University, College of Engineering, Southfield, MI 48075-1058. Offers architectural engineering (MS); automotive engineering (MS); civil engineering (MS); electrical and computer engineering (MS); engineering management (MEM); industrial engineering (MS); manufacturing systems (ME, DE); mechanical engineering (MS); mechatronic systems engineering (MS). Part-time and evening/weekend programs available. *Faculty:* 20 full-time (4 women), 12 part-time/adjunct (0 women). *Students:* 8 full-time (1 woman), 366 part-time (60 women); includes 29 Black or African American, non-Hispanic/Latino; 1 American Indian or Alaska Native, non-Hispanic/Latino; 36 Asian, non-Hispanic/Latino; 9 Hispanic/Latino; 4 Two or more races, non-Hispanic/Latino, 81 international. Average age 32. 398 applicants, 48% accepted, 87 enrolled. In 2010, 121 master's, 5 doctorates awarded. *Degree requirements:* For master's, thesis (for some programs). *Entrance requirements:* Additional exam requirements/recommendations for international students: Required—TOEFL (minimum score 550 paper-based; 213 computer-based; 79 iBT). *Application deadline:* For fall admission, 6/30 priority date for domestic students, 6/30 for international students; for spring admission, 11/15 priority date for domestic students, 11/15 for international students. Applications are processed on a rolling basis. Application fee: $50. Electronic applications accepted. *Financial support:* In 2010–11, 72 students received support. Federal Work-Study and institutionally sponsored loans available. Support available to part-time students. Financial award application deadline: 4/1; financial award applicants required to submit FAFSA. *Faculty research:* Advanced composite materials in bridges, strengthening existing bridges with carbon and glass fiber sheets, development of drive shafts using composite materials. *Unit head:* Dr. Nabil Grace, Interim Dean, 248-204-2500, Fax: 248-204-2509, E-mail: engrdean@ltu.edu. *Application contact:* Jane Rohrback, Director of Admissions, 248-204-3160, Fax: 248-204-2228, E-mail: admissions@ltu.edu.

Lehigh University, P.C. Rossin College of Engineering and Applied Science, Department of Industrial and Systems Engineering, Bethlehem, PA 18015. Offers analytical finance (MS); industrial and systems engineering (M Eng, MS); industrial engineering (PhD); management science and engineering (M Eng, MS); MBA/E. Part-time programs available. Postbaccalaureate distance learning degree programs offered (no on-campus study). *Faculty:* 15 full-time (2 women), 1 part-time/adjunct (0 women). *Students:* 77 full-time (27 women), 15 part-time (5 women); includes 3 minority (2 Black or African American, non-Hispanic/Latino; 1 Asian, non-Hispanic/Latino), 63 international. Average age 27. 636 applicants, 19% accepted, 39 enrolled. In 2010, 26 master's, 6 doctorates awarded. *Degree requirements:* For master's, thesis (MS); project (M Eng); for doctorate, comprehensive exam, thesis/dissertation. *Entrance requirements:* For master's and doctorate, GRE General Test. Additional exam requirements/recommendations for international students: Required—TOEFL (minimum score 550 paper-based; 213 computer-based; 79 iBT). *Application deadline:* For fall admission, 7/15 for domestic and international students; for spring admission, 12/1 for domestic and international students. Applications are processed on a rolling basis. Application fee: $75. Electronic applications accepted. *Financial support:* In 2010–11, 28 students received support, including 3 fellowships with full tuition reimbursements available (averaging $17,460 per year), 16 research assistantships with full tuition reimbursements available (averaging $15,300 per year), 11 teaching assistantships with full tuition reimbursements available (averaging $18,360 per year); career-related internships or fieldwork, scholarships/grants, tuition waivers, and unspecified assistantships also available. Financial award application deadline: 1/15. *Faculty research:* Optimization, mathematical programming; logistics and supply chain, stochastic processes and simulation; computational optimization and high performance computing; financial engineering and robust optimization. Total annual research expenditures: $1.8 million. *Unit head:* Dr. Tamas Terlaky, Chair, 610-758-4050, Fax: 610-758-4886, E-mail: terlaky@lehigh.edu. *Application contact:* Rita R. Frey, Graduate Coordinator, 610-758-4051, Fax: 610-758-4886, E-mail: ise@lehigh.edu.

Louisiana State University and Agricultural and Mechanical College, Graduate School, College of Engineering, Department of Construction Management and Industrial Engineering, Baton Rouge, LA 70803. Offers engineering science (PhD); industrial engineering (MSIE). *Faculty:* 12 full-time (5 women), 1 part-time/adjunct (0 women). *Students:* 16 full-time (2 women), 2 part-time (0 women); includes 1 Black or African American, non-Hispanic/Latino, 15 international. Average age 24. 37 applicants, 65% accepted, 4 enrolled. In 2010, 7 master's awarded. Terminal master's awarded for partial completion of doctoral program. *Degree requirements:* For master's, thesis; for doctorate, thesis/dissertation. *Entrance requirements:* For master's and doctorate, GRE General Test, minimum GPA of 3.0. Additional exam requirements/recommendations for international students: Required—TOEFL (minimum score 550 paper-based; 213 computer-based; 79 iBT) or IELTS (minimum score 6.5). *Application deadline:* For fall admission, 1/25 priority date for domestic students, 5/15 for international students; for spring admission, 10/15 for international students. Applications are processed on a rolling basis. Application fee: $50 ($70 for international students). Electronic applications accepted. *Financial support:* In 2010–11, 10 students received support, including 8 research assistantships with partial tuition reimbursements available (averaging $11,760 per year), 3 teaching assistantships with partial tuition reimbursements available (averaging $10,962 per year); fellowships, Federal Work-Study, institutionally sponsored loans, health care benefits, and unspecified assistantships also available. Financial award application deadline: 5/1; financial award applicants required to submit FAFSA. *Faculty research:* Ergonomics and occupational health, information technology, production systems, supply management, construction safety and methods. Total annual research expenditures: $249,966. *Unit head:* Dr. Craig Harvey, Chair, 225-578-5112, Fax: 225-578-5109, E-mail: harvey@lsu.edu. *Application contact:* Dr. Pius Egbelu, Graduate Adviser, 225-578-5112, Fax: 225-578-5109, E-mail: pegbelu@eng.lsu.edu.

Louisiana Tech University, Graduate School, College of Engineering and Science, Department of Industrial Engineering, Ruston, LA 71272. Offers MS.

Mississippi State University, Bagley College of Engineering, Department of Industrial and Systems Engineering, Mississippi State, MS 39762. Offers engineering (PhD), including industrial engineering; industrial engineering (MS). Part-time programs available. Postbaccalaureate distance learning degree programs offered (no on-campus study). *Faculty:* 9 full-time (3 women), 1 part-time/adjunct (0 women). *Students:* 36 full-time (11 women), 44 part-time (6 women); includes 14 minority (6 Black or African American, non-Hispanic/Latino; 4 Asian, non-Hispanic/Latino; 4 Hispanic/Latino), 25 international. Average age 33. 76 applicants, 38% accepted, 20 enrolled. In 2010, 15 master's, 2 doctorates awarded. *Degree requirements:* For master's, thesis (for some programs), comprehensive oral or written exam; for doctorate, thesis/dissertation, candidacy exam. *Entrance requirements:* For master's, GRE General Test, minimum GPA of 3.0; for doctorate, GRE General Test, minimum GPA of 3.3. Additional exam requirements/recommendations for international students: Required—TOEFL (minimum score 550 paper-based; 213 computer-based; 79 iBT); Recommended—IELTS (minimum score 6.5). *Application deadline:* For fall admission, 7/1 for domestic students, 5/1 for international students; for spring admission, 11/1 for domestic students, 9/1 for international students. Applications are processed on a rolling basis. Application fee: $40. *Expenses:* Tuition, state resident: full-time $2730.50; part-time $304 per credit hour. Tuition, nonresident: full-time $6901; part-time $767 per credit hour. *Financial support:* In 2010–11, 16 research assistantships with full tuition reimbursements (averaging $14,070 per year), 7 teaching assistantships with full tuition reimbursements (averaging $11,078 per year) were awarded; Federal Work-Study, institutionally sponsored loans, and unspecified assistantships also available. Financial award application deadline: 4/1; financial award applicants required to submit FAFSA. *Faculty research:* Operations research, ergonomics, production systems, management systems, transportation. *Unit head:* Dr. Royce Bowden, Professor and Head, 662-325-3865, Fax: 662-325-7618, E-mail: bowden@ise.msstate.edu. *Application contact:* Dr. John Usher, Professor and Graduate Coordinator, 662-325-7624, Fax: 662-325-7618, E-mail: usher@ise.msstate.edu.

Montana State University, College of Graduate Studies, College of Engineering, Department of Mechanical and Industrial Engineering, Bozeman, MT 59717. Offers engineering (PhD), including industrial engineering option, mechanical engineering option; industrial and management engineering (MS); mechanical engineering (MS). Part-time programs available. *Faculty:* 16 full-time (2 women), 9 part-time/adjunct (2 women). *Students:* 18 full-time (0 women), 28 part-time (9 women); includes 3 minority (all Asian, non-Hispanic/Latino), 9 international. Average age 27. 51 applicants, 43% accepted, 12 enrolled. In 2010, 14 master's, 1 doctorate awarded. *Degree requirements:* For master's, comprehensive exam, thesis, oral exams; for doctorate, comprehensive exam, thesis/dissertation, qualifying exam. *Entrance requirements:* For master's, GRE, official transcript, minimum GPA of 3.0, demonstrated potential for success, statement of goals, three letters of recommendation, proof of funds affidavit; for doctorate, minimum undergraduate GPA of 3.0, 3.2 graduate; three letters of recommendation; statement of objectives. Additional exam requirements/recommendations for international students: Required—TOEFL or IELTS. *Application deadline:* For fall admission, 7/15 priority date for domestic students, 5/15 priority date for international students; for spring admission, 12/1 priority date for domestic students, 10/1 priority date for international students. Applications are processed on a rolling basis. Application fee: $30. Electronic applications accepted. *Expenses:* Tuition, state resident: full-time $5553.90. Tuition, nonresident: full-time $14,646. Required fees: $1233. *Financial support:* In 2010–11, 34 students received support, including 22 research assistantships with tuition reimbursements available (averaging $8,276 per year), 22 teaching assistantships with tuition reimbursements available (averaging $5,255 per year); health care benefits and unspecified assistantships also available. Support available to part-time students. Financial award application deadline: 3/1; financial award applicants required to submit FAFSA. *Faculty research:* Human factors engineering, energy, design and manufacture, systems modeling, materials and structures, measurement systems. Total annual research expenditures: $1 million. *Unit head:* Dr. Chris Jenkins, Head, 406-994-2203, Fax: 406-994-6292, E-mail: cjenkins@me.montana.edu. *Application contact:* Dr. Carl A. Fox, Vice Provost for Graduate Education, 406-994-4145, Fax: 406-994-7433, E-mail: gradstudy@montana.edu.

Montana Tech of The University of Montana, Graduate School, Project Engineering and Management Program, Butte, MT 59701-8997. Offers MPEM. Part-time and evening/weekend programs available. Postbaccalaureate distance learning degree programs offered (no on-campus study). *Faculty:* 1 full-time (0 women), 7 part-time/adjunct (1 woman). *Students:* 16 part-time (4 women); includes 1 American Indian or Alaska Native, non-Hispanic/Latino, 1 international. 5 applicants, 40% accepted, 0 enrolled. *Degree requirements:* For master's, comprehensive exam, final project presentation. *Entrance requirements:* For master's, minimum GPA of 3.0. Additional exam requirements/recommendations for international students: Required—TOEFL (minimum score 550 paper-based; 213 computer-based; 71 iBT). *Application deadline:* For fall admission, 4/1 priority date for domestic students, 3/1 priority date for international students; for spring admission, 10/1 priority date for domestic students, 7/1 priority date for international students. Applications are processed on a rolling basis. Application fee: $30. Electronic applications accepted. *Expenses:* Tuition, state resident: full-time $5084. Tuition, nonresident: full-time $15,104. *Financial support:* Application deadline: 4/1. *Unit head:* Dr. Kumar Ganesan, Director, 406-496-4239, Fax: 406-496-4650, E-mail: kganesan@mtech.edu. *Application contact:* Fred Sullivan, Administrator, Graduate School, 406-496-4304, Fax: 406-496-4710, E-mail: fsullivan@mtech.edu.

Morehead State University, Graduate Programs, College of Science and Technology, Department of Industrial and Engineering Technology, Morehead, KY 40351. Offers career and technical education (MS); engineering technology (MS). Part-time and evening/weekend programs available. *Degree requirements:* For master's, completion and defense of thesis or written and oral comprehensive exit exams. *Entrance requirements:* For master's, GRE, minimum undergraduate GPA of 3.0 in major. Additional exam requirements/recommendations for international students: Required—TOEFL (minimum score 500 paper-based; 173 computer-based). Electronic applications accepted.

Morgan State University, School of Graduate Studies, Clarence M. Mitchell, Jr. School of Engineering, Baltimore, MD 21251. Offers civil engineering (M Eng, D Eng); electrical engineering (M Eng, D Eng); industrial engineering (M Eng, D Eng); transportation (MS). Part-time and evening/weekend programs available. *Degree requirements:* For master's, thesis, comprehensive exam or equivalent; for doctorate, thesis/dissertation, comprehensive exam or equivalent. *Entrance requirements:* For master's, GRE, minimum undergraduate GPA of 2.5; for doctorate, GRE, minimum GPA of 3.0. Additional exam requirements/recommendations for international students: Required—TOEFL (minimum score 550 paper-based; 213 computer-based).

New Jersey Institute of Technology, Office of Graduate Studies, Newark College of Engineering, Department of Industrial and Manufacturing Engineering, Program in Industrial Engineering, Newark, NJ 07102. Offers MS, PhD. Part-time and evening/weekend programs available. *Students:* 27 full-time (6 women), 18 part-time (5 women); includes 4 Black or African American, non-Hispanic/Latino; 2 Asian, non-Hispanic/Latino; 6 Hispanic/Latino, 21 international. Average age 28. 112 applicants, 47% accepted, 19 enrolled. In 2010, 24 master's, 3 doctorates awarded. Terminal master's awarded for partial completion of doctoral program. *Degree requirements:* For master's, thesis or alternative; for doctorate, thesis/dissertation. *Entrance requirements:* For master's, GRE General Test; for doctorate, GRE General Test, minimum graduate GPA of 3.5. Additional exam requirements/recommendations for international students: Required—TOEFL (minimum score 550 paper-based; 213 computer-based; 79 iBT). *Application deadline:* For fall admission, 6/5 priority date for domestic students, 4/1 for international students; for spring admission, 11/15 for domestic and international students. Applications are processed on a rolling basis. Application fee: $65. Electronic applications accepted. *Expenses:* Tuition, state resident: full-time $14,724; part-time $818 per credit. Tuition, nonresident: full-time $20,304; part-time $1128 per credit. Required fees: $2272; $209 per credit. $103 per semester. One-time fee: $312 full-time; $212 part-time. *Financial support:* Fellowships with full and partial tuition reimbursements, research assistantships with full and partial tuition reimbursements, teaching assistantships with full and partial tuition reimbursements, career-related internships or fieldwork, Federal Work-Study, institutionally sponsored loans, and unspecified assistantships available. Financial award application deadline: 3/15. *Faculty research:* Knowledge-based systems, CAS/CAM simulation and interface, expert system. *Unit head:* Dr. Sanchoy K. Das, Director, 973-596-3654, Fax: 973-596-3652, E-mail: sanchoy.k.das@njit.edu. *Application contact:* Kathryn Kelly, Director of Admissions, 973-596-3300, Fax: 973-596-3461, E-mail: admissions@njit.edu.

New Mexico State University, Graduate School, College of Engineering, Department of Industrial Engineering, Las Cruces, NM 88003-8001. Offers MSIE, PhD. Part-time and evening/weekend programs available. Postbaccalaureate distance learning degree programs offered (no on-campus study). *Faculty:* 6 full-time (2 women). *Students:* 40 full-time (11 women), 76 part-time (24 women); includes 47 minority (6 Black or African American, non-Hispanic/Latino; 2 American Indian or Alaska Native, non-Hispanic/Latino; 3 Asian, non-Hispanic/Latino; 34 Hispanic/Latino; 2 Two or more races, non-Hispanic/Latino), 23 international. Average age 29. 109 applicants, 77% accepted, 54 enrolled. In 2010, 45 master's awarded. *Degree requirements:* For master's, thesis optional; for doctorate, comprehensive exam, thesis/dissertation. *Entrance requirements:* For doctorate, qualifying exam. Additional exam requirements/recommendations for international students: Required—TOEFL. *Application deadline:* For fall admission, 7/1 priority date for domestic students, 3/1 for international students; for spring admission, 11/1 for domestic students, 10/1 for international students. Applications are processed on a rolling basis. Application fee: $30 ($50 for international students). Electronic applications accepted. *Expenses:* Tuition, state resident: full-time $4536; part-time $242 per credit. Tuition, nonresident: full-time $15,816; part-time $712 per credit. Required fees: $636 per term. *Financial support:* In 2010–11, 16 students received support, including 6 research assistantships (averaging $5,267 per year), 8 teaching assistantships (averaging $7,519 per year); fellowships, career-related internships or fieldwork, Federal Work-Study, health care benefits, and unspecified assistantships also available. Financial award application deadline: 3/1. *Faculty research:* Simulation, stochastic modeling, optimization, systems engineering. *Unit head:* Dr. Edward Pines, Head, 575-646-4923, Fax: 575-646-2976, E-mail: epines@nmsu.edu. *Application contact:* Sarah Deyoe, Department Secretary, 575-646-4923, Fax: 575-646-2976, E-mail: sdeyoe@nmsu.edu.

North Carolina Agricultural and Technical State University, Graduate School, College of Engineering, Department of Industrial and Systems Engineering, Greensboro, NC 27411. Offers industrial engineering (MSIE, PhD). Part-time programs available. *Degree requirements:* For master's, thesis, project; for doctorate, thesis/dissertation. *Entrance requirements:* For master's, GRE General Test (recommended); for doctorate, GRE General Test. *Faculty research:* Human-machine systems engineering, management systems engineering, operations research and systems analysis, production systems engineering.

North Carolina State University, Graduate School, College of Engineering, Edward P. Fitts Department of Industrial and Systems Engineering, Raleigh, NC 27695. Offers industrial engineering (MIE, MS, PhD). PhD offered jointly with North Carolina Agricultural and Technical State University, The University of North Carolina at Charlotte. Part-time programs available. Terminal master's awarded for partial completion of doctoral program. *Degree requirements:* For master's, thesis optional; for doctorate, thesis/dissertation. *Entrance requirements:* For master's, GRE General Test, minimum GPA of 3.0; for doctorate, GRE General Test. Additional exam requirements/recommendations for international students: Required—TOEFL. Electronic applications accepted.

North Dakota State University, College of Graduate and Interdisciplinary Studies, College of Engineering and Architecture, Department of Industrial and Manufacturing Engineering, Fargo, ND 58108. Offers industrial and manufacturing engineering (PhD); industrial engineering and management (MS); manufacturing engineering (MS). Part-time programs available. *Faculty:* 13 full-time (2 women), 1 part-time/adjunct (0 women). *Students:* 29 full-time (5 women), 9 part-time (4 women), 35 international. Average age 26. 23 applicants, 52% accepted, 4 enrolled. In 2010, 4 master's awarded. *Degree requirements:* For doctorate, comprehensive exam, thesis/dissertation. *Entrance requirements:* For master's, GRE General Test, bachelor's degree in engineering; for doctorate, GRE General Test, master's degree in engineering. Additional exam requirements/recommendations for international students: Required—TOEFL (minimum score 550 paper-based; 213 computer-based; 79 iBT), TWE (minimum score 4). *Application deadline:* For fall admission, 3/1 priority date for domestic students, 3/1 for international students; for spring admission, 11/1 priority date for domestic students, 11/1 for international students. Applications are processed on a rolling basis. Application fee: $45 ($60 for international students). Electronic applications accepted. *Financial support:* In 2010–11, 2 fellowships with full tuition reimbursements (averaging $15,000 per year), 9 research assistantships with full tuition reimbursements (averaging $12,000 per year), 16 teaching assistantships with full tuition reimbursements (averaging $12,000 per year) were awarded; Federal Work-Study, institutionally sponsored loans, scholarships/grants, and unspecified assistantships also available. Financial award application deadline: 4/1. *Faculty research:* Electronics manufacturing, quality engineering, manufacturing process science, healthcare, lean manufacturing. Total annual research expenditures: $60,000. *Unit head:* Prof. Kambiz Farahmand, Chair, 701-231-7287, Fax: 701-231-7195, E-mail: kambiz.farahmand@ndsu.edu. *Application contact:* Dr. David A. Wittrock, Dean, 701-231-7033, Fax: 701-231-6524.

Northeastern University, College of Engineering, Department of Mechanical, Industrial, and Manufacturing Engineering, Boston, MA 02115-5096. Offers engineering management (MS); industrial engineering (MS, PhD); mechanical engineering (MS, PhD); operations research (MS). Part-time programs available. *Faculty:* 34 full-time (2 women), 7 part-time/adjunct (0 women). *Students:* 297 full-time (70 women), 103 part-time (20 women). 616 applicants, 77% accepted, 140 enrolled. In 2010, 107 master's, 5 doctorates awarded. *Degree requirements:* For master's, thesis (for some programs); for doctorate, thesis/dissertation, departmental qualifying exam. *Entrance requirements:* For master's and doctorate, GRE General Test. Additional exam requirements/recommendations for international students: Required—TOEFL (minimum score 550 paper-based; 213 computer-based; 80 iBT). *Application deadline:* For fall admission, 1/15 priority date for domestic and international students; for spring admission, 11/1 priority date for domestic students. Applications are processed on a rolling basis. Application fee: $50. Electronic applications accepted. *Financial support:* In 2010–11, 79 students received support, including 50 research assistantships with full tuition reimbursements available (averaging $18,325 per year), 33 teaching assistantships with full tuition reimbursements available (averaging $18,325 per year); fellowships with full tuition reimbursements available, career-related internships or fieldwork, Federal Work-Study, scholarships/grants, health care benefits, and unspecified assistantships also available. Support available to part-time students. Financial award application deadline: 1/15; financial award applicants required to submit FAFSA. *Faculty research:* Dry sliding instabilities, droplet deposition, combustion, manufacturing systems, nano-manufacturing, advanced materials processing, bio-nano robotics, burning speed measurement, virtual environments. *Unit head:* Dr. Hameed Metghalchi, Chairman, 617-373-2973, Fax: 617-373-2921. *Application contact:* Jeffery Hengel, Admissions Specialist, 617-373-2711, Fax: 617-373-2501, E-mail: grad-eng@coe.neu.edu.

Industrial/Management Engineering

Northern Illinois University, Graduate School, College of Engineering and Engineering Technology, Department of Industrial Engineering, De Kalb, IL 60115-2854. Offers MS. Part-time programs available. *Faculty:* 4 full-time (1 woman), 1 part-time/adjunct (0 women). *Students:* 26 full-time (8 women), 21 part-time (5 women); includes 1 Black or African American, non-Hispanic/Latino; 3 Asian, non-Hispanic/Latino; 3 Hispanic/Latino, 29 international. Average age 26. 101 applicants, 68% accepted, 21 enrolled. In 2010, 25 master's awarded. *Degree requirements:* For master's, comprehensive exam, thesis optional. *Entrance requirements:* For master's, GRE General Test, minimum GPA of 2.75. Additional exam requirements/recommendations for international students: Required—TOEFL (minimum score 550 paper-based; 213 computer-based). *Application deadline:* For fall admission, 6/1 for domestic students, 5/1 for international students; for spring admission, 11/1 for domestic students, 10/1 for international students. Applications are processed on a rolling basis. Application fee: $30. Electronic applications accepted. *Expenses:* Tuition, state resident: full-time $7200; part-time $300 per credit hour. Tuition, nonresident: full-time $14,400; part-time $600 per credit hour. Required fees: $79 per credit hour. *Financial support:* In 2010–11, 9 research assistantships, 8 teaching assistantships were awarded; fellowships, Federal Work-Study, scholarships/grants, tuition waivers (full), and staff assistantships also available. Support available to part-time students. Financial award applicants required to submit FAFSA. *Faculty research:* Assembly robots, engineering ethics, quality cost models, data mining. *Unit head:* Dr. Omar Ghrayeb, Chair, 815-753-1349, Fax: 815-753-0823. *Application contact:* Graduate School Office, 815-753-0395, E-mail: gradsch@niu.edu.

Northwestern University, McCormick School of Engineering and Applied Science, Department of Industrial Engineering and Management Sciences, Evanston, IL 60208. Offers engineering management (MEM); industrial engineering and management science (MS, PhD). MS and PhD admissions and degrees offered through The Graduate School. *Faculty:* 17 full-time (2 women). *Students:* 62 full-time (21 women); includes 2 minority (1 Hispanic/Latino; 1 Two or more races, non-Hispanic/Latino), 46 international. Average age 23. 233 applicants, 8% accepted, 7 enrolled. In 2010, 12 master's, 5 doctorates awarded. Terminal master's awarded for partial completion of doctoral program. *Degree requirements:* For master's, comprehensive exam; for doctorate, comprehensive exam, thesis/dissertation. *Entrance requirements:* For master's and doctorate, General Exam of GRE. Additional exam requirements/recommendations for international students: Required—TOEFL (minimum score 577 paper-based; 233 computer-based; 90 iBT), IELTS (minimum score 7). *Application deadline:* For fall admission, 12/31 for domestic and international students. Application fee: $75. Electronic applications accepted. *Financial support:* Fellowships with full tuition reimbursements, research assistantships with full tuition reimbursements, teaching assistantships with full tuition reimbursements, career-related internships or fieldwork, institutionally sponsored loans, health care benefits, and unspecified assistantships available. Financial award application deadline: 1/15; financial award applicants required to submit FAFSA. *Faculty research:* Decision and risk analysis, financial engineering, healthcare engineering, humanitarian logistics, optimization, organization behavior and technology management, production and logistics, social and organizational networks, statistics for enterprise engineering, stochastic modeling and simulation. Total annual research expenditures: $2.7 million. *Unit head:* Dr. Barry Nelson, Chair, 847-491-3747, Fax: 847-491-8005, E-mail: nelsonb@northwestern.edu. *Application contact:* Dr. Jeremy Staum, Admission Officer, 847-491-3383, Fax: 847-491-8005, E-mail: j-staum@northwestern.edu.

The Ohio State University, Graduate School, College of Engineering, Program in Industrial and Systems Engineering, Columbus, OH 43210. Offers industrial and systems engineering (MS, PhD); welding engineering (MS, MWE, PhD). *Faculty:* 39. *Students:* 69 full-time (21 women), 63 part-time (12 women); includes 4 Black or African American, non-Hispanic/Latino; 14 Asian, non-Hispanic/Latino; 9 Hispanic/Latino, 129 international. Average age 28. In 2010, 23 master's, 11 doctorates awarded. *Degree requirements:* For master's, thesis optional; for doctorate, thesis/dissertation. *Entrance requirements:* For master's and doctorate, GRE General Test. Additional exam requirements/recommendations for international students: Recommended—TOEFL (minimum score 600 paper-based; 250 computer-based). *Application deadline:* For fall admission, 8/15 priority date for domestic students, 11/1 priority date for international students; for winter admission, 12/1 priority date for domestic students, 7/1 priority date for international students; for spring admission, 3/1 priority date for domestic students, 2/1 priority date for international students. Applications are processed on a rolling basis. Application fee: $40 ($50 for international students). Electronic applications accepted. *Expenses:* Tuition, state resident: full-time $10,605. Tuition, nonresident: full-time $26,535. Tuition and fees vary according to course load and program. *Financial support:* Fellowships, research assistantships, teaching assistantships, career-related internships or fieldwork, Federal Work-Study, institutionally sponsored loans, and unspecified assistantships available. Support available to part-time students. *Unit head:* Julie L. Higle, Chair, 614-292-6239, E-mail: higle.1@osu.edu. *Application contact:* 614-292-9444, Fax: 614-292-3895, E-mail: domestic.grad@osu.edu.

Ohio University, Graduate College, Russ College of Engineering and Technology, Department of Industrial and Systems Engineering, Athens, OH 45701-2979. Offers M Eng Mgt, MS. Part-time and evening/weekend programs available. *Students:* 21 full-time (7 women), 25 part-time (2 women); includes 3 minority (1 Black or African American, non-Hispanic/Latino; 1 Asian, non-Hispanic/Latino; 1 Two or more races, non-Hispanic/Latino), 18 international. 50 applicants, 34% accepted, 5 enrolled. In 2010, 12 master's awarded. *Degree requirements:* For master's, comprehensive exam (for some programs), thesis optional, research project. *Entrance requirements:* For master's, GRE General Test. Additional exam requirements/recommendations for international students: Required—TOEFL (minimum score 550 paper-based; 80 iBT) or IELTS (minimum score 6.5). *Application deadline:* For fall admission, 3/1 priority date for domestic and international students; for winter admission, 9/1 priority date for domestic and international students; for spring admission, 1/1 priority date for domestic and international students. Applications are processed on a rolling basis. Application fee: $50 ($55 for international students). Electronic applications accepted. *Financial support:* In 2010–11, research assistantships with full tuition reimbursements (averaging $9,000 per year); Federal Work-Study, institutionally sponsored loans, tuition waivers (full), and unspecified assistantships also available. Financial award application deadline: 2/15; financial award applicants required to submit FAFSA. *Faculty research:* Software systems integration, human factors and ergonomics. Total annual research expenditures: $350,000. *Unit head:* Dr. Robert P. Judd, Chairman, 740-593-0106, Fax: 740-593-0778, E-mail: judd@ohio.edu. *Application contact:* Dr. Gursel Suer, Graduate Chairman, 740-593-1542, Fax: 740-593-0778, E-mail: suer@ohio.edu.

Ohio University, Graduate College, Russ College of Engineering and Technology, Program in Mechanical and Systems Engineering, Athens, OH 45701-2979. Offers industrial engineering (PhD); mechanical engineering (PhD). *Students:* 18 full-time (5 women), 5 part-time (0 women), 18 international. 7 applicants, 14% accepted, 1 enrolled. In 2010, 2 doctorates awarded. *Degree requirements:* For doctorate, comprehensive exam, thesis/dissertation. *Entrance requirements:* For doctorate, GRE General Test, MS in engineering or related field. Additional exam requirements/recommendations for international students: Required—TOEFL (minimum score 550 paper-based; 80 iBT) or IELTS (minimum score 6.5). *Application deadline:* For fall admission, 3/15 priority date for domestic and international students. Applications are processed on a rolling basis. Application fee: $50 ($55 for international students). Electronic applications accepted. *Financial support:* In 2010–11, 4 research assistantships with full tuition reimbursements (averaging $14,000 per year) were awarded; Federal Work-Study, institutionally sponsored loans, and unspecified assistantships also available. Financial award application deadline: 3/15; financial award applicants required to submit FAFSA. *Faculty research:* Material processing, expert systems, environmental geotechnical manufacturing, thermal systems, robotics. Total annual research expenditures: $1.8 million. *Unit head:* Dr. Shawn Ostermann, Associate Dean, 740-593-1482, Fax: 740-593-0659, E-mail: ostermann@ohio.edu. *Application contact:* Dr. Shawn Ostermann, Associate Dean, 740-593-1482, Fax: 740-593-0659, E-mail: ostermann@ohio.edu.

Oklahoma State University, College of Engineering, Architecture and Technology, School of Industrial Engineering and Management, Stillwater, OK 74078. Offers MS, PhD. Postbaccalaureate distance learning degree programs offered. *Faculty:* 26 full-time (2 women). *Students:* 99 full-time (23 women), 107 part-time (20 women); includes 1 Black or African American, non-Hispanic/Latino; 2 American Indian or Alaska Native, non-Hispanic/Latino; 4 Asian, non-Hispanic/Latino; 3 Hispanic/Latino, 157 international. Average age 28. 393 applicants, 45% accepted, 48 enrolled. In 2010, 47 master's, 6 doctorates awarded. *Degree requirements:* For master's, creative component or thesis; for doctorate, comprehensive exam, thesis/dissertation. *Entrance requirements:* For master's and doctorate, GRE or GMAT. Additional exam requirements/recommendations for international students: Required—TOEFL (minimum score 550 paper-based; 79 iBT). *Application deadline:* For fall admission, 3/1 priority date for international students; for spring admission, 8/1 priority date for international students. Applications are processed on a rolling basis. Application fee: $40 ($75 for international students). Electronic applications accepted. *Expenses:* Tuition, state resident: full-time $3716; part-time $154.85 per credit hour. Tuition, nonresident: full-time $14,892; part-time $621 per credit hour. Required fees: $2044; $85.20 per credit hour. One-time fee: $50. Tuition and fees vary according to course load and campus/location. *Financial support:* In 2010–11, 70 research assistantships (averaging $12,214 per year), 30 teaching assistantships (averaging $8,654 per year) were awarded; career-related internships or fieldwork, Federal Work-Study, scholarships/grants, health care benefits, tuition waivers (partial), and unspecified assistantships also available. Support available to part-time students. Financial award application deadline: 3/1; financial award applicants required to submit FAFSA. *Unit head:* Dr. William J. Kolarik, Head, 405-744-6055, Fax: 405-744-4654. *Application contact:* Dr. Gordon Emslie, Dean, 405-744-6368, Fax: 405-744-0355, E-mail: grad-i@okstate.edu.

Oregon State University, Graduate School, College of Engineering, School of Mechanical, Industrial, and Manufacturing Engineering, Corvallis, OR 97331. Offers human systems engineering (MS, PhD); industrial engineering (MS, PhD); information systems engineering (MS, PhD); manufacturing engineering (M Engr); manufacturing systems engineering (MS, PhD); materials science (MAIS, MS, PhD); mechanical engineering (MS, PhD); nano/micro fabrication (MS, PhD). Part-time programs available. Postbaccalaureate distance learning degree programs offered (minimal on-campus study). *Degree requirements:* For master's, thesis or alternative; for doctorate, thesis/dissertation. *Entrance requirements:* For master's, placement exam, minimum GPA of 3.0 in last 90 hours of course work; for doctorate, GRE, placement exam, minimum GPA of 3.0 in last 90 hours of course work. Additional exam requirements/recommendations for international students: Required—TOEFL (minimum score 550 paper-based; 213 computer-based). *Faculty research:* Computer-integrated manufacturing, human factors, robotics, decision support systems, simulation modeling and analysis.

Penn State University Park, Graduate School, College of Engineering, Department of Industrial and Manufacturing Engineering, State College, University Park, PA 16802-1503. Offers M Eng, MS, PhD.

Polytechnic Institute of NYU, Department of Interdisciplinary Studies, Major in Industrial Engineering, Brooklyn, NY 11201-2990. Offers MS. Part-time and evening/weekend programs available. *Students:* 41 full-time (14 women), 14 part-time (3 women); includes 2 Black or African American, non-Hispanic/Latino; 1 Asian, non-Hispanic/Latino; 1 Hispanic/Latino, 36 international. Average age 26. 90 applicants, 52% accepted, 26 enrolled. In 2010, 15 master's awarded. *Degree requirements:* For master's, comprehensive exam (for some programs), thesis (for some programs). *Entrance requirements:* For master's, BE or BS in engineering, physics, chemistry, mathematical sciences, or biological sciences or MBA. Additional exam requirements/recommendations for international students: Required—TOEFL (minimum score 550 paper-based; 213 computer-based; 80 iBT); Recommended—IELTS (minimum score 6.5). *Application deadline:* For fall admission, 7/31 priority date for domestic students, 4/30 priority date for international students; for spring admission, 12/31 priority date for domestic students, 11/30 priority date for international students. Applications are processed on a rolling basis. Application fee: $75. Electronic applications accepted. *Expenses:* Tuition: Full-time $21,492; part-time $1194 per credit. Required fees: $385 per semester. Tuition and fees vary according to course load. *Financial support:* Institutionally sponsored loans, scholarships/grants, and unspecified assistantships available. Support available to part-time students. Financial award applicants required to submit FAFSA. *Unit head:* Prof. Michael Greenstein, Department Head, 718-260-3835, E-mail: mgreenst@poly.edu. *Application contact:* JeanCarlo Bonilla, Director of Graduate Enrollment Management, 718-260-3182, Fax: 718-260-3624, E-mail: gradinfo@poly.edu.

Polytechnic Institute of NYU, Long Island Graduate Center, Graduate Programs, Department of Interdisciplinary Studies, Major in Industrial Engineering, Melville, NY 11747. Offers MS. Part-time and evening/weekend programs available. *Students:* 1 part-time (0 women). Average age 34. 1 applicant, 100% accepted, 1 enrolled. In 2010, 1 master's awarded. *Entrance requirements:* Additional exam requirements/recommendations for international students: Required—TOEFL (minimum score 550 paper-based; 213 computer-based; 80 iBT); Recommended—IELTS (minimum score 6.5). *Application deadline:* For fall admission, 7/31 priority date for domestic students, 4/30 priority date for international students; for spring admission, 12/31 priority date for domestic students, 11/30 priority date for international students. Applications are processed on a rolling basis. Application fee: $75. Electronic applications accepted. *Expenses:* Tuition: Full-time $21,492; part-time $1194 per credit. Required fees: $385 per semester. Tuition and fees vary according to course load. *Financial support:* Institutionally sponsored loans, scholarships/grants, and unspecified assistantships available. Support available to part-time students. *Application contact:* JeanCarlo Bonilla, Director of Graduate Enrollment Management, 718-260-3182, Fax: 718-260-3624, E-mail: gradinfo@poly.edu.

Polytechnic Institute of NYU, Long Island Graduate Center, Graduate Programs, Department of Mechanical and Aerospace Engineering, Melville, NY 11747. Offers aeronautics and astronautics (MS); industrial engineering (MS); manufacturing engineering (MS); mechanical engineering (MS). Part-time and evening/weekend programs available. *Students:* 1 full-time (0 women), all international. Average age 28. *Degree requirements:* For master's, comprehensive exam (for some programs), thesis (for some programs). *Entrance requirements:* Additional exam requirements/recommendations for international students: Required—TOEFL (minimum score 550 paper-based; 213 computer-based; 80 iBT); Recommended—IELTS (minimum score 6.5). *Application deadline:* For fall admission, 7/31 priority date for domestic students, 4/30 priority date for international students; for spring admission, 12/31 priority date for domestic students, 11/30 priority date for international students. Applications are processed on a rolling basis. Application fee: $75. Electronic applications accepted. *Expenses:* Tuition: Full-time $21,492; part-time $1194 per credit. Required fees: $385 per semester. Tuition and fees vary according to course load. *Financial support:* In 2010–11, 16 fellowships with tuition reimbursements (averaging $1,394 per year) were awarded; research assistantships with tuition reimbursements, institutionally sponsored loans, scholarships/grants, and unspecified assistantships also available. Support available to part-time students. Financial award applicants required to submit FAFSA. *Faculty research:* UV filter, fuel efficient hydrodynamic containment for gas core fission, turbulent boundary layer research. *Unit head:* Dr. George Vradis, Department Head, 718-260-3875, E-mail: gvradis@duke.poly.edu. *Application contact:* JeanCarlo Bonilla, Director of Graduate Enrollment Management, 718-260-3182, Fax: 718-260-3624, E-mail: gradinfo@poly.edu.

Polytechnic Institute of NYU, Westchester Graduate Center, Graduate Programs, Department of Interdisciplinary Studies, Major in Industrial Engineering, Hawthorne, NY 10532-1507. Offers MS. *Students:* 1 part-time (0 women). Average age 35. In 2010, 2 master's awarded. *Entrance requirements:* Additional exam requirements/recommendations for international students: Required—TOEFL (minimum score 550 paper-based; 213 computer-based; 80 iBT); Recommended—IELTS (minimum score 6.5). *Application deadline:* For fall admission, 7/31 priority date for domestic students, 4/30 priority date for international students; for spring admission, 12/31 priority date for domestic students, 11/30 priority date for international students. Applications are processed on a rolling basis. Application fee: $75. Electronic applications accepted. *Expenses:* Tuition: Full-time $21,492; part-time $1194 per credit. Required fees: $385 per semester. Tuition and fees vary according to course load. *Financial support:*

Institutionally sponsored loans, scholarships/grants, and unspecified assistantships available. Support available to part-time students. *Application contact:* JeanCarlo Bonilla, Director of Graduate Enrollment Management, 718-260-3182, Fax: 718-260-3624, E-mail: gradinfo@poly.edu.

Purdue University, College of Engineering, School of Industrial Engineering, West Lafayette, IN 47907-2023. Offers MS, MSIE, PhD. Part-time programs available. Postbaccalaureate distance learning degree programs offered (no on-campus study). Terminal master's awarded for partial completion of doctoral program. *Entrance requirements:* For master's and doctorate, GRE General Test, minimum GPA of 3.0. Additional exam requirements/recommendations for international students: Required—TOEFL (minimum score 570 paper-based; 220 computer-based); Recommended—TWE. Electronic applications accepted. *Faculty research:* Precision manufacturing process, computer-aided manufacturing, computer-aided process planning, knowledge-based systems, combinatorics.

Rensselaer Polytechnic Institute, Graduate School, School of Engineering, Program in Decision Sciences and Engineering Systems, Troy, NY 12180-3590. Offers industrial and systems engineering (PhD). Part-time programs available. *Faculty:* 12 full-time (2 women). *Students:* 21 full-time (8 women), 2 part-time (1 woman); includes 1 minority (Asian, non-Hispanic/Latino), 14 international. Average age 28. 62 applicants, 15% accepted, 4 enrolled. In 2010, 3 doctorates awarded. Terminal master's awarded for partial completion of doctoral program. *Degree requirements:* For doctorate, thesis/dissertation. *Entrance requirements:* For doctorate, GRE General Test (minimum score 550 verbal). Additional exam requirements/recommendations for international students: Required—TOEFL (minimum score 570 paper-based). *Application deadline:* For fall admission, 1/1 priority date for domestic students, 1/1 for international students; for spring admission, 8/15 for domestic and international students. Applications are processed on a rolling basis. Application fee: $75. Electronic applications accepted. *Expenses:* Tuition: Full-time $39,600; part-time $1650 per credit. Required fees: $1896. *Financial support:* In 2010–11, 20 students received support, including 1 fellowship with full tuition reimbursement available (averaging $20,000 per year), 10 research assistantships with full tuition reimbursements available, 9 teaching assistantships with full tuition reimbursements available (averaging $17,500 per year); career-related internships or fieldwork and institutionally sponsored loans also available. Financial award application deadline: 1/1. *Faculty research:* Decision support systems, simulation and modeling, statistical methods/computing, operations research, supply chain logistics. Total annual research expenditures: $1.3 million. *Unit head:* Dr. Charles J. Malmborg, Department Head, 518-276-2773, Fax: 518-276-8227, E-mail: malmbc@rpi.edu. *Application contact:* Mary Wagner, Graduate Coordinator, 518-276-2895, Fax: 518-276-8227, E-mail: wagnem@rpi.edu.

Rensselaer Polytechnic Institute, Graduate School, School of Engineering, Program in Industrial and Management Engineering, Troy, NY 12180-3590. Offers M Eng, MS. Part-time programs available. *Faculty:* 12 full-time (2 women). *Students:* 5 full-time (1 woman), 1 part-time (0 women); includes 1 minority (Asian, non-Hispanic/Latino), 2 international. 59 applicants, 7% accepted, 3 enrolled. In 2010, 8 master's awarded. *Degree requirements:* For master's, thesis (for some programs). *Entrance requirements:* For master's, GRE General Test (minimum score 550 verbal). Additional exam requirements/recommendations for international students: Required—TOEFL (minimum score 570 paper-based). *Application deadline:* For fall admission, 1/1 priority date for domestic students, 1/1 for international students; for spring admission, 8/15 for domestic and international students. Applications are processed on a rolling basis. Application fee: $75. Electronic applications accepted. *Expenses:* Tuition: Full-time $39,600; part-time $1650 per credit. Required fees: $1896. *Financial support:* Fellowships, research assistantships with full tuition reimbursements, teaching assistantships with full tuition reimbursements, career-related internships or fieldwork and institutionally sponsored loans available. Financial award application deadline: 1/1. *Faculty research:* Decision support systems, simulation and modeling, statistical methods/computing, operations research, supply chain logistics. Total annual research expenditures: $1.3 million. *Unit head:* Dr. Charles J. Malmborg, Department Head, 518-276-2895, Fax: 518-276-8227, E-mail: malmbc@rpi.edu. *Application contact:* Mary Wagner, Graduate Coordinator, 518-276-2895, Fax: 518-276-8227, E-mail: wagnem@rpi.edu.

Rochester Institute of Technology, Graduate Enrollment Services, Kate Gleason College of Engineering, Department of Industrial and Systems Engineering, Rochester, NY 14623-5603. Offers engineering management (ME); industrial engineering (ME, MS); manufacturing engineering (ME, MS); systems engineering (ME). Part-time programs available. *Students:* 60 full-time (20 women), 17 part-time (5 women); includes 4 Asian, non-Hispanic/Latino; 2 Hispanic/Latino, 48 international. Average age 26. 179 applicants, 49% accepted, 29 enrolled. In 2010, 49 master's awarded. *Degree requirements:* For master's, internship. *Entrance requirements:* For master's, GRE, minimum GPA of 3.0. Additional exam requirements/recommendations for international students: Required—TOEFL (minimum score 570 paper-based; 230 computer-based; 88 iBT) or IELTS (minimum score 6.5). *Application deadline:* For fall admission, 2/15 priority date for domestic and international students. Applications are processed on a rolling basis. Application fee: $50. *Expenses:* Tuition: Full-time $33,234; part-time $924 per credit hour. Required fees: $219. *Financial support:* In 2010–11, 63 students received support; research assistantships with partial tuition reimbursements available, teaching assistantships with partial tuition reimbursements available, career-related internships or fieldwork, institutionally sponsored loans, scholarships/grants, tuition waivers (partial), and unspecified assistantships available. Support available to part-time students. Financial award applicants required to submit FAFSA. *Faculty research:* Safety, manufacturing (CAM), simulation. *Unit head:* Dr. Michael Kuhl, Interim Department Head, 585-475-2134, E-mail: mekeie@rit.edu. *Application contact:* Diane Ellison, Assistant Vice President, Graduate Enrollment Services, 585-475-2229, Fax: 585-475-7164, E-mail: gradinfo@rit.edu.

Rutgers, The State University of New Jersey, New Brunswick, Graduate School-New Brunswick, Department of Industrial and Systems Engineering, Piscataway, NJ 08854-8097. Offers industrial and systems engineering (MS, PhD); information technology (MS); manufacturing systems engineering (MS); quality and reliability engineering (MS). Part-time and evening/weekend programs available. Terminal master's awarded for partial completion of doctoral program. *Degree requirements:* For master's, thesis or alternative, seminar; for doctorate, comprehensive exam, thesis/dissertation. *Entrance requirements:* For master's and doctorate, GRE General Test. Additional exam requirements/recommendations for international students: Required—TOEFL. *Expenses:* Tuition, state resident: full-time $7200; part-time $600 per credit. Tuition, nonresident: full-time $11,124; part-time $927 per credit. *Faculty research:* Production and manufacturing systems, quality and reliability engineering, systems engineering and aviation safety.

St. Mary's University, Graduate School, Department of Engineering, Program in Industrial Engineering, San Antonio, TX 78228-8507. Offers engineering computer applications (MS); engineering management (MS); industrial engineering (MS); operations research (MS); JD/MS. Part-time programs available. *Degree requirements:* For master's, comprehensive exam. *Entrance requirements:* For master's, GRE General Test, BS in science or engineering, minimum GPA of 3.0. Additional exam requirements/recommendations for international students: Required—TOEFL (minimum score 550 paper-based; 213 computer-based; 80 iBT). Electronic applications accepted. *Faculty research:* Robotics, artificial intelligence, manufacturing engineering.

Sam Houston State University, College of Arts and Sciences, Department of Agricultural Sciences, Huntsville, TX 77341. Offers agriculture (MS); industrial technology (MA). Part-time and evening/weekend programs available. *Students:* 28 full-time (9 women), 21 part-time (13 women); includes 1 Hispanic/Latino, 1 international. Average age 27. 18 applicants, 100% accepted, 17 enrolled. In 2010, 12 master's awarded. *Degree requirements:* For master's, thesis optional. *Entrance requirements:* For master's, GRE General Test, minimum GPA of 2.5. Additional exam requirements/recommendations for international students: Required—TOEFL (minimum score 550 paper-based; 213 computer-based; 79 iBT). *Application deadline:* For fall admission, 8/1 for domestic and international students; for spring admission, 12/1 for domestic and international students. Application fee: $20. Electronic applications accepted. *Expenses:* Tuition, state resident: full-time $1363; part-time $163 per credit hour. Tuition, nonresident: full-time $3856; part-time $473 per credit hour. *Financial support:* Teaching assistantships, career-related internships or fieldwork available. Financial award application deadline: 5/31; financial award applicants required to submit FAFSA. *Unit head:* Dr. Stanley F. Kelley, Chair, 936-294-1189, Fax: 936-294-1232, E-mail: sfkelley@shsu.edu. *Application contact:* Tammy Gray, Advisor, 936-294-1230, E-mail: dca_tag@shsu.edu.

San Jose State University, Graduate Studies and Research, Charles W. Davidson College of Engineering, Department of Industrial and Systems Engineering, San Jose, CA 95192-0001. Offers industrial and systems engineering (MS). Part-time programs available. *Degree requirements:* For master's, comprehensive exam. Electronic applications accepted.

South Dakota State University, Graduate School, College of Engineering, Department of Engineering Technology and Management, Brookings, SD 57007. Offers industrial management (MS). *Degree requirements:* For master's, comprehensive exam, thesis (for some programs), oral exam. *Entrance requirements:* Additional exam requirements/recommendations for international students: Required—TOEFL (minimum score 575 paper-based). *Faculty research:* Query, economic development, statistical process control, foreign business plans, operations management.

Southern Illinois University Edwardsville, Graduate School, School of Engineering, Department of Mechanical and Industrial Engineering, Program in Industrial Engineering, Edwardsville, IL 62026-0001. Offers MS. Part-time programs available. *Students:* 5 full-time (0 women), 9 part-time (1 woman); includes 5 minority (all Black or African American, non-Hispanic/Latino), 2 international. Average age 26. 14 applicants, 71% accepted. In 2010, 2 master's awarded. *Degree requirements:* For master's, thesis (for some programs), final exam. *Entrance requirements:* For master's, GRE (for applicants whose degree is from non-ABET accredited institution). Additional exam requirements/recommendations for international students: Required—TOEFL (minimum score 550 paper-based; 213 computer-based; 79 iBT), IELTS (minimum score 6.5). *Application deadline:* For fall admission, 7/22 for domestic students, 6/1 for international students; for spring admission, 12/9 for domestic students, 10/1 for international students. Applications are processed on a rolling basis. Electronic applications accepted. *Expenses:* Tuition, state resident: full-time $6012; part-time $1503 per semester. Tuition, nonresident: full-time $15,030; part-time $3758 per semester. Required fees: $1711; $675 per semester. *Financial support:* In 2010–11, 4 research assistantships with full tuition reimbursements (averaging $8,064 per year), 4 teaching assistantships with full tuition reimbursements (averaging $8,064 per year) were awarded; fellowships, career-related internships or fieldwork, Federal Work-Study, institutionally sponsored loans, scholarships/grants, traineeships, and unspecified assistantships also available. Support available to part-time students. Financial award application deadline: 3/1; financial award applicants required to submit FAFSA. *Unit head:* Dr. Felix Lee, Director, 618-650-2805, E-mail: hflee@siue.edu. *Application contact:* Dr. Felix Lee, Director, 618-650-2805, E-mail: hflee@siue.edu.

Southern Polytechnic State University, School of Engineering Technology and Management, Department of Industrial Engineering Technology, Marietta, GA 30060-2896. Offers quality assurance (MS, Graduate Certificate). Part-time and evening/weekend programs available. Postbaccalaureate distance learning degree programs offered (minimal on-campus study). *Faculty:* 2 full-time (1 woman), 5 part-time/adjunct (4 women). *Students:* 12 full-time (5 women), 63 part-time (23 women); includes 19 Black or African American, non-Hispanic/Latino; 4 Asian, non-Hispanic/Latino; 4 Hispanic/Latino; 1 Two or more races, non-Hispanic/Latino, 5 international. Average age 40. 31 applicants, 97% accepted, 24 enrolled. In 2010, 19 master's, 1 other advanced degree awarded. *Degree requirements:* For master's and Graduate Certificate, comprehensive exam (for some programs). *Entrance requirements:* For master's, 3 reference forms, minimum GPA of 2.7, statement of purpose; for Graduate Certificate, minimum GPA of 2.7, statement of purpose. Additional exam requirements/recommendations for international students: Required—TOEFL (minimum score 550 paper-based; 213 computer-based; 79 iBT), IELTS (minimum score 6.5). *Application deadline:* For fall admission, 7/1 priority date for domestic students, 5/1 priority date for international students; for spring admission, 11/1 priority date for domestic students, 9/1 priority date for international students. Applications are processed on a rolling basis. Application fee: $20. Electronic applications accepted. *Expenses:* Tuition, state resident: full-time $3690; part-time $205 per semester hour. Tuition, nonresident: full-time $13,428; part-time $746 per semester hour. Required fees: $598 per semester. *Financial support:* In 2010–11, 1 research assistantship with partial tuition reimbursement (averaging $1,500 per year) was awarded; career-related internships or fieldwork, scholarships/grants, and unspecified assistantships also available. Support available to part-time students. Financial award application deadline: 5/1; financial award applicants required to submit FAFSA. *Faculty research:* Application on industrial engineering to public sector, investigation of the response model method in robust design, effectiveness of online education, learning community, physical and mechanical properties of shape-wear garments to their functional performance, the advantage of tablet computer technology in a distance learning format, health care, BRIGE: Optimization Models for Public Health Policy. *Unit head:* Tom Ball, Chair, 678-915-7162, Fax: 678-915-4991, E-mail: tball@spsu.edu. *Application contact:* Nikki Palamiotis, Director of Graduate Studies, 678-915-4276, Fax: 678-915-7292, E-mail: npalamio@spsu.edu.

Stanford University, School of Engineering, Department of Management Science and Engineering, Stanford, CA 94305-9991. Offers management science and engineering (MS, PhD). Terminal master's awarded for partial completion of doctoral program. *Degree requirements:* For doctorate, thesis/dissertation, qualification procedure. *Entrance requirements:* For master's and doctorate, GRE General Test. Additional exam requirements/recommendations for international students: Required—TOEFL. Electronic applications accepted. *Expenses:* Tuition: Full-time $38,700; part-time $860 per unit. One-time fee: $200 full-time.

State University of New York at Binghamton, Graduate School, Thomas J. Watson School of Engineering and Applied Science, Department of Systems Science and Industrial Engineering, Binghamton, NY 13902-6000. Offers M Eng, MS, MSAT, PhD. Part-time and evening/weekend programs available. *Faculty:* 10 full-time (3 women), 2 part-time/adjunct (0 women). *Students:* 77 full-time (17 women), 91 part-time (16 women); includes 6 Black or African American, non-Hispanic/Latino; 2 American Indian or Alaska Native, non-Hispanic/Latino; 10 Asian, non-Hispanic/Latino; 3 Hispanic/Latino, 97 international. Average age 29. 149 applicants, 56% accepted, 44 enrolled. In 2010, 41 master's, 10 doctorates awarded. Terminal master's awarded for partial completion of doctoral program. *Degree requirements:* For master's, thesis or alternative; for doctorate, thesis/dissertation. *Entrance requirements:* For master's and doctorate, GRE General Test, GRE Subject Test. Additional exam requirements/recommendations for international students: Required—TOEFL. *Application deadline:* For fall admission, 4/15 priority date for domestic students, 1/15 priority date for international students; for spring admission, 11/1 for domestic students, 10/1 priority date for international students. Applications are processed on a rolling basis. Application fee: $60. Electronic applications accepted. *Financial support:* In 2010–11, 73 students received support, including 2 fellowships with full tuition reimbursements available (averaging $16,500 per year), 51 research assistantships with full tuition reimbursements available (averaging $16,500 per year), 14 teaching assistantships with full tuition reimbursements available (averaging $16,500 per year); career-related internships or fieldwork, Federal Work-Study, institutionally sponsored loans, scholarships/grants, health care benefits, tuition waivers (full and partial), and unspecified assistantships also available. Financial award application deadline: 2/15; financial award applicants required to submit FAFSA. *Faculty research:* Problem restructuring, protein modeling. *Unit head:* Dr. Nagen Nagarur, Chair, 607-777-3027, E-mail: nnagarur@binghamton.edu. *Application contact:* Catherine Smith, Recruiting and Admissions Coordinator, 607-777-2151, Fax: 607-777-2501, E-mail: cmsmith@binghamton.edu.

Texas A&M University, College of Engineering, Department of Industrial and Systems Engineering, College Station, TX 77843. Offers industrial and systems engineering (M Eng,

Industrial/Management Engineering

Texas A&M University (continued)
MS); industrial engineering (D Eng, PhD). Part-time programs available. Postbaccalaureate distance learning degree programs offered (no on-campus study). *Faculty:* 21. *Students:* 247 full-time (60 women), 28 part-time (5 women); includes 22 minority (5 Black or African American, non-Hispanic/Latino; 6 Asian, non-Hispanic/Latino; 11 Hispanic/Latino), 220 international. Average age 28. In 2010, 88 master's, 8 doctorates awarded. *Degree requirements:* For master's, comprehensive exam (for some programs), thesis optional; for doctorate, comprehensive exam, dissertation (PhD). *Entrance requirements:* For master's and doctorate, GRE General Test. Additional exam requirements/recommendations for international students: Required—TOEFL. *Application deadline:* For fall admission, 3/1 priority date for domestic and international students; for spring admission, 8/1 priority date for domestic and international students. Applications are processed on a rolling basis. Application fee: $50 ($75 for international students). Electronic applications accepted. *Financial support:* In 2010–11, fellowships with partial tuition reimbursements (averaging $25,000 per year), research assistantships with partial tuition reimbursements (averaging $12,000 per year), teaching assistantships with partial tuition reimbursements (averaging $12,000 per year) were awarded; career-related internships or fieldwork, scholarships/grants, and unspecified assistantships also available. Financial award application deadline: 2/1. *Faculty research:* Manufacturing systems, computer integration, operations research, logistics, simulation. *Unit head:* Dr. Guy Curry, Head, 979-845-5576, Fax: 979-458-4299, E-mail: g-curry@tamu.edu. *Application contact:* Judy Meeks, Administrative Assistant, Graduate Program, 979-845-5536, Fax: 979-458-4299.

Texas A&M University–Commerce, Graduate School, College of Business and Technology, Department of Industrial Engineering and Technology, Commerce, TX 75429-3011. Offers industrial technology (MS); technology management (MS). Part-time programs available. *Degree requirements:* For master's, comprehensive exam, thesis (for some programs). *Entrance requirements:* For master's, GMAT, GRE General Test. Electronic applications accepted. *Faculty research:* Environmental science, engineering microelectronics, natural sciences.

Texas A&M University–Kingsville, College of Graduate Studies, College of Engineering, Department of Mechanical and Industrial Engineering, Program in Industrial Engineering, Kingsville, TX 78363. Offers ME, MS. *Degree requirements:* For master's, comprehensive exam, thesis or alternative. *Entrance requirements:* For master's, GRE General Test, minimum GPA of 3.0. Additional exam requirements/recommendations for international students: Required—TOEFL. *Faculty research:* Robotics and automation, neural networks and fuzzy logic, systems engineering/simulation modeling, integrated manufacturing and production systems.

Texas Southern University, School of Science and Technology, Department of Industrial Technology, Houston, TX 77004-4584. Offers MS. *Faculty:* 1 full-time (0 women). *Students:* 4 full-time (1 woman), 1 (woman) part-time; includes all Black or African American, non-Hispanic/Latino. Average age 30. 3 applicants, 100% accepted, 3 enrolled. In 2010, 2 master's awarded. *Degree requirements:* For master's, comprehensive exam. *Entrance requirements:* For master's, GRE General Test, minimum GPA of 2.5. Additional exam requirements/recommendations for international students: Required—TOEFL. *Application deadline:* For fall admission, 7/1 for domestic and international students; for spring admission, 11/1 for domestic and international students. Applications are processed on a rolling basis. Application fee: $50 ($75 for international students). Electronic applications accepted. *Expenses:* Tuition, state resident: full-time $1875; part-time $100 per credit hour. Tuition, nonresident: full-time $6641; part-time $343 per credit hour. Tuition and fees vary according to course level, course load and degree level. *Financial support:* In 2010–11, 1 teaching assistantship (averaging $12,750 per year) was awarded; scholarships/grants and unspecified assistantships also available. Financial award application deadline: 5/1. Total annual research expenditures: $500,000. *Unit head:* Dr. Jesse Horner, Chair, 713-313-7144, E-mail: horner_je@tsu.edu. *Application contact:* Lulueua Nasser, Administrative Secretary, 713-313-7679, E-mail: nasser_la@tsu.edu.

Texas State University–San Marcos, Graduate School, College of Science, Department of Engineering Technology, Program in Industrial Technology, San Marcos, TX 78666. Offers MST. Part-time and evening/weekend programs available. *Faculty:* 7 full-time (1 woman). *Students:* 21 full-time (2 women), 23 part-time (3 women); includes 8 minority (2 Black or African American, non-Hispanic/Latino; 1 Asian, non-Hispanic/Latino; 3 Hispanic/Latino; 2 Two or more races, non-Hispanic/Latino), 6 international. Average age 29. 21 applicants, 95% accepted, 13 enrolled. In 2010, 15 master's awarded. *Degree requirements:* For master's, comprehensive exam, thesis optional. *Entrance requirements:* For master's, minimum GPA of 2.75 in last 60 hours of undergraduate work. Additional exam requirements/recommendations for international students: Required—TOEFL (minimum score 550 paper-based; 213 computer-based; 78 iBT). *Application deadline:* For fall admission, 6/15 priority date for domestic students, 6/1 priority date for international students; for spring admission, 10/15 priority date for domestic students, 10/1 priority date for international students. Applications are processed on a rolling basis. Application fee: $40 ($90 for international students). *Expenses:* Tuition, state resident: full-time $6024; part-time $251 per credit hour. Tuition, nonresident: full-time $13,536; part-time $564 per credit hour. Required fees: $1776; $50 per credit hour. $306 per semester. *Financial support:* In 2010–11, 11 students received support, including 4 research assistantships (averaging $5,464 per year), 5 teaching assistantships (averaging $5,476 per year); career-related internships or fieldwork, Federal Work-Study, and institutionally sponsored loans also available. Support available to part-time students. Financial award application deadline: 4/1; financial award applicants required to submit FAFSA. *Faculty research:* Attack of Concrete. Total annual research expenditures: $107,849. *Unit head:* Dr. Andy Batey, Interim Chair, 512-245-2137, Fax: 512-245-3052, E-mail: ab08@txstate.edu. *Application contact:* Dr. Gary Winek, Graduate Adviser, 512-245-2137, Fax: 512-245-3052, E-mail: gw04@txstate.edu.

Texas Tech University, Graduate School, Edward E. Whitacre Jr. College of Engineering, Department of Industrial Engineering, Lubbock, TX 79409. Offers industrial engineering (MSIE, PhD); manufacturing systems engineering (MSMSE); systems and engineering management (MSSEM, PhD). Part-time programs available. Postbaccalaureate distance learning degree programs offered (minimal on-campus study). *Faculty:* 12 full-time (3 women). *Students:* 79 full-time (13 women), 47 part-time (7 women); includes 1 Black or African American, non-Hispanic/Latino; 1 Asian, non-Hispanic/Latino; 2 Hispanic/Latino, 81 international. Average age 28. 282 applicants, 51% accepted, 31 enrolled. In 2010, 39 master's, 9 doctorates awarded. *Degree requirements:* For master's, thesis or alternative; for doctorate, thesis/dissertation. *Entrance requirements:* For master's and doctorate, GRE General Test, minimum GPA of 3.0. Additional exam requirements/recommendations for international students: Required—TOEFL (minimum score 550 paper-based; 213 computer-based; 79 iBT). *Application deadline:* For fall admission, 6/1 priority date for domestic students, 1/15 priority date for international students; for spring admission, 9/1 priority date for domestic students, 6/15 priority date for international students. Applications are processed on a rolling basis. Application fee: $50 ($75 for international students). Electronic applications accepted. *Expenses:* Tuition, state resident: full-time $5495.76; part-time $228.99 per credit hour. Tuition, nonresident: full-time $12,936; part-time $538.99 per credit hour. Required fees: $2674; $36 per credit hour. $905 per semester. *Financial support:* In 2010–11, 40 students received support, including 12 research assistantships with partial tuition reimbursements available (averaging $3,905 per year), 8 teaching assistantships with partial tuition reimbursements available (averaging $3,150 per year). Financial award application deadline: 4/15; financial award applicants required to submit FAFSA. *Faculty research:* Knowledge and engineering management, environmentally conscious manufacturing, biomechanical simulation, aviation security, supply chain management. Total annual research expenditures: $646,598. *Unit head:* Dr. Pat Patterson, Chair, 806-742-3543, Fax: 806-742-3411, E-mail: pat.patterson@ttu.edu. *Application contact:* Dr. Mario Beruvides, Professor, 806-742-3543, Fax: 806-742-3411, E-mail: mario.beruvides@ttu.edu.

Universidad de las Américas–Puebla, Division of Graduate Studies, School of Engineering, Program in Industrial Engineering, Puebla, Mexico. Offers industrial engineering (MS); production

management (M Adm). Part-time and evening/weekend programs available. *Degree requirements:* For master's, one foreign language, thesis. *Faculty research:* Textile industry, quality control.

Université de Moncton, Faculty of Engineering, Program in Industrial Engineering, Moncton, NB E1A 3E9, Canada. Offers M Sc A. *Degree requirements:* For master's, thesis, proficiency in French. *Faculty research:* Production systems, optimization, simulation and expert systems, modeling and warehousing systems, quality control.

Université du Québec à Trois-Rivières, Graduate Programs, Program in Industrial Engineering, Trois-Rivières, QC G9A 5H7, Canada. Offers M Sc, DESS. *Entrance requirements:* For degree, appropriate bachelor's degree, proficiency in French. *Faculty research:* Production.

Université Laval, Faculty of Sciences and Engineering, Programs in Industrial Engineering, Québec, QC G1K 7P4, Canada. Offers Diploma. Part-time programs available. *Entrance requirements:* For degree, knowledge of French. Electronic applications accepted.

University at Buffalo, the State University of New York, Graduate School, School of Engineering and Applied Sciences, Department of Industrial and Systems Engineering, Buffalo, NY 14260. Offers ME, MS, PhD. Part-time programs available. Postbaccalaureate distance learning degree programs offered (minimal on-campus study). *Faculty:* 12 full-time (1 woman), 3 part-time/adjunct (0 women). *Students:* 147 full-time (35 women), 18 part-time (5 women); includes 1 Black or African American, non-Hispanic/Latino; 4 Asian, non-Hispanic/Latino; 1 Hispanic/Latino, 123 international. Average age 27. 594 applicants, 36% accepted, 55 enrolled. In 2010, 32 master's, 3 doctorates awarded. Terminal master's awarded for partial completion of doctoral program. *Degree requirements:* For master's, comprehensive exam (for some programs), thesis or alternative; for doctorate, thesis/dissertation. *Entrance requirements:* For master's and doctorate, GRE General Test. Additional exam requirements/recommendations for international students: Required—TOEFL (minimum score 550 paper-based; 213 computer-based; 79 iBT). *Application deadline:* For fall admission, 2/1 priority date for domestic students; for spring admission, 8/1 for domestic students. Applications are processed on a rolling basis. Application fee: $50. Electronic applications accepted. *Financial support:* In 2010–11, 58 students received support, including 10 fellowships with full tuition reimbursements available (averaging $28,900 per year), 22 research assistantships with full and partial tuition reimbursements available (averaging $24,000 per year), 17 teaching assistantships with partial tuition reimbursements available (averaging $20,900 per year); Federal Work-Study, institutionally sponsored loans, tuition waivers (full and partial), and unspecified assistantships also available. Financial award application deadline: 2/1; financial award applicants required to submit FAFSA. *Faculty research:* Ergonomics, operations research, production systems, human factors. Total annual research expenditures: $7 million. *Unit head:* Dr. Rakesh Nagi, Chairman, 716-645-2357, Fax: 716-645-3302, E-mail: iegrad@buffalo.edu. *Application contact:* Dr. Victor Paquet, Director of Graduate Studies, 716-645-4712, Fax: 716-645-3302, E-mail: iegrad@buffalo.edu.

The University of Alabama in Huntsville, School of Graduate Studies, College of Engineering, Department of Industrial and Systems Engineering/Engineering Management, Huntsville, AL 35899. Offers industrial and systems engineering (PhD), including engineering management (MSE, PhD), industrial engineering, systems engineering (MSE, PhD); industrial engineering (MSE), including engineering management (MSE, PhD), missile systems engineering, modeling and simulation, rotorcraft systems engineering, systems engineering (MSE, PhD); operations research (MSOR). Part-time and evening/weekend programs available. Postbaccalaureate distance learning degree programs offered (minimal on-campus study). *Faculty:* 8 full-time (2 women), 4 part-time/adjunct (1 woman). *Students:* 11 full-time (2 women), 158 part-time (40 women); includes 26 minority (18 Black or African American, non-Hispanic/Latino; 2 American Indian or Alaska Native, non-Hispanic/Latino; 2 Asian, non-Hispanic/Latino; 3 Hispanic/Latino; 1 Two or more races, non-Hispanic/Latino), 8 international. Average age 36. 108 applicants, 64% accepted, 48 enrolled. In 2010, 30 master's, 5 doctorates awarded. *Degree requirements:* For master's, comprehensive exam, thesis or alternative, oral and written exams; for doctorate, comprehensive exam, thesis/dissertation, oral and written exams. *Entrance requirements:* For master's and doctorate, GRE General Test, minimum GPA of 3.0. Additional exam requirements/recommendations for international students: Required—TOEFL (minimum score 500 paper-based; 173 computer-based; 62 iBT). *Application deadline:* For fall admission, 7/15 for domestic students, 4/1 for international students; for spring admission, 11/30 for domestic students, 9/1 for international students. Applications are processed on a rolling basis. Application fee: $40 ($50 for international students). Electronic applications accepted. *Expenses:* Tuition, state resident: full-time $7250; part-time $407.75 per credit hour. Tuition, nonresident: full-time $17,358; part-time $970.05 per credit hour. Required fees: $246.80 per semester. Tuition and fees vary according to course load and program. *Financial support:* In 2010–11, 7 students received support, including 1 research assistantship with full tuition reimbursement available (averaging $10,340 per year), 6 teaching assistantships with full tuition reimbursements available (averaging $10,768 per year); career-related internships or fieldwork, Federal Work-Study, institutionally sponsored loans, scholarships/grants, health care benefits, and unspecified assistantships also available. Support available to part-time students. Financial award application deadline: 4/1; financial award applicants required to submit FAFSA. *Faculty research:* Engineering management, systems engineering, manufacturing, logistics, simulation. Total annual research expenditures: $7.8 million. *Unit head:* Dr. James Swain, Chair, 256-824-6749, Fax: 256-824-6733, E-mail: jswain@ise.uah.edu. *Application contact:* Kathy Biggs, Graduate Studies Admissions Manager, 256-824-6199, Fax: 256-824-6405, E-mail: deangrad@uah.edu.

The University of Arizona, College of Engineering, Department of Systems and Industrial Engineering, Program in Industrial Engineering, Tucson, AZ 85721. Offers MS. Part-time programs available. Postbaccalaureate distance learning degree programs offered. *Students:* 2 full-time (0 women), 3 part-time (all women); includes 2 Black or African American, non-Hispanic/Latino, 2 international. Average age 24. 25 applicants, 40% accepted. In 2010, 4 master's awarded. *Entrance requirements:* Additional exam requirements/recommendations for international students: Required—TOEFL (minimum score 575 paper-based; 233 computer-based; 80 iBT). *Application deadline:* For fall admission, 6/1 for domestic students, 12/1 for international students; for spring admission, 9/1 for domestic students, 6/1 for international students. Applications are processed on a rolling basis. Application fee: $75. Electronic applications accepted. *Expenses:* Tuition, state resident: full-time $7692. *Financial support:* Institutionally sponsored loans, scholarships/grants, and unspecified assistantships available. *Faculty research:* Operations research, manufacturing systems, quality and reliability, statistical/engineering design. *Unit head:* Dr. K. Larry Head, Head, 520-621-6551, E-mail: larry@sie.arizona.edu. *Application contact:* Linda Cramer, Graduate Secretary, 520-626-4644, Fax: 520-621-6555, E-mail: gradapp@sie.arizona.edu.

The University of Arizona, College of Engineering, Department of Systems and Industrial Engineering, Program in Systems and Industrial Engineering, Tucson, AZ 85721. Offers MS, PhD. Postbaccalaureate distance learning degree programs offered. *Students:* 22 full-time (4 women), 3 part-time (0 women), 21 international. Average age 29. 24 applicants, 75% accepted, 6 enrolled. In 2010, 2 doctorates awarded. *Degree requirements:* For doctorate, thesis/dissertation. *Entrance requirements:* For master's, GRE General Test (minimum score: 500 Verbal, 700 Quantitative), 3 letters of recommendation, letter of intent; for doctorate, GRE General Test (minimum score: 500 Verbal, 750 Quantitative), 3 letters of recommendation, letter of intent. Additional exam requirements/recommendations for international students: Required—TOEFL (minimum score 575 paper-based; 233 computer-based; 80 iBT). *Application deadline:* For fall admission, 6/1 for domestic students, 12/1 for international students; for spring admission, 9/1 for domestic students, 6/1 for international students. Applications are processed on a rolling basis. Application fee: $75. Electronic applications accepted. *Expenses:* Tuition, state resident: full-time $7692. *Financial support:* Tuition waivers (full) and unspecified assistantships available. *Faculty research:* Optimization, systems theory, logistics, transportation, embedded systems. *Unit head:* Dr. K. Larry Head, Head, 520-621-6551, E-mail: larry@sie.arizona.edu. *Application contact:* Linda Cramer, Graduate Secretary, 520-626-4644, Fax: 520-621-6555, E-mail: gradapp@sie.arizona.edu.

University of Arkansas, Graduate School, College of Engineering, Department of Industrial Engineering, Program in Industrial Engineering, Fayetteville, AR 72701-1201. Offers MSE, MSIE, PhD. *Students:* 23 full-time (8 women), 26 part-time (5 women); includes 2 minority (1 Asian, non-Hispanic/Latino; 1 Hispanic/Latino), 29 international. 61 applicants, 59% accepted. In 2010, 5 master's, 3 doctorates awarded. *Degree requirements:* For master's, thesis optional; for doctorate, one foreign language, thesis/dissertation. *Application deadline:* For fall admission, 4/1 for international students; for spring admission, 10/1 for international students. Applications are processed on a rolling basis. Application fee: $40 ($50 for international students). Electronic applications accepted. *Financial support:* In 2010–11, 3 fellowships, 39 research assistantships were awarded; teaching assistantships, career-related internships or fieldwork and Federal Work-Study also available. Support available to part-time students. Financial award application deadline: 4/1; financial award applicants required to submit FAFSA. *Unit head:* Dr. Kim Needy, Department Chairperson, 479-575-3157, Fax: 479-575-8431, E-mail: kneedy@uark.edu. *Application contact:* Dr. Justin Chimka, Graduate Coordinator, 479-575-7392, E-mail: jchimka@uark.edu.

University of California, Berkeley, Graduate Division, College of Engineering, Department of Industrial Engineering and Operations Research, Berkeley, CA 94720-1500. Offers M Eng, MS, D Eng, PhD. *Degree requirements:* For master's, comprehensive exam or thesis (MS); for doctorate, thesis/dissertation, qualifying exam. *Entrance requirements:* For master's and doctorate, GRE General Test, minimum GPA of 3.0, 3 letters of recommendation. *Faculty research:* Mathematical programming, robotics and manufacturing, linear and nonlinear optimization, production planning and scheduling, queuing theory.

University of Central Florida, College of Engineering and Computer Science, Department of Industrial Engineering and Management Systems, Orlando, FL 32816. Offers applied operations research (Certificate); design for usability (Certificate); industrial engineering (MSIE, PhD); industrial engineering and management systems (MS); industrial ergonomics and safety (Certificate); project engineering (Certificate); quality assurance (Certificate); systems engineering (Certificate); systems simulation for engineers (Certificate); training simulation (Certificate). Part-time and evening/weekend programs available. *Faculty:* 17 full-time (4 women), 6 part-time/adjunct (1 woman). *Students:* 112 full-time (31 women), 171 part-time (66 women); includes 79 minority (27 Black or African American, non-Hispanic/Latino; 17 Asian, non-Hispanic/Latino; 32 Hispanic/Latino; 1 Native Hawaiian or other Pacific Islander, non-Hispanic/Latino; 2 Two or more races, non-Hispanic/Latino), 72 international. Average age 33. 210 applicants, 74% accepted, 82 enrolled. In 2010, 65 master's, 7 doctorates, 34 other advanced degrees awarded. *Degree requirements:* For master's, thesis; for doctorate, thesis/dissertation, departmental qualifying exam, candidacy exam. *Entrance requirements:* For master's, GRE General Test, minimum GPA of 3.0 in last 60 hours of course work; for doctorate, minimum GPA of 3.5 in last 60 hours of course work. Additional exam requirements/recommendations for international students: Required—TOEFL. *Application deadline:* For fall admission, 7/15 priority date for domestic students; for spring admission, 12/1 priority date for domestic students. Application fee: $30. Electronic applications accepted. *Expenses:* Tuition, state resident: part-time $256.56 per credit hour. Tuition, nonresident: part-time $1011.52 per credit hour. Part-time tuition and fees vary according to program. *Financial support:* In 2010–11, 24 students received support, including 85 fellowships with partial tuition reimbursements available (averaging $7,300 per year), 19 research assistantships with partial tuition reimbursements available (averaging $8,500 per year), 6 teaching assistantships with partial tuition reimbursements available (averaging $12,200 per year); career-related internships or fieldwork, Federal Work-Study, institutionally sponsored loans, tuition waivers (partial), and unspecified assistantships also available. Financial award application deadline: 3/1; financial award applicants required to submit FAFSA. *Unit head:* Dr. Waldemar Karwowski, Chair, 407-823-2204, E-mail: wkar@mail.ucf.edu. *Application contact:* Dr. Waldemar Karwowski, Chair, 407-823-2204, E-mail: wkar@mail.ucf.edu.

University of Cincinnati, Graduate School, College of Engineering, Department of Mechanical, Industrial and Nuclear Engineering, Program in Industrial Engineering, Cincinnati, OH 45221. Offers MS, PhD, MBA/MS. Part-time and evening/weekend programs available. *Degree requirements:* For master's, oral exam, thesis defense; for doctorate, variable foreign language requirement, thesis/dissertation, oral exam. *Entrance requirements:* For master's and doctorate, GRE General Test. Additional exam requirements/recommendations for international students: Required—TOEFL (minimum score 575 paper-based; 233 computer-based). Electronic applications accepted. *Faculty research:* Operations research, engineering administration, safety.

University of Florida, Graduate School, College of Engineering, Department of Industrial and Systems Engineering, Gainesville, FL 32611. Offers ME, MS, PhD, Engr. Part-time and evening/weekend programs available. Postbaccalaureate distance learning degree programs offered (minimal on-campus study). *Faculty:* 14 full-time (1 woman), 2 part-time/adjunct (1 woman). *Students:* 176 full-time (42 women), 155 part-time (35 women); includes 13 Black or African American, non-Hispanic/Latino; 18 Asian, non-Hispanic/Latino; 30 Hispanic/Latino, 155 international. Average age 28. 644 applicants, 35% accepted, 98 enrolled. In 2010, 136 master's, 7 doctorates awarded. Terminal master's awarded for partial completion of doctoral program. *Degree requirements:* For master's, thesis (for some programs); for doctorate, comprehensive exam (for some programs), thesis/dissertation (for some programs). *Entrance requirements:* For master's and doctorate, GRE General Test, minimum GPA of 3.0; for Engr, GRE General Test. Additional exam requirements/recommendations for international students: Required—TOEFL (minimum score 550 paper-based; 213 computer-based; 80 iBT), IELTS (minimum score 6). *Application deadline:* For fall admission, 2/1 priority date for domestic students, 2/1 for international students; for spring admission, 8/1 for domestic and international students. Applications are processed on a rolling basis. Application fee: $30. Electronic applications accepted. *Expenses:* Tuition, state resident: full-time $10,915.92. Tuition, nonresident: full-time $28,309. *Financial support:* In 2010–11, 15 students received support, including 1 fellowship, 10 research assistantships (averaging $19,083 per year), 4 teaching assistantships (averaging $18,238 per year); career-related internships or fieldwork, Federal Work-Study, and unspecified assistantships also available. Financial award application deadline: 1/15; financial award applicants required to submit FAFSA. *Faculty research:* Operations research; financial engineering; logistics and supply chain management; energy, healthcare, and transportation applications of operations research. Total annual research expenditures: $1.7 million. *Unit head:* Dr. Joseph C. Hartman, Chair, 352-392-1464, Fax: 352-392-3537, E-mail: hartman@ise.ufl.edu. *Application contact:* Jonathan C. Smith, Graduate Coordinator, 352-392-1464, Fax: 352-392-9673, E-mail: colesmit@ufl.edu.

University of Houston, Cullen College of Engineering, Department of Industrial Engineering, Houston, TX 77204. Offers MIE, PhD. Part-time programs available. *Faculty:* 7 full-time (1 woman), 3 part-time/adjunct (0 women). *Students:* 75 full-time (20 women), 35 part-time (6 women); includes 3 Black or African American, non-Hispanic/Latino; 3 Asian, non-Hispanic/Latino; 3 Hispanic/Latino, 93 international. Average age 27. 135 applicants, 78% accepted, 22 enrolled. In 2010, 54 master's, 2 doctorates awarded. Terminal master's awarded for partial completion of doctoral program. *Degree requirements:* For master's, thesis (for some programs); for doctorate, thesis/dissertation, departmental qualifying exam. *Entrance requirements:* For master's and doctorate, GRE General Test. Additional exam requirements/recommendations for international students: Required—TOEFL; Recommended—IELTS. *Application deadline:* For fall admission, 5/1 for domestic and international students; for spring admission, 11/1 for domestic and international students. Application fee: $25 ($75 for international students). Electronic applications accepted. *Expenses:* Tuition, state resident: full-time $8592; part-time $358 per credit hour. Tuition, nonresident: full-time $16,032; part-time $668 per credit hour. Required fees: $2889. Tuition and fees vary according to course load and program. *Financial support:* In 2010–11, 9 research assistantships with partial tuition reimbursements (averaging $8,360 per year), 8 teaching assistantships with partial tuition reimbursements (averaging $8,800 per year) were awarded; career-related internships or fieldwork, Federal Work-Study, institutionally sponsored loans, scholarships/grants, health care benefits, and unspecified assistantships also available. Support available to part-time students. Financial award application deadline: 2/1. *Unit head:* Dr. Fritz Claydon, Chairperson (Acting), 713-743-4204, Fax: 713-743-4190, E-mail: fclaydon@uh.edu. *Application contact:* Jane Geanangel, Graduate Program Academic Records Coordinator, 713-743-4219.

University of Illinois at Chicago, Graduate College, College of Engineering, Department of Mechanical and Industrial Engineering, Program in Industrial Engineering, Chicago, IL 60607-7128. Offers MS. Part-time programs available. *Degree requirements:* For master's, thesis. *Entrance requirements:* For master's, GRE General Test, minimum GPA of 2.75. Additional exam requirements/recommendations for international students: Required—TOEFL. Electronic applications accepted. *Faculty research:* Systems modeling.

University of Illinois at Chicago, Graduate College, College of Engineering, Department of Mechanical and Industrial Engineering, Program in Industrial Engineering and Operations Research, Chicago, IL 60607-7128. Offers PhD. Part-time programs available. *Degree requirements:* For doctorate, thesis/dissertation. *Entrance requirements:* For doctorate, GRE General Test, minimum GPA of 2.75. Additional exam requirements/recommendations for international students: Required—TOEFL. Electronic applications accepted.

University of Illinois at Urbana–Champaign, Graduate College, College of Engineering, Department of Industrial and Enterprise Systems Engineering, Champaign, IL 61820. Offers industrial engineering (MS, PhD); systems and entrepreneurial engineering (MS, PhD); MBA/MS. *Faculty:* 20 full-time (5 women). *Students:* 47 full-time (12 women), 19 part-time (10 women); includes 1 minority (Black or African American, non-Hispanic/Latino), 50 international. 218 applicants, 4% accepted, 5 enrolled. In 2010, 18 master's, 4 doctorates awarded. *Entrance requirements:* For master's and doctorate, GRE, minimum GPA of 3.25. Additional exam requirements/recommendations for international students: Required—TOEFL (minimum score 613 paper-based; 257 computer-based; 103 iBT) or IELTS (minimum score 7). *Application deadline:* Applications are processed on a rolling basis. Application fee: $75 ($90 for international students). Electronic applications accepted. *Financial support:* In 2010–11, 3 fellowships, 42 research assistantships, 43 teaching assistantships were awarded; tuition waivers (full and partial) also available. *Unit head:* Jong-Shi Pang, Head, 217-244-5703, Fax: 217-244-5705, E-mail: jspang@illinois.edu. *Application contact:* Michelle D. Tipsword, Coordinator of Graduate Programs, 217-333-2730, Fax: 217-244-5705, E-mail: deiskamp@illinois.edu.

University of Illinois at Urbana–Champaign, Graduate College, College of Engineering, Department of Mechanical Science and Engineering, Champaign, IL 61820. Offers mechanical engineering (MS, PhD); theoretical and applied mechanics (MS, PhD); MS/MBA. *Faculty:* 51 full-time (4 women), 2 part-time/adjunct (0 women). *Students:* 325 full-time (37 women), 39 part-time (4 women); includes 1 Black or African American, non-Hispanic/Latino; 17 Asian, non-Hispanic/Latino; 13 Hispanic/Latino, 198 international. 587 applicants, 33% accepted, 88 enrolled. In 2010, 77 master's, 29 doctorates awarded. Terminal master's awarded for partial completion of doctoral program. *Entrance requirements:* For master's, GRE General Test, minimum GPA of 3.25; for doctorate, GRE General Test, minimum GPA of 3.5. Additional exam requirements/recommendations for international students: Required—TOEFL (minimum score 613 paper-based; 257 computer-based; 103 iBT). *Application deadline:* Applications are processed on a rolling basis. Application fee: $75 ($90 for international students). Electronic applications accepted. *Financial support:* In 2010–11, 42 fellowships, 244 research assistantships, 102 teaching assistantships were awarded; tuition waivers (full and partial) also available. *Faculty research:* Combustion and propulsion, design methodology, dynamic systems and controls, energy transfer, materials behavior and processing, manufacturing systems operations, management. *Unit head:* Placid Mathew Ferreira, Head, 217-333-0639, Fax: 217-244-6534, E-mail: pferreir@illinois.edu. *Application contact:* Kathy A. Smith, Admissions and Records Officer, 217-244-4539, Fax: 217-244-6534, E-mail: smith15@illinois.edu.

The University of Iowa, Graduate College, College of Engineering, Department of Industrial Engineering, Iowa City, IA 52242-1316. Offers engineering design and manufacturing (MS, PhD); ergonomics (MS, PhD); information and engineering management (MS, PhD); operations research (MS, PhD); quality engineering (MS, PhD). *Faculty:* 6 full-time (0 women). *Students:* 33 full-time (9 women); includes 2 minority (1 Black or African American, non-Hispanic/Latino; 1 Asian, non-Hispanic/Latino), 14 international. Average age 30. 57 applicants, 19% accepted, 8 enrolled. In 2010, 12 master's, 5 doctorates awarded. *Degree requirements:* For master's, thesis optional, exam; for doctorate, comprehensive exam, thesis/dissertation, final defense exam. *Entrance requirements:* For master's and doctorate, GRE General Test. Additional exam requirements/recommendations for international students: Required—TOEFL (minimum score 550 paper-based; 213 computer-based; 81 iBT). *Application deadline:* For fall admission, 7/15 for domestic students, 4/15 for international students; for spring admission, 12/1 for domestic students, 10/1 for international students. Applications are processed on a rolling basis. Application fee: $60 ($100 for international students). Electronic applications accepted. *Financial support:* In 2010–11, 2 fellowships with partial tuition reimbursements (averaging $30,450 per year), 20 research assistantships with partial tuition reimbursements (averaging $20,000 per year), 8 teaching assistantships with partial tuition reimbursements (averaging $16,630 per year) were awarded; career-related internships or fieldwork, scholarships/grants, and unspecified assistantships also available. Support available to part-time students. Financial award applicants required to submit FAFSA. *Faculty research:* Operations research; informatics; human factors engineering; manufacturing systems; human-machine interaction. Total annual research expenditures: $4.7 million. *Unit head:* Dr. Andrew Kusiak, Department Executive Officer, 319-335-5934, Fax: 319-335-5669, E-mail: andrew-kusiak@uiowa.edu. *Application contact:* Jennifer Rumping, Secretary, 319-335-5939, Fax: 319-335-5669, E-mail: indeng@engineering.uiowa.edu.

University of Louisville, J.B. Speed School of Engineering, Department of Industrial Engineering, Louisville, KY 40292-0001. Offers engineering management (M Eng); industrial engineering (M Eng, MS, PhD); logistics and distribution (Certificate). *Accreditation:* ABET (one or more programs are accredited). Part-time programs available. *Faculty:* 10 full-time (1 woman). *Students:* 45 full-time (11 women), 26 part-time (7 women); includes 5 Black or African American, non-Hispanic/Latino; 1 Asian, non-Hispanic/Latino; 1 Hispanic/Latino; 1 Two or more races, non-Hispanic/Latino, 18 international. Average age 28. 56 applicants, 32% accepted, 7 enrolled. In 2010, 25 master's, 4 doctorates awarded. Terminal master's awarded for partial completion of doctoral program. *Degree requirements:* For master's, comprehensive exam (for some programs), thesis or alternative; for doctorate, comprehensive exam, thesis/dissertation, minimum GPA of 3.0. *Entrance requirements:* For master's and doctorate, GRE General Test. Additional exam requirements/recommendations for international students: Required—TOEFL (minimum score 550 paper-based; 213 computer-based; 80 iBT), IELTS (minimum score 6.5). *Application deadline:* For fall admission, 5/1 priority date for domestic and international students; for spring admission, 11/1 priority date for domestic and international students. Applications are processed on a rolling basis. Application fee: $50. Electronic applications accepted. *Expenses:* Tuition, state resident: full-time $9144; part-time $508 per credit hour. Tuition, nonresident: full-time $19,026; part-time $1057 per credit hour. Tuition and fees vary according to program and reciprocity agreements. *Financial support:* In 2010–11, 15 students received support, including 7 fellowships with full tuition reimbursements available (averaging $20,000 per year), 2 research assistantships with full tuition reimbursements available (averaging $20,000 per year), 6 teaching assistantships with full tuition reimbursements available (averaging $20,000 per year). Financial award application deadline: 1/25; financial award applicants required to submit FAFSA. *Faculty research:* Optimization,computer simulation, logistics and distribution, ergonomics and human factors, advanced manufacturing process. Total annual research expenditures: $748,000. *Unit head:* Dr. John S. Usher, Chair, 502-852-6342, Fax: 502-852-5633, E-mail: usher@louisville.edu. *Application contact:* Dr. Michael Day, Associate Dean, 502-852-6195, Fax: 502-852-7294, E-mail: day@louisville.edu.

University of Manitoba, Faculty of Graduate Studies, Faculty of Engineering, Department of Mechanical and Manufacturing Engineering, Winnipeg, MB R3T 2N2, Canada. Offers M Eng, M Sc, PhD. *Degree requirements:* For master's, thesis; for doctorate, thesis/dissertation.

University of Massachusetts Amherst, Graduate School, College of Engineering, Department of Mechanical and Industrial Engineering, Program in Industrial Engineering and Operations

Industrial/Management Engineering

University of Massachusetts Amherst (continued)

Research, Amherst, MA 01003. Offers MS, PhD. Part-time programs available. *Students:* 23 full-time (7 women), 5 part-time (2 women); includes 1 minority (Hispanic/Latino), 17 international. Average age 31. 74 applicants, 43% accepted, 13 enrolled. In 2010, 9 master's awarded. Terminal master's awarded for partial completion of doctoral program. *Degree requirements:* For master's, thesis or alternative, project; for doctorate, comprehensive exam, thesis/dissertation. *Entrance requirements:* For master's and doctorate, GRE General Test. Additional exam requirements/recommendations for international students: Required—TOEFL (minimum score 550 paper-based; 213 computer-based; 80 iBT), IELTS (minimum score 6.5). *Application deadline:* For fall admission, 1/15 for domestic and international students; for spring admission, 10/1 for domestic and international students. Application fee: $50 ($65 for international students). Electronic applications accepted. *Expenses:* Tuition, state resident: full-time $2640. Required fees: $8282. One-time fee: $357 full-time. *Financial support:* Fellowships with full tuition reimbursements, research assistantships with full tuition reimbursements, teaching assistantships with full tuition reimbursements, career-related internships or fieldwork, Federal Work-Study, scholarships/grants, traineeships, health care benefits, tuition waivers, and unspecified assistantships available. Support available to part-time students. Financial award application deadline: 1/15; financial award applicants required to submit FAFSA. *Unit head:* Dr. David P. Schmidt, Graduate Program Director, 413-545-3827, Fax: 413-545-1027. *Application contact:* Jean M. Ames, Supervisor of Admissions, 413-545-0722, Fax: 413-577-0100, E-mail: gradadm@grad.umass.edu.

University of Massachusetts Amherst, Graduate School, Interdisciplinary Programs, Program in Industrial Engineering and Business Administration, Amherst, MA 01003. Offers MBA/MSIE. Part-time programs available. *Students:* 1 applicant, 0% accepted, 0 enrolled. *Entrance requirements:* Additional exam requirements/recommendations for international students: Required—TOEFL (minimum score 600 paper-based; 250 computer-based; 100 iBT), IELTS (minimum score 7). *Application deadline:* For fall admission, 1/15 for domestic and international students. Applications are processed on a rolling basis. Application fee: $50 ($65 for international students). Electronic applications accepted. *Expenses:* Tuition, state resident: full-time $2640. Required fees: $8282. One-time fee: $357 full-time. *Financial support:* Career-related internships or fieldwork, Federal Work-Study, scholarships/grants, traineeships, health care benefits, tuition waivers (full), and unspecified assistantships available. Support available to part-time students. *Unit head:* Dr. David P. Schmidt, Graduate Program Director, 413-545-3827, Fax: 413-545-1027. *Application contact:* Jean M. Ames, Supervisor of Admissions, 413-545-0722, Fax: 413-577-0010, E-mail: gradadm@grad.umass.edu.

University of Massachusetts Lowell, School of Health and Environment, Department of Work Environment, Lowell, MA 01854-2881. Offers cleaner production and pollution prevention (MS, Sc D); environmental risk assessment (Certificate); epidemiology (MS, Sc D); ergonomics and safety (MS, Sc D); identification and control of ergonomic hazards (Certificate); job stress and healthy job redesign (Certificate); occupational and environmental hygiene (MS, Sc D); radiological health physics and general work environment protection (Certificate); work environment policy (MS, Sc D). *Accreditation:* ABET (one or more programs are accredited). Part-time programs available. Terminal master's awarded for partial completion of doctoral program. *Degree requirements:* For master's, thesis optional; for doctorate, thesis/dissertation. *Entrance requirements:* For master's and doctorate, GRE General Test. Additional exam requirements/recommendations for international students: Required—TOEFL.

University of Memphis, Graduate School, Herff College of Engineering, Department of Mechanical Engineering, Memphis, TN 38152. Offers design and mechanical engineering (MS); energy systems (MS); industrial engineering (MS); mechanical engineering (PhD); mechanical systems (MS); power systems (MS). Part-time programs available. *Faculty:* 8 full-time (0 women). *Students:* 3 full-time (1 woman), 8 part-time (0 women); includes 2 Black or African American, non-Hispanic/Latino, 5 international. Average age 30. 11 applicants, 64% accepted, 3 enrolled. In 2010, 5 master's awarded. Terminal master's awarded for partial completion of doctoral program. *Degree requirements:* For master's, comprehensive exam, thesis; for doctorate, comprehensive exam, thesis/dissertation. *Entrance requirements:* For master's, GRE General Test, BS in mechanical engineering, minimum undergraduate GPA of 3.0. *Application deadline:* For fall admission, 8/1 for domestic students; for spring admission, 12/1 for domestic students. Application fee: $35 ($60 for international students). *Financial support:* In 2010–11, 6 students received support; fellowships with full tuition reimbursements available, research assistantships with full tuition reimbursements available, teaching assistantships with full tuition reimbursements available, career-related internships or fieldwork, Federal Work-Study, scholarships/grants, and unspecified assistantships available. Financial award application deadline: 2/15; financial award applicants required to submit FAFSA. *Faculty research:* Computational fluid dynamics, computational mechanics, integrated design, nondestructive testing, operations research. *Unit head:* Dr. John I. Hochstein, Chair, 901-678-2173, Fax: 901-678-5459, E-mail: jhochste@memphis.edu. *Application contact:* Dr. Teong Tan, Graduate Studies Coordinator, 901-678-3264, Fax: 901-678-5459, E-mail: ttan@memphis.edu.

University of Miami, Graduate School, College of Engineering, Department of Industrial Engineering, Coral Gables, FL 33124. Offers ergonomics (PhD); industrial engineering (MSIE, PhD); management of technology (MS); occupational ergonomics and safety (MS, MSOES), including environmental health and safety (MS), occupational ergonomics and safety (MSOES); MBA/MSIE. Part-time programs available. *Degree requirements:* For master's, thesis (for some programs); for doctorate, comprehensive exam, thesis/dissertation. *Entrance requirements:* For master's and doctorate, GRE General Test, minimum GPA of 3.0. Additional exam requirements/recommendations for international students: Required—TOEFL (minimum score 550 paper-based; 213 computer-based). *Faculty research:* Logistics, supply chain management, industrial applications of biomechanics and ergonomics, technology management, back pain, aging, operations research, manufacturing, safety, human reliability, energy assessment.

University of Michigan, Horace H. Rackham School of Graduate Studies, College of Engineering, Department of Industrial and Operations Engineering, Ann Arbor, MI 48109. Offers MS, MSE, PhD, MBA/MS, MBA/MSE. *Accreditation:* ABET. Part-time programs available. *Students:* 186 full-time (67 women), 8 part-time (1 woman). 587 applicants, 44% accepted, 132 enrolled. In 2010, 121 master's, 12 doctorates awarded. Terminal master's awarded for partial completion of doctoral program. *Degree requirements:* For doctorate, oral defense of dissertation, preliminary exams, qualifying exam. *Entrance requirements:* For master's, GRE General Test, minimum GPA of 3.2; for doctorate, GRE General Test, minimum GPA of 3.5. Additional exam requirements/recommendations for international students: Required—TOEFL. *Application deadline:* Applications are processed on a rolling basis. Application fee: $65 ($75 for international students). Electronic applications accepted. *Expenses:* Tuition, state resident: full-time $17,784; part-time $1116 per credit hour. Tuition, nonresident: full-time $35,944; part-time $2125 per credit hour. International tuition: $35,994 full-time. Required fees: $95 per semester. Tuition and fees vary according to course load, degree level and program. *Financial support:* In 2010–11, 71 students received support; fellowships, research assistantships, teaching assistantships, Federal Work-Study, institutionally sponsored loans, scholarships/grants, traineeships, health care benefits, and unspecified assistantships available. Financial award applicants required to submit FAFSA. *Faculty research:* Production/distribution/logistics, financial engineering and enterprise systems, ergonomics (physical and cognitive), stochastic processes, linear and nonlinear optimization, operations research. *Unit head:* Mark Daskin, Chair, 734-764-9422, Fax: 734-764-3451, E-mail: msdaskin@umich.edu. *Application contact:* Matt Irelan, Graduate Student Advisor/Program Coordinator, 734-764-6480, Fax: 734-764-3451, E-mail: mirelan@umich.edu.

University of Michigan–Dearborn, College of Engineering and Computer Science, Department of Industrial and Manufacturing Systems Engineering, Dearborn, MI 48128-1491. Offers engineering management (MS); industrial and systems engineering (MSE); information systems and technology (MS); information systems engineering (PhD); program and project management (MS); MBA/MSE. Part-time and evening/weekend programs available. *Faculty:* 13 full-time (0 women), 3 part-time/adjunct (0 women). *Students:* 23 full-time (8 women), 142 part-time (40 women); includes 14 Black or African American, non-Hispanic/Latino; 27 Asian, non-Hispanic/Latino; 8 Hispanic/Latino, 23 international. Average age 35. 81 applicants, 58% accepted, 47 enrolled. In 2010, 57 master's awarded. *Degree requirements:* For master's, thesis optional. *Entrance requirements:* For master's, bachelor's degree in applied mathematics, computer science, engineering, or physical science; minimum GPA of 3.0. Additional exam requirements/recommendations for international students: Required—TOEFL (minimum score 560 paper-based; 220 computer-based; 84 iBT). *Application deadline:* For fall admission, 8/1 priority date for domestic students, 4/1 for international students; for winter admission, 12/1 priority date for domestic students, 8/1 for international students; for spring admission, 4/1 for domestic students, 12/1 for international students. Applications are processed on a rolling basis. Application fee: $60. Electronic applications accepted. *Financial support:* Fellowships, research assistantships, teaching assistantships, Federal Work-Study available. Financial award application deadline: 4/1; financial award applicants required to submit FAFSA. *Faculty research:* Health care systems, data and knowledge management, human factors engineering, machine diagnostics, precision machining. *Unit head:* Dr. Armen Zakarian, Chair, 313-593-5361, Fax: 313-593-3692, E-mail: zakarian@umd.umich.edu. *Application contact:* Joey W. Woods, Graduate Program Assistant, 313-593-5361, Fax: 313-593-3692, E-mail: jwwoods@umd.umich.edu.

University of Minnesota, Twin Cities Campus, Institute of Technology, Department of Mechanical Engineering, Program in Industrial Engineering, Minneapolis, MN 55455-0213. Offers MSIE, PhD. Part-time programs available. *Degree requirements:* For doctorate, thesis/dissertation. *Entrance requirements:* For master's, GRE General Test, minimum GPA of 3.0; for doctorate, GRE General Test.

University of Missouri, Graduate School, College of Engineering, Department of Industrial and Manufacturing Systems Engineering, Columbia, MO 65211. Offers MS, PhD. *Degree requirements:* For master's, thesis or alternative; for doctorate, thesis/dissertation. *Entrance requirements:* For master's and doctorate, GRE General Test, minimum GPA of 3.0. Additional exam requirements/recommendations for international students: Required—TOEFL (minimum score 550 paper-based; 213 computer-based; 80 iBT).

University of Nebraska–Lincoln, Graduate College, College of Engineering, Department of Industrial and Management Systems Engineering, Lincoln, NE 68588. Offers engineering management (M Eng); industrial and management systems engineering (MS, PhD); manufacturing systems engineering (MS). Postbaccalaureate distance learning degree programs offered. *Degree requirements:* For master's, thesis optional; for doctorate, comprehensive exam, thesis/dissertation. *Entrance requirements:* For master's and doctorate, GRE. Additional exam requirements/recommendations for international students: Required—TOEFL (minimum score 525 paper-based; 195 computer-based). Electronic applications accepted. *Faculty research:* Ergonomics, occupational safety, quality control, industrial packaging, facility design.

University of New Haven, Graduate School, Tagliatela College of Engineering, Program in Industrial Engineering, West Haven, CT 06516-1916. Offers industrial engineering (MSIE); lean-Six Sigma (Certificate); quality engineering (Certificate). Part-time and evening/weekend programs available. *Degree requirements:* For master's, project or thesis. *Entrance requirements:* For master's, bachelor's degree in engineering. Additional exam requirements/recommendations for international students: Required—TOEFL (minimum score 520 paper-based; 190 computer-based; 70 iBT); Recommended—IELTS (minimum score 5.5). *Application deadline:* For fall admission, 5/31 for international students; for winter admission, 10/15 for international students; for spring admission, 1/15 for international students. Applications are processed on a rolling basis. Application fee: $50. Electronic applications accepted. *Financial support:* Research assistantships with partial tuition reimbursements, teaching assistantships with partial tuition reimbursements, career-related internships or fieldwork, Federal Work-Study, scholarships/grants, tuition waivers, and unspecified assistantships available. Support available to part-time students. Financial award applicants required to submit FAFSA. *Unit head:* Dr. Alexis Sommes, Coordinator, 203-932-7434. *Application contact:* Eloise Gormley, Director of Graduate Admissions, 203-932-7449, Fax: 203-932-7137, E-mail: gradinfo@newhaven.edu.

University of Oklahoma, College of Engineering, School of Industrial Engineering, Norman, OK 73019. Offers industrial engineering (MS, PhD), including engineering management (MS), general (MS). Part-time programs available. *Faculty:* 14 full-time (5 women). *Students:* 37 full-time (11 women), 23 part-time (7 women); includes 5 minority (3 Black or African American, non-Hispanic/Latino; 1 American Indian or Alaska Native, non-Hispanic/Latino; 1 Two or more races, non-Hispanic/Latino), 32 international. Average age 28. 58 applicants, 72% accepted, 12 enrolled. In 2010, 7 master's, 5 doctorates awarded. *Degree requirements:* For master's, comprehensive exam, thesis (for some programs); for doctorate, thesis/dissertation, qualifying exam. *Entrance requirements:* For master's and doctorate, GRE, minimum GPA of 3.0, 3 letters of reference, resume or curriculum vitae. Additional exam requirements/recommendations for international students: Required—TOEFL (minimum score 550 paper-based; 213 computer-based; 79 iBT). *Application deadline:* For fall admission, 6/1 priority date for domestic students, 4/1 for international students; for spring admission, 11/1 for domestic students, 9/1 for international students. Applications are processed on a rolling basis. Application fee: $40 ($90 for international students). Electronic applications accepted. *Expenses:* Tuition, state resident: full-time $3892.80; part-time $162.20 per credit hour. Tuition, nonresident: full-time $14,167; part-time $590.30 per credit hour. Required fees: $2523.40; $94.60 per credit hour. Tuition and fees vary according to course load and degree level. *Financial support:* In 2010–11, 48 students received support, including 12 research assistantships with partial tuition reimbursements available (averaging $13,300 per year), 10 teaching assistantships with partial tuition reimbursements available (averaging $10,350 per year); scholarships/grants and unspecified assistantships also available. Financial award application deadline: 5/1; financial award applicants required to submit FAFSA. *Faculty research:* Computational optimization, logistics and supply chain management, human factors, design and manufacturing, systems modeling, engineering education. Total annual research expenditures: $2.5 million. *Unit head:* Dr. Randa Shehab, Director, 405-325-3721, Fax: 405-325-7555, E-mail: rlshehab@ou.edu. *Application contact:* Amy J. Piper, Student Services Coordinator, 405-325-3721, Fax: 405-325-7555, E-mail: ajpiper@ou.edu.

University of Pittsburgh, School of Engineering, Department of Industrial Engineering, Pittsburgh, PA 15260. Offers MSIE, PhD. Part-time programs available. Postbaccalaureate distance learning degree programs offered. *Faculty:* 13 full-time (2 women), 12 part-time/adjunct (2 women). *Students:* 57 full-time (22 women), 28 part-time (0 women); includes 5 minority (1 Black or African American, non-Hispanic/Latino; 1 Asian, non-Hispanic/Latino; 3 Hispanic/Latino), 54 international. 311 applicants, 52% accepted, 33 enrolled. In 2010, 36 master's, 2 doctorates awarded. Terminal master's awarded for partial completion of doctoral program. *Degree requirements:* For master's, thesis optional; for doctorate, comprehensive exam, thesis/dissertation, final oral exams. *Entrance requirements:* For master's and doctorate, GRE General Test, minimum QPA of 3.0. Additional exam requirements/recommendations for international students: Required—TOEFL (minimum score 550 paper-based; 213 computer-based; 80 iBT). *Application deadline:* For fall admission, 3/1 priority date for domestic students; for spring admission, 7/1 priority date for domestic students. Applications are processed on a rolling basis. Application fee: $50. Electronic applications accepted. *Expenses:* Tuition, state resident: full-time $17,304; part-time $701 per credit. Tuition, nonresident: full-time $29,554; part-time $1210 per credit. Required fees: $740; $214 per term. Tuition and fees vary according to program. *Financial support:* In 2010–11, 19 students received support, including 5 fellowships with full tuition reimbursements available (averaging $26,000 per year), 36 research assistantships with full tuition reimbursements available (averaging $25,000 per year), 7 teaching assistantships with full tuition reimbursements available (averaging $24,000 per year); scholarships/grants and tuition waivers (full and partial) also available. Financial award application deadline: 4/15. *Faculty research:* Operations research, engineering management, computational intelligence, manufacturing, information systems. Total annual research expenditures: $4.5 million. *Unit head:* Dr. Bopaya Bidanda, Chairman, 412-624-9830, Fax:

412-624-9831. *Application contact:* Dr. Jayant Rajgopal, Graduate Coordinator, 412-624-9840, Fax: 412-624-9831, E-mail: rajgopal@engrng.pitt.edu.

University of Puerto Rico, Mayagüez Campus, Graduate Studies, College of Engineering, Department of Industrial Engineering, Mayagüez, PR 00681-9000. Offers industrial engineering (ME, MS); management systems engineering (ME). Part-time programs available. *Students:* 30 full-time (19 women), 6 part-time (2 women); includes 25 Hispanic/Latino, 11 international. 18 applicants, 50% accepted, 4 enrolled. In 2010, 2 master's awarded. *Degree requirements:* For master's, comprehensive exam, thesis, project. *Entrance requirements:* For master's, minimum GPA of 2.5; proficiency in English and Spanish; BS in engineering. Additional exam requirements/recommendations for international students: Required—TOEFL. *Application deadline:* For fall admission, 2/15 for domestic and international students; for spring admission, 9/15 for domestic and international students. Applications are processed on a rolling basis. Application fee: $25. *Expenses:* Tuition, state resident: full-time $1188. Tuition, nonresident: full-time $1188. International tuition: $6126 full-time. Tuition and fees vary according to course level and course load. *Financial support:* In 2010–11, 11 students received support, including fellowships (averaging $12,000 per year), 7 research assistantships (averaging $15,000 per year), 11 teaching assistantships (averaging $8,500 per year); Federal Work-Study and institutionally sponsored loans also available. Total annual research expenditures: $141,455. *Unit head:* Dr. Viviana Cesan??, Chairperson, 787-265-3819, Fax: 787-265-3820, E-mail: viviana.cesani@upr.edu. *Application contact:* Dr. Viviana Cesan??, Chairperson, 787-265-3819, Fax: 787-265-3820, E-mail: viviana.cesani@upr.edu.

University of Regina, Faculty of Graduate Studies and Research, Faculty of Engineering and Applied Science, Program in Industrial Systems Engineering, Regina, SK S4S 0A2, Canada. Offers M Eng, MA Sc, PhD. Part-time programs available. *Faculty:* 13 full-time (2 women). *Students:* 33 full-time (6 women), 4 part-time (0 women). 67 applicants, 55% accepted. In 2010, 7 master's awarded. *Degree requirements:* For master's, thesis (for some programs); for doctorate, thesis/dissertation. *Entrance requirements:* For doctorate, master's degree. Additional exam requirements/recommendations for international students: Required—TOEFL (minimum score 550 paper-based; 80 iBT). *Application deadline:* For fall admission, 3/31 for domestic and international students; for winter admission, 7/31 for domestic and international students; for spring admission, 11/30 for domestic and international students. Applications are processed on a rolling basis. Application fee: $100. Tuition and fees charges are reported in Canadian dollars. *Expenses:* Tuition, area resident: Full-time $3244.50 Canadian dollars; part-time $180.25 Canadian dollars per credit hour. International tuition: $4744.50 Canadian dollars full-time. Required fees: $494 Canadian dollars; $115.25 Canadian dollars per credit hour. $115.25 Canadian dollars per semester. Tuition and fees vary according to program. *Financial support:* In 2010–11, 3 fellowships (averaging $18,000 per year), 2 research assistantships (averaging $17,250 per year), 5 teaching assistantships (averaging $6,956 per year) were awarded; career-related internships or fieldwork and scholarships/grants also available. Financial award application deadline: 6/15. *Faculty research:* Stochastic systems simulation, metallurgy of welding, computer-aided engineering, finite element method of engineering systems, manufacturing systems. *Unit head:* Dr. Raphael Idem, Associate Dean, Research and Graduate Studies, 306-337-2696, E-mail: raphael.idem@uregina.ca. *Application contact:* Dr. Denise Stilling, Chair, Graduate Program Coordinator, 306-337-2696, Fax: 306-585-4855, E-mail: denise.stilling@uregina.ca.

University of Southern California, Graduate School, Viterbi School of Engineering, Daniel J. Epstein Department of Industrial and Systems Engineering, Los Angeles, CA 90089. Offers digital supply chain management (MS); engineering management (MS); engineering technology communication (Graduate Certificate); health systems operations (Graduate Certificate); industrial and systems engineering (MS, PhD, Engr); manufacturing engineering (MS); operations research engineering (MS); optimization and supply chain management (Graduate Certificate); product development engineering (MS); safety systems and security (MS); systems architecting and engineering (MS, Graduate Certificate); systems safety and security (Graduate Certificate); transportation systems (Graduate Certificate); MS/MBA. Part-time and evening/weekend programs available. Postbaccalaureate distance learning degree programs offered (no on-campus study). *Faculty:* 12 full-time (2 women), 21 part-time/adjunct (2 women). *Students:* 224 full-time (69 women), 143 part-time (32 women); includes 63 minority (6 Black or African American, non-Hispanic/Latino; 35 Asian, non-Hispanic/Latino; 17 Hispanic/Latino; 5 Two or more races, non-Hispanic/Latino), 253 international. 669 applicants, 45% accepted, 155 enrolled. In 2010, 98 master's, 7 doctorates awarded. Terminal master's awarded for partial completion of doctoral program. *Degree requirements:* For master's, thesis optional; for doctorate, thesis/dissertation. *Entrance requirements:* For master's and doctorate, GRE General Test. *Application deadline:* For fall admission, 12/1 priority date for domestic students, 11/1 priority date for international students; for spring admission, 9/15 priority date for domestic and international students. Applications are processed on a rolling basis. Application fee: $85. Electronic applications accepted. *Expenses:* Tuition: Full-time $31,240; part-time $1420 per unit. Required fees: $600. One-time fee: $35 full-time. Full-time tuition and fees vary according to degree level and program. *Financial support:* In 2010–11, fellowships with full tuition reimbursements (averaging $30,000 per year), research assistantships with full tuition reimbursements (averaging $20,000 per year), teaching assistantships with full tuition reimbursements (averaging $20,000 per year) were awarded; career-related internships or fieldwork, scholarships/grants, health care benefits, and unspecified assistantships also available. Financial award application deadline: 12/1; financial award applicants required to submit CSS PROFILE or FAFSA. *Faculty research:* Health systems, music cognition and retrieval, transportation and logistics, manufacturing and automation, engineering systems design, risk and economic analysis. Total annual research expenditures: $1 million. *Unit head:* Dr. F. Stan Settles, Chair, 213-740-4893, E-mail: isedept@usc.edu. *Application contact:* Evelyn Felina, Director of Student Affairs, 213-740-7549, E-mail: efelina@usc.edu.

University of South Florida, Graduate School, College of Engineering, Department of Industrial and Management Systems Engineering, Tampa, FL 33620-9951. Offers engineering management (MSEM, MSIE); engineering science (PhD); industrial engineering (MIE, MSIE, PhD). Part-time programs available. Postbaccalaureate distance learning degree programs offered (minimal on-campus study). *Faculty:* 4 full-time (1 woman), 1 part-time/adjunct (0 women). *Students:* 61 full-time (15 women), 71 part-time (19 women); includes 9 Black or African American, non-Hispanic/Latino; 3 Asian, non-Hispanic/Latino; 17 Hispanic/Latino; 1 Two or more races, non-Hispanic/Latino, 51 international. Average age 31. 125 applicants, 46% accepted, 32 enrolled. In 2010, 49 master's, 3 doctorates awarded. Terminal master's awarded for partial completion of doctoral program. *Degree requirements:* For master's, comprehensive exam, thesis (for some programs); for doctorate, comprehensive exam, thesis/dissertation, 2 tools of research as specified by dissertation committee. *Entrance requirements:* For master's, GRE General Test, minimum GPA of 3.0 in last 60 hours of coursework; for doctorate, GRE General Test, minimum GPA of 3.0 in last 60 hours of coursework or in master's program. Additional exam requirements/recommendations for international students: Required—TOEFL (minimum score 550 paper-based; 213 computer-based; 80 iBT). *Application deadline:* For fall admission, 2/15 for domestic students, 1/2 for international students; for spring admission, 10/15 for domestic students, 6/1 for international students. Application fee: $30. Electronic applications accepted. *Financial support:* In 2010–11, 21 research assistantships with partial tuition reimbursements (averaging $17,902 per year), 10 teaching assistantships with partial tuition reimbursements (averaging $29,517 per year) were awarded; tuition waivers (partial) also available. Financial award applicants required to submit FAFSA. *Faculty research:* Bio-health engineering, engineering health care systems, energy markets, nanotechnology and nanomanufacturing, transportation and logistics, innovation in education. Total annual research expenditures: $926,936. *Unit head:* Dr. Jose Zayas-Castro, Department Chair, 813-974-2269, Fax: 813-974-5953, E-mail: josezaya@usf.edu. *Application contact:* Dr. Michael Weng, Program Coordinator, 813-974-5575, Fax: 813-974-5953, E-mail: mxweng@usf.edu.

The University of Tennessee, Graduate School, College of Engineering, Department of Industrial and Information Engineering, Knoxville, TN 37966. Offers engineering management (MS); industrial engineering (MS, PhD); reliability and maintainability engineering (MS); MS/MBA. Part-time programs available. Postbaccalaureate distance learning degree programs offered (minimal on-campus study). *Faculty:* 8 full-time (1 woman), 6 part-time/adjunct (1 woman). *Students:* 40 full-time (12 women), 57 part-time (13 women); includes 9 Black or African American, non-Hispanic/Latino; 1 American Indian or Alaska Native, non-Hispanic/Latino; 6 Asian, non-Hispanic/Latino, 31 international. Average age 28. 61 applicants, 77% accepted, 11 enrolled. In 2010, 15 master's, 5 doctorates awarded. *Degree requirements:* For master's, thesis or alternative; for doctorate, comprehensive exam, thesis/dissertation. *Entrance requirements:* For master's, GRE General Test, Minimum GPA of 2.7 (US degree holders); 3.0 (International degree holders); for doctorate, GRE General Test, Minimum GPA of 3.0 (previous graduate course work). Additional exam requirements/recommendations for international students: Required—TOEFL (minimum score 550 paper-based; 213 computer-based). *Application deadline:* For fall admission, 2/1 priority date for domestic and international students; for spring admission, 6/15 for domestic and international students. Applications are processed on a rolling basis. Application fee: $35. Electronic applications accepted. *Expenses:* Tuition, state resident: full-time $7440; part-time $414 per credit hour. Tuition, nonresident: full-time $22,478; part-time $1250 per credit hour. Required fees: $922; $43 per credit hour. Tuition and fees vary according to program. *Financial support:* In 2010–11, 27 students received support, including 17 research assistantships with full tuition reimbursements available (averaging $12,372 per year), 11 teaching assistantships with full tuition reimbursements available (averaging $6,792 per year); career-related internships or fieldwork, Federal Work-Study, institutionally sponsored loans, health care benefits, and unspecified assistantships also available. Financial award application deadline: 2/1; financial award applicants required to submit FAFSA. *Faculty research:* Defense-oriented supply chain modeling; dependability and reliability of large computer networks; design of lean, reliable systems; new product development; operations research in the automotive industry. Total annual research expenditures: $839,000. *Unit head:* Dr. Rapinder Sawhney, Department Head, 865-974-3333, Fax: 865-974-0588, E-mail: sawhney@utk.edu. *Application contact:* Dr. Denise Jackson, Graduate Representative, 865-946-3248, E-mail: djackson@utk.edu.

The University of Tennessee at Chattanooga, Graduate School, College of Engineering and Computer Science, Program in Engineering, Chattanooga, TN 37403. Offers chemical engineering (MS Engr); civil engineering (MS Engr); computational engineering (MS Engr); electrical engineering (MS Engr); industrial engineering (MS Engr); mechanical engineering (MS Engr). Part-time and evening/weekend programs available. *Faculty:* 8 full-time (0 women). *Students:* 27 full-time (5 women), 31 part-time (6 women); includes 12 minority (7 Black or African American, non-Hispanic/Latino; 1 Asian, non-Hispanic/Latino; 4 Hispanic/Latino), 10 international. Average age 29. 43 applicants, 100% accepted, 26 enrolled. In 2010, 16 master's awarded. *Degree requirements:* For master's, comprehensive exam, thesis or alternative, engineering project. *Entrance requirements:* For master's, GRE General Test, minimum undergraduate GPA of 2.5 or 3.0 in last 30 hours of coursework. Additional exam requirements/recommendations for international students: Required—TOEFL (minimum score 550 paper-based; 213 computer-based; 79 iBT), IELTS (minimum score 6). *Application deadline:* For fall admission, 8/1 priority date for domestic students, 6/1 for international students; for spring admission, 12/1 priority date for domestic students, 10/1 for international students. Applications are processed on a rolling basis. Application fee: $35. Electronic applications accepted. *Financial support:* In 2010–11, 23 research assistantships with full and partial tuition reimbursements (averaging $5,500 per year) were awarded; career-related internships or fieldwork, scholarships/grants, and unspecified assistantships also available. Support available to part-time students. *Faculty research:* Quality control and reliability engineering, financial management, thermal science, energy conservation, structural analysis. Total annual research expenditures: $2.6 million. *Unit head:* Dr. Neslihan Alp, Director, 423-425-4032, Fax: 423-425-5229, E-mail: neslihan-alp@utc.edu. *Application contact:* Dr. Jerald Ainsworth, Dean of Graduate Studies, 423-425-4478, Fax: 423-425-5223, E-mail: jerald-ainsworth@utc.edu.

The University of Texas at Arlington, Graduate School, College of Engineering, Department of Industrial and Manufacturing Systems Engineering, Arlington, TX 76019. Offers engineering management (MS); industrial engineering (MS, PhD); logistics (MS); systems engineering (MS). Part-time and evening/weekend programs available. Postbaccalaureate distance learning degree programs offered (no on-campus study). *Faculty:* 10 full-time (4 women). *Students:* 127 full-time (37 women), 89 part-time (16 women); includes 30 minority (11 Black or African American, non-Hispanic/Latino; 11 Asian, non-Hispanic/Latino; 8 Hispanic/Latino), 138 international. 178 applicants, 89% accepted, 49 enrolled. In 2010, 25 master's awarded. Terminal master's awarded for partial completion of doctoral program. *Degree requirements:* For master's, comprehensive exam, thesis optional; for doctorate, comprehensive exam, thesis/dissertation. *Entrance requirements:* For master's and doctorate, GRE General Test, minimum GPA of 3.0. Additional exam requirements/recommendations for international students: Required—TOEFL (minimum score 550 paper-based; 213 computer-based). *Application deadline:* For fall admission, 6/6 for domestic students, 4/4 for international students; for spring admission, 10/15 for domestic students, 9/5 for international students. Applications are processed on a rolling basis. Application fee: $35 ($50 for international students). *Expenses:* Tuition, state resident: full-time $7500. Tuition, nonresident: full-time $13,080. International tuition: $13,250 full-time. *Financial support:* In 2010–11, 50 students received support, including 9 fellowships (averaging $1,000 per year), 17 research assistantships (averaging $8,400 per year), 15 teaching assistantships (averaging $9,000 per year); career-related internships or fieldwork, Federal Work-Study, institutionally sponsored loans, scholarships/grants, and unspecified assistantships also available. Financial award application deadline: 6/1; financial award applicants required to submit FAFSA. *Faculty research:* Manufacturing, healthcare logistics, environmental systems, operations research, statistics. *Unit head:* Dr. Donald H. Liles, Chair, 817-272-3092, Fax: 817-272-3406, E-mail: dliles@uta.edu. *Application contact:* Dr. Sheik Imrhan, Graduate Advisor, 817-272-3167, Fax: 817-272-3406, E-mail: imrhan@uta.edu.

The University of Texas at Austin, Graduate School, Cockrell School of Engineering, Department of Mechanical Engineering, Program in Operations Research and Industrial Engineering, Austin, TX 78712-1111. Offers MS, PhD. *Entrance requirements:* For master's and doctorate, GRE General Test. Additional exam requirements/recommendations for international students: Required—TOEFL.

The University of Texas at El Paso, Graduate School, College of Engineering, Department of Industrial Engineering, El Paso, TX 79968-0001. Offers industrial engineering (MS); manufacturing engineering (MS); systems engineering (MS, Certificate). Part-time and evening/weekend programs available. *Students:* 51 (11 women); includes 1 Asian, non-Hispanic/Latino; 42 Hispanic/Latino, 8 international. Average age 34. 38 applicants. In 2010, 46 master's awarded. *Degree requirements:* For master's, thesis optional. *Entrance requirements:* For master's, GRE General Test, minimum GPA of 3.0 in major. Additional exam requirements/recommendations for international students: Required—TOEFL. *Application deadline:* For fall admission, 7/1 priority date for domestic students, 3/1 for international students; for spring admission, 11/1 priority date for domestic students, 9/1 for international students. Applications are processed on a rolling basis. Application fee: $15 ($65 for international students). Electronic applications accepted. *Financial support:* In 2010–11, research assistantships with partial tuition reimbursements (averaging $21,125 per year), teaching assistantships with partial tuition reimbursements (averaging $16,900 per year) were awarded; fellowships with partial tuition reimbursements, Federal Work-Study, institutionally sponsored loans, scholarships/grants, and tuition waivers (partial) also available. Financial award application deadline: 3/15; financial award applicants required to submit FAFSA. *Faculty research:* Computer vision, automated inspection, simulation and modeling. *Unit head:* Dr. Rafael S. Gutierrez, Chair, 915-747-5450, Fax: 915-747-5019, E-mail: rsgutier@utep.edu. *Application contact:* Dr. Charles H. Ambler, Dean of the Graduate School, 915-747-5491 Ext. 7886, Fax: 915-747-5788, E-mail: cambler@utep.edu.

The University of Toledo, College of Graduate Studies, College of Engineering, Department of Mechanical, Industrial, and Manufacturing Engineering, Toledo, OH 43606-3390. Offers industrial engineering (MS, PhD); mechanical engineering (MS, PhD). Part-time programs available. Postbaccalaureate distance learning degree programs offered (minimal on-campus

Industrial/Management Engineering

The University of Toledo (continued)

study). *Degree requirements:* For master's, thesis optional; for doctorate, thesis/dissertation, qualifying exam. *Entrance requirements:* For master's, GRE General Test, minimum GPA of 3.0; for doctorate, GRE General Test, minimum GPA of 3.3. Additional exam requirements/recommendations for international students: Required—TOEFL (minimum score 550 paper-based; 213 computer-based; 80 iBT). Electronic applications accepted. *Expenses:* Tuition, state resident: full-time $11,426; part-time $476 per credit hour. Tuition, nonresident: full-time $21,660; part-time $903 per credit hour. One-time fee: $62. *Faculty research:* Computational and experimental thermal sciences, manufacturing process and systems, mechanics, materials, design, quality and management engineering systems.

University of Toronto, School of Graduate Studies, Physical Sciences Division, Faculty of Applied Science and Engineering, Department of Mechanical and Industrial Engineering, Toronto, ON M5S 1A1, Canada. Offers M Eng, MA Sc, PhD. Part-time programs available. *Degree requirements:* For master's, thesis (for some programs), oral exam/thesis defense (MA Sc); for doctorate, thesis/dissertation, thesis defense, qualifying examination. *Entrance requirements:* For master's, GRE (recommended), minimum B+ average in last 2 years of undergraduate study, 2 letters of reference, resume, must be a Canadian citizen or a permanent resident (M Eng); for doctorate, GRE (recommended), minimum B+ average, 2 letters of reference, resumé. Additional exam requirements/recommendations for international students: Required—TOEFL (580 paper-based, 237 computer-based), Michigan English Language Assessment Battery (85), IELTS (7) or COPE (4).

University of Washington, Graduate School, College of Engineering, Department of Industrial and Systems Engineering, Seattle, WA 98195-2650. Offers MS, PhD. Part-time programs available. Postbaccalaureate distance learning degree programs offered (no on-campus study). *Faculty:* 11 full-time (4 women), 6 part-time/adjunct (2 women). *Students:* 33 full-time (11 women), 8 part-time (1 woman); includes 1 Black or African American, non-Hispanic/Latino; 2 Asian, non-Hispanic/Latino, 25 international. Average age 29. 200 applicants, 25% accepted, 15 enrolled. In 2010, 6 master's, 3 doctorates awarded. Terminal master's awarded for partial completion of doctoral program. *Degree requirements:* For master's, thesis optional; for doctorate, comprehensive exam, thesis/dissertation, Qualifying, general, and final exams.. *Entrance requirements:* For master's, GRE General Test, Minimum GPA of 3.0; bachelor's degree in engineering, math, or science; transcripts; letters of recommendation; resume; statement of objectives.; for doctorate, GRE General Test, Minimum GPA of 3.0; transcripts; letters of recommendation; resume; statement of objectives.. Additional exam requirements/recommendations for international students: Required—TOEFL (minimum score 580 paper-based; 237 computer-based; 92 iBT); Recommended—IELTS (minimum score 7). *Application deadline:* For fall admission, 2/1 priority date for domestic students, 1/1 priority date for international students. Applications are processed on a rolling basis. Application fee: $75. Electronic applications accepted. *Financial support:* In 2010–11, 1 student received support, including 3 fellowships (averaging $14,751 per year), 10 research assistantships with full tuition reimbursements available (averaging $14,751 per year), 6 teaching assistantships with full tuition reimbursements available (averaging $14,751 per year); career-related internships or fieldwork, scholarships/grants, traineeships, and tuition waivers (full) also available. Financial award application deadline: 2/1; financial award applicants required to submit FAFSA. *Faculty research:* Manufacturing, operations research, supply chain systems, human interface technology, quality control, logistics systems, bio-industrial systems. Total annual research expenditures: $420,000. *Unit head:* Dr. Richard Lee Storch, Professor and Chair, 206-543-1427, Fax: 206-685-3072, E-mail: rlstorch@u.washington.edu. *Application contact:* Jennifer W. Tsai, Academic Counselor, 206-543-5041, Fax: 206-685-3072, E-mail: ieadvise@u.washington.edu.

University of Windsor, Faculty of Graduate Studies, Faculty of Engineering, Department of Industrial and Manufacturing Systems Engineering, Windsor, ON N9B 3P4, Canada. Offers industrial engineering (M Eng, MA Sc); manufacturing systems engineering (PhD). Part-time programs available. *Degree requirements:* For master's, thesis; for doctorate, comprehensive exam, thesis/dissertation. *Entrance requirements:* For master's, minimum B average; for doctorate, master's degree, minimum B average. Additional exam requirements/recommendations for international students: Required—TOEFL (minimum score 560 paper-based; 220 computer-based). Electronic applications accepted. *Faculty research:* Human factors, operations research.

University of Wisconsin–Madison, Graduate School, College of Engineering, Department of Industrial and Systems Engineering, Madison, WI 53706. Offers MS, PhD. Part-time programs available. *Faculty:* 21 full-time (6 women), 12 part-time/adjunct (4 women). *Students:* 158 full-time (55 women), 15 part-time (7 women); includes 8 Black or African American, non-Hispanic/Latino; 1 American Indian or Alaska Native, non-Hispanic/Latino; 5 Asian, non-Hispanic/Latino; 2 Hispanic/Latino, 120 international. Average age 27. 449 applicants, 24% accepted, 39 enrolled. In 2010, 55 master's, 8 doctorates awarded. Terminal master's awarded for partial completion of doctoral program. *Degree requirements:* For master's, thesis optional; for doctorate, comprehensive exam, thesis/dissertation. *Entrance requirements:* For master's, GRE General Test, minimum GPA of 3.0, BS in engineering or equivalent, course work in computer programming and statistics; for doctorate, GRE General Test, minimum GPA of 3.0. Additional exam requirements/recommendations for international students: Required—IELTS (minimum score 6); Recommended—TOEFL (minimum score 550 paper-based; 213 computer-based; 80 iBT). *Application deadline:* For fall admission, 2/1 priority date for domestic and international students; for spring admission, 10/1 priority date for domestic and international students. Application fee: $56. Electronic applications accepted. *Expenses:* Tuition, state resident: full-time $9887.36; part-time $617.96 per credit. Tuition, nonresident: full-time $24,054; part-time $1503.40 per credit. Required fees: $67.63 per credit. Tuition and fees vary according to reciprocity agreements. *Financial support:* In 2010–11, 87 students received support, including fellowships with full tuition reimbursements available (averaging $21,760 per year), 72 research assistantships with full tuition reimbursements available (averaging $40,800 per year), 15 teaching assistantships with full tuition reimbursements available (averaging $28,175 per year); career-related internships or fieldwork, Federal Work-Study, institutionally sponsored loans, scholarships/grants, traineeships, health care benefits, and unspecified assistantships also available. *Faculty research:* Human factors and ergonomics, manufacturing and production systems, health systems engineering, decision science/operations research, quality engineering. Total annual research expenditures: $10.2 million. *Unit head:* Dr. Vicki M. Bier, Chair, 608-262-2064, Fax: 608-262-8454, E-mail: bier@engr.wisc.edu. *Application contact:* Anne Duchek, Graduate Admissions Coordinator, 608-890-2765, Fax: 608-890-2204, E-mail: amduchek@engr.wisc.edu.

University of Wisconsin–Milwaukee, Graduate School, College of Engineering and Applied Science, Program in Engineering, Milwaukee, WI 53201-0413. Offers civil engineering (MS); electrical and computer engineering (MS); energy engineering (Certificate); engineering (PhD); engineering management (MS); engineering mechanics (MS); ergonomics (Certificate); industrial and management engineering (MS); manufacturing engineering (MS); materials engineering (MS); mechanical engineering (MS); MUP/MS. Part-time programs available. *Faculty:* 50 full-time (5 women). *Students:* 152 full-time (27 women), 115 part-time (23 women); includes 13 Black or African American, non-Hispanic/Latino; 3 American Indian or Alaska Native, non-Hispanic/Latino; 6 Asian, non-Hispanic/Latino; 10 Hispanic/Latino, 25 international. Average age 31. 236 applicants, 67% accepted, 55 enrolled. In 2010, 39 master's, 19 doctorates awarded. *Degree requirements:* For master's, comprehensive exam (for some programs), thesis or alternative; for doctorate, comprehensive exam, thesis/dissertation, internship. *Entrance requirements:* For master's, GRE, minimum GPA of 2.75; for doctorate, GRE, minimum GPA of 3.5. Additional exam requirements/recommendations for international students: Required—TOEFL (minimum score 550 paper-based; 79 iBT), IELTS (minimum score 6.5). *Application deadline:* For fall admission, 1/1 priority date for domestic students; for spring admission, 9/1 for domestic students. Applications are processed on a rolling basis. Application fee: $56 ($96

for international students). *Financial support:* In 2010–11, 3 fellowships, 55 research assistantships, 77 teaching assistantships were awarded; career-related internships or fieldwork, Federal Work-Study, unspecified assistantships, and project assistantships also available. Support available to part-time students. Financial award application deadline: 4/15. Total annual research expenditures: $6.2 million. *Unit head:* David Yu, Representative, 414-229-6169, E-mail: yu@uwm.edu. *Application contact:* Betty Warras, General Information Contact, 414-229-6169, Fax: 414-229-6967, E-mail: bwarras@uwm.edu.

University of Wisconsin–Stout, Graduate School, College of Technology, Engineering, and Management, MS Program in Risk Control, Menomonie, WI 54751. Offers MS. Part-time programs available. *Degree requirements:* For master's, thesis. *Entrance requirements:* For master's, minimum GPA of 3.0. Additional exam requirements/recommendations for international students: Required—TOEFL (minimum score 500 paper-based; 173 computer-based; 61 iBT). Electronic applications accepted. *Faculty research:* Environmental microbiology, water supply safety, facilities planning, industrial ventilation, bioterrorist.

Virginia Polytechnic Institute and State University, Graduate School, College of Engineering, Department of Industrial and Systems Engineering, Blacksburg, VA 24061. Offers human-system integration (Certificate); industrial and systems engineering (MEA, PhD); systems engineering (MS). *Faculty:* 25 full-time (4 women). *Students:* 135 full-time (39 women), 48 part-time (10 women); includes 7 Black or African American, non-Hispanic/Latino; 7 Asian, non-Hispanic/Latino; 2 Hispanic/Latino, 92 international. Average age 29. 392 applicants, 25% accepted, 42 enrolled. In 2010, 64 master's, 15 doctorates awarded. *Degree requirements:* For master's, comprehensive exam (for some programs), thesis (for some programs); for doctorate, comprehensive exam (for some programs), thesis/dissertation (for some programs). *Entrance requirements:* For master's and doctorate, GRE. Additional exam requirements/recommendations for international students: Required—TOEFL (minimum score 550 paper-based; 213 computer-based). *Application deadline:* For fall admission, 7/1 for domestic and international students; for spring admission, 12/1 for domestic and international students. Applications are processed on a rolling basis. Application fee: $65. Electronic applications accepted. *Expenses:* Tuition, area resident: Full-time $9399; part-time $488 per credit hour. Tuition, state resident: full-time $9399; part-time $488 per credit hour. Tuition; nonresident: full-time $17,854; part-time $957.75 per credit hour. International tuition: $17,854 full-time. Required fees: $1534. Full-time tuition and fees vary according to program. *Financial support:* In 2010–11, 8 fellowships with full tuition reimbursements (averaging $13,216 per year), 26 research assistantships with full tuition reimbursements (averaging $19,107 per year), 17 teaching assistantships with full tuition reimbursements (averaging $18,060 per year) were awarded; career-related internships or fieldwork, Federal Work-Study, scholarships/grants, health care benefits, and unspecified assistantships also available. Financial award application deadline: 1/15. Total annual research expenditures: $3.3 million. *Unit head:* Dr. Gaylon D. Taylor, UNIT HEAD, 540-231-4771, Fax: 540-231-3322, E-mail: don.taylor@vt.edu. *Application contact:* Jaime Camelio, Contact, 540-231-8976, Fax: 540-231-3322, E-mail: jcamelio@vt.edu.

Wayne State University, College of Engineering, Department of Industrial and Manufacturing Engineering, Program in Industrial Engineering, Detroit, MI 48202. Offers MS, PhD. *Faculty:* 10 full-time (0 women), 4 part-time/adjunct (0 women). *Students:* 55 full-time (13 women), 29 part-time (4 women); includes 11 minority (6 Black or African American, non-Hispanic/Latino; 4 Asian, non-Hispanic/Latino; 1 Hispanic/Latino), 47 international. Average age 31. 84 applicants, 44% accepted, 12 enrolled. In 2010, 20 master's, 2 doctorates awarded. *Degree requirements:* For master's, thesis optional; for doctorate, thesis/dissertation. *Entrance requirements:* For master's, baccalaureate degree in engineering from an ABET-accredited institution, minimum undergraduate GPA of 2.8; for doctorate, minimum graduate GPA of 3.5. Additional exam requirements/recommendations for international students: Required—TOEFL (minimum score 550 paper-based; 213 computer-based); Recommended—TWE (minimum score 6). *Application deadline:* For fall admission, 7/1 priority date for domestic students, 6/1 for international students; for winter admission, 10/1 for international students; for spring admission, 3/15 for domestic students, 2/1 for international students. Applications are processed on a rolling basis. Application fee: $30 ($50 for international students). Electronic applications accepted. *Expenses:* Tuition, state resident: full-time $7662; part-time $478.85 per credit hour. Tuition, nonresident: full-time $16,920; part-time $1057.55 per credit hour. Required fees: $571.20; $35.70 per credit hour. $188.05 per semester. Tuition and fees vary according to course load and program. *Financial support:* In 2010–11, 3 fellowships (averaging $21,288 per year), 12 research assistantships (averaging $16,353 per year), 8 teaching assistantships (averaging $17,546 per year) were awarded; career-related internships or fieldwork also available. *Faculty research:* Reliability and quality, technology management, manufacturing systems, operations research, concurrent engineering. *Unit head:* Kenneth Chelst, Chair, 313-577-3857, Fax: 313-577-8833, E-mail: aa1276@wayne.edu. *Application contact:* Ratna Chinnam, Graduate Director, 313-577-7846, E-mail: r_chinnam@wayne.edu.

Western Carolina University, Graduate School, Kimmel School of Construction Management and Technology, Department of Engineering and Technology, Cullowhee, NC 28723. Offers MS. Part-time programs available. *Degree requirements:* For master's, comprehensive exam. *Entrance requirements:* For master's, GRE, appropriate undergraduate degree with minimum GPA of 3.0, 3 letters of recommendation. Additional exam requirements/recommendations for international students: Required—TOEFL (minimum score 550 paper-based; 270 computer-based; 79 iBT). *Faculty research:* Electrophysiology, 3D graphics, digital signal processing, CAM and advanced machining, fluid power, polymer science, wireless communication.

Western Michigan University, Graduate College, College of Engineering and Applied Sciences, Department of Industrial and Manufacturing Engineering, Program in Industrial Engineering, Kalamazoo, MI 49008. Offers MSE, PhD. *Entrance requirements:* For master's, minimum GPA of 3.0.

Western New England University, School of Engineering, Department of Industrial and Manufacturing Engineering, Springfield, MA 01119. Offers production management (MSEM). Part-time and evening/weekend programs available. *Students:* 38 part-time (12 women); includes 1 Black or African American, non-Hispanic/Latino; 1 Asian, non-Hispanic/Latino; 1 Hispanic/Latino; 1 Two or more races, non-Hispanic/Latino, 2 international. *Degree requirements:* For master's, comprehensive exam, thesis optional. *Entrance requirements:* For master's, GRE, bachelor's degree in engineering or related field, two letters of recommendation, resume. *Application deadline:* Applications are processed on a rolling basis. Application fee: $30. *Expenses:* Tuition: Full-time $35,582. *Financial support:* Available to part-time students. Applicants required to submit FAFSA. *Faculty research:* Project scheduling, flexible manufacturing systems, facility layout, energy management. *Unit head:* Dr. Eric W. Haffner, Chair, 413-782-1272, E-mail: ehaffner@wnec.edu. *Application contact:* Matt Fox, Director of Recruiting and Marketing for Adult Learners, 413-782-1249, Fax: 413-782-1779, E-mail: ce@wnec.edu.

West Virginia University, College of Engineering and Mineral Resources, Department of Industrial and Management Systems Engineering, Program in Industrial Engineering, Morgantown, WV 26506. Offers engineering (MSE); industrial engineering (MSIE, PhD). Part-time programs available. *Degree requirements:* For master's, thesis or alternative; for doctorate, comprehensive exam, thesis/dissertation. *Entrance requirements:* For master's, GRE General Test, minimum GPA of 3.0 Regular; 2.75 Provisional; for doctorate, GRE General Test, minimum GPA of 3.5. Additional exam requirements/recommendations for international students: Required—TOEFL (minimum score 550 paper-based; 213 computer-based; 80 iBT). Electronic applications accepted. *Faculty research:* Production planning and control, quality control, robotics and CIMS, ergonomics, castings.

Wichita State University, Graduate School, College of Engineering, Department of Industrial and Manufacturing Engineering, Wichita, KS 67260. Offers MEM, MS, PhD. Part-time programs available. In 2010, 37 master's, 3 doctorates awarded. *Entrance requirements:* Additional exam requirements/recommendations for international students: Required—TOEFL. *Financial* *support:* Teaching assistantships available. *Unit head:* Dr. Krishna Krishnan, Chair, 316-978-3425, Fax: 316-978-3742, E-mail: krishna.krishnan@wichita.edu. *Application contact:* Dr. Krishna Krishnan, Chair, 316-978-3425, Fax: 316-978-3742, E-mail: krishna.krishnan@wichita.edu.

Youngstown State University, Graduate School, College of Science, Technology, Engineering and Mathematics, Department of Industrial and Systems Engineering, Youngstown, OH 44555-0001. Offers MSE.

Manufacturing Engineering

Arizona State University, College of Technology and Innovation, Department of Engineering Technology, Mesa, AZ 85212. Offers technology (alternative energy technologies) (MS); technology (electronic systems engineering technology) (MS); technology (integrated electronic systems) (MS); technology (manufacturing engineering technology) (MS). Part-time and evening/weekend programs available. *Faculty:* 15 full-time (2 women), 3 part-time/adjunct (0 women). *Students:* 40 full-time (5 women), 48 part-time (12 women); includes 23 minority (5 Black or African American, non-Hispanic/Latino; 9 Asian, non-Hispanic/Latino; 9 Hispanic/Latino), 27 international. Average age 30. 74 applicants, 77% accepted, 25 enrolled. In 2010, 19 master's awarded. *Degree requirements:* For master's, thesis or applied project and oral defense, final examination, interactive Program of Study (iPOS) submitted before completing 50 percent of required credit hours. *Entrance requirements:* For master's, bachelor's degree with minimum of 30 credit hours or equivalent in a technology area including course work applicable to the concentration being sought and minimum of 16 credit hours of math and science; industrial experience beyond bachelor's degree (recommended). Additional exam requirements/recommendations for international students: Required—TOEFL, IELTS, or Pearson Test of English. *Application deadline:* For fall admission, 7/1 for domestic and international students; for spring admission, 12/1 for domestic and international students. Applications are processed on a rolling basis. Application fee: $70 ($90 for international students). Electronic applications accepted. *Expenses:* Tuition, state resident: full-time $8510; part-time $608 per credit. Tuition, nonresident: full-time $16,542; part-time $919 per credit. Required fees: $339; $110 per credit. Part-time tuition and fees vary according to course load. *Financial support:* In 2010–11, 3 research assistantships with full and partial tuition reimbursements (averaging $9,918 per year) were awarded; fellowships with full and partial tuition reimbursements, teaching assistantships with full and partial tuition reimbursements, career-related internships or fieldwork, Federal Work-Study, scholarships/grants, health care benefits, tuition waivers (full and partial), and unspecified assistantships also available. Support available to part-time students. Financial award application deadline: 3/1; financial award applicants required to submit FAFSA. *Faculty research:* Manufacturing modeling and simulation 'smart' and composite materials, optimization of turbine engines, machinability and manufacturing processes design, fuel cells and other alternative energy sources. Total annual research expenditures: $795,837. *Unit head:* Dr. Scott Danielson, Chair, 480-727-1185, Fax: 480-727-1549, E-mail: sdanielson@asu.edu. *Application contact:* Graduate Admissions, 480-965-6113.

Boston University, College of Engineering, Department of Mechanical Engineering, Boston, MA 02215. Offers global manufacturing (MS); manufacturing engineering (M Eng, MS); mechanical engineering (M Eng, MS, PhD); MS/MBA. Part-time programs available. Postbaccalaureate distance learning degree programs offered (no on-campus study). *Faculty:* 38 full-time (5 women), 1 part-time/adjunct (0 women). *Students:* 91 full-time (13 women), 17 part-time (5 women); includes 11 minority (3 Black or African American, non-Hispanic/Latino; 1 American Indian or Alaska Native, non-Hispanic/Latino; 4 Asian, non-Hispanic/Latino; 3 Hispanic/Latino), 45 international. Average age 26. 298 applicants, 21% accepted, 30 enrolled. In 2010, 32 master's, 5 doctorates awarded. Terminal master's awarded for partial completion of doctoral program. *Degree requirements:* For master's, thesis (for some programs); for doctorate, comprehensive exam, thesis/dissertation. *Entrance requirements:* For master's and doctorate, GRE General Test. Additional exam requirements/recommendations for international students: Required—TOEFL (minimum score 550 paper-based; 213 computer-based; 84 iBT), IELTS (minimum score 6). *Application deadline:* For fall admission, 4/1 for domestic and international students; for spring admission, 10/1 for domestic and international students. Applications are processed on a rolling basis. Application fee: $70. Electronic applications accepted. *Expenses:* Tuition: Full-time $39,314; part-time $1228 per credit. Required fees: $40 per semester. *Financial support:* In 2010–11, 81 students received support, including 13 fellowships with full tuition reimbursements available (averaging $28,200 per year), 41 research assistantships with full tuition reimbursements available (averaging $18,800 per year), 19 teaching assistantships with full tuition reimbursements available (averaging $18,800 per year); career-related internships or fieldwork, Federal Work-Study, institutionally sponsored loans, scholarships/grants, and health care benefits also available. Financial award application deadline: 1/15; financial award applicants required to submit FAFSA. *Faculty research:* Acoustics, ultrasound, and vibrations; biomechanics; dynamics, control, and robotics; energy and thermofluid sciences; MEMS and nanotechnology. Total annual research expenditures: $11 million. *Unit head:* Dr. Ronald A. Roy, Chairman, 617-353-2814, Fax: 617-353-5866, E-mail: ronroy@bu.edu. *Application contact:* Stephen Doherty, Director of Graduate Programs, 617-353-9760, Fax: 617-353-0259, E-mail: enggrad@bu.edu.

Bowling Green State University, Graduate College, College of Technology, Department of Technology Systems, Bowling Green, OH 43403. Offers construction management (MIT); manufacturing technology (MIT). Part-time programs available. *Degree requirements:* For master's, thesis or alternative. *Entrance requirements:* For master's, GRE General Test. Additional exam requirements/recommendations for international students: Required—TOEFL. Electronic applications accepted.

Bradley University, Graduate School, College of Engineering and Technology, Department of Industrial and Manufacturing Engineering and Technology, Peoria, IL 61625-0002. Offers industrial engineering (MSIE); manufacturing engineering (MSIE). Part-time and evening/weekend programs available. *Degree requirements:* For master's, comprehensive exam, project. *Entrance requirements:* For master's, minimum GPA of 3.0. Additional exam requirements/recommendations for international students: Required—TOEFL (minimum score 550 paper-based; 213 computer-based; 79 iBT).

California State University, Northridge, Graduate Studies, College of Engineering and Computer Science, Department of Manufacturing Systems Engineering and Management, Northridge, CA 91330. Offers engineering automation (MS); engineering management (MS); manufacturing systems engineering (MS); materials engineering (MS). Postbaccalaureate distance learning degree programs offered. *Entrance requirements:* For master's, GRE (if cumulative undergraduate GPA less than 3.0).

Clemson University, Graduate School, College of Agriculture, Forestry and Life Sciences, Department of Food, Nutrition and Packaging Sciences, Program of Packaging Science, Clemson, SC 29634. Offers MS. *Faculty:* 7 full-time (2 women), 1 part-time/adjunct (0 women). *Students:* 8 full-time (7 women), 4 part-time (2 women); includes 1 Hispanic/Latino, 2 international. Average age 27. 18 applicants, 28% accepted, 5 enrolled. In 2010, 4 master's awarded. *Entrance requirements:* For master's, GRE General Test. *Application deadline:* For fall admission, 4/15 for international students; for spring admission, 9/15 for international students. Applications are processed on a rolling basis. Application fee: $70 ($80 for international students). Electronic applications accepted. *Expenses:* Contact institution. *Financial support:* In 2010–11, 7 students received support, including 6 teaching assistantships with partial tuition reimbursements available (averaging $9,000 per year); fellowships with full and partial tuition reimbursements available, research assistantships with partial tuition reimbursements available, career-related internships or fieldwork, institutionally sponsored loans, scholarships/grants, health care benefits, and unspecified assistantships also available. Support available to part-time students. Total annual research expenditures: $143,855. *Unit head:* Dr. Anthony Pometto, Department Chair, 864-656-4382, Fax: 864-656-0331, E-mail: pometto@clemson.edu. *Application contact:* Dr. Ron Thomas, Coordinator, 864-656-5697, Fax: 864-656-4395, E-mail: rthms@clemson.edu.

Cornell University, Graduate School, Graduate Fields of Engineering, Field of Operations Research and Information Engineering, Ithaca, NY 14853. Offers applied probability and statistics (PhD); manufacturing systems engineering (PhD); mathematical programming (PhD); operations research and industrial engineering (M Eng). *Faculty:* 35 full-time (5 women). *Students:* 162 full-time (46 women); includes 3 Black or African American, non-Hispanic/Latino; 14 Asian, non-Hispanic/Latino; 3 Hispanic/Latino, 117 international. Average age 23. 1,076 applicants, 34% accepted, 139 enrolled. In 2010, 85 master's, 6 doctorates awarded. *Degree requirements:* For doctorate, comprehensive exam, thesis/dissertation. *Entrance requirements:* For master's and doctorate, GRE General Test, 3 letters of recommendation. Additional exam requirements/recommendations for international students: Required—TOEFL (minimum score 600 paper-based; 250 computer-based; 100 iBT). *Application deadline:* For fall admission, 12/15 for domestic students. Application fee: $70. Electronic applications accepted. *Expenses:* Tuition: Full-time $29,500. Required fees: $76. Tuition and fees vary according to degree level and program. *Financial support:* In 2010–11, 44 students received support, including 12 fellowships with full tuition reimbursements available, 9 research assistantships with full tuition reimbursements available, 24 teaching assistantships with full tuition reimbursements available; institutionally sponsored loans, scholarships/grants, health care benefits, tuition waivers (full and partial), and unspecified assistantships also available. Financial award applicants required to submit FAFSA. *Faculty research:* Mathematical programming and combinatorial optimization, statistics, stochastic processes, mathematical finance, simulation, manufacturing, e-commerce. *Unit head:* Director of Graduate Studies, 607-255-9128, Fax: 607-255-9129. *Application contact:* Graduate Field Assistant, 607-255-9128, Fax: 607-255-9129, E-mail: orie@cornell.edu.

Dartmouth College, Thayer School of Engineering, Program in Manufacturing Systems, Hanover, NH 03755. Offers MS, PhD. *Faculty research:* Scheduling, production planning and control, facilities planning, project management, design for assembly and manufacturing.

East Carolina University, Graduate School, College of Technology and Computer Science, Department of Technology Systems, Greenville, NC 27858-4353. Offers computer network professional (Certificate); industrial technology (MS), including computer networking management, digital communications, industrial distribution and logistics, information security, manufacturing, performance improvement, planning; information assurance (Certificate); occupational safety (MS); technology management (PhD); Website developer (Certificate). *Entrance requirements:* For master's and Certificate, GRE General Test or MAT, minimum GPA of 2.5; for doctorate, GRE General Test, related work experience. *Expenses:* Tuition, state resident: full-time $3130; part-time $391.25 per credit hour. Tuition, nonresident: full-time $13,817; part-time $1727.13 per credit hour. Required fees: $1916; $239.50 per credit hour. Tuition and fees vary according to campus/location and program.

Eastern Kentucky University, The Graduate School, College of Business and Technology, Department of Technology, Richmond, KY 40475-3102. Offers industrial education (MS), including occupational training and development, technical administration, technology education; industrial technology (MS). Part-time and evening/weekend programs available. *Entrance requirements:* For master's, GRE General Test, minimum GPA of 2.5. *Faculty research:* Lunar excavation, computer networking, integrating academic and vocational education.

East Tennessee State University, School of Graduate Studies, College of Business and Technology, Department of Technology and Geomatics, Johnson City, TN 37614. Offers digital media (MS); engineering technology (MS); entrepreneurial leadership (MS, Certificate). Part-time programs available. *Faculty:* 19 full-time (2 women). *Students:* 22 full-time (5 women), 27 part-time (8 women); includes 13 minority (8 Black or African American, non-Hispanic/Latino; 2 Asian, non-Hispanic/Latino; 2 Hispanic/Latino; 1 Two or more races, non-Hispanic/Latino), 3 international. Average age 35. 34 applicants, 71% accepted, 8 enrolled. In 2010, 21 master's, 2 other advanced degrees awarded. *Degree requirements:* For master's, comprehensive exam, thesis optional, strategic experience, capstone. *Entrance requirements:* For master's, bachelor's degree in technical or related area, minimum GPA of 3.0. Additional exam requirements/recommendations for international students: Required—TOEFL (minimum score 550 paper-based; 213 computer-based; 79 iBT). *Application deadline:* For fall admission, 6/1 priority date for domestic students, 4/30 for international students; for spring admission, 11/1 for domestic students, 9/30 for international students. Application fee: $25 ($35 for international students). Electronic applications accepted. *Financial support:* In 2010–11, 10 research assistantships with full tuition reimbursements (averaging $5,500 per year), 1 teaching assistantship with full tuition reimbursement (averaging $5,500 per year) were awarded; career-related internships or fieldwork, institutionally sponsored loans, scholarships/grants, and unspecified assistantships also available. Financial award application deadline: 7/1; financial award applicants required to submit FAFSA. *Faculty research:* Computer-integrated manufacturing, technology education, CAD/CAM, organizational change. Total annual research expenditures: $136,039. *Unit head:* Dr. Keith V. Johnson, Chair, 423-439-7813, Fax: 423-439-7750, E-mail: johnsonk@etsu.edu. *Application contact:* Dr. Keith V. Johnson, Chair, 423-439-7813, Fax: 423-439-7750, E-mail: johnsonk@etsu.edu.

Florida State University, The Graduate School, FAMU-FSU College of Engineering, Department of Industrial and Manufacturing Engineering, Tallahassee, FL 32306. Offers industrial engineering (MS, PhD). *Faculty:* 10 full-time (1 woman), 1 (woman) part-time/adjunct. *Students:* 43 full-time (7 women), 2 part-time (1 woman); includes 10 Black or African American, non-Hispanic/Latino; 2 Asian, non-Hispanic/Latino; 2 Hispanic/Latino, 22 international. Average age 24. 84 applicants, 54% accepted, 13 enrolled. In 2010, 11 master's, 3 doctorates awarded. *Degree requirements:* For master's, thesis; for doctorate, thesis/dissertation, preliminary exam, qualifying exam. *Entrance requirements:* For master's, GRE General Test (minimum score of 400 Verbal and 650 Quantitative), minimum GPA of 3.0; for doctorate, GRE General Test (minimum score of 450 Verbal and 700 Quantitative), minimum GPA of 3.0 (without MS in industrial engineering), 3.4 (with MS in industrial engineering). Additional exam requirements/recommendations for international students: Required—TOEFL (minimum score 550 paper-based; 213 computer-based; 80 iBT). *Application deadline:* For fall admission, 7/1 for domestic and international students; for spring admission, 11/1 for domestic and international students. Applications are processed on a rolling basis. Application fee: $30. *Expenses:* Tuition, state resident: full-time $8238.24. *Financial support:* In 2010–11, 31 students received support, including fellowships with full tuition reimbursements available (averaging $18,000 per year), 22 research assistantships with full tuition reimbursements available (averaging $15,000 per year), 1 teaching assistantship with full tuition reimbursement available (averaging $15,000 per year); tuition waivers (full) also available. Financial award application deadline: 6/15. *Faculty research:* Precision manufacturing, composite manufacturing, green manufacturing, applied optimization, simulation. Total annual research expenditures: $3.7 million. *Unit head:* Dr. Chun Zhang, Chair

Manufacturing Engineering

Florida State University (continued)

and Professor, 850-410-6355, Fax: 850-410-6342, E-mail: chzhang@eng.fsu.edu. *Application contact:* Stephanie Salters, Office Manager, 850-410-6345, Fax: 850-410-6342, E-mail: salters@eng.fsu.edu.

Grand Valley State University, Padnos College of Engineering and Computing, School of Engineering, Allendale, MI 49401-9403. Offers electrical and computer engineering (MSE); manufacturing operations (MSE); mechanical engineering (MSE); product design and manufacturing engineering (MSE). Part-time and evening/weekend programs available. *Degree requirements:* For master's, project or thesis. *Entrance requirements:* For master's, engineering degree, minimum GPA of 3.0. Additional exam requirements/recommendations for international students: Required—TOEFL. Electronic applications accepted. *Faculty research:* Digital signal processing, computer aided design, computer aided manufacturing, manufacturing simulation, biomechanics, product design.

Illinois Institute of Technology, Graduate College, Armour College of Engineering, Department of Mechanical, Materials and Aerospace Engineering, Chicago, IL 60616-3793. Offers manufacturing engineering (MME, MS); materials science and engineering (MMME, MS, PhD); mechanical and aerospace engineering (MMAE, MS, PhD), including economics (MS), energy (MS), environment (MS). Part-time and evening/weekend programs available. Postbaccalaureate distance learning degree programs offered (minimal on-campus study). *Faculty:* 26 full-time (1 woman), 6 part-time/adjunct (1 woman). *Students:* 135 full-time (22 women), 45 part-time (4 women); includes 11 minority (1 American Indian or Alaska Native, non-Hispanic/Latino; 9 Asian, non-Hispanic/Latino; 1 Hispanic/Latino), 117 international. Average age 27. 693 applicants, 41% accepted, 63 enrolled. In 2010, 58 master's, 4 doctorates awarded. Terminal master's awarded for partial completion of doctoral program. *Degree requirements:* For master's, comprehensive exam (for some programs), thesis (for some programs); for doctorate, comprehensive exam, thesis/dissertation. *Entrance requirements:* For master's and doctorate, GRE General Test (minimum score 1000 Quantitative and Verbal, 3.0 Analytical Writing), minimum undergraduate GPA of 3.0. Additional exam requirements/recommendations for international students: Required—TOEFL (minimum score 523 paper-based; 70 iBT); Recommended—IELTS (minimum score 5.5). *Application deadline:* For fall admission, 5/1 for domestic and international students; for spring admission, 10/15 for domestic and international students. Applications are processed on a rolling basis. Application fee: $50. Electronic applications accepted. *Expenses:* Tuition: Full-time $18,576; part-time $1032 per credit hour. Required fees: $583 per semester. One-time fee: $150. Tuition and fees vary according to program and student level. *Financial support:* In 2010–11, 7 fellowships with full and partial tuition reimbursements (averaging $7,673 per year), 33 research assistantships with full and partial tuition reimbursements (averaging $8,141 per year), 15 teaching assistantships with full and partial tuition reimbursements (averaging $6,930 per year) were awarded; Federal Work-Study, institutionally sponsored loans, scholarships/grants, health care benefits, tuition waivers, and unspecified assistantships also available. Support available to part-time students. Financial award applicants required to submit FAFSA. *Faculty research:* Fluid dynamics, metallurgical and materials engineering, solids and structures, computational mechanics, theoretical mechanics. Total annual research expenditures: $2.4 million. *Unit head:* Dr. Jamal Yagoobi, Professor and Chairman, 312-567-3239, Fax: 312-567-7230, E-mail: yagoobi@iit.edu. *Application contact:* Deborah Gibson, Director, Graduate Admission, 866-472-3448, Fax: 312-567-3138, E-mail: inquiry.grad@iit.edu.

Instituto Tecnológico y de Estudios Superiores de Monterrey, Campus Monterrey, Graduate and Research Division, Programs in Engineering, Monterrey, Mexico. Offers applied statistics (M Eng); artificial intelligence (PhD); automation engineering (M Eng); chemical engineering (M Eng); civil engineering (M Eng); electrical engineering (M Eng); electronic engineering (M Eng); environmental engineering (M Eng); industrial engineering (M Eng, PhD); manufacturing engineering (M Eng); mechanical engineering (M Eng); systems and quality engineering (M Eng). M Eng program offered jointly with University of Waterloo; PhD in industrial engineering with Texas A&M University. Part-time and evening/weekend programs available. Terminal master's awarded for partial completion of doctoral program. *Degree requirements:* For master's, one foreign language, thesis; for doctorate, one foreign language, thesis/dissertation. *Entrance requirements:* For master's, EXADEP; for doctorate, GRE, master's degree in related field. Additional exam requirements/recommendations for international students: Required—TOEFL. *Faculty research:* Flexible manufacturing cells, materials, statistical methods, environmental prevention, control and evaluation.

Kansas State University, Graduate School, College of Engineering, Department of Industrial and Manufacturing Systems Engineering, Manhattan, KS 66506. Offers engineering management (MEM); industrial engineering (MS, PhD); operations research (MS). Part-time programs available. Postbaccalaureate distance learning degree programs offered. *Degree requirements:* For master's, thesis or alternative; for doctorate, thesis/dissertation. *Entrance requirements:* For master's, GRE General Test, bachelor's degree in engineering, mathematics, or physical science; for doctorate, GRE General Test, master's degree in engineering or industrial manufacturing. Additional exam requirements/recommendations for international students: Required—TOEFL. Electronic applications accepted. *Faculty research:* Ergonomics, healthcare systems engineering, manufacturing processes, operations research, engineering management.

Kettering University, Graduate School, Department of Industrial and Manufacturing Engineering, Flint, MI 48504. Offers engineering (MS). Part-time and evening/weekend programs available. Postbaccalaureate distance learning degree programs offered (no on-campus study). *Faculty:* 4 full-time (2 women), 1 part-time/adjunct (0 women). *Students:* 1 full-time (0 women), 8 part-time (2 women); includes 1 minority (Asian, non-Hispanic/Latino). Average age 29. 6 applicants, 67% accepted, 1 enrolled. In 2010, 3 master's awarded. *Degree requirements:* For master's, thesis optional. *Entrance requirements:* Additional exam requirements/recommendations for international students: Required—TOEFL (minimum score 550 paper-based; 213 computer-based; 79 iBT). *Application deadline:* For fall admission, 9/15 for domestic students, 6/15 for international students; for winter admission, 12/15 for domestic students, 9/5 for international students; for spring admission, 3/15 for domestic students, 12/5 for international students. Applications are processed on a rolling basis. Application fee: $0. Electronic applications accepted. *Expenses:* Tuition: Full-time $11,120; part-time $695 per credit hour. *Financial support:* In 2010–11, 6 students received support, including fellowships with full tuition reimbursements available (averaging $13,000 per year), research assistantships with full tuition reimbursements available (averaging $13,000 per year), teaching assistantships with full tuition reimbursements available (averaging $13,000 per year); Federal Work-Study, scholarships/grants, and tuition waivers (partial) also available. Support available to part-time students. Financial award application deadline: 7/15; financial award applicants required to submit CSS PROFILE or FAFSA. *Faculty research:* Machine part testing, geothermal system study, office procedure study. Total annual research expenditures: $12,247. *Unit head:* Dr. W. L. Scheller, Department Head, 810-762-7974, E-mail: wschelle@kettering.edu. *Application contact:* Bonnie Switzer, Admissions Representative, 810-762-7953, Fax: 810-762-9935, E-mail: bswitzer@kettering.edu.

Lawrence Technological University, College of Engineering, Southfield, MI 48075-1058. Offers architectural engineering (MS); automotive engineering (MS); civil engineering (MS); electrical and computer engineering (MS); engineering management (MEM); industrial engineering (MS); manufacturing systems (ME, DE); mechanical engineering (MS); mechatronic systems engineering (MS). Part-time and evening/weekend programs available. *Faculty:* 20 full-time (4 women), 12 part-time/adjunct (0 women). *Students:* 8 full-time (1 woman), 366 part-time (60 women); includes 29 Black or African American, non-Hispanic/Latino; 1 American Indian or Alaska Native, non-Hispanic/Latino; 36 Asian, non-Hispanic/Latino; 9 Hispanic/Latino; 4 Two or more races, non-Hispanic/Latino, 81 international. Average age 32. 398 applicants, 48% accepted, 87 enrolled. In 2010, 121 master's, 5 doctorates awarded. *Degree requirements:* For master's, thesis (for some programs). *Entrance requirements:* Additional exam requirements/recommendations for international students: Required—TOEFL (minimum score 550 paper-based; 213 computer-based; 79 iBT). *Application deadline:* For fall admission, 6/30 priority date for domestic students, 6/30 for international students; for spring admission, 11/15 priority date for domestic students, 11/15 for international students. Applications are processed on a rolling basis. Application fee: $50. Electronic applications accepted. *Financial support:* In 2010–11, 72 students received support. Federal Work-Study and institutionally sponsored loans available. Support available to part-time students. Financial award application deadline: 4/1; financial award applicants required to submit FAFSA. *Faculty research:* Advanced composite materials in bridges, strengthening existing bridges with carbon and glass fiber sheets, development of drive shafts using composite materials. *Unit head:* Dr. Nabil Grace, Interim Dean, 248-204-2500, Fax: 248-204-2509, E-mail: engrdean@ltu.edu. *Application contact:* Jane Rohrback, Director of Admissions, 248-204-3160, Fax: 248-204-2228, E-mail: admissions@ltu.edu.

Lehigh University, P.C. Rossin College of Engineering and Applied Science, Program in Manufacturing Systems Engineering, Bethlehem, PA 18015. Offers MS, MBA/E. Part-time and evening/weekend programs available. Postbaccalaureate distance learning degree programs offered (no on-campus study). *Students:* 1 full-time (0 women), 22 part-time (7 women); includes 2 minority (1 Black or African American, non-Hispanic/Latino; 1 Asian, non-Hispanic/Latino). Average age 34. 16 applicants, 19% accepted, 3 enrolled. In 2010, 10 master's awarded. *Degree requirements:* For master's, comprehensive exam, project or thesis. *Entrance requirements:* For master's, GRE General Test, minimum GPA of 2.75. Additional exam requirements/recommendations for international students: Required—TOEFL (minimum score 620 paper-based; 260 computer-based; 85 iBT). *Application deadline:* For fall admission, 7/15 for domestic and international students; for spring admission, 12/1 for domestic and international students. Applications are processed on a rolling basis. Application fee: $75. Electronic applications accepted. *Faculty research:* Manufacturing systems design, development, and implementation; accounting and management; agile/lean systems; supply chain issues; sustainable systems design; product design. *Unit head:* Dr. Keith M. Gardiner, Director, 610-758-5070, Fax: 610-758-6527, E-mail: kg03@lehigh.edu. *Application contact:* Carolyn C. Jones, Graduate Coordinator, 610-758-5157, Fax: 610-758-6527, E-mail: ccj1@lehigh.edu.

Massachusetts Institute of Technology, School of Engineering, Department of Mechanical Engineering, Cambridge, MA 02139. Offers manufacturing (M Eng); mechanical engineering (SM, PhD, Sc D, Mech E); naval architecture and marine engineering (SM, PhD, Sc D); naval engineering (Naval E); ocean engineering (SM, PhD, Sc D), including); oceanographic engineering (SM, PhD, Sc D); SM/MBA. *Faculty:* 69 full-time (9 women). *Students:* 521 full-time (92 women); includes 71 minority (11 Black or African American, non-Hispanic/Latino; 1 American Indian or Alaska Native, non-Hispanic/Latino; 35 Asian, non-Hispanic/Latino; 20 Hispanic/Latino; 4 Two or more races, non-Hispanic/Latino), 217 international. Average age 27. 1,036 applicants, 23% accepted, 148 enrolled. In 2010, 132 master's, 49 doctorates, 10 other advanced degrees awarded. Terminal master's awarded for partial completion of doctoral program. *Degree requirements:* For master's and other advanced degree, thesis; for doctorate, comprehensive exam, thesis/dissertation. *Entrance requirements:* For master's, doctorate, and other advanced degree, GRE General Test. Additional exam requirements/recommendations for international students: Required—IELTS (minimum score 7). *Application deadline:* For fall admission, 12/1 for domestic and international students. Application fee: $75. Electronic applications accepted. *Expenses:* Tuition: Full-time $38,940; part-time $605 per unit. Required fees: $272. *Financial support:* In 2010–11, 443 students received support, including 91 fellowships with tuition reimbursements available (averaging $29,306 per year), 324 research assistantships with tuition reimbursements available (averaging $28,071 per year), 35 teaching assistantships with tuition reimbursements available (averaging $30,517 per year); career-related internships or fieldwork, Federal Work-Study, institutionally sponsored loans, scholarships/grants, health care benefits, and unspecified assistantships also available. *Faculty research:* Mechanics: modeling, experimentation and computation; design, manufacturing, and product development; controls, instrumentation, and robotics; energy science and engineering; ocean science and engineering; bioengineering; micro and nano engineering. Total annual research expenditures: $45.5 million. *Unit head:* Prof. Mary C. Boyce, Department Head, 617-253-2201, Fax: 617-258-6156, E-mail: mehq@mit.edu. *Application contact:* Graduate Office, 617-253-2291, Fax: 617-258-5802, E-mail: me-gradoffice@mit.edu.

Michigan State University, The Graduate School, College of Agriculture and Natural Resources, School of Packaging, East Lansing, MI 48824. Offers MS, PhD. *Entrance requirements:* Additional exam requirements/recommendations for international students: Required—TOEFL. Electronic applications accepted.

Minnesota State University Mankato, College of Graduate Studies, College of Science, Engineering and Technology, Department of Automotive and Manufacturing Engineering Technology, Mankato, MN 56001. Offers manufacturing engineering technology (MS). *Students:* 9 full-time (0 women), 10 part-time (1 woman). *Degree requirements:* For master's, comprehensive exam, thesis. *Entrance requirements:* For master's, GRE General Test (if GPA less than 3.0), minimum GPA of 3.0 during previous 2 years. Additional exam requirements/recommendations for international students: Required—TOEFL. *Application deadline:* For fall admission, 7/1 priority date for domestic students; for spring admission, 11/1 for domestic students. Applications are processed on a rolling basis. Application fee: $40. Electronic applications accepted. *Financial support:* Research assistantships with full tuition reimbursements, teaching assistantships with full tuition reimbursements, unspecified assistantships available. Financial award application deadline: 3/15; financial award applicants required to submit FAFSA. *Unit head:* Dr. Bruce Jones, Graduate Coordinator, 507-389-6700. *Application contact:* 507-389-2321, E-mail: grad@mnsu.edu.

Missouri University of Science and Technology, Graduate School, Department of Engineering Management and Systems Engineering, Rolla, MO 65409. Offers engineering management (MS, DE, PhD); manufacturing engineering (M Eng, MS); systems engineering (MS, PhD). *Degree requirements:* For master's, thesis optional; for doctorate, comprehensive exam. *Entrance requirements:* For master's, GRE (minimum score 1150 verbal and quantitative, 4.5 writing); for doctorate, GRE (minimum score: 1100 verbal and quantitative, 3.5 writing). Additional exam requirements/recommendations for international students: Required—TOEFL (minimum score 580 paper-based; 213 computer-based). *Faculty research:* Management of technology, industrial engineering, manufacturing engineering, packaging engineering, quality engineering.

New Jersey Institute of Technology, Office of Graduate Studies, Newark College of Engineering, Department of Industrial and Manufacturing Engineering, Program in Manufacturing Engineering, Newark, NJ 07102. Offers MS. Part-time and evening/weekend programs available. *Students:* 5 full-time (0 women), 4 part-time (1 woman); includes 3 Asian, non-Hispanic/Latino; 3 Hispanic/Latino, 2 international. Average age 30. 15 applicants, 47% accepted, 2 enrolled. In 2010, 2 master's awarded. *Degree requirements:* For master's, thesis or alternative. *Entrance requirements:* For master's, GRE General Test. Additional exam requirements/recommendations for international students: Required—TOEFL (minimum score 550 paper-based; 213 computer-based; 79 iBT). *Application deadline:* For fall admission, 6/5 priority date for domestic students, 4/1 for international students; for spring admission, 11/15 for domestic and international students. Applications are processed on a rolling basis. Application fee: $65. Electronic applications accepted. *Expenses:* Tuition, state resident: full-time $14,724; part-time $818 per credit. Tuition, nonresident: full-time $20,304; part-time $1128 per credit. Required fees: $2272; $209 per credit. $103 per semester. One-time fee: $312 full-time; $212 part-time. *Financial support:* Fellowships with full and partial tuition reimbursements, research assistantships with full and partial tuition reimbursements, teaching assistantships with full and partial tuition reimbursements, career-related internships or fieldwork, Federal Work-Study, institutionally sponsored loans, and unspecified assistantships available. Financial award application deadline: 3/15. *Faculty research:* Knowledge-based systems, CAS/CAM simulation and interface, expert system. *Unit head:* Dr. Sanchoy Das, Director, 973-596-3654, Fax: 973-596-3652, E-mail: sanchoy.k.das@njit.edu. *Application contact:* Kathryn Kelly, Director of Admissions, 973-596-3300, Fax: 973-596-3461, E-mail: admissions@njit.edu.

North Carolina State University, Graduate School, College of Engineering, Integrated Manufacturing Systems Engineering Institute, Raleigh, NC 27695. Offers MIMS. Part-time programs available. *Degree requirements:* For master's, thesis optional. *Entrance requirements:* For master's, GRE. Additional exam requirements/recommendations for international students: Required—TOEFL. Electronic applications accepted. *Faculty research:* Mechatronics, manufacturing systems modeling, systems integration product and process engineering, logistics.

North Dakota State University, College of Graduate and Interdisciplinary Studies, College of Engineering and Architecture, Department of Industrial and Manufacturing Engineering, Fargo, ND 58108. Offers industrial and manufacturing engineering (PhD); industrial engineering and management (MS); manufacturing engineering (MS). Part-time programs available. *Faculty:* 13 full-time (2 women), 1 part-time/adjunct (0 women). *Students:* 29 full-time (5 women), 9 part-time (4 women), 35 international. Average age 26. 23 applicants, 52% accepted, 4 enrolled. In 2010, 4 master's awarded. *Degree requirements:* For doctorate, comprehensive exam, thesis/dissertation. *Entrance requirements:* For master's, GRE General Test, bachelor's degree in engineering; for doctorate, GRE General Test, master's degree in engineering. Additional exam requirements/recommendations for international students: Required—TOEFL (minimum score 550 paper-based; 213 computer-based; 79 iBT), TWE (minimum score 4). *Application deadline:* For fall admission, 3/1 priority date for domestic students, 3/1 for international students; for spring admission, 11/1 priority date for domestic students, 11/1 for international students. Applications are processed on a rolling basis. Application fee: $45 ($60 for international students). Electronic applications accepted. *Financial support:* In 2010–11, 2 fellowships with full tuition reimbursements (averaging $15,000 per year), 9 research assistantships with full tuition reimbursements (averaging $12,000 per year), 16 teaching assistantships with full tuition reimbursements (averaging $12,000 per year) were awarded; Federal Work-Study, institutionally sponsored loans, scholarships/grants, and unspecified assistantships also available. Financial award application deadline: 4/1. *Faculty research:* Electronics manufacturing, quality engineering, manufacturing process science, healthcare, lean manufacturing. Total annual research expenditures: $60,000. *Unit head:* Prof. Kambiz Farahmand, Chair, 701-231-7287, Fax: 701-231-7195, E-mail: kambiz.farahmand@ndsu.edu. *Application contact:* Dr. David A. Wittrock, Dean, 701-231-7033, Fax: 701-231-6524.

Northeastern University, College of Engineering, Department of Mechanical, Industrial, and Manufacturing Engineering, Boston, MA 02115-5096. Offers engineering management (MS); industrial engineering (MS, PhD); mechanical engineering (MS, PhD); operations research (MS). Part-time programs available. *Faculty:* 34 full-time (2 women), 7 part-time/adjunct (0 women). *Students:* 297 full-time (70 women), 103 part-time (20 women). 616 applicants, 77% accepted, 140 enrolled. In 2010, 107 master's, 5 doctorates awarded. *Degree requirements:* For master's, thesis (for some programs); for doctorate, thesis/dissertation, departmental qualifying exam. *Entrance requirements:* For master's and doctorate, GRE General Test. Additional exam requirements/recommendations for international students: Required—TOEFL (minimum score 550 paper-based; 213 computer-based; 80 iBT). *Application deadline:* For fall admission, 1/15 priority date for domestic and international students; for spring admission, 11/1 priority date for domestic students. Applications are processed on a rolling basis. Application fee: $50. Electronic applications accepted. *Financial support:* In 2010–11, 79 students received support, including 50 research assistantships with full tuition reimbursements available (averaging $18,325 per year), 33 teaching assistantships with full tuition reimbursements available (averaging $18,325 per year); fellowships with full tuition reimbursements available, career-related internships or fieldwork, Federal Work-Study, scholarships/grants, health care benefits, and unspecified assistantships also available. Support available to part-time students. Financial award application deadline: 1/15; financial award applicants required to submit FAFSA. *Faculty research:* Dry sliding instabilities, droplet deposition, combustion, manufacturing systems, nano-manufacturing, advanced materials processing, bio-nano robotics, burning speed measurement, virtual environments. *Unit head:* Dr. Hameed Metghalchi, Chairman, 617-373-2973, Fax: 617-373-2921. *Application contact:* Jeffery Hengel, Admissions Specialist, 617-373-2711, Fax: 617-373-2501, E-mail: grad-eng@coe.neu.edu.

Old Dominion University, Frank Batten College of Engineering and Technology, Program in Mechanical Engineering, Norfolk, VA 23529. Offers design and manufacturing (ME); mechanical engineering (ME, MS, D Eng, PhD). Part-time and evening/weekend programs available. Postbaccalaureate distance learning degree programs offered (no on-campus study). *Faculty:* 24 full-time (2 women). *Students:* 31 full-time (6 women), 42 part-time (8 women); includes 7 minority (3 Asian, non-Hispanic/Latino; 3 Hispanic/Latino; 1 Two or more races, non-Hispanic/Latino), 34 international. Average age 29. 50 applicants, 76% accepted, 7 enrolled. In 2010, 10 master's, 3 doctorates awarded. *Degree requirements:* For master's, comprehensive exam, thesis optional; for doctorate, thesis/dissertation, candidacy exam. *Entrance requirements:* For master's, GRE, minimum GPA of 3.0; for doctorate, GRE, minimum GPA of 3.5. Additional exam requirements/recommendations for international students: Required—TOEFL (minimum score 550 paper-based; 213 computer-based). *Application deadline:* For fall admission, 6/1 for domestic students, 2/15 priority date for international students; for spring admission, 11/1 for domestic students, 10/1 for international students. Applications are processed on a rolling basis. Application fee: $50. Electronic applications accepted. *Expenses:* Tuition, state resident: full-time $8592; part-time $358 per credit. Tuition, nonresident: full-time $21,672; part-time $903 per credit. Required fees: $119 per semester. One-time fee: $50. *Financial support:* In 2010–11, 12 students received support, including 5 fellowships with partial tuition reimbursements available (averaging $16,000 per year), 11 research assistantships with partial tuition reimbursements available (averaging $15,000 per year), 15 teaching assistantships with partial tuition reimbursements available (averaging $6,400 per year); career-related internships or fieldwork, institutionally sponsored loans, scholarships/grants, and unspecified assistantships also available. Financial award application deadline: 2/15; financial award applicants required to submit FAFSA. *Faculty research:* Computational applied mechanics, manufacturing, experimental stress analysis, systems dynamics and control, mechanical design. Total annual research expenditures: $975,887. *Unit head:* Dr. Jen-Kuang Huang, Chair, 757-683-3734, Fax: 757-683-5344, E-mail: jhuang@odu.edu. *Application contact:* Dr. Gene Hou, Graduate Program Director, 757-683-3728, Fax: 757-683-5344, E-mail: megpd@odu.edu.

Oregon State University, Graduate School, College of Engineering, School of Mechanical, Industrial, and Manufacturing Engineering, Corvallis, OR 97331. Offers human systems engineering (MS, PhD); industrial engineering (MS, PhD); information systems engineering (MS, PhD); manufacturing engineering (M Engr); manufacturing systems engineering (MS, PhD); materials science (MAIS, MS, PhD); mechanical engineering (MS, PhD); nano/micro fabrication (MS, PhD). Part-time programs available. Postbaccalaureate distance learning degree programs offered (minimal on-campus study). *Degree requirements:* For master's, thesis or alternative; for doctorate, thesis/dissertation. *Entrance requirements:* For master's, placement exam, minimum GPA of 3.0 in last 90 hours of course work; for doctorate, GRE, placement exam, minimum GPA of 3.0 in last 90 hours of course work. Additional exam requirements/recommendations for international students: Required—TOEFL (minimum score 550 paper-based; 213 computer-based). *Faculty research:* Computer-integrated manufacturing, human factors, robotics, decision support systems, simulation modeling and analysis.

Penn State University Park, Graduate School, College of Engineering, Department of Industrial and Manufacturing Engineering, State College, University Park, PA 16802-1503. Offers M Eng, MS, PhD.

Polytechnic Institute of NYU, Department of Interdisciplinary Studies, Major in Manufacturing Engineering, Brooklyn, NY 11201-2990. Offers MS. Part-time and evening/weekend programs available. *Students:* 7 full-time (1 woman), 6 part-time (3 women); includes 1 Black or African American, non-Hispanic/Latino; 1 Asian, non-Hispanic/Latino; 2 Hispanic/Latino, 3 international. Average age 29. 10 applicants, 20% accepted, 1 enrolled. In 2010, 18 master's awarded. *Degree requirements:* For master's, comprehensive exam (for some programs), thesis (for some programs). *Entrance requirements:* For master's, BE or BS in engineering, physics, chemistry, mathematical sciences, or biological sciences or MBA. Additional exam requirements/recommendations for international students: Required—TOEFL (minimum score 550 paper-

based; 213 computer-based; 80 iBT). Recommended—IELTS (minimum score 6.5). *Application deadline:* For fall admission, 7/31 priority date for domestic students, 4/30 priority date for international students; for spring admission, 12/31 priority date for domestic students, 11/30 priority date for international students. Applications are processed on a rolling basis. Application fee: $75. Electronic applications accepted. *Expenses:* Tuition: Full-time $21,492; part-time $1194 per credit. Required fees: $385 per semester. Tuition and fees vary according to course load. *Financial support:* Institutionally sponsored loans, scholarships/grants, and unspecified assistantships available. Support available to part-time students. Financial award applicants required to submit FAFSA. *Unit head:* Prof. Michael Greenstein, Department Head, 718-260-3835, E-mail: mgreenst@poly.edu. *Application contact:* JeanCarlo Bonilla, Director, Graduate Enrollment Management, 718-260-3182, Fax: 718-260-3624, E-mail: gradinfo@poly.edu.

Polytechnic Institute of NYU, Long Island Graduate Center, Graduate Programs, Department of Interdisciplinary Studies, Major in Manufacturing Engineering, Melville, NY 11747. Offers MS. Part-time and evening/weekend programs available. *Entrance requirements:* Additional exam requirements/recommendations for international students: Required—TOEFL (minimum score 550 paper-based; 213 computer-based; 80 iBT); Recommended—IELTS (minimum score 6.5). *Application deadline:* For fall admission, 7/31 priority date for domestic students, 4/30 priority date for international students; for spring admission, 12/31 priority date for domestic students, 11/30 priority date for international students. Applications are processed on a rolling basis. Application fee: $75. Electronic applications accepted. *Expenses:* Tuition: Full-time $21,492; part-time $1194 per credit. Required fees: $385 per semester. Tuition and fees vary according to course load. *Financial support:* Institutionally sponsored loans, scholarships/grants, and unspecified assistantships available. Support available to part-time students. *Application contact:* JeanCarlo Bonilla, Director of Graduate Enrollment Management, 718-260-3182, Fax: 718-260-3624, E-mail: gradinfo@poly.edu.

Polytechnic Institute of NYU, Long Island Graduate Center, Graduate Programs, Department of Mechanical and Aerospace Engineering, Melville, NY 11747. Offers aeronautics and astronautics (MS); industrial engineering (MS); manufacturing engineering (MS); mechanical engineering (MS). Part-time and evening/weekend programs available. *Students:* 1 full-time (0 women), all international. Average age 28. *Degree requirements:* For master's, comprehensive exam (for some programs), thesis (for some programs). *Entrance requirements:* Additional exam requirements/recommendations for international students: Required—TOEFL (minimum score 550 paper-based; 213 computer-based; 80 iBT); Recommended—IELTS (minimum score 6.5). *Application deadline:* For fall admission, 7/31 priority date for domestic students, 4/30 priority date for international students; for spring admission, 12/31 priority date for domestic students, 11/30 priority date for international students. Applications are processed on a rolling basis. Application fee: $75. Electronic applications accepted. *Expenses:* Tuition: Full-time $21,492; part-time $1194 per credit. Required fees: $385 per semester. Tuition and fees vary according to course load. *Financial support:* In 2010–11, 16 fellowships with tuition reimbursements (averaging $1,394 per year) were awarded; research assistantships with tuition reimbursements, institutionally sponsored loans, scholarships/grants, and unspecified assistantships also available. Support available to part-time students. Financial award applicants required to submit FAFSA. *Faculty research:* UV filter, fuel efficient hydrodynamic containment for gas core fission, turbulent boundary layer research. *Unit head:* Dr. George Vradis, Department Head, 718-260-3875, E-mail: gvradis@duke.poly.edu. *Application contact:* JeanCarlo Bonilla, Director of Graduate Enrollment Management, 718-260-3182, Fax: 718-260-3624, E-mail: gradinfo@poly.edu.

Polytechnic Institute of NYU, Westchester Graduate Center, Graduate Programs, Department of Interdisciplinary Studies, Major in Manufacturing Engineering, Hawthorne, NY 10532-1507. Offers MS. *Entrance requirements:* Additional exam requirements/recommendations for international students: Required—TOEFL (minimum score 550 paper-based; 213 computer-based; 80 iBT); Recommended—IELTS (minimum score 6.5). *Application deadline:* For fall admission, 7/31 priority date for domestic students, 4/30 priority date for international students; for spring admission, 12/31 priority date for domestic students, 11/30 priority date for international students. Applications are processed on a rolling basis. Application fee: $75. Electronic applications accepted. *Expenses:* Tuition: Full-time $21,492; part-time $1194 per credit. Required fees: $385 per semester. Tuition and fees vary according to course load. *Financial support:* Institutionally sponsored loans, scholarships/grants, and unspecified assistantships available. Support available to part-time students. *Application contact:* JeanCarlo Bonilla, Director of Graduate Enrollment Management, 718-260-3182, Fax: 718-260-3624, E-mail: gradinfo@poly.edu.

Polytechnic University of Puerto Rico, Graduate School, Hato Rey, PR 00919. Offers business administration (MBA), including computer information systems, general management, management of information systems, management of international enterprises; civil engineering (ME, MS); computer engineering (ME, MS); computer science (MCS, MS); electrical engineering (ME, MS); engineering management (MEM); environmental management (MEM); landscape architecture (M Land Arch); manufacturing competitiveness (MMC, MS); manufacturing engineering (ME, MS); mechanical engineering (M Mech E). Part-time and evening/weekend programs available. *Entrance requirements:* For master's, 3 letters of recommendation.

Portland State University, Graduate Studies, Maseeh College of Engineering and Computer Science, Department of Engineering and Technology Management, Portland, OR 97207-0751. Offers engineering and technology management (M Eng); engineering management (MS); manufacturing engineering (ME); manufacturing management (M Eng); systems science/engineering management (PhD); MS/MBA; MS/MS. Part-time and evening/weekend programs available. *Faculty:* 8 full-time (1 woman), 3 part-time/adjunct (2 women). *Students:* 50 full-time (13 women), 58 part-time (16 women); includes 13 Asian, non-Hispanic/Latino; 6 Hispanic/Latino, 51 international. Average age 35. 38 applicants, 76% accepted, 13 enrolled. In 2010, 42 master's awarded. *Degree requirements:* For master's, thesis optional; for doctorate, one foreign language, thesis/dissertation, oral and written exams. *Entrance requirements:* For master's, minimum GPA of 3.0 in upper-division course work, BS in civil engineering; for doctorate, GRE General Test, GRE Subject Test, minimum GPA of 3.0 in upper-division course work. Additional exam requirements/recommendations for international students: Required—TOEFL (minimum score 550 paper-based; 213 computer-based). *Application deadline:* For fall admission, 4/1 for domestic students, 3/1 for international students; for winter admission, 9/1 for domestic students, 7/1 for international students; for spring admission, 11/1 for domestic students, 9/1 for international students. Applications are processed on a rolling basis. Application fee: $50. *Expenses:* Tuition, state resident: full-time $8505; part-time $315 per credit. Tuition, nonresident: full-time $13,284; part-time $492 per credit. Required fees: $1482; $21 per credit. $99 per term. One-time fee: $120. Part-time tuition and fees vary according to course load and program. *Financial support:* In 2010–11, 3 teaching assistantships with full tuition reimbursements (averaging $8,916 per year) were awarded; research assistantships with full tuition reimbursements, career-related internships or fieldwork, Federal Work-Study, scholarships/grants, and unspecified assistantships also available. Support available to part-time students. Financial award application deadline: 3/1; financial award applicants required to submit FAFSA. *Faculty research:* Scheduling, hierarchical decision modeling, operations research, knowledge-based information systems. Total annual research expenditures: $1.1 million. *Unit head:* Dr. Dundar F. Kocaoglu, Chair, 503-725-4660, Fax: 503-725-4667, E-mail: kocaoglu@etm.pdx.edu. *Application contact:* Dr. Dundar F. Kocaoglu, Chair, 503-725-4660, Fax: 503-725-4667, E-mail: kocaoglu@etm.pdx.edu.

Rochester Institute of Technology, Graduate Enrollment Services, College of Applied Science and Technology, Department of Electrical, Computer and Telecommunications Engineering Technology, Program in Manufacturing and Mechanical Systems Integration, Rochester, NY 14623-5603. Offers MS. Part-time and evening/weekend programs available. *Students:* 20 full-time (1 woman), 14 part-time (0 women); includes 1 Asian, non-Hispanic/Latino; 1 Hispanic/Latino, 8 international. Average age 29. 11 applicants, 91% accepted, 9 enrolled. In 2010, 9 master's awarded. *Degree requirements:* For master's, thesis. *Entrance requirements:* For master's, GRE, minimum GPA of 3.0. Additional exam requirements/recommendations for

Manufacturing Engineering

Rochester Institute of Technology (continued)
international students: Required—TOEFL (minimum score 550 paper-based; 213 computer-based; 79 iBT) or IELTS (minimum score 6.5). *Application deadline:* For fall admission, 2/15 priority date for domestic and international students; for winter admission, 11/1 for domestic and international students; for spring admission, 2/1 for domestic and international students. Applications are processed on a rolling basis. *Expenses:* Tuition: Full-time $33,234; part-time $924 per credit hour. Required fees: $219. *Financial support:* In 2010–11, 26 students received support; research assistantships with partial tuition reimbursements available, teaching assistantships with partial tuition reimbursements available, career-related internships or fieldwork, scholarships/grants, and unspecified assistantships available. Support available to part-time students. Financial award application deadline: 2/15; financial award applicants required to submit FAFSA. *Faculty research:* Biodegradable plastics, health physics, nuclear engineering technology, solidworks, automative engineering, compression strength, protective package development. *Unit head:* Dr. S. Manian Ramkumar, Graduate Program Director, 585-475-6081, Fax: 585-475-5227, E-mail: smrmet@rit.edu. *Application contact:* Diane Ellison, Assistant Vice President, Graduate Enrollment Services, 585-475-2229, Fax: 585-475-7164, E-mail: gradinfo@rit.edu.

Rochester Institute of Technology, Graduate Enrollment Services, College of Applied Science and Technology, Department of Manufacturing and Mechanical Engineering Technology/Packaging Science, Rochester, NY 14623-5603. Offers MS. Part-time programs available. *Students:* 22 full-time (10 women), 7 part-time (3 women); includes 1 Black or African American, non-Hispanic/Latino; 1 Asian, non-Hispanic/Latino, 14 international. Average age 30. 22 applicants, 64% accepted, 7 enrolled. In 2010, 17 master's awarded. *Degree requirements:* For master's, thesis or alternative. *Entrance requirements:* For master's, minimum GPA of 3.0. Additional exam requirements/recommendations for international students: Required—TOEFL (minimum score 550 paper-based; 213 computer-based; 79 iBT) or IELTS (minimum score 6.5). *Application deadline:* For fall admission, 2/15 priority date for domestic and international students; for winter admission, 11/1 for domestic and international students; for spring admission, 2/1 for domestic and international students. Applications are processed on a rolling basis. *Expenses:* Tuition: Full-time $33,234; part-time $924 per credit hour. Required fees: $219. *Financial support:* In 2010–11, 22 students received support; research assistantships with partial tuition reimbursements available, teaching assistantships with partial tuition reimbursements available, career-related internships or fieldwork, scholarships/grants, and unspecified assistantships available. Support available to part-time students. Financial award application deadline: 2/15; financial award applicants required to submit FAFSA. *Faculty research:* Dynamics involved in logistics and the performance features of different materials; design, sustainability, mathematics, and marketing. *Unit head:* Deanna Jacobs, Program Chair, 585-475-6801, Fax: 585-475-5227, E-mail: dmjipk@rit.edu. *Application contact:* Diane Ellison, Assistant Vice President, Graduate Enrollment Services, 585-475-2229, Fax: 585-475-7164, E-mail: gradinfo@rit.edu.

Rochester Institute of Technology, Graduate Enrollment Services, Kate Gleason College of Engineering, Department of Design, Development and Manufacturing, Rochester, NY 14623-5603. Offers manufacturing leadership (MS); product development (MS). Part-time and evening/weekend programs available. *Students:* 3 full-time (all women), 62 part-time (6 women); includes 2 Black or African American, non-Hispanic/Latino; 2 Asian, non-Hispanic/Latino; 3 Hispanic/Latino, 4 international. Average age 37. 12 applicants, 83% accepted, 9 enrolled. In 2010, 24 master's awarded. *Degree requirements:* For master's, capstone. *Entrance requirements:* For master's, minimum GPA of 2.5. Additional exam requirements/recommendations for international students: Required—TOEFL (minimum score 570 paper-based; 230 computer-based; 88 iBT) or IELTS (minimum score 6.5). *Application deadline:* For fall admission, 2/15 priority date for domestic and international students. Applications are processed on a rolling basis. Application fee: $50. Electronic applications accepted. *Expenses:* Tuition: Full-time $33,234; part-time $924 per credit hour. Required fees: $219. *Financial support:* In 2010–11, 7 students received support. *Faculty research:* Computer-integrated manufacturing, industrial ergonomics, optics and photonics, micromachines, electrochemical heating, signal and image processing, cardiovascular biomechanics, robotics and control, VLSI design, electron beam lithography, computer architecture, multimedia information systems, object-oriented software development. *Unit head:* Mark Smith, Director, 585-475-7971, Fax: 585-475-7955, E-mail: mpdmail@rit.edu. *Application contact:* Diane Ellison, Assistant Vice President, Graduate Enrollment Services, 585-475-2229, Fax: 585-475-7164, E-mail: gradinfo@rit.edu.

Rochester Institute of Technology, Graduate Enrollment Services, Kate Gleason College of Engineering, Department of Industrial and Systems Engineering, Rochester, NY 14623-5603. Offers engineering management (ME); industrial engineering (ME, MS); manufacturing engineering (ME, MS); systems engineering (ME). Part-time programs available. *Students:* 60 full-time (20 women), 17 part-time (5 women); includes 4 Asian, non-Hispanic/Latino; 2 Hispanic/Latino, 48 international. Average age 26. 179 applicants, 49% accepted, 29 enrolled. In 2010, 49 master's awarded. *Degree requirements:* For master's, internship. *Entrance requirements:* For master's, GRE, minimum GPA of 3.0. Additional exam requirements/recommendations for international students: Required—TOEFL (minimum score 570 paper-based; 230 computer-based; 88 iBT) or IELTS (minimum score 6.5). *Application deadline:* For fall admission, 2/15 priority date for domestic and international students. Applications are processed on a rolling basis. Application fee: $50. *Expenses:* Tuition: Full-time $33,234; part-time $924 per credit hour. Required fees: $219. *Financial support:* In 2010–11, 63 students received support; research assistantships with partial tuition reimbursements available, teaching assistantships with partial tuition reimbursements available, career-related internships or fieldwork, institutionally sponsored loans, scholarships/grants, tuition waivers (partial), and unspecified assistantships available. Support available to part-time students. Financial award applicants required to submit FAFSA. *Faculty research:* Safety, manufacturing (CAM), simulation. *Unit head:* Dr. Michael Kuhl, Interim Department Head, 585-475-2134, E-mail: mekeie@rit.edu. *Application contact:* Diane Ellison, Assistant Vice President, Graduate Enrollment Services, 585-475-2229, Fax: 585-475-7164, E-mail: gradinfo@rit.edu.

Rochester Institute of Technology, Graduate Enrollment Services, Kate Gleason College of Engineering, Department of Microelectronic Engineering, Program in Microelectronic Manufacturing Engineering, Rochester, NY 14623-5603. Offers ME. Part-time programs available. *Students:* 4 full-time, 3 part-time (all women); includes 1 Black or African American, non-Hispanic/Latino, 4 international. Average age 32. 15 applicants, 60% accepted, 7 enrolled. In 2010, 7 master's awarded. *Entrance requirements:* Additional exam requirements/recommendations for international students: Required—TOEFL (minimum score 570 paper-based; 230 computer-based; 88 iBT) or IELTS (minimum score 6.5). *Application deadline:* For fall admission, 2/15 for domestic students, 2/15 priority date for international students. *Expenses:* Tuition: Full-time $33,234; part-time $924 per credit hour. Required fees: $219. *Financial support:* In 2010–11, 1 student received support. Available to part-time students. Applicants required to submit FAFSA. *Unit head:* Dr. Robert Pearson, Director, 585-475-2923, Fax: 585-475-5845, E-mail: eme@rit.edu. *Application contact:* Diane Ellison, Assistant Vice President, Graduate Enrollment Services, 585-475-2229, Fax: 585-475-7164, E-mail: gradinfo@rit.edu.

Southern Illinois University Carbondale, Graduate School, College of Engineering, Program in Manufacturing Systems, Carbondale, IL 62901-4701. Offers MS. *Degree requirements:* For master's, comprehensive exam, thesis. *Entrance requirements:* For master's, minimum GPA of 2.7. Additional exam requirements/recommendations for international students: Required—TOEFL. *Faculty research:* Computer-aided manufacturing, robotics, quality assurance.

Southern Methodist University, Bobby B. Lyle School of Engineering, Department of Mechanical Engineering, Dallas, TX 75205. Offers electronic and optical packaging (MS); manufacturing systems management (MS); mechanical engineering (MSME, PhD). Part-time and evening/weekend programs available. Postbaccalaureate distance learning degree programs offered (no on-campus study). *Faculty:* 13 full-time (2 women), 7 part-time/adjunct (1 woman). *Students:* 29 full-time (6 women), 27 part-time (9 women); includes 1 Black or African American, non-Hispanic/Latino; 3 Asian, non-Hispanic/Latino; 2 Hispanic/Latino, 20 international. Average age 31. 53 applicants, 98% accepted, 52 enrolled. In 2010, 8 master's, 3 doctorates awarded. Terminal master's awarded for partial completion of doctoral program. *Degree requirements:* For master's, thesis optional; for doctorate, thesis/dissertation, oral and written qualifying exams, oral final exam. *Entrance requirements:* For master's, GRE General Test, minimum GPA of 3.0 in last 2 years; bachelor's degree in engineering, mathematics, or sciences; for doctorate, preliminary counseling exam, minimum graduate GPA of 3.0, bachelor's degree in related field. Additional exam requirements/recommendations for international students: Required—TOEFL. *Application deadline:* For fall admission, 7/1 for domestic students, 5/15 for international students; for spring admission, 11/15 for domestic students, 9/1 for international students. Applications are processed on a rolling basis. Application fee: $75. *Financial support:* In 2010–11, 17 students received support, including 10 research assistantships with full and partial tuition reimbursements available (averaging $16,000 per year), 7 teaching assistantships with full and partial tuition reimbursements available (averaging $16,000 per year); Federal Work-Study, institutionally sponsored loans, and tuition waivers (full and partial) also available. Financial award applicants required to submit FAFSA. *Faculty research:* Design, systems, and controls; thermal and fluid sciences. Total annual research expenditures: $774,564. *Unit head:* Dr. Volkan Otugen, Chairman, 214-768-3200, Fax: 214-768-1473, E-mail: otugen@engr.smu.edu. *Application contact:* Marc Valerin, Director of Graduate and Executive Admissions, 214-768-3042, E-mail: valerin@engr.smu.edu.

Stevens Institute of Technology, Graduate School, Charles V. Schaefer Jr. School of Engineering, Department of Mechanical Engineering, Program in Integrated Product Development, Hoboken, NJ 07030. Offers armament engineering (M Eng); computer and electrical engineering (M Eng); manufacturing technologies (M Eng); systems reliability and design (M Eng). *Students:* 8 part-time (1 woman). Average age 26. *Unit head:* Dr. Constantin Chassapis, Director, 201-216-5564. *Application contact:* Graduate Admissions, 800-496-4935, Fax: 201-216-8044, E-mail: gradadmissions@stevens.edu.

Texas A&M University, College of Engineering, Department of Engineering Technology and Industrial Distribution, College Station, TX 77843. Offers industrial distribution (MID). *Faculty:* 8. *Students:* 25 full-time (3 women); includes 4 minority (all Hispanic/Latino). In 2010, 8 master's awarded. *Entrance requirements:* Additional exam requirements/recommendations for international students: Required—TOEFL. *Application deadline:* For fall admission, 3/1 priority date for domestic and international students; for spring admission, 8/1 priority date for domestic and international students. Applications are processed on a rolling basis. Application fee: $50 ($75 for international students). Electronic applications accepted. *Financial support:* Application deadline: 2/1. *Unit head:* Dr. Walter W. Buchanan, Head, 979-862-4945, E-mail: buchanan@entc.tamu.edu. *Application contact:* Dr. Walter W. Buchanan, Head, 979-862-4945, E-mail: buchanan@entc.tamu.edu.

Texas Tech University, Graduate School, Edward E. Whitacre Jr. College of Engineering, Department of Industrial Engineering, Lubbock, TX 79409. Offers industrial engineering (MSIE, PhD); manufacturing systems engineering (MSMSE); systems and engineering management (MSSEM, PhD). Part-time programs available. Postbaccalaureate distance learning degree programs offered (minimal on-campus study). *Faculty:* 12 full-time (3 women). *Students:* 79 full-time (13 women), 47 part-time (7 women); includes 1 Black or African American, non-Hispanic/Latino; 1 Asian, non-Hispanic/Latino; 2 Hispanic/Latino, 81 international. Average age 28. 282 applicants, 51% accepted, 31 enrolled. In 2010, 39 master's, 9 doctorates awarded. *Degree requirements:* For master's, thesis or alternative; for doctorate, thesis/dissertation. *Entrance requirements:* For master's and doctorate, GRE General Test, minimum GPA of 3.0. Additional exam requirements/recommendations for international students: Required—TOEFL (minimum score 550 paper-based; 213 computer-based; 79 iBT). *Application deadline:* For fall admission, 6/1 priority date for domestic students, 1/15 priority date for international students; for spring admission, 9/1 priority date for domestic students, 6/15 priority date for international students. Applications are processed on a rolling basis. Application fee: $50 ($75 for international students). Electronic applications accepted. *Expenses:* Tuition, state resident: full-time $5495.76; part-time $228.99 per credit hour. Tuition, nonresident: full-time $12,936; part-time $538.99 per credit hour. Required fees: $2674; $36 per credit hour. $905 per semester. *Financial support:* In 2010–11, 40 students received support, including 12 research assistantships with partial tuition reimbursements available (averaging $3,905 per year), 8 teaching assistantships with partial tuition reimbursements available (averaging $3,150 per year). Financial award application deadline: 4/15; financial award applicants required to submit FAFSA. *Faculty research:* Knowledge and engineering management, environmentally conscious manufacturing, biomechanical simulation, aviation security, supply chain management. Total annual research expenditures: $646,598. *Unit head:* Dr. Pat Patterson, Chair, 806-742-3543, Fax: 806-742-3411, E-mail: pat.patterson@ttu.edu. *Application contact:* Dr. Mario Beruvides, Professor, 806-742-3543, Fax: 806-742-3411, E-mail: mario.beruvides@ttu.edu.

Tufts University, Graduate School of Arts and Sciences, Graduate Certificate Programs, Manufacturing Engineering Program, Medford, MA 02155. Offers Certificate. Part-time and evening/weekend programs available. Electronic applications accepted. *Expenses:* Tuition: Full-time $39,624; part-time $3962 per course. Required fees: $40 per year. Full-time tuition and fees vary according to degree level, program and student level. Part-time tuition and fees vary according to course load.

Universidad Autonoma de Guadalajara, Graduate Programs, Guadalajara, Mexico. Offers administrative law and justice (LL M); advertising and corporate communications (MA); architecture (M Arch); business (MBA); computational science (MCC); education (Ed M, Ed D); English-Spanish translation (MA); entrepreneurship and management (MBA); integrated management of digital animation (MA); international business (MIB); international corporate law (LL M); internet technologies (MS); manufacturing systems (MMS); occupational health (MS); philosophy (MA, PhD); power electronics (MS); quality systems (MQS); renewable energy (MS); social evaluation of projects (MBA); strategic market research (MBA); tax law (MA); teaching mathematics (MA).

Universidad de las Américas–Puebla, Division of Graduate Studies, School of Engineering, Program in Manufacturing Administration, Puebla, Mexico. Offers MS. *Faculty research:* Operations research, construction.

University of Calgary, Faculty of Graduate Studies, Schulich School of Engineering, Department of Mechanical and Manufacturing Engineering, Calgary, AB T2N 1N4, Canada. Offers M Eng, M Sc, PhD. *Degree requirements:* For master's, thesis (for some programs); for doctorate, thesis/dissertation, candidacy exam. *Entrance requirements:* For master's, minimum GPA of 3.0; for doctorate, minimum GPA of 3.3. Additional exam requirements/recommendations for international students: Required—TOEFL (minimum score 550 paper-based; 213 computer-based), IELTS (minimum score 7). *Faculty research:* Thermofluids, solid mechanics, materials, biomechanics, manufacturing.

University of California, Los Angeles, Graduate Division, Henry Samueli School of Engineering and Applied Science, Department of Mechanical and Aerospace Engineering, Program in Manufacturing Engineering, Los Angeles, CA 90095-1597. Offers MS. *Students:* 5 applicants, 20% accepted, 0 enrolled. *Degree requirements:* For master's, comprehensive exam or thesis. *Entrance requirements:* For master's, GRE General Test, minimum GPA of 3.0. Additional exam requirements/recommendations for international students: Required—TOEFL (minimum score 560 paper-based; 87 iBT). *Application deadline:* For fall admission, 12/15 for domestic and international students; for winter admission, 10/1 for domestic students; for spring admission, 12/31 for domestic students. Application fee: $70 ($90 for international students). Electronic applications accepted. *Financial support:* Fellowships, research assistantships, teaching assistantships, Federal Work-Study, institutionally sponsored loans, and tuition waivers (full and partial) available. Financial award application deadline: 12/15; financial award applicants required to submit FAFSA. *Unit head:* Dr. Adrienne Lavine, Chair, 310-825-7468. *Application* *contact:* Angie Castillo, Student Affairs Officer, 310-825-7793, Fax: 310-206-4830, E-mail: angie@ea.ucla.edu.

University of Colorado at Colorado Springs, College of Engineering and Applied Science, Department of Mechanical and Aerospace Engineering, Colorado Springs, CO 80933-7150. Offers engineering management (ME); information operations (ME); manufacturing (ME); mechanical engineering (MS); software engineering (ME); space operations (ME); space systems (MS). Part-time and evening/weekend programs available. *Faculty:* 10 full-time (2 women). *Students:* 56 full-time (11 women), 26 part-time (6 women); includes 3 Black or African American, non-Hispanic/Latino; 4 Asian, non-Hispanic/Latino; 3 Hispanic/Latino, 1 international. Average age 32. 33 applicants, 76% accepted, 19 enrolled. In 2010, 26 master's awarded. *Degree requirements:* For master's, thesis optional. *Entrance requirements:* For master's, GRE General Test, bachelor's degree in engineering or related degree, minimum GPA of 3.0. Additional exam requirements/recommendations for international students: Required—TOEFL. *Application deadline:* For fall admission, 5/1 for domestic students; for spring admission, 10/1 for domestic students. Applications are processed on a rolling basis. Application fee: $60 ($75 for international students). *Expenses:* Tuition, state resident: full-time $7916. Tuition, nonresident: full-time $16,610. Tuition and fees vary according to course load, degree level, program, reciprocity agreements and student level. *Financial support:* Federal Work-Study and scholarships/grants available. Support available to part-time students. Financial award application deadline: 3/1; financial award applicants required to submit FAFSA. *Faculty research:* Neural networks, artificial intelligence, robust control, space operations, space propulsion. Total annual research expenditures: $69,367. *Unit head:* Dr. James Stevens, Chair, 719-255-3581, Fax: 719-255-3042, E-mail: jstevens@uccs.edu. *Application contact:* Siew Nylund, Academic Adviser, 719-255-3243, Fax: 719-255-3589, E-mail: snylund@eas.uccs.edu.

The University of Iowa, Graduate College, College of Engineering, Department of Industrial Engineering, Iowa City, IA 52242-1316. Offers engineering design and manufacturing (MS, PhD); ergonomics (MS, PhD); information and engineering management (MS, PhD); operations research (MS, PhD); quality engineering (MS, PhD). *Faculty:* 6 full-time (0 women). *Students:* 33 full-time (9 women); includes 2 minority (1 Black or African American, non-Hispanic/Latino; 1 Asian, non-Hispanic/Latino), 14 international. Average age 30. 57 applicants, 19% accepted, 8 enrolled. In 2010, 12 master's, 5 doctorates awarded. *Degree requirements:* For master's, thesis optional, exam; for doctorate, comprehensive exam, thesis/dissertation, final defense exam. *Entrance requirements:* For master's and doctorate, GRE General Test. Additional exam requirements/recommendations for international students: Required—TOEFL (minimum score 550 paper-based; 213 computer-based; 81 iBT). *Application deadline:* For fall admission, 7/15 for domestic students, 4/15 for international students; for spring admission, 12/1 for domestic students, 10/1 for international students. Applications are processed on a rolling basis. Application fee: $60 ($100 for international students). Electronic applications accepted. *Financial support:* In 2010–11, 2 fellowships with partial tuition reimbursements (averaging $30,450 per year), 20 research assistantships with partial tuition reimbursements (averaging $20,000 per year), 8 teaching assistantships with partial tuition reimbursements (averaging $16,630 per year) were awarded; career-related internships or fieldwork, scholarships/grants, and unspecified assistantships also available. Support available to part-time students. Financial award applicants required to submit FAFSA. *Faculty research:* Operations research; informatics; human factors engineering; manufacturing systems; human-machine interaction. Total annual research expenditures: $4.7 million. *Unit head:* Dr. Andrew Kusiak, Department Executive Officer, 319-335-5934, Fax: 319-335-5669, E-mail: andrew-kusiak@uiowa.edu. *Application contact:* Jennifer Rumping, Secretary, 319-335-5939, Fax: 319-335-5669, E-mail: indeng@engineering.uiowa.edu.

University of Kentucky, Graduate School, College of Engineering, Program in Manufacturing Systems Engineering, Lexington, KY 40506-0032. Offers MSMSE. *Degree requirements:* For master's, comprehensive exam. *Entrance requirements:* For master's, GRE General Test, minimum undergraduate GPA of 2.75. Additional exam requirements/recommendations for international students: Required—TOEFL (minimum score 550 paper-based; 213 computer-based). Electronic applications accepted. *Faculty research:* Manufacturing processes and equipment, manufacturing systems and control, computer-aided design and manufacturing, automation in manufacturing, electric manufacturing and packaging.

University of Manitoba, Faculty of Graduate Studies, Faculty of Engineering, Department of Mechanical and Manufacturing Engineering, Winnipeg, MB R3T 2N2, Canada. Offers M Eng, M Sc, PhD. *Degree requirements:* For master's, thesis; for doctorate, thesis/dissertation.

University of Maryland, College Park, Academic Affairs, A. James Clark School of Engineering, Department of Mechanical Engineering, College Park, MD 20742. Offers electronic packaging and reliability (MS, PhD); manufacturing and design (MS, PhD); mechanics and materials (MS, PhD); reliability engineering (M Eng, MS, PhD); thermal and fluid sciences (MS, PhD). Part-time and evening/weekend programs available. Postbaccalaureate distance learning degree programs offered. *Faculty:* 79 full-time (7 women), 21 part-time/adjunct (1 woman). *Students:* 219 full-time (31 women), 73 part-time (10 women); includes 44 minority (11 Black or African American, non-Hispanic/Latino; 2 American Indian or Alaska Native, non-Hispanic/Latino; 21 Asian, non-Hispanic/Latino; 8 Hispanic/Latino; 2 Two or more races, non-Hispanic/Latino), 138 international. 520 applicants, 18% accepted, 63 enrolled. In 2010, 31 master's, 31 doctorates awarded. *Degree requirements:* For master's, thesis optional; for doctorate, thesis/dissertation, qualifying exam. *Entrance requirements:* For master's, GRE General Test, 3 letters of recommendation; for doctorate, GRE General Test, minimum GPA of 3.0. Additional exam requirements/recommendations for international students: Required—TOEFL. *Application deadline:* For fall admission, 5/15 for domestic students, 2/1 for international students; for spring admission, 10/1 for domestic students, 6/1 for international students. Applications are processed on a rolling basis. Application fee: $75. Electronic applications accepted. *Expenses:* Tuition, area resident: Part-time $471 per credit hour. Tuition, state resident: part-time $471 per credit hour. Tuition, nonresident: part-time $1016 per credit hour. Required fees: $337 per term. *Financial support:* In 2010–11, 3 fellowships with full and partial tuition reimbursements (averaging $19,975 per year), 166 research assistantships (averaging $23,679 per year), 12 teaching assistantships (averaging $17,644 per year) were awarded; Federal Work-Study and scholarships/grants also available. Support available to part-time students. Financial award applicants required to submit FAFSA. *Faculty research:* Injection molding, electronic packaging, fluid mechanics, product engineering. Total annual research expenditures: $17.4 million. *Unit head:* Dr. B. Balachandran, Interim Chair, 301-405-5297, E-mail: balab@umd.edu. *Application contact:* Dr. Charles A. Caramello, Graduate Director, 301-405-0358, Fax: 301-314-9305, E-mail: ccaramel@umd.edu.

University of Memphis, Graduate School, Herff College of Engineering, Department of Engineering Technology, Memphis, TN 38152. Offers computer engineering technology (MS); electronics engineering technology (MS); manufacturing engineering technology (MS). Part-time and evening/weekend programs available. *Faculty:* 5 full-time (0 women). *Students:* 4 full-time (1 woman), 6 part-time (1 woman); includes 4 Black or African American, non-Hispanic/Latino, 2 international. Average age 38. 2 applicants, 50% accepted, 1 enrolled. *Degree requirements:* For master's, comprehensive exam, thesis optional. *Entrance requirements:* For master's, GRE General Test, minimum undergraduate GPA of 2.5. *Application deadline:* For fall admission, 8/1 for domestic students; for spring admission, 12/1 for domestic students. Applications are processed on a rolling basis. Application fee: $25 ($50 for international students). Electronic applications accepted. *Financial support:* In 2010–11, 5 students received support; research assistantships with full tuition reimbursements available, career-related internships or fieldwork, Federal Work-Study, scholarships/grants, and unspecified assistantships available. Financial award application deadline: 2/15; financial award applicants required to submit FAFSA. *Faculty research:* Teacher education services-technology education; flexible manufacturing control systems; embedded, dedicated, and real-time computer systems; network, Internet, and Web-based programming; analog and digital electronic communication systems. *Unit head:* Deborah J. Hochstein, Chairman, 901-678-2225, Fax: 901-678-5145, E-mail: dhochstn@memphis.edu.

Application contact: Carl R. Williams, Coordinator of Graduate Studies, 901-678-3296, Fax: 901-678-5145, E-mail: crwillia@memphis.edu.

University of Michigan–Dearborn, College of Engineering and Computer Science, Interdisciplinary Programs, Program in Manufacturing Systems Engineering, Dearborn, MI 48128-1491. Offers MSE. Part-time and evening/weekend programs available. *Faculty:* 1 full-time (0 women). *Students:* 2 full-time (1 woman), 10 part-time (1 woman); includes 3 minority (all Black or African American, non-Hispanic/Latino), 1 international. Average age 30. 8 applicants, 63% accepted, 2 enrolled. In 2010, 3 master's awarded. *Degree requirements:* For master's, thesis optional. *Entrance requirements:* For master's, bachelor's degree in applied mathematics, computer science, engineering, or physical science; minimum GPA of 3.0. Additional exam requirements/recommendations for international students: Required—TOEFL (minimum score 560 paper-based; 220 computer-based; 84 iBT). *Application deadline:* For fall admission, 8/1 priority date for domestic students, 4/1 for international students; for winter admission, 12/1 priority date for domestic students, 8/1 for international students; for spring admission, 4/1 priority date for domestic students, 12/1 for international students. Applications are processed on a rolling basis. Application fee: $60 ($75 for international students). Electronic applications accepted. *Financial support:* Scholarships/grants and unspecified assistantships available. Financial award application deadline: 4/1; financial award applicants required to submit FAFSA. *Faculty research:* Toolwear metrology, paper handling, grinding wheel imbalance, machine mission. *Unit head:* Dr. Pankaj K. Mallick, Director/Professor, 313-593-5119, Fax: 313-593-5386, E-mail: pkm@umich.edu. *Application contact:* Sherry Boyd, Intermediate Administrative Assistant, 313-593-5582, Fax: 313-593-5386, E-mail: idpgrad@umd.umich.edu.

University of Missouri, Graduate School, College of Engineering, Department of Industrial and Manufacturing Systems Engineering, Columbia, MO 65211. Offers MS, PhD. *Degree requirements:* For master's, thesis or alternative; for doctorate, thesis/dissertation. *Entrance requirements:* For master's and doctorate, GRE General Test, minimum GPA of 3.0. Additional exam requirements/recommendations for international students: Required—TOEFL (minimum score 550 paper-based; 213 computer-based; 80 iBT).

University of Nebraska–Lincoln, Graduate College, College of Engineering, Department of Industrial and Management Systems Engineering, Lincoln, NE 68588. Offers engineering management (M Eng); industrial and management systems engineering (MS, PhD); manufacturing systems engineering (MS). Postbaccalaureate distance learning degree programs offered. *Degree requirements:* For master's, thesis optional; for doctorate, comprehensive exam, thesis/dissertation. *Entrance requirements:* For master's and doctorate, GRE. Additional exam requirements/recommendations for international students: Required—TOEFL (minimum score 525 paper-based; 195 computer-based). Electronic applications accepted. *Faculty research:* Ergonomics, occupational safety, quality control, industrial packaging, facility design.

University of New Mexico, Graduate School, School of Engineering, Manufacturing Engineering Program, Albuquerque, NM 87131-2039. Offers MEME, MBA/MEME. Part-time programs available. *Students:* 2 full-time (0 women), 4 part-time (0 women); includes 1 American Indian or Alaska Native, non-Hispanic/Latino; 2 Hispanic/Latino, 1 international. Average age 31. 6 applicants, 67% accepted, 2 enrolled. In 2010, 1 master's awarded. *Degree requirements:* For master's, 500 hours relevant industry experience, paid or unpaid. *Entrance requirements:* For master's, GRE General Test (minimum score: 400 verbal, 600 quantitative, 3.5 analytical writing), minimum GPA of 3.0. Additional exam requirements/recommendations for international students: Required—TOEFL (minimum score 550 paper-based; 213 computer-based; 79 iBT). *Application deadline:* For fall admission, 7/30 priority date for domestic students, 3/1 for international students; for spring admission, 11/30 priority date for domestic students, 8/1 for international students. Application fee: $50. Electronic applications accepted. *Expenses:* Tuition, state resident: full-time $5991; part-time $251 per credit hour. Tuition, nonresident: full-time $14,405; part-time $800.20 per credit hour. Tuition and fees vary according to course level, course load, program and reciprocity agreements. *Financial support:* In 2010–11, 2 students received support, including 1 teaching assistantship (averaging $5,045 per year); career-related internships or fieldwork and health care benefits also available. Support available to part-time students. Financial award application deadline: 3/1; financial award applicants required to submit FAFSA. *Faculty research:* Robotics, automation control and machine vision, microsystems and microgrippers, semiconductor manufacturing and metrology, cross-training and operations of technicians and engineers. Total annual research expenditures: $1.1 million. *Unit head:* Dr. John E. Wood, Director, 505-272-7000, Fax: 505-272-7152, E-mail: jw@unm.edu. *Application contact:* Arden L. Ballantine, Information Contact, 505-272-7000, Fax: 505-272-7152, E-mail: aballant@unm.edu.

University of St. Thomas, Graduate Studies, School of Engineering, St. Paul, MN 55105-1096. Offers manufacturing engineering and operations (MS); mechanical engineering (MS); medical device development (Certificate); regulatory science (MS); software engineering (MS); software management (MS); software systems (MSS); systems engineering (MS); technology management (MS). *Accreditation:* ABET (one or more programs are accredited). *Entrance requirements:* For master's, resume, official transcripts. Additional exam requirements/recommendations for international students: Required—TOEFL (minimum score 550 paper-based). *Application deadline:* For fall admission, 8/1 priority date for domestic students; for spring admission, 1/1 priority date for domestic students. Applications are processed on a rolling basis. Application fee: $30. Electronic applications accepted. *Expenses:* Contact institution. *Financial support:* Fellowships, research assistantships, institutionally sponsored loans and scholarships/grants available. Support available to part-time students. Financial award application deadline: 4/1; financial award applicants required to submit FAFSA. *Unit head:* Don Weinkauf, Dean, 651-962-5760, Fax: 651-962-6419, E-mail: dhweinkauf@stthomas.edu. *Application contact:* Joyce A. Taylor, Graduate Programs Coordinator, 651-962-5756, Fax: 651-962-6419, E-mail: jataylor1@stthomas.edu.

University of Southern California, Graduate School, Viterbi School of Engineering, Daniel J. Epstein Department of Industrial and Systems Engineering, Los Angeles, CA 90089. Offers digital supply chain management (MS); engineering management (MS); engineering technology communication (Graduate Certificate); health systems operations (Graduate Certificate); industrial and systems engineering (MS, PhD, Engr); manufacturing engineering (MS); operations research engineering (MS); optimization and supply chain management (Graduate Certificate); product development engineering (MS); safety systems and security (MS); systems architecting and engineering (MS, Graduate Certificate); systems safety and security (Graduate Certificate); transportation systems (Graduate Certificate); MS/MBA. Part-time and evening/weekend programs available. Postbaccalaureate distance learning degree programs offered (no on-campus study). *Faculty:* 12 full-time (2 women), 21 part-time/adjunct (2 women). *Students:* 224 full-time (69 women), 143 part-time (32 women); includes 63 minority (6 Black or African American, non-Hispanic/Latino; 35 Asian, non-Hispanic/Latino; 17 Hispanic/Latino; 5 Two or more races, non-Hispanic/Latino), 253 international. 669 applicants, 45% accepted, 155 enrolled. In 2010, 98 master's, 7 doctorates awarded. Terminal master's awarded for partial completion of doctoral program. *Degree requirements:* For master's, thesis optional; for doctorate, thesis/dissertation. *Entrance requirements:* For master's and doctorate, GRE General Test. *Application deadline:* For fall admission, 12/1 priority date for domestic students, 11/1 priority date for international students; for spring admission, 9/15 priority date for domestic and international students. Applications are processed on a rolling basis. Application fee: $85. Electronic applications accepted. *Expenses:* Tuition: Full-time $31,240; part-time $1420 per unit. Required fees: $600. One-time fee: $35 full-time. Full-time tuition and fees vary according to degree level and program. *Financial support:* In 2010–11, fellowships with full tuition reimbursements (averaging $30,000 per year), research assistantships with full tuition reimbursements (averaging $20,000 per year), teaching assistantships with full tuition reimbursements (averaging $20,000 per year) were awarded; career-related internships or fieldwork, scholarships/grants, health care benefits, and unspecified assistantships also available. Financial award application deadline: 12/1; financial award applicants required to submit CSS PROFILE or FAFSA. *Faculty research:* Health systems, music cognition and retrieval, transportation and logistics, manufacturing and automation, engineering systems design, risk and economic

Manufacturing Engineering

University of Southern California (continued)
analysis. Total annual research expenditures: $1 million. *Unit head:* Dr. F. Stan Settles, Chair, 213-740-4893, E-mail: isedept@usc.edu. *Application contact:* Evelyn Felina, Director of Student Affairs, 213-740-7549, E-mail: efelina@usc.edu.

University of Southern Maine, School of Applied Science, Engineering, and Technology, Department of Technology, Portland, ME 04104-9300. Offers manufacturing systems (MS). *Entrance requirements:* Additional exam requirements/recommendations for international students: Required—TOEFL. Electronic applications accepted.

The University of Texas at El Paso, Graduate School, College of Engineering, Department of Industrial Engineering, El Paso, TX 79968-0001. Offers industrial engineering (MS); manufacturing engineering (MS); systems engineering (MS, Certificate). Part-time and evening/weekend programs available. *Students:* 51 (11 women); includes 1 Asian, non-Hispanic/Latino; 42 Hispanic/Latino, 8 international. Average age 34. 38 applicants. In 2010, 46 master's awarded. *Degree requirements:* For master's, thesis optional. *Entrance requirements:* For master's, GRE General Test, minimum GPA of 3.0 in major. Additional exam requirements/recommendations for international students: Required—TOEFL. *Application deadline:* For fall admission, 7/1 priority date for domestic students, 3/1 for international students; for spring admission, 11/1 priority date for domestic students, 9/1 for international students. Applications are processed on a rolling basis. Application fee: $15 ($65 for international students). Electronic applications accepted. *Financial support:* In 2010–11, research assistantships with partial tuition reimbursements (averaging $21,125 per year), teaching assistantships with partial tuition reimbursements (averaging $16,900 per year) were awarded; fellowships with partial tuition reimbursements, Federal Work-Study, institutionally sponsored loans, scholarships/grants, and tuition waivers (partial) also available. Financial award application deadline: 3/15; financial award applicants required to submit FAFSA. *Faculty research:* Computer vision, automated inspection, simulation and modeling. *Unit head:* Dr. Rafael S. Gutierrez, Chair, 915-747-5450, Fax: 915-747-5019, E-mail: rsgutier@utep.edu. *Application contact:* Dr. Charles H. Ambler, Dean of the Graduate School, 915-747-5491 Ext. 7886, Fax: 915-747-5788, E-mail: cambler@utep.edu.

The University of Texas at San Antonio, College of Engineering, Department of Mechanical Engineering, San Antonio, TX 78249-0617. Offers advanced manufacturing and enterprise engineering (MS); mechanical engineering (MS). Part-time and evening/weekend programs available. *Faculty:* 15 full-time (1 woman), 3 part-time/adjunct (0 women). *Students:* 49 full-time (5 women), 46 part-time (7 women); includes 17 minority (3 Asian, non-Hispanic/Latino; 13 Hispanic/Latino; 1 Two or more races, non-Hispanic/Latino), 43 international. Average age 27. 65 applicants, 78% accepted, 28 enrolled. In 2010, 27 master's awarded. *Degree requirements:* For master's, comprehensive exam (for some programs), thesis (for some programs). *Entrance requirements:* For master's, GRE General Test, minimum GPA of 3.0 in last 60 hours of undergraduate degree. Additional exam requirements/recommendations for international students: Required—TOEFL (minimum score 500 paper-based; 173 computer-based; 61 iBT), IELTS (minimum score 5). *Application deadline:* For fall admission, 7/1 for domestic students, 4/1 for international students; for spring admission, 11/1 for domestic students, 9/1 for international students. Applications are processed on a rolling basis. Application fee: $45 ($80 for international students). Electronic applications accepted. *Expenses:* Tuition, state resident: full-time $4172; part-time $231.75 per credit hour. Tuition, nonresident: full-time $15,332; part-time $851.75 per credit hour. *Financial support:* In 2010–11, 33 students received support, including 1 fellowship (averaging $42,000 per year), 26 research assistantships (averaging $12,257 per year); career-related internships or fieldwork, scholarships/grants, tuition waivers, and unspecified assistantships also available. Support available to part-time students. Financial award application deadline: 3/31. Total annual research expenditures: $1.1 million. *Unit head:* Dr. Efstathios E. Michaelides, Department Chair, 210-458-5580, Fax: 210-458-6504, E-mail: stathis.michaelides@utsa.edu. *Application contact:* Veronica Ramirez, Assistant Dean of the Graduate School, 210-458-4330, Fax: 210-458-4332, E-mail: graduatestudies@utsa.edu.

See Display on next page and Close-Up on page 453.
See also Displays on pages 547 and 548 and Close-Ups on pages 559 and 561.

The University of Texas–Pan American, College of Science and Engineering, Department of Manufacturing Engineering, Edinburg, TX 78539. Offers MS.

University of Toronto, School of Graduate Studies, Physical Sciences Division, Advanced Design and Manufacturing Institute, Toronto, ON M5S 1A1, Canada. Offers M Eng. Program offered jointly with McMaster University, Queen's University, the University of Waterloo, and the University of Western Ontario; available only to Canadian citizens and permanent residents of Canada. Part-time programs available.

University of Windsor, Faculty of Graduate Studies, Faculty of Engineering, Department of Industrial and Manufacturing Systems Engineering, Windsor, ON N9B 3P4, Canada. Offers industrial engineering (M Eng, MA Sc); manufacturing systems engineering (PhD). Part-time programs available. *Degree requirements:* For master's, thesis; for doctorate, comprehensive exam, thesis/dissertation. *Entrance requirements:* For master's, minimum B average; for doctorate, master's degree, minimum B average. Additional exam requirements/recommendations for international students: Required—TOEFL (minimum score 560 paper-based; 220 computer-based). Electronic applications accepted. *Faculty research:* Human factors, operations research.

University of Wisconsin–Madison, Graduate School, College of Engineering, Manufacturing Systems Engineering Program, Madison, WI 53706. Offers MS. Part-time programs available. Postbaccalaureate distance learning degree programs offered (minimal on-campus study). *Faculty:* 32 part-time/adjunct (6 women). *Students:* 30 full-time (4 women), 6 part-time (0 women); includes 2 Asian, non-Hispanic/Latino; 1 Hispanic/Latino, 26 international. Average age 27. 40 applicants, 38% accepted. In 2010, 7 master's awarded. *Degree requirements:* For master's, thesis (for some programs), independent research projects. *Entrance requirements:* For master's, GRE General Test. Additional exam requirements/recommendations for international students: Required—TOEFL. *Application deadline:* For fall admission, 6/15 priority date for domestic students; for spring admission, 10/31 priority date for domestic students. Applications are processed on a rolling basis. Application fee: $45. Electronic applications accepted. *Expenses:* Tuition, state resident: full-time $9887.36; part-time $617.96 per credit. Tuition, nonresident: full-time $24,054; part-time $1503.40 per credit. Required fees: $67.63 per credit. Tuition and fees vary according to reciprocity agreements. *Financial support:* In 2010–11, 10 students received support, including 8 fellowships with tuition reimbursements available (averaging $16,500 per year), 2 research assistantships with tuition reimbursements available (averaging $19,000 per year); career-related internships or fieldwork, Federal Work-Study, institutionally sponsored loans, and unspecified assistantships also available. *Faculty research:* CAD/CAM, rapid prototyping, lead time reduction, quick response manufacturing. Total annual research expenditures: $250,000. *Unit head:* Ananth Krishnamurthy, Director, 608-262-0921, Fax: 608-265-4017, E-mail: ananth@engr.wisc.edu. *Application contact:* John Loeffelholz, Administrative Assistant, 608-262-0921, Fax: 608-265-4017, E-mail: mse@engr.wisc.edu.

University of Wisconsin–Milwaukee, Graduate School, College of Engineering and Applied Science, Program in Engineering, Milwaukee, WI 53201-0413. Offers civil engineering (MS); electrical and computer engineering (MS); energy engineering (Certificate); engineering (PhD); engineering management (MS); engineering mechanics (MS); ergonomics (Certificate); industrial and management engineering (MS); manufacturing engineering (MS); materials engineering (MS); mechanical engineering (MS); MUP/MS. Part-time programs available. *Faculty:* 50 full-time (5 women). *Students:* 152 full-time (27 women), 115 part-time (23 women); includes 13 Black or African American, non-Hispanic/Latino; 3 American Indian or Alaska Native, non-Hispanic/Latino; 6 Asian, non-Hispanic/Latino; 10 Hispanic/Latino, 25 international. Average age 31. 236 applicants, 67% accepted, 55 enrolled. In 2010, 39 master's, 19 doctorates awarded. *Degree requirements:* For master's, comprehensive exam (for some programs), thesis or alternative; for doctorate, comprehensive exam, thesis/dissertation, internship. *Entrance requirements:* For master's, GRE, minimum GPA of 2.75; for doctorate, GRE, minimum GPA of 3.5. Additional exam requirements/recommendations for international students: Required—TOEFL (minimum score 550 paper-based; 79 iBT), IELTS (minimum score 6.5). *Application deadline:* For fall admission, 1/1 priority date for domestic students; for spring admission, 9/1 for domestic students. Applications are processed on a rolling basis. Application fee: $56 ($96 for international students). *Financial support:* In 2010–11, 3 fellowships, 55 research assistantships, 77 teaching assistantships were awarded; career-related internships or fieldwork, Federal Work-Study, unspecified assistantships, and project assistantships also available. Support available to part-time students. Financial award application deadline: 4/15. Total annual research expenditures: $6.2 million. *Unit head:* David Yu, Representative, 414-229-6169, E-mail: yu@uwm.edu. *Application contact:* Betty Warras, General Information Contact, 414-229-6169, Fax: 414-229-6967, E-mail: bwarras@uwm.edu.

University of Wisconsin–Stout, Graduate School, College of Technology, Engineering, and Management, Program in Manufacturing Engineering, Menomonie, WI 54751. Offers MS. Postbaccalaureate distance learning degree programs offered (minimal on-campus study). *Degree requirements:* For master's, thesis. *Entrance requirements:* For master's, minimum GPA of 3.0. Additional exam requirements/recommendations for international students: Required—TOEFL (minimum score 500 paper-based; 173 computer-based; 61 iBT). Electronic applications accepted. *Faculty research:* General ceramics patents, metal matrix composites, solidification processing, high temperature processing.

Villanova University, College of Engineering, Department of Mechanical Engineering, Villanova, PA 19085-1699. Offers electro-mechanical systems (Certificate); machinery dynamics (Certificate); mechanical engineering (MSME); nonlinear dynamics and control (Certificate); thermofluid systems (Certificate). Part-time and evening/weekend programs available. Postbaccalaureate distance learning degree programs offered (no on-campus study). *Faculty:* 21 full-time (2 women), 15 part-time/adjunct (1 woman). *Students:* 17 full-time (2 women), 52 part-time (8 women); includes 1 Black or African American, non-Hispanic/Latino; 6 Asian, non-Hispanic/Latino; 2 Hispanic/Latino, 6 international. 48 applicants, 63% accepted, 14 enrolled. In 2010, 20 master's awarded. *Degree requirements:* For master's, thesis optional. *Entrance requirements:* For master's, GRE General Test (for applicants with degrees from foreign universities), BME, minimum GPA of 3.0. Additional exam requirements/recommendations for international students: Required—TOEFL (minimum score 600 paper-based; 250 computer-based; 100 iBT). *Application deadline:* For fall admission, 7/1 priority date for domestic students, 4/1 priority date for international students; for spring admission, 11/1 for domestic students, 10/1 for international students. Applications are processed on a rolling basis. Application fee: $50. Electronic applications accepted. *Expenses:* Tuition: Part-time $700 per credit. Part-time tuition and fees vary according to degree level and program. *Financial support:* In 2010–11, research assistantships with full tuition reimbursements (averaging $13,500 per year); Federal Work-Study, tuition waivers (full), and unspecified assistantships also available. Support available to part-time students. Financial award application deadline: 1/15. *Faculty research:* Composite materials, power plant systems, fluid mechanics, automated manufacturing, dynamic analysis. Total annual research expenditures: $1.6 million. *Unit head:* Dr. C. Nataraj, Chairperson, 610-519-4980, Fax: 610-519-7312. *Application contact:* College of Engineering Graduate Programs Office, 610-519-5840, Fax: 610-519-5859, E-mail: engineering.grad@villanova.edu.

Wayne State University, College of Engineering, Department of Industrial and Manufacturing Engineering, Program in Manufacturing Engineering, Detroit, MI 48202. Offers MS. *Faculty:* 9 full-time (0 women), 4 part-time/adjunct (0 women). *Students:* 2 full-time (0 women), 3 part-time (0 women); includes 2 Black or African American, non-Hispanic/Latino, 2 international. Average age 25. 7 applicants, 86% accepted, 3 enrolled. In 2010, 7 master's awarded. *Degree requirements:* For master's, thesis optional. *Entrance requirements:* For master's, minimum undergraduate GPA of 2.8, Baccalaureate degree in engineering from an ABET institution. Additional exam requirements/recommendations for international students: Required—TOEFL (minimum score 550 paper-based; 213 computer-based); Recommended—TWE (minimum score 6). *Application deadline:* For fall admission, 7/1 priority date for domestic students, 6/1 for international students; for winter admission, 10/1 for international students; for spring admission, 3/15 for domestic students, 2/1 for international students. Applications are processed on a rolling basis. Application fee: $30 ($50 for international students). *Expenses:* Tuition, state resident: full-time $7662; part-time $478.85 per credit hour. Tuition, nonresident: full-time $16,920; part-time $1057.55 per credit hour. Required fees: $571.20; $35.70 per credit hour. $188.05 per semester. Tuition and fees vary according to course load and program. *Financial support:* Fellowships, research assistantships, teaching assistantships, career-related internships or fieldwork available. *Faculty research:* Design for manufacturing, machine tools, manufacturing processes, material selection for manufacturing, manufacturing systems. *Unit head:* Kenneth Chelst, Chair, 313-577-3857, Fax: 313-577-8833, E-mail: aa1276@wayne.edu. *Application contact:* Ratna Chinnam, Graduate Director, 313-577-7846, E-mail: r_chinnam@wayne.edu.

Western Illinois University, School of Graduate Studies, College of Business and Technology, Department of Engineering Technology, Macomb, IL 61455-1390. Offers manufacturing engineering systems (MS). Part-time programs available. *Students:* 18 full-time (2 women), 4 part-time (0 women); includes 3 minority (all Black or African American, non-Hispanic/Latino), 9 international. Average age 27. 21 applicants, 71% accepted. In 2010, 11 master's awarded. *Degree requirements:* For master's, thesis or alternative. *Entrance requirements:* Additional exam requirements/recommendations for international students: Required—TOEFL (minimum score 550 paper-based; 213 computer-based; 80 iBT). *Application deadline:* Applications are processed on a rolling basis. Application fee: $30. Electronic applications accepted. *Expenses:* Tuition, state resident: full-time $6370; part-time $265.40 per credit hour. Tuition, nonresident: full-time $12,740; part-time $530.80 per credit hour. Required fees: $75.67 per credit hour. *Financial support:* In 2010–11, 5 students received support, including 5 research assistantships with full tuition reimbursements available (averaging $7,280 per year). Financial award applicants required to submit FAFSA. *Unit head:* Dr. Ray Diez, Chairperson, 309-298-1091. *Application contact:* Evelyn Hoing, Assistant Director of Graduate Studies, 309-298-1806, Fax: 309-298-2345, E-mail: grad-office@wiu.edu.

Western Michigan University, Graduate College, College of Engineering and Applied Sciences, Department of Industrial and Manufacturing Engineering, Program in Manufacturing Engineering, Kalamazoo, MI 49008. Offers MS. *Entrance requirements:* For master's, GRE General Test, minimum GPA of 3.0.

Western New England University, School of Engineering, Department of Industrial and Manufacturing Engineering, Springfield, MA 01119. Offers production management (MSEM). Part-time and evening/weekend programs available. *Students:* 38 part-time (12 women); includes 1 Black or African American, non-Hispanic/Latino; 1 Asian, non-Hispanic/Latino; 1 Hispanic/Latino; 1 Two or more races, non-Hispanic/Latino, 2 international. *Degree requirements:* For master's, comprehensive exam, thesis optional. *Entrance requirements:* For master's, GRE, bachelor's degree in engineering or related field, two letters of recommendation, resume. *Application deadline:* Applications are processed on a rolling basis. Application fee: $30. *Expenses:* Tuition: Full-time $35,582. *Financial support:* Available to part-time students. Applicants required to submit FAFSA. *Faculty research:* Project scheduling, flexible manufacturing systems, facility layout, energy management. *Unit head:* Dr. Eric W. Haffner, Chair, 413-782-1272, E-mail: ehaffner@wnec.edu. *Application contact:* Matt Fox, Director of Recruiting and Marketing for Adult Learners, 413-782-1249, Fax: 413-782-1779, E-mail: ce@wnec.edu.

Western New England University, School of Engineering, Master's Program in Engineering Management, Springfield, MA 01119. Offers business and engineering information systems (MSEM); general engineering management (MSEM); production and manufacturing systems (MSEM); quality engineering (MSEM). Evening/weekend programs available. Postbaccalaureate distance learning degree programs offered (no on-campus study). *Degree requirements:* For master's, thesis optional. *Expenses:* Tuition: Full-time $35,582.

Wichita State University, Graduate School, College of Engineering, Department of Industrial and Manufacturing Engineering, Wichita, KS 67260. Offers MEM, MS, PhD. Part-time programs available. In 2010, 37 master's, 3 doctorates awarded. *Entrance requirements:* Additional exam requirements/recommendations for international students: Required—TOEFL. *Financial support:* Teaching assistantships available. *Unit head:* Dr. Krishna Krishnan, Chair, 316-978-3425, Fax: 316-978-3742, E-mail: krishna.krishnan@wichita.edu. *Application contact:* Dr. Krishna Krishnan, Chair, 316-978-3425, Fax: 316-978-3742, E-mail: krishna.krishnan@wichita.edu.

Worcester Polytechnic Institute, Graduate Studies and Research, Department of Mechanical Engineering, Program in Manufacturing Engineering, Worcester, MA 01609-2280. Offers MS, PhD. Part-time and evening/weekend programs available. *Faculty:* 2 full-time (0 women). *Students:* 14 full-time (3 women), 18 part-time (3 women); includes 1 Black or African American, non-Hispanic/Latino; 1 Hispanic/Latino; 2 Native Hawaiian or other Pacific Islander, non-Hispanic/Latino, 9 international. 41 applicants, 88% accepted, 14 enrolled. In 2010, 23 master's, 3 doctorates awarded. *Degree requirements:* For master's, thesis optional; for doctorate, comprehensive exam, thesis/dissertation, research proposal. *Entrance requirements:* For master's and doctorate, GRE-required for International applicants, 3 letters of recommendation. Additional exam requirements/recommendations for international students: Required—TOEFL (minimum score 550 paper-based; 213 computer-based; 79 iBT), IELTS (minimum score 6.5). *Application deadline:* For fall admission, 1/1 priority date for domestic and international students; for spring admission, 10/1 priority date for domestic and international students. Applications are processed on a rolling basis. Application fee: $70. Electronic applications accepted. *Expenses:* Tuition: Full-time $20,862; part-time $1159 per term. One-time fee: $15. *Financial support:* Career-related internships or fieldwork, institutionally sponsored loans, scholarships/grants, and unspecified assistantships available. Financial award application deadline: 1/1; financial award applicants required to submit FAFSA. *Faculty research:* Manufacturing processes and systems, design for manufacturability, CAD/CAM applications, surface metrology, materials processing. *Unit head:* Dr. Kevin Rong, Director, 508-831-6088, Fax: 508-831-5673, E-mail: rong@wpi.edu. *Application contact:* Susan Milkman, Graduate Secretary, 508-831-6088, Fax: 508-831-5673, E-mail: smilkman@wpi.edu.

Worcester Polytechnic Institute, Graduate Studies and Research, Programs in Interdisciplinary Studies, Worcester, MA 01609-2280. Offers bioscience administration (MS); impact engineering (MS); manufacturing engineering management (MS); power systems management (MS); social science (PhD); systems modeling (MS). Part-time and evening/weekend programs available. *Faculty:* 1 part-time/adjunct (0 women). *Students:* 6 full-time (1 woman), 146 part-time (25 women); includes 1 Black or African American, non-Hispanic/Latino; 6 Hispanic/Latino; 11 Native Hawaiian or other Pacific Islander, non-Hispanic/Latino, 1 international. 151 applicants, 76% accepted, 79 enrolled. In 2010, 47 master's awarded. *Degree requirements:* For master's, thesis; for doctorate, comprehensive exam, thesis/dissertation. *Entrance requirements:* For master's and doctorate, 3 letters of recommendation. Additional exam requirements/recommendations for international students: Required—TOEFL (minimum score 550 paper-based; 213 computer-based; 79 iBT), IELTS (minimum score 6.5). *Application deadline:* For fall admission, 1/1 priority date for domestic students, 1/1 for international students; for spring admission, 10/1 priority date for domestic students, 10/1 for international students. Application fee: $70. *Expenses:* Tuition: Full-time $20,862; part-time $1159 per term. One-time fee: $15. *Financial support:* Institutionally sponsored loans, scholarships/grants, and unspecified assistantships available. Financial award application deadline: 1/1; financial award applicants required to submit FAFSA. *Unit head:* Dr. Fred J. Looft, Head, 508-831-5231, Fax: 508-831-5491, E-mail: fjlooft@wpi.edu. *Application contact:* Lynne Dougherty, Administrative Assistant, 508-831-5301, Fax: 508-831-5717, E-mail: grad@wpi.edu.

Pharmaceutical Engineering

New Jersey Institute of Technology, Office of Graduate Studies, Newark College of Engineering, Department of Chemical Engineering, Interdisciplinary Program in Pharmaceutical Engineering, Newark, NJ 07102. Offers MS. Part-time and evening/weekend programs available. *Students:* 58 full-time (23 women), 21 part-time (7 women); includes 5 Black or African American, non-Hispanic/Latino; 1 American Indian or Alaska Native, non-Hispanic/Latino; 11 Asian, non-Hispanic/Latino; 4 Hispanic/Latino, 50 international. Average age 26. 172 applicants, 56% accepted, 20 enrolled. In 2010, 35 master's awarded. *Degree requirements:* For master's, thesis optional. *Entrance requirements:* For master's, GRE General Test. Additional exam requirements/recommendations for international students: Required—TOEFL (minimum score 550 paper-based; 213 computer-based; 79 iBT). *Application deadline:* For fall admission, 6/5 priority date for domestic students, 4/1 for international students; for spring admission, 11/15 for domestic and international students. Applications are processed on a rolling basis. Application fee: $65. Electronic applications accepted. *Expenses:* Tuition, state resident: full-time $14,724; part-time $818 per credit. Tuition, nonresident: full-time $20,304; part-time $1128 per credit. Required fees: $2272; $209 per credit. $103 per semester. One-time fee: $312 full-time; $212 part-time. *Financial support:* Fellowships with full and partial tuition reimbursements, research assistantships with full and partial tuition reimbursements, teaching assistantships with full and partial tuition reimbursements, career-related internships or fieldwork, Federal Work-Study, institutionally sponsored loans, and unspecified assistantships available. Financial award application deadline: 3/15. *Unit head:* Dr. Piero Armenante, Director, 973-596-3548, Fax: 973-596-8436, E-mail: piero.armenante@njit.edu. *Application contact:* Kathryn Kelly, Director of Admissions, 973-596-3300, Fax: 973-596-3461, E-mail: admissions@njit.edu.

Reliability Engineering

Arizona State University, Ira A. Fulton School of Engineering, ASU Engineering Online Programs, Tempe, AZ 85287. Offers construction (MS); embedded systems (M Eng); enterprise systems innovation and management (MSE); modeling and simulation (M Eng); quality and reliability engineering (M Eng); software engineering (MSE); systems engineering (M Eng). *Expenses:* Tuition, state resident: full-time $8510; part-time $608 per credit. Tuition, nonresident: full-time $16,542; part-time $919 per credit. Required fees: $339; $110 per credit. Part-time tuition and fees vary according to course load.

The University of Arizona, College of Engineering, Department of Systems and Industrial Engineering, Program in Reliability and Quality Engineering, Tucson, AZ 85721. Offers MS. Part-time programs available. Postbaccalaureate distance learning degree programs offered. *Students:* 1 (woman) full-time, all international. Average age 27. 1 applicant, 0% accepted, 0 enrolled. *Entrance requirements:* Additional exam requirements/recommendations for international students: Required—TOEFL (minimum score 550 paper-based; 213 computer-based; 79 iBT). *Application deadline:* Applications are processed on a rolling basis. Application fee: $75. Electronic applications accepted. *Expenses:* Tuition, state resident: full-time $7692. *Financial support:* Unspecified assistantships available. *Unit head:* Dr. K. Larry Head, Head, 520-621-6551, E-mail: larry@sie.arizona.edu. *Application contact:* Graduate Secretary, 520-626-4644, Fax: 520-621-6555, E-mail: gradapp@sie.arizona.edu.

University of Maryland, College Park, Academic Affairs, A. James Clark School of Engineering, Department of Continuing and Distance Learning in Engineering, College Park, MD 20742. Offers engineering (M Eng), including aerospace engineering, chemical engineering, civil engineering, electrical engineering, engineering, fire protection engineering, materials science and engineering, mechanical engineering, reliability engineering, systems engineering. *Faculty:* 4 full-time (1 woman), 11 part-time/adjunct (1 woman). *Students:* 56 full-time (15 women), 428 part-time (88 women); includes 153 minority (59 Black or African American, non-Hispanic/Latino; 63 Asian, non-Hispanic/Latino; 24 Hispanic/Latino; 7 Two or more races, non-Hispanic/Latino), 55 international. 551 applicants, 82% accepted, 360 enrolled. In 2010, 130 master's awarded. *Application deadline:* For fall admission, 8/15 for domestic students, 1/10 for international students; for spring admission, 12/15 for domestic students, 6/1 for international students. Applications are processed on a rolling basis. Application fee: $75. Electronic applications accepted. *Expenses:* Tuition, area resident: Part-time $471 per credit hour. Tuition, state resident: part-time $471 per credit hour. Tuition, nonresident: part-time $1016 per credit hour. Required fees: $337 per term. *Financial support:* In 2010–11, 2 research assistantships (averaging $20,285 per year), 7 teaching assistantships (averaging $16,962 per year) were awarded. *Unit head:* Dr. Darryll Pines, Dean, 301-405-0376, Fax: 301-314-5908, E-mail: pines@umd.edu. *Application contact:* Dr. Charles A. Caramello, Dean of the Graduate School, 301-405-0358, Fax: 301-314-9305, E-mail: ccaramel@umd.edu.

University of Maryland, College Park, Academic Affairs, A. James Clark School of Engineering, Department of Mechanical Engineering, Reliability Engineering Program, College Park, MD 20742. Offers M Eng, MS, PhD. Part-time and evening/weekend programs available. Postbaccalaureate distance learning degree programs offered. *Students:* 32 full-time (8 women), 28 part-time (6 women); includes 6 minority (3 Black or African American, non-Hispanic/Latino; 3 Hispanic/Latino), 21 international. 37 applicants, 38% accepted, 14 enrolled. In 2010, 5 master's, 7 doctorates awarded. *Degree requirements:* For master's, thesis optional; for doctorate, thesis/dissertation. *Entrance requirements:* For master's, GRE General Test, 3 letters of recommendation; for doctorate, GRE General Test, minimum GPA of 3.0. Additional exam requirements/recommendations for international students: Required—TOEFL. *Application deadline:* For fall admission, 5/1 for domestic students, 2/1 for international students; for spring admission, 10/1 for domestic students, 6/1 for international students. Applications are processed on a rolling basis. Application fee: $75. Electronic applications accepted. *Expenses:* Tuition, area resident: Part-time $471 per credit hour. Tuition, state resident: part-time $471 per credit hour. Tuition, nonresident: part-time $1016 per credit hour. Required fees: $337 per term. *Financial support:* In 2010–11, 10 research assistantships (averaging $22,943 per year), 2 teaching assistantships (averaging $17,544 per year) were awarded; fellowships, career-related internships or fieldwork also available. Financial award applicants required to submit FAFSA. *Faculty research:* Electron linear acceleration, x-ray and imaging. *Unit head:* Dr. Aris Christou, Professor and Chair, 301-405-5208, Fax: 301-314-9601, E-mail: christou@umd.edu. *Application contact:* Dr. Charles A. Caramello, Dean of Graduate School, 301-405-0358, Fax: 301-314-9305.

The University of Tennessee, Graduate School, College of Engineering, Department of Chemical Engineering, Knoxville, TN 37996. Offers chemical engineering (MS, PhD); reliability and maintainability engineering (MS); MS/MBA. Part-time programs available. *Faculty:* 12 full-time (1 woman), 17 part-time/adjunct (0 women). *Students:* 35 full-time (12 women), 5 part-time (1 woman); includes 1 American Indian or Alaska Native, non-Hispanic/Latino; 2 Asian, non-Hispanic/Latino, 27 international. Average age 24. 73 applicants, 18% accepted, 8 enrolled. In 2010, 4 master's, 3 doctorates awarded. *Degree requirements:* For master's, thesis or alternative; for doctorate, comprehensive exam, thesis/dissertation. *Entrance requirements:* For master's, GRE General Test, Minimum GPA of 2.7 (US degree holders); 3.0 (International degree holders); for doctorate, GRE General Test, Minimum GPA of 3.0 (previous graduate course work). Additional exam requirements/recommendations for international students: Required—TOEFL (minimum score 550 paper-based; 213 computer-based). *Application deadline:* For fall admission, 2/1 priority date for domestic and international students; for spring admission, 6/15 for domestic and international students. Applications are processed on a rolling basis. Application fee: $35. Electronic applications accepted. *Expenses:* Tuition, state resident: full-time $7440; part-time $414 per credit hour. Tuition, nonresident: full-time $22,478; part-time $1250 per credit hour. Required fees: $922; $43 per credit hour. Tuition and fees vary according to program. *Financial support:* In 2010–11, 33 students received support, including 26 research assistantships with full tuition reimbursements available (averaging $22,020 per year), 11 teaching assistantships with full tuition reimbursements available (averaging $20,760 per year); career-related internships or fieldwork, Federal Work-Study, institutionally sponsored loans, health care benefits, and unspecified assistantships also available. Financial award application deadline: 2/1; financial award applicants required to submit FAFSA. *Faculty research:* Bio-fuels; engineering of soft, functional and structural materials; fuel cells and energy storage devices; molecular and cellular bioengineering; molecular modeling and simulations. Total annual research expenditures: $2.8 million. *Unit head:* Dr. Bamin Khomami, Head, 865-974-2421, Fax: 865-974-7076, E-mail: bkhomami@utk.edu. *Application contact:* Dr. Paul Frymier, Graduate Program Coordinator, 865-974-4961, Fax: 865-974-7076, E-mail: pdf@utk.edu.

The University of Tennessee, Graduate School, College of Engineering, Department of Electrical Engineering and Computer Science, Knoxville, TN 37996. Offers computer engineering (MS, PhD); computer science (MS, PhD); electrical engineering (MS, PhD); reliability and maintainability engineering (MS); MS/MBA. Part-time programs available. *Faculty:* 39 full-time (7 women), 14 part-time/adjunct (0 women). *Students:* 174 full-time (35 women), 43 part-time (6 women); includes 2 Black or African American, non-Hispanic/Latino; 3 Asian, non-Hispanic/Latino; 2 Hispanic/Latino, 114 international. Average age 29. 644 applicants, 12% accepted, 51 enrolled. In 2010, 42 master's, 21 doctorates awarded. *Degree requirements:* For master's, thesis or alternative; for doctorate, comprehensive exam, thesis/dissertation. *Entrance requirements:* For master's, GRE General Test, Minimum GPA of 2.7 (US degree holders); 3.0 (International degree holders); 3-References; Personal statement; for doctorate, GRE General Test, Minimum GPA of 3.0 (previous graduate degree); 3-References; Personal statement. Additional exam requirements/recommendations for international students: Required—TOEFL (minimum score 550 paper-based; 213 computer-based). *Application deadline:* For fall admission, 2/1 priority date for domestic and international students; for spring admission, 6/15 for domestic and international students. Applications are processed on a rolling basis. Application fee: $35. Electronic applications accepted. *Expenses:* Tuition, state resident: full-time $7440; part-time $414 per credit hour. Tuition, nonresident: full-time $22,478; part-time $1250 per credit hour. Required fees: $922; $43 per credit hour. Tuition and fees vary according to program. *Financial support:* In 2010–11, 148 students received support, including 13 fellowships with full tuition reimbursements available (averaging $12,312 per year), 100 research assistantships with full tuition reimbursements available (averaging $16,248 per year), 91 teaching assistantships with full tuition reimbursements available (averaging $12,996 per year); career-related internships or fieldwork, Federal Work-Study, institutionally sponsored loans, health care benefits, and unspecified assistantships also available. Financial award application deadline: 2/1; financial award applicants required to submit FAFSA. *Faculty research:* Artificial intelligence and visualization; microelectronics, mixed-signal electronics, VLSI; embedded systems; scientific and distributed computing; computer vision, robotics, and image processing; power electronics, power systems, communications. Total annual research expenditures: $10.7 million. *Unit head:* Dr. Kevin Tomsovic, Head, 865-974-3461, Fax: 865-974-5483, E-mail: tomsovic@eecs.utk.edu. *Application contact:* Dr. Lynne E. Parker, Associate Head, 865-974-4394, Fax: 865-974-5483, E-mail: parker@eecs.utk.edu.

The University of Tennessee, Graduate School, College of Engineering, Department of Industrial and Information Engineering, Knoxville, TN 37966. Offers engineering management (MS); industrial engineering (MS, PhD); reliability and maintainability engineering (MS); MS/MBA. Part-time programs available. Postbaccalaureate distance learning degree programs offered (minimal on-campus study). *Faculty:* 8 full-time (1 woman), 6 part-time/adjunct (1 woman). *Students:* 40 full-time (12 women), 57 part-time (13 women); includes 9 Black or African American, non-Hispanic/Latino; 1 American Indian or Alaska Native, non-Hispanic/Latino; 6 Asian, non-Hispanic/Latino, 31 international. Average age 28. 61 applicants, 77% accepted, 11 enrolled. In 2010, 15 master's, 5 doctorates awarded. *Degree requirements:* For master's, thesis or alternative; for doctorate, comprehensive exam, thesis/dissertation. *Entrance requirements:* For master's, GRE General Test, Minimum GPA of 2.7 (US degree holders); 3.0 (International degree holders); for doctorate, GRE General Test, Minimum GPA of 3.0 (previous graduate course work). Additional exam requirements/recommendations for international students: Required—TOEFL (minimum score 550 paper-based; 213 computer-based). *Application deadline:* For fall admission, 2/1 priority date for domestic and international students; for spring admission, 6/15 for domestic and international students. Applications are processed on a rolling basis. Application fee: $35. Electronic applications accepted. *Expenses:* Tuition, state resident: full-time $7440; part-time $414 per credit hour. Tuition, nonresident: full-time $22,478; part-time $1250 per credit hour. Required fees: $922; $43 per credit hour. Tuition and fees vary according to program. *Financial support:* In 2010–11, 27 students received support, including 17 research assistantships with full tuition reimbursements available (averaging $12,372 per year), 11 teaching assistantships with full tuition reimbursements available (averaging $6,792 per year); career-related internships or fieldwork, Federal Work-Study, institutionally sponsored loans, health care benefits, and unspecified assistantships also available. Financial award application deadline: 2/1; financial award applicants required to submit FAFSA. *Faculty research:* Defense-oriented supply chain modeling; dependability and reliability of large computer networks; design of lean, reliable systems; new product development; operations research in the automotive industry. Total annual research expenditures: $839,000. *Unit head:* Dr. Rapinder Sawhney, Department Head, 865-974-3333, Fax: 865-974-0588, E-mail: sawhney@utk.edu. *Application contact:* Dr. Denise Jackson, Graduate Representative, 865-946-3248, E-mail: djackson@utk.edu.

The University of Tennessee, Graduate School, College of Engineering, Department of Materials Science and Engineering, Knoxville, TN 37996-2200. Offers materials science and engineering (MS, PhD); polymer engineering (MS, PhD); reliability and maintainability engineering (MS); MS/MBA. Part-time programs available. *Faculty:* 31 full-time (2 women), 4 part-time/adjunct (2 women). *Students:* 80 full-time (15 women), 12 part-time (1 woman); includes 4 Black or African American, non-Hispanic/Latino; 3 Asian, non-Hispanic/Latino; 3 Hispanic/Latino, 54 international. Average age 22. 187 applicants, 20% accepted, 27 enrolled. In 2010, 10 master's, 13 doctorates awarded. *Degree requirements:* For master's, thesis or alternative; for doctorate, comprehensive exam, thesis/dissertation. *Entrance requirements:* For master's, GRE General Test, Minimum GPA of 2.7 (US degree holders); 3.0 (International degree holders); 3-References; for doctorate, GRE General Test, Minimum GPA of 3.0 (previous graduate course work); 3-References. Additional exam requirements/recommendations for international students: Required—TOEFL (minimum score 550 paper-based; 213 computer-based). *Application deadline:* For fall admission, 2/1 priority date for domestic and international students; for spring admission, 6/15 for domestic and international students. Applications are processed on a rolling basis. Application fee: $35. Electronic applications accepted. *Expenses:*

Tuition, state resident: full-time $7440; part-time $414 per credit hour. Tuition, nonresident: full-time $22,478; part-time $1250 per credit hour. Required fees: $922; $43 per credit hour. Tuition and fees vary according to program. *Financial support:* In 2010–11, 73 students received support, including 5 fellowships with full tuition reimbursements available (averaging $9,996 per year), 84 research assistantships with full tuition reimbursements available (averaging $19,272 per year), 12 teaching assistantships with full tuition reimbursements available (averaging $19,752 per year); career-related internships or fieldwork, Federal Work-Study, institutionally sponsored loans, health care benefits, and unspecified assistantships also available. Financial award application deadline: 2/1; financial award applicants required to submit FAFSA. *Faculty research:* Biomaterials; functional materials electronic, magnetic and optical; high temperature materials; mechanical behavior of materials; neutron materials science. Total annual research expenditures: $7.4 million. *Unit head:* Dr. George Pharr, Head, 865-974-5336, Fax: 865-974-4115, E-mail: pharr@utk.edu. *Application contact:* Dr. Roberto S. Benson, Associate Head, 865-974-5347, Fax: 865-974-4115, E-mail: rbenson1@utk.edu.

The University of Tennessee, Graduate School, College of Engineering, Department of Nuclear and Radiological Engineering, Knoxville, TN 37996. Offers nuclear engineering (MS, PhD); reliability and maintainability engineering (MS); MS/MBA. Part-time programs available. Postbaccalaureate distance learning degree programs offered (minimal on-campus study). *Faculty:* 14 full-time (1 woman), 54 part-time/adjunct (2 women). *Students:* 68 full-time (7 women), 30 part-time (4 women); includes 3 Black or African American, non-Hispanic/Latino; 2 Asian, non-Hispanic/Latino; 1 Hispanic/Latino, 9 international. Average age 30. 108 applicants, 56% accepted, 35 enrolled. In 2010, 11 master's, 5 doctorates awarded. *Degree requirements:* For master's, thesis or alternative; for doctorate, comprehensive exam, thesis/dissertation. *Entrance requirements:* For master's, GRE General Test, Minimum GPA of 2.7 (US degree holders); 3.0 (International degree holders); for doctorate, GRE General Test, Minimum GPA of 3.0 (previous graduate course work). Additional exam requirements/recommendations for international students: Required—TOEFL (minimum score 550 paper-based; 213 computer-based). *Application deadline:* For fall admission, 2/1 priority date for domestic and international students; for spring admission, 6/15 for domestic and international students. Applications are processed on a rolling basis. Application fee: $35. Electronic applications accepted. *Expenses:* Tuition, state resident: full-time $7440; part-time $414 per credit hour. Tuition, nonresident: full-time $22,478; part-time $1250 per credit hour. Required fees: $922; $43 per credit hour. Tuition and fees vary according to program. *Financial support:* In 2010–11, 63 students received support, including 16 fellowships with full tuition reimbursements available (averaging $25,200 per year), 46 research assistantships with full tuition reimbursements available (averaging $25,200 per year), 12 teaching assistantships with full tuition reimbursements available (averaging $25,200 per year); career-related internships or fieldwork, Federal Work-Study, institutionally sponsored loans, health care benefits, and unspecified assistantships also available. Financial award application deadline: 2/1; financial award applicants required to submit FAFSA. *Faculty research:* Heat transfer and fluid dynamics; instrumentation, sensors and controls; nuclear materials and nuclear security; radiological engineering; reactor system design and safety. Total annual research expenditures: $4.5 million. *Unit head:* Dr. Harold L. Dodds, Head, 865-974-2525, Fax: 865-974-0668, E-mail: hdj@utk.edu. *Application contact:* Dr. Masood Parang, Associate Dean of Student Affairs, 865-974-2454, Fax: 865-974-9871, E-mail: mparang@utk.edu.

Safety Engineering

Embry-Riddle Aeronautical University–Prescott, Program in Safety Science, Prescott, AZ 86301-3720. Offers MSSS. *Faculty:* 5 full-time (1 woman). *Students:* 45 full-time (11 women), 4 part-time (2 women); includes 6 minority (1 Black or African American, non-Hispanic/Latino; 3 Hispanic/Latino; 2 Two or more races, non-Hispanic/Latino), 9 international. Average age 28. 38 applicants, 63% accepted, 15 enrolled. In 2010, 17 master's awarded. *Degree requirements:* For master's, thesis (for some programs). *Entrance requirements:* Additional exam requirements/recommendations for international students: Required—TOEFL (minimum score 550 paper-based; 213 computer-based; 79 iBT). *Application deadline:* For fall admission, 8/1 priority date for domestic students; for spring admission, 12/1 priority date for domestic students. Applications are processed on a rolling basis. Application fee: $50. Electronic applications accepted. *Expenses:* Tuition: Full-time $14,040; part-time $1170 per credit hour. *Financial support:* In 2010–11, 36 students received support, including 8 research assistantships with full and partial tuition reimbursements available (averaging $1,215 per year); career-related internships or fieldwork, Federal Work-Study, and unspecified assistantships also available. Support available to part-time students. Financial award application deadline: 4/15; financial award applicants required to submit FAFSA. *Unit head:* Dr. Gary Northam, Dean, College of Aviation, 928-777-3964, Fax: 928-777-6958. *Application contact:* Debra Cates-Foster, Graduate Admissions Coordinator, 928-777-6687, E-mail: debra.cates@erau.edu.

Indiana University Bloomington, School of Health, Physical Education and Recreation, Department of Applied Health Science, Bloomington, IN 47405-7000. Offers health behavior (PhD); health promotion (MS); human development/family studies (MS); nutrition science (MS); public health (MPH); safety management (MS); school and college health programs (MS). *Accreditation:* CEPH (one or more programs are accredited). *Faculty:* 24 full-time (12 women). *Students:* 143 full-time (105 women), 32 part-time (20 women); includes 36 Black or African American, non-Hispanic/Latino; 2 American Indian or Alaska Native, non-Hispanic/Latino; 2 Asian, non-Hispanic/Latino; 7 Hispanic/Latino; 1 Two or more races, non-Hispanic/Latino, 28 international. Average age 30. 135 applicants, 80% accepted, 73 enrolled. In 2010, 49 master's, 7 doctorates awarded. *Degree requirements:* For master's, thesis optional; for doctorate, thesis/dissertation. *Entrance requirements:* For master's, GRE (MS in nutrition science), 3 recommendations; for doctorate, GRE, 3 recommendations. Additional exam requirements/recommendations for international students: Required—TOEFL (minimum score 550 paper-based; 213 computer-based; 79 iBT). *Application deadline:* For fall admission, 4/30 priority date for domestic students, 12/1 priority date for international students; for spring admission, 11/15 priority date for domestic students, 9/1 priority date for international students. Application fee: $55 ($65 for international students). *Financial support:* Fellowships, research assistantships with full and partial tuition reimbursements, teaching assistantships with full and partial tuition reimbursements, career-related internships or fieldwork, Federal Work-Study, institutionally sponsored loans, scholarships/grants, tuition waivers (partial), and fee remissions available. Financial award application deadline: 3/1. *Faculty research:* Cancer education, HIV/AIDS and drug education, public health, parent-child interactions, safety education. Total annual research expenditures: $2.8 million. *Unit head:* Dr. Mohammad R. Torabi, Chair, 812-855-4808, Fax: 812-855-3936, E-mail: torabi@indiana.edu. *Application contact:* Dr. Mohammad R. Torabi, Chair, 812-855-4808, Fax: 812-855-3936, E-mail: torabi@indiana.edu.

Murray State University, College of Health Sciences and Human Services, Program in Occupational Safety and Health, Murray, KY 42071. Offers environmental science (MS); industrial hygiene (MS); safety management (MS). *Accreditation:* ABET. Part-time programs available. *Degree requirements:* For master's, comprehensive exam, thesis optional, professional internship. Electronic applications accepted. *Faculty research:* Light effects on plant growth, ergonomics, toxic effects of pets' pesticides, traffic safety.

National University, Academic Affairs, School of Engineering and Technology, Department of Applied Engineering, La Jolla, CA 92037-1011. Offers database administration (MS); engineering management (MS); environmental engineering (MS), homeland security and safety engineering (MS); system engineering (MS); wireless communications (MS). Part-time and evening/weekend programs available. Postbaccalaureate distance learning degree programs offered (no on-campus study). *Faculty:* 6 full-time (1 woman), 69 part-time/adjunct (12 women). *Students:* 82 full-time (16 women), 153 part-time (35 women); includes 87 minority (18 Black or African American, non-Hispanic/Latino; 1 American Indian or Alaska Native, non-Hispanic/Latino; 34 Asian, non-Hispanic/Latino; 28 Hispanic/Latino; 2 Native Hawaiian or other Pacific Islander, non-Hispanic/Latino; 4 Two or more races, non-Hispanic/Latino), 60 international. Average age 31. 166 applicants, 100% accepted, 106 enrolled. In 2010, 79 master's awarded. *Degree requirements:* For master's, thesis. *Entrance requirements:* For master's, interview, minimum GPA of 2.5. Additional exam requirements/recommendations for international students: Required—TOEFL (minimum score 550 paper-based; 213 computer-based; 79 iBT), IELTS (minimum score 6). *Application deadline:* Applications are processed on a rolling basis. Application fee: $60 ($65 for international students). Electronic applications accepted. *Expenses:* Tuition: Full-time $9450; part-time $350 per unit. Required fees: $350 per unit. One-time fee: $60. *Financial support:* Career-related internships or fieldwork, institutionally sponsored loans, scholarships/grants, and tuition waivers (partial) available. Support available to part-time students. Financial award application deadline: 6/30; financial award applicants required to submit FAFSA. *Unit head:* Dr. Shekar Viswanathan, Chair and Associate Professor, 858-309-8416, Fax: 858-309-3420, E-mail: sviswana@nu.edu. *Application contact:* Dominick Giovanniello, Associate Regional Dean—San Diego, 800-NAT-UNIV, Fax: 858-541-7792, E-mail: dgiovann@nu.edu.

New Jersey Institute of Technology, Office of Graduate Studies, Newark College of Engineering, Department of Industrial and Manufacturing Engineering, Program in Occupational Safety and Health Engineering, Newark, NJ 07102. Offers MS. Part-time and evening/weekend programs available. *Students:* 6 full-time (1 woman), 7 part-time (4 women); includes 3 Black or African American, non-Hispanic/Latino; 3 Asian, non-Hispanic/Latino; 1 Hispanic/Latino, 2 international. Average age 33. 11 applicants, 27% accepted, 3 enrolled. *Degree requirements:* For master's, thesis or alternative. *Entrance requirements:* For master's, GRE General Test. Additional exam requirements/recommendations for international students: Required—TOEFL (minimum score 550 paper-based; 213 computer-based; 79 iBT). *Application deadline:* For fall admission, 6/5 priority date for domestic students, 4/1 for international students; for spring admission, 11/15 for domestic and international students. Applications are processed on a rolling basis. Application fee: $65. Electronic applications accepted. *Expenses:* Tuition, state resident: full-time $14,724; part-time $818 per credit. Tuition, nonresident: full-time $20,304; part-time $1128 per credit. Required fees: $2272; $209 per credit. $103 per semester. One-time fee: $312 full-time; $212 part-time. *Financial support:* Fellowships with full and partial tuition reimbursements, research assistantships with full and partial tuition reimbursements, teaching assistantships with full and partial tuition reimbursements, career-related internships or fieldwork, Federal Work-Study, institutionally sponsored loans, and unspecified assistantships available. Financial award application deadline: 3/15. *Faculty research:* Human factors engineering, manufacturing systems, materials, manufacturing automation and computer integration. *Unit head:* Dr. Rajpal Sodhi, Interim Chair, 973-596-3362, E-mail: rajpal.s.sodhi@njit.edu. *Application contact:* Kathryn Kelly, Director of Admissions, 973-596-3300, Fax: 973-596-3461, E-mail: admissions@njit.edu.

The University of Alabama at Birmingham, School of Engineering, Program in Engineering, Birmingham, AL 35294. Offers advanced safety engineering and management (M Eng); construction engineering management (M Eng); information engineering and management (M Eng). *Students:* 4 full-time (2 women), 170 part-time (42 women); includes 62 minority (46 Black or African American, non-Hispanic/Latino; 1 American Indian or Alaska Native, non-Hispanic/Latino; 8 Asian, non-Hispanic/Latino; 6 Hispanic/Latino; 1 Two or more races, non-Hispanic/Latino), 4 international. Average age 36. 99 applicants, 97% accepted, 81 enrolled. In 2010, 78 master's awarded. *Expenses:* Tuition, state resident: full-time $5482. Tuition, nonresident: full-time $12,430. Tuition and fees vary according to program. *Unit head:* Dr. Melinda Lalor, Dean, 205-934-8410. *Application contact:* Julie Bryant, Director of Graduate Admissions, 205-934-8227, Fax: 205-934-8413, E-mail: jbryant@uab.edu.

University of Minnesota, Duluth, Graduate School, Swenson College of Science and Engineering, Department of Mechanical and Industrial Engineering, Duluth, MN 55812-2496. Offers engineering management (MSEM); environmental health and safety (MEHS). Part-time and evening/weekend programs available. Postbaccalaureate distance learning degree programs offered (no on-campus study). *Degree requirements:* For master's, comprehensive exam, thesis or alternative, capstone design project (MSEM), field project (MEHS). *Entrance requirements:* For master's, GRE (MEHS), interview (MEHS), letters of recommendation. Additional exam requirements/recommendations for international students: Required—TOEFL (minimum score 550 paper-based; 213 computer-based). *Faculty research:* Transportation, ergonomics, toxicology, supply chain management, automation and robotics.

University of Southern California, Graduate School, Viterbi School of Engineering, Daniel J. Epstein Department of Industrial and Systems Engineering, Los Angeles, CA 90089. Offers digital supply chain management (MS); engineering management (MS); engineering technology communication (Graduate Certificate); health systems operations (Graduate Certificate); industrial and systems engineering (MS, PhD, Engr); manufacturing engineering (MS); operations research engineering (MS); optimization and supply chain management (Graduate Certificate); product development engineering (MS); safety systems and security (MS); systems architecting and engineering (MS, Graduate Certificate); systems safety and security (Graduate Certificate); transportation systems (Graduate Certificate); MS/MBA. Part-time and evening/weekend programs available. Postbaccalaureate distance learning degree programs offered (no on-campus study). *Faculty:* 12 full-time (2 women), 21 part-time/adjunct (2 women). *Students:* 224 full-time (69 women), 143 part-time (32 women); includes 63 minority (6 Black or African American, non-Hispanic/Latino; 35 Asian, non-Hispanic/Latino; 17 Hispanic/Latino; 5 Two or more races, non-Hispanic/Latino), 253 international. 669 applicants, 45% accepted, 155 enrolled. In 2010, 98 master's, 7 doctorates awarded. Terminal master's awarded for partial completion of doctoral program. *Degree requirements:* For master's, thesis optional; for doctorate, thesis/dissertation. *Entrance requirements:* For master's and doctorate, GRE General Test. *Application deadline:* For fall admission, 12/1 priority date for domestic students, 11/1 priority date for international students; for spring admission, 9/15 priority date for domestic and international students. Applications are processed on a rolling basis. Application fee: $85. Electronic applications accepted. *Expenses:* Tuition: Full-time $31,240; part-time $1420 per unit. Required fees: $600. One-time fee: $35 full-time. Full-time tuition and fees vary according to degree level and program. *Financial support:* In 2010–11, fellowships with full tuition reimbursements (averaging $30,000 per year), research assistantships with full tuition reimbursements (averaging $20,000 per year), teaching assistantships with full tuition reimbursements (averaging $20,000 per year) were awarded; career-related internships or fieldwork, scholarships/grants, health care benefits, and unspecified assistantships also available. Financial award application deadline: 12/1; financial award applicants required to submit CSS PROFILE or FAFSA. *Faculty research:* Health systems, music cognition and retrieval, transportation and logistics, manufacturing and automation, engineering systems design, risk and economic

Safety Engineering

University of Southern California (continued)
analysis. Total annual research expenditures: $1 million. *Unit head:* Dr. F. Stan Settles, Chair, 213-740-4893, E-mail: isedept@usc.edu. *Application contact:* Evelyn Felina, Director of Student Affairs, 213-740-7549, E-mail: efelina@usc.edu.

West Virginia University, College of Engineering and Mineral Resources, Department of Industrial and Management Systems Engineering, Program in Safety Management, Morgantown, WV 26506. Offers MS. *Accreditation:* ABET. *Degree requirements:* For master's, comprehensive exam, thesis optional. *Entrance requirements:* For master's, minimum GPA of 3.0 for regular admission; 2.75 for provisional. Additional exam requirements/recommendations for international students: Required—TOEFL (minimum score 550 paper-based; 213 computer-based; 80 iBT). Electronic applications accepted.

Systems Engineering

Air Force Institute of Technology, Graduate School of Engineering and Management, Department of Aeronautics and Astronautics, Dayton, OH 45433-7765. Offers aeronautical engineering (MS, PhD); astronautical engineering (MS, PhD); materials science (MS, PhD); space operations (MS); systems engineering (MS, PhD). *Accreditation:* ABET (one or more programs are accredited). Part-time programs available. *Degree requirements:* For master's, thesis; for doctorate, thesis/dissertation. *Entrance requirements:* For master's and doctorate, GRE General Test, minimum GPA of 3.0, U.S. citizenship. *Faculty research:* Computational fluid dynamics, experimental aerodynamics, computational structural mechanics, experimental structural mechanics, aircraft and spacecraft stability and control.

The American University of Athens, School of Graduate Studies, Athens, Greece. Offers biomedical sciences (MS); business (MBA); business communication (MA); computer sciences (MS); engineering and applied sciences (MS); politics and policy making (MA); systems engineering (MS); telecommunications (MS). *Entrance requirements:* For master's, resume, 2 recommendation letters. Additional exam requirements/recommendations for international students: Required—TOEFL (minimum score 550 paper-based; 213 computer-based). *Faculty research:* Nanotechnology, environmental sciences, rock mechanics, human skin studies, Monte Carlo algorithms and software.

Arizona State University, Ira A. Fulton School of Engineering, ASU Engineering Online Programs, Tempe, AZ 85287. Offers construction (MS); embedded systems (M Eng); enterprise systems innovation and management (MSE); modeling and simulation (M Eng); quality and reliability engineering (M Eng); software engineering (MSE); systems engineering (M Eng). *Expenses:* Tuition, state resident: full-time $8510; part-time $608 per credit. Tuition, nonresident: full-time $16,542; part-time $919 per credit. Required fees: $339; $110 per credit. Part-time tuition and fees vary according to course load.

Auburn University, Graduate School, Ginn College of Engineering, Department of Industrial and Systems Engineering, Auburn University, AL 36849. Offers MISE, MS, PhD. Part-time programs available. *Faculty:* 10 full-time (1 woman), 4 part-time/adjunct (0 women). *Students:* 89 full-time (21 women), 49 part-time (13 women); includes 12 Black or African American, non-Hispanic/Latino; 3 Asian, non-Hispanic/Latino; 1 Hispanic/Latino, 66 international. Average age 29. 252 applicants, 62% accepted, 50 enrolled. In 2010, 20 master's, 7 doctorates awarded. *Degree requirements:* For master's, thesis (MS); for doctorate, thesis/dissertation. *Entrance requirements:* For master's and doctorate, GRE General Test. *Application deadline:* For fall admission, 7/7 for domestic students; for spring admission, 11/24 for domestic students. Applications are processed on a rolling basis. Application fee: $50 ($60 for international students). *Expenses:* Tuition, state resident: full-time $7002. Tuition, nonresident: full-time $21,898. International tuition: $22,116 full-time. Required fees: $892. Tuition and fees vary according to course load and program. *Financial support:* Fellowships, research assistantships, teaching assistantships, Federal Work-Study available. Support available to part-time students. Financial award application deadline: 3/15; financial award applicants required to submit FAFSA. *Unit head:* Dr. Alice E. Smith, Chair, 334-844-1401. *Application contact:* Dr. George Flowers, Dean of the Graduate School, 334-844-2125.

Boston University, College of Engineering, Division of Systems Engineering, Boston, MA 02215. Offers M Eng, MS, PhD. Part-time programs available. *Students:* 35 full-time (4 women), 2 part-time (1 woman), 32 international. Average age 27. 133 applicants, 15% accepted, 14 enrolled. In 2010, 2 master's, 2 doctorates awarded. Terminal master's awarded for partial completion of doctoral program. *Degree requirements:* For master's, thesis (for some programs); for doctorate, comprehensive exam, thesis/dissertation. *Entrance requirements:* For master's and doctorate, GRE General Test. Additional exam requirements/recommendations for international students: Required—TOEFL (minimum score 550 paper-based; 213 computer-based; 84 iBT), IELTS (minimum score 6). *Application deadline:* For fall admission, 4/1 for domestic and international students; for spring admission, 10/1 for domestic and international students. Applications are processed on a rolling basis. Application fee: $70. Electronic applications accepted. *Expenses:* Tuition: Full-time $39,314; part-time $1228 per credit. Required fees: $40 per semester. *Financial support:* In 2010–11, 29 students received support, including 7 fellowships with full tuition reimbursements available (averaging $28,200 per year), 17 research assistantships with full tuition reimbursements available (averaging $18,800 per year), 3 teaching assistantships with full tuition reimbursements available (averaging $18,800 per year); career-related internships or fieldwork, Federal Work-Study, institutionally sponsored loans, scholarships/grants, traineeships, and health care benefits also available. Financial award application deadline: 1/15; financial award applicants required to submit FAFSA. *Faculty research:* Communication, network, sensing, and information systems; control systems, automation, and robotics; discrete event, queuing, hybrid, and complex systems; optimization and algorithms; production, service, distribution, and energy systems. *Unit head:* Dr. Christos Cassandras, Division Head, 617-353-7154, Fax: 617-353-5548, E-mail: cgc@bu.edu. *Application contact:* Stephen Doherty, Director of Graduate Programs, 617-353-9760, Fax: 617-353-0259, E-mail: enggrad@bu.edu.

California Institute of Technology, Division of Engineering and Applied Science, Option in Control and Dynamical Systems, Pasadena, CA 91125-0001. Offers MS, PhD. *Faculty:* 2 full-time (0 women). *Students:* 25 full-time (6 women). 97 applicants, 8% accepted, 3 enrolled. In 2010, 3 doctorates awarded. *Degree requirements:* For doctorate, thesis/dissertation. *Application deadline:* For fall admission, 1/15 for domestic students. Application fee: $0. *Financial support:* In 2010–11, 8 fellowships, 13 research assistantships, 2 teaching assistantships were awarded. *Faculty research:* Robustness, multivariable and nonlinear systems, optimal control, decentralized control, modeling and system identification for robust control. *Unit head:* Dr. Houman Owhadi, Academic Officer, 626-395-4547, E-mail: owhadi@caltech.edu. *Application contact:* Natalie Gilmore, Assistant Dean of Graduate Studies, 626-395-3812, Fax: 626-577-9246, E-mail: ngilmore@caltech.edu.

California State University, Fullerton, Graduate Studies, College of Engineering and Computer Science, Department of Electrical Engineering, Fullerton, CA 92834-9480. Offers electrical engineering (MS); systems engineering (MS). Part-time programs available. *Students:* 48 full-time (10 women), 120 part-time (26 women); includes 2 Black or African American, non-Hispanic/Latino; 35 Asian, non-Hispanic/Latino; 3 Hispanic/Latino; 1 Two or more races, non-Hispanic/Latino, 92 international. Average age 27. 238 applicants, 66% accepted, 54 enrolled. In 2010, 43 master's awarded. *Degree requirements:* For master's, comprehensive exam, project or thesis. *Entrance requirements:* For master's, GRE General Test, GRE Subject Test, minimum undergraduate GPA of 2.5, 3.0 graduate. Application fee: $55. *Financial support:* Career-related internships or fieldwork, Federal Work-Study, institutionally sponsored loans, and scholarships/grants available. Support available to part-time students. Financial award application deadline: 3/1; financial award applicants required to submit FAFSA. *Unit head:* Dr. Mostafa Shiva, Chair, 657-278-3013. *Application contact:* Admissions/Applications, 657-278-2371.

California State University, Northridge, Graduate Studies, College of Engineering and Computer Science, Department of Manufacturing Systems Engineering and Management, Northridge, CA 91330. Offers engineering automation (MS); engineering management (MS); manufacturing systems engineering (MS); materials engineering (MS). Postbaccalaureate distance learning degree programs offered. *Entrance requirements:* For master's, GRE (if cumulative undergraduate GPA less than 3.0).

Carleton University, Faculty of Graduate Studies, Faculty of Engineering and Design, Ottawa-Carleton Institute for Electrical Engineering, Department of Systems and Computer Engineering, Ottawa, ON K1S 5B6, Canada. Offers electrical engineering (MA Sc, PhD); information and systems science (M Sc); technology innovation management (M Eng, MA Sc). PhD program offered jointly with University of Ottawa. *Degree requirements:* For master's, thesis optional. *Entrance requirements:* For master's, honors degree. Additional exam requirements/recommendations for international students: Required—TOEFL. *Faculty research:* Design manufacturing management; network design, protocols, and performance; software engineering; wireless and satellite communications.

Carnegie Mellon University, Carnegie Institute of Technology, Information Networking Institute, Pittsburgh, PA 15213. Offers information networking (MS); information security technology and management (MS); information technology—information security (MS); information technology—mobility (MS); information technology—software management (MS). *Degree requirements:* For master's, thesis optional. *Entrance requirements:* For master's, GRE General Test, bachelor's degree in computer science, computer engineering, or electrical engineering, or related technology degree; programming skills (C/C++ fluency for some programs). Additional exam requirements/recommendations for international students: Required—TOEFL. *Faculty research:* Computer forensics and incident response; dependable systems, embedded systems, mobile systems, and sensor networks; computer and information networks, network and information security, human and socio-economic factors in secure system design; wireless sensor networks, survivable embedded systems, signal processing/compression; strategic management, international strategic management, group dynamics and decision-making structures, simulated competitive environments.

Case Western Reserve University, School of Graduate Studies, Case School of Engineering, Department of Electrical Engineering and Computer Science, Cleveland, OH 44106. Offers computer engineering (MS, PhD); computing and information sciences (MS, PhD); electrical engineering (MS, PhD); systems and control engineering (MS, PhD). Part-time and evening/weekend programs available. Postbaccalaureate distance learning degree programs offered (minimal on-campus study). *Faculty:* 33 full-time (2 women). *Students:* 190 full-time (31 women), 26 part-time (4 women); includes 3 Black or African American, non-Hispanic/Latino; 6 Asian, non-Hispanic/Latino, 128 international. In 2010, 32 master's, 13 doctorates awarded. Terminal master's awarded for partial completion of doctoral program. *Degree requirements:* For master's, thesis; for doctorate, thesis/dissertation, qualifying exam, teaching experience. *Entrance requirements:* For master's and doctorate, GRE General Test. Additional exam requirements/recommendations for international students: Required—TOEFL. *Application deadline:* For fall admission, 2/1 for domestic students; for spring admission, 11/1 for domestic students. Applications are processed on a rolling basis. Application fee: $50. *Financial support:* Fellowships with full and partial tuition reimbursements, research assistantships with full and partial tuition reimbursements, teaching assistantships, career-related internships or fieldwork, Federal Work-Study, and institutionally sponsored loans available. Support available to part-time students. Financial award application deadline: 3/1; financial award applicants required to submit FAFSA. *Faculty research:* Applied artificial intelligence, automation, computer-aided design and testing of digital systems. Total annual research expenditures: $6.8 million. *Unit head:* Michael Branicky, Department Chair, 216-368-6888, E-mail: branicky@case.edu. *Application contact:* David Easler, Student Affairs Coordinator, 216-368-4080, Fax: 216-368-2801, E-mail: david.easler@case.edu.

Colorado School of Mines, Graduate School, Division of Engineering, Golden, CO 80401. Offers engineering systems (ME, MS, PhD). Part-time programs available. *Faculty:* 39 full-time (7 women), 21 part-time/adjunct (4 women). *Students:* 171 full-time (34 women), 53 part-time (5 women); includes 1 Black or African American, non-Hispanic/Latino; 1 American Indian or Alaska Native, non-Hispanic/Latino; 9 Asian, non-Hispanic/Latino; 12 Hispanic/Latino, 41 international. Average age 30. 245 applicants, 74% accepted, 73 enrolled. In 2010, 69 master's, 4 doctorates awarded. *Degree requirements:* For master's, thesis (for some programs); for doctorate, one foreign language, comprehensive exam, thesis/dissertation. *Entrance requirements:* For master's and doctorate, GRE General Test. Additional exam requirements/recommendations for international students: Required—TOEFL (minimum score 550 paper-based; 213 computer-based; 80 iBT). *Application deadline:* For fall admission, 1/15 priority date for domestic and international students; for spring admission, 10/15 priority date for domestic and international students. Application fee: $50 ($70 for international students). Electronic applications accepted. *Expenses:* Tuition, state resident: full-time $11,550; part-time $641 per credit. Tuition, nonresident: full-time $25,980; part-time $1444 per credit. Required fees: $1874; $937 per semester. *Financial support:* In 2010–11, 102 students received support, including 29 fellowships with full tuition reimbursements available (averaging $20,000 per year), 53 research assistantships with full tuition reimbursements available (averaging $20,000 per year), 20 teaching assistantships with full tuition reimbursements available (averaging $20,000 per year); scholarships/grants, health care benefits, and unspecified assistantships also available. Financial award application deadline: 1/15; financial award applicants required to submit FAFSA. *Faculty research:* Geotechnical engineering, offshore mechanics, analytical design, process simulation, health monitoring. Total annual research expenditures: $2.3 million. *Unit head:* Dr. Kevin Moore, Division Director, 303-273-3899, Fax: 303-273-3602, E-mail: kmoore@mines.edu. *Application contact:* Sara Perna, Administrative Assistant, 303-384-2394, Fax: 303-273-3602, E-mail: sperna@mines.edu.

Colorado State University–Pueblo, College of Education, Engineering and Professional Studies, Department of Engineering, Pueblo, CO 81001-4901. Offers industrial and systems engineering (MS). *Degree requirements:* For master's, thesis optional. *Entrance requirements:* For master's, GRE General Test. Additional exam requirements/recommendations for international students: Required—TOEFL (minimum score 500 paper-based). *Faculty research:* Nanotechnology, applied operations, research transportation, decision analysis.

Colorado Technical University Colorado Springs, Graduate Studies, Program in Systems Engineering, Colorado Springs, CO 80907-3896. Offers MS.

Colorado Technical University Denver, Program in Systems Engineering, Greenwood Village, CO 80111. Offers MS.

Concordia University, School of Graduate Studies, Faculty of Engineering and Computer Science, Concordia Institute for Information Systems Engineering (CIISE), Montréal, QC H3G 1M8, Canada. Offers 3D graphics and game development (Certificate); information systems security (M Eng, MA Sc); quality systems engineering (M Eng, MA Sc); service engineering and network management (Certificate).

Cornell University, Graduate School, Graduate Fields of Engineering, Field of Systems Engineering, Ithaca, NY 14853-0001. Offers M Eng. *Faculty:* 19 full-time (2 women). *Students:* 99 full-time (15 women); includes 3 Black or African American, non-Hispanic/Latino; 19 Asian, non-Hispanic/Latino; 8 Hispanic/Latino, 10 international. Average age 25. 93 applicants, 89% accepted, 72 enrolled. In 2010, 41 master's awarded. *Degree requirements:* For master's, thesis. *Entrance requirements:* For master's, GRE General Test. Additional exam requirements/recommendations for international students: Required—TOEFL (minimum score 600 paper-based; 250 computer-based; 77 iBT). *Application deadline:* For fall admission, 2/1 priority date for domestic students. Application fee: $70. *Expenses:* Tuition: Full-time $29,500. Required fees: $76. Tuition and fees vary according to degree level and program. *Financial support:* In 2010–11, 1 fellowship with full and partial tuition reimbursement, 1 research assistantship with full and partial tuition reimbursement were awarded; teaching assistantships with full and partial tuition reimbursements, institutionally sponsored loans, scholarships/grants, health care benefits, tuition waivers (full and partial), and unspecified assistantships also available. Financial award applicants required to submit FAFSA. *Faculty research:* Space systems, systems engineering of mechanical and aerospace systems, multi-echelon inventory theory, math modeling of complex systems, chain supply integration. *Unit head:* Director of Graduate Studies, 607-255-8998, Fax: 607-255-9004, E-mail: systemseng@cornell.edu. *Application contact:* Graduate Field Assistant, 607-255-8998, Fax: 607-255-9004, E-mail: systemseng@cornell.edu.

Embry-Riddle Aeronautical University–Daytona, Daytona Beach Campus Graduate Program, Department of Human Factors and Systems, Daytona Beach, FL 32114-3900. Offers human factors engineering (MSHFS); systems engineering (MSHFS). Part-time and evening/weekend programs available. *Faculty:* 6 full-time (2 women). *Students:* 40 full-time (15 women), 15 part-time (8 women); includes 13 minority (3 Black or African American, non-Hispanic/Latino; 1 American Indian or Alaska Native, non-Hispanic/Latino; 7 Hispanic/Latino; 2 Two or more races, non-Hispanic/Latino), 4 international. Average age 26. 38 applicants, 71% accepted, 22 enrolled. In 2010, 4 master's awarded. *Degree requirements:* For master's, thesis, practicum, qualifying oral exam. *Entrance requirements:* For master's, minimum GPA of 2.5. Additional exam requirements/recommendations for international students: Required—TOEFL (minimum score 550 paper-based; 213 computer-based; 79 iBT). *Application deadline:* For fall admission, 8/1 priority date for domestic students; for spring admission, 12/1 priority date for domestic students. Applications are processed on a rolling basis. Application fee: $50. *Expenses:* Tuition: Full-time $14,040; part-time $1170 per credit hour. *Financial support:* In 2010–11, 20 students received support, including 5 research assistantships with full and partial tuition reimbursements available (averaging $4,504 per year), 2 teaching assistantships with full and partial tuition reimbursements available (averaging $4,504 per year); career-related internships or fieldwork and unspecified assistantships also available. Financial award application deadline: 4/15; financial award applicants required to submit FAFSA. *Unit head:* Dr. Shawn Doherty, Graduate Program Coordinator, 386-226-6249, E-mail: shawn.doherty@erau.edu. *Application contact:* Keith Deaton, Director, International and Graduate Admissions, 800-388-3728, Fax: 386-226-7070, E-mail: graduate.admissions@erau.edu.

Florida Institute of Technology, Graduate Programs, College of Engineering, Engineering Systems Department, Melbourne, FL 32901-6975. Offers engineering management (MS); systems engineering (MS, PhD). Part-time and evening/weekend programs available. *Faculty:* 5 full-time (0 women). *Students:* 21 full-time (4 women), 47 part-time (10 women); includes 8 minority (3 Black or African American, non-Hispanic/Latino; 2 Asian, non-Hispanic/Latino; 2 Hispanic/Latino; 1 Two or more races, non-Hispanic/Latino), 16 international. Average age 35. 106 applicants, 62% accepted, 16 enrolled. In 2010, 87 master's awarded. *Degree requirements:* For master's, comprehensive exam (for some programs), thesis optional, portfolio of competencies and summary of career relevance. *Entrance requirements:* For master's, GRE General Test (if GPA less than 3.0), BS in engineering, minimum GPA of 3.0, 2 letters of recommendation, resume, bachelor's degree from ABET-accredited program, statement of objectives. Additional exam requirements/recommendations for international students: Required—TOEFL (minimum score 550 paper-based; 213 computer-based; 79 iBT). *Application deadline:* For fall admission, 4/1 for international students; for spring admission, 9/30 for international students. Applications are processed on a rolling basis. Application fee: $50. Electronic applications accepted. *Expenses:* Tuition: Part-time $1040 per credit hour. Tuition and fees vary according to campus/location. *Financial support:* In 2010–11, 1 research assistantship with full and partial tuition reimbursement (averaging $16,245 per year) was awarded; career-related internships or fieldwork, institutionally sponsored loans, unspecified assistantships, and tuition remissions also available. Support available to part-time students. Financial award application deadline: 3/1; financial award applicants required to submit FAFSA. *Faculty research:* System/software engineering, simulation and analytical modeling, project management, multimedia tools, quality. *Unit head:* Dr. Muzaffar A. Shaikh, Department Head, 321-674-7345, Fax: 321-674-7136, E-mail: mshaikh@fit.edu. *Application contact:* Cheryl A. Brown, Associate Director of Graduate Admissions, 321-674-7581, Fax: 321-723-9468, E-mail: cbrown@fit.edu.

George Mason University, Volgenau School of Engineering, Department of Civil, Environmental, and Infrastructure Engineering, Fairfax, VA 22030. Offers civil and infrastructure engineering (MS, PhD); civil infrastructure and security engineering (Certificate); leading technical enterprises (Certificate); sustainability and the environment (Certificate); water resources engineering (Certificate). Part-time and evening/weekend programs available. *Faculty:* 9 full-time (4 women), 18 part-time/adjunct (1 woman). *Students:* 15 full-time (4 women), 62 part-time (13 women); includes 7 Black or African American, non-Hispanic/Latino; 9 Asian, non-Hispanic/Latino; 4 Hispanic/Latino; 2 Two or more races, non-Hispanic/Latino, 6 international. Average age 32. 77 applicants, 70% accepted, 29 enrolled. In 2010, 13 master's, 1 doctorate, 2 other advanced degrees awarded. *Degree requirements:* For master's, thesis (for some programs), 30 credits, departmental seminars; for doctorate, thesis/dissertation, qualifying exams. *Entrance requirements:* For master's, GRE or GMAT. Additional exam requirements/recommendations for international students: Required—TOEFL (minimum score 570 paper-based; 230 computer-based; 88 iBT). *Application deadline:* For fall admission, 3/15 priority date for domestic students, 3/15 for international students; for spring admission, 11/1 for domestic students, 10/1 for international students. Application fee: $100. Electronic applications accepted. *Expenses:* Tuition, state resident: full-time $8192; part-time $440 per credit hour. Tuition, nonresident: full-time $22,952; part-time $1055 per credit hour. Required fees: $2364; $99 per credit hour. *Financial support:* In 2010–11, 13 students received support, including 1 fellowship (averaging $18,000 per year), 2 research assistantships with full and partial tuition reimbursements available (averaging $13,924 per year), 10 teaching assistantships with full and partial tuition reimbursements available (averaging $10,468 per year); career-related internships or fieldwork, Federal Work-Study, scholarships/grants, unspecified assistantships, and health care benefits (full-time research or teaching assistantship recipients) also available. Financial award application deadline: 3/1; financial award applicants required to submit FAFSA. *Faculty research:* Evolutionary design, infrastructure security, intelligent transportation systems, national transportation networks, water quality modeling. Total annual research expenditures: $177,807. *Unit head:* Dr. Michael Bronzini, Chair, 703-993-1504, Fax: 703-993-1521. *Application contact:* Lisa Nolder, Graduate Student Services Director, 703-993-1499, E-mail: snolder@gmu.edu.

George Mason University, Volgenau School of Engineering, Department of Computer Science, Fairfax, VA 22030. Offers biometrics (Certificate); computer games technology (Certificate); computer networking (Certificate); computer science (MS, PhD); data mining (Certificate); database management (Certificate); electronic commerce (Certificate); foundations of information systems (Certificate); information engineering (Certificate); information security and assurance (MS, Certificate); information systems (MS); intelligent agents (Certificate); software architecture (Certificate); software engineering (MS, Certificate); systems engineering (MS); Web-based software engineering (Certificate). MS program offered jointly with Old Dominion University, University of Virginia, Virginia Commonwealth University, and Virginia Polytechnic Institute and State University. Part-time and evening/weekend programs available. Postbaccalaureate distance learning degree programs offered. *Faculty:* 42 full-time (9 women), 20 part-time/adjunct (1 woman). *Students:* 124 full-time (37 women), 453 part-time (103 women); includes 14 Black or African American, non-Hispanic/Latino; 66 Asian, non-Hispanic/Latino; 13 Hispanic/Latino; 3 Two or more races, non-Hispanic/Latino, 206 international. Average age 30. 904 applicants, 53% accepted, 150 enrolled. In 2010, 203 master's, 4 doctorates, 20 other advanced degrees awarded. *Degree requirements:* For master's, thesis optional; for doctorate, comprehensive exam, thesis/dissertation. *Entrance requirements:* For master's, GRE General Test, minimum GPA of 3.0 in last 60 hours, 3 letters of recommendation; for doctorate, GRE, 4-year BA, academic work in computer science, 3 letters of recommendation, statement of career goals and aspirations. Additional exam requirements/recommendations for international students: Required—TOEFL (minimum score 570 paper-based; 230 computer-based; 88 iBT). *Application deadline:* For fall admission, 4/15 priority date for domestic students, 1/15 for international students; for spring admission, 11/15 for domestic students. Application fee: $100. Electronic applications accepted. *Expenses:* Tuition, state resident: full-time $8192; part-time $440 per credit hour. Tuition, nonresident: full-time $22,952; part-time $1055 per credit hour. Required fees: $2364; $99 per credit hour. *Financial support:* In 2010–11, 101 students received support, including 3 fellowships (averaging $18,000 per year), 52 research assistantships (averaging $15,078 per year), 47 teaching assistantships (averaging $10,983 per year); career-related internships or fieldwork, Federal Work-Study, scholarships/grants, unspecified assistantships, and health care benefits (full-time research or teaching assistantship recipients) also available. Financial award application deadline: 3/1; financial award applicants required to submit FAFSA. *Faculty research:* Artificial intelligence, image processing/graphics, parallel/distributed systems, software engineering systems. Total annual research expenditures: $1.3 million. *Unit head:* Dr. Arun Sood, Director, 703-993-1524, Fax: 703-993-1710, E-mail: asood@gmu.edu. *Application contact:* Jay Shapiro, Professor, 703-993-1485, E-mail: jshapiro@gmu.edu.

George Mason University, Volgenau School of Engineering, Department of Systems Engineering and Operations Research, Fairfax, VA 22030. Offers architecture-based systems integration (Certificate); command, control, communication, computing and intelligence (Certificate); computational modeling (Certificate); discovery, design and innovation (Certificate); military operations research (Certificate); operations research (MS); systems engineering (MS); systems engineering analysis and architecture (Certificate); systems engineering and operations research (PhD); systems engineering of software intensive systems (Certificate). MS programs offered jointly with Old Dominion University, University of Virginia, Virginia Commonwealth University, and Virginia Polytechnic Institute and State University. Part-time and evening/weekend programs available. *Faculty:* 16 full-time (4 women), 11 part-time/adjunct (4 women). *Students:* 27 full-time (2 women), 175 part-time (39 women); includes 10 Black or African American, non-Hispanic/Latino; 2 American Indian or Alaska Native, non-Hispanic/Latino; 19 Asian, non-Hispanic/Latino; 9 Hispanic/Latino, 17 international. Average age 33. 132 applicants, 72% accepted, 53 enrolled. In 2010, 76 master's, 1 doctorate, 25 other advanced degrees awarded. *Degree requirements:* For master's, thesis optional; for doctorate, comprehensive exam, thesis/dissertation, qualifying exams. *Entrance requirements:* For master's, GRE General Test, 3 letters of recommendation, resume; for doctorate, GRE, undergraduate and graduate transcripts, 3 letters of reference, resume, statement of career goals and aspirations, self assessment of background. Additional exam requirements/recommendations for international students: Required—TOEFL (minimum score 570 paper-based; 230 computer-based; 88 iBT). *Application deadline:* For fall admission, 3/15 priority date for domestic students, 2/15 priority date for international students; for spring admission, 10/1 for domestic and international students. Application fee: $100. Electronic applications accepted. *Expenses:* Tuition, state resident: full-time $8192; part-time $440 per credit hour. Tuition, nonresident: full-time $22,952; part-time $1055 per credit hour. Required fees: $2364; $99 per credit hour. *Financial support:* In 2010–11, 11 students received support, including 6 research assistantships with full and partial tuition reimbursements available (averaging $15,982 per year), 5 teaching assistantships with full and partial tuition reimbursements available (averaging $10,661 per year); career-related internships or fieldwork, Federal Work-Study, scholarships/grants, unspecified assistantships, and health care benefits (full-time research or teaching assistantship recipients) also available. Financial award application deadline: 3/1; financial award applicants required to submit FAFSA. *Faculty research:* Requirements engineering, signal processing, systems architecture, data fusion. Total annual research expenditures: $1.3 million. *Unit head:* Dr. Ariela Sofer, Chairman, 703-993-1692, Fax: 703-993-1521, E-mail: asofer@gmu.edu. *Application contact:* Dr. K. C. Chang, Graduate Coordinator, 703-993-1639, E-mail: kchang@gmu.edu.

The George Washington University, School of Engineering and Applied Science, Department of Engineering Management and Systems Engineering, Washington, DC 20052. Offers MS, D Sc, App Sc, Engr, Graduate Certificate. Part-time and evening/weekend programs available. *Faculty:* 15 full-time (1 woman), 17 part-time/adjunct (2 women). *Students:* 132 full-time (40 women), 1,148 part-time (276 women); includes 291 minority (126 Black or African American, non-Hispanic/Latino; 7 American Indian or Alaska Native, non-Hispanic/Latino; 96 Asian, non-Hispanic/Latino; 55 Hispanic/Latino; 5 Native Hawaiian or other Pacific Islander, non-Hispanic/Latino; 2 Two or more races, non-Hispanic/Latino), 119 international. Average age 35. 496 applicants, 87% accepted, 260 enrolled. In 2010, 336 master's, 21 doctorates, 138 other advanced degrees awarded. *Degree requirements:* For master's, thesis optional; for doctorate, one foreign language, thesis/dissertation, final and qualifying exams, submission of articles; for other advanced degree, professional project. *Entrance requirements:* For master's, appropriate bachelor's degree, minimum GPA of 2.7, second semester calculus; for doctorate, appropriate master's degree, minimum GPA of 3.5, 2 letters of recommendation; for other advanced degree, appropriate master's degree, minimum GPA of 3.4. Additional exam requirements/recommendations for international students: Required—TOEFL or The George Washington University English as a Foreign Language Test. *Application deadline:* For fall admission, 3/1 for domestic students; for spring admission, 10/1 for domestic students. Applications are processed on a rolling basis. Application fee: $75. *Financial support:* In 2010–11, 35 students received support; fellowships with tuition reimbursements available, research assistantships, teaching assistantships with tuition reimbursements available, career-related internships or fieldwork and institutionally sponsored loans available. Financial award application deadline: 3/1; financial award applicants required to submit FAFSA. *Faculty research:* Artificial intelligence and expert systems, human factors engineering and systems analysis. Total annual research expenditures: $421,800. *Unit head:* Dr. Thomas Mazzuchi, Chair, 202-994-7424, Fax: 202-994-0245, E-mail: mazzu@gwu.edu. *Application contact:* Adina Lav, Marketing, Recruiting and Admissions, 202-994-5827, Fax: 202-994-0909, E-mail: engineering@gwu.edu.

Georgia Institute of Technology, Graduate Studies and Research, College of Engineering, School of Industrial and Systems Engineering, Program in Industrial and Systems Engineering, Atlanta, GA 30332-0001. Offers algorithms, combinatorics, and optimization (PhD); industrial and systems engineering (PhD); industrial engineering (MS, MSIE); statistics (MS Stat). Part-time programs available. Terminal master's awarded for partial completion of doctoral program. *Degree requirements:* For master's, thesis optional; for doctorate, thesis/dissertation. *Entrance requirements:* For master's and doctorate, GRE General Test, minimum GPA of 3.0. Additional exam requirements/recommendations for international students: Required—TOEFL. Electronic applications accepted. *Faculty research:* Computer-integrated manufacturing systems, materials handling systems, production and distribution.

Harrisburg University of Science and Technology, Program in Information Systems Engineering and Management, Harrisburg, PA 17101. Offers digital government specialization

Systems Engineering

Harrisburg University of Science and Technology *(continued)*
(MS); digital health specialization (MS); entrepreneurship specialization (MS). Part-time programs available. *Faculty:* 1 full-time (0 women), 2 part-time/adjunct (0 women). *Students:* 4 full-time (2 women), 16 part-time (5 women); includes 5 Black or African American, non-Hispanic/Latino; 2 Hispanic/Latino. Average age 30. 18 applicants, 83% accepted, 11 enrolled. *Degree requirements:* For master's, comprehensive exam, thesis optional. *Entrance requirements:* For master's, baccalaureate degree. Additional exam requirements/recommendations for international students: Required—TOEFL (minimum score 520 paper-based; 200 computer-based; 80 iBT). *Application deadline:* For fall admission, 8/1 priority date for domestic students, 7/1 priority date for international students. Applications are processed on a rolling basis. Application fee: $0. Electronic applications accepted. *Expenses:* Tuition: Full-time $19,500; part-time $700 per credit hour. *Financial support:* In 2010–11, 2 students received support. Scholarships/grants available. Financial award applicants required to submit FAFSA. *Unit head:* Dr. Amjad Umar, Director and Professor, 717-901-5141, Fax: 717-901-3141, E-mail: aumar@harrisburgu.edu. *Application contact:* Timothy Dawson, Information Contact, 717-901-5158, Fax: 717-901-3158, E-mail: admissions@harrisburgu.edu.

Indiana University–Purdue University Fort Wayne, College of Engineering, Technology, and Computer Science, Department of Engineering, Fort Wayne, IN 46805-1499. Offers computer engineering (MS); electrical engineering (MS); mechanical engineering (MS); systems engineering (MS). Part-time programs available. *Faculty:* 18 full-time (3 women). *Students:* 7 full-time (0 women), 31 part-time (7 women); includes 4 minority (1 Black or African American, non-Hispanic/Latino; 2 Asian, non-Hispanic/Latino; 1 Hispanic/Latino), 4 international. Average age 28. 21 applicants, 95% accepted, 18 enrolled. In 2010, 9 master's awarded. *Entrance requirements:* For master's, minimum GPA of 3.0, bachelor's degree in engineering discipline. Additional exam requirements/recommendations for international students: Required—TOEFL (minimum score 550 paper-based; 213 computer-based; 77 iBT); Recommended—TWE. *Application deadline:* For fall admission, 7/15 priority date for domestic students, 5/15 priority date for international students; for spring admission, 12/1 priority date for domestic students, 10/15 priority date for international students. Applications are processed on a rolling basis. Application fee: $55 ($60 for international students). Electronic applications accepted. *Expenses:* Tuition, state resident: full-time $4824; part-time $268 per credit. Tuition, nonresident: full-time $11,625; part-time $646 per credit. Required fees: $555; $30.85 per credit. Tuition and fees vary according to course load. *Financial support:* In 2010–11, 5 research assistantships with partial tuition reimbursements (averaging $12,740 per year), 3 teaching assistantships with partial tuition reimbursements (averaging $12,740 per year) were awarded. Financial award application deadline: 3/1; financial award applicants required to submit FAFSA. *Faculty research:* Worm-scanning strategies, measuring the acceleration of gravity. Total annual research expenditures: $129,186. *Unit head:* Dr. Donald Mueller, Chair, 260-481-5707, Fax: 260-481-6281, E-mail: mueller@engr.ipfw.edu. *Application contact:* Dr. Donald Mueller, Chair, 260-481-5707, Fax: 260-481-6281, E-mail: mueller@engr.ipfw.edu.

Instituto Tecnológico y de Estudios Superiores de Monterrey, Campus Chihuahua, Graduate Programs, Chihuahua, Mexico. Offers computer systems engineering (Ingeniero); electrical engineering (Ingeniero); electromechanical engineering (Ingeniero); electronic engineering (Ingeniero); engineering administration (MEA); industrial engineering (MIE, Ingeniero); international trade (MIT); mechanical engineering (Ingeniero).

Instituto Tecnológico y de Estudios Superiores de Monterrey, Campus Monterrey, Graduate and Research Division, Programs in Engineering, Monterrey, Mexico. Offers applied statistics (M Eng); artificial intelligence (PhD); automation engineering (M Eng); chemical engineering (M Eng); civil engineering (M Eng); electrical engineering (M Eng); electronic engineering (M Eng); environmental engineering (M Eng); industrial engineering (M Eng, PhD); manufacturing engineering (M Eng); mechanical engineering (M Eng); systems and quality engineering (M Eng). M Eng program offered jointly with University of Waterloo; PhD in industrial engineering with Texas A&M University. Part-time and evening/weekend programs available. Terminal master's awarded for partial completion of doctoral program. *Degree requirements:* For master's, one foreign language, thesis; for doctorate, one foreign language, thesis/dissertation. *Entrance requirements:* For master's, EXADEP; for doctorate, GRE, master's degree in related field. Additional exam requirements/recommendations for international students: Required—TOEFL. *Faculty research:* Flexible manufacturing cells, materials, statistical methods, environmental prevention, control and evaluation.

Iowa State University of Science and Technology, Graduate College, College of Engineering, Program in Systems Engineering, Ames, IA 50011. Offers M Eng. *Students:* 1 full-time (0 women), 34 part-time (6 women); includes 8 Black or African American, non-Hispanic/Latino; 3 Asian, non-Hispanic/Latino, 3 international. 23 applicants, 83% accepted, 7 enrolled. In 2010, 35 master's awarded. *Entrance requirements:* Additional exam requirements/recommendations for international students: Required—TOEFL (minimum score 550 paper-based; 79 iBT), IELTS (minimum score 6.5). *Application deadline:* Applications are processed on a rolling basis. Application fee: $40 ($90 for international students). Electronic applications accepted. *Financial support:* Research assistantships with full and partial tuition reimbursements, teaching assistantships with full and partial tuition reimbursements, scholarships/grants, health care benefits, and unspecified assistantships available. *Unit head:* Dr. Douglas D. Gemmill, Supervisory Committee Chair, 515-294-8731, Fax: 515-294-3524, E-mail: syseng@iastate.edu. *Application contact:* Dr. Douglas D. Gemmill, Supervisory Committee Chair, 515-294-8731, Fax: 515-294-3524, E-mail: syseng@iastate.edu.

The Johns Hopkins University, Engineering for Professionals, Part-time Program in Systems Engineering, Baltimore, MD 21218-2699. Offers MS, Graduate Certificate, Post-Master's Certificate. Part-time and evening/weekend programs available. Postbaccalaureate distance learning degree programs offered (no on-campus study). *Faculty:* 33 part-time/adjunct (3 women). *Students:* 2 full-time (0 women), 624 part-time (154 women); includes 219 minority (56 Black or African American, non-Hispanic/Latino; 3 American Indian or Alaska Native, non-Hispanic/Latino; 105 Asian, non-Hispanic/Latino; 47 Hispanic/Latino; 2 Native Hawaiian or other Pacific Islander, non-Hispanic/Latino; 6 Two or more races, non-Hispanic/Latino), 5 international. Average age 33. 208 applicants, 89% accepted, 141 enrolled. In 2010, 112 master's, 26 other advanced degrees awarded. *Application deadline:* Applications are processed on a rolling basis. Application fee: $75. Electronic applications accepted. *Unit head:* Dr. Ronald R. Luman, Program Chair, 443-778-5239, E-mail: ronald.luman@jhuapl.edu. *Application contact:* Priyanka Dwivedi, Admissions Manager, 410-516-2300, Fax: 410-579-8049, E-mail: pdwived1@jhu.edu.

Lehigh University, P.C. Rossin College of Engineering and Applied Science, Department of Industrial and Systems Engineering, Bethlehem, PA 18015. Offers analytical finance (MS); industrial and systems engineering (M Eng, MS); industrial engineering (PhD); management science and engineering (M Eng, MS); MBA/E. Part-time programs available. Postbaccalaureate distance learning degree programs offered (no on-campus study). *Faculty:* 15 full-time (2 women), 1 part-time/adjunct (0 women). *Students:* 77 full-time (27 women), 15 part-time (5 women); includes 3 minority (2 Black or African American, non-Hispanic/Latino; 1 Asian, non-Hispanic/Latino), 63 international. Average age 27. 636 applicants, 19% accepted, 39 enrolled. In 2010, 26 master's, 6 doctorates awarded. *Degree requirements:* For master's, thesis (MS); project (M Eng); for doctorate, comprehensive exam, thesis/dissertation. *Entrance requirements:* For master's and doctorate, GRE General Test. Additional exam requirements/recommendations for international students: Required—TOEFL (minimum score 550 paper-based; 213 computer-based; 79 iBT). *Application deadline:* For fall admission, 7/15 for domestic and international students; for spring admission, 12/1 for domestic and international students. Applications are processed on a rolling basis. Application fee: $75. Electronic applications accepted. *Financial support:* In 2010–11, 28 students received support, including 3 fellowships with full tuition reimbursements available (averaging $17,460 per year), 16 research assistantships with full tuition reimbursements available (averaging $15,300 per year), 11 teaching assistantships with full tuition reimbursements available (averaging $18,360 per year); career-related internships or fieldwork, scholarships/grants, tuition waivers, and unspecified assistantships also available. Financial award application deadline: 1/15. *Faculty research:* Optimization, mathematical programming; logistics and supply chain, stochastic processes and simulation; computational optimization and high performance computing; financial engineering and robust optimization. Total annual research expenditures: $1.8 million. *Unit head:* Dr. Tamas Terlaky, Chair, 610-758-4050, Fax: 610-758-4886, E-mail: terlaky@lehigh.edu. *Application contact:* Rita R. Frey, Graduate Coordinator, 610-758-4051, Fax: 610-758-4886, E-mail: ise@lehigh.edu.

Lehigh University, P.C. Rossin College of Engineering and Applied Science, Program in Manufacturing Systems Engineering, Bethlehem, PA 18015. Offers MS, MBA/E. Part-time and evening/weekend programs available. Postbaccalaureate distance learning degree programs offered (no on-campus study). *Students:* 1 full-time (0 women), 22 part-time (7 women); includes 2 minority (1 Black or African American, non-Hispanic/Latino; 1 Asian, non-Hispanic/Latino). Average age 34. 16 applicants, 19% accepted, 3 enrolled. In 2010, 10 master's awarded. *Degree requirements:* For master's, comprehensive exam, project or thesis. *Entrance requirements:* For master's, GRE General Test, minimum GPA of 2.75. Additional exam requirements/recommendations for international students: Required—TOEFL (minimum score 620 paper-based; 260 computer-based; 85 iBT). *Application deadline:* For fall admission, 7/15 for domestic and international students; for spring admission, 12/1 for domestic and international students. Applications are processed on a rolling basis. Application fee: $75. Electronic applications accepted. *Faculty research:* Manufacturing systems design, development, and implementation; accounting and management; agile/lean systems; supply chain issues; sustainable systems design; product design. *Unit head:* Dr. Keith M. Gardiner, Director, 610-758-5070, Fax: 610-758-6527, E-mail: kg03@lehigh.edu. *Application contact:* Carolyn C. Jones, Graduate Coordinator, 610-758-5157, Fax: 610-758-6527, E-mail: ccj1@lehigh.edu.

Loyola Marymount University, College of Business Administration, MBA/MS Program in Systems Engineering, Los Angeles, CA 90045. Offers MBA/MS. Part-time programs available. *Faculty:* 57 full-time (16 women), 9 part-time/adjunct (2 women). *Students:* 10 full-time (4 women), 3 part-time (1 woman); includes 2 Black or African American, non-Hispanic/Latino; 2 Hispanic/Latino. Average age 30. 6 applicants, 50% accepted, 3 enrolled. *Entrance requirements:* Additional exam requirements/recommendations for international students: Required—TOEFL (minimum score 600 paper-based; 250 computer-based; 100 iBT). *Application deadline:* For fall admission, 7/15 for domestic students; for spring admission, 12/15 for domestic students. Application fee: $50. Electronic applications accepted. *Expenses:* Contact institution. *Financial support:* In 2010–11, 6 students received support. Career-related internships or fieldwork, institutionally sponsored loans, scholarships/grants, and unspecified assistantships available. Financial award application deadline: 6/30; financial award applicants required to submit FAFSA. *Unit head:* Dr. Dennis Draper, Dean, 310-338-7504, E-mail: ddraper@lmu.edu. *Application contact:* Dr. Rachelle Katz, Associate Dean and Director of MBA Program, 310-338-2848, E-mail: rkatz@lmu.edu.

Loyola Marymount University, College of Science and Engineering, Department of Systems Engineering and Engineering Management, Program in System Engineering Leadership, Los Angeles, CA 90045-2659. Offers MS, MS/MBA. *Faculty:* 2 full-time (0 women), 3 part-time/adjunct (1 woman). *Students:* 10 full-time (4 women), 3 part-time (1 woman); includes 2 Black or African American, non-Hispanic/Latino; 2 Hispanic/Latino. Average age 30. 6 applicants, 50% accepted, 3 enrolled. In 2010, 4 master's awarded. *Degree requirements:* For master's, thesis. *Entrance requirements:* For master's, GMAT, personal statement, resume, letters of recommendation. Additional exam requirements/recommendations for international students: Required—TOEFL (minimum score 550 paper-based; 213 computer-based; 80 iBT). *Application deadline:* For fall admission, 7/15 for domestic students; for spring admission, 12/15 for domestic students. Applications are processed on a rolling basis. Application fee: $50. Electronic applications accepted. *Financial support:* In 2010–11, 6 students received support. Scholarships/grants and unspecified assistantships available. Support available to part-time students. Financial award application deadline: 6/1; financial award applicants required to submit FAFSA. Total annual research expenditures: $312,678. *Unit head:* Dr. Frederick S. Brown, Graduate Director, 310-338-7878, E-mail: fbrown@lmu.edu. *Application contact:* Chake H. Kouyoumjian, Associate Dean for Graduate Studies, 310-338-2721, Fax: 310-338-6086, E-mail: ckouyoum@lmu.edu.

Loyola Marymount University, College of Science and Engineering, Department of Systems Engineering and Engineering Management, Program in Systems Engineering, Los Angeles, CA 90045. Offers MS. *Faculty:* 2 full-time (0 women), 3 part-time/adjunct (1 woman). *Students:* 13 full-time (4 women), 16 part-time (3 women); includes 3 Black or African American, non-Hispanic/Latino; 8 Asian, non-Hispanic/Latino; 5 Hispanic/Latino, 4 international. Average age 32. 33 applicants, 39% accepted, 7 enrolled. In 2010, 13 master's awarded. *Degree requirements:* For master's, thesis. *Entrance requirements:* For master's, personal statement, resume, letters of recommendation. Additional exam requirements/recommendations for international students: Required—TOEFL (minimum score 550 paper-based; 213 computer-based; 80 iBT). *Application deadline:* For fall admission, 7/15 for domestic students; for spring admission, 12/15 for domestic students. Applications are processed on a rolling basis. Application fee: $50. Electronic applications accepted. *Financial support:* In 2010–11, 13 students received support, including 5 research assistantships (averaging $3,236 per year); scholarships/grants and unspecified assistantships also available. Support available to part-time students. Financial award applicants required to submit FAFSA. Total annual research expenditures: $312,678. *Unit head:* Dr. Frederick S. Brown, Program Director, 310-338-7878, E-mail: fbrown@lmu.edu. *Application contact:* Chake H. Kouyoumjian, Associate Dean of Graduate Studies, 310-338-2721, Fax: 310-338-6086, E-mail: graduate@lmu.edu.

Massachusetts Institute of Technology, School of Engineering, Engineering Systems Division, Cambridge, MA 02139-4307. Offers engineering and management (SM); engineering systems (SM, PhD); logistics (M Eng); technology and policy (SM); technology, management and policy (PhD); SM/MBA. *Faculty:* 22 full-time (7 women). *Students:* 271 full-time (78 women); includes 39 minority (5 Black or African American, non-Hispanic/Latino; 27 Asian, non-Hispanic/Latino; 6 Hispanic/Latino; 1 Two or more races, non-Hispanic/Latino), 105 international. Average age 31. 927 applicants, 28% accepted, 185 enrolled. In 2010, 169 master's, 10 doctorates awarded. *Degree requirements:* For master's, thesis; for doctorate, comprehensive exam, thesis/dissertation. *Entrance requirements:* For master's, GRE General Test (or GMAT for some programs); for doctorate, GRE General Test. Additional exam requirements/recommendations for international students: Required—IELTS (minimum score 7.5). Application fee: $75. *Expenses:* Contact institution. *Financial support:* In 2010–11, 217 students received support, including 36 fellowships with tuition reimbursements available (averaging $25,594 per year), 95 research assistantships with tuition reimbursements available (averaging $27,695 per year), 15 teaching assistantships with tuition reimbursements available (averaging $25,802 per year); career-related internships or fieldwork, Federal Work-Study, institutionally sponsored loans, scholarships/grants, health care benefits, and unspecified assistantships also available. *Faculty research:* Critical infrastructures; extended enterprises; energy and sustainability; health care delivery; humans and technology; uncertainty and dynamics; design and implementation; networks and flows; policy and standards. Total annual research expenditures: $13.2 million. *Unit head:* Prof. Yossi Sheffi, Director, 617-253-1764, E-mail: esdinquiries@mit.edu. *Application contact:* Graduate Admissions, 617-253-1182, E-mail: esdgrad@mit.edu.

Mississippi State University, Bagley College of Engineering, Department of Industrial and Systems Engineering, Mississippi State, MS 39762. Offers engineering (PhD), including industrial engineering; industrial engineering (MS). Part-time programs available. Postbaccalaureate distance learning degree programs offered (no on-campus study). *Faculty:* 9 full-time (3 women), 1 part-time/adjunct (0 women). *Students:* 36 full-time (11 women), 44 part-time (6 women); includes 14 minority (6 Black or African American, non-Hispanic/Latino; 4 Asian, non-Hispanic/Latino; 4 Hispanic/Latino), 25 international. Average age 33. 76 applicants, 38% accepted, 20 enrolled. In 2010, 15 master's, 2 doctorates awarded. *Degree requirements:* For master's, thesis (for some programs), comprehensive oral or written exam; for doctorate, thesis/dissertation, candidacy exam. *Entrance requirements:* For master's, GRE General Test, minimum GPA of 3.0; for doctorate, GRE General Test, minimum GPA of 3.3. Additional exam requirements/recommendations for international students: Required—TOEFL (minimum score 550 paper-based; 213 computer-based; 79 iBT); Recommended—IELTS (minimum score 6.5). *Application deadline:* For fall admission, 7/1 for domestic students, 5/1 for international students; for spring admission, 11/1 for domestic students, 9/1 for international students. Applications are processed on a rolling basis. Application fee: $40. *Expenses:* Tuition, state resident: full-time $2730.50; part-time $304 per credit hour. Tuition, nonresident: full-time $6901; part-time $767 per credit hour. *Financial support:* In 2010–11, 16 research assistantships with full tuition reimbursements (averaging $14,070 per year), 7 teaching assistantships with full tuition reimbursements (averaging $11,078 per year) were awarded; Federal Work-Study, institutionally sponsored loans, and unspecified assistantships also available. Financial award application deadline: 4/1; financial award applicants required to submit FAFSA. *Faculty research:* Operations research, ergonomics, production systems, management systems, transportation. *Unit head:* Dr. Royce Bowden, Professor and Head, 662-325-3865, Fax: 662-325-7618, E-mail: bowden@ise.msstate.edu. *Application contact:* Dr. John Usher, Professor and Graduate Coordinator, 662-325-7624, Fax: 662-325-7618, E-mail: usher@ise.msstate.edu.

Missouri University of Science and Technology, Graduate School, Department of Engineering Management and Systems Engineering, Rolla, MO 65409. Offers engineering management (MS, DE, PhD); manufacturing engineering (M Eng, MS); systems engineering (MS, PhD). *Degree requirements:* For master's, thesis optional; for doctorate, comprehensive exam. *Entrance requirements:* For master's, GRE (minimum score 1150 verbal and quantitative, 4.5 writing); for doctorate, GRE (minimum score: 1100 verbal and quantitative, 3.5 writing). Additional exam requirements/recommendations for international students: Required—TOEFL (minimum score 580 paper-based; 213 computer-based). *Faculty research:* Management of technology, industrial engineering, manufacturing engineering, packaging engineering, quality engineering.

National University, Academic Affairs, School of Engineering and Technology, Department of Applied Engineering, La Jolla, CA 92037-1011. Offers database administration (MS); engineering management (MS); environmental engineering (MS); homeland security and safety engineering (MS); system engineering (MS); wireless communications (MS). Part-time and evening/weekend programs available. Postbaccalaureate distance learning degree programs offered (no on-campus study). *Faculty:* 6 full-time (1 woman), 69 part-time/adjunct (12 women). *Students:* 82 full-time (16 women), 153 part-time (35 women); includes 87 minority (18 Black or African American, non-Hispanic/Latino; 1 American Indian or Alaska Native, non-Hispanic/Latino; 34 Asian, non-Hispanic/Latino; 28 Hispanic/Latino; 2 Native Hawaiian or other Pacific Islander, non-Hispanic/Latino; 4 Two or more races, non-Hispanic/Latino), 60 international. Average age 31. 166 applicants, 100% accepted, 106 enrolled. In 2010, 79 master's awarded. *Degree requirements:* For master's, thesis. *Entrance requirements:* For master's, interview, minimum GPA of 2.5. Additional exam requirements/recommendations for international students: Required—TOEFL (minimum score 550 paper-based; 213 computer-based; 79 iBT), IELTS (minimum score 6). *Application deadline:* Applications are processed on a rolling basis. Application fee: $60 ($65 for international students). Electronic applications accepted. *Expenses:* Tuition: Full-time $9450; part-time $350 per unit. Required fees: $350 per unit. One-time fee: $60. *Financial support:* Career-related internships or fieldwork, institutionally sponsored loans, scholarships/grants, and tuition waivers (partial) available. Support available to part-time students. Financial award application deadline: 6/30; financial award applicants required to submit FAFSA. *Unit head:* Dr. Shekar Viswanathan, Chair and Associate Professor, 858-309-8416, Fax: 858-309-3420, E-mail: sviswana@nu.edu. *Application contact:* Dominick Giovanniello, Associate Regional Dean—San Diego, 800-NAT-UNIV, Fax: 858-541-7792, E-mail: dgiovann@nu.edu.

Naval Postgraduate School, Graduate Programs, Department of Systems Engineering, Monterey, CA 93943. Offers systems engineering (MS, PhD, Certificate); systems engineering and analysis (MS); systems engineering management (MS). Program only open to commissioned officers of the United States and friendly nations and selected United States federal civilian employees. Part-time programs available. *Degree requirements:* For master's, thesis.

North Carolina Agricultural and Technical State University, Graduate School, College of Engineering, Department of Industrial and Systems Engineering, Greensboro, NC 27411. Offers industrial engineering (MSIE, PhD). Part-time programs available. *Degree requirements:* For master's, thesis, project; for doctorate, thesis/dissertation. *Entrance requirements:* For master's, GRE General Test (recommended); for doctorate, GRE General Test. *Faculty research:* Human-machine systems engineering, management systems engineering, operations research and systems analysis, production systems engineering.

Oakland University, Graduate Study and Lifelong Learning, School of Engineering and Computer Science, Department of Computer Science and Engineering, Rochester, MI 48309-4401. Offers computer science (MS); embedded systems (MS); information systems engineering (MS); software engineering (MS). Part-time and evening/weekend programs available. *Entrance requirements:* For master's, minimum GPA of 3.0 for unconditional admission. Electronic applications accepted. *Expenses:* Contact institution. *Faculty research:* Cyber security, 3D imaging of neurochemicals in rat brains.

Oakland University, Graduate Study and Lifelong Learning, School of Engineering and Computer Science, Department of Industrial and Systems Engineering, Program in Systems Engineering, Rochester, MI 48309-4401. Offers MS, PhD. *Degree requirements:* For doctorate, thesis/dissertation. *Entrance requirements:* For master's and doctorate, minimum GPA of 3.0 for unconditional admission. Additional exam requirements/recommendations for international students: Required—TOEFL (minimum score 550 paper-based; 213 computer-based). Electronic applications accepted. *Expenses:* Contact institution.

The Ohio State University, Graduate School, College of Engineering, Program in Industrial and Systems Engineering, Columbus, OH 43210. Offers industrial and systems engineering (MS, PhD); welding engineering (MS, MWE, PhD). *Faculty:* 39. *Students:* 69 full-time (21 women), 63 part-time (12 women); includes 4 Black or African American, non-Hispanic/Latino; 14 Asian, non-Hispanic/Latino; 9 Hispanic/Latino, 129 international. Average age 28. In 2010, 23 master's, 11 doctorates awarded. *Degree requirements:* For master's, thesis optional; for doctorate, thesis/dissertation. *Entrance requirements:* For master's and doctorate, GRE General Test. Additional exam requirements/recommendations for international students: Recommended—TOEFL (minimum score 600 paper-based; 250 computer-based). *Application deadline:* For fall admission, 8/15 priority date for domestic students, 11/1 priority date for international students; for winter admission, 12/1 priority date for domestic students, 7/1 priority date for international students; for spring admission, 3/1 priority date for domestic students, 2/1 priority date for international students. Applications are processed on a rolling basis. Application fee: $40 ($50 for international students). Electronic applications accepted. *Expenses:* Tuition, state resident: full-time $10,605. Tuition, nonresident: full-time $26,535. Tuition and fees vary according to course load and program. *Financial support:* Fellowships, research assistantships, teaching assistantships, career-related internships or fieldwork, Federal Work-Study, institutionally sponsored loans, and unspecified assistantships available. Support available to part-time students. *Unit head:* Julie L. Higle, Chair, 614-292-6239, E-mail: higle.1@osu.edu. *Application contact:* 614-292-9444, Fax: 614-292-3895, E-mail: domestic.grad@osu.edu.

Ohio University, Graduate College, Russ College of Engineering and Technology, Department of Industrial and Systems Engineering, Athens, OH 45701-2979. Offers M Eng Mgt, MS. Part-time and evening/weekend programs available. *Students:* 21 full-time (7 women), 25 part-time (2 women); includes 3 minority (1 Black or African American, non-Hispanic/Latino; 1 Asian, non-Hispanic/Latino; 1 Two or more races, non-Hispanic/Latino), 18 international. 50 applicants, 34% accepted, 5 enrolled. In 2010, 12 master's awarded. *Degree requirements:* For master's, comprehensive exam (for some programs), thesis optional, research project. *Entrance requirements:* For master's, GRE General Test. Additional exam requirements/recommendations for international students: Required—TOEFL (minimum score 550 paper-based; 80 iBT) or IELTS (minimum score 6.5). *Application deadline:* For fall admission, 3/1 priority date for domestic and international students; for winter admission, 9/1 priority date for domestic and international students; for spring admission, 1/1 priority date for domestic and international students. Applications are processed on a rolling basis. Application fee: $50 ($55 for international students). Electronic applications accepted. *Financial support:* In 2010–11, research assistantships with full tuition reimbursements (averaging $9,000 per year); Federal Work-Study, institutionally sponsored loans, tuition waivers (full), and unspecified assistantships also available. Financial award application deadline: 2/15; financial award applicants required to submit FAFSA. *Faculty research:* Software systems integration, human factors and ergonomics. Total annual research expenditures: $350,000. *Unit head:* Dr. Robert P. Judd, Chairman, 740-593-0106, Fax: 740-593-0778, E-mail: judd@ohio.edu. *Application contact:* Dr. Gursel Suer, Graduate Chairman, 740-593-1542, Fax: 740-593-0778, E-mail: suer@ohio.edu.

Old Dominion University, Frank Batten College of Engineering and Technology, Program in Engineering Management and Systems Engineering, Norfolk, VA 23529. Offers D Eng. Part-time and evening/weekend programs available. Postbaccalaureate distance learning degree programs offered (no on-campus study). *Faculty:* 14 full-time (3 women), 3 part-time/adjunct (0 women). *Students:* 2 full-time (0 women), 10 part-time (1 woman); includes 3 minority (1 Black or African American, non-Hispanic/Latino; 1 American Indian or Alaska Native, non-Hispanic/Latino; 1 Hispanic/Latino). Average age 43. *Degree requirements:* For doctorate, thesis/dissertation, candidacy exam. *Entrance requirements:* For doctorate, GRE, resume, letters of recommendation, minimum GPA of 3.0, interview. Additional exam requirements/recommendations for international students: Required—TOEFL (minimum score 550 paper-based; 213 computer-based; 79 iBT). *Application deadline:* For fall admission, 6/1 priority date for domestic students, 4/15 for international students; for spring admission, 11/1 priority date for domestic students, 2/1 for international students. Applications are processed on a rolling basis. Application fee: $40. Electronic applications accepted. *Expenses:* Tuition, state resident: full-time $8592; part-time $358 per credit. Tuition, nonresident: full-time $21,672; part-time $903 per credit. Required fees: $119 per semester. One-time fee: $50. *Financial support:* In 2010–11, research assistantships with full and partial tuition reimbursements (averaging $20,000 per year), teaching assistantships with full and partial tuition reimbursements (averaging $20,000 per year) were awarded; fellowships, career-related internships or fieldwork and tuition waivers also available. Support available to part-time students. Financial award application deadline: 2/15; financial award applicants required to submit FAFSA. *Faculty research:* Project management, systems engineering, modeling and simulation, virtual collaboration environments, multidisciplinary designs. Total annual research expenditures: $3.2 million. *Unit head:* Dr. Resit Unal, Department Chair, 757-683-4558, Fax: 757-683-5640, E-mail: enmagpd@odu.edu. *Application contact:* Ariel Pinto, Graduate Program Director, 757-683-4218, Fax: 757-683-5640, E-mail: enmagpd@odu.edu.

Old Dominion University, Frank Batten College of Engineering and Technology, Program in Systems Engineering, Norfolk, VA 23529. Offers ME. Part-time and evening/weekend programs available. Postbaccalaureate distance learning degree programs offered (no on-campus study). *Faculty:* 14 full-time (3 women), 3 part-time/adjunct (0 women). *Students:* 5 full-time (0 women), 28 part-time (6 women); includes 11 minority (7 Black or African American, non-Hispanic/Latino; 1 Asian, non-Hispanic/Latino; 2 Hispanic/Latino; 1 Two or more races, non-Hispanic/Latino), 2 international. Average age 35. 5 applicants, 100% accepted, 4 enrolled. In 2010, 8 master's awarded. *Degree requirements:* For master's, comprehensive exam, project. *Entrance requirements:* For master's, GRE, minimum GPA of 3.0. Additional exam requirements/recommendations for international students: Required—TOEFL (minimum score 550 paper-based; 213 computer-based; 79 iBT). *Application deadline:* For fall admission, 6/1 priority date for domestic students, 4/15 for international students; for spring admission, 11/1 priority date for domestic students, 2/1 for international students. Applications are processed on a rolling basis. Application fee: $40. Electronic applications accepted. *Expenses:* Tuition, state resident: full-time $8592; part-time $358 per credit. Tuition, nonresident: full-time $21,672; part-time $903 per credit. Required fees: $119 per semester. One-time fee: $50. *Financial support:* In 2010–11, research assistantships with partial tuition reimbursements (averaging $20,000 per year), teaching assistantships with partial tuition reimbursements (averaging $20,000 per year) were awarded; fellowships, career-related internships or fieldwork, scholarships/grants, and tuition waivers (partial) also available. Support available to part-time students. Financial award application deadline: 2/15; financial award applicants required to submit FAFSA. *Faculty research:* System of systems engineering, complex systems, optimization. Total annual research expenditures: $3.2 million. *Unit head:* Dr. Resit Unal, Chair, 757-683-4558, Fax: 757-683-5640, E-mail: enmagpd@odu.edu. *Application contact:* Ariel Pinto, Graduate Program Director, 757-683-4218, Fax: 757-683-5640, E-mail: enmagpd@odu.edu.

Oregon State University, Graduate School, College of Engineering, School of Mechanical, Industrial, and Manufacturing Engineering, Corvallis, OR 97331. Offers human systems engineering (MS, PhD); industrial engineering (MS, PhD); information systems engineering (MS, PhD); manufacturing engineering (M Engr); manufacturing systems engineering (MS, PhD); materials science (MAIS, MS, PhD); mechanical engineering (MS, PhD); nano/micro fabrication (MS, PhD). Part-time programs available. Postbaccalaureate distance learning degree programs offered (minimal on-campus study). *Degree requirements:* For master's, thesis or alternative; for doctorate, thesis/dissertation. *Entrance requirements:* For master's, placement exam, minimum GPA of 3.0 in last 90 hours of course work; for doctorate, GRE, placement exam, minimum GPA of 3.0 in last 90 hours of course work. Additional exam requirements/recommendations for international students: Required—TOEFL (minimum score 550 paper-based; 213 computer-based). *Faculty research:* Computer-integrated manufacturing, human factors, robotics, decision support systems, simulation modeling and analysis.

Polytechnic Institute of NYU, Department of Electrical and Computer Engineering, Major in Systems Engineering, Brooklyn, NY 11201-2990. Offers MS. Part-time and evening/weekend programs available. *Students:* 7 full-time (3 women), 2 part-time (both women); includes 3 Black or African American, non-Hispanic/Latino; 2 Asian, non-Hispanic/Latino, 4 international. Average age 26. 17 applicants, 59% accepted, 6 enrolled. In 2010, 2 master's awarded. *Degree requirements:* For master's, comprehensive exam (for some programs), thesis (for some programs). *Entrance requirements:* For master's, BS in electrical engineering. Additional exam requirements/recommendations for international students: Required—TOEFL (minimum score 550 paper-based; 213 computer-based; 80 iBT); Recommended—IELTS (minimum score 6.5). *Application deadline:* For fall admission, 7/31 priority date for domestic students, 4/30 priority date for international students; for spring admission, 12/31 priority date for domestic students, 11/30 priority date for international students. Applications are processed on a rolling basis. Application fee: $75. Electronic applications accepted. *Expenses:* Tuition: Full-time $21,492; part-time $1194 per credit. Required fees: $385 per semester. Tuition and fees vary according to course load. *Financial support:* Fellowships, research assistantships, teaching assistantships, institutionally sponsored loans, scholarships/grants, and unspecified assistantships available. Support available to part-time students. Financial award applicants required to submit FAFSA. *Unit head:* Dr. Jonathan Chao, Head, 718-260-3478, Fax: 718-260-3302, E-mail: chao@poly.edu. *Application contact:* JeanCarlo Bonilla, Director, Graduate Enrollment Management, 718-260-3182, Fax: 718-260-3624.

Polytechnic Institute of NYU, Long Island Graduate Center, Graduate Programs, Department of Computer Science and Engineering, Melville, NY 11747. Offers computer science (MS); information systems engineering (MS). Part-time and evening/weekend programs available. *Faculty:* 5 part-time/adjunct (0 women). *Students:* 2 full-time (1 woman), 27 part-time (4 women); includes 2 Black or African American, non-Hispanic/Latino; 10 Asian, non-Hispanic/Latino; 2 Hispanic/Latino, 1 international. Average age 32. 22 applicants, 73% accepted, 10 enrolled. In 2010, 11 master's awarded. *Degree requirements:* For master's, comprehensive exam (for some programs), thesis (for some programs). *Entrance requirements:* Additional exam requirements/recommendations for international students: Required—TOEFL (minimum score 550 paper-based; 213 computer-based; 80 iBT); Recommended—IELTS (minimum score 6.5). *Application deadline:* For fall admission, 7/31 priority date for domestic students, 4/30 priority date for international students; for spring admission, 12/31 priority date for domestic students, 11/30 priority date for international students. Applications are processed on a rolling basis. Application fee: $75. Electronic applications accepted. *Expenses:* Tuition: Full-time $21,492; part-time $1194 per credit. Required fees: $385 per semester. Tuition and

Systems Engineering

Polytechnic Institute of NYU, Long Island Graduate Center (continued)
fees vary according to course load. *Financial support:* In 2010–11, 36 fellowships (averaging $2,037 per year) were awarded; institutionally sponsored loans, scholarships/grants, and unspecified assistantships also available. Support available to part-time students. Financial award applicants required to submit FAFSA. *Faculty research:* Ultra-wideband electromagnetics, high resolution space-time signal, medical image compression, microwave-plasma interaction. *Unit head:* Dr. Keith W. Ross, Department Head, 718-260-3859, E-mail: ross@poly.edu. *Application contact:* JeanCarlo Bonilla, Director of Graduate Enrollment Management, 718-260-3182, Fax: 718-260-3624, E-mail: gradinfo@poly.edu.

Polytechnic Institute of NYU, Long Island Graduate Center, Graduate Programs, Department of Electrical and Computer Engineering, Program in Systems Engineering, Melville, NY 11747. Offers MS. Part-time and evening/weekend programs available. *Students:* 15 part-time (1 woman); includes 3 Black or African American, non-Hispanic/Latino; 3 Asian, non-Hispanic/Latino. Average age 30. 8 applicants, 100% accepted, 5 enrolled. In 2010, 4 master's awarded. *Degree requirements:* For master's, comprehensive exam (for some programs), thesis (for some programs). *Entrance requirements:* Additional exam requirements/recommendations for international students: Required—TOEFL (minimum score 550 paper-based; 213 computer-based; 80 iBT); Recommended—IELTS (minimum score 6.5). *Application deadline:* For fall admission, 7/31 priority date for domestic students, 4/30 priority date for international students; for spring admission, 12/31 priority date for domestic students, 11/30 priority date for international students. Applications are processed on a rolling basis. Application fee: $75. Electronic applications accepted. *Expenses:* Tuition: Full-time $21,492; part-time $1194 per credit. Required fees: $385 per semester. Tuition and fees vary according to course load. *Financial support:* Institutionally sponsored loans, scholarships/grants, and unspecified assistantships available. Support available to part-time students. *Unit head:* Dr. Jonathan Chao, Department Head, 718-260-3302, E-mail: chao@poly.edu. *Application contact:* JeanCarlo Bonilla, Director of Graduate Enrollment Management, 718-260-3182, Fax: 718-260-3624, E-mail: gradinfo@poly.edu.

Portland State University, Graduate Studies, Maseeh College of Engineering and Computer Science, Program in Systems Engineering, Portland, OR 97207-0751. Offers systems engineering (M Eng); systems engineering fundamentals (Certificate). Postbaccalaureate distance learning degree programs offered (no on-campus study). *Students:* 1 full-time (0 women), 10 part-time (2 women); includes 3 minority (2 Asian, non-Hispanic/Latino; 1 Hispanic/Latino). Average age 36. 5 applicants, 100% accepted, 4 enrolled. In 2010, 2 master's awarded. *Degree requirements:* For master's, internship/project. *Entrance requirements:* For master's, 3 years of engineering experience, bachelor's degree in engineering, minimum undergraduate GPA of 3.0 in upper division courses. Additional exam requirements/recommendations for international students: Required—TOEFL (minimum score 550 paper-based; 213 computer-based). *Application deadline:* Applications are processed on a rolling basis. Application fee: $50. *Expenses:* Tuition, state resident: full-time $8505; part-time $315 per credit. Tuition, nonresident: full-time $13,284; part-time $492 per credit. Required fees: $1482; $21 per credit. $99 per term. One-time fee: $120. Part-time tuition and fees vary according to course load and program. *Financial support:* Federal Work-Study, scholarships/grants, and unspecified assistantships available. *Unit head:* Dr. Herman Migliore, Director, 503-725-4262, Fax: 503-725-4298, E-mail: herm@cecs.pdx.edu. *Application contact:* Herman Migliore, Assistant Dean for Enrollment, 503-725-4262, Fax: 503-725-4298, E-mail: herm@cecs.pdx.edu.

Regis University, College for Professional Studies, School of Computer and Information Sciences, Denver, CO 80221-1099. Offers database administration with Oracle (Certificate); database development (Certificate); database technologies (M Sc); enterprise Java software development (Certificate); enterprise resource planning (Certificate); executive information technologies (Certificate); information assurance (M Sc, Certificate); information technology management (M Sc); software engineering (M Sc, Certificate); software engineering and database technologies (M Sc); storage area networks (Certificate); systems engineering (M Sc, Certificate). Offered at Boulder Campus, Northwest Denver Campus, Southeast Denver Campus, Fort Collins Campus, Colorado Springs Campus, and Broomfield Campus. Part-time and evening/weekend programs available. Postbaccalaureate distance learning degree programs offered (no on-campus study). *Degree requirements:* For master's, thesis, final research project. *Entrance requirements:* For master's, 2 years of related experience, resume, interview; for Certificate, 2 years of related experience, resumé. Additional exam requirements/recommendations for international students: Required—TOEFL (minimum score 213 computer-based), TWE (minimum score 5), TOEFL or university-based test. Electronic applications accepted. *Expenses:* Contact institution. *Faculty research:* Secure Virtual Laboratory Architecture, Joint IA project with W2C06 Institute, Information Policy, OLTP and OLAP Technologies, knowledge management, software architectures.

Rensselaer Polytechnic Institute, Graduate School, School of Engineering, Program in Computer and Systems Engineering, Troy, NY 12180-3590. Offers M Eng, MS, PhD. Part-time programs available. *Faculty:* 40 full-time (5 women), 5 part-time/adjunct (2 women). *Students:* 11 full-time (0 women), 20 part-time (0 women), 7 international. 82 applicants, 23% accepted, 10 enrolled. In 2010, 11 master's, 4 doctorates awarded. Terminal master's awarded for partial completion of doctoral program. *Degree requirements:* For master's, thesis (for some programs); for doctorate, thesis/dissertation. *Entrance requirements:* For master's, GRE; for doctorate, GRE, qualifying exam, candidacy exam. Additional exam requirements/recommendations for international students: Required—TOEFL (minimum score 570 paper-based; 89 iBT). *Application deadline:* For fall admission, 1/15 priority date for domestic and international students; for spring admission, 8/15 priority date for domestic and international students. Applications are processed on a rolling basis. Application fee: $75. Electronic applications accepted. *Expenses:* Tuition: Full-time $39,600; part-time $1650 per credit. Required fees: $1896. *Financial support:* In 2010–11, 2 fellowships with full tuition reimbursements (averaging $22,000 per year), 7 research assistantships with full tuition reimbursements (averaging $21,000 per year), 2 teaching assistantships (averaging $17,500 per year) were awarded; career-related internships or fieldwork, institutionally sponsored loans, and unspecified assistantships also available. Financial award application deadline: 1/15. *Faculty research:* Multimedia via ATM, mobile robotics, thermophotovoltaic devices, microelectronic interconnections, agile manufacturing. Total annual research expenditures: $3.5 million. *Unit head:* Dr. Kim L. Boyer, Head, 518-276-2150, Fax: 518-276-6261, E-mail: kim@ecse.rpi.edu. *Application contact:* Ann Bruno, Manager of Student Services and Graduate Enrollment, 518-276-2554, Fax: 518-276-4403, E-mail: ann@ecse.rpi.edu.

Rensselaer Polytechnic Institute, Graduate School, School of Engineering, Program in Decision Sciences and Engineering Systems, Troy, NY 12180-3590. Offers industrial and systems engineering (PhD). Part-time programs available. *Faculty:* 12 full-time (2 women). *Students:* 21 full-time (8 women), 2 part-time (1 woman); includes 1 minority (Asian, non-Hispanic/Latino), 14 international. Average age 28. 62 applicants, 15% accepted, 4 enrolled. In 2010, 3 doctorates awarded. Terminal master's awarded for partial completion of doctoral program. *Degree requirements:* For doctorate, thesis/dissertation. *Entrance requirements:* For doctorate, GRE General Test (minimum score 550 verbal). Additional exam requirements/recommendations for international students: Required—TOEFL (minimum score 570 paper-based). *Application deadline:* For fall admission, 1/1 priority date for domestic students, 1/1 for international students; for spring admission, 8/15 for domestic and international students. Applications are processed on a rolling basis. Application fee: $75. Electronic applications accepted. *Expenses:* Tuition: Full-time $39,600; part-time $1650 per credit. Required fees: $1896. *Financial support:* In 2010–11, 20 students received support, including 1 fellowship with full tuition reimbursement available (averaging $20,000 per year), 10 research assistantships with full tuition reimbursements available, 9 teaching assistantships with full tuition reimbursements available (averaging $17,500 per year); career-related internships or fieldwork and institutionally sponsored loans also available. Financial award application deadline: 1/1. *Faculty research:* Decision support systems, simulation and modeling, statistical methods/

computing, operations research, supply chain logistics. Total annual research expenditures: $1.3 million. *Unit head:* Dr. Charles J. Malmborg, Department Head, 518-276-2773, Fax: 518-276-8227, E-mail: malmbc@rpi.edu. *Application contact:* Mary Wagner, Graduate Coordinator, 518-276-2895, Fax: 518-276-8227, E-mail: wagnem@rpi.edu.

Rensselaer Polytechnic Institute, Graduate School, School of Engineering, Program in Systems Engineering and Technology Management, Troy, NY 12180-3590. Offers M Eng. Part-time programs available. *Faculty:* 12 full-time (2 women). *Students:* 1 part-time (0 women); minority (Asian, non-Hispanic/Latino). 3 applicants, 33% accepted, 1 enrolled. In 2010, 3 master's awarded. *Degree requirements:* For master's, thesis (for some programs). *Entrance requirements:* For master's, GRE General Test (minimum score 550 Verbal). Additional exam requirements/recommendations for international students: Required—TOEFL (minimum score 570 paper-based). *Application deadline:* For fall admission, 1/1 priority date for domestic students, 1/1 for international students; for spring admission, 8/15 for domestic and international students. Applications are processed on a rolling basis. Application fee: $75. Electronic applications accepted. *Expenses:* Tuition: Full-time $39,600; part-time $1650 per credit. Required fees: $1896. *Financial support:* Fellowships, research assistantships, teaching assistantships, career-related internships or fieldwork and institutionally sponsored loans available. Financial award application deadline: 1/1. *Faculty research:* Decision support systems, simulation and modeling, statistical methods/computing, operations research, supply chain logistics. Total annual research expenditures: $1.3 million. *Unit head:* Dr. Charles J. Malmborg, Department Head, 518-276-2895, Fax: 518-276-8227, E-mail: malmbc@rpi.edu. *Application contact:* Mary Wagner, Graduate Coordinator, 518-276-2895, Fax: 518-276-8227, E-mail: wagnem@rpi.edu.

Rochester Institute of Technology, Graduate Enrollment Services, Kate Gleason College of Engineering, Department of Design, Development and Manufacturing, Program in Product Development, Rochester, NY 14623-5603. Offers MS. Part-time and evening/weekend programs available. *Students:* 44 part-time (1 woman); includes 1 Asian, non-Hispanic/Latino; 1 Hispanic/Latino. Average age 37. 4 applicants, 75% accepted, 2 enrolled. In 2010, 11 master's awarded. *Entrance requirements:* For master's, undergraduate degree in engineering or related field, minimum GPA of 3.0; 5 years experience in product development. Additional exam requirements/recommendations for international students: Required—TOEFL (minimum score 570 paper-based; 230 computer-based; 88 iBT) or IELTS (minimum score 6.5). *Application deadline:* For fall admission, 2/15 priority date for domestic and international students. Application fee: $50. *Expenses:* Contact institution. *Financial support:* Applicants required to submit FAFSA. *Faculty research:* Platform element dynamics in a multi-product development environment, applying self-organizing principles to product development in a globally-distributed environment, collaborative design and development to accelerate durable goods design and manufacturing. *Unit head:* Mark Smith, Director, 585-475-7971, Fax: 585-475-7955, E-mail: mpdmail@rit.edu. *Application contact:* Diane Ellison, Assistant Vice President, Graduate Enrollment Services, 585-475-2229, Fax: 585-475-7164, E-mail: gradinfo@rit.edu.

Rochester Institute of Technology, Graduate Enrollment Services, Kate Gleason College of Engineering, Department of Industrial and Systems Engineering, Rochester, NY 14623-5603. Offers engineering management (ME); industrial engineering (ME, MS); manufacturing engineering (ME, MS); systems engineering (ME). Part-time programs available. *Students:* 60 full-time (20 women), 17 part-time (5 women); includes 4 Asian, non-Hispanic/Latino; 2 Hispanic/Latino, 48 international. Average age 26. 179 applicants, 49% accepted, 29 enrolled. In 2010, 49 master's awarded. *Degree requirements:* For master's, internship. *Entrance requirements:* For master's, GRE, minimum GPA of 3.0. Additional exam requirements/recommendations for international students: Required—TOEFL (minimum score 570 paper-based; 230 computer-based; 88 iBT) or IELTS (minimum score 6.5). *Application deadline:* For fall admission, 2/15 priority date for domestic and international students. Applications are processed on a rolling basis. Application fee: $50. *Expenses:* Tuition: Full-time $33,234; part-time $924 per credit hour. Required fees: $219. *Financial support:* In 2010–11, 63 students received support; research assistantships with partial tuition reimbursements available, teaching assistantships with partial tuition reimbursements available, career-related internships or fieldwork, institutionally sponsored loans, scholarships/grants, tuition waivers (partial), and unspecified assistantships available. Support available to part-time students. Financial award applicants required to submit FAFSA. *Faculty research:* Safety, manufacturing (CAM), simulation. *Unit head:* Dr. Michael Kuhl, Interim Department Head, 585-475-2134, E-mail: mekeie@rit.edu. *Application contact:* Diane Ellison, Assistant Vice President, Graduate Enrollment Services, 585-475-2229, Fax: 585-475-7164, E-mail: gradinfo@rit.edu.

Rochester Institute of Technology, Graduate Enrollment Services, Kate Gleason College of Engineering, Department of Microsystems Engineering, Rochester, NY 14623-5603. Offers PhD. Part-time programs available. *Students:* 26 full-time (6 women), 13 part-time (1 woman); includes 1 Black or African American, non-Hispanic/Latino; 1 Hispanic/Latino, 15 international. Average age 30. 35 applicants, 23% accepted, 6 enrolled. In 2010, 3 doctorates awarded. *Degree requirements:* For doctorate, comprehensive exam, thesis/dissertation. *Entrance requirements:* For doctorate, GRE. Additional exam requirements/recommendations for international students: Required—TOEFL (minimum score 570 paper-based; 230 computer-based; 88 iBT) or IELTS (minimum score 6.5). *Application deadline:* For fall admission, 2/15 priority date for domestic and international students. Application fee: $50. *Expenses:* Tuition: Full-time $33,234; part-time $924 per credit hour. Required fees: $219. *Financial support:* In 2010–11, 35 students received support; fellowships with full tuition reimbursements available, research assistantships with partial tuition reimbursements available, teaching assistantships with partial tuition reimbursements available, career-related internships or fieldwork, institutionally sponsored loans, scholarships/grants, health care benefits, and unspecified assistantships available. Support available to part-time students. Financial award applicants required to submit FAFSA. *Faculty research:* Scaling-driven nanoelectronics, MEMS (micro-electro-mechanical systems); photonics and nanophotonics imaging, communications, and sensing research; photovoltaics research in silicon, organic, and stacked solar cells and thrmovoltaics; microfluids research on the behavior, control, and manipulation of fluids at the micro-scale. *Unit head:* Dr. Bruce Smith, Director, 585-475-2058, Fax: 585-475-6879, E-mail: bwsemc@rit.edu. *Application contact:* Diane Ellison, Assistant Vice President, Graduate Enrollment Services, 585-475-2229, Fax: 585-475-7164, E-mail: gradinfo@rit.edu.

Rutgers, The State University of New Jersey, New Brunswick, Graduate School-New Brunswick, Department of Industrial and Systems Engineering, Piscataway, NJ 08854-8097. Offers industrial and systems engineering (MS, PhD); information technology (MS); manufacturing systems engineering (MS); quality and reliability engineering (MS). Part-time and evening/weekend programs available. Terminal master's awarded for partial completion of doctoral program. *Degree requirements:* For master's, thesis or alternative, seminar; for doctorate, comprehensive exam, thesis/dissertation. *Entrance requirements:* For master's and doctorate, GRE General Test. Additional exam requirements/recommendations for international students: Required—TOEFL. *Expenses:* Tuition, state resident: full-time $7200; part-time $600 per credit. Tuition, nonresident: full-time $11,124; part-time $927 per credit. *Faculty research:* Production and manufacturing systems, quality and reliability engineering, systems engineering and aviation safety.

San Jose State University, Graduate Studies and Research, Charles W. Davidson College of Engineering, Department of Industrial and Systems Engineering, San Jose, CA 95192-0001. Offers industrial and systems engineering (MS). Part-time programs available. *Degree requirements:* For master's, comprehensive exam. Electronic applications accepted.

Southern Methodist University, Bobby B. Lyle School of Engineering, Department of Engineering Management, Information, and Systems, Dallas, TX 75275. Offers applied science (MS); engineering management (MSEM, DE); information engineering and management (MSIEM); operations research (MS, PhD); systems engineering (MS, PhD). Part-time and evening/weekend programs available. Postbaccalaureate distance learning degree programs offered. *Faculty:* 8 full-time (1 woman), 22 part-time/adjunct (1 woman). *Students:* 47 full-time (12 women), 348 part-time (75 women); includes 114 minority (31 Black or African American, non-Hispanic/Latino; 2 American Indian or Alaska Native, non-Hispanic/Latino; 34 Asian, non-Hispanic/Latino; 44 Hispanic/Latino; 2 Native Hawaiian or other Pacific Islander, non-Hispanic/Latino; 1 Two or more races, non-Hispanic/Latino), 51 international. Average age 33. 208 applicants, 67% accepted, 92 enrolled. In 2010, 130 master's, 6 doctorates awarded. Terminal master's awarded for partial completion of doctoral program. *Degree requirements:* For master's, thesis optional; for doctorate, thesis/dissertation, oral and written qualifying exams. *Entrance requirements:* For master's, minimum GPA of 3.0 in last 2 years; bachelor's degree in engineering, mathematics, sciences, or technical area; for doctorate, GRE General Test (operations research, engineering management), bachelor's degree in related field. Additional exam requirements/recommendations for international students: Required—TOEFL. *Application deadline:* For fall admission, 7/1 for domestic students, 5/15 for international students; for spring admission, 11/15 for domestic students, 9/1 for international students. Applications are processed on a rolling basis. Application fee: $75. *Financial support:* In 2010–11, 6 students received support, including 4 research assistantships with full tuition reimbursements available (averaging $18,000 per year), 2 teaching assistantships with full tuition reimbursements available (averaging $18,000 per year); tuition waivers (full) also available. *Faculty research:* Telecommunications, decision systems, information engineering, operations research, software. Total annual research expenditures: $275,851. *Unit head:* Dr. Richard S. Barr, Chair, 214-768-1772, Fax: 214-768-1112, E-mail: emis@lyle.smu.edu. *Application contact:* Marc Valerin, Director of Graduate and Executive Admissions, 214-768-3042, E-mail: valerin@lyle.smu.edu.

Southern Polytechnic State University, Division of Engineering, Marietta, GA 30060-2896. Offers systems engineering (MS, Advanced Certificate, Graduate Certificate). Part-time and evening/weekend programs available. *Faculty:* 3 full-time (1 woman), 4 part-time/adjunct (3 women). *Students:* 8 full-time (0 women), 42 part-time (9 women); includes 12 Black or African American, non-Hispanic/Latino; 2 Asian, non-Hispanic/Latino; 3 Hispanic/Latino, 2 international. Average age 39. 15 applicants, 93% accepted, 11 enrolled. In 2010, 12 master's awarded. *Entrance requirements:* Additional exam requirements/recommendations for international students: Required—TOEFL (minimum score 550 paper-based; 213 computer-based; 79 iBT), IELTS (minimum score 6.5). *Application deadline:* For fall admission, 7/1 priority date for domestic students, 5/1 priority date for international students; for spring admission, 11/1 priority date for domestic students, 9/1 priority date for international students. Applications are processed on a rolling basis. Application fee: $20. Electronic applications accepted. *Expenses:* Tuition, state resident: full-time $3690; part-time $205 per semester hour. Tuition, nonresident: full-time $13,428; part-time $746 per semester hour. Required fees: $598 per semester. *Unit head:* Dr. Tom Currin, Associate Dean, 678-915-7482, Fax: 678-915-5527, E-mail: tcurrin@spsu.edu. *Application contact:* Nikki Palamiotis, Director of Graduate Studies, 678-915-4276, Fax: 678-915-7292, E-mail: npalamio@spsu.edu.

Stevens Institute of Technology, Graduate School, School of Systems and Enterprises, Program in Systems Engineering, Hoboken, NJ 07030. Offers agile systems and enterprises (Certificate); systems and supportability engineering (Certificate); systems engineering (M Eng, PhD); systems engineering management (Certificate). *Students:* 34 full-time (11 women), 156 part-time (29 women); includes 5 Black or African American, non-Hispanic/Latino; 19 Asian, non-Hispanic/Latino; 10 Hispanic/Latino, 20 international. Average age 34. *Unit head:* Dr. Charles L. Suffel, Dean of the Graduate School, 201-216-5234, Fax: 201-216-8044, E-mail: csuffel@stevens-tech.edu. *Application contact:* Graduate Admissions, 800-496-4935, Fax: 201-216-8044, E-mail: gradadmissions@stevens.edu.

Stony Brook University, State University of New York, Graduate School, College of Engineering and Applied Sciences, Department of Computer Science, Program in Information Systems Engineering, Stony Brook, NY 11794. Offers MS. *Students:* 1 part-time (0 women). 13 applicants, 0% accepted. *Expenses:* Tuition, state resident: full-time $8370; part-time $349 per credit. Tuition, nonresident: full-time $13,780; part-time $574 per credit. Required fees: $994. *Unit head:* Prof. Arie Kauffman, Chairman, 631-632-8470. *Application contact:* Graduate Director, 631-632-8462, Fax: 631-632-8334.

Texas Tech University, Graduate School, Edward E. Whitacre Jr. College of Engineering, Department of Industrial Engineering, Lubbock, TX 79409. Offers industrial engineering (MSIE, PhD); manufacturing systems engineering (MSMSE); systems and engineering management (MSSEM, PhD). Part-time programs available. Postbaccalaureate distance learning degree programs offered (minimal on-campus study). *Faculty:* 12 full-time (3 women). *Students:* 79 full-time (13 women), 47 part-time (7 women); includes 1 Black or African American, non-Hispanic/Latino; 1 Asian, non-Hispanic/Latino; 2 Hispanic/Latino, 81 international. Average age 28. 282 applicants, 51% accepted, 31 enrolled. In 2010, 39 master's, 9 doctorates awarded. *Degree requirements:* For master's, thesis or alternative; for doctorate, thesis/dissertation. *Entrance requirements:* For master's and doctorate, GRE General Test, minimum GPA of 3.0. Additional exam requirements/recommendations for international students: Required—TOEFL (minimum score 550 paper-based; 213 computer-based; 79 iBT). *Application deadline:* For fall admission, 6/1 priority date for domestic students, 1/15 priority date for international students; for spring admission, 9/1 priority date for domestic students, 6/15 priority date for international students. Applications are processed on a rolling basis. Application fee: $50 ($75 for international students). Electronic applications accepted. *Expenses:* Tuition, state resident: full-time $5495.76; part-time $228.99 per credit hour. Tuition, nonresident: full-time $12,936; part-time $538.99 per credit hour. Required fees: $2674; $36 per credit hour. $905 per semester. *Financial support:* In 2010–11, 40 students received support, including 12 research assistantships with partial tuition reimbursements available (averaging $3,905 per year), 8 teaching assistantships with partial tuition reimbursements available (averaging $3,150 per year). Financial award application deadline: 4/15; financial award applicants required to submit FAFSA. *Faculty research:* Knowledge and engineering management, environmentally conscious manufacturing, biomechanical simulation, aviation security, supply chain management. Total annual research expenditures: $646,598. *Unit head:* Dr. Pat Patterson, Chair, 806-742-3543, Fax: 806-742-3411, E-mail: pat.patterson@ttu.edu. *Application contact:* Dr. Mario Beruvides, Professor, 806-742-3543, Fax: 806-742-3411, E-mail: mario.beruvides@ttu.edu.

The University of Alabama in Huntsville, School of Graduate Studies, College of Engineering, Department of Industrial and Systems Engineering/Engineering Management, Huntsville, AL 35899. Offers industrial and systems engineering (PhD), including engineering management (MSE, PhD), industrial engineering, systems engineering (MSE, PhD); industrial engineering (MSE), including engineering management (MSE, PhD), missile systems engineering, modeling and simulation, rotorcraft systems engineering, systems engineering (MSE, PhD); operations research (MSOR). Part-time and evening/weekend programs available. Postbaccalaureate distance learning degree programs offered (minimal on-campus study). *Faculty:* 8 full-time (2 women), 4 part-time/adjunct (1 woman). *Students:* 11 full-time (2 women), 158 part-time (40 women); includes 26 minority (18 Black or African American, non-Hispanic/Latino; 2 American Indian or Alaska Native, non-Hispanic/Latino; 2 Asian, non-Hispanic/Latino; 3 Hispanic/Latino; 1 Two or more races, non-Hispanic/Latino), 8 international. Average age 36. 108 applicants, 64% accepted, 48 enrolled. In 2010, 30 master's, 5 doctorates awarded. *Degree requirements:* For master's, comprehensive exam, thesis or alternative, oral and written exams; for doctorate, comprehensive exam, thesis/dissertation, oral and written exams. *Entrance requirements:* For master's and doctorate, GRE General Test, minimum GPA of 3.0. Additional exam requirements/recommendations for international students: Required—TOEFL (minimum score 500 paper-based; 173 computer-based; 62 iBT). *Application deadline:* For fall admission, 7/15 for domestic students, 4/1 for international students; for spring admission, 11/30 for domestic students, 9/1 for international students. Applications are processed on a rolling basis. Application fee: $40 ($50 for international students). Electronic applications accepted. *Expenses:* Tuition, state resident: full-time $7250; part-time $407.75 per credit hour. Tuition, nonresident: full-time $17,358; part-time $970.05 per credit hour. Required fees: $246.80 per semester. Tuition and fees vary according to course load and program. *Financial support:* In 2010–11, 7 students received support, including 1 research assistantship with full tuition reimbursement available (averaging $10,340 per year), 6 teaching assistantships with full tuition reimbursements available (averaging $10,768 per year); career-related internships or fieldwork, Federal Work-Study, institutionally sponsored loans, scholarships/grants, health care benefits, and unspecified assistantships also available. Support available to part-time students. Financial award application deadline: 4/1; financial award applicants required to submit FAFSA. *Faculty research:* Engineering management, systems engineering, manufacturing, logistics, simulation. Total annual research expenditures: $7.8 million. *Unit head:* Dr. James Swain, Chair, 256-824-6749, Fax: 256-824-6733, E-mail: jswain@ise.uah.edu. *Application contact:* Kathy Biggs, Graduate Studies Admissions Manager, 256-824-6199, Fax: 256-824-6405, E-mail: deangrad@uah.edu.

University of Alberta, Faculty of Graduate Studies and Research, Department of Electrical and Computer Engineering, Edmonton, AB T6G 2E1, Canada. Offers communications (M Eng, M Sc, PhD); computer engineering (M Eng, M Sc, PhD); electromagnetics (M Eng, M Sc, PhD); nanotechnology and microdevices (M Eng, M Sc, PhD); power/power electronics (M Eng, M Sc, PhD); systems (M Eng, M Sc, PhD). Terminal master's awarded for partial completion of doctoral program. *Degree requirements:* For master's, thesis; for doctorate, thesis/dissertation. *Entrance requirements:* Additional exam requirements/recommendations for international students: Required—TOEFL. Electronic applications accepted. *Faculty research:* Controls, communications, microelectronics, electromagnetics.

The University of Arizona, College of Engineering, Department of Systems and Industrial Engineering, Program in Systems and Industrial Engineering, Tucson, AZ 85721. Offers MS, PhD. Postbaccalaureate distance learning degree programs offered. *Students:* 22 full-time (4 women), 3 part-time (0 women), 21 international. Average age 29. 24 applicants, 75% accepted, 6 enrolled. In 2010, 2 doctorates awarded. *Degree requirements:* For doctorate, thesis/dissertation. *Entrance requirements:* For master's, GRE General Test (minimum score: 500 Verbal, 700 Quantitative), 3 letters of recommendation, letter of intent; for doctorate, GRE General Test (minimum score: 500 Verbal, 750 Quantitative), 3 letters of recommendation, letter of intent. Additional exam requirements/recommendations for international students: Required—TOEFL (minimum score 575 paper-based; 233 computer-based; 80 iBT). *Application deadline:* For fall admission, 6/1 for domestic students, 12/1 for international students; for spring admission, 9/1 for domestic students, 6/1 for international students. Applications are processed on a rolling basis. Application fee: $75. Electronic applications accepted. *Expenses:* Tuition, state resident: full-time $7692. *Financial support:* Tuition waivers (full) and unspecified assistantships available. *Faculty research:* Optimization, systems theory, logistics, transportation, embedded systems. *Unit head:* Dr. K. Larry Head, Head, 520-621-6551, E-mail: larry@sie.arizona.edu. *Application contact:* Linda Cramer, Graduate Secretary, 520-626-4644, Fax: 520-621-6555, E-mail: gradapp@sie.arizona.edu.

The University of Arizona, College of Engineering, Department of Systems and Industrial Engineering, Program in Systems Engineering, Tucson, AZ 85721. Offers MS, PhD. Part-time programs available. *Students:* 11 full-time (4 women), 9 part-time (0 women); includes 10 minority (4 Black or African American, non-Hispanic/Latino; 1 Asian, non-Hispanic/Latino; 4 Hispanic/Latino; 1 Two or more races, non-Hispanic/Latino). Average age 32. 20 applicants, 60% accepted, 9 enrolled. In 2010, 7 master's awarded. *Entrance requirements:* For master's, GRE General Test (minimum score: 500 Verbal, 700 Quantitative), 3 letters of recommendation, letter of intent; for doctorate, GRE General Test (minimum score: 500 Verbal, 750 Quantitative), minimum GPA of 3.5, 3 letters of recommendation, letter of intent. Additional exam requirements/recommendations for international students: Required—TOEFL (minimum score 575 paper-based; 233 computer-based; 80 iBT). *Application deadline:* For fall admission, 6/1 for domestic students, 12/1 for international students; for spring admission, 10/1 for domestic students, 6/1 for international students. Applications are processed on a rolling basis. Application fee: $75. Electronic applications accepted. *Expenses:* Tuition, state resident: full-time $7692. *Financial support:* Institutionally sponsored loans, scholarships/grants, and unspecified assistantships available. *Faculty research:* Man/machine systems, optimal control, algorithmic probability. *Unit head:* Dr. K. Larry Head, Head, 520-621-6551, E-mail: larry@sie.arizona.edu. *Application contact:* Linda Cramer, Graduate Secretary, 520-626-4644, Fax: 520-621-6555, E-mail: gradapp@sie.arizona.edu.

University of Arkansas at Little Rock, Graduate School, George W. Donaghey College of Engineering and Information Technology, Department of Systems Engineering, Little Rock, AR 72204-1099. Offers Graduate Certificate.

University of Central Florida, College of Engineering and Computer Science, Department of Industrial Engineering and Management Systems, Orlando, FL 32816. Offers applied operations research (Certificate); design for usability (Certificate); industrial engineering (MSIE, PhD); industrial engineering and management systems (MS); industrial ergonomics and safety (Certificate); project engineering (Certificate); quality assurance (Certificate); systems engineering (Certificate); systems simulation for engineers (Certificate); training simulation (Certificate). Part-time and evening/weekend programs available. *Faculty:* 17 full-time (4 women), 6 part-time/adjunct (1 woman). *Students:* 112 full-time (31 women), 171 part-time (66 women); includes 79 minority (27 Black or African American, non-Hispanic/Latino; 17 Asian, non-Hispanic/Latino; 32 Hispanic/Latino; 1 Native Hawaiian or other Pacific Islander, non-Hispanic/Latino; 2 Two or more races, non-Hispanic/Latino), 72 international. Average age 33. 210 applicants, 74% accepted, 82 enrolled. In 2010, 65 master's, 7 doctorates, 34 other advanced degrees awarded. *Degree requirements:* For master's, thesis; for doctorate, thesis/dissertation, departmental qualifying exam, candidacy exam. *Entrance requirements:* For master's, GRE General Test, minimum GPA of 3.0 in last 60 hours of course work; for doctorate, minimum GPA of 3.5 in last 60 hours of course work. Additional exam requirements/recommendations for international students: Required—TOEFL. *Application deadline:* For fall admission, 7/15 priority date for domestic students; for spring admission, 12/1 priority date for domestic students. Application fee: $30. Electronic applications accepted. *Expenses:* Tuition, state resident: part-time $256.56 per credit hour. Tuition, nonresident: part-time $1011.52 per credit hour. Part-time tuition and fees vary according to program. *Financial support:* In 2010–11, 24 students received support, including 85 fellowships with partial tuition reimbursements available (averaging $7,300 per year), 19 research assistantships with partial tuition reimbursements available (averaging $8,500 per year), 6 teaching assistantships with partial tuition reimbursements available (averaging $12,200 per year); career-related internships or fieldwork, Federal Work-Study, institutionally sponsored loans, tuition waivers (partial), and unspecified assistantships also available. Financial award application deadline: 3/1; financial award applicants required to submit FAFSA. *Unit head:* Dr. Waldemar Karwowski, Chair, 407-823-2204, E-mail: wkar@mail.ucf.edu. *Application contact:* Dr. Waldemar Karwowski, Chair, 407-823-2204, E-mail: wkar@mail.ucf.edu.

University of Denver, School of Engineering and Computer Science, Department of Computer Science, Denver, CO 80208. Offers computer science (MS, PhD); computer science systems engineering (MS). Part-time programs available. *Faculty:* 11 full-time (2 women), 2 part-time/adjunct (1 woman). *Students:* 2 full-time (1 woman), 80 part-time (12 women); includes 11 minority (2 Black or African American, non-Hispanic/Latino; 3 Asian, non-Hispanic/Latino; 6 Hispanic/Latino), 18 international. Average age 33. 43 applicants, 72% accepted, 7 enrolled. In 2010, 16 master's, 2 doctorates awarded. *Degree requirements:* For doctorate, variable foreign language requirement, comprehensive exam, thesis/dissertation, reading competency in two languages, modern typesetting system, or additional coursework. *Entrance requirements:* For master's and doctorate, GRE General Test. Additional exam requirements/recommendations for international students: Required—TOEFL (minimum score 550 paper-based; 80 iBT). *Application deadline:* Applications are processed on a rolling basis. Application fee: $60. Electronic applications accepted. *Expenses:* Tuition: Full-time $35,604; part-time $29,670 per year. Required fees: $687 per year. Tuition and fees vary according to program. *Financial support:* In 2010–11, 2 research assistantships with full and partial tuition reimbursements (averaging $18,297 per year), 8 teaching assistantships with full and partial tuition reimbursements (averaging $18,297 per year) were awarded; fellowships with full and partial tuition reimbursements, career-related internships or fieldwork, Federal Work-Study, institutionally sponsored loans, scholarships/grants, and unspecified assistantships also available. Financial award application deadline: 3/1; financial award applicants required to submit FAFSA. *Faculty research:* Gaming, UML designs, STAMP. *Unit head:* Dr. Kimon Valavanis, Chair, 303-871-

Systems Engineering

University of Denver (continued)
2586, E-mail: kimon.valavanis@du.edu. *Application contact:* Information Contact, 303-871-2458, E-mail: info@cs.du.edu.

University of Florida, Graduate School, College of Engineering, Department of Industrial and Systems Engineering, Gainesville, FL 32611. Offers ME, MS, PhD, Engr. Part-time and evening/weekend programs available. Postbaccalaureate distance learning degree programs offered (minimal on-campus study). *Faculty:* 14 full-time (1 woman), 2 part-time/adjunct (1 woman). *Students:* 176 full-time (42 women), 155 part-time (35 women); includes 13 Black or African American, non-Hispanic/Latino; 18 Asian, non-Hispanic/Latino; 30 Hispanic/Latino, 155 international. Average age 28. 644 applicants, 35% accepted, 98 enrolled. In 2010, 136 master's, 7 doctorates awarded. Terminal master's awarded for partial completion of doctoral program. *Degree requirements:* For master's, thesis (for some programs); for doctorate, comprehensive exam (for some programs), thesis/dissertation (for some programs). *Entrance requirements:* For master's and doctorate, GRE General Test, minimum GPA of 3.0; for Engr, GRE General Test. Additional exam requirements/recommendations for international students: Required—TOEFL (minimum score 550 paper-based; 213 computer-based; 80 iBT), IELTS (minimum score 6). *Application deadline:* For fall admission, 2/1 priority date for domestic students, 2/1 for international students; for spring admission, 8/1 for domestic and international students. Applications are processed on a rolling basis. Application fee: $30. Electronic applications accepted. *Expenses:* Tuition, state resident: full-time $10,915.92. Tuition, nonresident: full-time $28,309. *Financial support:* In 2010–11, 15 students received support, including 1 fellowship, 10 research assistantships (averaging $19,083 per year), 4 teaching assistantships (averaging $18,238 per year); career-related internships or fieldwork, Federal Work-Study, and unspecified assistantships also available. Financial award application deadline: 1/15; financial award applicants required to submit FAFSA. *Faculty research:* Operations research; financial engineering; logistics and supply chain management; energy, healthcare, and transportation applications of operations research. Total annual research expenditures: $1.7 million. *Unit head:* Dr. Joseph C. Hartman, Chair, 352-392-1464, Fax: 352-392-3537, E-mail: hartman@ise.ufl.edu. *Application contact:* Jonathan C. Smith, Graduate Coordinator, 352-392-1464, Fax: 352-392-9673, E-mail: colesmit@ufl.edu.

University of Houston–Clear Lake, School of Science and Computer Engineering, Program in System Engineering, Houston, TX 77058-1098. Offers MS. *Entrance requirements:* Additional exam requirements/recommendations for international students: Required—TOEFL (minimum score 550 paper-based; 213 computer-based).

University of Illinois at Urbana–Champaign, Graduate College, College of Engineering, Department of Industrial and Enterprise Systems Engineering, Champaign, IL 61820. Offers industrial engineering (MS, PhD); systems and entrepreneurial engineering (MS, PhD); MBA/MS. *Faculty:* 20 full-time (5 women). *Students:* 47 full-time (12 women), 19 part-time (10 women); includes 1 minority (Black or African American, non-Hispanic/Latino), 50 international. 218 applicants, 4% accepted, 5 enrolled. In 2010, 18 master's, 4 doctorates awarded. *Entrance requirements:* For master's and doctorate, GRE, minimum GPA of 3.25. Additional exam requirements/recommendations for international students: Required—TOEFL (minimum score 613 paper-based; 257 computer-based; 103 iBT) or IELTS (minimum score 7). *Application deadline:* Applications are processed on a rolling basis. Application fee: $75 ($90 for international students). Electronic applications accepted. *Financial support:* In 2010–11, 3 fellowships, 42 research assistantships, 43 teaching assistantships were awarded; tuition waivers (full and partial) also available. *Unit head:* Jong-Shi Pang, Head, 217-244-5703, Fax: 217-244-5705, E-mail: jspang@illinois.edu. *Application contact:* Michelle D. Tipsword, Coordinator of Graduate Programs, 217-333-2730, Fax: 217-244-5705, E-mail: deiskamp@illinois.edu.

University of Maryland, Baltimore County, Graduate School, College of Engineering and Information Technology, Department of Computer Science and Electrical Engineering, Program in Systems Engineering, Baltimore, MD 21250. Offers MS, Postbaccalaureate Certificate. Part-time programs available. *Students:* 6 full-time (1 woman), 28 part-time (2 women); includes 12 minority (6 Black or African American, non-Hispanic/Latino; 3 Asian, non-Hispanic/Latino; 3 Hispanic/Latino). Average age 32. 22 applicants, 95% accepted, 14 enrolled. In 2010, 7 master's, 5 other advanced degrees awarded. *Degree requirements:* For master's, comprehensive exam (for some programs), thesis optional. *Entrance requirements:* For master's, BS in engineering or information technology with minimum GPA of 3.0. Additional exam requirements/recommendations for international students: Required—TOEFL (minimum score 550 paper-based; 213 computer-based; 80 iBT). *Application deadline:* For fall admission, 7/1 for domestic and international students; for spring admission, 12/1 for domestic and international students. Applications are processed on a rolling basis. Application fee: $50. Electronic applications accepted. *Financial support:* Career-related internships or fieldwork, Federal Work-Study, scholarships/grants, health care benefits, tuition waivers (partial), and unspecified assistantships available. Support available to part-time students. Financial award application deadline: 6/30; financial award applicants required to submit FAFSA. *Faculty research:* Systems architecture design, modeling and simulation, design and risk analysis, system integrations test, management and engineering projects. *Unit head:* Dr. Gary Carter, Professor and Chair, 410-455-3500, Fax: 410-455-3969, E-mail: carter@cs.umbc.edu. *Application contact:* Dr. Ted M. Foster, Professor of Practice and Assistant Dean, COEIT; Graduate Program Director, 410-455-1564, Fax: 410-455-3559, E-mail: tfoster@umbc.edu.

University of Maryland, College Park, Academic Affairs, A. James Clark School of Engineering, Department of Continuing and Distance Learning in Engineering, College Park, MD 20742. Offers engineering (M Eng), including aerospace engineering, chemical engineering, civil engineering, electrical engineering, engineering, fire protection engineering, materials science and engineering, mechanical engineering, reliability engineering, systems engineering. *Faculty:* 4 full-time (1 woman), 11 part-time/adjunct (1 woman). *Students:* 56 full-time (15 women), 428 part-time (88 women); includes 153 minority (59 Black or African American, non-Hispanic/Latino; 63 Asian, non-Hispanic/Latino; 24 Hispanic/Latino; 7 Two or more races, non-Hispanic/Latino), 55 international. 551 applicants, 82% accepted, 360 enrolled. In 2010, 130 master's awarded. *Application deadline:* For fall admission, 8/15 for domestic students, 1/10 for international students; for spring admission, 12/15 for domestic students, 6/1 for international students. Applications are processed on a rolling basis. Application fee: $75. Electronic applications accepted. *Expenses:* Tuition, area resident: Part-time $471 per credit hour. Tuition, state resident: part-time $471 per credit hour. Tuition, nonresident: part-time $1016 per credit hour. Required fees: $337 per term. *Financial support:* In 2010–11, 2 research assistantships (averaging $20,285 per year), 7 teaching assistantships (averaging $16,962 per year) were awarded. *Unit head:* Dr. Darryll Pines, Dean, 301-405-0376, Fax: 301-314-5908, E-mail: pines@umd.edu. *Application contact:* Dr. Charles A. Caramello, Dean of the Graduate School, 301-405-0358, Fax: 301-314-9305, E-mail: ccaramel@umd.edu.

University of Maryland, College Park, Academic Affairs, A. James Clark School of Engineering, Systems Engineering Program, College Park, MD 20742. Offers M Eng, MS. Part-time and evening/weekend programs available. *Faculty:* 79 full-time (14 women), 11 part-time/adjunct (3 women). *Students:* 10 full-time (3 women), 2 part-time (1 woman); includes 4 minority (1 Black or African American, non-Hispanic/Latino; 3 Asian, non-Hispanic/Latino), 4 international. 48 applicants, 31% accepted, 8 enrolled. *Degree requirements:* For master's, thesis optional. *Entrance requirements:* For master's, GRE General Test, minimum GPA of 3.0. *Application deadline:* For fall admission, 3/15 for domestic students, 2/1 for international students. Applications are processed on a rolling basis. Application fee: $75. Electronic applications accepted. *Expenses:* Tuition, area resident: Part-time $471 per credit hour. Tuition, state resident: part-time $471 per credit hour. Tuition, nonresident: part-time $1016 per credit hour. Required fees: $337 per term. *Financial support:* In 2010–11, 1 fellowship with tuition reimbursement (averaging $32,851 per year), 3 research assistantships with tuition reimbursements (averaging $16,882 per year) were awarded; teaching assistantships with tuition reimbursements, Federal Work-Study and scholarships/grants also available. Support available to part-time students. Financial award applicants required to submit FAFSA. *Faculty research:* Automation, computer, information, manufacturing, and process systems. Total annual research expenditures: $9.5 million. *Unit head:* Dr. Reza Ghodssi, Director, 301-405-8158, Fax: 301-314-9920, E-mail: ghodssi@umd.edu. *Application contact:* Dean of Graduate School, 301-405-0358, Fax: 301-314-9305.

University of Michigan–Dearborn, College of Engineering and Computer Science, Department of Industrial and Manufacturing Systems Engineering, Dearborn, MI 48128-1491. Offers engineering management (MS); industrial and systems engineering (MSE); information systems and technology (MS); information systems engineering (PhD); program and project management (MS); MBA/MSE. Part-time and evening/weekend programs available. *Faculty:* 13 full-time (0 women), 3 part-time/adjunct (0 women). *Students:* 23 full-time (8 women), 142 part-time (40 women); includes 14 Black or African American, non-Hispanic/Latino; 27 Asian, non-Hispanic/Latino; 8 Hispanic/Latino, 23 international. Average age 35. 81 applicants, 58% accepted, 47 enrolled. In 2010, 57 master's awarded. *Degree requirements:* For master's, thesis optional. *Entrance requirements:* For master's, bachelor's degree in applied mathematics, computer science, engineering, or physical science; minimum GPA of 3.0. Additional exam requirements/recommendations for international students: Required—TOEFL (minimum score 560 paper-based; 220 computer-based; 84 iBT). *Application deadline:* For fall admission, 8/1 priority date for domestic students, 4/1 for international students; for winter admission, 12/1 priority date for domestic students, 8/1 for international students; for spring admission, 4/1 for domestic students, 12/1 for international students. Applications are processed on a rolling basis. Application fee: $60. Electronic applications accepted. *Financial support:* Fellowships, research assistantships, teaching assistantships, Federal Work-Study available. Financial award application deadline: 4/1; financial award applicants required to submit FAFSA. *Faculty research:* Health care systems, data and knowledge management, human factors engineering, machine diagnostics, precision machining. *Unit head:* Dr. Armen Zakarian, Chair, 313-593-5361, Fax: 313-593-3692, E-mail: zakarian@umd.umich.edu. *Application contact:* Joey W. Woods, Graduate Program Assistant, 313-593-5361, Fax: 313-593-3692, E-mail: jwwoods@umd.umich.edu.

University of Michigan–Dearborn, College of Engineering and Computer Science, Interdisciplinary Programs, Program in Information Systems Engineering, Dearborn, MI 48128-1491. Offers PhD. Part-time and evening/weekend programs available. *Faculty:* 1 full-time (0 women). *Students:* 12 full-time (2 women), 5 part-time (0 women); includes 1 Asian, non-Hispanic/Latino, 6 international. Average age 32. 13 applicants, 31% accepted, 4 enrolled. *Degree requirements:* For doctorate, thesis/dissertation. *Entrance requirements:* For doctorate, GRE. Additional exam requirements/recommendations for international students: Required—TOEFL (minimum score 560 paper-based; 220 computer-based; 84 iBT). *Application deadline:* For fall admission, 8/1 priority date for domestic students, 4/1 priority date for international students; for winter admission, 12/1 priority date for domestic students, 8/1 priority date for international students; for spring admission, 4/1 priority date for domestic students, 12/1 priority date for international students. Applications are processed on a rolling basis. Application fee: $60 ($75 for international students). Electronic applications accepted. *Financial support:* In 2010–11, 1 research assistantship (averaging $19,000 per year) was awarded; scholarships/grants and unspecified assistantships also available. Financial award applicants required to submit FAFSA. *Unit head:* Dr. Pankaj K. Mallick, Director/Professor, 313-593-5119, Fax: 313-593-5386, E-mail: pkm@umich.edu. *Application contact:* Sherry Boyd, Intermediate Administrative Assistant, 313-593-5582, Fax: 313-593-5386, E-mail: idpgrad@umd.umich.edu.

University of Minnesota, Twin Cities Campus, Institute of Technology, Technological Leadership Institute, Program in Infrastructure Systems Engineering, Minneapolis, MN 55455-0213. Offers MSISE. Evening/weekend programs available. *Degree requirements:* For master's, capstone project. *Entrance requirements:* For master's, minimum of one year of work experience in related field, undergraduate degree in civil engineering or related field, minimum GPA of 3.0. Additional exam requirements/recommendations for international students: Required—TOEFL (minimum score 580 paper-based; 240 computer-based; 90 iBT). Electronic applications accepted. *Expenses:* Contact institution. *Faculty research:* Water distribution, pavement maintenance and management, traffic management systems, infrastructure systems maintenance and management.

University of New Haven, Graduate School, Tagliatela College of Engineering, Program in Computer and Information Science, West Haven, CT 06516-1916. Offers computer science (MS, Certificate), including advanced applications (MS), computer applications (Certificate), computer programming (Certificate), computer systems (MS), computing (Certificate), database and information systems (MS), network administration (Certificate), network systems (MS), software engineering and development (MS). Part-time and evening/weekend programs available. *Students:* 54 full-time (12 women), 25 part-time (4 women); includes 1 Black or African American, non-Hispanic/Latino; 3 Asian, non-Hispanic/Latino, 51 international. Average age 28. 204 applicants, 100% accepted, 40 enrolled. In 2010, 19 master's, 1 other advanced degree awarded. *Degree requirements:* For master's, thesis or alternative. *Entrance requirements:* Additional exam requirements/recommendations for international students: Required—TOEFL (minimum score 520 paper-based; 190 computer-based; 70 iBT); Recommended—IELTS (minimum score 5.5). *Application deadline:* For fall admission, 5/31 for international students; for winter admission, 10/15 for international students; for spring admission, 1/15 for international students. Applications are processed on a rolling basis. Application fee: $50. Electronic applications accepted. *Financial support:* Research assistantships with partial tuition reimbursements, teaching assistantships with partial tuition reimbursements, career-related internships or fieldwork, Federal Work-Study, scholarships/grants, tuition waivers, and unspecified assistantships available. Support available to part-time students. Financial award applicants required to submit FAFSA. *Unit head:* Dr. Tahany Fergany, Coordinator, 203-932-7067. *Application contact:* Eloise Gormley, Director of Graduate Admissions, 203-932-7449, Fax: 203-932-7137, E-mail: gradinfo@newhaven.edu.

The University of North Carolina at Charlotte, Graduate School, The William States Lee College of Engineering, Department of Civil and Environmental Engineering, Charlotte, NC 28223-0001. Offers civil engineering (MSCE); infrastructure and environmental systems (PhD), including infrastructure and environmental systems design. Part-time and evening/weekend programs available. *Faculty:* 20 full-time (2 women). *Students:* 44 full-time (13 women), 48 part-time (15 women); includes 11 minority (4 Black or African American, non-Hispanic/Latino; 1 American Indian or Alaska Native, non-Hispanic/Latino; 6 Hispanic/Latino), 29 international. Average age 29. 45 applicants, 69% accepted, 20 enrolled. In 2010, 10 master's, 3 doctorates awarded. Terminal master's awarded for partial completion of doctoral program. *Degree requirements:* For master's, thesis or alternative, thesis or project. *Entrance requirements:* For master's, GRE General Test, minimum GPA of 3.0 in undergraduate major, 2.75 overall. Additional exam requirements/recommendations for international students: Required—TOEFL (minimum score 550 paper-based; 220 computer-based; 83 iBT). *Application deadline:* For fall admission, 7/1 for domestic students, 5/1 for international students; for spring admission, 11/1 for domestic students, 10/1 for international students. Applications are processed on a rolling basis. Application fee: $55. Electronic applications accepted. *Expenses:* Tuition, state resident: full-time $3464. Tuition, nonresident: full-time $14,297. Required fees: $2094. Tuition and fees vary according to course load. *Financial support:* In 2010–11, 46 students received support, including 2 fellowships (averaging $28,347 per year), 19 research assistantships (averaging $5,352 per year), 25 teaching assistantships (averaging $6,166 per year); career-related internships or fieldwork, Federal Work-Study, institutionally sponsored loans, scholarships/grants, and administrative assistantship also available. Support available to part-time students. Financial award application deadline: 4/1; financial award applicants required to submit FAFSA. *Faculty research:* Structural composite materials, storm water systems, natural and man-made disaster reduction engineering, older drivers and nighttime driving, soil contamination and transport. Total annual research expenditures: $1.3 million. *Unit head:* Dr. David T. Young, Chair, 704-687-4175, Fax: 704-687-6953, E-mail: dyoung@.uncc.edu. *Application contact:* Kathy B. Giddings, Director of Graduate Admissions, 704-687-5503, Fax: 704-687-3279, E-mail: gradadm@uncc.edu.

University of Pennsylvania, School of Engineering and Applied Science, Department of Electrical and Systems Engineering, Philadelphia, PA 19104. Offers MSE, PhD. Part-time programs available. *Faculty:* 27 full-time (2 women), 9 part-time/adjunct (0 women). *Students:* 155 full-time (37 women), 42 part-time (4 women); includes 2 Black or African American, non-Hispanic/Latino; 15 Asian, non-Hispanic/Latino; 1 Hispanic/Latino, 137 international. 724 applicants, 33% accepted, 111 enrolled. In 2010, 59 master's, 1 doctorate awarded. Terminal master's awarded for partial completion of doctoral program. *Degree requirements:* For master's, thesis optional; for doctorate, comprehensive exam, thesis/dissertation. *Entrance requirements:* For master's and doctorate, GRE General Test. Additional exam requirements/recommendations for international students: Required—TOEFL. *Application deadline:* For fall admission, 6/1 priority date for domestic students, 5/1 priority date for international students; for spring admission, 11/1 priority date for domestic students, 10/1 priority date for international students. Applications are processed on a rolling basis. Application fee: $70. Electronic applications accepted. *Expenses:* Tuition: Full-time $25,660; part-time $4758 per course. Required fees: $2152; $270 per course. Tuition and fees vary according to course load, degree level and program. *Financial support:* Fellowships, research assistantships, teaching assistantships, institutionally sponsored loans, scholarships/grants, traineeships, health care benefits, and unspecified assistantships available. *Faculty research:* Electro-optics, microwave and millimeter-wave optics, solid-state and chemical electronics, electromagnetic propagation, telecommunications. *Application contact:* Nichole Wood, Graduate Coordinator, 215-898-9390, E-mail: woodn@seas.upenn.edu.

University of Regina, Faculty of Graduate Studies and Research, Faculty of Engineering and Applied Science, Program in Industrial Systems Engineering, Regina, SK S4S 0A2, Canada. Offers M Eng, MA Sc, PhD. Part-time programs available. *Faculty:* 13 full-time (2 women). *Students:* 33 full-time (6 women), 4 part-time (0 women). 67 applicants, 55% accepted. In 2010, 7 master's awarded. *Degree requirements:* For master's, thesis (for some programs); for doctorate, thesis/dissertation. *Entrance requirements:* For doctorate, master's degree. Additional exam requirements/recommendations for international students: Required—TOEFL (minimum score 550 paper-based; 80 iBT). *Application deadline:* For fall admission, 3/31 for domestic and international students; for winter admission, 7/31 for domestic and international students; for spring admission, 11/30 for domestic and international students. Applications are processed on a rolling basis. Application fee: $100. Tuition and fees charges are reported in Canadian dollars. *Expenses:* Tuition, area resident: Full-time $3244.50 Canadian dollars; part-time $180.25 Canadian dollars per credit hour. International tuition: $4744.50 Canadian dollars full-time. Required fees: $494 Canadian dollars; $115.25 Canadian dollars per credit hour. $115.25 Canadian dollars per semester. Tuition and fees vary according to program. *Financial support:* In 2010–11, 3 fellowships (averaging $18,000 per year), 2 research assistantships (averaging $17,250 per year), 5 teaching assistantships (averaging $6,956 per year) were awarded; career-related internships or fieldwork and scholarships/grants also available. Financial award application deadline: 6/15. *Faculty research:* Stochastic systems simulation, metallurgy of welding, computer-aided engineering, finite element method of engineering systems, manufacturing systems. *Unit head:* Dr. Raphael Idem, Associate Dean, Research and Graduate Studies, 306-337-2696, E-mail: raphael.idem@uregina.ca. *Application contact:* Dr. Denise Stilling, Chair, Graduate Program Coordinator, 306-337-2696, Fax: 306-585-4855, E-mail: denise.stilling@uregina.ca.

University of Regina, Faculty of Graduate Studies and Research, Faculty of Engineering and Applied Science, Program in Petroleum Systems Engineering, Regina, SK S4S 0A2, Canada. Offers M Eng, MA Sc, PhD. Part-time programs available. *Faculty:* 7 full-time (1 woman). *Students:* 32 full-time (5 women), 6 part-time (1 woman). 91 applicants, 30% accepted. In 2010, 8 master's, 2 doctorates awarded. *Degree requirements:* For master's, thesis; for doctorate, thesis/dissertation. *Entrance requirements:* Additional exam requirements/recommendations for international students: Required—TOEFL (minimum score 550 paper-based; 80 iBT). *Application deadline:* For fall admission, 3/31 for domestic and international students; for winter admission, 7/31 for domestic and international students; for spring admission, 11/30 for domestic and international students. Application fee: $100. Electronic applications accepted. Tuition and fees charges are reported in Canadian dollars. *Expenses:* Tuition, area resident: Full-time $3244.50 Canadian dollars; part-time $180.25 Canadian dollars per credit hour. International tuition: $4744.50 Canadian dollars full-time. Required fees: $494 Canadian dollars; $115.25 Canadian dollars per credit hour. $115.25 Canadian dollars per semester. Tuition and fees vary according to program. *Financial support:* In 2010–11, 3 fellowships (averaging $19,000 per year), 2 research assistantships (averaging $17,250 per year), 7 teaching assistantships (averaging $6,853 per year) were awarded; career-related internships or fieldwork and scholarships/grants also available. Financial award application deadline: 6/15. *Faculty research:* Enhanced oil recovery, production engineering, reservoir engineering, surface thermodynamics, geostatistics. *Unit head:* Dr. Raphael Idem, Associate Dean, Research and Graduate Studies, 306-337-3287, Fax: 306-585-4855, E-mail: raphael.idem@uregina.ca. *Application contact:* Dr. Farshid Torabi, Chair, Graduate Program Coordinator, 306-337-3287, Fax: 306-585-4855, E-mail: farshid.torabi@uregina.ca.

University of Regina, Faculty of Graduate Studies and Research, Faculty of Engineering and Applied Science, Program in Process Systems Engineering, Regina, SK S4S 0A2, Canada. Offers M Eng, MA Sc, PhD. Part-time programs available. *Faculty:* 1 full-time (0 women). *Students:* 27 full-time (4 women), 1 part-time (0 women). 12 applicants, 42% accepted. In 2010, 1 master's awarded. *Degree requirements:* For master's, thesis (for some programs); for doctorate, thesis/dissertation. *Entrance requirements:* Additional exam requirements/recommendations for international students: Required—TOEFL (minimum score 550 paper-based; 80 iBT). *Application deadline:* For fall admission, 3/31 for domestic and international students; for winter admission, 7/31 for domestic and international students; for spring admission, 11/30 for domestic and international students. Application fee: $100. Electronic applications accepted. Tuition and fees charges are reported in Canadian dollars. *Expenses:* Tuition, area resident: Full-time $3244.50 Canadian dollars; part-time $180.25 Canadian dollars per credit hour. International tuition: $4744.50 Canadian dollars full-time. Required fees: $494 Canadian dollars; $115.25 Canadian dollars per credit hour. $115.25 Canadian dollars per semester. Tuition and fees vary according to program. *Financial support:* In 2010–11, 2 fellowships (averaging $18,000 per year), 2 research assistantships (averaging $16,500 per year) were awarded; teaching assistantships, career-related internships or fieldwork and scholarships/grants also available. Financial award application deadline: 6/15. *Faculty research:* Membrane separation technologies, advanced reaction engineering, advanced transport phenomena, advanced heat transfer, advanced mass transfer. *Unit head:* Dr. Raphael Idem, Associate Dean, Research and Graduate Studies, 306-585-4470, Fax: 306-585-4855, E-mail: raphael.idem@uregina.ca. *Application contact:* Dr. David deMontigny, Chair, Graduate Program Coordinator, 306-337-2277, Fax: 306-585-4855, E-mail: david.demontigny@uregina.ca.

University of St. Thomas, Graduate Studies, School of Engineering, St. Paul, MN 55105-1096. Offers manufacturing engineering and operations (MS); mechanical engineering (MS); medical device development (Certificate); regulatory science (MS); software engineering (MS); software management (MS); software systems (MSS); systems engineering (MS); technology management (MS). *Accreditation:* ABET (one or more programs are accredited). *Entrance requirements:* For master's, resume, official transcripts. Additional exam requirements/recommendations for international students: Required—TOEFL (minimum score 550 paper-based). *Application deadline:* For fall admission, 8/1 priority date for domestic students; for spring admission, 1/1 priority date for domestic students. Applications are processed on a rolling basis. Application fee: $30. Electronic applications accepted. *Expenses:* Contact institution. *Financial support:* Fellowships, research assistantships, institutionally sponsored loans and scholarships/grants available. Support available to part-time students. Financial award application deadline: 4/1; financial award applicants required to submit FAFSA. *Unit head:* Don Weinkauf, Dean, 651-962-5760, Fax: 651-962-6419, E-mail: dhweinkauf@stthomas.edu. *Application contact:* Joyce A. Taylor, Graduate Programs Coordinator, 651-962-5756, Fax: 651-962-6419, E-mail: jataylor1@stthomas.edu.

University of Southern California, Graduate School, Viterbi School of Engineering, Daniel J. Epstein Department of Industrial and Systems Engineering, Los Angeles, CA 90089. Offers digital supply chain management (MS); engineering management (MS); engineering technology communication (Graduate Certificate); health systems operations (Graduate Certificate); industrial and systems engineering (MS, PhD, Engr); manufacturing engineering (MS); operations research engineering (MS); optimization and supply chain management (Graduate Certificate); product development engineering (MS); safety systems and security (MS); systems architecting and engineering (MS, Graduate Certificate); systems safety and security (Graduate Certificate); transportation systems (Graduate Certificate); MS/MBA. Part-time and evening/weekend programs available. Postbaccalaureate distance learning degree programs offered (no on-campus study). *Faculty:* 12 full-time (2 women), 21 part-time/adjunct (2 women). *Students:* 224 full-time (69 women), 143 part-time (32 women); includes 63 minority (6 Black or African American, non-Hispanic/Latino; 35 Asian, non-Hispanic/Latino; 17 Hispanic/Latino; 5 Two or more races, non-Hispanic/Latino), 253 international. 669 applicants, 45% accepted, 155 enrolled. In 2010, 98 master's, 7 doctorates awarded. Terminal master's awarded for partial completion of doctoral program. *Degree requirements:* For master's, thesis optional; for doctorate, thesis/dissertation. *Entrance requirements:* For master's and doctorate, GRE General Test. *Application deadline:* For fall admission, 12/1 priority date for domestic students, 11/1 priority date for international students; for spring admission, 9/15 priority date for domestic and international students. Applications are processed on a rolling basis. Application fee: $85. Electronic applications accepted. *Expenses:* Tuition: Full-time $31,240; part-time $1420 per unit. Required fees: $600. One-time fee: $35 full-time. Full-time tuition and fees vary according to degree level and program. *Financial support:* In 2010–11, fellowships with full tuition reimbursements (averaging $30,000 per year), research assistantships with full tuition reimbursements (averaging $20,000 per year), teaching assistantships with full tuition reimbursements (averaging $20,000 per year) were awarded; career-related internships or fieldwork, scholarships/grants, health care benefits, and unspecified assistantships also available. Financial award application deadline: 12/1; financial award applicants required to submit CSS PROFILE or FAFSA. *Faculty research:* Health systems, music cognition and retrieval, transportation and logistics, manufacturing and automation, engineering systems design, risk and economic analysis. Total annual research expenditures: $1 million. *Unit head:* Dr. F. Stan Settles, Chair, 213-740-4893, E-mail: isedept@usc.edu. *Application contact:* Evelyn Felina, Director of Student Affairs, 213-740-7549, E-mail: efelina@usc.edu.

The University of Texas at Arlington, Graduate School, College of Engineering, Department of Industrial and Manufacturing Systems Engineering, Program in Systems Engineering, Arlington, TX 76019. Offers MS. *Students:* 1 full-time (0 women), 27 part-time (5 women); includes 5 minority (2 Black or African American, non-Hispanic/Latino; 1 Asian, non-Hispanic/Latino; 2 Hispanic/Latino), 1 international. 9 applicants, 89% accepted, 5 enrolled. In 2010, 7 master's awarded. *Expenses:* Tuition, state resident: full-time $7500. Tuition, nonresident: full-time $13,080. International tuition: $13,250 full-time. *Unit head:* Dr. Donald H. Liles, Chair, 817-272-3092, Fax: 817-272-3406, E-mail: dliles@uta.edu. *Application contact:* Dr. Sheik Imrhan, Graduate Advisor, 817-272-3167, Fax: 817-272-3406, E-mail: imrhan@uta.edu.

The University of Texas at Dallas, Erik Jonsson School of Engineering and Computer Science, Program in Mechanical Engineering, Richardson, TX 75080. Offers mechanical systems engineering (MSME); microelectromechanical systems (MSME). Part-time and evening/weekend programs available. *Faculty:* 4 full-time (1 woman). *Students:* 11 full-time (4 women), 2 part-time (0 women); includes 1 minority (Hispanic/Latino), 7 international. Average age 27. 82 applicants, 37% accepted, 7 enrolled. *Degree requirements:* For master's, thesis or major design project. *Entrance requirements:* For master's, GRE General Test, minimum GPA of 3.0 in related bachelor's degree. Additional exam requirements/recommendations for international students: Required—TOEFL (minimum score 550 paper-based; 215 computer-based). *Application deadline:* For fall admission, 7/15 for domestic students, 5/1 priority date for international students; for spring admission, 11/15 for domestic students, 9/1 priority date for international students. Applications are processed on a rolling basis. Application fee: $50 ($100 for international students). Electronic applications accepted. *Expenses:* Tuition, state resident: full-time $10,248; part-time $569 per credit hour. Tuition, nonresident: full-time $18,544; part-time $1030 per credit hour. Tuition and fees vary according to course load. *Financial support:* In 2010–11, 9 students received support, including 4 research assistantships with partial tuition reimbursements available (averaging $15,292 per year), 3 teaching assistantships with partial tuition reimbursements available (averaging $14,850 per year); career-related internships or fieldwork, Federal Work-Study, institutionally sponsored loans, scholarships/grants, and unspecified assistantships also available. Support available to part-time students. Financial award application deadline: 4/30; financial award applicants required to submit FAFSA. *Faculty research:* Nano-materials and nano-electronic devices, biomedical devices, nonlinear systems and controls, semiconductor and oxide surfaces, flexible electronics. *Unit head:* Dr. Mario Rotea, Department Head, 972-883-2720, Fax: 972-883-2813, E-mail: rotea@utdallas.edu. *Application contact:* Dr. Matthew Goeckner, Associate Department Head, 972-883-4293, Fax: 972-883-2813, E-mail: gradecs@utdallas.edu.

The University of Texas at El Paso, Graduate School, College of Engineering, Department of Industrial Engineering, El Paso, TX 79968-0001. Offers industrial engineering (MS); manufacturing engineering (MS); systems engineering (MS, Certificate). Part-time and evening/weekend programs available. *Students:* 51 (11 women); includes 1 Asian, non-Hispanic/Latino; 42 Hispanic/Latino, 8 international. Average age 34. 38 applicants. In 2010, 46 master's awarded. *Degree requirements:* For master's, thesis optional. *Entrance requirements:* For master's, GRE General Test, minimum GPA of 3.0 in major. Additional exam requirements/recommendations for international students: Required—TOEFL. *Application deadline:* For fall admission, 7/1 priority date for domestic students, 3/1 for international students; for spring admission, 11/1 priority date for domestic students, 9/1 for international students. Applications are processed on a rolling basis. Application fee: $15 ($65 for international students). Electronic applications accepted. *Financial support:* In 2010–11, research assistantships with partial tuition reimbursements (averaging $21,125 per year), teaching assistantships with partial tuition reimbursements (averaging $16,900 per year) were awarded; fellowships with partial tuition reimbursements, Federal Work-Study, institutionally sponsored loans, scholarships/grants, and tuition waivers (partial) also available. Financial award application deadline: 3/15; financial award applicants required to submit FAFSA. *Faculty research:* Computer vision, automated inspection, simulation and modeling. *Unit head:* Dr. Rafael S. Gutierrez, Chair, 915-747-5450, Fax: 915-747-5019, E-mail: rsgutier@utep.edu. *Application contact:* Dr. Charles H. Ambler, Dean of the Graduate School, 915-747-5491 Ext. 7886, Fax: 915-747-5788, E-mail: cambler@utep.edu.

University of Virginia, School of Engineering and Applied Science, Department of Systems and Information Engineering, Charlottesville, VA 22903. Offers ME, MS, PhD, ME/MBA. Postbaccalaureate distance learning degree programs offered (no on-campus study). *Faculty:* 16 full-time (1 woman). *Students:* 78 full-time (21 women), 5 part-time (1 woman); includes 3 Black or African American, non-Hispanic/Latino; 6 Asian, non-Hispanic/Latino; 5 Hispanic/Latino; 4 Two or more races, non-Hispanic/Latino, 31 international. Average age 28. 121 applicants, 32% accepted, 24 enrolled. In 2010, 63 master's, 6 doctorates awarded. *Degree requirements:* For master's, comprehensive exam (for some programs); for doctorate, comprehensive exam, thesis/dissertation. *Entrance requirements:* For master's, GRE General Test, 3 letters of recommendation; for doctorate, GRE General Test, 3 letters of recommendation; essay. Additional exam requirements/recommendations for international students: Required—TOEFL (minimum score 650 paper-based; 250 computer-based; 90 iBT), IELTS (minimum score 7). *Application deadline:* For fall admission, 8/1 for domestic students, 4/1 for international students; for winter admission, 12/1 for domestic students, 8/1 for international students; for spring admission, 5/1 for domestic students, 1/1 for international students. Applications are processed on a rolling basis. Application fee: $60. Electronic applications accepted. *Financial support:* Fellowships, research assistantships, teaching assistantships available. Financial award application deadline: 1/15; financial award applicants required to submit FAFSA. *Faculty research:* Systems integration, human factors, computational statistics and simulation, risk and decision analysis, optimization and control. *Unit head:* Barry Horowitz, Chair, 434-924-5393, Fax: 434-982-2972. *Application contact:* Departmental Office, 434-924-5393, Fax: 434-982-2972, E-mail: siegradadministration@virginia.edu.

Systems Engineering

University of Waterloo, Graduate Studies, Faculty of Engineering, Department of Systems Design Engineering, Waterloo, ON N2L 3G1, Canada. Offers M Eng, MA Sc, PhD. Part-time programs available. *Degree requirements:* For master's, research project or thesis; for doctorate, comprehensive exam, thesis/dissertation. *Entrance requirements:* For master's, honors degree, minimum B average, resumé; for doctorate, master's degree, minimum A- average. Additional exam requirements/recommendations for international students: Required—TOEFL, TWE. Electronic applications accepted. *Faculty research:* Ergonomics, human factors and biomedical engineering, modeling and simulation, pattern analysis, machine intelligence and robotics.

University of Wisconsin–Madison, Graduate School, College of Engineering, Department of Industrial and Systems Engineering, Madison, WI 53706. Offers MS, PhD. Part-time programs available. *Faculty:* 21 full-time (6 women), 12 part-time/adjunct (4 women). *Students:* 158 full-time (55 women), 15 part-time (7 women); includes 8 Black or African American, non-Hispanic/Latino; 1 American Indian or Alaska Native, non-Hispanic/Latino; 5 Asian, non-Hispanic/Latino; 2 Hispanic/Latino, 120 international. Average age 27. 449 applicants, 24% accepted, 39 enrolled. In 2010, 55 master's, 8 doctorates awarded. Terminal master's awarded for partial completion of doctoral program. *Degree requirements:* For master's, thesis optional; for doctorate, comprehensive exam, thesis/dissertation. *Entrance requirements:* For master's, GRE General Test, minimum GPA of 3.0, BS in engineering or equivalent, course work in computer programming and statistics; for doctorate, GRE General Test, minimum GPA of 3.0. Additional exam requirements/recommendations for international students: Required—IELTS (minimum score 6); Recommended—TOEFL (minimum score 550 paper-based; 213 computer-based; 80 iBT). *Application deadline:* For fall admission, 2/1 priority date for domestic and international students; for spring admission, 10/1 priority date for domestic and international students. Application fee: $56. Electronic applications accepted. *Expenses:* Tuition, state resident: full-time $9887.36; part-time $617.96 per credit. Tuition, nonresident: full-time $24,054; part-time $1503.40 per credit. Required fees: $67.63 per credit. Tuition and fees vary according to reciprocity agreements. *Financial support:* In 2010–11, 87 students received support, including fellowships with full tuition reimbursements available (averaging $21,760 per year), 72 research assistantships with full tuition reimbursements available (averaging $40,800 per year), 15 teaching assistantships with full tuition reimbursements available (averaging $28,175 per year); career-related internships or fieldwork, Federal Work-Study, institutionally sponsored loans, scholarships/grants, traineeships, health care benefits, and unspecified assistantships also available. *Faculty research:* Human factors and ergonomics, manufacturing and production systems, health systems engineering, decision science/operations research, quality engineering. Total annual research expenditures: $10.2 million. *Unit head:* Dr. Vicki M. Bier, Chair, 608-262-2064, Fax: 608-262-8454, E-mail: bier@engr.wisc.edu. *Application contact:* Anne Duchek, Graduate Admissions Coordinator, 608-890-2765, Fax: 608-890-2204, E-mail: amduchek@engr.wisc.edu.

Virginia Polytechnic Institute and State University, Graduate School, College of Engineering, Department of Civil and Environmental Engineering, Blacksburg, VA 24061. Offers civil engineering (M Eng, MS, PhD); civil infrastructure systems (Certificate); environmental engineering (MS); environmental sciences and engineering (MS); transportation systems engineering (Certificate); treatment process engineering (Certificate); urban hydrology and stormwater management (Certificate); water quality management (Certificate). *Accreditation:* ABET (one or more programs are accredited). *Faculty:* 44 full-time (8 women), 1 part-time/adjunct (0 women). *Students:* 320 full-time (108 women), 70 part-time (20 women); includes 9 Black or African American, non-Hispanic/Latino; 15 Asian, non-Hispanic/Latino; 13 Hispanic/Latino, 126 international. Average age 27. 639 applicants, 44% accepted, 121 enrolled. In 2010, 97 master's, 18 doctorates awarded. *Degree requirements:* For master's, comprehensive exam (for some programs), thesis (for some programs); for doctorate, comprehensive exam (for some programs), thesis/dissertation (for some programs). *Entrance requirements:* For

master's and doctorate, GRE. Additional exam requirements/recommendations for international students: Required—TOEFL (minimum score 550 paper-based; 213 computer-based). *Application deadline:* For fall admission, 7/1 for domestic and international students; for spring admission, 12/1 for domestic and international students. Applications are processed on a rolling basis. Application fee: $65. Electronic applications accepted. *Expenses:* Tuition, area resident: Full-time $9399; part-time $488 per credit hour. Tuition, state resident: full-time $9399; part-time $488 per credit hour. Tuition, nonresident: full-time $17,854; part-time $957.75 per credit hour. International tuition: $17,854 full-time. Required fees: $1534. Full-time tuition and fees vary according to program. *Financial support:* In 2010–11, 35 fellowships with full tuition reimbursements (averaging $5,861 per year), 82 research assistantships with full tuition reimbursements (averaging $20,397 per year), 33 teaching assistantships with full tuition reimbursements (averaging $14,542 per year) were awarded; career-related internships or fieldwork, Federal Work-Study, scholarships/grants, health care benefits, and unspecified assistantships also available. Financial award application deadline: 1/15. *Faculty research:* Construction, environmental geotechnical hydrosystems, structures and transportation engineering. Total annual research expenditures: $12.2 million. *Unit head:* Dr. Sam Easterling, UNIT HEAD, 540-231-5143, Fax: 540-231-7532, E-mail: seaster@vt.edu. *Application contact:* Marc Widdowson, Contact, 540-231-7153, Fax: 540-231-7532, E-mail: mwiddows@vt.edu.

Virginia Polytechnic Institute and State University, Graduate School, College of Engineering, Department of Industrial and Systems Engineering, Program in Systems Engineering, Blacksburg, VA 24061. Offers MS. *Students:* 17 part-time (5 women); includes 1 Black or African American, non-Hispanic/Latino; 1 Asian, non-Hispanic/Latino. Average age 27. In 2010, 5 master's awarded. *Degree requirements:* For master's, comprehensive exam (for some programs), thesis (for some programs). *Entrance requirements:* For master's, GRE. Additional exam requirements/recommendations for international students: Required—TOEFL (minimum score 550 paper-based; 213 computer-based). *Application deadline:* For fall admission, 7/1 for domestic and international students; for spring admission, 12/1 for domestic and international students. Applications are processed on a rolling basis. Application fee: $65. Electronic applications accepted. *Expenses:* Tuition, area resident: Full-time $9399; part-time $488 per credit hour. Tuition, state resident: full-time $9399; part-time $488 per credit hour. Tuition, nonresident: full-time $17,854; part-time $957.75 per credit hour. International tuition: $17,854 full-time. Required fees: $1534. Full-time tuition and fees vary according to program. *Financial support:* Career-related internships or fieldwork, Federal Work-Study, scholarships/grants, health care benefits, and unspecified assistantships available. Financial award application deadline: 1/15. *Unit head:* Dr. Kostantinos P. Triantis, UNIT HEAD, 703-538-8446, Fax: 540-231-7248, E-mail: triantis@vt.edu. *Application contact:* Jeny Beausoliel, Contact, 703-538-8431, Fax: 540-231-7248, E-mail: jeny15@vt.edu.

Western International University, Graduate Programs in Business, Master of Science Program in Information System Engineering, Phoenix, AZ 85021-2718. Offers MS. Part-time and evening/weekend programs available. Postbaccalaureate distance learning degree programs offered (no on-campus study). *Entrance requirements:* For master's, minimum GPA of 2.75. Additional exam requirements/recommendations for international students: Required—TOEFL (minimum score 550 paper-based; 213 computer-based; 79 iBT), TWE (minimum score 5), or IELTS. Electronic applications accepted.

West Virginia University Institute of Technology, College of Engineering, Program in Control Systems Engineering, Montgomery, WV 25136. Offers MS. Part-time programs available. *Degree requirements:* For master's, thesis or alternative, fieldwork. *Entrance requirements:* For master's, GRE General Test, minimum GPA of 3.0. Additional exam requirements/recommendations for international students: Required—TOEFL. *Faculty research:* Process control.

THE UNIVERSITY OF TEXAS AT SAN ANTONIO

Master of Science in Advanced Manufacturing and Enterprise Engineering

Programs of Study	The Master of Science program in Advanced Manufacturing and Enterprise Engineering (M.S. in AMEE) at the University of Texas at San Antonio (UTSA) is designed to offer individuals the opportunity for continued study toward positions of leadership in industry and academia and for continuing technical education in a more specialized area. The M.S. AMEE is truly an interdisciplinary program founded on the strong collaboration of the Departments of Mechanical Engineering, Electrical and Computer Engineering; Information Systems and Technology Management; Management Science and Statistics; Computer Science; and the Center for Advanced Manufacturing and Lean Systems (CAMLS). Graduate students are exposed to research problems through interaction with the industry member of CAMLS and its state-of-the-art laboratory facilities. The program is offered with a thesis or nonthesis option.
	Advanced manufacturing, as the core component of enterprise systems, encompasses effective and efficient integration and synthesis of automation technologies, human resources, and decision-making models that facilitate design, planning, scheduling, and control of production of goods and provision of services. Enterprise engineering is defined as the body of knowledge, principles, and practices having to do with the analysis, design, implementation, and operation of an enterprise.
	Graduates of this program will have the fundamental knowledge and understanding of the operational complexity of enterprises, manufacturing and business process improvement/optimization, and integrated product/process/system design. In addition, graduates will have the cognitive skills to critically evaluate the potential benefits of alternative manufacturing strategies; to use virtual/simulated platforms to facilitate and improve business processes; and to analyze enterprise systems as systems of interacting units, components, and subsystems.
Research Facilities	In addition to its own dedicated Engineering Building, the College of Engineering operates out of UTSA's $84 million, 227,000-square-foot Biotechnology, Sciences and Engineering Building (BSE), which opened in 2006. The BSE features high-tech classrooms, state-of-the-art laboratories, and modern computing networks. The second phase of this project—the $90 million, 150,000-square-foot Applied Engineering and Technology Building (AET) opened in the fall of 2009. A teaching and research facility, the AET features the most sophisticated technology for an information-intensive environment.
	Students in the program have access to a wide range of equipment and resources, including a flexible manufacturing and lean systems lab, manufacturing systems and automation lab, robotics and intelligent machines lab, sustainable manufacturing systems lab, and an advanced machining cell at the engineering machine shop.
Financial Aid	Various forms of financial support and fellowships, including graduate teaching assistantships (GTA), graduate research assistantships (GRA), and tuition scholarships are available for qualified applicants. Additional financial aid information can be found at http://www.graduateschool.utsa.edu/prospective_students/detail/financing_your_future/.
Cost of Study	For the 2011–12 academic year, tuition and fees for a full-time graduate degree student (9 semester hours) are approximately $3149 per semester for Texas residents and $8783 per semester for nonresidents. Some courses and programs have additional fees. Please view the following Web sites for more information: http://www.utsa.edu/fiscalservices/tuition.html and http://www.graduateschool.utsa.edu/prospective_students/detail/graduate_tuition_and_fees.
Living and Housing Costs	University on-campus housing is available and includes apartment-style living at four complexes—Chisholm Hall, University Oaks, Laurel Village, and Chaparral Village. Off-campus housing is also available and includes many apartments adjacent to the University as well as a large number located within a 5-mile drive. The rate for a one-bedroom apartment is approximately $500 per month.
Student Group	In the 2010 fall semester, the University enrolled more than 30,000 students, of whom more than 4,000 were graduate students. Students in the program have the opportunity to join a number of student organizations related to their field of study: the American Institute of Aeronautics and Astronautics; American Society of Heating, Refrigerating, and Air-Conditioning Engineers; American Society of Mechanical Engineers; Materials Research Society; Society of Automotive Engineers; Society of Manufacturing Engineers; Society of Women Engineers; and the Texas Society of Professional Engineers.
Location	San Antonio, with a population of 1.5 million, is one of the nation's major metropolitan areas. As the home of the Alamo and numerous other missions built by the Franciscans, the city is historically and culturally diverse. The Guadalupe Cultural Arts Center, McNay Art Museum, the San Antonio Museum of Art, and the Witte Museum enrich the city. The performing arts are represented by the San Antonio Symphony, the annual Tejano Music Festival and Tejano Music Awards, and performances by opera and ballet companies. Also notable are Sea World, Six Flags Fiesta Texas, Brackenridge Park, the Botanical Gardens, and the downtown Riverwalk. The San Antonio Zoo has the third-largest collection in North America. A city landmark is the Tower of the Americas, which was built for the 1968 World's Fair. San Antonio is home to the National Basketball Association's Spurs, league champions in 2000, 2003, 2005, and 2007. Numerous nearby lakes allow almost year-round outdoor activity, and the beaches of the Texas Gulf coast are within a 2-hour drive. San Antonio is home to numerous festivals throughout the year, including the Fiesta San Antonio and the Rodeo with activities such as parades, fairs, and concerts.
The University	The University was founded in 1969 and has since become a comprehensive metropolitan institution. Its research expenditures place it in the top 25 percent of public universities in Texas. The University has entered a new building and recruitment phase with a view to greatly expand the research effort in the engineering and science. UTSA Roadrunners football is slated to compete as an NCAA Division I FCS independent in August 2011 and is expected to transition to the Division I FBS by 2013.
Applying	Applicants must meet University-wide graduate admission requirements and must also comply with general University regulations. Due to the multidisciplinary nature of the program, the Graduate Advisor of Record (GAR), in consultation with the Mechanical Engineering Graduate Program Committee and the Department Chair, will evaluate each student's transcript and determine any course deficiencies on a case-by-case basis. Students admitted with course deficiencies will be required to take additional courses within their program of study to make up the deficiencies. Courses taken to make up deficiencies may not count toward the graduate degree. Applicants who have insufficient preparation for the program, or who lack certain supporting documentation, may be admitted on a conditional basis. Additional information regarding admissions requirements and application procedures can be found at http://engineering.utsa.edu/graduate/admissions.php.
	The application deadline for domestic applicants is July 1 for the fall term and November 1 for the spring term. For international applicants, the deadline is April 1 for the fall term and September 1 for the spring term.
Correspondence and Information	For application information:

For application information:
The Graduate School
The University of Texas at San Antonio
One UTSA Circle
San Antonio, Texas 78249
Phone: 210-458-4330
Web site: http://www.graduateschool.utsa.edu

For program information:
Department of Mechanical Engineering
The University of Texas at San Antonio
One UTSA Circle
San Antonio, Texas 78249
Phone: 210-458-7614
E-mail: Can.Saygin@utsa.edu
Web site: http://engineering.utsa.edu/graduate/ms-amee.php

The University of Texas at San Antonio

THE FACULTY AND THEIR RESEARCH

Professors

Ronald Bagley, Ph.D., Air Force Tech. Material characterization, engineering mathematics. E-mail: Ronald.Bagley@utsa.edu.

F. Frank Chen, Ph.D., Missouri–Columbia. Lean manufacturing, flexible manufacturing, supply chain management. E-mail: FF.Chen@utsa.edu.

Hai-Chao Han, Ph.D., Xi'an Jiaotong (China) and California, San Diego. Cardiovascular biomechanics, mechanical modeling and analysis, tissue remodeling. E-mail: HaiChao.Han@utsa.edu.

Harry Millwater, Ph.D., Texas at Austin. Risk assessment, probabilistic life prediction, engine health monitoring. E-mail: Harry.Millwater@utsa.edu.

Amir Karimi, Ph.D., Kentucky; PE. Metastable thermodynamics, phase change heat transfer, thermal systems. E-mail: Amir.Karimi@utsa.edu.

Yesh P. Singh, D.Eng., Wisconsin–Milwaukee; PE. Design of machine elements, customized higher-pair linkages. E-mail: Yesh.Singh@utsa.edu.

Xiaodu Wang, Ph.D., Yokohama National (Japan). Tissue biomechanics, bone remodeling and tissue quality, micro/nanomechanics of materials. E-mail: Xiaodu.Wang@utsa.edu.

Associate Professors

Yusheng Feng, Ph.D., Texas at Austin. Computational and applied math, statistical mechanics and biophysics, cancer treatment simulation. E-mail: Yusheng.Feng@utsa.edu.

Randall Manteufel, Ph.D., MIT. Reliability analysis, performance assessment, thermal-fluid systems. E-mail: Randall.Manteufel@utsa.edu.

Brent Nowak, Ph.D., Texas at Austin. Robotics and intelligent machines, sensors and sensing systems, electromechanical system. E-mail: Brent.Nowak@utsa.edu.

Can Saygin, Ph.D., Middle East Technical (Turkey). Manufacturing engineering, shop floor control and automation, distributed decision-making. E-mail: Can.Saygin@utsa.edu.

Assistant Professors

Kiran Bhaganagar, Ph.D., Cornell. Direct numerical simulation, turbulence, flow in natural systems. E-mail: Kiran.Bhaganagar@utsa.edu.

Zhi-Gang Feng, Ph.D., Tulane. Multiphase flow, computational fluid dynamics, heat and mass transfer. E-mail: Zhigang.Feng@utsa.edu.

John Foster, Ph.D., Purdue. Viscoplasticity and dynamic fracture peridynamics.

Hung-Da Wan, Ph.D., Virginia Tech. Lean manufacturing, enterprise engineering, flexible manufacturing systems. E-mail: Hungda.Wan@utsa.edu.

Xiaowei Zeng, Ph.D., George Washington. Cell mechanics, cell-substrate interactions, bone mechanics, meshfree method, cohesive zone method, multiscale modeling and simulation.

Section 15
Management of Engineering and Technology

This section contains a directory of institutions offering graduate work in management of engineering and technology, followed by in-depth entries submitted by institutions that chose to prepare detailed program descriptions. Additional information about programs listed in the directory but not augmented by an in-depth entry may be obtained by writing directly to the dean of a graduate school or chair of a department at the address given in the directory.

For programs offering related work, in the other guides in this series:

Graduate Programs in the Humanities, Arts & Social Sciences

See *Applied Arts and Design, Architecture, Economics,* and *Sociology, Anthropology, and Archaeology*

Graduate Programs in the Biological Sciences

See *Ecology, Environmental Biology,* and *Evolutionary Biology and Biophysics (Radiation Biology)*

Graduate Programs in Business, Education, Health, Information Studies, Law & Social Work

See *Business Administration and Management, Health Services (Health Services Management and Hospital Administration), Law,* and *Public Health*

CONTENTS

Construction Management

The American University in Dubai, Master in Business Administration Program, Dubai, United Arab Emirates. Offers general (MBA); healthcare management (MBA); international finance (MBA); international marketing (MBA); management of construction enterprises (MBA). Part-time and evening/weekend programs available. *Degree requirements:* For master's, thesis optional. *Entrance requirements:* For master's, GMAT, Interview. Additional exam requirements/recommendations for international students: Required—TOEFL (minimum score 550 paper-based; 213 computer-based; 79 iBT). Electronic applications accepted.

Arizona State University, Ira A. Fulton School of Engineering, ASU Engineering Online Programs, Tempe, AZ 85287. Offers construction (MS); embedded systems (M Eng); enterprise systems innovation and management (MSE); modeling and simulation (M Eng); quality and reliability engineering (M Eng); software engineering (MSE); systems engineering (M Eng). *Expenses:* Tuition, state resident: full-time $8510; part-time $608 per credit. Tuition, nonresident: full-time $16,542; part-time $919 per credit. Required fees: $339; $110 per credit. Part-time tuition and fees vary according to course load.

Arizona State University, Ira A. Fulton School of Engineering, Del E. Webb School of Construction, Tempe, AZ 85287-5306. Offers civil, environmental and sustainable engineering (MS, MSE, PhD); construction (MS, MSE, PhD); construction engineering (MSE). Part-time and evening/weekend programs available. Postbaccalaureate distance learning degree programs offered (minimal on-campus study). *Faculty:* 40 full-time (4 women), 6 part-time/adjunct (1 woman). *Students:* 149 full-time (51 women), 85 part-time (17 women); includes 32 minority (6 Black or African American, non-Hispanic/Latino; 2 American Indian or Alaska Native, non-Hispanic/Latino; 13 Asian, non-Hispanic/Latino; 10 Hispanic/Latino; 1 Native Hawaiian or other Pacific Islander, non-Hispanic/Latino), 69 international. Average age 29. 379 applicants, 53% accepted, 77 enrolled. In 2010, 44 master's, 10 doctorates awarded. Terminal master's awarded for partial completion of doctoral program. *Degree requirements:* For master's, thesis optional, comprehensive exams (MSE); interactive Program of Study (iPOS) submitted before completing 50 percent of required credit hours; for doctorate, comprehensive exam, thesis/dissertation, interactive Program of Study (iPOS) submitted before completing 50 percent of required credit hours. *Entrance requirements:* For master's, GRE, minimum GPA of 3.0 or equivalent in last 2 years of work leading to bachelor's degree; for doctorate, GRE, minimum GPA of 3.0 in last 2 years of work leading to bachelor's degree, 3.2 in all graduate-level coursework with master's degree; 3 letters of recommendation; resume/curriculum vitae; letter of intent; thesis (if applicable); statement of research interests. Additional exam requirements/recommendations for international students: Required—TOEFL, IELTS, or Pearson Test of English. *Application deadline:* For fall admission, 1/1 for domestic and international students; for spring admission, 7/1 for domestic and international students. Application fee: $70 ($90 for international students). Electronic applications accepted. *Expenses:* Contact institution. *Financial support:* In 2010–11, 67 research assistantships with full and partial tuition reimbursements (averaging $16,393 per year), 17 teaching assistantships with full and partial tuition reimbursements (averaging $13,812 per year) were awarded; fellowships with full and partial tuition reimbursements, career-related internships or fieldwork, institutionally sponsored loans, scholarships/grants, traineeships, and tuition waivers (full and partial) also available. Financial award application deadline: 3/1; financial award applicants required to submit FAFSA. *Faculty research:* Water purification, transportation (safety and materials), construction management, environmental biotechnology, environmental nanotechnology, earth systems engineering and management, SMART innovations, project performance metrics, and underground infrastructure. Total annual research expenditures: $8.5 million. *Unit head:* Dr. G. Edward Gibson, Director, 480-965-7972, E-mail: edd.gibson@asu.edu. *Application contact:* Graduate Admissions, 480-965-6113.

Auburn University, Graduate School, College of Architecture, Design, and Construction, Department of Building Science, Auburn University, AL 36849. Offers building science (MBS); construction management (MBS). *Faculty:* 18 full-time (1 woman), 3 part-time/adjunct (1 woman). *Students:* 23 full-time (6 women), 25 part-time (3 women); includes 1 Black or African American, non-Hispanic/Latino; 2 Hispanic/Latino, 4 international. Average age 27. 83 applicants, 60% accepted, 42 enrolled. In 2010, 7 master's awarded. *Entrance requirements:* For master's, GRE General Test. *Application deadline:* For fall admission, 7/7 for domestic students; for spring admission, 11/24 for domestic students. Applications are processed on a rolling basis. Application fee: $50 ($60 for international students). Electronic applications accepted. *Expenses:* Tuition, state resident: full-time $7002. Tuition, nonresident: full-time $21,898. International tuition: $22,116 full-time. Required fees: $892. Tuition and fees vary according to course load and program. *Financial support:* Application deadline: 3/15. *Unit head:* Dr. Richard Burt, Head, 334-844-5260. *Application contact:* Dr. George Flowers, Dean of the Graduate School, 334-844-2125.

Bowling Green State University, Graduate College, College of Technology, Department of Technology Systems, Bowling Green, OH 43403. Offers construction management (MIT); manufacturing technology (MIT). Part-time programs available. *Degree requirements:* For master's, thesis or alternative. *Entrance requirements:* For master's, GRE General Test. Additional exam requirements/recommendations for international students: Required—TOEFL. Electronic applications accepted.

Brigham Young University, Graduate Studies, Ira A. Fulton College of Engineering and Technology, School of Technology, Provo, UT 84602-1001. Offers construction management (MS); information technology (MS); manufacturing systems (MS); technology and engineering education (MS). *Faculty:* 26 full-time (0 women). *Students:* 29 full-time (3 women), 6 part-time (0 women); includes 1 Black or African American, non-Hispanic/Latino; 7 American Indian or Alaska Native, non-Hispanic/Latino; 1 Asian, non-Hispanic/Latino; 3 Hispanic/Latino, 3 international. Average age 25. 14 applicants, 71% accepted, 6 enrolled. In 2010, 10 master's awarded. *Degree requirements:* For master's, thesis. *Entrance requirements:* For master's, GRE General Test, GMAT of GRE (Construction Management emphasis), minimum GPA of 3.0 in last 60 hours of course work. Additional exam requirements/recommendations for international students: Required—TOEFL (minimum score 580 paper-based; 237 computer-based; 85 iBT). *Application deadline:* For fall admission, 2/15 for domestic and international students; for winter admission, 9/15 for domestic and international students; for spring admission, 2/15 for domestic and international students. Application fee: $50. Electronic applications accepted. *Expenses:* Tuition: Full-time $5580; part-time $310 per credit hour. Tuition and fees vary according to program and student's religious affiliation. *Financial support:* In 2010–11, 34 students received support, including 13 research assistantships (averaging $3,498 per year), 6 teaching assistantships (averaging $3,000 per year); fellowships, career-related internships or fieldwork and scholarships/grants also available. Financial award application deadline: 2/1; financial award applicants required to submit FAFSA. *Faculty research:* Real time process control in IT, electronic physical design, processing and non-linear systems, networking, computerized systems in CM. Total annual research expenditures: $238,500. *Unit head:* Val D. Hawks, Director, 801-422-6300, Fax: 801-422-0490, E-mail: hawksv@byu.edu. *Application contact:* Ronald E. Terry, Graduate Coordinator, 801-422-4297, Fax: 801-422-0490, E-mail: ralowe@byu.edu.

California State University, East Bay, Office of Academic Programs and Graduate Studies, College of Science, Engineering Department, Hayward, CA 94542-3000. Offers construction management (MS); engineering management (MS). *Faculty:* 4 full-time (2 women). *Students:* 30 full-time (12 women), 62 part-time (12 women); includes 24 minority (4 Black or African American, non-Hispanic/Latino; 9 Asian, non-Hispanic/Latino; 11 Hispanic/Latino), 30 international. Average age 32. 92 applicants, 78% accepted, 27 enrolled. In 2010, 23 master's awarded. *Entrance requirements:* For master's, GRE or GMAT, minimum GPA of 2.5. Additional exam requirements/recommendations for international students: Required—TOEFL (minimum score 550 paper-based; 213 computer-based). *Application deadline:* For fall admission, 6/30 for domestic and international students. Application fee: $55. Electronic applications accepted. *Financial support:* Federal Work-Study and institutionally sponsored loans available. Support available to part-time students. Financial award application deadline: 3/2; financial award applicants required to submit FAFSA. *Unit head:* Dr. Saeid Motavalli, Chair, 510-885-2654, Fax: 510-885-2678, E-mail: saeid.motavalli@csueastbay.edu. *Application contact:* Dr. Donna Wiley, Interim Associate Director, 510-885-2928, Fax: 510-885-4777, E-mail: donna.wiley@csueastbay.edu.

Carnegie Mellon University, College of Fine Arts, School of Architecture, Pittsburgh, PA 15213-3891. Offers architectural engineering construction management (M Sc); architecture (MSA); architecture, engineering, and construction management (PhD); building performance and diagnostics (M Sc, PhD); computational design (M Sc, PhD); sustainable design (M Sc); urban design (M Sc). Terminal master's awarded for partial completion of doctoral program. *Degree requirements:* For doctorate, thesis/dissertation. *Entrance requirements:* For master's and doctorate, GRE General Test. Additional exam requirements/recommendations for international students: Required—TOEFL.

Central Connecticut State University, School of Graduate Studies, School of Technology, Department of Manufacturing and Construction Management, New Britain, CT 06050-4010. Offers construction management (MS, Certificate); lean manufacturing and Six Sigma (Certificate); supply chain and logistics (Certificate); technology management (MS). Part-time and evening/weekend programs available. *Faculty:* 19 full-time (4 women), 25 part-time/adjunct (1 woman). *Students:* 15 full-time (4 women), 78 part-time (16 women); includes 19 minority (10 Black or African American, non-Hispanic/Latino; 5 Asian, non-Hispanic/Latino; 3 Hispanic/Latino; 1 Two or more races, non-Hispanic/Latino), 5 international. Average age 38. 67 applicants, 76% accepted, 34 enrolled. In 2010, 24 master's awarded. *Degree requirements:* For master's, comprehensive exam, thesis or alternative; for Certificate, qualifying exam. *Entrance requirements:* For master's, minimum undergraduate GPA of 2.7. Additional exam requirements/recommendations for international students: Required—TOEFL. *Application deadline:* For fall admission, 7/1 for domestic students; for spring admission, 12/1 for domestic students. Applications are processed on a rolling basis. Application fee: $50. Electronic applications accepted. *Expenses:* Tuition, area resident: Full-time $5012; part-time $470 per credit. Tuition, state resident: full-time $7518; part-time $482 per credit. Tuition, nonresident: full-time $13,962; part-time $482 per credit. Required fees: $3772. One-time fee: $62 part-time. *Financial support:* In 2010–11, 5 students received support, including 5 research assistantships; career-related internships or fieldwork, Federal Work-Study, scholarships/grants, and unspecified assistantships also available. Support available to part-time students. Financial award application deadline: 2/15; financial award applicants required to submit FAFSA. *Faculty research:* All aspects of middle management, technical supervision in the workplace. *Unit head:* Dr. Jacob Kovel, Chair, 860-832-1830. *Application contact:* Dr. Jacob Kovel, Chair, 860-832-1830.

Clemson University, Graduate School, College of Architecture, Arts, and Humanities, Department of Construction Science and Management, Clemson, SC 29634. Offers MCSM. Part-time programs available. *Faculty:* 5 full-time (2 women). *Students:* 10 full-time (2 women), 5 part-time (0 women), 4 international. Average age 30. 30 applicants, 57% accepted, 7 enrolled. In 2010, 17 master's awarded. *Degree requirements:* For master's, thesis optional. *Entrance requirements:* For master's, GRE General Test, one year of construction experience, current resume. Additional exam requirements/recommendations for international students: Required—TOEFL. *Application deadline:* For fall admission, 1/1 for domestic students, 4/15 for international students; for spring admission, 9/1 for domestic students, 9/15 for international students. Application fee: $70 ($80 for international students). Electronic applications accepted. *Expenses:* Tuition, state resident: full-time $6492; part-time $400 per credit hour. Tuition, nonresident: full-time $13,634; part-time $800 per credit hour. Required fees: $262 per semester. Part-time tuition and fees vary according to course load and program. *Financial support:* In 2010–11, 8 students received support, including 8 teaching assistantships with partial tuition reimbursements available (averaging $5,688 per year); career-related internships or fieldwork, institutionally sponsored loans, scholarships/grants, health care benefits, and unspecified assistantships also available. Support available to part-time students. Financial award applicants required to submit FAFSA. *Faculty research:* Construction best practices, productivity improvement, women issues in construction, construction project management. Total annual research expenditures: $8,378. *Unit head:* Roger Liska, Chair, 864-656-0181, Fax: 864-656-0204, E-mail: riggor@clemson.edu. *Application contact:* Roger Liska, 864-656-0181, Fax: 864-656-0204, E-mail: riggor@clemson.edu.

Colorado State University, Graduate School, College of Applied Human Sciences, Department of Construction Management, Fort Collins, CO 80523-1584. Offers MS. Part-time and evening/weekend programs available. *Faculty:* 11 full-time (4 women), 1 part-time/adjunct (0 women). *Students:* 21 full-time (5 women), 37 part-time (5 women); includes 2 minority (1 Black or African American, non-Hispanic/Latino; 1 Hispanic/Latino), 3 international. Average age 35. 51 applicants, 59% accepted, 23 enrolled. In 2010, 19 master's awarded. *Degree requirements:* For master's, thesis optional, professional paper, article for journal or proceedings with faculty advisor. *Entrance requirements:* For master's, GRE, BA/BS from accredited institution, minimum GPA of 3.0. Additional exam requirements/recommendations for international students: Required—TOEFL (minimum score 550 paper-based; 213 computer-based; 80 iBT). *Application deadline:* For fall admission, 2/15 for domestic and international students. Application fee: $50. Electronic applications accepted. *Expenses:* Tuition, state resident: full-time $7434; part-time $413 per credit. Tuition, nonresident: full-time $19,022; part-time $1057 per credit. Required fees: $1729; $88 per credit. *Financial support:* In 2010–11, 13 students received support, including 6 research assistantships (averaging $7,252 per year), 7 teaching assistantships with full tuition reimbursements available (averaging $17,135 per year); fellowships, scholarships/grants and unspecified assistantships also available. Financial award application deadline: 3/1; financial award applicants required to submit FAFSA. *Faculty research:* Sustainable construction management, construction materials science, information technology and transfer, renewable energy systems, Internet project management. Total annual research expenditures: $150,762. *Unit head:* Dr. Mostafa M. Khattab, Interim Head, 970-491-6808, Fax: 970-491-2473, E-mail: mostafa.khattab@colostate.edu. *Application contact:* Kristen Haller, Graduate Program Advisor, 970-491-7355, Fax: 970-491-2473, E-mail: Kristen.Haller@colostate.edu.

Columbia University, Fu Foundation School of Engineering and Applied Science, Department of Civil Engineering and Engineering Mechanics, New York, NY 10027. Offers civil engineering (MS, Eng Sc D, PhD, Engr); construction engineering and management (MS); engineering mechanics (MS, Eng Sc D, PhD, Engr). Part-time programs available. Postbaccalaureate distance learning degree programs offered (no on-campus study). *Faculty:* 16 full-time (1 woman), 25 part-time/adjunct (3 women). *Students:* 96 full-time (19 women), 42 part-time (14 women); includes 25 minority (3 Black or African American, non-Hispanic/Latino; 11 Asian, non-Hispanic/Latino; 10 Hispanic/Latino; 1 Two or more races, non-Hispanic/Latino), 70 international. Average age 27. 265 applicants, 35% accepted, 59 enrolled. In 2010, 67 master's, 29 doctorates, 2 other advanced degrees awarded. Terminal master's awarded for partial completion of doctoral program. *Degree requirements:* For doctorate, thesis/dissertation, qualifying exam. *Entrance requirements:* For master's, doctorate, and Engr, GRE General Test. Additional exam requirements/recommendations for international students: Required—TOEFL, IELTS. *Application deadline:* For fall admission, 12/1 priority date for domestic and international students; for spring admission, 10/1 priority date for domestic and international students. Application fee: $95. Electronic applications accepted. *Financial support:* In 2010–11, 39 students received support, including 5 fellowships with full tuition reimbursements available (averaging $30,660 per year), 23 research assistantships with full tuition reimbursements available (averaging $30,660 per year), 11 teaching assistantships with full tuition reimbursements available (averaging $30,660 per year); traineeships and health care benefits also available. Financial award application deadline: 12/1; financial award applicants required to submit FAFSA. *Faculty research:* Motion monitoring of Manhattan Bridge, lightweight concrete panels, simulation of life of well sealant, intercultural knowledge system dynamics, corrosion monitoring of New York City bridges. *Unit head:* Dr. Raimondo Betti, Professor and Department

Chairman, 212-854-6388, Fax: 212-854-7081, E-mail: betti@civil.columbia.edu. *Application contact:* Rene B. Testa, Professor, 212-854-3143, Fax: 212-854-6267, E-mail: testa@civil.columbia.edu.

Columbia University, School of Continuing Education, Program in Construction Administration, New York, NY 10027. Offers MS. Part-time and evening/weekend programs available. *Degree requirements:* For master's, minimum GPA of 3.0 or internship. *Entrance requirements:* For master's, bachelor's degree, minimum GPA of 3.0. Electronic applications accepted.

Drexel University, School of Technology and Professional Studies, Philadelphia, PA 19104-2875. Offers construction management (MS); engineering technology (MS); food science (MS); hospitality management (MS); professional studies: creativity studies (MS); professional studies: e-learning leadership (MS); professional studies: homeland security management (MS); project management (MS); property management (MS); sport management (MS). Postbaccalaureate distance learning degree programs offered.

Eastern Michigan University, Graduate School, College of Technology, School of Engineering Technology, Program in Construction Management, Ypsilanti, MI 48197. Offers MS. Part-time and evening/weekend programs available. Postbaccalaureate distance learning degree programs offered (minimal on-campus study). *Students:* 14 full-time (2 women), 18 part-time (7 women); includes 4 minority (all Black or African American, non-Hispanic/Latino), 7 international. Average age 31. In 2010, 12 master's awarded. *Entrance requirements:* Additional exam requirements/recommendations for international students: Required—TOEFL. *Application deadline:* Applications are processed on a rolling basis. Application fee: $35. *Financial support:* Fellowships, research assistantships with full tuition reimbursements, teaching assistantships with full tuition reimbursements, career-related internships or fieldwork, Federal Work-Study, institutionally sponsored loans, scholarships/grants, tuition waivers (partial), and unspecified assistantships available. Support available to part-time students. Financial award applicants required to submit FAFSA. *Unit head:* Dr. James Stein, Program Coordinator, 734-487-1940, Fax: 734-487-8755, E-mail: jstein@emich.edu. *Application contact:* Dr. James Stein, Program Coordinator, 734-487-1940, Fax: 734-487-8755, E-mail: jstein@emich.edu.

Florida International University, College of Engineering and Computing, Department of Construction Management, Miami, FL 33175. Offers MS. Part-time and evening/weekend programs available. *Faculty:* 6 full-time (0 women), 8 part-time/adjunct (0 women). *Students:* 69 full-time (26 women), 103 part-time (25 women); includes 29 Black or African American, non-Hispanic/Latino; 1 American Indian or Alaska Native, non-Hispanic/Latino; 5 Asian, non-Hispanic/Latino; 66 Hispanic/Latino, 27 international. Average age 30. 264 applicants, 40% accepted, 82 enrolled. In 2010, 106 master's awarded. *Degree requirements:* For master's, thesis optional. *Entrance requirements:* For master's, minimum GPA of 3.0 in upper-level course work. Additional exam requirements/recommendations for international students: Required—TOEFL (minimum score 550 paper-based; 80 iBT). *Application deadline:* For fall admission, 6/1 for domestic students, 4/1 for international students; for spring admission, 10/1 for domestic students, 9/1 for international students. Applications are processed on a rolling basis. Application fee: $30. Electronic applications accepted. *Financial support:* In 2010–11, 5 students received support. Institutionally sponsored loans, scholarships/grants, and unspecified assistantships available. Financial award application deadline: 3/1; financial award applicants required to submit FAFSA. *Faculty research:* Information technology, construction organizations, contracts and partnerships in construction, construction education, concrete technology. *Unit head:* Dr. Irtishad Ahmad, Chair, Construction Management Department, 305-348-3045, Fax: 305-348-6255, E-mail: irtishad.ahmad@fiu.edu. *Application contact:* Maria Parrilla, Graduate Admissions Assistant, 305-348-1890, Fax: 305-348-6142, E-mail: grad_eng@fiu.edu.

Harrisburg University of Science and Technology, Program in Project Management, Harrisburg, PA 17101. Offers construction services (MS); governmental services (MS); information technology (MS). Part-time and evening/weekend programs available. *Faculty:* 1 full-time (0 women), 3 part-time/adjunct (0 women). *Students:* 11 part-time (2 women); includes 1 Black or African American, non-Hispanic/Latino; 1 Asian, non-Hispanic/Latino; 1 Hispanic/Latino, 1 international. Average age 30. 24 applicants, 75% accepted. In 2010, 7 master's awarded. *Entrance requirements:* For master's, BS, BBA. Additional exam requirements/recommendations for international students: Required—TOEFL (minimum score 520 paper-based; 200 computer-based; 80 iBT). *Application deadline:* For fall admission, 8/1 priority date for domestic students, 7/1 priority date for international students. Applications are processed on a rolling basis. Application fee: $0. Electronic applications accepted. *Expenses:* Tuition: Full-time $19,500; part-time $700 per credit hour. *Financial support:* Scholarships/grants available. Financial award applicants required to submit FAFSA. *Unit head:* Dr. Amjad Umar, Director and Professor, 717-901-5141, Fax: 717-901-3141, E-mail: aumar@harrisburgu.edu. *Application contact:* Timothy Dawson, Information Contact, 717-901-5158, Fax: 717-901-3158, E-mail: admissions@harrisburgu.edu.

Illinois Institute of Technology, Graduate College, Armour College of Engineering, Department of Civil, Architectural and Environmental Engineering, Chicago, IL 60616-3793. Offers architectural engineering (M Arch E); civil engineering (MS, PhD), including architectural engineering (MS), construction engineering and management (MS), geoenvironmental engineering (MS), geotechnical engineering (MS), structural engineering (MS), transportation engineering (MS); construction engineering and management (MCEM); environmental engineering (M Env E, PhD); geoenvironmental engineering (M Geoenv E); geotechnical engineering (MGE); public works (MPW); structural engineering (MSE); transportation engineering (M Trans E). Part-time and evening/weekend programs available. Postbaccalaureate distance learning degree programs offered (minimal on-campus study). *Faculty:* 15 full-time (1 woman), 13 part-time/adjunct (1 woman). *Students:* 159 full-time (63 women), 109 part-time (22 women); includes 30 minority (9 Black or African American, non-Hispanic/Latino; 16 Asian, non-Hispanic/Latino; 5 Hispanic/Latino), 126 international. Average age 27. 453 applicants, 66% accepted, 98 enrolled. In 2010, 76 master's, 1 doctorate awarded. Terminal master's awarded for partial completion of doctoral program. *Degree requirements:* For master's, thesis (for some programs); for doctorate, comprehensive exam, thesis/dissertation. *Entrance requirements:* For master's, GRE General Test (minimum score 900 Quantitative and Verbal, 2.5 Analytical Writing), minimum undergraduate GPA of 3.0; for doctorate, GRE General Test (minimum score 1000 Quantitative and Verbal, 3.0 Analytical Writing), minimum undergraduate GPA of 3.0. Additional exam requirements/recommendations for international students: Required—TOEFL (minimum score 523 paper-based; 70 iBT); Recommended—IELTS (minimum score 5.5). *Application deadline:* For fall admission, 5/1 for domestic and international students; for spring admission, 10/15 for domestic and international students. Applications are processed on a rolling basis. Application fee: $50. Electronic applications accepted. *Expenses:* Tuition: Full-time $18,576; part-time $1032 per credit hour. Required fees: $583 per semester. One-time fee: $150. Tuition and fees vary according to program and student level. *Financial support:* In 2010–11, 13 research assistantships with full and partial tuition reimbursements (averaging $9,453 per year), 19 teaching assistantships with full and partial tuition reimbursements (averaging $3,163 per year) were awarded; fellowships with full and partial tuition reimbursements, Federal Work-Study, institutionally sponsored loans, scholarships/grants, health care benefits, tuition waivers (partial), and unspecified assistantships also available. Support available to part-time students. Financial award applicants required to submit FAFSA. *Faculty research:* Structural, architectural, geotechnical and geoenvironmental engineering; construction engineering and management; transportation engineering; environmental engineering and public works. Total annual research expenditures: $763,042. *Unit head:* Dr. Jamshid Mohammadi, Professor and Chairman, 312-567-3629, Fax: 312-567-3519, E-mail: mohammadi@iit.edu. *Application contact:* Deborah Gibson, Director, Graduate Admission, 866-472-3448, Fax: 312-567-3138, E-mail: inquiry.grad@iit.edu.

Indiana University–Purdue University Fort Wayne, College of Engineering, Technology, and Computer Science, Program in Technology, Fort Wayne, IN 46805-1499. Offers facilities and construction management (MS); industrial technology/manufacturing (MS); information technology/advanced computer applications (MS). Part-time programs available. *Faculty:* 12 full-time (6 women), 1 part-time/adjunct (0 women). *Students:* 4 full-time (2 women), 14 part-time (1 woman); includes 3 minority (2 Asian, non-Hispanic/Latino; 1 Hispanic/Latino), 2 international. Average age 32. 5 applicants, 100% accepted, 2 enrolled. In 2010, 4 master's awarded. *Entrance requirements:* For master's, minimum GPA of 3.0. Additional exam requirements/recommendations for international students: Required—TOEFL (minimum score 550 paper-based; 213 computer-based; 77 iBT), TWE. *Application deadline:* For fall admission, 7/15 for domestic students, 5/15 for international students; for spring admission, 12/1 for domestic students, 10/15 for international students. Applications are processed on a rolling basis. Application fee: $55 ($60 for international students). Electronic applications accepted. *Expenses:* Tuition, state resident: full-time $4824; part-time $268 per credit. Tuition, nonresident: full-time $11,625; part-time $646 per credit. Required fees: $555; $30.85 per credit. Tuition and fees vary according to course load. *Financial support:* Career-related internships or fieldwork, scholarships/grants, and unspecified assistantships available. Support available to part-time students. Financial award application deadline: 3/1; financial award applicants required to submit FAFSA. *Unit head:* Dr. Max Yen, Dean, 260-481-6839, Fax: 260-481-5734, E-mail: yens@ipfw.edu. *Application contact:* Dr. Gary Steffen, Chair, 260-481-6344, Fax: 260-481-5734, E-mail: steffen@ipfw.edu.

Instituto Tecnologico de Santo-Domingo, Graduate School, Area of Engineering, Santo Domingo, Dominican Republic. Offers construction administration (MS, Certificate); data telecommunications (M Eng, MS, Certificate); industrial engineering (M Eng, Certificate); industrial management (M Mgmt); information technology (Certificate); maintenance engineering (M Eng); occupational hazard prevention (M Mgmt); production management (Certificate); quantitative methods (Certificate); sanitary and environmental engineering (M Eng); structural engineering (M Eng); systems engineering and electronic data processing (Certificate); transportation (Certificate).

Marquette University, Graduate School, College of Engineering, Department of Civil and Environmental Engineering, Milwaukee, WI 53201-1881. Offers construction and public works management (MS, PhD); construction engineering and management (Certificate); environmental/water resources engineering (MS, PhD); structural design (Certificate); structural/geotechnical engineering (MS, PhD); transportation planning and engineering (MS, PhD); waste and wastewater treatment processes (Certificate). Part-time and evening/weekend programs available. *Faculty:* 13 full-time (0 women), 3 part-time/adjunct (0 women). *Students:* 20 full-time (4 women), 12 part-time (1 woman); includes 1 minority (Black or African American, non-Hispanic/Latino), 12 international. Average age 27. 66 applicants, 64% accepted, 9 enrolled. In 2010, 8 master's, 1 doctorate awarded. Terminal master's awarded for partial completion of doctoral program. *Degree requirements:* For master's, comprehensive exam, thesis or alternative; for doctorate, thesis/dissertation. *Entrance requirements:* For master's, GRE General Test (recommended), minimum GPA of 3.0, official transcripts from all current and previous colleges/universities except Marquette, three letters of recommendation; for doctorate, GRE General Test, minimum GPA of 3.0, official transcripts from all current and previous colleges/universities except Marquette, three letters of recommendation, brief statement of purpose, submission of any English-language publications authored by applicant (strongly recommended). Additional exam requirements/recommendations for international students: Required—TOEFL (minimum score 530 paper-based; 78 computer-based). *Application deadline:* For fall admission, 6/1 priority date for domestic students. Applications are processed on a rolling basis. Application fee: $50. Electronic applications accepted. *Expenses:* Tuition: Full-time $16,290; part-time $905 per credit hour. Tuition and fees vary according to program. *Financial support:* In 2010–11, 13 students received support, including 4 fellowships with tuition reimbursements available, 4 research assistantships with tuition reimbursements available, 10 teaching assistantships with tuition reimbursements available; Federal Work-Study, institutionally sponsored loans, scholarships/grants, and tuition waivers (full and partial) also available. Support available to part-time students. Financial award application deadline: 2/15. *Faculty research:* Highway safety, highway performance, and intelligent transportation systems; surface mount technology; watershed management. Total annual research expenditures: $662,392. *Unit head:* Dr. Thomas Wenzel, Chair, 414-288-7030, Fax: 414-288-7521, E-mail: thomas.wenzel@marquette.edu. *Application contact:* Dr. Stephen M. Heinrich, Director of Graduate Studies, 414-288-5466, E-mail: stephen.heinrich@marquette.edu.

Michigan State University, The Graduate School, College of Agriculture and Natural Resources and College of Social Science, School of Planning, Design and Construction, East Lansing, MI 48824. Offers construction management (MS, PhD); environmental design (MA); interior design and facilities management (MA); international planning studies (MIPS); urban and regional planning (MURP). *Degree requirements:* For master's, thesis or alternative. *Entrance requirements:* Additional exam requirements/recommendations for international students: Required—TOEFL. Electronic applications accepted.

Missouri State University, Graduate College, College of Business Administration, Department of Technology and Construction Management, Springfield, MO 65897. Offers MS. Part-time programs available. *Degree requirements:* For master's, thesis or alternative. *Entrance requirements:* For master's, GRE or GMAT, minimum GPA of 2.75. Additional exam requirements/recommendations for international students: Required—TOEFL (minimum score 550 paper-based; 213 computer-based; 79 iBT). Electronic applications accepted. *Expenses:* Tuition, state resident: full-time $3348; part-time $186 per credit hour. Tuition, nonresident: full-time $6696; part-time $372 per credit hour. Required fees: $238 per semester. Tuition and fees vary according to course level, course load and program.

New York University, School of Continuing and Professional Studies, Schack Institute of Real Estate, Program in Construction Management, New York, NY 10012-1019. Offers construction management (Advanced Certificate); construction management for the development process (MS); project management (MS). Part-time and evening/weekend programs available. *Faculty:* 5 full-time (1 woman), 20 part-time/adjunct (2 women). *Students:* 15 full-time (4 women), 45 part-time (8 women); includes 2 Black or African American, non-Hispanic/Latino; 1 American Indian or Alaska Native, non-Hispanic/Latino; 3 Asian, non-Hispanic/Latino; 3 Hispanic/Latino, 12 international. Average age 32. 53 applicants, 60% accepted, 15 enrolled. In 2010, 32 master's, 16 other advanced degrees awarded. *Degree requirements:* For master's, capstone project. *Entrance requirements:* For master's, GRE General Test or GMAT (for recent graduates), resume, 2 letters of recommendation, essay, professional experience. Additional exam requirements/recommendations for international students: Required—TOEFL (minimum score 600 paper-based; 250 computer-based; 100 iBT). *Application deadline:* For fall admission, 2/1 priority date for domestic and international students; for spring admission, 10/15 priority date for domestic students, 8/15 priority date for international students. Applications are processed on a rolling basis. Application fee: $75. Electronic applications accepted. *Financial support:* In 2010–11, 36 students received support, including 36 fellowships (averaging $1,980 per year); scholarships/grants also available. Support available to part-time students. Financial award application deadline: 3/1; financial award applicants required to submit FAFSA. *Unit head:* James Stuckey, Divisional Dean, 212-992-3335, Fax: 212-992-3686, E-mail: james.stuckey@nyu.edu. *Application contact:* Jennifer Monahan, Assistant Director, 212-992-3335, Fax: 212-992-3686, E-mail: jm189@nyu.edu.

North Carolina Agricultural and Technical State University, Graduate School, School of Technology, Department of Construction Management and Occupational Safety and Health, Greensboro, NC 27411. Offers construction management (MSIT); occupational safety and health (MSIT).

North Dakota State University, College of Graduate and Interdisciplinary Studies, College of Engineering and Architecture, Department of Construction Management and Engineering, Fargo, ND 58108. Offers construction management (MS). *Students:* 23 full-time (4 women), 14 part-time (1 woman); includes 1 Asian, non-Hispanic/Latino, 12 international. 22 applicants, 82% accepted, 7 enrolled. *Entrance requirements:* Additional exam requirements/recommendations for international students: Required—TOEFL (minimum score 525 paper-based; 197 computer-based; 71 iBT). *Application deadline:* Applications are processed on a

Construction Management

North Dakota State University (continued)
rolling basis. Application fee: $45 ($60 for international students). Electronic applications accepted. *Unit head:* Dr. Charles McIntyre, Chair, 701-231-7879, Fax: 701-231-7431, E-mail: charles.mcintyre@ndsu.edu. *Application contact:* Dr. David A. Wittrock, Dean, 701-231-7033, Fax: 701-231-6524.

Norwich University, School of Graduate and Continuing Studies, Program in Civil Engineering, Northfield, VT 05663. Offers construction management (MCE); geo-technical (MCE); structural (MCE); water/environmental (MCE). Evening/weekend programs available. *Faculty:* 20 full-time (3 women). *Students:* 78 full-time (19 women); includes 5 Black or African American, non-Hispanic/Latino; 4 Asian, non-Hispanic/Latino; 7 Hispanic/Latino. Average age 35. 107 applicants, 88% accepted, 90 enrolled. In 2010, 78 master's awarded. *Entrance requirements:* For master's, minimum GPA of 2.75. Additional exam requirements/recommendations for international students: Required—TOEFL (minimum score 550 paper-based; 213 computer-based; 83 iBT). *Application deadline:* For fall admission, 8/10 for domestic and international students; for spring admission, 2/6 for domestic and international students. Application fee: $50. *Expenses:* Tuition: Full-time $17,380; part-time $645 per credit. Tuition and fees vary according to program. *Financial support:* Scholarships/grants available. Financial award applicants required to submit FAFSA. *Unit head:* Dr. Thomas Descoteaux, Program Director, 802-485-2730, Fax: 802-485-2533, E-mail: tdescote@norwich.edu. *Application contact:* Shelley W. Brown, Director of Business Partnership, 802-485-2784, Fax: 802-485-2533, E-mail: sbrown@norwich.edu.

Philadelphia University, School of Architecture, Program in Construction Management, Philadelphia, PA 19144. Offers MS.

Polytechnic Institute of NYU, Department of Civil Engineering, Major in Construction Management, Brooklyn, NY 11201-2990. Offers MS. *Students:* 35 full-time (13 women), 59 part-time (12 women); includes 10 Black or African American, non-Hispanic/Latino; 9 Asian, non-Hispanic/Latino; 5 Hispanic/Latino, 27 international. Average age 30. 79 applicants, 62% accepted, 27 enrolled. In 2010, 40 master's awarded. *Degree requirements:* For master's, comprehensive exam (for some programs), thesis (for some programs). *Entrance requirements:* Additional exam requirements/recommendations for international students: Required—TOEFL (minimum score 550 paper-based; 213 computer-based; 80 iBT); Recommended—IELTS (minimum score 6.5). *Application deadline:* For fall admission, 7/31 priority date for domestic students, 4/30 priority date for international students; for spring admission, 12/31 priority date for domestic students, 10/30 priority date for international students. Applications are processed on a rolling basis. Application fee: $75. Electronic applications accepted. *Expenses:* Tuition: Full-time $21,492; part-time $1194 per credit. Required fees: $385 per semester. Tuition and fees vary according to course load. *Financial support:* Institutionally sponsored loans, scholarships/grants, and unspecified assistantships available. Support available to part-time students. *Unit head:* Dr. Lawrence Chiarelli, Head, 718-260-4040, Fax: 718-260-3433, E-mail: lchiarel@poly.edu. *Application contact:* JeanCarlo Bonilla, Director, Graduate Enrollment Management, 718-260-3182, Fax: 718-260-3624, E-mail: gradinfo@poly.edu.

Polytechnic Institute of NYU, Department of Technology Management, Brooklyn, NY 11201-2990. Offers construction management (Advanced Certificate); electronic business management (Advanced Certificate); entrepreneurship (Advanced Certificate); human resources management (Advanced Certificate); information management (Advanced Certificate); management (MS); management of technology (MS); organizational behavior (MS, Advanced Certificate); project management (Advanced Certificate); technology management (MBA, PhD, Advanced Certificate); telecommunications and information management (MS); telecommunications management (Advanced Certificate). Part-time and evening/weekend programs available. *Faculty:* 7 full-time (2 women), 28 part-time/adjunct (4 women). *Students:* 224 full-time (93 women), 106 part-time (38 women); includes 15 Black or African American, non-Hispanic/Latino; 41 Asian, non-Hispanic/Latino; 10 Hispanic/Latino, 158 international. Average age 30. 370 applicants, 60% accepted, 120 enrolled. In 2010, 173 master's, 1 doctorate awarded. *Degree requirements:* For master's, comprehensive exam (for some programs), thesis (for some programs); for doctorate, comprehensive exam, thesis/dissertation. *Entrance requirements:* For master's, GMAT, minimum B average in undergraduate course work. Additional exam requirements/recommendations for international students: Required—TOEFL (minimum score 550 paper-based; 213 computer-based; 80 iBT); Recommended—IELTS (minimum score 6.5). *Application deadline:* For fall admission, 7/31 priority date for domestic students, 4/30 priority date for international students; for spring admission, 12/31 priority date for domestic students, 11/30 priority date for international students. Applications are processed on a rolling basis. Application fee: $75. Electronic applications accepted. *Expenses:* Tuition: Full-time $21,492; part-time $1194 per credit. Required fees: $385 per semester. Tuition and fees vary according to course load. *Financial support:* In 2010–11, 1 fellowship (averaging $26,400 per year) was awarded; research assistantships, teaching assistantships, institutionally sponsored loans, scholarships/grants, and unspecified assistantships also available. Support available to part-time students. *Unit head:* Prof. Bharadwaj Rao, Head, 718-260-3617, Fax: 718-260-3874, E-mail: brao@poly.edu. *Application contact:* JeanCarlo Bonilla, Director of Graduate Enrollment Management, 718-260-3182, Fax: 718-260-3624, E-mail: gradinfo@poly.edu.

Polytechnic Institute of NYU, Long Island Graduate Center, Graduate Programs, Department of Civil Engineering, Major in Construction Management, Melville, NY 11747. Offers MS. Part-time and evening/weekend programs available. *Students:* 4 part-time (2 women). Average age 29. 3 applicants, 100% accepted, 3 enrolled. *Entrance requirements:* Additional exam requirements/recommendations for international students: Required—TOEFL (minimum score 550 paper-based; 213 computer-based; 80 iBT); Recommended—IELTS (minimum score 6.5). *Application deadline:* For fall admission, 7/31 priority date for domestic students, 4/30 priority date for international students; for spring admission, 12/31 priority date for domestic students, 11/30 priority date for international students. Applications are processed on a rolling basis. Application fee: $75. Electronic applications accepted. *Expenses:* Tuition: Full-time $21,492; part-time $1194 per credit. Required fees: $385 per semester. Tuition and fees vary according to course load. *Financial support:* Institutionally sponsored loans, scholarships/grants, and unspecified assistantships available. Support available to part-time students. *Unit head:* Dr. Lawrence Chiarelli, Department Head, 718-260-4040, E-mail: lchiarel@duke.poly.edu. *Application contact:* JeanCarlo Bonilla, Director of Graduate Enrollment Management, 718-260-3182, Fax: 718-260-3624, E-mail: gradinfo@poly.edu.

Polytechnic University of Puerto Rico, Miami Campus, Graduate School, Miami, FL 33166. Offers accounting (MBA); business administration (MBA); construction management (MEM); environmental management (MEM); finance (MBA); human resources management (MBA); logistics and supply chain management (MBA); management of international enterprises (MBA); manufacturing management (MEM); marketing management (MBA); project management (MBA). Part-time and evening/weekend programs available. Postbaccalaureate distance learning degree programs offered (no on-campus study). *Entrance requirements:* For master's, minimum GPA of 3.0. Electronic applications accepted.

Polytechnic University of Puerto Rico, Orlando Campus, Graduate School, Winter Park, FL 32792. Offers accounting (MBA); business administration (MBA); construction management (MEM); engineering management (MEM); environmental management (MEM); finance (MBA); human resources management (MBA); management of international enterprises (MBA); management of technology (MBA); manufacturing management (MEM). Part-time and evening/weekend programs available. Postbaccalaureate distance learning degree programs offered (no on-campus study). *Entrance requirements:* For master's, minimum GPA of 3.0. Electronic applications accepted.

Roger Williams University, School of Engineering, Computing and Construction Management, Bristol, RI 02809. Offers construction management (MSCM).

Rowan University, Graduate School, College of Engineering, Department of Civil and Environmental Engineering, Program in Construction Management, Glassboro, NJ 08028-1701. Offers MS. *Entrance requirements:* For master's, GRE General Test. Additional exam requirements/recommendations for international students: Required—TOEFL. *Application deadline:* Applications are processed on a rolling basis. Application fee: $65 ($200 for international students). Electronic applications accepted. *Expenses:* Tuition, area resident: Part-time $602 per semester hour. Tuition, nonresident: part-time $602 per semester hour. Required fees: $100 per semester hour. One-time fee: $10 part-time. *Unit head:* Kauser Jahan, Chair, 856-256-5323, E-mail: jahan@rowan.edu. *Application contact:* Dr. Ralph Dusseau, Program Adviser, 856-256-5332.

South Dakota School of Mines and Technology, Graduate Division, Program in Construction Management, Rapid City, SD 57701-3995. Offers MS.

Southern Polytechnic State University, School of Architecture, Civil Engineering Technology and Construction, Department of Construction Management, Marietta, GA 30060-2896. Offers MS. Part-time and evening/weekend programs available. *Faculty:* 8 full-time (1 woman), 2 part-time/adjunct (0 women). *Students:* 24 full-time (6 women), 7 part-time (0 women); includes 10 Black or African American, non-Hispanic/Latino; 1 Hispanic/Latino, 5 international. Average age 35. 21 applicants, 76% accepted, 9 enrolled. In 2010, 15 master's awarded. *Degree requirements:* For master's, thesis or alternative. *Entrance requirements:* For master's, GMAT or GRE, 3 reference forms, minimum GPA of 2.75. Additional exam requirements/recommendations for international students: Required—TOEFL (minimum score 550 paper-based; 213 computer-based; 79 iBT), IELTS (minimum score 6.5). *Application deadline:* For fall admission, 7/1 priority date for domestic students, 5/1 priority date for international students; for spring admission, 11/1 priority date for domestic students, 9/1 priority date for international students. Applications are processed on a rolling basis. Application fee: $20. Electronic applications accepted. *Expenses:* Tuition, state resident: full-time $3690; part-time $205 per semester hour. Tuition, nonresident: full-time $13,428; part-time $746 per semester hour. Required fees: $598 per semester. *Financial support:* Research assistantships with tuition reimbursements, career-related internships or fieldwork, scholarships/grants, and unspecified assistantships available. Support available to part-time students. Financial award application deadline: 5/1; financial award applicants required to submit FAFSA. *Faculty research:* Environmental construction and green building techniques, risk management, bidding strategies in construction, construction worker safety, building automation and performance measurements. Total annual research expenditures: $115,000. *Unit head:* Dr. Khalid M. Siddiqi, Chair, 678-915-7221, Fax: 678-915-4966, E-mail: ksiddiqi@spsu.edu. *Application contact:* Nikki Palamiotis, Director of Graduate Studies, 678-915-4276, Fax: 678-915-7292, E-mail: npalamio@spsu.edu.

State University of New York College of Environmental Science and Forestry, Department of Sustainable Construction Management and Engineering, Syracuse, NY 13210-2779. Offers construction management (MPS, MS, PhD); engineered wood products and structures (MPS, MS, PhD); tropical timbers wood science and technology (MPS, MS, PhD); wood anatomy and ultrastructure (MPS, MS, PhD); wood treatments (MPS, MS, PhD). *Degree requirements:* For master's, thesis (for some programs); for doctorate, comprehensive exam, thesis/dissertation. *Entrance requirements:* For master's and doctorate, GRE General Test, minimum GPA of 3.0. Additional exam requirements/recommendations for international students: Required—TOEFL (minimum score 550 paper-based; 213 computer-based; 80 iBT), IELTS (minimum score 6). *Expenses:* Tuition, state resident: full-time $8370; part-time $349 per credit hour. Tuition, nonresident: full-time $13,780. Required fees: $30.30 per credit hour. $20 per year.

Stevens Institute of Technology, Graduate School, Charles V. Schaefer Jr. School of Engineering, Department of Civil, Environmental, and Ocean Engineering, Program in Construction Management, Hoboken, NJ 07030. Offers construction accounting/estimating (Certificate); construction engineering (Certificate); construction law/disputes (Certificate); construction management (MS); construction/quality management (Certificate). *Students:* 23 full-time (4 women), 29 part-time (3 women); includes 2 Black or African American, non-Hispanic/Latino; 6 Asian, non-Hispanic/Latino, 18 international. Average age 28. 21 applicants, 100% accepted. *Degree requirements:* For master's, thesis optional. *Entrance requirements:* For master's, GMAT, GRE General Test. Additional exam requirements/recommendations for international students: Required—TOEFL. *Application deadline:* Applications are processed on a rolling basis. Application fee: $50. Electronic applications accepted. *Unit head:* Henry Dobbelaar, Head, 201-216-5340. *Application contact:* Dr. David A. Vaccari, Director, 201-216-5570, Fax: 201-216-5352, E-mail: dvaccari@stevens.edu.

Texas A&M University, College of Architecture, Department of Construction Science, College Station, TX 77843. Offers construction management (MS). *Faculty:* 15. *Students:* 50 full-time (17 women), 5 part-time (0 women); includes 6 minority (2 Asian, non-Hispanic/Latino; 4 Hispanic/Latino), 38 international. Average age 30. In 2010, 52 master's awarded. *Degree requirements:* For master's, comprehensive exam. *Entrance requirements:* For master's, GRE General Test. Additional exam requirements/recommendations for international students: Required—TOEFL. *Application deadline:* For fall admission, 4/1 priority date for domestic students; for winter admission, 1/1 priority date for domestic students; for spring admission, 9/1 priority date for domestic students. Applications are processed on a rolling basis. Application fee: $50 ($75 for international students). Electronic applications accepted. *Financial support:* In 2010–11, fellowships with partial tuition reimbursements (averaging $1,000 per year), research assistantships with partial tuition reimbursements (averaging $9,000 per year), teaching assistantships with partial tuition reimbursements (averaging $9,000 per year) were awarded. Financial award application deadline: 4/1; financial award applicants required to submit FAFSA. *Faculty research:* Fire safety, housing foundations, construction project management, quality management. *Unit head:* Joe Horlen, JD, Head, 979-458-3477, E-mail: jhorlen@tamu.edu. *Application contact:* Joe Horlen, JD, Head, 979-458-3477, E-mail: jhorlen@tamu.edu.

Texas A&M University, College of Engineering, Zachry Department of Civil Engineering, College Station, TX 77843. Offers coastal and ocean engineering (M Eng, MS, D Eng, PhD); construction engineering and management (M Eng, MS, D Eng, PhD); environmental engineering (M Eng, MS, D Eng, PhD); geotechnical engineering (M Eng, MS, D Eng, PhD); materials engineering (M Eng, MS, D Eng, PhD); structural engineering (M Eng, MS, D Eng, PhD); transportation engineering (M Eng, MS, D Eng, PhD); water resources engineering (M Eng, MS, D Eng, PhD). Part-time programs available. *Faculty:* 57. *Students:* 384 full-time (81 women), 35 part-time (7 women); includes 35 minority (3 Black or African American, non-Hispanic/Latino; 1 American Indian or Alaska Native, non-Hispanic/Latino; 14 Asian, non-Hispanic/Latino; 17 Hispanic/Latino), 263 international. Average age 29. In 2010, 136 master's, 26 doctorates awarded. *Degree requirements:* For master's, thesis (MS); for doctorate, dissertation (PhD), internship (D Eng). *Entrance requirements:* For master's and doctorate, GRE General Test. Additional exam requirements/recommendations for international students: Required—TOEFL. *Application deadline:* Applications are processed on a rolling basis. Application fee: $50 ($75 for international students). Electronic applications accepted. *Financial support:* In 2010–11, fellowships (averaging $4,500 per year), research assistantships (averaging $14,000 per year), teaching assistantships (averaging $14,400 per year) were awarded; career-related internships or fieldwork and institutionally sponsored loans also available. Financial award application deadline: 4/15; financial award applicants required to submit FAFSA. *Unit head:* Dr. Tony Cahill, Head, 979-845-3858, E-mail: tcahill@civil.tamu.edu. *Application contact:* Graduate Advisor, 979-845-7435, Fax: 979-845-6156, E-mail: info@civil.tamu.edu.

Universidad de las Américas–Puebla, Division of Graduate Studies, School of Engineering, Program in Construction Management, Puebla, Mexico. Offers M Adm. Part-time and evening/weekend programs available. *Degree requirements:* For master's, one foreign language, thesis. *Faculty research:* Building structures, budget, project management.

University of Arkansas at Little Rock, Graduate School, College of Business Administration, Little Rock, AR 72204-1099. Offers accountancy (M Acc, Graduate Certificate); business administration (MBA); construction management (Graduate Certificate); management (Graduate Certificate); management information system (MIS); management information systems (Graduate Certificate); management information systems leadership (Graduate Certificate); taxation (MS, Graduate Certificate). *Accreditation:* AACSB. Part-time and evening/weekend programs available. *Entrance requirements:* For master's, GMAT, minimum undergraduate GPA of 2.7.

Additional exam requirements/recommendations for international students: Required—TOEFL (minimum score 525 paper-based; 195 computer-based).

University of California, Berkeley, UC Berkeley Extension, Certificate Programs in Engineering, Construction and Facilities Management, Berkeley, CA 94720-1500. Offers construction management (Certificate); HVAC (Certificate); integrated circuit design and techniques (online) (Certificate). Postbaccalaureate distance learning degree programs offered.

University of Denver, Daniels College of Business, Franklin L. Burns School of Real Estate and Construction Management, Denver, CO 80208. Offers construction management (IMBA, MS); real estate (IMBA, MBA, MS); real estate and construction management (EMS). Part-time and evening/weekend programs available. *Faculty:* 8 full-time (1 woman), 8 part-time/adjunct (2 women). *Students:* 40 full-time (8 women), 65 part-time (11 women); includes 11 minority (4 Black or African American, non-Hispanic/Latino; 3 Asian, non-Hispanic/Latino; 4 Hispanic/Latino), 14 international. Average age 32. 91 applicants, 77% accepted, 41 enrolled. In 2010, 62 master's awarded. *Entrance requirements:* For master's, GRE General Test or GMAT. Additional exam requirements/recommendations for international students: Required—TOEFL (minimum score 570 paper-based; 88 iBT). *Application deadline:* For fall admission, 11/15 priority date for domestic students; for spring admission, 10/15 priority date for domestic students. Applications are processed on a rolling basis. Application fee: $100. Electronic applications accepted. *Expenses:* Tuition: Full-time $35,604; part-time $29,670 per year. Required fees: $687 per year. Tuition and fees vary according to program. *Financial support:* In 2010–11, 3 teaching assistantships with full and partial tuition reimbursements (averaging $1,966 per year) were awarded; career-related internships or fieldwork, Federal Work-Study, institutionally sponsored loans, scholarships/grants, and unspecified assistantships also available. Support available to part-time students. Financial award application deadline: 3/15; financial award applicants required to submit FAFSA. *Unit head:* Dr. Mark Levine, Director, 303-871-2142, E-mail: mark.levine@du.edu. *Application contact:* Victoria Chen, Graduate Admissions Manager, 303-871-3826, E-mail: victoria.chen@du.edu.

University of Houston, College of Technology, Department of Engineering Technology, Houston, TX 77204. Offers construction management (MS); engineering technology (MS); network communications (M Tech). Part-time programs available. *Faculty:* 14 full-time (5 women), 6 part-time/adjunct (2 women). *Students:* 48 full-time (11 women), 38 part-time (8 women); includes 9 Black or African American, non-Hispanic/Latino; 6 Asian, non-Hispanic/Latino; 6 Hispanic/Latino, 39 international. Average age 28. 56 applicants, 88% accepted, 34 enrolled. In 2010, 27 master's awarded. *Degree requirements:* For master's, project or thesis (most programs). *Entrance requirements:* For master's, GRE. Additional exam requirements/recommendations for international students: Required—TOEFL (minimum score 550 paper-based; 79 iBT). *Application deadline:* For fall admission, 7/1 for domestic students, 4/1 for international students; for spring admission, 12/1 for domestic students, 10/1 for international students. Applications are processed on a rolling basis. Application fee: $75 ($150 for international students). Electronic applications accepted. *Expenses:* Tuition, state resident: full-time $8592; part-time $358 per credit hour. Tuition, nonresident: full-time $16,032; part-time $668 per credit hour. Required fees: $2889. Tuition and fees vary according to course load and program. *Financial support:* In 2010–11, 7 research assistantships with partial tuition reimbursements (averaging $10,531 per year), 18 teaching assistantships with partial tuition reimbursements (averaging $7,179 per year) were awarded. *Unit head:* Heidar Malki, Chairperson, 713-743-4075, Fax: 713-743-4032, E-mail: malki@uh.edu. *Application contact:* Tiffany Roosa, Graduate Advisor, 713-743-4100, Fax: 713-743-4151, E-mail: troosa@uh.edu.

The University of Kansas, Graduate Studies, School of Engineering, Department of Civil, Environmental, and Architectural Engineering, Program in Construction Management, Lawrence, KS 66045. Offers MCM. Part-time and evening/weekend programs available. *Faculty:* 3 full-time (0 women). *Students:* 1 full-time (0 women), 3 part-time (1 woman). Average age 28. 10 applicants, 20% accepted, 1 enrolled. In 2010, 4 master's awarded. *Degree requirements:* For master's, thesis or alternative, exam. *Entrance requirements:* For master's, GRE. Additional exam requirements/recommendations for international students: Required—TOEFL. *Application deadline:* For fall admission, 7/1 priority date for domestic students, 3/1 priority date for international students; for spring admission, 12/1 priority date for domestic students, 8/15 priority date for international students. Applications are processed on a rolling basis. Application fee: $55 ($65 for international students). Electronic applications accepted. *Expenses:* Tuition, state resident: full-time $7092; part-time $295.50 per credit hour. Tuition, nonresident: full-time $16,590; part-time $691.25 per credit hour. Required fees: $858; $71.49 per credit hour. Tuition and fees vary according to course load, campus/location and program. *Financial support:* Career-related internships or fieldwork available. Financial award application deadline: 2/7. *Faculty research:* Construction engineering, construction management. *Unit head:* Craig D. Adams, Chair, 785-864-2700, Fax: 785-864-5631, E-mail: adamscd@ku.edu. *Application contact:* Bruce M. McEnroe, Graduate Advisor, 785-864-2925, Fax: 785-864-2925, E-mail: mcenroe@ku.edu.

University of Nevada, Las Vegas, Graduate College, Howard R. Hughes College of Engineering, Department of Construction Management, Las Vegas, NV 89154-4054. Offers MS. *Faculty:* 2 full-time (0 women). *Students:* 9 full-time (1 woman), 7 part-time (3 women); includes 2 minority (both Two or more races, non-Hispanic/Latino), 5 international. Average age 31. 14 applicants, 86% accepted, 6 enrolled. In 2010, 8 master's awarded. *Entrance requirements:* Additional exam requirements/recommendations for international students: Required—TOEFL (minimum score 550 paper-based; 213 computer-based; 80 iBT), IELTS (minimum score 7). *Application deadline:* For fall admission, 6/15 priority date for domestic and international students; for spring admission, 11/15 priority date for domestic and international students. Applications are processed on a rolling basis. Application fee: $60 ($95 for international students). Electronic applications accepted. *Expenses:* Tuition, area resident: Part-time $239.50 per credit. Tuition, state resident: part-time $239.50 per credit. Tuition, nonresident: part-time $503 per credit. Required fees: $108 per semester. Tuition and fees vary according to course load, program and reciprocity agreements. *Financial support:* In 2010–11, 3 students received support, including 3 teaching assistantships with partial tuition reimbursements available (averaging $10,000 per year); institutionally sponsored loans, scholarships/grants, health care benefits, and unspecified assistantships also available. Financial award application deadline: 3/1. *Faculty research:* Sustainable construction, construction safety, infrastructure project performance, construction education, construction performance improvement. *Unit head:* Dr. David Shields, Director/ Associate Professor, 702-895-1461, Fax: 702-895-4966, E-mail: david.shields@unlv.edu. *Application contact:* Graduate College Admissions Evaluator, 702-895-3320, Fax: 702-895-4180, E-mail: gradcollege@unlv.edu.

University of New Mexico, Graduate School, School of Engineering, Department of Civil Engineering, Program in Construction Management, Albuquerque, NM 87131-2039. Offers MCM. Part-time programs available. *Students:* 1 full-time (0 women), 7 part-time (1 woman); includes 2 American Indian or Alaska Native, non-Hispanic/Latino; 1 Hispanic/Latino. Average age 40. 12 applicants, 42% accepted, 4 enrolled. In 2010, 2 master's awarded. *Degree requirements:* For master's, comprehensive exam, thesis optional. *Entrance requirements:* For master's, GMAT (minimum score 500), minimum GPA of 3.0; courses in statistics, elements of calculus, engineering economy, and construction contracting. Additional exam requirements/recommendations for international students: Required—TOEFL (minimum score 550 paper-based; 213 computer-based; 79 iBT). *Application deadline:* For fall admission, 7/15 for domestic students, 3/1 for international students; for spring admission, 11/10 for domestic students, 8/1 for international students. Applications are processed on a rolling basis. Application fee: $50. Electronic applications accepted. *Expenses:* Tuition, state resident: full-time $5991; part-time $251 per credit hour. Tuition, nonresident: full-time $14,405; part-time $800.20 per credit hour. Tuition and fees vary according to course level, course load, program and reciprocity agreements. *Financial support:* In 2010–11, 2 students received support. Scholarships/grants, health care benefits, and unspecified assistantships available. Support available to part-time students. Financial award application deadline: 3/1; financial award applicants required to submit FAFSA. *Faculty research:* Applied industry research and training, integration of the design/construction continuum, leadership in project management, life-cycle costing, production management and productivity management, project delivery methods, sustainable asset management, sustainable design and construction. Total annual research expenditures: $3 million. *Unit head:* Dr. John C. Stormont, Chair, 505-277-2722, Fax: 505-277-1988, E-mail: jcstorm@unm.edu. *Application contact:* Josie Gibson, Professional Academic Advisor, 505-277-2722, Fax: 505-277-1988, E-mail: civil@unm.edu.

University of North Florida, Coggin College of Business, MBA Program, Jacksonville, FL 32224. Offers accounting (MBA); construction management (MBA); e-commerce (MBA); economics (MBA); finance (MBA); human resource management (MBA); international business (MBA); logistics (MBA); management applications (MBA). *Accreditation:* AACSB. Part-time and evening/weekend programs available. *Faculty:* 17 full-time (5 women), 1 part-time/adjunct (0 women). *Students:* 137 full-time (56 women), 268 part-time (112 women); includes 17 Black or African American, non-Hispanic/Latino; 21 Asian, non-Hispanic/Latino; 12 Hispanic/Latino; 3 Two or more races, non-Hispanic/Latino, 29 international. Average age 30. 250 applicants, 57% accepted, 94 enrolled. In 2010, 173 master's awarded. *Entrance requirements:* For master's, GMAT or GRE, U.S. bachelor's degree from regionally-accredited university or equivalent foreign degree. Additional exam requirements/recommendations for international students: Required—TOEFL (minimum score 550 paper-based; 213 computer-based; 79 iBT). *Application deadline:* For fall admission, 7/1 priority date for domestic students, 5/1 for international students; for spring admission, 11/1 priority date for domestic students, 10/1 for international students. Applications are processed on a rolling basis. Application fee: $30. *Expenses:* Tuition, state resident: full-time $7646.40; part-time $318.60 per credit hour. Tuition, nonresident: full-time $23,502; part-time $979.24 per credit hour. Required fees: $1208.88; $50.37 per credit hour. Tuition and fees vary according to course load and program. *Financial support:* In 2010–11, 40 students received support; research assistantships, teaching assistantships, Federal Work-Study and tuition waivers (partial) available. Support available to part-time students. Financial award application deadline: 4/1; financial award applicants required to submit FAFSA. *Faculty research:* Performance measures, costing, and inventory issues in logistics and supply chain management; inter-organizational systems; international management and marketing practices; e-commerce; organizational learning and socialization processes. Total annual research expenditures: $9,024. *Unit head:* Dr. C. Bruce Kavan, Chair, 904-620-2780, Fax: 904-620-2832. *Application contact:* Cheryl Campbell, Graduate Advisor, 904-620-2575, Fax: 904-620-2832, E-mail: ccampbell@unf.edu.

University of Oklahoma, College of Architecture, Division of Construction Science, Norman, OK 73019-0390. Offers construction administration (MS). Part-time and evening/weekend programs available. *Faculty:* 2 full-time (1 woman). *Students:* 13 full-time (4 women), 13 part-time (2 women); includes 6 minority (1 Black or African American, non-Hispanic/Latino; 1 American Indian or Alaska Native, non-Hispanic/Latino; 2 Hispanic/Latino; 2 Two or more races, non-Hispanic/Latino), 3 international. Average age 31. 19 applicants, 74% accepted, 12 enrolled. In 2010, 10 master's awarded. *Degree requirements:* For master's, thesis or alternative, portfolio, project. *Entrance requirements:* For master's, GRE General Test, portfolio. Additional exam requirements/recommendations for international students: Required—TOEFL (minimum score 600 paper-based; 250 computer-based; 79 iBT). *Application deadline:* For fall admission, 4/1 for domestic and international students; for spring admission, 11/1 for domestic students, 9/1 for international students. Applications are processed on a rolling basis. Application fee: $40 ($90 for international students). Electronic applications accepted. *Expenses:* Tuition, state resident: full-time $3892.80; part-time $162.20 per credit hour. Tuition, nonresident: full-time $14,167; part-time $590.30 per credit hour. Required fees: $2523.40; $94.60 per credit hour. Tuition and fees vary according to course load and degree level. *Financial support:* In 2010–11, 19 students received support, including 42 research assistantships with partial tuition reimbursements available (averaging $11,025 per year), 3 teaching assistantships with partial tuition reimbursements available (averaging $10,641 per year); career-related internships or fieldwork, scholarships/grants, tuition waivers (partial), and unspecified assistantships also available. Support available to part-time students. Financial award applicants required to submit FAFSA. *Faculty research:* Online education, highway construction, lean construction, Hispanic construction worker design/safety, online instructional design. *Unit head:* Kenneth Robson, Director, 405-325-6404, Fax: 405-325-7558, E-mail: krobson@ou.edu. *Application contact:* Richard C. Ryan, Professor, 405-325-3976, Fax: 405-325-7558, E-mail: rryan@ou.edu.

University of Southern California, Graduate School, Viterbi School of Engineering, Sonny Astani Department of Civil Engineering, Los Angeles, CA 90089. Offers applied mechanics (MS); civil engineering (MS, PhD); computer-aided engineering (ME, Graduate Certificate); construction management (MCM); engineering technology commercialization (Graduate Certificate); environmental engineering (MS, PhD); environmental quality management (ME); structural design (ME); sustainable cities (Graduate Certificate); transportation systems (MS, Graduate Certificate); water and waste management (MS). Part-time and evening/weekend programs available. *Faculty:* 16 full-time (2 women), 35 part-time/adjunct (5 women). *Students:* 190 full-time (52 women), 81 part-time (20 women); includes 54 minority (2 Black or African American, non-Hispanic/Latino; 42 Asian, non-Hispanic/Latino; 9 Hispanic/Latino; 1 Two or more races, non-Hispanic/Latino), 149 international. 541 applicants, 43% accepted, 100 enrolled. In 2010, 74 master's, 10 doctorates awarded. Terminal master's awarded for partial completion of doctoral program. *Degree requirements:* For master's, thesis optional; for doctorate, thesis/dissertation. *Entrance requirements:* For master's and doctorate, GRE General Test. *Application deadline:* For fall admission, 12/1 priority date for domestic and international students; for spring admission, 9/15 for domestic students, 9/15 priority date for international students. Applications are processed on a rolling basis. Application fee: $85. Electronic applications accepted. *Expenses:* Tuition: Full-time $31,240; part-time $1420 per unit. Required fees: $600. One-time fee: $35 full-time. Full-time tuition and fees vary according to degree level and program. *Financial support:* In 2010–11, fellowships with full tuition reimbursements (averaging $30,000 per year), research assistantships with full tuition reimbursements (averaging $20,000 per year), teaching assistantships with full tuition reimbursements (averaging $20,000 per year) were awarded; career-related internships or fieldwork, scholarships/grants, health care benefits, and unspecified assistantships also available. Financial award application deadline: 12/1; financial award applicants required to submit CSS PROFILE or FAFSA. *Faculty research:* Geotechnical engineering, transportation engineering, structural engineering, construction management, environmental engineering, water resources. Total annual research expenditures: $5 million. *Unit head:* Dr. Jean-Pierre Bardet, Chair, 213-740-0603, Fax: 213-744-1426, E-mail: ceedept@usc.edu. *Application contact:* Jennifer A. Gerson, Director of Student Affairs, 213-740-0573, Fax: 213-740-8662, E-mail: jgerson@usc.edu.

The University of Texas at El Paso, Graduate School, College of Engineering, Department of Civil Engineering, El Paso, TX 79968-0001. Offers civil engineering (MS, PhD); construction management (MS); construction mangement (Certificate); environmental engineering (MEENE, MSENE). Part-time and evening/weekend programs available. *Students:* 113 (36 women); includes 2 Asian, non-Hispanic/Latino; 62 Hispanic/Latino, 36 international. Average age 34. In 2010, 14 master's, 9 doctorates awarded. *Degree requirements:* For master's, thesis optional. *Entrance requirements:* For master's, GRE General Test, minimum GPA of 3.0. Additional exam requirements/recommendations for international students: Required—TOEFL. *Application deadline:* For fall admission, 7/1 priority date for domestic students, 3/1 for international students; for spring admission, 11/1 priority date for domestic students, 9/1 for international students. Applications are processed on a rolling basis. Application fee: $15 ($65 for international students). Electronic applications accepted. *Financial support:* In 2010–11, research assistantships with partial tuition reimbursements (averaging $21,125 per year), teaching assistantships with partial tuition reimbursements (averaging $16,900 per year) were awarded; fellowships with partial tuition reimbursements, career-related internships or fieldwork, Federal Work-Study, institutionally sponsored loans, scholarships/grants, tuition waivers (partial), and stipends also available. Financial award application deadline: 3/15; financial award applicants required to submit FAFSA. *Faculty research:* On-site wastewater treatment systems, wastewater reuse, disinfection by-product control, water resources, membrane filtration. *Unit head:* Wen-Whai Li, Chair, 915-747-5464, E-mail: wli@utep.edu. *Application contact:* Dr. Charles H. Ambler,

Construction Management

The University of Texas at El Paso (continued)
Dean of the Graduate School, 915-747-5491 Ext. 7886, Fax: 915-747-5788, E-mail: cambler@utep.edu.

The University of Texas at San Antonio, College of Business, Department of Finance, San Antonio, TX 78249-0617. Offers business finance (MBA); construction science and management (MS); finance (MS); real estate finance (MBA). Part-time and evening/weekend programs available. *Faculty:* 10 full-time (1 woman). *Students:* 24 full-time (6 women), 58 part-time (11 women); includes 21 minority (1 Black or African American, non-Hispanic/Latino; 4 Asian, non-Hispanic/Latino; 15 Hispanic/Latino; 1 Two or more races, non-Hispanic/Latino), 8 international. Average age 29. 56 applicants, 52% accepted, 17 enrolled. In 2010, 38 master's awarded. *Degree requirements:* For master's, comprehensive exam (for some programs), thesis (for some programs). *Entrance requirements:* For master's, GMAT, minimum GPA of 3.0. Additional exam requirements/recommendations for international students: Required—TOEFL (minimum score 500 paper-based; 173 computer-based; 61 iBT), IELTS (minimum score 5). *Application deadline:* For fall admission, 7/1 for domestic students, 4/1 for international students; for spring admission, 11/1 for domestic students, 9/1 for international students. Applications are processed on a rolling basis. Application fee: $45 ($85 for international students). Electronic applications accepted. *Expenses:* Tuition, state resident: full-time $4172; part-time $231.75 per credit hour. Tuition, nonresident: full-time $15,332; part-time $851.75 per credit hour. *Financial support:* In 2010–11, 6 students received support, including 7 research assistantships (averaging $16,052 per year), 38 teaching assistantships (averaging $9,767 per year); career-related internships or fieldwork, scholarships/grants, tuition waivers, and unspecified assistantships also available. Support available to part-time students. *Faculty research:* Capital markets, corporate finance, asset pricing and investments, international finance, real estate, finance. *Unit head:* Dr. Lalatendu Misra, PhD, Chair, 210-458-6315, Fax: 210-458-6320, E-mail: kfairchild@utsa.edu. *Application contact:* Veronica Ramirez, Assistant Dean of the Graduate School, 210-458-4330, Fax: 210-458-4332, E-mail: graduatestudies@utsa.edu.

University of Washington, Graduate School, College of Built Environments, Department of Construction Management, Seattle, WA 98195. Offers MSCM. Part-time and evening/weekend programs available. *Degree requirements:* For master's, thesis or alternative. *Entrance requirements:* For master's, GRE General Test, minimum GPA of 3.0. Additional exam requirements/recommendations for international students: Required—TOEFL. Electronic applications accepted. *Faculty research:* Business practices, delivery methods, materials, productivity.

Wentworth Institute of Technology, Construction Management Program, Boston, MA 02115-5998. Offers MS. Part-time and evening/weekend programs available. *Faculty:* 5 full-time (1 woman), 4 part-time/adjunct (2 women). *Students:* 28 part-time (3 women); includes 3 Black or African American, non-Hispanic/Latino; 1 Asian, non-Hispanic/Latino; 1 Hispanic/Latino. Average age 36. 32 applicants, 97% accepted, 28 enrolled. *Degree requirements:* For master's, thesis optional. *Entrance requirements:* For master's, GRE or GMAT. Additional exam requirements/recommendations for international students: Required—TOEFL (minimum score 525 paper-based; 197 computer-based). *Application deadline:* For fall admission, 5/1 for domestic students. Application fee: $50. *Expenses:* Tuition: Full-time $31,200; part-time $1130 per credit hour.

Required fees: $1000. *Financial support:* Application deadline: 5/1. *Unit head:* Carl Sciple, Director, 617-989-4817, Fax: 617-989-4399, E-mail: sciplec@wit.edu. *Application contact:* Jacklyn Haas, Associate Director of Admissions for Continuing Education, 617-989-4258, Fax: 617-989-4399, E-mail: haasj@wit.edu.

See Display below and Close-Up on page 495.

Western Carolina University, Graduate School, Kimmel School of Construction Management and Technology, Department of Construction Management, Cullowhee, NC 28723. Offers MCM. Part-time and evening/weekend programs available. Postbaccalaureate distance learning degree programs offered. *Entrance requirements:* For master's, GRE or GMAT, appropriate undergraduate degree, resume, letters of recommendation, work experience. Additional exam requirements/recommendations for international students: Required—TOEFL (minimum score 550 paper-based; 270 computer-based; 79 iBT). *Faculty research:* Hazardous waste management, energy management and conservation, engineering materials, refrigeration and air conditioning systems.

Western Michigan University, Graduate College, College of Engineering and Applied Sciences, Department of Civil and Construction Engineering, Kalamazoo, MI 49008. Offers civil engineering (MS), including construction engineering and management, structural engineering, transportation engineering. *Entrance requirements:* For master's, minimum GPA of 3.0.

Worcester Polytechnic Institute, Graduate Studies and Research, Department of Civil and Environmental Engineering, Worcester, MA 01609-2280. Offers civil and environmental engineering (Advanced Certificate, Graduate Certificate); civil engineering (ME, MS, PhD); construction project management (MS); environmental engineering (MS); master builder environmental engineering (M Eng). Part-time and evening/weekend programs available. Postbaccalaureate distance learning degree programs offered (no on-campus study). *Faculty:* 11 full-time (1 woman), 2 part-time/adjunct (1 woman). *Students:* 46 full-time (21 women), 42 part-time (10 women); includes 1 Black or African American, non-Hispanic/Latino; 5 Asian, non-Hispanic/Latino; 1 Hispanic/Latino; 4 Native Hawaiian or other Pacific Islander, non-Hispanic/Latino, 18 international. 135 applicants, 74% accepted, 36 enrolled. In 2010, 26 master's, 2 doctorates awarded. *Degree requirements:* For master's, thesis optional; for doctorate, comprehensive exam, thesis/dissertation. *Entrance requirements:* For master's and doctorate, GRE (recommended), 3 letters of recommendation. Additional exam requirements/recommendations for international students: Required—TOEFL (minimum score 550 paper-based; 213 computer-based; 79 iBT), IELTS (minimum score 6.5). *Application deadline:* For fall admission, 1/1 priority date for domestic and international students; for spring admission, 10/1 priority date for domestic and international students. Applications are processed on a rolling basis. Application fee: $70. Electronic applications accepted. *Expenses:* Tuition: Full-time $20,862; part-time $1159 per term. One-time fee: $15. *Financial support:* Career-related internships or fieldwork, institutionally sponsored loans, scholarships/grants, and unspecified assistantships available. Financial award application deadline: 1/1; financial award applicants required to submit FAFSA. *Faculty research:* Environmental engineering and sustainability, pavement engineering technology, impact mechanics and engineering. *Unit head:* Dr. Tahar El-Korchi, Interim Head, 508-831-5530, Fax: 508-831-5808, E-mail: tek@wpi.edu. *Application contact:* Dr. Paul Mathisen, Graduate Coordinator, 508-831-5530, Fax: 508-831-5808, E-mail: mathisen@wpi.edu.

Energy Management and Policy

Holy Names University, Graduate Division, Department of Business, Oakland, CA 94619-1699. Offers energy and environment management (MBA); finance (MBA); management and leadership (MBA); marketing (MBA); sports management (MBA). Part-time and evening/weekend programs available. *Faculty:* 3 full-time (2 women), 4 part-time/adjunct (1 woman). *Students:* 67 full-time (40 women); includes 28 Black or African American, non-Hispanic/Latino; 7 Asian, non-Hispanic/Latino; 5 Hispanic/Latino, 2 international. Average age 33. 24 applicants, 75% accepted, 7 enrolled. In 2010, 29 master's awarded. *Entrance requirements:* For master's, minimum undergraduate GPA of 2.6 overall, 3.0 in major. Additional exam requirements/recommendations for international students: Required—TOEFL (minimum score 550 paper-based; 213 computer-based; 80 iBT). *Application deadline:* For fall admission, 8/1 priority date for domestic students, 8/1 for international students; for spring admission, 12/1 priority date for domestic students, 12/1 for international students. Applications are processed on a rolling basis. Application fee: $0. *Expenses:* Tuition: Full-time $13,788; part-time $766 per credit. Required fees: $340; $170 per semester. *Financial support:* In 2010–11, 19 students received support. Available to part-time students. Application deadline: 3/2. *Faculty research:* Business ethics, sustainable economics, accounting models, cross-cultural management, diversity in organizations. *Unit head:* Dr. Marcia Frideger, Program Director, 510-436-1205, E-mail: frideger@hnu.edu. *Application contact:* 800-430-1351, Fax: 510-436-1325, E-mail: admissions@hnu.edu.

Indiana University Bloomington, School of Public and Environmental Affairs, Environmental Science Programs, Bloomington, IN 47405-7000. Offers applied ecology (MSES); energy (MSES); environmental chemistry, toxicology, and risk assessment (MSES); environmental science (PhD); specialized environmental science (MSES); water resources (MSES); JD/MSES; MSES/MS. Part-time programs available. *Faculty:* 17 full-time, 8 part-time/adjunct. *Students:* 87 full-time (49 women), 2 part-time (1 woman); includes 1 Black or African American, non-Hispanic/Latino; 1 American Indian or Alaska Native, non-Hispanic/Latino; 10 Asian, non-Hispanic/Latino; 5 Hispanic/Latino, 11 international. Average age 26. 79 applicants, 29 enrolled. In 2010, 53 master's, 10 doctorates awarded. Terminal master's awarded for partial completion of doctoral program. *Degree requirements:* For master's, thesis optional; for doctorate, comprehensive exam, thesis/dissertation. *Entrance requirements:* For master's, GRE General Test or GMAT, official transcripts, 3 letters of recommendation, resume, personal statement, departmental questions; for doctorate, GRE General Test or LSAT and TOEFL (Intl.), official transcripts, 3 letters of recommendation, resume or curriculum vitae, statement of purpose, application, application fee, residence classification (Intl.). Additional exam requirements/recommendations for international students: Required—TOEFL (minimum score 600 paper-based; 96 iBT); Recommended—IELTS (minimum score 7). *Application deadline:* For fall admission, 5/1 for domestic students, 12/1 for international students; for spring admission, 11/1 for domestic and international students. Applications are processed on a rolling basis. Application fee: $55 ($65 for international students). Electronic applications accepted. *Financial support:* Fellowships with partial tuition reimbursements, research assistantships with partial tuition reimbursements, teaching assistantships with partial tuition reimbursements, career-related internships or fieldwork, Federal Work-Study, scholarships/grants, health care benefits, and unspecified assistantships available. Financial award application deadline: 2/1; financial award applicants required to submit FAFSA. *Faculty research:* Applied ecology, bio-geo chemistry, toxicology, wetlands ecology, environmental microbiology, forest ecology, environmental chemistry. *Unit head:* Jennifer J. Forney, Director, Graduate Student Servies, 812-855-9485, Fax: 812-856-3665, E-mail: speampo@indiana.edu. *Application contact:* Audrey Whittaker, Admissions Assistant, 812-855-2840, Fax: 812-856-3665, E-mail: speaapps@indiana.edu.

Indiana University Bloomington, School of Public and Environmental Affairs, Public Affairs Programs, Bloomington, IN 47405-7000. Offers comparative and international affairs (MPA); economic development (MPA); energy (MPA); environmental policy (PhD); environmental policy and natural resource management (MPA); information systems (MPA); local government management (MPA); nonprofit management (MPA, Certificate); policy analysis (MPA); public finance (PhD); public financial administration (MPA); public management (MPA, PhD); public policy analysis (PhD); specialized public affairs (MPA); sustainability and sustainable development (MPA); JD/MPA; MPA/MIS; MPA/MLS; MSES/MPA. *Accreditation:* NASPAA (one or more programs are accredited). Part-time programs available. *Faculty:* 31 full-time, 15 part-time/adjunct. *Students:* 466 full-time (261 women); includes 11 Black or African American, non-Hispanic/Latino; 2 American Indian or Alaska Native, non-Hispanic/Latino; 42 Asian, non-Hispanic/Latino; 1 Hispanic/Latino, 65 international. Average age 26. 650 applicants, 218 enrolled. In 2010, 166 master's, 10 doctorates awarded. *Degree requirements:* For master's, Core classes and capstone; for doctorate, comprehensive exam, thesis/dissertation. *Entrance requirements:* For master's, GRE General Test or GMAT, official transcripts, 3 letters of recommendation, resume, personal statement, departmental questions; for doctorate, GRE General Test or LSAT and TOEFL (intl), official transcripts, 3 letters of recommendation, resume or curriculum vitae, statement of purpose, application, application fee, residence classification (intl.). Additional exam requirements/recommendations for international students: Required—TOEFL (minimum score 600 paper-based; 96 iBT); Recommended—IELTS (minimum score 7). *Application deadline:* For fall admission, 5/1 priority date for domestic students, 12/1 priority date for international students. Applications are processed on a rolling basis. Application fee: $55 ($65 for international students). Electronic applications accepted. *Financial support:* Fellowships with partial tuition reimbursements, research assistantships with partial tuition reimbursements, teaching assistantships with partial tuition reimbursements, career-related internships or fieldwork, Federal Work-Study, scholarships/grants, health care benefits, unspecified assistantships, and Service Corps programs available. Financial award application deadline: 2/1; financial award applicants required to submit FAFSA. *Faculty research:* Comparative and international affairs, environmental policy and resource management, policy analysis, public finance, public management, urban management, nonprofit management, energy policy, social policy, public finance. *Unit head:* Jennifer Forney, Director of Graduate Student Services, 812-855-9485, Fax: 812-856-3665, E-mail: speampo@indiana.edu. *Application contact:* Audrey Whitaker, Admissions Assistant, 812-855-2840, E-mail: speaapps@indiana.edu.

Instituto Tecnologico de Santo Domingo, Graduate School, Area of Basic And Environmental Sciences, Santo Domingo, Dominican Republic. Offers environmental science (M En S), including environmental education, environmental management, marine resources, natural resources management; mathematics (MS, PhD); renewable energy technology (MS, Certificate).

New York Institute of Technology, Graduate Division, School of Engineering and Computing Sciences, Program in Energy Management, Old Westbury, NY 11568-8000. Offers energy management (MS); energy technology (Advanced Certificate); environmental management (Advanced Certificate); facilities management (Advanced Certificate). Part-time and evening/weekend programs available. Postbaccalaureate distance learning degree programs offered. *Students:* 57 full-time (12 women), 104 part-time (17 women); includes 31 minority (12 Black or African American, non-Hispanic/Latino; 2 American Indian or Alaska Native, non-Hispanic/Latino; 6 Asian, non-Hispanic/Latino; 11 Hispanic/Latino), 38 international. Average age 32. In 2010, 48 master's, 34 other advanced degrees awarded. *Degree requirements:* For master's, comprehensive exam, thesis or alternative. *Entrance requirements:* For master's, minimum QPA of 2.85. Additional exam requirements/recommendations for international students: Required—TOEFL (minimum score 550 paper-based; 213 computer-based). *Application deadline:* For fall admission, 7/1 priority date for domestic students; for spring admission, 12/1 priority date for domestic students. Applications are processed on a rolling basis. Application fee: $50. Electronic applications accepted. *Expenses:* Tuition: Part-time $835 per credit. *Financial support:* Fellowships, research assistantships with partial tuition reimbursements, institutionally sponsored loans, tuition waivers (full and partial), and unspecified assistantships available. Support available to part-time students. Financial award applicants required to submit FAFSA. *Unit head:* Dr. Robert Amundsen, Director, 516-686-7578, E-mail: ramundse@nyit.edu. *Application contact:* Dr. Jacquelyn Nealon, Vice President for Enrollment Services, 516-686-7925, Fax: 516-686-7597, E-mail: jnealon@nyit.edu.

Santa Clara University, School of Engineering, Program in Electrical Engineering, Santa Clara, CA 95053. Offers analog circuit design (Certificate); ASIC design and test (Certificate); digital signal processing (Certificate); electrical engineering (MS, PhD, Engineer); fundamentals of electrical engineering (Certificate); microwave and antennas (Certificate); renewable energy (Certificate). Part-time and evening/weekend programs available. *Students:* 54 full-time (14 women), 123 part-time (20 women); includes 62 minority (1 Black or African American, non-Hispanic/Latino; 55 Asian, non-Hispanic/Latino; 5 Hispanic/Latino; 1 Two or more races, non-Hispanic/Latino), 61 international. Average age 31. 161 applicants, 60% accepted, 49 enrolled. In 2010, 51 master's, 2 doctorates, 3 other advanced degrees awarded. *Degree requirements:* For master's, thesis (for some programs); for doctorate, thesis/dissertation; for other advanced degree, thesis. *Entrance requirements:* For master's, GRE (waiver may be available), transcript; for doctorate, GRE, master's degree or equivalent; for other advanced degree, master's degree, published paper. Additional exam requirements/recommendations for international students: Required—TOEFL (minimum score 550 paper-based; 213 computer-based; 79 iBT). *Application deadline:* For fall admission, 8/12 for domestic students, 7/15 for international students; for winter admission, 10/28 for domestic students, 9/23 for international students; for spring admission, 2/25 for domestic students, 1/21 for international students. Applications are processed on a rolling basis. Application fee: $60. Electronic applications accepted. *Expenses:* Contact institution. *Financial support:* Research assistantships, teaching assistantships available. Financial award application deadline: 3/2; financial award applicants required to submit FAFSA. *Faculty research:* Thermal and electrical nanoscale transport (TENT). Total annual research expenditures: $1.3 million. *Unit head:* Dr. Alex Zecevic, Associate Dean for Graduate Studies, 408-554-2394, E-mail: azecevic@scu.edu. *Application contact:* Stacey Tinker, Director of Enrollment Management, 408-554-4748, Fax: 408-554-4323, E-mail: stinker@scu.edu.

Université du Québec, Institut National de la Recherche Scientifique, Graduate Programs, Research Center—Energy, Materials and Telecommunications, Québec, QC G1K 9A9, Canada. Offers energy and materials science (M Sc, PhD); telecommunications (M Sc, PhD). Programs given in French; PhD programs offered jointly with Université du Québec à Trois-Rivières. Part-time programs available. *Faculty:* 40. *Students:* 171 full-time (44 women), 6 part-time (1 woman), 88 international. Average age 32. In 2010, 15 master's, 23 doctorates awarded. *Degree requirements:* For master's, thesis optional; for doctorate, thesis/dissertation. *Entrance requirements:* For master's, appropriate bachelor's degree, proficiency in French; for doctorate, appropriate master's degree, proficiency in French. *Application deadline:* For fall admission, 3/30 for domestic and international students; for winter admission, 11/1 for domestic and international students; for spring admission, 3/1 for domestic and international students. Application fee: $30. *Financial support:* Fellowships, research assistantships, teaching assistantships available. *Faculty research:* New energy sources, plasmas, fusion. *Unit head:* Jean-Claude Kieffer, Director, 450-929-8100, E-mail: kieffer@emt.inrs.ca. *Application contact:* Yvonne Boisvert, Registrar, 418-654-3861, Fax: 418-654-3858, E-mail: registrariat@adm.inrs.ca.

University of California, Berkeley, Graduate Division, Group in Energy and Resources, Berkeley, CA 94720-1500. Offers MA, MS, PhD. *Degree requirements:* For master's, project or thesis; for doctorate, one foreign language, thesis/dissertation, qualifying exam. *Entrance requirements:* For master's and doctorate, GRE General Test, minimum GPA of 3.0, 3 letters of recommendation. *Faculty research:* Technical, economic, environmental, and institutional aspects of energy conservation in residential and commercial buildings; international patterns of energy use; renewable energy sources; assessment of valuation of energy and environmental resources pricing.

University of Colorado Denver, Business School, Program in Global Energy Management, Denver, CO 80217. Offers MS. Postbaccalaureate distance learning degree programs offered (minimal on-campus study). *Students:* 76 full-time (17 women), 2 part-time; includes 7 Black or African American, non-Hispanic/Latino; 2 American Indian or Alaska Native, non-Hispanic/Latino; 1 Asian, non-Hispanic/Latino; 4 Hispanic/Latino, 1 international. Average age 33. 41 applicants, 85% accepted, 26 enrolled. *Degree requirements:* For master's, 36 semester credit hours. *Entrance requirements:* For master's, GMAT if less than three years of experience in the energy industry and no undergraduate degree in energy sciences or engineering, minimum of 5 years' experience in energy industry. Additional exam requirements/recommendations for international students: Required—TOEFL. *Application deadline:* For fall admission, 10/1 for domestic students; for spring admission, 5/10 for domestic students. Application fee: $50. Electronic applications accepted. *Expenses:* Contact institution. *Financial support:* Application deadline: 4/1. *Unit head:* John Turner, Director, 303-605-6211, E-mail: john.turner@ucdenver.edu. *Application contact:* Shelly Townley, Admissions Coordinator, 303-556-5956, Fax: 303-556-5904, E-mail: shelly.townley@ucdenver.edu.

University of Delaware, College of Human Services, Education and Public Policy, Center for Energy and Environmental Policy, Newark, DE 19716. Offers environmental and energy policy (MEEP, PhD); urban affairs and public policy (MA, PhD), including community development and nonprofit leadership (MA), energy and environmental policy (MA), governance, planning and management (PhD), historic preservation (MA), social and urban policy (PhD), technology, environment and society (PhD). *Degree requirements:* For master's, analytical paper or thesis; for doctorate, comprehensive exam, thesis/dissertation. *Entrance requirements:* For master's, GRE General Test, minimum GPA of 3.0; for doctorate, GRE General Test, minimum GPA of 3.5. Additional exam requirements/recommendations for international students: Required—TOEFL. Electronic applications accepted. *Faculty research:* Sustainable development, renewable energy, climate change, environmental policy, environmental justice, disaster policy.

University of Denver, University College, Denver, CO 80208. Offers arts and culture (MLS, Certificate), including art, literature, and culture, arts development and program management (Certificate), creative writing; environmental policy and management (MAS, Certificate), including energy and sustainability (Certificate), environmental assessment of nuclear power (Certificate), environmental health and safety (Certificate), environmental management, natural resource management (Certificate); geographic information systems (MAS, Certificate); global affairs (MLS, Certificate), including translation studies, world history and culture; healthcare leadership (MPH, Certificate), including healthcare policy, law, and ethics, medical and healthcare information technologies, strategic management of healthcare; information and communications technology (MCIS, Certificate), including database design and administration (Certificate), geographic information systems (MCIS), information security systems security (Certificate), information systems security (MCIS), project management (MCIS, MPS, Certificate), software design and administration (Certificate), software design and programming (MCIS), technology management, telecommunications technology (MCIS), Web design and development; leadership and organizations (MPS, Certificate), including human capital in organizations, philanthropic leadership, project management (MCIS, MPS, Certificate), strategic innovation and change; organizational and professional communication (MPS, Certificate), including alternative dispute resolution, organizational communication, organizational development and training, public relations and marketing; security management (MAS, Certificate), including emergency planning and response, information security (MAS), organizational security; strategic human resource management (MPS, Certificate), including global human resources (MPS), human resource management and development (MPS). Part-time and evening/weekend programs available. Postbaccalaureate distance learning degree programs offered (no on-campus study). *Faculty:* 7 full-time (2 women), 212 part-time/adjunct (83 women). *Students:* 52 full-time (19 women), 1,044 part-time (625 women); includes 196 minority (81 Black or African American, non-Hispanic/Latino; 7 American Indian or Alaska Native, non-Hispanic/Latino; 30 Asian, non-Hispanic/Latino; 66 Hispanic/Latino; 3 Native Hawaiian or other Pacific Islander, non-Hispanic/Latino; 9 Two or more races, non-Hispanic/Latino), 76 international. Average age 36. 488 applicants, 91% accepted, 339 enrolled. In 2010, 286 master's, 130 other advanced degrees awarded. *Entrance requirements:* Additional exam requirements/recommendations for international students: Required—TOEFL (minimum score 550 paper-based; 80 iBT). *Application deadline:*

Energy Management and Policy

University of Denver (continued)
For fall admission, 6/22 priority date for domestic students, 6/10 priority date for international students; for winter admission, 9/15 priority date for domestic students, 9/6 priority date for international students; for spring admission, 2/3 priority date for domestic students, 12/15 priority date for international students. Applications are processed on a rolling basis. Application fee: $75. Electronic applications accepted. *Expenses:* Contact institution. *Financial support:* Applicants required to submit FAFSA. *Unit head:* Dr. James Davis, Dean, 303-871-2291, Fax: 303-871-4047, E-mail: jdavis@du.edu. *Application contact:* Information Contact, 303-871-3155, Fax: 303-871-4047, E-mail: ucolinfo@du.edu.

University of Illinois at Urbana–Champaign, Graduate College, College of Agricultural, Consumer and Environmental Sciences, Program in Bioenergy, Champaign, IL 61820. Offers MS. Applications are only accepted for the fall semester. *Students:* 12 full-time (2 women); includes 1 Asian, non-Hispanic/Latino, 3 international. 10 applicants, 80% accepted, 6 enrolled. *Degree requirements:* For master's, internship. *Entrance requirements:* For master's, GRE, baccalaureate degree in recognized field of biological, physical, agricultural, socio-economic or engineering science. Additional exam requirements/recommendations for international students: Required—TOEFL (minimum score 590 paper-based; 243 computer-based). Application fee: $75 ($90 for international students). Electronic applications accepted. *Unit head:* Hans Blaschek, Director, 217-244-9270, E-mail: blascheck@illinois.edu. *Application contact:* Hans Blaschek, Director, 217-244-9270, E-mail: blascheck@illinois.edu.

University of Phoenix, School of Business, Phoenix, AZ 85034-7209. Offers accounting (MBA, MSA); business administration (MBA); energy management (MBA); global management (MBA); health care management (MBA); human resources management (MM); international management (MM); management (MM); marketing (MBA); project management (MBA); public administration (MPA); technology management (MBA). Programs are offered at the online campus. Evening/weekend programs available. Postbaccalaureate distance learning degree programs offered. *Students:* 20,237 full-time (12,641 women); includes 6,424 minority (4,376 Black or African American, non-Hispanic/Latino; 150 American Indian or Alaska Native, non-Hispanic/Latino; 546 Asian, non-Hispanic/Latino; 1,137 Hispanic/Latino; 155 Native Hawaiian or other Pacific Islander, non-Hispanic/Latino; 60 Two or more races, non-Hispanic/Latino), 1,149 international. Average age 39. *Entrance requirements:* For master's, minimum undergraduate GPA of 2.5 from accredited university, 3 years of work experience, citizen of the United States or have valid visa. Additional exam requirements/recommendations for international students: Required—TOEFL (minimum paper score 550, computer score 213, iBT 79), Test of English for International Communication, or IELTS. *Application deadline:* Applications are processed on a rolling basis. Application fee: $45. Electronic applications accepted. *Expenses:* Tuition: Full-time $16,440. One-time fee: $45 full-time. Full-time tuition and fees vary according to course load, degree level, campus/location and program. *Financial support:* Scholarships/grants available. Financial award applicants required to submit FAFSA. *Unit head:* Dr. Bill Berry, Director, 480-557-1824, E-mail: bill.berry@phoenix.edu. *Application contact:* Dr. Bill Berry, Director, 480-557-1824, E-mail: bill.berry@phoenix.edu.

University of Phoenix–Puerto Rico Campus, School of Business, Guaynabo, PR 00968. Offers accounting (MBA); energy management (MBA); global management (MBA); human resource management (MBA); marketing (MBA); project management (MBA); small business administration (MBA). Evening/weekend programs available. *Degree requirements:* For master's, thesis (for some programs). *Entrance requirements:* For master's, minimum undergraduate GPA of 3.0, 3 years work experience. Additional exam requirements/recommendations for international students: Required—TOEFL (minimum score 550 paper-based; 213 computer-based; 79 iBT). Electronic applications accepted.

University of Tulsa, Graduate School, Collins College of Business, Master of Business Administration Program, Tulsa, OK 74104-3189. Offers accounting (MBA); business administration (MBA); energy management (MBA); finance (MBA); international business (MBA); management information systems (MBA); taxation (MBA); JD/MBA; MBA/MSCS; MBA/MSF. *Accreditation:* AACSB. Part-time and evening/weekend programs available. *Faculty:* 32 full-time (6 women). *Students:* 39 full-time (14 women), 40 part-time (16 women); includes 7 minority (1 Black or African American, non-Hispanic/Latino; 2 Asian, non-Hispanic/Latino; 4 Hispanic/Latino), 9 international. Average age 26. 73 applicants, 55% accepted, 18 enrolled. In 2010, 55 master's awarded. *Entrance requirements:* For master's, GMAT. Additional exam requirements/recommendations for international students: Required—TOEFL (minimum score 575 paper-based; 232 computer-based; 90 iBT), IELTS (minimum score 6.5). *Application deadline:* Applications are processed on a rolling basis. Application fee: $40. Electronic applications accepted. *Expenses:* Tuition: Full-time $16,902; part-time $939 per credit hour. Required fees: $1020; $4 per credit hour. Tuition and fees vary according to course load. *Financial support:* In 2010–11, 56 students received support, including 23 fellowships (averaging $4,872 per year), 4 research assistantships (averaging $9,323 per year), 29 teaching assistantships (averaging $10,642 per year); career-related internships or fieldwork, institutionally sponsored loans, scholarships/grants, health care benefits, tuition waivers (full and partial), and unspecified assistantships also available. Support available to part-time students. Financial award application deadline: 2/1; financial award applicants required to submit FAFSA. *Faculty research:* Accounting, energy management, finance, international business, management information systems, taxation. *Unit head:* Dr. Linda Nichols, Associate Dean of the Collins College of Business, 918-631-2242, Fax: 918-631-2142, E-mail: linda-nichols@utulsa.edu. *Application contact:* Dr. Linda Nichols, Associate Dean of the Collins College of Business, 918-631-2242, Fax: 918-631-2142, E-mail: linda-nichols@utulsa.edu.

University of Washington, Graduate School, College of Forest Resources, Seattle, WA 98195. Offers bioresource science and engineering (MS, PhD); environmental horticulture (MEH); environmental horticulture and urban forestry (MS, PhD); forest ecology (MS, PhD); forest management (MFR); forest soils (MS, PhD); forest systems and bioenergy (MS, PhD); restoration ecology (MS, PhD); social sciences (MS, PhD); sustainable resource management (MS, PhD); wildlife science (MS, PhD); MFR/MAIS; MPA/MS. *Accreditation:* SAF. *Degree requirements:* For master's, thesis (for some programs); for doctorate, comprehensive exam (for some programs), thesis/dissertation. *Entrance requirements:* For master's and doctorate, GRE, minimum GPA of 3.0. Additional exam requirements/recommendations for international students: Required—TOEFL. Electronic applications accepted. *Faculty research:* Ecosystem analysis, silviculture and forest protection, paper science and engineering, environmental horticulture and urban forestry, natural resource policy and economics.

Engineering Management

Air Force Institute of Technology, Graduate School of Engineering and Management, Department of Systems and Engineering Management, Dayton, OH 45433-7765. Offers cost analysis (MS); environmental and engineering management (MS); environmental engineering science (MS); information resource/systems management (MS). *Accreditation:* ABET. Part-time programs available. *Degree requirements:* For master's, thesis. *Entrance requirements:* For master's, GRE, GMAT, minimum GPA of 3.0.

American University of Beirut, Graduate Programs, Faculty of Engineering and Architecture, Beirut, Lebanon. Offers applied energy (MME); civil engineering (ME, PhD); electrical and computer engineering (ME, PhD); engineering management (MEM); environmental and water resources (ME); environmental and water resources engineering (PhD); environmental technology (MSES); mechagical engineering (ME, PhD); urban design (MUD); urban planning and policy (MUP). Part-time programs available. *Faculty:* 57 full-time (12 women), 3 part-time/adjunct (0 women). *Students:* 261 full-time (92 women), 58 part-time (20 women). Average age 25. 272 applicants, 79% accepted, 108 enrolled. In 2010, 70 master's, 1 doctorate awarded. *Degree requirements:* For master's, one foreign language, comprehensive exam, thesis (for some programs); for doctorate, one foreign language, comprehensive exam, thesis/dissertation, publications. *Entrance requirements:* For master's, GRE (for electrical and computer engineering), letters of recommendation; for doctorate, GRE, letters of recommendation, master's degree, transcripts, curriculum vitae, interview. Additional exam requirements/recommendations for international students: Required—TOEFL (minimum score 600 paper-based; 250 computer-based; 100 iBT), IELTS (minimum score 7.5). *Application deadline:* For fall admission, 2/5 priority date for domestic and international students; for spring admission, 11/1 priority date for domestic students, 11/1 for international students. Applications are processed on a rolling basis. Application fee: $50. Electronic applications accepted. *Expenses:* Tuition: Full-time $12,294; part-time $683 per credit. Required fees: $499; $499 per credit. Tuition and fees vary according to course load and program. *Financial support:* In 2010–11, 10 fellowships with full tuition reimbursements (averaging $24,800 per year), 33 research assistantships with full tuition reimbursements (averaging $24,800 per year), 70 teaching assistantships with full tuition reimbursements (averaging $9,800 per year) were awarded; career-related internships or fieldwork, institutionally sponsored loans, scholarships/grants, health care benefits, and unspecified assistantships also available. Total annual research expenditures: $586,131. *Unit head:* Fadl H. Moukalled, Acting Dean, 961-135-0000 Ext. 3400, Fax: 961-174-4462, E-mail: memouk@aub.edu.lb. *Application contact:* Dr. Salim Kanaan, Director, Admissions Office, 961-135-0000 Ext. 2594, Fax: 961-175-0775, E-mail: sk00@aub.edu.lb.

California National University for Advanced Studies, College of Quality and Engineering Management, Northridge, CA 91325. Offers MEM. Part-time programs available. *Entrance requirements:* For master's, minimum GPA of 3.0.

California State Polytechnic University, Pomona, Academic Affairs, College of Engineering, Program in Engineering Management, Pomona, CA 91768-2557. Offers MS. *Students:* 4 full-time (1 woman), 31 part-time (10 women); includes 19 minority (7 Asian, non-Hispanic/Latino; 10 Hispanic/Latino; 2 Two or more races, non-Hispanic/Latino), 1 international. Average age 32. 47 applicants, 49% accepted, 16 enrolled. In 2010, 12 master's awarded. *Degree requirements:* For master's, thesis or project. *Application deadline:* Applications are processed on a rolling basis. Application fee: $55. Electronic applications accepted. *Expenses:* Tuition, state resident: full-time $5386; part-time $2850 per year. Tuition, nonresident: full-time $12,082; part-time $248 per credit. Required fees: $577; $248 per credit. $577 per year. Tuition and fees vary according to course load and program. *Unit head:* Dr. Abdul B. Sadat, Chair/Graduate Coordinator, 909-869-2555, E-mail: absadat@csupomona.edu. *Application contact:* Scott J. Duncan, Director, Admissions, 909-869-3258, E-mail: sjduncan@csupomona.edu.

California State University, East Bay, Office of Academic Programs and Graduate Studies, College of Science, Engineering Department, Hayward, CA 94542-3000. Offers construction management (MS); engineering management (MS). *Faculty:* 4 full-time (2 women). *Students:* 30 full-time (12 women), 62 part-time (12 women); includes 24 minority (4 Black or African American, non-Hispanic/Latino; 9 Asian, non-Hispanic/Latino; 11 Hispanic/Latino), 30 international. Average age 32. 92 applicants, 78% accepted, 27 enrolled. In 2010, 23 master's awarded. *Entrance requirements:* For master's, GRE or GMAT, minimum GPA of 2.5. Additional exam requirements/recommendations for international students: Required—TOEFL (minimum score 550 paper-based; 213 computer-based). *Application deadline:* For fall admission, 6/30 for domestic and international students. Application fee: $55. Electronic applications accepted. *Financial support:* Federal Work-Study and institutionally sponsored loans available. Support available to part-time students. Financial award application deadline: 3/2; financial award applicants required to submit FAFSA. *Unit head:* Dr. Saeid Motavalli, Chair, 510-885-2654, Fax: 510-885-2678, E-mail: saeid.motavalli@csueastbay.edu. *Application contact:* Dr. Donna Wiley, Interim Associate Director, 510-885-2928, Fax: 510-885-4777, E-mail: donna.wiley@csueastbay.edu.

California State University, Long Beach, Graduate Studies, College of Engineering, Department of Mechanical and Aerospace Engineering, Long Beach, CA 90840. Offers aerospace engineering (MSAE); engineering and industrial applied mathematics (PhD); interdisciplinary engineering (MSE); management engineering (MSE); mechanical engineering (MSME). Part-time programs available. *Faculty:* 14 full-time (3 women), 6 part-time/adjunct (0 women). *Students:* 44 full-time (1 woman), 56 part-time (8 women); includes 1 Black or African American, non-Hispanic/Latino; 1 American Indian or Alaska Native, non-Hispanic/Latino; 30 Asian, non-Hispanic/Latino; 15 Hispanic/Latino, 15 international. Average age 28. 169 applicants, 41% accepted, 25 enrolled. In 2010, 32 master's awarded. *Entrance requirements:* Additional exam requirements/recommendations for international students: Required—TOEFL. *Application deadline:* For fall admission, 7/1 for domestic students. Application fee: $55. Electronic applications accepted. *Financial support:* Career-related internships or fieldwork, Federal Work-Study, institutionally sponsored loans, scholarships/grants, and unspecified assistantships available. Financial award application deadline: 3/2. *Faculty research:* Unsteady turbulent flows, solar energy, energy conversion, CAD/CAM, computer-assisted instruction. *Unit head:* Dr. Hamid Hefazi, Chair, 562-985-1502, Fax: 562-985-1564, E-mail: hefazi@csulb.edu. *Application contact:* Dr. Hamid Rahai, Graduate Advisor, 562-985-5132, Fax: 562-985-4408, E-mail: rahai@csulb.edu.

California State University, Northridge, Graduate Studies, College of Engineering and Computer Science, Department of Manufacturing Systems Engineering and Management, Northridge, CA 91330. Offers engineering automation (MS); engineering management (MS); manufacturing systems engineering (MS); materials engineering (MS). Postbaccalaureate distance learning degree programs offered. *Entrance requirements:* For master's, GRE (if cumulative undergraduate GPA less than 3.0).

Case Western Reserve University, School of Graduate Studies, Case School of Engineering, The Institute for the Integration of Management and Engineering, Cleveland, OH 44106. Offers MEM. *Students:* 30 full-time (7 women); includes 3 Black or African American, non-Hispanic/Latino; 2 Asian, non-Hispanic/Latino, 10 international. In 2010, 40 master's awarded. *Entrance requirements:* Additional exam requirements/recommendations for international students: Required—TOEFL (minimum score 100 computer-based), IELTS (minimum score 7.5). *Application deadline:* For fall admission, 5/1 for domestic students, 2/1 for international students. *Financial support:* In 2010–11, 37 fellowships (averaging $14,300 per year) were awarded; scholarships/grants also available. *Unit head:* Suzette Williamson, Executive Director, 216-368-0598, Fax: 216-368-0144, E-mail: sxwll@cwru.edu. *Application contact:* Ramona David, Program Assistant, 216-368-0596, Fax: 216-368-0144, E-mail: rxd47@cwru.edu.

The Catholic University of America, School of Engineering, Program in Engineering Management, Washington, DC 20064. Offers MSE, Certificate. Part-time programs available. *Faculty:* 5 part-time/adjunct (0 women). *Students:* 14 full-time (5 women), 15 part-time (7 women); includes 1 Hispanic/Latino, 14 international. Average age 29. 52 applicants, 52%

accepted, 15 enrolled. In 2010, 31 master's awarded. *Degree requirements:* For master's, thesis optional. *Entrance requirements:* For master's and Certificate, statement of purpose, official copies of academic transcripts, three letters of recommendation. Additional exam requirements/recommendations for international students: Required—TOEFL (minimum score 580 paper-based; 237 computer-based). *Application deadline:* For fall admission, 8/1 priority date for domestic students, 7/15 for international students; for spring admission, 12/1 priority date for domestic students, 10/15 for international students. Applications are processed on a rolling basis. Application fee: $55. Electronic applications accepted. *Expenses:* Contact institution. *Financial support:* Fellowships, research assistantships, teaching assistantships, Federal Work-Study, scholarships/grants, tuition waivers (full and partial), and unspecified assistantships available. Financial award application deadline: 2/1; financial award applicants required to submit FAFSA. *Faculty research:* Engineering management and organization, project and systems engineering management, technology management. *Unit head:* Jeffrey E. Giangiuli, Director, 202-319-5191, Fax: 202-319-6860, E-mail: giangiuli@cua.edu. *Application contact:* Andrew Woodall, Director of Graduate Admissions, 202-319-5057, Fax: 202-319-6533, E-mail: cua-admissions@cua.edu.

Clarkson University, Graduate School, School of Business, Program in Engineering and Global Operations Management, Potsdam, NY 13699. Offers MS. Part-time and evening/weekend programs available. *Students:* 21 part-time (6 women); includes 2 minority (both Hispanic/Latino). Average age 38. 4 applicants, 100% accepted, 4 enrolled. In 2010, 14 master's awarded. *Entrance requirements:* For master's, GMAT or GRE, transcripts of all college coursework, resume, personal statement, three letters of recommendation. Additional exam requirements/recommendations for international students: Required—TOEFL (minimum score 550 paper-based; 213 computer-based; 80 iBT), IELTS (minimum score 6.5), TSE required for some. *Application deadline:* For fall admission, 1/30 priority date for domestic and international students; for spring admission, 9/1 priority date for domestic and international students. Applications are processed on a rolling basis. Application fee: $25 ($35 for international students). Electronic applications accepted. *Expenses:* Tuition: Part-time $1136 per credit hour. *Financial support:* In 2010–11, 1 student received support. Scholarships/grants available. *Faculty research:* Global supply chain management, business-to-business marketing, operations strategy, engineering economics process control. *Unit head:* Dr. Kenneth DaRin, Director, 315-268-5982, Fax: 315-268-3810, E-mail: kdarin@clarkson.edu. *Application contact:* Karen Fuhr, Assistant to the Graduate Director, 315-268-6613, Fax: 315-268-3810, E-mail: fuhrk@clarkson.edu.

Colorado School of Mines, Graduate School, Division of Economics and Business, Golden, CO 80401. Offers engineering and technology management (MS); mineral economics (MS, PhD). Part-time programs available. *Faculty:* 12 full-time (3 women), 8 part-time/adjunct (1 woman). *Students:* 121 full-time (22 women), 23 part-time (5 women); includes 1 Black or African American, non-Hispanic/Latino; 2 American Indian or Alaska Native, non-Hispanic/Latino; 1 Asian, non-Hispanic/Latino; 6 Hispanic/Latino, 31 international. Average age 29. 179 applicants, 72% accepted, 63 enrolled. In 2010, 70 master's, 3 doctorates awarded. *Degree requirements:* For master's, thesis (for some programs); for doctorate, comprehensive exam, thesis/dissertation. *Entrance requirements:* For master's and doctorate, GRE General Test. Additional exam requirements/recommendations for international students: Required—TOEFL (minimum score 550 paper-based; 213 computer-based; 80 iBT). *Application deadline:* For fall admission, 1/15 priority date for domestic and international students; for spring admission, 10/15 priority date for domestic and international students. Application fee: $50 ($70 for international students). Electronic applications accepted. *Expenses:* Tuition, state resident: full-time $11,550; part-time $641 per credit. Tuition, nonresident: full-time $25,980; part-time $1444 per credit. Required fees: $1874; $937 per semester. *Financial support:* In 2010–11, 45 students received support, including 6 fellowships with full tuition reimbursements available (averaging $20,000 per year), 11 research assistantships with full tuition reimbursements available (averaging $20,000 per year), 28 teaching assistantships with full tuition reimbursements available (averaging $20,000 per year); scholarships/grants, health care benefits, and unspecified assistantships also available. Financial award application deadline: 1/15; financial award applicants required to submit FAFSA. *Faculty research:* International trade, resource and environmental economics, energy economics, operations research. Total annual research expenditures: $137,815. *Unit head:* Dr. Rod Eggert, Division Head, 303-273-3981, Fax: 303-273-3416, E-mail: reggert@mines.edu. *Application contact:* Kathleen A. Feighny, Administrative Faculty, 303-273-3979, Fax: 303-273-3416, E-mail: kfeighny@mines.edu.

Cornell University, Graduate School, Graduate Fields of Engineering, Field of Civil and Environmental Engineering, Ithaca, NY 14853-0001. Offers engineering management (M Eng, MS, PhD); environmental engineering (M Eng, MS, PhD); environmental fluid mechanics and hydrology (M Eng, MS, PhD); environmental systems engineering (M Eng, MS, PhD); geotechnical engineering (M Eng, MS, PhD); remote sensing (M Eng, MS, PhD); structural engineering (M Eng, MS, PhD); structural mechanics (M Eng, MS); transportation engineering (MS, PhD); transportation systems engineering (M Eng); water resource systems (M Eng, MS, PhD). *Faculty:* 36 full-time (4 women). *Students:* 148 full-time (48 women); includes 3 Black or African American, non-Hispanic/Latino; 1 American Indian or Alaska Native, non-Hispanic/Latino; 16 Asian, non-Hispanic/Latino; 16 Hispanic/Latino, 60 international. Average age 24. 390 applicants, 56% accepted, 76 enrolled. In 2010, 93 master's, 5 doctorates awarded. Terminal master's awarded for partial completion of doctoral program. *Degree requirements:* For master's, thesis (MS); for doctorate, comprehensive exam, thesis/dissertation. *Entrance requirements:* For master's and doctorate, GRE General Test (recommended), 2 letters of recommendation. Additional exam requirements/recommendations for international students: Required—TOEFL (minimum score 600 paper-based; 250 computer-based; 77 iBT). *Application deadline:* For fall admission, 1/15 priority date for domestic students; for spring admission, 10/15 for domestic students. Application fee: $70. Electronic applications accepted. *Expenses:* Tuition: Full-time $29,500. Required fees: $76. Tuition and fees vary according to degree level and program. *Financial support:* In 2010–11, 50 students received support, including 17 fellowships with full tuition reimbursements available, 33 research assistantships with full tuition reimbursements available, 15 teaching assistantships with full tuition reimbursements available; institutionally sponsored loans, scholarships/grants, health care benefits, tuition waivers (full and partial), and unspecified assistantships also available. Financial award applicants required to submit FAFSA. *Faculty research:* Environmental engineering, geotechnical engineering, remote sensing, environmental fluid mechanics and hydrology, structural engineering. *Unit head:* Director of Graduate Studies, 607-255-7560, Fax: 607-255-9004. *Application contact:* Graduate Field Assistant, 607-255-7560, Fax: 607-255-9004, E-mail: cee_grad@cornell.edu.

Dallas Baptist University, College of Business, Business Administration Program, Dallas, TX 75211-9299. Offers accounting (MBA); business communication (MBA); conflict resolution management (MBA); e-business (MBA); entrepreneurship (MBA); finance (MBA); health care management (MBA); international business (MBA); leading the non-profit organization (MBA); management (MBA); management information systems (MBA); marketing (MBA); project management (MBA); technology and engineering management (MBA). *Accreditation:* ACBSP. Part-time and evening/weekend programs available. *Entrance requirements:* For master's, GMAT, minimum GPA of 3.0. Additional exam requirements/recommendations for international students: Required—TOEFL, IELTS. Electronic applications accepted. *Expenses:* Tuition: Full-time $11,394; part-time $633 per credit hour. *Faculty research:* Sports management, services marketing, retailing, strategic management, financial planning/investments.

Dartmouth College, Thayer School of Engineering, Program in Engineering Management, Hanover, NH 03755. Offers MEM, MBA/MEM. *Degree requirements:* For master's, design experience. *Entrance requirements:* For master's, GRE General Test. Additional exam requirements/recommendations for international students: Required—TOEFL.

Drexel University, College of Engineering, Program in Engineering Management, Philadelphia, PA 19104-2875. Offers MS, Certificate. Part-time and evening/weekend programs available. Postbaccalaureate distance learning degree programs offered (no on-campus study). *Degree*

requirements: For master's, thesis optional. *Entrance requirements:* For master's, minimum GPA of 3.0. Additional exam requirements/recommendations for international students: Required—TOEFL. Electronic applications accepted. *Faculty research:* Quality, operations research and management, ergonomics, applied statistics.

Duke University, Graduate School, Pratt School of Engineering, Distributed Master of Engineering Management Program (d-MEMP), durham, NC 27708-0271. Offers MEM. Part-time and evening/weekend programs available. Postbaccalaureate distance learning degree programs offered (minimal on-campus study). *Faculty:* 15 full-time (5 women), 12 part-time/adjunct (1 woman). *Students:* 32 part-time (10 women); includes 9 minority (8 Asian, non-Hispanic/Latino; 1 Hispanic/Latino), 3 international. 22 applicants, 77% accepted, 16 enrolled. *Entrance requirements:* For master's, GRE General Test, resume, 3 letters of recommendation, statement of purpose. Additional exam requirements/recommendations for international students: Required—TOEFL. *Application deadline:* For fall admission, 6/15 for domestic students. Application fee: $75. Electronic applications accepted. *Expenses:* Contact institution. *Faculty research:* Entrepreneurship, innovation and product development, project management, operations and supply chain management, financial engineering. *Unit head:* Dr. Brad Fox, Executive Director, Professional Masters Programs, 919-660-5516, Fax: 919-660-5456, E-mail: brad.fox@duke.edu. *Application contact:* Erin Degerman, Admissions Coordinator, 919-668-6789, Fax: 919-660-5456, E-mail: erin.degerman@duke.edu.

Duke University, Graduate School, Pratt School of Engineering, Master of Engineering Management Program, Durham, NC 27708-0271. Offers MEM. Part-time programs available. Postbaccalaureate distance learning degree programs offered. *Faculty:* 15 full-time (5 women), 12 part-time/adjunct (1 woman). *Students:* 175 full-time (53 women), 6 part-time (1 woman); includes 31 minority (6 Black or African American, non-Hispanic/Latino; 2 American Indian or Alaska Native, non-Hispanic/Latino; 21 Asian, non-Hispanic/Latino; 2 Hispanic/Latino), 94 international. Average age 24. 1,877 applicants, 18% accepted, 136 enrolled. In 2010, 132 master's awarded. *Entrance requirements:* For master's, GRE General Test, resume, 3 letters of recommendation, statement of purpose. Additional exam requirements/recommendations for international students: Required—TOEFL. *Application deadline:* For fall admission, 6/15 for domestic students, 3/15 for international students; for spring admission, 11/1 for domestic students, 9/1 for international students. Application fee: $75. Electronic applications accepted. *Expenses:* Contact institution. *Financial support:* Merit scholarships available. *Faculty research:* Entrepreneurship, innovation and product development, project management, operations and supply chain management, financial engineering. *Unit head:* Dr. Bradley A. Fox, Executive Director, 919-660-5455, Fax: 919-660-5456, E-mail: brad.fox@duke.edu. *Application contact:* Erin Degerman, Admissions Coordinator, 919-668-6789, E-mail: erin.degerman@duke.edu.

Eastern Michigan University, Graduate School, College of Technology, School of Engineering Technology, Program in Engineering Management, Ypsilanti, MI 48197. Offers MS. Part-time and evening/weekend programs available. Postbaccalaureate distance learning degree programs offered (minimal on-campus study). *Students:* 25 full-time (7 women), 101 part-time (14 women); includes 14 minority (7 Black or African American, non-Hispanic/Latino; 1 American Indian or Alaska Native, non-Hispanic/Latino; 2 Asian, non-Hispanic/Latino; 4 Hispanic/Latino), 27 international. Average age 32. In 2010, 55 master's awarded. *Entrance requirements:* Additional exam requirements/recommendations for international students: Required—TOEFL. *Application deadline:* Applications are processed on a rolling basis. Application fee: $35. *Financial support:* Fellowships, research assistantships with full tuition reimbursements, teaching assistantships with full tuition reimbursements, career-related internships or fieldwork, Federal Work-Study, institutionally sponsored loans, scholarships/grants, tuition waivers (partial), and unspecified assistantships available. Support available to part-time students. Financial award applicants required to submit FAFSA. *Unit head:* Dr. Muhammad Ahmad, Program Coordinator, 734-487-2040, Fax: 734-487-8755, E-mail: mahmed@emich.edu. *Application contact:* Dr. Muhammad Ahmad, Program Coordinator, 734-487-2040, Fax: 734-487-8755, E-mail: mahmed@emich.edu.

Florida Institute of Technology, Graduate Programs, College of Engineering, Engineering Systems Department, Melbourne, FL 32901-6975. Offers engineering management (MS); systems engineering (MS, PhD). Part-time and evening/weekend programs available. *Faculty:* 5 full-time (0 women). *Students:* 21 full-time (4 women), 47 part-time (10 women); includes 8 minority (3 Black or African American, non-Hispanic/Latino; 2 Asian, non-Hispanic/Latino; 2 Hispanic/Latino; 1 Two or more races, non-Hispanic/Latino), 16 international. Average age 35. 106 applicants, 62% accepted, 16 enrolled. In 2010, 87 master's awarded. *Degree requirements:* For master's, comprehensive exam (for some programs), thesis optional, portfolio of competencies and summary of career relevance. *Entrance requirements:* For master's, GRE General Test (if GPA less than 3.0), BS in engineering, minimum GPA of 3.0, 2 letters of recommendation, resume, bachelor's degree from ABET-accredited program, statement of objectives. Additional exam requirements/recommendations for international students: Required—TOEFL (minimum score 550 paper-based; 213 computer-based; 79 iBT). *Application deadline:* For fall admission, 4/1 for international students; for spring admission, 9/30 for international students. Applications are processed on a rolling basis. Application fee: $50. Electronic applications accepted. *Expenses:* Tuition: Part-time $1040 per credit hour. Tuition and fees vary according to campus/location. *Financial support:* In 2010–11, 1 research assistantship with full and partial tuition reimbursement (averaging $16,245 per year) was awarded; career-related internships or fieldwork, institutionally sponsored loans, unspecified assistantships, and tuition remissions also available. Support available to part-time students. Financial award application deadline: 3/1; financial award applicants required to submit FAFSA. *Faculty research:* System/software engineering, simulation and analytical modeling, project management, multimedia tools, quality. *Unit head:* Dr. Muzaffar A. Shaikh, Department Head, 321-674-7345, Fax: 321-674-7136, E-mail: mshaikh@fit.edu. *Application contact:* Cheryl A. Brown, Associate Director of Graduate Admissions, 321-674-7581, Fax: 321-723-9468, E-mail: cbrown@fit.edu.

Florida Institute of Technology, Graduate Programs, Extended Studies Division, Melbourne, FL 32901-6975. Offers acquisition and contract management (MS); aerospace engineering (MS); business administration (MBA); computer information systems (MS); computer science (MS); electrical engineering (MS); engineering management (MS); human resources management (MS); logistics management (MS), including humanitarian and disaster relief logistics; management (MS), including acquisition and contract management, e-business, human resources management, information systems, logistics management, management, transportation management; material acquisition management (MS); mechanical engineering (MS); operations research (MS); project management (MS), including information systems, operations research; public administration (MPA); quality management (MS); software engineering (MS); space systems (MS); space systems management (MS); systems management (MS), including information systems, operations research. Part-time and evening/weekend programs available. Postbaccalaureate distance learning degree programs offered (no on-campus study). *Faculty:* 11 full-time (3 women), 118 part-time/adjunct (24 women). *Students:* 69 full-time (23 women), 907 part-time (369 women); includes 385 minority (242 Black or African American, non-Hispanic/Latino; 15 American Indian or Alaska Native, non-Hispanic/Latino; 44 Asian, non-Hispanic/Latino; 52 Hispanic/Latino; 3 Native Hawaiian or other Pacific Islander, non-Hispanic/Latino; 29 Two or more races, non-Hispanic/Latino), 17 international. 517 applicants, 49% accepted, 245 enrolled. In 2010, 430 degrees awarded. *Degree requirements:* For master's, comprehensive exam (for some programs), capstone course. *Entrance requirements:* For master's, GMAT or resume showing 8 years of supervised experience, minimum GPA of 3.0, 2 letters of recommendation, resume. Additional exam requirements/recommendations for international students: Required—TOEFL (minimum score 550 paper-based; 213 computer-based; 79 iBT). *Application deadline:* For fall admission, 4/1 for international students; for spring admission, 9/30 for international students. Applications are processed on a rolling basis. Application fee: $50. Electronic applications accepted. *Expenses:* Contact institution. *Financial support:* Application deadline: 3/1. *Unit head:* Dr. Theodore Richardson, Senior Associate Dean, 321-674-8123, Fax: 321-674-7597, E-mail: trichardson@

Engineering Management

Florida Institute of Technology (continued)

fit.edu. *Application contact:* Carolyn Farrior, Director of Graduate Admissions, Online Learning and Off-Campus Programs, 321-674-7118, Fax: 321-674-8216, E-mail: cfarrior@fit.edu.

Gannon University, School of Graduate Studies, College of Engineering and Business, School of Engineering and Computer Science, Program in Engineering Management, Erie, PA 16541-0001. Offers MSEM. Part-time and evening/weekend programs available. *Students:* 25 full-time (2 women), 8 part-time (0 women); includes 1 Asian, non-Hispanic/Latino, 26 international. Average age 27. 62 applicants, 81% accepted, 7 enrolled. In 2010, 12 master's awarded. *Degree requirements:* For master's, comprehensive exam, thesis. *Entrance requirements:* For master's, GRE or GMAT, bachelor's degree in engineering, minimum QPA of 2.5. Additional exam requirements/recommendations for international students: Required—TOEFL (minimum score 79 iBT). *Application deadline:* Applications are processed on a rolling basis. Application fee: $25. Electronic applications accepted. *Expenses:* Tuition: Full-time $14,670; part-time $815 per credit. Required fees: $430; $18 per credit. Tuition and fees vary according to class time, course load, degree level, campus/location and program. *Financial support:* Scholarships/grants available. Financial award application deadline: 7/1; financial award applicants required to submit FAFSA. *Unit head:* Dr. Scott Steinbrink, Chair, 814-871-5302, E-mail: steinbri001@gannon.edu. *Application contact:* Kara Morgan, Assistant Director of Graduate Admissions, 814-871-5831, Fax: 814-871-5827, E-mail: graduate@gannon.edu.

The George Washington University, School of Engineering and Applied Science, Department of Engineering Management and Systems Engineering, Washington, DC 20052. Offers MS, D Sc, App Sc, Engr, Graduate Certificate. Part-time and evening/weekend programs available. *Faculty:* 15 full-time (1 woman), 17 part-time/adjunct (2 women). *Students:* 132 full-time (40 women), 1,148 part-time (276 women); includes 291 minority (126 Black or African American, non-Hispanic/Latino; 7 American Indian or Alaska Native, non-Hispanic/Latino; 96 Asian, non-Hispanic/Latino; 55 Hispanic/Latino; 5 Native Hawaiian or other Pacific Islander, non-Hispanic/Latino; 2 Two or more races, non-Hispanic/Latino), 119 international. Average age 35. 496 applicants, 87% accepted, 260 enrolled. In 2010, 336 master's, 21 doctorates, 138 other advanced degrees awarded. *Degree requirements:* For master's, thesis optional; for doctorate, one foreign language, thesis/dissertation, final and qualifying exams, submission of articles; for other advanced degree, professional project. *Entrance requirements:* For master's, appropriate bachelor's degree, minimum GPA of 2.7, second semester calculus; for doctorate, appropriate master's degree, minimum GPA of 3.5, 2 letters of recommendation; for other advanced degree, appropriate master's degree, minimum GPA of 3.4. Additional exam requirements/recommendations for international students: Required—TOEFL or The George Washington University English as a Foreign Language Test. *Application deadline:* For fall admission, 3/1 for domestic students; for spring admission, 10/1 for domestic students. Applications are processed on a rolling basis. Application fee: $75. *Financial support:* In 2010–11, 35 students received support; fellowships with tuition reimbursements available, research assistantships, teaching assistantships with tuition reimbursements available, career-related internships or fieldwork and institutionally sponsored loans available. Financial award application deadline: 3/1; financial award applicants required to submit FAFSA. *Faculty research:* Artificial intelligence and expert systems, human factors engineering and systems analysis. Total annual research expenditures: $421,800. *Unit head:* Dr. Thomas Mazzuchi, Chair, 202-994-7424, Fax: 202-994-0245, E-mail: mazzu@gwu.edu. *Application contact:* Adina Lav, Marketing, Recruiting and Admissions, 202-994-5827, Fax: 202-994-0909, E-mail: engineering@gwu.edu.

Instituto Tecnológico y de Estudios Superiores de Monterrey, Campus Chihuahua, Graduate Programs, Chihuahua, Mexico. Offers computer systems engineering (Ingeniero); electrical engineering (Ingeniero); electromechanical engineering (Ingeniero); electronic engineering (Ingeniero); engineering administration (MEA); industrial engineering (MIE, Ingeniero); international trade (MIT); mechanical engineering (Ingeniero).

International Technological University, Program in Engineering Management, Santa Clara, CA 95050. Offers MEM.

The Johns Hopkins University, G. W. C. Whiting School of Engineering, Program in Engineering Management, Baltimore, MD 21218-2699. Offers biomaterials (MSEM); communications science (MSEM); computer science (MSEM); fluid mechanics (MSEM); materials science and engineering (MSEM); mechanical engineering (MSEM); mechanics and materials (MSEM); nano-biotechnology (MSEM); nanomaterials and nanotechnology (MSEM); probability and statistics (MSEM); smart product and device design (MSEM); systems analysis, management and environmental policy (MSEM). *Students:* 32 full-time (5 women), 4 part-time (0 women); includes 7 minority (3 Black or African American, non-Hispanic/Latino; 3 Asian, non-Hispanic/Latino; 1 Hispanic/Latino), 11 international. Average age 23. 110 applicants, 60% accepted, 27 enrolled. In 2010, 6 master's awarded. *Entrance requirements:* For master's, GRE, 3 letters of recommendation, resume. Additional exam requirements/recommendations for international students: Required—TOEFL (minimum score 600 paper-based; 250 computer-based; 100 iBT) or IELTS (minimum score 7). *Application deadline:* For fall admission, 1/15 priority date for domestic students, 1/15 for international students; for spring admission, 9/15 priority date for domestic students, 9/15 for international students. Applications are processed on a rolling basis. Application fee: $75. Electronic applications accepted. *Financial support:* Fellowships, health care benefits available. *Unit head:* Dr. Edward R. Scheinerman, Interim Director/Vice Dean for Education, School of Engineering/Professor, Applied Mathematics and Statistics, 410-516-7395, Fax: 410-516-4880, E-mail: ers@jhu.edu. *Application contact:* Dennis McIver, Coordinator of Graduate Admissions, 410-516-8174, Fax: 410-516-0780, E-mail: graduateadmissions@jhu.edu.

Kansas State University, Graduate School, College of Engineering, Department of Industrial and Manufacturing Systems Engineering, Manhattan, KS 66506. Offers engineering management (MEM); industrial engineering (MS, PhD); operations research (MS). Part-time programs available. Postbaccalaureate distance learning degree programs offered. *Degree requirements:* For master's, thesis or alternative; for doctorate, thesis/dissertation. *Entrance requirements:* For master's, GRE General Test, bachelor's degree in engineering, mathematics, or physical science; for doctorate, GRE General Test, master's degree in engineering or industrial manufacturing. Additional exam requirements/recommendations for international students: Required—TOEFL. Electronic applications accepted. *Faculty research:* Ergonomics, healthcare systems engineering, manufacturing processes, operations research, engineering management.

Kettering University, Graduate School, Department of Business, Flint, MI 48504. Offers MBA, MS. *Accreditation:* ACBSP. Part-time and evening/weekend programs available. Postbaccalaureate distance learning degree programs offered (no on-campus study). *Faculty:* 8 full-time (3 women), 6 part-time/adjunct (0 women). *Students:* 8 full-time (2 women), 262 part-time (90 women); includes 52 minority (35 Black or African American, non-Hispanic/Latino; 1 American Indian or Alaska Native, non-Hispanic/Latino; 6 Asian, non-Hispanic/Latino; 10 Hispanic/Latino), 7 international. Average age 33. 80 applicants, 81% accepted, 31 enrolled. In 2010, 106 master's awarded. *Entrance requirements:* Additional exam requirements/recommendations for international students: Required—TOEFL (minimum score 550 paper-based; 213 computer-based; 79 iBT). *Application deadline:* For fall admission, 9/15 for domestic students, 6/15 for international students; for winter admission, 12/15 for domestic students, 9/15 for international students; for spring admission, 3/15 for domestic students, 12/15 for international students. Applications are processed on a rolling basis. Electronic applications accepted. *Expenses:* Tuition: Full-time $11,120; part-time $695 per credit hour. *Financial support:* In 2010–11, 108 students received support, including fellowships with full tuition reimbursements available (averaging $13,000 per year), research assistantships with full tuition reimbursements available (averaging $13,000 per year), teaching assistantships with full tuition reimbursements available (averaging $13,000 per year); Federal Work-Study, scholarships/grants, and tuition waivers (partial) also available. Support available to part-time students. Financial award application deadline: 7/15. *Faculty research:* Entrepreneurship. Total annual research expenditures: $19,876. *Unit head:* Dr. Tony Hain, Associate Provost, Graduate Studies, Continuing Education & Sponsored Research, 810-762-9616, Fax: 810-762-9935, E-mail: thain@kettering.edu. *Application contact:* Bonnie Switzer, Admissions Representative, 810-762-7953, Fax: 810-762-9935, E-mail: bswitzer@kettering.edu.

Lamar University, College of Graduate Studies, College of Engineering, Department of Industrial Engineering, Beaumont, TX 77710. Offers engineering management (MEM); industrial engineering (ME, MES, DE). *Faculty:* 4 full-time (0 women). *Students:* 43 full-time (7 women), 8 part-time (1 woman); includes 3 Black or African American, non-Hispanic/Latino; 4 Asian, non-Hispanic/Latino; 3 Hispanic/Latino, 28 international. Average age 29. 61 applicants, 66% accepted, 9 enrolled. In 2010, 10 master's awarded. *Degree requirements:* For doctorate, thesis/dissertation. *Entrance requirements:* For master's and doctorate, GRE General Test. Additional exam requirements/recommendations for international students: Required—TOEFL. *Application deadline:* For fall admission, 5/15 priority date for domestic students; for spring admission, 10/1 priority date for domestic students. Applications are processed on a rolling basis. Application fee: $25 ($50 for international students). *Expenses:* Tuition, state resident: full-time $4160; part-time $208 per credit hour. Tuition, nonresident: full-time $10,360; part-time $518 per credit hour. *Financial support:* In 2010–11, 2 fellowships (averaging $6,000 per year), 4 research assistantships (averaging $1,000 per year), 2 teaching assistantships (averaging $4,500 per year) were awarded. Financial award application deadline: 4/1. *Faculty research:* Process simulation, total quality management, ergonomics and safety, scheduling. *Unit head:* Dr. Victor Zaloom, Chair, 409-880-8804, Fax: 409-880-8121. *Application contact:* Dr. Hsing-Wei Chu, Professor, 409-880-8804, Fax: 409-880-8121.

Lawrence Technological University, College of Engineering, Southfield, MI 48075-1058. Offers architectural engineering (MS); automotive engineering (MS); civil engineering (MS); electrical and computer engineering (MS); engineering management (MEM); industrial engineering (MS); manufacturing systems (ME, DE); mechanical engineering (MS); mechatronic systems engineering (MS). Part-time and evening/weekend programs available. *Faculty:* 20 full-time (4 women), 12 part-time/adjunct (0 women). *Students:* 8 full-time (1 woman), 366 part-time (60 women); includes 29 Black or African American, non-Hispanic/Latino; 1 American Indian or Alaska Native, non-Hispanic/Latino; 36 Asian, non-Hispanic/Latino; 9 Hispanic/Latino; 4 Two or more races, non-Hispanic/Latino, 81 international. Average age 32. 398 applicants, 48% accepted, 87 enrolled. In 2010, 121 master's, 5 doctorates awarded. *Degree requirements:* For master's, thesis (for some programs). *Entrance requirements:* Additional exam requirements/recommendations for international students: Required—TOEFL (minimum score 550 paper-based; 213 computer-based; 79 iBT). *Application deadline:* For fall admission, 6/30 priority date for domestic students, 6/30 for international students; for spring admission, 11/15 priority date for domestic students, 11/15 for international students. Applications are processed on a rolling basis. Application fee: $50. Electronic applications accepted. *Financial support:* In 2010–11, 72 students received support. Federal Work-Study and institutionally sponsored loans available. Support available to part-time students. Financial award application deadline: 4/1; financial award applicants required to submit FAFSA. *Faculty research:* Advanced composite materials in bridges, strengthening existing bridges with carbon and glass fiber sheets, development of drive shafts using composite materials. *Unit head:* Dr. Nabil Grace, Interim Dean, 248-204-2500, Fax: 248-204-2509, E-mail: engrdean@ltu.edu. *Application contact:* Jane Rohrback, Director of Admissions, 248-204-3160, Fax: 248-204-2228, E-mail: admissions@ltu.edu.

Lehigh University, P.C. Rossin College of Engineering and Applied Science, Department of Industrial and Systems Engineering, Bethlehem, PA 18015. Offers analytical finance (MS); industrial and systems engineering (M Eng, MS); industrial engineering (PhD); management science and engineering (M Eng, MS); MBA/E. Part-time programs available. Postbaccalaureate distance learning degree programs offered (no on-campus study). *Faculty:* 15 full-time (2 women), 1 part-time/adjunct (0 women). *Students:* 77 full-time (27 women), 15 part-time (5 women); includes 3 minority (2 Black or African American, non-Hispanic/Latino; 1 Asian, non-Hispanic/Latino), 63 international. Average age 27. 636 applicants, 19% accepted, 39 enrolled. In 2010, 26 master's, 6 doctorates awarded. *Degree requirements:* For master's, thesis (MS); project (M Eng); for doctorate, comprehensive exam, thesis/dissertation. *Entrance requirements:* For master's and doctorate, GRE General Test. Additional exam requirements/recommendations for international students: Required—TOEFL (minimum score 550 paper-based; 213 computer-based; 79 iBT). *Application deadline:* For fall admission, 7/15 for domestic and international students; for spring admission, 12/1 for domestic and international students. Applications are processed on a rolling basis. Application fee: $75. Electronic applications accepted. *Financial support:* In 2010–11, 28 students received support, including 3 fellowships with full tuition reimbursements available (averaging $17,460 per year), 16 research assistantships with full tuition reimbursements available (averaging $15,300 per year), 11 teaching assistantships with full tuition reimbursements available (averaging $18,360 per year); career-related internships or fieldwork, scholarships/grants, tuition waivers, and unspecified assistantships also available. Financial award application deadline: 1/15. *Faculty research:* Optimization, mathematical programming; logistics and supply chain, stochastic processes and simulation; computational optimization and high performance computing; financial engineering and robust optimization. Total annual research expenditures: $1.8 million. *Unit head:* Dr. Tamas Terlaky, Chair, 610-758-4050, Fax: 610-758-4886, E-mail: terlaky@lehigh.edu. *Application contact:* Rita R. Frey, Graduate Coordinator, 610-758-4051, Fax: 610-758-4886, E-mail: ise@lehigh.edu.

Long Island University, C.W. Post Campus, College of Information and Computer Science, Department of Computer Science/Management Engineering, Brookville, NY 11548-1300. Offers information systems (MS); information technology education (MS); management engineering (MS). Part-time and evening/weekend programs available. *Degree requirements:* For master's, comprehensive exam, thesis or alternative. *Entrance requirements:* For master's, bachelor's degree in science, mathematics, or engineering; minimum GPA of 2.5. Additional exam requirements/recommendations for international students: Required—TOEFL (minimum score 500 paper-based; 173 computer-based). Electronic applications accepted. *Faculty research:* Inductive music learning, re-engineering business process, technology and ethics.

Loyola Marymount University, College of Science and Engineering, Department of Systems Engineering and Engineering Management, Program in System Engineering Leadership, Los Anegles, CA 90045-2659. Offers MS, MS/MBA. *Faculty:* 2 full-time (0 women), 3 part-time/adjunct (1 woman). *Students:* 10 full-time (4 women), 3 part-time (1 woman); includes 2 Black or African American, non-Hispanic/Latino; 2 Hispanic/Latino. Average age 30. 6 applicants, 50% accepted, 3 enrolled. In 2010, 4 master's awarded. *Degree requirements:* For master's, thesis. *Entrance requirements:* For master's, GMAT, personal statement, resume, letters of recommendation. Additional exam requirements/recommendations for international students: Required—TOEFL (minimum score 550 paper-based; 213 computer-based; 80 iBT). *Application deadline:* For fall admission, 7/15 for domestic students; for spring admission, 12/15 for domestic students. Applications are processed on a rolling basis. Application fee: $50. Electronic applications accepted. *Financial support:* In 2010–11, 6 students received support. Scholarships/grants and unspecified assistantships available. Support available to part-time students. Financial award application deadline: 6/1; financial award applicants required to submit FAFSA. Total annual research expenditures: $312,678. *Unit head:* Dr. Frederick S. Brown, Graduate Director, 310-338-7878, E-mail: fbrown@lmu.edu. *Application contact:* Chake H. Kouyoumjian, Associate Dean for Graduate Studies, 310-338-2721, Fax: 310-338-6086, E-mail: ckouyoum@lmu.edu.

Marquette University, Graduate School, College of Engineering, Department of Mechanical Engineering, Milwaukee, WI 53201-1881. Offers engineering innovation (Certificate); engineering management (MSEM); mechanical engineering (MS, PhD); new product and process development (Certificate). Part-time and evening/weekend programs available. *Faculty:* 16 full-time (0 women), 2 part-time/adjunct (0 women). *Students:* 26 full-time (7 women), 40 part-time (2 women); includes 4 minority (1 Black or African American, non-Hispanic/Latino; 1 Asian, non-Hispanic/Latino; 2 Hispanic/Latino), 15 international. Average age 29. 65 applicants, 68% accepted, 13 enrolled. In 2010, 9 master's, 1 doctorate awarded. Terminal master's awarded for partial completion of doctoral program. *Degree requirements:* For master's, comprehensive exam, thesis (for some programs); for doctorate, comprehensive exam, thesis/dissertation, qualifying exam. *Entrance requirements:* For master's, GRE General Test, minimum

GPA of 3.0, official transcripts from all current and previous colleges/universities except Marquette, three letters of recommendation; for doctorate, GRE General Test, minimum GPA of 3.0, official transcripts from all current and previous colleges/universities except Marquette, three letters of recommendation, statement of purpose, copies of any published work. Additional exam requirements/recommendations for international students: Required—TOEFL (minimum score 530 paper-based; 78 computer-based). *Application deadline:* For fall admission, 8/1 priority date for domestic students; for spring admission, 1/1 priority date for domestic students. Applications are processed on a rolling basis. Application fee: $50. Electronic applications accepted. *Expenses:* Tuition: Full-time $16,290; part-time $905 per credit hour. Tuition and fees vary according to program. *Financial support:* In 2010–11, 19 students received support, including 2 research assistantships with tuition reimbursements available, 12 teaching assistantships with tuition reimbursements available; fellowships with tuition reimbursements available, Federal Work-Study, institutionally sponsored loans, scholarships/grants, and tuition waivers (full and partial) also available. Support available to part-time students. Financial award application deadline: 2/15. *Faculty research:* Computer-integrated manufacturing, energy conversion, simulation modeling and optimization, applied mechanics, metallurgy. Total annual research expenditures: $901,053. *Unit head:* Dr. Kyle Kim, Chair, 414-288-7259, Fax: 414-288-7790, E-mail: kyle.kim@marquette.edu. *Application contact:* Dr. James Rice, Director of Graduate Studies, 414-288-5405, Fax: 414-288-7790, E-mail: nicholas.nigro@marquette.edu.

Marquette University, Graduate School, Program in Public Service, Milwaukee, WI 53201-1881. Offers criminal justice administration (MLS); dispute resolution (MDR, MLS); engineering (MLS); health care administration (MLS); law enforcement leadership and management (Certificate); leadership studies (Certificate); non-profit sector (MLS); public service (MAPS, MLS); sports leadership (MLS). Part-time and evening/weekend programs available. Postbaccalaureate distance learning degree programs offered (no on-campus study). *Faculty:* 3 full-time (2 women), 29 part-time/adjunct (11 women). *Students:* 27 full-time (13 women), 134 part-time (84 women); includes 29 minority (21 Black or African American, non-Hispanic/Latino; 1 American Indian or Alaska Native, non-Hispanic/Latino; 1 Asian, non-Hispanic/Latino; 6 Hispanic/Latino), 1 international. Average age 38. 108 applicants, 78% accepted, 36 enrolled. In 2010, 11 master's, 12 Certificates awarded. *Degree requirements:* For master's, comprehensive exam (for some programs). *Entrance requirements:* For master's, GRE General Test (preferred), GMAT, or LSAT, official transcripts from all current and previous colleges/universities except Marquette, three letters of recommendation, statement of purpose. Additional exam requirements/recommendations for international students: Required—TOEFL. *Application deadline:* Applications are processed on a rolling basis. Application fee: $50. Electronic applications accepted. *Expenses:* Tuition: Full-time $16,290; part-time $905 per credit hour. Tuition and fees vary according to program. *Financial support:* In 2010–11, 1 fellowship, 1 research assistantship were awarded; teaching assistantships. Financial award application deadline: 2/15. *Unit head:* Dr. Johnette Caulfield, Adjunct Assistant Professor and Director of Graduate Programs, 414-288-5556, E-mail: jay.caulfield@marquette.edu. *Application contact:* Erin Fox, Assistant Director for Recruitment, 414-288-5319, Fax: 414-288-1902, E-mail: erin.fox@marquette.edu.

Marshall University, Academic Affairs Division, College of Information Technology and Engineering, Weisberg Division of Engineering and Computer Science, Huntington, WV 25755. Offers engineering (MSE); information systems (MS). Part-time and evening/weekend programs available. *Faculty:* 10 full-time (1 woman), 1 part-time/adjunct (0 women). *Students:* 21 full-time (2 women), 29 part-time (3 women); includes 3 Black or African American, non-Hispanic/Latino; 2 Asian, non-Hispanic/Latino, 16 international. Average age 29. In 2010, 15 master's awarded. *Degree requirements:* For master's, final project, oral exam. *Entrance requirements:* For master's, GMAT or GRE General Test, minimum undergraduate GPA of 2.75. Application fee: $40. *Financial support:* Tuition waivers (full) available. Support available to part-time students. Financial award application deadline: 8/1; financial award applicants required to submit FAFSA. *Unit head:* Dr. Bill Pierson, Chair, 304-696-2695, E-mail: pierson@marshall.edu. *Application contact:* Information Contact, 304-746-1900, Fax: 304-746-1902, E-mail: services@marshall.edu.

Massachusetts Institute of Technology, School of Engineering, Engineering Systems Division, Cambridge, MA 02139-4307. Offers engineering and management (SM); engineering systems (SM, PhD); logistics (M Eng); technology and policy (SM); technology, management and policy (PhD); SM/MBA. *Faculty:* 22 full-time (7 women). *Students:* 271 full-time (78 women); includes 39 minority (5 Black or African American, non-Hispanic/Latino; 27 Asian, non-Hispanic/Latino; 6 Hispanic/Latino; 1 Two or more races, non-Hispanic/Latino), 105 international. Average age 31. 927 applicants, 28% accepted, 185 enrolled. In 2010, 169 master's, 10 doctorates awarded. *Degree requirements:* For master's, thesis; for doctorate, comprehensive exam, thesis/dissertation. *Entrance requirements:* For master's, GRE General Test (or GMAT for some programs); for doctorate, GRE General Test. Additional exam requirements/recommendations for international students: Required—IELTS (minimum score 7.5). Application fee: $75. *Expenses:* Contact institution. *Financial support:* In 2010–11, 217 students received support, including 36 fellowships with tuition reimbursements available (averaging $25,594 per year), 95 research assistantships with tuition reimbursements available (averaging $27,695 per year), 15 teaching assistantships with tuition reimbursements available (averaging $25,802 per year); career-related internships or fieldwork, Federal Work-Study, institutionally sponsored loans, scholarships/grants, health care benefits, and unspecified assistantships also available. *Faculty research:* Critical infrastructures; extended enterprises; energy and sustainability; health care delivery; humans and technology; uncertainty and dynamics; design and implementation; networks and flows; policy and standards. Total annual research expenditures: $13.2 million. *Unit head:* Prof. Yossi Sheffi, Director, 617-253-1764, E-mail: esdinquiries@mit.edu. *Application contact:* Graduate Admissions, 617-253-1182, E-mail: esdgrad@mit.edu.

McNeese State University, Doré School of Graduate Studies, College of Engineering and Engineering Technology, Lake Charles, LA 70609. Offers chemical engineering (M Eng); civil engineering (M Eng); electrical engineering (M Eng); engineering management (M Eng); mechanical engineering (M Eng). Part-time and evening/weekend programs available. *Faculty:* 15 full-time (1 woman). *Students:* 37 full-time (10 women), 18 part-time (1 woman); includes 5 minority (3 Black or African American, non-Hispanic/Latino; 1 American Indian or Alaska Native, non-Hispanic/Latino; 1 Two or more races, non-Hispanic/Latino), 43 international. In 2010, 28 master's awarded. *Degree requirements:* For master's, thesis or alternative. *Entrance requirements:* For master's, GRE, minimum undergraduate GPA of 3.0. Additional exam requirements/recommendations for international students: Required—TOEFL (minimum score 560 paper-based; 220 computer-based; 83 iBT). *Application deadline:* For fall admission, 5/15 priority date for domestic and international students; for spring admission, 10/15 priority date for domestic and international students. Applications are processed on a rolling basis. Application fee: $20 ($30 for international students). Tuition and fees vary according to course load. *Financial support:* Federal Work-Study available. Support available to part-time students. Financial award application deadline: 5/1. *Unit head:* Dr. Nikos Kiritsis, Dean, 337-475-5875, Fax: 337-475-5237, E-mail: nikosk@mcneese.edu.

Mercer University, Graduate Studies, Macon Campus, School of Engineering, Macon, GA 31207-0003. Offers biomedical engineering (MSE); computer engineering (MSE); electrical engineering (MSE); engineering management (MSE); environmental engineering (MSE); environmental systems (MS); mechanical engineering (MSE); software engineering (MSE); software systems (MS); technical communications management (MS); technical management (MS). Part-time and evening/weekend programs available. Postbaccalaureate distance learning degree programs offered (no on-campus study). *Faculty:* 18 full-time (4 women), 1 part-time/adjunct (0 women). *Students:* 11 full-time (2 women), 100 part-time (22 women); includes 26 minority (13 Black or African American, non-Hispanic/Latino; 12 Asian, non-Hispanic/Latino; 1 Hispanic/Latino), 3 international. Average age 32. In 2010, 46 master's awarded. *Degree requirements:* For master's, thesis or alternative. *Entrance requirements:* For master's, minimum undergraduate GPA of 3.0. Additional exam requirements/recommendations for international students: Required—TOEFL. *Application deadline:* For fall admission, 7/1 for domestic students; for spring admission, 11/15 for domestic students. Applications are processed on a rolling basis. Application fee: $35 ($50 for international students). Electronic applications accepted. *Expenses:* Contact institution. *Financial support:* Federal Work-Study available. *Unit head:* Dr. Wade H. Shaw, Dean, 478-301-2459, Fax: 478-301-5593, E-mail: shaw_wh@mercer.edu. *Application contact:* Greg Lofton, Graduate Program Coordinator, 478-301-5480, Fax: 478-301-5434, E-mail: lofton_g@mercer.edu.

Milwaukee School of Engineering, Rader School of Business, Program in Engineering Management, Milwaukee, WI 53202-3109. Offers MS. Part-time and evening/weekend programs available. *Faculty:* 3 full-time (1 woman), 8 part-time/adjunct (1 woman). *Students:* 6 full-time (1 woman), 73 part-time (16 women); includes 2 Black or African American, non-Hispanic/Latino; 1 American Indian or Alaska Native, non-Hispanic/Latino; 2 Asian, non-Hispanic/Latino; 1 Hispanic/Latino, 8 international. Average age 26. 18 applicants, 67% accepted, 8 enrolled. In 2010, 46 master's awarded. *Degree requirements:* For master's, thesis or alternative, thesis defense or capstone project. *Entrance requirements:* For master's, GRE General Test or GMAT, BS in engineering, science, management or related field. Additional exam requirements/recommendations for international students: Required—TOEFL (minimum score 79 iBT). *Application deadline:* Applications are processed on a rolling basis. Application fee: $30. Electronic applications accepted. *Expenses:* Tuition: Full-time $17,550; part-time $650 per credit. One-time fee: $75. *Financial support:* In 2010–11, 19 students received support, including 2 research assistantships (averaging $15,000 per year). Financial award applicants required to submit FAFSA. *Faculty research:* Operations, project management, quality marketing. *Unit head:* Dr. Kathy Faggiani, Director, 414-277-2711, Fax: 414-277-7279, E-mail: faggiani@msoe.com. *Application contact:* Sarah K. Winchowky, Graduate Admissions Director, 800-321-6763, Fax: 414-277-7475, E-mail: wp@msoe.edu.

Missouri University of Science and Technology, Graduate School, Department of Engineering Management and Systems Engineering, Rolla, MO 65409. Offers engineering management (MS, DE, PhD); manufacturing engineering (M Eng, MS); systems engineering (MS, PhD). *Degree requirements:* For master's, thesis optional; for doctorate, comprehensive exam. *Entrance requirements:* For master's, GRE (minimum score 1150 verbal and quantitative, 4.5 writing); for doctorate, GRE (minimum score: 1100 verbal and quantitative, 3.5 writing). Additional exam requirements/recommendations for international students: Required—TOEFL (minimum score 580 paper-based; 213 computer-based). *Faculty research:* Management of technology, industrial engineering, manufacturing engineering, packaging engineering, quality engineering.

National University, Academic Affairs, School of Engineering and Technology, Department of Applied Engineering, La Jolla, CA 92037-1011. Offers database administration (MS); engineering management (MS); environmental engineering (MS); homeland security and safety engineering (MS); system engineering (MS); wireless communications (MS). Part-time and evening/weekend programs available. Postbaccalaureate distance learning degree programs offered (no on-campus study). *Faculty:* 6 full-time (1 woman), 69 part-time/adjunct (12 women). *Students:* 82 full-time (16 women), 153 part-time (35 women); includes 87 minority (18 Black or African American, non-Hispanic/Latino; 1 American Indian or Alaska Native, non-Hispanic/Latino; 34 Asian, non-Hispanic/Latino; 28 Hispanic/Latino; 2 Native Hawaiian or other Pacific Islander, non-Hispanic/Latino; 4 Two or more races, non-Hispanic/Latino), 60 international. Average age 31. 166 applicants, 100% accepted, 106 enrolled. In 2010, 79 master's awarded. *Degree requirements:* For master's, thesis. *Entrance requirements:* For master's, interview, minimum GPA of 2.5. Additional exam requirements/recommendations for international students: Required—TOEFL (minimum score 550 paper-based; 213 computer-based; 79 iBT), IELTS (minimum score 6). *Application deadline:* Applications are processed on a rolling basis. Application fee: $60 ($65 for international students). Electronic applications accepted. *Expenses:* Tuition: Full-time $9450; part-time $350 per unit. Required fees: $350 per unit. One-time fee: $60. *Financial support:* Career-related internships or fieldwork, institutionally sponsored loans, scholarships/grants, and tuition waivers (partial) available. Support available to part-time students. Financial award application deadline: 6/30; financial award applicants required to submit FAFSA. *Unit head:* Dr. Shekar Viswanathan, Chair and Associate Professor, 858-309-8416, Fax: 858-309-3420, E-mail: sviswana@nu.edu. *Application contact:* Dominick Giovanniello, Associate Regional Dean—San Diego, 800-NAT-UNIV, Fax: 858-541-7792, E-mail: dgiovann@nu.edu.

New Jersey Institute of Technology, Office of Graduate Studies, Newark College of Engineering, Department of Industrial and Manufacturing Engineering, Program in Engineering Management, Newark, NJ 07102. Offers MS. Part-time and evening/weekend programs available. *Students:* 65 full-time (15 women), 135 part-time (31 women); includes 24 Black or African American, non-Hispanic/Latino; 1 American Indian or Alaska Native, non-Hispanic/Latino; 20 Asian, non-Hispanic/Latino; 36 Hispanic/Latino, 66 international. Average age 30. 209 applicants, 62% accepted, 51 enrolled. In 2010, 132 master's awarded. *Degree requirements:* For master's, thesis or alternative. *Entrance requirements:* For master's, GRE General Test. Additional exam requirements/recommendations for international students: Required—TOEFL (minimum score 550 paper-based; 213 computer-based; 79 iBT). *Application deadline:* For fall admission, 6/5 priority date for domestic students, 4/1 for international students; for spring admission, 11/15 for domestic and international students. Applications are processed on a rolling basis. Application fee: $65. Electronic applications accepted. *Expenses:* Tuition, state resident: full-time $14,724; part-time $818 per credit. Tuition, nonresident: full-time $20,304; part-time $1128 per credit. Required fees: $2272; $209 per credit. $103 per semester. One-time fee: $312 full-time; $212 part-time. *Financial support:* Fellowships with full and partial tuition reimbursements, research assistantships with full and partial tuition reimbursements, teaching assistantships with full and partial tuition reimbursements, career-related internships or fieldwork, Federal Work-Study, institutionally sponsored loans, and unspecified assistantships available. Financial award application deadline: 3/15. *Unit head:* Dr. Rajpal Sodhi, Interim Chair, 973-596-3362, E-mail: rajpal.s.sodhi@njit.edu. *Application contact:* Kathryn Kelly, Director of Admissions, 973-596-3300, Fax: 973-596-3461, E-mail: admissions@njit.edu.

New Mexico Institute of Mining and Technology, Graduate Studies, Program in Engineering Management, Socorro, NM 87801. Offers MEM. Part-time programs available.

Northeastern University, College of Engineering, Department of Mechanical, Industrial, and Manufacturing Engineering, Boston, MA 02115-5096. Offers engineering management (MS); industrial engineering (MS, PhD); mechanical engineering (MS, PhD); operations research (MS). Part-time programs available. *Faculty:* 34 full-time (2 women), 7 part-time/adjunct (0 women). *Students:* 297 full-time (70 women), 103 part-time (20 women). 616 applicants, 77% accepted, 140 enrolled. In 2010, 107 master's, 5 doctorates awarded. *Degree requirements:* For master's, thesis (for some programs); for doctorate, thesis/dissertation, departmental qualifying exam. *Entrance requirements:* For master's and doctorate, GRE General Test. Additional exam requirements/recommendations for international students: Required—TOEFL (minimum score 550 paper-based; 213 computer-based; 80 iBT). *Application deadline:* For fall admission, 1/15 priority date for domestic and international students; for spring admission, 11/1 priority date for domestic students. Applications are processed on a rolling basis. Application fee: $50. Electronic applications accepted. *Financial support:* In 2010–11, 79 students received support, including 50 research assistantships with full tuition reimbursements available (averaging $18,325 per year), 33 teaching assistantships with full tuition reimbursements available (averaging $18,325 per year); fellowships with full tuition reimbursements available, career-related internships or fieldwork, Federal Work-Study, scholarships/grants, health care benefits, and unspecified assistantships also available. Support available to part-time students. Financial award application deadline: 1/15; financial award applicants required to submit FAFSA. *Faculty research:* Dry sliding instabilities, droplet deposition, combustion, manufacturing systems, nano-manufacturing, advanced materials processing, bio-nano robotics, burning speed measurement, virtual environments. *Unit head:* Dr. Hameed Metghalchi, Chairman, 617-373-2973, Fax: 617-373-2921. *Application contact:* Jeffery Hengel, Admissions Specialist, 617-373-2711, Fax: 617-373-2501, E-mail: grad-eng@coe.neu.edu.

Northwestern University, McCormick School of Engineering and Applied Science, Department of Industrial Engineering and Management Sciences, Program in Engineering Management, Evanston, IL 60208. Offers MEM. Part-time and evening/weekend programs available. *Faculty:*

Engineering Management

Northwestern University (continued)
9 full-time (0 women), 8 part-time/adjunct (1 woman). *Students:* 135 full-time (40 women), 37 part-time (9 women); includes 45 minority (5 Black or African American, non-Hispanic/Latino; 30 Asian, non-Hispanic/Latino; 9 Hispanic/Latino; 1 Two or more races, non-Hispanic/Latino), 46 international. Average age 34. In 2010, 81 master's awarded. *Entrance requirements:* For master's, 3 years of work experience. Additional exam requirements/recommendations for international students: Required—TOEFL (minimum score 550 paper-based; 213 computer-based; 80 iBT), IELTS (minimum score 7). *Application deadline:* For fall admission, 8/15 priority date for domestic students, 7/1 priority date for international students; for winter admission, 11/15 priority date for domestic students, 11/1 priority date for international students; for spring admission, 2/15 priority date for domestic students, 2/1 priority date for international students. Applications are processed on a rolling basis. Application fee: $50. Electronic applications accepted. *Expenses:* Contact institution. *Financial support:* Institutionally sponsored loans available. Financial award application deadline: 12/31; financial award applicants required to submit FAFSA. *Faculty research:* Supply chain and operations management, design and innovation, project and process management. *Unit head:* Dr. Bruce Ankenman, Director, 847-491-5674, Fax: 847-491-5980, E-mail: ankenman@northwestern.edu. *Application contact:* Susan Fox, Associate Director, 847-491-5584, Fax: 847-491-5980, E-mail: s-fox@northwestern.edu.

Oakland University, Graduate Study and Lifelong Learning, School of Engineering and Computer Science, Department of Industrial and Systems Engineering, Program in Engineering Management, Rochester, MI 48309-4401. Offers MS. *Entrance requirements:* Additional exam requirements/recommendations for international students: Required—TOEFL (minimum score 550 paper-based; 213 computer-based). Electronic applications accepted. *Expenses:* Contact institution.

Old Dominion University, Frank Batten College of Engineering and Technology, Program in Engineering Management, Norfolk, VA 23529. Offers MEM, MS, PhD. Part-time and evening/weekend programs available. Postbaccalaureate distance learning degree programs offered (no on-campus study). *Faculty:* 14 full-time (3 women), 3 part-time/adjunct (0 women). *Students:* 47 full-time (15 women), 251 part-time (38 women); includes 57 minority (32 Black or African American, non-Hispanic/Latino; 9 Asian, non-Hispanic/Latino; 9 Hispanic/Latino; 1 Native Hawaiian or other Pacific Islander, non-Hispanic/Latino; 6 Two or more races, non-Hispanic/Latino), 40 international. Average age 32. 146 applicants, 86% accepted, 71 enrolled. In 2010, 125 master's, 7 doctorates awarded. *Degree requirements:* For master's, comprehensive exam, thesis optional, project; for doctorate, thesis/dissertation, candidacy exam. *Entrance requirements:* For master's, GRE, minimum GPA of 3.0; for doctorate, GRE, resume, letters of recommendation, minimum GPA of 3.0. Additional exam requirements/recommendations for international students: Required—TOEFL (minimum score 550 paper-based; 213 computer-based; 79 iBT). *Application deadline:* For fall admission, 6/1 priority date for domestic students, 4/15 for international students; for spring admission, 11/1 priority date for domestic students, 2/1 for international students. Applications are processed on a rolling basis. Application fee: $40. Electronic applications accepted. *Expenses:* Tuition, state resident: full-time $8592; part-time $358 per credit. Tuition, nonresident: full-time $21,672; part-time $903 per credit. Required fees: $119 per semester. One-time fee: $50. *Financial support:* In 2010–11, research assistantships with full and partial tuition reimbursements (averaging $20,000 per year), teaching assistantships with full and partial tuition reimbursements (averaging $20,000 per year) were awarded; fellowships, career-related internships or fieldwork, scholarships/grants, and tuition waivers (partial) also available. Support available to part-time students. Financial award application deadline: 2/15; financial award applicants required to submit FAFSA. *Faculty research:* Project management, systems engineering, modeling and simulation, virtual collaborative environments, multidisciplinary designs. Total annual research expenditures: $3.2 million. *Unit head:* Dr. Resit Unal, Chair, 757-683-4558, Fax: 757-683-5640, E-mail: runal@odu.edu. *Application contact:* Ariel Pinto, Graduate Program Director, 757-683-4218, Fax: 757-683-5640, E-mail: enmagpd@odu.edu.

Old Dominion University, Frank Batten College of Engineering and Technology, Program in Engineering Management and Systems Engineering, Norfolk, VA 23529. Offers D Eng. Part-time and evening/weekend programs available. Postbaccalaureate distance learning degree programs offered (no on-campus study). *Faculty:* 14 full-time (3 women), 3 part-time/adjunct (0 women). *Students:* 2 full-time (0 women), 10 part-time (1 woman); includes 3 minority (1 Black or African American, non-Hispanic/Latino; 1 American Indian or Alaska Native, non-Hispanic/Latino; 1 Hispanic/Latino). Average age 43. *Degree requirements:* For doctorate, thesis/dissertation, candidacy exam. *Entrance requirements:* For doctorate, GRE, resume, letters of recommendation, minimum GPA of 3.0, interview. Additional exam requirements/recommendations for international students: Required—TOEFL (minimum score 550 paper-based; 213 computer-based; 79 iBT). *Application deadline:* For fall admission, 6/1 priority date for domestic students, 4/15 for international students; for spring admission, 11/1 priority date for domestic students, 2/1 for international students. Applications are processed on a rolling basis. Application fee: $40. Electronic applications accepted. *Expenses:* Tuition, state resident: full-time $8592; part-time $358 per credit. Tuition, nonresident: full-time $21,672; part-time $903 per credit. Required fees: $119 per semester. One-time fee: $50. *Financial support:* In 2010–11, research assistantships with full and partial tuition reimbursements (averaging $20,000 per year), teaching assistantships with full and partial tuition reimbursements (averaging $20,000 per year) were awarded; fellowships, career-related internships or fieldwork and tuition waivers also available. Support available to part-time students. Financial award application deadline: 2/15; financial award applicants required to submit FAFSA. *Faculty research:* Project management, systems engineering, modeling and simulation, virtual collaboration environments, multidisciplinary designs. Total annual research expenditures: $3.2 million. *Unit head:* Dr. Resit Unal, Department Chair, 757-683-4558, Fax: 757-683-5640, E-mail: enmagpd@odu.edu. *Application contact:* Ariel Pinto, Graduate Program Director, 757-683-4218, Fax: 757-683-5640, E-mail: enmagpd@odu.edu.

Point Park University, School of Arts and Sciences, Department of Natural Science and Engineering Technology, Pittsburgh, PA 15222-1984. Offers engineering management (MS); environmental studies (MS). Part-time and evening/weekend programs available. *Faculty:* 4 full-time, 4 part-time/adjunct. *Students:* 7 full-time (4 women), 17 part-time (6 women); includes 5 minority (4 Black or African American, non-Hispanic/Latino; 1 Hispanic/Latino), 2 international. Average age 35. 36 applicants, 69% accepted, 11 enrolled. In 2010, 18 master's awarded. *Degree requirements:* For master's, comprehensive exam (for some programs), thesis or alternative. *Entrance requirements:* For master's, minimum QPA of 2.75, 2 letters of recommendation, minimum B average in engineering technology or a related field, official undergraduate transcript, statement of intent, resume. Additional exam requirements/recommendations for international students: Required—TOEFL. *Application deadline:* Applications are processed on a rolling basis. Application fee: $30. Electronic applications accepted. *Expenses:* Tuition: Full-time $12,456; part-time $692 per credit. Required fees: $630; $35 per credit. *Financial support:* In 2010–11, 16 students received support, including 1 teaching assistantship with full tuition reimbursement available (averaging $6,400 per year); scholarships/grants also available. Financial award application deadline: 4/15; financial award applicants required to submit FAFSA. *Unit head:* Dr. Mark Farrell, Chair, 412-392-3879, Fax: 421-392-3962, E-mail: mfarrell@pointpark.edu. *Application contact:* Misty Williams, Recruiter/Counselor, 412-392-3826, Fax: 412-392-6164, E-mail: mdwilliams@pointpark.edu.

Polytechnic University of Puerto Rico, Graduate School, Hato Rey, PR 00919. Offers business administration (MBA), including computer information systems, general management, management of information systems, management of international enterprises; civil engineering (ME, MS); computer engineering (ME, MS); computer science (MCS, MS); electrical engineering (ME, MS); engineering management (MEM); environmental management (MEM); landscape architecture (M Land Arch); manufacturing competitiveness (MMC, MS); manufacturing engineering (ME, MS); mechanical engineering (M Mech E). Part-time and evening/weekend programs available. *Entrance requirements:* For master's, 3 letters of recommendation.

Polytechnic University of Puerto Rico, Orlando Campus, Graduate School, Winter Park, FL 32792. Offers accounting (MBA); business administration (MBA); construction management (MEM); engineering management (MEM); environmental management (MEM); finance (MBA); human resources management (MBA); management of international enterprises (MBA); management of technology (MBA); manufacturing management (MEM). Part-time and evening/weekend programs available. Postbaccalaureate distance learning degree programs offered (no on-campus study). *Entrance requirements:* For master's, minimum GPA of 3.0. Electronic applications accepted.

Portland State University, Graduate Studies, Maseeh College of Engineering and Computer Science, Department of Civil and Environmental Engineering, Portland, OR 97207-0751. Offers civil and environmental engineering (M Eng, MS, PhD); civil and environmental engineering management (M Eng); environmental sciences and resources (PhD); systems science (PhD). Part-time and evening/weekend programs available. *Faculty:* 13 full-time (2 women), 3 part-time/adjunct (1 woman). *Students:* 48 full-time (17 women), 47 part-time (15 women); includes 1 Black or African American, non-Hispanic/Latino; 8 Asian, non-Hispanic/Latino; 5 Hispanic/Latino, 16 international. Average age 30. 98 applicants, 66% accepted, 32 enrolled. In 2010, 8 master's awarded. *Degree requirements:* For master's, thesis or alternative, oral exam; for doctorate, one foreign language, thesis/dissertation, oral and written exams. *Entrance requirements:* For master's, minimum GPA of 3.0 in upper-division course work, BS in civil engineering or allied field; for doctorate, GRE General Test, GRE Subject Test, minimum GPA of 3.0 in upper-division course work, master's in civil and environmental engineering, 2 years full-time graduate work beyond master's degree. Additional exam requirements/recommendations for international students: Required—TOEFL (minimum score 550 paper-based; 213 computer-based). *Application deadline:* For fall admission, 4/1 for domestic students, 4/11 for international students; for winter admission, 9/1 for domestic and international students; for spring admission, 11/1 for domestic and international students. Applications are processed on a rolling basis. Application fee: $50. *Expenses:* Tuition, state resident: full-time $8505; part-time $315 per credit. Tuition, nonresident: full-time $13,284; part-time $492 per credit. Required fees: $1482; $21 per credit. $99 per term. One-time fee: $120. Part-time tuition and fees vary according to course load and program. *Financial support:* In 2010–11, 15 research assistantships with tuition reimbursements (averaging $11,169 per year), 1 teaching assistantship with full tuition reimbursement (averaging $19,012 per year) were awarded; career-related internships or fieldwork, Federal Work-Study, scholarships/grants, and unspecified assistantships also available. Support available to part-time students. Financial award application deadline: 3/1; financial award applicants required to submit FAFSA. *Faculty research:* Structures, water resources, geotechnical engineering, environmental engineering, transportation. Total annual research expenditures: $2.4 million. *Unit head:* Scott Wells, Chair, 503-725-4282, Fax: 503-725-4298, E-mail: wellss@pdx.edu. *Application contact:* Marianne Stupfel-Wallace, Information Contact, 503-725-4244, Fax: 503-725-4298, E-mail: ceedept@cecs.pdx.edu.

Portland State University, Graduate Studies, Maseeh College of Engineering and Computer Science, Department of Engineering and Technology Management, Portland, OR 97207-0751. Offers engineering and technology management (M Eng); engineering management (MS); manufacturing engineering (ME); manufacturing management (M Eng); systems science/engineering management (PhD); MS/MBA; MS/MS. Part-time and evening/weekend programs available. *Faculty:* 8 full-time (1 woman), 3 part-time/adjunct (2 women). *Students:* 50 full-time (13 women), 58 part-time (16 women); includes 13 Asian, non-Hispanic/Latino; 6 Hispanic/Latino, 51 international. Average age 35. 38 applicants, 76% accepted, 13 enrolled. In 2010, 42 master's awarded. *Degree requirements:* For master's, thesis optional; for doctorate, one foreign language, thesis/dissertation, oral and written exams. *Entrance requirements:* For master's, minimum GPA of 3.0 in upper-division course work, BS in civil engineering; for doctorate, GRE General Test, GRE Subject Test, minimum GPA of 3.0 in upper-division course work. Additional exam requirements/recommendations for international students: Required—TOEFL (minimum score 550 paper-based; 213 computer-based). *Application deadline:* For fall admission, 4/1 for domestic students, 3/1 for international students; for winter admission, 9/1 for domestic students, 7/1 for international students; for spring admission, 11/1 for domestic students, 9/1 for international students. Applications are processed on a rolling basis. Application fee: $50. *Expenses:* Tuition, state resident: full-time $8505; part-time $315 per credit. Tuition, nonresident: full-time $13,284; part-time $492 per credit. Required fees: $1482; $21 per credit. $99 per term. One-time fee: $120. Part-time tuition and fees vary according to course load and program. *Financial support:* In 2010–11, 3 teaching assistantships with full tuition reimbursements (averaging $8,916 per year) were awarded; research assistantships with full tuition reimbursements, career-related internships or fieldwork, Federal Work-Study, scholarships/grants, and unspecified assistantships also available. Support available to part-time students. Financial award application deadline: 3/1; financial award applicants required to submit FAFSA. *Faculty research:* Scheduling, hierarchical decision modeling, operations research, knowledge-based information systems. Total annual research expenditures: $1.1 million. *Unit head:* Dr. Dundar F. Kocaoglu, Chair, 503-725-4660, Fax: 503-725-4667, E-mail: kocaoglu@etm.pdx.edu. *Application contact:* Dr. Dundar F. Kocaoglu, Chair, 503-725-4660, Fax: 503-725-4667, E-mail: kocaoglu@etm.pdx.edu.

Portland State University, Graduate Studies, Systems Science Program, Portland, OR 97207-0751. Offers computational intelligence (Certificate); computer modeling and simulation (Certificate); systems science (MS); systems science/anthropology (PhD); systems science/business administration (PhD); systems science/civil engineering (PhD); systems science/economics (PhD); systems science/engineering management (PhD); systems science/general (PhD); systems science/mathematical sciences (PhD); systems science/mechanical engineering (PhD); systems science/psychology (PhD); systems science/sociology (PhD). *Faculty:* 4 full-time (0 women), 1 part-time/adjunct (0 women). *Students:* 15 full-time (4 women), 35 part-time (11 women); includes 1 American Indian or Alaska Native, non-Hispanic/Latino; 1 Asian, non-Hispanic/Latino; 1 Two or more races, non-Hispanic/Latino, 4 international. Average age 39. 8 applicants, 88% accepted, 5 enrolled. In 2010, 2 master's, 4 doctorates awarded. *Degree requirements:* For doctorate, variable foreign language requirement, thesis/dissertation. *Entrance requirements:* For master's, 2 letters of recommendation; for doctorate, GMAT, GRE General Test, minimum undergraduate GPA of 3.0. Additional exam requirements/recommendations for international students: Required—TOEFL. *Application deadline:* For fall admission, 2/1 for domestic students; for spring admission, 11/1 for domestic students. Application fee: $50. *Expenses:* Tuition, state resident: full-time $8505; part-time $315 per credit. Tuition, nonresident: full-time $13,284; part-time $492 per credit. Required fees: $1482; $21 per credit. $99 per term. One-time fee: $120. Part-time tuition and fees vary according to course load and program. *Financial support:* In 2010–11, 1 research assistantship with full tuition reimbursement (averaging $7,704 per year) was awarded; teaching assistantships with full tuition reimbursements, career-related internships or fieldwork, Federal Work-Study, scholarships/grants, and unspecified assistantships also available. Support available to part-time students. Financial award application deadline: 3/1; financial award applicants required to submit FAFSA. *Faculty research:* Systems theory and methodology, artificial intelligence neural networks, information theory, nonlinear dynamics/chaos, modeling and simulation. *Unit head:* George Lendaris, Acting Director, 503-725-4960. *Application contact:* Dawn Sharafi, Administrative Assistant, 503-725-4960, E-mail: dawn@sysc.pdx.edu.

Rensselaer Polytechnic Institute, Graduate School, Lally School of Management and Technology, Troy, NY 12180-3590. Offers business (MBA); financial engineering and risk analysis (MS); management (MS, PhD); technology, commercialization, and entrepreneurship (MS). *Accreditation:* AACSB. Part-time and evening/weekend programs available. *Faculty:* 44 full-time (10 women), 19 part-time/adjunct (0 women). *Students:* 189 full-time (82 women), 162 part-time (40 women); includes 65 minority (22 Black or African American, non-Hispanic/Latino; 34 Asian, non-Hispanic/Latino; 9 Hispanic/Latino), 92 international. Average age 28. 507 applicants, 56% accepted, 150 enrolled. In 2010, 263 master's, 7 doctorates awarded. *Degree requirements:* For doctorate, thesis/dissertation. *Entrance requirements:* For master's, GMAT, 2 letters of recommendation, resume; for doctorate, GMAT or GRE General Test, 2 letters of recommendation. Additional exam requirements/recommendations for international students: Required—TOEFL (minimum score 600 paper-based; 250 computer-based; 100 iBT); Recommended—IELTS (minimum score 7). *Application deadline:* For fall admission, 3/15 priority date for domestic and international students. Applications are processed on a rolling basis. Application fee: $75. Electronic applications accepted. *Expenses:* Tuition: Full-time $39,600; part-time $1650 per credit. Required fees: $1896. *Financial support:* Fellowships with partial tuition reimbursements, career-related internships or fieldwork, institutionally sponsored loans, scholarships/grants, and assistantships are for Ph D students only available. Financial award application deadline: 3/15; financial award applicants required to submit FAFSA. *Faculty research:* Technological entrepreneurship, operations management, new product development and marketing, finance and financial engineering and risk analytics, information systems. *Unit head:* Dr. Iftekhar Hasan, Acting Dean/Professor, 518-276-6586, Fax: 518-276-2665, E-mail: lallymba@rpi.edu. *Application contact:* Michele M. Martens, Manager of Graduate Programs, 518-276-6586, Fax: 518-276-8190, E-mail: lallymba@rpi.edu.

Robert Morris University, Graduate Studies, School of Engineering, Mathematics and Science, Moon Township, PA 15108-1189. Offers engineering management (MS). Part-time and evening/weekend programs available. *Entrance requirements:* For master's, letters of recommendation. Additional exam requirements/recommendations for international students: Required—TOEFL (minimum score 550 paper-based; 213 computer-based; 79 iBT). Electronic applications accepted. *Expenses:* Contact institution.

Rochester Institute of Technology, Graduate Enrollment Services, Kate Gleason College of Engineering, Department of Design, Development and Manufacturing, Program in Product Development, Rochester, NY 14623-5603. Offers MS. Part-time and evening/weekend programs available. *Students:* 44 part-time (1 woman); includes 1 Asian, non-Hispanic/Latino; 1 Hispanic/Latino. Average age 37. 4 applicants, 75% accepted, 2 enrolled. In 2010, 11 master's awarded. *Entrance requirements:* For master's, undergraduate degree in engineering or related field, minimum GPA of 3.0, 5 years experience in product development. Additional exam requirements/recommendations for international students: Required—TOEFL (minimum score 570 paper-based; 230 computer-based; 88 iBT) or IELTS (minimum score 6.5). *Application deadline:* For fall admission, 2/15 priority date for domestic and international students. Application fee: $50. *Expenses:* Contact institution. *Financial support:* Applicants required to submit FAFSA. *Faculty research:* Platform element dynamics in a multi-product development environment, applying self-organizing principles to product development in a globally-distributed environment, collaborative design and development to accelerate durable goods design and manufacturing. *Unit head:* Mark Smith, Director, 585-475-7971, Fax: 585-475-7955, E-mail: mpdmail@rit.edu. *Application contact:* Diane Ellison, Assistant Vice President, Graduate Enrollment Services, 585-475-2229, Fax: 585-475-7164, E-mail: gradinfo@rit.edu.

Rochester Institute of Technology, Graduate Enrollment Services, Kate Gleason College of Engineering, Department of Industrial and Systems Engineering, Rochester, NY 14623-5603. Offers engineering management (ME); industrial engineering (ME, MS); manufacturing engineering (ME, MS); systems engineering (ME). Part-time programs available. *Students:* 60 full-time (20 women), 17 part-time (5 women); includes 4 Asian, non-Hispanic/Latino; 2 Hispanic/Latino, 48 international. Average age 26. 179 applicants, 49% accepted, 29 enrolled. In 2010, 49 master's awarded. *Degree requirements:* For master's, internship. *Entrance requirements:* For master's, GRE, minimum GPA of 3.0. Additional exam requirements/recommendations for international students: Required—TOEFL (minimum score 570 paper-based; 230 computer-based; 88 iBT) or IELTS (minimum score 6.5). *Application deadline:* For fall admission, 2/15 priority date for domestic and international students. Applications are processed on a rolling basis. Application fee: $50. *Expenses:* Tuition: Full-time $33,234; part-time $924 per credit hour. Required fees: $219. *Financial support:* In 2010–11, 63 students received support; research assistantships with partial tuition reimbursements available, teaching assistantships with partial tuition reimbursements available, career-related internships or fieldwork, institutionally sponsored loans, scholarships/grants, tuition waivers (partial), and unspecified assistantships available. Support available to part-time students. Financial award applicants required to submit FAFSA. *Faculty research:* Safety, manufacturing (CAM), simulation. *Unit head:* Dr. Michael Kuhl, Interim Department Head, 585-475-2134, E-mail: mekeie@rit.edu. *Application contact:* Diane Ellison, Assistant Vice President, Graduate Enrollment Services, 585-475-2229, Fax: 585-475-7164, E-mail: gradinfo@rit.edu.

Rose-Hulman Institute of Technology, Faculty of Engineering and Applied Sciences, Department of Engineering Management, Terre Haute, IN 47803-3999. Offers MS. Part-time and evening/weekend programs available. Postbaccalaureate distance learning degree programs offered (minimal on-campus study). *Faculty:* 3 full-time (0 women), 2 part-time/adjunct (1 woman). *Students:* 22 full-time (6 women), 28 part-time (6 women); includes 2 minority (both Asian, non-Hispanic/Latino), 13 international. Average age 26. 30 applicants, 90% accepted, 20 enrolled. In 2010, 34 master's awarded. *Degree requirements:* For master's, integrated project. *Entrance requirements:* For master's, GRE, minimum GPA of 3.0. Additional exam requirements/recommendations for international students: Required—TOEFL (minimum score 580 paper-based; 237 computer-based; 92 iBT). *Application deadline:* For fall admission, 2/1 priority date for domestic students. Applications are processed on a rolling basis. Application fee: $0. *Expenses:* Tuition: Full-time $35,595; part-time $1038 per credit hour. *Financial support:* In 2010–11, 17 students received support; fellowships with full and partial tuition reimbursements available available. *Faculty research:* Entrepreneurship, management of technology, manufacturing systems, project management, technology forecasting. *Unit head:* Dr. Craig Downing, Interim Chairman, 812-877-8822, Fax: 812-877-8878, E-mail: craig.downing@rose-hulman.edu. *Application contact:* Dr. Daniel J. Moore, Associate Dean of the Faculty, 812-877-8110, Fax: 812-877-8061, E-mail: daniel.j.moore@rose-hulman.edu.

Rowan University, Graduate School, College of Engineering, Program in Engineering Management, Glassboro, NJ 08028-1701. Offers MEM. Part-time and evening/weekend programs available. *Students:* 1 (woman) full-time. Average age 23. 1 applicant, 100% accepted, 1 enrolled. *Degree requirements:* For master's, thesis. *Entrance requirements:* For master's, GRE General Test. Additional exam requirements/recommendations for international students: Required—TOEFL. *Application deadline:* Applications are processed on a rolling basis. Application fee: $65 ($200 for international students). Electronic applications accepted. *Expenses:* Tuition, area resident: Part-time $602 per semester hour. Tuition, nonresident: part-time $602 per semester hour. Required fees: $100 per semester hour. One-time fee: $10 part-time. *Financial support:* Career-related internships or fieldwork, scholarships/grants, health care benefits, and unspecified assistantships available. *Unit head:* Dr. Horacio Sosa, Dean, College of Graduate and Continuing Education, 856-256-4747, Fax: 856-256-5638, E-mail: sosa@rowan.edu. *Application contact:* Karen Haynes, Graduate Coordinator, 856-256-4052, E-mail: haynes@rowan.edu.

St. Cloud State University, School of Graduate Studies, College of Science and Engineering, Program in Engineering Management, St. Cloud, MN 56301-4498. Offers MEM. *Degree requirements:* For master's, thesis or alternative. *Entrance requirements:* For master's, GRE General Test, minimum GPA of 2.75. Additional exam requirements/recommendations for international students: Required—Michigan English Language Assessment Battery; Recommended—TOEFL (minimum score 550 paper-based; 213 computer-based), IELTS (minimum score 6.5). Electronic applications accepted.

Saint Martin's University, Graduate Programs, Program in Engineering Management, Lacey, WA 98503. Offers M Eng Mgt. Part-time and evening/weekend programs available. *Faculty:* 1 full-time (0 women), 1 part-time/adjunct (0 women). *Students:* 8 full-time (1 woman), 4 part-time (all women); includes 2 minority (both Asian, non-Hispanic/Latino), 1 international. Average age 27. 3 applicants, 67% accepted, 1 enrolled. In 2010, 4 master's awarded. *Degree requirements:* For master's, comprehensive exam (for some programs), thesis optional. *Entrance requirements:* For master's, minimum GPA of 2.8 or professional engineer license. Additional exam requirements/recommendations for international students: Required—TOEFL (minimum score 525 paper-based). *Application deadline:* For fall admission, 8/1 priority date for domestic and international students; for spring admission, 12/1 priority date for domestic and international students. Applications are processed on a rolling basis. Application fee: $35. *Financial support:* In 2010–11, 3 students received support; fellowships, research assistantships, Federal Work-Study available. Support available to part-time students. Financial award application deadline: 3/1; financial award applicants required to submit FAFSA. *Faculty research:* Highway safety management, transportation, hydraulics, database structure. *Unit head:* Bill Phillips, Director, 360-438-4320, Fax: 560-438-4522, E-mail: bphillips@stmartin.edu. *Application contact:* Hopie Lopez, Administrative Assistant, 360-438-4320, Fax: 360-438-4548, E-mail: hlopez@stmartin.edu.

St. Mary's University, Graduate School, Department of Engineering, Program in Engineering Systems Management, San Antonio, TX 78228-8507. Offers MS. Part-time programs available. Postbaccalaureate distance learning degree programs offered (no on-campus study). *Degree requirements:* For master's, comprehensive exam. *Entrance requirements:* For master's, GRE or GMAT. Additional exam requirements/recommendations for international students: Required—TOEFL (minimum score 550 paper-based; 213 computer-based; 80 iBT). Electronic applications accepted.

St. Mary's University, Graduate School, Department of Engineering, Program in Industrial Engineering, San Antonio, TX 78228-8507. Offers engineering computer applications (MS); engineering management (MS); industrial engineering (MS); operations research (MS); JD/MS. Part-time programs available. *Degree requirements:* For master's, comprehensive exam. *Entrance requirements:* For master's, GRE General Test, BS in science or engineering, minimum GPA of 3.0. Additional exam requirements/recommendations for international students: Required—TOEFL (minimum score 550 paper-based; 213 computer-based; 80 iBT). Electronic applications accepted. *Faculty research:* Robotics, artificial intelligence, manufacturing engineering.

Santa Clara University, School of Engineering, Program in Engineering Management, Santa Clara, CA 95053. Offers MS. Part-time and evening/weekend programs available. *Students:* 83 full-time (31 women), 168 part-time (43 women); includes 78 minority (6 Black or African American, non-Hispanic/Latino; 58 Asian, non-Hispanic/Latino; 10 Hispanic/Latino; 2 Native Hawaiian or other Pacific Islander, non-Hispanic/Latino; 2 Two or more races, non-Hispanic/Latino), 110 international. Average age 29. 158 applicants, 78% accepted, 59 enrolled. In 2010, 75 master's awarded. *Degree requirements:* For master's, thesis (for some programs). *Entrance requirements:* For master's, GRE (waiver may be available), transcript. Additional exam requirements/recommendations for international students: Required—TOEFL (minimum score 550 paper-based; 213 computer-based; 79 iBT). *Application deadline:* For fall admission, 8/12 for domestic students, 7/15 for international students; for winter admission, 10/28 for domestic students, 9/23 for international students; for spring admission, 2/25 for domestic students, 1/21 for international students. Applications are processed on a rolling basis. Application fee: $60. Electronic applications accepted. *Expenses:* Contact institution. *Financial support:* Research assistantships, teaching assistantships available. Financial award application deadline: 3/2; financial award applicants required to submit FAFSA. *Unit head:* Dr. Alex Zecevic, PhD, Associate Dean for Graduate Studies, 408-554-2394, E-mail: azecevic@scu.edu. *Application contact:* Stacey Tinker, Director of Enrollment Management, 408-554-4748, Fax: 408-554-4323, E-mail: stinker@scu.edu.

South Dakota School of Mines and Technology, Graduate Division, Program in Engineering Management, Rapid City, SD 57701-3995. Offers MS. Program offered jointly with The University of South Dakota. Part-time programs available. *Entrance requirements:* For master's, GMAT. Additional exam requirements/recommendations for international students: Required—TOEFL, TWE. Electronic applications accepted.

Southern Methodist University, Bobby B. Lyle School of Engineering, Department of Engineering Management, Information, and Systems, Dallas, TX 75275. Offers applied science (MS); engineering management (MSEM, DE); information engineering and management (MSIEM); operations research (MS, PhD); systems engineering (MS, PhD). Part-time and evening/weekend programs available. Postbaccalaureate distance learning degree programs offered. *Faculty:* 8 full-time (1 woman), 22 part-time/adjunct (1 woman). *Students:* 47 full-time (12 women), 348 part-time (75 women); includes 114 minority (31 Black or African American, non-Hispanic/Latino; 2 American Indian or Alaska Native, non-Hispanic/Latino; 34 Asian, non-Hispanic/Latino; 44 Hispanic/Latino; 2 Native Hawaiian or other Pacific Islander, non-Hispanic/Latino; 1 Two or more races, non-Hispanic/Latino), 51 international. Average age 33. 208 applicants, 67% accepted, 92 enrolled. In 2010, 130 master's, 6 doctorates awarded. Terminal master's awarded for partial completion of doctoral program. *Degree requirements:* For master's, thesis optional; for doctorate, thesis/dissertation, oral and written qualifying exams. *Entrance requirements:* For master's, minimum GPA of 3.0 in last 2 years; bachelor's degree in engineering, mathematics, sciences, or technical area; for doctorate, GRE General Test (operations research, engineering management), bachelor's degree in related field. Additional exam requirements/recommendations for international students: Required—TOEFL. *Application deadline:* For fall admission, 7/1 for domestic students, 5/15 for international students; for spring admission, 11/15 for domestic students, 9/1 for international students. Applications are processed on a rolling basis. Application fee: $75. *Financial support:* In 2010–11, 6 students received support, including 4 research assistantships with full tuition reimbursements available (averaging $18,000 per year), 2 teaching assistantships with full tuition reimbursements available (averaging $18,000 per year); tuition waivers (full) also available. *Faculty research:* Telecommunications, decision systems, information engineering, operations research, software. Total annual research expenditures: $275,851. *Unit head:* Dr. Richard S. Barr, Chair, 214-768-1772, Fax: 214-768-1112, E-mail: emis@lyle.smu.edu. *Application contact:* Marc Valerin, Director of Graduate and Executive Admissions, 214-768-3042, E-mail: valerin@lyle.smu.edu.

Stanford University, School of Engineering, Department of Management Science and Engineering, Stanford, CA 94305-9991. Offers management science and engineering (MS, PhD). Terminal master's awarded for partial completion of doctoral program. *Degree requirements:* For doctorate, thesis/dissertation, qualification procedure. *Entrance requirements:* For master's and doctorate, GRE General Test. Additional exam requirements/recommendations for international students: Required—TOEFL. Electronic applications accepted. *Expenses:* Tuition: Full-time $38,700; part-time $860 per unit. One-time fee: $200 full-time.

Stevens Institute of Technology, Graduate School, School of Systems and Enterprises, Program in Engineering Management, Hoboken, NJ 07030. Offers M Eng, PhD. *Students:* 35 full-time (8 women), 49 part-time (13 women); includes 5 Black or African American, non-Hispanic/Latino; 8 Asian, non-Hispanic/Latino; 6 Hispanic/Latino, 22 international. Average age 30. *Unit head:* Dr. Charles L. Suffel, Dean of the Graduate School, 201-216-5234, Fax: 201-216-8044, E-mail: csuffel@stevens-tech.edu. *Application contact:* Graduate Admissions, 800-496-4935, Fax: 201-216-8044, E-mail: gradadmissions@stevens.edu.

Stevens Institute of Technology, Graduate School, Wesley J. Howe School of Technology Management, Program in Business Administration, Hoboken, NJ 07030. Offers engineering management (MBA); financial engineering (MBA); information management (MBA); information technology in financial services (MBA); information technology in the pharmaceutical industry (MBA); information technology outsourcing (MBA); pharmaceutical management (MBA); project management (MBA); technology management (MBA); telecommunications management (MBA).

Syracuse University, L. C. Smith College of Engineering and Computer Science, Program in Engineering Management, Syracuse, NY 13244. Offers MS. Part-time and evening/weekend programs available. *Students:* 72 full-time (28 women), 19 part-time (3 women); includes 5 minority (4 Asian, non-Hispanic/Latino; 1 Hispanic/Latino), 64 international. Average age 26. 114 applicants, 46% accepted, 23 enrolled. In 2010, 18 master's awarded. *Entrance requirements:* Additional exam requirements/recommendations for international students: Required—TOEFL (minimum score 100 iBT). *Application deadline:* For fall admission, 7/1 priority date for domestic students, 6/1 priority date for international students. Applications are processed on a rolling basis. Application fee: $75. Electronic applications accepted. *Expenses:*

Engineering Management

Syracuse University (continued)

Tuition: Part-time $1162 per credit. *Financial support:* Fellowships with full tuition reimbursements, research assistantships with full and partial tuition reimbursements, teaching assistantships with full and partial tuition reimbursements, tuition waivers (partial) available. Financial award application deadline: 1/1. *Unit head:* Fred Carranti, Program Director, 315-443-4346. *Application contact:* Kathy Datthyn-Madigan, Information Contact, 315-443-4367, E-mail: kjdatthy@syr.edu.

Texas Tech University, Graduate School, Edward E. Whitacre Jr. College of Engineering, Department of Industrial Engineering, Lubbock, TX 79409. Offers industrial engineering (MSIE, PhD); manufacturing systems engineering (MSMSE); systems and engineering management (MSSEM, PhD). Part-time programs available. Postbaccalaureate distance learning degree programs offered (minimal on-campus study). *Faculty:* 12 full-time (3 women). *Students:* 79 full-time (13 women), 47 part-time (7 women); includes 1 Black or African American, non-Hispanic/Latino; 1 Asian, non-Hispanic/Latino; 2 Hispanic/Latino, 81 international. Average age 28. 282 applicants, 51% accepted, 31 enrolled. In 2010, 39 master's, 9 doctorates awarded. *Degree requirements:* For master's, thesis or alternative; for doctorate, thesis/dissertation. *Entrance requirements:* For master's and doctorate, GRE General Test, minimum GPA of 3.0. Additional exam requirements/recommendations for international students: Required—TOEFL (minimum score 550 paper-based; 213 computer-based; 79 iBT). *Application deadline:* For fall admission, 6/1 priority date for domestic students, 1/15 priority date for international students; for spring admission, 9/1 priority date for domestic students, 6/15 priority date for international students. Applications are processed on a rolling basis. Application fee: $50 ($75 for international students). Electronic applications accepted. *Expenses:* Tuition, state resident: full-time $5495.76; part-time $228.99 per credit hour. Tuition, nonresident: full-time $12,936; part-time $538.99 per credit hour. Required fees: $2674; $36 per credit hour. $905 per semester. *Financial support:* In 2010–11, 40 students received support, including 12 research assistantships with partial tuition reimbursements available (averaging $3,905 per year), 8 teaching assistantships with partial tuition reimbursements available (averaging $3,150 per year). Financial award application deadline: 4/15; financial award applicants required to submit FAFSA. *Faculty research:* Knowledge and engineering management, environmentally conscious manufacturing, biomechanical simulation, aviation security, supply chain management. Total annual research expenditures: $646,598. *Unit head:* Dr. Pat Patterson, Chair, 806-742-3543, Fax: 806-742-3411, E-mail: pat.patterson@ttu.edu. *Application contact:* Dr. Mario Beruvides, Professor, 806-742-3543, Fax: 806-742-3411, E-mail: mario.beruvides@ttu.edu.

Tufts University, School of Engineering, The Gordon Institute, Medford, MA 02155. Offers MSEM. Part-time programs available. *Entrance requirements:* Additional exam requirements/recommendations for international students: Required—TOEFL (minimum score 550 paper-based; 213 computer-based; 80 iBT). Electronic applications accepted. *Expenses:* Contact institution.

Union Graduate College, School of Engineering and Computer Science, Schenectady, NY 12308-3107. Offers computer science (MS); electrical engineering (MS); engineering and management systems (MS); mechanical engineering (MS). Part-time and evening/weekend programs available. *Faculty:* 3 full-time (0 women), 9 part-time/adjunct (0 women). *Students:* 15 full-time (1 woman), 89 part-time (13 women); includes 1 Black or African American, non-Hispanic/Latino; 1 American Indian or Alaska Native, non-Hispanic/Latino; 7 Asian, non-Hispanic/Latino; 6 Hispanic/Latino, 2 international. Average age 27. 52 applicants, 79% accepted, 39 enrolled. In 2010, 24 master's awarded. *Degree requirements:* For master's, capstone course. *Entrance requirements:* For master's, minimum GPA of 3.0, letters of recommendation. Additional exam requirements/recommendations for international students: Required—TOEFL (minimum score 550 paper-based; 213 computer-based). *Application deadline:* Applications are processed on a rolling basis. Application fee: $60. Electronic applications accepted. *Expenses:* Contact institution. *Financial support:* Research assistantships, Federal Work-Study, scholarships/grants, health care benefits, and tuition waivers (full and partial) available. Support available to part-time students. Financial award applicants required to submit FAFSA. *Unit head:* Robert Kozik, Dean, 515-631-9881, Fax: 518-631-9902, E-mail: kozikr@union.edu. *Application contact:* Diane Trzaskos, Coordinator, Admissions, 518-631-9837, Fax: 518-631-9901, E-mail: trzaskod@uniongraduatecollege.edu.

Université de Sherbrooke, Faculty of Engineering, Programs in Engineering Management, Sherbrooke, QC J1K 2R1, Canada. Offers M Eng, Diploma. Part-time and evening/weekend programs available. *Entrance requirements:* For master's and Diploma, bachelor's degree in engineering, 1 year of practical experience. Electronic applications accepted.

The University of Akron, Graduate School, College of Engineering, Program in Engineering (Management Specialization), Akron, OH 44325. Offers MS. *Students:* 2 full-time (0 women), 5 part-time (0 women); includes 2 Asian, non-Hispanic/Latino, 1 international. Average age 26. 11 applicants, 36% accepted, 2 enrolled. In 2010, 5 master's awarded. *Degree requirements:* For master's, engineering report. *Entrance requirements:* For master's, GRE, minimum GPA of 2.75, two letters of recommendation, statement of purpose, resume. Additional exam requirements/recommendations for international students: Required—TOEFL (minimum score 550 paper-based; 213 computer-based; 79 iBT). *Application deadline:* Applications are processed on a rolling basis. Application fee: $30 ($40 for international students). Electronic applications accepted. *Expenses:* Tuition, state resident: full-time $6800; part-time $378 per credit hour. Tuition, nonresident: full-time $11,644; part-time $647 per credit hour. Required fees: $1265. One-time fee: $30 full-time. *Unit head:* Dr. Subramaniya Hariharan, Coordinator, 330-972-6580, E-mail: hari@uakron.edu. *Application contact:* Dr. Subramaniya Hariharan, Coordinator, 330-972-6580, E-mail: hari@uakron.edu.

The University of Alabama in Huntsville, School of Graduate Studies, College of Engineering, Department of Industrial and Systems Engineering/Engineering Management, Huntsville, AL 35899. Offers industrial and systems engineering (PhD), including engineering management (MSE, PhD), industrial engineering, systems engineering (MSE, PhD); industrial engineering (MSE), including engineering management (MSE, PhD), missile systems engineering, modeling and simulation, rotorcraft systems engineering, systems engineering (MSE, PhD); operations research (MSOR). Part-time and evening/weekend programs available. Postbaccalaureate distance learning degree programs offered (minimal on-campus study). *Faculty:* 8 full-time (2 women), 4 part-time/adjunct (1 woman). *Students:* 11 full-time (2 women), 158 part-time (40 women); includes 26 minority (18 Black or African American, non-Hispanic/Latino; 2 American Indian or Alaska Native, non-Hispanic/Latino; 2 Asian, non-Hispanic/Latino; 3 Hispanic/Latino; 1 Two or more races, non-Hispanic/Latino), 8 international. Average age 36. 108 applicants, 64% accepted, 48 enrolled. In 2010, 30 master's, 5 doctorates awarded. *Degree requirements:* For master's, comprehensive exam, thesis or alternative, oral and written exams; for doctorate, comprehensive exam, thesis/dissertation, oral and written exams. *Entrance requirements:* For master's and doctorate, GRE General Test, minimum GPA of 3.0. Additional exam requirements/recommendations for international students: Required—TOEFL (minimum score 500 paper-based; 173 computer-based; 62 iBT). *Application deadline:* For fall admission, 7/15 for domestic students, 4/1 for international students; for spring admission, 11/30 for domestic students, 9/1 for international students. Applications are processed on a rolling basis. Application fee: $40 ($50 for international students). Electronic applications accepted. *Expenses:* Tuition, state resident: full-time $7250; part-time $407.75 per credit hour. Tuition, nonresident: full-time $17,358; part-time $970.05 per credit hour. Required fees: $246.80 per semester. Tuition and fees vary according to course load and program. *Financial support:* In 2010–11, 7 students received support, including 1 research assistantship with full tuition reimbursement available (averaging $10,340 per year), 6 teaching assistantships with full tuition reimbursements available (averaging $10,768 per year); career-related internships or fieldwork, Federal Work-Study, institutionally sponsored loans, scholarships/grants, health care benefits, and unspecified assistantships also available. Support available to part-time students. Financial award application deadline: 4/1; financial award applicants required to submit FAFSA. *Faculty research:* Engineering management, systems engineering, manufacturing, logistics, simulation. Total annual research expenditures: $7.8 million. *Unit head:* Dr. James Swain, Chair, 256-824-6749, Fax: 256-824-6733, E-mail: jswain@ise.uah.edu. *Application contact:* Kathy Biggs, Graduate Studies Admissions Manager, 256-824-6199, Fax: 256-824-6405, E-mail: deangrad@uah.edu.

University of Alaska Anchorage, School of Engineering, Program in Engineering Management, Anchorage, AK 99508. Offers MS. Part-time and evening/weekend programs available. *Degree requirements:* For master's, comprehensive exam (for some programs), thesis optional. *Entrance requirements:* For master's, BS in engineering or science, work experience in engineering or science. Additional exam requirements/recommendations for international students: Required—TOEFL (minimum score 550 paper-based; 213 computer-based). *Faculty research:* Engineering economy, long-range forecasting, multicriteria design making, project management process and training.

University of Alaska Anchorage, School of Engineering, Program in Science Management, Anchorage, AK 99508. Offers MS. Part-time and evening/weekend programs available. *Degree requirements:* For master's, comprehensive exam (for some programs), thesis (for some programs). *Entrance requirements:* For master's, GRE General Test, BS in engineering or scientific field. Additional exam requirements/recommendations for international students: Required—TOEFL (minimum score 550 paper-based; 213 computer-based). *Faculty research:* Engineering economy, long-range forecasting, multicriteria decision making, project management process and training.

University of Alaska Fairbanks, College of Engineering and Mines, Department of Civil and Environmental Engineering, Engineering and Science Management Program, Fairbanks, AK 99775. Offers engineering management (MS, PhD); science management (MS). Part-time programs available. *Students:* 4 part-time (1 woman). Average age 34. 3 applicants, 33% accepted, 1 enrolled. In 2010, 1 master's awarded. *Degree requirements:* For master's, comprehensive exam, thesis or alternative, oral exam; for doctorate, comprehensive exam, thesis/dissertation, oral exam, oral defense. *Entrance requirements:* For doctorate, GRE General Test. Additional exam requirements/recommendations for international students: Required—TOEFL (minimum score 550 paper-based; 213 computer-based; 80 iBT). *Application deadline:* For fall admission, 6/1 for domestic students, 3/1 for international students; for spring admission, 10/15 for domestic students, 9/1 for international students. Applications are processed on a rolling basis. Application fee: $60. Electronic applications accepted. *Expenses:* Tuition, state resident: full-time $5688; part-time $316 per credit. Tuition, nonresident: full-time $11,628; part-time $646 per credit. Required fees: $289 per semester. Tuition and fees vary according to course load and reciprocity agreements. *Financial support:* Fellowships, research assistantships, teaching assistantships, career-related internships or fieldwork, Federal Work-Study, scholarships/grants, health care benefits, and unspecified assistantships available. Support available to part-time students. Financial award application deadline: 7/1; financial award applicants required to submit FAFSA. *Faculty research:* Traffic studies, decision analysis, application of optimization, transportation safety. *Unit head:* Dr. Robert A. Perkins, Program Coordinator, 907-474-7694, Fax: 907-474-6087, E-mail: raperkins@alaska.edu. *Application contact:* Dr. Robert A. Perkins, Program Coordinator, 907-474-7694, Fax: 907-474-6087, E-mail: raperkins@alaska.edu.

University of Alberta, Faculty of Graduate Studies and Research, Department of Mechanical Engineering, Edmonton, AB T6G 2E1, Canada. Offers engineering management (M Eng); mechanical engineering (M Eng, M Sc, PhD); MBA/M Eng. Part-time programs available. *Degree requirements:* For master's, thesis; for doctorate, thesis/dissertation. *Entrance requirements:* For master's and doctorate, minimum GPA of 7.0 on a 9.0 scale. Additional exam requirements/recommendations for international students: Required—TOEFL (minimum score 580 paper-based; 237 computer-based). *Faculty research:* Combustion and environmental issues, advanced materials, computational fluid dynamics, biomedical, acoustics and vibrations.

University of California, Berkeley, Graduate Division, College of Engineering, Department of Civil and Environmental Engineering, Berkeley, CA 94720-1500. Offers engineering and project management (M Eng, MS, D Eng, PhD); environmental engineering (M Eng, MS, D Eng, PhD); geoengineering (M Eng, MS, D Eng, PhD); structural engineering, mechanics and materials (M Eng, MS, D Eng, PhD); transportation engineering (M Eng, MS, D Eng, PhD); M Arch/MS; MCP/MS; MPP/MS. *Degree requirements:* For master's, comprehensive exam or thesis (MS); for doctorate, thesis/dissertation, qualifying exam. *Entrance requirements:* For master's, GRE General Test, minimum GPA of 3.0, 3 letters of recommendation; for doctorate, GRE General Test, minimum GPA of 3.5, 3 letters of recommendation. Additional exam requirements/recommendations for international students: Required—TOEFL (minimum score 570 paper-based; 230 computer-based). Electronic applications accepted.

University of Colorado at Colorado Springs, College of Engineering and Applied Science, Department of Mechanical and Aerospace Engineering, Colorado Springs, CO 80933-7150. Offers engineering management (ME); information operations (ME); manufacturing (ME); mechanical engineering (MS); software engineering (ME); space operations (ME); space systems (MS). Part-time and evening/weekend programs available. *Faculty:* 10 full-time (2 women). *Students:* 56 full-time (11 women), 26 part-time (6 women); includes 3 Black or African American, non-Hispanic/Latino; 4 Asian, non-Hispanic/Latino; 3 Hispanic/Latino, 1 international. Average age 32. 33 applicants, 76% accepted, 19 enrolled. In 2010, 26 master's awarded. *Degree requirements:* For master's, thesis optional. *Entrance requirements:* For master's, GRE General Test, bachelor's degree in engineering or related degree, minimum GPA of 3.0. Additional exam requirements/recommendations for international students: Required—TOEFL. *Application deadline:* For fall admission, 5/1 for domestic students; for spring admission, 10/1 for domestic students. Applications are processed on a rolling basis. Application fee: $60 ($75 for international students). *Expenses:* Tuition, state resident: full-time $7916. Tuition, nonresident: full-time $16,610. Tuition and fees vary according to course load, degree level, program, reciprocity agreements and student level. *Financial support:* Federal Work-Study and scholarships/grants available. Support available to part-time students. Financial award application deadline: 3/1; financial award applicants required to submit FAFSA. *Faculty research:* Neural networks, artificial intelligence, robust control, space operations, space propulsion. Total annual research expenditures: $69,367. *Unit head:* Dr. James Stevens, Chair, 719-255-3581, Fax: 719-255-3042, E-mail: jstevens@uccs.edu. *Application contact:* Siew Nylund, Academic Adviser, 719-255-3243, Fax: 719-255-3589, E-mail: snylund@eas.uccs.edu.

University of Colorado Boulder, Graduate School, College of Engineering and Applied Science, Engineering Management Program, Boulder, CO 80309. Offers operations and logistics (ME); quality and process (ME); research and development (ME). *Students:* 53 full-time (16 women), 72 part-time (16 women); includes 20 minority (2 Black or African American, non-Hispanic/Latino; 1 American Indian or Alaska Native, non-Hispanic/Latino; 11 Asian, non-Hispanic/Latino; 5 Hispanic/Latino; 1 Two or more races, non-Hispanic/Latino), 15 international. Average age 34. 55 applicants, 2 enrolled. In 2010, 47 master's awarded. *Entrance requirements:* For master's, minimum undergraduate GPA of 3.0. *Application deadline:* For fall admission, 2/15 for domestic students, 12/1 for international students; for spring admission, 8/15 for domestic students, 5/1 for international students. Application fee: $50 ($60 for international students). *Financial support:* In 2010–11, 2 fellowships (averaging $3,500 per year), 2 research assistantships (averaging $16,862 per year) were awarded. *Faculty research:* Quality and process, research and development, operations and logistics.

University of Dayton, Graduate School, School of Engineering, Engineering Management and Systems Department, Dayton, OH 45469-1300. Offers engineering management (MSEM); management science (MSMS). Part-time and evening/weekend programs available. Postbaccalaureate distance learning degree programs offered (no on-campus study). *Faculty:* 3 full-time (0 women), 8 part-time/adjunct (2 women). *Students:* 56 full-time (16 women), 56 part-time (14 women); includes 17 minority (13 Black or African American, non-Hispanic/Latino; 2 Asian, non-Hispanic/Latino; 1 Hispanic/Latino; 1 Two or more races, non-Hispanic/Latino), 23 international. Average age 31. 81 applicants, 74% accepted, 25 enrolled. In 2010,

41 master's awarded. *Degree requirements:* For master's, thesis, 7 core courses (for MSEM); 5 electives/5 core courses (for MSMS). *Entrance requirements:* For master's, bachelor's degree. Additional exam requirements/recommendations for international students: Required—TOEFL (minimum score 550 paper-based; 213 computer-based; 80 iBT). *Application deadline:* For fall admission, 8/1 for domestic students, 3/1 priority date for international students; for winter admission, 7/1 priority date for international students; for spring admission, 1/1 priority date for international students. Applications are processed on a rolling basis. Application fee: $0. Electronic applications accepted. *Expenses:* Tuition: Full-time $7800; part-time $650 per credit hour. *Financial support:* Applicants required to submit FAFSA. *Faculty research:* OPS research, simulation, reliability. Total annual research expenditures: $70,621. *Unit head:* Dr. Patrick Sweeney, Chair, 937-229-2238. *Application contact:* Alexander Popovski, Associate Director of International and Graduate Admissions, 937-229-2357, Fax: 937-229-4729, E-mail: alex.popovski@notes.udayton.edu.

University of Detroit Mercy, College of Engineering and Science, Program in Engineering Management, Detroit, MI 48221. Offers M Eng Mgt. Evening/weekend programs available. *Degree requirements:* For master's, thesis or alternative.

University of Idaho, College of Graduate Studies, College of Engineering, Department of Civil Engineering, Program in Engineering Management, Moscow, ID 83844-2282. Offers M Engr. *Students:* 2 full-time, 28 part-time. Average age 39. In 2010, 7 master's awarded. *Application deadline:* Applications are processed on a rolling basis. Application fee: $60. Electronic applications accepted. *Expenses:* Tuition, nonresident: part-time $580 per credit. Required fees: $306 per credit. *Financial support:* Applicants required to submit FAFSA. *Unit head:* Dr. Richard J. Nielsen, Department Chair. *Application contact:* Dr. Richard J. Nielsen, Department Chair.

The University of Kansas, Graduate Studies, School of Engineering, Program in Engineering Management, Overland Park, KS 66213. Offers MS. Part-time and evening/weekend programs available. Postbaccalaureate distance learning degree programs offered (no on-campus study). *Faculty:* 3 full-time (1 woman), 10 part-time/adjunct (1 woman). *Students:* 8 full-time (2 women), 140 part-time (19 women); includes 29 minority (10 Black or African American, non-Hispanic/Latino; 1 American Indian or Alaska Native, non-Hispanic/Latino; 12 Asian, non-Hispanic/Latino; 6 Hispanic/Latino), 23 international. Average age 33. 39 applicants, 69% accepted, 19 enrolled. In 2010, 29 master's awarded. *Degree requirements:* For master's, exam. *Entrance requirements:* For master's, minimum GPA of 3.0, 2 years of industrial experience. Additional exam requirements/recommendations for international students: Required—TOEFL (minimum score 600 paper-based; 250 computer-based; 100 iBT). *Application deadline:* Applications are processed on a rolling basis. Application fee: $55 ($65 for international students). Electronic applications accepted. *Expenses:* Tuition, state resident: full-time $7092; part-time $295.50 per credit hour. Tuition, nonresident: full-time $16,590; part-time $691.25 per credit hour. Required fees: $858; $71.49 per credit hour. Tuition and fees vary according to course load, campus/location and program. *Faculty research:* Project management, systems analysis, high performance teams, manufacturing systems, strategic analysis. *Unit head:* Herbert R. Tuttle, Director, 913-897-8561, Fax: 913-897-8682, E-mail: emgt@ku.edu. *Application contact:* Parveen Mozaffar, Academic Services Coordinator, 913-897-8560, Fax: 913-897-8682, E-mail: emgt@ku.edu.

University of Louisiana at Lafayette, College of Engineering, Department of Engineering and Technology Management, Lafayette, LA 70504. Offers MSET. Part-time and evening/weekend programs available. *Degree requirements:* For master's, comprehensive exam, thesis or alternative. *Entrance requirements:* For master's, GRE General Test, minimum GPA of 2.85. Additional exam requirements/recommendations for international students: Required—TOEFL (minimum score 550 paper-based; 213 computer-based). Electronic applications accepted. *Faculty research:* Mathematical programming, production management forecasting.

University of Louisville, J.B. Speed School of Engineering, Department of Industrial Engineering, Louisville, KY 40292-0001. Offers engineering management (M Eng); industrial engineering (M Eng, MS, PhD); logistics and distribution (Certificate). *Accreditation:* ABET (one or more programs are accredited). Part-time programs available. *Faculty:* 10 full-time (1 woman). *Students:* 45 full-time (11 women), 26 part-time (7 women); includes 5 Black or African American, non-Hispanic/Latino; 1 Asian, non-Hispanic/Latino; 1 Hispanic/Latino; 1 Two or more races, non-Hispanic/Latino, 18 international. Average age 28. 56 applicants, 32% accepted, 7 enrolled. In 2010, 25 master's, 4 doctorates awarded. Terminal master's awarded for partial completion of doctoral program. *Degree requirements:* For master's, comprehensive exam (for some programs), thesis or alternative; for doctorate, comprehensive exam, thesis/dissertation, minimum GPA of 3.0. *Entrance requirements:* For master's and doctorate, GRE General Test. Additional exam requirements/recommendations for international students: Required—TOEFL (minimum score 550 paper-based; 213 computer-based; 80 iBT), IELTS (minimum score 6.5). *Application deadline:* For fall admission, 5/1 priority date for domestic and international students; for spring admission, 11/1 priority date for domestic and international students. Applications are processed on a rolling basis. Application fee: $50. Electronic applications accepted. *Expenses:* Tuition, state resident: full-time $9144; part-time $508 per credit hour. Tuition, nonresident: full-time $19,026; part-time $1057 per credit hour. Tuition and fees vary according to program and reciprocity agreements. *Financial support:* In 2010–11, 15 students received support, including 7 fellowships with full tuition reimbursements available (averaging $20,000 per year), 2 research assistantships with full tuition reimbursements available (averaging $20,000 per year), 6 teaching assistantships with full tuition reimbursements available (averaging $20,000 per year). Financial award application deadline: 1/25; financial award applicants required to submit FAFSA. *Faculty research:* Optimization,computer simulation, logistics and distribution, ergonomics and human factors, advanced manufacturing process. Total annual research expenditures: $748,000. *Unit head:* Dr. John S. Usher, Chair, 502-852-6342, Fax: 502-852-5633, E-mail: usher@louisville.edu. *Application contact:* Dr. Michael Day, Associate Dean, 502-852-6195, Fax: 502-852-7294, E-mail: day@louisville.edu.

The University of Manchester, School of Mechanical, Aerospace and Civil Engineering, Manchester, United Kingdom. Offers advanced manufacturing technology (M Ent); aerospace engineering (M Phil, M Sc, PhD); civil engineering (M Phil, M Sc, PhD); environmental engineering (M Phil, PhD); management of projects (M Phil, M Sc, PhD); mechanical engineering (M Phil, M Sc, PhD); mechanical engineering design (M Ent); nuclear engineering (M Phil, D Eng, PhD).

University of Maryland, Baltimore County, Graduate School, College of Engineering and Information Technology, Department of Computer Science and Electrical Engineering, Program in Engineering Management, Baltimore, MD 21250. Offers MS, Postbaccalaureate Certificate. Part-time programs available. *Students:* 12 full-time (4 women), 73 part-time (24 women); includes 24 minority (15 Black or African American, non-Hispanic/Latino; 4 Asian, non-Hispanic/Latino; 5 Hispanic/Latino), 13 international. Average age 30. 44 applicants, 77% accepted, 19 enrolled. In 2010, 23 master's, 14 other advanced degrees awarded. *Degree requirements:* For master's, comprehensive exam (for some programs), thesis optional. *Entrance requirements:* For master's, BS in engineering or information technology with minimum GPA of 3.0. Additional exam requirements/recommendations for international students: Required—TOEFL (minimum score 550 paper-based; 213 computer-based; 80 iBT). *Application deadline:* For fall admission, 7/1 for domestic and international students; for spring admission, 12/1 for domestic and international students. Applications are processed on a rolling basis. Application fee: $50. Electronic applications accepted. *Financial support:* Career-related internships or fieldwork, Federal Work-Study, scholarships/grants, health care benefits, tuition waivers (partial), and unspecified assistantships available. Support available to part-time students. Financial award application deadline: 6/30; financial award applicants required to submit FAFSA. *Faculty research:* Regulatory engineering, environmental engineering, systems engineering, advanced manufacturing, chemical engineering. *Unit head:* Dr. Gary Carter, Professor and Chair, 410-455-3500, Fax: 410-455-3969, E-mail: carter@cs.umbc.edu. *Application contact:* Dr. Ted M. Foster, Professor of Practice and Assistant Dean, COEIT; Graduate Program Director, 410-455-1564, Fax: 410-455-3559, E-mail: tfoster@umbc.edu.

University of Massachusetts Amherst, Graduate School, Interdisciplinary Programs, Program in Environmental Engineering and Business Administration, Amherst, MA 01003. Offers MS Envr E/MBA. Part-time programs available. *Students:* 1 applicant, 0% accepted, 0 enrolled. *Entrance requirements:* Additional exam requirements/recommendations for international students: Required—TOEFL (minimum score 600 paper-based; 250 computer-based; 100 iBT), IELTS (minimum score 7). *Application deadline:* For fall admission, 2/1 for domestic and international students. Applications are processed on a rolling basis. Application fee: $50 ($65 for international students). Electronic applications accepted. *Expenses:* Tuition, state resident: full-time $2640. Required fees: $8282. One-time fee: $357 full-time. *Financial support:* Career-related internships or fieldwork, Federal Work-Study, scholarships/grants, traineeships, health care benefits, tuition waivers (full), and unspecified assistantships available. Support available to part-time students. *Unit head:* Dr. David Ahlfeld, Graduate Program Director, 413-545-2681, Fax: 413-545-2840. *Application contact:* Jean M. Ames, Supervisor of Admissions, 413-545-0722, Fax: 413-577-0010, E-mail: gradadm@grad.umass.edu.

University of Massachusetts Amherst, Graduate School, Interdisciplinary Programs, Program in Industrial Engineering and Business Administration, Amherst, MA 01003. Offers MBA/MSIE. Part-time programs available. *Students:* 1 applicant, 0% accepted, 0 enrolled. *Entrance requirements:* Additional exam requirements/recommendations for international students: Required—TOEFL (minimum score 600 paper-based; 250 computer-based; 100 iBT), IELTS (minimum score 7). *Application deadline:* For fall admission, 1/15 for domestic and international students. Applications are processed on a rolling basis. Application fee: $50 ($65 for international students). Electronic applications accepted. *Expenses:* Tuition, state resident: full-time $2640. Required fees: $8282. One-time fee: $357 full-time. *Financial support:* Career-related internships or fieldwork, Federal Work-Study, scholarships/grants, traineeships, health care benefits, tuition waivers (full), and unspecified assistantships available. Support available to part-time students. *Unit head:* Dr. David P. Schmidt, Graduate Program Director, 413-545-3827, Fax: 413-545-1027. *Application contact:* Jean M. Ames, Supervisor of Admissions, 413-545-0722, Fax: 413-577-0010, E-mail: gradadm@grad.umass.edu.

University of Massachusetts Amherst, Graduate School, Interdisciplinary Programs, Program in Mechanical Engineering and Business Administration, Amherst, MA 01003. Offers MSME/MBA. Part-time programs available. *Students:* 1 full-time (0 women); minority (Two or more races, non-Hispanic/Latino). Average age 25. 2 applicants, 50% accepted, 1 enrolled. *Entrance requirements:* Additional exam requirements/recommendations for international students: Required—TOEFL (minimum score 600 paper-based; 250 computer-based; 100 iBT), IELTS (minimum score 7). *Application deadline:* For fall admission, 1/15 for domestic and international students. Applications are processed on a rolling basis. Application fee: $50 ($65 for international students). Electronic applications accepted. *Expenses:* Tuition, state resident: full-time $2640. Required fees: $8282. One-time fee: $357 full-time. *Financial support:* Career-related internships or fieldwork, Federal Work-Study, scholarships/grants, traineeships, health care benefits, tuition waivers (full), and unspecified assistantships available. Support available to part-time students. *Unit head:* Dr. David P. Schmidt, Graduate Program Director, 413-545-3827, Fax: 413-545-1027. *Application contact:* Jean M. Ames, Supervisor of Admissions, 413-545-0722, Fax: 413-577-0010, E-mail: gradadm@grad.umass.edu.

University of Michigan–Dearborn, College of Engineering and Computer Science, Department of Industrial and Manufacturing Systems Engineering, Dearborn, MI 48128-1491. Offers engineering management (MS); industrial and systems engineering (MSE); information systems and technology (MS); information systems engineering (PhD); program and project management (MS); MBA/MSE. Part-time and evening/weekend programs available. *Faculty:* 13 full-time (0 women), 3 part-time/adjunct (0 women). *Students:* 23 full-time (8 women), 142 part-time (40 women); includes 14 Black or African American, non-Hispanic/Latino; 27 Asian, non-Hispanic/Latino; 8 Hispanic/Latino, 23 international. Average age 35. 81 applicants, 58% accepted, 47 enrolled. In 2010, 57 master's awarded. *Degree requirements:* For master's, thesis optional. *Entrance requirements:* For master's, bachelor's degree in applied mathematics, computer science, engineering, or physical science; minimum GPA of 3.0. Additional exam requirements/recommendations for international students: Required—TOEFL (minimum score 560 paper-based; 220 computer-based; 84 iBT). *Application deadline:* For fall admission, 8/1 priority date for domestic students, 4/1 for international students; for winter admission, 12/1 priority date for domestic students, 8/1 for international students; for spring admission, 4/1 for domestic students, 12/1 for international students. Applications are processed on a rolling basis. Application fee: $60. Electronic applications accepted. *Financial support:* Fellowships, research assistantships, teaching assistantships, Federal Work-Study available. Financial award application deadline: 4/1; financial award applicants required to submit FAFSA. *Faculty research:* Health care systems, data and knowledge management, human factors engineering, machine diagnostics, precision machining. *Unit head:* Dr. Armen Zakarian, Chair, 313-593-5361, Fax: 313-593-3692, E-mail: zakarian@umd.umich.edu. *Application contact:* Joey W. Woods, Graduate Program Assistant, 313-593-5361, Fax: 313-593-3692, E-mail: jwwoods@umd.umich.edu.

University of Minnesota, Duluth, Graduate School, Swenson College of Science and Engineering, Department of Mechanical and Industrial Engineering, Duluth, MN 55812-2496. Offers engineering management (MSEM); environmental health and safety (MEHS). Part-time and evening/weekend programs available. Postbaccalaureate distance learning degree programs offered (no on-campus study). *Degree requirements:* For master's, comprehensive exam, thesis or alternative, capstone design project (MSEM), field project (MEHS). *Entrance requirements:* For master's, GRE (MEHS), interview (MEHS), letters of recommendation. Additional exam requirements/recommendations for international students: Required—TOEFL (minimum score 550 paper-based; 213 computer-based). *Faculty research:* Transportation, ergonomics, toxicology, supply chain management, automation and robotics.

University of Nebraska–Lincoln, Graduate College, College of Engineering, Department of Industrial and Management Systems Engineering, Lincoln, NE 68588. Offers engineering management (M Eng); industrial and management systems engineering (MS, PhD); manufacturing systems engineering (MS). Postbaccalaureate distance learning degree programs offered. *Degree requirements:* For master's, thesis optional; for doctorate, comprehensive exam, thesis/dissertation. *Entrance requirements:* For master's and doctorate, GRE. Additional exam requirements/recommendations for international students: Required—TOEFL (minimum score 525 paper-based; 195 computer-based). Electronic applications accepted. *Faculty research:* Ergonomics, occupational safety, quality control, industrial packaging, facility design.

University of New Brunswick Fredericton, School of Graduate Studies, Faculty of Business Administration, Fredericton, NB E3B 5A3, Canada. Offers business administration (MBA); engineering management (MBA); entrepreneurship (MBA); sports and recreation management (MBA); MBA/LL B. Part-time programs available. *Faculty:* 23 full-time (3 women), 5 part-time/adjunct (2 women). *Students:* 43 full-time (18 women), 35 part-time (20 women). In 2010, 29 master's awarded. *Degree requirements:* For master's, thesis optional. *Entrance requirements:* For master's, GMAT (550 minimum score), minimum GPA of 3.0; 3-5 years work experience. Additional exam requirements/recommendations for international students: Required—TOEFL (minimum score 580 paper-based; 92 iBT), IELTS (minimum score 7), TOEFL or IELTS. *Application deadline:* For fall admission, 3/1 priority date for domestic students. Applications are processed on a rolling basis. Application fee: $50 Canadian dollars. *Expenses:* Tuition, area resident: Full-time $3708; part-time $927 per term. International tuition: $6300 full-time. Required fees: $50 per term. *Financial support:* In 2010–11, 4 research assistantships (averaging $4,500 per year), 13 teaching assistantships (averaging $2,250 per year) were awarded. *Faculty research:* Accounting and auditing practices, human resource management, the non-profit sector, marketing, strategic management, entrepreneurship, investment practices, supply chain management, and operations management. *Unit head:* Judy Roy, Director of Graduate Studies, 506-458-7307, Fax: 506-453-3561, E-mail: jroy@unb.ca. *Application contact:* Marilyn Davis, Acting Graduate Secretary, 506-453-4766, Fax: 506-453-3561, E-mail: mbacontact@unb.ca.

Engineering Management

University of New Haven, Graduate School, Tagliatela College of Engineering, Program in Engineering and Operations Management, West Haven, CT 06516-1916. Offers MS. *Students:* 13 full-time (3 women), 24 part-time (0 women); includes 3 Black or African American, non-Hispanic/Latino; 3 Asian, non-Hispanic/Latino; 2 Hispanic/Latino, 3 international. Average age 34. 25 applicants, 92% accepted, 20 enrolled. In 2010, 8 master's awarded. *Entrance requirements:* For master's, five or more years' experience in a supervisory role in engineering, technical staff support, engineering or systems management, project management, systems engineering, manufacturing, logistics, industrial engineering, military operations, or quality assurance. Additional exam requirements/recommendations for international students: Required—TOEFL (minimum score 520 paper-based; 190 computer-based; 70 iBT); Recommended—IELTS (minimum score 5.5). *Application deadline:* For fall admission, 5/31 for international students; for winter admission, 10/15 for international students; for spring admission, 1/15 for international students. Application fee: $50. *Unit head:* Dr. Barry Farbrother, Dean, 203-932-7167. *Application contact:* Eloise Gormley, Director of Graduate Admissions, 203-932-7449, Fax: 203-932-7137, E-mail: gradinfo@newhaven.edu.

University of New Orleans, Graduate School, College of Engineering, Program in Engineering Management, New Orleans, LA 70148. Offers MS, Certificate. *Degree requirements:* For master's, thesis optional. *Entrance requirements:* For master's, GRE General Test, minimum GPA of 3.0. Additional exam requirements/recommendations for international students: Required—TOEFL (minimum score 550 paper-based; 213 computer-based; 79 iBT). Electronic applications accepted.

The University of North Carolina at Charlotte, Graduate School, The William States Lee College of Engineering, Program in Engineering Management, Charlotte, NC 28223-0001. Offers MS. Part-time and evening/weekend programs available. *Degree requirements:* For master's, thesis optional. *Entrance requirements:* For master's, GRE General Test or GMAT. Additional exam requirements/recommendations for international students: Required—TOEFL (minimum score 575 paper-based; 230 computer-based; 83 iBT). *Application deadline:* For fall admission, 7/1 for domestic students, 5/1 for international students; for spring admission, 11/1 for domestic students, 10/1 for international students. Applications are processed on a rolling basis. Application fee: $55. Electronic applications accepted. *Expenses:* Tuition, state resident: full-time $3464. Tuition, nonresident: full-time $14,297. Required fees: $2094. Tuition and fees vary according to course load. *Financial support:* Teaching assistantships, career-related internships or fieldwork, Federal Work-Study, institutionally sponsored loans, scholarships/grants, and unspecified assistantships available. Support available to part-time students. Financial award application deadline: 4/1; financial award applicants required to submit FAFSA. *Unit head:* Dr. S. Gary Teng, Director, 704-687-3989, Fax: 704-687-3616, E-mail: sgteng@uncc.edu. *Application contact:* Kathy B. Giddings, Director of Graduate Admissions, 704-687-5503, Fax: 704-687-3279, E-mail: gradadm@uncc.edu.

University of Oklahoma, College of Engineering, School of Industrial Engineering, Norman, OK 73019. Offers industrial engineering (MS, PhD), including engineering management (MS), general (MS). Part-time programs available. *Faculty:* 14 full-time (5 women). *Students:* 37 full-time (11 women), 23 part-time (7 women); includes 5 minority (3 Black or African American, non-Hispanic/Latino; 1 American Indian or Alaska Native, non-Hispanic/Latino; 1 Two or more races, non-Hispanic/Latino), 32 international. Average age 28. 58 applicants, 72% accepted, 12 enrolled. In 2010, 7 master's, 5 doctorates awarded. *Degree requirements:* For master's, comprehensive exam, thesis (for some programs); for doctorate, thesis/dissertation, qualifying exam. *Entrance requirements:* For master's and doctorate, GRE, minimum GPA of 3.0, 3 letters of reference, resume or curriculum vitae. Additional exam requirements/recommendations for international students: Required—TOEFL (minimum score 550 paper-based; 213 computer-based; 79 iBT). *Application deadline:* For fall admission, 6/1 priority date for domestic students, 4/1 for international students; for spring admission, 11/1 for domestic students, 9/1 for international students. Applications are processed on a rolling basis. Application fee: $40 ($90 for international students). Electronic applications accepted. *Expenses:* Tuition, state resident: full-time $3892.80; part-time $162.20 per credit hour. Tuition, nonresident: full-time $14,167; part-time $590.30 per credit hour. Required fees: $2523.40; $94.60 per credit hour. Tuition and fees vary according to course load and degree level. *Financial support:* In 2010–11, 48 students received support, including 12 research assistantships with partial tuition reimbursements available (averaging $13,300 per year), 10 teaching assistantships with partial tuition reimbursements available (averaging $10,350 per year); scholarships/grants and unspecified assistantships also available. Financial award application deadline: 5/1; financial award applicants required to submit FAFSA. *Faculty research:* Computational optimization, logistics and supply chain management, human factors, design and manufacturing, systems modeling, engineering education. Total annual research expenditures: $2.5 million. *Unit head:* Dr. Randa Shehab, Director, 405-325-3721, Fax: 405-325-7555, E-mail: rlshehab@ou.edu. *Application contact:* Amy J. Piper, Student Services Coordinator, 405-325-3721, Fax: 405-325-7555, E-mail: ajpiper@ou.edu.

University of Ottawa, Faculty of Graduate and Postdoctoral Studies, Faculty of Engineering, Engineering Management Program, Ottawa, ON K1N 6N5, Canada. Offers engineering management (M Eng); information technology (Certificate); project management (Certificate). *Degree requirements:* For master's, thesis or alternative. *Entrance requirements:* For master's and Certificate, honors degree or equivalent, minimum B average. Electronic applications accepted.

University of St. Thomas, Graduate Studies, School of Engineering, St. Paul, MN 55105-1096. Offers manufacturing engineering and operations (MS); mechanical engineering (MS); medical device development (Certificate); regulatory science (MS); software engineering (MS); software management (MS); software systems (MSS); systems engineering (MS); technology management (MS). *Accreditation:* ABET (one or more programs are accredited). *Entrance requirements:* For master's, resume, official transcripts. Additional exam requirements/recommendations for international students: Required—TOEFL (minimum score 550 paper-based). *Application deadline:* For fall admission, 8/1 priority date for domestic students; for spring admission, 1/1 priority date for domestic students. Applications are processed on a rolling basis. Application fee: $30. Electronic applications accepted. *Expenses:* Contact institution. *Financial support:* Fellowships, research assistantships, institutionally sponsored loans and scholarships/grants available. Support available to part-time students. Financial award application deadline: 4/1; financial award applicants required to submit FAFSA. *Unit head:* Don Weinkauf, Dean, 651-962-5760, Fax: 651-962-6419, E-mail: dhweinkauf@stthomas.edu. *Application contact:* Joyce A. Taylor, Graduate Programs Coordinator, 651-962-5756, Fax: 651-962-6419, E-mail: jataylor1@stthomas.edu.

University of Southern California, Graduate School, Viterbi School of Engineering, Daniel J. Epstein Department of Industrial and Systems Engineering, Los Angeles, CA 90089. Offers digital supply chain management (MS); engineering management (MS); engineering technology communication (Graduate Certificate); health systems operations (Graduate Certificate); industrial and systems engineering (MS, PhD, Engr); manufacturing engineering (MS); operations research engineering (MS); optimization and supply chain management (Graduate Certificate); product development engineering (MS); safety systems and security (MS); systems architecting and engineering (MS, Graduate Certificate); systems safety and security (Graduate Certificate); transportation systems (Graduate Certificate); MS/MBA. Part-time and evening/weekend programs available. Postbaccalaureate distance learning degree programs offered (no on-campus study). *Faculty:* 12 full-time (2 women), 21 part-time/adjunct (2 women). *Students:* 224 full-time (69 women), 143 part-time (32 women); includes 63 minority (6 Black or African American, non-Hispanic/Latino; 35 Asian, non-Hispanic/Latino; 17 Hispanic/Latino; 5 Two or more races, non-Hispanic/Latino), 253 international. 669 applicants, 45% accepted, 155 enrolled. In 2010, 98 master's, 7 doctorates awarded. Terminal master's awarded for partial completion of doctoral program. *Degree requirements:* For master's, thesis optional; for doctorate, thesis/dissertation. *Entrance requirements:* For master's and doctorate, GRE General Test. *Application deadline:* For fall admission, 12/1 priority date for domestic students, 11/1 priority date for international students; for spring admission, 9/15 priority date for domestic and

international students. Applications are processed on a rolling basis. Application fee: $85. Electronic applications accepted. *Expenses:* Tuition: Full-time $31,240; part-time $1420 per unit. Required fees: $600. One-time fee: $35 full-time. Full-time tuition and fees vary according to degree level and program. *Financial support:* In 2010–11, fellowships with full tuition reimbursements (averaging $30,000 per year), research assistantships with full tuition reimbursements (averaging $20,000 per year), teaching assistantships with full tuition reimbursements (averaging $20,000 per year) were awarded; career-related internships or fieldwork, scholarships/grants, health care benefits, and unspecified assistantships also available. Financial award application deadline: 12/1; financial award applicants required to submit CSS PROFILE or FAFSA. *Faculty research:* Health systems, music cognition and retrieval, transportation and logistics, manufacturing and automation, engineering systems design, risk and economic analysis. Total annual research expenditures: $1 million. *Unit head:* Dr. F. Stan Settles, Chair, 213-740-4893, E-mail: isedept@usc.edu. *Application contact:* Evelyn Felina, Director of Student Affairs, 213-740-7549, E-mail: efelina@usc.edu.

University of Southern California, Graduate School, Viterbi School of Engineering, Department of Aerospace and Mechanical Engineering, Los Angeles, CA 90089. Offers aerospace and mechanical engineering: computational fluid and solid mechanics (MS); aerospace and mechanical engineering: dynamics and control (MS); aerospace engineering (MS, PhD, Engr), including aerospace engineering (PhD, Engr); green technologies (MS); mechanical engineering (MS, PhD, Engr), including mechanical engineering (PhD, Engr); product development engineering (MS). Part-time and evening/weekend programs available. Postbaccalaureate distance learning degree programs offered (no on-campus study). *Faculty:* 22 full-time (3 women), 19 part-time/adjunct (2 women). *Students:* 238 full-time (33 women), 214 part-time (30 women); includes 115 minority (10 Black or African American, non-Hispanic/Latino; 67 Asian, non-Hispanic/Latino; 32 Hispanic/Latino; 6 Two or more races, non-Hispanic/Latino), 151 international. 691 applicants, 43% accepted, 124 enrolled. In 2010, 107 master's, 11 doctorates, 1 other advanced degree awarded. Terminal master's awarded for partial completion of doctoral program. *Degree requirements:* For master's, thesis optional; for doctorate, thesis/dissertation. *Entrance requirements:* For master's, doctorate, and Engr, GRE General Test. *Application deadline:* For fall admission, 12/1 priority date for domestic and international students; for winter admission, 9/15 priority date for domestic and international students; for spring admission, 9/15 priority date for domestic and international students. Applications are processed on a rolling basis. Application fee: $85. Electronic applications accepted. *Expenses:* Tuition: Full-time $31,240; part-time $1420 per unit. Required fees: $600. One-time fee: $35 full-time. Full-time tuition and fees vary according to degree level and program. *Financial support:* In 2010–11, fellowships with full tuition reimbursements (averaging $30,000 per year), research assistantships with full tuition reimbursements (averaging $20,000 per year), teaching assistantships with full tuition reimbursements (averaging $20,000 per year) were awarded; career-related internships or fieldwork, scholarships/grants, health care benefits, and unspecified assistantships also available. Financial award application deadline: 12/1; financial award applicants required to submit CSS PROFILE or FAFSA. *Faculty research:* Mechanics and materials, aerodynamics of air/ground vehicles, gas dynamics, aerosols, astronautics and space science, geophysical and microgravity flows, planetary physics, power MEMs and MEMS vacuum pumps, heat transfer and combustion. Total annual research expenditures: $5 million. *Unit head:* Dr. Geoffrey Spedding, Chair, 213-740-5324, E-mail: ame@usc.edu. *Application contact:* Samantha Graves, Student Service Advisor, 213-740-1735, E-mail: smgraves@usc.edu.

University of South Florida, Graduate School, College of Engineering, Department of Industrial and Management Systems Engineering, Tampa, FL 33620-9951. Offers engineering management (MSEM, MSIE); engineering science (PhD); industrial engineering (MIE, MSIE, PhD). Part-time programs available. Postbaccalaureate distance learning degree programs offered (minimal on-campus study). *Faculty:* 4 full-time (1 woman), 1 part-time/adjunct (0 women). *Students:* 61 full-time (15 women), 71 part-time (19 women); includes 9 Black or African American, non-Hispanic/Latino; 3 Asian, non-Hispanic/Latino; 17 Hispanic/Latino; 1 Two or more races, non-Hispanic/Latino, 51 international. Average age 31. 125 applicants, 46% accepted, 32 enrolled. In 2010, 49 master's, 3 doctorates awarded. Terminal master's awarded for partial completion of doctoral program. *Degree requirements:* For master's, comprehensive exam, thesis (for some programs); for doctorate, comprehensive exam, thesis/dissertation, 2 tools of research as specified by dissertation committee. *Entrance requirements:* For master's, GRE General Test, minimum GPA of 3.0 in last 60 hours of coursework; for doctorate, GRE General Test, minimum GPA of 3.0 in last 60 hours of coursework or in master's program. Additional exam requirements/recommendations for international students: Required—TOEFL (minimum score 550 paper-based; 213 computer-based; 80 iBT). *Application deadline:* For fall admission, 2/15 for domestic students, 1/2 for international students; for spring admission, 10/15 for domestic students, 6/1 for international students. Application fee: $30. Electronic applications accepted. *Financial support:* In 2010–11, 21 research assistantships with partial tuition reimbursements (averaging $17,902 per year), 10 teaching assistantships with partial tuition reimbursements (averaging $29,517 per year) were awarded; tuition waivers (partial) also available. Financial award applicants required to submit FAFSA. *Faculty research:* Bio-health engineering, engineering health care systems, energy markets, nanotechnology and nanomanufacturing, transportation and logistics, innovation in education. Total annual research expenditures: $926,936. *Unit head:* Dr. Jose Zayas-Castro, Department Chair, 813-974-2269, Fax: 813-974-5953, E-mail: josezaya@usf.edu. *Application contact:* Dr. Michael Weng, Program Coordinator, 813-974-5575, Fax: 813-974-5953, E-mail: mxweng@usf.edu.

The University of Tennessee, Graduate School, College of Engineering, Department of Industrial and Information Engineering, Knoxville, TN 37966. Offers engineering management (MS); industrial engineering (MS, PhD); reliability and maintainability engineering (MS); MS/MBA. Part-time programs available. Postbaccalaureate distance learning degree programs offered (minimal on-campus study). *Faculty:* 8 full-time (1 woman), 6 part-time/adjunct (1 woman). *Students:* 40 full-time (12 women), 57 part-time (13 women); includes 9 Black or African American, non-Hispanic/Latino; 1 American Indian or Alaska Native, non-Hispanic/Latino; 6 Asian, non-Hispanic/Latino, 31 international. Average age 28. 61 applicants, 77% accepted, 11 enrolled. In 2010, 15 master's, 5 doctorates awarded. *Degree requirements:* For master's, thesis or alternative; for doctorate, comprehensive exam, thesis/dissertation. *Entrance requirements:* For master's, GRE General Test, Minimum GPA of 2.7 (US degree holders); 3.0 (International degree holders); for doctorate, GRE General Test, Minimum GPA of 3.0 (previous graduate course work). Additional exam requirements/recommendations for international students: Required—TOEFL (minimum score 550 paper-based; 213 computer-based). *Application deadline:* For fall admission, 2/1 priority date for domestic and international students; for spring admission, 6/15 for domestic and international students. Applications are processed on a rolling basis. Application fee: $35. Electronic applications accepted. *Expenses:* Tuition, state resident: full-time $7440; part-time $414 per credit hour. Tuition, nonresident: full-time $22,478; part-time $1250 per credit hour. Required fees: $922; $43 per credit hour. Tuition and fees vary according to program. *Financial support:* In 2010–11, 27 students received support, including 17 research assistantships with full tuition reimbursements available (averaging $12,372 per year), 11 teaching assistantships with full tuition reimbursements available (averaging $6,792 per year); career-related internships or fieldwork, Federal Work-Study, institutionally sponsored loans, health care benefits, and unspecified assistantships also available. Financial award application deadline: 2/1; financial award applicants required to submit FAFSA. *Faculty research:* Defense-oriented supply chain modeling; dependability and reliability of large computer networks; design of lean, reliable systems; new product development; operations research in the automotive industry. Total annual research expenditures: $839,000. *Unit head:* Dr. Rapinder Sawhney, Department Head, 865-974-3333, Fax: 865-974-0588, E-mail: sawhney@utk.edu. *Application contact:* Dr. Denise Jackson, Graduate Representative, 865-946-3248, E-mail: djackson@utk.edu.

The University of Tennessee at Chattanooga, Graduate School, College of Engineering and Computer Science, Program in Engineering Management, Chattanooga, TN 37403. Offers engineering management (MS); fundamentals of engineering management (Graduate

Certificate); power systems management (Graduate Certificate); project and value management (Graduate Certificate); quality management (Graduate Certificate). Postbaccalaureate distance learning degree programs offered (no on-campus study). *Faculty:* 4 full-time (1 woman). *Students:* 15 full-time (4 women), 77 part-time (13 women); includes 8 Black or African American, non-Hispanic/Latino; 1 Asian, non-Hispanic/Latino; 1 Hispanic/Latino, 11 international. Average age 32. 29 applicants, 100% accepted, 20 enrolled. In 2010, 23 master's, 20 other advanced degrees awarded. *Degree requirements:* For master's, thesis. *Entrance requirements:* For master's, GRE General Test, letters of recommendation; minimum undergraduate GPA of 2.5 overall or 3.0 in senior year. Additional exam requirements/recommendations for international students: Required—TOEFL (minimum score 550 paper-based; 213 computer-based; 79 iBT), IELTS (minimum score 6). *Application deadline:* For fall admission, 8/1 priority date for domestic students, 6/1 for international students; for spring admission, 12/1 priority date for domestic students, 10/1 for international students. Applications are processed on a rolling basis. Application fee: $35. Electronic applications accepted. *Financial support:* In 2010–11, 5 research assistantships with full and partial tuition reimbursements (averaging $5,500 per year) were awarded; career-related internships or fieldwork, scholarships/grants, and unspecified assistantships also available. Support available to part-time students. *Faculty research:* Plant layout design, lean manufacturing, six sigma, value management, product development. *Unit head:* Dr. Neslihan Alp, Director, 423-425-4032, Fax: 423-425-5229, E-mail: neslihan-alp@utc.edu. *Application contact:* Dr. Jerald Ainsworth, Dean of Graduate Studies, 423-425-4478, Fax: 423-425-5223, E-mail: jerald-ainsworth@utc.edu.

The University of Tennessee Space Institute, Graduate Programs, Program in Industrial Engineering (Engineering Management), Tullahoma, TN 37388-9700. Offers engineering management (MS, PhD). Part-time programs available. Postbaccalaureate distance learning degree programs offered (no on-campus study). *Faculty:* 1 full-time (0 women), 2 part-time/adjunct (1 woman). *Students:* 7 full-time (4 women), 40 part-time (12 women); includes 9 minority (6 Black or African American, non-Hispanic/Latino; 3 Asian, non-Hispanic/Latino), 2 international. 9 applicants, 89% accepted, 5 enrolled. In 2010, 10 master's awarded. *Degree requirements:* For master's, thesis (for some programs). *Entrance requirements:* Additional exam requirements/recommendations for international students: Required—TOEFL (minimum score 550 paper-based; 213 computer-based), IELTS (minimum score 6.5). *Application deadline:* For fall admission, 2/1 for international students; for spring admission, 6/15 for international students. Applications are processed on a rolling basis. Application fee: $35. Electronic applications accepted. *Financial support:* In 2010–11, 4 research assistantships with full tuition reimbursements (averaging $17,791 per year) were awarded; fellowships, career-related internships or fieldwork, Federal Work-Study, institutionally sponsored loans, health care benefits, tuition waivers (full and partial), and unspecified assistantships also available. Financial award applicants required to submit FAFSA. *Unit head:* Dr. Greg Sedrick, Degree Program Chairman, 931-393-7293, Fax: 931-393-7201, E-mail: gsedrick@utsi.edu. *Application contact:* Dee Merriman, Coordinator III, 931-393-7213, Fax: 931-393-7211, E-mail: dmerrima@utsi.edu.

The University of Texas at Arlington, Graduate School, College of Engineering, Department of Industrial and Manufacturing Systems Engineering, Program in Engineering Management, Arlington, TX 76019. Offers MS. Part-time and evening/weekend programs available. Postbaccalaureate distance learning degree programs offered (minimal on-campus study). *Students:* 31 full-time (10 women), 19 part-time (16 women); includes 9 minority (3 Black or African American, non-Hispanic/Latino; 2 Asian, non-Hispanic/Latino; 4 Hispanic/Latino), 29 international. 52 applicants, 90% accepted, 16 enrolled. In 2010, 11 master's awarded. *Degree requirements:* For master's, comprehensive exam, thesis optional. *Entrance requirements:* For master's, GRE, 3 years of full-time work experience, minimum GPA of 3.0. Additional exam requirements/recommendations for international students: Required—TOEFL (minimum score 550 paper-based; 213 computer-based). *Application deadline:* For fall admission, 6/6 for domestic students, 4/4 for international students; for spring admission, 10/15 for domestic students, 9/5 for international students. Application fee: $35 ($50 for international students). *Expenses:* Tuition, state resident: full-time $7500. Tuition, nonresident: full-time $13,080. International tuition: $13,250 full-time. *Financial support:* Fellowships, research assistantships, teaching assistantships, career-related internships or fieldwork, Federal Work-Study, institutionally sponsored loans, scholarships/grants, and unspecified assistantships available. Financial award application deadline: 6/1; financial award applicants required to submit FAFSA. *Unit head:* Dr. Donald H. Liles, Chair, 817-272-3092, Fax: 817-272-3406, E-mail: dliles@uta.edu. *Application contact:* Dr. Donald H. Liles, Chair, 817-272-3092, Fax: 817-272-3092, E-mail: dliles@uta.edu.

University of Waterloo, Graduate Studies, Faculty of Engineering, Department of Management Sciences, Waterloo, ON N2L 3G1, Canada. Offers applied operations research (MA Sc, MMS, PhD); information systems (MA Sc, MMS, PhD); management of technology (MA Sc, MMS, PhD). Part-time programs available. Postbaccalaureate distance learning degree programs offered (no on-campus study). *Degree requirements:* For master's, research paper or thesis; for doctorate, comprehensive exam, thesis/dissertation. *Entrance requirements:* For master's, GMAT or GRE, honors degree, minimum B average, resume; for doctorate, GMAT or GRE, master's degree, minimum A- average, resumé. Additional exam requirements/recommendations for international students: Required—TOEFL, TWE. *Faculty research:* Operations research, manufacturing systems, scheduling, information systems.

University of Wisconsin–Madison, Graduate School, Wisconsin School of Business, Wisconsin Full-Time MBA Program, Madison, WI 53706-1380. Offers applied security analysis (MBA); arts administration (MBA); brand and product management (MBA); corporate finance and investment banking (MBA); entrepreneurial management (MBA); marketing research (MBA); operations and technology management (MBA); real estate (MBA); risk management and insurance (MBA); strategic human resource management (MBA); strategic management in the life and engineering sciences (MBA); supply chain management (MBA). *Faculty:* 32 full-time (4 women), 17 part-time/adjunct (3 women). *Students:* 242 full-time (74 women); includes 16 Black or African American, non-Hispanic/Latino; 3 American Indian or Alaska Native, non-Hispanic/Latino; 16 Asian, non-Hispanic/Latino; 12 Hispanic/Latino, 29 international. Average age 28. 526 applicants, 32% accepted, 117 enrolled. In 2010, 106 master's awarded. *Entrance requirements:* For master's, GMAT, bachelor's or equivalent degree, 2 years of work experience, letters of recommendation. Additional exam requirements/recommendations for international students: Required—TOEFL (minimum score 600 paper-based; 250 computer-based; 100 iBT), IELTS. *Application deadline:* For fall admission, 11/4 for domestic students, 11/1 for international students; for winter admission, 2/5 for domestic and international students; for spring admission, 5/15 for domestic students, 4/5 for international students. Applications are processed on a rolling basis. Application fee: $56. Electronic applications accepted. *Expenses:* Tuition, state resident: full-time $9887.36; part-time $617.96 per credit. Tuition, nonresident: full-time $24,054; part-time $1503.40 per credit. Required fees: $67.63 per credit. Tuition and fees vary according to reciprocity agreements. *Financial support:* In 2010–11, 103 students received support, including 13 fellowships with full and partial tuition reimbursements available (averaging $15,000 per year), 53 research assistantships with full tuition reimbursements available (averaging $8,000 per year), 35 teaching assistantships with full tuition reimbursements available (averaging $11,000 per year); scholarships/grants, health care benefits, and unspecified assistantships also available. Financial award application deadline: 4/5; financial award applicants required to submit FAFSA. *Faculty research:* Market consequences of International Financial Reporting Standards (IFRS), inter-firm relationships and strategic partnerships, application of Bayesian statistical methods and applied probability models to understanding individuals' behaviors in the context of customer relationship management (CRM) applications, liquidity provision and the structure of financial markets, strategic management of global startups. *Unit head:* Prof. Kenneth A. Kavajecz, PhD, Associate Dean of Master's Programs, 608-265-3494, Fax: 608-265-4192, E-mail: kkavajecz@bus.wisc.edu. *Application contact:* Maria Reis, Assistant Director of MBA Marketing and Recruiting, 608-262-4000, Fax: 608-265-4192, E-mail: mreis@bus.wisc.edu.

University of Wisconsin–Milwaukee, Graduate School, College of Engineering and Applied Science, Program in Engineering, Milwaukee, WI 53201-0413. Offers civil engineering (MS); electrical and computer engineering (MS); energy engineering (Certificate); engineering (PhD); engineering management (MS); engineering mechanics (MS); ergonomics (Certificate); industrial and management engineering (MS); manufacturing engineering (MS); materials engineering (MS); mechanical engineering (MS); MUP/MS. Part-time programs available. *Faculty:* 50 full-time (5 women). *Students:* 152 full-time (27 women), 115 part-time (23 women); includes 13 Black or African American, non-Hispanic/Latino; 3 American Indian or Alaska Native, non-Hispanic/Latino; 6 Asian, non-Hispanic/Latino; 10 Hispanic/Latino, 25 international. Average age 31. 236 applicants, 67% accepted, 55 enrolled. In 2010, 39 master's, 19 doctorates awarded. *Degree requirements:* For master's, comprehensive exam (for some programs), thesis or alternative; for doctorate, comprehensive exam, thesis/dissertation, internship. *Entrance requirements:* For master's, GRE, minimum GPA of 2.75; for doctorate, GRE, minimum GPA of 3.5. Additional exam requirements/recommendations for international students: Required—TOEFL (minimum score 550 paper-based; 79 iBT), IELTS (minimum score 6.5). *Application deadline:* For fall admission, 1/1 priority date for domestic students; for spring admission, 9/1 for domestic students. Applications are processed on a rolling basis. Application fee: $56 ($96 for international students). *Financial support:* In 2010–11, 3 fellowships, 55 research assistantships, 77 teaching assistantships were awarded; career-related internships or fieldwork, Federal Work-Study, unspecified assistantships, and project assistantships also available. Support available to part-time students. Financial award application deadline: 4/15. Total annual research expenditures: $6.2 million. *Unit head:* David Yu, Representative, 414-229-6169, E-mail: yu@uwm.edu. *Application contact:* Betty Warras, General Information Contact, 414-229-6169, Fax: 414-229-6967, E-mail: bwarras@uwm.edu.

Valparaiso University, Graduate School, College of Business Administration, Valparaiso, IN 46383. Offers business administration (MBA); engineering management (MEM); management (Certificate); JD/MBA; MSN/MBA. *Accreditation:* AACSB. Part-time and evening/weekend programs available. Postbaccalaureate distance learning degree programs offered (minimal on-campus study). *Faculty:* 15 part-time/adjunct (4 women). *Students:* 25 full-time (11 women), 48 part-time (18 women); includes 10 minority (4 Black or African American, non-Hispanic/Latino; 1 Asian, non-Hispanic/Latino; 4 Hispanic/Latino; 1 Two or more races, non-Hispanic/Latino), 4 international. Average age 31. In 2010, 29 master's, 4 other advanced degrees awarded. *Entrance requirements:* For master's, GMAT, GRE, minimum GPA of 3.0. Additional exam requirements/recommendations for international students: Required—TOEFL (minimum score 550 paper-based; 213 computer-based; 80 iBT). *Application deadline:* Applications are processed on a rolling basis. Application fee: $30 ($50 for international students). Electronic applications accepted. *Expenses:* Contact institution. *Financial support:* Available to part-time students. Applicants required to submit FAFSA. *Unit head:* Bruce MacLean, Director of Graduate Programs in Management, 219-465-7952, Fax: 219-464-5789, E-mail: bruce.macLean@valpo.edu. *Application contact:* Cindy Scanlan, Assistant Director of Graduate Programs in Management, 219-465-7952, Fax: 219-464-5789, E-mail: cindy.scanlan@valpo.edu.

Virginia Polytechnic Institute and State University, VT Online, Blacksburg, VA 24061. Offers aerospace engineering (MS); business information systems (Graduate Certificate); career and technical education (MS); computer engineering (M Eng, MS); decision support systems (Graduate Certificate); eLearning leadership (MA); electrical engineering (M Eng, MS); engineering administration (MEA); environmental politics and policy (Graduate Certificate); foundations of political analysis (Graduate Certificate); health product risk management (Graduate Certificate); information policy and society (Graduate Certificate); information security (Graduate Certificate); instructional technology (MA); liberal arts (Graduate Certificate); life sciences: health product risk management (MS); natural resources (MNR, Graduate Certificate); networking (Graduate Certificate); nonprofit and nongovernmental organization management (Graduate Certificate); ocean engineering (MS); political science (MA); security studies (Graduate Certificate); software development (Graduate Certificate). *Expenses:* Tuition, area resident: Full-time $9399; part-time $488 per credit hour. Tuition, state resident: full-time $9399; part-time $488 per credit hour. Tuition, nonresident: full-time $17,854; part-time $957.75 per credit hour. International tuition: $17,854 full-time. Required fees: $1534. Full-time tuition and fees vary according to program.

Walden University, Graduate Programs, School of Management, Minneapolis, MN 55401. Offers accounting (MS), including cpa emphasis, professional track, self-designed; accounting and management (MS), including self-designed, strategic management; applied management and decision sciences (PhD), including accounting, engineering management, finance, general applied management and decision sciences, information systems management, knowledge management, leadership and organizational change, learning management, operations research, self-designed program in applied management and design sciences; business information management (MISM); enterprise information security (MISM); entrepreneurship (MBA, DBA); finance (MBA, DBA); global management (MS); global supply chain management (DBA); health informatics (MISM); healthcare management (MBA, MS); healthcare system improvement (MBA); human resource management (MBA, MS), including functional human resource management (MS), human resource management (MS), integrating functional and strategic human resource management (MS), organizational strategy (MS); information systems (MS); information systems management (DBA); information technology (MS), including information security, software engineering; international business (MBA, DBA); IT strategy and governance (MISM); leadership (MBA, MS, DBA), including entrepreneurship (MS), general management (MS), human resources leadership (MS), innovation and technology (MS), leader development (MS), leading sustainability (MS), project management (MS), self-designed (MS); managers as leaders (MS); managing global software and service supply chains (MISM); marketing (MBA, DBA); project management (MBA, MS); research strategies (MS); risk management (MBA); self-designed (MBA, DBA); social impact management (DBA); strategy and operations (MS); sustainable futures (MBA); sustainable management (MS); technology (MBA); technology entrepreneurship (DBA); technology management (MS). Part-time and evening/weekend programs available. Postbaccalaureate distance learning degree programs offered (minimal on-campus study). *Faculty:* 22 full-time (8 women), 291 part-time/adjunct (100 women). *Students:* 3,705 full-time (1,956 women), 976 part-time (549 women); includes 2,432 minority (2,021 Black or African American, non-Hispanic/Latino; 32 American Indian or Alaska Native, non-Hispanic/Latino; 137 Asian, non-Hispanic/Latino; 193 Hispanic/Latino; 5 Native Hawaiian or other Pacific Islander, non-Hispanic/Latino; 44 Two or more races, non-Hispanic/Latino), 302 international. Average age 40. In 2010, 658 master's, 86 doctorates awarded. *Degree requirements:* For doctorate, thesis/dissertation (for some programs), residency. *Entrance requirements:* For master's, bachelor's degree or equivalent in related field; minimum GPA of 2.5; official transcripts; goal statement; access to computer and Internet; for doctorate, master's degree or equivalent in related field; minimum GPA of 3.0; 3 years of related professional/academic experience (preferred). Additional exam requirements/recommendations for international students: Required—TOEFL (minimum score 550 paper-based; 213 computer-based), IELTS (minimum score 6.5), TOEFL, IELTS, or Michigan English Language Assessment Battery (minimum score 82). *Application deadline:* Applications are processed on a rolling basis. Application fee: $50. Electronic applications accepted. *Expenses:* Tuition: Full-time $10,274; part-time $445 per credit. Tuition and fees vary according to course load, degree level and program. *Financial support:* Fellowships, Federal Work-Study, scholarships/grants, unspecified assistantships, and family tuition reduction, active duty/veteran tuition reduction, group tuition reduction, interest-free payment plans available. Support available to part-time students. Financial award applicants required to submit FAFSA. *Unit head:* Dr. William Schulz, Associate Dean, 800-925-3368. *Application contact:* Jennifer Hall, Vice President of Enrollment Management, 866-4-WALDEN, E-mail: info@waldenu.edu.

Washington State University Spokane, Graduate Programs, Program in Engineering Management, Spokane, WA 99210. Offers METM. *Faculty:* 6. *Students:* 19 full-time (7 women). *Degree requirements:* For master's, comprehensive exam (for some programs), thesis (for some programs), project. *Entrance requirements:* For master's, GMAT, minimum GPA of 3.0, 3 letters of recommendation, resume. *Application deadline:* For fall admission, 1/10 priority date for domestic students, 1/10 for international students; for spring admission, 7/1 priority date for domestic students, 7/1 for international students. Application fee: $50. *Financial support:* Application deadline: 4/1. *Faculty research:* Operations research for decision analysis quality

Engineering Management

Washington State University Spokane (continued)
control and liability, analytical techniques to formulating decisions. *Unit head:* Dr. Hal Rumsey, Program Director, 509-358-7936, E-mail: rumsey@wsu.edu. *Application contact:* Graduate School Admissions, 800-GRADWSU, Fax: 509-335-1949, E-mail: gradsch@wsu.edu.

Wayne State University, College of Engineering, Department of Industrial and Manufacturing Engineering, Program in Engineering Management, Detroit, MI 48202. Offers MS. *Faculty:* 9 full-time (0 women), 4 part-time/adjunct (0 women). *Students:* 19 full-time (5 women), 36 part-time (10 women); includes 14 minority (7 Black or African American, non-Hispanic/Latino; 6 Asian, non-Hispanic/Latino; 1 Hispanic/Latino), 2 international. Average age 36. 12 applicants, 42% accepted, 3 enrolled. In 2010, 16 master's awarded. *Degree requirements:* For master's, thesis optional. *Entrance requirements:* For master's, GRE (if baccalaureate if not from an ABET accredited institution), minimum undergraduate GPA of 2.8; 3 years experience as an engineer or technical leader. Additional exam requirements/recommendations for international students: Required—TOEFL (minimum score 550 paper-based; 213 computer-based); Recommended—TWE (minimum score 6). *Application deadline:* For fall admission, 7/1 priority date for domestic students, 6/1 for international students; for winter admission, 10/1 for international students; for spring admission, 3/15 for domestic students, 2/1 for international students. Applications are processed on a rolling basis. Application fee: $30 ($50 for international students). Electronic applications accepted. *Expenses:* Tuition, state resident: full-time $7662; part-time $478.85 per credit hour. Tuition, nonresident: full-time $16,920; part-time $1057.55 per credit hour. Required fees: $571.20; $35.70 per credit hour. $188.05 per semester. Tuition and fees vary according to course load and program. *Financial support:* In 2010–11, 20 students received support; fellowships, research assistantships, teaching assistantships, career-related internships or fieldwork and tuition waivers (full) available. *Faculty research:* Technology and change management, quality/reliability, manufacturing systems/infrastructure. *Unit head:* Kenneth Chelst, Chair, 313-577-3857, Fax: 313-577-8833, E-mail: aa1276@wayne.edu. *Application contact:* Ratna Chinnam, Graduate Director, 313-577-7846, E-mail: r_chinnam@wayne.edu.

Webster University, College of Arts and Sciences, Department of Biological Sciences, Program in Professional Science Management and Leadership, St. Louis, MO 63119-3194. Offers MA. *Entrance requirements:* Additional exam requirements/recommendations for international students: Required—TOEFL. *Expenses:* Tuition: Part-time $585 per credit hour. Tuition and fees vary according to degree level, campus/location and program.

Western Michigan University, Graduate College, College of Engineering and Applied Sciences, Department of Industrial and Manufacturing Engineering, Program in Engineering Management, Kalamazoo, MI 49008. Offers MS. *Entrance requirements:* For master's, minimum GPA of 3.0.

Western New England University, School of Engineering, Master's Program in Engineering Management, Springfield, MA 01119. Offers business and engineering information systems (MSEM); general engineering management (MSEM); production and manufacturing systems (MSEM); quality engineering (MSEM). Evening/weekend programs available. Postbaccalaureate distance learning degree programs offered (no on-campus study). *Degree requirements:* For master's, thesis optional. *Expenses:* Tuition: Full-time $35,582.

Western New England University, School of Engineering, PhD Program in Engineering Management, Springfield, MA 01119. Offers PhD. Evening/weekend programs available. *Expenses:* Tuition: Full-time $35,582.

Widener University, Graduate Programs in Engineering, Program in Engineering Management, Chester, PA 19013-5792. Offers M Eng. Part-time and evening/weekend programs available. *Students:* 2 full-time (0 women), 5 part-time (1 woman); includes 2 Black or African American, non-Hispanic/Latino, 3 international. Average age 26. In 2010, 1 master's awarded. *Degree requirements:* For master's, thesis optional. *Application deadline:* For fall admission, 8/1 priority date for domestic students; for spring admission, 12/1 for domestic students. Applications are processed on a rolling basis. Application fee: $25 ($300 for international students). *Financial support:* Application deadline: 3/15. *Unit head:* Nora J. Kogut, Assistant Dean, 610-499-4037, Fax: 610-499-4059, E-mail: njkogut@widener.edu. *Application contact:* Christine M. Weist, Assistant to Associate Provost for Graduate Studies, 610-499-4351, Fax: 610-499-4277, E-mail: christine.m.weist@widener.edu.

Wilkes University, College of Graduate and Professional Studies, College of Science and Engineering, Division of Engineering and Physics, Wilkes-Barre, PA 18766-0002. Offers electrical engineering (MSEE); engineering management (MS); mechanical engineering (MS). Part-time programs available. *Students:* 13 full-time (1 woman), 15 part-time (2 women); includes 1 Asian, non-Hispanic/Latino; 1 Two or more races, non-Hispanic/Latino, 8 international. Average age 28. In 2010, 25 master's awarded. *Entrance requirements:* For master's, GRE General Test. Additional exam requirements/recommendations for international students: Required—TOEFL (minimum score 550 paper-based; 213 computer-based; 79 iBT). *Application deadline:* Applications are processed on a rolling basis. Application fee: $45 ($65 for international students). Electronic applications accepted. Tuition and fees vary according to degree level and program. *Financial support:* Federal Work-Study and unspecified assistantships available. Financial award application deadline: 3/1; financial award applicants required to submit FAFSA. *Unit head:* Dr. Rodney Ridley, Director, 570-408-4824, Fax: 570-408-7846, E-mail: rodney.ridley@wilkes.edu. *Application contact:* Kathleen Houlihan, Director of Graduate Studies, 570-408-3235, Fax: 570-408-7846, E-mail: kathleen.houlihan@wilkes.edu.

Ergonomics and Human Factors

Arizona State University, College of Technology and Innovation, Department of Technology Management, Mesa, AZ 85212. Offers technology (aviation management and human factors) (MS); technology (environmental technology management) (MS); technology (global technology and development) (MS); technology (graphic information technology) (MS); technology (management of technology) (MS). Part-time and evening/weekend programs available. Postbaccalaureate distance learning degree programs offered (minimal on-campus study). *Faculty:* 13 full-time (3 women), 6 part-time/adjunct (2 women). *Students:* 56 full-time (16 women), 212 part-time (95 women); includes 61 minority (14 Black or African American, non-Hispanic/Latino; 8 American Indian or Alaska Native, non-Hispanic/Latino; 14 Asian, non-Hispanic/Latino; 21 Hispanic/Latino; 4 Two or more races, non-Hispanic/Latino), 27 international. Average age 36. 124 applicants, 77% accepted, 58 enrolled. In 2010, 35 master's awarded. *Degree requirements:* For master's, thesis or applied project and oral defense; interactive Program of Study (iPOS) submitted before completing 50 percent of required credit hours. *Entrance requirements:* For master's, GRE, minimum GPA of 3.0 or equivalent in last 2 years of work leading to bachelor's degree. Additional exam requirements/recommendations for international students: Required—TOEFL, IELTS, or Pearson Test of English. *Application deadline:* For fall admission, 7/1 for domestic and international students; for spring admission, 12/1 for domestic and international students. Applications are processed on a rolling basis. Application fee: $70 ($90 for international students). Electronic applications accepted. *Expenses:* Tuition, state resident: full-time $8510; part-time $608 per credit. Tuition, nonresident: full-time $16,542; part-time $919 per credit. Required fees: $339; $110 per credit. Part-time tuition and fees vary according to course load. *Financial support:* In 2010–11, 3 research assistantships with full and partial tuition reimbursements (averaging $12,729 per year), 1 teaching assistantship with full and partial tuition reimbursement (averaging $14,125 per year) were awarded; career-related internships or fieldwork, Federal Work-Study, scholarships/grants, health care benefits, tuition waivers (full and partial), and unspecified assistantships also available. Support available to part-time students. Financial award application deadline: 3/1; financial award applicants required to submit FAFSA. *Faculty research:* Digital imaging, digital publishing, Internet development/e-commerce, information aviation human factors, pilot selection, databases, multimedia, commercial digital photography, digital workflow, computer graphics modeling and animation, information design, sociotechnology, visual and technical literacy, environmental management, quality management, project management, industrial ethics, hazardous materials, environmental chemistry. Total annual research expenditures: $755,686. *Unit head:* Dr. Mitzi Montoya, Vice Provost and Dean, 480-727-1955, Fax: 480-727-1538, E-mail: mitzi.montoya@asu.edu. *Application contact:* Graduate Admissions, 480-965-6113.

Bentley University, McCallum Graduate School of Business, Program in Human Factors in Information Design, Waltham, MA 02452-4705. Offers MSHFID. Part-time and evening/weekend programs available. Postbaccalaureate distance learning degree programs offered (minimal on-campus study). *Faculty:* 74 full-time (22 women), 21 part-time/adjunct (5 women). *Students:* 7 full-time (5 women), 81 part-time (46 women); includes 16 minority (2 Black or African American, non-Hispanic/Latino; 1 American Indian or Alaska Native, non-Hispanic/Latino; 6 Asian, non-Hispanic/Latino; 5 Hispanic/Latino; 2 Two or more races, non-Hispanic/Latino), 3 international. Average age 34. 53 applicants, 79% accepted, 29 enrolled. *Entrance requirements:* For master's, GMAT or GRE General Test. Additional exam requirements/recommendations for international students: Required—TOEFL (minimum score 600 paper-based; 250 computer-based; 100 iBT) or IELTS (minimum score 7). *Application deadline:* For fall admission, 12/1 priority date for domestic and international students; for spring admission, 10/1 priority date for domestic and international students. Applications are processed on a rolling basis. Application fee: $50. Electronic applications accepted. *Expenses:* Tuition: Full-time $28,224; part-time $1176 per credit. Required fees: $404. Part-time tuition and fees vary according to course load. *Financial support:* In 2010–11, 13 students received support. Scholarships/grants and unspecified assistantships available. Financial award application deadline: 6/1; financial award applicants required to submit CSS PROFILE or FAFSA. *Faculty research:* Usability engineering, ethnography, human-computer interaction, project management, user experience. *Unit head:* Dr. William M. Gribbons, Director, 781-891-2926, E-mail: wgribbons@bentley.edu. *Application contact:* Sharon Hill, Director of Graduate Admissions, 781-891-2108, Fax: 781-891-2464, E-mail: bentleygraduateadmissions@bentley.edu.

California State University, Long Beach, Graduate Studies, College of Liberal Arts, Department of Psychology, Long Beach, CA 90840. Offers human factors (MS); industrial/organizational psychology (MS); psychology (MA). Part-time and evening/weekend programs available. *Faculty:* 18 full-time (5 women), 1 part-time/adjunct (0 women). *Students:* 43 full-time (31 women), 27 part-time (17 women); includes 4 Black or African American, non-Hispanic/Latino; 10 Asian, non-Hispanic/Latino; 11 Hispanic/Latino, 2 international. Average age 27. 203 applicants, 16% accepted, 30 enrolled. In 2010, 19 master's awarded. *Degree requirements:* For master's, comprehensive exam, thesis. *Entrance requirements:* For master's, GRE General Test, GRE Subject Test. *Application deadline:* For fall admission, 3/1 for domestic students. Applications are processed on a rolling basis. Application fee: $55. Electronic applications accepted. *Financial support:* Federal Work-Study, institutionally sponsored loans, and scholarships/grants available. Financial award application deadline: 3/2. *Faculty research:* Physiological psychology, social and personality psychology, community-clinical psychology, industrial-organizational psychology, developmental psychology. *Unit head:* Dr. Kenneth Green, Chair, 562-985-5049, Fax: 562-985-8004, E-mail: kgreen@csulb.edu. *Application contact:* Dr. Kenneth Green, Chair, 562-985-5049, Fax: 562-985-8004, E-mail: kgreen@csulb.edu.

California State University, Northridge, Graduate Studies, College of Social and Behavioral Sciences, Department of Psychology, Northridge, CA 91330. Offers clinical psychology (MA); general-experimental psychology (MA); human factors and applied experimental psychology (MA). *Degree requirements:* For master's, thesis. *Entrance requirements:* For master's, GRE General Test, GRE Subject Test, minimum GPA of 3.0, letters of recommendation. Additional exam requirements/recommendations for international students: Required—TOEFL.

The Catholic University of America, School of Arts and Sciences, Department of Psychology, Washington, DC 20064. Offers applied experimental psychology (PhD); clinical psychology (PhD); general psychology (MA); human factors (MA); MA/JD. *Accreditation:* APA (one or more programs are accredited). Part-time programs available. *Faculty:* 12 full-time (6 women), 7 part-time/adjunct (2 women). *Students:* 39 full-time (25 women), 31 part-time (28 women); includes 6 Black or African American, non-Hispanic/Latino; 4 Asian, non-Hispanic/Latino; 4 Hispanic/Latino, 1 international. Average age 29. 229 applicants, 22% accepted, 17 enrolled. In 2010, 22 master's, 8 doctorates awarded. *Degree requirements:* For master's, comprehensive exam, thesis (for some programs); for doctorate, comprehensive exam, thesis/dissertation. *Entrance requirements:* For master's, GRE General Test, statement of purpose, official copies of academic transcripts, three letters of recommendation; for doctorate, GRE General Test, GRE Subject Test, statement of purpose, official copies of academic transcripts, three letters of recommendation. Additional exam requirements/recommendations for international students: Required—TOEFL (minimum score 580 paper-based; 237 computer-based). *Application deadline:* For fall admission, 8/1 priority date for domestic students, 7/15 for international students; for spring admission, 12/1 priority date for domestic students, 10/15 for international students. Applications are processed on a rolling basis. Application fee: $55. Electronic applications accepted. *Expenses:* Tuition: Full-time $33,580; part-time $1315 per credit hour. Required fees: $80; $40 per semester hour. One-time fee: $425. *Financial support:* Fellowships, research assistantships, teaching assistantships, Federal Work-Study, scholarships/grants, tuition waivers (full and partial), and unspecified assistantships available. Financial award application deadline: 2/1; financial award applicants required to submit FAFSA. *Faculty research:* Clinical psychology, applied cognitive science, psychopathology, cognitive neuroscience, psychotherapy. Total annual research expenditures: $409,988. *Unit head:* Dr. Marc M. Sebrechts, Chair, 202-319-5750, Fax: 202-319-6263, E-mail: sebrechts@cua.edu. *Application contact:* Andrew Woodall, Director of Graduate Admissions, 202-319-5057, Fax: 202-319-6533, E-mail: cua-admissions@cua.edu.

Clemson University, Graduate School, College of Business and Behavioral Science, Department of Psychology, Program in Human Factors Psychology, Clemson, SC 29634. Offers PhD. *Students:* 14 full-time (8 women), 1 part-time (0 women); includes 1 Two or more races, non-Hispanic/Latino. Average age 28. 17 applicants, 35% accepted, 4 enrolled. In 2010, 6 doctorates awarded. *Degree requirements:* For doctorate, thesis/dissertation. *Entrance requirements:* For doctorate, GRE General Test. Additional exam requirements/recommendations for international students: Required—TOEFL. *Application deadline:* For fall admission, 1/15 for domestic students. Applications are processed on a rolling basis. Application fee: $70 ($80 for international students). Electronic applications accepted. *Expenses:* Contact institution. *Financial support:* In 2010–11, 14 students received support, including 3 fellowships with full and partial tuition reimbursements available (averaging $7,167 per year), 5 research assistantships with partial tuition reimbursements available (averaging $13,400 per year), 9 teaching assistantships with partial tuition reimbursements available (averaging $12,000 per year); career-related internships or fieldwork, institutionally sponsored loans, scholarships/grants, health care benefits, and unspecified assistantships also available. Support available to part-time students. *Faculty research:* Transportation safety, human factors in health care, human-computer interaction, ergonomics, vision and visual performance. *Unit head:* Dr. Patrick Raymark, Chair, 864-656-4715, Fax: 864-656-0358, E-mail: praymar@clemson.edu. *Application contact:* Dr. Lee Gugerty, 864-656-4467, Fax: 864-656-0358, E-mail: gugerty@clemson.edu.

Cornell University, Graduate School, Graduate Fields of Human Ecology, Field of Design and Environmental Analysis, Ithaca, NY 14853. Offers applied research in human-environment relations (MS); facilities planning and management (MS); housing and design (MS); human factors and ergonomics (MS); human-environment relations (MS); interior design (MA, MPS). *Faculty:* 15 full-time (6 women). *Students:* 27 full-time (22 women); includes 2 Black or African American, non-Hispanic/Latino; 6 Asian, non-Hispanic/Latino, 7 international. Average age 25. 83 applicants, 27% accepted, 21 enrolled. In 2010, 29 master's awarded. *Degree requirements:* For master's, thesis. *Entrance requirements:* For master's, GRE General Test, portfolio or slides of recent work; bachelor's degree in interior design, architecture or related design discipline; 2 letters of recommendation. Additional exam requirements/recommendations for international students: Required—TOEFL (minimum score 600 paper-based; 250 computer-based; 105 iBT). *Application deadline:* For fall admission, 2/1 priority date for domestic students. Application fee: $70. Electronic applications accepted. *Expenses:* Tuition: Full-time $29,500. Required fees: $76. Tuition and fees vary according to degree level and program. *Financial support:* In 2010–11, 13 students received support, including 3 fellowships with full tuition reimbursements available, 2 research assistantships with full tuition reimbursements available, 13 teaching assistantships with full tuition reimbursements available; institutionally sponsored loans, scholarships/grants, health care benefits, tuition waivers (full and partial), and unspecified assistantships also available. Financial award applicants required to submit FAFSA. *Faculty research:* Facility planning and management, environmental psychology, housing, interior design, ergonomics and human factors. *Unit head:* Director of Graduate Studies, 607-255-2168, Fax: 607-255-0305. *Application contact:* Graduate Field Assistant, 607-255-2168, Fax: 607-255-0305, E-mail: deagrad@cornell.edu.

Embry-Riddle Aeronautical University–Daytona, Daytona Beach Campus Graduate Program, Department of Human Factors and Systems, Daytona Beach, FL 32114-3900. Offers human factors engineering (MSHFS); systems engineering (MSHFS). Part-time and evening/weekend programs available. *Faculty:* 6 full-time (2 women). *Students:* 40 full-time (15 women), 15 part-time (8 women); includes 13 minority (3 Black or African American, non-Hispanic/Latino; 1 American Indian or Alaska Native, non-Hispanic/Latino; 7 Hispanic/Latino; 2 Two or more races, non-Hispanic/Latino), 4 international. Average age 26. 38 applicants, 71% accepted, 22 enrolled. In 2010, 4 master's awarded. *Degree requirements:* For master's, thesis, practicum, qualifying oral exam. *Entrance requirements:* For master's, minimum GPA of 2.5. Additional exam requirements/recommendations for international students: Required—TOEFL (minimum score 550 paper-based; 213 computer-based; 79 iBT). *Application deadline:* For fall admission, 8/1 priority date for domestic students; for spring admission, 12/1 priority date for domestic students. Applications are processed on a rolling basis. Application fee: $50. *Expenses:* Tuition: Full-time $14,040; part-time $1170 per credit hour. *Financial support:* In 2010–11, 20 students received support, including 5 research assistantships with full and partial tuition reimbursements available (averaging $4,504 per year), 2 teaching assistantships with full and partial tuition reimbursements available (averaging $4,504 per year); career-related internships or fieldwork and unspecified assistantships also available. Financial award application deadline: 4/15; financial award applicants required to submit FAFSA. *Unit head:* Dr. Shawn Doherty, Graduate Program Coordinator, 386-226-6249, E-mail: shawn.doherty@erau.edu. *Application contact:* Keith Deaton, Director, International and Graduate Admissions, 800-388-3728, Fax: 386-226-7070, E-mail: graduate.admissions@erau.edu.

Florida Institute of Technology, Graduate Programs, College of Aeronautics, Melbourne, FL 32901-6975. Offers airport development and management (MSA); applied aviation safety option (MSA); aviation human factors (MS); human factors in aeronautics (MS). Part-time and evening/weekend programs available. *Faculty:* 9 full-time (0 women). *Students:* 23 full-time (3 women), 11 part-time (3 women); includes 3 minority (2 Asian, non-Hispanic/Latino; 1 Hispanic/Latino), 15 international. Average age 26. 36 applicants, 53% accepted, 9 enrolled. In 2010, 15 master's awarded. *Degree requirements:* For master's, thesis (for some programs). *Entrance requirements:* For master's, GRE, minimum GPA of 3.0, 3 letters of recommendation, resume, statement of objectives. Additional exam requirements/recommendations for international students: Required—TOEFL (minimum score 550 paper-based; 213 computer-based; 79 iBT). *Application deadline:* For fall admission, 4/1 for international students; for spring admission, 9/30 for international students. Applications are processed on a rolling basis. Application fee: $50. Electronic applications accepted. *Expenses:* Tuition: Part-time $1040 per credit hour. Tuition and fees vary according to campus/location. *Financial support:* Career-related internships or fieldwork, institutionally sponsored loans, tuition waivers (partial), and tuition remissions available. Support available to part-time students. Financial award application deadline: 3/1; financial award applicants required to submit FAFSA. *Faculty research:* Aircraft cockpit design, medical human factors, operating room human factors, hypobaric chamber operations and effects, aviation professional education. Total annual research expenditures: $98,763. *Unit head:* Dr. Winston E. Scott, Dean, 321-674-8971, Fax: 321-674-7368, E-mail: wscott@fit.edu. *Application contact:* Cheryl A. Brown, Associate Director of Graduate Admissions, 321-674-7581, Fax: 321-723-9468, E-mail: cbrown@fit.edu.

Georgia Institute of Technology, Graduate Studies and Research, College of Computing, Atlanta, GA 30332-0001. Offers algorithms, combinatorics, and optimization (PhD); computational science and engineering (MS, PhD); computer science (MS, MSCS, PhD); human computer interaction (MSHCI); human-centered computing (PhD); information security (MS). Part-time programs available. Postbaccalaureate distance learning degree programs offered. Terminal master's awarded for partial completion of doctoral program. *Degree requirements:* For master's, thesis optional; for doctorate, comprehensive exam, thesis/dissertation. *Entrance requirements:* For master's, GRE General Test, GRE Subject Test, minimum GPA of 3.0; for doctorate, GRE General Test, GRE Subject Test, minimum GPA of 3.3. Additional exam requirements/recommendations for international students: Required—TOEFL. *Faculty research:* Computer systems, graphics, intelligent systems and artificial intelligence, networks and telecommunications, software engineering.

Georgia Institute of Technology, Graduate Studies and Research, College of Sciences, School of Psychology, Atlanta, GA 30332-0001. Offers human computer interaction (MSHCI); psychology (MS, MS Psy, PhD), including engineering psychology (PhD), experimental psychology (PhD), industrial/organizational psychology (PhD). Terminal master's awarded for partial completion of doctoral program. *Degree requirements:* For master's, thesis; for doctorate, thesis/dissertation. *Entrance requirements:* For master's and doctorate, GRE General Test, GRE Subject Test, minimum GPA of 3.0. Additional exam requirements/recommendations for international students: Required—TOEFL. Electronic applications accepted. *Faculty research:* Experimental, industrial-organizational, and engineering psychology; cognitive aging and processes; leadership; human factors.

Indiana University Bloomington, School of Health, Physical Education and Recreation, Department of Kinesiology, Bloomington, IN 47405-7000. Offers adapted physical education (MS); applied sport science (MS); athletic administration/sport management (MS); athletic training (MS); biomechanics (MS); ergonomics (MS); exercise physiology (MS); fitness management (MS); human performance (PhD); motor learning/control (MS). Part-time programs available. *Faculty:* 28 full-time (11 women). *Students:* 142 full-time (63 women), 29 part-time (11 women); includes 21 minority (12 Black or African American, non-Hispanic/Latino; 1 American Indian or Alaska Native, non-Hispanic/Latino; 1 Asian, non-Hispanic/Latino; 5 Hispanic/Latino; 2 Two or more races, non-Hispanic/Latino), 28 international. Average age 28. 193 applicants, 59% accepted, 56 enrolled. In 2010, 57 master's, 8 doctorates awarded. Terminal master's awarded for partial completion of doctoral program. *Degree requirements:* For master's, thesis optional; for doctorate, variable foreign language requirement, thesis/dissertation. *Entrance requirements:* For master's, GRE General Test, minimum GPA of 2.8; for doctorate, GRE General Test, minimum graduate GPA of 3.5, undergraduate 3.0. *Application deadline:* For fall admission, 1/1 for international students; for spring admission, 9/1 for international students. Applications are processed on a rolling basis. Application fee: $55 ($65 for international students). *Financial support:* Fellowships, research assistantships with full tuition reimbursements, teaching assistantships with full tuition reimbursements, career-related internships or fieldwork, Federal Work-Study, institutionally sponsored loans, scholarships/grants, tuition waivers (partial), and fee remissions available. Financial award application deadline: 3/1. *Faculty research:* Exercise physiology and biochemistry, sports biomechanics, human motor control, adaptation of fitness and exercise to special populations. *Unit head:* Dr. Donetta Cothran, Chairperson, 812-855-3114. *Application contact:* Program Office, 812-855-5523, Fax: 812-855-9417, E-mail: kines@indiana.edu.

Missouri Western State University, Program in Applied Science, St. Joseph, MO 64507-2294. Offers chemistry (MAS); engineering technology management (MAS); human factors and usability testing (MAS); information technology management (MAS). *Expenses:* Tuition, state resident: full-time $5544; part-time $308 per credit hour. Tuition, nonresident: full-time $10,206; part-time $567 per credit hour. Required fees: $30 per semester. One-time fee: $45 full-time.

New York University, Graduate School of Arts and Science, Department of Environmental Medicine, New York, NY 10012-1019. Offers environmental health sciences (MS, PhD), including biostatistics (PhD), environmental hygiene (MS), epidemiology (PhD), ergonomics and biomechanics (PhD), exposure assessment and health effects (PhD), molecular toxicology/carcinogenesis (PhD), toxicology. Part-time programs available. *Faculty:* 26 full-time (7 women). *Students:* 53 full-time (38 women), 10 part-time (3 women); includes 3 Black or African American, non-Hispanic/Latino; 4 Asian, non-Hispanic/Latino; 5 Hispanic/Latino, 23 international. Average age 30. 60 applicants, 48% accepted, 14 enrolled. In 2010, 8 master's, 5 doctorates awarded. Terminal master's awarded for partial completion of doctoral program. *Degree requirements:* For master's, thesis or alternative; for doctorate, one foreign language, thesis/dissertation, oral and written exams. *Entrance requirements:* For master's and doctorate, GRE General Test, GRE Subject Test, minimum GPA of 3.0; bachelor's degree in biological, physical, or engineering science. Additional exam requirements/recommendations for international students: Required—TOEFL. *Application deadline:* For fall admission, 12/15 for domestic students. Application fee: $90. *Financial support:* Fellowships with tuition reimbursements, teaching assistantships with tuition reimbursements, career-related internships or fieldwork, Federal Work-Study, institutionally sponsored loans, and health care benefits available. Financial award application deadline: 12/15; financial award applicants required to submit FAFSA. *Unit head:* Dr. Max Costa, Chair, 845-731-3661, Fax: 845-351-4510, E-mail: ehs@env.med.nyu.edu. *Application contact:* Dr. Jerome J. Solomon, Director of Graduate Studies, 845-731-3661, Fax: 845-351-4510, E-mail: ehs@env.med.nyu.edu.

North Carolina State University, Graduate School, College of Humanities and Social Sciences, Department of Psychology, Raleigh, NC 27695. Offers developmental psychology (PhD); ergonomics and experimental psychology (PhD); industrial/organizational psychology (PhD); psychology in the public interest (PhD); school psychology (PhD). *Accreditation:* APA. *Degree requirements:* For doctorate, comprehensive exam, thesis/dissertation. *Entrance requirements:* For doctorate, GRE General Test, GRE Subject Test (industrial/organizational psychology), MAT (recommended), minimum GPA of 3.0 in major. Electronic applications accepted. *Faculty research:* Cognitive and social development (human factors, families, the workplace, community issues and health, aging).

Old Dominion University, College of Sciences, Doctoral Program in Psychology, Norfolk, VA 23529. Offers applied experimental psychology (PhD); human factors psychology (PhD); industrial/organizational psychology (PhD). *Faculty:* 21 full-time (9 women). *Students:* 32 full-time (21 women), 12 part-time (8 women); includes 2 minority (1 Black or African American, non-Hispanic/Latino; 1 Hispanic/Latino), 4 international. Average age 29. 59 applicants, 24% accepted, 12 enrolled. In 2010, 1 doctorate awarded. *Degree requirements:* For doctorate, thesis/dissertation, candidacy exam. *Entrance requirements:* For doctorate, GRE General Test, GRE Subject Test, 3 recommendation letters. Additional exam requirements/recommendations for international students: Required—TOEFL (minimum score 550 paper-based). *Application deadline:* For winter admission, 1/5 for domestic and international students. Application fee: $50. Electronic applications accepted. *Expenses:* Tuition, state resident: full-time $8592; part-time $358 per credit. Tuition, nonresident: full-time $21,672; part-time $903 per credit. Required fees: $119 per semester. One-time fee: $50. *Financial support:* In 2010–11, 33 students received support, including 4 fellowships with full tuition reimbursements available (averaging $18,000 per year), 4 research assistantships with full tuition reimbursements available (averaging $12,000 per year), 25 teaching assistantships with full tuition reimbursements available (averaging $12,000 per year). Financial award application deadline: 1/15. *Faculty research:* Human factors, industrial psychology, organizational psychology, applied experimental (health, developmental, quantitative). Total annual research expenditures: $978,563. *Unit head:* Dr. Bryan E. Porter, Graduate Program Director, 757-683-4458, Fax: 757-683-5087, E-mail: bporter@odu.edu. *Application contact:* Dr. Bryan E. Porter, Graduate Program Director, 757-683-4458, Fax: 757-683-5087, E-mail: bporter@odu.edu.

Tufts University, School of Engineering, Department of Mechanical Engineering, Medford, MA 02155. Offers human factors (MS); mechanical engineering (ME, MS, PhD). Part-time programs available. Terminal master's awarded for partial completion of doctoral program. *Degree requirements:* For master's, thesis; for doctorate, thesis/dissertation. *Entrance requirements:* For master's and doctorate, GRE General Test. Additional exam requirements/recommendations for international students: Required—TOEFL (minimum score 550 paper-based; 213 computer-based; 80 iBT). Electronic applications accepted. *Expenses:* Tuition: Full-time $39,624; part-time $3962 per course. Required fees: $40 per year. Full-time tuition and fees vary according to degree level, program and student level. Part-time tuition and fees vary according to course load.

Université de Montréal, Faculty of Medicine, Programs in Ergonomics, Montréal, QC H3C 3J7, Canada. Offers occupational therapy (DESS). Program offered jointly with École Polytechnique de Montréal.

Université du Québec à Montréal, Graduate Programs, Program in Ergonomics in Occupational Health and Safety, Montréal, QC H3C 3P8, Canada. Offers Diploma. Part-time programs available. *Entrance requirements:* For degree, appropriate bachelor's degree or equivalent, proficiency in French.

The University of Alabama, Graduate School, College of Human Environmental Sciences, Program in Human Environmental Science, Tuscaloosa, AL 35487. Offers family financial planning and counseling (MS); interactive technology (MS); quality management (MS); restaurant and meeting management (MS); rural community health (MS); sport management (MS). *Faculty:* 1 full-time (0 women). *Students:* 67 full-time (39 women), 86 part-time (52 women); includes 47 minority (40 Black or African American, non-Hispanic/Latino; 3 Hispanic/Latino; 4 Two or more races, non-Hispanic/Latino), 1 international. Average age 34. 112 applicants, 78% accepted, 64 enrolled. In 2010, 64 master's awarded. *Degree requirements:* For master's, comprehensive exam. *Entrance requirements:* For master's, GRE (for some specializations), minimum GPA of 3.0. Additional exam requirements/recommendations for international students: Required—TOEFL. *Application deadline:* Applications are processed on a rolling basis. Application fee: $50 ($60 for international students). Electronic applications accepted. *Expenses:* Tuition, state resident: full-time $7900. Tuition, nonresident: full-time $20,500. *Faculty research:* Hospitality management, sports medicine education, technology and education. *Unit head:* Dr. Milla D. Boschung, Dean, 205-348-6250, Fax: 205-348-1786, E-mail: mboschun@ches.ua.edu. *Application contact:* Dr. Stuart Usdan, Associate Dean, 205-348-6150, Fax: 205-348-3789, E-mail: susdan@ches.ua.edu.

Ergonomics and Human Factors

University of Central Florida, College of Engineering and Computer Science, Department of Industrial Engineering and Management Systems, Orlando, FL 32816. Offers applied operations research (Certificate); design for usability (Certificate); industrial engineering (MSIE, PhD); industrial engineering and management systems (MS); industrial ergonomics and safety (Certificate); project engineering (Certificate); quality assurance (Certificate); systems engineering (Certificate); systems simulation for engineers (Certificate); training simulation (Certificate). Part-time and evening/weekend programs available. *Faculty:* 17 full-time (4 women), 6 part-time/adjunct (1 woman). *Students:* 112 full-time (31 women), 171 part-time (66 women); includes 79 minority (27 Black or African American, non-Hispanic/Latino; 17 Asian, non-Hispanic/Latino; 32 Hispanic/Latino; 1 Native Hawaiian or other Pacific Islander, non-Hispanic/Latino; 2 Two or more races, non-Hispanic/Latino), 72 international. Average age 33. 210 applicants, 74% accepted, 82 enrolled. In 2010, 65 master's, 7 doctorates, 34 other advanced degrees awarded. *Degree requirements:* For master's, thesis; for doctorate, thesis/dissertation, departmental qualifying exam, candidacy exam. *Entrance requirements:* For master's, GRE General Test, minimum GPA of 3.0 in last 60 hours of course work; for doctorate, minimum GPA of 3.5 in last 60 hours of course work. Additional exam requirements/recommendations for international students: Required—TOEFL. *Application deadline:* For fall admission, 7/15 priority date for domestic students; for spring admission, 12/1 priority date for domestic students. Application fee: $30. Electronic applications accepted. *Expenses:* Tuition, state resident: part-time $256.56 per credit hour. Tuition, nonresident: part-time $1011.52 per credit hour. Part-time tuition and fees vary according to program. *Financial support:* In 2010–11, 24 students received support, including 85 fellowships with partial tuition reimbursements available (averaging $7,300 per year), 19 research assistantships with partial tuition reimbursements available (averaging $8,500 per year), 6 teaching assistantships with partial tuition reimbursements available (averaging $12,200 per year); career-related internships or fieldwork, Federal Work-Study, institutionally sponsored loans, tuition waivers (partial), and unspecified assistantships also available. Financial award application deadline: 3/1; financial award applicants required to submit FAFSA. *Unit head:* Dr. Waldemar Karwowski, Chair, 407-823-2204, E-mail: wkar@mail.ucf.edu. *Application contact:* Dr. Waldemar Karwowski, Chair, 407-823-2204, E-mail: wkar@mail.ucf.edu.

University of Cincinnati, Graduate School, College of Medicine, Graduate Programs in Biomedical Sciences, Department of Environmental Health, Cincinnati, OH 45221. Offers environmental and industrial hygiene (MS, PhD); environmental and occupational medicine (MS); environmental genetics and molecular toxicology (MS, PhD); epidemiology and biostatistics (MS, PhD); occupational safety and ergonomics (MS, PhD). *Accreditation:* ABET (one or more programs are accredited). Terminal master's awarded for partial completion of doctoral program. *Degree requirements:* For master's, thesis; for doctorate, thesis/dissertation, qualifying exam. *Entrance requirements:* For master's, GRE General Test, bachelor's degree in science; for doctorate, GRE General Test. Additional exam requirements/recommendations for international students: Required—TOEFL (minimum score 600 paper-based; 250 computer-based; 100 iBT). Electronic applications accepted. *Faculty research:* Carcinogens and mutagenesis, pulmonary studies, reproduction and development.

University of Illinois at Urbana–Champaign, Institute of Aviation, Champaign, IL 61820. Offers human factors (MS). *Students:* 11 full-time (8 women), 6 international. 18 applicants, 28% accepted, 4 enrolled. In 2010, 3 master's awarded. *Entrance requirements:* For master's, GRE, minimum undergraduate GPA of 3.0 for last 60 hours. Additional exam requirements/recommendations for international students: Required—TOEFL. *Application deadline:* Applications are processed on a rolling basis. Application fee: $75 ($90 for international students). Electronic applications accepted. *Financial support:* In 2010–11, 5 research assistantships, 3 teaching assistantships were awarded; fellowships, tuition waivers (full and partial) also available. *Unit head:* Alex Kirlik, Acting Head, 217-244-8972, E-mail: kirlik@illinois.edu. *Application contact:* Peter Vlach, Information Systems Specialist, 217-265-9456, E-mail: pvlach@illinois.edu.

The University of Iowa, Graduate College, College of Engineering, Department of Industrial Engineering, Iowa City, IA 52242-1316. Offers engineering design and manufacturing (MS, PhD); ergonomics (MS, PhD); information and engineering management (MS, PhD); operations research (MS, PhD); quality engineering (MS, PhD). *Faculty:* 6 full-time (0 women). *Students:* 33 full-time (9 women); includes 2 minority (1 Black or African American, non-Hispanic/Latino; 1 Asian, non-Hispanic/Latino), 14 international. Average age 30. 57 applicants, 19% accepted, 8 enrolled. In 2010, 12 master's, 5 doctorates awarded. *Degree requirements:* For master's, thesis optional, exam; for doctorate, comprehensive exam, thesis/dissertation, final defense exam. *Entrance requirements:* For master's and doctorate, GRE General Test. Additional exam requirements/recommendations for international students: Required—TOEFL (minimum score 550 paper-based; 213 computer-based; 81 iBT). *Application deadline:* For fall admission, 7/15 for domestic students, 4/15 for international students; for spring admission, 12/1 for domestic students, 10/1 for international students. Applications are processed on a rolling basis. Application fee: $60 ($100 for international students). Electronic applications accepted. *Financial support:* In 2010–11, 2 fellowships with partial tuition reimbursements (averaging $30,450 per year), 20 research assistantships with partial tuition reimbursements (averaging $20,000 per year), 8 teaching assistantships with partial tuition reimbursements (averaging $16,630 per year) were awarded; career-related internships or fieldwork, scholarships/grants, and unspecified assistantships also available. Support available to part-time students. Financial award applicants required to submit FAFSA. *Faculty research:* Operations research; informatics; human factors engineering; manufacturing systems; human-machine interaction. Total annual research expenditures: $4.7 million. *Unit head:* Dr. Andrew Kusiak, Department Executive Officer, 319-335-5934, Fax: 319-335-5669, E-mail: andrew-kusiak@uiowa.edu. *Application contact:* Jennifer Rumping, Secretary, 319-335-5939, Fax: 319-335-5669, E-mail: indeng@engineering.uiowa.edu.

University of Massachusetts Lowell, School of Health and Environment, Department of Work Environment, Lowell, MA 01854-2881. Offers cleaner production and pollution prevention (MS, Sc D); environmental risk assessment (Certificate); epidemiology (MS, Sc D); ergonomics and safety (MS, Sc D); identification and control of ergonomic hazards (Certificate); job stress and healthy job redesign (Certificate); occupational and environmental hygiene (MS, Sc D); radiological health physics and general work environment protection (Certificate); work environment policy (MS, Sc D). *Accreditation:* ABET (one or more programs are accredited). Part-time programs available. Terminal master's awarded for partial completion of doctoral program. *Degree requirements:* For master's, thesis optional; for doctorate, thesis/dissertation. *Entrance requirements:* For master's and doctorate, GRE General Test. Additional exam requirements/recommendations for international students: Required—TOEFL.

University of Miami, Graduate School, College of Engineering, Department of Industrial Engineering, Program in Occupational Ergonomics and Safety, Coral Gables, FL 33124. Offers environmental health and safety (MS); occupational ergonomics and safety (MSOES). Part-time programs available. *Degree requirements:* For master's, thesis optional. *Entrance requirements:* For master's, GRE General Test, minimum GPA of 3.0. Additional exam requirements/recommendations for international students: Required—TOEFL (minimum score 550 paper-based; 213 computer-based). Electronic applications accepted. *Faculty research:* Noise, heat stress, water pollution.

University of Wisconsin–Milwaukee, Graduate School, College of Engineering and Applied Science, Program in Engineering, Milwaukee, WI 53201-0413. Offers civil engineering (MS); electrical and computer engineering (MS); energy engineering (Certificate); engineering (PhD); engineering management (MS); engineering mechanics (MS); ergonomics (Certificate); industrial and management engineering (MS); manufacturing engineering (MS); materials engineering (MS); mechanical engineering (MS); MUP/MS. Part-time programs available. *Faculty:* 50 full-time (5 women). *Students:* 152 full-time (27 women), 115 part-time (23 women); includes 13 Black or African American, non-Hispanic/Latino; 3 American Indian or Alaska Native, non-Hispanic/Latino; 6 Asian, non-Hispanic/Latino; 10 Hispanic/Latino, 25 international. Average age 31. 236 applicants, 67% accepted, 55 enrolled. In 2010, 39 master's, 19 doctorates awarded. *Degree requirements:* For master's, comprehensive exam (for some programs), thesis or alternative; for doctorate, comprehensive exam, thesis/dissertation, internship. *Entrance requirements:* For master's, GRE, minimum GPA of 2.75; for doctorate, GRE, minimum GPA of 3.5. Additional exam requirements/recommendations for international students: Required—TOEFL (minimum score 550 paper-based; 79 iBT), IELTS (minimum score 6.5). *Application deadline:* For fall admission, 1/1 priority date for domestic students; for spring admission, 9/1 for domestic students. Applications are processed on a rolling basis. Application fee: $56 ($96 for international students). *Financial support:* In 2010–11, 3 fellowships, 55 research assistantships, 77 teaching assistantships were awarded; career-related internships or fieldwork, Federal Work-Study, unspecified assistantships, and project assistantships also available. Support available to part-time students. Financial award application deadline: 4/15. Total annual research expenditures: $6.2 million. *Unit head:* David Yu, Representative, 414-229-6169, E-mail: yu@uwm.edu. *Application contact:* Betty Warras, General Information Contact, 414-229-6169, Fax: 414-229-6967, E-mail: bwarras@uwm.edu.

University of Wisconsin–Milwaukee, Graduate School, College of Health Sciences, Department of Occupational Therapy, Milwaukee, WI 53201-0413. Offers ergonomics (Certificate); occupational therapy (MS); therapeutic recreation (Certificate). *Accreditation:* AOTA. *Faculty:* 10 full-time (6 women). *Students:* 40 full-time (37 women), 3 part-time (all women), 6 international. Average age 25. 19 applicants, 37% accepted, 1 enrolled. In 2010, 38 master's awarded. *Degree requirements:* For master's, thesis or alternative. *Entrance requirements:* Additional exam requirements/recommendations for international students: Required—TOEFL (minimum score 550 paper-based; 79 iBT), IELTS (minimum score 6.5). *Application deadline:* For fall admission, 1/1 priority date for domestic students; for spring admission, 9/1 for domestic students. Applications are processed on a rolling basis. Application fee: $45 ($75 for international students). *Financial support:* Fellowships, research assistantships, teaching assistantships, unspecified assistantships available. Support available to part-time students. Financial award application deadline: 4/15. Total annual research expenditures: $53,814. *Unit head:* Virginia Stoffel, Representative, 414-229-5583, Fax: 414-229-5100, E-mail: stoffelv@uwm.edu. *Application contact:* Virginia Stoffel, Representative, 414-229-5583, Fax: 414-229-5100, E-mail: stoffelv@uwm.edu.

Wright State University, School of Graduate Studies, College of Engineering and Computer Science, Programs in Engineering, Program in Biomedical and Human Factors Engineering, Dayton, OH 45435. Offers biomedical engineering (MSE); human factors engineering (MSE). Part-time programs available. *Degree requirements:* For master's, thesis or course option alternative. *Entrance requirements:* Additional exam requirements/recommendations for international students: Required—TOEFL. *Faculty research:* Medical imaging, functional electrical stimulation, implantable aids, man-machine interfaces, expert systems.

Wright State University, School of Graduate Studies, College of Science and Mathematics, Department of Psychology, Program in Human Factors and Industrial/Organizational Psychology, Dayton, OH 45435. Offers MS, PhD. *Degree requirements:* For master's, thesis; for doctorate, thesis/dissertation.

Management of Technology

Air Force Institute of Technology, Graduate School of Engineering and Management, Department of Operational Sciences, Dayton, OH 45433-7765. Offers logistics management (MS); operations research (MS, PhD); space operations (MS). Part-time programs available. *Degree requirements:* For master's, thesis; for doctorate, thesis/dissertation. *Entrance requirements:* For doctorate, GRE General Test, minimum GPA of 3.0, U.S. citizenship. *Faculty research:* Optimization, simulation, combat modeling and analysis, reliability and maintainability, resource scheduling.

Alliant International University–San Diego, Marshall Goldsmith School of Management, Business and Management Division, San Diego, CA 92131-1799. Offers business administration (MBA); information and technology management (DBA); international business (MIBA, DBA), including finance (DBA), marketing (DBA); strategic business (DBA); sustainable management (MBA); MBA/MA; MBA/PhD. Part-time and evening/weekend programs available. *Degree requirements:* For doctorate, thesis/dissertation. *Entrance requirements:* For master's, GMAT, minimum GPA of 3.0; for doctorate, GMAT, minimum GPA of 3.3. Additional exam requirements/recommendations for international students: Required—TOEFL (minimum score 550 paper-based; 213 computer-based), TWE (minimum score 5). Electronic applications accepted. *Faculty research:* Consumer behavior, international business, strategic management, information systems.

The American University in Cairo, School of Sciences and Engineering, Department of Electronics Engineering, Cairo, Egypt. Offers electronics engineering (M Eng, MS); management of technology (M Eng).

Arizona State University, College of Technology and Innovation, Department of Technology Management, Mesa, AZ 85212. Offers technology (aviation management and human factors) (MS); technology (environmental technology management) (MS); technology (global technology and development) (MS); technology (graphic information technology) (MS); technology (management of technology) (MS). Part-time and evening/weekend programs available. Postbaccalaureate distance learning degree programs offered (minimal on-campus study). *Faculty:* 13 full-time (3 women), 6 part-time/adjunct (2 women). *Students:* 56 full-time (16 women), 212 part-time (95 women); includes 61 minority (14 Black or African American, non-Hispanic/Latino; 8 American Indian or Alaska Native, non-Hispanic/Latino; 14 Asian, non-Hispanic/Latino; 21 Hispanic/Latino; 4 Two or more races, non-Hispanic/Latino), 27 international. Average age 36. 124 applicants, 77% accepted, 58 enrolled. In 2010, 35 master's awarded. *Degree requirements:* For master's, thesis or applied project and oral defense; interactive Program of Study (iPOS) submitted before completing 50 percent of required credit hours. *Entrance requirements:* For master's, GRE, minimum GPA of 3.0 or equivalent in last 2 years of work leading to bachelor's degree. Additional exam requirements/recommendations for international students: Required—TOEFL, IELTS, or Pearson Test of English. *Application deadline:* For fall admission, 7/1 for domestic and international students; for spring admission, 12/1 for domestic and international students. Applications are processed on a rolling basis. Application fee: $70 ($90 for international students). Electronic applications accepted. *Expenses:* Tuition, state resident: full-time $8510; part-time $608 per credit. Tuition, nonresident: full-time $16,542; part-time $919 per credit. Required fees: $339; $110 per credit. Part-time tuition and fees vary according to course load. *Financial support:* In 2010–11, 3 research assistantships with full and partial tuition reimbursements (averaging $12,729 per year), 1 teaching assistantship with full and partial tuition reimbursement (averaging $14,125 per year) were awarded; career-related internships or fieldwork, Federal Work-Study, scholarships/grants, health care benefits, tuition waivers (full and partial), and unspecified assistantships also available. Support available to part-time students. Financial award application deadline: 3/1; financial award applicants required to submit FAFSA. *Faculty research:* Digital imaging, digital publishing, Internet development/e-commerce, information aviation human factors, pilot selection, databases, multimedia, commercial digital photography, digital workflow, computer graphics modeling and animation, information design, sociotechnology, visual and technical literacy, environmental management, quality management, project management, industrial ethics, hazardous materials, environmental chemistry. Total annual research expenditures: $755,686. *Unit head:* Dr. Mitzi Montoya, Vice Provost and Dean, 480-727-1955, Fax: 480-727-1538, E-mail: mitzi.montoya@asu.edu. *Application contact:* Graduate Admissions, 480-965-6113.

Athabasca University, Centre for Innovative Management, St. Albert, AB T8N 1B4, Canada. Offers business administration (MBA); information technology management (MBA), including policing concentration; management (GDM); project management (MBA, GDM). Part-time and evening/weekend programs available. Postbaccalaureate distance learning degree programs offered (no on-campus study). *Degree requirements:* For master's, thesis or alternative, applied project. *Entrance requirements:* For master's, 3-8 years of managerial experience, 3 years with undergraduate degree, 5 years managerial experience with professional designation, 8-10 years management experience (on exception). Electronic applications accepted. *Expenses:* Contact institution. *Faculty research:* Human resources, project management, operations research, information technology management, corporate stewardship, energy management.

Boston University, Metropolitan College, Department of Administrative Sciences, Boston, MA 02215. Offers banking and financial management (MSM); business continuity in emergency management (MSM); economics development and tourism management (MSAS); electronic commerce, systems, and technology (MSAS); financial economics (MSAS); innovation and technology (MSAS); insurance management (MSM); international market management (MSM); multinational commerce (MSAS); project management (MSM). *Accreditation:* AACSB. Part-time and evening/weekend programs available. Postbaccalaureate distance learning degree programs offered (no on-campus study). *Faculty:* 14 full-time (2 women), 22 part-time/adjunct (2 women). *Students:* 107 full-time (51 women), 786 part-time (356 women); includes 130 minority (55 Black or African American, non-Hispanic/Latino; 1 American Indian or Alaska Native, non-Hispanic/Latino; 30 Asian, non-Hispanic/Latino; 36 Hispanic/Latino; 1 Native Hawaiian or other Pacific Islander, non-Hispanic/Latino; 7 Two or more races, non-Hispanic/Latino), 175 international. Average age 33. 398 applicants, 87% accepted, 180 enrolled. In 2010, 154 master's awarded. *Degree requirements:* For master's, thesis optional. *Entrance requirements:* For master's, 1 year of work experience, minimum GPA of 3.0. Additional exam requirements/recommendations for international students: Required—TOEFL (minimum score 560 paper-based; 220 computer-based; 84 iBT). *Application deadline:* Applications are processed on a rolling basis. Application fee: $70. Electronic applications accepted. *Expenses:* Tuition: Full-time $39,314; part-time $1228 per credit. Required fees: $40 per semester. *Financial support:* In 2010–11, 15 students received support, including 7 research assistantships with partial tuition reimbursements available (averaging $10,000 per year); career-related internships or fieldwork, Federal Work-Study, and unspecified assistantships also available. *Faculty research:* International business, innovative process. *Unit head:* Dr. Kip Becker, Chairman, 617-353-3016, E-mail: adminsc@bu.edu. *Application contact:* Lucille Dicker, Administrative Sciences Department, 617-353-3016, E-mail: adminsc@bu.edu.

California Lutheran University, Graduate Studies, School of Management, Thousand Oaks, CA 91360-2787. Offers business (IMBA); computer science (MS); econometrics (MBA); economics (MS); entrepreneurship (MBA, Certificate); finance (MBA, Certificate); financial planning (MBA, Certificate); information systems and technology (MS); information technology management (MBA, Certificate); international business (MBA, Certificate); management and organization behavior (MBA); management and organizational behavior (Certificate); marketing (MBA, Certificate); microeconomics (MBA); nonprofit and social enterprise (MBA). Part-time and evening/weekend programs available. Postbaccalaureate distance learning degree programs offered (no on-campus study). *Faculty:* 12 full-time (3 women), 27 part-time/adjunct (6 women). *Students:* 350 full-time (162 women), 262 part-time (99 women); includes 21 Black or African American, non-Hispanic/Latino; 44 Asian, non-Hispanic/Latino; 56 Hispanic/Latino; 4 Native Hawaiian or other Pacific Islander, non-Hispanic/Latino; 12 Two or more races, non-Hispanic/Latino, 185 international. Average age 32. 379 applicants, 74% accepted, 138 enrolled. In 2010, 231 master's awarded. *Entrance requirements:* For master's, GMAT, interview, minimum GPA of 3.0. *Application deadline:* Applications are processed on a rolling basis. Application fee: $50. *Expenses:* Contact institution. *Unit head:* Dr. Charles Maxey, Dean, 805-493-3360. *Application contact:* 805-493-3127, Fax: 805-493-3542, E-mail: clugrad@clunet.edu.

California State University, Los Angeles, Graduate Studies, College of Engineering, Computer Science, and Technology, Department of Technology, Los Angeles, CA 90032-8530. Offers industrial and technical studies (MA). Part-time and evening/weekend programs available. *Faculty:* 2 part-time/adjunct (0 women). *Students:* 10 full-time (2 women), 19 part-time (2 women); includes 10 minority (2 Black or African American, non-Hispanic/Latino; 4 Asian, non-Hispanic/Latino; 4 Hispanic/Latino), 11 international. Average age 33. 13 applicants, 100% accepted, 9 enrolled. In 2010, 12 master's awarded. *Entrance requirements:* For master's, minimum GPA of 2.5. Additional exam requirements/recommendations for international students: Required—TOEFL (minimum score 550 paper-based). *Application deadline:* For fall admission, 5/1 for domestic and international students. Applications are processed on a rolling basis. Application fee: $55. *Financial support:* Federal Work-Study available. Support available to part-time students. Financial award application deadline: 3/1. *Unit head:* Dr. Benjamin Lee, Chair, 323-343-4550, Fax: 323-343-4571, E-mail: blee10@calstatela.edu. *Application contact:* Dr. Alan Muchlinski, Dean of Graduate Studies, 323-343-3820, Fax: 323-343-5653, E-mail: amuchli@exchange.calstatela.edu.

Cambridge College, School of Management, Cambridge, MA 02138-5304. Offers business negotiation and conflict resolution (M Mgt); general business (M Mgt); health care informatics (M Mgt); health care management (M Mgt); leadership in human and organizational dynamics (M Mgt); non-profit and public organization management (M Mgt); small business development (M Mgt); technology management (M Mgt). Part-time and evening/weekend programs available. *Faculty:* 6 full-time (3 women), 54 part-time/adjunct (26 women). *Students:* 222 full-time (121 women), 175 part-time (110 women); includes 127 minority (89 Black or African American, non-Hispanic/Latino; 2 American Indian or Alaska Native, non-Hispanic/Latino; 9 Asian, non-Hispanic/Latino; 25 Hispanic/Latino; 2 Two or more races, non-Hispanic/Latino), 125 international. Average age 37. In 2010, 221 master's awarded. *Degree requirements:* For master's, thesis, seminars. *Entrance requirements:* For master's, resume, 2 professional references. Additional exam requirements/recommendations for international students: Required—TOEFL (minimum score 550 paper-based; 213 computer-based; 79 iBT); Recommended—IELTS (minimum score 6). *Application deadline:* Applications are processed on a rolling basis. Application fee: $30. Electronic applications accepted. *Expenses:* Contact institution. *Financial support:* Career-related internships or fieldwork, Federal Work-Study, and scholarships/grants available. Financial award applicants required to submit FAFSA. *Faculty research:* Negotiation, mediation and conflict resolution; leadership; management of diverse organizations; case studies and simulation methodologies for management education, digital as a second language; social networking for digital immigrants, non-profit and public management. *Unit head:* Dr. Mary Ann Joseph, Acting Dean, 617-873-0227, E-mail: maryann.joseph@cambridgecollege.edu. *Application contact:* Elaine M. Lapomardo, Dean of Enrollment Management, 617-873-0274, Fax: 617-349-3561, E-mail: elaine.lapomardo@cambridgecollege.edu.

Capella University, School of Business and Technology, Minneapolis, MN 55402. Offers accounting (MBA), including system design and programming; business (Certificate), including human resource management (MS, PhD, Certificate); information technology management (MS, PhD, Certificate); leadership (MBA, MS, PhD, Certificate); finance (MBA); general business (MBA); health care management (MBA); information technology (MS, Certificate), including

general information technology (MS), information security, network architecture and design (MS), professional projects management (Certificate), project management and leadership (MS), system design and development (MS),); information technology management (MBA); marketing (MBA); organization and management (MBA, MS, PhD), including general business (PhD), general organization and management (MBA, MS), human resource management (MS, PhD, Certificate), information technology management (MS, PhD, Certificate), leadership (MBA, MS, PhD, Certificate); project management (MBA). Part-time and evening/weekend programs available. Postbaccalaureate distance learning degree programs offered (minimal on-campus study). Terminal master's awarded for partial completion of doctoral program. *Degree requirements:* For master's, thesis optional, integrative project; for doctorate, comprehensive exam, thesis/dissertation. *Entrance requirements:* Additional exam requirements/recommendations for international students: Required—TOEFL (minimum score 550 paper-based; 213 computer-based), TWE (minimum score 4). Electronic applications accepted. *Expenses:* Tuition: Full-time $11,880; part-time $440 per credit hour. *Faculty research:* Business policies: strategic, corporate, and financial management; interplay of technological, organizational and social change.

Carleton University, Faculty of Graduate Studies, Faculty of Engineering and Design, Ottawa-Carleton Institute for Electrical Engineering, Department of Systems and Computer Engineering, Program in Technology Innovation Management, Ottawa, ON K1S 5B6, Canada. Offers M Eng, MA Sc. *Degree requirements:* For master's, thesis optional. *Entrance requirements:* For master's, honors degree. Additional exam requirements/recommendations for international students: Required—TOEFL.

Carnegie Mellon University, Mellon College of Science, Department of Chemistry, Pittsburgh, PA 15213-3891. Offers biotechnology and management (MS); chemistry (PhD), including bioinorganic, bioorganic, organic and materials, biophysics and spectroscopy, computational and theoretical, polymer; colloids, polymers and surfaces (MS). Part-time programs available. Terminal master's awarded for partial completion of doctoral program. *Degree requirements:* For doctorate, thesis/dissertation, departmental qualifying and oral exams, teaching experience. *Entrance requirements:* For master's, GRE General Test; for doctorate, GRE General Test, GRE Subject Test. Additional exam requirements/recommendations for international students: Required—TOEFL. Electronic applications accepted. *Faculty research:* Physical and theoretical chemistry, chemical synthesis, biophysical/bioinorganic chemistry.

Central Connecticut State University, School of Graduate Studies, School of Technology, Department of Manufacturing and Construction Management, New Britain, CT 06050-4010. Offers construction management (MS, Certificate); lean manufacturing and Six Sigma (Certificate); supply chain and logistics (Certificate); technology management (MS). Part-time and evening/weekend programs available. *Faculty:* 19 full-time (4 women), 25 part-time/adjunct (1 woman). *Students:* 15 full-time (4 women), 78 part-time (16 women); includes 19 minority (10 Black or African American, non-Hispanic/Latino; 5 Asian, non-Hispanic/Latino; 3 Hispanic/Latino; 1 Two or more races, non-Hispanic/Latino), 5 international. Average age 38. 67 applicants, 76% accepted, 34 enrolled. In 2010, 24 master's awarded. *Degree requirements:* For master's, comprehensive exam, thesis or alternative; for Certificate, qualifying exam. *Entrance requirements:* For master's, minimum undergraduate GPA of 2.7. Additional exam requirements/recommendations for international students: Required—TOEFL. *Application deadline:* For fall admission, 7/1 for domestic students; for spring admission, 12/1 for domestic students. Applications are processed on a rolling basis. Application fee: $50. Electronic applications accepted. *Expenses:* Tuition, area resident: Full-time $5012; part-time $470 per credit. Tuition, state resident: full-time $7518; part-time $482 per credit. Tuition, nonresident: full-time $13,962; part-time $482 per credit. Required fees: $3772. One-time fee: $62 part-time. *Financial support:* In 2010–11, 5 students received support, including 5 research assistantships; career-related internships or fieldwork, Federal Work-Study, scholarships/grants, and unspecified assistantships also available. Support available to part-time students. Financial award application deadline: 2/15; financial award applicants required to submit FAFSA. *Faculty research:* All aspects of middle management, technical supervision in the workplace. *Unit head:* Dr. Jacob Kovel, Chair, 860-832-1830. *Application contact:* Dr. Jacob Kovel, Chair, 860-832-1830.

Champlain College, Graduate Studies, Burlington, VT 05402-0670. Offers business (MBA); digital forensic management (MS); education (M Ed); emergent media (MFA); health care management (MS); law (MS); managing innovation and information technology (MS); mediation and applied conflict studies (MS). Part-time programs available. Postbaccalaureate distance learning degree programs offered (no on-campus study). *Faculty:* 14 full-time (0 women), 24 part-time/adjunct (9 women). *Students:* 304 full-time (144 women), 2 part-time (both women). Average age 30. 271 applicants, 90% accepted, 216 enrolled. In 2010, 8 master's awarded. *Degree requirements:* For master's, capstone project. *Entrance requirements:* Additional exam requirements/recommendations for international students: Required—TOEFL. *Application deadline:* For fall admission, 8/1 priority date for domestic and international students; for spring admission, 1/1 priority date for domestic and international students. Applications are processed on a rolling basis. Application fee: $50. Electronic applications accepted. *Expenses:* Tuition: Part-time $740 per credit hour. Part-time tuition and fees vary according to program. *Financial support:* Applicants required to submit FAFSA. *Unit head:* Dr. Donald Haggerty, Associate Provost, Graduate Studies, 802-865-6403, Fax: 802-865-6447. *Application contact:* Jon Walsh, Assistant Vice President, Graduate Admission, 800-570-5858, E-mail: walsh@champlain.edu.

City University of Seattle, Graduate Division, School of Management, Bellevue, WA 98005. Offers accounting (Certificate); change leadership (MBA, Certificate); computer systems (MS); finance (Certificate); financial management (MBA); general management (MBA); general management-Europe (MBA); global marketing (MBA); human resources management (Certificate); individualized study (MBA); information security (MS); information systems (MBA); leadership (MA); marketing (MBA, Certificate); project management (MBA, MS, Certificate); sustainable business (Certificate); technology management (MBA, Certificate). Part-time and evening/weekend programs available. Postbaccalaureate distance learning degree programs offered (no on-campus study). *Entrance requirements:* Additional exam requirements/recommendations for international students: Required—TOEFL (minimum score 540 paper-based; 207 computer-based); Recommended—IELTS. Electronic applications accepted.

Coleman University, Program in Business and Technology Management, San Diego, CA 92123. Offers MS. Evening/weekend programs available. Postbaccalaureate distance learning degree programs offered (no on-campus study). *Entrance requirements:* For master's, bachelor's degree, minimum GPA of 3.0. Additional exam requirements/recommendations for international students: Required—TOEFL (minimum score 500 paper-based; 173 computer-based).

Colorado School of Mines, Graduate School, Division of Economics and Business, Golden, CO 80401. Offers engineering and technology management (MS); mineral economics (MS, PhD). Part-time programs available. *Faculty:* 12 full-time (3 women), 8 part-time/adjunct (1 woman). *Students:* 121 full-time (22 women), 23 part-time (5 women); includes 1 Black or African American, non-Hispanic/Latino; 2 American Indian or Alaska Native, non-Hispanic/Latino; 1 Asian, non-Hispanic/Latino; 6 Hispanic/Latino, 31 international. Average age 29. 179 applicants, 72% accepted, 63 enrolled. In 2010, 70 master's, 3 doctorates awarded. *Degree requirements:* For master's, thesis (for some programs); for doctorate, comprehensive exam, thesis/dissertation. *Entrance requirements:* For master's and doctorate, GRE General Test. Additional exam requirements/recommendations for international students: Required—TOEFL (minimum score 550 paper-based; 213 computer-based; 80 iBT). *Application deadline:* For fall admission, 1/15 priority date for domestic and international students; for spring admission, 10/15 priority date for domestic and international students. Application fee: $50 ($70 for international students). Electronic applications accepted. *Expenses:* Tuition, state resident: full-time $11,550; part-time $641 per credit. Tuition, nonresident: full-time $25,980; part-time $1444 per credit. Required fees: $1874; $937 per semester. *Financial support:* In 2010–11, 45 students received support, including 6 fellowships with full tuition reimbursements available (averaging $20,000 per year), 11 research assistantships with full tuition reimbursements

Management of Technology

Colorado School of Mines (continued)
available (averaging $20,000 per year), 28 teaching assistantships with full tuition reimbursements available (averaging $20,000 per year); scholarships/grants, health care benefits, and unspecified assistantships also available. Financial award application deadline: 1/15; financial award applicants required to submit FAFSA. *Faculty research:* International trade, resource and environmental economics, energy economics, operations research. Total annual research expenditures: $137,815. *Unit head:* Dr. Rod Eggert, Division Head, 303-273-3981, Fax: 303-273-3416, E-mail: reggert@mines.edu. *Application contact:* Kathleen A. Feighny, Administrative Faculty, 303-273-3979, Fax: 303-273-3416, E-mail: kfeighny@mines.edu.

Colorado Technical University Colorado Springs, Graduate Studies, Program in Management, Colorado Springs, CO 80907-3896. Offers accounting (MBA, MSA); business administration (MBA); finance (MBA); human resources management (MBA); logistics/supply chain management (MBA); management (DM); marketing (MBA); mediation and dispute resolution (MBA); operations management (MBA); project management (MBA); technology management (MBA). Part-time and evening/weekend programs available. Postbaccalaureate distance learning degree programs offered. *Degree requirements:* For master's, thesis or alternative; for doctorate, thesis/dissertation. *Entrance requirements:* For doctorate, minimum graduate GPA of 3.0, 5 years of related work experience. *Faculty research:* Sexual harassment, performance evaluation, critical thinking.

Colorado Technical University Denver, Programs in Business Administration and Management, Greenwood Village, CO 80111. Offers accounting (MBA); business administration (MBA); business administration and management (EMBA); finance (MBA); human resource management (MBA); marketing (MBA); mediation and dispute resolution (MBA); operations management (MBA); project management (MBA); technology management (MBA). Part-time and evening/weekend programs available. *Degree requirements:* For master's, thesis or alternative. *Entrance requirements:* For master's, minimum undergraduate GPA of 3.0, resume.

Colorado Technical University Sioux Falls, Programs in Business Administration and Management, Sioux Falls, SD 57108. Offers business administration (MBA); business management (MSM); health science management (MSM); human resources management (MSM); information technology (MSM); organizational leadership (MSM); project management (MBA); technology management (MBA). Evening/weekend programs available. *Degree requirements:* For master's, thesis optional. *Entrance requirements:* For master's, minimum 2 years work experience, resume.

Columbia University, School of Continuing Education, Program in Technology Management, New York, NY 10027. Offers Exec MS. Part-time and evening/weekend programs available. *Entrance requirements:* For master's, minimum undergraduate GPA of 3.0. Additional exam requirements/recommendations for international students: Required—American Language Program placement test. Electronic applications accepted. *Faculty research:* Information systems, management.

Dallas Baptist University, College of Business, Business Administration Program, Dallas, TX 75211-9299. Offers accounting (MBA); business communication (MBA); conflict resolution management (MBA); e-business (MBA); entrepreneurship (MBA); finance (MBA); health care management (MBA); international business (MBA); leading the non-profit organization (MBA); management (MBA); management information systems (MBA); marketing (MBA); project management (MBA); technology and engineering management (MBA). *Accreditation:* ACBSP. Part-time and evening/weekend programs available. *Entrance requirements:* For master's, GMAT, minimum GPA of 3.0. Additional exam requirements/recommendations for international students: Required—TOEFL, IELTS. Electronic applications accepted. *Expenses:* Tuition: Full-time $11,394; part-time $633 per credit hour. *Faculty research:* Sports management, services marketing, retailing, strategic management, financial planning/investments.

DePaul University, College of Computing and Digital Media, Chicago, IL 60604. Offers animation (MA, MFA); applied technology (MS); business information technology (MS); cinema (MFA); cinema production (MS); computational finance (MS); computer and information sciences (PhD); computer game development (MS); computer graphics and motion technology (MS); computer information and network security (MS); computer science (MS); e-commerce technology (MS); human-computer interaction (MS); information systems (MS); information technology (MA); information technology project management (MS); network engineering and management (MS); predictive analytics (MS); screenwriting (MFA); software engineering (MS); JD/MA; JD/MS. Part-time and evening/weekend programs available. Postbaccalaureate distance learning degree programs offered (no on-campus study). *Faculty:* 51 full-time (11 women), 50 part-time/adjunct (9 women). *Students:* 952 full-time (230 women), 927 part-time (226 women); includes 557 minority (205 Black or African American, non-Hispanic/Latino; 2 American Indian or Alaska Native, non-Hispanic/Latino; 167 Asian, non-Hispanic/Latino; 136 Hispanic/Latino; 7 Native Hawaiian or other Pacific Islander, non-Hispanic/Latino; 40 Two or more races, non-Hispanic/Latino), 292 international. Average age 31. 896 applicants, 70% accepted, 324 enrolled. In 2010, 417 master's, 6 doctorates awarded. *Degree requirements:* For master's, thesis (for some programs); for doctorate, comprehensive exam, thesis/dissertation. *Entrance requirements:* For master's, GRE or GMAT (MS in computational finance only), bachelor's degree, resume (MS in predictive analytics only), IT experience (MS in information technology project management only), portfolio review (MFA); for doctorate, GRE, master's degree in computer science. Additional exam requirements/recommendations for international students: Required—TOEFL (minimum score 550 paper-based; 213 computer-based; 80 iBT), IELTS (minimum score 6.5), Pearson Test of English (minimum score 53). *Application deadline:* For fall admission, 8/15 priority date for domestic students, 6/1 priority date for international students; for winter admission, 12/15 priority date for domestic students, 9/15 priority date for international students; for spring admission, 3/1 priority date for domestic students, 12/15 priority date for international students. Applications are processed on a rolling basis. Application fee: $25. Electronic applications accepted. *Expenses:* Contact institution. *Financial support:* In 2010–11, 102 students received support, including 4 fellowships with full tuition reimbursements available (averaging $24,435 per year), 6 research assistantships (averaging $21,100 per year), 92 teaching assistantships with full and partial tuition reimbursements available (averaging $6,904 per year); Federal Work-Study, scholarships/grants, tuition waivers (full and partial), and unspecified assistantships also available. Support available to part-time students. Financial award application deadline: 4/30; financial award applicants required to submit FAFSA. *Faculty research:* Bioinformatics, visual computing, graphics and animation, high performance and scientific computing, databases. Total annual research expenditures: $1.4 million. *Unit head:* Dr. David Miller, Dean, 312-362-8381, Fax: 312-362-5185. *Application contact:* Dr. Liz Friedman, Assistant Dean of Student Services, 312-362-8714, Fax: 312-362-5179, E-mail: efriedm2@cdm.depaul.edu.

East Carolina University, Graduate School, College of Technology and Computer Science, Department of Technology Systems, Greenville, NC 27858-4353. Offers computer network professional (Certificate); industrial technology (MS), including computer networking management, digital communications, industrial distribution and logistics, information security, manufacturing, performance improvement, planning; information assurance (Certificate); occupational safety (MS); technology management (PhD); Website developer (Certificate). *Entrance requirements:* For master's and Certificate, GRE General Test or MAT, minimum GPA of 2.5; for doctorate, GRE General Test, related work experience. *Expenses:* Tuition, state resident: full-time $3130; part-time $391.25 per credit hour. Tuition, nonresident: full-time $13,817; part-time $1727.13 per credit hour. Required fees: $1916; $239.50 per credit hour. Tuition and fees vary according to campus/location and program.

Eastern Michigan University, Graduate School, College of Technology, Program in Technology, Ypsilanti, MI 48197. Offers PhD. Part-time and evening/weekend programs available. *Students:* 6 full-time (3 women), 48 part-time (19 women); includes 7 minority (5 Black or African American, non-Hispanic/Latino; 1 Asian, non-Hispanic/Latino; 1 Hispanic/Latino), 15 international. Average age 39. 55 applicants, 22% accepted, 8 enrolled. In 2010, 2 doctorates awarded. *Degree requirements:* For doctorate, comprehensive exam, thesis/dissertation. *Entrance requirements:* For doctorate, GRE. Additional exam requirements/recommendations for international students: Required—TOEFL. *Application deadline:* For fall admission, 2/15 for domestic and international students; for winter admission, 10/15 for domestic and international students. Applications are processed on a rolling basis. Application fee: $35. *Financial support:* Fellowships, research assistantships with full and partial tuition reimbursements, teaching assistantships with full and partial tuition reimbursements, career-related internships or fieldwork, Federal Work-Study, institutionally sponsored loans, scholarships/grants, tuition waivers (partial), and unspecified assistantships available. Support available to part-time students. Financial award applicants required to submit FAFSA. *Unit head:* Dr. Morell Boone, Dean, 734-487-0354, Fax: 734-487-0843, E-mail: mboone@emich.edu. *Application contact:* Dr. Morell Boone, Dean, 734-487-0354, Fax: 734-487-0843, E-mail: mboone@emich.edu.

École Polytechnique de Montréal, Graduate Programs, Department of Mathematics and Industrial Engineering, Montréal, QC H3C 3A7, Canada. Offers ergonomy (M Eng, M Sc A, DESS); mathematical method in CA engineering (M Eng, M Sc A, PhD); operational research (M Eng, M Sc A, PhD); production (M Eng, M Sc A); technology management (M Eng, M Sc A). DESS program offered jointly with HEC Montreal and Université de Montréal. Part-time programs available. *Degree requirements:* For master's, one foreign language, thesis. *Entrance requirements:* For master's, minimum GPA of 2.75. *Faculty research:* Use of computers in organizations.

Embry-Riddle Aeronautical University–Worldwide, Worldwide Headquarters, Program in Technical Management, Daytona Beach, FL 32114-3900. Offers MSTM. Part-time and evening/weekend programs available. Postbaccalaureate distance learning degree programs offered. *Faculty:* 4 full-time (1 woman), 50 part-time/adjunct (15 women). *Students:* 21 full-time (2 women), 40 part-time (6 women); includes 18 minority (7 Black or African American, non-Hispanic/Latino; 1 Asian, non-Hispanic/Latino; 9 Hispanic/Latino; 1 Two or more races, non-Hispanic/Latino), 1 international. Average age 39. 14 applicants, 36% accepted, 3 enrolled. In 2010, 71 master's awarded. *Degree requirements:* For master's, thesis (for some programs). *Entrance requirements:* For master's, GMAT. *Application deadline:* Applications are processed on a rolling basis. Application fee: $50. Electronic applications accepted. *Financial support:* In 2010–11, 6 students received support. Applicants required to submit FAFSA. *Unit head:* Dr. Kees Rietsema, Chair, 602-904-1285, E-mail: rietsd37@erau.edu. *Application contact:* Linda Dammer, Director of Admissions, 386-226-6396 Ext. 1, Fax: 386-226-6984, E-mail: worldwide@erau.edu.

Fairfield University, School of Engineering, Fairfield, CT 06824-5195. Offers electrical and computer engineering (MS); management of technology (MS); mechanical engineering (MS); software engineering (MS). Part-time and evening/weekend programs available. *Faculty:* 8 full-time (1 woman), 11 part-time/adjunct (0 women). *Students:* 31 full-time (12 women), 98 part-time (20 women); includes 28 minority (5 Black or African American, non-Hispanic/Latino; 17 Asian, non-Hispanic/Latino; 4 Hispanic/Latino; 1 Native Hawaiian or other Pacific Islander, non-Hispanic/Latino; 1 Two or more races, non-Hispanic/Latino), 26 international. Average age 35. 120 applicants, 55% accepted, 15 enrolled. In 2010, 52 master's awarded. *Degree requirements:* For master's, thesis, capstone course. *Entrance requirements:* For master's, interview, minimum GPA of 2.8, resume, 2 recommendations. Additional exam requirements/recommendations for international students: Required—TOEFL (minimum score 550 paper-based; 213 computer-based; 80 iBT). *Application deadline:* For fall admission, 5/15 for international students; for spring admission, 10/15 for international students. Applications are processed on a rolling basis. Application fee: $60. Electronic applications accepted. *Expenses:* Contact institution. *Financial support:* In 2010–11, 25 students received support. Unspecified assistantships available. Financial award applicants required to submit FAFSA. *Faculty research:* Vehicle dynamics, image processing, multimedia in instruction, thermal packaging, character recognition, photovoltaics and nanotechnology, Web technology. *Unit head:* Dr. Jack Beal, Dean, 203-254-4000 Ext. 4147, Fax: 203-254-4013, E-mail: jwbeal@fairfield.edu. *Application contact:* Marianne Gumpper, Director of Graduate and Continuing Studies Admissions, 203-254-4184, Fax: 203-254-4073, E-mail: gradadmis@fairfield.edu.

Fairleigh Dickinson University, College at Florham, Silberman College of Business, Departments of Management, Marketing, and Entrepreneurial Studies, Program in Management, Madison, NJ 07940-1099. Offers evolving technology (Certificate); management (MBA); MBA/MA. *Students:* 7 full-time (5 women), 33 part-time (20 women), 4 international. Average age 30. 32 applicants, 72% accepted, 9 enrolled. In 2010, 14 master's awarded. *Application deadline:* Applications are processed on a rolling basis. Application fee: $40.

Florida Institute of Technology, Graduate Programs, Nathan M. Bisk College of Business, Online Programs, Melbourne, FL 32901-6975. Offers accounting (MBA); accounting and finance (MBA); finance (MBA); healthcare management (MBA); information technology (MS); information technology management (MBA); Internet marketing (MBA); management (MBA); marketing (MBA); project management (MBA). Part-time and evening/weekend programs available. Postbaccalaureate distance learning degree programs offered (no on-campus study). *Faculty:* 32 part-time/adjunct (8 women). *Students:* 4 full-time (1 woman), 1,062 part-time (499 women); includes 373 minority (244 Black or African American, non-Hispanic/Latino; 8 American Indian or Alaska Native, non-Hispanic/Latino; 37 Asian, non-Hispanic/Latino; 76 Hispanic/Latino; 8 Native Hawaiian or other Pacific Islander, non-Hispanic/Latino), 39 international. Average age 37. 299 applicants, 167 enrolled. In 2010, 134 master's awarded. *Entrance requirements:* For master's, GMAT or resume showing 8 years of supervised experience, 2 letters of recommendation, resume, competency in math past college algebra. Additional exam requirements/recommendations for international students: Required—TOEFL (minimum score 550 paper-based; 213 computer-based; 79 iBT). *Application deadline:* For fall admission, 4/1 for international students; for spring admission, 9/30 for international students. Applications are processed on a rolling basis. Application fee: $50. Electronic applications accepted. *Expenses:* Contact institution. *Financial support:* Available to part-time students. Application deadline: 3/1. *Unit head:* Dr. Mary S. Bonhomme, Dean, Florida Tech Online Associate Provost for Online Learning, 321-674-8202, Fax: 321-674-8216, E-mail: bonhomme@fit.edu. *Application contact:* Carolyn Farrior, Director of Graduate Admissions Online Learning and Off Campus Programs, 321-674-7118, Fax: 321-674-8216, E-mail: cfarrior@fit.edu.

George Mason University, School of Management, Program in Technology Management, Fairfax, VA 22030. Offers MS. Evening/weekend programs available. *Faculty:* 80 full-time (26 women), 51 part-time/adjunct (15 women). *Students:* 44 full-time (9 women); includes 2 Black or African American, non-Hispanic/Latino; 3 Asian, non-Hispanic/Latino; 2 Hispanic/Latino, 2 international. Average age 39. In 2010, 48 master's awarded. *Entrance requirements:* For master's, GMAT, 2 letters of recommendation, resume. Additional exam requirements/recommendations for international students: Required—TOEFL (minimum score 570 paper-based; 230 computer-based; 88 iBT), IELTS. *Application deadline:* For spring admission, 10/1 for domestic students. Applications are processed on a rolling basis. Application fee: $100. Electronic applications accepted. *Expenses:* Contact institution. *Financial support:* Application deadline: 3/1. *Faculty research:* Leadership careers in technology-oriented businesses, achieving success in the technology marketplace, emphasizing technology leadership and management, technology innovation, commercialization, methods and approaches of systems thinking. *Unit head:* Dr. David Kravitz, Chair, 703-993-1781, E-mail: dkravitz@gmu.edu. *Application contact:* Edward Lewis, Director, 703-993-4833, E-mail: elewis9@gmu.edu.

George Mason University, School of Public Policy, Program in Public Policy, Arlington, VA 22201. Offers MPP, PhD. Part-time programs available. *Faculty:* 66 full-time (24 women), 15 part-time/adjunct (3 women). *Students:* 153 full-time (78 women), 368 part-time (188 women); includes 31 Black or African American, non-Hispanic/Latino; 22 Asian, non-Hispanic/Latino; 24 Hispanic/Latino; 2 Two or more races, non-Hispanic/Latino, 68 international. Average age 31. 508 applicants, 62% accepted, 143 enrolled. In 2010, 133 master's, 15 doctorates awarded. *Degree requirements:* For master's, thesis or alternative; for doctorate, comprehensive exam, thesis/dissertation. *Entrance requirements:* For master's, GRE (for students seeking merit-based scholarships), minimum GPA of 3.0, resume, 2 letters of recommendation, goals statement; for doctorate, GMAT or GRE General Test, resume, writing sample, 2 letters of recommendation. Additional exam requirements/recommendations for international students: Required—TOEFL (minimum score 570 paper-based; 230 computer-based; 88 iBT). *Application deadline:* For fall admission, 6/1 priority date for domestic students, 5/1 priority date for international students; for spring admission, 12/1 priority date for domestic students, 11/1 priority date for international students. Applications are processed on a rolling basis. Application fee: $100. Electronic applications accepted. *Expenses:* Contact institution. *Financial support:* In 2010–11, 42 students received support, including 2 fellowships with full tuition reimbursements available (averaging $18,000 per year), 40 research assistantships with full and partial tuition reimbursements available (averaging $18,153 per year), 2 teaching assistantships with full and partial tuition reimbursements available (averaging $10,408 per year); career-related internships or fieldwork, Federal Work-Study, scholarships/grants, unspecified assistantships, and health care benefits (full-time research or teaching assistantship recipients) also available. Financial award application deadline: 3/1; financial award applicants required to submit FAFSA. *Unit head:* Dr. Catherine Rudder, Director of MPP Program, 703-993-8099, E-mail: spp@gmu.edu. *Application contact:* Tennille Haegele, Director, Graduate Admissions, 703-993–3183, Fax: 703-993-4876, E-mail: thaegele@gmu.edu.

The George Washington University, School of Business, Department of Information Systems and Technology Management, Washington, DC 20052. Offers information and decision systems (PhD); information systems (MSIST); information systems development (MSIST); information systems management (MBA); information systems project management (MSIST); management information systems (MSIST); management of science, technology, and innovation (MBA, PhD). Programs also offered in Ashburn and Arlington, VA. Part-time and evening/weekend programs available. *Faculty:* 12 full-time (4 women), 5 part-time/adjunct (1 woman). *Students:* 93 full-time (33 women), 141 part-time (46 women); includes 31 Black or African American, non-Hispanic/Latino; 1 American Indian or Alaska Native, non-Hispanic/Latino; 28 Asian, non-Hispanic/Latino; 17 Hispanic/Latino; 1 Native Hawaiian or other Pacific Islander, non-Hispanic/Latino, 40 international. Average age 33. 201 applicants, 68% accepted, 67 enrolled. In 2010, 89 master's, 2 doctorates awarded. *Entrance requirements:* For master's, GMAT. Additional exam requirements/recommendations for international students: Required—TOEFL. *Application deadline:* For fall admission, 4/1 priority date for domestic students; for spring admission, 10/1 for domestic students. Applications are processed on a rolling basis. Application fee: $75. *Financial support:* In 2010–11, 35 students received support; fellowships, teaching assistantships, career-related internships or fieldwork, Federal Work-Study, institutionally sponsored loans, and tuition waivers available. Financial award application deadline: 4/1. *Faculty research:* Expert systems, decision support systems. *Unit head:* Richard G. Donnelly, Chair, 202-994-4364, E-mail: rgd@gwu.edu. *Application contact:* Kristin Williams, Assistant Vice President for Graduate and Special Enrollment Management, 202-994-0467, Fax: 202-994-0371, E-mail: ksw@gwu.edu.

Georgia Institute of Technology, Graduate Studies and Research, College of Management, Program in Business Administration, Atlanta, GA 30332-0001. Offers accounting (MBA); e-commerce (Certificate); engineering entrepreneurship (MBA); entrepreneurship (Certificate); finance (MBA); information technology management (MBA); international business (MBA, Certificate); management of technology (Certificate); marketing (MBA); operations management (MBA); organizational behavior (MBA); strategic management (MBA). *Accreditation:* AACSB.

Georgia Institute of Technology, Graduate Studies and Research, College of Management, Program in Management of Technology, Atlanta, GA 30332-0001. Offers EMBA. Part-time and evening/weekend programs available. *Degree requirements:* For master's, study abroad. *Entrance requirements:* For master's, GMAT, 5 years of professional work experience. Additional exam requirements/recommendations for international students: Required—TOEFL. Electronic applications accepted. *Expenses:* Contact institution. *Faculty research:* Innovation management, technology analysis, operations management.

Golden Gate University, Ageno School of Business, San Francisco, CA 94105-2968. Offers accounting (MBA); business administration (EMBA, MBA, PMBA, DBA); finance (MBA, MS, Certificate); financial planning (MS, Certificate); healthcare information systems (Certificate); human resource management (MBA, MS); human resources management (Certificate); information systems (MS); information technology (MBA); information technology management (Certificate); integrated marketing and communications (MS, Certificate); international business (MBA); management (MBA); marketing (MBA, MS, Certificate); operations supply chain management (Certificate); psychology (MA, Certificate); public administration (EMPA); public relations (MS, Certificate); technical market analysis (Certificate); JD/MBA. Part-time and evening/weekend programs available. *Faculty:* 16 full-time (4 women), 241 part-time/adjunct (72 women). *Students:* 421 full-time (235 women), 744 part-time (425 women); includes 526 minority (114 Black or African American, non-Hispanic/Latino; 2 American Indian or Alaska Native, non-Hispanic/Latino; 296 Asian, non-Hispanic/Latino; 73 Hispanic/Latino; 29 Native Hawaiian or other Pacific Islander, non-Hispanic/Latino; 12 Two or more races, non-Hispanic/Latino), 109 international. Average age 32. 681 applicants, 78% accepted, 270 enrolled. In 2010, 550 master's, 13 doctorates awarded. *Degree requirements:* For doctorate, thesis/dissertation. *Entrance requirements:* For master's, GMAT (MBA), minimum GPA of 2.5 (MS). Additional exam requirements/recommendations for international students: Required—TOEFL. *Application deadline:* For fall admission, 5/15 for domestic and international students; for winter admission, 1/15 for domestic and international students; for spring admission, 9/15 for domestic and international students. Applications are processed on a rolling basis. Application fee: $70 ($110 for international students). Electronic applications accepted. *Expenses:* Contact institution. *Financial support:* Career-related internships or fieldwork, Federal Work-Study, institutionally sponsored loans, and scholarships/grants available. Support available to part-time students. Financial award applicants required to submit FAFSA. *Unit head:* Dr. Paul Fouts, Dean, 415-442-7026, Fax: 415-442-6579. *Application contact:* Angela Melero, Enrollment Services, 415-442-7800, Fax: 415-442-7807, E-mail: info@ggu.edu.

Harding University, College of Business Administration, Searcy, AR 72149-0001. Offers health care management (MBA); information technology management (MBA); international business (MBA); leadership and organizational management (MBA). *Accreditation:* ACBSP. Part-time and evening/weekend programs available. Postbaccalaureate distance learning degree programs offered (no on-campus study). *Faculty:* 30 part-time/adjunct (6 women). *Students:* 85 full-time (49 women), 133 part-time (52 women); includes 35 minority (27 Black or African American, non-Hispanic/Latino; 1 American Indian or Alaska Native, non-Hispanic/Latino; 4 Asian, non-Hispanic/Latino; 1 Hispanic/Latino; 1 Native Hawaiian or other Pacific Islander, non-Hispanic/Latino; 1 Two or more races, non-Hispanic/Latino), 29 international. Average age 30. 52 applicants, 94% accepted, 44 enrolled. In 2010, 100 master's awarded. *Degree requirements:* For master's, portfolio. *Entrance requirements:* For master's, minimum GPA of 3.0, 2 letters of recommendation, resume. Additional exam requirements/recommendations for international students: Required—TOEFL (minimum score 550 paper-based; 213 computer-based; 80 iBT). *Application deadline:* For fall admission, 8/1 priority date for domestic and international students; for spring admission, 12/1 priority date for domestic and international students. Applications are processed on a rolling basis. Application fee: $35. *Expenses:* Tuition: Full-time $10,098; part-time $561 per credit hour. Required fees: $22.50 per credit hour. *Financial support:* In 2010–11, 19 students received support. Unspecified assistantships available. Financial award application deadline: 7/30; financial award applicants required to submit FAFSA. *Unit head:* Glen Metheny, Director of Graduate Studies, 501-279-5851, Fax: 501-279-4805, E-mail: gmetheny@harding.edu. *Application contact:* Melanie Kiihnl, Recruiting Manager/Director of Marketing, 501-279-4523, Fax: 501-279-4805, E-mail: mba@harding.edu.

Harrisburg University of Science and Technology, Program in Project Management, Harrisburg, PA 17101. Offers construction services (MS); governmental services (MS); information technology (MS). Part-time and evening/weekend programs available. *Faculty:* 1 full-time (0 women), 3 part-time/adjunct (0 women). *Students:* 11 part-time (2 women); includes 1 Black or African American, non-Hispanic/Latino; 1 Asian, non-Hispanic/Latino; 1 Hispanic/Latino, 1

international. Average age 30. 24 applicants, 75% accepted. In 2010, 7 master's awarded. *Entrance requirements:* For master's, BS, BBA. Additional exam requirements/recommendations for international students: Required—TOEFL (minimum score 520 paper-based; 200 computer-based; 80 iBT). *Application deadline:* For fall admission, 8/1 priority date for domestic students, 7/1 priority date for international students. Applications are processed on a rolling basis. Application fee: $0. Electronic applications accepted. *Expenses:* Tuition: Full-time $19,500; part-time $700 per credit hour. *Financial support:* Scholarships/grants available. Financial award applicants required to submit FAFSA. *Unit head:* Dr. Amjad Umar, Director and Professor, 717-901-5141, Fax: 717-901-3141, E-mail: aumar@harrisburgu.edu. *Application contact:* Timothy Dawson, Information Contact, 717-901-5158, Fax: 717-901-3158, E-mail: admissions@harrisburgu.edu.

Harvard University, Graduate School of Arts and Sciences, Program in Information, Technology and Management, Cambridge, MA 02138. Offers PhD. *Expenses:* Tuition: Full-time $34,976. Required fees: $1166. Full-time tuition and fees vary according to program.

Harvard University, Harvard Business School, Doctoral Programs in Management, Boston, MA 02163. Offers accounting and management (DBA); business economics (PhD); health policy management (PhD); management (DBA); marketing (DBA); organizational behavior (PhD); science, technology and management (PhD); strategy (DBA); technology and operations management (DBA). *Degree requirements:* For doctorate, comprehensive exam (for some programs), thesis/dissertation. *Entrance requirements:* For doctorate, GRE General Test or GMAT. Additional exam requirements/recommendations for international students: Required—TOEFL. *Expenses:* Tuition: Full-time $34,976. Required fees: $1166. Full-time tuition and fees vary according to program.

Herzing University Online, Program in Business Administration, Milwaukee, WI 53203. Offers accounting (MBA); business administration (MBA); business management (MBA); healthcare management (MBA); human resources (MBA); marketing (MBA); project management (MBA); technology management (MBA). Postbaccalaureate distance learning degree programs offered (no on-campus study).

Hodges University, Graduate Programs, Naples, FL 34119. Offers business administration (MBA); computer information technology (MS); criminal justice (MCJ); education (MPS); information systems management (MIS); interdisciplinary (MPS); legal studies (MS); management (MSM); mental health counseling (MS); psychology (MPS); public administration (MPA). Part-time and evening/weekend programs available. Postbaccalaureate distance learning degree programs offered (no on-campus study). *Faculty:* 25 full-time (9 women), 5 part-time/adjunct (4 women). *Students:* 27 full-time (15 women), 228 part-time (146 women); includes 76 minority (35 Black or African American, non-Hispanic/Latino; 5 Asian, non-Hispanic/Latino; 36 Hispanic/Latino). Average age 36. 92 applicants, 91% accepted, 81 enrolled. In 2010, 92 master's awarded. *Degree requirements:* For master's, comprehensive exam (for some programs), thesis (for some programs). *Entrance requirements:* For master's, in-house entrance exam. *Application deadline:* Applications are processed on a rolling basis. Application fee: $50. Electronic applications accepted. *Expenses:* Tuition: Full-time $16,605; part-time $615 per credit hour. Required fees: $190 per trimester. *Financial support:* In 2010–11, 200 students received support. Federal Work-Study and scholarships/grants available. Financial award application deadline: 7/9; financial award applicants required to submit FAFSA. *Unit head:* Terry McMahan, President, 239-513-1122, Fax: 239-598-6253, E-mail: tmcmahan@hodges.edu. *Application contact:* Rita Lampus, Vice President of Student Enrollment Management, 239-513-1122, Fax: 239-598-6253, E-mail: rlampus@hodges.edu.

Idaho State University, Office of Graduate Studies, College of Technology, Department of Human Resource Training and Development, Pocatello, ID 83209-8380. Offers MTD. Part-time and evening/weekend programs available. *Degree requirements:* For master's, comprehensive exam, thesis optional, statistical procedures. *Entrance requirements:* For master's, GRE or MAT, minimum GPA of 3.0 in upper-division courses. Additional exam requirements/recommendations for international students: Required—TOEFL (minimum score 550 paper-based; 213 computer-based; 80 iBT). Electronic applications accepted. *Faculty research:* Learning styles, instructional methodology, leadership administration.

Illinois State University, Graduate School, College of Applied Science and Technology, Department of Technology, Normal, IL 61790-2200. Offers MS. *Degree requirements:* For master's, thesis or alternative. *Entrance requirements:* For master's, GRE General Test, minimum GPA of 2.8. *Faculty research:* National Center for Engineering and Technology Education, Illinois Manufacturing Extension Center Field Office hosting, model for the professional development of K-12 technology education teachers, Illinois State University Illinois Mathematics and Science Partnership, Illinois University council for career and technical education.

Indiana State University, College of Graduate and Professional Studies, Program in Technology Management, Terre Haute, IN 47809. Offers PhD. Postbaccalaureate distance learning degree programs offered (minimal on-campus study). *Degree requirements:* For doctorate, thesis/dissertation. *Entrance requirements:* For doctorate, GRE or GMAT, minimum graduate GPA of 3.5, 6000 hours of occupational experience. Electronic applications accepted. *Faculty research:* Production management, quality control, human resource development, construction project management, lean manufacturing.

Instituto Centroamericano de Administración de Empresas, Graduate Programs, La Garita, Costa Rica. Offers agribusiness management (MIAM); business administration (EMBA); finance (MBA); real estate management (MGREM); sustainable development (MBA); technology (MBA). *Degree requirements:* For master's, comprehensive exam, essay. *Entrance requirements:* For master's, GMAT or GRE General Test, fluency in Spanish, interview, letters of recommendation, minimum 1 year of work experience. Electronic applications accepted. *Faculty research:* Competitiveness, production.

Instituto Tecnológico y de Estudios Superiores de Monterrey, Campus Central de Veracruz, Graduate Programs, Córdoba, Mexico. Offers administration (MA); administration of information technologies (MTI); computer sciences (MCC); education (MEE); educational institution administration (MAD); educational technology (MTE); electronic commerce (MCE); finance (MAF); humanistic studies (MEH); international business for Latin America (MNL); marketing (MMT); science (MCP); technology management (MTT). Part-time and evening/weekend programs available. Postbaccalaureate distance learning degree programs offered (minimal on-campus study). *Degree requirements:* For master's, thesis (for some programs). *Entrance requirements:* For master's, PAEP College Board. Electronic applications accepted.

Instituto Tecnológico y de Estudios Superiores de Monterrey, Campus Cuernavaca, Programs in Information Science, Temixco, Mexico. Offers administration of information technology (MATI); computer science (MCC, DCC); information technology (MTI).

Instituto Tecnológico y de Estudios Superiores de Monterrey, Campus Irapuato, Graduate Programs, Irapuato, Mexico. Offers administration (MBA); administration of information technology (MAIT); administration of telecommunications (MAT); architecture (M Arch); computer science (MCS); education (M Ed); educational administration (MEA); educational innovation and technology (DEIT); educational technology (MET); electronic commerce (MBA); environmental administration and planning (MEAP); environmental systems (MES); finances (MBA); humanistic studies (MHS); international management for Latin American executives (MIMLAE); library and information science (MLIS); manufacturing quality management (MMQM); marketing research (MBA).

Iona College, Hagan School of Business, Department of Information and Decision Technology Management, New Rochelle, NY 10801-1890. Offers information systems (MBA, PMC). Part-time and evening/weekend programs available. *Faculty:* 5 full-time (0 women), 4 part-time/adjunct (0 women). *Students:* 6 full-time (1 woman), 15 part-time (4 women); includes 2 minority (1 Black or African American, non-Hispanic/Latino; 1 Hispanic/Latino), 1 international. Average

Management of Technology

Iona College (continued)
age 30. 8 applicants, 88% accepted, 5 enrolled. In 2010, 9 master's awarded. *Entrance requirements:* For master's, GMAT, 2 letters of recommendation; for PMC, GMAT. Additional exam requirements/recommendations for international students: Required—TOEFL (minimum score 550 paper-based; 213 computer-based). *Application deadline:* Applications are processed on a rolling basis. Application fee: $50. Electronic applications accepted. *Expenses:* Contact institution. *Financial support:* Scholarships/grants, tuition waivers (partial), and unspecified assistantships available. Support available to part-time students. Financial award application deadline: 4/15; financial award applicants required to submit FAFSA. *Faculty research:* Fuzzy sets, risk management, computer security, competence set analysis, investment strategies. *Unit head:* Dr. Robert Richardson, Chairman, 914-637-7726, E-mail: rrichardson@iona.edu. *Application contact:* Ben Fan, Director of MBA Admissions, 914-633-2289, Fax: 914-637-2708, E-mail: sfan@iona.edu.

The Johns Hopkins University, Engineering for Professionals, Part-time Program in Technical Management, Baltimore, MD 21218-2699. Offers MS, Graduate Certificate, Post-Master's Certificate. Part-time and evening/weekend programs available. *Faculty:* 37 part-time/adjunct (13 women). *Students:* 3 full-time (1 woman), 145 part-time (40 women); includes 51 minority (25 Black or African American, non-Hispanic/Latino; 16 Asian, non-Hispanic/Latino; 7 Hispanic/Latino; 3 Two or more races, non-Hispanic/Latino), 7 international. Average age 35. 42 applicants, 90% accepted, 34 enrolled. In 2010, 47 master's, 2 other advanced degrees awarded. *Application deadline:* Applications are processed on a rolling basis. Application fee: $75. Electronic applications accepted. *Financial support:* Institutionally sponsored loans available. *Unit head:* Dr. Joseph J. Suter, Program Chair, 443-778-5826, E-mail: joseph.suter@jhuapl.edu. *Application contact:* Priyanka Dwivedi, Admissions Manager, 410-516-2300, Fax: 410-579-8049, E-mail: pdwived1@jhu.edu.

Jones International University, School of Business, Centennial, CO 80112. Offers accounting (MBA); business communication (MABC); entrepreneurship (MABC, MBA); finance (MBA); global enterprise management (MBA); health care management (MBA); information security management (MBA); information technology management (MBA); leadership and influence (MABC); leading the customer-driven organization (MABC); negotiation and conflict management (MBA); project management (MABC, MBA). Program only offered online. Part-time and evening/weekend programs available. Postbaccalaureate distance learning degree programs offered (no on-campus study). *Degree requirements:* For master's, capstone project. *Entrance requirements:* For master's, minimum cumulative GPA of 2.5. Additional exam requirements/recommendations for international students: Recommended—TOEFL (minimum score 550 paper-based; 213 computer-based). Electronic applications accepted.

La Salle University, School of Arts and Sciences, Program in Information Technology Leadership, Philadelphia, PA 19141-1199. Offers MS.

Lawrence Technological University, College of Management, Southfield, MI 48075-1058. Offers business administration (MBA, DBA); business administration international (MBA); global leadership and management (MS); global operations and project management (MS); information systems (MS); information technology (DM); operations management (MS). *Accreditation:* ACBSP. Part-time and evening/weekend programs available. *Faculty:* 14 full-time (6 women), 53 part-time/adjunct (14 women). *Students:* 7 full-time (2 women), 584 part-time (258 women); includes 137 Black or African American, non-Hispanic/Latino; 2 American Indian or Alaska Native, non-Hispanic/Latino; 51 Asian, non-Hispanic/Latino; 10 Hispanic/Latino; 8 Two or more races, non-Hispanic/Latino, 48 international. Average age 35. 431 applicants, 54% accepted, 151 enrolled. In 2010, 216 master's, 12 doctorates awarded. *Degree requirements:* For master's, thesis (for some programs). *Entrance requirements:* For master's, GMAT. Additional exam requirements/recommendations for international students: Required—TOEFL (minimum score 550 paper-based; 213 computer-based; 79 iBT). *Application deadline:* For fall admission, 6/30 priority date for domestic students, 6/30 for international students; for spring admission, 11/15 priority date for domestic students, 11/15 for international students. Applications are processed on a rolling basis. Application fee: $50. Electronic applications accepted. *Financial support:* In 2010–11, 142 students received support. Federal Work-Study and institutionally sponsored loans available. Support available to part-time students. Financial award application deadline: 4/1; financial award applicants required to submit FAFSA. *Unit head:* Dr. Lou DeGennaro, Dean, 248-204-3050, E-mail: degennaro@ltu.edu. *Application contact:* Jane Rohrback, Director of Admissions, 248-204-3160, Fax: 248-204-2228, E-mail: admissions@ltu.edu.

Lewis University, College of Business, Graduate School of Management, Program in Business Administration, Romeoville, IL 60446. Offers accounting (MBA); custom elective option (MBA); e-business (MBA); finance (MBA); healthcare management (MBA); human resources management (MBA); information security (MBA); international business (MBA); management information systems (MBA); marketing (MBA); project management (MBA); technology and operations management (MBA). Part-time and evening/weekend programs available. *Students:* 119 full-time (66 women), 204 part-time (104 women); includes 55 Black or African American, non-Hispanic/Latino; 9 Asian, non-Hispanic/Latino; 30 Hispanic/Latino; 1 Native Hawaiian or other Pacific Islander, non-Hispanic/Latino, 9 international. Average age 28. In 2010, 111 master's awarded. *Entrance requirements:* For master's, interview, bachelor's degree, resume, 2 recommendations. Additional exam requirements/recommendations for international students: Required—TOEFL (minimum score 550 paper-based; 213 computer-based). *Application deadline:* For fall admission, 8/15 priority date for domestic students, 5/1 priority date for international students; for spring admission, 11/15 priority date for international students. Applications are processed on a rolling basis. Application fee: $40. Electronic applications accepted. *Expenses:* Tuition: Full-time $13,320; part-time $740 per credit hour. Tuition and fees vary according to program. *Financial support:* Career-related internships or fieldwork, Federal Work-Study, scholarships/grants, and unspecified assistantships available. Financial award application deadline: 5/1; financial award applicants required to submit FAFSA. *Unit head:* Dr. Maureen Culleeney, Academic Program Director, 815-838-0500 Ext. 5631, E-mail: culleema@lewisu.edu. *Application contact:* Michele Ryan, Director of Admission, 815-838-0500 Ext. 5384, E-mail: gsm@lewisu.edu.

Marist College, Graduate Programs, School of Computer Science and Mathematics, Poughkeepsie, NY 12601-1387. Offers computer science/software development (MS); information systems (MS, Adv C); technology management (MS). Part-time and evening/weekend programs available. Postbaccalaureate distance learning degree programs offered (minimal on-campus study). *Entrance requirements:* For master's, resume. Additional exam requirements/recommendations for international students: Required—TOEFL (minimum score 550 paper-based; 213 computer-based; 80 iBT); Recommended—IELTS (minimum score 6.5). Electronic applications accepted. *Faculty research:* Data quality, artificial intelligence, imaging, analysis of algorithms, distributed systems and applications.

Marist College, Graduate Programs, School of Management and School of Computer Science and Mathematics, Program in Technology Management, Poughkeepsie, NY 12601-1387. Offers MS. Part-time and evening/weekend programs available. Postbaccalaureate distance learning degree programs offered (minimal on-campus study). *Entrance requirements:* For master's, GMAT or GRE, minimum undergraduate GPA of 3.0, 2 letters of recommendation, resume, professional experience. Additional exam requirements/recommendations for international students: Required—TOEFL (minimum score 550 paper-based; 213 computer-based; 80 iBT); Recommended—IELTS (minimum score 6.5). Electronic applications accepted.

Marquette University, Graduate School, College of Engineering, Department of Biomedical Engineering, Milwaukee, WI 53201-1881. Offers biocomputing (ME); bioimaging (ME); bioinstrumentation (ME); bioinstrumentation/computers (MS, PhD); biomechanics (ME); biomechanics/biomaterials (MS, PhD); biorehabilitation (ME); functional imaging (PhD); healthcare technologies management (MS); rehabilitation bioengineering (PhD); systems physiology (MS, PhD). Part-time and evening/weekend programs available. *Faculty:* 15 full-time (5 women), 5 part-time/adjunct (2 women). *Students:* 59 full-time (18 women), 27 part-time (9 women); includes 8 minority (1 American Indian or Alaska Native, non-Hispanic/Latino; 5 Asian, non-Hispanic/Latino; 1 Hispanic/Latino; 1 Native Hawaiian or other Pacific Islander, non-Hispanic/Latino), 24 international. Average age 27. 128 applicants, 30% accepted, 14 enrolled. In 2010, 8 master's awarded. Terminal master's awarded for partial completion of doctoral program. *Degree requirements:* For master's, comprehensive exam, thesis; for doctorate, comprehensive exam, thesis/dissertation, dissertation defense, qualifying exam. *Entrance requirements:* For master's, GRE General Test, minimum GPA of 3.0, official transcripts from all current and previous colleges/universities except Marquette, three letters of recommendation, brief statement of purpose that includes proposed area of research specialization, interview with the M.E. program director, one year of post-baccalaureate professional work experience; for doctorate, GRE General Test, minimum GPA of 3.0, official transcripts from all current and previous colleges/universities except Marquette, three letters of recommendation, brief statement of purpose that includes proposed area of research specialization. Additional exam requirements/recommendations for international students: Required—TOEFL (minimum score 530 paper-based; 78 computer-based). *Application deadline:* For fall admission, 2/15 priority date for domestic students; for spring admission, 11/15 priority date for domestic students. Applications are processed on a rolling basis. Application fee: $50. Electronic applications accepted. *Expenses:* Tuition: Full-time $16,290; part-time $905 per credit hour. Tuition and fees vary according to program. *Financial support:* In 2010–11, 50 students received support, including 8 fellowships with full tuition reimbursements available, 4 research assistantships with full tuition reimbursements available, 7 teaching assistantships with full tuition reimbursements available; Federal Work-Study, institutionally sponsored loans, and scholarships/grants also available. Support available to part-time students. Financial award application deadline: 2/15. *Faculty research:* Cell and organ physiology, signal processing, gait analysis, orthopedic rehabilitation engineering, telemedicine. Total annual research expenditures: $1.8 million. *Unit head:* Dr. Kristina Ropella, Chair, 414-288-3375, Fax: 414-288-7938, E-mail: kristina.ropella@marquette.edu. *Application contact:* Erin Fox, Assistant Chair, 414-288-7182, Fax: 414-288-1902, E-mail: erin.fox@marquette.edu.

Marshall University, Academic Affairs Division, College of Information Technology and Engineering, Division of Applied Science and Technology, Program in Technology Management, Huntington, WV 25755. Offers MS. Part-time and evening/weekend programs available. *Students:* 28 full-time (5 women), 31 part-time (4 women); includes 2 Black or African American, non-Hispanic/Latino, 19 international. Average age 33. In 2010, 6 master's awarded. *Degree requirements:* For master's, final project, oral exam. *Entrance requirements:* For master's, GRE General Test or GMAT, minimum undergraduate GPA of 2.5. Application fee: $40. *Financial support:* Tuition waivers (full) available. Support available to part-time students. Financial award application deadline: 8/1; financial award applicants required to submit FAFSA. *Unit head:* Dr. Tracy Christofero, Program Coordinator, 304-746-2078, E-mail: christofero@marshall.edu. *Application contact:* Information Contact, 304-746-1900, Fax: 304-746-1902, E-mail: services@marshall.edu.

Mercer University, Graduate Studies, Macon Campus, School of Engineering, Macon, GA 31207-0003. Offers biomedical engineering (MSE); computer engineering (MSE); electrical engineering (MSE); engineering management (MSE); environmental engineering (MSE); environmental systems (MS); mechanical engineering (MSE); software engineering (MSE); software systems (MS); technical communications management (MS); technical management (MS). Part-time and evening/weekend programs available. Postbaccalaureate distance learning degree programs offered (no on-campus study). *Faculty:* 18 full-time (4 women), 1 part-time/adjunct (0 women). *Students:* 11 full-time (2 women), 100 part-time (22 women); includes 26 minority (13 Black or African American, non-Hispanic/Latino; 12 Asian, non-Hispanic/Latino; 1 Hispanic/Latino), 3 international. Average age 32. In 2010, 46 master's awarded. *Degree requirements:* For master's, thesis or alternative. *Entrance requirements:* For master's, minimum undergraduate GPA of 3.0. Additional exam requirements/recommendations for international students: Required—TOEFL. *Application deadline:* For fall admission, 7/1 for domestic students; for spring admission, 11/15 for domestic students. Applications are processed on a rolling basis. Application fee: $35 ($50 for international students). Electronic applications accepted. *Expenses:* Contact institution. *Financial support:* Federal Work-Study available. *Unit head:* Dr. Wade H. Shaw, Dean, 478-301-2459, Fax: 478-301-5593, E-mail: shaw_wh@mercer.edu. *Application contact:* Greg Lofton, Graduate Program Coordinator, 478-301-5480, Fax: 478-301-5434, E-mail: lofton_g@mercer.edu.

Murray State University, College of Science, Engineering and Technology, Program in Management of Technology, Murray, KY 42071. Offers MS. Part-time and evening/weekend programs available. *Degree requirements:* For master's, comprehensive exam. *Entrance requirements:* Additional exam requirements/recommendations for international students: Required—TOEFL (computer-based 273) or IELTS. *Faculty research:* Environmental, hydrology, groundworks.

National University, Academic Affairs, School of Business and Management, Department of Leadership and Business Administration, La Jolla, CA 92037-1011. Offers alternative dispute resolution (MBA); e-business (MBA); financial management (MBA); human resource management (MBA); human resources management (MA); international business (MBA); knowledge management (MS); marketing (MBA); organizational leadership (MBA, MS); technology management (MBA). Part-time and evening/weekend programs available. Postbaccalaureate distance learning degree programs offered (no on-campus study). *Faculty:* 16 full-time (4 women), 126 part-time/adjunct (39 women). *Students:* 119 full-time (81 women), 410 part-time (202 women); includes 176 minority (81 Black or African American, non-Hispanic/Latino; 1 American Indian or Alaska Native, non-Hispanic/Latino; 31 Asian, non-Hispanic/Latino; 52 Hispanic/Latino; 4 Native Hawaiian or other Pacific Islander, non-Hispanic/Latino; 7 Two or more races, non-Hispanic/Latino), 303 international. Average age 38. 219 applicants, 100% accepted, 160 enrolled. In 2010, 95 master's awarded. *Degree requirements:* For master's, thesis. *Entrance requirements:* For master's, interview, minimum GPA of 2.5. Additional exam requirements/recommendations for international students: Required—TOEFL (minimum score 550 paper-based; 213 computer-based; 79 iBT), IELTS (minimum score 6). *Application deadline:* Applications are processed on a rolling basis. Application fee: $60 ($65 for international students). Electronic applications accepted. *Expenses:* Tuition: Full-time $9450; part-time $350 per unit. Required fees: $350 per unit. One-time fee: $60. *Financial support:* Career-related internships or fieldwork, institutionally sponsored loans, scholarships/grants, and tuition waivers (partial) available. Support available to part-time students. Financial award application deadline: 6/30; financial award applicants required to submit FAFSA. *Unit head:* Dr. Bruce Buchowicz, Chair, 858-642-8439, Fax: 858-642-8406, E-mail: bbuchowicz@nu.edu. *Application contact:* Dominick Giovanniello, Associate Regional Dean—San Diego, 800-NAT-UNIV, Fax: 858-541-7792, E-mail: dgiovann@nu.edu.

National University, Academic Affairs, School of Engineering and Technology, Department of Computer Science and Information Systems, La Jolla, CA 92037-1011. Offers computer science (MS); information systems (MS); software engineering (MS); technology management (MS). Part-time and evening/weekend programs available. Postbaccalaureate distance learning degree programs offered (no on-campus study). *Faculty:* 8 full-time (1 woman), 90 part-time/adjunct (13 women). *Students:* 60 full-time (12 women), 146 part-time (40 women); includes 365 minority (25 Black or African American, non-Hispanic/Latino; 21 Asian, non-Hispanic/Latino; 14 Hispanic/Latino; 2 Native Hawaiian or other Pacific Islander, non-Hispanic/Latino; 303 Two or more races, non-Hispanic/Latino), 54 international. Average age 32. 138 applicants, 100% accepted, 79 enrolled. In 2010, 79 master's awarded. *Degree requirements:* For master's, thesis. *Entrance requirements:* For master's, interview, minimum GPA of 2.5. Additional exam requirements/recommendations for international students: Required—TOEFL (minimum score 550 paper-based; 213 computer-based; 79 iBT), IELTS (minimum score 6). *Application deadline:* Applications are processed on a rolling basis. Application fee: $60 ($65 for international students). Electronic applications accepted. *Expenses:* Tuition: Full-time $9450; part-time $350 per unit. Required fees: $350 per unit. One-time fee: $60. *Financial support:* Career-related internships or fieldwork, institutionally sponsored loans, scholarships/grants, and tuition waivers (partial) available. Support available to part-time students. Financial award application deadline: 6/30; financial award applicants required to submit FAFSA. *Unit head:* Dr. Alireza M. Farahani, Chair and Instructor, 858-309-3438, Fax: 858-309-3420, E-mail: afarahan@nu.edu. *Application contact:* Dominick Giovanniello, Associate Regional Dean—San Diego, 800-NAT-UNIV, Fax: 858-541-7792, E-mail: dgiovann@nu.edu.

New Jersey Institute of Technology, Office of Graduate Studies, School of Management, Program in Management of Technology, Newark, NJ 07102. Offers MS. Part-time and evening/weekend programs available. *Students:* 1 full-time; includes Hispanic/Latino. Average age 32.Terminal master's awarded for partial completion of doctoral program. *Degree requirements:* For master's, thesis optional. *Entrance requirements:* For master's, GMAT. Additional exam requirements/recommendations for international students: Required—TOEFL (minimum score 550 paper-based; 213 computer-based; 79 iBT). *Application deadline:* For fall admission, 6/5 priority date for domestic students, 4/1 for international students; for spring admission, 11/15 for domestic and international students. Applications are processed on a rolling basis. Application fee: $65. Electronic applications accepted. *Expenses:* Tuition, state resident: full-time $14,724; part-time $818 per credit. Tuition, nonresident: full-time $20,304; part-time $1128 per credit. Required fees: $2272; $209 per credit. $103 per semester. One-time fee: $312 full-time; $212 part-time. *Financial support:* Fellowships with full and partial tuition reimbursements, research assistantships with full and partial tuition reimbursements, teaching assistantships with full and partial tuition reimbursements, career-related internships or fieldwork, Federal Work-Study, institutionally sponsored loans, and unspecified assistantships available. Financial award application deadline: 3/15; financial award applicants required to submit FAFSA. *Unit head:* Dr. Robert English, Chair, 973-596-3224, Fax: 973-596-3074, E-mail: robert.english@njit.edu. *Application contact:* Kathryn Kelly, Director of Admissions, 973-596-3300, Fax: 973-596-3461, E-mail: admissions@njit.edu.

North Carolina Agricultural and Technical State University, Graduate School, School of Technology, Department of Graphic Communication Systems and Technological Studies, Greensboro, NC 27411. Offers industrial arts education (MS); technology education (MS); technology management (PhD); vocational-industrial education (MS); workforce development director (MS). *Accreditation:* NCATE (one or more programs are accredited). Part-time and evening/weekend programs available. *Degree requirements:* For master's, comprehensive exam, thesis or alternative, qualifying exam. *Entrance requirements:* For master's, GRE General Test, minimum GPA of 3.0.

North Carolina Agricultural and Technical State University, Graduate School, School of Technology, Department of Manufacturing Systems, Greensboro, NC 27411. Offers industrial technology (MS, MSIT); safety and driver education (MS). Part-time and evening/weekend programs available. *Degree requirements:* For master's, comprehensive exam, thesis or alternative, qualifying exam. *Entrance requirements:* For master's, GRE General Test, minimum GPA of 3.0.

North Carolina State University, Graduate School, College of Textiles, Program in Textile Technology Management, Raleigh, NC 27695. Offers PhD. *Degree requirements:* For doctorate, one foreign language, thesis/dissertation, cumulative exams. *Entrance requirements:* For doctorate, GRE or GMAT. Electronic applications accepted. *Faculty research:* Niche markets, supply chain, globalization, logistics.

Northern Kentucky University, Office of Graduate Programs, College of Informatics, Program in Computer Information Technology, Highland Heights, KY 41099. Offers MSCIT. Part-time and evening/weekend programs available. *Faculty:* 6 full-time (1 woman). *Students:* 14 full-time (2 women), 25 part-time (10 women); includes 6 minority (3 Black or African American, non-Hispanic/Latino; 2 Asian, non-Hispanic/Latino; 1 Hispanic/Latino), 2 international. Average age 35. 41 applicants, 66% accepted, 17 enrolled. In 2010, 1 master's awarded. *Degree requirements:* For master's, thesis optional. *Entrance requirements:* For master's, GRE, minimum GPA of 2.5, computer science or related undergraduate degree, letter of intent, resume. Additional exam requirements/recommendations for international students: Required—TOEFL (minimum score 550 paper-based; 213 computer-based; 79 iBT); Recommended—IELTS (minimum score 6.5). *Application deadline:* For fall admission, 8/1 for domestic students, 6/1 for international students; for spring admission, 12/1 for domestic students, 10/1 for international students. Applications are processed on a rolling basis. Application fee: $40. Electronic applications accepted. *Expenses:* Tuition, state resident: full-time $7254; part-time $403 per credit hour. Tuition, nonresident: full-time $12,492; part-time $694 per credit hour. Tuition and fees vary according to degree level and program. *Financial support:* Scholarships/grants and unspecified assistantships available. Financial award applicants required to submit FAFSA. *Faculty research:* Data privacy, software security, database security, mobile and wireless networks, network security. *Unit head:* Dr. Traian Marius Truta, Coordinator, 859-572-7551, E-mail: trutat1@nku.edu. *Application contact:* Dr. Peg Griffin, Director of Graduate Programs, 859-572-6934, Fax: 859-572-6670, E-mail: griffinp@nku.edu.

OGI School of Science & Engineering at Oregon Health & Science University, Graduate Studies, Department of Management in Science and Technology, Beaverton, OR 97006-8921. Offers health care management (Certificate); management in science and technology (MS, Certificate). Part-time and evening/weekend programs available. *Degree requirements:* For master's, thesis. *Entrance requirements:* For master's, 2 years of work experience. Additional exam requirements/recommendations for international students: Recommended—TOEFL (minimum score 625 paper-based; 263 computer-based). Electronic applications accepted.

Old Dominion University, College of Business and Public Administration, MBA Program, Norfolk, VA 23529. Offers business and economic forecasting (MBA); financial analysis and valuation (MBA); information technology and enterprise integration (MBA); international business (MBA); maritime and port management (MBA); public administration (MBA). *Accreditation:* AACSB. Part-time and evening/weekend programs available. *Faculty:* 66 full-time (15 women), 6 part-time/adjunct (1 woman). *Students:* 74 full-time (32 women), 166 part-time (62 women); includes 45 minority (21 Black or African American, non-Hispanic/Latino; 1 American Indian or Alaska Native, non-Hispanic/Latino; 8 Asian, non-Hispanic/Latino; 10 Hispanic/Latino; 1 Native Hawaiian or other Pacific Islander, non-Hispanic/Latino; 4 Two or more races, non-Hispanic/Latino), 19 international. Average age 31. 169 applicants, 52% accepted, 61 enrolled. In 2010, 100 master's awarded. *Entrance requirements:* For master's, GMAT, letter of reference, resume, coursework in calculus, essay. Additional exam requirements/recommendations for international students: Required—TOEFL (minimum score 550 paper-based; 213 computer-based; 80 iBT). *Application deadline:* For fall admission, 6/1 priority date for domestic students, 4/15 priority date for international students; for spring admission, 11/1 priority date for domestic students, 10/1 priority date for international students. Applications are processed on a rolling basis. Application fee: $50. Electronic applications accepted. *Expenses:* Tuition, state resident: full-time $8592; part-time $358 per credit. Tuition, nonresident: full-time $21,672; part-time $903 per credit. Required fees: $119 per semester. One-time fee: $50. *Financial support:* In 2010–11, 44 students received support, including 90 research assistantships with partial tuition reimbursements available (averaging $3,200 per year); career-related internships or fieldwork, scholarships/grants, and unspecified assistantships also available. Support available to part-time students. Financial award application deadline: 2/15; financial award applicants required to submit FAFSA. *Faculty research:* International business, buyer behavior, financial markets, strategy, operations research. *Unit head:* Dr. Larry Filer, Graduate Program Director, 757-683-3585, Fax: 757-683-5750, E-mail: mbainfo@odu.edu. *Application contact:* Shanna Wood, MBA Program Manager, 757-683-3585, Fax: 757-683-5750, E-mail: mbainfo@odu.edu.

Oregon Health & Science University, School of Medicine, Graduate Programs in Medicine, Department of Management in Science and Technology, Portland, OR 97239-3098. Offers healthcare management (MBA, MS). Part-time programs available. *Faculty:* 4 full-time (2 women), 59 part-time/adjunct (21 women). *Students:* 115 (63 women); includes 2 Black or African American, non-Hispanic/Latino; 1 American Indian or Alaska Native, non-Hispanic/Latino; 11 Asian, non-Hispanic/Latino; 3 Hispanic/Latino; 1 Native Hawaiian or other Pacific Islander, non-Hispanic/Latino, 10 international. Average age 39. 13 applicants, 69% accepted, 2 enrolled. In 2010, 7 master's awarded. *Degree requirements:* For master's, thesis optional. *Entrance requirements:* For master's, GRE General Test (minimum scores: 500 Verbal/600 Quantitative/4.5 Analytical) or GMAT. Additional exam requirements/recommendations for international students: Required—TOEFL. *Application deadline:* For fall admission, 7/15 for domestic and international students; for winter admission, 10/15 for domestic and international students; for spring admission, 1/15 for domestic and international students. Applications are processed on a rolling basis. Application fee: $65. Electronic applications accepted. *Financial support:* Health care benefits available. *Unit head:* Colm Joyce, Director of Admissions & Marketing, 503-346-0376, E-mail: hcmanagement@ohsu.edu. *Application contact:* Program Coordinator, 503-346-0375, E-mail: hcmanagement@ohsu.edu.

Pacific Lutheran University, Division of Graduate Studies, School of Business, Tacoma, WA 98447. Offers business administration (MBA), including technology and innovation management. *Accreditation:* AACSB. Part-time and evening/weekend programs available. *Entrance requirements:* For master's, GMAT. Additional exam requirements/recommendations for international students: Required—TOEFL (minimum score 550 paper-based; 213 computer-based).

Pacific States University, College of Business, Los Angeles, CA 90006. Offers accounting (MBA); business administration (DBA); finance (MBA); international business (MBA); management of information technology (MBA); real estate management (MBA). Part-time and evening/weekend programs available. Postbaccalaureate distance learning degree programs offered (no on-campus study). *Faculty:* 4 full-time (1 woman), 13 part-time/adjunct (0 women). *Students:* 130 full-time (55 women); includes 1 Black or African American, non-Hispanic/Latino; 7 Asian, non-Hispanic/Latino; 3 Native Hawaiian or other Pacific Islander, non-Hispanic/Latino, 115 international. Average age 31. 42 applicants, 83% accepted, 33 enrolled. In 2010, 67 master's awarded. *Degree requirements:* For doctorate, comprehensive exam, thesis/dissertation. *Entrance requirements:* For master's, minimum undergraduate GPA of 2.5 during last 90 hours of course work. Additional exam requirements/recommendations for international students: Required—TOEFL (minimum score 133 computer-based; 45 iBT), IELTS (minimum score 4.5). *Application deadline:* For fall admission, 8/15 priority date for domestic students; for winter admission, 10/15 priority date for domestic students; for spring admission, 1/15 priority date for domestic students. Applications are processed on a rolling basis. Application fee: $100. *Expenses:* Tuition: Full-time $8280; part-time $345 per credit hour. Required fees: $150 per quarter. *Financial support:* Scholarships/grants available. Financial award applicants required to submit FAFSA. *Unit head:* Dr. Chase C. Lee, Director, 888-200-0383, Fax: 323-731-2383, E-mail: admission@psuca.edu. *Application contact:* Zolzaya Enkhbayar, Assistant Director of Admissions, 323-731-2383, Fax: 323-731-7276, E-mail: admissions@psuca.edu.

Polytechnic Institute of NYU, Department of Finance and Risk Engineering, Brooklyn, NY 11201-2990. Offers financial engineering (MS, Advanced Certificate), including capital markets (MS), computational finance (MS), financial technology (MS); financial technology management (Advanced Certificate); organizational behavior (Advanced Certificate); risk management (Advanced Certificate); technology management (Advanced Certificate). Part-time and evening/weekend programs available. *Faculty:* 6 full-time (1 woman), 24 part-time/adjunct (5 women). *Students:* 126 full-time (45 women), 61 part-time (15 women); includes 4 Black or African American, non-Hispanic/Latino; 17 Asian, non-Hispanic/Latino; 1 Hispanic/Latino, 130 international. Average age 27. 528 applicants, 44% accepted, 67 enrolled. In 2010, 154 master's awarded. *Degree requirements:* For master's, comprehensive exam (for some programs), thesis (for some programs). *Entrance requirements:* For master's, GMAT, minimum B average in undergraduate course work. Additional exam requirements/recommendations for international students: Required—TOEFL (minimum score 550 paper-based; 213 computer-based; 80 iBT); Recommended—IELTS (minimum score 6.5). *Application deadline:* For fall admission, 7/31 priority date for domestic students, 4/30 priority date for international students; for spring admission, 12/31 priority date for domestic students, 11/30 priority date for international students. Applications are processed on a rolling basis. Application fee: $75. Electronic applications accepted. *Expenses:* Tuition: Full-time $21,492; part-time $1194 per credit. Required fees: $385 per semester. Tuition and fees vary according to course load. *Financial support:* Institutionally sponsored loans, scholarships/grants, and unspecified assistantships available. Support available to part-time students. Financial award applicants required to submit FAFSA. *Unit head:* Prof. Charles S. Tapiero, Academic Director, 718-260-3653, Fax: 718-260-3874, E-mail: ctapiero@poly.edu. *Application contact:* JeanCarlo Bonilla, Director, Graduate Enrollment Management, 718-260-3182, Fax: 718-260-3624.

Polytechnic Institute of NYU, Department of Technology Management, Major in Management of Technology, Brooklyn, NY 11201-2990. Offers MS. *Students:* 89 full-time (27 women), 20 part-time (5 women); includes 13 Asian, non-Hispanic/Latino; 3 Hispanic/Latino, 39 international. Average age 30. 108 applicants, 59% accepted, 42 enrolled. In 2010, 31 master's awarded. *Degree requirements:* For master's, comprehensive exam (for some programs), thesis (for some programs). *Entrance requirements:* For master's, GMAT, minimum B average in undergraduate course work. Additional exam requirements/recommendations for international students: Required—TOEFL (minimum score 550 paper-based; 213 computer-based; 80 iBT); Recommended—IELTS (minimum score 6.5). *Application deadline:* For fall admission, 7/31 priority date for domestic students, 4/30 priority date for international students; for spring admission, 12/31 priority date for domestic students, 11/30 priority date for international students. Applications are processed on a rolling basis. Application fee: $75. Electronic applications accepted. *Expenses:* Tuition: Full-time $21,492; part-time $1194 per credit. Required fees: $385 per semester. Tuition and fees vary according to course load. *Financial support:* Institutionally sponsored loans, scholarships/grants, and unspecified assistantships available. Support available to part-time students. Financial award applicants required to submit FAFSA. *Unit head:* Prof. Bharadwaj Rao, Head, 718-260-3617, Fax: 718-260-3874, E-mail: brao@poly.edu. *Application contact:* JeanCarlo Bonilla, Director of Graduate Enrollment Management, 718-260-3182, Fax: 718-260-3624, E-mail: gradinfo@poly.edu.

Polytechnic Institute of NYU, Department of Technology Management, Major in Technology Management, Brooklyn, NY 11201-2990. Offers MBA, PhD. *Students:* 1 (woman) full-time, 4 part-time (1 woman); includes 1 Hispanic/Latino, 2 international. Average age 35. 19 applicants, 32% accepted, 1 enrolled. In 2010, 1 doctorate awarded. *Entrance requirements:* Additional exam requirements/recommendations for international students: Required—TOEFL (minimum score 550 paper-based; 213 computer-based; 80 iBT); Recommended—IELTS (minimum score 6.5). *Application deadline:* For fall admission, 7/31 priority date for domestic students, 4/30 priority date for international students; for spring admission, 12/31 priority date for domestic students, 11/30 priority date for international students. Applications are processed on a rolling basis. Application fee: $75. Electronic applications accepted. *Expenses:* Tuition: Full-time $21,492; part-time $1194 per credit. Required fees: $385 per semester. Tuition and fees vary according to course load. *Financial support:* Institutionally sponsored loans, scholarships/grants, and unspecified assistantships available. Support available to part-time students. *Unit head:* Bharadwaj Rao, Head, 718-260-3617, Fax: 718-260-3874, E-mail: brao@poly.edu. *Application contact:* JeanCarlo Bonilla, Director, Graduate Enrollment Management, 718-260-3182, Fax: 718-260-3624, E-mail: gradinfo@poly.edu.

Polytechnic Institute of NYU, Long Island Graduate Center, Graduate Programs, Department of Technology Management, Major in Management, Melville, NY 11747. Offers MS. Part-time and evening/weekend programs available. *Faculty:* 3 part-time/adjunct (0 women). *Students:* 5 part-time (2 women); includes 2 minority (both Asian, non-Hispanic/Latino). Average age 39. 14 applicants, 64% accepted, 4 enrolled. In 2010, 4 master's awarded. *Degree requirements:* For master's, comprehensive exam (for some programs), thesis (for some programs). *Entrance requirements:* Additional exam requirements/recommendations for international students: Required—TOEFL (minimum score 550 paper-based; 213 computer-based; 80 iBT); Recommended—IELTS (minimum score 6.5). *Application deadline:* For fall admission, 7/31 priority date for domestic students, 4/30 priority date for international students; for spring admission, 12/31 priority date for domestic students, 11/30 priority date for international students. Applications are processed on a rolling basis. Application fee: $75. Electronic applications accepted. *Expenses:* Tuition: Full-time $21,492; part-time $1194 per credit. Required

Management of Technology

Polytechnic Institute of NYU, Long Island Graduate Center *(continued)*
fees: $385 per semester. Tuition and fees vary according to course load. *Financial support:* Institutionally sponsored loans, scholarships/grants, and unspecified assistantships available. Support available to part-time students. Financial award applicants required to submit FAFSA. *Unit head:* Dr. Bharadwaj Rao, Department Head, 718-260-3617, E-mail: brao@poly.edu. *Application contact:* JeanCarlo Bonilla, Director of Graduate Enrollment Management, 718-260-3182, Fax: 718-260-3624, E-mail: gradinfo@poly.edu.

Polytechnic Institute of NYU, Long Island Graduate Center, Graduate Programs, Department of Technology Management, Major in Management of Technology, Melville, NY 11747. Offers MS. Part-time and evening/weekend programs available. *Students:* 1 part-time (0 women); minority (Asian, non-Hispanic/Latino). Average age 37. 6 applicants, 67% accepted. *Entrance requirements:* Additional exam requirements/recommendations for international students: Required—TOEFL (minimum score 550 paper-based; 213 computer-based; 80 iBT); Recommended—IELTS (minimum score 6.5). *Application deadline:* For fall admission, 7/31 priority date for domestic students, 4/30 priority date for international students; for spring admission, 12/31 priority date for domestic students, 11/30 priority date for international students. Applications are processed on a rolling basis. Application fee: $75. Electronic applications accepted. *Expenses:* Tuition: Full-time $21,492; part-time $1194 per credit. Required fees: $385 per semester. Tuition and fees vary according to course load. *Financial support:* Institutionally sponsored loans, scholarships/grants, and unspecified assistantships available. Support available to part-time students. *Unit head:* Dr. Bharadwaj Rao, Department Head, 718-260-3617, E-mail: brao@poly.edu. *Application contact:* JeanCarlo Bonilla, Director of Graduate Enrollment Management, 718-260-3182, Fax: 718-260-3624, E-mail: gradinfo@poly.edu.

Polytechnic Institute of NYU, Westchester Graduate Center, Graduate Programs, Department of Technology Management, Major in Management, Hawthorne, NY 10532-1507. Offers MS. Part-time and evening/weekend programs available. *Faculty:* 5 part-time/adjunct (1 woman). *Students:* 5 part-time (1 woman). Average age 35. 1 applicant, 100% accepted, 0 enrolled. In 2010, 13 master's awarded. *Degree requirements:* For master's, comprehensive exam (for some programs), thesis (for some programs). *Entrance requirements:* Additional exam requirements/recommendations for international students: Required—TOEFL (minimum score 550 paper-based; 213 computer-based; 80 iBT); Recommended—IELTS (minimum score 6.5). *Application deadline:* For fall admission, 7/31 priority date for domestic students, 4/30 priority date for international students; for spring admission, 12/31 priority date for domestic students, 11/30 priority date for international students. Applications are processed on a rolling basis. Application fee: $75. Electronic applications accepted. *Expenses:* Tuition: Full-time $21,492; part-time $1194 per credit. Required fees: $385 per semester. Tuition and fees vary according to course load. *Financial support:* Institutionally sponsored loans, scholarships/grants, and unspecified assistantships available. Support available to part-time students. *Unit head:* Dr. Bharadwaj Rao, Department Head, 718-260-3617, E-mail: brao@poly.edu. *Application contact:* JeanCarlo Bonilla, Director of Graduate Enrollment Management, 718-260-3182, Fax: 718-260-3624, E-mail: gradinfo@poly.edu.

Polytechnic Institute of NYU, Westchester Graduate Center, Graduate Programs, Department of Technology Management, Major in Management of Technology, Hawthorne, NY 10532-1507. Offers MS. *Students:* 1 full-time (0 women), 6 part-time (1 woman); includes 2 minority (1 Black or African American, non-Hispanic/Latino; 1 Asian, non-Hispanic/Latino), 1 international. Average age 35. In 2010, 9 master's awarded. *Entrance requirements:* Additional exam requirements/recommendations for international students: Required—TOEFL (minimum score 550 paper-based; 213 computer-based; 80 iBT); Recommended—IELTS (minimum score 6.5). *Application deadline:* For fall admission, 7/31 priority date for domestic students, 4/30 priority date for international students; for spring admission, 12/31 priority date for domestic students, 11/30 priority date for international students. Applications are processed on a rolling basis. Application fee: $75. Electronic applications accepted. *Expenses:* Tuition: Full-time $21,492; part-time $1194 per credit. Required fees: $385 per semester. Tuition and fees vary according to course load. *Financial support:* Institutionally sponsored loans, scholarships/grants, and unspecified assistantships available. Support available to part-time students. *Unit head:* Dr. Bharadwaj Rao, Department Head, 718-260-3617, E-mail: brao@poly.edu. *Application contact:* JeanCarlo Bonilla, Director of Graduate Enrollment Management, 718-260-3182, Fax: 718-260-3624, E-mail: gradinfo@poly.edu.

Polytechnic University of Puerto Rico, Graduate School, Hato Rey, PR 00919. Offers business administration (MBA), including computer information systems, general management, management of information systems, management of international enterprises; civil engineering (ME, MS); computer engineering (ME, MS); computer science (MCS, MS); electrical engineering (ME, MS); engineering management (MEM); environmental management (MEM); landscape architecture (M Land Arch); manufacturing competitiveness (MMC, MS); manufacturing engineering (ME, MS); mechanical engineering (M Mech E). Part-time and evening/weekend programs available. *Entrance requirements:* For master's, 3 letters of recommendation.

Polytechnic University of Puerto Rico, Orlando Campus, Graduate School, Winter Park, FL 32792. Offers accounting (MBA); business administration (MBA); construction management (MEM); engineering management (MEM); environmental management (MEM); finance (MBA); human resources management (MBA); management of international enterprises (MBA); management of technology (MBA); manufacturing management (MEM). Part-time and evening/weekend programs available. Postbaccalaureate distance learning degree programs offered (no on-campus study). *Entrance requirements:* For master's, minimum GPA of 3.0. Electronic applications accepted.

Portland State University, Graduate Studies, Maseeh College of Engineering and Computer Science, Department of Engineering and Technology Management, Portland, OR 97207-0751. Offers engineering and technology management (M Eng); engineering management (MS); manufacturing engineering (ME); manufacturing management (M Eng); systems science/engineering management (PhD); MS/MBA; MS/MS. Part-time and evening/weekend programs available. *Faculty:* 8 full-time (1 woman), 3 part-time/adjunct (2 women). *Students:* 50 full-time (13 women), 58 part-time (16 women); includes 13 Asian, non-Hispanic/Latino; 6 Hispanic/Latino, 51 international. Average age 35. 38 applicants, 76% accepted, 13 enrolled. In 2010, 42 master's awarded. *Degree requirements:* For master's, thesis optional; for doctorate, one foreign language, thesis/dissertation, oral and written exams. *Entrance requirements:* For master's, minimum GPA of 3.0 in upper-division course work, BS in civil engineering; for doctorate, GRE General Test, GRE Subject Test, minimum GPA of 3.0 in upper-division course work. Additional exam requirements/recommendations for international students: Required—TOEFL (minimum score 550 paper-based; 213 computer-based). *Application deadline:* For fall admission, 4/1 for domestic students, 3/1 for international students; for winter admission, 9/1 for domestic students, 7/1 for international students; for spring admission, 11/1 for domestic students, 9/1 for international students. Applications are processed on a rolling basis. Application fee: $50. *Expenses:* Tuition, state resident: full-time $8505; part-time $315 per credit. Tuition, nonresident: full-time $13,284; part-time $492 per credit. Required fees: $1482; $21 per credit. $99 per term. One-time fee: $120. Part-time tuition and fees vary according to course load and program. *Financial support:* In 2010–11, 3 teaching assistantships with full tuition reimbursements (averaging $8,916 per year) were awarded; research assistantships with full tuition reimbursements, career-related internships or fieldwork, Federal Work-Study, scholarships/grants, and unspecified assistantships also available. Support available to part-time students. Financial award application deadline: 3/1; financial award applicants required to submit FAFSA. *Faculty research:* Scheduling, hierarchical decision modeling, operations research, knowledge-based information systems. Total annual research expenditures: $1.1 million. *Unit head:* Dr. Dundar F. Kocaoglu, Chair, 503-725-4660, Fax: 503-725-4667, E-mail: kocaoglu@etm.pdx.edu. *Application contact:* Dr. Dundar F. Kocaoglu, Chair, 503-725-4660, Fax: 503-725-4667, E-mail: kocaoglu@etm.pdx.edu.

Regis University, College for Professional Studies, School of Management, Denver, CO 80221-1099. Offers accounting (MS, Certificate); executive international management (Certificate); executive leadership (Certificate); executive project management (Certificate); finance and accounting (MBA); general business administration (MBA); health care management (MBA); human resource management and leadership (MSOL); information technology leadership and management (MSOL); international business (MBA); marketing (MBA); operations management (MBA); organizational leadership and management (MSOL); project leadership and management (MSOL); project management (Certificate); strategic business management (Certificate); strategic human resource management (Certificate); strategic management (MBA). Offered at Colorado Springs Campus, Northwest Denver Campus, Southeast Denver Campus, Fort Collins Campus, Broomfield Campus, Henderson (Nevada) Campus, and Summerlin (Nevada) Campus and online. Part-time and evening/weekend programs available. Postbaccalaureate distance learning degree programs offered (no on-campus study). *Degree requirements:* For master's, thesis optional, capstone project. *Entrance requirements:* For master's, GMAT or essays, interview, 2 years of full-time business work experience, resume; for Certificate, GMAT. Additional exam requirements/recommendations for international students: Required—TOEFL, TOEFL or university-based test; Recommended—TWE (minimum score 5). Electronic applications accepted. *Faculty research:* Impact of Info Technology on Small Business Regulation of Accounting, International Project financing, Mineral Development, Delivery of Healthcare to rural indigenos communities.

Rollins College, Crummer Graduate School of Business, Winter Park, FL 32789-4499. Offers entrepreneurship (MBA); finance (MBA); international business (MBA); management (MBA); marketing (MBA); operations and technology management (MBA). *Accreditation:* AACSB. Part-time and evening/weekend programs available. Postbaccalaureate distance learning degree programs offered (minimal on-campus study). *Faculty:* 22 full-time (3 women), 5 part-time/adjunct (3 women). *Students:* 303 full-time (117 women), 130 part-time (49 women); includes 111 minority (30 Black or African American, non-Hispanic/Latino; 1 American Indian or Alaska Native, non-Hispanic/Latino; 29 Asian, non-Hispanic/Latino; 50 Hispanic/Latino; 1 Two or more races, non-Hispanic/Latino), 29 international. Average age 32. 484 applicants, 42% accepted, 131 enrolled. In 2010, 223 master's awarded. *Entrance requirements:* For master's, GMAT, interview. Additional exam requirements/recommendations for international students: Required—TOEFL (minimum score 550 paper-based; 213 computer-based; 80 iBT). *Application deadline:* Applications are processed on a rolling basis. Application fee: $50. Electronic applications accepted. *Expenses:* Contact institution. *Financial support:* In 2010–11, 112 students received support, including 95 fellowships, 56 research assistantships (averaging $2,400 per year); career-related internships or fieldwork, scholarships/grants, and unspecified assistantships also available. Support available to part-time students. Financial award applicants required to submit FAFSA. *Faculty research:* Sustainability, world financial markets, international business, market research, strategic marketing. *Unit head:* Dr. Craig M. McAllaster, Dean, 407-646-2249, Fax: 407-646-1550, E-mail: cmcallaster@rollins.edu. *Application contact:* Linda Puritz, Student Admissions Office, 407-646-2405, Fax: 407-646-1550, E-mail: mbaadmissions@rollins.edu.

Rutgers, The State University of New Jersey, Newark, Rutgers Business School–Newark and New Brunswick, Doctoral Programs in Management, Newark, NJ 07102. Offers accounting (PhD); accounting information systems (PhD); economics (PhD); finance (PhD); individualized study (PhD); information technology (PhD); international business (PhD); management science (PhD); marketing science (PhD); organizational management (PhD); science, technology and management (PhD); supply chain management (PhD). *Faculty:* 143 full-time (36 women), 2 part-time/adjunct (0 women). *Students:* 117 full-time (42 women), 1 (woman) part-time; includes 8 Black or African American, non-Hispanic/Latino; 14 Asian, non-Hispanic/Latino; 3 Hispanic/Latino, 68 international. Average age 33. 355 applicants, 14% accepted, 35 enrolled. In 2010, 8 doctorates awarded. *Degree requirements:* For doctorate, comprehensive exam, thesis/dissertation. *Entrance requirements:* For doctorate, GRE or GMAT. Additional exam requirements/recommendations for international students: Required—TOEFL (minimum score 550 paper-based; 213 computer-based; 79 iBT). *Application deadline:* For fall admission, 3/1 for domestic and international students; for spring admission, 10/15 for domestic and international students. Application fee: $65. Electronic applications accepted. *Expenses:* Tuition, state resident: part-time $600 per credit. Tuition, nonresident: full-time $10,694. *Financial support:* In 2010–11, 52 students received support, including 7 fellowships (averaging $18,000 per year), 4 research assistantships with tuition reimbursements available (averaging $23,112 per year), 41 teaching assistantships with tuition reimbursements available (averaging $23,112 per year); health care benefits also available. Financial award application deadline: 3/1. *Unit head:* Dr. Glenn Shafer, Director, 973-353-1604, Fax: 973-353-5691, E-mail: gshafer@rbs.rutgers.edu. *Application contact:* Information Contact, 973-353-5371, Fax: 973-353-5691, E-mail: phdinfo@andromeda.rutgers.edu.

St. Ambrose University, College of Business, Program in Information Technology Management, Davenport, IA 52803-2898. Offers MSITM. Part-time programs available. *Faculty:* 3 full-time (0 women). *Students:* 3 full-time (1 woman), 8 part-time (4 women); includes 1 minority (Black or African American, non-Hispanic/Latino). Average age 33. 4 applicants, 100% accepted, 3 enrolled. In 2010, 5 master's awarded. *Degree requirements:* For master's, thesis (for some programs), practica. *Entrance requirements:* For master's, GRE or GMAT, minimum GPA of 2.8. Additional exam requirements/recommendations for international students: Required—TOEFL. *Application deadline:* For fall admission, 8/15 priority date for domestic students; for winter admission, 12/15 priority date for domestic students; for spring admission, 1/1 priority date for domestic students. Applications are processed on a rolling basis. Application fee: $25. Electronic applications accepted. *Expenses:* Tuition: Full-time $13,230; part-time $735 per credit hour. Required fees: $60 per semester. Tuition and fees vary according to degree level, program and reciprocity agreements. *Financial support:* In 2010–11, 5 students received support; research assistantships with partial tuition reimbursements available, career-related internships or fieldwork, scholarships/grants, and unspecified assistantships available. Financial award application deadline: 3/15; financial award applicants required to submit FAFSA. *Unit head:* Kenneth R. Grenier, Director, 563-333-6173, Fax: 563-333-6268, E-mail: grenierkennethr@sau.edu. *Application contact:* Deborah K. Bennett, Administrative Assistant, 563-333-6266, Fax: 563-333-6268, E-mail: bennettdeborahk@sau.edu.

Santa Clara University, Leavey School of Business, Program in Business Administration, Santa Clara, CA 95053. Offers accounting (MBA); entrepreneurship (MBA); executive business administration (EMBA); finance (MBA); food and agribusiness (MBA); international business (MBA); leading people and organizations (MBA); managing technology and innovation (MBA); marketing management (MBA); supply chain management (MBA). *Accreditation:* AACSB. Part-time and evening/weekend programs available. *Students:* 229 full-time (80 women), 748 part-time (244 women); includes 354 minority (14 Black or African American, non-Hispanic/Latino; 1 American Indian or Alaska Native, non-Hispanic/Latino; 287 Asian, non-Hispanic/Latino; 42 Hispanic/Latino; 5 Native Hawaiian or other Pacific Islander, non-Hispanic/Latino; 5 Two or more races, non-Hispanic/Latino), 209 international. Average age 32. 334 applicants, 76% accepted, 191 enrolled. In 2010, 307 master's awarded. *Degree requirements:* For master's, thesis or alternative. *Entrance requirements:* For master's, GMAT, GRE. Additional exam requirements/recommendations for international students: Required—TOEFL (minimum score 600 paper-based; 250 computer-based; 100 iBT). *Application deadline:* For fall admission, 6/1 for domestic and international students; for spring admission, 1/19 for domestic students, 1/17 for international students. Applications are processed on a rolling basis. Application fee: $75 ($100 for international students). Electronic applications accepted. *Expenses:* Contact institution. *Financial support:* In 2010–11, 350 students received support; fellowships with partial tuition reimbursements available, research assistantships with partial tuition reimbursements available, career-related internships or fieldwork, Federal Work-Study, institutionally sponsored loans, scholarships/grants, health care benefits, and unspecified assistantships available. Support available to part-time students. Financial award application deadline: 6/1; financial award applicants required to submit FAFSA. *Unit head:* Elizabeth B. Ford, Senior Assistant Dean, 408-554-2752, Fax: 408-554-4571, E-mail: eford@scu.edu. *Application contact:*

Molly Mulally, Assistant Director, Graduate Business Admissions, 408-554-4539, Fax: 408-554-4571, E-mail: mbaadmissions@scu.edu.

Seton Hall University, Stillman School of Business, Programs in Business Administration, South Orange, NJ 07079-2697. Offers accounting (MBA); finance (MBA); information technology management (MBA); international business (MBA); management (MBA); marketing (MBA); sport management (MBA); supply chain management (MBA). Part-time and evening/weekend programs available. *Faculty:* 35 full-time (8 women), 11 part-time/adjunct (1 woman). *Students:* 93 full-time (33 women), 165 part-time (76 women); includes 26 Black or African American, non-Hispanic/Latino; 39 Asian, non-Hispanic/Latino; 8 Hispanic/Latino. Average age 29. 404 applicants, 74% accepted, 258 enrolled. In 2010, 203 master's awarded. *Degree requirements:* For master's, 20 hours of community service (Social Responsibility Project). *Entrance requirements:* For master's, GMAT or CPA, Advanced degree such as PhD, MD, JD, DVM, DDS, PharmD, MBA from an AACSB institution, MS in a business discipline and a minimum GPA of 3.0. Additional exam requirements/recommendations for international students: Required—TOEFL (minimum: 254 computer, 102 iBT), IELTS or Pearson Test of English (PTE). *Application deadline:* For fall admission, 5/31 priority date for domestic students, 3/31 priority date for international students; for spring admission, 10/31 priority date for domestic students, 9/30 priority date for international students. Applications are processed on a rolling basis. Application fee: $75. Electronic applications accepted. *Financial support:* In 2010–11, research assistantships with full tuition reimbursements (averaging $35,610 per year); career-related internships or fieldwork, Federal Work-Study, scholarships/grants, and unspecified assistantships also available. Support available to part-time students. Financial award application deadline: 6/30; financial award applicants required to submit FAFSA. *Faculty research:* Financial, hedge funds, international business, legal issues, disclosure and branding. *Unit head:* Dr. Joyce A. Strawser, Associate Dean for Undergraduate and MBA Curricula, 973-761-9225, Fax: 973-761-9217, E-mail: strawsjo@shu.edu. *Application contact:* Catherine Bianchi, Director of Graduate Admissions, 973-761-9262, Fax: 973-761-9208, E-mail: catherine.bianchi@shu.edu.

Simon Fraser University, Graduate Studies, Faculty of Business Administration, Burnaby, BC V5A 1S6, Canada. Offers business administration (EMBA, PhD); financial management (MA); general business (MBA); global asset and wealth management (MBA); management of technology/biotechnology (MBA); MBA/MRM. *Accreditation:* AACSB. Postbaccalaureate distance learning degree programs offered. *Degree requirements:* For master's, thesis or written project. *Entrance requirements:* For master's, minimum GPA of 3.0. Additional exam requirements/recommendations for international students: Required—TOEFL. *Expenses:* Contact institution. *Faculty research:* Leadership, marketing and technology, wealth management.

South Dakota School of Mines and Technology, Graduate Division, Program in Engineering Management, Rapid City, SD 57701-3995. Offers MS. Program offered jointly with The University of South Dakota. Part-time programs available. *Entrance requirements:* For master's, GMAT. Additional exam requirements/recommendations for international students: Required—TOEFL, TWE. Electronic applications accepted.

Southeast Missouri State University, School of Graduate Studies, Department of Industrial and Engineering Technology, Cape Girardeau, MO 63701-4799. Offers industrial management (MS); technology management (MS). Part-time programs available. Postbaccalaureate distance learning degree programs offered (no on-campus study). *Faculty:* 11 full-time (1 woman). *Students:* 42 full-time (8 women), 24 part-time (1 woman); includes 1 minority (Black or African American, non-Hispanic/Latino), 37 international. Average age 27. 60 applicants, 97% accepted, 24 enrolled. In 2010, 6 master's awarded. *Degree requirements:* For master's, comprehensive exam (for some programs), thesis (for some programs), minimum GPA of 3.0; thesis and oral exam or comprehensive exam and applied research project. *Entrance requirements:* For master's, GRE or GMAT if undergraduate GPA below 2.7, undergraduate degree in an engineering, technology, or a related field or portfolio of experience and prerequisite course work. Additional exam requirements/recommendations for international students: Required—TOEFL (minimum score 550 paper-based; 213 computer-based; 79 iBT); Recommended—IELTS (minimum score 6). *Application deadline:* For fall admission, 8/1 for domestic students, 6/1 for international students; for spring admission, 11/21 for domestic students, 10/1 for international students. Applications are processed on a rolling basis. Application fee: $25 ($35 for international students). Electronic applications accepted. *Expenses:* Tuition, state resident: full-time $4698; part-time $261 per credit hour. Tuition, nonresident: full-time $8379; part-time $465.50 per credit hour. *Financial support:* In 2010–11, 40 students received support, including 12 teaching assistantships with full tuition reimbursements available (averaging $7,600 per year); career-related internships or fieldwork, Federal Work-Study, institutionally sponsored loans, scholarships/grants, tuition waivers (full), and unspecified assistantships also available. Financial award application deadline: 6/30; financial award applicants required to submit FAFSA. *Faculty research:* Supply chain management, lean manufacturing, energy conservation, telecommunications, graphic communications, ISQ/Q5 9000, SAP (enterprise resource planning), automatic control systems. *Unit head:* Dr. Chris McGowan, Interim, Chairperson, 573-651-2163, E-mail: cwmcgowan@semo.edu. *Application contact:* Gail Amick, Administrative Secretary, 573-651-2049, Fax: 573-651-2001, E-mail: gamick2@semo.edu.

State University of New York Institute of Technology, School of Business, Program in Business Administration in Technology Management, Utica, NY 13504-3050. Offers technology management (MBA). *Entrance requirements:* For master's, GMAT, minimum GPA of 3.0. Additional exam requirements/recommendations for international students: Required—TOEFL (minimum score 550 paper-based; 213 computer-based). *Faculty research:* Technology management, writing schools, leadership, new products.

Stevens Institute of Technology, Graduate School, Wesley J. Howe School of Technology Management, Doctoral Program in Technology Management, Hoboken, NJ 07030. Offers information management (PhD); technology management (PhD); telecommunications management (PhD). Part-time and evening/weekend programs available. Postbaccalaureate distance learning degree programs offered (minimal on-campus study). *Students:* 22 full-time (9 women), 66 part-time (11 women); includes 1 Black or African American, non-Hispanic/Latino; 14 Asian, non-Hispanic/Latino; 8 Hispanic/Latino, 23 international. Average age 34. 66 applicants, 70% accepted. *Entrance requirements:* Additional exam requirements/recommendations for international students: Required—TOEFL. *Application deadline:* Applications are processed on a rolling basis. Application fee: $50. Electronic applications accepted. *Financial support:* Research assistantships, teaching assistantships, institutionally sponsored loans available. *Unit head:* Richard Reilly, Director, 201-216-5383. *Application contact:* Graduate Admissions, 800-496-4935, Fax: 201-216-8044, E-mail: gradadmissions@stevens.edu.

Stevens Institute of Technology, Graduate School, Wesley J. Howe School of Technology Management, Program in Business Administration for Experienced Professionals, Hoboken, NJ 07030. Offers technology management (EMBA).

Stevens Institute of Technology, Graduate School, Wesley J. Howe School of Technology Management, Program in Management, Hoboken, NJ 07030. Offers general management (MS); global innovation management (MS); human resource management (MS); information management (MS); project management (MS); technology commercialization (MS); technology management (MS). Part-time programs available. *Students:* 15 full-time (6 women), 35 part-time (15 women); includes 1 Black or African American, non-Hispanic/Latino; 5 Asian, non-Hispanic/Latino; 6 Hispanic/Latino, 12 international. Average age 31. *Degree requirements:* For master's, thesis optional. *Entrance requirements:* For master's, GMAT, GRE General Test. Additional exam requirements/recommendations for international students: Required—TOEFL. *Application deadline:* Applications are processed on a rolling basis. Application fee: $50. Electronic applications accepted. *Financial support:* Unspecified assistantships available. *Faculty research:* Industrial economics. *Unit head:* Elizabeth Watson, Director, 201-216-5081. *Application contact:* Graduate Admissions, 800-496-4935, Fax: 201-216-8044, E-mail: gradadmissions@stevens.edu.

Stevens Institute of Technology, Graduate School, Wesley J. Howe School of Technology Management, Program in Technology Management for Experienced Professionals, Hoboken, NJ 07030. Offers EMTM, MS, Certificate. Part-time and evening/weekend programs available. Postbaccalaureate distance learning degree programs offered. *Entrance requirements:* For master's, GMAT, GRE General Test. Additional exam requirements/recommendations for international students: Required—TOEFL. Electronic applications accepted. *Expenses:* Contact institution.

Stevens Institute of Technology, Graduate School, Wesley J. Howe School of Technology Management, Program in Telecommunications Management, Hoboken, NJ 07030. Offers business (MS); global innovation management (MS); management of wireless networks (MS); online security, technology and business (MS); project management (MS); technical management (MS); telecommunications management (PhD, Certificate). *Students:* 26 full-time (6 women), 92 part-time (15 women); includes 8 Black or African American, non-Hispanic/Latino; 9 Asian, non-Hispanic/Latino; 9 Hispanic/Latino, 25 international. Average age 33. 154 applicants, 91% accepted. *Degree requirements:* For master's, thesis optional; for doctorate, thesis/dissertation. *Entrance requirements:* For master's and doctorate, GMAT, GRE General Test. Additional exam requirements/recommendations for international students: Required—TOEFL. *Application deadline:* Applications are processed on a rolling basis. Application fee: $50. Electronic applications accepted. *Unit head:* Audrey Kames Curtis, Director, 201-216-5524. *Application contact:* Sharen Glennon, Administrative Assistant, 201-216-8322, Fax: 201-216-8355, E-mail: sglennon@stevens-tech.edu.

Stevenson University, Program in Business and Technology Management, Stevenson, MD 21153. Offers MS. *Students:* 20 full-time (15 women), 53 part-time (27 women); includes 17 Black or African American, non-Hispanic/Latino; 3 Asian, non-Hispanic/Latino, 2 international. In 2010, 24 master's awarded. *Degree requirements:* For master's, capstone course. *Expenses:* Tuition: Part-time $560 per credit. Required fees: $100 per semester. Part-time tuition and fees vary according to program. *Unit head:* Steve Engorn, Program Coordinator, Business and Technology Management, 443-352-4220, Fax: 443-394-0538, E-mail: sengorn@stevenson.edu. *Application contact:* Angela Scagliola, Director, Recruitment and Admissions, 443-352-4414, Fax: 443-352-4440, E-mail: ascagliola@stevenson.edu.

Stony Brook University, State University of New York, Graduate School, College of Business, Program in Technology Management, Stony Brook, NY 11794. Offers MS. Program conducted mostly in Korea. Evening/weekend programs available. Postbaccalaureate distance learning degree programs offered. In 2010, 25 master's awarded. *Entrance requirements:* For master's, GMAT or GRE General Test, 3 years of work experience, minimum GPA of 3.0, letters of recommendation. Additional exam requirements/recommendations for international students: Required—TOEFL (minimum score 550 paper-based; 213 computer-based). Application fee: $100. *Expenses:* Tuition, state resident: full-time $8370; part-time $349 per credit. Tuition, nonresident: full-time $13,780; part-time $574 per credit. Required fees: $994. *Unit head:* Dr. Manuel London, Interim Dean, 631-632-7180. *Application contact:* Dr. Owen Carroll, Director, Graduate Program, 631-632-7171, E-mail: tcarroll@notes.cc.sunysb.edu.

Stony Brook University, State University of New York, Graduate School, College of Engineering and Applied Sciences, Department of Technology and Society, Program in Global Operations Management, Stony Brook, NY 11794. Offers MS. Postbaccalaureate distance learning degree programs offered. *Application deadline:* For fall admission, 2/1 for domestic students; for spring admission, 10/1 for domestic students. Electronic applications accepted. *Expenses:* Tuition, state resident: full-time $8370; part-time $349 per credit. Tuition, nonresident: full-time $13,780; part-time $574 per credit. Required fees: $994. *Unit head:* Dr. David Ferguson, Chairman, 631-632-8770, E-mail: david.ferguson@stonybrook.edu. *Application contact:* Dr. Sheldon Reaven, Graduate Director, 631-632-8765, Fax: 631-632-7809, E-mail: sheldon.raven@sunysb.edu.

Sullivan University, School of Business, Louisville, KY 40205. Offers business administration (MBA); collaborative leadership (MSCL); conflict management (MSCM); dispute resolution (MSDR); executive business administration (EMBA); human resource leadership (MSHRL); information technology (MSMIT); management (PhD); management and information technology (MBIT); pharmacy (Pharm D). Part-time programs available. Postbaccalaureate distance learning degree programs offered (no on-campus study). *Faculty:* 13 full-time (7 women), 11 part-time/adjunct (4 women). *Students:* 429 full-time (239 women), 322 part-time (198 women); includes 275 minority (152 Black or African American, non-Hispanic/Latino; 5 American Indian or Alaska Native, non-Hispanic/Latino; 31 Asian, non-Hispanic/Latino; 5 Hispanic/Latino; 56 Native Hawaiian or other Pacific Islander, non-Hispanic/Latino; 26 Two or more races, non-Hispanic/Latino), 15 international. In 2010, 133 master's awarded. *Entrance requirements:* Additional exam requirements/recommendations for international students: Required—TOEFL. *Application deadline:* Applications are processed on a rolling basis. Application fee: $100. *Unit head:* Dr. Eric S. Harter, Dean of Graduate School, 502-456-6504, Fax: 502-456-0040, E-mail: eharter@sullivan.edu. *Application contact:* Beverly Horsley, Admissions Officer, 502-456-6505, Fax: 502-456-0040, E-mail: bhorsley@sullivan.edu.

Teachers College, Columbia University, Graduate Faculty of Education, Department of Math, Science and Technology, Program in Technology Specialist, New York, NY 10027-6696. Offers MA. *Expenses:* Tuition: Full-time $28,272; part-time $1178 per credit. Required fees: $756; $378 per semester. *Unit head:* Dr. Ellen Meier, Program Coordinator, 212-678-3829, E-mail: ebm15@columbia.edu. *Application contact:* Deanna Ghozati, Admissions Contact, 212-678-3710.

Texas A&M University–Commerce, Graduate School, College of Business and Technology, Department of Industrial Engineering and Technology, Commerce, TX 75429-3011. Offers industrial technology (MS); technology management (MS). Part-time programs available. *Degree requirements:* For master's, comprehensive exam, thesis (for some programs). *Entrance requirements:* For master's, GMAT, GRE General Test. Electronic applications accepted. *Faculty research:* Environmental science, engineering microelectronics, natural sciences.

Texas State University–San Marcos, Graduate School, College of Science, Department of Engineering Technology, San Marcos, TX 78666. Offers industrial technology (MST). Part-time and evening/weekend programs available. *Faculty:* 7 full-time (1 woman). *Students:* 21 full-time (2 women), 23 part-time (3 women); includes 8 minority (2 Black or African American, non-Hispanic/Latino; 1 Asian, non-Hispanic/Latino; 3 Hispanic/Latino; 2 Two or more races, non-Hispanic/Latino), 6 international. Average age 29. 21 applicants, 95% accepted, 13 enrolled. In 2010, 15 master's awarded. *Degree requirements:* For master's, comprehensive exam, thesis optional. *Entrance requirements:* For master's, minimum GPA of 2.75 in last 60 hours of undergraduate work. Additional exam requirements/recommendations for international students: Required—TOEFL (minimum score 550 paper-based; 213 computer-based; 78 iBT). *Application deadline:* For fall admission, 6/15 priority date for domestic students, 6/1 priority date for international students; for spring admission, 10/15 priority date for domestic students, 10/1 priority date for international students. Applications are processed on a rolling basis. Application fee: $40 ($90 for international students). Electronic applications accepted. *Expenses:* Tuition, state resident: full-time $6024; part-time $251 per credit hour. Tuition, nonresident: full-time $13,536; part-time $564 per credit hour. Required fees: $1776; $50 per credit hour. $306 per semester. *Financial support:* In 2010–11, 11 students received support, including 4 research assistantships (averaging $5,463 per year), 5 teaching assistantships (averaging $5,476 per year); career-related internships or fieldwork, Federal Work-Study, institutionally sponsored loans, scholarships/grants, health care benefits, and unspecified assistantships also available. Support available to part-time students. Financial award application deadline: 4/1; financial award applicants required to submit FAFSA. *Faculty research:* Attack of Concrete. Total annual research expenditures: $107,849. *Unit head:* Dr. Andy Batey, Interim Chair, 512-245-2137, Fax: 512-245-3052, E-mail: ab08@txstate.edu. *Application contact:* Dr. Gary Winek, Graduate Adviser, 512-245-2137, Fax: 512-245-3052, E-mail: gw04@txstate.edu.

Trevecca Nazarene University, Graduate Division, Graduate Business Programs, Nashville, TN 37210-2877. Offers business administration (MBA); information technology (MBA); management (MSM). Evening/weekend programs available. *Faculty:* 6 full-time (1 woman), 1

Management of Technology

Trevecca Nazarene University (continued)

part-time/adjunct (0 women). *Students:* 69 full-time (31 women), 25 part-time (16 women); includes 28 minority (24 Black or African American, non-Hispanic/Latino; 1 American Indian or Alaska Native, non-Hispanic/Latino; 1 Native Hawaiian or other Pacific Islander, non-Hispanic/Latino; 2 Two or more races, non-Hispanic/Latino). Average age 35. In 2010, 62 master's awarded. *Entrance requirements:* For master's, GMAT, proficiency exam (quantitative skills), minimum GPA of 2.5, resume, employer letter of recommendation, 2 letters of recommendation, written business analysis. Additional exam requirements/recommendations for international students: Required—TOEFL (minimum score 550 paper-based; 213 computer-based). *Application deadline:* Applications are processed on a rolling basis. Application fee: $25. *Expenses:* Contact institution. *Financial support:* Applicants required to submit FAFSA. *Unit head:* Dr. Jon Burch, Director of Graduate Management Program, 615-248-1529, Fax: 615-248-1700, E-mail: management@trevecca.edu. *Application contact:* College of Lifelong Learning, 615-248-1200, E-mail: cll@trevecca.edu.

University at Albany, State University of New York, School of Business, Department of Information Technology Management, Albany, NY 12222-0001. Offers MBA. *Degree requirements:* For master's, field study project. *Entrance requirements:* For master's, GMAT. Additional exam requirements/recommendations for international students: Required—TOEFL (minimum score 550 paper-based; 213 computer-based). Electronic applications accepted. *Faculty research:* Data quality, expert systems, collaborative technology, expert information systems.

University of Advancing Technology, Master of Science Program in Technology, Tempe, AZ 85283-1042. Offers advancing computer science (MS); emerging technologies (MS); game production and management (MS); information assurance (MS); technology leadership (MS). *Faculty:* 9 full-time (3 women), 3 part-time/adjunct (1 woman). *Students:* 55 full-time (9 women), 4 part-time (1 woman). Average age 25. In 2010, 5 master's awarded. *Degree requirements:* For master's, project or thesis. *Entrance requirements:* Additional exam requirements/recommendations for international students: Required—TOEFL (minimum score 550 paper-based). *Application deadline:* For fall admission, 8/15 priority date for domestic students, 7/15 priority date for international students; for winter admission, 12/15 priority date for domestic students, 11/15 priority date for international students; for spring admission, 4/1 priority date for domestic students, 3/1 priority date for international students. Applications are processed on a rolling basis. Application fee: $100 ($250 for international students). Electronic applications accepted. *Expenses:* Tuition: Full-time $18,300. *Financial support:* Career-related internships or fieldwork, Federal Work-Study, and scholarships/grants available. Financial award applicants required to submit FAFSA. *Faculty research:* Artificial intelligence, fractals, organizational management. *Unit head:* Robert Marshall, Dean of Graduate Education, 602-383-8283, Fax: 602-383-8222, E-mail: rmarshall@uat.edu. *Application contact:* Information Contact, 800-658-5744, Fax: 602-383-8222.

The University of Akron, Graduate School, College of Business Administration, Department of Management, Program in Management of Technology, Akron, OH 44325. Offers MBA. *Students:* 3 full-time (1 woman), 8 part-time (1 woman), 2 international. Average age 46. 7 applicants, 71% accepted, 4 enrolled. In 2010, 4 master's awarded. *Entrance requirements:* For master's, GMAT, minimum GPA of 2.75, two letters of recommendation, statement of purpose, resume. Additional exam requirements/recommendations for international students: Required—TOEFL (minimum score 550 paper-based; 213 computer-based; 79 iBT). *Application deadline:* For fall admission, 7/15 for domestic and international students; for spring admission, 11/15 for domestic and international students. Application fee: $30 ($40 for international students). Electronic applications accepted. *Expenses:* Tuition, state resident: full-time $6800; part-time $378 per credit hour. Tuition, nonresident: full-time $11,644; part-time $647 per credit hour. Required fees: $1265. One-time fee: $30 full-time. *Unit head:* Head. *Application contact:* Dr. Susan Hanlon, Director of Graduate Business Programs, 330-972-7043, Fax: 330-972-6588, E-mail: shanlon@uakron.edu.

University of Arkansas at Little Rock, Graduate School, College of Business Administration, Little Rock, AR 72204-1099. Offers accountancy (M Acc, Graduate Certificate); business administration (MBA); construction management (Graduate Certificate); management (Graduate Certificate); management information system (MIS); management information systems (Graduate Certificate); management information systems leadership (Graduate Certificate); taxation (MS, Graduate Certificate). *Accreditation:* AACSB. Part-time and evening/weekend programs available. *Entrance requirements:* For master's, GMAT, minimum undergraduate GPA of 2.7. Additional exam requirements/recommendations for international students: Required—TOEFL (minimum score 525 paper-based; 195 computer-based).

University of Bridgeport, School of Engineering, Department of Technology Management, Bridgeport, CT 06604. Offers MS. *Degree requirements:* For master's, thesis optional. *Entrance requirements:* Additional exam requirements/recommendations for international students: Recommended—TOEFL (minimum score 550 paper-based; 213 computer-based; 80 iBT), IELTS (minimum score 6.5). Electronic applications accepted. *Expenses:* Tuition: Full-time $22,000; part-time $575 per credit hour. Required fees: $90 per semester. Tuition and fees vary according to course level, course load and program. *Faculty research:* CAD/CAM.

University of California, Santa Cruz, Division of Graduate Studies, Jack Baskin School of Engineering, Department of Technology and Information Management, Santa Cruz, CA 95064. Offers MS, PhD. *Students:* 7 full-time (1 woman), 3 part-time (1 woman), 5 international. Average age 33. 17 applicants, 35% accepted, 3 enrolled. Terminal master's awarded for partial completion of doctoral program. *Degree requirements:* For master's, thesis, 2 seminars; for doctorate, thesis/dissertation, 2 seminars. *Entrance requirements:* For master's and doctorate, GRE General Test; GRE Subject Test preferably in computer science, engineering, physics, or mathematics (highly recommended), minimum GPA of 3.5. Additional exam requirements/recommendations for international students: Required—TOEFL (minimum score 570 paper-based; 230 computer-based; 89 iBT); Recommended—IELTS (minimum score 8). *Application deadline:* For fall admission, 1/3 for domestic and international students. Application fee: $70 ($90 for international students). Electronic applications accepted. *Financial support:* Fellowships, research assistantships, teaching assistantships, institutionally sponsored loans and tuition waivers available. Financial award applicants required to submit FAFSA. *Faculty research:* Integration of information systems, technology, and business management. *Unit head:* Carol Mullane, Graduate Program Advisor, 831-459-2576, E-mail: mullane@soe.ucsc.edu. *Application contact:* Carol Mullane, Graduate Program Advisor, 831-459-2576, E-mail: mullane@soe.ucsc.edu.

University of Central Missouri, The Graduate School, College of Science and Technology, Warrensburg, MO 64093. Offers applied mathematics (MS); aviation safety (MS); biology (MS); computer science (MS); environmental studies (MA); industrial management (MS); mathematics (MS); technology (MS); technology management (PhD). PhD is offered jointly with Indiana State University. Part-time programs available. Postbaccalaureate distance learning degree programs offered. *Entrance requirements:* Additional exam requirements/recommendations for international students: Required—TOEFL (minimum score 550 paper-based; 79 computer-based). Electronic applications accepted.

University of Colorado Denver, Business School, Program in Information Systems, Denver, CO 80217. Offers accounting and information systems audit and control (MS); business intelligence (MS); enterprise technology management (PhD); health information technology management (MS); web and mobile computing (MS). Part-time and evening/weekend programs available. Postbaccalaureate distance learning degree programs offered (no on-campus study). *Students:* 55 full-time (13 women), 30 part-time (13 women); includes 3 Black or African American, non-Hispanic/Latino; 8 Asian, non-Hispanic/Latino; 3 Hispanic/Latino, 13 international. Average age 34. 30 applicants, 80% accepted, 15 enrolled. In 2010, 13 master's awarded. *Degree requirements:* For master's, 30 credit hours. *Entrance requirements:* For master's, GMAT. Additional exam requirements/recommendations for international students: Required—TOEFL (minimum score 525 paper-based; 197 computer-based; 71 iBT). *Application deadline:*

For fall admission, 4/1 priority date for domestic students, 3/15 priority date for international students; for spring admission, 10/1 priority date for domestic and international students. Application fee: $50 ($75 for international students). Electronic applications accepted. *Expenses:* Contact institution. *Financial support:* Federal Work-Study and scholarships/grants available. Support available to part-time students. Financial award application deadline: 4/1; financial award applicants required to submit FAFSA. *Faculty research:* Human-computer interaction, expert systems, database management, electronic commerce, object-oriented software development. *Unit head:* Dr. Jahangir Karimi, Director, 303-315-8430, E-mail: jahangir.karimi@ucdenver.edu. *Application contact:* Shelly Townley, Admissions Director, Graduate Programs, 303-315-8202, E-mail: shelly.townley@ucdenver.edu.

University of Colorado Denver, Business School, Program in Management and Organization, Denver, CO 80217. Offers communications management (MS); enterprise technology management (MS); entrepreneurship and innovation (MS); global management (MS); human resources management (MS); leadership (MS); quantitative decision methods (MS); sports and entertainment management (MS); strategic management (MS); sustainability management (MS). *Accreditation:* AACSB. Part-time and evening/weekend programs available. Postbaccalaureate distance learning degree programs offered (no on-campus study). *Students:* 34 full-time (21 women), 9 part-time (2 women); includes 3 Asian, non-Hispanic/Latino; 5 Hispanic/Latino. Average age 33. 28 applicants, 61% accepted, 10 enrolled. In 2010, 20 master's awarded. *Degree requirements:* For master's, 30 semester hours (12 of required courses, 12 of management electives, and 6 of free electives). *Entrance requirements:* For master's, GMAT. Additional exam requirements/recommendations for international students: Required—TOEFL (minimum score 525 paper-based; 197 computer-based; 71 iBT). *Application deadline:* For fall admission, 4/1 priority date for domestic students, 3/15 priority date for international students; for spring admission, 10/1 priority date for domestic and international students. Application fee: $50 ($75 for international students). Electronic applications accepted. *Expenses:* Contact institution. *Financial support:* Federal Work-Study and scholarships/grants available. Support available to part-time students. Financial award application deadline: 4/1; financial award applicants required to submit FAFSA. *Faculty research:* Human resource management, management of catastrophe, turnaround strategies. *Unit head:* Dr. Kenneth Bettenhausen, Associate Professor/Director, 303-315-8425, E-mail: kenneth.bettehausen@ucdenver.edu. *Application contact:* Shelly Townley, Admissions Director, Graduate Programs, 303-315-8202, E-mail: shelly.townley@ucdenver.edu.

University of Dallas, Graduate School of Management, Irving, TX 75062-4736. Offers accounting (MBA, MM, MS); business management (MBA, MM); corporate finance (MBA, MM); financial services (MBA); global business (MBA, MM); health services management (MBA, MM); human resource management (MBA, MM); information assurance (MBA, MM, MS); information technology (MBA, MM, MS); information technology service management (MBA, MM, MS); marketing management (MBA, MM); organization development (MBA, MM); project management (MBA, MM); sports and entertainment management (MBA, MM); strategic leadership (MBA, MM); supply chain management (MBA); supply chain management and market logistics (MM). *Accreditation:* ACBSP. Part-time and evening/weekend programs available. Postbaccalaureate distance learning degree programs offered (no on-campus study). *Entrance requirements:* Additional exam requirements/recommendations for international students: Required—TOEFL. Electronic applications accepted. *Expenses:* Contact institution.

University of Delaware, Alfred Lerner College of Business and Economics, Department of Accounting and Management Information Systems and Department of Electrical and Computer Engineering, Program in Information Systems and Technology Management, Newark, DE 19716. Offers MS. Part-time and evening/weekend programs available. *Entrance requirements:* For master's, GRE or GMAT, 2 letters of recommendation, resume, minimum GPA of 2.75. Additional exam requirements/recommendations for international students: Required—TOEFL (minimum score 600 paper-based; 250 computer-based). *Faculty research:* Security, developer trust, XML.

University of Denver, University College, Denver, CO 80208. Offers arts and culture (MLS, Certificate), including art, literature, and culture, arts development and program management (Certificate), creative writing; environmental policy and management (MAS, Certificate), including energy and sustainability (Certificate), environmental assessment of nuclear power (Certificate), environmental health and safety (Certificate), environmental management, natural resource management (Certificate); geographic information systems (MAS, Certificate); global affairs (MLS, Certificate), including translation studies, world history and culture; healthcare leadership (MPH, Certificate), including healthcare policy, law, and ethics, medical and healthcare information technologies, strategic management of healthcare; information and communications technology (MCIS, Certificate), including database design and administration (Certificate), geographic information systems (MCIS), information security systems security (Certificate), information systems security (MCIS), project management (MCIS, MPS, Certificate), software design and administration (Certificate), software design and programming (MCIS), technology management, telecommunications technology (MCIS), Web design and development; leadership and organizations (MPS, Certificate), including human capital in organizations, philanthropic leadership, project management (MCIS, MPS, Certificate), strategic innovation and change; organizational and professional communication (MPS, Certificate), including alternative dispute resolution, organizational communication, organizational development and training, public relations and marketing; security management (MAS, Certificate), including emergency planning and response, information security (MAS), organizational security; strategic human resource management (MPS, Certificate), including global human resources (MPS), human resource management and development (MPS). Part-time and evening/weekend programs available. Postbaccalaureate distance learning degree programs offered (no on-campus study). *Faculty:* 7 full-time (2 women), 212 part-time/adjunct (83 women). *Students:* 52 full-time (19 women), 1,044 part-time (625 women); includes 196 minority (81 Black or African American, non-Hispanic/Latino; 7 American Indian or Alaska Native, non-Hispanic/Latino; 30 Asian, non-Hispanic/Latino; 66 Hispanic/Latino; 3 Native Hawaiian or other Pacific Islander, non-Hispanic/Latino; 9 Two or more races, non-Hispanic/Latino), 76 international. Average age 36. 488 applicants, 91% accepted, 339 enrolled. In 2010, 286 master's, 130 other advanced degrees awarded. *Entrance requirements:* Additional exam requirements/recommendations for international students: Required—TOEFL (minimum score 550 paper-based; 80 iBT). *Application deadline:* For fall admission, 6/22 priority date for domestic students, 6/10 priority date for international students; for winter admission, 9/15 priority date for domestic students, 9/6 priority date for international students; for spring admission, 2/3 priority date for domestic students, 12/15 priority date for international students. Applications are processed on a rolling basis. Application fee: $75. Electronic applications accepted. *Expenses:* Contact institution. *Financial support:* Applicants required to submit FAFSA. *Unit head:* Dr. James Davis, Dean, 303-871-2291, Fax: 303-871-4047, E-mail: jdavis@du.edu. *Application contact:* Information Contact, 303-871-3155, Fax: 303-871-4047, E-mail: ucolinfo@du.edu.

University of Illinois at Urbana–Champaign, Graduate College, College of Agricultural, Consumer and Environmental Sciences, Department of Agricultural and Biological Engineering, Champaign, IL 61820. Offers agricultural and biological engineering (MS, PhD); technical systems management (MS, PSM). *Faculty:* 20 full-time (2 women). *Students:* 48 full-time (10 women), 3 part-time (1 woman); includes 2 Hispanic/Latino, 39 international. 57 applicants, 28% accepted, 11 enrolled. In 2010, 6 master's, 4 doctorates awarded. *Entrance requirements:* For master's and doctorate, minimum GPA of 3.0. Additional exam requirements/recommendations for international students: Required—TOEFL (minimum score 570 paper-based; 230 computer-based; 88 iBT) or IELTS (minimum score 6.5). *Application deadline:* Applications are processed on a rolling basis. Application fee: $75 ($90 for international students). Electronic applications accepted. *Financial support:* In 2010–11, 6 fellowships, 42 research assistantships, 3 teaching assistantships were awarded; tuition waivers (full and partial) also available. *Unit head:* Kuan Chong Ting, Head, 217-333-3570, Fax: 217-244-0323, E-mail: kcting@illinois.edu. *Application contact:* Ronda Sullivan, Assistant to the Head, 217-333-3570, Fax: 217-244-0323, E-mail: rsully@illinois.edu.

University of Illinois at Urbana–Champaign, Graduate College, College of Business, Department of Business Administration, Champaign, IL 61820. Offers business administration (MS, PhD); technology management (MS). *Accreditation:* AACSB. *Faculty:* 44 full-time (8 women), 5 part-time/adjunct (1 woman). *Students:* 98 full-time (36 women), 11 part-time (4 women); includes 6 Asian, non-Hispanic/Latino, 91 international. 344 applicants, 24% accepted, 58 enrolled. In 2010, 46 master's, 10 doctorates awarded. *Entrance requirements:* For master's, minimum GPA of 3.0; for doctorate, GMAT or GRE, minimum GPA of 3.0. Additional exam requirements/recommendations for international students: Required—TOEFL (minimum score 550 paper-based; 231 computer-based; 79 iBT) or IELTS (6.5). *Application deadline:* Applications are processed on a rolling basis. Application fee: $75 ($90 for international students). Electronic applications accepted. *Expenses:* Contact institution. *Financial support:* In 2010–11, 24 fellowships, 38 research assistantships, 16 teaching assistantships were awarded; tuition waivers (full and partial) also available. *Unit head:* William J. Qualls, Interim Head, 217-265-0794, Fax: 217-244-7969, E-mail: wqualls@illinois.edu. *Application contact:* J. E. Miller, Coordinator of Graduate Programs, 217-244-8002, Fax: 217-244-7969, E-mail: j-miller@illinois.edu.

University of Maryland University College, Graduate School of Management and Technology, Technology Management Program, Adelphi, MD 20783. Offers MS, Certificate. Program held entirely online. Part-time and evening/weekend programs available. Postbaccalaureate distance learning degree programs offered (no on-campus study). *Students:* 9 full-time (5 women), 614 part-time (298 women); includes 303 minority (238 Black or African American, non-Hispanic/Latino; 1 American Indian or Alaska Native, non-Hispanic/Latino; 29 Asian, non-Hispanic/Latino; 29 Hispanic/Latino; 6 Two or more races, non-Hispanic/Latino), 7 international. Average age 38. 132 applicants, 100% accepted, 80 enrolled. In 2010, 170 master's, 76 other advanced degrees awarded. *Degree requirements:* For master's, thesis or alternative, capstone course. *Application deadline:* Applications are processed on a rolling basis. Application fee: $50. Electronic applications accepted. *Financial support:* Federal Work-Study and scholarships/grants available. Support available to part-time students. Financial award application deadline: 6/1; financial award applicants required to submit FAFSA. *Unit head:* Dr. Joyce Shirazi, Chair, Information and Technology Systems, 240-684-2400, Fax: 240-684-2401, E-mail: jshirazi@umuc.edu. *Application contact:* Coordinator, Graduate Admissions, 800-888-8682, Fax: 240-684-2151, E-mail: newgrad@umuc.edu.

University of Miami, Graduate School, College of Engineering, Department of Industrial Engineering, Coral Gables, FL 33124. Offers ergonomics (PhD); industrial engineering (MSIE, PhD); management of technology (MS); occupational ergonomics and safety (MS, MSOES), including environmental health and safety (MS), occupational ergonomics and safety (MSOES); MBA/MSIE. Part-time programs available. *Degree requirements:* For master's, thesis (for some programs); for doctorate, comprehensive exam, thesis/dissertation. *Entrance requirements:* For master's and doctorate, GRE General Test, minimum GPA of 3.0. Additional exam requirements/recommendations for international students: Required—TOEFL (minimum score 550 paper-based; 213 computer-based). *Faculty research:* Logistics, supply chain management, industrial applications of biomechanics and ergonomics, technology management, back pain, aging, operations research, manufacturing, safety, human reliability, energy assessment.

University of Minnesota, Twin Cities Campus, Institute of Technology, Technological Leadership Institute, Program in Management of Technology, Minneapolis, MN 55455-0213. Offers MSMOT. Evening/weekend programs available. *Degree requirements:* For master's, thesis, capstone project. *Entrance requirements:* For master's, 5 years of work experience in high-tech company, preferably in Twin Cities area; demonstrated technological leadership ability. Additional exam requirements/recommendations for international students: Required—TOEFL (minimum score 580 paper-based; 240 computer-based; 90 iBT). Electronic applications accepted. *Expenses:* Contact institution. *Faculty research:* Operations management, strategic management, technology foresight, marketing, business analysis.

University of New Hampshire, Graduate School, Whittemore School of Business and Economics, Department of Business Administration, Program in Management of Technology, Durham, NH 03824. Offers MS, Postbaccalaureate Certificate. Part-time programs available. *Application deadline:* For fall admission, 6/1 for domestic students, 4/1 for international students; for spring admission, 12/1 for domestic students. Application fee: $65. *Financial support:* Fellowships, research assistantships, teaching assistantships available. *Application contact:* Holly Hurwitch, Administrative Assistant, 603-862-0277, E-mail: management.technology@unh.edu.

University of New Mexico, Robert O. Anderson Graduate School of Management, Department of Finance, International, Technology and Entrepreneurship, Albuquerque, NM 87131-1221. Offers finance (MBA); international management (MBA); international management in Latin America (MBA); management of technology (MBA). Part-time and evening/weekend programs available. *Entrance requirements:* For master's, GMAT or GRE (can be waived in some instances). Additional exam requirements/recommendations for international students: Required—TOEFL (minimum score 550 paper-based; 213 computer-based; 79 iBT). Electronic applications accepted. *Expenses:* Tuition, state resident: full-time $5991; part-time $251 per credit hour. Tuition, nonresident: full-time $14,405; part-time $800.20 per credit hour. Tuition and fees vary according to course level, course load, program and reciprocity agreements. *Faculty research:* Corporate finance, investments, management in Latin America, management of technology, entrepreneurship.

University of North Dakota, Graduate School, College of Business and Public Administration, Department of Technology, Grand Forks, ND 58202. Offers MSIT. Part-time programs available. *Faculty:* 3 full-time (1 woman), 1 part-time/adjunct (0 women). *Students:* 3 full-time (1 woman), 8 part-time (2 women), 3 international. Average age 32. 6 applicants, 100% accepted, 6 enrolled. In 2010, 2 master's awarded. *Degree requirements:* For master's, comprehensive exam (for some programs), thesis optional. *Entrance requirements:* For master's, minimum GPA of 2.75. Additional exam requirements/recommendations for international students: Required—TOEFL (minimum score 550 paper-based; 213 computer-based; 79 iBT); IELTS (minimum score 6.5). *Application deadline:* For fall admission, 8/1 priority date for domestic students, 8/1 for international students; for spring admission, 12/1 priority date for domestic students, 12/1 for international students. Applications are processed on a rolling basis. Application fee: $35. Electronic applications accepted. *Expenses:* Tuition, state resident: full-time $5857; part-time $306.74 per credit. Tuition, nonresident: full-time $15,666; part-time $729.77 per credit. Required fees: $53.42 per credit. Tuition and fees vary according to course load, program and reciprocity agreements. *Financial support:* In 2010–11, 4 students received support, including 3 teaching assistantships with full and partial tuition reimbursements available; fellowships with full and partial tuition reimbursements available, research assistantships with full and partial tuition reimbursements available, Federal Work-Study, institutionally sponsored loans, scholarships/grants, health care benefits, tuition waivers (full and partial), and unspecified assistantships also available. Support available to part-time students. Financial award application deadline: 3/15; financial award applicants required to submit FAFSA. *Unit head:* Dr. Dave Yearwood, Graduate Director, 701-777-2249, Fax: 701-777-4320, E-mail: yearwood@und.edu. *Application contact:* Matt Anderson, Admissions Specialist, 701-777-2947, Fax: 701-777-3619, E-mail: matthew.anderson@gradschool.und.edu.

University of Pennsylvania, School of Engineering and Applied Science, Executive Master's in Technology Management Program, Philadelphia, PA 19104. Offers EMBA. Program offered jointly with The Wharton School. Part-time and evening/weekend programs available. *Students:* 3 full-time (1 woman), 129 part-time (19 women); includes 6 Black or African American, non-Hispanic/Latino; 33 Asian, non-Hispanic/Latino; 5 Hispanic/Latino, 6 international. 69 applicants, 72% accepted, 45 enrolled. In 2010, 34 master's awarded. *Application deadline:* For fall admission, 4/1 priority date for domestic students. Application fee: $70. *Expenses:* Tuition: Full-time $25,660; part-time $4758 per course. Required fees: $2152; $270 per course. Tuition and fees vary according to course load, degree level and program.

University of Phoenix, School of Business, Phoenix, AZ 85034-7209. Offers accounting (MBA, MSA); business administration (MBA); energy management (MBA); global management (MBA); health care management (MBA); human resources management (MM); international management (MM); management (MM); marketing (MBA); project management (MBA); public administration (MPA); technology management (MBA). Programs are offered at the online campus. Evening/weekend programs available. Postbaccalaureate distance learning degree programs offered. *Students:* 20,237 full-time (12,641 women); includes 6,424 minority (4,376 Black or African American, non-Hispanic/Latino; 150 American Indian or Alaska Native, non-Hispanic/Latino; 546 Asian, non-Hispanic/Latino; 1,137 Hispanic/Latino; 155 Native Hawaiian or other Pacific Islander, non-Hispanic/Latino; 60 Two or more races, non-Hispanic/Latino), 1,149 international. Average age 39. *Entrance requirements:* For master's, minimum undergraduate GPA of 2.5 from accredited university, 3 years of work experience, citizen of the United States or have valid visa. Additional exam requirements/recommendations for international students: Required—TOEFL (minimum paper score 550, computer score 213, iBT 79), Test of English for International Communication, or IELTS. *Application deadline:* Applications are processed on a rolling basis. Application fee: $45. Electronic applications accepted. *Expenses:* Tuition: Full-time $16,440. One-time fee: $45 full-time. Full-time tuition and fees vary according to course load, degree level, campus/location and program. *Financial support:* Scholarships/grants available. Financial award applicants required to submit FAFSA. *Unit head:* Dr. Bill Berry, Director, 480-557-1824, E-mail: bill.berry@phoenix.edu. *Application contact:* Dr. Bill Berry, Director, 480-557-1824, E-mail: bill.berry@phoenix.edu.

University of Phoenix–Atlanta Campus, College of Information Systems and Technology, Sandy Springs, GA 30350-4153. Offers information systems (MIS); technology management (MBA). Evening/weekend programs available. *Degree requirements:* For master's, thesis (for some programs). *Entrance requirements:* For master's, 3 years of work experience, minimum undergraduate GPA of 3.0. Additional exam requirements/recommendations for international students: Required—TOEFL (minimum score 550 paper-based; 213 computer-based; 79 iBT). Electronic applications accepted.

University of Phoenix–Augusta Campus, College of Information Systems and Technology, Augusta, GA 30909-4583. Offers information systems (MIS); technology management (MBA).

University of Phoenix–Austin Campus, College of Information Systems and Technology, Austin, TX 78759. Offers information systems (MIS); technology management (MBA).

University of Phoenix–Birmingham Campus, College of Information Systems and Technology, Birmingham, AL 35244. Offers information systems (MIS); technology management (MBA).

University of Phoenix–Boston Campus, College of Information Systems and Technology, Braintree, MA 02184-4949. Offers technology management (MBA). Evening/weekend programs available. *Degree requirements:* For master's, thesis (for some programs). *Entrance requirements:* For master's, minimum GPA of 3.0, 3 years of work experience. Additional exam requirements/recommendations for international students: Required—TOEFL (minimum score 550 paper-based; 213 computer-based; 79 iBT). Electronic applications accepted.

University of Phoenix–Central Florida Campus, College of Information Systems and Technology, Maitland, FL 32751-7057. Offers management (MIS); technology management (MBA). Evening/weekend programs available. *Degree requirements:* For master's, thesis (for some programs). *Entrance requirements:* For master's, minimum undergraduate GPA of 3.0, 3 years work experience. Additional exam requirements/recommendations for international students: Required—TOEFL (minimum score 550 paper-based; 213 computer-based; 79 iBT). Electronic applications accepted.

University of Phoenix–Central Massachusetts Campus, College of Information Systems and Technology, Westborough, MA 01581-3906. Offers technology management (MBA). Evening/weekend programs available. *Degree requirements:* For master's, thesis (for some programs). *Entrance requirements:* For master's, minimum undergraduate GPA of 3.0, 3 years of work experience. Additional exam requirements/recommendations for international students: Required—TOEFL (minimum score 550 paper-based; 213 computer-based; 79 iBT). Electronic applications accepted.

University of Phoenix–Central Valley Campus, College of Information Systems and Technology, Fresno, CA 93720-1562. Offers information systems (MIS); technology management (MBA).

University of Phoenix–Charlotte Campus, College of Information Systems and Technology, Charlotte, NC 28273-3409. Offers information systems (MIS); information systems management (MISM); technology management (MBA). Evening/weekend programs available. *Degree requirements:* For master's, thesis (for some programs). *Entrance requirements:* For master's, minimum undergraduate GPA of 3.0, 3 years work experience. Additional exam requirements/recommendations for international students: Required—TOEFL (minimum score 550 paper-based; 213 computer-based; 79 iBT). Electronic applications accepted.

University of Phoenix–Chattanooga Campus, College of Information Systems and Technology, Chattanooga, TN 37421-3707. Offers information systems (MIS); technology management (MBA). Postbaccalaureate distance learning degree programs offered.

University of Phoenix–Cheyenne Campus, College of Information Systems and Technology, Cheyenne, WY 82009. Offers information systems (MIS); technology management (MBA).

University of Phoenix–Chicago Campus, College of Information Systems and Technology, Schaumburg, IL 60173-4399. Offers e-business (MBA); information systems (MIS); management (MM); technology management (MBA). Evening/weekend programs available. *Degree requirements:* For master's, thesis (for some programs). *Entrance requirements:* For master's, 3 years of work experience, minimum undergraduate GPA of 3.0. Additional exam requirements/recommendations for international students: Required—TOEFL (minimum score 550 paper-based; 213 computer-based; 79 iBT). Electronic applications accepted.

University of Phoenix–Cincinnati Campus, College of Information Systems and Technology, West Chester, OH 45069-4875. Offers electronic business (MBA); information systems (MIS); technology management (MBA). Evening/weekend programs available. Postbaccalaureate distance learning degree programs offered. *Degree requirements:* For master's, thesis (for some programs). *Entrance requirements:* For master's, minimum undergraduate GPA of 2.5, 3 years of work experience. Additional exam requirements/recommendations for international students: Required—TOEFL (minimum score 550 paper-based; 213 computer-based; 79 iBT). Electronic applications accepted.

University of Phoenix–Cleveland Campus, College of Information Systems and Technology, Independence, OH 44131-2194. Offers information management (MIS); technology management (MBA). Evening/weekend programs available. Postbaccalaureate distance learning degree programs offered (no on-campus study). *Degree requirements:* For master's, thesis (for some programs). *Entrance requirements:* For master's, minimum undergraduate GPA of 3.0, 3 years of work experience. Additional exam requirements/recommendations for international students: Required—TOEFL (minimum score 550 paper-based; 213 computer-based; 79 iBT). Electronic applications accepted.

University of Phoenix–Columbia Campus, College of Information Systems and Technology, Columbia, SC 29223. Offers technology management (MBA).

University of Phoenix–Columbus Georgia Campus, College of Information Systems and Technology, Columbus, GA 31904-6321. Offers e-business (MBA); information systems (MIS); technology management (MBA). Evening/weekend programs available. Postbaccalaureate distance learning degree programs offered. *Degree requirements:* For master's, thesis (for some programs). *Entrance requirements:* For master's, minimum undergraduate GPA of 3.0, 3 years of work experience. Additional exam requirements/recommendations for international

Management of Technology

University of Phoenix–Columbus Georgia Campus (continued)
students: Required—TOEFL (minimum score 550 paper-based; 213 computer-based; 79 iBT). Electronic applications accepted.

University of Phoenix–Columbus Ohio Campus, College of Information Systems and Technology, Columbus, OH 43240-4032. Offers information systems (MIS); technology management (MBA). Postbaccalaureate distance learning degree programs offered.

University of Phoenix–Dallas Campus, College of Information Systems and Technology, Dallas, TX 75251-2009. Offers e-business (MBA); information systems (MIS); technology management (MBA). Evening/weekend programs available. *Degree requirements:* For master's, thesis (for some programs). *Entrance requirements:* For master's, minimum undergraduate GPA of 3.0, 3 years of work experience. Additional exam requirements/recommendations for international students: Required—TOEFL (minimum score 550 paper-based; 213 computer-based; 79 iBT). Electronic applications accepted.

University of Phoenix–Denver Campus, College of Information Systems and Technology, Lone Tree, CO 80124-5453. Offers e-business (MBA); management (MIS); technology management (MBA). Evening/weekend programs available. Postbaccalaureate distance learning degree programs offered. *Degree requirements:* For master's, thesis (for some programs). *Entrance requirements:* For master's, minimum undergraduate GPA of 3.0, 3 years of work experience. Additional exam requirements/recommendations for international students: Required—TOEFL (minimum score 550 paper-based; 213 computer-based; 79 iBT). Electronic applications accepted.

University of Phoenix–Des Moines Campus, College of Information Systems and Technology, Des Moines, IA 50266. Offers information systems (MIS); technology management (MBA). Postbaccalaureate distance learning degree programs offered.

University of Phoenix–Eastern Washington Campus, College of Information Systems and Technology, Spokane Valley, WA 99212-2531. Offers technology management (MBA).

University of Phoenix–Harrisburg Campus, College of Information Systems and Technology, Harrisburg, PA 17112. Offers information systems (MIS); technology management (MBA). Postbaccalaureate distance learning degree programs offered.

University of Phoenix–Hawaii Campus, College of Information Systems and Technology, Honolulu, HI 96813-4317. Offers information systems (MIS); technology management (MBA). Evening/weekend programs available. *Degree requirements:* For master's, thesis (for some programs). *Entrance requirements:* For master's, minimum undergraduate GPA of 3.0, 3 years of work experience. Additional exam requirements/recommendations for international students: Required—TOEFL (minimum score 550 paper-based; 213 computer-based; 79 iBT). Electronic applications accepted.

University of Phoenix–Houston Campus, College of Information Systems and Technology, Houston, TX 77079-2004. Offers e-business (MBA); information systems (MIS); technology management (MBA). Evening/weekend programs available. Postbaccalaureate distance learning degree programs offered. *Degree requirements:* For master's, comprehensive exam (for some programs), thesis. *Entrance requirements:* For master's, minimum undergraduate GPA of 3.0, 3 years of work experience. Additional exam requirements/recommendations for international students: Required—TOEFL (minimum score 550 paper-based; 213 computer-based; 79 iBT). Electronic applications accepted.

University of Phoenix–Idaho Campus, College of Information Systems and Technology, Meridian, ID 83642-3014. Offers information systems (MIS); technology management (MBA). Evening/weekend programs available. *Degree requirements:* For master's, thesis (for some programs). *Entrance requirements:* For master's, minimum undergraduate GPA of 3.0, 3 years of work experience. Additional exam requirements/recommendations for international students: Required—TOEFL (minimum score 550 paper-based; 213 computer-based). Electronic applications accepted.

University of Phoenix–Indianapolis Campus, College of Information Systems and Technology, Indianapolis, IN 46250-932. Offers information systems (MIS); technology management (MBA). Evening/weekend programs available. *Degree requirements:* For master's, thesis (for some programs). *Entrance requirements:* For master's, minimum undergraduate GPA of 3.0, 3 years of work experience. Additional exam requirements/recommendations for international students: Required—TOEFL (minimum score 550 paper-based; 213 computer-based). Electronic applications accepted.

University of Phoenix–Jersey City Campus, College of Information Systems and Technology, Jersey City, NJ 07310. Offers information systems (MIS); technology management (MBA). Postbaccalaureate distance learning degree programs offered.

University of Phoenix–Kansas City Campus, College of Information Systems and Technology, Kansas City, MO 64131-4517. Offers management (MIS); technology management (MBA). Evening/weekend programs available. *Degree requirements:* For master's, thesis (for some programs). *Entrance requirements:* For master's, minimum undergraduate GPA of 3.0, 3 years of work experience. Additional exam requirements/recommendations for international students: Required—TOEFL (minimum score 550 paper-based; 213 computer-based). Electronic applications accepted.

University of Phoenix–Las Vegas Campus, College of Information Systems and Technology, Las Vegas, NV 89128. Offers information systems (MIS); technology management (MBA). Evening/weekend programs available. *Degree requirements:* For master's, thesis (for some programs). *Entrance requirements:* For master's, minimum undergraduate GPA of 3.0, 3 years of work experience. Additional exam requirements/recommendations for international students: Required—TOEFL (minimum score 550 paper-based; 213 computer-based; 79 iBT). Electronic applications accepted.

University of Phoenix–Louisiana Campus, College of Information Systems and Technology, Metairie, LA 70001-2082. Offers information systems/management (MIS); technology management (MBA). Evening/weekend programs available. *Degree requirements:* For master's, thesis (for some programs). *Entrance requirements:* For master's, minimum undergraduate GPA of 3.0, 3 years work experience. Additional exam requirements/recommendations for international students: Required—TOEFL (minimum score 550 paper-based; 213 computer-based). Electronic applications accepted.

University of Phoenix–Louisville Campus, College of Information Systems and Technology, Louisville, KY 40223-3839. Offers technology management (MBA). Postbaccalaureate distance learning degree programs offered.

University of Phoenix–Madison Campus, College of Information Systems and Technology, Madison, WI 53718-2416. Offers information systems (MIS); management (MIS); technology management (MBA).

University of Phoenix–Maryland Campus, College of Information Systems and Technology, Columbia, MD 21045-5424. Offers information systems (MIS); technology management (MBA). Evening/weekend programs available. *Degree requirements:* For master's, thesis (for some programs). *Entrance requirements:* For master's, minimum undergraduate GPA of 3.0, 3 years of work experience. Additional exam requirements/recommendations for international students: Required—TOEFL (minimum score 550 paper-based; 213 computer-based; 79 iBT). Electronic applications accepted.

University of Phoenix–Memphis Campus, College of Information Systems and Technology, Cordova, TN 38018. Offers information systems (MIS); technology management (MBA).

University of Phoenix–Minneapolis/St. Louis Park Campus, College of Information Systems and Technology, St. Louis Park, MN 55426. Offers technology management (MBA).

University of Phoenix–Nashville Campus, College of Information Systems and Technology, Nashville, TN 37214-5048. Offers technology management (MBA). Evening/weekend programs available. *Degree requirements:* For master's, thesis (for some programs). *Entrance requirements:* For master's, 3 years of work experience, minimum undergraduate GPA of 3.0. Additional exam requirements/recommendations for international students: Required—TOEFL (minimum score 550 paper-based; 213 computer-based; 79 iBT). Electronic applications accepted.

University of Phoenix–New Mexico Campus, College of Information Systems and Technology, Albuquerque, NM 87113-1570. Offers e-business (MBA); information systems (MIS); technology management (MBA). Evening/weekend programs available. *Degree requirements:* For master's, thesis (for some programs). *Entrance requirements:* For master's, minimum undergraduate GPA of 3.0, 3 years of work experience. Additional exam requirements/recommendations for international students: Required—TOEFL (minimum score 550 paper-based; 213 computer-based; 79 iBT). Electronic applications accepted.

University of Phoenix–Northern Nevada Campus, College of Information Systems and Technology, Reno, NV 89521-5862. Offers information systems (MIS); technology management (MBA).

University of Phoenix–Northwest Arkansas Campus, College of Information Systems and Technology, Rogers, AR 72756-9615. Offers information systems (MIS); technology management (MBA).

University of Phoenix–Oklahoma City Campus, College of Information Systems and Technology, Oklahoma City, OK 73116-8244. Offers e-business (MBA); technology management (MBA). Evening/weekend programs available. *Degree requirements:* For master's, thesis (for some programs). *Entrance requirements:* For master's, minimum undergraduate GPA of 3.0, 3 years of work experience. Additional exam requirements/recommendations for international students: Required—TOEFL (minimum score 550 paper-based; 213 computer-based; 79 iBT). Electronic applications accepted.

University of Phoenix–Omaha Campus, College of Information Systems and Technology, Omaha, NE 68154-5240. Offers information systems (MIS); technology management (MBA).

University of Phoenix–Oregon Campus, College of Information Systems and Technology, Tigard, OR 97223. Offers information systems (MIS); technology management (MBA). Evening/weekend programs available. *Degree requirements:* For master's, thesis (for some programs). *Entrance requirements:* For master's, minimum undergraduate GPA of 2.5, 3 years work experience. Additional exam requirements/recommendations for international students: Required—TOEFL (minimum score 550 paper-based; 213 computer-based; 79 iBT). Electronic applications accepted.

University of Phoenix–Philadelphia Campus, College of Information Systems and Technology, Wayne, PA 19087-2121. Offers information systems (MIS); technology management (MBA). Evening/weekend programs available. *Degree requirements:* For master's, thesis (for some programs). *Entrance requirements:* For master's, 3 years of work experience, minimum undergraduate GPA of 3.0. Additional exam requirements/recommendations for international students: Required—TOEFL (minimum score 550 paper-based; 213 computer-based; 79 iBT). Electronic applications accepted.

University of Phoenix–Pittsburgh Campus, College of Information Systems and Technology, Pittsburgh, PA 15276. Offers e-business (MBA); information systems (MIS); technology management (MBA). Evening/weekend programs available. *Degree requirements:* For master's, thesis (for some programs). *Entrance requirements:* For master's, minimum undergraduate GPA of 3.0, 3 years work experience. Additional exam requirements/recommendations for international students: Required—TOEFL (minimum score 550 paper-based; 213 computer-based; 79 iBT). Electronic applications accepted.

University of Phoenix–Puerto Rico Campus, College of Information Systems and Technology, Guaynabo, PR 00968. Offers technology management (MBA). Evening/weekend programs available. *Degree requirements:* For master's, thesis (for some programs). *Entrance requirements:* For master's, minimum undergraduate GPA of 3.0, 3 years of work experience. Additional exam requirements/recommendations for international students: Required—TOEFL (minimum score 550 paper-based; 213 computer-based; 79 iBT). Electronic applications accepted.

University of Phoenix–Raleigh Campus, College of Information Systems and Technology, Raleigh, NC 27606. Offers information systems and technology (MIS); management (MIS); technology management (MBA).

University of Phoenix–Richmond Campus, College of Information Systems and Technology, Richmond, VA 23230. Offers information systems (MIS); technology management (MBA). Evening/weekend programs available. *Degree requirements:* For master's, thesis (for some programs). *Entrance requirements:* For master's, minimum undergraduate GPA of 3.0, 3 years work experience. Additional exam requirements/recommendations for international students: Required—TOEFL (minimum score 500 paper-based; 213 computer-based; 79 iBT). Electronic applications accepted.

University of Phoenix–Sacramento Valley Campus, College of Information Systems and Technology, Sacramento, CA 95833-3632. Offers management (MIS); technology management (MBA). Evening/weekend programs available. *Degree requirements:* For master's, thesis (for some programs). *Entrance requirements:* For master's, minimum undergraduate GPA of 3.0, 3 years work experience. Additional exam requirements/recommendations for international students: Required—TOEFL (minimum score 550 paper-based; 213 computer-based; 79 iBT). Electronic applications accepted.

University of Phoenix–San Antonio Campus, College of Information Systems and Technology, San Antonio, TX 78230. Offers information systems (MIS); technology management (MBA).

University of Phoenix–San Diego Campus, College of Information Systems and Technology, San Diego, CA 92123. Offers management (MIS); technology management (MBA). Evening/weekend programs available. *Degree requirements:* For master's, thesis (for some programs). *Entrance requirements:* For master's, minimum undergraduate GPA of 3.0, 3 years work experience. Additional exam requirements/recommendations for international students: Required—TOEFL (minimum score 550 paper-based; 213 computer-based; 79 iBT). Electronic applications accepted.

University of Phoenix–Savannah Campus, College of Information Systems and Technology, Savannah, GA 31405-7400. Offers information systems and technology (MIS); technology management (MBA).

University of Phoenix–Southern Arizona Campus, College of Information Systems and Technology, Tucson, AZ 85711. Offers information systems (MIS); technology management (MBA). Evening/weekend programs available. *Degree requirements:* For master's, thesis (for some programs). *Entrance requirements:* For master's, minimum undergraduate GPA of 3.0, 3 years of work experience. Additional exam requirements/recommendations for international students: Required—TOEFL (minimum score 550 paper-based; 213 computer-based; 79 iBT). Electronic applications accepted.

University of Phoenix–Southern Colorado Campus, College of Information Systems and Technology, Colorado Springs, CO 80919-2335. Offers technology management (MBA). Evening/weekend programs available. *Degree requirements:* For master's, thesis (for some programs). *Entrance requirements:* For master's, minimum undergraduate GPA of 3.0, 3 years of work experience. Additional exam requirements/recommendations for international students: Required—TOEFL (minimum score 550 paper-based; 213 computer-based; 79 iBT). Electronic applications accepted.

University of Phoenix–Springfield Campus, College of Information Systems and Technology, Springfield, MO 65804-7211. Offers information systems (MIS); technology management (MBA).

University of Phoenix–Tulsa Campus, College of Information Systems and Technology, Tulsa, OK 74134-1412. Offers information systems and technology (MIS); technology management (MBA).

University of Phoenix–Utah Campus, School of Business, Salt Lake City, UT 84123-4617. Offers accounting (MBA); business administration (MBA); global management (MBA); human resource management (MBA, MM); management (MM); marketing (MBA); technology management (MBA). Evening/weekend programs available. *Degree requirements:* For master's, thesis (for some programs). *Entrance requirements:* For master's, minimum undergraduate GPA of 3.0, 3 years of work experience. Additional exam requirements/recommendations for international students: Required—TOEFL (minimum score 550 paper-based; 213 computer-based; 79 iBT). Electronic applications accepted.

University of Phoenix–Vancouver Campus, John Sperling School of Business, College of Information Systems and Technology, Burnaby, BC V5C 6G9, Canada. Offers technology management (MBA). Evening/weekend programs available. *Degree requirements:* For master's, thesis (for some programs). *Entrance requirements:* For master's, minimum undergraduate GPA of 3.0, 3 years of work experience. Additional exam requirements/recommendations for international students: Required—TOEFL (minimum score 550 paper-based; 213 computer-based; 79 iBT). Electronic applications accepted.

University of Phoenix–West Florida Campus, College of Information Systems and Technology, Temple Terrace, FL 33637. Offers information systems (MIS); technology management (MBA). Evening/weekend programs available. *Degree requirements:* For master's, thesis (for some programs). *Entrance requirements:* For master's, minimum undergraduate GPA of 3.0, 3 years work experience. Additional exam requirements/recommendations for international students: Required—TOEFL (minimum score 550 paper-based; 213 computer-based; 79 iBT). Electronic applications accepted.

University of Portland, Dr. Robert B. Pamplin, Jr. School of Business, Portland, OR 97203-5798. Offers business administration (MBA); entrepreneurship (MBA); finance (MBA, MS); health care management (MBA); marketing (MBA); nonprofit management (EMBA); operations and technology management (MBA); sustainability (MBA). *Accreditation:* AACSB. Part-time and evening/weekend programs available. *Faculty:* 12 full-time (2 women), 7 part-time/adjunct (2 women). *Students:* 55 full-time (24 women), 81 part-time (29 women); includes 18 minority (2 Black or African American, non-Hispanic/Latino; 8 Asian, non-Hispanic/Latino; 5 Hispanic/Latino; 3 Two or more races, non-Hispanic/Latino), 23 international. Average age 30. In 2010, 55 master's awarded. *Entrance requirements:* For master's, GMAT, minimum GPA of 3.0, resume, 2 letters of recommendation. Additional exam requirements/recommendations for international students: Required—TOEFL (minimum score 570 paper-based; 89 iBT), IELTS (minimum score 7). *Application deadline:* For fall admission, 7/15 priority date for domestic and international students; for spring admission, 12/15 priority date for domestic and international students. Applications are processed on a rolling basis. Application fee: $50. *Expenses:* Contact institution. *Financial support:* Federal Work-Study, scholarships/grants, and tuition waivers (partial) available. Support available to part-time students. Financial award application deadline: 3/1; financial award applicants required to submit FAFSA. *Unit head:* Dr. Howard Feldman, Associate Dean, 503-943-7224, E-mail: feldman@up.edu. *Application contact:* Melissa McCarthy, Academic Specialist, 503-943-7225, E-mail: mccarthy@up.edu.

University of St. Thomas, Graduate Studies, School of Engineering, St. Paul, MN 55105-1096. Offers manufacturing engineering and operations (MS); mechanical engineering (MS); medical device development (Certificate); regulatory science (MS); software engineering (MS); software management (MS); software systems (MSS); systems engineering (MS); technology management (MS). *Accreditation:* ABET (one or more programs are accredited). *Entrance requirements:* For master's, resume, official transcripts. Additional exam requirements/recommendations for international students: Required—TOEFL (minimum score 550 paper-based). *Application deadline:* For fall admission, 8/1 priority date for domestic students; for spring admission, 1/1 priority date for domestic students. Applications are processed on a rolling basis. Application fee: $30. Electronic applications accepted. *Expenses:* Contact institution. *Financial support:* Fellowships, research assistantships, institutionally sponsored loans and scholarships/grants available. Support available to part-time students. Financial award application deadline: 4/1; financial award applicants required to submit FAFSA. *Unit head:* Don Weinkauf, Dean, 651-962-5760, Fax: 651-962-6419, E-mail: dhweinkauf@stthomas.edu. *Application contact:* Joyce A. Taylor, Graduate Programs Coordinator, 651-962-5756, Fax: 651-962-6419, E-mail: jataylor1@stthomas.edu.

The University of Texas at San Antonio, College of Business, General Business Program, San Antonio, TX 78249-0617. Offers accounting (PhD); business (MBA); finance (PhD); information systems (MBA); information technology (PhD); international business (MBA); management accounting (MBA); management and organization studies (PhD); management of technology (MBA); marketing (PhD); marketing management (MBA); taxation (MBA). Part-time and evening/weekend programs available. *Students:* 159 full-time (59 women), 124 part-time (43 women); includes 82 minority (9 Black or African American, non-Hispanic/Latino; 2 American Indian or Alaska Native, non-Hispanic/Latino; 17 Asian, non-Hispanic/Latino; 50 Hispanic/Latino; 1 Native Hawaiian or other Pacific Islander, non-Hispanic/Latino; 3 Two or more races, non-Hispanic/Latino), 39 international. Average age 32. 330 applicants, 46% accepted, 105 enrolled. In 2010, 85 master's, 9 doctorates awarded. *Degree requirements:* For master's, comprehensive exam (for some programs), thesis (for some programs). *Entrance requirements:* For master's, GMAT. Additional exam requirements/recommendations for international students: Required—TOEFL (minimum score 500 paper-based; 173 computer-based; 61 iBT), IELTS (minimum score 5). *Application deadline:* For fall admission, 7/1 for domestic students, 4/1 for international students; for spring admission, 11/1 for domestic students, 9/1 for international students. Application fee: $45 ($80 for international students). *Expenses:* Tuition, state resident: full-time $4172; part-time $231.75 per credit hour. Tuition, nonresident: full-time $15,332; part-time $851.75 per credit hour. *Financial support:* In 2010–11, 282 research assistantships (averaging $13,930 per year), 74 teaching assistantships (averaging $9,284 per year) were awarded; scholarships/grants, tuition waivers, and unspecified assistantships also available. Support available to part-time students. *Unit head:* Dr. Lynda Y. de la Vinna, Dean, 210-458-4317, Fax: 210-458-4308, E-mail: lynda.delavina@utsa.edu. *Application contact:* Veronica Ramirez, Assistant Dean of the Graduate School, 210-458-4330, Fax: 210-458-4332, E-mail: graduatestudies@utsa.edu.

University of Toronto, School of Graduate Studies, Life Sciences Division, Program in Management of Innovation, Toronto, ON M5S 1A1, Canada. Offers MMI.

University of Washington, Graduate School, Michael G. Foster School of Business, Seattle, WA 98195-3200. Offers auditing and assurance (MP Acc); business (PhD); business administration (evening) (MBA); business administration (full-time) (MBA); executive business administration (MBA); global business administration (MBA); global executive business administration (MBA); taxation (MP Acc); technology management (MBA); JD/MBA; MBA/MAIS; MBA/MHA. *Accreditation:* AACSB. Part-time and evening/weekend programs available. Terminal master's awarded for partial completion of doctoral program. *Degree requirements:* For doctorate, comprehensive exam, thesis/dissertation. *Entrance requirements:* For master's, GMAT; for doctorate, GMAT, GRE. Additional exam requirements/recommendations for international students: Required—TOEFL (minimum score 600 paper-based; 250 computer-based). Electronic applications accepted. *Expenses:* Contact institution. *Faculty research:* Finance, marketing, organizational behavior, information technology, strategy.

University of Waterloo, Graduate Studies, Centre for Business, Entrepreneurship and Technology, Waterloo, ON N2L 3G1, Canada. Offers MBET. *Entrance requirements:* For master's, honors degree. Additional exam requirements/recommendations for international students: Required—TOEFL (minimum score 550 paper-based; 213 computer-based), TWE. Electronic applications accepted.

University of Waterloo, Graduate Studies, Faculty of Engineering, Department of Management Sciences, Waterloo, ON N2L 3G1, Canada. Offers applied operations research (MA Sc, MMS, PhD); information systems (MA Sc, MMS, PhD); management of technology (MA Sc, MMS, PhD). Part-time programs available. Postbaccalaureate distance learning degree programs offered (no on-campus study). *Degree requirements:* For master's, research paper or thesis; for doctorate, comprehensive exam, thesis/dissertation. *Entrance requirements:* For master's, GMAT or GRE, honors degree, minimum B average, resume; for doctorate, GMAT or GRE, master's degree, minimum A- average, resumé. Additional exam requirements/recommendations for international students: Required—TOEFL, TWE. *Faculty research:* Operations research, manufacturing systems, scheduling, information systems.

University of Wisconsin–Madison, Graduate School, Wisconsin School of Business, Wisconsin Full-Time MBA Program, Madison, WI 53706-1380. Offers applied security analysis (MBA); arts administration (MBA); brand and product management (MBA); corporate finance and investment banking (MBA); entrepreneurial management (MBA); marketing research (MBA); operations and technology management (MBA); real estate (MBA); risk management and insurance (MBA); strategic human resource management (MBA); strategic management in the life and engineering sciences (MBA); supply chain management (MBA). *Faculty:* 32 full-time (4 women), 17 part-time/adjunct (3 women). *Students:* 242 full-time (74 women); includes 16 Black or African American, non-Hispanic/Latino; 3 American Indian or Alaska Native, non-Hispanic/Latino; 16 Asian, non-Hispanic/Latino; 12 Hispanic/Latino, 29 international. Average age 28. 526 applicants, 32% accepted, 117 enrolled. In 2010, 106 master's awarded. *Entrance requirements:* For master's, GMAT, bachelor's or equivalent degree, 2 years of work experience, letters of recommendation. Additional exam requirements/recommendations for international students: Required—TOEFL (minimum score 600 paper-based; 250 computer-based; 100 iBT), IELTS. *Application deadline:* For fall admission, 11/4 for domestic students, 11/1 for international students; for winter admission, 2/5 for domestic and international students; for spring admission, 5/15 for domestic students, 4/5 for international students. Applications are processed on a rolling basis. Application fee: $56. Electronic applications accepted. *Expenses:* Tuition, state resident: full-time $9887.36; part-time $617.96 per credit. Tuition, nonresident: full-time $24,054; part-time $1503.40 per credit. Required fees: $67.63 per credit. Tuition and fees vary according to reciprocity agreements. *Financial support:* In 2010–11, 103 students received support, including 13 fellowships with full and partial tuition reimbursements available (averaging $15,000 per year), 53 research assistantships with full tuition reimbursements available (averaging $8,000 per year), 35 teaching assistantships with full tuition reimbursements available (averaging $11,000 per year); scholarships/grants, health care benefits, and unspecified assistantships also available. Financial award application deadline: 4/5; financial award applicants required to submit FAFSA. *Faculty research:* Market consequences of International Financial Reporting Standards (IFRS), inter-firm relationships and strategic partnerships, application of Bayesian statistical methods and applied probability models to understanding individuals' behaviors in the context of customer relationship management (CRM) applications, liquidity provision and the structure of financial markets, strategic management of global startups. *Unit head:* Prof. Kenneth A. Kavajecz, PhD, Associate Dean of Master's Programs, 608-265-3494, Fax: 608-265-4192, E-mail: kkavajecz@bus.wisc.edu. *Application contact:* Maria Reis, Assistant Director of MBA Marketing and Recruiting, 608-262-4000, Fax: 608-265-4192, E-mail: mreis@bus.wisc.edu.

University of Wisconsin–Stout, Graduate School, College of Technology, Engineering, and Management, Program in Technology Management, Menomonie, WI 54751. Offers MS. Part-time programs available. *Degree requirements:* For master's, thesis. *Entrance requirements:* For master's, minimum GPA of 2.75. Additional exam requirements/recommendations for international students: Required—TOEFL (minimum score 500 paper-based; 173 computer-based; 61 iBT). Electronic applications accepted. *Faculty research:* Miniature engines, solid modeling, packaging, lean manufacturing, supply chain management.

University of Wisconsin–Whitewater, School of Graduate Studies, College of Business and Economics, Program in Business Administration, Whitewater, WI 53190-1790. Offers finance (MBA); human resource management (MBA); information technology management (MBA); international business (MBA); management (MBA); marketing (MBA); operations and supply chain management (MBA). *Accreditation:* AACSB. Part-time and evening/weekend programs available. Postbaccalaureate distance learning degree programs offered (no on-campus study). *Degree requirements:* For master's, thesis or alternative. *Entrance requirements:* For master's, GMAT, minimum AACSB index of 1000, minimum GPA of 2.75. Additional exam requirements/recommendations for international students: Required—TOEFL (minimum score 550 paper-based; 213 computer-based). Electronic applications accepted. *Faculty research:* Interface between social institutions and individual behavior, technology and innovation management, occupational mental health, workplace deviance and workplace romance.

Walden University, Graduate Programs, School of Management, Minneapolis, MN 55401. Offers accounting (MS), including cpa emphasis, professional track, self-designed; accounting and management (MS), including self-designed, strategic management; applied management and decision sciences (PhD), including accounting, engineering management, finance, general applied management and decision sciences, information systems management, knowledge management, leadership and organizational change, learning management, operations research, self-designed program in applied management and design sciences; business information management (MISM); enterprise information security (MISM); entrepreneurship (MBA, DBA); finance (MBA, DBA); global management (MS); global supply chain management (DBA); health informatics (MISM); healthcare management (MBA, MS); healthcare system improvement (MBA); human resource management (MBA, MS), including functional human resource management (MS), human resource management (MS), integrating functional and strategic human resource management (MS), organizational strategy (MS); information systems (MS); information systems management (DBA); information technology (MS), including information security, software engineering; international business (MBA, DBA); IT strategy and governance (MISM); leadership (MBA, MS, DBA), including entrepreneurship (MS), general management (MS), human resources leadership (MS), innovation and technology (MS), leader development (MS), leading sustainability (MS), project management (MS), self-designed (MS); managers as leaders (MS); managing global software and service supply chains (MISM); marketing (MBA, DBA); project management (MBA, MS); research strategies (MS); risk management (MBA); self-designed (MBA, DBA); social impact management (DBA); strategy and operations (MS); sustainable futures (MBA); sustainable management (MS); technology (MBA); technology entrepreneurship (DBA); technology management (MS). Part-time and evening/weekend programs available. Postbaccalaureate distance learning degree programs offered (minimal on-campus study). *Faculty:* 22 full-time (8 women), 291 part-time/adjunct (100 women). *Students:* 3,705 full-time (1,956 women), 976 part-time (549 women); includes 2,432 minority (2,021 Black or African American, non-Hispanic/Latino; 32 American Indian or Alaska Native, non-Hispanic/Latino; 137 Asian, non-Hispanic/Latino; 193 Hispanic/Latino; 5 Native Hawaiian or other Pacific Islander, non-Hispanic/Latino; 44 Two or more races, non-Hispanic/Latino), 302 international. Average age 40. In 2010, 658 master's, 86 doctorates awarded. *Degree requirements:* For doctorate, thesis/dissertation (for some programs), residency. *Entrance requirements:* For master's, bachelor's degree or equivalent in related field; minimum GPA of 2.5; official transcripts; goal statement; access to computer and Internet; for doctorate, master's degree or equivalent in related field; minimum GPA of 3.0; 3 years of related professional/academic experience (preferred). Additional exam requirements/recommendations for international students: Required—TOEFL (minimum score 550 paper-based; 213 computer-based), IELTS (minimum score 6.5), TOEFL, IELTS, or Michigan English Language Assessment Battery (minimum score 82). *Application deadline:* Applications are processed on a rolling basis. Application fee: $50. Electronic applications accepted. *Expenses:* Tuition: Full-time

Management of Technology

Walden University (continued)
$10,274; part-time $445 per credit. Tuition and fees vary according to course load, degree level and program. *Financial support:* Fellowships, Federal Work-Study, scholarships/grants, unspecified assistantships, and family tuition reduction, active duty/veteran tuition reduction, group tuition reduction, interest-free payment plans available. Support available to part-time students. Financial award applicants required to submit FAFSA. *Unit head:* Dr. William Schulz, Associate Dean, 800-925-3368. *Application contact:* Jennifer Hall, Vice President of Enrollment Management, 866-4-WALDEN, E-mail: info@waldenu.edu.

Western Kentucky University, Graduate Studies, Ogden College of Science and Engineering, Department of Architectural and Manufacturing Sciences, Bowling Green, KY 42101. Offers technology management (MS).

Westminster College, The Bill and Vieve Gore School of Business, Salt Lake City, UT 84105-3697. Offers accountancy (M Acc); business administration (MBA, Certificate); technology management (MBATM). *Accreditation:* ACBSP. Part-time and evening/weekend programs available. Postbaccalaureate distance learning degree programs offered (minimal on-campus study). *Faculty:* 35 full-time (9 women), 22 part-time/adjunct (4 women). *Students:* 175 full-time (44 women), 242 part-time (61 women); includes 2 Black or African American, non-Hispanic/Latino; 2 American Indian or Alaska Native, non-Hispanic/Latino; 8 Asian, non-Hispanic/Latino; 6 Hispanic/Latino; 2 Two or more races, non-Hispanic/Latino, 6 international. Average age 32. 342 applicants, 46% accepted, 113 enrolled. In 2010, 196 master's, 75 other advanced degrees awarded. *Degree requirements:* For master's, international trip, minimum grade of C in all classes. *Entrance requirements:* For master's, GMAT, 2 professional recommendations, employer letter of support, personal resume, essay questions, official transcripts. Additional exam requirements/recommendations for international students: Required—TOEFL (minimum score 600 paper-based; 250 computer-based; 100 iBT), IELTS (minimum score 7). *Application deadline:* Applications are processed on a rolling basis. Application fee: $50. Electronic applications accepted. *Expenses:* Contact institution. *Financial support:* In 2010–11, 222 students received support. Career-related internships or fieldwork and tuition reimbursement, tuition remission available. Support available to part-time students. Financial award applicants required to submit FAFSA. *Faculty research:* Innovation and entrepreneurship, business strategy

and change, financial analysis and capital budgeting, leadership development. Total annual research expenditures: $100,000. *Unit head:* Gary Daynes, Dean, 801-832-2600, Fax: 801-832-3106, E-mail: gdaynes@westminstercollege.edu. *Application contact:* Joel Bauman, Vice President of Enrollment Services, 801-832-2200, Fax: 801-832-3101, E-mail: admission@westminstercollege.edu.

Wilfrid Laurier University, Faculty of Graduate and Postdoctoral Studies, School of Business and Economics, Department of Business, Waterloo, ON N2L 3C5, Canada. Offers accounting (PhD); finance (M Fin); financial economics (PhD); marketing (PhD); operations and supply chain management (PhD); organizational behavior and human resource management (M Sc); organizational behaviour and human resource management (PhD); supply chain management (M Sc); technology management (EMTM). Part-time and evening/weekend programs available. *Faculty:* 67 full-time (20 women), 12 part-time/adjunct (4 women). *Students:* 20 full-time (11 women), 1 part-time (0 women), 5 international. 80 applicants, 28% accepted, 3 enrolled. In 2010, 6 master's, 1 doctorate awarded. *Degree requirements:* For master's, thesis optional; for doctorate, comprehensive exam, thesis/dissertation. *Entrance requirements:* For master's, GMAT, 4-year honors degree with minimum B+ average; for doctorate, GMAT, master's degree, minimum B+ average. Additional exam requirements/recommendations for international students: Required—TOEFL (minimum score 89 iBT). *Application deadline:* For fall admission, 1/15 priority date for domestic and international students. Application fee: $125. Electronic applications accepted. Tuition and fees charges are reported in Canadian dollars. *Expenses:* Tuition, area resident: Full-time $15,300 Canadian dollars; part-time $1200 Canadian dollars per credit. International tuition: $21,300 Canadian dollars full-time. Required fees: $650 Canadian dollars; $100 Canadian dollars per credit. Tuition and fees vary according to course load, degree level, campus/location and program. *Financial support:* In 2010–11, 27 fellowships, 1 research assistantship, 27 teaching assistantships were awarded; career-related internships or fieldwork, scholarships/grants, health care benefits, and unspecified assistantships also available. *Faculty research:* Financial economics, management and organizational behavior, operations and supply chain management. *Unit head:* Dr. Hamid Noori, Director, 519-884-0710 Ext. 2571, Fax: 519-884-2357, E-mail: sbephdmasters@wlu.ca. *Application contact:* Jennifer Williams, Graduate Admission & Records Officer, 519-884-0710 Ext. 3536, Fax: 519-884-1020, E-mail: gradstudies@wlu.ca.

Operations Research

Air Force Institute of Technology, Graduate School of Engineering and Management, Department of Operational Sciences, Dayton, OH 45433-7765. Offers logistics management (MS); operations research (MS, PhD); space operations (MS). Part-time programs available. *Degree requirements:* For master's, thesis; for doctorate, thesis/dissertation. *Entrance requirements:* For doctorate, GRE General Test, minimum GPA of 3.0, U.S. citizenship. *Faculty research:* Optimization, simulation, combat modeling and analysis, reliability and maintainability, resource scheduling.

Bowling Green State University, Graduate College, College of Arts and Sciences, Department of Computer Science, Bowling Green, OH 43403. Offers computer science (MS), including operations research, parallel and distributed computing, software engineering. Part-time programs available. *Degree requirements:* For master's, thesis or alternative. *Entrance requirements:* For master's, GRE General Test. Additional exam requirements/recommendations for international students: Required—TOEFL. Electronic applications accepted. *Faculty research:* Artificial intelligence, real time and concurrent programming languages, behavioral aspects of computing, network protocols.

California State University, East Bay, Office of Academic Programs and Graduate Studies, College of Business and Economics, Department of Information Technology Management, Hayward, CA 94542-3000. Offers MBA. Part-time and evening/weekend programs available. *Faculty:* 37 full-time (7 women), 8 part-time/adjunct (3 women). *Students:* Average age 32. *Degree requirements:* For master's, comprehensive exam or thesis. *Entrance requirements:* For master's, GMAT, minimum GPA of 2.75. Additional exam requirements/recommendations for international students: Required—TOEFL (minimum score 550 paper-based; 213 computer-based). *Application deadline:* For fall admission, 6/30 for domestic and international students. Application fee: $55. Electronic applications accepted. *Financial support:* Career-related internships or fieldwork, Federal Work-Study, and institutionally sponsored loans available. Support available to part-time students. Financial award application deadline: 3/2; financial award applicants required to submit FAFSA. *Unit head:* Dr. Xinjian Lu, Chair, 510-885-3307, Fax: 510-885-2165, E-mail: xinjian.lu@csueastbay.edu. *Application contact:* Donna Wiley, Interim Associate Director, 510-885-2928, Fax: 510-885-4777.

Carnegie Mellon University, Tepper School of Business, Program in Operations Research, Pittsburgh, PA 15213-3891. Offers PhD. *Degree requirements:* For doctorate, thesis/dissertation. *Entrance requirements:* For doctorate, GMAT or GRE General Test.

Case Western Reserve University, Weatherhead School of Management, Department of Operations, Management Program, Cleveland, OH 44106. Offers operations research (MSM); supply chain (MSM); MBA/MSM. *Accreditation:* AACSB. Part-time and evening/weekend programs available. *Entrance requirements:* For master's, GMAT or GRE, 3 letters of recommendation, resume. Additional exam requirements/recommendations for international students: Required—TOEFL (minimum score 600 paper-based; 250 computer-based). *Faculty research:* Supply chain management, operations management, operations/finance interface optimization, scheduling.

Claremont Graduate University, Graduate Programs, School of Mathematical Sciences, Claremont, CA 91711-6160. Offers computational and systems biology (PhD); computational mathematics and numerical analysis (MA, MS); computational science (PhD); engineering and industrial applied mathematics (PhD); mathematics (PhD); operations research and statistics (MA, MS); physical applied mathematics (MA, MS); pure mathematics (MA, MS); scientific computing (MA, MS); systems and control theory (MA, MS). Part-time programs available. *Faculty:* 6 full-time (0 women). *Students:* 50 full-time (15 women), 11 part-time (1 woman); includes 2 Black or African American, non-Hispanic/Latino; 9 Asian, non-Hispanic/Latino; 7 Hispanic/Latino; 3 Two or more races, non-Hispanic/Latino, 13 international. Average age 36. In 2010, 17 master's, 11 doctorates awarded. Terminal master's awarded for partial completion of doctoral program. *Entrance requirements:* For master's and doctorate, GRE General Test. Additional exam requirements/recommendations for international students: Required—TOEFL (minimum score 550 paper-based; 213 computer-based; 80 iBT). *Application deadline:* For fall admission, 2/1 priority date for domestic students. Applications are processed on a rolling basis. Application fee: $60. Electronic applications accepted. *Expenses:* Tuition: Full-time $35,748; part-time $1554 per unit. Required fees: $215 per semester. *Financial support:* Fellowships, research assistantships, Federal Work-Study, institutionally sponsored loans, scholarships/grants, and tuition waivers (full and partial) available. Support available to part-time students. Financial award application deadline: 2/15; financial award applicants required to submit FAFSA. *Unit head:* John Angus, Dean, 909-621-8080, Fax: 909-607-8261, E-mail: john.angus@cgu.edu. *Application contact:* Susan Townzen, Program Coordinator, 909-621-8080, Fax: 909-607-8261, E-mail: susan.n.townzen@cgu.edu.

Clemson University, Graduate School, College of Engineering and Science, Department of Mathematical Sciences, Clemson, SC 29634. Offers applied and pure mathematics (MS,

PhD); computational mathematics (MS, PhD); operations research (MS, PhD); statistics (MS, PhD). Part-time programs available. *Faculty:* 48 full-time (13 women), 12 part-time/adjunct (4 women). *Students:* 127 full-time (51 women), 5 part-time (2 women); includes 2 Black or African American, non-Hispanic/Latino; 1 American Indian or Alaska Native, non-Hispanic/Latino; 1 Two or more races, non-Hispanic/Latino, 36 international. Average age 26. 163 applicants, 79% accepted, 51 enrolled. In 2010, 27 master's, 5 doctorates awarded. *Degree requirements:* For master's, thesis optional, final project; for doctorate, thesis/dissertation, qualifying exams. *Entrance requirements:* For master's and doctorate, GRE General Test. Additional exam requirements/recommendations for international students: Required—TOEFL. *Application deadline:* For fall admission, 1/15 priority date for domestic and international students; for spring admission, 10/1 priority date for domestic students, 9/15 priority date for international students. Applications are processed on a rolling basis. Application fee: $70 ($80 for international students). Electronic applications accepted. *Expenses:* Tuition, state resident: full-time $6492; part-time $400 per credit hour. Tuition, nonresident: full-time $13,634; part-time $800 per credit hour. Required fees: $262 per semester. Part-time tuition and fees vary according to course load and program. *Financial support:* In 2010–11, 110 students received support, including 2 fellowships with full and partial tuition reimbursements available (averaging $6,000 per year), 8 research assistantships with partial tuition reimbursements available (averaging $19,823 per year), 101 teaching assistantships with partial tuition reimbursements available (averaging $17,582 per year); career-related internships or fieldwork, institutionally sponsored loans, scholarships/grants, health care benefits, and unspecified assistantships also available. Support available to part-time students. Financial award application deadline: 4/15. *Faculty research:* Applied and computational analysis, cryptography, discrete mathematics, optimization, statistics. Total annual research expenditures: $823,404. *Unit head:* Dr. Robert L. Taylor, Chair, 864-656-5240, Fax: 864-656-5230, E-mail: rtaylo2@clemson.edu. *Application contact:* Dr. K.B. Kulasekera, Graduate Coordinator, 864-656-5231, Fax: 864-656-5230, E-mail: kk@clemson.edu.

The College of William and Mary, Faculty of Arts and Sciences, Department of Computer Science, Program in Computational Operations Research, Williamsburg, VA 23187-8795. Offers computer science (MS), including operations research. Part-time programs available. *Faculty:* 9 full-time (2 women), 2 part-time/adjunct (1 woman). *Students:* 19 full-time (6 women), 7 international. Average age 26. 25 applicants, 80% accepted, 10 enrolled. In 2010, 9 master's awarded. *Degree requirements:* For master's, research project. *Entrance requirements:* For master's, GRE General Test, minimum GPA of 2.5. Additional exam requirements/recommendations for international students: Required—TOEFL. *Application deadline:* For fall admission, 3/1 priority date for domestic students, 3/15 priority date for international students; for spring admission, 11/1 for domestic and international students. Applications are processed on a rolling basis. Application fee: $45. Electronic applications accepted. *Expenses:* Tuition, state resident: full-time $6400; part-time $345 per credit hour. Tuition, nonresident: full-time $19,720; part-time $920 per credit hour. Required fees: $4368. *Financial support:* In 2010–11, 13 students received support, including 6 fellowships (averaging $9,000 per year), 7 teaching assistantships with full tuition reimbursements available (averaging $11,500 per year); scholarships/grants, tuition waivers (full), and unspecified assistantships also available. Financial award application deadline: 3/1; financial award applicants required to submit FAFSA. *Faculty research:* Metaheuristics, reliability, optimization, statistics, networks. *Unit head:* Dr. Rex Kincaid, Professor, 757-221-2038, Fax: 757-221-1717, E-mail: rrkinc@math.wm.edu. *Application contact:* Vanessa Godwin, Administrative Director, 757-221-3455, Fax: 757-221-1717, E-mail: cor@cs.wm.edu.

Columbia University, Fu Foundation School of Engineering and Applied Science, Department of Industrial Engineering and Operations Research, New York, NY 10027. Offers financial engineering (MS); industrial engineering (Engr); industrial engineering and operations research (MS, Eng Sc D, PhD); MS/MBA. Part-time and evening/weekend programs available. Postbaccalaureate distance learning degree programs offered (no on-campus study). *Faculty:* 22 full-time (3 women), 23 part-time/adjunct (1 woman). *Students:* 295 full-time (81 women), 115 part-time (36 women); includes 23 minority (19 Asian, non-Hispanic/Latino; 3 Hispanic/Latino; 1 Two or more races, non-Hispanic/Latino), 352 international. Average age 26. 1,492 applicants, 21% accepted, 183 enrolled. In 2010, 258 master's, 7 doctorates, 1 other advanced degree awarded. *Degree requirements:* For doctorate, thesis/dissertation, oral and written qualifying exams. *Entrance requirements:* For master's, doctorate, and Engr, GRE General Test. Additional exam requirements/recommendations for international students: Required—TOEFL, IELTS. *Application deadline:* For fall admission, 12/1 priority date for domestic and international students; for spring admission, 10/1 priority date for domestic and international students. Application fee: $95. Electronic applications accepted. *Financial support:* In 2010–11, 59 students received support, including 12 fellowships (averaging $1,700 per year), 27 research assistantships with full tuition reimbursements available (averaging $30,765 per year), 20 teaching assistantships with full tuition reimbursements available (averaging $30,765 per year); career-related internships or fieldwork and health care benefits also available. Financial award application deadline: 12/1; financial award applicants required to submit FAFSA. *Faculty research:* Combinatorial optimization and mathematical programming; financial engineering; supply chain management and inventory theory; applied probability; queuing theory; scheduling, and simulation. *Unit head:* Dr. Cliff S. Stein, Professor and Department Chairman, 212-854-5238, Fax: 212-854-8103, E-mail: cliff@ieor.columbia.edu. *Application contact:* Adina Berrios Brooks, Student Affairs Manager, 212-854-1934, Fax: 212-854-8103, E-mail: admit@ieor.columbia.edu.

Cornell University, Graduate School, Graduate Fields of Engineering, Field of Operations Research and Information Engineering, Ithaca, NY 14853. Offers applied probability and statistics (PhD); manufacturing systems engineering (PhD); mathematical programming (PhD); operations research and industrial engineering (M Eng). *Faculty:* 35 full-time (5 women). *Students:* 162 full-time (46 women); includes 3 Black or African American, non-Hispanic/Latino; 14 Asian, non-Hispanic/Latino; 3 Hispanic/Latino, 117 international. Average age 23. 1,076 applicants, 34% accepted, 139 enrolled. In 2010, 85 master's, 6 doctorates awarded. *Degree requirements:* For doctorate, comprehensive exam, thesis/dissertation. *Entrance requirements:* For master's and doctorate, GRE General Test, 3 letters of recommendation. Additional exam requirements/recommendations for international students: Required—TOEFL (minimum score 600 paper-based; 250 computer-based; 100 iBT). *Application deadline:* For fall admission, 12/15 for domestic students. Application fee: $70. Electronic applications accepted. *Expenses:* Tuition: Full-time $29,500. Required fees: $76. Tuition and fees vary according to degree level and program. *Financial support:* In 2010–11, 44 students received support, including 12 fellowships with full tuition reimbursements available, 9 research assistantships with full tuition reimbursements available, 24 teaching assistantships with full tuition reimbursements available; institutionally sponsored loans, scholarships/grants, health care benefits, tuition waivers (full and partial), and unspecified assistantships also available. Financial award applicants required to submit FAFSA. *Faculty research:* Mathematical programming and combinatorial optimization, statistics, stochastic processes, mathematical finance, simulation, manufacturing, e-commerce. *Unit head:* Director of Graduate Studies, 607-255-9128, Fax: 607-255-9129. *Application contact:* Graduate Field Assistant, 607-255-9128, Fax: 607-255-9129, E-mail: orie@cornell.edu.

École Polytechnique de Montréal, Graduate Programs, Department of Mathematics and Industrial Engineering, Montréal, QC H3C 3A7, Canada. Offers ergonomy (M Eng, M Sc A, DESS); mathematical method in CA engineering (M Eng, M Sc A, PhD); operational research (M Eng, M Sc A, PhD); production (M Eng, M Sc A); technology management (M Eng, M Sc A). DESS program offered jointly with HEC Montreal and Université de Montréal. Part-time programs available. *Degree requirements:* For master's, one foreign language, thesis. *Entrance requirements:* For master's, minimum GPA of 2.75. *Faculty research:* Use of computers in organizations.

Florida Institute of Technology, Graduate Programs, College of Science, Department of Mathematical Sciences, Melbourne, FL 32901-6975. Offers applied mathematics (MS, PhD); operations research (MS, PhD). Part-time and evening/weekend programs available. *Faculty:* 8 full-time (1 woman). *Students:* 29 full-time (9 women), 17 part-time (2 women); includes 5 minority (3 Black or African American, non-Hispanic/Latino; 1 Asian, non-Hispanic/Latino; 1 Hispanic/Latino), 21 international. Average age 32. 70 applicants, 69% accepted, 12 enrolled. In 2010, 5 master's, 3 doctorates awarded. *Degree requirements:* For master's, comprehensive exam (for some programs), thesis optional; for doctorate, comprehensive exam, thesis/dissertation, Preliminary Exam. *Entrance requirements:* For master's, minimum GPA of 3.0, computer programming literacy; for doctorate, minimum GPA of 3.2, resume, 3 letters of recommendation, statement of objectives. Additional exam requirements/recommendations for international students: Required—TOEFL (minimum score 550 paper-based; 213 computer-based; 79 iBT). *Application deadline:* For fall admission, 4/1 for international students; for spring admission, 9/30 for international students. Applications are processed on a rolling basis. Application fee: $50. Electronic applications accepted. *Expenses:* Tuition: Part-time $1040 per credit hour. Tuition and fees vary according to campus/location. *Financial support:* In 2010–11, 16 teaching assistantships with full and partial tuition reimbursements (averaging $8,933 per year) were awarded; research assistantships, career-related internships or fieldwork, institutionally sponsored loans, tuition waivers (partial), unspecified assistantships, and tuition remissions also available. Support available to part-time students. Financial award application deadline: 3/1; financial award applicants required to submit FAFSA. *Faculty research:* Real analysis, numerical analysis, statistics, data analysis, combinatorics, artificial intelligence, simulation. Total annual research expenditures: $78,876. *Unit head:* Dr. Semen Koksal, Department Head, 321-674-8765, Fax: 321-674-7412, E-mail: skoksal@fit.edu. *Application contact:* Cheryl A. Brown, Associate Director of Graduate Admissions, 321-674-7581, Fax: 321-723-9468, E-mail: cbrown@fit.edu.

Florida Institute of Technology, Graduate Programs, Extended Studies Division, Melbourne, FL 32901-6975. Offers acquisition and contract management (MS); aerospace engineering (MS); business administration (MBA); computer information systems (MS); computer science (MS); electrical engineering (MS); engineering management (MS); human resources management (MS); logistics management (MS), including humanitarian and disaster relief logistics; management (MS), including acquisition and contract management, e-business, human resources management, information systems, logistics management, management, transportation management; material acquisition management (MS); mechanical engineering (MS); operations research (MS); project management (MS), including information systems, operations research; public administration (MPA); quality management (MS); software engineering (MS); space systems (MS); space systems management (MS); systems management (MS), including information systems, operations research. Part-time and evening/weekend programs available. Postbaccalaureate distance learning degree programs offered (no on-campus study). *Faculty:* 11 full-time (3 women), 118 part-time/adjunct (24 women). *Students:* 69 full-time (23 women), 907 part-time (369 women); includes 385 minority (242 Black or African American, non-Hispanic/Latino; 15 American Indian or Alaska Native, non-Hispanic/Latino; 44 Asian, non-Hispanic/Latino; 52 Hispanic/Latino; 3 Native Hawaiian or other Pacific Islander, non-Hispanic/Latino; 29 Two or more races, non-Hispanic/Latino), 17 international. 517 applicants, 49% accepted, 245 enrolled. In 2010, 430 degrees awarded. *Degree requirements:* For master's, comprehensive exam (for some programs), capstone course. *Entrance requirements:* For master's, GMAT or resume showing 8 years of supervised experience, minimum GPA of 3.0, 2 letters of recommendation, resume. Additional exam requirements/recommendations for international students: Required—TOEFL (minimum score 550 paper-based; 213 computer-based; 79 iBT). *Application deadline:* For fall admission, 4/1 for international students; for spring admission, 9/30 for international students. Applications are processed on a rolling basis. Application fee: $50. Electronic applications accepted. *Expenses:* Contact institution. *Financial support:* Application deadline: 3/1. *Unit head:* Dr. Theodore Richardson, Senior Associate Dean, 321-674-8123, Fax: 321-674-7597, E-mail: trichardson@fit.edu. *Application contact:* Carolyn Farrior, Director of Graduate Admissions, Online Learning and Off-Campus Programs, 321-674-7118, Fax: 321-674-8216, E-mail: cfarrior@fit.edu.

George Mason University, Volgenau School of Engineering, Department of Systems Engineering and Operations Research, Fairfax, VA 22030. Offers architecture-based systems integration (Certificate); command, control, communication, computing and intelligence (Certificate); computational modeling (Certificate); discovery, design and innovation (Certificate); military operations research (Certificate); operations research (MS); systems engineering (MS); systems engineering analysis and architecture (Certificate); systems engineering and operations research (PhD); systems engineering of software intensive systems (Certificate). MS programs offered jointly with Old Dominion University, University of Virginia, Virginia Commonwealth University, and Virginia Polytechnic Institute and State University. Part-time and evening/weekend programs available. *Faculty:* 16 full-time (4 women), 11 part-time/adjunct (4 women). *Students:* 27 full-time (2 women), 175 part-time (39 women); includes 10 Black or African American, non-Hispanic/Latino; 2 American Indian or Alaska Native, non-Hispanic/Latino; 19 Asian, non-Hispanic/Latino; 9 Hispanic/Latino, 17 international. Average age 33. 132 applicants, 72% accepted, 53 enrolled. In 2010, 76 master's, 1 doctorate, 25 other advanced degrees awarded. *Degree requirements:* For master's, thesis optional; for doctorate, comprehensive exam, thesis/dissertation, qualifying exams. *Entrance requirements:* For master's, GRE General Test, 3 letters of recommendation, resume; for doctorate, GRE, undergraduate and graduate transcripts, 3 letters of reference, resume, statement of career goals and aspirations, self assessment of background. Additional exam requirements/recommendations for international students: Required—TOEFL (minimum score 570 paper-based; 230 computer-based; 88 iBT). *Application deadline:* For fall admission, 3/15 priority date for domestic students, 2/15 priority date for international students; for spring admission, 10/1 for domestic and international students. Application fee: $100. Electronic applications accepted. *Expenses:* Tuition, state resident: full-time $8192; part-time $440 per credit hour. Tuition, nonresident: full-time $22,952; part-time $1055 per credit hour. Required fees: $2364; $99 per credit hour. *Financial support:* In 2010–11, 11 students received support, including 6 research assistantships with full and partial tuition reimbursements available (averaging $15,982 per year), 5 teaching assistantships with full and partial tuition reimbursements available (averaging $10,661 per year); career-related internships or fieldwork, Federal Work-Study, scholarships/grants, unspecified assistantships, and health care benefits (full-time research or teaching assistantship recipients) also available. Financial award application deadline: 3/1; financial award applicants required to submit FAFSA. *Faculty research:* Requirements engineering, signal processing, systems architecture, data fusion. Total annual research expenditures: $1.3 million. *Unit head:* Dr. Ariela Sofer, Chairman, 703-993-1692, Fax: 703-993-1521, E-mail: asofer@gmu.edu. *Application contact:* Dr. K. C. Chang, Graduate Coordinator, 703-993-1639, E-mail: kchang@gmu.edu.

Georgia Institute of Technology, Graduate Studies and Research, College of Engineering, School of Industrial and Systems Engineering, Program in Operations Research, Atlanta, GA 30332-0001. Offers MSOR, PhD. Part-time programs available. *Entrance requirements:* For master's, GRE General Test, minimum GPA of 3.0. Additional exam requirements/recommendations for international students: Required—TOEFL. Electronic applications accepted. *Faculty research:* Linear and nonlinear deterministic models in operations research, mathematical statistics, design of experiments.

Georgia State University, J. Mack Robinson College of Business, Department of Managerial Sciences, Atlanta, GA 30302-3083. Offers business analysis (MBA, MS); decision sciences (PhD); entrepreneurship (MBA); human resources management (MBA, MS); management (MBA, PhD); operations management (MBA, MS); organization change (MS); personnel employee relations (PhD); strategic management (PhD). *Accreditation:* AACSB. Part-time and evening/weekend programs available. *Degree requirements:* For doctorate, thesis/dissertation. *Entrance requirements:* For master's and doctorate, GMAT. Additional exam requirements/recommendations for international students: Required—TOEFL (minimum score 610 paper-based; 255 computer-based; 101 iBT). Electronic applications accepted. *Faculty research:* Abusive supervision, entrepreneurship, time series and neural networks, organizational controls, inventory control systems.

HEC Montreal, School of Business Administration, Master of Science Programs in Administration, Program in Business Analytics, Montréal, QC H3T 2A7, Canada. Offers M Sc. Part-time programs available. *Students:* 6 full-time (1 woman), 2 part-time (1 woman). 10 applicants, 90% accepted, 3 enrolled. *Degree requirements:* For master's, one foreign language, thesis. *Application deadline:* For fall admission, 3/15 for domestic and international students; for winter admission, 9/15 for domestic and international students. Application fee: $78. Electronic applications accepted. *Expenses:* Tuition, area resident: Part-time $68.93 per credit. Tuition, state resident: full-time $2481.48; part-time $188.92 per credit. Tuition, nonresident: full-time $6801; part-time $482.06 per course. International tuition: $17,354.16 full-time. Required fees: $1309.50; $30.28 per credit. $93.45 per term. Tuition and fees vary according to degree level and program. *Financial support:* Research assistantships, teaching assistantships, scholarships/grants available. Financial award application deadline: 9/2. *Unit head:* Claude Laurin, Director, 514-340-6485, Fax: 514-340-6880, E-mail: claude.laurin@hec.ca. *Application contact:* Francine Blais, Administrative Director, 514-340-6112, Fax: 514-340-6411, E-mail: francine.blais@hec.ca.

Idaho State University, Office of Graduate Studies, College of Engineering, Mechanical Engineering Department, Pocatello, ID 83209-8060. Offers measurement and control engineering (MS); mechanical engineering (MS). Part-time programs available. *Degree requirements:* For master's, comprehensive exam (for some programs), 2 semesters of seminar; thesis or project. *Entrance requirements:* For master's, GRE. Additional exam requirements/recommendations for international students: Required—TOEFL (minimum score 550 paper-based; 213 computer-based; 80 iBT). Electronic applications accepted. *Faculty research:* Modeling and identification of biomedical systems, intelligent systems and adaptive control, active flow control of turbo machinery, validation of advanced computational codes for thermal fluid interactions, development of methodologies for the assessment of passive safety system performance in advanced reactors, alternative energy research (wind, solar, hydrogen).

Indiana University–Purdue University Fort Wayne, College of Arts and Sciences, Department of Mathematical Sciences, Fort Wayne, IN 46805-1499. Offers applied mathematics (MS); applied statistics (Certificate); mathematics (MS); operations research (MS); teaching (MAT). Part-time and evening/weekend programs available. *Faculty:* 18 full-time (4 women), 1 (woman) part-time/adjunct. *Students:* 3 full-time (0 women), 17 part-time (6 women). Average age 33. 12 applicants, 100% accepted, 12 enrolled. In 2010, 4 master's, 3 other advanced degrees awarded. *Entrance requirements:* For master's, minimum GPA of 3.0, major or minor in mathematics, three letters of recommendation. Additional exam requirements/recommendations for international students: Required—TOEFL (minimum score 550 paper-based; 213 computer-based; 77 iBT); Recommended—TWE. *Application deadline:* For fall admission, 8/1 priority date for domestic students, 7/1 priority date for international students; for spring admission, 12/1 for domestic students, 10/1 for international students. Applications are processed on a rolling basis. Application fee: $55 ($60 for international students). Electronic applications accepted. *Expenses:* Tuition, state resident: full-time $4824; part-time $268 per credit. Tuition, nonresident: full-time $11,625; part-time $646 per credit. Required fees: $555; $30.85 per credit. Tuition and fees vary according to course load. *Financial support:* In 2010–11, 9 teaching assistantships with partial tuition reimbursements (averaging $12,740 per year) were awarded; scholarships/grants and unspecified assistantships also available. Support available to part-time students. Financial award application deadline: 3/1; financial award applicants required to submit FAFSA. *Faculty research:* Axis-supported external fields, discipline of doubt, t-design graphs. *Unit head:* Dr. David A. Legg, Chair, 260-481-6222, Fax: 260-481-0155, E-mail: legg@ipfw.edu. *Application contact:* Dr. W. Douglas Weakley, Director of Graduate Studies, 260-481-6233, Fax: 260-481-0155, E-mail: weakley@ipfw.edu.

Iowa State University of Science and Technology, Graduate College, College of Engineering, Department of Industrial and Manufacturing Systems Engineering, Ames, IA 50011. Offers industrial engineering (M Eng, MS, PhD); operations research (MS); systems engineering (M Eng). *Faculty:* 14 full-time (2 women). *Students:* 50 full-time (12 women), 54 part-time (9 women); includes 3 Black or African American, non-Hispanic/Latino; 1 Asian, non-Hispanic/Latino; 1 Hispanic/Latino, 50 international. 142 applicants, 22% accepted, 10 enrolled. In 2010, 6 master's, 4 doctorates awarded. *Degree requirements:* For master's, thesis or alternative; for doctorate, thesis/dissertation. *Entrance requirements:* For master's and doctorate, GRE General Test. Additional exam requirements/recommendations for international students: Required—TOEFL (minimum score 550 paper-based; 79 iBT), IELTS (minimum score 6.5). *Application deadline:* For fall admission, 1/15 priority date for international students; for spring admission, 7/15 priority date for international students. Application fee: $40 ($90 for international students). Electronic applications accepted. *Financial support:* In 2010–11, 23 research assistantships with full and partial tuition reimbursements (averaging $6,292 per year), 6 teaching assistantships with full and partial tuition reimbursements (averaging $4,298 per year) were awarded; fellowships, scholarships/grants, health care benefits, and unspecified assistantships also available. *Faculty research:* Economic modeling, valuation techniques, robotics, digital controls, systems reliability. *Unit head:* Dr. Gary Mirka, Chair, 515-294-8661,

Operations Research

Iowa State University of Science and Technology (continued)
Fax: 515-294-3524. *Application contact:* Dr. Sarah Ryan, Director of Graduate Studies, 515-294-4347, E-mail: smryan@iastate.edu.

The Johns Hopkins University, G. W. C. Whiting School of Engineering, Department of Applied Mathematics and Statistics, Baltimore, MD 21218-2699. Offers computational medicine (PhD); discrete mathematics (MA, MSE, PhD); financial mathematics (MSE); operations research/optimization/decision science (MA, MSE, PhD); statistics/probability/stochastic processes (MA, MSE, PhD). *Faculty:* 17 full-time (3 women), 4 part-time/adjunct (0 women). *Students:* 72 full-time (27 women), 3 part-time (0 women); includes 10 minority (1 Black or African American, non-Hispanic/Latino; 7 Asian, non-Hispanic/Latino; 2 Two or more races, non-Hispanic/Latino), 51 international. Average age 25. 306 applicants, 47% accepted, 36 enrolled. In 2010, 26 master's, 7 doctorates awarded. Terminal master's awarded for partial completion of doctoral program. *Degree requirements:* For master's, thesis (for some programs); for doctorate, thesis/dissertation, oral exam, introductory exam. *Entrance requirements:* For master's and doctorate, GRE General Test, GRE Subject Test. Additional exam requirements/recommendations for international students: Required—TOEFL (minimum score 600 paper-based; 250 computer-based; 100 iBT). *Application deadline:* For fall admission, 1/15 for domestic and international students; for spring admission, 9/15 for domestic and international students. Application fee: $75. Electronic applications accepted. *Financial support:* In 2010–11, 40 students received support, including 9 fellowships with full tuition reimbursements available (averaging $19,800 per year), 19 research assistantships with full tuition reimbursements available (averaging $1,800 per year), 9 teaching assistantships with full tuition reimbursements available (averaging $1,800 per year); Federal Work-Study, institutionally sponsored loans, scholarships/grants, health care benefits, tuition waivers (partial), and unspecified assistantships also available. Financial award application deadline: 1/15. *Faculty research:* Discrete mathematics, probability, statistics, optimization and operations research, scientific computation, financial mathematics. Total annual research expenditures: $1.3 million. *Unit head:* Dr. Daniel Q. Naiman, Chair, 410-516-7203, Fax: 410-516-7459, E-mail: daniel.naiman@jhu.edu. *Application contact:* Kristin Bechtel, Academic Program Coordinator, 410-516-7198, Fax: 410-516-7459, E-mail: kbechtel@jhu.edu.

Kansas State University, Graduate School, College of Engineering, Department of Industrial and Manufacturing Systems Engineering, Manhattan, KS 66506. Offers engineering management (MEM); industrial engineering (MS, PhD); operations research (MS). Part-time programs available. Postbaccalaureate distance learning degree programs offered. *Degree requirements:* For master's, thesis or alternative; for doctorate, thesis/dissertation. *Entrance requirements:* For master's, GRE General Test, bachelor's degree in engineering, mathematics, or physical science; for doctorate, GRE General Test, master's degree in engineering or industrial manufacturing. Additional exam requirements/recommendations for international students: Required—TOEFL. Electronic applications accepted. *Faculty research:* Ergonomics, healthcare systems engineering, manufacturing processes, operations research, engineering management.

Massachusetts Institute of Technology, Operations Research Center, Cambridge, MA 02139-4307. Offers SM, PhD. *Faculty:* 45 full-time (8 women). *Students:* 52 full-time (11 women); includes 5 minority (4 Asian, non-Hispanic/Latino; 1 Hispanic/Latino), 26 international. Average age 26. 224 applicants, 9% accepted, 9 enrolled. In 2010, 13 master's, 5 doctorates awarded. Terminal master's awarded for partial completion of doctoral program. *Degree requirements:* For master's, thesis, writing exam; for doctorate, comprehensive exam, thesis/dissertation, qualifying exam, writing exam. *Entrance requirements:* For master's and doctorate, GRE General Test. Additional exam requirements/recommendations for international students: Required—TOEFL (minimum score 600 paper-based; 250 computer-based; 100 iBT), IELTS (minimum score 7). *Application deadline:* For fall admission, 12/15 for domestic and international students. Application fee: $75. Electronic applications accepted. *Expenses:* Tuition: Full-time $38,940; part-time $605 per unit. Required fees: $272. *Financial support:* In 2010–11, 51 students received support, including 5 fellowships (averaging $23,821 per year), 35 research assistantships (averaging $28,777 per year), 11 teaching assistantships (averaging $31,352 per year); Federal Work-Study, institutionally sponsored loans, scholarships/grants, health care benefits, tuition waivers, and unspecified assistantships also available. Financial award application deadline: 12/15. *Faculty research:* Probability, mathematical programming, statistics, stochastic processes and healthcare. *Unit head:* Dr. Dimitris J. Bertsimas, Co-Director, 617-253-3601, Fax: 617-258-9214, E-mail: orc-www@mit.edu. *Application contact:* Laura A. Rose, Admissions Coordinator, 617-253-9303, Fax: 617-258-9214, E-mail: lrose@mit.edu.

Naval Postgraduate School, Graduate Programs, Department of Operations Research, Monterey, CA 93943. Offers MS, PhD. Program only open to commissioned officers of the United States and friendly nations and selected United States federal civilian employees. Part-time programs available. *Degree requirements:* For master's, thesis; for doctorate, one foreign language, thesis/dissertation.

Naval Postgraduate School, Graduate Programs, Program in Undersea Warfare, Monterey, CA 93943. Offers applied science (MS); electrical engineering (MS); engineering acoustics (MS); operations research (MS); physical oceanography (MS). Program only open to commissioned officers of the United States and friendly nations and selected United States federal civilian employees. Part-time programs available. *Degree requirements:* For master's, thesis.

New Mexico Institute of Mining and Technology, Graduate Studies, Department of Mathematics, Socorro, NM 87801. Offers applied math (PhD); mathematics (MS); operations research (MS). *Degree requirements:* For master's, thesis optional; for doctorate, thesis/dissertation. *Entrance requirements:* For master's, GRE General Test. Additional exam requirements/recommendations for international students: Required—TOEFL (minimum score 540 paper-based; 207 computer-based). *Faculty research:* Applied mathematics, differential equations, industrial mathematics, numerical analysis, stochastic processes.

North Carolina State University, Graduate School, College of Engineering and College of Physical and Mathematical Sciences, Program in Operations Research, Raleigh, NC 27695. Offers MOR, MS, PhD. Part-time programs available. *Degree requirements:* For master's, thesis (for some programs), thesis (MS); for doctorate, thesis/dissertation, comprehensive oral and written exams. *Entrance requirements:* For master's, GRE General Test, minimum GPA of 2.7; for doctorate, GRE General Test, minimum GPA of 3.0. Additional exam requirements/recommendations for international students: Required—TOEFL. Electronic applications accepted. *Faculty research:* Queuing analysis, simulation, inventory theory, supply chain management, mathematical programming.

North Carolina State University, Graduate School, College of Management, Institute for Advanced Analytics, Raleigh, NC 27695. Offers analytics (MS). *Entrance requirements:* For master's, GRE General Test. Additional exam requirements/recommendations for international students: Required—TOEFL. Electronic applications accepted.

North Dakota State University, College of Graduate and Interdisciplinary Studies, College of Science and Mathematics, Department of Computer Science, Fargo, ND 58108. Offers computer science (MS, PhD); operations research (MS); software engineering (MS, PhD, Certificate). Part-time programs available. *Faculty:* 14 full-time (1 woman). *Students:* 100 full-time (19 women), 109 part-time (32 women); includes 3 Black or African American, non-Hispanic/Latino; 1 American Indian or Alaska Native, non-Hispanic/Latino; 8 Asian, non-Hispanic/Latino; 2 Hispanic/Latino, 161 international. Average age 24. 220 applicants, 34% accepted, 31 enrolled. In 2010, 30 master's, 2 doctorates awarded. *Degree requirements:* For master's, comprehensive exam, thesis optional; for doctorate, thesis/dissertation, qualifying exam. *Entrance requirements:* For master's, minimum GPA of 3.0, BS in computer science or related field; for doctorate, minimum GPA of 3.25, MS in computer science or related field. Additional exam requirements/recommendations for international students: Required—TOEFL (minimum score 550 paper-based; 213 computer-based; 79 iBT). *Application deadline:* For fall admission, 8/15 priority date for domestic students, 8/15 for international students; for spring admission, 12/15

priority date for domestic students, 12/15 for international students. Application fee: $45 ($60 for international students). *Financial support:* In 2010–11, 37 research assistantships with full tuition reimbursements (averaging $10,000 per year), 17 teaching assistantships with full tuition reimbursements (averaging $4,500 per year) were awarded; career-related internships or fieldwork, Federal Work-Study, institutionally sponsored loans, and tuition waivers (full) also available. Financial award application deadline: 4/15. *Faculty research:* Networking, software engineering, artificial intelligence, database, programming languages. Total annual research expenditures: $366,434. *Unit head:* Dr. Brian Slator, Head, 701-231-8562, Fax: 701-231-8255. *Application contact:* Dr. Ken R. Nygard, Graduate Coordinator, 701-231-9460, Fax: 701-231-8255, E-mail: kendall.nygard@ndsu.edu.

Northeastern University, College of Engineering, Department of Mechanical, Industrial, and Manufacturing Engineering, Boston, MA 02115-5096. Offers engineering management (MS); industrial engineering (MS, PhD); mechanical engineering (MS, PhD); operations research (MS). Part-time programs available. *Faculty:* 34 full-time (2 women), 7 part-time/adjunct (0 women). *Students:* 297 full-time (70 women), 103 part-time (20 women). 616 applicants, 77% accepted, 140 enrolled. In 2010, 107 master's, 5 doctorates awarded. *Degree requirements:* For master's, thesis (for some programs); for doctorate, thesis/dissertation, departmental qualifying exam. *Entrance requirements:* For master's and doctorate, GRE General Test. Additional exam requirements/recommendations for international students: Required—TOEFL (minimum score 550 paper-based; 213 computer-based; 80 iBT). *Application deadline:* For fall admission, 1/15 priority date for domestic and international students; for spring admission, 11/1 priority date for domestic students. Applications are processed on a rolling basis. Application fee: $50. Electronic applications accepted. *Financial support:* In 2010–11, 79 students received support, including 50 research assistantships with full tuition reimbursements available (averaging $18,325 per year), 33 teaching assistantships with full tuition reimbursements available (averaging $18,325 per year); fellowships with full tuition reimbursements available, career-related internships or fieldwork, Federal Work-Study, scholarships/grants, health care benefits, and unspecified assistantships also available. Support available to part-time students. Financial award application deadline: 1/15; financial award applicants required to submit FAFSA. *Faculty research:* Dry sliding instabilities, droplet deposition, combustion, manufacturing systems, nano-manufacturing, advanced materials processing, bio-nano robotics, burning speed measurement, virtual environments. *Unit head:* Dr. Hameed Metghalchi, Chairman, 617-373-2973, Fax: 617-373-2921. *Application contact:* Jeffery Hengel, Admissions Specialist, 617-373-2711, Fax: 617-373-2501, E-mail: grad-eng@coe.neu.edu.

Northeastern University, College of Science, Department of Mathematics, Boston, MA 02115-5096. Offers applied mathematics (MS); mathematics (MS, PhD); operations research (MSOR). Part-time and evening/weekend programs available. *Faculty:* 39 full-time (5 women), 15 part-time/adjunct (7 women). *Students:* 52 full-time (16 women), 3 part-time (2 women). 164 applicants, 58% accepted, 14 enrolled. In 2010, 6 master's, 7 doctorates awarded. *Degree requirements:* For master's, thesis (for some programs); for doctorate, thesis/dissertation, qualifying exams. *Entrance requirements:* For master's and doctorate, GRE Subject Test, GRE General Test. Additional exam requirements/recommendations for international students: Required—TOEFL. *Application deadline:* For fall admission, 2/1 priority date for domestic and international students. Applications are processed on a rolling basis. Application fee: $50. Electronic applications accepted. *Financial support:* In 2010–11, 26 teaching assistantships with tuition reimbursements (averaging $17,345 per year) were awarded; research assistantships with tuition reimbursements, Federal Work-Study, institutionally sponsored loans, tuition waivers (full and partial), and unspecified assistantships also available. Financial award application deadline: 3/1; financial award applicants required to submit FAFSA. *Faculty research:* Algebra and singularities, combinatorics, topology, probability and statistics, geometric analysis and partial differential equations. *Unit head:* Dr. Jerzy Weyman, Graduate Coordinator, 617-373-5513, Fax: 617-373-5658, E-mail: j.weyman@neu.edu. *Application contact:* Jo-Anne Dickinson, Admissions Contact, 617-373-5990, Fax: 617-373-7281, E-mail: gsas@neu.edu.

The Ohio State University, Graduate School, Max M. Fisher College of Business, Program in Business Operational Excellence, Columbus, OH 43210. Offers MBOE. *Students:* 22 full-time (7 women); includes 3 Black or African American, non-Hispanic/Latino; 1 Asian, non-Hispanic/Latino; 1 Hispanic/Latino, 1 international. Average age 41. In 2010, 10 master's awarded. *Entrance requirements:* Additional exam requirements/recommendations for international students: Required—TOEFL. *Expenses:* Tuition, state resident: full-time $10,605. Tuition, nonresident: full-time $26,535. Tuition and fees vary according to course load and program. *Application contact:* Graduate Admissions, 614-292-9444, Fax: 614-292-3895, E-mail: domestic.grad@osu.edu.

Oregon State University, Graduate School, College of Science, Department of Statistics, Corvallis, OR 97331. Offers operations research (MA, MS); statistics (MA, MS, PhD). Part-time programs available. *Degree requirements:* For master's, consulting experience; for doctorate, thesis/dissertation, consulting experience. *Entrance requirements:* For master's and doctorate, minimum GPA of 3.0 in last 90 hours. Additional exam requirements/recommendations for international students: Required—TOEFL. *Faculty research:* Analysis of enumerative data, nonparametric statistics, asymptotics, experimental design, generalized regression models, linear model theory, reliability theory, survival analysis, wildlife and general survey methodology.

Princeton University, Graduate School, School of Engineering and Applied Science, Department of Operations Research and Financial Engineering, Princeton, NJ 08544-1019. Offers M Eng, MSE, PhD. Terminal master's awarded for partial completion of doctoral program. *Degree requirements:* For master's, thesis (MSE); for doctorate, thesis/dissertation, general exam. *Entrance requirements:* For master's and doctorate, GRE General Test, official transcript(s), 3 letters of recommendation, personal statement. Additional exam requirements/recommendations for international students: Required—TOEFL. Electronic applications accepted. *Faculty research:* Applied and computational mathematics; financial mathematics; optimization, queuing theory, and machine learning; statistics and stochastic analysis; transportation and logistics.

Rutgers, The State University of New Jersey, New Brunswick, Graduate School-New Brunswick, Program in Operations Research, Piscataway, NJ 08854-8097. Offers PhD. Part-time programs available. *Degree requirements:* For doctorate, comprehensive exam, thesis/dissertation, qualifying exam. *Entrance requirements:* For doctorate, GRE General Test, GRE Subject Test. Electronic applications accepted. *Expenses:* Tuition, state resident: full-time $7200; part-time $600 per credit. Tuition, nonresident: full-time $11,124; part-time $927 per credit. *Faculty research:* Mathematical programming, combinatorial optimization, graph theory, stochastic modeling, queuing theory.

St. Mary's University, Graduate School, Department of Engineering, Program in Industrial Engineering, San Antonio, TX 78228-8507. Offers engineering computer applications (MS); engineering management (MS); industrial engineering (MS); operations research (MS); JD/MS. Part-time programs available. *Degree requirements:* For master's, comprehensive exam. *Entrance requirements:* For master's, GRE General Test, BS in science or engineering, minimum GPA of 3.0. Additional exam requirements/recommendations for international students: Required—TOEFL (minimum score 550 paper-based; 213 computer-based; 80 iBT). Electronic applications accepted. *Faculty research:* Robotics, artificial intelligence, manufacturing engineering.

Southern Methodist University, Bobby B. Lyle School of Engineering, Department of Engineering Management, Information, and Systems, Dallas, TX 75275. Offers applied science (MS); engineering management (MSEM, DE); information engineering and management (MSIEM); operations research (MS, PhD); systems engineering (MS, PhD). Part-time and evening/weekend programs available. Postbaccalaureate distance learning degree programs offered. *Faculty:* 8 full-time (1 woman), 22 part-time/adjunct (1 woman). *Students:* 47 full-time (12 women), 348 part-time (75 women); includes 114 minority (31 Black or African American, non-Hispanic/Latino; 2 American Indian or Alaska Native, non-Hispanic/Latino; 34 Asian, non-Hispanic/Latino; 44 Hispanic/Latino; 2 Native Hawaiian or other Pacific Islander, non-

Hispanic/Latino; 1 Two or more races, non-Hispanic/Latino), 51 international. Average age 33. 208 applicants, 67% accepted, 92 enrolled. In 2010, 130 master's, 6 doctorates awarded. Terminal master's awarded for partial completion of doctoral program. *Degree requirements:* For master's, thesis optional; for doctorate, thesis/dissertation, oral and written qualifying exams. *Entrance requirements:* For master's, minimum GPA of 3.0 in last 2 years; bachelor's degree in engineering, mathematics, sciences, or technical area; for doctorate, GRE General Test (operations research, engineering management), bachelor's degree in related field. Additional exam requirements/recommendations for international students: Required—TOEFL. *Application deadline:* For fall admission, 7/1 for domestic students, 5/15 for international students; for spring admission, 11/15 for domestic students, 9/1 for international students. Applications are processed on a rolling basis. Application fee: $75. *Financial support:* In 2010–11, 6 students received support, including 4 research assistantships with full tuition reimbursements available (averaging $18,000 per year), 2 teaching assistantships with full tuition reimbursements available (averaging $18,000 per year); tuition waivers (full) also available. *Faculty research:* Telecommunications, decision systems, information engineering, operations research, software. Total annual research expenditures: $275,851. *Unit head:* Dr. Richard S. Barr, Chair, 214-768-1772, Fax: 214-768-1112, E-mail: emis@lyle.smu.edu. *Application contact:* Marc Valerin, Director of Graduate and Executive Admissions, 214-768-3042, E-mail: valerin@lyle.smu.edu.

The University of Alabama in Huntsville, School of Graduate Studies, College of Engineering, Department of Industrial and Systems Engineering/Engineering Management, Program in Operations Research, Huntsville, AL 35899. Offers MSOR. Part-time and evening/weekend programs available. Postbaccalaureate distance learning degree programs offered (minimal on-campus study). *Faculty:* 6 full-time (2 women), 4 part-time/adjunct (1 woman). *Students:* 1 (woman) full-time, 3 part-time (1 woman); includes 1 minority (Black or African American, non-Hispanic/Latino). Average age 31. 9 applicants, 44% accepted, 2 enrolled. In 2010, 3 master's awarded. *Degree requirements:* For master's, comprehensive exam, thesis or alternative, oral and written exams. *Entrance requirements:* For master's, GRE General Test, minimum GPA of 3.0, 6 hours of course work in applied or mathematical statistics and calculus. Additional exam requirements/recommendations for international students: Required—TOEFL (minimum score 500 paper-based; 173 computer-based; 62 iBT). *Application deadline:* For fall admission, 7/15 for domestic students, 4/1 for international students; for spring admission, 11/30 for domestic students, 9/1 for international students. Applications are processed on a rolling basis. Application fee: $40 ($50 for international students). Electronic applications accepted. *Expenses:* Tuition, state resident: full-time $7250; part-time $407.75 per credit hour. Tuition, nonresident: full-time $17,358; part-time $970.05 per credit hour. Required fees: $246.80 per semester. Tuition and fees vary according to course load and program. *Financial support:* In 2010–11, 1 teaching assistantship with full tuition reimbursement (averaging $8,450 per year) was awarded; career-related internships or fieldwork, Federal Work-Study, institutionally sponsored loans, scholarships/grants, health care benefits, and unspecified assistantships also available. Support available to part-time students. Financial award application deadline: 4/1; financial award applicants required to submit FAFSA. *Faculty research:* Simulation, manufacturing systems, system ergonomics, logistics. *Unit head:* Dr. James Swain, Chair, 256-824-6749, Fax: 256-824-6733, E-mail: jswain@ise.uah.edu. *Application contact:* Kathy Biggs, Manager, 256-824-6199, Fax: 256-824-6405, E-mail: deangrad@uah.edu.

University of Arkansas, Graduate School, College of Engineering, Department of Industrial Engineering, Fayetteville, AR 72701-1201. Offers industrial engineering (MSE, MSIE, PhD); operations management (MS); operations research (MSE, MSOR). *Faculty:* 10 full-time (1 woman), 26 part-time/adjunct (1 woman). *Students:* 47 full-time (18 women), 460 part-time (118 women); includes 99 minority (64 Black or African American, non-Hispanic/Latino; 6 American Indian or Alaska Native, non-Hispanic/Latino; 17 Asian, non-Hispanic/Latino; 11 Hispanic/Latino; 1 Native Hawaiian or other Pacific Islander, non-Hispanic/Latino), 45 international. 198 applicants, 83% accepted. In 2010, 216 master's, 3 doctorates awarded. *Degree requirements:* For master's, thesis optional; for doctorate, one foreign language, thesis/dissertation. *Application deadline:* For fall admission, 4/1 for international students; for spring admission, 10/1 for international students. Applications are processed on a rolling basis. Application fee: $40 ($50 for international students). Electronic applications accepted. *Financial support:* In 2010–11, 4 fellowships, 41 research assistantships were awarded; teaching assistantships, career-related internships or fieldwork and Federal Work-Study also available. Support available to part-time students. Financial award application deadline: 4/1; financial award applicants required to submit FAFSA. *Unit head:* Dr. Kim Needy, Departmental Chair, 479-575-3157, Fax: 479-575-8431, E-mail: kneedy@uark.edu. *Application contact:* Dr. Justin Chimka, Graduate Coordinator, 479-575-6756, E-mail: jchimka@uark.edu.

The University of British Columbia, Sauder School of Business, Master of Management in Operations Research, Vancouver, BC V6T 1Z1, Canada. Offers MM. *Degree requirements:* For master's, course work and industry project. *Entrance requirements:* For master's, GMAT or GRE, strong quantitative or analytical background, bachelor's degree or recognized equivalent from an accredited university-level institution, minimum of B+ average in undergraduate upper-level course work. Additional exam requirements/recommendations for international students: Required—TOEFL, IELTS or Michigan English Language Assessment Battery. Electronic applications accepted. *Expenses:* Contact institution. *Faculty research:* Operations and Logistics.

University of California, Berkeley, Graduate Division, College of Engineering, Department of Industrial Engineering and Operations Research, Berkeley, CA 94720-1500. Offers M Eng, MS, D Eng, PhD. *Degree requirements:* For master's, comprehensive exam or thesis (MS); for doctorate, thesis/dissertation, qualifying exam. *Entrance requirements:* For master's and doctorate, GRE General Test, minimum GPA of 3.0, 3 letters of recommendation. *Faculty research:* Mathematical programming, robotics and manufacturing, linear and nonlinear optimization, production planning and scheduling, queuing theory.

University of Central Florida, College of Engineering and Computer Science, Department of Industrial Engineering and Management Systems, Orlando, FL 32816. Offers applied operations research (Certificate); design for usability (Certificate); industrial engineering (MSIE, PhD); industrial engineering and management systems (MS); industrial ergonomics and safety (Certificate); project engineering (Certificate); quality assurance (Certificate); systems engineering (Certificate); systems simulation for engineers (Certificate); training simulation (Certificate). Part-time and evening/weekend programs available. *Faculty:* 17 full-time (4 women), 6 part-time/adjunct (1 woman). *Students:* 112 full-time (31 women), 171 part-time (66 women); includes 79 minority (27 Black or African American, non-Hispanic/Latino; 17 Asian, non-Hispanic/Latino; 32 Hispanic/Latino; 1 Native Hawaiian or other Pacific Islander, non-Hispanic/Latino; 2 Two or more races, non-Hispanic/Latino), 72 international. Average age 33. 210 applicants, 74% accepted, 82 enrolled. In 2010, 65 master's, 7 doctorates, 34 other advanced degrees awarded. *Degree requirements:* For master's, thesis; for doctorate, thesis/dissertation, departmental qualifying exam, candidacy exam. *Entrance requirements:* For master's, GRE General Test, minimum GPA of 3.0 in last 60 hours of course work; for doctorate, minimum GPA of 3.5 in last 60 hours of course work. Additional exam requirements/recommendations for international students: Required—TOEFL. *Application deadline:* For fall admission, 7/15 priority date for domestic students; for spring admission, 12/1 priority date for domestic students. Application fee: $30. Electronic applications accepted. *Expenses:* Tuition, state resident: part-time $256.56 per credit hour. Tuition, nonresident: part-time $1011.52 per credit hour. Part-time tuition and fees vary according to program. *Financial support:* In 2010–11, 24 students received support, including 85 fellowships with partial tuition reimbursements available (averaging $7,300 per year), 19 research assistantships with partial tuition reimbursements available (averaging $8,500 per year), 6 teaching assistantships with partial tuition reimbursements available (averaging $12,200 per year); career-related internships or fieldwork, Federal Work-Study, institutionally sponsored loans, tuition waivers (partial), and unspecified assistantships also available. Financial award application deadline: 3/1; financial award applicants required to submit FAFSA. *Unit head:* Dr. Waldemar Karwowski, Chair, 407-823-2204, E-mail: wkar@mail.ucf.edu. *Application contact:* Dr. Waldemar Karwowski, Chair, 407-823-2204, E-mail: wkar@mail.ucf.edu.

University of Colorado Boulder, Graduate School, College of Engineering and Applied Science, Engineering Management Program, Boulder, CO 80309. Offers operations and logistics (ME); quality and process (ME); research and development (ME). *Students:* 53 full-time (16 women), 72 part-time (16 women); includes 20 minority (2 Black or African American, non-Hispanic/Latino; 1 American Indian or Alaska Native, non-Hispanic/Latino; 11 Asian, non-Hispanic/Latino; 5 Hispanic/Latino; 1 Two or more races, non-Hispanic/Latino), 15 international. Average age 34. 55 applicants, 2 enrolled. In 2010, 47 master's awarded. *Entrance requirements:* For master's, minimum undergraduate GPA of 3.0. *Application deadline:* For fall admission, 2/15 for domestic students, 12/1 for international students; for spring admission, 8/15 for domestic students, 5/1 for international students. Application fee: $50 ($60 for international students). *Financial support:* In 2010–11, 2 fellowships (averaging $3,500 per year), 2 research assistantships (averaging $16,862 per year) were awarded. *Faculty research:* Quality and process, research and development, operations and logistics.

University of Delaware, College of Agriculture and Natural Resources, Operations Research Program, Newark, DE 19716. Offers MS, PhD. Part-time programs available. Terminal master's awarded for partial completion of doctoral program. *Degree requirements:* For master's, thesis, oral exam; for doctorate, thesis/dissertation, qualifying exam. *Entrance requirements:* For master's and doctorate, GRE General Test, 3 letters of recommendation, program language/s, engineering calculus. Additional exam requirements/recommendations for international students: Required—TOEFL. Electronic applications accepted. *Faculty research:* Simulation and modeling-production scheduling and optimization, agricultural production and resource economics, transportation engineering, statistical quality control.

University of Illinois at Chicago, Graduate College, College of Engineering, Department of Mechanical and Industrial Engineering, Program in Industrial Engineering and Operations Research, Chicago, IL 60607-7128. Offers PhD. Part-time programs available. *Degree requirements:* For doctorate, thesis/dissertation. *Entrance requirements:* For doctorate, GRE General Test, minimum GPA of 2.75. Additional exam requirements/recommendations for international students: Required—TOEFL. Electronic applications accepted.

The University of Iowa, Graduate College, College of Engineering, Department of Industrial Engineering, Iowa City, IA 52242-1316. Offers engineering design and manufacturing (MS, PhD); ergonomics (MS, PhD); information and engineering management (MS, PhD); operations research (MS, PhD); quality engineering (MS, PhD). *Faculty:* 6 full-time (0 women). *Students:* 33 full-time (9 women); includes 2 minority (1 Black or African American, non-Hispanic/Latino; 1 Asian, non-Hispanic/Latino), 14 international. Average age 30. 57 applicants, 19% accepted, 8 enrolled. In 2010, 12 master's, 5 doctorates awarded. *Degree requirements:* For master's, thesis optional, exam; for doctorate, comprehensive exam, thesis/dissertation, final defense exam. *Entrance requirements:* For master's and doctorate, GRE General Test. Additional exam requirements/recommendations for international students: Required—TOEFL (minimum score 550 paper-based; 213 computer-based; 81 iBT). *Application deadline:* For fall admission, 7/15 for domestic students, 4/15 for international students; for spring admission, 12/1 for domestic students, 10/1 for international students. Applications are processed on a rolling basis. Application fee: $60 ($100 for international students). Electronic applications accepted. *Financial support:* In 2010–11, 2 fellowships with partial tuition reimbursements (averaging $30,450 per year), 20 research assistantships with partial tuition reimbursements (averaging $20,000 per year), 8 teaching assistantships with partial tuition reimbursements (averaging $16,630 per year) were awarded; career-related internships or fieldwork, scholarships/grants, and unspecified assistantships also available. Support available to part-time students. Financial award applicants required to submit FAFSA. *Faculty research:* Operations research; informatics; human factors engineering; manufacturing systems; human-machine interaction. Total annual research expenditures: $4.7 million. *Unit head:* Dr. Andrew Kusiak, Department Executive Officer, 319-335-5934, Fax: 319-335-5669, E-mail: andrew-kusiak@uiowa.edu. *Application contact:* Jennifer Rumping, Secretary, 319-335-5939, Fax: 319-335-5669, E-mail: indeng@engineering.uiowa.edu.

University of Massachusetts Amherst, Graduate School, College of Engineering, Department of Mechanical and Industrial Engineering, Program in Industrial Engineering and Operations Research, Amherst, MA 01003. Offers MS, PhD. Part-time programs available. *Students:* 23 full-time (7 women), 5 part-time (2 women); includes 1 minority (Hispanic/Latino), 17 international. Average age 31. 74 applicants, 43% accepted, 13 enrolled. In 2010, 9 master's awarded. Terminal master's awarded for partial completion of doctoral program. *Degree requirements:* For master's, thesis or alternative, project; for doctorate, comprehensive exam, thesis/dissertation. *Entrance requirements:* For master's and doctorate, GRE General Test. Additional exam requirements/recommendations for international students: Required—TOEFL (minimum score 550 paper-based; 213 computer-based; 80 iBT), IELTS (minimum score 6.5). *Application deadline:* For fall admission, 1/15 for domestic and international students; for spring admission, 10/1 for domestic and international students. Application fee: $50 ($65 for international students). Electronic applications accepted. *Expenses:* Tuition, state resident: full-time $2640. Required fees: $8282. One-time fee: $357 full-time. *Financial support:* Fellowships with full tuition reimbursements, research assistantships with full tuition reimbursements, teaching assistantships with full tuition reimbursements, career-related internships or fieldwork, Federal Work-Study, scholarships/grants, traineeships, health care benefits, tuition waivers, and unspecified assistantships available. Support available to part-time students. Financial award application deadline: 1/15; financial award applicants required to submit FAFSA. *Unit head:* Dr. David P. Schmidt, Graduate Program Director, 413-545-3827, Fax: 413-545-1027. *Application contact:* Jean M. Ames, Supervisor of Admissions, 413-545-0722, Fax: 413-577-0100, E-mail: gradadm@grad.umass.edu.

University of Michigan, Horace H. Rackham School of Graduate Studies, College of Engineering, Department of Industrial and Operations Engineering, Ann Arbor, MI 48109. Offers MS, MSE, PhD, MBA/MS, MBA/MSE. *Accreditation:* ABET. Part-time programs available. *Students:* 186 full-time (67 women), 8 part-time (1 woman). 587 applicants, 44% accepted, 132 enrolled. In 2010, 121 master's, 12 doctorates awarded. Terminal master's awarded for partial completion of doctoral program. *Degree requirements:* For doctorate, oral defense of dissertation, preliminary exams, qualifying exam. *Entrance requirements:* For master's, GRE General Test, minimum GPA of 3.2; for doctorate, GRE General Test, minimum GPA of 3.5. Additional exam requirements/recommendations for international students: Required—TOEFL. *Application deadline:* Applications are processed on a rolling basis. Application fee: $65 ($75 for international students). Electronic applications accepted. *Expenses:* Tuition, state resident: full-time $17,784; part-time $1116 per credit hour. Tuition, nonresident: full-time $35,944; part-time $2125 per credit hour. International tuition: $35,994 full-time. Required fees: $95 per semester. Tuition and fees vary according to course load, degree level and program. *Financial support:* In 2010–11, 71 students received support; fellowships, research assistantships, teaching assistantships, Federal Work-Study, institutionally sponsored loans, scholarships/grants, traineeships, health care benefits, and unspecified assistantships available. Financial award applicants required to submit FAFSA. *Faculty research:* Production/distribution/logistics, financial engineering and enterprise systems, ergonomics (physical and cognitive), stochastic processes, linear and nonlinear optimization, operations research. *Unit head:* Mark Daskin, Chair, 734-764-9422, Fax: 734-764-3451, E-mail: msdaskin@umich.edu. *Application contact:* Matt Irelan, Graduate Student Advisor/Program Coordinator, 734-764-6480, Fax: 734-764-3451, E-mail: mirelan@umich.edu.

The University of North Carolina at Chapel Hill, Graduate School, College of Arts and Sciences, Department of Operations Research, Chapel Hill, NC 27599. Offers MS, PhD. *Degree requirements:* For master's, comprehensive exam; for doctorate, comprehensive exam, thesis/dissertation. *Entrance requirements:* For master's and doctorate, GRE General Test, minimum GPA of 3.0.

Operations Research

University of Southern California, Graduate School, Viterbi School of Engineering, Daniel J. Epstein Department of Industrial and Systems Engineering, Los Angeles, CA 90089. Offers digital supply chain management (MS); engineering management (MS); engineering technology communication (Graduate Certificate); health systems operations (Graduate Certificate); industrial and systems engineering (MS, PhD, Engr); manufacturing engineering (MS); operations research engineering (MS); optimization and supply chain management (Graduate Certificate); product development engineering (MS); safety systems and security (MS); systems architecting and engineering (MS, Graduate Certificate); systems safety and security (Graduate Certificate); transportation systems (Graduate Certificate); MS/MBA. Part-time and evening/weekend programs available. Postbaccalaureate distance learning degree programs offered (no on-campus study). *Faculty:* 12 full-time (2 women), 21 part-time/adjunct (2 women). *Students:* 224 full-time (69 women), 143 part-time (32 women); includes 63 minority (6 Black or African American, non-Hispanic/Latino; 35 Asian, non-Hispanic/Latino; 17 Hispanic/Latino; 5 Two or more races, non-Hispanic/Latino), 253 international. 669 applicants, 45% accepted, 155 enrolled. In 2010, 98 master's, 7 doctorates awarded. Terminal master's awarded for partial completion of doctoral program. *Degree requirements:* For master's, thesis optional; for doctorate, thesis/dissertation. *Entrance requirements:* For master's and doctorate, GRE General Test. *Application deadline:* For fall admission, 12/1 priority date for domestic students, 11/1 priority date for international students; for spring admission, 9/15 priority date for domestic and international students. Applications are processed on a rolling basis. Application fee: $85. Electronic applications accepted. *Expenses:* Tuition: Full-time $31,240; part-time $1420 per unit. Required fees: $600. One-time fee: $35 full-time. Full-time tuition and fees vary according to degree level and program. *Financial support:* In 2010–11, fellowships with full tuition reimbursements (averaging $30,000 per year), research assistantships with full tuition reimbursements (averaging $20,000 per year), teaching assistantships with full tuition reimbursements (averaging $20,000 per year) were awarded; career-related internships or fieldwork, scholarships/grants, health care benefits, and unspecified assistantships also available. Financial award application deadline: 12/1; financial award applicants required to submit CSS PROFILE or FAFSA. *Faculty research:* Health systems, music cognition and retrieval, transportation and logistics, manufacturing and automation, engineering systems design, risk and economic analysis. Total annual research expenditures: $1 million. *Unit head:* Dr. F. Stan Settles, Chair, 213-740-4893, E-mail: isedept@usc.edu. *Application contact:* Evelyn Felina, Director of Student Affairs, 213-740-7549, E-mail: efelina@usc.edu.

The University of Texas at Austin, Graduate School, Cockrell School of Engineering, Department of Mechanical Engineering, Program in Operations Research and Industrial Engineering, Austin, TX 78712-1111. Offers MS, PhD. *Entrance requirements:* For master's and doctorate, GRE General Test. Additional exam requirements/recommendations for international students: Required—TOEFL.

University of Waterloo, Graduate Studies, Faculty of Engineering, Department of Management Sciences, Waterloo, ON N2L 3G1, Canada. Offers applied operations research (MA Sc, MMS, PhD); information systems (MA Sc, MMS, PhD); management of technology (MA Sc, MMS, PhD). Part-time programs available. Postbaccalaureate distance learning degree programs offered (no on-campus study). *Degree requirements:* For master's, research paper or thesis; for doctorate, comprehensive exam, thesis/dissertation. *Entrance requirements:* For master's, GMAT or GRE, honors degree, minimum B average, resume; for doctorate, GMAT or GRE, master's degree, minimum A- average, resumé. Additional exam requirements/recommendations for international students: Required—TOEFL, TWE. *Faculty research:* Operations research, manufacturing systems, scheduling, information systems.

Virginia Commonwealth University, Graduate School, College of Humanities and Sciences, Department of Mathematics and Applied Mathematics, Program in Statistical Sciences and Operations Research, Richmond, VA 23284-9005. Offers MS. *Students:* 20 applicants, 70% accepted, 11 enrolled. *Entrance requirements:* For master's, GRE General Test, 30 undergraduate credits in mathematics, statistics, or operations research, including calculus I and II, multivariate calculus, linear algebra, probability and statistics. Additional exam requirements/recommendations for international students: Required—TOEFL (minimum score 600 paper-based; 250 computer-based; 100 iBT); Recommended—IELTS (minimum score 6.5). *Application deadline:* For fall admission, 3/1 for domestic students; for spring admission, 10/15 for domestic students. Applications are processed on a rolling basis. Application fee: $50. Electronic applications accepted. *Expenses:* Tuition, state resident: full-time $4308; part-time $479 per credit hour. Tuition, nonresident: full-time $8942; part-time $994 per credit hour. Required fees: $2000; $85 per credit hour. Tuition and fees vary according to course level, course load, degree level, campus/location and program. *Unit head:* Dr. D'Arcy P. Mays, Chair, 804-828-1301 Ext. 151. *Application contact:* Dr. Edward L. Boone, Director, Master???s Programs in Statistical Sciences and Operations Research, 804-828-4637, E-mail: jawood@vcu.edu.

Technology and Public Policy

Arizona State University, College of Liberal Arts and Sciences, Program in Science and Technology Policy, Tempe, AZ 85287-6505. Offers PSM. Fall admission only. *Faculty:* 18 full-time (6 women). *Students:* 3 full-time (2 women), 2 part-time (1 woman); includes 1 minority (Two or more races, non-Hispanic/Latino). Average age 33. 7 applicants, 100% accepted, 4 enrolled. *Degree requirements:* For master's, thesis or alternative, internship, applied project, interactive Program of Study (iPOS) submitted before completing 50 percent of required credit hours. *Entrance requirements:* For master's, GRE, bachelor's degree (or equivalent) or graduate degree from regionally-accredited college or university or of recognized standing; minimum GPA of 3.0 or equivalent in last 2 years of work leading to bachelor's degree; 3 letters of recommendation; personal statement; current resume. Additional exam requirements/recommendations for international students: Required—TOEFL, IELTS, or Pearson Test of English. *Application deadline:* For fall admission, 4/1 priority date for domestic and international students. Application fee: $70 ($90 for international students). Electronic applications accepted. *Expenses:* Contact institution. *Financial support:* Institutionally sponsored loans available. Financial award application deadline: 3/1; financial award applicants required to submit FAFSA. *Unit head:* Dr. Clark Miller, Program Chair, 480-965-1778, E-mail: clark.miller@asu.edu. *Application contact:* Graduate Admissions, 480-965-6113.

Carnegie Mellon University, Carnegie Institute of Technology, Department of Civil and Environmental Engineering, Pittsburgh, PA 15213. Offers advanced infrastructure systems (MS, PhD); civil and environmental engineering (MS, PhD); civil and environmental engineering/engineering and public policy (PhD); civil engineering (MS, PhD); computational mechanics (MS, PhD); computational science and engineering (MS, PhD); environmental engineering (MS, PhD); environmental management and science (MS, PhD). Part-time programs available. *Faculty:* 20 full-time (3 women), 15 part-time/adjunct (5 women). *Students:* 144 full-time (67 women), 8 part-time (2 women); includes 4 Black or African American, non-Hispanic/Latino; 1 American Indian or Alaska Native, non-Hispanic/Latino; 9 Asian, non-Hispanic/Latino, 99 international. Average age 26. 388 applicants, 66% accepted, 80 enrolled. In 2010, 62 master's, 8 doctorates awarded. Terminal master's awarded for partial completion of doctoral program. *Degree requirements:* For master's, thesis optional; for doctorate, comprehensive exam, thesis/dissertation, qualifying exam, public defense of dissertation. *Entrance requirements:* For master's and doctorate, GRE General Test. Additional exam requirements/recommendations for international students: Required—TOEFL (minimum score 84 iBT). *Application deadline:* For fall admission, 1/15 priority date for domestic and international students; for spring admission, 9/30 priority date for domestic and international students. Application fee: $65. Electronic applications accepted. *Financial support:* In 2010–11, 134 students received support, including 27 fellowships with full and partial tuition reimbursements available (averaging $21,708 per year), 42 research assistantships with full and partial tuition reimbursements available (averaging $24,474 per year); tuition waivers (partial) and unspecified assistantships also available. Financial award application deadline: 1/15. *Faculty research:* Advanced infrastructure systems; environmental engineering science and management; mechanics, materials, and computing; green design; global sustainable construction. Total annual research expenditures: $4.7 million. *Unit head:* Dr. James H. Garrett, Head, 412-268-2941, Fax: 412-268-7813, E-mail: garrett@cmu.edu. *Application contact:* Maxine A. Leffard, Director of the Graduate Program, 412-268-5673, Fax: 412-268-7813, E-mail: ce-admissions@andrew.cmu.edu.

Carnegie Mellon University, Carnegie Institute of Technology, Department of Engineering and Public Policy, Pittsburgh, PA 15213-3891. Offers PhD. *Degree requirements:* For doctorate, thesis/dissertation. *Entrance requirements:* For doctorate, GRE General Test, BS in physical sciences or engineering. Additional exam requirements/recommendations for international students: Required—TOEFL. *Faculty research:* Issues in energy and environmental policy, IT and telecommunications policy, risk analysis and communication, management of technological innovation, security and engineered civil systems.

See Display on next page and Close-Up on page 493.

Eastern Michigan University, Graduate School, College of Technology, School of Technology Studies, Program in Technology Studies, Ypsilanti, MI 48197. Offers interdisciplinary technology (MLS); technology studies (MS). Part-time and evening/weekend programs available. Postbaccalaureate distance learning degree programs offered (minimal on-campus study). *Students:* 27 full-time (3 women), 72 part-time (21 women); includes 21 minority (17 Black or African American, non-Hispanic/Latino; 3 Asian, non-Hispanic/Latino; 1 Hispanic/Latino), 5 international. Average age 36. In 2010, 23 master's awarded. *Degree requirements:* For master's, thesis optional. *Entrance requirements:* For master's, GRE General Test, minimum GPA of 2.6. Additional exam requirements/recommendations for international students: Required—TOEFL. *Application deadline:* Applications are processed on a rolling basis. Application fee: $35. *Financial support:* Fellowships, research assistantships with full tuition reimbursements, teaching assistantships with full tuition reimbursements, career-related internships or fieldwork, Federal Work-Study, institutionally sponsored loans, scholarships/grants, tuition waivers (partial), and unspecified assistantships available. Support available to part-time students. Financial award applicants required to submit FAFSA. *Unit head:* Dr. Denise Pilato, Program Coordinator, 734-487-1161, Fax: 734-487-7690, E-mail: denise.pilato@emich.edu. *Application contact:* Dr. Denise Pilato, Program Coordinator, 734-487-1161, Fax: 734-487-7690, E-mail: denise.pilato@emich.edu.

The George Washington University, Elliott School of International Affairs, Program in International Science and Technology Policy, Washington, DC 20052. Offers MA, JD/MA. Part-time and evening/weekend programs available. *Students:* 26 full-time (10 women), 18 part-time (8 women); includes 4 Asian, non-Hispanic/Latino; 4 Hispanic/Latino, 3 international. Average age 29. 35 applicants, 77% accepted, 18 enrolled. In 2010, 8 master's awarded. *Degree requirements:* For master's, one foreign language, capstone project. *Entrance requirements:* For master's, GRE General Test. Additional exam requirements/recommendations for international students: Required—TOEFL. *Application deadline:* For fall admission, 2/1 for domestic students; for spring admission, 10/1 for domestic students. Application fee: $75. Electronic applications accepted. *Financial support:* In 2010–11, 15 students received support; fellowships with tuition reimbursements available, research assistantships with tuition reimbursements available, career-related internships or fieldwork, Federal Work-Study, institutionally sponsored loans, and tuition waivers (full and partial) available. Financial award application deadline: 1/15; financial award applicants required to submit FAFSA. *Faculty research:* Science policy, space policy, risk assessment, technology transfer, energy policy. *Unit head:* Dr. Nicholas Vonortas, Director, 202-994-6458, E-mail: vonortas@gwu.edu. *Application contact:* Jeff V. Miles, Director of Graduate Admissions, 202-994-7050, Fax: 202-994-9537, E-mail: esiagrad@gwu.edu.

Massachusetts Institute of Technology, School of Engineering, Engineering Systems Division, Cambridge, MA 02139-4307. Offers engineering and management (SM); engineering systems (SM, PhD); logistics (M Eng); technology and policy (SM); technology, management and policy (PhD); SM/MBA. *Faculty:* 22 full-time (7 women). *Students:* 271 full-time (78 women); includes 39 minority (5 Black or African American, non-Hispanic/Latino; 27 Asian, non-Hispanic/Latino; 6 Hispanic/Latino; 1 Two or more races, non-Hispanic/Latino), 105 international. Average age 31. 927 applicants, 28% accepted, 185 enrolled. In 2010, 169 master's, 10 doctorates awarded. *Degree requirements:* For master's, thesis; for doctorate, comprehensive exam, thesis/dissertation. *Entrance requirements:* For master's, GRE General Test (or GMAT for some programs); for doctorate, GRE General Test. Additional exam requirements/recommendations for international students: Required—IELTS (minimum score 7.5). Application fee: $75. *Expenses:* Contact institution. *Financial support:* In 2010–11, 217 students received support, including 36 fellowships with tuition reimbursements available (averaging $25,594 per year), 95 research assistantships with tuition reimbursements available (averaging $27,695 per year), 15 teaching assistantships with tuition reimbursements available (averaging $25,802 per year); career-related internships or fieldwork, Federal Work-Study, institutionally sponsored loans, scholarships/grants, health care benefits, and unspecified assistantships also available. *Faculty research:* Critical infrastructures; extended enterprises; energy and sustainability; health care delivery; humans and technology; uncertainty and dynamics; design and implementation; networks and flows; policy and standards. Total annual research expenditures: $13.2 million. *Unit head:* Prof. Yossi Sheffi, Director, 617-253-1764, E-mail: esdinquiries@mit.edu. *Application contact:* Graduate Admissions, 617-253-1182, E-mail: esdgrad@mit.edu.

Massachusetts Institute of Technology, School of Humanities, Arts, and Social Sciences, Program in Science, Technology, and Society, Cambridge, MA 02139. Offers history, anthropology, and science, technology and society (PhD). *Faculty:* 13 full-time (5 women). *Students:* 28 full-time (17 women); includes 4 minority (1 Black or African American, non-Hispanic/Latino; 1 American Indian or Alaska Native, non-Hispanic/Latino; 1 Asian, non-Hispanic/Latino; 1 Two or more races, non-Hispanic/Latino), 7 international. Average age 30. 146 applicants, 6% accepted, 5 enrolled. In 2010, 1 doctorate awarded. *Degree requirements:* For doctorate, comprehensive exam, thesis/dissertation. *Entrance requirements:* For doctorate, GRE General Test. Additional exam requirements/recommendations for international students: Required—TOEFL (minimum score 577 paper-based; 233 computer-based; 90 iBT), IELTS (minimum score 7). *Application deadline:* For fall admission, 1/1 for domestic and international students. Application fee: $75. Electronic applications accepted. *Expenses:* Tuition: Full-time $38,940; part-time $605 per unit. Required fees: $272. *Financial support:* In 2010–11, 25 students received support, including 19 fellowships with tuition reimbursements available (averaging $31,612 per year), 1 research assistantship (averaging $30,697 per year), 6 teaching assistantships with tuition reimbursements available (averaging $31,405 per year); Federal Work-Study, institutionally sponsored loans, scholarships/grants, traineeships, health care benefits, and unspecified assistantships also available. *Faculty research:* History of science; history of technology; sociology of science and technology; anthropology of science and technology; science, technology, and society; aeronautics and astronautics; humans and automation. Total annual research expenditures: $472,000. *Unit head:* Prof. David A. Mindell, Director, 617-253-4062, Fax: 617-258-8118, E-mail: stsprogram@mit.edu. *Application contact:* Karen Gardner, Academic Administrator, 617-253-9759, Fax: 617-258-8118, E-mail: hasts@mit.edu.

Rensselaer Polytechnic Institute, Graduate School, School of Humanities, Arts, and Social Sciences, Program in Science and Technology Studies, Troy, NY 12180-3590. Offers design studies (MS, PhD); policy studies (MS, PhD); science studies (MS, PhD); sustainability studies (MS, PhD); technology studies (MS, PhD). *Faculty:* 15 full-time (5 women). *Students:* 20 full-time (5 women), 4 part-time (2 women); includes 2 Black or African American, non-Hispanic/Latino; 1 Asian, non-Hispanic/Latino, 4 international. Average age 27. 19 applicants, 42% accepted, 5 enrolled. In 2010, 2 master's, 1 doctorate awarded. Terminal master's awarded for partial completion of doctoral program. *Degree requirements:* For master's, thesis (for some programs); for doctorate, comprehensive exam, thesis/dissertation. *Entrance requirements:* For master's and doctorate, GRE General Test. Additional exam requirements/recommendations for international students: Required—TOEFL (minimum score 600 paper-based; 250 computer-based). *Application deadline:* For fall admission, 1/15 priority date for domestic students, 1/15 for international students. Applications are processed on a rolling basis. Application fee: $75. Electronic applications accepted. *Expenses:* Tuition: Full-time $39,600; part-time $1650 per credit. Required fees: $1896. *Financial support:* In 2010–11, 22 students received support, including 6 fellowships with tuition reimbursements available (averaging $19,800 per year), 2 research assistantships with full tuition reimbursements available (averaging $19,800 per year), 11 teaching assistantships with full tuition reimbursements available (averaging $19,800 per year); career-related internships or fieldwork, institutionally sponsored loans, and tuition waivers (partial) also available. Financial award application deadline: 1/15. *Faculty research:* Communities and technology, social dimensions of IT and biotechnology, ethics and policy, design. Total annual research expenditures: $75,000. *Unit head:* Dr. Sharon Anderson-Gold, Chair, 518-276-8837, Fax: 518-276-2659, E-mail: anders@rpi.edu. *Application contact:* Dr. Edward J. Woodhouse, Director of Graduate Studies, 518-276-8506, Fax: 518-276-2659, E-mail: woodhouse@rpi.edu.

Rochester Institute of Technology, Graduate Enrollment Services, College of Liberal Arts, Department of Science, Technology and Society/Public Policy, Rochester, NY 14623-5603. Offers science, technology and public policy (MS). Part-time programs available. *Students:* 6 full-time (3 women), 6 part-time (3 women), 2 international. Average age 27. 15 applicants, 80% accepted, 4 enrolled. In 2010, 3 master's awarded. *Degree requirements:* For master's, thesis. *Entrance requirements:* For master's, GRE General Test, minimum GPA of 3.0. Additional exam requirements/recommendations for international students: Required—TOEFL (minimum score 570 paper-based; 230 computer-based; 88 iBT) or IELTS (minimum score 6.5). *Application deadline:* For fall admission, 2/15 priority date for domestic and international students; for winter admission, 11/1 for domestic and international students; for spring admission, 2/1 for domestic and international students. Applications are processed on a rolling basis. Electronic applications accepted. *Expenses:* Tuition: Full-time $33,234; part-time $924 per credit hour. Required fees: $219. *Financial support:* In 2010–11, 9 students received support; research assistantships with partial tuition reimbursements available, teaching assistantships with partial tuition reimbursements available, career-related internships or fieldwork, scholarships/grants, and unspecified assistantships available. Support available to part-time students. Financial award applicants required to submit FAFSA. *Faculty research:* Environmental policy, information and communications policy, energy policy, biotechnology policy. *Unit head:* Dr. James Winebrake, Chair, 585-475-4648, Fax: 585-475-2510, E-mail: james.winebrake@rit.edu. *Application contact:* Diane Ellison, Assistant Vice President, Graduate Enrollment Services, 585-475-2229, Fax: 585-475-7164, E-mail: gradinfo@rit.edu.

St. Cloud State University, School of Graduate Studies, College of Science and Engineering, Department of Environmental and Technological Studies, St. Cloud, MN 56301-4498. Offers

MS. *Degree requirements:* For master's, thesis or alternative. *Entrance requirements:* For master's, minimum GPA of 2.75. Additional exam requirements/recommendations for international students: Required—TOEFL (minimum score 550 paper-based; 213 computer-based), Michigan English Language Assessment Battery; Recommended—IELTS (minimum score 6.5). Electronic applications accepted.

Stony Brook University, State University of New York, Graduate School, College of Engineering and Applied Sciences, Department of Technology and Society, Program in Technology, Policy, and Innovation, Stony Brook, NY 11794-3760. Offers PhD. *Degree requirements:* For doctorate, comprehensive exam, thesis/dissertation. *Entrance requirements:* For doctorate, GRE General Test, minimum undergraduate GPA of 3.0. Additional exam requirements/recommendations for international students: Required—TOEFL. *Application deadline:* For fall admission, 2/1 for domestic and international students. *Expenses:* Tuition, state resident: full-time $8370; part-time $349 per credit. Tuition, nonresident: full-time $13,780; part-time $574 per credit. Required fees: $994. *Unit head:* Dr. David Ferguson. *Application contact:* Dr. Sheldon Reaven, Graduate Director, 631-632-8765, Fax: 631-632-7809, E-mail: sheldon.reaven@sunysb.edu.

University of Minnesota, Twin Cities Campus, Graduate School, Hubert H. Humphrey School of Public Affairs, Program in Science, Technology, and Environmental Policy, Minneapolis, MN 55455-0213. Offers MS, JD/MS. Part-time programs available. *Degree requirements:* For master's, thesis. *Entrance requirements:* For master's, GRE General Test, undergraduate training in the biological or physical sciences or engineering, minimum undergraduate GPA of 3.0. Additional exam requirements/recommendations for international students: Required—TOEFL (minimum score 600 paper-based; 250 computer-based; 100 iBT). Electronic applications accepted. *Faculty research:* Economics, history, philosophy, and politics of science and technology; organization and management of science and technology.

University of South Africa, College of Human Sciences, Pretoria, South Africa. Offers adult education (M Ed); African languages (MA, PhD); African politics (MA, PhD); Afrikaans (MA, PhD); ancient history (MA, PhD); ancient Near Eastern studies (MA, PhD); anthropology (MA, PhD); applied linguistics (MA); Arabic (MA, PhD); archaeology (MA); art history (MA); Biblical archaeology (MA); Biblical studies (M Th, D Th, PhD); Christian spirituality (M Th, D Th); church history (M Th, D Th); classical studies (MA, PhD); clinical psychology (MA); communication (MA, PhD); comparative education (M Ed, Ed D); consulting psychology (D Admin, D Com, PhD); curriculum studies (M Ed, Ed D); development studies (M Admin, MA, D Admin, PhD); didactics (M Ed, Ed D); education (M Tech); education management (M Ed, Ed D); educational psychology (M Ed); English (MA); environmental education (M Ed); French (MA, PhD); German (MA, PhD); Greek (MA); guidance and counseling (M Ed); health studies (MA, PhD), including health sciences education (MA), health services management (MA), medical and surgical nursing science (critical care general) (MA), midwifery and neonatal nursing science (MA), trauma and emergency care (MA); history (MA, PhD); history of education (Ed D); inclusive education (M Ed, Ed D); information and communications technology policy and regulation (MA); information science (MA, MIS, PhD); international politics (MA, PhD); Islamic studies (MA, PhD); Italian (MA, PhD); Judaica (MA, PhD); linguistics (MA, PhD); mathematical education (M Ed); mathematics education (MA); missiology (M Th, D Th); modern Hebrew (MA, PhD); musicology (MA, MMus, D Mus, PhD); natural science education (M Ed); New Testament (M Th, D Th); Old Testament (D Th); pastoral therapy (M Th, D Th); philosophy (MA); philosophy of education (M Ed, Ed D); politics (MA, PhD); Portuguese (MA, PhD); practical theology (M Th, D Th); psychology (MA, MS, PhD); psychology of education (M Ed, Ed D); public health (MA); religious studies (MA, D Th, PhD); Romance languages (MA); Russian (MA, PhD); Semitic languages (MA, PhD); social behavior studies in HIV/AIDS (MA); social science (mental health) (MA); social science in development studies (MA); social science in psychology (MA); social science in social work (MA); social science in sociology (MA); social work (MSW, DSW, PhD); socio-education (M Ed, Ed D); sociolinguistics (MA); sociology (MA, PhD); Spanish (MA, PhD); systematic theology (M Th, D Th); TESOL (teaching

Technology and Public Policy

University of South Africa (continued)
English to speakers of other languages) (MA); theological ethics (M Th, D Th); theory of literature (MA, PhD); urban ministries (D Th); urban ministry (M Th).

The University of Texas at Austin, Graduate School, Program in Technology Commercialization, Austin, TX 78712-1111. Offers MS. Twelve month program, beginning in May, with classes held every other Friday and Saturday. Evening/weekend programs available. Postbaccalaureate distance learning degree programs offered (no on-campus study). *Degree requirements:* For master's, year-long global teaming project. *Entrance requirements:* For master's, GRE General Test, or GMAT. Additional exam requirements/recommendations for international students: Required—TOEFL (minimum score 550 paper-based; 213 computer-based; 79 iBT). Electronic applications accepted. *Expenses:* Contact institution. *Faculty research:* Technology transfer; entrepreneurship; commercialization; research, development and innovation.

Western Illinois University, School of Graduate Studies, College of Business and Technology, Department of Engineering Technology, Macomb, IL 61455-1390. Offers manufacturing engineering systems (MS). Part-time programs available. *Students:* 18 full-time (2 women), 4 part-time (0 women); includes 3 minority (all Black or African American, non-Hispanic/Latino), 9 international. Average age 27. 21 applicants, 71% accepted. In 2010, 11 master's awarded. *Degree requirements:* For master's, thesis or alternative. *Entrance requirements:* Additional exam requirements/recommendations for international students: Required—TOEFL (minimum score 550 paper-based; 213 computer-based; 80 iBT). *Application deadline:* Applications are processed on a rolling basis. Application fee: $30. Electronic applications accepted. *Expenses:* Tuition, state resident: full-time $6370; part-time $265.40 per credit hour. Tuition, nonresident: full-time $12,740; part-time $530.80 per credit hour. Required fees: $75.67 per credit hour. *Financial support:* In 2010–11, 5 students received support, including 5 research assistantships with full tuition reimbursements available (averaging $7,280 per year). Financial award applicants required to submit FAFSA. *Unit head:* Dr. Ray Diez, Chairperson, 309-298-1091. *Application contact:* Evelyn Hoing, Assistant Director of Graduate Studies, 309-298-1806, Fax: 309-298-2345, E-mail: grad-office@wiu.edu.

Carnegie Mellon

CARNEGIE MELLON UNIVERSITY

Department of Engineering and Public Policy

Program of Study	A broad range of critical problems require analysis and skills at the interface between technology and society. The graduate program in the Department of Engineering and Public Policy is designed to prepare students to adapt and extend the perspectives and tools of engineering and science to these problems. While students receive a considerable amount of training and experience in social science and in techniques of social analysis, the Department's philosophical and methodological roots remain in engineering.
	The primary degree offered is a research-oriented Ph.D. In preparing for the Ph.D., students may elect to earn a joint M.S. with one of the traditional engineering departments. Terminal M.S. programs are not recommended.
	Graduate students take three types of courses: engineering and science courses, primarily offered by the engineering departments of Carnegie Institute of Technology (the College of Engineering); courses in social sciences and social analysis offered by the H. John Heinz III College, the School of Humanities and Social Sciences, and the Tepper School of Business; and courses offered by the Department of Engineering and Public Policy, including, at a minimum, a one-semester course in project management and a four-course sequence on applied policy analysis. Candidates for the Ph.D. degree should expect to spend at least three years or the equivalent in graduate study. Part-time Ph.D. degree candidates must devote at least one academic year to full-time graduate study.
	The Department of Engineering and Public Policy subscribes firmly to the belief that the Ph.D. is a research degree. Research undertaken in fulfillment of the requirements for a Ph.D. must make a fundamental and generalizable contribution toward the definition, understanding, or solution of a class of problems in the area of technology and public policy. While faculty members assist students in defining and developing their research problems, responsibility in this area lies primarily with the student.
	Faculty research and interest are currently focused on policy problems in energy and environmental systems; information and communication; risk analysis and communication; and the management of technical innovation and R&D policy. The Department also addresses issues in technology and economic development, focusing in particular on China, India, Mexico, and Brazil; the domestic security aspects of engineered civil systems; and various issues in technology, organizations, and social networks. The Department frequently undertakes the development of new software tools for the support of policy analysis and research and sometimes studies issues in arms control and defense policy. Faculty members maintain many close ties in their areas of interest with industrial and public sector organizations, and many members act as consultants to industry and government agencies. Students are encouraged to make full use of these faculty ties in defining and developing their research problems.
	Specific details on degree requirements are included in the descriptive literature available from the Department.
Research Facilities	The University has excellent computer and library facilities. In addition, research facilities are available through the Heinz College, the Tepper School of Business, the Robotics Institute, and the Institute for Complex Engineered Systems.
Financial Aid	The Department strives to provide financial aid for the majority of its qualified doctoral students.
Cost of Study	Tuition is $37,800 for the 2011–12 academic year.
Living and Housing Costs	The estimated cost for living expenses for 2011–12, including housing, transportation, books and supplies, and incidentals, is $26,600. All graduate students live off campus in areas near the University.
Student Group	The graduate enrollment at Carnegie Mellon University totals more than 5,000 students, who come from colleges and universities throughout the United States and from many countries. In 2010, more than 2,000 graduate degrees were awarded, including 251 doctorates. The current enrollment in the Department is 98 graduate students and 84 undergraduates.
Student Outcomes	Since 1978, 191 students have graduated with a Ph.D. degree and 36 have graduated with an M.S. degree. Graduates are currently employed in policy research in think tanks, consulting firms, and nongovernmental organizations (27 percent); as university faculty members and postdoctoral research fellows (40 percent); in private-sector firms (17 percent); and in government and national labs (16 percent).
Location	Pittsburgh offers many valuable resources to students working on problems in the area of technology and society. It is a dynamic, working city that has been revitalized in the past few decades and has developed an outstanding cultural life. Excellent cultural opportunities are available, including museums, orchestras, opera, drama, and dance, and there are active groups in the fine arts and folk crafts. The city has a good botanical garden, a zoo, many fine parks, and excellent public radio and television. The countryside around Pittsburgh provides opportunities for outdoor activities in all seasons.
The University and The Department	Carnegie Mellon University has developed an international reputation as an outstanding environment in which to conduct interdisciplinary research on problems in the area of technology and society. The Department of Engineering and Public Policy maintains a vigorous intellectual interaction with the engineering departments and special programs of the Carnegie Institute of Technology, the School of Computer Science, the H. John Heinz III College, the College of Humanities and Social Sciences, and the Tepper School of Business. In addition to these, the University includes the Mellon College of Science and the College of Fine Arts.
Applying	All entering students must hold the equivalent of an undergraduate degree in engineering, physical science, or mathematics. Students with education or experience beyond the bachelor's degree are particularly encouraged to apply. Applications are welcome at any time, but they are usually processed between December and March for fall admission. Students are urged to take the General Test of the Graduate Record Examinations (the test is required for international students). In addition to filing the formal application, each student is asked to submit a letter describing his or her background and probable area(s) of research interest. Correspondence about the details of the program is encouraged.
Correspondence and Information	Victoria Finney, Graduate Program Administrator Department of Engineering and Public Policy Carnegie Mellon University Pittsburgh, Pennsylvania 15213 Phone: 412-268-2670 E-mail: eppadmt@andrew.cmu.edu Web site: http://www.epp.cmu.edu/

Carnegie Mellon University

THE FACULTY AND THEIR RESEARCH

Peter Adams, Professor of Civil and Environmental Engineering and of Engineering and Public Policy; Ph.D., Caltech. Climatic effects of atmospheric particulate matter (aerosols), global and regional models of atmospheric chemistry, air quality in developing countries.

Jay Apt, Professor of Technology, Tepper School of Business, and of Engineering and Public Policy; Director, Carnegie Mellon Electricity Industry Center; Ph.D., MIT. Structure, economics, and control of the electric power system; public communication of natural and human-caused planetary change.

V. S. Arunachalam, Distinguished Service Professor of Engineering and Public Policy; Ph.D., Wales. Technology for economic development, energy and communication technology.

Inês L. Azevedo, Assistant Research Professor of Engineering and Public Policy and Executive Director of Climate and Energy Decision Making; Ph.D., Carnegie Mellon. Energy and climate policy, decision-making under uncertainty, sustainable energy systems.

Michel Bézy, Distinguished Service Professor of Engineering and Public Policy; Ph.D., UCL (Belgium). Strategic use of digital information, innovation management, ICT for development.

Alfred Blumstein, J. Erik Jonsson University Professor of Urban Systems and Operations Research, H. John Heinz III College, and Professor of Engineering and Public Policy; Ph.D., Cornell. Methodologies for public systems analysis, criminology, and criminal justice.

Serguey Braguinsky, Associate Professor of Social and Decision Sciences and of Engineering and Public Policy; Ph.D., Keio (Japan). Economics of innovation, entrepreneurship, and growth; development economics; institutional economics.

Wändi Bruine de Bruin, Assistant Professor of Social and Decision Sciences and of Engineering and Public Policy; Ph.D., Carnegie Mellon. Judgment and decision making, risk perception and communication, individual differences in decision-making competence, health decision making, environmental decision making.

Kathleen M. Carley, Professor of Computation, Organization, and Society; Engineering and Public Policy; Institute for Software Research; Social and Decision Sciences; the Heinz College; and the Tepper School of Business; Ph.D., Harvard. Dynamic network analysis, agent-based systems, complexity, diffusion, nuclear deterrence, information assurance and knowledge management.

Elizabeth A. Casman, Associate Research Professor of Engineering and Public Policy; Ph.D., Johns Hopkins. Environmental and microbial risk assessment, infectious disease transmission, health policy, risk communication, water resources.

Jared L. Cohon, President of Carnegie Mellon; Professor of Civil and Environmental Engineering and of Engineering and Public Policy; Ph.D., MIT. Environmental and energy systems analysis, multi-criteria decision making.

Lorrie Faith Cranor, Associate Professor of Computer Science and of Engineering and Public Policy; D.Sc., Washington (St. Louis). Usable privacy and security, online privacy, privacy enhancing technology, usability of privacy and security software, technology policy, social impact of computers.

Neil M. Donahue, Professor of Chemistry, Chemical Engineering, and Engineering and Public Policy; Ph.D., MIT. Chemical processes in air pollution and fine particles.

David J. Farber, Distinguished Career Professor of the School of Computer Science and of Public Policy; D.Sc. (hon.), Stevens. Information and telecommunication technology and policy.

Pedro Ferreira, Assistant Research Professor of Engineering and Public Policy and of the Heinz College; Ph.D., Carnegie Mellon. Telecommunications technology, policy and management; economics of information technology and networks.

Paul S. Fischbeck, Professor of Social and Decision Sciences and of Engineering and Public Policy; Ph.D., Stanford. Bayesian decision theory, geographic information systems, subjective probability assessment, system reliability, military decision making.

Baruch Fischhoff, Howard Heinz University Professor of Social and Decision Sciences and of Engineering and Public Policy; Ph.D., Hebrew (Jerusalem). Judgment and decision making, risk management, risk perception and communication, environmental benefits assessment, historical and expert judgment, adolescent decision making, homeland security, medical decision making, political and behavioral foundations of formal analysis.

Eden S. Fisher, Professor of the Practice of Engineering and Public Policy and Executive Director of Engineering and Technology Innovation Management Program; Ph.D., Carnegie Mellon. Technology planning, innovation management, design for sustainability, innovation education.

Erica R. H. Fuchs, Assistant Professor of Engineering and Public Policy; Ph.D., MIT. Geography of design; international technology and operations management; innovation and industrial policy; automotive and semiconductor telecom/computing industries, especially optoelectronics; China.

W. Michael Griffin, Executive Director of the Green Design Institute; Assistant Research Professor of Engineering and Public Policy and of the Tepper School of Business; Ph.D., Rhode Island. Renewable energy systems analysis, uncertainty in life cycle analysis.

Alex Hills, Distinguished Service Professor of Engineering and Public Policy; Ph.D., Carnegie Mellon. Telecommunications in the developing world; remote and rural telecommunications systems; wireless communications technology, including LAN, MAN, and WAN; telecommunications policy and regulation.

David A. Hounshell, David M. Roderick Professor of Technology and Social Change; Professor of Social and Decision Sciences and of Engineering and Public Policy; Ph.D., Delaware. Study of innovation in its engineering, scientific, business, organizational, and regulatory contexts.

Marija D. Ilic, Professor of Electrical and Computer Engineering and of Engineering and Public Policy; D.Sc., Washington (St. Louis). Modeling and control of electric power and other large-scale systems.

Paulina Jaramillo, Assistant Research Professor of Engineering and Public Policy; Executive Director of the RenewElec Project; Ph.D., Carnegie Mellon. Energy system analysis, life cycle assessment, green design, renewable electricity.

Deanna H. Matthews, Assistant Teaching Professor and Associate Department Head for Undergraduate Affairs, Engineering and Public Policy; Ph.D., Carnegie Mellon. Life-cycle assessment, green design, K–12 engineering and science education.

H. Scott Matthews, Professor of Civil and Environmental Engineering and of Engineering and Public Policy; Ph.D., Carnegie Mellon. Life-cycle assessment of energy, transportation and information infrastructure, energy sensing, methods for and uncertainty assessment of environmental footprinting.

Francis C. McMichael, Professor Emeritus, Departments of Civil and Environmental Engineering and of Engineering and Public Policy; Ph.D., Caltech. Industrial and municipal solid-waste management, landfills, product design for the environment, engineering economics, risk analysis, source reduction, and recycling.

Jeremy J. Michalek, Associate Professor of Mechanical Engineering and of Engineering and Public Policy; Ph.D., Michigan. Systems optimization, design for market systems, green design, vehicle electrification, environmental policy.

Benoît Morel, Associate Teaching Professor of Engineering and Public Policy; Ph.D., Geneva. Cyber security, international security, nonlinear dynamical modeling, environmental studies, arms control (technical aspects), space policy, complexity theory.

M. Granger Morgan, University and Lord Chair Professor of Engineering; Head, Department of Engineering and Public Policy; Professor of Electrical and Computer Engineering and of the Heinz College; Director of the Center for Climate and Energy Decision Making; and Deputy Director of the Carnegie Mellon Electricity Industry Center; Ph.D., California, San Diego. Technology and public policy, analysis and treatment of uncertainty, health and environmental risk analysis and communication, climate decision making, electric power systems and policy.

Indira Nair, Professor Emeritus of Engineering and Public Policy; Ph.D., Northwestern University. Health and environmental risk assessment, engineering education, pre-college and public science education, ethics of technology.

Spyros N. Pandis, Research Professor of Chemical Engineering and of Engineering and Public Policy; Ph.D., Caltech. Air pollution, atmospheric chemistry, aerosol science.

Jon M. Peha, Professor of Engineering and Public Policy and of Electrical and Computer Engineering; Ph.D., Stanford. Technical and policy issues of telecommunications, including spectrum management, Internet architecture and policy, public safety and homeland security, e-commerce and payment systems, information technology for developing countries.

Adrian Perrig, Professor of Electrical and Computer Engineering and of Engineering and Public Policy; Ph.D., Carnegie Mellon. Computer and communications security, applied cryptography, trusted computing technologies, secure operating systems.

Henry R. Piehler, Professor Emeritus of Materials Sciences and Engineering, of Engineering and Public Policy, and of Biomedical Engineering; Sc.D., MIT. Deformation processing and the mechanical behavior of materials, powder processing, clad, coated, and composite materials, biomaterials and medical devices, product liability litigation and standardization processes, productivity and innovation.

Allen L. Robinson, Professor of Mechanical Engineering and of Engineering and Public Policy; Ph.D., Berkeley. Air pollution, atmospheric chemistry, aerosol science, climate change, biomass energy.

Edward S. Rubin, Professor of Engineering and Public Policy and of Mechanical Engineering; Ph.D., Stanford. Integrated energy–environmental–economic modeling and analysis of electric power systems, global climate change mitigation, carbon sequestration, environmental technology innovation.

Marvin A. Sirbu, Professor of Engineering and Public Policy, Industrial Administration, and Electrical and Computer Engineering; D.Sc., MIT. Telecommunication technology, policy and management regulation and industrial structure, economic impacts of information and communication technologies.

Mitchell J. Small, H. John Heinz III Professor of Environmental Engineering; Professor and Associate Department Head for Graduate Affairs of Engineering and Public Policy; and Professor of Civil and Environmental Engineering; Ph.D., Michigan. Environmental policy and decision support, modeling sustainability, water and air quality, statistical analysis and uncertainty, carbon sequestration monitoring and risk.

Sarosh N. Talukdar, Professor Emeritus of Electrical and Computer Engineering and of Engineering and Public Policy; Ph.D., Purdue. Electrical power systems, autonomous agents, distributed control, market design.

Joel A. Tarr, Richard S. Caliguiri University Professor of History and Policy; Professor of History, Engineering and Public Policy, and the Heinz College; Ph.D.; Northwestern. Development of the urban infrastructure, urban technology, environmental trends, problems, and regulatory policies.

Francisco Veloso, Professor of Engineering and Public Policy; Ph.D., MIT. Technology policy and management, supply chain decisions, innovation and entrepreneurship, automotive industry.

Jay Whitacre, Assistant Professor of Materials Science and Engineering and of Engineering and Public Policy; Ph.D., Michigan. Sustainable energy solutions with a focus on both materials and policy issues surrounding energy generation and storage technology.

Robert White, Professor Emeritus of Electrical and Computer Engineering and of Engineering and Public Policy; Ph.D., Stanford. Technology Policy.

Additional information on this list of faculty members, as well as adjunct and other faculty members, can be found on the Department Web site at http://www.epp.cmu.edu/.

WENTWORTH INSTITUTE OF TECHNOLOGY

Master of Science in Construction Management

Programs of Study	Wentworth Institute of Technology offers a Master of Science in Construction Management (MSCM) through the Institute's College of Architecture, Design, and Construction Management in collaboration with the College of Professional and Continuing Education. This professional master's degree program is designed to educate construction professionals in advanced management principles and in construction management issues, topics, practices, and research. Graduates of the program are prepared to assume advanced managerial and leadership positions in construction-related careers.
	The completion of the 30-credit or 36-credit program (including a 6-credit optional thesis) is required for the master's degree. This program is a part-time, evening program (6 credits per semester). The courses are taught in a hybrid model (some course work completed face-to-face, and other course work completed online).
	The MSCM program examines general management principles and practices. The program explores advanced construction management issues specific to the built environment, and it uses a combination of technologies and team instruction as well as leading academic and industry experts in the delivery of this unique program. Students are exposed to research methodologies and creative problem solving, and they are encouraged to publish their scholarly works in relevant journals.
	Wentworth's MSCM program is noted for the close interaction and valuable insights its students gain from industry professionals. The students are exposed to leaders in the field by partnering faculty members with industry experts in the classroom, which brings real-world case studies into the classroom.
Research Facilities	The Alumni Library, with over 75,000 volumes, supports the Wentworth community in teaching, learning, and scholarship by providing resources and services that anticipate and respond to changing information and research needs. As part of the consortium Fenway Libraries Online (FLO), Wentworth has access to the New England Library Information Network (NELINET), a regional member of OCLC, an international bibliographic service which is shared by about 60,000 libraries in 96 countries around the world, and a member of the cataloguing services of the Library of Congress.
	Wentworth distributes laptops to all students and faculty members to promote digital learning and to support instruction. Laptops include high-end software that is customized for the MSCM program.
Financial Aid	Financial aid is available to MSCM students in the form of loans. If students are interested in pursuing financial aid they should submit the Free Application for Federal Student Aid (FAFSA) form online at www.fafsa.ed.gov.
Cost of Study	Tuition for 2011–12 is $1130 per credit hour. This tuition cost includes a laptop with industry-specific software and all textbooks.
Living and Housing Costs	On-campus housing is not available to students. Students seeking off-campus housing options should contact Wentworth's Office of Housing and Residential Life at 617-989-4160 for information on housing in the Boston area.
Student Group	More than 3,800 students (3,285 full-time undergraduates) from 33 states and 46 countries attend Wentworth. The College of Professional and Continuing Education serves over 1,000 students in degree programs, graduate and professional certificates, and a number of corporate and workforce training programs.
Student Outcomes	The MSCM program enrolled its first class in the fall of 2010. Currently enrolled students average fifteen years in the construction industry and hold careers as project managers, senior project managers, and business owners.
Location	Wentworth Institute of Technology is located in Boston, Massachusetts. The city offers students many different cultural, entertainment, and educational options. Wentworth is conveniently located around the Massachusetts Bay Transit Authority (MBTA or "the T"), which allows students to easily access public transportation.
The Institute	Founded in 1904, Wentworth Institute of Technology is an independent, coeducational, nationally ranked institution offering career-focused education through eighteen bachelor degree programs in areas such as architecture, computer science, construction management, design, engineering, engineering technology, and management. In addition, Wentworth offers master's degrees in architecture and construction management. For over a century, Wentworth has been a leader in higher education, as it is known for its academic excellence, community service, and support for the economic growth of the region. The Institute is distinguished by its high-quality classroom instruction and its practical application of technology through extensive laboratory and studio training. This curriculum is combined with on-the-job experience received through Wentworth's cooperative education program (co-op); being one of the most comprehensive of its kind in the nation. Located in the heart of Boston, the 31-acre campus provides an intimate and supportive learning environment, offering both academic and residential facilities with four separate colleges housing more than fifteen departments.
Applying	The admissions process is administered on a rolling basis. An admissions decision will be rendered by the Director of the MSCM program once all application materials are received. Applicants must submit the online application (www.wit.edu/apply), a current resume demonstrating at least one year of construction management experience, two letters of recommendation from their current or prior supervisors, and undergraduate transcripts from all colleges attended.
	Applicants who have not completed a bachelor's degree in Construction Management at an ACCE-accredited program must also demonstrate proficiency in the following content areas, as they are the prerequisite requirements: general business management, accounting, construction project management, construction estimating, and construction scheduling.
	Applicants can demonstrate proficiency by submitting a petition for prior learning assessment, or by taking additional course work in these specific content areas.
	Questions about the prerequisite requirements can be directed to the Director of the MSCM program (see below).
	Questions about the application process can be directed to the admissions counselors within the College of Professional and Continuing Education (see below).

Correspondence and Information

College of Professional and Continuing Education
Larry Carr, Dean, College of Professional and Continuing
  Education
Wentworth Institute of Technology
550 Huntington Avenue
Boston, Massachusetts 02115
Phone: 617-989-4300
Fax: 617-989-4399
E-mail: CPCE@wit.edu
Web site: http://www.wit.edu/continuinged

College of Architecture, Design, and Construction
Management
Glenn Wiggins, Dean College of Architecture, Design, and
  Construction Management
Carl Sciple, Director, M.S. in Construction Management
Wentworth Institute of Technology
550 Huntington Avenue
Boston, Massachusetts 02115
Phone: 617-989-4817
Fax: 617-989-4399
E-mail: sciplec@wit.edu
Web site: http://www.wit.edu/mscm

Wentworth Institute of Technology

THE FACULTY

Joshua Anderson, M.S.
Michael Dunlop, Assistant Professor; Ed.D.
Ronald E. Fionte, M.B.A.
Mark H. Hasso, Professor; Ph.D., PE
Mary Kaitlin McSally, Esq., J.D.,
Thom L. Neff, Ph.D.
Hossein Noorian, M.B.A.
Cathy Shanks, Esq., J.D.,
Cindy Stevens, Associate Professor; Ph.D.

Section 16
Materials Sciences and Engineering

This section contains a directory of institutions offering graduate work in materials sciences and engineering, followed by an in-depth entry submitted by an institution that chose to prepare a detailed program description. Additional information about programs listed in the directory but not augmented by an in-depth entry may be obtained by writing directly to the dean of a graduate school or chair of a department at the address given in the directory.

For programs offering related work, see also in this book *Agricultural Engineering and Bioengineering, Biomedical Engineering and Biotechnology, Engineering and Applied Sciences,* and *Geological, Mineral/Mining, and Petroleum Engineering.* In another guide in this series:

Graduate Programs in the Physical Sciences, Mathematics, Agricultural Sciences, the Environment & Natural Resources

See *Chemistry and Geosciences*

CONTENTS

Program Directories

Close-Ups and Displays

See also:

Ceramic Sciences and Engineering

Alfred University, Graduate School, New York State College of Ceramics, School of Engineering, Alfred, NY 14802-1205. Offers biomedical materials engineering science (MS); ceramic engineering (MS); ceramics (PhD); electrical engineering (MS); glass science (MS, PhD); materials science and engineering (MS, PhD); mechanical engineering (MS). *Degree requirements:* For master's, thesis; for doctorate, thesis/dissertation. *Entrance requirements:* Additional exam requirements/recommendations for international students: Required—TOEFL (minimum score 590 paper-based; 243 computer-based). Electronic applications accepted. *Expenses:* Contact institution. *Faculty research:* Fine-particle technology, x-ray diffraction, superconductivity, electronic materials.

Missouri University of Science and Technology, Graduate School, Department of Materials Science and Engineering, Rolla, MO 65409. Offers ceramic engineering (MS, DE, PhD); metallurgical engineering (MS, PhD). *Degree requirements:* For master's, thesis optional; for doctorate, comprehensive exam. *Entrance requirements:* For master's, GRE (minimum combined score 1100, 600 verbal, 3.5 writing); for doctorate, GRE (minimum score: quantitative 600, writing 3.5). Additional exam requirements/recommendations for international students: Required—TOEFL (minimum score 570 paper-based; 230 computer-based).

Rensselaer Polytechnic Institute, Graduate School, School of Engineering, Program in Materials Science and Engineering, Troy, NY 12180. Offers ceramics and glass science (M Eng, MS, PhD); composites (M Eng, MS, PhD); electronic materials (M Eng, MS, PhD); metallurgy (M Eng, MS, PhD); polymers (M Eng, MS, PhD). Part-time programs available. *Faculty:* 16 full-time (2 women). *Students:* 57 full-time (13 women), 6 part-time (1 woman), 37 international. Average age 24. 304 applicants, 15% accepted, 16 enrolled. In 2010, 5 master's, 6 doctorates awarded. Terminal master's awarded for partial completion of doctoral program. *Degree requirements:* For master's, thesis; for doctorate, comprehensive exam, thesis/ dissertation. *Entrance requirements:* For master's and doctorate, GRE. Additional exam requirements/recommendations for international students: Required—TOEFL (minimum score 570 paper-based; 230 computer-based; 100 iBT). *Application deadline:* For fall admission, 1/15 priority date for domestic and international students; for spring admission, 8/31 priority date for domestic and international students. Applications are processed on a rolling basis. Application fee: $75. Electronic applications accepted. *Expenses:* Tuition: Full-time $39,600; part-time $1650 per credit. Required fees: $1896. *Financial support:* In 2010–11, 56 students received support, including 2 fellowships with full tuition reimbursements available (averaging $26,250 per year), 41 research assistantships with full tuition reimbursements available (averaging $26,250 per year), 13 teaching assistantships with full tuition reimbursements available (averaging $17,500 per year); career-related internships or fieldwork, institutionally sponsored loans, and unspecified assistantships also available. Financial award application deadline: 2/1. *Faculty research:* Materials processing, nanostructural materials, materials for microelectronics, composite materials, computational materials. Total annual research expenditures: $3.6 million. *Unit head:* Dr. Robert Hull, Department Head, 518-276-6373, Fax: 518-276-8554, E-mail: hullr2@rpi.edu. *Application contact:* Dr. Pawel Keblinski, Admissions Coordinator, 518-276-6858, Fax: 518-276-8554, E-mail: keblip@rpi.edu.

University of Cincinnati, Graduate School, College of Engineering, Department of Chemical and Materials Engineering, Program in Materials Science and Metallurgical Engineering, Cincinnati, OH 45221. Offers ceramic science and engineering (MS, PhD); materials science and engineering (MS, PhD); metallurgical engineering (MS, PhD); polymer science and engineering (MS, PhD). Evening/weekend programs available. *Degree requirements:* For master's, thesis optional; for doctorate, one foreign language, comprehensive exam, thesis/ dissertation, oral English proficiency exam. *Entrance requirements:* For master's and doctorate, GRE General Test, BS in related field, minimum undergraduate GPA of 3.0. Additional exam requirements/recommendations for international students: Required—TOEFL (minimum score 550 paper-based; 213 computer-based). Electronic applications accepted. *Expenses:* Contact institution.

University of Washington, Graduate School, College of Engineering, Department of Materials Science and Engineering, Seattle, WA 98195-2120. Offers ceramic engineering (PhD); materials science and engineering (MS, MSE, PhD); materials science and engineering and nanotechnology (PhD). Part-time programs available. *Faculty:* 24 full-time (4 women). *Students:* 55 full-time (14 women), 9 part-time (2 women); includes 2 Black or African American, non-Hispanic/Latino; 7 Asian, non-Hispanic/Latino; 2 Hispanic/Latino, 22 international. Average age 30. 246 applicants, 11% accepted, 11 enrolled. In 2010, 3 master's, 9 doctorates awarded. *Degree requirements:* For master's, comprehensive exam, thesis optional; for doctorate, comprehensive exam, thesis/dissertation, Qualifying evaluation, general and final exams. *Entrance requirements:* For master's and doctorate, GRE General Test, minimum GPA of 3.0. Additional exam requirements/ recommendations for international students: Required—TOEFL (minimum score 580 paper-based; 237 computer-based; 92 iBT); Recommended—IELTS (minimum score 7). *Application deadline:* For fall admission, 1/15 priority date for domestic students, 12/15 priority date for international students. Application fee: $75. Electronic applications accepted. *Financial support:* In 2010–11, 3 students received support, including 7 fellowships with full tuition reimbursements available (averaging $22,500 per year), 39 research assistantships with full tuition reimbursements available (averaging $16,407 per year), 8 teaching assistantships with full tuition reimbursements available (averaging $16,362 per year); career-related internships or fieldwork, Federal Work-Study, institutionally sponsored loans, scholarships/grants, health care benefits, unspecified assistantships, and stipend supplements also available. Financial award application deadline: 1/15; financial award applicants required to submit FAFSA. *Faculty research:* Biomimetics and biomaterials; electronic, optical and magnetic materials; eco-materials and materials for energy applications; ceramics, metals, composites, and polymers. Total annual research expenditures: $8.8 million. *Unit head:* Dr. Alex Jen, Professor and Chair, 206-543-2600, Fax: 206-543-3100, E-mail: ajen@uw.edu. *Application contact:* Kathleen A. Elkins, Academic Counselor, 206-616-6581, Fax: 206-543-3100, E-mail: kelkins@uw.edu.

Electronic Materials

Colorado School of Mines, Graduate School, Department of Metallurgical and Materials Engineering, Golden, CO 80401. Offers materials science (MS, PhD); metallurgical and materials engineering (ME, MS, PhD). Part-time programs available. *Faculty:* 35 full-time (3 women), 5 part-time/adjunct (0 women). *Students:* 65 full-time (16 women), 5 part-time (1 woman); includes 2 American Indian or Alaska Native, non-Hispanic/Latino; 1 Asian, non-Hispanic/ Latino; 2 Hispanic/Latino; 1 Two or more races, non-Hispanic/Latino, 18 international. Average age 30. 95 applicants, 36% accepted, 28 enrolled. In 2010, 12 master's, 6 doctorates awarded. *Degree requirements:* For master's, thesis (for some programs); for doctorate, comprehensive exam, thesis/dissertation. *Entrance requirements:* For master's and doctorate, GRE General Test. Additional exam requirements/recommendations for international students: Required—TOEFL (minimum score 550 paper-based; 213 computer-based; 80 iBT). *Application deadline:* For fall admission, 1/15 priority date for domestic and international students; for spring admission, 10/15 priority date for domestic and international students. Application fee: $50 ($70 for international students). Electronic applications accepted. *Expenses:* Tuition: state resident: full-time $11,550; part-time $641 per credit. Tuition, nonresident: full-time $25,980; part-time $1444 per credit. Required fees: $1874; $937 per semester. *Financial support:* In 2010–11, 53 students received support, including 6 fellowships with full tuition reimbursements available (averaging $20,000 per year), 44 research assistantships with full tuition reimbursements available (averaging $20,000 per year), 3 teaching assistantships with full tuition reimbursements available (averaging $20,000 per year); scholarships/grants, health care benefits, and unspecified assistantships also available. Financial award application deadline: 1/15; financial award applicants required to submit FAFSA. Total annual research expenditures: $6.3 million. *Unit head:* Dr. Michael Kaufman, Interim Department Head, 303-273-3009, Fax: 303-273-3795, E-mail: mkaufman@mines.edu. *Application contact:* Susan Ballantype, Program Assistant, 303-273-3660, Fax: 303-273-3795, E-mail: susan.ballantyne@is.mines.edu.

Massachusetts Institute of Technology, School of Engineering, Department of Materials Science and Engineering, Cambridge, MA 02139. Offers archaeological materials (PhD, Sc D); bio- and polymeric materials (PhD, Sc D); electronic, photonic and magnetic materials (PhD, Sc D); emerging, fundamental and computational studies in materials science (Sc D); emerging, fundamental, and computational studies in materials science (PhD); materials engineering (Mat E); materials science and engineering (M Eng, SM, PhD, Sc D); metallurgical engineering (Met E); structural and environmental materials (PhD, Sc D); SM/MBA. *Faculty:* 34 full-time (8 women). *Students:* 196 full-time (52 women); includes 32 minority (2 Black or African American, non-Hispanic/Latino; 20 Asian, non-Hispanic/Latino; 7 Hispanic/Latino; 3 Two or more races, non-Hispanic/Latino), 113 international. Average age 26. 507 applicants, 15% accepted, 41 enrolled. In 2010, 22 master's, 38 doctorates awarded. Terminal master's awarded for partial completion of doctoral program. *Degree requirements:* For master's and other advanced degree, thesis; for doctorate, comprehensive exam, thesis/dissertation. *Entrance requirements:* For master's, doctorate, and other advanced degree, GRE General Test. Additional exam requirements/recommendations for international students: Required—IELTS (minimum score 7). *Application deadline:* For fall admission, 12/15 for domestic and international students. Application fee: $75. Electronic applications accepted. *Expenses:* Tuition: Full-time $38,940; part-time $605 per unit. Required fees: $272.. *Financial support:* In 2010–11, 183 students received support, including 52 fellowships with tuition reimbursements available (averaging $32,695 per year), 124 research assistantships with tuition reimbursements available (averaging $27,409 per year), 8 teaching assistantships with tuition reimbursements available (averaging $31,861 per year); career-related internships or fieldwork, Federal Work-Study, institutionally sponsored loans, scholarships/grants, health care benefits, and unspecified assistantships also available. *Faculty research:* Thermodynamics and kinetics of phase transformations; structure of all materials classes: metals, ceramics, semiconductors, polymers, biomaterials; influence of processing on materials structure; structure ??? property relationships (electrical, magnetic, optical, mechanical); materials in extreme environments. Total annual research expenditures: $28.1 million. *Unit head:* Prof. Edwin L. Thomas, Department Head, 617-253-3300, Fax: 617-252-1775. *Application contact:* Angelita Mireles, Graduate Admissions, 617-253-3302, E-mail: dmse-admissions@mit.edu.

Northwestern University, McCormick School of Engineering and Applied Science, Department of Electrical Engineering and Computer Science and Department of Materials Science and Engineering, Program in Electronic Materials, Evanston, IL 60208. Offers MS, PhD, Certificate. Part-time programs available. *Faculty:* 11 full-time (1 woman). Terminal master's awarded for partial completion of doctoral program. *Degree requirements:* For master's, thesis; for doctorate, comprehensive exam, thesis/dissertation. *Financial support:* Fellowships with tuition reimbursements, research assistantships with tuition reimbursements, teaching assistantships with tuition reimbursements available. *Faculty research:* Electronic optical magnetic materials and devices. Total annual research expenditures: $5.8 million. *Unit head:* Prof. Bruce W. Wessels, Director, 847-491-3219, Fax: 847-491-7820, E-mail: b-wessels@northwestern.edu. *Application contact:* Allen Taflove, Admission Officer, 847-491-4127, Fax: 847-491-4455, E-mail: taflove@ece.northwestern.edu.

Princeton University, Princeton Institute for the Science and Technology of Materials (PRISM), Princeton, NJ 08544-1019. Offers materials (PhD).

University of Arkansas, Graduate School, Interdisciplinary Program in Microelectronics and Photonics, Fayetteville, AR 72701-1201. Offers MS, PhD. *Students:* 7 full-time (2 women), 44 part-time (4 women); includes 8 minority (6 Black or African American, non-Hispanic/Latino; 2 Asian, non-Hispanic/Latino), 17 international. 10 applicants, 100% accepted. In 2010, 4 master's, 2 doctorates awarded. *Degree requirements:* For doctorate, thesis/dissertation. *Application deadline:* For fall admission, 4/1 for international students; for spring admission, 10/1 for international students. Applications are processed on a rolling basis. Application fee: $40 ($50 for international students). Electronic applications accepted. *Financial support:* In 2010–11, 5 fellowships with tuition reimbursements, 17 research assistantships, 3 teaching assistantships were awarded. Financial award application deadline: 4/1; financial award applicants required to submit FAFSA. *Unit head:* Dr. Ken Vickers, Head, 479-575-2875, Fax: 479-575-4580, E-mail: vickers@uark.edu. *Application contact:* Graduate Admissions, 479-575-6246, Fax: 479-575-5908, E-mail: gradinfo@uark.edu.

Materials Engineering

Arizona State University, Ira A. Fulton School of Engineering, Department of Mechanical and Aerospace Engineering, Tempe, AZ 85281. Offers aerospace engineering (MS, MSE, PhD); chemical engineering (MS, MSE, PhD); materials science and engineering (MS, PhD); mechanical engineering (MS, MSE, PhD). Part-time and evening/weekend programs available. Postbaccalaureate distance learning degree programs offered (minimal on-campus study). *Faculty:* 50 full-time (10 women), 13 part-time/adjunct (3 women). *Students:* 258 full-time (47 women), 114 part-time (29 women); includes 48 minority (3 Black or African American, non-Hispanic/Latino; 2 American Indian or Alaska Native, non-Hispanic/Latino; 15 Asian, non-Hispanic/Latino; 27 Hispanic/Latino; 1 Two or more races, non-Hispanic/Latino), 164 international. Average age 28. 721 applicants, 58% accepted, 119 enrolled. In 2010, 55 master's, 29 doctorates awarded. Terminal master's awarded for partial completion of doctoral program. *Degree requirements:* For master's, thesis and oral defense (MS); applied project or comprehensive exam (MSE); interactive Program of Study (iPOS) submitted before completing 50 percent of required credit hours; for doctorate, comprehensive exam, thesis/dissertation, interactive Program of Study (iPOS) submitted before completing 50 percent of required credit hours. *Entrance requirements:* For master's, GRE, minimum GPA of 3.0 or equivalent in last 2 years of work leading to bachelor's degree; for doctorate, GRE, minimum GPA of 3.0 in last 2 years of work leading to bachelor's degree. Additional exam requirements/recommendations for international students: Required—TOEFL, IELTS, or Pearson Test of English. *Application deadline:* For fall admission, 1/31 for domestic and international students; for spring admission, 7/1 for domestic and international students. Application fee: $70 ($90 for international students). Electronic applications accepted. *Expenses:* Contact institution. *Financial support:* In 2010–11, 120 research assistantships with partial tuition reimbursements (averaging $15,353 per year), 34 teaching assistantships with partial tuition reimbursements (averaging $13,861 per year) were awarded; fellowships with full and partial tuition reimbursements, institutionally sponsored loans, scholarships/grants, and tuition waivers (full and partial) also available. Financial award application deadline: 3/1; financial award applicants required to submit FAFSA. *Faculty research:* Electronic materials and packaging, materials for energy (batteries), adaptive/intelligent materials and structures, multiscale fluid mechanics, membranes, therapeutics and bioseparations, flexible structures, nanostructured materials, and micro/nano transport. Total annual research expenditures: $17.5 million. *Unit head:* Dr. Kyle D. Squires, Director, 480-965-3957, E-mail: squires@asu.edu. *Application contact:* Graduate Admissions, 480-965-6113.

Auburn University, Graduate School, Ginn College of Engineering, Department of Mechanical Engineering, Program in Materials Engineering, Auburn University, AL 36849. Offers M Mtl E, MS, PhD. *Faculty:* 29 full-time (0 women), 2 part-time/adjunct (0 women). *Students:* 16 full-time (6 women), 33 part-time (8 women); includes 1 Black or African American, non-Hispanic/Latino, 33 international. Average age 31. 62 applicants, 15% accepted, 5 enrolled. In 2010, 5 master's, 6 doctorates awarded. *Degree requirements:* For master's, thesis (MS), oral exam; for doctorate, one foreign language, thesis/dissertation. *Entrance requirements:* For master's and doctorate, GRE General Test. *Application deadline:* For fall admission, 7/7 for domestic students; for spring admission, 11/24 for domestic students. Applications are processed on a rolling basis. Application fee: $50 ($60 for international students). Electronic applications accepted. *Expenses:* Tuition, state resident: full-time $7002. Tuition, nonresident: full-time $21,898. International tuition: $22,116 full-time. Required fees: $892. Tuition and fees vary according to course load and program. *Financial support:* Fellowships, research assistantships, teaching assistantships, Federal Work-Study available. Support available to part-time students. Financial award application deadline: 3/15; financial award applicants required to submit FAFSA. *Faculty research:* Smart materials. *Unit head:* Dr. Bryan Chin, Head, 334-844-3322. *Application contact:* Dr. George Flowers, Dean of the Graduate School, 334-844-2125.

Boise State University, Graduate College, College of Engineering, Department of Materials Science and Engineering, Boise, ID 83725-0399. Offers M Engr, MS.

Boston University, College of Engineering, Division of Materials Science and Engineering, Boston, MA 02215. Offers M Eng, MS, PhD. Part-time programs available. *Students:* 33 full-time (8 women), 1 (woman) part-time; includes 4 minority (3 Asian, non-Hispanic/Latino; 1 Hispanic/Latino), 17 international. Average age 26. 92 applicants, 26% accepted, 13 enrolled. In 2010, 1 master's, 3 doctorates awarded. Terminal master's awarded for partial completion of doctoral program. *Degree requirements:* For master's, thesis (for some programs); for doctorate, comprehensive exam, thesis/dissertation. *Entrance requirements:* For master's and doctorate, GRE General Test. Additional exam requirements/recommendations for international students: Required—TOEFL (minimum score 550 paper-based; 213 computer-based; 84 iBT), IELTS (minimum score 6). *Application deadline:* For fall admission, 4/1 for domestic and international students; for spring admission, 10/1 for domestic and international students. Applications are processed on a rolling basis. Application fee: $70. Electronic applications accepted. *Expenses:* Tuition: Full-time $39,314; part-time $1228 per credit. Required fees: $40 per semester. *Financial support:* In 2010–11, 23 students received support, including 2 fellowships with full tuition reimbursements available (averaging $28,200 per year), 15 research assistantships with full tuition reimbursements available (averaging $18,800 per year), 4 teaching assistantships with full tuition reimbursements available (averaging $18,800 per year); career-related internships or fieldwork, Federal Work-Study, institutionally sponsored loans, scholarships/grants, traineeships, and health care benefits also available. Financial award application deadline: 1/15; financial award applicants required to submit FAFSA. *Faculty research:* Biomaterials; electronic and photonic materials; materials for energy and environment; nanomaterials. *Unit head:* Dr. Uday Pal, Division Head, 617-353-7708, Fax: 617-353-5548, E-mail: upal@bu.edu. *Application contact:* Stephen Doherty, Director of Graduate Programs, 617-353-9760, Fax: 617-353-0259, E-mail: enggrad@bu.edu.

California State University, Northridge, Graduate Studies, College of Engineering and Computer Science, Department of Manufacturing Systems Engineering and Management, Northridge, CA 91330. Offers engineering automation (MS); engineering management (MS); manufacturing systems engineering (MS); materials engineering (MS). Postbaccalaureate distance learning degree programs offered. *Entrance requirements:* For master's, GRE (if cumulative undergraduate GPA less than 3.0).

Carleton University, Faculty of Graduate Studies, Faculty of Engineering and Design, Department of Mechanical and Aerospace Engineering, Ottawa, ON K1S 5B6, Canada. Offers aerospace engineering (M Eng, MA Sc, PhD); materials engineering (M Eng, MA Sc); mechanical engineering (M Eng, MA Sc, PhD). *Degree requirements:* For master's, thesis optional; for doctorate, thesis/dissertation. *Entrance requirements:* For master's, honors degree; for doctorate, MA Sc or M Eng. Additional exam requirements/recommendations for international students: Required—TOEFL. *Faculty research:* Thermal fluids engineering, heat transfer, vehicle engineering.

Carnegie Mellon University, Carnegie Institute of Technology, Department of Materials Science and Engineering, Pittsburgh, PA 15213-3891. Offers MS, PhD. Part-time programs available. Terminal master's awarded for partial completion of doctoral program. *Degree requirements:* For master's, exam; for doctorate, thesis/dissertation, qualifying exam. *Entrance requirements:* For master's and doctorate, GRE General Test. Additional exam requirements/recommendations for international students: Required—TOEFL. *Faculty research:* Materials characterization, process metallurgy, high strength alloys, growth kinetics, ceramics.

Case Western Reserve University, School of Graduate Studies, Case School of Engineering, Department of Materials Science and Engineering, Cleveland, OH 44106. Offers materials science and engineering (MS, PhD). Part-time programs available. Postbaccalaureate distance learning degree programs offered (no on-campus study). *Faculty:* 11 full-time (0 women). *Students:* 45 full-time (11 women), 3 part-time (1 woman); includes 1 Asian, non-Hispanic/Latino, 39 international. In 2010, 3 master's, 9 doctorates awarded. Terminal master's awarded for partial completion of doctoral program. *Degree requirements:* For master's, thesis (for

some programs); for doctorate, thesis/dissertation, qualifying exam, teaching experience. *Entrance requirements:* For master's and doctorate, GRE General Test. Additional exam requirements/recommendations for international students: Required—TOEFL. *Application deadline:* For fall admission, 2/15 priority date for domestic students; for spring admission, 9/15 for domestic students. Applications are processed on a rolling basis. Application fee: $50. *Financial support:* Fellowships with full and partial tuition reimbursements, research assistantships with full and partial tuition reimbursements, teaching assistantships available. Financial award application deadline: 4/30; financial award applicants required to submit FAFSA. *Faculty research:* Surface hardening of steels and other alloys, chemistry and structure of surfaces, microstructural and mechanical property characterization, materials for energy applications, thermodynamics and kinetics of materials, performance and reliability of materials. Total annual research expenditures: $3.6 million. *Unit head:* Dr. James D. McGuffin-Cawley, Department Chair, 216-368-6482, Fax: 216-368-4224, E-mail: emse.info@case.edu. *Application contact:* Theresa Claytor, Student Affairs Coordinator, 216-368-8555, Fax: 216-368-8555, E-mail: esme.info@case.edu.

The Catholic University of America, School of Engineering, Department of Materials Science and Engineering, Washington, DC 20064. Offers MS. Part-time programs available. *Students:* 1 full-time. Average age 31. 6 applicants, 33% accepted, 1 enrolled. *Degree requirements:* For master's, thesis optional. *Entrance requirements:* For master's, GRE (minimum score 1250), minimum GPA of 3.0, statement of purpose, official copies of academic transcripts. Additional exam requirements/recommendations for international students: Required—TOEFL (minimum score 580 paper-based; 237 computer-based). *Application deadline:* For fall admission, 8/1 for domestic students, 7/15 for international students; for spring admission, 12/1 for domestic students, 10/15 for international students. Applications are processed on a rolling basis. Application fee: $55. Electronic applications accepted. *Expenses:* Tuition: Full-time $33,580; part-time $1315 per credit hour. Required fees: $80; $40 per semester hour. One-time fee: $425. *Financial support:* Fellowships, research assistantships, teaching assistantships, Federal Work-Study, scholarships/grants, tuition waivers (full and partial), and unspecified assistantships available. Financial award application deadline: 2/1; financial award applicants required to submit FAFSA. *Unit head:* Dr. Biprodas Dutta, Director, 202-319-5535, Fax: 202-319-4469, E-mail: duttab@cua.edu. *Application contact:* Andrew Woodall, Director of Graduate Admissions, 202-319-5057, Fax: 202-319-6533, E-mail: cua-admissions@cua.edu.

Clemson University, Graduate School, College of Engineering and Science, School of Materials Science and Engineering, Clemson, SC 29634. Offers MS, PhD. Part-time programs available. *Faculty:* 14 full-time (2 women), 6 part-time/adjunct (0 women). *Students:* 59 full-time (22 women), 1 part-time (0 women); includes 1 Black or African American, non-Hispanic/Latino, 33 international. Average age 27. 130 applicants, 45% accepted, 20 enrolled. In 2010, 11 master's, 8 doctorates awarded. Terminal master's awarded for partial completion of doctoral program. *Degree requirements:* For master's, thesis; for doctorate, comprehensive exam, thesis/dissertation. *Entrance requirements:* For master's and doctorate, GRE General Test. Additional exam requirements/recommendations for international students: Required—TOEFL. *Application deadline:* For fall admission, 2/1 for domestic students; for spring admission, 9/1 for domestic students. Applications are processed on a rolling basis. Application fee: $70 ($80 for international students). Electronic applications accepted. *Expenses:* Tuition, state resident: full-time $6492; part-time $400 per credit hour. Tuition, nonresident: full-time $13,634; part-time $800 per credit hour. Required fees: $262 per semester. Part-time tuition and fees vary according to course load and program. *Financial support:* In 2010–11, 52 students received support, including 2 fellowships with full and partial tuition reimbursements available (averaging $10,500 per year), 43 research assistantships with partial tuition reimbursements available (averaging $17,275 per year), 15 teaching assistantships with partial tuition reimbursements available (averaging $12,600 per year); career-related internships or fieldwork, institutionally sponsored loans, scholarships/grants, health care benefits, and unspecified assistantships also available. Support available to part-time students. Financial award applicants required to submit FAFSA. Total annual research expenditures: $2.5 million. *Unit head:* Dr. Kathleen Richardson, Chair and Director of the School of Materials Science and Engineering, 864-656-3311, Fax: 864-656-5973, E-mail: richar3@clemson.edu. *Application contact:* Dr. Gary C. Lickfield, Graduate Program Coordinator, 864-656-5964, Fax: 864-656-5973, E-mail: lgary@clemson.edu.

Colorado School of Mines, Graduate School, Department of Metallurgical and Materials Engineering, Golden, CO 80401. Offers materials science (MS, PhD); metallurgical and materials engineering (ME, MS, PhD). Part-time programs available. *Faculty:* 35 full-time (3 women), 5 part-time/adjunct (0 women). *Students:* 65 full-time (16 women), 5 part-time (1 woman); includes 2 American Indian or Alaska Native, non-Hispanic/Latino; 1 Asian, non-Hispanic/Latino; 2 Hispanic/Latino; 1 Two or more races, non-Hispanic/Latino, 18 international. Average age 30. 95 applicants, 36% accepted, 28 enrolled. In 2010, 12 master's, 6 doctorates awarded. *Degree requirements:* For master's, thesis (for some programs); for doctorate, comprehensive exam, thesis/dissertation. *Entrance requirements:* For master's and doctorate, GRE General Test. Additional exam requirements/recommendations for international students: Required—TOEFL (minimum score 550 paper-based; 213 computer-based; 80 iBT). *Application deadline:* For fall admission, 1/15 priority date for domestic and international students; for spring admission, 10/15 priority date for domestic and international students. Application fee: $50 ($70 for international students). Electronic applications accepted. *Expenses:* Tuition, state resident: full-time $11,550; part-time $641 per credit. Tuition, nonresident: full-time $25,980; part-time $1444 per credit. Required fees: $1874; $937 per semester. *Financial support:* In 2010–11, 53 students received support, including 6 fellowships with full tuition reimbursements available (averaging $20,000 per year), 44 research assistantships with full tuition reimbursements available (averaging $20,000 per year), 3 teaching assistantships with full tuition reimbursements available (averaging $20,000 per year); scholarships/grants, health care benefits, and unspecified assistantships also available. Financial award application deadline: 1/15; financial award applicants required to submit FAFSA. Total annual research expenditures: $6.3 million. *Unit head:* Dr. Michael Kaufman, Interim Department Head, 303-273-3009, Fax: 303-273-3795, E-mail: mkaufman@mines.edu. *Application contact:* Susan Ballantype, Program Assistant, 303-273-3660, Fax: 303-273-3795, E-mail: susan.ballantyne@is.mines.edu.

Columbia University, Fu Foundation School of Engineering and Applied Science, Department of Applied Physics and Applied Mathematics, New York, NY 10027. Offers applied physics (Eng Sc D); applied physics and applied mathematics (MS, PhD, Engr); materials science and engineering (MS, Eng Sc D, PhD); medical physics (MS). Part-time programs available. Postbaccalaureate distance learning degree programs offered (no on-campus study). *Faculty:* 32 full-time (2 women), 23 part-time/adjunct (2 women). *Students:* 126 full-time (28 women), 23 part-time (5 women); includes 14 minority (2 Black or African American, non-Hispanic/Latino; 8 Asian, non-Hispanic/Latino; 1 Hispanic/Latino; 3 Two or more races, non-Hispanic/Latino), 60 international. Average age 28. 344 applicants, 22% accepted, 36 enrolled. In 2010, 56 master's, 13 doctorates awarded. Terminal master's awarded for partial completion of doctoral program. *Degree requirements:* For master's, comprehensive exam; for doctorate, thesis/dissertation, qualifying exam. *Entrance requirements:* For master's, GRE General Test, GRE Subject Test (strongly recommended); for doctorate, GRE General Test, GRE Subject Test (applied physics); for Engr, GRE General Test. Additional exam requirements/recommendations for international students: Required—TOEFL, IELTS. *Application deadline:* For fall admission, 12/1 priority date for domestic and international students; for spring admission, 10/1 priority date for domestic and international students. Application fee: $95. Electronic applications accepted. *Financial support:* In 2010–11, 73 students received support, including 3 fellowships with full tuition reimbursements available (averaging $30,000 per year), 53 research assistantships with full tuition reimbursements available (averaging $30,667 per year), 17 teaching assistantships with full tuition reimbursements available (averaging $30,667 per year). Financial award application deadline: 12/1; financial award applicants required to submit FAFSA. *Faculty research:* Plasma, solid state, optical and laser physics; atmospheric, oceanic and earth

Materials Engineering

Columbia University (continued)
physics; computational math and applied mathematics; materials science and engineering. *Unit head:* Dr. Irving P. Herman, Professor and Department Chairman, 212-854-4457, E-mail: seasinfo.apam@columbia.edu. *Application contact:* Montserrat Fernandez-Pinkley, Student Services Coordinator, 212-854-4457, Fax: 212-854-8257, E-mail: mf2157@columbia.edu.

Cornell University, Graduate School, Graduate Fields of Engineering, Field of Materials Science and Engineering, Ithaca, NY 14853. Offers materials engineering (M Eng, PhD); materials science (M Eng, PhD). *Faculty:* 45 full-time (5 women). *Students:* 75 full-time (25 women); includes 1 Black or African American, non-Hispanic/Latino; 11 Asian, non-Hispanic/Latino; 4 Hispanic/Latino, 37 international. Average age 26. 343 applicants, 23% accepted, 40 enrolled. In 2010, 20 master's, 9 doctorates awarded. *Degree requirements:* For doctorate, comprehensive exam, thesis/dissertation. *Entrance requirements:* For master's and doctorate, GRE General Test, 3 letters of recommendation. Additional exam requirements/recommendations for international students: Required—TOEFL (minimum score 550 paper-based; 213 computer-based; 77 iBT). *Application deadline:* For fall admission, 1/15 priority date for domestic students. Application fee: $70. Electronic applications accepted. *Expenses:* Tuition: Full-time $29,500. Required fees: $76. Tuition and fees vary according to degree level and program. *Financial support:* In 2010–11, 48 students received support, including 17 fellowships with full tuition reimbursements available, 30 research assistantships with full tuition reimbursements available, 7 teaching assistantships with full tuition reimbursements available; institutionally sponsored loans, scholarships/grants, health care benefits, tuition waivers (full and partial), and unspecified assistantships also available. Financial award applicants required to submit FAFSA. *Faculty research:* Ceramics, complex fluids, glass, metals, polymers semiconductors. *Unit head:* Director of Graduate Studies, 607-255-9159, Fax: 607-255-2365. *Application contact:* Graduate Field Assistant, 607-255-9159, Fax: 607-255-2365, E-mail: matsci@cornell.edu.

Dalhousie University, Faculty of Engineering, Department of Materials Engineering, Halifax, NS B3H 1Z1, Canada. Offers M Eng, MA Sc, PhD. *Degree requirements:* For master's, thesis; for doctorate, thesis/dissertation. *Entrance requirements:* Additional exam requirements/recommendations for international students: Required—TOEFL, IELTS, CANTEST, CAEL, or Michigan English Language Assessment Battery. Electronic applications accepted. *Faculty research:* Ceramic and metal matrix composites, electron microscopy, electrolysis in molten salt, fracture mechanics, electronic materials.

Dartmouth College, Thayer School of Engineering, Program in Materials Sciences and Engineering, Hanover, NH 03755. Offers MS, PhD. *Degree requirements:* For master's, thesis; for doctorate, thesis/dissertation, candidacy oral exam. *Entrance requirements:* For master's and doctorate, GRE General Test. *Application deadline:* For fall admission, 1/1 priority date for domestic students. Application fee: $45. *Financial support:* Fellowships, research assistantships, teaching assistantships, career-related internships or fieldwork, Federal Work-Study, institutionally sponsored loans, and tuition waivers (full and partial) available. Financial award application deadline: 1/15. *Faculty research:* Electronic and magnetic materials, microstructural evolution, biomaterials and nanostructures, laser-material interactions, nano composites. Total annual research expenditures: $2.2 million. *Unit head:* Dr. Joseph J. Helbie, Dean, 603-646-2238, Fax: 603-646-2580, E-mail: joseph.j.helbie@dartmouth.edu. *Application contact:* Candace S. Potter, Graduate Admissions Administrator, 603-646-3844, Fax: 603-646-1620, E-mail: candace.potter@dartmouth.edu.

Drexel University, College of Engineering, Department of Materials Engineering, Philadelphia, PA 19104-2875. Offers MS, PhD. Part-time and evening/weekend programs available. Terminal master's awarded for partial completion of doctoral program. *Degree requirements:* For master's, thesis or alternative; for doctorate, thesis/dissertation. *Entrance requirements:* For master's, minimum GPA of 3.0; for doctorate, minimum GPA of 3.0, MS. Additional exam requirements/recommendations for international students: Required—TOEFL. Electronic applications accepted. *Faculty research:* Composite science; polymer and biomedical engineering; solidification; near net shape processing, including powder metallurgy.

Duke University, Graduate School, Pratt School of Engineering, Master of Engineering Program, Durham, NC 27708-0271. Offers biomedical engineering (M Eng); civil engineering (M Eng); electrical and computer engineering (M Eng); environmental engineering (M Eng); materials science and engineering (M Eng); mechanical engineering (M Eng); photonics and optical sciences (M Eng). Part-time programs available. *Faculty:* 123 full-time, 1 part-time/adjunct. *Students:* 9 full-time (4 women); includes 2 minority (both Asian, non-Hispanic/Latino), 3 international. Average age 24. *Entrance requirements:* For master's, GRE General Test, resume, 3 letters of recommendation, statement of purpose. Additional exam requirements/recommendations for international students: Required—TOEFL. *Application deadline:* For fall admission, 6/15 for domestic students, 2/15 for international students; for spring admission, 11/1 for domestic students, 9/1 for international students. Application fee: $75. *Financial support:* Merit scholarships/grants available. *Unit head:* Dr. Bradley A. Fox, Executive Director, 919-660-5455, Fax: 919-660-5456. *Application contact:* Erin Degerman, Admissions Coordinator, 919-668-6789, Fax: 919-660-5456, E-mail: erin.degerman@duke.edu.

Florida International University, College of Engineering and Computing, Department of Mechanical and Materials Engineering, Materials Science and Engineering Program, Miami, FL 33175. Offers MS, PhD. Part-time and evening/weekend programs available. *Students:* 27 full-time (0 women), 17 part-time (1 woman); includes 1 Hispanic/Latino, 26 international. Average age 27. 136 applicants, 21% accepted, 22 enrolled. In 2010, 9 master's, 2 doctorates awarded. Terminal master's awarded for partial completion of doctoral program. *Degree requirements:* For master's, thesis or alternative; for doctorate, comprehensive exam, thesis/dissertation. *Entrance requirements:* For master's, GRE, 3 letters of recommendation, minimum undergraduate GPA of 3.0 in upper-level course work; for doctorate, GRE, minimum GPA of 3.0, 3 letters of recommendation, letter of intent. Additional exam requirements/recommendations for international students: Required—TOEFL (minimum score 550 paper-based; 80 iBT). *Application deadline:* For fall admission, 6/1 for domestic students, 4/1 for international students; for spring admission, 10/1 for domestic students, 9/1 for international students. Applications are processed on a rolling basis. Application fee: $30. Electronic applications accepted. *Financial support:* Institutionally sponsored loans, scholarships/grants, and unspecified assistantships available. Financial award application deadline: 3/1; financial award applicants required to submit FAFSA. *Unit head:* Dr. Cesar Levy, Chair, Mechanical and Materials Engineering Department, 305-348-1932, Fax: 305-348-1932, E-mail: cesar.levy@fiu.edu. *Application contact:* Maria Parrilla, Graduate Admissions Assistant, 305-348-1890, Fax: 305-348-6142, E-mail: grad_eng@fiu.edu.

Georgia Institute of Technology, Graduate Studies and Research, College of Engineering, School of Materials Science and Engineering, Atlanta, GA 30332-0001. Offers biomedical engineering (MS Bio E); materials science and engineering (MS, PhD); polymers (MS Poly). Terminal master's awarded for partial completion of doctoral program. *Degree requirements:* For master's, thesis (for some programs); for doctorate, comprehensive exam, thesis/dissertation. *Entrance requirements:* For master's and doctorate, GRE General Test. Additional exam requirements/recommendations for international students: Required—TOEFL (minimum score 620 paper-based; 260 computer-based). Electronic applications accepted. *Faculty research:* Nanomaterials, biomaterials, computational materials science, mechanical behavior, advanced engineering materials.

Illinois Institute of Technology, Graduate College, Armour College of Engineering, Department of Mechanical, Materials and Aerospace Engineering, Chicago, IL 60616-3793. Offers manufacturing engineering (MME, MS); materials science and engineering (MMME, MS, PhD); mechanical and aerospace engineering (MMAE, MS, PhD), including economics (MS), energy (MS), environment (MS). Part-time and evening/weekend programs available. Postbaccalaureate distance learning degree programs offered (minimal on-campus study). *Faculty:* 26 full-time (1 woman), 6 part-time/adjunct (1 woman). *Students:* 135 full-time (22 women), 45 part-time (4 women); includes 11 minority (1 American Indian or Alaska Native, non-Hispanic/

Latino; 9 Asian, non-Hispanic/Latino; 1 Hispanic/Latino), 117 international. Average age 27. 693 applicants, 41% accepted, 63 enrolled. In 2010, 58 master's, 4 doctorates awarded. Terminal master's awarded for partial completion of doctoral program. *Degree requirements:* For master's, comprehensive exam (for some programs), thesis (for some programs); for doctorate, comprehensive exam, thesis/dissertation. *Entrance requirements:* For master's and doctorate, GRE General Test (minimum score 1000 Quantitative and Verbal, 3.0 Analytical Writing), minimum undergraduate GPA of 3.0. Additional exam requirements/recommendations for international students: Required—TOEFL (minimum score 523 paper-based; 70 iBT); Recommended—IELTS (minimum score 5.5). *Application deadline:* For fall admission, 5/1 for domestic and international students; for spring admission, 10/15 for domestic and international students. Applications are processed on a rolling basis. Application fee: $50. Electronic applications accepted. *Expenses:* Tuition: Full-time $18,576; part-time $1032 per credit hour. Required fees: $583 per semester. One-time fee: $150. Tuition and fees vary according to program and student level. *Financial support:* In 2010–11, 7 fellowships with full and partial tuition reimbursements (averaging $7,673 per year), 33 research assistantships with full and partial tuition reimbursements (averaging $8,141 per year), 15 teaching assistantships with full and partial tuition reimbursements (averaging $6,930 per year) were awarded; Federal Work-Study, institutionally sponsored loans, scholarships/grants, health care benefits, tuition waivers, and unspecified assistantships also available. Support available to part-time students. Financial award applicants required to submit FAFSA. *Faculty research:* Fluid dynamics, metallurgical and materials engineering, solids and structures, computational mechanics, theoretical mechanics. Total annual research expenditures: $2.4 million. *Unit head:* Dr. Jamal Yagoobi, Professor and Chairman, 312-567-3239, Fax: 312-567-7230, E-mail: yagoobi@iit.edu. *Application contact:* Deborah Gibson, Director, Graduate Admission, 866-472-3448, Fax: 312-567-3138, E-mail: inquiry.grad@iit.edu.

Instituto Tecnológico y de Estudios Superiores de Monterrey, Campus Estado de México, Professional and Graduate Division, Estado de Mexico, Mexico. Offers administration of information technologies (MITA); architecture (M Arch); business administration (GMBA, MBA); computer sciences (MCS, PhD); education (M Ed); educational institution administration (MAD); educational technology and innovation (PhD); electronic commerce (MEC); environmental systems (MS); finance (MAF); humanistic studies (MHS); information sciences and knowledge management (MISKM); information systems (MS); manufacturing systems (MS); marketing (MEM); quality systems and productivity (MS); science and materials engineering (PhD); telecommunications management (MTM). Part-time programs available. Postbaccalaureate distance learning degree programs offered (minimal on-campus study). *Degree requirements:* For master's, one foreign language; thesis (for some programs); for doctorate, one foreign language, thesis/dissertation. *Entrance requirements:* For master's, E-PAEP 500, interview; for doctorate, E-PAEP 500, research proposal. Additional exam requirements/recommendations for international students: Required—TOEFL (minimum score 550 paper-based). *Faculty research:* Surface treatments by plasmas, mechanical properties, robotics, graphical computing, mechatronics security protocols.

Iowa State University of Science and Technology, Graduate College, College of Engineering and College of Liberal Arts and Sciences, Department of Materials Science and Engineering, Ames, IA 50011. Offers MS, PhD. *Faculty:* 31 full-time (4 women), 1 part-time/adjunct (0 women). *Students:* 81 full-time (23 women), 12 part-time (2 women); includes 1 Black or African American, non-Hispanic/Latino; 1 American Indian or Alaska Native, non-Hispanic/Latino; 2 Asian, non-Hispanic/Latino; 2 Hispanic/Latino, 50 international. 211 applicants, 17% accepted, 25 enrolled. In 2010, 8 master's, 13 doctorates awarded. *Degree requirements:* For master's, thesis; for doctorate, thesis/dissertation. *Entrance requirements:* For master's and doctorate, GRE General Test. Additional exam requirements/recommendations for international students: Required—TOEFL (minimum score 550 paper-based; 79 iBT), IELTS (minimum score 6.5). *Application deadline:* For fall admission, 1/15 priority date for domestic and international students; for spring admission, 8/15 priority date for domestic and international students. Application fee: $40 ($90 for international students). Electronic applications accepted. *Financial support:* In 2010–11, 57 research assistantships with full and partial tuition reimbursements (averaging $17,300 per year), 3 teaching assistantships with full and partial tuition reimbursements (averaging $17,300 per year) were awarded; fellowships, scholarships/grants, health care benefits, and unspecified assistantships also available. *Unit head:* Dr. Richard Lesar, Chair, 515-294-1841, Fax: 515-204-5444, E-mail: gradmse@iastate.edu. *Application contact:* Dr. Alan Russell, Director of Graduate Education, 515-294-3204, E-mail: gradmse@iastate.edu.

The Johns Hopkins University, Engineering for Professionals, Part-time Program in Materials Science and Engineering, Baltimore, MD 21218-2699. Offers M Mat SE, MSE. Part-time and evening/weekend programs available. *Faculty:* 6 part-time/adjunct (1 woman). *Students:* 11 part-time (5 women); includes 5 minority (3 Black or African American, non-Hispanic/Latino; 1 Asian, non-Hispanic/Latino; 1 Two or more races, non-Hispanic/Latino). Average age 30. 2 applicants, 50% accepted, 1 enrolled. In 2010, 6 master's awarded. *Application deadline:* Applications are processed on a rolling basis. Application fee: $75. Electronic applications accepted. *Financial support:* Institutionally sponsored loans available. *Unit head:* Dr. Robert C. Cammarata, Program Chair, 410-516-5462, Fax: 410-516-5293, E-mail: rcc@jhu.edu. *Application contact:* Priyanka Dwivedi, Admissions Manager, 410-516-2300, Fax: 410-579-8049, E-mail: pdwived1@jhu.edu.

The Johns Hopkins University, G. W. C. Whiting School of Engineering, Department of Materials Science and Engineering, Baltimore, MD 21218-2699. Offers M Mat SE, MSE, PhD. Part-time and evening/weekend programs available. *Faculty:* 14 full-time (3 women), 1 part-time/adjunct (0 women). *Students:* 43 full-time (11 women), 1 part-time (0 women); includes 9 minority (1 American Indian or Alaska Native, non-Hispanic/Latino; 6 Asian, non-Hispanic/Latino; 2 Hispanic/Latino), 13 international. Average age 27. 173 applicants, 17% accepted, 12 enrolled. In 2010, 10 master's, 6 doctorates awarded. Terminal master's awarded for partial completion of doctoral program. *Degree requirements:* For master's, thesis, oral exam; for doctorate, thesis/dissertation, oral exam, thesis defense. *Entrance requirements:* For master's and doctorate, GRE General Test. Additional exam requirements/recommendations for international students: Required—TOEFL (minimum score 600 paper-based; 250 computer-based). *Application deadline:* For fall admission, 1/15 priority date for domestic and international students; for spring admission, 10/15 priority date for domestic and international students. Application fee: $0 ($75 for international students). Electronic applications accepted. *Financial support:* In 2010–11, 5 fellowships with full tuition reimbursements (averaging $31,600 per year), 34 research assistantships with full tuition reimbursements (averaging $29,800 per year), 3 teaching assistantships with full tuition reimbursements (averaging $24,600 per year) were awarded; Federal Work-Study, institutionally sponsored loans, health care benefits, tuition waivers (full), and unspecified assistantships also available. Financial award application deadline: 3/15. *Faculty research:* Thin films, nanomaterials, biomaterials, materials characterization, electronic materials. Total annual research expenditures: $5.1 million. *Unit head:* Dr. Howard E. Katz, Chair, 410-516-6141, Fax: 410-516-5293, E-mail: hekatz@jhu.edu. *Application contact:* Jeanine Majewski, Academic Coordinator, 410-516-8760, Fax: 410-516-5293, E-mail: dmse.admissions@jhu.edu.

The Johns Hopkins University, G. W. C. Whiting School of Engineering, Program in Engineering Management, Baltimore, MD 21218-2699. Offers biomaterials (MSEM); communications science (MSEM); computer science (MSEM); fluid mechanics (MSEM); materials science and engineering (MSEM); mechanical engineering (MSEM); mechanics and materials (MSEM); nano-biotechnology (MSEM); nanomaterials and nanotechnology (MSEM); probability and statistics (MSEM); smart product and device design (MSEM); systems analysis, management and environmental policy (MSEM). *Students:* 32 full-time (5 women), 4 part-time (0 women); includes 7 minority (3 Black or African American, non-Hispanic/Latino; 3 Asian, non-Hispanic/Latino; 1 Hispanic/Latino), 11 international. Average age 23. 110 applicants, 60% accepted, 27 enrolled. In 2010, 6 master's awarded. *Entrance requirements:* For master's, GRE, 3 letters of recommendation, resume. Additional exam requirements/recommendations for international students: Required—TOEFL (minimum score 600 paper-based; 250 computer-based; 100 iBT) or IELTS (minimum score 7). *Application deadline:* For fall admission, 1/15 priority date for domestic students, 1/15 for international students; for spring admission, 9/15 priority date for domestic students, 9/15 for international students. Applications are processed on a rolling basis. Application fee: $75. Electronic applications accepted. *Financial support:* Fellowships, health care benefits available. *Unit head:* Dr. Edward R. Scheinerman, Interim Director/Vice Dean for Education, School of Engineering/Professor, Applied Mathematics and Statistics, 410-516-7395, Fax: 410-516-4880, E-mail: ers@jhu.edu. *Application contact:* Dennis McIver, Coordinator of Graduate Admissions, 410-516-8174, Fax: 410-516-0780, E-mail: graduateadmissions@jhu.edu.

Lehigh University, P.C. Rossin College of Engineering and Applied Science, Department of Materials Science and Engineering, Bethlehem, PA 18015. Offers materials science and engineering (M Eng, MS, PhD); photonics (MS); polymer science/engineering (M Eng, MS, PhD); MBA/E. Part-time programs available. *Faculty:* 13 full-time (3 women), 1 part-time/adjunct (0 women). *Students:* 27 full-time (4 women), 4 part-time (1 woman); includes 1 minority (Asian, non-Hispanic/Latino), 14 international. Average age 26. 411 applicants, 2% accepted, 7 enrolled. In 2010, 8 master's, 2 doctorates awarded. *Degree requirements:* For master's, thesis; for doctorate, comprehensive exam, thesis/dissertation. *Entrance requirements:* For master's and doctorate, GRE General Test, minimum GPA of 3.0. Additional exam requirements/recommendations for international students: Required—TOEFL (minimum score 487 paper-based; 216 computer-based; 85 iBT). *Application deadline:* For fall admission, 1/15 priority date for domestic students, 1/15 for international students; for spring admission, 12/1 priority date for domestic students, 12/1 for international students. Applications are processed on a rolling basis. Application fee: $75. Electronic applications accepted. *Financial support:* In 2010–11, 7 fellowships with full and partial tuition reimbursements (averaging $22,400 per year), 21 research assistantships with full tuition reimbursements (averaging $22,449 per year), 5 teaching assistantships with partial tuition reimbursements (averaging $17,512 per year) were awarded; career-related internships or fieldwork, Federal Work-Study, institutionally sponsored loans, scholarships/grants, and unspecified assistantships also available. Support available to part-time students. Financial award application deadline: 1/15. *Faculty research:* Metals, ceramics, crystals, polymers, fatigue crack propagation. Total annual research expenditures: $4.3 million. *Unit head:* Dr. Helen Chan, Chairperson, 610-758-5554, Fax: 610-758-4244, E-mail: hmc0@lehigh.edu. *Application contact:* Anne Marie Lobley, Graduate Administrative Coordinator, 610-758-4222, Fax: 610-758-4244, E-mail: amme@lehigh.edu.

Massachusetts Institute of Technology, School of Engineering, Department of Civil and Environmental Engineering, Cambridge, MA 02139. Offers biological oceanography (PhD, Sc D); chemical oceanography (PhD, Sc D); civil and environmental engineering (M Eng, SM, PhD, Sc D); civil and environmental systems (PhD, Sc D); civil engineering (PhD, Sc D, CE); coastal engineering (PhD, Sc D); construction engineering and management (PhD, Sc D); environmental biology (PhD, Sc D); environmental chemistry (PhD, Sc D); environmental engineering (PhD, Sc D); environmental fluid mechanics (PhD, Sc D); geotechnical and geoenvironmental engineering (PhD, Sc D); hydrology (PhD, Sc D); information technology (PhD, Sc D); oceanographic engineering (PhD, Sc D); structures and materials (PhD, Sc D); transportation (PhD, Sc D); SM/MBA. *Faculty:* 36 full-time (6 women). *Students:* 181 full-time (56 women); includes 27 minority (3 Black or African American, non-Hispanic/Latino; 10 Asian, non-Hispanic/Latino; 10 Hispanic/Latino; 4 Two or more races, non-Hispanic/Latino), 93 international. Average age 26. 525 applicants, 29% accepted, 74 enrolled. In 2010, 85 master's, 18 doctorates, 2 other advanced degrees awarded. *Degree requirements:* For master's and CE, thesis; for doctorate, comprehensive exam, thesis/dissertation. *Entrance requirements:* For master's and doctorate, GRE General Test. Additional exam requirements/recommendations for international students: Required—TOEFL (minimum score 577 paper-based; 233 computer-based; 90 iBT), IELTS (minimum score 7). *Application deadline:* For fall admission, 1/2 for domestic and international students. Application fee: $75. Electronic applications accepted. *Expenses:* Tuition: Full-time $38,940; part-time $605 per unit. Required fees: $272. *Financial support:* In 2010–11, 146 students received support, including 50 fellowships with tuition reimbursements available (averaging $21,808 per year), 90 research assistantships with tuition reimbursements available (averaging $28,452 per year), 20 teaching assistantships with tuition reimbursements available (averaging $27,842 per year); career-related internships or fieldwork, Federal Work-Study, institutionally sponsored loans, scholarships/grants, health care benefits, and unspecified assistantships also available. *Faculty research:* Environmental chemistry; environmental microbiology; environmental fluid mechanics and coastal engineering; geotechnical engineering and geomechanics; hydrology and hydroclimatology; mechanics of materials and structures; operations research/supply chain; transportation. Total annual research expenditures: $19.5 million. *Unit head:* Prof. Andrew Whittle, Department Head, 617-253-7101. *Application contact:* Patricia Glidden, Graduate Admissions Coordinator, 617-253-7119, Fax: 617-258-6775, E-mail: cee-admissions@mit.edu.

Massachusetts Institute of Technology, School of Engineering, Department of Materials Science and Engineering, Cambridge, MA 02139. Offers archaeological materials (PhD, Sc D); bio- and polymeric materials (PhD, Sc D); electronic, photonic and magnetic materials (PhD, Sc D); emerging, fundamental and computational studies in materials science (Sc D); emerging, fundamental, and computational studies in materials science (PhD); materials engineering (Mat E); materials science and engineering (M Eng, SM, PhD, Sc D); metallurgical engineering (Met E); structural and environmental materials (PhD, Sc D); SM/MBA. *Faculty:* 34 full-time (8 women). *Students:* 196 full-time (52 women); includes 32 minority (2 Black or African American, non-Hispanic/Latino; 20 Asian, non-Hispanic/Latino; 7 Hispanic/Latino; 3 Two or more races, non-Hispanic/Latino), 113 international. Average age 26. 507 applicants, 15% accepted, 41 enrolled. In 2010, 22 master's, 38 doctorates awarded. Terminal master's awarded for partial completion of doctoral program. *Degree requirements:* For master's and other advanced degree, thesis; for doctorate, comprehensive exam, thesis/dissertation. *Entrance requirements:* For master's, doctorate, and other advanced degree, GRE General Test. Additional exam requirements/recommendations for international students: Required—IELTS (minimum score 7). *Application deadline:* For fall admission, 12/15 for domestic and international students. Application fee: $75. Electronic applications accepted. *Expenses:* Tuition: Full-time $38,940; part-time $605 per unit. Required fees: $272. *Financial support:* In 2010–11, 183 students received support, including 52 fellowships with tuition reimbursements available (averaging $32,695 per year), 124 research assistantships with tuition reimbursements available (averaging $27,409 per year), 8 teaching assistantships with tuition reimbursements available (averaging $31,861 per year); career-related internships or fieldwork, Federal Work-Study, institutionally sponsored loans, scholarships/grants, health care benefits, and unspecified assistantships also available. *Faculty research:* Thermodynamics and kinetics of phase transformations; structure of all materials classes: metals, ceramics, semiconductors, polymers, biomaterials; influence of processing on materials structure; structure ??? property relationships (electrical, magnetic, optical, mechanical); materials in extreme environments. Total annual research expenditures: $28.1 million. *Unit head:* Prof. Edwin L. Thomas, Department Head, 617-253-3300, Fax: 617-252-1775. *Application contact:* Angelita Mireles, Graduate Admissions, 617-253-3302, E-mail: dmse-admissions@mit.edu.

McGill University, Faculty of Graduate and Postdoctoral Studies, Faculty of Engineering, Department of Civil Engineering and Applied Mechanics, Montréal, QC H3A 2T5, Canada. Offers environmental engineering (M Eng, M Sc, PhD); fluid mechanics (M Sc); fluid mechanics and hydraulic engineering (M Eng, PhD); materials engineering (M Eng, PhD); rehabilitation of urban infrastructure (M Eng, PhD); soil behavior (M Eng, PhD); soil mechanics and foundations (M Eng, PhD); structures and structural mechanics (M Eng, PhD); water resources (M Sc); water resources engineering (M Eng, PhD).

McGill University, Faculty of Graduate and Postdoctoral Studies, Faculty of Engineering, Department of Mining and Materials Engineering, Montréal, QC H3A 2T5, Canada. Offers materials engineering (M Eng, PhD); mining engineering (M Eng, M Sc, PhD, Diploma).

McMaster University, School of Graduate Studies, Faculty of Engineering, Department of Materials Science and Engineering, Hamilton, ON L8S 4M2, Canada. Offers materials engineering (M Eng, MA Sc, PhD); materials science (M Eng, PhD). *Degree requirements:* For master's, thesis; for doctorate, comprehensive exam, thesis/dissertation. *Entrance requirements:* Additional exam requirements/recommendations for international students: Required—TOEFL (minimum score 550 paper-based; 213 computer-based). *Faculty research:* Localized corrosion of metals and alloys, electron microscopy, polymer synthesis and characterization, polymer reaction kinetics and engineering, polymer process modeling.

Michigan State University, The Graduate School, College of Engineering, Department of Chemical Engineering and Materials Science, East Lansing, MI 48824. Offers chemical engineering (MS, PhD); materials science and engineering (MS, PhD). *Entrance requirements:* Additional exam requirements/recommendations for international students: Required—TOEFL. Electronic applications accepted.

Michigan Technological University, Graduate School, College of Engineering, Department of Materials Science and Engineering, Houghton, MI 49931. Offers MS, PhD. Part-time programs available. Terminal master's awarded for partial completion of doctoral program. *Degree requirements:* For master's, comprehensive exam; for doctorate, comprehensive exam, thesis/dissertation. *Entrance requirements:* For master's, GRE. Additional exam requirements/recommendations for international students: Required—TOEFL (minimum score 550 paper-based; 213 computer-based). Electronic applications accepted. *Expenses:* Contact institution. *Faculty research:* Structure/property/processing relationships, microstructural characterization, alloy design, electronic/magnetic/photonic materials, materials and manufacturing processes.

New Jersey Institute of Technology, Office of Graduate Studies, College of Science and Liberal Arts, Department of Chemistry and Environmental Science, Program in Materials Science and Engineering, Newark, NJ 07102. Offers MS, PhD. Part-time and evening/weekend programs available. *Students:* 27 full-time (8 women), 3 part-time (0 women); includes 2 Black or African American, non-Hispanic/Latino; 5 Asian, non-Hispanic/Latino; 2 Hispanic/Latino, 17 international. Average age 30. 74 applicants, 36% accepted, 9 enrolled. In 2010, 4 master's, 5 doctorates awarded. Terminal master's awarded for partial completion of doctoral program. *Degree requirements:* For master's, thesis; for doctorate, thesis/dissertation. *Entrance requirements:* For master's, GRE General Test; for doctorate, GRE General Test, minimum graduate GPA of 3.5. Additional exam requirements/recommendations for international students: Required—TOEFL (minimum score 550 paper-based; 213 computer-based; 79 iBT). *Application deadline:* For fall admission, 6/5 priority date for domestic students, 4/1 for international students; for spring admission, 11/15 for domestic students, 10/15 for international students. Applications are processed on a rolling basis. Application fee: $65. Electronic applications accepted. *Expenses:* Tuition, state resident: full-time $14,724; part-time $818 per credit. Tuition, nonresident: full-time $20,304; part-time $1128 per credit. Required fees: $2272; $209 per credit. $103 per semester. One-time fee: $312 full-time; $212 part-time. *Financial support:* Fellowships with full and partial tuition reimbursements, research assistantships with full and partial tuition reimbursements, teaching assistantships with full and partial tuition reimbursements, career-related internships or fieldwork, Federal Work-Study, institutionally sponsored loans, and unspecified assistantships available. Financial award application deadline: 3/15. *Application contact:* Kathryn Kelly, Director of Admissions, 973-596-3300, Fax: 973-596-3461, E-mail: admissions@njit.edu.

New Mexico Institute of Mining and Technology, Graduate Studies, Department of Materials Engineering, Socorro, NM 87801. Offers MS, PhD. *Degree requirements:* For master's, thesis; for doctorate, thesis/dissertation. *Entrance requirements:* For master's, GRE General Test; for doctorate, GRE General Test, GRE Subject Test. Additional exam requirements/recommendations for international students: Required—TOEFL (minimum score 540 paper-based; 207 computer-based). *Faculty research:* Thin films, ceramics, damage studies from radiation, corrosion shock.

North Carolina State University, Graduate School, College of Engineering, Department of Materials Science and Engineering, Raleigh, NC 27695. Offers MMSE, MS, PhD. PhD offered jointly with The University of North Carolina at Charlotte. *Degree requirements:* For master's, thesis; for doctorate, thesis/dissertation. Electronic applications accepted. *Faculty research:* Processing and properties of wide band gap semiconductors, ferroelectric thin-film materials, ductility of nanocrystalline materials, computational materials science, defects in silicon-based devices.

Northwestern University, McCormick School of Engineering and Applied Science, Department of Materials Science and Engineering, Evanston, IL 60208. Offers integrated computational materials engineering (Certificate); materials science and engineering (MS, PhD). Admissions and degrees offered through The Graduate School. Part-time programs available. *Faculty:* 22 full-time (3 women), 1 (woman) part-time/adjunct. *Students:* 181 full-time (54 women); includes 31 minority (3 Black or African American, non-Hispanic/Latino; 19 Asian, non-Hispanic/Latino; 8 Hispanic/Latino; 1 Two or more races, non-Hispanic/Latino), 70 international. Average age 26. In 2010, 10 master's, 31 doctorates awarded. Terminal master's awarded for partial completion of doctoral program. *Degree requirements:* For master's, thesis optional, oral thesis defense; for doctorate, comprehensive exam, thesis/dissertation, oral defense of dissertation, preliminary evaluation, qualifying exam. *Entrance requirements:* For master's and doctorate, General Exam of GRE. Additional exam requirements/recommendations for international students: Required—TOEFL (minimum score 577 paper-based, 233 computer-based, 90 iBT) or IELTS (7). *Application deadline:* For fall admission, 12/31 for domestic and international students. Application fee: $60 ($75 for international students). Electronic applications accepted. *Financial support:* Fellowships with full tuition reimbursements, research assistantships with full tuition reimbursements, teaching assistantships with full tuition reimbursements, career-related internships or fieldwork, institutionally sponsored loans, health care benefits, and unspecified assistantships available. Financial award application deadline: 1/15; financial award applicants required to submit FAFSA. *Faculty research:* Biomaterials, cement, ceramics, composites, electrical properties, electron and ion microscopy, energy, materials design, materials processing, materials theory, mechanical properties, metals, molecular synthesis, nanomaterials, optical properties, phase transformation, polymers, scattering and diffraction, self-assembly, semiconductors, surfaces and interfaces, thin films. Total annual research expenditures: $28.3 million. *Unit head:* Dr. Michael Bedzyk, Chair, 847-491-3570, Fax: 847-491-7820, E-mail: bedzyk@northwestern.edu. *Application contact:* Dr. Chris Wolverton, Admissions Officer, 847-497-0593, Fax: 847-491-7820, E-mail: c-wolverton@northwestern.edu.

The Ohio State University, Graduate School, College of Engineering, Department of Materials Science and Engineering, Columbus, OH 43210. Offers materials science and engineering (MS, PhD); welding engineering (MS, MWE, PhD). *Faculty:* 26. *Students:* 69 full-time (12 women), 41 part-time (11 women); includes 2 Asian, non-Hispanic/Latino; 1 Hispanic/Latino, 53 international. Average age 26. In 2010, 25 master's, 11 doctorates awarded. *Degree requirements:* For master's, thesis; for doctorate, thesis/dissertation. *Entrance requirements:* For master's and doctorate, GRE (for graduates of foreign universities and holders of non-engineering degrees). Additional exam requirements/recommendations for international students: Recommended—TOEFL (minimum score 600 paper-based; 250 computer-based). *Application deadline:* For fall admission, 8/15 priority date for domestic students, 7/1 priority date for international students; for winter admission, 12/1 priority date for domestic students, 11/1 priority date for international students; for spring admission, 3/1 priority date for domestic students, 2/1 priority date for international students. Applications are processed on a rolling basis. Application fee: $40 ($50 for international students). Electronic applications accepted. *Expenses:* Tuition, state resident: full-time $10,605. Tuition, nonresident: full-time $26,535. Tuition and fees vary according to course load and program. *Financial support:* In 2010–11, fellowships (averaging $43,000 per year), research assistantships (averaging $40,700 per year) were awarded; teaching assistantships, career-related internships or fieldwork, scholarships/grants, and unspecified assistantships also available. *Faculty research:* Computational materials modeling, biomaterials, metallurgy, ceramics, advanced alloys/composites. Total annual research expenditures: $10 million. *Unit head:* Rudolph G. Buchheit,

Materials Engineering

The Ohio State University (continued)
Chair, 614-292-2553, Fax: 614-292-4668, E-mail: buchheit.8@osu.edu. *Application contact:* 614-292-9444, Fax: 614-292-3895, E-mail: domestic.grad@osu.edu.

Penn State University Park, Graduate School, College of Earth and Mineral Sciences, Department of Materials Science and Engineering, State College, University Park, PA 16802-1503. Offers MS, PhD.

Purdue University, College of Engineering, School of Materials Engineering, West Lafayette, IN 47907. Offers MSMSE, PhD. Part-time programs available. *Entrance requirements:* For master's and doctorate, minimum GPA of 3.0. Additional exam requirements/recommendations for international students: Required—TOEFL (minimum score 550 paper-based; 213 computer-based; 77 iBT); Recommended—TWE. Electronic applications accepted. *Faculty research:* Electronic behavior, mechanical behavior, thermodynamics, kinetics, phase transformations.

Rensselaer Polytechnic Institute, Graduate School, School of Engineering, Program in Materials Science and Engineering, Troy, NY 12180. Offers ceramics and glass science (M Eng, MS, PhD); composites (M Eng, MS, PhD); electronic materials (M Eng, MS, PhD); metallurgy (M Eng, MS, PhD); polymers (M Eng, MS, PhD). Part-time programs available. *Faculty:* 16 full-time (2 women). *Students:* 57 full-time (13 women), 6 part-time (1 woman), 37 international. Average age 24. 304 applicants, 15% accepted, 16 enrolled. In 2010, 5 master's, 6 doctorates awarded. Terminal master's awarded for partial completion of doctoral program. *Degree requirements:* For master's, thesis; for doctorate, comprehensive exam, thesis/dissertation. *Entrance requirements:* For master's and doctorate, GRE. Additional exam requirements/recommendations for international students: Required—TOEFL (minimum score 570 paper-based; 230 computer-based; 100 iBT). *Application deadline:* For fall admission, 1/15 priority date for domestic and international students; for spring admission, 8/31 priority date for domestic and international students. Applications are processed on a rolling basis. Application fee: $75. Electronic applications accepted. *Expenses:* Tuition: Full-time $39,600; part-time $1650 per credit. Required fees: $1896. *Financial support:* In 2010–11, 56 students received support, including 2 fellowships with full tuition reimbursements available (averaging $26,250 per year), 41 research assistantships with full tuition reimbursements available (averaging $26,250 per year), 13 teaching assistantships with full tuition reimbursements available (averaging $17,500 per year); career-related internships or fieldwork, institutionally sponsored loans, and unspecified assistantships also available. Financial award application deadline: 2/1. *Faculty research:* Materials processing, nanostructural materials, materials for microelectronics, composite materials, computational materials. Total annual research expenditures: $3.6 million. *Unit head:* Dr. Robert Hull, Department Head, 518-276-6373, Fax: 518-276-8554, E-mail: hullr2@rpi.edu. *Application contact:* Dr. Pawel Keblinski, Admissions Coordinator, 518-276-6858, Fax: 518-276-8554, E-mail: keblip@rpi.edu.

Rochester Institute of Technology, Graduate Enrollment Services, College of Science, Health Sciences and Sustainability, Center for Materials Science and Engineering, Rochester, NY 14623-5603. Offers MS. Part-time and evening/weekend programs available. *Students:* 15 full-time (4 women), 10 part-time (4 women); includes 2 Asian, non-Hispanic/Latino; 1 Hispanic/Latino, 12 international. Average age 28. 33 applicants, 67% accepted, 6 enrolled. In 2010, 8 master's awarded. *Degree requirements:* For master's, thesis or project. *Entrance requirements:* For master's, GRE (recommended), minimum GPA of 3.0. Additional exam requirements/recommendations for international students: Required—TOEFL (minimum score 575 paper-based; 233 computer-based; 90 iBT) or IELTS (minimum score 6.5). *Application deadline:* For fall admission, 2/15 priority date for domestic and international students; for winter admission, 11/1 for domestic students, 10/1 for international students; for spring admission, 2/1 for domestic students, 1/1 for international students. Applications are processed on a rolling basis. Application fee: $50. Electronic applications accepted. *Expenses:* Tuition: Full-time $33,234; part-time $924 per credit hour. Required fees: $219. *Financial support:* In 2010–11, 10 students received support; research assistantships with partial tuition reimbursements available, teaching assistantships with partial tuition reimbursements available, career-related internships or fieldwork, scholarships/grants, tuition waivers (partial), and unspecified assistantships available. Support available to part-time students. Financial award application deadline: 7/29; financial award applicants required to submit FAFSA. *Faculty research:* VUV modification of polymers, stress and morphology of sputtered copper films, MRI applications to materials problems. *Unit head:* Dr. KSV Santhanam, Program Director, 585-475-2920, Fax: 585-475-2800, E-mail: ksssch@rit.edu. *Application contact:* Diane Ellison, Assistant Vice President, Graduate Enrollment Services, 585-475-2229, Fax: 585-475-7164, E-mail: gradinfo@rit.edu.

Rutgers, The State University of New Jersey, New Brunswick, Graduate School-New Brunswick, Program in Materials Science and Engineering, Piscataway, NJ 08854-8097. Offers MS, PhD. Part-time programs available. *Degree requirements:* For master's, thesis; for doctorate, comprehensive exam, thesis/dissertation. *Entrance requirements:* For master's and doctorate, GRE General Test. Electronic applications accepted. *Expenses:* Tuition, state resident: full-time $7200; part-time $600 per credit. Tuition, nonresident: full-time $11,124; part-time $927 per credit. *Faculty research:* Ceramic processing, nanostructured materials, electrical and structural ceramics, fiber optics.

San Jose State University, Graduate Studies and Research, Charles W. Davidson College of Engineering, Department of Chemical and Materials Engineering, Program in Materials Engineering, San Jose, CA 95192-0001. Offers MS. Part-time programs available. *Degree requirements:* For master's, thesis or alternative. *Entrance requirements:* For master's, GRE. Additional exam requirements/recommendations for international students: Required—TOEFL. Electronic applications accepted. *Faculty research:* Electronic materials, thin films, electron microscopy, fiber composites, polymeric materials.

Santa Clara University, School of Engineering, Program in Mechanical Engineering, Santa Clara, CA 95053. Offers controls (Certificate); dynamics (Certificate); materials engineering (Certificate); mechanical design analysis (Certificate); mechanical engineering (MS, PhD, Engineer); mechatronics systems engineering (Certificate); technology jump-start (Certificate); thermofluids (Certificate). Part-time and evening/weekend programs available. *Students:* 33 full-time (4 women), 55 part-time (6 women); includes 30 minority (21 Asian, non-Hispanic/Latino; 6 Hispanic/Latino; 1 Native Hawaiian or other Pacific Islander, non-Hispanic/Latino; 2 Two or more races, non-Hispanic/Latino), 15 international. Average age 28. 82 applicants, 71% accepted, 29 enrolled. In 2010, 19 master's awarded. *Degree requirements:* For master's, thesis (for some programs); for doctorate, thesis/dissertation; for other advanced degree, thesis. *Entrance requirements:* For master's, GRE (waiver may be available), transcript; for doctorate, GRE, master's degree or equivalent; for other advanced degree, master's degree, published paper. Additional exam requirements/recommendations for international students: Required—TOEFL (minimum score 550 paper-based; 213 computer-based; 79 iBT). *Application deadline:* For fall admission, 8/12 for domestic students, 7/15 for international students; for winter admission, 10/28 for domestic students, 9/23 for international students; for spring admission, 2/25 for domestic students, 1/21 for international students. Applications are processed on a rolling basis. Application fee: $60. Electronic applications accepted. *Expenses:* Contact institution. *Financial support:* Research assistantships, teaching assistantships available. Financial award application deadline: 3/2; financial award applicants required to submit FAFSA. *Faculty research:* Development of small satellite design, tests and operations technology. Total annual research expenditures: $585,448. *Unit head:* Dr. Alex Zecevic, Associate Dean for Graduate Studies, 408-554-2394, E-mail: azecevic@scu.edu. *Application contact:* Stacey Tinker, Director of Admissions, Graduate Engineering, 408-554-4748, Fax: 408-554-4323, E-mail: stinker@scu.edu.

South Dakota School of Mines and Technology, Graduate Division, Doctoral Program in Materials Engineering and Science, Rapid City, SD 57701-3995. Offers PhD. Part-time programs available. *Degree requirements:* For doctorate, thesis/dissertation. *Entrance requirements:* For doctorate, GRE General Test, minimum graduate GPA of 3.0, 3 letters of recommendation. Additional exam requirements/recommendations for international students: Required—TOEFL,

TWE. Electronic applications accepted. *Faculty research:* Thermophysical properties of solids, development of multiphase materials and composites, concrete technology, electronic polymer materials.

South Dakota School of Mines and Technology, Graduate Division, Master's Program in Materials Engineering and Science, Rapid City, SD 57701-3995. Offers MS. *Entrance requirements:* For master's, GRE General Test. Additional exam requirements/recommendations for international students: Required—TOEFL, TWE. Electronic applications accepted.

Stanford University, School of Engineering, Department of Materials Science and Engineering, Stanford, CA 94305-9991. Offers MS, PhD, Eng. Terminal master's awarded for partial completion of doctoral program. *Degree requirements:* For doctorate, thesis/dissertation; for Eng, thesis. *Entrance requirements:* For master's, doctorate, and Eng, GRE General Test. Additional exam requirements/recommendations for international students: Required—TOEFL. Electronic applications accepted. *Expenses:* Tuition: Full-time $38,700; part-time $860 per unit. One-time fee: $200 full-time.

State University of New York at Binghamton, Graduate School, Thomas J. Watson School of Engineering and Applied Science and School of Arts and Sciences, Materials Science and Engineering Program, Binghamton, NY 13902-6000. Offers MS, PhD. *Faculty:* 3 full-time (0 women). *Students:* 16 full-time (7 women), 31 part-time (7 women); includes 2 Asian, non-Hispanic/Latino, 34 international. Average age 29. 32 applicants, 34% accepted, 8 enrolled. In 2010, 1 master's, 6 doctorates awarded. Application fee: $60. *Financial support:* In 2010–11, 31 students received support, including 21 research assistantships with full tuition reimbursements available (averaging $16,500 per year), 9 teaching assistantships with full tuition reimbursements available (averaging $16,500 per year); career-related internships or fieldwork, Federal Work-Study, institutionally sponsored loans, scholarships/grants, health care benefits, tuition waivers (full and partial), and unspecified assistantships also available. Financial award application deadline: 2/15; financial award applicants required to submit FAFSA. *Unit head:* Dr. Stanley Whittingham, Director, 607-777-4623, E-mail: stanwhit@binghamton.edu. *Application contact:* Catherine Smith, Recruiting and Admissions Coordinator, 607-777-2151, Fax: 607-777-2501, E-mail: cmsmith@binghamton.edu.

Stevens Institute of Technology, Graduate School, Charles V. Schaefer Jr. School of Engineering, Department of Chemical Engineering and Materials Science, Program in Materials Science, Hoboken, NJ 07030. Offers M Eng, PhD. *Students:* 35 full-time (13 women), 4 part-time (0 women); includes 3 Asian, non-Hispanic/Latino, 28 international. Average age 25.*Unit head:* Henry Du, Director, 201-216-5262, Fax: 201-216-8306, E-mail: hdu@stevens.edu. *Application contact:* Graduate Admissions, 800-496-4935, Fax: 201-216-8044, E-mail: gradadmissions@stevens.edu.

Stony Brook University, State University of New York, Graduate School, College of Engineering and Applied Sciences, Department of Materials Science and Engineering, Stony Brook, NY 11794. Offers MS, PhD. *Faculty:* 13 full-time (3 women), 8 part-time/adjunct (1 woman). *Students:* 104 full-time (33 women), 7 part-time (1 woman); includes 3 Black or African American, non-Hispanic/Latino; 8 Asian, non-Hispanic/Latino; 2 Hispanic/Latino, 79 international. Average age 28. 176 applicants, 45% accepted, 30 enrolled. In 2010, 17 master's, 6 doctorates awarded. *Degree requirements:* For master's, thesis or alternative; for doctorate, comprehensive exam, thesis/dissertation. *Entrance requirements:* For master's and doctorate, GRE General Test, minimum undergraduate GPA of 3.0. Additional exam requirements/recommendations for international students: Required—TOEFL. *Application deadline:* For fall admission, 1/15 for domestic students. Application fee: $100. *Expenses:* Tuition, state resident: full-time $8370; part-time $349 per credit. Tuition, nonresident: full-time $13,780; part-time $574 per credit. Required fees: $994. *Financial support:* In 2010–11, 40 research assistantships, 12 teaching assistantships were awarded; fellowships also available. *Faculty research:* Electronic materials, biomaterials, synchrotron topography. Total annual research expenditures: $3.1 million. *Unit head:* Dr. Michael Dudley, Chairman, 631-632-8484. *Application contact:* Dr. Miriam Rafailovich, Director, 631-632-8484, Fax: 631-632-8052, E-mail: mrafailovich.nsf@notes.cc.sunysb.edu.

Texas A&M University, College of Engineering, Zachry Department of Civil Engineering, College Station, TX 77843. Offers coastal and ocean engineering (M Eng, MS, D Eng, PhD); construction engineering and management (M Eng, MS, D Eng, PhD); environmental engineering (M Eng, MS, D Eng, PhD); geotechnical engineering (M Eng, MS, D Eng, PhD); materials engineering (M Eng, MS, D Eng, PhD); structural engineering (M Eng, MS, D Eng, PhD); transportation engineering (M Eng, MS, D Eng, PhD); water resources engineering (M Eng, MS, D Eng, PhD). Part-time programs available. *Faculty:* 57. *Students:* 384 full-time (81 women), 35 part-time (7 women); includes 35 minority (3 Black or African American, non-Hispanic/Latino; 1 American Indian or Alaska Native, non-Hispanic/Latino; 14 Asian, non-Hispanic/Latino; 17 Hispanic/Latino), 263 international. Average age 29. In 2010, 136 master's, 26 doctorates awarded. *Degree requirements:* For master's, thesis (MS); for doctorate, dissertation (PhD), internship (D Eng). *Entrance requirements:* For master's and doctorate, GRE General Test. Additional exam requirements/recommendations for international students: Required—TOEFL. *Application deadline:* Applications are processed on a rolling basis. Application fee: $50 ($75 for international students). Electronic applications accepted. *Financial support:* In 2010–11, fellowships (averaging $4,500 per year), research assistantships (averaging $14,000 per year), teaching assistantships (averaging $14,400 per year) were awarded; career-related internships or fieldwork and institutionally sponsored loans also available. Financial award application deadline: 4/15; financial award applicants required to submit FAFSA. *Unit head:* Dr. Tony Cahill, Head, 979-845-3858, E-mail: tcahill@civil.tamu.edu. *Application contact:* Graduate Advisor, 979-845-7435, Fax: 979-845-6156, E-mail: info@civil.tamu.edu.

Tuskegee University, Graduate Programs, College of Engineering, Architecture and Physical Sciences, Program in Material Science and Engineering, Tuskegee, AL 36088. Offers PhD. *Students:* 12 full-time (5 women), 4 part-time (1 woman); includes 7 Black or African American, non-Hispanic/Latino, 9 international. Average age 30. 5 applicants, 20% accepted, 1 enrolled. *Entrance requirements:* Additional exam requirements/recommendations for international students: Required—TOEFL (minimum score 500 paper-based; 69 computer-based). *Application deadline:* For fall admission, 7/15 for domestic students. Applications are processed on a rolling basis. Application fee: $25 ($35 for international students). *Expenses:* Tuition: Full-time $16,100; part-time $665 per credit hour. Required fees: $650. *Financial support:* Application deadline: 4/15. *Unit head:* Dr. Shaik Jeelani, Head, 334-727-8375. *Application contact:* Dr. Robert L. Laney, Vice President/Director of Admissions and Enrollment Management, 334-727-8580, Fax: 334-727-5750, E-mail: planey@tuskegee.edu.

The University of Alabama, Graduate School, College of Engineering, Department of Metallurgical and Materials Engineering, Tuscaloosa, AL 35487. Offers MS Met E, PhD. Phd offered jointly with The University of Alabama at Birmingham. *Faculty:* 8 full-time (2 women). *Students:* 19 full-time (2 women), 3 part-time (0 women); includes 1 minority (Black or African American, non-Hispanic/Latino), 10 international. Average age 26. 19 applicants, 26% accepted, 3 enrolled. In 2010, 3 master's, 7 doctorates awarded. *Degree requirements:* For master's, thesis or alternative; for doctorate, thesis/dissertation. *Entrance requirements:* For master's, GRE General Test, minimum GPA of 3.0 in last 60 hours; for doctorate, GRE General Test, minimum graduate GPA of 3.0, graduate degree. Additional exam requirements/recommendations for international students: Required—TOEFL (minimum score 550 paper-based; 213 computer-based). *Application deadline:* For fall admission, 7/1 priority date for domestic students. Applications are processed on a rolling basis. Application fee: $50 ($60 for international students). Electronic applications accepted. *Expenses:* Tuition, state resident: full-time $7900. Tuition, nonresident: full-time $20,500. *Financial support:* In 2010–11, 3 fellowships (averaging $15,000 per year), 14 research assistantships (averaging $14,700 per year), 6 teaching assistantships (averaging $12,250 per year) were awarded; Federal Work-Study and unspecified assistantships also available. *Faculty research:* Thermodynamics, molten metals processing, casting and solidification, mechanical properties of materials, thin films and nanostructures, electrochemistry, corrosion and alloy development. Total annual research expenditures: $1.9

million. *Unit head:* Dr. Ramana G. Reddy, Head and ACIPCO Professor, 205-348-4246, Fax: 205-348-2164. *Application contact:* Dr. Su Gupta, Associate Professor, 205-348-4272, Fax: 205-348-2164, E-mail: sgupta@eng.ua.edu.

The University of Alabama at Birmingham, School of Engineering, Program in Materials Engineering, Birmingham, AL 35294. Offers MS Mt E, PhD. PhD offered jointly with The University of Alabama (Tuscaloosa). *Students:* 24 full-time (5 women), 5 part-time (1 woman); includes 8 minority (6 Black or African American, non-Hispanic/Latino; 2 Asian, non-Hispanic/Latino), 7 international. Average age 27. 15 applicants, 60% accepted, 9 enrolled. In 2010, 8 master's, 2 doctorates awarded. *Degree requirements:* For master's, comprehensive exam, project/thesis; for doctorate, comprehensive exam, thesis/dissertation. *Entrance requirements:* For master's and doctorate, GRE General Test. *Application deadline:* Applications are processed on a rolling basis. Application fee: $35 ($60 for international students). Electronic applications accepted. *Expenses:* Tuition, state resident: full-time $5482. Tuition, nonresident: full-time $12,430. Tuition and fees vary according to program. *Financial support:* In 2010–11, 10 fellowships with full and partial tuition reimbursements (averaging $12,500 per year), 8 research assistantships with full tuition reimbursements (averaging $12,500 per year) were awarded; career-related internships or fieldwork, Federal Work-Study, and institutionally sponsored loans also available. Support available to part-time students. *Faculty research:* Casting metallurgy, microgravity solidification, thin film techniques, ceramics/glass processing, biomedical materials processing. *Unit head:* Dr. J. Barry Andrews, Chair, 205-934-8460, Fax: 205-934-8485, E-mail: barry@uab.edu. *Application contact:* Julie Bryant, Director of Graduate Admissions, 205-934-8227, Fax: 205-934-8413, E-mail: jbryant@uab.edu.

University of Alberta, Faculty of Graduate Studies and Research, Department of Chemical and Materials Engineering, Edmonton, AB T6G 2E1, Canada. Offers chemical engineering (M Eng, M Sc, PhD); materials engineering (M Eng, M Sc, PhD); process control (M Eng, M Sc, PhD); welding (M Eng). Part-time programs available. Postbaccalaureate distance learning degree programs offered (minimal on-campus study). Terminal master's awarded for partial completion of doctoral program. *Degree requirements:* For master's, thesis; for doctorate, thesis/dissertation. *Faculty research:* Advanced materials and polymers, catalytic and reaction engineering, mineral processing, physical metallurgy, fluid mechanics.

The University of Arizona, College of Engineering, Department of Materials Science and Engineering, Tucson, AZ 85721. Offers MS, PhD. Part-time programs available. *Faculty:* 10 full-time (3 women), 2 part-time/adjunct (0 women). *Students:* 37 full-time (16 women), 14 part-time (6 women); includes 14 minority (1 American Indian or Alaska Native, non-Hispanic/Latino; 1 Asian, non-Hispanic/Latino; 7 Hispanic/Latino; 5 Two or more races, non-Hispanic/Latino), 15 international. Average age 29. 82 applicants, 20% accepted, 6 enrolled. In 2010, 5 master's, 5 doctorates awarded. *Degree requirements:* For master's, thesis (for some programs); for doctorate, comprehensive exam, thesis/dissertation. *Entrance requirements:* For master's and doctorate, GRE General Test, 3 letters of recommendation, statement of purpose. Additional exam requirements/recommendations for international students: Required—TOEFL (minimum score 550 paper-based; 213 computer-based). *Application deadline:* Applications are processed on a rolling basis. Application fee: $75. Electronic applications accepted. *Expenses:* Tuition, state resident: full-time $7692. *Financial support:* In 2010–11, 25 research assistantships with full tuition reimbursements (averaging $23,789 per year), 2 teaching assistantships with full tuition reimbursements (averaging $23,586 per year) were awarded; institutionally sponsored loans, scholarships/grants, health care benefits, tuition waivers (full), and unspecified assistantships also available. Financial award application deadline: 12/31. *Faculty research:* High-technology ceramics, optical materials, electronic materials, chemical metallurgy, science of materials. Total annual research expenditures: $1.9 million. *Unit head:* Dr. Joseph H. Simmons, Head, 520-621-6070, Fax: 520-621-8059, E-mail: simmons@mse.arizona.edu. *Application contact:* Information Contact, 520-626-6762, Fax: 520-621-8059, E-mail: msed@email.arizona.edu.

The University of British Columbia, Faculty of Applied Science, Department of Materials Engineering, Vancouver, BC V6T 1Z1, Canada. Offers materials and metallurgy (M Sc, PhD); metals and materials engineering (MA Sc, PhD). *Degree requirements:* For master's, comprehensive exam, thesis; for doctorate, comprehensive exam, thesis/dissertation. *Entrance requirements:* Additional exam requirements/recommendations for international students: Required—TOEFL (minimum score 560 paper-based; 220 computer-based; 83 iBT). Electronic applications accepted. Tuition charges are reported in Canadian dollars. *Expenses:* Tuition, area resident: Full-time $4179 Canadian dollars. International tuition: $7344 Canadian dollars full-time. *Faculty research:* Electroslag melting, mathematical modeling, solidification and hydrometallurgy.

University of California, Berkeley, Graduate Division, College of Engineering, Department of Materials Science and Engineering, Berkeley, CA 94720-1500. Offers engineering (M Eng, MS, D Eng, PhD); engineering science (M Eng, MS, PhD). *Degree requirements:* For master's, comprehensive exam or thesis (MS); for doctorate, comprehensive exam, thesis/dissertation, qualifying exam. *Entrance requirements:* For master's and doctorate, GRE General Test, minimum GPA of 3.0, 3 letters of recommendation. Additional exam requirements/recommendations for international students: Required—TOEFL (minimum score 230 computer-based). *Faculty research:* Ceramics, biomaterials, structural, electronic, magnetic and optical materials.

University of California, Davis, College of Engineering, Program in Materials Science and Engineering, Davis, CA 95616. Offers MS, PhD. Terminal master's awarded for partial completion of doctoral program. *Degree requirements:* For master's, comprehensive exam (for some programs), thesis (for some programs); for doctorate, comprehensive exam, thesis/dissertation. *Entrance requirements:* Additional exam requirements/recommendations for international students: Required—TOEFL (minimum score 550 paper-based; 213 computer-based).

University of California, Irvine, School of Engineering, Department of Chemical Engineering and Materials Science, Irvine, CA 92697. Offers chemical and biochemical engineering (MS, PhD); materials science and engineering (MS, PhD). Part-time programs available. *Students:* 77 full-time (24 women), 3 part-time (1 woman); includes 22 minority (1 American Indian or Alaska Native, non-Hispanic/Latino; 16 Asian, non-Hispanic/Latino; 3 Hispanic/Latino; 1 Native Hawaiian or other Pacific Islander, non-Hispanic/Latino; 1 Two or more races, non-Hispanic/Latino), 32 international. Average age 28. 300 applicants, 27% accepted, 26 enrolled. In 2010, 24 master's, 8 doctorates awarded. Terminal master's awarded for partial completion of doctoral program. *Degree requirements:* For doctorate, thesis/dissertation. *Entrance requirements:* For master's and doctorate, GRE General Test, minimum GPA of 3.0, 3 letters of recommendation. Additional exam requirements/recommendations for international students: Required—TOEFL (minimum score 550 paper-based; 213 computer-based). *Application deadline:* For fall admission, 1/15 priority date for domestic students, 1/15 for international students. Applications are processed on a rolling basis. Application fee: $80 ($100 for international students). Electronic applications accepted. *Financial support:* Fellowships with tuition reimbursements, research assistantships with full tuition reimbursements, teaching assistantships with tuition reimbursements, institutionally sponsored loans, traineeships, health care benefits, and unspecified assistantships available. Financial award application deadline: 3/1; financial award applicants required to submit FAFSA. *Faculty research:* Molecular biotechnology, nano-bio-materials, biophotonics, synthesis, superplasticity and mechanical behavior, characterization of advanced and nanostructural materials. *Unit head:* Prof. Albert Yee, Chair, 949-824-7320, Fax: 949-824-2541, E-mail: albert.yee@uci.edu. *Application contact:* Grace Hai-Chin Chau, Academic Program/Graduate Admission Coordinator, 949-824-3887, Fax: 949-824-2541, E-mail: chaug@uci.edu.

University of California, Irvine, School of Engineering, Program in Materials Engineering and Manufacturing Technology, Irvine, CA 92697. Offers engineering (MS, PhD). Part-time programs available. *Students:* 16 full-time (4 women), 4 part-time (2 women); includes 6 minority (all Asian, non-Hispanic/Latino), 10 international. Average age 28. 17 applicants, 53% accepted, 5 enrolled. In 2010, 3 master's, 2 doctorates awarded. *Entrance requirements:* For master's and doctorate, GRE General Test, 3 letters of recommendation, minimum GPA of 3.0. Additional exam requirements/recommendations for international students: Required—TOEFL (minimum score 550 paper-based; 213 computer-based). *Application deadline:* For fall admission, 1/15 priority date for domestic students, 1/15 for international students. Applications are processed on a rolling basis. Application fee: $80 ($100 for international students). Electronic applications accepted. *Financial support:* Fellowships with tuition reimbursements, research assistantships with full tuition reimbursements, teaching assistantships with tuition reimbursements, institutionally sponsored loans, traineeships, health care benefits, and unspecified assistantships available. Financial award application deadline: 3/1; financial award applicants required to submit FAFSA. *Faculty research:* Advanced materials, microelectronic and photonic devices and packaging, biomedical devices, MEMS, thin film materials, nanotechnology. *Unit head:* Dr. Andrew Asher Shapiro, Associate Adjunct Professor, 949-393-7311, Fax: 949-824-5055, E-mail: aashapir@uci.edu. *Application contact:* Jean Harmony Bennett, Academic Counselor, 949-824-6475, Fax: 949-824-3440, E-mail: jean.bennett@uci.edu.

University of California, Los Angeles, Graduate Division, Henry Samueli School of Engineering and Applied Science, Department of Materials Science and Engineering, Los Angeles, CA 90095-1595. Offers MS, PhD. *Faculty:* 12 full-time (3 women). *Students:* 111 full-time (25 women); includes 3 Black or African American, non-Hispanic/Latino; 15 Asian, non-Hispanic/Latino; 3 Hispanic/Latino, 60 international. 183 applicants, 49% accepted, 40 enrolled. In 2010, 20 master's, 21 doctorates awarded. *Degree requirements:* For master's, comprehensive exam or thesis; for doctorate, thesis/dissertation, qualifying exams. *Entrance requirements:* For master's, GRE General Test, minimum GPA of 3.0; for doctorate, GRE General Test, minimum GPA of 3.25. Additional exam requirements/recommendations for international students: Required—TOEFL (minimum score 560 paper-based; 220 computer-based; 87 iBT). *Application deadline:* For fall admission, 12/15 for domestic and international students. Application fee: $70 ($90 for international students). Electronic applications accepted. *Financial support:* In 2010–11, 42 fellowships, 302 research assistantships, 33 teaching assistantships were awarded; Federal Work-Study, institutionally sponsored loans, and tuition waivers (full and partial) also available. Financial award application deadline: 1/15; financial award applicants required to submit FAFSA. Total annual research expenditures: $6.5 million. *Unit head:* Dr. Jenn-Ming Yang, Chair, 310-825-2758, E-mail: jyang@seas.ucla.edu. *Application contact:* Paradee Chularee, Student Affairs Officer, 310-825-8913, Fax: 310-206-7353, E-mail: paradee@ea.ucla.edu.

University of California, Riverside, Graduate Division, Graduate Materials Science and Engineering Program, Riverside, CA 92521. Offers MS, PhD. *Faculty:* 40. *Students:* 15 full-time (5 women); includes 1 Black or African American, non-Hispanic/Latino; 6 Asian, non-Hispanic/Latino. Average age 27. 60 applicants, 30% accepted, 8 enrolled. *Entrance requirements:* For master's and doctorate, GRE. Additional exam requirements/recommendations for international students: Required—TOEFL (minimum score 550 paper-based; 213 computer-based; 80 iBT). *Application deadline:* For fall admission, 1/5 priority date for domestic students. Application fee: $0 ($100 for international students). Electronic applications accepted. *Financial support:* In 2010–11, 8 students received support; fellowships, research assistantships, teaching assistantships, scholarships/grants, health care benefits, and unspecified assistantships available. Financial award application deadline: 1/5. *Unit head:* MSE Program Office, 951-827-3392, Fax: 951-827-3188, E-mail: mse-program@engr.ucr.edu. *Application contact:* Graduate Admissions, 951-827-3392, Fax: 951-827-3188, E-mail: mse-program@engr.ucr.edu.

University of California, Santa Barbara, Graduate Division, College of Engineering, Department of Materials, Santa Barbara, CA 93106-5050. Offers MS, PhD, MS/PhD. *Faculty:* 28 full-time (3 women), 4 part-time/adjunct (0 women). *Students:* 125 full-time (27 women); includes 28 Asian, non-Hispanic/Latino; 3 Hispanic/Latino; 1 Native Hawaiian or other Pacific Islander, non-Hispanic/Latino. Average age 26. 321 applicants, 25% accepted, 37 enrolled. In 2010, 5 master's, 20 doctorates awarded. Terminal master's awarded for partial completion of doctoral program. *Degree requirements:* For doctorate, comprehensive exam, thesis/dissertation. *Entrance requirements:* For master's and doctorate, GRE General Test. Additional exam requirements/recommendations for international students: Required—TOEFL (minimum score 600 paper-based; 100 iBT), IELTS (minimum score 7). *Application deadline:* For fall admission, 1/7 priority date for domestic and international students; for winter admission, 11/1 priority date for domestic and international students; for spring admission, 1/1 priority date for domestic and international students. Application fee: $70 ($90 for international students). Electronic applications accepted. *Financial support:* In 2010–11, 105 students received support, including 48 fellowships with full and partial tuition reimbursements available (averaging $11,846 per year), 97 research assistantships with full and partial tuition reimbursements available (averaging $14,386 per year), 21 teaching assistantships with partial tuition reimbursements available (averaging $3,824 per year); career-related internships or fieldwork, scholarships/grants, tuition waivers (full), and unspecified assistantships also available. Financial award application deadline: 3/2; financial award applicants required to submit FAFSA. *Faculty research:* Electronic and photonic materials, inorganic materials, macromolecular and biomolecular materials, structural materials. Total annual research expenditures: $5.8 million. *Unit head:* Dr. James S. Speck, Chair and Professor, 805-893-4362, Fax: 805-893-8486, E-mail: speck@mrl.ucsb.edu. *Application contact:* Oura Neak, Graduate Program Assistant, 805-893-4601, Fax: 805-893-8486, E-mail: mtrl-applications@engineering.ucsb.edu.

University of Central Florida, College of Engineering and Computer Science, Department of Mechanical, Materials, and Aerospace Engineering, Program in Materials Science and Engineering, Orlando, FL 32816. Offers MSMSE, PhD. *Students:* 41 full-time (9 women), 13 part-time (4 women); includes 1 Black or African American, non-Hispanic/Latino; 1 American Indian or Alaska Native, non-Hispanic/Latino; 3 Asian, non-Hispanic/Latino; 4 Hispanic/Latino, 28 international. Average age 28. 40 applicants, 50% accepted, 9 enrolled. In 2010, 15 master's, 7 doctorates awarded. *Degree requirements:* For master's, thesis or alternative; for doctorate, thesis/dissertation, candidacy exam, departmental qualifying exam. *Application deadline:* For fall admission, 7/15 priority date for domestic students; for spring admission, 12/1 priority date for domestic students. Application fee: $30. Electronic applications accepted. *Expenses:* Tuition, state resident: part-time $256.56 per credit hour. Tuition, nonresident: part-time $1011.52 per credit hour. Part-time tuition and fees vary according to program. *Financial support:* In 2010–11, 31 students received support, including 13 fellowships (averaging $1,600 per year), 34 research assistantships (averaging $9,800 per year), 5 teaching assistantships (averaging $8,100 per year).

University of Cincinnati, Graduate School, College of Engineering, Department of Chemical and Materials Engineering, Cincinnati, OH 45221. Offers chemical engineering (MS, PhD); materials science and metallurgical engineering (MS, PhD), including ceramic science and engineering, materials science and engineering, metallurgical engineering, polymer science and engineering. Part-time and evening/weekend programs available. Terminal master's awarded for partial completion of doctoral program. *Degree requirements:* For master's, thesis; for doctorate, thesis/dissertation. *Entrance requirements:* For master's and doctorate, GRE General Test. Additional exam requirements/recommendations for international students: Required—TOEFL. Electronic applications accepted. *Faculty research:* Process synthesis, aerosol processes, clean coal technology, membrane technology.

University of Cincinnati, Graduate School, College of Engineering, Department of Chemical and Materials Engineering, Program in Materials Science and Metallurgical Engineering, Program in Materials Science and Engineering, Cincinnati, OH 45221. Offers MS, PhD. Evening/weekend programs available. *Degree requirements:* For master's, thesis optional; for doctorate, one foreign language, comprehensive exam, thesis/dissertation, oral English proficiency exam. *Entrance requirements:* For master's and doctorate, GRE General Test, BS in related field, minimum undergraduate GPA of 3.0. Additional exam requirements/recommendations for international students: Required—TOEFL. Electronic applications accepted. *Faculty research:* Polymer characterization, surface analysis, and adhesion; mechanical behavior of high-temperature materials; composites; electrochemistry of materials.

Materials Engineering

University of Connecticut, Graduate School, School of Engineering, Department of Metallurgy and Materials Engineering, Storrs, CT 06269. Offers MS, PhD. Terminal master's awarded for partial completion of doctoral program. *Degree requirements:* For master's, comprehensive exam, thesis or alternative; for doctorate, thesis/dissertation. *Entrance requirements:* For master's and doctorate, GRE General Test, GRE Subject Test. Additional exam requirements/recommendations for international students: Required—TOEFL (minimum score 550 paper-based; 213 computer-based). Electronic applications accepted. *Faculty research:* Microsegregation and coarsening, fatigue crack, electron-dislocation interaction.

University of Dayton, Graduate School, School of Engineering, Department of Materials Engineering, Dayton, OH 45469-1300. Offers MS Mat E, DE, PhD. Part-time and evening/weekend programs available. *Faculty:* 2 full-time (0 women), 11 part-time/adjunct (0 women). *Students:* 48 full-time (20 women), 8 part-time (1 woman); includes 6 minority (3 Black or African American, non-Hispanic/Latino; 1 Asian, non-Hispanic/Latino; 2 Hispanic/Latino), 17 international. Average age 30. 28 applicants, 100% accepted, 14 enrolled. In 2010, 13 master's, 7 doctorates awarded. *Degree requirements:* For master's, thesis optional; for doctorate, variable foreign language requirement, thesis/dissertation, departmental qualifying exam. *Entrance requirements:* Additional exam requirements/recommendations for international students: Required—TOEFL (minimum score 550 paper-based; 213 computer-based; 80 iBT). *Application deadline:* For fall admission, 8/1 for domestic students, 3/1 priority date for international students; for winter admission, 7/1 priority date for international students; for spring admission, 1/1 priority date for international students. Applications are processed on a rolling basis. Application fee: $0 ($50 for international students). Electronic applications accepted. *Expenses:* Tuition: Full-time $7800; part-time $650 per credit hour. *Financial support:* In 2010–11, 1 fellowship (averaging $27,500 per year), 10 research assistantships with full tuition reimbursements (averaging $18,397 per year) were awarded. Financial award applicants required to submit FAFSA. *Faculty research:* Ultra-fine microstructure by rapid hot-compaction of Armstrong-process titanium powder, diffusion during synthesis of titanium alloys by means of power metallurgy. Total annual research expenditures: $37,397. *Unit head:* Dr. Daniel Eylon, Director, 937-229-2679, E-mail: deylon@udayton.edu. *Application contact:* Alexander Popovski, Associate Director of Graduate and International Admissions, 937-229-3725, Fax: 937-229-4729, E-mail: alex.popovski@notes.udayton.edu.

University of Delaware, College of Engineering, Department of Materials Science and Engineering, Newark, DE 19716. Offers MMSE, PhD. Terminal master's awarded for partial completion of doctoral program. *Degree requirements:* For master's, thesis; for doctorate, thesis/dissertation. *Entrance requirements:* For master's and doctorate, GRE General Test, 3 letters of recommendation, minimum GPA of 3.2. Additional exam requirements/recommendations for international students: Required—TOEFL. Electronic applications accepted. *Faculty research:* Thin films and self assembly, drug delivery and tissue engineering, biomaterials and nanocomposites, semiconductor and oxide interfaces, electronic and magnetic materials.

University of Denver, School of Engineering and Computer Science, Department of Mechanical and Materials Engineering, Denver, CO 80208. Offers bioengineering (MS); engineering (MS, PhD); interdisciplinary engineering (PhD); materials science (MS, PhD); mechanical engineering (MS, PhD); nanoscale science and engineering (PhD). Part-time programs available. *Faculty:* 8 full-time (1 woman), 5 part-time/adjunct (1 woman). *Students:* 3 full-time (1 woman), 21 part-time (5 women), 7 international. Average age 33. 63 applicants, 65% accepted, 5 enrolled. In 2010, 5 master's, 1 doctorate awarded. Terminal master's awarded for partial completion of doctoral program. *Degree requirements:* For master's, thesis or alternative; for doctorate, comprehensive exam, thesis/dissertation. *Entrance requirements:* For master's and doctorate, GRE General Test. Additional exam requirements/recommendations for international students: Required—TOEFL (minimum score 550 paper-based; 80 iBT). *Application deadline:* Applications are processed on a rolling basis. Application fee: $60. Electronic applications accepted. *Expenses:* Tuition: Full-time $35,604; part-time $29,670 per year. Required fees: $687 per year. Tuition and fees vary according to program. *Financial support:* In 2010–11, 7 research assistantships with full and partial tuition reimbursements (averaging $10,795 per year), 5 teaching assistantships with full and partial tuition reimbursements (averaging $13,230 per year) were awarded; Federal Work-Study, scholarships/grants, and unspecified assistantships also available. Financial award applicants required to submit FAFSA. *Faculty research:* Aerosols, biomechanics, composite materials, photo optics, drug delivery. *Unit head:* Dr. Daniel Armentrout, Chair, 303-871-3580, Fax: 303-871-4450, E-mail: darmentr@du.edu. *Application contact:* Renee Carvalho, Assistant to the Chair, 303-871-2107, Fax: 303-871-4450, E-mail: renee.carvalho@du.edu.

University of Florida, Graduate School, College of Engineering, Department of Materials Science and Engineering, Gainesville, FL 32611. Offers ME, MS, PhD, Engr, JD/MS. Part-time programs available. *Faculty:* 26 full-time (6 women), 2 part-time/adjunct (0 women). *Students:* 304 full-time (48 women), 50 part-time (13 women); includes 12 Black or African American, non-Hispanic/Latino; 13 Asian, non-Hispanic/Latino; 11 Hispanic/Latino, 200 international. Average age 27. 577 applicants, 57% accepted, 95 enrolled. In 2010, 43 master's, 37 doctorates awarded. Terminal master's awarded for partial completion of doctoral program. *Degree requirements:* For master's, comprehensive exam, thesis; for doctorate, comprehensive exam, thesis/dissertation; for Engr, thesis optional. *Entrance requirements:* For master's and doctorate, GRE General Test, minimum GPA of 3.0; for Engr, GRE General Test. Additional exam requirements/recommendations for international students: Required—TOEFL (minimum score 550 paper-based; 213 computer-based; 80 iBT), IELTS (minimum score 6). *Application deadline:* For fall admission, 7/1 priority date for domestic students, 5/1 for international students; for spring admission, 11/1 for domestic students, 9/1 for international students. Applications are processed on a rolling basis. Application fee: $30. Electronic applications accepted. *Expenses:* Tuition, state resident: full-time $10,915.92. Tuition, nonresident: full-time $28,309. *Financial support:* In 2010–11, 180 students received support, including 4 fellowships, 176 research assistantships (averaging $22,263 per year). Financial award applicants required to submit FAFSA. *Faculty research:* Polymeric system, biomaterials and biomimetics; inorganic and organic electronic materials; functional ceramic materials for energy systems and microelectronic applications; advanced metallic systems for aerospace, transportation and biological applications; nuclear materials. Total annual research expenditures: $8.5 million. *Unit head:* Simon R. Phillpot, PhD, Chair, 352-846-3782, Fax: 352-392-7219, E-mail: sphil@mse.ufl.edu. *Application contact:* Jack Mecholsky, PhD, Graduate Coordinator, 352-846-3306, Fax: 352-846-1182, E-mail: jmech@mse.ufl.edu.

University of Illinois at Chicago, Graduate College, College of Engineering, Department of Civil and Materials Engineering, Chicago, IL 60607-7128. Offers civil engineering (MS, PhD); materials engineering (MS, PhD). Evening/weekend programs available. *Degree requirements:* For master's, thesis (for some programs); for doctorate, thesis/dissertation, preliminary and qualifying exams. *Entrance requirements:* For master's and doctorate, GRE General Test, minimum GPA of 3.0. Additional exam requirements/recommendations for international students: Required—TOEFL. Electronic applications accepted. *Faculty research:* Transportation and geotechnical engineering, damage and anisotropic behavior, steel processing.

University of Illinois at Urbana–Champaign, Graduate College, College of Engineering, Department of Materials Science and Engineering, Champaign, IL 61820. Offers MS, PhD, MS/MBA, PhD/MBA. *Faculty:* 23 full-time (3 women), 3 part-time/adjunct (0 women). *Students:* 154 full-time (38 women), 5 part-time (1 woman); includes 18 Asian, non-Hispanic/Latino; 2 Hispanic/Latino, 84 international. 336 applicants, 23% accepted, 29 enrolled. In 2010, 5 master's, 29 doctorates awarded. *Entrance requirements:* For master's and doctorate, GRE, minimum GPA of 3.0. Additional exam requirements/recommendations for international students: Required—TOEFL (minimum score 613 paper-based; 257 computer-based; 103 iBT) or IELTS (minimum score 7). *Application deadline:* Applications are processed on a rolling basis. Application fee: $75 ($90 for international students). Electronic applications accepted. *Financial support:* In 2010–11, 21 fellowships, 141 research assistantships, 15 teaching assistantships were awarded; tuition waivers (full and partial) also available. *Unit head:* David G. Cahill, Head, 217-333-6753, Fax: 217-244-1631, E-mail: d-cahill@illinois.edu. *Application contact:*

Michelle L. Malloch, Office Support Associate, 217-333-8517, Fax: 217-333-2736, E-mail: malloch@illinois.edu.

University of Maryland, College Park, Academic Affairs, A. James Clark School of Engineering, Department of Continuing and Distance Learning in Engineering, College Park, MD 20742. Offers engineering (M Eng), including aerospace engineering, chemical engineering, civil engineering, electrical engineering, engineering, fire protection engineering, materials science and engineering, mechanical engineering, reliability engineering, systems engineering. *Faculty:* 4 full-time (1 woman), 11 part-time/adjunct (1 woman). *Students:* 56 full-time (15 women), 428 part-time (88 women); includes 153 minority (59 Black or African American, non-Hispanic/Latino; 63 Asian, non-Hispanic/Latino; 24 Hispanic/Latino; 7 Two or more races, non-Hispanic/Latino), 55 international. 551 applicants, 82% accepted, 360 enrolled. In 2010, 130 master's awarded. *Application deadline:* For fall admission, 8/15 for domestic students, 1/10 for international students; for spring admission, 12/15 for domestic students, 6/1 for international students. Applications are processed on a rolling basis. Application fee: $75. Electronic applications accepted. *Expenses:* Tuition, area resident: Part-time $471 per credit hour. Tuition, state resident: part-time $471 per credit hour. Tuition, nonresident: part-time $1016 per credit hour. Required fees: $337 per term. *Financial support:* In 2010–11, 2 research assistantships (averaging $20,285 per year), 7 teaching assistantships (averaging $16,962 per year) were awarded. *Unit head:* Dr. Darryll Pines, Dean, 301-405-0376, Fax: 301-314-5908, E-mail: pines@umd.edu. *Application contact:* Dr. Charles A. Caramello, Dean of the Graduate School, 301-405-0358, Fax: 301-314-9305, E-mail: ccaramel@umd.edu.

University of Maryland, College Park, Academic Affairs, A. James Clark School of Engineering, Department of Materials and Nuclear Engineering, Materials Science and Engineering Program, College Park, MD 20742. Offers MS, PhD. Part-time and evening/weekend programs available. Postbaccalaureate distance learning degree programs offered. *Students:* 55 full-time (11 women), 12 part-time (6 women); includes 14 minority (7 Black or African American, non-Hispanic/Latino; 5 Asian, non-Hispanic/Latino; 2 Hispanic/Latino), 20 international. 232 applicants, 10% accepted, 7 enrolled. In 2010, 4 master's, 10 doctorates awarded. *Degree requirements:* For master's, comprehensive exam, thesis optional, research paper; for doctorate, thesis/dissertation, oral exam. *Entrance requirements:* For master's and doctorate, GRE General Test, minimum B+ average in undergraduate course work. Additional exam requirements/recommendations for international students: Required—TOEFL. *Application deadline:* For fall admission, 2/1 for domestic and international students; for spring admission, 8/1 for domestic students, 6/1 for international students. Applications are processed on a rolling basis. Application fee: $75. Electronic applications accepted. *Expenses:* Tuition, area resident: Part-time $471 per credit hour. Tuition, state resident: part-time $471 per credit hour. Tuition, nonresident: part-time $1016 per credit hour. Required fees: $337 per term. *Financial support:* In 2010–11, 2 fellowships with full tuition reimbursements (averaging $27,835 per year), 46 research assistantships (averaging $24,019 per year), 5 teaching assistantships (averaging $19,461 per year) were awarded. Financial award applicants required to submit FAFSA. *Unit head:* Robert Briber, Chair, 301-405-7313, E-mail: rbriber@umd.edu. *Application contact:* Dr. Charles A. Caramello, Dean of Graduate School, 301-405-0358, Fax: 301-314-9305, E-mail: ccaramel@umd.edu.

University of Maryland, College Park, Academic Affairs, A. James Clark School of Engineering, Department of Mechanical Engineering, College Park, MD 20742. Offers electronic packaging and reliability (MS, PhD); manufacturing and design (MS, PhD); mechanics and materials (MS, PhD); reliability engineering (M Eng, MS, PhD); thermal and fluid sciences (MS, PhD). Part-time and evening/weekend programs available. Postbaccalaureate distance learning degree programs offered. *Faculty:* 79 full-time (7 women), 21 part-time/adjunct (1 woman). *Students:* 219 full-time (31 women), 73 part-time (10 women); includes 44 minority (11 Black or African American, non-Hispanic/Latino; 2 American Indian or Alaska Native, non-Hispanic/Latino; 21 Asian, non-Hispanic/Latino; 8 Hispanic/Latino; 2 Two or more races, non-Hispanic/Latino), 138 international. 520 applicants, 18% accepted, 63 enrolled. In 2010, 31 master's, 31 doctorates awarded. *Degree requirements:* For master's, thesis optional; for doctorate, thesis/dissertation, qualifying exam. *Entrance requirements:* For master's, GRE General Test, 3 letters of recommendation; for doctorate, GRE General Test, minimum GPA of 3.0. Additional exam requirements/recommendations for international students: Required—TOEFL. *Application deadline:* For fall admission, 5/15 for domestic students, 2/1 for international students; for spring admission, 10/1 for domestic students, 6/1 for international students. Applications are processed on a rolling basis. Application fee: $75. Electronic applications accepted. *Expenses:* Tuition, area resident: Part-time $471 per credit hour. Tuition, state resident: part-time $471 per credit hour. Tuition, nonresident: part-time $1016 per credit hour. Required fees: $337 per term. *Financial support:* In 2010–11, 3 fellowships with full and partial tuition reimbursements (averaging $19,975 per year), 166 research assistantships (averaging $23,679 per year), 12 teaching assistantships (averaging $17,644 per year) were awarded; Federal Work-Study and scholarships/grants also available. Support available to part-time students. Financial award applicants required to submit FAFSA. *Faculty research:* Injection molding, electronic packaging, fluid mechanics, product engineering. Total annual research expenditures: $17.4 million. *Unit head:* Dr. B. Balachandran, Interim Chair, 301-405-5297, E-mail: balab@umd.edu. *Application contact:* Dr. Charles A. Caramello, Graduate Director, 301-405-0358, Fax: 301-314-9305, E-mail: ccaramel@umd.edu.

University of Massachusetts Lowell, James B. Francis College of Engineering, Department of Plastics Engineering, Lowell, MA 01854-2881. Offers elastomers (Graduate Certificate); medical plastics design and manufacturing (Graduate Certificate); plastics design (Graduate Certificate); plastics engineering (MS Eng, D Eng, PhD), including coatings and adhesives (MS Eng), plastics materials (MS Eng), plastics processing (MS Eng), product design (MS Eng); plastics engineering fundamentals (Graduate Certificate); plastics materials (Graduate Certificate); plastics processing (Graduate Certificate); polymer science/plastics engineering (PhD). Part-time programs available. Terminal master's awarded for partial completion of doctoral program. *Degree requirements:* For master's, thesis optional; for doctorate, comprehensive exam, thesis/dissertation. *Entrance requirements:* For master's and doctorate, GRE General Test. Additional exam requirements/recommendations for international students: Required—TOEFL.

University of Michigan, Horace H. Rackham School of Graduate Studies, College of Engineering, Department of Materials Science and Engineering, Ann Arbor, MI 48109. Offers MS, PhD. Part-time programs available. *Students:* 101 full-time (26 women), 1 part-time (0 women). 353 applicants, 24% accepted, 31 enrolled. In 2010, 14 master's, 9 doctorates awarded. *Degree requirements:* For master's, thesis, oral defense of thesis; for doctorate, thesis/dissertation, oral defense of dissertation, written exam. *Entrance requirements:* For master's, GRE General Test, minimum GPA of 3.0 in related field; for doctorate, GRE General Test, minimum GPA of 3.0 in related field, master's degree. Additional exam requirements/recommendations for international students: Required—TOEFL. *Application deadline:* Applications are processed on a rolling basis. Application fee: $65 ($75 for international students). Electronic applications accepted. *Expenses:* Tuition, state resident: full-time $17,784; part-time $1116 per credit hour. Tuition, nonresident: full-time $35,944; part-time $2125 per credit hour. International tuition: $35,994 full-time. Required fees: $95 per semester. Tuition and fees vary according to course load, degree level and program. *Financial support:* Fellowships, research assistantships, teaching assistantships available. Financial award applicants required to submit FAFSA. *Faculty research:* Soft materials (polymers, biomaterials); computational materials science; structural materials; electronic and optical materials; nanocomposite materials. *Unit head:* Peter Green, Department Chair, 734-763-2445, Fax: 734-763-4788. *Application contact:* Renee Hilgendorf, Graduate Program Coordinator, 734-763-9790, Fax: 734-763-4788, E-mail: reneeh@umich.edu.

See Display on page 514 and Close-Up on page 523.

University of Minnesota, Twin Cities Campus, Institute of Technology, Department of Chemical Engineering and Materials Science, Program in Materials Science and Engineering, Minneapolis, MN 55455-0132. Offers M Mat SE, MS Mat SE, PhD. Part-time programs available. Terminal master's awarded for partial completion of doctoral program. *Degree requirements:* For master's, thesis; for doctorate, thesis/dissertation. *Entrance requirements:* For master's and doctorate, GRE General Test. *Faculty research:* Fracture micromechanics, hydrogen embrittlement, polymer physics, microelectric materials, corrosion science.

University of Nebraska–Lincoln, Graduate College, College of Engineering, Department of Mechanical Engineering, Lincoln, NE 68588. Offers chemical and materials engineering (PhD); mechanical engineering (MS, PhD), including materials science engineering (MS), metallurgical engineering (MS). *Degree requirements:* For master's, thesis optional; for doctorate, comprehensive exam, thesis/dissertation. *Entrance requirements:* For master's and doctorate, GRE General Test. Additional exam requirements/recommendations for international students: Required—TOEFL (minimum score 550 paper-based; 213 computer-based). Electronic applications accepted. *Faculty research:* Robotics for planetary exploration, vehicle crashworthiness, transient heat conduction, laser beam/particle interactions.

See Display on page 543 and Close-Up on page 557.

University of Nevada, Las Vegas, Graduate College, Howard R. Hughes College of Engineering, Department of Mechanical Engineering, Las Vegas, NV 89154-4027. Offers aerospace engineering (MS); biomedical engineering (MS); materials and nuclear engineering (MS); mechanical engineering (MSE, PhD). Part-time programs available. *Faculty:* 17 full-time (0 women), 10 part-time/adjunct (0 women). *Students:* 43 full-time (6 women), 24 part-time (6 women); includes 24 minority (1 Black or African American, non-Hispanic/Latino; 4 Asian, non-Hispanic/Latino; 1 Hispanic/Latino; 1 Native Hawaiian or other Pacific Islander, non-Hispanic/Latino; 17 Two or more races, non-Hispanic/Latino), 24 international. Average age 30. 32 applicants, 84% accepted, 15 enrolled. In 2010, 10 master's, 4 doctorates awarded. *Degree requirements:* For master's, comprehensive exam, thesis (for some programs), project; for doctorate, comprehensive exam, thesis/dissertation. *Entrance requirements:* For master's and doctorate, GRE General Test. Additional exam requirements/recommendations for international students: Required—TOEFL (minimum score 550 paper-based; 213 computer-based; 80 iBT), IELTS (minimum score 7). *Application deadline:* For fall admission, 5/1 priority date for domestic and international students; for spring admission, 10/1 priority date for domestic and international students. Applications are processed on a rolling basis. Application fee: $60 ($95 for international students). Electronic applications accepted. *Expenses:* Tuition, area resident: Part-time $239.50 per credit. Tuition, state resident: part-time $239.50 per credit. Tuition, nonresident: part-time $503 per credit. Required fees: $108 per semester. Tuition and fees vary according to course load, program and reciprocity agreements. *Financial support:* In 2010–11, 37 students received support, including 21 research assistantships with partial tuition reimbursements available (averaging $13,335 per year), 16 teaching assistantships with partial tuition reimbursements available (averaging $11,000 per year); institutionally sponsored loans, scholarships/grants, health care benefits, and unspecified assistantships also available. Financial award application deadline: 3/1. *Faculty research:* Dynamics and control systems; energy systems including renewable and nuclear; computational fluid and solid mechanics; structures, materials and manufacturing; vibrations and acoustics. Total annual research expenditures: $3 million. *Unit head:* Dr. Woosoon Yim, Chair/Professor, 702-895-0956, Fax: 702-895-3936, E-mail: wy@me.unlv.edu. *Application contact:* Graduate College Admissions Evaluator, 702-895-3320, Fax: 702-895-4180, E-mail: gradcollege@unlv.edu.

University of Nevada, Reno, Graduate School, College of Engineering, Department of Chemical and Materials Engineering, Program in Materials Science and Engineering, Reno, NV 89557. Offers MS, PhD. Terminal master's awarded for partial completion of doctoral program. *Degree requirements:* For master's, thesis; for doctorate, one foreign language, thesis/dissertation. *Entrance requirements:* For master's, minimum GPA of 2.75; for doctorate, GRE, minimum GPA of 3.0. Additional exam requirements/recommendations for international students: Required—TOEFL (minimum score 500 paper-based; 173 computer-based; 61 iBT), IELTS (minimum score 6). Electronic applications accepted. *Expenses:* Tuition, state resident: full-time $2219; part-time $246 per credit. Tuition, nonresident: part-time $510 per credit. International tuition: $9009 full-time. Required fees: $59 per term. One-time fee: $101. Tuition and fees vary according to course load. *Faculty research:* Hydrometallurgy, applied surface chemistry, mineral processing, mineral bioprocessing, ceramics.

University of Pennsylvania, School of Engineering and Applied Science, Department of Materials Science and Engineering, Philadelphia, PA 19104. Offers MSE, PhD, MSE/MBA. Part-time programs available. *Faculty:* 14 full-time (3 women), 1 part-time/adjunct (0 women). *Students:* 93 full-time (30 women), 9 part-time (1 woman); includes 10 Asian, non-Hispanic/Latino; 1 Hispanic/Latino, 64 international. 331 applicants, 27% accepted, 50 enrolled. In 2010, 19 master's, 10 doctorates awarded. Terminal master's awarded for partial completion of doctoral program. *Degree requirements:* For master's, thesis; for doctorate, thesis/dissertation. *Entrance requirements:* Additional exam requirements/recommendations for international students: Required—TOEFL. *Application deadline:* For fall admission, 6/1 priority date for domestic students, 5/1 priority date for international students; for spring admission, 11/1 priority date for domestic students, 10/1 priority date for international students. Applications are processed on a rolling basis. Application fee: $70. Electronic applications accepted. *Expenses:* Tuition: Full-time $25,660; part-time $4758 per course. Required fees: $2152; $270 per course. Tuition and fees vary according to course load, degree level and program. *Financial support:* Fellowships, research assistantships, teaching assistantships, institutionally sponsored loans, scholarships/grants, traineeships, health care benefits, and unspecified assistantships available. *Faculty research:* Advanced metallic, ceramic, and polymeric materials for device applications; micromechanics and structure of interfaces; thin film electronic materials; physics and chemistry of solids. *Application contact:* Irene Clements, Graduate Coordinator, 215-898-8337, E-mail: ipc@lrsm.upenn.edu.

University of Southern California, Graduate School, Viterbi School of Engineering, Mork Family Department of Chemical Engineering and Materials Science, Los Angeles, CA 90089. Offers chemical engineering (MS, PhD, Engr); materials engineering (MS); materials science (MS, PhD, Engr); petroleum engineering (MS, PhD, Engr); smart oilfield technologies (MS, Graduate Certificate). *Faculty:* 19 full-time (3 women), 9 part-time/adjunct (1 woman). *Students:* 235 full-time (77 women), 77 part-time (25 women); includes 43 minority (6 Black or African American, non-Hispanic/Latino; 25 Asian, non-Hispanic/Latino; 11 Hispanic/Latino; 1 Two or more races, non-Hispanic/Latino), 213 international. 643 applicants, 36% accepted, 118 enrolled. In 2010, 37 master's, 19 doctorates, 4 other advanced degrees awarded. Terminal master's awarded for partial completion of doctoral program. *Degree requirements:* For master's, thesis optional; for doctorate, thesis/dissertation. *Entrance requirements:* For master's and doctorate, GRE General Test. *Application deadline:* For fall admission, 12/1 priority date for domestic and international students; for spring admission, 9/1 priority date for domestic and international students. Applications are processed on a rolling basis. Application fee: $85. Electronic applications accepted. *Expenses:* Contact institution. *Financial support:* In 2010–11, fellowships with full tuition reimbursements (averaging $30,000 per year), research assistantships with full tuition reimbursements (averaging $20,000 per year), teaching assistantships with full tuition reimbursements (averaging $20,000 per year) were awarded; career-related internships or fieldwork, scholarships/grants, health care benefits, and unspecified assistantships also available. Financial award application deadline: 12/1; financial award applicants required to submit CSS PROFILE or FAFSA. *Faculty research:* Heterogeneous materials and porous media, statistical mechanics, molecular simulation, polymer science and engineering, advanced materials, reaction engineering and catalysis, membrane processes and separation, biochemical engineering, cell culture, bioreactor modeling, petroleum engineering. Total annual research expenditures: $11.6 million. *Unit head:* Dr. Theodore Tsotsis, Chair, 213-740-2227, E-mail: chedept@usc.edu. *Application contact:* Karen Woo, Student Services Advisor, 213-740-2227, E-mail: karenwoo@usc.edu.

The University of Tennessee, Graduate School, College of Engineering, Department of Materials Science and Engineering, Program in Materials Science and Engineering, Knoxville, TN 37996. Offers MS, PhD. *Faculty:* 26 full-time (1 woman), 4 part-time/adjunct (2 women). *Students:* 72 full-time (14 women), 11 part-time (1 woman); includes 2 Black or African American, non-Hispanic/Latino; 3 Asian, non-Hispanic/Latino; 3 Hispanic/Latino, 51 international. Average age 22. 140 applicants, 26% accepted, 25 enrolled. In 2010, 5 master's, 9 doctorates awarded. *Degree requirements:* For master's, thesis or alternative; for doctorate, comprehensive exam, thesis/dissertation. *Entrance requirements:* For master's, GRE General Test, Minimum GPA of 2.7 (US degree holders); 3.0 (International degree holders); 3-References; for doctorate, GRE General Test, Minimum GPA of 3.0 (previous graduate course work); 3-References. Additional exam requirements/recommendations for international students: Required—TOEFL (minimum score 550 paper-based; 213 computer-based). *Application deadline:* For fall admission, 2/1 priority date for domestic and international students; for spring admission, 6/15 for domestic and international students. Applications are processed on a rolling basis. Application fee: $35. Electronic applications accepted. *Expenses:* Tuition, state resident: full-time $7440; part-time $414 per credit hour. Tuition, nonresident: full-time $22,478; part-time $1250 per credit hour. Required fees: $922; $43 per credit hour. Tuition and fees vary according to program. *Financial support:* In 2010–11, 66 students received support, including 4 fellowships with full tuition reimbursements available (averaging $9,996 per year), 76 research assistantships with full tuition reimbursements available (averaging $19,272 per year), 11 teaching assistantships with full tuition reimbursements available (averaging $19,752 per year); career-related internships or fieldwork, Federal Work-Study, institutionally sponsored loans, health care benefits, and unspecified assistantships also available. Financial award application deadline: 2/1; financial award applicants required to submit FAFSA. *Faculty research:* Biomaterials; functional materials electronic, magnetic and optical; high temperature materials; mechanical behavior of materials; neutron materials science. *Unit head:* Dr. George Pharr, Head, 865-974-5336, Fax: 865-974-4115, E-mail: pharr@utk.edu. *Application contact:* Dr. Roberto S. Benson, Associate Head, 865-974-5347, Fax: 865-974-4115, E-mail: rbenson1@utk.edu.

The University of Tennessee Space Institute, Graduate Programs, Program in Materials Science and Engineering, Tullahoma, TN 37388-9700. Offers MS. *Faculty:* 4 full-time (1 woman). *Students:* 5 full-time (0 women), 1 part-time (0 women); includes 1 minority (Asian, non-Hispanic/Latino), 2 international. 3 applicants, 100% accepted, 1 enrolled. In 2010, 1 master's awarded. *Entrance requirements:* Additional exam requirements/recommendations for international students: Required—TOEFL (minimum score 550 paper-based; 213 computer-based; 80 iBT), IELTS (minimum score 6.5). *Application deadline:* For fall admission, 2/1 for international students; for spring admission, 6/15 for international students. Applications are processed on a rolling basis. Application fee: $35. Electronic applications accepted. *Financial support:* In 2010–11, 5 research assistantships with full tuition reimbursements (averaging $17,791 per year) were awarded; fellowships, career-related internships or fieldwork, Federal Work-Study, institutionally sponsored loans, health care benefits, tuition waivers (full and partial), and unspecified assistantships also available. *Unit head:* Dr. William Hofmeister, Degree Program Chairman, 931-393-7466, Fax: 931-393-7437, E-mail: whofmeis@utsi.edu. *Application contact:* Dee Merriman, Coordinator III, 931-393-7213, Fax: 931-393-7211, E-mail: dmerrima@utsi.edu.

The University of Texas at Arlington, Graduate School, College of Engineering, Department of Materials Science and Engineering, Arlington, TX 76019. Offers M Engr, MS, PhD. *Faculty:* 8 full-time (0 women). *Students:* 45 full-time (13 women), 13 part-time (3 women); includes 4 minority (1 Black or African American, non-Hispanic/Latino; 3 Asian, non-Hispanic/Latino), 48 international. 33 applicants, 61% accepted, 11 enrolled. In 2010, 21 master's, 5 doctorates awarded. Terminal master's awarded for partial completion of doctoral program. *Degree requirements:* For master's, comprehensive exam (for some programs), thesis optional; for doctorate, comprehensive exam, thesis/dissertation optional. *Entrance requirements:* For master's, GRE General Test, minimum GPA of 3.0; for doctorate, GRE General Test, minimum GPA of 3.5. Additional exam requirements/recommendations for international students: Required—TOEFL (minimum score 550 paper-based; 213 computer-based). *Application deadline:* For fall admission, 6/6 for domestic students, 4/4 for international students; for spring admission, 10/15 for domestic students, 9/5 for international students. Applications are processed on a rolling basis. Application fee: $35 ($50 for international students). *Expenses:* Tuition, state resident: full-time $7500. Tuition, nonresident: full-time $13,080. International tuition: $13,250 full-time. *Financial support:* In 2010–11, 27 students received support, including 4 fellowships (averaging $1,000 per year), 10 research assistantships (averaging $16,000 per year), 13 teaching assistantships (averaging $16,000 per year); scholarships/grants and unspecified assistantships also available. Financial award application deadline: 6/1; financial award applicants required to submit FAFSA. *Faculty research:* Electronic materials, conductive polymer, composites biomaterial, structural materials. Total annual research expenditures: $400,000. *Unit head:* Dr. Efstathios Meletis, Chair, 817-272-2398, Fax: 817-272-2538, E-mail: meletis@uta.edu. *Application contact:* Dr. Choong-Un Kim, Graduate Adviser, 817-272-5497, Fax: 817-272-2538, E-mail: choongun@uta.edu.

The University of Texas at Austin, Graduate School, Cockrell School of Engineering, Program in Materials Science and Engineering, Austin, TX 78712-1111. Offers MS, PhD. Part-time programs available. *Degree requirements:* For master's, thesis (for some programs); for doctorate, thesis/dissertation. *Entrance requirements:* For master's and doctorate, GRE General Test. Additional exam requirements/recommendations for international students: Required—TOEFL (minimum score 550 paper-based; 213 computer-based). Electronic applications accepted.

The University of Texas at Dallas, Erik Jonsson School of Engineering and Computer Science, Programs in Materials Science and Engineering, Richardson, TX 75080. Offers MS, PhD. Part-time and evening/weekend programs available. *Faculty:* 11 full-time (1 woman). *Students:* 49 full-time (11 women), 8 part-time (3 women); includes 9 minority (1 Black or African American, non-Hispanic/Latino; 2 Asian, non-Hispanic/Latino; 6 Hispanic/Latino), 35 international. Average age 28. 56 applicants, 41% accepted, 9 enrolled. In 2010, 3 master's, 2 doctorates awarded. *Degree requirements:* For master's, thesis or major design project; for doctorate, thesis/dissertation. *Entrance requirements:* For master's, GRE General Test, minimum GPA of 3.0 in related bachelor's degree; for doctorate, GRE General Test, minimum GPA of 3.5. Additional exam requirements/recommendations for international students: Required—TOEFL (minimum score 550 paper-based; 215 computer-based). *Application deadline:* For fall admission, 7/15 for domestic students, 5/1 priority date for international students; for spring admission, 11/15 for domestic students, 9/1 priority date for international students. Applications are processed on a rolling basis. Application fee: $50 ($100 for international students). Electronic applications accepted. *Expenses:* Tuition, state resident: full-time $10,248; part-time $569 per credit hour. Tuition, nonresident: full-time $18,544; part-time $1030 per credit hour. Tuition and fees vary according to course load. *Financial support:* In 2010–11, 41 students received support, including 45 research assistantships with partial tuition reimbursements available (averaging $17,450 per year), 1 teaching assistantship with partial tuition reimbursement available (averaging $16,619 per year); career-related internships or fieldwork, Federal Work-Study, institutionally sponsored loans, scholarships/grants, and unspecified assistantships also available. Support available to part-time students. Financial award application deadline: 4/30; financial award applicants required to submit FAFSA. *Faculty research:* Graphene-based semiconducting materials, neuro-inspired computational paradigms, electronic materials with emphasis on dielectrics, energy harvesting (photovoltaics, Li-ion batteries), biosensors and H2 storage materials. *Unit head:* Dr. Yves Chabal, Department Head, 972-883-5751, Fax: 972-883-5725, E-mail: chabal@utdallas.edu. *Application contact:* Tonya Griffin, Administrative Services Officer, 972-883-5764, Fax: 972-883-5725, E-mail: gradecs@utdallas.edu.

The University of Texas at El Paso, Graduate School, College of Engineering, Department of Metallurgical and Materials Engineering, El Paso, TX 79968-0001. Offers materials science and engineering (PhD); metallurgical and materials engineering (MS). Part-time and evening/weekend programs available. *Students:* 15 (3 women); includes 1 Asian, non-Hispanic/Latino; 9 Hispanic/Latino, 3 international. Average age 34. In 2010, 1 master's awarded. *Degree requirements:* For master's, thesis. *Entrance requirements:* For master's, GRE General Test. Additional exam requirements/recommendations for international students: Required—TOEFL.

Materials Engineering

The University of Texas at El Paso (continued)

Application deadline: For fall admission, 7/1 priority date for domestic students, 3/1 for international students; for spring admission, 11/1 priority date for domestic students, 9/1 for international students. Applications are processed on a rolling basis. Application fee: $15 ($65 for international students). Electronic applications accepted. *Financial support:* In 2010–11, research assistantships with partial tuition reimbursements (averaging $21,125 per year), teaching assistantships with partial tuition reimbursements (averaging $16,900 per year) were awarded; fellowships with partial tuition reimbursements, career-related internships or fieldwork, Federal Work-Study, institutionally sponsored loans, scholarships/grants, and tuition waivers (partial) also available. Financial award application deadline: 3/15; financial award applicants required to submit FAFSA. *Unit head:* Dr. Lawrence E. Murr, Chairperson, 915-747-5468, Fax: 915-747-8036, E-mail: fekberg@utep.edu. *Application contact:* Dr. Charles H. Ambler, Dean of the Graduate School, 915-747-5491 Ext. 7886, Fax: 915-747-5788, E-mail: cambler@utep.edu.

The University of Texas at El Paso, Graduate School, Interdisciplinary Program in Materials Science and Engineering, El Paso, TX 79968-0001. Offers PhD. Part-time and evening/weekend programs available. *Students:* 20 (6 women); includes 2 Black or African American, non-Hispanic/Latino; 1 Asian, non-Hispanic/Latino; 8 Hispanic/Latino, 8 international. Average age 34. In 2010, 5 doctorates awarded. *Degree requirements:* For doctorate, thesis/dissertation. *Entrance requirements:* For doctorate, GRE, letters of recommendation. Additional exam requirements/recommendations for international students: Required—TOEFL; Recommended—IELTS. *Application deadline:* For fall admission, 8/1 priority date for domestic students, 3/1 for international students; for spring admission, 11/1 priority date for domestic students, 9/1 for international students. Applications are processed on a rolling basis. Application fee: $45 ($80 for international students). Electronic applications accepted. *Financial support:* In 2010–11, research assistantships with partial tuition reimbursements (averaging $22,500 per year), teaching assistantships with partial tuition reimbursements (averaging $1,800 per year) were awarded; fellowships with partial tuition reimbursements, institutionally sponsored loans, scholarships/grants, health care benefits, tuition waivers (partial), and unspecified assistantships also available. Support available to part-time students. Financial award application deadline: 3/15; financial award applicants required to submit FAFSA. *Unit head:* Dr. Lawrence E. Murr, Director, 915-747-8002, Fax: 915-747-8036, E-mail: fekberg@utep.edu. *Application contact:* Dr. Patricia D. Witherspoon, Dean of the Graduate School, 915-747-5491, Fax: 915-747-5788, E-mail: withersp@utep.edu.

University of Toronto, School of Graduate Studies, Physical Sciences Division, Faculty of Applied Science and Engineering, Department of Materials Science and Engineering, Toronto, ON M5S 1A1, Canada. Offers M Eng, MA Sc, PhD. Part-time programs available. *Degree requirements:* For master's, thesis (for some programs), oral presentation/thesis defense (MA Sc), qualifying exam; for doctorate, thesis/dissertation. *Entrance requirements:* For master's, BA Sc or B Sc degree in materials science and engineering, 2 letters of reference; for doctorate, MA Sc degree or equivalent, 2 letters of reference, minimum B+ average in last 2 years. Additional exam requirements/recommendations for international students: Required—TOEFL (minimum score 580 paper-based), TWE (minimum score 4).

University of Utah, Graduate School, College of Engineering, Department of Materials Science and Engineering, Salt Lake City, UT 84112. Offers MS, PhD. *Faculty:* 8 full-time (1 woman), 1 part-time/adjunct (0 women). *Students:* 32 full-time (3 women), 10 part-time (2 women); includes 1 minority (Asian, non-Hispanic/Latino), 25 international. Average age 29. 84 applicants, 14% accepted, 11 enrolled. In 2010, 5 master's, 4 doctorates awarded. Terminal master's awarded for partial completion of doctoral program. *Degree requirements:* For master's, thesis; for doctorate, thesis/dissertation, exam. *Entrance requirements:* For master's, GRE General Test, minimum GPA of 3.0; for doctorate, GRE General Test, minimum GPA of 3.0. Additional exam requirements/recommendations for international students: Required—TOEFL (minimum score 570 paper-based; 230 computer-based; 88 iBT), IELTS (minimum score 7). *Application deadline:* For fall admission, 1/15 for domestic students, 12/15 for international students; for spring admission, 9/1 for domestic students, 10/1 for international students. Applications are processed on a rolling basis. Application fee: $55 ($65 for international students). Electronic applications accepted. *Expenses:* Contact institution. *Financial support:* In 2010–11, 33 research assistantships (averaging $20,000 per year) were awarded; career-related internships or fieldwork and Federal Work-Study also available. Financial award application deadline: 2/5; financial award applicants required to submit FAFSA. *Faculty research:* Solid oxide fuel cells, computational nanostructures, computational polymers, biomaterials, electronic materials, nanomaterials. Total annual research expenditures: $2.8 million. *Unit head:* Dr. Anil V. Virkar, Chair, 801-581-6863, Fax: 801-581-4816, E-mail: anil.virkar@utah.edu. *Application contact:* Ashley Christensen, Academic Program Specialist, 801-581-6863, Fax: 801-581-4816, E-mail: ashley.christensen@utah.edu.

University of Washington, Graduate School, College of Engineering, Department of Materials Science and Engineering, Seattle, WA 98195-2120. Offers ceramic engineering (PhD); materials science and engineering (MS, MSE, PhD); materials science and engineering and nanotechnology (PhD). Part-time programs available. *Faculty:* 24 full-time (4 women). *Students:* 55 full-time (14 women), 9 part-time (2 women); includes 2 Black or African American, non-Hispanic/Latino; 7 Asian, non-Hispanic/Latino; 2 Hispanic/Latino, 22 international. Average age 30. 246 applicants, 11% accepted, 11 enrolled. In 2010, 3 master's, 9 doctorates awarded. *Degree requirements:* For master's, comprehensive exam, thesis optional; for doctorate, comprehensive exam, thesis/dissertation, Qualifying evaluation, general and final exams. *Entrance requirements:* For master's and doctorate, GRE General Test, minimum GPA of 3.0. Additional exam requirements/recommendations for international students: Required—TOEFL (minimum score 580 paper-based; 237 computer-based; 92 iBT); Recommended—IELTS (minimum score 7). *Application deadline:* For fall admission, 1/15 priority date for domestic students, 12/15 priority date for international students. Application fee: $75. Electronic applications accepted. *Financial support:* In 2010–11, 3 students received support, including 7 fellowships with full tuition reimbursements available (averaging $22,500 per year), 39 research assistantships with full tuition reimbursements available (averaging $16,407 per year), 8 teaching assistantships with full tuition reimbursements available (averaging $16,362 per year); career-related internships or fieldwork, Federal Work-Study, institutionally sponsored loans, scholarships/grants, health care benefits, unspecified assistantships, and stipend supplements also available. Financial award application deadline: 1/15; financial award applicants required to submit FAFSA. *Faculty research:* Biomimetics and biomaterials; electronic, optical and magnetic materials; eco-materials and materials for energy applications; ceramics, metals, composites, and polymers. Total annual research expenditures: $8.8 million. *Unit head:* Dr. Alex Jen, Professor and Chair, 206-543-2600, Fax: 206-543-3100, E-mail: ajen@uw.edu. *Application contact:* Kathleen A. Elkins, Academic Counselor, 206-616-6581, Fax: 206-543-3100, E-mail: kelkins@uw.edu.

The University of Western Ontario, Faculty of Graduate Studies, Physical Sciences Division, Faculty of Engineering, London, ON N6A 5B8, Canada. Offers chemical and biochemical engineering (ME Sc, PhD); civil and environmental engineering (M Eng, ME Sc, PhD); electrical and computer engineering (M Eng, ME Sc, PhD); mechanical and materials engineering (M Eng, ME Sc, PhD). Part-time programs available. Terminal master's awarded for partial completion of doctoral program. *Degree requirements:* For master's, thesis; for doctorate, thesis/dissertation. *Entrance requirements:* For master's, minimum B average; for doctorate, minimum B+ average. *Faculty research:* Wind, geotechnical, chemical reactor engineering, applied electrostatics, biochemical engineering.

University of Windsor, Faculty of Graduate Studies, Faculty of Engineering, Department of Mechanical, Automotive, and Materials Engineering, Windsor, ON N9B 3P4, Canada. Offers engineering materials (M Eng, MA Sc, PhD); mechanical engineering (M Eng, MA Sc, PhD). Part-time programs available. *Degree requirements:* For master's, thesis; for doctorate, comprehensive exam, thesis/dissertation. *Entrance requirements:* For master's, minimum B average; for doctorate, master's degree, minimum B average. Additional exam requirements/recommendations for international students: Required—TOEFL (minimum score 600 paper-based; 250 computer-based). Electronic applications accepted. *Faculty research:* Thermofluids, applied mechanics, materials engineering.

University of Wisconsin–Madison, Graduate School, College of Engineering, Department of Materials Science and Engineering, Madison, WI 53706-1380. Offers materials engineering (MS, PhD). Part-time programs available. *Faculty:* 20 full-time (4 women). *Students:* 19 full-time (3 women). Average age 25. 34 applicants, 3% accepted, 1 enrolled. Terminal master's awarded for partial completion of doctoral program. *Degree requirements:* For master's, thesis; for doctorate, comprehensive exam, thesis/dissertation. *Entrance requirements:* For master's and doctorate, GRE General Test. Additional exam requirements/recommendations for international students: Required—TOEFL (minimum score 580 paper-based; 237 computer-based). *Application deadline:* For fall admission, 7/1 priority date for domestic students, 1/1 priority date for international students; for spring admission, 10/15 priority date for domestic and international students. Applications are processed on a rolling basis. Application fee: $56. Electronic applications accepted. *Expenses:* Tuition, state resident: full-time $9887.36; part-time $617.96 per credit. Tuition, nonresident: full-time $24,054; part-time $1503.40 per credit. Required fees: $67.63 per credit. Tuition and fees vary according to reciprocity agreements. *Financial support:* In 2010–11, 1 fellowship with tuition reimbursement (averaging $20,760 per year), 3 research assistantships with tuition reimbursements (averaging $20,184 per year) were awarded; teaching assistantships with tuition reimbursements. Financial award application deadline: 1/15. *Faculty research:* Materials characterization, electronic materials, metallurgy, computational materials science, nanotechnology. Total annual research expenditures: $16.3 million. *Unit head:* Dr. Susan Elizabeth Babcock, Chair, 608-262-1821, Fax: 608-262-8353, E-mail: mat_engr@engr.wisc.edu. *Application contact:* Lynn J. Neis, University Services Program Associate B, 608-262-3732, Fax: 608-262-8353, E-mail: lynn@engr.wisc.edu.

University of Wisconsin–Milwaukee, Graduate School, College of Engineering and Applied Science, Program in Engineering, Milwaukee, WI 53201-0413. Offers civil engineering (MS); electrical and computer engineering (MS); energy engineering (Certificate); engineering (PhD); engineering management (MS); engineering mechanics (MS); ergonomics (Certificate); industrial and management engineering (MS); manufacturing engineering (MS); materials engineering (MS); mechanical engineering (MS); MUP/MS. Part-time programs available. *Faculty:* 50 full-time (5 women). *Students:* 152 full-time (27 women), 115 part-time (23 women); includes 13 Black or African American, non-Hispanic/Latino; 3 American Indian or Alaska Native, non-Hispanic/Latino; 6 Asian, non-Hispanic/Latino; 10 Hispanic/Latino, 25 international. Average age 31. 236 applicants, 67% accepted, 55 enrolled. In 2010, 39 master's, 19 doctorates awarded. *Degree requirements:* For master's, comprehensive exam (for some programs), thesis or alternative; for doctorate, comprehensive exam, thesis/dissertation, internship. *Entrance requirements:* For master's, GRE, minimum GPA of 2.75; for doctorate, GRE, minimum GPA of 3.5. Additional exam requirements/recommendations for international students: Required—TOEFL (minimum score 550 paper-based; 79 iBT), IELTS (minimum score 6.5). *Application deadline:* For fall admission, 1/1 priority date for domestic students; for spring admission, 9/1 for domestic students. Applications are processed on a rolling basis. Application fee: $56 ($96 for international students). *Financial support:* In 2010–11, 3 fellowships, 55 research assistantships, 77 teaching assistantships were awarded; career-related internships or fieldwork, Federal Work-Study, unspecified assistantships, and project assistantships also available. Support available to part-time students. Financial award application deadline: 4/15. Total annual research expenditures: $6.2 million. *Unit head:* David Yu, Representative, 414-229-6169, E-mail: yu@uwm.edu. *Application contact:* Betty Warras, General Information Contact, 414-229-6169, Fax: 414-229-6967, E-mail: bwarras@uwm.edu.

Virginia Polytechnic Institute and State University, Graduate School, College of Engineering, Department of Materials Science and Engineering, Blacksburg, VA 24061. Offers M Eng, MS, PhD. *Faculty:* 14 full-time (4 women). *Students:* 56 full-time (7 women), 3 part-time (1 woman); includes 3 Asian, non-Hispanic/Latino; 1 Hispanic/Latino, 27 international. Average age 28. 207 applicants, 12% accepted, 14 enrolled. In 2010, 5 master's, 9 doctorates awarded. *Degree requirements:* For master's, comprehensive exam (for some programs), thesis (for some programs); for doctorate, comprehensive exam (for some programs), thesis/dissertation (for some programs). *Entrance requirements:* For master's and doctorate, GRE. Additional exam requirements/recommendations for international students: Required—TOEFL (minimum score 550 paper-based; 213 computer-based). *Application deadline:* For fall admission, 7/1 for domestic and international students; for spring admission, 12/1 for domestic and international students. Applications are processed on a rolling basis. Application fee: $65. Electronic applications accepted. *Expenses:* Tuition, area resident: Full-time $9399; part-time $488 per credit hour. Tuition, state resident: full-time $9399; part-time $488 per credit hour. Tuition, nonresident: full-time $17,854; part-time $957.75 per credit hour. International tuition: $17,854 full-time. Required fees: $1534. Full-time tuition and fees vary according to program. *Financial support:* In 2010–11, 1 fellowship with full tuition reimbursement (averaging $7,500 per year), 23 research assistantships with full tuition reimbursements (averaging $23,993 per year), 2 teaching assistantships with full tuition reimbursements (averaging $23,679 per year) were awarded; career-related internships or fieldwork, Federal Work-Study, scholarships/grants, health care benefits, and unspecified assistantships also available. Financial award application deadline: 1/15. Total annual research expenditures: $5.2 million. *Unit head:* Dr. David E. Clark, UNIT HEAD, 540-231-6640, Fax: 540-231-8819, E-mail: dclark@vt.edu. *Application contact:* Gary Pickrell, Contact, 540-231-3504, Fax: 540-231-8919, E-mail: pickrell@vt.edu.

Washington State University, Graduate School, College of Engineering and Architecture, School of Mechanical and Materials Engineering, Program in Material Science Engineering, Pullman, WA 99164. Offers MS. *Faculty:* 29. *Students:* 27 full-time (6 women), 3 part-time (1 woman); includes 1 Black or African American, non-Hispanic/Latino; 1 American Indian or Alaska Native, non-Hispanic/Latino; 2 Asian, non-Hispanic/Latino; 1 Hispanic/Latino, 13 international. 133 applicants, 10% accepted, 3 enrolled. *Degree requirements:* For master's, comprehensive exam (for some programs), thesis. *Entrance requirements:* For master's, GRE, statement of purpose, three letters of recommendation, transcripts. Additional exam requirements/recommendations for international students: Required—TOEFL, IELTS. *Application deadline:* For fall admission, 1/10 for domestic and international students; for spring admission, 7/1 for domestic and international students. Applications are processed on a rolling basis. Application fee: $50. Electronic applications accepted. *Expenses:* Tuition, state resident: full-time $8552; part-time $443 per credit. Tuition, nonresident: full-time $21,650; part-time $1083 per credit. Required fees: $846. *Financial support:* In 2010–11, fellowships (averaging $2,500 per year), research assistantships with tuition reimbursements (averaging $13,917 per year) were awarded. Financial award application deadline: 2/10. Total annual research expenditures: $2.2 million. *Unit head:* Dr. Matthew McCluskey, Chair, 509-335-5356, Fax: 509-335-4662, E-mail: mattmcc@wsu.edu. *Application contact:* Graduate School Admissions, 800-GRADWSU, Fax: 509-335-1949, E-mail: gradsch@wsu.edu.

Wayne State University, College of Engineering, Department of Chemical Engineering and Materials Science, Program in Materials Science and Engineering, Detroit, MI 48202. Offers materials science and engineering (MS, PhD); polymer engineering (Certificate). Part-time programs available. *Faculty:* 8 full-time (2 women), 2 part-time/adjunct (0 women). *Students:* 14 full-time (3 women), 2 part-time (1 woman), 14 international. Average age 27. 22 applicants, 32% accepted, 2 enrolled. In 2010, 1 master's, 2 doctorates awarded. Terminal master's awarded for partial completion of doctoral program. *Degree requirements:* For master's, thesis optional; for doctorate, thesis/dissertation. *Entrance requirements:* For master's, GRE (if applying for financial support), recommendations; resume; for doctorate, GRE (if applying for financial support), recommendations; resume, personal statement. Additional exam requirements/recommendations for international students: Required—TOEFL (minimum score 550 paper-based; 213 computer-based); Recommended—TWE (minimum score 6). *Application deadline:* For fall admission, 7/1 priority date for domestic students, 6/1 for international students; for winter admission, 10/1 for international students; for spring admission, 3/15 for domestic students, 2/1 for international students. Applications are processed on a rolling basis. Application fee: $30 ($50 for international students). Electronic applications accepted. *Expenses:* Tuition, state resident: full-time $7662; part-time $478.85 per credit hour. Tuition, nonresident: full-time $16,920; part-time $1057.55 per credit hour. Required fees: $571.20; $35.70 per credit hour. $188.05 per semester. Tuition and fees vary according to course load and program. *Financial support:* In 2010–11, 6 research assistantships (averaging $16,221 per year), 5 teaching assistantships (averaging $16,984 per year) were awarded; fellowships also available. Financial award application deadline: 2/15. *Faculty research:* Polymer science, rheology, fatigue in metals, metal matrix composites, ceramics. *Unit head:* Charles Manke, Chair, 313-577-3849, Fax: 313-577-3810, E-mail: emanke@chem1.eng.wayne.edu. *Application contact:* Rangaramanujam Kannan, Associate Professor, 313-577-3800, E-mail: rkannan@che.eng.wayne.edu.

Worcester Polytechnic Institute, Graduate Studies and Research, Department of Mechanical Engineering, Program in Materials Science and Engineering, Worcester, MA 01609-2280. Offers MS, PhD. Part-time and evening/weekend programs available. *Faculty:* 4 full-time (1 woman), 1 part-time/adjunct (0 women). *Students:* 38 full-time (12 women), 7 part-time (4 women); includes 1 American Indian or Alaska Native, non-Hispanic/Latino; 3 Native Hawaiian or other Pacific Islander, non-Hispanic/Latino, 31 international. 71 applicants, 86% accepted, 13 enrolled. In 2010, 14 master's, 5 doctorates awarded. *Degree requirements:* For master's, thesis; for doctorate, comprehensive exam, thesis/dissertation. *Entrance requirements:* For master's and doctorate, GRE General Test (recommended). Required for International applicants, 3 letters of recommendation. Additional exam requirements/recommendations for international students: Required—TOEFL (minimum score 550 paper-based; 213 computer-based; 79 iBT), IELTS (minimum score 6.5). *Application deadline:* For fall admission, 1/1 priority date for domestic students, 1/1 for international students; for spring admission, 10/1 priority date for domestic students, 10/1 for international students. Applications are processed on a rolling basis. Application fee: $70. Electronic applications accepted. *Expenses:* Tuition: Full-time $20,862; part-time $1159 per term. One-time fee: $15. *Financial support:* Career-related internships or fieldwork, institutionally sponsored loans, scholarships/grants, and unspecified assistantships available. Financial award application deadline: 1/1; financial award applicants required to submit FAFSA. *Faculty research:* Metals processing, nanomaterials, reliability analysis, surface metrology, biopolymers. *Unit head:* Dr. Richard D. Sisson, Director, 508-831-5633, Fax: 508-831-5178, E-mail: sisson@wpi.edu. *Application contact:* Rita Shilansky, Graduate Secretary, 508-831-5633, Fax: 508-831-5178, E-mail: rita@wpi.edu.

Wright State University, School of Graduate Studies, College of Engineering and Computer Science, Programs in Engineering, Program in Mechanical and Materials Engineering, Dayton, OH 45435. Offers materials science and engineering (MSE); mechanical engineering (MSE). *Degree requirements:* For master's, thesis or course option alternative. *Entrance requirements:* Additional exam requirements/recommendations for international students: Required—TOEFL.

Materials Sciences

Air Force Institute of Technology, Graduate School of Engineering and Management, Department of Aeronautics and Astronautics, Dayton, OH 45433-7765. Offers aeronautical engineering (MS, PhD); astronautical engineering (MS, PhD); materials science (MS, PhD); space operations (MS); systems engineering (MS, PhD). *Accreditation:* ABET (one or more programs are accredited). Part-time programs available. *Degree requirements:* For master's, thesis; for doctorate, thesis/dissertation. *Entrance requirements:* For master's and doctorate, GRE General Test, minimum GPA of 3.0, U.S. citizenship. *Faculty research:* Computational fluid dynamics, experimental aerodynamics, computational structural mechanics, experimental structural mechanics, aircraft and spacecraft stability and control.

Air Force Institute of Technology, Graduate School of Engineering and Management, Department of Engineering Physics, Dayton, OH 45433-7765. Offers applied physics (MS, PhD); electro-optics (MS, PhD); materials science (PhD); nuclear engineering (MS, PhD); space physics (MS). Part-time programs available. *Degree requirements:* For master's, thesis; for doctorate, thesis/dissertation. *Entrance requirements:* For master's and doctorate, GRE General Test, minimum GPA of 3.0, U.S. citizenship. *Faculty research:* High-energy lasers, space physics, nuclear weapon effects, semiconductor physics.

Alabama Agricultural and Mechanical University, School of Graduate Studies, School of Arts and Sciences, Department of Physics, Huntsville, AL 35811. Offers physics (MS, PhD), including applied physics (PhD), materials science (PhD), optics/lasers (PhD). Part-time and evening/weekend programs available. *Degree requirements:* For doctorate, thesis/dissertation. *Entrance requirements:* For master's and doctorate, GRE General Test. Additional exam requirements/recommendations for international students: Required—TOEFL (minimum score 500 paper-based; 173 computer-based; 61 iBT). Electronic applications accepted.

Alfred University, Graduate School, New York State College of Ceramics, School of Engineering, Alfred, NY 14802-1205. Offers biomedical materials engineering science (MS); ceramic engineering (MS); ceramics (PhD); electrical engineering (MS); glass science (MS, PhD); materials science and engineering (MS, PhD); mechanical engineering (MS). *Degree requirements:* For master's, thesis; for doctorate, thesis/dissertation. *Entrance requirements:* Additional exam requirements/recommendations for international students: Required—TOEFL (minimum score 590 paper-based; 243 computer-based). Electronic applications accepted. *Expenses:* Contact institution. *Faculty research:* Fine-particle technology, x-ray diffraction, superconductivity, electronic materials.

Arizona State University, Ira A. Fulton School of Engineering, Department of Mechanical and Aerospace Engineering, Tempe, AZ 85281. Offers aerospace engineering (MS, MSE, PhD); chemical engineering (MS, MSE, PhD); materials science and engineering (MS, PhD); mechanical engineering (MS, MSE, PhD). Part-time and evening/weekend programs available. Postbaccalaureate distance learning degree programs offered (minimal on-campus study). *Faculty:* 50 full-time (10 women), 13 part-time/adjunct (3 women). *Students:* 258 full-time (47 women), 114 part-time (29 women); includes 48 minority (3 Black or African American, non-Hispanic/Latino; 2 American Indian or Alaska Native, non-Hispanic/Latino; 15 Asian, non-Hispanic/Latino; 27 Hispanic/Latino; 1 Two or more races, non-Hispanic/Latino), 164 international. Average age 28. 721 applicants, 58% accepted, 119 enrolled. In 2010, 55 master's, 29 doctorates awarded. Terminal master's awarded for partial completion of doctoral program. *Degree requirements:* For master's, thesis and oral defense (MS); applied project or comprehensive exam (MSE); interactive Program of Study (iPOS) submitted before completing 50 percent of required credit hours; for doctorate, comprehensive exam, thesis/dissertation, interactive Program of Study (iPOS) submitted before completing 50 percent of required credit hours. *Entrance requirements:* For master's, GRE, minimum GPA of 3.0 or equivalent in last 2 years of work leading to bachelor's degree; for doctorate, GRE, minimum GPA of 3.0 in last 2 years of work leading to bachelor's degree. Additional exam requirements/recommendations for international students: Required—TOEFL, IELTS, or Pearson Test of English. *Application deadline:* For fall admission, 1/31 for domestic and international students; for spring admission, 7/1 for domestic and international students. Application fee: $70 ($90 for international students). Electronic applications accepted. *Expenses:* Contact institution. *Financial support:* In 2010–11, 120 research assistantships with partial tuition reimbursements (averaging $15,353 per year), 34 teaching assistantships with partial tuition reimbursements (averaging $13,861 per year) were awarded; fellowships with full and partial tuition reimbursements, institutionally sponsored loans, scholarships/grants, and tuition waivers (full and partial) also available. Financial award application deadline: 3/1; financial award applicants required to submit FAFSA. *Faculty research:* Electronic materials and packaging, materials for energy (batteries), adaptive/intelligent materials and structures, multiscale fluid mechanics, membranes, therapeutics and bioseparations, flexible structures, nanostructured materials, and micro/nano transport. Total annual research expenditures: $17.5 million. *Unit head:* Dr. Kyle D. Squires, Director, 480-965-3957, E-mail: squires@asu.edu. *Application contact:* Graduate Admissions, 480-965-6113.

Boston University, College of Engineering, Division of Materials Science and Engineering, Boston, MA 02215. Offers M Eng, MS, PhD. Part-time programs available. *Students:* 33 full-time (8 women), 1 (woman) part-time; includes 4 minority (3 Asian, non-Hispanic/Latino; 1 Hispanic/Latino), 17 international. Average age 26. 92 applicants, 26% accepted, 13 enrolled. In 2010, 1 master's, 3 doctorates awarded. Terminal master's awarded for partial completion of doctoral program. *Degree requirements:* For master's, thesis (for some programs); for doctorate, comprehensive exam, thesis/dissertation. *Entrance requirements:* For master's and doctorate, GRE General Test. Additional exam requirements/recommendations for international students: Required—TOEFL (minimum score 550 paper-based; 213 computer-based; 84 iBT), IELTS (minimum score 6). *Application deadline:* For fall admission, 4/1 for domestic and international students; for spring admission, 10/1 for domestic and international students. Applications are processed on a rolling basis. Application fee: $70. Electronic applications accepted. *Expenses:* Tuition: Full-time $39,314; part-time $1228 per credit. Required fees: $40 per semester. *Financial support:* In 2010–11, 23 students received support, including 2 fellowships with full tuition reimbursements available (averaging $28,200 per year), 15 research assistantships with full tuition reimbursements available (averaging $18,800 per year), 4 teaching assistantships with full tuition reimbursements available (averaging $18,800 per year); career-related internships or fieldwork, Federal Work-Study, institutionally sponsored loans, scholarships/grants, traineeships, and health care benefits also available. Financial award application deadline: 1/15; financial award applicants required to submit FAFSA. *Faculty research:* Biomaterials; electronic and photonic materials; materials for energy and environment; nanomaterials. *Unit head:* Dr. Uday Pal, Division Head, 617-353-7708, Fax: 617-353-5548, E-mail: upal@bu.edu. *Application contact:* Stephen Doherty, Director of Graduate Programs, 617-353-9760, Fax: 617-353-0259, E-mail: enggrad@bu.edu.

Brown University, Graduate School, Division of Engineering, Program in Materials Science and Engineering, Providence, RI 02912. Offers Sc M, PhD. *Degree requirements:* For doctorate, thesis/dissertation, preliminary exam.

California Institute of Technology, Division of Engineering and Applied Science, Option in Materials Science, Pasadena, CA 91125-0001. Offers MS, PhD. *Faculty:* 6 full-time (2 women). *Students:* 57 full-time (14 women). 198 applicants, 10% accepted, 6 enrolled. In 2010, 4 master's, 6 doctorates awarded. *Degree requirements:* For doctorate, thesis/dissertation. *Application deadline:* For fall admission, 1/15 for domestic students. Application fee: $0. *Financial support:* In 2010–11, 13 fellowships, 40 research assistantships, 7 teaching assistantships were awarded. *Faculty research:* Mechanical properties, physical properties, kinetics of phase transformations, metastable phases, transmission electron microscopy. *Unit head:* Dr. Brent Fultz, Academic Officer, 626-395-2170, E-mail: btf@caltech.edu. *Application contact:* Natalie Gilmore, Assistant Dean of Graduate Studies, 626-395-3812, Fax: 626-577-9246, E-mail: ngilmore@caltech.edu.

Carnegie Mellon University, Carnegie Institute of Technology, Department of Materials Science and Engineering, Pittsburgh, PA 15213-3891. Offers MS, PhD. Part-time programs available. Terminal master's awarded for partial completion of doctoral program. *Degree requirements:* For master's, exam; for doctorate, thesis/dissertation, qualifying exam. *Entrance requirements:* For master's and doctorate, GRE General Test. Additional exam requirements/recommendations for international students: Required—TOEFL. *Faculty research:* Materials characterization, process metallurgy, high strength alloys, growth kinetics, ceramics.

Case Western Reserve University, School of Graduate Studies, Case School of Engineering, Department of Materials Science and Engineering, Cleveland, OH 44106. Offers materials science and engineering (MS, PhD). Part-time programs available. Postbaccalaureate distance learning degree programs offered (no on-campus study). *Faculty:* 11 full-time (0 women). *Students:* 45 full-time (11 women), 3 part-time (1 woman); includes 1 Asian, non-Hispanic/Latino, 39 international. In 2010, 3 master's, 9 doctorates awarded. Terminal master's awarded for partial completion of doctoral program. *Degree requirements:* For master's, thesis (for some programs); for doctorate, thesis/dissertation, qualifying exam, teaching experience. *Entrance requirements:* For master's and doctorate, GRE General Test. Additional exam requirements/recommendations for international students: Required—TOEFL. *Application deadline:* For fall admission, 2/15 priority date for domestic students; for spring admission, 9/15 for domestic students. Applications are processed on a rolling basis. Application fee: $50. *Financial support:* Fellowships with full and partial tuition reimbursements, research assistantships with full and partial tuition reimbursements, teaching assistantships available. Financial award application deadline: 4/30; financial award applicants required to submit FAFSA. *Faculty research:* Surface hardening of steels and other alloys, chemistry and structure of surfaces, microstructural and mechanical property characterization, materials for energy applications, thermodynamics and kinetics of materials, performance and reliability of materials. Total annual research expenditures: $3.6 million. *Unit head:* Dr. James D. McGuffin-Cawley, Department Chair, 216-368-6482, Fax: 216-368-4224, E-mail: emse.info@case.edu. *Application contact:* Theresa Claytor, Student Affairs Coordinator, 216-368-8555, Fax: 216-368-8555, E-mail: esme.info@case.edu.

The Catholic University of America, School of Engineering, Department of Materials Science and Engineering, Washington, DC 20064. Offers MS. Part-time programs available. *Students:* 1 full-time. Average age 31. 6 applicants, 33% accepted, 1 enrolled. *Degree requirements:* For master's, thesis optional. *Entrance requirements:* For master's, GRE (minimum score 1250), minimum GPA of 3.0, statement of purpose, official copies of academic transcripts. Additional exam requirements/recommendations for international students: Required—TOEFL (minimum score 580 paper-based; 237 computer-based). *Application deadline:* For fall admission, 8/1 for domestic students, 7/15 for international students; for spring admission, 12/1 for domestic students, 10/15 for international students. Applications are processed on a rolling basis. Application fee: $55. Electronic applications accepted. *Expenses:* Tuition: Full-time $33,580; part-time $1315 per credit hour. Required fees: $80; $40 per semester hour. One-time fee: $425. *Financial support:* Fellowships, research assistantships, teaching assistantships, Federal Work-Study, scholarships/grants, tuition waivers (full and partial), and unspecified assistantships available. Financial award application deadline: 2/1; financial award applicants required to submit FAFSA. *Unit head:* Dr. Biprodas Dutta, Director, 202-319-5535, Fax: 202-319-4469, E-mail: duttab@cua.edu. *Application contact:* Andrew Woodall, Director of Graduate Admissions, 202-319-5057, Fax: 202-319-6533, E-mail: cua-admissions@cua.edu.

Central Michigan University, College of Graduate Studies, College of Science and Technology, Department of Physics, Program in the Science of Advanced Materials, Mount Pleasant, MI 48859. Offers PhD. *Students:* 3 full-time (0 women), 10 part-time (4 women); includes 1 Asian, non-Hispanic/Latino, 8 international. *Degree requirements:* For doctorate, comprehensive exam, thesis/dissertation. *Entrance requirements:* For doctorate, GRE. *Application deadline:* For fall admission, 2/1 for domestic and international students. Application fee: $35 ($45 for inter-

Materials Sciences

Central Michigan University (continued)

national students). Electronic applications accepted. *Expenses:* Tuition, state resident: full-time $8208; part-time $456 per credit hour. Tuition, nonresident: full-time $13,788; part-time $766 per credit hour. One-time fee: $25. *Financial support:* Research assistantships with tuition reimbursements, teaching assistantships with tuition reimbursements, unspecified assistantships and out-of-state merit awards, non-resident graduate awards available. *Faculty research:* Electronic properties of nanomaterials, polymers for energy and for environmental applications, inorganic materials synthesis, magnetic properties from first-principles, and nano devices for biomedical applications and environmental remediation. *Unit head:* Dr. Koblar Alan Jackson, Chairperson, 989-774-3321, Fax: 989-774-2697, E-mail: jacks1ka@cmich.edu. *Application contact:* Jessica Lapp, Program Coordinator, 989-774-2221, Fax: 989-774-2697, E-mail: jessica.lapp@cmich.edu.

Clemson University, Graduate School, College of Engineering and Science, School of Materials Science and Engineering, Clemson, SC 29634. Offers MS, PhD. Part-time programs available. *Faculty:* 14 full-time (2 women), 6 part-time/adjunct (0 women). *Students:* 59 full-time (22 women), 1 part-time (0 women); includes 1 Black or African American, non-Hispanic/Latino, 33 international. Average age 27. 130 applicants, 45% accepted, 20 enrolled. In 2010, 11 master's, 8 doctorates awarded. Terminal master's awarded for partial completion of doctoral program. *Degree requirements:* For master's, thesis; for doctorate, comprehensive exam, thesis/dissertation. *Entrance requirements:* For master's and doctorate, GRE General Test. Additional exam requirements/recommendations for international students: Required—TOEFL. *Application deadline:* For fall admission, 2/1 for domestic students; for spring admission, 9/1 for domestic students. Applications are processed on a rolling basis. Application fee: $70 ($80 for international students). Electronic applications accepted. *Expenses:* Tuition, state resident: full-time $6492; part-time $400 per credit hour. Tuition, nonresident: full-time $13,634; part-time $800 per credit hour. Required fees: $262 per semester. Part-time tuition and fees vary according to course load and program. *Financial support:* In 2010–11, 52 students received support, including 2 fellowships with full and partial tuition reimbursements available (averaging $10,500 per year), 43 research assistantships with partial tuition reimbursements available (averaging $17,275 per year), 15 teaching assistantships with partial tuition reimbursements available (averaging $12,600 per year); career-related internships or fieldwork, institutionally sponsored loans, scholarships/grants, health care benefits, and unspecified assistantships also available. Support available to part-time students. Financial award applicants required to submit FAFSA. Total annual research expenditures: $2.5 million. *Unit head:* Dr. Kathleen Richardson, Chair and Director of the School of Materials Science and Engineering, 864-656-3311, Fax: 864-656-5973, E-mail: richar3@clemson.edu. *Application contact:* Dr. Gary C. Lickfield, Graduate Program Coordinator, 864-656-5964, Fax: 864-656-5973, E-mail: lgary@clemson.edu.

Colorado School of Mines, Graduate School, Department of Metallurgical and Materials Engineering, Golden, CO 80401. Offers materials science (MS, PhD); metallurgical and materials engineering (ME, MS, PhD). Part-time programs available. *Faculty:* 35 full-time (3 women), 5 part-time/adjunct (0 women). *Students:* 65 full-time (16 women), 5 part-time (1 woman); includes 2 American Indian or Alaska Native, non-Hispanic/Latino; 1 Asian, non-Hispanic/Latino; 2 Hispanic/Latino; 1 Two or more races, non-Hispanic/Latino, 18 international. Average age 30. 95 applicants, 36% accepted, 28 enrolled. In 2010, 12 master's, 6 doctorates awarded. *Degree requirements:* For master's, thesis (for some programs); for doctorate, comprehensive exam, thesis/dissertation. *Entrance requirements:* For master's and doctorate, GRE General Test. Additional exam requirements/recommendations for international students: Required—TOEFL (minimum score 550 paper-based; 213 computer-based; 80 iBT). *Application deadline:* For fall admission, 1/15 priority date for domestic and international students; for spring admission, 10/15 priority date for domestic and international students. Application fee: $50 ($70 for international students). Electronic applications accepted. *Expenses:* Tuition, state resident: full-time $11,550; part-time $641 per credit. Tuition, nonresident: full-time $25,980; part-time $1444 per credit. Required fees: $1874; $937 per semester. *Financial support:* In 2010–11, 53 students received support, including 6 fellowships with full tuition reimbursements available (averaging $20,000 per year), 44 research assistantships with full tuition reimbursements available (averaging $20,000 per year), 3 teaching assistantships with full tuition reimbursements available (averaging $20,000 per year); scholarships/grants, health care benefits, and unspecified assistantships also available. Financial award application deadline: 1/15; financial award applicants required to submit FAFSA. Total annual research expenditures: $6.3 million. *Unit head:* Dr. Michael Kaufman, Interim Department Head, 303-273-3009, Fax: 303-273-3795, E-mail: mkaufman@mines.edu. *Application contact:* Susan Ballantype, Program Assistant, 303-273-3660, Fax: 303-273-3795, E-mail: susan.ballantyne@is.mines.edu.

Colorado School of Mines, Graduate School, Program in Materials Science, Golden, CO 80401. Offers MS, PhD. Part-time programs available. *Students:* 53 full-time (9 women), 10 part-time (4 women); includes 2 Asian, non-Hispanic/Latino; 2 Hispanic/Latino, 24 international. Average age 30. 64 applicants, 22% accepted, 10 enrolled. In 2010, 10 master's, 3 doctorates awarded. *Degree requirements:* For master's, thesis (for some programs); for doctorate, comprehensive exam, thesis/dissertation. *Entrance requirements:* For master's and doctorate, GRE General Test. Additional exam requirements/recommendations for international students: Required—TOEFL (minimum score 550 paper-based; 213 computer-based; 80 iBT). *Application deadline:* For fall admission, 1/15 priority date for domestic and international students; for spring admission, 10/15 priority date for domestic and international students. Application fee: $50 ($70 for international students). Electronic applications accepted. *Expenses:* Tuition, state resident: full-time $11,550; part-time $641 per credit. Tuition, nonresident: full-time $25,980; part-time $1444 per credit. Required fees: $1874; $937 per semester. *Financial support:* In 2010–11, 53 students received support, including 3 fellowships with full tuition reimbursements available (averaging $20,000 per year), 40 research assistantships with full tuition reimbursements available (averaging $20,000 per year), 10 teaching assistantships with full tuition reimbursements available (averaging $20,000 per year); scholarships/grants, health care benefits, and unspecified assistantships also available. Financial award application deadline: 1/15; financial award applicants required to submit FAFSA. *Faculty research:* Ceramics processing, solar and electronic materials, optical properties of surfaces and interfaces, materials synthesis, metal and alloy processing. *Unit head:* Dr. Michael Kaufman, Interim Department Head, 303-273-3009, Fax: 303-273-3795, E-mail: mkaufman@mines.edu. *Application contact:* Susan Ballantyne, Program Assistant, 303-273-3660, Fax: 303-273-3795, E-mail: susan.ballantyne@is.mines.edu.

Columbia University, Fu Foundation School of Engineering and Applied Science, Department of Applied Physics and Applied Mathematics, New York, NY 10027. Offers applied physics (Eng Sc D); applied physics and applied mathematics (MS, PhD, Engr); materials science and engineering (MS, Eng Sc D, PhD); medical physics (MS). Part-time programs available. Postbaccalaureate distance learning degree programs offered (no on-campus study). *Faculty:* 32 full-time (2 women), 23 part-time/adjunct (2 women). *Students:* 126 full-time (28 women), 23 part-time (5 women); includes 14 minority (2 Black or African American, non-Hispanic/Latino; 8 Asian, non-Hispanic/Latino; 1 Hispanic/Latino; 3 Two or more races, non-Hispanic/Latino), 60 international. Average age 28. 344 applicants, 22% accepted, 36 enrolled. In 2010, 56 master's, 13 doctorates awarded. Terminal master's awarded for partial completion of doctoral program. *Degree requirements:* For master's, comprehensive exam; for doctorate, thesis/dissertation, qualifying exam. *Entrance requirements:* For master's, GRE General Test, GRE Subject Test (strongly recommended); for doctorate, GRE General Test, GRE Subject Test (applied physics); for Engr, GRE General Test. Additional exam requirements/recommendations for international students: Required—TOEFL, IELTS. *Application deadline:* For fall admission, 12/1 priority date for domestic and international students; for spring admission, 10/1 priority date for domestic and international students. Application fee: $95. Electronic applications accepted. *Financial support:* In 2010–11, 73 students received support, including 3 fellowships with full tuition reimbursements available (averaging $30,000 per year), 53 research assistantships with full tuition reimbursements available (averaging $30,667 per year), 17 teaching assistantships with full tuition reimbursements available (averaging $30,667 per year). Financial award application deadline: 12/1; financial award applicants required to submit FAFSA. *Faculty research:* Plasma, solid state, optical and laser physics; atmospheric, oceanic and earth physics; computational math and applied mathematics; materials science and engineering. *Unit head:* Dr. Irving P. Herman, Professor and Department Chairman, 212-854-4457, E-mail: seasinfo.apam@columbia.edu. *Application contact:* Montserrat Fernandez-Pinkley, Student Services Coordinator, 212-854-4457, Fax: 212-854-8257, E-mail: mf2157@columbia.edu.

Cornell University, Graduate School, Graduate Fields of Engineering, Field of Materials Science and Engineering, Ithaca, NY 14853. Offers materials engineering (M Eng, PhD); materials science (M Eng, PhD). *Faculty:* 45 full-time (5 women). *Students:* 75 full-time (25 women); includes 1 Black or African American, non-Hispanic/Latino; 11 Asian, non-Hispanic/Latino; 4 Hispanic/Latino, 37 international. Average age 26. 343 applicants, 23% accepted, 40 enrolled. In 2010, 20 master's, 9 doctorates awarded. *Degree requirements:* For doctorate, comprehensive exam, thesis/dissertation. *Entrance requirements:* For master's and doctorate, GRE General Test, 3 letters of recommendation. Additional exam requirements/recommendations for international students: Required—TOEFL (minimum score 550 paper-based; 213 computer-based; 77 iBT). *Application deadline:* For fall admission, 1/15 priority date for domestic students. Application fee: $70. Electronic applications accepted. *Expenses:* Tuition: Full-time $29,500. Required fees: $76. Tuition and fees vary according to degree level and program. *Financial support:* In 2010–11, 48 students received support, including 17 fellowships with full tuition reimbursements available, 30 research assistantships with full tuition reimbursements available, 7 teaching assistantships with full tuition reimbursements available; institutionally sponsored loans, scholarships/grants, health care benefits, tuition waivers (full and partial), and unspecified assistantships also available. Financial award applicants required to submit FAFSA. *Faculty research:* Ceramics, complex fluids, glass, metals, polymers semiconductors. *Unit head:* Director of Graduate Studies, 607-255-9159, Fax: 607-255-2365. *Application contact:* Graduate Field Assistant, 607-255-9159, Fax: 607-255-2365, E-mail: matsci@cornell.edu.

Dartmouth College, Thayer School of Engineering, Program in Materials Sciences and Engineering, Hanover, NH 03755. Offers MS, PhD. *Degree requirements:* For master's, thesis; for doctorate, thesis/dissertation, candidacy oral exam. *Entrance requirements:* For master's and doctorate, GRE General Test. *Application deadline:* For fall admission, 1/1 priority date for domestic students. Application fee: $45. *Financial support:* Fellowships, research assistantships, teaching assistantships, career-related internships or fieldwork, Federal Work-Study, institutionally sponsored loans, and tuition waivers (full and partial) available. Financial award application deadline: 1/15. *Faculty research:* Electronic and magnetic materials, microstructural evolution, biomaterials and nanostructures, laser-material interactions, nano composites. Total annual research expenditures: $2.2 million. *Unit head:* Dr. Joseph J. Helbie, Dean, 603-646-2238, Fax: 603-646-2580, E-mail: joseph.j.helbie@dartmouth.edu. *Application contact:* Candace S. Potter, Graduate Admissions Administrator, 603-646-3844, Fax: 603-646-1620, E-mail: candace.potter@dartmouth.edu.

Duke University, Graduate School, Pratt School of Engineering, Department of Mechanical Engineering and Materials Science, Durham, NC 27708. Offers materials science (MS, PhD); mechanical engineering (MS, PhD); JD/MS. Part-time programs available. *Faculty:* 26 full-time. *Students:* 73 full-time (14 women); includes 4 Asian, non-Hispanic/Latino; 1 Hispanic/Latino, 26 international. 247 applicants, 32% accepted, 27 enrolled. In 2010, 5 master's, 7 doctorates awarded. Terminal master's awarded for partial completion of doctoral program. *Degree requirements:* For master's, thesis optional; for doctorate, thesis/dissertation. *Entrance requirements:* For master's and doctorate, GRE General Test. Additional exam requirements/recommendations for international students: Required—TOEFL (minimum score 550 paper-based; 213 computer-based; 83 iBT), IELTS (minimum score 7). *Application deadline:* For fall admission, 12/8 priority date for domestic and international students; for spring admission, 11/1 for domestic students. Application fee: $75. Electronic applications accepted. *Financial support:* Fellowships, research assistantships, teaching assistantships, Federal Work-Study available. Financial award application deadline: 12/8. *Unit head:* Stefan Zauscher, Director of Graduate Studies, 919-660-5310, Fax: 919-660-8963, E-mail: kparrish@duke.edu. *Application contact:* Elizabeth Hutton, Director of Admissions, 919-684-3913, Fax: 919-684-2277, E-mail: grad-admissions@duke.edu.

Duke University, Graduate School, Pratt School of Engineering, Master of Engineering Program, Durham, NC 27708-0271. Offers biomedical engineering (M Eng); civil engineering (M Eng); electrical and computer engineering (M Eng); environmental engineering (M Eng); materials science and engineering (M Eng); mechanical engineering (M Eng); photonics and optical sciences (M Eng). Part-time programs available. *Faculty:* 123 full-time, 1 part-time/adjunct. *Students:* 9 full-time (4 women); includes 2 minority (both Asian, non-Hispanic/Latino), 3 international. Average age 24. *Entrance requirements:* For master's, GRE General Test, resume, 3 letters of recommendation, statement of purpose. Additional exam requirements/recommendations for international students: Required—TOEFL. *Application deadline:* For fall admission, 6/15 for domestic students, 2/15 for international students; for spring admission, 11/1 for domestic students, 9/1 for international students. Application fee: $75. *Financial support:* Merit scholarships/grants available. *Unit head:* Dr. Bradley A. Fox, Executive Director, 919-660-5455, Fax: 919-660-5456. *Application contact:* Erin Degerman, Admissions Coordinator, 919-668-6789, Fax: 919-660-5456, E-mail: erin.degerman@duke.edu.

Florida International University, College of Engineering and Computing, Department of Mechanical and Materials Engineering, Materials Science and Engineering Program, Miami, FL 33175. Offers MS, PhD. Part-time and evening/weekend programs available. *Students:* 27 full-time (0 women), 17 part-time (1 woman); includes 1 Hispanic/Latino, 26 international. Average age 27. 136 applicants, 21% accepted, 22 enrolled. In 2010, 9 master's, 2 doctorates awarded. Terminal master's awarded for partial completion of doctoral program. *Degree requirements:* For master's, thesis or alternative; for doctorate, comprehensive exam, thesis/dissertation. *Entrance requirements:* For master's, GRE, 3 letters of recommendation, minimum undergraduate GPA of 3.0 in upper-level course work; for doctorate, GRE, minimum GPA of 3.0, 3 letters of recommendation, letter of intent. Additional exam requirements/recommendations for international students: Required—TOEFL (minimum score 550 paper-based; 80 iBT). *Application deadline:* For fall admission, 6/1 for domestic students, 4/1 for international students; for spring admission, 10/1 for domestic students, 9/1 for international students. Applications are processed on a rolling basis. Application fee: $30. Electronic applications accepted. *Financial support:* Institutionally sponsored loans, scholarships/grants, and unspecified assistantships available. Financial award application deadline: 3/1; financial award applicants required to submit FAFSA. *Unit head:* Dr. Cesar Levy, Chair, Mechanical and Materials Engineering Department, 305-348-1932, Fax: 305-348-1932, E-mail: cesar.levy@fiu.edu. *Application contact:* Maria Parrilla, Graduate Admissions Assistant, 305-348-1890, Fax: 305-348-6142, E-mail: grad_eng@fiu.edu.

Florida State University, The Graduate School, College of Arts and Sciences, Department of Chemistry and Biochemistry, Tallahassee, FL 32306-4390. Offers analytical chemistry (MS, PhD); biochemistry (MS, PhD); inorganic chemistry (MS, PhD); materials chemistry (PhD); organic chemistry (MS, PhD); physical chemistry (MS, PhD). *Faculty:* 38 full-time (5 women), 3 part-time/adjunct (0 women). *Students:* 142 full-time (46 women), 8 part-time (4 women); includes 12 minority (6 Black or African American, non-Hispanic/Latino; 3 Asian, non-Hispanic/Latino; 3 Hispanic/Latino), 68 international. Average age 25. 299 applicants, 17% accepted, 19 enrolled. In 2010, 10 master's, 20 doctorates awarded. Terminal master's awarded for partial completion of doctoral program. *Degree requirements:* For master's, comprehensive exam (for some programs), thesis (for some programs), cumulative exams; for doctorate, comprehensive exam (for some programs), thesis/dissertation, cumulative exams. *Entrance requirements:* For master's and doctorate, GRE General Test, minimum B average in undergraduate course work. Additional exam requirements/recommendations for international students: Required—TOEFL (minimum score 550 paper-based; 213 computer-based; 80 iBT). *Application deadline:* For fall admission, 12/15 priority date for domestic and international students; for spring admission, 9/15 for domestic and international students. Applications are processed on a rolling basis. Application fee: $30. Electronic applications accepted. *Expenses:* Tuition, state resident: full-time $8238.24. *Financial support:* In 2010–11, 150 students received support, including fellowships with full tuition reimbursements available (averaging $20,000 per year), 50 research assistantships with full tuition reimbursements available (averaging $20,000 per year), 100 teaching assistantships with full tuition reimbursements available (averaging $20,000 per year). Financial award application deadline: 12/15; financial award applicants required to submit FAFSA. *Faculty research:* Materials synthesis including polymers, natural products; catalysis, NMR; mass spectrometry; optical spectroscopy, scattering techniques, computational chemistry, separation technology; nanostructured materials including metallic, semiconducting and magnetic nanocrystals; nanoscience interfaced with biology; supramolecular materials for solar energy conversion. Total annual research expenditures: $5.6 million. *Unit head:* Dr. Timothy Logan, Chairman, 850-644-1244, Fax: 850-644-8281, E-mail: gradinfo@chem.fsu.edu. *Application contact:* Dr. Tyler McQuade, Chair, Graduate Admissions Committee, 888-525-9286, Fax: 850-644-0465, E-mail: gradinfo@chem.fsu.edu.

Florida State University, The Graduate School, Interdisciplinary Program in Materials Science, Tallahassee, FL 32306. Offers computational materials science and mechanics (MS); functional materials (MS); nanoscale materials, composite materials, and interfaces (MS); polymers and bio-inspired materials (MS). *Faculty:* 38 full-time (5 women). *Students:* 9 full-time (3 women), 4 international. 14 applicants, 71% accepted, 4 enrolled. In 2010, 2 master's awarded. *Degree requirements:* For master's, thesis. *Entrance requirements:* For master's, GRE General Test (minimum score 1100 verbal and quantitative), minimum GPA of 3.0, 3 letters of recommendation. Additional exam requirements/recommendations for international students: Required—TOEFL (minimum score 80 iBT). *Application deadline:* For fall admission, 7/1 for domestic students, 5/1 for international students; for spring admission, 11/1 for domestic students, 9/1 for international students. Applications are processed on a rolling basis. Application fee: $25. Electronic applications accepted. *Expenses:* Tuition, state resident: full-time $8238.24. *Financial support:* In 2010–11, 1 student received support, including 8 research assistantships with full tuition reimbursements available (averaging $22,900 per year), 1 teaching assistantship with full tuition reimbursement available (averaging $23,000 per year); fellowships also available. Financial award application deadline: 1/15. *Faculty research:* Magnetism and magnetic materials, composites, superconductors, polymers, computations, nanotechnology. *Unit head:* Prof. Eric Hellstrom, Director, 850-645-7489, Fax: 850-645-7754, E-mail: hellstrom@asc.magnet.fsu.edu. *Application contact:* Todd Kramer, Admissions Coordinator, 850-410-6425, Fax: 850-410-6486, E-mail: krameto@eng.fsu.edu.

Georgetown University, Graduate School of Arts and Sciences, Department of Chemistry, Washington, DC 20057. Offers analytical chemistry (PhD); biochemistry (PhD); computational chemistry (PhD); inorganic chemistry (PhD); materials chemistry (PhD); organic chemistry (PhD); physical chemistry (PhD); theoretical chemistry (PhD). Terminal master's awarded for partial completion of doctoral program. *Degree requirements:* For doctorate, comprehensive exam, thesis/dissertation. *Entrance requirements:* For doctorate, GRE General Test. Additional exam requirements/recommendations for international students: Required—TOEFL.

The George Washington University, Columbian College of Arts and Sciences, Department of Chemistry, Washington, DC 20052. Offers analytical chemistry (MS, PhD); inorganic chemistry (MS, PhD); materials science (MS, PhD); organic chemistry (MS, PhD); physical chemistry (MS, PhD). Part-time and evening/weekend programs available. *Faculty:* 15 full-time (4 women), 5 part-time/adjunct (2 women). *Students:* 21 full-time (10 women), 10 part-time (5 women); includes 3 Asian, non-Hispanic/Latino; 1 Hispanic/Latino, 9 international. Average age 28. 33 applicants, 45% accepted, 7 enrolled. In 2010, 4 master's, 2 doctorates awarded. Terminal master's awarded for partial completion of doctoral program. *Degree requirements:* For master's, comprehensive exam, thesis or alternative; for doctorate, thesis/dissertation, general exam. *Entrance requirements:* For master's and doctorate, GRE General Test, interview, minimum GPA of 3.0. Additional exam requirements/recommendations for international students: Required—TOEFL (minimum score 550 paper-based; 213 computer-based; 80 iBT). *Application deadline:* For fall admission, 1/15 priority date for domestic and international students; for spring admission, 9/1 priority date for domestic and international students. Applications are processed on a rolling basis. Application fee: $75. Electronic applications accepted. *Financial support:* In 2010–11, 27 students received support; fellowships with tuition reimbursements available, research assistantships, teaching assistantships with tuition reimbursements available, Federal Work-Study and tuition waivers available. Financial award application deadline: 1/15. *Unit head:* Dr. Michael King, Chair, 202-994-6488. *Application contact:* Information Contact, 202-994-6121, E-mail: gwchem@gwu.edu.

Illinois Institute of Technology, Graduate College, Armour College of Engineering, Department of Mechanical, Materials and Aerospace Engineering, Chicago, IL 60616-3793. Offers manufacturing engineering (MME, MS); materials science and engineering (MMME, MS, PhD); mechanical and aerospace engineering (MMAE, MS, PhD), including economics (MS), energy (MS), environment (MS). Part-time and evening/weekend programs available. Postbaccalaureate distance learning degree programs offered (minimal on-campus study). *Faculty:* 26 full-time (1 woman), 6 part-time/adjunct (1 woman). *Students:* 135 full-time (22 women), 45 part-time (4 women); includes 11 minority (1 American Indian or Alaska Native, non-Hispanic/Latino; 9 Asian, non-Hispanic/Latino; 1 Hispanic/Latino), 117 international. Average age 27. 693 applicants, 41% accepted, 63 enrolled. In 2010, 58 master's, 4 doctorates awarded. Terminal master's awarded for partial completion of doctoral program. *Degree requirements:* For master's, comprehensive exam (for some programs), thesis (for some programs); for doctorate, comprehensive exam, thesis/dissertation. *Entrance requirements:* For master's and doctorate, GRE General Test (minimum score 1000 Quantitative and Verbal, 3.0 Analytical Writing), minimum undergraduate GPA of 3.0. Additional exam requirements/recommendations for international students: Required—TOEFL (minimum score 523 paper-based; 70 iBT); Recommended—IELTS (minimum score 5.5). *Application deadline:* For fall admission, 5/1 for domestic and international students; for spring admission, 10/15 for domestic and international students. Applications are processed on a rolling basis. Application fee: $50. Electronic applications accepted. *Expenses:* Tuition: Full-time $18,576; part-time $1032 per credit hour. Required fees: $583 per semester. One-time fee: $150. Tuition and fees vary according to program and student level. *Financial support:* In 2010–11, 7 fellowships with full and partial tuition reimbursements (averaging $7,673 per year), 33 research assistantships with full and partial tuition reimbursements (averaging $8,141 per year), 15 teaching assistantships with full and partial tuition reimbursements (averaging $6,930 per year) were awarded; Federal Work-Study, institutionally sponsored loans, scholarships/grants, health care benefits, tuition waivers, and unspecified assistantships also available. Support available to part-time students. Financial award applicants required to submit FAFSA. *Faculty research:* Fluid dynamics, metallurgical and materials engineering, solids and structures, computational mechanics, theoretical mechanics. Total annual research expenditures: $2.4 million. *Unit head:* Dr. Jamal Yagoobi, Professor and Chairman, 312-567-3239, Fax: 312-567-7230, E-mail: yagoobi@iit.edu. *Application contact:* Deborah Gibson, Director, Graduate Admission, 866-472-3448, Fax: 312-567-3138, E-mail: inquiry.grad@iit.edu.

Illinois Institute of Technology, Graduate College, College of Science and Letters, Department of Biological, Chemical and Physical Sciences, Chemistry Division, Chicago, IL 60616. Offers analytical chemistry (M Ch); chemistry (M Chem, MS, PhD); materials and chemical synthesis (M Ch). Part-time and evening/weekend programs available. Postbaccalaureate distance learning degree programs offered (no on-campus study). *Faculty:* 13 full-time (5 women), 2 part-time/adjunct (0 women). *Students:* 29 full-time (11 women), 46 part-time (20 women); includes 26 minority (1 Black or African American, non-Hispanic/Latino; 2 Asian, non-Hispanic/Latino; 23 Hispanic/Latino), 23 international. Average age 30. 157 applicants, 46% accepted, 18 enrolled. In 2010, 11 master's, 3 doctorates awarded. Terminal master's awarded for partial completion of doctoral program. *Degree requirements:* For master's, comprehensive exam, thesis (for some programs); for doctorate, comprehensive exam, thesis/dissertation. *Entrance requirements:* For master's, GRE General Test (minimum score 1000 Quantitative and Verbal, 2.5 Analytical Writing), minimum undergraduate GPA of 3.0; for doctorate, GRE General Test (minimum score 1100 Quantitative and Verbal, 3.0 Analytical Writing), GRE Subject Test, minimum undergraduate GPA of 3.0. Additional exam requirements/recommendations for international students: Required—TOEFL (minimum score 523 paper-based; 213 computer-based; 70 iBT);

Recommended—IELTS. *Application deadline:* For fall admission, 5/1 for domestic and international students; for spring admission, 10/15 for domestic and international students. Applications are processed on a rolling basis. Application fee: $40. Electronic applications accepted. *Expenses:* Tuition: Full-time $18,576; part-time $1032 per credit hour. Required fees: $583 per semester. One-time fee: $150. Tuition and fees vary according to program and student level. *Financial support:* In 2010–11, 2 fellowships with full and partial tuition reimbursements (averaging $7,750 per year), 3 research assistantships with full and partial tuition reimbursements (averaging $5,950 per year), 13 teaching assistantships with full and partial tuition reimbursements (averaging $7,173 per year) were awarded; Federal Work-Study, institutionally sponsored loans, scholarships/grants, health care benefits, tuition waivers (partial), and unspecified assistantships also available. Support available to part-time students. Financial award applicants required to submit FAFSA. *Faculty research:* Synthesis and analysis of inorganic nanoparticles; synthetic and mechanistic organic chemistry; synthesis of penicillin-related compounds; design, synthesis and property studies of nanomaterials for applications in chemical sensing, energy storage and biomedical usage; scanning probe microscopy. Total annual research expenditures: $356,146. *Unit head:* Dr. Rong Wang, Associate Chair, 312-567-3121, Fax: 312-567-3494, E-mail: wangr@iit.edu. *Application contact:* Deborah Gibson, Director, Graduate Admission, 866-472-3448, Fax: 312-567-3138, E-mail: inquiry.grad@iit.edu.

Indiana University Bloomington, University Graduate School, College of Arts and Sciences, Department of Chemistry, Bloomington, IN 47405. Offers analytical chemistry (PhD); chemical biology chemistry (PhD); chemistry (MAT); inorganic chemistry (PhD); materials chemistry (PhD); organic chemistry (PhD); physical chemistry (PhD). *Faculty:* 42 full-time (4 women). *Students:* 224 full-time (77 women); includes 19 minority (7 Black or African American, non-Hispanic/Latino; 1 American Indian or Alaska Native, non-Hispanic/Latino; 8 Asian, non-Hispanic/Latino; 3 Hispanic/Latino), 68 international. Average age 27. 270 applicants, 39% accepted, 31 enrolled. In 2010, 1 master's, 20 doctorates awarded. Terminal master's awarded for partial completion of doctoral program. *Degree requirements:* For master's, thesis; for doctorate, thesis/dissertation. *Entrance requirements:* For master's and doctorate, GRE General Test, GRE Subject Test. Additional exam requirements/recommendations for international students: Required—TOEFL. *Application deadline:* For fall admission, 1/15 priority date for domestic students, 12/15 for international students. Applications are processed on a rolling basis. Application fee: $55 ($65 for international students). *Financial support:* In 2010–11, 200 students received support, including 10 fellowships with full tuition reimbursements available, 76 research assistantships with full tuition reimbursements available, 111 teaching assistantships with full tuition reimbursements available; Federal Work-Study and institutionally sponsored loans also available. *Faculty research:* Synthesis of complex natural products, organic reaction mechanisms, organic electrochemistry, transitive-metal chemistry, solid-state and surface chemistry. Total annual research expenditures: $7.7 million. *Unit head:* David Giedroc, Chairperson, 812-855-6239, E-mail: chemchair@indiana.edu. *Application contact:* Daneil Mindiola, Director of Graduate Admissions, 812-855-2069, Fax: 812-855-8385, E-mail: mindiola@indiana.edu.

Instituto Tecnológico y de Estudios Superiores de Monterrey, Campus Estado de México, Professional and Graduate Division, Estado de Mexico, Mexico. Offers administration of information technologies (MITA); architecture (M Arch); business administration (GMBA, MBA); computer sciences (MCS, PhD); education (M Ed); educational institution administration (MAD); educational technology and innovation (PhD); electronic commerce (MEC); environmental systems (MS); finance (MAF); humanistic studies (MHS); information sciences and knowledge management (MISKM); information systems (MS); manufacturing systems (MS); marketing (MEM); quality systems and productivity (MS); science and materials engineering (PhD); telecommunications management (MTM). Part-time programs available. Postbaccalaureate distance learning degree programs offered (minimal on-campus study). *Degree requirements:* For master's, one foreign language, thesis (for some programs); for doctorate, one foreign language, thesis/dissertation. *Entrance requirements:* For master's, E-PAEP 500, interview; for doctorate, E-PAEP 500, research proposal. Additional exam requirements/recommendations for international students: Required—TOEFL (minimum score 550 paper-based). *Faculty research:* Surface treatments by plasmas, mechanical properties, robotics, graphical computing, mechatronics security protocols.

Iowa State University of Science and Technology, Graduate College, College of Engineering and College of Liberal Arts and Sciences, Department of Materials Science and Engineering, Ames, IA 50011. Offers MS, PhD. *Faculty:* 31 full-time (4 women), 1 part-time/adjunct (0 women). *Students:* 81 full-time (23 women), 12 part-time (2 women); includes 1 Black or African American, non-Hispanic/Latino; 1 American Indian or Alaska Native, non-Hispanic/Latino; 2 Asian, non-Hispanic/Latino; 2 Hispanic/Latino, 50 international. 211 applicants, 17% accepted, 25 enrolled. In 2010, 8 master's, 13 doctorates awarded. *Degree requirements:* For master's, thesis; for doctorate, thesis/dissertation. *Entrance requirements:* For master's and doctorate, GRE General Test. Additional exam requirements/recommendations for international students: Required—TOEFL (minimum score 550 paper-based; 79 iBT), IELTS (minimum score 6.5). *Application deadline:* For fall admission, 1/15 priority date for domestic and international students; for spring admission, 8/15 priority date for domestic and international students. Application fee: $40 ($90 for international students). Electronic applications accepted. *Financial support:* In 2010–11, 57 research assistantships with full and partial tuition reimbursements (averaging $17,300 per year), 3 teaching assistantships with full and partial tuition reimbursements (averaging $17,300 per year) were awarded; fellowships, scholarships/grants, health care benefits, and unspecified assistantships also available. *Unit head:* Dr. Richard Lesar, Chair, 515-294-1841, Fax: 515-204-5444, E-mail: gradmse@iastate.edu. *Application contact:* Dr. Alan Russell, Director of Graduate Education, 515-294-3204, E-mail: gradmse@iastate.edu.

Jackson State University, Graduate School, College of Science, Engineering and Technology, Department of Technology, Jackson, MS 39217. Offers hazardous materials management (MS); technology education (MS Ed). Part-time and evening/weekend programs available. *Faculty:* 3 full-time (1 woman). *Students:* 36 full-time (19 women), 34 part-time (19 women); includes 61 Black or African American, non-Hispanic/Latino; 2 Asian, non-Hispanic/Latino, 3 international. Average age 36. In 2010, 6 master's awarded. *Degree requirements:* For master's, comprehensive exam, thesis or alternative. *Entrance requirements:* For master's, GRE General Test. Additional exam requirements/recommendations for international students: Required—TOEFL (minimum score 520 paper-based; 195 computer-based; 67 iBT). *Application deadline:* For fall admission, 3/1 priority date for domestic students, 3/1 for international students; for spring admission, 10/1 for domestic and international students. Applications are processed on a rolling basis. Application fee: $25. *Expenses:* Tuition, state resident: full-time $5050; part-time $281 per credit hour. Tuition, nonresident: full-time $12,380; part-time $689 per credit hour. *Financial support:* Career-related internships or fieldwork, Federal Work-Study, scholarships/grants, and unspecified assistantships available. Support available to part-time students. Financial award application deadline: 3/1; financial award applicants required to submit FAFSA. *Unit head:* Dr. John Colonias, Acting Chair, 601-968-2466, Fax: 601-979-4110, E-mail: john.a.colonias@jsums.edu. *Application contact:* Sharlene Wilson, Director of Graduate Admissions, 601-979-2455, Fax: 601-979-4325, E-mail: sharlene.f.wilson@jsums.edu.

The Johns Hopkins University, Engineering for Professionals, Part-time Program in Materials Science and Engineering, Baltimore, MD 21218-2699. Offers M Mat SE, MSE. Part-time and evening/weekend programs available. *Faculty:* 6 part-time/adjunct (1 woman). *Students:* 11 part-time (5 women); includes 5 minority (3 Black or African American, non-Hispanic/Latino; 1 Asian, non-Hispanic/Latino; 1 Two or more races, non-Hispanic/Latino). Average age 30. 2 applicants, 50% accepted, 1 enrolled. In 2010, 6 master's awarded. *Application deadline:* Applications are processed on a rolling basis. Application fee: $75. Electronic applications accepted. *Financial support:* Institutionally sponsored loans available. *Unit head:* Dr. Robert C. Cammarata, Program Chair, 410-516-5462, Fax: 410-516-5293, E-mail: rcc@jhu.edu. *Application contact:* Priyanka Dwivedi, Admissions Manager, 410-516-2300, Fax: 410-579-8049, E-mail: pdwived1@jhu.edu.

Materials Sciences

The Johns Hopkins University, G. W. C. Whiting School of Engineering, Department of Materials Science and Engineering, Baltimore, MD 21218-2699. Offers M Mat SE, MSE, PhD. Part-time and evening/weekend programs available. *Faculty:* 14 full-time (3 women), 1 part-time/adjunct (0 women). *Students:* 43 full-time (11 women), 1 part-time (0 women); includes 9 minority (1 American Indian or Alaska Native, non-Hispanic/Latino; 6 Asian, non-Hispanic/Latino; 2 Hispanic/Latino), 13 international. Average age 27. 173 applicants, 17% accepted, 12 enrolled. In 2010, 10 master's, 6 doctorates awarded. Terminal master's awarded for partial completion of doctoral program. *Degree requirements:* For master's, thesis, oral exam; for doctorate, thesis/dissertation, oral exam, thesis defense. *Entrance requirements:* For master's and doctorate, GRE General Test. Additional exam requirements/recommendations for international students: Required—TOEFL (minimum score 600 paper-based; 250 computer-based). *Application deadline:* For fall admission, 1/15 priority date for domestic and international students; for spring admission, 10/15 priority date for domestic and international students. Application fee: $0 ($75 for international students). Electronic applications accepted. *Financial support:* In 2010–11, 5 fellowships with full tuition reimbursements (averaging $31,600 per year), 34 research assistantships with full tuition reimbursements (averaging $29,800 per year), 3 teaching assistantships with full tuition reimbursements (averaging $24,600 per year) were awarded; Federal Work-Study, institutionally sponsored loans, health care benefits, tuition waivers (full), and unspecified assistantships also available. Financial award application deadline: 3/15. *Faculty research:* Thin films, nanomaterials, biomaterials, materials characterization, electronic materials. Total annual research expenditures: $5.1 million. *Unit head:* Dr. Howard E. Katz, Chair, 410-516-6141, Fax: 410-516-5293, E-mail: hekatz@jhu.edu. *Application contact:* Jeanine Majewski, Academic Coordinator, 410-516-8760, Fax: 410-516-5293, E-mail: dmse.admissions@jhu.edu.

The Johns Hopkins University, G. W. C. Whiting School of Engineering, Program in Engineering Management, Baltimore, MD 21218-2699. Offers biomaterials (MSEM); communications science (MSEM); computer science (MSEM); fluid mechanics (MSEM); materials science and engineering (MSEM); mechanical engineering (MSEM); mechanics and materials (MSEM); nano-biotechnology (MSEM); nanomaterials and nanotechnology (MSEM); probability and statistics (MSEM); smart product and device design (MSEM); systems analysis, management and environmental policy (MSEM). *Students:* 32 full-time (5 women), 4 part-time (0 women); includes 7 minority (3 Black or African American, non-Hispanic/Latino; 3 Asian, non-Hispanic/Latino; 1 Hispanic/Latino), 11 international. Average age 23. 110 applicants, 60% accepted, 27 enrolled. In 2010, 6 master's awarded. *Entrance requirements:* For master's, GRE, 3 letters of recommendation, resume. Additional exam requirements/recommendations for international students: Required—TOEFL (minimum score 600 paper-based; 250 computer-based; 100 iBT) or IELTS (minimum score 7). *Application deadline:* For fall admission, 1/15 priority date for domestic students, 1/15 for international students; for spring admission, 9/15 priority date for domestic students, 9/15 for international students. Applications are processed on a rolling basis. Application fee: $75. Electronic applications accepted. *Financial support:* Fellowships, health care benefits available. *Unit head:* Dr. Edward R. Scheinerman, Interim Director/Vice Dean for Education, School of Engineering/Professor, Applied Mathematics and Statistics, 410-516-7395, Fax: 410-516-4880, E-mail: ers@jhu.edu. *Application contact:* Dennis McIver, Coordinator of Graduate Admissions, 410-516-8174, Fax: 410-516-0780, E-mail: graduateadmissions@jhu.edu.

Lehigh University, P.C. Rossin College of Engineering and Applied Science, Department of Materials Science and Engineering, Bethlehem, PA 18015. Offers materials science and engineering (M Eng, MS, PhD); photonics (MS); polymer science/engineering (M Eng, MS, PhD); MBA/E. Part-time programs available. *Faculty:* 13 full-time (3 women), 1 part-time/adjunct (0 women). *Students:* 27 full-time (4 women), 4 part-time (1 woman); includes 1 minority (Asian, non-Hispanic/Latino), 14 international. Average age 26. 411 applicants, 2% accepted, 7 enrolled. In 2010, 8 master's, 2 doctorates awarded. *Degree requirements:* For master's, thesis; for doctorate, comprehensive exam, thesis/dissertation. *Entrance requirements:* For master's and doctorate, GRE General Test, minimum GPA of 3.0. Additional exam requirements/recommendations for international students: Required—TOEFL (minimum score 487 paper-based; 216 computer-based; 85 iBT). *Application deadline:* For fall admission, 1/15 priority date for domestic students, 1/15 for international students; for spring admission, 12/1 priority date for domestic students, 12/1 for international students. Applications are processed on a rolling basis. Application fee: $75. Electronic applications accepted. *Financial support:* In 2010–11, 7 fellowships with full and partial tuition reimbursements (averaging $22,400 per year), 21 research assistantships with full tuition reimbursements (averaging $22,449 per year), 5 teaching assistantships with partial tuition reimbursements (averaging $17,512 per year) were awarded; career-related internships or fieldwork, Federal Work-Study, institutionally sponsored loans, scholarships/grants, and unspecified assistantships also available. Support available to part-time students. Financial award application deadline: 1/15. *Faculty research:* Metals, ceramics, crystals, polymers, fatigue crack propagation. Total annual research expenditures: $4.3 million. *Unit head:* Dr. Helen Chan, Chairperson, 610-758-5554, Fax: 610-758-4244, E-mail: hmc0@lehigh.edu. *Application contact:* Anne Marie Lobley, Graduate Administrative Coordinator, 610-758-4222, Fax: 610-758-4244, E-mail: amme@lehigh.edu.

Massachusetts Institute of Technology, School of Engineering, Department of Materials Science and Engineering, Cambridge, MA 02139. Offers archaeological materials (PhD, Sc D); bio- and polymeric materials (PhD, Sc D); electronic, photonic and magnetic materials (PhD, Sc D); emerging, fundamental and computational studies in materials science (Sc D); emerging, fundamental, and computational studies in materials science (PhD); materials engineering (Mat E); materials science and engineering (M Eng, SM, PhD, Sc D); metallurgical engineering (Met E); structural and environmental materials (PhD, Sc D); SM/MBA. *Faculty:* 34 full-time (8 women). *Students:* 196 full-time (52 women); includes 32 minority (2 Black or African American, non-Hispanic/Latino; 20 Asian, non-Hispanic/Latino; 7 Hispanic/Latino; 3 Two or more races, non-Hispanic/Latino), 113 international. Average age 26. 507 applicants, 15% accepted, 41 enrolled. In 2010, 22 master's, 38 doctorates awarded. Terminal master's awarded for partial completion of doctoral program. *Degree requirements:* For master's and other advanced degree, thesis; for doctorate, comprehensive exam, thesis/dissertation. *Entrance requirements:* For master's, doctorate, and other advanced degree, GRE General Test. Additional exam requirements/recommendations for international students: Required—IELTS (minimum score 7). *Application deadline:* For fall admission, 12/15 for domestic and international students. Application fee: $75. Electronic applications accepted. *Expenses:* Tuition: Full-time $38,940; part-time $605 per unit. Required fees: $272. *Financial support:* In 2010–11, 183 students received support, including 52 fellowships with tuition reimbursements available (averaging $32,695 per year), 124 research assistantships with tuition reimbursements available (averaging $27,409 per year), 8 teaching assistantships with tuition reimbursements available (averaging $31,861 per year); career-related internships or fieldwork, Federal Work-Study, institutionally sponsored loans, scholarships/grants, health care benefits, and unspecified assistantships also available. *Faculty research:* Thermodynamics and kinetics of phase transformations; structure of all materials classes: metals, ceramics, semiconductors, polymers, biomaterials; influence of processing on materials structure; structure ??? property relationships (electrical, magnetic, optical, mechanical); materials in extreme environments. Total annual research expenditures: $28.1 million. *Unit head:* Prof. Edwin L. Thomas, Department Head, 617-253-3300, Fax: 617-252-1775. *Application contact:* Angelita Mireles, Graduate Admissions, 617-253-3302, E-mail: dmse-admissions@mit.edu.

McMaster University, School of Graduate Studies, Faculty of Engineering, Department of Materials Science and Engineering, Hamilton, ON L8S 4M2, Canada. Offers materials engineering (M Eng, MA Sc, PhD); materials science (M Eng, PhD). *Degree requirements:* For master's, thesis; for doctorate, comprehensive exam, thesis/dissertation. *Entrance requirements:* Additional exam requirements/recommendations for international students: Required—TOEFL (minimum score 550 paper-based; 213 computer-based). *Faculty research:* Localized corrosion of metals and alloys, electron microscopy, polymer synthesis and characterization, polymer reaction kinetics and engineering, polymer process modeling.

Michigan State University, The Graduate School, College of Engineering, Department of Chemical Engineering and Materials Science, East Lansing, MI 48824. Offers chemical engineering (MS, PhD); materials science and engineering (MS, PhD). *Entrance requirements:* Additional exam requirements/recommendations for international students: Required—TOEFL. Electronic applications accepted.

Missouri State University, Graduate College, College of Natural and Applied Sciences, Department of Physics, Astronomy, and Materials Science, Springfield, MO 65897. Offers materials science (MS); physics, astronomy, and materials science (MNAS); secondary education (MS Ed), including physics. Part-time programs available. *Degree requirements:* For master's, comprehensive exam, thesis. *Entrance requirements:* For master's, GRE (MS, MNAS), minimum undergraduate GPA of 3.0 (MS and MNAS), 9-12 teaching certification (MS Ed). Additional exam requirements/recommendations for international students: Required—TOEFL (minimum score 550 paper-based; 213 computer-based; 79 iBT). Electronic applications accepted. *Expenses:* Tuition, state resident: full-time $3348; part-time $186 per credit hour. Tuition, nonresident: full-time $6696; part-time $372 per credit hour. Required fees: $238 per semester. Tuition and fees vary according to course level, course load and program. *Faculty research:* Nanocomposites, ferroelectricity, infrared focal plane array sensors, biosensors, pulsating stars.

New Jersey Institute of Technology, Office of Graduate Studies, College of Science and Liberal Arts, Department of Chemistry and Environmental Science, Program in Materials Science and Engineering, Newark, NJ 07102. Offers MS, PhD. Part-time and evening/weekend programs available. *Students:* 27 full-time (8 women), 3 part-time (0 women); includes 2 Black or African American, non-Hispanic/Latino; 5 Asian, non-Hispanic/Latino; 2 Hispanic/Latino, 17 international. Average age 30. 74 applicants, 36% accepted, 9 enrolled. In 2010, 4 master's, 5 doctorates awarded. Terminal master's awarded for partial completion of doctoral program. *Degree requirements:* For master's, thesis; for doctorate, thesis/dissertation. *Entrance requirements:* For master's, GRE General Test; for doctorate, GRE General Test, minimum graduate GPA of 3.5. Additional exam requirements/recommendations for international students: Required—TOEFL (minimum score 550 paper-based; 213 computer-based; 79 iBT). *Application deadline:* For fall admission, 6/5 priority date for domestic students, 4/1 for international students; for spring admission, 11/15 for domestic students, 10/15 for international students. Applications are processed on a rolling basis. Application fee: $65. Electronic applications accepted. *Expenses:* Tuition, state resident: full-time $14,724; part-time $818 per credit. Tuition, nonresident: full-time $20,304; part-time $1128 per credit. Required fees: $2272; $209 per credit. $103 per semester. One-time fee: $312 full-time; $212 part-time. *Financial support:* Fellowships with full and partial tuition reimbursements, research assistantships with full and partial tuition reimbursements, teaching assistantships with full and partial tuition reimbursements, career-related internships or fieldwork, Federal Work-Study, institutionally sponsored loans, and unspecified assistantships available. Financial award application deadline: 3/15. *Application contact:* Kathryn Kelly, Director of Admissions, 973-596-3300, Fax: 973-596-3461, E-mail: admissions@njit.edu.

Norfolk State University, School of Graduate Studies, School of Science and Technology, Department of Chemistry, Norfolk, VA 23504. Offers materials science (MS). *Entrance requirements:* Additional exam requirements/recommendations for international students: Required—TOEFL (minimum score 500 paper-based).

North Carolina State University, Graduate School, College of Engineering, Department of Materials Science and Engineering, Raleigh, NC 27695. Offers MMSE, MS, PhD. PhD offered jointly with The University of North Carolina at Charlotte. *Degree requirements:* For master's, thesis; for doctorate, thesis/dissertation. Electronic applications accepted. *Faculty research:* Processing and properties of wide band gap semiconductors, ferroelectric thin-film materials, ductility of nanocrystalline materials, computational materials science, defects in silicon-based devices.

North Dakota State University, College of Graduate and Interdisciplinary Studies, Interdisciplinary Program in Materials and Nanotechnology, Fargo, ND 58108. Offers PhD. *Students:* 11 full-time (2 women), 2 part-time (0 women), 7 international. 10 applicants, 50% accepted, 5 enrolled. In 2010, 1 doctorate awarded. *Entrance requirements:* For doctorate, GRE General Test. Additional exam requirements/recommendations for international students: Required—TOEFL (minimum score 525 paper-based; 197 computer-based; 71 iBT). *Application deadline:* For fall admission, 5/1 for international students; for spring admission, 8/1 for international students. Application fee: $45 ($60 for international students). *Unit head:* Dr. Erik Hobbie, Director, 701-231-7049, E-mail: erik.hobbie@ndsu.edu. *Application contact:* Dr. Erik Hobbe, Director, 701-231-7049, E-mail: erik.hobbie@ndsu.edu.

Northwestern University, McCormick School of Engineering and Applied Science, Department of Civil and Environmental Engineering, Evanston, IL 60208-3109. Offers environmental engineering and science (MS, PhD); geotechnical engineering (MS, PhD); mechanics of materials and solids (MS, PhD); project management (MS, PhD); structural engineering and materials (MS, PhD); theoretical and applied mechanics (MS, PhD), including fluid mechanics, solid mechanics; transportation systems analysis and planning (MS, PhD). MS and PhD admissions and degrees offered through The Graduate School. Part-time programs available. Terminal master's awarded for partial completion of doctoral program. *Degree requirements:* For master's, thesis (for some programs); for doctorate, thesis/dissertation. *Entrance requirements:* For master's and doctorate, GRE General Test, minimum 2 letters of recommendation, transcripts from all academic institutions attended. Additional exam requirements/recommendations for international students: Required—TOEFL (minimum score 600 paper-based; 250 computer-based; 100 iBT), IELTS (minimum score 7). Electronic applications accepted. *Faculty research:* Environmental engineering and science, geotechnics, mechanics of materials and solids, structural engineering and materials, transportation systems analysis and planning.

Northwestern University, McCormick School of Engineering and Applied Science, Department of Materials Science and Engineering, Evanston, IL 60208. Offers integrated computational materials engineering (Certificate); materials science and engineering (MS, PhD). Admissions and degrees offered through The Graduate School. Part-time programs available. *Faculty:* 22 full-time (3 women), 1 (woman) part-time/adjunct. *Students:* 181 full-time (54 women); includes 31 minority (3 Black or African American, non-Hispanic/Latino; 19 Asian, non-Hispanic/Latino; 8 Hispanic/Latino; 1 Two or more races, non-Hispanic/Latino), 70 international. Average age 26. In 2010, 10 master's, 31 doctorates awarded. Terminal master's awarded for partial completion of doctoral program. *Degree requirements:* For master's, thesis optional, oral thesis defense; for doctorate, comprehensive exam, thesis/dissertation, oral defense of dissertation, preliminary evaluation, qualifying exam. *Entrance requirements:* For master's and doctorate, General Exam of GRE. Additional exam requirements/recommendations for international students: Required—TOEFL (minimum score 577 paper-based, 233 computer-based, 90 iBT) or IELTS (7). *Application deadline:* For fall admission, 12/31 for domestic and international students. Application fee: $60 ($75 for international students). Electronic applications accepted. *Financial support:* Fellowships with full tuition reimbursements, research assistantships with full tuition reimbursements, teaching assistantships with full tuition reimbursements, career-related internships or fieldwork, institutionally sponsored loans, health care benefits, and unspecified assistantships available. Financial award application deadline: 1/15; financial award applicants required to submit FAFSA. *Faculty research:* Biomaterials, cement, ceramics, composites, electrical properties, electron and ion microscopy, energy, materials design, materials processing, materials theory, mechanical properties, metals, molecular synthesis, nanomaterials, optical properties, phase transformation, polymers, scattering and diffraction, self-assembly, semiconductors, surfaces and interfaces, thin films. Total annual research expenditures: $28.3 million. *Unit head:* Dr. Michael Bedzyk, Chair, 847-491-3570, Fax: 847-491-7820, E-mail: bedzyk@northwestern.edu. *Application contact:* Dr. Chris Wolverton, Admissions Officer, 847-497-0593, Fax: 847-491-7820, E-mail: c-wolverton@northwestern.edu.

The Ohio State University, Graduate School, College of Engineering, Department of Materials Science and Engineering, Columbus, OH 43210. Offers materials science and engineering (MS, PhD); welding engineering (MS, MWE, PhD). *Faculty:* 26. *Students:* 69 full-time (12 women), 41 part-time (11 women); includes 2 Asian, non-Hispanic/Latino; 1 Hispanic/Latino, 53 international. Average age 26. In 2010, 25 master's, 11 doctorates awarded. *Degree requirements:* For master's, thesis; for doctorate, thesis/dissertation. *Entrance requirements:* For master's and doctorate, GRE (for graduates of foreign universities and holders of non-engineering degrees). Additional exam requirements/recommendations for international students: Recommended—TOEFL (minimum score 600 paper-based; 250 computer-based). *Application deadline:* For fall admission, 8/15 priority date for domestic students, 7/1 priority date for international students; for winter admission, 12/1 priority date for domestic students, 11/1 priority date for international students; for spring admission, 3/1 priority date for domestic students, 2/1 priority date for international students. Applications are processed on a rolling basis. Application fee: $40 ($50 for international students). Electronic applications accepted. *Expenses:* Tuition, state resident: full-time $10,605. Tuition, nonresident: full-time $26,535. Tuition and fees vary according to course load and program. *Financial support:* In 2010–11, fellowships (averaging $43,000 per year), research assistantships (averaging $40,700 per year) were awarded; teaching assistantships, career-related internships or fieldwork, scholarships/grants, and unspecified assistantships also available. *Faculty research:* Computational materials modeling, biomaterials, metallurgy, ceramics, advanced alloys/composites. Total annual research expenditures: $10 million. *Unit head:* Rudolph G. Buchheit, Chair, 614-292-2553, Fax: 614-292-4668, E-mail: buchheit.8@osu.edu. *Application contact:* 614-292-9444, Fax: 614-292-3895, E-mail: domestic.grad@osu.edu.

Oregon State University, Graduate School, College of Engineering, School of Mechanical, Industrial, and Manufacturing Engineering, Program in Materials Science, Corvallis, OR 97331. Offers MAIS, MS, PhD. *Degree requirements:* For master's, thesis or alternative. *Entrance requirements:* For master's, GRE General Test, minimum GPA of 3.0 in last 90 hours of course work. Additional exam requirements/recommendations for international students: Required—TOEFL (minimum score 550 paper-based; 213 computer-based).

Penn State University Park, Graduate School, College of Earth and Mineral Sciences, Department of Materials Science and Engineering, State College, University Park, PA 16802-1503. Offers MS, PhD.

Princeton University, Princeton Institute for the Science and Technology of Materials (PRISM), Princeton, NJ 08544-1019. Offers materials (PhD).

Rensselaer Polytechnic Institute, Graduate School, School of Engineering, Program in Materials Science and Engineering, Troy, NY 12180. Offers ceramics and glass science (M Eng, MS, PhD); composites (M Eng, MS, PhD); electronic materials (M Eng, MS, PhD); metallurgy (M Eng, MS, PhD); polymers (M Eng, MS, PhD). Part-time programs available. *Faculty:* 16 full-time (2 women). *Students:* 57 full-time (13 women), 6 part-time (1 woman), 37 international. Average age 24. 304 applicants, 15% accepted, 16 enrolled. In 2010, 5 master's, 6 doctorates awarded. Terminal master's awarded for partial completion of doctoral program. *Degree requirements:* For master's, thesis; for doctorate, comprehensive exam, thesis/dissertation. *Entrance requirements:* For master's and doctorate, GRE. Additional exam requirements/recommendations for international students: Required—TOEFL (minimum score 570 paper-based; 230 computer-based; 100 iBT). *Application deadline:* For fall admission, 1/15 priority date for domestic and international students; for spring admission, 8/31 priority date for domestic and international students. Applications are processed on a rolling basis. Application fee: $75. Electronic applications accepted. *Expenses:* Tuition: Full-time $39,600; part-time $1650 per credit. Required fees: $1896. *Financial support:* In 2010–11, 56 students received support, including 2 fellowships with full tuition reimbursements available (averaging $26,250 per year), 41 research assistantships with full tuition reimbursements available (averaging $26,250 per year), 13 teaching assistantships with full tuition reimbursements available (averaging $17,500 per year); career-related internships or fieldwork, institutionally sponsored loans, and unspecified assistantships also available. Financial award application deadline: 2/1. *Faculty research:* Materials processing, nanostructural materials, materials for microelectronics, composite materials, computational materials. Total annual research expenditures: $3.6 million. *Unit head:* Dr. Robert Hull, Department Head, 518-276-6373, Fax: 518-276-8554, E-mail: hullr2@rpi.edu. *Application contact:* Dr. Pawel Keblinski, Admissions Coordinator, 518-276-6858, Fax: 518-276-8554, E-mail: keblip@rpi.edu.

Rice University, Graduate Programs, George R. Brown School of Engineering, Department of Mechanical Engineering and Materials Science, Houston, TX 77251-1892. Offers materials science (MMS, MS, PhD); mechanical engineering (MME, MS, PhD); MBA/ME. Part-time programs available. Terminal master's awarded for partial completion of doctoral program. *Degree requirements:* For master's, comprehensive exam, thesis; for doctorate, comprehensive exam, thesis/dissertation. *Entrance requirements:* For master's and doctorate, GRE General Test, minimum GPA of 3.0. Additional exam requirements/recommendations for international students: Required—TOEFL (minimum score 600 paper-based; 250 computer-based; 90 iBT), IELTS (minimum score 7). Electronic applications accepted. *Faculty research:* Heat transfer, biomedical engineering, fluid dynamics, aero-astronautics, control systems/robotics, materials science.

Rochester Institute of Technology, Graduate Enrollment Services, College of Science, Health Sciences and Sustainability, Center for Materials Science and Engineering, Rochester, NY 14623-5603. Offers MS. Part-time and evening/weekend programs available. *Students:* 15 full-time (4 women), 10 part-time (4 women); includes 2 Asian, non-Hispanic/Latino; 1 Hispanic/Latino, 12 international. Average age 28. 33 applicants, 67% accepted, 6 enrolled. In 2010, 8 master's awarded. *Degree requirements:* For master's, thesis or project. *Entrance requirements:* For master's, GRE (recommended), minimum GPA of 3.0. Additional exam requirements/recommendations for international students: Required—TOEFL (minimum score 575 paper-based; 233 computer-based; 90 iBT) or IELTS (minimum score 6.5). *Application deadline:* For fall admission, 2/15 priority date for domestic and international students; for winter admission, 11/1 for domestic students, 10/1 for international students; for spring admission, 2/1 for domestic students, 1/1 for international students. Applications are processed on a rolling basis. Application fee: $50. Electronic applications accepted. *Expenses:* Tuition: Full-time $33,234; part-time $924 per credit hour. Required fees: $219. *Financial support:* In 2010–11, 10 students received support; research assistantships with partial tuition reimbursements available, teaching assistantships with partial tuition reimbursements available, career-related internships or fieldwork, scholarships/grants, tuition waivers (partial), and unspecified assistantships available. Support available to part-time students. Financial award application deadline: 7/29; financial award applicants required to submit FAFSA. *Faculty research:* VUV modification of polymers, stress and morphology of sputtered copper films, MRI applications to materials problems. *Unit head:* Dr. KSV Santhanam, Program Director, 585-475-2920, Fax: 585-475-2800, E-mail: ksssch@rit.edu. *Application contact:* Diane Ellison, Assistant Vice President, Graduate Enrollment Services, 585-475-2229, Fax: 585-475-7164, E-mail: gradinfo@rit.edu.

Royal Military College of Canada, Division of Graduate Studies and Research, Engineering Division, Program in Chemical and Materials Science, Kingston, ON K7K 7B4, Canada. Offers M Sc, PhD. *Degree requirements:* For master's, thesis; for doctorate, comprehensive exam, thesis/dissertation. *Entrance requirements:* For master's, honours degree with second-class standing; for doctorate, master's degree. Electronic applications accepted.

Rutgers, The State University of New Jersey, New Brunswick, Graduate School-New Brunswick, Program in Materials Science and Engineering, Piscataway, NJ 08854-8097. Offers MS, PhD. Part-time programs available. *Degree requirements:* For master's, thesis; for doctorate, comprehensive exam, thesis/dissertation. *Entrance requirements:* For master's and doctorate, GRE General Test. Electronic applications accepted. *Expenses:* Tuition, state resident: full-time $7200; part-time $600 per credit. Tuition, nonresident: full-time $11,124; part-time $927 per credit. *Faculty research:* Ceramic processing, nanostructured materials, electrical and structural ceramics, fiber optics.

School of the Art Institute of Chicago, Graduate Division, Department of Fiber and Material Studies, Chicago, IL 60603-3103. Offers MFA. *Accreditation:* NASAD. *Entrance requirements:* Additional exam requirements/recommendations for international students: Required—TOEFL, IELTS.

South Dakota School of Mines and Technology, Graduate Division, Doctoral Program in Materials Engineering and Science, Rapid City, SD 57701-3995. Offers PhD. Part-time programs available. *Degree requirements:* For doctorate, thesis/dissertation. *Entrance requirements:* For doctorate, GRE General Test, minimum graduate GPA of 3.0, 3 letters of recommendation. Additional exam requirements/recommendations for international students: Required—TOEFL, TWE. Electronic applications accepted. *Faculty research:* Thermophysical properties of solids, development of multiphase materials and composites, concrete technology, electronic polymer materials.

South Dakota School of Mines and Technology, Graduate Division, Master's Program in Materials Engineering and Science, Rapid City, SD 57701-3995. Offers MS. *Entrance requirements:* For master's, GRE General Test. Additional exam requirements/recommendations for international students: Required—TOEFL, TWE. Electronic applications accepted.

Stanford University, School of Engineering, Department of Materials Science and Engineering, Stanford, CA 94305-9991. Offers MS, PhD, Eng. Terminal master's awarded for partial completion of doctoral program. *Degree requirements:* For doctorate, thesis/dissertation; for Eng, thesis. *Entrance requirements:* For master's, doctorate, and Eng, GRE General Test. Additional exam requirements/recommendations for international students: Required—TOEFL. Electronic applications accepted. *Expenses:* Tuition: Full-time $38,700; part-time $860 per unit. One-time fee: $200 full-time.

State University of New York at Binghamton, Graduate School, Thomas J. Watson School of Engineering and Applied Science and School of Arts and Sciences, Materials Science and Engineering Program, Binghamton, NY 13902-6000. Offers MS, PhD. *Faculty:* 3 full-time (0 women). *Students:* 16 full-time (7 women), 31 part-time (7 women); includes 2 Asian, non-Hispanic/Latino, 34 international. Average age 29. 32 applicants, 34% accepted, 8 enrolled. In 2010, 1 master's, 6 doctorates awarded. Application fee: $60. *Financial support:* In 2010–11, 31 students received support, including 21 research assistantships with full tuition reimbursements available (averaging $16,500 per year), 9 teaching assistantships with full tuition reimbursements available (averaging $16,500 per year); career-related internships or fieldwork, Federal Work-Study, institutionally sponsored loans, scholarships/grants, health care benefits, tuition waivers (full and partial), and unspecified assistantships also available. Financial award application deadline: 2/15; financial award applicants required to submit FAFSA. *Unit head:* Dr. Stanley Whittingham, Director, 607-777-4623, E-mail: stanwhit@binghamton.edu. *Application contact:* Catherine Smith, Recruiting and Admissions Coordinator, 607-777-2151, Fax: 607-777-2501, E-mail: cmsmith@binghamton.edu.

Stony Brook University, State University of New York, Graduate School, College of Engineering and Applied Sciences, Department of Materials Science and Engineering, Stony Brook, NY 11794. Offers MS, PhD. *Faculty:* 13 full-time (3 women), 8 part-time/adjunct (1 woman). *Students:* 104 full-time (33 women), 7 part-time (1 woman); includes 3 Black or African American, non-Hispanic/Latino; 8 Asian, non-Hispanic/Latino; 2 Hispanic/Latino, 79 international. Average age 28. 176 applicants, 45% accepted, 30 enrolled. In 2010, 17 master's, 6 doctorates awarded. *Degree requirements:* For master's, thesis or alternative; for doctorate, comprehensive exam, thesis/dissertation. *Entrance requirements:* For master's and doctorate, GRE General Test, minimum undergraduate GPA of 3.0. Additional exam requirements/recommendations for international students: Required—TOEFL. *Application deadline:* For fall admission, 1/15 for domestic students. Application fee: $100. *Expenses:* Tuition, state resident: full-time $8370; part-time $349 per credit. Tuition, nonresident: full-time $13,780; part-time $574 per credit. Required fees: $994. *Financial support:* In 2010–11, 40 research assistantships, 12 teaching assistantships were awarded; fellowships also available. *Faculty research:* Electronic materials, biomaterials, synchrotron topography. Total annual research expenditures: $3.1 million. *Unit head:* Dr. Michael Dudley, Chairman, 631-632-8484. *Application contact:* Dr. Miriam Rafailovich, Director, 631-632-8484, Fax: 631-632-8052, E-mail: mrafailovich.nsf@notes.cc.sunysb.edu.

Texas A&M Health Science Center, Baylor College of Dentistry, Graduate Division, Department of Biomaterials Science, College Station, TX 77840. Offers MS. Part-time programs available. *Degree requirements:* For master's, thesis. *Entrance requirements:* For master's, GRE General Test, DDS or DMD or BS in engineering. Additional exam requirements/recommendations for international students: Required—TOEFL. *Faculty research:* Titanium casting for dental applications, mechanical properties of dental ceramics, metal-ceramic adhesion, fatigue failure of dental implants, orthodontic materials, laser welding.

Texas State University–San Marcos, Graduate School, College of Science, Program in Material Physics, San Marcos, TX 78666. Offers PhD. *Faculty:* 6 full-time (2 women), 1 part-time/adjunct (0 women). *Students:* 3 full-time (0 women), 1 part-time (0 women); includes 1 minority (Hispanic/Latino), 1 international. Average age 28. 3 applicants, 100% accepted, 2 enrolled. *Entrance requirements:* Additional exam requirements/recommendations for international students: Required—TOEFL (minimum score 550 paper-based; 213 computer-based; 78 iBT). *Application deadline:* For fall admission, 6/15 for domestic students, 6/1 for international students; for spring admission, 10/15 for domestic students, 10/1 for international students. Applications are processed on a rolling basis. Application fee: $40 ($90 for international students). Electronic applications accepted. *Expenses:* Tuition, state resident: full-time $6024; part-time $251 per credit hour. Tuition, nonresident: full-time $13,536; part-time $564 per credit hour. Required fees: $1776; $50 per credit hour. $306 per semester. *Financial support:* In 2010–11, 3 students received support, including 1 research assistantship (averaging $5,076 per year), 1 teaching assistantship (averaging $5,076 per year); Federal Work-Study, institutionally sponsored loans, scholarships/grants, health care benefits, and unspecified assistantships also available. Support available to part-time students. *Faculty research:* Micropower chip plan, uniflow SE bypass, high performance FET, growth of expitaxial, layer suprlattices, geteronintegration. Total annual research expenditures: $383,881. *Unit head:* Dr. David Donnelly, Graduate Advisor, 512-245-2131, E-mail: donnelly@txstate.edu. *Application contact:* Dr. J. Michael Willoughby, Dean of Graduate School, 512-245-2581, Fax: 512-245-8365, E-mail: gradcollege@txstate.edu.

Trent University, Graduate Studies, Program in Materials Science, Peterborough, ON K9J 7B8, Canada. Offers M Sc.

Université du Québec, Institut National de la Recherche Scientifique, Graduate Programs, Research Center—Energy, Materials and Telecommunications, Québec, QC G1K 9A9, Canada. Offers energy and materials science (M Sc, PhD); telecommunications (M Sc, PhD). Programs given in French; PhD programs offered jointly with Université du Québec à Trois-Rivières. Part-time programs available. *Faculty:* 40. *Students:* 171 full-time (44 women), 6 part-time (1 woman), 88 international. Average age 32. In 2010, 15 master's, 23 doctorates awarded. *Degree requirements:* For master's, thesis optional; for doctorate, thesis/dissertation. *Entrance requirements:* For master's, appropriate bachelor's degree, proficiency in French; for doctorate, appropriate master's degree, proficiency in French. *Application deadline:* For fall admission, 3/30 for domestic and international students; for winter admission, 11/1 for domestic and international students; for spring admission, 3/1 for domestic and international students. Application fee: $30. *Financial support:* Fellowships, research assistantships, teaching assistantships available. *Faculty research:* New energy sources, plasmas, fusion. *Unit head:* Jean-Claude Kieffer, Director, 450-929-8100, E-mail: kieffer@emt.inrs.ca. *Application contact:* Yvonne Boisvert, Registrar, 418-654-3861, Fax: 418-654-3858, E-mail: registrariat@adm.inrs.ca.

University at Buffalo, the State University of New York, Graduate School, School of Dental Medicine, Graduate Programs in Dental Medicine, Department of Oral Diagnostic Sciences, Buffalo, NY 14260. Offers biomaterials (MS). Part-time programs available. *Degree requirements:* For master's, thesis. *Entrance requirements:* Additional exam requirements/recommendations for international students: Required—TOEFL (minimum score 79 iBT). Electronic applications accepted. *Faculty research:* Bioengineering, surface science, bioadhesion, regulatory sterilization.

Materials Sciences

The University of Alabama, Graduate School, College of Engineering and College of Arts and Sciences, Tri-Campus Materials Science PhD Program, Tuscaloosa, AL 35487. Offers PhD. Program offered jointly with The University of Alabama at Birmingham, The University of Alabama in Huntsville. *Students:* 9 full-time (2 women), 2 part-time (1 woman); includes 3 minority (2 Black or African American, non-Hispanic/Latino; 1 Asian, non-Hispanic/Latino), 7 international. Average age 27. 15 applicants, 20% accepted, 0 enrolled. In 2010, 1 doctorate awarded. *Degree requirements:* For doctorate, comprehensive exam, thesis/dissertation. *Entrance requirements:* For doctorate, GRE General Test. Additional exam requirements/recommendations for international students: Required—TOEFL (minimum score 550 paper-based; 213 computer-based). *Application deadline:* For fall admission, 2/28 priority date for domestic and international students; for spring admission, 10/30 priority date for domestic students, 9/30 priority date for international students. Applications are processed on a rolling basis. Application fee: $50 ($60 for international students). Electronic applications accepted. *Expenses:* Tuition, state resident: full-time $7900. Tuition, nonresident: full-time $20,500. *Financial support:* In 2010–11, 4 research assistantships with full tuition reimbursements (averaging $19,500 per year) were awarded; career-related internships or fieldwork and unspecified assistantships also available. Financial award application deadline: 2/28. *Faculty research:* Magnetic multilayers, metals casting, molecular electronics, conducting polymers, metals physics, electrodeposition. *Unit head:* Prof. Garry Warren, Campus Coordinator, 205-348-4337, E-mail: gwarren@coe.eng.ua.edu. *Application contact:* Dr. David A. Francko, Dean, 205-348-8280, Fax: 205-348-0400, E-mail: dfrancko@ua.edu.

The University of Alabama at Birmingham, School of Engineering, Joint Materials Science PhD Program, Birmingham, AL 35294. Offers PhD. Program offered jointly with The University of Alabama (Tuscaloosa), The University of Alabama in Huntsville. *Degree requirements:* For doctorate, thesis/dissertation. *Entrance requirements:* For doctorate, GRE General Test. *Expenses:* Tuition, state resident: full-time $5482. Tuition, nonresident: full-time $12,430. Tuition and fees vary according to program. *Financial support:* In 2010–11, fellowships with full and partial tuition reimbursements (averaging $12,500 per year), research assistantships with full tuition reimbursements (averaging $12,500 per year) were awarded; career-related internships or fieldwork, Federal Work-Study, and institutionally sponsored loans also available. Support available to part-time students. Financial award application deadline: 4/1. *Faculty research:* Biocompatibility studies with biomaterials, microgravity solidification of proteins and metals, analysis of microelectronic materials, thin film analysis using TEM. *Unit head:* Dr. J. Barry Andrews, Chair, 205-934-8460, Fax: 205-934-8485, E-mail: barry@uab.edu. *Application contact:* Julie Bryant, Director of Graduate Admissions, 205-934-8227, Fax: 205-934-8413, E-mail: jbryant@uab.edu.

The University of Alabama in Huntsville, School of Graduate Studies, Interdisciplinary Studies, Interdisciplinary Program in Materials Science, Huntsville, AL 35899. Offers MS, PhD. PhD offered jointly with The University of Alabama and The University of Alabama at Birmingham. Part-time and evening/weekend programs available. *Faculty:* 20 full-time (1 woman). *Students:* 5 full-time (3 women), 2 part-time (both women); includes 1 Black or African American, non-Hispanic/Latino, 2 international. Average age 31. 13 applicants, 46% accepted, 5 enrolled. In 2010, 3 master's, 2 doctorates awarded. *Degree requirements:* For master's, comprehensive exam, thesis or alternative, oral and written exams; for doctorate, comprehensive exam, thesis/dissertation, oral and written exams. *Entrance requirements:* For master's, GRE General Test, minimum GPA of 3.0; for doctorate, GRE General Test, bachelor's degree in engineering or physical science, minimum GPA of 3.0. Additional exam requirements/recommendations for international students: Required—TOEFL (minimum score 500 paper-based; 173 computer-based; 62 iBT). *Application deadline:* For fall admission, 7/15 for domestic students, 4/1 for international students; for spring admission, 11/30 for domestic students, 9/1 for international students. Applications are processed on a rolling basis. Application fee: $40 ($50 for international students). Electronic applications accepted. *Expenses:* Tuition, state resident: full-time $7250; part-time $407.75 per credit hour. Tuition, nonresident: full-time $17,358; part-time $970.05 per credit hour. Required fees: $246.80 per semester. Tuition and fees vary according to course load and program. *Financial support:* In 2010–11, 3 students received support, including 1 research assistantship with full and partial tuition reimbursement available (averaging $12,000 per year), 2 teaching assistantships with full and partial tuition reimbursements available (averaging $11,116 per year); career-related internships or fieldwork, Federal Work-Study, institutionally sponsored loans, scholarships/grants, health care benefits, and unspecified assistantships also available. Support available to part-time students. Financial award application deadline: 4/1; financial award applicants required to submit FAFSA. *Faculty research:* Materials structure and properties; materials processing; mechanical behavior; macromolecular materials; electronic, optical, and magnetic materials. *Unit head:* Dr. Michael Banish, Coordinator, 256-824-6810, Fax: 256-824-6349, E-mail: banishm@uah.edu. *Application contact:* Kathy Biggs, Graduate Studies Admissions Manager, 256-824-6199, Fax: 256-824-6405, E-mail: deangrad@uah.edu.

The University of Arizona, College of Engineering, Department of Materials Science and Engineering, Tucson, AZ 85721. Offers MS, PhD. Part-time programs available. *Faculty:* 10 full-time (3 women), 2 part-time/adjunct (0 women). *Students:* 37 full-time (16 women), 14 part-time (6 women); includes 14 minority (1 American Indian or Alaska Native, non-Hispanic/Latino; 1 Asian, non-Hispanic/Latino; 7 Hispanic/Latino; 5 Two or more races, non-Hispanic/Latino), 15 international. Average age 29. 82 applicants, 20% accepted, 6 enrolled. In 2010, 5 master's, 5 doctorates awarded. *Degree requirements:* For master's, thesis (for some programs); for doctorate, comprehensive exam, thesis/dissertation. *Entrance requirements:* For master's and doctorate, GRE General Test, 3 letters of recommendation, statement of purpose. Additional exam requirements/recommendations for international students: Required—TOEFL (minimum score 550 paper-based; 213 computer-based). *Application deadline:* Applications are processed on a rolling basis. Application fee: $75. Electronic applications accepted. *Expenses:* Tuition, state resident: full-time $7692. *Financial support:* In 2010–11, 25 research assistantships with full tuition reimbursements (averaging $23,789 per year), 2 teaching assistantships with full tuition reimbursements (averaging $23,586 per year) were awarded; institutionally sponsored loans, scholarships/grants, health care benefits, tuition waivers (full), and unspecified assistantships also available. Financial award application deadline: 12/31. *Faculty research:* High-technology ceramics, optical materials, electronic materials, chemical metallurgy, science of materials. Total annual research expenditures: $1.9 million. *Unit head:* Dr. Joseph H. Simmons, Head, 520-621-6070, Fax: 520-621-8059, E-mail: simmons@mse.arizona.edu. *Application contact:* Information Contact, 520-626-6762, Fax: 520-621-8059, E-mail: msed@email.arizona.edu.

The University of British Columbia, Faculty of Applied Science, Department of Materials Engineering, Vancouver, BC V6T 1Z1, Canada. Offers materials and metallurgy (M Sc, PhD); metals and materials engineering (MA Sc, PhD). *Degree requirements:* For master's, comprehensive exam, thesis; for doctorate, comprehensive exam, thesis/dissertation. *Entrance requirements:* Additional exam requirements/recommendations for international students: Required—TOEFL (minimum score 560 paper-based; 220 computer-based; 83 iBT). Electronic applications accepted. Tuition charges are reported in Canadian dollars. *Expenses:* Tuition, area resident: Full-time $4179 Canadian dollars. International tuition: $7344 Canadian dollars full-time. *Faculty research:* Electroslag melting, mathematical modeling, solidification and hydrometallurgy.

University of California, Berkeley, Graduate Division, College of Engineering, Department of Materials Science and Engineering, Berkeley, CA 94720-1500. Offers engineering (M Eng, MS, D Eng, PhD); engineering science (M Eng, MS, PhD). *Degree requirements:* For master's, comprehensive exam or thesis (MS); for doctorate, comprehensive exam, thesis/dissertation, qualifying exam. *Entrance requirements:* For master's and doctorate, GRE General Test, minimum GPA of 3.0, 3 letters of recommendation. Additional exam requirements/recommendations for international students: Required—TOEFL (minimum score 230 computer-based). *Faculty research:* Ceramics, biomaterials, structural, electronic, magnetic and optical materials.

University of California, Davis, College of Engineering, Program in Materials Science and Engineering, Davis, CA 95616. Offers MS, PhD. Terminal master's awarded for partial completion of doctoral program. *Degree requirements:* For master's, comprehensive exam (for some programs), thesis (for some programs); for doctorate, comprehensive exam, thesis/dissertation. *Entrance requirements:* Additional exam requirements/recommendations for international students: Required—TOEFL (minimum score 550 paper-based; 213 computer-based).

University of California, Irvine, School of Engineering, Department of Chemical Engineering and Materials Science, Irvine, CA 92697. Offers chemical and biochemical engineering (MS, PhD); materials science and engineering (MS, PhD). Part-time programs available. *Students:* 77 full-time (24 women), 3 part-time (1 woman); includes 22 minority (1 American Indian or Alaska Native, non-Hispanic/Latino; 16 Asian, non-Hispanic/Latino; 3 Hispanic/Latino; 1 Native Hawaiian or other Pacific Islander, non-Hispanic/Latino; 1 Two or more races, non-Hispanic/Latino), 32 international. Average age 28. 300 applicants, 27% accepted, 26 enrolled. In 2010, 24 master's, 8 doctorates awarded. Terminal master's awarded for partial completion of doctoral program. *Degree requirements:* For doctorate, thesis/dissertation. *Entrance requirements:* For master's and doctorate, GRE General Test, minimum GPA of 3.0, 3 letters of recommendation. Additional exam requirements/recommendations for international students: Required—TOEFL (minimum score 550 paper-based; 213 computer-based). *Application deadline:* For fall admission, 1/15 priority date for domestic students, 1/15 for international students. Applications are processed on a rolling basis. Application fee: $80 ($100 for international students). Electronic applications accepted. *Financial support:* Fellowships with tuition reimbursements, research assistantships with full tuition reimbursements, teaching assistantships with tuition reimbursements, institutionally sponsored loans, traineeships, health care benefits, and unspecified assistantships available. Financial award application deadline: 3/1; financial award applicants required to submit FAFSA. *Faculty research:* Molecular bio-technology, nano-bio-materials, biophotonics, synthesis, superplasticity and mechanical behavior, characterization of advanced and nanostructural materials. *Unit head:* Prof. Albert Yee, Chair, 949-824-7320, Fax: 949-824-2541, E-mail: albert.yee@uci.edu. *Application contact:* Grace Hai-Chin Chau, Academic Program/Graduate Admission Coordinator, 949-824-3887, Fax: 949-824-2541, E-mail: chaug@uci.edu.

University of California, Irvine, School of Physical Sciences, Department of Chemistry and Department of Physics and Astronomy, Program in Chemical and Materials Physics (CHAMP), Irvine, CA 92697. Offers MS, PhD. *Students:* 58 full-time (14 women); includes 13 minority (6 Asian, non-Hispanic/Latino; 5 Hispanic/Latino; 2 Two or more races, non-Hispanic/Latino), 11 international. Average age 28. 49 applicants, 35% accepted, 9 enrolled. In 2010, 4 master's, 8 doctorates awarded. *Degree requirements:* For doctorate, thesis/dissertation. *Entrance requirements:* For master's and doctorate, GRE General Test, GRE Subject Test, minimum GPA of 3.0. *Application deadline:* For fall admission, 1/15 priority date for domestic students, 1/15 for international students. Applications are processed on a rolling basis. Application fee: $80 ($100 for international students). Electronic applications accepted. *Financial support:* Fellowships, research assistantships with full tuition reimbursements, teaching assistantships, institutionally sponsored loans, traineeships, health care benefits, and unspecified assistantships available. Financial award application deadline: 3/1; financial award applicants required to submit FAFSA. *Unit head:* Craig Martens, ChaMP Co-director, 949-824-5141, E-mail: cmartens@uci.edu. *Application contact:* Philip Collins, ChaMP Advisor, 949-824-9961, E-mail: collinsp@uci.edu.

University of California, Los Angeles, Graduate Division, Henry Samueli School of Engineering and Applied Science, Department of Materials Science and Engineering, Los Angeles, CA 90095-1595. Offers MS, PhD. *Faculty:* 12 full-time (3 women). *Students:* 111 full-time (25 women); includes 3 Black or African American, non-Hispanic/Latino; 15 Asian, non-Hispanic/Latino; 3 Hispanic/Latino, 60 international. 183 applicants, 49% accepted, 40 enrolled. In 2010, 20 master's, 21 doctorates awarded. *Degree requirements:* For master's, comprehensive exam or thesis; for doctorate, thesis/dissertation, qualifying exams. *Entrance requirements:* For master's, GRE General Test, minimum GPA of 3.0; for doctorate, GRE General Test, minimum GPA of 3.25. Additional exam requirements/recommendations for international students: Required—TOEFL (minimum score 560 paper-based; 220 computer-based; 87 iBT). *Application deadline:* For fall admission, 12/15 for domestic and international students. Application fee: $70 ($90 for international students). Electronic applications accepted. *Financial support:* In 2010–11, 42 fellowships, 302 research assistantships, 33 teaching assistantships were awarded; Federal Work-Study, institutionally sponsored loans, and tuition waivers (full and partial) also available. Financial award application deadline: 1/15; financial award applicants required to submit FAFSA. Total annual research expenditures: $6.5 million. *Unit head:* Dr. Jenn-Ming Yang, Chair, 310-825-2758, E-mail: jyang@seas.ucla.edu. *Application contact:* Paradee Chularee, Student Affairs Officer, 310-825-8913, Fax: 310-206-7353, E-mail: paradee@ea.ucla.edu.

University of California, Riverside, Graduate Division, Graduate Materials Science and Engineering Program, Riverside, CA 92521. Offers MS, PhD. *Faculty:* 40. *Students:* 15 full-time (5 women); includes 1 Black or African American, non-Hispanic/Latino; 6 Asian, non-Hispanic/Latino. Average age 27. 60 applicants, 30% accepted, 8 enrolled. *Entrance requirements:* For master's and doctorate, GRE. Additional exam requirements/recommendations for international students: Required—TOEFL (minimum score 550 paper-based; 213 computer-based; 80 iBT). *Application deadline:* For fall admission, 1/5 priority date for domestic students. Application fee: $0 ($100 for international students). Electronic applications accepted. *Financial support:* In 2010–11, 8 students received support; fellowships, research assistantships, teaching assistantships, scholarships/grants, health care benefits, and unspecified assistantships available. Financial award application deadline: 1/5. *Unit head:* MSE Program Office, 951-827-3392, Fax: 951-827-3188, E-mail: mse-program@engr.ucr.edu. *Application contact:* Graduate Admissions, 951-827-3392, Fax: 951-827-3188, E-mail: mse-program@engr.ucr.edu.

University of California, San Diego, Office of Graduate Studies, Materials Science and Engineering Program, La Jolla, CA 92093. Offers MS, PhD. *Degree requirements:* For doctorate, thesis/dissertation. *Entrance requirements:* For master's and doctorate, GRE General Test, minimum GPA of 3.0. Additional exam requirements/recommendations for international students: Required—TOEFL. Electronic applications accepted.

University of California, Santa Barbara, Graduate Division, College of Engineering, Department of Materials, Santa Barbara, CA 93106-5050. Offers MS, PhD, MS/PhD. *Faculty:* 28 full-time (3 women), 4 part-time/adjunct (0 women). *Students:* 125 full-time (27 women); includes 28 Asian, non-Hispanic/Latino; 3 Hispanic/Latino; 1 Native Hawaiian or other Pacific Islander, non-Hispanic/Latino. Average age 26. 321 applicants, 25% accepted, 37 enrolled. In 2010, 5 master's, 20 doctorates awarded. Terminal master's awarded for partial completion of doctoral program. *Degree requirements:* For doctorate, comprehensive exam, thesis/dissertation. *Entrance requirements:* For master's and doctorate, GRE General Test. Additional exam requirements/recommendations for international students: Required—TOEFL (minimum score 600 paper-based; 100 iBT), IELTS (minimum score 7). *Application deadline:* For fall admission, 1/7 priority date for domestic and international students; for winter admission, 11/1 priority date for domestic and international students; for spring admission, 1/1 priority date for domestic and international students. Application fee: $70 ($90 for international students). Electronic applications accepted. *Financial support:* In 2010–11, 105 students received support, including 48 fellowships with full and partial tuition reimbursements available (averaging $11,846 per year), 97 research assistantships with full and partial tuition reimbursements available (averaging $14,386 per year), 21 teaching assistantships with partial tuition reimbursements available (averaging $3,824 per year); career-related internships or fieldwork, scholarships/grants, tuition waivers (full), and unspecified assistantships also available. Financial award application deadline: 3/2; financial award applicants required to submit FAFSA. *Faculty research:* Electronic and photonic materials, inorganic materials, macromolecular and biomolecular materials, structural materials. Total annual research expenditures: $5.8 million. *Unit head:* Dr. James S. Speck, Chair and Professor, 805-893-4362, Fax: 805-893-8486, E-mail: speck@mrl.ucsb.edu.

Application contact: Oura Neak, Graduate Program Assistant, 805-893-4601, Fax: 805-893-8486, E-mail: mtrl-applications@engineering.ucsb.edu.

University of Central Florida, College of Engineering and Computer Science, Department of Mechanical, Materials, and Aerospace Engineering, Program in Materials Science and Engineering, Orlando, FL 32816. Offers MSMSE, PhD. *Students:* 41 full-time (9 women), 13 part-time (4 women); includes 1 Black or African American, non-Hispanic/Latino; 1 American Indian or Alaska Native, non-Hispanic/Latino; 3 Asian, non-Hispanic/Latino; 4 Hispanic/Latino, 28 international. Average age 28. 40 applicants, 50% accepted, 9 enrolled. In 2010, 15 master's, 7 doctorates awarded. *Degree requirements:* For master's, thesis or alternative; for doctorate, thesis/dissertation, candidacy exam, departmental qualifying exam. *Application deadline:* For fall admission, 7/15 priority date for domestic students; for spring admission, 12/1 priority date for domestic students. Application fee: $30. Electronic applications accepted. *Expenses:* Tuition, state resident: part-time $256.56 per credit hour. Tuition, nonresident: part-time $1011.52 per credit hour. Part-time tuition and fees vary according to program. *Financial support:* In 2010–11, 31 students received support, including 13 fellowships (averaging $1,600 per year), 34 research assistantships (averaging $9,800 per year), 5 teaching assistantships (averaging $8,100 per year).

University of Cincinnati, Graduate School, College of Engineering, Department of Chemical and Materials Engineering, Cincinnati, OH 45221. Offers chemical engineering (MS, PhD); materials science and metallurgical engineering (MS, PhD), including ceramic science and engineering, materials science and engineering, metallurgical engineering, polymer science and engineering. Part-time and evening/weekend programs available. Terminal master's awarded for partial completion of doctoral program. *Degree requirements:* For master's, thesis; for doctorate, thesis/dissertation. *Entrance requirements:* For master's and doctorate, GRE General Test. Additional exam requirements/recommendations for international students: Required—TOEFL. Electronic applications accepted. *Faculty research:* Process synthesis, aerosol processes, clean coal technology, membrane technology.

University of Cincinnati, Graduate School, College of Engineering, Department of Chemical and Materials Engineering, Program in Materials Science and Metallurgical Engineering, Program in Materials Science and Engineering, Cincinnati, OH 45221. Offers MS, PhD. Evening/weekend programs available. *Degree requirements:* For master's, thesis optional; for doctorate, one foreign language, comprehensive exam, thesis/dissertation, oral English proficiency exam. *Entrance requirements:* For master's and doctorate, GRE General Test, BS in related field, minimum undergraduate GPA of 3.0. Additional exam requirements/recommendations for international students: Required—TOEFL. Electronic applications accepted. *Faculty research:* Polymer characterization, surface analysis, and adhesion; mechanical behavior of high-temperature materials; composites; electrochemistry of materials.

University of Connecticut, Graduate School, School of Engineering, Department of Chemical, Materials and Biomolecular Engineering, Field of Materials Science and Engineering, Storrs, CT 06269. Offers MS, PhD. Terminal master's awarded for partial completion of doctoral program. *Degree requirements:* For master's, comprehensive exam; for doctorate, thesis/dissertation. *Entrance requirements:* For master's and doctorate, GRE General Test, GRE Subject Test. Additional exam requirements/recommendations for international students: Required—TOEFL (minimum score 550 paper-based; 213 computer-based). Electronic applications accepted.

University of Connecticut, Institute of Materials Science, Storrs, CT 06269. Offers MS, PhD.

University of Delaware, College of Engineering, Department of Materials Science and Engineering, Newark, DE 19716. Offers MMSE, PhD. Terminal master's awarded for partial completion of doctoral program. *Degree requirements:* For master's, thesis; for doctorate, thesis/dissertation. *Entrance requirements:* For master's and doctorate, GRE General Test, 3 letters of recommendation, minimum GPA of 3.2. Additional exam requirements/recommendations for international students: Required—TOEFL. Electronic applications accepted. *Faculty research:* Thin films and self assembly, drug delivery and tissue engineering, biomaterials and nanocomposites, semiconductor and oxide interfaces, electronic and magnetic materials.

University of Denver, School of Engineering and Computer Science, Department of Mechanical and Materials Engineering, Denver, CO 80208. Offers bioengineering (MS); engineering (MS, PhD); interdisciplinary engineering (PhD); materials science (MS, PhD); mechanical engineering (MS, PhD); nanoscale science and engineering (PhD). Part-time programs available. *Faculty:* 8 full-time (1 woman), 5 part-time/adjunct (1 woman). *Students:* 3 full-time (1 woman), 21 part-time (5 women), 7 international. Average age 33. 63 applicants, 65% accepted, 5 enrolled. In 2010, 5 master's, 1 doctorate awarded. Terminal master's awarded for partial completion of doctoral program. *Degree requirements:* For master's, thesis or alternative; for doctorate, comprehensive exam, thesis/dissertation. *Entrance requirements:* For master's and doctorate, GRE General Test. Additional exam requirements/recommendations for international students: Required—TOEFL (minimum score 550 paper-based; 80 iBT). *Application deadline:* Applications are processed on a rolling basis. Application fee: $60. Electronic applications accepted. *Expenses:* Tuition: Full-time $35,604; part-time $29,670 per year. Required fees: $687 per year. Tuition and fees vary according to program. *Financial support:* In 2010–11, 7 research assistantships with full and partial tuition reimbursements (averaging $10,795 per year), 5 teaching assistantships with full and partial tuition reimbursements (averaging $13,230 per year) were awarded; Federal Work-Study, scholarships/grants, and unspecified assistantships also available. Financial award applicants required to submit FAFSA. *Faculty research:* Aerosols, biomechanics, composite materials, photo optics, drug delivery. *Unit head:* Dr. Daniel Armentrout, Chair, 303-871-3580, Fax: 303-871-4450, E-mail: darmentr@du.edu. *Application contact:* Renee Carvalho, Assistant to the Chair, 303-871-2107, Fax: 303-871-4450, E-mail: renee.carvalho@du.edu.

University of Florida, Graduate School, College of Engineering, Department of Materials Science and Engineering, Gainesville, FL 32611. Offers ME, MS, PhD, Engr, JD/MS. Part-time programs available. *Faculty:* 26 full-time (6 women), 2 part-time/adjunct (0 women). *Students:* 304 full-time (48 women), 50 part-time (13 women); includes 12 Black or African American, non-Hispanic/Latino; 13 Asian, non-Hispanic/Latino; 11 Hispanic/Latino, 200 international. Average age 27. 577 applicants, 57% accepted, 95 enrolled. In 2010, 43 master's, 37 doctorates awarded. Terminal master's awarded for partial completion of doctoral program. *Degree requirements:* For master's, comprehensive exam, thesis; for doctorate, comprehensive exam, thesis/dissertation; for Engr, thesis optional. *Entrance requirements:* For master's and doctorate, GRE General Test, minimum GPA of 3.0; for Engr, GRE General Test. Additional exam requirements/recommendations for international students: Required—TOEFL (minimum score 550 paper-based; 213 computer-based; 80 iBT), IELTS (minimum score 6). *Application deadline:* For fall admission, 7/1 priority date for domestic students, 5/1 for international students; for spring admission, 11/1 for domestic students, 9/1 for international students. Applications are processed on a rolling basis. Application fee: $30. Electronic applications accepted. *Expenses:* Tuition, state resident: full-time $10,915.92. Tuition, nonresident: full-time $28,309. *Financial support:* In 2010–11, 180 students received support, including 4 fellowships, 176 research assistantships (averaging $22,263 per year). Financial award applicants required to submit FAFSA. *Faculty research:* Polymeric system, biomaterials and biomimetics; inorganic and organic electronic materials; functional ceramic materials for energy systems and microelectronic applications; advanced metallic systems for aerospace, transportation and biological applications; nuclear materials. Total annual research expenditures: $8.5 million. *Unit head:* Simon R. Phillpot, PhD, Chair, 352-846-3782, Fax: 352-392-7219, E-mail: sphil@mse.ufl.edu. *Application contact:* Jack Mecholsky, PhD, Graduate Coordinator, 352-846-3306, Fax: 352-846-1182, E-mail: jmech@mse.ufl.edu.

University of Idaho, College of Graduate Studies, College of Engineering, Department of Chemical and Materials Engineering, Program in Materials Science and Engineering, Moscow, ID 83844-2282. Offers materials science and engineering (MS, PhD); metallurgical engineering (MS); mining engineering (PhD). *Students:* 8 full-time. Average age 30. In 2010, 2 master's, 1 doctorate awarded. *Application deadline:* Applications are processed on a rolling basis. Application fee: $60. Electronic applications accepted. *Expenses:* Tuition, nonresident: part-time $580 per credit. Required fees: $306 per credit. *Financial support:* Applicants required to submit FAFSA. *Unit head:* Dr. Wudneh Admassu, Chair, 208-885-6376. *Application contact:* Dr. Wudneh Admassu, Chair, 208-885-6376.

University of Illinois at Urbana–Champaign, Graduate College, College of Engineering, Department of Materials Science and Engineering, Champaign, IL 61820. Offers MS, PhD, MS/MBA, PhD/MBA. *Faculty:* 23 full-time (3 women), 3 part-time/adjunct (0 women). *Students:* 154 full-time (38 women), 5 part-time (1 woman); includes 18 Asian, non-Hispanic/Latino; 2 Hispanic/Latino, 84 international. 336 applicants, 23% accepted, 29 enrolled. In 2010, 5 master's, 29 doctorates awarded. *Entrance requirements:* For master's and doctorate, GRE, minimum GPA of 3.0. Additional exam requirements/recommendations for international students: Required—TOEFL (minimum score 613 paper-based; 257 computer-based; 103 iBT) or IELTS (minimum score 7). *Application deadline:* Applications are processed on a rolling basis. Application fee: $75 ($90 for international students). Electronic applications accepted. *Financial support:* In 2010–11, 21 fellowships, 141 research assistantships, 15 teaching assistantships were awarded; tuition waivers (full and partial) also available. *Unit head:* David G. Cahill, Head, 217-333-6753, Fax: 217-244-1631, E-mail: d-cahill@illinois.edu. *Application contact:* Michelle L. Malloch, Office Support Associate, 217-333-8517, Fax: 217-333-2736, E-mail: malloch@illinois.edu.

University of Kentucky, Graduate School, College of Engineering, Program in Materials Science, Lexington, KY 40506-0032. Offers materials science and engineering (MSMAE, PhD). *Degree requirements:* For master's, comprehensive exam, thesis optional; for doctorate, comprehensive exam, thesis/dissertation. *Entrance requirements:* For master's, GRE General Test, minimum undergraduate GPA of 2.75; for doctorate, GRE General Test, minimum undergraduate GPA of 3.0. Additional exam requirements/recommendations for international students: Required—TOEFL (minimum score 550 paper-based; 213 computer-based). Electronic applications accepted. *Faculty research:* Physical and mechanical metallurgy, computational material engineering, polymers and composites, high-temperature ceramics, powder metallurgy.

The University of Manchester, School of Chemistry, Manchester, United Kingdom. Offers biological chemistry (PhD); chemistry (M Ent, M Phil, M Sc, D Ent, PhD); inorganic chemistry (PhD); materials chemistry (PhD); nanoscience (PhD); nuclear fission (PhD); organic chemistry (PhD); physical chemistry (PhD); theoretical chemistry (PhD).

The University of Manchester, School of Materials, Manchester, United Kingdom. Offers advanced aerospace materials engineering (M Sc); advanced metallic systems (PhD); biomedical materials (M Phil, M Sc, PhD); ceramics and glass (M Phil, M Sc, PhD); composite materials (M Sc, PhD); corrosion and protection (M Phil, M Sc, PhD); materials (M Phil, PhD); metallic materials (M Phil, M Sc, PhD); nanostructural materials (M Phil, M Sc, PhD); paper science (M Phil, M Sc, PhD); polymer science and engineering (M Phil, M Sc, PhD); technical textiles (M Sc); textile design, fashion and management (M Phil, M Sc, PhD); textile science and technology (M Phil, M Sc, PhD); textiles (M Phil, PhD); textiles and fashion (M Ent).

University of Maryland, College Park, Academic Affairs, A. James Clark School of Engineering, Department of Continuing and Distance Learning in Engineering, College Park, MD 20742. Offers engineering (M Eng), including aerospace engineering, chemical engineering, civil engineering, electrical engineering, engineering, fire protection engineering, materials science and engineering, mechanical engineering, reliability engineering, systems engineering. *Faculty:* 4 full-time (1 woman), 11 part-time/adjunct (1 woman). *Students:* 56 full-time (15 women), 428 part-time (88 women); includes 153 minority (59 Black or African American, non-Hispanic/Latino; 63 Asian, non-Hispanic/Latino; 24 Hispanic/Latino; 7 Two or more races, non-Hispanic/Latino), 55 international. 551 applicants, 82% accepted, 360 enrolled. In 2010, 130 master's awarded. *Application deadline:* For fall admission, 8/15 for domestic students, 1/10 for international students; for spring admission, 12/15 for domestic students, 6/1 for international students. Applications are processed on a rolling basis. Application fee: $75. Electronic applications accepted. *Expenses:* Tuition, area resident: Part-time $471 per credit hour. Tuition, state resident: part-time $471 per credit hour. Tuition, nonresident: part-time $1016 per credit hour. Required fees: $337 per term. *Financial support:* In 2010–11, 2 research assistantships (averaging $20,285 per year), 7 teaching assistantships (averaging $16,962 per year) were awarded. *Unit head:* Dr. Darryll Pines, Dean, 301-405-0376, Fax: 301-314-5908, E-mail: pines@umd.edu. *Application contact:* Dr. Charles A. Caramello, Dean of the Graduate School, 301-405-0358, Fax: 301-314-9305, E-mail: ccaramel@umd.edu.

University of Maryland, College Park, Academic Affairs, A. James Clark School of Engineering, Department of Materials and Nuclear Engineering, Materials Science and Engineering Program, College Park, MD 20742. Offers MS, PhD. Part-time and evening/weekend programs available. Postbaccalaureate distance learning degree programs offered. *Students:* 55 full-time (11 women), 12 part-time (6 women); includes 14 minority (7 Black or African American, non-Hispanic/Latino; 5 Asian, non-Hispanic/Latino; 2 Hispanic/Latino), 20 international. 232 applicants, 10% accepted, 7 enrolled. In 2010, 4 master's, 10 doctorates awarded. *Degree requirements:* For master's, comprehensive exam, thesis optional, research paper; for doctorate, thesis/dissertation, oral exam. *Entrance requirements:* For master's and doctorate, GRE General Test, minimum B+ average in undergraduate course work. Additional exam requirements/recommendations for international students: Required—TOEFL. *Application deadline:* For fall admission, 2/1 for domestic and international students; for spring admission, 8/1 for domestic students, 6/1 for international students. Applications are processed on a rolling basis. Application fee: $75. Electronic applications accepted. *Expenses:* Tuition, area resident: Part-time $471 per credit hour. Tuition, state resident: part-time $471 per credit hour. Tuition, nonresident: part-time $1016 per credit hour. Required fees: $337 per term. *Financial support:* In 2010–11, 2 fellowships with full tuition reimbursements (averaging $27,835 per year), 46 research assistantships (averaging $24,019 per year), 5 teaching assistantships (averaging $19,461 per year) were awarded. Financial award applicants required to submit FAFSA. *Unit head:* Robert Briber, Chair, 301-405-7313, E-mail: rbriber@umd.edu. *Application contact:* Dr. Charles A. Caramello, Dean of Graduate School, 301-405-0358, Fax: 301-314-9305, E-mail: ccaramel@umd.edu.

University of Michigan, Horace H. Rackham School of Graduate Studies, College of Engineering, Department of Materials Science and Engineering, Ann Arbor, MI 48109. Offers MS, PhD. Part-time programs available. *Students:* 101 full-time (26 women), 1 part-time (0 women). 353 applicants, 24% accepted, 31 enrolled. In 2010, 14 master's, 9 doctorates awarded. *Degree requirements:* For master's, thesis, oral defense of thesis; for doctorate, thesis/dissertation, oral defense of dissertation, written exam. *Entrance requirements:* For master's, GRE General Test, minimum GPA of 3.0 in related field; for doctorate, GRE General Test, minimum GPA of 3.0 in related field, master's degree. Additional exam requirements/recommendations for international students: Required—TOEFL. *Application deadline:* Applications are processed on a rolling basis. Application fee: $65 ($75 for international students). Electronic applications accepted. *Expenses:* Tuition, state resident: full-time $17,784; part-time $1116 per credit hour. Tuition, nonresident: full-time $35,944; part-time $2125 per credit hour. International tuition: $35,994 full-time. Required fees: $95 per semester. Tuition and fees vary according to course load, degree level and program. *Financial support:* Fellowships, research assistantships, teaching assistantships available. Financial award applicants required to submit FAFSA. *Faculty research:* Soft materials (polymers, biomaterials); computational materials science; structural materials; electronic and optical materials; nanocomposite materials. *Unit head:* Peter Green, Department Chair, 734-763-2445, Fax: 734-763-4788. *Application contact:* Renee Hilgendorf, Graduate Program Coordinator, 734-763-9790, Fax: 734-763-4788, E-mail: reneeh@umich.edu.

See Display on next page and Close-Up on page 523.

University of Minnesota, Twin Cities Campus, Institute of Technology, Department of Chemical Engineering and Materials Science, Program in Materials Science and Engineering, Min-

Materials Sciences

University of Minnesota, Twin Cities Campus (continued)
neapolis, MN 55455-0132. Offers M Mat SE, MS Mat SE, PhD. Part-time programs available. Terminal master's awarded for partial completion of doctoral program. *Degree requirements:* For master's, thesis; for doctorate, thesis/dissertation. *Entrance requirements:* For master's and doctorate, GRE General Test. *Faculty research:* Fracture micromechanics, hydrogen embrittlement, polymer physics, microelectric materials, corrosion science.

University of Nebraska–Lincoln, Graduate College, College of Arts and Sciences, Department of Chemistry, Lincoln, NE 68588. Offers analytical chemistry (PhD); biochemistry (PhD); chemistry (MS); inorganic chemistry (PhD); materials chemistry (PhD); organic chemistry (PhD); physical chemistry (PhD). *Degree requirements:* For master's, one foreign language, thesis optional, departmental qualifying exam; for doctorate, one foreign language, comprehensive exam, thesis/dissertation, departmental qualifying exams. *Entrance requirements:* For master's and doctorate, GRE. Additional exam requirements/recommendations for international students: Required—TOEFL (minimum score 550 paper-based; 213 computer-based). Electronic applications accepted. *Faculty research:* Bioorganic and bioinorganic chemistry, biophysical and bioanalytical chemistry, structure-function of DNA and proteins, organometallics, mass spectrometry.

University of New Brunswick Fredericton, School of Graduate Studies, Faculty of Engineering, Department of Civil Engineering, Fredericton, NB E3B 5A3, Canada. Offers construction engineering and management (M Eng, M Sc E, PhD); environmental engineering (M Eng, M Sc E, PhD); environmental studies (M Eng); geotechnical engineering (M Eng, M Sc E, PhD); groundwater/hydrology (M Eng, M Sc E, PhD); materials (M Eng, M Sc E, PhD); pavements (M Eng, M Sc E, PhD); structures (M Eng, M Sc E, PhD); transportation (M Eng, M Sc E, PhD). Part-time programs available. *Faculty:* 13 full-time (1 woman), 7 part-time/adjunct (1 woman). *Students:* 34 full-time (8 women), 16 part-time (2 women). In 2010, 16 master's, 6 doctorates awarded. *Degree requirements:* For master's, thesis, proposal; for doctorate, comprehensive exam, thesis/dissertation, qualifying exam; proposal; 27 credit hours of courses. *Entrance requirements:* For master's, minimum GPA of 3.0; B Sc E in civil engineering or related engineering degree; for doctorate, minimum GPA of 3.0; graduate degree in engineering or applied science. Additional exam requirements/recommendations for international students: Required—TWE (minimum score 4), TOEFL (minimum score 580 paper-based; 237 computer-based) or IELTS (minimum score 7.5). *Application deadline:* For fall admission, 5/1 priority date for domestic students; for winter admission, 11/1 priority date for domestic students. Applications are processed on a rolling basis. Application fee: $50 Canadian dollars. *Expenses:* Tuition, area resident: Full-time $3708; part-time $927 per term. International tuition: $6300 full-time. Required fees: $50 per term. *Financial support:* In 2010–11, 52 research assistantships (averaging $7,000 per year), 46 teaching assistantships (averaging $2,000 per year) were awarded; career-related internships or fieldwork and scholarships/grants also available. *Faculty research:* Construction engineering and management; materials and infrastructure renewal; highway and pavement research; structures and solid mechanics; geotechnical, soil; structure interaction; transportation and planning; environment, solid waste management. *Unit head:* Dr. Eric Hildebrand, Director of Graduate Studies, 506-453-5113, Fax: 506-453-3568, E-mail: edh@unb.ca. *Application contact:* Joyce Moore, Graduate Secretary, 506-452-6127, Fax: 506-453-3568, E-mail: civil-grad@unb.ca.

University of New Hampshire, Graduate School, College of Engineering and Physical Sciences, Program in Materials Science, Durham, NH 03824. Offers MS, PhD. *Faculty:* 3 full-time (0 women). *Students:* 9 full-time (6 women), 3 part-time (0 women); includes 1 minority (Two or more races, non-Hispanic/Latino), 11 international. Average age 27. 28 applicants, 43% accepted, 2 enrolled. In 2010, 1 doctorate awarded. *Degree requirements:* For master's, thesis or alternative. *Entrance requirements:* For master's, GRE. Additional exam requirements/recommendations for international students: Required—TOEFL (minimum score 550 paper-based; 213 computer-based; 80 iBT). *Application deadline:* For fall admission, 4/1 priority date

for domestic students, 4/1 for international students. Applications are processed on a rolling basis. Application fee: $65. Electronic applications accepted. *Financial support:* In 2010–11, 11 students received support, including 10 research assistantships, 1 teaching assistantship; fellowships, Federal Work-Study, scholarships/grants, and tuition waivers (full and partial) also available. Support available to part-time students. Financial award application deadline: 2/15. *Unit head:* Dr. Glenn Miller, Chairperson, 603-862-2456. *Application contact:* Katie Makem-Boucher, Administrative Assistant, 603-862-2669, E-mail: materials.science@unh.edu.

The University of North Carolina at Chapel Hill, Graduate School, College of Arts and Sciences, Curriculum in Applied Sciences and Engineering, Chapel Hill, NC 27599. Offers materials science (MS, PhD). *Faculty:* 31 full-time. *Students:* 19 full-time (10 women); includes 15 minority (2 Black or African American, non-Hispanic/Latino; 13 Asian, non-Hispanic/Latino), 1 international. Average age 23. 39 applicants, 33% accepted, 7 enrolled. In 2010, 1 master's, 2 doctorates awarded. Terminal master's awarded for partial completion of doctoral program. *Degree requirements:* For doctorate, thesis/dissertation. *Entrance requirements:* For master's, GRE General Test, minimum GPA of 3.0; for doctorate, GRE General Test. *Application deadline:* For fall admission, 4/15 priority date for domestic students; for winter admission, 10/15 for domestic students; for spring admission, 4/15 priority date for domestic students. Application fee: $60. Electronic applications accepted. *Financial support:* In 2010–11, 13 students received support, including 10 research assistantships with full tuition reimbursements available (averaging $18,000 per year), 5 teaching assistantships with full tuition reimbursements available (averaging $13,950 per year); scholarships/grants, tuition waivers (full), and unspecified assistantships also available. Financial award application deadline: 3/1. *Faculty research:* Scanning tunneling microscopy, magnetic resonance, carbon nanotubes, thin films, biomaterials, nano-materials, nanotechnology, polymeric materials, electronic and optic materials, tissue engineering. *Unit head:* Prof. Sean Washburn, Chair, 919-962-6293, Fax: 919-962-3341, E-mail: materials_science@unc.edu. *Application contact:* Admissions, 919-962-6293, Fax: 919-962-3341, E-mail: materials_science@unc.edu.

University of North Texas, Toulouse Graduate School, College of Engineering, Department of Materials Science and Engineering, Denton, TX 76203. Offers MS, PhD. Part-time programs available. *Degree requirements:* For master's, comprehensive exam, thesis optional; for doctorate, thesis/dissertation. *Entrance requirements:* For master's and doctorate, GRE General Test. Additional exam requirements/recommendations for international students: Recommended—TOEFL (minimum score 550 paper-based; 213 computer-based). *Application deadline:* Applications are processed on a rolling basis. Electronic applications accepted. *Expenses:* Tuition, state resident: full-time $4298; part-time $239 per credit hour. Tuition, nonresident: full-time $10,782; part-time $549 per credit hour. Required fees: $1292; $270 per credit hour. *Financial support:* Fellowships, research assistantships with tuition reimbursements, teaching assistantships, scholarships/grants available. *Faculty research:* Polymers, electronic materials, ceramics, metals, nanomaterials. *Application contact:* Graduate Advisor, 940-369-7714, Fax: 940-565-4824.

University of Pennsylvania, School of Engineering and Applied Science, Department of Materials Science and Engineering, Philadelphia, PA 19104. Offers MSE, PhD, MSE/MBA. Part-time programs available. *Faculty:* 14 full-time (3 women), 1 part-time/adjunct (0 women). *Students:* 93 full-time (30 women), 9 part-time (1 woman); includes 10 Asian, non-Hispanic/Latino; 1 Hispanic/Latino, 64 international. 331 applicants, 27% accepted, 50 enrolled. In 2010, 19 master's, 10 doctorates awarded. Terminal master's awarded for partial completion of doctoral program. *Degree requirements:* For master's, thesis; for doctorate, thesis/dissertation. *Entrance requirements:* Additional exam requirements/recommendations for international students: Required—TOEFL. *Application deadline:* For fall admission, 6/1 priority date for domestic students; 5/1 priority date for international students; for spring admission, 11/1 priority date for domestic students, 10/1 priority date for international students. Applications are processed on a rolling basis. Application fee: $70. Electronic applications accepted. *Expenses:* Tuition: Full-time $25,660; part-time $4758 per course. Required fees: $2152; $270 per course. Tuition and fees vary according to course load, degree level and program. *Financial support:* Fellowships, research assistantships, teaching assistantships, institutionally sponsored loans, scholarships/grants, traineeships, health care benefits, and unspecified assistantships available. *Faculty research:* Advanced metallic, ceramic, and polymeric materials for device applications; micromechanics and structure of interfaces; thin film electronic materials; physics and chemistry of solids. *Application contact:* Irene Clements, Graduate Coordinator, 215-898-8337, E-mail: ipc@lrsm.upenn.edu.

University of Pittsburgh, School of Engineering, Department of Mechanical Engineering and Materials Science, Pittsburgh, PA 15260. Offers MSME, PhD. Part-time programs available. Postbaccalaureate distance learning degree programs offered. *Faculty:* 27 full-time (4 women), 30 part-time/adjunct (4 women). *Students:* 91 full-time (14 women), 104 part-time (16 women); includes 9 minority (5 Black or African American, non-Hispanic/Latino; 2 Asian, non-Hispanic/Latino; 2 Hispanic/Latino), 55 international. 394 applicants, 31% accepted, 55 enrolled. In 2010, 36 master's, 12 doctorates awarded. Terminal master's awarded for partial completion of doctoral program. *Degree requirements:* For master's, thesis optional; for doctorate, comprehensive exam, thesis/dissertation, final oral exams. *Entrance requirements:* For master's and doctorate, minimum QPA of 3.0. Additional exam requirements/recommendations for international students: Required—TOEFL (minimum score 550 paper-based; 230 computer-based). *Application deadline:* For fall admission, 3/1 priority date for domestic students; for spring admission, 7/1 priority date for domestic students. Applications are processed on a rolling basis. Application fee: $50. Electronic applications accepted. *Expenses:* Tuition, state resident: full-time $17,304; part-time $701 per credit. Tuition, nonresident: full-time $29,554; part-time $1210 per credit. Required fees: $740; $214 per term. Tuition and fees vary according to program. *Financial support:* In 2010–11, 75 students received support, including 11 fellowships with full tuition reimbursements available (averaging $26,000 per year), 49 research assistantships with full tuition reimbursements available (averaging $25,000 per year), 27 teaching assistantships with full tuition reimbursements available (averaging $24,000 per year); scholarships/grants and tuition waivers (full and partial) also available. Financial award application deadline: 4/15. *Faculty research:* Smart materials and structure solid mechanics, computational fluid dynamics, multiphase bio-fluid dynamics, mechanical vibration analysis. Total annual research expenditures: $6.7 million. *Unit head:* Dr. Minking K. Chyu, Chairman, 412-624-9784, Fax: 412-624-4846. *Application contact:* Dr. Patrick Smelinski, Graduate Coordinator, 412-624-9788, Fax: 412-624-4846, E-mail: pat.smel@pitt.edu.

University of Rochester, Hajim School of Engineering and Applied Sciences, Program in Materials Science, Rochester, NY 14627. Offers MS, PhD. Terminal master's awarded for partial completion of doctoral program. *Degree requirements:* For master's, comprehensive exam, thesis optional; for doctorate, thesis/dissertation, preliminary and qualifying exams. *Entrance requirements:* For master's and doctorate, GRE. Additional exam requirements/recommendations for international students: Required—TOEFL.

University of Southern California, Graduate School, Viterbi School of Engineering, Mork Family Department of Chemical Engineering and Materials Science, Los Angeles, CA 90089. Offers chemical engineering (MS, PhD, Engr); materials engineering (MS); materials science (MS, PhD, Engr); petroleum engineering (MS, PhD, Engr); smart oilfield technologies (MS, Graduate Certificate). *Faculty:* 19 full-time (3 women), 9 part-time/adjunct (1 woman). *Students:* 235 full-time (77 women), 77 part-time (25 women); includes 43 minority (6 Black or African American, non-Hispanic/Latino; 25 Asian, non-Hispanic/Latino; 11 Hispanic/Latino; 1 Two or more races, non-Hispanic/Latino), 213 international. 643 applicants, 36% accepted, 118 enrolled. In 2010, 37 master's, 19 doctorates, 4 other advanced degrees awarded. Terminal master's awarded for partial completion of doctoral program. *Degree requirements:* For master's, thesis optional; for doctorate, thesis/dissertation. *Entrance requirements:* For master's and doctorate, GRE General Test. *Application deadline:* For fall admission, 12/1 priority date for domestic and international students; for spring admission, 9/1 priority date for domestic and international students. Applications are processed on a rolling basis. Application fee: $85. Electronic applications accepted. *Expenses:* Contact institution. *Financial support:* In 2010–11, fellowships with full tuition reimbursements (averaging $30,000 per year), research assistantships with full tuition reimbursements (averaging $20,000 per year), teaching assistantships with full tuition reimbursements (averaging $20,000 per year) were awarded; career-related internships or fieldwork, scholarships/grants, health care benefits, and unspecified assistantships also available. Financial award application deadline: 12/1; financial award applicants required to submit CSS PROFILE or FAFSA. *Faculty research:* Heterogeneous materials and porous media, statistical mechanics, molecular simulation, polymer science and engineering, advanced materials, reaction engineering and catalysis, membrane processes and separation, biochemical engineering, cell culture, bioreactor modeling, petroleum engineering. Total annual research expenditures: $11.6 million. *Unit head:* Dr. Theodore Tsotsis, Chair, 213-740-2227, E-mail: chedept@usc.edu. *Application contact:* Karen Woo, Student Services Advisor, 213-740-2227, E-mail: karenwoo@usc.edu.

The University of Tennessee, Graduate School, College of Engineering, Department of Materials Science and Engineering, Program in Materials Science and Engineering, Knoxville, TN 37996. Offers MS, PhD. *Faculty:* 26 full-time (1 woman), 4 part-time/adjunct (2 women). *Students:* 72 full-time (14 women), 11 part-time (1 woman); includes 2 Black or African American, non-Hispanic/Latino; 3 Asian, non-Hispanic/Latino; 3 Hispanic/Latino, 51 international. Average age 22. 140 applicants, 26% accepted, 25 enrolled. In 2010, 5 master's, 9 doctorates awarded. *Degree requirements:* For master's, thesis or alternative; for doctorate, comprehensive exam, thesis/dissertation. *Entrance requirements:* For master's, GRE General Test, Minimum GPA of 2.7 (US degree holders); 3.0 (International degree holders); 3-References; for doctorate, GRE General Test, Minimum GPA of 3.0 (previous graduate course work); 3-References. Additional exam requirements/recommendations for international students: Required—TOEFL (minimum score 550 paper-based; 213 computer-based). *Application deadline:* For fall admission, 2/1 priority date for domestic and international students; for spring admission, 6/15 for domestic and international students. Applications are processed on a rolling basis. Application fee: $35. Electronic applications accepted. *Expenses:* Tuition, state resident: full-time $7440; part-time $414 per credit hour. Tuition, nonresident: full-time $22,478; part-time $1250 per credit hour. Required fees: $922; $43 per credit hour. Tuition and fees vary according to program. *Financial support:* In 2010–11, 66 students received support, including 4 fellowships with full tuition reimbursements available (averaging $9,996 per year), 76 research assistantships with full tuition reimbursements available (averaging $19,272 per year), 11 teaching assistantships with full tuition reimbursements available (averaging $19,752 per year); career-related internships or fieldwork, Federal Work-Study, institutionally sponsored loans, health care benefits, and unspecified assistantships also available. Financial award application deadline: 2/1; financial award applicants required to submit FAFSA. *Faculty research:* Biomaterials; functional materials electronic, magnetic and optical; high temperature materials; mechanical behavior of materials; neutron materials science. *Unit head:* Dr. George Pharr, Head, 865-974-5336, Fax: 865-974-4115, E-mail: pharr@utk.edu. *Application contact:* Dr. Roberto S. Benson, Associate Head, 865-974-5347, Fax: 865-974-4115, E-mail: rbenson1@utk.edu.

The University of Tennessee Space Institute, Graduate Programs, Program in Materials Science and Engineering, Tullahoma, TN 37388-9700. Offers MS. *Faculty:* 4 full-time (1 woman). *Students:* 5 full-time (0 women), 1 part-time (0 women); includes 1 minority (Asian, non-Hispanic/Latino), 2 international. 3 applicants, 100% accepted, 1 enrolled. In 2010, 1 master's awarded. *Entrance requirements:* Additional exam requirements/recommendations for international students: Required—TOEFL (minimum score 550 paper-based; 213 computer-based; 80 iBT), IELTS (minimum score 6.5). *Application deadline:* For fall admission, 2/1 for international students; for spring admission, 6/15 for international students. Applications are processed on a rolling basis. Application fee: $35. Electronic applications accepted. *Financial support:* In 2010–11, 5 research assistantships with full tuition reimbursements (averaging $17,791 per year) were awarded; fellowships, career-related internships or fieldwork, Federal Work-Study, institutionally sponsored loans, health care benefits, tuition waivers (full and partial), and unspecified assistantships also available. *Unit head:* Dr. William Hofmeister, Degree Program Chairman, 931-393-7466, Fax: 931-393-7437, E-mail: whofmeis@utsi.edu. *Application contact:* Dee Merriman, Coordinator III, 931-393-7213, Fax: 931-393-7211, E-mail: dmerrima@utsi.edu.

The University of Texas at Arlington, Graduate School, College of Engineering, Department of Materials Science and Engineering, Arlington, TX 76019. Offers M Engr, MS, PhD. *Faculty:* 8 full-time (0 women). *Students:* 45 full-time (13 women), 13 part-time (3 women); includes 4 minority (1 Black or African American, non-Hispanic/Latino; 3 Asian, non-Hispanic/Latino), 48 international. 33 applicants, 61% accepted, 11 enrolled. In 2010, 21 master's, 5 doctorates awarded. Terminal master's awarded for partial completion of doctoral program. *Degree requirements:* For master's, comprehensive exam (for some programs), thesis optional; for doctorate, comprehensive exam, thesis/dissertation optional. *Entrance requirements:* For master's, GRE General Test, minimum GPA of 3.0; for doctorate, GRE General Test, minimum GPA of 3.5. Additional exam requirements/recommendations for international students: Required—TOEFL (minimum score 550 paper-based; 213 computer-based). *Application deadline:* For fall admission, 6/6 for domestic students, 4/4 for international students; for spring admission, 10/15 for domestic students, 9/5 for international students. Applications are processed on a rolling basis. Application fee: $35 ($50 for international students). *Expenses:* Tuition, state resident: full-time $7500. Tuition, nonresident: full-time $13,080. International tuition: $13,250 full-time. *Financial support:* In 2010–11, 27 students received support, including 4 fellowships (averaging $1,000 per year), 10 research assistantships (averaging $16,000 per year), 13 teaching assistantships (averaging $16,000 per year); scholarships/grants and unspecified assistantships also available. Financial award application deadline: 6/1; financial award applicants required to submit FAFSA. *Faculty research:* Electronic materials, conductive polymer, composites biomaterial, structural materials. Total annual research expenditures: $400,000. *Unit head:* Dr. Efstathios Meletis, Chair, 817-272-2398, Fax: 817-272-2538, E-mail: meletis@uta.edu. *Application contact:* Dr. Choong-Un Kim, Graduate Adviser, 817-272-5497, Fax: 817-272-2538, E-mail: choongun@uta.edu.

The University of Texas at Austin, Graduate School, Cockrell School of Engineering, Program in Materials Science and Engineering, Austin, TX 78712-1111. Offers MS, PhD. Part-time programs available. *Degree requirements:* For master's, thesis (for some programs); for doctorate, thesis/dissertation. *Entrance requirements:* For master's and doctorate, GRE General Test. Additional exam requirements/recommendations for international students: Required—TOEFL (minimum score 550 paper-based; 213 computer-based). Electronic applications accepted.

The University of Texas at Dallas, Erik Jonsson School of Engineering and Computer Science, Programs in Materials Science and Engineering, Richardson, TX 75080. Offers MS, PhD. Part-time and evening/weekend programs available. *Faculty:* 11 full-time (1 woman). *Students:* 49 full-time (11 women), 8 part-time (3 women); includes 9 minority (1 Black or African American, non-Hispanic/Latino; 2 Asian, non-Hispanic/Latino; 6 Hispanic/Latino), 35 international. Average age 28. 56 applicants, 41% accepted, 9 enrolled. In 2010, 3 master's, 2 doctorates awarded. *Degree requirements:* For master's, thesis or major design project; for doctorate, thesis/dissertation. *Entrance requirements:* For master's, GRE General Test, minimum GPA of 3.0 in related bachelor's degree; for doctorate, GRE General Test, minimum GPA of 3.5. Additional exam requirements/recommendations for international students: Required—TOEFL (minimum score 550 paper-based; 215 computer-based). *Application deadline:* For fall admission, 7/15 for domestic students, 5/1 priority date for international students; for spring admission, 11/15 for domestic students, 9/1 priority date for international students. Applications are processed on a rolling basis. Application fee: $50 ($100 for international students). Electronic applications accepted. *Expenses:* Tuition, state resident: full-time $10,248; part-time $569 per credit hour. Tuition, nonresident: full-time $18,544; part-time $1030 per credit hour. Tuition and fees vary according to course load. *Financial support:* In 2010–11, 41 students received support, including 45 research assistantships with partial tuition reimbursements available (averaging $17,450 per year), 1 teaching assistantship with partial tuition reimbursement available (averaging $16,619 per year); career-related internships or fieldwork, Federal Work-Study, institutionally sponsored loans, scholarships/grants, and unspecified assistantships also available. Support available to part-time students. Financial award application deadline: 4/30; financial award applicants required to submit FAFSA. *Faculty research:* Graphene-based semiconducting materials, neuro-inspired computational paradigms, electronic materials with emphasis on dielectrics, energy harvesting (photovoltaics, Li-ion batteries), biosensors and H2 storage materials. *Unit head:* Dr. Yves Chabal, Department Head, 972-883-5751, Fax: 972-883-5725, E-mail: chabal@utdallas.edu. *Application contact:* Tonya Griffin, Administrative Services Officer, 972-883-5764, Fax: 972-883-5725, E-mail: gradecs@utdallas.edu.

The University of Texas at El Paso, Graduate School, College of Engineering, Department of Metallurgical and Materials Engineering, El Paso, TX 79968-0001. Offers materials science and engineering (PhD); metallurgical and materials engineering (MS). Part-time and evening/weekend programs available. *Students:* 15 (3 women); includes 1 Asian, non-Hispanic/Latino; 9 Hispanic/Latino, 3 international. Average age 34. In 2010, 1 master's awarded. *Degree requirements:* For master's, thesis. *Entrance requirements:* For master's, GRE General Test. Additional exam requirements/recommendations for international students: Required—TOEFL. *Application deadline:* For fall admission, 7/1 priority date for domestic students, 3/1 for international students; for spring admission, 11/1 priority date for domestic students, 9/1 for international students. Applications are processed on a rolling basis. Application fee: $15 ($65 for international students). Electronic applications accepted. *Financial support:* In 2010–11, research assistantships with partial tuition reimbursements (averaging $21,125 per year), teaching assistantships with partial tuition reimbursements (averaging $16,900 per year) were awarded; fellowships with partial tuition reimbursements, career-related internships or fieldwork, Federal Work-Study, institutionally sponsored loans, scholarships/grants, and tuition waivers (partial) also available. Financial award application deadline: 3/15; financial award applicants required to submit FAFSA. *Unit head:* Dr. Lawrence E. Murr, Chairperson, 915-747-5468, Fax: 915-747-8036, E-mail: fekberg@utep.edu. *Application contact:* Dr. Charles H. Ambler, Dean of the Graduate School, 915-747-5491 Ext. 7886, Fax: 915-747-5788, E-mail: cambler@utep.edu.

The University of Texas at El Paso, Graduate School, Interdisciplinary Program in Materials Science and Engineering, El Paso, TX 79968-0001. Offers PhD. Part-time and evening/weekend programs available. *Students:* 20 (6 women); includes 2 Black or African American, non-Hispanic/Latino; 1 Asian, non-Hispanic/Latino; 8 Hispanic/Latino, 8 international. Average age 34. In 2010, 5 doctorates awarded. *Degree requirements:* For doctorate, thesis/dissertation. *Entrance requirements:* For doctorate, GRE, letters of recommendation. Additional exam requirements/recommendations for international students: Required—TOEFL; Recommended—IELTS. *Application deadline:* For fall admission, 8/1 priority date for domestic students, 3/1 for international students; for spring admission, 11/1 priority date for domestic students, 9/1 for international students. Applications are processed on a rolling basis. Application fee: $45 ($80 for international students). Electronic applications accepted. *Financial support:* In 2010–11, research assistantships with partial tuition reimbursements (averaging $22,500 per year), teaching assistantships with partial tuition reimbursements (averaging $1,800 per year) were awarded; fellowships with partial tuition reimbursements, institutionally sponsored loans, scholarships/grants, health care benefits, tuition waivers (partial), and unspecified assistantships also available. Support available to part-time students. Financial award application deadline: 3/15; financial award applicants required to submit FAFSA. *Unit head:* Dr. Lawrence E. Murr, Director, 915-747-8002, Fax: 915-747-8036, E-mail: fekberg@utep.edu. *Application contact:* Dr. Patricia D. Witherspoon, Dean of the Graduate School, 915-747-5491, Fax: 915-747-5788, E-mail: withersp@utep.edu.

University of Toronto, School of Graduate Studies, Physical Sciences Division, Faculty of Applied Science and Engineering, Department of Materials Science and Engineering, Toronto, ON M5S 1A1, Canada. Offers M Eng, MA Sc, PhD. Part-time programs available. *Degree requirements:* For master's, thesis (for some programs), oral presentation/thesis defense (MA Sc), qualifying exam; for doctorate, thesis/dissertation. *Entrance requirements:* For master's, BA Sc or B Sc degree in materials science and engineering, 2 letters of reference; for doctorate,

Materials Sciences

University of Toronto (continued)
MA Sc degree or equivalent, 2 letters of reference, minimum B+ average in last 2 years. Additional exam requirements/recommendations for international students: Required—TOEFL (minimum score 580 paper-based), TWE (minimum score 4).

University of Utah, Graduate School, College of Engineering, Department of Materials Science and Engineering, Salt Lake City, UT 84112. Offers MS, PhD. *Faculty:* 8 full-time (1 woman), 1 part-time/adjunct (0 women). *Students:* 32 full-time (3 women), 10 part-time (2 women); includes 1 minority (Asian, non-Hispanic/Latino), 25 international. Average age 29. 84 applicants, 14% accepted, 11 enrolled. In 2010, 5 master's, 4 doctorates awarded. Terminal master's awarded for partial completion of doctoral program. *Degree requirements:* For master's, thesis; for doctorate, thesis/dissertation, exam. *Entrance requirements:* For master's, GRE General Test, minimum GPA of 3.0; for doctorate, GRE General Test, minimum GPA of 3.0. Additional exam requirements/recommendations for international students: Required—TOEFL (minimum score 570 paper-based; 230 computer-based; 88 iBT), IELTS (minimum score 7). *Application deadline:* For fall admission, 1/15 for domestic students, 12/15 for international students; for spring admission, 9/1 for domestic students, 10/1 for international students. Applications are processed on a rolling basis. Application fee: $55 ($65 for international students). Electronic applications accepted. *Expenses:* Contact institution. *Financial support:* In 2010–11, 33 research assistantships (averaging $20,000 per year) were awarded; career-related internships or fieldwork and Federal Work-Study also available. Financial award application deadline: 2/5; financial award applicants required to submit FAFSA. *Faculty research:* Solid oxide fuel cells, computational nanostructures, computational polymers, biomaterials, electronic materials, nanomaterials. Total annual research expenditures: $2.8 million. *Unit head:* Dr. Anil V. Virkar, Chair, 801-581-6863, Fax: 801-581-4816, E-mail: anil.virkar@utah.edu. *Application contact:* Ashley Christensen, Academic Program Specialist, 801-581-6863, Fax: 801-581-4816, E-mail: ashley.christensen@utah.edu.

University of Vermont, Graduate College, College of Engineering and Mathematics, Program in Materials Science, Burlington, VT 05405. Offers MS, PhD. *Students:* 12 (4 women), 7 international. 33 applicants, 15% accepted, 1 enrolled. In 2010, 2 doctorates awarded. *Degree requirements:* For master's, thesis or alternative; for doctorate, thesis/dissertation. *Entrance requirements:* Additional exam requirements/recommendations for international students: Required—TOEFL (minimum score 550 paper-based; 213 computer-based; 80 iBT). *Application deadline:* For fall admission, 4/1 priority date for domestic students. Applications are processed on a rolling basis. Application fee: $40. Electronic applications accepted. *Expenses:* Tuition, state resident: part-time $537 per credit hour. Tuition, nonresident: part-time $1355 per credit hour. *Financial support:* Research assistantships, teaching assistantships available. Financial award application deadline: 3/1. *Unit head:* Dr. R. Hendrick, Coordinator, 802-656-2644. *Application contact:* Dr. R. Hendrick, Coordinator, 802-656-2644.

University of Virginia, School of Engineering and Applied Science, Department of Materials Science and Engineering, Charlottesville, VA 22903. Offers materials science (MMSE, MS, PhD). Part-time programs available. Postbaccalaureate distance learning degree programs offered (no on-campus study). *Faculty:* 22 full-time (2 women). *Students:* 42 full-time (16 women), 1 part-time (0 women); includes 1 Black or African American, non-Hispanic/Latino; 4 Asian, non-Hispanic/Latino, 9 international. Average age 27. 104 applicants, 17% accepted, 9 enrolled. In 2010, 8 master's, 4 doctorates awarded. Terminal master's awarded for partial completion of doctoral program. *Degree requirements:* For master's, comprehensive exam, thesis (for some programs); for doctorate, comprehensive exam, thesis/dissertation. *Entrance requirements:* For master's and doctorate, GRE General Test, three recommendations. Additional exam requirements/recommendations for international students: Required—TOEFL. *Application deadline:* For fall admission, 1/15 for domestic and international students. Applications are processed on a rolling basis. Application fee: $60. Electronic applications accepted. *Financial support:* Fellowships, research assistantships, teaching assistantships available. Financial award application deadline: 1/15; financial award applicants required to submit FAFSA. *Faculty research:* Environmental effects on material behavior, electronic materials, metals, polymers, tribology. *Unit head:* William C. Johnson, Chair, 434-982-5641, Fax: 434-982-5660. *Application contact:* Kathryn C. Thornton, Assistant Dean for Graduate Programs, 434-924-3897, Fax: 434-982-2214, E-mail: seas-grad-admission@cs.virginia.edu.

University of Washington, Graduate School, College of Engineering, Department of Materials Science and Engineering, Seattle, WA 98195-2120. Offers ceramic engineering (PhD); materials science and engineering (MS, MSE, PhD); materials science and engineering and nanotechnology (PhD). Part-time programs available. *Faculty:* 24 full-time (4 women). *Students:* 55 full-time (14 women), 9 part-time (2 women); includes 2 Black or African American, non-Hispanic/Latino; 7 Asian, non-Hispanic/Latino; 2 Hispanic/Latino, 22 international. Average age 30. 246 applicants, 11% accepted, 11 enrolled. In 2010, 3 master's, 9 doctorates awarded. *Degree requirements:* For master's, comprehensive exam, thesis optional; for doctorate, comprehensive exam, thesis/dissertation, Qualifying evaluation, general and final exams. *Entrance requirements:* For master's and doctorate, GRE General Test, minimum GPA of 3.0. Additional exam requirements/recommendations for international students: Required—TOEFL (minimum score 580 paper-based; 237 computer-based; 92 iBT); Recommended—IELTS (minimum score 7). *Application deadline:* For fall admission, 1/15 priority date for domestic students, 12/15 priority date for international students. Application fee: $75. Electronic applications accepted. *Financial support:* In 2010–11, 3 students received support, including 7 fellowships with full tuition reimbursements available (averaging $22,500 per year), 39 research assistantships with full tuition reimbursements available (averaging $16,407 per year), 8 teaching assistantships with full tuition reimbursements available (averaging $16,362 per year); career-related internships or fieldwork, Federal Work-Study, institutionally sponsored loans, scholarships/grants, health care benefits, unspecified assistantships, and stipend supplements also available. Financial award application deadline: 1/15; financial award applicants required to submit FAFSA. *Faculty research:* Biomimetics and biomaterials; electronic, optical and magnetic materials; eco-materials and materials for energy applications; ceramics, metals, composites, and polymers. Total annual research expenditures: $8.8 million. *Unit head:* Dr. Alex Jen, Professor and Chair, 206-543-2600, Fax: 206-543-3100, E-mail: ajen@uw.edu. *Application contact:* Kathleen A. Elkins, Academic Counselor, 206-616-6581, Fax: 206-543-3100, E-mail: kelkins@uw.edu.

University of Wisconsin–Madison, Graduate School, College of Engineering, Materials Science Program, Madison, WI 53704. Offers MS, PhD. Part-time programs available. *Faculty:* 75 full-time (15 women). *Students:* 92 full-time (20 women); includes 1 American Indian or Alaska Native, non-Hispanic/Latino; 36 Asian, non-Hispanic/Latino; 14 Hispanic/Latino. Average age 29. 447 applicants, 9% accepted, 16 enrolled. In 2010, 18 master's, 18 doctorates awarded. Terminal master's awarded for partial completion of doctoral program. *Degree requirements:* For master's, thesis or alternative; for doctorate, comprehensive exam, thesis/dissertation. *Entrance requirements:* For master's and doctorate, GRE General Test. Additional exam requirements/recommendations for international students: Required—TOEFL (minimum score 550 paper-based; 213 computer-based; 80 iBT). *Application deadline:* For fall admission, 7/1 for domestic and international students; for spring admission, 11/1 for domestic and international students. Applications are processed on a rolling basis. Application fee: $56. Electronic applications accepted. *Expenses:* Tuition, state resident: full-time $9887.36; part-time $617.96 per credit. Tuition, nonresident: full-time $24,054; part-time $1503.40 per credit. Required fees: $67.63 per credit. Tuition and fees vary according to reciprocity agreements. *Financial support:* In 2010–11, 5 fellowships with full tuition reimbursements (averaging $22,440 per year), 86 research assistantships with full tuition reimbursements (averaging $20,400 per year), 1 teaching assistantship with tuition reimbursement (averaging $28,175 per year) were awarded; traineeships, health care benefits, and unspecified assistantships also available. Financial award application deadline: 1/15. *Faculty research:* Electronic materials, polymers and biomaterials, nanotechnology and nanoscience, structural and mechanical materials, magnetic and superconducting materials, ceramics, metals, computational and theoretical modeling of materials, photonics and optical materials, materials for energy or environmental technology. *Unit head:* Ray Vanderby, Director, 608-265-3032, Fax: 608-262-8353, E-mail: matsciad@engr.wisc.edu. *Application contact:* Diana J. Rhoads, University Services Program Associate, 608-263-1795, Fax: 608-262-8353, E-mail: rhoads@engr.wisc.edu.

Vanderbilt University, School of Engineering, Interdisciplinary Program in Materials Science, Nashville, TN 37240-1001. Offers M Eng, MS, PhD. Part-time programs available. *Faculty:* 43 full-time (6 women), 2 part-time/adjunct (0 women). *Students:* 32 full-time (12 women); includes 1 Asian, non-Hispanic/Latino; 5 Hispanic/Latino, 9 international. Average age 26. 73 applicants, 12% accepted, 6 enrolled. In 2010, 8 doctorates awarded. Terminal master's awarded for partial completion of doctoral program. *Degree requirements:* For master's, thesis; for doctorate, thesis/dissertation. *Entrance requirements:* For master's and doctorate, GRE General Test. *Application deadline:* For fall admission, 1/15 for domestic students; for spring admission, 11/1 for domestic students. Application fee: $0. Electronic applications accepted. *Financial support:* In 2010–11, 8 fellowships with tuition reimbursements (averaging $30,000 per year), 10 research assistantships with tuition reimbursements (averaging $19,800 per year), 8 teaching assistantships with tuition reimbursements (averaging $18,000 per year) were awarded; institutionally sponsored loans and tuition waivers (partial) also available. Support available to part-time students. Financial award application deadline: 1/15. *Faculty research:* Nanostructure materials, materials physics, surface and interface science, materials synthesis, biomaterials. *Unit head:* Dr. D. Greg Walker, Director, 615-343-6959, Fax: 615-343-6687, E-mail: greg.walker@vanderbilt.edu. *Application contact:* Sarah R. Satterwhite, Administrative Assistant, 615-343-6868, Fax: 615-322-3202, E-mail: sarah.m.ross@vanderbilt.edu.

Virginia Polytechnic Institute and State University, Graduate School, College of Engineering, Department of Materials Science and Engineering, Blacksburg, VA 24061. Offers M Eng, MS, PhD. *Faculty:* 14 full-time (4 women). *Students:* 56 full-time (7 women), 3 part-time (1 woman); includes 3 Asian, non-Hispanic/Latino; 1 Hispanic/Latino, 27 international. Average age 28. 207 applicants, 12% accepted, 14 enrolled. In 2010, 5 master's, 9 doctorates awarded. *Degree requirements:* For master's, comprehensive exam (for some programs), thesis (for some programs); for doctorate, comprehensive exam (for some programs), thesis/dissertation (for some programs). *Entrance requirements:* For master's and doctorate, GRE. Additional exam requirements/recommendations for international students: Required—TOEFL (minimum score 550 paper-based; 213 computer-based). *Application deadline:* For fall admission, 7/1 for domestic and international students; for spring admission, 12/1 for domestic and international students. Applications are processed on a rolling basis. Application fee: $65. Electronic applications accepted. *Expenses:* Tuition, area resident: Full-time $9399; part-time $488 per credit hour. Tuition, state resident: full-time $9399; part-time $488 per credit hour. Tuition, nonresident: full-time $17,854; part-time $957.75 per credit hour. International tuition: $17,854 full-time. Required fees: $1534. Full-time tuition and fees vary according to program. *Financial support:* In 2010–11, 1 fellowship with full tuition reimbursement (averaging $7,500 per year), 23 research assistantships with full tuition reimbursements (averaging $23,993 per year), 2 teaching assistantships with full tuition reimbursements (averaging $23,679 per year) were awarded; career-related internships or fieldwork, Federal Work-Study, scholarships/grants, health care benefits, and unspecified assistantships also available. Financial award application deadline: 1/15. Total annual research expenditures: $5.2 million. *Unit head:* Dr. David E. Clark, UNIT HEAD, 540-231-6640, Fax: 540-231-8819, E-mail: dclark@vt.edu. *Application contact:* Gary Pickrell, Contact, 540-231-3504, Fax: 540-231-8919, E-mail: pickrell@vt.edu.

Washington State University, Graduate School, College of Engineering and Architecture, School of Mechanical and Materials Engineering, Program in Material Science Engineering, Pullman, WA 99164. Offers MS. *Faculty:* 29. *Students:* 27 full-time (6 women), 3 part-time (1 woman); includes 1 Black or African American, non-Hispanic/Latino; 1 American Indian or Alaska Native, non-Hispanic/Latino; 2 Asian, non-Hispanic/Latino; 1 Hispanic/Latino, 13 international. 133 applicants, 10% accepted, 3 enrolled. *Degree requirements:* For master's, comprehensive exam (for some programs), thesis. *Entrance requirements:* For master's, GRE, statement of purpose, three letters of recommendation, transcripts. Additional exam requirements/recommendations for international students: Required—TOEFL, IELTS. *Application deadline:* For fall admission, 1/10 for domestic and international students; for spring admission, 7/1 for domestic and international students. Applications are processed on a rolling basis. Application fee: $50. Electronic applications accepted. *Expenses:* Tuition, state resident: full-time $8552; part-time $443 per credit. Tuition, nonresident: full-time $21,650; part-time $1083 per credit. Required fees: $846. *Financial support:* In 2010–11, fellowships (averaging $2,500 per year), research assistantships with tuition reimbursements (averaging $13,917 per year) were awarded. Financial award application deadline: 2/10. Total annual research expenditures: $2.2 million. *Unit head:* Dr. Matthew McCluskey, Chair, 509-335-5356, Fax: 509-335-4662, E-mail: mattmcc@wsu.edu. *Application contact:* Graduate School Admissions, 800-GRADWSU, Fax: 509-335-1949, E-mail: gradsch@wsu.edu.

Washington State University, Graduate School, College of Sciences, Program in Materials Science, Pullman, WA 99164. Offers PhD. *Faculty:* 10. *Students:* 24 full-time (8 women), 1 part-time (0 women); includes 1 Asian, non-Hispanic/Latino; 2 Hispanic/Latino, 10 international. Average age 30. 49 applicants, 22% accepted, 7 enrolled. In 2010, 3 doctorates awarded. *Degree requirements:* For doctorate, comprehensive exam, thesis/dissertation, oral exam, written exam. *Entrance requirements:* For doctorate, minimum GPA of 3.0, 3 letters of recommendation. Additional exam requirements/recommendations for international students: Required—TOEFL. *Application deadline:* For fall admission, 1/15 priority date for domestic students, 3/1 for international students; for spring admission, 7/1 priority date for domestic students, 7/1 for international students. Applications are processed on a rolling basis. Application fee: $50. *Expenses:* Tuition, state resident: full-time $8552; part-time $443 per credit. Tuition, nonresident: full-time $21,650; part-time $1083 per credit. Required fees: $846. *Financial support:* In 2010–11, fellowships (averaging $2,000 per year), research assistantships with full and partial tuition reimbursements (averaging $13,917 per year), teaching assistantships with full and partial tuition reimbursements (averaging $13,056 per year) were awarded; career-related internships or fieldwork, Federal Work-Study, institutionally sponsored loans, and teaching associateships also available. Financial award application deadline: 4/1. *Faculty research:* Thin films, materials characterization, mechanical properties, materials processing, electrical and optical behavior. *Unit head:* Dr. K. W. Hipps, Chair, 509-835-2942, E-mail: hipps@wsu.edu. *Application contact:* Graduate School Admissions, 800-GRADWSU, Fax: 509-335-1949, E-mail: gradsch@wsu.edu.

Wayne State University, College of Engineering, Department of Chemical Engineering and Materials Science, Program in Materials Science and Engineering, Detroit, MI 48202. Offers materials science and engineering (MS, PhD); polymer engineering (Certificate). Part-time programs available. *Faculty:* 8 full-time (2 women), 2 part-time/adjunct (0 women). *Students:* 14 full-time (3 women), 2 part-time (1 woman), 14 international. Average age 27. 22 applicants, 32% accepted, 2 enrolled. In 2010, 1 master's, 2 doctorates awarded. Terminal master's awarded for partial completion of doctoral program. *Degree requirements:* For master's, thesis optional; for doctorate, thesis/dissertation. *Entrance requirements:* For master's, GRE (if applying for financial support), recommendations; resume; for doctorate, GRE (if applying for financial support), recommendations; resume, personal statement. Additional exam requirements/recommendations for international students: Required—TOEFL (minimum score 550 paper-based; 213 computer-based); Recommended—TWE (minimum score 6). *Application deadline:* For fall admission, 7/1 priority date for domestic students, 6/1 for international students; for winter admission, 10/1 for international students; for spring admission, 3/15 for domestic students, 2/1 for international students. Applications are processed on a rolling basis. Application fee: $30 ($50 for international students). Electronic applications accepted. *Expenses:* Tuition, state resident: full-time $7662; part-time $478.85 per credit hour. Tuition, nonresident: full-time $16,920; part-time $1057.55 per credit hour. Required fees: $571.20; $35.70 per credit hour. $188.05 per semester. Tuition and fees vary according to course load and program. *Financial support:* In 2010–11, 6 research assistantships (averaging $16,221 per year), 5 teaching assistantships (averaging $16,984 per year) were awarded; fellowships also available. Financial award application deadline: 2/15. *Faculty research:* Polymer science, rheology, fatigue in metals, metal matrix composites, ceramics. *Unit head:* Charles Manke, Chair, 313-577-3849,

Fax: 313-577-3810, E-mail: emanke@chem1.eng.wayne.edu. *Application contact:* Rangaramanujam Kannan, Associate Professor, 313-577-3800, E-mail: rkannan@che.eng.wayne.edu.

Worcester Polytechnic Institute, Graduate Studies and Research, Department of Mechanical Engineering, Program in Materials Process Engineering, Worcester, MA 01609-2280. Offers MS. Part-time and evening/weekend programs available. *Students:* 1 (woman) full-time, 5 part-time (2 women); includes 1 Native Hawaiian or other Pacific Islander, non-Hispanic/Latino, 1 international. 6 applicants, 83% accepted, 3 enrolled. *Degree requirements:* For master's, thesis optional. *Entrance requirements:* For master's, GRE required for all International applicants, 3 letters of recommendation. Additional exam requirements/recommendations for international students: Required—TOEFL (minimum score 550 paper-based; 213 computer-based). *Application deadline:* For fall admission, 1/1 priority date for domestic and international students; for spring admission, 10/1 priority date for domestic and international students. Applications are processed on a rolling basis. Application fee: $70. Electronic applications accepted. *Expenses:* Tuition: Full-time $20,862; part-time $1159 per term. One-time fee: $15. *Financial support:* Application deadline: 1/1. *Unit head:* Dr. Richard D. Sisson, Director, 508-831-5633, Fax: 508-831-5178, E-mail: sisson@wpi.edu. *Application contact:* Rita Shilansky, Graduate Secretary, 508-831-5633, Fax: 508-831-5178, E-mail: rita@wpi.edu.

Worcester Polytechnic Institute, Graduate Studies and Research, Department of Mechanical Engineering, Program in Materials Science and Engineering, Worcester, MA 01609-2280. Offers MS, PhD. Part-time and evening/weekend programs available. *Faculty:* 4 full-time (1 woman), 1 part-time/adjunct (0 women). *Students:* 38 full-time (12 women), 7 part-time (4 women); includes 1 American Indian or Alaska Native, non-Hispanic/Latino; 3 Native Hawaiian or other Pacific Islander, non-Hispanic/Latino, 31 international. 71 applicants, 86% accepted, 13 enrolled. In 2010, 14 master's, 5 doctorates awarded. *Degree requirements:* For master's, thesis; for doctorate, comprehensive exam, thesis/dissertation. *Entrance requirements:* For master's and doctorate, GRE General Test (recommended). Required for International applicants, 3 letters of recommendation. Additional exam requirements/recommendations for international students: Required—TOEFL (minimum score 550 paper-based; 213 computer-based; 79 iBT), IELTS (minimum score 6.5). *Application deadline:* For fall admission, 1/1 priority date for domestic students, 1/1 for international students; for spring admission, 10/1 priority date for domestic students, 10/1 for international students. Applications are processed on a rolling basis. Application fee: $70. Electronic applications accepted. *Expenses:* Tuition: Full-time $20,862; part-time $1159 per term. One-time fee: $15. *Financial support:* Career-related internships or fieldwork, institutionally sponsored loans, scholarships/grants, and unspecified assistantships available. Financial award application deadline: 1/1; financial award applicants required to submit FAFSA. *Faculty research:* Metals processing, nanomaterials, reliability analysis, surface metrology, biopolymers. *Unit head:* Dr. Richard D. Sisson, Director, 508-831-5633, Fax: 508-831-5178, E-mail: sisson@wpi.edu. *Application contact:* Rita Shilansky, Graduate Secretary, 508-831-5633, Fax: 508-831-5178, E-mail: rita@wpi.edu.

Wright State University, School of Graduate Studies, College of Engineering and Computer Science, Programs in Engineering, Program in Mechanical and Materials Engineering, Dayton, OH 45435. Offers materials science and engineering (MSE); mechanical engineering (MSE). *Degree requirements:* For master's, thesis or course option alternative. *Entrance requirements:* Additional exam requirements/recommendations for international students: Required—TOEFL.

Metallurgical Engineering and Metallurgy

Colorado School of Mines, Graduate School, Department of Metallurgical and Materials Engineering, Golden, CO 80401. Offers materials science (MS, PhD); metallurgical and materials engineering (ME, MS, PhD). Part-time programs available. *Faculty:* 35 full-time (3 women), 5 part-time/adjunct (0 women). *Students:* 65 full-time (16 women), 5 part-time (1 woman); includes 2 American Indian or Alaska Native, non-Hispanic/Latino; 1 Asian, non-Hispanic/Latino; 2 Hispanic/Latino; 1 Two or more races, non-Hispanic/Latino, 18 international. Average age 30. 95 applicants, 36% accepted, 28 enrolled. In 2010, 12 master's, 6 doctorates awarded. *Degree requirements:* For master's, thesis (for some programs); for doctorate, comprehensive exam, thesis/dissertation. *Entrance requirements:* For master's and doctorate, GRE General Test. Additional exam requirements/recommendations for international students: Required—TOEFL (minimum score 550 paper-based; 213 computer-based; 80 iBT). *Application deadline:* For fall admission, 1/15 priority date for domestic and international students; for spring admission, 10/15 priority date for domestic and international students. Application fee: $50 ($70 for international students). Electronic applications accepted. *Expenses:* Tuition, state resident: full-time $11,550; part-time $641 per credit. Tuition, nonresident: full-time $25,980; part-time $1444 per credit. Required fees: $1874; $937 per semester. *Financial support:* In 2010–11, 53 students received support, including 6 fellowships with full tuition reimbursements available (averaging $20,000 per year), 44 research assistantships with full tuition reimbursements available (averaging $20,000 per year), 3 teaching assistantships with full tuition reimbursements available (averaging $20,000 per year); scholarships/grants, health care benefits, and unspecified assistantships also available. Financial award application deadline: 1/15; financial award applicants required to submit FAFSA. Total annual research expenditures: $6.3 million. *Unit head:* Dr. Michael Kaufman, Interim Department Head, 303-273-3009, Fax: 303-273-3795, E-mail: mkaufman@mines.edu. *Application contact:* Susan Ballantype, Program Assistant, 303-273-3660, Fax: 303-273-3795, E-mail: susan.ballantyne@is.mines.edu.

Columbia University, Fu Foundation School of Engineering and Applied Science, Department of Earth and Environmental Engineering, New York, NY 10027. Offers earth and environmental engineering (MS, Eng Sc D, PhD); metallurgical engineering (Engr); mining engineering (Engr); MS/MBA. Part-time programs available. Postbaccalaureate distance learning degree programs offered (minimal on-campus study). *Faculty:* 12 full-time (1 woman), 6 part-time/adjunct (0 women). *Students:* 47 full-time (18 women), 14 part-time (9 women); includes 5 minority (1 American Indian or Alaska Native, non-Hispanic/Latino; 2 Asian, non-Hispanic/Latino; 1 Hispanic/Latino; 1 Two or more races, non-Hispanic/Latino), 30 international. Average age 29. 192 applicants, 14% accepted, 12 enrolled. In 2010, 28 master's, 8 doctorates awarded. Terminal master's awarded for partial completion of doctoral program. *Degree requirements:* For master's, thesis; for doctorate, thesis/dissertation, qualifying exam. *Entrance requirements:* For master's, doctorate, and Engr, GRE General Test. Additional exam requirements/recommendations for international students: Required—TOEFL, IELTS. *Application deadline:* For fall admission, 12/1 priority date for domestic and international students; for spring admission, 10/1 priority date for domestic and international students. Application fee: $95. Electronic applications accepted. *Financial support:* In 2010–11, 39 students received support, including 6 fellowships with full and partial tuition reimbursements available (averaging $16,478 per year), 26 research assistantships with full tuition reimbursements available (averaging $27,733 per year), 7 teaching assistantships with full tuition reimbursements available (averaging $22,500 per year); health care benefits and unspecified assistantships also available. Financial award application deadline: 12/1; financial award applicants required to submit FAFSA. *Faculty research:* Sustainable energy and materials, waste to energy, water resources and climate risks, environmental health engineering, life cycle analysis. *Unit head:* Dr. Klaus S. Lackner, Maurice Ewing and J. Lamar Worzel Professor of Geophysics and Department Chairman, 212-854-0304, Fax: 212-854-7081, E-mail: kl2010@columbia.edu. *Application contact:* Gary Hill, Administrative Assistant, 212-854-2905, Fax: 212-854-7081, E-mail: gh2206@columbia.edu.

Massachusetts Institute of Technology, School of Engineering, Department of Materials Science and Engineering, Cambridge, MA 02139. Offers archaeological materials (PhD, Sc D); bio- and polymeric materials (PhD, Sc D); electronic, photonic and magnetic materials (PhD, Sc D); emerging, fundamental and computational studies in materials science (Sc D); emerging, fundamental, and computational studies in materials science (PhD); materials engineering (Mat E); materials science and engineering (M Eng, SM, PhD, Sc D); metallurgical engineering (Met E); structural and environmental materials (PhD, Sc D); SM/MBA. *Faculty:* 34 full-time (8 women). *Students:* 196 full-time (52 women); includes 32 minority (2 Black or African American, non-Hispanic/Latino; 20 Asian, non-Hispanic/Latino; 7 Hispanic/Latino; 3 Two or more races, non-Hispanic/Latino), 113 international. Average age 26. 507 applicants, 15% accepted, 41 enrolled. In 2010, 22 master's, 38 doctorates awarded. Terminal master's awarded for partial completion of doctoral program. *Degree requirements:* For master's and other advanced degree, thesis; for doctorate, comprehensive exam, thesis/dissertation. *Entrance requirements:* For master's, doctorate, and other advanced degree, GRE General Test. Additional exam requirements/recommendations for international students: Required—IELTS (minimum score 7). *Application deadline:* For fall admission, 12/15 for domestic and international students. Application fee: $75. Electronic applications accepted. *Expenses:* Tuition: Full-time $38,940; part-time $605 per unit. Required fees: $272. *Financial support:* In 2010–11, 183 students received support, including 52 fellowships with tuition reimbursements available (averaging $32,695 per year), 124 research assistantships with tuition reimbursements available (averaging $27,409 per year), 8 teaching assistantships with tuition reimbursements available (averaging $31,861 per year); career-related internships or fieldwork, Federal Work-Study, institutionally sponsored loans, scholarships/grants, health care benefits, and unspecified assistantships also available. *Faculty research:* Thermodynamics and kinetics of phase transformations; structure of all materials classes: metals, ceramics, semiconductors, polymers, biomaterials; influence of processing on materials structure; structure ??? property relationships (electrical, magnetic, optical, mechanical); materials in extreme environments. Total annual research expenditures: $28.1 million. *Unit head:* Prof. Edwin L. Thomas, Department Head, 617-253-3300, Fax: 617-252-1775. *Application contact:* Angelita Mireles, Graduate Admissions, 617-253-3302, E-mail: dmse-admissions@mit.edu.

Michigan Technological University, Graduate School, College of Engineering, Department of Materials Science and Engineering, Houghton, MI 49931. Offers MS, PhD. Part-time programs available. Terminal master's awarded for partial completion of doctoral program. *Degree requirements:* For master's, comprehensive exam; for doctorate, comprehensive exam, thesis/dissertation. *Entrance requirements:* For master's, GRE. Additional exam requirements/recommendations for international students: Required—TOEFL (minimum score 550 paper-based; 213 computer-based). Electronic applications accepted. *Expenses:* Contact institution. *Faculty research:* Structure/property/processing relationships, microstructural characterization, alloy design, electronic/magnetic/photonic materials, materials and manufacturing processes.

Missouri University of Science and Technology, Graduate School, Department of Materials Science and Engineering, Rolla, MO 65409. Offers ceramic engineering (MS, DE, PhD); metallurgical engineering (MS, PhD). *Degree requirements:* For master's, thesis optional; for doctorate, comprehensive exam. *Entrance requirements:* For master's, GRE (minimum combined score 1100, 600 verbal, 3.5 writing); for doctorate, GRE (minimum score: quantitative 600, writing 3.5). Additional exam requirements/recommendations for international students: Required—TOEFL (minimum score 570 paper-based; 230 computer-based).

Montana Tech of The University of Montana, Graduate School, Metallurgical/Mineral Processing Engineering Programs, Butte, MT 59701-8997. Offers MS. Part-time programs available. *Faculty:* 6 full-time (0 women). *Students:* 5 full-time (3 women), 2 part-time (0 women). 3 applicants, 67% accepted, 2 enrolled. In 2010, 2 master's awarded. *Degree requirements:* For master's, comprehensive exam (for some programs), thesis optional. *Entrance requirements:* For master's, GRE General Test, minimum GPA of 3.0. Additional exam requirements/recommendations for international students: Required—TOEFL (minimum score 525 paper-based; 195 computer-based; 71 iBT). *Application deadline:* For fall admission, 4/1 priority date for domestic students, 3/1 priority date for international students; for spring admission, 10/1 priority date for domestic students, 7/1 priority date for international students. Applications are processed on a rolling basis. Application fee: $30. Electronic applications accepted. *Expenses:* Tuition, state resident: full-time $5084. Tuition, nonresident: full-time $15,104. *Financial support:* In 2010–11, 5 students received support, including 5 teaching assistantships with partial tuition reimbursements available (averaging $5,000 per year); research assistantships with partial tuition reimbursements available, career-related internships or fieldwork, tuition waivers (full and partial), and unspecified assistantships also available. Financial award application deadline: 4/1; financial award applicants required to submit FAFSA. *Faculty research:* Stabilizing hazardous waste, decontamination of metals by melt refining, ultraviolet enhancement of stabilization reactions, extractive metallurgy, fuel cells. *Unit head:* Dr. Courtney Young, Department Head, 406-496-4158, Fax: 406-496-4664, E-mail: cyoung@mtech.edu. *Application contact:* Fred Sullivan, Administrator, Graduate School, 406-496-4304, Fax: 406-496-4710, E-mail: fsullivan@mtech.edu.

The Ohio State University, Graduate School, College of Engineering, Department of Materials Science and Engineering, Program in Welding Engineering, Columbus, OH 43210. Offers MS, MWE, PhD. *Faculty:* 25. *Students:* 17 full-time (2 women), 20 part-time (2 women); includes 1 Black or African American, non-Hispanic/Latino; 1 Asian, non-Hispanic/Latino; 1 Two or more races, non-Hispanic/Latino, 9 international. Average age 29. In 2010, 6 master's, 1 doctorate awarded. *Degree requirements:* For master's, thesis optional; for doctorate, thesis/dissertation. *Entrance requirements:* For master's and doctorate, GRE General Test or engineering degree. Additional exam requirements/recommendations for international students: Recommended—TOEFL (minimum score 600 paper-based; 250 computer-based). *Application deadline:* For fall admission, 8/15 priority date for domestic students, 7/1 priority date for international students; for winter admission, 12/1 priority date for domestic students, 11/1 priority date for international students; for spring admission, 3/1 priority date for domestic students, 2/1 priority date for international students. Applications are processed on a rolling basis. Application fee: $40 ($50 for international students). Electronic applications accepted. *Expenses:* Tuition, state resident: full-time $10,605. Tuition, nonresident: full-time $26,535. Tuition and fees vary according to course load and program. *Financial support:* Fellowships, research assistantships, teaching assistantships, Federal Work-Study and institutionally sponsored loans available. Support available to part-time students. *Unit head:* Avaraham Benatar, Graduate Studies Committee Chair, 614-292-2466, Fax: 614-292-7852, E-mail: benatar.1@osu.edu. *Application contact:* 614-292-9444, Fax: 614-292-3895, E-mail: domestic.grad@osu.edu.

The Ohio State University, Graduate School, College of Engineering, Program in Industrial and Systems Engineering, Columbus, OH 43210. Offers industrial and systems engineering (MS, PhD); welding engineering (MS, MWE, PhD). *Faculty:* 39. *Students:* 69 full-time (21 women), 63 part-time (12 women); includes 4 Black or African American, non-Hispanic/Latino; 14 Asian, non-Hispanic/Latino; 9 Hispanic/Latino, 129 international. Average age 28. In 2010, 23 master's, 11 doctorates awarded. *Degree requirements:* For master's, thesis optional; for doctorate, thesis/dissertation. *Entrance requirements:* For master's and doctorate, GRE General Test. Additional exam requirements/recommendations for international students: Recommended—

Metallurgical Engineering and Metallurgy

The Ohio State University (continued)
TOEFL (minimum score 600 paper-based; 250 computer-based). *Application deadline:* For fall admission, 8/15 priority date for domestic students, 11/1 priority date for international students; for winter admission, 12/1 priority date for domestic students, 7/1 priority date for international students; for spring admission, 3/1 priority date for domestic students, 2/1 priority date for international students. Applications are processed on a rolling basis. Application fee: $40 ($50 for international students). Electronic applications accepted. *Expenses:* Tuition, state resident: full-time $10,605. Tuition, nonresident: full-time $26,535. Tuition and fees vary according to course load and program. *Financial support:* Fellowships, research assistantships, teaching assistantships, career-related internships or fieldwork, Federal Work-Study, institutionally sponsored loans, and unspecified assistantships available. Support available to part-time students. *Unit head:* Julie L. Higle, Chair, 614-292-6239, E-mail: higle.1@osu.edu. *Application contact:* 614-292-9444, Fax: 614-292-3895, E-mail: domestic.grad@osu.edu.

Rensselaer Polytechnic Institute, Graduate School, School of Engineering, Program in Materials Science and Engineering, Troy, NY 12180. Offers ceramics and glass science (M Eng, MS, PhD); composites (M Eng, MS, PhD); electronic materials (M Eng, MS, PhD); metallurgy (M Eng, MS, PhD); polymers (M Eng, MS, PhD). Part-time programs available. *Faculty:* 16 full-time (2 women). *Students:* 57 full-time (13 women), 6 part-time (1 woman), 37 international. Average age 24. 304 applicants, 15% accepted, 16 enrolled. In 2010, 5 master's, 6 doctorates awarded. Terminal master's awarded for partial completion of doctoral program. *Degree requirements:* For master's, thesis; for doctorate, comprehensive exam, thesis/dissertation. *Entrance requirements:* For master's and doctorate, GRE. Additional exam requirements/recommendations for international students: Required—TOEFL (minimum score 570 paper-based; 230 computer-based; 100 iBT). *Application deadline:* For fall admission, 1/15 priority date for domestic and international students; for spring admission, 8/31 priority date for domestic and international students. Applications are processed on a rolling basis. Application fee: $75. Electronic applications accepted. *Expenses:* Tuition: Full-time $39,600; part-time $1650 per credit. Required fees: $1896. *Financial support:* In 2010–11, 56 students received support, including 2 fellowships with full tuition reimbursements available (averaging $26,250 per year), 41 research assistantships with full tuition reimbursements available (averaging $26,250 per year), 13 teaching assistantships with full tuition reimbursements available (averaging $17,500 per year); career-related internships or fieldwork, institutionally sponsored loans, and unspecified assistantships also available. Financial award application deadline: 2/1. *Faculty research:* Materials processing, nanostructural materials, materials for microelectronics, composite materials, computational materials. Total annual research expenditures: $3.6 million. *Unit head:* Dr. Robert Hull, Department Head, 518-276-6373, Fax: 518-276-8554, E-mail: hullr2@rpi.edu. *Application contact:* Dr. Pawel Keblinski, Admissions Coordinator, 518-276-6858, Fax: 518-276-8554, E-mail: keblip@rpi.edu.

Université Laval, Faculty of Sciences and Engineering, Department of Mining, Metallurgical and Materials Engineering, Programs in Metallurgical Engineering, Québec, QC G1K 7P4, Canada. Offers M Sc, PhD. Terminal master's awarded for partial completion of doctoral program. *Degree requirements:* For master's, thesis; for doctorate, comprehensive exam, thesis/dissertation. *Entrance requirements:* For master's and doctorate, knowledge of French and English. Electronic applications accepted.

The University of Alabama, Graduate School, College of Engineering, Department of Metallurgical and Materials Engineering, Tuscaloosa, AL 35487. Offers MS Met E, PhD. Phd offered jointly with The University of Alabama at Birmingham. *Faculty:* 8 full-time (2 women). *Students:* 19 full-time (2 women), 3 part-time (0 women); includes 1 minority (Black or African American, non-Hispanic/Latino), 10 international. Average age 26. 19 applicants, 26% accepted, 3 enrolled. In 2010, 3 master's, 7 doctorates awarded. *Degree requirements:* For master's, thesis or alternative; for doctorate, thesis/dissertation. *Entrance requirements:* For master's, GRE General Test, minimum GPA of 3.0 in last 60 hours; for doctorate, GRE General Test, minimum graduate GPA of 3.0, graduate degree. Additional exam requirements/recommendations for international students: Required—TOEFL (minimum score 550 paper-based; 213 computer-based). *Application deadline:* For fall admission, 7/1 priority date for domestic students. Applications are processed on a rolling basis. Application fee: $50 ($60 for international students). Electronic applications accepted. *Expenses:* Tuition, state resident: full-time $7900. Tuition, nonresident: full-time $20,500. *Financial support:* In 2010–11, 3 fellowships (averaging $15,000 per year), 14 research assistantships (averaging $14,700 per year), 6 teaching assistantships (averaging $12,250 per year) were awarded; Federal Work-Study and unspecified assistantships also available. *Faculty research:* Thermodynamics, molten metals processing, casting and solidification, mechanical properties of materials, thin films and nanostructures, electrochemistry, corrosion and alloy development. Total annual research expenditures: $1.9 million. *Unit head:* Dr. Ramana G. Reddy, Head and ACIPCO Professor, 205-348-4246, Fax: 205-348-2164. *Application contact:* Dr. Su Gupta, Associate Professor, 205-348-4272, Fax: 205-348-2164, E-mail: sgupta@eng.ua.edu.

The University of British Columbia, Faculty of Applied Science, Department of Materials Engineering, Vancouver, BC V6T 1Z1, Canada. Offers materials and metallurgy (M Sc, PhD); metals and materials engineering (MA Sc, PhD). *Degree requirements:* For master's, comprehensive exam, thesis; for doctorate, comprehensive exam, thesis/dissertation. *Entrance requirements:* Additional exam requirements/recommendations for international students: Required—TOEFL (minimum score 560 paper-based; 220 computer-based; 83 iBT). Electronic applications accepted. Tuition charges are reported in Canadian dollars. *Expenses:* Tuition, area resident: Full-time $4179 Canadian dollars. International tuition: $7344 Canadian dollars full-time. *Faculty research:* Electroslag melting, mathematical modeling, solidification and hydrometallurgy.

University of Cincinnati, Graduate School, College of Engineering, Department of Chemical and Materials Engineering, Cincinnati, OH 45221. Offers chemical engineering (MS, PhD); materials science and metallurgical engineering (MS, PhD), including ceramic science and engineering, materials science and engineering, metallurgical engineering, polymer science and engineering. Part-time and evening/weekend programs available. Terminal master's awarded for partial completion of doctoral program. *Degree requirements:* For master's, thesis; for doctorate, thesis/dissertation. *Entrance requirements:* For master's and doctorate, GRE General Test. Additional exam requirements/recommendations for international students: Required—TOEFL. Electronic applications accepted. *Faculty research:* Process synthesis, aerosol processes, clean coal technology, membrane technology.

University of Cincinnati, Graduate School, College of Engineering, Department of Chemical and Materials Engineering, Program in Materials Science and Metallurgical Engineering, Program in Metallurgical Engineering, Cincinnati, OH 45221. Offers MS, PhD. *Degree requirements:* For master's, thesis optional; for doctorate, one foreign language, comprehensive exam, thesis/dissertation, oral English proficiency exam. *Entrance requirements:* For master's and doctorate, GRE General Test, BS in related field, minimum undergraduate GPA of 3.0. Additional exam requirements/recommendations for international students: Required—TOEFL. Electronic applications accepted. *Faculty research:* Polymer characterization, surface analysis, and adhesion; high-temperature coatings and physical chemistry of materials.

University of Connecticut, Graduate School, School of Engineering, Department of Metallurgy and Materials Engineering, Storrs, CT 06269. Offers MS, PhD. Terminal master's awarded for partial completion of doctoral program. *Degree requirements:* For master's, comprehensive exam, thesis or alternative; for doctorate, thesis/dissertation. *Entrance requirements:* For master's and doctorate, GRE General Test, GRE Subject Test. Additional exam requirements/recommendations for international students: Required—TOEFL (minimum score 550 paper-based; 213 computer-based). Electronic applications accepted. *Faculty research:* Microsegregation and coarsening, fatigue crack, electron-dislocation interaction.

University of Idaho, College of Graduate Studies, College of Engineering, Department of Chemical and Materials Engineering, Program in Materials Science and Engineering, Moscow, ID 83844-2282. Offers materials science and engineering (MS, PhD); metallurgical engineering (MS); mining engineering (PhD). *Students:* 8 full-time. Average age 30. In 2010, 2 master's, 1 doctorate awarded. *Application deadline:* Applications are processed on a rolling basis. Application fee: $60. Electronic applications accepted. *Expenses:* Tuition, nonresident: part-time $580 per credit. Required fees: $306 per credit. *Financial support:* Applicants required to submit FAFSA. *Unit head:* Dr. Wudneh Admassu, Chair, 208-885-6376. *Application contact:* Dr. Wudneh Admassu, Chair, 208-885-6376.

The University of Manchester, School of Materials, Manchester, United Kingdom. Offers advanced aerospace materials engineering (M Sc); advanced metallic systems (PhD); biomedical materials (M Phil, M Sc, PhD); ceramics and glass (M Phil, M Sc, PhD); composite materials (M Sc, PhD); corrosion and protection (M Phil, M Sc, PhD); materials (M Phil, PhD); metallic materials (M Phil, M Sc, PhD); nanostructural materials (M Phil, M Sc, PhD); paper science (M Phil, M Sc, PhD); polymer science and engineering (M Phil, M Sc, PhD); technical textiles (M Sc); textile design, fashion and management (M Phil, M Sc, PhD); textile science and technology (M Phil, M Sc, PhD); textiles (M Phil, PhD); textiles and fashion (M Ent).

University of Nebraska–Lincoln, Graduate College, College of Engineering, Department of Mechanical Engineering, Lincoln, NE 68588. Offers chemical and materials engineering (PhD); mechanical engineering (MS, PhD), including materials science engineering (MS), metallurgical engineering (MS). *Degree requirements:* For master's, thesis optional; for doctorate, comprehensive exam, thesis/dissertation. *Entrance requirements:* For master's and doctorate, GRE General Test. Additional exam requirements/recommendations for international students: Required—TOEFL (minimum score 550 paper-based; 213 computer-based). Electronic applications accepted. *Faculty research:* Robotics for planetary exploration, vehicle crashworthiness, transient heat conduction, laser beam/particle interactions.

See Display on page 543 and Close-Up on page 557.

University of Nevada, Reno, Graduate School, College of Engineering, Department of Chemical and Materials Engineering, Program in Materials Science and Engineering, Reno, NV 89557. Offers MS, PhD. Terminal master's awarded for partial completion of doctoral program. *Degree requirements:* For master's, thesis; for doctorate, one foreign language, thesis/dissertation. *Entrance requirements:* For master's, minimum GPA of 2.75; for doctorate, GRE, minimum GPA of 3.0. Additional exam requirements/recommendations for international students: Required—TOEFL (minimum score 500 paper-based; 173 computer-based; 61 iBT), IELTS (minimum score 6). Electronic applications accepted. *Expenses:* Tuition, state resident: full-time $2219; part-time $246 per credit. Tuition, nonresident: part-time $510 per credit. International tuition: $9009 full-time. Required fees: $59 per term. One-time fee: $101. Tuition and fees vary according to course load. *Faculty research:* Hydrometallurgy, applied surface chemistry, mineral processing, mineral bioprocessing, ceramics.

The University of Texas at El Paso, Graduate School, College of Engineering, Department of Metallurgical and Materials Engineering, El Paso, TX 79968-0001. Offers materials science and engineering (PhD); metallurgical and materials engineering (MS). Part-time and evening/weekend programs available. *Students:* 15 (3 women); includes 1 Asian, non-Hispanic/Latino; 9 Hispanic/Latino, 3 international. Average age 34. In 2010, 1 master's awarded. *Degree requirements:* For master's, thesis. *Entrance requirements:* For master's, GRE General Test. Additional exam requirements/recommendations for international students: Required—TOEFL. *Application deadline:* For fall admission, 7/1 priority date for domestic students, 3/1 for international students; for spring admission, 11/1 priority date for domestic students, 9/1 for international students. Applications are processed on a rolling basis. Application fee: $15 ($65 for international students). Electronic applications accepted. *Financial support:* In 2010–11, research assistantships with partial tuition reimbursements (averaging $21,125 per year), teaching assistantships with partial tuition reimbursements (averaging $16,900 per year) were awarded; fellowships with partial tuition reimbursements, career-related internships or fieldwork, Federal Work-Study, institutionally sponsored loans, scholarships/grants, and tuition waivers (partial) also available. Financial award application deadline: 3/15; financial award applicants required to submit FAFSA. *Unit head:* Dr. Lawrence E. Murr, Chairperson, 915-747-5468, Fax: 915-747-8036, E-mail: fekberg@utep.edu. *Application contact:* Dr. Charles H. Ambler, Dean of the Graduate School, 915-747-5491 Ext. 7886, Fax: 915-747-5788, E-mail: cambler@utep.edu.

University of Utah, Graduate School, College of Mines and Earth Sciences, Department of Metallurgical Engineering, Salt Lake City, UT 84112. Offers ME, MS, PhD. Part-time programs available. *Faculty:* 8 full-time (0 women), 2 part-time/adjunct (0 women). *Students:* 45 full-time (14 women), 11 part-time (0 women); includes 4 minority (3 Asian, non-Hispanic/Latino; 1 Hispanic/Latino), 44 international. Average age 29. 33 applicants, 61% accepted, 10 enrolled. In 2010, 9 master's, 3 doctorates awarded. Terminal master's awarded for partial completion of doctoral program. *Degree requirements:* For master's, thesis; for doctorate, comprehensive exam, thesis/dissertation. *Entrance requirements:* For master's and doctorate, GRE General Test (required), minimum GPA of 3.0. Additional exam requirements/recommendations for international students: Required—TOEFL (minimum score 530 paper; 197 computer) or IELTS (minimum 5.5). *Application deadline:* For fall admission, 4/1 for domestic students, 4/1 priority date for international students; for spring admission, 11/1 priority date for domestic and international students. Applications are processed on a rolling basis. Application fee: $55 ($65 for international students). Electronic applications accepted. *Expenses:* Tuition, area resident: Part-time $179.19 per credit hour. Tuition, state resident: full-time $4384. Tuition, nonresident: full-time $16,684; part-time $630.67 per credit hour. Required fees: $350 per semester. Tuition and fees vary according to course load, degree level and program. *Financial support:* In 2010–11, 1 student received support, including 2 fellowships with full and partial tuition reimbursements available (averaging $16,500 per year), 46 research assistantships with full and partial tuition reimbursements available (averaging $15,969 per year); institutionally sponsored loans also available. Financial award application deadline: 2/15; financial award applicants required to submit FAFSA. *Faculty research:* Physical metallurgy, mathematical modeling, mineral processing, chemical metallurgy nanoscience and technology. Total annual research expenditures: $2.4 million. *Unit head:* Dr. Jan D. Miller, Chair, 801-581-5160, Fax: 801-581-4937, E-mail: jan.miller@utah.edu. *Application contact:* Kay Argyle, Executive Secretary, 801-581-6386, Fax: 801-581-4937, E-mail: kay.argyle@utah.edu.

Wayne State University, College of Engineering, Department of Chemical Engineering and Materials Science, Detroit, MI 48202. Offers chemical engineering (MS, PhD); materials science and engineering (MS, PhD, Certificate), including materials science and engineering (MS, PhD), polymer engineering (Certificate); metallurgical engineering (MS, PhD). Part-time programs available. *Faculty:* 8 full-time (2 women), 2 part-time/adjunct (0 women). *Students:* 32 full-time (10 women); 10 part-time (4 women); includes 4 minority (3 Asian, non-Hispanic/Latino; 1 Hispanic/Latino), 29 international. Average age 28. 50 applicants, 42% accepted, 7 enrolled. In 2010, 7 master's, 5 doctorates awarded. Terminal master's awarded for partial completion of doctoral program. *Degree requirements:* For master's, thesis optional; for doctorate, thesis/dissertation. *Entrance requirements:* For master's, GRE (if applying for financial support), letters of recommendation; resume; for doctorate, GRE (if applying for financial support), recommendations; resume personal statement. Additional exam requirements/recommendations for international students: Required—TOEFL (minimum score 550 paper-based; 213 computer-based), TWE (minimum score 6). *Application deadline:* For fall admission, 7/1 priority date for domestic students, 6/1 for international students; for winter admission, 10/1 for international students; for spring admission, 2/1 for international students. Applications are processed on a rolling basis. Application fee: $30 ($50 for international students). Electronic applications accepted. *Expenses:* Tuition, state resident: full-time $7662; part-time $478.85 per credit hour. Tuition, nonresident: full-time $16,920; part-time $1057.55 per credit hour. Required fees: $571.20; $35.70 per credit hour. $188.05 per semester. Tuition and fees vary according to course load and program. *Financial support:* In 2010–11, 1 fellowship, 14 research assistantships, 10 teaching assistantships were awarded. *Faculty research:* Polymer solutions and processing, catalysis, environmental transport, waste minimization, transport in biological systems. *Unit head:* Charles Manke, Chair, 313-577-3849, Fax: 313-577-3810, E-mail: emanke@chem1.eng.wayne.edu. *Application contact:* Dr. Yinlun Huang, Graduate Director, 313-577-3800, E-mail: yhuang@wayne.edu.

Polymer Science and Engineering

California Polytechnic State University, San Luis Obispo, College of Science and Mathematics, Department of Chemistry and Biochemistry, San Luis Obispo, CA 93407. Offers polymers and coating science (MS). Part-time programs available. *Students:* 3 full-time (0 women), 7 part-time (3 women); includes 2 minority (1 Black or African American, non-Hispanic/Latino; 1 Asian, non-Hispanic/Latino). Average age 24. 5 applicants, 80% accepted, 1 enrolled. *Degree requirements:* For master's, comprehensive oral exam. *Entrance requirements:* For master's, minimum GPA of 2.5 in last 90 quarter units of course work. Additional exam requirements/recommendations for international students: Required—TOEFL (minimum score 550 paper-based; 213 computer-based) or IELTS (minimum score 6). *Application deadline:* For fall admission, 7/1 for domestic students, 11/30 for international students; for winter admission, 11/1 for domestic students, 6/30 for international students; for spring admission, 2/1 for domestic students. Applications are processed on a rolling basis. Application fee: $55. Electronic applications accepted. *Expenses:* Tuition, state resident: full-time $5386; part-time $3124 per year. Tuition, nonresident: full-time $11,160; part-time $248 per unit. Required fees: $2250; $614 per term. One-time fee: $2250 full-time; $1842 part-time. *Financial support:* Career-related internships or fieldwork, Federal Work-Study, and scholarships/grants available. Support available to part-time students. Financial award application deadline: 3/2; financial award applicants required to submit FAFSA. *Faculty research:* Polymer physical chemistry and analysis, polymer synthesis, coatings formulation. *Unit head:* Dr. Ray Fernando, Graduate Coordinator, 805-756-2395, Fax: 805-756-5500, E-mail: rhfernan@calpoly.edu. *Application contact:* Dr. James Maraviglia, Assistant Vice President for Admissions, Recruitment and Financial Aid, 805-756-2311, Fax: 805-756-5400, E-mail: admissions@calpoly.edu.

Carnegie Mellon University, Carnegie Institute of Technology, Department of Chemical Engineering and Department of Chemistry, Program in Colloids, Polymers and Surfaces, Pittsburgh, PA 15213-3891. Offers MS. Part-time and evening/weekend programs available. *Entrance requirements:* For master's, GRE General Test, GRE Subject Test. Additional exam requirements/recommendations for international students: Required—TOEFL. *Faculty research:* Surface phenomena, polymer rheology, solubilization phenomena, colloid transport phenomena, polymer synthesis.

Carnegie Mellon University, Mellon College of Science, Department of Chemistry, Pittsburgh, PA 15213-3891. Offers biotechnology and management (MS); chemistry (PhD), including bioinorganic, bioorganic, organic and materials, biophysics and spectroscopy, computational and theoretical, polymer; colloids, polymers and surfaces (MS). Part-time programs available. Terminal master's awarded for partial completion of doctoral program. *Degree requirements:* For doctorate, thesis/dissertation, departmental qualifying and oral exams, teaching experience. *Entrance requirements:* For master's, GRE General Test; for doctorate, GRE General Test, GRE Subject Test. Additional exam requirements/recommendations for international students: Required—TOEFL. Electronic applications accepted. *Faculty research:* Physical and theoretical chemistry, chemical synthesis, biophysical/bioinorganic chemistry.

Case Western Reserve University, School of Graduate Studies, Case School of Engineering, Department of Macromolecular Science and Engineering, Cleveland, OH 44106. Offers MS, PhD, MD/PhD. Part-time programs available. *Faculty:* 12 full-time (3 women). *Students:* 48 full-time (13 women), 5 part-time (1 woman); includes 1 Black or African American, non-Hispanic/Latino; 1 American Indian or Alaska Native, non-Hispanic/Latino; 3 Asian, non-Hispanic/Latino; 1 Hispanic/Latino, 25 international. In 2010, 2 master's, 9 doctorates awarded. Terminal master's awarded for partial completion of doctoral program. *Degree requirements:* For master's, thesis; for doctorate, thesis/dissertation, qualifying exam, teaching experience. *Entrance requirements:* For master's and doctorate, GRE General Test. Additional exam requirements/recommendations for international students: Required—TOEFL. *Application deadline:* For fall admission, 2/28 priority date for domestic students; for spring admission, 10/1 priority date for domestic students. Applications are processed on a rolling basis. Application fee: $50. *Financial support:* Fellowships with full tuition reimbursements, research assistantships with full and partial tuition reimbursements, teaching assistantships available. Financial award applicants required to submit FAFSA. *Faculty research:* Synthesis and molecular design; processing, modeling and simulation, structure-property relationships. Total annual research expenditures: $5.8 million. *Unit head:* Dr. David Schiraldi, Department Chair, 216-368-4243, Fax: 216-368-4202, E-mail: das44@case.edu. *Application contact:* Theresa Claytor, Student Affairs Coordinator, 216-368-8555, Fax: 216-368-8555, E-mail: theresa.claytor@case.edu.

Cornell University, Graduate School, Graduate Fields of Engineering, Field of Chemical Engineering, Ithaca, NY 14853-0001. Offers advanced materials processing (M Eng, MS, PhD); applied mathematics and computational methods (M Eng, MS, PhD); biochemical engineering (M Eng, MS, PhD); chemical reaction engineering (M Eng, MS, PhD); classical and statistical thermodynamics (M Eng, MS, PhD); fluid dynamics, rheology and biorheology (M Eng, MS, PhD); heat and mass transfer (M Eng, MS, PhD); kinetics and catalysis (M Eng, MS, PhD); polymers (M Eng, MS, PhD); surface science (M Eng, MS, PhD). *Faculty:* 29 full-time (2 women). *Students:* 116 full-time (34 women); includes 1 Black or African American, non-Hispanic/Latino; 17 Asian, non-Hispanic/Latino; 5 Hispanic/Latino, 45 international. Average age 24. 392 applicants, 35% accepted, 70 enrolled. In 2010, 35 master's, 17 doctorates awarded. *Degree requirements:* For master's, thesis (MS); for doctorate, comprehensive exam, thesis/dissertation. *Entrance requirements:* For master's and doctorate, GRE General Test, 2 letters of recommendation. Additional exam requirements/recommendations for international students: Required—TOEFL (minimum score 600 paper-based; 237 computer-based; 77 iBT). *Application deadline:* For fall admission, 1/15 priority date for domestic students. Application fee: $70. Electronic applications accepted. *Expenses:* Tuition: Full-time $29,500. Required fees: $76. Tuition and fees vary according to degree level and program. *Financial support:* In 2010–11, 67 students received support, including 20 fellowships with full tuition reimbursements available, 40 research assistantships with full tuition reimbursements available, 13 teaching assistantships with full tuition reimbursements available; institutionally sponsored loans, scholarships/grants, health care benefits, tuition waivers (full and partial), and unspecified assistantships also available. Financial award applicants required to submit FAFSA. *Faculty research:* Biochemical, biomedical and metabolic engineering; fluid and polymer dynamics; surface science and chemical kinetics; electronics materials; microchemical systems and nanotechnology. *Unit head:* Director of Graduate Studies, 607-255-4550. *Application contact:* Graduate Field Assistant, 607-255-4550, E-mail: dgs@cheme.cornell.edu.

Cornell University, Graduate School, Graduate Fields of Human Ecology, Field of Textiles, Ithaca, NY 14853. Offers apparel design (MA, MPS); fiber science (MS, PhD); polymer science (MS, PhD); textile science (MS, PhD). *Faculty:* 19 full-time (7 women). *Students:* 20 full-time (15 women); includes 1 Black or African American, non-Hispanic/Latino; 1 Asian, non-Hispanic/Latino, 9 international. Average age 28. 41 applicants, 29% accepted, 9 enrolled. In 2010, 5 master's, 3 doctorates awarded. *Degree requirements:* For master's, thesis (MA, MS), project paper (MPS); for doctorate, comprehensive exam, thesis/dissertation. *Entrance requirements:* For master's, GRE General Test, 2 letters of recommendation, portfolio (functional apparel design); for doctorate, GRE General Test, 2 letters of recommendation. Additional exam requirements/recommendations for international students: Required—TOEFL (minimum score 600 paper-based; 250 computer-based; 77 iBT). *Application deadline:* For fall admission, 3/1 for domestic students; for spring admission, 10/1 for domestic students. Application fee: $70. Electronic applications accepted. *Expenses:* Tuition: Full-time $29,500. Required fees: $76. Tuition and fees vary according to degree level and program. *Financial support:* In 2010–11, 19 students received support, including 2 fellowships with full tuition reimbursements available, 7 research assistantships with full tuition reimbursements available, 8 teaching assistantships with full tuition reimbursements available; institutionally sponsored loans, scholarships/grants, health care benefits, tuition waivers (full and partial), and unspecified assistantships also available. Financial award applicants required to submit FAFSA. *Faculty research:* Apparel design, consumption, mass customization, 3-D body scanning. *Unit head:* Director of Graduate Studies, 607-255-3151, Fax: 607-255-1093. *Application contact:* Graduate Field Assistant, 607-255-3151, Fax: 607-255-1093, E-mail: textiles_grad@cornell.edu.

DePaul University, College of Liberal Arts and Sciences, Department of Chemistry, Chicago, IL 60614. Offers biochemistry (MS); chemistry (MS); polymer chemistry and coatings technology (MS). Part-time and evening/weekend programs available. *Degree requirements:* For master's, thesis (for some programs), oral exam (for select programs). *Entrance requirements:* For master's, GRE Subject Test (chemistry), GRE General Test, BS in chemistry or equivalent. Additional exam requirements/recommendations for international students: Required—TOEFL (minimum score 590 paper-based; 243 computer-based). Electronic applications accepted. *Faculty research:* Computational chemistry, organic synthesis, inorganic synthesis, polymer synthesis, biochemistry.

Eastern Michigan University, Graduate School, College of Technology, School of Engineering Technology, Program in Polymers and Coatings Technology, Ypsilanti, MI 48197. Offers polymer technology (MS). Part-time and evening/weekend programs available. Postbaccalaureate distance learning degree programs offered (minimal on-campus study). *Students:* 1 full-time (0 women), 17 part-time (6 women); includes 3 Asian, non-Hispanic/Latino, 6 international. Average age 30. In 2010, 7 master's awarded. *Degree requirements:* For master's, thesis optional. *Entrance requirements:* For master's, GRE General Test, BS in chemistry, minimum GPA of 2.6. Additional exam requirements/recommendations for international students: Required—TOEFL. *Application deadline:* Applications are processed on a rolling basis. Application fee: $35. *Financial support:* Fellowships, research assistantships with full tuition reimbursements, teaching assistantships with full tuition reimbursements, career-related internships or fieldwork, Federal Work-Study, institutionally sponsored loans, scholarships/grants, tuition waivers (partial), and unspecified assistantships available. Support available to part-time students. Financial award applicants required to submit FAFSA. *Unit head:* Dr. Jamil Baghdachi, Program Coordinator, 734-487-3192, Fax: 734-487-8755, E-mail: jamil.baghdachi@emich.edu. *Application contact:* Dr. Jamil Baghdachi, Program Coordinator, 734-487-3192, Fax: 734-487-8755, E-mail: jamil.baghdachi@emich.edu.

Florida State University, The Graduate School, Interdisciplinary Program in Materials Science, Tallahassee, FL 32306. Offers computational materials science and mechanics (MS); functional materials (MS); nanoscale materials, composite materials, and interfaces (MS); polymers and bio-inspired materials (MS). *Faculty:* 38 full-time (5 women). *Students:* 9 full-time (3 women), 4 international. 14 applicants, 71% accepted, 4 enrolled. In 2010, 2 master's awarded. *Degree requirements:* For master's, thesis. *Entrance requirements:* For master's, GRE General Test (minimum score 1100 verbal and quantitative), minimum GPA of 3.0, 3 letters of recommendation. Additional exam requirements/recommendations for international students: Required—TOEFL (minimum score 80 iBT). *Application deadline:* For fall admission, 7/1 for domestic students, 5/1 for international students; for spring admission, 11/1 for domestic students, 9/1 for international students. Applications are processed on a rolling basis. Application fee: $25. Electronic applications accepted. *Expenses:* Tuition, state resident: full-time $8238.24. *Financial support:* In 2010–11, 1 student received support, including 8 research assistantships with full tuition reimbursements available (averaging $22,900 per year), 1 teaching assistantship with full tuition reimbursement available (averaging $23,000 per year); fellowships also available. Financial award application deadline: 1/15. *Faculty research:* Magnetism and magnetic materials, composites, superconductors, polymers, computations, nanotechnology. *Unit head:* Prof. Eric Hellstrom, Director, 850-645-7489, Fax: 850-645-7754, E-mail: hellstrom@asc.magnet.fsu.edu. *Application contact:* Todd Kramer, Admissions Coordinator, 850-410-6425, Fax: 850-410-6486, E-mail: krameto@eng.fsu.edu.

Georgia Institute of Technology, Graduate Studies and Research, College of Engineering, Multidisciplinary Program in Polymers, Atlanta, GA 30332-0001. Offers MS Poly. *Degree requirements:* For master's, thesis. *Entrance requirements:* For master's, minimum GPA of 2.7. Additional exam requirements/recommendations for international students: Required—TOEFL.

Georgia Institute of Technology, Graduate Studies and Research, College of Engineering, School of Polymer, Textile, and Fiber Engineering, Atlanta, GA 30332-0001. Offers polymer, textile and fiber engineering (MS, PhD); polymers (MS Poly). *Degree requirements:* For master's, thesis (for some programs); for doctorate, comprehensive exam, thesis/dissertation. *Entrance requirements:* For master's, GRE, minimum GPA of 2.7; for doctorate, GRE, minimum GPA of 3.0. Additional exam requirements/recommendations for international students: Required—TOEFL (minimum score 550 paper-based; 213 computer-based). Electronic applications accepted. *Faculty research:* Energy conservation, environmental control, engineered fibrous structures, polymer synthesis and degradation, high performance organic-carbon-ceramic fibers.

Lehigh University, College of Arts and Sciences, Department of Physics, Bethlehem, PA 18015. Offers photonics (MS); physics (MS, PhD); polymer science (MS, PhD). Part-time programs available. *Faculty:* 17 full-time (1 woman). *Students:* 42 full-time (14 women), 2 part-time (0 women); includes 1 minority (Black or African American, non-Hispanic/Latino), 17 international. Average age 26. 73 applicants, 15% accepted, 8 enrolled. In 2010, 19 master's, 5 doctorates awarded. *Degree requirements:* For doctorate, comprehensive exam, thesis/dissertation. *Entrance requirements:* Additional exam requirements/recommendations for international students: Required—TOEFL (minimum score 213 computer-based; 85 iBT). *Application deadline:* For fall admission, 2/15 priority date for domestic and international students. Applications are processed on a rolling basis. Application fee: $75. Electronic applications accepted. *Financial support:* In 2010–11, 44 students received support, including 5 fellowships with full tuition reimbursements available (averaging $23,000 per year), 19 research assistantships with full tuition reimbursements available (averaging $22,180 per year), 20 teaching assistantships with full tuition reimbursements available (averaging $22,180 per year); career-related

Polymer Science and Engineering

Lehigh University (continued)

internships or fieldwork, Federal Work-Study, institutionally sponsored loans, scholarships/grants, tuition waivers (full and partial), and unspecified assistantships also available. Support available to part-time students. Financial award application deadline: 1/15. *Faculty research:* Condensed matter physics; atomic, molecular and optical physics; plasma physics; nonlinear optics and photonics; astronomy and astrophysics. Total annual research expenditures: $3.5 million. *Unit head:* Dr. Volkmar Dierolf, Chair, 610-758-3915, Fax: 610-758-5730, E-mail: vod2@lehigh.edu. *Application contact:* Dr. Ivan Biaggio, Graduate Admissions Officer, 610-758-4916, Fax: 610-758-5730, E-mail: ivb2@lehigh.edu.

Lehigh University, P.C. Rossin College of Engineering and Applied Science and College of Arts and Sciences, Center for Polymer Science and Engineering, Bethlehem, PA 18015. Offers M Eng, MS, PhD. Part-time and evening/weekend programs available. Postbaccalaureate distance learning degree programs offered (no on-campus study). *Students:* 5 full-time (1 woman), 8 part-time (2 women); includes 1 minority (Hispanic/Latino), 2 international. Average age 33. In 2010, 3 master's, 1 doctorate awarded. Terminal master's awarded for partial completion of doctoral program. *Degree requirements:* For master's, thesis (for some programs); for doctorate, thesis/dissertation. *Entrance requirements:* For master's and doctorate, GRE General Test. Additional exam requirements/recommendations for international students: Required—TOEFL (minimum score 487 paper-based; 216 computer-based; 85 iBT). *Application deadline:* For fall admission, 7/15 for domestic students, 1/15 for international students; for spring admission, 12/1 for domestic and international students. Applications are processed on a rolling basis. Application fee: $75. Electronic applications accepted. *Financial support:* In 2010–11, 3 students received support, including 5 research assistantships (averaging $24,200 per year), teaching assistantships (averaging $24,200 per year). Financial award application deadline: 1/15. *Faculty research:* Polymer colloids, polymer coatings, blends and composites, polymer interfaces, emulsion polymer. *Unit head:* Dr. Raymond A. Pearson, Director, 610-758-3857, Fax: 610-758-3526, E-mail: rp02@lehigh.edu. *Application contact:* James E. Roberts, Chair, Polymer Education Committee, 610-758-4841, Fax: 610-758-6536, E-mail: jer1@lehigh.edu.

Lehigh University, P.C. Rossin College of Engineering and Applied Science, Department of Materials Science and Engineering, Bethlehem, PA 18015. Offers materials science and engineering (M Eng, MS, PhD); photonics (MS); polymer science/engineering (M Eng, MS, PhD); MBA/E. Part-time programs available. *Faculty:* 13 full-time (3 women), 1 part-time/adjunct (0 women). *Students:* 27 full-time (4 women), 4 part-time (1 woman); includes 1 minority (Asian, non-Hispanic/Latino), 14 international. Average age 26. 411 applicants, 2% accepted, 7 enrolled. In 2010, 8 master's, 2 doctorates awarded. *Degree requirements:* For master's, thesis; for doctorate, comprehensive exam, thesis/dissertation. *Entrance requirements:* For master's and doctorate, GRE General Test, minimum GPA of 3.0. Additional exam requirements/recommendations for international students: Required—TOEFL (minimum score 487 paper-based; 216 computer-based; 85 iBT). *Application deadline:* For fall admission, 1/15 priority date for domestic students, 1/15 for international students; for spring admission, 12/1 priority date for domestic students, 12/1 for international students. Applications are processed on a rolling basis. Application fee: $75. Electronic applications accepted. *Financial support:* In 2010–11, 7 fellowships with full and partial tuition reimbursements (averaging $22,400 per year), 21 research assistantships with full tuition reimbursements (averaging $22,449 per year), 5 teaching assistantships with partial tuition reimbursements (averaging $17,512 per year) were awarded; career-related internships or fieldwork, Federal Work-Study, institutionally sponsored loans, scholarships/grants, and unspecified assistantships also available. Support available to part-time students. Financial award application deadline: 1/15. *Faculty research:* Metals, ceramics, crystals, polymers, fatigue crack propagation. Total annual research expenditures: $4.3 million. *Unit head:* Dr. Helen Chan, Chairperson, 610-758-5554, Fax: 610-758-4244, E-mail: hmc0@lehigh.edu. *Application contact:* Anne Marie Lobley, Graduate Administrative Coordinator, 610-758-4222, Fax: 610-758-4244, E-mail: amme@lehigh.edu.

Lehigh University, P.C. Rossin College of Engineering and Applied Science, Department of Mechanical Engineering and Mechanics, Bethlehem, PA 18015. Offers computational engineering and mechanics (MS, PhD); mechanical engineering (M Eng, MS, PhD, MBA/E); polymer science/engineering (M Eng, MS, PhD, MBA/E); MBA/E. Part-time and evening/weekend programs available. Postbaccalaureate distance learning degree programs offered. *Faculty:* 24 full-time (0 women). *Students:* 106 full-time (12 women), 34 part-time (2 women); includes 7 minority (3 Black or African American, non-Hispanic/Latino; 3 Asian, non-Hispanic/Latino; 1 Hispanic/Latino), 71 international. Average age 26. 408 applicants, 29% accepted, 59 enrolled. In 2010, 23 master's, 7 doctorates awarded. Terminal master's awarded for partial completion of doctoral program. *Degree requirements:* For master's, thesis; for doctorate, thesis/dissertation, general exam. *Entrance requirements:* Additional exam requirements/recommendations for international students: Required—TOEFL (minimum score 550 paper-based; 213 computer-based; 79 iBT). *Application deadline:* For fall admission, 7/15 for domestic and international students; for spring admission, 12/1 for domestic and international students. Applications are processed on a rolling basis. Application fee: $75. Electronic applications accepted. *Financial support:* In 2010–11, 74 students received support, including 9 fellowships with full and partial tuition reimbursements available (averaging $23,280 per year), 23 research assistantships with full and partial tuition reimbursements available (averaging $20,700 per year), 24 teaching assistantships with full and partial tuition reimbursements available (averaging $24,480 per year); unspecified assistantships and Dean's doctoral assistantships also available. Financial award application deadline: 1/15. *Faculty research:* Thermofluids, dynamic systems, CAD/CAM, computational mechanics, solid mechanics. Total annual research expenditures: $3.3 million. *Unit head:* Dr. D. Gary Harlow, Chairman, 610-758-4102, Fax: 610-758-6224, E-mail: dgh0@lehigh.edu. *Application contact:* Jo Ann M. Casciano, Graduate Coordinator, 610-758-4107, Fax: 610-758-6224, E-mail: jmc4@lehigh.edu.

Massachusetts Institute of Technology, School of Engineering, Department of Materials Science and Engineering, Cambridge, MA 02139. Offers archaeological materials (PhD, Sc D); bio- and polymeric materials (PhD, Sc D); electronic, photonic and magnetic materials (PhD, Sc D); emerging, fundamental and computational studies in materials science (Sc D); emerging, fundamental, and computational studies in materials science (PhD); materials engineering (Mat E); materials science and engineering (M Eng, SM, PhD, Sc D); metallurgical engineering (Met E); structural and environmental materials (PhD, Sc D); SM/MBA. *Faculty:* 34 full-time (8 women). *Students:* 196 full-time (52 women); includes 32 minority (2 Black or African American, non-Hispanic/Latino; 20 Asian, non-Hispanic/Latino; 7 Hispanic/Latino; 3 Two or more races, non-Hispanic/Latino), 113 international. Average age 26. 507 applicants, 15% accepted, 41 enrolled. In 2010, 22 master's, 38 doctorates awarded. Terminal master's awarded for partial completion of doctoral program. *Degree requirements:* For master's and other advanced degree, thesis; for doctorate, comprehensive exam, thesis/dissertation. *Entrance requirements:* For master's, doctorate, and other advanced degree, GRE General Test. Additional exam requirements/recommendations for international students: Required—IELTS (minimum score 7). *Application deadline:* For fall admission, 12/15 for domestic and international students. Application fee: $75. Electronic applications accepted. *Expenses:* Tuition: Full-time $38,940; part-time $605 per unit. Required fees: $272. *Financial support:* In 2010–11, 183 students received support, including 52 fellowships with tuition reimbursements available (averaging $32,695 per year), 124 research assistantships with tuition reimbursements available (averaging $27,409 per year), 8 teaching assistantships with tuition reimbursements available (averaging $31,861 per year); career-related internships or fieldwork, Federal Work-Study, institutionally sponsored loans, scholarships/grants, health care benefits, and unspecified assistantships also available. *Faculty research:* Thermodynamics and kinetics of phase transformations; structure of all materials classes: metals, ceramics, semiconductors, polymers, biomaterials; influence of processing on materials structure; structure ??? property relationships (electrical, magnetic, optical, mechanical); materials in extreme environments. Total annual research expenditures: $28.1 million. *Unit head:* Prof. Edwin L. Thomas, Department Head, 617-253-3300, Fax: 617-252-1775. *Application contact:* Angelita Mireles, Graduate Admissions, 617-253-3302, E-mail: dmse-admissions@mit.edu.

North Carolina State University, Graduate School, College of Textiles, Program in Fiber and Polymer Science, Raleigh, NC 27695. Offers PhD. *Degree requirements:* For doctorate, one foreign language, thesis/dissertation, cumulative exams. *Entrance requirements:* For doctorate, GRE. Electronic applications accepted. *Faculty research:* Polymer science, fiber mechanics, medical textiles, nanotechnology.

North Dakota State University, College of Graduate and Interdisciplinary Studies, College of Science and Mathematics, Department of Coatings and Polymeric Materials, Fargo, ND 58108. Offers MS, PhD. Part-time programs available. *Students:* 18 full-time (5 women), 11 part-time (2 women); includes 1 Asian, non-Hispanic/Latino, 16 international. 23 applicants, 22% accepted, 4 enrolled. In 2010, 3 doctorates awarded. Terminal master's awarded for partial completion of doctoral program. *Degree requirements:* For master's, thesis, cumulative exams; for doctorate, comprehensive exam, thesis/dissertation, cumulative exams. *Entrance requirements:* For master's and doctorate, BS in chemistry or chemical engineering, minimum GPA of 3.0. Additional exam requirements/recommendations for international students: Required—TOEFL (minimum score 550 paper-based; 213 computer-based). *Application deadline:* Applications are processed on a rolling basis. Application fee: $45 ($60 for international students). Electronic applications accepted. *Financial support:* Fellowships, research assistantships with full tuition reimbursements, teaching assistantships with full tuition reimbursements, Federal Work-Study, institutionally sponsored loans, scholarships/grants, health care benefits, and tuition waivers (full) available. Support available to part-time students. Financial award application deadline: 3/15. *Faculty research:* Nanomaterials, combinatorial materials science. Total annual research expenditures: $1.2 million. *Unit head:* Dr. Stuart Croll, Chair, 701-231-7633, Fax: 701-231-8439. *Application contact:* Dr. Dean C. Webster, Assistant Professor, 701-231-8709, Fax: 701-231-8439, E-mail: dean.webster@ndsu.edu.

Polytechnic Institute of NYU, Department of Chemical and Biological Engineering, Major in Polymer Science and Engineering, Brooklyn, NY 11201-2990. Offers MS. *Degree requirements:* For master's, comprehensive exam (for some programs), thesis (for some programs). *Entrance requirements:* Additional exam requirements/recommendations for international students: Required—TOEFL (minimum score 550 paper-based; 213 computer-based; 80 iBT); Recommended—IELTS (minimum score 6.5). *Application deadline:* For fall admission, 7/31 priority date for domestic students, 4/30 priority date for international students; for spring admission, 12/31 priority date for domestic students, 10/30 priority date for international students. Applications are processed on a rolling basis. Application fee: $75. Electronic applications accepted. *Expenses:* Tuition: Full-time $21,492; part-time $1194 per credit. Required fees: $385 per semester. Tuition and fees vary according to course load. *Unit head:* Dr. Walter Zurawsky, Department Head, 718-260-3600. *Application contact:* JeanCarlo Bonilla, Dir. Graduate Enrollment Management, 718-260-3182, Fax: 718-260-3624.

Rensselaer Polytechnic Institute, Graduate School, School of Engineering, Program in Materials Science and Engineering, Troy, NY 12180. Offers ceramics and glass science (M Eng, MS, PhD); composites (M Eng, MS, PhD); electronic materials (M Eng, MS, PhD); metallurgy (M Eng, MS, PhD); polymers (M Eng, MS, PhD). Part-time programs available. *Faculty:* 16 full-time (2 women). *Students:* 57 full-time (13 women), 6 part-time (1 woman), 37 international. Average age 24. 304 applicants, 15% accepted, 16 enrolled. In 2010, 5 master's, 6 doctorates awarded. Terminal master's awarded for partial completion of doctoral program. *Degree requirements:* For master's, thesis; for doctorate, comprehensive exam, thesis/dissertation. *Entrance requirements:* For master's and doctorate, GRE. Additional exam requirements/recommendations for international students: Required—TOEFL (minimum score 570 paper-based; 230 computer-based; 100 iBT). *Application deadline:* For fall admission, 1/15 priority date for domestic and international students; for spring admission, 8/31 priority date for domestic and international students. Applications are processed on a rolling basis. Application fee: $75. Electronic applications accepted. *Expenses:* Tuition: Full-time $39,600; part-time $1650 per credit. Required fees: $1896. *Financial support:* In 2010–11, 56 students received support, including 2 fellowships with full tuition reimbursements available (averaging $26,250 per year), 41 research assistantships with full tuition reimbursements available (averaging $26,250 per year), 13 teaching assistantships with full tuition reimbursements available (averaging $17,500 per year); career-related internships or fieldwork, institutionally sponsored loans, and unspecified assistantships also available. Financial award application deadline: 2/1. *Faculty research:* Materials processing, nanostructural materials, materials for microelectronics, composite materials, computational materials. Total annual research expenditures: $3.6 million. *Unit head:* Dr. Robert Hull, Department Head, 518-276-6373, Fax: 518-276-8554, E-mail: hullr2@rpi.edu. *Application contact:* Dr. Pawel Keblinski, Admissions Coordinator, 518-276-6858, Fax: 518-276-8554, E-mail: keblip@rpi.edu.

Stevens Institute of Technology, Graduate School, Charles V. Schaefer Jr. School of Engineering, Department of Chemistry, Chemical Biology and Biomedical Engineering, Hoboken, NJ 07030. Offers analytical chemistry (PhD, Certificate); bioinformatics (PhD, Certificate); biomedical chemistry (Certificate); biomedical engineering (M Eng, Certificate); chemical biology (MS, PhD, Certificate); chemical physiology (Certificate); chemistry (MS, PhD); organic chemistry (PhD); physical chemistry (PhD); polymer chemistry (PhD, Certificate). Part-time and evening/weekend programs available. Postbaccalaureate distance learning degree programs offered (no on-campus study). *Students:* 66 full-time (35 women), 25 part-time (7 women); includes 2 Black or African American, non-Hispanic/Latino; 14 Asian, non-Hispanic/Latino; 8 Hispanic/Latino, 31 international. Average age 26. 109 applicants, 68% accepted. Terminal master's awarded for partial completion of doctoral program. *Degree requirements:* For master's, thesis or alternative; for doctorate, one foreign language, thesis/dissertation; for Certificate, project or thesis. *Entrance requirements:* Additional exam requirements/recommendations for international students: Required—TOEFL. *Application deadline:* Applications are processed on a rolling basis. Application fee: $50. Electronic applications accepted. *Financial support:* Fellowships, research assistantships, teaching assistantships available. Financial award application deadline: 4/1. *Faculty research:* Biochemical reaction engineering, polymerization engineering, reactor design, biochemical process control and synthesis. *Unit head:* Philip Leopold, Director, 201-216-8957, Fax: 201-216-8196, E-mail: pleopold@stevens.edu. *Application contact:* Graduate Admissions, 800-496-4935, Fax: 201-216-8044, E-mail: gradadmissions@stevens.edu.

The University of Akron, Graduate School, College of Engineering, Program in Engineering (Polymer Specialization), Akron, OH 44325. Offers MS. *Students:* 1 applicant, 100% accepted, 0 enrolled. *Degree requirements:* For master's, thesis. *Entrance requirements:* For master's, GRE, minimum GPA of 2.75, three letters of recommendation, statement of purpose, resume. Additional exam requirements/recommendations for international students: Required—TOEFL (minimum score 550 paper-based; 213 computer-based; 79 iBT). *Application deadline:* Applications are processed on a rolling basis. Application fee: $30 ($40 for international students). Electronic applications accepted. *Expenses:* Tuition, state resident: full-time $6800; part-time $378 per credit hour. Tuition, nonresident: full-time $11,644; part-time $647 per credit hour. Required fees: $1265. One-time fee: $30 full-time. *Unit head:* Dr. Subramaniya Hariharan, Coordinator, 330-972-6580, E-mail: hari@uakron.edu. *Application contact:* Director of Graduate Studies.

The University of Akron, Graduate School, College of Polymer Science and Polymer Engineering, Department of Polymer Engineering, Akron, OH 44325. Offers MS, PhD. Part-time and evening/weekend programs available. *Faculty:* 13 full-time (0 women), 2 part-time/adjunct (0 women). *Students:* 72 full-time (21 women), 5 part-time (0 women); includes 2 Black or African American, non-Hispanic/Latino; 1 Hispanic/Latino, 59 international. Average age 27. 100 applicants, 29% accepted, 17 enrolled. In 2010, 3 master's, 10 doctorates awarded. *Degree requirements:* For master's, thesis, basic engineering exam; for doctorate, one foreign language, thesis/dissertation, candidacy exam. *Entrance requirements:* For master's and doctorate, GRE, bachelor's degree in engineering or physical science, minimum GPA of 2.75 (3.0 in last two years), three letters of recommendation. Additional exam requirements/recommendations for international students: Required—TOEFL (minimum score 550 paper-based; 213 computer-based; 79 iBT). *Application deadline:* For fall admission, 1/15 priority date for domestic and international students. Application fee: $30 ($40 for international students).

Electronic applications accepted. *Expenses:* Tuition, state resident: full-time $6800; part-time $378 per credit hour. Tuition, nonresident: full-time $11,644; part-time $647 per credit hour. Required fees: $1265. One-time fee: $30 full-time. *Financial support:* In 2010–11, 68 research assistantships with full tuition reimbursements were awarded; unspecified assistantships also available. *Faculty research:* Processing and properties of multi-functional polymeric materials, nanomaterials and nanocomposites, micro and nano-scale materials processing, novel self-assembled polymeric materials for energy applications, coating materials and coating technology. Total annual research expenditures: $4.8 million. *Unit head:* Dr. Sadhan Jana, Chair, 330-972-8293, E-mail: janas@uakron.edu. *Application contact:* Sarah Thorley, Coordinator of Academic Program, 330-972-8845, E-mail: sarah3@uakron.edu.

The University of Akron, Graduate School, College of Polymer Science and Polymer Engineering, Department of Polymer Science, Akron, OH 44325. Offers MS, PhD. Part-time and evening/weekend programs available. *Faculty:* 14 full-time (2 women), 2 part-time/adjunct (0 women). *Students:* 87 full-time (20 women), 23 part-time (10 women); includes 2 Black or African American, non-Hispanic/Latino; 3 Asian, non-Hispanic/Latino, 78 international. Average age 28. 160 applicants, 23% accepted, 33 enrolled. In 2010, 11 doctorates awarded. Terminal master's awarded for partial completion of doctoral program. *Degree requirements:* For master's, thesis; for doctorate, one foreign language, thesis/dissertation, cumulative exam, seminars. *Entrance requirements:* For master's and doctorate, GRE, minimum GPA of 3.0, three letters of recommendation, statement of purpose. Additional exam requirements/recommendations for international students: Required—TOEFL (minimum score 550 paper-based; 213 computer-based; 79 iBT). *Application deadline:* For fall admission, 12/1 priority date for domestic students, 12/15 priority date for international students. Application fee: $30 ($40 for international students). Electronic applications accepted. *Expenses:* Tuition, state resident: full-time $6800; part-time $378 per credit hour. Tuition, nonresident: full-time $11,644; part-time $647 per credit hour. Required fees: $1265. One-time fee: $30 full-time. *Financial support:* In 2010–11, 1 fellowship with full tuition reimbursement, 93 research assistantships with full tuition reimbursements were awarded; scholarships/grants also available. *Faculty research:* Synthesis of polymers, structure of polymers, physical properties of polymers, engineering and technological properties of polymers, elastomers. Total annual research expenditures: $4.6 million. *Unit head:* Dr. Ali Dhinojwala, Chair, 330-972-6246, E-mail: ali4@uakron.edu. *Application contact:* Melissa Bowman, Coordinator, Academic Programs, 330-972-7532, E-mail: mb8@uakron.edu.

University of Cincinnati, Graduate School, College of Engineering, Department of Chemical and Materials Engineering, Program in Materials Science and Metallurgical Engineering, Cincinnati, OH 45221. Offers ceramic science and engineering (MS, PhD); materials science and engineering (MS, PhD); metallurgical engineering (MS, PhD); polymer science and engineering (MS, PhD). Evening/weekend programs available. *Degree requirements:* For master's, thesis optional; for doctorate, one foreign language, comprehensive exam, thesis/dissertation, oral English proficiency exam. *Entrance requirements:* For master's and doctorate, GRE General Test, BS in related field, minimum undergraduate GPA of 3.0. Additional exam requirements/recommendations for international students: Required—TOEFL (minimum score 550 paper-based; 213 computer-based). Electronic applications accepted. *Expenses:* Contact institution.

University of Connecticut, Institute of Materials Science, Polymer Program, Storrs, CT 06269-3136. Offers polymer science and engineering (MS, PhD). Part-time programs available. Terminal master's awarded for partial completion of doctoral program. *Degree requirements:* For master's, thesis (for some programs); for doctorate, one foreign language, comprehensive exam, thesis/dissertation. *Entrance requirements:* For master's and doctorate, GRE General Test. Additional exam requirements/recommendations for international students: Required—TOEFL (minimum score 550 paper-based; 213 computer-based; 80 iBT), IELTS (minimum score 6.5). Electronic applications accepted. *Faculty research:* Nanomaterials and nanotechnology, biomaterials and sensors, synthesis, electronic/photonic materials, solar cells and fuel cells, structure and function of proteins, biodegradable polymers, molecular simulations, drug targeting and delivery.

The University of Manchester, School of Materials, Manchester, United Kingdom. Offers advanced aerospace materials engineering (M Sc); advanced metallic systems (PhD); biomedical materials (M Phil, M Sc, PhD); ceramics and glass (M Phil, M Sc, PhD); composite materials (M Sc, PhD); corrosion and protection (M Phil, M Sc, PhD); materials (M Phil, PhD); metallic materials (M Phil, M Sc, PhD); nanostructural materials (M Phil, M Sc, PhD); paper science (M Phil, M Sc, PhD); polymer science and engineering (M Phil, M Sc, PhD); technical textiles (M Sc); textile design, fashion and management (M Phil, M Sc, PhD); textile science and technology (M Phil, M Sc, PhD); textiles (M Phil, PhD); textiles and fashion (M Ent).

University of Massachusetts Amherst, Graduate School, College of Natural Sciences, Department of Polymer Science and Engineering, Amherst, MA 01003. Offers MS, PhD. *Faculty:* 18 full-time (1 woman). *Students:* 111 full-time (41 women), 5 part-time (1 woman); includes 5 minority (4 Asian, non-Hispanic/Latino; 1 Two or more races, non-Hispanic/Latino), 58 international. Average age 26. 193 applicants, 23% accepted, 27 enrolled. In 2010, 7 master's, 9 doctorates awarded. Terminal master's awarded for partial completion of doctoral program. *Degree requirements:* For master's, thesis or alternative; for doctorate, comprehensive exam, thesis/dissertation. *Entrance requirements:* For master's and doctorate, GRE General Test. Additional exam requirements/recommendations for international students: Required—TOEFL (minimum score 550 paper-based; 213 computer-based; 80 iBT); IELTS (minimum score 6.5). *Application deadline:* For fall admission, 2/1 for domestic and international students. Applications are processed on a rolling basis. Application fee: $50 ($65 for international students). Electronic applications accepted. *Expenses:* Tuition, state resident: full-time $2640. Required fees: $8282. One-time fee: $357 full-time. *Financial support:* In 2010–11, 6 fellowships with full tuition reimbursements (averaging $16,926 per year), 110 research assistantships with full tuition reimbursements (averaging $19,894 per year), 19 teaching assistantships with full tuition reimbursements (averaging $1,657 per year) were awarded; career-related internships or fieldwork, Federal Work-Study, scholarships/grants, traineeships, health care benefits, tuition waivers (full), and unspecified assistantships also available. Support available to part-time students. Financial award application deadline: 2/1; financial award applicants required to submit FAFSA. *Unit head:* Dr. Alfred J. Crosby, Graduate Program Director, 413-577-9120, Fax: 413-545-0082. *Application contact:* Jean M. Ames, Supervisor of Admissions, 413-545-0722, Fax: 413-577-0010, E-mail: gradadm@grad.umass.edu.

University of Massachusetts Lowell, College of Arts and Sciences, Department of Chemistry, Program in Polymer Science, Lowell, MA 01854-2881. Offers MS. *Degree requirements:* For master's, thesis. *Entrance requirements:* For master's, GRE General Test. Electronic applications accepted.

University of Massachusetts Lowell, James B. Francis College of Engineering, Department of Plastics Engineering, Lowell, MA 01854-2881. Offers elastomers (Graduate Certificate); medical plastics design and manufacturing (Graduate Certificate); plastics design (Graduate Certificate); plastics engineering (MS Eng, D Eng, PhD), including coatings and adhesives (MS Eng), plastics materials (MS Eng), plastics processing (MS Eng), product design (MS Eng); plastics engineering fundamentals (Graduate Certificate); plastics materials (Graduate Certificate); plastics processing (Graduate Certificate); polymer science/plastics engineering (PhD). Part-time programs available. Terminal master's awarded for partial completion of doctoral program. *Degree requirements:* For master's, thesis optional; for doctorate, comprehensive exam, thesis/dissertation. *Entrance requirements:* For master's and doctorate, GRE General Test. Additional exam requirements/recommendations for international students: Required—TOEFL.

University of Missouri–Kansas City, College of Arts and Sciences, Department of Chemistry, Kansas City, MO 64110-2499. Offers analytical chemistry (MS, PhD); inorganic chemistry (MS, PhD); organic chemistry (MS, PhD); physical chemistry (MS, PhD); polymer chemistry (MS, PhD). PhD (interdisciplinary) offered through the School of Graduate Studies. Part-time and evening/weekend programs available. *Faculty:* 17 full-time (3 women). *Students:* 5 part-time (2 women); includes 1 minority (Black or African American, non-Hispanic/Latino). Average age 37. 19 applicants, 37% accepted, 1 enrolled. In 2010, 4 master's awarded. *Degree requirements:* For master's, thesis (for some programs); for doctorate, thesis/dissertation. *Entrance requirements:* For master's, equivalent of American Chemical Society approved bachelor's degree in chemistry; for doctorate, GRE General Test, equivalent of American Chemical Society approved bachelor's degree in chemistry. Additional exam requirements/recommendations for international students: Required—TOEFL (minimum score 550 paper-based; 213 computer-based; 80 iBT), TWE. *Application deadline:* For fall admission, 4/15 for domestic and international students; for spring admission, 10/15 for domestic and international students. Applications are processed on a rolling basis. Application fee: $45 ($50 for international students). Electronic applications accepted. *Expenses:* Tuition, state resident: full-time $5522.40; part-time $306.80 per credit hour. Tuition, nonresident: full-time $7128; part-time $792 per credit hour. Required fees: $261.15 per term. *Financial support:* In 2010–11, 7 research assistantships with partial tuition reimbursements (averaging $18,311 per year), 16 teaching assistantships with partial tuition reimbursements (averaging $16,906 per year) were awarded; Federal Work-Study, institutionally sponsored loans, and scholarships/grants also available. Support available to part-time students. Financial award application deadline: 3/1; financial award applicants required to submit FAFSA. *Faculty research:* Molecular spectroscopy, characterization and synthesis of materials and compounds, computational chemistry, natural products, drug delivery systems and anti-tumor agents. Total annual research expenditures: $729,815. *Unit head:* Dr. Kathleen V. Kilway, Chair, 816-235-2289, Fax: 816-235-5502. *Application contact:* Graduate Recruiting Committee, 816-235-2272, Fax: 816-235-5502, E-mail: umkc-chemdept@umkc.edu.

University of Southern Mississippi, Graduate School, College of Science and Technology, School of Polymers and High Performance Materials, Hattiesburg, MS 39406-0001. Offers polymer science (MS); polymer science and engineering (MS, PhD), including polymer science and engineering (PhD), sports and high performance materials. *Faculty:* 14 full-time (1 woman), 1 part-time/adjunct (0 women). *Students:* 70 full-time (20 women), 4 part-time (2 women); includes 2 Black or African American, non-Hispanic/Latino; 1 American Indian or Alaska Native, non-Hispanic/Latino; 2 Asian, non-Hispanic/Latino, 20 international. Average age 28. 86 applicants, 23% accepted, 17 enrolled. In 2010, 2 master's, 15 doctorates awarded. Terminal master's awarded for partial completion of doctoral program. *Degree requirements:* For master's, comprehensive exam, thesis; for doctorate, comprehensive exam, thesis/dissertation, original proposal. *Entrance requirements:* For master's, GRE General Test, minimum GPA of 2.75; for doctorate, GRE General Test, minimum GPA of 3.5. Additional exam requirements/recommendations for international students: Required—TOEFL, IELTS. *Application deadline:* For fall admission, 3/1 priority date for domestic students, 3/1 for international students. Applications are processed on a rolling basis. Application fee: $50. Electronic applications accepted. *Financial support:* In 2010–11, 60 research assistantships with full tuition reimbursements (averaging $20,000 per year), 15 teaching assistantships with full tuition reimbursements (averaging $10,000 per year) were awarded; fellowships, Federal Work-Study, scholarships/grants, health care benefits, and unspecified assistantships also available. Financial award application deadline: 3/15; financial award applicants required to submit FAFSA. *Faculty research:* Water-soluble polymers; polymer composites; coatings; solid-state, laser-initiated polymerization. *Unit head:* Dr. Robert Lochhead, Chair, 601-266-4868, Fax: 601-266-6178. *Application contact:* Dr. Brett Calhoun, Director, Graduate Studies, 601-266-4868.

University of South Florida, Graduate School, College of Arts and Sciences, Department of Chemistry, Tampa, FL 33620-9951. Offers analytical chemistry (MS, PhD); biochemistry (MS, PhD); computational chemistry (MS, PhD); environmental chemistry (MS, PhD); inorganic chemistry (MS, PhD); organic chemistry (MS); physical chemistry (MS, PhD); polymer chemistry (PhD). Part-time programs available. *Faculty:* 15 full-time (1 woman). *Students:* 120 full-time (42 women), 9 part-time (2 women); includes 7 Black or African American, non-Hispanic/Latino; 8 Asian, non-Hispanic/Latino; 8 Hispanic/Latino, 62 international. Average age 29. 1,118 applicants, 4% accepted, 20 enrolled. In 2010, 4 master's, 14 doctorates awarded. Terminal master's awarded for partial completion of doctoral program. *Degree requirements:* For master's, comprehensive exam, thesis (for some programs); for doctorate, 2 foreign languages, comprehensive exam, thesis/dissertation. *Entrance requirements:* For master's, GRE General Test or GMAT, minimum GPA of 3.0. Additional exam requirements/recommendations for international students: Required—TOEFL (minimum score 550 paper-based; 213 computer-based). *Application deadline:* For fall admission, 2/15 priority date for domestic students, 1/2 priority date for international students; for spring admission, 10/1 priority date for domestic students, 6/1 priority date for international students. Applications are processed on a rolling basis. Application fee: $30. Electronic applications accepted. *Financial support:* In 2010–11, 39 research assistantships (averaging $14,359 per year), 99 teaching assistantships with tuition reimbursements (averaging $15,094 per year) were awarded; unspecified assistantships also available. Financial award application deadline: 6/30. *Faculty research:* Synthesis, bio-organic chemistry, bioinorganic chemistry, environmental chemistry, NMR. Total annual research expenditures: $3.9 million. *Unit head:* Dr. Randy Larsen, Chairperson, 813-974-4129, Fax: 813-974-3203, E-mail: rlarsen@cas.usf.edu. *Application contact:* Patricia Muisener, Director, 813-974-1730, Fax: 813-974-3203, E-mail: muisener@cas.usf.edu.

The University of Tennessee, Graduate School, College of Engineering, Department of Materials Science and Engineering, Program in Polymer Engineering, Knoxville, TN 37996. Offers MS, PhD. *Faculty:* 5 full-time (1 woman). *Students:* 8 full-time (1 woman), 1 part-time (0 women); includes 2 Black or African American, non-Hispanic/Latino, 3 international. Average age 22. 47 applicants, 4% accepted, 2 enrolled. In 2010, 5 master's, 4 doctorates awarded. *Degree requirements:* For master's, thesis or alternative; for doctorate, comprehensive exam, thesis/dissertation. *Entrance requirements:* For master's, GRE General Test, Minimum GPA of 2.7 (US degree holders); 3.0 (International degree holders); 3-References; for doctorate, GRE General Test, Minimum GPA of 3.0 (previous graduate course work); 3-References. Additional exam requirements/recommendations for international students: Required—TOEFL (minimum score 550 paper-based; 213 computer-based). *Application deadline:* For fall admission, 2/1 priority date for domestic and international students; for spring admission, 6/15 for domestic and international students. Applications are processed on a rolling basis. Application fee: $35. Electronic applications accepted. *Expenses:* Tuition, state resident: full-time $7440; part-time $414 per credit hour. Tuition, nonresident: full-time $22,478; part-time $1250 per credit hour. Required fees: $922; $43 per credit hour. Tuition and fees vary according to program. *Financial support:* In 2010–11, 7 students received support, including 1 fellowship with full tuition reimbursement available (averaging $9,996 per year), 8 research assistantships with full tuition reimbursements available (averaging $19,272 per year), 1 teaching assistantship with full tuition reimbursement available (averaging $19,752 per year); career-related internships or fieldwork, Federal Work-Study, institutionally sponsored loans, health care benefits, and unspecified assistantships also available. Financial award application deadline: 2/1; financial award applicants required to submit FAFSA. *Faculty research:* Polymer chemistry, processing, and characterization. *Unit head:* Dr. George Pharr, Head, 865-974-5336, Fax: 865-974-4115, E-mail: pharr@utk.edu. *Application contact:* Dr. Roberto S. Benson, Associate Head, 865-974-5347, Fax: 865-974-4115, E-mail: rbenson1@utk.edu.

University of Wisconsin–Madison, Graduate School, College of Engineering, Department of Mechanical Engineering, Madison, WI 53706-1380. Offers energy systems (ME); engine systems (ME); mechanical engineering (MS, PhD); polymers (ME). Part-time programs available. Postbaccalaureate distance learning degree programs offered (no on-campus study). *Faculty:* 33 full-time (3 women), 1 part-time/adjunct (0 women). *Students:* 181 full-time (17 women), 54 part-time (6 women); includes 3 Black or African American, non-Hispanic/Latino; 9 Asian, non-Hispanic/Latino; 8 Hispanic/Latino. Average age 25. 652 applicants, 19% accepted, 68 enrolled. In 2010, 62 master's, 14 doctorates awarded. Terminal master's awarded for partial completion of doctoral program. *Degree requirements:* For master's, thesis optional; for doctorate,

Polymer Science and Engineering

University of Wisconsin–Madison (continued)
thesis/dissertation, qualifying exam, preliminary exam. *Entrance requirements:* For master's, GRE, BS in mechanical engineering or related field, minimum GPA of 3.0 in last 60 hours of course work; for doctorate, GRE, BS in mechanical engineering or related field, minimum undergraduate GPA of 3.0 in last 60 hours of course work. Additional exam requirements/recommendations for international students: Required—TOEFL (minimum score 550 paper-based; 213 computer-based; 80 iBT). *Application deadline:* For fall admission, 5/1 for domestic students, 6/1 for international students; for spring admission, 11/30 for domestic students, 10/1 for international students. Applications are processed on a rolling basis. Application fee: $56. Electronic applications accepted. *Expenses:* Tuition, state resident: full-time $9887.36; part-time $617.96 per credit. Tuition, nonresident: full-time $24,054; part-time $1503.40 per credit. Required fees: $67.63 per credit. Tuition and fees vary according to reciprocity agreements. *Financial support:* In 2010–11, 14 fellowships with full tuition reimbursements (averaging $22,224 per year), 148 research assistantships with full tuition reimbursements (averaging $19,596 per year), 45 teaching assistantships with full tuition reimbursements (averaging $8,595 per year) were awarded; career-related internships or fieldwork, institutionally sponsored loans, scholarships/grants, traineeships, health care benefits, and unspecified assistantships also available. *Faculty research:* Design and manufacturing, materials processing, combustion, energy systems nanotechnology. Total annual research expenditures: $10 million. *Unit head:* Roxann L. Engelstad, Chair, 608-262-5745, Fax: 608-265-2316, E-mail: engelsta@engr.wisc.edu. *Application contact:* Roxann L. Engelstad, Chair, 608-262-5745, Fax: 608-265-2316, E-mail: engelsta@engr.wisc.edu.

Wayne State University, College of Engineering, Department of Chemical Engineering and Materials Science, Program in Materials Science and Engineering, Detroit, MI 48202. Offers materials science and engineering (MS, PhD); polymer engineering (Certificate). Part-time programs available. *Faculty:* 8 full-time (2 women), 2 part-time/adjunct (0 women). *Students:* 14 full-time (3 women), 2 part-time (1 woman), 14 international. Average age 27. 22 applicants, 32% accepted, 2 enrolled. In 2010, 1 master's, 2 doctorates awarded. Terminal master's awarded for partial completion of doctoral program. *Degree requirements:* For master's, thesis optional; for doctorate, thesis/dissertation. *Entrance requirements:* For master's, GRE (if applying for financial support), recommendations; resume; for doctorate, GRE (if applying for financial support), recommendations; resume, personal statement. Additional exam requirements/recommendations for international students: Required—TOEFL (minimum score 550 paper-based; 213 computer-based); Recommended—TWE (minimum score 6). *Application deadline:* For fall admission, 7/1 priority date for domestic students, 6/1 for international students; for winter admission, 10/1 for international students; for spring admission, 3/15 for domestic students, 2/1 for international students. Applications are processed on a rolling basis. Application fee: $30 ($50 for international students). Electronic applications accepted. *Expenses:* Tuition, state resident: full-time $7662; part-time $478.85 per credit hour. Tuition, nonresident: full-time $16,920; part-time $1057.55 per credit hour. Required fees: $571.20; $35.70 per credit hour. $188.05 per semester. Tuition and fees vary according to course load and program. *Financial support:* In 2010–11, 6 research assistantships (averaging $16,221 per year), 5 teaching assistantships (averaging $16,984 per year) were awarded; fellowships also available. Financial award application deadline: 2/15. *Faculty research:* Polymer science, rheology, fatigue in metals, metal matrix composites, ceramics. *Unit head:* Charles Manke, Chair, 313-577-3849, Fax: 313-577-3810, E-mail: emanke@chem1.eng.wayne.edu. *Application contact:* Rangaramanujam Kannan, Associate Professor, 313-577-3800, E-mail: rkannan@che.eng.wayne.edu.

UNIVERSITY OF MICHIGAN

College of Engineering
Department of Materials Science and Engineering

Programs of Study	The Department of Materials Science and Engineering offers Master of Science in Engineering (M.S.E.) and Ph.D. programs leading to degrees in materials science and engineering. Students may emphasize work in various materials categories or phenomena, although the Department encourages a broad graduate educational experience. Course offerings include basic materials courses in structure of materials, thermodynamics, diffusion, phase transformations, mechanical behavior, and materials characterization. Courses also exist in many areas of special interest, such as corrosion, composites, deformation processing, and failure analysis. The M.S.E. degree, typically completed in one to two years, requires 30 credit hours of graduate study. A research project of up to 6 credit hours or a master's thesis of 9–11 credit hours is included within this total and often forms the basis for the student's Ph.D. written examination. The Ph.D. degree, usually completed in four to five years beyond the B.S. degree, requires 18 credit hours of courses beyond the M.S.E. degree, passing grades on a written examination based on advanced undergraduate and graduate-level course material, a research-based oral examination, satisfactory completion of research, and defense of the doctoral dissertation. A precandidate must complete at least 18 credit hours of graded graduate course work registered as a Rackham student while in residence on the Ann Arbor campus. Master's students must complete at least one-half of the minimum required credit hours on the home campus. Each student is also required to complete one teaching assignment prior to the completion of the Ph.D. degree.

Faculty interests are diverse (see the reverse of this page) and fall into five main categories: inorganic materials, organic and biomaterials, electronic materials, structural materials, and computational materials science. Many additional research activities exist in collaboration with other departments and graduate programs.

Research Facilities
The Department occupies approximately 50,000 square feet, primarily in the H. H. Dow Building, but also in the adjacent G. G. Brown Building and the nearby Space Research and Gerstacker Buildings. Research facilities include world-class laboratories for electron microscopy and X-ray diffraction, ion-beam characterization and modification of materials, thin-film deposition, and solid-state device research. Modern instrumentation is added regularly. The Electron Microbeam Analysis Laboratory (EMAL) is a user facility that provides a broad spectrum of analytical equipment for the microstructural and microchemical characterization of materials. The facility includes two dual-beam focused ion beam (FIB) systems; four scanning electron microscopes (SEM); two environmental SEMs; three transmission electron microscopes (TEM) equipped with STEM, XEDS, and EELS; one X-ray photoelectron spectroscopy (XPS) system; and two atomic force microscopes (AFM). The J. D. Hanawalt X-ray Diffraction Laboratory offers several Rigaku, Phillips, and Siemens X-ray diffractometers. The Michigan Ion Beam Laboratory includes facilities for Rutherford backscattering spectrometry, ion channeling, nuclear reaction analysis, elastic recoil detection, and ion implantation for most of the elements of the periodic table, over a wide energy range. The Lurie Nanofabrication Facility offers complete capabilities for the fabrication and characterization of solid-state materials, devices, and circuits using silicon and compound semiconductors, and organic materials.

Financial Aid
Qualified applicants are eligible for fellowships and teaching or research assistantships that pay stipends of up to $26,553 per calendar year in 2011–12 plus tuition remission and some fringe benefits. Students funded by faculty advisers as research assistants work on research problems that are appropriate for their thesis topic. Teaching and research assistantships carry certain defined responsibilities that are adjusted to the needs of the student and the Department.

Cost of Study
The 2011–12 tuition fee for full-time students is $10,630 per term for Michigan residents and $20,003 per term for nonresidents.

Living and Housing Costs
A residence hall contract for room and board for the 2011–12 fall and winter terms ranges in cost from $9242 for a double to $12,530 for a single. Family housing units cost from $845 per month for an unfurnished one-bedroom unit to $1241 per month for a furnished three-bedroom unit. Prices include all utilities except telephone.

Many graduate students live in privately owned off-campus housing, which varies in expense depending on its proximity to the University. Food costs and local restaurant prices are typical of those in smaller cities in the Midwest.

Student Group
The Department has 127 full-time graduate students and 2 part-time students from local industry and research laboratories. Approximately 60 percent of the students are from the United States, and 40 percent are from abroad. Most students receive financial aid from the Department. The Department also has about 140 undergraduate students. The College of Engineering currently enrolls 8,522 students in twelve engineering departments/divisions and more than sixty engineering fields of study. The current total student enrollment on the Ann Arbor campus is approximately 42,000. The student-based Michigan Materials Society is very active.

Location
Ann Arbor is a cultural and cosmopolitan community of approximately 105,000 about 40 miles west of Detroit in southeastern Michigan. Ann Arbor offers world-class orchestras, dance companies, dramatic artists, and musical performers throughout the year. The internationally renowned May Festival of classical music and the Ann Arbor Folk Festival are held annually. Ann Arbor art fairs attract 500,000 patrons from across the nation every July. Recreational facilities are extensive, both on campus and throughout the community.

The University and The College
The University of Michigan, one of the nation's most distinguished state universities, is internationally recognized in all of its schools and colleges. The 6,275 faculty members and 42,000 students work in a modern environment that includes more than 275 research units. Michigan consistently ranks as a national leader in total research expenditures. The College of Engineering, of which the Department is a part, awards about 1,250 B.S., 1,030 M.S., and 250 Ph.D. degrees annually. There are more than 400 faculty members, 500 supporting staff members, 91 research faculty, and more than 65,000 alumni. Many of the programs in the College are rated among the ten best in the nation, and the College itself is often ranked among the top five engineering schools and colleges.

Applying
Applications are accepted for either the fall (September) or winter (January) terms; however, most students are admitted in the fall term. Applications for fall admission should be received by December 15 if financial support is required. Additional information on admission may be obtained from the Department or from the Horace H. Rackham School of Graduate Studies.

Correspondence and Information
Graduate Program Office
Department of Materials Science and Engineering
College of Engineering
University of Michigan
Ann Arbor, Michigan 48109-2136
Phone: 734-763-9790
Web site: http:// www.mse.engin.umich.edu

Horace H. Rackham School of Graduate Studies
Mail Office
University of Michigan
Ann Arbor, Michigan 48109

University of Michigan

THE FACULTY AND THEIR RESEARCH

John Allison, Professor of Materials Science and Engineering, Ph.D., Carnegie-Mellon, 1982. Understanding the inter-relationships between processing, microstructure and properties in advanced metallic materials and the utilization of this knowledge to engineer metallic materials for use in engineering applications.

Michael Atzmon, Professor of Materials Science and Engineering and Nuclear Engineering and Radiological Sciences; Ph.D., Caltech, 1985. Phase transformations and mechanical behavior of nonequilibrium metal alloys.

Akram Boukai, Assistant Professor of Materials Science and Engineering; Ph.D., Caltech, 2008. Growth and characterization of nanomaterials for energy and electronic applications.

Samantha Daly, Assistant Professor of Materials Science and Engineering; Ph.D., Caltech, 2007. Multi-scale material characterization, with application to active materials, high temperature ceramics.

Rodney C. Ewing, Professor of Materials Science and Engineering, Geological Sciences and Nuclear Engineering and Radiological Sciences; Ph.D., Stanford, 1974. Radiation effects in complex ceramics and minerals, crystal chemistry of actinides, nuclear materials.

Steven Forrest, Professor of Materials Science and Engineering, Electrical Engineering and Computer Science, Physics, and Vice President for Research; Ph.D., Michigan, 1979. Theory, growth, and characterization of organic and III-V semiconductors for optoelectronic device applications.

Amit K. Ghosh, Professor of Materials Science and Engineering and Mechanical Engineering; Ph.D., MIT, 1972. Superplasticity, deformation processing, advanced metallic materials, composites and laminates, friction stir processing.

Sharon C. Glotzer, Professor of Materials Science and Engineering, Chemical Engineering, and Physics; Ph.D., Boston University, 1993. Soft materials, polymers, dense liquids, glasses, colloids, and liquid crystals.

Rachel S. Goldman, Professor of Materials Science and Engineering, Electrical Engineering and Computer Science, and Physics; Ph.D., California, San Diego, 1995. Atomic-scale design of electronic materials; strain relaxation, alloy formation, and diffusion; correlations between microstructure and electronic and optical properties of semiconductor films, nanostructures, and heterostructures.

Peter Green, Professor and Chair of Materials Science and Engineering; Ph.D., Cornell, 1985. Polymer physics, oxide glasses, nanocomposites, thin films.

John W. Halloran, Alfred Holmes White Collegiate Professor of Materials Science and Engineering; Ph.D., MIT, 1977. Ceramics, rapid prototyping, electromagnetic materials, fuel cells, hydrogen and carbon.

J. Wayne Jones, Professor of Materials Science and Engineering; Ph.D., Vanderbilt, 1977. Fatigue of structural alloys for transportation and energy systems. Lightweight alloys.

John Kieffer, Professor of Materials Science and Engineering; Ph.D., Clausthal (Germany), 1985. Molecular design of materials for energy, photonics, and structural applications.

Jinsang Kim, Associate Professor of Materials Science and Engineering and Chemical Engineering; Ph.D., MIT, 2001. Functional polymers for biomedical and optoelectronic applications..

Emmanouil Kioupakis, Assistant Professor of Materials Science and Engineering; Ph.D., Berkeley, 2008. Computational study of novel materials for energy applications.

Nicholas Kotov, Professor of Materials Science and Engineering and Chemical Engineering; Ph.D., Moscow State, 1990. Applications of nanostructured materials to biology and medicine, self-organization of nanocolloidal systems.

Joerg Lahann, Professor of Materials Science and Engineering; Ph.D., RWTH Aachen,1998. Designer surfaces, advanced polymers, biomimetic materials, microfluidic devices, engineered cellular microenvironments, nanoscale self-assembly.

Richard M. Laine, Professor of Materials Science and Engineering, Macromolecular Science and Engineering, and Chemistry; Ph.D., USC, 1973. Inorganic and organometallic precursors, materials chemistry, catalysis.

Victor Li, Professor of Materials Science and Engineering and Civil and Environmental Engineering; Ph.D., Brown, 1981. Fiber reinforced cementitious composites, micromechanics, self-healing design, sustainable material development.

Brian Love, Professor of Materials Science and Engineering; Ph.D., SMU, 1990. Photopolymerization, chemorheology, tissue engineering, proteins as polymers.

John F. Mansfield, Associate Research Scientist; Ph.D., Bristol (England), 1983. Analytical electron microscopy of metals, semiconductors, and superconductors.

Emmanuelle Marquis, Assistant Professor of Materials Science and Engineering; Ph.D. Northwestern, 2002. Microstructure evolution, atomic scale characterization.

Jyotirmoy Mazumder, Robert H. Lurie Professor of Materials Science and Engineering and Mechanical Engineering; Ph.D., Imperial College (London), 1978. Laser-aided manufacturing, atom to application for nonequilibrium synthesis, mathematical modeling, spectroscopic and optical diagnostics of laser materials interaction.

Joanna Mirecki Millunchick, Professor of Materials Science and Engineering; Ph.D., Northwestern, 1995. Growth and characterization of thin films, directed self-assembly, and nanomanufacturing.

Xiaoqing Pan, Professor of Materials Science and Engineering and Director of EMAL; Ph.D., Saarlandes (Germany), 1991. High-resolution electron microscopy, structural-property relationships of materials interfaces, thin-film growth and characterization.

Pierre Ferdinand P. Poudeu, Assistant Professor of Materials Science and Engineering; Ph.D., Dresden University of Technology, 2004. Design, synthesis, and evaluation of solid-state inorganic materials with the goal to (1) discover new materials with significantly useful technological applications combining multiple interesting physical properties and (2) to understand and control the interplay between coexisting functionalities.

Richard E. Robertson, Professor of Materials Science and Engineering and Macromolecular Science and Engineering; Ph.D., Caltech, 1960. Polymer structure, molecular dynamics and fracture, fiber composite properties, composite design and manufacturing.

Anne Marie Sastry, Professor of Materials Science and Engineering and Mechanical Engineering; Ph.D., Cornell, 1994. Battery design, biomaterials, disordered microstructures, nanomanufacturing.

Max Shtein, Associate Professor of Materials Science and Engineering; Ph.D., Princeton, 2004. Optoelectronic materials and devices; thin-film processing; energy.

Katsuyo Thornton, Associate Professor of Materials Science and Engineering; Ph.D., Chicago, 1997. Computational materials science, nano- and microstructures, materials for energy.

Michael D. Thouless, Professor of Materials Science and Engineering and Mechanical Engineering and Applied Mechanics; Ph.D., Berkeley, 1984. Mechanics of materials and interfaces; physics of adhesion and fracture.

Anish Tuteja, Assistant Professor of Materials Science and Engineering; Ph.D., Michigan State, 2006. Surface and interfacial science; functional polymer nanocomposites.

Anton Van der Ven, Associate Professor of Materials Science and Engineering; Ph.D., MIT, 2000. Electronic structure methods (density functional theory), with techniques from statistical mechanics to calculate thermodynamic and kinetic properties of new materials.

Lumin Wang, Professor of Materials Science and Engineering and Nuclear Engineering and Radiological Sciences, and Director of Electron Microbeam Analysis Laboratory, Ph.D., Wisconsin–Madison, 1988. Radiation effects, Ion-beam processing of nanostructured materials, transmission electron microscopy.

Gary S. Was, Professor of Materials Science and Engineering, and Nuclear Engineering and Radiological Sciences; Sc.D., MIT, 1980. Ion-solid interactions, radiation effects, stress corrosion cracking, hydrogen embrittlement.

Steven M. Yalisove, Professor; Ph.D., Pennsylvania, 1986. Ultrafast laser/material interaction; atomic scale assembly and characterization.

Students working in the Van Vlack Undergraduate Lab.

The Lurie Carillon Tower on North Campus.

Section 17
Mechanical Engineering and Mechanics

This section contains a directory of institutions offering graduate work in mechanical engineering and mechanics, followed by in-depth entries submitted by institutions that chose to prepare detailed program descriptions. Additional information about programs listed in the directory but not augmented by an in-depth entry may be obtained by writing directly to the dean of a graduate school or chair of a department at the address given in the directory.

For programs offering related work, see also in this book *Engineering and Applied Sciences, Management of Engineering and Technology,* and *Materials Sciences and Engineering.* In another guide in this series:

Graduate Programs in the Physical Sciences, Mathematics, Agricultural Sciences, the Environment & Natural Resources
See *Geosciences and Physics*

CONTENTS

Program Directories

Close-Ups and Displays

Mechanical Engineering

Alfred University, Graduate School, New York State College of Ceramics, School of Engineering, Alfred, NY 14802-1205. Offers biomedical materials engineering science (MS); ceramic engineering (MS); ceramics (PhD); electrical engineering (MS); glass science (MS, PhD); materials science and engineering (MS, PhD); mechanical engineering (MS). *Degree requirements:* For master's, thesis; for doctorate, thesis/dissertation. *Entrance requirements:* Additional exam requirements/recommendations for international students: Required—TOEFL (minimum score 590 paper-based; 243 computer-based). Electronic applications accepted. *Expenses:* Contact institution. *Faculty research:* Fine-particle technology, x-ray diffraction, superconductivity, electronic materials.

The American University in Cairo, School of Sciences and Engineering, Department of Mechanical Engineering, Cairo, Egypt. Offers mechanical engineering (MS); product development and systems management (M Eng).

American University of Beirut, Graduate Programs, Faculty of Engineering and Architecture, Beirut, Lebanon. Offers applied energy (MME); civil engineering (ME, PhD); electrical and computer engineering (ME, PhD); engineering management (MEM); environmental and water resources (ME); environmental and water resources engineering (PhD); environmental technology (MSES); mechanical engineering (ME, PhD); urban design (MUD); urban planning and policy (MUP). Part-time programs available. *Faculty:* 57 full-time (12 women), 3 part-time/adjunct (0 women). *Students:* 261 full-time (92 women), 58 part-time (20 women). Average age 25. 272 applicants, 79% accepted, 108 enrolled. In 2010, 70 master's, 1 doctorate awarded. *Degree requirements:* For master's, one foreign language, comprehensive exam, thesis (for some programs); for doctorate, one foreign language, comprehensive exam, thesis/dissertation, publications. *Entrance requirements:* For master's, GRE (for electrical and computer engineering), letters of recommendation; for doctorate, GRE, letters of recommendation, master's degree, transcripts, curriculum vitae, interview. Additional exam requirements/recommendations for international students: Required—TOEFL (minimum score 600 paper-based; 250 computer-based; 100 iBT), IELTS (minimum score 7.5). *Application deadline:* For fall admission, 2/5 priority date for domestic and international students; for spring admission, 11/1 priority date for domestic students, 11/1 for international students. Applications are processed on a rolling basis. Application fee: $50. Electronic applications accepted. *Expenses:* Tuition: Full-time $12,294; part-time $683 per credit. Required fees: $499; $499 per credit. Tuition and fees vary according to course load and program. *Financial support:* In 2010–11, 10 fellowships with full tuition reimbursements (averaging $24,800 per year), 33 research assistantships with full tuition reimbursements (averaging $24,800 per year), 70 teaching assistantships with full tuition reimbursements (averaging $9,800 per year) were awarded; career-related internships or fieldwork, institutionally sponsored loans, scholarships/grants, health care benefits, and unspecified assistantships also available. Total annual research expenditures: $586,131. *Unit head:* Fadl H. Moukalled, Acting Dean, 961-135-0000 Ext. 3400, Fax: 961-174-4462, E-mail: memouk@aub.edu.lb. *Application contact:* Dr. Salim Kanaan, Director, Admissions Office, 961-135-0000 Ext. 2594, Fax: 961-175-0775, E-mail: sk00@aub.edu.lb.

American University of Sharjah, Graduate Programs, Sharjah, United Arab Emirates. Offers business (EMBA, GEMPA, MBA); chemical engineering (MS Ch E); civil engineering (MSCE); computer engineering (MS); electrical engineering (MSEE); mechanical engineering (MSME); mechatronics engineering (MS); public administration (MPA); teaching English to speakers of other languages (MA); translation and interpreting (MA); urban planning (MUP). Part-time and evening/weekend programs available. *Entrance requirements:* For master's, GMAT (MBA). Additional exam requirements/recommendations for international students: Required—TOEFL (minimum score 550 paper-based; 213 computer-based; 80 iBT), TWE (minimum score 5). Electronic applications accepted. *Faculty research:* Chemical engineering, civil engineering, computer engineering, electrical engineering, linguistics, translation.

Arizona State University, College of Technology and Innovation, Department of Engineering Technology, Mesa, AZ 85212. Offers technology (alternative energy technologies) (MS); technology (electronic systems engineering technology) (MS); technology (integrated electronic systems) (MS); technology (manufacturing engineering technology) (MS). Part-time and evening/weekend programs available. *Faculty:* 15 full-time (2 women), 3 part-time/adjunct (0 women). *Students:* 40 full-time (5 women), 48 part-time (12 women); includes 23 minority (5 Black or African American, non-Hispanic/Latino; 9 Asian, non-Hispanic/Latino; 9 Hispanic/Latino), 27 international. Average age 30. 74 applicants, 77% accepted, 25 enrolled. In 2010, 19 master's awarded. *Degree requirements:* For master's, thesis or applied project and oral defense, final examination, interactive Program of Study (iPOS) submitted before completing 50 percent of required credit hours. *Entrance requirements:* For master's, bachelor's degree with minimum of 30 credit hours or equivalent in a technology area including course work applicable to the concentration being sought and minimum of 16 credit hours of math and science; industrial experience beyond bachelor's degree (recommended). Additional exam requirements/recommendations for international students: Required—TOEFL, IELTS, or Pearson Test of English. *Application deadline:* For fall admission, 7/1 for domestic and international students; for spring admission, 12/1 for domestic and international students. Applications are processed on a rolling basis. Application fee: $70 ($90 for international students). Electronic applications accepted. *Expenses:* Tuition, state resident: full-time $8510; part-time $608 per credit. Tuition, nonresident: full-time $16,542; part-time $919 per credit. Required fees: $339; $110 per credit. Part-time tuition and fees vary according to course load. *Financial support:* In 2010–11, 3 research assistantships with full and partial tuition reimbursements (averaging $9,918 per year) were awarded; fellowships with full and partial tuition reimbursements, teaching assistantships with full and partial tuition reimbursements, career-related internships or fieldwork, Federal Work-Study, scholarships/grants, health care benefits, tuition waivers (full and partial), and unspecified assistantships also available. Support available to part-time students. Financial award application deadline: 3/1; financial award applicants required to submit FAFSA. *Faculty research:* Manufacturing modeling and simulation 'smart' and composite materials, optimization of turbine engines, machinability and manufacturing processes design, fuel cells and other alternative energy sources. Total annual research expenditures: $795,837. *Unit head:* Dr. Scott Danielson, Chair, 480-727-1185, Fax: 480-727-1549, E-mail: sdanielson@asu.edu. *Application contact:* Graduate Admissions, 480-965-6113.

Arizona State University, Ira A. Fulton School of Engineering, Department of Mechanical and Aerospace Engineering, Tempe, AZ 85281. Offers aerospace engineering (MS, MSE, PhD); chemical engineering (MS, MSE, PhD); materials science and engineering (MS, PhD); mechanical engineering (MS, MSE, PhD). Part-time and evening/weekend programs available. Postbaccalaureate distance learning degree programs offered (minimal on-campus study). *Faculty:* 50 full-time (10 women), 13 part-time/adjunct (3 women). *Students:* 258 full-time (47 women), 114 part-time (29 women); includes 48 minority (3 Black or African American, non-Hispanic/Latino; 2 American Indian or Alaska Native, non-Hispanic/Latino; 15 Asian, non-Hispanic/Latino; 27 Hispanic/Latino; 1 Two or more races, non-Hispanic/Latino), 164 international. Average age 28. 721 applicants, 58% accepted, 119 enrolled. In 2010, 55 master's, 29 doctorates awarded. Terminal master's awarded for partial completion of doctoral program. *Degree requirements:* For master's, thesis and oral defense (MS); applied project or comprehensive exam (MSE); interactive Program of Study (iPOS) submitted before completing 50 percent of required credit hours; for doctorate, comprehensive exam, thesis/dissertation, interactive Program of Study (iPOS) submitted before completing 50 percent of required credit hours. *Entrance requirements:* For master's, GRE, minimum GPA of 3.0 or equivalent in last 2 years of work leading to bachelor's degree; for doctorate, GRE, minimum GPA of 3.0 in last 2 years of work leading to bachelor's degree. Additional exam requirements/recommendations for international students: Required—TOEFL, IELTS, or Pearson Test of English. *Application deadline:* For fall admission, 1/31 for domestic and international students; for spring admission, 7/1 for domestic and international students. Application fee: $70 ($90 for international students). Electronic applications accepted. *Expenses:* Contact institution. *Financial support:* In 2010–11, 120 research assistantships with partial tuition reimbursements (averaging $15,353 per year), 34 teaching assistantships with partial tuition reimbursements (averaging $13,861 per year) were awarded; fellowships with full and partial tuition reimbursements, institutionally sponsored loans, scholarships/grants, and tuition waivers (full and partial) also available. Financial award application deadline: 3/1; financial award applicants required to submit FAFSA. *Faculty research:* Electronic materials and packaging, materials for energy (batteries), adaptive/intelligent materials and structures, multiscale fluid mechanics, membranes, therapeutics and bioseparations, flexible structures, nanostructured materials, and micro/nano transport. Total annual research expenditures: $17.5 million. *Unit head:* Dr. Kyle D. Squires, Director, 480-965-3957, E-mail: squires@asu.edu. *Application contact:* Graduate Admissions, 480-965-6113.

Auburn University, Graduate School, Ginn College of Engineering, Department of Mechanical Engineering, Auburn University, AL 36849. Offers materials engineering (M Mtl E, MS, PhD); mechanical engineering (MME, MS, PhD). Part-time programs available. *Faculty:* 29 full-time (0 women), 2 part-time/adjunct (0 women). *Students:* 65 full-time (10 women), 85 part-time (10 women); includes 3 Black or African American, non-Hispanic/Latino; 1 American Indian or Alaska Native, non-Hispanic/Latino; 2 Asian, non-Hispanic/Latino; 1 Hispanic/Latino, 89 international. Average age 28. 237 applicants, 41% accepted, 21 enrolled. In 2010, 14 master's, 11 doctorates awarded. *Degree requirements:* For master's, thesis (for some programs); for doctorate, one foreign language, thesis/dissertation. *Entrance requirements:* For master's and doctorate, GRE General Test. *Application deadline:* For fall admission, 7/7 for domestic students; for spring admission, 11/24 for domestic students. Applications are processed on a rolling basis. Application fee: $50 ($60 for international students). *Expenses:* Tuition, state resident: full-time $7002. Tuition, nonresident: full-time $21,898. International tuition: $22,116 full-time. Required fees: $892. Tuition and fees vary according to course load and program. *Financial support:* Fellowships, research assistantships, teaching assistantships, Federal Work-Study available. Support available to part-time students. Financial award application deadline: 3/15; financial award applicants required to submit FAFSA. *Faculty research:* Engineering mechanics, experimental mechanics, engineering design, engineering acoustics, engineering optics. *Unit head:* Dr. Jeff Suhling, Chair, 334-844-3332. *Application contact:* Dr. George Flowers, Dean of the Graduate School, 334-844-2125.

Baylor University, Graduate School, School of Engineering and Computer Science, Department of Engineering, Waco, TX 76798. Offers biomedical engineering (MSBE); electrical and computer engineering (MSECE, PhD); engineering (ME); mechanical engineering (MSME). *Faculty:* 14 full-time (1 woman). *Students:* 30 full-time (4 women), 6 part-time (0 women); includes 9 minority (3 Black or African American, non-Hispanic/Latino; 2 Asian, non-Hispanic/Latino; 1 Hispanic/Latino; 3 Two or more races, non-Hispanic/Latino), 7 international. In 2010, 7 master's awarded. *Unit head:* Dr. Mike Thompson, Graduate Director, 254-710-4188. *Application contact:* Linda Keer, Administrative Assistant, 254-710-4188, Fax: 254-710-3870, E-mail: linda_kerr@baylor.edu.

Boise State University, Graduate College, College of Engineering, Department of Mechanical and Biomedical Engineering, Boise, ID 83725-0399. Offers mechanical engineering (M Engr, MS). Part-time and evening/weekend programs available. *Degree requirements:* For master's, thesis. *Entrance requirements:* For master's, GRE General Test, minimum GPA of 3.0. Additional exam requirements/recommendations for international students: Required—TOEFL. Electronic applications accepted.

Boston University, College of Engineering, Department of Mechanical Engineering, Boston, MA 02215. Offers global manufacturing (MS); manufacturing engineering (M Eng, MS); mechanical engineering (M Eng, MS, PhD); MS/MBA. Part-time programs available. Postbaccalaureate distance learning degree programs offered (no on-campus study). *Faculty:* 38 full-time (5 women), 1 part-time/adjunct (0 women). *Students:* 91 full-time (13 women), 17 part-time (5 women); includes 11 minority (3 Black or African American, non-Hispanic/Latino; 1 American Indian or Alaska Native, non-Hispanic/Latino; 4 Asian, non-Hispanic/Latino; 3 Hispanic/Latino), 45 international. Average age 26. 298 applicants, 21% accepted, 30 enrolled. In 2010, 32 master's, 5 doctorates awarded. Terminal master's awarded for partial completion of doctoral program. *Degree requirements:* For master's, thesis (for some programs); for doctorate, comprehensive exam, thesis/dissertation. *Entrance requirements:* For master's and doctorate, GRE General Test. Additional exam requirements/recommendations for international students: Required—TOEFL (minimum score 550 paper-based; 213 computer-based; 84 iBT), IELTS (minimum score 6). *Application deadline:* For fall admission, 4/1 for domestic and international students; for spring admission, 10/1 for domestic and international students. Applications are processed on a rolling basis. Application fee: $70. Electronic applications accepted. *Expenses:* Tuition: Full-time $39,314; part-time $1228 per credit. Required fees: $40 per semester. *Financial support:* In 2010–11, 81 students received support, including 13 fellowships with full tuition reimbursements available (averaging $28,200 per year), 41 research assistantships with full tuition reimbursements available (averaging $18,800 per year), 19 teaching assistantships with full tuition reimbursements available (averaging $18,800 per year); career-related internships or fieldwork, Federal Work-Study, institutionally sponsored loans, scholarships/grants, and health care benefits also available. Financial award application deadline: 1/15; financial award applicants required to submit FAFSA. *Faculty research:* Acoustics, ultrasound, and vibrations; biomechanics; dynamics, control, and robotics; energy and thermofluid sciences; MEMS and nanotechnology. Total annual research expenditures: $11 million. *Unit head:* Dr. Ronald A. Roy, Chairman, 617-353-2814, Fax: 617-353-5866, E-mail: ronroy@bu.edu. *Application contact:* Stephen Doherty, Director of Graduate Programs, 617-353-9760, Fax: 617-353-0259, E-mail: enggrad@bu.edu.

Bradley University, Graduate School, College of Engineering and Technology, Department of Mechanical Engineering, Peoria, IL 61625-0002. Offers MSME. Part-time and evening/weekend programs available. *Degree requirements:* For master's, comprehensive exam, thesis optional. *Entrance requirements:* For master's, minimum GPA of 3.0. Additional exam requirements/recommendations for international students: Required—TOEFL (minimum score 550 paper-based; 213 computer-based; 79 iBT). *Faculty research:* Ground-coupled heat pumps, robotic end-effectors, power plant optimization.

Brigham Young University, Graduate Studies, Ira A. Fulton College of Engineering and Technology, Department of Mechanical Engineering, Provo, UT 84602. Offers MS, PhD. *Faculty:* 26 full-time (1 woman), 1 part-time/adjunct (0 women). *Students:* 127 full-time (13 women), 8 part-time (0 women); includes 1 American Indian or Alaska Native, non-Hispanic/Latino; 3 Asian, non-Hispanic/Latino; 2 Hispanic/Latino, 8 international. Average age 26. 73 applicants, 73% accepted, 41 enrolled. In 2010, 35 master's, 3 doctorates awarded. Terminal master's awarded for partial completion of doctoral program. *Degree requirements:* For master's, thesis; for doctorate, comprehensive exam, thesis/dissertation. *Entrance requirements:* For master's and doctorate, GRE General Test, minimum GPA of 3.0 in last 60 hours of upper-division course work. Additional exam requirements/recommendations for international students: Required—IELTS (minimum score 7), TOEFL (minimum scores: paper-based 580; iBT 85 with minimums of speaking 22, listening, reading, writing 21. *Application deadline:* For fall admission, 1/15 for domestic and international students; for winter admission, 9/15 for domestic and international students; for spring admission, 1/15 for domestic and international students. Application fee: $50. Electronic applications accepted. *Expenses:* Tuition: Full-time $5580; part-time $310 per credit hour. Tuition and fees vary according to program and student's religious affiliation. *Financial support:* In 2010–11, 3 students received support, including 17 fellowships with full tuition reimbursements available (averaging $3,650 per year), 41 research assistantships with full tuition reimbursements available (averaging $11,300 per year), 26 teaching assistantships with full and partial tuition reimbursements available (averaging $4,600 per year); scholarships/grants and unspecified assistantships also available. Financial award application deadline: 1/15; financial award applicants required to submit FAFSA. *Faculty research:* Combustion, composite materials, advanced design methods and optimization, electronics heat transfer, acoustic noise controls and robotics. Total annual research expenditures: $1.2 million. *Unit head:* Dr. Timothy W. McLain, Chair, 801-422-2625, Fax: 801-422-0516, E-mail: tmclaine@et.byu.edu. *Application contact:* Miriam Busch, Graduate Advisor, 801-422-2624, Fax: 801-422-0516, E-mail: mbusch@byu.edu.

Brown University, Graduate School, Division of Engineering, Program in Mechanics of Solids, Providence, RI 02912. Offers Sc M, PhD. *Degree requirements:* For doctorate, thesis/dissertation, preliminary exam.

Bucknell University, Graduate Studies, College of Engineering, Department of Mechanical Engineering, Lewisburg, PA 17837. Offers MS, MSME. Part-time programs available. *Degree requirements:* For master's, thesis. *Entrance requirements:* For master's, GRE General Test, GRE Subject Test, minimum GPA of 2.8. Additional exam requirements/recommendations for international students: Required—TOEFL. *Expenses:* Tuition: Full-time $36,992; part-time $4624 per course. *Faculty research:* Heat pump performance, microprocessors in heat engine testing, computer-aided design.

California Institute of Technology, Division of Engineering and Applied Science, Option in Mechanical Engineering, Pasadena, CA 91125-0001. Offers MS, PhD, Engr. *Faculty:* 8 full-time (3 women). *Students:* 42 full-time (11 women). 299 applicants, 10% accepted, 10 enrolled. In 2010, 6 master's, 14 doctorates awarded. *Degree requirements:* For doctorate, thesis/dissertation. *Application deadline:* For fall admission, 1/1 for domestic students. Application fee: $0. *Financial support:* In 2010–11, 15 fellowships, 27 research assistantships, 5 teaching assistantships were awarded. *Faculty research:* Design, mechanics, thermal and fluids engineering, jet propulsion. *Unit head:* Dr. Kaushik Bhattacharya, Executive Officer, 626-395-8306, E-mail: bhatta@caltech.edu. *Application contact:* Natalie Gilmore, Assistant Dean of Graduate Studies, 626-395-3812, Fax: 626-577-9246, E-mail: ngilmore@caltech.edu.

California Polytechnic State University, San Luis Obispo, College of Engineering, Department of Mechanical Engineering, San Luis Obispo, CA 93407. Offers MS. Part-time programs available. *Faculty:* 2 full-time (0 women). *Students:* 37 full-time (2 women), 13 part-time (1 woman); includes 14 minority (1 American Indian or Alaska Native, non-Hispanic/Latino; 9 Asian, non-Hispanic/Latino; 4 Hispanic/Latino). Average age 25. 53 applicants, 70% accepted, 21 enrolled. In 2010, 23 master's awarded. *Degree requirements:* For master's, comprehensive exam (for some programs), thesis (for some programs). *Entrance requirements:* For master's, GRE, minimum GPA of 3.0 in last 90 quarter units of course work, 3 letters of recommendation. Additional exam requirements/recommendations for international students: Required—TOEFL (minimum score 550 paper-based; 213 computer-based) or IELTS (minimum score 6). *Application deadline:* For fall admission, 12/1 for domestic students, 11/30 for international students; for winter admission, 11/1 for domestic students, 6/30 for international students; for spring admission, 2/1 for domestic students. Applications are processed on a rolling basis. Application fee: $55. Electronic applications accepted. *Expenses:* Tuition, state resident: full-time $5386; part-time $3124 per year. Tuition, nonresident: full-time $11,160; part-time $248 per unit. Required fees: $2250; $614 per term. One-time fee: $2250 full-time; $1842 part-time. *Financial support:* Fellowships, research assistantships, teaching assistantships, career-related internships or fieldwork, Federal Work-Study, and scholarships/grants available. Support available to part-time students. Financial award application deadline: 3/2; financial award applicants required to submit FAFSA. *Faculty research:* Mechatronics, robotics, thermosciences, mechanics and stress analysis, composite materials. *Unit head:* Dr. Saeed Niku, Graduate Coordinator, 805-756-1376, Fax: 805-756-1137, E-mail: sniku@calpoly.edu. *Application contact:* Dr. Saeed Niku, Graduate Coordinator, 805-756-1376, Fax: 805-756-1137, E-mail: sniku@calpoly.edu.

California State Polytechnic University, Pomona, Academic Affairs, College of Engineering, Program in Mechanical Engineering, Pomona, CA 91768-2557. Offers MS. *Students:* 7 full-time (2 women), 43 part-time (7 women); includes 23 minority (1 Black or African American, non-Hispanic/Latino; 12 Asian, non-Hispanic/Latino; 9 Hispanic/Latino; 1 Two or more races, non-Hispanic/Latino), 8 international. Average age 32. 69 applicants, 52% accepted, 22 enrolled. In 2010, 2 master's awarded. *Application deadline:* Applications are processed on a rolling basis. Application fee: $55. Electronic applications accepted. *Expenses:* Tuition, state resident: full-time $5386; part-time $2850 per year. Tuition, nonresident: full-time $12,082; part-time $248 per credit. Required fees: $577; $248 per credit. $577 per year. Tuition and fees vary according to course load and program. *Unit head:* Dr. Hassan M. Rejali, Chair/Graduate Coordinator, 909-869-2575, E-mail: hmrejali@csupomona.edu. *Application contact:* Scott J. Duncan, Director, Admissions, 909-869-3258, E-mail: sjduncan@csupomona.edu.

California State University, Fresno, Division of Graduate Studies, College of Engineering and Computer Science, Program in Mechanical Engineering, Fresno, CA 93740-8027. Offers MS. Offered at Edwards Air Force Base. Part-time programs available. *Degree requirements:* For master's, thesis or alternative. *Entrance requirements:* For master's, GRE General Test, minimum GPA of 2.7. Additional exam requirements/recommendations for international students: Required—TOEFL. Electronic applications accepted. *Faculty research:* Flowmeter calibration, digital camera calibration.

California State University, Fullerton, Graduate Studies, College of Engineering and Computer Science, Department of Mechanical Engineering, Fullerton, CA 92834-9480. Offers MS. Part-time programs available. *Students:* 18 full-time (2 women), 40 part-time (2 women); includes 1 Black or African American, non-Hispanic/Latino; 15 Asian, non-Hispanic/Latino; 8 Hispanic/Latino, 18 international. Average age 28. 100 applicants, 62% accepted, 28 enrolled. In 2010, 10 master's awarded. *Degree requirements:* For master's, comprehensive exam, project or thesis. *Entrance requirements:* For master's, minimum undergraduate GPA of 2.5. Application fee: $55. *Financial support:* Career-related internships or fieldwork, Federal Work-Study, institutionally sponsored loans, and scholarships/grants available. Support available to part-time students. Financial award application deadline: 3/1; financial award applicants required to submit FAFSA. *Unit head:* Dr. Hossein Moini, Chair, 657-278-4304. *Application contact:* Admissions/Applications, 657-278-2371.

California State University, Long Beach, Graduate Studies, College of Engineering, Department of Mechanical and Aerospace Engineering, Long Beach, CA 90840. Offers aerospace engineering (MSAE); engineering and industrial applied mathematics (PhD); interdisciplinary engineering (MSE); management engineering (MSE); mechanical engineering (MSME). Part-time programs available. *Faculty:* 14 full-time (3 women), 6 part-time/adjunct (0 women). *Students:* 44 full-time (1 woman), 56 part-time (8 women); includes 1 Black or African American, non-Hispanic/Latino; 1 American Indian or Alaska Native, non-Hispanic/Latino; 30 Asian, non-Hispanic/Latino; 15 Hispanic/Latino, 15 international. Average age 28. 169 applicants, 41% accepted, 25 enrolled. In 2010, 32 master's awarded. *Entrance requirements:* Additional exam requirements/recommendations for international students: Required—TOEFL. *Application deadline:* For fall admission, 7/1 for domestic students. Application fee: $55. Electronic applications accepted. *Financial support:* Career-related internships or fieldwork, Federal Work-Study, institutionally sponsored loans, scholarships/grants, and unspecified assistantships available. Financial award application deadline: 3/2. *Faculty research:* Unsteady turbulent flows, solar energy, energy conversion, CAD/CAM, computer-assisted instruction. *Unit head:* Dr. Hamid Hefazi, Chair, 562-985-1502, Fax: 562-985-1564, E-mail: hefazi@csulb.edu. *Application contact:* Dr. Hamid Rahai, Graduate Advisor, 562-985-5132, Fax: 562-985-4408, E-mail: rahai@csulb.edu.

California State University, Los Angeles, Graduate Studies, College of Engineering, Computer Science, and Technology, Department of Mechanical Engineering, Los Angeles, CA 90032-8530. Offers MS. Part-time and evening/weekend programs available. *Faculty:* 6 full-time (2 women), 1 part-time/adjunct (0 women). *Students:* 25 full-time (3 women), 41 part-time (6 women); includes 28 minority (1 Black or African American, non-Hispanic/Latino; 9 Asian, non-Hispanic/Latino; 18 Hispanic/Latino), 30 international. Average age 28. 48 applicants, 100% accepted, 29 enrolled. In 2010, 17 master's awarded. *Degree requirements:* For master's, comprehensive exam or thesis. *Entrance requirements:* For master's, minimum GPA of 2.75. Additional exam requirements/recommendations for international students: Required—TOEFL

(minimum score 550 paper-based). *Application deadline:* For fall admission, 5/1 for domestic and international students. Applications are processed on a rolling basis. Application fee: $55. Electronic applications accepted. *Financial support:* Federal Work-Study available. Support available to part-time students. Financial award application deadline: 3/1. *Faculty research:* Mechanical design, thermal systems, solar-powered vehicle. *Unit head:* Dr. Darrell Guillaume, Chair, 323-343-4490, Fax: 323-343-5004, E-mail: dguilla@calstatela.edu. *Application contact:* Dr. Alan Muchlinski, Dean of Graduate Studies, 323-343-3820, Fax: 323-343-5653, E-mail: amuchli@exchange.calstatela.edu.

California State University, Northridge, Graduate Studies, College of Engineering and Computer Science, Department of Mechanical Engineering, Northridge, CA 91330. Offers MS. Part-time and evening/weekend programs available. *Degree requirements:* For master's, thesis or project. *Entrance requirements:* Additional exam requirements/recommendations for international students: Required—TOEFL.

California State University, Sacramento, Graduate Studies, College of Engineering and Computer Science, Department of Mechanical Engineering, Sacramento, CA 95819. Offers MS. Evening/weekend programs available. *Degree requirements:* For master's, thesis or alternative, writing proficiency exam. *Entrance requirements:* Additional exam requirements/recommendations for international students: Required—TOEFL. Electronic applications accepted.

Carleton University, Faculty of Graduate Studies, Faculty of Engineering and Design, Department of Mechanical and Aerospace Engineering, Ottawa, ON K1S 5B6, Canada. Offers aerospace engineering (M Eng, MA Sc, PhD); materials engineering (M Eng, MA Sc); mechanical engineering (M Eng, MA Sc, PhD). *Degree requirements:* For master's, thesis optional; for doctorate, thesis/dissertation. *Entrance requirements:* For master's, honors degree; for doctorate, MA Sc or M Eng. Additional exam requirements/recommendations for international students: Required—TOEFL. *Faculty research:* Thermal fluids engineering, heat transfer, vehicle engineering.

Carnegie Mellon University, Carnegie Institute of Technology, Department of Mechanical Engineering, Pittsburgh, PA 15213-3891. Offers MS, PhD. Part-time and evening/weekend programs available. Terminal master's awarded for partial completion of doctoral program. *Degree requirements:* For master's, thesis (for some programs); for doctorate, thesis/dissertation (for some programs), qualifying exam. *Entrance requirements:* For master's and doctorate, GRE General Test. Additional exam requirements/recommendations for international students: Required—TOEFL. *Faculty research:* Combustion, design, fluid, and thermal sciences; computational fluid dynamics; energy and environment; solid mechanics; systems and controls; materials and manufacturing.

Case Western Reserve University, School of Graduate Studies, Case School of Engineering, Department of Mechanical and Aerospace Engineering, Cleveland, OH 44106. Offers MS, PhD, MD/PhD. Part-time programs available. Postbaccalaureate distance learning degree programs offered (no on-campus study). *Faculty:* 12 full-time (3 women). *Students:* 70 full-time (9 women), 20 part-time (4 women); includes 3 Black or African American, non-Hispanic/Latino; 2 American Indian or Alaska Native, non-Hispanic/Latino; 6 Asian, non-Hispanic/Latino; 1 Hispanic/Latino; 1 Two or more races, non-Hispanic/Latino, 33 international. In 2010, 22 master's, 1 doctorate awarded. *Degree requirements:* For master's, thesis (for some programs); for doctorate, thesis/dissertation, qualifying exam, teaching experience. *Entrance requirements:* For master's and doctorate, GRE General Test. Additional exam requirements/recommendations for international students: Required—TOEFL. *Application deadline:* For fall admission, 7/1 priority date for domestic students. Applications are processed on a rolling basis. Application fee: $50. *Financial support:* Fellowships with full and partial tuition reimbursements, research assistantships with full and partial tuition reimbursements, teaching assistantships, institutionally sponsored loans and tuition waivers (full and partial) available. Financial award application deadline: 3/1; financial award applicants required to submit FAFSA. *Faculty research:* Musculoskeletal biomechanics, combustion diagnostics and computation, mechanical behavior of advanced materials and nanostructures, biorobotics. Total annual research expenditures: $4.1 million. *Unit head:* Dr. Iwan Alexander, Department Chair, 216-368-6045, Fax: 216-368-6445, E-mail: ida2@case.edu. *Application contact:* Carla Wilson, Student Affairs Coordinator, 216-368-4580, Fax: 216-368-3007, E-mail: cxw75@case.edu.

The Catholic University of America, School of Engineering, Department of Mechanical Engineering, Washington, DC 20064. Offers MME, MSE, PhD. Part-time programs available. *Faculty:* 7 full-time (0 women). *Students:* 5 full-time (0 women), 16 part-time (1 woman); includes 1 Black or African American, non-Hispanic/Latino, 5 international. Average age 34. 14 applicants, 79% accepted, 3 enrolled. In 2010, 5 master's awarded. *Degree requirements:* For master's, thesis (for some programs); for doctorate, comprehensive exam, thesis/dissertation, oral exams. *Entrance requirements:* For master's and doctorate, statement of purpose, official copies of academic transcripts, three letters of recommendation. Additional exam requirements/recommendations for international students: Required—TOEFL (minimum score 580 paper-based; 237 computer-based). *Application deadline:* For fall admission, 8/1 priority date for domestic students, 7/15 for international students; for spring admission, 12/1 priority date for domestic students, 10/15 for international students. Applications are processed on a rolling basis. Application fee: $55. Electronic applications accepted. *Expenses:* Contact institution. *Financial support:* Fellowships, research assistantships, teaching assistantships, Federal Work-Study, scholarships/grants, tuition waivers (full and partial), and unspecified assistantships available. Financial award application deadline: 2/1; financial award applicants required to submit FAFSA. *Faculty research:* Fluid mechanics, dynamics, acoustics, computational mechanics, solar winds. Total annual research expenditures: $523,041. *Unit head:* Dr. Sen Nieh, Chair, 202-319-5170, Fax: 202-319-5173, E-mail: nieh@cua.edu. *Application contact:* Andrew Woodall, Director of Graduate Admissions, 202-319-5057, Fax: 202-319-6533, E-mail: cua-admissions@cua.edu.

City College of the City University of New York, Graduate School, Grove School of Engineering, Department of Mechanical Engineering, New York, NY 10031-9198. Offers ME, MS, PhD. PhD program offered jointly with Graduate School and University Center of the City University of New York. Part-time programs available. *Degree requirements:* For master's, thesis optional; for doctorate, one foreign language, comprehensive exam, thesis/dissertation. *Entrance requirements:* For master's and doctorate, GRE General Test. Additional exam requirements/recommendations for international students: Required—TOEFL (minimum score 500 paper-based; 173 computer-based). *Faculty research:* Bio-heat and mass transfer, bone mechanics, fracture mechanics, heat transfer in computer parts, mechanisms design.

Clarkson University, Graduate School, Wallace H. Coulter School of Engineering, Department of Mechanical and Aeronautical Engineering, Potsdam, NY 13699. Offers mechanical engineering (ME, MS, PhD). Part-time programs available. *Faculty:* 22 full-time (3 women). *Students:* 61 full-time (7 women); includes 3 minority (1 Asian, non-Hispanic/Latino; 1 Hispanic/Latino; 1 Two or more races, non-Hispanic/Latino), 27 international. Average age 27. 112 applicants, 63% accepted, 13 enrolled. In 2010, 10 master's, 4 doctorates awarded. Terminal master's awarded for partial completion of doctoral program. *Degree requirements:* For master's, thesis; for doctorate, comprehensive exam, thesis/dissertation, departmental qualifying exam. *Entrance requirements:* For master's and doctorate, GRE, transcripts of all college coursework, resume, personal statement, three letters of recommendation. Additional exam requirements/recommendations for international students: Required—TOEFL (minimum score 550 paper-based; 213 computer-based; 80 iBT), IELTS (minimum score 6.5). *Application deadline:* For fall admission, 1/30 priority date for domestic and international students; for spring admission, 9/1 priority date for domestic and international students. Applications are processed on a rolling basis. Application fee: $25 ($35 for international students). Electronic applications accepted. *Expenses:* Tuition: Part-time $1136 per credit hour. *Financial support:* In 2010–11, 53 students received support, including 5 fellowships with full tuition reimbursements available (averaging $21,580 per year), 37 research assistantships with full tuition reimbursements available (averaging $21,580 per year), 17 teaching assistantships with full tuition reimbursements available (averaging $21,580 per year); scholarships/grants, tuition waivers (partial),

Mechanical Engineering

Clarkson University (continued)
and unspecified assistantships also available. *Faculty research:* Electrostatic forces, intelligent systems, airflow study, acoustic measurement, cloud sampling, battle radar. Total annual research expenditures: $2.6 million. *Unit head:* Dr. Daryush Aidun, Chair, 315-268-6586, Fax: 315-268-6695, E-mail: dka@clarkson.edu. *Application contact:* Kelly Sharlow, Assistant to the Dean, 315-268-7929, Fax: 315-268-4494, E-mail: ksharlow@clarkson.edu.

Clemson University, Graduate School, College of Engineering and Science, Department of Mechanical Engineering, Clemson, SC 29634. Offers MS, PhD. *Faculty:* 34 full-time (1 woman), 3 part-time/adjunct (0 women). *Students:* 154 full-time (15 women), 17 part-time (1 woman); includes 9 minority (3 Black or African American, non-Hispanic/Latino; 5 Asian, non-Hispanic/Latino; 1 Two or more races, non-Hispanic/Latino), 111 international. Average age 26. 334 applicants, 55% accepted, 41 enrolled. In 2010, 49 master's, 8 doctorates awarded. *Degree requirements:* For master's, thesis; for doctorate, thesis/dissertation. *Entrance requirements:* For master's and doctorate, GRE General Test. Additional exam requirements/recommendations for international students: Required—TOEFL. *Application deadline:* For fall admission, 6/1 for domestic students. Applications are processed on a rolling basis. Application fee: $70 ($80 for international students). Electronic applications accepted. *Expenses:* Contact institution. *Financial support:* In 2010–11, 136 students received support, including 6 fellowships with partial tuition reimbursements available (averaging $11,167 per year), 76 research assistantships with partial tuition reimbursements available (averaging $14,850 per year), 59 teaching assistantships with partial tuition reimbursements available (averaging $8,994 per year); career-related internships or fieldwork, institutionally sponsored loans, scholarships/grants, health care benefits, and unspecified assistantships also available. Support available to part-time students. Financial award applicants required to submit FAFSA. *Faculty research:* Thermal sciences, fluid mechanics, automated manufacturing and robotics, materials engineering. Total annual research expenditures: $3.1 million. *Unit head:* Dr. Donald Beasley, ME Department Chair, 864-656-5622, Fax: 864-656-4435, E-mail: debsl@exchange.clemson.edu. *Application contact:* Dr. Richard Miller, Coordinator, 864-656-6248, Fax: 864-656-4435, E-mail: rm@clemson.edu.

Cleveland State University, College of Graduate Studies, Fenn College of Engineering, Department of Civil and Environmental Engineering, Cleveland, OH 44115. Offers accelerated program civil engineering (MS); accelerated program environmental engineering (MS); civil engineering (MS, D Eng); engineering mechanics (MS); environmental engineering (MS). Part-time and evening/weekend programs available. *Faculty:* 9 full-time (1 woman), 1 part-time/adjunct (0 women). *Students:* 8 full-time (0 women), 43 part-time (9 women); includes 2 Black or African American, non-Hispanic/Latino; 2 Asian, non-Hispanic/Latino; 1 Hispanic/Latino, 16 international. Average age 26. 67 applicants, 61% accepted, 14 enrolled. In 2010, 13 master's, 2 doctorates awarded. *Degree requirements:* For master's, project or thesis; for doctorate, comprehensive exam, thesis/dissertation, candidacy and qualifying exams. *Entrance requirements:* For master's, GRE General Test, GRE Subject Test, minimum GPA of 2.75; for doctorate, GRE General Test, GRE Subject Test, minimum GPA of 3.25. Additional exam requirements/recommendations for international students: Required—TOEFL (minimum score 525 paper-based; 197 computer-based). *Application deadline:* For fall admission, 7/15 priority date for domestic students. Applications are processed on a rolling basis. Application fee: $30. *Expenses:* Tuition, state resident: full-time $8447; part-time $469 per credit hour. Tuition, nonresident: full-time $16,020; part-time $890 per credit hour. Required fees: $50. *Financial support:* In 2010–11, 9 research assistantships with full and partial tuition reimbursements (averaging $3,920 per year) were awarded; teaching assistantships with tuition reimbursements, career-related internships or fieldwork, scholarships/grants, and unspecified assistantships also available. Financial award application deadline: 9/1. *Faculty research:* Solid-waste disposal, constitutive modeling, transportation, safety engineering. Total annual research expenditures: $800,000. *Unit head:* Dr. Stephen F. Duffy, Chairperson, 216-687-3874, Fax: 216-687-9280, E-mail: p.bosela@csuohio.edu. *Application contact:* Dr. Stephen F. Duffy, Chairperson, 216-687-3874, Fax: 216-687-9280, E-mail: p.bosela@csuohio.edu.

Cleveland State University, College of Graduate Studies, Fenn College of Engineering, Department of Mechanical Engineering, Cleveland, OH 44115. Offers MS, D Eng. Part-time programs available. *Faculty:* 9 full-time (0 women). *Students:* 13 full-time (4 women), 57 part-time (14 women); includes 1 Black or African American, non-Hispanic/Latino; 2 Asian, non-Hispanic/Latino; 1 Hispanic/Latino, 32 international. Average age 26. 117 applicants, 56% accepted, 13 enrolled. In 2010, 22 master's awarded. *Degree requirements:* For master's, project or thesis; for doctorate, thesis/dissertation, candidacy and qualifying exams. *Entrance requirements:* For master's, GRE General Test, minimum GPA of 3.0; for doctorate, GRE General Test, minimum GPA of 3.25. Additional exam requirements/recommendations for international students: Required—TOEFL (minimum score 525 paper-based; 197 computer-based). *Application deadline:* For fall admission, 7/15 priority date for domestic students; for spring admission, 12/15 priority date for domestic students. Applications are processed on a rolling basis. Application fee: $30. *Expenses:* Tuition, state resident: full-time $8447; part-time $469 per credit hour. Tuition, nonresident: full-time $16,020; part-time $890 per credit hour. Required fees: $50. *Financial support:* In 2010–11, 22 students received support, including 9 research assistantships with full and partial tuition reimbursements available (averaging $3,480 per year); teaching assistantships with partial tuition reimbursements available, career-related internships or fieldwork, Federal Work-Study, institutionally sponsored loans, and unspecified assistantships also available. Support available to part-time students. *Faculty research:* Fluid piezoelectric sensors, laser-optical inspection simulation of forging and forming processes, multiphase flow and heat transfer, turbulent flows. *Unit head:* Dr. William J. Atherton, Interim Chair, 216-687-2595, Fax: 216-687-5375, E-mail: w.atherton@csuohio.edu. *Application contact:* Dr. William J. Atherton, Interim Chair, 216-687-2595, Fax: 216-687-5375, E-mail: w.atherton@csuohio.edu.

Colorado State University, Graduate School, College of Engineering, Department of Mechanical Engineering, Fort Collins, CO 80523-1374. Offers ME, MS, PhD. Part-time and evening/weekend programs available. Postbaccalaureate distance learning degree programs offered (no on-campus study). *Faculty:* 19 full-time (2 women), 1 part-time/adjunct (0 women). *Students:* 52 full-time (5 women), 62 part-time (5 women); includes 7 minority (2 Asian, non-Hispanic/Latino; 3 Hispanic/Latino; 1 Native Hawaiian or other Pacific Islander, non-Hispanic/Latino; 1 Two or more races, non-Hispanic/Latino), 33 international. Average age 30. 114 applicants, 37% accepted, 25 enrolled. In 2010, 20 master's, 7 doctorates awarded. Terminal master's awarded for partial completion of doctoral program. *Degree requirements:* For master's, comprehensive exam, thesis, oral exam; for doctorate, comprehensive exam, thesis/dissertation, preliminary exams, diagnostic exams, defense as final exam. *Entrance requirements:* For master's, GRE General Test (minimum score 1200 verbal and quantitative, 4.5 analytical), minimum GPA of 3.0, BS/BA from ABET-accredited institution, 3 letters of recommendation, curriculum vitae/resume; for doctorate, GRE General Test (minimum score of 1200 on Verbal and Quantitative sections and 4.5 on the Analytical section), minimum GPA of 3.0, 3 letters of recommendation, curriculum vitae, department application, statement of purpose, resume. Additional exam requirements/recommendations for international students: Required—TOEFL (minimum score 550 paper-based; 213 computer-based; 80 iBT). *Application deadline:* For fall admission, 1/15 priority date for domestic and international students; for spring admission, 4/1 priority date for domestic and international students. Application fee: $50. Electronic applications accepted. *Expenses:* Contact institution. *Financial support:* In 2010–11, 56 students received support, including 4 fellowships (averaging $22,144 per year), 36 research assistantships with tuition reimbursements available (averaging $14,244 per year), 16 teaching assistantships with tuition reimbursements available (averaging $11,069 per year); Federal Work-Study and scholarships/grants also available. Financial award application deadline: 1/15; financial award applicants required to submit FAFSA. *Faculty research:* Advanced materials processing and plasma engineering, energy conversion, dynamic and industrial systems, motorsport engineering, bioengineering. Total annual research expenditures: $4.3 million. *Unit head:* Dr. Susan P. James, Head, 970-491-6559, Fax: 970-491-3827, E-mail: susan.james@colostate.edu. *Application contact:* Karen Mueller, Graduate Coordinator, 970-491-3872, Fax: 970-491-3827, E-mail: karen.mueller@colostate.edu.

Columbia University, Fu Foundation School of Engineering and Applied Science, Department of Mechanical Engineering, New York, NY 10027. Offers MS, Eng Sc D, PhD, Engr. PhD offered through the Graduate School of Arts and Sciences. Part-time programs available. Postbaccalaureate distance learning degree programs offered (no on-campus study). *Faculty:* 15 full-time (1 woman), 9 part-time/adjunct (1 woman). *Students:* 128 full-time (22 women), 31 part-time (5 women); includes 21 minority (4 Black or African American, non-Hispanic/Latino; 12 Asian, non-Hispanic/Latino; 2 Hispanic/Latino; 3 Two or more races, non-Hispanic/Latino), 99 international. Average age 27. 374 applicants, 43% accepted, 60 enrolled. In 2010, 65 master's, 10 doctorates awarded. *Degree requirements:* For doctorate, thesis/dissertation, qualifying exam. *Entrance requirements:* For master's, GRE General Test, minimum GPA of 3.3; for doctorate and Engr, GRE General Test. Additional exam requirements/recommendations for international students: Required—TOEFL, IELTS. *Application deadline:* For fall admission, 12/1 priority date for domestic and international students; for spring admission, 10/1 priority date for domestic and international students. Application fee: $95. Electronic applications accepted. *Financial support:* In 2010–11, 75 students received support, including 8 fellowships with full tuition reimbursements available (averaging $35,000 per year), 53 research assistantships with full tuition reimbursements available (averaging $30,667 per year), 14 teaching assistantships with full tuition reimbursements available (averaging $30,667 per year); health care benefits also available. Financial award application deadline: 12/1; financial award applicants required to submit FAFSA. *Faculty research:* Biomechanics, solid mechanics, molecular biology, energy and tribology. *Unit head:* Dr. Y. Lawrence Yao, Professor and Department Chair, 212-854-2887, Fax: 212-854-3304, E-mail: yly1@columbia.edu. *Application contact:* Sandra Morris, Department Administrator, 212-854-6269, Fax: 212-854-3304, E-mail: swm16@columbia.edu.

Concordia University, School of Graduate Studies, Faculty of Engineering and Computer Science, Department of Mechanical and Industrial Engineering, Montréal, QC H3G 1M8, Canada. Offers composites (M Eng); industrial engineering (M Eng, MA Sc); mechanical engineering (M Eng, MA Sc, PhD, Certificate); software systems for industrial engineering (Certificate). M Eng in composites program offered jointly with École Polytechnique de Montréal. *Degree requirements:* For master's, variable foreign language requirement, thesis or alternative; for doctorate, comprehensive exam, thesis/dissertation. *Faculty research:* Mechanical systems, fluid control systems, thermofluids engineering and robotics, industrial control systems.

Cooper Union for the Advancement of Science and Art, Albert Nerken School of Engineering, New York, NY 10003-7120. Offers chemical engineering (ME); civil engineering (ME); electrical engineering (ME); mechanical engineering (ME). Part-time programs available. *Faculty:* 27 full-time (1 woman), 15 part-time/adjunct (2 women). *Students:* 57 full-time (15 women), 25 part-time (1 woman); includes 2 Black or African American, non-Hispanic/Latino; 1 American Indian or Alaska Native, non-Hispanic/Latino; 22 Asian, non-Hispanic/Latino; 2 Hispanic/Latino, 16 international. Average age 24. 72 applicants, 39% accepted, 27 enrolled. In 2010, 25 master's awarded. *Degree requirements:* For master's, thesis. *Entrance requirements:* For master's, GRE, BE, minimum GPA of 3.5. Additional exam requirements/recommendations for international students: Required—TOEFL (minimum score 600 paper-based; 250 computer-based; 100 iBT). *Application deadline:* For fall admission, 2/15 for domestic and international students. Application fee: $65. *Expenses:* Tuition: Full-time $35,000; part-time $1100 per credit. Required fees: $825 per semester. *Financial support:* Fellowships with full tuition reimbursements, career-related internships or fieldwork, Federal Work-Study, tuition waivers (full), and all admitted students receive full-tuition scholarships available. Support available to part-time students. Financial award application deadline: 5/1; financial award applicants required to submit CSS PROFILE or FAFSA. *Faculty research:* Civil infrastructure, imaging and sensing technology, biomedical engineering, encryption technology, process engineering. *Unit head:* Dr. Simon Ben-Avi, Acting Dean, 212-353-4285, E-mail: benavi@cooper.edu. *Application contact:* Student Contact, 212-353-4120, E-mail: admissions@cooper.edu.

Cornell University, Graduate School, Graduate Fields of Engineering, Field of Mechanical Engineering, Ithaca, NY 14853-0001. Offers biomechanical engineering (M Eng, MS, PhD); combustion (M Eng, MS, PhD); energy and power systems (M Eng, MS, PhD); fluid mechanics (M Eng, MS, PhD); heat transfer (M Eng, MS, PhD); materials and manufacturing engineering (M Eng, MS, PhD); mechanical systems and design (M Eng, MS, PhD); multiphase flows (M Eng, MS, PhD). *Faculty:* 51 full-time (7 women). *Students:* 150 full-time (33 women); includes 3 Black or African American, non-Hispanic/Latino; 24 Asian, non-Hispanic/Latino; 6 Hispanic/Latino, 45 international. Average age 24. 586 applicants, 25% accepted, 78 enrolled. In 2010, 60 master's, 3 doctorates awarded. Terminal master's awarded for partial completion of doctoral program. *Degree requirements:* For master's, project (M Eng), thesis (MS); for doctorate, one foreign language, comprehensive exam, thesis/dissertation, 2 semesters of teaching experience. *Entrance requirements:* For master's and doctorate, GRE General Test, 3 letters of recommendation. Additional exam requirements/recommendations for international students: Required—TOEFL (minimum score 550 paper-based; 213 computer-based; 77 iBT). *Application deadline:* For fall admission, 1/15 for domestic students; for spring admission, 11/1 for domestic students. Application fee: $70. Electronic applications accepted. *Expenses:* Tuition: Full-time $29,500. Required fees: $76. Tuition and fees vary according to degree level and program. *Financial support:* In 2010–11, 47 students received support, including 34 fellowships with full tuition reimbursements available, 57 research assistantships with full tuition reimbursements available, 14 teaching assistantships with full tuition reimbursements available; institutionally sponsored loans, scholarships/grants, health care benefits, tuition waivers (full and partial), and unspecified assistantships also available. Financial award applicants required to submit FAFSA. *Faculty research:* Combustion and heat transfer, fluid mechanics and CFD, system dynamics and control, biomechanics, manufacturing. *Unit head:* Director of Graduate Studies, 607-255-5250. *Application contact:* Graduate Field Assistant, 607-255-5250, E-mail: maegrad@cornell.edu.

Dalhousie University, Faculty of Engineering, Department of Mechanical Engineering, Halifax, NS B3J 2X4, Canada. Offers M Eng, MA Sc, PhD. *Degree requirements:* For master's, thesis; for doctorate, thesis/dissertation. *Entrance requirements:* Additional exam requirements/recommendations for international students: Required—TOEFL, IELTS, CANTEST, CAEL, or Michigan English Language Assessment Battery. Electronic applications accepted. *Faculty research:* Fluid dynamics and energy, system dynamics, naval architecture, MEMS, space structures.

Dartmouth College, Thayer School of Engineering, Program in Mechanical Engineering, Hanover, NH 03755. Offers MS, PhD. *Degree requirements:* For master's, thesis; for doctorate, thesis/dissertation, candidacy oral exam. *Entrance requirements:* For master's and doctorate, GRE General Test. *Application deadline:* For fall admission, 1/1 priority date for domestic students. Application fee: $45. *Financial support:* Fellowships, research assistantships, teaching assistantships, career-related internships or fieldwork, Federal Work-Study, institutionally sponsored loans, and tuition waivers (full and partial) available. Financial award application deadline: 1/15. *Faculty research:* Tribology, dynamics and control systems, thermal science and energy conversion, fluid mechanics and multi-phase flow, mobile robots. Total annual research expenditures: $383,799. *Unit head:* Dr. Joseph J. Helbie, Dean, 603-646-2238, Fax: 603-646-2580, E-mail: joseph.j.helbie@dartmouth.edu. *Application contact:* Candace S. Potter, Graduate Admissions Administrator, 603-646-3844, Fax: 603-646-1620, E-mail: candace.potter@dartmouth.edu.

Drexel University, College of Engineering, Department of Mechanical Engineering and Mechanics, Philadelphia, PA 19104-2875. Offers mechanical engineering (MS, PhD). Part-time and evening/weekend programs available. Terminal master's awarded for partial completion of doctoral program. *Degree requirements:* For master's, thesis optional; for doctorate, thesis/dissertation. *Entrance requirements:* For master's, minimum GPA of 3.0, BS in engineering or science; for doctorate, minimum GPA of 3.5, MS in engineering or science. Additional exam requirements/recommendations for international students: Required—TOEFL. Electronic applications accepted. *Faculty research:* Composites, dynamic systems and control, combustion and fuels, biomechanics, mechanics and thermal fluid sciences.

Duke University, Graduate School, Pratt School of Engineering, Department of Mechanical Engineering and Materials Science, Durham, NC 27708. Offers materials science (MS, PhD); mechanical engineering (MS, PhD); JD/MS. Part-time programs available. *Faculty:* 26 full-time. *Students:* 73 full-time (14 women); includes 4 Asian, non-Hispanic/Latino; 1 Hispanic/Latino, 26 international. 247 applicants, 32% accepted, 27 enrolled. In 2010, 5 master's, 7 doctorates awarded. Terminal master's awarded for partial completion of doctoral program. *Degree requirements:* For master's, thesis optional; for doctorate, thesis/dissertation. *Entrance requirements:* For master's and doctorate, GRE General Test. Additional exam requirements/recommendations for international students: Required—TOEFL (minimum score 550 paper-based; 213 computer-based; 83 iBT), IELTS (minimum score 7). *Application deadline:* For fall admission, 12/8 priority date for domestic and international students; for spring admission, 11/1 for domestic students. Application fee: $75. Electronic applications accepted. *Financial support:* Fellowships, research assistantships, teaching assistantships, Federal Work-Study available. Financial award application deadline: 12/8. *Unit head:* Stefan Zauscher, Director of Graduate Studies, 919-660-5310, Fax: 919-660-8963, E-mail: kparrish@duke.edu. *Application contact:* Elizabeth Hutton, Director of Admissions, 919-684-3913, Fax: 919-684-2277, E-mail: grad-admissions@duke.edu.

Duke University, Graduate School, Pratt School of Engineering, Master of Engineering Program, Durham, NC 27708-0271. Offers biomedical engineering (M Eng); civil engineering (M Eng); electrical and computer engineering (M Eng); environmental engineering (M Eng); materials science and engineering (M Eng); mechanical engineering (M Eng); photonics and optical sciences (M Eng). Part-time programs available. *Faculty:* 123 full-time, 1 part-time/adjunct. *Students:* 9 full-time (4 women); includes 2 minority (both Asian, non-Hispanic/Latino), 3 international. Average age 24. *Entrance requirements:* For master's, GRE General Test, resume, 3 letters of recommendation, statement of purpose. Additional exam requirements/recommendations for international students: Required—TOEFL. *Application deadline:* For fall admission, 6/15 for domestic students, 2/15 for international students; for spring admission, 11/1 for domestic students, 9/1 for international students. Application fee: $75. *Financial support:* Merit scholarships/grants available. *Unit head:* Dr. Bradley A. Fox, Executive Director, 919-660-5455, Fax: 919-660-5456. *Application contact:* Erin Degerman, Admissions Coordinator, 919-668-6789, Fax: 919-660-5456, E-mail: erin.degerman@duke.edu.

École Polytechnique de Montréal, Graduate Programs, Department of Mechanical Engineering, Montréal, QC H3C 3A7, Canada. Offers aerothermics (M Eng, M Sc A, PhD); applied mechanics (M Eng, M Sc A, PhD); tool design (M Eng, M Sc A, PhD). Part-time and evening/weekend programs available. *Degree requirements:* For master's, one foreign language, thesis; for doctorate, one foreign language, thesis/dissertation. *Entrance requirements:* For master's, minimum GPA of 2.75; for doctorate, minimum GPA of 3.0. *Faculty research:* Noise control and vibration, fatigue and creep, aerodynamics, composite materials, biomechanics, robotics.

Embry-Riddle Aeronautical University–Daytona, Daytona Beach Campus Graduate Program, Department of Mechanical Engineering, Daytona Beach, FL 32114-3900. Offers MSME. *Faculty:* 5 full-time (0 women). *Students:* 34 full-time (5 women), 2 part-time (1 woman); includes 7 minority (2 Black or African American, non-Hispanic/Latino; 1 American Indian or Alaska Native, non-Hispanic/Latino; 3 Asian, non-Hispanic/Latino; 1 Hispanic/Latino), 11 international. Average age 25. 45 applicants, 60% accepted, 17 enrolled. In 2010, 2 master's awarded. *Degree requirements:* For master's, thesis. *Entrance requirements:* Additional exam requirements/recommendations for international students: Required—TOEFL (minimum score 550 paper-based; 213 computer-based; 79 iBT). *Application deadline:* For fall admission, 8/1 priority date for domestic students; for spring admission, 12/1 priority date for domestic students. Applications are processed on a rolling basis. Application fee: $50. *Expenses:* Tuition: Full-time $14,040; part-time $1170 per credit hour. *Financial support:* In 2010–11, 19 students received support, including 4 research assistantships (averaging $6,598 per year), 10 teaching assistantships (averaging $6,598 per year). Financial award applicants required to submit FAFSA. *Unit head:* Dr. Charles Reinholtz, Department Chair, 386-323-8848, E-mail: charles.reinholtz@erau.edu. *Application contact:* Keith Deaton, Associate Director, International and Graduate Admissions, 800-388-3728, Fax: 386-226-7070, E-mail: graduate.admissions@erau.edu.

Fairfield University, School of Engineering, Fairfield, CT 06824-5195. Offers electrical and computer engineering (MS); management of technology (MS); mechanical engineering (MS); software engineering (MS). Part-time and evening/weekend programs available. *Faculty:* 8 full-time (1 woman), 11 part-time/adjunct (0 women). *Students:* 31 full-time (12 women), 98 part-time (20 women); includes 28 minority (5 Black or African American, non-Hispanic/Latino; 17 Asian, non-Hispanic/Latino; 4 Hispanic/Latino; 1 Native Hawaiian or other Pacific Islander, non-Hispanic/Latino; 1 Two or more races, non-Hispanic/Latino), 26 international. Average age 35. 120 applicants, 55% accepted, 15 enrolled. In 2010, 52 master's awarded. *Degree requirements:* For master's, thesis, capstone course. *Entrance requirements:* For master's, interview, minimum GPA of 2.8, resume, 2 recommendations. Additional exam requirements/recommendations for international students: Required—TOEFL (minimum score 550 paper-based; 213 computer-based; 80 iBT). *Application deadline:* For fall admission, 5/15 for international students; for spring admission, 10/15 for international students. Applications are processed on a rolling basis. Application fee: $60. Electronic applications accepted. *Expenses:* Contact institution. *Financial support:* In 2010–11, 25 students received support. Unspecified assistantships available. Financial award applicants required to submit FAFSA. *Faculty research:* Vehicle dynamics, image processing, multimedia in instruction, thermal packaging, character recognition, photovoltaics and nanotechnology, Web technology. *Unit head:* Dr. Jack Beal, Dean, 203-254-4000 Ext. 4147, Fax: 203-254-4013, E-mail: jwbeal@fairfield.edu. *Application contact:* Marianne Gumpper, Director of Graduate and Continuing Studies Admissions, 203-254-4184, Fax: 203-254-4073, E-mail: gradadmis@fairfield.edu.

Florida Agricultural and Mechanical University, Division of Graduate Studies, Research, and Continuing Education, FAMU-FSU College of Engineering, Department of Mechanical Engineering, Tallahassee, FL 32307-3200. Offers MS, PhD. *Degree requirements:* For master's, thesis optional; for doctorate, comprehensive exam, thesis/dissertation. *Entrance requirements:* For master's, GRE General Test, minimum GPA of 3.0. Additional exam requirements/recommendations for international students: Required—TOEFL (minimum score 550 paper-based; 213 computer-based). *Faculty research:* Fluid mechanical and heat transfer, thermodynamics, dynamics and controls, mechanics and materials.

Florida Atlantic University, College of Engineering and Computer Science, Department of Ocean and Mechanical Engineering, Boca Raton, FL 33431-0991. Offers mechanical engineering (MS, PhD); ocean engineering (MS, PhD). Part-time and evening/weekend programs available. *Faculty:* 23 full-time (1 woman), 3 part-time/adjunct (0 women). *Students:* 51 full-time (11 women), 42 part-time (9 women); includes 16 minority (4 Black or African American, non-Hispanic/Latino; 1 American Indian or Alaska Native, non-Hispanic/Latino; 2 Asian, non-Hispanic/Latino; 9 Hispanic/Latino), 25 international. Average age 29. 45 applicants, 60% accepted, 16 enrolled. In 2010, 23 master's, 1 doctorate awarded. Terminal master's awarded for partial completion of doctoral program. *Degree requirements:* For master's, thesis (for some programs); for doctorate, comprehensive exam, thesis/dissertation, qualifying exam. *Entrance requirements:* For master's and doctorate, GRE General Test, minimum GPA of 3.0. Additional exam requirements/recommendations for international students: Required—TOEFL. *Application deadline:* For fall admission, 7/1 priority date for domestic students, 2/15 for international students; for spring admission, 11/1 for domestic students, 7/15 for international students. Applications are processed on a rolling basis. Application fee: $30. *Expenses:* Tuition, area resident: Part-time $319.96 per credit. Tuition, state resident: part-time $319.96 per credit. Tuition, nonresident: part-time $926.42 per credit. *Financial support:* In 2010–11, research assistantships (averaging $15,000 per year); career-related internships or fieldwork, Federal Work-Study, scholarships/grants, and unspecified assistantships also available. Financial award application deadline: 1/10; financial award applicants required to submit FAFSA. *Faculty research:* Marine materials and corrosion, ocean structures, marine vehicles, acoustics and vibrations, hydrodynamics, coastal engineering. *Unit head:* Dr. Manhar Dhanak, Chairman, 954-924-7000, Fax: 954-924-7270, E-mail: dhanak@oe.fau.edu. *Application contact:* Dr. Manhar Dhanak, Chairman, 954-924-7000, Fax: 954-924-7270, E-mail: dhanak@oe.fau.edu.

Florida Institute of Technology, Graduate Programs, College of Engineering, Mechanical and Aerospace Engineering Department, Melbourne, FL 32901-6975. Offers aerospace engineering (MS, PhD); mechanical engineering (MS, PhD). Part-time programs available. *Faculty:* 13 full-time (0 women). *Students:* 59 full-time (3 women), 30 part-time (5 women); includes 7 minority (1 Black or African American, non-Hispanic/Latino; 1 Asian, non-Hispanic/Latino; 4 Hispanic/Latino; 1 Two or more races, non-Hispanic/Latino), 47 international. Average age 26. 183 applicants, 47% accepted, 24 enrolled. In 2010, 24 master's awarded. Terminal master's awarded for partial completion of doctoral program. *Degree requirements:* For master's, comprehensive exam (for some programs), thesis optional; for doctorate, comprehensive exam, thesis/dissertation, oral section of written exam, complete program of significant original research. *Entrance requirements:* For master's, GRE General Test, minimum GPA of 3.0, bachelor's degree from an ABET-accredited program, transcripts; for doctorate, GRE General Test, 3 letters of recommendation, minimum GPA of 3.2, resume, statement of objectives. Additional exam requirements/recommendations for international students: Required—TOEFL (minimum score 550 paper-based; 213 computer-based; 79 iBT). *Application deadline:* For fall admission, 4/1 for international students; for spring admission, 9/30 for international students. Applications are processed on a rolling basis. Application fee: $50. Electronic applications accepted. *Expenses:* Tuition: Part-time $1040 per credit hour. Tuition and fees vary according to campus/location. *Financial support:* In 2010–11, 4 research assistantships with full and partial tuition reimbursements (averaging $3,310 per year), 14 teaching assistantships with full and partial tuition reimbursements (averaging $2,362 per year) were awarded; career-related internships or fieldwork, institutionally sponsored loans, tuition waivers (partial), unspecified assistantships, and tuition remissions also available. Support available to part-time students. Financial award application deadline: 3/1; financial award applicants required to submit FAFSA. *Faculty research:* Dynamic systems, robotics, and controls; structures, solid mechanics, and materials; thermal-fluid sciences, optical tomography, composite/recycled materials. Total annual research expenditures: $924,059. *Unit head:* Dr. Pei-feng Hsu, Department Head, 321-674-8092, Fax: 321-674-8813, E-mail: phsu@fit.edu. *Application contact:* Cheryl A. Brown, Associate Director of Graduate Admissions, 321-674-7581, Fax: 321-723-9468, E-mail: cbrown@fit.eu.

Florida Institute of Technology, Graduate Programs, Extended Studies Division, Melbourne, FL 32901-6975. Offers acquisition and contract management (MS); aerospace engineering (MS); business administration (MBA); computer information systems (MS); computer science (MS); electrical engineering (MS); engineering management (MS); human resources management (MS); logistics management (MS), including humanitarian and disaster relief logistics; management (MS), including acquisition and contract management, e-business, human resources management, information systems, logistics management, management, transportation management; material acquisition management (MS); mechanical engineering (MS); operations research (MS); project management (MS), including information systems, operations research; public administration (MPA); quality management (MS); software engineering (MS); space systems (MS); space systems management (MS); systems management (MS), including information systems, operations research. Part-time and evening/weekend programs available. Postbaccalaureate distance learning degree programs offered (no on-campus study). *Faculty:* 11 full-time (3 women), 118 part-time/adjunct (24 women). *Students:* 69 full-time (23 women), 907 part-time (369 women); includes 385 minority (242 Black or African American, non-Hispanic/Latino; 15 American Indian or Alaska Native, non-Hispanic/Latino; 44 Asian, non-Hispanic/Latino; 52 Hispanic/Latino; 3 Native Hawaiian or other Pacific Islander, non-Hispanic/Latino; 29 Two or more races, non-Hispanic/Latino), 17 international. 517 applicants, 49% accepted, 245 enrolled. In 2010, 430 degrees awarded. *Degree requirements:* For master's, comprehensive exam (for some programs), capstone course. *Entrance requirements:* For master's, GMAT or resume showing 8 years of supervised experience, minimum GPA of 3.0, 2 letters of recommendation, resume. Additional exam requirements/recommendations for international students: Required—TOEFL (minimum score 550 paper-based; 213 computer-based; 79 iBT). *Application deadline:* For fall admission, 4/1 for international students; for spring admission, 9/30 for international students. Applications are processed on a rolling basis. Application fee: $50. Electronic applications accepted. *Expenses:* Contact institution. *Financial support:* Application deadline: 3/1. *Unit head:* Dr. Theodore Richardson, Senior Associate Dean, 321-674-8123, Fax: 321-674-7597, E-mail: trichardson@fit.edu. *Application contact:* Carolyn Farrior, Director of Graduate Admissions, Online Learning and Off-Campus Programs, 321-674-7118, Fax: 321-674-8216, E-mail: cfarrior@fit.edu.

Florida International University, College of Engineering and Computing, Department of Mechanical and Materials Engineering, Mechanical Engineering Program, Miami, FL 33175. Offers MS, PhD. Part-time and evening/weekend programs available. *Students:* 25 full-time (10 women), 3 part-time (1 woman); includes 2 Black or African American, non-Hispanic/Latino; 2 Asian, non-Hispanic/Latino; 15 Hispanic/Latino, 21 international. Average age 27. 50 applicants, 16% accepted, 7 enrolled. In 2010, 8 master's, 1 doctorate awarded. Terminal master's awarded for partial completion of doctoral program. *Degree requirements:* For master's, thesis or alternative; for doctorate, comprehensive exam, thesis/dissertation. *Entrance requirements:* For master's, minimum undergraduate GPA of 3.0 in upper level coursework, letters of recommendation, letter of intent; for doctorate, GRE, minimum undergraduate GPA of 3.0, 3 letters of recommendation, letter of intent. Additional exam requirements/recommendations for international students: Required—TOEFL (minimum score 550 paper-based; 80 iBT). *Application deadline:* For fall admission, 6/1 for domestic students, 4/1 for international students; for spring admission, 10/1 for domestic students, 9/1 for international students. Applications are processed on a rolling basis. Application fee: $30. Electronic applications accepted. *Financial support:* Institutionally sponsored loans, scholarships/grants, and unspecified assistantships available. Financial award application deadline: 3/1; financial award applicants required to submit FAFSA. *Unit head:* Dr. Cesar Levy, Chair, Mechanical and Materials Engineering Department, 305-348-0104, Fax: 305-348-1932, E-mail: cesar.levy@fiu.edu. *Application contact:* Maria Parrilla, Graduate Admissions Assistant, 305-348-1890, Fax: 305-348-6142, E-mail: grad_eng@fiu.edu.

Florida State University, The Graduate School, FAMU-FSU College of Engineering, Department of Mechanical Engineering, Tallahassee, FL 32310-6046. Offers mechanical engineering (MS, PhD); sustainable energy (MS). Part-time programs available. *Faculty:* 18 full-time (2 women), 4 part-time/adjunct (0 women). *Students:* 72 full-time (12 women); includes 12 Black or African American, non-Hispanic/Latino; 3 Hispanic/Latino, 26 international. 92 applicants, 52% accepted, 16 enrolled. In 2010, 11 master's, 6 doctorates awarded. Terminal master's awarded for partial completion of doctoral program. *Degree requirements:* For master's, thesis optional, 30 credit hours (27 course, 6 research) or 33 credit hours (for non-thesis); for doctorate, thesis/dissertation, 45 credit hours (21 course, 24 research). *Entrance requirements:* For master's and doctorate, GRE General Test, minimum GPA of 3.0, official transcripts, resume, personal statement, 3 letters of recommendation. Additional exam requirements/recommendations for international students: Required—TOEFL (minimum score 550 paper-based; 213 computer-based; 80 iBT), IELTS (minimum score 6.5), Michigan English Language Assessment Battery (minimum score 77). *Application deadline:* For fall admission, 5/1 for domestic and international students; for spring admission, 10/1 for domestic and international students. Applications are processed on a rolling basis. Application fee: $30. Electronic applications accepted. *Expenses:* Tuition, state resident: full-time $8238.24. *Financial support:* In 2010–11, 1 fellowship with full tuition reimbursement (averaging $30,000 per year), 50 research assistantships with full tuition reimbursements (averaging $20,000 per year), 10 teaching assistantships with full tuition reimbursements (averaging $20,000 per year) were awarded; career-related internships or fieldwork, institutionally sponsored loans, scholarships/grants, health care benefits, tuition waivers (partial), and unspecified assistantships also available. Support available to part-time students. Financial award applicants required to submit FAFSA. *Faculty research:* Aero-propulsion, superconductivity, smart materials, nano-materials, intelligent robotic systems, robotic locomotion, sustainable energy. Total annual research expenditures: $5 million. *Unit head:* Dr. Chiang Shih, Chair, 850-410-6321, Fax: 850-410-6337, E-mail: shih@eng.fsu.edu.

Mechanical Engineering

Florida State University (continued)

Application contact: George Green, Coordinator of Graduate Studies, 850-410-6196, Fax: 850-410-6337, E-mail: ggreen@eng.fsu.edu.

Gannon University, School of Graduate Studies, College of Engineering and Business, School of Engineering and Computer Science, Program in Mechanical Engineering, Erie, PA 16541-0001. Offers MSME. Part-time and evening/weekend programs available. *Students:* 26 full-time (0 women), 10 part-time (3 women), 21 international. Average age 24. 113 applicants, 81% accepted, 8 enrolled. In 2010, 27 master's awarded. *Degree requirements:* For master's, comprehensive exam, thesis or project. *Entrance requirements:* For master's, GRE or GMAT, bachelor's degree in mechanical engineering, minimum QPA of 2.5. Additional exam requirements/recommendations for international students: Required—TOEFL (minimum score 79 iBT). *Application deadline:* Applications are processed on a rolling basis. Application fee: $25. Electronic applications accepted. *Expenses:* Tuition: Full-time $14,670; part-time $815 per credit. Required fees: $430; $18 per credit. Tuition and fees vary according to class time, course load, degree level, campus/location and program. *Financial support:* Career-related internships or fieldwork, scholarships/grants, traineeships, and unspecified assistantships available. Financial award application deadline: 7/1; financial award applicants required to submit FAFSA. *Unit head:* Dr. Scott Steinbrink, Chair, 814-871-5302, E-mail: steinbri001@gannon.edu. *Application contact:* Kara Morgan, Assistant Director of Graduate Admissions, 814-871-5831, Fax: 814-871-5827, E-mail: graduate@gannon.edu.

The George Washington University, School of Engineering and Applied Science, Department of Mechanical and Aerospace Engineering, Washington, DC 20052. Offers MS, D Sc, App Sc, Engr, Graduate Certificate. Part-time and evening/weekend programs available. *Faculty:* 13 full-time (1 woman), 14 part-time/adjunct (2 women). *Students:* 45 full-time (13 women), 28 part-time (3 women); includes 4 Black or African American, non-Hispanic/Latino; 1 American Indian or Alaska Native, non-Hispanic/Latino; 5 Asian, non-Hispanic/Latino; 3 Hispanic/Latino, 27 international. Average age 28. 95 applicants, 84% accepted, 19 enrolled. In 2010, 11 master's, 4 doctorates, 1 other advanced degree awarded. *Degree requirements:* For master's, thesis optional; for doctorate, thesis/dissertation, final and qualifying exams. *Entrance requirements:* For master's, appropriate bachelor's degree, minimum GPA of 3.0; for doctorate, appropriate bachelor's or master's degree, minimum GPA of 3.4, GRE if highest earned degree is BS; for other advanced degree, appropriate master's degree, minimum GPA of 3.0. Additional exam requirements/recommendations for international students: Required—TOEFL or The George Washington University English as a Foreign Language Test. *Application deadline:* For fall admission, 3/1 priority date for domestic students; for spring admission, 10/1 for domestic students. Applications are processed on a rolling basis. Application fee: $75. *Financial support:* In 2010–11, 51 students received support; fellowships with tuition reimbursements available, research assistantships, teaching assistantships with tuition reimbursements available, career-related internships or fieldwork and institutionally sponsored loans available. Financial award application deadline: 3/1; financial award applicants required to submit FAFSA. *Unit head:* Dr. Michael Plesniak, Chairman, 202-994-6749, E-mail: maeng@gwu.edu. *Application contact:* Adina Lav, Marketing, Recruiting and Admissions, 202-994-5827, Fax: 202-994-0909, E-mail: engineering@gwu.edu.

Georgia Institute of Technology, Graduate Studies and Research, College of Engineering, George W. Woodruff School of Mechanical Engineering, Program in Mechanical Engineering, Atlanta, GA 30332-0001. Offers biomedical engineering (MS Bio E); mechanical engineering (MS, MSME, PhD). Part-time programs available. Postbaccalaureate distance learning degree programs offered (no on-campus study). Terminal master's awarded for partial completion of doctoral program. *Degree requirements:* For master's, thesis optional; for doctorate, comprehensive exam, thesis/dissertation. *Entrance requirements:* For master's and doctorate, GRE General Test, minimum GPA of 3.0. Additional exam requirements/recommendations for international students: Required—TOEFL. Electronic applications accepted. *Faculty research:* Automation and mechatronics; computer-aided engineering and design; micro-electronic mechanical systems; heat transfer, combustion and energy systems; fluid mechanics.

Georgia Southern University, Jack N. Averitt College of Graduate Studies, Allen E. Paulson College of Science and Technology, Department of Mechanical and Electrical Engineering Technology, Statesboro, GA 30460. Offers M Tech, MSAE, Certificate. Part-time and evening/weekend programs available. *Students:* 33 full-time (8 women), 20 part-time (3 women); includes 14 Black or African American, non-Hispanic/Latino; 4 Hispanic/Latino; 4 Two or more races, non-Hispanic/Latino, 6 international. Average age 27. 11 applicants, 100% accepted, 6 enrolled. In 2010, 7 master's awarded. *Degree requirements:* For master's, comprehensive exam, thesis optional. *Entrance requirements:* For master's, GRE. Additional exam requirements/recommendations for international students: Required—TOEFL (minimum score 550 paper-based; 213 computer-based; 80 iBT). *Application deadline:* For fall admission, 3/1 priority date for domestic and international students; for spring admission, 10/1 priority date for domestic students, 10/1 for international students. Applications are processed on a rolling basis. Application fee: $50. Electronic applications accepted. *Expenses:* Tuition, state resident: full-time $6000; part-time $250 per semester hour. Tuition, nonresident: full-time $23,976; part-time $999 per semester hour. Required fees: $1644. *Financial support:* In 2010–11, 37 students received support, including 4 research assistantships with partial tuition reimbursements available (averaging $7,200 per year); tuition waivers (partial) and unspecified assistantships also available. Financial award application deadline: 4/15; financial award applicants required to submit FAFSA. *Faculty research:* Interdisciplinary research in computational mechanics, experimental and computational biofuel combustion and tribology, mechatronics and control, thermomechanical and thermofluid finite element modeling, information technology. Total annual research expenditures: $458,293. *Unit head:* Dr. Mohammad S. Davoud, Chair, 912-478-0540, Fax: 912-478-1455, E-mail: mdavoud@georgiasouthern.edu. *Application contact:* Dr. Charles Ziglar, Coordinator for Graduate Student Recruitment, 912-478-5635, Fax: 912-478-0740, E-mail: gradadmissions@georgiasouthern.edu.

Graduate School and University Center of the City University of New York, Graduate Studies, Program in Engineering, New York, NY 10016-4039. Offers biomedical engineering (PhD); chemical engineering (PhD); civil engineering (PhD); electrical engineering (PhD); mechanical engineering (PhD). *Degree requirements:* For doctorate, thesis/dissertation. *Entrance requirements:* For doctorate, GRE General Test. Additional exam requirements/recommendations for international students: Required—TOEFL. Electronic applications accepted.

Grand Valley State University, Padnos College of Engineering and Computing, School of Engineering, Allendale, MI 49401-9403. Offers electrical and computer engineering (MSE); manufacturing operations (MSE); mechanical engineering (MSE); product design and manufacturing engineering (MSE). Part-time and evening/weekend programs available. *Degree requirements:* For master's, project or thesis. *Entrance requirements:* For master's, engineering degree, minimum GPA of 3.0. Additional exam requirements/recommendations for international students: Required—TOEFL. Electronic applications accepted. *Faculty research:* Digital signal processing, computer aided design, computer aided manufacturing, manufacturing simulation, biomechanics, product design.

Howard University, College of Engineering, Architecture, and Computer Sciences, School of Engineering and Computer Science, Department of Mechanical Engineering, Washington, DC 20059-0002. Offers M Eng, PhD. *Degree requirements:* For master's, comprehensive exam, thesis; for doctorate, one foreign language, comprehensive exam, thesis/dissertation, 2 terms of residency. *Entrance requirements:* For master's and doctorate, GRE General Test, minimum GPA of 3.0. Additional exam requirements/recommendations for international students: Required—TOEFL (minimum score 213 computer-based). Electronic applications accepted. *Faculty research:* The dynamics and control of large flexible space structures, optimization of space structures.

Idaho State University, Office of Graduate Studies, College of Engineering, Mechanical Engineering Department, Pocatello, ID 83209-8060. Offers measurement and control engineering (MS); mechanical engineering (MS). Part-time programs available. *Degree requirements:* For master's, comprehensive exam (for some programs), 2 semesters of seminar; thesis or project. *Entrance requirements:* For master's, GRE. Additional exam requirements/recommendations for international students: Required—TOEFL (minimum score 550 paper-based; 213 computer-based; 80 iBT). Electronic applications accepted. *Faculty research:* Modeling and identification of biomedical systems, intelligent systems and adaptive control, active flow control of turbo machinery, validation of advanced computational codes for thermal fluid interactions, development of methodologies for the assessment of passive safety system performance in advanced reactors, alternative energy research (wind, solar, hydrogen).

Illinois Institute of Technology, Graduate College, Armour College of Engineering, Department of Mechanical, Materials and Aerospace Engineering, Chicago, IL 60616-3793. Offers manufacturing engineering (MME, MS); materials science and engineering (MMME, MS, PhD); mechanical and aerospace engineering (MMAE, MS, PhD), including economics (MS), energy (MS), environment (MS). Part-time and evening/weekend programs available. Postbaccalaureate distance learning degree programs offered (minimal on-campus study). *Faculty:* 26 full-time (1 woman), 6 part-time/adjunct (1 woman). *Students:* 135 full-time (22 women), 45 part-time (4 women); includes 11 minority (1 American Indian or Alaska Native, non-Hispanic/Latino; 9 Asian, non-Hispanic/Latino; 1 Hispanic/Latino), 117 international. Average age 27. 693 applicants, 41% accepted, 63 enrolled. In 2010, 58 master's, 4 doctorates awarded. Terminal master's awarded for partial completion of doctoral program. *Degree requirements:* For master's, comprehensive exam (for some programs), thesis (for some programs); for doctorate, comprehensive exam, thesis/dissertation. *Entrance requirements:* For master's and doctorate, GRE General Test (minimum score 1000 Quantitative and Verbal, 3.0 Analytical Writing), minimum undergraduate GPA of 3.0. Additional exam requirements/recommendations for international students: Required—TOEFL (minimum score 523 paper-based; 70 iBT); Recommended—IELTS (minimum score 5.5). *Application deadline:* For fall admission, 5/1 for domestic and international students; for spring admission, 10/15 for domestic and international students. Applications are processed on a rolling basis. Application fee: $50. Electronic applications accepted. *Expenses:* Tuition: Full-time $18,576; part-time $1032 per credit hour. Required fees: $583 per semester. One-time fee: $150. Tuition and fees vary according to program and student level. *Financial support:* In 2010–11, 7 fellowships with full and partial tuition reimbursements (averaging $7,673 per year), 33 research assistantships with full and partial tuition reimbursements (averaging $8,141 per year), 15 teaching assistantships with full and partial tuition reimbursements (averaging $6,930 per year) were awarded; Federal Work-Study, institutionally sponsored loans, scholarships/grants, health care benefits, tuition waivers, and unspecified assistantships also available. Support available to part-time students. Financial award applicants required to submit FAFSA. *Faculty research:* Fluid dynamics, metallurgical and materials engineering, solids and structures, computational mechanics, theoretical mechanics. Total annual research expenditures: $2.4 million. *Unit head:* Dr. Jamal Yagoobi, Professor and Chairman, 312-567-3239, Fax: 312-567-7230, E-mail: yagoobi@iit.edu. *Application contact:* Deborah Gibson, Director, Graduate Admission, 866-472-3448, Fax: 312-567-3138, E-mail: inquiry.grad@iit.edu.

Indiana University–Purdue University Fort Wayne, College of Engineering, Technology, and Computer Science, Department of Engineering, Fort Wayne, IN 46805-1499. Offers computer engineering (MS); electrical engineering (MS); mechanical engineering (MS); systems engineering (MS). Part-time programs available. *Faculty:* 18 full-time (3 women). *Students:* 7 full-time (0 women), 31 part-time (7 women); includes 4 minority (1 Black or African American, non-Hispanic/Latino; 2 Asian, non-Hispanic/Latino; 1 Hispanic/Latino), 4 international. Average age 28. 21 applicants, 95% accepted, 18 enrolled. In 2010, 9 master's awarded. *Entrance requirements:* For master's, minimum GPA of 3.0, bachelor's degree in engineering discipline. Additional exam requirements/recommendations for international students: Required—TOEFL (minimum score 550 paper-based; 213 computer-based; 77 iBT); Recommended—TWE. *Application deadline:* For fall admission, 7/15 priority date for domestic students, 5/15 priority date for international students; for spring admission, 12/1 priority date for domestic students, 10/15 priority date for international students. Applications are processed on a rolling basis. Application fee: $55 ($60 for international students). Electronic applications accepted. *Expenses:* Tuition, state resident: full-time $4824; part-time $268 per credit. Tuition, nonresident: full-time $11,625; part-time $646 per credit. Required fees: $555; $30.85 per credit. Tuition and fees vary according to course load. *Financial support:* In 2010–11, 5 research assistantships with partial tuition reimbursements (averaging $12,740 per year), 3 teaching assistantships with partial tuition reimbursements (averaging $12,740 per year) were awarded. Financial award application deadline: 3/1; financial award applicants required to submit FAFSA. *Faculty research:* Worm-scanning strategies, measuring the acceleration of gravity. Total annual research expenditures: $129,186. *Unit head:* Dr. Donald Mueller, Chair, 260-481-5707, Fax: 260-481-6281, E-mail: mueller@engr.ipfw.edu. *Application contact:* Dr. Donald Mueller, Chair, 260-481-5707, Fax: 260-481-6281, E-mail: mueller@engr.ipfw.edu.

Indiana University–Purdue University Indianapolis, School of Engineering and Technology, Department of Mechanical Engineering, Indianapolis, IN 46202-2896. Offers biomedical engineering (MS Bm E); computer-aided mechanical engineering (Certificate); mechanical engineering (MSME, PhD). Part-time programs available. *Students:* 22 full-time (6 women), 30 part-time (3 women); includes 4 minority (2 Black or African American, non-Hispanic/Latino; 2 Asian, non-Hispanic/Latino), 26 international. Average age 28. In 2010, 26 master's awarded. *Degree requirements:* For master's, thesis optional. *Entrance requirements:* For master's, GRE. Additional exam requirements/recommendations for international students: Required—TOEFL. *Application deadline:* For fall admission, 7/1 for domestic students. Application fee: $55 ($65 for international students). *Financial support:* Fellowships with tuition reimbursements, research assistantships with full and partial tuition reimbursements, tuition waivers (full and partial) available. Financial award application deadline: 3/1. *Faculty research:* Computational fluid dynamics, heat transfer, finite-element methods, composites, biomechanics. *Unit head:* Dr. Hasan Akay, Chairman, 317-274-9717, Fax: 317-274-9744. *Application contact:* Valerie Diemer, Graduate Program, 317-278-4960, Fax: 317-278-1671, E-mail: grad@engr.iupui.edu.

Instituto Tecnológico y de Estudios Superiores de Monterrey, Campus Chihuahua, Graduate Programs, Chihuahua, Mexico. Offers computer systems engineering (Ingeniero); electrical engineering (Ingeniero); electromechanical engineering (Ingeniero); electronic engineering (Ingeniero); engineering administration (MEA); industrial engineering (MIE, Ingeniero); international trade (MIT); mechanical engineering (Ingeniero).

Instituto Tecnológico y de Estudios Superiores de Monterrey, Campus Monterrey, Graduate and Research Division, Programs in Engineering, Monterrey, Mexico. Offers applied statistics (M Eng); artificial intelligence (PhD); automation engineering (M Eng); chemical engineering (M Eng); civil engineering (M Eng); electrical engineering (M Eng); electronic engineering (M Eng); environmental engineering (M Eng); industrial engineering (M Eng, PhD); manufacturing engineering (M Eng); mechanical engineering (M Eng); systems and quality engineering (M Eng). M Eng program offered jointly with University of Waterloo; PhD in industrial engineering with Texas A&M University. Part-time and evening/weekend programs available. Terminal master's awarded for partial completion of doctoral program. *Degree requirements:* For master's, one foreign language, thesis; for doctorate, one foreign language, thesis/dissertation. *Entrance requirements:* For master's, EXADEP; for doctorate, GRE, master's degree in related field. Additional exam requirements/recommendations for international students: Required—TOEFL. *Faculty research:* Flexible manufacturing cells, materials, statistical methods, environmental prevention, control and evaluation.

Iowa State University of Science and Technology, Graduate College, College of Engineering, Department of Mechanical Engineering, Ames, IA 50011. Offers mechanical engineering (MS, PhD); mechanical engineering (coursework only) (M Eng); systems engineering (M Eng). *Faculty:* 32 full-time (3 women), 1 (woman) part-time/adjunct. *Students:* 150 full-time (21 women), 84 part-time (5 women); includes 6 Black or African American, non-Hispanic/Latino; 2 American Indian or Alaska Native, non-Hispanic/Latino; 6 Asian, non-Hispanic/Latino; 1 Hispanic/Latino, 88 international. 288 applicants, 21% accepted, 32 enrolled. In 2010, 35 master's, 11 doctorates awarded. *Degree requirements:* For master's, thesis or alternative; for doctorate, thesis/dissertation. *Entrance requirements:* For master's and doctorate, GRE General Test, resume. Additional exam requirements/recommendations for international students: Required—TOEFL (minimum score 570 paper-based; 79 iBT), IELTS (minimum score 6.5). *Application deadline:* For fall admission, 1/10 priority date for domestic and international students; for spring admission, 8/10 priority date for domestic and international students. Application fee: $40 ($90 for international students). Electronic applications accepted. *Financial support:* In 2010–11, 87 research assistantships with full and partial tuition reimbursements (averaging $11,460 per year), 24 teaching assistantships with full and partial tuition reimbursements (averaging $6,801 per year) were awarded; fellowships, scholarships/grants, health care benefits, and unspecified assistantships also available. *Unit head:* Dr. Thomas Heindel, Interim Chair, 515-294-3891, E-mail: megradinfo@iastate.edu. *Application contact:* Dr. Sriram Sundararajan, Director of Graduate Education, 515-294-1050, E-mail: megradinfo@iastate.edu.

The Johns Hopkins University, Engineering for Professionals, Part-time Program in Mechanical Engineering, Baltimore, MD 21218-2699. Offers MME. Part-time and evening/weekend programs available. *Faculty:* 9 part-time/adjunct (0 women). *Students:* 2 full-time (1 woman), 97 part-time (16 women); includes 10 minority (5 Black or African American, non-Hispanic/Latino; 4 Asian, non-Hispanic/Latino; 1 Hispanic/Latino), 2 international. Average age 27. 22 applicants, 86% accepted, 17 enrolled. In 2010, 32 master's awarded. *Application deadline:* Applications are processed on a rolling basis. Application fee: $75. Electronic applications accepted. *Financial support:* Institutionally sponsored loans available. *Unit head:* Dr. Lester Su, Program Chair, 410-516-7754, Fax: 410-516-7254, E-mail: lsu@jhu.edu. *Application contact:* Priyanka Dwivedi, Admissions Manager, 410-516-2300, Fax: 410-579-8049, E-mail: pdwived1@jhu.edu.

The Johns Hopkins University, G. W. C. Whiting School of Engineering, Department of Mechanical Engineering, Baltimore, MD 21218-2681. Offers MSE, PhD. *Faculty:* 18 full-time (3 women), 13 part-time/adjunct (1 woman). *Students:* 95 full-time (20 women), 2 part-time (1 woman); includes 5 minority (1 Black or African American, non-Hispanic/Latino; 2 Asian, non-Hispanic/Latino; 2 Hispanic/Latino), 51 international. Average age 26. 247 applicants, 36% accepted, 31 enrolled. In 2010, 18 master's, 17 doctorates awarded. Terminal master's awarded for partial completion of doctoral program. *Degree requirements:* For master's, thesis (for some programs); for doctorate, comprehensive exam, thesis/dissertation, oral exam. *Entrance requirements:* For master's and doctorate, GRE General Test. Additional exam requirements/recommendations for international students: Required—TOEFL or IELTS. *Application deadline:* For fall admission, 12/15 priority date for domestic and international students; for spring admission, 10/15 priority date for domestic and international students. Application fee: $25. Electronic applications accepted. *Financial support:* In 2010–11, 55 students received support, including 16 fellowships with full tuition reimbursements available (averaging $27,531 per year), 45 research assistantships with full tuition reimbursements available (averaging $25,400 per year); Federal Work-Study, institutionally sponsored loans, scholarships/grants, health care benefits, tuition waivers (partial), and unspecified assistantships also available. Support available to part-time students. Financial award application deadline: 12/15. *Faculty research:* Microscale/nanoscale science and engineering, computational engineering, aerospace and marine systems, robotics and human-machine interaction, energy and the environment, mechanics and materials. Total annual research expenditures: $5.5 million. *Unit head:* Dr. Kevin Hemker, Chair, 410-516-6451, Fax: 410-516-7254, E-mail: hemker@jhu.edu. *Application contact:* Mike Bernard, Academic Program Administrator, 410-516-7154, Fax: 410-516-7254, E-mail: megrad@jhu.edu.

The Johns Hopkins University, G. W. C. Whiting School of Engineering, Program in Engineering Management, Baltimore, MD 21218-2699. Offers biomaterials (MSEM); communications science (MSEM); computer science (MSEM); fluid mechanics (MSEM); materials science and engineering (MSEM); mechanical engineering (MSEM); mechanics and materials (MSEM); nano-biotechnology (MSEM); nanomaterials and nanotechnology (MSEM); probability and statistics (MSEM); smart product and device design (MSEM); systems analysis, management and environmental policy (MSEM). *Students:* 32 full-time (5 women), 4 part-time (0 women); includes 7 minority (3 Black or African American, non-Hispanic/Latino; 3 Asian, non-Hispanic/Latino; 1 Hispanic/Latino), 11 international. Average age 23. 110 applicants, 60% accepted, 27 enrolled. In 2010, 6 master's awarded. *Entrance requirements:* For master's, GRE, 3 letters of recommendation, resume. Additional exam requirements/recommendations for international students: Required—TOEFL (minimum score 600 paper-based; 250 computer-based; 100 iBT) or IELTS (minimum score 7). *Application deadline:* For fall admission, 1/15 priority date for domestic students, 1/15 for international students; for spring admission, 9/15 priority date for domestic students, 9/15 for international students. Applications are processed on a rolling basis. Application fee: $75. Electronic applications accepted. *Financial support:* Fellowships, health care benefits available. *Unit head:* Dr. Edward R. Scheinerman, Interim Director/Vice Dean for Education, School of Engineering/Professor, Applied Mathematics and Statistics, 410-516-7395, Fax: 410-516-4880, E-mail: ers@jhu.edu. *Application contact:* Dennis McIver, Coordinator of Graduate Admissions, 410-516-8174, Fax: 410-516-0780, E-mail: graduateadmissions@jhu.edu.

Kansas State University, Graduate School, College of Engineering, Department of Mechanical and Nuclear Engineering, Manhattan, KS 66506. Offers mechanical engineering (MS, PhD); nuclear engineering (MS, PhD). *Degree requirements:* For master's, thesis or alternative; for doctorate, comprehensive exam, thesis/dissertation. *Entrance requirements:* For master's, GRE General Test, minimum GPA of 3.0 in physics, mathematics, and chemistry; for doctorate, GRE General Test, master's degree in mechanical engineering. Additional exam requirements/recommendations for international students: Required—TOEFL. Electronic applications accepted. *Faculty research:* Radiation detection and protection, heat and mass transfer, machine design, control systems, nuclear reactor physics and engineering.

Kettering University, Graduate School, Mechanical Engineering Department, Flint, MI 48504. Offers engineering (MS). Part-time and evening/weekend programs available. Postbaccalaureate distance learning degree programs offered (no on-campus study). *Faculty:* 11 full-time (1 woman), 1 part-time/adjunct (0 women). *Students:* 1 full-time (0 women), 37 part-time (3 women); includes 2 minority (1 Asian, non-Hispanic/Latino; 1 Hispanic/Latino), 5 international. Average age 29. 29 applicants, 41% accepted, 6 enrolled. In 2010, 19 master's awarded. *Degree requirements:* For master's, thesis optional. *Entrance requirements:* Additional exam requirements/recommendations for international students: Required—TOEFL (minimum score 550 paper-based; 213 computer-based; 79 iBT). *Application deadline:* For fall admission, 9/15 for domestic students, 6/15 for international students; for winter admission, 12/15 for domestic students, 9/15 for international students, for spring admission, 3/15 for domestic students, 12/15 for international students. Applications are processed on a rolling basis. Electronic applications accepted. *Expenses:* Tuition: Full-time $11,120; part-time $695 per credit hour. *Financial support:* In 2010–11, 21 students received support, including fellowships with full tuition reimbursements available (averaging $13,000 per year), research assistantships with full tuition reimbursements available (averaging $13,000 per year), teaching assistantships with full tuition reimbursements available (averaging $13,000 per year); Federal Work-Study, scholarships/grants, and tuition waivers (partial) also available. Support available to part-time students. Financial award application deadline: 7/15; financial award applicants required to submit CSS PROFILE or FAFSA. *Faculty research:* Fuel cells, chemical agents, crash safety, bio-gas, sustainable energy. Total annual research expenditures: $3.9 million. *Unit head:* Dr. K. Joel Berry, Department Head, 810-762-7833, Fax: 810-762-7860, E-mail: jberry@kettering.edu. *Application contact:* Bonnie Switzer, Graduate Admissions Officer, 810-762-7953, Fax: 810-762-9935, E-mail: bswitzer@kettering.edu.

Lamar University, College of Graduate Studies, College of Engineering, Department of Mechanical Engineering, Beaumont, TX 77710. Offers ME, MES, DE. Part-time programs available. *Faculty:* 8 full-time (1 woman). *Students:* 53 full-time (2 women), 29 part-time (2 women); includes 4 Asian, non-Hispanic/Latino, 62 international. Average age 25. 75 applicants, 63% accepted, 11 enrolled. In 2010, 30 master's awarded. Terminal master's awarded for partial completion of doctoral program. *Degree requirements:* For master's, comprehensive exam (for some programs), thesis (for some programs); for doctorate, thesis/dissertation. *Entrance requirements:* For master's and doctorate, GRE General Test. Additional exam requirements/recommendations for international students: Required—TOEFL. *Application deadline:* For fall admission, 5/15 priority date for domestic students; for spring admission, 10/1 priority date for domestic students. Applications are processed on a rolling basis. Application fee: $25 ($50 for international students). *Expenses:* Tuition, state resident: full-time $4160; part-time $208 per credit hour. Tuition, nonresident: full-time $10,360; part-time $518 per credit hour. *Financial support:* In 2010–11, 2 fellowships (averaging $7,200 per year), 4 research assistantships, 5 teaching assistantships were awarded; tuition waivers (partial) also available. Financial award application deadline: 4/1. *Faculty research:* Materials combustion, mechanical and multiphysics study in micro-electronics, structural instability/reliability, mechanics of micro electronics. *Unit head:* Dr. Malur N. Srinivasan, Chair, 409-880-8094, Fax: 409-880-8121, E-mail: srinivasmn@hal.lamar.edu. *Application contact:* Dr. James L. Thomas, Director of Recruitment, 409-880-7870, Fax: 409-880-8121, E-mail: thomasjl@hal.lamar.edu.

Lawrence Technological University, College of Engineering, Southfield, MI 48075-1058. Offers architectural engineering (MS); automotive engineering (MS); civil engineering (MS); electrical and computer engineering (MS); engineering management (MEM); industrial engineering (MS); manufacturing systems (ME, DE); mechanical engineering (MS); mechatronic systems engineering (MS). Part-time and evening/weekend programs available. *Faculty:* 20 full-time (4 women), 12 part-time/adjunct (0 women). *Students:* 8 full-time (1 woman), 366 part-time (60 women); includes 29 Black or African American, non-Hispanic/Latino; 1 American Indian or Alaska Native, non-Hispanic/Latino; 36 Asian, non-Hispanic/Latino; 9 Hispanic/Latino; 4 Two or more races, non-Hispanic/Latino, 81 international. Average age 32. 398 applicants, 48% accepted, 87 enrolled. In 2010, 121 master's, 5 doctorates awarded. *Degree requirements:* For master's, thesis (for some programs). *Entrance requirements:* Additional exam requirements/recommendations for international students: Required—TOEFL (minimum score 550 paper-based; 213 computer-based; 79 iBT). *Application deadline:* For fall admission, 6/30 priority date for domestic students, 6/30 for international students; for spring admission, 11/15 priority date for domestic students, 11/15 for international students. Applications are processed on a rolling basis. Application fee: $50. Electronic applications accepted. *Financial support:* In 2010–11, 72 students received support. Federal Work-Study and institutionally sponsored loans available. Support available to part-time students. Financial award application deadline: 4/1; financial award applicants required to submit FAFSA. *Faculty research:* Advanced composite materials in bridges, strengthening existing bridges with carbon and glass fiber sheets, development of drive shafts using composite materials. *Unit head:* Dr. Nabil Grace, Interim Dean, 248-204-2500, Fax: 248-204-2509, E-mail: engrdean@ltu.edu. *Application contact:* Jane Rohrback, Director of Admissions, 248-204-3160, Fax: 248-204-2228, E-mail: admissions@ltu.edu.

Lehigh University, P.C. Rossin College of Engineering and Applied Science, Department of Mechanical Engineering and Mechanics, Bethlehem, PA 18015. Offers computational engineering and mechanics (MS, PhD); mechanical engineering (M Eng, MS, PhD, MBA/E); polymer science/engineering (M Eng, MS, PhD, MBA/E); MBA/E. Part-time and evening/weekend programs available. Postbaccalaureate distance learning degree programs offered. *Faculty:* 24 full-time (0 women). *Students:* 106 full-time (12 women), 34 part-time (2 women); includes 7 minority (3 Black or African American, non-Hispanic/Latino; 3 Asian, non-Hispanic/Latino; 1 Hispanic/Latino), 71 international. Average age 26. 408 applicants, 29% accepted, 59 enrolled. In 2010, 23 master's, 7 doctorates awarded. Terminal master's awarded for partial completion of doctoral program. *Degree requirements:* For master's, thesis; for doctorate, thesis/dissertation, general exam. *Entrance requirements:* Additional exam requirements/recommendations for international students: Required—TOEFL (minimum score 550 paper-based; 213 computer-based; 79 iBT). *Application deadline:* For fall admission, 7/15 for domestic and international students; for spring admission, 12/1 for domestic and international students. Applications are processed on a rolling basis. Application fee: $75. Electronic applications accepted. *Financial support:* In 2010–11, 74 students received support, including 9 fellowships with full and partial tuition reimbursements available (averaging $23,280 per year), 23 research assistantships with full and partial tuition reimbursements available (averaging $20,700 per year), 24 teaching assistantships with full and partial tuition reimbursements available (averaging $24,480 per year); unspecified assistantships and Dean's doctoral assistantships also available. Financial award application deadline: 1/15. *Faculty research:* Thermofluids, dynamic systems, CAD/CAM, computational mechanics, solid mechanics. Total annual research expenditures: $3.3 million. *Unit head:* Dr. D. Gary Harlow, Chairman, 610-758-4102, Fax: 610-758-6224, E-mail: dgh0@lehigh.edu. *Application contact:* Jo Ann M. Casciano, Graduate Coordinator, 610-758-4107, Fax: 610-758-6224, E-mail: jmc4@lehigh.edu.

Louisiana State University and Agricultural and Mechanical College, Graduate School, College of Engineering, Department of Mechanical Engineering, Baton Rouge, LA 70803. Offers MSME, PhD. Part-time programs available. *Faculty:* 27 full-time (1 woman). *Students:* 94 full-time (8 women), 7 part-time (0 women); includes 6 Black or African American, non-Hispanic/Latino; 3 Asian, non-Hispanic/Latino; 1 Hispanic/Latino, 73 international. Average age 28. 92 applicants, 67% accepted, 12 enrolled. In 2010, 8 master's, 8 doctorates awarded. Terminal master's awarded for partial completion of doctoral program. *Degree requirements:* For master's, thesis; for doctorate, thesis/dissertation. *Entrance requirements:* For master's and doctorate, GRE General Test, minimum GPA of 3.0. Additional exam requirements/recommendations for international students: Required—TOEFL (minimum score 550 paper-based; 213 computer-based; 79 iBT) or IELTS (minimum score 6.5). *Application deadline:* For fall admission, 1/25 priority date for domestic students, 2/15 priority date for international students; for spring admission, 10/15 for international students. Applications are processed on a rolling basis. Application fee: $50 ($70 for international students). Electronic applications accepted. *Financial support:* In 2010–11, 8 students received support, including 13 fellowships with full and partial tuition reimbursements available (averaging $19,992 per year), 66 research assistantships with partial tuition reimbursements available (averaging $16,528 per year), 16 teaching assistantships with partial tuition reimbursements available (averaging $9,379 per year); Federal Work-Study, institutionally sponsored loans, health care benefits, tuition waivers (full and partial), and unspecified assistantships also available. Financial award applicants required to submit FAFSA. *Faculty research:* Computer-aided design, thermal and fluid sciences materials engineering, fluid mechanics, combustion and microsystems engineering. Total annual research expenditures: $1.9 million. *Unit head:* Dr. Dimitris Nikitopoulos, Chair, 225-578-5900, E-mail: medimi@egateway.lsu.edu. *Application contact:* Dr. Eyassu Woldesenbet, Graduate Adviser, 225-578-5900, Fax: 225 578-5924, E-mail: woldesen@me.lsu.edu.

Louisiana Tech University, Graduate School, College of Engineering and Science, Department of Mechanical Engineering, Ruston, LA 71272. Offers MS, PhD. Part-time programs available. Terminal master's awarded for partial completion of doctoral program. *Degree requirements:* For master's, thesis; for doctorate, thesis/dissertation. *Entrance requirements:* For master's, GRE General Test, minimum GPA of 3.0 in last 60 hours; for doctorate, minimum graduate GPA of 3.25 (with MS) or GRE General Test. Additional exam requirements/recommendations for international students: Required—TOEFL. *Faculty research:* Engineering management, facilities planning, thermodynamics, automated manufacturing, micromanufacturing.

Loyola Marymount University, College of Science and Engineering, Department of Mechanical Engineering, Program in Mechanical Engineering, Los Angeles, CA 90045-2659. Offers MSE. *Faculty:* 6 full-time (0 women). *Students:* 9 full-time (2 women), 3 part-time (0 women); includes 1 Black or African American, non-Hispanic/Latino; 3 Asian, non-Hispanic/Latino; 3 Hispanic/Latino; 1 Native Hawaiian or other Pacific Islander, non-Hispanic/Latino. Average age 29. 13 applicants, 77% accepted, 5 enrolled. In 2010, 17 master's awarded. *Degree requirements:* For master's, thesis or alternative. *Entrance requirements:* For master's, letters of recommendation, undergraduate degree in mechanical engineering or related field from ABET-accredited university, computer proficiency. Additional exam requirements/recommendations for international students: Required—TOEFL (minimum score 550 paper-based; 213 computer-based; 80 iBT). *Application deadline:* Applications are processed on a rolling basis. Application fee: $50. Electronic applications accepted. *Financial support:* In

Mechanical Engineering

Loyola Marymount University (continued)
2010–11, 7 students received support. Federal Work-Study, scholarships/grants, and laboratory assistantships available. Support available to part-time students. Financial award application deadline: 6/1; financial award applicants required to submit FAFSA. Total annual research expenditures: $312,678. *Unit head:* Dr. Nader Saniei, Chair, 310-338-7378, E-mail: nader.saniei@lmu.edu. *Application contact:* Dr. Matthew T. Siniawski, Graduate Director, 310-338-5849, E-mail: matthew.siniawski@lmu.edu.

Manhattan College, Graduate Division, School of Engineering, Program in Mechanical Engineering, Riverdale, NY 10471. Offers MS. Part-time and evening/weekend programs available. *Faculty:* 7 full-time (0 women), 3 part-time/adjunct (0 women). *Students:* 14 full-time (1 woman), 9 part-time (2 women); includes 1 Black or African American, non-Hispanic/Latino; 1 Hispanic/Latino, 7 international. Average age 26. 28 applicants, 64% accepted, 15 enrolled. In 2010, 7 master's awarded. *Degree requirements:* For master's, thesis or alternative. *Entrance requirements:* For master's, GRE (recommended), minimum GPA of 3.0. Additional exam requirements/recommendations for international students: Required—TOEFL (minimum score 550 paper-based; 213 computer-based; 80 iBT), IELTS (minimum score 6). *Application deadline:* For fall admission, 8/10 priority date for domestic students, 8/10 for international students; for spring admission, 1/7 for domestic and international students. Applications are processed on a rolling basis. Application fee: $50. *Financial support:* In 2010–11, 5 students received support, including 5 teaching assistantships with partial tuition reimbursements available (averaging $4,000 per year); unspecified assistantships also available. Financial award application deadline: 2/1. *Faculty research:* Thermal analysis of rocket thrust chambers, quality of wood, biomechanics/structural analysis of cacti, orthodontic research. *Unit head:* Dr. Bahman Litkouhi, Chairman, 718-862-7927, Fax: 718-862-7163, E-mail: mechdept@manhattan.edu. *Application contact:* Kathy Balaj, Information Contact, 718-862-7145, Fax: 718-862-7163, E-mail: kathy.balaj@manhattan.edu.

Marquette University, Graduate School, College of Engineering, Department of Mechanical Engineering, Milwaukee, WI 53201-1881. Offers engineering innovation (Certificate); engineering management (MSEM); mechanical engineering (MS, PhD); new product and process development (Certificate). Part-time and evening/weekend programs available. *Faculty:* 16 full-time (0 women), 2 part-time/adjunct (0 women). *Students:* 26 full-time (7 women), 40 part-time (2 women); includes 4 minority (1 Black or African American, non-Hispanic/Latino; 1 Asian, non-Hispanic/Latino; 2 Hispanic/Latino), 15 international. Average age 29. 65 applicants, 68% accepted, 13 enrolled. In 2010, 9 master's, 1 doctorate awarded. Terminal master's awarded for partial completion of doctoral program. *Degree requirements:* For master's, comprehensive exam, thesis (for some programs); for doctorate, comprehensive exam, thesis/dissertation, qualifying exam. *Entrance requirements:* For master's, GRE General Test, minimum GPA of 3.0, official transcripts from all current and previous colleges/universities except Marquette, three letters of recommendation; for doctorate, GRE General Test, minimum GPA of 3.0, official transcripts from all current and previous colleges/universities except Marquette, three letters of recommendation, statement of purpose, copies of any published work. Additional exam requirements/recommendations for international students: Required—TOEFL (minimum score 530 paper-based; 78 computer-based). *Application deadline:* For fall admission, 8/1 priority date for domestic students; for spring admission, 1/1 priority date for domestic students. Applications are processed on a rolling basis. Application fee: $50. Electronic applications accepted. *Expenses:* Tuition: Full-time $16,290; part-time $905 per credit hour. Tuition and fees vary according to program. *Financial support:* In 2010–11, 19 students received support, including 2 research assistantships with tuition reimbursements available, 12 teaching assistantships with tuition reimbursements available; fellowships with tuition reimbursements available, Federal Work-Study, institutionally sponsored loans, scholarships/grants, and tuition waivers (full and partial) also available. Support available to part-time students. Financial award application deadline: 2/15. *Faculty research:* Computer-integrated manufacturing, energy conversion, simulation modeling and optimization, applied mechanics, metallurgy. Total annual research expenditures: $901,053. *Unit head:* Dr. Kyle Kim, Chair, 414-288-7259, Fax: 414-288-7790, E-mail: kyle.kim@marquette.edu. *Application contact:* Dr. James Rice, Director of Graduate Studies, 414-288-5405, Fax: 414-288-7790, E-mail: nicholas.nigro@marquette.edu.

Massachusetts Institute of Technology, School of Engineering, Department of Mechanical Engineering, Cambridge, MA 02139. Offers manufacturing (M Eng); mechanical engineering (SM, PhD, Sc D, Mech E); naval architecture and marine engineering (SM, PhD, Sc D); naval engineering (Naval E); ocean engineering (SM, PhD, Sc D), including); oceanographic engineering (SM, PhD, Sc D); SM/MBA. *Faculty:* 69 full-time (9 women). *Students:* 521 full-time (92 women); includes 71 minority (11 Black or African American, non-Hispanic/Latino; 1 American Indian or Alaska Native, non-Hispanic/Latino; 35 Asian, non-Hispanic/Latino; 20 Hispanic/Latino; 4 Two or more races, non-Hispanic/Latino), 217 international. Average age 27. 1,036 applicants, 23% accepted, 148 enrolled. In 2010, 132 master's, 49 doctorates, 10 other advanced degrees awarded. Terminal master's awarded for partial completion of doctoral program. *Degree requirements:* For master's and other advanced degree, thesis; for doctorate, comprehensive exam, thesis/dissertation. *Entrance requirements:* For master's, doctorate, and other advanced degree, GRE General Test. Additional exam requirements/recommendations for international students: Required—IELTS (minimum score 7). *Application deadline:* For fall admission, 12/1 for domestic and international students. Application fee: $75. Electronic applications accepted. *Expenses:* Tuition: Full-time $38,940; part-time $605 per unit. Required fees: $272. *Financial support:* In 2010–11, 443 students received support, including 91 fellowships with tuition reimbursements available (averaging $29,306 per year), 324 research assistantships with tuition reimbursements available (averaging $28,071 per year), 35 teaching assistantships with tuition reimbursements available (averaging $30,517 per year); career-related internships or fieldwork, Federal Work-Study, institutionally sponsored loans, scholarships/grants, health care benefits, and unspecified assistantships also available. *Faculty research:* Mechanics: modeling, experimentation and computation; design, manufacturing, and product development; controls, instrumentation, and robotics; energy science and engineering; ocean science and engineering; bioengineering; micro and nano engineering. Total annual research expenditures: $45.5 million. *Unit head:* Prof. Mary C. Boyce, Department Head, 617-253-2201, Fax: 617-258-6156, E-mail: mehq@mit.edu. *Application contact:* Graduate Office, 617-253-2291, Fax: 617-258-5802, E-mail: me-gradoffice@mit.edu.

McGill University, Faculty of Graduate and Postdoctoral Studies, Faculty of Engineering, Department of Mechanical Engineering, Montréal, QC H3A 2T5, Canada. Offers aerospace (M Eng); manufacturing management (MMM); mechanical engineering (M Eng, M Sc, PhD).

McMaster University, School of Graduate Studies, Faculty of Engineering, Department of Mechanical Engineering, Hamilton, ON L8S 4M2, Canada. Offers M Eng, MA Sc, PhD. M Eng degree offered as part of the Advanced Design and Manufacturing Institute (ADMI) group collaboration with the University of Toronto, University of Western Ontario, and University of Waterloo. *Degree requirements:* For master's, thesis; for doctorate, comprehensive exam, thesis/dissertation. *Entrance requirements:* Additional exam requirements/recommendations for international students: Required—TOEFL (minimum score 550 paper-based; 213 computer-based). *Faculty research:* Manufacturing engineering, dimensional metrology, micro-fluidics, multi-phase flow and heat transfer, process modeling simulation.

McNeese State University, Doré School of Graduate Studies, College of Engineering and Engineering Technology, Lake Charles, LA 70609. Offers chemical engineering (M Eng); civil engineering (M Eng); electrical engineering (M Eng); engineering management (M Eng); mechanical engineering (M Eng). Part-time and evening/weekend programs available. *Faculty:* 15 full-time (1 woman). *Students:* 37 full-time (10 women), 18 part-time (1 woman); includes 5 minority (3 Black or African American, non-Hispanic/Latino; 1 American Indian or Alaska Native, non-Hispanic/Latino; 1 Two or more races, non-Hispanic/Latino), 43 international. In 2010, 28 master's awarded. *Degree requirements:* For master's, thesis or alternative. *Entrance requirements:* For master's, GRE, minimum undergraduate GPA of 3.0. Additional exam requirements/recommendations for international students: Required—TOEFL (minimum score

560 paper-based; 220 computer-based; 83 iBT). *Application deadline:* For fall admission, 5/15 priority date for domestic and international students; for spring admission, 10/15 priority date for domestic and international students. Applications are processed on a rolling basis. Application fee: $20 ($30 for international students). Tuition and fees vary according to course load. *Financial support:* Federal Work-Study available. Support available to part-time students. Financial award application deadline: 5/1. *Unit head:* Dr. Nikos Kiritsis, Dean, 337-475-5875, Fax: 337-475-5237, E-mail: nikosk@mcneese.edu.

Memorial University of Newfoundland, School of Graduate Studies, Faculty of Engineering and Applied Science, St. John's, NL A1C 5S7, Canada. Offers civil engineering (M Eng, PhD); electrical and computer engineering (M Eng, PhD); mechanical engineering (M Eng, PhD); ocean and naval architecture engineering (M Eng, PhD). Part-time programs available. *Degree requirements:* For master's, thesis; for doctorate, comprehensive exam, thesis/dissertation, oral thesis defense. *Entrance requirements:* For master's, 2nd class degree; for doctorate, master's degree in engineering. Electronic applications accepted. *Faculty research:* Engineering analysis, environmental and hydrotechnical studies, manufacturing and robotics, mechanics, structures and materials.

Mercer University, Graduate Studies, Macon Campus, School of Engineering, Macon, GA 31207-0003. Offers biomedical engineering (MSE); computer engineering (MSE); electrical engineering (MSE); engineering management (MSE); environmental engineering (MSE); environmental systems (MS); mechanical engineering (MSE); software engineering (MSE); software systems (MS); technical communications management (MS); technical management (MS). Part-time and evening/weekend programs available. Postbaccalaureate distance learning degree programs offered (no on-campus study). *Faculty:* 18 full-time (4 women), 1 part-time/adjunct (0 women). *Students:* 11 full-time (2 women), 100 part-time (22 women); includes 26 minority (13 Black or African American, non-Hispanic/Latino; 12 Asian, non-Hispanic/Latino; 1 Hispanic/Latino), 3 international. Average age 32. In 2010, 46 master's awarded. *Degree requirements:* For master's, thesis or alternative. *Entrance requirements:* For master's, minimum undergraduate GPA of 3.0. Additional exam requirements/recommendations for international students: Required—TOEFL. *Application deadline:* For fall admission, 7/1 for domestic students; for spring admission, 11/15 for domestic students. Applications are processed on a rolling basis. Application fee: $35 ($50 for international students). Electronic applications accepted. *Expenses:* Contact institution. *Financial support:* Federal Work-Study available. *Unit head:* Dr. Wade H. Shaw, Dean, 478-301-2459, Fax: 478-301-5593, E-mail: shaw_wh@mercer.edu. *Application contact:* Greg Lofton, Graduate Program Coordinator, 478-301-5480, Fax: 478-301-5434, E-mail: lofton_g@mercer.edu.

Michigan State University, The Graduate School, College of Engineering, Department of Mechanical Engineering, East Lansing, MI 48824. Offers engineering mechanics (MS, PhD); mechanical engineering (MS, PhD). *Entrance requirements:* For master's, GRE General Test. Additional exam requirements/recommendations for international students: Required—TOEFL. Electronic applications accepted.

Michigan Technological University, Graduate School, College of Engineering, Department of Mechanical Engineering-Engineering Mechanics, Program in Mechanical Engineering, Houghton, MI 49931. Offers mechanical engineering (MS); mechanical engineering-engineering mechanics (PhD). Part-time programs available. Postbaccalaureate distance learning degree programs offered (minimal on-campus study). Terminal master's awarded for partial completion of doctoral program. *Degree requirements:* For master's, comprehensive exam (for some programs), thesis (for some programs); for doctorate, comprehensive exam, thesis/dissertation. *Entrance requirements:* For master's, GRE; for doctorate, GRE, MS (preferred). Additional exam requirements/recommendations for international students: Required—TOEFL (minimum score 637 paper-based; 270 computer-based). Electronic applications accepted. *Expenses:* Contact institution.

Mississippi State University, Bagley College of Engineering, Department of Mechanical Engineering, Mississippi State, MS 39762. Offers engineering (PhD), including mechanical engineering; mechanical engineering (MS). Part-time programs available. Postbaccalaureate distance learning degree programs offered (minimal on-campus study). *Faculty:* 21 full-time (2 women), 1 part-time/adjunct (0 women). *Students:* 72 full-time (10 women), 9 part-time (2 women); includes 7 minority (6 Black or African American, non-Hispanic/Latino; 1 Hispanic/Latino), 25 international. Average age 27. 125 applicants, 26% accepted, 24 enrolled. In 2010, 9 master's, 8 doctorates awarded. *Degree requirements:* For master's, thesis optional, oral exam; for doctorate, thesis/dissertation, qualifying exam, preliminary exam, dissertation defense. *Entrance requirements:* For master's and doctorate, GRE General Test, minimum GPA of 2.75. Additional exam requirements/recommendations for international students: Required—TOEFL (minimum score 550 paper-based; 213 computer-based; 79 iBT); Recommended—IELTS (minimum score 6.5). *Application deadline:* For fall admission, 7/1 for domestic students, 5/1 for international students; for spring admission, 11/1 for domestic students, 9/1 for international students. Applications are processed on a rolling basis. Application fee: $40. Electronic applications accepted. *Expenses:* Tuition, state resident: full-time $2730.50; part-time $304 per credit hour. Tuition, nonresident: full-time $6901; part-time $767 per credit hour. *Financial support:* In 2010–11, 31 research assistantships with full tuition reimbursements (averaging $14,692 per year), 2 teaching assistantships with full tuition reimbursements (averaging $13,500 per year) were awarded; career-related internships or fieldwork, Federal Work-Study, institutionally sponsored loans, scholarships/grants, and unspecified assistantships also available. Financial award application deadline: 4/1; financial award applicants required to submit FAFSA. *Faculty research:* Fatigue and fracture, heat transfer, fluid dynamics, manufacturing systems, materials. Total annual research expenditures: $11 million. *Unit head:* Dr. Steve Daniewicz, Professor and Interim Head, 662-325-7322, Fax: 662-325-7223, E-mail: Daniewicz@me.msstate.edu. *Application contact:* Dr. David Marcum, Professor and Graduate Coordinator, 662-325-2423, Fax: 662-325-7692, E-mail: marcum@cavs.msstate.edu.

Missouri University of Science and Technology, Graduate School, Department of Mechanical and Aerospace Engineering, Rolla, MO 65409. Offers aerospace engineering (MS, PhD); mechanical engineering (MS, DE, PhD). Part-time and evening/weekend programs available. Terminal master's awarded for partial completion of doctoral program. *Degree requirements:* For master's, thesis optional; for doctorate, comprehensive exam, thesis/dissertation. *Entrance requirements:* For master's, GRE General Test (minimum score 1100 verbal and quantitative, writing 3.5), minimum GPA of 3.0; for doctorate, GRE General Test (minimum score: verbal and quantitative 1100, writing 3.5), minimum GPA of 3.5. Additional exam requirements/recommendations for international students: Required—TOEFL. Electronic applications accepted. *Faculty research:* Dynamics and controls, acoustics, computational fluid dynamics, space mechanics, hypersonics.

Montana State University, College of Graduate Studies, College of Engineering, Department of Mechanical and Industrial Engineering, Bozeman, MT 59717. Offers engineering (PhD), including industrial engineering option, mechanical engineering option; industrial and management engineering (MS); mechanical engineering (MS). Part-time programs available. *Faculty:* 16 full-time (2 women), 9 part-time/adjunct (2 women). *Students:* 18 full-time (0 women), 28 part-time (9 women); includes 3 minority (all Asian, non-Hispanic/Latino), 9 international. Average age 27. 51 applicants, 43% accepted, 12 enrolled. In 2010, 14 master's, 1 doctorate awarded. *Degree requirements:* For master's, comprehensive exam, thesis, oral exams; for doctorate, comprehensive exam, thesis/dissertation, qualifying exam. *Entrance requirements:* For master's, GRE, official transcript, minimum GPA of 3.0, demonstrated potential for success, statement of goals, three letters of recommendation, proof of funds affidavit; for doctorate, minimum undergraduate GPA of 3.0, 3.2 graduate; three letters of recommendation; statement of objectives. Additional exam requirements/recommendations for international students: Required—TOEFL or IELTS. *Application deadline:* For fall admission, 7/15 priority date for domestic students, 5/15 priority date for international students; for spring admission, 12/1 priority date for domestic students, 10/1 priority date for international students. Applications are processed on a rolling basis. Application fee: $30. Electronic applications accepted. *Expenses:* Tuition, state resident: full-time $5553.90. Tuition, nonresident: full-time $14,646. Required fees: $1233. *Financial support:* In 2010–11, 34 students received support, including 22 research assistantships with tuition reimbursements available (averaging $8,276 per year), 22 teaching assistantships with tuition reimbursements available (averaging $5,255 per year); health care benefits and unspecified assistantships also available. Support available to part-time students. Financial award application deadline: 3/1; financial award applicants required to submit FAFSA. *Faculty research:* Human factors engineering, energy, design and manufacture, systems modeling, materials and structures, measurement systems. Total annual research expenditures: $1 million. *Unit head:* Dr. Chris Jenkins, Head, 406-994-2203, Fax: 406-994-6292, E-mail: cjenkins@me.montana.edu. *Application contact:* Dr. Carl A. Fox, Vice Provost for Graduate Education, 406-994-4145, Fax: 406-994-7433, E-mail: gradstudy@montana.edu.

Naval Postgraduate School, Graduate Programs, Department of Mechanical and Astronautical Engineering, Monterey, CA 93943. Offers MS, D Eng, PhD, Eng. Program only open to commissioned officers of the United States and friendly nations and selected United States federal civilian employees. *Accreditation:* ABET (one or more programs are ,accredited). Part-time programs available. Postbaccalaureate distance learning degree programs offered. *Degree requirements:* For master's and Eng, thesis; for doctorate, one foreign language, thesis/dissertation.

New Jersey Institute of Technology, Office of Graduate Studies, Newark College of Engineering, Department of Mechanical Engineering, Newark, NJ 07102. Offers MS, PhD, Engineer. Part-time and evening/weekend programs available. *Faculty:* 28 full-time (1 woman), 17 part-time/adjunct (3 women). *Students:* 176 full-time (28 women), 189 part-time (46 women); includes 37 Black or African American, non-Hispanic/Latino; 1 American Indian or Alaska Native, non-Hispanic/Latino; 40 Asian, non-Hispanic/Latino; 48 Hispanic/Latino, 138 international. Average age 29. 621 applicants, 50% accepted, 115 enrolled. In 2010, 198 master's, 7 doctorates awarded. Terminal master's awarded for partial completion of doctoral program. *Degree requirements:* For master's, thesis optional; for doctorate, thesis/dissertation. *Entrance requirements:* For master's, GRE General Test; for doctorate, GRE General Test, minimum graduate GPA of 3.5. Additional exam requirements/recommendations for international students: Required—TOEFL (minimum score 550 paper-based; 213 computer-based; 79 iBT). *Application deadline:* For fall admission, 6/5 priority date for domestic students, 4/1 for international students; for spring admission, 11/15 for domestic and international students. Applications are processed on a rolling basis. Application fee: $65. Electronic applications accepted. *Expenses:* Tuition, state resident: full-time $14,724; part-time $818 per credit. Tuition, nonresident: full-time $20,304; part-time $1128 per credit. Required fees: $2272; $209 per credit. $103 per semester. One-time fee: $312 full-time; $212 part-time. *Financial support:* Fellowships with full and partial tuition reimbursements, research assistantships with full and partial tuition reimbursements, teaching assistantships with full and partial tuition reimbursements, career-related internships or fieldwork, Federal Work-Study, institutionally sponsored loans, and unspecified assistantships available. Financial award application deadline: 3/15. *Faculty research:* Energy systems, structural mechanics, electromechanical systems. Total annual research expenditures: $4.5 million. *Unit head:* Dr. Rajpal S. Sodhi, Interim Chair, 973-596-3333, E-mail: rajpal.s.sodhi@njit.edu. *Application contact:* Kathryn Kelly, Director of Admissions, 973-596-3300, Fax: 973-596-3461, E-mail: admissions@njit.edu.

New Mexico State University, Graduate School, College of Engineering, Department of Mechanical Engineering, Las Cruces, NM 88003-8001. Offers MSME, PhD. Postbaccalaureate distance learning degree programs offered (no on-campus study). *Faculty:* 15 full-time (1 woman), 8 part-time (1 woman); includes 10 minority (1 Black or African American, non-Hispanic/Latino; 9 Hispanic/Latino), 36 international. Average age 28. 81 applicants, 84% accepted, 24 enrolled. In 2010, 13 master's, 4 doctorates awarded. *Degree requirements:* For master's, thesis (for some programs); for doctorate, thesis/dissertation, 2 research tools. *Entrance requirements:* For master's, minimum GPA of 3.0; for

doctorate, qualifying exam, minimum GPA of 3.0. *Application deadline:* For fall admission, 7/1 priority date for domestic students; for spring admission, 11/1 for domestic students. Applications are processed on a rolling basis. Application fee: $30 ($50 for international students). Electronic applications accepted. *Expenses:* Tuition, state resident: full-time $4536; part-time $242 per credit. Tuition, nonresident: full-time $15,816; part-time $712 per credit. Required fees: $636 per term. *Financial support:* In 2010–11, 24 research assistantships with partial tuition reimbursements (averaging $14,663 per year), 20 teaching assistantships with partial tuition reimbursements (averaging $8,417 per year) were awarded; fellowships with partial tuition reimbursements, career-related internships or fieldwork, Federal Work-Study, scholarships/grants, and health care benefits also available. Support available to part-time students. Financial award application deadline: 3/1. *Faculty research:* Computational mechanics; robotics; CAD/CAM; control, dynamics, and solid mechanics; interconnection engineering; heat transfer; composites. *Unit head:* Dr. Thomas Burton, Head, 575-646-3501, Fax: 575-646-6111, E-mail: tdburton@nmsu.edu. *Application contact:* Dr. Thomas Burton, Head, 575-646-3501, Fax: 575-646-6111, E-mail: tdburton@nmsu.edu.

North Carolina Agricultural and Technical State University, Graduate School, College of Engineering, Department of Mechanical and Chemical Engineering, Greensboro, NC 27411. Offers chemical engineering (MS Ch E); mechanical engineering (MSME, PhD). Part-time programs available. *Degree requirements:* For master's, comprehensive exam, thesis optional, dual exam, qualifying exam, thesis defense; for doctorate, thesis/dissertation. *Entrance requirements:* For doctorate, GRE. *Faculty research:* Composites, smart materials and sensors, mechanical systems modeling and finite element analysis, computational fluid dynamics and engine research, design and manufacturing.

North Carolina State University, Graduate School, College of Engineering, Department of Mechanical and Aerospace Engineering, Program in Mechanical Engineering, Raleigh, NC 27695. Offers MS, PhD. Part-time programs available. Postbaccalaureate distance learning degree programs offered (no on-campus study). *Degree requirements:* For master's, thesis optional, oral exam; for doctorate, thesis/dissertation, oral and preliminary exams. *Entrance requirements:* For master's and doctorate, GRE General Test. Additional exam requirements/recommendations for international students: Required—TOEFL (minimum score 550 paper-based; 213 computer-based). Electronic applications accepted. *Faculty research:* Vibration and control, fluid dynamics, thermal sciences, structures and materials, aerodynamics acoustics.

See Display below and Close-Up on page 555.

North Dakota State University, College of Graduate and Interdisciplinary Studies, College of Engineering and Architecture, Department of Mechanical Engineering and Applied Mechanics, Fargo, ND 58108. Offers MS, PhD. Part-time programs available. *Faculty:* 15 full-time (1 woman), 1 part-time/adjunct (0 women). *Students:* 39 full-time (8 women), 18 part-time (2 women); includes 1 Asian, non-Hispanic/Latino, 25 international. Average age 28. 74 applicants, 41% accepted, 14 enrolled. In 2010, 11 master's awarded. *Degree requirements:* For master's, thesis; for doctorate, comprehensive exam, thesis/dissertation. *Entrance requirements:* For master's and doctorate, minimum GPA of 3.0. Additional exam requirements/recommendations for international students: Required—TOEFL (minimum score 550 paper-based). *Application deadline:* For fall admission, 7/1 priority date for domestic students, 5/1 priority date for international students; for spring admission, 12/1 priority date for domestic students, 9/1 priority date for international students. Applications are processed on a rolling basis. Application fee: $45 ($60 for international students). Electronic applications accepted. *Financial support:* In 2010–11, 20 students received support, including research assistantships with full tuition reimbursements available (averaging $9,000 per year), teaching assistantships with full tuition reimbursements available (averaging $9,000 per year); career-related internships or fieldwork, Federal Work-Study, and institutionally sponsored loans also available. Financial award application deadline: 2/15. *Faculty research:* Thermodynamics, finite element analysis, automotive systems, robotics, nanotechnology. Total annual research expenditures: $530,000.

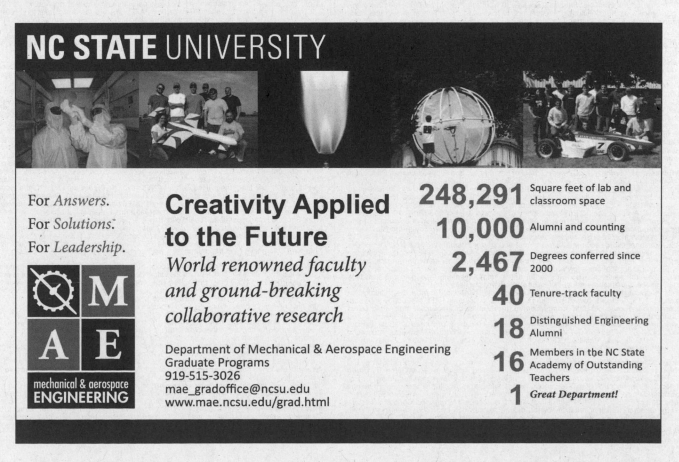

Mechanical Engineering

North Dakota State University (continued)

Unit head: Dr. Alan Kallmeyer, Chair, 701-231-8836, Fax: 701-231-8913, E-mail: alan.kallmeyer@ndsu.edu. *Application contact:* Dr. David A. Wittrock, Dean, 701-231-7033, Fax: 701-231-6524.

Northeastern University, College of Engineering, Department of Mechanical, Industrial, and Manufacturing Engineering, Boston, MA 02115-5096. Offers engineering management (MS); industrial engineering (MS, PhD); mechanical engineering (MS, PhD); operations research (MS). Part-time programs available. *Faculty:* 34 full-time (2 women), 7 part-time/adjunct (0 women). *Students:* 297 full-time (70 women), 103 part-time (20 women). 616 applicants, 77% accepted, 140 enrolled. In 2010, 107 master's, 5 doctorates awarded. *Degree requirements:* For master's, thesis (for some programs); for doctorate, thesis/dissertation, departmental qualifying exam. *Entrance requirements:* For master's and doctorate, GRE General Test. Additional exam requirements/recommendations for international students: Required—TOEFL (minimum score 550 paper-based; 213 computer-based; 80 iBT). *Application deadline:* For fall admission, 1/15 priority date for domestic and international students; for spring admission, 11/1 priority date for domestic students. Applications are processed on a rolling basis. Application fee: $50. Electronic applications accepted. *Financial support:* In 2010–11, 79 students received support, including 50 research assistantships with full tuition reimbursements available (averaging $18,325 per year), 33 teaching assistantships with full tuition reimbursements available (averaging $18,325 per year); fellowships with full tuition reimbursements available, career-related internships or fieldwork, Federal Work-Study, scholarships/grants, health care benefits, and unspecified assistantships also available. Support available to part-time students. Financial award application deadline: 1/15; financial award applicants required to submit FAFSA. *Faculty research:* Dry sliding instabilities, droplet deposition, combustion, manufacturing systems, nano-manufacturing, advanced materials processing, bio-nano robotics, burning speed measurement, virtual environments. *Unit head:* Dr. Hameed Metghalchi, Chairman, 617-373-2973, Fax: 617-373-2921. *Application contact:* Jeffery Hengel, Admissions Specialist, 617-373-2711, Fax: 617-373-2501, E-mail: grad-eng@coe.neu.edu.

Northern Arizona University, Graduate College, College of Engineering, Forestry and Natural Sciences, Programs in Engineering, Flagstaff, AZ 86011. Offers civil and environmental engineering (M Eng); civil engineering (MSE); computer science (MSE); electrical engineering (M Eng, MSE); engineering (M Eng, MSE); environmental engineering (M Eng, MSE); mechanical engineering (M Eng, MSE). Part-time programs available. Postbaccalaureate distance learning degree programs offered (no on-campus study). *Faculty:* 42 full-time (12 women). *Students:* 19 full-time (3 women), 15 part-time (2 women); includes 6 minority (2 American Indian or Alaska Native, non-Hispanic/Latino; 3 Hispanic/Latino; 1 Two or more races, non-Hispanic/Latino), 7 international. Average age 28. 21 applicants, 48% accepted, 4 enrolled. In 2010, 15 master's awarded. *Degree requirements:* For master's, thesis. *Entrance requirements:* For master's, GRE General Test. Additional exam requirements/recommendations for international students: Required—TOEFL (minimum score 550 paper-based; 213 computer-based; 80 iBT), IELTS (minimum score 7). *Application deadline:* For fall admission, 3/1 priority date for domestic and international students; for spring admission, 9/15 priority date for domestic and international students. Applications are processed on a rolling basis. Application fee: $65. Electronic applications accepted. *Financial support:* In 2010–11, 3 research assistantships with partial tuition reimbursements (averaging $14,541 per year), 12 teaching assistantships with partial tuition reimbursements (averaging $12,863 per year) were awarded; career-related internships or fieldwork, Federal Work-Study, scholarships/grants, health care benefits, and unspecified assistantships also available. Financial award applicants required to submit FAFSA. *Unit head:* Dr. Ernesto Penado, Chair, 928-523-9453, Fax: 928-523-2300, E-mail: ernesto.penado@nau.edu. *Application contact:* Natasha Kypfer, Program Coordinator, 928-523-1447, Fax: 928-523-2300, E-mail: egrmasters@nau.edu.

Northern Illinois University, Graduate School, College of Engineering and Engineering Technology, Department of Mechanical Engineering, De Kalb, IL 60115-2854. Offers MS. Part-time programs available. *Faculty:* 9 full-time (0 women). *Students:* 43 full-time (2 women), 23 part-time (3 women); includes 1 Asian, non-Hispanic/Latino; 2 Two or more races, non-Hispanic/Latino, 37 international. Average age 23. 147 applicants, 50% accepted, 24 enrolled. In 2010, 20 master's awarded. *Degree requirements:* For master's, comprehensive exam, thesis optional. *Entrance requirements:* For master's, GRE General Test, minimum GPA of 2.75. Additional exam requirements/recommendations for international students: Required—TOEFL (minimum score 550 paper-based; 213 computer-based). *Application deadline:* For fall admission, 6/1 for domestic students, 5/1 for international students; for spring admission, 11/1 for domestic students, 10/1 for international students. Applications are processed on a rolling basis. Application fee: $30. Electronic applications accepted. *Expenses:* Tuition, state resident: full-time $7200; part-time $300 per credit hour. Tuition, nonresident: full-time $14,400; part-time $600 per credit hour. Required fees: $79 per credit hour. *Financial support:* In 2010–11, 6 research assistantships with full tuition reimbursements, 16 teaching assistantships with full tuition reimbursements were awarded; fellowships with full tuition reimbursements, Federal Work-Study, scholarships/grants, tuition waivers (full), and staff assistantships also available. Support available to part-time students. Financial award applicants required to submit FAFSA. *Faculty research:* Robotics, nonlinear dynamic systems, piezo mechanics, quartz resonators, sheet metal forming. *Unit head:* Dr. Simon Song, Chair, 815-753-9970, Fax: 815-753-0416, E-mail: smsong@ceet.niu.edu. *Application contact:* Graduate School Office, 815-753-0395, E-mail: gradsch@niu.edu.

Northwestern University, McCormick School of Engineering and Applied Science, Department of Mechanical Engineering, Evanston, IL 60208. Offers MS, PhD. MS and PhD degrees offered through The Graduate School. Part-time programs available. *Faculty:* 21 full-time (5 women). *Students:* 111 full-time (20 women), 2 part-time (0 women); includes 15 minority (11 Asian, non-Hispanic/Latino; 2 Hispanic/Latino; 2 Two or more races, non-Hispanic/Latino), 53 international. Average age 26. 287 applicants, 18% accepted, 21 enrolled. In 2010, 21 master's, 15 doctorates awarded. Terminal master's awarded for partial completion of doctoral program. *Degree requirements:* For master's, thesis optional; for doctorate, comprehensive exam, thesis/dissertation. *Entrance requirements:* For master's and doctorate, General Exam of GRE. Additional exam requirements/recommendations for international students: Required—TOEFL (minimum score 577 paper-based, 233 computer-based, 90 iBT) or IELTS. *Application deadline:* For fall admission, 12/31 for domestic and international students. Application fee: $75. Electronic applications accepted. *Financial support:* Fellowships with full tuition reimbursements, research assistantships with partial tuition reimbursements, teaching assistantships with full tuition reimbursements, career-related internships or fieldwork, institutionally sponsored loans, health care benefits, and unspecified assistantships available. Financial award application deadline: 1/15; financial award applicants required to submit FAFSA. *Faculty research:* Experimental, theoretical and computational mechanics of materials; fluid mechanics; manufacturing processes; robotics and control; micro-electromechanical systems and nanotechnology. Total annual research expenditures: $8.9 million. *Unit head:* Dr. Cate Brinson, Chair, 847-467-2347, Fax: 847-491-3915, E-mail: cbrinson@northwestern.edu. *Application contact:* Dr. Jian Cao, Admission Officer, 847-467-1032, Fax: 847-491-3915, E-mail: jcao@northwestern.edu.

Oakland University, Graduate Study and Lifelong Learning, School of Engineering and Computer Science, Department of Mechanical Engineering, Rochester, MI 48309-4401. Offers MS, PhD. Part-time and evening/weekend programs available. *Entrance requirements:* For master's, minimum GPA of 3.0 for unconditional admission. Additional exam requirements/recommendations for international students: Required—TOEFL (minimum score 550 paper-based; 213 computer-based). Electronic applications accepted. *Expenses:* Contact institution. *Faculty research:* Efficient reliability-based design optimization and robust design methods, mechanical loading and Bunc, automotive research, industrial mentorship.

The Ohio State University, Graduate School, College of Engineering, Department of Mechanical and Aerospace Engineering, Columbus, OH 43210. Offers mechanical engineering (MS, PhD); nuclear engineering (MS, PhD). *Faculty:* 62. *Students:* 259 full-time (41 women), 123 part-time (17 women); includes 4 Black or African American, non-Hispanic/Latino; 14 Asian, non-Hispanic/Latino; 9 Hispanic/Latino, 129 international. Average age 27. In 2010, 62 master's, 28 doctorates awarded. *Degree requirements:* For doctorate, thesis/dissertation. *Entrance requirements:* For master's, GRE General Test or U.S. engineering degree with minimum GPA of 3.3; for doctorate, GRE General Test or U.S. engineering degree with minimum GPA of 3.75. Additional exam requirements/recommendations for international students: Recommended—TOEFL (minimum score 600 paper-based; 250 computer-based). *Application deadline:* For fall admission, 8/15 priority date for domestic students, 7/1 priority date for international students; for winter admission, 12/1 priority date for domestic students, 11/1 priority date for international students; for spring admission, 3/1 priority date for domestic students, 2/1 priority date for international students. Applications are processed on a rolling basis. Application fee: $40 ($50 for international students). Electronic applications accepted. *Expenses:* Tuition, state resident: full-time $10,605. Tuition, nonresident: full-time $26,535. Tuition and fees vary according to course load and program. *Financial support:* Fellowships, research assistantships, teaching assistantships, career-related internships or fieldwork, Federal Work-Study, institutionally sponsored loans, and unspecified assistantships available. Support available to part-time students. *Unit head:* Krishnaswamy Srinivasan, Chair, 614-292-0503, E-mail: srinivasan.3@osu.edu. *Application contact:* 614-292-9444, Fax: 614-292-3895, E-mail: domestic.grad@osu.edu.

Ohio University, Graduate College, Russ College of Engineering and Technology, Department of Mechanical Engineering, Athens, OH 45701-2979. Offers biomedical engineering (MS); mechanical engineering (MS), including CAD/CAM, design, energy, manufacturing, materials, robotics, thermofluids. Part-time programs available. *Students:* 29 full-time (3 women), 4 part-time (1 woman); includes 3 minority (1 Black or African American, non-Hispanic/Latino; 1 Hispanic/Latino; 1 Two or more races, non-Hispanic/Latino), 12 international. 40 applicants, 73% accepted, 11 enrolled. In 2010, 4 master's awarded. *Degree requirements:* For master's, comprehensive exam (for some programs), thesis; for doctorate, comprehensive exam, thesis/dissertation. *Entrance requirements:* For master's, GRE, BS in engineering or science, minimum GPA of 2.8; for doctorate, GRE. Additional exam requirements/recommendations for international students: Required—TOEFL (minimum score 550 paper-based; 80 iBT) or IELTS (minimum score 6.5). *Application deadline:* For fall admission, 2/15 priority date for domestic and international students. Applications are processed on a rolling basis. Application fee: $50 ($55 for international students). Electronic applications accepted. *Financial support:* In 2010–11, research assistantships with tuition reimbursements (averaging $14,000 per year), teaching assistantships with tuition reimbursements (averaging $14,000 per year) were awarded; career-related internships or fieldwork, Federal Work-Study, institutionally sponsored loans, tuition waivers (full and partial), and unspecified assistantships also available. Financial award application deadline: 2/15; financial award applicants required to submit FAFSA. *Faculty research:* Biomedical, energy and the environment, materials and manufacturing, bioengineering. *Unit head:* Dr. Greg Kremer, Chairman, 740-593-1561, Fax: 740-593-0476, E-mail: kremer@bobcat.ent.ohiou.edu. *Application contact:* Dr. Frank F. Kraft, Graduate Chairman, 740-597-1478, Fax: 740-593-0476, E-mail: kraft@ohio.edu.

Ohio University, Graduate College, Russ College of Engineering and Technology, Program in Mechanical and Systems Engineering, Athens, OH 45701-2979. Offers industrial engineering (PhD); mechanical engineering (PhD). *Students:* 18 full-time (5 women), 5 part-time (0 women), 18 international. 7 applicants, 14% accepted, 1 enrolled. In 2010, 2 doctorates awarded. *Degree requirements:* For doctorate, comprehensive exam, thesis/dissertation. *Entrance requirements:* For doctorate, GRE General Test, MS in engineering or related field. Additional exam requirements/recommendations for international students: Required—TOEFL (minimum score 550 paper-based; 80 iBT) or IELTS (minimum score 6.5). *Application deadline:* For fall admission, 3/15 priority date for domestic and international students. Applications are processed on a rolling basis. Application fee: $50 ($55 for international students). Electronic applications accepted. *Financial support:* In 2010–11, 4 research assistantships with full tuition reimbursements (averaging $14,000 per year) were awarded; Federal Work-Study, institutionally sponsored loans, and unspecified assistantships also available. Financial award application deadline: 3/15; financial award applicants required to submit FAFSA. *Faculty research:* Material processing, expert systems, environmental geotechnical manufacturing, thermal systems, robotics. Total annual research expenditures: $1.8 million. *Unit head:* Dr. Shawn Ostermann, Associate Dean, 740-593-1482, Fax: 740-593-0659, E-mail: ostermann@ohio.edu. *Application contact:* Dr. Shawn Ostermann, Associate Dean, 740-593-1482, Fax: 740-593-0659, E-mail: ostermann@ohio.edu.

Oklahoma State University, College of Engineering, Architecture and Technology, School of Mechanical and Aerospace Engineering, Stillwater, OK 74078. Offers mechanical and aerospace engineering (MS, PhD); mechanical engineering (MS, PhD). Postbaccalaureate distance learning degree programs offered. *Faculty:* 25 full-time (2 women), 1 part-time/adjunct (0 women). *Students:* 89 full-time (10 women), 92 part-time (8 women); includes 1 American Indian or Alaska Native, non-Hispanic/Latino; 1 Asian, non-Hispanic/Latino; 1 Hispanic/Latino, 146 international. Average age 26. 297 applicants, 30% accepted, 48 enrolled. In 2010, 54 master's, 3 doctorates awarded. *Degree requirements:* For master's, thesis or alternative; for doctorate, comprehensive exam, thesis/dissertation. *Entrance requirements:* For master's and doctorate, GRE or GMAT. Additional exam requirements/recommendations for international students: Required—TOEFL (minimum score 550 paper-based; 79 iBT). *Application deadline:* For fall admission, 3/1 priority date for international students; for spring admission, 8/1 priority date for international students. Applications are processed on a rolling basis. Application fee: $40 ($75 for international students). Electronic applications accepted. *Expenses:* Tuition, state resident: full-time $3716; part-time $154.85 per credit hour. Tuition, nonresident: full-time $14,892; part-time $621 per credit hour. Required fees: $2044; $85.20 per credit hour. One-time fee: $50. Tuition and fees vary according to course load and campus/location. *Financial support:* In 2010–11, 92 research assistantships (averaging $10,986 per year), 69 teaching assistantships (averaging $7,403 per year) were awarded; career-related internships or fieldwork, Federal Work-Study, scholarships/grants, health care benefits, tuition waivers (partial), and unspecified assistantships also available. Support available to part-time students. Financial award application deadline: 3/1; financial award applicants required to submit FAFSA. *Unit head:* Dr. Lawrence L. Hoberock, Head, 405-744-5900, Fax: 405-744-7873. *Application contact:* Dr. Gordon Emslie, Dean, 405-744-6368, Fax: 405-744-0355, E-mail: grad-i@okstate.edu.

Old Dominion University, Frank Batten College of Engineering and Technology, Program in Mechanical Engineering, Norfolk, VA 23529. Offers design and manufacturing (ME); mechanical engineering (ME, MS, D Eng, PhD). Part-time and evening/weekend programs available. Postbaccalaureate distance learning degree programs offered (no on-campus study). *Faculty:* 24 full-time (2 women). *Students:* 31 full-time (6 women), 42 part-time (8 women); includes 7 minority (3 Asian, non-Hispanic/Latino; 3 Hispanic/Latino; 1 Two or more races, non-Hispanic/Latino), 34 international. Average age 29. 50 applicants, 76% accepted, 7 enrolled. In 2010, 10 master's, 3 doctorates awarded. *Degree requirements:* For master's, comprehensive exam, thesis optional; for doctorate, thesis/dissertation, candidacy exam. *Entrance requirements:* For master's, GRE, minimum GPA of 3.0; for doctorate, GRE, minimum GPA of 3.5. Additional exam requirements/recommendations for international students: Required—TOEFL (minimum score 550 paper-based; 213 computer-based). *Application deadline:* For fall admission, 6/1 for domestic students, 2/15 priority date for international students; for spring admission, 11/1 for domestic students, 10/1 for international students. Applications are processed on a rolling basis. Application fee: $50. Electronic applications accepted. *Expenses:* Tuition, state resident: full-time $8592; part-time $358 per credit. Tuition, nonresident: full-time $21,672; part-time $903 per credit. Required fees: $119 per semester. One-time fee: $50. *Financial support:* In 2010–11, 12 students received support, including 5 fellowships with partial tuition reimbursements available (averaging $16,000 per year), 11 research assistantships with partial tuition reimbursements available (averaging $15,000 per year), 15 teaching assistantships with partial tuition reimbursements available (averaging $6,400 per year); career-related internships or fieldwork, institutionally sponsored loans, scholarships/grants, and unspecified assistantships also available. Financial award application deadline: 2/15; financial award applicants required to submit FAFSA. *Faculty research:* Computational applied mechanics, manufacturing, experimental stress analysis, systems dynamics and control, mechanical design. Total annual research expenditures: $975,887. *Unit head:* Dr. Jen-Kuang Huang, Chair, 757-683-3734, Fax: 757-683-5344, E-mail: jhuang@odu.edu. *Application contact:* Dr. Gene Hou, Graduate Program Director, 757-683-3728, Fax: 757-683-5344, E-mail: megpd@odu.edu.

Oregon State University, Graduate School, College of Engineering, School of Mechanical, Industrial, and Manufacturing Engineering, Corvallis, OR 97331. Offers human systems engineering (MS, PhD); industrial engineering (MS, PhD); information systems engineering (MS, PhD); manufacturing engineering (M Engr); manufacturing systems engineering (MS, PhD); materials science (MAIS, MS, PhD); mechanical engineering (MS, PhD); nano/micro fabrication (MS, PhD). Part-time programs available. Postbaccalaureate distance learning degree programs offered (minimal on-campus study). *Degree requirements:* For master's, thesis or alternative; for doctorate, thesis/dissertation. *Entrance requirements:* For master's, placement exam, minimum GPA of 3.0 in last 90 hours of course work; for doctorate, GRE, placement exam, minimum GPA of 3.0 in last 90 hours of course work. Additional exam requirements/recommendations for international students: Required—TOEFL (minimum score 550 paper-based; 213 computer-based). *Faculty research:* Computer-integrated manufacturing, human factors, robotics, decision support systems, simulation modeling and analysis.

Penn State University Park, Graduate School, College of Engineering, Department of Mechanical and Nuclear Engineering, State College, University Park, PA 16802-1503. Offers M Eng, MS, PhD. *Faculty research:* Reactor safety, radiation damage, advanced controls, radiation instrumentation, computational methods.

Polytechnic Institute of NYU, Department of Mechanical and Aerospace Engineering, Major in Mechanical Engineering, Brooklyn, NY 11201-2990. Offers MS, PhD. Part-time and evening/weekend programs available. *Students:* 45 full-time (5 women), 19 part-time (6 women); includes 9 Asian, non-Hispanic/Latino; 2 Hispanic/Latino, 36 international. Average age 25. 168 applicants, 54% accepted, 34 enrolled. In 2010, 14 master's awarded. *Degree requirements:* For master's, comprehensive exam (for some programs), thesis (for some programs); for doctorate, comprehensive exam, thesis/dissertation. *Entrance requirements:* For master's, BE or BS in engineering, physics, chemistry, mathematical sciences, or biological sciences or MBA. Additional exam requirements/recommendations for international students: Required—TOEFL (minimum score 550 paper-based; 213 computer-based; 80 iBT); Recommended—IELTS (minimum score 6.5). *Application deadline:* For fall admission, 7/31 priority date for domestic students, 4/30 priority date for international students; for spring admission, 12/31 priority date for domestic students, 11/30 priority date for international students. Applications are processed on a rolling basis. Application fee: $75. Electronic applications accepted. *Expenses:* Tuition: Full-time $21,492; part-time $1194 per credit. Required fees: $385 per semester. Tuition and fees vary according to course load. *Financial support:* Institutionally sponsored loans, scholarships/grants, and unspecified assistantships available. Support available to part-time students. Financial award applicants required to submit FAFSA. *Unit head:* Dr. George Vradis, Head, 718-260-3875, Fax: 718-260-3532, E-mail: gvradis@poly.edu. *Application contact:* JeanCarlo Bonilla, Director of Graduate Enrollment Management, 718-260-3182, Fax: 718-260-3624, E-mail: gradinfo@poly.edu.

Polytechnic Institute of NYU, Long Island Graduate Center, Graduate Programs, Department of Mechanical and Aerospace Engineering, Melville, NY 11747. Offers aeronautics and astronautics (MS); industrial engineering (MS); manufacturing engineering (MS); mechanical engineering (MS). Part-time and evening/weekend programs available. *Students:* 1 full-time (0 women), all international. Average age 28. *Degree requirements:* For master's, comprehensive exam (for some programs), thesis (for some programs). *Entrance requirements:* Additional exam requirements/recommendations for international students: Required—TOEFL (minimum score 550 paper-based; 213 computer-based; 80 iBT); Recommended—IELTS (minimum score 6.5). *Application deadline:* For fall admission, 7/31 priority date for domestic students, 4/30 priority date for international students; for spring admission, 12/31 priority date for domestic students, 11/30 priority date for international students. Applications are processed on a rolling basis. Application fee: $75. Electronic applications accepted. *Expenses:* Tuition: Full-time $21,492; part-time $1194 per credit. Required fees: $385 per semester. Tuition and fees vary according to course load. *Financial support:* In 2010–11, 16 fellowships with tuition reimbursements (averaging $1,394 per year) were awarded; research assistantships with tuition reimbursements, institutionally sponsored loans, scholarships/grants, and unspecified assistantships also available. Support available to part-time students. Financial award applicants required to submit FAFSA. *Faculty research:* UV filter, fuel efficient hydrodynamic containment for gas core fission, turbulent boundary layer research. *Unit head:* Dr. George Vradis, Department Head, 718-260-3875, E-mail: gvradis@duke.poly.edu. *Application contact:* JeanCarlo Bonilla, Director of Graduate Enrollment Management, 718-260-3182, Fax: 718-260-3624, E-mail: gradinfo@poly.edu.

Polytechnic University of Puerto Rico, Graduate School, Hato Rey, PR 00919. Offers business administration (MBA), including computer information systems, general management, management of information systems, management of international enterprises; civil engineering (ME, MS); computer engineering (ME, MS); computer science (MCS, MS); electrical engineering (ME, MS); engineering management (MEM); environmental management (MEM); landscape architecture (M Land Arch); manufacturing competitiveness (MMC, MS); manufacturing engineering (ME, MS); mechanical engineering (M Mech E). Part-time and evening/weekend programs available. *Entrance requirements:* For master's, 3 letters of recommendation.

Portland State University, Graduate Studies, Maseeh College of Engineering and Computer Science, Department of Mechanical Engineering, Portland, OR 97207-0751. Offers M Eng, MS, PhD. Part-time and evening/weekend programs available. *Faculty:* 14 full-time (1 woman), 1 part-time/adjunct (0 women). *Students:* 26 full-time (1 woman), 25 part-time (5 women); includes 1 Black or African American, non-Hispanic/Latino; 2 Asian, non-Hispanic/Latino; 2 Hispanic/Latino, 7 international. Average age 29. 29 applicants, 52% accepted, 14 enrolled. In 2010, 20 master's awarded. *Degree requirements:* For master's, thesis or alternative; for doctorate, one foreign language, thesis/dissertation, oral and written exams. *Entrance requirements:* For master's, minimum GPA of 3.0 in upper-division course work, BS in mechanical engineering or allied field; for doctorate, GRE General Test, GRE Subject Test, minimum GPA of 3.0 in upper-division course work. Additional exam requirements/recommendations for international students: Required—TOEFL (minimum score 550 paper-based; 213 computer-based). *Application deadline:* For fall admission, 4/1 for domestic students, 3/1 for international students; for winter admission, 9/1 for domestic students, 8/1 for international students; for spring admission, 11/1 for domestic students, 10/1 for international students. Applications are processed on a rolling basis. Application fee: $50. *Expenses:* Tuition, state resident: full-time $8505; part-time $315 per credit. Tuition, nonresident: full-time $13,284; part-time $492 per credit. Required fees: $1482; $21 per credit. $99 per term. One-time fee: $120. Part-time tuition and fees vary according to course load and program. *Financial support:* In 2010–11, 4 research assistantships with full tuition reimbursements (averaging $16,184 per year) were awarded; teaching assistantships with full tuition reimbursements, Federal Work-Study, scholarships/grants, and unspecified assistantships also available. Support available to part-time students. Financial award application deadline: 3/1; financial award applicants required to submit FAFSA. *Faculty research:* Mechanical system modeling, indoor air quality, manufacturing process, computational fluid dynamics, building science. Total annual research expenditures: $1.1 million. *Unit head:* Gerald Recktenwald, Chair, 503-725-4290, Fax: 503-725-4298, E-mail: gerry@me.pdx.edu. *Application contact:* Gerald Recktenwald, Chair, 503-725-4290, Fax: 503-725-4298, E-mail: gerry@me.pdx.edu.

Portland State University, Graduate Studies, Systems Science Program, Portland, OR 97207-0751. Offers computational intelligence (Certificate); computer modeling and simulation (Certificate); systems science (MS); systems science/anthropology (PhD); systems science/business administration (PhD); systems science/civil engineering (PhD); systems science/economics (PhD); systems science/engineering management (PhD); systems science/general (PhD); systems science/mathematical sciences (PhD); systems science/mechanical engineering (PhD); systems science/psychology (PhD); systems science/sociology (PhD). *Faculty:* 4 full-time (0 women), 1 part-time/adjunct (0 women). *Students:* 15 full-time (4 women), 35 part-time (11 women); includes 1 American Indian or Alaska Native, non-Hispanic/Latino; 1 Asian, non-Hispanic/Latino; 1 Two or more races, non-Hispanic/Latino, 4 international. Average age 39. 8 applicants, 88% accepted, 5 enrolled. In 2010, 2 master's, 4 doctorates awarded. *Degree requirements:* For doctorate, variable foreign language requirement, thesis/dissertation. *Entrance requirements:* For master's, 2 letters of recommendation; for doctorate, GMAT, GRE General Test, minimum undergraduate GPA of 3.0. Additional exam requirements/recommendations for international students: Required—TOEFL. *Application deadline:* For fall admission, 2/1 for domestic students; for spring admission, 11/1 for domestic students. Application fee: $50. *Expenses:* Tuition, state resident: full-time $8505; part-time $315 per credit. Tuition, nonresident: full-time $13,284; part-time $492 per credit. Required fees: $1482; $21 per credit. $99 per term. One-time fee: $120. Part-time tuition and fees vary according to course load and program. *Financial support:* In 2010–11, 1 research assistantship with full tuition reimbursement (averaging $7,704 per year) was awarded; teaching assistantships with full tuition reimbursements, career-related internships or fieldwork, Federal Work-Study, scholarships/grants, and unspecified assistantships also available. Support available to part-time students. Financial award application deadline: 3/1; financial award applicants required to submit FAFSA. *Faculty research:* Systems theory and methodology, artificial intelligence neural networks, information theory, nonlinear dynamics/chaos, modeling and simulation. *Unit head:* George Lendaris, Acting Director, 503-725-4960. *Application contact:* Dawn Sharafi, Administrative Assistant, 503-725-4960, E-mail: dawn@sysc.pdx.edu.

Princeton University, Graduate School, School of Engineering and Applied Science, Department of Mechanical and Aerospace Engineering, Princeton, NJ 08544. Offers M Eng, MSE, PhD. Terminal master's awarded for partial completion of doctoral program. *Degree requirements:* For master's, thesis (MSE); for doctorate, thesis/dissertation, general exam. *Entrance requirements:* For master's, GRE General Test, 3 letters of recommendation; for doctorate, GRE General Test, official transcript(s), 3 letters of recommendation, personal statement. Additional exam requirements/recommendations for international students: Required—TOEFL. Electronic applications accepted. *Faculty research:* Bioengineering and bio-mechanics; combustion, energy conversion, and climate; fluid mechanics, dynamics, and control systems; lasers and applied physics; materials and mechanical systems.

Purdue University, College of Engineering, School of Mechanical Engineering, West Lafayette, IN 47907-2088. Offers MS, MSE, MSME, PhD, Certificate. MS and PhD degree programs in biomedical engineering offered jointly with School of Electrical and Computer Engineering and School of Chemical Engineering. Part-time programs available. Postbaccalaureate distance learning degree programs offered (no on-campus study). *Entrance requirements:* For master's and doctorate, GRE General Test, minimum GPA of 3.2. Additional exam requirements/recommendations for international students: Required—TOEFL (minimum score 575 paper-based; 233 computer-based; 77 iBT); Recommended—TWE. Electronic applications accepted. *Faculty research:* Design, manufacturing, thermal/fluid sciences, mechanics, electromechanical systems.

Purdue University Calumet, Graduate Studies Office, School of Engineering, Mathematics, and Science, Department of Engineering, Hammond, IN 46323-2094. Offers computer engineering (MSE); electrical engineering (MSE); engineering (MS); mechanical engineering (MSE). Evening/weekend programs available. *Entrance requirements:* Additional exam requirements/recommendations for international students: Required—TOEFL. Application fee: $30. *Expenses:* Tuition, state resident: full-time $6867. Tuition, nonresident: full-time $14,157. *Financial support:* Career-related internships or fieldwork available. Financial award application deadline: 3/1. *Unit head:* Dr. Kaliappan Gopalan, Head, 219-989-2685, E-mail: gopalan@purduecal.edu. *Application contact:* Janice Novosel, Engineering Graduate Program Secretary, 219-989-3106, E-mail: janice.novosel@purduecal.edu.

Queen's University at Kingston, School of Graduate Studies and Research, Faculty of Applied Science, Department of Mechanical and Materials Engineering, Kingston, ON K7L 3N6, Canada. Offers M Eng, M Sc, M Sc Eng, PhD. Part-time programs available. *Degree requirements:* For master's, thesis optional; for doctorate, comprehensive exam, thesis/dissertation. *Entrance requirements:* Additional exam requirements/recommendations for international students: Required—TOEFL. Electronic applications accepted. *Faculty research:* Dynamics and control systems, manufacturing and design, materials and engineering, heat transferring fluid dynamics, energy systems and combustion.

Rensselaer at Hartford, Department of Engineering, Program in Mechanical Engineering, Hartford, CT 06120-2991. Offers ME, MS. Part-time and evening/weekend programs available. *Degree requirements:* For master's, thesis optional. *Entrance requirements:* For master's, GRE. Additional exam requirements/recommendations for international students: Required—TOEFL (minimum score 600 paper-based; 250 computer-based; 100 iBT).

Rensselaer Polytechnic Institute, Graduate School, School of Engineering, Program in Mechanical Engineering, Troy, NY 12180-3590. Offers M Eng, MS, PhD. Part-time programs available. Postbaccalaureate distance learning degree programs offered. *Faculty:* 18 full-time (4 women), 2 part-time/adjunct (0 women). *Students:* 104 full-time (17 women), 13 part-time (1 woman); includes 6 Hispanic/Latino, 69 international. Average age 27. 201 applicants, 45% accepted, 26 enrolled. In 2010, 13 master's, 18 doctorates awarded. *Degree requirements:* For master's, thesis (for some programs); for doctorate, thesis/dissertation. *Entrance requirements:* For master's and doctorate, GRE. Additional exam requirements/recommendations for international students: Required—TOEFL (minimum score 600 paper-based; 250 computer-based; 100 iBT). *Application deadline:* For fall admission, 1/15 priority date for domestic and international students; for spring admission, 1/15 for domestic students, 1/15 priority date for international students. Applications are processed on a rolling basis. Application fee: $75. Electronic applications accepted. *Expenses:* Tuition: Full-time $39,600; part-time $1650 per credit. Required fees: $1896. *Financial support:* In 2010–11, 101 students received support, including 12 fellowships with full tuition reimbursements available (averaging $25,000 per year), 48 research assistantships with full tuition reimbursements available (averaging $17,500 per year), 41 teaching assistantships with full tuition reimbursements available (averaging $17,500 per year); unspecified assistantships also available. Financial award application deadline: 2/1. *Faculty research:* Tribology, advanced composite materials, energy and combustion systems, computer-aided and optimal design, manufacturing. Total annual research expenditures: $6.2 million. *Unit head:* Dr. Timothy Wei, Head, 518-276-6351, Fax: 518-276-6025, E-mail: weit@rpi.edu. *Application contact:* Dr. Thierry A. Blanchet, Associate Chair for Graduate Studies, 518-276-8697, Fax: 518-276-2623, E-mail: blanct@rpi.edu.

Rice University, Graduate Programs, George R. Brown School of Engineering, Department of Mechanical Engineering and Materials Science, Houston, TX 77251-1892. Offers materials science (MMS, MS, PhD); mechanical engineering (MME, MS, PhD); MBA/ME. Part-time programs available. Terminal master's awarded for partial completion of doctoral program. *Degree requirements:* For master's, comprehensive exam, thesis; for doctorate, comprehensive exam, thesis/dissertation. *Entrance requirements:* For master's and doctorate, GRE General Test, minimum GPA of 3.0. Additional exam requirements/recommendations for international students: Required—TOEFL (minimum score 600 paper-based; 250 computer-based; 90 iBT), IELTS (minimum score 7). Electronic applications accepted. *Faculty research:* Heat transfer, biomedical engineering, fluid dynamics, aero-astronautics, control systems/robotics, materials science.

Rochester Institute of Technology, Graduate Enrollment Services, College of Applied Science and Technology, Department of Electrical, Computer and Telecommunications Engineering Technology, Program in Manufacturing and Mechanical Systems Integration, Rochester, NY 14623-5603. Offers MS. Part-time and evening/weekend programs available. *Students:* 20 full-time (1 woman), 14 part-time (0 women); includes 1 Asian, non-Hispanic/Latino; 1 Hispanic/Latino, 8 international. Average age 29. 11 applicants, 91% accepted, 9 enrolled. In 2010, 9

Mechanical Engineering

Rochester Institute of Technology (continued)

master's awarded. *Degree requirements:* For master's, thesis. *Entrance requirements:* For master's, GRE, minimum GPA of 3.0. Additional exam requirements/recommendations for international students: Required—TOEFL (minimum score 550 paper-based; 213 computer-based; 79 iBT) or IELTS (minimum score 6.5). *Application deadline:* For fall admission, 2/15 priority date for domestic and international students; for winter admission, 11/1 for domestic and international students; for spring admission, 2/1 for domestic and international students. Applications are processed on a rolling basis. *Expenses:* Tuition: Full-time $33,234; part-time $924 per credit hour. Required fees: $219. *Financial support:* In 2010–11, 26 students received support; research assistantships with partial tuition reimbursements available, teaching assistantships with partial tuition reimbursements available, career-related internships or fieldwork, scholarships/grants, and unspecified assistantships available. Support available to part-time students. Financial award application deadline: 2/15; financial award applicants required to submit FAFSA. *Faculty research:* Biodegradable plastics, health physics, nuclear engineering technology, solidworks, automotive engineering, compression strength, protective package development. *Unit head:* Dr. S. Manian Ramkumar, Graduate Program Director, 585-475-6081, Fax: 585-475-5227, E-mail: smrmet@rit.edu. *Application contact:* Diane Ellison, Assistant Vice President, Graduate Enrollment Services, 585-475-2229, Fax: 585-475-7164, E-mail: gradinfo@rit.edu.

Rochester Institute of Technology, Graduate Enrollment Services, Kate Gleason College of Engineering, Department of Mechanical Engineering, Rochester, NY 14623-5603. Offers ME, MS. Part-time programs available. *Students:* 55 full-time (6 women), 40 part-time (3 women); includes 1 American Indian or Alaska Native, non-Hispanic/Latino; 1 Asian, non-Hispanic/Latino; 1 Hispanic/Latino, 27 international. Average age 26. 148 applicants, 53% accepted, 35 enrolled. In 2010, 57 master's awarded. *Degree requirements:* For master's, thesis optional. *Entrance requirements:* For master's, GRE, minimum GPA of 3.0. Additional exam requirements/recommendations for international students: Required—TOEFL (minimum score 570 paper-based; 230 computer-based; 88 iBT) or IELTS (minimum score 6.5). *Application deadline:* For fall admission, 2/15 priority date for domestic and international students; for winter admission, 10/15 for domestic and international students; for spring admission, 2/1 for domestic and international students. Applications are processed on a rolling basis. Application fee: $50. Electronic applications accepted. *Expenses:* Tuition: Full-time $33,234; part-time $924 per credit hour. Required fees: $219. *Financial support:* In 2010–11, 86 students received support; research assistantships with partial tuition reimbursements available, teaching assistantships with partial tuition reimbursements available, career-related internships or fieldwork, institutionally sponsored loans, scholarships/grants, and unspecified assistantships available. Support available to part-time students. Financial award applicants required to submit FAFSA. *Faculty research:* Aerospace systems, unmanned aircraft design, fabrication and testing, automotive systems, assistive device technologies, artificial organ engineering, biomedical device engineering, microscale heat and mass transfer, thermoelectric energy, energy systems for developing countries. *Unit head:* Dr. Edward Hensel, Department Head, 585-475-5181, Fax: 585-475-7710, E-mail: echeme@rit.edu. *Application contact:* Diane Ellison, Assistant Vice President, Graduate Enrollment Services, 585-475-2229, Fax: 585-475-7164, E-mail: gradinfo@rit.edu.

Rose-Hulman Institute of Technology, Faculty of Engineering and Applied Sciences, Department of Mechanical Engineering, Terre Haute, IN 47803-3999. Offers MS. Part-time programs available. Postbaccalaureate distance learning degree programs offered (minimal on-campus study). *Faculty:* 24 full-time (3 women). *Students:* 5 full-time (0 women), 8 part-time (0 women); includes 1 minority (Asian, non-Hispanic/Latino), 3 international. Average age 24. 11 applicants, 100% accepted, 5 enrolled. In 2010, 9 master's awarded. *Degree requirements:* For master's, thesis. *Entrance requirements:* For master's, GRE, minimum GPA of 3.0. Additional exam requirements/recommendations for international students: Required—TOEFL (minimum score 580 paper-based; 237 computer-based; 92 iBT). *Application deadline:* For fall admission, 2/1 priority date for domestic students. Applications are processed on a rolling basis. Application fee: $0. *Expenses:* Tuition: Full-time $35,595; part-time $1038 per credit hour. *Financial support:* In 2010–11, 8 students received support; fellowships with full and partial tuition reimbursements available, research assistantships with full and partial tuition reimbursements available, institutionally sponsored loans, scholarships/grants, and tuition waivers (full and partial) available. *Faculty research:* Dynamics of large flexible space structures, finite-element analysis, system simulation and optimization, mechanical design, fracture mechanics and fatigue. Total annual research expenditures: $30,457. *Unit head:* Dr. David J. Purdy, Chairman, 812-877-8320, Fax: 812-877-3198. *Application contact:* Dr. Daniel J. Moore, Associate Dean of the Faculty, 812-877-8110, Fax: 812-877-8061, E-mail: daniel.j.moore@rose-hulman.edu.

Rowan University, Graduate School, College of Engineering, Department of Mechanical Engineering, Glassboro, NJ 08028-1701. Offers MS. Part-time and evening/weekend programs available. *Faculty:* 8 full-time (1 woman). *Students:* 2 full-time (1 woman), 3 part-time (0 women); includes 1 Asian, non-Hispanic/Latino. Average age 24. 4 applicants, 75% accepted, 2 enrolled. In 2010, 4 master's awarded. *Entrance requirements:* For master's, GRE General Test. Additional exam requirements/recommendations for international students: Required—TOEFL. *Application deadline:* Applications are processed on a rolling basis. Application fee: $65 ($200 for international students). Electronic applications accepted. *Expenses:* Tuition, area resident: Part-time $602 per semester hour. Tuition, nonresident: part-time $602 per semester hour. Required fees: $100 per semester hour. One-time fee: $10 part-time. *Unit head:* Dr. Steve Chin, Dean, 856-256-5301. *Application contact:* Dr. Ralph Dusseau, Program Adviser, 856-256-5332.

Royal Military College of Canada, Division of Graduate Studies and Research, Engineering Division, Department of Mechanical Engineering, Kingston, ON K7K 7B4, Canada. Offers M Eng, MA Sc, PhD. *Degree requirements:* For master's, thesis; for doctorate, comprehensive exam, thesis/dissertation. *Entrance requirements:* For master's, honours degree with second-class standing; for doctorate, master's degree. Electronic applications accepted.

Rutgers, The State University of New Jersey, New Brunswick, Graduate School-New Brunswick, Program in Mechanical and Aerospace Engineering, Piscataway, NJ 08854-8097. Offers design and control (MS, PhD); fluid mechanics (MS, PhD); solid mechanics (MS, PhD); thermal sciences (MS, PhD). Part-time and evening/weekend programs available. *Degree requirements:* For master's, thesis (for some programs); for doctorate, thesis/dissertation. *Entrance requirements:* For master's, GRE General Test, BS in mechanical/aerospace engineering or related field; for doctorate, GRE General Test, MS in mechanical/aerospace engineering or related field. Additional exam requirements/recommendations for international students: Required—TOEFL. Electronic applications accepted. *Expenses:* Tuition, state resident: full-time $7200; part-time $600 per credit. Tuition, nonresident: full-time $11,124; part-time $927 per credit. *Faculty research:* Combustion, propulsion, thermal transport, crystal plasticity, optimization, fabrication, nanoidentation.

St. Cloud State University, School of Graduate Studies, College of Science and Engineering, Program in Mechanical Engineering, St. Cloud, MN 56301-4498. Offers MS. *Degree requirements:* For master's, thesis or alternative. *Entrance requirements:* For master's, GRE General Test, minimum GPA of 2.75. Additional exam requirements/recommendations for international students: Required—Michigan English Language Assessment Battery; Recommended—TOEFL (minimum score 550 paper-based; 213 computer-based), IELTS (minimum score 6.5). Electronic applications accepted.

San Diego State University, Graduate and Research Affairs, College of Engineering, Department of Mechanical Engineering, San Diego, CA 92182. Offers engineering sciences and applied mechanics (PhD); manufacture and design (MS); mechanical engineering (MS). PhD offered jointly with University of California, San Diego and Department of Aerospace Engineering and Engineering Mechanics. Evening/weekend programs available. *Degree requirements:* For master's, comprehensive exam (for some programs), thesis (for some programs); for doctorate, thesis/dissertation. *Entrance requirements:* For master's, GRE General Test; for doctorate, GRE, 3 letters of recommendation. Additional exam requirements/recommendations for international students: Required—TOEFL. Electronic applications accepted. *Faculty research:* Energy analysis and diagnosis, seawater pump design, space-related research.

San Jose State University, Graduate Studies and Research, Charles W. Davidson College of Engineering, Department of Mechanical and Aerospace Engineering, Program in Mechanical Engineering, San Jose, CA 95192-0001. Offers MS. Part-time programs available. *Degree requirements:* For master's, thesis optional. *Entrance requirements:* For master's, GRE. Additional exam requirements/recommendations for international students: Required—TOEFL. Electronic applications accepted. *Faculty research:* Gas dynamics, mechanics/vibrations, heat transfer, structural analysis, two-phase fluid flow.

Santa Clara University, School of Engineering, Program in Mechanical Engineering, Santa Clara, CA 95053. Offers controls (Certificate); dynamics (Certificate); materials engineering (Certificate); mechanical design analysis (Certificate); mechanical engineering (MS, PhD, Engineer); mechatronics systems engineering (Certificate); technology jump-start (Certificate); thermofluids (Certificate). Part-time and evening/weekend programs available. *Students:* 33 full-time (4 women), 55 part-time (6 women); includes 30 minority (21 Asian, non-Hispanic/Latino; 6 Hispanic/Latino; 1 Native Hawaiian or other Pacific Islander, non-Hispanic/Latino; 2 Two or more races, non-Hispanic/Latino), 15 international. Average age 28. 82 applicants, 71% accepted, 29 enrolled. In 2010, 19 master's awarded. *Degree requirements:* For master's, thesis (for some programs); for doctorate, thesis/dissertation; for other advanced degree, thesis. *Entrance requirements:* For master's, GRE (waiver may be available), transcript; for doctorate, GRE, master's degree or equivalent; for other advanced degree, master's degree, published paper. Additional exam requirements/recommendations for international students: Required—TOEFL (minimum score 550 paper-based; 213 computer-based; 79 iBT). *Application deadline:* For fall admission, 8/12 for domestic students, 7/15 for international students; for winter admission, 10/28 for domestic students, 9/23 for international students; for spring admission, 2/25 for domestic students, 1/21 for international students. Applications are processed on a rolling basis. Application fee: $60. Electronic applications accepted. *Expenses:* Contact institution. *Financial support:* Research assistantships, teaching assistantships available. Financial award application deadline: 3/2; financial award applicants required to submit FAFSA. *Faculty research:* Development of small satellite design, tests and operations technology. Total annual research expenditures: $585,448. *Unit head:* Dr. Alex Zecevic, Associate Dean for Graduate Studies, 408-554-2394, E-mail: azecevic@scu.edu. *Application contact:* Stacey Tinker, Director of Admissions, Graduate Engineering, 408-554-4748, Fax: 408-554-4323, E-mail: stinker@scu.edu.

South Carolina State University, School of Graduate Studies, Department of Civil and Mechanical Engineering Technology and Nuclear Engineering, Orangeburg, SC 29117-0001. Offers transportation (MS). Part-time and evening/weekend programs available. *Degree requirements:* For master's, comprehensive exam, thesis, departmental qualifying exam. *Entrance requirements:* For master's, GRE. Electronic applications accepted. *Faculty research:* Societal competence, relationship of parent-child interaction to adult, rehabilitation evaluation, vocation, language assessment of rural children.

South Dakota School of Mines and Technology, Graduate Division, Department of Mechanical Engineering, Rapid City, SD 57701-3995. Offers MS, PhD. Part-time programs available. *Entrance requirements:* Additional exam requirements/recommendations for international students: Required—TOEFL, TWE. Electronic applications accepted. *Faculty research:* Advanced composite materials, robotics, computer-integrated manufacturing, enhanced heat transfer, dynamic systems controls.

South Dakota State University, Graduate School, College of Engineering, Department of Mechanical Engineering, Brookings, SD 57007. Offers engineering (MS). Part-time programs available. *Degree requirements:* For master's, thesis (for some programs), oral exam. *Entrance requirements:* Additional exam requirements/recommendations for international students: Required—TOEFL (minimum score 525 paper-based; 197 computer-based; 71 iBT). *Faculty research:* Thermo-fluid science, solid mechanics and dynamics, industrial and quality control engineering, bioenergy.

Southern Illinois University Carbondale, Graduate School, College of Engineering, Department of Mechanical Engineering and Energy Processes, Carbondale, IL 62901-4701. Offers MS. *Degree requirements:* For master's, comprehensive exam, thesis or alternative. *Entrance requirements:* For master's, GRE General Test, minimum GPA of 2.7. Additional exam requirements/recommendations for international students: Required—TOEFL. *Faculty research:* Coal conversion and processing, combustion, materials science and engineering, mechanical system dynamics.

Southern Illinois University Edwardsville, Graduate School, School of Engineering, Department of Mechanical and Industrial Engineering, Program in Mechanical Engineering, Edwardsville, IL 62026-0001. Offers MS. Part-time programs available. *Students:* 14 full-time (2 women), 14 part-time (3 women); includes 1 minority (Black or African American, non-Hispanic/Latino), 14 international. Average age 26. 39 applicants, 82% accepted. In 2010, 11 master's awarded. *Degree requirements:* For master's, comprehensive exam (for some programs), thesis (for some programs). *Entrance requirements:* Additional exam requirements/recommendations for international students: Required—TOEFL (minimum score 550 paper-based; 213 computer-based; 79 iBT), IELTS (minimum score 6.5). *Application deadline:* For fall admission, 7/22 for domestic students, 6/1 for international students; for spring admission, 12/9 for domestic students, 10/1 for international students. Applications are processed on a rolling basis. Application fee: $30. Electronic applications accepted. *Expenses:* Tuition, state resident: full-time $6012; part-time $1503 per semester. Tuition, nonresident: full-time $15,030; part-time $3758 per semester. Required fees: $1711; $675 per semester. *Financial support:* In 2010–11, 1 fellowship with tuition reimbursement (averaging $8,370 per year), 8 research assistantships with full tuition reimbursements (averaging $8,064 per year), 14 teaching assistantships with full tuition reimbursements (averaging $8,064 per year) were awarded; career-related internships or fieldwork, Federal Work-Study, institutionally sponsored loans, scholarships/grants, traineeships, and unspecified assistantships also available. Support available to part-time students. Financial award application deadline: 3/1; financial award applicants required to submit FAFSA. *Unit head:* Dr. Kegin Gu, Chair, 618-650-3389, E-mail: kgu@siue.edu. *Application contact:* Dr. Terry Yan, Program Director, 618-650-3463, E-mail: xyan@siue.edu.

Southern Methodist University, Bobby B. Lyle School of Engineering, Department of Mechanical Engineering, Dallas, TX 75205. Offers electronic and optical packaging (MS); manufacturing systems management (MS); mechanical engineering (MSME, PhD). Part-time and evening/weekend programs available. Postbaccalaureate distance learning degree programs offered (no on-campus study). *Faculty:* 13 full-time (2 women), 7 part-time/adjunct (1 woman). *Students:* 29 full-time (6 women), 27 part-time (9 women); includes 1 Black or African American, non-Hispanic/Latino; 3 Asian, non-Hispanic/Latino; 2 Hispanic/Latino, 20 international. Average age 31. 53 applicants, 98% accepted, 52 enrolled. In 2010, 8 master's, 3 doctorates awarded. Terminal master's awarded for partial completion of doctoral program. *Degree requirements:* For master's, thesis optional; for doctorate, thesis/dissertation, oral and written qualifying exams, oral final exam. *Entrance requirements:* For master's, GRE General Test, minimum GPA of 3.0 in last 2 years; bachelor's degree in engineering, mathematics, or sciences; for doctorate, preliminary counseling exam, minimum graduate GPA of 3.0, bachelor's degree in related field. Additional exam requirements/recommendations for international students: Required—TOEFL. *Application deadline:* For fall admission, 7/1 for domestic students, 5/15 for international students; for spring admission, 11/15 for domestic students, 9/1 for international students. Applications are processed on a rolling basis. Application fee: $75. *Financial support:* In 2010–11, 17 students received support, including 10 research assistantships with full and partial tuition reimbursements available (averaging $16,000 per year), 7 teaching assistantships with full and partial tuition reimbursements available (averaging $16,000 per year); Federal Work-Study, institutionally sponsored loans, and tuition waivers (full and partial) also available. Financial award applicants required to submit FAFSA. *Faculty research:* Design, systems, and controls; thermal and fluid sciences. Total annual research expenditures: $774,564.

Unit head: Dr. Volkan Otugen, Chairman, 214-768-3200, Fax: 214-768-1473, E-mail: otugen@engr.smu.edu. *Application contact:* Marc Valerin, Director of Graduate and Executive Admissions, 214-768-3042, E-mail: valerin@engr.smu.edu.

Stanford University, School of Engineering, Department of Mechanical Engineering, Stanford, CA 94305-9991. Offers biomechanical engineering (MS); mechanical engineering (MS, PhD, Eng); product design (MS). *Degree requirements:* For doctorate, thesis/dissertation; for Eng, thesis. *Entrance requirements:* For master's, GRE General Test, undergraduate degree in engineering, math or sciences; for doctorate and Eng, GRE General Test, MS in engineering, math or sciences. Additional exam requirements/recommendations for international students: Required—TOEFL. *Expenses:* Tuition: Full-time $38,700; part-time $860 per unit. One-time fee: $200 full-time.

State University of New York at Binghamton, Graduate School, Thomas J. Watson School of Engineering and Applied Science, Department of Mechanical Engineering, Binghamton, NY 13902-6000. Offers M Eng, MS, PhD. Part-time and evening/weekend programs available. *Faculty:* 16 full-time (0 women), 1 part-time/adjunct (0 women). *Students:* 54 full-time (6 women), 35 part-time (5 women); includes 1 Black or African American, non-Hispanic/Latino; 5 Asian, non-Hispanic/Latino; 1 Hispanic/Latino, 46 international. Average age 26. 82 applicants, 56% accepted, 28 enrolled. In 2010, 12 master's, 6 doctorates awarded. *Degree requirements:* For master's, thesis or alternative; for doctorate, thesis/dissertation. *Entrance requirements:* For master's and doctorate, GRE General Test, GRE Subject Test. Additional exam requirements/recommendations for international students: Required—TOEFL. *Application deadline:* For fall admission, 4/15 priority date for domestic students, 1/15 priority date for international students; for spring admission, 11/1 for domestic students, 10/1 priority date for international students. Applications are processed on a rolling basis. Application fee: $60. Electronic applications accepted. *Financial support:* In 2010–11, 50 students received support, including 33 research assistantships with full tuition reimbursements available (averaging $16,500 per year), 15 teaching assistantships with full tuition reimbursements available (averaging $16,500 per year); fellowships with full tuition reimbursements available, career-related internships or fieldwork, Federal Work-Study, institutionally sponsored loans, scholarships/grants, health care benefits, tuition waivers (full), and unspecified assistantships also available. Financial award application deadline: 2/15; financial award applicants required to submit FAFSA. *Unit head:* Dr. James M. Pitarresi, Chairperson, 607-777-4037, E-mail: jmp@binghamton.edu. *Application contact:* Catherine Smith, Recruiting and Admissions Coordinator, 607-777-2151, Fax: 607-777-2501, E-mail: cmsmith@binghamton.edu.

Stevens Institute of Technology, Graduate School, Charles V. Schaefer Jr. School of Engineering, Department of Mechanical Engineering, Hoboken, NJ 07030. Offers advanced manufacturing (Certificate); air pollution technology (Certificate); computational fluid mechanics and heat transfer (Certificate); design and production management (Certificate); integrated product development (M Eng), including armament engineering, computer and electrical engineering, manufacturing technologies, systems reliability and design; mechanical engineering (M Eng, PhD), including manufacturing systems (M Eng), pharmaceutical manufacturing systems (M Eng), product design (M Eng), thermal engineering (M Eng); pharmaceutical manufacturing (M Eng, MS, Certificate); power generation (Certificate); product architecture and engineering (M Eng); robotics and control (Certificate); structural analysis and design (Certificate); vibration and noise control (Certificate). Part-time and evening/weekend programs available. *Students:* 305 full-time (70 women), 143 part-time (27 women); includes 5 Black or African American, non-Hispanic/Latino; 36 Asian, non-Hispanic/Latino; 19 Hispanic/Latino, 253 international. Average age 26. 104 applicants, 63% accepted.Terminal master's awarded for partial completion of doctoral program. *Degree requirements:* For master's, thesis optional; for doctorate, variable foreign language requirement, thesis/dissertation; for Certificate, project or thesis. *Entrance requirements:* Additional exam requirements/recommendations for international students: Required—TOEFL. *Application deadline:* Applications are processed on a rolling basis. Application fee: $50. Electronic applications accepted. *Financial support:* Fellowships, research assistantships, teaching assistantships, Federal Work-Study, institutionally sponsored loans, and unspecified assistantships available. Financial award application deadline: 4/15. *Faculty research:* Acoustics, incineration, CAD/CAM, computational fluid dynamics and heat transfer, robotics. *Unit head:* Dr. Constantin Chassapis, Director, 201-216-5564. *Application contact:* Graduate Admissions, 800-496-4935, Fax: 201-216-8044, E-mail: gradadmissions@stevens.edu.

Stony Brook University, State University of New York, Graduate School, College of Engineering and Applied Sciences, Department of Mechanical Engineering, Stony Brook, NY 11794. Offers MS, PhD. Evening/weekend programs available. *Faculty:* 17 full-time (0 women), 5 part-time/adjunct (0 women). *Students:* 70 full-time (9 women), 21 part-time (3 women); includes 3 Black or African American, non-Hispanic/Latino; 15 Asian, non-Hispanic/Latino; 1 Hispanic/Latino, 51 international. Average age 27. 207 applicants, 20% accepted, 32 enrolled. In 2010, 30 master's, 3 doctorates awarded. *Degree requirements:* For master's, thesis or alternative; for doctorate, comprehensive exam, thesis/dissertation. *Entrance requirements:* For master's, GRE General Test, minimum GPA of 3.0; for doctorate, GRE General Test, minimum GPA of 3.5. Additional exam requirements/recommendations for international students: Required—TOEFL. *Application deadline:* For fall admission, 1/15 for domestic students. Application fee: $100. *Expenses:* Tuition, state resident: full-time $8370; part-time $349 per credit. Tuition, nonresident: full-time $13,780; part-time $574 per credit. Required fees: $994. *Financial support:* In 2010–11, 9 research assistantships, 15 teaching assistantships were awarded; fellowships also available. *Faculty research:* Atmospheric sciences, thermal fluid sciences, solid mechanics. Total annual research expenditures: $708,233. *Unit head:* Dr. Fu-Pen Chiang, Chairman, 631-632-8310. *Application contact:* Dr. John Kincaid, Director, 631-632-8305, Fax: 631-632-8720, E-mail: jkincaid@ccmail.sunysb.edu.

Syracuse University, L. C. Smith College of Engineering and Computer Science, Program in Mechanical and Aerospace Engineering, Syracuse, NY 13244. Offers MS, PhD. *Students:* 97 full-time (17 women), 15 part-time (2 women); includes 10 minority (1 Black or African American, non-Hispanic/Latino; 6 Asian, non-Hispanic/Latino; 3 Hispanic/Latino), 78 international. Average age 26. 155 applicants, 57% accepted, 43 enrolled. In 2010, 15 master's, 3 doctorates awarded. *Degree requirements:* For master's, project or thesis; for doctorate, thesis/dissertation. *Entrance requirements:* For master's and doctorate, GRE General Test. Additional exam requirements/recommendations for international students: Required—TOEFL (minimum score 100 iBT). *Application deadline:* For fall admission, 7/1 priority date for domestic students, 6/1 priority date for international students. Applications are processed on a rolling basis. Application fee: $75. Electronic applications accepted. *Expenses:* Tuition: Part-time $1162 per credit. *Financial support:* Fellowships with full tuition reimbursements, research assistantships with full and partial tuition reimbursements, teaching assistantships with full and partial tuition reimbursements, scholarships/grants and tuition waivers (partial) available. Financial award application deadline: 1/1. *Faculty research:* Solid mechanics and materials, fluid mechanics, thermal sciences, controls and robotics. *Unit head:* Dr. Alan Levy, Chair, 315-443-4311, Fax: 315-443-9099. *Application contact:* Kathy Datthyn-Madigan, Information Contact, 315-443-4367, E-mail: kjdatthy@syr.edu.

Temple University, College of Engineering, Department of Mechanical Engineering, Philadelphia, PA 19122-6096. Offers MSE. Part-time and evening/weekend programs available. *Faculty:* 14 full-time (4 women). *Students:* 12 full-time (6 women), 7 part-time (0 women); includes 1 American Indian or Alaska Native, non-Hispanic/Latino; 2 Asian, non-Hispanic/Latino, 11 international. 42 applicants, 52% accepted, 7 enrolled. In 2010, 11 master's awarded. *Degree requirements:* For master's, thesis optional. *Entrance requirements:* For master's, GRE General Test, minimum GPA of 3.0. Additional exam requirements/recommendations for international students: Required—TOEFL (minimum score 550 paper-based; 213 computer-based; 79 iBT). *Application deadline:* For fall admission, 7/1 priority date for domestic students, 12/15 for international students; for spring admission, 11/1 priority date for domestic students, 8/1 for international students. Applications are processed on a rolling basis. Application fee: $50. Electronic applications accepted. *Financial support:* In 2010–11, 1 research assistantship with full tuition reimbursement, 8 teaching assistantships with full tuition reimbursements were awarded; fellowships, Federal Work-Study also available. Financial award application deadline: 1/15; financial award applicants required to submit FAFSA. *Faculty research:* Rapid solidification by melt spinning, microfracture analysis of dental materials, failure detection methods. Total annual research expenditures: $1 million. *Unit head:* Dr. Mohammad Kiani, Chair, 215-204-4644, Fax: 215-204-4956, E-mail: mkiani@temple.edu. *Application contact:* Dr. Mohammad Kiani, Chair, 215-204-4644, Fax: 215-204-4956, E-mail: mkiani@temple.edu.

Tennessee Technological University, Graduate School, College of Engineering, Department of Mechanical Engineering, Cookeville, TN 38505. Offers MS, PhD. Part-time programs available. *Faculty:* 25 full-time (2 women). *Students:* 13 full-time (0 women), 12 part-time (0 women); includes 1 Black or African American, non-Hispanic/Latino; 4 Asian, non-Hispanic/Latino. Average age 28. 34 applicants, 47% accepted, 10 enrolled. In 2010, 7 master's awarded. *Degree requirements:* For master's, thesis. *Entrance requirements:* For master's, GRE. Additional exam requirements/recommendations for international students: Required—TOEFL (minimum score 550 paper-based; 79 iBT), IELTS (minimum score 5.5). *Application deadline:* For fall admission, 8/1 for domestic students, 5/1 for international students; for spring admission, 12/1 for domestic students, 10/1 for international students. Application fee: $25 ($30 for international students). Electronic applications accepted. *Expenses:* Tuition, state resident: full-time $7934; part-time $388 per credit hour. Tuition, nonresident: full-time $19,758; part-time $962 per credit hour. *Financial support:* In 2010–11, fellowships (averaging $8,000 per year), 20 research assistantships (averaging $8,190 per year), 8 teaching assistantships (averaging $6,711 per year) were awarded. Financial award application deadline: 4/1. *Faculty research:* Energy-related systems, design, acoustics and acoustical systems. *Unit head:* Dr. Darrell A. Hoy, Interim Chairperson, 931-372-3233, Fax: 931-372-3497. *Application contact:* Shelia K. Kendrick, Coordinator of Graduate Admissions, 931-372-3808, Fax: 931-372-3497, E-mail: skendrick@tntech.edu.

Texas A&M University, College of Engineering, Department of Mechanical Engineering, College Station, TX 77843. Offers M Eng, MS, D Eng, PhD. *Faculty:* 58. *Students:* 384 full-time (80 women), 36 part-time (6 women); includes 57 minority (9 Black or African American, non-Hispanic/Latino; 1 American Indian or Alaska Native, non-Hispanic/Latino; 16 Asian, non-Hispanic/Latino; 31 Hispanic/Latino), 272 international. Average age 24. In 2010, 88 master's, 20 doctorates awarded. *Degree requirements:* For master's, thesis (MS); for doctorate, dissertation (PhD). *Entrance requirements:* For master's, GRE General Test, minimum undergraduate GPA of 3.0; for doctorate, GRE General Test, minimum graduate GPA of 3.5. Additional exam requirements/recommendations for international students: Required—TOEFL (minimum score 570 paper-based). *Application deadline:* For fall admission, 2/1 priority date for domestic students; for spring admission, 11/1 for domestic students. Applications are processed on a rolling basis. Application fee: $50 ($75 for international students). Electronic applications accepted. *Financial support:* In 2010–11, fellowships with partial tuition reimbursements (averaging $5,000 per year), research assistantships with partial tuition reimbursements (averaging $14,000 per year), teaching assistantships (averaging $14,000 per year) were awarded; institutionally sponsored loans also available. Financial award application deadline: 3/1; financial award applicants required to submit FAFSA. *Faculty research:* Thermal/fluid sciences, materials/manufacturing and controls systems. *Unit head:* Dennis O'Neal, Head, 979-845-5337, E-mail: doneal@tamu.edu. *Application contact:* Missy Cornett, Senior Academic Advisor I, 979-845-1270, Fax: 979-845-3081, E-mail: mcornett@tamu.edu.

Texas A&M University–Kingsville, College of Graduate Studies, College of Engineering, Department of Mechanical and Industrial Engineering, Program in Mechanical Engineering, Kingsville, TX 78363. Offers ME, MS. *Degree requirements:* For master's, comprehensive exam, thesis or alternative. *Entrance requirements:* For master's, GRE General Test, minimum GPA of 3.0. Additional exam requirements/recommendations for international students: Required—TOEFL. *Faculty research:* Intelligent systems and controls; neural networks and fuzzy logic; robotics and automation; biomass, cogeneration, and enhanced heat transfer.

Texas Tech University, Graduate School, Edward E. Whitacre Jr. College of Engineering, Department of Mechanical Engineering, Lubbock, TX 79409. Offers MSME, PhD. Part-time programs available. *Faculty:* 19 full-time (2 women), 1 (woman) part-time/adjunct. *Students:* 78 full-time (10 women), 10 part-time (1 woman); includes 4 Hispanic/Latino, 44 international. Average age 25. 157 applicants, 37% accepted, 20 enrolled. In 2010, 32 master's, 12 doctorates awarded. *Degree requirements:* For master's, thesis or alternative; for doctorate, thesis/dissertation. *Entrance requirements:* For master's and doctorate, GRE General Test, minimum GPA of 3.0, 3 letters of recommendation, statement of purpose. Additional exam requirements/recommendations for international students: Required—TOEFL (minimum score 550 paper-based; 213 computer-based; 79 iBT). *Application deadline:* For fall admission, 6/1 priority date for domestic students, 1/15 priority date for international students; for spring admission, 9/1 priority date for domestic students, 6/15 priority date for international students. Applications are processed on a rolling basis. Application fee: $50 ($75 for international students). Electronic applications accepted. *Expenses:* Tuition, state resident: full-time $5495.76; part-time $228.99 per credit hour. Tuition, nonresident: full-time $12,936; part-time $538.99 per credit hour. Required fees: $2674; $36 per credit hour. $905 per semester. *Financial support:* In 2010–11, 77 students received support, including 23 research assistantships with partial tuition reimbursements available (averaging $4,171 per year), 10 teaching assistantships with partial tuition reimbursements available (averaging $2,691 per year). Financial award application deadline: 4/15; financial award applicants required to submit FAFSA. *Faculty research:* Dynamics and control, energy systems, materials, experimental and computational fluid mechanics, bioengineering. Total annual research expenditures: $2.2 million. *Unit head:* Dr. Jharna Chaudhuri, Chair, 806-742-3563, Fax: 806-742-3540, E-mail: jharna.chandhuri@ttu.edu. *Application contact:* Dr. Sira P. Parameswaran, Graduate Advisor, 806-742-3563 Ext. 247, Fax: 806-742-3540, E-mail: sira.parameswaran@ttu.edu.

Trine University, Allen School of Engineering and Technology, Angola, IN 46703-1764. Offers civil engineering (ME); mechanical engineering (ME). Part-time and evening/weekend programs available. *Degree requirements:* For master's, comprehensive exam, thesis. *Faculty research:* CAD, computer aided MFG, computer numerical control, parametric modeling, megatronics.

Tufts University, School of Engineering, Department of Mechanical Engineering, Medford, MA 02155. Offers human factors (MS); mechanical engineering (ME, MS, PhD). Part-time programs available. Terminal master's awarded for partial completion of doctoral program. *Degree requirements:* For master's, thesis; for doctorate, thesis/dissertation. *Entrance requirements:* For master's and doctorate, GRE General Test. Additional exam requirements/recommendations for international students: Required—TOEFL (minimum score 550 paper-based; 213 computer-based; 80 iBT). Electronic applications accepted. *Expenses:* Tuition: Full-time $39,624; part-time $3962 per course. Required fees: $40 per year. Full-time tuition and fees vary according to degree level, program and student level. Part-time tuition and fees vary according to course load.

Tuskegee University, Graduate Programs, College of Engineering, Architecture and Physical Sciences, Department of Mechanical Engineering, Tuskegee, AL 36088. Offers MSME. *Faculty:* 11 full-time (0 women). *Students:* 19 full-time (4 women), 2 part-time (1 woman); includes 4 Black or African American, non-Hispanic/Latino, 15 international. Average age 29. In 2010, 7 master's awarded. *Degree requirements:* For master's, thesis or alternative. *Entrance requirements:* For master's, GRE General Test, GRE Subject Test. Additional exam requirements/recommendations for international students: Required—TOEFL (minimum score 500 paper-based; 69 computer-based). *Application deadline:* For fall admission, 7/15 for domestic students. Applications are processed on a rolling basis. Application fee: $25 ($35 for international students). *Expenses:* Tuition: Full-time $16,100; part-time $665 per credit hour. Required fees: $650. *Financial support:* Fellowships, research assistantships, teaching assistantships, career-related internships or fieldwork, Federal Work-Study, and institutionally sponsored loans available. Support available to part-time students. Financial award application deadline: 4/15. *Faculty research:* Superalloys, fatigue and surface machinery, energy management, solar energy. *Unit head:* Dr. Pradosh Ray, Head, 334-727-8989. *Application contact:* Dr. Robert L. Laney, Vice

Mechanical Engineering

Tuskegee University *(continued)*
President/Director of Admissions and Enrollment Management, 334-727-8580, Fax: 334-727-5750, E-mail: planey@tuskegee.edu.

Union Graduate College, School of Engineering and Computer Science, Schenectady, NY 12308-3107. Offers computer science (MS); electrical engineering (MS); engineering and management systems (MS); mechanical engineering (MS). Part-time and evening/weekend programs available. *Faculty:* 3 full-time (0 women), 9 part-time/adjunct (0 women). *Students:* 15 full-time (1 woman), 89 part-time (13 women); includes 1 Black or African American, non-Hispanic/Latino; 1 American Indian or Alaska Native, non-Hispanic/Latino; 7 Asian, non-Hispanic/Latino; 6 Hispanic/Latino, 2 international. Average age 27. 52 applicants, 79% accepted, 39 enrolled. In 2010, 24 master's awarded. *Degree requirements:* For master's, capstone course. *Entrance requirements:* For master's, minimum GPA of 3.0, letters of recommendation. Additional exam requirements/recommendations for international students: Required—TOEFL (minimum score 550 paper-based; 213 computer-based). *Application deadline:* Applications are processed on a rolling basis. Application fee: $60. Electronic applications accepted. *Expenses:* Contact institution. *Financial support:* Research assistantships, Federal Work-Study, scholarships/grants, health care benefits, and tuition waivers (full and partial) available. Support available to part-time students. Financial award applicants required to submit FAFSA. *Unit head:* Robert Kozik, Dean, 515-631-9881, Fax: 518-631-9902, E-mail: kozikr@union.edu. *Application contact:* Diane Trzaskos, Coordinator, Admissions, 518-631-9837, Fax: 518-631-9901, E-mail: trzaskod@uniongraduatecollege.edu.

Université de Moncton, Faculty of Engineering, Program in Mechanical Engineering, Moncton, NB E1A 3E9, Canada. Offers M Sc A. *Degree requirements:* For master's, thesis, proficiency in French. *Faculty research:* Composite materials, thermal energy systems, control systems, fluid mechanics and heat transfer, CAD/CAM and robotics.

Université de Sherbrooke, Faculty of Engineering, Department of Mechanical Engineering, Sherbrooke, QC J1K 2R1, Canada. Offers M Sc A, PhD. *Degree requirements:* For master's, one foreign language, thesis; for doctorate, comprehensive exam, thesis/dissertation. *Entrance requirements:* For master's, bachelor's degree in engineering or equivalent; for doctorate, master's degree in engineering or equivalent. Electronic applications accepted. *Faculty research:* Acoustics, aerodynamics, vehicle dynamics, composite materials, heat transfer.

Université Laval, Faculty of Sciences and Engineering, Department of Mechanical Engineering, Programs in Mechanical Engineering, Québec, QC G1K 7P4, Canada. Offers M Sc, PhD. Part-time programs available. Terminal master's awarded for partial completion of doctoral program. *Degree requirements:* For master's, thesis; for doctorate, comprehensive exam, thesis/dissertation. *Entrance requirements:* For master's and doctorate, knowledge of French. Electronic applications accepted.

University at Buffalo, the State University of New York, Graduate School, School of Engineering and Applied Sciences, Department of Mechanical and Aerospace Engineering, Buffalo, NY 14260. Offers aerospace engineering (ME, MS, PhD); mechanical engineering (ME, MS, PhD). Part-time programs available. *Faculty:* 29 full-time (4 women), 10 part-time/adjunct (0 women). *Students:* 184 full-time (16 women), 63 part-time (4 women); includes 3 Black or African American, non-Hispanic/Latino; 11 Asian, non-Hispanic/Latino; 3 Hispanic/Latino, 128 international. Average age 26. 848 applicants, 17% accepted, 53 enrolled. In 2010, 52 master's, 9 doctorates awarded. Terminal master's awarded for partial completion of doctoral program. *Degree requirements:* For master's, comprehensive exam, project or thesis; for doctorate, thesis/dissertation. *Entrance requirements:* For master's and doctorate, GRE General Test, GRE Subject Test. Additional exam requirements/recommendations for international students: Required—TOEFL (minimum score 79 iBT). *Application deadline:* For fall admission, 1/15 for domestic and international students; for spring admission, 9/15 for domestic and international students. Applications are processed on a rolling basis. Application fee: $50. *Financial support:* In 2010–11, 73 students received support, including 4 fellowships with full tuition reimbursements available (averaging $28,900 per year), 17 research assistantships with full tuition reimbursements available (averaging $24,000 per year), 30 teaching assistantships with full tuition reimbursements available (averaging $20,900 per year); Federal Work-Study, institutionally sponsored loans, tuition waivers (partial), and unspecified assistantships also available. Financial award application deadline: 1/15; financial award applicants required to submit FAFSA. *Faculty research:* Fluid and thermal sciences, systems and design, mechanics and materials. Total annual research expenditures: $5.5 million. *Unit head:* Dr. Gary Dargush, Chair, 716-645-2593, Fax: 716-645-2883, E-mail: gdargush@buffalo.edu. *Application contact:* Dr. Susan Hua, Director of Graduate Studies, 716-645-1471, Fax: 716-645-3875, E-mail: zhua@.buffalo.edu.

The University of Akron, Graduate School, College of Engineering, Department of Mechanical Engineering, Akron, OH 44325. Offers MS, PhD. Part-time and evening/weekend programs available. *Faculty:* 22 full-time (1 woman), 5 part-time/adjunct (0 women). *Students:* 60 full-time (11 women), 33 part-time (3 women); includes 1 Black or African American, non-Hispanic/Latino; 1 Asian, non-Hispanic/Latino; 1 Two or more races, non-Hispanic/Latino, 43 international. Average age 28. 87 applicants, 66% accepted, 21 enrolled. In 2010, 11 master's, 5 doctorates awarded. Terminal master's awarded for partial completion of doctoral program. *Degree requirements:* For master's, thesis optional; for doctorate, one foreign language, thesis/dissertation, candidacy exam, qualifying exam. *Entrance requirements:* For master's, GRE, minimum GPA of 2.75, hold a baccalaureate degree in Engineering, three letters of recommendation, statement of purpose, resume; for doctorate, GRE, minimum GPA of 3.0 with bachelor's degree, 3.5 with master's degree; three letters of recommendation, statement of purpose, resume. Additional exam requirements/recommendations for international students: Required—TOEFL (minimum score 550 paper-based; 213 computer-based; 79 iBT). *Application deadline:* Applications are processed on a rolling basis. Application fee: $30 ($40 for international students). Electronic applications accepted. *Expenses:* Tuition, state resident: full-time $6800; part-time $378 per credit hour. Tuition, nonresident: full-time $11,644; part-time $647 per credit hour. Required fees: $1265. One-time fee: $30 full-time. *Financial support:* In 2010–11, 2 fellowships with full tuition reimbursements, 19 research assistantships with full tuition reimbursements, 27 teaching assistantships with full tuition reimbursements were awarded. *Faculty research:* Materials science, tribology and lubrication, vibration and dynamic analysis, solid mechanics, MEMS and NEMS, bio-mechanics. Total annual research expenditures: $921,655. *Unit head:* Dr. Celal Batur, Chair, 330-972-7367, E-mail: batur@uakron.edu. *Application contact:* Dr. Celal Batur, Chair, 330-972-7367, E-mail: batur@uakron.edu.

The University of Alabama, Graduate School, College of Engineering, Department of Mechanical Engineering, Tuscaloosa, AL 35487. Offers MS, PhD. Part-time programs available. *Faculty:* 19 full-time (2 women). *Students:* 46 full-time (6 women), 16 part-time (1 woman); includes 5 minority (3 Black or African American, non-Hispanic/Latino; 2 Asian, non-Hispanic/Latino), 23 international. Average age 28. 74 applicants, 61% accepted, 18 enrolled. In 2010, 16 master's, 6 doctorates awarded. Terminal master's awarded for partial completion of doctoral program. *Degree requirements:* For master's, comprehensive exam, thesis (for some programs); for doctorate, comprehensive exam, thesis/dissertation. *Entrance requirements:* For master's, GRE General Test (waived for ABET accredited engineering degree), minimum GPA of 3.0; for doctorate, GRE General Test (waived for ABET-accredited engineering degree), minimum GPA of 3.0 with MS, 3.3 without MS. Additional exam requirements/recommendations for international students: Required—TOEFL (minimum score 600 paper-based). *Application deadline:* For fall admission, 7/1 priority date for domestic students, 1/15 priority date for international students; for spring admission, 11/1 priority date for domestic students, 6/1 priority date for international students. Applications are processed on a rolling basis. Application fee: $50 ($60 for international students). Electronic applications accepted. *Expenses:* Tuition, state resident: full-time $7900. Tuition, nonresident: full-time $20,500. *Financial support:* In 2010–11, 32 students received support, including 5 fellowships with full tuition reimbursements available (averaging $15,000 per year), 14 research assistantships with full tuition reimbursements available (averaging $15,000 per year), 13 teaching assistantships with full tuition

reimbursements available (averaging $12,000 per year); career-related internships or fieldwork and unspecified assistantships also available. Financial award application deadline: 3/30. *Faculty research:* Thermal/fluids, robotics, numerical modeling, energy conservation, energy and combustion systems, internal combustion engines, manufacturing, vehicular systems, solid mechanics and materials. Total annual research expenditures: $2.7 million. *Unit head:* Dr. Robert P. Taylor, Head and Professor, 205-348-4078, Fax: 205-348-6419, E-mail: btaylor2@eng.ua.edu. *Application contact:* Dr. Will Schreiber, Coordinator and Professor, 205-348-1650, Fax: 205-348-6419, E-mail: wschreiber@eng.ua.edu.

The University of Alabama at Birmingham, School of Engineering, Program in Mechanical Engineering, Birmingham, AL 35294. Offers MSME. *Students:* 9 full-time (0 women), 4 part-time (0 women); includes 2 minority (1 Black or African American, non-Hispanic/Latino; 1 Asian, non-Hispanic/Latino), 5 international. Average age 27. 21 applicants, 86% accepted, 6 enrolled. In 2010, 9 master's awarded. *Expenses:* Tuition, state resident: full-time $5482. Tuition, nonresident: full-time $12,430. Tuition and fees vary according to program. *Unit head:* Dr. Bharat K. Soni, Chair, 205-934-8460. *Application contact:* Julie Bryant, Director of Graduate Admissions, 205-934-8227, Fax: 205-934-8413, E-mail: jbryant@uab.edu.

The University of Alabama in Huntsville, School of Graduate Studies, College of Engineering, Department of Mechanical and Aerospace Engineering, Huntsville, AL 35899. Offers aerospace engineering (MSE), including missile systems engineering, rotorcraft systems engineering; aerospace systems engineering (MS, PhD); mechanical engineering (MSE, PhD). Part-time and evening/weekend programs available. *Faculty:* 19 full-time (1 woman), 4 part-time/adjunct (1 woman). *Students:* 50 full-time (10 women), 126 part-time (18 women); includes 15 minority (4 Black or African American, non-Hispanic/Latino; 2 American Indian or Alaska Native, non-Hispanic/Latino; 5 Asian, non-Hispanic/Latino; 4 Hispanic/Latino), 12 international. Average age 30. 134 applicants, 69% accepted, 59 enrolled. In 2010, 31 master's, 1 doctorate awarded. *Degree requirements:* For master's, comprehensive exam, thesis or alternative, oral and written exams; for doctorate, comprehensive exam, thesis/dissertation, oral and written exams. *Entrance requirements:* For master's, GRE General Test, BSE, minimum GPA of 3.0; for doctorate, GRE General Test, minimum GPA of 3.0. Additional exam requirements/recommendations for international students: Required—TOEFL (minimum score 500 paper-based; 173 computer-based; 62 iBT). *Application deadline:* For fall admission, 7/15 for domestic students, 4/1 for international students; for spring admission, 1/30 for domestic students, 9/1 for international students. Applications are processed on a rolling basis. Application fee: $40 ($50 for international students). Electronic applications accepted. *Expenses:* Tuition, state resident: full-time $7250; part-time $407.75 per credit hour. Tuition, nonresident: full-time $17,358; part-time $970.05 per credit hour. Required fees: $246.80 per semester. Tuition and fees vary according to course load and program. *Financial support:* In 2010–11, 34 students received support, including 19 research assistantships with full tuition reimbursements available (averaging $12,545 per year), 15 teaching assistantships with full tuition reimbursements available (averaging $10,840 per year); career-related internships or fieldwork, Federal Work-Study, institutionally sponsored loans, scholarships/grants, health care benefits, and unspecified assistantships also available. Support available to part-time students. Financial award application deadline: 4/1; financial award applicants required to submit FAFSA. *Faculty research:* Combustion, fluid dynamics, materials and structures, propulsion, laser diagnostics. Total annual research expenditures: $20.8 million. *Unit head:* Dr. Robert Frederick, Interim Chair, 256-824-7200, Fax: 256-824-6758, E-mail: robert.frederick@uah.edu. *Application contact:* Kathy Biggs, Graduate Studies Admissions Manager, 256-824-6199, Fax: 256-824-6405, E-mail: deangrad@uah.edu.

University of Alaska Fairbanks, College of Engineering and Mines, Department of Mechanical Engineering, Fairbanks, AK 99775-5905. Offers engineering (PhD); mechanical engineering (MS). Part-time programs available. *Faculty:* 9 full-time (0 women). *Students:* 12 full-time (3 women), 4 part-time (0 women); includes 3 minority (1 Black or African American, non-Hispanic/Latino; 1 Asian, non-Hispanic/Latino; 1 Two or more races, non-Hispanic/Latino), 7 international. Average age 29. 24 applicants, 29% accepted, 5 enrolled. In 2010, 2 master's, 1 doctorate awarded. Terminal master's awarded for partial completion of doctoral program. *Degree requirements:* For master's, comprehensive exam, thesis or alternative; for doctorate, comprehensive exam, thesis/dissertation, oral exam, oral defense. *Entrance requirements:* For master's and doctorate, GRE General Test. Additional exam requirements/recommendations for international students: Required—TOEFL (minimum score 550 paper-based; 213 computer-based; 80 iBT). *Application deadline:* For fall admission, 6/1 for domestic students, 3/1 for international students; for spring admission, 10/15 for domestic students, 9/1 for international students. Applications are processed on a rolling basis. Application fee: $60. Electronic applications accepted. *Expenses:* Tuition, state resident: full-time $5688; part-time $316 per credit. Tuition, nonresident: full-time $11,628; part-time $646 per credit. Required fees: $289 per semester. Tuition and fees vary according to course load and reciprocity agreements. *Financial support:* In 2010–11, 3 research assistantships with tuition reimbursements (averaging $13,721 per year), 5 teaching assistantships with tuition reimbursements (averaging $7,302 per year) were awarded; fellowships with tuition reimbursements, career-related internships or fieldwork, Federal Work-Study, scholarships/grants, health care benefits, and unspecified assistantships also available. Support available to part-time students. Financial award application deadline: 7/1; financial award applicants required to submit FAFSA. *Faculty research:* Cold regions engineering, fluid mechanics, heat transfer, energy systems, indoor air quality. *Unit head:* Dr. Jonah Lee, Department Chair, 907-474-7136, Fax: 907-474-6141, E-mail: fymech@uaf.edu. *Application contact:* Dr. Jonah Lee, Department Chair, 907-474-7136, Fax: 907-474-6141, E-mail: fymech@uaf.edu.

University of Alberta, Faculty of Graduate Studies and Research, Department of Mechanical Engineering, Edmonton, AB T6G 2E1, Canada. Offers engineering management (M Eng); mechanical engineering (M Eng, M Sc, PhD); MBA/M Eng. Part-time programs available. *Degree requirements:* For master's, thesis; for doctorate, thesis/dissertation. *Entrance requirements:* For master's and doctorate, minimum GPA of 7.0 on a 9.0 scale. Additional exam requirements/recommendations for international students: Required—TOEFL (minimum score 580 paper-based; 237 computer-based). *Faculty research:* Combustion and environmental issues, advanced materials, computational fluid dynamics, biomedical, acoustics and vibrations.

The University of Arizona, College of Engineering, Department of Aerospace and Mechanical Engineering, Program in Mechanical Engineering, Tucson, AZ 85721. Offers MS, PhD. Part-time programs available. *Students:* 59 full-time (11 women), 8 part-time (0 women); includes 4 minority (all Hispanic/Latino), 41 international. Average age 28. 64 applicants, 69% accepted, 16 enrolled. In 2010, 23 master's, 5 doctorates awarded. *Degree requirements:* For master's, thesis or alternative; for doctorate, one foreign language, thesis/dissertation. *Entrance requirements:* For master's and doctorate, GRE General Test, minimum GPA of 3.25, 3 letters of recommendation, statement of purpose. Additional exam requirements/recommendations for international students: Required—TOEFL (minimum score 550 paper-based; 213 computer-based; 79 iBT). *Application deadline:* For fall admission, 6/1 for domestic students, 12/1 for international students; for spring admission, 10/1 for domestic students, 6/1 for international students. Applications are processed on a rolling basis. Application fee: $75. Electronic applications accepted. *Expenses:* Tuition, state resident: full-time $7692. *Financial support:* Research assistantships, teaching assistantships, unspecified assistantships available. *Faculty research:* Fluid mechanics, structures, computer-aided design, stability and control, probabilistic design. *Unit head:* Dr. Ara Arabyan, Interim Department Head, 520-621-2116, Fax: 520-621-8191, E-mail: arabyan@email.arizona.edu. *Application contact:* Barbara Heefner, Graduate Secretary, 520-621-4692, Fax: 520-621-8191, E-mail: heefner@email.arizona.edu.

University of Arkansas, Graduate School, College of Engineering, Department of Mechanical Engineering, Fayetteville, AR 72701-1201. Offers MSE, MSME, PhD. Part-time programs available. Postbaccalaureate distance learning degree programs offered. *Students:* 15 full-time (1 woman), 20 part-time (0 women); includes 4 minority (1 Black or African American, non-Hispanic/Latino; 3 Asian, non-Hispanic/Latino), 17 international. 40 applicants, 65% accepted.

In 2010, 11 master's, 8 doctorates awarded. *Degree requirements:* For master's, thesis optional; for doctorate, one foreign language, thesis/dissertation. *Application deadline:* For fall admission, 4/1 for international students; for spring admission, 10/1 for international students. Applications are processed on a rolling basis. Application fee: $40 ($50 for international students). Electronic applications accepted. *Financial support:* In 2010–11, 5 fellowships, 16 research assistantships, 2 teaching assistantships were awarded; career-related internships or fieldwork and Federal Work-Study also available. Support available to part-time students. Financial award application deadline: 4/1; financial award applicants required to submit FAFSA. *Unit head:* Dr. Matt Gordon, Departmental Chair, 479-575-4153, Fax: 479-575-6982, E-mail: mhg@uark.edu. *Application contact:* Dr. Rick Couvillion, Graduate Coordinator, 479-575-4155, E-mail: rjc@uark.edu.

University of Bridgeport, School of Engineering, Department of Mechanical Engineering, Bridgeport, CT 06604. Offers MS. *Degree requirements:* For master's, thesis optional. *Entrance requirements:* Additional exam requirements/recommendations for international students: Recommended—TOEFL (minimum score 550 paper-based; 213 computer-based; 80 iBT), IELTS (minimum score 6.5). Electronic applications accepted. *Expenses:* Tuition: Full-time $22,000; part-time $575 per credit hour. Required fees: $90 per semester. Tuition and fees vary according to course level, course load and program. *Faculty research:* Residual stress in composite material resins, helicopter composite structure and dynamic components, water spray cooling, heat transfer.

The University of British Columbia, Faculty of Applied Science, Program in Mechanical Engineering, Vancouver, BC V6T 1Z1, Canada. Offers M Eng, MA Sc, PhD. *Degree requirements:* For master's, thesis; for doctorate, comprehensive exam, thesis/dissertation, 33 credits beyond bachelor's degree. *Entrance requirements:* For master's, bachelor's degree, minimum B+ average; for doctorate, master's degree, minimum B+ average. Additional exam requirements/recommendations for international students: Required—TOEFL (minimum score 580 paper-based; 237 computer-based; 93 iBT), IELTS (minimum score 6.5), GRE (recommended); Recommended—TWE. Electronic applications accepted. Tuition charges are reported in Canadian dollars. *Expenses:* Tuition; area resident: Full-time $4179 Canadian dollars. International tuition: $7344 Canadian dollars full-time. *Faculty research:* Applied mechanics, manufacturing, robotics and controls, thermodynamics and combustion, fluid/aerodynamics, acoustics.

University of Calgary, Faculty of Graduate Studies, Schulich School of Engineering, Department of Mechanical and Manufacturing Engineering, Calgary, AB T2N 1N4, Canada. Offers M Eng, M Sc, PhD. *Degree requirements:* For master's, thesis (for some programs); for doctorate, thesis/dissertation, candidacy exam. *Entrance requirements:* For master's, minimum GPA of 3.0; for doctorate, minimum GPA of 3.3. Additional exam requirements/recommendations for international students: Required—TOEFL (minimum score 550 paper-based; 213 computer-based), IELTS (minimum score 7). *Faculty research:* Thermofluids, solid mechanics, materials, biomechanics, manufacturing.

University of California, Berkeley, Graduate Division, College of Engineering, Department of Mechanical Engineering, Berkeley, CA 94720-1500. Offers M Eng, MS, D Eng, PhD. *Degree requirements:* For master's, comprehensive exam or thesis (MS); for doctorate, thesis/dissertation, preliminary and qualifying exams. *Entrance requirements:* For master's and doctorate, GRE General Test, minimum GPA of 3.0, 3 letters of recommendation. Additional exam requirements/recommendations for international students: Required—TOEFL.

University of California, Davis, College of Engineering, Program in Mechanical and Aeronautical Engineering, Davis, CA 95616. Offers aeronautical engineering (M Engr, MS, D Engr, PhD, Certificate); mechanical engineering (M Engr, MS, D Engr, PhD, Certificate); M Engr/MBA. *Degree requirements:* For master's, comprehensive exam (for some programs), thesis (for some programs); for doctorate, thesis/dissertation. *Entrance requirements:* For master's and doctorate, GRE General Test, minimum GPA of 3.0. Additional exam requirements/recommendations for international students: Required—TOEFL (minimum score 550 paper-based; 213 computer-based). Electronic applications accepted.

University of California, Irvine, School of Engineering, Department of Mechanical and Aerospace Engineering, Irvine, CA 92697. Offers MS, PhD. Part-time programs available. *Students:* 125 full-time (19 women), 13 part-time (3 women); includes 38 minority (25 Asian, non-Hispanic/Latino; 12 Hispanic/Latino; 1 Two or more races, non-Hispanic/Latino), 57 international. Average age 28. 399 applicants, 35% accepted, 43 enrolled. In 2010, 31 master's, 11 doctorates awarded. Terminal master's awarded for partial completion of doctoral program. *Degree requirements:* For doctorate, thesis/dissertation. *Entrance requirements:* For master's and doctorate, GRE General Test, minimum GPA of 3.0, 3 letters of recommendation. Additional exam requirements/recommendations for international students: Required—TOEFL (minimum score 550 paper-based; 213 computer-based). *Application deadline:* For fall admission, 1/15 priority date for domestic students, 1/15 for international students. Applications are processed on a rolling basis. Application fee: $80 ($100 for international students). Electronic applications accepted. *Financial support:* Fellowships with tuition reimbursements, research assistantships with full tuition reimbursements, teaching assistantships with tuition reimbursements, institutionally sponsored loans, traineeships, health care benefits, and unspecified assistantships available. Financial award application deadline: 3/1; financial award applicants required to submit FAFSA. *Faculty research:* Thermal and fluid sciences, combustion and propulsion, control systems, robotics, lightweight structures. *Unit head:* Prof. Derek Dunn-Rankin, Chair, 949-824-8745, Fax: 949-824-8585, E-mail: ddunnran@uci.edu. *Application contact:* Lousie Yeager, Graduate Coordinator, 949-824-7984, Fax: 949-824-8585, E-mail: lyeager@uci.edu.

University of California, Los Angeles, Graduate Division, Henry Samueli School of Engineering and Applied Science, Department of Mechanical and Aerospace Engineering, Program in Mechanical Engineering, Los Angeles, CA 90095-1597. Offers MS, PhD. *Faculty:* 31 full-time (2 women). *Students:* 208 full-time (33 women); includes 2 Black or African American, non-Hispanic/Latino; 51 Asian, non-Hispanic/Latino; 10 Hispanic/Latino, 69 international. 389 applicants, 45% accepted, 67 enrolled. In 2010, 78 master's, 17 doctorates awarded. *Degree requirements:* For master's, comprehensive exam or thesis; for doctorate, thesis/dissertation, qualifying exams. *Entrance requirements:* For master's, GRE General Test, minimum GPA of 3.0; for doctorate, GRE General Test, minimum GPA of 3.25. Additional exam requirements/recommendations for international students: Required—TOEFL (minimum score 560 paper-based; 87 iBT). *Application deadline:* For fall admission, 12/15 for domestic and international students; for winter admission, 10/1 for domestic students; for spring admission, 12/31 for domestic students. Application fee: $70 ($90 for international students). Electronic applications accepted. *Financial support:* Fellowships, research assistantships, teaching assistantships, Federal Work-Study, institutionally sponsored loans, and tuition waivers (full and partial) available. Financial award application deadline: 1/5; financial award applicants required to submit FAFSA. *Unit head:* Dr. Adrienne Lavine, Chair, 310-825-7468. *Application contact:* Angie Castillo, Student Affairs Officer, 310-825-7793, Fax: 310-206-4830, E-mail: angie@ea.ucla.edu.

University of California, Merced, Division of Graduate Studies, School of Natural Sciences, Merced, CA 95343. Offers applied mathematics (MS, PhD); biological engineering and small-scale technologies (MS, PhD); environmental systems (MS, PhD); mechanical engineering and applied mechanics (MS, PhD); physics and chemistry (PhD); quantitative and systems biology (MS, PhD).

University of California, Riverside, Graduate Division, Department of Mechanical Engineering, Riverside, CA 92521. Offers MS, PhD. Part-time programs available. Terminal master's awarded for partial completion of doctoral program. *Degree requirements:* For master's, comprehensive exam or thesis, seminar in mechanical engineering; for doctorate, comprehensive exam, thesis/dissertation, seminar in mechanical engineering. *Entrance requirements:* Additional exam requirements/recommendations for international students: Required—TOEFL (minimum score 550 paper-based; 213 computer-based; 80 iBT). *Faculty research:* Advanced robotics

and machine design, air quality modeling group, computational fluid dynamics, computational mechanics and materials, biomaterials and nanotechnology laboratory.

University of California, San Diego, Office of Graduate Studies, Department of Mechanical and Aerospace Engineering, Program in Mechanical Engineering, La Jolla, CA 92093. Offers MS, PhD. Part-time programs available. *Degree requirements:* For master's, comprehensive exam or thesis; for doctorate, thesis/dissertation, qualifying exam. *Entrance requirements:* For master's and doctorate, GRE General Test, minimum GPA of 3.0. Additional exam requirements/recommendations for international students: Required—TOEFL. Electronic applications accepted. *Faculty research:* Combustion engineering, environmental mechanics, magnetic recording, materials processing, computational fluid dynamics.

University of California, Santa Barbara, Graduate Division, College of Engineering, Department of Mechanical Engineering, Santa Barbara, CA 93106-5070. Offers computational science and engineering (MS, PhD); mechanical engineering (MS, PhD); MS/PhD. *Faculty:* 27 full-time (4 women), 7 part-time/adjunct (3 women). *Students:* 76 full-time (11 women); includes 1 Black or African American, non-Hispanic/Latino; 18 Asian, non-Hispanic/Latino; 2 Hispanic/Latino. Average age 27. 270 applicants, 11% accepted, 15 enrolled. In 2010, 7 master's, 8 doctorates awarded. *Degree requirements:* For master's, thesis; for doctorate, comprehensive exam, thesis/dissertation. *Entrance requirements:* For master's and doctorate, GRE. Additional exam requirements/recommendations for international students: Required—TOEFL (minimum score 550 paper-based; 80 iBT), IELTS (minimum score 7). *Application deadline:* For fall admission, 1/1 for domestic and international students. Application fee: $70 ($90 for international students). Electronic applications accepted. *Financial support:* In 2010–11, 72 students received support, including 18 fellowships with full and partial tuition reimbursements available (averaging $11,139 per year), 57 research assistantships with full and partial tuition reimbursements available (averaging $13,711 per year), 45 teaching assistantships with full and partial tuition reimbursements available (averaging $9,120 per year); scholarships/grants, health care benefits, tuition waivers (full and partial), and unspecified assistantships also available. Financial award application deadline: 1/1; financial award applicants required to submit FAFSA. *Faculty research:* Micro/nanoscale technology; computational science and engineering; dynamics systems, controls and robotics; thermofluid sciences, solid mechanics, materials, and structures. *Unit head:* Dr. Kimberly Turner, Chair, 805-893-8080, Fax: 805-893-8651, E-mail: turner@engineering.ucsb.edu. *Application contact:* Laura L. Reynolds, Staff Graduate Program Advisor, 805-893-2239, Fax: 805-893-8651, E-mail: megrad@engineering.ucsb.edu.

University of Central Florida, College of Engineering and Computer Science, Department of Mechanical, Materials, and Aerospace Engineering, Program in Mechanical Engineering, Orlando, FL 32816. Offers CAD/CAM technology (Certificate); HVAC engineering (Certificate); mechanical engineering (MSME, PhD). *Students:* 82 full-time (10 women), 64 part-time (4 women); includes 4 Black or African American, non-Hispanic/Latino; 12 Asian, non-Hispanic/Latino; 16 Hispanic/Latino; 1 Two or more races, non-Hispanic/Latino, 40 international. Average age 27. 119 applicants, 71% accepted, 49 enrolled. In 2010, 19 master's, 9 doctorates awarded. *Degree requirements:* For master's, thesis or alternative; for doctorate, thesis/dissertation, candidacy exam, departmental qualifying exam. *Application deadline:* For fall admission, 7/15 priority date for domestic students; for spring admission, 12/1 priority date for domestic students. Electronic applications accepted. *Expenses:* Tuition, state resident: part-time $256.56 per credit hour. Tuition, nonresident: part-time $1011.52 per credit hour. Part-time tuition and fees vary according to program. *Financial support:* In 2010–11, 50 students received support, including 7 fellowships (averaging $2,500 per year), 38 research assistantships (averaging $6,000 per year), 29 teaching assistantships (averaging $10,100 per year); career-related internships or fieldwork, institutionally sponsored loans, scholarships/grants, tuition waivers (partial), and unspecified assistantships also available.

University of Cincinnati, Graduate School, College of Engineering, Department of Mechanical, Industrial and Nuclear Engineering, Program in Mechanical Engineering, Cincinnati, OH 45221. Offers MS, PhD. Evening/weekend programs available. Terminal master's awarded for partial completion of doctoral program. *Degree requirements:* For master's, oral exam or thesis defense; for doctorate, variable foreign language requirement, thesis/dissertation. *Entrance requirements:* For master's and doctorate, GRE General Test. Additional exam requirements/recommendations for international students: Required—TOEFL (minimum score 575 paper-based; 233 computer-based). Electronic applications accepted. *Faculty research:* Signature analysis, structural analysis, energy, design, robotics.

University of Colorado at Colorado Springs, College of Engineering and Applied Science, Department of Mechanical and Aerospace Engineering, Colorado Springs, CO 80933-7150. Offers engineering management (ME); information operations (ME); manufacturing (ME); mechanical engineering (MS); software engineering (ME); space operations (ME); space systems (MS). Part-time and evening/weekend programs available. *Faculty:* 10 full-time (2 women). *Students:* 56 full-time (11 women), 26 part-time (6 women); includes 3 Black or African American, non-Hispanic/Latino; 4 Asian, non-Hispanic/Latino; 3 Hispanic/Latino, 1 international. Average age 32. 33 applicants, 76% accepted, 19 enrolled. In 2010, 26 master's awarded. *Degree requirements:* For master's, thesis optional. *Entrance requirements:* For master's, GRE General Test, bachelor's degree in engineering or related degree, minimum GPA of 3.0. Additional exam requirements/recommendations for international students: Required—TOEFL. *Application deadline:* For fall admission, 5/1 for domestic students; for spring admission, 10/1 for domestic students. Applications are processed on a rolling basis. Application fee: $60 ($75 for international students). *Expenses:* Tuition, state resident: full-time $7916. Tuition, nonresident: full-time $16,610. Tuition and fees vary according to course load, degree level, program, reciprocity agreements and student level. *Financial support:* Federal Work-Study and scholarships/grants available. Support available to part-time students. Financial award application deadline: 3/1; financial award applicants required to submit FAFSA. *Faculty research:* Neural networks, artificial intelligence, robust control, space operations, space propulsion. Total annual research expenditures: $69,367. *Unit head:* Dr. James Stevens, Chair, 719-255-3581, Fax: 719-255-3042, E-mail: jstevens@uccs.edu. *Application contact:* Siew Nylund, Academic Adviser, 719-255-3243, Fax: 719-255-3589, E-mail: snylund@eas.uccs.edu.

University of Colorado Boulder, Graduate School, College of Engineering and Applied Science, Department of Mechanical Engineering, Boulder, CO 80309. Offers ME, MS, PhD. Part-time programs available. *Faculty:* 24 full-time (5 women). *Students:* 198 full-time (37 women), 24 part-time (2 women); includes 22 minority (1 Black or African American, non-Hispanic/Latino; 2 American Indian or Alaska Native, non-Hispanic/Latino; 11 Asian, non-Hispanic/Latino; 6 Hispanic/Latino; 2 Two or more races, non-Hispanic/Latino), 57 international. Average age 26. 324 applicants, 19% accepted, 54 enrolled. In 2010, 56 master's, 18 doctorates awarded. Terminal master's awarded for partial completion of doctoral program. *Degree requirements:* For master's, comprehensive exam, thesis optional; for doctorate, comprehensive exam, thesis/dissertation, final and preliminary exams. *Entrance requirements:* For master's and doctorate, minimum undergraduate GPA of 3.0. Additional exam requirements/recommendations for international students: Required—TOEFL. *Application deadline:* For fall admission, 1/15 priority date for domestic students, 12/1 for international students; for spring admission, 10/15 for domestic students, 9/1 for international students. Applications are processed on a rolling basis. Application fee: $50 ($60 for international students). *Financial support:* In 2010–11, 37 fellowships with full tuition reimbursements (averaging $11,900 per year), 72 research assistantships with full tuition reimbursements (averaging $16,054 per year), 18 teaching assistantships with full tuition reimbursements (averaging $14,537 per year) were awarded; career-related internships or fieldwork also available. Financial award application deadline: 1/15. *Faculty research:* Thermal science, fluid mechanics, solid mechanics, materials science, interactive design and manufacturing. Total annual research expenditures: $8.1 million.

University of Colorado Denver, College of Engineering and Applied Science, Department of Bioengineering, Aurora, CO 80045-2560. Offers bioengineering (PhD); clinical imaging (MS); device design and entrepreneurship (MS); research (MS). Part-time programs available. *Faculty:*

Mechanical Engineering

University of Colorado Denver (continued)
3 full-time (1 woman). *Students:* 13 full-time (2 women), 1 part-time; includes 1 Black or African American, non-Hispanic/Latino; 1 Asian, non-Hispanic/Latino; 1 Hispanic/Latino. Average age 30. 15 applicants, 100% accepted, 12 enrolled.Terminal master's awarded for partial completion of doctoral program. *Degree requirements:* For master's, thesis or alternative, 30 credit hours; for doctorate, comprehensive exam, thesis/dissertation, 36 credit hours of classwork (18 core, 18 elective), additional 30 hours of thesis work, three formal examinations, approval of dissertations. *Entrance requirements:* For master's, GRE (recommended); for doctorate, GRE. Additional exam requirements/recommendations for international students: Required—TOEFL (minimum score 550 paper-based; 213 computer-based; 79 iBT), TOEFL (minimum 250 CBT/600 PBT/100IBT) for Ph D. *Application deadline:* For fall admission, 4/30 for domestic students. Application fee: $50. Electronic applications accepted. *Expenses:* Contact institution. *Financial support:* Fellowships, research assistantships, teaching assistantships, Federal Work-Study available. Financial award application deadline: 4/1; financial award applicants required to submit FAFSA. *Faculty research:* Imaging and biophotonics, cardiovascular biomechanics and hemodynamics, orthopedic biomechanics, ophthalmology, neuroscience engineering. *Unit head:* Dr. Robin Shandas, Chair, 303-724-4196, E-mail: robin.shandas@ucdenver.edu. *Application contact:* Dr. Robin Shandas, Chair, 303-724-4196, E-mail: robin.shandas@ucdenver.edu.

University of Colorado Denver, College of Engineering and Applied Science, Department of Mechanical Engineering, Denver, CO 80217. Offers mechanical engineering (MS). Part-time and evening/weekend programs available. *Faculty:* 8 full-time (0 women), 2 part-time/adjunct (both women). *Students:* 44 full-time (4 women), 11 part-time (1 woman); includes 3 Black or African American, non-Hispanic/Latino; 5 Asian, non-Hispanic/Latino; 2 Hispanic/Latino, 18 international. Average age 29. 47 applicants, 49% accepted, 15 enrolled. In 2010, 9 master's awarded. *Degree requirements:* For master's, comprehensive exam, thesis or alternative. *Entrance requirements:* For master's, GRE. Additional exam requirements/recommendations for international students: Required—TOEFL (minimum score 525 paper-based; 197 computer-based). *Application deadline:* For fall admission, 4/1 for domestic students; for spring admission, 10/1 for domestic students. Applications are processed on a rolling basis. Application fee: $50 ($75 for international students). Electronic applications accepted. *Expenses:* Contact institution. *Financial support:* Research assistantships, teaching assistantships, career-related internships or fieldwork and Federal Work-Study available. Financial award application deadline: 4/1; financial award applicants required to submit FAFSA. *Faculty research:* Applied and computational mechanics, bioengineering, energy systems, tribology, micro/mesofluidics and biomechanics, vehicle dynamics. *Unit head:* Dr. Sam Welch, Chair, 303-556-8488, Fax: 303-556-6371, E-mail: sam.welch@ucdenver.edu. *Application contact:* Petrina Morgan, Program Assistant, 303-556-8516, E-mail: petrina.morgan@ucdenver.edu.

University of Colorado Denver, College of Engineering and Applied Science, Master of Engineering Program, Denver, CO 80217-3364. Offers civil engineering (M Eng); electrical engineering (M Eng); mechanical engineering (M Eng). Part-time programs available. *Students:* 26 full-time (9 women), 31 part-time (8 women); includes 1 Black or African American, non-Hispanic/Latino; 3 Asian, non-Hispanic/Latino; 1 Hispanic/Latino, 2 international. Average age 36. 22 applicants, 77% accepted, 14 enrolled. In 2010, 23 master's awarded. *Degree requirements:* For master's, comprehensive exam, thesis, 27 credit hours of course work, 3 credit hours of report or thesis work. *Entrance requirements:* For master's, GRE (required for those with GPA below 2.75), transcripts, references, statement of purpose. Additional exam requirements/recommendations for international students: Required—TOEFL (minimum score 525 paper-based; 71 iBT). *Application deadline:* For fall admission, 7/15 for domestic students, 6/15 for international students; for spring admission, 12/1 for domestic students, 11/1 for international students. Applications are processed on a rolling basis. Application fee: $50 ($75 for international students). Electronic applications accepted. *Expenses:* Contact institution. *Financial support:* Federal Work-Study and scholarships/grants available. Financial award application deadline: 4/1; financial award applicants required to submit FAFSA. *Faculty research:* Civil, electrical and mechanical engineering.

University of Connecticut, Graduate School, School of Engineering, Department of Mechanical Engineering, Storrs, CT 06269. Offers MS, PhD. Terminal master's awarded for partial completion of doctoral program. *Degree requirements:* For master's, comprehensive exam, thesis or alternative; for doctorate, thesis/dissertation. *Entrance requirements:* For master's and doctorate, GRE General Test, GRE Subject Test. Additional exam requirements/recommendations for international students: Required—TOEFL (minimum score 550 paper-based; 213 computer-based). Electronic applications accepted. *Faculty research:* Design, applied mechanics, dynamics and control, energy and thermal sciences, manufacturing.

University of Dayton, Graduate School, School of Engineering, Department of Mechanical and Aerospace Engineering, Dayton, OH 45469-1300. Offers aerospace engineering (MSAE, DE, PhD); mechanical engineering (MSME, DE, PhD); renewable and clean energy (MS). Part-time programs available. Postbaccalaureate distance learning degree programs offered (no on-campus study). *Faculty:* 16 full-time (2 women), 11 part-time/adjunct (1 woman). *Students:* 113 full-time (22 women), 26 part-time (6 women); includes 15 minority (6 Black or African American, non-Hispanic/Latino; 3 Asian, non-Hispanic/Latino; 6 Hispanic/Latino), 47 international. Average age 28. 113 applicants, 84% accepted, 50 enrolled. In 2010, 30 master's, 7 doctorates awarded. Terminal master's awarded for partial completion of doctoral program. *Degree requirements:* For master's, thesis optional; for doctorate, variable foreign language requirement, thesis/dissertation, departmental qualifying exam. *Entrance requirements:* Additional exam requirements/recommendations for international students: Required—TOEFL (minimum score 550 paper-based; 213 computer-based; 80 iBT). *Application deadline:* For fall admission, 8/1 priority date for domestic students, 6/1 priority date for international students; for winter admission, 9/1 priority date for international students; for spring admission, 3/1 priority date for international students. Applications are processed on a rolling basis. Application fee: $0. Electronic applications accepted. *Expenses:* Tuition: Full-time $7800; part-time $650 per credit hour. *Financial support:* In 2010–11, 25 students received support, including 29 research assistantships with full tuition reimbursements available (averaging $11,000 per year), 7 teaching assistantships with full tuition reimbursements available (averaging $9,100 per year). Financial award applicants required to submit FAFSA. *Faculty research:* Jet engine combustion, surface coating friction and wear, aircraft thermal management, aerospace fuels, energy efficient buildings, energy efficient manufacturing, renewable energy. Total annual research expenditures: $1.2 million. *Unit head:* Dr. Kelly Kissock, Chair, 937-229-2999, Fax: 937-229-4766, E-mail: kelly.kissock@udayton.edu. *Application contact:* Dr. Vinod Jain, Graduate Program Director, 937-229-2992, Fax: 937-229-4766, E-mail: vinod.jain@notes.udayton.edu.

University of Delaware, College of Engineering, Department of Mechanical Engineering, Newark, DE 19716. Offers MEM, MSME, PhD. Part-time programs available. Terminal master's awarded for partial completion of doctoral program. *Degree requirements:* For master's, thesis (for some programs); for doctorate, thesis/dissertation. *Entrance requirements:* For master's and doctorate, GRE General Test. Additional exam requirements/recommendations for international students: Required—TOEFL (minimum score 600 paper-based; 250 computer-based). Electronic applications accepted. *Faculty research:* Biomedical engineering, clean energy, composites and nanotechnology, robotics and controls, fluid mechanics.

University of Denver, School of Engineering and Computer Science, Department of Mechanical and Materials Engineering, Denver, CO 80208. Offers bioengineering (MS); engineering (MS, PhD); interdisciplinary engineering (PhD); materials science (MS, PhD); mechanical engineering (MS, PhD); nanoscale science and engineering (PhD). Part-time programs available. *Faculty:* 8 full-time (1 woman), 5 part-time/adjunct (1 woman). *Students:* 3 full-time (1 woman), 21 part-time (5 women), 7 international. Average age 33. 63 applicants, 65% accepted, 5 enrolled. In 2010, 5 master's, 1 doctorate awarded. Terminal master's awarded for partial completion of doctoral program. *Degree requirements:* For master's, thesis or alternative; for doctorate, comprehensive exam, thesis/dissertation. *Entrance requirements:* For master's and doctorate, GRE General Test. Additional exam requirements/recommendations for international students: Required—TOEFL (minimum score 550 paper-based; 80 iBT). *Application deadline:* Applications are processed on a rolling basis. Application fee: $60. Electronic applications accepted. *Expenses:* Tuition: Full-time $35,604; part-time $29,670 per year. Required fees: $687 per year. Tuition and fees vary according to program. *Financial support:* In 2010–11, 7 research assistantships with full and partial tuition reimbursements (averaging $10,795 per year), 5 teaching assistantships with full and partial tuition reimbursements (averaging $13,230 per year) were awarded; Federal Work-Study, scholarships/grants, and unspecified assistantships also available. Financial award applicants required to submit FAFSA. *Faculty research:* Aerosols, biomechanics, composite materials, photo optics, drug delivery. *Unit head:* Dr. Daniel Armentrout, Chair, 303-871-3580, Fax: 303-871-4450, E-mail: darmentr@du.edu. *Application contact:* Renee Carvalho, Assistant to the Chair, 303-871-2107, Fax: 303-871-4450, E-mail: renee.carvalho@du.edu.

University of Detroit Mercy, College of Engineering and Science, Department of Mechanical Engineering, Detroit, MI 48221. Offers mechanical engineering (ME, DE). Evening/weekend programs available. *Degree requirements:* For doctorate, thesis/dissertation. *Faculty research:* CAD/CAM.

University of Florida, Graduate School, College of Engineering, Department of Mechanical and Aerospace Engineering, Gainesville, FL 32611. Offers aerospace engineering (ME, MS, PhD, Engr); mechanical engineering (ME, MS, PhD, Engr). Part-time programs available. *Faculty:* 49 full-time (4 women). *Students:* 380 full-time (45 women), 76 part-time (7 women); includes 9 Black or African American, non-Hispanic/Latino; 20 Asian, non-Hispanic/Latino; 25 Hispanic/Latino, 210 international. Average age 26. 790 applicants, 32% accepted, 139 enrolled. In 2010, 102 master's, 28 doctorates awarded. *Degree requirements:* For master's, thesis (for some programs); for doctorate, comprehensive exam, thesis/dissertation; for Engr, thesis. *Entrance requirements:* For master's and doctorate, GRE General Test, minimum GPA of 3.0; for Engr, GRE General Test. Additional exam requirements/recommendations for international students: Required—TOEFL (minimum score 550 paper-based; 213 computer-based; 80 iBT), IELTS (minimum score 6). *Application deadline:* Applications are processed on a rolling basis. Application fee: $30. Electronic applications accepted. *Expenses:* Tuition, state resident: full-time $10,915.92. Tuition, nonresident: full-time $28,309. *Financial support:* In 2010–11, 203 students received support, including 5 fellowships, 197 research assistantships (averaging $21,150 per year), 1 teaching assistantship (averaging $18,540 per year); institutionally sponsored loans and unspecified assistantships also available. Support available to part-time students. Financial award applicants required to submit FAFSA. *Faculty research:* Thermal sciences, design, controls and robotics, manufacturing, energy transport and utilization. *Unit head:* David W. Hahn, PhD, Chair, 352-392-0807, Fax: 352-392-1071, E-mail: dwhahn@ufl.edu. *Application contact:* David W. Mikolaitis, PhD, Graduate Coordinator, 352-392-7632, Fax: 352-392-7303, E-mail: mollusk@ufl.edu.

University of Hawaii at Manoa, Graduate Division, College of Engineering, Department of Mechanical Engineering, Honolulu, HI 96822. Offers MS, PhD. Part-time programs available. *Faculty:* 19 full-time (0 women). *Students:* 43 full-time (7 women), 8 part-time (1 woman); includes 19 minority (10 Asian, non-Hispanic/Latino; 2 Native Hawaiian or other Pacific Islander, non-Hispanic/Latino; 7 Two or more races, non-Hispanic/Latino), 19 international. Average age 28. 50 applicants, 66% accepted, 21 enrolled. In 2010, 10 master's, 3 doctorates awarded. *Degree requirements:* For master's, comprehensive exam, thesis; for doctorate, comprehensive exam, thesis/dissertation. *Entrance requirements:* For master's and doctorate, GRE General Test. Additional exam requirements/recommendations for international students: Required—TOEFL (minimum score 550 paper-based; 213 computer-based; 79 iBT), IELTS (minimum score 5). *Application deadline:* For fall admission, 3/1 for domestic students, 1/15 for international students; for spring admission, 9/1 for domestic students, 8/1 for international students. Applications are processed on a rolling basis. Application fee: $60. *Financial support:* In 2010–11, 9 fellowships (averaging $956 per year), 31 research assistantships (averaging $19,974 per year), 4 teaching assistantships (averaging $15,558 per year) were awarded; tuition waivers (full) also available. Financial award application deadline: 8/31; financial award applicants required to submit FAFSA. *Faculty research:* Materials and manufacturing; mechanics, systems and control; thermal and fluid sciences. Total annual research expenditures: $472,000. *Application contact:* Beei-Huan Chao, Graduate Chairperson, 808-956-7167, Fax: 808-956-2373, E-mail: bchao@wiliki.eng.hawaii.edu.

University of Houston, Cullen College of Engineering, Department of Mechanical Engineering, Houston, TX 77204. Offers MME, MSME, PhD. Part-time programs available. *Faculty:* 22 full-time (1 woman), 2 part-time/adjunct (0 women). *Students:* 79 full-time (9 women), 29 part-time (6 women); includes 2 Black or African American, non-Hispanic/Latino; 5 Asian, non-Hispanic/Latino; 3 Hispanic/Latino; 1 Two or more races, non-Hispanic/Latino, 77 international. Average age 26. 145 applicants, 53% accepted, 27 enrolled. In 2010, 18 master's, 5 doctorates awarded. Terminal master's awarded for partial completion of doctoral program. *Degree requirements:* For master's, thesis (for some programs); for doctorate, thesis/dissertation, departmental qualifying exam. *Entrance requirements:* For master's and doctorate, GRE General Test. Additional exam requirements/recommendations for international students: Required—TOEFL. *Application deadline:* For fall admission, 5/1 for domestic students, 3/1 for international students; for spring admission, 11/1 for domestic students, 10/1 for international students. Application fee: $25 ($75 for international students). *Expenses:* Tuition, state resident: full-time $8592; part-time $358 per credit hour. Tuition, nonresident: full-time $16,032; part-time $668 per credit hour. Required fees: $2889. Tuition and fees vary according to course load and program. *Financial support:* In 2010–11, 3 fellowships with partial tuition reimbursements (averaging $4,334 per year), 28 research assistantships with partial tuition reimbursements (averaging $12,240 per year), 5 teaching assistantships with partial tuition reimbursements (averaging $10,952 per year) were awarded; career-related internships or fieldwork, Federal Work-Study, institutionally sponsored loans, scholarships/grants, health care benefits, and unspecified assistantships also available. Support available to part-time students. Financial award application deadline: 3/10. *Unit head:* Dr. David Zimmerman, Interim Chairperson, 713-743-4520, Fax: 713-743-4503, E-mail: dzimmerman@uh.edu. *Application contact:* Jane Geanangel, Academic Advisor, 713-743-4219.

University of Illinois at Chicago, Graduate College, College of Engineering, Department of Mechanical and Industrial Engineering, Chicago, IL 60607-7128. Offers energy engineering (MEE); industrial engineering (MS); industrial engineering and operations research (PhD); mechanical engineering (MS, PhD), including fluids engineering, mechanical analysis and design, thermomechanical and power engineering. Part-time programs available. *Degree requirements:* For doctorate, thesis/dissertation. *Entrance requirements:* For master's and doctorate, GRE General Test, minimum GPA of 2.75. Additional exam requirements/recommendations for international students: Required—TOEFL. Electronic applications accepted.

University of Illinois at Urbana–Champaign, Graduate College, College of Engineering, Department of Mechanical Science and Engineering, Champaign, IL 61820. Offers mechanical engineering (MS, PhD); theoretical and applied mechanics (MS, PhD); MS/MBA. *Faculty:* 51 full-time (4 women), 2 part-time/adjunct (0 women). *Students:* 325 full-time (37 women), 39 part-time (4 women); includes 1 Black or African American, non-Hispanic/Latino; 17 Asian, non-Hispanic/Latino; 13 Hispanic/Latino, 198 international. 587 applicants, 33% accepted, 88 enrolled. In 2010, 77 master's, 29 doctorates awarded. Terminal master's awarded for partial completion of doctoral program. *Entrance requirements:* For master's, GRE General Test, minimum GPA of 3.25; for doctorate, GRE General Test, minimum GPA of 3.5. Additional exam requirements/recommendations for international students: Required—TOEFL (minimum score 613 paper-based; 257 computer-based; 103 iBT). *Application deadline:* Applications are processed on a rolling basis. Application fee: $75 ($90 for international students). Electronic applications accepted. *Financial support:* In 2010–11, 42 fellowships, 244 research assistantships, 102 teaching assistantships were awarded; tuition waivers (full and partial) also available. *Faculty research:* Combustion and propulsion, design methodology, dynamic systems and controls, energy transfer, materials behavior and processing, manufacturing systems operations, management. *Unit head:* Placid Mathew Ferreira, Head, 217-333-0639, Fax: 217-244-6534, E-mail: pferreir@illinois.edu. *Application contact:* Kathy A. Smith, Admissions and Records Officer, 217-244-4539, Fax: 217-244-6534, E-mail: smith15@illinois.edu.

The University of Iowa, Graduate College, College of Engineering, Department of Mechanical Engineering, Iowa City, IA 52242-1316. Offers MS, PhD. *Faculty:* 13 full-time (1 woman). *Students:* 56 full-time (8 women); includes 2 minority (both Asian, non-Hispanic/Latino), 30 international. Average age 27. 104 applicants, 29% accepted, 13 enrolled. In 2010, 10 master's, 8 doctorates awarded. *Degree requirements:* For master's, oral exam or thesis; for doctorate, comprehensive exam, thesis/dissertation. *Entrance requirements:* For master's and doctorate, GRE. Additional exam requirements/recommendations for international students: Required—TOEFL (minimum score 550 paper-based; 213 computer-based; 81 iBT). *Application deadline:* For fall admission, 7/15 for domestic students, 4/15 for international students; for spring admission, 12/1 for domestic students, 10/1 for international students. Applications are processed on a rolling basis. Application fee: $60 ($100 for international students). Electronic applications accepted. *Financial support:* In 2010–11, 48 research assistantships with partial tuition reimbursements (averaging $21,930 per year), 19 teaching assistantships with partial tuition reimbursements (averaging $16,575 per year) were awarded; fellowships with partial tuition reimbursements, traineeships and unspecified assistantships also available. Financial award applicants required to submit FAFSA. *Faculty research:* Computer simulation methodology; biomechanics; dynamics; solid mechanics; fluid dynamics. Total annual research expenditures: $6.4 million. *Unit head:* Dr. Andrew Kusiak, Departmental Executive Officer, 319-335-5934, Fax: 319-335-5669, E-mail: andrew-kusiak@uiowa.edu. *Application contact:* Jennifer Rumping, Secretary, 319-335-5668, Fax: 319-335-5669, E-mail: mech_eng@engineering.uiowa.edu.

The University of Kansas, Graduate Studies, School of Engineering, Department of Mechanical Engineering, Lawrence, KS 66045. Offers MS, DE, PhD. Part-time programs available. *Faculty:* 17 full-time (4 women). *Students:* 47 full-time (9 women), 9 part-time (1 woman); includes 5 minority (2 Asian, non-Hispanic/Latino; 1 Hispanic/Latino; 2 Two or more races, non-Hispanic/Latino), 21 international. Average age 26. 61 applicants, 38% accepted, 10 enrolled. In 2010, 9 master's, 1 doctorate awarded. *Degree requirements:* For master's, thesis or alternative, exam; for doctorate, comprehensive exam, thesis/dissertation. *Entrance requirements:* For master's, minimum GPA of 3.0; for doctorate, minimum GPA of 3.5. Additional exam requirements/recommendations for international students: Required—TOEFL. *Application deadline:* For fall admission, 6/1 priority date for domestic students, 3/31 priority date for international students; for spring admission, 11/1 priority date for domestic students, 9/30 priority date for international students. Applications are processed on a rolling basis. Application fee: $55 ($65 for international students). Electronic applications accepted. *Expenses:* Tuition, state resident: full-time $7092; part-time $295.50 per credit hour. Tuition, nonresident: full-time $16,590; part-time $691.25 per credit hour. Required fees: $858; $71.49 per credit hour. Tuition and fees vary according to course load, campus/location and program. *Financial support:* Fellowships with full and partial tuition reimbursements, research assistantships with full and partial tuition reimbursements, teaching assistantships with full and partial tuition reimbursements, career-related internships or fieldwork available. Financial award application deadline: 5/15. *Faculty research:* Heat transfer, energy analysis, computer-aided design, biomedical engineering, computational mathematics. *Unit head:* Ronald Dougherty, Chair, 785-864-3181, E-mail: kume@ku.edu. *Application contact:* Glen Marotz, Associate Dean, 785-864-2941, Fax: 785-864-5445, E-mail: gama@ku.edu.

University of Kentucky, Graduate School, College of Engineering, Program in Mechanical Engineering, Lexington, KY 40506-0032. Offers MSME, PhD. *Degree requirements:* For master's, comprehensive exam, thesis optional; for doctorate, comprehensive exam, thesis/dissertation. *Entrance requirements:* For master's, GRE General Test, minimum undergraduate GPA of 2.75; for doctorate, GRE General Test, minimum undergraduate GPA of 3.0. Additional exam requirements/recommendations for international students: Required—TOEFL (minimum score 550 paper-based; 213 computer-based). Electronic applications accepted. *Faculty research:* Combustion, computational fluid dynamics, design and systems, manufacturing, thermal and fluid sciences.

University of Louisiana at Lafayette, College of Engineering, Department of Mechanical Engineering, Lafayette, LA 70504. Offers MSE. Evening/weekend programs available. *Degree requirements:* For master's, comprehensive exam, thesis or alternative. *Entrance requirements:* For master's, GRE General Test, BS in mechanical engineering, minimum GPA of 2.85. Additional exam requirements/recommendations for international students: Required—TOEFL (minimum score 550 paper-based; 213 computer-based). Electronic applications accepted. *Faculty research:* CAD/CAM, machine design and vibration, thermal science.

University of Louisville, J.B. Speed School of Engineering, Department of Mechanical Engineering, Louisville, KY 40292-0001. Offers M Eng, MS, PhD. *Accreditation:* ABET (one or more programs are accredited). Part-time programs available. *Faculty:* 17 full-time (2 women). *Students:* 75 full-time (12 women), 21 part-time (1 woman); includes 7 Asian, non-Hispanic/Latino; 3 Hispanic/Latino; 2 Two or more races, non-Hispanic/Latino, 12 international. Average age 27. 31 applicants, 68% accepted, 10 enrolled. In 2010, 57 master's awarded. Terminal master's awarded for partial completion of doctoral program. *Degree requirements:* For master's, comprehensive exam (for some programs), thesis or alternative; for doctorate, comprehensive exam, thesis/dissertation, minimum GPA of 3.0. *Entrance requirements:* For master's and doctorate, GRE General Test. Additional exam requirements/recommendations for international students: Required—TOEFL (minimum score 550 paper-based; 213 computer-based; 80 iBT), IELTS (minimum score 6.5). *Application deadline:* For fall admission, 5/1 priority date for domestic and international students; for spring admission, 11/1 priority date for domestic and international students. Applications are processed on a rolling basis. Application fee: $50. Electronic applications accepted. *Expenses:* Tuition, state resident: full-time $9144; part-time $508 per credit hour. Tuition, nonresident: full-time $19,026; part-time $1057 per credit hour. Tuition and fees vary according to program and reciprocity agreements. *Financial support:* In 2010–11, 16 students received support, including 1 fellowship with full tuition reimbursement available (averaging $22,000 per year), 4 research assistantships with full tuition reimbursements available (averaging $22,500 per year), 11 teaching assistantships with full tuition reimbursements available (averaging $20,000 per year). Financial award application deadline: 1/25; financial award applicants required to submit FAFSA. *Faculty research:* Aerospace and automotive engineering, air pollution control, biomechanics and rehabilitation engineering, computer-aided design, micro and nanotechnology. Total annual research expenditures: $1.3 million. *Unit head:* Dr. Glen Prater, Chair, 502-852-6331, Fax: 502-852-6053, E-mail: gprater@louisville.edu. *Application contact:* Dr. Michael Day, Associate Dean, 502-852-6195, Fax: 502-852-7294, E-mail: day@louisville.edu.

University of Maine, Graduate School, College of Engineering, Department of Mechanical Engineering, Orono, ME 04469. Offers MS, PhD. *Faculty:* 11 full-time (0 women), 4 part-time/adjunct (3 women). *Students:* 17 full-time (2 women), 6 part-time (1 woman), 11 international. Average age 32. 34 applicants, 38% accepted, 7 enrolled. In 2010, 3 master's, 2 doctorates awarded. *Degree requirements:* For master's, thesis (for some programs). *Entrance requirements:* For master's and doctorate, GRE General Test. Additional exam requirements/recommendations for international students: Required—TOEFL. *Application deadline:* For fall admission, 2/1 priority date for domestic students. Applications are processed on a rolling basis. Application fee: $65. Electronic applications accepted. *Expenses:* Tuition, state resident: full-time $400. Tuition, nonresident: full-time $1050. *Financial support:* In 2010–11, 17 research assistantships with tuition reimbursements (averaging $16,800 per year), 2 teaching assistantships with tuition reimbursements (averaging $12,790 per year) were awarded; Federal Work-Study and tuition waivers (full and partial) also available. Financial award application deadline: 3/1. *Faculty research:* Higher order beam and plate theories, dynamic response of structural systems, heat transfer in window systems, forced convection heat transfer in gas turbine passages, effect of parallel space heating systems on utility load management. *Unit head:* Dr. Moshen Shahinpoor, Chair, 207-581-2120, Fax: 207-581-2379. *Application contact:* Scott G.

Delcourt, Associate Dean of the Graduate School, 207-581-3291, Fax: 207-581-3232, E-mail: graduate@maine.edu.

The University of Manchester, School of Mechanical, Aerospace and Civil Engineering, Manchester, United Kingdom. Offers advanced manufacturing technology (M Ent); aerospace engineering (M Phil, M Sc, PhD); civil engineering (M Phil, M Sc, PhD); environmental engineering (M Phil, PhD); management of projects (M Phil, M Sc, PhD); mechanical engineering (M Phil, M Sc, PhD); mechanical engineering design (M Ent); nuclear engineering (M Phil, D Eng, PhD).

University of Manitoba, Faculty of Graduate Studies, Faculty of Engineering, Department of Mechanical and Manufacturing Engineering, Winnipeg, MB R3T 2N2, Canada. Offers M Eng, M Sc, PhD. *Degree requirements:* For master's, thesis; for doctorate, thesis/dissertation.

University of Maryland, Baltimore County, Graduate School, College of Engineering and Information Technology, Department of Mechanical Engineering, Baltimore, MD 21250. Offers computational thermal/fluid dynamics (Postbaccalaureate Certificate); mechanical engineering (MS, PhD); mechatronics (Postbaccalaureate Certificate). Part-time programs available. *Faculty:* 17 full-time (3 women), 3 part-time/adjunct (0 women). *Students:* 66 full-time (12 women), 23 part-time (4 women); includes 17 minority (6 Black or African American, non-Hispanic/Latino; 5 Asian, non-Hispanic/Latino; 3 Hispanic/Latino; 3 Two or more races, non-Hispanic/Latino), 31 international. Average age 30. 46 applicants, 74% accepted, 22 enrolled. In 2010, 8 master's, 7 doctorates, 3 other advanced degrees awarded. *Degree requirements:* For master's, comprehensive exam (for some programs), thesis (for some programs); for doctorate, comprehensive exam, thesis/dissertation. *Entrance requirements:* For master's, GRE General Test, minimum GPA of 3.0; for doctorate, GRE General Test, minimum overall GPA of 3.3; bachelor's degree in mechanical, aerospace, civil, industrial, or chemical engineering. Additional exam requirements/recommendations for international students: Required—TOEFL (minimum score 550 paper-based; 250 computer-based; 80 iBT). *Application deadline:* For fall admission, 6/1 for domestic students, 1/1 for international students; for spring admission, 11/1 for domestic students, 6/1 for international students. Applications are processed on a rolling basis. Application fee: $50. Electronic applications accepted. *Financial support:* In 2010–11, 4 fellowships with full tuition reimbursements (averaging $15,000 per year), 20 research assistantships with full tuition reimbursements (averaging $20,000 per year), 20 teaching assistantships with full tuition reimbursements (averaging $17,000 per year) were awarded; career-related internships or fieldwork, Federal Work-Study, scholarships/grants, health care benefits, tuition waivers (partial), and unspecified assistantships also available. Support available to part-time students. Financial award application deadline: 6/30; financial award applicants required to submit FAFSA. *Faculty research:* Design and manufacturing, thermal fluids, solid mechanics and materials, biomechanics. Total annual research expenditures: $1.7 million. *Unit head:* Dr. Brian Reed, Professor and Interim Chair, 410-455-3313, Fax: 410-455-1052, E-mail: reedb@umbc.edu. *Application contact:* Dr. Marc Zupan, Associate Professor and Graduate Program Director, 410-455-6822, Fax: 410-455-1052, E-mail: mzupan@umbc.edu.

University of Maryland, College Park, Academic Affairs, A. James Clark School of Engineering, Department of Continuing and Distance Learning in Engineering, College Park, MD 20742. Offers engineering (M Eng), including aerospace engineering, chemical engineering, civil engineering, electrical engineering, engineering, fire protection engineering, materials science and engineering, mechanical engineering, reliability engineering, systems engineering. *Faculty:* 4 full-time (1 woman), 11 part-time/adjunct (1 woman). *Students:* 56 full-time (15 women), 428 part-time (88 women); includes 153 minority (59 Black or African American, non-Hispanic/Latino; 63 Asian, non-Hispanic/Latino; 24 Hispanic/Latino; 7 Two or more races, non-Hispanic/Latino), 55 international. 551 applicants, 82% accepted, 360 enrolled. In 2010, 130 master's awarded. *Application deadline:* For fall admission, 8/15 for domestic students, 1/10 for international students; for spring admission, 12/15 for domestic students, 6/1 for international students. Applications are processed on a rolling basis. Application fee: $75. Electronic applications accepted. *Expenses:* Tuition, area resident: Part-time $471 per credit hour. Tuition, state resident: part-time $471 per credit hour. Tuition, nonresident: part-time $1016 per credit hour. Required fees: $337 per term. *Financial support:* In 2010–11, 2 research assistantships (averaging $20,285 per year), 7 teaching assistantships (averaging $16,962 per year) were awarded. *Unit head:* Dr. Darryll Pines, Dean, 301-405-0376, Fax: 301-314-5908, E-mail: pines@umd.edu. *Application contact:* Dr. Charles A. Caramello, Dean of the Graduate School, 301-405-0358, Fax: 301-314-9305, E-mail: ccaramel@umd.edu.

University of Maryland, College Park, Academic Affairs, A. James Clark School of Engineering, Department of Mechanical Engineering, College Park, MD 20742. Offers electronic packaging and reliability (MS, PhD); manufacturing and design (MS, PhD); mechanics and materials (MS, PhD); reliability engineering (M Eng, MS, PhD); thermal and fluid sciences (MS, PhD). Part-time and evening/weekend programs available. Postbaccalaureate distance learning degree programs offered. *Faculty:* 79 full-time (7 women), 21 part-time/adjunct (1 woman). *Students:* 219 full-time (31 women), 73 part-time (10 women); includes 44 minority (11 Black or African American, non-Hispanic/Latino; 2 American Indian or Alaska Native, non-Hispanic/Latino; 21 Asian, non-Hispanic/Latino; 8 Hispanic/Latino; 2 Two or more races, non-Hispanic/Latino), 138 international. 520 applicants, 18% accepted, 63 enrolled. In 2010, 31 master's, 31 doctorates awarded. *Degree requirements:* For master's, thesis optional; for doctorate, thesis/dissertation, qualifying exam. *Entrance requirements:* For master's, GRE General Test, 3 letters of recommendation; for doctorate, GRE General Test, minimum GPA of 3.0. Additional exam requirements/recommendations for international students: Required—TOEFL. *Application deadline:* For fall admission, 5/15 for domestic students, 2/1 for international students; for spring admission, 10/1 for domestic students, 6/1 for international students. Applications are processed on a rolling basis. Application fee: $75. Electronic applications accepted. *Expenses:* Tuition, area resident: Part-time $471 per credit hour. Tuition, state resident: part-time $471 per credit hour. Tuition, nonresident: part-time $1016 per credit hour. Required fees: $337 per term. *Financial support:* In 2010–11, 3 fellowships with full and partial tuition reimbursements (averaging $19,975 per year), 166 research assistantships (averaging $23,679 per year), 12 teaching assistantships (averaging $17,644 per year) were awarded; Federal Work-Study and scholarships/grants also available. Support available to part-time students. Financial award applicants required to submit FAFSA. *Faculty research:* Injection molding, electronic packaging, fluid mechanics, product engineering. Total annual research expenditures: $17.4 million. *Unit head:* Dr. B. Balachandran, Interim Chair, 301-405-5297, E-mail: balab@umd.edu. *Application contact:* Dr. Charles A. Caramello, Graduate Director, 301-405-0358, Fax: 301-314-9305, E-mail: ccaramel@umd.edu.

University of Massachusetts Amherst, Graduate School, College of Engineering, Department of Mechanical and Industrial Engineering, Program in Mechanical Engineering, Amherst, MA 01003. Offers MSME, PhD. Part-time programs available. *Students:* 64 full-time (17 women), 16 part-time (1 woman); includes 3 minority (1 Asian, non-Hispanic/Latino; 1 Hispanic/Latino; 1 Native Hawaiian or other Pacific Islander, non-Hispanic/Latino), 37 international. Average age 27. 206 applicants, 46% accepted, 19 enrolled. In 2010, 10 master's, 2 doctorates awarded. Terminal master's awarded for partial completion of doctoral program. *Degree requirements:* For master's, thesis or alternative, project; for doctorate, comprehensive exam, thesis/dissertation. *Entrance requirements:* For master's and doctorate, GRE General Test. Additional exam requirements/recommendations for international students: Required—TOEFL (minimum score 550 paper-based; 213 computer-based; 80 iBT), IELTS (minimum score 6.5). *Application deadline:* For fall admission, 1/15 for domestic and international students; for spring admission, 10/1 for domestic and international students. Applications are processed on a rolling basis. Application fee: $50 ($65 for international students). Electronic applications accepted. *Expenses:* Tuition, state resident: full-time $2640. Required fees: $8282. One-time fee: $357 full-time. *Financial support:* Fellowships with full tuition reimbursements, research assistantships with full tuition reimbursements, teaching assistantships with full tuition reimbursements, career-related internships or fieldwork, Federal Work-Study, scholarships/grants, traineeships, health care benefits, tuition waivers, and unspecified assistantships available. Support available to part-time students. Financial award application deadline: 1/15; financial award

Mechanical Engineering

University of Massachusetts Amherst (continued)

applicants required to submit FAFSA. *Unit head:* Dr. David P. Schmidt, Director, 413-545-3827, Fax: 413-545-1027. *Application contact:* Jean M. Ames, Supervisor of Admissions, 413-545-0722, Fax: 413-577-0100, E-mail: gradadml@grad.umass.edu.

University of Massachusetts Amherst, Graduate School, Interdisciplinary Programs, Program in Mechanical Engineering and Business Administration, Amherst, MA 01003. Offers MSME/MBA. Part-time programs available. *Students:* 1 full-time (0 women); minority (Two or more races, non-Hispanic/Latino). Average age 25. 2 applicants, 50% accepted, 1 enrolled. *Entrance requirements:* Additional exam requirements/recommendations for international students: Required—TOEFL (minimum score 600 paper-based; 250 computer-based; 100 iBT), IELTS (minimum score 7). *Application deadline:* For fall admission, 1/15 for domestic and international students. Applications are processed on a rolling basis. Application fee: $50 ($65 for international students). Electronic applications accepted. *Expenses:* Tuition, state resident: full-time $2640. Required fees: $8282. One-time fee: $357 full-time. *Financial support:* Career-related internships or fieldwork, Federal Work-Study, scholarships/grants, traineeships, health care benefits, tuition waivers (full), and unspecified assistantships available. Support available to part-time students. *Unit head:* Dr. David P. Schmidt, Graduate Program Director, 413-545-3827, Fax: 413-545-1027. *Application contact:* Jean M. Ames, Supervisor of Admissions, 413-545-0722, Fax: 413-577-0010, E-mail: gradadm@grad.umass.edu.

University of Massachusetts Dartmouth, Graduate School, College of Engineering, Program in Mechanical Engineering, North Dartmouth, MA 02747-2300. Offers MS. Part-time programs available. *Faculty:* 10 full-time (1 woman), 2 part-time/adjunct (0 women). *Students:* 18 full-time (4 women), 20 part-time (0 women); includes 1 Hispanic/Latino, 14 international. Average age 27. 29 applicants, 66% accepted, 12 enrolled. In 2010, 5 master's awarded. *Degree requirements:* For master's, thesis or alternative. *Entrance requirements:* For master's, GRE General Test, minimum undergraduate GPA of 3.0, 3 letters of recommendation. Additional exam requirements/recommendations for international students: Required—TOEFL (minimum score 500 paper-based). *Application deadline:* For fall admission, 4/20 priority date for domestic students, 2/20 priority date for international students; for spring admission, 11/15 priority date for domestic students, 9/15 priority date for international students. Applications are processed on a rolling basis. Application fee: $40 ($60 for international students). Electronic applications accepted. *Expenses:* Tuition, state resident: full-time $2071; part-time $86 per credit. Tuition, nonresident: full-time $8099; part-time $337 per credit. Required fees: $9446; $394 per credit. One-time fee: $75. Part-time tuition and fees vary according to class time, course load, degree level and reciprocity agreements. *Financial support:* In 2010–11, 12 research assistantships with full tuition reimbursements (averaging $7,964 per year), 7 teaching assistantships with full tuition reimbursements (averaging $8,827 per year) were awarded; Federal Work-Study and unspecified assistantships also available. Support available to part-time students. Financial award application deadline: 3/1. *Faculty research:* Biofluid mechanics, universal design, heat and mass transfer, computer simulation, volcanic flows. Total annual research expenditures: $507,182. *Unit head:* Dr. John Rice, Director, 508-999-8498, E-mail: jrice@umassd.edu. *Application contact:* Elan Turcotte-Shamski, Graduate Admissions Officer, 508-999-8604, Fax: 508-999-8183, E-mail: graduate@umassd.edu.

University of Massachusetts Lowell, James B. Francis College of Engineering, Department of Mechanical Engineering, Lowell, MA 01854-2881. Offers MS Eng, D Eng, PhD. Part-time programs available. *Degree requirements:* For master's, thesis or alternative; for doctorate, 2 foreign languages, comprehensive exam, thesis/dissertation. *Entrance requirements:* For master's and doctorate, GRE General Test. Additional exam requirements/recommendations for international students: Required—TOEFL (minimum score 560 paper-based; 215 computer-based). Electronic applications accepted. *Faculty research:* Composites, heat transfer.

University of Memphis, Graduate School, Herff College of Engineering, Department of Mechanical Engineering, Memphis, TN 38152. Offers design and mechanical engineering (MS); energy systems (MS); industrial engineering (MS); mechanical engineering (PhD); mechanical systems (MS); power systems (MS). Part-time programs available. *Faculty:* 8 full-time (0 women). *Students:* 3 full-time (1 woman), 8 part-time (0 women); includes 2 Black or African American, non-Hispanic/Latino, 5 international. Average age 30. 11 applicants, 64% accepted, 3 enrolled. In 2010, 5 master's awarded. Terminal master's awarded for partial completion of doctoral program. *Degree requirements:* For master's, comprehensive exam, thesis; for doctorate, comprehensive exam, thesis/dissertation. *Entrance requirements:* For master's, GRE General Test, BS in mechanical engineering, minimum undergraduate GPA of 3.0. *Application deadline:* For fall admission, 8/1 for domestic students; for spring admission, 12/1 for domestic students. Application fee: $35 ($60 for international students). *Financial support:* In 2010–11, 6 students received support; fellowships with full tuition reimbursements available, research assistantships with full tuition reimbursements available, teaching assistantships with full tuition reimbursements available, career-related internships or fieldwork, Federal Work-Study, scholarships/grants, and unspecified assistantships available. Financial award application deadline: 2/15; financial award applicants required to submit FAFSA. *Faculty research:* Computational fluid dynamics, computational mechanics, integrated design, nondestructive testing, operations research. *Unit head:* Dr. John I. Hochstein, Chair, 901-678-2173, Fax: 901-678-5459, E-mail: jhochste@memphis.edu. *Application contact:* Dr. Teong Tan, Graduate Studies Coordinator, 901-678-3264, Fax: 901-678-5459, E-mail: ttan@memphis.edu.

University of Miami, Graduate School, College of Engineering, Department of Mechanical and Aerospace Engineering, Coral Gables, FL 33124. Offers MSME, PhD. Part-time programs available. *Degree requirements:* For master's, thesis (for some programs); for doctorate, comprehensive exam, thesis/dissertation. *Entrance requirements:* For master's and doctorate, GRE General Test, minimum GPA of 3.0. Additional exam requirements/recommendations for international students: Required—TOEFL (minimum score 550 paper-based; 213 computer-based). Electronic applications accepted. *Faculty research:* Internal combustion engines, heat transfer, hydrogen energy, controls, fuel cells.

University of Michigan, Horace H. Rackham School of Graduate Studies, College of Engineering, Department of Mechanical Engineering, Ann Arbor, MI 48109. Offers MSE, PhD. Part-time programs available. *Students:* 429 full-time (54 women), 14 part-time (2 women). 1,071 applicants, 42% accepted, 184 enrolled. In 2010, 105 master's, 39 doctorates awarded. Terminal master's awarded for partial completion of doctoral program. *Degree requirements:* For master's, thesis optional; for doctorate, thesis/dissertation, oral defense of dissertation, preliminary and qualifying exams. *Entrance requirements:* For master's, GRE General Test, undergraduate degree in same or relevant field; for doctorate, GRE General Test. Additional exam requirements/recommendations for international students: Required—TOEFL (minimum score 560 paper-based; 220 computer-based). *Application deadline:* Applications are processed on a rolling basis. Application fee: $65 ($75 for international students). Electronic applications accepted. *Expenses:* Tuition, state resident: full-time $17,784; part-time $1116 per credit hour. Tuition, nonresident: full-time $35,944; part-time $2125 per credit hour. International tuition: $35,994 full-time. Required fees: $95 per semester. Tuition and fees vary according to course load, degree level and program. *Financial support:* Fellowships, research assistantships, teaching assistantships, institutionally sponsored loans, health care benefits, tuition waivers (full), and unspecified assistantships available. *Faculty research:* Design and manufacturing, systems and controls, combustion and heat transfer, materials and solid mechanics, dynamics and vibrations, biosystems, fluid mechanics, microsystems, environmental sustainabilities. *Unit head:* Kon-Well Wang, Department Chair, 734-764-8464, E-mail: kwwang@umich.edu. *Application contact:* Cynthia Quann-White, Graduate Admissions and Program Coordinator, 734-763-9223, Fax: 734-647-7303, E-mail: me.grad.application@umich.edu.

University of Michigan–Dearborn, College of Engineering and Computer Science, Department of Mechanical Engineering, Dearborn, MI 48128. Offers MSE. Part-time and evening/weekend programs available. Postbaccalaureate distance learning degree programs offered (no on-campus study). *Faculty:* 18 full-time (1 woman), 3 part-time/adjunct (0 women). *Students:* 10 full-time (0 women), 56 part-time (4 women); includes 1 Black or African American, non-Hispanic/Latino; 8 Asian, non-Hispanic/Latino; 2 Hispanic/Latino, 15 international. Average age 28. 37 applicants, 73% accepted, 13 enrolled. In 2010, 30 master's awarded. *Degree requirements:* For master's, thesis optional. *Entrance requirements:* For master's, BS/BSE in mechanical engineering and/or applied mathematics, minimum GPA of 3.0 or equivalent. Additional exam requirements/recommendations for international students: Required—TOEFL (minimum score 560 paper-based; 220 computer-based; 84 iBT), IELTS, or Michigan English Language Assessment Battery. *Application deadline:* For fall admission, 7/1 priority date for domestic students, 4/1 for international students; for winter admission, 11/1 priority date for domestic students, 8/1 for international students; for spring admission, 3/1 priority date for domestic students, 12/1 for international students. Applications are processed on a rolling basis. Application fee: $60 ($75 for international students). Electronic applications accepted. *Financial support:* In 2010–11, 5 students received support, including 5 research assistantships with full tuition reimbursements available (averaging $14,700 per year), 5 teaching assistantships (averaging $3,400 per year); Federal Work-Study, scholarships/grants, health care benefits, and unspecified assistantships also available. Financial award application deadline: 4/1; financial award applicants required to submit FAFSA. *Faculty research:* Combustion, fatigue, fracture/damage mechanics, noise and vibration, vehicle climate control. *Unit head:* Dr. Ben Q. Li, Chair, 313-593-5241, Fax: 313-593-3851, E-mail: benqli@umich.edu. *Application contact:* Rebekah S. Awood, Graduate Secretary, 313-593-5241, Fax: 313-593-3851, E-mail: rsdew@umd.umich.edu.

University of Minnesota, Twin Cities Campus, Institute of Technology, Department of Mechanical Engineering, Minneapolis, MN 55455-0213. Offers industrial engineering (MSIE, PhD); mechanical engineering (MSME, PhD). Part-time programs available. *Degree requirements:* For doctorate, thesis/dissertation. *Entrance requirements:* For master's, GRE General Test, minimum GPA of 3.0; for doctorate, GRE General Test.

University of Missouri, Graduate School, College of Engineering, Department of Mechanical and Aerospace Engineering, Columbia, MO 65211. Offers MS, PhD. *Degree requirements:* For master's, thesis; for doctorate, one foreign language, thesis/dissertation. *Entrance requirements:* For master's and doctorate, GRE General Test, minimum GPA of 3.0. Additional exam requirements/recommendations for international students: Required—TOEFL (minimum score 500 paper-based; 173 computer-based; 61 iBT).

University of Missouri–Kansas City, School of Computing and Engineering, Kansas City, MO 64110-2499. Offers civil engineering (MS); computer and electrical engineering (PhD); computer science (MS), including bioinformatics, software engineering, telecommunications networking; computer science and informatics (PhD); computing (PhD); electrical engineering (MS); engineering (PhD); mechanical engineering (MS); telecommunications (PhD). PhD (interdisciplinary) offered through the School of Graduate Studies. Part-time programs available. *Faculty:* 36 full-time (5 women), 21 part-time/adjunct (0 women). *Students:* 160 full-time (32 women), 194 part-time (41 women); includes 21 minority (5 Black or African American, non-Hispanic/Latino; 9 Asian, non-Hispanic/Latino; 6 Hispanic/Latino; 1 Two or more races, non-Hispanic/Latino), 273 international. Average age 25. 440 applicants, 55% accepted, 104 enrolled. In 2010, 135 master's awarded. *Degree requirements:* For doctorate, thesis/dissertation. *Entrance requirements:* For master's, GRE General Test, minimum GPA of 3.0, 3 letters of recommendation from professors; for doctorate, GRE General Test, minimum GPA of 3.5. Additional exam requirements/recommendations for international students: Required—TOEFL (minimum score 550 paper-based; 213 computer-based; 80 iBT). *Application deadline:* For fall admission, 1/15 priority date for domestic students, 1/15 for international students. Applications are processed on a rolling basis. Application fee: $45 ($50 for international students). *Expenses:* Tuition, state resident: full-time $5522.40; part-time $306.80 per credit hour. Tuition, nonresident: full-time $7128; part-time $792 per credit hour. Required fees: $261.15 per term. *Financial support:* In 2010–11, 35 research assistantships with partial tuition reimbursements (averaging $14,340 per year), 20 teaching assistantships with partial tuition reimbursements (averaging $13,351 per year) were awarded; career-related internships or fieldwork, Federal Work-Study, scholarships/grants, tuition waivers (partial), and unspecified assistantships also available. Support available to part-time students. Financial award application deadline: 3/1; financial award applicants required to submit FAFSA. *Faculty research:* Algorithms, bioinformatics and medical informatics, biomechanics/biomaterials, civil engineering materials, networking and telecommunications, thermal science. Total annual research expenditures: $1.1 million. *Unit head:* Dr. Kevin Z. Truman, Dean, 816-235-2399, Fax: 816-235-5159. *Application contact:* Dr. Kevin Z. Truman, Dean, 816-235-2399, Fax: 816-235-5159.

University of Nebraska–Lincoln, Graduate College, College of Engineering, Department of Mechanical Engineering, Lincoln, NE 68588. Offers chemical and materials engineering (PhD); mechanical engineering (MS, PhD), including materials science engineering (MS), metallurgical engineering (MS). *Degree requirements:* For master's, thesis optional; for doctorate, comprehensive exam, thesis/dissertation. *Entrance requirements:* For master's and doctorate, GRE General Test. Additional exam requirements/recommendations for international students: Required—TOEFL (minimum score 550 paper-based; 213 computer-based). Electronic applications accepted. *Faculty research:* Robotics for planetary exploration, vehicle crashworthiness, transient heat conduction, laser beam/particle interactions.

See Display on next page and Close-Up on page 557.

University of Nevada, Las Vegas, Graduate College, Howard R. Hughes College of Engineering, Department of Mechanical Engineering, Las Vegas, NV 89154-4027. Offers aerospace engineering (MS); biomedical engineering (MS); materials and nuclear engineering (MS); mechanical engineering (MSE, PhD). Part-time programs available. *Faculty:* 17 full-time (0 women), 10 part-time/adjunct (0 women). *Students:* 43 full-time (6 women), 24 part-time (6 women); includes 24 minority (1 Black or African American, non-Hispanic/Latino; 4 Asian, non-Hispanic/Latino; 1 Hispanic/Latino; 1 Native Hawaiian or other Pacific Islander, non-Hispanic/Latino; 17 Two or more races, non-Hispanic/Latino), 24 international. Average age 30. 32 applicants, 84% accepted, 15 enrolled. In 2010, 10 master's, 4 doctorates awarded. *Degree requirements:* For master's, comprehensive exam, thesis (for some programs), project; for doctorate, comprehensive exam, thesis/dissertation. *Entrance requirements:* For master's and doctorate, GRE General Test. Additional exam requirements/recommendations for international students: Required—TOEFL (minimum score 550 paper-based; 213 computer-based; 80 iBT), IELTS (minimum score 7). *Application deadline:* For fall admission, 5/1 priority date for domestic and international students; for spring admission, 10/1 priority date for domestic and international students. Applications are processed on a rolling basis. Application fee: $60 ($95 for international students). Electronic applications accepted. *Expenses:* Tuition, area resident: Part-time $239.50 per credit. Tuition, state resident: part-time $239.50 per credit. Tuition, nonresident: part-time $503 per credit. Required fees: $108 per semester. Tuition and fees vary according to course load, program and reciprocity agreements. *Financial support:* In 2010–11, 37 students received support, including 21 research assistantships with partial tuition reimbursements available (averaging $13,335 per year), 16 teaching assistantships with partial tuition reimbursements available (averaging $11,000 per year); institutionally sponsored loans, scholarships/grants, health care benefits, and unspecified assistantships also available. Financial award application deadline: 3/1. *Faculty research:* Dynamics and control systems; energy systems including renewable and nuclear; computational fluid and solid mechanics; structures, materials and manufacturing; vibrations and acoustics. Total annual research expenditures: $3 million. *Unit head:* Dr. Woosoon Yim, Chair/Professor, 702-895-0956, Fax: 702-895-3936, E-mail: wy@me.unlv.edu. *Application contact:* Graduate College Admissions Evaluator, 702-895-3320, Fax: 702-895-4180, E-mail: gradcollege@unlv.edu.

University of Nevada, Reno, Graduate School, College of Engineering, Department of Mechanical Engineering, Reno, NV 89557. Offers MS, PhD. Terminal master's awarded for partial completion of doctoral program. *Degree requirements:* For master's, thesis optional; for doctorate, thesis/dissertation. *Entrance requirements:* For master's, GRE General Test, minimum

UNIVERSITY OF NEBRASKA-LINCOLN
DEPARTMENT OF MECHANICAL & MATERIALS ENGINEERING

In 2011, the UNL Department of Mechanical Engineering and Department of Engineering Mechanics merged. We offer graduate programs leading to M.S. and Ph.D. degrees and faculty expertise in all areas of mechanical engineering and applied mechanics, including biomedical engineering, energy, materials, and micro/nanotechnology.

OUR GRADUATE STUDENTS:

- Approximately 83 full-time graduate students
- Diverse student population: 60% percent are international
- More than 65% percent supported by research assistantships, teaching assistantships & fellowships

W342 NH • P.O. Box 880526 • Lincoln, NE 68588-0526
www.engineering.unl.edu • www.mme.unl.edu
(402) 472-2375

Nebraska Engineering

UNIVERSITY OF Nebraska Lincoln

The University of Nebraska-Lincoln is an equal opportunity educator and employer.

GPA of 2.75; for doctorate, GRE General Test, minimum GPA of 3.0. Additional exam requirements/recommendations for international students: Required—TOEFL (minimum score 500 paper-based; 173 computer-based; 61 iBT), IELTS (minimum score 6). Electronic applications accepted. *Expenses:* Tuition, state resident: full-time $2219; part-time $246 per credit. Tuition, nonresident: part-time $510 per credit. International tuition: $9009 full-time. Required fees: $59 per term. One-time fee: $101. Tuition and fees vary according to course load. *Faculty research:* Composite, solid, fluid, thermal, and smart materials.

University of New Brunswick Fredericton, School of Graduate Studies, Faculty of Engineering, Department of Mechanical Engineering, Fredericton, NB E3B 5A3, Canada. Offers applied mechanics (M Eng, M Sc E, PhD); mechanical engineering (M Eng, M Sc E, PhD). Part-time programs available. *Faculty:* 14 full-time (1 woman), 2 part-time/adjunct (0 women). *Students:* 44 full-time (6 women), 4 part-time (0 women). In 2010, 10 master's, 2 doctorates awarded. *Degree requirements:* For master's, thesis; for doctorate, comprehensive exam, thesis/dissertation, qualifying exam. *Entrance requirements:* For master's, minimum GPA of 3.0; B Sc E; for doctorate, minimum GPA of 3.0; M Sc E. Additional exam requirements/recommendations for international students: Required—TOEFL (minimum score 550 paper-based), IELTS, TWE (minimum score 4). *Application deadline:* For fall admission, 3/1 priority date for domestic students. Applications are processed on a rolling basis. Application fee: $50 Canadian dollars. *Expenses:* Tuition, area resident: Full-time $3708; part-time $927 per term. International tuition: $6300 full-time. Required fees: $50 per term. *Financial support:* In 2010–11, 61 research assistantships, 51 teaching assistantships were awarded. *Faculty research:* Analysis of gross motor activities as a means of assessing upper limb prosthesis, distance determination algorithms and their applications, void nucleation in automotive aluminum alloy, robot kinematics, micromechanics, analysis of human walking, plastic linjection molding, green nanotechnology, mechatronics, fatigue assessment of structures, ocean renewable energy. *Unit head:* Dr. Zengtao Chen, Director of Graduate Studies, 506-458-7784, Fax: 506-453-5025, E-mail: ztchen@unb.ca. *Application contact:* Susan Shea-Perrott, Graduate Secretary, 506-458-7742, Fax: 506-453-5025, E-mail: susan@unb.ca.

University of New Hampshire, Graduate School, College of Engineering and Physical Sciences, Department of Mechanical Engineering, Durham, NH 03824. Offers mechanical engineering (MS, PhD); systems design (PhD). Part-time programs available. *Faculty:* 14 full-time (1 woman). *Students:* 18 full-time (2 women), 34 part-time (4 women); includes 1 minority (Two or more races, non-Hispanic/Latino), 12 international. Average age 29. 45 applicants, 69% accepted, 13 enrolled. In 2010, 11 master's, 1 doctorate awarded. *Degree requirements:* For master's, thesis or alternative; for doctorate, thesis/dissertation. *Entrance requirements:* For master's and doctorate, GRE. Additional exam requirements/recommendations for international students: Required—TOEFL (minimum score 550 paper-based; 213 computer-based; 80 iBT). *Application deadline:* For fall admission, 4/1 priority date for domestic students, 4/1 for international students; for spring admission, 12/1 for domestic students. Applications are processed on a rolling basis. Application fee: $65. Electronic applications accepted. *Financial support:* In 2010–11, 32 students received support, including 1 fellowship, 14 research assistantships, 15 teaching assistantships; Federal Work-Study, scholarships/grants, and tuition waivers (full and partial) also available. Support available to part-time students. Financial award application deadline: 2/15. *Faculty research:* Solid mechanics, dynamics, materials science, dynamic systems, automatic control. *Unit head:* Dr. Todd Gross, Chairperson, 603-862-2445. *Application contact:* Tracey Harvey, Administrative Assistant, 603-862-1353, E-mail: mechanical.engineering@unh.edu.

University of New Haven, Graduate School, Tagliatela College of Engineering, Program in Mechanical Engineering, West Haven, CT 06516-1916. Offers MS. Part-time and evening/weekend programs available. *Degree requirements:* For master's, thesis. *Entrance requirements:* Additional exam requirements/recommendations for international students: Required—TOEFL (minimum score 520 paper-based; 190 computer-based; 70 iBT); Recommended—IELTS (minimum score 5.5). *Application deadline:* For fall admission, 5/31 for international students; for winter admission, 10/15 for international students; for spring admission, 1/15 for international students. Applications are processed on a rolling basis. Application fee: $50. Electronic applications accepted. *Financial support:* Research assistantships with partial tuition reimbursements, teaching assistantships with partial tuition reimbursements, career-related internships or fieldwork, Federal Work-Study, scholarships/grants, tuition waivers, and unspecified assistantships available. Support available to part-time students. Financial award applicants required to submit FAFSA. *Unit head:* Dr. Stephen Ross, Coordinator, 203-932-7408. *Application contact:* Eloise Gormley, Director of Graduate Admissions, 203-932-7449, Fax: 203-932-7137, E-mail: gradinfo@newhaven.edu.

University of New Mexico, Graduate School, School of Engineering, Department of Mechanical Engineering, Albuquerque, NM 87131-2039. Offers MS, PhD. Part-time programs available. *Faculty:* 19 full-time (3 women), 6 part-time/adjunct (0 women). *Students:* 47 full-time (5 women), 29 part-time (3 women); includes 3 Asian, non-Hispanic/Latino; 22 Hispanic/Latino, 7 international. Average age 29. 52 applicants, 29% accepted, 14 enrolled. In 2010, 11 master's awarded. Terminal master's awarded for partial completion of doctoral program. *Degree requirements:* For master's, thesis optional; for doctorate, comprehensive exam, thesis/dissertation. *Entrance requirements:* For master's and doctorate, GRE. Additional exam requirements/recommendations for international students: Required—TOEFL (minimum score 550 paper-based; 210 computer-based; 80 iBT). *Application deadline:* For fall admission, 7/30 for domestic students, 3/1 for international students; for spring admission, 11/30 for domestic students, 8/1 for international students. Applications are processed on a rolling basis. Application fee: $50. Electronic applications accepted. *Expenses:* Tuition, state resident: full-time $5991; part-time $251 per credit hour. Tuition, nonresident: full-time $14,405; part-time $800.20 per credit hour. Tuition and fees vary according to course level, course load, program and reciprocity agreements. *Financial support:* In 2010–11, 49 students received support, including 1 fellowship (averaging $10,000 per year), 33 research assistantships with full and partial tuition reimbursements available (averaging $15,740 per year), 13 teaching assistantships with full and partial tuition reimbursements available (averaging $7,066 per year); scholarships/grants, health care benefits, and unspecified assistantships also available. Financial award application deadline: 3/1; financial award applicants required to submit FAFSA. *Faculty research:* Engineering mechanics and materials (including solid mechanics and materials science), mechanical sciences and engineering (including dynamic systems, controls and robotics), thermal sciences and engineering. Total annual research expenditures: $811,981. *Unit head:* Dr. Yu-Lin Shen, Chairperson, 505-277-6286, Fax: 505-277-1571, E-mail: shenyl@unm.edu. *Application contact:* Dr. Nader D. Ebrahimi, Director of Graduate Programs, 505-277-2761, Fax: 505-277-1571, E-mail: ebrahimi@unm.edu.

University of New Orleans, Graduate School, College of Engineering, Concentration in Mechanical Engineering, New Orleans, LA 70148. Offers MS. *Degree requirements:* For master's, thesis optional. *Entrance requirements:* For master's, GRE General Test, minimum GPA of 3.0. Additional exam requirements/recommendations for international students: Required—TOEFL (minimum score 550 paper-based; 213 computer-based; 79 iBT). Electronic applications accepted. *Faculty research:* Two-phase flow instabilities, thermal-hydrodynamic modeling, solar energy, heat transfer from sprays, boundary integral techniques in mechanics.

The University of North Carolina at Charlotte, Graduate School, The William States Lee College of Engineering, Department of Mechanical Engineering and Engineering Science, Charlotte, NC 28223-0001. Offers engineering (MS); mechanical engineering (MSE, MSME, PhD). Evening/weekend programs available. *Faculty:* 36 full-time (5 women), 1 (woman) part-time/adjunct. *Students:* 70 full-time (11 women), 69 part-time (12 women); includes 17 minority (10 Black or African American, non-Hispanic/Latino; 5 Asian, non-Hispanic/Latino; 1 Hispanic/Latino; 1 Two or more races, non-Hispanic/Latino), 63 international. Average age 28. 116 applicants, 73% accepted, 25 enrolled. In 2010, 32 master's, 6 doctorates awarded. *Degree requirements:* For master's, thesis; for doctorate, thesis/dissertation. *Entrance requirements:* For master's, GRE General Test, minimum GPA of 3.0 in undergraduate major, 2.75 overall; for doctorate, GRE General Test, 3 letters of reference from faculty or professionals.

Mechanical Engineering

The University of North Carolina at Charlotte (continued)

Additional exam requirements/recommendations for international students: Required—TOEFL (minimum score 557 paper-based; 220 computer-based; 83 iBT). *Application deadline:* For fall admission, 7/1 for domestic students, 5/1 for international students; for spring admission, 11/1 for domestic students, 10/1 for international students. Applications are processed on a rolling basis. Application fee: $55. Electronic applications accepted. *Expenses:* Tuition, state resident: full-time $3464. Tuition, nonresident: full-time $14,297. Required fees: $2094. Tuition and fees vary according to course load. *Financial support:* In 2010–11, 67 students received support, including 1 fellowship (averaging $38,750 per year), 30 research assistantships (averaging $9,468 per year), 36 teaching assistantships (averaging $9,757 per year); career-related internships or fieldwork, Federal Work-Study, institutionally sponsored loans, scholarships/grants, and unspecified assistantships also available. Support available to part-time students. Financial award application deadline: 4/1; financial award applicants required to submit FAFSA. *Faculty research:* Precision metrology, bioengineering/cell preservation, computational mechanics/computational modeling, materials processing, precision design. Total annual research expenditures: $2.8 million. *Unit head:* Dr. Scott Smith, Chair, 704-687-8350, Fax: 704-687-8345, E-mail: kssmith@uncc.edu. *Application contact:* Kathy B. Giddings, Director of Graduate Admissions, 704-687-5503, Fax: 704-687-3279, E-mail: gradadm@uncc.edu.

University of North Dakota, Graduate School, School of Engineering and Mines, Department of Mechanical Engineering, Grand Forks, ND 58202. Offers M Engr, MS. Part-time programs available. *Faculty:* 8 full-time (0 women), 3 part-time/adjunct (0 women). *Students:* 12 full-time (1 woman), 17 part-time (1 woman); includes 2 minority (both Asian, non-Hispanic/Latino), 7 international. Average age 26. 33 applicants, 48% accepted, 11 enrolled. In 2010, 5 master's awarded. *Degree requirements:* For master's, comprehensive exam, thesis or alternative. *Entrance requirements:* For master's, GRE General Test, minimum GPA of 3.0 (MS), 2.5 (M Engr). Additional exam requirements/recommendations for international students: Required—TOEFL (minimum score 550 paper-based; 213 computer-based; 79 iBT), IELTS (minimum score 6.5). *Application deadline:* For fall admission, 2/1 priority date for domestic and international students; for spring admission, 10/1 priority date for domestic and international students. Applications are processed on a rolling basis. Application fee: $35. Electronic applications accepted. *Expenses:* Tuition, state resident: full-time $5857; part-time $306.74 per credit. Tuition, nonresident: full-time $15,666; part-time $729.77 per credit. Required fees: $53.42 per credit. Tuition and fees vary according to course load, program and reciprocity agreements. *Financial support:* In 2010–11, 21 students received support, including 13 research assistantships with full and partial tuition reimbursements available (averaging $8,500 per year), 8 teaching assistantships with full and partial tuition reimbursements available (averaging $6,941 per year); fellowships with full and partial tuition reimbursements available, career-related internships or fieldwork, Federal Work-Study, institutionally sponsored loans, scholarships/grants, health care benefits, tuition waivers (full and partial), and unspecified assistantships also available. Support available to part-time students. Financial award application deadline: 3/15; financial award applicants required to submit FAFSA. *Faculty research:* Energy conversion, dynamics, control, manufacturing processes with special emphasis on machining, stress vibration analysis. Total annual research expenditures: $503,152. *Unit head:* Dr. Mathew Cavalli, Director, 701-777-2571, Fax: 701-777-4838, E-mail: mathew.cavalli@mail.und.edu. *Application contact:* Staci Wells, Admissions Associate, 701-777-2945, Fax: 701-777-3619, E-mail: staci.wells@gradschool.und.edu.

University of North Florida, College of Computing, Engineering, and Construction, School of Engineering, Jacksonville, FL 32224. Offers MSCE, MSEE, MSME. Part-time programs available. *Faculty:* 15 full-time (2 women). *Students:* 5 full-time (2 women), 41 part-time (5 women); includes 2 Black or African American, non-Hispanic/Latino; 1 Asian, non-Hispanic/Latino; 4 Hispanic/Latino; 1 Two or more races, non-Hispanic/Latino, 6 international. Average age 29. 45 applicants, 40% accepted, 13 enrolled. In 2010, 3 master's awarded. *Application deadline:* For fall admission, 7/1 for domestic students, 5/1 for international students; for spring admission, 11/1 for domestic students, 10/1 for international students. Application fee: $30. *Expenses:* Tuition, state resident: full-time $7646.40; part-time $318.60 per credit hour. Tuition, nonresident: full-time $23,502; part-time $979.24 per credit hour. Required fees: $1208.88; $50.37 per credit hour. Tuition and fees vary according to course load and program. *Financial support:* In 2010–11, 16 students received support, including research assistantships (averaging $2,669 per year), teaching assistantships (averaging $451 per year); Federal Work-Study, scholarships/grants, tuition waivers, and unspecified assistantships also available. Financial award application deadline: 4/1; financial award applicants required to submit FAFSA. Total annual research expenditures: $2.9 million. *Unit head:* Gerald Merckel, Associate Dean, 904-620-1390, E-mail: gmerckel@unf.edu. *Application contact:* Lillith Richardson, Assistant Director, The Graduate School, 904-320-1360, Fax: 904-620-1362, E-mail: graduateschool@unf.edu.

University of Notre Dame, Graduate School, College of Engineering, Department of Aerospace and Mechanical Engineering, Notre Dame, IN 46556. Offers aerospace and mechanical engineering (M Eng, PhD); aerospace engineering (MS Aero E); mechanical engineering (MEME, MSME). Terminal master's awarded for partial completion of doctoral program. *Degree requirements:* For master's, comprehensive exam, thesis or alternative; for doctorate, thesis/dissertation, candidacy exam. *Entrance requirements:* For master's and doctorate, GRE General Test. Additional exam requirements/recommendations for international students: Required—TOEFL (minimum score 600 paper-based; 250 computer-based; 80 iBT). Electronic applications accepted. *Faculty research:* Aerodynamics/fluid dynamics, design and manufacturing, controls/robotics, solid mechanics or biomechanics/biomaterials.

University of Oklahoma, College of Engineering, School of Aerospace and Mechanical Engineering, Program in Mechanical Engineering, Norman, OK 73019. Offers mechanical engineering (MS, PhD), including combustion, controls, fluid mechanics, general, heat transfer, solid mechanics. Part-time programs available. *Students:* 38 full-time (0 women), 18 part-time (2 women); includes 6 minority (1 Black or African American, non-Hispanic/Latino; 2 American Indian or Alaska Native, non-Hispanic/Latino; 3 Asian, non-Hispanic/Latino), 28 international. Average age 28. 39 applicants, 31% accepted, 8 enrolled. In 2010, 20 master's, 7 doctorates awarded. *Degree requirements:* For master's, comprehensive exam, thesis or alternative; for doctorate, comprehensive exam, thesis/dissertation optional, combined general and qualifying exam. *Entrance requirements:* For master's, GRE General Test, BS in engineering or physical sciences; for doctorate, GRE General Test, MS in mechanical engineering or equivalent. Additional exam requirements/recommendations for international students: Required—TOEFL (minimum score 600 paper-based; 250 computer-based; 100 iBT). *Application deadline:* For fall admission, 6/1 priority date for domestic students, 4/1 for international students; for spring admission, 11/1 for domestic students, 9/1 for international students. Applications are processed on a rolling basis. Application fee: $40 ($90 for international students). Electronic applications accepted. *Expenses:* Tuition, state resident: full-time $3892.80; part-time $162.20 per credit hour. Tuition, nonresident: full-time $14,167; part-time $590.30 per credit hour. Required fees: $2523.40; $94.60 per credit hour. Tuition and fees vary according to course load and degree level. *Financial support:* In 2010–11, 50 students received support. Unspecified assistantships available. Financial award application deadline: 3/1; financial award applicants required to submit FAFSA. *Faculty research:* Dynamics; controls and robotics; materials, design and manufacturing; structures; thermal-fluid systems. *Unit head:* Farrokh Mistree, Director, 405-325-5011, Fax: 405-325-1088, E-mail: farrokh.mistree@ou.edu. *Application contact:* Dr. David P. Miller, Graduate Liaison, 405-325-1094, Fax: 405-325-1088, E-mail: dpmiller@ou.edu.

University of Ottawa, Faculty of Graduate and Postdoctoral Studies, Faculty of Engineering, Ottawa-Carleton Institute for Mechanical and Aerospace Engineering, Ottawa, ON K1N 6N5, Canada. Offers M Eng, MA Sc, PhD. MA Sc, M Eng, PhD offered jointly with Carleton University. *Degree requirements:* For master's, thesis or alternative; for doctorate, thesis/dissertation, seminar series, qualifying exam. *Entrance requirements:* For master's, honors degree or equivalent, minimum B average; for doctorate, master's degree, minimum B+ average. Electronic applications accepted. *Faculty research:* Fluid mechanics-heat transfer, solid mechanics, design, manufacturing and control.

University of Pennsylvania, School of Engineering and Applied Science, Department of Mechanical Engineering and Applied Mechanics, Philadelphia, PA 19104. Offers applied mechanics (MSE, PhD); mechanical engineering (MSE, PhD). Part-time programs available. *Faculty:* 20 full-time (3 women), 9 part-time/adjunct (0 women). *Students:* 92 full-time (14 women), 20 part-time (4 women); includes 5 Black or African American, non-Hispanic/Latino; 8 Asian, non-Hispanic/Latino; 2 Hispanic/Latino, 41 international. 439 applicants, 37% accepted, 70 enrolled. In 2010, 46 master's, 6 doctorates awarded. *Degree requirements:* For master's, thesis optional; for doctorate, thesis/dissertation. *Entrance requirements:* Additional exam requirements/recommendations for international students: Required—TOEFL. *Application deadline:* For fall admission, 1/2 priority date for domestic students. Applications are processed on a rolling basis. Application fee: $70. Electronic applications accepted. *Expenses:* Tuition: Full-time $25,660; part-time $4758 per course. Required fees: $2152; $270 per course. Tuition and fees vary according to course load, degree level and program. *Financial support:* Fellowships, research assistantships, teaching assistantships, institutionally sponsored loans, scholarships/grants, traineeships, health care benefits, and unspecified assistantships available. *Faculty research:* Heat transfer, fluid mechanics, energy conversion, solid mechanics, dynamics of mechanisms and robots.

University of Pittsburgh, School of Engineering, Department of Mechanical Engineering and Materials Science, Pittsburgh, PA 15260. Offers MSME, PhD. Part-time programs available. Postbaccalaureate distance learning degree programs offered. *Faculty:* 27 full-time (4 women), 30 part-time/adjunct (4 women). *Students:* 91 full-time (14 women), 104 part-time (16 women); includes 9 minority (5 Black or African American, non-Hispanic/Latino; 2 Asian, non-Hispanic/Latino; 2 Hispanic/Latino), 55 international. 394 applicants, 31% accepted, 55 enrolled. In 2010, 36 master's, 12 doctorates awarded. Terminal master's awarded for partial completion of doctoral program. *Degree requirements:* For master's, thesis optional; for doctorate, comprehensive exam, thesis/dissertation, final oral exams. *Entrance requirements:* For master's and doctorate, minimum QPA of 3.0. Additional exam requirements/recommendations for international students: Required—TOEFL (minimum score 550 paper-based; 230 computer-based). *Application deadline:* For fall admission, 3/1 priority date for domestic students; for spring admission, 7/1 priority date for domestic students. Applications are processed on a rolling basis. Application fee: $50. Electronic applications accepted. *Expenses:* Tuition, state resident: full-time $17,304; part-time $701 per credit. Tuition, nonresident: full-time $29,554; part-time $1210 per credit. Required fees: $740; $214 per term. Tuition and fees vary according to program. *Financial support:* In 2010–11, 75 students received support, including 11 fellowships with full tuition reimbursements available (averaging $26,000 per year), 49 research assistantships with full tuition reimbursements available (averaging $25,000 per year), 27 teaching assistantships with full tuition reimbursements available (averaging $24,000 per year); scholarships/grants and tuition waivers (full and partial) also available. Financial award application deadline: 4/15. *Faculty research:* Smart materials and structure solid mechanics, computational fluid dynamics, multiphase bio-fluid dynamics, mechanical vibration analysis. Total annual research expenditures: $6.7 million. *Unit head:* Dr. Minking K. Chyu, Chairman, 412-624-9784, Fax: 412-624-4846. *Application contact:* Dr. Patrick Smelinski, Graduate Coordinator, 412-624-9788, Fax: 412-624-4846, E-mail: pat.smel@pitt.edu.

University of Puerto Rico, Mayagüez Campus, Graduate Studies, College of Engineering, Department of Mechanical Engineering, Mayagüez, PR 00681-9000. Offers ME, MS. Part-time programs available. *Students:* 57 full-time (12 women), 15 part-time (1 woman); includes 53 Hispanic/Latino, 18 international. 22 applicants, 86% accepted, 5 enrolled. In 2010, 8 master's awarded. *Degree requirements:* For master's, comprehensive exam, thesis. *Entrance requirements:* For master's, BS in mechanical engineering or the equivalent; minimum GPA of 2.75, 3.0 in field of specialty. Additional exam requirements/recommendations for international students: Required—TOEFL. *Application deadline:* For fall admission, 2/15 for domestic and international students; for spring admission, 9/15 for domestic and international students. Applications are processed on a rolling basis. Application fee: $25. *Expenses:* Tuition, state resident: full-time $1188. Tuition, nonresident: full-time $1188. International tuition: $6126 full-time. Tuition and fees vary according to course level and course load. *Financial support:* In 2010–11, 28 students received support, including fellowships (averaging $12,000 per year), 26 research assistantships (averaging $15,000 per year), 28 teaching assistantships (averaging $8,500 per year); Federal Work-Study and institutionally sponsored loans also available. *Faculty research:* Metallurgy, hybrid vehicles, manufacturing, thermal and fluid sciences, HVAC. Total annual research expenditures: $1.2 million. *Unit head:* Dr. Gustavo Gutierrez, Director, 787-832-4040 Ext. 2496, Fax: 787-265-3817, E-mail: ggutierr@me.uprm.edu. *Application contact:* Yolanda Perez, Graduate Program Secretary, 787-832-4040 Ext. 3659, Fax: 787-265-3817, E-mail: yolanda.perez4@upr.edu.

University of Rochester, Hajim School of Engineering and Applied Sciences, Department of Mechanical Engineering, Rochester, NY 14627. Offers mechanical engineering (MS, PhD). Part-time programs available. Terminal master's awarded for partial completion of doctoral program. *Degree requirements:* For master's, comprehensive exam, thesis optional; for doctorate, thesis/dissertation, preliminary and qualifying exams. *Entrance requirements:* For master's and doctorate, GRE. Additional exam requirements/recommendations for international students: Required—TOEFL.

University of St. Thomas, Graduate Studies, School of Engineering, St. Paul, MN 55105-1096. Offers manufacturing engineering and operations (MS); mechanical engineering (MS); medical device development (Certificate); regulatory science (MS); software engineering (MS); software management (MS); software systems (MSS); systems engineering (MS); technology management (MS). *Accreditation:* ABET (one or more programs are accredited). *Entrance requirements:* For master's, resume, official transcripts. Additional exam requirements/recommendations for international students: Required—TOEFL (minimum score 550 paper-based). *Application deadline:* For fall admission, 8/1 priority date for domestic students; for spring admission, 1/1 priority date for domestic students. Applications are processed on a rolling basis. Application fee: $30. Electronic applications accepted. *Expenses:* Contact institution. *Financial support:* Fellowships, research assistantships, institutionally sponsored loans and scholarships/grants available. Support available to part-time students. Financial award application deadline: 4/1; financial award applicants required to submit FAFSA. *Unit head:* Don Weinkauf, Dean, 651-962-5760, Fax: 651-962-6419, E-mail: dhweinkauf@stthomas.edu. *Application contact:* Joyce A. Taylor, Graduate Programs Coordinator, 651-962-5756, Fax: 651-962-6419, E-mail: jatayIor1@stthomas.edu.

University of Saskatchewan, College of Graduate Studies and Research, College of Engineering, Department of Mechanical Engineering, Saskatoon, SK S7N 5A2, Canada. Offers M Sc, PhD. *Degree requirements:* For master's, thesis (for some programs); for doctorate, thesis/dissertation. *Entrance requirements:* For master's and doctorate, GRE. Additional exam requirements/recommendations for international students: Required—TOEFL.

University of South Alabama, Graduate School, College of Engineering, Department of Mechanical Engineering, Mobile, AL 36688-0002. Offers MSME. *Faculty:* 7 full-time (2 women). *Students:* 12 full-time (1 woman), 9 part-time (1 woman); includes 3 minority (1 Asian, non-Hispanic/Latino; 2 Hispanic/Latino), 7 international. 33 applicants, 33% accepted, 5 enrolled. In 2010, 5 master's awarded. *Degree requirements:* For master's, project or thesis. *Entrance requirements:* For master's, GRE General Test, BS in engineering, minimum GPA of 3.0. *Application deadline:* For fall admission, 7/15 priority date for domestic students, 6/15 priority date for international students; for spring admission, 12/1 priority date for domestic students, 11/1 priority date for international students. Applications are processed on a rolling basis. Application fee: $35. *Expenses:* Tuition, state resident: part-time $300 per credit hour. Tuition, nonresident: part-time $600 per credit hour. Required fees: $150 per semester. *Financial support:* Research assistantships, career-related internships or fieldwork and institutionally sponsored loans available. Support available to part-time students. Financial award application deadline: 4/1. *Unit head:* Dr. David Nelson, Chair, 251-460-6168. *Application contact:* Dr. David Nelson, Chair, 251-460-6168.

University of South Carolina, The Graduate School, College of Engineering and Computing, Department of Mechanical Engineering, Columbia, SC 29208. Offers ME, MS, PhD. Part-time and evening/weekend programs available. Postbaccalaureate distance learning degree programs offered. *Degree requirements:* For master's, thesis (for some programs); for doctorate, thesis/dissertation. *Entrance requirements:* For master's and doctorate, GRE General Test. Additional exam requirements/recommendations for international students: Required—TOEFL (minimum score 600 paper-based; 250 computer-based). Electronic applications accepted. *Faculty research:* Heat exchangers, computer vision measurements in solid mechanics and bio-mechanics, robot dynamics and control.

University of Southern California, Graduate School, Viterbi School of Engineering, Department of Aerospace and Mechanical Engineering, Los Angeles, CA 90089. Offers aerospace and mechanical engineering: computational fluid and solid mechanics (MS); aerospace and mechanical engineering: dynamics and control (MS); aerospace engineering (MS, PhD, Engr), including aerospace engineering (PhD, Engr); green technologies (MS); mechanical engineering (MS, PhD, Engr), including mechanical engineering (PhD, Engr); product development engineering (MS). Part-time and evening/weekend programs available. Postbaccalaureate distance learning degree programs offered (no on-campus study). *Faculty:* 22 full-time (3 women), 19 part-time/adjunct (2 women). *Students:* 238 full-time (33 women), 214 part-time (30 women); includes 115 minority (10 Black or African American, non-Hispanic/Latino; 67 Asian, non-Hispanic/Latino; 32 Hispanic/Latino; 6 Two or more races, non-Hispanic/Latino), 151 international. 691 applicants, 43% accepted, 124 enrolled. In 2010, 107 master's, 11 doctorates, 1 other advanced degree awarded. Terminal master's awarded for partial completion of doctoral program. *Degree requirements:* For master's, thesis optional; for doctorate, thesis/dissertation. *Entrance requirements:* For master's, doctorate, and Engr, GRE General Test. *Application deadline:* For fall admission, 12/1 priority date for domestic and international students; for winter admission, 9/15 priority date for domestic and international students; for spring admission, 9/15 priority date for domestic and international students. Applications are processed on a rolling basis. Application fee: $85. Electronic applications accepted. *Expenses:* Tuition: Full-time $31,240; part-time $1420 per unit. Required fees: $600. One-time fee: $35 full-time. Full-time tuition and fees vary according to degree level and program. *Financial support:* In 2010–11, fellowships with full tuition reimbursements (averaging $30,000 per year), research assistantships with full tuition reimbursements (averaging $20,000 per year), teaching assistantships with full tuition reimbursements (averaging $20,000 per year) were awarded; career-related internships or fieldwork, scholarships/grants, health care benefits, and unspecified assistantships also available. Financial award application deadline: 12/1; financial award applicants required to submit CSS PROFILE or FAFSA. *Faculty research:* Mechanics and materials, aerodynamics of air/ground vehicles, gas dynamics, aerosols, astronautics and space science, geophysical and microgravity flows, planetary physics, power MEMs and MEMS vacuum pumps, heat transfer and combustion. Total annual research expenditures: $5 million. *Unit head:* Dr. Geoffrey Spedding, Chair, 213-740-5324, E-mail: ame@usc.edu. *Application contact:* Samantha Graves, Student Service Advisor, 213-740-1735, E-mail: smgraves@usc.edu.

University of South Florida, Graduate School, College of Engineering, Department of Mechanical Engineering, Tampa, FL 33620-9951. Offers ME, MME, MSES, MSME, PhD. Part-time programs available. *Faculty:* 13 full-time (1 woman). *Students:* 67 full-time (10 women), 22 part-time (2 women); includes 3 Black or African American, non-Hispanic/Latino; 8 Asian, non-Hispanic/Latino; 7 Hispanic/Latino; 1 Two or more races, non-Hispanic/Latino, 32 international. Average age 28. 101 applicants, 67% accepted, 33 enrolled. In 2010, 18 master's, 1 doctorate awarded. Terminal master's awarded for partial completion of doctoral program. *Degree requirements:* For master's, comprehensive exam, thesis or alternative; for doctorate, comprehensive exam, thesis/dissertation, 2 tools of research as specified by dissertation committee. *Entrance requirements:* For master's, GRE General Test (minimum score 1100 verbal and quantitative), minimum GPA of 3.0 in last 60 hours of coursework, BSME or equivalent; for doctorate, GRE General Test (minimum score: 1100 Verbal and Quantitative), BSME, MSME or equivalent. Additional exam requirements/recommendations for international students: Required—TOEFL (minimum score 550 paper-based; 213 computer-based). *Application deadline:* For fall admission, 2/15 for domestic students, 1/2 for international students; for spring admission, 10/15 for domestic students, 6/1 for international students. Application fee: $30. Electronic applications accepted. *Financial support:* In 2010–11, 33 research assistantships with tuition reimbursements (averaging $13,073 per year), 26 teaching assistantships with partial tuition reimbursements (averaging $14,890 per year) were awarded. Financial award applicants required to submit FAFSA. *Faculty research:* Robot sensors, rehabilitation engineering, mechatronics, vibrations, composites. Total annual research expenditures: $2.7 million. *Application contact:* Muhammad Rahman, Director, 813-974-5625, Fax: 813-974-3539, E-mail: rahman@eng.usf.edu.

The University of Tennessee, Graduate School, College of Engineering, Department of Mechanical, Aerospace and Biomedical Engineering, Program in Mechanical Engineering, Knoxville, TN 37996. Offers MS, PhD, MS/MBA. Part-time programs available. Postbaccalaureate distance learning degree programs offered (minimal on-campus study). *Faculty:* 14 full-time (0 women), 8 part-time/adjunct (0 women). *Students:* 47 full-time (3 women), 44 part-time (2 women); includes 2 Black or African American, non-Hispanic/Latino; 1 American Indian or Alaska Native, non-Hispanic/Latino; 3 Asian, non-Hispanic/Latino; 1 Hispanic/Latino, 23 international. Average age 30. 112 applicants, 54% accepted, 22 enrolled. In 2010, 15 master's, 3 doctorates awarded. *Degree requirements:* For master's, thesis or alternative; for doctorate, comprehensive exam, thesis/dissertation. *Entrance requirements:* For master's, GRE General Test, Minimum GPA of 2.7 (US degree holders); 3.0 (International degree holders); 3-References; Statement of purpose; for doctorate, GRE General Test, Minimum GPA of 3.0 (previous graduate course work); 3-References; Statement of purpose. Additional exam requirements/recommendations for international students: Required—TOEFL (minimum score 550 paper-based; 213 computer-based). *Application deadline:* For fall admission, 2/1 priority date for domestic and international students; for spring admission, 6/15 for domestic and international students. Applications are processed on a rolling basis. Application fee: $35. Electronic applications accepted. *Expenses:* Tuition, state resident: full-time $7440; part-time $414 per credit hour. Tuition, nonresident: full-time $22,478; part-time $1250 per credit hour. Required fees: $922; $43 per credit hour. Tuition and fees vary according to program. *Financial support:* In 2010–11, 28 students received support, including 3 fellowships with full tuition reimbursements available (averaging $12,000 per year), 27 research assistantships with full tuition reimbursements available (averaging $15,480 per year), 14 teaching assistantships with full tuition reimbursements available (averaging $10,500 per year); career-related internships or fieldwork, Federal Work-Study, institutionally sponsored loans, health care benefits, and unspecified assistantships also available. Financial award application deadline: 2/1; financial award applicants required to submit FAFSA. *Faculty research:* Automotive systems and technology; combustion and emissions; alternative fuels; electromechanical actuators; nanomechanics, nanomaterials, and nanotechnology. *Unit head:* Dr. William Hamel, Head, 865-974-5115, Fax: 865-974-5274, E-mail: whamel@utk.edu. *Application contact:* Dr. Gary V. Smith, Associate Head, 865-974-5271, Fax: 865-974-5274, E-mail: gvsmith@utk.edu.

The University of Tennessee at Chattanooga, Graduate School, College of Engineering and Computer Science, Program in Engineering, Chattanooga, TN 37403. Offers chemical engineering (MS Engr); civil engineering (MS Engr); computational engineering (MS Engr); electrical engineering (MS Engr); industrial engineering (MS Engr); mechanical engineering (MS Engr). Part-time and evening/weekend programs available. *Faculty:* 8 full-time (0 women). *Students:* 27 full-time (5 women), 31 part-time (6 women); includes 12 minority (7 Black or African American, non-Hispanic/Latino; 1 Asian, non-Hispanic/Latino; 4 Hispanic/Latino), 10 international. Average age 29. 43 applicants, 100% accepted, 26 enrolled. In 2010, 16 master's awarded. *Degree requirements:* For master's, comprehensive exam, thesis or alternative, engineering project. *Entrance requirements:* For master's, GRE General Test, minimum undergraduate GPA of 2.5 or 3.0 in last 30 hours of coursework. Additional exam requirements/recommendations for international students: Required—TOEFL (minimum score 550 paper-

based; 213 computer-based; 79 iBT), IELTS (minimum score 6). *Application deadline:* For fall admission, 8/1 priority date for domestic students, 6/1 for international students; for spring admission, 12/1 priority date for domestic students, 10/1 for international students. Applications are processed on a rolling basis. Application fee: $35. Electronic applications accepted. *Financial support:* In 2010–11, 23 research assistantships with full and partial tuition reimbursements (averaging $5,500 per year) were awarded; career-related internships or fieldwork, scholarships/grants, and unspecified assistantships also available. Support available to part-time students. *Faculty research:* Quality control and reliability engineering, financial management, thermal science, energy conservation, structural analysis. Total annual research expenditures: $2.6 million. *Unit head:* Dr. Neslihan Alp, Director, 423-425-4032, Fax: 423-425-5229, E-mail: neslihan-alp@utc.edu. *Application contact:* Dr. Jerald Ainsworth, Dean of Graduate Studies; 423-425-4478, Fax: 423-425-5223, E-mail: jerald-ainsworth@utc.edu.

The University of Tennessee Space Institute, Graduate Programs, Program in Mechanical Engineering, Tullahoma, TN 37388-9700. Offers MS, PhD. Part-time programs available. *Faculty:* 5 full-time (0 women), 12 part-time/adjunct (0 women). *Students:* 7 full-time (1 woman), 20 part-time (0 women); includes 1 minority (Asian, non-Hispanic/Latino), 5 international. 3 applicants, 100% accepted, 3 enrolled. In 2010, 7 master's, 1 doctorate awarded. Terminal master's awarded for partial completion of doctoral program. *Degree requirements:* For master's, thesis (for some programs); for doctorate, one foreign language, thesis/dissertation. *Entrance requirements:* For master's and doctorate, GRE General Test. Additional exam requirements/recommendations for international students: Required—TOEFL (minimum score 550 paper-based; 213 computer-based), IELTS (minimum score 6.5). *Application deadline:* For fall admission, 2/1 for international students; for spring admission, 6/15 for international students. Applications are processed on a rolling basis. Application fee: $35. Electronic applications accepted. *Financial support:* In 2010–11, 1 fellowship (averaging $350 per year), 6 research assistantships with full tuition reimbursements (averaging $17,791 per year) were awarded; career-related internships or fieldwork, Federal Work-Study, institutionally sponsored loans, health care benefits, tuition waivers (full and partial), and unspecified assistantships also available. Financial award applicants required to submit FAFSA. *Unit head:* Dr. Trevor Moeller, Degree Program Chairman, 931-393-7351, Fax: 931-393-7437, E-mail: tmoeller@utsi.edu. *Application contact:* Dee Merriman, Coordinator III, 931-393-7213, Fax: 931-393-7211, E-mail: dmerrima@utsi.edu.

The University of Texas at Arlington, Graduate School, College of Engineering, Department of Mechanical and Aerospace Engineering, Program in Mechanical Engineering, Arlington, TX 76019. Offers M Engr, MS, PhD. Part-time and evening/weekend programs available. Post-baccalaureate distance learning degree programs offered (minimal on-campus study). *Faculty:* 14 full-time (2 women). *Students:* 126 full-time (13 women), 58 part-time (4 women); includes 18 minority (3 Black or African American, non-Hispanic/Latino; 6 Asian, non-Hispanic/Latino; 9 Hispanic/Latino), 125 international. 155 applicants, 84% accepted, 52 enrolled. In 2010, 38 master's, 8 doctorates awarded. *Degree requirements:* For master's, thesis optional; for doctorate, comprehensive exam, thesis/dissertation. *Entrance requirements:* For master's, GRE General Test, minimum GPA of 3.0; for doctorate, GRE General Test, minimum GPA of 3.5. Additional exam requirements/recommendations for international students: Required—TOEFL (minimum score 550 paper-based; 213 computer-based). *Application deadline:* For fall admission, 6/1 for domestic students, 4/1 for international students; for spring admission, 10/5 for domestic students, 9/15 for international students. Applications are processed on a rolling basis. Application fee: $35 ($50 for international students). *Expenses:* Tuition, state resident: full-time $7500. Tuition, nonresident: full-time $13,080. International tuition: $13,250 full-time. *Financial support:* In 2010–11, 61 students received support, including 1 fellowship with partial tuition reimbursement available (averaging $1,000 per year), 10 research assistantships with partial tuition reimbursements available (averaging $13,500 per year), 20 teaching assistant-ships with partial tuition reimbursements available (averaging $14,400 per year); institutionally sponsored loans, scholarships/grants, health care benefits, and unspecified assistantships also available. Financial award application deadline: 6/1; financial award applicants required to submit FAFSA. *Unit head:* Dr. Erian Armanios, Chair, 817-272-2603, Fax: 817-272-5010, E-mail: armanios@uta.edu. *Application contact:* Dr. Albert Tong, Graduate Advisor, 817-272-2297, Fax: 817-272-2952, E-mail: tong@uta.edu.

The University of Texas at Austin, Graduate School, Cockrell School of Engineering, Department of Mechanical Engineering, Austin, TX 78712-1111. Offers mechanical engineering (MS, PhD); operations research and industrial engineering (MS, PhD). *Entrance requirements:* For master's and doctorate, GRE General Test. Additional exam requirements/recommendations for international students: Required—TOEFL.

The University of Texas at Dallas, Erik Jonsson School of Engineering and Computer Science, Program in Mechanical Engineering, Richardson, TX 75080. Offers mechanical systems engineering (MSME); microelectromechanical systems (MSME). Part-time and evening/weekend programs available. *Faculty:* 4 full-time (1 woman). *Students:* 11 full-time (4 women), 2 part-time (0 women); includes 1 minority (Hispanic/Latino), 7 international. Average age 27. 82 applicants, 37% accepted, 7 enrolled. *Degree requirements:* For master's, thesis or major design project. *Entrance requirements:* For master's, GRE General Test, minimum GPA of 3.0 in related bachelor's degree. Additional exam requirements/recommendations for international students: Required—TOEFL (minimum score 550 paper-based; 215 computer-based). *Application deadline:* For fall admission, 7/15 for domestic students, 5/1 priority date for international students; for spring admission, 11/15 for domestic students, 9/1 priority date for international students. Applications are processed on a rolling basis. Application fee: $50 ($100 for international students). Electronic applications accepted. *Expenses:* Tuition, state resident: full-time $10,248; part-time $569 per credit hour. Tuition, nonresident: full-time $18,544; part-time $1030 per credit hour. Tuition and fees vary according to course load. *Financial support:* In 2010–11, 9 students received support, including 4 research assistantships with partial tuition reimbursements available (averaging $15,292 per year), 3 teaching assistant-ships with partial tuition reimbursements available (averaging $14,850 per year); career-related internships or fieldwork, Federal Work-Study, institutionally sponsored loans, scholarships/grants, and unspecified assistantships also available. Support available to part-time students. Financial award application deadline: 4/30; financial award applicants required to submit FAFSA. *Faculty research:* Nano-materials and nano-electronic devices, biomedical devices, nonlinear systems and controls, semiconductor and oxide surfaces, flexible electronics. *Unit head:* Dr. Mario Rotea, Department Head, 972-883-2720, Fax: 972-883-2813, E-mail: rotea@utdallas.edu. *Application contact:* Dr. Matthew Goeckner, Associate Department Head, 972-883-4293, Fax: 972-883-2813, E-mail: gradecs@utdallas.edu.

The University of Texas at El Paso, Graduate School, College of Engineering, Department of Mechanical Engineering, El Paso, TX 79968-0001. Offers MS. Part-time and evening/weekend programs available. *Students:* 52 (4 women); includes 2 Asian, non-Hispanic/Latino; 18 Hispanic/Latino, 30 international. Average age 34. In 2010, 16 master's awarded. *Degree requirements:* For master's, thesis optional. *Entrance requirements:* For master's, GRE, minimum GPA of 3.0, letter of reference. Additional exam requirements/recommendations for international students: Required—TOEFL; Recommended—IELTS. *Application deadline:* For fall admission, 8/1 priority date for domestic students, 3/1 for international students; for spring admission, 11/1 priority date for domestic students, 9/1 for international students. Applications are processed on a rolling basis. Application fee: $45 ($80 for international students). Electronic applications accepted. *Financial support:* In 2010–11, research assistantships with partial tuition reimbursements (averaging $21,125 per year), teaching assistantships with partial tuition reimbursements (averaging $16,900 per year) were awarded; fellowships with partial tuition reimbursements, institutionally sponsored loans, scholarships/grants, health care benefits, tuition waivers (partial), and unspecified assistantships also available. Support available to part-time students. Financial award application deadline: 3/15; financial award applicants required to submit FAFSA. *Unit head:* Dr. Louis Everett, Chair, 915-747-5450 Ext. 7987, Fax: 915-747-5019, E-mail: leverett@utep.edu. *Application contact:* Dr. Patricia D. Witherspoon, Dean of the Graduate School, 915-747-5491, Fax: 915-747-5788, E-mail: withersp@utep.edu.

Mechanical Engineering

The University of Texas at San Antonio, College of Engineering, Department of Mechanical Engineering, San Antonio, TX 78249-0617. Offers advanced manufacturing and enterprise engineering (MS); mechanical engineering (MS). Part-time and evening/weekend programs available. *Faculty:* 15 full-time (1 woman), 3 part-time/adjunct (0 women). *Students:* 49 full-time (5 women), 46 part-time (7 women); includes 17 minority (3 Asian, non-Hispanic/Latino; 13 Hispanic/Latino; 1 Two or more races, non-Hispanic/Latino), 43 international. Average age 27. 65 applicants, 78% accepted, 28 enrolled. In 2010, 27 master's awarded. *Degree requirements:* For master's, comprehensive exam (for some programs), thesis (for some programs). *Entrance requirements:* For master's, GRE General Test, minimum GPA of 3.0 in last 60 hours of undergraduate degree. Additional exam requirements/recommendations for international students: Required—TOEFL (minimum score 500 paper-based; 173 computer-based; 61 iBT), IELTS (minimum score 5). *Application deadline:* For fall admission, 7/1 for domestic students, 4/1 for international students; for spring admission, 11/1 for domestic students, 9/1 for international students. Applications are processed on a rolling basis. Application fee: $45 ($80 for international students). Electronic applications accepted. *Expenses:* Tuition, state resident: full-time $4172; part-time $231.75 per credit hour. Tuition, nonresident: full-time $15,332; part-time $851.75 per credit hour. *Financial support:* In 2010–11, 33 students received support, including 1 fellowship (averaging $42,000 per year), 26 research assistantships (averaging $12,257 per year); career-related internships or fieldwork, scholarships/grants, tuition waivers, and unspecified assistantships also available. Support available to part-time students. Financial award application deadline: 3/31. Total annual research expenditures: $1.1 million. *Unit head:* Dr. Efstathios E. Michaelides, Department Chair, 210-458-5580, Fax: 210-458-6504, E-mail: stathis.michaelides@utsa.edu. *Application contact:* Veronica Ramirez, Assistant Dean of the Graduate School, 210-458-4330, Fax: 210-458-4332, E-mail: graduatestudies@utsa.edu.

See M.S. Display on next page and Close-Up on page 559 and Ph.D. Display on page 548 and Close-Up on page 561. See also Display on page 441 and Close-Up on page 453.

The University of Texas at Tyler, College of Engineering and Computer Science, Department of Mechanical Engineering, Tyler, TX 75799-0001. Offers MS. Part-time and evening/weekend programs available. *Degree requirements:* For master's, engineering project. *Entrance requirements:* For master's, GRE or GMAT, bachelor's degree in engineering. *Faculty research:* Mechatronics vibration analysis, fluid dynamics, electronics and instrumentation, manufacturing processes, optics, computational fluid dynamics, signal processing, high voltage related studies, real time systems, semiconductors.

The University of Texas–Pan American, College of Science and Engineering, Department of Mechanical Engineering, Edinburg, TX 78539. Offers MS.

The University of Toledo, College of Graduate Studies, College of Engineering, Department of Mechanical, Industrial, and Manufacturing Engineering, Toledo, OH 43606-3390. Offers industrial engineering (MS, PhD); mechanical engineering (MS, PhD). Part-time programs available. Postbaccalaureate distance learning degree programs offered (minimal on-campus study). *Degree requirements:* For master's, thesis optional; for doctorate, thesis/dissertation, qualifying exam. *Entrance requirements:* For master's, GRE General Test, minimum GPA of 3.0; for doctorate, GRE General Test, minimum GPA of 3.3. Additional exam requirements/recommendations for international students: Required—TOEFL (minimum score 550 paper-based; 213 computer-based; 80 iBT). Electronic applications accepted. *Expenses:* Tuition, state resident: full-time $11,426; part-time $476 per credit hour. Tuition, nonresident: full-time $21,660; part-time $903 per credit hour. One-time fee: $62. *Faculty research:* Computational and experimental thermal sciences, manufacturing process and systems, mechanics, materials, design, quality and management engineering systems.

University of Toronto, School of Graduate Studies, Physical Sciences Division, Faculty of Applied Science and Engineering, Department of Mechanical and Industrial Engineering, Toronto, ON M5S 1A1, Canada. Offers M Eng, MA Sc, PhD. Part-time programs available. *Degree requirements:* For master's, thesis (for some programs), oral exam/thesis defense (MA Sc); for doctorate, thesis/dissertation, thesis defense, qualifying examination. *Entrance requirements:* For master's, GRE (recommended), minimum B+ average in last 2 years of undergraduate study, 2 letters of reference, resume, must be a Canadian citizen or a permanent resident (M Eng); for doctorate, GRE (recommended), minimum B+ average, 2 letters of reference, resumé. Additional exam requirements/recommendations for international students: Required—TOEFL (580 paper-based, 237 computer-based), Michigan English Language Assessment Battery (85), IELTS (7) or COPE (4).

University of Tulsa, Graduate School, College of Engineering and Natural Sciences, Department of Mechanical Engineering, Tulsa, OK 74104-3189. Offers ME, MSE, PhD. Part-time programs available. *Faculty:* 9 full-time (0 women). *Students:* 23 full-time (1 woman), 12 part-time (2 women); includes 1 minority (Asian, non-Hispanic/Latino), 21 international. Average age 27. 19 applicants, 53% accepted, 5 enrolled. In 2010, 11 master's, 2 doctorates awarded. Terminal master's awarded for partial completion of doctoral program. *Degree requirements:* For master's, thesis (MSE); for doctorate, thesis/dissertation. *Entrance requirements:* For master's and doctorate, GRE General Test. Additional exam requirements/recommendations for international students: Required—TOEFL (minimum score 550 paper-based; 213 computer-based; 80 iBT), IELTS (minimum score 6). *Application deadline:* Applications are processed on a rolling basis. Application fee: $40. Electronic applications accepted. *Expenses:* Tuition: Full-time $16,902; part-time $939 per credit hour. Required fees: $1020; $4 per credit hour. Tuition and fees vary according to course load. *Financial support:* In 2010–11, 28 students received support, including 6 fellowships with full and partial tuition reimbursements available (averaging $2,158 per year), 24 research assistantships with full and partial tuition reimbursements available (averaging $10,894 per year), 12 teaching assistantships with full and partial tuition reimbursements available (averaging $8,149 per year); career-related internships or fieldwork, Federal Work-Study, scholarships/grants, health care benefits, tuition waivers (full and partial), and unspecified assistantships also available. Support available to part-time students. Financial award application deadline: 2/1; financial award applicants required to submit FAFSA. *Faculty research:* Erosion and corrosion, solid mechanics, composite material, computational fluid dynamics, coiled tubing mechanics. Total annual research expenditures: $3.4 million. *Unit head:* Dr. Edmund F. Rybicki, Chairperson, 918-631-2996, Fax: 918-631-2397, E-mail: ed-rybicki@utulsa.edu. *Application contact:* Dr. Siamack A. Shirazi, Adviser, 918-631-3001, Fax: 918-631-2397, E-mail: grad@utulsa.edu.

University of Utah, Graduate School, College of Engineering, Department of Mechanical Engineering, Salt Lake City, UT 84112. Offers M Phil, MS, PhD. Part-time programs available. *Faculty:* 28 full-time (4 women), 4 part-time/adjunct (0 women). *Students:* 140 full-time (7 women), 68 part-time (5 women); includes 12 minority (1 American Indian or Alaska Native, non-Hispanic/Latino; 6 Asian, non-Hispanic/Latino; 4 Hispanic/Latino; 1 Two or more races, non-Hispanic/Latino), 53 international. Average age 28. 181 applicants, 58% accepted, 62 enrolled. In 2010, 71 master's, 7 doctorates awarded. Terminal master's awarded for partial completion of doctoral program. *Degree requirements:* For master's, comprehensive exam (for some programs), thesis (for some programs); for doctorate, comprehensive exam, thesis/dissertation, qualifying exam. *Entrance requirements:* For master's and doctorate, GRE General Test, minimum GPA of 3.0, statement of purpose, 3 letters of recommendation. Additional exam requirements/recommendations for international students: Required—TOEFL (minimum score 590 paper-based; 243 computer-based; 96 iBT). *Application deadline:* For fall admission, 4/1 priority date for domestic students, 12/1 priority date for international students; for spring admission, 11/1 priority date for domestic students. Application fee: $55 ($65 for international students). Electronic applications accepted. *Expenses:* Contact institution. *Financial support:* In 2010–11, 110 students received support, including 9 fellowships with full tuition reimbursements available (averaging $24,972 per year), 53 research assistantships with full and partial tuition reimbursements available (averaging $12,640 per year), 48 teaching assistantships with full and partial tuition reimbursements available (averaging $11,200 per year); institutionally sponsored loans, traineeships, health care benefits, and unspecified assistantships also available. Financial award application deadline: 1/15; financial award applicants required to submit FAFSA. *Faculty research:* Thermal science and energy systems, robotics, design and fatigue, automated manufacturing, ergonomics and safety. Total annual research expenditures: $2.8 million. *Unit head:* Dr. Timothy Ameel, Chair, 801-585-9730, Fax: 801-585-9826, E-mail: ameel@mech.utah.edu. *Application contact:* Dr. Eric Pardyjak, Director of Graduate Studies, 801-585-6414, Fax: 801-585-9826, E-mail: pardyjak@mech.utah.edu.

University of Vermont, Graduate College, College of Engineering and Mathematics, Department of Mechanical Engineering, Burlington, VT 05405. Offers MS, PhD. *Students:* 29 (7 women); includes 1 Asian, non-Hispanic/Latino, 7 international. 24 applicants, 42% accepted, 2 enrolled. In 2010, 3 master's, 2 doctorates awarded. *Degree requirements:* For master's, thesis; for doctorate, thesis/dissertation. *Entrance requirements:* Additional exam requirements/recommendations for international students: Required—TOEFL (minimum score 550 paper-based; 213 computer-based; 80 iBT). *Application deadline:* For fall admission, 2/1 priority date for domestic students. Applications are processed on a rolling basis. Application fee: $40. Electronic applications accepted. *Expenses:* Tuition, state resident: part-time $537 per credit hour. Tuition, nonresident: part-time $1355 per credit hour. *Financial support:* Fellowships, research assistantships, teaching assistantships available. Financial award application deadline: 3/1. *Unit head:* Dr. Jeff Marshall, Director, 802-656-3333. *Application contact:* Prof. Douglas Fletcher, Coordinator, 802-656-3333.

University of Victoria, Faculty of Graduate Studies, Faculty of Engineering, Department of Mechanical Engineering, Victoria, BC V8W 2Y2, Canada. Offers M Eng, MA Sc, PhD. Part-time programs available. *Degree requirements:* For master's, thesis (for some programs); for doctorate, thesis/dissertation, candidacy exam. *Entrance requirements:* For master's, minimum B average in undergraduate course work. Additional exam requirements/recommendations for international students: Required—TOEFL (minimum score 575 paper-based; 233 computer-based), IELTS (minimum score 7). Electronic applications accepted. *Faculty research:* CAD/CAM, energy systems, cryofuels, fuel cell technology, computational mechanics.

University of Virginia, School of Engineering and Applied Science, Department of Mechanical and Aerospace Engineering, Charlottesville, VA 22903. Offers ME, MS, PhD. Postbaccalaureate distance learning degree programs offered (no on-campus study). *Faculty:* 20 full-time (3 women), 2 part-time/adjunct (0 women). *Students:* 80 full-time (8 women), 3 part-time (0 women); includes 4 Asian, non-Hispanic/Latino, 22 international. Average age 27. 167 applicants, 15% accepted, 16 enrolled. In 2010, 18 master's, 4 doctorates awarded. *Degree requirements:* For master's, thesis (MS); for doctorate, comprehensive exam, thesis/dissertation. *Entrance requirements:* For master's and doctorate, GRE General Test, 3 letters of recommendation. Additional exam requirements/recommendations for international students: Required—TOEFL (minimum score 650 paper-based; 250 computer-based; 90 iBT), IELTS (minimum score 7). *Application deadline:* For fall admission, 8/1 for domestic students, 4/1 for international students; for winter admission, 12/1 for domestic students, 8/1 for international students; for spring admission, 5/1 for domestic students, 1/1 for international students. Applications are processed on a rolling basis. Application fee: $60. Electronic applications accepted. *Financial support:* Fellowships, research assistantships, teaching assistantships available. Financial award application deadline: 1/15; financial award applicants required to submit FAFSA. *Faculty research:* Solid mechanics, dynamical systems and control, thermofluids. *Unit head:* Hossein Haj-Hariri, Chair, 434-924-7424, Fax: 434-982-2037, E-mail: mae-adm@virginia.edu. *Application contact:* Graduate Secretary, 434-924-7425, Fax: 434-982-2037, E-mail: mae-adm@virginia.edu.

University of Washington, Graduate School, College of Engineering, Department of Mechanical Engineering, Seattle, WA 98195-2600. Offers MS, MSE, MSME, PhD. Part-time programs available. Postbaccalaureate distance learning degree programs offered (minimal on-campus study). *Faculty:* 38 full-time (5 women), 13 part-time/adjunct (1 woman). *Students:* 139 full-time (26 women), 92 part-time (13 women); includes 6 Black or African American, non-Hispanic/Latino; 1 American Indian or Alaska Native, non-Hispanic/Latino; 22 Asian, non-Hispanic/Latino; 9 Hispanic/Latino, 52 international. Average age 24. 328 applicants, 53% accepted, 56 enrolled. In 2010, 54 master's, 9 doctorates awarded. *Degree requirements:* For master's, thesis optional; for doctorate, comprehensive exam, thesis/dissertation, Qualifying, general, and final exams.. *Entrance requirements:* For master's, GRE General Test: minimum 450 Verbal (350 if English is not a native language), 650 Quantitative, and 4.0 Analytical Writing (3.5 if English is not a native language)., Minimum GPA of at least 3.00 (prefer overall undergraduate GPA of at least 3.2). Letters of recommendation, statement of purpose, and professional experience (if applicable).; for doctorate, GRE General Test: minimum 450 Verbal (350 if English is not a native language), 650 Quantitative, and 4.0 Analytical Writing (3.5 if English is not a native language)., Minimum GPA of at least 3.00 (prefer overall undergraduate GPA of at least 3.2 and MS grade point average of 3.5 or better). Letters of recommendation, statement of purpose, and professional experience (if applicable).. Additional exam requirements/recommendations for international students: Required—TOEFL (minimum score 580 paper-based; 237 computer-based; 92 iBT). *Application deadline:* For fall admission, 1/15 priority date for domestic and international students; for winter admission, 11/1 for domestic students, 9/1 priority date for international students; for spring admission, 2/1 for domestic students, 1/1 priority date for international students. Applications are processed on a rolling basis. Application fee: $75. Electronic applications accepted. *Financial support:* In 2010–11, 6 students received support, including 22 fellowships with partial tuition reimbursements available (averaging $21,762 per year), 71 research assistantships with full tuition reimbursements available (averaging $16,812 per year), 17 teaching assistantships with full tuition reimbursements available (averaging $14,517 per year); Federal Work-Study and health care benefits also available. Financial award application deadline: 1/15; financial award applicants required to submit FAFSA. *Faculty research:* Environmentally sensitive energy conversion; health systems and biotechnology; mechatronics; advanced materials, structures and manufacturing. Total annual research expenditures: $9.3 million. *Unit head:* Dr. Per Reinhall, Professor and Chair, 206-543-5090, Fax: 206-685-8047, E-mail: reinhall@u.washington.edu. *Application contact:* Maria Tovar Hopper, Graduate Academic Adviser, 206-543-7963, Fax: 206-685-8047, E-mail: mariah3@u.washington.edu.

University of Waterloo, Graduate Studies, Faculty of Engineering, Department of Mechanical and Mechatronics Engineering, Waterloo, ON N2L 3G1, Canada. Offers mechanical engineering (M Eng, MA Sc, PhD); mechanical engineering design and manufacturing (M Eng). Part-time and evening/weekend programs available. *Degree requirements:* For master's, research paper or thesis; for doctorate, comprehensive exam, thesis/dissertation. *Entrance requirements:* For master's, honors degree, minimum B average, resume; for doctorate, master's degree, minimum A- average, resumé. Additional exam requirements/recommendations for international students: Required—TOEFL (minimum score 550 paper-based; 213 computer-based), TWE (minimum score 4). Electronic applications accepted. *Faculty research:* Fluid mechanics, thermal engineering, solid mechanics, automation and control, materials engineering.

The University of Western Ontario, Faculty of Graduate Studies, Physical Sciences Division, Faculty of Engineering, London, ON N6A 5B8, Canada. Offers chemical and biochemical engineering (ME Sc, PhD); civil and environmental engineering (M Eng, ME Sc, PhD); electrical and computer engineering (M Eng, ME Sc, PhD); mechanical and materials engineering (M Eng, ME Sc, PhD). Part-time programs available. Terminal master's awarded for partial completion of doctoral program. *Degree requirements:* For master's, thesis; for doctorate, thesis/dissertation. *Entrance requirements:* For master's, minimum B average; for doctorate, minimum B+ average. *Faculty research:* Wind, geotechnical, chemical reactor engineering, applied electrostatics, biochemical engineering.

University of Windsor, Faculty of Graduate Studies, Faculty of Engineering, Department of Mechanical, Automotive, and Materials Engineering, Windsor, ON N9B 3P4, Canada. Offers engineering materials (M Eng, MA Sc, PhD); mechanical engineering (M Eng, MA Sc, PhD). Part-time programs available. *Degree requirements:* For master's, thesis; for doctorate, comprehensive exam, thesis/dissertation. *Entrance requirements:* For master's, minimum B average; for doctorate, master's degree, minimum B average. Additional exam requirements/

recommendations for international students: Required—TOEFL (minimum score 600 paper-based; 250 computer-based). Electronic applications accepted. *Faculty research:* Thermofluids, applied mechanics, materials engineering.

University of Wisconsin–Madison, Graduate School, College of Engineering, Department of Mechanical Engineering, Madison, WI 53706-1380. Offers energy systems (ME); engine systems (ME); mechanical engineering (MS, PhD); polymers (ME). Part-time programs available. Postbaccalaureate distance learning degree programs offered (no on-campus study). *Faculty:* 33 full-time (3 women), 1 part-time/adjunct (0 women). *Students:* 181 full-time (17 women), 54 part-time (6 women); includes 3 Black or African American, non-Hispanic/Latino; 9 Asian, non-Hispanic/Latino; 8 Hispanic/Latino. Average age 25. 652 applicants, 19% accepted, 68 enrolled. In 2010, 62 master's, 14 doctorates awarded. Terminal master's awarded for partial completion of doctoral program. *Degree requirements:* For master's, thesis optional; for doctorate, thesis/dissertation, qualifying exam, preliminary exam. *Entrance requirements:* For master's, GRE, BS in mechanical engineering or related field, minimum GPA of 3.0 in last 60 hours of course work; for doctorate, GRE, BS in mechanical engineering or related field, minimum undergraduate GPA of 3.0 in last 60 hours of course work. Additional exam requirements/recommendations for international students: Required—TOEFL (minimum score 550 paper-based; 213 computer-based; 80 iBT). *Application deadline:* For fall admission, 5/1 for domestic students, 6/1 for international students; for spring admission, 11/30 for domestic students, 10/1 for international students. Applications are processed on a rolling basis. Application fee: $56. Electronic applications accepted. *Expenses:* Tuition, state resident: full-time $9887.36; part-time $617.96 per credit. Tuition, nonresident: full-time $24,054; part-time $1503.40 per credit. Required fees: $67.63 per credit. Tuition and fees vary according to reciprocity agreements. *Financial support:* In 2010–11, 14 fellowships with full tuition reimbursements (averaging $22,224 per year), 148 research assistantships with full tuition reimbursements (averaging $19,596 per year), 45 teaching assistantships with full tuition reimbursements (averaging $8,595 per year) were awarded; career-related internships or fieldwork, institutionally sponsored loans, scholarships/grants, traineeships, health care benefits, and unspecified assistantships also available. *Faculty research:* Design and manufacturing, materials processing, combustion, energy systems nanotechnology. Total annual research expenditures: $10 million. *Unit head:* Roxann L. Engelstad, Chair, 608-262-5745, Fax: 608-265-2316, E-mail: engelsta@engr.wisc.edu. *Application contact:* Roxann L. Engelstad, Chair, 608-262-5745, Fax: 608-265-2316, E-mail: engelsta@engr.wisc.edu.

University of Wisconsin–Milwaukee, Graduate School, College of Engineering and Applied Science, Program in Engineering, Milwaukee, WI 53201-0413. Offers civil engineering (MS); electrical and computer engineering (MS); energy engineering (Certificate); engineering (PhD); engineering management (MS); engineering mechanics (MS); ergonomics (Certificate); industrial and management engineering (MS); manufacturing engineering (MS); materials engineering (MS); mechanical engineering (MS); MUP/MS. Part-time programs available. *Faculty:* 50 full-time (5 women). *Students:* 152 full-time (27 women), 115 part-time (23 women); includes 13 Black or African American, non-Hispanic/Latino; 3 American Indian or Alaska Native, non-Hispanic/Latino; 6 Asian, non-Hispanic/Latino; 10 Hispanic/Latino, 25 international. Average age 31. 236 applicants, 67% accepted, 55 enrolled. In 2010, 39 master's, 19 doctorates awarded. *Degree requirements:* For master's, comprehensive exam (for some programs), thesis or alternative; for doctorate, comprehensive exam, thesis/dissertation, internship. *Entrance requirements:* For master's, GRE, minimum GPA of 2.75; for doctorate, GRE, minimum GPA of 3.5. Additional exam requirements/recommendations for international students: Required—TOEFL (minimum score 550 paper-based; 79 iBT), IELTS (minimum score 6.5). *Application deadline:* For fall admission, 1/1 priority date for domestic students; for spring admission, 9/1 for domestic students. Applications are processed on a rolling basis. Application fee: $56 ($96 for international students). *Financial support:* In 2010–11, 3 fellowships, 55 research assistantships, 77 teaching assistantships were awarded; career-related internships or fieldwork, Federal Work-Study, unspecified assistantships, and project assistantships also available. Support available to part-time students. Financial award application deadline: 4/15. Total annual research expenditures: $6.2 million. *Unit head:* David Yu, Representative, 414-229-6169, E-mail: yu@uwm.edu. *Application contact:* Betty Warras, General Information Contact, 414-229-6169, Fax: 414-229-6967, E-mail: bwarras@uwm.edu.

University of Wyoming, College of Engineering and Applied Sciences, Department of Mechanical Engineering, Laramie, WY 82070. Offers MS, PhD. Terminal master's awarded for partial completion of doctoral program. *Degree requirements:* For master's, thesis; for doctorate, thesis/dissertation. *Entrance requirements:* For master's, GRE General Test (minimum score 900), minimum GPA of 3.0; for doctorate, GRE General Test (minimum score: 1000), minimum GPA of 3.0. Additional exam requirements/recommendations for international students: Required—TOEFL (minimum score 550 paper-based; 215 computer-based). Electronic applications accepted. *Faculty research:* Composite materials, thermal and fluid sciences, continuum mechanics, material science.

Utah State University, School of Graduate Studies, College of Engineering, Department of Mechanical and Aerospace Engineering, Logan, UT 84322. Offers aerospace engineering (MS, PhD); mechanical engineering (ME, MS, PhD). Terminal master's awarded for partial completion of doctoral program. *Degree requirements:* For master's, thesis (for some programs); for doctorate, thesis/dissertation. *Entrance requirements:* For master's, GRE General Test, minimum GPA of 3.0; for doctorate, GRE General Test, minimum GPA of 3.3. Additional exam requirements/recommendations for international students: Required—TOEFL. *Faculty research:* In-space instruments, cryogenic cooling, thermal science, space structures, composite materials.

Vanderbilt University, School of Engineering, Department of Mechanical Engineering, Nashville, TN 37240-1001. Offers M Eng, MS, PhD. MS and PhD offered through the Graduate School. Part-time programs available. *Faculty:* 16 full-time (1 woman). *Students:* 62 full-time (9 women); includes 2 Black or African American, non-Hispanic/Latino; 1 Asian, non-Hispanic/Latino, 18 international. Average age 27. 188 applicants, 7% accepted, 6 enrolled. In 2010, 2 master's, 4 doctorates awarded. Terminal master's awarded for partial completion of doctoral program. *Degree requirements:* For master's, comprehensive exam, thesis; for doctorate, comprehensive exam, thesis/dissertation. *Entrance requirements:* For master's and doctorate, GRE General Test. Additional exam requirements/recommendations for international students: Required—TOEFL (minimum score 550 paper-based; 220 computer-based); Recommended—TWE (minimum score 4). *Application deadline:* For fall admission, 1/15 for domestic students; for spring admission, 11/1 for domestic students. Applications are processed on a rolling basis. Application fee: $0. Electronic applications accepted. *Financial support:* In 2010–11, 6 fellowships with full tuition reimbursements (averaging $24,516 per year), 28 research assistantships with full tuition reimbursements (averaging $22,916 per year), 10 teaching assistantships with full tuition reimbursements (averaging $22,316 per year) were awarded; institutionally sponsored loans, health care benefits, and tuition waivers (full) also available. Support available to part-time students. Financial award application deadline: 1/15. *Faculty research:* Active noise and vibration control, robotics, mesoscale and microscale energy conversions, laser diagnostics, combustion. Total annual research expenditures: $3.1 million. *Unit head:* Dr. Robert W. Pitz, Chair, 615-322-2413, Fax: 615-343-6687, E-mail: robert.w.pitz@vanderbilt.edu. *Application contact:* Dr. Nilanjan Sarkar, Director of Graduate Studies, 615-343-7219, Fax: 615-343-6687, E-mail: nilanjan.sarkar@vanderbilt.edu.

Villanova University, College of Engineering, Department of Electrical and Computer Engineering, Program in Electrical Engineering, Villanova, PA 19085-1699. Offers electric power systems (Certificate); electrical engineering (MSEE); electro mechanical systems (Certificate); high frequency systems (Certificate); intelligent control systems (Certificate); wireless and digital communications (Certificate). Part-time and evening/weekend programs available. *Students:* 9 full-time (1 woman), 55 part-time (11 women); includes 5 Black or African American, non-Hispanic/Latino; 6 Asian, non-Hispanic/Latino; 1 Hispanic/Latino, 16 international. 54 applicants, 63% accepted, 18 enrolled. In 2010, 16 master's awarded. *Degree requirements:* For master's, thesis optional. *Entrance requirements:* For master's, GRE General Test (for applicants with degrees from foreign universities), BEE, minimum GPA of 3.0. Additional

Mechanical Engineering

exam requirements/recommendations for international students: Required—TOEFL (minimum score 600 paper-based; 250 computer-based; 100 iBT). *Application deadline:* For fall admission, 8/1 for domestic students, 4/1 for international students; for spring admission, 12/1 for domestic students, 8/1 for international students. Applications are processed on a rolling basis. Application fee: $50. *Expenses:* Tuition: Part-time $700 per credit. Part-time tuition and fees vary according to degree level and program. *Financial support:* In 2010–11, research assistantships with full and partial tuition reimbursements (averaging $13,500 per year); Federal Work-Study, scholarships/grants, tuition waivers (full and partial), and unspecified assistantships also available. Support available to part-time students. Financial award application deadline: 1/15. *Faculty research:* Signal processing, communications, antennas, devices. *Unit head:* Dr. Pritpal Singh, Chairman, 610-519-4971, Fax: 610-519-4436. *Application contact:* College of Engineering, Graduate Programs Office, 610-519-5840, Fax: 610-519-5859, E-mail: engineering.grad@villanova.edu.

Villanova University, College of Engineering, Department of Mechanical Engineering, Villanova, PA 19085-1699. Offers electro-mechanical systems (Certificate); machinery dynamics (Certificate); mechanical engineering (MSME); nonlinear dynamics and control (Certificate); thermofluid systems (Certificate). Part-time and evening/weekend programs available. Post-baccalaureate distance learning degree programs offered (no on-campus study). *Faculty:* 21 full-time (2 women), 15 part-time/adjunct (1 woman). *Students:* 17 full-time (2 women), 52 part-time (8 women); includes 1 Black or African American, non-Hispanic/Latino; 6 Asian, non-Hispanic/Latino; 2 Hispanic/Latino, 6 international. 48 applicants, 63% accepted, 14 enrolled. In 2010, 20 master's awarded. *Degree requirements:* For master's, thesis optional. *Entrance requirements:* For master's, GRE General Test (for applicants with degrees from foreign universities), BME, minimum GPA of 3.0. Additional exam requirements/recommendations for international students: Required—TOEFL (minimum score 600 paper-based; 250 computer-based; 100 iBT). *Application deadline:* For fall admission, 7/1 priority date for domestic students, 4/1 priority date for international students; for spring admission, 11/1 for domestic students, 10/1 for international students. Applications are processed on a rolling basis. Application fee: $50. Electronic applications accepted. *Expenses:* Tuition: Part-time $700 per credit. Part-time tuition and fees vary according to degree level and program. *Financial support:* In 2010–11, research assistantships with full tuition reimbursements (averaging $13,500 per year); Federal Work-Study, tuition waivers (full), and unspecified assistantships also available. Support available to part-time students. Financial award application deadline: 1/15. *Faculty research:* Composite materials, power plant systems, fluid mechanics, automated manufacturing, dynamic analysis. Total annual research expenditures: $1.6 million. *Unit head:* Dr. C. Nataraj, Chairperson, 610-519-4980, Fax: 610-519-7312. *Application contact:* College of Engineering Graduate Programs Office, 610-519-5840, Fax: 610-519-5859, E-mail: engineering.grad@villanova.edu.

Virginia Commonwealth University, Graduate School, School of Engineering, Department of Mechanical Engineering, Richmond, VA 23284-9005. Offers MS, PhD. *Faculty:* 9 full-time (1 woman). *Entrance requirements:* For master's and doctorate, GRE. Additional exam requirements/recommendations for international students: Required—TOEFL (minimum score 600 paper-based; 250 computer-based; 100 iBT). *Application deadline:* For fall admission, 2/1 priority date for domestic students; for spring admission, 11/15 for domestic students. Application fee: $50. Electronic applications accepted. *Expenses:* Tuition, state resident: full-time $4308; part-time $479 per credit hour. Tuition, nonresident: full-time $8942; part-time $994 per credit hour. Required fees: $2000; $85 per credit hour. Tuition and fees vary according to course level, course load, degree level, campus/location and program. *Financial support:* Applicants required to submit FAFSA. *Unit head:* Dr. Rosalyn S. Hobson, Associate Dean for Graduate Studies, 804-828-8308, Fax: 804-827-7030, E-mail: rhobson@vcu.edu. *Application contact:* Dr. Karla M. Mossi, Director, Graduate Programs in Mechanical Engineering, 804-827-5275, E-mail: kmmossi@vcu.edu.

Virginia Polytechnic Institute and State University, Graduate School, College of Engineering, Department of Mechanical Engineering, Blacksburg, VA 24061. Offers M Eng, MS, PhD. *Faculty:* 49 full-time (5 women). *Students:* 242 full-time (29 women), 30 part-time (2 women); includes 4 Black or African American, non-Hispanic/Latino; 14 Asian, non-Hispanic/Latino; 1 Hispanic/Latino, 79 international. Average age 27. 432 applicants, 29% accepted, 87 enrolled. In 2010, 50 master's, 16 doctorates awarded. *Degree requirements:* For master's, comprehensive exam (for some programs), thesis (for some programs); for doctorate, comprehensive exam (for some programs), thesis/dissertation (for some programs). *Entrance requirements:* For master's and doctorate, GRE. Additional exam requirements/recommendations for international students: Required—TOEFL (minimum score 550 paper-based; 213 computer-based). *Application deadline:* For fall admission, 7/1 for domestic and international students; for spring admission, 12/1 for domestic and international students. Applications are processed on a rolling basis. Application fee: $65. Electronic applications accepted. *Expenses:* Tuition, area resident: Full-time $9399; part-time $488 per credit hour. Tuition, state resident: full-time $9399; part-time $488 per credit hour. Tuition, nonresident: full-time $17,854; part-time $957.75 per credit hour. International tuition: $17,854 full-time. Required fees: $1534. Full-time tuition and fees vary according to program. *Financial support:* In 2010–11, 4 fellowships with full tuition reimbursements (averaging $29,555 per year), 23 research assistantships with full tuition reimbursements (averaging $24,673 per year), 20 teaching assistantships with full tuition reimbursements (averaging $18,256 per year) were awarded; career-related internships or fieldwork, Federal Work-Study, scholarships/grants, health care benefits, and unspecified assistantships also available. Financial award application deadline: 1/15. *Faculty research:* Turbomachinery, CAD/CAM, thermofluid sciences, controls, mechanical system dynamics. Total annual research expenditures: $16 million. *Unit head:* Dr. Kenneth S. Ball, UNIT HEAD, 540-231-6661, Fax: 540-231-9100, E-mail: ball@vt.edu. *Application contact:* Mary Kasarda, Contact, 540-231-8552, Fax: 540-231-9100, E-mail: maryk@vt.edu.

Washington State University, Graduate School, College of Engineering and Architecture, School of Mechanical and Materials Engineering, Program in Mechanical Engineering, Pullman, WA 99164. Offers MS, PhD. Part-time programs available. *Faculty:* 32. *Students:* 57 full-time (11 women), 18 part-time (3 women); includes 2 Black or African American, non-Hispanic/Latino; 1 Hispanic/Latino, 42 international. Average age 32. 137 applicants, 28% accepted, 15 enrolled. In 2010, 11 master's, 3 doctorates awarded. Terminal master's awarded for partial completion of doctoral program. *Degree requirements:* For master's, comprehensive exam (for some programs), thesis (for some programs), oral exam; for doctorate, comprehensive exam, thesis/dissertation, oral exam, qualifying exam. *Entrance requirements:* For master's, GRE (recommended), minimum GPA of 3.0, resume, 3 letters of recommendation with evaluation forms, student interest profile; for doctorate, minimum GPA of 3.4, resume, 3 letters of recommendation with evaluation forms, student interest profile. Additional exam requirements/recommendations for international students: Required—TOEFL, IELTS. *Application deadline:* For fall admission, 1/10 priority date for domestic students, 1/10 for international students; for spring admission, 7/1 priority date for domestic students, 7/1 for international students. Applications are processed on a rolling basis. Application fee: $50. Electronic applications accepted. *Expenses:* Tuition, state resident: full-time $8552; part-time $443 per credit. Tuition, nonresident: full-time $21,650; part-time $1083 per credit. Required fees: $846. *Financial support:* In 2010–11, 38 students received support, including 3 fellowships (averaging $3,252 per year), 19 research assistantships with full tuition reimbursements available (averaging $13,917 per year), 15 teaching assistantships with full tuition reimbursements available (averaging $13,056 per year); career-related internships or fieldwork, Federal Work-Study, institutionally sponsored loans, scholarships/grants, health care benefits, and unspecified assistantships also available. Financial award application deadline: 4/1; financial award applicants required to submit FAFSA. *Faculty research:* Thermal and fluid sciences, solid mechanics, manufacturing, MEMS, computer-aided design. Total annual research expenditures: $2.2 million. *Unit head:* Dr. Hussein M. Zbib, Director, 509-335-8654, Fax: 509-335-4662, E-mail: director@mme.wsu.edu. *Application contact:* Graduate School Admissions, 800-GRADWSU, Fax: 509-335-1949, E-mail: gradsch@wsu.edu.

Washington State University Tri-Cities, Graduate Programs, College of Engineering and Computer Science, Richland, WA 99352. Offers computer science (MS, PhD); electrical and computer engineering (PhD); electrical engineering (MS); mechanical engineering (MS, PhD). Part-time programs available. *Faculty:* 28. *Students:* 4 full-time (0 women), 25 part-time (8 women); includes 2 Black or African American, non-Hispanic/Latino, 1 international. *Degree requirements:* For master's, comprehensive exam, thesis (for some programs); for doctorate, comprehensive exam, thesis/dissertation, oral exam. *Entrance requirements:* For master's and doctorate, GRE, minimum GPA of 3.0, 3 letters of recommendation. Additional exam requirements/recommendations for international students: Required—TOEFL (minimum score 550 paper-based; 213 computer-based). *Application deadline:* For fall admission, 1/10 priority date for domestic students, 1/10 for international students; for spring admission, 7/1 priority date for domestic students, 7/1 for international students. Application fee: $50. *Financial support:* Application deadline: 3/1. *Faculty research:* Positive ion track structure, biological systems computer simulations. *Unit head:* Dr. Ali Saberi, Chair, 509-372-7178, E-mail: sidra@eecs.wsu.edu. *Application contact:* Dr. Scott Hudson, Associate Director, 509-372-7254, Fax: 509-335-1949, E-mail: hudson@tricity.wsu.edu.

Washington State University Vancouver, Graduate Programs, School of Engineering and Computer Science, Vancouver, WA 98686. Offers computer science (MS); mechanical engineering (MS). Part-time programs available. *Faculty:* 9. *Students:* 14 full-time (1 woman), 5 part-time (1 woman); includes 1 Asian, non-Hispanic/Latino, 5 international. In 2010, 4 master's awarded. *Degree requirements:* For master's, comprehensive exam (for some programs), thesis, research project. *Entrance requirements:* For master's, minimum GPA of 3.0, 3 letters of recommendation with evaluation forms, resume. Additional exam requirements/recommendations for international students: Required—TOEFL (minimum score 550 paper-based). *Application deadline:* For fall admission, 1/10 priority date for domestic students, 1/10 for international students; for spring admission, 7/1 priority date for domestic students, 7/1 for international students. Applications are processed on a rolling basis. Application fee: $50. *Financial support:* In 2010–11, research assistantships with full tuition reimbursements (averaging $14,634 per year), teaching assistantships with full tuition reimbursements (averaging $13,383 per year) were awarded; health care benefits and unspecified assistantships also available. Financial award application deadline: 2/15. *Faculty research:* Software design, artificial intelligence, sensor networks, robotics, nanotechnology. Total annual research expenditures: $3.4 million. *Unit head:* Dr. Hakan Gurocak, Director, 360-546-9637, Fax: 360-546-9438, E-mail: hgurocak@vancouver.wsu.edu. *Application contact:* Peggy Moore, Academic Coordinator, 360-546-9638, Fax: 360-546-9438, E-mail: moorep@vancouver.wsu.edu.

Washington University in St. Louis, School of Engineering and Applied Science, Department of Mechanical, Aerospace and Structural Engineering, St. Louis, MO 63130-4899. Offers MS, D Sc, PhD. Part-time programs available. Terminal master's awarded for partial completion of doctoral program. *Degree requirements:* For master's, thesis optional; for doctorate, thesis/dissertation optional. *Entrance requirements:* For master's, GRE; for doctorate, GRE General Test, departmental qualifying exam. *Faculty research:* Aerosols science and technology, applied mechanics, biomechanics and biomedical engineering, design, dynamic systems, combustion science, composite materials, materials science.

Wayne State University, College of Engineering, Department of Mechanical Engineering, Detroit, MI 48202. Offers MS, PhD. *Faculty:* 12 full-time (0 women), 4 part-time/adjunct (0 women). *Students:* 92 full-time (13 women), 48 part-time (10 women); includes 15 minority (5 Black or African American, non-Hispanic/Latino; 7 Asian, non-Hispanic/Latino; 1 Hispanic/Latino; 2 Two or more races, non-Hispanic/Latino), 87 international. Average age 29. 145 applicants, 54% accepted, 26 enrolled. In 2010, 49 master's, 4 doctorates awarded. *Degree requirements:* For master's, thesis optional; for doctorate, thesis/dissertation. *Entrance requirements:* For master's, GRE (if BS degree is not from an ABET accredited university), minimum undergraduate GPA of 3.0; for doctorate, GRE, minimum graduate GPA of 3.5. Additional exam requirements/recommendations for international students: Required—TOEFL (minimum score 550 paper-based; 213 computer-based); Recommended—TWE (minimum score 6). *Application deadline:* For fall admission, 7/1 priority date for domestic students, 6/1 for international students; for winter admission, 10/1 for international students; for spring admission, 3/15 for domestic students, 2/1 for international students. Applications are processed on a rolling basis. Application fee: $30 ($50 for international students). Electronic applications accepted. *Expenses:* Tuition, state resident: full-time $7662; part-time $478.85 per credit hour. Tuition, nonresident: full-time $16,920; part-time $1057.55 per credit hour. Required fees: $571.20; $35.70 per credit hour. $188.05 per semester. Tuition and fees vary according to course load and program. *Financial support:* In 2010–11, 5 fellowships (averaging $14,057 per year), 20 research assistantships (averaging $17,459 per year), 10 teaching assistantships (averaging $16,984 per year) were awarded; career-related internships or fieldwork, Federal Work-Study, and tuition waivers (full and partial) also available. Financial award application deadline: 2/28. *Faculty research:* Acoustics and vibrations/noise control, engine combustion and emission controls, advanced materials and structures, computational fluid mechanics, material processing and manufacturing. Total annual research expenditures: $5.5 million. *Unit head:* Dr. Trilochan Singh, Chair, 313-577-3702, Fax: 313-577-8789, E-mail: tsingh@wayne.edu. *Application contact:* Emmanuel Ayorinde, Graduate Director, 313-577-5548, E-mail: ayorinde@eng.wayne.edu.

Western Michigan University, Graduate College, College of Engineering and Applied Sciences, Department of Mechanical and Aeronautical Engineering, Kalamazoo, MI 49008. Offers mechanical engineering (MSE, PhD). Part-time programs available. *Degree requirements:* For master's, thesis optional; for doctorate, thesis/dissertation, oral exam. *Entrance requirements:* For master's, minimum GPA of 3.0; for doctorate, GRE General Test, minimum GPA of 3.0. *Faculty research:* Computational fluid dynamics, manufacturing process designs, composite materials, thermal fluid flow, experimental stress analysis.

Western New England University, School of Engineering, Department of Mechanical Engineering, Springfield, MA 01119. Offers MSE. Part-time and evening/weekend programs available. *Students:* 6 part-time (1 woman); includes 1 Hispanic/Latino. Average age 29. In 2010, 1 master's awarded. *Degree requirements:* For master's, comprehensive exam, thesis optional. *Entrance requirements:* For master's, GRE, bachelor's degree in engineering or related field. *Application deadline:* Applications are processed on a rolling basis. Application fee: $30. *Expenses:* Tuition: Full-time $35,582. *Financial support:* Available to part-time students. Application deadline: 4/1. *Faculty research:* Low-loss fluid mixing, flow separation delay and alleviation, high-lift airfoils, ejector research, compact heat exchangers. *Unit head:* Dr. Said Dini, Chair, 413-782-1272, E-mail: sdini@wnec.edu. *Application contact:* Douglas Kenyon, Assistant Vice President, Graduate Studies and Continuing Education, 413-782-1249, Fax: 413-782-1779, E-mail: ce@wnec.edu.

West Virginia University, College of Engineering and Mineral Resources, Department of Mechanical and Aerospace Engineering, Program in Mechanical Engineering, Morgantown, WV 26506. Offers MSME, PhD. Part-time programs available. Terminal master's awarded for partial completion of doctoral program. *Degree requirements:* For master's, thesis; for doctorate, comprehensive exam, thesis/dissertation, qualifying exam, proposal and defense. *Entrance requirements:* For master's and doctorate, GRE Subject Test, minimum GPA of 3.0, 3 references. Additional exam requirements/recommendations for international students: Required—TOEFL. *Faculty research:* Thermal sciences, material sciences, automatic controls, mechanical/structure design.

Wichita State University, Graduate School, College of Engineering, Department of Mechanical Engineering, Wichita, KS 67260. Offers MS, PhD. Part-time programs available. *Unit head:* Dr. David Koert, Acting Chair, 316-978-3402, Fax: 316-978-3236, E-mail: david.koert@wichita.edu. *Application contact:* Dr. T. S. Ravigururajan, Graduate Coordinator, 316-978-3402, E-mail: ts.ravi@wichita.edu.

Widener University, Graduate Programs in Engineering, Program in Mechanical Engineering, Chester, PA 19013-5792. Offers M Eng. Part-time and evening/weekend programs available. *Students:* 2 full-time (0 women), 3 part-time (0 women); includes 1 Black or African American, non-Hispanic/Latino, 1 international. Average age 27. In 2010, 1 master's awarded. *Degree requirements:* For master's, thesis optional. *Application deadline:* For fall admission, 8/1 priority date for domestic students; for spring admission, 12/1 for domestic students. Applications are processed on a rolling basis. Application fee: $25 ($300 for international students). *Financial support:* Teaching assistantships with full tuition reimbursements, unspecified assistantships available. Financial award application deadline: 3/15. *Faculty research:* Computational fluid mechanics, thermal and solar engineering, energy conversion, composite materials, solid mechanics. *Unit head:* Dr. Maria Slomiana, Chairman, 610-499-4062, Fax: 610-449-4059, E-mail: maria.slomiana@widener.edu. *Application contact:* Dr. Maria Slomiana, Chairman, 610-499-4062, Fax: 610-449-4059, E-mail: maria.slomiana@widener.edu.

Wilkes University, College of Graduate and Professional Studies, College of Science and Engineering, Division of Engineering and Physics, Wilkes-Barre, PA 18766-0002. Offers electrical engineering (MSEE); engineering management (MS); mechanical engineering (MS). Part-time programs available. *Students:* 13 full-time (1 woman), 15 part-time (2 women); includes 1 Asian, non-Hispanic/Latino; 1 Two or more races, non-Hispanic/Latino, 8 international. Average age 28. In 2010, 25 master's awarded. *Entrance requirements:* For master's, GRE General Test. Additional exam requirements/recommendations for international students: Required—TOEFL (minimum score 550 paper-based; 213 computer-based; 79 iBT). *Application deadline:* Applications are processed on a rolling basis. Application fee: $45 ($65 for international students). Electronic applications accepted. Tuition and fees vary according to degree level and program. *Financial support:* Federal Work-Study and unspecified assistantships available. Financial award application deadline: 3/1; financial award applicants required to submit FAFSA. *Unit head:* Dr. Rodney Ridley, Director, 570-408-4824, Fax: 570-408-7846, E-mail: rodney.ridley@wilkes.edu. *Application contact:* Kathleen Houlihan, Director of Graduate Studies, 570-408-3235, Fax: 570-408-7846, E-mail: kathleen.houlihan@wilkes.edu.

Woods Hole Oceanographic Institution, MIT/WHOI Joint Program in Oceanography/Applied Ocean Science and Engineering, Woods Hole, MA 02543-1541. Offers applied ocean sciences (PhD); biological oceanography (PhD, Sc D); chemical oceanography (PhD, Sc D); civil and environmental and oceanographic engineering (PhD); electrical and oceanographic engineering (PhD); geochemistry (PhD); geophysics (PhD); marine biology (PhD); marine geochemistry (PhD, Sc D); marine geology (PhD, Sc D); marine geophysics (PhD); mechanical and oceanographic engineering (PhD); ocean engineering (PhD); oceanographic engineering (M Eng, MS, PhD, Sc D, Eng); paleoceanography (PhD); physical oceanography (PhD, Sc D). MS, PhD, Sc D offered jointly with Massachusetts Institute of Technology. Terminal master's awarded for partial completion of doctoral program. *Degree requirements:* For master's and Eng, thesis (for some programs); for doctorate, thesis/dissertation. *Entrance requirements:* For master's, GRE General Test; for doctorate, GRE General Test, GRE Subject Test. Additional exam requirements/recommendations for international students: Required—TOEFL. Electronic applications accepted.

Worcester Polytechnic Institute, Graduate Studies and Research, Department of Mechanical Engineering, Worcester, MA 01609-2280. Offers manufacturing engineering (MS, PhD); materials process engineering (MS); materials science and engineering (MS, PhD); mechanical engineering (MS, PhD, Graduate Certificate). Part-time and evening/weekend programs available. Postbaccalaureate distance learning degree programs offered (minimal on-campus study). *Faculty:* 27 full-time (4 women), 3 part-time/adjunct (0 women). *Students:* 94 full-time (16 women), 41 part-time (9 women); includes 2 Black or African American, non-Hispanic/Latino; 3 Hispanic/Latino; 10 Native Hawaiian or other Pacific Islander, non-Hispanic/Latino, 28 international. 251 applicants, 82% accepted, 76 enrolled. In 2010, 48 master's, 1 doctorate awarded. *Degree requirements:* For master's, thesis optional; for doctorate, comprehensive exam, thesis/dissertation. *Entrance requirements:* For master's, GRE (recommended), BS in mechanical engineering or related field, 3 letters of recommendation; for doctorate, GRE (recommended), MS in mechanical engineering or related field, 3 letters of recommendation, statement of purpose. Additional exam requirements/recommendations for international students: Required—TOEFL (minimum score 550 paper-based; 213 computer-based; 79 iBT), IELTS (minimum score 6.5). *Application deadline:* For fall admission, 1/1 priority date for domestic and international students; for spring admission, 10/1 priority date for domestic and international students. Applications are processed on a rolling basis. Application fee: $70. Electronic applications accepted. *Expenses:* Tuition: Full-time $20,862; part-time $1159 per term. One-time fee: $15. *Financial support:* Career-related internships or fieldwork, institutionally sponsored loans, scholarships/grants, and unspecified assistantships available. Financial award application deadline: 1/1; financial award applicants required to submit FAFSA. *Faculty research:* Theoretical, numerical and experimental work in rarefied gas and plasma dynamics; electric propulsion; multiphase flows; rotating flows; turbomachinery; fluid-structure interactions; structural analysis; nonlinear dynamics and control; cooperative control in network systems; random vibrations; biomechanics and biomaterials; mesh generation for biomedical imaging; robotics and biorobotics; materials processing; mechanics of granular materials; laser holography; MEMS; computer-aided engineering. *Unit head:* Dr. John Sullivan, Interim Head, 508-831-5556, Fax: 508-831-5680, E-mail: sullivan@wpi.edu. *Application contact:* Dr. Mark Richman, Graduate Coordinator, 508-831-5556, Fax: 508-831-5680, E-mail: mrichman@wpi.edu.

Wright State University, School of Graduate Studies, College of Engineering and Computer Science, Programs in Engineering, Program in Mechanical and Materials Engineering, Dayton, OH 45435. Offers materials science and engineering (MSE); mechanical engineering (MSE). *Degree requirements:* For master's, thesis or course option alternative. *Entrance requirements:* Additional exam requirements/recommendations for international students: Required—TOEFL.

Yale University, Graduate School of Arts and Sciences, School of Engineering and Applied Science, Department of Mechanical Engineering, New Haven, CT 06520. Offers MS, PhD. Terminal master's awarded for partial completion of doctoral program. *Degree requirements:* For doctorate, thesis/dissertation, exam. *Entrance requirements:* For master's and doctorate, GRE General Test. Additional exam requirements/recommendations for international students: Required—TOEFL. *Faculty research:* Mechanics of fluids, mechanics of solids/material science.

Youngstown State University, Graduate School, College of Science, Technology, Engineering and Mathematics, Department of Mechanical Engineering, Youngstown, OH 44555-0001. Offers MSE. Part-time and evening/weekend programs available. *Degree requirements:* For master's, thesis optional. *Entrance requirements:* For master's, minimum GPA of 2.75 in field. Additional exam requirements/recommendations for international students: Required—TOEFL. *Faculty research:* Kinematics and dynamics of machines, computational and experimental heat transfer, machine controls and mechanical design.

Mechanics

Brown University, Graduate School, Division of Engineering, Program in Mechanics of Solids, Providence, RI 02912. Offers Sc M, PhD. *Degree requirements:* For doctorate, thesis/dissertation, preliminary exam.

California Institute of Technology, Division of Engineering and Applied Science, Option in Applied Mechanics, Pasadena, CA 91125-0001. Offers MS, PhD. *Faculty:* 1 full-time (0 women). *Students:* 4 full-time (1 woman). 4 applicants, 0% accepted, 0 enrolled. In 2010, 1 master's awarded. *Degree requirements:* For doctorate, thesis/dissertation. *Application deadline:* For fall admission, 1/1 for domestic students. Application fee: $0. *Financial support:* In 2010–11, 2 fellowships, 2 research assistantships, 1 teaching assistantship were awarded. *Faculty research:* Elasticity, mechanics of quasi-static and dynamic fracture, dynamics and mechanical vibrations, stability and control. *Unit head:* Dr. Thomas H. Heaton, Academic Officer, 626-395-4232, E-mail: heaton@caltech.edu. *Application contact:* Natalie Gilmore, Assistant Dean of Graduate Studies, 626-395-3812, Fax: 626-577-9246, E-mail: ngilmore@caltech.edu.

California State University, Fullerton, Graduate Studies, College of Engineering and Computer Science, Department of Civil Engineering and Engineering Mechanics, Fullerton, CA 92834-9480. Offers MS. Part-time programs available. *Students:* 88 full-time (14 women), 82 part-time (22 women); includes 2 Black or African American, non-Hispanic/Latino; 60 Asian, non-Hispanic/Latino; 21 Hispanic/Latino; 3 Two or more races, non-Hispanic/Latino, 24 international. Average age 29. 238 applicants, 63% accepted, 91 enrolled. In 2010, 40 master's awarded. *Degree requirements:* For master's, comprehensive exam, project or thesis. *Entrance requirements:* For master's, minimum undergraduate GPA of 2.5. Application fee: $55. *Financial support:* Career-related internships or fieldwork, Federal Work-Study, institutionally sponsored loans, and scholarships/grants available. Support available to part-time students. Financial award application deadline: 3/1; financial award applicants required to submit FAFSA. *Faculty research:* Soil-structure interaction, finite-element analysis, computer-aided analysis and design. *Unit head:* Dr. Pinaki Chakrabarti, Chair, 657-278-3016. *Application contact:* Admissions/Applications, 657-278-2371.

Carnegie Mellon University, Carnegie Institute of Technology, Department of Civil and Environmental Engineering, Pittsburgh, PA 15213. Offers advanced infrastructure systems (MS, PhD); civil and environmental engineering (MS, PhD); civil and environmental engineering/engineering and public policy (PhD); civil engineering (MS, PhD); computational mechanics (MS, PhD); computational science and engineering (MS, PhD); environmental engineering (MS, PhD); environmental management and science (MS, PhD). Part-time programs available. *Faculty:* 20 full-time (3 women), 15 part-time/adjunct (5 women). *Students:* 144 full-time (67 women), 8 part-time (2 women); includes 4 Black or African American, non-Hispanic/Latino; 1 American Indian or Alaska Native, non-Hispanic/Latino; 9 Asian, non-Hispanic/Latino, 99 international. Average age 26. 388 applicants, 66% accepted, 80 enrolled. In 2010, 62 master's, 8 doctorates awarded. Terminal master's awarded for partial completion of doctoral program. *Degree requirements:* For master's, thesis optional; for doctorate, comprehensive exam, thesis/dissertation, qualifying exam, public defense of dissertation. *Entrance requirements:* For master's and doctorate, GRE General Test. Additional exam requirements/recommendations for international students: Required—TOEFL (minimum score 84 iBT). *Application deadline:* For fall admission, 1/15 priority date for domestic and international students; for spring admission, 9/30 priority date for domestic and international students. Application fee: $65. Electronic applications accepted. *Financial support:* In 2010–11, 134 students received support, including 27 fellowships with full and partial tuition reimbursements available (averaging $21,708 per year), 42 research assistantships with full and partial tuition reimbursements available (averaging $24,474 per year); tuition waivers (partial) and unspecified assistantships also available. Financial award application deadline: 1/15. *Faculty research:* Advanced infrastructure systems; environmental engineering science and management; mechanics, materials, and computing; green design; global sustainable construction. Total annual research expenditures: $4.7 million. *Unit head:* Dr. James H. Garrett, Head, 412-268-2941, Fax: 412-268-7813, E-mail: garrett@cmu.edu. *Application contact:* Maxine A. Leffard, Director of the Graduate Program, 412-268-5673, Fax: 412-268-7813, E-mail: ce-admissions@andrew.cmu.edu.

Columbia University, Fu Foundation School of Engineering and Applied Science, Department of Civil Engineering and Engineering Mechanics, New York, NY 10027. Offers civil engineering (MS, Eng Sc D, PhD, Engr); construction engineering and management (MS); engineering mechanics (MS, Eng Sc D, PhD, Engr). Part-time programs available. Postbaccalaureate distance learning degree programs offered (no on-campus study). *Faculty:* 16 full-time (1 woman), 25 part-time/adjunct (3 women). *Students:* 96 full-time (19 women), 42 part-time (14 women); includes 25 minority (3 Black or African American, non-Hispanic/Latino; 11 Asian, non-Hispanic/Latino; 10 Hispanic/Latino; 1 Two or more races, non-Hispanic/Latino), 70 international. Average age 27. 265 applicants, 35% accepted, 59 enrolled. In 2010, 67 master's, 29 doctorates, 2 other advanced degrees awarded. Terminal master's awarded for partial completion of doctoral program. *Degree requirements:* For doctorate, thesis/dissertation, qualifying exam. *Entrance requirements:* For master's, doctorate, and Engr, GRE General Test. Additional exam requirements/recommendations for international students: Required—TOEFL, IELTS. *Application deadline:* For fall admission, 12/1 priority date for domestic and international students; for spring admission, 10/1 priority date for domestic and international students. Application fee: $95. Electronic applications accepted. *Financial support:* In 2010–11, 39 students received support, including 5 fellowships with full tuition reimbursements available (averaging $30,660 per year), 23 research assistantships with full tuition reimbursements available (averaging $30,660 per year), 11 teaching assistantships with full tuition reimbursements available (averaging $30,660 per year); traineeships and health care benefits also available. Financial award application deadline: 12/1; financial award applicants required to submit FAFSA. *Faculty research:* Motion monitoring of Manhattan Bridge, lightweight concrete panels, simulation of life of well sealant, intercultural knowledge system dynamics, corrosion monitoring of New York City bridges. *Unit head:* Dr. Raimondo Betti, Professor and Department Chairman, 212-854-6388, Fax: 212-854-7081, E-mail: betti@civil.columbia.edu. *Application contact:* Rene B. Testa, Professor, 212-854-3143, Fax: 212-854-6267, E-mail: testa@civil.columbia.edu.

Cornell University, Graduate School, Graduate Fields of Engineering, Field of Theoretical and Applied Mechanics, Ithaca, NY 14853-0001. Offers advanced composites and structures (M Eng); dynamics and space mechanics (MS, PhD); fluid mechanics (MS, PhD); mechanics of materials (MS, PhD); solid mechanics (MS, PhD). *Faculty:* 23 full-time (1 woman). *Students:* 32 full-time (8 women), 22 international. Average age 25. 38 applicants, 39% accepted, 9 enrolled. In 2010, 1 master's, 2 doctorates awarded. *Degree requirements:* For master's, thesis (MS); for doctorate, one foreign language, comprehensive exam, thesis/dissertation, teaching experience. *Entrance requirements:* For master's and doctorate, GRE General Test, 3 letters of recommendation. Additional exam requirements/recommendations for international students: Required—TOEFL (minimum score 600 paper-based; 237 computer-based; 77 iBT). *Application deadline:* For fall admission, 1/15 for domestic students. Application fee: $70. Electronic applications accepted. *Expenses:* Tuition: Full-time $29,500. Required fees: $76. Tuition and fees vary according to degree level and program. *Financial support:* In 2010–11, 5 fellowships with full tuition reimbursements, 7 research assistantships with full tuition reimbursements, 16 teaching assistantships with full tuition reimbursements were awarded; institutionally sponsored loans, scholarships/grants, health care benefits, and unspecified assistantships also available. *Faculty research:* Biomathematics, bio-fluids, animal locomotion; non-linear dynamics, celestial mechanics, control; mechanics of materials, computational mechanics; experimental mechanics; non-linear elasticity, granular materials, phase transitions. *Unit head:* Director of Graduate Studies, 607-255-5062, Fax: 607-255-2011. *Application contact:* Graduate Field Assistant, 607-255-5062, Fax: 607-255-2011, E-mail: tam_grad@cornell.edu.

Drexel University, College of Engineering, Department of Mechanical Engineering and Mechanics, Philadelphia, PA 19104-2875. Offers mechanical engineering (MS, PhD). Part-time and evening/weekend programs available. Terminal master's awarded for partial completion of doctoral program. *Degree requirements:* For master's, thesis optional; for doctorate, thesis/dissertation. *Entrance requirements:* For master's, minimum GPA of 3.0, BS in engineering or science; for doctorate, minimum GPA of 3.5, MS in engineering or science. Additional exam requirements/recommendations for international students: Required—TOEFL. Electronic applications accepted. *Faculty research:* Composites, dynamic systems and control, combustion and fuels, biomechanics, mechanics and thermal fluid sciences.

École Polytechnique de Montréal, Graduate Programs, Department of Mechanical Engineering, Montréal, QC H3C 3A7, Canada. Offers aerothermics (M Eng, M Sc A, PhD); applied mechanics (M Eng, M Sc A, PhD); tool design (M Eng, M Sc A, PhD). Part-time and evening/weekend programs available. *Degree requirements:* For master's, one foreign language, thesis; for doctorate, one foreign language, thesis/dissertation. *Entrance requirements:* For master's, minimum GPA of 2.75; for doctorate, minimum GPA of 3.0. *Faculty research:* Noise control and vibration, fatigue and creep, aerodynamics, composite materials, biomechanics, robotics.

Georgia Institute of Technology, Graduate Studies and Research, College of Engineering, School of Civil and Environmental Engineering, Program in Engineering Science and Mechanics, Atlanta, GA 30332-0001. Offers MS, MSESM, PhD. Part-time programs available. Terminal master's awarded for partial completion of doctoral program. *Degree requirements:* For doctorate, thesis/dissertation. *Entrance requirements:* For master's, GRE; for doctorate, GRE, minimum GPA of 3.2. Additional exam requirements/recommendations for international students: Required—TOEFL. *Faculty research:* Bioengineering, structural mechanics, solid mechanics, dynamics.

Iowa State University of Science and Technology, Graduate College, College of Engineering, Department of Aerospace Engineering and Engineering Mechanics, Ames, IA 50011. Offers aerospace engineering (M Eng, MS, PhD); engineering mechanics (M Eng, MS, PhD). *Faculty:* 34 full-time (1 woman), 3 part-time/adjunct (0 women). *Students:* 47 full-time (8 women), 12 part-time (2 women); includes 2 Asian, non-Hispanic/Latino; 1 Hispanic/Latino, 31 international. 86 applicants, 12% accepted, 5 enrolled. In 2010, 9 master's, 3 doctorates awarded. *Degree requirements:* For master's, thesis (for some programs); for doctorate, thesis/dissertation. *Entrance requirements:* For master's and doctorate, GRE General Test, resume. Additional exam requirements/recommendations for international students: Required—TOEFL (minimum score 550 paper-based; 80 iBT), IELTS (minimum score 6.5). *Application deadline:* For fall admission, 1/1 priority date for domestic and international students; for spring admission, 9/1 priority date for domestic and international students. Application fee: $40 ($90 for international students). Electronic applications accepted. *Financial support:* In 2010–11, 26 research assistantships with full and partial tuition reimbursements (averaging $6,250 per year), 18 teaching assistantships with full and partial tuition reimbursements (averaging $6,164 per year) were awarded; fellowships, scholarships/grants, health care benefits, and unspecified assistantships also available. *Unit head:* Dr. Thomas Rudolphi, Interim Chair, 515-294-5666, E-mail: aere_@iastate.edu. *Application contact:* Dr. Alric Rothmayer, Director of Graduate Education, 515-294-8851, E-mail: aere_info@iastate.edu.

The Johns Hopkins University, G. W. C. Whiting School of Engineering, Program in Engineering Management, Baltimore, MD 21218-2699. Offers biomaterials (MSEM); communications science (MSEM); computer science (MSEM); fluid mechanics (MSEM); materials science and engineering (MSEM); mechanical engineering (MSEM); mechanics and materials (MSEM); nano-biotechnology (MSEM); nanomaterials and nanotechnology (MSEM); probability and statistics (MSEM); smart product and device design (MSEM); systems analysis, management and environmental policy (MSEM). *Students:* 32 full-time (5 women), 4 part-time (0 women); includes 7 minority (3 Black or African American, non-Hispanic/Latino; 3 Asian, non-Hispanic/Latino; 1 Hispanic/Latino), 11 international. Average age 23. 110 applicants, 60% accepted, 27 enrolled. In 2010, 6 master's awarded. *Entrance requirements:* For master's, GRE, 3 letters of recommendation, resume. Additional exam requirements/recommendations for international students: Required—TOEFL (minimum score 600 paper-based; 250 computer-based; 100 iBT) or IELTS (minimum score 7). *Application deadline:* For fall admission, 1/15 priority date for domestic students, 1/15 for international students; for spring admission, 9/15 priority date for domestic students, 9/15 for international students. Applications are processed on a rolling basis. Application fee: $75. Electronic applications accepted. *Financial support:* Fellowships, health care benefits available. *Unit head:* Dr. Edward R. Scheinerman, Interim Director/Vice Dean for Education, School of Engineering/Professor, Applied Mathematics and Statistics, 410-516-7395, Fax: 410-516-4880, E-mail: ers@jhu.edu. *Application contact:* Dennis McIver, Coordinator of Graduate Admissions, 410-516-8174, Fax: 410-516-0780, E-mail: graduateadmissions@jhu.edu.

Lehigh University, P.C. Rossin College of Engineering and Applied Science, Department of Mechanical Engineering and Mechanics, Bethlehem, PA 18015. Offers computational engineering and mechanics (MS, PhD); mechanical engineering (M Eng, MS, PhD, MBA/E); polymer science/engineering (M Eng, MS, PhD, MBA/E); MBA/E. Part-time and evening/weekend programs available. Postbaccalaureate distance learning degree programs offered. *Faculty:* 24 full-time (0 women). *Students:* 106 full-time (12 women), 34 part-time (2 women); includes 7 minority (3 Black or African American, non-Hispanic/Latino; 3 Asian, non-Hispanic/Latino; 1 Hispanic/Latino), 71 international. Average age 26. 408 applicants, 29% accepted, 59 enrolled. In 2010, 23 master's, 7 doctorates awarded. Terminal master's awarded for partial completion of doctoral program. *Degree requirements:* For master's, thesis; for doctorate, thesis/dissertation, general exam. *Entrance requirements:* Additional exam requirements/recommendations for international students: Required—TOEFL (minimum score 550 paper-based; 213 computer-based; 79 iBT). *Application deadline:* For fall admission, 7/15 for domestic and international students; for spring admission, 12/1 for domestic and international students. Applications are processed on a rolling basis. Application fee: $75. Electronic applications accepted. *Financial support:* In 2010–11, 74 students received support, including 9 fellowships with full and partial tuition reimbursements available (averaging $23,280 per year), 23 research assistantships with full and partial tuition reimbursements available (averaging $20,700 per year), 24 teaching assistantships with full and partial tuition reimbursements available (averaging $24,480 per year); unspecified assistantships and Dean's doctoral assistantships also available. Financial award application deadline: 1/15. *Faculty research:* Thermofluids, dynamic systems, CAD/CAM, computational mechanics, solid mechanics. Total annual research expenditures: $3.3 million. *Unit head:* Dr. D. Gary Harlow, Chairman, 610-758-4102, Fax: 610-758-6224, E-mail: dgh0@lehigh.edu. *Application contact:* Jo Ann M. Casciano, Graduate Coordinator, 610-758-4107, Fax: 610-758-6224, E-mail: jmc4@lehigh.edu.

Louisiana State University and Agricultural and Mechanical College, Graduate School, College of Engineering, Department of Civil and Environmental Engineering, Baton Rouge, LA 70803. Offers environmental engineering (MSCE, PhD); geotechnical engineering (MSCE, PhD); structural engineering and mechanics (MSCE, PhD); transportation engineering (MSCE, PhD); water resources (MSCE, PhD). Part-time programs available. *Faculty:* 29 full-time (3 women). *Students:* 89 full-time (19 women), 35 part-time (8 women); includes 2 Black or African American, non-Hispanic/Latino; 1 American Indian or Alaska Native, non-Hispanic/Latino; 3 Asian, non-Hispanic/Latino; 3 Hispanic/Latino, 65 international. Average age 29. 96 applicants, 65% accepted, 16 enrolled. In 2010, 20 master's, 8 doctorates awarded. *Degree requirements:* For master's, thesis optional; for doctorate, one foreign language, thesis/dissertation. *Entrance requirements:* For master's and doctorate, GRE General Test, minimum GPA of 3.0. Additional exam requirements/recommendations for international students: Required—TOEFL (minimum score 550 paper-based; 213 computer-based; 79 iBT) or IELTS (minimum score 6.5). *Application deadline:* For fall admission, 1/25 priority date for domestic students, 5/15 for international students; for spring admission, 10/15 for international students. Applications are processed on a rolling basis. Application fee: $50 ($70 for international students). Electronic applications accepted. *Financial support:* In 2010–11, 89 students received support, including 2 fellowships with full and partial tuition reimbursements available (averaging $24,418 per year), 75 research assistantships with full and partial tuition reimbursements available (averaging $16,115 per year), 3 teaching assistantships with full and partial tuition reimbursements available (averaging $12,843 per year); career-related internships or fieldwork, institutionally sponsored loans, scholarships/grants, and health care benefits also available. Financial award application deadline: 3/1; financial award applicants required to submit FAFSA. *Faculty research:* Mechanics and structures, environmental, geotechnical transportation, water resources. Total annual research expenditures: $2.6 million. *Unit head:* Dr. George Z. Voyiadjis, Chair/Professor, 225-578-8668, Fax: 225-578-9176, E-mail: cegzv@lsu.edu. *Application contact:* Dr. Clinton Willson, Professor, 225-578-8652, E-mail: cwillson@lsu.edu.

McGill University, Faculty of Graduate and Postdoctoral Studies, Faculty of Engineering, Department of Civil Engineering and Applied Mechanics, Montréal, QC H3A 2T5, Canada. Offers environmental engineering (M Eng, M Sc, PhD); fluid mechanics (M Sc); fluid mechanics and hydraulic engineering (M Eng, PhD); materials engineering (M Eng, PhD); rehabilitation of urban infrastructure (M Eng, PhD); soil behavior (M Eng, PhD); soil mechanics and foundations (M Eng, PhD); structures and structural mechanics (M Eng, PhD); water resources (M Sc); water resources engineering (M Eng, PhD).

Michigan State University, The Graduate School, College of Engineering, Department of Mechanical Engineering, East Lansing, MI 48824. Offers engineering mechanics (MS, PhD); mechanical engineering (MS, PhD). *Entrance requirements:* For master's, GRE General Test. Additional exam requirements/recommendations for international students: Required—TOEFL. Electronic applications accepted.

Michigan Technological University, Graduate School, College of Engineering, Department of Mechanical Engineering-Engineering Mechanics, Program in Engineering Mechanics, Houghton, MI 49931. Offers MS. Part-time programs available. *Degree requirements:* For master's, comprehensive exam (for some programs), thesis (for some programs). *Entrance requirements:* For master's, GRE. Additional exam requirements/recommendations for international students: Required—TOEFL (minimum score 637 paper-based; 270 computer-based). Electronic applications accepted. *Expenses:* Contact institution.

Missouri University of Science and Technology, Graduate School, Department of Civil, Architectural, and Environmental Engineering, Rolla, MO 65409. Offers civil engineering (MS, DE, PhD); construction engineering (MS, DE, PhD); environmental engineering (MS); fluid mechanics (MS, DE, PhD); geotechnical engineering (MS, DE, PhD); hydrology and hydraulic engineering (MS, DE, PhD). Part-time and evening/weekend programs available. Terminal master's awarded for partial completion of doctoral program. *Degree requirements:* For master's, thesis optional; for doctorate, comprehensive exam, thesis/dissertation. *Entrance requirements:* For master's, GRE General Test (minimum combined score 1100), minimum GPA of 3.0; for doctorate, GRE General Test (minimum score: verbal and quantitative 400, writing 3.5), minimum GPA of 3.0. Additional exam requirements/recommendations for international students: Required—TOEFL. Electronic applications accepted. *Faculty research:* Earthquake engineering, structural optimization and control systems, structural health monitoring/damage detection, soil-structure interaction, soil mechanics and foundation engineering.

Montana State University, College of Graduate Studies, College of Engineering, Department of Civil Engineering, Bozeman, MT 59717. Offers civil engineering (MS); construction engineering management (MCEM); engineering (PhD), including applied mechanics option, civil engineering option. Part-time programs available. *Faculty:* 19 full-time (2 women), 5 part-time/adjunct (1 woman). *Students:* 26 full-time (6 women), 21 part-time (6 women); includes 2 minority (1 American Indian or Alaska Native, non-Hispanic/Latino; 1 Two or more races, non-Hispanic/Latino), 1 international. Average age 27. 43 applicants, 44% accepted, 17 enrolled. In 2010, 15 master's, 1 doctorate awarded. *Degree requirements:* For master's, comprehensive exam, thesis (for some programs); for doctorate, comprehensive exam, thesis/dissertation. *Entrance requirements:* For master's and doctorate, GRE General Test. Additional exam requirements/recommendations for international students: Required—TOEFL (minimum score 550 paper-based; 213 computer-based). *Application deadline:* For fall admission, 7/15 priority date for domestic students, 5/15 priority date for international students; for spring admission, 12/1 priority date for domestic students, 10/1 priority date for international students. Applications are processed on a rolling basis. Application fee: $30. Electronic applications accepted. *Expenses:* Tuition, state resident: full-time $5553.90. Tuition, nonresident: full-time $14,646. Required fees: $1233. *Financial support:* In 2010–11, 20 students received support, including 1 fellowship (averaging $15,000 per year), 5 research assistantships with partial tuition reimbursements available (averaging $12,000 per year), 6 teaching assistantships with partial tuition reimbursements available (averaging $8,000 per year); scholarships/grants and tuition waivers (partial) also available. Financial award application deadline: 3/1; financial award applicants required to submit FAFSA. *Faculty research:* Snow and ice mechanics, biofilm engineering, transportation, structural and geo materials, water resources. Total annual research expenditures: $54,392. *Unit head:* Dr. Brett Gunnick, Head, 406-994-2111, Fax: 406-994-6105, E-mail: bgunnick@ce.montana.edu. *Application contact:* Dr. Carl A. Fox, Vice Provost for Graduate Education, 406-994-4145, Fax: 406-994-7433, E-mail: gradstudy@montana.edu.

New Mexico Institute of Mining and Technology, Graduate Studies, Program in Engineering Science in Mechanics, Socorro, NM 87801. Offers advanced mechanics (MS); explosives engineering (MS). *Degree requirements:* For master's, thesis (for some programs). *Entrance requirements:* For master's, GRE General Test. Additional exam requirements/recommendations for international students: Required—TOEFL (minimum score 540 paper-based; 207 computer-based). *Faculty research:* Vibrations, fluid-structure interactions.

North Dakota State University, College of Graduate and Interdisciplinary Studies, College of Engineering and Architecture, Department of Mechanical Engineering and Applied Mechanics, Fargo, ND 58108. Offers MS, PhD. Part-time programs available. *Faculty:* 15 full-time (1 woman), 1 part-time/adjunct (0 women). *Students:* 39 full-time (8 women), 18 part-time (2 women); includes 1 Asian, non-Hispanic/Latino, 25 international. Average age 28. 74 applicants, 41% accepted, 14 enrolled. In 2010, 11 master's awarded. *Degree requirements:* For master's, thesis; for doctorate, comprehensive exam, thesis/dissertation. *Entrance requirements:* For master's and doctorate, minimum GPA of 3.0. Additional exam requirements/recommendations for international students: Required—TOEFL (minimum score 550 paper-based). *Application deadline:* For fall admission, 7/1 priority date for domestic students, 5/1 priority date for international students; for spring admission, 12/1 priority date for domestic students, 9/1 priority date for international students. Applications are processed on a rolling basis. Application fee: $45 ($60 for international students). Electronic applications accepted. *Financial support:* In 2010–11, 20 students received support, including research assistantships with full tuition reimbursements available (averaging $9,000 per year), teaching assistantships with full tuition reimbursements available (averaging $9,000 per year); career-related internships or fieldwork, Federal Work-Study, and institutionally sponsored loans also available. Financial award application deadline: 2/15. *Faculty research:* Thermodynamics, finite element analysis, automotive systems, robotics, nanotechnology. Total annual research expenditures: $530,000. *Unit head:* Dr. Alan Kallmeyer, Chair, 701-231-8836, Fax: 701-231-8913, E-mail: alan.kallmeyer@ndsu.edu. *Application contact:* Dr. David A. Wittrock, Dean, 701-231-7033, Fax: 701-231-6524.

Northwestern University, McCormick School of Engineering and Applied Science, Department of Civil and Environmental Engineering, Program in Theoretical and Applied Mechanics, Evanston, IL 60208. Offers fluid mechanics (MS, PhD); solid mechanics (MS, PhD). Admissions and degrees offered through The Graduate School. Terminal master's awarded for partial completion of doctoral program. *Degree requirements:* For master's, thesis; for doctorate, thesis/dissertation. *Entrance requirements:* For master's, GRE General Test, minimum 2 letters of recommendation; for doctorate, GRE General Test, minimum 2 letters of recommendation, transcripts from all academic institutions attended. Additional exam requirements/recommendations for international students: Required—TOEFL (minimum score 600 paper-based; 250 computer-based; 100 iBT), IELTS (minimum score 7), TOEFL (internet-based)

speaking score of 26. Electronic applications accepted. *Faculty research:* Composite materials, computational mechanics, fracture and damage mechanics, geophysics, nondestructive evaluation.

Ohio University, Graduate College, Russ College of Engineering and Technology, Department of Civil Engineering, Athens, OH 45701-2979. Offers civil engineering (PhD); construction (MS); environmental (MS); geotechnical and geoenvironmental (MS); mechanics (MS); structures (MS); transportation (MS); water resources and structures (MS). Part-time programs available. *Students:* 29 full-time (6 women), 5 part-time (1 woman); includes 2 minority (1 Hispanic/Latino; 1 Two or more races, non-Hispanic/Latino), 16 international. 52 applicants, 83% accepted, 14 enrolled. In 2010, 7 master's awarded. *Degree requirements:* For master's, comprehensive exam (for some programs), thesis or alternative; for doctorate, comprehensive exam, thesis/dissertation. *Entrance requirements:* For master's, GRE General Test, minimum GPA of 3.0, 3 letters of recommendation; for doctorate, GRE General Test. Additional exam requirements/recommendations for international students: Required—TOEFL (minimum score 550 paper-based; 80 iBT) or IELTS (minimum score 6.5). *Application deadline:* For fall admission, 5/1 priority date for domestic students, 2/1 priority date for international students; for winter admission, 8/1 priority date for domestic students, 4/1 priority date for international students; for spring admission, 2/1 priority date for domestic students, 7/1 priority date for international students. Applications are processed on a rolling basis. Application fee: $50 ($55 for international students). Electronic applications accepted. *Financial support:* Research assistantships with full tuition reimbursements, teaching assistantships with full tuition reimbursements, Federal Work-Study, institutionally sponsored loans, scholarships/grants, and unspecified assistantships available. Financial award application deadline: 3/15; financial award applicants required to submit FAFSA. *Faculty research:* Noise abatement, materials and environment, highway infrastructure, subsurface investigation (pavements, pipes, bridges). *Unit head:* Dr. Gayle F. Mitchell, Chair, 740-593-0430, Fax: 740-593-0625, E-mail: mitchelg@ohio.edu. *Application contact:* Dr. Shad M. Sargand, Graduate Chair, 740-593-1465, Fax: 740-593-0625, E-mail: sargand@ohio.edu.

Penn State University Park, Graduate School, College of Engineering, Department of Engineering Science and Mechanics, State College, University Park, PA 16802-1503. Offers M Eng, MS, PhD.

Rutgers, The State University of New Jersey, New Brunswick, Graduate School-New Brunswick, Program in Mechanics, Piscataway, NJ 08854-8097. Offers MS, PhD. Part-time programs available. Terminal master's awarded for partial completion of doctoral program. *Degree requirements:* For master's, thesis optional, qualifying exam; for doctorate, thesis/dissertation, qualifying exam. *Entrance requirements:* For master's and doctorate, GRE General Test, GRE Subject Test (recommended). Additional exam requirements/recommendations for international students: Required—TOEFL. Electronic applications accepted. *Expenses:* Tuition, state resident: full-time $7200; part-time $600 per credit. Tuition, nonresident: full-time $11,124; part-time $927 per credit. *Faculty research:* Continuum mechanics, constitutive theory, thermodynamics, visolasticity, liquid crystal theory.

San Diego State University, Graduate and Research Affairs, College of Engineering, Department of Aerospace Engineering and Engineering Mechanics, San Diego, CA 92182. Offers aerospace engineering (MS); engineering mechanics (MS); engineering sciences and applied mechanics (PhD); flight dynamics (MS); fluid dynamics (MS). PhD offered jointly with University of California, San Diego and Department of Mechanical Engineering. Terminal master's awarded for partial completion of doctoral program. *Degree requirements:* For master's, comprehensive exam (for some programs), thesis (for some programs); for doctorate, thesis/dissertation. *Entrance requirements:* For master's, GRE General Test; for doctorate, GRE, 3 letters of recommendation. Additional exam requirements/recommendations for international students: Required—TOEFL. Electronic applications accepted. *Faculty research:* Organized structures in post-stall flow over wings/three dimensional separated flow, airfoil growth effect, probabilities, structural mechanics.

Southern Illinois University Carbondale, Graduate School, College of Engineering, Department of Civil and Environmental Engineering, Carbondale, IL 62901-4701. Offers civil engineering (MS). *Degree requirements:* For master's, comprehensive exam, thesis. *Entrance requirements:* For master's, minimum GPA of 2.7. Additional exam requirements/recommendations for international students: Required—TOEFL. *Faculty research:* Composite materials, wastewater treatment, solid waste disposal, slurry transport, geotechnical engineering.

Southern Illinois University Carbondale, Graduate School, College of Engineering, Program in Engineering Science, Carbondale, IL 62901-4701. Offers electrical systems (PhD); fossil energy (PhD); mechanics (PhD). *Degree requirements:* For doctorate, thesis/dissertation. *Entrance requirements:* For doctorate, GRE General Test, minimum GPA of 3.5. Additional exam requirements/recommendations for international students: Required—TOEFL.

The University of Alabama, Graduate School, College of Engineering, Department of Aerospace Engineering and Mechanics, Tuscaloosa, AL 35487. Offers aerospace engineering (MAE); engineering science and mechanics (MES, PhD). Part-time programs available. Post-baccalaureate distance learning degree programs offered (no on-campus study). *Faculty:* 14 full-time (1 woman). *Students:* 14 full-time (3 women), 35 part-time (5 women); includes 2 minority (both Hispanic/Latino), 17 international. Average age 29. 47 applicants, 72% accepted, 11 enrolled. In 2010, 10 master's, 4 doctorates awarded. Terminal master's awarded for partial completion of doctoral program. *Degree requirements:* For master's, comprehensive exam (for some programs), thesis (for some programs); for doctorate, comprehensive exam, thesis/dissertation, 1 year residency. *Entrance requirements:* For master's and doctorate, GRE, minimum undergraduate GPA of 3.0. Additional exam requirements/recommendations for international students: Required—TOEFL (minimum score 550 paper-based). *Application deadline:* For fall admission, 7/1 priority date for domestic students, 1/15 priority date for international students; for spring admission, 11/1 priority date for domestic students, 6/1 priority date for international students. Applications are processed on a rolling basis. Application fee: $50 ($60 for international students). Electronic applications accepted. *Expenses:* Tuition, state resident: full-time $7900. Tuition, nonresident: full-time $20,500. *Financial support:* In 2010–11, 18 students received support, including fellowships with full tuition reimbursements available (averaging $20,000 per year), research assistantships with full tuition reimbursements available (averaging $18,375 per year), teaching assistantships with full tuition reimbursements available (averaging $18,375 per year); Federal Work-Study, institutionally sponsored loans, scholarships/grants, health care benefits, and unspecified assistantships also available. Financial award application deadline: 2/15. *Faculty research:* Intelligent computer systems, genetic algorithms, neural networks, impact and penetration mechanics, spacecraft dynamics and controls. Total annual research expenditures: $959,591. *Unit head:* Dr. Stanley E. Jones, Interim Department Head and Cudworth Professor, 205-348-7242, Fax: 205-348-7240, E-mail: sejones@eng.ua.edu. *Application contact:* Dr. John E. Jackson, Professor, 205-348-7306, Fax: 208-348-7240, E-mail: johnjackson@eng.ua.edu.

The University of Arizona, College of Engineering, Department of Civil Engineering and Engineering Mechanics, Tucson, AZ 85721. Offers civil engineering (MS, PhD); engineering mechanics (MS, PhD). Part-time programs available. *Faculty:* 10 full-time (1 woman), 1 part-time/adjunct (0 women). *Students:* 57 full-time (14 women), 40 part-time (6 women); includes 21 minority (6 Black or African American, non-Hispanic/Latino; 2 Asian, non-Hispanic/Latino; 4 Hispanic/Latino; 9 Two or more races, non-Hispanic/Latino), 36 international. Average age 29. 74 applicants, 46% accepted, 7 enrolled. In 2010, 7 master's, 6 doctorates awarded. *Degree requirements:* For master's, thesis; for doctorate, thesis/dissertation, departmental qualifying exam. *Entrance requirements:* For master's, GRE General Test, 3 letters of recommendation, statement of purpose; for doctorate, GRE General Test, minimum GPA of 3.5, 3 letters of recommendation, statement of purpose. Additional exam requirements/recommendations for international students: Required—TOEFL (minimum score 550 paper-based; 213 computer-based; 79 iBT). *Application deadline:* For fall admission, 6/1 for domestic students, 12/1 for international students; for spring admission, 10/1 for domestic students, 6/1

Mechanics

The University of Arizona (continued)
for international students. Applications are processed on a rolling basis. Application fee: $75. Electronic applications accepted. *Expenses:* Tuition, state resident: full-time $7692. *Financial support:* In 2010–11, 24 research assistantships with full tuition reimbursements (averaging $23,586 per year), 7 teaching assistantships with full tuition reimbursements (averaging $23,586 per year) were awarded; institutionally sponsored loans, scholarships/grants, health care benefits, tuition waivers (partial), and unspecified assistantships also available. Financial award application deadline: 4/1. *Faculty research:* Constitutive modeling, rehabilitation of structures, groundwater, earthquake engineering, hazardous waste treatment. Total annual research expenditures: $1.1 million. *Unit head:* Kevin E. Lansey, Department Head, 520-621-6564, E-mail: lansey@engr.arizona.edu. *Application contact:* Graduate Coordinator, 520-621-2266, Fax: 520-621-2550, E-mail: ceemg@engr.arizona.edu.

University of California, Berkeley, Graduate Division, College of Engineering, Department of Civil and Environmental Engineering, Berkeley, CA 94720-1500. Offers engineering and project management (M Eng, MS, D Eng, PhD); environmental engineering (M Eng, MS, D Eng, PhD); geoengineering (M Eng, MS, D Eng, PhD); structural engineering, mechanics and materials (M Eng, MS, D Eng, PhD); transportation engineering (M Eng, MS, D Eng, PhD); M Arch/MS; MCP/MS; MPP/MS. *Degree requirements:* For master's, comprehensive exam or thesis (MS); for doctorate, thesis/dissertation, qualifying exam. *Entrance requirements:* For master's, GRE General Test, minimum GPA of 3.0, 3 letters of recommendation; for doctorate, GRE General Test, minimum GPA of 3.5, 3 letters of recommendation. Additional exam requirements/recommendations for international students: Required—TOEFL (minimum score 570 paper-based; 230 computer-based). Electronic applications accepted.

University of California, Merced, Division of Graduate Studies, School of Natural Sciences, Merced, CA 95343. Offers applied mathematics (MS, PhD); biological engineering and small-scale technologies (MS, PhD); environmental systems (MS, PhD); mechanical engineering and applied mechanics (MS, PhD); physics and chemistry (PhD); quantitative and systems biology (MS, PhD).

University of California, San Diego, Office of Graduate Studies, Department of Mechanical and Aerospace Engineering, Program in Applied Mechanics, La Jolla, CA 92093. Offers MS, PhD. PhD offered jointly with San Diego State University. Part-time programs available. *Degree requirements:* For master's, comprehensive exam or thesis; for doctorate, thesis/dissertation, qualifying exam. *Entrance requirements:* For master's and doctorate, GRE General Test, minimum GPA of 3.0. Additional exam requirements/recommendations for international students: Required—TOEFL. Electronic applications accepted. *Faculty research:* Combustion engineering, environmental mechanics, magnetic recording, materials processing, computational fluid dynamics.

University of Cincinnati, Graduate School, College of Engineering, Department of Aerospace Engineering and Engineering Mechanics, Cincinnati, OH 45221. Offers MS, PhD. Part-time programs available. Terminal master's awarded for partial completion of doctoral program. *Degree requirements:* For master's, project or thesis; for doctorate, thesis/dissertation. *Entrance requirements:* For master's and doctorate, GRE General Test. Additional exam requirements/recommendations for international students: Required—TOEFL (minimum score 550 paper-based; 213 computer-based). Electronic applications accepted. *Faculty research:* Computational fluid mechanics/propulsion, large space structures, dynamics and guidance of VTOL vehicles.

University of Dayton, Graduate School, School of Engineering, Department of Civil and Environmental Engineering and Engineering Mechanics, Dayton, OH 45469-1300. Offers engineering mechanics (MSEM); environmental engineering (MSCE); geotechnical engineering (MSCE); structural engineering (MSCE); transportation engineering (MSCE); water resources engineering (MSCE). Part-time programs available. *Faculty:* 7 full-time (2 women), 2 part-time/adjunct (0 women). *Students:* 10 full-time (5 women), 7 part-time (2 women); includes 2 minority (both Black or African American, non-Hispanic/Latino), 6 international. Average age 27. 23 applicants, 43% accepted, 4 enrolled. In 2010, 5 master's awarded. *Degree requirements:* For master's, thesis optional. *Entrance requirements:* For master's, minimum GPA of 3.0 in undergraduate work. Additional exam requirements/recommendations for international students: Required—TOEFL (minimum score 550 paper-based; 213 computer-based; 80 iBT). *Application deadline:* For fall admission, 8/1 for domestic students, 3/1 priority date for international students; for winter admission, 7/1 priority date for international students; for spring admission, 1/1 priority date for international students. Applications are processed on a rolling basis. Application fee: $0 ($50 for international students). Electronic applications accepted. *Expenses:* Tuition: Full-time $7800; part-time $650 per credit hour. *Financial support:* In 2010–11, 2 research assistantships (averaging $10,600 per year) were awarded. Financial award applicants required to submit FAFSA. *Faculty research:* Physical modeling of hydraulic systems, finite element methods, mechanics of composite materials, transportation systems safety, biological treatment processes. Total annual research expenditures: $200,000. *Unit head:* Dr. Donald V. Chase, Chair, 937-229-3847, Fax: 937-229-3491, E-mail: donald.chase@notes.udayton.edu. *Application contact:* Alexander Popovski, Associate Director of International and Graduate Admissions, 937-229-2357, Fax: 937-229-4729, E-mail: alex.popovski@notes.udayton.edu.

University of Illinois at Urbana–Champaign, Graduate College, College of Engineering, Department of Mechanical Science and Engineering, Champaign, IL 61820. Offers mechanical engineering (MS, PhD); theoretical and applied mechanics (MS, PhD); MS/MBA. *Faculty:* 51 full-time (4 women), 2 part-time/adjunct (0 women). *Students:* 325 full-time (37 women), 39 part-time (4 women); includes 1 Black or African American, non-Hispanic/Latino; 17 Asian, non-Hispanic/Latino; 13 Hispanic/Latino, 198 international. 587 applicants, 33% accepted, 88 enrolled. In 2010, 77 master's, 29 doctorates awarded. Terminal master's awarded for partial completion of doctoral program. *Entrance requirements:* For master's, GRE General Test, minimum GPA of 3.25; for doctorate, GRE General Test, minimum GPA of 3.5. Additional exam requirements/recommendations for international students: Required—TOEFL (minimum score 613 paper-based; 257 computer-based; 103 iBT). *Application deadline:* Applications are processed on a rolling basis. Application fee: $75 ($90 for international students). Electronic applications accepted. *Financial support:* In 2010–11, 42 fellowships, 244 research assistantships, 102 teaching assistantships were awarded; tuition waivers (full and partial) also available. *Faculty research:* Combustion and propulsion, design methodology, dynamic systems and controls, energy transfer, materials behavior and processing, manufacturing systems operations, management. *Unit head:* Placid Mathew Ferreira, Head, 217-333-0639, Fax: 217-244-6534, E-mail: pferreir@illinois.edu. *Application contact:* Kathy A. Smith, Admissions and Records Officer, 217-244-4539, Fax: 217-244-6534, E-mail: smith15@illinois.edu.

University of Maryland, College Park, Academic Affairs, A. James Clark School of Engineering, Department of Mechanical Engineering, College Park, MD 20742. Offers electronic packaging and reliability (MS, PhD); manufacturing and design (MS, PhD); mechanics and materials (MS, PhD); reliability engineering (M Eng, MS, PhD); thermal and fluid sciences (MS, PhD). Part-time and evening/weekend programs available. Postbaccalaureate distance learning degree programs offered. *Faculty:* 79 full-time (7 women), 21 part-time/adjunct (1 woman). *Students:* 219 full-time (31 women), 73 part-time (10 women); includes 44 minority (11 Black or African American, non-Hispanic/Latino; 2 American Indian or Alaska Native, non-Hispanic/Latino; 21 Asian, non-Hispanic/Latino; 8 Hispanic/Latino; 2 Two or more races, non-Hispanic/Latino), 138 international. 520 applicants, 18% accepted, 63 enrolled. In 2010, 31 master's, 31 doctorates awarded. *Degree requirements:* For master's, thesis optional; for doctorate, thesis/dissertation, qualifying exam. *Entrance requirements:* For master's, GRE General Test, 3 letters of recommendation; for doctorate, GRE General Test, minimum GPA of 3.0. Additional exam requirements/recommendations for international students: Required—TOEFL. *Application deadline:* For fall admission, 5/15 for domestic students, 2/1 for international students; for spring admission, 10/1 for domestic students, 6/1 for international students. Applications are processed on a rolling basis. Application fee: $75. Electronic applications accepted. *Expenses:* Tuition, area resident: Part-time $471 per credit hour. Tuition, state resident: part-time $471 per credit hour. Tuition, nonresident: part-time $1016 per credit hour. Required fees: $337 per term. *Financial support:* In 2010–11, 3 fellowships with full and partial tuition reimbursements (averaging $19,975 per year), 166 research assistantships (averaging $23,679 per year), 12 teaching assistantships (averaging $17,644 per year) were awarded; Federal Work-Study and scholarships/grants also available. Support available to part-time students. Financial award applicants required to submit FAFSA. *Faculty research:* Injection molding, electronic packaging, fluid mechanics, product engineering. Total annual research expenditures: $17.4 million. *Unit head:* Dr. B. Balachandran, Interim Chair, 301-405-5297, E-mail: balab@umd.edu. *Application contact:* Dr. Charles A. Caramello, Graduate Director, 301-405-0358, Fax: 301-314-9305, E-mail: ccaramel@umd.edu.

University of Massachusetts Lowell, College of Arts and Sciences, Department of Physics and Applied Physics, Program in Applied Physics, Lowell, MA 01854-2881. Offers applied mechanics (PhD); applied physics (MS, PhD), including optical sciences (MS). Terminal master's awarded for partial completion of doctoral program. *Degree requirements:* For master's, thesis; for doctorate, 2 foreign languages, thesis/dissertation. *Entrance requirements:* For master's, GRE General Test, 3 letters of reference; for doctorate, GRE General Test, transcripts, 3 letters of reference. Additional exam requirements/recommendations for international students: Required—TOEFL.

University of Minnesota, Twin Cities Campus, Institute of Technology, Department of Aerospace Engineering and Mechanics, Minneapolis, MN 55455-0213. Offers aerospace engineering (M Aero E); aerospace engineering and mechanics (MS, PhD). Part-time programs available. *Degree requirements:* For doctorate, thesis/dissertation. *Entrance requirements:* Additional exam requirements/recommendations for international students: Required—TOEFL (minimum score 550 paper-based; 213 computer-based). Electronic applications accepted. *Faculty research:* Fluid mechanics, solid and continuum fluid mechanics, computational mechanics, aerospace systems.

University of Nebraska–Lincoln, Graduate College, College of Engineering, Department of Engineering Mechanics, Lincoln, NE 68588. Offers MS, PhD. *Degree requirements:* For master's, thesis optional; for doctorate, comprehensive exam, thesis/dissertation. *Entrance requirements:* For master's and doctorate, GRE. Additional exam requirements/recommendations for international students: Required—TOEFL (minimum score 550 paper-based; 213 computer-based). Electronic applications accepted. *Faculty research:* Polymer mechanics, piezoelectric materials, meshless methods, smart materials, fracture mechanics.

University of New Brunswick Fredericton, School of Graduate Studies, Faculty of Engineering, Department of Mechanical Engineering, Fredericton, NB E3B 5A3, Canada. Offers applied mechanics (M Eng, M Sc E, PhD); mechanical engineering (M Eng, M Sc E, PhD). Part-time programs available. *Faculty:* 14 full-time (1 woman), 2 part-time/adjunct (0 women). *Students:* 44 full-time (6 women), 4 part-time (0 women). In 2010, 10 master's, 2 doctorates awarded. *Degree requirements:* For master's, thesis; for doctorate, comprehensive exam, thesis/dissertation, qualifying exam. *Entrance requirements:* For master's, minimum GPA of 3.0; B Sc E; for doctorate, minimum GPA of 3.0; M Sc E. Additional exam requirements/recommendations for international students: Required—TOEFL (minimum score 550 paper-based), IELTS, TWE (minimum score 4). *Application deadline:* For fall admission, 3/1 priority date for domestic students. Applications are processed on a rolling basis. Application fee: $50 Canadian dollars. *Expenses:* Tuition, area resident: Full-time $3708; part-time $927 per term. International tuition: $6300 full-time. Required fees: $50 per term. *Financial support:* In 2010–11, 61 research assistantships, 51 teaching assistantships were awarded. *Faculty research:* Analysis of gross motor activities as a means of assessing upper limb prosthesis, distance determination algorithms and their applications, void nucleation in automotive aluminum alloy, robot kinematics, micromechanics, analysis of human walking, plastic linjection molding, green nanotechnology, mechatronics, fatigue assessment of strucutures, ocean renewable energy. *Unit head:* Dr. Zengtao Chen, Director of Graduate Studies, 506-458-7784, Fax: 506-453-5025, E-mail: ztchen@unb.ca. *Application contact:* Susan Shea-Perrott, Graduate Secretary, 506-458-7742, Fax: 506-453-5025, E-mail: susan@unb.ca.

University of Pennsylvania, School of Engineering and Applied Science, Department of Mechanical Engineering and Applied Mechanics, Philadelphia, PA 19104. Offers applied mechanics (MSE, PhD); mechanical engineering (MSE, PhD). Part-time programs available. *Faculty:* 20 full-time (3 women), 9 part-time/adjunct (0 women). *Students:* 92 full-time (14 women), 20 part-time (4 women); includes 5 Black or African American, non-Hispanic/Latino; 8 Asian, non-Hispanic/Latino; 2 Hispanic/Latino, 41 international. 439 applicants, 37% accepted, 70 enrolled. In 2010, 46 master's, 6 doctorates awarded. *Degree requirements:* For master's, thesis optional; for doctorate, thesis/dissertation. *Entrance requirements:* Additional exam requirements/recommendations for international students: Required—TOEFL. *Application deadline:* For fall admission, 1/2 priority date for domestic students. Applications are processed on a rolling basis. Application fee: $70. Electronic applications accepted. *Expenses:* Tuition: Full-time $25,660; part-time $4758 per course. Required fees: $2152; $270 per course. Tuition and fees vary according to course load, degree level and program. *Financial support:* Fellowships, research assistantships, teaching assistantships, institutionally sponsored loans, scholarships/grants, traineeships, health care benefits, and unspecified assistantships also available. *Faculty research:* Heat transfer, fluid mechanics, energy conversion, solid mechanics, dynamics of mechanisms and robots.

University of Southern California, Graduate School, Viterbi School of Engineering, Sonny Astani Department of Civil Engineering, Los Angeles, CA 90089. Offers applied mechanics (MS); civil engineering (MS, PhD); computer-aided engineering (ME, Graduate Certificate); construction management (MCM); engineering technology commercialization (Graduate Certificate); environmental engineering (MS, PhD); environmental quality management (ME); structural design (ME); sustainable cities (Graduate Certificate); transportation systems (MS, Graduate Certificate); water and waste management (MS). Part-time and evening/weekend programs available. *Faculty:* 16 full-time (2 women), 35 part-time/adjunct (5 women). *Students:* 190 full-time (52 women), 81 part-time (20 women); includes 54 minority (2 Black or African American, non-Hispanic/Latino; 42 Asian, non-Hispanic/Latino; 9 Hispanic/Latino; 1 Two or more races, non-Hispanic/Latino), 149 international. 541 applicants, 43% accepted, 100 enrolled. In 2010, 74 master's, 10 doctorates awarded. Terminal master's awarded for partial completion of doctoral program. *Degree requirements:* For master's, thesis optional; for doctorate, thesis/dissertation. *Entrance requirements:* For master's and doctorate, GRE General Test. *Application deadline:* For fall admission, 12/1 priority date for domestic and international students; for spring admission, 9/15 for domestic students, 9/15 priority date for international students. Applications are processed on a rolling basis. Application fee: $85. Electronic applications accepted. *Expenses:* Tuition: Full-time $31,240; part-time $1420 per unit. Required fees: $600. One-time fee: $35 full-time. Full-time tuition and fees vary according to degree level and program. *Financial support:* In 2010–11, fellowships with full tuition reimbursements (averaging $30,000 per year), research assistantships with full tuition reimbursements (averaging $20,000 per year), teaching assistantships with full tuition reimbursements (averaging $20,000 per year) were awarded; career-related internships or fieldwork, scholarships/grants, health care benefits, and unspecified assistantships also available. Financial award application deadline: 12/1; financial award applicants required to submit CSS PROFILE or FAFSA. *Faculty research:* Geotechnical engineering, transportation engineering, structural engineering, construction management, environmental engineering, water resources. Total annual research expenditures: $5 million. *Unit head:* Dr. Jean-Pierre Bardet, Chair, 213-740-0603, Fax: 213-744-1426, E-mail: ceedept@usc.edu. *Application contact:* Jennifer A. Gerson, Director of Student Affairs, 213-740-0573, Fax: 213-740-8662, E-mail: jgerson@usc.edu.

The University of Tennessee Space Institute, Graduate Programs, Program in Engineering Sciences and Mechanics, Tullahoma, TN 37388-9700. Offers engineering sciences (MS, PhD); mechanics (MS, PhD). Part-time programs available. *Faculty:* 5 full-time (0 women), 12 part-time/adjunct (0 women). *Students:* 3 full-time (1 woman), 3 part-time (0 women), 1 international. 1 applicant, 100% accepted, 1 enrolled. In 2010, 1 master's awarded. *Degree requirements:* For master's, thesis (for some programs); for doctorate, one foreign language, thesis/dissertation. *Entrance requirements:* Additional exam requirements/recommendations for international students: Required—TOEFL (minimum score 550 paper-based; 213 computer-based), IELTS (minimum score 6.5). *Application deadline:* For fall admission, 2/1 for international students; for spring admission, 6/15 for international students. Applications are processed on a rolling basis. Application fee: $35. Electronic applications accepted. *Financial support:* In 2010–11, 2 research assistantships with full tuition reimbursements (averaging $17,791 per year) were awarded; fellowships with full and partial tuition reimbursements, career-related internships or fieldwork, Federal Work-Study, institutionally sponsored loans, health care benefits, tuition waivers (full and partial), and unspecified assistantships also available. Financial award applicants required to submit FAFSA. *Unit head:* Dr. Trevor Meller, Degree Program Chairman, 931-393-7351, Fax: 931-393-7437, E-mail: tmoeller@utsi.edu. *Application contact:* Dee Merriman, Coordinator III, 931-393-7213, Fax: 931-393-7211, E-mail: dmerrima@utsi.edu.

The University of Texas at Austin, Graduate School, Cockrell School of Engineering, Department of Aerospace Engineering and Engineering Mechanics, Program in Engineering Mechanics, Austin, TX 78712-1111. Offers MS, PhD. *Degree requirements:* For doctorate, one foreign language, thesis/dissertation, qualifying exam. *Entrance requirements:* For master's and doctorate, GRE General Test.

University of Wisconsin–Madison, Graduate School, College of Engineering, Department of Engineering Physics, Madison, WI 53706-1380. Offers engineering mechanics (MS, PhD); nuclear engineering and engineering physics (MS, PhD). Part-time programs available. Post-baccalaureate distance learning degree programs offered (minimal on-campus study). Terminal master's awarded for partial completion of doctoral program. *Degree requirements:* For master's, thesis optional; for doctorate, thesis/dissertation. *Entrance requirements:* For master's and doctorate, GRE General Test, minimum GPA of 3.0 in last 60 hours, appropriate bachelor's degree. Additional exam requirements/recommendations for international students: Required—TOEFL (minimum score 600 paper-based; 245 computer-based). Electronic applications accepted. *Expenses:* Tuition, state resident: full-time $9887.36; part-time $617.96 per credit. Tuition, nonresident: full-time $24,054; part-time $1503.40 per credit. Required fees: $67.63 per credit. Tuition and fees vary according to reciprocity agreements. *Faculty research:* Fission reactor engineering and safety, plasma physics and fusion technology, plasma processing and ion implantation, nanotechnology, engineering mechanics and astronautics.

University of Wisconsin–Milwaukee, Graduate School, College of Engineering and Applied Science, Program in Engineering, Milwaukee, WI 53201-0413. Offers civil engineering (MS); electrical and computer engineering (MS); energy engineering (Certificate); engineering (PhD); engineering management (MS); engineering mechanics (MS); ergonomics (Certificate); industrial and management engineering (MS); manufacturing engineering (MS); materials engineering (MS); mechanical engineering (MS); MUP/MS. Part-time programs available. *Faculty:* 50 full-time (5 women). *Students:* 152 full-time (27 women), 115 part-time (23 women); includes 13 Black or African American, non-Hispanic/Latino; 3 American Indian or Alaska Native, non-Hispanic/Latino; 6 Asian, non-Hispanic/Latino; 10 Hispanic/Latino, 25 international. Average age 31. 236 applicants, 67% accepted, 55 enrolled. In 2010, 39 master's, 19 doctorates awarded. *Degree requirements:* For master's, comprehensive exam (for some programs), thesis or alternative; for doctorate, comprehensive exam, thesis/dissertation. *Entrance requirements:* For master's, GRE, minimum GPA of 2.75; for doctorate, GRE, minimum GPA of 3.5. Additional exam requirements/recommendations for international students: Required—TOEFL (minimum score 550 paper-based; 79 iBT), IELTS (minimum score 6.5). *Application deadline:* For fall admission, 1/1 priority date for domestic students; for spring admission, 9/1 for domestic students. Applications are processed on a rolling basis. Application fee: $56 ($96 for international students). *Financial support:* In 2010–11, 3 fellowships, 55 research assistantships, 77 teaching assistantships were awarded; career-related internships or fieldwork, Federal Work-Study, unspecified assistantships, and project assistantships also available. Support available to part-time students. Financial award application deadline: 4/15. Total annual research expenditures: $6.2 million. *Unit head:* David Yu, Representative, 414-229-6169, E-mail: yu@uwm.edu. *Application contact:* Betty Warras, General Information Contact, 414-229-6169, Fax: 414-229-6967, E-mail: bwarras@uwm.edu.

Virginia Polytechnic Institute and State University, Graduate School, College of Engineering, Department of Engineering Science and Mechanics, Blacksburg, VA 24061. Offers computational engineering science and mechanics (Certificate); engineering mechanics (MS, PhD). Part-time programs available. *Faculty:* 26 full-time (2 women). *Students:* 81 full-time (17 women), 9 part-time (1 woman); includes 1 Black or African American, non-Hispanic/Latino; 1 Asian, non-Hispanic/Latino; 1 Hispanic/Latino, 64 international. Average age 28. 70 applicants, 49% accepted, 21 enrolled. In 2010, 9 master's, 10 doctorates awarded. Terminal master's awarded for partial completion of doctoral program. *Median time to degree:* Of those who began their doctoral program in fall 2002, 98% received their degree in 8 years or less. *Degree requirements:* For master's, thesis optional, 21-30 credit hours; for doctorate, comprehensive exam, thesis/dissertation, 45 credit hours. *Entrance requirements:* For master's and doctorate, GRE General Test. Additional exam requirements/recommendations for international students: Required—TOEFL (minimum score 550 paper-based; 213 computer-based). *Application deadline:* For fall admission, 7/1 for domestic and international students; for spring admission, 12/1 for domestic and international students. Applications are processed on a rolling basis. Application fee: $65. Electronic applications accepted. *Expenses:* Tuition, area resident: Full-time $9399; part-time $488 per credit hour. Tuition, state resident: full-time $9399; part-time $488 per credit hour. Tuition, nonresident: full-time $17,854; part-time $957.75 per credit hour. International tuition: $17,854 full-time. Required fees: $1534. Full-time tuition and fees vary according to program. *Financial support:* In 2010–11, 2 students received support, including 4 fellowships with tuition reimbursements available (averaging $28,342 per year), 31 research assistantships with full tuition reimbursements available (averaging $21,583 per year), 19 teaching assistantships with full tuition reimbursements available (averaging $17,903 per year); career-related internships or fieldwork, Federal Work-Study, scholarships/grants, health care benefits, and unspecified assistantships also available. Financial award application deadline: 12/31. *Faculty research:* Solid mechanics and materials, fluid mechanics, dynamics and vibrations, composite materials, computational mechanics and finite element methods. Total annual research expenditures: $3.1 million. *Unit head:* Dr. Ishwar K. Puri, Professor and Department Head, 540-231-3243, Fax: 540-231-4574. *Application contact:* Lisa L Smith, Information Contact, 540-231-4935, Fax: 540-231-4574, E-mail: lisas@vt.edu.

NC STATE UNIVERSITY

NORTH CAROLINA STATE UNIVERSITY

College of Engineering
Department of Mechanical and Aerospace Engineering

Programs of Study	The Department of Mechanical and Aerospace Engineering (MAE) at North Carolina State University is the largest in the state and among the largest and most prominent in the nation. The MAE Department is housed in a new state-of-the-art building on the University's beautiful Centennial Campus. The strengths of the Department lie in the thermal sciences, particularly thermal fluids, fluid mechanics, and combustion; mechanical sciences, including manufacturing mechanics, structural dynamics, and materials and controls; and the aerospace sciences, particularly aerodynamics, aircraft design, space flight dynamics, space systems design, hypersonics, propulsion, flight research using UAVs, and computational fluid dynamics. The Department offers the Master of Science (M.S.) degree in both mechanical engineering (ME) and aerospace engineering (AE) with a thesis or nonthesis option and the Doctor of Philosophy (Ph.D.) degree in both ME and AE. Nonthesis M.S. degrees in both mechanical engineering and aerospace engineering are offered through distance education. The Department also offers an accelerated B.S./M.S. degree in both mechanical engineering and aerospace engineering and an en route Ph.D. program that provides a direct path from the B.S. degree to the Ph.D., awarding the M.S. on the way to the Ph.D.
Research Facilities	The Department houses several facilities that support research activities. Included in these facilities are instruments and equipment associated with the centers and laboratories of the MAE Department. The Precision Engineering Center is a multidisciplinary research center that performs research in metrology (sensors and measurement systems), innovative precision fabrication processes, and real-time process control. The Flight Research Laboratory conducts state-of-the-art research in UAV propulsion integration and control. Laboratory facilities in Aerospace Engineering include computational hypersonic aerodynamics and propulsion, spacecraft structures, navigation and control, and composite materials and fabrication.
	The Sound and Vibration Laboratory encompasses a range of graduate research activities in the areas of acoustics and mechanical vibration. The laboratory has a new large anechoic chamber as well as computational and data acquisition equipment. The Adaptive Structures Laboratory conducts basic and applied research on shape memory alloys. The Optical Sensing and Monitoring Laboratory conducts research in fiber optic sensors for structural health monitoring of composite structures. The Computational Fluid-Particle Dynamics Laboratory conducts research in areas such as two-phase flow, blood rheology, microscale flows, particle dynamics, and cell biology.
	The Applied Energy Research Laboratory conducts research in experimental fluid mechanics, heat transfer, and combustion, and collaborates with the North Carolina Solar Center on alternative energy initiatives. As a facility established to promote the implementation of solar technologies, the North Carolina Solar Center, operating in conjunction with the NCSU Solar House, has a variety of resources that support this function. The Energy analysis and Diagnostic Laboratory conducts research and development in energy efficiency as well as alternative energy sources.
Financial Aid	The Department of Mechanical and Aerospace Engineering offers a number of graduate research and teaching assistantships ranging from $15,000 to $26,000 per year. A limited number of fellowships are also available.
Cost of Study	Tuition and fees for full-time study in 2011–12 are $4420.49 per semester for North Carolina residents and $9614.15 per semester for nonresidents. Students taking fewer than 9 credits pay reduced amounts. Both North Carolina State residents and out-of-state students appointed as teaching or research assistants have all tuition and health insurance covered.
Living and Housing Costs	On-campus dormitory facilities are provided for unmarried graduate students. In 2011–12, the rent for double occupancy rooms starts at $2420 per semester. Accommodations in the newest residence hall for graduate students cost $2755 per semester (Wolf Village). Apartments for married students in King Village rent for $560 per month for a studio, $620 for a one-bedroom apartment, and $715 for a two-bedroom apartment.
Student Group	The Department of Mechanical and Aerospace Engineering has an enrollment of 1,328 undergraduate students and 361 graduate students. Most graduate students find full- or part-time support through fellowships, assistantships, and special duties with research organizations in the area.
Location	Raleigh, the state capital, has a population of 405,791. Nearby is the Research Triangle Park, one of the largest and fastest-growing research institutions of its type in the country. The Raleigh metro area population is 1,742,816. The University's concert series has more subscribers than any other in the United States. Excellent sports and recreational facilities are also available.
The University and The College	North Carolina State University is the principal technological institution of the University of North Carolina System. Its largest schools are the Colleges of Engineering, Agriculture and Life Sciences, Physical and Mathematical Sciences, and Humanities and Social Sciences. Total enrollment in the Department of Mechanical and Aerospace Engineering is 1,695. A strong cooperative relationship exists with nearby Duke University and the University of North Carolina at Chapel Hill, as well as with the Research Triangle Park. The Department has 39 tenure track faculty members and 8 instructors with professorial rank. Some of their current research areas are listed on the back of this page.
Applying	Application submission deadlines for fall and spring semesters, respectively, are June 25 and November 25 for U.S. citizens and March 1 and July 15 for international applicants. Application forms may be downloaded from http://www2.acs.ncsu.edu/grad/applygrad.htm. Electronic submission of applications is required. An applicant desiring to visit the campus may request information concerning travel allowances by writing to the Director of Graduate Programs. Students may apply for fellowships or assistantships in their application for admission. For further information, students should write to the University address.
Correspondence and Information	Director of Graduate Programs Department of Mechanical and Aerospace Engineering North Carolina State University Box 7910 Raleigh, North Carolina 27695-7910 Phone: 919-515-3026 Web site: http://www.mae.ncsu.edu/

North Carolina State University

THE FACULTY AND THEIR RESEARCH

G. D. Buckner, Professor; Ph.D., Texas at Austin, 1996. Electromechanical systems; intelligent system identification and control; applications, including active vehicle suspension systems, magnetic bearings, and machine operations. (e-mail: greg_buckner@ncsu.edu)

F. R. DeJarnette, Professor; Ph.D., Virginia Tech, 1965. Engineering and computational methods in aerothermodynamics. (e-mail: dejar@eos.ncsu.edu)

T. A. Dow, Professor; Ph.D., Northwestern, 1972. Precision mechanism/machine design, process development (machining, grinding, polishing), actuator design/control (mechatronic, piezoelectric), metrology, nanotechnology. (e-mail: thomas_dow@ncsu.edu)

T. Echekki, Professor; Ph.D., Stanford, 1993. Direct numerical simulation and large eddy simulation of turbulent combustion, combustion theory and dynamics. (e-mail: techekk@eos.ncsu.edu)

H. M. Eckerlin, Professor; Ph.D., North Carolina State, 1972. Industrial energy conservation/management, solar-active/passive/photovoltaic, renewable energy, steam generation, incineration. (e-mail: eckerlin@eos.ncsu.edu)

J. R. Edwards Jr., Professor; Ph.D., North Carolina State, 1993. CFD, 2-D and 3-D compressible flows, chemically reacting and multiphase flows, turbulence modeling. (e-mail: jredward@eos.ncsu.edu)

J. W. Eischen, Associate Professor; Ph.D., Stanford, 1986. Computational solid mechanics, elasticity, fracture mechanics, structural dynamics. (e-mail: eischen@eos.ncsu.edu)

T. Fang, Assistant Professor; Ph.D., Illinois, 2007. Combustion and propulsion, internal combustion engines, exhaust emissions and air pollution control, alternative fuels, renewable energy, spray and atomization, laser diagnostics for reacting flows, energy conversion systems. (e-mail: tfang2@ncsu.edu)

S. Ferguson, Assistant Professor; Ph.D., Buffalo, 2008. Design theory, reconfigurability, multidisciplinary/multiobjective optimization. (e-mail: smfergu2@ncsu.edu)

A. Gopalarathnam, Associate Professor; Ph.D., Illinois at Urbana-Champaign, 1999. Applied aerodynamics, flight mechanics, aircraft design, design methodologies. (e-mail: agopalar@eos.ncsu.edu)

R. D. Gould, Professor and Head; Ph.D., Purdue, 1987. Experimental heat transfer, electronic cooling, fluid mechanics, combustion, turbulence, nonintrusive optical diagnostics. (e-mail: gould@eos.ncsu.edu)

C. E. Hall Jr., Associate Professor; Ph.D., Ohio State, 1986. Flight dynamics and control, nonlinear control theory, RPV system design and flight testing. (e-mail: chall@skyraider.mae.ncsu.edu)

H. A. Hassan, Professor; Ph.D., Illinois at Urbana-Champaign, 1956. Fluid mechanics, aerodynamics, combustion, transition, turbulence, Monte Carlo methods, CFD. (e-mail: hassan@eos.ncsu.edu)

H. Y. Huang, Assistant Professor; Ph.D., Pittsburgh, 2004. Degradation mechanisms in rechargeable battery cathode materials via theoretical and computational approaches. (e-mail: hshuang@ncsu.edu)

X. Jiang, Associate Professor; Ph.D., Tsinghua (Beijing), 1997. High-frequency ultrasound bioimaging, developing electromechanical devices for extreme environments, new smart-material structures for energy conversion (harvesting, sensing, actuation). (e-mail: xjiang5@ncsu.edu)

R. F. Keltie, Professor; Ph.D., North Carolina State, 1978. Structural acoustics, vibration of rib-stiffened structures, acoustic radiation, mechanical vibrations. (e-mail: keltie@eos.ncsu.edu)

E. C. Klang, Associate Professor; Ph.D., Virginia Tech, 1983. Automotive engineering, analytical and experimental studies of composite materials, aerospace structural analysis. (e-mail: klang@eos.ncsu.edu)

C. Kleinstreuer, Professor; Ph.D., Vanderbilt, 1977. Computational biofluid mechanics; convection heat and mass transfer; two-phase flow, including microfluidics and system optimization. (e-mail: ck@eos.ncsu.edu; Web site: http://www.mae.ncsu.edu/research/ck_CFPDlab)

A. V. Kuznetsov, Professor; Ph.D., Russian Academy of Sciences, 1992. Heat transfer and fluid flow in porous media, modeling of solidification processing, macrosegregation and processes in the mushy zone during solidification of binary alloys. (e-mail: avkuznet@eos.ncsu.edu)

H. Luo, Associate Professor; Ph.D., Paris VI, 1989. Computational fluid dynamics, numerical methods, shock waves, parallel computing, multimaterial flows, mesh generation methods. (e-mail: hluo2@ncsu.edu)

K. M. Lyons, Professor; Ph.D., Yale, 1994. Experimental combustion, laser diagnostics, jet flames, turbulent mixing. (e-mail: lyons@eos.ncsu.edu)

A. P. Mazzoleni, Associate Professor; Ph.D., Wisconsin–Madison, 1992. Dynamics, vibrations, nonlinear systems, astronautics, spacecraft design. (e-mail: a_mazzoleni@ncsu.edu)

R. T. Nagel, Professor, Associate Department Head and Director of the Graduate Program; Ph.D., Connecticut, 1980. Acoustics, aeroacoustics, active noise control, experimental fluid mechanics. (e-mail: nagel@eos.ncsu.edu)

G. Ngaile, Associate Professor; Ph.D., Kumamoto (Japan), 1999. Tribology in manufacturing, modeling and optimization of manufacturing processes, material characterization, tool design. (e-mail: gngaile@unity.ncsu.edu)

B. O'Connor, Assistant Professor; Ph.D., Michigan, 2009. Organic solar cells, transistors, and light-emitting devices; unconventional device structures; low-cost and scalable fabrication methods for robust flexible electronics (displays, solar cells, sensors). (e-mail: kjpeters@eos.ncsu.edu)

K. J. Peters, Associate Professor; Ph.D., Michigan, 1996. Optical fiber sensors, structural health monitoring, composite materials. (e-mail: kjpeters@eos.ncsu.edu)

A. Rabiei, Associate Professor; Ph.D., Tokyo, 1997. Fracture mechanics, materials science, reliability and nondestructive evaluation of materials and structures, thin-film coatings, MEMS. (e-mail: arabiei@eos.ncsu.edu)

M. K. Ramasubramanian, Professor; Ph.D., Syracuse, 1987. Design, manufacturing, mechanics, behavior of paper and short-fiber composites, mechatronics design, unmanned autonomous vehicles, automotive mechatronics. (e-mail: rammk@eos.ncsu.edu)

P. I. Ro, Professor; Ph.D., MIT, 1989. Precision mechatronics, robotics, manufacturing automation, control theory, vehicle dynamics. (e-mail: ro@eos.ncsu.edu)

W. L. Roberts, Professor; Ph.D., Michigan, 1992. Experimental combustion, laser diagnostics, propulsion, turbulence-chemistry interactions. (e-mail: bill_roberts@eos.ncsu.edu)

A. Saveliev, Associate Professor; Ph.D., Moscow Institute of Physics and Technology, 1988, Non-thermal plasmas for pollution control and material synthesis, energy systems, fuel processing and gasification. (e-mail: avsaveli@ncsu.edu)

L. M. Silverberg, Professor, Associate Department Head, and Director of Undergraduate Programs, IMSE; Ph.D., Virginia Tech, 1983. Structural electrodynamics and control, electromechanical systems. (e-mail: silver@eos.ncsu.edu)

J. S. Strenkowski, Professor; Ph.D., Virginia, 1976. Finite-element analysis, nonlinear stresses, structural dynamics, computer-aided design and optimization. (e-mail: jsstren@eos.ncsu.edu)

R. H. Tolson, Langley Professor; Ph.D., Old Dominion, 1990. Space flight orbital and rigid body mechanics, guidance, navigation and control; planetary atmospheric aero-assisted mission aerodynamics and atmospheric modeling. (e-mail: rhtolson@ncsu.edu).

J. F. Tu, Professor; Ph.D., Michigan, 1991. Laser material processing, high speed machining/spindle technology, monitoring and modeling of manufacturing processes, precision engineering, control systems, mechatronics. (e-mail: jftu@unity.ncsu.edu)

T. Ward, Assistant Professor; Ph.D., California, Santa Barbara, 2003. Heat/mass transfer in multiphase flows, fluid mixing, electro-hydromechanics and dynamical systems. (e-mail: tward@ncsu.edu)

F. Wu, Professor; Ph.D., Berkeley, 1995. Robust and gain-scheduling control, control theory, applications including automotive engine, aircraft and missile control, smart-structure control. (e-mail: fwu@eos.ncsu.edu)

F. G. Yuan, Professor; Ph.D., Illinois at Urbana-Champaign, 1986. Structural health monitoring, microsensor design, failure analysis, fracture and life prediction of advanced materials and structures. (e-mail: yuan@eos.ncsu.edu)

Y. Zhu, Assistant Professor; Ph.D., Northwestern, 2005. MEMS/NEMS design, fabrication, and characterization; mechanics and material issues in nanostructures and thin films; experimental solid mechanics. (e-mail: yong_zhu@ncsu.edu).

M. A. Zikry, Professor; Ph.D., California, San Diego, 1990. Dynamics plasticity and fracture, constitutive relations for solids, computational solid mechanics. (e-mail: zikry@eos.ncsu.edu)

EMERITUS PROFESSORS

E. M. Afify, J. A. Bailey, M. A. Boles, J. A. Edwards, F J. Hale, F. D. Hart, T. H. Hodgson, R. R. Johnson, J. W. Leach, D. J. Maday, D. S. McRae, J. C. Mulligan, J. N. Perkins, L. H. Royster, F. Y. Sorrell, G. D. Walberg, C. F. Zorowski.

UNIVERSITY OF NEBRASKA–LINCOLN

College of Engineering
Department of Mechanical and Materials Engineering

Programs of Study

The Department of Mechanical and Materials Engineering offers programs leading to the M.S. and Ph.D. degrees. There are three primary areas of emphasis within the Department: thermal/fluids engineering, systems and design engineering, and materials science engineering.

The Department offers a broad program of study leading to the M.S. in mechanical engineering. The thesis-based program requires 24 hours of course work and at least 6 hours of thesis credit. Students may obtain an M.S. in mechanical engineering with a specialization in metallurgical engineering or, by taking a stronger materials course concentration, with a specialization in materials science engineering. It typically takes nineteen months to complete the master's program.

Students in the doctoral program may obtain the Doctor of Philosophy in engineering with a designated field of either mechanical engineering or chemical and materials engineering. A Ph.D. supervisory committee, in consultation with the student, arranges an appropriate program of doctoral course work. After the course work is substantially completed, the graduate student must pass a written comprehensive exam administered by the supervisory committee. In addition to the course work, doctoral students must complete a written Ph.D. dissertation with an oral presentation and defense. It typically requires three years of study after the M.S. to complete the Ph.D., but an M.S. is not required for admission.

Research Facilities

There are eight specialized research laboratories in the Department of Mechanical and Materials Engineering. The Computational Thermal-Fluid Sciences Laboratory is a state-of-the-art workstation facility for research using finite-difference, finite-element, and Green's functions methods applied to problems in fluid flow, heat transfer, combustion, and DNA replication. Design, simulation, and crash testing of roadside safety hardware are conducted at the Midwest Roadside Safety Facility. The Robotics and Mechatronics Laboratory performs research on surgical, industrial, planetary, mobile, and highway maintenance robots. The Central Facility for Electron Microscopy provides hands-on access, with training, to comprehensive, well-equipped electron microscopes, sample preparation, and related computing for surface and nanoscale observation and characterization of materials. It is supported by the University's Nebraska Center for Materials and Nanoscience. Measurement and characterization of the mechanical and physical properties of materials is the purview of the Physical/Mechanical Materials Characterization Laboratory. In the Thin Film Laboratory research is conducted on thin-film deposition and characterization, while work in the X-Ray Diffraction Laboratory focuses on powder and single-crystal X-ray diffraction.

Financial Aid

Approximately 65 percent of the Department's full-time graduate students are currently supported by research assistantships, teaching assistantships, and/or fellowships. Applicants with degrees from U.S. institutions and highly qualified international students are considered for such awards on a competitive basis. In addition to a monthly stipend, students holding research or teaching assistantships receive a tuition waiver so they pay only program and facilities fees.

Cost of Study

Tuition for graduate-level courses in 2011–12 ranged from $236–$380 per credit hour for Nebraska residents and $275–$978 per credit hour for nonresidents. Program and facilities fees are $267.60 per term if enrolled for 1 to 6 credit hours, $482 per term if enrolled 7 or more credit hours. Library and technology fees are $10.35 per credit hour. Students are expected to pay the program and facilities fees, library fee, engineering fee, course fees, registration fee, and international fees. N-Card charges and late fees may apply.

Living and Housing Costs

Most graduate students choose to live off-campus, but both residence halls and family housing are available. Three traditional residence halls have rooms reserved especially for graduate students. Apartment-style residence halls and apartments for married couples and parents are also available. For more information on campus housing, visit http://housing.unl.edu. Privately owned rental units within walking distance are also readily available; these units are advertised by the owners.

Student Group

The Department of Mechanical and Materials Engineering has approximately 52 full-time and 5 part-time graduate students. Approximately 65 percent of the mechanical engineering graduate students are supported either by the Department or research. The student population is diverse; currently 60 percent of the students in the Department are international.

Student Outcomes

M.S. and Ph.D. graduates readily find positions in a wide range of academic institutions, government agencies, consulting firms, and industries. National and international employers include Black & Veatch, Boeing, Caterpillar, Ford, General Electric, General Motors, Goodyear, Honda, Intel, McDonnell-Douglas, and Toyota. M.S. graduates also continue on to a Ph.D. at the University of Nebraska or elsewhere.

Location

Lincoln is located in the Great Plains and has the reputation of being one of the Midwest's most beloved cities with a population of more than 250,000 people. As Nebraska's state capitol and a University community, Lincoln provides the amenities of a big city and the serenity of country living. The city offers fine culinary and artistic experiences, a live music scene, numerous parks and bike trails, golf courses, and a friendly Midwestern attitude. The continental climate varies by season; winters are cold but relatively dry, and summers are hot and humid.

The University and The Department

The University of Nebraska–Lincoln (UNL) is the largest component of the University of Nebraska system. UNL began as a land-grant university chartered in 1869 and granted its first engineering degree in 1882. Mechanical engineering is one of eleven departments in the college and is the only mechanical engineering program in the state of Nebraska. The student population on the Lincoln campus is over 23,000 students and over 2,450 of those students are enrolled in engineering programs. Current enrollment in the Department of Mechanical and Materials Engineering is over 370 students.

Applying

Applications for an M.S. degree should specify the Department of Mechanical and Materials Engineering and the area of interest (thermal/fluids, systems/design, materials). Ph.D. applicants should specify engineering and the field area of mechanical engineering or of chemical and materials engineering. Ph.D. applicants need not have an M.S. degree.

Applicants to the M.S. or Ph.D. programs in mechanical engineering should have a B.S. degree in mechanical engineering or in a closely related field of engineering, science, or math.

Applicants to the M.S. in mechanical engineering with a metallurgical or materials specialization or the Ph.D. in engineering in the field of chemical and materials engineering are expected to have a B.S. degree in mechanical engineering or materials science or in a closely related field of engineering or science.

International applicants without degrees from U.S. institutions are required to take the TOEFL and GRE General Test. Faculty members in an applicant's area of interest evaluate each application on an individual basis. Applications are evaluated as they arrive, and full processing of an application may take about two months. Applicants who lack the background that is a prerequisite for required courses in their chosen program are informed of any required prerequisite courses in their letter of offer of admission.

Correspondence and Information

Dr. John D. Reid
Professor and Graduate Chair
Department of Mechanical and Materials Engineering
University of Nebraska–Lincoln
W359 NH
Lincoln, Nebraska 68588-0656
Phone: 402-472-3084
Fax: 402-472-1465
E-mail: megrad@unl.edu
Web site: http://www.engr.unl.edu/me/

University of Nebraska–Lincoln

THE FACULTY AND THEIR RESEARCH

J. P. Barton, Professor; Ph.D., Stanford, 1980. Laser beam/particle interactions, acoustics, electromagnetic wave theory, high-temperature gas dynamics, fluid mechanics, experimental methods, data acquisition and analysis.

K. Coen-Brown, Lecturer; M.S., Nebraska, 1989. Engineering education in the field of engineering graphics and computer modeling: computer-aided drafting and design, solid modeling, rendering, animation, and other three-dimensional visualization techniques.

K. D. Cole, Professor; Ph.D., Michigan State, 1986. Heat transfer and diffusion theory, Green's functions and symbolic computation, numerical modeling, thermal sensor technology, thermal conductivity measurements.

L. E. Ehlers, Associate Professor Emeritus; Ph.D., Oklahoma State, 1969. Fluid flow, wind energy, vibrations.

S. M. Farritor, Professor; Ph.D., MIT, 1998. Robotics for planetary exploration, design and control of mobile robot systems, industrial robot programming, mobile robot planning, modular design, computer-aided creative design.

J. Huang, Assistant Professor; Ph.D., UCLA, 2007. Polymer solar cells, organic field-effect transistors, organic photodetectors, organic spintronics, polymer light emitting diodes, nano-based sensors and capacitors.

G. Gogos, Professor; Ph.D., Pennsylvania, 1986. Computational heat transfer and fluid flow; perturbation methods; fundamental processes associated with vaporizing/combusting sprays with applications in liquid-fueled rocket engines, gas turbines, diesel engines, and industrial furnaces (evaporation/combustion of moving droplets, subcritical and supercritical droplet evaporation, transition of envelop to wake flames in burning droplets, droplet interactions, interaction of sprays and buoyant diffusion flames); natural convection; heat transfer and material deposition in rotational molding.

L. Gu, Assistant Professor, Ph.D., Florida, 2004. Computational mechanics with experimental validation, multiscale modeling, fluid-structure interaction, material characterization, traumatic brain injury, vascular mechanics including vascular remodeling, mechanism of in-stent restenosis and atherosclerosis, minimally invasive medical device design.

D. L. Johnson, Professor Emeritus; Ph.D., Nebraska, 1968. Corrosion/degradation and hydrogen permeation and diffusion in metallic and nonmetallic systems, metallurgical thermochemistry.

D. Y. S. Lou, Ludwickson Professor; Sc.D., MIT, 1967. Rarefied gas dynamics, heat conduction in rarefied gases, solar energy, thermal curing of composite materials, thermal manufacturing process analysis, thermal modeling of pulse combustors, heat transfer in phase change materials.

C. A. Nelson, Associate Professor; Ph.D., Purdue, 2005. Design and analysis of robotic and mechanical systems, robot-assisted surgery, design of novel medical devices, modular design, applied graph theory, rehabilitation engineering.

R. C. Nelson, Professor Emeritus; D.Sc., Colorado School of Mines, 1951. Powder metallurgy; biomaterials; the mechanical behavior of materials, including failure analysis.

J. D. Reid, Professor; Ph.D., Michigan State, 1990. Vehicle crashworthiness and roadside safety design, analysis, and simulation; vehicle dynamics; nonlinear, large deformation, finite-element analysis; computer simulation.

B. W. Robertson, Professor; Ph.D., Glasgow, 1979. Nanoscale and nanostructured materials; electron beam–induced fabrication of materials with nm-scale resolution; development and application of characterization methods and instrumentation for quantitative nm-scale electron microscopy and spectroscopy; plasma enhanced chemical vapor deposition of boron-carbide materials; novel materials for electronic, magnetic, and neutron detection, extreme radiation, and extreme temperature applications.

J. E. Shield, Professor; Ph.D., Iowa State, 1992. Microstructural evolution in materials during processing, rapid solidification processing, structure/property relationships in magnetic materials, order/disorder transformations in materials, nucleation and growth, materials characterization by X-ray and electron diffraction and electron microscopy.

W. M. Szydlowski, Associate Professor; Ph.D., Warsaw Technical, 1975. Analysis and synthesis of mechanisms, computer simulation of mechanical systems, dynamics of machinery (mechanical impact and mechanisms of intermittent motion with clearances in particular), redundant constraints in large mechanical systems, application of genetic algorithms to synthesis of mechanisms.

C. W. S. To, Professor; Ph.D., Southampton, 1980. Sound and vibration studies (acoustic pulsation in pipelines, railway noise and vibration, signal analysis, structural dynamics, random vibration, nonlinear and chaotic vibration), solid mechanics (linear and nonlinear finite-element methods with application to laminated composite shell structures and modeling of aorta dissection), system dynamics (nonlinear and rigid-body dynamics), controls (deterministic and stochastic), nanomechanics.

Z. Zhang, Associate Professor; Ph.D., Penn State, 2000. Numerical and experimental study of the laser-induced plasma and its application to pulsed laser deposition of thin films, numerical modeling of diesel particulate filters and other after-treatment devices, blast wave mitigation devices.

THE UNIVERSITY OF TEXAS AT SAN ANTONIO

Master of Science in Mechanical Engineering

Programs of Study

The Master of Science in Mechanical Engineering program is designed to offer students the opportunity to prepare for doctoral studies and leadership roles in government, industry, or research institutions. The program offers a thesis and a nonthesis option. In addition to satisfying the University-wide graduate admission requirements, admission is based on a combination of factors: a bachelor's degree in mechanical engineering or a related field from an accredited institution of higher education or proof of equivalent education at a foreign or unaccredited institution, satisfactory performance on the Graduate Record Examination (GRE), and satisfactory undergraduate grade point average (GPA) in engineering or relevant course work.

Research Facilities

In addition to its own dedicated Engineering Building, the College of Engineering operates out of UTSA's $84 million, 227,000-square-foot Biotechnology, Sciences and Engineering Building (BSE), which opened in 2006. The BSE features high-tech classrooms, state-of-the-art laboratories, and modern computing networks. The second phase of this project—the $90 million, 150,000-square-foot Applied Engineering and Technology Building (AET)—opened in the fall of 2009. A teaching and research facility, the AET features the most sophisticated technology for an information-intensive environment.

Students in the program also have access to the Cardiovascular Biomechanics Lab, Computational Bioengineering and Nanotechnology Lab, Computational Reliability and Visualization Lab, Flexible Manufacturing and Lean Systems Lab, Hard Tissue Biomechanics Lab, Manufacturing Systems and Automation Lab, Robotics and Intelligent Machines Lab, and the Sustainable Manufacturing Lab.

Excellent computer facilities are available with state-of-the-art software products including Ansys, Labview, Matlab, and Solidworks. A 192-core cluster supercomputer is available for computing as well as three student labs equipped with Windows-based PCs and a recently-developed advanced visualization lab.

Financial Aid

Various forms of financial support and fellowships, including graduate teaching assistantships and graduate research assistantships, and tuition scholarships are available for qualified applicants.

Cost of Study

For the 2011–12 academic year, tuition and fees for a full-time graduate degree student (9 semester hours) are approximately $3149 per semester for Texas residents and $8783 per semester for nonresidents. Some courses and programs have additional fees. Please view the following Web sites for more information: http://www.graduateschool.utsa.edu/prospective_students/detail/graduate_tuition_and_fees and http://www.utsa.edu/fiscalservices/tuition.html.

Living and Housing Costs

University on-campus housing is available and includes apartment-style living at four complexes—Chisholm Hall, University Oaks, Laurel Village, and Chaparral Village. Off-campus housing is also available and includes many apartments adjacent to the University as well as a large number located within a 5-mile drive. The rate for a one-bedroom apartment is approximately $500 per month.

Student Group

In the 2010 fall semester, the University enrolled more than 30,000 students, of whom more than 4,000 were graduate students. Students in the program have the opportunity to join a number of student organizations related to their field of study: the American Institute of Aeronautics and Astronautics; American Society of Heating, Refrigerating, and Air-Conditioning Engineers; American Society of Mechanical Engineers; Materials Research Society; Society of Automotive Engineers; Society of Manufacturing Engineers; Society of Women Engineers; and the Texas Society of Professional Engineers.

Location

San Antonio, with a population of 1.5 million, is one of the nation's major metropolitan areas. As the home of the Alamo and numerous other missions built by the Franciscans, the city is historically and culturally diverse. The Guadalupe Cultural Arts Center, McNay Art Museum, the San Antonio Museum of Art, and the Witte Museum enrich the city. The performing arts are represented by the San Antonio Symphony, the annual Tejano Music Festival and Tejano Music Awards, and performances by opera and ballet companies. Also notable are Sea World, Six Flags Fiesta Texas, Brackenridge Park, the Botanical Gardens, and the downtown Riverwalk. The San Antonio Zoo has the third-largest collection in North America. A city landmark is the Tower of the Americas, which was built for the 1968 World's Fair. San Antonio is home to the National Basketball Association's Spurs, league champions in 2000, 2003, 2005, and 2007. Numerous nearby lakes allow almost year-round outdoor activity, and the beaches of the Texas Gulf coast are within a 2-hour drive. San Antonio is home to numerous festivals throughout the year, including the Fiesta San Antonio and the Rodeo with activities such as parades, fairs, and concerts.

The University

The University was founded in 1969 and has since become a comprehensive metropolitan institution. Its research expenditures place it in the top 25 percent of public universities in Texas. The University has entered a new building and recruitment phase with a view to greatly expand the research effort in engineering and the sciences. UTSA Roadrunners football is slated to compete as an NCAA Division I FCS independent in August 2011 and is expected to transition to the Division I FBS subdivision by 2013.

Applying

In order to be eligible for admission without conditions as a graduate degree-seeking student, an applicant normally must: hold a baccalaureate degree from a regionally accredited college or university in the United States or have proof of equivalent training at a foreign institution, have a grade point average of at least 3.0 (on a 4.0 scale) in the last 60 semester credit hours of coursework, have completed at least 18 semester credit hours (12 of which must be at the upper-division level) in the area or areas in which the graduate degree is sought or in related areas as determined by the Graduate Program Committee for the proposed major, and be in good standing at the last institution attended. Students must list on the application for admission all colleges and universities attended and request that an official transcript from each institution be sent to the Graduate School.

The M.S. in Mechanical Engineering program requires that applicants submit a Graduate Studies Application (available online), general GRE scores, and TOEFEL scores for applicants who are not native English-speakers (minimum score 500 paper-based or 61 Internet-based). Letters of recommendation and a statement of purpose are optional.

The application deadline for domestic applicants is July 1 for the fall term and November 1 for the spring term. For international applicants, the deadline is April 1 for the fall term and September 1 for the spring term.

Correspondence and Information

For application information:
The Graduate School
The University of Texas at San Antonio
One UTSA Circle
San Antonio, Texas 78249
Phone: 210-458-4330
Web site: http://www.graduateschool.utsa.edu

For program information:
Department of Mechanical Engineering
The University of Texas at San Antonio
One UTSA Circle
San Antonio, Texas 78249
Phone: 210-458-7614
E-mail: can.saygin@utsa.edu
Web site: http://engineering.utsa.edu/~mechanical/

The University of Texas at San Antonio

THE FACULTY AND THEIR RESEARCH

Professors

Ronald Bagley, Ph.D., Air Force Tech. Material characterization, engineering mathematics. E-mail: Ronald.Bagley@utsa.edu.

F. Frank Chen, Ph.D., Missouri–Columbia. Lean manufacturing, flexible manufacturing, supply chain management. E-mail: FF.Chen@utsa.edu.

Hai-Chao Han, Ph.D., Xi'an Jiaotong (China) and California, San Diego. Cardiovascular biomechanics, mechanical modeling and analysis, tissue remodeling. E-mail: HaiChao.Han@utsa.edu.

Harry Millwater, Ph.D., Texas at Austin. Risk assessment, probabilistic life prediction, engine health monitoring. E-mail: Harry.Millwater@utsa.edu.

Amir Karimi, Ph.D., Kentucky; PE. Metastable thermodynamics, phase change heat transfer, thermal systems. E-mail: Amir.Karimi@utsa.edu.

Yesh P. Singh, D.Eng., Wisconsin–Milwaukee; PE. Design of machine elements, customized higher-pair linkages. E-mail: Yesh.Singh@utsa.edu.

Xiaodu Wang, Ph.D., Yokohama National (Japan). Tissue biomechanics, bone remodeling and tissue quality, micro/nanomechanics of materials. E-mail: Xiaodu.Wang@utsa.edu.

Associate Professors

Yusheng Feng, Ph.D., Texas at Austin. Computational and applied math, statistical mechanics and biophysics, cancer treatment simulation. E-mail: Yusheng.Feng@utsa.edu.

Randall Manteufel, Ph.D., MIT. Reliability analysis, performance assessment, thermal-fluid systems. E-mail: Randall.Manteufel@utsa.edu.

Brent Nowak, Ph.D., Texas at Austin. Robotics and intelligent machines, sensors and sensing systems, electromechanical system. E-mail: Brent.Nowak@utsa.edu.

Can Saygin, Ph.D., Middle East Technical (Turkey). Manufacturing engineering, shop floor control and automation, distributed decision-making. E-mail: Can.Saygin@utsa.edu.

Assistant Professors

Kiran Bhaganagar, Ph.D., Cornell. Direct numerical simulation, turbulence, flow in natural systems. E-mail: Kiran.Bhaganagar@utsa.edu.

Zhi-Gang Feng, Ph.D., Tulane. Multiphase flow, computational fluid dynamics, heat and mass transfer. E-mail: Zhigang.Feng@utsa.edu.

John Foster, Ph.D., Purdue. Viscoplasticity and dynamic fracture peridynamics.

Hung-Da Wan, Ph.D., Virginia Tech. Lean manufacturing, enterprise engineering, flexible manufacturing systems. E-mail: Hungda.Wan@utsa.edu.

Xiaowei Zeng, Ph.D., George Washington. Cell mechanics, cell-substrate interactions, bone mechanics, meshfree method, cohesive zone method, multiscale modeling and simulation.

THE UNIVERSITY OF TEXAS AT SAN ANTONIO

Ph.D. in Mechanical Engineering

Programs of Study	The Department of Mechanical Engineering at the University of Texas at San Antonio (USTA) offers advanced course work integrated with research, leading to the Doctor of Philosophy (Ph.D.) degree in mechanical engineering. The program has three concentrations: thermal and fluids systems, design and manufacturing systems, and mechanics and materials. The program is conducted jointly with the Southwest Research Institute and course work will be completed at both institutions. The Ph.D. in mechanical engineering will be awarded to candidates who have displayed an in-depth understanding of the subject matter and demonstrated the ability to make an original contribution to knowledge in their field of specialty. The degree requires 90 credits beyond the bachelor's degree or 60 credits beyond the master's degree, passing the qualifying exam, dissertation proposal, and dissertation defense and acceptance of the Ph.D. dissertation.
Research Facilities	In addition to its own dedicated Engineering Building, the College of Engineering operates out of UTSA's $84 million, 227,000-square-foot Biotechnology, Sciences and Engineering Building (BSE), which opened in 2006. The BSE features high-tech classrooms, state-of-the-art laboratories, and modern computing networks. The second phase of this project—the $90 million, 150,000-square-foot Applied Engineering and Technology Building (AET)—opened in the fall of 2009. A teaching and research facility, the AET features the most sophisticated technology for an information-intensive environment.
	Students in the program also have access to the Cardiovascular Biomechanics Lab, Computational Bioengineering and Nanotechnology Lab, Computational Reliability and Visualization Lab, Flexible Manufacturing and Lean Systems Lab, Hard Tissue Biomechanics Lab, Manufacturing Systems and Automation Lab, Robotics and Intelligent Machines Lab, and the Sustainable Manufacturing Lab.
	Excellent computer facilities are available with state-of-the-art software products including Ansys, Labview, Matlab, and Solidworks. A 192-core cluster supercomputer is available for computing as well as three student labs equipped with Windows-based PCs and a recently-developed advanced visualization lab.
Financial Aid	Various forms of financial support and fellowships, including graduate teaching assistantships and graduate research assistantships (GTA and GRA), Valero Competitive Research Scholar, Valero Research Fellow, and tuition scholarships are available for qualified applicants.
Cost of Study	For the 2011–12 academic year, tuition and fees for a full-time graduate degree student (9 semester hours) are approximately $3149 per semester for Texas residents and $8783 per semester for nonresidents. Some courses and programs have additional fees. Please view the following Web sites for more information: http://www.utsa.edu/fiscalservices/tuition.html and http://www.graduateschool.utsa.edu/prospective_students/detail/graduate_tuition_and_fees.
Living and Housing Costs	University on-campus housing is available and includes apartment-style living at four complexes—Chisholm Hall, University Oaks, Laurel Village, and Chaparral Village. Off-campus housing is also available and includes many apartments adjacent to the University as well as a large number located within a 5-mile drive. The rate for a one-bedroom apartment is approximately $500 per month.
Student Group	In the 2010 fall semester, the University enrolled more than 30,000 students, of whom more than 4,000 were graduate students. Students in the program have the opportunity to be part of a number of student organizations related to their field of study: the American Institute of Aeronautics and Astronautics; American Society of Heating, Refrigerating, and Air-Conditioning Engineers; American Society of Mechanical Engineers; Materials Research Society; Society of Automotive Engineers; Society of Manufacturing Engineers; Society of Women Engineers; and the Texas Society of Professional Engineers.
Location	San Antonio, with a population of 1.5 million, is one of the nation's major metropolitan areas. As the home of the Alamo and numerous other missions built by the Franciscans, the city is historically and culturally diverse. The Guadalupe Cultural Arts Center, McNay Art Museum, the San Antonio Museum of Art, and the Witte Museum enrich the city. The performing arts are represented by the San Antonio Symphony, the annual Tejano Music Festival and Tejano Music Awards, and performances by opera and ballet companies. Also notable are Sea World, Six Flags Fiesta Texas, Brackenridge Park, the Botanical Gardens, and the downtown Riverwalk. Numerous nearby lakes allow almost year-round outdoor activity, and the beaches of the Texas Gulf coast are within a 2-hour drive. San Antonio is home to numerous festivals throughout the year, including the Fiesta San Antonio and the Rodeo with activities such as parades, fairs, and concerts.
The University	The University was founded in 1969 and has since become a comprehensive metropolitan institution. Its research expenditures place it in the top 25 percent of public universities in Texas. The University has entered a new building and recruitment phase with a view to greatly expand the research effort in engineering and the sciences. UTSA Roadrunners football is slated to compete as an NCAA Division I FCS independent in August 2011 and is expected to transition to the Division I FBS subdivision by 2013.
Applying	All graduate students must meet the University admission requirements as outlined in the graduate catalog. Students whose native language is not English must achieve a minimum score of 550 on the Test of English as a Foreign Language (TOEFL) or 6.5 on the International English Language Testing System (IELTS). Normally, a student must hold a master's degree in mechanical engineering or in a related field with a GPA of 3.0 or better before being granted admission to the program. Outstanding students who do not hold a master's degree may enter the program on provisional status directly upon receiving a bachelor's degree in mechanical engineering or a closely related field, with the special approval of the Graduate Programs Committee. The Graduate Programs Committee will evaluate each applicant, approve the necessary requirements, and recommend corrective actions on a case-by-case basis.
	The application deadline for the fall term is February 1.
Correspondence and Information	For application information: The Graduate School The University of Texas at San Antonio One UTSA Circle San Antonio, Texas 78249 Phone: 210-458-4330 Web site: http://www.graduateschool.usta.edu	For program information: Department of Mechanical Engineering The University of Texas at San Antonio One UTSA Circle San Antonio, Texas 78249 Phone: 210-458-7614 E-mail: Can.Saygin@utsa.edu Web site: http://engineering.utsa.edu/graduate/ phd-mechanical-engineering.php

The University of Texas at San Antonio

THE FACULTY AND THEIR RESEARCH

Professors

Ronald Bagley, Ph.D., Air Force Tech. Material characterization, engineering mathematics. E-mail: Ronald.Bagley@utsa.edu.

F. Frank Chen, Ph.D., Missouri–Columbia. Lean manufacturing, flexible manufacturing, supply chain management. E-mail: FF.Chen@utsa.edu.

Hai-Chao Han, Ph.D., Xi'an Jiaotong (China) and California, San Diego. Cardiovascular biomechanics, mechanical modeling and analysis, tissue remodeling. E-mail: HaiChao.Han@utsa.edu.

Harry Millwater, Ph.D., Texas at Austin. Risk assessment, probabilistic life prediction, engine health monitoring. E-mail: Harry.Millwater@utsa.edu.

Amir Karimi, Ph.D., Kentucky; PE. Metastable thermodynamics, phase change heat transfer, thermal systems. E-mail: Amir.Karimi@utsa.edu.

Yesh P. Singh, D.Eng., Wisconsin–Milwaukee; PE. Design of machine elements, customized higher-pair linkages. E-mail: Yesh.Singh@utsa.edu.

Xiaodu Wang, Ph.D., Yokohama National (Japan). Tissue biomechanics, bone remodeling and tissue quality, micro/nanomechanics of materials. E-mail: Xiaodu.Wang@utsa.edu.

Associate Professors

Yusheng Feng, Ph.D., Texas at Austin. Computational and applied math, statistical mechanics and biophysics, cancer treatment simulation. E-mail: Yusheng.Feng@utsa.edu.

Randall Manteufel, Ph.D., MIT. Reliability analysis, performance assessment, thermal-fluid systems. E-mail: Randall.Manteufel@utsa.edu.

Brent Nowak, Ph.D., Texas at Austin. Robotics and intelligent machines, sensors and sensing systems, electromechanical system. E-mail: Brent.Nowak@utsa.edu.

Can Saygin, Ph.D., Middle East Technical (Turkey). Manufacturing engineering, shop floor control and automation, distributed decision-making. E-mail: Can.Saygin@utsa.edu.

Assistant Professors

Kiran Bhaganagar, Ph.D., Cornell. Direct numerical simulation, turbulence, flow in natural systems. E-mail: Kiran.Bhaganagar@utsa.edu.

Zhi-Gang Feng, Ph.D., Tulane. Multiphase flow, computational fluid dynamics, heat and mass transfer. E-mail: Zhigang.Feng@utsa.edu.

John Foster, Ph.D., Purdue. Viscoplasticity and dynamic fracture peridynamics.

Hung-Da Wan, Ph.D., Virginia Tech. Lean manufacturing, enterprise engineering, flexible manufacturing systems. E-mail: Hungda.Wan@utsa.edu.

Xiaowei Zeng, Ph.D., George Washington. Cell mechanics, cell-substrate interactions, bone mechanics, meshfree method, cohesive zone method, multiscale modeling and simulation.

Section 18
Ocean Engineering

This section contains a directory of institutions offering graduate work in ocean engineering. Additional information about programs listed in the directory may be obtained by writing directly to the dean of a graduate school or chair of a department at the address given in the directory.

For programs offering related work, see also in this book *Civil and Environmental Engineering* and *Engineering and Applied Sciences.* In the other guides in this series:

Graduate Programs in the Biological Sciences
See *Marine Biology*
Graduate Programs in the Physical Sciences, Mathematics, Agricultural Sciences, the Environment & Natural Resources

See *Environmental Sciences and Management* and *Marine Sciences and Oceanography*

CONTENTS

Program Directory

Ocean Engineering

Florida Atlantic University, College of Engineering and Computer Science, Department of Ocean and Mechanical Engineering, Boca Raton, FL 33431-0991. Offers mechanical engineering (MS, PhD); ocean engineering (MS, PhD). Part-time and evening/weekend programs available. *Faculty:* 23 full-time (1 woman), 3 part-time/adjunct (0 women). *Students:* 51 full-time (11 women), 42 part-time (9 women); includes 16 minority (4 Black or African American, non-Hispanic/Latino; 1 American Indian or Alaska Native, non-Hispanic/Latino; 2 Asian, non-Hispanic/Latino; 9 Hispanic/Latino), 25 international. Average age 29. 45 applicants, 60% accepted, 16 enrolled. In 2010, 23 master's, 1 doctorate awarded. Terminal master's awarded for partial completion of doctoral program. *Degree requirements:* For master's, thesis (for some programs); for doctorate, comprehensive exam, thesis/dissertation, qualifying exam. *Entrance requirements:* For master's and doctorate, GRE General Test, minimum GPA of 3.0. Additional exam requirements/recommendations for international students: Required—TOEFL. *Application deadline:* For fall admission, 7/1 priority date for domestic students, 2/15 for international students; for spring admission, 11/1 for domestic students, 7/15 for international students. Applications are processed on a rolling basis. Application fee: $30. *Expenses:* Tuition, area resident: Part-time $319.96 per credit. Tuition, state resident: part-time $319.96 per credit. Tuition, nonresident: part-time $926.42 per credit. *Financial support:* In 2010–11, research assistantships (averaging $15,000 per year); career-related internships or fieldwork, Federal Work-Study, scholarships/grants, and unspecified assistantships also available. Financial award application deadline: 1/10; financial award applicants required to submit FAFSA. *Faculty research:* Marine materials and corrosion, ocean structures, marine vehicles, acoustics and vibrations, hydrodynamics, coastal engineering. *Unit head:* Dr. Manhar Dhanak, Chairman, 954-924-7000, Fax: 954-924-7270, E-mail: dhanak@oe.fau.edu. *Application contact:* Dr. Manhar Dhanak, Chairman, 954-924-7000, Fax: 954-924-7270, E-mail: dhanak@oe.fau.edu.

Florida Institute of Technology, Graduate Programs, College of Engineering, Department of Marine and Environmental Systems, Program in Ocean Engineering, Melbourne, FL 32901-6975. Offers MS, PhD. Part-time programs available. *Faculty:* 11 full-time (0 women), 3 part-time/adjunct (0 women). *Students:* 19 full-time (4 women), 10 part-time (0 women); includes 1 American Indian or Alaska Native, non-Hispanic/Latino; 1 Asian, non-Hispanic/Latino; 1 Hispanic/Latino, 5 international. Average age 27. 38 applicants, 55% accepted, 6 enrolled. In 2010, 6 degrees awarded. *Degree requirements:* For master's, comprehensive exam (for some programs), thesis (for some programs); for doctorate, comprehensive exam, thesis/dissertation. *Entrance requirements:* For master's, GRE General Test, minimum GPA of 3.0, 3 letters of recommendation, resume, transcripts, statement of objectives; for doctorate, GRE General Test, minimum GPA of 3.3, resume, 3 letters of recommendation, statement of objectives, on-campus interview (highly recommended). Additional exam requirements/recommendations for international students: Required—TOEFL (minimum score 550 paper-based; 213 computer-based; 79 iBT). *Application deadline:* Applications are processed on a rolling basis. Application fee: $50. Electronic applications accepted. *Expenses:* Tuition: Part-time $1040 per credit hour. Tuition and fees vary according to campus/location. *Financial support:* In 2010–11, 5 fellowships with full and partial tuition reimbursements (averaging $7,240 per year), 5 research assistantships with full and partial tuition reimbursements (averaging $3,664 per year), 10 teaching assistantships with full and partial tuition reimbursements (averaging $6,670 per year) were awarded; career-related internships or fieldwork, institutionally sponsored loans, tuition waivers (partial), unspecified assistantships, and tuition remissions also available. Support available to part-time students. Financial award application deadline: 3/1; financial award applicants required to submit FAFSA. *Faculty research:* Underwater technology, materials and structures, coastal processes and engineering, marine vehicles and ocean systems, naval architecture. Total annual research expenditures: $1.7 million. *Unit head:* Dr. George Maul, Department Head, 321-674-7453, Fax: 321-674-7212, E-mail: gmaul@fit.edu. *Application contact:* Cheryl A. Brown, Associate Director of Graduate Admission, 321-674-7581, Fax: 321-723-9468, E-mail: cbrown@fit.edu.

Massachusetts Institute of Technology, School of Engineering, Department of Mechanical Engineering, Cambridge, MA 02139. Offers manufacturing (M Eng); mechanical engineering (SM, PhD, Sc D, Mech E); naval architecture and marine engineering (SM, PhD, Sc D); naval engineering (Naval E); ocean engineering (SM, PhD, Sc D), including); oceanographic engineering (SM, PhD, Sc D); SM/MBA. *Faculty:* 69 full-time (9 women). *Students:* 521 full-time (92 women); includes 71 minority (11 Black or African American, non-Hispanic/Latino; 1 American Indian or Alaska Native, non-Hispanic/Latino; 35 Asian, non-Hispanic/Latino; 20 Hispanic/Latino; 4 Two or more races, non-Hispanic/Latino), 217 international. Average age 27. 1,036 applicants, 23% accepted, 148 enrolled. In 2010, 132 master's, 49 doctorates, 10 other advanced degrees awarded. Terminal master's awarded for partial completion of doctoral program. *Degree requirements:* For master's and other advanced degree, thesis; for doctorate, comprehensive exam, thesis/dissertation. *Entrance requirements:* For master's, doctorate, and other advanced degree, GRE General Test. Additional exam requirements/recommendations for international students: Required—IELTS (minimum score 7). *Application deadline:* For fall admission, 12/1 for domestic and international students. Application fee: $75. Electronic applications accepted. *Expenses:* Tuition: Full-time $38,940; part-time $605 per unit. Required fees: $272. *Financial support:* In 2010–11, 443 students received support, including 91 fellowships with tuition reimbursements available (averaging $29,306 per year), 324 research assistantships with tuition reimbursements available (averaging $28,071 per year), 35 teaching assistantships with tuition reimbursements available (averaging $30,517 per year); career-related internships or fieldwork, Federal Work-Study, institutionally sponsored loans, scholarships/grants, health care benefits, and unspecified assistantships also available. *Faculty research:* Mechanics: modeling, experimentation and computation; design, manufacturing, and product development; controls, instrumentation, and robotics; energy science and engineering; ocean science and engineering; bioengineering; micro and nano engineering. Total annual research expenditures: $45.5 million. *Unit head:* Prof. Mary C. Boyce, Department Head, 617-253-2201, Fax: 617-258-6156, E-mail: mehq@mit.edu. *Application contact:* Graduate Office, 617-253-2291, Fax: 617-258-5802, E-mail: me-gradoffice@mit.edu.

Memorial University of Newfoundland, School of Graduate Studies, Faculty of Engineering and Applied Science, St. John's, NL A1C 5S7, Canada. Offers civil engineering (M Eng, PhD); electrical and computer engineering (M Eng, PhD); mechanical engineering (M Eng, PhD); ocean and naval architecture engineering (M Eng, PhD). Part-time programs available. *Degree requirements:* For master's, thesis; for doctorate, comprehensive exam, thesis/dissertation, oral thesis defense. *Entrance requirements:* For master's, 2nd class degree; for doctorate, master's degree in engineering. Electronic applications accepted. *Faculty research:* Engineering analysis, environmental and hydrotechnical studies, manufacturing and robotics, mechanics, structures and materials.

OGI School of Science & Engineering at Oregon Health & Science University, Graduate Studies, Science and Technology Center for Coastal and Land Margin Research, Beaverton, OR 97006-8921. Offers M Sc, PhD. Part-time programs available. *Entrance requirements:* For master's and doctorate, GRE General Test. Additional exam requirements/recommendations for international students: Required—TOEFL. Electronic applications accepted. *Faculty research:* Coastal marine observation and prediction science and technology.

Oregon State University, Graduate School, College of Engineering, School of Civil and Construction Engineering, Program in Coastal and Ocean Engineering, Corvallis, OR 97331. Offers M Oc E, MS, PhD. Part-time programs available. *Degree requirements:* For master's, thesis or alternative. *Entrance requirements:* For master's, GRE General Test, minimum GPA of 3.0 in last 90 hours. Additional exam requirements/recommendations for international students: Required—TOEFL. *Faculty research:* Beach erosion and coastal protection, loads on sea-based structures, ocean wave mechanics, wave forces on structures, breakwater behavior.

Princeton University, Graduate School, Department of Geosciences, Princeton, NJ 08544-1019. Offers atmospheric and oceanic sciences (PhD); geosciences (PhD); ocean sciences and marine biology (PhD). *Degree requirements:* For doctorate, one foreign language, thesis/dissertation. *Entrance requirements:* For doctorate, GRE General Test. Additional exam requirements/recommendations for international students: Required—TOEFL (minimum score 600 paper-based; 250 computer-based). Electronic applications accepted. *Faculty research:* Biogeochemistry, climate science, earth history, regional geology and tectonics, solid–earth geophysics.

Stevens Institute of Technology, Graduate School, Charles V. Schaefer Jr. School of Engineering, Department of Civil, Environmental, and Ocean Engineering, Program in Ocean Engineering, Hoboken, NJ 07030. Offers M Eng, PhD. *Students:* 19 full-time (3 women), 5 part-time (2 women); includes 1 Hispanic/Latino, 4 international. Average age 26. 18 applicants, 100% accepted. *Degree requirements:* For master's, thesis optional; for doctorate, variable foreign language requirement, thesis/dissertation. *Entrance requirements:* For doctorate, GRE. Additional exam requirements/recommendations for international students: Required—TOEFL. *Application deadline:* Applications are processed on a rolling basis. Application fee: $45. Electronic applications accepted. *Financial support:* Fellowships, research assistantships, teaching assistantships available. Financial award application deadline: 4/15. *Faculty research:* Estuarine oceanography, hydrodynamic and environmental processes, wave/ship interaction. *Unit head:* Dr. Richard I. Hires, Director, 201-216-5676, Fax: 201-216-5352, E-mail: rhires@stevens-tech.edu. *Application contact:* Dr. David A. Vaccari, Director, 201-216-5570, Fax: 201-216-5352, E-mail: dvaccari@stevens.edu.

Texas A&M University, College of Engineering, Zachry Department of Civil Engineering, College Station, TX 77843. Offers coastal and ocean engineering (M Eng, MS, D Eng, PhD); construction engineering and management (M Eng, MS, D Eng, PhD); environmental engineering (M Eng, MS, D Eng, PhD); geotechnical engineering (M Eng, MS, D Eng, PhD); materials engineering (M Eng, MS, D Eng, PhD); structural engineering (M Eng, MS, D Eng, PhD); transportation engineering (M Eng, MS, D Eng, PhD); water resources engineering (M Eng, MS, D Eng, PhD). Part-time programs available. *Faculty:* 57. *Students:* 384 full-time (81 women), 35 part-time (7 women); includes 35 minority (3 Black or African American, non-Hispanic/Latino; 1 American Indian or Alaska Native, non-Hispanic/Latino; 14 Asian, non-Hispanic/Latino; 17 Hispanic/Latino), 263 international. Average age 29. In 2010, 136 master's, 26 doctorates awarded. *Degree requirements:* For master's, thesis (MS); for doctorate, dissertation (PhD), internship (D Eng). *Entrance requirements:* For master's and doctorate, GRE General Test. Additional exam requirements/recommendations for international students: Required—TOEFL. *Application deadline:* Applications are processed on a rolling basis. Application fee: $50 ($75 for international students). Electronic applications accepted. *Financial support:* In 2010–11, fellowships (averaging $4,500 per year), research assistantships (averaging $14,000 per year), teaching assistantships (averaging $14,400 per year) were awarded; career-related internships or fieldwork and institutionally sponsored loans also available. Financial award application deadline: 4/15; financial award applicants required to submit FAFSA. *Unit head:* Dr. Tony Cahill, Head, 979-845-3858, E-mail: tcahill@civil.tamu.edu. *Application contact:* Graduate Advisor, 979-845-7435, Fax: 979-845-6156, E-mail: info@civil.tamu.edu.

University of Alaska Anchorage, School of Engineering, Program in Civil Engineering, Anchorage, AK 99508. Offers civil engineering (MCE, MS); port and coastal engineering (Certificate). Part-time and evening/weekend programs available. *Degree requirements:* For master's, thesis (for some programs). *Entrance requirements:* For master's, bachelor's degree in engineering. Additional exam requirements/recommendations for international students: Required—TOEFL (minimum score 550 paper-based; 213 computer-based). *Faculty research:* Structural engineering, engineering education, astronomical observations related to engineering.

University of California, San Diego, Office of Graduate Studies, Department of Electrical and Computer Engineering, La Jolla, CA 92093. Offers applied ocean science (MS, PhD); applied physics (MS, PhD); communication theory and systems (MS, PhD); computer engineering (MS, PhD); electrical engineering (M Eng); electronic circuits and systems (MS, PhD); intelligent systems, robotics and control (MS, PhD); photonics (MS, PhD); signal and image processing (MS, PhD). MS only offered to students who have been admitted to the PhD program. *Entrance requirements:* For master's and doctorate, GRE General Test. Electronic applications accepted.

University of California, San Diego, Office of Graduate Studies, Department of Mechanical and Aerospace Engineering, Program in Applied Ocean Science, La Jolla, CA 92093. Offers MS, PhD. Part-time programs available. *Degree requirements:* For master's, comprehensive exam or thesis; for doctorate, thesis/dissertation, qualifying exam. *Entrance requirements:* For master's and doctorate, GRE General Test, minimum GPA of 3.0. Additional exam requirements/recommendations for international students: Required—TOEFL. Electronic applications accepted.

University of Delaware, College of Earth, Ocean, and Environment, School of Marine Science and Policy, Newark, DE 19716. Offers marine policy (MMP); marine studies (MS, PhD), including marine biosciences, oceanography, physical ocean science and engineering; oceanography (PhD).

University of Delaware, College of Engineering, Department of Civil and Environmental Engineering, Newark, DE 19716. Offers environmental engineering (MAS, MCE, PhD); geotechnical engineering (MAS, MCE, PhD); ocean engineering (MAS, MCE, PhD); structural engineering (MAS, MCE, PhD); transportation engineering (MAS, MCE, PhD); water resource engineering (MAS, MCE, PhD). Part-time programs available. Terminal master's awarded for partial completion of doctoral program. *Degree requirements:* For master's, thesis; for doctorate, thesis/dissertation. *Entrance requirements:* For master's and doctorate, GRE General Test. Additional exam requirements/recommendations for international students: Required—TOEFL. Electronic applications accepted. *Faculty research:* Structural engineering and mechanics; transportation engineering; ocean engineering; soil mechanics and foundation; water resources and environmental engineering.

University of Florida, Graduate School, College of Engineering, Department of Civil and Coastal Engineering, Gainesville, FL 32611. Offers civil engineering (MCE, MS, PhD, Engr); coastal and oceanographic engineering (ME, MS, PhD, Engr). Part-time programs available. Postbaccalaureate distance learning degree programs offered (no on-campus study). *Faculty:* 29 full-time (2 women). *Students:* 238 full-time (55 women), 79 part-time (16 women); includes 12 Black or African American, non-Hispanic/Latino; 1 American Indian or Alaska Native, non-Hispanic/Latino; 11 Asian, non-Hispanic/Latino; 30 Hispanic/Latino, 115 international. Average age 27. 445 applicants, 60% accepted, 78 enrolled. In 2010, 115 master's, 23 doctorates awarded. Terminal master's awarded for partial completion of doctoral program. *Degree requirements:* For master's, thesis (for some programs); for doctorate, comprehensive exam, thesis/dissertation. *Entrance requirements:* For master's and doctorate, GRE General Test, minimum GPA of 3.0. Additional exam requirements/recommendations for international students: Required—TOEFL (minimum score 550 paper-based; 213 computer-based; 80 iBT), IELTS (minimum score 6). *Application deadline:* For fall admission, 8/1 priority date for domestic students, 1/31 for international students; for winter admission, 9/30 for international students; for spring admission, 12/1 for domestic students, 1/31 for international students. Applications are processed on a rolling basis. Application fee: $30. Electronic applications accepted. *Expenses:* Tuition, state resident: full-time $10,915.92. Tuition, nonresident: full-time $28,309. *Financial support:* In 2010–11, 118 students received support, including 14 fellowships, 85 research assistantships (averaging $20,326 per year), 19 teaching assistantships (averaging $14,158 per year); unspecified assistantships also available. Financial award application deadline: 1/31; financial award applicants required to submit FAFSA. *Faculty research:* Traffic congestion mitigation, wind mitigation, sustainable infrastructure materials, improved sensors for in situ measurements, storm surge modeling. Total annual research expenditures: $8.9 million. *Unit head:* Dr. Kirk Hatfield, Interim Department Chair, 352-392-9537 Ext. 1441, Fax:

352-392-3394, E-mail: khatf@ufl.edu. *Application contact:* Mange Tia, Graduate Coordinator, 352-392-9537 Ext. 1463, Fax: 352-392-3394, E-mail: tia@ce.ufl.edu.

University of Hawaii at Manoa, Graduate Division, School of Ocean and Earth Science and Technology, Department of Ocean and Resources Engineering, Honolulu, HI 96822. Offers MS, PhD. *Accreditation:* ABET (one or more programs are accredited). Part-time programs available. *Faculty:* 21 full-time (4 women), 3 part-time/adjunct (0 women). *Students:* 31 full-time (6 women), 2 part-time (0 women); includes 9 minority (5 Asian, non-Hispanic/Latino; 1 Hispanic/Latino; 2 Native Hawaiian or other Pacific Islander, non-Hispanic/Latino; 1 Two or more races, non-Hispanic/Latino), 8 international. Average age 31. 46 applicants, 59% accepted, 11 enrolled. In 2010, 5 master's, 2 doctorates awarded. *Degree requirements:* For master's, thesis optional, exams; for doctorate, comprehensive exam, thesis/dissertation, exams. *Entrance requirements:* For master's and doctorate, GRE General Test. Additional exam requirements/recommendations for international students: Required—TOEFL (minimum score 560 paper-based; 220 computer-based; 83 iBT), IELTS (minimum score 5). *Application deadline:* For fall admission, 3/15 for domestic students, 2/15 for international students; for spring admission, 9/15 for domestic students, 8/15 for international students. Application fee: $60. *Financial support:* In 2010–11, 1 fellowship (averaging $2,500 per year), 24 research assistantships (averaging $21,608 per year), 2 teaching assistantships (averaging $18,588 per year) were awarded; institutionally sponsored loans and tuition waivers (full) also available. Financial award application deadline: 3/1. *Faculty research:* Coastal and harbor engineering, near shore environmental ocean engineering, marine structures/naval architecture. Total annual research expenditures: $2.2 million. *Application contact:* Geno Pawlak, Graduate Chairperson, 808-956-7572, Fax: 808-956-3498, E-mail: pawlak@hawaii.edu.

University of Maine, Graduate School, Interdisciplinary Doctoral Program, Orono, ME 04469. Offers communication (PhD); functional genomics (PhD); mass communication (PhD); ocean engineering (PhD). Part-time and evening/weekend programs available. *Students:* 22 full-time (13 women), 25 part-time (14 women); includes 2 minority (1 Black or African American, non-Hispanic/Latino; 1 Asian, non-Hispanic/Latino), 4 international. Average age 37. 17 applicants, 41% accepted, 7 enrolled. In 2010, 10 doctorates awarded. *Degree requirements:* For doctorate, comprehensive exam, thesis/dissertation. *Entrance requirements:* For doctorate, GRE General Test. Additional exam requirements/recommendations for international students: Required—TOEFL. *Application deadline:* For fall admission, 4/1 for domestic students; for spring admission, 11/1 for domestic students. Applications are processed on a rolling basis. Application fee: $65. Electronic applications accepted. *Expenses:* Tuition, state resident: full-time $400. Tuition, nonresident: full-time $1050. *Unit head:* Scott G. Delcourt, Associate Dean of the Graduate School, 207-581-3291, Fax: 207-581-3232, E-mail: graduate@maine.edu. *Application contact:* Scott G. Delcourt, Associate Dean of the Graduate School, 207-581-3291, Fax: 207-581-3232, E-mail: graduate@maine.edu.

University of Michigan, Horace H. Rackham School of Graduate Studies, College of Engineering, Department of Naval Architecture and Marine Engineering, Ann Arbor, MI 48109. Offers concurrent marine design (M Eng); naval architecture and marine engineering (MS, MSE, PhD, Mar Eng, Nav Arch); MBA/MSE. Part-time programs available. *Students:* 88 full-time (15 women), 4 part-time (0 women). 110 applicants, 71% accepted, 52 enrolled. In 2010, 31 master's, 8 doctorates awarded. Terminal master's awarded for partial completion of doctoral program. *Degree requirements:* For master's, thesis (for some programs); for doctorate, comprehensive exam, thesis/dissertation, oral defense of dissertation, preliminary exams (written and oral); for other advanced degree, comprehensive exam, thesis, oral defense of thesis. *Entrance requirements:* For doctorate, GRE General Test, master's degree; for other advanced degree, GRE General Test. Additional exam requirements/recommendations for international students: Required—TOEFL (minimum score 560 paper-based; 220 computer-based). *Application deadline:* Applications are processed on a rolling basis. Application fee: $65 ($75 for international students). Electronic applications accepted. *Expenses:* Tuition, state resident: full-time $17,784; part-time $1116 per credit hour. Tuition, nonresident: full-time $35,944; part-time $2125 per credit hour. International tuition: $35,994 full-time. Required fees: $95 per semester. Tuition and fees vary according to course load, degree level and program. *Financial support:* Fellowships, research assistantships, teaching assistantships, career-related internships or fieldwork, Federal Work-Study, institutionally sponsored loans, scholarships/grants, and unspecified assistantships available. *Faculty research:* System and structural reliability, design and analysis of offshore structures and vehicles, marine systems design, remote sensing of ship wakes and sea surfaces, marine hydrodynamics, nonlinear seakeeping analysis. *Unit head:* Dr. Armin W. Troesch, Chair, 734-763-6644, Fax: 734-936-8820, E-mail: kdrake@engin.umich.edu. *Application contact:* Nathalie Fiveland, Unit Administrator, 734-936-0566, Fax: 734-936-8820, E-mail: fiveland@umich.edu.

University of New Hampshire, Graduate School, College of Engineering and Physical Sciences, Program in Ocean Engineering, Durham, NH 03824. Offers ocean engineering (MS, PhD); ocean mapping (MS, Postbaccalaureate Certificate). *Faculty:* 13 full-time (1 woman). *Students:* 18 full-time (4 women), 5 part-time (0 women); includes 1 minority (Hispanic/Latino), 14 international. Average age 30. 25 applicants, 88% accepted, 12 enrolled. In 2010, 2 master's, 5 other advanced degrees awarded. *Degree requirements:* For master's, thesis. *Entrance requirements:* Additional exam requirements/recommendations for international students: Required—TOEFL (minimum score 550 paper-based; 213 computer-based; 80 iBT). *Application deadline:* For fall admission, 4/1 priority date for domestic students; for spring admission, 12/1 for domestic students. Applications are processed on a rolling basis. Application fee: $65. Electronic applications accepted. *Financial support:* In 2010–11, 11 students received support, including 10 research assistantships, 1 teaching assistantship; fellowships, Federal Work-Study, scholarships/grants, and tuition waivers (full and partial) also available. Support available to part-time students. Financial award application deadline: 2/15. *Unit head:* Dr. Kenneth Baldwin, Chairperson, 603-862-1898. *Application contact:* Jennifer Bedsole, Information Contact, 603-862-0672, E-mail: ocean.engineering@unh.edu.

University of Rhode Island, Graduate School, College of Engineering, Department of Ocean Engineering, Narragansett, RI 02882. Offers MS, PhD. Part-time programs available. *Faculty:* 8 full-time (1 woman), 3 part-time/adjunct (1 woman). *Students:* 22 full-time (4 women), 19 part-time (3 women); includes 1 minority (Asian, non-Hispanic/Latino), 6 international. In 2010, 7 master's, 1 doctorate awarded. *Degree requirements:* For master's, comprehensive exam (for some programs), thesis optional; for doctorate, comprehensive exam, thesis/dissertation. *Entrance requirements:* For master's and doctorate, 2 letters of recommendation. Additional exam requirements/recommendations for international students: Required—TOEFL (minimum score 550 paper-based; 213 computer-based). *Application deadline:* For fall admission, 7/15 for domestic students, 2/1 for international students; for spring admission, 11/15 for domestic students, 7/15 for international students. Application fee: $65. Electronic applications accepted. *Expenses:* Tuition, state resident: full-time $9588; part-time $533 per credit hour. Tuition, nonresident: full-time $22,968; part-time $1276 per credit hour. Required fees: $1282; $68 per semester. Tuition and fees vary according to program. *Financial support:* In 2010–11, 1 research assistantship with full and partial tuition reimbursement (averaging $14,350 per year), 4 teaching assistantships with full and partial tuition reimbursements (averaging $12,157 per year) were awarded. Financial award application deadline: 2/1; financial award applicants required to submit FAFSA. *Faculty research:* Tele-presence technology for high bandwidth ship-to-shore link, wave-induced sediment transport, tsunami impact, geohazards, acoustical oceanography, underwater vehicle mechanical and control system design, deep sea drilling. Total annual research expenditures: $1.6 million. *Unit head:* Dr. James H. Miller, Chairman, 401-874-6540, Fax: 401-874-6837, E-mail: miller@uri.edu. *Application contact:* Dr. Christopher Baxter, Associate Professor, 401-874-6575, Fax: 401-874-6837, E-mail: baxter@oce.uri.edu.

Virginia Polytechnic Institute and State University, VT Online, Blacksburg, VA 24061. Offers aerospace engineering (MS); business information systems (Graduate Certificate); career and technical education (MS); computer engineering (M Eng, MS); decision support systems (Graduate Certificate); eLearning leadership (MA); electrical engineering (M Eng, MS); engineering administration (MEA); environmental politics and policy (Graduate Certificate); foundations of political analysis (Graduate Certificate); health product risk management (Graduate Certificate); information policy and society (Graduate Certificate); information security (Graduate Certificate); instructional technology (MA); liberal arts (Graduate Certificate); life sciences: health product risk management (MS); natural resources (MNR, Graduate Certificate); networking (Graduate Certificate); nonprofit and nongovernmental organization management (Graduate Certificate); ocean engineering (MS); political science (MA); security studies (Graduate Certificate); software development (Graduate Certificate). *Expenses:* Tuition, area resident: Full-time $9399; part-time $488 per credit hour. Tuition, state resident: full-time $9399; part-time $488 per credit hour. Tuition, nonresident: full-time $17,854; part-time $957.75 per credit hour. International tuition: $17,854 full-time. Required fees: $1534. Full-time tuition and fees vary according to program.

Woods Hole Oceanographic Institution, MIT/WHOI Joint Program in Oceanography/Applied Ocean Science and Engineering, Woods Hole, MA 02543-1541. Offers applied ocean sciences (PhD); biological oceanography (PhD, Sc D); chemical oceanography (PhD, Sc D); civil and environmental and oceanographic engineering (PhD); electrical and oceanographic engineering (PhD); geochemistry (PhD); geophysics (PhD); marine biology (PhD); marine geochemistry (PhD, Sc D); marine geology (PhD, Sc D); marine geophysics (PhD); mechanical and oceanographic engineering (PhD); ocean engineering (PhD); oceanographic engineering (M Eng, MS, PhD, Sc D, Eng); paleoceanography (PhD); physical oceanography (PhD, Sc D). MS, PhD, Sc D offered jointly with Massachusetts Institute of Technology. Terminal master's awarded for partial completion of doctoral program. *Degree requirements:* For master's and Eng, thesis (for some programs); for doctorate, thesis/dissertation. *Entrance requirements:* For master's, GRE General Test; for doctorate, GRE General Test, GRE Subject Test. Additional exam requirements/recommendations for international students: Required—TOEFL. Electronic applications accepted.

Section 19
Paper and Textile Engineering

This section contains a directory of institutions offering graduate work in paper and textile engineering. Additional information about programs listed in the directory may be obtained by writing directly to the dean of a graduate school or chair of a department at the address given in the directory.

For programs offering related work, see also in this book *Engineering and Applied Sciences* and *Materials Sciences and Engineering*. In another guide in this series:

Graduate Programs in the Humanities, Arts & Social Sciences
See *Family and Consumer Sciences (Clothing and Textiles)*

CONTENTS

Program Directories

Paper and Pulp Engineering

Miami University, Graduate School, School of Engineering and Applied Science, Department of Chemical and Paper Engineering, Oxford, OH 45056. Offers MS. *Students:* 9 full-time (4 women), 7 international. Average age 24. In 2010, 5 master's awarded. *Entrance requirements:* For master's, GRE General Test, minimum undergraduate GPA of 3.0 during previous 2 years or 2.75 overall. Additional exam requirements/recommendations for international students: Required—TOEFL. Application fee: $50. *Expenses:* Tuition, state resident: full-time $11,616; part-time $484 per credit hour. Tuition, nonresident: full-time $25,656; part-time $1069 per credit hour. Required fees: $528. *Financial support:* Fellowships, research assistantships, teaching assistantships, Federal Work-Study, health care benefits, tuition waivers (full), and unspecified assistantships available. Financial award application deadline: 3/1. *Unit head:* Dr. Shashi Lalvani, Chair, 513-529-0763, Fax: 513-529-0761, E-mail: lalvansb@muohio.edu. *Application contact:* Dr. Shashi Lalvani, Chair, 513-529-0763, Fax: 513-529-0761, E-mail: lalvansb@muohio.edu.

North Carolina State University, Graduate School, College of Natural Resources, Department of Wood and Paper Science, Raleigh, NC 27695. Offers MS, MWPS, PhD. Postbaccalaureate distance learning degree programs offered. *Degree requirements:* For master's, thesis optional; for doctorate, thesis/dissertation. *Entrance requirements:* For master's and doctorate, GRE General Test. Additional exam requirements/recommendations for international students: Required—TOEFL. Electronic applications accepted. *Faculty research:* Pulping, bleaching, recycling, papermaking, drying of wood.

Oregon State University, Graduate School, College of Forestry, Department of Wood Science and Engineering, Corvallis, OR 97331. Offers forest products (MAIS, MF, MS, PhD); wood science and technology (MF, MS, PhD). *Accreditation:* SAF (one or more programs are accredited). Part-time programs available. *Degree requirements:* For master's, thesis (for some programs); for doctorate, thesis/dissertation. *Entrance requirements:* For master's and doctorate, GRE General Test, minimum GPA of 3.0 in last 90 hours. Additional exam requirements/recommendations for international students: Required—TOEFL. *Faculty research:* Biodeterioration and preservation, timber engineering, process engineering and control, composite materials science, anatomy, chemistry and physical properties.

State University of New York College of Environmental Science and Forestry, Department of Paper and Bioprocess Engineering, Syracuse, NY 13210-2779. Offers environmental and resource engineering (MPS, MS, PhD). *Degree requirements:* For master's, thesis; for doctorate, comprehensive exam, thesis/dissertation. *Entrance requirements:* For master's and doctorate, GRE General Test, minimum GPA of 3.0. Additional exam requirements/recommendations for international students: Required—TOEFL (minimum score 550 paper-based; 213 computer-based; 80 iBT), IELTS (minimum score 6). *Expenses:* Tuition, state resident: full-time $8370; part-time $349 per credit hour. Tuition, nonresident: full-time $13,780. Required fees: $30.30 per credit hour. $20 per year.

The University of Manchester, School of Materials, Manchester, United Kingdom. Offers advanced aerospace materials engineering (M Sc); advanced metallic systems (PhD); biomedical materials (M Phil, M Sc, PhD); ceramics and glass (M Phil, M Sc, PhD); composite materials (M Sc, PhD); corrosion and protection (M Phil, M Sc, PhD); materials (M Phil, PhD); metallic materials (M Phil, M Sc, PhD); nanostructural materials (M Phil, M Sc, PhD); paper science (M Phil, M Sc, PhD); polymer science and engineering (M Phil, M Sc, PhD); technical textiles (M Sc); textile design, fashion and management (M Phil, M Sc, PhD); textile science and technology (M Phil, M Sc, PhD); textiles (M Phil, PhD); textiles and fashion (M Ent).

Western Michigan University, Graduate College, College of Engineering and Applied Sciences, Department of Paper Engineering, Chemical Engineering, and Imaging, Kalamazoo, MI 49008. Offers paper and imaging science and engineering (MS, PhD). *Degree requirements:* For master's, thesis optional; for doctorate, one foreign language, comprehensive exam, thesis/dissertation. *Entrance requirements:* For master's, minimum GPA of 3.0. *Faculty research:* Fiber recycling, paper machine wet end operations, paper coating.

Textile Sciences and Engineering

Auburn University, Graduate School, Interdepartmental Programs, Interdepartmental Program in Integrated Textile and Apparel Sciences, Auburn University, AL 36849. Offers PhD. *Faculty:* 23 full-time (16 women), 1 (woman) part-time/adjunct. *Students:* 12 full-time (5 women), 12 part-time (9 women); includes 1 Black or African American, non-Hispanic/Latino; 2 Asian, non-Hispanic/Latino, 16 international. Average age 29. 33 applicants, 55% accepted, 2 enrolled. In 2010, 3 doctorates awarded. *Application deadline:* For fall admission, 7/7 for domestic students; for spring admission, 11/24 for domestic students. Applications are processed on a rolling basis. Application fee: $50 ($60 for international students). *Expenses:* Tuition, state resident: full-time $7002. Tuition, nonresident: full-time $21,898. International tuition: $22,116 full-time. Required fees: $892. Tuition and fees vary according to course load and program. *Financial support:* Research assistantships, Federal Work-Study available. Support available to part-time students. Financial award application deadline: 3/15; financial award applicants required to submit FAFSA. *Faculty research:* Design and utilization of textile products, engineering and technology of textile production, textile material science, textile chemistry, use of resources. *Unit head:* Dr. Royall M. Broughton, Graduate Program Officer, 334-844-5460, E-mail: royalb@eng.auburn.edu. *Application contact:* Dr. George Flowers, Dean of the Graduate School, 334-844-2125.

Cornell University, Graduate School, Graduate Fields of Human Ecology, Field of Textiles, Ithaca, NY 14853. Offers apparel design (MA, MPS); fiber science (MS, PhD); polymer science (MS, PhD); textile science (MS, PhD). *Faculty:* 19 full-time (7 women). *Students:* 20 full-time (15 women); includes 1 Black or African American, non-Hispanic/Latino; 1 Asian, non-Hispanic/Latino, 9 international. Average age 28. 41 applicants, 29% accepted, 9 enrolled. In 2010, 5 master's, 3 doctorates awarded. *Degree requirements:* For master's, thesis (MA, MS), project paper (MPS); for doctorate, comprehensive exam, thesis/dissertation. *Entrance requirements:* For master's, GRE General Test, 2 letters of recommendation, portfolio (functional apparel design); for doctorate, GRE General Test, 2 letters of recommendation. Additional exam requirements/recommendations for international students: Required—TOEFL (minimum score 600 paper-based; 250 computer-based; 77 iBT). *Application deadline:* For fall admission, 3/1 for domestic students; for spring admission, 10/1 for domestic students. Application fee: $70. Electronic applications accepted. *Expenses:* Tuition: Full-time $29,500. Required fees: $76. Tuition and fees vary according to degree level and program. *Financial support:* In 2010–11, 19 students received support, including 2 fellowships with full tuition reimbursements available, 7 research assistantships with full tuition reimbursements available, 8 teaching assistantships with full tuition reimbursements available; institutionally sponsored loans, scholarships/grants, health care benefits, tuition waivers (full and partial), and unspecified assistantships also available. Financial award applicants required to submit FAFSA. *Faculty research:* Apparel design, consumption, mass customization, 3-D body scanning. *Unit head:* Director of Graduate Studies, 607-255-3151, Fax: 607-255-1093. *Application contact:* Graduate Field Assistant, 607-255-3151, Fax: 607-255-1093, E-mail: textiles_grad@cornell.edu.

Georgia Institute of Technology, Graduate Studies and Research, College of Engineering, School of Polymer, Textile, and Fiber Engineering, Atlanta, GA 30332-0001. Offers polymer, textile and fiber engineering (MS, PhD); polymers (MS Poly). *Degree requirements:* For master's, thesis (for some programs); for doctorate, comprehensive exam, thesis/dissertation. *Entrance requirements:* For master's, GRE, minimum GPA of 2.7; for doctorate, GRE, minimum GPA of 3.0. Additional exam requirements/recommendations for international students: Required—TOEFL (minimum score 550 paper-based; 213 computer-based). Electronic applications accepted. *Faculty research:* Energy conservation, environmental control, engineered fibrous structures, polymer synthesis and degradation, high performance organic-carbon-ceramic fibers.

North Carolina State University, Graduate School, College of Textiles, Department of Textile and Apparel Technology and Management, Raleigh, NC 27695. Offers MS, MT. *Degree requirements:* For master's, thesis optional. *Entrance requirements:* For master's, GRE. Electronic applications accepted. *Faculty research:* Textile and apparel products and processes, management systems, nonwovens, process simulation, structure design and analysis.

North Carolina State University, Graduate School, College of Textiles, Department of Textile Engineering, Chemistry, and Science, Program in Textile Chemistry, Raleigh, NC 27695. Offers MS. *Degree requirements:* For master's, thesis optional. *Entrance requirements:* For master's, GRE. Electronic applications accepted. *Faculty research:* Color science, polymer science, dye chemistry, fiber formation, wet processing technology.

North Carolina State University, Graduate School, College of Textiles, Department of Textile Engineering, Chemistry, and Science, Program in Textile Engineering, Raleigh, NC 27695. Offers MS. *Degree requirements:* For master's, thesis optional. *Entrance requirements:* For master's, GRE. Electronic applications accepted. *Faculty research:* Electro-mechanical design, inventory and supply chain control, textile composites, biomedical textile appliations, pollution prevention.

North Carolina State University, Graduate School, College of Textiles, Program in Fiber and Polymer Science, Raleigh, NC 27695. Offers PhD. *Degree requirements:* For doctorate, one foreign language, thesis/dissertation, cumulative exams. *Entrance requirements:* For doctorate, GRE. Electronic applications accepted. *Faculty research:* Polymer science, fiber mechanics, medical textiles, nanotechnology.

Philadelphia University, School of Engineering and Textiles, Program in Textile Engineering, Philadelphia, PA 19144. Offers MS, PhD. Part-time programs available. *Entrance requirements:* For master's, GRE, minimum GPA of 2.8; for doctorate, master's degree. Additional exam requirements/recommendations for international students: Required—TOEFL (minimum score 550 paper-based; 213 computer-based; 79 iBT). Electronic applications accepted.

University of Massachusetts Dartmouth, Graduate School, College of Engineering, Department of Materials and Textiles, North Dartmouth, MA 02747-2300. Offers textile chemistry (MS); textile technology (MS). Part-time programs available. *Faculty:* 6 full-time (0 women). *Students:* 7 full-time (2 women), 4 part-time (0 women); includes 1 Hispanic/Latino, 9 international. Average age 27. 14 applicants, 79% accepted, 4 enrolled. In 2010, 4 master's awarded. *Degree requirements:* For master's, thesis. *Entrance requirements:* For master's, GRE General Test, 3 letters of recommendation. Additional exam requirements/recommendations for international students: Required—TOEFL (minimum score 500 paper-based). *Application deadline:* For fall admission, 4/20 priority date for domestic students, 2/20 priority date for international students; for spring admission, 11/15 priority date for domestic students, 9/15 priority date for international students. Applications are processed on a rolling basis. Application fee: $40 ($60 for international students). Electronic applications accepted. *Expenses:* Tuition, state resident: full-time $2071; part-time $86 per credit. Tuition, nonresident: full-time $8099; part-time $337 per credit. Required fees: $9446; $394 per credit. One-time fee: $75. Part-time tuition and fees vary according to class time, course load, degree level and reciprocity agreements. *Financial support:* In 2010–11, 4 research assistantships with full tuition reimbursements (averaging $7,792 per year), 1 teaching assistantship with full tuition reimbursement (averaging $6,000 per year) were awarded; Federal Work-Study also available. Support available to part-time students. Financial award application deadline: 3/1; financial award applicants required to submit FAFSA. *Faculty research:* Flock fundamentals, nanofibers, bio-active fabrics, high stress elastic materials, nano-engineered fire resistant composite fibers. Total annual research expenditures: $3.6 million. *Unit head:* Dr. Qinguo Fan, Director, 508-999-9147, Fax: 508-999-9139, E-mail: qfan@umassd.edu. *Application contact:* Elan Turcotte-Shamski, Graduate Admissions Officer, 508-999-8604, Fax: 508-999-8183, E-mail: graduate@umassd.edu.

The University of Texas at Austin, Graduate School, College of Natural Sciences, School of Human Ecology, Program in Textile and Apparel Technology, Austin, TX 78712-1111. Offers MS.

Section 20
Telecommunications

This section contains a directory of institutions offering graduate work in telecommunications. Additional information about programs listed in the directory may be obtained by writing directly to the dean of a graduate school or chair of a department at the address given in the directory.

For programs offering related work, see also in this book *Computer Science and Information Technology* and *Engineering and Applied Sciences*. In the other guides in this series:

Graduate Programs in the Humanities, Arts & Social Sciences
See *Communication and Media*
Graduate Programs in Business, Education, Health, Information Studies, Law & Social Work
See *Business Administration and Management*

CONTENTS

Program Directories

Telecommunications

The American University of Athens, School of Graduate Studies, Athens, Greece. Offers biomedical sciences (MS); business (MBA); business communication (MA); computer sciences (MS); engineering and applied sciences (MS); politics and policy making (MA); systems engineering (MS); telecommunications (MS). *Entrance requirements:* For master's, resume, 2 recommendation letters. Additional exam requirements/recommendations for international students: Required—TOEFL (minimum score 550 paper-based; 213 computer-based). *Faculty research:* Nanotechnology, environmental sciences, rock mechanics, human skin studies, Monte Carlo algorithms and software.

Ball State University, Graduate School, College of Communication, Information, and Media, Department of Telecommunications, Muncie, IN 47306-1099. Offers digital storytelling (MA). *Faculty:* 7. *Students:* 29 full-time (8 women), 13 part-time (2 women); includes 7 minority (2 Black or African American, non-Hispanic/Latino; 3 Hispanic/Latino; 2 Two or more races, non-Hispanic/Latino), 4 international. 28 applicants, 64% accepted, 12 enrolled. In 2010, 7 master's awarded. Application fee: $50. *Expenses:* Tuition, state resident: full-time $6160; part-time $299 per credit hour. Tuition, nonresident: full-time $16,020; part-time $783 per credit hour. Required fees: $2278; $95 per credit hour. *Financial support:* In 2010–11, 11 teaching assistantships with full tuition reimbursements (averaging $7,966 per year) were awarded. *Unit head:* Timothy Pollard, Chairperson, 765-285-1480, Fax: 765-285-9278, E-mail: tpollard@bsu.edu. *Application contact:* Dr. Robert Morris, Associate Provost for Research and Dean of the Graduate School, 765-285-4723, Fax: 765-285-1328, E-mail: rmorris@bsu.edu.

Boston University, Metropolitan College, Department of Computer Science, Program in Telecommunications, Boston, MA 02215. Offers security (MS). Part-time and evening/weekend programs available. *Faculty:* 10 full-time (0 women), 30 part-time/adjunct (3 women). *Students:* 8 part-time (0 women); includes 2 minority (1 Asian, non-Hispanic/Latino; 1 Hispanic/Latino), 1 international. Average age 38. 6 applicants, 83% accepted, 1 enrolled. In 2010, 3 master's awarded. *Entrance requirements:* For master's, 3 letters of recommendation, resume. Additional exam requirements/recommendations for international students: Required—TOEFL. *Application deadline:* For fall admission, 6/1 priority date for international students; for spring admission, 10/1 priority date for international students. Applications are processed on a rolling basis. Application fee: $70. Electronic applications accepted. *Expenses:* Tuition: Full-time $39,314; part-time $1228 per credit. Required fees: $40 per semester. *Financial support:* Research assistantships with partial tuition reimbursements, career-related internships or fieldwork and unspecified assistantships available. Support available to part-time students. Financial award applicants required to submit FAFSA. *Unit head:* Dr. Lubomir Chitkushev, Chairman, 617-353-2566, Fax: 617-353-2367, E-mail: csinfo@bu.edu. *Application contact:* Camille Kardoose, Program Coordinator, 617-353-2566, Fax: 617-353-2367, E-mail: cgkardoo@bu.edu.

California Miramar University, Program in Telecommunications Management, San Diego, CA 92126. Offers MST.

Claremont Graduate University, Graduate Programs, School of Information Systems and Technology, Claremont, CA 91711-6160. Offers electronic commerce (MS, PhD); health information management (MS); information systems (Certificate); knowledge management (MS, PhD); systems development (MS, PhD); telecommunications and networking (MS, PhD); MBA/MS. Part-time programs available. *Faculty:* 6 full-time (1 woman), 1 part-time/adjunct (0 women). *Students:* 87 full-time (24 women), 22 part-time (8 women); includes 31 minority (6 Black or African American, non-Hispanic/Latino; 1 American Indian or Alaska Native, non-Hispanic/Latino; 18 Asian, non-Hispanic/Latino; 3 Hispanic/Latino; 1 Native Hawaiian or other Pacific Islander, non-Hispanic/Latino; 2 Two or more races, non-Hispanic/Latino), 37 international. Average age 37. In 2010, 30 master's, 6 doctorates awarded. *Degree requirements:* For doctorate, comprehensive exam, thesis/dissertation, portfolio. *Entrance requirements:* For master's and doctorate, GMAT, GRE General Test. Additional exam requirements/recommendations for international students: Required—TOEFL (minimum score 550 paper-based; 213 computer-based; 80 iBT). *Application deadline:* For fall admission, 2/1 priority date for domestic students. Applications are processed on a rolling basis. Application fee: $60. Electronic applications accepted. *Expenses:* Tuition: Full-time $35,748; part-time $1554 per unit. Required fees: $215 per semester. *Financial support:* Fellowships, research assistantships, teaching assistantships, Federal Work-Study, institutionally sponsored loans, and scholarships/grants available. Support available to part-time students. Financial award application deadline: 2/15; financial award applicants required to submit FAFSA. *Faculty research:* GPSS, man-machine interaction, organizational aspects of computing, implementation of information systems, information systems practice. *Unit head:* Terry Ryan, Dean, 909-607-9591, Fax: 909-621-8564, E-mail: terry.ryan@cgu.edu. *Application contact:* Matt Hutter, Director of External Affairs, 909-621-3180, Fax: 909-621-8564, E-mail: matt.hutter@cgu.edu.

Drexel University, College of Engineering, Department of Electrical and Computer Engineering, Program in Telecommunications Engineering, Philadelphia, PA 19104-2875. Offers MSEE. *Entrance requirements:* For master's, BS in electrical engineering or physics, minimum GPA of 3.0. Additional exam requirements/recommendations for international students: Required—TOEFL. Electronic applications accepted.

Florida International University, College of Engineering and Computing, Department of Electrical and Computer Engineering, Miami, FL 33175. Offers computer engineering (MS); electrical engineering (MS, PhD); telecommunications and networking (MS). Part-time and evening/weekend programs available. *Faculty:* 18 full-time (0 women), 6 part-time/adjunct (0 women). *Students:* 98 full-time (17 women), 31 part-time (1 woman); includes 5 Black or African American, non-Hispanic/Latino; 3 Asian, non-Hispanic/Latino; 24 Hispanic/Latino, 83 international. Average age 30. 350 applicants, 23% accepted, 63 enrolled. In 2010, 46 master's, 12 doctorates awarded. Terminal master's awarded for partial completion of doctoral program. *Degree requirements:* For master's, thesis optional; for doctorate, comprehensive exam, thesis/dissertation. *Entrance requirements:* For master's, minimum undergraduate GPA of 3.0 in upper-level coursework, resume, letters of recommendation, letter of intent; for doctorate, GRE General Test, minimum graduate GPA of 3.3, resume, letters of recommendation, letter of intent. Additional exam requirements/recommendations for international students: Required—TOEFL (minimum score 550 paper-based; 80 iBT). *Application deadline:* For fall admission, 6/1 for domestic students, 4/1 for international students; for spring admission, 10/1 for domestic students, 9/1 for international students. Applications are processed on a rolling basis. Application fee: $30. Electronic applications accepted. *Financial support:* Institutionally sponsored loans, scholarships/grants, and unspecified assistantships available. Financial award application deadline: 3/1; financial award applicants required to submit FAFSA. *Unit head:* Dr. Kang Yen, Chair, Electrical and Computer Engineering Department, 305-348-3037, Fax: 305-348-3707, E-mail: yenk@fiu.edu. *Application contact:* Maria Parrilla, Graduate Admissions Assistant, 305-348-1980, Fax: 305-348-6142, E-mail: grad_eng@fiu.edu.

Florida International University, College of Engineering and Computing, School of Computing and Information Sciences, Program in Telecommunications and Networking, Miami, FL 33175. Offers MS. Part-time and evening/weekend programs available. *Students:* 19 full-time (3 women), 25 part-time (6 women); includes 4 Black or African American, non-Hispanic/Latino; 2 Asian, non-Hispanic/Latino; 16 Hispanic/Latino, 14 international. Average age 33. 142 applicants, 22% accepted, 24 enrolled. In 2010, 18 master's awarded. *Entrance requirements:* For master's, minimum undergraduate GPA of 3.0 in upper-level coursework. Additional exam requirements/recommendations for international students: Required—TOEFL (minimum score 550 paper-based; 80 iBT). *Application deadline:* For fall admission, 6/1 for domestic students, 4/1 for international students; for spring admission, 10/1 for domestic students, 9/1 for international students. Applications are processed on a rolling basis. Application fee: $30. Electronic applications accepted. *Financial support:* Institutionally sponsored loans and scholarships/grants available. Financial award application deadline: 3/1; financial award applicants required to

submit FAFSA. *Faculty research:* Wireless networks and mobile computing, high-performance routers and switches, network-centric middleware components, distributed systems, networked databases. *Unit head:* Dr. Jainendra Navlakha, Director, School of Computing and Information Sciences, 305-348-2026, Fax: 305-348-3549, E-mail: navlakha@cis.fiu.edu. *Application contact:* Maria Parrilla, Graduate Admissions Assistant, 305-348-1890, Fax: 305-348-6142, E-mail: grad_eng@fiu.edu.

Franklin Pierce University, Graduate Studies, Rindge, NH 03461-0060. Offers curriculum and instruction (M Ed); emerging network technology (Graduate Certificate); health administration (MBA, Graduate Certificate); human resource management (MBA, Graduate Certificate); information technology management (MS); leadership (MBA, DA); nursing (MS); physical therapy (DPT); physician assistant studies (MPAS); special education (M Ed); sports management (MS). *Accreditation:* APTA. Part-time programs available. Postbaccalaureate distance learning degree programs offered (no on-campus study). *Faculty:* 28 full-time (18 women), 72 part-time/adjunct (44 women). *Students:* 100 full-time (63 women), 487 part-time (306 women); includes 42 minority (25 Black or African American, non-Hispanic/Latino; 10 Asian, non-Hispanic/Latino; 6 Hispanic/Latino; 1 Two or more races, non-Hispanic/Latino), 67 international. Average age 38. 227 applicants, 97% accepted, 185 enrolled. In 2010, 76 master's, 46 doctorates awarded. *Degree requirements:* For master's, concentrated original research projects; student teaching; fieldwork and/or internship; leadership project; Praxis 1&2 (M.Ed) for doctorate, concentrated original research projects, clinical fieldwork and/or internship, leadership project. *Entrance requirements:* For master's, minimum GPA of 2.5, 3 letters of recommendation For MBA: Competencies in accounting, economics, statistics, and computer skills through life experience or undergraduate coursework For M.Ed.: Certification/e-portfolio, No grade < C in education courses For MSN: License to practice as RN; for doctorate, BA/BS, completion of the GRE, 3 letters of recommendation, personal mission statement, interview; writing sample (for DA program) For DPT: 80 hours of observation/work in PT settings, completion of anatomy, chemistry, physics, an statistics, all > 3.0 GPA For DA: 2.8 cum. GPA, Master's degree completion. Additional exam requirements/recommendations for international students: Required—TOEFL (minimum score 550 paper-based; 195 computer-based; 61 iBT). *Application deadline:* Applications are processed on a rolling basis. Application fee: $0. Electronic applications accepted. *Expenses:* Tuition: Part-time $573 per credit hour. Part-time tuition and fees vary according to degree level and program. *Financial support:* In 2010–11, 121 students received support, including 32 teaching assistantships with full and partial tuition reimbursements available (averaging $8,000 per year); career-related internships or fieldwork and unspecified assistantships also available. Support available to part-time students. Financial award applicants required to submit FAFSA. *Faculty research:* Evidence-based practice in sports physical therapy, human resource management in economic crisis, leadership in nursing, innovation in sports facility management, differentiated learning and understanding by design. *Unit head:* Dr. Patricia Brown, Interim Dean of Graduate and Professional Studies, 603-899-4316, Fax: 603-229-4580, E-mail: brownp@franklinpierce.edu.

George Mason University, Volgenau School of Engineering, Department of Electrical and Computer Engineering, Fairfax, VA 22030. Offers advanced networking protocols for telecommunications (Certificate); communications and networking (Certificate); computer engineering (MS); computer forensics (MS); electrical and computer engineering (PhD); electrical engineering (MS); network technology and applications (Certificate); networks, system integration and testing (Certificate); signal processing (Certificate); telecom systems modeling (Certificate); telecommunications (MS); telecommunications forensics and security (Certificate); VLSI design/manufacturing (Certificate); wireless communication (Certificate). MS program offered jointly with Old Dominion University, University of Virginia, Virginia Commonwealth University, and Virginia Polytechnic Institute and State University. Part-time and evening/weekend programs available. *Faculty:* 33 full-time (4 women), 39 part-time/adjunct (4 women). *Students:* 106 full-time (27 women), 336 part-time (64 women); includes 24 Black or African American, non-Hispanic/Latino; 1 American Indian or Alaska Native, non-Hispanic/Latino; 54 Asian, non-Hispanic/Latino; 20 Hispanic/Latino; 1 Two or more races, non-Hispanic/Latino, 172 international. Average age 30. 506 applicants, 71% accepted, 142 enrolled. In 2010, 145 master's, 3 doctorates, 61 other advanced degrees awarded. *Degree requirements:* For master's, thesis optional; for doctorate, comprehensive exam, thesis or scholarly paper. *Entrance requirements:* For master's, GMAT or GRE General Test, letters of recommendation, resume; for doctorate, GRE/GMAT, personal goal statement, 2 transcripts, letter of recommendation. Additional exam requirements/recommendations for international students: Required—TOEFL (minimum score 570 paper-based; 230 computer-based; 88 iBT). *Application deadline:* For fall admission, 7/15 priority date for domestic and international students; for spring admission, 12/1 for domestic and international students. Applications are processed on a rolling basis. Application fee: $100. Electronic applications accepted. *Expenses:* Tuition, state resident: full-time $8192; part-time $440 per credit hour. Tuition, nonresident: full-time $22,952; part-time $1055 per credit hour. Required fees: $2364; $99 per credit hour. *Financial support:* In 2010–11, 74 students received support, including 2 fellowships with full tuition reimbursements available (averaging $18,000 per year), 26 research assistantships with full and partial tuition reimbursements available (averaging $14,648 per year), 46 teaching assistantships with full and partial tuition reimbursements available (averaging $10,946 per year); career-related internships or fieldwork, Federal Work-Study, scholarships/grants, unspecified assistantships, and health care benefits (full-time research or teaching assistantship recipients) also available. Financial award application deadline: 3/1; financial award applicants required to submit FAFSA. *Faculty research:* Communication networks, signal processing, system failure diagnosis, multiprocessors, material processing using microwave energy. Total annual research expenditures: $3.4 million. *Unit head:* Dr. Andre Manitius, Chairperson, 703-993-1569, Fax: 703-993-1601, E-mail: ece@gmu.edu. *Application contact:* Jessica Skinner, Associate Dean, 703-993-1569, E-mail: jskinne6@gmu.edu.

The George Washington University, School of Engineering and Applied Science, Department of Electrical and Computer Engineering, Washington, DC 20052. Offers electrical and computer engineering (MS, D Sc); telecommunication and computers (MS). Part-time and evening/weekend programs available. *Faculty:* 24 full-time (2 women), 9 part-time/adjunct (0 women). *Students:* 101 full-time (19 women), 114 part-time (20 women); includes 12 Black or African American, non-Hispanic/Latino; 23 Asian, non-Hispanic/Latino; 2 Hispanic/Latino; 1 Native Hawaiian or other Pacific Islander, non-Hispanic/Latino, 112 international. Average age 29. 339 applicants, 81% accepted, 69 enrolled. In 2010, 65 master's, 14 doctorates awarded. *Degree requirements:* For master's, thesis optional; for doctorate, comprehensive exam, thesis/dissertation, dissertation defense, qualifying exam. *Entrance requirements:* For master's, appropriate bachelor's degree, minimum GPA of 3.0; for doctorate, appropriate bachelor's or master's degree, minimum GPA of 3.3, GRE if highest earned degree is BS. Additional exam requirements/recommendations for international students: Required—TOEFL or The George Washington University English as a Foreign Language Test. *Application deadline:* For fall admission, 3/1 priority date for domestic students; for spring admission, 10/1 for domestic students. Applications are processed on a rolling basis. Application fee: $75. *Financial support:* In 2010–11, 39 students received support; fellowships with tuition reimbursements available, research assistantships, teaching assistantships with tuition reimbursements available, career-related internships or fieldwork and institutionally sponsored loans available. Financial award application deadline: 3/1; financial award applicants required to submit FAFSA. *Faculty research:* Computer graphics, multimedia systems. *Unit head:* Can E. Korman, Chair, 202-994-4952, E-mail: korman@gwu.edu. *Application contact:* Adina Lav, Marketing, Recruiting and Admissions, 202-994-5827, Fax: 202-994-0909, E-mail: engineering@gwu.edu.

Illinois Institute of Technology, Graduate College, Armour College of Engineering, Department of Electrical and Computer Engineering, Chicago, IL 60616-3793. Offers biomedical imaging and signals (MBMI); computer engineering (MS, PhD); electrical and computer engineering (MECE); electrical engineering (MS, PhD); electricity markets (MEM); network engineering

(MNE); power engineering (MPE); telecommunications and software engineering (MTSE); VLSI and microelectronics (MVM). Part-time and evening/weekend programs available. Postbaccalaureate distance learning degree programs offered (minimal on-campus study). *Faculty:* 26 full-time (3 women), 2 part-time/adjunct (0 women). *Students:* 456 full-time (77 women), 140 part-time (17 women); includes 25 minority (4 Black or African American, non-Hispanic/Latino; 15 Asian, non-Hispanic/Latino; 4 Hispanic/Latino; 2 Two or more races, non-Hispanic/Latino), 488 international. Average age 26. 1,407 applicants, 68% accepted, 217 enrolled. In 2010, 214 master's, 17 doctorates awarded. Terminal master's awarded for partial completion of doctoral program. *Degree requirements:* For master's, comprehensive exam (for some programs), thesis (for some programs); for doctorate, comprehensive exam, thesis/dissertation. *Entrance requirements:* For master's and doctorate, GRE General Test (minimum score 1100 Quantitative and Verbal, 3.5 Analytical Writing), minimum undergraduate GPA of 3.0. Additional exam requirements/recommendations for international students: Required—TOEFL (minimum score 523 paper-based; 70 iBT); Recommended—IELTS (minimum score 5.5). *Application deadline:* For fall admission, 5/1 for domestic and international students; for spring admission, 10/15 for domestic and international students. Applications are processed on a rolling basis. Application fee: $50. Electronic applications accepted. *Expenses:* Tuition: Full-time $18,576; part-time $1032 per credit hour. Required fees: $583 per semester. One-time fee: $150. Tuition and fees vary according to program and student level. *Financial support:* In 2010–11, 1 fellowship with full and partial tuition reimbursement (averaging $1,090 per year), 52 research assistantships with full and partial tuition reimbursements (averaging $9,530 per year), 24 teaching assistantships with full and partial tuition reimbursements (averaging $9,092 per year) were awarded; career-related internships or fieldwork, Federal Work-Study, institutionally sponsored loans, scholarships/grants, health care benefits, tuition waivers (full), and unspecified assistantships also available. Support available to part-time students. Financial award applicants required to submit FAFSA. *Faculty research:* Communication systems, computer systems and micro-electronics, electromagnetics and electronics, power and control systems, signal and image processing. Total annual research expenditures: $5.6 million. *Unit head:* Dr. Geoffrey Williamson, Interim Chair, 312-567-5960, Fax: 312-567-8976, E-mail: williamson@iit.edu. *Application contact:* Deborah Gibson, Director, Graduate Admission, 866-472-3448, Fax: 312-567-3138, E-mail: inquiry.grad@iit.edu.

Illinois Institute of Technology, Graduate College, College of Science and Letters, Department of Computer Science, Chicago, IL 60616-3793. Offers business (MCS); computer networking and telecommunications (MCS); computer science (MCS, MS, PhD); information systems (MCS); software engineering (MCS); teaching (MST). Part-time and evening/weekend programs available. Postbaccalaureate distance learning degree programs offered (no on-campus study). *Faculty:* 29 full-time (6 women), 3 part-time/adjunct (0 women). *Students:* 262 full-time (62 women), 132 part-time (27 women); includes 44 minority (3 Black or African American, non-Hispanic/Latino; 7 Asian, non-Hispanic/Latino; 34 Hispanic/Latino), 340 international. Average age 26. 974 applicants, 71% accepted, 148 enrolled. In 2010, 138 master's, 5 doctorates awarded. Terminal master's awarded for partial completion of doctoral program. *Degree requirements:* For master's, thesis optional; for doctorate, comprehensive exam, thesis/dissertation. *Entrance requirements:* For master's, GRE General Test (minimum scores 1000 Quantitative and Verbal, 3.0 Analytical Writing), minimum undergraduate GPA of 3.0; for doctorate, GRE General Test (minimum scores 1100 Quantitative and Verbal, 3.5 Analytical Writing), minimum undergraduate GPA of 3.0. Additional exam requirements/recommendations for international students: Required—TOEFL (minimum score 523 paper-based; 70 iBT). *Application deadline:* For fall admission, 5/1 for domestic and international students; for spring admission, 10/15 for domestic and international students. Applications are processed on a rolling basis. Application fee: $50. Electronic applications accepted. *Expenses:* Tuition: Full-time $18,576; part-time $1032 per credit hour. Required fees: $583 per semester. One-time fee: $150. Tuition and fees vary according to program and student level. *Financial support:* In 2010–11, 15 research assistantships with full and partial tuition reimbursements (averaging $10,380 per year), 21 teaching assistantships with full and partial tuition reimbursements (averaging $12,452 per year) were awarded; fellowships with partial tuition reimbursements, career-related internships or fieldwork, Federal Work-Study, institutionally sponsored loans, scholarships/grants, traineeships, health care benefits, tuition waivers (partial), and unspecified assistantships also available. Support available to part-time students. Financial award applicants required to submit FAFSA. *Faculty research:* Algorithms, data structures, artificial intelligences, computer architecture, computer graphics, computer networking and telecommunications. Total annual research expenditures: $1.8 million. *Unit head:* Dr. Xian-He Sun, Chair/Professor, 312-567-5260, Fax: 312-567-5067, E-mail: sun@cs.iit.edu. *Application contact:* Debbie Gibson, Director, Graduate Admission, 866-472-3448, Fax: 312-567-3138, E-mail: inquiry.grad@iit.edu.

Indiana University Bloomington, University Graduate School, College of Arts and Sciences, Department of Telecommunications, Program in Telecommunications, Bloomington, IN 47405-7000. Offers MA, MS. *Students:* 24 full-time (13 women), 13 part-time (2 women); includes 4 minority (1 Black or African American, non-Hispanic/Latino; 1 Asian, non-Hispanic/Latino; 1 Hispanic/Latino; 1 Two or more races, non-Hispanic/Latino), 12 international. Average age 28. 38 applicants, 61% accepted, 16 enrolled. In 2010, 10 master's awarded. *Degree requirements:* For master's, comprehensive exam (for some programs), thesis (for some programs). *Entrance requirements:* For master's, GRE General Test. Application fee: $55 ($65 for international students). *Unit head:* Tamera Theodore, Graduate Secretary, 812-855-2017, E-mail: ttheodor@indiana.edu. *Application contact:* Tamera Theodore, Graduate Secretary, 812-855-2017, E-mail: ttheodor@indiana.edu.

Instituto Tecnologico de Santo Domingo, Graduate School, Area of Engineering, Santo Domingo, Dominican Republic. Offers construction administration (MS, Certificate); data telecommunications (M Eng, MS, Certificate); industrial engineering (M Eng, Certificate); industrial management (M Mgmt); information technology (Certificate); maintenance engineering (M Eng); occupational hazard prevention (M Mgmt); production management (Certificate); quantitative methods (Certificate); sanitary and environmental engineering (M Eng); structural engineering (M Eng); systems engineering and electronic data processing (Certificate); transportation (Certificate).

Iona College, School of Arts and Science, Program in Computer Science, New Rochelle, NY 10801-1890. Offers computer science (MS); telecommunications (MS). Part-time and evening/weekend programs available. *Faculty:* 8 full-time (3 women), 3 part-time/adjunct (0 women). *Students:* 1 full-time (0 women), 15 part-time (5 women); includes 3 minority (2 Black or African American, non-Hispanic/Latino; 1 Hispanic/Latino), 1 international. Average age 35. 6 applicants, 83% accepted, 5 enrolled. In 2010, 13 master's awarded. *Degree requirements:* For master's, thesis or alternative. *Entrance requirements:* For master's, minimum GPA of 3.0. Additional exam requirements/recommendations for international students: Required—TOEFL (minimum score 550 paper-based; 213 computer-based). *Application deadline:* Applications are processed on a rolling basis. Application fee: $50. Electronic applications accepted. *Expenses:* Contact institution. *Financial support:* Tuition waivers (partial) and unspecified assistantships available. Support available to part-time students. Financial award application deadline: 4/15; financial award applicants required to submit FAFSA. *Faculty research:* Telecommunications, expert systems, graph isomorphism, algorithms, formal verification of hardware. *Unit head:* Dr. Robert Schiaffino, Chair, 914-633-2338, E-mail: rschiaffino@iona.edu. *Application contact:* Veronica Jarek-Prinz, Director of Graduate Admissions, 914-633-2420, Fax: 914-633-2277, E-mail: vjarekprinz@iona.edu.

The Johns Hopkins University, Engineering for Professionals, Part-Time Program in Computer Science, Baltimore, MD 21218-2699. Offers bioinformatics (MS); computer science (MS, Post-Master's Certificate); telecommunications and networking (MS). Part-time and evening/weekend programs available. Postbaccalaureate distance learning degree programs offered (no on-campus study). *Faculty:* 58 part-time/adjunct (5 women). *Students:* 16 full-time (5 women), 428 part-time (54 women); includes 131 minority (24 Black or African American, non-Hispanic/Latino; 81 Asian, non-Hispanic/Latino; 16 Hispanic/Latino; 1 Native Hawaiian or other Pacific Islander, non-Hispanic/Latino; 9 Two or more races, non-Hispanic/Latino), 16

international. Average age 29. 133 applicants, 87% accepted, 74 enrolled. In 2010, 153 master's, 2 other advanced degrees awarded. *Application deadline:* Applications are processed on a rolling basis. Application fee: $75. Electronic applications accepted. *Financial support:* Institutionally sponsored loans available. *Unit head:* Dr. Thomas A. Longstaff, Program Chair, 443-778-9389, E-mail: thomas.longstaff@jhuapl.edu. *Application contact:* Priyanka Dwivedi, Admissions Manager, 410-516-2300, Fax: 410-579-8049, E-mail: pdwived1@jhu.edu.

Michigan State University, The Graduate School, College of Communication Arts and Sciences, Department of Telecommunication, Information Studies, and Media, East Lansing, MI 48824. Offers digital media arts and technology (MA); information and telecommunication management (MA); information, policy and society (MA); serious game design (MA). *Entrance requirements:* Additional exam requirements/recommendations for international students: Required—TOEFL. Electronic applications accepted.

National University, Academic Affairs, School of Engineering and Technology, Department of Applied Engineering, La Jolla, CA 92037-1011. Offers database administration (MS); engineering management (MS); environmental engineering (MS); homeland security and safety engineering (MS); system engineering (MS); wireless communications (MS). Part-time and evening/weekend programs available. Postbaccalaureate distance learning degree programs offered (no on-campus study). *Faculty:* 6 full-time (1 woman), 69 part-time/adjunct (12 women). *Students:* 82 full-time (16 women), 153 part-time (35 women); includes 87 minority (18 Black or African American, non-Hispanic/Latino; 1 American Indian or Alaska Native, non-Hispanic/Latino; 34 Asian, non-Hispanic/Latino; 28 Hispanic/Latino; 2 Native Hawaiian or other Pacific Islander, non-Hispanic/Latino; 4 Two or more races, non-Hispanic/Latino), 60 international. Average age 31. 166 applicants, 100% accepted, 106 enrolled. In 2010, 79 master's awarded. *Degree requirements:* For master's, thesis. *Entrance requirements:* For master's, interview, minimum GPA of 2.5. Additional exam requirements/recommendations for international students: Required—TOEFL (minimum score 550 paper-based; 213 computer-based; 79 iBT), IELTS (minimum score 6). *Application deadline:* Applications are processed on a rolling basis. Application fee: $60 ($65 for international students). Electronic applications accepted. *Expenses:* Tuition: Full-time $9450; part-time $350 per unit. Required fees: $350 per unit. One-time fee: $60. *Financial support:* Career-related internships or fieldwork, institutionally sponsored loans, scholarships/grants, and tuition waivers (partial) available. Support available to part-time students. Financial award application deadline: 6/30; financial award applicants required to submit FAFSA. *Unit head:* Dr. Shekar Viswanathan, Chair and Associate Professor, 858-309-8416, Fax: 858-309-3420, E-mail: sviswana@nu.edu. *Application contact:* Dominick Giovanniello, Associate Regional Dean—San Diego, 800-NAT-UNIV, Fax: 858-541-7792, E-mail: dgiovann@nu.edu.

Ohio University, Graduate College, Scripps College of Communication, J. Warren McClure School of Information and Telecommunication Systems, Athens, OH 45701-2979. Offers MCTP. Part-time programs available. *Students:* 21 full-time (4 women), 4 part-time (2 women); includes 2 minority (both Asian, non-Hispanic/Latino), 16 international. 25 applicants, 88% accepted, 13 enrolled. In 2010, 12 master's awarded. *Degree requirements:* For master's, comprehensive exam (for some programs), thesis (for some programs). *Entrance requirements:* For master's, GRE or GMAT, minimum cumulative GPA of 3.0. Additional exam requirements/recommendations for international students: Required—TOEFL (minimum score 550 paper-based; 80 iBT) or IELTS (minimum score 6.5). *Application deadline:* For fall admission, 2/1 priority date for domestic students, 12/15 priority date for international students. Applications are processed on a rolling basis. Application fee: $50 ($55 for international students). Electronic applications accepted. *Financial support:* Research assistantships with full and partial tuition reimbursements, institutionally sponsored loans and unspecified assistantships available. Financial award application deadline: 2/1; financial award applicants required to submit FAFSA. *Faculty research:* Voice and data networks, with special emphasis on the interaction of technology and policy issues in the successful design, deployment, and operation of complex networks and information systems. Total annual research expenditures: $200,000. *Unit head:* Philip D. Campbell, Associate Professor and Director, 740-593-4907, Fax: 740-593-4889, E-mail: campbell@ohio.edu. *Application contact:* Dr. Phyllis W. Bernt, Professor and Associate Director for Graduate Studies, 740-593-0020, Fax: 740-593-4889, E-mail: bernt@ohio.edu.

Pace University, Seidenberg School of Computer Science and Information Systems, New York, NY 10038. Offers computer communications and networks (Certificate); computer science (MS); computing studies (DPS); information systems (MS); Internet technologies for e-commerce (MS); Internet technology (MS); object-oriented programming (Certificate); security and information assurance (Certificate); software development and engineering (MS); telecommunications (MS, Certificate). Part-time and evening/weekend programs available. *Entrance requirements:* For master's, GRE General Test. Additional exam requirements/recommendations for international students: Required—TOEFL. Electronic applications accepted. *Expenses:* Contact institution.

Polytechnic Institute of NYU, Department of Electrical and Computer Engineering, Major in Telecommunication Networks, Brooklyn, NY 11201-2990. Offers MS. Part-time and evening/weekend programs available. *Students:* 48 full-time (7 women), 22 part-time (3 women); includes 2 Black or African American, non-Hispanic/Latino; 4 Asian, non-Hispanic/Latino; 4 Hispanic/Latino, 46 international. 119 applicants, 54% accepted, 24 enrolled. In 2010, 39 master's awarded. *Degree requirements:* For master's, comprehensive exam (for some programs), thesis (for some programs). *Entrance requirements:* For master's, BS in electrical engineering. Additional exam requirements/recommendations for international students: Required—TOEFL (minimum score 550 paper-based; 213 computer-based; 80 iBT); Recommended—IELTS (minimum score 6.5). *Application deadline:* For fall admission, 7/31 priority date for domestic students, 4/30 priority date for international students; for spring admission, 12/31 priority date for domestic students, 11/30 priority date for international students. Applications are processed on a rolling basis. Application fee: $75. Electronic applications accepted. *Expenses:* Tuition: Full-time $21,492; part-time $1194 per credit. Required fees: $385 per semester. Tuition and fees vary according to course load. *Financial support:* Fellowships, research assistantships, teaching assistantships, institutionally sponsored loans, scholarships/grants, and unspecified assistantships available. Support available to part-time students. Financial award applicants required to submit FAFSA. *Unit head:* Dr. Jonathan Chao, Head, 718-260-3478, Fax: 718-260-3302, E-mail: chao@poly.edu. *Application contact:* JeanCarlo Bonilla, Director, Graduate Enrollment Management, 718-260-3182, Fax: 718-260-3624.

Polytechnic Institute of NYU, Long Island Graduate Center, Graduate Programs, Department of Electrical and Computer Engineering, Major in Telecommunication Networks, Melville, NY 11747. Offers MS. Part-time and evening/weekend programs available. *Students:* 1 part-time (0 women). Average age 37. 2 applicants, 50% accepted, 1 enrolled. In 2010, 3 master's awarded. *Degree requirements:* For master's, comprehensive exam (for some programs), thesis (for some programs). *Entrance requirements:* Additional exam requirements/recommendations for international students: Required—TOEFL (minimum score 550 paper-based; 213 computer-based; 80 iBT); Recommended—IELTS (minimum score 6.5). *Application deadline:* For fall admission, 7/31 priority date for domestic students, 4/30 priority date for international students; for spring admission, 12/31 priority date for domestic students, 11/30 priority date for international students. Applications are processed on a rolling basis. Application fee: $75. Electronic applications accepted. *Expenses:* Tuition: Full-time $21,492; part-time $1194 per credit. Required fees: $385 per semester. Tuition and fees vary according to course load. *Financial support:* Institutionally sponsored loans, scholarships/grants, and unspecified assistantships available. Support available to part-time students. Financial award applicants required to submit FAFSA. *Unit head:* Dr. Jonathan Chao, Department Head, 718-260-3302, E-mail: chao@poly.edu. *Application contact:* JeanCarlo Bonilla, Director of Graduate Enrollment Management, 718-260-3182, Fax: 718-260-3624, E-mail: gradinfo@poly.edu.

Polytechnic Institute of NYU, Westchester Graduate Center, Graduate Programs, Department of Electrical and Computer Engineering, Major in Telecommunication Networks, Hawthorne, NY 10532-1507. Offers MS. Part-time and evening/weekend programs available.

Telecommunications

Polytechnic Institute of NYU, Westchester Graduate Center *(continued)*
Students: 1 part-time (0 women). Average age 32. 2 applicants, 100% accepted, 1 enrolled. In 2010, 3 master's awarded. *Degree requirements:* For master's, thesis (for some programs). *Entrance requirements:* Additional exam requirements/recommendations for international students: Required—TOEFL (minimum score 550 paper-based; 213 computer-based; 80 iBT); Recommended—IELTS (minimum score 6.5). *Application deadline:* For fall admission, 7/31 priority date for domestic students, 4/30 priority date for international students; for spring admission, 12/31 priority date for domestic students, 11/30 priority date for international students. Applications are processed on a rolling basis. Application fee: $75. Electronic applications accepted. *Expenses:* Tuition: Full-time $21,492; part-time $1194 per credit. Required fees: $385 per semester. Tuition and fees vary according to course load. *Financial support:* Institutionally sponsored loans, scholarships/grants, and unspecified assistantships available. Support available to part-time students. *Unit head:* Dr. Jonathan Chao, Department Head, 718-260-3302, E-mail: chao@poly.edu. *Application contact:* JeanCarlo Bonilla, Director of Graduate Enrollment Management, 718-260-3182, Fax: 718-260-3624, E-mail: gradinfo@poly.edu.

Rochester Institute of Technology, Graduate Enrollment Services, College of Applied Science and Technology, Department of Electrical, Computer and Telecommunications Engineering Technology, Program of Telecommunications Engineering Technology, Rochester, NY 14623-5603. Offers MS. Part-time and evening/weekend programs available. Postbaccalaureate distance learning degree programs offered (no on-campus study). *Students:* 42 full-time (12 women), 27 part-time (5 women); includes 2 Black or African American, non-Hispanic/Latino; 1 Asian, non-Hispanic/Latino; 3 Hispanic/Latino; 1 Two or more races, non-Hispanic/Latino, 51 international. Average age 29. 109 applicants, 52% accepted, 22 enrolled. In 2010, 16 master's awarded. *Degree requirements:* For master's, thesis or alternative. *Entrance requirements:* For master's, GRE. Additional exam requirements/recommendations for international students: Required—TOEFL (minimum score 570 paper-based; 230 computer-based; 89 iBT) or IELTS (minimum score 6.5). *Application deadline:* For fall admission, 2/15 priority date for domestic and international students; for winter admission, 11/1 for domestic and international students; for spring admission, 2/1 for domestic and international students. Applications are processed on a rolling basis. Electronic applications accepted. *Expenses:* Tuition: Full-time $33,234; part-time $924 per credit hour. Required fees: $219. *Financial support:* In 2010–11, 47 students received support; research assistantships with partial tuition reimbursements available, teaching assistantships, career-related internships or fieldwork, scholarships/grants, and unspecified assistantships available. Support available to part-time students. Financial award application deadline: 2/15; financial award applicants required to submit FAFSA. *Unit head:* Warren Koontz, Program Chair, 585-475-5706, E-mail: telecom@cast-fc.rit.edu. *Application contact:* Diane Ellison, Assistant Vice President, Graduate Enrollment Services, 585-475-2229, Fax: 585-475-7164, E-mail: gradinfo@rit.edu.

Roosevelt University, Graduate Division, College of Arts and Sciences, Department of Computer Science and Telecommunications, Program in Telecommunications, Chicago, IL 60605. Offers MST. Part-time and evening/weekend programs available. *Entrance requirements:* For master's, GRE. *Faculty research:* Coding theory, mathematical models, network design, simulation models.

Saint Mary's University of Minnesota, Schools of Graduate and Professional Programs, Graduate School of Business and Technology, Information Technology Management Program, Winona, MN 55987-1399. Offers MS. *Unit head:* Paula Justich, Director, 612-728-5165, E-mail: pjustich@smumn.edu. *Application contact:* Yasin Alsaidi, Director of Admissions for Graduate and Professional Programs, 612-728-5207, Fax: 612-728-5121, E-mail: yalsaidi@smumn.edu.

Southern Methodist University, Bobby B. Lyle School of Engineering, Department of Electrical Engineering, Dallas, TX 75275-0338. Offers electrical engineering (MSEE, PhD); telecommunications (MS). Part-time and evening/weekend programs available. Postbaccalaureate distance learning degree programs offered (no on-campus study). *Faculty:* 12 full-time (1 woman), 9 part-time/adjunct (0 women). *Students:* 83 full-time (9 women), 61 part-time (10 women); includes 5 Black or African American, non-Hispanic/Latino; 10 Asian, non-Hispanic/Latino; 5 Hispanic/Latino, 97 international. Average age 28. 270 applicants, 49% accepted, 46 enrolled. In 2010, 60 master's, 3 doctorates awarded. Terminal master's awarded for partial completion of doctoral program. *Degree requirements:* For master's, thesis optional; for doctorate, thesis/dissertation, oral and written qualifying exams, oral final exam. *Entrance requirements:* For master's, GRE General Test, minimum GPA of 3.0 in last 2 years; bachelor's degree in engineering, mathematics, or sciences; for doctorate, preliminary counseling exam, minimum GPA of 3.0, bachelor's degree in related field. Additional exam requirements/recommendations for international students: Required—TOEFL. *Application deadline:* For fall admission, 7/1 priority date for domestic students, 5/15 for international students; for spring admission, 11/15 for domestic students, 9/1 for international students. Applications are processed on a rolling basis. Application fee: $75. Electronic applications accepted. *Financial support:* In 2010–11, 38 students received support, including 22 research assistantships with full tuition reimbursements available (averaging $19,200 per year), 16 teaching assistantships with full tuition reimbursements available (averaging $14,400 per year); unspecified assistantships also available. Financial award application deadline: 5/15; financial award applicants required to submit FAFSA. *Faculty research:* Mobile communications, optical communications, digital signal processing, photonics. *Unit head:* Dr. Marc P. Christensen, Chair, 214-768-3113, Fax: 214-768-3573, E-mail: mpc@lyle.smu.edu. *Application contact:* Marc Valerin, Director of Graduate and Executive Admissions, 214-768-3042, Fax: 214-768-3778, E-mail: valerin@lyle.smu.edu.

State University of New York Institute of Technology, School of Information Systems and Engineering Technology, Program in Telecommunications, Utica, NY 13504-3050. Offers MS. Part-time and evening/weekend programs available. *Degree requirements:* For master's, thesis, project or capstone. *Entrance requirements:* For master's, GRE General Test, minimum GPA of 3.0, letters of recommendation (3). Additional exam requirements/recommendations for international students: Required—TOEFL (minimum score 550 paper-based; 213 computer-based). *Faculty research:* Network design/simulation/management, wireless telecommunication systems, international telecommunications policy and management, information assurance, disaster recovery.

Stevens Institute of Technology, Graduate School, Wesley J. Howe School of Technology Management, Program in Telecommunications Management, Hoboken, NJ 07030. Offers business (MS); global innovation management (MS); management of wireless networks (MS); online security, technology and business (MS); project management (MS); technical management (MS); telecommunications management (PhD, Certificate). *Students:* 26 full-time (6 women), 92 part-time (15 women); includes 8 Black or African American, non-Hispanic/Latino; 9 Asian, non-Hispanic/Latino; 9 Hispanic/Latino, 25 international. Average age 33. 154 applicants, 91% accepted. *Degree requirements:* For master's, thesis optional; for doctorate, thesis/dissertation. *Entrance requirements:* For master's and doctorate, GMAT, GRE General Test. Additional exam requirements/recommendations for international students: Required—TOEFL. *Application deadline:* Applications are processed on a rolling basis. Application fee: $50. Electronic applications accepted. *Unit head:* Audrey Kames Curtis, Director, 201-216-5524. *Application contact:* Sharen Glennon, Administrative Assistant, 201-216-8322, Fax: 201-216-8355, E-mail: sglennon@stevens-tech.edu.

Stratford University, School of Graduate Studies, Falls Church, VA 22043. Offers accounting (MS); business administration (IMBA, MBA); enterprise business management (MS); entrepreneurial management (MS); information assurance (MS); information systems (MS); software engineering (MS); telecommunications (MS). Part-time and evening/weekend programs available. Postbaccalaureate distance learning degree programs offered (no on-campus study). *Degree requirements:* For master's, comprehensive exam, capstone project. *Entrance requirements:* For master's, baccalaureate degree. Additional exam requirements/

recommendations for international students: Required—TOEFL (minimum score 500 paper-based; 173 computer-based; 61 iBT). Electronic applications accepted.

Syracuse University, School of Information Studies, Program in Telecommunications and Network Management, Syracuse, NY 13244. Offers MS, MS/CAS. Part-time and evening/weekend programs available. Postbaccalaureate distance learning degree programs offered (minimal on-campus study). *Students:* 48 full-time (13 women), 33 part-time (5 women); includes 10 minority (4 Black or African American, non-Hispanic/Latino; 1 Asian, non-Hispanic/Latino; 5 Hispanic/Latino), 44 international. Average age 29. 103 applicants, 68% accepted, 33 enrolled. In 2010, 21 master's awarded. *Degree requirements:* For master's, internship or research project. *Entrance requirements:* For master's, GRE General Test. Additional exam requirements/recommendations for international students: Required—TOEFL (minimum score 100 iBT). *Application deadline:* For fall admission, 2/1 priority date for domestic and international students; for spring admission, 10/15 priority date for domestic and international students. Applications are processed on a rolling basis. Application fee: $75. Electronic applications accepted. *Expenses:* Tuition: Part-time $1162 per credit. *Financial support:* Fellowships with full tuition reimbursements, research assistantships with partial tuition reimbursements, teaching assistantships with partial tuition reimbursements, career-related internships or fieldwork and Federal Work-Study available. Financial award application deadline: 1/1. *Faculty research:* Multimedia, information resources management. *Unit head:* Martha Garcia-Marillo, Director, 315-443-2911, Fax: 315-443-6886, E-mail: mgarciam@syr.edu. *Application contact:* Susan Corieri, Director of Enrollment Management, 315-443-2575, E-mail: ischool@syr.edu.

Universidad del Turabo, Graduate Programs, School of Engineering, Program in Telecommunication and Network Administration, Gurabo, PR 00778-3030. Offers MS.

Université du Québec, Institut National de la Recherche Scientifique, Graduate Programs, Research Center—Energy, Materials and Telecommunications, Québec, QC G1K 9A9, Canada. Offers energy and materials science (M Sc, PhD); telecommunications (M Sc, PhD). Programs given in French; PhD programs offered jointly with Université du Québec à Trois-Rivières. Part-time programs available. *Faculty:* 40. *Students:* 171 full-time (44 women), 6 part-time (1 woman), 88 international. Average age 32. In 2010, 15 master's, 23 doctorates awarded. *Degree requirements:* For master's, thesis optional; for doctorate, thesis/dissertation. *Entrance requirements:* For master's, appropriate bachelor's degree, proficiency in French; for doctorate, appropriate master's degree, proficiency in French. *Application deadline:* For fall admission, 3/30 for domestic and international students; for winter admission, 11/1 for domestic and international students; for spring admission, 3/1 for domestic and international students. Application fee: $30. *Financial support:* Fellowships, research assistantships, teaching assistantships available. *Faculty research:* New energy sources, plasmas, fusion. *Unit head:* Jean-Claude Kieffer, Director, 450-929-8100, E-mail: kieffer@emt.inrs.ca. *Application contact:* Yvonne Boisvert, Registrar, 418-654-3861, Fax: 418-654-3858, E-mail: registrariat@adm.inrs.ca.

University of Alberta, Faculty of Graduate Studies and Research, Department of Electrical and Computer Engineering, Edmonton, AB T6G 2E1, Canada. Offers communications (M Eng, M Sc, PhD); computer engineering (M Eng, M Sc, PhD); electromagnetics (M Eng, M Sc, PhD); nanotechnology and microdevices (M Eng, M Sc, PhD); power/power electronics (M Eng, M Sc, PhD); systems (M Eng, M Sc, PhD). Terminal master's awarded for partial completion of doctoral program. *Degree requirements:* For master's, thesis; for doctorate, thesis/dissertation. *Entrance requirements:* Additional exam requirements/recommendations for international students: Required—TOEFL. Electronic applications accepted. *Faculty research:* Controls, communications, microelectronics, electromagnetics.

University of Arkansas, Graduate School, College of Engineering, Department of Electrical Engineering, Fayetteville, AR 72701-1201. Offers electrical engineering (MSEE, PhD); telecommunications engineering (MS Tc E). *Students:* 19 full-time (3 women), 58 part-time (8 women); includes 3 minority (2 Black or African American, non-Hispanic/Latino; 1 Asian, non-Hispanic/Latino), 48 international. 74 applicants, 58% accepted. In 2010, 11 master's, 8 doctorates awarded. *Degree requirements:* For master's, thesis optional; for doctorate, one foreign language, thesis/dissertation. *Entrance requirements:* For master's and doctorate, GRE General Test. *Application deadline:* For fall admission, 4/1 for international students; for spring admission, 10/1 for international students. Applications are processed on a rolling basis. Application fee: $40 ($50 for international students). Electronic applications accepted. *Financial support:* In 2010–11, 9 fellowships with tuition reimbursements, 51 research assistantships, 7 teaching assistantships were awarded; career-related internships or fieldwork and Federal Work-Study also available. Support available to part-time students. Financial award application deadline: 4/1; financial award applicants required to submit FAFSA. *Unit head:* Dr. Juan Balda, Department Chair, 479-575-3005, Fax: 479-575-7967, E-mail: jbalda@uark.edu. *Application contact:* Dr. Randy Brown, Graduate Coordinator, 479-575-6581, E-mail: rlb02@uark.edu.

University of California, San Diego, Office of Graduate Studies, Department of Electrical and Computer Engineering, La Jolla, CA 92093. Offers applied ocean science (MS, PhD); applied physics (MS, PhD); communication theory and systems (MS, PhD); computer engineering (MS, PhD); electrical engineering (M Eng); electronic circuits and systems (MS, PhD); intelligent systems, robotics and control (MS, PhD); photonics (MS, PhD); signal and image processing (MS, PhD). MS only offered to students who have been admitted to the PhD program. *Entrance requirements:* For master's and doctorate, GRE General Test. Electronic applications accepted.

University of California, Santa Cruz, Division of Graduate Studies, Jack Baskin School of Engineering, Program in Computer Engineering, Santa Cruz, CA 95064. Offers computer engineering (MS, PhD); network engineering (MS). Part-time programs available. *Students:* 77 full-time (15 women), 6 part-time (1 woman); includes 16 minority (1 Black or African American, non-Hispanic/Latino; 1 American Indian or Alaska Native, non-Hispanic/Latino; 9 Asian, non-Hispanic/Latino; 5 Hispanic/Latino), 23 international. Average age 31. 103 applicants, 24% accepted, 13 enrolled. In 2010, 8 master's, 8 doctorates awarded. Terminal master's awarded for partial completion of doctoral program. *Degree requirements:* For master's, thesis; for doctorate, comprehensive exam, thesis/dissertation, oral qualifying exams. *Entrance requirements:* For master's and doctorate, GRE General Test, GRE Subject Test. Additional exam requirements/recommendations for international students: Required—TOEFL (minimum score 570 paper-based; 230 computer-based; 89 iBT); Recommended—IELTS (minimum score 8). *Application deadline:* For fall admission, 1/3 for domestic and international students. Application fee: $70 ($90 for international students). Electronic applications accepted. *Financial support:* Fellowships, research assistantships, teaching assistantships, institutionally sponsored loans and tuition waivers available. Financial award applicants required to submit FAFSA. *Faculty research:* Computer-aided design of digital systems, networks, robotics and control, sensing and interaction. *Unit head:* Carol Mullane, Graduate Program Coordinator, 831-459-2576, E-mail: mullane@soe.ucsc.edu. *Application contact:* Carol Mullane, Graduate Program Coordinator, 831-459-2576, E-mail: mullane@soe.ucsc.edu.

University of Colorado Boulder, Graduate School, College of Engineering and Applied Science, Interdisciplinary Telecommunications Program, Boulder, CO 80309. Offers MS, JD/MS, MBA/MS. Part-time programs available. Postbaccalaureate distance learning degree programs offered. *Students:* 96 full-time (10 women), 34 part-time (5 women); includes 7 minority (1 Black or African American, non-Hispanic/Latino; 5 Asian, non-Hispanic/Latino; 1 Hispanic/Latino), 91 international. Average age 27. 160 applicants, 38 enrolled. In 2010, 71 master's awarded. *Degree requirements:* For master's, comprehensive exam, thesis or alternative. *Entrance requirements:* For master's, minimum undergraduate GPA of 3.0. *Application deadline:* For fall admission, 6/15 priority date for domestic students, 3/15 for international students; for spring admission, 11/1 for domestic students, 10/1 for international students. Applications are processed on a rolling basis. Application fee: $50 ($60 for international students). *Financial support:* In 2010–11, 14 fellowships (averaging $1,709 per year), 2 research assistantships (averaging $12,197 per year) were awarded; career-related internships or fieldwork also available. *Faculty research:* Technology, planning, and management of telecommunications systems. Total annual research expenditures: $18,152.

University of Denver, University College, Denver, CO 80208. Offers arts and culture (MLS, Certificate), including art, literature, and culture, arts development and program management (Certificate), creative writing; environmental policy and management (MAS, Certificate), including energy and sustainability (Certificate), environmental assessment of nuclear power (Certificate), environmental health and safety (Certificate), environmental management, natural resource management (Certificate); geographic information systems (MAS, Certificate); global affairs (MLS, Certificate), including translation studies, world history and culture; healthcare leadership (MPH, Certificate), including healthcare policy, law, and ethics, medical and healthcare information technologies, strategic management of healthcare; information and communications technology (MCIS, Certificate), including database design and administration (Certificate), geographic information systems (MCIS), information security systems security (Certificate), information systems security (MCIS), project management (MCIS, MPS, Certificate), software design and administration (Certificate), software design and programming (MCIS), technology management, telecommunications technology (MCIS), Web design and development; leadership and organizations (MPS, Certificate), including human capital in organizations, philanthropic leadership, project management (MCIS, MPS, Certificate), strategic innovation and change; organizational and professional communication (MPS, Certificate), including alternative dispute resolution, organizational communication, organizational development and training, public relations and marketing; security management (MAS, Certificate), including emergency planning and response, information security (MAS), organizational security; strategic human resource management (MPS, Certificate), including global human resources (MPS), human resource management and development (MPS). Part-time and evening/weekend programs available. Postbaccalaureate distance learning degree programs offered (no on-campus study). *Faculty:* 7 full-time (2 women), 212 part-time/adjunct (83 women). *Students:* 52 full-time (19 women), 1,044 part-time (625 women); includes 196 minority (81 Black or African American, non-Hispanic/Latino; 7 American Indian or Alaska Native, non-Hispanic/Latino; 30 Asian, non-Hispanic/Latino; 66 Hispanic/Latino; 3 Native Hawaiian or other Pacific Islander, non-Hispanic/Latino; 9 Two or more races, non-Hispanic/Latino), 76 international. Average age 36. 488 applicants, 91% accepted, 339 enrolled. In 2010, 286 master's, 130 other advanced degrees awarded. *Entrance requirements:* Additional exam requirements/recommendations for international students: Required—TOEFL (minimum score 550 paper-based; 80 iBT). *Application deadline:* For fall admission, 6/22 priority date for domestic students, 6/10 priority date for international students; for winter admission, 9/15 priority date for domestic students, 9/6 priority date for international students; for spring admission, 2/3 priority date for domestic students, 12/15 priority date for international students. Applications are processed on a rolling basis. Application fee: $75. Electronic applications accepted. *Expenses:* Contact institution. *Financial support:* Applicants required to submit FAFSA. *Unit head:* Dr. James Davis, Dean, 303-871-2291, Fax: 303-871-4047, E-mail: jdavis@du.edu. *Application contact:* Information Contact, 303-871-3155, Fax: 303-871-4047, E-mail: ucolinfo@du.edu.

University of Hawaii at Manoa, Graduate Division, College of Social Sciences, School of Communications, Program in Telecommunication and Information Resource Management, Honolulu, HI 96822. Offers Graduate Certificate. Part-time programs available. *Students:* 1 part-time (0 women), all international. Average age 29. In 2010, 5 Graduate Certificates awarded. *Entrance requirements:* Additional exam requirements/recommendations for international students: Required—TOEFL (minimum score 500 paper-based; 173 computer-based; 61 iBT), IELTS (minimum score 5). *Application deadline:* For fall admission, 5/1 for domestic and international students; for spring admission, 10/1 for domestic and international students. Application fee: $60. *Application contact:* Norman Okamura, Director, 808-956-2895, Fax: 808-956-5591, E-mail: tirm@hawaii.edu.

University of Houston, College of Technology, Department of Engineering Technology, Houston, TX 77204. Offers construction management (MS); engineering technology (MS); network communications (M Tech). Part-time programs available. *Faculty:* 14 full-time (5 women), 6 part-time/adjunct (2 women). *Students:* 48 full-time (11 women), 38 part-time (8 women); includes 9 Black or African American, non-Hispanic/Latino; 6 Asian, non-Hispanic/Latino; 6 Hispanic/Latino, 39 international. Average age 28. 56 applicants, 88% accepted, 34 enrolled. In 2010, 27 master's awarded. *Degree requirements:* For master's, project or thesis (most programs). *Entrance requirements:* For master's, GRE. Additional exam requirements/recommendations for international students: Required—TOEFL (minimum score 550 paper-based; 79 iBT). *Application deadline:* For fall admission, 7/1 for domestic students, 4/1 for international students; for spring admission, 12/1 for domestic students, 10/1 for international students. Applications are processed on a rolling basis. Application fee: $75 ($150 for international students). Electronic applications accepted. *Expenses:* Tuition, state resident: full-time $8592; part-time $358 per credit hour. Tuition, nonresident: full-time $16,032; part-time $668 per credit hour. Required fees: $2889. Tuition and fees vary according to course load and program. *Financial support:* In 2010–11, 7 research assistantships with partial tuition reimbursements (averaging $10,531 per year), 18 teaching assistantships with partial tuition reimbursements (averaging $7,179 per year) were awarded. *Unit head:* Heidar Malki, Chairperson, 713-743-4075, Fax: 713-743-4032, E-mail: malki@uh.edu. *Application contact:* Tiffany Roosa, Graduate Advisor, 713-743-4100, Fax: 713-743-4151, E-mail: troosa@uh.edu.

University of Louisiana at Lafayette, College of Engineering, Department of Electrical and Computer Engineering, Program in Telecommunications, Lafayette, LA 70504. Offers MSTC. *Degree requirements:* For master's, thesis or alternative. *Entrance requirements:* For master's, GRE General Test, minimum GPA of 2.75. Additional exam requirements/recommendations for international students: Required—TOEFL (minimum score 550 paper-based; 213 computer-based). Electronic applications accepted.

University of Maryland, College Park, Academic Affairs, A. James Clark School of Engineering, Department of Electrical and Computer Engineering, Program in Telecommunications, College Park, MD 20742. Offers MS. Part-time and evening/weekend programs available. *Students:* 122 full-time (41 women), 22 part-time (6 women); includes 17 minority (6 Black or African American, non-Hispanic/Latino; 7 Asian, non-Hispanic/Latino; 3 Hispanic/Latino; 1 Two or more races, non-Hispanic/Latino), 116 international. 431 applicants, 48% accepted, 76 enrolled. In 2010, 69 master's awarded. *Degree requirements:* For master's, thesis or alternative. *Entrance requirements:* For master's, GRE General Test, minimum GPA of 3.0, professional experience. Additional exam requirements/recommendations for international students: Required—TOEFL. *Application deadline:* For fall admission, 5/1 for domestic students, 2/1 for international students. Applications are processed on a rolling basis. Application fee: $75. Electronic applications accepted. *Expenses:* Tuition, area resident: Part-time $471 per credit hour. Tuition, state resident: part-time $471 per credit hour. Tuition, nonresident: part-time $1016 per credit hour. Required fees: $337 per term. *Financial support:* In 2010–11, 1 fellowship with full tuition reimbursement (averaging $27,500 per year), 1 research assistantship (averaging $17,544 per year), 21 teaching assistantships (averaging $16,333 per year) were awarded. Financial award applicants required to submit FAFSA. *Unit head:* Asante Dumisani Shakuur, Associate Director, 301-405-8189, Fax: 301-314-9324, E-mail: ashakuur@eng.umd.edu. *Application contact:* Charles A. Caramello, Dean of Graduate School, 301-405-0358, Fax: 301-314-9305, E-mail: ccaramel@umd.edu.

University of Massachusetts Dartmouth, Graduate School, College of Engineering, Department of Electrical and Computer Engineering, North Dartmouth, MA 02747-2300. Offers acoustics (Postbaccalaureate Certificate); communications (Postbaccalaureate Certificate); computer engineering (MS, PhD); computer systems engineering (Postbaccalaureate Certificate); digital signal processing (Postbaccalaureate Certificate); electrical engineering (MS, PhD); electrical engineering systems (Postbaccalaureate Certificate). Part-time programs available. *Faculty:* 17 full-time (3 women), 3 part-time/adjunct (0 women). *Students:* 32 full-time (6 women), 48 part-time (13 women); includes 2 Black or African American, non-Hispanic/Latino; 1 American Indian or Alaska Native, non-Hispanic/Latino; 4 Asian, non-Hispanic/Latino, 47 international. Average age 29. 97 applicants, 84% accepted, 19 enrolled. In 2010, 17 master's, 1 other advanced degree awarded. *Degree requirements:* For master's, culminating project or thesis; for doctorate, comprehensive exam, thesis/dissertation. *Entrance requirements:* For master's, GRE, minimum undergraduate GPA of 3.0, 3 letters of recommendation; for doctorate, GRE. Additional exam requirements/recommendations for international students: Required—TOEFL (minimum score 550 paper-based; 213 computer-based). *Application deadline:* For fall admission, 2/1 priority date for domestic students, 12/1 for international students; for spring admission, 11/1 priority date for domestic students, 9/1 for international students. Applications are processed on a rolling basis. Application fee: $40 ($60 for international students). Electronic applications accepted. *Expenses:* Tuition, state resident: full-time $2071; part-time $86 per credit. Tuition, nonresident: full-time $8099; part-time $337 per credit. Required fees: $9446; $394 per credit. One-time fee: $75. Part-time tuition and fees vary according to class time, course load, degree level and reciprocity agreements. *Financial support:* In 2010–11, 2 fellowships with full tuition reimbursements (averaging $16,000 per year), 14 research assistantships with full tuition reimbursements (averaging $11,096 per year), 9 teaching assistantships with full tuition reimbursements (averaging $12,500 per year) were awarded; Federal Work-Study and unspecified assistantships also available. Support available to part-time students. Financial award application deadline: 3/1; financial award applicants required to submit FAFSA. *Faculty research:* Speech acoustics, marine applications, signals and systems, applied electromagnetics, intelligent agency. Total annual research expenditures: $1.1 million. *Unit head:* Dr. Karen Payton, Director, 508-999-8434, Fax: 508-999-8489, E-mail: kpayton@umassd.edu. *Application contact:* Elan Turcotte-Shamski, Graduate Admissions Officer, 508-999-8604, Fax: 508-999-8183, E-mail: graduate@umassd.edu.

University of Missouri–Kansas City, School of Computing and Engineering, Kansas City, MO 64110-2499. Offers civil engineering (MS); computer and electrical engineering (PhD); computer science (MS), including bioinformatics, software engineering, telecommunications networking; computer science and informatics (PhD); computing (PhD); electrical engineering (MS); engineering (PhD); mechanical engineering (MS); telecommunications (PhD). PhD (interdisciplinary) offered through the School of Graduate Studies. Part-time programs available. *Faculty:* 36 full-time (5 women), 21 part-time/adjunct (0 women). *Students:* 160 full-time (32 women), 194 part-time (41 women); includes 21 minority (5 Black or African American, non-Hispanic/Latino; 9 Asian, non-Hispanic/Latino; 6 Hispanic/Latino; 1 Two or more races, non-Hispanic/Latino), 273 international. Average age 25. 440 applicants, 55% accepted, 104 enrolled. In 2010, 135 master's awarded. *Degree requirements:* For doctorate, thesis/dissertation. *Entrance requirements:* For master's, GRE General Test, minimum GPA of 3.0, 3 letters of recommendation from professors; for doctorate, GRE General Test, minimum GPA of 3.5. Additional exam requirements/recommendations for international students: Required—TOEFL (minimum score 550 paper-based; 213 computer-based; 80 iBT). *Application deadline:* For fall admission, 1/15 priority date for domestic students, 1/15 for international students. Applications are processed on a rolling basis. Application fee: $45 ($50 for international students). *Expenses:* Tuition, state resident: full-time $5522.40; part-time $306.80 per credit hour. Tuition, nonresident: full-time $7128; part-time $792 per credit hour. Required fees: $261.15 per term. *Financial support:* In 2010–11, 35 research assistantships with partial tuition reimbursements (averaging $14,340 per year), 20 teaching assistantships with partial tuition reimbursements (averaging $13,351 per year) were awarded; career-related internships or fieldwork, Federal Work-Study, scholarships/grants, tuition waivers (partial), and unspecified assistantships also available. Support available to part-time students. Financial award application deadline: 3/1; financial award applicants required to submit FAFSA. *Faculty research:* Algorithms, bioinformatics and medical informatics, biomechanics/biomaterials, civil engineering materials, networking and telecommunications, thermal science. Total annual research expenditures: $1.1 million. *Unit head:* Dr. Kevin Z. Truman, Dean, 816-235-2399, Fax: 816-235-5159. *Application contact:* Dr. Kevin Z. Truman, Dean, 816-235-2399, Fax: 816-235-5159.

University of Oklahoma, College of Engineering, Department of Electrical and Computer Engineering, Program in Telecommunications Engineering, Tulsa, OK 74135. Offers MS. Part-time programs available. *Students:* 8 full-time (4 women), 1 (woman) part-time, all international. Average age 24. 15 applicants, 80% accepted, 3 enrolled. In 2010, 2 master's awarded. *Entrance requirements:* Additional exam requirements/recommendations for international students: Required—TOEFL (minimum score 550 paper-based; 213 computer-based; 79 iBT). *Application deadline:* For fall admission, 4/1 for domestic and international students; for spring admission, 11/1 for domestic students, 9/1 for international students. Application fee: $40 ($90 for international students). Electronic applications accepted. *Expenses:* Tuition, state resident: full-time $3892.80; part-time $162.20 per credit hour. Tuition, nonresident: full-time $14,167; part-time $590.30 per credit hour. Required fees: $2523.40; $94.60 per credit hour. Tuition and fees vary according to course load and degree level. *Financial support:* In 2010–11, 3 students received support. Career-related internships or fieldwork, scholarships/grants, health care benefits, tuition waivers (partial), and unspecified assistantships available. *Faculty research:* Optical communications and networks, wireless communications and networking, telecommunications security, photonic systems, information theory. *Unit head:* Dr. James Sluss, Director, 405-325-4721, Fax: 405-325-7066, E-mail: sluss@ou.edu. *Application contact:* Pramode Verma, Director/Graduate Liaison, 918-660-3236, Fax: 918-660-3238, E-mail: pverma@ou.edu.

University of Oklahoma, Gaylord College of Journalism and Mass Communication, Program in Journalism and Mass Communication, Norman, OK 73019-0390. Offers advertising and public relations (MA); information gathering and distribution (MA); mass communication management and policy (MA); professional writing (MA); telecommunications and new technologies (MA). Part-time programs available. *Students:* 21 full-time (16 women), 26 part-time (13 women); includes 7 minority (4 Black or African American, non-Hispanic/Latino; 2 American Indian or Alaska Native, non-Hispanic/Latino; 1 Hispanic/Latino), 6 international. Average age 27. 29 applicants, 76% accepted, 10 enrolled. In 2010, 20 master's awarded. *Degree requirements:* For master's, thesis optional. *Entrance requirements:* For master's, GRE General Test, minimum GPA of 3.2, 9 hours of course work in journalism, course work in statistics. Additional exam requirements/recommendations for international students: Required—TOEFL (minimum score 600 paper-based; 250 computer-based; 100 iBT), TWE (minimum score 5). *Application deadline:* For fall admission, 2/1 for domestic students, 4/1 for international students; for spring admission, 11/1 for domestic students, 9/1 for international students. Application fee: $40 ($90 for international students). Electronic applications accepted. *Expenses:* Tuition, state resident: full-time $3892.80; part-time $162.20 per credit hour. Tuition, nonresident: full-time $14,167; part-time $590.30 per credit hour. Required fees: $2523.40; $94.60 per credit hour. Tuition and fees vary according to course load and degree level. *Financial support:* In 2010–11, 30 students received support. Career-related internships or fieldwork, scholarships/grants, health care benefits, and unspecified assistantships available. *Faculty research:* Organizational management, strategic communications, rhetorical theories and mass communication, interactive messaging and audience response; mass media history and law. *Unit head:* Dr. Joe Foote, Dean, 405-325-2721, Fax: 405-325-7565, E-mail: jfoote@ou.edu. *Application contact:* Kelly Storm, Graduate Advisor, 405-325-2722, Fax: 405-325-7565, E-mail: kstorm@ou.edu.

University of Pennsylvania, School of Engineering and Applied Science, Telecommunications and Networking Program, Philadelphia, PA 19104. Offers MSE. Part-time programs available. *Students:* 58 full-time (8 women), 9 part-time (3 women); includes 1 Black or African American, non-Hispanic/Latino; 3 Asian, non-Hispanic/Latino, 61 international. 169 applicants, 51% accepted, 38 enrolled. In 2010, 39 master's awarded. *Application deadline:* For fall admission, 6/1 for domestic students, 5/1 for international students; for spring admission, 11/1 for domestic students, 10/1 for international students. Application fee: $70. Electronic applications accepted. *Expenses:* Tuition: Full-time $25,660; part-time $4758 per course. Required fees: $2152; $270 per course. Tuition and fees vary according to course load, degree level and program.

University of Pittsburgh, School of Information Sciences, Telecommunications and Networking Program, Pittsburgh, PA 15260. Offers telecommunications (MST, PhD, Certificate). Part-time and evening/weekend programs available. *Faculty:* 6 full-time (0 women), 1 part-time/adjunct (0 women). *Students:* 46 full-time (9 women), 11 part-time (1 woman); includes 1 Black or

Telecommunications

University of Pittsburgh (continued)
African American, non-Hispanic/Latino; 2 Asian, non-Hispanic/Latino, 41 international. 68 applicants, 90% accepted, 15 enrolled. In 2010, 18 master's, 4 doctorates awarded. *Degree requirements:* For master's, thesis optional; for doctorate, comprehensive exam, thesis/ dissertation. *Entrance requirements:* For master's, GRE General Test, undergraduate degree with minimum GPA of 3.0; previous course work in computer programming, calculus, and probability; for doctorate, GRE, master's degree; minimum GPA of 3.3; course work in computer programming (2 languages), differential and integral calculus, and probability and statistics; for Certificate, MSIS, MST from accredited university. Additional exam requirements/ recommendations for international students: Required—TOEFL (minimum score 550 paper-based; 0 computer-based; 80 iBT). *Application deadline:* For fall admission, 1/15 priority date for domestic and international students; for winter admission, 9/15 priority date for domestic students, 6/15 for international students; for spring admission, 1/15 priority date for domestic students, 12/15 priority date for international students. Applications are processed on a rolling basis. Application fee: $50. Electronic applications accepted. *Expenses:* Contact institution. *Financial support:* Fellowships with full and partial tuition reimbursements, research assistant-ships with full and partial tuition reimbursements, teaching assistantships, career-related internships or fieldwork, scholarships/grants, health care benefits, tuition waivers (full and partial), and unspecified assistantships available. Financial award application deadline: 1/15; financial award applicants required to submit FAFSA. *Faculty research:* Telecommunication systems, telecommunications policy, network design and management, wireless information systems, network security. *Unit head:* Dr. David Tipper, Program Chair, 412-624-9421, Fax: 412-624-2788, E-mail: tipper@tele.pitt.edu. *Application contact:* Shabana Reza, Student Recruiting Coordinator, 412-624-3988, Fax: 412-624-5231, E-mail: teleinq@sis.pitt.edu.

University of Southern California, Graduate School, Viterbi School of Engineering, Daniel J. Epstein Department of Industrial and Systems Engineering, Los Angeles, CA 90089. Offers digital supply chain management (MS); engineering management (MS); engineering technology communication (Graduate Certificate); health systems operations (Graduate Certificate); industrial and systems engineering (MS, PhD, Engr); manufacturing engineering (MS); operations research engineering (MS); optimization and supply chain management (Graduate Certificate); product development engineering (MS); safety systems and security (MS); systems architecting and engineering (MS, Graduate Certificate); systems safety and security (Graduate Certificate); transportation systems (Graduate Certificate); MS/MBA. Part-time and evening/ weekend programs available. Postbaccalaureate distance learning degree programs offered (no on-campus study). *Faculty:* 12 full-time (2 women), 21 part-time/adjunct (2 women). *Students:* 224 full-time (69 women), 143 part-time (32 women); includes 63 minority (6 Black or African American, non-Hispanic/Latino; 35 Asian, non-Hispanic/Latino; 17 Hispanic/Latino; 5 Two or more races, non-Hispanic/Latino), 253 international. 669 applicants, 45% accepted, 155 enrolled. In 2010, 98 master's, 7 doctorates awarded. Terminal master's awarded for partial completion of doctoral program. *Degree requirements:* For master's, thesis optional; for doctorate, thesis/dissertation. *Entrance requirements:* For master's and doctorate, GRE General Test. *Application deadline:* For fall admission, 12/1 priority date for domestic students, 11/1 priority date for international students; for spring admission, 9/15 priority date for domestic and international students. Applications are processed on a rolling basis. Application fee: $85. Electronic applications accepted. *Expenses:* Tuition: Full-time $31,240; part-time $1420 per unit. Required fees: $600. One-time fee: $35 full-time. Full-time tuition and fees vary according to degree level and program. *Financial support:* In 2010–11, fellowships with full tuition reimbursements (averaging $30,000 per year), research assistantships with full tuition reimburse-ments (averaging $20,000 per year), teaching assistantships with full tuition reimbursements (averaging $20,000 per year) were awarded; career-related internships or fieldwork, scholarships/ grants, health care benefits, and unspecified assistantships also available. Financial award application deadline: 12/1; financial award applicants required to submit CSS PROFILE or FAFSA. *Faculty research:* Health systems, music cognition and retrieval, transportation and logistics, manufacturing and automation, engineering systems design, risk and economic analysis. Total annual research expenditures: $1 million. *Unit head:* Dr. F. Stan Settles, Chair, 213-740-4893, E-mail: isedept@usc.edu. *Application contact:* Evelyn Felina, Director of Student Affairs, 213-740-7549, E-mail: efelina@usc.edu.

University of Southern California, Graduate School, Viterbi School of Engineering, Ming Hsieh Department of Electrical Engineering, Los Angeles, CA 90089. Offers computer engineering (MS, PhD); electric power (MS); electrical engineering (MS, PhD, Engr); engineering technology commercialization (Graduate Certificate); multimedia and creative technologies (MS); telecommunications (MS); VLSI design (MS); wireless health technology (MS). Part-time programs available. Postbaccalaureate distance learning degree programs offered (no on-campus study). *Faculty:* 56 full-time (3 women), 31 part-time/adjunct (1 woman). *Students:* 886 full-time (171 women), 605 part-time (100 women); includes 209 minority (20 Black or African American, non-Hispanic/Latino; 145 Asian, non-Hispanic/Latino; 36 Hispanic/Latino; 8

Two or more races, non-Hispanic/Latino), 1,003 international. 2,986 applicants, 36% accepted, 461 enrolled. In 2010, 351 master's, 41 doctorates, 2 other advanced degrees awarded. Terminal master's awarded for partial completion of doctoral program. *Degree requirements:* For master's, thesis optional; for doctorate, thesis/dissertation. *Entrance requirements:* For master's and doctorate, GRE General Test. *Application deadline:* For fall admission, 12/1 priority date for domestic and international students; for spring admission, 9/15 priority date for domestic and international students. Applications are processed on a rolling basis. Application fee: $85. Electronic applications accepted. *Expenses:* Tuition: Full-time $31,240; part-time $1420 per unit. Required fees: $600. One-time fee: $35 full-time. Full-time tuition and fees vary according to degree level and program. *Financial support:* In 2010–11, fellowships with full tuition reimbursements (averaging $30,000 per year), research assistantships with full tuition reimbursements (averaging $20,000 per year), teaching assistantships with full tuition reimburse-ments (averaging $20,000 per year) were awarded; career-related internships or fieldwork, scholarships/grants, health care benefits, and unspecified assistantships also available. Financial award application deadline: 12/1; financial award applicants required to submit CSS PROFILE or FAFSA. *Faculty research:* Communications, computer engineering and networks, control systems, integrated circuits and systems, electromagnetics and energy conversion, micro electro-mechanical systems and nanotechnology, photonics and quantum electronics, plasma research, signal and image processing. Total annual research expenditures: $18 million. *Unit head:* Dr. Alexander A. Sawchuk, Chair, 213-740-4447, E-mail: studentinfo@ee.usc.edu. *Application contact:* Diane Demetras, Director of Student Affairs, 213-740-4447, E-mail: studentinfo@ee.usc.edu.

The University of Texas at Dallas, Erik Jonsson School of Engineering and Computer Science, Department of Electrical Engineering, Richardson, TX 75080. Offers computer engineering (MS, PhD); electrical engineering (MSEE, PhD); microelectronics (MSEE, PhD); telecommunications (MSEE, MSTE, PhD). Part-time and evening/weekend programs available. *Faculty:* 43 full-time (2 women). *Students:* 404 full-time (78 women), 186 part-time (32 women); includes 85 minority (11 Black or African American, non-Hispanic/Latino; 56 Asian, non-Hispanic/ Latino; 17 Hispanic/Latino; 1 Two or more races, non-Hispanic/Latino), 406 international. Average age 27. 1,612 applicants, 44% accepted, 188 enrolled. In 2010, 152 master's, 31 doctorates awarded. *Degree requirements:* For master's, thesis or major design project; for doctorate, thesis/dissertation. *Entrance requirements:* For master's, GRE General Test, minimum GPA of 3.0 in related bachelor's degree; for doctorate, GRE General Test, minimum GPA of 3.5. Additional exam requirements/recommendations for international students: Required— TOEFL (minimum score 550 paper-based; 215 computer-based). *Application deadline:* For fall admission, 7/15 for domestic students, 5/1 priority date for international students; for spring admission, 11/15 for domestic students, 9/1 priority date for international students. Applications are processed on a rolling basis. Application fee: $50 ($100 for international students). Electronic applications accepted. *Expenses:* Tuition, state resident: full-time $10,248; part-time $569 per credit hour. Tuition, nonresident: full-time $18,544; part-time $1030 per credit hour. Tuition and fees vary according to course load. *Financial support:* In 2010–11, 211 students received support, including 5 fellowships with partial tuition reimbursements available (averaging $15,960 per year), 129 research assistantships with partial tuition reimbursements available (averaging $16,317 per year), 43 teaching assistantships with partial tuition reimbursements available (averaging $15,206 per year); Federal Work-Study, institutionally sponsored loans, scholarships/grants, unspecified assistantships, and cooperative positions also available. Support available to part-time students. Financial award application deadline: 4/30; financial award applicants required to submit FAFSA. *Faculty research:* Semiconductor device manufacturing, photonics devices and systems, signal processing and language technology, nano-fabrication, energy efficient digital systems. *Unit head:* Dr. John H.L. Hansen, Department Head, 972-883-6755, Fax: 972-883-2710, E-mail: john.hansen@utdallas.edu. *Application contact:* Kathy Gribble, Graduate Program Coordinator, 972-883-2649, Fax: 972-883-2710, E-mail: gradecs@ utdallas.edu.

Widener University, Graduate Programs in Engineering, Program Telecommunications Engineering, Chester, PA 19013-5792. Offers M Eng. Part-time and evening/weekend programs available. *Students:* 1 full-time (0 women), 2 part-time (0 women), 2 international. Average age 30. In 2010, 1 master's awarded. *Degree requirements:* For master's, thesis optional. *Application deadline:* For fall admission, 8/1 priority date for domestic students; for spring admission, 12/1 for domestic students. Applications are processed on a rolling basis. Application fee: $25 ($300 for international students). *Financial support:* Teaching assistantships with full tuition reimbursements, unspecified assistantships available. Financial award application deadline: 3/15. *Faculty research:* Signal and image processing, electromagnetics, telecommunications and computer network. *Unit head:* Dr. Bryen E. Lorenz, Chairman, Department of Electrical/ Telecommunication Engineering, 610-499-4064, Fax: 610-499-4059, E-mail: bryen.f.lorenz@ widener.edu. *Application contact:* Dr. Bryen E. Lorenz, Chairman, Department of Electrical/ Telecommunication Engineering, 610-499-4064, Fax: 610-499-4059, E-mail: bryen.f.lorenz@ widener.edu.

Telecommunications Management

Alaska Pacific University, Graduate Programs, Business Administration Department, Programs in Information and Communication Technology, Anchorage, AK 99508-4672. Offers MBAICT. Part-time and evening/weekend programs available. *Degree requirements:* For master's, capstone course. *Entrance requirements:* For master's, GMAT or GRE General Test, minimum GPA of 3.0.

Boston University, Metropolitan College, Department of Computer Science, Program in Telecommunications, Boston, MA 02215. Offers security (MS). Part-time and evening/ weekend programs available. *Faculty:* 10 full-time (0 women), 30 part-time/adjunct (3 women). *Students:* 8 part-time (0 women); includes 2 minority (1 Asian, non-Hispanic/Latino; 1 Hispanic/ Latino), 1 international. Average age 38. 6 applicants, 83% accepted, 1 enrolled. In 2010, 3 master's awarded. *Entrance requirements:* For master's, 3 letters of recommendation, resume. Additional exam requirements/recommendations for international students: Required—TOEFL. *Application deadline:* For fall admission, 6/1 priority date for international students; for spring admission, 10/1 priority date for international students. Applications are processed on a rolling basis. Application fee: $70. Electronic applications accepted. *Expenses:* Tuition: Full-time $39,314; part-time $1228 per credit. Required fees: $40 per semester. *Financial support:* Research assistantships with partial tuition reimbursements, career-related internships or fieldwork and unspecified assistantships available. Support available to part-time students. Financial award applicants required to submit FAFSA. *Unit head:* Dr. Lubomir Chitkushev, Chairman, 617-353-2566, Fax: 617-353-2367, E-mail: csinfo@bu.edu. *Application contact:* Camille Kardoose, Program Coordinator, 617-353-2566, Fax: 617-353-2367, E-mail: cgkardoo@ bu.edu.

California Miramar University, Program in Telecommunications Management, San Diego, CA 92126. Offers MST.

Capitol College, Graduate Programs, Laurel, MD 20708-9759. Offers business administration (MBA); computer science (MS); electrical engineering (MS); information and telecommunications systems management (MS); information architecture (MS); network security (MS). Part-time and evening/weekend programs available. Postbaccalaureate distance learning degree programs offered (no on-campus study). *Entrance requirements:* For master's, minimum GPA of 3.0. Electronic applications accepted.

Carnegie Mellon University, Carnegie Institute of Technology, Information Networking Institute, Pittsburgh, PA 15213. Offers information networking (MS); information security technology and management (MS); information technology—information security (MS); information technology— mobility (MS); information technology—software management (MS). *Degree requirements:* For master's, thesis optional. *Entrance requirements:* For master's, GRE General Test, bachelor's degree in computer science, computer engineering, or electrical engineering, or related technology degree; programming skills (C/C++ fluency for some programs). Additional exam requirements/recommendations for international students: Required—TOEFL. *Faculty research:* Computer forensics and incident response; dependable systems, embedded systems, mobile systems, and sensor networks; computer and information networks, network and information security, human and socio-economic factors in secure system design; wireless sensor networks, survivable embedded systems, signal processing/compression; strategic management, international strategic management, group dynamics and decision-making structures, simulated competitive environments.

Concordia University, School of Graduate Studies, Faculty of Engineering and Computer Science, Concordia Institute for Information Systems Engineering (CIISE), Montréal, QC H3G 1M8, Canada. Offers 3D graphics and game development (Certificate); information systems security (M Eng, MA Sc); quality systems engineering (M Eng, MA Sc); service engineering and network management (Certificate).

George Mason University, Volgenau School of Engineering, Department of Electrical and Computer Engineering, Fairfax, VA 22030. Offers advanced networking protocols for telecommunications (Certificate); communications and networking (Certificate); computer engineering (MS); computer forensics (MS); electrical and computer engineering (PhD); electrical engineering (MS); network technology and applications (Certificate); networks, system integration and testing (Certificate); signal processing (Certificate); telecom systems modeling (Certificate); telecommunications (MS); telecommunications forensics and security (Certificate); VLSI design/ manufacturing (Certificate); wireless communication (Certificate). MS program offered jointly with Old Dominion University, University of Virginia, Virginia Commonwealth University, and Virginia Polytechnic Institute and State University. Part-time and evening/weekend programs available. *Faculty:* 33 full-time (4 women), 39 part-time/adjunct (4 women). *Students:* 106 full-time (27 women), 336 part-time (64 women); includes 24 Black or African American, non-Hispanic/Latino; 1 American Indian or Alaska Native, non-Hispanic/Latino; 54 Asian, non-Hispanic/Latino; 20 Hispanic/Latino; 1 Two or more races, non-Hispanic/Latino, 172 international. Average age 30. 506 applicants, 71% accepted, 142 enrolled. In 2010, 145 master's, 3 doctorates, 61 other advanced degrees awarded. *Degree requirements:* For master's, thesis optional; for doctorate, comprehensive exam, thesis or scholarly paper. *Entrance requirements:* For master's, GMAT or GRE General Test, letters of recommendation, resume; for doctorate, GRE/GMAT, personal goal statement, 2 transcripts, letter of recommendation. Additional exam requirements/recommendations for international students: Required—TOEFL (minimum score 570 paper-based; 230 computer-based; 88 iBT). *Application deadline:* For fall admission, 7/15 priority date for domestic and international students; for spring admission, 12/1 for domestic and international students. Applications are processed on a rolling basis. Application fee: $100. Electronic applications accepted. *Expenses:* Tuition, state resident: full-time $8192; part-time $440 per credit hour. Tuition, nonresident: full-time $22,952; part-time $1055 per credit hour. Required fees: $2364; $99 per credit hour. *Financial support:* In 2010–11, 74 students received support, including 2 fellowships with full tuition reimbursements available (averaging $18,000 per year), 26 research assistantships with full and partial tuition reimbursements available (averaging $14,648 per year), 46 teaching assistantships with full and partial tuition reimbursements available (averaging $10,946 per year); career-related internships or fieldwork, Federal Work-Study, scholarships/grants, unspecified assistantships, and health care benefits (full-time research or teaching assistantship recipients) also available. Financial award application deadline: 3/1; financial award applicants required to submit FAFSA. *Faculty research:* Communication networks, signal processing, system failure diagnosis, multiprocessors, material processing using microwave energy. Total annual research expenditures: $3.4 million. *Unit head:* Dr. Andre Manitius, Chairperson, 703-993-1569, Fax: 703-993-1601, E-mail: ece@gmu.edu. *Application contact:* Jessica Skinner, Associate Dean, 703-993-1569, E-mail: jskinne6@gmu.edu.

Hawai'i Pacific University, College of Business Administration, Program in Information Systems, Honolulu, HI 96813. Offers knowledge management (MSIS); software engineering (MSIS); telecommunications security (MSIS).

Instituto Tecnológico y de Estudios Superiores de Monterrey, Campus Ciudad de México, Division of Engineering and Architecture, Ciudad de Mexico, Mexico. Offers management (MA); telecommunications (MA). Part-time and evening/weekend programs available. Postbaccalaureate distance learning degree programs offered (minimal on-campus study). *Faculty research:* Telecommunications; informatics; technology development; computer systems.

Instituto Tecnológico y de Estudios Superiores de Monterrey, Campus Ciudad Obregón, Program in Administration of Telecommunications, Ciudad Obregón, Mexico. Offers MAT.

Instituto Tecnológico y de Estudios Superiores de Monterrey, Campus Estado de México, Professional and Graduate Division, Estado de Mexico, Mexico. Offers administration of information technologies (MITA); architecture (M Arch); business administration (GMBA, MBA); computer sciences (MCS, PhD); education (M Ed); educational institution administration (MAD); educational technology and innovation (PhD); electronic commerce (MEC); environmental systems (MS); finance (MAF); humanistic studies (MHS); information sciences and knowledge management (MISKM); information systems (MS); manufacturing systems (MS); marketing (MEM); quality systems and productivity (MS); science and materials engineering (PhD); telecommunications management (MTM). Part-time programs available. Postbaccalaureate distance learning degree programs offered (minimal on-campus study). *Degree requirements:* For master's, one foreign language, thesis (for some programs); for doctorate, one foreign language, thesis/dissertation. *Entrance requirements:* For master's, E-PAEP 500, interview; for doctorate, E-PAEP 500, research proposal. Additional exam requirements/recommendations for international students: Required—TOEFL (minimum score 550 paper-based). *Faculty research:* Surface treatments by plasmas, mechanical properties, robotics, graphical computing, mechatronics security protocols.

Instituto Tecnológico y de Estudios Superiores de Monterrey, Campus Irapuato, Graduate Programs, Irapuato, Mexico. Offers administration (MBA); administration of information technology (MAIT); administration of telecommunications (MAT); architecture (M Arch); computer science (MCS); education (M Ed); educational administration (MEA); educational innovation and technology (DEIT); educational technology (MET); electronic commerce (MBA); environmental administration and planning (MEAP); environmental systems (MES); finances (MBA); humanistic studies (MHS); international management for Latin American executives (MIMLAE); library and information science (MLIS); manufacturing quality management (MMQM); marketing research (MBA).

Morgan State University, School of Graduate Studies, College of Liberal Arts, Department of Telecommunications Management, Baltimore, MD 21251. Offers MS. *Degree requirements:* For master's, comprehensive exam. *Entrance requirements:* For master's, GRE. Additional exam requirements/recommendations for international students: Required—TOEFL (minimum score 550 paper-based; 213 computer-based).

Murray State University, College of Business and Public Affairs, Program in Telecommunications Systems Management, Murray, KY 42071. Offers MS. *Entrance requirements:* For master's, GMAT or GRE. Additional exam requirements/recommendations for international students: Required—TOEFL (minimum score 213 computer-based). *Faculty research:* Network security, emergency management communications, network economies.

Northeastern University, College of Engineering, Program in Telecommunication Systems Management, Boston, MA 02115-5096. Offers MS. Part-time programs available. *Students:* 82 full-time (21 women), 3 part-time (0 women). Average age 25. 124 applicants, 81% accepted, 19 enrolled. In 2010, 57 master's awarded. *Entrance requirements:* For master's, GRE General Test. Additional exam requirements/recommendations for international students: Required—TOEFL (minimum score 550 paper-based; 213 computer-based). *Application deadline:* For fall admission, 1/15 for domestic and international students. Applications are processed on a rolling basis. Application fee: $50. Electronic applications accepted. *Financial support:* In 2010–11, 2 students received support, including 1 fellowship (averaging $18,325 per year), 1 research assistantship (averaging $18,325 per year); teaching assistantships, career-related internships or fieldwork, Federal Work-Study, scholarships/grants, health care benefits, tuition waivers, and unspecified assistantships also available. Support available to part-time students. Financial award application deadline: 1/15; financial award applicants required to submit FAFSA. *Faculty research:* Information theory, wireless grids, IP telephony architecture. *Unit head:* Dr. Peter O'Reilly, Director, 617-373-5548, Fax: 617-373-2501. *Application contact:* Stephen L. Gibson, Associate Director, 617-373-2711, Fax: 617-373-2501, E-mail: grad-eng@coe.neu.edu.

Oklahoma State University, Spears School of Business, Department of Management Science and Information Systems, Stillwater, OK 74078. Offers management information systems (MS); management science and information systems (PhD); telecommunications management (MS). Part-time programs available. Postbaccalaureate distance learning degree programs offered. *Faculty:* 17 full-time (3 women), 2 part-time/adjunct (0 women). *Students:* 64 full-time (12 women), 75 part-time (15 women); includes 4 Black or African American, non-Hispanic/Latino; 4 American Indian or Alaska Native, non-Hispanic/Latino; 1 Asian, non-Hispanic/Latino, 74 international. Average age 29. 252 applicants, 36% accepted, 36 enrolled. In 2010, 68 master's, 1 doctorate awarded. *Degree requirements:* For master's, thesis or alternative; for doctorate, comprehensive exam, thesis/dissertation. *Entrance requirements:* For master's and doctorate, GRE or GMAT. Additional exam requirements/recommendations for international students: Required—TOEFL (minimum score 550 paper-based; 79 iBT). *Application deadline:* For fall admission, 3/1 priority date for international students; for spring admission, 8/1 priority date for international students. Applications are processed on a rolling basis. Application fee: $40 ($75 for international students). Electronic applications accepted. *Expenses:* Tuition, state resident: full-time $3716; part-time $154.85 per credit hour. Tuition, nonresident: full-time $14,892; part-time $621 per credit hour. Required fees: $2044; $85.20 per credit hour. One-time fee: $50. Tuition and fees vary according to course load and campus/location. *Financial support:* In 2010–11, 1 research assistantship (averaging $4,200 per year), 12 teaching assistantships (averaging $12,460 per year) were awarded; career-related internships or fieldwork, Federal Work-Study, scholarships/grants, health care benefits, tuition waivers (partial), and unspecified assistantships also available. Support available to part-time students. Financial award application deadline: 3/1; financial award applicants required to submit FAFSA. *Unit head:* Dr. Rick Wilson, Head, 405-744-3551, Fax: 405-744-5180. *Application contact:* Dr. Gordon Emslie, Dean, 405-744-6368, Fax: 405-744-0355, E-mail: grad-i@okstate.edu.

Polytechnic Institute of NYU, Department of Technology Management, Major in Telecommunications and Information Management, Brooklyn, NY 11201-2990. Offers MS. *Students:* 1 full-time (0 women). Average age 34. 1 applicant, 0% accepted, 0 enrolled. In 2010, 3 master's awarded. *Degree requirements:* For master's, comprehensive exam (for some programs), thesis (for some programs). *Entrance requirements:* For master's, GMAT, minimum B average in undergraduate course work. Additional exam requirements/recommendations for international students: Required—TOEFL (minimum score 550 paper-based; 213 computer-based; 80 iBT); Recommended—IELTS (minimum score 6.5). *Application deadline:* For fall admission, 7/31 priority date for domestic students, 4/30 priority date for international students; for spring admission, 12/31 priority date for domestic students, 11/30 priority date for international students. Applications are processed on a rolling basis. Application fee: $75. Electronic applications accepted. *Expenses:* Tuition: Full-time $21,492; part-time $1194 per credit. Required fees: $385 per semester. Tuition and fees vary according to course load. *Financial support:* Institutionally sponsored loans, scholarships/grants, and unspecified assistantships available. Support available to part-time students. Financial award applicants required to submit FAFSA. *Unit head:* Prof. Bharadwaj Rao, Head, 718-260-3617, Fax: 718-260-3874, E-mail: ro@poly.edu. *Application contact:* JeanCarlo Bonilla, Director of Graduate Enrollment Management, 718-260-3182, Fax: 718-260-3624, E-mail: gradinfo@poly.edu.

San Diego State University, Graduate and Research Affairs, College of Professional Studies and Fine Arts, School of Communication, San Diego, CA 92182. Offers advertising and public relations (MA); critical-cultural studies (MA); interaction studies (MA); intercultural and international studies (MA); new media studies (MA); news and information studies (MA); telecommunications and media management (MA). *Degree requirements:* For master's, thesis. *Entrance requirements:* For master's, GRE General Test, 3 letters of recommendation. Additional exam requirements/recommendations for international students: Required—TOEFL. Electronic applications accepted.

Stevens Institute of Technology, Graduate School, Wesley J. Howe School of Technology Management, Doctoral Program in Technology Management, Hoboken, NJ 07030. Offers information management (PhD); technology management (PhD); telecommunications management (PhD). Part-time and evening/weekend programs available. Postbaccalaureate distance learning degree programs offered (minimal on-campus study). *Students:* 22 full-time (9 women), 66 part-time (11 women); includes 1 Black or African American, non-Hispanic/Latino; 14 Asian, non-Hispanic/Latino; 8 Hispanic/Latino, 23 international. Average age 34. 66 applicants, 70% accepted. *Entrance requirements:* Additional exam requirements/recommendations for international students: Required—TOEFL. *Application deadline:* Applications are processed on a rolling basis. Application fee: $50. Electronic applications accepted. *Financial support:* Research assistantships, teaching assistantships, institutionally sponsored loans available. *Unit head:* Richard Reilly, Director, 201-216-5383. *Application contact:* Graduate Admissions, 800-496-4935, Fax: 201-216-8044, E-mail: gradadmissions@stevens.edu.

Stevens Institute of Technology, Graduate School, Wesley J. Howe School of Technology Management, Program in Business Administration, Hoboken, NJ 07030. Offers engineering management (MBA); financial engineering (MBA); information management (MBA); information technology in financial services (MBA); information technology in the pharmaceutical industry (MBA); information technology outsourcing (MBA); pharmaceutical management (MBA); project management (MBA); technology management (MBA); telecommunications management (MBA).

Stevens Institute of Technology, Graduate School, Wesley J. Howe School of Technology Management, Program in Information Systems, Hoboken, NJ 07030. Offers computer science (MS); e-commerce (MS); enterprise systems (MS); entrepreneurial information technology (MS); information architecture (MS); information management (MS, Certificate); information security (MS); information technology in financial services industry (MS); information technology in the pharmaceutical industry (MS); information technology outsourcing management (MS); project management (MS, Certificate); software engineering (MS); telecommunications (MS). *Degree requirements:* For master's, thesis optional. *Entrance requirements:* For master's, GMAT, GRE General Test. Additional exam requirements/recommendations for international students: Required—TOEFL. Electronic applications accepted.

Stevens Institute of Technology, Graduate School, Wesley J. Howe School of Technology Management, Program in Telecommunications Management, Hoboken, NJ 07030. Offers business (MS); global innovation management (MS); management of wireless networks (MS); online security, technology and business (MS); project management (MS); technical management (MS); telecommunications management (PhD, Certificate). *Students:* 26 full-time (6 women), 92 part-time (15 women); includes 8 Black or African American, non-Hispanic/Latino; 9 Asian, non-Hispanic/Latino; 9 Hispanic/Latino, 25 international. Average age 33. 154 applicants, 91% accepted. *Degree requirements:* For master's, thesis optional; for doctorate, thesis/dissertation. *Entrance requirements:* For master's and doctorate, GMAT, GRE General Test. Additional exam requirements/recommendations for international students: Required—TOEFL. *Application deadline:* Applications are processed on a rolling basis. Application fee: $50. Electronic applications accepted. *Unit head:* Audrey Kames Curtis, Director, 201-216-5524. *Application contact:* Sharen Glennon, Administrative Assistant, 201-216-8322, Fax: 201-216-8355, E-mail: sglennon@stevens-tech.edu.

Strayer University, Graduate Studies, Washington, DC 20005-2603. Offers accounting (MS); acquisition (MBA); business administration (MBA); communications technology (MS); educational management (M Ed); finance (MBA); health services administration (MHSA); hospitality and tourism management (MBA); human resource management (MBA); information systems (MS), including computer security management, decision support system management, enterprise resource management, network management, software engineering management, systems development management; management (MBA); management information systems (MS); marketing (MBA); professional accounting (MS), including accounting information systems, controllership, taxation; public administration (MPA); supply chain management (MBA); technology in education (M Ed). Programs also offered at campus locations in Birmingham, AL; Chamblee, GA; Cobb County, GA; Morrow, GA; White Marsh, MD; Charleston, SC; Columbia, SC; Greensboro, NC; Greenville, SC; Lexington, KY; Louisville, KY; Nashville, TN; North Raleigh, NC; Washington, DC. Part-time and evening/weekend programs available. Postbaccalaureate distance learning degree programs offered (minimal on-campus study). *Degree requirements:* For master's, thesis. *Entrance requirements:* For master's, GMAT, GRE General Test, bachelor's degree from an accredited college or university, minimum undergraduate GPA of 2.75. Electronic applications accepted.

Syracuse University, School of Information Studies, Program in Information Systems and Telecommunications Management, Syracuse, NY 13244. Offers CAS. Part-time and evening/weekend programs available. Postbaccalaureate distance learning degree programs offered. *Students:* 2 full-time (1 woman), 7 part-time (3 women); includes 4 minority (2 Black or African American, non-Hispanic/Latino; 2 Hispanic/Latino). Average age 34. 13 applicants, 92% accepted, 3 enrolled. In 2010, 13 CASs awarded. *Entrance requirements:* Additional exam requirements/recommendations for international students: Required—TOEFL (minimum score 100 iBT). *Application deadline:* For fall admission, 2/1 priority date for domestic and international students; for spring admission, 10/15 priority date for domestic and international students. Applications are processed on a rolling basis. Application fee: $75. Electronic applications accepted. *Expenses:* Tuition: Part-time $1162 per credit. *Financial support:* Fellowships with full tuition reimbursements, research assistantships with partial tuition reimbursements,

Telecommunications Management

Syracuse University (continued)

teaching assistantships with partial tuition reimbursements available. Financial award application deadline: 1/1; financial award applicants required to submit FAFSA. *Unit head:* David Dischiave, Director, 315-443-4681, Fax: 315-443-6886, E-mail: ddischia@syr.edu. *Application contact:* Susan Corieri, Director of Enrollment Management, 315-443-2575, E-mail: ischool@syr.edu.

Syracuse University, School of Information Studies, Program in Telecommunications and Network Management, Syracuse, NY 13244. Offers MS, MS/CAS. Part-time and evening/weekend programs available. Postbaccalaureate distance learning degree programs offered (minimal on-campus study). *Students:* 48 full-time (13 women), 33 part-time (5 women); includes 10 minority (4 Black or African American, non-Hispanic/Latino; 1 Asian, non-Hispanic/Latino; 5 Hispanic/Latino), 44 international. Average age 29. 103 applicants, 68% accepted, 33 enrolled. In 2010, 21 master's awarded. *Degree requirements:* For master's, internship or research project. *Entrance requirements:* For master's, GRE General Test. Additional exam requirements/recommendations for international students: Required—TOEFL (minimum score 100 iBT). *Application deadline:* For fall admission, 2/1 priority date for domestic and international students; for spring admission, 10/15 priority date for domestic and international students. Applications are processed on a rolling basis. Application fee: $75. Electronic applications accepted. *Expenses:* Tuition: Part-time $1162 per credit. *Financial support:* Fellowships with full tuition reimbursements, research assistantships with partial tuition reimbursements, teaching assistantships with partial tuition reimbursements, career-related internships or fieldwork and Federal Work-Study available. Financial award application deadline: 1/1. *Faculty research:* Multimedia, information resources management. *Unit head:* Martha Garcia-Marillo, Director, 315-443-2911, Fax: 315-443-6886, E-mail: mgarciam@syr.edu. *Application contact:* Susan Corieri, Director of Enrollment Management, 315-443-2575, E-mail: ischool@syr.edu.

University of Colorado Boulder, Graduate School, College of Engineering and Applied Science, Interdisciplinary Telecommunications Program, Boulder, CO 80309. Offers MS, JD/MS, MBA/MS. Part-time programs available. Postbaccalaureate distance learning degree programs offered. *Students:* 96 full-time (10 women), 34 part-time (5 women); includes 7 minority (1 Black or African American, non-Hispanic/Latino; 5 Asian, non-Hispanic/Latino; 1 Hispanic/Latino), 91 international. Average age 27. 160 applicants, 38 enrolled. In 2010, 71 master's awarded. *Degree requirements:* For master's, comprehensive exam, thesis or alternative. *Entrance requirements:* For master's, minimum undergraduate GPA of 3.0. *Application deadline:* For fall admission, 6/15 priority date for domestic students, 3/15 for international students; for spring admission, 11/1 for domestic students, 10/1 for international students. Applications are processed on a rolling basis. Application fee: $50 ($60 for international students). *Financial support:* In 2010–11, 14 fellowships (averaging $1,709 per year), 2 research assistantships (averaging $12,197 per year) were awarded; career-related internships or fieldwork also available. *Faculty research:* Technology, planning, and management of telecommunications systems. Total annual research expenditures: $18,152.

University of New Haven, Graduate School, School of Business, Program in Business Administration, West Haven, CT 06516-1916. Offers accounting (MBA, Certificate), including CPA (MBA); business management (Certificate); business policy and strategy (MBA); finance (MBA), including CFA; global marketing (MBA); human resource management (Certificate); human resources management (MBA); international business (Certificate); marketing (Certificate); sports management (MBA); telecommunications management (Certificate); MBA/MPA. Part-time and evening/weekend programs available. *Students:* 158 full-time (80 women), 150 part-time (70 women); includes 36 Black or African American, non-Hispanic/Latino; 2 American Indian or Alaska Native, non-Hispanic/Latino; 19 Asian, non-Hispanic/Latino; 16 Hispanic/Latino, 82 international. Average age 32. 162 applicants, 99% accepted, 85 enrolled. In 2010, 141 master's, 16 other advanced degrees awarded. *Degree requirements:* For master's, thesis or alternative. *Entrance requirements:* For master's, GMAT. Additional exam requirements/recommendations for international students: Required—TOEFL (minimum score 520 paper-based; 190 computer-based; 70 iBT), IELTS (minimum score 5.5). *Application deadline:* For fall admission, 5/31 for international students; for winter admission, 10/15 for international students; for spring admission, 1/15 for international students. Applications are processed on a rolling basis. Application fee: $50. Electronic applications accepted. *Expenses:* Contact institution. *Financial support:* Research assistantships with partial tuition reimbursements, teaching assistantships with partial tuition reimbursements, Federal Work-Study, scholarships/grants, health care benefits, tuition waivers, and unspecified assistantships available. Support available to part-time students. Financial award applicants required to submit FAFSA. *Unit head:* Charles Coleman, Chairman, 203-932-7375. *Application contact:* Eloise Gormley, Director of Graduate Admissions, 203-932-7449, Fax: 203-932-7137, E-mail: gradinfo@newhaven.edu.

University of Pennsylvania, School of Engineering and Applied Science, Telecommunications and Networking Program, Philadelphia, PA 19104. Offers MSE. Part-time programs available. *Students:* 58 full-time (8 women), 9 part-time (3 women); includes 1 Black or African American, non-Hispanic/Latino; 3 Asian, non-Hispanic/Latino, 61 international. 169 applicants, 51% accepted, 38 enrolled. In 2010, 39 master's awarded. *Application deadline:* For fall admission, 6/1 for domestic students, 5/1 for international students; for spring admission, 11/1 for domestic students, 10/1 for international students. Application fee: $70. Electronic applications accepted. *Expenses:* Tuition: Full-time $25,660; part-time $4758 per course. Required fees: $2152; $270 per course. Tuition and fees vary according to course load, degree level and program.

University of San Francisco, School of Business and Professional Studies, Masagung Graduate School of Management, Program in Business Administration, San Francisco, CA 94117-1080. Offers business economics (MBA); e-business (MBA); entrepreneurship (MBA); finance (MBA); international business (MBA); management (MBA); marketing (MBA); telecommunications management and policy (MBA); JD/MBA; MSN/MBA. *Accreditation:* AACSB. *Faculty:* 17 full-time (4 women), 16 part-time/adjunct (7 women). *Students:* 263 full-time (130 women), 11 part-time (6 women); includes 98 minority (3 Black or African American, non-

Hispanic/Latino; 65 Asian, non-Hispanic/Latino; 18 Hispanic/Latino; 3 Native Hawaiian or other Pacific Islander, non-Hispanic/Latino; 9 Two or more races, non-Hispanic/Latino), 43 international. Average age 29. 503 applicants, 60% accepted, 80 enrolled. In 2010, 115 master's awarded. *Entrance requirements:* For master's, GMAT, minimum undergraduate GPA of 3.2. Additional exam requirements/recommendations for international students: Required—TOEFL. *Application deadline:* For fall admission, 7/1 priority date for domestic students; for spring admission, 11/30 for domestic students. Applications are processed on a rolling basis. Application fee: $55 ($65 for international students). *Expenses:* Tuition: Full-time $20,070; part-time $1115 per credit hour. Tuition and fees vary according to course load, degree level and program. *Financial support:* In 2010–11, 156 students received support; fellowships available. Financial award application deadline: 3/2; financial award applicants required to submit FAFSA. *Faculty research:* International financial markets, technology transfer licensing, international marketing, strategic planning. Total annual research expenditures: $50,000. *Unit head:* Kelly Brookes, Director, 415-422-2221, Fax: 415-422-6315. *Application contact:* Director, MBA Program, 415-422-2221, Fax: 415-422-6315, E-mail: mba@usfca.edu.

University of South Africa, College of Human Sciences, Pretoria, South Africa. Offers adult education (M Ed); African languages (MA, PhD); African politics (MA, PhD); Afrikaans (MA, PhD); ancient history (MA, PhD); ancient Near Eastern studies (MA, PhD); anthropology (MA, PhD); applied linguistics (MA); Arabic (MA, PhD); archaeology (MA); art history (MA); Biblical archaeology (MA); Biblical studies (M Th, D Th, PhD); Christian spirituality (M Th, D Th); church history (M Th, D Th); classical studies (MA, PhD); clinical psychology (MA); communication (MA, PhD); comparative education (M Ed, Ed D); consulting psychology (D Admin, D Com, PhD); curriculum studies (M Ed, Ed D); development studies (M Admin, MA, D Admin, PhD); didactics (M Ed, Ed D); education (M Tech); education management (M Ed, Ed D); educational psychology (M Ed); English (MA); environmental education (M Ed); French (MA, PhD); German (MA, PhD); Greek (MA); guidance and counseling (M Ed); health studies (MA, PhD), including health sciences education (MA), health services management (MA), medical and surgical nursing science (critical care general) (MA), midwifery and neonatal nursing science (MA), trauma and emergency care (MA); history (MA, PhD); history of education (Ed D); inclusive education (M Ed, Ed D); information and communications technology policy and regulation (MA); information science (MA, MIS, PhD); international politics (MA, PhD); Islamic studies (MA, PhD); Italian (MA, PhD); Judaica (MA, PhD); linguistics (MA, PhD); mathematical education (M Ed); mathematics education (MA); missiology (M Th, D Th); modern Hebrew (MA, PhD); musicology (MA, MMus, D Mus, PhD); natural science education (M Ed); New Testament (M Th, D Th); Old Testament (D Th); pastoral therapy (M Th, D Th); philosophy (MA); philosophy of education (M Ed, Ed D); politics (MA, PhD); Portuguese (MA, PhD); practical theology (M Th, D Th); psychology (MA, MS, PhD); psychology of education (M Ed, Ed D); public health (MA); religious studies (MA, D Th, PhD); Romance languages (MA); Russian (MA, PhD); Semitic languages (MA, PhD); social behavior studies in HIV/AIDS (MA); social science (mental health) (MA); social science in development studies (MA); social science in psychology (MA); social science in social work (MA); social science in sociology (MA); social work (MSW, DSW, PhD); socio-education (M Ed, Ed D); sociolinguistics (MA); sociology (MA, PhD); Spanish (MA, PhD); systematic theology (M Th, D Th); TESOL (teaching English to speakers of other languages) (MA); theological ethics (M Th, D Th); theory of literature (MA, PhD); urban ministries (D Th); urban ministry (M Th).

University of Wisconsin–Stout, Graduate School, College of Technology, Engineering, and Management, Program in Information and Communication Technologies, Menomonie, WI 54751. Offers MS. Part-time programs available. Postbaccalaureate distance learning degree programs offered (minimal on-campus study). *Degree requirements:* For master's, thesis. *Entrance requirements:* For master's, minimum GPA of 2.75. Additional exam requirements/recommendations for international students: Required—TOEFL (minimum score 500 paper-based; 173 computer-based; 61 iBT). Electronic applications accepted.

Webster University, George Herbert Walker School of Business and Technology, Department of Business, St. Louis, MO 63119-3194. Offers business (MA); business and organizational security management (MBA); computer resources and information management (MBA); environmental management (MBA); finance (MA, MBA); health services management (MBA); human resources development (MBA); human resources management (MBA); international business (MA, MBA); management and leadership (MBA); marketing (MBA); procurement and acquisitions management (MBA); telecommunications management (MBA). *Accreditation:* ACBSP. Part-time and evening/weekend programs available. Postbaccalaureate distance learning degree programs offered (no on-campus study). *Degree requirements:* For master's, comprehensive exam (for some programs), thesis (for some programs). *Entrance requirements:* Additional exam requirements/recommendations for international students: Required—TOEFL. *Expenses:* Tuition: Part-time $585 per credit hour. Tuition and fees vary according to degree level, campus/location and program.

Webster University, George Herbert Walker School of Business and Technology, Department of Management, St. Louis, MO 63119-3194. Offers business and organizational security management (MA); computer resources and information management (MA); environmental management (MS); government contracting (Certificate); health care management (MA); health services management (MA); human resources development (MA); human resources management (MA); management (DM); management and leadership (MA); marketing (MA); nonprofit management (Certificate); procurement and acquisitions management (MA); public administration (MA); quality management (MA); space systems operations management (MS); telecommunications management (MA). *Accreditation:* ACBSP. Part-time and evening/weekend programs available. Postbaccalaureate distance learning degree programs offered (no on-campus study). *Degree requirements:* For master's, thesis (for some programs); for doctorate, thesis/dissertation, written exam. *Entrance requirements:* For doctorate, GMAT, 3 years of work experience, MBA. Additional exam requirements/recommendations for international students: Required—TOEFL. *Expenses:* Tuition: Part-time $585 per credit hour. Tuition and fees vary according to degree level, campus/location and program.

APPENDIXES

Institutional Changes
Since the 2011 Edition

Following is an alphabetical listing of institutions that have recently closed, merged with other institutions, or changed their names or status. In the case of a name change, the former name appears first, followed by the new name.

Alliance Theological Seminary (Nyack, NY): now listed as a unit of Nyack College (Nyack, NY)

American InterContinental University (Houston, TX): name changed to American InterContinental University Houston

American InterContinental University Buckhead Campus (Atlanta, GA): closed

American InterContinental University Dunwoody Campus (Atlanta, GA): name changed to American InterContinental University Atlanta

American InterContinental University–London (London, United Kingdom): name changed to American InterContinental University London

Arkansas State University - Jonesboro (State University, AR): name changed to Arkansas State University

Bard Graduate Center for Studies in the Decorative Arts, Design, and Culture (New York, NY): name changed to Bard Graduate Center: Decorative Arts, Design History, Material Culture

Birmingham-Southern College (Birmingham, AL): no longer offers graduate degrees

California School of Podiatric Medicine at Samuel Merritt College (Oakland, CA): name changed to California School of Podiatric Medicine at Samuel Merritt University

Church of God Theological Seminary (Cleveland, TN): name changed to Pentecostal Theological Seminary

Clarke College (Dubuque, IA): name changed to Clarke University

College of Santa Fe (Santa Fe, NM): name changed to Santa Fe University of Art and Design and no longer offers graduate degrees

Dongguk Royal University (Los Angeles, CA): name changed to Dongguk University Los Angeles

Embry-Riddle Aeronautical University (Prescott, AZ): name changed to Embry-Riddle Aeronautical University–Prescott

Embry-Riddle Aeronautical University (Daytona Beach, FL): name changed to Embry-Riddle Aeronautical University–Daytona

Embry-Riddle Aeronautical University Worldwide (Daytona Beach, FL): name changed to Embry-Riddle Aeronautical University—Worldwide

Emily Carr Institute of Art & Design (Vancouver, BC, Canada): name changed to Emily Carr University of Art & Design

Emmanuel School of Religion (Johnson City, TN): name changed to Emmanuel Christian Seminary

Everest University (Clearwater, FL): no longer a campus of Everest University

Framingham State College (Framingham, MA): name changed to Framingham State University

Hannibal-LaGrange College (Hannibal, MO): name changed to Hannibal-LaGrange University

Hebrew Union College–Jewish Institute of Religion (Los Angeles, CA): merged into a single entry for Hebrew Union College–Jewish Institute of Religion (New York, NY) by request from the institution

Hebrew Union College–Jewish Institute of Religion (Cincinnati, OH): merged into a single entry for Hebrew Union College–Jewish Institute of Religion (New York, NY) by request from the institution

Jesuit School of Theology at Berkeley (Berkeley, CA): now listed as a unit of Santa Clara University (Santa Clara, CA)

Johnson Bible College (Knoxville, TN): name changed to Johnson University

Keller Graduate School of Management (Long Island City, NY): now listed as a unit of DeVry College of New York (Long Island City, NY)

Keller Graduate School of Management (New York, NY): now listed as a unit of DeVry University Manhattan Extension Site (New York, NY)

Lancaster Bible College & Graduate School (Lancaster, PA): name changed to Lancaster Bible College

Medical College of Georgia (Augusta, GA): name changed to Georgia Health Sciences University

Mennonite Brethren Biblical Seminary (Fresno, CA): name changed to Fresno Pacific Biblical Seminary and now a unit of Fresno Pacific University (Fresno, CA)

Meritus University (Fredericton, NB, Canada): closed

Mount Mercy College (Cedar Rapids, IA): name changed to Mount Mercy University

Mount Sinai School of Medicine of New York University (New York, NY): name changed to Mount Sinai School of Medicine

Northeastern Ohio Universities College of Medicine and Pharmacy (Rootstown, OH): name changed to Northeastern Ohio Universities Colleges of Medicine and Pharmacy

Polytechnic University of the Americas–Miami Campus (Miami, FL): name changed to Polytechnic University of Puerto Rico, Miami Campus

Polytechnic University of the Americas–Orlando Campus (Winter Park, FL): name changed to Polytechnic University of Puerto Rico, Orlando Campus

Salem State College (Salem, MA): name changed to Salem State University

Sherman College of Straight Chiropractic (Spartanburg, SC): name changed to Sherman College of Chiropractic

Union Theological Seminary and Presbyterian School of Christian Education (Richmond, VA): name changed to Union Presbyterian Seminary

University of Colorado at Boulder (Boulder, CO): name changed to University of Colorado Boulder

University of Phoenix–Western Washington Campus (Tukwila, WA): merged into a single entry for University of Phoenix–Washington Campus (Seattle, WA)

Vassar College (Poughkeepsie, NY): no longer offers graduate degrees

Western New England College (Springfield, MA): name changed to Western New England University

Western States Chiropractic College (Portland, OR): name changed to University of Western States

Westfield State College (Westfield, MA): name changed to Westfield State University

Westminster Choir College of Rider University (Princeton, NJ): name changed to Westminster Choir College and now a unit of Rider University (Lawrenceville, NJ)

West Suburban College of Nursing (Oak Park, IL): name changed to Resurrection University

Worcester State College (Worcester, MA): name changed to Worcester State University

Abbreviations Used in the Guides

The following list includes abbreviations of degree names used in the profiles in the 2012 edition of the guides. Because some degrees (e.g., Doctor of Education) can be abbreviated in more than one way (e.g., D.Ed. or Ed.D.), and because the abbreviations used in the guides reflect the preferences of the individual colleges and universities, the list may include two or more abbreviations for a single degree.

Degrees

A Mus D	Doctor of Musical Arts
AC	Advanced Certificate
AD	Artist's Diploma Doctor of Arts
ADP	Artist's Diploma
Adv C	Advanced Certificate
Adv M	Advanced Master
AGC	Advanced Graduate Certificate
AGSC	Advanced Graduate Specialist Certificate
ALM	Master of Liberal Arts
AM	Master of Arts
AMBA	Accelerated Master of Business Administration Aviation Master of Business Administration
AMRS	Master of Arts in Religious Studies
APC	Advanced Professional Certificate
APMPH	Advanced Professional Master of Public Health
App Sc	Applied Scientist
App Sc D	Doctor of Applied Science
Au D	Doctor of Audiology
B Th	Bachelor of Theology
CAES	Certificate of Advanced Educational Specialization
CAGS	Certificate of Advanced Graduate Studies
CAL	Certificate in Applied Linguistics
CALS	Certificate of Advanced Liberal Studies
CAMS	Certificate of Advanced Management Studies
CAPS	Certificate of Advanced Professional Studies
CAS	Certificate of Advanced Studies
CASPA	Certificate of Advanced Study in Public Administration
CASR	Certificate in Advanced Social Research
CATS	Certificate of Achievement in Theological Studies
CBHS	Certificate in Basic Health Sciences
CBS	Graduate Certificate in Biblical Studies
CCJA	Certificate in Criminal Justice Administration
CCSA	Certificate in Catholic School Administration
CCTS	Certificate in Clinical and Translational Science
CE	Civil Engineer
CEM	Certificate of Environmental Management
CET	Certificate in Educational Technologies
CGS	Certificate of Graduate Studies
Ch E	Chemical Engineer
CM	Certificate in Management
CMH	Certificate in Medical Humanities
CMM	Master of Church Ministries
CMS	Certificate in Ministerial Studies
CNM	Certificate in Nonprofit Management
CP	Certificate in Performance
CPASF	Certificate Program for Advanced Study in Finance
CPC	Certificate in Professional Counseling Certificate in Publication and Communication
CPH	Certificate in Public Health
CPM	Certificate in Public Management
CPS	Certificate of Professional Studies
CScD	Doctor of Clinical Science
CSD	Certificate in Spiritual Direction
CSS	Certificate of Special Studies
CTS	Certificate of Theological Studies
CURP	Certificate in Urban and Regional Planning
D Admin	Doctor of Administration
D Arch	Doctor of Architecture
D Com	Doctor of Commerce
D Couns	Doctor of Counseling
D Div	Doctor of Divinity
D Ed	Doctor of Education
D Ed Min	Doctor of Educational Ministry
D Eng	Doctor of Engineering
D Engr	Doctor of Engineering
D Ent	Doctor of Enterprise
D Env	Doctor of Environment
D Law	Doctor of Law
D Litt	Doctor of Letters
D Med Sc	Doctor of Medical Science
D Min	Doctor of Ministry
D Miss	Doctor of Missiology
D Mus	Doctor of Music
D Mus A	Doctor of Musical Arts
D Phil	Doctor of Philosophy
D Prof	Doctor of Professional Studies
D Ps	Doctor of Psychology
D Sc	Doctor of Science
D Sc D	Doctor of Science in Dentistry
D Sc IS	Doctor of Science in Information Systems
D Sc PA	Doctor of Science in Physician Assistant Studies
D Th	Doctor of Theology
D Th P	Doctor of Practical Theology
DA	Doctor of Accounting Doctor of Arts
DA Ed	Doctor of Arts in Education
DAH	Doctor of Arts in Humanities
DAOM	Doctorate in Acupuncture and Oriental Medicine
DAST	Diploma of Advanced Studies in Teaching

DBA	Doctor of Business Administration
DBH	Doctor of Behavioral Health
DBL	Doctor of Business Leadership
DBS	Doctor of Buddhist Studies
DC	Doctor of Chiropractic
DCC	Doctor of Computer Science
DCD	Doctor of Communications Design
DCL	Doctor of Civil Law Doctor of Comparative Law
DCM	Doctor of Church Music
DCN	Doctor of Clinical Nutrition
DCS	Doctor of Computer Science
DDN	Diplôme du Droit Notarial
DDS	Doctor of Dental Surgery
DE	Doctor of Education Doctor of Engineering
DED	Doctor of Economic Development
DEIT	Doctor of Educational Innovation and Technology
DEL	Doctor of Executive Leadership
DEM	Doctor of Educational Ministry
DEPD	Diplôme Études Spécialisées
DES	Doctor of Engineering Science
DESS	Diplôme Études Supérieures Spécialisées
DFA	Doctor of Fine Arts
DGP	Diploma in Graduate and Professional Studies
DH Ed	Doctor of Health Education
DH Sc	Doctor of Health Sciences
DHA	Doctor of Health Administration
DHCE	Doctor of Health Care Ethics
DHL	Doctor of Hebrew Letters Doctor of Hebrew Literature
DHS	Doctor of Health Science
DHSc	Doctor of Health Science
Dip CS	Diploma in Christian Studies
DIT	Doctor of Industrial Technology
DJ Ed	Doctor of Jewish Education
DJS	Doctor of Jewish Studies
DLS	Doctor of Liberal Studies
DM	Doctor of Management Doctor of Music
DMA	Doctor of Musical Arts
DMD	Doctor of Dental Medicine
DME	Doctor of Manufacturing Management Doctor of Music Education
DMEd	Doctor of Music Education
DMFT	Doctor of Marital and Family Therapy
DMH	Doctor of Medical Humanities
DML	Doctor of Modern Languages
DMP	Doctorate in Medical Physics
DMPNA	Doctor of Management Practice in Nurse Anesthesia
DN Sc	Doctor of Nursing Science
DNAP	Doctor of Nurse Anesthesia Practice
DNP	Doctor of Nursing Practice
DNS	Doctor of Nursing Science
DO	Doctor of Osteopathy
DOT	Doctor of Occupational Therapy
DPA	Doctor of Public Administration
DPC	Doctor of Pastoral Counseling
DPDS	Doctor of Planning and Development Studies
DPH	Doctor of Public Health
DPM	Doctor of Plant Medicine Doctor of Podiatric Medicine
DPPD	Doctor of Policy, Planning, and Development
DPS	Doctor of Professional Studies
DPT	Doctor of Physical Therapy
DPTSc	Doctor of Physical Therapy Science
Dr DES	Doctor of Design
Dr OT	Doctor of Occupational Therapy
Dr PH	Doctor of Public Health
Dr Sc PT	Doctor of Science in Physical Therapy
DRSc	Doctor of Regulatory Science
DS	Doctor of Science
DS Sc	Doctor of Social Science
DSJS	Doctor of Science in Jewish Studies
DSL	Doctor of Strategic Leadership
DSW	Doctor of Social Work
DTL	Doctor of Talmudic Law
DV Sc	Doctor of Veterinary Science
DVM	Doctor of Veterinary Medicine
DWS	Doctor of Worship Studies
EAA	Engineer in Aeronautics and Astronautics
ECS	Engineer in Computer Science
Ed D	Doctor of Education
Ed DCT	Doctor of Education in College Teaching
Ed L D	Doctor of Education Leadership
Ed M	Master of Education
Ed S	Specialist in Education
Ed Sp	Specialist in Education
EDB	Executive Doctorate in Business
EDM	Executive Doctorate in Management
EDSPC	Education Specialist
EE	Electrical Engineer
EJD	Executive Juris Doctor
EMBA	Executive Master of Business Administration
EMFA	Executive Master of Forensic Accounting
EMHA	Executive Master of Health Administration
EMIB	Executive Master of International Business
EML	Executive Master of Leadership
EMPA	Executive Master of Public Administration
EMPP	Executive Master's of Public Policy
EMS	Executive Master of Science
EMTM	Executive Master of Technology Management
Eng	Engineer
Eng Sc D	Doctor of Engineering Science

Engr	Engineer	**M Ad Ed**	Master of Adult Education
Ex Doc	Executive Doctor of Pharmacy	**M Adm**	Master of Administration
Exec Ed D	Executive Doctor of Education	**M Adm Mgt**	Master of Administrative Management
Exec MBA	Executive Master of Business Administration	**M Admin**	Master of Administration
Exec MPA	Executive Master of Public Administration	**M ADU**	Master of Architectural Design and Urbanism
Exec MPH	Executive Master of Public Health	**M Adv**	Master of Advertising
Exec MS	Executive Master of Science	**M Aero E**	Master of Aerospace Engineering
G Dip	Graduate Diploma	**M AEST**	Master of Applied Environmental Science and Technology
GBC	Graduate Business Certificate	**M Ag**	Master of Agriculture
GCE	Graduate Certificate in Education	**M Ag Ed**	Master of Agricultural Education
GDM	Graduate Diploma in Management	**M Agr**	Master of Agriculture
GDPA	Graduate Diploma in Public Administration	**M Anesth Ed**	Master of Anesthesiology Education
GDRE	Graduate Diploma in Religious Education	**M App Comp Sc**	Master of Applied Computer Science
GEMBA	Global Executive Master of Business Administration	**M App St**	Master of Applied Statistics
GEMPA	Gulf Executive Master of Public Administration	**M Appl Stat**	Master of Applied Statistics
GM Acc	Graduate Master of Accountancy	**M Aq**	Master of Aquaculture
GMBA	Global Master of Business Administration	**M Arc**	Master of Architecture
GPD	Graduate Performance Diploma	**M Arch**	Master of Architecture
GSS	Graduate Special Certificate for Students in Special Situations	**M Arch I**	Master of Architecture I
		M Arch II	Master of Architecture II
IEMBA	International Executive Master of Business Administration	**M Arch E**	Master of Architectural Engineering
IM Acc	Integrated Master of Accountancy	**M Arch H**	Master of Architectural History
IMA	Interdisciplinary Master of Arts	**M Bioethics**	Master in Bioethics
IMBA	International Master of Business Administration	**M Biomath**	Master of Biomathematics
IMES	International Master's in Environmental Studies	**M Ch**	Master of Chemistry
		M Ch E	Master of Chemical Engineering
Ingeniero	Engineer	**M Chem**	Master of Chemistry
JCD	Doctor of Canon Law	**M Cl D**	Master of Clinical Dentistry
JCL	Licentiate in Canon Law	**M Cl Sc**	Master of Clinical Science
JD	Juris Doctor	**M Comp**	Master of Computing
JSD	Doctor of Juridical Science Doctor of Jurisprudence Doctor of the Science of Law	**M Comp E**	Master of Computer Engineering
		M Comp Sc	Master of Computer Science
JSM	Master of Science of Law	**M Coun**	Master of Counseling
L Th	Licenciate in Theology	**M Dent**	Master of Dentistry
LL B	Bachelor of Laws	**M Dent Sc**	Master of Dental Sciences
LL CM	Master of Laws in Comparative Law	**M Des**	Master of Design
LL D	Doctor of Laws	**M Des S**	Master of Design Studies
LL M	Master of Laws	**M Div**	Master of Divinity
LL M in Tax	Master of Laws in Taxation	**M Ec**	Master of Economics
LL M CL	Master of Laws (Common Law)	**M Econ**	Master of Economics
M Ac	Master of Accountancy Master of Accounting Master of Acupuncture	**M Ed**	Master of Education
		M Ed T	Master of Education in Teaching
M Ac OM	Master of Acupuncture and Oriental Medicine	**M En**	Master of Engineering Master of Environmental Science
M Acc	Master of Accountancy Master of Accounting	**M En S**	Master of Environmental Sciences
M Acct	Master of Accountancy Master of Accounting	**M Eng**	Master of Engineering
		M Eng Mgt	Master of Engineering Management
M Accy	Master of Accountancy	**M Engr**	Master of Engineering
M Actg	Master of Accounting	**M Ent**	Master of Enterprise
M Acy	Master of Accountancy	**M Env**	Master of Environment
M Ad	Master of Administration	**M Env Des**	Master of Environmental Design

M Env E	Master of Environmental Engineering
M Env Sc	Master of Environmental Science
M Fin	Master of Finance
M Geo E	Master of Geological Engineering
M Geoenv E	Master of Geoenvironmental Engineering
M Geog	Master of Geography
M Hum	Master of Humanities
M Hum Svcs	Master of Human Services
M IBD	Master of Integrated Building Delivery
M IDST	Master's in Interdisciplinary Studies
M Kin	Master of Kinesiology
M Land Arch	Master of Landscape Architecture
M Litt	Master of Letters
M Mat SE	Master of Material Science and Engineering
M Math	Master of Mathematics
M Mech E	Master of Mechanical Engineering
M Med Sc	Master of Medical Science
M Mgmt	Master of Management
M Mgt	Master of Management
M Min	Master of Ministries
M Mtl E	Master of Materials Engineering
M Mu	Master of Music
M Mus	Master of Music
M Mus Ed	Master of Music Education
M Music	Master of Music
M Nat Sci	Master of Natural Science
M Oc E	Master of Oceanographic Engineering
M Pet E	Master of Petroleum Engineering
M Pharm	Master of Pharmacy
M Phil	Master of Philosophy
M Phil F	Master of Philosophical Foundations
M Pl	Master of Planning
M Plan	Master of Planning
M Pol	Master of Political Science
M Pr Met	Master of Professional Meteorology
M Prob S	Master of Probability and Statistics
M Psych	Master of Psychology
M Pub	Master of Publishing
M Rel	Master of Religion
M S Ed	Master of Science Education
M Sc	Master of Science
M Sc A	Master of Science (Applied)
M Sc AHN	Master of Science in Applied Human Nutrition
M Sc BMC	Master of Science in Biomedical Communications
M Sc CS	Master of Science in Computer Science
M Sc E	Master of Science in Engineering
M Sc Eng	Master of Science in Engineering
M Sc Engr	Master of Science in Engineering
M Sc F	Master of Science in Forestry
M Sc FE	Master of Science in Forest Engineering
M Sc Geogr	Master of Science in Geography

M Sc N	Master of Science in Nursing
M Sc OT	Master of Science in Occupational Therapy
M Sc P	Master of Science in Planning
M Sc Pl	Master of Science in Planning
M Sc PT	Master of Science in Physical Therapy
M Sc T	Master of Science in Teaching
M SEM	Master of Sustainable Environmental Management
M Serv Soc	Master of Social Service
M Soc	Master of Sociology
M Sp Ed	Master of Special Education
M Stat	Master of Statistics
M Sys Sc	Master of Systems Science
M Tax	Master of Taxation
M Tech	Master of Technology
M Th	Master of Theology
M Tox	Master of Toxicology
M Trans E	Master of Transportation Engineering
M Urb	Master of Urban Planning
M Vet Sc	Master of Veterinary Science
MA	Master of Accounting Master of Administration Master of Arts
MA Missions	Master of Arts in Missions
MA Comm	Master of Arts in Communication
MA Ed	Master of Arts in Education
MA Ed Ad	Master of Arts in Educational Administration
MA Ext	Master of Agricultural Extension
MA Islamic	Master of Arts in Islamic Studies
MA Military Studies	Master of Arts in Military Studies
MA Min	Master of Arts in Ministry
MA Miss	Master of Arts in Missiology
MA Past St	Master of Arts in Pastoral Studies
MA Ph	Master of Arts in Philosophy
MA Psych	Master of Arts in Psychology
MA Sc	Master of Applied Science
MA Sp	Master of Arts (Spirituality)
MA Th	Master of Arts in Theology
MA-R	Master of Arts (Research)
MAA	Master of Administrative Arts Master of Applied Anthropology Master of Applied Arts Master of Arts in Administration
MAAA	Master of Arts in Arts Administration
MAAAP	Master of Arts Administration and Policy
MAAE	Master of Arts in Art Education
MAAT	Master of Arts in Applied Theology Master of Arts in Art Therapy
MAB	Master of Agribusiness
MABC	Master of Arts in Biblical Counseling Master of Arts in Business Communication
MABE	Master of Arts in Bible Exposition
MABL	Master of Arts in Biblical Languages

MABM	Master of Agribusiness Management
MABS	Master of Arts in Biblical Studies
MABT	Master of Arts in Bible Teaching
MAC	Master of Accountancy Master of Accounting Master of Arts in Communication Master of Arts in Counseling
MACC	Master of Arts in Christian Counseling Master of Arts in Clinical Counseling
MACCM	Master of Arts in Church and Community Ministry
MACCT	Master of Accounting
MACD	Master of Arts in Christian Doctrine
MACE	Master of Arts in Christian Education
MACFM	Master of Arts in Children's and Family Ministry
MACH	Master of Arts in Church History
MACI	Master of Arts in Curriculum and Instruction
MACIS	Master of Accounting and Information Systems
MACJ	Master of Arts in Criminal Justice
MACL	Master of Arts in Christian Leadership
MACM	Master of Arts in Christian Ministries Master of Arts in Christian Ministry Master of Arts in Church Music Master of Arts in Counseling Ministries
MACN	Master of Arts in Counseling
MACO	Master of Arts in Counseling
MAcOM	Master of Acupuncture and Oriental Medicine
MACP	Master of Arts in Counseling Psychology
MACS	Master of Arts in Catholic Studies
MACSE	Master of Arts in Christian School Education
MACT	Master of Arts in Christian Thought Master of Arts in Communications and Technology
MAD	Master in Educational Institution Administration Master of Art and Design
MADR	Master of Arts in Dispute Resolution
MADS	Master of Animal and Dairy Science Master of Applied Disability Studies
MAE	Master of Aerospace Engineering Master of Agricultural Economics Master of Agricultural Education Master of Architectural Engineering Master of Art Education Master of Arts in Education Master of Arts in English
MAEd	Master of Arts Education
MAEL	Master of Arts in Educational Leadership
MAEM	Master of Arts in Educational Ministries
MAEN	Master of Arts in English
MAEP	Master of Arts in Economic Policy
MAES	Master of Arts in Environmental Sciences
MAET	Master of Arts in English Teaching
MAF	Master of Arts in Finance
MAFE	Master of Arts in Financial Economics
MAFLL	Master of Arts in Foreign Language and Literature
MAFM	Master of Accounting and Financial Management
MAFS	Master of Arts in Family Studies
MAG	Master of Applied Geography

MAGU	Master of Urban Analysis and Management
MAH	Master of Arts in Humanities
MAHA	Master of Arts in Humanitarian Assistance Master of Arts in Humanitarian Studies
MAHCM	Master of Arts in Health Care Mission
MAHG	Master of American History and Government
MAHL	Master of Arts in Hebrew Letters
MAHN	Master of Applied Human Nutrition
MAHSR	Master of Applied Health Services Research
MAIA	Master of Arts in International Administration
MAIB	Master of Arts in International Business
MAICS	Master of Arts in Intercultural Studies
MAIDM	Master of Arts in Interior Design and Merchandising
MAIH	Master of Arts in Interdisciplinary Humanities
MAIOP	Master of Arts in Industrial/Organizational Psychology
MAIPCR	Master of Arts in International Peace and Conflict Management
MAIS	Master of Arts in Intercultural Studies Master of Arts in Interdisciplinary Studies Master of Arts in International Studies
MAIT	Master of Administration in Information Technology Master of Applied Information Technology
MAJ	Master of Arts in Journalism
MAJ Ed	Master of Arts in Jewish Education
MAJCS	Master of Arts in Jewish Communal Service
MAJE	Master of Arts in Jewish Education
MAJS	Master of Arts in Jewish Studies
MAL	Master in Agricultural Leadership
MALA	Master of Arts in Liberal Arts
MALD	Master of Arts in Law and Diplomacy
MALER	Master of Arts in Labor and Employment Relations
MALM	Master of Arts in Leadership Evangelical Mobilization
MALP	Master of Arts in Language Pedagogy
MALPS	Master of Arts in Liberal and Professional Studies
MALS	Master of Arts in Liberal Studies
MALT	Master of Arts in Learning and Teaching
MAM	Master of Acquisition Management Master of Agriculture and Management Master of Applied Mathematics Master of Arts in Management Master of Arts in Ministry Master of Arts Management Master of Avian Medicine
MAMB	Master of Applied Molecular Biology
MAMC	Master of Arts in Mass Communication Master of Arts in Ministry and Culture Master of Arts in Ministry for a Multicultural Church Master of Arts in Missional Christianity
MAME	Master of Arts in Missions/Evangelism
MAMFC	Master of Arts in Marriage and Family Counseling
MAMFCC	Master of Arts in Marriage, Family, and Child Counseling

MAMFT	Master of Arts in Marriage and Family Therapy
MAMHC	Master of Arts in Mental Health Counseling
MAMI	Master of Arts in Missions
MAMS	Master of Applied Mathematical Sciences Master of Arts in Ministerial Studies Master of Arts in Ministry and Spirituality
MAMT	Master of Arts in Mathematics Teaching
MAN	Master of Applied Nutrition
MANP	Master of Applied Natural Products
MANT	Master of Arts in New Testament
MAOL	Master of Arts in Organizational Leadership
MAOM	Master of Acupuncture and Oriental Medicine Master of Arts in Organizational Management
MAOT	Master of Arts in Old Testament
MAP	Master of Applied Psychology Master of Arts in Planning Master of Psychology Master of Public Administration
MAP Min	Master of Arts in Pastoral Ministry
MAPA	Master of Arts in Public Administration
MAPC	Master of Arts in Pastoral Counseling Master of Arts in Professional Counseling
MAPE	Master of Arts in Political Economy
MAPL	Master of Arts in Pastoral Leadership
MAPM	Master of Arts in Pastoral Ministry Master of Arts in Pastoral Music Master of Arts in Practical Ministry
MAPP	Master of Arts in Public Policy
MAPPS	Master of Arts in Asia Pacific Policy Studies
MAPS	Master of Arts in Pastoral Counseling/Spiritual Formation Master of Arts in Pastoral Studies Master of Arts in Public Service
MAPT	Master of Practical Theology
MAPW	Master of Arts in Professional Writing
MAR	Master of Arts in Religion
Mar Eng	Marine Engineer
MARC	Master of Arts in Rehabilitation Counseling
MARE	Master of Arts in Religious Education
MARL	Master of Arts in Religious Leadership
MARS	Master of Arts in Religious Studies
MAS	Master of Accounting Science Master of Actuarial Science Master of Administrative Science Master of Advanced Study Master of Aeronautical Science Master of American Studies Master of Applied Science Master of Applied Statistics Master of Archival Studies
MASA	Master of Advanced Studies in Architecture
MASD	Master of Arts in Spiritual Direction
MASE	Master of Arts in Special Education
MASF	Master of Arts in Spiritual Formation
MASJ	Master of Arts in Systems of Justice
MASL	Master of Arts in School Leadership
MASLA	Master of Advanced Studies in Landscape Architecture

MASM	Master of Aging Services Management Master of Arts in Specialized Ministries
MASP	Master of Applied Social Psychology Master of Arts in School Psychology
MASPAA	Master of Arts in Sports and Athletic Administration
MASS	Master of Applied Social Science Master of Arts in Social Science
MAST	Master of Arts in Science Teaching
MASW	Master of Aboriginal Social Work
MAT	Master of Arts in Teaching Master of Arts in Theology Master of Athletic Training Master's in Administration of Telecommunications
Mat E	Materials Engineer
MATCM	Master of Acupuncture and Traditional Chinese Medicine
MATDE	Master of Arts in Theology, Development, and Evangelism
MATDR	Master of Territorial Management and Regional Development
MATE	Master of Arts for the Teaching of English
MATESL	Master of Arts in Teaching English as a Second Language
MATESOL	Master of Arts in Teaching English to Speakers of Other Languages
MATF	Master of Arts in Teaching English as a Foreign Language/Intercultural Studies
MATFL	Master of Arts in Teaching Foreign Language
MATH	Master of Arts in Therapy
MATI	Master of Administration of Information Technology
MATL	Master of Arts in Teacher Leadership Master of Arts in Teaching of Languages Master of Arts in Transformational Leadership
MATM	Master of Arts in Teaching of Mathematics
MATS	Master of Arts in Theological Studies Master of Arts in Transforming Spirituality
MATSL	Master of Arts in Teaching a Second Language
MAUA	Master of Arts in Urban Affairs
MAUD	Master of Arts in Urban Design
MAURP	Master of Arts in Urban and Regional Planning
MAWSHP	Master of Arts in Worship
MAYM	Master of Arts in Youth Ministry
MB	Master of Bioinformatics Master of Biology
MBA	Master of Business Administration
MBA-AM	Master of Business Administration in Aviation Management
MBA-EP	Master of Business Administration–Experienced Professionals
MBAA	Master of Business Administration in Aviation
MBAE	Master of Biological and Agricultural Engineering Master of Biosystems and Agricultural Engineering
MBAH	Master of Business Administration in Health
MBAi	Master of Business Administration–International

MBAICT	Master of Business Administration in Information and Communication Technology
MBATM	Master of Business Administration in Technology Management
MBC	Master of Building Construction
MBE	Master of Bilingual Education Master of Bioengineering Master of Bioethics Master of Biological Engineering Master of Biomedical Engineering Master of Business and Engineering Master of Business Economics Master of Business Education
MBET	Master of Business, Entrepreneurship and Technology
MBiotech	Master of Biotechnology
MBIT	Master of Business Information Technology
MBL	Master of Business Law Master of Business Leadership
MBLE	Master in Business Logistics Engineering
MBMI	Master of Biomedical Imaging and Signals
MBMSE	Master of Business Management and Software Engineering
MBOE	Master of Business Operational Excellence
MBS	Master of Biblical Studies Master of Biological Science Master of Biomedical Sciences Master of Bioscience Master of Building Science
MBT	Master of Biblical and Theological Studies Master of Biomedical Technology Master of Biotechnology Master of Business Taxation
MC	Master of Communication Master of Counseling Master of Cybersecurity
MC Ed	Master of Continuing Education
MC Sc	Master of Computer Science
MCA	Master of Arts in Applied Criminology Master of Commercial Aviation
MCAM	Master of Computational and Applied Mathematics
MCC	Master of Computer Science
MCCS	Master of Crop and Soil Sciences
MCD	Master of Communications Disorders Master of Community Development
MCE	Master in Electronic Commerce Master of Christian Education Master of Civil Engineering Master of Control Engineering
MCEM	Master of Construction Engineering Management
MCH	Master of Chemical Engineering
MCHE	Master of Chemical Engineering
MCIS	Master of Communication and Information Studies Master of Computer and Information Science Master of Computer Information Systems
MCIT	Master of Computer and Information Technology
MCJ	Master of Criminal Justice
MCJA	Master of Criminal Justice Administration
MCL	Master in Communication Leadership Master of Canon Law Master of Comparative Law
MCM	Master of Christian Ministry Master of Church Music Master of City Management Master of Communication Management Master of Community Medicine Master of Construction Management Master of Contract Management Master of Corporate Media
MCMP	Master of City and Metropolitan Planning
MCMS	Master of Clinical Medical Science
MCN	Master of Clinical Nutrition
MCP	Master of City Planning Master of Community Planning Master of Counseling Psychology Master of Cytopathology Practice Master of Science in Quality Systems and Productivity
MCPC	Master of Arts in Chaplaincy and Pastoral Care
MCPD	Master of Community Planning and Development
MCR	Master in Clinical Research
MCRP	Master of City and Regional Planning
MCRS	Master of City and Regional Studies
MCS	Master of Christian Studies Master of Clinical Science Master of Combined Sciences Master of Communication Studies Master of Computer Science Master of Consumer Science
MCSE	Master of Computer Science and Engineering
MCSL	Master of Catholic School Leadership
MCSM	Master of Construction Science/Management
MCST	Master of Science in Computer Science and Information Technology
MCTP	Master of Communication Technology and Policy
MCTS	Master of Clinical and Translational Science
MCVS	Master of Cardiovascular Science
MD	Doctor of Medicine
MDA	Master of Development Administration Master of Dietetic Administration
MDB	Master of Design-Build
MDE	Master of Developmental Economics Master of Distance Education Master of the Education of the Deaf
MDH	Master of Dental Hygiene
MDM	Master of Design Methods Master of Digital Media
MDP	Master of Development Practice
MDR	Master of Dispute Resolution
MDS	Master of Dental Surgery
ME	Master of Education Master of Engineering Master of Entrepreneurship Master of Evangelism
ME Sc	Master of Engineering Science
MEA	Master of Educational Administration Master of Engineering Administration

Peterson's Graduate Programs in Engineering & Applied Sciences 2012

MEAP	Master of Environmental Administration and Planning
MEBT	Master in Electronic Business Technologies
MEC	Master of Electronic Commerce
MECE	Master of Electrical and Computer Engineering
Mech E	Mechanical Engineer
MED	Master of Education of the Deaf
MEDS	Master of Environmental Design Studies
MEE	Master in Education
	Master of Electrical Engineering
	Master of Energy Engineering
	Master of Environmental Engineering
MEEM	Master of Environmental Engineering and Management
MEENE	Master of Engineering in Environmental Engineering
MEEP	Master of Environmental and Energy Policy
MEERM	Master of Earth and Environmental Resource Management
MEH	Master in Humanistic Studies
	Master of Environmental Horticulture
MEHS	Master of Environmental Health and Safety
MEIM	Master of Entertainment Industry Management
MEL	Master of Educational Leadership
	Master of English Literature
MELP	Master of Environmental Law and Policy
MEM	Master of Ecosystem Management
	Master of Electricity Markets
	Master of Engineering Management
	Master of Environmental Management
	Master of Marketing
MEME	Master of Engineering in Manufacturing Engineering
	Master of Engineering in Mechanical Engineering
MENG	Master of Arts in English
MENVEGR	Master of Environmental Engineering
MEP	Master of Engineering Physics
MEPC	Master of Environmental Pollution Control
MEPD	Master of Education–Professional Development
	Master of Environmental Planning and Design
MER	Master of Employment Relations
MES	Master of Education and Science
	Master of Engineering Science
	Master of Environment and Sustainability
	Master of Environmental Science
	Master of Environmental Studies
	Master of Environmental Systems
	Master of Special Education
MESM	Master of Environmental Science and Management
MET	Master of Educational Technology
	Master of Engineering Technology
	Master of Entertainment Technology
	Master of Environmental Toxicology
Met E	Metallurgical Engineer
METM	Master of Engineering and Technology Management
MF	Master of Finance
	Master of Forestry
MFA	Master of Fine Arts
MFAM	Master in Food Animal Medicine
MFAS	Master of Fisheries and Aquatic Science
MFAW	Master of Fine Arts in Writing
MFC	Master of Forest Conservation
MFCS	Master of Family and Consumer Sciences
MFE	Master of Financial Economics
	Master of Financial Engineering
	Master of Forest Engineering
MFG	Master of Functional Genomics
MFHD	Master of Family and Human Development
MFM	Master of Financial Mathematics
MFMS	Master's in Food Microbiology and Safety
MFPE	Master of Food Process Engineering
MFR	Master of Forest Resources
MFRC	Master of Forest Resources and Conservation
MFS	Master of Food Science
	Master of Forensic Sciences
	Master of Forest Science
	Master of Forest Studies
	Master of French Studies
MFST	Master of Food Safety and Technology
MFT	Master of Family Therapy
	Master of Food Technology
MFWB	Master of Fishery and Wildlife Biology
MFWCB	Master of Fish, Wildlife and Conservation Biology
MFWS	Master of Fisheries and Wildlife Sciences
MFYCS	Master of Family, Youth and Community Sciences
MG	Master of Genetics
MGA	Master of Global Affairs
	Master of Governmental Administration
MGC	Master of Genetic Counseling
MGD	Master of Graphic Design
MGE	Master of Geotechnical Engineering
MGEM	Master of Global Entrepreneurship and Management
MGH	Master of Geriatric Health
MGIS	Master of Geographic Information Science
	Master of Geographic Information Systems
MGM	Master of Global Management
MGP	Master of Gestion de Projet
MGPS	Master of Global Policy Studies
MGREM	Master of Global Real Estate Management
MGS	Master of Gerontological Studies
	Master of Global Studies
MH	Master of Humanities
MH Ed	Master of Health Education
MH Sc	Master of Health Sciences
MHA	Master of Health Administration
	Master of Healthcare Administration
	Master of Hospital Administration
	Master of Hospitality Administration
MHA/MCRP	Master of Healthcare Administration/Master of City and Regional Planning
MHAD	Master of Health Administration
MHB	Master of Human Behavior
MHCA	Master of Health Care Administration

MHCI	Master of Human-Computer Interaction
MHCL	Master of Health Care Leadership
MHE	Master of Health Education Master of Human Ecology
MHE Ed	Master of Home Economics Education
MHEA	Master of Higher Education Administration
MHHS	Master of Health and Human Services
MHI	Master of Health Informatics Master of Healthcare Innovation
MHIIM	Master of Health Informatics and Information Management
MHIS	Master of Health Information Systems
MHK	Master of Human Kinetics
MHL	Master of Hebrew Literature
MHM	Master of Healthcare Management
MHMS	Master of Health Management Systems
MHP	Master of Health Physics Master of Heritage Preservation Master of Historic Preservation
MHPA	Master of Heath Policy and Administration
MHPE	Master of Health Professions Education
MHR	Master of Human Resources
MHRD	Master in Human Resource Development
MHRIR	Master of Human Resources and Industrial Relations
MHRLR	Master of Human Resources and Labor Relations
MHRM	Master of Human Resources Management
MHS	Master of Health Science Master of Health Sciences Master of Health Studies Master of Hispanic Studies Master of Human Services Master of Humanistic Studies
MHSA	Master of Health Services Administration
MHSM	Master of Health Systems Management
MI	Master of Instruction
MI Arch	Master of Interior Architecture
MI St	Master of Information Studies
MIA	Master of Interior Architecture Master of International Affairs
MIAA	Master of International Affairs and Administration
MIAM	Master of International Agribusiness Management
MIB	Master of International Business
MIBA	Master of International Business Administration
MICM	Master of International Construction Management
MID	Master of Industrial Design Master of Industrial Distribution Master of Interior Design Master of International Development
MIE	Master of Industrial Engineering
MIH	Master of Integrative Health
MIHTM	Master of International Hospitality and Tourism Management
MIJ	Master of International Journalism
MILR	Master of Industrial and Labor Relations
MiM	Master in Management

MIM	Master of Industrial Management Master of Information Management Master of International Management
MIMLAE	Master of International Management for Latin American Executives
MIMS	Master of Information Management and Systems Master of Integrated Manufacturing Systems
MIP	Master of Infrastructure Planning Master of Intellectual Property
MIPER	Master of International Political Economy of Resources
MIPP	Master of International Policy and Practice Master of International Public Policy
MIPS	Master of International Planning Studies
MIR	Master of Industrial Relations Master of International Relations
MIS	Master of Industrial Statistics Master of Information Science Master of Information Systems Master of Integrated Science Master of Interdisciplinary Studies Master of International Service Master of International Studies
MISE	Master of Industrial and Systems Engineering
MISKM	Master of Information Sciences and Knowledge Management
MISM	Master of Information Systems Management
MIT	Master in Teaching Master of Industrial Technology Master of Information Technology Master of Initial Teaching Master of International Trade Master of Internet Technology
MITA	Master of Information Technology Administration
MITM	Master of Information Technology and Management
MITO	Master of Industrial Technology and Operations
MJ	Master of Journalism Master of Jurisprudence
MJ Ed	Master of Jewish Education
MJA	Master of Justice Administration
MJM	Master of Justice Management
MJS	Master of Judicial Studies Master of Juridical Science
MKM	Master of Knowledge Management
ML	Master of Latin
ML Arch	Master of Landscape Architecture
MLA	Master of Landscape Architecture Master of Liberal Arts
MLAS	Master of Laboratory Animal Science Master of Liberal Arts and Sciences
MLAUD	Master of Landscape Architecture in Urban Development
MLD	Master of Leadership Development
MLE	Master of Applied Linguistics and Exegesis
MLER	Master of Labor and Employment Relations
MLHR	Master of Labor and Human Resources
MLI Sc	Master of Library and Information Science
MLIS	Master of Library and Information Science Master of Library and Information Studies

MLM	Master of Library Media
MLRHR	Master of Labor Relations and Human Resources
MLS	Master of Leadership Studies
	Master of Legal Studies
	Master of Liberal Studies
	Master of Library Science
	Master of Life Sciences
MLSP	Master of Law and Social Policy
MLT	Master of Language Technologies
MLTCA	Master of Long Term Care Administration
MM	Master of Management
	Master of Ministry
	Master of Missiology
	Master of Music
MM Ed	Master of Music Education
MM Sc	Master of Medical Science
MM St	Master of Museum Studies
MMA	Master of Marine Affairs
	Master of Media Arts
	Master of Musical Arts
MMAE	Master of Mechanical and Aerospace Engineering
MMAS	Master of Military Art and Science
MMB	Master of Microbial Biotechnology
MMBA	Managerial Master of Business Administration
MMC	Master of Manufacturing Competitiveness
	Master of Mass Communications
	Master of Music Conducting
MMCM	Master of Music in Church Music
MMCSS	Master of Mathematical Computational and Statistical Sciences
MME	Master of Manufacturing Engineering
	Master of Mathematics Education
	Master of Mathematics for Educators
	Master of Mechanical Engineering
	Master of Medical Engineering
	Master of Mining Engineering
	Master of Music Education
MMF	Master of Mathematical Finance
MMFT	Master of Marriage and Family Therapy
MMG	Master of Management
MMH	Master of Management in Hospitality
	Master of Medical Humanities
MMI	Master of Management of Innovation
MMIS	Master of Management Information Systems
MMM	Master of Manufacturing Management
	Master of Marine Management
	Master of Medical Management
MMME	Master of Metallurgical and Materials Engineering
MMP	Master of Management Practice
	Master of Marine Policy
	Master of Medical Physics
	Master of Music Performance
MMPA	Master of Management and Professional Accounting
MMQM	Master of Manufacturing Quality Management
MMR	Master of Marketing Research
MMRM	Master of Marine Resources Management

MMS	Master of Management Science
	Master of Management Studies
	Master of Manufacturing Systems
	Master of Marine Studies
	Master of Materials Science
	Master of Medical Science
	Master of Medieval Studies
	Master of Modern Studies
MMSE	Master of Manufacturing Systems Engineering
MMSM	Master of Music in Sacred Music
MMT	Master in Marketing
	Master of Management
	Master of Math for Teaching
	Master of Music Teaching
	Master of Music Therapy
	Master's in Marketing Technology
MMus	Master of Music
MN	Master of Nursing
	Master of Nutrition
MN NP	Master of Nursing in Nurse Practitioner
MNA	Master of Nonprofit Administration
	Master of Nurse Anesthesia
MNAL	Master of Nonprofit Administration and Leadership
MNAS	Master of Natural and Applied Science
MNCM	Master of Network and Communications Management
MNE	Master of Network Engineering
	Master of Nuclear Engineering
MNL	Master in International Business for Latin America
MNM	Master of Nonprofit Management
MNO	Master of Nonprofit Organization
MNPL	Master of Not-for-Profit Leadership
MNpS	Master of Nonprofit Studies
MNR	Master of Natural Resources
MNRES	Master of Natural Resources and Environmental Studies
MNRM	Master of Natural Resource Management
MNRS	Master of Natural Resource Stewardship
MNS	Master of Natural Science
MO	Master of Oceanography
MOD	Master of Organizational Development
MOGS	Master of Oil and Gas Studies
MOH	Master of Occupational Health
MOL	Master of Organizational Leadership
MOM	Master of Oriental Medicine
MOR	Master of Operations Research
MOT	Master of Occupational Therapy
MP	Master of Physiology
	Master of Planning
MP Ac	Master of Professional Accountancy
MP Acc	Master of Professional Accountancy
	Master of Professional Accounting
	Master of Public Accounting
MP Aff	Master of Public Affairs
MP Th	Master of Pastoral Theology

MPA	Master of Physician Assistant Master of Professional Accountancy Master of Professional Accounting Master of Public Administration Master of Public Affairs
MPAC	Master of Professional Accounting
MPAID	Master of Public Administration and International Development
MPAP	Master of Physician Assistant Practice Master of Public Affairs and Politics
MPAS	Master of Physician Assistant Science Master of Physician Assistant Studies
MPC	Master of Pastoral Counseling Master of Professional Communication Master of Professional Counseling
MPD	Master of Product Development Master of Public Diplomacy
MPDS	Master of Planning and Development Studies
MPE	Master of Physical Education Master of Power Engineering
MPEM	Master of Project Engineering and Management
MPH	Master of Public Health
MPH/MCRP	Master of Public Health/Mster of Community and Regional Planning
MPHE	Master of Public Health Education
MPHTM	Master of Public Health and Tropical Medicine
MPIA	Master in International Affairs Master of Public and International Affairs
MPM	Master of Pastoral Ministry Master of Pest Management Master of Policy Management Master of Practical Ministries Master of Project Management Master of Public Management
MPNA	Master of Public and Nonprofit Administration
MPO	Master of Prosthetics and Orthotics
MPOD	Master of Positive Organizational Development
MPP	Master of Public Policy
MPPA	Master of Public Policy Administration Master of Public Policy and Administration
MPPAL	Master of Public Policy, Administration and Law
MPPM	Master of Public and Private Management Master of Public Policy and Management
MPPPM	Master of Plant Protection and Pest Management
MPRTM	Master of Parks, Recreation, and Tourism Management
MPS	Master of Pastoral Studies Master of Perfusion Science Master of Planning Studies Master of Political Science Master of Preservation Studies Master of Prevention Science Master of Professional Studies Master of Public Service
MPSA	Master of Public Service Administration
MPSRE	Master of Professional Studies in Real Estate
MPT	Master of Pastoral Theology Master of Physical Therapy
MPVM	Master of Preventive Veterinary Medicine
MPW	Master of Professional Writing Master of Public Works

MQM	Master of Quality Management
MQS	Master of Quality Systems
MR	Master of Recreation Master of Retailing
MRA	Master in Research Administration
MRC	Master of Rehabilitation Counseling
MRCP	Master of Regional and City Planning Master of Regional and Community Planning
MRD	Master of Rural Development
MRE	Master of Real Estate Master of Religious Education
MRED	Master of Real Estate Development
MREM	Master of Resource and Environmental Management
MRLS	Master of Resources Law Studies
MRM	Master of Resources Management
MRP	Master of Regional Planning
MRS	Master of Religious Studies
MRSc	Master of Rehabilitation Science
MS	Master of Science
MS Cmp E	Master of Science in Computer Engineering
MS Kin	Master of Science in Kinesiology
MS Acct	Master of Science in Accounting
MS Accy	Master of Science in Accountancy
MS Aero E	Master of Science in Aerospace Engineering
MS Ag	Master of Science in Agriculture
MS Arch	Master of Science in Architecture
MS Arch St	Master of Science in Architectural Studies
MS Bio E	Master of Science in Bioengineering Master of Science in Biomedical Engineering
MS Bm E	Master of Science in Biomedical Engineering
MS Ch E	Master of Science in Chemical Engineering
MS Chem	Master of Science in Chemistry
MS Cp E	Master of Science in Computer Engineering
MS Eco	Master of Science in Economics
MS Econ	Master of Science in Economics
MS Ed	Master of Science in Education
MS EI	Master of Science in Educational Leadership and Administration
MS En E	Master of Science in Environmental Engineering
MS Eng	Master of Science in Engineering
MS Engr	Master of Science in Engineering
MS Env E	Master of Science in Environmental Engineering
MS Exp Surg	Master of Science in Experimental Surgery
MS Int A	Master of Science in International Affairs
MS Mat E	Master of Science in Materials Engineering
MS Mat SE	Master of Science in Material Science and Engineering
MS Met E	Master of Science in Metallurgical Engineering
MS Mgt	Master of Science in Management
MS Min	Master of Science in Mining
MS Min E	Master of Science in Mining Engineering
MS Mt E	Master of Science in Materials Engineering

MS Otal	Master of Science in Otalrynology
MS Pet E	Master of Science in Petroleum Engineering
MS Phys	Master of Science in Physics
MS Poly	Master of Science in Polymers
MS Psy	Master of Science in Psychology
MS Pub P	Master of Science in Public Policy
MS Sc	Master of Science in Social Science
MS Sp Ed	Master of Science in Special Education
MS Stat	Master of Science in Statistics
MS Surg	Master of Science in Surgery
MS Tax	Master of Science in Taxation
MS Tc E	Master of Science in Telecommunications Engineering
MS-R	Master of Science (Research)
MSA	Master of School Administration
	Master of Science Administration
	Master of Science in Accountancy
	Master of Science in Accounting
	Master of Science in Administration
	Master of Science in Aeronautics
	Master of Science in Agriculture
	Master of Science in Anesthesia
	Master of Science in Architecture
	Master of Science in Aviation
	Master of Sports Administration
MSA Phy	Master of Science in Applied Physics
MSAA	Master of Science in Astronautics and Aeronautics
MSAAE	Master of Science in Aeronautical and Astronautical Engineering
MSABE	Master of Science in Agricultural and Biological Engineering
MSAC	Master of Science in Acupuncture
MSACC	Master of Science in Accounting
MSaCS	Master of Science in Applied Computer Science
MSAE	Master of Science in Aeronautical Engineering
	Master of Science in Aerospace Engineering
	Master of Science in Applied Economics
	Master of Science in Applied Engineering
	Master of Science in Architectural Engineering
	Master of Science in Art Education
MSAH	Master of Science in Allied Health
MSAL	Master of Sport Administration and Leadership
MSAM	Master of Science in Applied Mathematics
MSANR	Master of Science in Agriculture and Natural Resources Systems Management
MSAPM	Master of Security Analysis and Portfolio Management
MSAS	Master of Science in Applied Statistics
	Master of Science in Architectural Studies
MSAT	Master of Science in Accounting and Taxation
	Master of Science in Advanced Technology
	Master of Science in Athletic Training
MSB	Master of Science in Bible
	Master of Science in Business
MSBA	Master of Science in Business Administration
	Master of Science in Business Analysis
MSBAE	Master of Science in Biological and Agricultural Engineering
	Master of Science in Biosystems and Agricultural Engineering
MSBC	Master of Science in Building Construction
MSBE	Master of Science in Biological Engineering
	Master of Science in Biomedical Engineering
MSBENG	Master of Science in Bioengineering
MSBIT	Master of Science in Business Information Technology
MSBM	Master of Sport Business Management
MSBME	Master of Science in Biomedical Engineering
MSBMS	Master of Science in Basic Medical Science
MSBS	Master of Science in Biomedical Sciences
MSC	Master of Science in Commerce
	Master of Science in Communication
	Master of Science in Computers
	Master of Science in Counseling
	Master of Science in Criminology
MSCC	Master of Science in Christian Counseling
	Master of Science in Community Counseling
MSCD	Master of Science in Communication Disorders
	Master of Science in Community Development
MSCE	Master of Science in Civil Engineering
	Master of Science in Clinical Epidemiology
	Master of Science in Computer Engineering
	Master of Science in Continuing Education
MSCEE	Master of Science in Civil and Environmental Engineering
MSCF	Master of Science in Computational Finance
MSChE	Master of Science in Chemical Engineering
MSCI	Master of Science in Clinical Investigation
	Master of Science in Curriculum and Instruction
MSCIS	Master of Science in Computer and Information Systems
	Master of Science in Computer Information Science
	Master of Science in Computer Information Systems
MSCIT	Master of Science in Computer Information Technology
MSCJ	Master of Science in Criminal Justice
MSCJA	Master of Science in Criminal Justice Administration
MSCJPS	Master of Science in Criminal Justice and Public Safety
MSCJS	Master of Science in Crime and Justice Studies
MSCL	Master of Science in Collaborative Leadership
MSCLS	Master of Science in Clinical Laboratory Studies
MSCM	Master of Science in Church Management
	Master of Science in Conflict Management
	Master of Science in Construction Management
MScM	Master of Science in Management
MSCM	Master of Supply Chain Management
MSCNU	Master of Science in Clinical Nutrition
MSCP	Master of Science in Clinical Psychology
	Master of Science in Computer Engineering
	Master of Science in Counseling Psychology

MSCPE	Master of Science in Computer Engineering
MSCPharm	Master of Science in Pharmacy
MSCPI	Master in Strategic Planning for Critical Infrastructures
MSCR	Master of Science in Clinical Research
MSCRP	Master of Science in City and Regional Planning Master of Science in Community and Regional Planning
MSCS	Master of Science in Clinical Science Master of Science in Computer Science
MSCSD	Master of Science in Communication Sciences and Disorders
MSCSE	Master of Science in Computer Science and Engineering
MSCTE	Master of Science in Career and Technical Education
MSD	Master of Science in Dentistry Master of Science in Design Master of Science in Dietetics
MSDR	Master of Dispute Resolution
MSE	Master of Science Education Master of Science in Economics Master of Science in Education Master of Science in Engineering Master of Science in Engineering Management Master of Software Engineering Master of Special Education Master of Structural Engineering
MSECE	Master of Science in Electrical and Computer Engineering
MSED	Master of Sustainable Economic Development
MSEE	Master of Science in Electrical Engineering Master of Science in Environmental Engineering
MSEH	Master of Science in Environmental Health
MSEL	Master of Science in Educational Leadership
MSEM	Master of Science in Engineering Management Master of Science in Engineering Mechanics Master of Science in Environmental Management
MSENE	Master of Science in Environmental Engineering
MSEO	Master of Science in Electro-Optics
MSEP	Master of Science in Economic Policy
MSEPA	Master of Science in Economics and Policy Analysis
MSES	Master of Science in Embedded Software Engineering Master of Science in Engineering Science Master of Science in Environmental Science Master of Science in Environmental Studies
MSESM	Master of Science in Engineering Science and Mechanics
MSET	Master of Science in Educational Technology Master of Science in Engineering Technology
MSEV	Master of Science in Environmental Engineering
MSEVH	Master of Science in Environmental Health and Safety
MSF	Master of Science in Finance Master of Science in Forestry Master of Spiritual Formation
MSFA	Master of Science in Financial Analysis
MSFAM	Master of Science in Family Studies
MSFCS	Master of Science in Family and Consumer Science
MSFE	Master of Science in Financial Engineering
MSFOR	Master of Science in Forestry
MSFP	Master of Science in Financial Planning
MSFS	Master of Science in Financial Sciences Master of Science in Forensic Science
MSFSB	Master of Science in Financial Services and Banking
MSFT	Master of Science in Family Therapy
MSGC	Master of Science in Genetic Counseling
MSH	Master of Science in Health Master of Science in Hospice
MSHA	Master of Science in Health Administration
MSHCA	Master of Science in Health Care Administration
MSHCI	Master of Science in Human Computer Interaction
MSHCPM	Master of Science in Health Care Policy and Management
MSHE	Master of Science in Health Education
MSHES	Master of Science in Human Environmental Sciences
MSHFID	Master of Science in Human Factors in Information Design
MSHFS	Master of Science in Human Factors and Systems
MSHI	Master of Science in Health Informatics
MSHP	Master of Science in Health Professions Master of Science in Health Promotion
MSHR	Master of Science in Human Resources
MSHRL	Master of Science in Human Resource Leadership
MSHRM	Master of Science in Human Resource Management
MSHROD	Master of Science in Human Resources and Organizational Development
MSHS	Master of Science in Health Science Master of Science in Health Services Master of Science in Health Systems Master of Science in Homeland Security
MSHT	Master of Science in History of Technology
MSI	Master of Science in Information Master of Science in Instruction
MSIA	Master of Science in Industrial Administration Master of Science in Information Assurance and Computer Security
MSIB	Master of Science in International Business
MSIDM	Master of Science in Interior Design and Merchandising
MSIDT	Master of Science in Information Design and Technology
MSIE	Master of Science in Industrial Engineering Master of Science in International Economics
MSIEM	Master of Science in Information Engineering and Management
MSIID	Master of Science in Information and Instructional Design
MSIM	Master of Science in Information Management Master of Science in International Management

MSIMC	Master of Science in Integrated Marketing Communications
MSIR	Master of Science in Industrial Relations
MSIS	Master of Science in Information Science Master of Science in Information Systems Master of Science in Interdisciplinary Studies
MSISE	Master of Science in Infrastructure Systems Engineering
MSISM	Master of Science in Information Systems Management
MSISPM	Master of Science in Information Security Policy and Management
MSIST	Master of Science in Information Systems Technology
MSIT	Master of Science in Industrial Technology Master of Science in Information Technology Master of Science in Instructional Technology
MSITM	Master of Science in Information Technology Management
MSJ	Master of Science in Journalism Master of Science in Jurisprudence
MSJC	Master of Social Justice and Criminology
MSJE	Master of Science in Jewish Education
MSJFP	Master of Science in Juvenile Forensic Psychology
MSJJ	Master of Science in Juvenile Justice
MSJPS	Master of Science in Justice and Public Safety
MSJS	Master of Science in Jewish Studies
MSK	Master of Science in Kinesiology
MSL	Master of School Leadership Master of Science in Leadership Master of Science in Limnology Master of Strategic Leadership Master of Studies in Law
MSLA	Master of Science in Landscape Architecture Master of Science in Legal Administration
MSLD	Master of Science in Land Development
MSLFS	Master of Science in Life Sciences
MSLP	Master of Speech-Language Pathology
MSLS	Master of Science in Library Science
MSLSCM	Master of Science in Logistics and Supply Chain Management
MSLT	Master of Second Language Teaching
MSM	Master of Sacred Ministry Master of Sacred Music Master of School Mathematics Master of Science in Management Master of Science in Mathematics Master of Science in Organization Management Master of Security Management
MSMA	Master of Science in Marketing Analysis
MSMAE	Master of Science in Materials Engineering
MSMC	Master of Science in Mass Communications
MSME	Master of Science in Mathematics Education Master of Science in Mechanical Engineering
MSMFE	Master of Science in Manufacturing Engineering
MSMFT	Master of Science in Marriage and Family Therapy
MSMIS	Master of Science in Management Information Systems

MSMIT	Master of Science in Management and Information Technology
MSMOT	Master of Science in Management of Technology
MSMS	Master of Science in Management Science Master of Science in Medical Sciences
MSMSE	Master of Science in Manufacturing Systems Engineering Master of Science in Material Science and Engineering Master of Science in Mathematics and Science Education
MSMT	Master of Science in Management and Technology Master of Science in Medical Technology
MSMus	Master of Sacred Music
MSN	Master of Science in Nursing
MSN-R	Master of Science in Nursing (Research)
MSNA	Master of Science in Nurse Anesthesia
MSNE	Master of Science in Nuclear Engineering
MSNED	Master of Science in Nurse Education
MSNM	Master of Science in Nonprofit Management
MSNS	Master of Science in Natural Science Master of Science in Nutritional Science
MSOD	Master of Science in Organizational Development
MSOEE	Master of Science in Outdoor and Environmental Education
MSOES	Master of Science in Occupational Ergonomics and Safety
MSOH	Master of Science in Occupational Health
MSOL	Master of Science in Organizational Leadership
MSOM	Master of Science in Operations Management Master of Science in Organization and Management Master of Science in Oriental Medicine
MSOR	Master of Science in Operations Research
MSOT	Master of Science in Occupational Technology Master of Science in Occupational Therapy
MSP	Master of Science in Pharmacy Master of Science in Planning Master of Science in Psychology Master of Speech Pathology
MSPA	Master of Science in Physician Assistant Master of Science in Professional Accountancy
MSPAS	Master of Science in Physician Assistant Studies
MSPC	Master of Science in Professional Communications Master of Science in Professional Counseling
MSPE	Master of Science in Petroleum Engineering
MSPG	Master of Science in Psychology
MSPH	Master of Science in Public Health
MSPH/M Ed	Master of Science in Public Health/Master of Education
MSPH/MCRP	Master of Science in Public Health/Msater of City and Regional Planning
MSPH/MSIS	Master of Science in Public Health/Master of Science in Information Science
MSPH/MSLS	Master of Science in Public Health/Master of Science in Library Science
MSPHR	Master of Science in Pharmacy

MSPM	Master of Science in Professional Management Master of Science in Project Management
MSPNGE	Master of Science in Petroleum and Natural Gas Engineering
MSPS	Master of Science in Pharmaceutical Science Master of Science in Political Science Master of Science in Psychological Services
MSPT	Master of Science in Physical Therapy
MSpVM	Master of Specialized Veterinary Medicine
MSR	Master of Science in Radiology Master of Science in Reading
MSRA	Master of Science in Recreation Administration
MSRC	Master of Science in Resource Conservation
MSRE	Master of Science in Real Estate Master of Science in Religious Education
MSRED	Master of Science in Real Estate Development
MSRLS	Master of Science in Recreation and Leisure Studies
MSRMP	Master of Science in Radiological Medical Physics
MSRS	Master of Science in Rehabilitation Science
MSS	Master of Science in Software Master of Social Science Master of Social Services Master of Software Systems Master of Sports Science Master of Strategic Studies
MSSA	Master of Science in Social Administration
MSSCP	Master of Science in Science Content and Process
MSSD	Master of Science in Sustainable Design
MSSE	Master of Science in Software Engineering Master of Science in Space Education Master of Science in Special Education
MSSEM	Master of Science in Systems and Engineering Management
MSSI	Master of Science in Security Informatics Master of Science in Strategic Intelligence
MSSL	Master of Science in School Leadership Master of Science in Strategic Leadership
MSSLP	Master of Science in Speech-Language Pathology
MSSM	Master of Science in Sports Medicine
MSSP	Master of Science in Social Policy
MSSPA	Master of Science in Student Personnel Administration
MSSS	Master of Science in Safety Science Master of Science in Systems Science
MSST	Master of Science in Security Technologies
MSSW	Master of Science in Social Work
MSSWE	Master of Science in Software Engineering
MST	Master of Science and Technology Master of Science in Taxation Master of Science in Teaching Master of Science in Technology Master of Science in Telecommunications Master of Science Teaching
MSTC	Master of Science in Technical Communication Master of Science in Telecommunications
MSTCM	Master of Science in Traditional Chinese Medicine
MSTE	Master of Science in Telecommunications Engineering Master of Science in Transportation Engineering
MSTM	Master of Science in Technical Management
MSTOM	Master of Science in Traditional Oriental Medicine
MSUD	Master of Science in Urban Design
MSW	Master of Social Work
MSWE	Master of Software Engineering
MSWREE	Master of Science in Water Resources and Environmental Engineering
MSX	Master of Science in Exercise Science
MT	Master of Taxation Master of Teaching Master of Technology Master of Textiles
MTA	Master of Tax Accounting Master of Teaching Arts Master of Tourism Administration
MTCM	Master of Traditional Chinese Medicine
MTD	Master of Training and Development
MTE	Master in Educational Technology
MTESOL	Master in Teaching English to Speakers of Other Languages
MTHM	Master of Tourism and Hospitality Management
MTI	Master of Information Technology
MTIM	Master of Trust and Investment Management
MTL	Master of Talmudic Law
MTM	Master of Technology Management Master of Telecommunications Management Master of the Teaching of Mathematics
MTMH	Master of Tropical Medicine and Hygiene
MTOM	Master of Traditional Oriental Medicine
MTP	Master of Transpersonal Psychology
MTPC	Master of Technical and Professional Communication
MTR	Master of Translational Research
MTS	Master of Theological Studies
MTSC	Master of Technical and Scientific Communication
MTSE	Master of Telecommunications and Software Engineering
MTT	Master in Technology Management
MTX	Master of Taxation
MUA	Master of Urban Affairs
MUD	Master of Urban Design
MUEP	Master of Urban and Environmental Planning
MUP	Master of Urban Planning
MUPDD	Master of Urban Planning, Design, and Development
MUPP	Master of Urban Planning and Policy
MUPRED	Master of Urban Planning and Real Estate Development
MURP	Master of Urban and Regional Planning Master of Urban and Rural Planning
MURPL	Master of Urban and Regional Planning
MUS	Master of Urban Studies
MVM	Master of VLSI and Microelectronics

MVP	Master of Voice Pedagogy
MVPH	Master of Veterinary Public Health
MVS	Master of Visual Studies
MWC	Master of Wildlife Conservation
MWE	Master in Welding Engineering
MWPS	Master of Wood and Paper Science
MWR	Master of Water Resources
MWS	Master of Women's Studies Master of Worship Studies
MZS	Master of Zoological Science
Nav Arch	Naval Architecture
Naval E	Naval Engineer
ND	Doctor of Naturopathic Medicine
NE	Nuclear Engineer
Nuc E	Nuclear Engineer
OD	Doctor of Optometry
OTD	Doctor of Occupational Therapy
PBME	Professional Master of Biomedical Engineering
PD	Professional Diploma
PGC	Post-Graduate Certificate
PGD	Postgraduate Diploma
Ph L	Licentiate of Philosophy
Pharm D	Doctor of Pharmacy
PhD	Doctor of Philosophy
PhD Otal	Doctor of Philosophy in Otalrynology
PhD Surg	Doctor of Philosophy in Surgery
PhDEE	Doctor of Philosophy in Electrical Engineering
PM Sc	Professional Master of Science
PMBA	Professional Master of Business Administration
PMC	Post Master Certificate
PMD	Post-Master's Diploma
PMS	Professional Master of Science Professional Master's
Post-Doctoral MS	Post-Doctoral Master of Science
Post-MSN Certificate	Post-Master of Science in Nursing Certificate
PPDPT	Postprofessional Doctor of Physical Therapy
PSM	Professional Master of Science Professional Science Master's
Psy D	Doctor of Psychology
Psy M	Master of Psychology
Psy S	Specialist in Psychology
Psya D	Doctor of Psychoanalysis
Re Dir	Director of Recreation
Rh D	Doctor of Rehabilitation
S Psy S	Specialist in Psychological Services
Sc D	Doctor of Science
Sc M	Master of Science
SCCT	Specialist in Community College Teaching
ScDPT	Doctor of Physical Therapy Science
SD	Doctor of Science Specialist Degree
SJD	Doctor of Juridical Science
SLPD	Doctor of Speech-Language Pathology
SM	Master of Science
SM Arch S	Master of Science in Architectural Studies
SM Vis S	Master of Science in Visual Studies
SMBT	Master of Science in Building Technology
SP	Specialist Degree
Sp C	Specialist in Counseling
Sp Ed	Specialist in Education
Sp LIS	Specialist in Library and Information Science
SPA	Specialist in Arts
SPCM	Special in Church Music
Spec	Specialist's Certificate
Spec M	Specialist in Music
SPEM	Special in Educational Ministries
SPS	School Psychology Specialist
Spt	Specialist Degree
SPTH	Special in Theology
SSP	Specialist in School Psychology
STB	Bachelor of Sacred Theology
STD	Doctor of Sacred Theology
STL	Licentiate of Sacred Theology
STM	Master of Sacred Theology
TDPT	Transitional Doctor of Physical Therapy
Th D	Doctor of Theology
Th M	Master of Theology
VMD	Doctor of Veterinary Medicine
WEMBA	Weekend Executive Master of Business Administration
XMA	Executive Master of Arts
XMBA	Executive Master of Business Administration

INDEXES

Close-Ups and Displays

Directories and Subject Areas

Following is an alphabetical listing of directories and subject areas. Also listed are cross-references for subject area names not used in the directory structure of the guides, for example, "Arabic (*see* Near and Middle Eastern Languages)."

Graduate Programs in the Humanities, Arts & Social Sciences

Addictions/Substance Abuse Counseling
Administration (*see* Arts Administration; Public Administration)
African-American Studies
African Languages and Literatures (*see* African Studies)
African Studies
Agribusiness (*see* Agricultural Economics and Agribusiness)
Agricultural Economics and Agribusiness
Alcohol Abuse Counseling (*see* Addictions/Substance Abuse Counseling)
American Indian/Native American Studies
American Studies
Anthropology
Applied Arts and Design—General
Applied Behavior Analysis
Applied Economics
Applied History (*see* Public History)
Applied Psychology
Applied Social Research
Arabic (*see* Near and Middle Eastern Languages)
Arab Studies (*see* Near and Middle Eastern Studies)
Archaeology
Architectural History
Architecture
Archives Administration (*see* Public History)
Area and Cultural Studies (*see* African-American Studies; African Studies; American Indian/Native American Studies; American Studies; Asian-American Studies; Asian Studies; Canadian Studies; Cultural Studies; East European and Russian Studies; Ethnic Studies; Folklore; Gender Studies; Hispanic Studies; Holocaust Studies; Jewish Studies; Latin American Studies; Near and Middle Eastern Studies; Northern Studies; Pacific Area/Pacific Rim Studies; Western European Studies; Women's Studies)
Art/Fine Arts
Art History
Arts Administration
Arts Journalism
Art Therapy
Asian-American Studies
Asian Languages
Asian Studies
Behavioral Sciences (*see* Psychology)
Bible Studies (*see* Religion; Theology)
Biological Anthropology
Black Studies (*see* African-American Studies)
Broadcasting (*see* Communication; Film, Television, and Video Production)
Broadcast Journalism
Building Science
Canadian Studies
Celtic Languages
Ceramics (*see* Art/Fine Arts)
Child and Family Studies

Child Development
Chinese
Chinese Studies (*see* Asian Languages; Asian Studies)
Christian Studies (*see* Missions and Missiology; Religion; Theology)
Cinema (*see* Film, Television, and Video Production)
City and Regional Planning (*see* Urban and Regional Planning)
Classical Languages and Literatures (*see* Classics)
Classics
Clinical Psychology
Clothing and Textiles
Cognitive Psychology (*see* Psychology—General; Cognitive Sciences)
Cognitive Sciences
Communication—General
Community Affairs (*see* Urban and Regional Planning; Urban Studies)
Community Planning (*see* Architecture; Environmental Design; Urban and Regional Planning; Urban Design; Urban Studies)
Community Psychology (*see* Social Psychology)
Comparative and Interdisciplinary Arts
Comparative Literature
Composition (*see* Music)
Computer Art and Design
Conflict Resolution and Mediation/Peace Studies
Consumer Economics
Corporate and Organizational Communication
Corrections (*see* Criminal Justice and Criminology)
Counseling (*see* Counseling Psychology; Pastoral Ministry and Counseling)
Counseling Psychology
Crafts (*see* Art/Fine Arts)
Creative Arts Therapies (*see* Art Therapy; Therapies—Dance, Drama, and Music)
Criminal Justice and Criminology
Cultural Anthropology
Cultural Studies
Dance
Decorative Arts
Demography and Population Studies
Design (*see* Applied Arts and Design; Architecture; Art/Fine Arts; Environmental Design; Graphic Design; Industrial Design; Interior Design; Textile Design; Urban Design)
Developmental Psychology
Diplomacy (*see* International Affairs)
Disability Studies
Drama Therapy (*see* Therapies—Dance, Drama, and Music)
Dramatic Arts (*see* Theater)
Drawing (*see* Art/Fine Arts)
Drug Abuse Counseling (*see* Addictions/Substance Abuse Counseling)
Drug and Alcohol Abuse Counseling (*see* Addictions/Substance Abuse Counseling)
East Asian Studies (*see* Asian Studies)
East European and Russian Studies
Economic Development
Economics
Educational Theater (*see* Theater; Therapies—Dance, Drama, and Music)
Emergency Management
English
Environmental Design
Ethics
Ethnic Studies
Ethnomusicology (*see* Music)
Experimental Psychology
Family and Consumer Sciences—General
Family Studies (*see* Child and Family Studies)

Family Therapy (*see* Child and Family Studies; Clinical Psychology; Counseling Psychology; Marriage and Family Therapy)
Filmmaking (*see* Film, Television, and Video Production)
Film Studies (*see* Film, Television, and Video Production)
Film, Television, and Video Production
Film, Television, and Video Theory and Criticism
Fine Arts (*see* Art/Fine Arts)
Folklore
Foreign Languages (*see* specific language)
Foreign Service (*see* International Affairs; International Development)
Forensic Psychology
Forensic Sciences
Forensics (*see* Speech and Interpersonal Communication)
French
Gender Studies
General Studies (*see* Liberal Studies)
Genetic Counseling
Geographic Information Systems
Geography
German
Gerontology
Graphic Design
Greek (*see* Classics)
Health Communication
Health Psychology
Hebrew (*see* Near and Middle Eastern Languages)
Hebrew Studies (*see* Jewish Studies)
Hispanic and Latin American Languages
Hispanic Studies
Historic Preservation
History
History of Art (*see* Art History)
History of Medicine
History of Science and Technology
Holocaust and Genocide Studies
Home Economics (*see* Family and Consumer Sciences—General)
Homeland Security
Household Economics, Sciences, and Management (*see* Family and Consumer Sciences—General)
Human Development
Humanities
Illustration
Industrial and Labor Relations
Industrial and Organizational Psychology
Industrial Design
Interdisciplinary Studies
Interior Design
International Affairs
International Development
International Economics
International Service (*see* International Affairs; International Development)
International Trade Policy
Internet and Interactive Multimedia
Interpersonal Communication (*see* Speech and Interpersonal Communication)
Interpretation (*see* Translation and Interpretation)
Islamic Studies (*see* Near and Middle Eastern Studies; Religion)
Italian
Japanese
Japanese Studies (*see* Asian Languages; Asian Studies; Japanese)
Jewelry (*see* Art/Fine Arts)
Jewish Studies
Journalism
Judaic Studies (*see* Jewish Studies; Religion)
Labor Relations (*see* Industrial and Labor Relations)
Landscape Architecture
Latin American Studies

Latin (*see* Classics)
Law Enforcement (*see* Criminal Justice and Criminology)
Liberal Studies
Lighting Design
Linguistics
Literature (*see* Classics; Comparative Literature; specific language)
Marriage and Family Therapy
Mass Communication
Media Studies
Medical Illustration
Medieval and Renaissance Studies
Metalsmithing (*see* Art/Fine Arts)
Middle Eastern Studies (*see* Near and Middle Eastern Studies)
Military and Defense Studies
Mineral Economics
Ministry (*see* Pastoral Ministry and Counseling; Theology)
Missions and Missiology
Motion Pictures (*see* Film, Television, and Video Production)
Museum Studies
Music
Musicology (*see* Music)
Music Therapy (*see* Therapies—Dance, Drama, and Music)
National Security
Native American Studies (*see* American Indian/Native American Studies)
Near and Middle Eastern Languages
Near and Middle Eastern Studies
Near Environment (*see* Family and Consumer Sciences)
Northern Studies
Organizational Psychology (*see* Industrial and Organizational Psychology)
Oriental Languages (*see* Asian Languages)
Oriental Studies (*see* Asian Studies)
Pacific Area/Pacific Rim Studies
Painting (*see* Art/Fine Arts)
Pastoral Ministry and Counseling
Philanthropic Studies
Philosophy
Photography
Playwriting (*see* Theater; Writing)
Policy Studies (*see* Public Policy)
Political Science
Population Studies (*see* Demography and Population Studies)
Portuguese
Printmaking (*see* Art/Fine Arts)
Product Design (*see* Industrial Design)
Psychoanalysis and Psychotherapy
Psychology—General
Public Administration
Public Affairs
Public History
Public Policy
Public Speaking (*see* Mass Communication; Rhetoric; Speech and Interpersonal Communication)
Publishing
Regional Planning (*see* Architecture; Urban and Regional Planning; Urban Design; Urban Studies)
Rehabilitation Counseling
Religion
Renaissance Studies (*see* Medieval and Renaissance Studies)
Rhetoric
Romance Languages
Romance Literatures (*see* Romance Languages)
Rural Planning and Studies
Rural Sociology
Russian
Scandinavian Languages
School Psychology
Sculpture (*see* Art/Fine Arts)

Security Administration (see Criminal Justice and Criminology)
Slavic Languages
Slavic Studies (see East European and Russian Studies; Slavic Languages)
Social Psychology
Social Sciences
Sociology
Southeast Asian Studies (see Asian Studies)
Soviet Studies (see East European and Russian Studies; Russian)
Spanish
Speech and Interpersonal Communication
Sport Psychology
Studio Art (see Art/Fine Arts)
Substance Abuse Counseling (see Addictions/Substance Abuse Counseling)
Survey Methodology
Sustainable Development
Technical Communication
Technical Writing
Telecommunications (see Film, Television, and Video Production)
Television (see Film, Television, and Video Production)
Textile Design
Textiles (see Clothing and Textiles; Textile Design)
Thanatology
Theater
Theater Arts (see Theater)
Theology
Therapies—Dance, Drama, and Music
Translation and Interpretation
Transpersonal and Humanistic Psychology
Urban and Regional Planning
Urban Design
Urban Planning (see Architecture; Urban and Regional Planning; Urban Design; Urban Studies)
Urban Studies
Video (see Film, Television, and Video Production)
Visual Arts (see Applied Arts and Design; Art/Fine Arts; Film, Television, and Video Production; Graphic Design; Illustration; Photography)
Western European Studies
Women's Studies
World Wide Web (see Internet and Interactive Multimedia)
Writing

Graduate Programs in the Biological Sciences

Anatomy
Animal Behavior
Bacteriology
Behavioral Sciences (see Biopsychology; Neuroscience; Zoology)
Biochemistry
Biological and Biomedical Sciences—General
Biological Chemistry (see Biochemistry)
Biological Oceanography (see Marine Biology)
Biophysics
Biopsychology
Botany
Breeding (see Botany; Plant Biology; Genetics)
Cancer Biology/Oncology
Cardiovascular Sciences
Cell Biology
Cellular Physiology (see Cell Biology; Physiology)
Computational Biology
Conservation (see Conservation Biology; Environmental Biology)
Conservation Biology
Crop Sciences (see Botany; Plant Biology)

Cytology (see Cell Biology)
Developmental Biology
Dietetics (see Nutrition)
Ecology
Embryology (see Developmental Biology)
Endocrinology (see Physiology)
Entomology
Environmental Biology
Evolutionary Biology
Foods (see Nutrition)
Genetics
Genomic Sciences
Histology (see Anatomy; Cell Biology)
Human Genetics
Immunology
Infectious Diseases
Laboratory Medicine (see Immunology; Microbiology; Pathology)
Life Sciences (see Biological and Biomedical Sciences)
Marine Biology
Medical Microbiology
Medical Sciences (see Biological and Biomedical Sciences)
Medical Science Training Programs (see Biological and Biomedical Sciences)
Microbiology
Molecular Biology
Molecular Biophysics
Molecular Genetics
Molecular Medicine
Molecular Pathogenesis
Molecular Pathology
Molecular Pharmacology
Molecular Physiology
Molecular Toxicology
Neural Sciences (see Biopsychology; Neurobiology; Neuroscience)
Neurobiology
Neuroendocrinology (see Biopsychology; Neurobiology; Neuroscience; Physiology)
Neuropharmacology (see Biopsychology; Neurobiology; Neuroscience; Pharmacology)
Neurophysiology (see Biopsychology; Neurobiology; Neuroscience; Physiology)
Neuroscience
Nutrition
Oncology (see Cancer Biology/Oncology)
Organismal Biology (see Biological and Biomedical Sciences; Zoology)
Parasitology
Pathobiology
Pathology
Pharmacology
Photobiology of Cells and Organelles (see Botany; Cell Biology; Plant Biology)
Physiological Optics (see Physiology)
Physiology
Plant Biology
Plant Molecular Biology
Plant Pathology
Plant Physiology
Pomology (see Botany; Plant Biology)
Psychobiology (see Biopsychology)
Psychopharmacology (see Biopsychology; Neuroscience; Pharmacology)
Radiation Biology
Reproductive Biology
Sociobiology (see Evolutionary Biology)
Structural Biology
Systems Biology
Teratology
Theoretical Biology (see Biological and Biomedical Sciences)
Therapeutics (see Pharmacology)

Toxicology
Translational Biology
Tropical Medicine (*see* Parasitology)
Virology
Wildlife Biology (*see* Zoology)
Zoology

Graduate Programs in the Physical Sciences, Mathematics, Agricultural Sciences, the Environment & Natural Resources

Acoustics
Agricultural Sciences
Agronomy and Soil Sciences
Analytical Chemistry
Animal Sciences
Applied Mathematics
Applied Physics
Applied Statistics
Aquaculture
Astronomy
Astrophysical Sciences (*see* Astrophysics; Atmospheric Sciences; Meteorology; Planetary and Space Sciences)
Astrophysics
Atmospheric Sciences
Biological Oceanography (*see* Marine Affairs; Marine Sciences; Oceanography)
Biomathematics
Biometry
Biostatistics
Chemical Physics
Chemistry
Computational Sciences
Condensed Matter Physics
Dairy Science (*see* Animal Sciences)
Earth Sciences (*see* Geosciences)
Environmental Management and Policy
Environmental Sciences
Environmental Studies (*see* Environmental Management and Policy)
Experimental Statistics (*see* Statistics)
Fish, Game, and Wildlife Management
Food Science and Technology
Forestry
General Science (*see* specific topics)
Geochemistry
Geodetic Sciences
Geological Engineering (*see* Geology)
Geological Sciences (*see* Geology)
Geology
Geophysical Fluid Dynamics (*see* Geophysics)
Geophysics
Geosciences
Horticulture
Hydrogeology
Hydrology
Inorganic Chemistry
Limnology
Marine Affairs
Marine Geology
Marine Sciences
Marine Studies (*see* Marine Affairs; Marine Geology; Marine Sciences; Oceanography)
Mathematical and Computational Finance

Mathematical Physics
Mathematical Statistics (*see* Applied Statistics; Statistics)
Mathematics
Meteorology
Mineralogy
Natural Resource Management (*see* Environmental Management and Policy; Natural Resources)
Natural Resources
Nuclear Physics (*see* Physics)
Ocean Engineering (*see* Marine Affairs; Marine Geology; Marine Sciences; Oceanography)
Oceanography
Optical Sciences
Optical Technologies (*see* Optical Sciences)
Optics (*see* Applied Physics; Optical Sciences; Physics)
Organic Chemistry
Paleontology
Paper Chemistry (*see* Chemistry)
Photonics
Physical Chemistry
Physics
Planetary and Space Sciences
Plant Sciences
Plasma Physics
Poultry Science (*see* Animal Sciences)
Radiological Physics (*see* Physics)
Range Management (*see* Range Science)
Range Science
Resource Management (*see* Environmental Management and Policy; Natural Resources)
Solid-Earth Sciences (*see* Geosciences)
Space Sciences (*see* Planetary and Space Sciences)
Statistics
Theoretical Chemistry
Theoretical Physics
Viticulture and Enology
Water Resources

Graduate Programs in Engineering & Applied Sciences

Aeronautical Engineering (*see* Aerospace/Aeronautical Engineering)
Aerospace/Aeronautical Engineering
Aerospace Studies (*see* Aerospace/Aeronautical Engineering)
Agricultural Engineering
Applied Mechanics (*see* Mechanics)
Applied Science and Technology
Architectural Engineering
Artificial Intelligence/Robotics
Astronautical Engineering (*see* Aerospace/Aeronautical Engineering)
Automotive Engineering
Aviation
Biochemical Engineering
Bioengineering
Bioinformatics
Biological Engineering (*see* Bioengineering)
Biomedical Engineering
Biosystems Engineering
Biotechnology
Ceramic Engineering (*see* Ceramic Sciences and Engineering)
Ceramic Sciences and Engineering
Ceramics (*see* Ceramic Sciences and Engineering)
Chemical Engineering
Civil Engineering
Computer and Information Systems Security
Computer Engineering

Computer Science
Computing Technology (see Computer Science)
Construction Engineering
Construction Management
Database Systems
Electrical Engineering
Electronic Materials
Electronics Engineering (see Electrical Engineering)
Energy and Power Engineering
Energy Management and Policy
Engineering and Applied Sciences
Engineering and Public Affairs (see Technology and Public Policy)
Engineering and Public Policy (see Energy Management and Policy; Technology and Public Policy)
Engineering Design
Engineering Management
Engineering Mechanics (see Mechanics)
Engineering Metallurgy (see Metallurgical Engineering and Metallurgy)
Engineering Physics
Environmental Design (see Environmental Engineering)
Environmental Engineering
Ergonomics and Human Factors
Financial Engineering
Fire Protection Engineering
Food Engineering (see Agricultural Engineering)
Game Design and Development
Gas Engineering (see Petroleum Engineering)
Geological Engineering
Geophysics Engineering (see Geological Engineering)
Geotechnical Engineering
Hazardous Materials Management
Health Informatics
Health Systems (see Safety Engineering; Systems Engineering)
Highway Engineering (see Transportation and Highway Engineering)
Human-Computer Interaction
Human Factors (see Ergonomics and Human Factors)
Hydraulics
Hydrology (see Water Resources Engineering)
Industrial Engineering (see Industrial/Management Engineering)
Industrial/Management Engineering
Information Science
Internet Engineering
Macromolecular Science (see Polymer Science and Engineering)
Management Engineering (see Engineering Management; Industrial/Management Engineering)
Management of Technology
Manufacturing Engineering
Marine Engineering (see Civil Engineering)
Materials Engineering
Materials Sciences
Mechanical Engineering
Mechanics
Medical Informatics
Metallurgical Engineering and Metallurgy
Metallurgy (see Metallurgical Engineering and Metallurgy)
Mineral/Mining Engineering
Modeling and Simulation
Nanotechnology
Nuclear Engineering
Ocean Engineering
Operations Research
Paper and Pulp Engineering
Petroleum Engineering
Pharmaceutical Engineering
Plastics Engineering (see Polymer Science and Engineering)
Polymer Science and Engineering
Public Policy (see Energy Management and Policy; Technology and Public Policy)

Reliability Engineering
Robotics (see Artificial Intelligence/Robotics)
Safety Engineering
Software Engineering
Solid-State Sciences (see Materials Sciences)
Structural Engineering
Surveying Science and Engineering
Systems Analysis (see Systems Engineering)
Systems Engineering
Systems Science
Technology and Public Policy
Telecommunications
Telecommunications Management
Textile Sciences and Engineering
Textiles (see Textile Sciences and Engineering)
Transportation and Highway Engineering
Urban Systems Engineering (see Systems Engineering)
Waste Management (see Hazardous Materials Management)
Water Resources Engineering

Graduate Programs in Business, Education, Health, Information Studies, Law & Social Work

Accounting
Actuarial Science
Acupuncture and Oriental Medicine
Acute Care/Critical Care Nursing
Administration (see Business Administration and Management; Educational Administration; Health Services Management and Hospital Administration; Industrial and Manufacturing Management; Nursing and Healthcare Administration; Pharmaceutical Administration; Sports Management)
Adult Education
Adult Nursing
Advanced Practice Nursing (see Family Nurse Practitioner Studies)
Advertising and Public Relations
Agricultural Education
Alcohol Abuse Counseling (see Counselor Education)
Allied Health—General
Allied Health Professions (see Clinical Laboratory Sciences/Medical Technology; Clinical Research; Communication Disorders; Dental Hygiene; Emergency Medical Services; Occupational Therapy; Physical Therapy; Physician Assistant Studies; Rehabilitation Sciences)
Allopathic Medicine
Anesthesiologist Assistant Studies
Archival Management and Studies
Art Education
Athletics Administration (see Kinesiology and Movement Studies)
Athletic Training and Sports Medicine
Audiology (see Communication Disorders)
Aviation Management
Banking (see Finance and Banking)
Bioethics
Business Administration and Management—General
Business Education
Child-Care Nursing (see Maternal and Child/Neonatal Nursing)
Chiropractic
Clinical Laboratory Sciences/Medical Technology
Clinical Research
Communication Disorders
Community College Education
Community Health
Community Health Nursing

Computer Education
Continuing Education (*see* Adult Education)
Counseling (*see* Counselor Education)
Counselor Education
Curriculum and Instruction
Dental and Oral Surgery (*see* Oral and Dental Sciences)
Dental Assistant Studies (*see* Dental Hygiene)
Dental Hygiene
Dental Services (*see* Dental Hygiene)
Dentistry
Developmental Education
Distance Education Development
Drug Abuse Counseling (*see* Counselor Education)
Early Childhood Education
Educational Leadership and Administration
Educational Measurement and Evaluation
Educational Media/Instructional Technology
Educational Policy
Educational Psychology
Education—General
Education of the Blind (*see* Special Education)
Education of the Deaf (*see* Special Education)
Education of the Gifted
Education of the Hearing Impaired (*see* Special Education)
Education of the Learning Disabled (*see* Special Education)
Education of the Mentally Retarded (*see* Special Education)
Education of the Physically Handicapped (*see* Special Education)
Education of Students with Severe/Multiple Disabilities
Education of the Visually Handicapped (*see* Special Education)
Electronic Commerce
Elementary Education
Emergency Medical Services
English as a Second Language
English Education
Entertainment Management
Entrepreneurship
Environmental and Occupational Health
Environmental Education
Environmental Law
Epidemiology
Exercise and Sports Science
Exercise Physiology (*see* Kinesiology and Movement Studies)
Facilities and Entertainment Management
Family Nurse Practitioner Studies
Finance and Banking
Food Services Management (*see* Hospitality Management)
Foreign Languages Education
Forensic Nursing
Foundations and Philosophy of Education
Gerontological Nursing
Guidance and Counseling (*see* Counselor Education)
Health Education
Health Law
Health Physics/Radiological Health
Health Promotion
Health-Related Professions (*see* individual allied health professions)
Health Services Management and Hospital Administration
Health Services Research
Hearing Sciences (*see* Communication Disorders)
Higher Education
HIV/AIDS Nursing
Home Economics Education
Hospice Nursing
Hospital Administration (*see* Health Services Management and Hospital Administration)
Hospitality Management
Hotel Management (*see* Travel and Tourism)
Human Resources Development
Human Resources Management

Human Services
Industrial Administration (*see* Industrial and Manufacturing Management)
Industrial and Manufacturing Management
Industrial Education (*see* Vocational and Technical Education)
Industrial Hygiene
Information Studies
Instructional Technology (*see* Educational Media/Instructional Technology)
Insurance
Intellectual Property Law
International and Comparative Education
International Business
International Commerce (*see* International Business)
International Economics (*see* International Business)
International Health
International Trade (*see* International Business)
Investment and Securities (*see* Business Administration and Management; Finance and Banking; Investment Management)
Investment Management
Junior College Education (*see* Community College Education)
Kinesiology and Movement Studies
Laboratory Medicine (*see* Clinical Laboratory Sciences/Medical Technology)
Law
Legal and Justice Studies
Leisure Services (*see* Recreation and Park Management)
Leisure Studies
Library Science
Logistics
Management (*see* Business Administration and Management)
Management Information Systems
Management Strategy and Policy
Marketing
Marketing Research
Maternal and Child Health
Maternal and Child/Neonatal Nursing
Mathematics Education
Medical Imaging
Medical Nursing (*see* Medical/Surgical Nursing)
Medical Physics
Medical/Surgical Nursing
Medical Technology (*see* Clinical Laboratory Sciences/Medical Technology)
Medicinal and Pharmaceutical Chemistry
Medicinal Chemistry (*see* Medicinal and Pharmaceutical Chemistry)
Medicine (*see* Allopathic Medicine; Naturopathic Medicine; Osteopathic Medicine; Podiatric Medicine)
Middle School Education
Midwifery (*see* Nurse Midwifery)
Movement Studies (*see* Kinesiology and Movement Studies)
Multilingual and Multicultural Education
Museum Education
Music Education
Naturopathic Medicine
Nonprofit Management
Nuclear Medical Technology (*see* Clinical Laboratory Sciences/Medical Technology)
Nurse Anesthesia
Nurse Midwifery
Nurse Practitioner Studies (*see* Family Nurse Practitioner Studies)
Nursery School Education (*see* Early Childhood Education)
Nursing Administration (*see* Nursing and Healthcare Administration)
Nursing and Healthcare Administration
Nursing Education
Nursing—General
Nursing Informatics
Occupational Education (*see* Vocational and Technical Education)

Occupational Health (*see* Environmental and Occupational Health; Occupational Health Nursing)

Occupational Health Nursing

Occupational Therapy

Oncology Nursing

Optometry

Oral and Dental Sciences

Oral Biology (*see* Oral and Dental Sciences)

Oral Pathology (*see* Oral and Dental Sciences)

Organizational Behavior

Organizational Management

Oriental Medicine and Acupuncture (*see* Acupuncture and Oriental Medicine)

Orthodontics (*see* Oral and Dental Sciences)

Osteopathic Medicine

Parks Administration (*see* Recreation and Park Management)

Pediatric Nursing

Pedontics (*see* Oral and Dental Sciences)

Perfusion

Personnel (*see* Human Resources Development; Human Resources Management; Organizational Behavior; Organizational Management; Student Affairs)

Pharmaceutical Administration

Pharmaceutical Chemistry (*see* Medicinal and Pharmaceutical Chemistry)

Pharmaceutical Sciences

Pharmacy

Philosophy of Education (*see* Foundations and Philosophy of Education)

Physical Education

Physical Therapy

Physician Assistant Studies

Physiological Optics (*see* Vision Sciences)

Podiatric Medicine

Preventive Medicine (*see* Community Health and Public Health)

Project Management

Psychiatric Nursing

Public Health—General

Public Health Nursing (*see* Community Health Nursing)

Public Relations (*see* Advertising and Public Relations)

Quality Management

Quantitative Analysis

Radiological Health (*see* Health Physics/Radiological Health)

Reading Education

Real Estate

Recreation and Park Management

Recreation Therapy (*see* Recreation and Park Management)

Rehabilitation Sciences

Rehabilitation Therapy (*see* Physical Therapy)

Religious Education

Remedial Education (*see* Special Education)

Restaurant Administration (*see* Hospitality Management)

School Nursing

Science Education

Secondary Education

Social Sciences Education

Social Studies Education (*see* Social Sciences Education)

Social Work

Special Education

Speech-Language Pathology and Audiology (*see* Communication Disorders)

Sports Management

Sports Medicine (*see* Athletic Training and Sports Medicine)

Sports Psychology and Sociology (*see* Kinesiology and Movement Studies)

Student Affairs

Substance Abuse Counseling (*see* Counselor Education)

Supply Chain Management

Surgical Nursing (*see* Medical/Surgical Nursing)

Sustainability Management

Systems Management (*see* Management Information Systems)

Taxation

Teacher Education (*see* specific subject areas)

Teaching English as a Second Language (*see* English as a Second Language)

Technical Education (*see* Vocational and Technical Education)

Teratology (*see* Environmental and Occupational Health)

Therapeutics (*see* Pharmaceutical Sciences; Pharmacy)

Transcultural Nursing

Transportation Management

Travel and Tourism

Urban Education

Veterinary Medicine

Veterinary Sciences

Vision Sciences

Vocational and Technical Education

Vocational Counseling (*see* Counselor Education)

Women's Health Nursing

Directories and Subject Areas in This Book

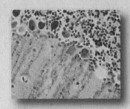

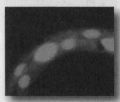
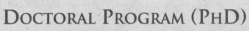

AMIT SOOD | sports business major

BE A BILLIKEN

Find out how the breadth and depth of the fully accredited undergraduate and graduate programs at Saint Louis University's **JOHN COOK SCHOOL OF BUSINESS** will give you the knowledge and tools necessary for success in today's global and highly technical business world.

— + Visit **BeABilliken.com** for more information on our undergraduate business programs and to see what life is like as a Billiken.

To learn about our graduate business programs, attend an open house or visit **gradbiz.slu.edu.** + ————————

SAINT LOUIS UNIVERSITY

CONCENTRATIONS IN THE JOHN COOK SCHOOL OF BUSINESS

Accounting

Economics

Entrepreneurship

Finance

Information Technology Management

International Business

Leadership and Change Management

Marketing

Sports Business

GRADUATE PROGRAMS IN THE JOHN COOK SCHOOL OF BUSINESS

One-Year MBA

Part-Time MBA

Master of Supply Chain Management

Master of Accounting

Executive Master of International Business

Post-MBA Certificate

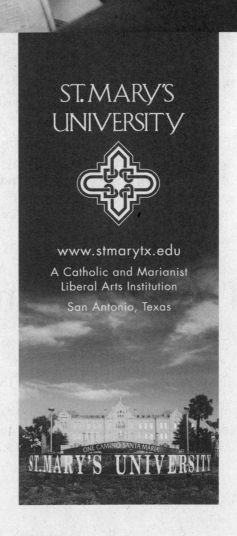

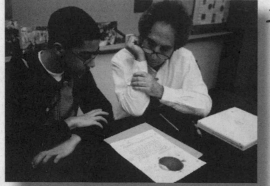